AMERICAN
COST
OF
LIVING
SURVEY

Third Edition

AMERICAN COST OF LIVING SURVEY

Third Edition

A Compilation of Price Data for Nearly 580 Goods and Services in 506 U.S. Cities from More Than 100 Sources

Arsen J. Darnay

GALE GROUP

THOMSON LEARNING

Detroit • New York • San Diego • San Francisco
Boston • New Haven, Conn. • Waterville, Maine
London • Munich

Arsen J. Darnay, Editor

Editorial Code & Data Inc. Staff

Robert S. Lazich, Helen S. Fisher, and Susan Turner, Contributing Editors
Sherae R. Carroll, Data Entry Associate

Gale Group Staff

Jason B. Baldwin, Coordinating Editor
Mary Beth Trimper, Production Director
Nekita McKee, Buyer

Kenn Zorn, Product Design Manager
Mike Logusz, Graphic Artist

This book is printed on recycled paper that meets Environmental Protection Agency Standards.

The paper used in this publication meets the minimum requirements of American National Standard for Information Sciences—Permanence Paper for Printed Library Materials, ANSI Z39.48-1984.

Copyright © 2002
Gale Group
27500 Drake Road
Farmington Hills, MI 48331-3535

ISBN 0-7876-1162-X
ISSN 1071-099X

Printed in the United States of America

TABLE OF CONTENTS

STATE LISTING OF CITIES

INTRODUCTION

American Cost of Living Survey, third edition (*ACLS*) is a compilation of reported prices for more than 560 products and services in 506 cities in the United States drawn from more than 110 sources, including federal and state statistical reports, city surveys, association databases, and the periodicals literature. The large number of items and communities covered ensures that cost of living data are now available to individuals, librarians, researchers, and analysts in a single, comprehensive, easy-to-use volume.

ACLS responds to a perennial need. People are curious about the cost of things and current and future trends in the economy. National series about the Gross Domestic Product and other economic indicators provide an insight into the general performance of the economy. But data at the local level are difficult to obtain; the Consumer Price Index (CPI) covers major cities but does not permit comparisons *between and among* cities and is unavailable for smaller communities. *ACLS* provides a convenient and current bridge between the relatively accessible "global" scale and the "local" scale where, after all, everybody lives.

ACLS is, therefore, an excellent tool for those seeking cost of living information and those asked to supply it (librarians, counselors, employers, analysts, and others).

Uses of *ACLS* are many and varied. For example:

- People considering a move to another part of the United States can use the book to see how the move may affect their standard of living.

- Companies relocating employees can use *ACLS* to determine appropriate levels of compensation adjustment.

- Parents deciding the costs of education for their college-bound offspring can use *ACLS* to determine living costs in other areas.

- Individuals and organizations seeking adjustments in compensation—or organizations defending the levels of compensation they offer—can both use *ACLS* as a basis for analysis.

• Investors, market researchers, developers, and government agencies, similarly, will find well-organized data in *ACLS* to fill in the often missing information on local cost of living.

Making comparisons among locations can bring interesting differences to light. For example, in the first quarter of 2001, the price of a bottle of Gallo Chablis Blanc wine in Amarillo, Texas, was $5.40; the same product in Atlanta, Georgia, cost $5.99; and in Albequerque, NM, $6.56. A comparison of phone line installation charges for businesses in 1997 shows that in Alexandria, Louisiana, the cost was $85; in Allentown, Pennsylvania, $75; and in Akron, Ohio, $56.32. For those considering attending a public university, the total average cost for one year in a four-year public university in Abilene, Texas, is $5464; in Altoona, Pennsylvania, $9124; in Ann Arbor, Michigan, $8195; and in Bloomington, Indiana, $7392. Delivering a child by Cesarean costs $14716 in Allentown, Pennsylvania; $11587 in Bakersfield, California; and $10722 in Appleton, Wisconsin. Obtaining information on such differences can aid the typical consumer in making decisions on where to live, where to look for employment, where to send children to college, and where to obtain medical care.

* * *

The remainder of this introduction presents a discussion of subjects covered, geographical coverage, periods of coverage, methodology of compilation, the consumer price index, arrangement and format, and sources.

SUBJECTS COVERED

ACLS contains more than 105,000 entries for the average prices of more than 560 items in 506 cities in the United States. For each community, if available, items are arranged under the following major topics:

Alcoholic Beverages	Entertainment	Personal Services
Appliances	Funerals	Pets
Banking and Money	Groceries	Restaurant Food
Business Expenses	Goods and Services	Taxes
Charity	Health Care	Transportation
Child Care	Household Goods	Travel
Clothing	Housing	Utilities
Communications	Insurance and Pensions	Weddings
Education	Legal Fees	
Energy and Fuels	Personal Goods	

Under each of these major topics, price information for more specific items within the broader topic is provided. A listing of these items, alphabetically arranged within each major topic, is provided in the *List of Items Covered* which appears on p. xxvii.

Energy and Fuels. Energy substances—including natural gas, gasoline, and fuel oil—are placed under *Energy and Fuels*. The notable exception is electric power: all entries dealing with electric power have been placed under *Utilities* because, in general, people associate electric power with the "local utility."

Utilities. Included under the heading of *Utilities* are electric power costs as well as costs associated with water and similar services that are regulated or franchised. The chief exception is telephone service, which is classified under *Communications*.

Costs versus Expenditures. The majority of items shown are costs as they would be experienced by people buying the product or service. Some data shown are followed by the abbreviation *exp*. These indicate measured *levels of expenditure* on the item on a per capita basis or annual basis.

Prices for Two or More Periods. In some cases prices for the same item were obtained for more than one period, sometimes from the same sources, sometimes from different sources. In these instances, both prices are shown, with the most recent period shown last. These data may be useful in tracking changes in price over a period of time.

ACCRA Indexes. For cities that are part of the ACCRA cost of living survey (discussed more fully below), the ACCRA composite index is shown as the first item; component indices are also shown under major topics.

The ACCRA indices measure the relative price levels for consumer goods and services in the areas that participate in the ACCRA survey. The average of all participating cities is defined as 100. For each community, the community's index is read as a percentage of the average of all places. The values are always on either side of 100, e.g., 95.6 or 105.2. A value less than 100 indicates an area where the price levels are *less* than the average of all places surveyed. A value greater than 100 indicates that price levels, on average, are *higher* than average prices of all places participating in the ACCRA survey.

GEOGRAPHIC COVERAGE

ACLS provides information on 506 cities. At least one city is covered in every state. For many cities, data are reported for metropolitan areas, e.g., Allentown-Bethlehem-Easton, PA, NJ. In this case, as in others, the cities listed second or third in order are also listed alphabetically in the *Table of Contents*. Thus, Bethlehem, PA and Easton, NJ can both be found separately in alphabetical order; page references, however, are to the Allentown-Bethlehem-Easton metropolitan area.

Geographical access to the data is provided, first, in the *Table of Contents*, where the cities are arranged in alphabetical order. Immediately following the *Table of Contents* is a *List of Cities by State.* Cities are listed alphabetically by state. Cost of living data for some items are only available at the state or regional level. The methods used to "allocate" such data to cities are described below under *Methodology of Compilation*.

Coverage of cities also varies depending on the data available. For most communities, many specific items are available. For others, reporting is more sparse. However, only communities in which data were available for most major categories are included in *ACLS*.

PERIODS OF COVERAGE

ACLS coverage extends from 1995 up to and including mid-2001. The majority of entries, however, are from the period 1998 to 2001. The dates reproduced with each entry refer either to the date of collection or, if not available from the source, the date of the source itself. To the extent possible, the time periods of data collection are reported in the *List of Sources* which concludes *ACLS*.

METHODOLOGY OF COMPILATION

Geographical Selection. The editors initially selected 300 metropolitan statistical areas (MSAs) for coverage using 2000 Census of Population data. All research and data acquisition efforts were then aimed at obtaining information for at least the targeted MSAs. One major source (ACCRA—discussed more fully below) provided data for many (but not all) of the targeted MSAs. ACCRA data were also available for cities that were not on the original target list. These cities were added to the list. Similarly, the number of communities covered grew as other sources came to light. The final list of communities was edited to conform to a single naming convention. Descriptive tags (such as "MSA," "Area," and others) were removed so that the database, once sorted, would not display variants of the same city name. The final result was a "master list" of cities to be included.

Data Acquisition. Data were obtained from a variety of sources using many methods. Data arrived on paper as well as on magnetic media. Mailings, telephone contacts, special arrangements, literature and web searches were used to locate and to obtain data. Sources were classified by the geographical level of the data (city, metro area, state, region) and each item within each source was assigned to one of the major topics used.

Data Allocation. Some interesting data were obtainable only at the state level (e.g., driver's license fees, education costs), at the Census region level (e.g., funeral costs), and in one case (weddings), at the national level. The editors decided to include the national average costs for wedding because inquiries determined that these costs were fairly consistent across the nation. If alternative sources for such categories could not be located, data were "allocated" to cities on the master list by using the state of each city and the known state composition of regions as a guide.

An obvious consequence of this method is that items marked as having a regional or a state-level source are not as accurate as items that have a city-level source. This is generally true except for those items where the price is controlled at the state level, e.g., driver's license fees or tuition at state educational institutions. In the case of many cities, data from regional/state as well as city-level sources are shown side-by-side, permitting some judgment on the accuracy of the regional/state or regional/city items.

Accuracy of Data. In all cases, data are reported exactly as obtained from the sources. The quality and accuracy of the data are obviously variable and depend on the methods used by the sources themselves. Data assigned from state or regional sources to cities were not changed in the process of allocation in any way.

COST OF LIVING VS. CONSUMER PRICE INDEX

ACLS does ***not*** report on the Consumer Price Index (CPI). A detailed listing of CPI data is available from another Gale title: *Economic Indicators Handbook.*

The difference between *cost of living* and the CPI is confusing for many people. For this reason, a brief outline of the differences is provided here.

The CPI measures price change from ***one period to the next within the same city*** (or in the Nation). A cost of living index measures differences in the price of goods and services ***between cities within the same period***. To see how prices have changed in Chicago between 1998 and 2000, one would use the CPI. To see how Chicago compares with Dallas in cost of living, one would use a cost of living index or data such as those reported in *ACLS.*

ARRANGEMENT AND FORMAT

ACLS is arranged alphabetically by city. The city name and its state appear in boldface type at the head of a column of entries. The first item under each city name is usually the composite cost of living index attributed to that city by ACCRA.

Major topics covered are sorted alphabetically and appear in boldface print and initial caps, e.g., **Alcoholic Beverages**. Specific items covered within the major topic are arranged alphabetically.

The "Per" column typically contains a measurement, such as pound, month, or hour.

The "Value" column contains average prices represented in dollars or in fractions of dollars.

The "Date" column indicates the date on which that particular price was charged for that item, or in some cases, the date of the source material consulted. In some cases, there are two prices or price ranges given for a particular item; these reflect different dates from different source materials which included some of the same products, or the difference in price between a brand-name product and a generic product.

The "Ref." (for Reference) column contains numbers to be used when consulting the *List of Sources* section of *ACLS*. Each reference number is followed by a letter representing the geographical level for which data were reported in the source materials: s = State, r = Region, c = City or Metropolitan area.

A list of abbreviations used in *ACLS* is provided below.

SOURCES

General. More than 110 sources were used to compile *ACLS*. These included newspapers, magazines, government reports and publications, and surveys or other reports compiled by independent governmental agencies.

In addition to governmental sources, *ACLS* cites significant databases that are copyrighted and are included by special arrangement with the originators or publishers. Some of these sources are mentioned in the acknowledgments below. One source, ACCRA, represents what might well be described as the spine of the *ACLS-3* database by providing a large number of items for a large number of cities.

ACCRA. A large database was obtained by a special arrangement with ACCRA, the association of applied community researchers (formerly the American Chambers of Commerce Research Association). ACCRA is an affiliate of the American Chamber of Commerce Executives and the American Economic Development Council. ACCRA produces the *ACCRA Cost of Living Index* in cooperation with chambers of commerce or analogous organizations in 300 urban areas. Participation in the survey is voluntary and communities covered also change from one reporting period to the next.

In addition to price information, ACCRA provides a weighted **cost of living index** for the city as a whole ("composite index") and for components of expenditure (e.g., "grocery items," "utilities," etc.). These indexes are also included in *ACLS*. The user should note that these indexes are specifically built to reflect "differentials for a mid-management standard of living." The use of ACCRA indexes, therefore, should not be applied indiscriminately to other groupings, e.g., "clerical workers" or "all urban consumers".

All sources are cited by number in each entry of *ACLS* in the column headed by the abbreviation "Ref." The reference numbers can be used as a guide to the sources shown in the *List of Sources*. A given source may be cited more than once if several different issues of the same source were used. This applies especially to periodicals.

Source entries include comments and notes that are useful for further interpretation of the data. Wherever possible, the address and telephone number of the publisher, association, or agency have been provided as a convenience for further research.

ACKNOWLEDGMENTS

A compilation like *ACLS* would not be possible without the help of numerous people who provided information, took time to discuss the availability of data, made useful referrals, and otherwise lent the editors a helping hand.

Furthermore, each source—whether containing many entries or just a few that filled a gap—was valued and appreciated.

The editors, therefore, would like to thank all those who made a contribution. Without intending to slight any contributor, we would like to acknowledge the unusual efforts on our behalf of the following persons/organizations:

- ACCRA
- American Public Transit Association (APTA)
- Bellcore, Inc.
- National Association of Realtors (NAR)
- National Association of Regulatory Utility Commissioners (NARUC)
- National Funeral Directors Association

COMMENTS AND SUGGESTIONS

Comments on *ACLS* and suggestions for improvement of its usefulness, format, and coverage are always welcome. Although every effort is made to maintain accuracy, errors may occasionally occur; the editors would be grateful if these are called to their attention. Please contact:

Editors

American Cost of Living Survey

Gale Group

27500 Drake Road

Farmington Hills, MI 48331-3535

248-699-GALE

ABBREVIATIONS

The following abbreviations are used throughout *American Cost of Living Survey*, 3rd edition.

<	less than
4Q	Fourth Quarter
ABA	American Bar Association
ACCRA	American Chamber of Commerce Researchers Association
addl	additional
adm	Admission
APTA	American Public Transit Association
ARM	Adjustable rate mortgage
br	bedroom
BTU	British Thermal Unit
c	city, metro
cf	cubic foot
chg	charge
conv	Convertible
CPI	Consumer Price Index
cu ft	cubic foot
DL	Driver's License
DOE	Department of Energy
doz	dozen
EIA	Energy Information Administration
exc	except, excluding
exp	expenditures
FHFB	Federal Housing Finance Board
FHWA	Federal Highway Administration
ft	foot
FTC	Federal Trade Commission
gal	gallon
gov't	government
HMO	Health Maintenance Organization

in	inch
inc	including
inst	Installation
KWh	Kilowatt hour
lab	labor
lb	pound
mg	milligram
mi	mile
mil	million
min	minimum, minute
min lab chg	Minimum labor charge
misc	miscellaneous
ml	milliliter
mos	month
NARUC	National Association of Regulatory Utility Commissioners
NFDA	National Funeral Directors Association
orig	Origination, original
oz	ounce
pk	package
priv	private
r	region
s	state
sq ft	square foot
therm	Equivalent to 100,000 BTU
unfurn	Unfurnished
USDA	United States Department of Agriculture
yr	year

LIST OF ITEMS COVERED

This listing shows all categories of items contained in *American Cost of Living Survey*, 3rd Edition. Items are arranged in alphabetical order under topic headings as they appear in the body of the book.

Average annual expenditures
Composite, ACCRA index

Alcoholic Beverages
Alcoholic beverage purchases
Beer, Heineken, 12-oz, ex deposit
J & B Scotch
Malt beverages, all types, all sizes, any origin
Wine, Livingston or Gallo, Chablis blanc
Wine, red and white table, all sizes, any origin

Appliances
Appliance repair, service call, washing machine
Major appliances, expenditures on
Small appliances, housewares, expenditures on

Banking and Money
Mortgage interest and charges paid
Mortgage principal paid on owned property
Mortgage rate, incl. points and orig. fee, 30-yr. conv.
  fixed or ARM
Vehicle finance charges paid

Business Expenses
Business travel, car rental
Business travel, food
Business travel, hotel
Medical office space cost
Office space, 11-20 storey building
Office space, 2-4 storey building
Office space, 5-10 storey building
Office space, central business district, Class A
Office space, outside central business district, Class
  A

Charity
Cash contributions, expenditures

Child Care
Child care fee, one year old
Child care fee, six year old
Child care fee, three year old
Child raising cost, total
Child's child care and education
Child's clothing
Child's food
Child's health care
Child's housing

Child's personal care, reading
Daycare
Daycare, 3-year old, 5 days, 8 hrs/day
Infant care, federal child care center
Nannies: criminal background check

Clothing
Apparel and services purchases
Boys' brief, cotton
Boys, 2 to 15, expenditures on
Children under 2, expenditures on
Footwear, expenditures on
Girls, 2 to 15, expenditures on
Men and boys, expenditures on
Men, 16 and over, expenditures on
Shirt, man's dress shirt
Slacks, man's "No Wrinkles" khaki
Women, 16 and over, expenditures on

Communications
Cable modem installation, Adelphi
Cable modem installation, AT&T-BIS
Cable modem installation, Bresnan
Cable modem installation, Cablevision Systems
Cable modem installation, Charter
Cable modem installation, Comcast
Cable modem installation, Cox
Cable modem installation, Intermedia
Cable modem installation, Jones Intercable
Cable modem installation, Marcus
Cable modem installation, Media One
Cable modem installation, Time Warner
Cable modem rate, cable subscriber, Adelphi
Cable modem rate, cable subscriber, AT&T-BIS
Cable modem rate, cable subscriber, Bresnan
Cable modem rate, cable subscriber, Cablevision
  Systems
Cable modem rate, cable subscriber, Century
Cable modem rate, cable subscriber, Charter
Cable modem rate, cable subscriber, Comcast
Cable modem rate, cable subscriber, Cox
Cable modem rate, cable subscriber, Intermedia
Cable modem rate, cable subscriber, Jones
  Intercable

Fountain grass (pennisetum)
Hanging basket (10 in)
Hardy geranium (geranium)
Hosta (hosta)
Lilac (syrubga vulgaris)
Miscellaneous purchases
Rhododendron (rhododendron)
Sage (salvia)
Snowblower, single stage
Wintercreeper euonymus (euonymus fortunei)

Groceries

Groceries, ACCRA Index
American processed cheese
Antibiotic ointment, Polysporin
Apples
Apples, red delicious
Baby food, strained vegetables or fruit, lowest price
Bacon
Bacon, sliced
Bakery products, expenditures on
Bananas
Beans, dried, any type, all sizes
Beef for stew, boneless
Beef or hamburger, ground
Beef, expenditures on
Bologna, all beef or mixed
Box of cereal
Bread, French
Bread, white
Bread, white, 20 oz loaf
Bread, white, pan
Bread, whole wheat, pan
Broccoli
Butter, salted, grade AA, stick
Butter, yoghurt, cheese, etc, expenditures on
Cabbage
Cereals and bakery product purchases
Cereals and cereal products, expenditures on
Cheddar cheese
Cheddar cheese, mild
Cheddar cheese, natural
Cheerios, 10 oz box
Cheese, Kraft grated Parmesan
Chicken breast, bone-in
Chicken legs, bone-in
Chicken, fresh, whole
Chicken, whole fryer
Chops, boneless,
Chuck roast, graded and ungraded, excl U.S. prime and choice
Chuck roast, U.S. choice, boneless
Cigarettes, Winston, Kings
Coca cola, 2l bottle
Coffee, 100%, ground roast, all sizes
Coffee, instant, plain, regular, all sizes

Coffee, vacuum-packed
Cola, non diet,
Cookies, chocolate chip
Corn Flakes, Kellogg's or Post Toasties
Corn oil, Mazola, 32 oz
Corn, frozen, whole kernel, lowest price
Cost of food, family of four
Crackers, soda, salted
Dairy product purchases
Detergent (Tide), 33 oz
Dishwashing soap (Joy), 28 oz
Eggs, expenditures on
Eggs, Grade A or AA
Eggs, grade A, large
Eggs, grade AA, large
Fats and oils, expenditures on
Fish and seafood, expenditures on
Flour, all purpose
Flour, white, all purpose
Food (excl fruit and vegetables), eaten at home, purchases
Food cooked on trips, expenditures on
Food purchases
Food purchases, eaten away from home
Food purchases, food eaten at home
Fresh fruits, expenditures on
Fresh milk and cream, expenditures on
Fresh vegetables, expenditures on
Fruit and vegetable purchases
Grade A large eggs
Grapefruit
Grapes, Thompson, seedless
Ground beef, 100% beef
Ground beef, lean and extra lean
Ground chuck
Ground chuck, 100% beef
Ham, boneless, excl canned
Ham, rump or shank half, bone-in, smoked
Head of lettuce
Ice cream, prepackaged, bulk, regular
Juice (12-oz can)
Ketchup (Heinz), 20 oz.
Lemons
Lettuce, iceberg
Loaf of bread
Margarine, Blue Bonnet or Parkay, stick
Margarine, soft, tubs
Mayonnaise, Kraft, 32 oz
Meats, poultry, fish, and egg purchases
Milk, fresh, low fat,
Milk, fresh, whole, fortified
Milk, whole
Nonalcoholic beverages, expenditures on
Orange juice, frozen concentrate
Orange juice, Minute Maid frozen

Oranges, Navel
Oranges, Valencia
Peaches
Peaches, halves or slices, Hunt's, Del Monte, or
Libby's
Peanut butter, creamy, all sizes
Pears, Anjou
Peas, green, Del Monte or Green Giant
Pork chops, center cut, bone-in
Pork sausage, fresh, loose
Pork shoulder picnic, bone-in, smoked
Pork, expenditures on
Potato chips
Potatoes, frozen, french fried
Potatoes, russet
Potatoes, white or red
Potatoes, white, all types
Poultry, expenditures on
Processed fruits, expenditures on
Processed vegetables, expenditures on
Red Delicious apples
Rice, white, long grain, uncooked
Round roast, graded and ungraded, excl U.S. prime
and choice
Round roast, U.S. choice, boneless
Round steak, graded and ungraded, excl U.S. prime
and choice
Sausage, Jimmy Dean/Owens pork
Shortening, vegetable oil blends
Shortening, vegetable, Crisco
Sirloin steak
Sirloin steak, graded and ungraded, excl U.S. prime
and choice
Sirloin tip roast
Soda (Coke), 2 liter bottle
Soft drink, Coca Cola, ex deposit
Spaghetti and macaroni
Steak, round, U.S. choice, boneless
Steak, sirloin, U.S. choice, boneless
Steak, T-bone
Steak, T-bone, U.S. choice, bone-in
Strawberries, dry pint
Sugar and other sweets, expenditures on
Sugar, cane or beet
Sugar, white, 33-80 ounce package
Sugar, white, all sizes
Tobacco products and smoking supplies purchases
Tomatoes, field grown
Tomatoes, Hunt's or Del Monte
Tuna, chunk, light
Tuna, light, chunk
Turkey, frozen, whole
Vegetable oil, Crisco, 32 oz
Whole fryer
Whole milk

Yogurt, natural, fruit flavored
Health Care
Health care, ACCRA Index
Cardiac catheterization, ave hospital/physician
charges
Childbirth, Cesarean delivery
Childbirth, vaginal delivery
Dentist's fee, adult teeth cleaning and periodic oral
exam
Doctor's fee, routine exam, established patient
Drugs, expenditures on
Health care purchases
Health insurance expenditures
Home health care aide cost, licensed agency
Hospital bed, semi private room
Hospital care, private room
Hysterectomy, laproscopically-assisted, ave
hospital/physician charges
Hysterectomy, vaginal, ave hospital and physician
charges
Laser eye surgery
Medicaid dispensing fee
Medical services expenditures
Medical supplies, expenditures on
Nursing home care
Nursing home costs, private room
Nursing home stay, private room
Plastic surgery, breast augmentation
Plastic surgery, breast lift
Plastic surgery, facelift
Plastic surgery, hair transplantation
Plastic surgery, lip augmentation
Plastic surgery, lower body lift
Plastic surgery, thigh lift
Household Goods
Dishwashing powder, Cascade
Floor coverings, expenditures on
Furniture, expenditures on
Hockey mask
House paint
Household furnishings and equipment purchases
Household textiles, expenditures on
Lamp
Laundry and cleaning supplies, expenditures on
Poinsettia, fake
Shirt, flannel
Tissues, facial, Kleenex brand
TV stand
Housing
Housing, ACCRA Index
Apartment rent
Apartment rent, 2 bedroom
Condominium ave price
Home price, existing, ave
Home price, median

Home price, single family, ave
Home purchase, 2,000 sq ft
Home value, median
Home, 2200 sq ft, 4-br, 2-bath, 2-car garage, average
Home, suburban, 2,200 square feet
House payment, principal and interest, 25% down payment
House, 2-story, 2,400 sq ft, 2-car garage, new
House, 2400 sq ft, 8000 sq ft lot, new, urban, utilities
Household operation expenditures
Housekeeping supplies purchases
Housing, expenditures on
Lodging expenditures
Maintenance, repairs, insurance expenditures
Monthly rental value of owned home
Owned dwellings, expenditures own
Rent expenditures
Rent, apartment, 2 br, 1 1/2-2 baths, unfurn, 950 sq ft, water
Rental unit, 1 bedroom, with utilities
Rental unit, 2 bedroom, with utilities
Rental unit, 3 bedroom, with utilities
Rental unit, 4 bedroom, with utilities
Shelter, expenditures on
Single-family home ave price
Single-family home rent
Single-family home, ave construction cost
Single-family home, purchase price
Two-bedroom apartment rent

Insurance and Pensions

Auto insurance
Auto insurance premium
Auto insurance, no teens
Life and other personal insurance purchases
Medigap health insurance, Plan H
Medigap health insurance, Plan I
Medigap health insurance, Plan J
Pensions and Social Security, expenditures on
Personal insurance and pensions, expenditures on

Legal Fees

Combination hunting and fishing license
Divorce, filing fee
Driver's license fee
Fishing license
Hunting license
Parking in front of hydrant, fine
Parking in loading zone, fine
Parking meter violation, fine

Personal Goods

Deodorant (Secret), 1.7 oz
Personal care products and services purchases
Shampoo, Alberto VO5
Toothpaste, Crest or Colgate

Personal Services

Detective service, finding a missing person

Dry cleaning, man's 2-pc suit
Man's haircut, barbershop, no styling
Navel piercing
Personal services, household, expenditures on
Personal trainer
Tatooing
Tongue piercing
Woman's shampoo, trim, blow-dry, no style-change

Pets

Kennel charges, dog
Pets, dog day care service
Pets, toys, and playground equipment, expenditures on

Restaurant Food

Cheeseburger, 1/4-lb, large fries, medium soft drink, excl tax
Chicken, fried, thigh and drumstick, KFC/Church's
Fine restaurant meal
Hamburger with cheese, McDonald's
McDonald Quarterpounder
Pizza, Pizza Hut or Pizza Inn
Starbucks latte

Taxes

Federal income taxes paid
Personal taxes, expenditures on
Property taxes paid
State and local income taxes paid

Transportation

Transportation, ACCRA Index
Auto operation, annual cost
Automobile insurance
Bus fare, one-way
Bus fare, to central business district
Cars and trucks, new, expenditures on
Cars and trucks, used, expenditures on
Commuter rail, one-way
Diesel at the pump
Ferry boat transit fare, one-way
Gas and oil for transportation
Gasoline and motor oil purchases
Gasoline before-tax price (cents)
Heavy rail transit fare, one-way
Household transportation expenditures
Light rail transit fare, one-way
Maintenance and repair expenditures
Monorail transit fare, one-way
Motorcycle license fee
Parking at airport, lowest rate
Public transit expenditures
Public transportation, expenditures on
Subway token
Tire balance, computer or spin balance, front
Transportation purchases
Trolley bus transit fare, one-way
Vehicle expenses

Abilene, TX

Item	Per	Value	Date	Ref.
Composite, ACCRA index		92.50	3/01	4c
Alcoholic Beverages				
Alcoholic beverage purchases	yr	253	1999	30r
Beer, Heineken, 12-oz, ex deposit	6	6.63	3/01	4c
J & B Scotch	750-ml	21.51	3/01	4c
Malt beverages, all types, all sizes, any origin	16 oz	0.96	7/01	11r
Wine, Livingston or Gallo, Chablis blanc	1.5 liter	4.85	3/01	4c
Appliances				
Appliance repair, service call, washing machine	min lab chg	43.63	3/01	4c
Major appliances, expenditures on	yr	172	1999	30r
Small appliances, housewares, expenditures on	yr	81	1999	30r
Banking and Money				
Mortgage interest and charges paid	yr	2039	1999	30r
Mortgage principal paid on owned property	yr	1026	1999	30r
Mortgage rate, incl. points and orig. fee, 30-yr. conv. fixed or ARM	mos	6.94	3/01	4c
Vehicle finance charges paid	yr	365	1999	30r
Charity				
Cash contributions, expenditures	yr	1127	1999	30r
Child Care				
Child raising cost, total, age 0-2	yr	8540	1999	60r
Child raising cost, total, age 3-5	yr	8780	1999	60r
Child raising cost, total, age 6-8	yr	8820	1999	60r
Child raising cost, total, age 9-11	yr	8800	1999	60r
Child raising cost, total, age 12-14	yr	9510	1999	60r
Child raising cost, total, age 15-17	yr	9740	1999	60r
Child's child care and education, age 0-2	yr	1380	1999	60r
Child's child care and education, age 3-5	yr	1520	1999	60r
Child's child care and education, age 6-8	yr	990	1999	60r
Child's child care and education, age 9-11	yr	650	1999	60r
Child's child care and education, age 12-14	yr	490	1999	60r
Child's child care and education, age 15-17	yr	840	1999	60r
Child's clothing, age 0-2	yr	480	1999	60r
Child's clothing, age 3-5	yr	470	1999	60r
Child's clothing, age 6-8	yr	520	1999	60r
Child's clothing, age 9-11	yr	570	1999	60r
Child's clothing, age 12-14	yr	950	1999	60r
Child's clothing, age 15-17	yr	850	1999	60r
Child's food, age 0-2	yr	1000	1999	60r
Child's food, age 3-5	yr	1160	1999	60r
Child's food, age 6-8	yr	1490	1999	60r
Child's food, age 9-11	yr	1770	1999	60r
Child's food, age 12-14	yr	1770	1999	60r
Child's food, age 15-17	yr	1980	1999	60r
Child's health care, age 0-2	yr	620	1999	60r
Child's health care, age 3-5	yr	590	1999	60r
Child's health care, age 6-8	yr	680	1999	60r
Child's health care, age 9-11	yr	720	1999	60r
Child's health care, age 12-14	yr	730	1999	60r
Child's health care, age 15-17	yr	760	1999	60r
Child's housing, age 0-2	yr	3070	1999	60r
Child's housing, age 3-5	yr	3050	1999	60r
Child's housing, age 6-8	yr	3010	1999	60r
Child's housing, age 9-11	yr	2850	1999	60r
Child's housing, age 12-14	yr	3040	1999	60r
Child's housing, age 15-17	yr	2650	1999	60r
Child's personal care, reading, age 0-2	yr	910	1999	60r
Child's personal care, reading, age 3-5	yr	930	1999	60r
Child's personal care, reading, age 6-8	yr	960	1999	60r
Child's personal care, reading, age 9-11	yr	1000	1999	60r

Item	Per	Value	Date	Ref.
Child Care - continued				
Child's personal care, reading, age 12-14	yr	1170	1999	60r
Child's personal care, reading, age 15-17	yr	950	1999	60r
Clothing				
Apparel and services purchases	yr	1610	1999	30r
Boys' brief, cotton	3	6.19	3/01	4c
Boys, 2 to 15, expenditures on	yr	89	1999	30r
Children under 2, expenditures on	yr	79	1999	30r
Footwear, expenditures on	yr	283	1999	30r
Girls, 2 to 15, expenditures on	yr	103	1999	30r
Men and boys, expenditures on	yr	351	1999	30r
Men, 16 and over, expenditures on	yr	262	1999	30r
Shirt, man's dress shirt		26.50	3/01	4c
Slacks, man's "No Wrinkles" khaki		30.99	3/01	4c
Women, 16 and over, expenditures on	yr	538	1999	30r
Communications				
Cable modem installation, AT&T-BIS		150.00	6/99	103s
Cable modem installation, Marcus		499.00	6/99	103s
Cable modem installation, Time Warner		75.00-225.00	6/99	103s
Cable modem rate, cable subscriber, AT&T-BIS	mos	39.95	6/99	103s
Cable modem rate, cable subscriber, Marcus	mos	14.95-49.95	6/99	103s
Cable modem rate, cable subscriber, Time Warner	mos	39.95-49.95	6/99	103s
Cable modem rate, non-cable subscriber, Marcus	mos	60.95	6/99	103s
Cable modem rate, non-cable subscriber, Time Warner	mos	39.95-54.95	6/99	103s
Newspaper subscription, daily and Sunday delivery	mos	15.50	3/01	4c
Phone line, single, business, field visit	inst.	71.90	12/97	17s
Phone line, single, business, no field visit	inst.	57.30	12/97	17s
Phone line, single, residence, field visit	inst.	52.95	12/97	17s
Phone line, single, residence, no field visit	inst.	38.35	12/97	17s
Postage and stationery, expenditures on	yr	104	1999	30r
Postal rate, express mail, up to half-pound		12.45	7/01	108r
Postal rate, letter, first class, first ounce		0.34	7/01	108r
Postal rate, letter, two ounces		0.57	7/01	108r
Postal rate, post card		0.21	7/01	108r
Postal rate, priority mail, two pounds		3.95	7/01	108r
Postal rate, priority mail, up to one pound		3.50	7/01	108r
Telephone bill, family of three	mos	17.94	3/01	4c
Telephone services, expenditures on	yr	860	1999	30r
Education				
Board, 4-year private college/university	yr	2198	1996	38s
Board, 4-year public college/university	yr	1759	1996	38s
Education expenditures	yr	431	1999	30r
Room, 4-year private college/university	yr	2000	1996	38s
Room, 4-year public college/university	yr	1885	1996	38s
Total cost, 4-year private college/university	yr	13156	1996	38s
Total cost, 4-year public college/university	yr	5464	1996	38s
Tuition, 2-year public college/university, in state	yr	771	1996	38s
Tuition, 4-year private college/university, in state	yr	8959	1996	38s
Tuition, 4-year public college/university	yr	1820	1996	38s
Energy and Fuels				
Electricity	KWh	0.09	7/01	11r
Electricity	500 KWhs	47.29	7/01	11r

Values are in dollars or fractions of dollars. In the column headed *Ref*, references are shown to sources. Each reference is followed by a letter. These refer to the geographical level for which data were reported: s=State, r=Region, and c=City or metro. The abbreviation *ex* is used to mean *except* or *excluding*; *exp* stands for *expenditures*. For other abbreviations and further explanations, please see the Introduction.

Abilene, TX - continued

Item	Per	Value	Date	Ref.
Energy and Fuels				
Energy, combined forms, 2400 sq ft	mos	125.20	3/01	4c
Fuel oil #2	gal	1.43	7/01	11r
Fuel oil and other fuels, expenditures on	yr	45	1999	30r
Gas, natural, commercial rate	1000 cf	6.94	11/00	88s
Gas, regular unleaded, cash, self-service	gal	1.33	3/01	4c
Gasoline, all types	gal	1.60	7/01	11r
Gasoline, unleaded midgrade	gal	1.65	7/01	11r
Gasoline, unleaded premium	gal	1.74	7/01	11r
Natural gas, expenditures on	yr	164	1999	30r
Utility (piped) gas, therm		1.01	7/01	11r
Utility (piped) gas, 40 therms		44.29	7/01	11r
Utility (piped) gas, 100 therms		97.44	7/01	11r
Entertainment				
Bowling, Saturday evening rate	line	2.50	3/01	4c
Entertainment purchases	yr	1574	1999	30r
Fees and admissions paid	yr	371	1999	30r
Monopoly game, Parker Brothers', No. 9	game	11.21	3/01	4c
Movie, first-run, Saturday, evening	adm.	6.58	3/01	4c
Reading purchases	yr	121	1999	30r
Television, radios, sound equipment, expenditures on	yr	561	1999	30r
Tennis balls, yellow, Wilson or Penn, 3	can	2.25	3/01	4c
Funerals				
Total cost of funeral		5842.28	1/99	78r
Acknowledgement cards		28.35	1/99	78r
Casket		2494.29	1/99	78r
Cosmetology, hair, other preparation		109.22	1/99	78r
Embalming		361.42	1/99	78r
Funeral at funeral home		349.20	1/99	78r
Hearse (local)		161.91	1/99	78r
Professional service charges		1116.50	1/99	78r
Service car/van		65.56	1/99	78r
Transfer of remains to funeral home		143.56	1/99	78r
Vault		785.25	1/99	78r
Visitation/viewing		227.02	1/99	78r
Groceries				
Groceries, ACCRA Index		86.70	3/01	4c
American processed cheese	lb	3.50	7/01	11r
Antibiotic ointment, Polysporin	0.5 oz	4.74	3/01	4c
Baby food, strained vegetables or fruit, lowest price	4-4.5 oz	0.28	3/01	4c
Bakery products, expenditures on	yr	261	1999	30r
Bananas	lb	0.42	3/01	4c
Bananas	lb	0.47	7/01	11r
Beans, dried, any type, all sizes	lb	0.63	7/01	11r
Beef for stew, boneless	lb	2.86	7/01	11r
Beef or hamburger, ground	lb	1.31	3/01	4c
Beef, expenditures on	yr	210	1999	30r
Bologna, all beef or mixed	lb	2.29	7/01	11r
Bread, French	lb	1.66	7/01	11r
Bread, white	loaf	0.64	3/01	4c
Bread, white, pan	lb	0.87	7/01	11r
Bread, whole wheat, pan	lb	1.38	7/01	11r
Broccoli	lb	1.04	7/01	11r
Butter, salted, grade AA, stick	lb	2.26	7/01	11r
Butter, yoghurt, cheese, etc, expenditures on	yr	170	1999	30r
Cabbage	lb	0.42	7/01	11r
Cereals and cereal products, expenditures on	yr	140	1999	30r
Cheddar cheese, natural	lb	3.75	7/01	11r
Cheese, Kraft grated Parmesan	8 oz	3.47	3/01	4c
Chicken breast, bone-in	lb	1.85	7/01	11r
Chicken legs, bone-in	lb	1.34	7/01	11r
Chicken, fresh, whole	lb	1.05	7/01	11r
Chicken, whole fryer	lb	0.85	3/01	4c
Chops, boneless,	lb	4.13	7/01	11r
Chuck roast, graded and ungraded, excl U.S. prime and choice	lb	2.35	7/01	11r
Chuck roast, U.S. choice, boneless	lb	2.67	7/01	11r
Cigarettes, Winston, Kings	carton	28.47	3/01	4c
Coffee, 100%, ground roast, all sizes	lb	2.88	7/01	11r

Abilene, TX - continued

Item	Per	Value	Date	Ref.
Groceries - continued				
Coffee, instant, plain, regular, all sizes	16 oz	9.25	7/01	11r
Coffee, vacuum-packed	13 oz	2.26	3/01	4c
Cola, non diet,	2 liter	1.11	7/01	11r
Corn Flakes, Kellogg's or Post Toasties	18 oz	2.15	3/01	4c
Corn, frozen, whole kernel, lowest price	16 oz	1.20	3/01	4c
Crackers, soda, salted	lb	1.70	7/01	11r
Dairy product purchases	yr	282	1999	30r
Eggs, expenditures on	yr	32	1999	30r
Eggs, Grade A or AA	dozen	1.05	3/01	4c
Fats and oils, expenditures on	yr	79	1999	30r
Fish and seafood, expenditures on	yr	99	1999	30r
Flour, white, all purpose	lb	0.32	7/01	11r
Food (excl fruit and vegetables), eaten at home, purchases	yr	815	1999	30r
Food cooked on trips, expenditures on	yr	36	1999	30r
Food purchases	yr	4533	1999	30r
Food purchases, eaten away from home	yr	1873	1999	30r
Food purchases, food eaten at home	yr	2660	1999	30r
Fresh fruits, expenditures on	yr	128	1999	30r
Fresh milk and cream, expenditures on	yr	112	1999	30r
Fresh vegetables, expenditures on	yr	131	1999	30r
Fruit and vegetable purchases	yr	438	1999	30r
Grapefruit	lb	0.59	7/01	11r
Grapes, Thompson, seedless	lb	2.12	7/01	11r
Ground beef, 100% beef	lb	1.76	7/01	11r
Ground beef, lean and extra lean	lb	2.60	7/01	11r
Ground chuck, 100% beef	lb	2.08	7/01	11r
Ham, boneless, excl canned	lb	2.71	7/01	11r
Ham, rump or shank half, bone-in, smoked	lb	2.19	7/01	11r
Ice cream, prepackaged, bulk, regular	1/2 gal	3.93	7/01	11r
Lemons	lb	1.32	7/01	11r
Lettuce, iceberg	head	0.99	3/01	4c
Lettuce, iceberg	lb	0.76	7/01	11r
Margarine, Blue Bonnet or Parkay, stick	lb	0.82	3/01	4c
Milk, fresh, low fat,	gal	2.75	7/01	11r
Milk, fresh, whole, fortified	gal	2.97	7/01	11r
Milk, whole	1/2 gal	1.52	3/01	4c
Nonalcoholic beverages, expenditures on	yr	228	1999	30r
Orange juice, frozen concentrate	16 oz	1.95	7/01	11r
Orange juice, Minute Maid frozen	12 oz	1.42	3/01	4c
Oranges, Navel	lb	0.73	7/01	11r
Oranges, Valencia	lb	0.55	7/01	11r
Peaches, halves or slices, Hunt's, Del Monte, or Libby's	29 oz	1.74	3/01	4c
Peanut butter, creamy, all sizes	lb	1.83	7/01	11r
Pears, Anjou	lb	0.98	7/01	11r
Peas, green, Del Monte or Green Giant	15 oz	0.59	3/01	4c
Pork chops, center cut, bone-in	lb	3.33	7/01	11r
Pork sausage, fresh, loose	lb	2.59	7/01	11r
Pork shoulder picnic, bone-in, smoked	lb	1.12	7/01	11r
Pork, expenditures on	yr	162	1999	30r
Potato chips	16 oz	3.59	7/01	11r
Potatoes, frozen, french fried	lb	1.00	7/01	11r
Potatoes, white or red	10 lb	2.45	3/01	4c
Potatoes, white, all types	lb	0.44	7/01	11r
Poultry, expenditures on	yr	137	1999	30r
Processed fruits, expenditures on	yr	97	1999	30r
Processed vegetables, expenditures on	yr	82	1999	30r
Rice, white, long grain, uncooked	lb	0.51	7/01	11r
Round roast, graded and ungraded, excl U.S. prime and choice	lb	2.96	7/01	11r
Round steak, graded and ungraded, excl U.S. prime and choice	lb	3.11	7/01	11r
Sausage, Jimmy Dean/Owens pork	lb	2.61	3/01	4c
Shortening, vegetable, Crisco	3 lb	2.92	3/01	4c
Sirloin steak, graded and ungraded, excl U.S. prime and choice	lb	4.23	7/01	11r
Soft drink, Coca Cola, ex deposit	2 liter	1.11	3/01	4c
Spaghetti and macaroni	lb	0.78	7/01	11r
Steak, round, U.S. choice, boneless	lb	3.56	7/01	11r
Steak, sirloin, U.S. choice, boneless	lb	5.65	7/01	11r
Steak, T-bone	lb	5.37	3/01	4c

Values are in dollars or fractions of dollars. In the column headed *Ref*, references are shown to sources. Each reference is followed by a letter. These refer to the geographical level for which data were reported: s=State, r=Region, and c=City or metro. The abbreviation *ex* is used to mean *except* or *excluding*; *exp* stands for expenditures. For other abbreviations and further explanations, please see the Introduction.

Abilene, TX - continued

Item	Per	Value	Date	Ref.
Groceries				
Strawberries, dry pint	12 oz	1.50	7/01	11r
Sugar and other sweets, expenditures on	yr	99	1999	30r
Sugar, cane or beet	4 lbs	1.42	3/01	4c
Sugar, white, 33-80 ounce package	lb	0.39	7/01	11r
Sugar, white, all sizes	lb	0.42	7/01	11r
Tobacco products and smoking supplies purchases	yr	288	1999	30r
Tomatoes, field grown	lb	1.43	7/01	11r
Tomatoes, Hunt's or Del Monte	14.5 oz	0.90	3/01	4c
Tuna, chunk, light	6 oz	0.54	3/01	4c
Tuna, light, chunk	lb	1.77	7/01	11r
Turkey, frozen, whole	lb	1.05	7/01	11r
Goods and Services				
Miscellaneous goods and services, ACCRA Index		97.70	3/01	4c
B&B Japanese maple (acer japonicum)	gal	79.98-99.00	4/00	93r
Boxwood (buxus)	2 gal	12.98-18.99	4/00	93r
Christmas tree, noble fir		40-60	2000	65s
Daylilly (hemerocallis)	gal	7.96-11.00	4/00	93r
Flat of annuals		13.99-27.99	4/00	93r
Fountain grass (pennisetum)	gal	6.96-9.00	4/00	93r
Hanging basket (10 in)		9.99-24.99	4/00	93r
Hardy geranium (geranium)	gal	5.96-8.00	4/00	93r
Hosta (hosta)	gal	8.96-12.99	4/00	93r
Lilac (syrubga vulgaris)	2 gal	13.00-19.99	4/00	93r
Rhododendron (rhododendron)	2 gal	12.98-29.99	4/00	93r
Sage (salvia)	gal	5.96-8.00	4/00	93r
Wintercreeper euonymus (euonymus fortunei)	2 gal	13.00-18.99	4/00	93r
Hunting license	yr	19.00	4/01	34s
Health Care				
Health care, ACCRA Index		91.80	3/01	4c
Cardiac catheterization, ave hospital/ physician charges		20140	1998	77s
Childbirth, Cesarean delivery		11587	1997	13r
Childbirth, vaginal delivery		6725	1997	13r
Dentist's fee, adult teeth cleaning and periodic oral exam	visit	68.00	3/01	4c
Doctor's fee, routine exam, established patient	visit	51.75	3/01	4c
Drugs, expenditures on	yr	399	1999	30r
Health care purchases	yr	1971	1999	30r
Health insurance expenditures	yr	933	1999	30r
Hospital care, private room	day	457.25	3/01	4c
Hysterectomy, laproscopically-assisted, ave hospital/physician charges		15700	1998	76s
Hysterectomy, vaginal, ave hospital and physician charges		12180	1998	76s
Medicaid dispensing fee		5.27	1999	87s
Medical services expenditures	yr	547	1999	30r
Medical supplies, expenditures on	yr	91	1999	30r
Household Goods				
Dishwashing powder, Cascade	50 oz	3.32	3/01	4c
Floor coverings, expenditures on	yr	44	1999	30r
Furniture, expenditures on	yr	335	1999	30r
Household furnishings and equipment purchases	yr	1328	1999	30r
Household textiles, expenditures on	yr	89	1999	30r
Laundry and cleaning supplies, expenditures on	yr	113	1999	30r

Abilene, TX - continued

Item	Per	Value	Date	Ref.
Household Goods - continued				
Tissues, facial, Kleenex brand	175	1.20	3/01	4c
Housing				
Housing, ACCRA Index		86.10	3/01	4c
Home price, existing, ave		160100	10/00	90r
Home value, median		112000	2001	53s
House, 2400 sq ft, 8000 sq ft lot, new, urban, utilities	total	183000	3/01	4c
House payment, principal and interest, 25% down payment	mos	908	3/01	4c
Household operation expenditures	yr	553	1999	30r
Housekeeping supplies purchases	yr	473	1999	30r
Housing, expenditures on	yr	10303	1999	30r
Maintenance, repairs, insurance expenditures	yr	699	1999	30r
Monthly rental value of owned home	mos	505	1999	30r
Owned dwellings, expenditures own	yr	3465	1999	30r
Rent expenditures	yr	1641	1999	30r
Rent, apartment, 2 br, 1 1/2-2 baths, unfurn, 950 sq ft, water	mos	544	3/01	4c
Rental unit, 1 bedroom, with utilities	mos	376	4/01	41c
Rental unit, 2 bedroom, with utilities	mos	485	4/01	41c
Rental unit, 3 bedroom, with utilities	mos	654	4/01	41c
Rental unit, 4 bedroom, with utilities	mos	795	4/01	41c
Shelter, expenditures on	yr	5467	1999	30r
Insurance and Pensions				
Life and other personal insurance purchases	yr	414	1999	30r
Pensions and Social Security, expenditures on	yr	2635	1999	30r
Personal insurance and pensions, expenditures on	yr	3048	1999	30r
Legal Fees				
Divorce, filing fee		150.00-200.00	4/01	35s
Driver's license fee	orig	24.00	1999	48s
Driver's license fee	renew	20.00	1999	48s
Fishing license	yr	19.00	4/01	34s
Personal Goods				
Personal care products and services purchases	yr	393	1999	30r
Shampoo, Alberto VO5	15 oz	1.03	3/01	4c
Toothpaste, Crest or Colgate	6-7 oz	2.12	3/01	4c
Personal Services				
Dry cleaning, man's 2-pc suit		5.83	3/01	4c
Man's haircut, barbershop, no styling		9.58	3/01	4c
Personal services, household, expenditures on	yr	258	1999	30r
Woman's shampoo, trim, blow-dry, no style-change		25.99	3/01	4c
Pets				
Pets, toys, and playground equipment, expenditures on	yr	306	1999	30r
Restaurant Food				
Chicken, fried, thigh and drumstick, KFC/Church's		2.48	3/01	4c
Hamburger with cheese, McDonald's	1/4 lb	2.05	3/01	4c
Pizza, Pizza Hut or Pizza Inn	11-12 in	9.69	3/01	4c
Taxes				
Federal income taxes paid	yr	2047	1999	30r
Personal taxes, expenditures on	yr	2554	1999	30r
Property taxes paid	yr	726	1999	30r
State and local income taxes paid	yr	363	1999	30r
Transportation				
Transportation, ACCRA Index		96.60	3/01	4c
Cars and trucks, new, expenditures on	yr	1648	1999	30r
Cars and trucks, used, expenditures on	yr	1651	1999	30r
Diesel at the pump	gal	1.18	10/99	73s
Gasoline and motor oil purchases	yr	1052	1999	30r

Values are in dollars or fractions of dollars. In the column headed *Ref*, references are shown to sources. Each reference is followed by a letter. These refer to the geographical level for which data were reported: s=State, r=Region, and c=City or metro. The abbreviation *ex* is used to mean *except* or *excluding*; *exp* stands for expenditures. For other abbreviations and further explanations, please see the Introduction.

Abilene, TX - continued

Item	Per	Value	Date	Ref.
Transportation				
Gasoline before-tax price (cents)	gal	101.30	10/00	43s
Maintenance and repair expenditures	yr	621	1999	30r
Public transportation, expenditures on	yr	298	1999	30r
Tire balance, computer or spin balance, front	wheel	7.87	3/01	4c
Transportation purchases	yr	6738	1999	30r
Vehicle expenses, miscellaneous, purchases	yr	2033	1999	30r
Vehicle insurance payments	yr	696	1999	30r
Vehicle purchases (net outlay)	yr	3354	1999	30r
Vehicle rental, lease expenditures	yr	352	1999	30r
Utilities				
Utilities, ACCRA Index		99.80	3/01	4c
Electrical bill, average	mos	87.17	9/00	9s
Electricity, 2400 sq ft, new home	mos	125.20	3/01	4c
Electricity, expenditures on	yr	1115	1999	30r
Electricity, summer, 250 KWh	mos	22.23	2/96	96c
Electricity, summer, 500 KWh	mos	38.45	2/96	96c
Electricity, summer, 750 KWh	mos	54.68	2/96	96c
Electricity, summer, 1000 KWh	mos	70.91	2/96	96c
Electricity cost, average	KWh	6.48	9/00	9s
Water and other public services, expenditures on	yr	298	1999	30r
Weddings				
Wedding (national average cost)		19936	2000	33r
Attendants' gifts		321	1998	33r
Bridal attendants' apparel (5 persons)		824	2000	33r
Bride's headpiece/veil		173	1998	33r
Bride's wedding dress		859	1998	33r
Clergy, religious facility fee		242	1998	33r
Engagement ring		3177	1998	33r
Flowers		789	1998	33r
Groom's formalwear rental		99	2000	33r
Limousine		410	1998	33r
Marriage license cost		36.00	4/01	35s
Men's formalwear (ushers, best man)		469	2000	33r
Mother of bride apparel		241	2000	33r
Music		866	1998	33r
Photography and videography		1368	1998	33r
Rehearsal dinner		728	1998	33r
Wedding invitations and announcements		341	1998	33r
Wedding reception		7968	2000	33r
Wedding rings (bride and groom)		1060	1998	33r

Akron, OH

Item	Per	Value	Date	Ref.
Average annual expenditures	yr	35369	1999	30r
Composite, ACCRA index		101.70	3/01	4c
Alcoholic Beverages				
Alcoholic beverage purchases	yr	304	1999	30r
Beer, Heineken, 12-oz, ex deposit	6	7.49	3/01	4c
J & B Scotch	750-ml	21.30	3/01	4c
Malt beverages, all types, all sizes, any origin	16 oz	0.93	7/01	11r
Wine, Livingston or Gallo, Chablis blanc	1.5 liter	5.49	3/01	4c
Wine, red and white table, all sizes, any origin	liter	7.04	7/01	11r
Appliances				
Appliance repair, service call, washing machine	min lab chg	37.05	3/01	4c
Major appliances, expenditures on	yr	165	1999	30r
Small appliances, housewares, expenditures on	yr	90	1999	30r
Banking and Money				
Mortgage interest and charges paid	yr	2277	1999	30r
Mortgage principal paid on owned property	yr	1230	1999	30r
Mortgage rate, incl. points and orig. fee, 30-yr. conv. fixed or ARM	mos	6.91	3/01	4c
Vehicle finance charges paid	yr	328	1999	30r
Business Expenses				
Business travel, car rental	day	51	2001	3c

Akron, OH - continued

Item	Per	Value	Date	Ref.
Business Expenses - continued				
Business travel, food	day	44	2001	3c
Business travel, hotel	day	88	2001	3c
Charity				
Cash contributions, expenditures	yr	1126	1999	30r
Child Care				
Child raising cost, total, age 0-2	yr	7890	1999	60r
Child raising cost, total, age 3-5	yr	8130	1999	60r
Child raising cost, total, age 6-8	yr	8170	1999	60r
Child raising cost, total, age 9-11	yr	8190	1999	60r
Child raising cost, total, age 12-14	yr	8890	1999	60r
Child raising cost, total, age 15-17	yr	9050	1999	60r
Child's child care and education, age 0-2	yr	1240	1999	60r
Child's child care and education, age 3-5	yr	1370	1999	60r
Child's child care and education, age 6-8	yr	880	1999	60r
Child's child care and education, age 9-11	yr	570	1999	60r
Child's child care and education, age 12-14	yr	420	1999	60r
Child's child care and education, age 15-17	yr	720	1999	60r
Child's clothing, age 0-2	yr	410	1999	60r
Child's clothing, age 3-5	yr	400	1999	60r
Child's clothing, age 6-8	yr	450	1999	60r
Child's clothing, age 9-11	yr	500	1999	60r
Child's clothing, age 12-14	yr	840	1999	60r
Child's clothing, age 15-17	yr	740	1999	60r
Child's food, age 0-2	yr	960	1999	60r
Child's food, age 3-5	yr	1120	1999	60r
Child's food, age 6-8	yr	1430	1999	60r
Child's food, age 9-11	yr	1710	1999	60r
Child's food, age 12-14	yr	1710	1999	60r
Child's food, age 15-17	yr	1920	1999	60r
Child's health care, age 0-2	yr	520	1999	60r
Child's health care, age 3-5	yr	500	1999	60r
Child's health care, age 6-8	yr	570	1999	60r
Child's health care, age 9-11	yr	610	1999	60r
Child's health care, age 12-14	yr	630	1999	60r
Child's health care, age 15-17	yr	650	1999	60r
Child's housing, age 0-2	yr	2860	1999	60r
Child's housing, age 3-5	yr	2840	1999	60r
Child's housing, age 6-8	yr	2800	1999	60r
Child's housing, age 9-11	yr	2650	1999	60r
Child's housing, age 12-14	yr	2840	1999	60r
Child's housing, age 15-17	yr	2440	1999	60r
Child's personal care, reading, age 0-2	yr	880	1999	60r
Child's personal care, reading, age 3-5	yr	900	1999	60r
Child's personal care, reading, age 6-8	yr	930	1999	60r
Child's personal care, reading, age 9-11	yr	970	1999	60r
Child's personal care, reading, age 12-14	yr	1150	1999	60r
Child's personal care, reading, age 15-17	yr	920	1999	60r
Clothing				
Apparel and services purchases	yr	1607	1999	30r
Boys' brief, cotton	3	5.84	3/01	4c
Boys, 2 to 15, expenditures on	yr	91	1999	30r
Children under 2, expenditures on	yr	59	1999	30r
Footwear, expenditures on	yr	285	1999	30r
Girls, 2 to 15, expenditures on	yr	116	1999	30r
Men and boys, expenditures on	yr	433	1999	30r
Men, 16 and over, expenditures on	yr	341	1999	30r
Shirt, man's dress shirt		24.30	3/01	4c
Slacks, man's "No Wrinkles" khaki		44.00	3/01	4c
Women, 16 and over, expenditures on	yr	490	1999	30r
Communications				
Cable modem installation, Adelphi		54.90	6/99	103s
Cable modem installation, Media One		100.00	6/99	103s
Cable modem installation, Time Warner		75.00-225.00	6/99	103s
Cable modem rate, cable subscriber, Adelphi	mos	34.95	6/99	103s
Cable modem rate, cable subscriber, Media One	mos	34.95-39.95	6/99	103s
Cable modem rate, cable subscriber, Time Warner	mos	39.95-49.95	6/99	103s

Values are in dollars or fractions of dollars. In the column headed *Ref*, references are shown to sources. Each reference is followed by a letter. These refer to the geographical level for which data were reported: s=State, r=Region, and c=City or metro. The abbreviation *ex* is used to mean *except* or *excluding*; *exp* stands for *expenditures*. For other abbreviations and further explanations, please see the Introduction.

Akron, OH - continued

Item	Per	Value	Date	Ref.
Communications				
Cable modem rate, non-cable subscriber, Adelphi	mos	44.95	6/99	103s
Cable modem rate, non-cable subscriber, Media One	mos	49.95	6/99	103s
Cable modem rate, non-cable subscriber, Time Warner	mos	39.95-54.95	6/99	103s
Newspaper subscription, daily and Sunday delivery	mos	15.22	3/01	4c
Phone line, single, business, field visit	inst.	56.32	12/97	17s
Phone line, single, business, no field visit	inst.	56.32	12/97	17s
Phone line, single, residence, field visit	inst.	31.10	12/97	17s
Phone line, single, residence, no field visit	inst.	31.10	12/97	17s
Postage and stationery, expenditures on	yr	140	1999	30r
Postal rate, express mail, up to half-pound		12.45	7/01	108r
Postal rate, letter, first class, first ounce		0.34	7/01	108r
Postal rate, letter, two ounces		0.57	7/01	108r
Postal rate, post card		0.21	7/01	108r
Postal rate, priority mail, two pounds		3.95	7/01	108r
Postal rate, priority mail, up to one pound		3.50	7/01	108r
Telephone bill, family of three	mos	19.95	3/01	4c
Telephone services, expenditures on	yr	830	1999	30r
Education				
Board, 4-year private college/university	yr	2414	1996	38s
Board, 4-year public college/university	yr	2181	1996	38s
Education expenditures	yr	583	1999	30r
Room, 4-year private college/university	yr	2349	1996	38s
Room, 4-year public college/university	yr	2386	1996	38s
Total cost, 4-year private college/university	yr	17139	1996	38s
Total cost, 4-year public college/university	yr	8169	1996	38s
Tuition, 2-year public college/university, in state	yr	2261	1996	38s
Tuition, 4-year private college/university, in state	yr	12377	1996	38s
Tuition, 4-year public college/university	yr	3603	1996	38s
Energy and Fuels				
Electricity	500 KWhs	46.59	7/01	11r
Energy, combined forms, 2400 sq ft	mos	154.96	3/01	4c
Energy, exc. electricity, 2400 sq ft	mos	74.10	3/01	4c
Fuel oil #2	gal	1.27	7/01	11r
Fuel oil and other fuels, expenditures on	yr	68	1999	30r
Gas, natural, commercial rate	1000 cf	8.65	11/00	88s
Gas, regular unleaded, cash, self-service	gal	1.50	3/01	4c
Gasoline, unleaded midgrade	gal	1.79	7/01	11r
Gasoline, unleaded premium	gal	1.86	7/01	11r
Gasoline, unleaded regular	gal	1.58	7/01	11r
Natural gas, expenditures on	yr	389	1999	30r
Utility (piped) gas, therm		0.81	7/01	11r
Utility (piped) gas, 40 therms		38.01	7/01	11r
Utility (piped) gas, 100 therms		81.75	7/01	11r
Entertainment				
Bowling, Saturday evening rate	line	2.83	3/01	4c
Entertainment purchases	yr	1984	1999	30r
Fees and admissions paid	yr	444	1999	30r
Monopoly game, Parker Brothers', No. 9	game	11.99	3/01	4c
Movie, first-run, Saturday, evening	adm.	7.25	3/01	4c
Television, radios, sound equipment, expenditures on	yr	580	1999	30r
Tennis balls, yellow, Wilson or Penn, 3	can	2.05	3/01	4c
Funerals				
Cosmetology, hair, other preparation		178.32	1/99	78r
Embalming		408.19	1/99	78r
Funeral at funeral home		362.13	1/99	78r
Professional service charges		1375.51	1/99	78r
Transfer of remains to funeral home		155.92	1/99	78r
Visitation/viewing		294.38	1/99	78r
Groceries				
Groceries, ACCRA Index		106.20	3/01	4c
Antibiotic ointment, Polysporin	0.5 oz	4.91	3/01	4c

Akron, OH - continued

Item	Per	Value	Date	Ref.
Groceries - continued				
Baby food, strained vegetables or fruit, lowest price	4-4.5 oz	0.45	3/01	4c
Bacon, sliced	lb	3.15	7/01	11r
Bakery products, expenditures on	yr	281	1999	30r
Bananas	lb	0.42	3/01	4c
Bananas	lb	0.48	7/01	11r
Beans, dried, any type, all sizes	lb	0.61	7/01	11r
Beef for stew, boneless	lb	3.08	7/01	11r
Beef or hamburger, ground	lb	1.92	3/01	4c
Beef, expenditures on	yr	217	1999	30r
Bologna, all beef or mixed	lb	2.52	7/01	11r
Bread, white	loaf	1.09	3/01	4c
Bread, white, pan	lb	1.06	7/01	11r
Broccoli	lb	0.91	7/01	11r
Butter, salted, grade AA, stick	lb	3.04	7/01	11r
Butter, yoghurt, cheese, etc, expenditures on	yr	183	1999	30r
Cereals and bakery product purchases	yr	430	1999	30r
Cereals and cereal products, expenditures on	yr	149	1999	30r
Cheese, Kraft grated Parmesan	8 oz	3.58	3/01	4c
Chicken, fresh, whole	lb	1.07	7/01	11r
Chicken, whole fryer	lb	1.24	3/01	4c
Chops, boneless,	lb	3.64	7/01	11r
Chuck roast, U.S. choice, boneless	lb	2.47	7/01	11r
Cigarettes, Winston, Kings	carton	25.37	3/01	4c
Coffee, 100%, ground roast, all sizes	lb	2.69	7/01	11r
Coffee, vacuum-packed	13 oz	2.77	3/01	4c
Cookies, chocolate chip	lb	2.87	7/01	11r
Corn Flakes, Kellogg's or Post Toasties	18 oz	2.86	3/01	4c
Corn, frozen, whole kernel, lowest price	16 oz	1.31	3/01	4c
Dairy product purchases	yr	304	1999	30r
Eggs, expenditures on	yr	26	1999	30r
Eggs, Grade A or AA	dozen	1.10	3/01	4c
Eggs, grade A, large	dozen	0.88	7/01	11r
Fats and oils, expenditures on	yr	75	1999	30r
Fish and seafood, expenditures on	yr	72	1999	30r
Food (excl fruit and vegetables), eaten at home, purchases	yr	887	1999	30r
Food cooked on trips, expenditures on	yr	44	1999	30r
Food purchases	yr	4802	1999	30r
Food purchases, eaten away from home	yr	2069	1999	30r
Food purchases, food eaten at home	yr	2733	1999	30r
Fresh fruits, expenditures on	yr	138	1999	30r
Fresh milk and cream, expenditures on	yr	120	1999	30r
Fresh vegetables, expenditures on	yr	126	1999	30r
Grapefruit	lb	0.66	7/01	11r
Grapes, Thompson, seedless	lb	1.64	7/01	11r
Ground beef, 100% beef	lb	1.64	7/01	11r
Ground beef, lean and extra lean	lb	2.16	7/01	11r
Ground chuck, 100% beef	lb	2.13	7/01	11r
Ham, boneless, excl canned	lb	2.62	7/01	11r
Ice cream, prepackaged, bulk, regular	1/2 gal	3.35	7/01	11r
Lemons	lb	1.19	7/01	11r
Lettuce, iceberg	head	1.13	3/01	4c
Lettuce, iceberg	lb	0.73	7/01	11r
Margarine, Blue Bonnet or Parkay, stick	lb	0.95	3/01	4c
Margarine, soft, tubs	lb	0.89	7/01	11r
Meats, poultry, fish, and egg purchases	yr	671	1999	30r
Milk, fresh, whole, fortified	gal	2.71	7/01	11r
Milk, whole	1/2 gal	1.60	3/01	4c
Nonalcoholic beverages, expenditures on	yr	239	1999	30r
Orange juice, Minute Maid frozen	12 oz	1.66	3/01	4c
Oranges, Navel	lb	0.80	7/01	11r
Oranges, Valencia	lb	0.66	7/01	11r
Peaches, halves or slices, Hunt's, Del Monte, or Libby's	29 oz	1.67	3/01	4c
Pears, Anjou	lb	0.93	7/01	11r
Peas, green, Del Monte or Green Giant	15 oz	0.77	3/01	4c
Pork chops, center cut, bone-in	lb	3.63	7/01	11r
Pork, expenditures on	yr	150	1999	30r
Potato chips	16 oz	3.52	7/01	11r
Potatoes, frozen, french fried	lb	1.08	7/01	11r

Values are in dollars or fractions of dollars. In the column headed *Ref*, references are shown to sources. Each reference is followed by a letter. These refer to the geographical level for which data were reported: s=State, r=Region, and c=City or metro. The abbreviation *ex* is used to mean *except* or *excluding*; *exp* stands for *expenditures*. For other abbreviations and further explanations, please see the Introduction.

5

Akron, OH - continued

Item	Per	Value	Date	Ref.
Groceries				
Potatoes, white or red	10 lb	2.85	3/01	4c
Potatoes, white, all types	lb	0.33	7/01	11r
Poultry, expenditures on	yr	108	1999	30r
Processed fruits, expenditures on	yr	98	1999	30r
Processed vegetables, expenditures on	yr	80	1999	30r
Round roast, U.S. choice, boneless	lb	3.07	7/01	11r
Round steak, graded and ungraded, excl U.S. prime and choice	lb	3.41	7/01	11r
Sausage, Jimmy Dean/Owens pork	lb	3.45	3/01	4c
Shortening, vegetable oil blends	lb	1.13	7/01	11r
Shortening, vegetable, Crisco	3 lb	3.09	3/01	4c
Soft drink, Coca Cola, ex deposit	2 liter	1.26	3/01	4c
Spaghetti and macaroni	lb	0.80	7/01	11r
Steak, round, U.S. choice, boneless	lb	3.23	7/01	11r
Steak, T-bone	lb	7.63	3/01	4c
Steak, T-bone, U.S. choice, bone-in	lb	6.68	7/01	11r
Strawberries, dry pint	12 oz	1.32	7/01	11r
Sugar and other sweets, expenditures on	yr	114	1999	30r
Sugar, cane or beet	4 lbs	1.30	3/01	4c
Sugar, white, 33-80 ounce package	lb	0.42	7/01	11r
Sugar, white, all sizes	lb	0.43	7/01	11r
Tobacco products and smoking supplies purchases	yr	331	1999	30r
Tomatoes, field grown	lb	1.46	7/01	11r
Tomatoes, Hunt's or Del Monte	14.5 oz	0.93	3/01	4c
Tuna, chunk, light	6 oz	0.83	3/01	4c
Tuna, light, chunk	lb	1.80	7/01	11r
Turkey, frozen, whole	lb	1.15	7/01	11r
Goods and Services				
Miscellaneous goods and services, ACCRA Index		103.20	3/01	4c
B&B Japanese maple (acer japonicum)	gal	29.99-169.99	4/00	93r
Boxwood (buxus)	2 gal	18.99-39.99	4/00	93r
Daylilly (hemerocallis)	gal	4.99-25.00	4/00	93r
Flat of annuals		11.98-24.99	4/00	93r
Fountain grass (pennisetum)	gal	5.98-12.98	4/00	93r
Hanging basket (10 in)		12.99-27.99	4/00	93r
Hardy geranium (geranium)	gal	7.99-9.99	4/00	93r
Hosta (hosta)	gal	6.00-25.00	4/00	93r
Lilac (syrubga vulgaris)	2 gal	14.99-24.99	4/00	93r
Miscellaneous purchases	yr	865	1999	30r
Rhododendron (rhododendron)	2 gal	23.98-42.99	4/00	93r
Sage (salvia)	gal	6.00-9.99	4/00	93r
Wintercreeper euonymus (euonymus fortunei)	2 gal	16.00-169.99	4/00	93r
Hunting license	yr	15.00	4/01	34s
Health Care				
Health care, ACCRA Index		101.80	3/01	4c
Cardiac catheterization, ave hospital/physician charges		11760	1998	77s
Childbirth, Cesarean delivery		10722	1997	13r
Childbirth, vaginal delivery		6223	1997	13r
Dentist's fee, adult teeth cleaning and periodic oral exam	visit	78.60	3/01	4c
Doctor's fee, routine exam, established patient	visit	51.60	3/01	4c
Drugs, expenditures on	yr	394	1999	30r
Health care purchases	yr	2048	1999	30r
Health insurance expenditures	yr	978	1999	30r
Hospital care, private room	day	586.40	3/01	4c

Akron, OH - continued

Item	Per	Value	Date	Ref.
Health Care - continued				
Hysterectomy, laproscopically-assisted, ave hospital/physician charges		11730	1998	76s
Hysterectomy, vaginal, ave hospital and physician charges		9640	1998	76s
Medicaid dispensing fee		3.70	1999	87s
Medical services expenditures	yr	554	1999	30r
Medical supplies, expenditures on	yr	122	1999	30r
Plastic surgery, breast augmentation		3184	2000	7r
Plastic surgery, breast lift		3585	2000	7r
Plastic surgery, facelift		4999	2000	7r
Plastic surgery, hair transplantation		3105	2000	7r
Plastic surgery, lip augmentation		1290	2000	7r
Plastic surgery, lower body lift		8135	2000	7r
Plastic surgery, thigh lift		3839	2000	7r
Household Goods				
Dishwashing powder, Cascade	50 oz	3.43	3/01	4c
Floor coverings, expenditures on	yr	52	1999	30r
Furniture, expenditures on	yr	344	1999	30r
Household furnishings and equipment purchases	yr	1475	1999	30r
Household textiles, expenditures on	yr	109	1999	30r
Laundry and cleaning supplies, expenditures on	yr	134	1999	30r
Tissues, facial, Kleenex brand	175	1.22	3/01	4c
Housing				
Housing, ACCRA Index		90.40	3/01	4c
Home, 2200 sq ft, 4-br, 2-bath, 2-car garage, average		154000	2000	47c
Home price, existing, ave		144400	10/00	90r
Home value, median		96000	2001	53s
House, 2400 sq ft, 8000 sq ft lot, new, urban, utilities	total	192200	3/01	4c
House payment, principal and interest, 25% down payment	mos	950	3/01	4c
Household operation expenditures	yr	542	1999	30r
Housekeeping supplies purchases	yr	508	1999	30r
Lodging expenditures	yr	430	1999	30r
Maintenance, repairs, insurance expenditures	yr	853	1999	30r
Monthly rental value of owned home	mos	547	1999	30r
Owned dwellings, expenditures own	yr	4282	1999	30r
Rent expenditures	yr	1558	1999	30r
Rent, apartment, 2 br, 1 1/2-2 baths, unfurn, 950 sq ft, water	mos	580	3/01	4c
Rental unit, 1 bedroom, with utilities	mos	469	4/01	41c
Rental unit, 2 bedroom, with utilities	mos	602	4/01	41c
Rental unit, 3 bedroom, with utilities	mos	753	4/01	41c
Rental unit, 4 bedroom, with utilities	mos	845	4/01	41c
Shelter, expenditures on	yr	6270	1999	30r
Insurance and Pensions				
Life and other personal insurance purchases	yr	387	1999	30r
Pensions and Social Security, expenditures on	yr	2968	1999	30r
Legal Fees				
Divorce, filing fee		100.00	4/01	35s
Driver's license fee	renew	14.50	1999	48s
Driver's license fee	orig	14.50	1999	48s
Fishing license	yr	15.00	4/01	34s
Personal Goods				
Personal care products and services purchases	yr	385	1999	30r
Shampoo, Alberto VO5	15 oz	1.13	3/01	4c
Toothpaste, Crest or Colgate	6-7 oz	2.75	3/01	4c
Personal Services				
Dry cleaning, man's 2-pc suit		7.89	3/01	4c
Man's haircut, barbershop, no styling		9.40	3/01	4c
Personal services, household, expenditures on	yr	300	1999	30r

Values are in dollars or fractions of dollars. In the column headed *Ref*, references are shown to sources. Each reference is followed by a letter. These refer to the geographical level for which data were reported: s=State, r=Region, and c=City or metro. The abbreviation *ex* is used to mean *except* or *excluding*; *exp* stands for *expenditures*. For other abbreviations and further explanations, please see the Introduction.

Akron, OH - continued

Item	Per	Value	Date	Ref.
Personal Services				
Woman's shampoo, trim, blow-dry, no style-change		19.60	3/01	4c
Pets				
Pets, toys, and playground equipment, expenditures on	yr	375	1999	30r
Restaurant Food				
Chicken, fried, thigh and drumstick, KFC/Church's		3.15	3/01	4c
Hamburger with cheese, McDonald's	1/4 lb	2.23	3/01	4c
Pizza, Pizza Hut or Pizza Inn	11-12 in	7.99	3/01	4c
Taxes				
Federal income taxes paid	yr	2326	1999	30r
Personal taxes, expenditures on	yr	3223	1999	30r
Property taxes paid	yr	1152	1999	30r
State and local income taxes paid	yr	753	1999	30r
Transportation				
Transportation, ACCRA Index		104.40	3/01	4c
Bus fare, one-way	trip	1.00	2000	1c
Bus fare, to central business district	1-way	1.00	3/01	4c
Cars and trucks, new, expenditures on	yr	1280	1999	30r
Cars and trucks, used, expenditures on	yr	1763	1999	30r
Diesel at the pump	gal	1.25	10/99	73s
Gasoline and motor oil purchases	yr	1036	1999	30r
Gasoline before-tax price (cents)	gal	109.50	10/00	43s
Maintenance and repair expenditures	yr	594	1999	30r
Public transportation, expenditures on	yr	341	1999	30r
Tire balance, computer or spin balance, front	wheel	8.29	3/01	4c
Transportation purchases	yr	6617	1999	30r
Vehicle expenses, miscellaneous, purchases	yr	2159	1999	30r
Vehicle insurance payments	yr	701	1999	30r
Vehicle purchases (net outlay)	yr	3081	1999	30r
Vehicle rental, lease expenditures	yr	536	1999	30r
Utilities				
Utilities, ACCRA Index		122.10	3/01	4c
Electrical bill, average	mos	72.83	9/00	9s
Electricity, expenditures on	yr	841	1999	30r
Electricity, summer, 250 KWh	mos	30.95	2/96	96c
Electricity, summer, 500 KWh	mos	58.64	2/96	96c
Electricity, summer, 750 KWh	mos	86.44	2/96	96c
Electricity, summer, 1000 KWh	mos	114.25	2/96	96c
Electricity and other, mixed, 2400 sq ft, new home	mos	80.86	3/01	4c
Electricity cost, average	KWh	6.59	9/00	9s
Utilities, fuels, and public services purchased	yr	2401	1999	30r
Water and other public services, expenditures on	yr	273	1999	30r
Weddings				
Wedding (national average cost)		19936	2000	33r
Wedding (regional average total cost)		16195	1997	110r
Attendants' gifts		321	1998	33r
Bridal attendants' apparel (5 persons)		824	2000	33r
Bride's headpiece/veil		173	1998	33r
Bride's wedding dress		859	1998	33r
Clergy, religious facility fee		242	1998	33r
Engagement ring		3177	1998	33r
Flowers		789	1998	33r
Groom's formalwear rental		99	2000	33r
Limousine		410	1998	33r
Marriage license cost		45.00	4/01	35s
Men's formalwear (ushers, best man)		469	2000	33r
Mother of bride apparel		241	2000	33r
Music		866	1998	33r
Photography and videography		1368	1998	33r
Rehearsal dinner		728	1998	33r
Wedding invitations and announcements		341	1998	33r
Wedding reception		7968	2000	33r
Wedding rings (bride and groom)		1060	1998	33r

Albany, GA

Item	Per	Value	Date	Ref.
Composite, ACCRA index		92.80	3/01	4c
Alcoholic Beverages				
Alcoholic beverage purchases	yr	253	1999	30r
Beer, Heineken, 12-oz, ex deposit	6	7.25	3/01	4c
J & B Scotch	750-ml	18.32	3/01	4c
Malt beverages, all types, all sizes, any origin	16 oz	0.96	7/01	11r
Wine, Livingston or Gallo, Chablis blanc	1.5 liter	6.32	3/01	4c
Appliances				
Appliance repair, service call, washing machine	min lab chg	42.98	3/01	4c
Major appliances, expenditures on	yr	172	1999	30r
Small appliances, housewares, expenditures on	yr	81	1999	30r
Banking and Money				
Mortgage interest and charges paid	yr	2039	1999	30r
Mortgage principal paid on owned property	yr	1026	1999	30r
Mortgage rate, incl. points and orig. fee, 30-yr. conv. fixed or ARM	mos	7.04	3/01	4c
Vehicle finance charges paid	yr	365	1999	30r
Charity				
Cash contributions, expenditures	yr	1127	1999	30r
Child Care				
Child raising cost, total, age 0-2	yr	8540	1999	60r
Child raising cost, total, age 3-5	yr	8780	1999	60r
Child raising cost, total, age 6-8	yr	8820	1999	60r
Child raising cost, total, age 9-11	yr	8800	1999	60r
Child raising cost, total, age 12-14	yr	9510	1999	60r
Child raising cost, total, age 15-17	yr	9740	1999	60r
Child's child care and education, age 0-2	yr	1380	1999	60r
Child's child care and education, age 3-5	yr	1520	1999	60r
Child's child care and education, age 6-8	yr	990	1999	60r
Child's child care and education, age 9-11	yr	650	1999	60r
Child's child care and education, age 12-14	yr	490	1999	60r
Child's child care and education, age 15-17	yr	840	1999	60r
Child's clothing, age 0-2	yr	480	1999	60r
Child's clothing, age 3-5	yr	470	1999	60r
Child's clothing, age 6-8	yr	520	1999	60r
Child's clothing, age 9-11	yr	570	1999	60r
Child's clothing, age 12-14	yr	950	1999	60r
Child's clothing, age 15-17	yr	850	1999	60r
Child's food, age 0-2	yr	1000	1999	60r
Child's food, age 3-5	yr	1160	1999	60r
Child's food, age 6-8	yr	1490	1999	60r
Child's food, age 9-11	yr	1770	1999	60r
Child's food, age 12-14	yr	1770	1999	60r
Child's food, age 15-17	yr	1980	1999	60r
Child's health care, age 0-2	yr	620	1999	60r
Child's health care, age 3-5	yr	590	1999	60r
Child's health care, age 6-8	yr	680	1999	60r
Child's health care, age 9-11	yr	720	1999	60r
Child's health care, age 12-14	yr	730	1999	60r
Child's health care, age 15-17	yr	760	1999	60r
Child's housing, age 0-2	yr	3070	1999	60r
Child's housing, age 3-5	yr	3050	1999	60r
Child's housing, age 6-8	yr	3010	1999	60r
Child's housing, age 9-11	yr	2850	1999	60r
Child's housing, age 12-14	yr	3040	1999	60r
Child's housing, age 15-17	yr	2650	1999	60r
Child's personal care, reading, age 0-2	yr	910	1999	60r
Child's personal care, reading, age 3-5	yr	930	1999	60r
Child's personal care, reading, age 6-8	yr	960	1999	60r
Child's personal care, reading, age 9-11	yr	1000	1999	60r
Child's personal care, reading, age 12-14	yr	1170	1999	60r
Child's personal care, reading, age 15-17	yr	950	1999	60r
Clothing				
Apparel and services purchases	yr	1610	1999	30r
Boys' brief, cotton	3	4.48	3/01	4c
Boys, 2 to 15, expenditures on	yr	89	1999	30r
Children under 2, expenditures on	yr	79	1999	30r
Footwear, expenditures on	yr	283	1999	30r

Values are in dollars or fractions of dollars. In the column headed *Ref*, references are shown to sources. Each reference is followed by a letter. These refer to the geographical level for which data were reported: s=State, r=Region, and c=City or metro. The abbreviation *ex* is used to mean *except* or *excluding*; *exp* stands for *expenditures*. For other abbreviations and further explanations, please see the Introduction.

Albany, GA - continued

Item	Per	Value	Date	Ref.
Clothing				
Girls, 2 to 15, expenditures on	yr	103	1999	30r
Men and boys, expenditures on	yr	351	1999	30r
Men, 16 and over, expenditures on	yr	262	1999	30r
Shirt, man's dress shirt		28.20	3/01	4c
Slacks, man's "No Wrinkles" khaki		34.99	3/01	4c
Women, 16 and over, expenditures on	yr	538	1999	30r
Communications				
Cable modem installation, Charter		99.00-169.00	6/99	103s
Cable modem installation, Comcast		95.00	6/99	103s
Cable modem installation, Intermedia		149.95	6/99	103s
Cable modem installation, Media One		100.00	6/99	103s
Cable modem rate, cable subscriber, Charter	mos	49.95-79.95	6/99	103s
Cable modem rate, cable subscriber, Comcast	mos	39.95	6/99	103s
Cable modem rate, cable subscriber, Intermedia	mos	49.95	6/99	103s
Cable modem rate, cable subscriber, Media One	mos	34.95-39.95	6/99	103s
Cable modem rate, non-cable subscriber, Charter	mos	59.95-89.95	6/99	103s
Cable modem rate, non-cable subscriber, Comcast	mos	49.95	6/99	103s
Cable modem rate, non-cable subscriber, Intermedia	mos	54.95	6/99	103s
Cable modem rate, non-cable subscriber, Media One	mos	49.95	6/99	103s
Newspaper subscription, daily and Sunday delivery	mos	12.15	3/01	4c
Phone line, single, business, field visit	inst.	58.25	12/97	17s
Phone line, single, business, no field visit	inst.	58.25	12/97	17s
Phone line, single, residence, field visit	inst.	42.50	12/97	17s
Phone line, single, residence, no field visit	inst.	42.50	12/97	17s
Postage and stationery, expenditures on	yr	104	1999	30r
Postal rate, express mail, up to half-pound		12.45	7/01	108r
Postal rate, letter, first class, first ounce		0.34	7/01	108r
Postal rate, letter, two ounces		0.57	7/01	108r
Postal rate, post card		0.21	7/01	108r
Postal rate, priority mail, two pounds		3.95	7/01	108r
Postal rate, priority mail, up to one pound		3.50	7/01	108r
Telephone bill, family of three	mos	26.45	3/01	4c
Telephone services, expenditures on	yr	860	1999	30r
Education				
Board, 4-year private college/university	yr	2267	1996	38s
Board, 4-year public college/university	yr	1877	1996	38s
Education expenditures	yr	431	1999	30r
Room, 4-year private college/university	yr	2719	1996	38s
Room, 4-year public college/university	yr	1712	1996	38s
Total cost, 4-year private college/university	yr	15194	1996	38s
Total cost, 4-year public college/university	yr	5691	1996	38s
Tuition, 2-year public college/university, in state	yr	1062	1996	38s
Tuition, 4-year private college/university, in state	yr	10208	1996	38s
Tuition, 4-year public college/university	yr	2103	1996	38s
Energy and Fuels				
Electricity	KWh	0.09	7/01	11r
Electricity	500 KWhs	47.29	7/01	11r
Energy, combined forms, 2400 sq ft	mos	110.40	3/01	4c
Fuel oil #2	gal	1.43	7/01	11r
Fuel oil and other fuels, expenditures on	yr	45	1999	30r
Gas, regular unleaded, cash, self-service	gal	1.24	3/01	4c
Gasoline, all types	gal	1.60	7/01	11r
Gasoline, unleaded midgrade	gal	1.65	7/01	11r
Gasoline, unleaded premium	gal	1.74	7/01	11r
Natural gas, expenditures on	yr	164	1999	30r
Utility (piped) gas, therm		1.01	7/01	11r
Utility (piped) gas, 40 therms		44.29	7/01	11r
Utility (piped) gas, 100 therms		97.44	7/01	11r

Albany, GA - continued

Item	Per	Value	Date	Ref.
Entertainment				
Bowling, Saturday evening rate	line	2.79	3/01	4c
Entertainment purchases	yr	1574	1999	30r
Fees and admissions paid	yr	371	1999	30r
Monopoly game, Parker Brothers', No. 9	game	9.44	3/01	4c
Movie, first-run, Saturday, evening	adm.	6.50	3/01	4c
Reading purchases	yr	121	1999	30r
Television, radios, sound equipment, expenditures on	yr	561	1999	30r
Tennis balls, yellow, Wilson or Penn, 3	can	1.94	3/01	4c
Funerals				
Total cost of funeral		5922.53	1/99	78r
Acknowledgement cards		63.43	1/99	78r
Casket		2258.77	1/99	78r
Cosmetology, hair, other preparation		127.09	1/99	78r
Embalming		393.49	1/99	78r
Funeral at funeral home		367.50	1/99	78r
Hearse (local)		169.66	1/99	78r
Professional service charges		1211.32	1/99	78r
Service car/van		80.69	1/99	78r
Transfer of remains to funeral home		144.25	1/99	78r
Vault		803.50	1/99	78r
Visitation/viewing		302.83	1/99	78r
Groceries				
Groceries, ACCRA Index		98.40	3/01	4c
American processed cheese	lb	3.50	7/01	11r
Antibiotic ointment, Polysporin	0.5 oz	4.41	3/01	4c
Baby food, strained vegetables or fruit, lowest price	4-4.5 oz	0.42	3/01	4c
Bakery products, expenditures on	yr	261	1999	30r
Bananas	lb	0.53	3/01	4c
Bananas	lb	0.47	7/01	11r
Beans, dried, any type, all sizes	lb	0.63	7/01	11r
Beef for stew, boneless	lb	2.86	7/01	11r
Beef or hamburger, ground	lb	1.77	3/01	4c
Beef, expenditures on	yr	210	1999	30r
Bologna, all beef or mixed	lb	2.29	7/01	11r
Bread, French	lb	1.66	7/01	11r
Bread, white	loaf	0.95	3/01	4c
Bread, white, pan	lb	0.87	7/01	11r
Bread, whole wheat, pan	lb	1.38	7/01	11r
Broccoli	lb	1.04	7/01	11r
Butter, salted, grade AA, stick	lb	2.26	7/01	11r
Butter, yoghurt, cheese, etc, expenditures on	yr	170	1999	30r
Cabbage	lb	0.42	7/01	11r
Cereals and cereal products, expenditures on	yr	140	1999	30r
Cheddar cheese, natural	lb	3.75	7/01	11r
Cheese, Kraft grated Parmesan	8 oz	3.03	3/01	4c
Chicken breast, bone-in	lb	1.85	7/01	11r
Chicken legs, bone-in	lb	1.34	7/01	11r
Chicken, fresh, whole	lb	1.05	7/01	11r
Chicken, whole fryer	lb	0.95	3/01	4c
Chops, boneless,	lb	4.13	7/01	11r
Chuck roast, graded and ungraded, excl U.S. prime and choice	lb	2.35	7/01	11r
Chuck roast, U.S. choice, boneless	lb	2.67	7/01	11r
Cigarettes, Winston, Kings	carton	25.15	3/01	4c
Coffee, 100%, ground roast, all sizes	lb	2.88	7/01	11r
Coffee, instant, plain, regular, all sizes	16 oz	9.25	7/01	11r
Coffee, vacuum-packed	13 oz	2.47	3/01	4c
Cola, non diet	2 liter	1.11	7/01	11r
Corn Flakes, Kellogg's or Post Toasties	18 oz	2.97	3/01	4c
Corn, frozen, whole kernel, lowest price	16 oz	1.09	3/01	4c
Crackers, soda, salted	lb	1.70	7/01	11r
Dairy product purchases	yr	282	1999	30r
Eggs, expenditures on	yr	32	1999	30r
Eggs, Grade A or AA	dozen	1.21	3/01	4c
Fats and oils, expenditures on	yr	79	1999	30r
Fish and seafood, expenditures on	yr	99	1999	30r
Flour, white, all purpose	lb	0.32	7/01	11r

Values are in dollars or fractions of dollars. In the column headed *Ref*, references are shown to sources. Each reference is followed by a letter. These refer to the geographical level for which data were reported: s=State, r=Region, and c=City or metro. The abbreviation *ex* is used to mean *except* or *excluding*; *exp* stands for expenditures. For other abbreviations and further explanations, please see the Introduction.

Albany, GA - continued

Item	Per	Value	Date	Ref.
Groceries				
Food (excl fruit and vegetables), eaten at home, purchases	yr	815	1999	30r
Food cooked on trips, expenditures on	yr	36	1999	30r
Food purchases	yr	4533	1999	30r
Food purchases, eaten away from home	yr	1873	1999	30r
Food purchases, food eaten at home	yr	2660	1999	30r
Fresh fruits, expenditures on	yr	128	1999	30r
Fresh milk and cream, expenditures on	yr	112	1999	30r
Fresh vegetables, expenditures on	yr	131	1999	30r
Fruit and vegetable purchases	yr	438	1999	30r
Grapefruit	lb	0.59	7/01	11r
Grapes, Thompson, seedless	lb	2.12	7/01	11r
Ground beef, 100% beef	lb	1.76	7/01	11r
Ground beef, lean and extra lean	lb	2.60	7/01	11r
Ground chuck, 100% beef	lb	2.08	7/01	11r
Ham, boneless, excl canned	lb	2.71	7/01	11r
Ham, rump or shank half, bone-in, smoked	lb	2.19	7/01	11r
Ice cream, prepackaged, bulk, regular	1/2 gal	3.93	7/01	11r
Lemons	lb	1.32	7/01	11r
Lettuce, iceberg	head	1.03	3/01	4c
Lettuce, iceberg	lb	0.76	7/01	11r
Margarine, Blue Bonnet or Parkay, stick	lb	0.59	3/01	4c
Milk, fresh, low fat,	gal	2.75	7/01	11r
Milk, fresh, whole, fortified	gal	2.97	7/01	11r
Milk, whole	1/2 gal	1.85	3/01	4c
Nonalcoholic beverages, expenditures on	yr	228	1999	30r
Orange juice, frozen concentrate	16 oz	1.95	7/01	11r
Orange juice, Minute Maid frozen	12 oz	1.53	3/01	4c
Oranges, Navel	lb	0.73	7/01	11r
Oranges, Valencia	lb	0.55	7/01	11r
Peaches, halves or slices, Hunt's, Del Monte, or Libby's	29 oz	1.45	3/01	4c
Peanut butter, creamy, all sizes	lb	1.83	7/01	11r
Pears, Anjou	lb	0.98	7/01	11r
Peas, green, Del Monte or Green Giant	15 oz	0.66	3/01	4c
Pork chops, center cut, bone-in	lb	3.33	7/01	11r
Pork sausage, fresh, loose	lb	2.59	7/01	11r
Pork shoulder picnic, bone-in, smoked	lb	1.12	7/01	11r
Pork, expenditures on	yr	162	1999	30r
Potato chips	16 oz	3.59	7/01	11r
Potatoes, frozen, french fried	lb	1.00	7/01	11r
Potatoes, white or red	10 lb	2.83	3/01	4c
Potatoes, white, all types	lb	0.44	7/01	11r
Poultry, expenditures on	yr	137	1999	30r
Processed fruits, expenditures on	yr	97	1999	30r
Processed vegetables, expenditures on	yr	82	1999	30r
Rice, white, long grain, uncooked	lb	0.51	7/01	11r
Round roast, graded and ungraded, excl U.S. prime and choice	lb	2.96	7/01	11r
Round steak, graded and ungraded, excl U.S. prime and choice	lb	3.11	7/01	11r
Sausage, Jimmy Dean/Owens pork	lb	2.69	3/01	4c
Shortening, vegetable, Crisco	3 lb	3.09	3/01	4c
Sirloin steak, graded and ungraded, excl U.S. prime and choice	lb	4.23	7/01	11r
Soft drink, Coca Cola, ex deposit	2 liter	1.23	3/01	4c
Spaghetti and macaroni	lb	0.78	7/01	11r
Steak, round, U.S. choice, boneless	lb	3.56	7/01	11r
Steak, sirloin, U.S. choice, boneless	lb	5.65	7/01	11r
Steak, T-bone	lb	7.45	7/01	11r
Strawberries, dry pint	12 oz	1.50	7/01	11r
Sugar and other sweets, expenditures on	yr	99	1999	30r
Sugar, cane or beet	4 lbs	1.53	3/01	4c
Sugar, white, 33-80 ounce package	lb	0.39	7/01	11r
Sugar, white, all sizes	lb	0.42	7/01	11r
Tobacco products and smoking supplies purchases	yr	288	1999	30r
Tomatoes, field grown	lb	1.43	7/01	11r
Tomatoes, Hunt's or Del Monte	14.5 oz	0.79	3/01	4c
Tuna, chunk, light	6 oz	0.53	3/01	4c
Tuna, light, chunk	lb	1.77	7/01	11r
Turkey, frozen, whole	lb	1.05	7/01	11r

Albany, GA - continued

Item	Per	Value	Date	Ref.
Goods and Services				
Miscellaneous goods and services, ACCRA Index		98.10	3/01	4c
B&B Japanese maple (acer japonicum)	gal	49.98-129.00	4/00	93r
Boxwood (buxus)	2 gal	12.99-16.99	4/00	93r
Daylilly (hemerocallis)	gal	4.99-8.99	4/00	93r
Flat of annuals		11.00-13.92	4/00	93r
Fountain grass (pennisetum)	gal	5.98-7.98	4/00	93r
Hanging basket (10 in)		7.99-14.98	4/00	93r
Hardy geranium (geranium)	gal	5.98-8.00	4/00	93r
Hosta (hosta)	gal	4.99-10.98	4/00	93r
Lilac (syrubga vulgaris)	2 gal	12.99-21.99	4/00	93r
Rhododendron (rhododendron)	2 gal	14.99-24.99	4/00	93r
Sage (salvia)	gal	5.98-6.99	4/00	93r
Wintercreeper euonymus (euonymus fortunei)	2 gal	7.99-89.99	4/00	93r
Hunting license	yr	10.00	4/01	34s
Health Care				
Health care, ACCRA Index		87.40	3/01	4c
Cardiac catheterization, ave hospital/physician charges		14190	1998	77s
Childbirth, Cesarean delivery		11587	1997	13r
Childbirth, vaginal delivery		6725	1997	13r
Dentist's fee, adult teeth cleaning and periodic oral exam	visit	58.00	3/01	4c
Doctor's fee, routine exam, established patient	visit	61.80	3/01	4c
Drugs, expenditures on	yr	399	1999	30r
Health care purchases	yr	1971	1999	30r
Health insurance expenditures	yr	933	1999	30r
Hospital care, private room	day	316.00	3/01	4c
Hysterectomy, laproscopically-assisted, ave hospital/physician charges		16760	1998	76s
Hysterectomy, vaginal, ave hospital and physician charges		11160	1998	76s
Medicaid dispensing fee		4.63	1999	87s
Medical services expenditures	yr	547	1999	30r
Medical supplies, expenditures on	yr	91	1999	30r
Plastic surgery, breast augmentation		2870	2000	7r
Plastic surgery, breast lift		3649	2000	7r
Plastic surgery, facelift		5008	2000	7r
Plastic surgery, hair transplantation		3425	2000	7r
Plastic surgery, lip augmentation		1227	2000	7r
Plastic surgery, lower body lift		4793	2000	7r
Plastic surgery, thigh lift		3862	2000	7r
Household Goods				
Dishwashing powder, Cascade	50 oz	3.43	3/01	4c
Floor coverings, expenditures on	yr	44	1999	30r
Furniture, expenditures on	yr	335	1999	30r
Household furnishings and equipment purchases	yr	1328	1999	30r
Household textiles, expenditures on	yr	89	1999	30r
Laundry and cleaning supplies, expenditures on	yr	113	1999	30r
Tissues, facial, Kleenex brand	175	1.33	3/01	4c
Housing				
Housing, ACCRA Index		84.30	3/01	4c
Home price, existing, ave		160100	10/00	90r
Home value, median		131000	2001	53s
House, 2400 sq ft, 8000 sq ft lot, new, urban, utilities	total	182600	3/01	4c

Values are in dollars or fractions of dollars. In the column headed *Ref*, references are shown to sources. Each reference is followed by a letter. These refer to the geographical level for which data were reported: s=State, r=Region, and c=City or metro. The abbreviation *ex* is used to mean *except* or *excluding*; *exp* stands for *expenditures*. For other abbreviations and further explanations, please see the Introduction.

Albany, GA - continued

Item	Per	Value	Date	Ref.
Housing				
House payment, principal and interest, 25% down payment	mos	915	3/01	4c
Household operation expenditures	yr	553	1999	30r
Housekeeping supplies purchases	yr	473	1999	30r
Housing, expenditures on	yr	10303	1999	30r
Maintenance, repairs, insurance expenditures	yr	699	1999	30r
Monthly rental value of owned home	mos	505	1999	30r
Owned dwellings, expenditures own	yr	3465	1999	30r
Rent expenditures	yr	1641	1999	30r
Rent, apartment, 2 br, 1 1/2-2 baths, unfurn, 950 sq ft, water	mos	465	3/01	4c
Rental unit, 1 bedroom, with utilities	mos	361	4/01	41c
Rental unit, 2 bedroom, with utilities	mos	440	4/01	41c
Rental unit, 3 bedroom, with utilities	mos	601	4/01	41c
Rental unit, 4 bedroom, with utilities	mos	651	4/01	41c
Shelter, expenditures on	yr	5467	1999	30r
Insurance and Pensions				
Life and other personal insurance purchases	yr	414	1999	30r
Pensions and Social Security, expenditures on	yr	2635	1999	30r
Personal insurance and pensions, expenditures on	yr	3048	1999	30r
Legal Fees				
Divorce, filing fee		65.00-85.00	4/01	35s
Driver's license fee	renew	15.00	1999	48s
Driver's license fee	orig	16.50	1999	48s
Personal Goods				
Personal care products and services purchases	yr	393	1999	30r
Shampoo, Alberto VO5	15 oz	1.11	3/01	4c
Toothpaste, Crest or Colgate	6-7 oz	2.48	3/01	4c
Personal Services				
Dry cleaning, man's 2-pc suit		6.82	3/01	4c
Man's haircut, barbershop, no styling		9.75	3/01	4c
Personal services, household, expenditures on	yr	258	1999	30r
Woman's shampoo, trim, blow-dry, no style-change		26.60	3/01	4c
Pets				
Pets, toys, and playground equipment, expenditures on	yr	306	1999	30r
Restaurant Food				
Chicken, fried, thigh and drumstick, KFC/ Church's		2.59	3/01	4c
Hamburger with cheese, McDonald's	1/4 lb	2.19	3/01	4c
Pizza, Pizza Hut or Pizza Inn	11-12 in	9.49	3/01	4c
Taxes				
Federal income taxes paid	yr	2047	1999	30r
Personal taxes, expenditures on	yr	2554	1999	30r
Property taxes paid	yr	726	1999	30r
State and local income taxes paid	yr	363	1999	30r
Transportation				
Transportation, ACCRA Index		91.60	3/01	4c
Bus fare, one-way	trip	0.70	2000	1c
Cars and trucks, new, expenditures on	yr	1648	1999	30r
Cars and trucks, used, expenditures on	yr	1651	1999	30r
Diesel at the pump	gal	1.10	10/99	73s
Gasoline and motor oil purchases	yr	1052	1999	30r
Gasoline before-tax price (cents)	gal	102.00	10/00	43s
Maintenance and repair expenditures	yr	621	1999	30r
Public transportation, expenditures on	yr	298	1999	30r
Tire balance, computer or spin balance, front	wheel	7.62	3/01	4c
Transportation purchases	yr	6738	1999	30r
Vehicle expenses, miscellaneous, purchases	yr	2033	1999	30r
Vehicle insurance payments	yr	696	1999	30r
Vehicle purchases (net outlay)	yr	3354	1999	30r

Albany, GA - continued

Item	Per	Value	Date	Ref.
Transportation - continued				
Vehicle rental, lease expenditures	yr	352	1999	30r
Utilities				
Utilities, ACCRA Index		94.70	3/01	4c
Electrical bill, average	mos	79.83	9/00	9s
Electricity, 2400 sq ft, new home	mos	110.40	3/01	4c
Electricity, expenditures on	yr	1115	1999	30r
Electricity cost, average	KWh	6.10	9/00	9s
Water and other public services, expenditures on	yr	298	1999	30r
Weddings				
Wedding (national average cost)		19936	2000	33r
Wedding (regional average total cost)		16293	1997	110r
Attendants' gifts		321	1998	33r
Bridal attendants' apparel (5 persons)		824	2000	33r
Bride's headpiece/veil		173	1998	33r
Bride's wedding dress		859	1998	33r
Clergy, religious facility fee		242	1998	33r
Engagement ring		3177	1998	33r
Flowers		789	1998	33r
Groom's formalwear rental		99	2000	33r
Limousine		410	1998	33r
Marriage license cost		40.00	4/01	35s
Men's formalwear (ushers, best man)		469	2000	33r
Mother of bride apparel		241	2000	33r
Music		866	1998	33r
Photography and videography		1368	1998	33r
Rehearsal dinner		728	1998	33r
Wedding invitations and announcements		341	1998	33r
Wedding reception		7968	2000	33r
Wedding rings (bride and groom)		1060	1998	33r

Albany-Schenectady-Troy, NY

Item	Per	Value	Date	Ref.
Average annual expenditures	yr	37971	1999	30r
Alcoholic Beverages				
Alcoholic beverage purchases	yr	368	1999	30r
Wine, red and white table, all sizes, any origin	liter	9.64	7/01	11r
Appliances				
Major appliances, expenditures on	yr	194	1999	30r
Small appliances, housewares, expenditures on	yr	93	1999	30r
Banking and Money				
Mortgage interest and charges paid	yr	2622	1999	30r
Mortgage principal paid on owned property	yr	1262	1999	30r
Vehicle finance charges paid	yr	240	1999	30r
Charity				
Cash contributions, expenditures	yr	1001	1999	30r
Child Care				
Child raising cost, total, age 0-2	yr	8670	1999	60r
Child raising cost, total, age 3-5	yr	8910	1999	60r
Child raising cost, total, age 6-8	yr	9040	1999	60r
Child raising cost, total, age 9-11	yr	9100	1999	60r
Child raising cost, total, age 12-14	yr	9890	1999	60r
Child raising cost, total, age 15-17	yr	10010	1999	60r
Child's child care and education, age 0-2	yr	1070	1999	60r
Child's child care and education, age 3-5	yr	1190	1999	60r
Child's child care and education, age 6-8	yr	740	1999	60r
Child's child care and education, age 9-11	yr	470	1999	60r
Child's child care and education, age 12-14	yr	350	1999	60r
Child's child care and education, age 15-17	yr	590	1999	60r
Child's clothing, age 0-2	yr	480	1999	60r
Child's clothing, age 3-5	yr	470	1999	60r
Child's clothing, age 6-8	yr	520	1999	60r
Child's clothing, age 9-11	yr	570	1999	60r
Child's clothing, age 12-14	yr	970	1999	60r
Child's clothing, age 15-17	yr	870	1999	60r
Child's food, age 0-2	yr	1130	1999	60r

Values are in dollars or fractions of dollars. In the column headed *Ref*, references are shown to sources. Each reference is followed by a letter. These refer to the geographical level for which data were reported: s=State, r=Region, and c=City or metro. The abbreviation *ex* is used to mean *except* or *excluding*; *exp* stands for expenditures. For other abbreviations and further explanations, please see the Introduction.

Albany-Schenectady-Troy, NY - continued

Item	Per	Value	Date	Ref.
Child Care				
Child's food, age 3-5	yr	1290	1999	60r
Child's food, age 6-8	yr	1640	1999	60r
Child's food, age 9-11	yr	1930	1999	60r
Child's food, age 12-14	yr	1940	1999	60r
Child's food, age 15-17	yr	2150	1999	60r
Child's health care, age 0-2	yr	550	1999	60r
Child's health care, age 3-5	yr	530	1999	60r
Child's health care, age 6-8	yr	610	1999	60r
Child's health care, age 9-11	yr	650	1999	60r
Child's health care, age 12-14	yr	660	1999	60r
Child's health care, age 15-17	yr	690	1999	60r
Child's housing, age 0-2	yr	3555	1999	60r
Child's housing, age 3-5	yr	3530	1999	60r
Child's housing, age 6-8	yr	3490	1999	60r
Child's housing, age 9-11	yr	3340	1999	60r
Child's housing, age 12-14	yr	3530	1999	60r
Child's housing, age 15-17	yr	3140	1999	60r
Child's personal care, reading, age 0-2	yr	920	1999	60r
Child's personal care, reading, age 3-5	yr	950	1999	60r
Child's personal care, reading, age 6-8	yr	980	1999	60r
Child's personal care, reading, age 9-11	yr	1020	1999	60r
Child's personal care, reading, age 12-14	yr	1190	1999	60r
Child's personal care, reading, age 15-17	yr	970	1999	60r
Nannies: criminal background check		74	1998	84s
Clothing				
Apparel and services purchases	yr	1831	1999	30r
Boys, 2 to 15, expenditures on	yr	92	1999	30r
Children under 2, expenditures on	yr	63	1999	30r
Footwear, expenditures on	yr	300	1999	30r
Girls, 2 to 15, expenditures on	yr	101	1999	30r
Men and boys, expenditures on	yr	446	1999	30r
Men, 16 and over, expenditures on	yr	354	1999	30r
Women, 16 and over, expenditures on	yr	584	1999	30r
Communications				
Cable modem installation, Adelphi		54.90	6/99	103s
Cable modem installation, Cablevision Systems		150.00	6/99	103s
Cable modem installation, Time Warner		75.00-225.00	6/99	103s
Cable modem rate, cable subscriber, Adelphi	mos	34.95	6/99	103s
Cable modem rate, cable subscriber, Cablevision Systems	mos	44.95	6/99	103s
Cable modem rate, cable subscriber, Century	mos	39.95	6/99	103s
Cable modem rate, cable subscriber, Time Warner	mos	39.95-49.95	6/99	103s
Cable modem rate, non-cable subscriber, Adelphi	mos	44.95	6/99	103s
Cable modem rate, non-cable subscriber, Cablevision Systems	mos	54.95	6/99	103s
Cable modem rate, non-cable subscriber, Time Warner	mos	39.95-54.95	6/99	103s
Phone line, single, business, field visit	inst.	142.76	12/97	17s
Phone line, single, business, no field visit	inst.	106.05	12/97	17s
Phone line, single, residence, field visit	inst.	102.78	12/97	17s
Phone line, single, residence, no field visit	inst.	55.00	12/97	17s
Postage and stationery, expenditures on	yr	138	1999	30r
Postal rate, express mail, up to half-pound		12.45	7/01	108r
Postal rate, letter, first class, first ounce		0.34	7/01	108r
Postal rate, letter, two ounces		0.57	7/01	108r
Postal rate, post card		0.21	7/01	108r
Postal rate, priority mail, two pounds		3.95	7/01	108r
Postal rate, priority mail, up to one pound		3.50	7/01	108r
Telephone services, expenditures on	yr	830	1999	30r
Education				
Board, 4-year private college/university	yr	3255	1996	38s
Board, 4-year public college/university	yr	2310	1996	38s
Education expenditures	yr	877	1999	30r
Room, 4-year private college/university	yr	3724	1996	38s
Room, 4-year public college/university	yr	2937	1996	38s
Total cost, 4-year private college/university	yr	20831	1996	38s
Total cost, 4-year public college/university	yr	8960	1996	38s

Albany-Schenectady-Troy, NY - continued

Item	Per	Value	Date	Ref.
Education - continued				
Tuition, 2-year public college/university, in state	yr	2427	1996	38s
Tuition, 4-year private college/university, in state	yr	13852	1996	38s
Tuition, 4-year public college/university	yr	3714	1996	38s
Energy and Fuels				
Electricity	KWh	0.12	7/01	11r
Fuel oil #2	gal	1.31	7/01	11r
Fuel oil and other fuels, expenditures on	yr	207	1999	30r
Gasoline, all types	gal	1.80	7/01	11r
Gasoline, unleaded midgrade	gal	1.85	7/01	11r
Gasoline, unleaded premium	gal	1.91	7/01	11r
Gasoline, unleaded regular	gal	1.71	7/01	11r
Natural gas, expenditures on	yr	368	1999	30r
Utility (piped) gas, therm		1.08	7/01	11r
Utility (piped) gas, 40 therms		50.87	7/01	11r
Utility (piped) gas, 100 therms		111.06	7/01	11r
Entertainment				
Entertainment purchases	yr	1821	1999	30r
Fees and admissions paid	yr	511	1999	30r
Television, radios, sound equipment, expenditures on	yr	650	1999	30r
Funerals				
Total cost of funeral		5813.50	1/99	78r
Acknowledgement cards		28.32	1/99	78r
Casket		2082.20	1/99	78r
Cosmetology, hair, other preparation		169.59	1/99	78r
Embalming		465.60	1/99	78r
Funeral at funeral home		339.56	1/99	78r
Hearse (local)		183.96	1/99	78r
Professional service charges		1157.85	1/99	78r
Service car/van		100.41	1/99	78r
Transfer of remains to funeral home		158.66	1/99	78r
Vault		766.31	1/99	78r
Visitation/viewing		361.04	1/99	78r
Groceries				
Apples, red delicious	lb	0.95	7/01	11r
Bacon, sliced	lb	3.44	7/01	11r
Bakery products, expenditures on	yr	310	1999	30r
Bananas	lb	0.55	7/01	11r
Beef, expenditures on	yr	236	1999	30r
Bread, white, pan	lb	1.09	7/01	11r
Butter, yoghurt, cheese, etc, expenditures on	yr	214	1999	30r
Cereals and bakery product purchases	yr	474	1999	30r
Cereals and cereal products, expenditures on	yr	164	1999	30r
Chicken legs, bone-in	lb	1.23	7/01	11r
Chicken, fresh, whole	lb	1.13	7/01	11r
Chuck roast, U.S. choice, boneless	lb	2.79	7/01	11r
Coffee, 100%, ground roast, all sizes	lb	3.40	7/01	11r
Dairy product purchases	yr	342	1999	30r
Eggs, expenditures on	yr	34	1999	30r
Eggs, grade A, large	dozen	0.82	7/01	11r
Fats and oils, expenditures on	yr	80	1999	30r
Fish and seafood, expenditures on	yr	123	1999	30r
Food (excl fruit and vegetables), eaten at home, purchases	yr	838	1999	30r
Food cooked on trips, expenditures on	yr	48	1999	30r
Food purchases	yr	5314	1999	30r
Food purchases, eaten away from home	yr	2313	1999	30r
Food purchases, food eaten at home	yr	3001	1999	30r
Fresh fruits, expenditures on	yr	169	1999	30r
Fresh milk and cream, expenditures on	yr	128	1999	30r
Fresh vegetables, expenditures on	yr	164	1999	30r
Grapefruit	lb	0.67	7/01	11r
Grapes, Thompson, seedless	lb	2.18	7/01	11r
Ground beef, lean and extra lean	lb	2.66	7/01	11r
Ground chuck, 100% beef	lb	2.04	7/01	11r
Lettuce, iceberg	lb	0.76	7/01	11r
Meats, poultry, fish, and egg purchases	yr	808	1999	30r

Values are in dollars or fractions of dollars. In the column headed *Ref*, references are shown to sources. Each reference is followed by a letter. These refer to the geographical level for which data were reported: s=State, r=Region, and c=City or metro. The abbreviation *ex* is used to mean *except* or *excluding*; *exp* stands for *expenditures*. For other abbreviations and further explanations, please see the Introduction.

Albany-Schenectady-Troy, NY - continued

Item	Per	Value	Date	Ref.
Groceries				
Nonalcoholic beverages, expenditures on	yr	225	1999	30r
Orange juice, frozen concentrate	16 oz	1.88	7/01	11r
Oranges, Navel	lb	0.79	7/01	11r
Oranges, Valencia	lb	0.56	7/01	11r
Peaches	lb	1.16	7/01	11r
Peanut butter, creamy, all sizes	lb	2.01	7/01	11r
Pears, Anjou	lb	1.16	7/01	11r
Pork chops, center cut, bone-in	lb	3.57	7/01	11r
Pork, expenditures on	yr	146	1999	30r
Potato chips	16 oz	3.37	7/01	11r
Potatoes, white, all types	lb	0.42	7/01	11r
Poultry, expenditures on	yr	158	1999	30r
Processed fruits, expenditures on	yr	124	1999	30r
Processed vegetables, expenditures on	yr	82	1999	30r
Round roast, U.S. choice, boneless	lb	3.04	7/01	11r
Spaghetti and macaroni	lb	1.04	7/01	11r
Steak, sirloin, U.S. choice, boneless	lb	5.39	7/01	11r
Strawberries, dry pint	12 oz	1.51	7/01	11r
Sugar and other sweets, expenditures on	yr	110	1999	30r
Sugar, white, 33-80 ounce package	lb	0.46	7/01	11r
Sugar, white, all sizes	lb	0.47	7/01	11r
Tobacco products and smoking supplies purchases	yr	309	1999	30r
Yogurt, natural, fruit flavored	8 oz	0.79	7/01	11r
Goods and Services				
B&B Japanese maple (acer japonicum)	gal	38.99-125.00	4/00	93r
Boxwood (buxus)	2 gal	15.99-49.95	4/00	93r
Daylilly (hemerocallis)	gal	4.95	4/00	93r
Flat of annuals		8.00-14.99	4/00	93r
Fountain grass (pennisetum)	gal	6.99-9.99	4/00	93r
Hanging basket (10 in)		12.95-19.99	4/00	93r
Hardy geranium (geranium)	gal	6.95-7.99	4/00	93r
Hosta (hosta)	gal	4.95	4/00	93r
Lilac (syrubga vulgaris)	2 gal	17.99-74.95	4/00	93r
Miscellaneous purchases	yr	872	1999	30r
Rhododendron (rhododendron)	2 gal	23.99-54.95	4/00	93r
Sage (salvia)	gal	6.95-7.99	4/00	93r
Wintercreeper euonymus (euonymus fortunei)	2 gal	14.99-23.95	4/00	93r
Hunting license	yr	11.00	4/01	34s
Health Care				
Cardiac catheterization, ave hospital/physician charges		12750	1998	77s
Childbirth, Cesarean delivery		14716	1997	13r
Childbirth, vaginal delivery		8541	1997	13r
Drugs, expenditures on	yr	296	1999	30r
Health care purchases	yr	1788	1999	30r
Health insurance expenditures	yr	875	1999	30r
Hysterectomy, laproscopically-assisted, ave hospital/physician charges		13460	1998	76s
Hysterectomy, vaginal, ave hospital and physician charges		10310	1998	76s
Medicaid dispensing fee		3.50-4.50	1999	87s
Medical services expenditures	yr	516	1999	30r
Medical supplies, expenditures on	yr	102	1999	30r
Plastic surgery, breast augmentation		4232	2000	7r
Plastic surgery, breast lift		4605	2000	7r
Plastic surgery, facelift		6964	2000	7r
Plastic surgery, hair transplantation		4193	2000	7r
Plastic surgery, lip augmentation		1675	2000	7r
Plastic surgery, lower body lift		6611	2000	7r

Albany-Schenectady-Troy, NY - continued

Item	Per	Value	Date	Ref.
Health Care - continued				
Plastic surgery, thigh lift		4751	2000	7r
Household Goods				
Floor coverings, expenditures on	yr	59	1999	30r
Furniture, expenditures on	yr	388	1999	30r
Household furnishings and equipment purchases	yr	1567	1999	30r
Household textiles, expenditures on	yr	112	1999	30r
Laundry and cleaning supplies, expenditures on	yr	104	1999	30r
Housing				
Home price, existing, ave		180800	10/00	90r
Home value, median		179000	2001	53s
Household operation expenditures	yr	581	1999	30r
Housekeeping supplies purchases	yr	474	1999	30r
Lodging expenditures	yr	550	1999	30r
Maintenance, repairs, insurance expenditures	yr	835	1999	30r
Monthly rental value of owned home	mos	663	1999	30r
Owned dwellings, expenditures own	yr	5209	1999	30r
Rent expenditures	yr	2390	1999	30r
Rental unit, 1 bedroom, with utilities	mos	494	4/01	41c
Rental unit, 2 bedroom, with utilities	mos	607	4/01	41c
Rental unit, 3 bedroom, with utilities	mos	762	4/01	41c
Rental unit, 4 bedroom, with utilities	mos	851	4/01	41c
Shelter, expenditures on	yr	8149	1999	30r
Insurance and Pensions				
Auto insurance premium	yr	1113.55	1999	57s
Life and other personal insurance purchases	yr	424	1999	30r
Pensions and Social Security, expenditures on	yr	3037	1999	30r
Legal Fees				
Divorce, filing fee		270.00	4/01	35s
Driver's license fee	renew	25.00	1999	48s
Driver's license fee	orig	25.00	1999	48s
Fishing license	yr	14.00	4/01	34s
Personal Goods				
Personal care products and services purchases	yr	399	1999	30r
Personal Services				
Personal services, household, expenditures on	yr	271	1999	30r
Pets				
Pets, toys, and playground equipment, expenditures on	yr	325	1999	30r
Taxes				
Federal income taxes paid	yr	2606	1999	30r
Personal taxes, expenditures on	yr	3567	1999	30r
Property taxes paid	yr	1752	1999	30r
State and local income taxes paid	yr	694	1999	30r
Transportation				
Cars and trucks, new, expenditures on	yr	1496	1999	30r
Cars and trucks, used, expenditures on	yr	1251	1999	30r
Diesel at the pump	gal	1.33	10/99	73s
Gasoline and motor oil purchases	yr	901	1999	30r
Gasoline before-tax price (cents)	gal	110.70	10/00	43s
Maintenance and repair expenditures	yr	618	1999	30r
Public transportation, expenditures on	yr	575	1999	30r
Transportation purchases	yr	6503	1999	30r
Vehicle expenses, miscellaneous, purchases	yr	2266	1999	30r
Vehicle insurance payments	yr	824	1999	30r
Vehicle purchases (net outlay)	yr	2761	1999	30r
Vehicle rental, lease expenditures	yr	584	1999	30r
Travel				
Hotel room	night	139.88	2/01	95s

Values are in dollars or fractions of dollars. In the column headed *Ref*, references are shown to sources. Each reference is followed by a letter. These refer to the geographical level for which data were reported: s=State, r=Region, and c=City or metro. The abbreviation *ex* is used to mean *except* or *excluding*; *exp* stands for expenditures. For other abbreviations and further explanations, please see the Introduction.

Albany-Schenectady-Troy, NY - continued

Item	Per	Value	Date	Ref.
Utilities				
Electrical bill, average	mos	71.50	9/00	9s
Electricity, expenditures on	yr	837	1999	30r
Electricity cost, average	KWh	11.34	9/00	9s
Utilities, fuels, and public services purchased	yr	2457	1999	30r
Water and other public services, expenditures on	yr	215	1999	30r
Weddings				
Wedding (national average cost)		19936	2000	33r
Wedding (regional average total cost)		29454	1997	110r
Attendants' gifts		321	1998	33r
Bridal attendants' apparel (5 persons)		824	2000	33r
Bride's headpiece/veil		173	1998	33r
Bride's wedding dress		859	1998	33r
Clergy, religious facility fee		242	1998	33r
Engagement ring		3177	1998	33r
Flowers		789	1998	33r
Groom's formalwear rental		99	2000	33r
Limousine		410	1998	33r
Marriage license cost		25.00	4/01	35s
Men's formalwear (ushers, best man)		469	2000	33r
Mother of bride apparel		241	2000	33r
Music		866	1998	33r
Photography and videography		1368	1998	33r
Rehearsal dinner		728	1998	33r
Wedding invitations and announcements		341	1998	33r
Wedding reception		7968	2000	33r
Wedding rings (bride and groom)		1060	1998	33r

Albuquerque, NM

Item	Per	Value	Date	Ref.
Composite, ACCRA index		100.60	3/01	4c
Alcoholic Beverages				
Beer, Heineken, 12-oz, ex deposit	6	7.54	3/01	4c
J & B Scotch	750-ml	19.93	3/01	4c
Wine, Livingston or Gallo, Chablis blanc	1.5 liter	6.56	3/01	4c
Appliances				
Appliance repair, service call, washing machine	min lab chg	33.80	3/01	4c
Banking and Money				
Mortgage rate, incl. points and orig. fee, 30-yr. conv. fixed or ARM	mos	6.84	3/01	4c
Business Expenses				
Business travel, car rental	day	55	2001	3c
Business travel, food	day	43	2001	3c
Business travel, hotel	day	90	2001	3c
Child Care				
Daycare	mos	341	1998	37c
Daycare, 3-year old, 5 days, 8 hrs/day	mos	341	1998	85c
Clothing				
Boys' brief, cotton	3	5.18	3/01	4c
Shirt, man's dress shirt		24.95	3/01	4c
Slacks, man's "No Wrinkles" khaki		34.50	3/01	4c
Communications				
Newspaper subscription, daily and Sunday delivery	mos	11.25	3/01	4c
Phone line, single, business, field visit	inst.	53.95	12/97	17s
Phone line, single, business, no field visit	inst.	53.95	12/97	17s
Phone line, single, residence, field visit	inst.	30.00	12/97	17s
Phone line, single, residence, no field visit	inst.	30.00	12/97	17s
Postal rate, express mail, up to half-pound		12.45	7/01	108r
Postal rate, letter, first class, first ounce		0.34	7/01	108r
Postal rate, letter, two ounces		0.57	7/01	108r
Postal rate, post card		0.21	7/01	108r
Postal rate, priority mail, two pounds		3.95	7/01	108r
Postal rate, priority mail, up to one pound		3.50	7/01	108r
Telephone bill, business, basic rate	mos	51.27	12/97	18c
Telephone bill, family of three	mos	18.31	3/01	4c

Albuquerque, NM - continued

Item	Per	Value	Date	Ref.
Communications - continued				
Telephone bill, residential, basic rate	mos	16.16	12/97	18c
Education				
Board, 4-year private college/university	yr	2282	1996	38s
Board, 4-year public college/university	yr	1854	1996	38s
Room, 4-year private college/university	yr	2289	1996	38s
Room, 4-year public college/university	yr	1504	1996	38s
Total cost, 4-year private college/university	yr	14355	1996	38s
Total cost, 4-year public college/university	yr	5298	1996	38s
Tuition, 2-year public college/university, in state	yr	690	1996	38s
Tuition, 4-year private college/university, in state	yr	9784	1996	38s
Tuition, 4-year public college/university	yr	1940	1996	38s
Energy and Fuels				
Energy, combined forms, 2400 sq ft	mos	123.76	3/01	4c
Energy, exc. electricity, 2400 sq ft	mos	61.06	3/01	4c
Gas, cooking, winter, 10 therms	mos	12.21	2/96	98c
Gas, cooking, winter, 30 therms	mos	18.62	2/96	98c
Gas, cooking, winter, 50 therms	mos	25.03	2/96	98c
Gas, heating, winter, average use	mos	48.74	2/96	98c
Gas, regular unleaded, cash, self-service	gal	1.57	3/01	4c
Entertainment				
Bowling, Saturday evening rate	line	2.67	3/01	4c
Monopoly game, Parker Brothers', No. 9	game	13.97	3/01	4c
Movie, first-run, Saturday, evening	adm.	7.56	3/01	4c
Tennis balls, yellow, Wilson or Penn, 3	can	2.16	3/01	4c
Funerals				
Total cost of funeral		5401.08	1/99	78r
Acknowledgement cards		33.64	1/99	78r
Casket		2170.43	1/99	78r
Cosmetology, hair, other preparation		136.32	1/99	78r
Embalming		319.13	1/99	78r
Funeral at funeral home		370.21	1/99	78r
Hearse (local)		161.04	1/99	78r
Professional service charges		963.15	1/99	78r
Service car/van		133.99	1/99	78r
Transfer of remains to funeral home		159.82	1/99	78r
Vault		778.07	1/99	78r
Visitation/viewing		175.28	1/99	78r
Groceries				
Groceries, ACCRA Index		107.20	3/01	4c
Antibiotic ointment, Polysporin	0.5 oz	4.94	3/01	4c
Baby food, strained vegetables or fruit, lowest price	4-4.5 oz	0.39	3/01	4c
Bananas	lb	0.49	3/01	4c
Beef or hamburger, ground	lb	1.47	3/01	4c
Bread, white	loaf	0.96	3/01	4c
Cheese, Kraft grated Parmesan	8 oz	4.29	3/01	4c
Chicken, whole fryer	lb	0.85	3/01	4c
Cigarettes, Winston, Kings	carton	28.97	3/01	4c
Coffee, vacuum-packed	13 oz	3.05	3/01	4c
Corn Flakes, Kellogg's or Post Toasties	18 oz	3.53	3/01	4c
Corn, frozen, whole kernel, lowest price	16 oz	1.39	3/01	4c
Eggs, Grade A or AA	dozen	0.96	3/01	4c
Lettuce, iceberg	head	1.09	3/01	4c
Margarine, Blue Bonnet or Parkay, stick	lb	0.89	3/01	4c
Milk, whole	1/2 gal	1.97	3/01	4c
Orange juice, Minute Maid frozen	12 oz	1.73	3/01	4c
Peaches, halves or slices, Hunt's, Del Monte, or Libby's	29 oz	1.59	3/01	4c
Peas, green, Del Monte or Green Giant	15 oz	0.75	3/01	4c
Potatoes, white or red	10 lb	2.13	3/01	4c
Sausage, Jimmy Dean/Owens pork	lb	3.55	3/01	4c
Shortening, vegetable, Crisco	3 lb	3.46	3/01	4c
Soft drink, Coca Cola, ex deposit	2 liter	1.29	3/01	4c
Steak, T-bone	lb	5.67	3/01	4c
Sugar, cane or beet	4 lbs	1.68	3/01	4c
Tomatoes, Hunt's or Del Monte	14.5 oz	0.99	3/01	4c
Tuna, chunk, light	6 oz	0.77	3/01	4c

Values are in dollars or fractions of dollars. In the column headed *Ref*, references are shown to sources. Each reference is followed by a letter. These refer to the geographical level for which data were reported: s=State, r=Region, and c=City or metro. The abbreviation *ex* is used to mean *except* or *excluding*; *exp* stands for expenditures. For other abbreviations and further explanations, please see the Introduction.

Albuquerque, NM - continued

Item	Per	Value	Date	Ref.
Goods and Services				
Miscellaneous goods and services, ACCRA Index		99.10	3/01	4c
Hunting license	yr	25.00	4/01	34s
Health Care				
Health care, ACCRA Index		101.60	3/01	4c
Cardiac catheterization, ave hospital/ physician charges		15920	1998	77s
Childbirth, Cesarean delivery		11587	1997	13r
Childbirth, vaginal delivery		6725	1997	13r
Dentist's fee, adult teeth cleaning and periodic oral exam	visit	79.60	3/01	4c
Doctor's fee, routine exam, established patient	visit	54.87	3/01	4c
Hospital care, private room	day	507.39	3/01	4c
Hysterectomy, laproscopically-assisted, ave hospital/physician charges		11750	1998	76s
Hysterectomy, vaginal, ave hospital and physician charges		8980	1998	76s
Medicaid dispensing fee		4.00	1999	87s
Household Goods				
Dishwashing powder, Cascade	50 oz	4.23	3/01	4c
Tissues, facial, Kleenex brand	175	1.75	3/01	4c
Housing				
Housing, ACCRA Index		98.70	3/01	4c
Home, 2200 sq ft, 4-br, 2-bath, 2-car garage, average		190800	2000	47c
Home value, median		119000	2001	53s
House, 2400 sq ft, 8000 sq ft lot, new, urban, utilities	total	206321	3/01	4c
House payment, principal and interest, 25% down payment	mos	1013	3/01	4c
Rent, apartment, 2 br, 1 1/2-2 baths, unfurn, 950 sq ft, water	mos	697	3/01	4c
Rental unit, 1 bedroom, with utilities	mos	473	4/01	41c
Rental unit, 2 bedroom, with utilities	mos	592	4/01	41c
Rental unit, 3 bedroom, with utilities	mos	816	4/01	41c
Rental unit, 4 bedroom, with utilities	mos	963	4/01	41c
Legal Fees				
Combination hunting and fishing license	yr	37.50	4/01	34s
Driver's license fee	renew	10.00	1999	48s
Driver's license fee	orig	10.00	1999	48s
Fishing license	yr	25.00	4/01	34s
Personal Goods				
Shampoo, Alberto VO5	15 oz	1.39	3/01	4c
Toothpaste, Crest or Colgate	6-7 oz	2.79	3/01	4c
Personal Services				
Dry cleaning, man's 2-pc suit		5.53	3/01	4c
Man's haircut, barbershop, no styling		8.50	3/01	4c
Woman's shampoo, trim, blow-dry, no style-change		26.60	3/01	4c
Restaurant Food				
Chicken, fried, thigh and drumstick, KFC/Church's		2.56	3/01	4c
Hamburger with cheese, McDonald's	1/4 lb	2.29	3/01	4c
Pizza, Pizza Hut or Pizza Inn	11-12 in	8.99	3/01	4c
Transportation				
Transportation, ACCRA Index		100.90	3/01	4c
Bus fare, one-way	trip	0.75	2000	1c
Bus fare, to central business district	1-way	0.75	3/01	4c
Diesel at the pump	gal	1.22	10/99	73s
Gasoline before-tax price (cents)	gal	115.20	10/00	43s
Tire balance, computer or spin balance, front	wheel	7.53	3/01	4c
Utilities				
Utilities, ACCRA Index		99.00	3/01	4c
Electrical bill, average	mos	46.92	9/00	9s
Electricity, summer, 250 KWh	mos	23.47	2/96	96c
Electricity, summer, 500 KWh	mos	46.57	2/96	96c

Albuquerque, NM - continued

Item	Per	Value	Date	Ref.
Utilities - continued				
Electricity, summer, 750 KWh	mos	69.67	2/96	96c
Electricity, summer, 1000 KWh	mos	92.77	2/96	96c
Electricity and other, mixed, 2400 sq ft, new home	mos	62.70	3/01	4c
Electricity cost, average	KWh	6.30	9/00	9s
Weddings				
Wedding (national average cost)		19936	2000	33r
Attendants' gifts		321	1998	33r
Bridal attendants' apparel (5 persons)		824	2000	33r
Bride's headpiece/veil		173	1998	33r
Bride's wedding dress		859	1998	33r
Clergy, religious facility fee		242	1998	33r
Engagement ring		3177	1998	33r
Flowers		789	1998	33r
Groom's formalwear rental		99	2000	33r
Limousine		410	1998	33r
Marriage license cost		25.00	4/01	35s
Men's formalwear (ushers, best man)		469	2000	33r
Mother of bride apparel		241	2000	33r
Music		866	1998	33r
Photography and videography		1368	1998	33r
Rehearsal dinner		728	1998	33r
Wedding invitations and announcements		341	1998	33r
Wedding reception		7968	2000	33r
Wedding rings (bride and groom)		1060	1998	33r

Alexandria, LA

Item	Per	Value	Date	Ref.
Alcoholic Beverages				
Alcoholic beverage purchases	yr	253	1999	30r
Malt beverages, all types, all sizes, any origin	16 oz	0.96	7/01	11r
Appliances				
Major appliances, expenditures on	yr	172	1999	30r
Small appliances, housewares, expenditures on	yr	81	1999	30r
Banking and Money				
Mortgage interest and charges paid	yr	2039	1999	30r
Mortgage principal paid on owned property	yr	1026	1999	30r
Vehicle finance charges paid	yr	365	1999	30r
Charity				
Cash contributions, expenditures	yr	1127	1999	30r
Child Care				
Child raising cost, total, age 0-2	yr	8540	1999	60r
Child raising cost, total, age 3-5	yr	8780	1999	60r
Child raising cost, total, age 6-8	yr	8820	1999	60r
Child raising cost, total, age 9-11	yr	8800	1999	60r
Child raising cost, total, age 12-14	yr	9510	1999	60r
Child raising cost, total, age 15-17	yr	9740	1999	60r
Child's child care and education, age 0-2	yr	1380	1999	60r
Child's child care and education, age 3-5	yr	1520	1999	60r
Child's child care and education, age 6-8	yr	990	1999	60r
Child's child care and education, age 9-11	yr	650	1999	60r
Child's child care and education, age 12-14	yr	490	1999	60r
Child's child care and education, age 15-17	yr	840	1999	60r
Child's clothing, age 0-2	yr	480	1999	60r
Child's clothing, age 3-5	yr	470	1999	60r
Child's clothing, age 6-8	yr	520	1999	60r
Child's clothing, age 9-11	yr	570	1999	60r
Child's clothing, age 12-14	yr	950	1999	60r
Child's clothing, age 15-17	yr	850	1999	60r
Child's food, age 0-2	yr	1000	1999	60r
Child's food, age 3-5	yr	1160	1999	60r
Child's food, age 6-8	yr	1490	1999	60r
Child's food, age 9-11	yr	1770	1999	60r
Child's food, age 12-14	yr	1770	1999	60r
Child's food, age 15-17	yr	1980	1999	60r
Child's health care, age 0-2	yr	620	1999	60r
Child's health care, age 3-5	yr	590	1999	60r

Values are in dollars or fractions of dollars. In the column headed *Ref*, references are shown to sources. Each reference is followed by a letter. These refer to the geographical level for which data were reported: s=State, r=Region, and c=City or metro. The abbreviation *ex* is used to mean *except* or *excluding*; *exp* stands for *expenditures*. For other abbreviations and further explanations, please see the Introduction.

Alexandria, LA - continued

Item	Per	Value	Date	Ref.
Child Care				
Child's health care, age 6-8	yr	680	1999	60r
Child's health care, age 9-11	yr	720	1999	60r
Child's health care, age 12-14	yr	730	1999	60r
Child's health care, age 15-17	yr	760	1999	60r
Child's housing, age 0-2	yr	3070	1999	60r
Child's housing, age 3-5	yr	3050	1999	60r
Child's housing, age 6-8	yr	3010	1999	60r
Child's housing, age 9-11	yr	2850	1999	60r
Child's housing, age 12-14	yr	3040	1999	60r
Child's housing, age 15-17	yr	2650	1999	60r
Child's personal care, reading, age 0-2	yr	910	1999	60r
Child's personal care, reading, age 3-5	yr	930	1999	60r
Child's personal care, reading, age 6-8	yr	960	1999	60r
Child's personal care, reading, age 9-11	yr	1000	1999	60r
Child's personal care, reading, age 12-14	yr	1170	1999	60r
Child's personal care, reading, age 15-17	yr	950	1999	60r
Clothing				
Apparel and services purchases	yr	1610	1999	30r
Boys, 2 to 15, expenditures on	yr	89	1999	30r
Children under 2, expenditures on	yr	79	1999	30r
Footwear, expenditures on	yr	283	1999	30r
Girls, 2 to 15, expenditures on	yr	103	1999	30r
Men and boys, expenditures on	yr	351	1999	30r
Men, 16 and over, expenditures on	yr	262	1999	30r
Women, 16 and over, expenditures on	yr	538	1999	30r
Communications				
Phone line, single, business, field visit	inst.	85.00	12/97	17s
Phone line, single, business, no field visit	inst.	85.00	12/97	17s
Phone line, single, residence, field visit	inst.	41.00	12/97	17s
Phone line, single, residence, no field visit	inst.	41.00	12/97	17s
Postage and stationery, expenditures on	yr	104	1999	30r
Postal rate, express mail, up to half-pound		12.45	7/01	108r
Postal rate, letter, first class, first ounce		0.34	7/01	108r
Postal rate, letter, two ounces		0.57	7/01	108r
Postal rate, post card		0.21	7/01	108r
Postal rate, priority mail, two pounds		3.95	7/01	108r
Postal rate, priority mail, up to one pound		3.50	7/01	108r
Telephone services, expenditures on	yr	860	1999	30r
Education				
Board, 4-year private college/university	yr	2440	1996	38s
Board, 4-year public college/university	yr	1806	1996	38s
Education expenditures	yr	431	1999	30r
Room, 4-year private college/university	yr	2906	1996	38s
Room, 4-year public college/university	yr	1464	1996	38s
Total cost, 4-year private college/university	yr	17796	1996	38s
Total cost, 4-year public college/university	yr	5491	1996	38s
Tuition, 2-year public college/university, in state	yr	1031	1996	38s
Tuition, 4-year private college/university, in state	yr	12449	1996	38s
Tuition, 4-year public college/university	yr	2221	1996	38s
Energy and Fuels				
Electricity	KWh	0.09	7/01	11r
Electricity	500 KWhs	47.29	7/01	11r
Fuel oil #2	gal	1.43	7/01	11r
Fuel oil and other fuels, expenditures on	yr	45	1999	30r
Gas, natural, commercial rate	1000 cf	8.75	11/00	88s
Gasoline, all types	gal	1.60	7/01	11r
Gasoline, unleaded midgrade	gal	1.65	7/01	11r
Gasoline, unleaded premium	gal	1.74	7/01	11r
Natural gas, expenditures on	yr	164	1999	30r
Utility (piped) gas, therm		1.01	7/01	11r
Utility (piped) gas, 40 therms		44.29	7/01	11r
Utility (piped) gas, 100 therms		97.44	7/01	11r
Entertainment				
Entertainment purchases	yr	1574	1999	30r
Fees and admissions paid	yr	371	1999	30r
Reading purchases	yr	121	1999	30r

Alexandria, LA - continued

Item	Per	Value	Date	Ref.
Entertainment - continued				
Television, radios, sound equipment, expenditures on	yr	561	1999	30r
Funerals				
Total cost of funeral		5842.28	1/99	78r
Acknowledgement cards		28.35	1/99	78r
Casket		2494.29	1/99	78r
Cosmetology, hair, other preparation		109.22	1/99	78r
Embalming		361.42	1/99	78r
Funeral at funeral home		349.20	1/99	78r
Hearse (local)		161.91	1/99	78r
Professional service charges		1116.50	1/99	78r
Service car/van		65.56	1/99	78r
Transfer of remains to funeral home		143.56	1/99	78r
Vault		785.25	1/99	78r
Visitation/viewing		227.02	1/99	78r
Groceries				
American processed cheese	lb	3.50	7/01	11r
Bakery products, expenditures on	yr	261	1999	30r
Bananas	lb	0.47	7/01	11r
Beans, dried, any type, all sizes	lb	0.63	7/01	11r
Beef for stew, boneless	lb	2.86	7/01	11r
Beef, expenditures on	yr	210	1999	30r
Bologna, all beef or mixed	lb	2.29	7/01	11r
Bread, French	lb	1.66	7/01	11r
Bread, white, pan	lb	0.87	7/01	11r
Bread, whole wheat, pan	lb	1.38	7/01	11r
Broccoli	lb	1.04	7/01	11r
Butter, salted, grade AA, stick	lb	2.26	7/01	11r
Butter, yoghurt, cheese, etc, expenditures on	yr	170	1999	30r
Cabbage	lb	0.42	7/01	11r
Cereals and cereal products, expenditures on	yr	140	1999	30r
Cheddar cheese, natural	lb	3.75	7/01	11r
Chicken breast, bone-in	lb	1.85	7/01	11r
Chicken legs, bone-in	lb	1.34	7/01	11r
Chicken, fresh, whole	lb	1.05	7/01	11r
Chops, boneless,	lb	4.13	7/01	11r
Chuck roast, graded and ungraded, excl U.S. prime and choice	lb	2.35	7/01	11r
Chuck roast, U.S. choice, boneless	lb	2.67	7/01	11r
Coffee, 100%, ground roast, all sizes	lb	2.88	7/01	11r
Coffee, instant, plain, regular, all sizes	16 oz	9.25	7/01	11r
Cola, non diet,	2 liter	1.11	7/01	11r
Crackers, soda, salted	lb	1.70	7/01	11r
Dairy product purchases	yr	282	1999	30r
Eggs, expenditures on	yr	32	1999	30r
Fats and oils, expenditures on	yr	79	1999	30r
Fish and seafood, expenditures on	yr	99	1999	30r
Flour, white, all purpose	lb	0.32	7/01	11r
Food (excl fruit and vegetables), eaten at home, purchases	yr	815	1999	30r
Food cooked on trips, expenditures on	yr	36	1999	30r
Food purchases	yr	4533	1999	30r
Food purchases, eaten away from home	yr	1873	1999	30r
Food purchases, food eaten at home	yr	2660	1999	30r
Fresh fruits, expenditures on	yr	128	1999	30r
Fresh milk and cream, expenditures on	yr	112	1999	30r
Fresh vegetables, expenditures on	yr	131	1999	30r
Fruit and vegetable purchases	yr	438	1999	30r
Grapefruit	lb	0.59	7/01	11r
Grapes, Thompson, seedless	lb	2.12	7/01	11r
Ground beef, 100% beef	lb	1.76	7/01	11r
Ground beef, lean and extra lean	lb	2.60	7/01	11r
Ground chuck, 100% beef	lb	2.08	7/01	11r
Ham, boneless, excl canned	lb	2.71	7/01	11r
Ham, rump or shank half, bone-in, smoked	lb	2.19	7/01	11r
Ice cream, prepackaged, bulk, regular	1/2 gal	3.93	7/01	11r
Lemons	lb	1.32	7/01	11r
Lettuce, iceberg	lb	0.76	7/01	11r
Milk, fresh, low fat,	gal	2.75	7/01	11r
Milk, fresh, whole, fortified	gal	2.97	7/01	11r

Values are in dollars or fractions of dollars. In the column headed *Ref*, references are shown to sources. Each reference is followed by a letter. These refer to the geographical level for which data were reported: s=State, r=Region, and c=City or metro. The abbreviation *ex* is used to mean *except* or *excluding*; *exp* stands for *expenditures*. For other abbreviations and further explanations, please see the Introduction.

Alexandria, LA - continued

Item	Per	Value	Date	Ref.
Groceries				
Nonalcoholic beverages, expenditures on	yr	228	1999	30r
Orange juice, frozen concentrate	16 oz	1.95	7/01	11r
Oranges, Navel	lb	0.73	7/01	11r
Oranges, Valencia	lb	0.55	7/01	11r
Peanut butter, creamy, all sizes	lb	1.83	7/01	11r
Pears, Anjou	lb	0.98	7/01	11r
Pork chops, center cut, bone-in	lb	3.33	7/01	11r
Pork sausage, fresh, loose	lb	2.59	7/01	11r
Pork shoulder picnic, bone-in, smoked	lb	1.12	7/01	11r
Pork, expenditures on	yr	162	1999	30r
Potato chips	16 oz	3.59	7/01	11r
Potatoes, frozen, french fried	lb	1.00	7/01	11r
Potatoes, white, all types	lb	0.44	7/01	11r
Poultry, expenditures on	yr	137	1999	30r
Processed fruits, expenditures on	yr	97	1999	30r
Processed vegetables, expenditures on	yr	82	1999	30r
Rice, white, long grain, uncooked	lb	0.51	7/01	11r
Round roast, graded and ungraded, excl U.S. prime and choice	lb	2.96	7/01	11r
Round steak, graded and ungraded, excl U.S. prime and choice	lb	3.11	7/01	11r
Sirloin steak, graded and ungraded, excl U.S. prime and choice	lb	4.23	7/01	11r
Spaghetti and macaroni	lb	0.78	7/01	11r
Steak, round, U.S. choice, boneless	lb	3.56	7/01	11r
Steak, sirloin, U.S. choice, boneless	lb	5.65	7/01	11r
Strawberries, dry pint	12 oz	1.50	7/01	11r
Sugar and other sweets, expenditures on	yr	99	1999	30r
Sugar, white, 33-80 ounce package	lb	0.39	7/01	11r
Sugar, white, all sizes	lb	0.42	7/01	11r
Tobacco products and smoking supplies purchases	yr	288	1999	30r
Tomatoes, field grown	lb	1.43	7/01	11r
Tuna, light, chunk	lb	1.77	7/01	11r
Turkey, frozen, whole	lb	1.05	7/01	11r
Goods and Services				
B&B Japanese maple (acer japonicum)	gal	79.98-99.00	4/00	93r
Boxwood (buxus)	2 gal	12.98-18.99	4/00	93r
Daylilly (hemerocallis)	gal	7.96-11.00	4/00	93r
Flat of annuals		13.99-27.99	4/00	93r
Fountain grass (pennisetum)	gal	6.96-9.00	4/00	93r
Hanging basket (10 in)		9.99-24.99	4/00	93r
Hardy geranium (geranium)	gal	5.96-8.00	4/00	93r
Hosta (hosta)	gal	8.96-12.99	4/00	93r
Lilac (syrubga vulgaris)	2 gal	13.00-19.99	4/00	93r
Rhododendron (rhododendron)	2 gal	12.98-29.99	4/00	93r
Sage (salvia)	gal	5.96-8.00	4/00	93r
Wintercreeper euonymus (euonymus fortunei)	2 gal	13.00-18.99	4/00	93r
Hunting license	yr	15.00	4/01	34s
Health Care				
Cardiac catheterization, ave hospital/ physician charges		15650	1998	77s
Childbirth, Cesarean delivery		11587	1997	13r
Childbirth, vaginal delivery		6725	1997	13r
Drugs, expenditures on	yr	399	1999	30r
Health care purchases	yr	1971	1999	30r
Health insurance expenditures	yr	933	1999	30r
Hysterectomy, laproscopically-assisted, ave hospital/physician charges		14600	1998	76s

Alexandria, LA - continued

Item	Per	Value	Date	Ref.
Health Care - continued				
Hysterectomy, vaginal, ave hospital and physician charges		10520	1998	76s
Medicaid dispensing fee		5.77	1999	87s
Medical services expenditures	yr	547	1999	30r
Medical supplies, expenditures on	yr	91	1999	30r
Household Goods				
Floor coverings, expenditures on	yr	44	1999	30r
Furniture, expenditures on	yr	335	1999	30r
Household furnishings and equipment purchases	yr	1328	1999	30r
Household textiles, expenditures on	yr	89	1999	30r
Laundry and cleaning supplies, expenditures on	yr	113	1999	30r
Housing				
Home price, existing, ave		160100	10/00	90r
Home value, median		108000	2001	53s
Household operation expenditures	yr	553	1999	30r
Housekeeping supplies purchases	yr	473	1999	30r
Housing, expenditures on	yr	10303	1999	30r
Maintenance, repairs, insurance expenditures	yr	699	1999	30r
Monthly rental value of owned home	mos	505	1999	30r
Owned dwellings, expenditures own	yr	3465	1999	30r
Rent expenditures	yr	1641	1999	30r
Rental unit, 1 bedroom, with utilities	mos	354	4/01	41c
Rental unit, 2 bedroom, with utilities	mos	444	4/01	41c
Rental unit, 3 bedroom, with utilities	mos	615	4/01	41c
Rental unit, 4 bedroom, with utilities	mos	625	4/01	41c
Shelter, expenditures on	yr	5467	1999	30r
Insurance and Pensions				
Auto insurance premium	yr	965.15	1999	57s
Life and other personal insurance purchases	yr	414	1999	30r
Pensions and Social Security, expenditures on	yr	2635	1999	30r
Personal insurance and pensions, expenditures on	yr	3048	1999	30r
Legal Fees				
Divorce, filing fee		162.00	4/01	35s
Driver's license fee	renew	12.50	1999	48s
Driver's license fee	orig	18.00	1999	48s
Fishing license	yr	9.50	4/01	34s
Personal Goods				
Personal care products and services purchases	yr	393	1999	30r
Personal Services				
Personal services, household, expenditures on	yr	258	1999	30r
Pets				
Pets, toys, and playground equipment, expenditures on	yr	306	1999	30r
Taxes				
Federal income taxes paid	yr	2047	1999	30r
Personal taxes, expenditures on	yr	2554	1999	30r
Property taxes paid	yr	726	1999	30r
State and local income taxes paid	yr	363	1999	30r
Transportation				
Cars and trucks, new, expenditures on	yr	1648	1999	30r
Cars and trucks, used, expenditures on	yr	1651	1999	30r
Diesel at the pump	gal	1.19	10/99	73s
Gasoline and motor oil purchases	yr	1052	1999	30r
Gasoline before-tax price (cents)	gal	102.70	10/00	43s
Maintenance and repair expenditures	yr	621	1999	30r
Public transportation, expenditures on	yr	298	1999	30r
Transportation purchases	yr	6738	1999	30r
Vehicle expenses, miscellaneous, purchases	yr	2033	1999	30r
Vehicle insurance payments	yr	696	1999	30r
Vehicle purchases (net outlay)	yr	3354	1999	30r

Values are in dollars or fractions of dollars. In the column headed *Ref*, references are shown to sources. Each reference is followed by a letter. These refer to the geographical level for which data were reported: s=State, r=Region, and c=City or metro. The abbreviation *ex* is used to mean *except* or *excluding*; *exp* stands for *expenditures*. For other abbreviations and further explanations, please see the Introduction.

Alexandria, LA - continued

Item	Per	Value	Date	Ref.
Transportation				
Vehicle rental, lease expenditures	yr	352	1999	30r
Utilities				
Electrical bill, average	mos	87.50	9/00	9s
Electricity, expenditures on	yr	1115	1999	30r
Electricity cost, average	KWh	6.35	9/00	9s
Water and other public services, expenditures on	yr	298	1999	30r
Weddings				
Wedding (national average cost)		19936	2000	33r
Attendants' gifts		321	1998	33r
Bridal attendants' apparel (5 persons)		824	2000	33r
Bride's headpiece/veil		173	1998	33r
Bride's wedding dress		859	1998	33r
Clergy, religious facility fee		242	1998	33r
Engagement ring		3177	1998	33r
Flowers		789	1998	33r
Groom's formalwear rental		99	2000	33r
Limousine		410	1998	33r
Marriage license cost		25.00	4/01	35s
Men's formalwear (ushers, best man)		469	2000	33r
Mother of bride apparel		241	2000	33r
Music		866	1998	33r
Photography and videography		1368	1998	33r
Rehearsal dinner		728	1998	33r
Wedding invitations and announcements		341	1998	33r
Wedding reception		7968	2000	33r
Wedding rings (bride and groom)		1060	1998	33r

Allentown-Bethlehem-Easton, PA-NJ

Item	Per	Value	Date	Ref.
Average annual expenditures	yr	37971	1999	30r
Alcoholic Beverages				
Alcoholic beverage purchases	yr	368	1999	30r
Wine, red and white table, all sizes, any origin	liter	9.64	7/01	11r
Appliances				
Major appliances, expenditures on	yr	194	1999	30r
Small appliances, housewares, expenditures on	yr	93	1999	30r
Banking and Money				
Mortgage interest and charges paid	yr	2622	1999	30r
Mortgage principal paid on owned property	yr	1262	1999	30r
Vehicle finance charges paid	yr	240	1999	30r
Charity				
Cash contributions, expenditures	yr	1001	1999	30r
Child Care				
Child raising cost, total, age 0-2	yr	8670	1999	60r
Child raising cost, total, age 3-5	yr	8910	1999	60r
Child raising cost, total, age 6-8	yr	9040	1999	60r
Child raising cost, total, age 9-11	yr	9100	1999	60r
Child raising cost, total, age 12-14	yr	9890	1999	60r
Child raising cost, total, age 15-17	yr	10010	1999	60r
Child's child care and education, age 0-2	yr	1070	1999	60r
Child's child care and education, age 3-5	yr	1190	1999	60r
Child's child care and education, age 6-8	yr	740	1999	60r
Child's child care and education, age 9-11	yr	470	1999	60r
Child's child care and education, age 12-14	yr	350	1999	60r
Child's child care and education, age 15-17	yr	590	1999	60r
Child's clothing, age 0-2	yr	480	1999	60r
Child's clothing, age 3-5	yr	470	1999	60r
Child's clothing, age 6-8	yr	520	1999	60r
Child's clothing, age 9-11	yr	570	1999	60r
Child's clothing, age 12-14	yr	970	1999	60r
Child's clothing, age 15-17	yr	870	1999	60r
Child's food, age 0-2	yr	1130	1999	60r
Child's food, age 3-5	yr	1290	1999	60r
Child's food, age 6-8	yr	1640	1999	60r
Child's food, age 9-11	yr	1930	1999	60r

Allentown-Bethlehem-Easton, PA-NJ - continued

Item	Per	Value	Date	Ref.
Child Care - continued				
Child's food, age 12-14	yr	1940	1999	60r
Child's food, age 15-17	yr	2150	1999	60r
Child's health care, age 0-2	yr	550	1999	60r
Child's health care, age 3-5	yr	530	1999	60r
Child's health care, age 6-8	yr	610	1999	60r
Child's health care, age 9-11	yr	650	1999	60r
Child's health care, age 12-14	yr	660	1999	60r
Child's health care, age 15-17	yr	690	1999	60r
Child's housing, age 0-2	yr	3555	1999	60r
Child's housing, age 3-5	yr	3530	1999	60r
Child's housing, age 6-8	yr	3490	1999	60r
Child's housing, age 9-11	yr	3340	1999	60r
Child's housing, age 12-14	yr	3530	1999	60r
Child's housing, age 15-17	yr	3140	1999	60r
Child's personal care, reading, age 0-2	yr	920	1999	60r
Child's personal care, reading, age 3-5	yr	950	1999	60r
Child's personal care, reading, age 6-8	yr	980	1999	60r
Child's personal care, reading, age 9-11	yr	1020	1999	60r
Child's personal care, reading, age 12-14	yr	1190	1999	60r
Child's personal care, reading, age 15-17	yr	970	1999	60r
Clothing				
Apparel and services purchases	yr	1831	1999	30r
Boys, 2 to 15, expenditures on	yr	92	1999	30r
Children under 2, expenditures on	yr	63	1999	30r
Footwear, expenditures on	yr	300	1999	30r
Girls, 2 to 15, expenditures on	yr	101	1999	30r
Men and boys, expenditures on	yr	446	1999	30r
Men, 16 and over, expenditures on	yr	354	1999	30r
Women, 16 and over, expenditures on	yr	584	1999	30r
Communications				
Cable modem installation, Adelphi		54.90	6/99	103s
Cable modem installation, Comcast		95.00	6/99	103s
Cable modem rate, cable subscriber, Adelphi	mos	34.95	6/99	103s
Cable modem rate, cable subscriber, Comcast	mos	39.95	6/99	103s
Cable modem rate, non-cable subscriber, Adelphi	mos	44.95	6/99	103s
Cable modem rate, non-cable subscriber, Comcast	mos	49.95	6/99	103s
Phone line, single, business, field visit	inst.	75.00	12/97	17s
Phone line, single, business, no field visit	inst.	75.00	12/97	17s
Phone line, single, residence, field visit	inst.	40.00	12/97	17s
Phone line, single, residence, no field visit	inst.	40.00	12/97	17s
Postage and stationery, expenditures on	yr	138	1999	30r
Postal rate, express mail, up to half-pound		12.45	7/01	108r
Postal rate, letter, first class, first ounce		0.34	7/01	108r
Postal rate, letter, two ounces		0.57	7/01	108r
Postal rate, post card		0.21	7/01	108r
Postal rate, priority mail, two pounds		3.95	7/01	108r
Postal rate, priority mail, up to one pound		3.50	7/01	108r
Telephone services, expenditures on	yr	830	1999	30r
Education				
Board, 4-year private college/university	yr	2822	1996	38s
Board, 4-year public college/university	yr	2174	1996	38s
Education expenditures	yr	877	1999	30r
Room, 4-year private college/university	yr	2943	1996	38s
Room, 4-year public college/university	yr	2227	1996	38s
Total cost, 4-year private college/university	yr	19876	1996	38s
Total cost, 4-year public college/university	yr	9124	1996	38s
Tuition, 2-year public college/university, in state	yr	1909	1996	38s
Tuition, 4-year private college/university, in state	yr	14111	1996	38s
Tuition, 4-year public college/university	yr	4723	1996	38s
Energy and Fuels				
Electricity	KWh	0.12	7/01	11r
Fuel oil #2	gal	1.31	7/01	11r
Fuel oil and other fuels, expenditures on	yr	207	1999	30r
Gas, natural, commercial rate	1000 cf	5.96	11/00	88s
Gasoline, all types	gal	1.80	7/01	11r

Values are in dollars or fractions of dollars. In the column headed *Ref*, references are shown to sources. Each reference is followed by a letter. These refer to the geographical level for which data were reported: s=State, r=Region, and c=City or metro. The abbreviation *ex* is used to mean *except* or *excluding*; *exp* stands for *expenditures*. For other abbreviations and further explanations, please see the Introduction.

Allentown-Bethlehem-Easton, PA-NJ - continued

Item	Per	Value	Date	Ref.
Energy and Fuels				
Gasoline, unleaded midgrade	gal	1.85	7/01	11r
Gasoline, unleaded premium	gal	1.91	7/01	11r
Gasoline, unleaded regular	gal	1.71	7/01	11r
Natural gas, expenditures on	yr	368	1999	30r
Utility (piped) gas, therm		1.08	7/01	11r
Utility (piped) gas, 40 therms		50.87	7/01	11r
Utility (piped) gas, 100 therms		111.06	7/01	11r
Entertainment				
Entertainment purchases	yr	1821	1999	30r
Fees and admissions paid	yr	511	1999	30r
Television, radios, sound equipment, expenditures on	yr	650	1999	30r
Funerals				
Total cost of funeral		5813.50	1/99	78r
Acknowledgement cards		28.32	1/99	78r
Casket		2082.20	1/99	78r
Cosmetology, hair, other preparation		169.59	1/99	78r
Embalming		465.60	1/99	78r
Funeral at funeral home		339.56	1/99	78r
Hearse (local)		183.96	1/99	78r
Professional service charges		1157.85	1/99	78r
Service car/van		100.41	1/99	78r
Transfer of remains to funeral home		158.66	1/99	78r
Vault		766.31	1/99	78r
Visitation/viewing		361.04	1/99	78r
Groceries				
Apples, red delicious	lb	0.95	7/01	11r
Bacon, sliced	lb	3.44	7/01	11r
Bakery products, expenditures on	yr	310	1999	30r
Bananas	lb	0.55	7/01	11r
Beef, expenditures on	yr	236	1999	30r
Bread, white, pan	lb	1.09	7/01	11r
Butter, yoghurt, cheese, etc, expenditures on	yr	214	1999	30r
Cereals and bakery product purchases	yr	474	1999	30r
Cereals and cereal products, expenditures on	yr	164	1999	30r
Chicken legs, bone-in	lb	1.23	7/01	11r
Chicken, fresh, whole	lb	1.13	7/01	11r
Chuck roast, U.S. choice, boneless	lb	2.79	7/01	11r
Coffee, 100%, ground roast, all sizes	lb	3.40	7/01	11r
Dairy product purchases	yr	342	1999	30r
Eggs, expenditures on	yr	34	1999	30r
Eggs, grade A, large	dozen	0.82	7/01	11r
Fats and oils, expenditures on	yr	80	1999	30r
Fish and seafood, expenditures on	yr	123	1999	30r
Food (excl fruit and vegetables), eaten at home, purchases	yr	838	1999	30r
Food cooked on trips, expenditures on	yr	48	1999	30r
Food purchases	yr	5314	1999	30r
Food purchases, eaten away from home	yr	2313	1999	30r
Food purchases, food eaten at home	yr	3001	1999	30r
Fresh fruits, expenditures on	yr	169	1999	30r
Fresh milk and cream, expenditures on	yr	128	1999	30r
Fresh vegetables, expenditures on	yr	164	1999	30r
Grapefruit	lb	0.67	7/01	11r
Grapes, Thompson, seedless	lb	2.18	7/01	11r
Ground beef, lean and extra lean	lb	2.66	7/01	11r
Ground chuck, 100% beef	lb	2.04	7/01	11r
Lettuce, iceberg	lb	0.76	7/01	11r
Meats, poultry, fish, and egg purchases	yr	808	1999	30r
Nonalcoholic beverages, expenditures on	yr	225	1999	30r
Orange juice, frozen concentrate	16 oz	1.88	7/01	11r
Oranges, Navel	lb	0.79	7/01	11r
Oranges, Valencia	lb	0.56	7/01	11r
Peaches	lb	1.16	7/01	11r
Peanut butter, creamy, all sizes	lb	2.01	7/01	11r
Pears, Anjou	lb	1.16	7/01	11r
Pork chops, center cut, bone-in	lb	3.57	7/01	11r
Pork, expenditures on	yr	146	1999	30r
Potato chips	16 oz	3.37	7/01	11r
Potatoes, white, all types	lb	0.42	7/01	11r

Allentown-Bethlehem-Easton, PA-NJ - continued

Item	Per	Value	Date	Ref.
Groceries - continued				
Poultry, expenditures on	yr	158	1999	30r
Processed fruits, expenditures on	yr	124	1999	30r
Processed vegetables, expenditures on	yr	82	1999	30r
Round roast, U.S. choice, boneless	lb	3.04	7/01	11r
Spaghetti and macaroni	lb	1.04	7/01	11r
Steak, sirloin, U.S. choice, boneless	lb	5.39	7/01	11r
Strawberries, dry pint	12 oz	1.51	7/01	11r
Sugar and other sweets, expenditures on	yr	110	1999	30r
Sugar, white, 33-80 ounce package	lb	0.46	7/01	11r
Sugar, white, all sizes	lb	0.47	7/01	11r
Tobacco products and smoking supplies purchases	yr	309	1999	30r
Yogurt, natural, fruit flavored	8 oz	0.79	7/01	11r
Goods and Services				
B&B Japanese maple (acer japonicum)	gal	38.99-125.00	4/00	93r
Boxwood (buxus)	2 gal	15.99-49.95	4/00	93r
Daylilly (hemerocallis)	gal	4.95	4/00	93r
Flat of annuals		8.00-14.99	4/00	93r
Fountain grass (pennisetum)	gal	6.99-9.99	4/00	93r
Hanging basket (10 in)		12.95-19.99	4/00	93r
Hardy geranium (geranium)	gal	6.95-7.99	4/00	93r
Hosta (hosta)	gal	4.95	4/00	93r
Lilac (syrubga vulgaris)	2 gal	17.99-74.95	4/00	93r
Miscellaneous purchases	yr	872	1999	30r
Rhododendron (rhododendron)	2 gal	23.99-54.95	4/00	93r
Sage (salvia)	gal	6.95-7.99	4/00	93r
Wintercreeper euonymus (euonymus fortunei)	2 gal	14.99-23.95	4/00	93r
Hunting license	yr	20.00	4/01	34s
Health Care				
Cardiac catheterization, ave hospital/physician charges		13870	1998	77s
Childbirth, Cesarean delivery		14716	1997	13r
Childbirth, vaginal delivery		8541	1997	13r
Drugs, expenditures on	yr	296	1999	30r
Health care purchases	yr	1788	1999	30r
Health insurance expenditures	yr	875	1999	30r
Hysterectomy, laproscopically-assisted, ave hospital/physician charges		14760	1998	76s
Hysterectomy, vaginal, ave hospital and physician charges		9270	1998	76s
Medicaid dispensing fee		4.00	1999	87s
Medical services expenditures	yr	516	1999	30r
Medical supplies, expenditures on	yr	102	1999	30r
Plastic surgery, breast augmentation		4232	2000	7r
Plastic surgery, breast lift		4605	2000	7r
Plastic surgery, facelift		6964	2000	7r
Plastic surgery, hair transplantation		4193	2000	7r
Plastic surgery, lip augmentation		1675	2000	7r
Plastic surgery, lower body lift		6611	2000	7r
Plastic surgery, thigh lift		4751	2000	7r
Household Goods				
Floor coverings, expenditures on	yr	59	1999	30r
Furniture, expenditures on	yr	388	1999	30r
Household furnishings and equipment purchases	yr	1567	1999	30r
Household textiles, expenditures on	yr	112	1999	30r
Laundry and cleaning supplies, expenditures on	yr	104	1999	30r

Values are in dollars or fractions of dollars. In the column headed *Ref*, references are shown to sources. Each reference is followed by a letter. These refer to the geographical level for which data were reported: s=State, r=Region, and c=City or metro. The abbreviation *ex* is used to mean *except* or *excluding*; *exp* stands for *expenditures*. For other abbreviations and further explanations, please see the Introduction.

Allentown-Bethlehem-Easton, PA-NJ - continued

Item	Per	Value	Date	Ref.
Housing				
Home price, existing, ave		180800	10/00	90r
Home value, median		115000	2001	53s
Household operation expenditures	yr	581	1999	30r
Housekeeping supplies purchases	yr	474	1999	30r
Lodging expenditures	yr	550	1999	30r
Maintenance, repairs, insurance expenditures	yr	835	1999	30r
Monthly rental value of owned home	mos	663	1999	30r
Owned dwellings, expenditures own	yr	5209	1999	30r
Rent expenditures	yr	2390	1999	30r
Rental unit, 1 bedroom, with utilities	mos	511	4/01	41c
Rental unit, 2 bedroom, with utilities	mos	608	4/01	41c
Rental unit, 3 bedroom, with utilities	mos	792	4/01	41c
Rental unit, 4 bedroom, with utilities	mos	889	4/01	41c
Shelter, expenditures on	yr	8149	1999	30r
Insurance and Pensions				
Life and other personal insurance purchases	yr	424	1999	30r
Pensions and Social Security, expenditures on	yr	3037	1999	30r
Legal Fees				
Divorce, filing fee		65.00	4/01	35s
Driver's license fee	orig	29.00	1999	48s
Driver's license fee	renew	24.00	1999	48s
Fishing license	yr	17.00	4/01	34s
Personal Goods				
Personal care products and services purchases	yr	399	1999	30r
Personal Services				
Personal services, household, expenditures on	yr	271	1999	30r
Pets				
Pets, toys, and playground equipment, expenditures on	yr	325	1999	30r
Taxes				
Federal income taxes paid	yr	2606	1999	30r
Personal taxes, expenditures on	yr	3567	1999	30r
Property taxes paid	yr	1752	1999	30r
State and local income taxes paid	yr	694	1999	30r
Transportation				
Cars and trucks, new, expenditures on	yr	1496	1999	30r
Cars and trucks, used, expenditures on	yr	1251	1999	30r
Diesel at the pump	gal	1.31	10/99	73s
Gasoline and motor oil purchases	yr	901	1999	30r
Gasoline before-tax price (cents)	gal	106.60	10/00	43s
Maintenance and repair expenditures	yr	618	1999	30r
Public transportation, expenditures on	yr	575	1999	30r
Transportation purchases	yr	6503	1999	30r
Vehicle expenses, miscellaneous, purchases	yr	2266	1999	30r
Vehicle insurance payments	yr	824	1999	30r
Vehicle purchases (net outlay)	yr	2761	1999	30r
Vehicle rental, lease expenditures	yr	584	1999	30r
Utilities				
Electrical bill, average	mos	69.16	9/00	9s
Electricity, expenditures on	yr	837	1999	30r
Electricity, summer, 250 KWh	mos	27.97	2/96	96c
Electricity, summer, 500 KWh	mos	47.60	2/96	96c
Electricity, summer, 750 KWh	mos	67.24	2/96	96c
Electricity, summer, 1000 KWh	mos	85.69	2/96	96c
Electricity cost, average	KWh	5.08	9/00	9s
Utilities, fuels, and public services purchased	yr	2457	1999	30r
Water and other public services, expenditures on	yr	215	1999	30r
Weddings				
Wedding (national average cost)		19936	2000	33r
Wedding (regional average total cost)		29454	1997	110r
Attendants' gifts		321	1998	33r
Bridal attendants' apparel (5 persons)		824	2000	33r

Allentown-Bethlehem-Easton, PA-NJ - continued

Item	Per	Value	Date	Ref.
Weddings - continued				
Bride's headpiece/veil		173	1998	33r
Bride's wedding dress		859	1998	33r
Clergy, religious facility fee		242	1998	33r
Engagement ring		3177	1998	33r
Flowers		789	1998	33r
Groom's formalwear rental		99	2000	33r
Limousine		410	1998	33r
Marriage license cost		25.00-40.00	4/01	35s
Men's formalwear (ushers, best man)		469	2000	33r
Mother of bride apparel		241	2000	33r
Music		866	1998	33r
Photography and videography		1368	1998	33r
Rehearsal dinner		728	1998	33r
Wedding invitations and announcements		341	1998	33r
Wedding reception		7968	2000	33r
Wedding rings (bride and groom)		1060	1998	33r

Altoona, PA

Item	Per	Value	Date	Ref.
Average annual expenditures	yr	37971	1999	30r
Alcoholic Beverages				
Alcoholic beverage purchases	yr	368	1999	30r
Wine, red and white table, all sizes, any origin	liter	9.64	7/01	11r
Appliances				
Major appliances, expenditures on	yr	194	1999	30r
Small appliances, housewares, expenditures on	yr	93	1999	30r
Banking and Money				
Mortgage interest and charges paid	yr	2622	1999	30r
Mortgage principal paid on owned property	yr	1262	1999	30r
Vehicle finance charges paid	yr	240	1999	30r
Charity				
Cash contributions, expenditures	yr	1001	1999	30r
Child Care				
Child raising cost, total, age 0-2	yr	8670	1999	60r
Child raising cost, total, age 3-5	yr	8910	1999	60r
Child raising cost, total, age 6-8	yr	9040	1999	60r
Child raising cost, total, age 9-11	yr	9100	1999	60r
Child raising cost, total, age 12-14	yr	9890	1999	60r
Child raising cost, total, age 15-17	yr	10010	1999	60r
Child's child care and education, age 0-2	yr	1070	1999	60r
Child's child care and education, age 3-5	yr	1190	1999	60r
Child's child care and education, age 6-8	yr	740	1999	60r
Child's child care and education, age 9-11	yr	470	1999	60r
Child's child care and education, age 12-14	yr	350	1999	60r
Child's child care and education, age 15-17	yr	590	1999	60r
Child's clothing, age 0-2	yr	480	1999	60r
Child's clothing, age 3-5	yr	470	1999	60r
Child's clothing, age 6-8	yr	520	1999	60r
Child's clothing, age 9-11	yr	570	1999	60r
Child's clothing, age 12-14	yr	970	1999	60r
Child's clothing, age 15-17	yr	870	1999	60r
Child's food, age 0-2	yr	1130	1999	60r
Child's food, age 3-5	yr	1290	1999	60r
Child's food, age 6-8	yr	1640	1999	60r
Child's food, age 9-11	yr	1930	1999	60r
Child's food, age 12-14	yr	1940	1999	60r
Child's food, age 15-17	yr	2150	1999	60r
Child's health care, age 0-2	yr	550	1999	60r
Child's health care, age 3-5	yr	530	1999	60r
Child's health care, age 6-8	yr	610	1999	60r
Child's health care, age 9-11	yr	650	1999	60r
Child's health care, age 12-14	yr	660	1999	60r
Child's health care, age 15-17	yr	690	1999	60r
Child's housing, age 0-2	yr	3555	1999	60r
Child's housing, age 3-5	yr	3530	1999	60r
Child's housing, age 6-8	yr	3490	1999	60r

Values are in dollars or fractions of dollars. In the column headed *Ref*, references are shown to sources. Each reference is followed by a letter. These refer to the geographical level for which data were reported: s=State, r=Region, and c=City or metro. The abbreviation *ex* is used to mean *except* or *excluding*; *exp* stands for *expenditures*. For other abbreviations and further explanations, please see the Introduction.

Altoona, PA - continued

Item	Per	Value	Date	Ref.
Child Care				
Child's housing, age 9-11	yr	3340	1999	60r
Child's housing, age 12-14	yr	3530	1999	60r
Child's housing, age 15-17	yr	3140	1999	60r
Child's personal care, reading, age 0-2	yr	920	1999	60r
Child's personal care, reading, age 3-5	yr	950	1999	60r
Child's personal care, reading, age 6-8	yr	980	1999	60r
Child's personal care, reading, age 9-11	yr	1020	1999	60r
Child's personal care, reading, age 12-14	yr	1190	1999	60r
Child's personal care, reading, age 15-17	yr	970	1999	60r
Clothing				
Apparel and services purchases	yr	1831	1999	30r
Boys, 2 to 15, expenditures on	yr	92	1999	30r
Children under 2, expenditures on	yr	63	1999	30r
Footwear, expenditures on	yr	300	1999	30r
Girls, 2 to 15, expenditures on	yr	101	1999	30r
Men and boys, expenditures on	yr	446	1999	30r
Men, 16 and over, expenditures on	yr	354	1999	30r
Women, 16 and over, expenditures on	yr	584	1999	30r
Communications				
Cable modem installation, Adelphi		54.90	6/99	103s
Cable modem installation, Comcast		95.00	6/99	103s
Cable modem rate, cable subscriber, Adelphi	mos	34.95	6/99	103s
Cable modem rate, cable subscriber, Comcast	mos	39.95	6/99	103s
Cable modem rate, non-cable subscriber, Adelphi	mos	44.95	6/99	103s
Cable modem rate, non-cable subscriber, Comcast	mos	49.95	6/99	103s
Phone line, single, business, field visit	inst.	75.00	12/97	17s
Phone line, single, business, no field visit	inst.	75.00	12/97	17s
Phone line, single, residence, field visit	inst.	40.00	12/97	17s
Phone line, single, residence, no field visit	inst.	40.00	12/97	17s
Postage and stationery, expenditures on	yr	138	1999	30r
Postal rate, express mail, up to half-pound		12.45	7/01	108r
Postal rate, letter, first class, first ounce		0.34	7/01	108r
Postal rate, letter, two ounces		0.57	7/01	108r
Postal rate, post card		0.21	7/01	108r
Postal rate, priority mail, two pounds		3.95	7/01	108r
Postal rate, priority mail, up to one pound		3.50	7/01	108r
Telephone services, expenditures on	yr	830	1999	30r
Education				
Board, 4-year private college/university	yr	2822	1996	38s
Board, 4-year public college/university	yr	2174	1996	38s
Education expenditures	yr	877	1999	30r
Room, 4-year private college/university	yr	2943	1996	38s
Room, 4-year public college/university	yr	2227	1996	38s
Total cost, 4-year private college/university	yr	19876	1996	38s
Total cost, 4-year public college/university	yr	9124	1996	38s
Tuition, 2-year public college/university, in state	yr	1909	1996	38s
Tuition, 4-year private college/university, in state	yr	14111	1996	38s
Tuition, 4-year public college/university	yr	4723	1996	38s
Energy and Fuels				
Electricity	KWh	0.12	7/01	11r
Fuel oil #2	gal	1.31	7/01	11r
Fuel oil and other fuels, expenditures on	yr	207	1999	30r
Gas, natural, commercial rate	1000 cf	5.96	11/00	88s
Gasoline, all types	gal	1.80	7/01	11r
Gasoline, unleaded midgrade	gal	1.85	7/01	11r
Gasoline, unleaded premium	gal	1.91	7/01	11r
Gasoline, unleaded regular	gal	1.71	7/01	11r
Natural gas, expenditures on	yr	368	1999	30r
Utility (piped) gas, therm		1.08	7/01	11r
Utility (piped) gas, 40 therms		50.87	7/01	11r
Utility (piped) gas, 100 therms		111.06	7/01	11r
Entertainment				
Entertainment purchases	yr	1821	1999	30r
Fees and admissions paid	yr	511	1999	30r

Altoona, PA - continued

Item	Per	Value	Date	Ref.
Entertainment - continued				
Television, radios, sound equipment, expenditures on	yr	650	1999	30r
Funerals				
Total cost of funeral		5813.50	1/99	78r
Acknowledgement cards		28.32	1/99	78r
Casket		2082.20	1/99	78r
Cosmetology, hair, other preparation		169.59	1/99	78r
Embalming		465.60	1/99	78r
Funeral at funeral home		339.56	1/99	78r
Hearse (local)		183.96	1/99	78r
Professional service charges		1157.85	1/99	78r
Service car/van		100.41	1/99	78r
Transfer of remains to funeral home		158.66	1/99	78r
Vault		766.31	1/99	78r
Visitation/viewing		361.04	1/99	78r
Groceries				
Apples, red delicious	lb	0.95	7/01	11r
Bacon, sliced	lb	3.44	7/01	11r
Bakery products, expenditures on	yr	310	1999	30r
Bananas	lb	0.55	7/01	11r
Beef, expenditures on	yr	236	1999	30r
Bread, white, pan	lb	1.09	7/01	11r
Butter, yoghurt, cheese, etc, expenditures on	yr	214	1999	30r
Cereals and bakery product purchases	yr	474	1999	30r
Cereals and cereal products, expenditures on	yr	164	1999	30r
Chicken legs, bone-in	lb	1.23	7/01	11r
Chicken, fresh, whole	lb	1.13	7/01	11r
Chuck roast, U.S. choice, boneless	lb	2.79	7/01	11r
Coffee, 100%, ground roast, all sizes	lb	3.40	7/01	11r
Dairy product purchases	yr	342	1999	30r
Eggs, expenditures on	yr	34	1999	30r
Eggs, grade A, large	dozen	0.82	7/01	11r
Fats and oils, expenditures on	yr	80	1999	30r
Fish and seafood, expenditures on	yr	123	1999	30r
Food (excl fruit and vegetables), eaten at home, purchases	yr	838	1999	30r
Food cooked on trips, expenditures on	yr	48	1999	30r
Food purchases	yr	5314	1999	30r
Food purchases, eaten away from home	yr	2313	1999	30r
Food purchases, food eaten at home	yr	3001	1999	30r
Fresh fruits, expenditures on	yr	169	1999	30r
Fresh milk and cream, expenditures on	yr	128	1999	30r
Fresh vegetables, expenditures on	yr	164	1999	30r
Grapefruit	lb	0.67	7/01	11r
Grapes, Thompson, seedless	lb	2.18	7/01	11r
Ground beef, lean and extra lean	lb	2.66	7/01	11r
Ground chuck, 100% beef	lb	2.04	7/01	11r
Lettuce, iceberg	lb	0.76	7/01	11r
Meats, poultry, fish, and egg purchases	yr	808	1999	30r
Nonalcoholic beverages, expenditures on	yr	225	1999	30r
Orange juice, frozen concentrate	16 oz	1.88	7/01	11r
Oranges, Navel	lb	0.79	7/01	11r
Oranges, Valencia	lb	0.56	7/01	11r
Peaches	lb	1.16	7/01	11r
Peanut butter, creamy, all sizes	lb	2.01	7/01	11r
Pears, Anjou	lb	1.16	7/01	11r
Pork chops, center cut, bone-in	lb	3.57	7/01	11r
Pork, expenditures on	yr	146	1999	30r
Potato chips	16 oz	3.37	7/01	11r
Potatoes, white, all types	lb	0.42	7/01	11r
Poultry, expenditures on	yr	158	1999	30r
Processed fruits, expenditures on	yr	124	1999	30r
Processed vegetables, expenditures on	yr	82	1999	30r
Round roast, U.S. choice, boneless	lb	3.04	7/01	11r
Spaghetti and macaroni	lb	1.04	7/01	11r
Steak, sirloin, U.S. choice, boneless	lb	5.39	7/01	11r
Strawberries, dry pint	12 oz	1.51	7/01	11r
Sugar and other sweets, expenditures on	yr	110	1999	30r
Sugar, white, 33-80 ounce package	lb	0.46	7/01	11r
Sugar, white, all sizes	lb	0.47	7/01	11r

Values are in dollars or fractions of dollars. In the column headed *Ref*, references are shown to sources. Each reference is followed by a letter. These refer to the geographical level for which data were reported: s=State, r=Region, and c=City or metro. The abbreviation *ex* is used to mean *except* or *excluding*; *exp* stands for *expenditures*. For other abbreviations and further explanations, please see the Introduction.

Altoona, PA - continued

Item	Per	Value	Date	Ref.
Groceries				
Tobacco products and smoking supplies purchases	yr	309	1999	30r
Yogurt, natural, fruit flavored	8 oz	0.79	7/01	11r
Goods and Services				
B&B Japanese maple (acer japonicum)	gal	38.99-125.00	4/00	93r
Boxwood (buxus)	2 gal	15.99-49.95	4/00	93r
Daylily (hemerocallis)	gal	4.95	4/00	93r
Flat of annuals		8.00-14.99	4/00	93r
Fountain grass (pennisetum)	gal	6.99-9.99	4/00	93r
Hanging basket (10 in)		12.95-19.99	4/00	93r
Hardy geranium (geranium)	gal	6.95-7.99	4/00	93r
Hosta (hosta)	gal	4.95	4/00	93r
Lilac (syrubga vulgaris)	2 gal	17.99-74.95	4/00	93r
Miscellaneous purchases	yr	872	1999	30r
Rhododendron (rhododendron)	2 gal	23.99-54.95	4/00	93r
Sage (salvia)	gal	6.95-7.99	4/00	93r
Wintercreeper euonymus (euonymus fortunei)	2 gal	14.99-23.95	4/00	93r
Hunting license	yr	20.00	4/01	34s
Health Care				
Cardiac catheterization, ave hospital/ physician charges		13870	1998	77s
Childbirth, Cesarean delivery		14716	1997	13r
Childbirth, vaginal delivery		8541	1997	13r
Drugs, expenditures on	yr	296	1999	30r
Health care purchases	yr	1788	1999	30r
Health insurance expenditures	yr	875	1999	30r
Hysterectomy, laproscopically-assisted, ave hospital/physician charges		14760	1998	76s
Hysterectomy, vaginal, ave hospital and physician charges		9270	1998	76s
Medicaid dispensing fee		4.00	1999	87s
Medical services expenditures	yr	516	1999	30r
Medical supplies, expenditures on	yr	102	1999	30r
Plastic surgery, breast augmentation		4232	2000	7r
Plastic surgery, breast lift		4605	2000	7r
Plastic surgery, facelift		6964	2000	7r
Plastic surgery, hair transplantation		4193	2000	7r
Plastic surgery, lip augmentation		1675	2000	7r
Plastic surgery, lower body lift		6611	2000	7r
Plastic surgery, thigh lift		4751	2000	7r
Household Goods				
Floor coverings, expenditures on	yr	59	1999	30r
Furniture, expenditures on	yr	388	1999	30r
Household furnishings and equipment purchases	yr	1567	1999	30r
Household textiles, expenditures on	yr	112	1999	30r
Laundry and cleaning supplies, expenditures on	yr	104	1999	30r
Housing				
Home price, existing, ave		180800	10/00	90r
Home value, median		115000	2001	53s
Household operation expenditures	yr	581	1999	30r
Housekeeping supplies purchases	yr	474	1999	30r
Lodging expenditures	yr	550	1999	30r
Maintenance, repairs, insurance expenditures	yr	835	1999	30r
Monthly rental value of owned home	mos	663	1999	30r
Owned dwellings, expenditures own	yr	5209	1999	30r
Rent expenditures	yr	2390	1999	30r
Rental unit, 1 bedroom, with utilities	mos	365	4/01	41c

Altoona, PA - continued

Item	Per	Value	Date	Ref.
Housing - continued				
Rental unit, 2 bedroom, with utilities	mos	438	4/01	41c
Rental unit, 3 bedroom, with utilities	mos	571	4/01	41c
Rental unit, 4 bedroom, with utilities	mos	639	4/01	41c
Shelter, expenditures on	yr	8149	1999	30r
Insurance and Pensions				
Life and other personal insurance purchases	yr	424	1999	30r
Pensions and Social Security, expenditures on	yr	3037	1999	30r
Legal Fees				
Divorce, filing fee		65.00	4/01	35s
Driver's license fee	renew	24.00	1999	48s
Driver's license fee	orig	29.00	1999	48s
Fishing license	yr	17.00	4/01	34s
Personal Goods				
Personal care products and services purchases	yr	399	1999	30r
Personal Services				
Personal services, household, expenditures on	yr	271	1999	30r
Pets				
Pets, toys, and playground equipment, expenditures on	yr	325	1999	30r
Taxes				
Federal income taxes paid	yr	2606	1999	30r
Personal taxes, expenditures on	yr	3567	1999	30r
Property taxes paid	yr	1752	1999	30r
State and local income taxes paid	yr	694	1999	30r
Transportation				
Bus fare, one-way	trip	1.25	2000	1c
Cars and trucks, new, expenditures on	yr	1496	1999	30r
Cars and trucks, used, expenditures on	yr	1251	1999	30r
Diesel at the pump	gal	1.31	10/99	73s
Gasoline and motor oil purchases	yr	901	1999	30r
Gasoline before-tax price (cents)	gal	106.60	10/00	43s
Maintenance and repair expenditures	yr	618	1999	30r
Public transportation, expenditures on	yr	575	1999	30r
Transportation purchases	yr	6503	1999	30r
Vehicle expenses, miscellaneous, purchases	yr	2266	1999	30r
Vehicle insurance payments	yr	824	1999	30r
Vehicle purchases (net outlay)	yr	2761	1999	30r
Vehicle rental, lease expenditures	yr	584	1999	30r
Utilities				
Electrical bill, average	mos	69.16	9/00	9s
Electricity, expenditures on	yr	837	1999	30r
Electricity cost, average	KWh	5.08	9/00	9s
Utilities, fuels, and public services purchased	yr	2457	1999	30r
Water and other public services, expenditures on	yr	215	1999	30r
Weddings				
Wedding (national average cost)		19936	2000	33r
Wedding (regional average total cost)		29454	1997	110r
Attendants' gifts		321	1998	33r
Bridal attendants' apparel (5 persons)		824	2000	33r
Bride's headpiece/veil		173	1998	33r
Bride's wedding dress		859	1998	33r
Clergy, religious facility fee		242	1998	33r
Engagement ring		3177	1998	33r
Flowers		789	1998	33r
Groom's formalwear rental		99	2000	33r
Limousine		410	1998	33r
Marriage license cost		25.00-40.00	4/01	35s
Men's formalwear (ushers, best man)		469	2000	33r
Mother of bride apparel		241	2000	33r
Music		866	1998	33r
Photography and videography		1368	1998	33r
Rehearsal dinner		728	1998	33r

Values are in dollars or fractions of dollars. In the column headed *Ref*, references are shown to sources. Each reference is followed by a letter. These refer to the geographical level for which data were reported: s=State, r=Region, and c=City or metro. The abbreviation *ex* is used to mean *except* or *excluding*; *exp* stands for *expenditures*. For other abbreviations and further explanations, please see the Introduction.

Altoona, PA - continued

Item	Per	Value	Date	Ref.
Weddings				
Wedding invitations and announcements		341	1998	33r
Wedding reception		7968	2000	33r
Wedding rings (bride and groom)		1060	1998	33r

Amarillo, TX

Item	Per	Value	Date	Ref.
Composite, ACCRA index		92.70	3/01	4c
Alcoholic Beverages				
Alcoholic beverage purchases	yr	253	1999	30r
Beer, Heineken, 12-oz, ex deposit	6	6.82	3/01	4c
J & B Scotch	750-ml	20.03	3/01	4c
Malt beverages, all types, all sizes, any origin	16 oz	0.96	7/01	11r
Wine, Livingston or Gallo, Chablis blanc	1.5 liter	5.40	3/01	4c
Appliances				
Appliance repair, service call, washing machine	min lab chg	35.39	3/01	4c
Major appliances, expenditures on	yr	172	1999	30r
Small appliances, housewares, expenditures on	yr	81	1999	30r
Banking and Money				
Mortgage interest and charges paid	yr	2039	1999	30r
Mortgage principal paid on owned property	yr	1026	1999	30r
Mortgage rate, incl. points and orig. fee, 30-yr. conv. fixed or ARM	mos	6.98	3/01	4c
Vehicle finance charges paid	yr	365	1999	30r
Charity				
Cash contributions, expenditures	yr	1127	1999	30r
Child Care				
Child raising cost, total, age 0-2	yr	8540	1999	60r
Child raising cost, total, age 3-5	yr	8780	1999	60r
Child raising cost, total, age 6-8	yr	8820	1999	60r
Child raising cost, total, age 9-11	yr	8800	1999	60r
Child raising cost, total, age 12-14	yr	9510	1999	60r
Child raising cost, total, age 15-17	yr	9740	1999	60r
Child's child care and education, age 0-2	yr	1380	1999	60r
Child's child care and education, age 3-5	yr	1520	1999	60r
Child's child care and education, age 6-8	yr	990	1999	60r
Child's child care and education, age 9-11	yr	650	1999	60r
Child's child care and education, age 12-14	yr	490	1999	60r
Child's child care and education, age 15-17	yr	840	1999	60r
Child's clothing, age 0-2	yr	480	1999	60r
Child's clothing, age 3-5	yr	470	1999	60r
Child's clothing, age 6-8	yr	520	1999	60r
Child's clothing, age 9-11	yr	570	1999	60r
Child's clothing, age 12-14	yr	950	1999	60r
Child's clothing, age 15-17	yr	850	1999	60r
Child's food, age 0-2	yr	1000	1999	60r
Child's food, age 3-5	yr	1160	1999	60r
Child's food, age 6-8	yr	1490	1999	60r
Child's food, age 9-11	yr	1770	1999	60r
Child's food, age 12-14	yr	1770	1999	60r
Child's food, age 15-17	yr	1980	1999	60r
Child's health care, age 0-2	yr	620	1999	60r
Child's health care, age 3-5	yr	590	1999	60r
Child's health care, age 6-8	yr	680	1999	60r
Child's health care, age 9-11	yr	720	1999	60r
Child's health care, age 12-14	yr	730	1999	60r
Child's health care, age 15-17	yr	760	1999	60r
Child's housing, age 0-2	yr	3070	1999	60r
Child's housing, age 3-5	yr	3050	1999	60r
Child's housing, age 6-8	yr	3010	1999	60r
Child's housing, age 9-11	yr	2850	1999	60r
Child's housing, age 12-14	yr	3040	1999	60r
Child's housing, age 15-17	yr	2650	1999	60r
Child's personal care, reading, age 0-2	yr	910	1999	60r
Child's personal care, reading, age 3-5	yr	930	1999	60r
Child's personal care, reading, age 6-8	yr	960	1999	60r
Child's personal care, reading, age 9-11	yr	1000	1999	60r
Child's personal care, reading, age 12-14	yr	1170	1999	60r

Amarillo, TX - continued

Item	Per	Value	Date	Ref.
Child Care - continued				
Child's personal care, reading, age 15-17	yr	950	1999	60r
Clothing				
Apparel and services purchases	yr	1610	1999	30r
Boys' brief, cotton	3	4.20	3/01	4c
Boys, 2 to 15, expenditures on	yr	89	1999	30r
Children under 2, expenditures on	yr	79	1999	30r
Footwear, expenditures on	yr	283	1999	30r
Girls, 2 to 15, expenditures on	yr	103	1999	30r
Men and boys, expenditures on	yr	351	1999	30r
Men, 16 and over, expenditures on	yr	262	1999	30r
Shirt, man's dress shirt		20.50	3/01	4c
Slacks, man's "No Wrinkles" khaki		35.59	3/01	4c
Women, 16 and over, expenditures on	yr	538	1999	30r
Communications				
Cable modem installation, AT&T-BIS		150.00	6/99	103s
Cable modem installation, Marcus		499.00	6/99	103s
Cable modem installation, Time Warner		75.00-225.00	6/99	103s
Cable modem rate, cable subscriber, AT&T-BIS	mos	39.95	6/99	103s
Cable modem rate, cable subscriber, Marcus	mos	14.95-49.95	6/99	103s
Cable modem rate, cable subscriber, Time Warner	mos	39.95-49.95	6/99	103s
Cable modem rate, non-cable subscriber, Marcus	mos	60.95	6/99	103s
Cable modem rate, non-cable subscriber, Time Warner	mos	39.95-54.95	6/99	103s
Newspaper subscription, daily and Sunday delivery	mos	10.25	3/01	4c
Phone line, single, business, field visit	inst.	71.90	12/97	17s
Phone line, single, business, no field visit	inst.	57.30	12/97	17s
Phone line, single, residence, field visit	inst.	52.95	12/97	17s
Phone line, single, residence, no field visit	inst.	38.35	12/97	17s
Postage and stationery, expenditures on	yr	104	1999	30r
Postal rate, express mail, up to half-pound		12.45	7/01	108r
Postal rate, letter, first class, first ounce		0.34	7/01	108r
Postal rate, letter, two ounces		0.57	7/01	108r
Postal rate, post card		0.21	7/01	108r
Postal rate, priority mail, two pounds		3.95	7/01	108r
Postal rate, priority mail, up to one pound		3.50	7/01	108r
Telephone bill, business, basic rate	mos	21.30	12/97	18c
Telephone bill, family of three	mos	17.39	3/01	4c
Telephone bill, residential, basic rate	mos	9.10	12/97	18c
Telephone services, expenditures on	yr	860	1999	30r
Education				
Board, 4-year private college/university	yr	2198	1996	38s
Board, 4-year public college/university	yr	1759	1996	38s
Education expenditures	yr	431	1999	30r
Room, 4-year private college/university	yr	2000	1996	38s
Room, 4-year public college/university	yr	1885	1996	38s
Total cost, 4-year private college/university	yr	13156	1996	38s
Total cost, 4-year public college/university	yr	5464	1996	38s
Tuition, 2-year public college/university, in state	yr	771	1996	38s
Tuition, 4-year private college/university, in state	yr	8959	1996	38s
Tuition, 4-year public college/university	yr	1820	1996	38s
Energy and Fuels				
Electricity	KWh	0.09	7/01	11r
Electricity	500 KWhs	47.29	7/01	11r
Energy, combined forms, 2400 sq ft	mos	111.80	3/01	4c
Energy, exc. electricity, 2400 sq ft	mos	48.54	3/01	4c
Fuel oil #2	gal	1.43	7/01	11r
Fuel oil and other fuels, expenditures on	yr	45	1999	30r
Gas, cooking, winter, 10 therms	mos	8.66	2/96	98c
Gas, cooking, winter, 30 therms	mos	15.67	2/96	98c
Gas, cooking, winter, 50 therms	mos	22.58	2/96	98c
Gas, heating, winter, average use	mos	49.16	2/96	98c

Values are in dollars or fractions of dollars. In the column headed *Ref*, references are shown to sources. Each reference is followed by a letter. These refer to the geographical level for which data were reported: s=State, r=Region, and c=City or metro. The abbreviation *ex* is used to mean *except* or *excluding*; *exp* stands for *expenditures*. For other abbreviations and further explanations, please see the Introduction.

Amarillo, TX - continued

Item	Per	Value	Date	Ref.
Energy and Fuels				
Gas, natural, commercial rate	1000 cf	6.94	11/00	88s
Gas, regular unleaded, cash, self-service	gal	1.30	3/01	4c
Gasoline, all types	gal	1.60	7/01	11r
Gasoline, unleaded midgrade	gal	1.65	7/01	11r
Gasoline, unleaded premium	gal	1.74	7/01	11r
Natural gas, expenditures on	yr	164	1999	30r
Utility (piped) gas, therm		1.01	7/01	11r
Utility (piped) gas, 40 therms		44.29	7/01	11r
Utility (piped) gas, 100 therms		97.44	7/01	11r
Entertainment				
Bowling, Saturday evening rate	line	2.40	3/01	4c
Entertainment purchases	yr	1574	1999	30r
Fees and admissions paid	yr	371	1999	30r
Monopoly game, Parker Brothers', No. 9	game	8.59	3/01	4c
Movie, first-run, Saturday, evening	adm.	6.63	3/01	4c
Reading purchases	yr	121	1999	30r
Television, radios, sound equipment, expenditures on	yr	561	1999	30r
Tennis balls, yellow, Wilson or Penn, 3	can	2.08	3/01	4c
Funerals				
Total cost of funeral		5842.28	1/99	78r
Acknowledgement cards		28.35	1/99	78r
Casket		2494.29	1/99	78r
Cosmetology, hair, other preparation		109.22	1/99	78r
Embalming		361.42	1/99	78r
Funeral at funeral home		349.20	1/99	78r
Hearse (local)		161.91	1/99	78r
Professional service charges		1116.50	1/99	78r
Service car/van		65.56	1/99	78r
Transfer of remains to funeral home		143.56	1/99	78r
Vault		785.25	1/99	78r
Visitation/viewing		227.02	1/99	78r
Groceries				
Groceries, ACCRA Index		92.20	3/01	4c
American processed cheese	lb	3.50	7/01	11r
Antibiotic ointment, Polysporin	0.5 oz	4.21	3/01	4c
Baby food, strained vegetables or fruit, lowest price	4-4.5 oz	0.32	3/01	4c
Bakery products, expenditures on	yr	261	1999	30r
Bananas	lb	0.48	3/01	4c
Bananas	lb	0.47	7/01	11r
Beans, dried, any type, all sizes	lb	0.63	7/01	11r
Beef for stew, boneless	lb	2.86	7/01	11r
Beef or hamburger, ground	lb	1.81	3/01	4c
Beef, expenditures on	yr	210	1999	30r
Bologna, all beef or mixed	lb	2.29	7/01	11r
Bread, French	lb	1.66	7/01	11r
Bread, white	loaf	0.68	3/01	4c
Bread, white, pan	lb	0.87	7/01	11r
Bread, whole wheat, pan	lb	1.38	7/01	11r
Broccoli	lb	1.04	7/01	11r
Butter, salted, grade AA, stick	lb	2.26	7/01	11r
Butter, yoghurt, cheese, etc, expenditures on	yr	170	1999	30r
Cabbage	lb	0.42	7/01	11r
Cereals and cereal products, expenditures on	yr	140	1999	30r
Cheddar cheese, natural	lb	3.75	7/01	11r
Cheese, Kraft grated Parmesan	8 oz	4.21	3/01	4c
Chicken breast, bone-in	lb	1.85	7/01	11r
Chicken legs, bone-in	lb	1.34	7/01	11r
Chicken, fresh, whole	lb	1.05	7/01	11r
Chicken, whole fryer	lb	0.86	3/01	4c
Chops, boneless	lb	4.13	7/01	11r
Chuck roast, graded and ungraded, excl U.S. prime and choice	lb	2.35	7/01	11r
Chuck roast, U.S. choice, boneless	lb	2.67	7/01	11r
Cigarettes, Winston, Kings	carton	27.91	3/01	4c
Coffee, 100%, ground roast, all sizes	lb	2.88	7/01	11r
Coffee, instant, plain, regular, all sizes	16 oz	9.25	7/01	11r
Coffee, vacuum-packed	13 oz	2.19	3/01	4c
Cola, non diet	2 liter	1.11	7/01	11r

Amarillo, TX - continued

Item	Per	Value	Date	Ref.
Groceries - continued				
Corn Flakes, Kellogg's or Post Toasties	18 oz	1.82	3/01	4c
Corn, frozen, whole kernel, lowest price	16 oz	1.16	3/01	4c
Crackers, soda, salted	lb	1.70	7/01	11r
Dairy product purchases	yr	282	1999	30r
Eggs, expenditures on	yr	32	1999	30r
Eggs, Grade A or AA	dozen	1.16	3/01	4c
Fats and oils, expenditures on	yr	79	1999	30r
Fish and seafood, expenditures on	yr	99	1999	30r
Flour, white, all purpose	lb	0.32	7/01	11r
Food (excl fruit and vegetables), eaten at home, purchases	yr	815	1999	30r
Food cooked on trips, expenditures on	yr	36	1999	30r
Food purchases	yr	4533	1999	30r
Food purchases, eaten away from home	yr	1873	1999	30r
Food purchases, food eaten at home	yr	2660	1999	30r
Fresh fruits, expenditures on	yr	128	1999	30r
Fresh milk and cream, expenditures on	yr	112	1999	30r
Fresh vegetables, expenditures on	yr	131	1999	30r
Fruit and vegetable purchases	yr	438	1999	30r
Grapefruit	lb	0.59	7/01	11r
Grapes, Thompson, seedless	lb	2.12	7/01	11r
Ground beef, 100% beef	lb	1.76	7/01	11r
Ground beef, lean and extra lean	lb	2.60	7/01	11r
Ground chuck, 100% beef	lb	2.08	7/01	11r
Ham, boneless, excl canned	lb	2.71	7/01	11r
Ham, rump or shank half, bone-in, smoked	lb	2.19	7/01	11r
Ice cream, prepackaged, bulk, regular	1/2 gal	3.93	7/01	11r
Lemons	lb	1.32	7/01	11r
Lettuce, iceberg	head	1.24	3/01	4c
Lettuce, iceberg	lb	0.76	7/01	11r
Margarine, Blue Bonnet or Parkay, stick	lb	0.90	3/01	4c
Milk, fresh, low fat,	gal	2.75	7/01	11r
Milk, fresh, whole, fortified	gal	2.97	7/01	11r
Milk, whole	1/2 gal	1.46	3/01	4c
Nonalcoholic beverages, expenditures on	yr	228	1999	30r
Orange juice, frozen concentrate	16 oz	1.95	7/01	11r
Orange juice, Minute Maid frozen	12 oz	1.54	3/01	4c
Oranges, Navel	lb	0.73	7/01	11r
Oranges, Valencia	lb	0.55	7/01	11r
Peaches, halves or slices, Hunt's, Del Monte, or Libby's	29 oz	1.61	3/01	4c
Peanut butter, creamy, all sizes	lb	1.83	7/01	11r
Pears, Anjou	lb	0.98	7/01	11r
Peas, green, Del Monte or Green Giant	15 oz	0.68	3/01	4c
Pork chops, center cut, bone-in	lb	3.33	7/01	11r
Pork sausage, fresh, loose	lb	2.59	7/01	11r
Pork shoulder picnic, bone-in, smoked	lb	1.12	7/01	11r
Pork, expenditures on	yr	162	1999	30r
Potato chips	16 oz	3.59	7/01	11r
Potatoes, frozen, french fried	lb	1.00	7/01	11r
Potatoes, white or red	10 lb	2.24	3/01	4c
Potatoes, white, all types	lb	0.44	7/01	11r
Poultry, expenditures on	yr	137	1999	30r
Processed fruits, expenditures on	yr	97	1999	30r
Processed vegetables, expenditures on	yr	82	1999	30r
Rice, white, long grain, uncooked	lb	0.51	7/01	11r
Round roast, graded and ungraded, excl U.S. prime and choice	lb	2.96	7/01	11r
Round steak, graded and ungraded, excl U.S. prime and choice	lb	3.11	7/01	11r
Sausage, Jimmy Dean/Owens pork	lb	3.01	3/01	4c
Shortening, vegetable, Crisco	3 lb	2.69	3/01	4c
Sirloin steak, graded and ungraded, excl U.S. prime and choice	lb	4.23	7/01	11r
Soft drink, Coca Cola, ex deposit	2 liter	1.11	3/01	4c
Spaghetti and macaroni	lb	0.78	7/01	11r
Steak, round, U.S. choice, boneless	lb	3.56	7/01	11r
Steak, sirloin, U.S. choice, boneless	lb	5.65	7/01	11r
Steak, T-bone	lb	6.76	3/01	4c
Strawberries, dry pint	12 oz	1.50	7/01	11r
Sugar and other sweets, expenditures on	yr	99	1999	30r
Sugar, cane or beet	4 lbs	1.53	3/01	4c

Values are in dollars or fractions of dollars. In the column headed *Ref*, references are shown to sources. Each reference is followed by a letter. These refer to the geographical level for which data were reported: s=State, r=Region, and c=City or metro. The abbreviation *ex* is used to mean *except* or *excluding*; *exp* stands for *expenditures*. For other abbreviations and further explanations, please see the Introduction.

Amarillo, TX - continued

Item	Per	Value	Date	Ref.
Groceries				
Sugar, white, 33-80 ounce package	lb	0.39	7/01	11r
Sugar, white, all sizes	lb	0.42	7/01	11r
Tobacco products and smoking supplies purchases	yr	288	1999	30r
Tomatoes, field grown	lb	1.43	7/01	11r
Tomatoes, Hunt's or Del Monte	14.5 oz	0.89	3/01	4c
Tuna, chunk, light	6 oz	0.62	3/01	4c
Tuna, light, chunk	lb	1.77	7/01	11r
Turkey, frozen, whole	lb	1.05	7/01	11r
Goods and Services				
Miscellaneous goods and services, ACCRA Index		91.50	3/01	4c
B&B Japanese maple (acer japonicum)	gal	79.98-99.00	4/00	93r
Boxwood (buxus)	2 gal	12.98-18.99	4/00	93r
Christmas tree, noble fir		40-60	2000	65s
Daylily (hemerocallis)	gal	7.96-11.00	4/00	93r
Flat of annuals		13.99-27.99	4/00	93r
Fountain grass (pennisetum)	gal	6.96-9.00	4/00	93r
Hanging basket (10 in)		9.99-24.99	4/00	93r
Hardy geranium (geranium)	gal	5.96-8.00	4/00	93r
Hosta (hosta)	gal	8.96-12.99	4/00	93r
Lilac (syrubga vulgaris)	2 gal	13.00-19.99	4/00	93r
Rhododendron (rhododendron)	2 gal	12.98-29.99	4/00	93r
Sage (salvia)	gal	5.96-8.00	4/00	93r
Wintercreeper euonymus (euonymus fortunei)	2 gal	13.00-18.99	4/00	93r
Hunting license	yr	19.00	4/01	34s
Health Care				
Health care, ACCRA Index		92.30	3/01	4c
Cardiac catheterization, ave hospital/physician charges		20140	1998	77s
Childbirth, Cesarean delivery		11587	1997	13r
Childbirth, vaginal delivery		6725	1997	13r
Dentist's fee, adult teeth cleaning and periodic oral exam	visit	67.80	3/01	4c
Doctor's fee, routine exam, established patient	visit	57.20	3/01	4c
Drugs, expenditures on	yr	399	1999	30r
Health care purchases	yr	1971	1999	30r
Health insurance expenditures	yr	933	1999	30r
Hospital care, private room	day	415.00	3/01	4c
Hysterectomy, laproscopically-assisted, ave hospital/physician charges		15700	1998	76s
Hysterectomy, vaginal, ave hospital and physician charges		12180	1998	76s
Medicaid dispensing fee		5.27	1999	87s
Medical services expenditures	yr	547	1999	30r
Medical supplies, expenditures on	yr	91	1999	30r
Household Goods				
Dishwashing powder, Cascade	50 oz	3.17	3/01	4c
Floor coverings, expenditures on	yr	44	1999	30r
Furniture, expenditures on	yr	335	1999	30r
Household furnishings and equipment purchases	yr	1328	1999	30r
Household textiles, expenditures on	yr	89	1999	30r
Laundry and cleaning supplies, expenditures on	yr	113	1999	30r
Tissues, facial, Kleenex brand	175	1.33	3/01	4c

Amarillo, TX - continued

Item	Per	Value	Date	Ref.
Housing				
Housing, ACCRA Index		92.20	3/01	4c
Home, 2200 sq ft, 4-br, 2-bath, 2-car garage, average		145625	2000	47c
Home price, existing, ave		160100	10/00	90r
Home value, median		112000	2001	53s
House, 2400 sq ft, 8000 sq ft lot, new, urban, utilities	total	194733	3/01	4c
House payment, principal and interest, 25% down payment	mos	970	3/01	4c
Household operation expenditures	yr	553	1999	30r
Housekeeping supplies purchases	yr	473	1999	30r
Housing, expenditures on	yr	10303	1999	30r
Maintenance, repairs, insurance expenditures	yr	699	1999	30r
Monthly rental value of owned home	mos	505	1999	30r
Owned dwellings, expenditures own	yr	3465	1999	30r
Rent expenditures	yr	1641	1999	30r
Rent, apartment, 2 br, 1 1/2-2 baths, unfurn, 950 sq ft, water	mos	590	3/01	4c
Rental unit, 1 bedroom, with utilities	mos	361	4/01	41c
Rental unit, 2 bedroom, with utilities	mos	449	4/01	41c
Rental unit, 3 bedroom, with utilities	mos	626	4/01	41c
Rental unit, 4 bedroom, with utilities	mos	738	4/01	41c
Shelter, expenditures on	yr	5467	1999	30r
Insurance and Pensions				
Life and other personal insurance purchases	yr	414	1999	30r
Pensions and Social Security, expenditures on	yr	2635	1999	30r
Personal insurance and pensions, expenditures on	yr	3048	1999	30r
Legal Fees				
Divorce, filing fee		150.00-200.00	4/01	35s
Driver's license fee	orig	24.00	1999	48s
Driver's license fee	renew	20.00	1999	48s
Fishing license	yr	19.00	4/01	34s
Personal Goods				
Personal care products and services purchases	yr	393	1999	30r
Shampoo, Alberto VO5	15 oz	0.94	3/01	4c
Toothpaste, Crest or Colgate	6-7 oz	2.06	3/01	4c
Personal Services				
Dry cleaning, man's 2-pc suit		6.60	3/01	4c
Man's haircut, barbershop, no styling		10.20	3/01	4c
Personal services, household, expenditures on	yr	258	1999	30r
Woman's shampoo, trim, blow-dry, no style-change		25.17	3/01	4c
Pets				
Pets, toys, and playground equipment, expenditures on	yr	306	1999	30r
Restaurant Food				
Chicken, fried, thigh and drumstick, KFC/Church's		2.47	3/01	4c
Hamburger with cheese, McDonald's	1/4 lb	2.19	3/01	4c
Pizza, Pizza Hut or Pizza Inn	11-12 in	9.69	3/01	4c
Taxes				
Federal income taxes paid	yr	2047	1999	30r
Personal taxes, expenditures on	yr	2554	1999	30r
Property taxes paid	yr	726	1999	30r
State and local income taxes paid	yr	363	1999	30r
Transportation				
Transportation, ACCRA Index		101.30	3/01	4c
Cars and trucks, new, expenditures on	yr	1648	1999	30r
Cars and trucks, used, expenditures on	yr	1651	1999	30r
Diesel at the pump	gal	1.18	10/99	73s
Gasoline and motor oil purchases	yr	1052	1999	30r
Gasoline before-tax price (cents)	gal	101.30	10/00	43s

Values are in dollars or fractions of dollars. In the column headed *Ref*, references are shown to sources. Each reference is followed by a letter. These refer to the geographical level for which data were reported: s=State, r=Region, and c=City or metro. The abbreviation *ex* is used to mean *except* or *excluding*; *exp* stands for *expenditures*. For other abbreviations and further explanations, please see the Introduction.

Amarillo, TX - continued

Item	Per	Value	Date	Ref.
Transportation				
Maintenance and repair expenditures	yr	621	1999	30r
Public transportation, expenditures on	yr	298	1999	30r
Tire balance, computer or spin balance, front	wheel	9.00	3/01	4c
Transportation purchases	yr	6738	1999	30r
Vehicle expenses, miscellaneous, purchases	yr	2033	1999	30r
Vehicle insurance payments	yr	696	1999	30r
Vehicle purchases (net outlay)	yr	3354	1999	30r
Vehicle rental, lease expenditures	yr	352	1999	30r
Utilities				
Utilities, ACCRA Index		90.00	3/01	4c
Electrical bill, average	mos	87.17	9/00	9s
Electricity, expenditures on	yr	1115	1999	30r
Electricity, summer, 250 KWh	mos	18.81	2/96	96c
Electricity, summer, 500 KWh	mos	32.97	2/96	96c
Electricity, summer, 750 KWh	mos	47.13	2/96	96c
Electricity, summer, 1000 KWh	mos	61.29	2/96	96c
Electricity and other, mixed, 2400 sq ft, new home	mos	63.26	3/01	4c
Electricity cost, average	KWh	6.48	9/00	9s
Water and other public services, expenditures on	yr	298	1999	30r
Weddings				
Wedding (national average cost)		19936	2000	33r
Attendants' gifts		321	1998	33r
Bridal attendants' apparel (5 persons)		824	2000	33r
Bride's headpiece/veil		173	1998	33r
Bride's wedding dress		859	1998	33r
Clergy, religious facility fee		242	1998	33r
Engagement ring		3177	1998	33r
Flowers		789	1998	33r
Groom's formalwear rental		99	2000	33r
Limousine		410	1998	33r
Marriage license cost		36.00	4/01	35s
Men's formalwear (ushers, best man)		469	2000	33r
Mother of bride apparel		241	2000	33r
Music		866	1998	33r
Photography and videography		1368	1998	33r
Rehearsal dinner		728	1998	33r
Wedding invitations and announcements		341	1998	33r
Wedding reception		7968	2000	33r
Wedding rings (bride and groom)		1060	1998	33r

Anchorage, AK

Item	Per	Value	Date	Ref.
Average annual expenditures	yr	40662	1999	30r
Composite, ACCRA index		123.00	3/01	4c
Alcoholic Beverages				
Alcoholic beverage purchases	yr	508	1999	30c
Beer, Heineken, 12-oz, ex deposit	6	7.97	3/01	4c
J & B Scotch	750-ml	25.43	3/01	4c
Malt beverages, all types, all sizes, any origin	16 oz	0.94	7/01	11r
Wine, Livingston or Gallo, Chablis blanc	1.5 liter	6.10	3/01	4c
Wine, red and white table, all sizes, any origin	liter	6.00	7/01	11r
Appliances				
Appliance repair, service call, washing machine	min lab chg	45.16	3/01	4c
Major appliances, expenditures on	yr	167	1999	30r
Small appliances, housewares, expenditures on	yr	105	1999	30r
Banking and Money				
Mortgage interest and charges paid	yr	3368	1999	30r
Mortgage principal paid on owned property	yr	1677	1999	30r
Mortgage rate, incl. points and orig. fee, 30-yr. conv. fixed or ARM	mos	7.20	3/01	4c
Vehicle finance charges paid	yr	311	1999	30r
Charity				
Cash contributions, expenditures	yr	1225	1999	30c

Anchorage, AK - continued

Item	Per	Value	Date	Ref.
Child Care				
Child raising cost, total, age 0-2	yr	9140	1999	60r
Child raising cost, total, age 3-5	yr	9370	1999	60r
Child raising cost, total, age 6-8	yr	9450	1999	60r
Child raising cost, total, age 9-11	yr	9470	1999	60r
Child raising cost, total, age 12-14	yr	10170	1999	60r
Child raising cost, total, age 15-17	yr	10360	1999	60r
Child's child care and education, age 0-2	yr	1250	1999	60r
Child's child care and education, age 3-5	yr	1380	1999	60r
Child's child care and education, age 6-8	yr	890	1999	60r
Child's child care and education, age 9-11	yr	580	1999	60r
Child's child care and education, age 12-14	yr	430	1999	60r
Child's child care and education, age 15-17	yr	730	1999	60r
Child's clothing, age 0-2	yr	430	1999	60r
Child's clothing, age 3-5	yr	420	1999	60r
Child's clothing, age 6-8	yr	470	1999	60r
Child's clothing, age 9-11	yr	520	1999	60r
Child's clothing, age 12-14	yr	870	1999	60r
Child's clothing, age 15-17	yr	770	1999	60r
Child's food, age 0-2	yr	1120	1999	60r
Child's food, age 3-5	yr	1280	1999	60r
Child's food, age 6-8	yr	1640	1999	60r
Child's food, age 9-11	yr	1930	1999	60r
Child's food, age 12-14	yr	1940	1999	60r
Child's food, age 15-17	yr	2150	1999	60r
Child's health care, age 0-2	yr	490	1999	60r
Child's health care, age 3-5	yr	470	1999	60r
Child's health care, age 6-8	yr	530	1999	60r
Child's health care, age 9-11	yr	570	1999	60r
Child's health care, age 12-14	yr	580	1999	60r
Child's health care, age 15-17	yr	610	1999	60r
Child's housing, age 0-2	yr	3630	1999	60r
Child's housing, age 3-5	yr	3610	1999	60r
Child's housing, age 6-8	yr	3570	1999	60r
Child's housing, age 9-11	yr	3410	1999	60r
Child's housing, age 12-14	yr	3600	1999	60r
Child's housing, age 15-17	yr	3210	1999	60r
Child's personal care, reading, age 0-2	yr	1040	1999	60r
Child's personal care, reading, age 3-5	yr	1060	1999	60r
Child's personal care, reading, age 6-8	yr	1090	1999	60r
Child's personal care, reading, age 9-11	yr	1130	1999	60r
Child's personal care, reading, age 12-14	yr	1300	1999	60r
Child's personal care, reading, age 15-17	yr	1080	1999	60r
Clothing				
Apparel and services purchases	yr	1957	1999	30c
Boys' brief, cotton	3	6.13	3/01	4c
Boys, 2 to 15, expenditures on	yr	80	1999	30r
Children under 2, expenditures on	yr	74	1999	30r
Footwear, expenditures on	yr	307	1999	30r
Girls, 2 to 15, expenditures on	yr	101	1999	30r
Men and boys, expenditures on	yr	443	1999	30r
Men, 16 and over, expenditures on	yr	363	1999	30r
Shirt, man's dress shirt		36.20	3/01	4c
Slacks, man's "No Wrinkles" khaki		46.00	3/01	4c
Women, 16 and over, expenditures on	yr	594	1999	30r
Communications				
Newspaper subscription, daily and Sunday delivery	mos	11.25	3/01	4c
Postage and stationery, expenditures on	yr	150	1999	30r
Postal rate, express mail, up to half-pound		12.45	7/01	108r
Postal rate, letter, first class, first ounce		0.34	7/01	108r
Postal rate, letter, two ounces		0.57	7/01	108r
Postal rate, post card		0.21	7/01	108r
Postal rate, priority mail, two pounds		3.95	7/01	108r
Postal rate, priority mail, up to one pound		3.50	7/01	108r
Telephone bill, family of three	mos	15.10	3/01	4c
Telephone services, expenditures on	yr	825	1999	30r
Education				
Board, 4-year private college/university	yr	2745	1996	38s
Board, 4-year public college/university	yr	1937	1996	38s
Education expenditures	yr	576	1999	30c
Room, 4-year private college/university	yr	1879	1996	38s

Values are in dollars or fractions of dollars. In the column headed *Ref*, references are shown to sources. Each reference is followed by a letter. These refer to the geographical level for which data were reported: s=State, r=Region, and c=City or metro. The abbreviation *ex* is used to mean *except* or *excluding*; *exp* stands for expenditures. For other abbreviations and further explanations, please see the Introduction.

Anchorage, AK - continued

Item	Per	Value	Date	Ref.
Education				
Room, 4-year public college/university	yr	2238	1996	38s
Total cost, 4-year private college/university	yr	12917	1996	38s
Total cost, 4-year public college/university	yr	6665	1996	38s
Tuition, 2-year public college/university, in state	yr	2120	1996	38s
Tuition, 4-year private college/university, in state	yr	8293	1996	38s
Tuition, 4-year public college/university	yr	2489	1996	38s
Energy and Fuels				
Electricity	KWh	0.11	7/01	11r
Electricity	500 KWhs	48.23	7/01	11r
Energy, combined forms, 2400 sq ft	mos	103.92	3/01	4c
Energy, exc. electricity, 2400 sq ft	mos	51.46	3/01	4c
Fuel oil and other fuels, expenditures on	yr	35	1999	30r
Gas, cooking, winter, 10 therms	mos	7.73	2/96	98c
Gas, cooking, winter, 30 therms	mos	14.11	2/96	98c
Gas, cooking, winter, 50 therms	mos	20.51	2/96	98c
Gas, heating, winter, average use	mos	100.43	2/96	98c
Gas, natural, commercial rate	1000 cf	2.11	11/00	88s
Gas, regular unleaded, cash, self-service	gal	1.61	3/01	4c
Gasoline, all types	gal	1.91	7/01	11r
Gasoline, unleaded premium	gal	2.05	7/01	11r
Gasoline, unleaded regular	gal	1.83	7/01	11r
Natural gas, expenditures on	yr	255	1999	30r
Utility (piped) gas, therm		0.98	7/01	11r
Utility (piped) gas, 40 therms		40.74	7/01	11r
Utility (piped) gas, 100 therms		96.80	7/01	11r
Entertainment				
Bowling, Saturday evening rate	line	3.10	3/01	4c
Entertainment purchases	yr	3561	1999	30c
Fees and admissions paid	yr	545	1999	30r
Monopoly game, Parker Brothers', No. 9	game	14.08	3/01	4c
Movie, first-run, Saturday, evening	adm.	7.81	3/01	4c
Reading purchases	yr	312	1999	30c
Television, radios, sound equipment, expenditures on	yr	624	1999	30r
Tennis balls, yellow, Wilson or Penn, 3	can	2.70	3/01	4c
Funerals				
Total cost of funeral		5401.08	1/99	78r
Acknowledgement cards		33.64	1/99	78r
Casket		2170.43	1/99	78r
Cosmetology, hair, other preparation		136.32	1/99	78r
Embalming		319.13	1/99	78r
Funeral at funeral home		370.21	1/99	78r
Hearse (local)		161.04	1/99	78r
Professional service charges		963.15	1/99	78r
Service car/van		133.99	1/99	78r
Transfer of remains to funeral home		159.82	1/99	78r
Vault		778.07	1/99	78r
Visitation/viewing		175.28	1/99	78r
Groceries				
Groceries, ACCRA Index		127.90	3/01	4c
Antibiotic ointment, Polysporin	0.5 oz	4.39	3/01	4c
Apples, red delicious	lb	0.84	7/01	11r
Baby food, strained vegetables or fruit, lowest price	4-4.5 oz	0.42	3/01	4c
Bacon, sliced	lb	3.38	7/01	11r
Bakery products, expenditures on	yr	299	1999	30r
Bananas	lb	0.95	3/01	4c
Bananas	lb	0.54	7/01	11r
Beans, dried, any type, all sizes	lb	0.76	7/01	11r
Beef or hamburger, ground	lb	2.12	3/01	4c
Beef, expenditures on	yr	222	1999	30r
Bread, white	loaf	0.94	3/01	4c
Bread, white, pan	lb	0.99	7/01	11r
Butter, yoghurt, cheese, etc, expenditures on	yr	211	1999	30r
Cereals and bakery product purchases	yr	466	1999	30r
Cereals and cereal products, expenditures on	yr	168	1999	30r

Anchorage, AK - continued

Item	Per	Value	Date	Ref.
Groceries - continued				
Cheese, Kraft grated Parmesan	8 oz	3.78	3/01	4c
Chicken breast, bone-in	lb	2.45	7/01	11r
Chicken, fresh, whole	lb	1.19	7/01	11r
Chicken, whole fryer	lb	1.35	3/01	4c
Chops, boneless,	lb	4.00	7/01	11r
Chuck roast, graded and ungraded, excl U.S. prime and choice	lb	2.55	7/01	11r
Cigarettes, Winston, Kings	carton	43.59	3/01	4c
Coffee, 100%, ground roast, all sizes	lb	3.80	7/01	11r
Coffee, vacuum-packed	13 oz	4.05	3/01	4c
Cookies, chocolate chip	lb	2.83	7/01	11r
Corn Flakes, Kellogg's or Post Toasties	18 oz	3.16	3/01	4c
Corn, frozen, whole kernel, lowest price	16 oz	1.42	3/01	4c
Cost of food, family of four	week	99.17	12/99	21c
Dairy product purchases	yr	408	1999	30c
Eggs, expenditures on	yr	39	1999	30r
Eggs, Grade A or AA	dozen	1.65	3/01	4c
Eggs, grade AA, large	dozen	1.23	7/01	11r
Fats and oils, expenditures on	yr	88	1999	30r
Fish and seafood, expenditures on	yr	121	1999	30r
Food (excl fruit and vegetables), eaten at home, purchases	yr	1313	1999	30c
Food cooked on trips, expenditures on	yr	64	1999	30r
Food purchases	yr	6267	1999	30c
Food purchases, eaten away from home	yr	2345	1999	30c
Food purchases, food eaten at home	yr	3922	1999	30c
Fresh fruits, expenditures on	yr	186	1999	30r
Fresh milk and cream, expenditures on	yr	130	1999	30r
Fresh vegetables, expenditures on	yr	177	1999	30r
Fruit and vegetable purchases	yr	699	1999	30c
Grapefruit	lb	0.68	7/01	11r
Grapes, Thompson, seedless	lb	2.42	7/01	11r
Ground beef, lean and extra lean	lb	2.46	7/01	11r
Ice cream, prepackaged, bulk, regular	1/2 gal	3.62	7/01	11r
Lettuce, iceberg	head	2.24	3/01	4c
Lettuce, iceberg	lb	0.63	7/01	11r
Margarine, Blue Bonnet or Parkay, stick	lb	0.72	3/01	4c
Meats, poultry, fish, and egg purchases	yr	761	1999	30r
Milk, fresh, low fat	gal	2.80	7/01	11r
Milk, fresh, whole, fortified	gal	2.88	7/01	11r
Milk, whole	1/2 gal	2.35	3/01	4c
Nonalcoholic beverages, expenditures on	yr	258	1999	30r
Orange juice, Minute Maid frozen	12 oz	1.56	3/01	4c
Oranges, Navel	lb	0.97	7/01	11r
Oranges, Valencia	lb	0.43	7/01	11r
Peaches	lb	1.38	7/01	11r
Peaches, halves or slices, Hunt's, Del Monte, or Libby's	29 oz	1.60	3/01	4c
Peanut butter, creamy, all sizes	lb	2.14	7/01	11r
Peas, green, Del Monte or Green Giant	15 oz	0.75	3/01	4c
Pork chops, center cut, bone-in	lb	3.83	7/01	11r
Pork, expenditures on	yr	141	1999	30r
Potatoes, white or red	10 lb	3.99	3/01	4c
Potatoes, white, all types	lb	0.37	7/01	11r
Poultry, expenditures on	yr	146	1999	30r
Processed fruits, expenditures on	yr	118	1999	30r
Processed vegetables, expenditures on	yr	81	1999	30r
Round roast, graded and ungraded, excl U.S. prime and choice	lb	3.07	7/01	11r
Round roast, U.S. choice, boneless	lb	3.37	7/01	11r
Round steak, graded and ungraded, excl U.S. prime and choice	lb	3.51	7/01	11r
Sausage, Jimmy Dean/Owens pork	lb	4.65	3/01	4c
Shortening, vegetable, Crisco	3 lb	3.36	3/01	4c
Sirloin steak, graded and ungraded, excl U.S. prime and choice	lb	4.67	7/01	11r
Soft drink, Coca Cola, ex deposit	2 liter	1.79	3/01	4c
Steak, sirloin, U.S. choice, boneless	lb	6.20	7/01	11r
Steak, T-bone	lb	7.52	3/01	4c
Strawberries, dry pint	12 oz	1.79	7/01	11r
Sugar and other sweets, expenditures on	yr	124	1999	30r
Sugar, cane or beet	4 lbs	1.94	3/01	4c

Values are in dollars or fractions of dollars. In the column headed *Ref*, references are shown to sources. Each reference is followed by a letter. These refer to the geographical level for which data were reported: s=State, r=Region, and c=City or metro. The abbreviation *ex* is used to mean *except* or *excluding*; *exp* stands for expenditures. For other abbreviations and further explanations, please see the Introduction.

Anchorage, AK - continued

Item	Per	Value	Date	Ref.
Groceries				
Sugar, white, all sizes	lb	0.46	7/01	11r
Tobacco products and smoking supplies purchases	yr	419	1999	30c
Tomatoes, field grown	lb	1.17	7/01	11r
Tomatoes, Hunt's or Del Monte	14.5 oz	0.81	3/01	4c
Tuna, chunk, light	6 oz	0.83	3/01	4c
Tuna, light, chunk	lb	2.05	7/01	11r
Goods and Services				
Miscellaneous goods and services, ACCRA Index		122.10	3/01	4c
B&B Japanese maple (acer japonicum)	gal	39.99	4/00	93r
Boxwood (buxus)	2 gal	14.99-24.99	4/00	93r
Daylilly (hemerocallis)	gal	6.99-8.99	4/00	93r
Flat of annuals		16.68	4/00	93r
Fountain grass (pennisetum)	gal	7.99-11.99	4/00	93r
Hanging basket (10 in)		29.99	4/00	93r
Hardy geranium (geranium)	gal	6.99-11.99	4/00	93r
Hosta (hosta)	gal	6.99-18.99	4/00	93r
Lilac (syrubga vulgaris)	2 gal	14.99-17.99	4/00	93r
Miscellaneous purchases	yr	1070	1999	30r
Rhododendron (rhododendron)	2 gal	14.99	4/00	93r
Sage (salvia)	gal	6.99	4/00	93r
Wintercreeper euonymus (euonymus fortunei)	2 gal	14.99-22.99	4/00	93r
Hunting license	yr	25.00	4/01	34s
Health Care				
Health care, ACCRA Index		157.30	3/01	4c
Childbirth, Cesarean delivery		11587	1997	13r
Childbirth, vaginal delivery		6725	1997	13r
Dentist's fee, adult teeth cleaning and periodic oral exam	visit	133.71	3/01	4c
Doctor's fee, routine exam, established patient	visit	87.43	3/01	4c
Drugs, expenditures on	yr	309	1999	30r
Health care purchases	yr	2324	1999	30c
Health insurance expenditures	yr	868	1999	30r
Hospital care, private room	day	821.00	3/01	4c
Hysterectomy, vaginal, ave hospital and physician charges		12380	1998	76s
Medicaid dispensing fee		3.45-11.46	1999	87s
Medical services expenditures	yr	580	1999	30r
Medical supplies, expenditures on	yr	112	1999	30r
Household Goods				
Dishwashing powder, Cascade	50 oz	3.58	3/01	4c
Floor coverings, expenditures on	yr	49	1999	30r
Furniture, expenditures on	yr	444	1999	30r
Household furnishings and equipment purchases	yr	2573	1999	30c
Household textiles, expenditures on	yr	141	1999	30r
Laundry and cleaning supplies, expenditures on	yr	128	1999	30r
Tissues, facial, Kleenex brand	175	1.46	3/01	4c
Housing				
Housing, ACCRA Index		131.30	3/01	4c
Apartment rent	mos	747	3/00	6c
Home price, existing, ave		239400	10/00	90r
Home value, median		148000	2001	53s
House, 2400 sq ft, 8000 sq ft lot, new, urban, utilities	total	267991	3/01	4c
House payment, principal and interest, 25% down payment	mos	1364	3/01	4c
Household operation expenditures	yr	957	1999	30c
Housekeeping supplies purchases	yr	700	1999	30c

Anchorage, AK - continued

Item	Per	Value	Date	Ref.
Housing - continued				
Housing, expenditures on	yr	17366	1999	30c
Lodging expenditures	yr	575	1999	30r
Maintenance, repairs, insurance expenditures	yr	939	1999	30r
Monthly rental value of owned home	mos	662	1999	30r
Owned dwellings, expenditures own	yr	6163	1999	30c
Rent expenditures	yr	3367	1999	30c
Rent, apartment, 2 br, 1 1/2-2 baths, unfurn, 950 sq ft, water	mos	883	3/01	4c
Rental unit, 1 bedroom, with utilities	mos	599	4/01	41c
Rental unit, 2 bedroom, with utilities	mos	794	4/01	41c
Rental unit, 3 bedroom, with utilities	mos	1105	4/01	41c
Rental unit, 4 bedroom, with utilities	mos	1304	4/01	41c
Shelter, expenditures on	yr	10522	1999	30c
Single-family home rent	mos	1312	12/99	21c
Two-bedroom apartment rent	mos	739	12/99	21c
Insurance and Pensions				
Auto insurance premium	yr	922.74	1999	57s
Life and other personal insurance purchases	yr	574	1999	30c
Pensions and Social Security, expenditures on	yr	4568	1999	30c
Personal insurance and pensions, expenditures on	yr	5141	1999	30c
Legal Fees				
Driver's license fee	orig	15.00	1999	48s
Driver's license fee	renew	15.00	1999	48s
Personal Goods				
Personal care products and services purchases	yr	524	1999	30c
Shampoo, Alberto VO5	15 oz	1.18	3/01	4c
Toothpaste, Crest or Colgate	6-7 oz	2.40	3/01	4c
Personal Services				
Dry cleaning, man's 2-pc suit		9.95	3/01	4c
Man's haircut, barbershop, no styling		13.00	3/01	4c
Personal services, household, expenditures on	yr	353	1999	30r
Woman's shampoo, trim, blow-dry, no style-change		31.22	3/01	4c
Pets				
Pets, toys, and playground equipment, expenditures on	yr	358	1999	30r
Restaurant Food				
Chicken, fried, thigh and drumstick, KFC/Church's		3.22	3/01	4c
Hamburger with cheese, McDonald's	1/4 lb	2.87	3/01	4c
Pizza, Pizza Hut or Pizza Inn	11-12 in	10.99	3/01	4c
Taxes				
Federal income taxes paid	yr	3200	1999	30r
Personal taxes, expenditures on	yr	4153	1999	30r
Property taxes paid	yr	923	1999	30r
State and local income taxes paid	yr	812	1999	30r
Transportation				
Transportation, ACCRA Index		110.20	3/01	4c
Bus fare, to central business district	1-way	1.00	3/01	4c
Cars and trucks, new, expenditures on	yr	1534	1999	30r
Cars and trucks, used, expenditures on	yr	1593	1999	30r
Gasoline and motor oil purchases	yr	1300	1999	30c
Gasoline before-tax price (cents)	gal	146.80	10/00	43s
Maintenance and repair expenditures	yr	797	1999	30r
Motorcycle license fee	orig	15.00	1999	49s
Motorcycle license fee	renew	15.00	1999	49s
Public transportation, expenditures on	yr	981	1999	30c
Tire balance, computer or spin balance, front	wheel	8.66	3/01	4c
Transportation purchases	yr	9284	1999	30c
Vehicle expenses, miscellaneous, purchases	yr	3191	1999	30c
Vehicle insurance payments	yr	811	1999	30r
Vehicle purchases (net outlay)	yr	3812	1999	30c
Vehicle rental, lease expenditures	yr	666	1999	30r

Values are in dollars or fractions of dollars. In the column headed *Ref*, references are shown to sources. Each reference is followed by a letter. These refer to the geographical level for which data were reported: s=State, r=Region, and c=City or metro. The abbreviation *ex* is used to mean *except* or *excluding*; *exp* stands for *expenditures*. For other abbreviations and further explanations, please see the Introduction.

Anchorage, AK - continued

Item	Per	Value	Date	Ref.
Utilities				
Utilities, ACCRA Index		83.00	3/01	4c
Electrical bill, average	mos	76.33	9/00	9s
Electricity, expenditures on	yr	725	1999	30r
Electricity and other, mixed, 2400 sq ft, new home	mos	52.46	3/01	4c
Electricity cost, average	KWh	9.80	9/00	9s
Utilities, fuels, and public services purchased	yr	2179	1999	30r
Water and other public services, expenditures on	yr	339	1999	30r
Weddings				
Wedding (national average cost)		19936	2000	33r
Wedding (regional average total cost)		18918	1997	110r
Attendants' gifts		321	1998	33r
Bridal attendants' apparel (5 persons)		824	2000	33r
Bride's headpiece/veil		173	1998	33r
Bride's wedding dress		859	1998	33r
Clergy, religious facility fee		242	1998	33r
Engagement ring		3177	1998	33r
Flowers		789	1998	33r
Groom's formalwear rental		99	2000	33r
Limousine		410	1998	33r
Marriage license cost		25.00	4/01	35s
Men's formalwear (ushers, best man)		469	2000	33r
Mother of bride apparel		241	2000	33r
Music		866	1998	33r
Photography and videography		1368	1998	33r
Rehearsal dinner		728	1998	33r
Wedding invitations and announcements		341	1998	33r
Wedding reception		7968	2000	33r
Wedding rings (bride and groom)		1060	1998	33r

Ann Arbor, MI

Item	Per	Value	Date	Ref.
Average annual expenditures	yr	35369	1999	30r
Alcoholic Beverages				
Alcoholic beverage purchases	yr	304	1999	30r
Malt beverages, all types, all sizes, any origin	16 oz	0.93	7/01	11r
Wine, red and white table, all sizes, any origin	liter	7.04	7/01	11r
Appliances				
Major appliances, expenditures on	yr	165	1999	30r
Small appliances, housewares, expenditures on	yr	90	1999	30r
Banking and Money				
Mortgage interest and charges paid	yr	2277	1999	30r
Mortgage principal paid on owned property	yr	1230	1999	30r
Vehicle finance charges paid	yr	328	1999	30r
Charity				
Cash contributions, expenditures	yr	1126	1999	30r
Child Care				
Child raising cost, total, age 0-2	yr	7890	1999	60r
Child raising cost, total, age 3-5	yr	8130	1999	60r
Child raising cost, total, age 6-8	yr	8170	1999	60r
Child raising cost, total, age 9-11	yr	8190	1999	60r
Child raising cost, total, age 12-14	yr	8890	1999	60r
Child raising cost, total, age 15-17	yr	9050	1999	60r
Child's child care and education, age 0-2	yr	1240	1999	60r
Child's child care and education, age 3-5	yr	1370	1999	60r
Child's child care and education, age 6-8	yr	880	1999	60r
Child's child care and education, age 9-11	yr	570	1999	60r
Child's child care and education, age 12-14	yr	420	1999	60r
Child's child care and education, age 15-17	yr	720	1999	60r
Child's clothing, age 0-2	yr	410	1999	60r
Child's clothing, age 3-5	yr	400	1999	60r
Child's clothing, age 6-8	yr	450	1999	60r
Child's clothing, age 9-11	yr	500	1999	60r
Child's clothing, age 12-14	yr	840	1999	60r
Child's clothing, age 15-17	yr	740	1999	60r

Ann Arbor, MI - continued

Item	Per	Value	Date	Ref.
Child Care - continued				
Child's food, age 0-2	yr	960	1999	60r
Child's food, age 3-5	yr	1120	1999	60r
Child's food, age 6-8	yr	1430	1999	60r
Child's food, age 9-11	yr	1710	1999	60r
Child's food, age 12-14	yr	1710	1999	60r
Child's food, age 15-17	yr	1920	1999	60r
Child's health care, age 0-2	yr	520	1999	60r
Child's health care, age 3-5	yr	500	1999	60r
Child's health care, age 6-8	yr	570	1999	60r
Child's health care, age 9-11	yr	610	1999	60r
Child's health care, age 12-14	yr	630	1999	60r
Child's health care, age 15-17	yr	650	1999	60r
Child's housing, age 0-2	yr	2860	1999	60r
Child's housing, age 3-5	yr	2840	1999	60r
Child's housing, age 6-8	yr	2800	1999	60r
Child's housing, age 9-11	yr	2650	1999	60r
Child's housing, age 12-14	yr	2840	1999	60r
Child's housing, age 15-17	yr	2440	1999	60r
Child's personal care, reading, age 0-2	yr	880	1999	60r
Child's personal care, reading, age 3-5	yr	900	1999	60r
Child's personal care, reading, age 6-8	yr	930	1999	60r
Child's personal care, reading, age 9-11	yr	970	1999	60r
Child's personal care, reading, age 12-14	yr	1150	1999	60r
Child's personal care, reading, age 15-17	yr	920	1999	60r
Clothing				
Apparel and services purchases	yr	1607	1999	30r
Boys, 2 to 15, expenditures on	yr	91	1999	30r
Children under 2, expenditures on	yr	59	1999	30r
Footwear, expenditures on	yr	285	1999	30r
Girls, 2 to 15, expenditures on	yr	116	1999	30r
Men and boys, expenditures on	yr	433	1999	30r
Men, 16 and over, expenditures on	yr	341	1999	30r
Women, 16 and over, expenditures on	yr	490	1999	30r
Communications				
Cable modem installation, Bresnan		99.95	6/99	103s
Cable modem installation, Comcast		95.00	6/99	103s
Cable modem installation, Media One		100.00	6/99	103s
Cable modem rate, cable subscriber, Bresnan	mos	39.95	6/99	103s
Cable modem rate, cable subscriber, Comcast	mos	39.95	6/99	103s
Cable modem rate, cable subscriber, Media One	mos	34.95-39.95	6/99	103s
Cable modem rate, non-cable subscriber, Bresnan	mos	49.95	6/99	103s
Cable modem rate, non-cable subscriber, Comcast	mos	49.95	6/99	103s
Cable modem rate, non-cable subscriber, Media One	mos	49.95	6/99	103s
Phone line, single, business, field visit	inst.	42.00	12/97	17s
Phone line, single, business, no field visit	inst.	42.00	12/97	17s
Phone line, single, residence, field visit	inst.	42.00	12/97	17s
Phone line, single, residence, no field visit	inst.	42.00	12/97	17s
Postage and stationery, expenditures on	yr	140	1999	30r
Postal rate, express mail, up to half-pound		12.45	7/01	108r
Postal rate, letter, first class, first ounce		0.34	7/01	108r
Postal rate, letter, two ounces		0.57	7/01	108r
Postal rate, post card		0.21	7/01	108r
Postal rate, priority mail, two pounds		3.95	7/01	108r
Postal rate, priority mail, up to one pound		3.50	7/01	108r
Telephone bill, business, basic rate	mos	13.04	12/97	18c
Telephone bill, residential, basic rate	mos	10.40	12/97	18c
Telephone services, expenditures on	yr	830	1999	30r
Education				
Board, 4-year private college/university	yr	2182	1996	38s
Board, 4-year public college/university	yr	2276	1996	38s
Education expenditures	yr	583	1999	30r
Room, 4-year private college/university	yr	1974	1996	38s
Room, 4-year public college/university	yr	2024	1996	38s
Total cost, 4-year private college/university	yr	13331	1996	38s
Total cost, 4-year public college/university	yr	8195	1996	38s

Values are in dollars or fractions of dollars. In the column headed *Ref*, references are shown to sources. Each reference is followed by a letter. These refer to the geographical level for which data were reported: s=State, r=Region, and c=City or metro. The abbreviation *ex* is used to mean *except* or *excluding*; *exp* stands for *expenditures*. For other abbreviations and further explanations, please see the Introduction.

Ann Arbor, MI - continued

Item	Per	Value	Date	Ref.
Education				
Tuition, 2-year public college/university, in state	yr	1529	1996	38s
Tuition, 4-year private college/university, in state	yr	9176	1996	38s
Tuition, 4-year public college/university	yr	3895	1996	38s
Energy and Fuels				
Electricity	500 KWhs	46.59	7/01	11r
Fuel oil #2	gal	1.27	7/01	11r
Fuel oil and other fuels, expenditures on	yr	68	1999	30r
Gas, natural, commercial rate	1000 cf	4.91	11/00	88s
Gasoline, unleaded midgrade	gal	1.79	7/01	11r
Gasoline, unleaded premium	gal	1.86	7/01	11r
Gasoline, unleaded regular	gal	1.58	7/01	11r
Natural gas, expenditures on	yr	389	1999	30r
Utility (piped) gas, therm		0.81	7/01	11r
Utility (piped) gas, 40 therms		38.01	7/01	11r
Utility (piped) gas, 100 therms		81.75	7/01	11r
Entertainment				
Entertainment purchases	yr	1984	1999	30r
Fees and admissions paid	yr	444	1999	30r
Television, radios, sound equipment, expenditures on	yr	580	1999	30r
Funerals				
Cosmetology, hair, other preparation		178.32	1/99	78r
Embalming		408.19	1/99	78r
Funeral at funeral home		362.13	1/99	78r
Professional service charges		1375.51	1/99	78r
Transfer of remains to funeral home		155.92	1/99	78r
Visitation/viewing		294.38	1/99	78r
Groceries				
Bacon, sliced	lb	3.15	7/01	11r
Bakery products, expenditures on	yr	281	1999	30r
Bananas	lb	0.48	7/01	11r
Beans, dried, any type, all sizes	lb	0.61	7/01	11r
Beef for stew, boneless	lb	3.08	7/01	11r
Beef, expenditures on	yr	217	1999	30r
Bologna, all beef or mixed	lb	2.52	7/01	11r
Bread, white, pan	lb	1.06	7/01	11r
Broccoli	lb	0.91	7/01	11r
Butter, salted, grade AA, stick	lb	3.04	7/01	11r
Butter, yoghurt, cheese, etc, expenditures on	yr	183	1999	30r
Cereals and bakery product purchases	yr	430	1999	30r
Cereals and cereal products, expenditures on	yr	149	1999	30r
Chicken, fresh, whole	lb	1.07	7/01	11r
Chops, boneless,	lb	3.64	7/01	11r
Chuck roast, U.S. choice, boneless	lb	2.47	7/01	11r
Coffee, 100%, ground roast, all sizes	lb	2.69	7/01	11r
Cookies, chocolate chip	lb	2.87	7/01	11r
Dairy product purchases	yr	304	1999	30r
Eggs, expenditures on	yr	26	1999	30r
Eggs, grade A, large	dozen	0.88	7/01	11r
Fats and oils, expenditures on	yr	75	1999	30r
Fish and seafood, expenditures on	yr	72	1999	30r
Food (excl fruit and vegetables), eaten at home, purchases	yr	887	1999	30r
Food cooked on trips, expenditures on	yr	44	1999	30r
Food purchases	yr	4802	1999	30r
Food purchases, eaten away from home	yr	2069	1999	30r
Food purchases, food eaten at home	yr	2733	1999	30r
Fresh fruits, expenditures on	yr	138	1999	30r
Fresh milk and cream, expenditures on	yr	120	1999	30r
Fresh vegetables, expenditures on	yr	126	1999	30r
Grapefruit	lb	0.66	7/01	11r
Grapes, Thompson, seedless	lb	1.64	7/01	11r
Ground beef, 100% beef	lb	1.64	7/01	11r
Ground beef, lean and extra lean	lb	2.16	7/01	11r
Ground chuck, 100% beef	lb	2.13	7/01	11r
Ham, boneless, excl canned	lb	2.62	7/01	11r

Ann Arbor, MI - continued

Item	Per	Value	Date	Ref.
Groceries - continued				
Ice cream, prepackaged, bulk, regular	1/2 gal	3.35	7/01	11r
Lemons	lb	1.19	7/01	11r
Lettuce, iceberg	lb	0.73	7/01	11r
Margarine, soft, tubs	lb	0.89	7/01	11r
Meats, poultry, fish, and egg purchases	yr	671	1999	30r
Milk, fresh, whole, fortified	gal	2.71	7/01	11r
Nonalcoholic beverages, expenditures on	yr	239	1999	30r
Oranges, Navel	lb	0.80	7/01	11r
Oranges, Valencia	lb	0.66	7/01	11r
Pears, Anjou	lb	0.93	7/01	11r
Pork chops, center cut, bone-in	lb	3.63	7/01	11r
Pork, expenditures on	yr	150	1999	30r
Potato chips	16 oz	3.52	7/01	11r
Potatoes, frozen, french fried	lb	1.08	7/01	11r
Potatoes, white, all types	lb	0.33	7/01	11r
Poultry, expenditures on	yr	108	1999	30r
Processed fruits, expenditures on	yr	98	1999	30r
Processed vegetables, expenditures on	yr	80	1999	30r
Round roast, U.S. choice, boneless	lb	3.07	7/01	11r
Round steak, graded and ungraded, excl U.S. prime and choice	lb	3.41	7/01	11r
Shortening, vegetable oil blends	lb	1.13	7/01	11r
Spaghetti and macaroni	lb	0.80	7/01	11r
Steak, round, U.S. choice, boneless	lb	3.23	7/01	11r
Steak, T-bone, U.S. choice, bone-in	lb	6.68	7/01	11r
Strawberries, dry pint	12 oz	1.32	7/01	11r
Sugar and other sweets, expenditures on	yr	114	1999	30r
Sugar, white, 33-80 ounce package	lb	0.42	7/01	11r
Sugar, white, all sizes	lb	0.43	7/01	11r
Tobacco products and smoking supplies purchases	yr	331	1999	30r
Tomatoes, field grown	lb	1.46	7/01	11r
Tuna, light, chunk	lb	1.80	7/01	11r
Turkey, frozen, whole	lb	1.15	7/01	11r
Goods and Services				
B&B Japanese maple (acer japonicum)	gal	29.99-169.99	4/00	93r
Boxwood (buxus)	2 gal	18.99-39.99	4/00	93r
Daylilly (hemerocallis)	gal	4.99-25.00	4/00	93r
Flat of annuals		11.98-24.99	4/00	93r
Fountain grass (pennisetum)	gal	5.98-12.98	4/00	93r
Hanging basket (10 in)		12.99-27.99	4/00	93r
Hardy geranium (geranium)	gal	7.99-9.99	4/00	93r
Hosta (hosta)	gal	6.00-25.00	4/00	93r
Lilac (syrubga vulgaris)	2 gal	14.99-24.99	4/00	93r
Miscellaneous purchases	yr	865	1999	30r
Rhododendron (rhododendron)	2 gal	23.98-42.99	4/00	93r
Sage (salvia)	gal	6.00-9.99	4/00	93r
Snowblower, single stage		400-600	12/00	99s
Wintercreeper euonymus (euonymus fortunei)	2 gal	16.00-169.99	4/00	93r
Hunting license	yr	14.00	4/01	34s
Health Care				
Cardiac catheterization, ave hospital/physician charges		11830	1998	77s
Childbirth, Cesarean delivery		10722	1997	13r
Childbirth, vaginal delivery		6223	1997	13r
Drugs, expenditures on	yr	394	1999	30r
Health care purchases	yr	2048	1999	30r
Health insurance expenditures	yr	978	1999	30r

Values are in dollars or fractions of dollars. In the column headed *Ref*, references are shown to sources. Each reference is followed by a letter. These refer to the geographical level for which data were reported: s=State, r=Region, and c=City or metro. The abbreviation *ex* is used to mean *except* or *excluding*; *exp* stands for *expenditures*. For other abbreviations and further explanations, please see the Introduction.

Ann Arbor, MI - continued

Item	Per	Value	Date	Ref.
Health Care				
Hysterectomy, laproscopically-assisted, ave hospital/physician charges		13820	1998	76s
Hysterectomy, vaginal, ave hospital and physician charges		8780	1998	76s
Medicaid dispensing fee		3.72	1999	87s
Medical services expenditures	yr	554	1999	30r
Medical supplies, expenditures on	yr	122	1999	30r
Plastic surgery, breast augmentation		3184	2000	7r
Plastic surgery, breast lift		3585	2000	7r
Plastic surgery, facelift		4999	2000	7r
Plastic surgery, hair transplantation		3105	2000	7r
Plastic surgery, lip augmentation		1290	2000	7r
Plastic surgery, lower body lift		8135	2000	7r
Plastic surgery, thigh lift		3839	2000	7r
Household Goods				
Floor coverings, expenditures on	yr	52	1999	30r
Furniture, expenditures on	yr	344	1999	30r
Household furnishings and equipment purchases	yr	1475	1999	30r
Household textiles, expenditures on	yr	109	1999	30r
Laundry and cleaning supplies, expenditures on	yr	134	1999	30r
Housing				
Home, 2200 sq ft, 4-br, 2-bath, 2-car garage, average		345531	2000	47c
Home price, existing, ave		144400	10/00	90r
Home value, median		135000	2001	53s
Household operation expenditures	yr	542	1999	30r
Housekeeping supplies purchases	yr	508	1999	30r
Lodging expenditures	yr	430	1999	30r
Maintenance, repairs, insurance expenditures	yr	853	1999	30r
Monthly rental value of owned home	mos	547	1999	30r
Owned dwellings, expenditures own	yr	4282	1999	30r
Rent expenditures	yr	1558	1999	30r
Rental unit, 1 bedroom, with utilities	mos	596	4/01	41c
Rental unit, 2 bedroom, with utilities	mos	736	4/01	41c
Rental unit, 3 bedroom, with utilities	mos	965	4/01	41c
Rental unit, 4 bedroom, with utilities	mos	1082	4/01	41c
Shelter, expenditures on	yr	6270	1999	30r
Insurance and Pensions				
Life and other personal insurance purchases	yr	387	1999	30r
Pensions and Social Security, expenditures on	yr	2968	1999	30r
Legal Fees				
Divorce, filing fee		65.00	4/01	35s
Driver's license fee	renew	5.00	1999	48s
Driver's license fee	orig	20.00	1999	48s
Fishing license	yr	14.00	4/01	34s
Personal Goods				
Personal care products and services purchases	yr	385	1999	30r
Personal Services				
Personal services, household, expenditures on	yr	300	1999	30r
Pets				
Pets, toys, and playground equipment, expenditures on	yr	375	1999	30r
Taxes				
Federal income taxes paid	yr	2326	1999	30r
Personal taxes, expenditures on	yr	3223	1999	30r
Property taxes paid	yr	1152	1999	30r
State and local income taxes paid	yr	753	1999	30r
Transportation				
Bus fare, one-way	trip	0.75	2000	1c
Cars and trucks, new, expenditures on	yr	1280	1999	30r
Cars and trucks, used, expenditures on	yr	1763	1999	30r

Ann Arbor, MI - continued

Item	Per	Value	Date	Ref.
Transportation - continued				
Diesel at the pump	gal	1.19	10/99	73s
Gasoline and motor oil purchases	yr	1036	1999	30r
Gasoline before-tax price (cents)	gal	111.50	10/00	43s
Maintenance and repair expenditures	yr	594	1999	30r
Public transportation, expenditures on	yr	341	1999	30r
Transportation purchases	yr	6617	1999	30r
Vehicle expenses, miscellaneous, purchases	yr	2159	1999	30r
Vehicle insurance payments	yr	701	1999	30r
Vehicle purchases (net outlay)	yr	3081	1999	30r
Vehicle rental, lease expenditures	yr	536	1999	30r
Utilities				
Electrical bill, average	mos	55.00	9/00	9s
Electricity, expenditures on	yr	841	1999	30r
Electricity cost, average	KWh	7.00	9/00	9s
Utilities, fuels, and public services purchased	yr	2401	1999	30r
Water and other public services, expenditures on	yr	273	1999	30r
Weddings				
Wedding (national average cost)		19936	2000	33r
Wedding (regional average total cost)		16195	1997	110r
Attendants' gifts		321	1998	33r
Bridal attendants' apparel (5 persons)		824	2000	33r
Bride's headpiece/veil		173	1998	33r
Bride's wedding dress		859	1998	33r
Clergy, religious facility fee		242	1998	33r
Engagement ring		3177	1998	33r
Flowers		789	1998	33r
Groom's formalwear rental		99	2000	33r
Limousine		410	1998	33r
Marriage license cost		20.00	4/01	35s
Men's formalwear (ushers, best man)		469	2000	33r
Mother of bride apparel		241	2000	33r
Music		866	1998	33r
Photography and videography		1368	1998	33r
Rehearsal dinner		728	1998	33r
Wedding invitations and announcements		341	1998	33r
Wedding reception		7968	2000	33r
Wedding rings (bride and groom)		1060	1998	33r

Anniston, AL

Item	Per	Value	Date	Ref.
Alcoholic Beverages				
Alcoholic beverage purchases	yr	253	1999	30r
Malt beverages, all types, all sizes, any origin	16 oz	0.96	7/01	11r
Appliances				
Major appliances, expenditures on	yr	172	1999	30r
Small appliances, housewares, expenditures on	yr	81	1999	30r
Banking and Money				
Mortgage interest and charges paid	yr	2039	1999	30r
Mortgage principal paid on owned property	yr	1026	1999	30r
Vehicle finance charges paid	yr	365	1999	30r
Charity				
Cash contributions, expenditures	yr	1127	1999	30r
Child Care				
Child raising cost, total, age 0-2	yr	8540	1999	60r
Child raising cost, total, age 3-5	yr	8780	1999	60r
Child raising cost, total, age 6-8	yr	8820	1999	60r
Child raising cost, total, age 9-11	yr	8800	1999	60r
Child raising cost, total, age 12-14	yr	9510	1999	60r
Child raising cost, total, age 15-17	yr	9740	1999	60r
Child's child care and education, age 0-2	yr	1380	1999	60r
Child's child care and education, age 3-5	yr	1520	1999	60r
Child's child care and education, age 6-8	yr	990	1999	60r
Child's child care and education, age 9-11	yr	650	1999	60r
Child's child care and education, age 12-14	yr	490	1999	60r
Child's child care and education, age 15-17	yr	840	1999	60r
Child's clothing, age 0-2	yr	480	1999	60r

Values are in dollars or fractions of dollars. In the column headed *Ref*, references are shown to sources. Each reference is followed by a letter. These refer to the geographical level for which data were reported: s=State, r=Region, and c=City or metro. The abbreviation *ex* is used to mean *except* or *excluding*; *exp* stands for *expenditures*. For other abbreviations and further explanations, please see the Introduction.

Anniston, AL - continued

Item	Per	Value	Date	Ref.
Child Care				
Child's clothing, age 3-5	yr	470	1999	60r
Child's clothing, age 6-8	yr	520	1999	60r
Child's clothing, age 9-11	yr	570	1999	60r
Child's clothing, age 12-14	yr	950	1999	60r
Child's clothing, age 15-17	yr	850	1999	60r
Child's food, age 0-2	yr	1000	1999	60r
Child's food, age 3-5	yr	1160	1999	60r
Child's food, age 6-8	yr	1490	1999	60r
Child's food, age 9-11	yr	1770	1999	60r
Child's food, age 12-14	yr	1770	1999	60r
Child's food, age 15-17	yr	1980	1999	60r
Child's health care, age 0-2	yr	620	1999	60r
Child's health care, age 3-5	yr	590	1999	60r
Child's health care, age 6-8	yr	680	1999	60r
Child's health care, age 9-11	yr	720	1999	60r
Child's health care, age 12-14	yr	730	1999	60r
Child's health care, age 15-17	yr	760	1999	60r
Child's housing, age 0-2	yr	3070	1999	60r
Child's housing, age 3-5	yr	3050	1999	60r
Child's housing, age 6-8	yr	3010	1999	60r
Child's housing, age 9-11	yr	2850	1999	60r
Child's housing, age 12-14	yr	3040	1999	60r
Child's housing, age 15-17	yr	2650	1999	60r
Child's personal care, reading, age 0-2	yr	910	1999	60r
Child's personal care, reading, age 3-5	yr	930	1999	60r
Child's personal care, reading, age 6-8	yr	960	1999	60r
Child's personal care, reading, age 9-11	yr	1000	1999	60r
Child's personal care, reading, age 12-14	yr	1170	1999	60r
Child's personal care, reading, age 15-17	yr	950	1999	60r
Clothing				
Apparel and services purchases	yr	1610	1999	30r
Boys, 2 to 15, expenditures on	yr	89	1999	30r
Children under 2, expenditures on	yr	79	1999	30r
Footwear, expenditures on	yr	283	1999	30r
Girls, 2 to 15, expenditures on	yr	103	1999	30r
Men and boys, expenditures on	yr	351	1999	30r
Men, 16 and over, expenditures on	yr	262	1999	30r
Women, 16 and over, expenditures on	yr	538	1999	30r
Communications				
Phone line, single, business, field visit	inst.	69.00	12/97	17s
Phone line, single, business, no field visit	inst.	69.00	12/97	17s
Phone line, single, residence, field visit	inst.	40.00	12/97	17s
Phone line, single, residence, no field visit	inst.	40.00	12/97	17s
Postage and stationery, expenditures on	yr	104	1999	30r
Postal rate, express mail, up to half-pound		12.45	7/01	108r
Postal rate, letter, first class, first ounce		0.34	7/01	108r
Postal rate, letter, two ounces		0.57	7/01	108r
Postal rate, post card		0.21	7/01	108r
Postal rate, priority mail, two pounds		3.95	7/01	108r
Postal rate, priority mail, up to one pound		3.50	7/01	108r
Telephone services, expenditures on	yr	860	1999	30r
Education				
Board, 4-year private college/university	yr	2256	1996	38s
Board, 4-year public college/university	yr	1739	1996	38s
Education expenditures	yr	431	1999	30r
Room, 4-year private college/university	yr	1799	1996	38s
Room, 4-year public college/university	yr	1757	1996	38s
Total cost, 4-year private college/university	yr	11635	1996	38s
Total cost, 4-year public college/university	yr	5737	1996	38s
Tuition, 2-year public college/university, in state	yr	1317	1996	38s
Tuition, 4-year private college/university, in state	yr	7580	1996	38s
Tuition, 4-year public college/university	yr	2240	1996	38s
Energy and Fuels				
Electricity	KWh	0.09	7/01	11r
Electricity	500 KWhs	47.29	7/01	11r
Fuel oil #2	gal	1.43	7/01	11r
Fuel oil and other fuels, expenditures on	yr	45	1999	30r

Anniston, AL - continued

Item	Per	Value	Date	Ref.
Energy and Fuels - continued				
Gas, natural, commercial rate	1000 cf	9.50	11/00	88s
Gasoline, all types	gal	1.60	7/01	11r
Gasoline, unleaded midgrade	gal	1.65	7/01	11r
Gasoline, unleaded premium	gal	1.74	7/01	11r
Natural gas, expenditures on	yr	164	1999	30r
Utility (piped) gas, therm		1.01	7/01	11r
Utility (piped) gas, 40 therms		44.29	7/01	11r
Utility (piped) gas, 100 therms		97.44	7/01	11r
Entertainment				
Entertainment purchases	yr	1574	1999	30r
Fees and admissions paid	yr	371	1999	30r
Reading purchases	yr	121	1999	30r
Television, radios, sound equipment, expenditures on	yr	561	1999	30r
Groceries				
American processed cheese	lb	3.50	7/01	11r
Bakery products, expenditures on	yr	261	1999	30r
Bananas	lb	0.47	7/01	11r
Beans, dried, any type, all sizes	lb	0.63	7/01	11r
Beef for stew, boneless	lb	2.86	7/01	11r
Beef, expenditures on	yr	210	1999	30r
Bologna, all beef or mixed	lb	2.29	7/01	11r
Bread, French	lb	1.66	7/01	11r
Bread, white, pan	lb	0.87	7/01	11r
Bread, whole wheat, pan	lb	1.38	7/01	11r
Broccoli	lb	1.04	7/01	11r
Butter, salted, grade AA, stick	lb	2.26	7/01	11r
Butter, yoghurt, cheese, etc, expenditures on	yr	170	1999	30r
Cabbage	lb	0.42	7/01	11r
Cereals and cereal products, expenditures on	yr	140	1999	30r
Cheddar cheese, natural	lb	3.75	7/01	11r
Chicken breast, bone-in	lb	1.85	7/01	11r
Chicken legs, bone-in	lb	1.34	7/01	11r
Chicken, fresh, whole	lb	1.05	7/01	11r
Chops, boneless,	lb	4.13	7/01	11r
Chuck roast, graded and ungraded, excl U.S. prime and choice	lb	2.35	7/01	11r
Chuck roast, U.S. choice, boneless	lb	2.67	7/01	11r
Coffee, 100%, ground roast, all sizes	lb	2.88	7/01	11r
Coffee, instant, plain, regular, all sizes	16 oz	9.25	7/01	11r
Cola, non diet,	2 liter	1.11	7/01	11r
Crackers, soda, salted	lb	1.70	7/01	11r
Dairy product purchases	yr	282	1999	30r
Eggs, expenditures on	yr	32	1999	30r
Fats and oils, expenditures on	yr	79	1999	30r
Fish and seafood, expenditures on	yr	99	1999	30r
Flour, white, all purpose	lb	0.32	7/01	11r
Food (excl fruit and vegetables), eaten at home, purchases	yr	815	1999	30r
Food cooked on trips, expenditures on	yr	36	1999	30r
Food purchases	yr	4533	1999	30r
Food purchases, eaten away from home	yr	1873	1999	30r
Food purchases, food eaten at home	yr	2660	1999	30r
Fresh fruits, expenditures on	yr	128	1999	30r
Fresh milk and cream, expenditures on	yr	112	1999	30r
Fresh vegetables, expenditures on	yr	131	1999	30r
Fruit and vegetable purchases	yr	438	1999	30r
Grapefruit	lb	0.59	7/01	11r
Grapes, Thompson, seedless	lb	2.12	7/01	11r
Ground beef, 100% beef	lb	1.76	7/01	11r
Ground beef, lean and extra lean	lb	2.60	7/01	11r
Ground chuck, 100% beef	lb	2.08	7/01	11r
Ham, boneless, excl canned	lb	2.71	7/01	11r
Ham, rump or shank half, bone-in, smoked	lb	2.19	7/01	11r
Ice cream, prepackaged, bulk, regular	1/2 gal	3.93	7/01	11r
Lemons	lb	1.32	7/01	11r
Lettuce, iceberg	lb	0.76	7/01	11r
Milk, fresh, low fat,	gal	2.75	7/01	11r
Milk, fresh, whole, fortified	gal	2.97	7/01	11r
Nonalcoholic beverages, expenditures on	yr	228	1999	30r

Values are in dollars or fractions of dollars. In the column headed *Ref*, references are shown to sources. Each reference is followed by a letter. These refer to the geographical level for which data were reported: s=State, r=Region, and c=City or metro. The abbreviation *ex* is used to mean *except* or *excluding*; *exp* stands for expenditures. For other abbreviations and further explanations, please see the Introduction.

Anniston, AL - continued

Item	Per	Value	Date	Ref.
Groceries				
Orange juice, frozen concentrate	16 oz	1.95	7/01	11r
Oranges, Navel	lb	0.73	7/01	11r
Oranges, Valencia	lb	0.55	7/01	11r
Peanut butter, creamy, all sizes	lb	1.83	7/01	11r
Pears, Anjou	lb	0.98	7/01	11r
Pork chops, center cut, bone-in	lb	3.33	7/01	11r
Pork sausage, fresh, loose	lb	2.59	7/01	11r
Pork shoulder picnic, bone-in, smoked	lb	1.12	7/01	11r
Pork, expenditures on	yr	162	1999	30r
Potato chips	16 oz	3.59	7/01	11r
Potatoes, frozen, french fried	lb	1.00	7/01	11r
Potatoes, white, all types	lb	0.44	7/01	11r
Poultry, expenditures on	yr	137	1999	30r
Processed fruits, expenditures on	yr	97	1999	30r
Processed vegetables, expenditures on	yr	82	1999	30r
Rice, white, long grain, uncooked	lb	0.51	7/01	11r
Round roast, graded and ungraded, excl U.S. prime and choice	lb	2.96	7/01	11r
Round steak, graded and ungraded, excl U.S. prime and choice	lb	3.11	7/01	11r
Sirloin steak, graded and ungraded, excl U.S. prime and choice	lb	4.23	7/01	11r
Spaghetti and macaroni	lb	0.78	7/01	11r
Steak, round, U.S. choice, boneless	lb	3.56	7/01	11r
Steak, sirloin, U.S. choice, boneless	lb	5.65	7/01	11r
Strawberries, dry pint	12 oz	1.50	7/01	11r
Sugar and other sweets, expenditures on	yr	99	1999	30r
Sugar, white, 33-80 ounce package	lb	0.39	7/01	11r
Sugar, white, all sizes	lb	0.42	7/01	11r
Tobacco products and smoking supplies purchases	yr	288	1999	30r
Tomatoes, field grown	lb	1.43	7/01	11r
Tuna, light, chunk	lb	1.77	7/01	11r
Turkey, frozen, whole	lb	1.05	7/01	11r
Goods and Services				
Hunting license	yr	16.00	4/01	34s
Health Care				
Cardiac catheterization, ave hospital/ physician charges		15260	1998	77s
Childbirth, Cesarean delivery		11587	1997	13r
Childbirth, vaginal delivery		6725	1997	13r
Drugs, expenditures on	yr	399	1999	30r
Health care purchases	yr	1971	1999	30r
Health insurance expenditures	yr	933	1999	30r
Hysterectomy, laproscopically-assisted, ave hospital/physician charges		16780	1998	76s
Hysterectomy, vaginal, ave hospital and physician charges		10990	1998	76s
Medicaid dispensing fee		5.40	1999	87s
Medical services expenditures	yr	547	1999	30r
Medical supplies, expenditures on	yr	91	1999	30r
Household Goods				
Floor coverings, expenditures on	yr	44	1999	30r
Furniture, expenditures on	yr	335	1999	30r
Household furnishings and equipment purchases	yr	1328	1999	30r
Household textiles, expenditures on	yr	89	1999	30r
Laundry and cleaning supplies, expenditures on	yr	113	1999	30r
Housing				
Home price, existing, ave		160100	10/00	90r
Home value, median		115000	2001	53s
Household operation expenditures	yr	553	1999	30r
Housekeeping supplies purchases	yr	473	1999	30r
Housing, expenditures on	yr	10303	1999	30r
Maintenance, repairs, insurance expenditures	yr	699	1999	30r
Monthly rental value of owned home	mos	505	1999	30r
Owned dwellings, expenditures own	yr	3465	1999	30r
Rent expenditures	yr	1641	1999	30r

Anniston, AL - continued

Item	Per	Value	Date	Ref.
Housing - continued				
Rental unit, 1 bedroom, with utilities	mos	312	4/01	41c
Rental unit, 2 bedroom, with utilities	mos	390	4/01	41c
Rental unit, 3 bedroom, with utilities	mos	544	4/01	41c
Rental unit, 4 bedroom, with utilities	mos	616	4/01	41c
Shelter, expenditures on	yr	5467	1999	30r
Insurance and Pensions				
Life and other personal insurance purchases	yr	414	1999	30r
Pensions and Social Security, expenditures on	yr	2635	1999	30r
Personal insurance and pensions, expenditures on	yr	3048	1999	30r
Legal Fees				
Divorce, filing fee		146.00-193.00	4/01	35s
Driver's license fee	renew	18.50	1999	48s
Driver's license fee	orig	18.50	1999	48s
Personal Goods				
Personal care products and services purchases	yr	393	1999	30r
Personal Services				
Personal services, household, expenditures on	yr	258	1999	30r
Pets				
Pets, toys, and playground equipment, expenditures on	yr	306	1999	30r
Taxes				
Federal income taxes paid	yr	2047	1999	30r
Personal taxes, expenditures on	yr	2554	1999	30r
Property taxes paid	yr	726	1999	30r
State and local income taxes paid	yr	363	1999	30r
Transportation				
Cars and trucks, new, expenditures on	yr	1648	1999	30r
Cars and trucks, used, expenditures on	yr	1651	1999	30r
Diesel at the pump	gal	1.19	10/99	73s
Gasoline and motor oil purchases	yr	1052	1999	30r
Gasoline before-tax price (cents)	gal	104.10	10/00	43s
Maintenance and repair expenditures	yr	621	1999	30r
Public transportation, expenditures on	yr	298	1999	30r
Transportation purchases	yr	6738	1999	30r
Vehicle expenses, miscellaneous, purchases	yr	2033	1999	30r
Vehicle insurance payments	yr	696	1999	30r
Vehicle purchases (net outlay)	yr	3354	1999	30r
Vehicle rental, lease expenditures	yr	352	1999	30r
Utilities				
Electrical bill, average	mos	83.42	9/00	9s
Electricity, expenditures on	yr	1115	1999	30r
Electricity cost, average	KWh	5.60	9/00	9s
Water and other public services, expenditures on	yr	298	1999	30r
Weddings				
Wedding (national average cost)		19936	2000	33r
Attendants' gifts		321	1998	33r
Bridal attendants' apparel (5 persons)		824	2000	33r
Bride's headpiece/veil		173	1998	33r
Bride's wedding dress		859	1998	33r
Clergy, religious facility fee		242	1998	33r
Engagement ring		3177	1998	33r
Flowers		789	1998	33r
Groom's formalwear rental		99	2000	33r
Limousine		410	1998	33r
Marriage license cost		25.00	4/01	35s
Men's formalwear (ushers, best man)		469	2000	33r
Mother of bride apparel		241	2000	33r
Music		866	1998	33r
Photography and videography		1368	1998	33r
Rehearsal dinner		728	1998	33r
Wedding invitations and announcements		341	1998	33r

Values are in dollars or fractions of dollars. In the column headed *Ref*, references are shown to sources. Each reference is followed by a letter. These refer to the geographical level for which data were reported: s=State, r=Region, and c=City or metro. The abbreviation *ex* is used to mean *except* or *excluding*; *exp* stands for expenditures. For other abbreviations and further explanations, please see the Introduction.

Anniston, AL - continued

Item	Per	Value	Date	Ref.
Weddings				
Wedding reception		7968	2000	33r
Wedding rings (bride and groom)		1060	1998	33r

Appleton-Oshkosh-Neenah, WI

Item	Per	Value	Date	Ref.
Average annual expenditures	yr	35369	1999	30r
Alcoholic Beverages				
Alcoholic beverage purchases	yr	304	1999	30r
Malt beverages, all types, all sizes, any origin	16 oz	0.93	7/01	11r
Wine, red and white table, all sizes, any origin	liter	7.04	7/01	11r
Appliances				
Major appliances, expenditures on	yr	165	1999	30r
Small appliances, housewares, expenditures on	yr	90	1999	30r
Banking and Money				
Mortgage interest and charges paid	yr	2277	1999	30r
Mortgage principal paid on owned property	yr	1230	1999	30r
Vehicle finance charges paid	yr	328	1999	30r
Charity				
Cash contributions, expenditures	yr	1126	1999	30r
Child Care				
Child raising cost, total, age 0-2	yr	7890	1999	60r
Child raising cost, total, age 3-5	yr	8130	1999	60r
Child raising cost, total, age 6-8	yr	8170	1999	60r
Child raising cost, total, age 9-11	yr	8190	1999	60r
Child raising cost, total, age 12-14	yr	8890	1999	60r
Child raising cost, total, age 15-17	yr	9050	1999	60r
Child's child care and education, age 0-2	yr	1240	1999	60r
Child's child care and education, age 3-5	yr	1370	1999	60r
Child's child care and education, age 6-8	yr	880	1999	60r
Child's child care and education, age 9-11	yr	570	1999	60r
Child's child care and education, age 12-14	yr	420	1999	60r
Child's child care and education, age 15-17	yr	720	1999	60r
Child's clothing, age 0-2	yr	410	1999	60r
Child's clothing, age 3-5	yr	400	1999	60r
Child's clothing, age 6-8	yr	450	1999	60r
Child's clothing, age 9-11	yr	500	1999	60r
Child's clothing, age 12-14	yr	840	1999	60r
Child's clothing, age 15-17	yr	740	1999	60r
Child's food, age 0-2	yr	960	1999	60r
Child's food, age 3-5	yr	1120	1999	60r
Child's food, age 6-8	yr	1430	1999	60r
Child's food, age 9-11	yr	1710	1999	60r
Child's food, age 12-14	yr	1710	1999	60r
Child's food, age 15-17	yr	1920	1999	60r
Child's health care, age 0-2	yr	520	1999	60r
Child's health care, age 3-5	yr	500	1999	60r
Child's health care, age 6-8	yr	570	1999	60r
Child's health care, age 9-11	yr	610	1999	60r
Child's health care, age 12-14	yr	630	1999	60r
Child's health care, age 15-17	yr	650	1999	60r
Child's housing, age 0-2	yr	2860	1999	60r
Child's housing, age 3-5	yr	2840	1999	60r
Child's housing, age 6-8	yr	2800	1999	60r
Child's housing, age 9-11	yr	2650	1999	60r
Child's housing, age 12-14	yr	2840	1999	60r
Child's housing, age 15-17	yr	2440	1999	60r
Child's personal care, reading, age 0-2	yr	880	1999	60r
Child's personal care, reading, age 3-5	yr	900	1999	60r
Child's personal care, reading, age 6-8	yr	930	1999	60r
Child's personal care, reading, age 9-11	yr	970	1999	60r
Child's personal care, reading, age 12-14	yr	1150	1999	60r
Child's personal care, reading, age 15-17	yr	920	1999	60r
Clothing				
Apparel and services purchases	yr	1607	1999	30r
Boys, 2 to 15, expenditures on	yr	91	1999	30r
Children under 2, expenditures on	yr	59	1999	30r

Item	Per	Value	Date	Ref.
Clothing - continued				
Footwear, expenditures on	yr	285	1999	30r
Girls, 2 to 15, expenditures on	yr	116	1999	30r
Men and boys, expenditures on	yr	433	1999	30r
Men, 16 and over, expenditures on	yr	341	1999	30r
Women, 16 and over, expenditures on	yr	490	1999	30r
Communications				
Cable modem installation, Bresnan		99.95	6/99	103s
Cable modem installation, Marcus		499.00	6/99	103s
Cable modem rate, cable subscriber, Bresnan	mos	39.95	6/99	103s
Cable modem rate, cable subscriber, Marcus	mos	14.95-49.95	6/99	103s
Cable modem rate, non-cable subscriber, Bresnan	mos	49.95	6/99	103s
Cable modem rate, non-cable subscriber, Marcus	mos	60.95	6/99	103s
Phone line, single, business, field visit	inst.	64.65	12/97	17s
Phone line, single, business, no field visit	inst.	64.65	12/97	17s
Phone line, single, residence, field visit	inst.	33.05	12/97	17s
Phone line, single, residence, no field visit	inst.	33.05	12/97	17s
Postage and stationery, expenditures on	yr	140	1999	30r
Postal rate, express mail, up to half-pound		12.45	7/01	108r
Postal rate, letter, first class, first ounce		0.34	7/01	108r
Postal rate, letter, two ounces		0.57	7/01	108r
Postal rate, post card		0.21	7/01	108r
Postal rate, priority mail, two pounds		3.95	7/01	108r
Postal rate, priority mail, up to one pound		3.50	7/01	108r
Telephone services, expenditures on	yr	830	1999	30r
Education				
Board, 4-year private college/university	yr	2271	1996	38s
Board, 4-year public college/university	yr	1527	1996	38s
Education expenditures	yr	583	1999	30r
Room, 4-year private college/university	yr	1812	1996	38s
Room, 4-year public college/university	yr	1706	1996	38s
Total cost, 4-year private college/university	yr	15652	1996	38s
Total cost, 4-year public college/university	yr	5847	1996	38s
Tuition, 2-year public college/university, in state	yr	1840	1996	38s
Tuition, 4-year private college/university, in state	yr	11569	1996	38s
Tuition, 4-year public college/university	yr	2614	1996	38s
Energy and Fuels				
Electricity	500 KWhs	46.59	7/01	11r
Fuel oil #2	gal	1.27	7/01	11r
Fuel oil and other fuels, expenditures on	yr	68	1999	30r
Gas, natural, commercial rate	1000 cf	7.32	11/00	88s
Gasoline, unleaded midgrade	gal	1.79	7/01	11r
Gasoline, unleaded premium	gal	1.86	7/01	11r
Gasoline, unleaded regular	gal	1.58	7/01	11r
Natural gas, expenditures on	yr	389	1999	30r
Utility (piped) gas, therm		0.81	7/01	11r
Utility (piped) gas, 40 therms		38.01	7/01	11r
Utility (piped) gas, 100 therms		81.75	7/01	11r
Entertainment				
Entertainment purchases	yr	1984	1999	30r
Fees and admissions paid	yr	444	1999	30r
Television, radios, sound equipment, expenditures on	yr	580	1999	30r
Funerals				
Cosmetology, hair, other preparation		178.32	1/99	78r
Embalming		408.19	1/99	78r
Funeral at funeral home		362.13	1/99	78r
Professional service charges		1375.51	1/99	78r
Transfer of remains to funeral home		155.92	1/99	78r
Visitation/viewing		294.38	1/99	78r
Groceries				
Bacon, sliced	lb	3.15	7/01	11r
Bakery products, expenditures on	yr	281	1999	30r

Values are in dollars or fractions of dollars. In the column headed *Ref*, references are shown to sources. Each reference is followed by a letter. These refer to the geographical level for which data were reported: s=State, r=Region, and c=City or metro. The abbreviation *ex* is used to mean *except* or *excluding*; *exp* stands for expenditures. For other abbreviations and further explanations, please see the Introduction.

Appleton-Oshkosh-Neenah, WI - continued

Item	Per	Value	Date	Ref.
Groceries				
Bananas	lb	0.48	7/01	11r
Beans, dried, any type, all sizes	lb	0.61	7/01	11r
Beef for stew, boneless	lb	3.08	7/01	11r
Beef, expenditures on	yr	217	1999	30r
Bologna, all beef or mixed	lb	2.52	7/01	11r
Bread, white, pan	lb	1.06	7/01	11r
Broccoli	lb	0.91	7/01	11r
Butter, salted, grade AA, stick	lb	3.04	7/01	11r
Butter, yoghurt, cheese, etc, expenditures on	yr	183	1999	30r
Cereals and bakery product purchases	yr	430	1999	30r
Cereals and cereal products, expenditures on	yr	149	1999	30r
Chicken, fresh, whole	lb	1.07	7/01	11r
Chops, boneless,	lb	3.64	7/01	11r
Chuck roast, U.S. choice, boneless	lb	2.47	7/01	11r
Coffee, 100%, ground roast, all sizes	lb	2.69	7/01	11r
Cookies, chocolate chip	lb	2.87	7/01	11r
Dairy product purchases	yr	304	1999	30r
Eggs, expenditures on	yr	26	1999	30r
Eggs, grade A, large	dozen	0.88	7/01	11r
Fats and oils, expenditures on	yr	75	1999	30r
Fish and seafood, expenditures on	yr	72	1999	30r
Food (excl fruit and vegetables), eaten at home, purchases	yr	887	1999	30r
Food cooked on trips, expenditures on	yr	44	1999	30r
Food purchases	yr	4802	1999	30r
Food purchases, eaten away from home	yr	2069	1999	30r
Food purchases, food eaten at home	yr	2733	1999	30r
Fresh fruits, expenditures on	yr	138	1999	30r
Fresh milk and cream, expenditures on	yr	120	1999	30r
Fresh vegetables, expenditures on	yr	126	1999	30r
Grapefruit	lb	0.66	7/01	11r
Grapes, Thompson, seedless	lb	1.64	7/01	11r
Ground beef, 100% beef	lb	1.64	7/01	11r
Ground beef, lean and extra lean	lb	2.16	7/01	11r
Ground chuck, 100% beef	lb	2.13	7/01	11r
Ham, boneless, excl canned	lb	2.62	7/01	11r
Ice cream, prepackaged, bulk, regular	1/2 gal	3.35	7/01	11r
Lemons	lb	1.19	7/01	11r
Lettuce, iceberg	lb	0.73	7/01	11r
Margarine, soft, tubs	lb	0.89	7/01	11r
Meats, poultry, fish, and egg purchases	yr	671	1999	30r
Milk, fresh, whole, fortified	gal	2.71	7/01	11r
Nonalcoholic beverages, expenditures on	yr	239	1999	30r
Oranges, Navel	lb	0.80	7/01	11r
Oranges, Valencia	lb	0.66	7/01	11r
Pears, Anjou	lb	0.93	7/01	11r
Pork chops, center cut, bone-in	lb	3.63	7/01	11r
Pork, expenditures on	yr	150	1999	30r
Potato chips	16 oz	3.52	7/01	11r
Potatoes, frozen, french fried	lb	1.08	7/01	11r
Potatoes, white, all types	lb	0.33	7/01	11r
Poultry, expenditures on	yr	108	1999	30r
Processed fruits, expenditures on	yr	98	1999	30r
Processed vegetables, expenditures on	yr	80	1999	30r
Round roast, U.S. choice, boneless	lb	3.07	7/01	11r
Round steak, graded and ungraded, excl U.S. prime and choice	lb	3.41	7/01	11r
Shortening, vegetable oil blends	lb	1.13	7/01	11r
Spaghetti and macaroni	lb	0.80	7/01	11r
Steak, round, U.S. choice, boneless	lb	3.23	7/01	11r
Steak, T-bone, U.S. choice, bone-in	lb	6.68	7/01	11r
Strawberries, dry pint	12 oz	1.32	7/01	11r
Sugar and other sweets, expenditures on	yr	114	1999	30r
Sugar, white, 33-80 ounce package	lb	0.42	7/01	11r
Sugar, white, all sizes	lb	0.43	7/01	11r
Tobacco products and smoking supplies purchases	yr	331	1999	30r
Tomatoes, field grown	lb	1.46	7/01	11r
Tuna, light, chunk	lb	1.80	7/01	11r
Turkey, frozen, whole	lb	1.15	7/01	11r

Appleton-Oshkosh-Neenah, WI - continued

Item	Per	Value	Date	Ref.
Goods and Services				
B&B Japanese maple (acer japonicum)	gal	29.99-169.99	4/00	93r
Boxwood (buxus)	2 gal	18.99-39.99	4/00	93r
Daylilly (hemerocallis)	gal	4.99-25.00	4/00	93r
Flat of annuals		11.98-24.99	4/00	93r
Fountain grass (pennisetum)	gal	5.98-12.98	4/00	93r
Hanging basket (10 in)		12.99-27.99	4/00	93r
Hardy geranium (geranium)	gal	7.99-9.99	4/00	93r
Hosta (hosta)	gal	6.00-25.00	4/00	93r
Lilac (syrubga vulgaris)	2 gal	14.99-24.99	4/00	93r
Miscellaneous purchases	yr	865	1999	30r
Rhododendron (rhododendron)	2 gal	23.98-42.99	4/00	93r
Sage (salvia)	gal	6.00-9.99	4/00	93r
Wintercreeper euonymus (euonymus fortunei)	2 gal	16.00-169.99	4/00	93r
Hunting license	yr	14.00	4/01	34s
Health Care				
Cardiac catheterization, ave hospital/ physician charges		13240	1998	77s
Childbirth, Cesarean delivery		10722	1997	13r
Childbirth, vaginal delivery		6223	1997	13r
Drugs, expenditures on	yr	394	1999	30r
Health care purchases	yr	2048	1999	30r
Health insurance expenditures	yr	978	1999	30r
Hysterectomy, laproscopically-assisted, ave hospital/physician charges		13270	1998	76s
Hysterectomy, vaginal, ave hospital and physician charges		9170	1998	76s
Laser eye surgery	eye	1950-2400	2000	63s
Medicaid dispensing fee		4.88-40.11	1999	87s
Medical services expenditures	yr	554	1999	30r
Medical supplies, expenditures on	yr	122	1999	30r
Plastic surgery, breast augmentation		3184	2000	7r
Plastic surgery, breast lift		3585	2000	7r
Plastic surgery, facelift		4999	2000	7r
Plastic surgery, hair transplantation		3105	2000	7r
Plastic surgery, lip augmentation		1290	2000	7r
Plastic surgery, lower body lift		8135	2000	7r
Plastic surgery, thigh lift		3839	2000	7r
Household Goods				
Floor coverings, expenditures on	yr	52	1999	30r
Furniture, expenditures on	yr	344	1999	30r
Household furnishings and equipment purchases	yr	1475	1999	30r
Household textiles, expenditures on	yr	109	1999	30r
Laundry and cleaning supplies, expenditures on	yr	134	1999	30r
Housing				
Home price, existing, ave		144400	10/00	90r
Home value, median		117000	2001	53s
Household operation expenditures	yr	542	1999	30r
Housekeeping supplies purchases	yr	508	1999	30r
Lodging expenditures	yr	430	1999	30r
Maintenance, repairs, insurance expenditures	yr	853	1999	30r
Monthly rental value of owned home	mos	547	1999	30r
Owned dwellings, expenditures own	yr	4282	1999	30r
Rent expenditures	yr	1558	1999	30r
Rental unit, 1 bedroom, with utilities	mos	400	4/01	41c

Values are in dollars or fractions of dollars. In the column headed *Ref*, references are shown to sources. Each reference is followed by a letter. These refer to the geographical level for which data were reported: s=State, r=Region, and c=City or metro. The abbreviation *ex* is used to mean *except* or *excluding*; *exp* stands for expenditures. For other abbreviations and further explanations, please see the Introduction.

Appleton-Oshkosh-Neenah, WI - continued

Item	Per	Value	Date	Ref.
Housing				
Rental unit, 2 bedroom, with utilities	mos	509	4/01	41c
Rental unit, 3 bedroom, with utilities	mos	641	4/01	41c
Rental unit, 4 bedroom, with utilities	mos	740	4/01	41c
Shelter, expenditures on	yr	6270	1999	30r
Insurance and Pensions				
Auto insurance premium	yr	603.84	1999	57s
Life and other personal insurance purchases	yr	387	1999	30r
Pensions and Social Security, expenditures on	yr	2968	1999	30r
Legal Fees				
Divorce, filing fee		142.00-150.00	4/01	35s
Driver's license fee	orig	18.00	1999	48s
Driver's license fee	renew	12.00	1999	48s
Fishing license	yr	14.00	4/01	34s
Personal Goods				
Personal care products and services purchases	yr	385	1999	30r
Personal Services				
Personal services, household, expenditures on	yr	300	1999	30r
Pets				
Pets, toys, and playground equipment, expenditures on	yr	375	1999	30r
Taxes				
Federal income taxes paid	yr	2326	1999	30r
Personal taxes, expenditures on	yr	3223	1999	30r
Property taxes paid	yr	1152	1999	30r
State and local income taxes paid	yr	753	1999	30r
Transportation				
Cars and trucks, new, expenditures on	yr	1280	1999	30r
Cars and trucks, used, expenditures on	yr	1763	1999	30r
Diesel at the pump	gal	1.34	10/99	73s
Gasoline and motor oil purchases	yr	1036	1999	30r
Gasoline before-tax price (cents)	gal	113.40	10/00	43s
Maintenance and repair expenditures	yr	594	1999	30r
Public transportation, expenditures on	yr	341	1999	30r
Transportation purchases	yr	6617	1999	30r
Vehicle expenses, miscellaneous, purchases	yr	2159	1999	30r
Vehicle insurance payments	yr	701	1999	30r
Vehicle purchases (net outlay)	yr	3081	1999	30r
Vehicle rental, lease expenditures	yr	536	1999	30r
Utilities				
Electrical bill, average	mos	52.08	9/00	9s
Electricity, expenditures on	yr	841	1999	30r
Electricity cost, average	KWh	5.69	9/00	9s
Utilities, fuels, and public services purchased	yr	2401	1999	30r
Water and other public services, expenditures on	yr	273	1999	30r
Weddings				
Wedding (national average cost)		19936	2000	33r
Wedding (regional average total cost)		16195	1997	110r
Attendants' gifts		321	1998	33r
Bridal attendants' apparel (5 persons)		824	2000	33r
Bride's headpiece/veil		173	1998	33r
Bride's wedding dress		859	1998	33r
Clergy, religious facility fee		242	1998	33r
Engagement ring		3177	1998	33r
Flowers		789	1998	33r
Groom's formalwear rental		99	2000	33r
Limousine		410	1998	33r
Marriage license cost		50.00-60.00	4/01	35s
Men's formalwear (ushers, best man)		469	2000	33r
Mother of bride apparel		241	2000	33r
Music		866	1998	33r
Photography and videography		1368	1998	33r

Appleton-Oshkosh-Neenah, WI - continued

Item	Per	Value	Date	Ref.
Weddings - continued				
Rehearsal dinner		728	1998	33r
Wedding invitations and announcements		341	1998	33r
Wedding reception		7968	2000	33r
Wedding rings (bride and groom)		1060	1998	33r

Asheville, NC

Item	Per	Value	Date	Ref.
Composite, ACCRA index		103.50	3/01	4c
Alcoholic Beverages				
Alcoholic beverage purchases	yr	253	1999	30r
Beer, Heineken, 12-oz, ex deposit	6	6.55	3/01	4c
J & B Scotch	750-ml	20.75	3/01	4c
Malt beverages, all types, all sizes, any origin	16 oz	0.96	7/01	11r
Wine, Livingston or Gallo, Chablis blanc	1.5 liter	5.87	3/01	4c
Appliances				
Appliance repair, service call, washing machine	min lab chg	45.68	3/01	4c
Major appliances, expenditures on	yr	172	1999	30r
Small appliances, housewares, expenditures on	yr	81	1999	30r
Banking and Money				
Mortgage interest and charges paid	yr	2039	1999	30r
Mortgage principal paid on owned property	yr	1026	1999	30r
Mortgage rate, incl. points and orig. fee, 30-yr. conv. fixed or ARM	mos	7.20	3/01	4c
Vehicle finance charges paid	yr	365	1999	30r
Charity				
Cash contributions, expenditures	yr	1127	1999	30r
Child Care				
Child raising cost, total, age 0-2	yr	8540	1999	60r
Child raising cost, total, age 3-5	yr	8780	1999	60r
Child raising cost, total, age 6-8	yr	8820	1999	60r
Child raising cost, total, age 9-11	yr	8800	1999	60r
Child raising cost, total, age 12-14	yr	9510	1999	60r
Child raising cost, total, age 15-17	yr	9740	1999	60r
Child's child care and education, age 0-2	yr	1380	1999	60r
Child's child care and education, age 3-5	yr	1520	1999	60r
Child's child care and education, age 6-8	yr	990	1999	60r
Child's child care and education, age 9-11	yr	650	1999	60r
Child's child care and education, age 12-14	yr	490	1999	60r
Child's child care and education, age 15-17	yr	840	1999	60r
Child's clothing, age 0-2	yr	480	1999	60r
Child's clothing, age 3-5	yr	470	1999	60r
Child's clothing, age 6-8	yr	520	1999	60r
Child's clothing, age 9-11	yr	570	1999	60r
Child's clothing, age 12-14	yr	950	1999	60r
Child's clothing, age 15-17	yr	850	1999	60r
Child's food, age 0-2	yr	1000	1999	60r
Child's food, age 3-5	yr	1160	1999	60r
Child's food, age 6-8	yr	1490	1999	60r
Child's food, age 9-11	yr	1770	1999	60r
Child's food, age 12-14	yr	1770	1999	60r
Child's food, age 15-17	yr	1980	1999	60r
Child's health care, age 0-2	yr	620	1999	60r
Child's health care, age 3-5	yr	590	1999	60r
Child's health care, age 6-8	yr	680	1999	60r
Child's health care, age 9-11	yr	720	1999	60r
Child's health care, age 12-14	yr	730	1999	60r
Child's health care, age 15-17	yr	760	1999	60r
Child's housing, age 0-2	yr	3070	1999	60r
Child's housing, age 3-5	yr	3050	1999	60r
Child's housing, age 6-8	yr	3010	1999	60r
Child's housing, age 9-11	yr	2850	1999	60r
Child's housing, age 12-14	yr	3040	1999	60r
Child's housing, age 15-17	yr	2650	1999	60r
Child's personal care, reading, age 0-2	yr	910	1999	60r
Child's personal care, reading, age 3-5	yr	930	1999	60r
Child's personal care, reading, age 6-8	yr	960	1999	60r
Child's personal care, reading, age 9-11	yr	1000	1999	60r

Values are in dollars or fractions of dollars. In the column headed *Ref*, references are shown to sources. Each reference is followed by a letter. These refer to the geographical level for which data were reported: s=State, r=Region, and c=City or metro. The abbreviation *ex* is used to mean *except* or *excluding*; *exp* stands for expenditures. For other abbreviations and further explanations, please see the Introduction.

Asheville, NC - continued

Item	Per	Value	Date	Ref.
Child Care				
Child's personal care, reading, age 12-14	yr	1170	1999	60r
Child's personal care, reading, age 15-17	yr	950	1999	60r
Clothing				
Apparel and services purchases	yr	1610	1999	30r
Boys' brief, cotton	3	3.27	3/01	4c
Boys, 2 to 15, expenditures on	yr	89	1999	30r
Children under 2, expenditures on	yr	79	1999	30r
Footwear, expenditures on	yr	283	1999	30r
Girls, 2 to 15, expenditures on	yr	103	1999	30r
Men and boys, expenditures on	yr	351	1999	30r
Men, 16 and over, expenditures on	yr	262	1999	30r
Shirt, man's dress shirt		25.75	3/01	4c
Slacks, man's "No Wrinkles" khaki		40.33	3/01	4c
Women, 16 and over, expenditures on	yr	538	1999	30r
Communications				
Cable modem installation, Intermedia		149.95	6/99	103s
Cable modem installation, Time Warner		75.00-225.00	6/99	103s
Cable modem rate, cable subscriber, Intermedia	mos	49.95	6/99	103s
Cable modem rate, cable subscriber, Time Warner	mos	39.95-49.95	6/99	103s
Cable modem rate, non-cable subscriber, Intermedia	mos	54.95	6/99	103s
Cable modem rate, non-cable subscriber, Time Warner	mos	39.95-54.95	6/99	103s
Newspaper subscription, daily and Sunday delivery	mos	15.22	3/01	4c
Phone line, single, business, field visit	inst.	65.00	12/97	17s
Phone line, single, business, no field visit	inst.	65.00	12/97	17s
Phone line, single, residence, field visit	inst.	42.75	12/97	17s
Phone line, single, residence, no field visit	inst.	42.75	12/97	17s
Postage and stationery, expenditures on	yr	104	1999	30r
Postal rate, express mail, up to half-pound		12.45	7/01	108r
Postal rate, letter, first class, first ounce		0.34	7/01	108r
Postal rate, letter, two ounces		0.57	7/01	108r
Postal rate, post card		0.21	7/01	108r
Postal rate, priority mail, two pounds		3.95	7/01	108r
Postal rate, priority mail, up to one pound		3.50	7/01	108r
Telephone bill, family of three	mos	16.56	3/01	4c
Telephone services, expenditures on	yr	860	1999	30r
Education				
Board, 4-year private college/university	yr	2316	1996	38s
Board, 4-year public college/university	yr	1737	1996	38s
Education expenditures	yr	431	1999	30r
Room, 4-year private college/university	yr	2128	1996	38s
Room, 4-year public college/university	yr	1742	1996	38s
Total cost, 4-year private college/university	yr	15428	1996	38s
Total cost, 4-year public college/university	yr	5119	1996	38s
Tuition, 4-year private college/university, in state	yr	10984	1996	38s
Tuition, 4-year public college/university	yr	1639	1996	38s
Energy and Fuels				
Electricity	500 KWhs	47.29	7/01	11r
Electricity	KWh	0.09	7/01	11r
Energy, combined forms, 2400 sq ft	mos	109.62	3/01	4c
Fuel oil #2	gal	1.43	7/01	11r
Fuel oil and other fuels, expenditures on	yr	45	1999	30r
Gas, natural, commercial rate	1000 cf	9.25	11/00	88s
Gas, regular unleaded, cash, self-service	gal	1.32	3/01	4c
Gasoline, all types	gal	1.60	7/01	11r
Gasoline, unleaded midgrade	gal	1.65	7/01	11r
Gasoline, unleaded premium	gal	1.74	7/01	11r
Natural gas, expenditures on	yr	164	1999	30r
Utility (piped) gas, therm		1.01	7/01	11r
Utility (piped) gas, 40 therms		44.29	7/01	11r
Utility (piped) gas, 100 therms		97.44	7/01	11r

Asheville, NC - continued

Item	Per	Value	Date	Ref.
Entertainment				
Bowling, Saturday evening rate	line	3.37	3/01	4c
Entertainment purchases	yr	1574	1999	30r
Fees and admissions paid	yr	371	1999	30r
Monopoly game, Parker Brothers', No. 9	game	9.99	3/01	4c
Movie, first-run, Saturday, evening	adm.	6.81	3/01	4c
Reading purchases	yr	121	1999	30r
Television, radios, sound equipment, expenditures on	yr	561	1999	30r
Tennis balls, yellow, Wilson or Penn, 3	can	2.07	3/01	4c
Funerals				
Total cost of funeral		5922.53	1/99	78r
Acknowledgement cards		63.43	1/99	78r
Casket		2258.77	1/99	78r
Cosmetology, hair, other preparation		127.09	1/99	78r
Embalming		393.49	1/99	78r
Funeral at funeral home		367.50	1/99	78r
Hearse (local)		169.66	1/99	78r
Professional service charges		1211.32	1/99	78r
Service car/van		80.69	1/99	78r
Transfer of remains to funeral home		144.25	1/99	78r
Vault		803.50	1/99	78r
Visitation/viewing		302.83	1/99	78r
Groceries				
Groceries, ACCRA Index		102.80	3/01	4c
American processed cheese	lb	3.50	7/01	11r
Antibiotic ointment, Polysporin	0.5 oz	4.29	3/01	4c
Baby food, strained vegetables or fruit, lowest price	4-4.5 oz	0.45	3/01	4c
Bakery products, expenditures on	yr	261	1999	30r
Bananas	lb	0.58	3/01	4c
Bananas	lb	0.47	7/01	11r
Beans, dried, any type, all sizes	lb	0.63	7/01	11r
Beef for stew, boneless	lb	2.86	7/01	11r
Beef or hamburger, ground	lb	1.99	3/01	4c
Beef, expenditures on	yr	210	1999	30r
Bologna, all beef or mixed	lb	2.29	7/01	11r
Bread, French	lb	1.66	7/01	11r
Bread, white	loaf	0.87	3/01	4c
Bread, white, pan	lb	0.87	7/01	11r
Bread, whole wheat, pan	lb	1.38	7/01	11r
Broccoli	lb	1.04	7/01	11r
Butter, salted, grade AA, stick	lb	2.26	7/01	11r
Butter, yoghurt, cheese, etc, expenditures on	yr	170	1999	30r
Cabbage	lb	0.42	7/01	11r
Cereals and cereal products, expenditures on	yr	140	1999	30r
Cheddar cheese, natural	lb	3.75	7/01	11r
Cheese, Kraft grated Parmesan	8 oz	3.53	3/01	4c
Chicken breast, bone-in	lb	1.85	7/01	11r
Chicken legs, bone-in	lb	1.34	7/01	11r
Chicken, fresh, whole	lb	1.05	7/01	11r
Chicken, whole fryer	lb	0.99	3/01	4c
Chops, boneless,	lb	4.13	7/01	11r
Chuck roast, graded and ungraded, excl U.S. prime and choice	lb	2.35	7/01	11r
Chuck roast, U.S. choice, boneless	lb	2.67	7/01	11r
Cigarettes, Winston, Kings	carton	27.70	3/01	4c
Coffee, 100%, ground roast, all sizes	lb	2.88	7/01	11r
Coffee, instant, plain, regular, all sizes	16 oz	9.25	7/01	11r
Coffee, vacuum-packed	13 oz	2.35	3/01	4c
Cola, non diet	2 liter	1.11	7/01	11r
Corn Flakes, Kellogg's or Post Toasties	18 oz	2.47	3/01	4c
Corn, frozen, whole kernel, lowest price	16 oz	1.24	3/01	4c
Crackers, soda, salted	lb	1.70	7/01	11r
Dairy product purchases	yr	282	1999	30r
Eggs, expenditures on	yr	32	1999	30r
Eggs, Grade A or AA	dozen	1.37	3/01	4c
Fats and oils, expenditures on	yr	79	1999	30r
Fish and seafood, expenditures on	yr	99	1999	30r
Flour, white, all purpose	lb	0.32	7/01	11r

Values are in dollars or fractions of dollars. In the column headed *Ref*, references are shown to sources. Each reference is followed by a letter. These refer to the geographical level for which data were reported: s=State, r=Region, and c=City or metro. The abbreviation *ex* is used to mean *except* or *excluding*; *exp* stands for expenditures. For other abbreviations and further explanations, please see the Introduction.

Asheville, NC - continued

Item	Per	Value	Date	Ref.
Groceries				
Food (excl fruit and vegetables), eaten at home, purchases	yr	815	1999	30r
Food cooked on trips, expenditures on	yr	36	1999	30r
Food purchases	yr	4533	1999	30r
Food purchases, eaten away from home	yr	1873	1999	30r
Food purchases, food eaten at home	yr	2660	1999	30r
Fresh fruits, expenditures on	yr	128	1999	30r
Fresh milk and cream, expenditures on	yr	112	1999	30r
Fresh vegetables, expenditures on	yr	131	1999	30r
Fruit and vegetable purchases	yr	438	1999	30r
Grapefruit	lb	0.59	7/01	11r
Grapes, Thompson, seedless	lb	2.12	7/01	11r
Ground beef, 100% beef	lb	1.76	7/01	11r
Ground beef, lean and extra lean	lb	2.60	7/01	11r
Ground chuck, 100% beef	lb	2.08	7/01	11r
Ham, boneless, excl canned	lb	2.71	7/01	11r
Ham, rump or shank half, bone-in, smoked	lb	2.19	7/01	11r
Ice cream, prepackaged, bulk, regular	1/2 gal	3.93	7/01	11r
Lemons	lb	1.32	7/01	11r
Lettuce, iceberg	head	1.25	3/01	4c
Lettuce, iceberg	lb	0.76	7/01	11r
Margarine, Blue Bonnet or Parkay, stick	lb	0.73	3/01	4c
Milk, fresh, low fat,	gal	2.75	7/01	11r
Milk, fresh, whole, fortified	gal	2.97	7/01	11r
Milk, whole	1/2 gal	1.84	3/01	4c
Nonalcoholic beverages, expenditures on	yr	228	1999	30r
Orange juice, frozen concentrate	16 oz	1.95	7/01	11r
Orange juice, Minute Maid frozen	12 oz	1.66	3/01	4c
Oranges, Navel	lb	0.73	7/01	11r
Oranges, Valencia	lb	0.55	7/01	11r
Peaches, halves or slices, Hunt's, Del Monte, or Libby's	29 oz	1.54	3/01	4c
Peanut butter, creamy, all sizes	lb	1.83	7/01	11r
Pears, Anjou	lb	0.98	7/01	11r
Peas, green, Del Monte or Green Giant	15 oz	0.66	3/01	4c
Pork chops, center cut, bone-in	lb	3.33	7/01	11r
Pork sausage, fresh, loose	lb	2.59	7/01	11r
Pork shoulder picnic, bone-in, smoked	lb	1.12	7/01	11r
Pork, expenditures on	yr	162	1999	30r
Potato chips	16 oz	3.59	7/01	11r
Potatoes, frozen, french fried	lb	1.00	7/01	11r
Potatoes, white or red	10 lb	2.45	3/01	4c
Potatoes, white, all types	lb	0.44	7/01	11r
Poultry, expenditures on	yr	137	1999	30r
Processed fruits, expenditures on	yr	97	1999	30r
Processed vegetables, expenditures on	yr	82	1999	30r
Rice, white, long grain, uncooked	lb	0.51	7/01	11r
Round roast, graded and ungraded, excl U.S. prime and choice	lb	2.96	7/01	11r
Round steak, graded and ungraded, excl U.S. prime and choice	lb	3.11	7/01	11r
Sausage, Jimmy Dean/Owens pork	lb	3.39	3/01	4c
Shortening, vegetable, Crisco	3 lb	3.03	3/01	4c
Sirloin steak, graded and ungraded, excl U.S. prime and choice	lb	4.23	7/01	11r
Soft drink, Coca Cola, ex deposit	2 liter	1.29	3/01	4c
Spaghetti and macaroni	lb	0.78	7/01	11r
Steak, round, U.S. choice, boneless	lb	3.56	7/01	11r
Steak, sirloin, U.S. choice, boneless	lb	5.65	7/01	11r
Steak, T-bone	lb	7.39	3/01	4c
Strawberries, dry pint	12 oz	1.50	7/01	11r
Sugar and other sweets, expenditures on	yr	99	1999	30r
Sugar, cane or beet	4 lbs	1.54	3/01	4c
Sugar, white, 33-80 ounce package	lb	0.39	7/01	11r
Sugar, white, all sizes	lb	0.42	7/01	11r
Tobacco products and smoking supplies purchases	yr	288	1999	30r
Tomatoes, field grown	lb	1.43	7/01	11r
Tomatoes, Hunt's or Del Monte	14.5 oz	0.83	3/01	4c
Tuna, chunk, light	6 oz	0.77	3/01	4c
Tuna, light, chunk	lb	1.77	7/01	11r
Turkey, frozen, whole	lb	1.05	7/01	11r

Asheville, NC - continued

Item	Per	Value	Date	Ref.
Goods and Services				
Miscellaneous goods and services, ACCRA Index		100.40	3/01	4c
B&B Japanese maple (acer japonicum)	gal	49.98-129.00	4/00	93r
Boxwood (buxus)	2 gal	12.99-16.99	4/00	93r
Daylilly (hemerocallis)	gal	4.99-8.99	4/00	93r
Flat of annuals		11.00-13.92	4/00	93r
Fountain grass (pennisetum)	gal	5.98-7.98	4/00	93r
Hanging basket (10 in)		7.99-14.98	4/00	93r
Hardy geranium (geranium)	gal	5.98-8.00	4/00	93r
Hosta (hosta)	gal	4.99-10.98	4/00	93r
Lilac (syrubga vulgaris)	2 gal	12.99-21.99	4/00	93r
Rhododendron (rhododendron)	2 gal	14.99-24.99	4/00	93r
Sage (salvia)	gal	5.98-6.99	4/00	93r
Wintercreeper euonymus (euonymus fortunei)	2 gal	7.99-89.99	4/00	93r
Hunting license	yr	15.00	4/01	34s
Health Care				
Health care, ACCRA Index		93.80	3/01	4c
Cardiac catheterization, ave hospital/ physician charges		12500	1998	77s
Childbirth, Cesarean delivery		11587	1997	13r
Childbirth, vaginal delivery		6725	1997	13r
Dentist's fee, adult teeth cleaning and periodic oral exam	visit	73.67	3/01	4c
Doctor's fee, routine exam, established patient	visit	61.75	3/01	4c
Drugs, expenditures on	yr	399	1999	30r
Health care purchases	yr	1971	1999	30r
Health insurance expenditures	yr	933	1999	30r
Hospital care, private room	day	290.00	3/01	4c
Hysterectomy, laproscopically-assisted, ave hospital/physician charges		12260	1998	76s
Hysterectomy, vaginal, ave hospital and physician charges		8440	1998	76s
Medicaid dispensing fee		5.60	1999	87s
Medical services expenditures	yr	547	1999	30r
Medical supplies, expenditures on	yr	91	1999	30r
Plastic surgery, breast augmentation		2870	2000	7r
Plastic surgery, breast lift		3649	2000	7r
Plastic surgery, facelift		5008	2000	7r
Plastic surgery, hair transplantation		3425	2000	7r
Plastic surgery, lip augmentation		1227	2000	7r
Plastic surgery, lower body lift		4793	2000	7r
Plastic surgery, thigh lift		3862	2000	7r
Household Goods				
Dishwashing powder, Cascade	50 oz	3.39	3/01	4c
Floor coverings, expenditures on	yr	44	1999	30r
Furniture, expenditures on	yr	335	1999	30r
Household furnishings and equipment purchases	yr	1328	1999	30r
Household textiles, expenditures on	yr	89	1999	30r
Laundry and cleaning supplies, expenditures on	yr	113	1999	30r
Tissues, facial, Kleenex brand	175	1.31	3/01	4c
Housing				
Housing, ACCRA Index		114.20	3/01	4c
Home, 2200 sq ft, 4-br, 2-bath, 2-car garage, average		159100	2000	47c
Home price, existing, ave		160100	10/00	90r
Home value, median		146000	2001	53s

Values are in dollars or fractions of dollars. In the column headed *Ref*, references are shown to sources. Each reference is followed by a letter. These refer to the geographical level for which data were reported: s=State, r=Region, and c=City or metro. The abbreviation *ex* is used to mean *except* or *excluding*; *exp* stands for expenditures. For other abbreviations and further explanations, please see the Introduction.

Asheville, NC - continued

Item	Per	Value	Date	Ref.
Housing				
House, 2400 sq ft, 8000 sq ft lot, new, urban, utilities	total	238725	3/01	4c
House payment, principal and interest, 25% down payment	mos	1215	3/01	4c
Household operation expenditures	yr	553	1999	30r
Housekeeping supplies purchases	yr	473	1999	30r
Housing, expenditures on	yr	10303	1999	30r
Maintenance, repairs, insurance expenditures	yr	699	1999	30r
Monthly rental value of owned home	mos	505	1999	30r
Owned dwellings, expenditures own	yr	3465	1999	30r
Rent expenditures	yr	1641	1999	30r
Rent, apartment, 2 br, 1 1/2-2 baths, unfurn, 950 sq ft, water	mos	691	3/01	4c
Rental unit, 1 bedroom, with utilities	mos	422	4/01	41c
Rental unit, 2 bedroom, with utilities	mos	550	4/01	41c
Rental unit, 3 bedroom, with utilities	mos	717	4/01	41c
Rental unit, 4 bedroom, with utilities	mos	773	4/01	41c
Shelter, expenditures on	yr	5467	1999	30r
Insurance and Pensions				
Life and other personal insurance purchases	yr	414	1999	30r
Pensions and Social Security, expenditures on	yr	2635	1999	30r
Personal insurance and pensions, expenditures on	yr	3048	1999	30r
Legal Fees				
Combination hunting and fishing license	yr	20.00	4/01	34s
Divorce, filing fee		80.00	4/01	35s
Driver's license fee	renew	10.00	1999	48s
Driver's license fee	orig	10.00	1999	48s
Fishing license	yr	15.00	4/01	34s
Personal Goods				
Personal care products and services purchases	yr	393	1999	30r
Shampoo, Alberto VO5	15 oz	1.01	3/01	4c
Toothpaste, Crest or Colgate	6-7 oz	2.19	3/01	4c
Personal Services				
Dry cleaning, man's 2-pc suit		8.21	3/01	4c
Man's haircut, barbershop, no styling		10.80	3/01	4c
Personal services, household, expenditures on	yr	258	1999	30r
Woman's shampoo, trim, blow-dry, no style-change		23.80	3/01	4c
Pets				
Pets, toys, and playground equipment, expenditures on	yr	306	1999	30r
Restaurant Food				
Chicken, fried, thigh and drumstick, KFC/Church's		2.75	3/01	4c
Hamburger with cheese, McDonald's	1/4 lb	2.09	3/01	4c
Pizza, Pizza Hut or Pizza Inn	11-12 in	9.65	3/01	4c
Taxes				
Federal income taxes paid	yr	2047	1999	30r
Personal taxes, expenditures on	yr	2554	1999	30r
Property taxes paid	yr	726	1999	30r
State and local income taxes paid	yr	363	1999	30r
Transportation				
Transportation, ACCRA Index		101.90	3/01	4c
Cars and trucks, new, expenditures on	yr	1648	1999	30r
Cars and trucks, used, expenditures on	yr	1651	1999	30r
Diesel at the pump	gal	1.19	10/99	73s
Gasoline and motor oil purchases	yr	1052	1999	30r
Gasoline before-tax price (cents)	gal	103.20	10/00	43s
Maintenance and repair expenditures	yr	621	1999	30r
Motorcycle license fee	renew	1.50	1999	49s
Motorcycle license fee	orig	1.50	1999	49s
Public transportation, expenditures on	yr	298	1999	30r
Tire balance, computer or spin balance, front	wheel	8.94	3/01	4c

Asheville, NC - continued

Item	Per	Value	Date	Ref.
Transportation - continued				
Transportation purchases	yr	6738	1999	30r
Vehicle expenses, miscellaneous, purchases	yr	2033	1999	30r
Vehicle insurance payments	yr	696	1999	30r
Vehicle purchases (net outlay)	yr	3354	1999	30r
Vehicle rental, lease expenditures	yr	352	1999	30r
Utilities				
Utilities, ACCRA Index		87.90	3/01	4c
Electrical bill, average	mos	83.66	9/00	9s
Electricity, 2400 sq ft, new home	mos	109.62	3/01	4c
Electricity, expenditures on	yr	1115	1999	30r
Electricity cost, average	KWh	6.40	9/00	9s
Water and other public services, expenditures on	yr	298	1999	30r
Weddings				
Wedding (national average cost)		19936	2000	33r
Wedding (regional average total cost)		16293	1997	110r
Attendants' gifts		321	1998	33r
Bridal attendants' apparel (5 persons)		824	2000	33r
Bride's headpiece/veil		173	1998	33r
Bride's wedding dress		859	1998	33r
Clergy, religious facility fee		242	1998	33r
Engagement ring		3177	1998	33r
Flowers		789	1998	33r
Groom's formalwear rental		99	2000	33r
Limousine		410	1998	33r
Marriage license cost		40.00	4/01	35s
Men's formalwear (ushers, best man)		469	2000	33r
Mother of bride apparel		241	2000	33r
Music		866	1998	33r
Photography and videography		1368	1998	33r
Rehearsal dinner		728	1998	33r
Wedding invitations and announcements		341	1998	33r
Wedding reception		7968	2000	33r
Wedding rings (bride and groom)		1060	1998	33r

Athens, GA

Item	Per	Value	Date	Ref.
Alcoholic Beverages				
Alcoholic beverage purchases	yr	253	1999	30r
Malt beverages, all types, all sizes, any origin	16 oz	0.96	7/01	11r
Appliances				
Major appliances, expenditures on	yr	172	1999	30r
Small appliances, housewares, expenditures on	yr	81	1999	30r
Banking and Money				
Mortgage interest and charges paid	yr	2039	1999	30r
Mortgage principal paid on owned property	yr	1026	1999	30r
Vehicle finance charges paid	yr	365	1999	30r
Charity				
Cash contributions, expenditures	yr	1127	1999	30r
Child Care				
Child raising cost, total, age 0-2	yr	8540	1999	60r
Child raising cost, total, age 3-5	yr	8780	1999	60r
Child raising cost, total, age 6-8	yr	8820	1999	60r
Child raising cost, total, age 9-11	yr	8800	1999	60r
Child raising cost, total, age 12-14	yr	9510	1999	60r
Child raising cost, total, age 15-17	yr	9740	1999	60r
Child's child care and education, age 0-2	yr	1380	1999	60r
Child's child care and education, age 3-5	yr	1520	1999	60r
Child's child care and education, age 6-8	yr	990	1999	60r
Child's child care and education, age 9-11	yr	650	1999	60r
Child's child care and education, age 12-14	yr	490	1999	60r
Child's child care and education, age 15-17	yr	840	1999	60r
Child's clothing, age 0-2	yr	480	1999	60r
Child's clothing, age 3-5	yr	470	1999	60r
Child's clothing, age 6-8	yr	520	1999	60r
Child's clothing, age 9-11	yr	570	1999	60r
Child's clothing, age 12-14	yr	950	1999	60r

Values are in dollars or fractions of dollars. In the column headed *Ref*, references are shown to sources. Each reference is followed by a letter. These refer to the geographical level for which data were reported: s=State, r=Region, and c=City or metro. The abbreviation *ex* is used to mean *except* or *excluding*; *exp* stands for *expenditures*. For other abbreviations and further explanations, please see the Introduction.

Athens, GA - continued

Item	Per	Value	Date	Ref.
Child Care				
Child's clothing, age 15-17	yr	850	1999	60r
Child's food, age 0-2	yr	1000	1999	60r
Child's food, age 3-5	yr	1160	1999	60r
Child's food, age 6-8	yr	1490	1999	60r
Child's food, age 9-11	yr	1770	1999	60r
Child's food, age 12-14	yr	1770	1999	60r
Child's food, age 15-17	yr	1980	1999	60r
Child's health care, age 0-2	yr	620	1999	60r
Child's health care, age 3-5	yr	590	1999	60r
Child's health care, age 6-8	yr	680	1999	60r
Child's health care, age 9-11	yr	720	1999	60r
Child's health care, age 12-14	yr	730	1999	60r
Child's health care, age 15-17	yr	760	1999	60r
Child's housing, age 0-2	yr	3070	1999	60r
Child's housing, age 3-5	yr	3050	1999	60r
Child's housing, age 6-8	yr	3010	1999	60r
Child's housing, age 9-11	yr	2850	1999	60r
Child's housing, age 12-14	yr	3040	1999	60r
Child's housing, age 15-17	yr	2650	1999	60r
Child's personal care, reading, age 0-2	yr	910	1999	60r
Child's personal care, reading, age 3-5	yr	930	1999	60r
Child's personal care, reading, age 6-8	yr	960	1999	60r
Child's personal care, reading, age 9-11	yr	1000	1999	60r
Child's personal care, reading, age 12-14	yr	1170	1999	60r
Child's personal care, reading, age 15-17	yr	950	1999	60r
Clothing				
Apparel and services purchases	yr	1610	1999	30r
Boys, 2 to 15, expenditures on	yr	89	1999	30r
Children under 2, expenditures on	yr	79	1999	30r
Footwear, expenditures on	yr	283	1999	30r
Girls, 2 to 15, expenditures on	yr	103	1999	30r
Men and boys, expenditures on	yr	351	1999	30r
Men, 16 and over, expenditures on	yr	262	1999	30r
Women, 16 and over, expenditures on	yr	538	1999	30r
Communications				
Cable modem installation, Charter		99.00-169.00	6/99	103s
Cable modem installation, Comcast		95.00	6/99	103s
Cable modem installation, Intermedia		149.95	6/99	103s
Cable modem installation, Media One		100.00	6/99	103s
Cable modem rate, cable subscriber, Charter	mos	49.95-79.95	6/99	103s
Cable modem rate, cable subscriber, Comcast	mos	39.95	6/99	103s
Cable modem rate, cable subscriber, Intermedia	mos	49.95	6/99	103s
Cable modem rate, cable subscriber, Media One	mos	34.95-39.95	6/99	103s
Cable modem rate, non-cable subscriber, Charter	mos	59.95-89.95	6/99	103s
Cable modem rate, non-cable subscriber, Comcast	mos	49.95	6/99	103s
Cable modem rate, non-cable subscriber, Intermedia	mos	54.95	6/99	103s
Cable modem rate, non-cable subscriber, Media One	mos	49.95	6/99	103s
Phone line, single, business, field visit	inst.	58.25	12/97	17s
Phone line, single, business, no field visit	inst.	58.25	12/97	17s
Phone line, single, residence, field visit	inst.	42.50	12/97	17s
Phone line, single, residence, no field visit	inst.	42.50	12/97	17s
Postage and stationery, expenditures on	yr	104	1999	30r
Postal rate, express mail, up to half-pound		12.45	7/01	108r
Postal rate, letter, first class, first ounce		0.34	7/01	108r
Postal rate, letter, two ounces		0.57	7/01	108r
Postal rate, post card		0.21	7/01	108r
Postal rate, priority mail, two pounds		3.95	7/01	108r
Postal rate, priority mail, up to one pound		3.50	7/01	108r
Telephone services, expenditures on	yr	860	1999	30r
Education				
Board, 4-year private college/university	yr	2267	1996	38s
Board, 4-year public college/university	yr	1877	1996	38s

Athens, GA - continued

Item	Per	Value	Date	Ref.
Education - continued				
Education expenditures	yr	431	1999	30r
Room, 4-year private college/university	yr	2719	1996	38s
Room, 4-year public college/university	yr	1712	1996	38s
Total cost, 4-year private college/university	yr	15194	1996	38s
Total cost, 4-year public college/university	yr	5691	1996	38s
Tuition, 2-year public college/university, in state	yr	1062	1996	38s
Tuition, 4-year private college/university, in state	yr	10208	1996	38s
Tuition, 4-year public college/university	yr	2103	1996	38s
Energy and Fuels				
Electricity	500 KWhs	47.29	7/01	11r
Electricity	KWh	0.09	7/01	11r
Fuel oil #2	gal	1.43	7/01	11r
Fuel oil and other fuels, expenditures on	yr	45	1999	30r
Gasoline, all types	gal	1.60	7/01	11r
Gasoline, unleaded midgrade	gal	1.65	7/01	11r
Gasoline, unleaded premium	gal	1.74	7/01	11r
Natural gas, expenditures on	yr	164	1999	30r
Utility (piped) gas, therm		1.01	7/01	11r
Utility (piped) gas, 40 therms		44.29	7/01	11r
Utility (piped) gas, 100 therms		97.44	7/01	11r
Entertainment				
Entertainment purchases	yr	1574	1999	30r
Fees and admissions paid	yr	371	1999	30r
Reading purchases	yr	121	1999	30r
Television, radios, sound equipment, expenditures on	yr	561	1999	30r
Funerals				
Total cost of funeral		5922.53	1/99	78r
Acknowledgement cards		63.43	1/99	78r
Casket		2258.77	1/99	78r
Cosmetology, hair, other preparation		127.09	1/99	78r
Embalming		393.49	1/99	78r
Funeral at funeral home		367.50	1/99	78r
Hearse (local)		169.66	1/99	78r
Professional service charges		1211.32	1/99	78r
Service car/van		80.69	1/99	78r
Transfer of remains to funeral home		144.25	1/99	78r
Vault		803.50	1/99	78r
Visitation/viewing		302.83	1/99	78r
Groceries				
American processed cheese	lb	3.50	7/01	11r
Bakery products, expenditures on	yr	261	1999	30r
Bananas	lb	0.47	7/01	11r
Beans, dried, any type, all sizes	lb	0.63	7/01	11r
Beef for stew, boneless	lb	2.86	7/01	11r
Beef, expenditures on	yr	210	1999	30r
Bologna, all beef or mixed	lb	2.29	7/01	11r
Bread, French	lb	1.66	7/01	11r
Bread, white, pan	lb	0.87	7/01	11r
Bread, whole wheat, pan	lb	1.38	7/01	11r
Broccoli	lb	1.04	7/01	11r
Butter, salted, grade AA, stick	lb	2.26	7/01	11r
Butter, yoghurt, cheese, etc, expenditures on	yr	170	1999	30r
Cabbage	lb	0.42	7/01	11r
Cereals and cereal products, expenditures on	yr	140	1999	30r
Cheddar cheese, natural	lb	3.75	7/01	11r
Chicken breast, bone-in	lb	1.85	7/01	11r
Chicken legs, bone-in	lb	1.34	7/01	11r
Chicken, fresh, whole	lb	1.05	7/01	11r
Chops, boneless,	lb	4.13	7/01	11r
Chuck roast, graded and ungraded, excl U.S. prime and choice	lb	2.35	7/01	11r
Chuck roast, U.S. choice, boneless	lb	2.67	7/01	11r
Coffee, 100%, ground roast, all sizes	lb	2.88	7/01	11r
Coffee, instant, plain, regular, all sizes	16 oz	9.25	7/01	11r
Cola, non diet,	2 liter	1.11	7/01	11r

Values are in dollars or fractions of dollars. In the column headed *Ref*, references are shown to sources. Each reference is followed by a letter. These refer to the geographical level for which data were reported: s=State, r=Region, and c=City or metro. The abbreviation *ex* is used to mean *except* or *excluding*; *exp* stands for *expenditures*. For other abbreviations and further explanations, please see the Introduction.

Athens, GA - continued

Item	Per	Value	Date	Ref.
Groceries				
Crackers, soda, salted	lb	1.70	7/01	11r
Dairy product purchases	yr	282	1999	30r
Eggs, expenditures on	yr	32	1999	30r
Fats and oils, expenditures on	yr	79	1999	30r
Fish and seafood, expenditures on	yr	99	1999	30r
Flour, white, all purpose	lb	0.32	7/01	11r
Food (excl fruit and vegetables), eaten at home, purchases	yr	815	1999	30r
Food cooked on trips, expenditures on	yr	36	1999	30r
Food purchases	yr	4533	1999	30r
Food purchases, eaten away from home	yr	1873	1999	30r
Food purchases, food eaten at home	yr	2660	1999	30r
Fresh fruits, expenditures on	yr	128	1999	30r
Fresh milk and cream, expenditures on	yr	112	1999	30r
Fresh vegetables, expenditures on	yr	131	1999	30r
Fruit and vegetable purchases	yr	438	1999	30r
Grapefruit	lb	0.59	7/01	11r
Grapes, Thompson, seedless	lb	2.12	7/01	11r
Ground beef, 100% beef	lb	1.76	7/01	11r
Ground beef, lean and extra lean	lb	2.60	7/01	11r
Ground chuck, 100% beef	lb	2.08	7/01	11r
Ham, boneless, excl canned	lb	2.71	7/01	11r
Ham, rump or shank half, bone-in, smoked	lb	2.19	7/01	11r
Ice cream, prepackaged, bulk, regular	1/2 gal	3.93	7/01	11r
Lemons	lb	1.32	7/01	11r
Lettuce, iceberg	lb	0.76	7/01	11r
Milk, fresh, low fat,	gal	2.75	7/01	11r
Milk, fresh, whole, fortified	gal	2.97	7/01	11r
Nonalcoholic beverages, expenditures on	yr	228	1999	30r
Orange juice, frozen concentrate	16 oz	1.95	7/01	11r
Oranges, Navel	lb	0.73	7/01	11r
Oranges, Valencia	lb	0.55	7/01	11r
Peanut butter, creamy, all sizes	lb	1.83	7/01	11r
Pears, Anjou	lb	0.98	7/01	11r
Pork chops, center cut, bone-in	lb	3.33	7/01	11r
Pork sausage, fresh, loose	lb	2.59	7/01	11r
Pork shoulder picnic, bone-in, smoked	lb	1.12	7/01	11r
Pork, expenditures on	yr	162	1999	30r
Potato chips	16 oz	3.59	7/01	11r
Potatoes, frozen, french fried	lb	1.00	7/01	11r
Potatoes, white, all types	lb	0.44	7/01	11r
Poultry, expenditures on	yr	137	1999	30r
Processed fruits, expenditures on	yr	97	1999	30r
Processed vegetables, expenditures on	yr	82	1999	30r
Rice, white, long grain, uncooked	lb	0.51	7/01	11r
Round roast, graded and ungraded, excl U.S. prime and choice	lb	2.96	7/01	11r
Round steak, graded and ungraded, excl U.S. prime and choice	lb	3.11	7/01	11r
Sirloin steak, graded and ungraded, excl U.S. prime and choice	lb	4.23	7/01	11r
Spaghetti and macaroni	lb	0.78	7/01	11r
Steak, round, U.S. choice, boneless	lb	3.56	7/01	11r
Steak, sirloin, U.S. choice, boneless	lb	5.65	7/01	11r
Strawberries, dry pint	12 oz	1.50	7/01	11r
Sugar and other sweets, expenditures on	yr	99	1999	30r
Sugar, white, 33-80 ounce package	lb	0.39	7/01	11r
Sugar, white, all sizes	lb	0.42	7/01	11r
Tobacco products and smoking supplies purchases	yr	288	1999	30r
Tomatoes, field grown	lb	1.43	7/01	11r
Tuna, light, chunk	lb	1.77	7/01	11r
Turkey, frozen, whole	lb	1.05	7/01	11r
Goods and Services				
B&B Japanese maple (acer japonicum)	gal	49.98-129.00	4/00	93r
Boxwood (buxus)	2 gal	12.99-16.99	4/00	93r
Daylilly (hemerocallis)	gal	4.99-8.99	4/00	93r
Flat of annuals		11.00-13.92	4/00	93r

Athens, GA - continued

Item	Per	Value	Date	Ref.
Goods and Services - continued				
Fountain grass (pennisetum)	gal	5.98-7.98	4/00	93r
Hanging basket (10 in)		7.99-14.98	4/00	93r
Hardy geranium (geranium)	gal	5.98-8.00	4/00	93r
Hosta (hosta)	gal	4.99-10.98	4/00	93r
Lilac (syrubga vulgaris)	2 gal	12.99-21.99	4/00	93r
Rhododendron (rhododendron)	2 gal	14.99-24.99	4/00	93r
Sage (salvia)	gal	5.98-6.99	4/00	93r
Wintercreeper euonymus (euonymus fortunei)	2 gal	7.99-89.99	4/00	93r
Hunting license	yr	10.00	4/01	34s
Health Care				
Cardiac catheterization, ave hospital/physician charges		14190	1998	77s
Childbirth, Cesarean delivery		11587	1997	13r
Childbirth, vaginal delivery		6725	1997	13r
Drugs, expenditures on	yr	399	1999	30r
Health care purchases	yr	1971	1999	30r
Health insurance expenditures	yr	933	1999	30r
Hysterectomy, laproscopically-assisted, ave hospital/physician charges		16760	1998	76s
Hysterectomy, vaginal, ave hospital and physician charges		11160	1998	76s
Medicaid dispensing fee		4.63	1999	87s
Medical services expenditures	yr	547	1999	30r
Medical supplies, expenditures on	yr	91	1999	30r
Plastic surgery, breast augmentation		2870	2000	7r
Plastic surgery, breast lift		3649	2000	7r
Plastic surgery, facelift		5008	2000	7r
Plastic surgery, hair transplantation		3425	2000	7r
Plastic surgery, lip augmentation		1227	2000	7r
Plastic surgery, lower body lift		4793	2000	7r
Plastic surgery, thigh lift		3862	2000	7r
Household Goods				
Floor coverings, expenditures on	yr	44	1999	30r
Furniture, expenditures on	yr	335	1999	30r
Household furnishings and equipment purchases	yr	1328	1999	30r
Household textiles, expenditures on	yr	89	1999	30r
Laundry and cleaning supplies, expenditures on	yr	113	1999	30r
Housing				
Home, 2200 sq ft, 4-br, 2-bath, 2-car garage, average		137975	2000	47c
Home price, existing, ave		160100	10/00	90r
Home value, median		131000	2001	53s
Household operation expenditures	yr	553	1999	30r
Housekeeping supplies purchases	yr	473	1999	30r
Housing, expenditures on	yr	10303	1999	30r
Maintenance, repairs, insurance expenditures	yr	699	1999	30r
Monthly rental value of owned home	mos	505	1999	30r
Owned dwellings, expenditures own	yr	3465	1999	30r
Rent expenditures	yr	1641	1999	30r
Rental unit, 1 bedroom, with utilities	mos	409	4/01	41c
Rental unit, 2 bedroom, with utilities	mos	529	4/01	41c
Rental unit, 3 bedroom, with utilities	mos	722	4/01	41c
Rental unit, 4 bedroom, with utilities	mos	870	4/01	41c
Shelter, expenditures on	yr	5467	1999	30r
Insurance and Pensions				
Life and other personal insurance purchases	yr	414	1999	30r
Pensions and Social Security, expenditures on	yr	2635	1999	30r

Values are in dollars or fractions of dollars. In the column headed *Ref*, references are shown to sources. Each reference is followed by a letter. These refer to the geographical level for which data were reported: s=State, r=Region, and c=City or metro. The abbreviation *ex* is used to mean *except* or *excluding*; *exp* stands for expenditures. For other abbreviations and further explanations, please see the Introduction.

Athens, GA - continued

Item	Per	Value	Date	Ref.
Insurance and Pensions				
Personal insurance and pensions, expenditures on	yr	3048	1999	30r
Legal Fees				
Divorce, filing fee		65.00-85.00	4/01	35s
Driver's license fee	orig	16.50	1999	48s
Driver's license fee	renew	15.00	1999	48s
Personal Goods				
Personal care products and services purchases	yr	393	1999	30r
Personal Services				
Personal services, household, expenditures on	yr	258	1999	30r
Pets				
Pets, toys, and playground equipment, expenditures on	yr	306	1999	30r
Taxes				
Federal income taxes paid	yr	2047	1999	30r
Personal taxes, expenditures on	yr	2554	1999	30r
Property taxes paid	yr	726	1999	30r
State and local income taxes paid	yr	363	1999	30r
Transportation				
Bus fare, one-way	trip	1.00	2000	1c
Cars and trucks, new, expenditures on	yr	1648	1999	30r
Cars and trucks, used, expenditures on	yr	1651	1999	30r
Diesel at the pump	gal	1.10	10/99	73s
Gasoline and motor oil purchases	yr	1052	1999	30r
Gasoline before-tax price (cents)	gal	102.00	10/00	43s
Maintenance and repair expenditures	yr	621	1999	30r
Public transportation, expenditures on	yr	298	1999	30r
Transportation purchases	yr	6738	1999	30r
Vehicle expenses, miscellaneous, purchases	yr	2033	1999	30r
Vehicle insurance payments	yr	696	1999	30r
Vehicle purchases (net outlay)	yr	3354	1999	30r
Vehicle rental, lease expenditures	yr	352	1999	30r
Utilities				
Electrical bill, average	mos	79.83	9/00	9s
Electricity, expenditures on	yr	1115	1999	30r
Electricity cost, average	KWh	6.10	9/00	9s
Water and other public services, expenditures on	yr	298	1999	30r
Weddings				
Wedding (national average cost)		19936	2000	33r
Wedding (regional average total cost)		16293	1997	110r
Attendants' gifts		321	1998	33r
Bridal attendants' apparel (5 persons)		824	2000	33r
Bride's headpiece/veil		173	1998	33r
Bride's wedding dress		859	1998	33r
Clergy, religious facility fee		242	1998	33r
Engagement ring		3177	1998	33r
Flowers		789	1998	33r
Groom's formalwear rental		99	2000	33r
Limousine		410	1998	33r
Marriage license cost		40.00	4/01	35s
Men's formalwear (ushers, best man)		469	2000	33r
Mother of bride apparel		241	2000	33r
Music		866	1998	33r
Photography and videography		1368	1998	33r
Rehearsal dinner		728	1998	33r
Wedding invitations and announcements		341	1998	33r
Wedding reception		7968	2000	33r
Wedding rings (bride and groom)		1060	1998	33r

Atlanta, GA

Item	Per	Value	Date	Ref.
Average annual expenditures	yr	38726	1999	30c
Composite, ACCRA index		101.80	3/01	4c
Alcoholic Beverages				
Alcoholic beverage purchases	yr	240	1999	30c
Beer, Heineken, 12-oz, ex deposit	6	7.39	3/01	4c
J & B Scotch	750-ml	21.14	3/01	4c
Malt beverages, all types, all sizes, any origin	16 oz	0.96	7/01	11r
Wine, Livingston or Gallo, Chablis blanc	1.5 liter	5.99	3/01	4c
Appliances				
Appliance repair, service call, washing machine	min lab chg	37.99	3/01	4c
Major appliances, expenditures on	yr	172	1999	30r
Small appliances, housewares, expenditures on	yr	81	1999	30r
Banking and Money				
Mortgage interest and charges paid	yr	2039	1999	30r
Mortgage principal paid on owned property	yr	1026	1999	30r
Mortgage rate, incl. points and orig. fee, 30-yr. conv. fixed or ARM	mos	6.80	3/01	4c
Vehicle finance charges paid	yr	365	1999	30r
Business Expenses				
Business travel, car rental	day	73	2001	3c
Business travel, food	day	58	2001	3c
Business travel, hotel	day	112	2001	3c
Medical office space cost	sq ft	106.79	2001	31c
Office space, 2-4 storey building	sq ft	93.56	2001	31c
Office space, 5-10 storey building	sq ft	82.64	2001	31c
Office space, 11-20 storey building	sq ft	79.43	2001	31c
Charity				
Cash contributions, expenditures	yr	1488	1999	30c
Child Care				
Child raising cost, total, age 0-2	yr	8540	1999	60r
Child raising cost, total, age 3-5	yr	8780	1999	60r
Child raising cost, total, age 6-8	yr	8820	1999	60r
Child raising cost, total, age 9-11	yr	8800	1999	60r
Child raising cost, total, age 12-14	yr	9510	1999	60r
Child raising cost, total, age 15-17	yr	9740	1999	60r
Child's child care and education, age 0-2	yr	1380	1999	60r
Child's child care and education, age 3-5	yr	1520	1999	60r
Child's child care and education, age 6-8	yr	990	1999	60r
Child's child care and education, age 9-11	yr	650	1999	60r
Child's child care and education, age 12-14	yr	490	1999	60r
Child's child care and education, age 15-17	yr	840	1999	60r
Child's clothing, age 0-2	yr	480	1999	60r
Child's clothing, age 3-5	yr	470	1999	60r
Child's clothing, age 6-8	yr	520	1999	60r
Child's clothing, age 9-11	yr	570	1999	60r
Child's clothing, age 12-14	yr	950	1999	60r
Child's clothing, age 15-17	yr	850	1999	60r
Child's food, age 0-2	yr	1000	1999	60r
Child's food, age 3-5	yr	1160	1999	60r
Child's food, age 6-8	yr	1490	1999	60r
Child's food, age 9-11	yr	1770	1999	60r
Child's food, age 12-14	yr	1770	1999	60r
Child's food, age 15-17	yr	1980	1999	60r
Child's health care, age 0-2	yr	620	1999	60r
Child's health care, age 3-5	yr	590	1999	60r
Child's health care, age 6-8	yr	680	1999	60r
Child's health care, age 9-11	yr	720	1999	60r
Child's health care, age 12-14	yr	730	1999	60r
Child's health care, age 15-17	yr	760	1999	60r
Child's housing, age 0-2	yr	3070	1999	60r
Child's housing, age 3-5	yr	3050	1999	60r
Child's housing, age 6-8	yr	3010	1999	60r
Child's housing, age 9-11	yr	2850	1999	60r
Child's housing, age 12-14	yr	3040	1999	60r
Child's housing, age 15-17	yr	2650	1999	60r
Child's personal care, reading, age 0-2	yr	910	1999	60r
Child's personal care, reading, age 3-5	yr	930	1999	60r
Child's personal care, reading, age 6-8	yr	960	1999	60r

Values are in dollars or fractions of dollars. In the column headed *Ref*, references are shown to sources. Each reference is followed by a letter. These refer to the geographical level for which data were reported: s=State, r=Region, and c=City or metro. The abbreviation *ex* is used to mean *except* or *excluding*; *exp* stands for *expenditures*. For other abbreviations and further explanations, please see the Introduction.

Atlanta, GA - continued

Item	Per	Value	Date	Ref.
Child Care				
Child's personal care, reading, age 9-11	yr	1000	1999	60r
Child's personal care, reading, age 12-14	yr	1170	1999	60r
Child's personal care, reading, age 15-17	yr	950	1999	60r
Clothing				
Apparel and services purchases	yr	1712	1999	30c
Boys' brief, cotton	3	4.38	3/01	4c
Boys, 2 to 15, expenditures on	yr	89	1999	30r
Children under 2, expenditures on	yr	79	1999	30r
Footwear, expenditures on	yr	283	1999	30r
Girls, 2 to 15, expenditures on	yr	103	1999	30r
Men and boys, expenditures on	yr	351	1999	30r
Men, 16 and over, expenditures on	yr	262	1999	30r
Shirt, man's dress shirt		26.50	3/01	4c
Slacks, man's "No Wrinkles" khaki		36.99	3/01	4c
Women, 16 and over, expenditures on	yr	538	1999	30r
Communications				
Cable modem installation, Charter		99.00-169.00	6/99	103s
Cable modem installation, Comcast		95.00	6/99	103s
Cable modem installation, Intermedia		149.95	6/99	103s
Cable modem installation, Media One		100.00	6/99	103s
Cable modem rate, cable subscriber, Charter	mos	49.95-79.95	6/99	103s
Cable modem rate, cable subscriber, Comcast	mos	39.95	6/99	103s
Cable modem rate, cable subscriber, Intermedia	mos	49.95	6/99	103s
Cable modem rate, cable subscriber, Media One	mos	34.95-39.95	6/99	103s
Cable modem rate, non-cable subscriber, Charter	mos	59.95-89.95	6/99	103s
Cable modem rate, non-cable subscriber, Comcast	mos	49.95	6/99	103s
Cable modem rate, non-cable subscriber, Intermedia	mos	54.95	6/99	103s
Cable modem rate, non-cable subscriber, Media One	mos	49.95	6/99	103s
Cellular phone service	mos	36.85	2/01	55c
Newspaper subscription, daily and Sunday delivery	mos	16.30	3/01	4c
Phone line, single, business, field visit	inst.	58.25	12/97	17s
Phone line, single, business, no field visit	inst.	58.25	12/97	17s
Phone line, single, residence, field visit	inst.	42.50	12/97	17s
Phone line, single, residence, no field visit	inst.	42.50	12/97	17s
Postage and stationery, expenditures on	yr	104	1999	30r
Postal rate, express mail, up to half-pound		12.45	7/01	108r
Postal rate, letter, first class, first ounce		0.34	7/01	108r
Postal rate, letter, two ounces		0.57	7/01	108r
Postal rate, post card		0.21	7/01	108r
Postal rate, priority mail, two pounds		3.95	7/01	108r
Postal rate, priority mail, up to one pound		3.50	7/01	108r
Telephone bill, business, basic rate	mos	48.30	12/97	18c
Telephone bill, family of three	mos	24.90	3/01	4c
Telephone bill, residential, basic rate	mos	16.15	12/97	18c
Telephone services, expenditures on	yr	860	1999	30r
Education				
Board, 4-year private college/university	yr	2267	1996	38s
Board, 4-year public college/university	yr	1877	1996	38s
Education expenditures	yr	545	1999	30c
Room, 4-year private college/university	yr	2719	1996	38s
Room, 4-year public college/university	yr	1712	1996	38s
Total cost, 4-year private college/university	yr	15194	1996	38s
Total cost, 4-year public college/university	yr	5691	1996	38s
Tuition, 2-year public college/university, in state	yr	1062	1996	38s
Tuition, 4-year private college/university, in state	yr	10208	1996	38s
Tuition, 4-year public college/university	yr	2103	1996	38s

Atlanta, GA - continued

Item	Per	Value	Date	Ref.
Energy and Fuels				
Electricity	500 KWhs	47.29	7/01	11r
Electricity	KWh	0.09	7/01	11c
Electricity	500 KWhs	42.17	7/01	11c
Energy, combined forms, 2400 sq ft	mos	106.22	3/01	4c
Fuel oil #2	gal	1.43	7/01	11r
Fuel oil and other fuels, expenditures on	yr	45	1999	30r
Gas, cooking, winter, 10 therms	mos	14.34	2/96	98c
Gas, cooking, winter, 30 therms	mos	24.91	2/96	98c
Gas, cooking, winter, 50 therms	mos	35.49	2/96	98c
Gas, heating, winter, average use	mos	93.62	2/96	98c
Gas, regular unleaded, cash, self-service	gal	1.26	3/01	4c
Gasoline, all types	gal	1.49	7/01	11c
Gasoline, unleaded midgrade	gal	1.53	7/01	11c
Gasoline, unleaded premium	gal	1.74	7/01	11r
Gasoline, unleaded regular	gal	1.42	7/01	11c
Natural gas, expenditures on	yr	164	1999	30r
Utility (piped) gas, therm		1.24	7/01	11c
Utility (piped) gas, 40 therms		44.29	7/01	11r
Utility (piped) gas, 100 therms		123.22	7/01	11c
Entertainment				
Bowling, Saturday evening rate	line	3.43	3/01	4c
Entertainment purchases	yr	1692	1999	30c
Fees and admissions paid	yr	371	1999	30r
Major League baseball ticket		19.78	2000	16c
Monopoly game, Parker Brothers', No. 9	game	9.70	3/01	4c
Movie, first-run, Saturday, evening	adm.	7.28	3/01	4c
Reading purchases	yr	121	1999	30r
Television, radios, sound equipment, expenditures on	yr	561	1999	30r
Tennis balls, yellow, Wilson or Penn, 3	can	2.62	3/01	4c
Funerals				
Total cost of funeral		5922.53	1/99	78r
Acknowledgement cards		63.43	1/99	78r
Casket		2258.77	1/99	78r
Cosmetology, hair, other preparation		127.09	1/99	78r
Embalming		393.49	1/99	78r
Funeral at funeral home		367.50	1/99	78r
Hearse (local)		169.66	1/99	78r
Professional service charges		1211.32	1/99	78r
Service car/van		80.69	1/99	78r
Transfer of remains to funeral home		144.25	1/99	78r
Vault		803.50	1/99	78r
Visitation/viewing		302.83	1/99	78r
Groceries				
Groceries, ACCRA Index		98.40	3/01	4c
American processed cheese	lb	3.50	7/01	11r
Antibiotic ointment, Polysporin	0.5 oz	4.03	3/01	4c
Apples	pound	1.26		29c
Baby food, strained vegetables or fruit, lowest price	4-4.5 oz	0.39	3/01	4c
Bakery products, expenditures on	yr	261	1999	30r
Bananas	lb	0.54	3/01	4c
Bananas	lb	0.47	7/01	11r
Beans, dried, any type, all sizes	lb	0.63	7/01	11r
Beef for stew, boneless	lb	2.86	7/01	11r
Beef or hamburger, ground	lb	1.86	3/01	4c
Beef, expenditures on	yr	210	1999	30r
Bologna, all beef or mixed	lb	2.29	7/01	11r
Bread, French	lb	1.66	7/01	11r
Bread, white	loaf	1.02	3/01	4c
Bread, white, pan	lb	0.87	7/01	11r
Bread, whole wheat, pan	lb	1.38	7/01	11r
Broccoli	lb	1.04	7/01	11r
Butter, salted, grade AA, stick	lb	2.26	7/01	11r
Butter, yoghurt, cheese, etc, expenditures on	yr	170	1999	30r
Cabbage	lb	0.42	7/01	11r
Cereals and bakery product purchases	yr	365	1999	30c
Cereals and cereal products, expenditures on	yr	140	1999	30r

Values are in dollars or fractions of dollars. In the column headed *Ref*, references are shown to sources. Each reference is followed by a letter. These refer to the geographical level for which data were reported: s=State, r=Region, and c=City or metro. The abbreviation *ex* is used to mean *except* or *excluding*; *exp* stands for expenditures. For other abbreviations and further explanations, please see the Introduction.

Atlanta, GA - continued

Item	Per	Value	Date	Ref.
Groceries				
Cheddar cheese, natural	lb	3.75	7/01	11r
Cheese, Kraft grated Parmesan	8 oz	3.28	3/01	4c
Chicken breast, bone-in	lb	1.85	7/01	11r
Chicken legs, bone-in	lb	1.34	7/01	11r
Chicken, fresh, whole	lb	1.05	7/01	11r
Chicken, whole fryer	lb	0.99	3/01	4c
Chops, boneless,	lb	4.13	7/01	11r
Chuck roast, graded and ungraded, excl U.S. prime and choice	lb	2.35	7/01	11r
Chuck roast, U.S. choice, boneless	lb	2.67	7/01	11r
Cigarettes, Winston, Kings	carton	25.29	3/01	4c
Coffee, 100%, ground roast, all sizes	lb	2.88	7/01	11r
Coffee, instant, plain, regular, all sizes	16 oz	9.25	7/01	11r
Coffee, vacuum-packed	13 oz	2.29	3/01	4c
Cola, non diet,	2 liter	1.11	7/01	11r
Corn Flakes, Kellogg's or Post Toasties	18 oz	2.50	3/01	4c
Corn, frozen, whole kernel, lowest price	16 oz	0.89	3/01	4c
Crackers, soda, salted	lb	1.70	7/01	11r
Dairy product purchases	yr	234	1999	30c
Detergent (Tide), 33 oz		3	12/00	72c
Dishwashing soap (Joy), 28 oz		2	12/00	72c
Eggs, expenditures on	yr	32	1999	30r
Eggs, Grade A or AA	dozen	1.26	3/01	4c
Fats and oils, expenditures on	yr	79	1999	30r
Fish and seafood, expenditures on	yr	99	1999	30r
Flour, white, all purpose	lb	0.32	7/01	11r
Food (excl fruit and vegetables), eaten at home, purchases	yr	727	1999	30c
Food cooked on trips, expenditures on	yr	36	1999	30r
Food purchases	yr	4449	1999	30c
Food purchases, eaten away from home	yr	2060	1999	30c
Food purchases, food eaten at home	yr	2390	1999	30c
Fresh fruits, expenditures on	yr	128	1999	30r
Fresh milk and cream, expenditures on	yr	112	1999	30r
Fresh vegetables, expenditures on	yr	131	1999	30r
Fruit and vegetable purchases	yr	438	1999	30r
Grapefruit	lb	0.59	7/01	11r
Grapes, Thompson, seedless	lb	2.12	7/01	11r
Ground beef, 100% beef	lb	1.76	7/01	11r
Ground beef, lean and extra lean	lb	2.60	7/01	11r
Ground chuck, 100% beef	lb	2.08	7/01	11r
Ham, boneless, excl canned	lb	2.71	7/01	11r
Ham, rump or shank half, bone-in, smoked	lb	2.19	7/01	11r
Ice cream, prepackaged, bulk, regular	1/2 gal	3.93	7/01	11r
Ketchup (Heinz), 20 oz.		1.00	12/00	72c
Lemons	lb	1.32	7/01	11r
Lettuce, iceberg	head	1.06	3/01	4c
Lettuce, iceberg	lb	0.76	7/01	11r
Margarine, Blue Bonnet or Parkay, stick	lb	0.79	3/01	4c
Meats, poultry, fish, and egg purchases	yr	649	1999	30c
Milk, fresh, low fat,	gal	2.75	7/01	11r
Milk, fresh, whole, fortified	gal	2.97	7/01	11r
Milk, whole	1/2 gal	1.99	3/01	4c
Nonalcoholic beverages, expenditures on	yr	228	1999	30r
Orange juice, frozen concentrate	16 oz	1.95	7/01	11r
Orange juice, Minute Maid frozen	12 oz	1.61	3/01	4c
Oranges, Navel	lb	0.73	7/01	11r
Oranges, Valencia	lb	0.55	7/01	11r
Peaches, halves or slices, Hunt's, Del Monte, or Libby's	29 oz	1.42	3/01	4c
Peanut butter, creamy, all sizes	lb	1.83	7/01	11r
Pears, Anjou	lb	0.98	7/01	11r
Peas, green, Del Monte or Green Giant	15 oz	0.65	3/01	4c
Pork chops, center cut, bone-in	lb	3.33	7/01	11r
Pork sausage, fresh, loose	lb	2.59	7/01	11r
Pork shoulder picnic, bone-in, smoked	lb	1.12	7/01	11r
Pork, expenditures on	yr	162	1999	30r
Potato chips	16 oz	3.59	7/01	11r
Potatoes, frozen, french fried	lb	1.00	7/01	11r
Potatoes, white or red	10 lb	2.72	3/01	4c
Potatoes, white, all types	lb	0.44	7/01	11r
Poultry, expenditures on	yr	137	1999	30r

Item	Per	Value	Date	Ref.
Groceries - continued				
Processed fruits, expenditures on	yr	97	1999	30r
Processed vegetables, expenditures on	yr	82	1999	30r
Rice, white, long grain, uncooked	lb	0.51	7/01	11r
Round roast, graded and ungraded, excl U.S. prime and choice	lb	2.96	7/01	11r
Round steak, graded and ungraded, excl U.S. prime and choice	lb	3.11	7/01	11r
Sausage, Jimmy Dean/Owens pork	lb	3.16	3/01	4c
Shortening, vegetable, Crisco	3 lb	3.17	3/01	4c
Sirloin steak, graded and ungraded, excl U.S. prime and choice	lb	4.23	7/01	11r
Soda (Coke), 2 liter bottle		1.00	12/00	72c
Soft drink, Coca Cola, ex deposit	2 liter	0.99	3/01	4c
Spaghetti and macaroni	lb	0.78	7/01	11r
Steak, round, U.S. choice, boneless	lb	3.56	7/01	11r
Steak, sirloin, U.S. choice, boneless	lb	5.65	7/01	11r
Steak, T-bone	lb	7.16	3/01	4c
Strawberries, dry pint	12 oz	1.50	7/01	11r
Sugar and other sweets, expenditures on	yr	99	1999	30r
Sugar, cane or beet	4 lbs	1.65	3/01	4c
Sugar, white, 33-80 ounce package	lb	0.39	7/01	11r
Sugar, white, all sizes	lb	0.42	7/01	11r
Tobacco products and smoking supplies purchases	yr	198	1999	30c
Tomatoes, field grown	lb	1.43	7/01	11r
Tomatoes, Hunt's or Del Monte	14.5 oz	0.86	3/01	4c
Tuna, chunk, light	6 oz	0.54	3/01	4c
Tuna, light, chunk	lb	1.77	7/01	11r
Turkey, frozen, whole	lb	1.05	7/01	11r
Goods and Services				
Miscellaneous goods and services, ACCRA Index		100.10	3/01	4c
B&B Japanese maple (acer japonicum)	gal	49.98-129.00	4/00	93r
Boxwood (buxus)	2 gal	12.99-16.99	4/00	93r
Daylily (hemerocallis)	gal	4.99-8.99	4/00	93r
Flat of annuals		11.00-13.92	4/00	93r
Fountain grass (pennisetum)	gal	5.98-7.98	4/00	93r
Hanging basket (10 in)		7.99-14.98	4/00	93r
Hardy geranium (geranium)	gal	5.98-8.00	4/00	93r
Hosta (hosta)	gal	4.99-10.98	4/00	93r
Lilac (syrubga vulgaris)	2 gal	12.99-21.99	4/00	93r
Miscellaneous purchases	yr	727	1999	30c
Rhododendron (rhododendron)	2 gal	14.99-24.99	4/00	93r
Sage (salvia)	gal	5.98-6.99	4/00	93r
Wintercreeper euonymus (euonymus fortunei)	2 gal	7.99-89.99	4/00	93r
Hunting license	yr	10.00	4/01	34s
Health Care				
Health care, ACCRA Index		109.20	3/01	4c
Cardiac catheterization, ave hospital/ physician charges		14190	1998	77s
Childbirth, Cesarean delivery		11587	1997	13r
Childbirth, vaginal delivery		6725	1997	13r
Dentist's fee, adult teeth cleaning and periodic oral exam	visit	93.22	3/01	4c
Doctor's fee, routine exam, established patient	visit	61.62	3/01	4c
Drugs, expenditures on	yr	399	1999	30r
Health care purchases	yr	1835	1999	30c
Health insurance expenditures	yr	933	1999	30r

Values are in dollars or fractions of dollars. In the column headed *Ref*, references are shown to sources. Each reference is followed by a letter. These refer to the geographical level for which data were reported: s=State, r=Region, and c=City or metro. The abbreviation *ex* is used to mean *except* or *excluding*; *exp* stands for expenditures. For other abbreviations and further explanations, please see the Introduction.

Atlanta, GA - continued

Item	Per	Value	Date	Ref.
Health Care				
Home health care aide cost, licensed agency	hour	15	2000	82c
Hospital care, private room	day	481.22	3/01	4c
Hysterectomy, laproscopically-assisted, ave hospital/physician charges		16760	1998	76s
Hysterectomy, vaginal, ave hospital and physician charges		11160	1998	76s
Medicaid dispensing fee		4.63	1999	87s
Medical services expenditures	yr	547	1999	30r
Medical supplies, expenditures on	yr	91	1999	30r
Nursing home costs, private room	day	110	2000	82c
Nursing home stay, private room	day	110	2000	83c
Plastic surgery, breast augmentation		2870	2000	7r
Plastic surgery, breast lift		3649	2000	7r
Plastic surgery, facelift		5008	2000	7r
Plastic surgery, hair transplantation		3425	2000	7r
Plastic surgery, lip augmentation		1227	2000	7r
Plastic surgery, lower body lift		4793	2000	7r
Plastic surgery, thigh lift		3862	2000	7r
Household Goods				
Dishwashing powder, Cascade	50 oz	2.72	3/01	4c
Floor coverings, expenditures on	yr	44	1999	30r
Furniture, expenditures on	yr	335	1999	30r
Hockey mask		1.00	12/00	72c
House paint	gal	9	12/00	72c
Household furnishings and equipment purchases	yr	1417	1999	30c
Household textiles, expenditures on	yr	89	1999	30r
Lamp		15	12/00	72c
Laundry and cleaning supplies, expenditures on	yr	113	1999	30r
Poinsettia, fake		3	12/00	72c
Shirt, flannel		5	12/00	72c
Tissues, facial, Kleenex brand	175	1.38	3/01	4c
TV stand		20	12/00	72c
Housing				
Housing, ACCRA Index		107.30	3/01	4c
Home, 2200 sq ft, 4-br, 2-bath, 2-car garage, average		237375	2000	47c
Home, suburban, 2,200 square feet		285300	2000	23c
Home price, existing, ave		160100	10/00	90r
Home value, median		131000	2001	53s
House, 2400 sq ft, 8000 sq ft lot, new, urban, utilities	total	230067	3/01	4c
House payment, principal and interest, 25% down payment	mos	1125	3/01	4c
Household operation expenditures	yr	793	1999	30c
Housekeeping supplies purchases	yr	340	1999	30c
Housing, expenditures on	yr	10303	1999	30r
Lodging expenditures	yr	508	1999	30c
Maintenance, repairs, insurance expenditures	yr	699	1999	30r
Monthly rental value of owned home	mos	505	1999	30r
Owned dwellings, expenditures own	yr	5397	1999	30c
Rent expenditures	yr	2230	1999	30c
Rent, apartment, 2 br, 1 1/2-2 baths, unfurn, 950 sq ft, water	mos	695	3/01	4c
Rental unit, 1 bedroom, with utilities	mos	682	4/01	41c
Rental unit, 2 bedroom, with utilities	mos	795	4/01	41c
Rental unit, 3 bedroom, with utilities	mos	1060	4/01	41c
Rental unit, 4 bedroom, with utilities	mos	1282	4/01	41c
Shelter, expenditures on	yr	8136	1999	30c
Insurance and Pensions				
Life and other personal insurance purchases	yr	503	1999	30c
Pensions and Social Security, expenditures on	yr	3020	1999	30c
Personal insurance and pensions, expenditures on	yr	3048	1999	30r
Legal Fees				
Divorce, filing fee		65.00-85.00	4/01	35s

Atlanta, GA - continued

Item	Per	Value	Date	Ref.
Legal Fees - continued				
Driver's license fee	orig	16.50	1999	48s
Driver's license fee	renew	15.00	1999	48s
Personal Goods				
Deodorant (Secret), 1.7 oz		1.50	12/00	72c
Personal care products and services purchases	yr	343	1999	30c
Shampoo, Alberto VO5	15 oz	0.93	3/01	4c
Toothpaste, Crest or Colgate	6-7 oz	2.59	3/01	4c
Personal Services				
Detective service, finding a missing person	hour	55	1999	22c
Dry cleaning, man's 2-pc suit		6.99	3/01	4c
Man's haircut, barbershop, no styling		10.22	3/01	4c
Personal services, household, expenditures on	yr	258	1999	30r
Woman's shampoo, trim, blow-dry, no style-change		27.50	3/01	4c
Pets				
Pets, toys, and playground equipment, expenditures on	yr	306	1999	30r
Restaurant Food				
Cheeseburger, 1/4-lb, large fries, medium soft drink, excl tax		4.48	1999	40c
Chicken, fried, thigh and drumstick, KFC/Church's		2.21	3/01	4c
Hamburger with cheese, McDonald's	1/4 lb	2.22	3/01	4c
Pizza, Pizza Hut or Pizza Inn	11-12 in	8.99	3/01	4c
Taxes				
Federal income taxes paid	yr	2047	1999	30r
Personal taxes, expenditures on	yr	2554	1999	30r
Property taxes paid	yr	726	1999	30r
State and local income taxes paid	yr	363	1999	30r
Transportation				
Transportation, ACCRA Index		102.80	3/01	4c
Bus fare, one-way	trip	1.50	2000	1c
Bus fare, to central business district	1-way	1.31	3/01	4c
Cars and trucks, new, expenditures on	yr	1648	1999	30r
Cars and trucks, used, expenditures on	yr	1651	1999	30r
Diesel at the pump	gal	1.10	10/99	73s
Gas and oil for transportation		1158	97-1998	102c
Gasoline and motor oil purchases	yr	1074	1999	30c
Gasoline before-tax price (cents)	gal	102.00	10/00	43s
Heavy rail transit fare, one-way	trip	1.50	2000	2c
Household transportation expenditures	yr	8513	97-1998	102c
Maintenance and repair expenditures	yr	621	1999	30r
Public transit expenditures		98	97-1998	102c
Public transportation, expenditures on	yr	346	1999	30c
Tire balance, computer or spin balance, front	wheel	9.11	3/01	4c
Transportation purchases	yr	8058	1999	30c
Vehicle expenses		2970	97-1998	102c
Vehicle expenses, miscellaneous, purchases	yr	2824	1999	30c
Vehicle insurance payments	yr	696	1999	30r
Vehicle purchase expense		4287	97-1998	102c
Vehicle purchases (net outlay)	yr	3354	1999	30r
Vehicle rental, lease expenditures	yr	352	1999	30r
Travel				
Car rental	day	79.50	2000	24c
Hotel room, ave	night	95.42	2000	70c
Utilities				
Utilities, ACCRA Index		90.80	3/01	4c
Electrical bill, average	mos	79.83	9/00	9s
Electricity, 2400 sq ft, new home	mos	106.22	3/01	4c
Electricity, expenditures on	yr	1115	1999	30r
Electricity, summer, 250 KWh	mos	23.23	2/96	97c
Electricity, summer, 500 KWh	mos	38.96	2/96	97c
Electricity, summer, 750 KWh	mos	53.99	2/96	97c
Electricity, summer, 1000 KWh	mos	68.03	2/96	97c
Electricity cost, average	KWh	6.10	9/00	9s
Utilities, fuels, and public services purchased	yr	3053	1999	30c

Values are in dollars or fractions of dollars. In the column headed *Ref*, references are shown to sources. Each reference is followed by a letter. These refer to the geographical level for which data were reported: s=State, r=Region, and c=City or metro. The abbreviation *ex* is used to mean *except* or *excluding*; *exp* stands for *expenditures*. For other abbreviations and further explanations, please see the Introduction.

Atlanta, GA - continued

Item	Per	Value	Date	Ref.
Utilities				
Water and other public services, expenditures on	yr	298	1999	30r
Weddings				
Wedding (national average cost)		19936	2000	33r
Wedding (regional average total cost)		16293	1997	110r
Attendants' gifts		321	1998	33r
Bridal attendants' apparel (5 persons)		824	2000	33r
Bride's headpiece/veil		173	1998	33r
Bride's wedding dress		859	1998	33r
Clergy, religious facility fee		242	1998	33r
Engagement ring		3177	1998	33r
Flowers		789	1998	33r
Groom's formalwear rental		99	2000	33r
Limousine		410	1998	33r
Marriage license cost		40.00	4/01	35s
Men's formalwear (ushers, best man)		469	2000	33r
Mother of bride apparel		241	2000	33r
Music		866	1998	33r
Photography and videography		1368	1998	33r
Rehearsal dinner		728	1998	33r
Wedding invitations and announcements		341	1998	33r
Wedding reception		7968	2000	33r
Wedding rings (bride and groom)		1060	1998	33r

Atlantic-Cape May, NJ

Item	Per	Value	Date	Ref.
Average annual expenditures	yr	37971	1999	30r
Alcoholic Beverages				
Alcoholic beverage purchases	yr	368	1999	30r
Wine, red and white table, all sizes, any origin	liter	9.64	7/01	11r
Appliances				
Major appliances, expenditures on	yr	194	1999	30r
Small appliances, housewares, expenditures on	yr	93	1999	30r
Banking and Money				
Mortgage interest and charges paid	yr	2622	1999	30r
Mortgage principal paid on owned property	yr	1262	1999	30r
Vehicle finance charges paid	yr	240	1999	30r
Charity				
Cash contributions, expenditures	yr	1001	1999	30r
Child Care				
Child raising cost, total, age 0-2	yr	8670	1999	60r
Child raising cost, total, age 3-5	yr	8910	1999	60r
Child raising cost, total, age 6-8	yr	9040	1999	60r
Child raising cost, total, age 9-11	yr	9100	1999	60r
Child raising cost, total, age 12-14	yr	9890	1999	60r
Child raising cost, total, age 15-17	yr	10010	1999	60r
Child's child care and education, age 0-2	yr	1070	1999	60r
Child's child care and education, age 3-5	yr	1190	1999	60r
Child's child care and education, age 6-8	yr	740	1999	60r
Child's child care and education, age 9-11	yr	470	1999	60r
Child's child care and education, age 12-14	yr	350	1999	60r
Child's child care and education, age 15-17	yr	590	1999	60r
Child's clothing, age 0-2	yr	480	1999	60r
Child's clothing, age 3-5	yr	470	1999	60r
Child's clothing, age 6-8	yr	520	1999	60r
Child's clothing, age 9-11	yr	570	1999	60r
Child's clothing, age 12-14	yr	970	1999	60r
Child's clothing, age 15-17	yr	870	1999	60r
Child's food, age 0-2	yr	1130	1999	60r
Child's food, age 3-5	yr	1290	1999	60r
Child's food, age 6-8	yr	1640	1999	60r
Child's food, age 9-11	yr	1930	1999	60r
Child's food, age 12-14	yr	1940	1999	60r
Child's food, age 15-17	yr	2150	1999	60r
Child's health care, age 0-2	yr	550	1999	60r
Child's health care, age 3-5	yr	530	1999	60r

Item	Per	Value	Date	Ref.
Child Care - continued				
Child's health care, age 6-8	yr	610	1999	60r
Child's health care, age 9-11	yr	650	1999	60r
Child's health care, age 12-14	yr	660	1999	60r
Child's health care, age 15-17	yr	690	1999	60r
Child's housing, age 0-2	yr	3555	1999	60r
Child's housing, age 3-5	yr	3530	1999	60r
Child's housing, age 6-8	yr	3490	1999	60r
Child's housing, age 9-11	yr	3340	1999	60r
Child's housing, age 12-14	yr	3530	1999	60r
Child's housing, age 15-17	yr	3140	1999	60r
Child's personal care, reading, age 0-2	yr	920	1999	60r
Child's personal care, reading, age 3-5	yr	950	1999	60r
Child's personal care, reading, age 6-8	yr	980	1999	60r
Child's personal care, reading, age 9-11	yr	1020	1999	60r
Child's personal care, reading, age 12-14	yr	1190	1999	60r
Child's personal care, reading, age 15-17	yr	970	1999	60r
Clothing				
Apparel and services purchases	yr	1831	1999	30r
Boys, 2 to 15, expenditures on	yr	92	1999	30r
Children under 2, expenditures on	yr	63	1999	30r
Footwear, expenditures on	yr	300	1999	30r
Girls, 2 to 15, expenditures on	yr	101	1999	30r
Men and boys, expenditures on	yr	446	1999	30r
Men, 16 and over, expenditures on	yr	354	1999	30r
Women, 16 and over, expenditures on	yr	584	1999	30r
Communications				
Cable modem installation, Adelphi		54.90	6/99	103s
Cable modem installation, Comcast		95.00	6/99	103s
Cable modem rate, cable subscriber, Adelphi	mos	34.95	6/99	103s
Cable modem rate, cable subscriber, Comcast	mos	39.95	6/99	103s
Cable modem rate, non-cable subscriber, Adelphi	mos	44.95	6/99	103s
Cable modem rate, non-cable subscriber, Comcast	mos	49.95	6/99	103s
Phone line, single, business, field visit	inst.	98.50	12/97	17s
Phone line, single, business, no field visit	inst.	79.50	12/97	17s
Phone line, single, residence, field visit	inst.	56.50	12/97	17s
Phone line, single, residence, no field visit	inst.	42.00	12/97	17s
Postage and stationery, expenditures on	yr	138	1999	30r
Postal rate, express mail, up to half-pound		12.45	7/01	108r
Postal rate, letter, first class, first ounce		0.34	7/01	108r
Postal rate, letter, two ounces		0.57	7/01	108r
Postal rate, post card		0.21	7/01	108r
Postal rate, priority mail, two pounds		3.95	7/01	108r
Postal rate, priority mail, up to one pound		3.50	7/01	108r
Telephone services, expenditures on	yr	830	1999	30r
Education				
Board, 4-year private college/university	yr	2959	1996	38s
Board, 4-year public college/university	yr	2052	1996	38s
Education expenditures	yr	877	1999	30r
Room, 4-year private college/university	yr	3226	1996	38s
Room, 4-year public college/university	yr	3101	1996	38s
Total cost, 4-year private college/university	yr	19751	1996	38s
Total cost, 4-year public college/university	yr	9125	1996	38s
Tuition, 2-year public college/university, in state	yr	1878	1996	38s
Tuition, 4-year private college/university, in state	yr	13566	1996	38s
Tuition, 4-year public college/university	yr	3972	1996	38s
Energy and Fuels				
Electricity	KWh	0.12	7/01	11r
Fuel oil #2	gal	1.31	7/01	11r
Fuel oil and other fuels, expenditures on	yr	207	1999	30r
Gas, natural, commercial rate	1000 cf	5.98	11/00	88s
Gasoline, all types	gal	1.80	7/01	11r
Gasoline, unleaded midgrade	gal	1.85	7/01	11r
Gasoline, unleaded premium	gal	1.91	7/01	11r
Gasoline, unleaded regular	gal	1.71	7/01	11r
Natural gas, expenditures on	yr	368	1999	30r

Values are in dollars or fractions of dollars. In the column headed *Ref*, references are shown to sources. Each reference is followed by a letter. These refer to the geographical level for which data were reported: s=State, r=Region, and c=City or metro. The abbreviation *ex* is used to mean *except* or *excluding*; *exp* stands for *expenditures*. For other abbreviations and further explanations, please see the Introduction.

Atlantic-Cape May, NJ - continued

Item	Per	Value	Date	Ref.
Energy and Fuels				
Utility (piped) gas, therm		1.08	7/01	11r
Utility (piped) gas, 40 therms		50.87	7/01	11r
Utility (piped) gas, 100 therms		111.06	7/01	11r
Entertainment				
Entertainment purchases	yr	1821	1999	30r
Fees and admissions paid	yr	511	1999	30r
Television, radios, sound equipment, expenditures on	yr	650	1999	30r
Funerals				
Total cost of funeral		5813.50	1/99	78r
Acknowledgement cards		28.32	1/99	78r
Casket		2082.20	1/99	78r
Cosmetology, hair, other preparation		169.59	1/99	78r
Embalming		465.60	1/99	78r
Funeral at funeral home		339.56	1/99	78r
Hearse (local)		183.96	1/99	78r
Professional service charges		1157.85	1/99	78r
Service car/van		100.41	1/99	78r
Transfer of remains to funeral home		158.66	1/99	78r
Vault		766.31	1/99	78r
Visitation/viewing		361.04	1/99	78r
Groceries				
Apples, red delicious	lb	0.95	7/01	11r
Bacon, sliced	lb	3.44	7/01	11r
Bakery products, expenditures on	yr	310	1999	30r
Bananas	lb	0.55	7/01	11r
Beef, expenditures on	yr	236	1999	30r
Bread, white, pan	lb	1.09	7/01	11r
Butter, yoghurt, cheese, etc, expenditures on	yr	214	1999	30r
Cereals and bakery product purchases	yr	474	1999	30r
Cereals and cereal products, expenditures on	yr	164	1999	30r
Chicken legs, bone-in	lb	1.23	7/01	11r
Chicken, fresh, whole	lb	1.13	7/01	11r
Chuck roast, U.S. choice, boneless	lb	2.79	7/01	11r
Coffee, 100%, ground roast, all sizes	lb	3.40	7/01	11r
Dairy product purchases	yr	342	1999	30r
Eggs, expenditures on	yr	34	1999	30r
Eggs, grade A, large	dozen	0.82	7/01	11r
Fats and oils, expenditures on	yr	80	1999	30r
Fish and seafood, expenditures on	yr	123	1999	30r
Food (excl fruit and vegetables), eaten at home, purchases	yr	838	1999	30r
Food cooked on trips, expenditures on	yr	48	1999	30r
Food purchases	yr	5314	1999	30r
Food purchases, eaten away from home	yr	2313	1999	30r
Food purchases, food eaten at home	yr	3001	1999	30r
Fresh fruits, expenditures on	yr	169	1999	30r
Fresh milk and cream, expenditures on	yr	128	1999	30r
Fresh vegetables, expenditures on	yr	164	1999	30r
Grapefruit	lb	0.67	7/01	11r
Grapes, Thompson, seedless	lb	2.18	7/01	11r
Ground beef, lean and extra lean	lb	2.66	7/01	11r
Ground chuck, 100% beef	lb	2.04	7/01	11r
Lettuce, iceberg	lb	0.76	7/01	11r
Meats, poultry, fish, and egg purchases	yr	808	1999	30r
Nonalcoholic beverages, expenditures on	yr	225	1999	30r
Orange juice, frozen concentrate	16 oz	1.88	7/01	11r
Oranges, Navel	lb	0.79	7/01	11r
Oranges, Valencia	lb	0.56	7/01	11r
Peaches	lb	1.16	7/01	11r
Peanut butter, creamy, all sizes	lb	2.01	7/01	11r
Pears, Anjou	lb	1.16	7/01	11r
Pork chops, center cut, bone-in	lb	3.57	7/01	11r
Pork, expenditures on	yr	146	1999	30r
Potato chips	16 oz	3.37	7/01	11r
Potatoes, white, all types	lb	0.42	7/01	11r
Poultry, expenditures on	yr	158	1999	30r
Processed fruits, expenditures on	yr	124	1999	30r
Processed vegetables, expenditures on	yr	82	1999	30r
Round roast, U.S. choice, boneless	lb	3.04	7/01	11r

Atlantic-Cape May, NJ - continued

Item	Per	Value	Date	Ref.
Groceries - continued				
Spaghetti and macaroni	lb	1.04	7/01	11r
Steak, sirloin, U.S. choice, boneless	lb	5.39	7/01	11r
Strawberries, dry pint	12 oz	1.51	7/01	11r
Sugar and other sweets, expenditures on	yr	110	1999	30r
Sugar, white, 33-80 ounce package	lb	0.46	7/01	11r
Sugar, white, all sizes	lb	0.47	7/01	11r
Tobacco products and smoking supplies purchases	yr	309	1999	30r
Yogurt, natural, fruit flavored	8 oz	0.79	7/01	11r
Goods and Services				
B&B Japanese maple (acer japonicum)	gal	38.99-125.00	4/00	93r
Boxwood (buxus)	2 gal	15.99-49.95	4/00	93r
Daylily (hemerocallis)	gal	4.95	4/00	93r
Flat of annuals		8.00-14.99	4/00	93r
Fountain grass (pennisetum)	gal	6.99-9.99	4/00	93r
Hanging basket (10 in)		12.95-19.99	4/00	93r
Hardy geranium (geranium)	gal	6.95-7.99	4/00	93r
Hosta (hosta)	gal	4.95	4/00	93r
Lilac (syrubga vulgaris)	2 gal	17.99-74.95	4/00	93r
Miscellaneous purchases	yr	872	1999	30r
Rhododendron (rhododendron)	2 gal	23.99-54.95	4/00	93r
Sage (salvia)	gal	6.95-7.99	4/00	93r
Wintercreeper euonymus (euonymus fortunei)	2 gal	14.99-23.95	4/00	93r
Hunting license	yr	22.50	4/01	34s
Health Care				
Cardiac catheterization, ave hospital/ physician charges		14680	1998	77s
Childbirth, Cesarean delivery		14716	1997	13r
Childbirth, vaginal delivery		8541	1997	13r
Drugs, expenditures on	yr	296	1999	30r
Health care purchases	yr	1788	1999	30r
Health insurance expenditures	yr	875	1999	30r
Hysterectomy, laproscopically-assisted, ave hospital/physician charges		18330	1998	76s
Hysterectomy, vaginal, ave hospital and physician charges		13620	1998	76s
Medicaid dispensing fee		3.73-4.07	1999	87s
Medical services expenditures	yr	516	1999	30r
Medical supplies, expenditures on	yr	102	1999	30r
Plastic surgery, breast augmentation		4232	2000	7r
Plastic surgery, breast lift		4605	2000	7r
Plastic surgery, facelift		6964	2000	7r
Plastic surgery, hair transplantation		4193	2000	7r
Plastic surgery, lip augmentation		1675	2000	7r
Plastic surgery, lower body lift		6611	2000	7r
Plastic surgery, thigh lift		4751	2000	7r
Household Goods				
Floor coverings, expenditures on	yr	59	1999	30r
Furniture, expenditures on	yr	388	1999	30r
Household furnishings and equipment purchases	yr	1567	1999	30r
Household textiles, expenditures on	yr	112	1999	30r
Laundry and cleaning supplies, expenditures on	yr	104	1999	30r
Housing				
Home price, existing, ave		180800	10/00	90r
Home value, median		213000	2001	53s
Household operation expenditures	yr	581	1999	30r
Housekeeping supplies purchases	yr	474	1999	30r

Values are in dollars or fractions of dollars. In the column headed *Ref*, references are shown to sources. Each reference is followed by a letter. These refer to the geographical level for which data were reported: s=State, r=Region, and c=City or metro. The abbreviation *ex* is used to mean *except* or *excluding*; *exp* stands for *expenditures*. For other abbreviations and further explanations, please see the Introduction.

Atlantic-Cape May, NJ - continued

Item	Per	Value	Date	Ref.
Housing				
Lodging expenditures	yr	550	1999	30r
Maintenance, repairs, insurance expenditures	yr	835	1999	30r
Monthly rental value of owned home	mos	663	1999	30r
Owned dwellings, expenditures own	yr	5209	1999	30r
Rent expenditures	yr	2390	1999	30r
Rental unit, 1 bedroom, with utilities	mos	582	4/01	41c
Rental unit, 2 bedroom, with utilities	mos	774	4/01	41c
Rental unit, 3 bedroom, with utilities	mos	970	4/01	41c
Rental unit, 4 bedroom, with utilities	mos	1108	4/01	41c
Shelter, expenditures on	yr	8149	1999	30r
Insurance and Pensions				
Auto insurance premium	yr	1292.76	1999	57s
Life and other personal insurance purchases	yr	424	1999	30r
Pensions and Social Security, expenditures on	yr	3037	1999	30r
Legal Fees				
Divorce, filing fee		65.00	4/01	35s
Driver's license fee	orig	18.00	1999	48s
Driver's license fee	renew	15.00	1999	48s
Fishing license	yr	22.50	4/01	34s
Personal Goods				
Personal care products and services purchases	yr	399	1999	30r
Personal Services				
Personal services, household, expenditures on	yr	271	1999	30r
Pets				
Pets, toys, and playground equipment, expenditures on	yr	325	1999	30r
Taxes				
Federal income taxes paid	yr	2606	1999	30r
Personal taxes, expenditures on	yr	3567	1999	30r
Property taxes paid	yr	1752	1999	30r
State and local income taxes paid	yr	694	1999	30r
Transportation				
Automobile insurance	yr	975.90	2000	79s
Cars and trucks, new, expenditures on	yr	1496	1999	30r
Cars and trucks, used, expenditures on	yr	1251	1999	30r
Diesel at the pump	gal	1.19	10/99	73s
Gasoline and motor oil purchases	yr	901	1999	30r
Gasoline before-tax price (cents)	gal	114.90	10/00	43s
Maintenance and repair expenditures	yr	618	1999	30r
Motorcycle license fee	renew	13.00	1999	49s
Motorcycle license fee	orig	15.00	1999	49s
Public transportation, expenditures on	yr	575	1999	30r
Transportation purchases	yr	6503	1999	30r
Vehicle expenses, miscellaneous, purchases	yr	2266	1999	30r
Vehicle insurance payments	yr	824	1999	30r
Vehicle purchases (net outlay)	yr	2761	1999	30r
Vehicle rental, lease expenditures	yr	584	1999	30r
Utilities				
Electrical bill, average	mos	74.08	9/00	9s
Electricity, expenditures on	yr	837	1999	30r
Electricity cost, average	KWh	8.91	9/00	9s
Utilities, fuels, and public services purchased	yr	2457	1999	30r
Water and other public services, expenditures on	yr	215	1999	30r
Weddings				
Wedding (national average cost)		19936	2000	33r
Wedding (regional average total cost)		29454	1997	110r
Attendants' gifts		321	1998	33r
Bridal attendants' apparel (5 persons)		824	2000	33r
Bride's headpiece/veil		173	1998	33r
Bride's wedding dress		859	1998	33r
Clergy, religious facility fee		242	1998	33r
Engagement ring		3177	1998	33r

Atlantic-Cape May, NJ - continued

Item	Per	Value	Date	Ref.
Weddings - continued				
Flowers		789	1998	33r
Groom's formalwear rental		99	2000	33r
Limousine		410	1998	33r
Marriage license cost		28.00	4/01	35s
Men's formalwear (ushers, best man)		469	2000	33r
Mother of bride apparel		241	2000	33r
Music		866	1998	33r
Photography and videography		1368	1998	33r
Rehearsal dinner		728	1998	33r
Wedding invitations and announcements		341	1998	33r
Wedding reception		7968	2000	33r
Wedding rings (bride and groom)		1060	1998	33r

Auburn-Opelica, AL

Item	Per	Value	Date	Ref.
Alcoholic Beverages				
Alcoholic beverage purchases	yr	253	1999	30r
Malt beverages, all types, all sizes, any origin	16 oz	0.96	7/01	11r
Appliances				
Major appliances, expenditures on	yr	172	1999	30r
Small appliances, housewares, expenditures on	yr	81	1999	30r
Banking and Money				
Mortgage interest and charges paid	yr	2039	1999	30r
Mortgage principal paid on owned property	yr	1026	1999	30r
Vehicle finance charges paid	yr	365	1999	30r
Charity				
Cash contributions, expenditures	yr	1127	1999	30r
Child Care				
Child raising cost, total, age 0-2	yr	8540	1999	60r
Child raising cost, total, age 3-5	yr	8780	1999	60r
Child raising cost, total, age 6-8	yr	8820	1999	60r
Child raising cost, total, age 9-11	yr	8800	1999	60r
Child raising cost, total, age 12-14	yr	9510	1999	60r
Child raising cost, total, age 15-17	yr	9740	1999	60r
Child's child care and education, age 0-2	yr	1380	1999	60r
Child's child care and education, age 3-5	yr	1520	1999	60r
Child's child care and education, age 6-8	yr	990	1999	60r
Child's child care and education, age 9-11	yr	650	1999	60r
Child's child care and education, age 12-14	yr	490	1999	60r
Child's child care and education, age 15-17	yr	840	1999	60r
Child's clothing, age 0-2	yr	480	1999	60r
Child's clothing, age 3-5	yr	470	1999	60r
Child's clothing, age 6-8	yr	520	1999	60r
Child's clothing, age 9-11	yr	570	1999	60r
Child's clothing, age 12-14	yr	950	1999	60r
Child's clothing, age 15-17	yr	850	1999	60r
Child's food, age 0-2	yr	1000	1999	60r
Child's food, age 3-5	yr	1160	1999	60r
Child's food, age 6-8	yr	1490	1999	60r
Child's food, age 9-11	yr	1770	1999	60r
Child's food, age 12-14	yr	1770	1999	60r
Child's food, age 15-17	yr	1980	1999	60r
Child's health care, age 0-2	yr	620	1999	60r
Child's health care, age 3-5	yr	590	1999	60r
Child's health care, age 6-8	yr	680	1999	60r
Child's health care, age 9-11	yr	720	1999	60r
Child's health care, age 12-14	yr	730	1999	60r
Child's health care, age 15-17	yr	760	1999	60r
Child's housing, age 0-2	yr	3070	1999	60r
Child's housing, age 3-5	yr	3050	1999	60r
Child's housing, age 6-8	yr	3010	1999	60r
Child's housing, age 9-11	yr	2850	1999	60r
Child's housing, age 12-14	yr	3040	1999	60r
Child's housing, age 15-17	yr	2650	1999	60r
Child's personal care, reading, age 0-2	yr	910	1999	60r
Child's personal care, reading, age 3-5	yr	930	1999	60r
Child's personal care, reading, age 6-8	yr	960	1999	60r
Child's personal care, reading, age 9-11	yr	1000	1999	60r

Values are in dollars or fractions of dollars. In the column headed *Ref*, references are shown to sources. Each reference is followed by a letter. These refer to the geographical level for which data were reported: s=State, r=Region, and c=City or metro. The abbreviation *ex* is used to mean *except* or *excluding*; *exp* stands for *expenditures*. For other abbreviations and further explanations, please see the Introduction.

Auburn-Opelica, AL - continued

Item	Per	Value	Date	Ref.
Child Care				
Child's personal care, reading, age 12-14	yr	1170	1999	60r
Child's personal care, reading, age 15-17	yr	950	1999	60r
Clothing				
Apparel and services purchases	yr	1610	1999	30r
Boys, 2 to 15, expenditures on	yr	89	1999	30r
Children under 2, expenditures on	yr	79	1999	30r
Footwear, expenditures on	yr	283	1999	30r
Girls, 2 to 15, expenditures on	yr	103	1999	30r
Men and boys, expenditures on	yr	351	1999	30r
Men, 16 and over, expenditures on	yr	262	1999	30r
Women, 16 and over, expenditures on	yr	538	1999	30r
Communications				
Phone line, single, business, field visit	inst.	69.00	12/97	17s
Phone line, single, business, no field visit	inst.	69.00	12/97	17s
Phone line, single, residence, field visit	inst.	40.00	12/97	17s
Phone line, single, residence, no field visit	inst.	40.00	12/97	17s
Postage and stationery, expenditures on	yr	104	1999	30r
Postal rate, express mail, up to half-pound		12.45	7/01	108r
Postal rate, letter, first class, first ounce		0.34	7/01	108r
Postal rate, letter, two ounces		0.57	7/01	108r
Postal rate, post card		0.21	7/01	108r
Postal rate, priority mail, two pounds		3.95	7/01	108r
Postal rate, priority mail, up to one pound		3.50	7/01	108r
Telephone services, expenditures on	yr	860	1999	30r
Education				
Board, 4-year private college/university	yr	2256	1996	38s
Board, 4-year public college/university	yr	1739	1996	38s
Education expenditures	yr	431	1999	30r
Room, 4-year private college/university	yr	1799	1996	38s
Room, 4-year public college/university	yr	1757	1996	38s
Total cost, 4-year private college/university	yr	11635	1996	38s
Total cost, 4-year public college/university	yr	5737	1996	38s
Tuition, 2-year public college/university, in state	yr	1317	1996	38s
Tuition, 4-year private college/university, in state	yr	7580	1996	38s
Tuition, 4-year public college/university	yr	2240	1996	38s
Energy and Fuels				
Electricity	500 KWhs	47.29	7/01	11r
Electricity	KWh	0.09	7/01	11r
Fuel oil #2	gal	1.43	7/01	11r
Fuel oil and other fuels, expenditures on	yr	45	1999	30r
Gas, natural, commercial rate	1000 cf	9.50	11/00	88s
Gasoline, all types	gal	1.60	7/01	11r
Gasoline, unleaded midgrade	gal	1.65	7/01	11r
Gasoline, unleaded premium	gal	1.74	7/01	11r
Natural gas, expenditures on	yr	164	1999	30r
Utility (piped) gas, therm		1.01	7/01	11r
Utility (piped) gas, 40 therms		44.29	7/01	11r
Utility (piped) gas, 100 therms		97.44	7/01	11r
Entertainment				
Entertainment purchases	yr	1574	1999	30r
Fees and admissions paid	yr	371	1999	30r
Reading purchases	yr	121	1999	30r
Television, radios, sound equipment, expenditures on	yr	561	1999	30r
Groceries				
American processed cheese	lb	3.50	7/01	11r
Bakery products, expenditures on	yr	261	1999	30r
Bananas	lb	0.47	7/01	11r
Beans, dried, any type, all sizes	lb	0.63	7/01	11r
Beef for stew, boneless	lb	2.86	7/01	11r
Beef, expenditures on	yr	210	1999	30r
Bologna, all beef or mixed	lb	2.29	7/01	11r
Bread, French	lb	1.66	7/01	11r
Bread, white, pan	lb	0.87	7/01	11r
Bread, whole wheat, pan	lb	1.38	7/01	11r
Broccoli	lb	1.04	7/01	11r

Auburn-Opelica, AL - continued

Item	Per	Value	Date	Ref.
Groceries - continued				
Butter, salted, grade AA, stick	lb	2.26	7/01	11r
Butter, yoghurt, cheese, etc, expenditures on	yr	170	1999	30r
Cabbage	lb	0.42	7/01	11r
Cereals and cereal products, expenditures on	yr	140	1999	30r
Cheddar cheese, natural	lb	3.75	7/01	11r
Chicken breast, bone-in	lb	1.85	7/01	11r
Chicken legs, bone-in	lb	1.34	7/01	11r
Chicken, fresh, whole	lb	1.05	7/01	11r
Chops, boneless,	lb	4.13	7/01	11r
Chuck roast, graded and ungraded, excl U.S. prime and choice	lb	2.35	7/01	11r
Chuck roast, U.S. choice, boneless	lb	2.67	7/01	11r
Coffee, 100%, ground roast, all sizes	lb	2.88	7/01	11r
Coffee, instant, plain, regular, all sizes	16 oz	9.25	7/01	11r
Cola, non diet,	2 liter	1.11	7/01	11r
Crackers, soda, salted	lb	1.70	7/01	11r
Dairy product purchases	yr	282	1999	30r
Eggs, expenditures on	yr	32	1999	30r
Fats and oils, expenditures on	yr	79	1999	30r
Fish and seafood, expenditures on	yr	99	1999	30r
Flour, white, all purpose	lb	0.32	7/01	11r
Food (excl fruit and vegetables), eaten at home, purchases	yr	815	1999	30r
Food cooked on trips, expenditures on	yr	36	1999	30r
Food purchases	yr	4533	1999	30r
Food purchases, eaten away from home	yr	1873	1999	30r
Food purchases, food eaten at home	yr	2660	1999	30r
Fresh fruits, expenditures on	yr	128	1999	30r
Fresh milk and cream, expenditures on	yr	112	1999	30r
Fresh vegetables, expenditures on	yr	131	1999	30r
Fruit and vegetable purchases	yr	438	1999	30r
Grapefruit	lb	0.59	7/01	11r
Grapes, Thompson, seedless	lb	2.12	7/01	11r
Ground beef, 100% beef	lb	1.76	7/01	11r
Ground beef, lean and extra lean	lb	2.60	7/01	11r
Ground chuck, 100% beef	lb	2.08	7/01	11r
Ham, boneless, excl canned	lb	2.71	7/01	11r
Ham, rump or shank half, bone-in, smoked	lb	2.19	7/01	11r
Ice cream, prepackaged, bulk, regular	1/2 gal	3.93	7/01	11r
Lemons	lb	1.32	7/01	11r
Lettuce, iceberg	lb	0.76	7/01	11r
Milk, fresh, low fat,	gal	2.75	7/01	11r
Milk, fresh, whole, fortified	gal	2.97	7/01	11r
Nonalcoholic beverages, expenditures on	yr	228	1999	30r
Orange juice, frozen concentrate	16 oz	1.95	7/01	11r
Oranges, Navel	lb	0.73	7/01	11r
Oranges, Valencia	lb	0.55	7/01	11r
Peanut butter, creamy, all sizes	lb	1.83	7/01	11r
Pears, Anjou	lb	0.98	7/01	11r
Pork chops, center cut, bone-in	lb	3.33	7/01	11r
Pork sausage, fresh, loose	lb	2.59	7/01	11r
Pork shoulder picnic, bone-in, smoked	lb	1.12	7/01	11r
Pork, expenditures on	yr	162	1999	30r
Potato chips	16 oz	3.59	7/01	11r
Potatoes, frozen, french fried	lb	1.00	7/01	11r
Potatoes, white, all types	lb	0.44	7/01	11r
Poultry, expenditures on	yr	137	1999	30r
Processed fruits, expenditures on	yr	97	1999	30r
Processed vegetables, expenditures on	yr	82	1999	30r
Rice, white, long grain, uncooked	lb	0.51	7/01	11r
Round roast, graded and ungraded, excl U.S. prime and choice	lb	2.96	7/01	11r
Round steak, graded and ungraded, excl U.S. prime and choice	lb	3.11	7/01	11r
Sirloin steak, graded and ungraded, excl U.S. prime and choice	lb	4.23	7/01	11r
Spaghetti and macaroni	lb	0.78	7/01	11r
Steak, round, U.S. choice, boneless	lb	3.56	7/01	11r
Steak, sirloin, U.S. choice, boneless	lb	5.65	7/01	11r
Strawberries, dry pint	12 oz	1.50	7/01	11r
Sugar and other sweets, expenditures on	yr	99	1999	30r

Values are in dollars or fractions of dollars. In the column headed *Ref*, references are shown to sources. Each reference is followed by a letter. These refer to the geographical level for which data were reported: s=State, r=Region, and c=City or metro. The abbreviation *ex* is used to mean *except* or *excluding*; *exp* stands for *expenditures*. For other abbreviations and further explanations, please see the Introduction.

Auburn-Opelica, AL - continued

Item	Per	Value	Date	Ref.
Groceries				
Sugar, white, 33-80 ounce package	lb	0.39	7/01	11r
Sugar, white, all sizes	lb	0.42	7/01	11r
Tobacco products and smoking supplies purchases	yr	288	1999	30r
Tomatoes, field grown	lb	1.43	7/01	11r
Tuna, light, chunk	lb	1.77	7/01	11r
Turkey, frozen, whole	lb	1.05	7/01	11r
Goods and Services				
Hunting license	yr	16.00	4/01	34s
Health Care				
Cardiac catheterization, ave hospital/ physician charges		15260	1998	77s
Childbirth, Cesarean delivery		11587	1997	13r
Childbirth, vaginal delivery		6725	1997	13r
Drugs, expenditures on	yr	399	1999	30r
Health care purchases	yr	1971	1999	30r
Health insurance expenditures	yr	933	1999	30r
Hysterectomy, laproscopically-assisted, ave hospital/physician charges		16780	1998	76s
Hysterectomy, vaginal, ave hospital and physician charges		10990	1998	76s
Medicaid dispensing fee		5.40	1999	87s
Medical services expenditures	yr	547	1999	30r
Medical supplies, expenditures on	yr	91	1999	30r
Household Goods				
Floor coverings, expenditures on	yr	44	1999	30r
Furniture, expenditures on	yr	335	1999	30r
Household furnishings and equipment purchases	yr	1328	1999	30r
Household textiles, expenditures on	yr	89	1999	30r
Laundry and cleaning supplies, expenditures on	yr	113	1999	30r
Housing				
Home price, existing, ave		160100	10/00	90r
Home value, median		115000	2001	53s
Household operation expenditures	yr	553	1999	30r
Housekeeping supplies purchases	yr	473	1999	30r
Housing, expenditures on	yr	10303	1999	30r
Maintenance, repairs, insurance expenditures	yr	699	1999	30r
Monthly rental value of owned home	mos	505	1999	30r
Owned dwellings, expenditures own	yr	3465	1999	30r
Rent expenditures	yr	1641	1999	30r
Rental unit, 1 bedroom, with utilities	mos	367	4/01	41c
Rental unit, 2 bedroom, with utilities	mos	471	4/01	41c
Rental unit, 3 bedroom, with utilities	mos	612	4/01	41c
Rental unit, 4 bedroom, with utilities	mos	774	4/01	41c
Shelter, expenditures on	yr	5467	1999	30r
Insurance and Pensions				
Life and other personal insurance purchases	yr	414	1999	30r
Pensions and Social Security, expenditures on	yr	2635	1999	30r
Personal insurance and pensions, expenditures on	yr	3048	1999	30r
Legal Fees				
Divorce, filing fee		146.00- 193.00	4/01	35s
Driver's license fee	orig	18.50	1999	48s
Driver's license fee	renew	18.50	1999	48s
Personal Goods				
Personal care products and services purchases	yr	393	1999	30r
Personal Services				
Personal services, household, expenditures on	yr	258	1999	30r

Auburn-Opelica, AL - continued

Item	Per	Value	Date	Ref.
Pets				
Pets, toys, and playground equipment, expenditures on	yr	306	1999	30r
Taxes				
Federal income taxes paid	yr	2047	1999	30r
Personal taxes, expenditures on	yr	2554	1999	30r
Property taxes paid	yr	726	1999	30r
State and local income taxes paid	yr	363	1999	30r
Transportation				
Cars and trucks, new, expenditures on	yr	1648	1999	30r
Cars and trucks, used, expenditures on	yr	1651	1999	30r
Diesel at the pump	gal	1.19	10/99	73s
Gasoline and motor oil purchases	yr	1052	1999	30r
Gasoline before-tax price (cents)	gal	104.10	10/00	43s
Maintenance and repair expenditures	yr	621	1999	30r
Public transportation, expenditures on	yr	298	1999	30r
Transportation purchases	yr	6738	1999	30r
Vehicle expenses, miscellaneous, purchases	yr	2033	1999	30r
Vehicle insurance payments	yr	696	1999	30r
Vehicle purchases (net outlay)	yr	3354	1999	30r
Vehicle rental, lease expenditures	yr	352	1999	30r
Utilities				
Electrical bill, average	mos	83.42	9/00	9s
Electricity, expenditures on	yr	1115	1999	30r
Electricity cost, average	KWh	5.60	9/00	9s
Water and other public services, expenditures on	yr	298	1999	30r
Weddings				
Wedding (national average cost)		19936	2000	33r
Attendants' gifts		321	1998	33r
Bridal attendants' apparel (5 persons)		824	2000	33r
Bride's headpiece/veil		173	1998	33r
Bride's wedding dress		859	1998	33r
Clergy, religious facility fee		242	1998	33r
Engagement ring		3177	1998	33r
Flowers		789	1998	33r
Groom's formalwear rental		99	2000	33r
Limousine		410	1998	33r
Marriage license cost		25.00	4/01	35s
Men's formalwear (ushers, best man)		469	2000	33r
Mother of bride apparel		241	2000	33r
Music		866	1998	33r
Photography and videography		1368	1998	33r
Rehearsal dinner		728	1998	33r
Wedding invitations and announcements		341	1998	33r
Wedding reception		7968	2000	33r
Wedding rings (bride and groom)		1060	1998	33r

Augusta-Aiken, GA-SC

Item	Per	Value	Date	Ref.
Composite, ACCRA index		94.20	12/00	5c
Alcoholic Beverages				
Alcoholic beverage purchases	yr	253	1999	30r
Beer, Heineken, 12-oz, ex deposit	6	7.48	12/00	5c
J & B Scotch	750-ml	22.52	12/00	5c
Malt beverages, all types, all sizes, any origin	16 oz	0.96	7/01	11r
Wine, Livingston or Gallo, Chablis blanc	1.5 liter	5.66	12/00	5c
Appliances				
Appliance repair, service call, washing machine	min lab chg	40.00	12/00	5c
Major appliances, expenditures on	yr	172	1999	30r
Small appliances, housewares, expenditures on	yr	81	1999	30r
Banking and Money				
Mortgage interest and charges paid	yr	2039	1999	30r
Mortgage principal paid on owned property	yr	1026	1999	30r
Mortgage rate, incl. points and orig. fee, 30-yr. conv. fixed or ARM	mos	7.96	12/00	5c
Vehicle finance charges paid	yr	365	1999	30r

Values are in dollars or fractions of dollars. In the column headed *Ref*, references are shown to sources. Each reference is followed by a letter. These refer to the geographical level for which data were reported: s=State, r=Region, and c=City or metro. The abbreviation *ex* is used to mean *except* or *excluding*; *exp* stands for *expenditures*. For other abbreviations and further explanations, please see the Introduction.

Augusta-Aiken, GA-SC - continued

Item	Per	Value	Date	Ref.
Charity				
Cash contributions, expenditures	yr	1127	1999	30r
Child Care				
Child raising cost, total, age 0-2	yr	8540	1999	60r
Child raising cost, total, age 3-5	yr	8780	1999	60r
Child raising cost, total, age 6-8	yr	8820	1999	60r
Child raising cost, total, age 9-11	yr	8800	1999	60r
Child raising cost, total, age 12-14	yr	9510	1999	60r
Child raising cost, total, age 15-17	yr	9740	1999	60r
Child's child care and education, age 0-2	yr	1380	1999	60r
Child's child care and education, age 3-5	yr	1520	1999	60r
Child's child care and education, age 6-8	yr	990	1999	60r
Child's child care and education, age 9-11	yr	650	1999	60r
Child's child care and education, age 12-14	yr	490	1999	60r
Child's child care and education, age 15-17	yr	840	1999	60r
Child's clothing, age 0-2	yr	480	1999	60r
Child's clothing, age 3-5	yr	470	1999	60r
Child's clothing, age 6-8	yr	520	1999	60r
Child's clothing, age 9-11	yr	570	1999	60r
Child's clothing, age 12-14	yr	950	1999	60r
Child's clothing, age 15-17	yr	850	1999	60r
Child's food, age 0-2	yr	1000	1999	60r
Child's food, age 3-5	yr	1160	1999	60r
Child's food, age 6-8	yr	1490	1999	60r
Child's food, age 9-11	yr	1770	1999	60r
Child's food, age 12-14	yr	1770	1999	60r
Child's food, age 15-17	yr	1980	1999	60r
Child's health care, age 0-2	yr	620	1999	60r
Child's health care, age 3-5	yr	590	1999	60r
Child's health care, age 6-8	yr	680	1999	60r
Child's health care, age 9-11	yr	720	1999	60r
Child's health care, age 12-14	yr	730	1999	60r
Child's health care, age 15-17	yr	760	1999	60r
Child's housing, age 0-2	yr	3070	1999	60r
Child's housing, age 3-5	yr	3050	1999	60r
Child's housing, age 6-8	yr	3010	1999	60r
Child's housing, age 9-11	yr	2850	1999	60r
Child's housing, age 12-14	yr	3040	1999	60r
Child's housing, age 15-17	yr	2650	1999	60r
Child's personal care, reading, age 0-2	yr	910	1999	60r
Child's personal care, reading, age 3-5	yr	930	1999	60r
Child's personal care, reading, age 6-8	yr	960	1999	60r
Child's personal care, reading, age 9-11	yr	1000	1999	60r
Child's personal care, reading, age 12-14	yr	1170	1999	60r
Child's personal care, reading, age 15-17	yr	950	1999	60r
Clothing				
Apparel and services purchases	yr	1610	1999	30r
Boys' brief, cotton	3	3.59	12/00	5c
Boys, 2 to 15, expenditures on	yr	89	1999	30r
Children under 2, expenditures on	yr	79	1999	30r
Footwear, expenditures on	yr	283	1999	30r
Girls, 2 to 15, expenditures on	yr	103	1999	30r
Men and boys, expenditures on	yr	351	1999	30r
Men, 16 and over, expenditures on	yr	262	1999	30r
Shirt, man's dress shirt		31.60	12/00	5c
Slacks, man's "No Wrinkles" khaki		36.20	12/00	5c
Women, 16 and over, expenditures on	yr	538	1999	30r
Communications				
Cable modem installation, Charter		99.00-169.00	6/99	103s
Cable modem installation, Comcast		95.00	6/99	103s
Cable modem installation, Intermedia		149.95	6/99	103s
Cable modem installation, Media One		100.00	6/99	103s
Cable modem rate, cable subscriber, Charter	mos	49.95-79.95	6/99	103s
Cable modem rate, cable subscriber, Comcast	mos	39.95	6/99	103s
Cable modem rate, cable subscriber, Intermedia	mos	49.95	6/99	103s
Cable modem rate, cable subscriber, Media One	mos	34.95-39.95	6/99	103s

Augusta-Aiken, GA-SC - continued

Item	Per	Value	Date	Ref.
Communications - continued				
Cable modem rate, non-cable subscriber, Charter	mos	59.95-89.95	6/99	103s
Cable modem rate, non-cable subscriber, Comcast	mos	49.95	6/99	103s
Cable modem rate, non-cable subscriber, Intermedia	mos	54.95	6/99	103s
Cable modem rate, non-cable subscriber, Media One	mos	49.95	6/99	103s
Newspaper subscription, daily and Sunday delivery	mos	12.00	12/00	5c
Phone line, single, business, field visit	inst.	58.25	12/97	17s
Phone line, single, business, no field visit	inst.	58.25	12/97	17s
Phone line, single, residence, field visit	inst.	42.50	12/97	17s
Phone line, single, residence, no field visit	inst.	42.50	12/97	17s
Postage and stationery, expenditures on	yr	104	1999	30r
Postal rate, express mail, up to half-pound		12.45	7/01	108r
Postal rate, letter, first class, first ounce		0.34	7/01	108r
Postal rate, letter, two ounces		0.57	7/01	108r
Postal rate, post card		0.21	7/01	108r
Postal rate, priority mail, two pounds		3.95	7/01	108r
Postal rate, priority mail, up to one pound		3.50	7/01	108r
Telephone bill, family of three	mos	21.98	12/00	5c
Telephone services, expenditures on	yr	860	1999	30r
Education				
Board, 4-year private college/university	yr	2267	1996	38s
Board, 4-year public college/university	yr	1877	1996	38s
Education expenditures	yr	431	1999	30r
Room, 4-year private college/university	yr	2719	1996	38s
Room, 4-year public college/university	yr	1712	1996	38s
Total cost, 4-year private college/university	yr	15194	1996	38s
Total cost, 4-year public college/university	yr	5691	1996	38s
Tuition, 2-year public college/university, in state	yr	1062	1996	38s
Tuition, 4-year private college/university, in state	yr	10208	1996	38s
Tuition, 4-year public college/university	yr	2103	1996	38s
Energy and Fuels				
Electricity	500 KWhs	47.29	7/01	11r
Electricity	KWh	0.09	7/01	11r
Energy, combined forms, 2400 sq ft	mos	102.09	12/00	5c
Energy, exc. electricity, 2400 sq ft	mos	40.58	12/00	5c
Fuel oil #2	gal	1.43	7/01	11r
Fuel oil and other fuels, expenditures on	yr	45	1999	30r
Gas, regular unleaded, cash, self-service	gal	1.29	12/00	5c
Gasoline, all types	gal	1.60	7/01	11r
Gasoline, unleaded midgrade	gal	1.65	7/01	11r
Gasoline, unleaded premium	gal	1.74	7/01	11r
Natural gas, expenditures on	yr	164	1999	30r
Utility (piped) gas, therm		1.01	7/01	11r
Utility (piped) gas, 40 therms		44.29	7/01	11r
Utility (piped) gas, 100 therms		97.44	7/01	11r
Entertainment				
Bowling, Saturday evening rate	line	3.16	12/00	5c
Entertainment purchases	yr	1574	1999	30r
Fees and admissions paid	yr	371	1999	30r
Monopoly game, Parker Brothers', No. 9	game	10.97	12/00	5c
Movie, first-run, Saturday, evening	adm.	6.25	12/00	5c
Reading purchases	yr	121	1999	30r
Television, radios, sound equipment, expenditures on	yr	561	1999	30r
Tennis balls, yellow, Wilson or Penn, 3	can	1.98	12/00	5c
Funerals				
Total cost of funeral		5922.53	1/99	78r
Acknowledgement cards		63.43	1/99	78r
Casket		2258.77	1/99	78r
Cosmetology, hair, other preparation		127.09	1/99	78r
Embalming		393.49	1/99	78r
Funeral at funeral home		367.50	1/99	78r
Hearse (local)		169.66	1/99	78r

Values are in dollars or fractions of dollars. In the column headed *Ref*, references are shown to sources. Each reference is followed by a letter. These refer to the geographical level for which data were reported: s=State, r=Region, and c=City or metro. The abbreviation *ex* is used to mean *except* or *excluding*; *exp* stands for *expenditures*. For other abbreviations and further explanations, please see the Introduction.

Augusta-Aiken, GA-SC - continued

Item	Per	Value	Date	Ref.
Funerals				
Professional service charges		1211.32	1/99	78r
Service car/van		80.69	1/99	78r
Transfer of remains to funeral home		144.25	1/99	78r
Vault		803.50	1/99	78r
Visitation/viewing		302.83	1/99	78r
Groceries				
Groceries, ACCRA Index		104.50	12/00	5c
American processed cheese	lb	3.50	7/01	11r
Antibiotic ointment, Polysporin	0.5 oz	4.43	12/00	5c
Baby food, strained vegetables or fruit, lowest price	4-4.5 oz	0.46	12/00	5c
Bakery products, expenditures on	yr	261	1999	30r
Bananas	lb	0.47	7/01	11r
Bananas	lb	0.47	7/01	5c
Beans, dried, any type, all sizes	lb	0.63	7/01	11r
Beef for stew, boneless	lb	2.86	7/01	11r
Beef or hamburger, ground	lb	1.19	12/00	5c
Beef, expenditures on	yr	210	1999	30r
Bologna, all beef or mixed	lb	2.29	7/01	11r
Bread, French	lb	1.66	7/01	11r
Bread, white	loaf	1.09	12/00	5c
Bread, white, pan	lb	0.87	7/01	11r
Bread, whole wheat, pan	lb	1.38	7/01	11r
Broccoli	lb	1.04	7/01	11r
Butter, salted, grade AA, stick	lb	2.26	7/01	11r
Butter, yoghurt, cheese, etc, expenditures on	yr	170	1999	30r
Cabbage	lb	0.42	7/01	11r
Cereals and cereal products, expenditures on	yr	140	1999	30r
Cheddar cheese, natural	lb	3.75	7/01	11r
Cheese, Kraft grated Parmesan	8 oz	3.53	12/00	5c
Chicken breast, bone-in	lb	1.85	7/01	11r
Chicken legs, bone-in	lb	1.34	7/01	11r
Chicken, fresh, whole	lb	1.05	7/01	11r
Chicken, whole fryer	lb	0.97	12/00	5c
Chops, boneless,	lb	4.13	7/01	11r
Chuck roast, graded and ungraded, excl U.S. prime and choice	lb	2.35	7/01	11r
Chuck roast, U.S. choice, boneless	lb	2.67	7/01	11r
Cigarettes, Winston, Kings	carton	27.70	12/00	5c
Coffee, 100%, ground roast, all sizes	lb	2.88	7/01	11r
Coffee, instant, plain, regular, all sizes	16 oz	9.25	7/01	11r
Coffee, vacuum-packed	13 oz	2.63	12/00	5c
Cola, non diet,	2 liter	1.11	7/01	11r
Corn Flakes, Kellogg's or Post Toasties	18 oz	2.87	12/00	5c
Corn, frozen, whole kernel, lowest price	16 oz	1.35	12/00	5c
Crackers, soda, salted	lb	1.70	7/01	11r
Dairy product purchases	yr	282	1999	30r
Eggs, expenditures on	yr	32	1999	30r
Eggs, Grade A or AA	dozen	1.07	12/00	5c
Fats and oils, expenditures on	yr	79	1999	30r
Fish and seafood, expenditures on	yr	99	1999	30r
Flour, white, all purpose	lb	0.32	7/01	11r
Food (excl fruit and vegetables), eaten at home, purchases	yr	815	1999	30r
Food cooked on trips, expenditures on	yr	36	1999	30r
Food purchases	yr	4533	1999	30r
Food purchases, eaten away from home	yr	1873	1999	30r
Food purchases, food eaten at home	yr	2660	1999	30r
Fresh fruits, expenditures on	yr	128	1999	30r
Fresh milk and cream, expenditures on	yr	112	1999	30r
Fresh vegetables, expenditures on	yr	131	1999	30r
Fruit and vegetable purchases	yr	438	1999	30r
Grapefruit	lb	0.59	7/01	11r
Grapes, Thompson, seedless	lb	2.12	7/01	11r
Ground beef, 100% beef	lb	1.76	7/01	11r
Ground beef, lean and extra lean	lb	2.60	7/01	11r
Ground chuck, 100% beef	lb	2.08	7/01	11r
Ham, boneless, excl canned	lb	2.71	7/01	11r
Ham, rump or shank half, bone-in, smoked	lb	2.19	7/01	11r
Ice cream, prepackaged, bulk, regular	1/2 gal	3.93	7/01	11r
Lemons	lb	1.32	7/01	11r

Augusta-Aiken, GA-SC - continued

Item	Per	Value	Date	Ref.
Groceries - continued				
Lettuce, iceberg	lb	0.76	7/01	11r
Lettuce, iceberg	head	1.05	12/00	5c
Margarine, Blue Bonnet or Parkay, stick	lb	0.61	12/00	5c
Milk, fresh, low fat,	gal	2.75	7/01	11r
Milk, fresh, whole, fortified	gal	2.97	7/01	11r
Milk, whole	1/2 gal	2.03	12/00	5c
Nonalcoholic beverages, expenditures on	yr	228	1999	30r
Orange juice, frozen concentrate	16 oz	1.95	7/01	11r
Orange juice, Minute Maid frozen	12 oz	1.51	12/00	5c
Oranges, Navel	lb	0.73	7/01	11r
Oranges, Valencia	lb	0.55	7/01	11r
Peaches, halves or slices, Hunt's, Del Monte, or Libby's	29 oz	1.59	12/00	5c
Peanut butter, creamy, all sizes	lb	1.83	7/01	11r
Pears, Anjou	lb	0.98	7/01	11r
Peas, green, Del Monte or Green Giant	15 oz	0.74	12/00	5c
Pork chops, center cut, bone-in	lb	3.33	7/01	11r
Pork sausage, fresh, loose	lb	2.59	7/01	11r
Pork shoulder picnic, bone-in, smoked	lb	1.12	7/01	11r
Pork, expenditures on	yr	162	1999	30r
Potato chips	16 oz	3.59	7/01	11r
Potatoes, frozen, french fried	lb	1.00	7/01	11r
Potatoes, white or red	10 lb	3.59	12/00	5c
Potatoes, white, all types	lb	0.44	7/01	11r
Poultry, expenditures on	yr	137	1999	30r
Processed fruits, expenditures on	yr	97	1999	30r
Processed vegetables, expenditures on	yr	82	1999	30r
Rice, white, long grain, uncooked	lb	0.51	7/01	11r
Round roast, graded and ungraded, excl U.S. prime and choice	lb	2.96	7/01	11r
Round steak, graded and ungraded, excl U.S. prime and choice	lb	3.11	7/01	11r
Sausage, Jimmy Dean/Owens pork	lb	3.31	12/00	5c
Shortening, vegetable, Crisco	3 lb	2.93	12/00	5c
Sirloin steak, graded and ungraded, excl U.S. prime and choice	lb	4.23	7/01	11r
Soft drink, Coca Cola, ex deposit	2 liter	1.15	12/00	5c
Spaghetti and macaroni	lb	0.78	7/01	11r
Steak, round, U.S. choice, boneless	lb	3.56	7/01	11r
Steak, sirloin, U.S. choice, boneless	lb	5.65	7/01	11r
Steak, T-bone	lb	7.63	12/00	5c
Strawberries, dry pint	12 oz	1.50	7/01	11r
Sugar and other sweets, expenditures on	yr	99	1999	30r
Sugar, cane or beet	4 lbs	1.63	12/00	5c
Sugar, white, 33-80 ounce package	lb	0.39	7/01	11r
Sugar, white, all sizes	lb	0.42	7/01	11r
Tobacco products and smoking supplies purchases	yr	288	1999	30r
Tomatoes, field grown	lb	1.43	7/01	11r
Tomatoes, Hunt's or Del Monte	14.5 oz	0.85	12/00	5c
Tuna, chunk, light	6 oz	0.85	12/00	5c
Tuna, light, chunk	lb	1.77	7/01	11r
Turkey, frozen, whole	lb	1.05	7/01	11r
Goods and Services				
Miscellaneous goods and services, ACCRA Index		98.50	12/00	5c
B&B Japanese maple (acer japonicum)	gal	49.98-129.00	4/00	93r
Boxwood (buxus)	2 gal	12.99-16.99	4/00	93r
Daylily (hemerocallis)	gal	4.99-8.99	4/00	93r
Flat of annuals		11.00-13.92	4/00	93r
Fountain grass (pennisetum)	gal	5.98-7.98	4/00	93r
Hanging basket (10 in)		7.99-14.98	4/00	93r
Hardy geranium (geranium)	gal	5.98-8.00	4/00	93r
Hosta (hosta)	gal	4.99-10.98	4/00	93r

Values are in dollars or fractions of dollars. In the column headed *Ref*, references are shown to sources. Each reference is followed by a letter. These refer to the geographical level for which data were reported: s=State, r=Region, and c=City or metro. The abbreviation *ex* is used to mean *except* or *excluding*; *exp* stands for expenditures. For other abbreviations and further explanations, please see the Introduction.

Augusta-Aiken, GA-SC - continued

Item	Per	Value	Date	Ref.
Goods and Services				
Lilac (syrubga vulgaris)	2 gal	12.99-21.99	4/00	93r
Rhododendron (rhododendron)	2 gal	14.99-24.99	4/00	93r
Sage (salvia)	gal	5.98-6.99	4/00	93r
Wintercreeper euonymus (euonymus fortunei)	2 gal	7.99-89.99	4/00	93r
Hunting license	yr	10.00	4/01	34s
Health Care				
Health care, ACCRA Index		98.40	12/00	5c
Cardiac catheterization, ave hospital/ physician charges		14190	1998	77s
Childbirth, Cesarean delivery		11587	1997	13r
Childbirth, vaginal delivery		6725	1997	13r
Dentist's fee, adult teeth cleaning and periodic oral exam	visit	66.60	12/00	5c
Doctor's fee, routine exam, established patient	visit	64.87	12/00	5c
Drugs, expenditures on	yr	399	1999	30r
Health care purchases	yr	1971	1999	30r
Health insurance expenditures	yr	933	1999	30r
Hospital care, private room	day	391.80	12/00	5c
Hysterectomy, laproscopically-assisted, ave hospital/physician charges		16760	1998	76s
Hysterectomy, vaginal ave hospital and physician charges		11160	1998	76s
Medicaid dispensing fee		4.63	1999	87s
Medical services expenditures	yr	547	1999	30r
Medical supplies, expenditures on	yr	91	1999	30r
Plastic surgery, breast augmentation		2870	2000	7r
Plastic surgery, breast lift		3649	2000	7r
Plastic surgery, facelift		5008	2000	7r
Plastic surgery, hair transplantation		3425	2000	7r
Plastic surgery, lip augmentation		1227	2000	7r
Plastic surgery, lower body lift		4793	2000	7r
Plastic surgery, thigh lift		3862	2000	7r
Household Goods				
Dishwashing powder, Cascade	50 oz	2.94	12/00	5c
Floor coverings, expenditures on	yr	44	1999	30r
Furniture, expenditures on	yr	335	1999	30r
Household furnishings and equipment purchases	yr	1328	1999	30r
Household textiles, expenditures on	yr	89	1999	30r
Laundry and cleaning supplies, expenditures on	yr	113	1999	30r
Tissues, facial, Kleenex brand	175	1.37	12/00	5c
Housing				
Housing, ACCRA Index		82.50	12/00	5c
Home price, existing, ave		160100	10/00	90r
Home value, median		131000	2001	53s
House, 2400 sq ft, 8000 sq ft lot, new, urban, utilities	total	168570	12/00	5c
House payment, principal and interest, 25% down payment	mos	924	12/00	5c
Household operation expenditures	yr	553	1999	30r
Housekeeping supplies purchases	yr	473	1999	30r
Housing, expenditures on	yr	10303	1999	30r
Maintenance, repairs, insurance expenditures	yr	699	1999	30r
Monthly rental value of owned home	mos	505	1999	30r
Owned dwellings, expenditures own	yr	3465	1999	30r
Rent expenditures	yr	1641	1999	30r
Rent, apartment, 2 br, 1 1/2-2 baths, unfurn, 950 sq ft, water	mos	583	12/00	5c
Rental unit, 1 bedroom, with utilities	mos	465	4/01	41c
Rental unit, 2 bedroom, with utilities	mos	548	4/01	41c
Rental unit, 3 bedroom, with utilities	mos	744	4/01	41c
Rental unit, 4 bedroom, with utilities	mos	880	4/01	41c
Shelter, expenditures on	yr	5467	1999	30r

Augusta-Aiken, GA-SC - continued

Item	Per	Value	Date	Ref.
Insurance and Pensions				
Life and other personal insurance purchases	yr	414	1999	30r
Pensions and Social Security, expenditures on	yr	2635	1999	30r
Personal insurance and pensions, expenditures on	yr	3048	1999	30r
Legal Fees				
Divorce, filing fee		65.00-85.00	4/01	35s
Driver's license fee	orig	16.50	1999	48s
Driver's license fee	renew	15.00	1999	48s
Personal Goods				
Personal care products and services purchases	yr	393	1999	30r
Shampoo, Alberto VO5	15 oz	1.02	12/00	5c
Toothpaste, Crest or Colgate	6-7 oz	2.12	12/00	5c
Personal Services				
Dry cleaning, man's 2-pc suit		6.08	12/00	5c
Man's haircut, barbershop, no styling		9.86	12/00	5c
Personal services, household, expenditures on	yr	258	1999	30r
Woman's shampoo, trim, blow-dry, no style-change		28.29	12/00	5c
Pets				
Pets, toys, and playground equipment, expenditures on	yr	306	1999	30r
Restaurant Food				
Chicken, fried, thigh and drumstick, KFC/ Church's		2.46	12/00	5c
Hamburger with cheese, McDonald's	1/4 lb	1.99	12/00	5c
Pizza, Pizza Hut or Pizza Inn	11-12 in	9.49	12/00	5c
Taxes				
Federal income taxes paid	yr	2047	1999	30r
Personal taxes, expenditures on	yr	2554	1999	30r
Property taxes paid	yr	726	1999	30r
State and local income taxes paid	yr	363	1999	30r
Transportation				
Transportation, ACCRA Index		95.50	12/00	5c
Cars and trucks, new, expenditures on	yr	1648	1999	30r
Cars and trucks, used, expenditures on	yr	1651	1999	30r
Diesel at the pump	gal	1.10	10/99	73s
Gasoline and motor oil purchases	yr	1052	1999	30r
Gasoline before-tax price (cents)	gal	102.00	10/00	43s
Maintenance and repair expenditures	yr	621	1999	30r
Public transportation, expenditures on	yr	298	1999	30r
Tire balance, computer or spin balance, front	wheel	8.41	12/00	5c
Transportation purchases	yr	6738	1999	30r
Vehicle expenses, miscellaneous, purchases	yr	2033	1999	30r
Vehicle insurance payments	yr	696	1999	30r
Vehicle purchases (net outlay)	yr	3354	1999	30r
Vehicle rental, lease expenditures	yr	352	1999	30r
Utilities				
Utilities, ACCRA Index		92.50	12/00	5c
Electrical bill, average	mos	79.83	9/00	9s
Electricity, expenditures on	yr	1115	1999	30r
Electricity and other, mixed, 2400 sq ft, new home	mos	61.51	12/00	5c
Electricity cost, average	KWh	6.10	9/00	9s
Water and other public services, expenditures on	yr	298	1999	30r
Weddings				
Wedding (national average cost)		19936	2000	33r
Wedding (regional average total cost)		16293	1997	110r
Attendants' gifts		321	1998	33r
Bridal attendants' apparel (5 persons)		824	2000	33r
Bride's headpiece/veil		173	1998	33r
Bride's wedding dress		859	1998	33r
Clergy, religious facility fee		242	1998	33r

Values are in dollars or fractions of dollars. In the column headed *Ref*, references are shown by sources. Each reference is followed by a letter. These refer to the geographical level for which data were reported: s=State, r=Region, and c=City or metro. The abbreviation *ex* is used to mean *except* or *excluding*; *exp* stands for expenditures. For other abbreviations and further explanations, please see the Introduction.

Augusta-Aiken, GA-SC - continued

Item	Per	Value	Date	Ref.
Weddings				
Engagement ring		3177	1998	33r
Flowers		789	1998	33r
Groom's formalwear rental		99	2000	33r
Limousine		410	1998	33r
Marriage license cost		40.00	4/01	35s
Men's formalwear (ushers, best man)		469	2000	33r
Mother of bride apparel		241	2000	33r
Music		866	1998	33r
Photography and videography		1368	1998	33r
Rehearsal dinner		728	1998	33r
Wedding invitations and announcements		341	1998	33r
Wedding reception		7968	2000	33r
Wedding rings (bride and groom)		1060	1998	33r

Austin-San Marcos, TX

Item	Per	Value	Date	Ref.
Alcoholic Beverages				
Alcoholic beverage purchases	yr	253	1999	30r
Malt beverages, all types, all sizes, any origin	16 oz	0.96	7/01	11r
Appliances				
Major appliances, expenditures on	yr	172	1999	30r
Small appliances, housewares, expenditures on	yr	81	1999	30r
Banking and Money				
Mortgage interest and charges paid	yr	2039	1999	30r
Mortgage principal paid on owned property	yr	1026	1999	30r
Vehicle finance charges paid	yr	365	1999	30r
Charity				
Cash contributions, expenditures	yr	1127	1999	30r
Child Care				
Child raising cost, total, age 0-2	yr	8540	1999	60r
Child raising cost, total, age 3-5	yr	8780	1999	60r
Child raising cost, total, age 6-8	yr	8820	1999	60r
Child raising cost, total, age 9-11	yr	8800	1999	60r
Child raising cost, total, age 12-14	yr	9510	1999	60r
Child raising cost, total, age 15-17	yr	9740	1999	60r
Child's child care and education, age 0-2	yr	1380	1999	60r
Child's child care and education, age 3-5	yr	1520	1999	60r
Child's child care and education, age 6-8	yr	990	1999	60r
Child's child care and education, age 9-11	yr	650	1999	60r
Child's child care and education, age 12-14	yr	490	1999	60r
Child's child care and education, age 15-17	yr	840	1999	60r
Child's clothing, age 0-2	yr	480	1999	60r
Child's clothing, age 3-5	yr	470	1999	60r
Child's clothing, age 6-8	yr	520	1999	60r
Child's clothing, age 9-11	yr	570	1999	60r
Child's clothing, age 12-14	yr	950	1999	60r
Child's clothing, age 15-17	yr	850	1999	60r
Child's food, age 0-2	yr	1000	1999	60r
Child's food, age 3-5	yr	1160	1999	60r
Child's food, age 6-8	yr	1490	1999	60r
Child's food, age 9-11	yr	1770	1999	60r
Child's food, age 12-14	yr	1770	1999	60r
Child's food, age 15-17	yr	1980	1999	60r
Child's health care, age 0-2	yr	620	1999	60r
Child's health care, age 3-5	yr	590	1999	60r
Child's health care, age 6-8	yr	680	1999	60r
Child's health care, age 9-11	yr	720	1999	60r
Child's health care, age 12-14	yr	730	1999	60r
Child's health care, age 15-17	yr	760	1999	60r
Child's housing, age 0-2	yr	3070	1999	60r
Child's housing, age 3-5	yr	3050	1999	60r
Child's housing, age 6-8	yr	3010	1999	60r
Child's housing, age 9-11	yr	2850	1999	60r
Child's housing, age 12-14	yr	3040	1999	60r
Child's housing, age 15-17	yr	2650	1999	60r
Child's personal care, reading, age 0-2	yr	910	1999	60r
Child's personal care, reading, age 3-5	yr	930	1999	60r
Child's personal care, reading, age 6-8	yr	960	1999	60r

Austin-San Marcos, TX - continued

Item	Per	Value	Date	Ref.
Child Care - continued				
Child's personal care, reading, age 9-11	yr	1000	1999	60r
Child's personal care, reading, age 12-14	yr	1170	1999	60r
Child's personal care, reading, age 15-17	yr	950	1999	60r
Clothing				
Apparel and services purchases	yr	1610	1999	30r
Boys, 2 to 15, expenditures on	yr	89	1999	30r
Children under 2, expenditures on	yr	79	1999	30r
Footwear, expenditures on	yr	283	1999	30r
Girls, 2 to 15, expenditures on	yr	103	1999	30r
Men and boys, expenditures on	yr	351	1999	30r
Men, 16 and over, expenditures on	yr	262	1999	30r
Women, 16 and over, expenditures on	yr	538	1999	30r
Communications				
Cable modem installation, AT&T-BIS		150.00	6/99	103s
Cable modem installation, Marcus		499.00	6/99	103s
Cable modem installation, Time Warner		75.00-225.00	6/99	103s
Cable modem rate, cable subscriber, AT&T-BIS	mos	39.95	6/99	103s
Cable modem rate, cable subscriber, Marcus	mos	14.95-49.95	6/99	103s
Cable modem rate, cable subscriber, Time Warner	mos	39.95-49.95	6/99	103s
Cable modem rate, non-cable subscriber, Marcus	mos	60.95	6/99	103s
Cable modem rate, non-cable subscriber, Time Warner	mos	39.95-54.95	6/99	103s
Phone line, single, business, field visit	inst.	71.90	12/97	17s
Phone line, single, business, no field visit	inst.	57.30	12/97	17s
Phone line, single, residence, field visit	inst.	52.95	12/97	17s
Phone line, single, residence, no field visit	inst.	38.35	12/97	17s
Postage and stationery, expenditures on	yr	104	1999	30r
Postal rate, express mail, up to half-pound		12.45	7/01	108r
Postal rate, letter, first class, first ounce		0.34	7/01	108r
Postal rate, letter, two ounces		0.57	7/01	108r
Postal rate, post card		0.21	7/01	108r
Postal rate, priority mail, two pounds		3.95	7/01	108r
Postal rate, priority mail, up to one pound		3.50	7/01	108r
Telephone services, expenditures on	yr	860	1999	30r
Education				
Board, 4-year private college/university	yr	2198	1996	38s
Board, 4-year public college/university	yr	1759	1996	38s
Education expenditures	yr	431	1999	30r
Room, 4-year private college/university	yr	2000	1996	38s
Room, 4-year public college/university	yr	1885	1996	38s
Total cost, 4-year private college/university	yr	13156	1996	38s
Total cost, 4-year public college/university	yr	5464	1996	38s
Tuition, 2-year public college/university, in state	yr	771	1996	38s
Tuition, 4-year private college/university, in state	yr	8959	1996	38s
Tuition, 4-year public college/university	yr	1820	1996	38s
Energy and Fuels				
Electricity	KWh	0.09	7/01	11r
Electricity	500 KWhs	47.29	7/01	11r
Fuel oil #2	gal	1.43	7/01	11r
Fuel oil and other fuels, expenditures on	yr	45	1999	30r
Gas, natural, commercial rate	1000 cf	6.94	11/00	88s
Gasoline, all types	gal	1.60	7/01	11r
Gasoline, unleaded midgrade	gal	1.65	7/01	11r
Gasoline, unleaded premium	gal	1.74	7/01	11r
Natural gas, expenditures on	yr	164	1999	30r
Utility (piped) gas, therm		1.01	7/01	11r
Utility (piped) gas, 40 therms		44.29	7/01	11r
Utility (piped) gas, 100 therms		97.44	7/01	11r
Entertainment				
Entertainment purchases	yr	1574	1999	30r
Fees and admissions paid	yr	371	1999	30r

Values are in dollars or fractions of dollars. In the column headed *Ref*, references are shown to sources. Each reference is followed by a letter. These refer to the geographical level for which data were reported: s=State, r=Region, and c=City or metro. The abbreviation *ex* is used to mean *except* or *excluding*; *exp* stands for *expenditures*. For other abbreviations and further explanations, please see the Introduction.

Austin-San Marcos, TX - continued

Item	Per	Value	Date	Ref.
Entertainment				
Reading purchases	yr	121	1999	30r
Television, radios, sound equipment, expenditures on	yr	561	1999	30r
Funerals				
Total cost of funeral		5842.28	1/99	78r
Acknowledgement cards		28.35	1/99	78r
Casket		2494.29	1/99	78r
Cosmetology, hair, other preparation		109.22	1/99	78r
Embalming		361.42	1/99	78r
Funeral at funeral home		349.20	1/99	78r
Hearse (local)		161.91	1/99	78r
Professional service charges		1116.50	1/99	78r
Service car/van		65.56	1/99	78r
Transfer of remains to funeral home		143.56	1/99	78r
Vault		785.25	1/99	78r
Visitation/viewing		227.02	1/99	78r
Groceries				
American processed cheese	lb	3.50	7/01	11r
Bakery products, expenditures on	yr	261	1999	30r
Bananas	lb	0.47	7/01	11r
Beans, dried, any type, all sizes	lb	0.63	7/01	11r
Beef for stew, boneless	lb	2.86	7/01	11r
Beef, expenditures on	yr	210	1999	30r
Bologna, all beef or mixed	lb	2.29	7/01	11r
Bread, French	lb	1.66	7/01	11r
Bread, white, pan	lb	0.87	7/01	11r
Bread, whole wheat, pan	lb	1.38	7/01	11r
Broccoli	lb	1.04	7/01	11r
Butter, salted, grade AA, stick	lb	2.26	7/01	11r
Butter, yoghurt, cheese, etc, expenditures on	yr	170	1999	30r
Cabbage	lb	0.42	7/01	11r
Cereals and cereal products, expenditures on	yr	140	1999	30r
Cheddar cheese, natural	lb	3.75	7/01	11r
Chicken breast, bone-in	lb	1.85	7/01	11r
Chicken legs, bone-in	lb	1.34	7/01	11r
Chicken, fresh, whole	lb	1.05	7/01	11r
Chops, boneless,	lb	4.13	7/01	11r
Chuck roast, graded and ungraded, excl U.S. prime and choice	lb	2.35	7/01	11r
Chuck roast, U.S. choice, boneless	lb	2.67	7/01	11r
Coffee, 100%, ground roast, all sizes	lb	2.88	7/01	11r
Coffee, instant, plain, regular, all sizes	16 oz	9.25	7/01	11r
Cola, non diet,	2 liter	1.11	7/01	11r
Crackers, soda, salted	lb	1.70	7/01	11r
Dairy product purchases	yr	282	1999	30r
Eggs, expenditures on	yr	32	1999	30r
Fats and oils, expenditures on	yr	79	1999	30r
Fish and seafood, expenditures on	yr	99	1999	30r
Flour, white, all purpose	lb	0.32	7/01	11r
Food (excl fruit and vegetables), eaten at home, purchases	yr	815	1999	30r
Food cooked on trips, expenditures on	yr	36	1999	30r
Food purchases	yr	4533	1999	30r
Food purchases, eaten away from home	yr	1873	1999	30r
Food purchases, food eaten at home	yr	2660	1999	30r
Fresh fruits, expenditures on	yr	128	1999	30r
Fresh milk and cream, expenditures on	yr	112	1999	30r
Fresh vegetables, expenditures on	yr	131	1999	30r
Fruit and vegetable purchases	yr	438	1999	30r
Grapefruit	lb	0.59	7/01	11r
Grapes, Thompson, seedless	lb	2.12	7/01	11r
Ground beef, 100% beef	lb	1.76	7/01	11r
Ground beef, lean and extra lean	lb	2.60	7/01	11r
Ground chuck, 100% beef	lb	2.08	7/01	11r
Ham, boneless, excl canned	lb	2.71	7/01	11r
Ham, rump or shank half, bone-in, smoked	lb	2.19	7/01	11r
Ice cream, prepackaged, bulk, regular	1/2 gal	3.93	7/01	11r
Lemons	lb	1.32	7/01	11r
Lettuce, iceberg	lb	0.76	7/01	11r
Milk, fresh, low fat,	gal	2.75	7/01	11r

Austin-San Marcos, TX - continued

Item	Per	Value	Date	Ref.
Groceries - continued				
Milk, fresh, whole, fortified	gal	2.97	7/01	11r
Nonalcoholic beverages, expenditures on	yr	228	1999	30r
Orange juice, frozen concentrate	16 oz	1.95	7/01	11r
Oranges, Navel	lb	0.73	7/01	11r
Oranges, Valencia	lb	0.55	7/01	11r
Peanut butter, creamy, all sizes	lb	1.83	7/01	11r
Pears, Anjou	lb	0.98	7/01	11r
Pork chops, center cut, bone-in	lb	3.33	7/01	11r
Pork sausage, fresh, loose	lb	2.59	7/01	11r
Pork shoulder picnic, bone-in, smoked	lb	1.12	7/01	11r
Pork, expenditures on	yr	162	1999	30r
Potato chips	16 oz	3.59	7/01	11r
Potatoes, frozen, french fried	lb	1.00	7/01	11r
Potatoes, white, all types	lb	0.44	7/01	11r
Poultry, expenditures on	yr	137	1999	30r
Processed fruits, expenditures on	yr	97	1999	30r
Processed vegetables, expenditures on	yr	82	1999	30r
Rice, white, long grain, uncooked	lb	0.51	7/01	11r
Round roast, graded and ungraded, excl U.S. prime and choice	lb	2.96	7/01	11r
Round steak, graded and ungraded, excl U.S. prime and choice	lb	3.11	7/01	11r
Sirloin steak, graded and ungraded, excl U.S. prime and choice	lb	4.23	7/01	11r
Spaghetti and macaroni	lb	0.78	7/01	11r
Steak, round, U.S. choice, boneless	lb	3.56	7/01	11r
Steak, sirloin, U.S. choice, boneless	lb	5.65	7/01	11r
Strawberries, dry pint	12 oz	1.50	7/01	11r
Sugar and other sweets, expenditures on	yr	99	1999	30r
Sugar, white, 33-80 ounce package	lb	0.39	7/01	11r
Sugar, white, all sizes	lb	0.42	7/01	11r
Tobacco products and smoking supplies purchases	yr	288	1999	30r
Tomatoes, field grown	lb	1.43	7/01	11r
Tuna, light, chunk	lb	1.77	7/01	11r
Turkey, frozen, whole	lb	1.05	7/01	11r
Goods and Services				
B&B Japanese maple (acer japonicum)	gal	79.98-99.00	4/00	93r
Boxwood (buxus)	2 gal	12.98-18.99	4/00	93r
Christmas tree, noble fir		40-60	2000	65s
Daylilly (hemerocallis)	gal	7.96-11.00	4/00	93r
Flat of annuals		13.99-27.99	4/00	93r
Fountain grass (pennisetum)	gal	6.96-9.00	4/00	93r
Hanging basket (10 in)		9.99-24.99	4/00	93r
Hardy geranium (geranium)	gal	5.96-8.00	4/00	93r
Hosta (hosta)	gal	8.96-12.99	4/00	93r
Lilac (syrubga vulgaris)	2 gal	13.00-19.99	4/00	93r
Rhododendron (rhododendron)	2 gal	12.98-29.99	4/00	93r
Sage (salvia)	gal	5.96-8.00	4/00	93r
Wintercreeper euonymus (euonymus fortunei)	2 gal	13.00-18.99	4/00	93r
Hunting license	yr	19.00	4/01	34s
Health Care				
Cardiac catheterization, ave hospital/ physician charges		20140	1998	77s
Childbirth, Cesarean delivery		11587	1997	13r
Childbirth, vaginal delivery		6725	1997	13r
Drugs, expenditures on	yr	399	1999	30r
Health care purchases	yr	1971	1999	30r
Health insurance expenditures	yr	933	1999	30r

Values are in dollars or fractions of dollars. In the column headed *Ref*, references are shown to sources. Each reference is followed by a letter. These refer to the geographical level for which data were reported: s=State, r=Region, and c=City or metro. The abbreviation *ex* is used to mean *except* or *excluding*; *exp* stands for expenditures. For other abbreviations and further explanations, please see the Introduction.

Austin-San Marcos, TX - continued

Item	Per	Value	Date	Ref.
Health Care				
Hysterectomy, laproscopically-assisted, ave hospital/physician charges		15700	1998	76s
Hysterectomy, vaginal, ave hospital and physician charges		12180	1998	76s
Medicaid dispensing fee		5.27	1999	87s
Medical services expenditures	yr	547	1999	30r
Medical supplies, expenditures on	yr	91	1999	30r
Household Goods				
Floor coverings, expenditures on	yr	44	1999	30r
Furniture, expenditures on	yr	335	1999	30r
Household furnishings and equipment purchases	yr	1328	1999	30r
Household textiles, expenditures on	yr	89	1999	30r
Laundry and cleaning supplies, expenditures on	yr	113	1999	30r
Housing				
Home price, existing, ave		160100	10/00	90r
Home value, median		112000	2001	53s
Household operation expenditures	yr	553	1999	30r
Housekeeping supplies purchases	yr	473	1999	30r
Housing, expenditures on	yr	10303	1999	30r
Maintenance, repairs, insurance expenditures	yr	699	1999	30r
Monthly rental value of owned home	mos	505	1999	30r
Owned dwellings, expenditures own	yr	3465	1999	30r
Rent expenditures	yr	1641	1999	30r
Rental unit, 1 bedroom, with utilities	mos	615	4/01	41c
Rental unit, 2 bedroom, with utilities	mos	819	4/01	41c
Rental unit, 3 bedroom, with utilities	mos	1137	4/01	41c
Rental unit, 4 bedroom, with utilities	mos	1344	4/01	41c
Shelter, expenditures on	yr	5467	1999	30r
Insurance and Pensions				
Life and other personal insurance purchases	yr	414	1999	30r
Pensions and Social Security, expenditures on	yr	2635	1999	30r
Personal insurance and pensions, expenditures on	yr	3048	1999	30r
Legal Fees				
Divorce, filing fee		150.00-200.00	4/01	35s
Driver's license fee	renew	20.00	1999	48s
Driver's license fee	orig	24.00	1999	48s
Fishing license	yr	19.00	4/01	34s
Personal Goods				
Personal care products and services purchases	yr	393	1999	30r
Personal Services				
Personal services, household, expenditures on	yr	258	1999	30r
Pets				
Pets, toys, and playground equipment, expenditures on	yr	306	1999	30r
Taxes				
Federal income taxes paid	yr	2047	1999	30r
Personal taxes, expenditures on	yr	2554	1999	30r
Property taxes paid	yr	726	1999	30r
State and local income taxes paid	yr	363	1999	30r
Transportation				
Cars and trucks, new, expenditures on	yr	1648	1999	30r
Cars and trucks, used, expenditures on	yr	1651	1999	30r
Diesel at the pump	gal	1.18	10/99	73s
Gasoline and motor oil purchases	yr	1052	1999	30r
Gasoline before-tax price (cents)	gal	101.30	10/00	43s
Maintenance and repair expenditures	yr	621	1999	30r
Public transportation, expenditures on	yr	298	1999	30r
Transportation purchases	yr	6738	1999	30r
Vehicle expenses, miscellaneous, purchases	yr	2033	1999	30r

Austin-San Marcos, TX - continued

Item	Per	Value	Date	Ref.
Transportation - continued				
Vehicle insurance payments	yr	696	1999	30r
Vehicle purchases (net outlay)	yr	3354	1999	30r
Vehicle rental, lease expenditures	yr	352	1999	30r
Utilities				
Electrical bill, average	mos	87.17	9/00	9s
Electricity, expenditures on	yr	1115	1999	30r
Electricity cost, average	KWh	6.48	9/00	9s
Water and other public services, expenditures on	yr	298	1999	30r
Weddings				
Wedding (national average cost)		19936	2000	33r
Attendants' gifts		321	1998	33r
Bridal attendants' apparel (5 persons)		824	2000	33r
Bride's headpiece/veil		173	1998	33r
Bride's wedding dress		859	1998	33r
Clergy, religious facility fee		242	1998	33r
Engagement ring		3177	1998	33r
Flowers		789	1998	33r
Groom's formalwear rental		99	2000	33r
Limousine		410	1998	33r
Marriage license cost		36.00	4/01	35s
Men's formalwear (ushers, best man)		469	2000	33r
Mother of bride apparel		241	2000	33r
Music		866	1998	33r
Photography and videography		1368	1998	33r
Rehearsal dinner		728	1998	33r
Wedding invitations and announcements		341	1998	33r
Wedding reception		7968	2000	33r
Wedding rings (bride and groom)		1060	1998	33r

Bakersfield, CA

Item	Per	Value	Date	Ref.
Average annual expenditures	yr	40662	1999	30r
Alcoholic Beverages				
Alcoholic beverage purchases	yr	372	1999	30r
Malt beverages, all types, all sizes, any origin	16 oz	0.94	7/01	11r
Wine, red and white table, all sizes, any origin	liter	6.00	7/01	11r
Appliances				
Major appliances, expenditures on	yr	167	1999	30r
Small appliances, housewares, expenditures on	yr	105	1999	30r
Banking and Money				
Mortgage interest and charges paid	yr	3368	1999	30r
Mortgage principal paid on owned property	yr	1677	1999	30r
Vehicle finance charges paid	yr	311	1999	30r
Business Expenses				
Business travel, car rental	day	46	2001	3c
Business travel, food	day	45	2001	3c
Business travel, hotel	day	85	2001	3c
Charity				
Cash contributions, expenditures	yr	1344	1999	30r
Child Care				
Child raising cost, total, age 0-2	yr	9140	1999	60r
Child raising cost, total, age 3-5	yr	9370	1999	60r
Child raising cost, total, age 6-8	yr	9450	1999	60r
Child raising cost, total, age 9-11	yr	9470	1999	60r
Child raising cost, total, age 12-14	yr	10170	1999	60r
Child raising cost, total, age 15-17	yr	10360	1999	60r
Child's child care and education, age 0-2	yr	1250	1999	60r
Child's child care and education, age 3-5	yr	1380	1999	60r
Child's child care and education, age 6-8	yr	890	1999	60r
Child's child care and education, age 9-11	yr	580	1999	60r
Child's child care and education, age 12-14	yr	430	1999	60r
Child's child care and education, age 15-17	yr	730	1999	60r
Child's clothing, age 0-2	yr	430	1999	60r
Child's clothing, age 3-5	yr	420	1999	60r

Values are in dollars or fractions of dollars. In the column headed *Ref*, references are shown to sources. Each reference is followed by a letter. These refer to the geographical level for which data were reported: s=State, r=Region, and c=City or metro. The abbreviation *ex* is used to mean *except* or *excluding*; *exp* stands for *expenditures*. For other abbreviations and further explanations, please see the Introduction.

Bakersfield, CA - continued

Item	Per	Value	Date	Ref.
Child Care				
Child's clothing, age 6-8	yr	470	1999	60r
Child's clothing, age 9-11	yr	520	1999	60r
Child's clothing, age 12-14	yr	870	1999	60r
Child's clothing, age 15-17	yr	770	1999	60r
Child's food, age 0-2	yr	1120	1999	60r
Child's food, age 3-5	yr	1280	1999	60r
Child's food, age 6-8	yr	1640	1999	60r
Child's food, age 9-11	yr	1930	1999	60r
Child's food, age 12-14	yr	1940	1999	60r
Child's food, age 15-17	yr	2150	1999	60r
Child's health care, age 0-2	yr	490	1999	60r
Child's health care, age 3-5	yr	470	1999	60r
Child's health care, age 6-8	yr	530	1999	60r
Child's health care, age 9-11	yr	570	1999	60r
Child's health care, age 12-14	yr	580	1999	60r
Child's health care, age 15-17	yr	610	1999	60r
Child's housing, age 0-2	yr	3630	1999	60r
Child's housing, age 3-5	yr	3610	1999	60r
Child's housing, age 6-8	yr	3570	1999	60r
Child's housing, age 9-11	yr	3410	1999	60r
Child's housing, age 12-14	yr	3600	1999	60r
Child's housing, age 15-17	yr	3210	1999	60r
Child's personal care, reading, age 0-2	yr	1040	1999	60r
Child's personal care, reading, age 3-5	yr	1060	1999	60r
Child's personal care, reading, age 6-8	yr	1090	1999	60r
Child's personal care, reading, age 9-11	yr	1130	1999	60r
Child's personal care, reading, age 12-14	yr	1300	1999	60r
Child's personal care, reading, age 15-17	yr	1080	1999	60r
Clothing				
Apparel and services purchases	yr	1863	1999	30r
Boys, 2 to 15, expenditures on	yr	80	1999	30r
Children under 2, expenditures on	yr	74	1999	30r
Footwear, expenditures on	yr	307	1999	30r
Girls, 2 to 15, expenditures on	yr	101	1999	30r
Men and boys, expenditures on	yr	443	1999	30r
Men, 16 and over, expenditures on	yr	363	1999	30r
Women, 16 and over, expenditures on	yr	594	1999	30r
Communications				
Cable modem installation, AT&T-BIS		150.00	6/99	103s
Cable modem installation, Charter		99.00-169.00	6/99	103s
Cable modem installation, Comcast		95.00	6/99	103s
Cable modem installation, Cox		99.00-174.95	6/99	103s
Cable modem installation, Media One		100.00	6/99	103s
Cable modem installation, Time Warner		75.00-225.00	6/99	103s
Cable modem rate, cable subscriber, AT&T-BIS	mos	39.95	6/99	103s
Cable modem rate, cable subscriber, Charter	mos	49.95-79.95	6/99	103s
Cable modem rate, cable subscriber, Comcast	mos	39.95	6/99	103s
Cable modem rate, cable subscriber, Cox	mos	29.95-44.95	6/99	103s
Cable modem rate, cable subscriber, Media One	mos	34.95-39.95	6/99	103s
Cable modem rate, cable subscriber, Time Warner	mos	39.95-49.95	6/99	103s
Cable modem rate, non-cable subscriber, Charter	mos	59.95-89.95	6/99	103s
Cable modem rate, non-cable subscriber, Comcast	mos	49.95	6/99	103s
Cable modem rate, non-cable subscriber, Cox	mos	42.95-54.95	6/99	103s
Cable modem rate, non-cable subscriber, Media One	mos	49.95	6/99	103s
Cable modem rate, non-cable subscriber, Time Warner	mos	39.95-54.95	6/99	103s
Phone line, single, business, field visit	inst.	70.75	12/97	17s
Phone line, single, business, no field visit	inst.	70.75	12/97	17s

Bakersfield, CA - continued

Item	Per	Value	Date	Ref.
Communications - continued				
Phone line, single, residence, field visit	inst.	34.75	12/97	17s
Phone line, single, residence, no field visit	inst.	34.75	12/97	17s
Postage and stationery, expenditures on	yr	150	1999	30r
Postal rate, express mail, up to half-pound		12.45	7/01	108r
Postal rate, letter, first class, first ounce		0.34	7/01	108r
Postal rate, letter, two ounces		0.57	7/01	108r
Postal rate, post card		0.21	7/01	108r
Postal rate, priority mail, two pounds		3.95	7/01	108r
Postal rate, priority mail, up to one pound		3.50	7/01	108r
Telephone services, expenditures on	yr	825	1999	30r
Education				
Board, 4-year private college/university	yr	2970	1996	38s
Board, 4-year public college/university	yr	2516	1996	38s
Education expenditures	yr	676	1999	30r
Room, 4-year private college/university	yr	3196	1996	38s
Room, 4-year public college/university	yr	3031	1996	38s
Total cost, 4-year private college/university	yr	20143	1996	38s
Total cost, 4-year public college/university	yr	8213	1996	38s
Tuition, 2-year public college/university, in state	yr	362	1996	38s
Tuition, 4-year private college/university, in state	yr	13977	1996	38s
Tuition, 4-year public college/university	yr	2666	1996	38s
Energy and Fuels				
Electricity	KWh	0.11	7/01	11r
Electricity	500 KWhs	48.23	7/01	11r
Fuel oil and other fuels, expenditures on	yr	35	1999	30r
Gas, natural, commercial rate	1000 cf	8.74	11/00	88s
Gasoline, all types	gal	1.91	7/01	11r
Gasoline, unleaded premium	gal	2.05	7/01	11r
Gasoline, unleaded regular	gal	1.83	7/01	11r
Natural gas, expenditures on	yr	255	1999	30r
Utility (piped) gas, therm		0.98	7/01	11r
Utility (piped) gas, 40 therms		40.74	7/01	11r
Utility (piped) gas, 100 therms		96.80	7/01	11r
Entertainment				
Entertainment purchases	yr	2139	1999	30r
Fees and admissions paid	yr	545	1999	30r
Television, radios, sound equipment, expenditures on	yr	624	1999	30r
Funerals				
Total cost of funeral		5401.08	1/99	78r
Acknowledgement cards		33.64	1/99	78r
Casket		2170.43	1/99	78r
Cosmetology, hair, other preparation		136.32	1/99	78r
Embalming		319.13	1/99	78r
Funeral at funeral home		370.21	1/99	78r
Hearse (local)		161.04	1/99	78r
Professional service charges		963.15	1/99	78r
Service car/van		133.99	1/99	78r
Transfer of remains to funeral home		159.82	1/99	78r
Vault		778.07	1/99	78r
Visitation/viewing		175.28	1/99	78r
Groceries				
Apples, red delicious	lb	0.84	7/01	11r
Bacon, sliced	lb	3.38	7/01	11r
Bakery products, expenditures on	yr	299	1999	30r
Bananas	lb	0.54	7/01	11r
Beans, dried, any type, all sizes	lb	0.76	7/01	11r
Beef, expenditures on	yr	222	1999	30r
Bread, white, pan	lb	0.99	7/01	11r
Butter, yoghurt, cheese, etc, expenditures on	yr	211	1999	30r
Cereals and bakery product purchases	yr	466	1999	30r
Cereals and cereal products, expenditures on	yr	168	1999	30r
Chicken breast, bone-in	lb	2.45	7/01	11r
Chicken, fresh, whole	lb	1.19	7/01	11r
Chops, boneless,	lb	4.00	7/01	11r

Values are in dollars or fractions of dollars. In the column headed *Ref*, references are shown to sources. Each reference is followed by a letter. These refer to the geographical level for which data were reported: s=State, r=Region, and c=City or metro. The abbreviation *ex* is used to mean *except* or *excluding*; *exp* stands for expenditures. For other abbreviations and further explanations, please see the Introduction.

Bakersfield, CA - continued

Item	Per	Value	Date	Ref.
Groceries				
Chuck roast, graded and ungraded, excl U.S. prime and choice	lb	2.55	7/01	11r
Coffee, 100%, ground roast, all sizes	lb	3.80	7/01	11r
Cookies, chocolate chip	lb	2.83	7/01	11r
Dairy product purchases	yr	341	1999	30r
Eggs, expenditures on	yr	39	1999	30r
Eggs, grade AA, large	dozen	1.23	7/01	11r
Fats and oils, expenditures on	yr	88	1999	30r
Fish and seafood, expenditures on	yr	121	1999	30r
Food (excl fruit and vegetables), eaten at home, purchases	yr	1001	1999	30r
Food cooked on trips, expenditures on	yr	64	1999	30r
Food purchases	yr	5312	1999	30r
Food purchases, eaten away from home	yr	2180	1999	30r
Food purchases, food eaten at home	yr	3132	1999	30r
Fresh fruits, expenditures on	yr	186	1999	30r
Fresh milk and cream, expenditures on	yr	130	1999	30r
Fresh vegetables, expenditures on	yr	177	1999	30r
Grapefruit	lb	0.68	7/01	11r
Grapes, Thompson, seedless	lb	2.42	7/01	11r
Ground beef, lean and extra lean	lb	2.46	7/01	11r
Ice cream, prepackaged, bulk, regular	1/2 gal	3.62	7/01	11r
Lettuce, iceberg	lb	0.63	7/01	11r
Meats, poultry, fish, and egg purchases	yr	761	1999	30r
Milk, fresh, low fat,	gal	2.80	7/01	11r
Milk, fresh, whole, fortified	gal	2.88	7/01	11r
Nonalcoholic beverages, expenditures on	yr	258	1999	30r
Oranges, Navel	lb	0.97	7/01	11r
Oranges, Valencia	lb	0.43	7/01	11r
Peaches	lb	1.38	7/01	11r
Peanut butter, creamy, all sizes	lb	2.14	7/01	11r
Pork chops, center cut, bone-in	lb	3.83	7/01	11r
Pork, expenditures on	yr	141	1999	30r
Potatoes, white, all types	lb	0.37	7/01	11r
Poultry, expenditures on	yr	146	1999	30r
Processed fruits, expenditures on	yr	118	1999	30r
Processed vegetables, expenditures on	yr	81	1999	30r
Round roast, graded and ungraded, excl U.S. prime and choice	lb	3.07	7/01	11r
Round roast, U.S. choice, boneless	lb	3.37	7/01	11r
Round steak, graded and ungraded, excl U.S. prime and choice	lb	3.51	7/01	11r
Sirloin steak, graded and ungraded, excl U.S. prime and choice	lb	4.67	7/01	11r
Steak, sirloin, U.S. choice, boneless	lb	6.20	7/01	11r
Strawberries, dry pint	12 oz	1.79	7/01	11r
Sugar and other sweets, expenditures on	yr	124	1999	30r
Sugar, white, all sizes	lb	0.46	7/01	11r
Tobacco products and smoking supplies purchases	yr	217	1999	30r
Tomatoes, field grown	lb	1.17	7/01	11r
Tuna, light, chunk	lb	2.05	7/01	11r
Goods and Services				
B&B Japanese maple (acer japonicum)	gal	39.99	4/00	93r
Boxwood (buxus)	2 gal	14.99- 24.99	4/00	93r
Christmas tree, noble fir		40-60	2000	65s
Daylily (hemerocallis)	gal	6.99- 8.99	4/00	93r
Flat of annuals		16.68	4/00	93r
Fountain grass (pennisetum)	gal	7.99- 11.99	4/00	93r
Hanging basket (10 in)		29.99	4/00	93r
Hardy geranium (geranium)	gal	6.99- 11.99	4/00	93r
Hosta (hosta)	gal	6.99- 18.99	4/00	93r
Lilac (syrubga vulgaris)	2 gal	14.99- 17.99	4/00	93r
Miscellaneous purchases	yr	1070	1999	30r
Rhododendron (rhododendron)	2 gal	14.99	4/00	93r
Sage (salvia)	gal	6.99	4/00	93r

Bakersfield, CA - continued

Item	Per	Value	Date	Ref.
Goods and Services - continued				
Wintercreeper euonymus (euonymus fortunei)	2 gal	14.99- 22.99	4/00	93r
Hunting license	yr	29.95	4/01	34s
Health Care				
Cardiac catheterization, ave hospital/ physician charges		24000	1998	77s
Childbirth, Cesarean delivery		11587	1997	13r
Childbirth, vaginal delivery		6725	1997	13r
Drugs, expenditures on	yr	309	1999	30r
Health care purchases	yr	1869	1999	30r
Health insurance expenditures	yr	868	1999	30r
Hysterectomy, laproscopically-assisted, ave hospital/physician charges		20760	1998	76s
Hysterectomy, vaginal, ave hospital and physician charges		14570	1998	76s
Medicaid dispensing fee		4.05	1999	87s
Medical services expenditures	yr	580	1999	30r
Medical supplies, expenditures on	yr	112	1999	30r
Household Goods				
Floor coverings, expenditures on	yr	49	1999	30r
Furniture, expenditures on	yr	444	1999	30r
Household furnishings and equipment purchases	yr	1768	1999	30r
Household textiles, expenditures on	yr	141	1999	30r
Laundry and cleaning supplies, expenditures on	yr	128	1999	30r
Housing				
Home, 2200 sq ft, 4-br, 2-bath, 2-car garage, average		171737	2000	47c
Home price, existing, ave		239400	10/00	90r
Home value, median		215000	2001	53s
Household operation expenditures	yr	781	1999	30r
Housekeeping supplies purchases	yr	513	1999	30r
Lodging expenditures	yr	575	1999	30r
Maintenance, repairs, insurance expenditures	yr	939	1999	30r
Monthly rental value of owned home	mos	662	1999	30r
Owned dwellings, expenditures own	yr	5231	1999	30r
Rent expenditures	yr	2709	1999	30r
Rental unit, 1 bedroom, with utilities	mos	419	4/01	41c
Rental unit, 2 bedroom, with utilities	mos	526	4/01	41c
Rental unit, 3 bedroom, with utilities	mos	731	4/01	41c
Rental unit, 4 bedroom, with utilities	mos	809	4/01	41c
Shelter, expenditures on	yr	8516	1999	30r
Insurance and Pensions				
Life and other personal insurance purchases	yr	355	1999	30r
Pensions and Social Security, expenditures on	yr	3636	1999	30r
Legal Fees				
Divorce, filing fee		182.00	4/01	35s
Driver's license fee	renew	15.00	1999	48s
Driver's license fee	orig	12.00	1999	48s
Personal Goods				
Personal care products and services purchases	yr	449	1999	30r
Personal Services				
Personal services, household, expenditures on	yr	353	1999	30r
Pets				
Pets, toys, and playground equipment, expenditures on	yr	358	1999	30r
Taxes				
Federal income taxes paid	yr	3200	1999	30r
Personal taxes, expenditures on	yr	4153	1999	30r
Property taxes paid	yr	923	1999	30r
State and local income taxes paid	yr	812	1999	30r

Values are in dollars or fractions of dollars. In the column headed *Ref*, references are shown to sources. Each reference is followed by a letter. These refer to the geographical level for which data were reported: s=State, r=Region, and c=City or metro. The abbreviation *ex* is used to mean *except* or *excluding*; *exp* stands for *expenditures*. For other abbreviations and further explanations, please see the Introduction.

Bakersfield, CA - continued

Item	Per	Value	Date	Ref.
Transportation				
Bus fare, one-way	trip	0.75	2000	1c
Cars and trucks, new, expenditures on	yr	1534	1999	30r
Cars and trucks, used, expenditures on	yr	1593	1999	30r
Diesel at the pump	gal	1.37	10/99	73s
Gasoline and motor oil purchases	yr	1129	1999	30r
Gasoline before-tax price (cents)	gal	128.80	10/00	43s
Maintenance and repair expenditures	yr	797	1999	30r
Public transportation, expenditures on	yr	530	1999	30r
Transportation purchases	yr	7423	1999	30r
Vehicle expenses, miscellaneous, purchases	yr	2585	1999	30r
Vehicle insurance payments	yr	811	1999	30r
Vehicle purchases (net outlay)	yr	3180	1999	30r
Vehicle rental, lease expenditures	yr	666	1999	30r
Utilities				
Electrical bill, average	mos	58.66	9/00	9s
Electricity, expenditures on	yr	725	1999	30r
Electricity cost, average	KWh	7.75	9/00	9s
Utilities, fuels, and public services purchased	yr	2179	1999	30r
Water and other public services, expenditures on	yr	339	1999	30r
Weddings				
Wedding (national average cost)		19936	2000	33r
Wedding (regional average total cost)		18918	1997	110r
Attendants' gifts		321	1998	33r
Bridal attendants' apparel (5 persons)		824	2000	33r
Bride's headpiece/veil		173	1998	33r
Bride's wedding dress		859	1998	33r
Clergy, religious facility fee		242	1998	33r
Engagement ring		3177	1998	33r
Flowers		789	1998	33r
Groom's formalwear rental		99	2000	33r
Limousine		410	1998	33r
Marriage license cost		50.00- 80.00	4/01	35s
Men's formalwear (ushers, best man)		469	2000	33r
Mother of bride apparel		241	2000	33r
Music		866	1998	33r
Photography and videography		1368	1998	33r
Rehearsal dinner		728	1998	33r
Wedding invitations and announcements		341	1998	33r
Wedding reception		7968	2000	33r
Wedding rings (bride and groom)		1060	1998	33r

Baltimore, MD

Item	Per	Value	Date	Ref.
Composite, ACCRA index		95.50	3/01	4c
Alcoholic Beverages				
Alcoholic beverage purchases	yr	371	1999	30c
Beer, Heineken, 12-oz, ex deposit	6	6.57	3/01	4c
J & B Scotch	750-ml	18.49	3/01	4c
Malt beverages, all types, all sizes, any origin	16 oz	0.96	7/01	11r
Wine, Livingston or Gallo, Chablis blanc	1.5 liter	5.49	3/01	4c
Appliances				
Appliance repair, service call, washing machine	min lab chg	44.59	3/01	4c
Major appliances, expenditures on	yr	172	1999	30r
Small appliances, housewares, expenditures on	yr	81	1999	30r
Banking and Money				
Mortgage interest and charges paid	yr	2039	1999	30r
Mortgage principal paid on owned property	yr	1026	1999	30r
Mortgage rate, incl. points and orig. fee, 30-yr. conv. fixed or ARM	mos	7.14	3/01	4c
Vehicle finance charges paid	yr	365	1999	30r
Business Expenses				
Business travel, car rental	day	68	2001	3c
Business travel, food	day	50	2001	3c
Business travel, hotel	day	97	2001	3c

Baltimore, MD - continued

Item	Per	Value	Date	Ref.
Business Expenses - continued				
Medical office space cost	sq ft	110.14	2001	31c
Office space, 2-4 storey building	sq ft	96.50	2001	31c
Office space, 5-10 storey building	sq ft	85.24	2001	31c
Office space, 11-20 storey building	sq ft	81.93	2001	31c
Charity				
Cash contributions, expenditures	yr	1122	1999	30c
Child Care				
Child raising cost, total, age 0-2	yr	8540	1999	60r
Child raising cost, total, age 3-5	yr	8780	1999	60r
Child raising cost, total, age 6-8	yr	8820	1999	60r
Child raising cost, total, age 9-11	yr	8800	1999	60r
Child raising cost, total, age 12-14	yr	9510	1999	60r
Child raising cost, total, age 15-17	yr	9740	1999	60r
Child's child care and education, age 0-2	yr	1380	1999	60r
Child's child care and education, age 3-5	yr	1520	1999	60r
Child's child care and education, age 6-8	yr	990	1999	60r
Child's child care and education, age 9-11	yr	650	1999	60r
Child's child care and education, age 12-14	yr	490	1999	60r
Child's child care and education, age 15-17	yr	840	1999	60r
Child's clothing, age 0-2	yr	480	1999	60r
Child's clothing, age 3-5	yr	470	1999	60r
Child's clothing, age 6-8	yr	520	1999	60r
Child's clothing, age 9-11	yr	570	1999	60r
Child's clothing, age 12-14	yr	950	1999	60r
Child's clothing, age 15-17	yr	850	1999	60r
Child's food, age 0-2	yr	1000	1999	60r
Child's food, age 3-5	yr	1160	1999	60r
Child's food, age 6-8	yr	1490	1999	60r
Child's food, age 9-11	yr	1770	1999	60r
Child's food, age 12-14	yr	1770	1999	60r
Child's food, age 15-17	yr	1980	1999	60r
Child's health care, age 0-2	yr	620	1999	60r
Child's health care, age 3-5	yr	590	1999	60r
Child's health care, age 6-8	yr	680	1999	60r
Child's health care, age 9-11	yr	720	1999	60r
Child's health care, age 12-14	yr	730	1999	60r
Child's health care, age 15-17	yr	760	1999	60r
Child's housing, age 0-2	yr	3070	1999	60r
Child's housing, age 3-5	yr	3050	1999	60r
Child's housing, age 6-8	yr	3010	1999	60r
Child's housing, age 9-11	yr	2850	1999	60r
Child's housing, age 12-14	yr	3040	1999	60r
Child's housing, age 15-17	yr	2650	1999	60r
Child's personal care, reading, age 0-2	yr	910	1999	60r
Child's personal care, reading, age 3-5	yr	930	1999	60r
Child's personal care, reading, age 6-8	yr	960	1999	60r
Child's personal care, reading, age 9-11	yr	1000	1999	60r
Child's personal care, reading, age 12-14	yr	1170	1999	60r
Child's personal care, reading, age 15-17	yr	950	1999	60r
Clothing				
Apparel and services purchases	yr	1660	1999	30c
Boys' brief, cotton	3	3.58	3/01	4c
Boys, 2 to 15, expenditures on	yr	89	1999	30r
Children under 2, expenditures on	yr	79	1999	30r
Footwear, expenditures on	yr	283	1999	30r
Girls, 2 to 15, expenditures on	yr	103	1999	30r
Men and boys, expenditures on	yr	351	1999	30r
Men, 16 and over, expenditures on	yr	262	1999	30r
Shirt, man's dress shirt		25.49	3/01	4c
Slacks, man's "No Wrinkles" khaki		31.99	3/01	4c
Women, 16 and over, expenditures on	yr	538	1999	30r
Communications				
Cable modem installation, Comcast		95.00	6/99	103s
Cable modem rate, cable subscriber, Comcast	mos	39.95	6/99	103s
Cable modem rate, non-cable subscriber, Comcast	mos	49.95	6/99	103s
Newspaper subscription, daily and Sunday delivery	mos	15.00	3/01	4c
Phone line, single, business, field visit	inst.	98.50	12/97	17s

Values are in dollars or fractions of dollars. In the column headed *Ref*, references are shown to sources. Each reference is followed by a letter. These refer to the geographical level for which data were reported: s=State, r=Region, and c=City or metro. The abbreviation *ex* is used to mean *except* or *excluding*; *exp* stands for expenditures. For other abbreviations and further explanations, please see the Introduction.

Baltimore, MD - continued

Item	Per	Value	Date	Ref.
Communications				
Phone line, single, business, no field visit	inst.	98.50	12/97	17s
Phone line, single, residence, field visit	inst.	48.00	12/97	17s
Phone line, single, residence, no field visit	inst.	48.00	12/97	17s
Postage and stationery, expenditures on	yr	104	1999	30r
Postal rate, express mail, up to half-pound		12.45	7/01	108r
Postal rate, letter, first class, first ounce		0.34	7/01	108r
Postal rate, letter, two ounces		0.57	7/01	108r
Postal rate, post card		0.21	7/01	108r
Postal rate, priority mail, two pounds		3.95	7/01	108r
Postal rate, priority mail, up to one pound		3.50	7/01	108r
Telephone bill, family of three	mos	22.48	3/01	4c
Telephone bill, residential, basic rate	mos	10.65	12/97	18c
Telephone services, expenditures on	yr	860	1999	30r
Education				
Board, 4-year private college/university	yr	3022	1996	38s
Board, 4-year public college/university	yr	2435	1996	38s
Education expenditures	yr	671	1999	30c
Room, 4-year private college/university	yr	3524	1996	38s
Room, 4-year public college/university	yr	2722	1996	38s
Total cost, 4-year private college/university	yr	21245	1996	38s
Total cost, 4-year public college/university	yr	8728	1996	38s
Tuition, 2-year public college/university, in state	yr	1967	1996	38s
Tuition, 4-year private college/university, in state	yr	14700	1996	38s
Tuition, 4-year public college/university	yr	3572	1996	38s
Energy and Fuels				
Electricity	KWh	0.09	7/01	11r
Electricity	500 KWhs	47.29	7/01	11r
Energy, combined forms, 2400 sq ft	mos	145.99	3/01	4c
Energy, exc. electricity, 2400 sq ft	mos	65.01	3/01	4c
Fuel oil #2	gal	1.43	7/01	11r
Fuel oil and other fuels, expenditures on	yr	45	1999	30r
Gas, cooking, winter, 10 therms	mos	16.13	2/96	98c
Gas, cooking, winter, 30 therms	mos	28.40	2/96	98c
Gas, cooking, winter, 50 therms	mos	40.68	2/96	98c
Gas, heating, winter, average use	mos	114.30	2/96	98c
Gas, natural, commercial rate	1000 cf	8.64	11/00	88s
Gas, regular unleaded, cash, self-service	gal	1.41	3/01	4c
Gasoline, all types	gal	1.60	7/01	11r
Gasoline, unleaded midgrade	gal	1.65	7/01	11r
Gasoline, unleaded premium	gal	1.74	7/01	11r
Natural gas, expenditures on	yr	164	1999	30r
Utility (piped) gas, therm		1.01	7/01	11r
Utility (piped) gas, 40 therms		44.29	7/01	11r
Utility (piped) gas, 100 therms		97.44	7/01	11r
Entertainment				
Bowling, Saturday evening rate	line	3.65	3/01	4c
Entertainment purchases	yr	2104	1999	30c
Fees and admissions paid	yr	371	1999	30r
Major League baseball ticket		19.52	2000	16c
Monopoly game, Parker Brothers', No. 9	game	10.35	3/01	4c
Movie, first-run, Saturday, evening	adm.	7.20	3/01	4c
Reading purchases	yr	129	1999	30c
Television, radios, sound equipment, expenditures on	yr	561	1999	30r
Tennis balls, yellow, Wilson or Penn, 3	can	2.05	3/01	4c
Funerals				
Total cost of funeral		5922.53	1/99	78r
Acknowledgement cards		63.43	1/99	78r
Casket		2258.77	1/99	78r
Cosmetology, hair, other preparation		127.09	1/99	78r
Embalming		393.49	1/99	78r
Funeral at funeral home		367.50	1/99	78r
Hearse (local)		169.66	1/99	78r
Professional service charges		1211.32	1/99	78r
Service car/van		80.69	1/99	78r
Transfer of remains to funeral home		144.25	1/99	78r
Vault		803.50	1/99	78r

Baltimore, MD - continued

Item	Per	Value	Date	Ref.
Funerals - continued				
Visitation/viewing		302.83	1/99	78r
Groceries				
Groceries, ACCRA Index		92.00	3/01	4c
American processed cheese	lb	3.50	7/01	11r
Antibiotic ointment, Polysporin	0.5 oz	4.16	3/01	4c
Baby food, strained vegetables or fruit, lowest price	4-4.5 oz	0.43	3/01	4c
Bakery products, expenditures on	yr	261	1999	30r
Bananas	lb	0.40	3/01	4c
Bananas	lb	0.47	7/01	11r
Beans, dried, any type, all sizes	lb	0.63	7/01	11r
Beef for stew, boneless	lb	2.86	7/01	11r
Beef or hamburger, ground	lb	1.45	3/01	4c
Beef, expenditures on	yr	210	1999	30r
Bologna, all beef or mixed	lb	2.29	7/01	11r
Bread, French	lb	1.66	7/01	11r
Bread, white	loaf	0.68	3/01	4c
Bread, white, pan	lb	0.87	7/01	11r
Bread, whole wheat, pan	lb	1.38	7/01	11r
Broccoli	lb	1.04	7/01	11r
Butter, salted, grade AA, stick	lb	2.26	7/01	11r
Butter, yoghurt, cheese, etc, expenditures on	yr	170	1999	30r
Cabbage	lb	0.42	7/01	11r
Cereals and cereal products, expenditures on	yr	140	1999	30r
Cheddar cheese, natural	lb	3.75	7/01	11r
Cheese, Kraft grated Parmesan	8 oz	3.39	3/01	4c
Chicken breast, bone-in	lb	1.85	7/01	11r
Chicken legs, bone-in	lb	1.34	7/01	11r
Chicken, fresh, whole	lb	1.05	7/01	11r
Chicken, whole fryer	lb	0.79	3/01	4c
Chops, boneless	lb	4.13	7/01	11r
Chuck roast, graded and ungraded, excl U.S. prime and choice	lb	2.35	7/01	11r
Chuck roast, U.S. choice, boneless	lb	2.67	7/01	11r
Cigarettes, Winston, Kings	carton	30.29	3/01	4c
Coffee, 100%, ground roast, all sizes	lb	2.88	7/01	11r
Coffee, instant, plain, regular, all sizes	16 oz	9.25	7/01	11r
Coffee, vacuum-packed	13 oz	2.74	3/01	4c
Cola, non diet	2 liter	1.11	7/01	11r
Corn Flakes, Kellogg's or Post Toasties	18 oz	2.23	3/01	4c
Corn, frozen, whole kernel, lowest price	16 oz	1.07	3/01	4c
Crackers, soda, salted	lb	1.70	7/01	11r
Dairy product purchases	yr	312	1999	30c
Eggs, expenditures on	yr	32	1999	30r
Eggs, Grade A or AA	dozen	1.09	3/01	4c
Fats and oils, expenditures on	yr	79	1999	30r
Fish and seafood, expenditures on	yr	99	1999	30r
Flour, white, all purpose	lb	0.32	7/01	11r
Food (excl fruit and vegetables), eaten at home, purchases	yr	913	1999	30c
Food cooked on trips, expenditures on	yr	36	1999	30r
Food purchases	yr	5165	1999	30c
Food purchases, eaten away from home	yr	2198	1999	30c
Food purchases, food eaten at home	yr	2967	1999	30c
Fresh fruits, expenditures on	yr	128	1999	30r
Fresh milk and cream, expenditures on	yr	112	1999	30r
Fresh vegetables, expenditures on	yr	131	1999	30r
Fruit and vegetable purchases	yr	502	1999	30c
Grapefruit	lb	0.59	7/01	11r
Grapes, Thompson, seedless	lb	2.12	7/01	11r
Ground beef, 100% beef	lb	1.76	7/01	11r
Ground beef, lean and extra lean	lb	2.60	7/01	11r
Ground chuck, 100% beef	lb	2.08	7/01	11r
Ham, boneless, excl canned	lb	2.71	7/01	11r
Ham, rump or shank half, bone-in, smoked	lb	2.19	7/01	11r
Ice cream, prepackaged, bulk, regular	1/2 gal	3.93	7/01	11r
Lemons	lb	1.32	7/01	11r
Lettuce, iceberg	head	1.29	3/01	4c
Lettuce, iceberg	lb	0.76	7/01	11r
Margarine, Blue Bonnet or Parkay, stick	lb	0.85	3/01	4c
Milk, fresh, low fat,	gal	2.75	7/01	11r

Values are in dollars or fractions of dollars. In the column headed *Ref*, references are shown to sources. Each reference is followed by a letter. These refer to the geographical level for which data were reported: s=State, r=Region, and c=City or metro. The abbreviation *ex* is used to mean *except* or *excluding*; *exp* stands for *expenditures*. For other abbreviations and further explanations, please see the Introduction.

Baltimore, MD - continued

Item	Per	Value	Date	Ref.
Groceries				
Milk, fresh, whole, fortified	gal	2.97	7/01	11r
Milk, whole	1/2 gal	1.68	3/01	4c
Nonalcoholic beverages, expenditures on	yr	228	1999	30r
Orange juice, frozen concentrate	16 oz	1.95	7/01	11r
Orange juice, Minute Maid frozen	12 oz	1.34	3/01	4c
Oranges, Navel	lb	0.73	7/01	11r
Oranges, Valencia	lb	0.55	7/01	11r
Peaches, halves or slices, Hunt's, Del Monte, or Libby's	29 oz	1.71	3/01	4c
Peanut butter, creamy, all sizes	lb	1.83	7/01	11r
Pears, Anjou	lb	0.98	7/01	11r
Peas, green, Del Monte or Green Giant	15 oz	0.49	3/01	4c
Pork chops, center cut, bone-in	lb	3.33	7/01	11r
Pork sausage, fresh, loose	lb	2.59	7/01	11r
Pork shoulder picnic, bone-in, smoked	lb	1.12	7/01	11r
Pork, expenditures on	yr	162	1999	30r
Potato chips	16 oz	3.59	7/01	11r
Potatoes, frozen, french fried	lb	1.00	7/01	11r
Potatoes, white or red	10 lb	2.15	3/01	4c
Potatoes, white, all types	lb	0.44	7/01	11r
Poultry, expenditures on	yr	137	1999	30r
Processed fruits, expenditures on	yr	97	1999	30r
Processed vegetables, expenditures on	yr	82	1999	30r
Rice, white, long grain, uncooked	lb	0.51	7/01	11r
Round roast, graded and ungraded, excl U.S. prime and choice	lb	2.96	7/01	11r
Round steak, graded and ungraded, excl U.S. prime and choice	lb	3.11	7/01	11r
Sausage, Jimmy Dean/Owens pork	lb	2.59	3/01	4c
Shortening, vegetable, Crisco	3 lb	3.51	3/01	4c
Sirloin steak, graded and ungraded, excl U.S. prime and choice	lb	4.23	7/01	11r
Soft drink, Coca Cola, ex deposit	2 liter	0.85	3/01	4c
Spaghetti and macaroni	lb	0.78	7/01	11r
Steak, round, U.S. choice, boneless	lb	3.56	7/01	11r
Steak, sirloin, U.S. choice, boneless	lb	5.65	7/01	11r
Steak, T-bone	lb	5.89	3/01	4c
Strawberries, dry pint	12 oz	1.50	7/01	11r
Sugar and other sweets, expenditures on	yr	99	1999	30r
Sugar, cane or beet	4 lbs	1.53	3/01	4c
Sugar, white, 33-80 ounce package	lb	0.39	7/01	11r
Sugar, white, all sizes	lb	0.42	7/01	11r
Tobacco products and smoking supplies purchases	yr	243	1999	30c
Tomatoes, field grown	lb	1.43	7/01	11r
Tomatoes, Hunt's or Del Monte	14.5 oz	0.88	3/01	4c
Tuna, chunk, light	6 oz	0.60	3/01	4c
Tuna, light, chunk	lb	1.77	7/01	11r
Turkey, frozen, whole	lb	1.05	7/01	11r
Goods and Services				
Miscellaneous goods and services, ACCRA Index		94.90	3/01	4c
B&B Japanese maple (acer japonicum)	gal	49.98-129.00	4/00	93r
Boxwood (buxus)	2 gal	12.99-16.99	4/00	93r
Daylilly (hemerocallis)	gal	4.99-8.99	4/00	93r
Flat of annuals		11.00-13.92	4/00	93r
Fountain grass (pennisetum)	gal	5.98-7.98	4/00	93r
Hanging basket (10 in)		7.99-14.98	4/00	93r
Hardy geranium (geranium)	gal	5.98-8.00	4/00	93r
Hosta (hosta)	gal	4.99-10.98	4/00	93r
Lilac (syrubga vulgaris)	2 gal	12.99-21.99	4/00	93r
Rhododendron (rhododendron)	2 gal	14.99-24.99	4/00	93r

Baltimore, MD - continued

Item	Per	Value	Date	Ref.
Goods and Services - continued				
Sage (salvia)	gal	5.98-6.99	4/00	93r
Wintercreeper euonymus (euonymus fortunei)	2 gal	7.99-89.99	4/00	93r
Hunting license	yr	15.50	4/01	34s
Health Care				
Health care, ACCRA Index		94.50	3/01	4c
Cardiac catheterization, ave hospital/ physician charges		11420	1998	77s
Childbirth, Cesarean delivery		11587	1997	13r
Childbirth, vaginal delivery		6725	1997	13r
Dentist's fee, adult teeth cleaning and periodic oral exam	visit	61.50	3/01	4c
Doctor's fee, routine exam, established patient	visit	57.00	3/01	4c
Drugs, expenditures on	yr	399	1999	30r
Health care purchases	yr	1581	1999	30c
Health insurance expenditures	yr	933	1999	30r
Home health care aide cost, licensed agency	hour	15	2000	82c
Hospital care, private room	day	571.00	3/01	4c
Hysterectomy, laproscopically-assisted, ave hospital/physician charges		11890	1998	76s
Hysterectomy, vaginal, ave hospital and physician charges		8120	1998	76s
Medicaid dispensing fee		4.21	1999	87s
Medical services expenditures	yr	547	1999	30r
Medical supplies, expenditures on	yr	91	1999	30r
Nursing home costs, private room	day	163	2000	82c
Nursing home stay, private room	day	163	2000	83c
Plastic surgery, breast augmentation		2870	2000	7r
Plastic surgery, breast lift		3649	2000	7r
Plastic surgery, facelift		5008	2000	7r
Plastic surgery, hair transplantation		3425	2000	7r
Plastic surgery, lip augmentation		1227	2000	7r
Plastic surgery, lower body lift		4793	2000	7r
Plastic surgery, thigh lift		3862	2000	7r
Household Goods				
Dishwashing powder, Cascade	50 oz	3.56	3/01	4c
Floor coverings, expenditures on	yr	44	1999	30r
Furniture, expenditures on	yr	335	1999	30r
Household furnishings and equipment purchases	yr	1697	1999	30c
Household textiles, expenditures on	yr	89	1999	30r
Laundry and cleaning supplies, expenditures on	yr	113	1999	30r
Tissues, facial, Kleenex brand	175	1.08	3/01	4c
Housing				
Housing, ACCRA Index		90.50	3/01	4c
Home, 2200 sq ft, 4-br, 2-bath, 2-car garage, average		206500	2000	47c
Home price, existing, ave		160100	10/00	90r
Home value, median		146000	2001	53s
House, 2400 sq ft, 8000 sq ft lot, new, urban, utilities	total	187898	3/01	4c
House payment, principal and interest, 25% down payment	mos	950	3/01	4c
Household operation expenditures	yr	606	1999	30c
Housekeeping supplies purchases	yr	661	1999	30c
Housing, expenditures on	yr	13489	1999	30c
Maintenance, repairs, insurance expenditures	yr	699	1999	30r
Monthly rental value of owned home	mos	505	1999	30r
Owned dwellings, expenditures own	yr	5756	1999	30c
Rent expenditures	yr	1784	1999	30c
Rent, apartment, 2 br, 1 1/2-2 baths, unfurn, 950 sq ft, water	mos	583	3/01	4c
Rental unit, 1 bedroom, with utilities	mos	542	4/01	41c
Rental unit, 2 bedroom, with utilities	mos	661	4/01	41c
Rental unit, 3 bedroom, with utilities	mos	875	4/01	41c
Rental unit, 4 bedroom, with utilities	mos	1001	4/01	41c
Shelter, expenditures on	yr	8169	1999	30c

Values are in dollars or fractions of dollars. In the column headed *Ref*, references are shown to sources. Each reference is followed by a letter. These refer to the geographical level for which data were reported: s=State, r=Region, and c=City or metro. The abbreviation *ex* is used to mean *except* or *excluding*; *exp* stands for expenditures. For other abbreviations and further explanations, please see the Introduction.

Baltimore, MD - continued

Item	Per	Value	Date	Ref.
Insurance and Pensions				
Life and other personal insurance purchases	yr	433	1999	30c
Pensions and Social Security, expenditures on	yr	3921	1999	30c
Personal insurance and pensions, expenditures on	yr	4354	1999	30c
Legal Fees				
Driver's license fee	orig	30.00	1999	48s
Driver's license fee	renew	20.00	1999	48s
Fishing license	yr	9.00	4/01	34s
Personal Goods				
Personal care products and services purchases	yr	462	1999	30c
Shampoo, Alberto VO5	15 oz	1.02	3/01	4c
Toothpaste, Crest or Colgate	6-7 oz	1.98	3/01	4c
Personal Services				
Dry cleaning, man's 2-pc suit		4.49	3/01	4c
Man's haircut, barbershop, no styling		8.20	3/01	4c
Personal services, household, expenditures on	yr	258	1999	30r
Woman's shampoo, trim, blow-dry, no style-change		28.40	3/01	4c
Pets				
Pets, toys, and playground equipment, expenditures on	yr	306	1999	30r
Restaurant Food				
Chicken, fried, thigh and drumstick, KFC/Church's		2.59	3/01	4c
Hamburger with cheese, McDonald's	1/4 lb	2.19	3/01	4c
Pizza, Pizza Hut or Pizza Inn	11-12 in	7.89	3/01	4c
Taxes				
Federal income taxes paid	yr	2047	1999	30r
Personal taxes, expenditures on	yr	2554	1999	30r
Property taxes paid	yr	726	1999	30r
State and local income taxes paid	yr	363	1999	30r
Transportation				
Transportation, ACCRA Index		99.70	3/01	4c
Bus fare, one-way	trip	1.35	2000	1c
Bus fare, to central business district	1-way	1.35	3/01	4c
Cars and trucks, new, expenditures on	yr	1648	1999	30r
Cars and trucks, used, expenditures on	yr	1651	1999	30r
Commuter rail, one-way	trip	3.25	2000	2c
Diesel at the pump	gal	1.29	10/99	73s
Gasoline and motor oil purchases	yr	1012	1999	30c
Gasoline before-tax price (cents)	gal	106.80	10/00	43s
Heavy rail transit fare, one-way	trip	1.35	2000	2c
Light rail transit fare, one-way	trip	1.35	2000	2c
Maintenance and repair expenditures	yr	621	1999	30r
Public transportation, expenditures on	yr	435	1999	30c
Tire balance, computer or spin balance, front	wheel	7.29	3/01	4c
Transportation purchases	yr	6347	1999	30c
Vehicle expenses, miscellaneous, purchases	yr	2100	1999	30c
Vehicle insurance payments	yr	696	1999	30r
Vehicle purchases (net outlay)	yr	2801	1999	30c
Vehicle purchases (net outlay)	yr	3354	1999	30r
Vehicle rental, lease expenditures	yr	352	1999	30r
Utilities				
Utilities, ACCRA Index		117.40	3/01	4c
Electrical bill, average	mos	83.58	9/00	9s
Electricity, expenditures on	yr	1115	1999	30r
Electricity, summer, 250 KWh	mos	26.17	2/96	97c
Electricity, summer, 500 KWh	mos	47.84	2/96	97c
Electricity, summer, 750 KWh	mos	64.63	2/96	97c
Electricity, summer, 1000 KWh	mos	81.41	2/96	97c
Electricity and other, mixed, 2400 sq ft, new home	mos	80.98	3/01	4c
Electricity cost, average	KWh	6.90	9/00	9s
Water and other public services, expenditures on	yr	298	1999	30r

Baltimore, MD - continued

Item	Per	Value	Date	Ref.
Weddings				
Wedding (national average cost)		19936	2000	33r
Wedding (regional average total cost)		16293	1997	110r
Attendants' gifts		321	1998	33r
Bridal attendants' apparel (5 persons)		824	2000	33r
Bride's headpiece/veil		173	1998	33r
Bride's wedding dress		859	1998	33r
Clergy, religious facility fee		242	1998	33r
Engagement ring		3177	1998	33r
Flowers		789	1998	33r
Groom's formalwear rental		99	2000	33r
Limousine		410	1998	33r
Marriage license cost		55.00	4/01	35s
Men's formalwear (ushers, best man)		469	2000	33r
Mother of bride apparel		241	2000	33r
Music		866	1998	33r
Photography and videography		1368	1998	33r
Rehearsal dinner		728	1998	33r
Wedding invitations and announcements		341	1998	33r
Wedding reception		7968	2000	33r
Wedding rings (bride and groom)		1060	1998	33r

Bangor, ME

Item	Per	Value	Date	Ref.
Average annual expenditures	yr	37971	1999	30r
Alcoholic Beverages				
Alcoholic beverage purchases	yr	368	1999	30r
Wine, red and white table, all sizes, any origin	liter	9.64	7/01	11r
Appliances				
Major appliances, expenditures on	yr	194	1999	30r
Small appliances, housewares, expenditures on	yr	93	1999	30r
Banking and Money				
Mortgage interest and charges paid	yr	2622	1999	30r
Mortgage principal paid on owned property	yr	1262	1999	30r
Vehicle finance charges paid	yr	240	1999	30r
Charity				
Cash contributions, expenditures on	yr	1001	1999	30r
Child Care				
Child raising cost, total, age 0-2	yr	8670	1999	60r
Child raising cost, total, age 3-5	yr	8910	1999	60r
Child raising cost, total, age 6-8	yr	9040	1999	60r
Child raising cost, total, age 9-11	yr	9100	1999	60r
Child raising cost, total, age 12-14	yr	9890	1999	60r
Child raising cost, total, age 15-17	yr	10010	1999	60r
Child's child care and education, age 0-2	yr	1070	1999	60r
Child's child care and education, age 3-5	yr	1190	1999	60r
Child's child care and education, age 6-8	yr	740	1999	60r
Child's child care and education, age 9-11	yr	470	1999	60r
Child's child care and education, age 12-14	yr	350	1999	60r
Child's child care and education, age 15-17	yr	590	1999	60r
Child's clothing, age 0-2	yr	480	1999	60r
Child's clothing, age 3-5	yr	470	1999	60r
Child's clothing, age 6-8	yr	520	1999	60r
Child's clothing, age 9-11	yr	570	1999	60r
Child's clothing, age 12-14	yr	970	1999	60r
Child's clothing, age 15-17	yr	870	1999	60r
Child's food, age 0-2	yr	1130	1999	60r
Child's food, age 3-5	yr	1290	1999	60r
Child's food, age 6-8	yr	1640	1999	60r
Child's food, age 9-11	yr	1930	1999	60r
Child's food, age 12-14	yr	1940	1999	60r
Child's food, age 15-17	yr	2150	1999	60r
Child's health care, age 0-2	yr	550	1999	60r
Child's health care, age 3-5	yr	530	1999	60r
Child's health care, age 6-8	yr	610	1999	60r
Child's health care, age 9-11	yr	650	1999	60r
Child's health care, age 12-14	yr	660	1999	60r
Child's health care, age 15-17	yr	690	1999	60r

Values are in dollars or fractions of dollars. In the column headed *Ref*, references are shown to sources. Each reference is followed by a letter. These refer to the geographical level for which data were reported: s=State, r=Region, and c=City or metro. The abbreviation *ex* is used to mean *except* or *excluding*; *exp* stands for *expenditures*. For other abbreviations and further explanations, please see the Introduction.

Bangor, ME - continued

Item	Per	Value	Date	Ref.
Child Care				
Child's housing, age 0-2	yr	3555	1999	60r
Child's housing, age 3-5	yr	3530	1999	60r
Child's housing, age 6-8	yr	3490	1999	60r
Child's housing, age 9-11	yr	3340	1999	60r
Child's housing, age 12-14	yr	3530	1999	60r
Child's housing, age 15-17	yr	3140	1999	60r
Child's personal care, reading, age 0-2	yr	920	1999	60r
Child's personal care, reading, age 3-5	yr	950	1999	60r
Child's personal care, reading, age 6-8	yr	980	1999	60r
Child's personal care, reading, age 9-11	yr	1020	1999	60r
Child's personal care, reading, age 12-14	yr	1190	1999	60r
Child's personal care, reading, age 15-17	yr	970	1999	60r
Clothing				
Apparel and services purchases	yr	1831	1999	30r
Boys, 2 to 15, expenditures on	yr	92	1999	30r
Children under 2, expenditures on	yr	63	1999	30r
Footwear, expenditures on	yr	300	1999	30r
Girls, 2 to 15, expenditures on	yr	101	1999	30r
Men and boys, expenditures on	yr	446	1999	30r
Men, 16 and over, expenditures on	yr	354	1999	30r
Women, 16 and over, expenditures on	yr	584	1999	30r
Communications				
Cable modem installation, Time Warner		75.00-225.00	6/99	103s
Cable modem rate, cable subscriber, Time Warner	mos	39.95-49.95	6/99	103s
Cable modem rate, non-cable subscriber, Time Warner	mos	39.95-54.95	6/99	103s
Phone line, single, business, field visit	inst.	110.00	12/97	17s
Phone line, single, business, no field visit	inst.	75.00	12/97	17s
Phone line, single, residence, field visit	inst.	101.00	12/97	17s
Phone line, single, residence, no field visit	inst.	75.00	12/97	17s
Postage and stationery, expenditures on	yr	138	1999	30r
Postal rate, express mail, up to half-pound		12.45	7/01	108r
Postal rate, letter, first class, first ounce		0.34	7/01	108r
Postal rate, letter, two ounces		0.57	7/01	108r
Postal rate, post card		0.21	7/01	108r
Postal rate, priority mail, two pounds		3.95	7/01	108r
Postal rate, priority mail, up to one pound		3.50	7/01	108r
Telephone services, expenditures on	yr	830	1999	30r
Education				
Board, 4-year private college/university	yr	2910	1996	38s
Board, 4-year public college/university	yr	2257	1996	38s
Education expenditures	yr	877	1999	30r
Room, 4-year private college/university	yr	2758	1996	38s
Room, 4-year public college/university	yr	2235	1996	38s
Total cost, 4-year private college/university	yr	21872	1996	38s
Total cost, 4-year public college/university	yr	7966	1996	38s
Tuition, 2-year public college/university, in state	yr	2381	1996	38s
Tuition, 4-year private college/university, in state	yr	16204	1996	38s
Tuition, 4-year public college/university	yr	3474	1996	38s
Energy and Fuels				
Electricity	KWh	0.12	7/01	11r
Fuel oil #2	gal	1.31	7/01	11r
Fuel oil and other fuels, expenditures on	yr	207	1999	30r
Gasoline, all types	gal	1.80	7/01	11r
Gasoline, unleaded midgrade	gal	1.85	7/01	11r
Gasoline, unleaded premium	gal	1.91	7/01	11r
Gasoline, unleaded regular	gal	1.71	7/01	11r
Natural gas, expenditures on	yr	368	1999	30r
Utility (piped) gas, therm		1.08	7/01	11r
Utility (piped) gas, 40 therms		50.87	7/01	11r
Utility (piped) gas, 100 therms		111.06	7/01	11r
Entertainment				
Entertainment purchases	yr	1821	1999	30r
Fees and admissions paid	yr	511	1999	30r

Bangor, ME - continued

Item	Per	Value	Date	Ref.
Entertainment - continued				
Television, radios, sound equipment, expenditures on	yr	650	1999	30r
Funerals				
Total cost of funeral		5776.91	1/99	78r
Acknowledgement cards		14.47	1/99	78r
Casket		2090.19	1/99	78r
Cosmetology, hair, other preparation		132.92	1/99	78r
Embalming		377.33	1/99	78r
Funeral at funeral home		352.43	1/99	78r
Hearse (local)		185.55	1/99	78r
Professional service charges		1289.95	1/99	78r
Service car/van		87.42	1/99	78r
Transfer of remains to funeral home		175.48	1/99	78r
Vault		729.40	1/99	78r
Visitation/viewing		341.76	1/99	78r
Groceries				
Apples, red delicious	lb	0.95	7/01	11r
Bacon, sliced	lb	3.44	7/01	11r
Bakery products, expenditures on	yr	310	1999	30r
Bananas	lb	0.55	7/01	11r
Beef, expenditures on	yr	236	1999	30r
Bread, white, pan	lb	1.09	7/01	11r
Butter, yoghurt, cheese, etc, expenditures on	yr	214	1999	30r
Cereals and bakery product purchases	yr	474	1999	30r
Cereals and cereal products, expenditures on	yr	164	1999	30r
Chicken legs, bone-in	lb	1.23	7/01	11r
Chicken, fresh, whole	lb	1.13	7/01	11r
Chuck roast, U.S. choice, boneless	lb	2.79	7/01	11r
Coffee, 100%, ground roast, all sizes	lb	3.40	7/01	11r
Dairy product purchases	yr	342	1999	30r
Eggs, expenditures on	yr	34	1999	30r
Eggs, grade A, large	dozen	0.82	7/01	11r
Fats and oils, expenditures on	yr	80	1999	30r
Fish and seafood, expenditures on	yr	123	1999	30r
Food (excl fruit and vegetables), eaten at home, purchases	yr	838	1999	30r
Food cooked on trips, expenditures on	yr	48	1999	30r
Food purchases	yr	5314	1999	30r
Food purchases, eaten away from home	yr	2313	1999	30r
Food purchases, food eaten at home	yr	3001	1999	30r
Fresh fruits, expenditures on	yr	169	1999	30r
Fresh milk and cream, expenditures on	yr	128	1999	30r
Fresh vegetables, expenditures on	yr	164	1999	30r
Grapefruit	lb	0.67	7/01	11r
Grapes, Thompson, seedless	lb	2.18	7/01	11r
Ground beef, lean and extra lean	lb	2.66	7/01	11r
Ground chuck, 100% beef	lb	2.04	7/01	11r
Lettuce, iceberg	lb	0.76	7/01	11r
Meats, poultry, fish, and egg purchases	yr	808	1999	30r
Nonalcoholic beverages, expenditures on	yr	225	1999	30r
Orange juice, frozen concentrate	16 oz	1.88	7/01	11r
Oranges, Navel	lb	0.79	7/01	11r
Oranges, Valencia	lb	0.56	7/01	11r
Peaches	lb	1.16	7/01	11r
Peanut butter, creamy, all sizes	lb	2.01	7/01	11r
Pears, Anjou	lb	1.16	7/01	11r
Pork chops, center cut, bone-in	lb	3.57	7/01	11r
Pork, expenditures on	yr	146	1999	30r
Potato chips	16 oz	3.37	7/01	11r
Potatoes, white, all types	lb	0.42	7/01	11r
Poultry, expenditures on	yr	158	1999	30r
Processed fruits, expenditures on	yr	124	1999	30r
Processed vegetables, expenditures on	yr	82	1999	30r
Round roast, U.S. choice, boneless	lb	3.04	7/01	11r
Spaghetti and macaroni	lb	1.04	7/01	11r
Steak, sirloin, U.S. choice, boneless	lb	5.39	7/01	11r
Strawberries, dry pint	12 oz	1.51	7/01	11r
Sugar and other sweets, expenditures on	yr	110	1999	30r
Sugar, white, 33-80 ounce package	lb	0.46	7/01	11r
Sugar, white, all sizes	lb	0.47	7/01	11r

Values are in dollars or fractions of dollars. In the column headed *Ref*, references are shown to sources. Each reference is followed by a letter. These refer to the geographical level for which data were reported: s=State, r=Region, and c=City or metro. The abbreviation *ex* is used to mean *except* or *excluding*; *exp* stands for *expenditures*. For other abbreviations and further explanations, please see the Introduction.

Bangor, ME - continued

Item	Per	Value	Date	Ref.
Groceries				
Tobacco products and smoking supplies purchases	yr	309	1999	30r
Yogurt, natural, fruit flavored	8 oz	0.79	7/01	11r
Goods and Services				
B&B Japanese maple (acer japonicum)	gal	38.99-125.00	4/00	93r
Boxwood (buxus)	2 gal	15.99-49.95	4/00	93r
Daylily (hemerocallis)	gal	4.95	4/00	93r
Flat of annuals		8.00-14.99	4/00	93r
Fountain grass (pennisetum)	gal	6.99-9.99	4/00	93r
Hanging basket (10 in)		12.95-19.99	4/00	93r
Hardy geranium (geranium)	gal	6.95-7.99	4/00	93r
Hosta (hosta)	gal	4.95	4/00	93r
Lilac (syrubga vulgaris)	2 gal	17.99-74.95	4/00	93r
Miscellaneous purchases	yr	872	1999	30r
Rhododendron (rhododendron)	2 gal	23.99-54.95	4/00	93r
Sage (salvia)	gal	6.95-7.99	4/00	93r
Wintercreeper euonymus (euonymus fortunei)	2 gal	14.99-23.95	4/00	93r
Hunting license	yr	19.00	4/01	34s
Health Care				
Cardiac catheterization, ave hospital/ physician charges		10740	1998	77s
Childbirth, Cesarean delivery		14716	1997	13r
Childbirth, vaginal delivery		8541	1997	13r
Drugs, expenditures on	yr	296	1999	30r
Health care purchases	yr	1788	1999	30r
Health insurance expenditures	yr	875	1999	30r
Hysterectomy, laproscopically-assisted, ave hospital/physician charges		11180	1998	76s
Hysterectomy, vaginal, ave hospital and physician charges		7810	1998	76s
Medicaid dispensing fee		3.35-5.35	1999	87s
Medical services expenditures	yr	516	1999	30r
Medical supplies, expenditures on	yr	102	1999	30r
Plastic surgery, breast augmentation		4232	2000	7r
Plastic surgery, breast lift		4605	2000	7r
Plastic surgery, facelift		6964	2000	7r
Plastic surgery, hair transplantation		4193	2000	7r
Plastic surgery, lip augmentation		1675	2000	7r
Plastic surgery, lower body lift		6611	2000	7r
Plastic surgery, thigh lift		4751	2000	7r
Household Goods				
Floor coverings, expenditures on	yr	59	1999	30r
Furniture, expenditures on	yr	388	1999	30r
Household furnishings and equipment purchases	yr	1567	1999	30r
Household textiles, expenditures on	yr	112	1999	30r
Laundry and cleaning supplies, expenditures on	yr	104	1999	30r
Housing				
Home, 2200 sq ft, 4-br, 2-bath, 2-car garage, average		158000	2000	47c
Home price, existing, ave		180800	10/00	90r
Home value, median		112000	2001	53s
Household operation expenditures	yr	581	1999	30r
Housekeeping supplies purchases	yr	474	1999	30r
Lodging expenditures	yr	550	1999	30r
Maintenance, repairs, insurance expenditures	yr	835	1999	30r
Monthly rental value of owned home	mos	663	1999	30r

Bangor, ME - continued

Item	Per	Value	Date	Ref.
Housing - continued				
Owned dwellings, expenditures own	yr	5209	1999	30r
Rent expenditures	yr	2390	1999	30r
Rental unit, 1 bedroom, with utilities	mos	432	4/01	41c
Rental unit, 2 bedroom, with utilities	mos	554	4/01	41c
Rental unit, 3 bedroom, with utilities	mos	724	4/01	41c
Rental unit, 4 bedroom, with utilities	mos	777	4/01	41c
Shelter, expenditures on	yr	8149	1999	30r
Insurance and Pensions				
Auto insurance premium	yr	542.81	1999	57s
Life and other personal insurance purchases	yr	424	1999	30r
Pensions and Social Security, expenditures on	yr	3037	1999	30r
Legal Fees				
Combination hunting and fishing license	yr	36.00	4/01	34s
Divorce, filing fee		60.00	4/01	35s
Driver's license fee	orig	35.00	1999	48s
Driver's license fee	renew	20.00	1999	48s
Fishing license	yr	19.00	4/01	34s
Personal Goods				
Personal care products and services purchases	yr	399	1999	30r
Personal Services				
Personal services, household, expenditures on	yr	271	1999	30r
Pets				
Pets, toys, and playground equipment, expenditures on	yr	325	1999	30r
Taxes				
Federal income taxes paid	yr	2606	1999	30r
Personal taxes, expenditures on	yr	3567	1999	30r
Property taxes paid	yr	1752	1999	30r
State and local income taxes paid	yr	694	1999	30r
Transportation				
Cars and trucks, new, expenditures on	yr	1496	1999	30r
Cars and trucks, used, expenditures on	yr	1251	1999	30r
Diesel at the pump	gal	1.32	10/99	73s
Gasoline and motor oil purchases	yr	901	1999	30r
Gasoline before-tax price (cents)	gal	117.60	10/00	43s
Maintenance and repair expenditures	yr	618	1999	30r
Public transportation, expenditures on	yr	575	1999	30r
Transportation purchases	yr	6503	1999	30r
Vehicle expenses, miscellaneous, purchases	yr	2266	1999	30r
Vehicle insurance payments	yr	824	1999	30r
Vehicle purchases (net outlay)	yr	2761	1999	30r
Vehicle rental, lease expenditures	yr	584	1999	30r
Utilities				
Electrical bill, average	mos	64.42	9/00	9s
Electricity, expenditures on	yr	837	1999	30r
Electricity, summer, 250 KWh	mos	31.93	2/96	97c
Electricity, summer, 500 KWh	mos	63.87	2/96	97c
Electricity, summer, 750 KWh	mos	95.80	2/96	97c
Electricity, summer, 1000 KWh	mos	127.73	2/96	97c
Electricity cost, average	KWh	10.12	9/00	9s
Utilities, fuels, and public services purchased	yr	2457	1999	30r
Water and other public services, expenditures on	yr	215	1999	30r
Weddings				
Wedding (national average cost)		19936	2000	33r
Wedding (regional average total cost)		29454	1997	110r
Attendants' gifts		321	1998	33r
Bridal attendants' apparel (5 persons)		824	2000	33r
Bride's headpiece/veil		173	1998	33r
Bride's wedding dress		859	1998	33r
Clergy, religious facility fee		242	1998	33r
Engagement ring		3177	1998	33r
Flowers		789	1998	33r
Groom's formalwear rental		99	2000	33r

Values are in dollars or fractions of dollars. In the column headed *Ref*, references are shown to sources. Each reference is followed by a letter. These refer to the geographical level for which data were reported: s=State, r=Region, and c=City or metro. The abbreviation *ex* is used to mean *except* or *excluding*; *exp* stands for *expenditures*. For other abbreviations and further explanations, please see the Introduction.

Bangor, ME - continued

Item	Per	Value	Date	Ref.
Weddings				
Limousine		410	1998	33r
Marriage license cost		20.00	4/01	35s
Men's formalwear (ushers, best man)		469	2000	33r
Mother of bride apparel		241	2000	33r
Music		866	1998	33r
Photography and videography		1368	1998	33r
Rehearsal dinner		728	1998	33r
Wedding invitations and announcements		341	1998	33r
Wedding reception		7968	2000	33r
Wedding rings (bride and groom)		1060	1998	33r

Barnstable-Yarmouth, MA

Item	Per	Value	Date	Ref.
Average annual expenditures	yr	37971	1999	30r
Alcoholic Beverages				
Alcoholic beverage purchases	yr	368	1999	30r
Wine, red and white table, all sizes, any origin	liter	9.64	7/01	11r
Appliances				
Major appliances, expenditures on	yr	194	1999	30r
Small appliances, housewares, expenditures on	yr	93	1999	30r
Banking and Money				
Mortgage interest and charges paid	yr	2622	1999	30r
Mortgage principal paid on owned property	yr	1262	1999	30r
Vehicle finance charges paid	yr	240	1999	30r
Charity				
Cash contributions, expenditures	yr	1001	1999	30r
Child Care				
Child raising cost, total, age 0-2	yr	8670	1999	60r
Child raising cost, total, age 3-5	yr	8910	1999	60r
Child raising cost, total, age 6-8	yr	9040	1999	60r
Child raising cost, total, age 9-11	yr	9100	1999	60r
Child raising cost, total, age 12-14	yr	9890	1999	60r
Child raising cost, total, age 15-17	yr	10010	1999	60r
Child's child care and education, age 0-2	yr	1070	1999	60r
Child's child care and education, age 3-5	yr	1190	1999	60r
Child's child care and education, age 6-8	yr	740	1999	60r
Child's child care and education, age 9-11	yr	470	1999	60r
Child's child care and education, age 12-14	yr	350	1999	60r
Child's child care and education, age 15-17	yr	590	1999	60r
Child's clothing, age 0-2	yr	480	1999	60r
Child's clothing, age 3-5	yr	470	1999	60r
Child's clothing, age 6-8	yr	520	1999	60r
Child's clothing, age 9-11	yr	570	1999	60r
Child's clothing, age 12-14	yr	970	1999	60r
Child's clothing, age 15-17	yr	870	1999	60r
Child's food, age 0-2	yr	1130	1999	60r
Child's food, age 3-5	yr	1290	1999	60r
Child's food, age 6-8	yr	1640	1999	60r
Child's food, age 9-11	yr	1930	1999	60r
Child's food, age 12-14	yr	1940	1999	60r
Child's food, age 15-17	yr	2150	1999	60r
Child's health care, age 0-2	yr	550	1999	60r
Child's health care, age 3-5	yr	530	1999	60r
Child's health care, age 6-8	yr	610	1999	60r
Child's health care, age 9-11	yr	650	1999	60r
Child's health care, age 12-14	yr	660	1999	60r
Child's health care, age 15-17	yr	690	1999	60r
Child's housing, age 0-2	yr	3555	1999	60r
Child's housing, age 3-5	yr	3530	1999	60r
Child's housing, age 6-8	yr	3490	1999	60r
Child's housing, age 9-11	yr	3340	1999	60r
Child's housing, age 12-14	yr	3530	1999	60r
Child's housing, age 15-17	yr	3140	1999	60r
Child's personal care, reading, age 0-2	yr	920	1999	60r
Child's personal care, reading, age 3-5	yr	950	1999	60r
Child's personal care, reading, age 6-8	yr	980	1999	60r
Child's personal care, reading, age 9-11	yr	1020	1999	60r

Barnstable-Yarmouth, MA - continued

Item	Per	Value	Date	Ref.
Child Care - continued				
Child's personal care, reading, age 12-14	yr	1190	1999	60r
Child's personal care, reading, age 15-17	yr	970	1999	60r
Clothing				
Apparel and services purchases	yr	1831	1999	30r
Boys, 2 to 15, expenditures on	yr	92	1999	30r
Children under 2, expenditures on	yr	63	1999	30r
Footwear, expenditures on	yr	300	1999	30r
Girls, 2 to 15, expenditures on	yr	101	1999	30r
Men and boys, expenditures on	yr	446	1999	30r
Men, 16 and over, expenditures on	yr	354	1999	30r
Women, 16 and over, expenditures on	yr	584	1999	30r
Communications				
Cable modem installation, Adelphi		54.90	6/99	103s
Cable modem installation, Media One		100.00	6/99	103s
Cable modem rate, cable subscriber, Adelphi	mos	34.95	6/99	103s
Cable modem rate, cable subscriber, Media One	mos	34.95-39.95	6/99	103s
Cable modem rate, non-cable subscriber, Adelphi	mos	44.95	6/99	103s
Cable modem rate, non-cable subscriber, Media One	mos	49.95	6/99	103s
Phone line, single, business, field visit	inst.	120.52	12/97	17s
Phone line, single, business, no field visit	inst.	93.02	12/97	17s
Phone line, single, residence, field visit	inst.	64.57	12/97	17s
Phone line, single, residence, no field visit	inst.	37.07	12/97	17s
Postage and stationery, expenditures on	yr	138	1999	30r
Postal rate, express mail, up to half-pound		12.45	7/01	108r
Postal rate, letter, first class, first ounce		0.34	7/01	108r
Postal rate, letter, two ounces		0.57	7/01	108r
Postal rate, post card		0.21	7/01	108r
Postal rate, priority mail, two pounds		3.95	7/01	108r
Postal rate, priority mail, up to one pound		3.50	7/01	108r
Telephone services, expenditures on	yr	830	1999	30r
Education				
Board, 4-year private college/university	yr	3244	1996	38s
Board, 4-year public college/university	yr	2042	1996	38s
Education expenditures	yr	877	1999	30r
Room, 4-year private college/university	yr	3688	1996	38s
Room, 4-year public college/university	yr	2462	1996	38s
Total cost, 4-year private college/university	yr	23335	1996	38s
Total cost, 4-year public college/university	yr	8757	1996	38s
Tuition, 2-year public college/university, in state	yr	2359	1996	38s
Tuition, 4-year private college/university, in state	yr	16403	1996	38s
Tuition, 4-year public college/university	yr	4253	1996	38s
Energy and Fuels				
Electricity	KWh	0.12	7/01	11r
Fuel oil #2	gal	1.31	7/01	11r
Fuel oil and other fuels, expenditures on	yr	207	1999	30r
Gas, natural, commercial rate	1000 cf	10.82	11/00	88s
Gasoline, all types	gal	1.80	7/01	11r
Gasoline, unleaded midgrade	gal	1.85	7/01	11r
Gasoline, unleaded premium	gal	1.91	7/01	11r
Gasoline, unleaded regular	gal	1.71	7/01	11r
Natural gas, expenditures on	yr	368	1999	30r
Utility (piped) gas, therm		1.08	7/01	11r
Utility (piped) gas, 40 therms		50.87	7/01	11r
Utility (piped) gas, 100 therms		111.06	7/01	11r
Entertainment				
Entertainment purchases	yr	1821	1999	30r
Fees and admissions paid	yr	511	1999	30r
Television, radios, sound equipment, expenditures on	yr	650	1999	30r
Funerals				
Total cost of funeral		5776.91	1/99	78r
Acknowledgement cards		14.47	1/99	78r
Casket		2090.19	1/99	78r
Cosmetology, hair, other preparation		132.92	1/99	78r

Values are in dollars or fractions of dollars. In the column headed *Ref*, references are shown to sources. Each reference is followed by a letter. These refer to the geographical level for which data were reported: s=State, r=Region, and c=City or metro. The abbreviation *ex* is used to mean *except* or *excluding*; *exp* stands for *expenditures*. For other abbreviations and further explanations, please see the Introduction.

Barnstable-Yarmouth, MA - continued

Item	Per	Value	Date	Ref.
Funerals				
Embalming		377.33	1/99	78r
Funeral at funeral home		352.43	1/99	78r
Hearse (local)		185.55	1/99	78r
Professional service charges		1289.95	1/99	78r
Service car/van		87.42	1/99	78r
Transfer of remains to funeral home		175.48	1/99	78r
Vault		729.40	1/99	78r
Visitation/viewing		341.76	1/99	78r
Groceries				
Apples, red delicious	lb	0.95	7/01	11r
Bacon, sliced	lb	3.44	7/01	11r
Bakery products, expenditures on	yr	310	1999	30r
Bananas	lb	0.55	7/01	11r
Beef, expenditures on	yr	236	1999	30r
Bread, white, pan	lb	1.09	7/01	11r
Butter, yoghurt, cheese, etc, expenditures on	yr	214	1999	30r
Cereals and bakery product purchases	yr	474	1999	30r
Cereals and cereal products, expenditures on	yr	164	1999	30r
Chicken legs, bone-in	lb	1.23	7/01	11r
Chicken, fresh, whole	lb	1.13	7/01	11r
Chuck roast, U.S. choice, boneless	lb	2.79	7/01	11r
Coffee, 100%, ground roast, all sizes	lb	3.40	7/01	11r
Dairy product purchases	yr	342	1999	30r
Eggs, expenditures on	yr	34	1999	30r
Eggs, grade A, large	dozen	0.82	7/01	11r
Fats and oils, expenditures on	yr	80	1999	30r
Fish and seafood, expenditures on	yr	123	1999	30r
Food (excl fruit and vegetables), eaten at home, purchases	yr	838	1999	30r
Food cooked on trips, expenditures on	yr	48	1999	30r
Food purchases	yr	5314	1999	30r
Food purchases, eaten away from home	yr	2313	1999	30r
Food purchases, food eaten at home	yr	3001	1999	30r
Fresh fruits, expenditures on	yr	169	1999	30r
Fresh milk and cream, expenditures on	yr	128	1999	30r
Fresh vegetables, expenditures on	yr	164	1999	30r
Grapefruit	lb	0.67	7/01	11r
Grapes, Thompson, seedless	lb	2.18	7/01	11r
Ground beef, lean and extra lean	lb	2.66	7/01	11r
Ground chuck, 100% beef	lb	2.04	7/01	11r
Lettuce, iceberg	lb	0.76	7/01	11r
Meats, poultry, fish, and egg purchases	yr	808	1999	30r
Nonalcoholic beverages, expenditures on	yr	225	1999	30r
Orange juice, frozen concentrate	16 oz	1.88	7/01	11r
Oranges, Navel	lb	0.79	7/01	11r
Oranges, Valencia	lb	0.56	7/01	11r
Peaches	lb	1.16	7/01	11r
Peanut butter, creamy, all sizes	lb	2.01	7/01	11r
Pears, Anjou	lb	1.16	7/01	11r
Pork chops, center cut, bone-in	lb	3.57	7/01	11r
Pork, expenditures on	yr	146	1999	30r
Potato chips	16 oz	3.37	7/01	11r
Potatoes, white, all types	lb	0.42	7/01	11r
Poultry, expenditures on	yr	158	1999	30r
Processed fruits, expenditures on	yr	124	1999	30r
Processed vegetables, expenditures on	yr	82	1999	30r
Round roast, U.S. choice, boneless	lb	3.04	7/01	11r
Spaghetti and macaroni	lb	1.04	7/01	11r
Steak, sirloin, U.S. choice, boneless	lb	5.39	7/01	11r
Strawberries, dry pint	12 oz	1.51	7/01	11r
Sugar and other sweets, expenditures on	yr	110	1999	30r
Sugar, white, 33-80 ounce package	lb	0.46	7/01	11r
Sugar, white, all sizes	lb	0.47	7/01	11r
Tobacco products and smoking supplies purchases	yr	309	1999	30r
Yogurt, natural, fruit flavored	8 oz	0.79	7/01	11r
Goods and Services				
B&B Japanese maple (acer japonicum)	gal	38.99-125.00	4/00	93r

Barnstable-Yarmouth, MA - continued

Item	Per	Value	Date	Ref.
Goods and Services - continued				
Boxwood (buxus)	2 gal	15.99-49.95	4/00	93r
Daylilly (hemerocallis)	gal	4.95	4/00	93r
Flat of annuals		8.00-14.99	4/00	93r
Fountain grass (pennisetum)	gal	6.99-9.99	4/00	93r
Hanging basket (10 in)		12.95-19.99	4/00	93r
Hardy geranium (geranium)	gal	6.95-7.99	4/00	93r
Hosta (hosta)	gal	4.95	4/00	93r
Lilac (syrubga vulgaris)	2 gal	17.99-74.95	4/00	93r
Miscellaneous purchases	yr	872	1999	30r
Rhododendron (rhododendron)	2 gal	23.99-54.95	4/00	93r
Sage (salvia)	gal	6.95-7.99	4/00	93r
Wintercreeper euonymus (euonymus fortunei)	2 gal	14.99-23.95	4/00	93r
Hunting license	yr	27.50	4/01	34s
Health Care				
Cardiac catheterization, ave hospital/physician charges		17080	1998	77s
Childbirth, Cesarean delivery		14716	1997	13r
Childbirth, vaginal delivery		8541	1997	13r
Drugs, expenditures on	yr	296	1999	30r
Health care purchases	yr	1788	1999	30r
Health insurance expenditures	yr	875	1999	30r
Hysterectomy, laproscopically-assisted, ave hospital/physician charges		13100	1998	76s
Hysterectomy, vaginal, ave hospital and physician charges		8780	1998	76s
Medicaid dispensing fee		3.00	1999	87s
Medical services expenditures	yr	516	1999	30r
Medical supplies, expenditures on	yr	102	1999	30r
Plastic surgery, breast augmentation		4232	2000	7r
Plastic surgery, breast lift		4605	2000	7r
Plastic surgery, facelift		6964	2000	7r
Plastic surgery, hair transplantation		4193	2000	7r
Plastic surgery, lip augmentation		1675	2000	7r
Plastic surgery, lower body lift		6611	2000	7r
Plastic surgery, thigh lift		4751	2000	7r
Household Goods				
Floor coverings, expenditures on	yr	59	1999	30r
Furniture, expenditures on	yr	388	1999	30r
Household furnishings and equipment purchases	yr	1567	1999	30r
Household textiles, expenditures on	yr	112	1999	30r
Laundry and cleaning supplies, expenditures on	yr	104	1999	30r
Housing				
Home price, existing, ave		180800	10/00	90r
Home value, median		261000	2001	53s
Household operation expenditures	yr	581	1999	30r
Housekeeping supplies purchases	yr	474	1999	30r
Lodging expenditures	yr	550	1999	30r
Maintenance, repairs, insurance expenditures	yr	835	1999	30r
Monthly rental value of owned home	mos	663	1999	30r
Owned dwellings, expenditures own	yr	5209	1999	30r
Rent expenditures	yr	2390	1999	30r
Rental unit, 1 bedroom, with utilities	mos	671	4/01	41c
Rental unit, 2 bedroom, with utilities	mos	896	4/01	41c
Rental unit, 3 bedroom, with utilities	mos	1122	4/01	41c
Rental unit, 4 bedroom, with utilities	mos	1256	4/01	41c
Shelter, expenditures on	yr	8149	1999	30r

Values are in dollars or fractions of dollars. In the column headed *Ref*, references are shown to sources. Each reference is followed by a letter. These refer to the geographical level for which data were reported: s=State, r=Region, and c=City or metro. The abbreviation *ex* is used to mean *except* or *excluding*; *exp* stands for expenditures. For other abbreviations and further explanations, please see the Introduction.

Barnstable-Yarmouth, MA - continued

Item	Per	Value	Date	Ref.
Insurance and Pensions				
Life and other personal insurance purchases	yr	424	1999	30r
Pensions and Social Security, expenditures on	yr	3037	1999	30r
Legal Fees				
Divorce, filing fee		100.00	4/01	35s
Driver's license fee	renew	33.75	1999	48s
Driver's license fee	orig	33.75	1999	48s
Fishing license	yr	27.50	4/01	34s
Personal Goods				
Personal care products and services purchases	yr	399	1999	30r
Personal Services				
Personal services, household, expenditures on	yr	271	1999	30r
Pets				
Pets, toys, and playground equipment, expenditures on	yr	325	1999	30r
Taxes				
Federal income taxes paid	yr	2606	1999	30r
Personal taxes, expenditures on	yr	3567	1999	30r
Property taxes paid	yr	1752	1999	30r
State and local income taxes paid	yr	694	1999	30r
Transportation				
Cars and trucks, new, expenditures on	yr	1496	1999	30r
Cars and trucks, used, expenditures on	yr	1251	1999	30r
Diesel at the pump	gal	1.32	10/99	73s
Gasoline and motor oil purchases	yr	901	1999	30r
Gasoline before-tax price (cents)	gal	118.70	10/00	43s
Maintenance and repair expenditures	yr	618	1999	30r
Public transportation, expenditures on	yr	575	1999	30r
Transportation purchases	yr	6503	1999	30r
Vehicle expenses, miscellaneous, purchases	yr	2266	1999	30r
Vehicle insurance payments	yr	824	1999	30r
Vehicle purchases (net outlay)	yr	2761	1999	30r
Vehicle rental, lease expenditures	yr	584	1999	30r
Travel				
Hotel room	night	111.15	2/01	95s
Utilities				
Electrical bill, average	mos	58.58	9/00	9s
Electricity, expenditures on	yr	837	1999	30r
Electricity cost, average	KWh	8.90	9/00	9s
Utilities, fuels, and public services purchased	yr	2457	1999	30r
Water and other public services, expenditures on	yr	215	1999	30r
Weddings				
Wedding (national average cost)		19936	2000	33r
Wedding (regional average total cost)		29454	1997	110r
Attendants' gifts		321	1998	33r
Bridal attendants' apparel (5 persons)		824	2000	33r
Bride's headpiece/veil		173	1998	33r
Bride's wedding dress		859	1998	33r
Clergy, religious facility fee		242	1998	33r
Engagement ring		3177	1998	33r
Flowers		789	1998	33r
Groom's formalwear rental		99	2000	33r
Limousine		410	1998	33r
Marriage license cost		25.00	4/01	35s
Men's formalwear (ushers, best man)		469	2000	33r
Mother of bride apparel		241	2000	33r
Music		866	1998	33r
Photography and videography		1368	1998	33r
Rehearsal dinner		728	1998	33r
Wedding invitations and announcements		341	1998	33r
Wedding reception		7968	2000	33r
Wedding rings (bride and groom)		1060	1998	33r

Baton Rouge, LA

Item	Per	Value	Date	Ref.
Composite, ACCRA index		104.60	3/01	4c
Alcoholic Beverages				
Alcoholic beverage purchases	yr	253	1999	30r
Beer, Heineken, 12-oz, ex deposit	6	6.61	3/01	4c
J & B Scotch	750-ml	19.68	3/01	4c
Malt beverages, all types, all sizes, any origin	16 oz	0.96	7/01	11r
Wine, Livingston or Gallo, Chablis blanc	1.5 liter	5.61	3/01	4c
Appliances				
Appliance repair, service call, washing machine	min lab chg	37.71	3/01	4c
Major appliances, expenditures on	yr	172	1999	30r
Small appliances, housewares, expenditures on	yr	81	1999	30r
Banking and Money				
Mortgage interest and charges paid	yr	2039	1999	30r
Mortgage principal paid on owned property	yr	1026	1999	30r
Mortgage rate, incl. points and orig. fee, 30-yr. conv. fixed or ARM	mos	6.85	3/01	4c
Vehicle finance charges paid	yr	365	1999	30r
Business Expenses				
Business travel, car rental	day	60	2001	3c
Business travel, food	day	42	2001	3c
Business travel, hotel	day	83	2001	3c
Charity				
Cash contributions, expenditures	yr	1127	1999	30r
Child Care				
Child raising cost, total, age 0-2	yr	8540	1999	60r
Child raising cost, total, age 3-5	yr	8780	1999	60r
Child raising cost, total, age 6-8	yr	8820	1999	60r
Child raising cost, total, age 9-11	yr	8800	1999	60r
Child raising cost, total, age 12-14	yr	9510	1999	60r
Child raising cost, total, age 15-17	yr	9740	1999	60r
Child's child care and education, age 0-2	yr	1380	1999	60r
Child's child care and education, age 3-5	yr	1520	1999	60r
Child's child care and education, age 6-8	yr	990	1999	60r
Child's child care and education, age 9-11	yr	650	1999	60r
Child's child care and education, age 12-14	yr	490	1999	60r
Child's child care and education, age 15-17	yr	840	1999	60r
Child's clothing, age 0-2	yr	480	1999	60r
Child's clothing, age 3-5	yr	470	1999	60r
Child's clothing, age 6-8	yr	520	1999	60r
Child's clothing, age 9-11	yr	570	1999	60r
Child's clothing, age 12-14	yr	950	1999	60r
Child's clothing, age 15-17	yr	850	1999	60r
Child's food, age 0-2	yr	1000	1999	60r
Child's food, age 3-5	yr	1160	1999	60r
Child's food, age 6-8	yr	1490	1999	60r
Child's food, age 9-11	yr	1770	1999	60r
Child's food, age 12-14	yr	1770	1999	60r
Child's food, age 15-17	yr	1980	1999	60r
Child's health care, age 0-2	yr	620	1999	60r
Child's health care, age 3-5	yr	590	1999	60r
Child's health care, age 6-8	yr	680	1999	60r
Child's health care, age 9-11	yr	720	1999	60r
Child's health care, age 12-14	yr	730	1999	60r
Child's health care, age 15-17	yr	760	1999	60r
Child's housing, age 0-2	yr	3070	1999	60r
Child's housing, age 3-5	yr	3050	1999	60r
Child's housing, age 6-8	yr	3010	1999	60r
Child's housing, age 9-11	yr	2850	1999	60r
Child's housing, age 12-14	yr	3040	1999	60r
Child's housing, age 15-17	yr	2650	1999	60r
Child's personal care, reading, age 0-2	yr	910	1999	60r
Child's personal care, reading, age 3-5	yr	930	1999	60r
Child's personal care, reading, age 6-8	yr	960	1999	60r
Child's personal care, reading, age 9-11	yr	1000	1999	60r
Child's personal care, reading, age 12-14	yr	1170	1999	60r
Child's personal care, reading, age 15-17	yr	950	1999	60r

Values are in dollars or fractions of dollars. In the column headed *Ref*, references are shown to sources. Each reference is followed by a letter. These refer to the geographical level for which data were reported: s=State, r=Region, and c=City or metro. The abbreviation *ex* is used to mean *except* or *excluding*; *exp* stands for *expenditures*. For other abbreviations and further explanations, please see the Introduction.

Baton Rouge, LA - continued

Item	Per	Value	Date	Ref.
Clothing				
Apparel and services purchases	yr	1610	1999	30r
Boys' brief, cotton	3	3.36	3/01	4c
Boys, 2 to 15, expenditures on	yr	89	1999	30r
Children under 2, expenditures on	yr	79	1999	30r
Footwear, expenditures on	yr	283	1999	30r
Girls, 2 to 15, expenditures on	yr	103	1999	30r
Men and boys, expenditures on	yr	351	1999	30r
Men, 16 and over, expenditures on	yr	262	1999	30r
Shirt, man's dress shirt		27.83	3/01	4c
Slacks, man's "No Wrinkles" khaki		48.00	3/01	4c
Women, 16 and over, expenditures on	yr	538	1999	30r
Communications				
Newspaper subscription, daily and Sunday delivery	mos	11.09	3/01	4c
Phone line, single, business, field visit	inst.	85.00	12/97	17s
Phone line, single, business, no field visit	inst.	85.00	12/97	17s
Phone line, single, residence, field visit	inst.	41.00	12/97	17s
Phone line, single, residence, no field visit	inst.	41.00	12/97	17s
Postage and stationery, expenditures on	yr	104	1999	30r
Postal rate, express mail, up to half-pound		12.45	7/01	108r
Postal rate, letter, first class, first ounce		0.34	7/01	108r
Postal rate, letter, two ounces		0.57	7/01	108r
Postal rate, post card		0.21	7/01	108r
Postal rate, priority mail, two pounds		3.95	7/01	108r
Postal rate, priority mail, up to one pound		3.50	7/01	108r
Telephone bill, business, basic rate	mos	36.76	12/97	18c
Telephone bill, family of three	mos	21.25	3/01	4c
Telephone bill, residential, basic rate	mos	12.64	12/97	18c
Telephone services, expenditures on	yr	860	1999	30r
Education				
Board, 4-year private college/university	yr	2440	1996	38s
Board, 4-year public college/university	yr	1806	1996	38s
Education expenditures	yr	431	1999	30r
Room, 4-year private college/university	yr	2906	1996	38s
Room, 4-year public college/university	yr	1464	1996	38s
Total cost, 4-year private college/university	yr	17796	1996	38s
Total cost, 4-year public college/university	yr	5491	1996	38s
Tuition, 2-year public college/university, in state	yr	1031	1996	38s
Tuition, 4-year private college/university, in state	yr	12449	1996	38s
Tuition, 4-year public college/university	yr	2221	1996	38s
Energy and Fuels				
Electricity	KWh	0.09	7/01	11r
Electricity	500 KWhs	47.29	7/01	11r
Energy, combined forms, 2400 sq ft	mos	155.48	3/01	4c
Fuel oil #2	gal	1.43	7/01	11r
Fuel oil and other fuels, expenditures on	yr	45	1999	30r
Gas, cooking, winter, 10 therms	mos	8.35	2/96	98c
Gas, cooking, winter, 30 therms	mos	24.24	2/96	98c
Gas, cooking, winter, 50 therms	mos	33.80	2/96	98c
Gas, heating, winter, average use	mos	66.79	2/96	98c
Gas, natural, commercial rate	1000 cf	8.75	11/00	88s
Gas, regular unleaded, cash, self-service	gal	1.34	3/01	4c
Gasoline, all types	gal	1.60	7/01	11r
Gasoline, unleaded midgrade	gal	1.65	7/01	11r
Gasoline, unleaded premium	gal	1.74	7/01	11r
Natural gas, expenditures on	yr	164	1999	30r
Utility (piped) gas, therm		1.01	7/01	11r
Utility (piped) gas, 40 therms		44.29	7/01	11r
Utility (piped) gas, 100 therms		97.44	7/01	11r
Entertainment				
Bowling, Saturday evening rate	line	3.08	3/01	4c
Entertainment purchases	yr	1574	1999	30r
Fees and admissions paid	yr	371	1999	30r
Monopoly game, Parker Brothers', No. 9	game	12.69	3/01	4c
Movie, first-run, Saturday, evening	adm.	6.53	3/01	4c
Reading purchases	yr	121	1999	30r

Baton Rouge, LA - continued

Item	Per	Value	Date	Ref.
Entertainment - continued				
Television, radios, sound equipment, expenditures on	yr	561	1999	30r
Tennis balls, yellow, Wilson or Penn, 3	can	2.06	3/01	4c
Funerals				
Total cost of funeral		5842.28	1/99	78r
Acknowledgement cards		28.35	1/99	78r
Casket		2494.29	1/99	78r
Cosmetology, hair, other preparation		109.22	1/99	78r
Embalming		361.42	1/99	78r
Funeral at funeral home		349.20	1/99	78r
Hearse (local)		161.91	1/99	78r
Professional service charges		1116.50	1/99	78r
Service car/van		65.56	1/99	78r
Transfer of remains to funeral home		143.56	1/99	78r
Vault		785.25	1/99	78r
Visitation/viewing		227.02	1/99	78r
Groceries				
Groceries, ACCRA Index		108.60	3/01	4c
American processed cheese	lb	3.50	7/01	11r
Antibiotic ointment, Polysporin	0.5 oz	4.79	3/01	4c
Baby food, strained vegetables or fruit, lowest price	4-4.5 oz	0.41	3/01	4c
Bakery products, expenditures on	yr	261	1999	30r
Bananas	lb	0.43	3/01	4c
Bananas	lb	0.47	7/01	11r
Beans, dried, any type, all sizes	lb	0.63	7/01	11r
Beef for stew, boneless	lb	2.86	7/01	11r
Beef or hamburger, ground	lb	1.90	3/01	4c
Beef, expenditures on	yr	210	1999	30r
Bologna, all beef or mixed	lb	2.29	7/01	11r
Bread, French	lb	1.66	7/01	11r
Bread, white	loaf	0.96	3/01	4c
Bread, white, pan	lb	0.87	7/01	11r
Bread, whole wheat, pan	lb	1.38	7/01	11r
Broccoli	lb	1.04	7/01	11r
Butter, salted, grade AA, stick	lb	2.26	7/01	11r
Butter, yoghurt, cheese, etc, expenditures on	yr	170	1999	30r
Cabbage	lb	0.42	7/01	11r
Cereals and cereal products, expenditures on	yr	140	1999	30r
Cheddar cheese, natural	lb	3.75	7/01	11r
Cheese, Kraft grated Parmesan	8 oz	4.54	3/01	4c
Chicken breast, bone-in	lb	1.85	7/01	11r
Chicken legs, bone-in	lb	1.34	7/01	11r
Chicken, fresh, whole	lb	1.05	7/01	11r
Chicken, whole fryer	lb	0.82	3/01	4c
Chops, boneless,	lb	4.13	7/01	11r
Chuck roast, graded and ungraded, excl U.S. prime and choice	lb	2.35	7/01	11r
Chuck roast, U.S. choice, boneless	lb	2.67	7/01	11r
Cigarettes, Winston, Kings	carton	33.11	3/01	4c
Coffee, 100%, ground roast, all sizes	lb	2.88	7/01	11r
Coffee, instant, plain, regular, all sizes	16 oz	9.25	7/01	11r
Coffee, vacuum-packed	13 oz	2.94	3/01	4c
Cola, non diet,	2 liter	1.11	7/01	11r
Corn Flakes, Kellogg's or Post Toasties	18 oz	3.19	3/01	4c
Corn, frozen, whole kernel, lowest price	16 oz	1.29	3/01	4c
Crackers, soda, salted	lb	1.70	7/01	11r
Dairy product purchases	yr	282	1999	30r
Eggs, expenditures on	yr	32	1999	30r
Eggs, Grade A or AA	dozen	1.19	3/01	4c
Fats and oils, expenditures on	yr	79	1999	30r
Fish and seafood, expenditures on	yr	99	1999	30r
Flour, white, all purpose	lb	0.32	7/01	11r
Food (excl fruit and vegetables), eaten at home, purchases	yr	815	1999	30r
Food cooked on trips, expenditures on	yr	36	1999	30r
Food purchases	yr	4533	1999	30r
Food purchases, eaten away from home	yr	1873	1999	30r
Food purchases, food eaten at home	yr	2660	1999	30r
Fresh fruits, expenditures on	yr	128	1999	30r

Values are in dollars or fractions of dollars. In the column headed *Ref*, references are shown to sources. Each reference is followed by a letter. These refer to the geographical level for which data were reported: s=State, r=Region, and c=City or metro. The abbreviation *ex* is used to mean *except* or *excluding*; *exp* stands for *expenditures*. For other abbreviations and further explanations, please see the Introduction.

Baton Rouge, LA - continued

Item	Per	Value	Date	Ref.
Groceries				
Fresh milk and cream, expenditures on	yr	112	1999	30r
Fresh vegetables, expenditures on	yr	131	1999	30r
Fruit and vegetable purchases	yr	438	1999	30r
Grapefruit	lb	0.59	7/01	11r
Grapes, Thompson, seedless	lb	2.12	7/01	11r
Ground beef, 100% beef	lb	1.76	7/01	11r
Ground beef, lean and extra lean	lb	2.60	7/01	11r
Ground chuck, 100% beef	lb	2.08	7/01	11r
Ham, boneless, excl canned	lb	2.71	7/01	11r
Ham, rump or shank half, bone-in, smoked	lb	2.19	7/01	11r
Ice cream, prepackaged, bulk, regular	1/2 gal	3.93	7/01	11r
Lemons	lb	1.32	7/01	11r
Lettuce, iceberg	head	1.08	3/01	4c
Lettuce, iceberg	lb	0.76	7/01	11r
Margarine, Blue Bonnet or Parkay, stick	lb	0.84	3/01	4c
Milk, fresh, low fat	gal	2.75	7/01	11r
Milk, fresh, whole, fortified	gal	2.97	7/01	11r
Milk, whole	1/2 gal	1.97	3/01	4c
Nonalcoholic beverages, expenditures on	yr	228	1999	30r
Orange juice, frozen concentrate	16 oz	1.95	7/01	11r
Orange juice, Minute Maid frozen	12 oz	1.86	3/01	4c
Oranges, Navel	lb	0.73	7/01	11r
Oranges, Valencia	lb	0.55	7/01	11r
Peaches, halves or slices, Hunt's, Del Monte, or Libby's	29 oz	1.71	3/01	4c
Peanut butter, creamy, all sizes	lb	1.83	7/01	11r
Pears, Anjou	lb	0.98	7/01	11r
Peas, green, Del Monte or Green Giant	15 oz	0.74	3/01	4c
Pork chops, center cut, bone-in	lb	3.33	7/01	11r
Pork sausage, fresh, loose	lb	2.59	7/01	11r
Pork shoulder picnic, bone-in, smoked	lb	1.12	7/01	11r
Pork, expenditures on	yr	162	1999	30r
Potato chips	16 oz	3.59	7/01	11r
Potatoes, frozen, french fried	lb	1.00	7/01	11r
Potatoes, white or red	10 lb	2.83	3/01	4c
Potatoes, white, all types	lb	0.44	7/01	11r
Poultry, expenditures on	yr	137	1999	30r
Processed fruits, expenditures on	yr	97	1999	30r
Processed vegetables, expenditures on	yr	82	1999	30r
Rice, white, long grain, uncooked	lb	0.51	7/01	11r
Round roast, graded and ungraded, excl U.S. prime and choice	lb	2.96	7/01	11r
Round steak, graded and ungraded, excl U.S. prime and choice	lb	3.11	7/01	11r
Sausage, Jimmy Dean/Owens pork	lb	3.30	3/01	4c
Shortening, vegetable, Crisco	3 lb	2.94	3/01	4c
Sirloin steak, graded and ungraded, excl U.S. prime and choice	lb	4.23	7/01	11r
Soft drink, Coca Cola, ex deposit	2 liter	1.40	3/01	4c
Spaghetti and macaroni	lb	0.78	7/01	11r
Steak, round, U.S. choice, boneless	lb	3.56	7/01	11r
Steak, sirloin, U.S. choice, boneless	lb	5.65	7/01	11r
Steak, T-bone	lb	6.52	3/01	4c
Strawberries, dry pint	12 oz	1.50	7/01	11r
Sugar and other sweets, expenditures on	yr	99	1999	30r
Sugar, cane or beet	4 lbs	1.84	3/01	4c
Sugar, white, 33-80 ounce package	lb	0.39	7/01	11r
Sugar, white, all sizes	lb	0.42	7/01	11r
Tobacco products and smoking supplies purchases	yr	288	1999	30r
Tomatoes, field grown	lb	1.43	7/01	11r
Tomatoes, Hunt's or Del Monte	14.5 oz	0.95	3/01	4c
Tuna, chunk, light	6 oz	0.75	3/01	4c
Tuna, light, chunk	lb	1.77	7/01	11r
Turkey, frozen, whole	lb	1.05	7/01	11r
Goods and Services				
Miscellaneous goods and services, ACCRA Index		103.90	3/01	4c
B&B Japanese maple (acer japonicum)	gal	79.98-99.00	4/00	93r
Boxwood (buxus)	2 gal	12.98-18.99	4/00	93r

Baton Rouge, LA - continued

Item	Per	Value	Date	Ref.
Goods and Services - continued				
Daylily (hemerocallis)	gal	7.96-11.00	4/00	93r
Flat of annuals		13.99-27.99	4/00	93r
Fountain grass (pennisetum)	gal	6.96-9.00	4/00	93r
Hanging basket (10 in)		9.99-24.99	4/00	93r
Hardy geranium (geranium)	gal	5.96-8.00	4/00	93r
Hosta (hosta)	gal	8.96-12.99	4/00	93r
Lilac (syrubga vulgaris)	2 gal	13.00-19.99	4/00	93r
Rhododendron (rhododendron)	2 gal	12.98-29.99	4/00	93r
Sage (salvia)	gal	5.96-8.00	4/00	93r
Wintercreeper euonymus (euonymus fortunei)	2 gal	13.00-18.99	4/00	93r
Hunting license	yr	15.00	4/01	34s
Health Care				
Health care, ACCRA Index		97.20	3/01	4c
Cardiac catheterization, ave hospital/ physician charges		15650	1998	77s
Childbirth, Cesarean delivery		11587	1997	13r
Childbirth, vaginal delivery		6725	1997	13r
Dentist's fee, adult teeth cleaning and periodic oral exam	visit	78.86	3/01	4c
Doctor's fee, routine exam, established patient	visit	54.71	3/01	4c
Drugs, expenditures on	yr	399	1999	30r
Health care purchases	yr	1971	1999	30r
Health insurance expenditures	yr	933	1999	30r
Hospital care, private room	day	406.33	3/01	4c
Hysterectomy, laproscopically-assisted, ave hospital/physician charges		14600	1998	76s
Hysterectomy, vaginal, ave hospital and physician charges		10520	1998	76s
Medicaid dispensing fee		5.77	1999	87s
Medical services expenditures	yr	547	1999	30r
Medical supplies, expenditures on	yr	91	1999	30r
Household Goods				
Dishwashing powder, Cascade	50 oz	3.79	3/01	4c
Floor coverings, expenditures on	yr	44	1999	30r
Furniture, expenditures on	yr	335	1999	30r
Household furnishings and equipment purchases	yr	1328	1999	30r
Household textiles, expenditures on	yr	89	1999	30r
Laundry and cleaning supplies, expenditures on	yr	113	1999	30r
Tissues, facial, Kleenex brand	175	1.60	3/01	4c
Housing				
Housing, ACCRA Index		99.10	3/01	4c
Home, 2200 sq ft, 4-br, 2-bath, 2-car garage, average		190225	2000	47c
Home price, existing, ave		160100	10/00	90r
Home value, median		108000	2001	53s
House, 2400 sq ft, 8000 sq ft lot, new, urban, utilities	total	216558	3/01	4c
House payment, principal and interest, 25% down payment	mos	1064	3/01	4c
Household operation expenditures	yr	553	1999	30r
Housekeeping supplies purchases	yr	473	1999	30r
Housing, expenditures on	yr	10303	1999	30r
Maintenance, repairs, insurance expenditures	yr	699	1999	30r
Monthly rental value of owned home	mos	505	1999	30r
Owned dwellings, expenditures own	yr	3465	1999	30r
Rent expenditures	yr	1641	1999	30r

Values are in dollars or fractions of dollars. In the column headed *Ref*, references are shown to sources. Each reference is followed by a letter. These refer to the geographical level for which data were reported: s=State, r=Region, and c=City or metro. The abbreviation *ex* is used to mean *except* or *excluding*; *exp* stands for expenditures. For other abbreviations and further explanations, please see the Introduction.

Baton Rouge, LA - continued

Item	Per	Value	Date	Ref.
Housing				
Rent, apartment, 2 br, 1 1/2-2 baths, unfurn, 950 sq ft, water	mos	578	3/01	4c
Rental unit, 1 bedroom, with utilities	mos	381	4/01	41c
Rental unit, 2 bedroom, with utilities	mos	473	4/01	41c
Rental unit, 3 bedroom, with utilities	mos	656	4/01	41c
Rental unit, 4 bedroom, with utilities	mos	775	4/01	41c
Shelter, expenditures on	yr	5467	1999	30r
Insurance and Pensions				
Auto insurance premium	yr	965.15	1999	57s
Life and other personal insurance purchases	yr	414	1999	30r
Pensions and Social Security, expenditures on	yr	2635	1999	30r
Personal insurance and pensions, expenditures on	yr	3048	1999	30r
Legal Fees				
Divorce, filing fee		162.00	4/01	35s
Driver's license fee	renew	12.50	1999	48s
Driver's license fee	orig	18.00	1999	48s
Fishing license	yr	9.50	4/01	34s
Personal Goods				
Personal care products and services purchases	yr	393	1999	30r
Shampoo, Alberto VO5	15 oz	1.30	3/01	4c
Toothpaste, Crest or Colgate	6-7 oz	3.30	3/01	4c
Personal Services				
Dry cleaning, man's 2-pc suit		7.59	3/01	4c
Man's haircut, barbershop, no styling		10.50	3/01	4c
Personal services, household, expenditures on	yr	258	1999	30r
Woman's shampoo, trim, blow-dry, no style-change		23.00	3/01	4c
Pets				
Pets, toys, and playground equipment, expenditures on	yr	306	1999	30r
Restaurant Food				
Chicken, fried, thigh and drumstick, KFC/Church's		2.69	3/01	4c
Hamburger with cheese, McDonald's	1/4 lb	1.99	3/01	4c
Pizza, Pizza Hut or Pizza Inn	11-12 in	10.43	3/01	4c
Taxes				
Federal income taxes paid	yr	2047	1999	30r
Personal taxes, expenditures on	yr	2554	1999	30r
Property taxes paid	yr	726	1999	30r
State and local income taxes paid	yr	363	1999	30r
Transportation				
Transportation, ACCRA Index		104.70	3/01	4c
Bus fare, to central business district	1-way	1.25	3/01	4c
Cars and trucks, new, expenditures on	yr	1648	1999	30r
Cars and trucks, used, expenditures on	yr	1651	1999	30r
Diesel at the pump	gal	1.19	10/99	73s
Gasoline and motor oil purchases	yr	1052	1999	30r
Gasoline before-tax price (cents)	gal	102.70	10/00	43s
Maintenance and repair expenditures	yr	621	1999	30r
Public transportation, expenditures on	yr	298	1999	30r
Tire balance, computer or spin balance, front	wheel	9.03	3/01	4c
Transportation purchases	yr	6738	1999	30r
Vehicle expenses, miscellaneous, purchases	yr	2033	1999	30r
Vehicle insurance payments	yr	696	1999	30r
Vehicle purchases (net outlay)	yr	3354	1999	30r
Vehicle rental, lease expenditures	yr	352	1999	30r
Utilities				
Utilities, ACCRA Index		123.30	3/01	4c
Electrical bill, average	mos	87.50	9/00	9s
Electricity, 2400 sq ft, new home	mos	155.48	3/01	4c
Electricity, expenditures on	yr	1115	1999	30r
Electricity, summer, 250 KWh	mos	25.04	2/96	97c
Electricity, summer, 500 KWh	mos	44.14	2/96	97c

Baton Rouge, LA - continued

Item	Per	Value	Date	Ref.
Utilities - continued				
Electricity, summer, 750 KWh	mos	63.23	2/96	97c
Electricity, summer, 1000 KWh	mos	82.32	2/96	97c
Electricity cost, average	KWh	6.35	9/00	9s
Water and other public services, expenditures on	yr	298	1999	30r
Weddings				
Wedding (national average cost)		19936	2000	33r
Attendants' gifts		321	1998	33r
Bridal attendants' apparel (5 persons)		824	2000	33r
Bride's headpiece/veil		173	1998	33r
Bride's wedding dress		859	1998	33r
Clergy, religious facility fee		242	1998	33r
Engagement ring		3177	1998	33r
Flowers		789	1998	33r
Groom's formalwear rental		99	2000	33r
Limousine		410	1998	33r
Marriage license cost		25.00	4/01	35s
Men's formalwear (ushers, best man)		469	2000	33r
Mother of bride apparel		241	2000	33r
Music		866	1998	33r
Photography and videography		1368	1998	33r
Rehearsal dinner		728	1998	33r
Wedding invitations and announcements		341	1998	33r
Wedding reception		7968	2000	33r
Wedding rings (bride and groom)		1060	1998	33r

Beaumont-Port Arthur, TX

Item	Per	Value	Date	Ref.
Alcoholic Beverages				
Alcoholic beverage purchases	yr	253	1999	30r
Malt beverages, all types, all sizes, any origin	16 oz	0.96	7/01	11r
Appliances				
Major appliances, expenditures on	yr	172	1999	30r
Small appliances, housewares, expenditures on	yr	81	1999	30r
Banking and Money				
Mortgage interest and charges paid	yr	2039	1999	30r
Mortgage principal paid on owned property	yr	1026	1999	30r
Vehicle finance charges paid	yr	365	1999	30r
Charity				
Cash contributions, expenditures	yr	1127	1999	30r
Child Care				
Child raising cost, total, age 0-2	yr	8540	1999	60r
Child raising cost, total, age 3-5	yr	8780	1999	60r
Child raising cost, total, age 6-8	yr	8820	1999	60r
Child raising cost, total, age 9-11	yr	8800	1999	60r
Child raising cost, total, age 12-14	yr	9510	1999	60r
Child raising cost, total, age 15-17	yr	9740	1999	60r
Child's child care and education, age 0-2	yr	1380	1999	60r
Child's child care and education, age 3-5	yr	1520	1999	60r
Child's child care and education, age 6-8	yr	990	1999	60r
Child's child care and education, age 9-11	yr	650	1999	60r
Child's child care and education, age 12-14	yr	490	1999	60r
Child's child care and education, age 15-17	yr	840	1999	60r
Child's clothing, age 0-2	yr	480	1999	60r
Child's clothing, age 3-5	yr	470	1999	60r
Child's clothing, age 6-8	yr	520	1999	60r
Child's clothing, age 9-11	yr	570	1999	60r
Child's clothing, age 12-14	yr	950	1999	60r
Child's clothing, age 15-17	yr	850	1999	60r
Child's food, age 0-2	yr	1000	1999	60r
Child's food, age 3-5	yr	1160	1999	60r
Child's food, age 6-8	yr	1490	1999	60r
Child's food, age 9-11	yr	1770	1999	60r
Child's food, age 12-14	yr	1770	1999	60r
Child's food, age 15-17	yr	1980	1999	60r
Child's health care, age 0-2	yr	620	1999	60r
Child's health care, age 3-5	yr	590	1999	60r

Values are in dollars or fractions of dollars. In the column headed *Ref*, references are shown to sources. Each reference is followed by a letter. These refer to the geographical level for which data were reported: s=State, r=Region, and c=City or metro. The abbreviation *ex* is used to mean *except* or *excluding*; *exp* stands for *expenditures*. For other abbreviations and further explanations, please see the Introduction.

Beaumont-Port Arthur, TX - continued

Item	Per	Value	Date	Ref.
Child Care				
Child's health care, age 6-8	yr	680	1999	60r
Child's health care, age 9-11	yr	720	1999	60r
Child's health care, age 12-14	yr	730	1999	60r
Child's health care, age 15-17	yr	760	1999	60r
Child's housing, age 0-2	yr	3070	1999	60r
Child's housing, age 3-5	yr	3050	1999	60r
Child's housing, age 6-8	yr	3010	1999	60r
Child's housing, age 9-11	yr	2850	1999	60r
Child's housing, age 12-14	yr	3040	1999	60r
Child's housing, age 15-17	yr	2650	1999	60r
Child's personal care, reading, age 0-2	yr	910	1999	60r
Child's personal care, reading, age 3-5	yr	930	1999	60r
Child's personal care, reading, age 6-8	yr	960	1999	60r
Child's personal care, reading, age 9-11	yr	1000	1999	60r
Child's personal care, reading, age 12-14	yr	1170	1999	60r
Child's personal care, reading, age 15-17	yr	950	1999	60r
Clothing				
Apparel and services purchases	yr	1610	1999	30r
Boys, 2 to 15, expenditures on	yr	89	1999	30r
Children under 2, expenditures on	yr	79	1999	30r
Footwear, expenditures on	yr	283	1999	30r
Girls, 2 to 15, expenditures on	yr	103	1999	30r
Men and boys, expenditures on	yr	351	1999	30r
Men, 16 and over, expenditures on	yr	262	1999	30r
Women, 16 and over, expenditures on	yr	538	1999	30r
Communications				
Cable modem installation, AT&T-BIS		150.00	6/99	103s
Cable modem installation, Marcus		499.00	6/99	103s
Cable modem installation, Time Warner		75.00-225.00	6/99	103s
Cable modem rate, cable subscriber, AT&T-BIS	mos	39.95	6/99	103s
Cable modem rate, cable subscriber, Marcus	mos	14.95-49.95	6/99	103s
Cable modem rate, cable subscriber, Time Warner	mos	39.95-49.95	6/99	103s
Cable modem rate, non-cable subscriber, Marcus	mos	60.95	6/99	103s
Cable modem rate, non-cable subscriber, Time Warner	mos	39.95-54.95	6/99	103s
Phone line, single, business, field visit	inst.	71.90	12/97	17s
Phone line, single, business, no field visit	inst.	57.30	12/97	17s
Phone line, single, residence, field visit	inst.	52.95	12/97	17s
Phone line, single, residence, no field visit	inst.	38.35	12/97	17s
Postage and stationery	yr	104	1999	30r
Postal rate, express mail, up to half-pound		12.45	7/01	108r
Postal rate, letter, first class, first ounce		0.34	7/01	108r
Postal rate, letter, two ounces		0.57	7/01	108r
Postal rate, post card		0.21	7/01	108r
Postal rate, priority mail, two pounds		3.95	7/01	108r
Postal rate, priority mail, up to one pound		3.50	7/01	108r
Telephone services, expenditures on	yr	860	1999	30r
Education				
Board, 4-year private college/university	yr	2198	1996	38s
Board, 4-year public college/university	yr	1759	1996	38s
Education expenditures	yr	431	1999	30r
Room, 4-year private college/university	yr	2000	1996	38s
Room, 4-year public college/university	yr	1885	1996	38s
Total cost, 4-year private college/university	yr	13156	1996	38s
Total cost, 4-year public college/university	yr	5464	1996	38s
Tuition, 2-year public college/university, in state	yr	771	1996	38s
Tuition, 4-year private college/university, in state	yr	8959	1996	38s
Tuition, 4-year public college/university	yr	1820	1996	38s
Energy and Fuels				
Electricity	KWh	0.09	7/01	11r
Electricity	500 KWhs	47.29	7/01	11r
Fuel oil #2	gal	1.43	7/01	11r

Beaumont-Port Arthur, TX - continued

Item	Per	Value	Date	Ref.
Energy and Fuels - continued				
Fuel oil and other fuels, expenditures on	yr	45	1999	30r
Gas, natural, commercial rate	1000 cf	6.94	11/00	88s
Gasoline, all types	gal	1.60	7/01	11r
Gasoline, unleaded midgrade	gal	1.65	7/01	11r
Gasoline, unleaded premium	gal	1.74	7/01	11r
Natural gas, expenditures on	yr	164	1999	30r
Utility (piped) gas, therm		1.01	7/01	11r
Utility (piped) gas, 40 therms		44.29	7/01	11r
Utility (piped) gas, 100 therms		97.44	7/01	11r
Entertainment				
Entertainment purchases	yr	1574	1999	30r
Fees and admissions paid	yr	371	1999	30r
Reading purchases	yr	121	1999	30r
Television, radios, sound equipment, expenditures on	yr	561	1999	30r
Funerals				
Total cost of funeral		5842.28	1/99	78r
Acknowledgement cards		28.35	1/99	78r
Casket		2494.29	1/99	78r
Cosmetology, hair, other preparation		109.22	1/99	78r
Embalming		361.42	1/99	78r
Funeral at funeral home		349.20	1/99	78r
Hearse (local)		161.91	1/99	78r
Professional service charges		1116.50	1/99	78r
Service car/van		65.56	1/99	78r
Transfer of remains to funeral home		143.56	1/99	78r
Vault		785.25	1/99	78r
Visitation/viewing		227.02	1/99	78r
Groceries				
American processed cheese	lb	3.50	7/01	11r
Bakery products, expenditures on	yr	261	1999	30r
Bananas	lb	0.47	7/01	11r
Beans, dried, any type, all sizes	lb	0.63	7/01	11r
Beef for stew, boneless	lb	2.86	7/01	11r
Beef, expenditures on	yr	210	1999	30r
Bologna, all beef or mixed	lb	2.29	7/01	11r
Bread, French	lb	1.66	7/01	11r
Bread, white, pan	lb	0.87	7/01	11r
Bread, whole wheat, pan	lb	1.38	7/01	11r
Broccoli	lb	1.04	7/01	11r
Butter, salted, grade AA, stick	lb	2.26	7/01	11r
Butter, yoghurt, cheese, etc, expenditures on	yr	170	1999	30r
Cabbage	lb	0.42	7/01	11r
Cereals and cereal products, expenditures on	yr	140	1999	30r
Cheddar cheese, natural	lb	3.75	7/01	11r
Chicken breast, bone-in	lb	1.85	7/01	11r
Chicken legs, bone-in	lb	1.34	7/01	11r
Chicken, fresh, whole	lb	1.05	7/01	11r
Chops, boneless,	lb	4.13	7/01	11r
Chuck roast, graded and ungraded, excl U.S. prime and choice	lb	2.35	7/01	11r
Chuck roast, U.S. choice, boneless	lb	2.67	7/01	11r
Coffee, 100%, ground roast, all sizes	lb	2.88	7/01	11r
Coffee, instant, plain, regular, all sizes	16 oz	9.25	7/01	11r
Cola, non diet	2 liter	1.11	7/01	11r
Crackers, soda, salted	lb	1.70	7/01	11r
Dairy product purchases	yr	282	1999	30r
Eggs, expenditures on	yr	32	1999	30r
Fats and oils, expenditures on	yr	79	1999	30r
Fish and seafood, expenditures on	yr	99	1999	30r
Flour, white, all purpose	lb	0.32	7/01	11r
Food (excl fruit and vegetables), eaten at home, purchases	yr	815	1999	30r
Food cooked on trips, expenditures on	yr	36	1999	30r
Food purchases	yr	4533	1999	30r
Food purchases, eaten away from home	yr	1873	1999	30r
Food purchases, food eaten at home	yr	2660	1999	30r
Fresh fruits, expenditures on	yr	128	1999	30r
Fresh milk and cream, expenditures on	yr	112	1999	30r
Fresh vegetables, expenditures on	yr	131	1999	30r

Values are in dollars or fractions of dollars. In the column headed *Ref*, references are shown to sources. Each reference is followed by a letter. These refer to the geographical level for which data were reported: s=State, r=Region, and c=City or metro. The abbreviation *ex* is used to mean *except* or *excluding*; *exp* stands for *expenditures*. For other abbreviations and further explanations, please see the Introduction.

Beaumont-Port Arthur, TX - continued

Item	Per	Value	Date	Ref.
Groceries				
Fruit and vegetable purchases	yr	438	1999	30r
Grapefruit	lb	0.59	7/01	11r
Grapes, Thompson, seedless	lb	2.12	7/01	11r
Ground beef, 100% beef	lb	1.76	7/01	11r
Ground beef, lean and extra lean	lb	2.60	7/01	11r
Ground chuck, 100% beef	lb	2.08	7/01	11r
Ham, boneless, excl canned	lb	2.71	7/01	11r
Ham, rump or shank half, bone-in, smoked	lb	2.19	7/01	11r
Ice cream, prepackaged, bulk, regular	1/2 gal	3.93	7/01	11r
Lemons	lb	1.32	7/01	11r
Lettuce, iceberg	lb	0.76	7/01	11r
Milk, fresh, low fat,	gal	2.75	7/01	11r
Milk, fresh, whole, fortified	gal	2.97	7/01	11r
Nonalcoholic beverages, expenditures on	yr	228	1999	30r
Orange juice, frozen concentrate	16 oz	1.95	7/01	11r
Oranges, Navel	lb	0.73	7/01	11r
Oranges, Valencia	lb	0.55	7/01	11r
Peanut butter, creamy, all sizes	lb	1.83	7/01	11r
Pears, Anjou	lb	0.98	7/01	11r
Pork chops, center cut, bone-in	lb	3.33	7/01	11r
Pork sausage, fresh, loose	lb	2.59	7/01	11r
Pork shoulder picnic, bone-in, smoked	lb	1.12	7/01	11r
Pork, expenditures on	yr	162	1999	30r
Potato chips	16 oz	3.59	7/01	11r
Potatoes, frozen, french fried	lb	1.00	7/01	11r
Potatoes, white, all types	lb	0.44	7/01	11r
Poultry, expenditures on	yr	137	1999	30r
Processed fruits, expenditures on	yr	97	1999	30r
Processed vegetables, expenditures on	yr	82	1999	30r
Rice, white, long grain, uncooked	lb	0.51	7/01	11r
Round roast, graded and ungraded, excl U.S. prime and choice	lb	2.96	7/01	11r
Round steak, graded and ungraded, excl U.S. prime and choice	lb	3.11	7/01	11r
Sirloin steak, graded and ungraded, excl U.S. prime and choice	lb	4.23	7/01	11r
Spaghetti and macaroni	lb	0.78	7/01	11r
Steak, round, U.S. choice, boneless	lb	3.56	7/01	11r
Steak, sirloin, U.S. choice, boneless	lb	5.65	7/01	11r
Strawberries, dry pint	12 oz	1.50	7/01	11r
Sugar and other sweets, expenditures on	yr	99	1999	30r
Sugar, white, 33-80 ounce package	lb	0.39	7/01	11r
Sugar, white, all sizes	lb	0.42	7/01	11r
Tobacco products and smoking supplies purchases	yr	288	1999	30r
Tomatoes, field grown	lb	1.43	7/01	11r
Tuna, light, chunk	lb	1.77	7/01	11r
Turkey, frozen, whole	lb	1.05	7/01	11r
Goods and Services				
B&B Japanese maple (acer japonicum)	gal	79.98-99.00	4/00	93r
Boxwood (buxus)	2 gal	12.98-18.99	4/00	93r
Christmas tree, noble fir		40-60	2000	65s
Daylilly (hemerocallis)	gal	7.96-11.00	4/00	93r
Flat of annuals		13.99-27.99	4/00	93r
Fountain grass (pennisetum)	gal	6.96-9.00	4/00	93r
Hanging basket (10 in)		9.99-24.99	4/00	93r
Hardy geranium (geranium)	gal	5.96-8.00	4/00	93r
Hosta (hosta)	gal	8.96-12.99	4/00	93r
Lilac (syrubga vulgaris)	2 gal	13.00-19.99	4/00	93r
Rhododendron (rhododendron)	2 gal	12.98-29.99	4/00	93r
Sage (salvia)	gal	5.96-8.00	4/00	93r

Beaumont-Port Arthur, TX - continued

Item	Per	Value	Date	Ref.
Goods and Services - continued				
Wintercreeper euonymus (euonymus fortunei)	2 gal	13.00-18.99	4/00	93r
Hunting license	yr	19.00	4/01	34s
Health Care				
Cardiac catheterization, ave hospital/ physician charges		20140	1998	77s
Childbirth, Cesarean delivery		11587	1997	13r
Childbirth, vaginal delivery		6725	1997	13r
Drugs, expenditures on	yr	399	1999	30r
Health care purchases	yr	1971	1999	30r
Health insurance expenditures	yr	933	1999	30r
Hysterectomy, laproscopically-assisted, ave hospital/physician charges		15700	1998	76s
Hysterectomy, vaginal, ave hospital and physician charges		12180	1998	76s
Medicaid dispensing fee		5.27	1999	87s
Medical services expenditures	yr	547	1999	30r
Medical supplies, expenditures on	yr	91	1999	30r
Household Goods				
Floor coverings, expenditures on	yr	44	1999	30r
Furniture, expenditures on	yr	335	1999	30r
Household furnishings and equipment purchases	yr	1328	1999	30r
Household textiles, expenditures on	yr	89	1999	30r
Laundry and cleaning supplies, expenditures on	yr	113	1999	30r
Housing				
Home price, existing, ave		160100	10/00	90r
Home value, median		112000	2001	53s
Household operation expenditures	yr	553	1999	30r
Housekeeping supplies purchases	yr	473	1999	30r
Housing, expenditures on	yr	10303	1999	30r
Maintenance, repairs, insurance expenditures	yr	699	1999	30r
Monthly rental value of owned home	mos	505	1999	30r
Owned dwellings, expenditures own	yr	3465	1999	30r
Rent expenditures	yr	1641	1999	30r
Rental unit, 1 bedroom, with utilities	mos	394	4/01	41c
Rental unit, 2 bedroom, with utilities	mos	480	4/01	41c
Rental unit, 3 bedroom, with utilities	mos	636	4/01	41c
Rental unit, 4 bedroom, with utilities	mos	673	4/01	41c
Shelter, expenditures on	yr	5467	1999	30r
Insurance and Pensions				
Life and other personal insurance purchases	yr	414	1999	30r
Pensions and Social Security, expenditures on	yr	2635	1999	30r
Personal insurance and pensions, expenditures on	yr	3048	1999	30r
Legal Fees				
Divorce, filing fee		150.00-200.00	4/01	35s
Driver's license fee	renew	20.00	1999	48s
Driver's license fee	orig	24.00	1999	48s
Fishing license	yr	19.00	4/01	34s
Personal Goods				
Personal care products and services purchases	yr	393	1999	30r
Personal Services				
Personal services, household, expenditures on	yr	258	1999	30r
Pets				
Pets, toys, and playground equipment, expenditures on	yr	306	1999	30r
Taxes				
Federal income taxes paid	yr	2047	1999	30r
Personal taxes, expenditures on	yr	2554	1999	30r
Property taxes paid	yr	726	1999	30r

Values are in dollars or fractions of dollars. In the column headed *Ref*, references are shown to sources. Each reference is followed by a letter. These refer to the geographical level for which data were reported: s=State, r=Region, and c=City or metro. The abbreviation *ex* is used to mean *except* or *excluding*; *exp* stands for *expenditures*. For other abbreviations and further explanations, please see the Introduction.

Beaumont-Port Arthur, TX - continued

Item	Per	Value	Date	Ref.
Taxes				
State and local income taxes paid	yr	363	1999	30r
Transportation				
Cars and trucks, new, expenditures on	yr	1648	1999	30r
Cars and trucks, used, expenditures on	yr	1651	1999	30r
Diesel at the pump	gal	1.18	10/99	73s
Gasoline and motor oil purchases	yr	1052	1999	30r
Gasoline before-tax price (cents)	gal	101.30	10/00	43s
Maintenance and repair expenditures	yr	621	1999	30r
Public transportation, expenditures on	yr	298	1999	30r
Transportation purchases	yr	6738	1999	30r
Vehicle expenses, miscellaneous, purchases	yr	2033	1999	30r
Vehicle insurance payments	yr	696	1999	30r
Vehicle purchases (net outlay)	yr	3354	1999	30r
Vehicle rental, lease expenditures	yr	352	1999	30r
Utilities				
Electrical bill, average	mos	87.17	9/00	9s
Electricity, expenditures on	yr	1115	1999	30r
Electricity, summer, 250 KWh	mos	23.76	2/96	96c
Electricity, summer, 500 KWh	mos	41.81	2/96	96c
Electricity, summer, 750 KWh	mos	59.87	2/96	96c
Electricity, summer, 1000 KWh	mos	77.92	2/96	96c
Electricity cost, average	KWh	6.48	9/00	9s
Water and other public services, expenditures on	yr	298	1999	30r
Weddings				
Wedding (national average cost)		19936	2000	33r
Attendants' gifts		321	1998	33r
Bridal attendants' apparel (5 persons)		824	2000	33r
Bride's headpiece/veil		173	1998	33r
Bride's wedding dress		859	1998	33r
Clergy, religious facility fee		242	1998	33r
Engagement ring		3177	1998	33r
Flowers		789	1998	33r
Groom's formalwear rental		99	2000	33r
Limousine		410	1998	33r
Marriage license cost		36.00	4/01	35s
Men's formalwear (ushers, best man)		469	2000	33r
Mother of bride apparel		241	2000	33r
Music		866	1998	33r
Photography and videography		1368	1998	33r
Rehearsal dinner		728	1998	33r
Wedding invitations and announcements		341	1998	33r
Wedding reception		7968	2000	33r
Wedding rings (bride and groom)		1060	1998	33r

Bellingham, WA

Item	Per	Value	Date	Ref.
Average annual expenditures	yr	40662	1999	30r
Composite, ACCRA index		108.70	12/00	5c
Alcoholic Beverages				
Alcoholic beverage purchases	yr	372	1999	30r
Beer, Heineken, 12-oz, ex deposit	6	6.85	12/00	5c
J & B Scotch	750-ml	22.50	12/00	5c
Malt beverages, all types, all sizes, any origin	16 oz	0.94	7/01	11r
Wine, Livingston or Gallo, Chablis blanc	1.5 liter	4.71	12/00	5c
Wine, red and white table, all sizes, any origin	liter	6.00	7/01	11r
Appliances				
Appliance repair, service call, washing machine	min lab chg	47.48	12/00	5c
Major appliances, expenditures on	yr	167	1999	30r
Small appliances, housewares, expenditures on	yr	105	1999	30r
Banking and Money				
Mortgage interest and charges paid	yr	3368	1999	30r
Mortgage principal paid on owned property	yr	1677	1999	30r
Mortgage rate, incl. points and orig. fee, 30-yr. conv. fixed or ARM	mos	7.77	12/00	5c

Bellingham, WA - continued

Item	Per	Value	Date	Ref.
Banking and Money - continued				
Vehicle finance charges paid	yr	311	1999	30r
Charity				
Cash contributions, expenditures	yr	1344	1999	30r
Child Care				
Child raising cost, total, age 0-2	yr	9140	1999	60r
Child raising cost, total, age 3-5	yr	9370	1999	60r
Child raising cost, total, age 6-8	yr	9450	1999	60r
Child raising cost, total, age 9-11	yr	9470	1999	60r
Child raising cost, total, age 12-14	yr	10170	1999	60r
Child raising cost, total, age 15-17	yr	10360	1999	60r
Child's child care and education, age 0-2	yr	1250	1999	60r
Child's child care and education, age 3-5	yr	1380	1999	60r
Child's child care and education, age 6-8	yr	890	1999	60r
Child's child care and education, age 9-11	yr	580	1999	60r
Child's child care and education, age 12-14	yr	430	1999	60r
Child's child care and education, age 15-17	yr	730	1999	60r
Child's clothing, age 0-2	yr	430	1999	60r
Child's clothing, age 3-5	yr	420	1999	60r
Child's clothing, age 6-8	yr	470	1999	60r
Child's clothing, age 9-11	yr	520	1999	60r
Child's clothing, age 12-14	yr	870	1999	60r
Child's clothing, age 15-17	yr	770	1999	60r
Child's food, age 0-2	yr	1120	1999	60r
Child's food, age 3-5	yr	1280	1999	60r
Child's food, age 6-8	yr	1640	1999	60r
Child's food, age 9-11	yr	1930	1999	60r
Child's food, age 12-14	yr	1940	1999	60r
Child's food, age 15-17	yr	2150	1999	60r
Child's health care, age 0-2	yr	490	1999	60r
Child's health care, age 3-5	yr	470	1999	60r
Child's health care, age 6-8	yr	530	1999	60r
Child's health care, age 9-11	yr	570	1999	60r
Child's health care, age 12-14	yr	580	1999	60r
Child's health care, age 15-17	yr	610	1999	60r
Child's housing, age 0-2	yr	3630	1999	60r
Child's housing, age 3-5	yr	3610	1999	60r
Child's housing, age 6-8	yr	3570	1999	60r
Child's housing, age 9-11	yr	3410	1999	60r
Child's housing, age 12-14	yr	3600	1999	60r
Child's housing, age 15-17	yr	3210	1999	60r
Child's personal care, reading, age 0-2	yr	1040	1999	60r
Child's personal care, reading, age 3-5	yr	1060	1999	60r
Child's personal care, reading, age 6-8	yr	1090	1999	60r
Child's personal care, reading, age 9-11	yr	1130	1999	60r
Child's personal care, reading, age 12-14	yr	1300	1999	60r
Child's personal care, reading, age 15-17	yr	1080	1999	60r
Clothing				
Apparel and services purchases	yr	1863	1999	30r
Boys' brief, cotton	3	5.36	12/00	5c
Boys, 2 to 15, expenditures on	yr	80	1999	30r
Children under 2, expenditures on	yr	74	1999	30r
Footwear, expenditures on	yr	307	1999	30r
Girls, 2 to 15, expenditures on	yr	101	1999	30r
Men and boys, expenditures on	yr	443	1999	30r
Men, 16 and over, expenditures on	yr	363	1999	30r
Shirt, man's dress shirt		30.83	12/00	5c
Slacks, man's "No Wrinkles" khaki		36.99	12/00	5c
Women, 16 and over, expenditures on	yr	594	1999	30r
Communications				
Cable modem installation, AT&T-BIS		150.00	6/99	103s
Cable modem rate, cable subscriber, AT&T-BIS	mos	39.95	6/99	103s
Newspaper subscription, daily and Sunday delivery	mos	12.39	12/00	5c
Phone line, single, business, field visit	inst.	48.00	12/97	17s
Phone line, single, business, no field visit	inst.	48.00	12/97	17s
Phone line, single, residence, field visit	inst.	31.00	12/97	17s
Phone line, single, residence, no field visit	inst.	31.00	12/97	17s
Postage and stationery, expenditures on	yr	150	1999	30r
Postal rate, express mail, up to half-pound		12.45	7/01	108r

Values are in dollars or fractions of dollars. In the column headed *Ref*, references are shown to sources. Each reference is followed by a letter. These refer to the geographical level for which data were reported: s=State, r=Region, and c=City or metro. The abbreviation *ex* is used to mean *except* or *excluding*; *exp* stands for expenditures. For other abbreviations and further explanations, please see the Introduction.

Bellingham, WA - continued

Item	Per	Value	Date	Ref.
Communications				
Postal rate, letter, first class, first ounce		0.34	7/01	108r
Postal rate, letter, two ounces		0.57	7/01	108r
Postal rate, post card		0.21	7/01	108r
Postal rate, priority mail, two pounds		3.95	7/01	108r
Postal rate, priority mail, up to one pound		3.50	7/01	108r
Telephone bill, family of three	mos	20.20	12/00	5c
Telephone services, expenditures on	yr	825	1999	30r
Education				
Board, 4-year private college/university	yr	2329	1996	38s
Board, 4-year public college/university	yr	2158	1996	38s
Education expenditures	yr	676	1999	30r
Room, 4-year private college/university	yr	2487	1996	38s
Room, 4-year public college/university	yr	2187	1996	38s
Total cost, 4-year private college/university	yr	18092	1996	38s
Total cost, 4-year public college/university	yr	7136	1996	38s
Tuition, 2-year public college/university, in state	yr	1369	1996	38s
Tuition, 4-year private college/university, in state	yr	13276	1996	38s
Tuition, 4-year public college/university	yr	2791	1996	38s
Energy and Fuels				
Electricity	500 KWhs	48.23	7/01	11r
Electricity	KWh	0.11	7/01	11r
Energy, combined forms, 2400 sq ft	mos	99.62	12/00	5c
Energy, exc. electricity, 2400 sq ft	mos	60.24	12/00	5c
Fuel oil and other fuels, expenditures on	yr	35	1999	30r
Gas, cooking, winter, 10 therms	mos	6.01	2/96	98c
Gas, cooking, winter, 30 therms	mos	18.02	2/96	98c
Gas, cooking, winter, 50 therms	mos	30.03	2/96	98c
Gas, heating, winter, average use	mos	70.84	2/96	98c
Gas, natural, commercial rate	1000 cf	6.89	11/00	88s
Gas, regular unleaded, cash, self-service	gal	1.78	12/00	5c
Gasoline, all types	gal	1.91	7/01	11r
Gasoline, unleaded premium	gal	2.05	7/01	11r
Gasoline, unleaded regular	gal	1.83	7/01	11r
Natural gas, expenditures on	yr	255	1999	30r
Utility (piped) gas, therm		0.98	7/01	11r
Utility (piped) gas, 40 therms		40.74	7/01	11r
Utility (piped) gas, 100 therms		96.80	7/01	11r
Entertainment				
Bowling, Saturday evening rate	line	2.75	12/00	5c
Entertainment purchases	yr	2139	1999	30r
Fees and admissions paid	yr	545	1999	30r
Monopoly game, Parker Brothers', No. 9	game	12.16	12/00	5c
Movie, first-run, Saturday, evening	adm.	7.00	12/00	5c
Television, radios, sound equipment, expenditures on	yr	624	1999	30r
Tennis balls, yellow, Wilson or Penn, 3	can	2.22	12/00	5c
Funerals				
Total cost of funeral		5401.08	1/99	78r
Acknowledgement cards		33.64	1/99	78r
Casket		2170.43	1/99	78r
Cosmetology, hair, other preparation		136.32	1/99	78r
Embalming		319.13	1/99	78r
Funeral at funeral home		370.21	1/99	78r
Hearse (local)		161.04	1/99	78r
Professional service charges		963.15	1/99	78r
Service car/van		133.99	1/99	78r
Transfer of remains to funeral home		159.82	1/99	78r
Vault		778.07	1/99	78r
Visitation/viewing		175.28	1/99	78r
Groceries				
Groceries, ACCRA Index		105.60	12/00	5c
Antibiotic ointment, Polysporin	0.5 oz	4.89	12/00	5c
Apples, red delicious	lb	0.84	7/01	11r
Baby food, strained vegetables or fruit, lowest price	4-4.5 oz	0.35	12/00	5c
Bacon, sliced	lb	3.38	7/01	11r

Bellingham, WA - continued

Item	Per	Value	Date	Ref.
Groceries - continued				
Bakery products, expenditures on	yr	299	1999	30r
Bananas	lb	0.54	7/01	11r
Bananas	lb	0.70	12/00	5c
Beans, dried, any type, all sizes	lb	0.76	7/01	11r
Beef or hamburger, ground	lb	1.53	12/00	5c
Beef, expenditures on	yr	222	1999	30r
Bread, white	loaf	0.75	12/00	5c
Bread, white, pan		0.99	7/01	11r
Butter, yoghurt, cheese, etc, expenditures on	yr	211	1999	30r
Cereals and bakery product purchases	yr	466	1999	30r
Cereals and cereal products, expenditures on	yr	168	1999	30r
Cheese, Kraft grated Parmesan	8 oz	4.25	12/00	5c
Chicken breast, bone-in	lb	2.45	7/01	11r
Chicken, fresh, whole	lb	1.19	7/01	11r
Chicken, whole fryer	lb	1.25	12/00	5c
Chops, boneless,	lb	4.00	7/01	11r
Chuck roast, graded and ungraded, excl U.S. prime and choice	lb	2.55	7/01	11r
Cigarettes, Winston, Kings	carton	37.85	12/00	5c
Coffee, 100%, ground roast, all sizes	lb	3.80	7/01	11r
Coffee, vacuum-packed	13 oz	3.70	12/00	5c
Cookies, chocolate chip	lb	2.83	7/01	11r
Corn Flakes, Kellogg's or Post Toasties	18 oz	2.87	12/00	5c
Corn, frozen, whole kernel, lowest price	16 oz	1.01	12/00	5c
Dairy product purchases	yr	341	1999	30r
Eggs, expenditures on	yr	39	1999	30r
Eggs, Grade A or AA	dozen	1.17	12/00	5c
Eggs, grade AA, large	dozen	1.23	7/01	11r
Fats and oils, expenditures on	yr	88	1999	30r
Fish and seafood, expenditures on	yr	121	1999	30r
Food (excl fruit and vegetables), eaten at home, purchases	yr	1001	1999	30r
Food cooked on trips, expenditures on	yr	64	1999	30r
Food purchases	yr	5312	1999	30r
Food purchases, eaten away from home	yr	2180	1999	30r
Food purchases, food eaten at home	yr	3132	1999	30r
Fresh fruits, expenditures on	yr	186	1999	30r
Fresh milk and cream, expenditures on	yr	130	1999	30r
Fresh vegetables, expenditures on	yr	177	1999	30r
Grapefruit	lb	0.68	7/01	11r
Grapes, Thompson, seedless	lb	2.42	7/01	11r
Ground beef, lean and extra lean	lb	2.46	7/01	11r
Ice cream, prepackaged, bulk, regular	1/2 gal	3.62	7/01	11r
Lettuce, iceberg	lb	0.63	7/01	11r
Lettuce, iceberg	head	1.10	12/00	5c
Margarine, Blue Bonnet or Parkay, stick	lb	0.64	12/00	5c
Meats, poultry, fish, and egg purchases	yr	761	1999	30r
Milk, fresh, low fat,	gal	2.80	7/01	11r
Milk, fresh, whole, fortified	gal	2.88	7/01	11r
Milk, whole	1/2 gal	1.86	12/00	5c
Nonalcoholic beverages, expenditures on	yr	258	1999	30r
Orange juice, Minute Maid frozen	12 oz	1.34	12/00	5c
Oranges, Navel	lb	0.97	7/01	11r
Oranges, Valencia	lb	0.43	7/01	11r
Peaches	lb	1.38	7/01	11r
Peaches, halves or slices, Hunt's, Del Monte, or Libby's	29 oz	1.80	12/00	5c
Peanut butter, creamy, all sizes	lb	2.14	7/01	11r
Peas, green, Del Monte or Green Giant	15 oz	0.78	12/00	5c
Pork chops, center cut, bone-in	lb	3.83	7/01	11r
Pork, expenditures on	yr	141	1999	30r
Potatoes, white or red	10 lb	1.88	12/00	5c
Potatoes, white, all types	lb	0.37	7/01	11r
Poultry, expenditures on	yr	146	1999	30r
Processed fruits, expenditures on	yr	118	1999	30r
Processed vegetables, expenditures on	yr	81	1999	30r
Round roast, graded and ungraded, excl U.S. prime and choice	lb	3.07	7/01	11r
Round roast, U.S. choice, boneless	lb	3.37	7/01	11r
Round steak, graded and ungraded, excl U.S. prime and choice	lb	3.51	7/01	11r

Values are in dollars or fractions of dollars. In the column headed *Ref*, references are shown to sources. Each reference is followed by a letter. These refer to the geographical level for which data were reported: s=State, r=Region, and c=City or metro. The abbreviation *ex* is used to mean *except* or *excluding*; *exp* stands for *expenditures*. For other abbreviations and further explanations, please see the Introduction.

Bellingham, WA - continued

Item	Per	Value	Date	Ref.
Groceries				
Sausage, Jimmy Dean/Owens pork	lb	3.61	12/00	5c
Shortening, vegetable, Crisco	3 lb	2.25	12/00	5c
Sirloin steak, graded and ungraded, excl U.S. prime and choice	lb	4.67	7/01	11r
Soft drink, Coca Cola, ex deposit	2 liter	1.15	12/00	5c
Steak, sirloin, U.S. choice, boneless	lb	6.20	7/01	11r
Steak, T-bone	lb	5.68	12/00	5c
Strawberries, dry pint	12 oz	1.79	7/01	11r
Sugar and other sweets, expenditures on	yr	124	1999	30r
Sugar, cane or beet	4 lbs	1.66	12/00	5c
Sugar, white, all sizes	lb	0.46	7/01	11r
Tobacco products and smoking supplies purchases	yr	217	1999	30r
Tomatoes, field grown	lb	1.17	7/01	11r
Tomatoes, Hunt's or Del Monte	14.5 oz	0.88	12/00	5c
Tuna, chunk, light	6 oz	0.78	12/00	5c
Tuna, light, chunk	lb	2.05	7/01	11r
Goods and Services				
Miscellaneous goods and services, ACCRA Index		106.00	12/00	5c
B&B Japanese maple (acer japonicum)	gal	39.99	4/00	93r
Boxwood (buxus)	2 gal	14.99-24.99	4/00	93r
Daylilly (hemerocallis)	gal	6.99-8.99	4/00	93r
Flat of annuals		16.68	4/00	93r
Fountain grass (pennisetum)	gal	7.99-11.99	4/00	93r
Hanging basket (10 in)		29.99	4/00	93r
Hardy geranium (geranium)	gal	6.99-11.99	4/00	93r
Hosta (hosta)	gal	6.99-18.99	4/00	93r
Lilac (syrubga vulgaris)	2 gal	14.99-17.99	4/00	93r
Miscellaneous purchases	yr	1070	1999	30r
Rhododendron (rhododendron)	2 gal	14.99	4/00	93r
Sage (salvia)	gal	6.99	4/00	93r
Wintercreeper euonymus (euonymus fortunei)	2 gal	14.99-22.99	4/00	93r
Hunting license	yr	30.00	4/01	34s
Health Care				
Health care, ACCRA Index		121.50	12/00	5c
Cardiac catheterization, ave hospital/ physician charges		13290	1998	77s
Childbirth, Cesarean delivery		11587	1997	13r
Childbirth, vaginal delivery		6725	1997	13r
Dentist's fee, adult teeth cleaning and periodic oral exam	visit	109.80	12/00	5c
Doctor's fee, routine exam, established patient	visit	61.80	12/00	5c
Drugs, expenditures on	yr	309	1999	30r
Health care purchases	yr	1869	1999	30r
Health insurance expenditures	yr	868	1999	30r
Hospital care, private room	day	465.00	12/00	5c
Hysterectomy, laproscopically-assisted, ave hospital/physician charges		10960	1998	76s
Hysterectomy, vaginal, ave hospital and physician charges		9000	1998	76s
Medicaid dispensing fee		3.98-4.92	1999	87s
Medical services expenditures	yr	580	1999	30r
Medical supplies, expenditures on	yr	112	1999	30r
Household Goods				
Dishwashing powder, Cascade	50 oz	2.94	12/00	5c
Floor coverings, expenditures on	yr	49	1999	30r
Furniture, expenditures on	yr	444	1999	30r
Household furnishings and equipment purchases	yr	1768	1999	30r
Household textiles, expenditures on	yr	141	1999	30r

Bellingham, WA - continued

Item	Per	Value	Date	Ref.
Household Goods - continued				
Laundry and cleaning supplies, expenditures on	yr	128	1999	30r
Tissues, facial, Kleenex brand	175	1.46	12/00	5c
Housing				
Housing, ACCRA Index		117.40	12/00	5c
Home price, existing, ave		239400	10/00	90r
Home value, median		195000	2001	53s
House, 2400 sq ft, 8000 sq ft lot, new, urban, utilities	total	253000	12/00	5c
House payment, principal and interest, 25% down payment	mos	1362	12/00	5c
Household operation expenditures	yr	781	1999	30r
Housekeeping supplies purchases	yr	513	1999	30r
Lodging expenditures	yr	575	1999	30r
Maintenance, repairs, insurance expenditures	yr	939	1999	30r
Monthly rental value of owned home	mos	662	1999	30r
Owned dwellings, expenditures own	yr	5231	1999	30r
Rent expenditures	yr	2709	1999	30r
Rent, apartment, 2 br, 1 1/2-2 baths, unfurn, 950 sq ft, water	mos	710	12/00	5c
Rental unit, 1 bedroom, with utilities	mos	520	4/01	41c
Rental unit, 2 bedroom, with utilities	mos	692	4/01	41c
Rental unit, 3 bedroom, with utilities	mos	956	4/01	41c
Rental unit, 4 bedroom, with utilities	mos	1133	4/01	41c
Shelter, expenditures on	yr	8516	1999	30r
Insurance and Pensions				
Life and other personal insurance purchases	yr	355	1999	30r
Pensions and Social Security, expenditures on	yr	3636	1999	30r
Legal Fees				
Divorce, filing fee		100.00	4/01	35s
Driver's license fee	orig	14.00	1999	48s
Driver's license fee	renew	14.00	1999	48s
Fishing license	yr	20.00	4/01	34s
Personal Goods				
Personal care products and services purchases	yr	449	1999	30r
Shampoo, Alberto VO5	15 oz	1.21	12/00	5c
Toothpaste, Crest or Colgate	6-7 oz	2.35	12/00	5c
Personal Services				
Dry cleaning, man's 2-pc suit		7.98	12/00	5c
Man's haircut, barbershop, no styling		11.25	12/00	5c
Personal services, household, expenditures on	yr	353	1999	30r
Woman's shampoo, trim, blow-dry, no style-change		26.40	12/00	5c
Pets				
Pets, toys, and playground equipment, expenditures on	yr	358	1999	30r
Restaurant Food				
Chicken, fried, thigh and drumstick, KFC/ Church's		2.99	12/00	5c
Hamburger with cheese, McDonald's	1/4 lb	2.19	12/00	5c
Pizza, Pizza Hut or Pizza Inn	11-12 in	9.99	12/00	5c
Taxes				
Federal income taxes paid	yr	3200	1999	30r
Personal taxes, expenditures on	yr	4153	1999	30r
Property taxes paid	yr	923	1999	30r
State and local income taxes paid	yr	812	1999	30r
Transportation				
Transportation, ACCRA Index		106.70	12/00	5c
Bus fare, to central business district	1-way	0.50	12/00	5c
Cars and trucks, new, expenditures on	yr	1534	1999	30r
Cars and trucks, used, expenditures on	yr	1593	1999	30r
Diesel at the pump	gal	1.37	10/99	73s
Gasoline and motor oil purchases	yr	1129	1999	30r

Values are in dollars or fractions of dollars. In the column headed *Ref*, references are shown to sources. Each reference is followed by a letter. These refer to the geographical level for which data were reported: s=State, r=Region, and c=City or metro. The abbreviation *ex* is used to mean *except* or *excluding*; *exp* stands for expenditures. For other abbreviations and further explanations, please see the Introduction.

Bellingham, WA - continued

Item	Per	Value	Date	Ref.
Transportation				
Gasoline before-tax price (cents)	gal	127.10	10/00	43s
Maintenance and repair expenditures	yr	797	1999	30r
Public transportation, expenditures on	yr	530	1999	30r
Tire balance, computer or spin balance, front	wheel	8.34	12/00	5c
Transportation purchases	yr	7423	1999	30r
Vehicle expenses, miscellaneous, purchases	yr	2585	1999	30r
Vehicle insurance payments	yr	811	1999	30r
Vehicle purchases (net outlay)	yr	3180	1999	30r
Vehicle rental, lease expenditures	yr	666	1999	30r
Utilities				
Utilities, ACCRA Index		89.50	12/00	5c
Electrical bill, average	mos	58.33	9/00	9s
Electricity, expenditures on	yr	725	1999	30r
Electricity and other, mixed, 2400 sq ft, new home	mos	39.38	12/00	5c
Electricity cost, average	KWh	4.47	9/00	9s
Utilities, fuels, and public services purchased	yr	2179	1999	30r
Water and other public services, expenditures on	yr	339	1999	30r
Weddings				
Wedding (national average cost)		19936	2000	33r
Wedding (regional average total cost)		18918	1997	110r
Attendants' gifts		321	1998	33r
Bridal attendants' apparel (5 persons)		824	2000	33r
Bride's headpiece/veil		173	1998	33r
Bride's wedding dress		859	1998	33r
Clergy, religious facility fee		242	1998	33r
Engagement ring		3177	1998	33r
Flowers		789	1998	33r
Groom's formalwear rental		99	2000	33r
Limousine		410	1998	33r
Marriage license cost		52.00	4/01	35s
Men's formalwear (ushers, best man)		469	2000	33r
Mother of bride apparel		241	2000	33r
Music		866	1998	33r
Photography and videography		1368	1998	33r
Rehearsal dinner		728	1998	33r
Wedding invitations and announcements		341	1998	33r
Wedding reception		7968	2000	33r
Wedding rings (bride and groom)		1060	1998	33r

Benton Harbor, MI

Item	Per	Value	Date	Ref.
Average annual expenditures	yr	35369	1999	30r
Alcoholic Beverages				
Alcoholic beverage purchases	yr	304	1999	30r
Malt beverages, all types, all sizes, any origin	16 oz	0.93	7/01	11r
Wine, red and white table, all sizes, any origin	liter	7.04	7/01	11r
Appliances				
Major appliances, expenditures on	yr	165	1999	30r
Small appliances, housewares, expenditures on	yr	90	1999	30r
Banking and Money				
Mortgage interest and charges paid	yr	2277	1999	30r
Mortgage principal paid on owned property	yr	1230	1999	30r
Vehicle finance charges paid	yr	328	1999	30r
Charity				
Cash contributions, expenditures on	yr	1126	1999	30r
Child Care				
Child raising cost, total, age 0-2	yr	7890	1999	60r
Child raising cost, total, age 3-5	yr	8130	1999	60r
Child raising cost, total, age 6-8	yr	8170	1999	60r
Child raising cost, total, age 9-11	yr	8190	1999	60r
Child raising cost, total, age 12-14	yr	8890	1999	60r
Child raising cost, total, age 15-17	yr	9050	1999	60r
Child's child care and education, age 0-2	yr	1240	1999	60r
Child's child care and education, age 3-5	yr	1370	1999	60r

Benton Harbor, MI - continued

Item	Per	Value	Date	Ref.
Child Care - continued				
Child's child care and education, age 6-8	yr	880	1999	60r
Child's child care and education, age 9-11	yr	570	1999	60r
Child's child care and education, age 12-14	yr	420	1999	60r
Child's child care and education, age 15-17	yr	720	1999	60r
Child's clothing, age 0-2	yr	410	1999	60r
Child's clothing, age 3-5	yr	400	1999	60r
Child's clothing, age 6-8	yr	450	1999	60r
Child's clothing, age 9-11	yr	500	1999	60r
Child's clothing, age 12-14	yr	840	1999	60r
Child's clothing, age 15-17	yr	740	1999	60r
Child's food, age 0-2	yr	960	1999	60r
Child's food, age 3-5	yr	1120	1999	60r
Child's food, age 6-8	yr	1430	1999	60r
Child's food, age 9-11	yr	1710	1999	60r
Child's food, age 12-14	yr	1710	1999	60r
Child's food, age 15-17	yr	1920	1999	60r
Child's health care, age 0-2	yr	520	1999	60r
Child's health care, age 3-5	yr	500	1999	60r
Child's health care, age 6-8	yr	570	1999	60r
Child's health care, age 9-11	yr	610	1999	60r
Child's health care, age 12-14	yr	630	1999	60r
Child's health care, age 15-17	yr	650	1999	60r
Child's housing, age 0-2	yr	2860	1999	60r
Child's housing, age 3-5	yr	2840	1999	60r
Child's housing, age 6-8	yr	2800	1999	60r
Child's housing, age 9-11	yr	2650	1999	60r
Child's housing, age 12-14	yr	2840	1999	60r
Child's housing, age 15-17	yr	2440	1999	60r
Child's personal care, reading, age 0-2	yr	880	1999	60r
Child's personal care, reading, age 3-5	yr	900	1999	60r
Child's personal care, reading, age 6-8	yr	930	1999	60r
Child's personal care, reading, age 9-11	yr	970	1999	60r
Child's personal care, reading, age 12-14	yr	1150	1999	60r
Child's personal care, reading, age 15-17	yr	920	1999	60r
Clothing				
Apparel and services purchases	yr	1607	1999	30r
Boys, 2 to 15, expenditures on	yr	91	1999	30r
Children under 2, expenditures on	yr	59	1999	30r
Footwear, expenditures on	yr	285	1999	30r
Girls, 2 to 15, expenditures on	yr	116	1999	30r
Men and boys, expenditures on	yr	433	1999	30r
Men, 16 and over, expenditures on	yr	341	1999	30r
Women, 16 and over, expenditures on	yr	490	1999	30r
Communications				
Cable modem installation, Bresnan		99.95	6/99	103s
Cable modem installation, Comcast		95.00	6/99	103s
Cable modem installation, Media One		100.00	6/99	103s
Cable modem rate, cable subscriber, Bresnan	mos	39.95	6/99	103s
Cable modem rate, cable subscriber, Comcast	mos	39.95	6/99	103s
Cable modem rate, cable subscriber, Media One	mos	34.95-39.95	6/99	103s
Cable modem rate, non-cable subscriber, Bresnan	mos	49.95	6/99	103s
Cable modem rate, non-cable subscriber, Comcast	mos	49.95	6/99	103s
Cable modem rate, non-cable subscriber, Media One	mos	49.95	6/99	103s
Phone line, single, business, field visit	inst.	42.00	12/97	17s
Phone line, single, business, no field visit	inst.	42.00	12/97	17s
Phone line, single, residence, field visit	inst.	42.00	12/97	17s
Phone line, single, residence, no field visit	inst.	42.00	12/97	17s
Postage and stationery, expenditures on	yr	140	1999	30r
Postal rate, express mail, up to half-pound		12.45	7/01	108r
Postal rate, letter, first class, first ounce		0.34	7/01	108r
Postal rate, letter, two ounces		0.57	7/01	108r
Postal rate, post card		0.21	7/01	108r
Postal rate, priority mail, two pounds		3.95	7/01	108r
Postal rate, priority mail, up to one pound		3.50	7/01	108r
Telephone services, expenditures on	yr	830	1999	30r

Values are in dollars or fractions of dollars. In the column headed *Ref*, references are shown to sources. Each reference is followed by a letter. These refer to the geographical level for which data were reported: s=State, r=Region, and c=City or metro. The abbreviation *ex* is used to mean *except* or *excluding*; *exp* stands for *expenditures*. For other abbreviations and further explanations, please see the Introduction.

Benton Harbor, MI - continued

Item	Per	Value	Date	Ref.
Education				
Board, 4-year private college/university	yr	2182	1996	38s
Board, 4-year public college/university	yr	2276	1996	38s
Education expenditures	yr	583	1999	30r
Room, 4-year private college/university	yr	1974	1996	38s
Room, 4-year public college/university	yr	2024	1996	38s
Total cost, 4-year private college/university	yr	13331	1996	38s
Total cost, 4-year public college/university	yr	8195	1996	38s
Tuition, 2-year public college/university, in state	yr	1529	1996	38s
Tuition, 4-year private college/university, in state	yr	9176	1996	38s
Tuition, 4-year public college/university	yr	3895	1996	38s
Energy and Fuels				
Electricity	500 KWhs	46.59	7/01	11r
Fuel oil #2	gal	1.27	7/01	11r
Fuel oil and other fuels, expenditures on	yr	68	1999	30r
Gas, natural, commercial rate	1000 cf	4.91	11/00	88s
Gasoline, unleaded midgrade	gal	1.79	7/01	11r
Gasoline, unleaded premium	gal	1.86	7/01	11r
Gasoline, unleaded regular	gal	1.58	7/01	11r
Natural gas, expenditures on	yr	389	1999	30r
Utility (piped) gas, therm		0.81	7/01	11r
Utility (piped) gas, 40 therms		38.01	7/01	11r
Utility (piped) gas, 100 therms		81.75	7/01	11r
Entertainment				
Entertainment purchases	yr	1984	1999	30r
Fees and admissions paid	yr	444	1999	30r
Television, radios, sound equipment, expenditures on	yr	580	1999	30r
Funerals				
Cosmetology, hair, other preparation		178.32	1/99	78r
Embalming		408.19	1/99	78r
Funeral at funeral home		362.13	1/99	78r
Professional service charges		1375.51	1/99	78r
Transfer of remains to funeral home		155.92	1/99	78r
Visitation/viewing		294.38	1/99	78r
Groceries				
Bacon, sliced	lb	3.15	7/01	11r
Bakery products, expenditures on	yr	281	1999	30r
Bananas	lb	0.48	7/01	11r
Beans, dried, any type, all sizes	lb	0.61	7/01	11r
Beef for stew, boneless	lb	3.08	7/01	11r
Beef, expenditures on	yr	217	1999	30r
Bologna, all beef or mixed	lb	2.52	7/01	11r
Bread, white, pan	lb	1.06	7/01	11r
Broccoli	lb	0.91	7/01	11r
Butter, salted, grade AA, stick	lb	3.04	7/01	11r
Butter, yoghurt, cheese, etc, expenditures on	yr	183	1999	30r
Cereals and bakery product purchases	yr	430	1999	30r
Cereals and cereal products, expenditures on	yr	149	1999	30r
Chicken, fresh, whole	lb	1.07	7/01	11r
Chops, boneless	lb	3.64	7/01	11r
Chuck roast, U.S. choice, boneless	lb	2.47	7/01	11r
Coffee, 100%, ground roast, all sizes	lb	2.69	7/01	11r
Cookies, chocolate chip	lb	2.87	7/01	11r
Dairy product purchases	yr	304	1999	30r
Eggs, expenditures on	yr	26	1999	30r
Eggs, grade A, large	dozen	0.88	7/01	11r
Fats and oils, expenditures on	yr	75	1999	30r
Fish and seafood, expenditures on	yr	72	1999	30r
Food (excl fruit and vegetables), eaten at home, purchases	yr	887	1999	30r
Food cooked on trips, expenditures on	yr	44	1999	30r
Food purchases	yr	4802	1999	30r
Food purchases, eaten away from home	yr	2069	1999	30r
Food purchases, food eaten at home	yr	2733	1999	30r
Fresh fruits, expenditures on	yr	138	1999	30r
Fresh milk and cream, expenditures on	yr	120	1999	30r

Benton Harbor, MI - continued

Item	Per	Value	Date	Ref.
Groceries - continued				
Fresh vegetables, expenditures on	yr	126	1999	30r
Grapefruit	lb	0.66	7/01	11r
Grapes, Thompson, seedless	lb	1.64	7/01	11r
Ground beef, 100% beef	lb	1.64	7/01	11r
Ground beef, lean and extra lean	lb	2.16	7/01	11r
Ground chuck, 100% beef	lb	2.13	7/01	11r
Ham, boneless, excl canned	lb	2.62	7/01	11r
Ice cream, prepackaged, bulk, regular	1/2 gal	3.35	7/01	11r
Lemons	lb	1.19	7/01	11r
Lettuce, iceberg	lb	0.73	7/01	11r
Margarine, soft, tubs	lb	0.89	7/01	11r
Meats, poultry, fish, and egg purchases	yr	671	1999	30r
Milk, fresh, whole, fortified	gal	2.71	7/01	11r
Nonalcoholic beverages, expenditures on	yr	239	1999	30r
Oranges, Navel	lb	0.80	7/01	11r
Oranges, Valencia	lb	0.66	7/01	11r
Pears, Anjou	lb	0.93	7/01	11r
Pork chops, center cut, bone-in	lb	3.63	7/01	11r
Pork, expenditures on	yr	150	1999	30r
Potato chips	16 oz	3.52	7/01	11r
Potatoes, frozen, french fried	lb	1.08	7/01	11r
Potatoes, white, all types	lb	0.33	7/01	11r
Poultry, expenditures on	yr	108	1999	30r
Processed fruits, expenditures on	yr	98	1999	30r
Processed vegetables, expenditures on	yr	80	1999	30r
Round roast, U.S. choice, boneless	lb	3.07	7/01	11r
Round steak, graded and ungraded, excl U.S. prime and choice	lb	3.41	7/01	11r
Shortening, vegetable oil blends	lb	1.13	7/01	11r
Spaghetti and macaroni	lb	0.80	7/01	11r
Steak, round, U.S. choice, boneless	lb	3.23	7/01	11r
Steak, T-bone, U.S. choice, bone-in	lb	6.68	7/01	11r
Strawberries, dry pint	12 oz	1.32	7/01	11r
Sugar and other sweets, expenditures on	yr	114	1999	30r
Sugar, white, 33-80 ounce package	lb	0.42	7/01	11r
Sugar, white, all sizes	lb	0.43	7/01	11r
Tobacco products and smoking supplies purchases	yr	331	1999	30r
Tomatoes, field grown	lb	1.46	7/01	11r
Tuna, light, chunk	lb	1.80	7/01	11r
Turkey, frozen, whole	lb	1.15	7/01	11r
Goods and Services				
B&B Japanese maple (acer japonicum)	gal	29.99-169.99	4/00	93r
Boxwood (buxus)	2 gal	18.99-39.99	4/00	93r
Daylily (hemerocallis)	gal	4.99-25.00	4/00	93r
Flat of annuals		11.98-24.99	4/00	93r
Fountain grass (pennisetum)	gal	5.98-12.98	4/00	93r
Hanging basket (10 in)		12.99-27.99	4/00	93r
Hardy geranium (geranium)	gal	7.99-9.99	4/00	93r
Hosta (hosta)	gal	6.00-25.00	4/00	93r
Lilac (syrubga vulgaris)	2 gal	14.99-24.99	4/00	93r
Miscellaneous purchases	yr	865	1999	30r
Rhododendron (rhododendron)	2 gal	23.98-42.99	4/00	93r
Sage (salvia)	gal	6.00-9.99	4/00	93r
Snowblower, single stage		400-600	12/00	99s
Wintercreeper euonymus (euonymus fortunei)	2 gal	16.00-169.99	4/00	93r
Hunting license	yr	14.00	4/01	34s

Values are in dollars or fractions of dollars. In the column headed *Ref*, references are shown to sources. Each reference is followed by a letter. These refer to the geographical level for which data were reported: s=State, r=Region, and c=City or metro. The abbreviation *ex* is used to mean *except* or *excluding*; *exp* stands for expenditures. For other abbreviations and further explanations, please see the Introduction.

Benton Harbor, MI - continued

Item	Per	Value	Date	Ref.
Health Care				
Cardiac catheterization, ave hospital/ physician charges		11830	1998	77s
Childbirth, Cesarean delivery		10722	1997	13r
Childbirth, vaginal delivery		6223	1997	13r
Drugs, expenditures on	yr	394	1999	30r
Health care purchases	yr	2048	1999	30r
Health insurance expenditures	yr	978	1999	30r
Hysterectomy, laproscopically-assisted, ave hospital/physician charges		13820	1998	76s
Hysterectomy, vaginal, ave hospital and physician charges		8780	1998	76s
Medicaid dispensing fee		3.72	1999	87s
Medical services expenditures	yr	554	1999	30r
Medical supplies, expenditures on	yr	122	1999	30r
Plastic surgery, breast augmentation		3184	2000	7r
Plastic surgery, breast lift		3585	2000	7r
Plastic surgery, facelift		4999	2000	7r
Plastic surgery, hair transplantation		3105	2000	7r
Plastic surgery, lip augmentation		1290	2000	7r
Plastic surgery, lower body lift		8135	2000	7r
Plastic surgery, thigh lift		3839	2000	7r
Household Goods				
Floor coverings, expenditures on	yr	52	1999	30r
Furniture, expenditures on	yr	344	1999	30r
Household furnishings and equipment purchases	yr	1475	1999	30r
Household textiles, expenditures on	yr	109	1999	30r
Laundry and cleaning supplies, expenditures on	yr	134	1999	30r
Housing				
Home price, existing, ave		144400	10/00	90r
Home value, median		135000	2001	53s
Household operation expenditures	yr	542	1999	30r
Housekeeping supplies purchases	yr	508	1999	30r
Lodging expenditures	yr	430	1999	30r
Maintenance, repairs, insurance expenditures	yr	853	1999	30r
Monthly rental value of owned home	mos	547	1999	30r
Owned dwellings, expenditures own	yr	4282	1999	30r
Rent expenditures	yr	1558	1999	30r
Rental unit, 1 bedroom, with utilities	mos	389	4/01	41c
Rental unit, 2 bedroom, with utilities	mos	511	4/01	41c
Rental unit, 3 bedroom, with utilities	mos	638	4/01	41c
Rental unit, 4 bedroom, with utilities	mos	716	4/01	41c
Shelter, expenditures on	yr	6270	1999	30r
Insurance and Pensions				
Life and other personal insurance purchases	yr	387	1999	30r
Pensions and Social Security, expenditures on	yr	2968	1999	30r
Legal Fees				
Divorce, filing fee		65.00	4/01	35s
Driver's license fee	renew	5.00	1999	48s
Driver's license fee	orig	20.00	1999	48s
Fishing license	yr	14.00	4/01	34s
Personal Goods				
Personal care products and services purchases	yr	385	1999	30r
Personal Services				
Personal services, household, expenditures on	yr	300	1999	30r
Pets				
Pets, toys, and playground equipment, expenditures on	yr	375	1999	30r
Taxes				
Federal income taxes paid	yr	2326	1999	30r
Personal taxes, expenditures on	yr	3223	1999	30r
Property taxes paid	yr	1152	1999	30r
State and local income taxes paid	yr	753	1999	30r

Benton Harbor, MI - continued

Item	Per	Value	Date	Ref.
Transportation				
Cars and trucks, new, expenditures on	yr	1280	1999	30r
Cars and trucks, used, expenditures on	yr	1763	1999	30r
Diesel at the pump	gal	1.19	10/99	73s
Gasoline and motor oil purchases	yr	1036	1999	30r
Gasoline before-tax price (cents)	gal	111.50	10/00	43s
Maintenance and repair expenditures	yr	594	1999	30r
Public transportation, expenditures on	yr	341	1999	30r
Transportation purchases	yr	6617	1999	30r
Vehicle expenses, miscellaneous, purchases	yr	2159	1999	30r
Vehicle insurance payments	yr	701	1999	30r
Vehicle purchases (net outlay)	yr	3081	1999	30r
Vehicle rental, lease expenditures	yr	536	1999	30r
Utilities				
Electrical bill, average	mos	55.00	9/00	9s
Electricity, expenditures on	yr	841	1999	30r
Electricity cost, average	KWh	7.00	9/00	9s
Utilities, fuels, and public services purchased	yr	2401	1999	30r
Water and other public services, expenditures on	yr	273	1999	30r
Weddings				
Wedding (national average cost)		19936	2000	33r
Wedding (regional average total cost)		16195	1997	110r
Attendants' gifts		321	1998	33r
Bridal attendants' apparel (5 persons)		824	2000	33r
Bride's headpiece/veil		173	1998	33r
Bride's wedding dress		859	1998	33r
Clergy, religious facility fee		242	1998	33r
Engagement ring		3177	1998	33r
Flowers		789	1998	33r
Groom's formalwear rental		99	2000	33r
Limousine		410	1998	33r
Marriage license cost		20.00	4/01	35s
Men's formalwear (ushers, best man)		469	2000	33r
Mother of bride apparel		241	2000	33r
Music		866	1998	33r
Photography and videography		1368	1998	33r
Rehearsal dinner		728	1998	33r
Wedding invitations and announcements		341	1998	33r
Wedding reception		7968	2000	33r
Wedding rings (bride and groom)		1060	1998	33r

Bergen-Passaic, NJ

Item	Per	Value	Date	Ref.
Average annual expenditures	yr	37971	1999	30r
Alcoholic Beverages				
Alcoholic beverage purchases	yr	368	1999	30r
Wine, red and white table, all sizes, any origin	liter	9.64	7/01	11r
Appliances				
Major appliances, expenditures on	yr	194	1999	30r
Small appliances, housewares, expenditures on	yr	93	1999	30r
Banking and Money				
Mortgage interest and charges paid	yr	2622	1999	30r
Mortgage principal paid on owned property	yr	1262	1999	30r
Vehicle finance charges paid	yr	240	1999	30r
Charity				
Cash contributions, expenditures	yr	1001	1999	30r
Child Care				
Child raising cost, total, age 0-2	yr	8670	1999	60r
Child raising cost, total, age 3-5	yr	8910	1999	60r
Child raising cost, total, age 6-8	yr	9040	1999	60r
Child raising cost, total, age 9-11	yr	9100	1999	60r
Child raising cost, total, age 12-14	yr	9890	1999	60r
Child raising cost, total, age 15-17	yr	10010	1999	60r
Child's child care and education, age 0-2	yr	1070	1999	60r
Child's child care and education, age 3-5	yr	1190	1999	60r
Child's child care and education, age 6-8	yr	740	1999	60r

Values are in dollars or fractions of dollars. In the column headed *Ref*, references are shown to sources. Each reference is followed by a letter. These refer to the geographical level for which data were reported: s=State, r=Region, and c=City or metro. The abbreviation *ex* is used to mean *except* or *excluding*; *exp* stands for expenditures. For other abbreviations and further explanations, please see the Introduction.

Bergen-Passaic, NJ - continued

Item	Per	Value	Date	Ref.
Child Care				
Child's child care and education, age 9-11	yr	470	1999	60r
Child's child care and education, age 12-14	yr	350	1999	60r
Child's child care and education, age 15-17	yr	590	1999	60r
Child's clothing, age 0-2	yr	480	1999	60r
Child's clothing, age 3-5	yr	470	1999	60r
Child's clothing, age 6-8	yr	520	1999	60r
Child's clothing, age 9-11	yr	570	1999	60r
Child's clothing, age 12-14	yr	970	1999	60r
Child's clothing, age 15-17	yr	870	1999	60r
Child's food, age 0-2	yr	1130	1999	60r
Child's food, age 3-5	yr	1290	1999	60r
Child's food, age 6-8	yr	1640	1999	60r
Child's food, age 9-11	yr	1930	1999	60r
Child's food, age 12-14	yr	1940	1999	60r
Child's food, age 15-17	yr	2150	1999	60r
Child's health care, age 0-2	yr	550	1999	60r
Child's health care, age 3-5	yr	530	1999	60r
Child's health care, age 6-8	yr	610	1999	60r
Child's health care, age 9-11	yr	650	1999	60r
Child's health care, age 12-14	yr	660	1999	60r
Child's health care, age 15-17	yr	690	1999	60r
Child's housing, age 0-2	yr	3555	1999	60r
Child's housing, age 3-5	yr	3530	1999	60r
Child's housing, age 6-8	yr	3490	1999	60r
Child's housing, age 9-11	yr	3340	1999	60r
Child's housing, age 12-14	yr	3530	1999	60r
Child's housing, age 15-17	yr	3140	1999	60r
Child's personal care, reading, age 0-2	yr	920	1999	60r
Child's personal care, reading, age 3-5	yr	950	1999	60r
Child's personal care, reading, age 6-8	yr	980	1999	60r
Child's personal care, reading, age 9-11	yr	1020	1999	60r
Child's personal care, reading, age 12-14	yr	1190	1999	60r
Child's personal care, reading, age 15-17	yr	970	1999	60r
Clothing				
Apparel and services purchases	yr	1831	1999	30r
Boys, 2 to 15, expenditures on	yr	92	1999	30r
Children under 2, expenditures on	yr	63	1999	30r
Footwear, expenditures on	yr	300	1999	30r
Girls, 2 to 15, expenditures on	yr	101	1999	30r
Men and boys, expenditures on	yr	446	1999	30r
Men, 16 and over, expenditures on	yr	354	1999	30r
Women, 16 and over, expenditures on	yr	584	1999	30r
Communications				
Cable modem installation, Adelphi		54.90	6/99	103s
Cable modem installation, Comcast		95.00	6/99	103s
Cable modem rate, cable subscriber, Adelphi	mos	34.95	6/99	103s
Cable modem rate, cable subscriber, Comcast	mos	39.95	6/99	103s
Cable modem rate, non-cable subscriber, Adelphi	mos	44.95	6/99	103s
Cable modem rate, non-cable subscriber, Comcast	mos	49.95	6/99	103s
Phone line, single, business, field visit	inst.	98.50	12/97	17s
Phone line, single, business, no field visit	inst.	79.50	12/97	17s
Phone line, single, residence, field visit	inst.	56.50	12/97	17s
Phone line, single, residence, no field visit	inst.	42.00	12/97	17s
Postage and stationery, expenditures on	yr	138	1999	30r
Postal rate, express mail, up to half-pound		12.45	7/01	108r
Postal rate, letter, first class, first ounce		0.34	7/01	108r
Postal rate, letter, two ounces		0.57	7/01	108r
Postal rate, post card		0.21	7/01	108r
Postal rate, priority mail, two pounds		3.95	7/01	108r
Postal rate, priority mail, up to one pound		3.50	7/01	108r
Telephone services, expenditures on	yr	830	1999	30r
Education				
Board, 4-year private college/university	yr	2959	1996	38s
Board, 4-year public college/university	yr	2052	1996	38s
Education expenditures	yr	877	1999	30r
Room, 4-year private college/university	yr	3226	1996	38s
Room, 4-year public college/university	yr	3101	1996	38s
Total cost, 4-year private college/university	yr	19751	1996	38s

Bergen-Passaic, NJ - continued

Item	Per	Value	Date	Ref.
Education - continued				
Total cost, 4-year public college/university	yr	9125	1996	38s
Tuition, 2-year public college/university, in state	yr	1878	1996	38s
Tuition, 4-year private college/university, in state	yr	13566	1996	38s
Tuition, 4-year public college/university	yr	3972	1996	38s
Energy and Fuels				
Electricity	KWh	0.12	7/01	11r
Fuel oil #2	gal	1.31	7/01	11r
Fuel oil and other fuels, expenditures on	yr	207	1999	30r
Gas, natural, commercial rate	1000 cf	5.98	11/00	88s
Gasoline, all types	gal	1.80	7/01	11r
Gasoline, unleaded midgrade	gal	1.85	7/01	11r
Gasoline, unleaded premium	gal	1.91	7/01	11r
Gasoline, unleaded regular	gal	1.71	7/01	11r
Natural gas, expenditures on	yr	368	1999	30r
Utility (piped) gas, therm		1.08	7/01	11r
Utility (piped) gas, 40 therms		50.87	7/01	11r
Utility (piped) gas, 100 therms		111.06	7/01	11r
Entertainment				
Entertainment purchases	yr	1821	1999	30r
Fees and admissions paid	yr	511	1999	30r
Television, radios, sound equipment, expenditures on	yr	650	1999	30r
Funerals				
Total cost of funeral		5813.50	1/99	78r
Acknowledgement cards		28.32	1/99	78r
Casket		2082.20	1/99	78r
Cosmetology, hair, other preparation		169.59	1/99	78r
Embalming		465.60	1/99	78r
Funeral at funeral home		339.56	1/99	78r
Hearse (local)		183.96	1/99	78r
Professional service charges		1157.85	1/99	78r
Service car/van		100.41	1/99	78r
Transfer of remains to funeral home		158.66	1/99	78r
Vault		766.31	1/99	78r
Visitation/viewing		361.04	1/99	78r
Groceries				
Apples, red delicious	lb	0.95	7/01	11r
Bacon, sliced	lb	3.44	7/01	11r
Bakery products, expenditures on	yr	310	1999	30r
Bananas	lb	0.55	7/01	11r
Beef, expenditures on	yr	236	1999	30r
Bread, white, pan	lb	1.09	7/01	11r
Butter, yoghurt, cheese, etc, expenditures on	yr	214	1999	30r
Cereals and bakery product purchases	yr	474	1999	30r
Cereals and cereal products, expenditures on	yr	164	1999	30r
Chicken legs, bone-in	lb	1.23	7/01	11r
Chicken, fresh, whole	lb	1.13	7/01	11r
Chuck roast, U.S. choice, boneless	lb	2.79	7/01	11r
Coffee, 100%, ground roast, all sizes	lb	3.40	7/01	11r
Dairy product purchases	yr	342	1999	30r
Eggs, expenditures on	yr	34	1999	30r
Eggs, grade A, large	dozen	0.82	7/01	11r
Fats and oils, expenditures on	yr	80	1999	30r
Fish and seafood, expenditures on	yr	123	1999	30r
Food (excl fruit and vegetables), eaten at home, purchases	yr	838	1999	30r
Food cooked on trips, expenditures on	yr	48	1999	30r
Food purchases	yr	5314	1999	30r
Food purchases, eaten away from home	yr	2313	1999	30r
Food purchases, food eaten at home	yr	3001	1999	30r
Fresh fruits, expenditures on	yr	169	1999	30r
Fresh milk and cream, expenditures on	yr	128	1999	30r
Fresh vegetables, expenditures on	yr	164	1999	30r
Grapefruit	lb	0.67	7/01	11r
Grapes, Thompson, seedless	lb	2.18	7/01	11r
Ground beef, lean and extra lean	lb	2.66	7/01	11r
Ground chuck, 100% beef	lb	2.04	7/01	11r

Values are in dollars or fractions of dollars. In the column headed *Ref*, references are shown to sources. Each reference is followed by a letter. These refer to the geographical level for which data were reported: s=State, r=Region, and c=City or metro. The abbreviation *ex* is used to mean *except* or *excluding*; *exp* stands for expenditures. For other abbreviations and further explanations, please see the Introduction.

Bergen-Passaic, NJ - continued

Item	Per	Value	Date	Ref.
Groceries				
Lettuce, iceberg	lb	0.76	7/01	11r
Meats, poultry, fish, and egg purchases	yr	808	1999	30r
Nonalcoholic beverages, expenditures on	yr	225	1999	30r
Orange juice, frozen concentrate	16 oz	1.88	7/01	11r
Oranges, Navel	lb	0.79	7/01	11r
Oranges, Valencia	lb	0.56	7/01	11r
Peaches	lb	1.16	7/01	11r
Peanut butter, creamy, all sizes	lb	2.01	7/01	11r
Pears, Anjou	lb	1.16	7/01	11r
Pork chops, center cut, bone-in	lb	3.57	7/01	11r
Pork, expenditures on	yr	146	1999	30r
Potato chips	16 oz	3.37	7/01	11r
Potatoes, white, all types	lb	0.42	7/01	11r
Poultry, expenditures on	yr	158	1999	30r
Processed fruits, expenditures on	yr	124	1999	30r
Processed vegetables, expenditures on	yr	82	1999	30r
Round roast, U.S. choice, boneless	lb	3.04	7/01	11r
Spaghetti and macaroni	lb	1.04	7/01	11r
Steak, sirloin, U.S. choice, boneless	lb	5.39	7/01	11r
Strawberries, dry pint	12 oz	1.51	7/01	11r
Sugar and other sweets, expenditures on	yr	110	1999	30r
Sugar, white, 33-80 ounce package	lb	0.46	7/01	11r
Sugar, white, all sizes	lb	0.47	7/01	11r
Tobacco products and smoking supplies purchases	yr	309	1999	30r
Yogurt, natural, fruit flavored	8 oz	0.79	7/01	11r
Goods and Services				
B&B Japanese maple (acer japonicum)	gal	38.99-125.00	4/00	93r
Boxwood (buxus)	2 gal	15.99-49.95	4/00	93r
Daylilly (hemerocallis)	gal	4.95	4/00	93r
Flat of annuals		8.00-14.99	4/00	93r
Fountain grass (pennisetum)	gal	6.99-9.99	4/00	93r
Hanging basket (10 in)		12.95-19.99	4/00	93r
Hardy geranium (geranium)	gal	6.95-7.99	4/00	93r
Hosta (hosta)	gal	4.95	4/00	93r
Lilac (syrubga vulgaris)	2 gal	17.99-74.95	4/00	93r
Miscellaneous purchases	yr	872	1999	30r
Rhododendron (rhododendron)	2 gal	23.99-54.95	4/00	93r
Sage (salvia)	gal	6.95-7.99	4/00	93r
Wintercreeper euonymus (euonymus fortunei)	2 gal	14.99-23.95	4/00	93r
Hunting license	yr	22.50	4/01	34s
Health Care				
Cardiac catheterization, ave hospital/ physician charges		14680	1998	77s
Childbirth, Cesarean delivery		14716	1997	13r
Childbirth, vaginal delivery		8541	1997	13r
Drugs, expenditures on	yr	296	1999	30r
Health care purchases	yr	1788	1999	30r
Health insurance expenditures	yr	875	1999	30r
Hysterectomy, laproscopically-assisted, ave hospital/physician charges		18330	1998	76s
Hysterectomy, vaginal, ave hospital and physician charges		13620	1998	76s
Medicaid dispensing fee		3.73-4.07	1999	87s
Medical services expenditures	yr	516	1999	30r
Medical supplies, expenditures on	yr	102	1999	30r
Plastic surgery, breast augmentation		4232	2000	7r
Plastic surgery, breast lift		4605	2000	7r
Plastic surgery, facelift		6964	2000	7r
Plastic surgery, hair transplantation		4193	2000	7r

Bergen-Passaic, NJ - continued

Item	Per	Value	Date	Ref.
Health Care - continued				
Plastic surgery, lip augmentation		1675	2000	7r
Plastic surgery, lower body lift		6611	2000	7r
Plastic surgery, thigh lift		4751	2000	7r
Household Goods				
Floor coverings, expenditures on	yr	59	1999	30r
Furniture, expenditures on	yr	388	1999	30r
Household furnishings and equipment purchases	yr	1567	1999	30r
Household textiles, expenditures on	yr	112	1999	30r
Laundry and cleaning supplies, expenditures on	yr	104	1999	30r
Housing				
Home price, existing, ave		180800	10/00	90r
Home value, median		213000	2001	53s
Household operation expenditures	yr	581	1999	30r
Housekeeping supplies purchases	yr	474	1999	30r
Lodging expenditures	yr	550	1999	30r
Maintenance, repairs, insurance expenditures	yr	835	1999	30r
Monthly rental value of owned home	mos	663	1999	30r
Owned dwellings, expenditures own	yr	5209	1999	30r
Rent expenditures	yr	2390	1999	30r
Rental unit, 1 bedroom, with utilities	mos	797	4/01	41c
Rental unit, 2 bedroom, with utilities	mos	934	4/01	41c
Rental unit, 3 bedroom, with utilities	mos	1244	4/01	41c
Rental unit, 4 bedroom, with utilities	mos	1535	4/01	41c
Shelter, expenditures on	yr	8149	1999	30r
Single-family home, purchase price		250200	2000	19c
Insurance and Pensions				
Auto insurance premium	yr	1292.76	1999	57s
Life and other personal insurance purchases	yr	424	1999	30r
Pensions and Social Security, expenditures on	yr	3037	1999	30r
Legal Fees				
Divorce, filing fee		65.00	4/01	35s
Driver's license fee	orig	18.00	1999	48s
Driver's license fee	renew	15.00	1999	48s
Fishing license	yr	22.50	4/01	34s
Personal Goods				
Personal care products and services purchases	yr	399	1999	30r
Personal Services				
Personal services, household, expenditures on	yr	271	1999	30r
Pets				
Pets, toys, and playground equipment, expenditures on	yr	325	1999	30r
Taxes				
Federal income taxes paid	yr	2606	1999	30r
Personal taxes, expenditures on	yr	3567	1999	30r
Property taxes paid	yr	1752	1999	30r
State and local income taxes paid	yr	694	1999	30r
Transportation				
Automobile insurance	yr	975.90	2000	79s
Cars and trucks, new, expenditures on	yr	1496	1999	30r
Cars and trucks, used, expenditures on	yr	1251	1999	30r
Diesel at the pump	gal	1.19	10/99	73s
Gasoline and motor oil purchases	yr	901	1999	30r
Gasoline before-tax price (cents)	gal	114.90	10/00	43s
Maintenance and repair expenditures	yr	618	1999	30r
Motorcycle license fee	orig	15.00	1999	49s
Motorcycle license fee	renew	13.00	1999	49s
Public transportation, expenditures on	yr	575	1999	30r
Transportation purchases	yr	6503	1999	30r
Vehicle expenses, miscellaneous, purchases	yr	2266	1999	30r
Vehicle insurance payments	yr	824	1999	30r
Vehicle purchases (net outlay)	yr	2761	1999	30r

Values are in dollars or fractions of dollars. In the column headed *Ref*, references are shown to sources. Each reference is followed by a letter. These refer to the geographical level for which data were reported: s=State, r=Region, and c=City or metro. The abbreviation *ex* is used to mean *except* or *excluding*; *exp* stands for *expenditures*. For other abbreviations and further explanations, please see the Introduction.

Bergen-Passaic, NJ - continued

Item	Per	Value	Date	Ref.
Transportation				
Vehicle rental, lease expenditures	yr	584	1999	30r
Utilities				
Electrical bill, average	mos	74.08	9/00	9s
Electricity, expenditures on	yr	837	1999	30r
Electricity cost, average	KWh	8.91	9/00	9s
Utilities, fuels, and public services purchased	yr	2457	1999	30r
Water and other public services, expenditures on	yr	215	1999	30r
Weddings				
Wedding (national average cost)		19936	2000	33r
Wedding (regional average total cost)		29454	1997	110r
Attendants' gifts		321	1998	33r
Bridal attendants' apparel (5 persons)		824	2000	33r
Bride's headpiece/veil		173	1998	33r
Bride's wedding dress		859	1998	33r
Clergy, religious facility fee		242	1998	33r
Engagement ring		3177	1998	33r
Flowers		789	1998	33r
Groom's formalwear rental		99	2000	33r
Limousine		410	1998	33r
Marriage license cost		28.00	4/01	35s
Men's formalwear (ushers, best man)		469	2000	33r
Mother of bride apparel		241	2000	33r
Music		866	1998	33r
Photography and videography		1368	1998	33r
Rehearsal dinner		728	1998	33r
Wedding invitations and announcements		341	1998	33r
Wedding reception		7968	2000	33r
Wedding rings (bride and groom)		1060	1998	33r

Billings, MT

Item	Per	Value	Date	Ref.
Composite, ACCRA index		98.00	3/01	4c
Alcoholic Beverages				
Beer, Heineken, 12-oz, ex deposit	6	7.48	3/01	4c
J & B Scotch	750-ml	23.77	3/01	4c
Wine, Livingston or Gallo, Chablis blanc	1.5 liter	5.75	3/01	4c
Appliances				
Appliance repair, service call, washing machine	min lab chg	47.20	3/01	4c
Banking and Money				
Mortgage rate, incl. points and orig. fee, 30-yr. conv. fixed or ARM	mos	7.04	3/01	4c
Child Care				
Daycare	mos	317	1998	37c
Daycare, 3-year old, 5 days, 8 hrs/day	mos	317	1998	85c
Clothing				
Boys' brief, cotton	3	4.04	3/01	4c
Shirt, man's dress shirt		28.49	3/01	4c
Slacks, man's "No Wrinkles" khaki		29.39	3/01	4c
Communications				
Newspaper subscription, daily and Sunday delivery	mos	19.57	3/01	4c
Phone line, single, business, field visit	inst.	61.40	12/97	17s
Phone line, single, business, no field visit	inst.	61.40	12/97	17s
Phone line, single, residence, field visit	inst.	25.00	12/97	17s
Phone line, single, residence, no field visit	inst.	25.00	12/97	17s
Postal rate, express mail, up to half-pound		12.45	7/01	108r
Postal rate, letter, first class, first ounce		0.34	7/01	108r
Postal rate, letter, two ounces		0.57	7/01	108r
Postal rate, post card		0.21	7/01	108r
Postal rate, priority mail, two pounds		3.95	7/01	108r
Postal rate, priority mail, up to one pound		3.50	7/01	108r
Telephone bill, business, basic rate	mos	38.69	12/97	18c
Telephone bill, family of three	mos	26.36	3/01	4c
Telephone bill, residential, basic rate	mos	13.84	12/97	18c

Billings, MT - continued

Item	Per	Value	Date	Ref.
Education				
Board, 4-year private college/university	yr	2128	1996	38s
Board, 4-year public college/university	yr	3609	1996	38s
Room, 4-year private college/university	yr	1388	1996	38s
Room, 4-year public college/university	yr	1778	1996	38s
Total cost, 4-year private college/university	yr	11062	1996	38s
Total cost, 4-year public college/university	yr	7754	1996	38s
Tuition, 2-year public college/university, in state	yr	1382	1996	38s
Tuition, 4-year private college/university, in state	yr	7545	1996	38s
Tuition, 4-year public college/university	yr	2367	1996	38s
Energy and Fuels				
Energy, combined forms, 2400 sq ft	mos	122.90	3/01	4c
Energy, exc. electricity, 2400 sq ft	mos	78.03	3/01	4c
Gas, cooking, winter, 10 therms	mos	8.15	2/96	98c
Gas, cooking, winter, 30 therms	mos	15.45	2/96	98c
Gas, cooking, winter, 50 therms	mos	22.76	2/96	98c
Gas, heating, winter, average use	mos	76.44	2/96	98c
Gas, natural, commercial rate	1000 cf	5.54	11/00	88s
Gas, regular unleaded, cash, self-service	gal	1.36	3/01	4c
Entertainment				
Bowling, Saturday evening rate	line	2.00	3/01	4c
Monopoly game, Parker Brothers', No. 9	game	10.15	3/01	4c
Movie, first-run, Saturday, evening	adm.	6.75	3/01	4c
Tennis balls, yellow, Wilson or Penn, 3	can	2.13	3/01	4c
Funerals				
Total cost of funeral		5401.08	1/99	78r
Acknowledgement cards		33.64	1/99	78r
Casket		2170.43	1/99	78r
Cosmetology, hair, other preparation		136.32	1/99	78r
Embalming		319.13	1/99	78r
Funeral at funeral home		370.21	1/99	78r
Hearse (local)		161.04	1/99	78r
Professional service charges		963.15	1/99	78r
Service car/van		133.99	1/99	78r
Transfer of remains to funeral home		159.82	1/99	78r
Vault		778.07	1/99	78r
Visitation/viewing		175.28	1/99	78r
Groceries				
Groceries, ACCRA Index		98.60	3/01	4c
Antibiotic ointment, Polysporin	0.5 oz	4.64	3/01	4c
Baby food, strained vegetables or fruit, lowest price	4-4.5 oz	0.34	3/01	4c
Bananas	lb	0.43	3/01	4c
Beef or hamburger, ground	lb	1.26	3/01	4c
Bread, white	loaf	0.89	3/01	4c
Cheese, Kraft grated Parmesan	8 oz	4.50	3/01	4c
Chicken, whole fryer	lb	0.87	3/01	4c
Cigarettes, Winston, Kings	carton	29.89	3/01	4c
Coffee, vacuum-packed	13 oz	3.13	3/01	4c
Corn Flakes, Kellogg's or Post Toasties	18 oz	3.03	3/01	4c
Corn, frozen, whole kernel, lowest price	16 oz	1.02	3/01	4c
Eggs, Grade A or AA	dozen	1.13	3/01	4c
Lettuce, iceberg	head	1.12	3/01	4c
Margarine, Blue Bonnet or Parkay, stick	lb	0.86	3/01	4c
Milk, whole	1/2 gal	1.63	3/01	4c
Orange juice, Minute Maid frozen	12 oz	1.51	3/01	4c
Peaches, halves or slices, Hunt's, Del Monte, or Libby's	29 oz	1.73	3/01	4c
Peas, green, Del Monte or Green Giant	15 oz	0.79	3/01	4c
Potatoes, white or red	10 lb	1.85	3/01	4c
Sausage, Jimmy Dean/Owens pork	lb	3.03	3/01	4c
Shortening, vegetable, Crisco	3 lb	3.24	3/01	4c
Soft drink, Coca Cola, ex deposit	2 liter	1.13	3/01	4c
Steak, T-bone	lb	5.68	3/01	4c
Sugar, cane or beet	4 lbs	1.68	3/01	4c
Tomatoes, Hunt's or Del Monte	14.5 oz	0.89	3/01	4c
Tuna, chunk, light	6 oz	0.57	3/01	4c

Values are in dollars or fractions of dollars. In the column headed *Ref*, references are shown to sources. Each reference is followed by a letter. These refer to the geographical level for which data were reported: s=State, r=Region, and c=City or metro. The abbreviation *ex* is used to mean *except* or *excluding*; *exp* stands for expenditures. For other abbreviations and further explanations, please see the Introduction.

Billings, MT - continued

Item	Per	Value	Date	Ref.
Goods and Services				
Miscellaneous goods and services, ACCRA Index		98.40	3/01	4c
Hunting license	yr	10.00	4/01	34s
Health Care				
Health care, ACCRA Index		103.80	3/01	4c
Cardiac catheterization, ave hospital/ physician charges		13700	1998	77s
Childbirth, Cesarean delivery		11587	1997	13r
Childbirth, vaginal delivery		6725	1997	13r
Dentist's fee, adult teeth cleaning and periodic oral exam	visit	74.00	3/01	4c
Doctor's fee, routine exam, established patient	visit	66.00	3/01	4c
Hospital care, private room	day	473.00	3/01	4c
Hysterectomy, laproscopically-assisted, ave hospital/physician charges		11400	1998	76s
Hysterectomy, vaginal, ave hospital and physician charges		8290	1998	76s
Medicaid dispensing fee		2.00-4.20	1999	87s
Household Goods				
Dishwashing powder, Cascade	50 oz	3.78	3/01	4c
Tissues, facial, Kleenex brand	175	1.38	3/01	4c
Housing				
Housing, ACCRA Index		94.10	3/01	4c
Home, 2200 sq ft, 4-br, 2-bath, 2-car garage, average		132950	2000	47c
Home value, median		108000	2001	53s
House, 2400 sq ft, 8000 sq ft lot, new, urban, utilities	total	202500	3/01	4c
House payment, principal and interest, 25% down payment	mos	1014	3/01	4c
Rent, apartment, 2 br, 1 1/2-2 baths, unfurn, 950 sq ft, water	mos	537	3/01	4c
Rental unit, 1 bedroom, with utilities	mos	389	4/01	41c
Rental unit, 2 bedroom, with utilities	mos	520	4/01	41c
Rental unit, 3 bedroom, with utilities	mos	699	4/01	41c
Rental unit, 4 bedroom, with utilities	mos	848	4/01	41c
Legal Fees				
Divorce, filing fee		230.00	4/01	35s
Driver's license fee	renew	16.00	1999	48s
Driver's license fee	orig	16.00	1999	48s
Fishing license	yr	17.00	4/01	34s
Personal Goods				
Shampoo, Alberto VO5	15 oz	1.31	3/01	4c
Toothpaste, Crest or Colgate	6-7 oz	2.60	3/01	4c
Personal Services				
Dry cleaning, man's 2-pc suit		9.37	3/01	4c
Man's haircut, barbershop, no styling		9.59	3/01	4c
Woman's shampoo, trim, blow-dry, no style-change		20.40	3/01	4c
Restaurant Food				
Chicken, fried, thigh and drumstick, KFC/ Church's		2.89	3/01	4c
Hamburger with cheese, McDonald's	1/4 lb	1.99	3/01	4c
Pizza, Pizza Hut or Pizza Inn	11-12 in	8.99	3/01	4c
Transportation				
Transportation, ACCRA Index		99.20	3/01	4c
Bus fare, to central business district	1-way	0.75	3/01	4c
Diesel at the pump	gal	1.35	10/99	73s
Gasoline before-tax price (cents)	gal	126.00	10/00	43s
Tire balance, computer or spin balance, front	wheel	8.80	3/01	4c
Travel				
Hotel room	night	54.24	2/01	94s
Utilities				
Utilities, ACCRA Index		103.50	3/01	4c
Electrical bill, average	mos	52.58	9/00	9s

Billings, MT - continued

Item	Per	Value	Date	Ref.
Utilities - continued				
Electricity and other, mixed, 2400 sq ft, new home	mos	44.87	3/01	4c
Electricity cost, average	KWh	5.92	9/00	9s
Water price	100 cf	1.31	2000	109c
Water price, dwelling unit	mos	25.72	2000	109c
Weddings				
Wedding (national average cost)		19936	2000	33r
Attendants' gifts		321	1998	33r
Bridal attendants' apparel (5 persons)		824	2000	33r
Bride's headpiece/veil		173	1998	33r
Bride's wedding dress		859	1998	33r
Clergy, religious facility fee		242	1998	33r
Engagement ring		3177	1998	33r
Flowers		789	1998	33r
Groom's formalwear rental		99	2000	33r
Limousine		410	1998	33r
Marriage license cost		30.25	4/01	35s
Men's formalwear (ushers, best man)		469	2000	33r
Mother of bride apparel		241	2000	33r
Music		866	1998	33r
Photography and videography		1368	1998	33r
Rehearsal dinner		728	1998	33r
Wedding invitations and announcements		341	1998	33r
Wedding reception		7968	2000	33r
Wedding rings (bride and groom)		1060	1998	33r

Biloxi-Gulfport-Pascagoula, MS

Item	Per	Value	Date	Ref.
Alcoholic Beverages				
Alcoholic beverage purchases	yr	253	1999	30r
Malt beverages, all types, all sizes, any origin	16 oz	0.96	7/01	11r
Appliances				
Major appliances, expenditures on	yr	172	1999	30r
Small appliances, housewares, expenditures on	yr	81	1999	30r
Banking and Money				
Mortgage interest and charges paid	yr	2039	1999	30r
Mortgage principal paid on owned property	yr	1026	1999	30r
Vehicle finance charges paid	yr	365	1999	30r
Charity				
Cash contributions, expenditures	yr	1127	1999	30r
Child Care				
Child raising cost, total, age 0-2	yr	8540	1999	60r
Child raising cost, total, age 3-5	yr	8780	1999	60r
Child raising cost, total, age 6-8	yr	8820	1999	60r
Child raising cost, total, age 9-11	yr	8800	1999	60r
Child raising cost, total, age 12-14	yr	9510	1999	60r
Child raising cost, total, age 15-17	yr	9740	1999	60r
Child's child care and education, age 0-2	yr	1380	1999	60r
Child's child care and education, age 3-5	yr	1520	1999	60r
Child's child care and education, age 6-8	yr	990	1999	60r
Child's child care and education, age 9-11	yr	650	1999	60r
Child's child care and education, age 12-14	yr	490	1999	60r
Child's child care and education, age 15-17	yr	840	1999	60r
Child's clothing, age 0-2	yr	480	1999	60r
Child's clothing, age 3-5	yr	470	1999	60r
Child's clothing, age 6-8	yr	520	1999	60r
Child's clothing, age 9-11	yr	570	1999	60r
Child's clothing, age 12-14	yr	950	1999	60r
Child's clothing, age 15-17	yr	850	1999	60r
Child's food, age 0-2	yr	1000	1999	60r
Child's food, age 3-5	yr	1160	1999	60r
Child's food, age 6-8	yr	1490	1999	60r
Child's food, age 9-11	yr	1770	1999	60r
Child's food, age 12-14	yr	1770	1999	60r
Child's food, age 15-17	yr	1980	1999	60r
Child's health care, age 0-2	yr	620	1999	60r
Child's health care, age 3-5	yr	590	1999	60r

Values are in dollars or fractions of dollars. In the column headed *Ref*, references are shown to sources. Each reference is followed by a letter. These refer to the geographical level for which data were reported: s=State, r=Region, and c=City or metro. The abbreviation *ex* is used to mean *except* or *excluding*; *exp* stands for *expenditures*. For other abbreviations and further explanations, please see the Introduction.

Biloxi-Gulfport-Pascagoula, MS - continued

Item	Per	Value	Date	Ref.
Child Care				
Child's health care, age 6-8	yr	680	1999	60r
Child's health care, age 9-11	yr	720	1999	60r
Child's health care, age 12-14	yr	730	1999	60r
Child's health care, age 15-17	yr	760	1999	60r
Child's housing, age 0-2	yr	3070	1999	60r
Child's housing, age 3-5	yr	3050	1999	60r
Child's housing, age 6-8	yr	3010	1999	60r
Child's housing, age 9-11	yr	2850	1999	60r
Child's housing, age 12-14	yr	3040	1999	60r
Child's housing, age 15-17	yr	2650	1999	60r
Child's personal care, reading, age 0-2	yr	910	1999	60r
Child's personal care, reading, age 3-5	yr	930	1999	60r
Child's personal care, reading, age 6-8	yr	960	1999	60r
Child's personal care, reading, age 9-11	yr	1000	1999	60r
Child's personal care, reading, age 12-14	yr	1170	1999	60r
Child's personal care, reading, age 15-17	yr	950	1999	60r
Clothing				
Apparel and services purchases	yr	1610	1999	30r
Boys, 2 to 15, expenditures on	yr	89	1999	30r
Children under 2, expenditures on	yr	79	1999	30r
Footwear, expenditures on	yr	283	1999	30r
Girls, 2 to 15, expenditures on	yr	103	1999	30r
Men and boys, expenditures on	yr	351	1999	30r
Men, 16 and over, expenditures on	yr	262	1999	30r
Women, 16 and over, expenditures on	yr	538	1999	30r
Communications				
Phone line, single, business, field visit	inst.	67.00	12/97	17s
Phone line, single, business, no field visit	inst.	67.00	12/97	17s
Phone line, single, residence, field visit	inst.	46.00	12/97	17s
Phone line, single, residence, no field visit	inst.	46.00	12/97	17s
Postage and stationery, expenditures on	yr	104	1999	30r
Postal rate, express mail, up to half-pound		12.45	7/01	108r
Postal rate, letter, first class, first ounce		0.34	7/01	108r
Postal rate, letter, two ounces		0.57	7/01	108r
Postal rate, post card		0.21	7/01	108r
Postal rate, priority mail, two pounds		3.95	7/01	108r
Postal rate, priority mail, up to one pound		3.50	7/01	108r
Telephone services, expenditures on	yr	860	1999	30r
Education				
Board, 4-year private college/university	yr	1536	1996	38s
Board, 4-year public college/university	yr	1568	1996	38s
Education expenditures	yr	431	1999	30r
Room, 4-year private college/university	yr	1582	1996	38s
Room, 4-year public college/university	yr	1399	1996	38s
Total cost, 4-year private college/university	yr	9901	1996	38s
Total cost, 4-year public college/university	yr	5425	1996	38s
Tuition, 2-year public college/university, in state	yr	941	1996	38s
Tuition, 4-year private college/university, in state	yr	6782	1996	38s
Tuition, 4-year public college/university	yr	2459	1996	38s
Energy and Fuels				
Electricity	500 KWhs	47.29	7/01	11r
Electricity	KWh	0.09	7/01	11r
Fuel oil #2	gal	1.43	7/01	11r
Fuel oil and other fuels, expenditures on	yr	45	1999	30r
Gas, natural, commercial rate	1000 cf	7.01	11/00	88s
Gasoline, all types	gal	1.60	7/01	11r
Gasoline, unleaded midgrade	gal	1.65	7/01	11r
Gasoline, unleaded premium	gal	1.74	7/01	11r
Natural gas, expenditures on	yr	164	1999	30r
Utility (piped) gas, therm		1.01	7/01	11r
Utility (piped) gas, 40 therms		44.29	7/01	11r
Utility (piped) gas, 100 therms		97.44	7/01	11r
Entertainment				
Entertainment purchases	yr	1574	1999	30r
Fees and admissions paid	yr	371	1999	30r
Reading purchases	yr	121	1999	30r

Biloxi-Gulfport-Pascagoula, MS - continued

Item	Per	Value	Date	Ref.
Entertainment - continued				
Television, radios, sound equipment, expenditures on	yr	561	1999	30r
Groceries				
American processed cheese	lb	3.50	7/01	11r
Bakery products, expenditures on	yr	261	1999	30r
Bananas	lb	0.47	7/01	11r
Beans, dried, any type, all sizes	lb	0.63	7/01	11r
Beef for stew, boneless	lb	2.86	7/01	11r
Beef, expenditures on	yr	210	1999	30r
Bologna, all beef or mixed	lb	2.29	7/01	11r
Bread, French	lb	1.66	7/01	11r
Bread, white, pan	lb	0.87	7/01	11r
Bread, whole wheat, pan	lb	1.38	7/01	11r
Broccoli	lb	1.04	7/01	11r
Butter, salted, grade AA, stick	lb	2.26	7/01	11r
Butter, yoghurt, cheese, etc, expenditures on	yr	170	1999	30r
Cabbage	lb	0.42	7/01	11r
Cereals and cereal products, expenditures on	yr	140	1999	30r
Cheddar cheese, natural	lb	3.75	7/01	11r
Chicken breast, bone-in	lb	1.85	7/01	11r
Chicken legs, bone-in	lb	1.34	7/01	11r
Chicken, fresh, whole	lb	1.05	7/01	11r
Chops, boneless	lb	4.13	7/01	11r
Chuck roast, graded and ungraded, excl U.S. prime and choice	lb	2.35	7/01	11r
Chuck roast, U.S. choice, boneless	lb	2.67	7/01	11r
Coffee, 100%, ground roast, all sizes	lb	2.88	7/01	11r
Coffee, instant, plain, regular, all sizes	16 oz	9.25	7/01	11r
Cola, non diet,	2 liter	1.11	7/01	11r
Crackers, soda, salted	lb	1.70	7/01	11r
Dairy product purchases	yr	282	1999	30r
Eggs, expenditures on	yr	32	1999	30r
Fats and oils, expenditures on	yr	79	1999	30r
Fish and seafood, expenditures on	yr	99	1999	30r
Flour, white, all purpose	lb	0.32	7/01	11r
Food (excl fruit and vegetables), eaten at home, purchases	yr	815	1999	30r
Food cooked on trips, expenditures on	yr	36	1999	30r
Food purchases	yr	4533	1999	30r
Food purchases, eaten away from home	yr	1873	1999	30r
Food purchases, food eaten at home	yr	2660	1999	30r
Fresh fruits, expenditures on	yr	128	1999	30r
Fresh milk and cream, expenditures on	yr	112	1999	30r
Fresh vegetables, expenditures on	yr	131	1999	30r
Fruit and vegetable purchases	yr	438	1999	30r
Grapefruit	lb	0.59	7/01	11r
Grapes, Thompson, seedless	lb	2.12	7/01	11r
Ground beef, 100% beef	lb	1.76	7/01	11r
Ground beef, lean and extra lean	lb	2.60	7/01	11r
Ground chuck, 100% beef	lb	2.08	7/01	11r
Ham, boneless, excl canned	lb	2.71	7/01	11r
Ham, rump or shank half, bone-in, smoked	lb	2.19	7/01	11r
Ice cream, prepackaged, bulk, regular	1/2 gal	3.93	7/01	11r
Lemons	lb	1.32	7/01	11r
Lettuce, iceberg	lb	0.76	7/01	11r
Milk, fresh, low fat	gal	2.75	7/01	11r
Milk, fresh, whole, fortified	gal	2.97	7/01	11r
Nonalcoholic beverages, expenditures on	yr	228	1999	30r
Orange juice, frozen concentrate	16 oz	1.95	7/01	11r
Oranges, Navel	lb	0.73	7/01	11r
Oranges, Valencia	lb	0.55	7/01	11r
Peanut butter, creamy, all sizes	lb	1.83	7/01	11r
Pears, Anjou	lb	0.98	7/01	11r
Pork chops, center cut, bone-in	lb	3.33	7/01	11r
Pork sausage, fresh, loose	lb	2.59	7/01	11r
Pork shoulder picnic, bone-in, smoked	lb	1.12	7/01	11r
Pork, expenditures on	yr	162	1999	30r
Potato chips	16 oz	3.59	7/01	11r
Potatoes, frozen, french fried	lb	1.00	7/01	11r
Potatoes, white, all types	lb	0.44	7/01	11r
Poultry, expenditures on	yr	137	1999	30r

Values are in dollars or fractions of dollars. In the column headed *Ref*, references are shown to sources. Each reference is followed by a letter. These refer to the geographical level for which data were reported: s=State, r=Region, and c=City or metro. The abbreviation *ex* is used to mean *except* or *excluding*; *exp* stands for *expenditures*. For other abbreviations and further explanations, please see the Introduction.

Biloxi-Gulfport-Pascagoula, MS - continued

Item	Per	Value	Date	Ref.
Groceries				
Processed fruits, expenditures on	yr	97	1999	30r
Processed vegetables, expenditures on	yr	82	1999	30r
Rice, white, long grain, uncooked	lb	0.51	7/01	11r
Round roast, graded and ungraded, excl U.S. prime and choice	lb	2.96	7/01	11r
Round steak, graded and ungraded, excl U.S. prime and choice	lb	3.11	7/01	11r
Sirloin steak, graded and ungraded, excl U.S. prime and choice	lb	4.23	7/01	11r
Spaghetti and macaroni	lb	0.78	7/01	11r
Steak, round, U.S. choice, boneless	lb	3.56	7/01	11r
Steak, sirloin, U.S. choice, boneless	lb	5.65	7/01	11r
Strawberries, dry pint	12 oz	1.50	7/01	11r
Sugar and other sweets, expenditures on	yr	99	1999	30r
Sugar, white, 33-80 ounce package	lb	0.39	7/01	11r
Sugar, white, all sizes	lb	0.42	7/01	11r
Tobacco products and smoking supplies purchases	yr	288	1999	30r
Tomatoes, field grown	lb	1.43	7/01	11r
Tuna, light, chunk	lb	1.77	7/01	11r
Turkey, frozen, whole	lb	1.05	7/01	11r
Goods and Services				
Hunting license	yr	18.00	4/01	34s
Health Care				
Cardiac catheterization, ave hospital/ physician charges		10310	1998	77s
Childbirth, Cesarean delivery		11587	1997	13r
Childbirth, vaginal delivery		6725	1997	13r
Drugs, expenditures on	yr	399	1999	30r
Health care purchases	yr	1971	1999	30r
Health insurance expenditures	yr	933	1999	30r
Hysterectomy, laproscopically-assisted, ave hospital/physician charges		14270	1998	76s
Hysterectomy, vaginal, ave hospital and physician charges		10020	1998	76s
Medicaid dispensing fee		4.91	1999	87s
Medical services expenditures	yr	547	1999	30r
Medical supplies, expenditures on	yr	91	1999	30r
Household Goods				
Floor coverings, expenditures on	yr	44	1999	30r
Furniture, expenditures on	yr	335	1999	30r
Household furnishings and equipment purchases	yr	1328	1999	30r
Household textiles, expenditures on	yr	89	1999	30r
Laundry and cleaning supplies, expenditures on	yr	113	1999	30r
Housing				
Home price, existing, ave		160100	10/00	90r
Home value, median		102000	2001	53s
Household operation expenditures	yr	553	1999	30r
Housekeeping supplies purchases	yr	473	1999	30r
Housing, expenditures on	yr	10303	1999	30r
Maintenance, repairs, insurance expenditures	yr	699	1999	30r
Monthly rental value of owned home	mos	505	1999	30r
Owned dwellings, expenditures own	yr	3465	1999	30r
Rent expenditures	yr	1641	1999	30r
Rental unit, 1 bedroom, with utilities	mos	470	4/01	41c
Rental unit, 2 bedroom, with utilities	mos	541	4/01	41c
Rental unit, 3 bedroom, with utilities	mos	754	4/01	41c
Rental unit, 4 bedroom, with utilities	mos	889	4/01	41c
Shelter, expenditures on	yr	5467	1999	30r
Insurance and Pensions				
Life and other personal insurance purchases	yr	414	1999	30r
Pensions and Social Security, expenditures on	yr	2635	1999	30r
Personal insurance and pensions, expenditures on	yr	3048	1999	30r

Biloxi-Gulfport-Pascagoula, MS - continued

Item	Per	Value	Date	Ref.
Legal Fees				
Combination hunting and fishing license	yr	18.00	4/01	34s
Driver's license fee	orig	20.00	1999	48s
Driver's license fee	renew	5.00	1999	48s
Fishing license	yr	12.00	4/01	34s
Personal Goods				
Personal care products and services purchases	yr	393	1999	30r
Personal Services				
Personal services, household, expenditures on	yr	258	1999	30r
Pets				
Pets, toys, and playground equipment, expenditures on	yr	306	1999	30r
Taxes				
Federal income taxes paid	yr	2047	1999	30r
Personal taxes, expenditures on	yr	2554	1999	30r
Property taxes paid	yr	726	1999	30r
State and local income taxes paid	yr	363	1999	30r
Transportation				
Cars and trucks, new, expenditures on	yr	1648	1999	30r
Cars and trucks, used, expenditures on	yr	1651	1999	30r
Diesel at the pump	gal	1.17	10/99	73s
Gasoline and motor oil purchases	yr	1052	1999	30r
Gasoline before-tax price (cents)	gal	108.40	10/00	43s
Maintenance and repair expenditures	yr	621	1999	30r
Motorcycle license fee	orig	5.00	1999	49s
Motorcycle license fee	renew	5.00	1999	49s
Public transportation, expenditures on	yr	298	1999	30r
Transportation purchases	yr	6738	1999	30r
Vehicle expenses, miscellaneous, purchases	yr	2033	1999	30r
Vehicle insurance payments	yr	696	1999	30r
Vehicle purchases (net outlay)	yr	3354	1999	30r
Vehicle rental, lease expenditures	yr	352	1999	30r
Utilities				
Electrical bill, average	mos	79.66	9/00	9s
Electricity, expenditures on	yr	1115	1999	30r
Electricity cost, average	KWh	5.69	9/00	9s
Water and other public services, expenditures on	yr	298	1999	30r
Weddings				
Wedding (national average cost)		19936	2000	33r
Attendants' gifts		321	1998	33r
Bridal attendants' apparel (5 persons)		824	2000	33r
Bride's headpiece/veil		173	1998	33r
Bride's wedding dress		859	1998	33r
Clergy, religious facility fee		242	1998	33r
Engagement ring		3177	1998	33r
Flowers		789	1998	33r
Groom's formalwear rental		99	2000	33r
Limousine		410	1998	33r
Marriage license cost		21.00	4/01	35s
Men's formalwear (ushers, best man)		469	2000	33r
Mother of bride apparel		241	2000	33r
Music		866	1998	33r
Photography and videography		1368	1998	33r
Rehearsal dinner		728	1998	33r
Wedding invitations and announcements		341	1998	33r
Wedding reception		7968	2000	33r
Wedding rings (bride and groom)		1060	1998	33r

Binghamton, NY

Item	Per	Value	Date	Ref.
Average annual expenditures	yr	37971	1999	30r
Alcoholic Beverages				
Alcoholic beverage purchases	yr	368	1999	30r
Wine, red and white table, all sizes, any origin	liter	9.64	7/01	11r

Values are in dollars or fractions of dollars. In the column headed *Ref*, references are shown to sources. Each reference is followed by a letter. These refer to the geographical level for which data were reported: s=State, r=Region, and c=City or metro. The abbreviation *ex* is used to mean *except* or *excluding*; *exp* stands for expenditures. For other abbreviations and further explanations, please see the Introduction.

Binghamton, NY - continued

Item	Per	Value	Date	Ref.
Appliances				
Major appliances, expenditures on	yr	194	1999	30r
Small appliances, housewares, expenditures on	yr	93	1999	30r
Banking and Money				
Mortgage interest and charges paid	yr	2622	1999	30r
Mortgage principal paid on owned property	yr	1262	1999	30r
Vehicle finance charges paid	yr	240	1999	30r
Charity				
Cash contributions, expenditures	yr	1001	1999	30r
Child Care				
Child raising cost, total, age 0-2	yr	8670	1999	60r
Child raising cost, total, age 3-5	yr	8910	1999	60r
Child raising cost, total, age 6-8	yr	9040	1999	60r
Child raising cost, total, age 9-11	yr	9100	1999	60r
Child raising cost, total, age 12-14	yr	9890	1999	60r
Child raising cost, total, age 15-17	yr	10010	1999	60r
Child's child care and education, age 0-2	yr	1070	1999	60r
Child's child care and education, age 3-5	yr	1190	1999	60r
Child's child care and education, age 6-8	yr	740	1999	60r
Child's child care and education, age 9-11	yr	470	1999	60r
Child's child care and education, age 12-14	yr	350	1999	60r
Child's child care and education, age 15-17	yr	590	1999	60r
Child's clothing, age 0-2	yr	480	1999	60r
Child's clothing, age 3-5	yr	470	1999	60r
Child's clothing, age 6-8	yr	520	1999	60r
Child's clothing, age 9-11	yr	570	1999	60r
Child's clothing, age 12-14	yr	970	1999	60r
Child's clothing, age 15-17	yr	870	1999	60r
Child's food, age 0-2	yr	1130	1999	60r
Child's food, age 3-5	yr	1290	1999	60r
Child's food, age 6-8	yr	1640	1999	60r
Child's food, age 9-11	yr	1930	1999	60r
Child's food, age 12-14	yr	1940	1999	60r
Child's food, age 15-17	yr	2150	1999	60r
Child's health care, age 0-2	yr	550	1999	60r
Child's health care, age 3-5	yr	530	1999	60r
Child's health care, age 6-8	yr	610	1999	60r
Child's health care, age 9-11	yr	650	1999	60r
Child's health care, age 12-14	yr	660	1999	60r
Child's health care, age 15-17	yr	690	1999	60r
Child's housing, age 0-2	yr	3555	1999	60r
Child's housing, age 3-5	yr	3530	1999	60r
Child's housing, age 6-8	yr	3490	1999	60r
Child's housing, age 9-11	yr	3340	1999	60r
Child's housing, age 12-14	yr	3530	1999	60r
Child's housing, age 15-17	yr	3140	1999	60r
Child's personal care, reading, age 0-2	yr	920	1999	60r
Child's personal care, reading, age 3-5	yr	950	1999	60r
Child's personal care, reading, age 6-8	yr	980	1999	60r
Child's personal care, reading, age 9-11	yr	1020	1999	60r
Child's personal care, reading, age 12-14	yr	1190	1999	60r
Child's personal care, reading, age 15-17	yr	970	1999	60r
Nannies: criminal background check		74	1998	84s
Clothing				
Apparel and services purchases	yr	1831	1999	30r
Boys, 2 to 15, expenditures on	yr	92	1999	30r
Children under 2, expenditures on	yr	63	1999	30r
Footwear, expenditures on	yr	300	1999	30r
Girls, 2 to 15, expenditures on	yr	101	1999	30r
Men and boys, expenditures on	yr	446	1999	30r
Men, 16 and over, expenditures on	yr	354	1999	30r
Women, 16 and over, expenditures on	yr	584	1999	30r
Communications				
Cable modem installation, Adelphi		54.90	6/99	103s
Cable modem installation, Cablevision Systems		150.00	6/99	103s
Cable modem installation, Time Warner		75.00-225.00	6/99	103s
Cable modem rate, cable subscriber, Adelphi	mos	34.95	6/99	103s

Binghamton, NY - continued

Item	Per	Value	Date	Ref.
Communications - continued				
Cable modem rate, cable subscriber, Cablevision Systems	mos	44.95	6/99	103s
Cable modem rate, cable subscriber, Century	mos	39.95	6/99	103s
Cable modem rate, cable subscriber, Time Warner	mos	39.95-49.95	6/99	103s
Cable modem rate, non-cable subscriber, Adelphi	mos	44.95	6/99	103s
Cable modem rate, non-cable subscriber, Cablevision Systems	mos	54.95	6/99	103s
Cable modem rate, non-cable subscriber, Time Warner	mos	39.95-54.95	6/99	103s
Phone line, single, business, field visit	inst.	142.76	12/97	17s
Phone line, single, business, no field visit	inst.	106.05	12/97	17s
Phone line, single, residence, field visit	inst.	102.78	12/97	17s
Phone line, single, residence, no field visit	inst.	55.00	12/97	17s
Postage and stationery, expenditures on	yr	138	1999	30r
Postal rate, express mail, up to half-pound		12.45	7/01	108r
Postal rate, letter, first class, first ounce		0.34	7/01	108r
Postal rate, letter, two ounces		0.57	7/01	108r
Postal rate, post card		0.21	7/01	108r
Postal rate, priority mail, two pounds		3.95	7/01	108r
Postal rate, priority mail, up to one pound		3.50	7/01	108r
Telephone bill, business, basic rate	mos	16.23	12/97	18c
Telephone bill, residential, basic rate	mos	16.65	12/97	18c
Telephone services, expenditures on	yr	830	1999	30r
Education				
Board, 4-year private college/university	yr	3255	1996	38s
Board, 4-year public college/university	yr	2310	1996	38s
Education expenditures	yr	877	1999	30r
Room, 4-year private college/university	yr	3724	1996	38s
Room, 4-year public college/university	yr	2937	1996	38s
Total cost, 4-year private college/university	yr	20831	1996	38s
Total cost, 4-year public college/university	yr	8960	1996	38s
Tuition, 2-year public college/university, in state	yr	2427	1996	38s
Tuition, 4-year private college/university, in state	yr	13852	1996	38s
Tuition, 4-year public college/university	yr	3714	1996	38s
Energy and Fuels				
Electricity	KWh	0.12	7/01	11r
Fuel oil #2	gal	1.31	7/01	11r
Fuel oil and other fuels, expenditures on	yr	207	1999	30r
Gasoline, all types	gal	1.80	7/01	11r
Gasoline, unleaded midgrade	gal	1.85	7/01	11r
Gasoline, unleaded premium	gal	1.91	7/01	11r
Gasoline, unleaded regular	gal	1.71	7/01	11r
Natural gas, expenditures on	yr	368	1999	30r
Utility (piped) gas, therm		1.08	7/01	11r
Utility (piped) gas, 40 therms		50.87	7/01	11r
Utility (piped) gas, 100 therms		111.06	7/01	11r
Entertainment				
Entertainment purchases	yr	1821	1999	30r
Fees and admissions paid	yr	511	1999	30r
Television, radios, sound equipment, expenditures on	yr	650	1999	30r
Funerals				
Total cost of funeral		5813.50	1/99	78r
Acknowledgement cards		28.32	1/99	78r
Casket		2082.20	1/99	78r
Cosmetology, hair, other preparation		169.59	1/99	78r
Embalming		465.60	1/99	78r
Funeral at funeral home		339.56	1/99	78r
Hearse (local)		183.96	1/99	78r
Professional service charges		1157.85	1/99	78r
Service car/van		100.41	1/99	78r
Transfer of remains to funeral home		158.66	1/99	78r
Vault		766.31	1/99	78r
Visitation/viewing		361.04	1/99	78r

Values are in dollars or fractions of dollars. In the column headed *Ref*, references are shown to sources. Each reference is followed by a letter. These refer to the geographical level for which data were reported: s=State, r=Region, and c=City or metro. The abbreviation *ex* is used to mean *except* or *excluding*; *exp* stands for *expenditures*. For other abbreviations and further explanations, please see the Introduction.

Binghamton, NY - continued

Item	Per	Value	Date	Ref.
Groceries				
Apples, red delicious	lb	0.95	7/01	11r
Bacon, sliced	lb	3.44	7/01	11r
Bakery products, expenditures on	yr	310	1999	30r
Bananas	lb	0.55	7/01	11r
Beef, expenditures on	yr	236	1999	30r
Bread, white, pan	lb	1.09	7/01	11r
Butter, yoghurt, cheese, etc, expenditures on	yr	214	1999	30r
Cereals and bakery product purchases	yr	474	1999	30r
Cereals and cereal products, expenditures on	yr	164	1999	30r
Chicken legs, bone-in	lb	1.23	7/01	11r
Chicken, fresh, whole	lb	1.13	7/01	11r
Chuck roast, U.S. choice, boneless	lb	2.79	7/01	11r
Coffee, 100%, ground roast, all sizes	lb	3.40	7/01	11r
Dairy product purchases	yr	342	1999	30r
Eggs, expenditures on	yr	34	1999	30r
Eggs, grade A, large	dozen	0.82	7/01	11r
Fats and oils, expenditures on	yr	80	1999	30r
Fish and seafood, expenditures on	yr	123	1999	30r
Food (excl fruit and vegetables), eaten at home, purchases	yr	838	1999	30r
Food cooked on trips, expenditures on	yr	48	1999	30r
Food purchases	yr	5314	1999	30r
Food purchases, eaten away from home	yr	2313	1999	30r
Food purchases, food eaten at home	yr	3001	1999	30r
Fresh fruits, expenditures on	yr	169	1999	30r
Fresh milk and cream, expenditures on	yr	128	1999	30r
Fresh vegetables, expenditures on	yr	164	1999	30r
Grapefruit	lb	0.67	7/01	11r
Grapes, Thompson, seedless	lb	2.18	7/01	11r
Ground beef, lean and extra lean	lb	2.66	7/01	11r
Ground chuck, 100% beef	lb	2.04	7/01	11r
Lettuce, iceberg	lb	0.76	7/01	11r
Meats, poultry, fish, and egg purchases	yr	808	1999	30r
Nonalcoholic beverages, expenditures on	yr	225	1999	30r
Orange juice, frozen concentrate	16 oz	1.88	7/01	11r
Oranges, Navel	lb	0.79	7/01	11r
Oranges, Valencia	lb	0.56	7/01	11r
Peaches	lb	1.16	7/01	11r
Peanut butter, creamy, all sizes	lb	2.01	7/01	11r
Pears, Anjou	lb	1.16	7/01	11r
Pork chops, center cut, bone-in	lb	3.57	7/01	11r
Pork, expenditures on	yr	146	1999	30r
Potato chips	16 oz	3.37	7/01	11r
Potatoes, white, all types	lb	0.42	7/01	11r
Poultry, expenditures on	yr	158	1999	30r
Processed fruits, expenditures on	yr	124	1999	30r
Processed vegetables, expenditures on	yr	82	1999	30r
Round roast, U.S. choice, boneless	lb	3.04	7/01	11r
Spaghetti and macaroni	lb	1.04	7/01	11r
Steak, sirloin, U.S. choice, boneless	lb	5.39	7/01	11r
Strawberries, dry pint	12 oz	1.51	7/01	11r
Sugar and other sweets, expenditures on	yr	110	1999	30r
Sugar, white, 33-80 ounce package	lb	0.46	7/01	11r
Sugar, white, all sizes	lb	0.47	7/01	11r
Tobacco products and smoking supplies purchases	yr	309	1999	30r
Yogurt, natural, fruit flavored	8 oz	0.79	7/01	11r
Goods and Services				
B&B Japanese maple (acer japonicum)	gal	38.99-125.00	4/00	93r
Boxwood (buxus)	2 gal	15.99-49.95	4/00	93r
Daylily (hemerocallis)	gal	4.95	4/00	93r
Flat of annuals		8.00-14.99	4/00	93r
Fountain grass (pennisetum)	gal	6.99-9.99	4/00	93r
Hanging basket (10 in)		12.95-19.99	4/00	93r
Hardy geranium (geranium)	gal	6.95-7.99	4/00	93r

Binghamton, NY - continued

Item	Per	Value	Date	Ref.
Goods and Services - continued				
Hosta (hosta)	gal	4.95	4/00	93r
Lilac (syrubga vulgaris)	2 gal	17.99-74.95	4/00	93r
Miscellaneous purchases	yr	872	1999	30r
Rhododendron (rhododendron)	2 gal	23.99-54.95	4/00	93r
Sage (salvia)	gal	6.95-7.99	4/00	93r
Wintercreeper euonymus (euonymus fortunei)	2 gal	14.99-23.95	4/00	93r
Hunting license	yr	11.00	4/01	34s
Health Care				
Cardiac catheterization, ave hospital/physician charges		12750	1998	77s
Childbirth, Cesarean delivery		14716	1997	13r
Childbirth, vaginal delivery		8541	1997	13r
Drugs, expenditures on	yr	296	1999	30r
Health care purchases	yr	1788	1999	30r
Health insurance expenditures	yr	875	1999	30r
Hysterectomy, laproscopically-assisted, ave hospital/physician charges		13460	1998	76s
Hysterectomy, vaginal, ave hospital and physician charges		10310	1998	76s
Medicaid dispensing fee		3.50-4.50	1999	87s
Medical services expenditures	yr	516	1999	30r
Medical supplies, expenditures on	yr	102	1999	30r
Plastic surgery, breast augmentation		4232	2000	7r
Plastic surgery, breast lift		4605	2000	7r
Plastic surgery, facelift		6964	2000	7r
Plastic surgery, hair transplantation		4193	2000	7r
Plastic surgery, lip augmentation		1675	2000	7r
Plastic surgery, lower body lift		6611	2000	7r
Plastic surgery, thigh lift		4751	2000	7r
Household Goods				
Floor coverings, expenditures on	yr	59	1999	30r
Furniture, expenditures on	yr	388	1999	30r
Household furnishings and equipment purchases	yr	1567	1999	30r
Household textiles, expenditures on	yr	112	1999	30r
Laundry and cleaning supplies, expenditures on	yr	104	1999	30r
Housing				
Home, 2200 sq ft, 4-br, 2-bath, 2-car garage, average		142450	2000	47c
Home price, existing, ave		180800	10/00	90c
Home value, median		179000	2001	53s
Household operation expenditures	yr	581	1999	30r
Housekeeping supplies purchases	yr	474	1999	30r
Lodging expenditures	yr	550	1999	30r
Maintenance, repairs, insurance expenditures	yr	835	1999	30r
Monthly rental value of owned home	mos	663	1999	30r
Owned dwellings, expenditures own	yr	5209	1999	30r
Rent expenditures	yr	2390	1999	30r
Rental unit, 1 bedroom, with utilities	mos	404	4/01	41c
Rental unit, 2 bedroom, with utilities	mos	504	4/01	41c
Rental unit, 3 bedroom, with utilities	mos	640	4/01	41c
Rental unit, 4 bedroom, with utilities	mos	718	4/01	41c
Shelter, expenditures on	yr	8149	1999	30r
Insurance and Pensions				
Auto insurance premium	yr	1113.55	1999	57s
Life and other personal insurance purchases	yr	424	1999	30r
Pensions and Social Security, expenditures on	yr	3037	1999	30r
Legal Fees				
Divorce, filing fee		270.00	4/01	35s
Driver's license fee	orig	25.00	1999	48s
Driver's license fee	renew	25.00	1999	48s

Values are in dollars or fractions of dollars. In the column headed *Ref*, references are shown to sources. Each reference is followed by a letter. These refer to the geographical level for which data were reported: s=State, r=Region, and c=City or metro. The abbreviation *ex* is used to mean *except* or *excluding*; *exp* stands for *expenditures*. For other abbreviations and further explanations, please see the Introduction.

Binghamton, NY - continued

Item	Per	Value	Date	Ref.
Legal Fees				
Fishing license	yr	14.00	4/01	34s
Personal Goods				
Personal care products and services purchases	yr	399	1999	30r
Personal Services				
Personal services, household, expenditures on	yr	271	1999	30r
Pets				
Pets, toys, and playground equipment, expenditures on	yr	325	1999	30r
Taxes				
Federal income taxes paid	yr	2606	1999	30r
Personal taxes, expenditures on	yr	3567	1999	30r
Property taxes paid	yr	1752	1999	30r
State and local income taxes paid	yr	694	1999	30r
Transportation				
Cars and trucks, new, expenditures on	yr	1496	1999	30r
Cars and trucks, used, expenditures on	yr	1251	1999	30r
Diesel at the pump	gal	1.33	10/99	73s
Gasoline and motor oil purchases	yr	901	1999	30r
Gasoline before-tax price (cents)	gal	110.70	10/00	43s
Maintenance and repair expenditures	yr	618	1999	30r
Public transportation, expenditures on	yr	575	1999	30r
Transportation purchases	yr	6503	1999	30r
Vehicle expenses, miscellaneous, purchases	yr	2266	1999	30r
Vehicle insurance payments	yr	824	1999	30r
Vehicle purchases (net outlay)	yr	2761	1999	30r
Vehicle rental, lease expenditures	yr	584	1999	30r
Travel				
Hotel room	night	139.88	2/01	95s
Utilities				
Electrical bill, average	mos	71.50	9/00	9s
Electricity, expenditures on	yr	837	1999	30r
Electricity, summer, 250 KWh	mos	40.60	2/96	96c
Electricity, summer, 500 KWh	mos	73.31	2/96	96c
Electricity, summer, 750 KWh	mos	106.04	2/96	96c
Electricity, summer, 1000 KWh	mos	138.77	2/96	96c
Electricity cost, average	KWh	11.34	9/00	9s
Utilities, fuels, and public services purchased	yr	2457	1999	30r
Water and other public services, expenditures on	yr	215	1999	30r
Weddings				
Wedding (national average cost)		19936	2000	33r
Wedding (regional average total cost)		29454	1997	110r
Attendants' gifts		321	1998	33r
Bridal attendants' apparel (5 persons)		824	2000	33r
Bride's headpiece/veil		173	1998	33r
Bride's wedding dress		859	1998	33r
Clergy, religious facility fee		242	1998	33r
Engagement ring		3177	1998	33r
Flowers		789	1998	33r
Groom's formalwear rental		99	2000	33r
Limousine		410	1998	33r
Marriage license cost		25.00	4/01	35s
Men's formalwear (ushers, best man)		469	2000	33r
Mother of bride apparel		241	2000	33r
Music		866	1998	33r
Photography and videography		1368	1998	33r
Rehearsal dinner		728	1998	33r
Wedding invitations and announcements		341	1998	33r
Wedding reception		7968	2000	33r
Wedding rings (bride and groom)		1060	1998	33r

Birmingham, AL

Item	Per	Value	Date	Ref.
Composite, ACCRA index		96.30	3/01	4c
Alcoholic Beverages				
Alcoholic beverage purchases	yr	253	1999	30r
Beer, Heineken, 12-oz, ex deposit	6	7.58	3/01	4c
J & B Scotch	750-ml	23.99	3/01	4c
Malt beverages, all types, all sizes, any origin	16 oz	0.96	7/01	11r
Wine, Livingston or Gallo, Chablis blanc	1.5 liter	6.10	3/01	4c
Appliances				
Appliance repair, service call, washing machine	min lab chg	40.75	3/01	4c
Major appliances, expenditures on	yr	172	1999	30r
Small appliances, housewares, expenditures on	yr	81	1999	30r
Banking and Money				
Mortgage interest and charges paid	yr	2039	1999	30r
Mortgage principal paid on owned property	yr	1026	1999	30r
Mortgage rate, incl. points and orig. fee, 30-yr. conv. fixed or ARM	mos	6.85	3/01	4c
Vehicle finance charges paid	yr	365	1999	30r
Business Expenses				
Business travel, car rental	day	42	2001	3c
Business travel, food	day	45	2001	3c
Business travel, hotel	day	103	2001	3c
Charity				
Cash contributions, expenditures	yr	1127	1999	30r
Child Care				
Child raising cost, total, age 0-2	yr	8540	1999	60r
Child raising cost, total, age 3-5	yr	8780	1999	60r
Child raising cost, total, age 6-8	yr	8820	1999	60r
Child raising cost, total, age 9-11	yr	8800	1999	60r
Child raising cost, total, age 12-14	yr	9510	1999	60r
Child raising cost, total, age 15-17	yr	9740	1999	60r
Child's child care and education, age 0-2	yr	1380	1999	60r
Child's child care and education, age 3-5	yr	1520	1999	60r
Child's child care and education, age 6-8	yr	990	1999	60r
Child's child care and education, age 9-11	yr	650	1999	60r
Child's child care and education, age 12-14	yr	490	1999	60r
Child's child care and education, age 15-17	yr	840	1999	60r
Child's clothing, age 0-2	yr	480	1999	60r
Child's clothing, age 3-5	yr	470	1999	60r
Child's clothing, age 6-8	yr	520	1999	60r
Child's clothing, age 9-11	yr	570	1999	60r
Child's clothing, age 12-14	yr	950	1999	60r
Child's clothing, age 15-17	yr	850	1999	60r
Child's food, age 0-2	yr	1000	1999	60r
Child's food, age 3-5	yr	1160	1999	60r
Child's food, age 6-8	yr	1490	1999	60r
Child's food, age 9-11	yr	1770	1999	60r
Child's food, age 12-14	yr	1770	1999	60r
Child's food, age 15-17	yr	1980	1999	60r
Child's health care, age 0-2	yr	620	1999	60r
Child's health care, age 3-5	yr	590	1999	60r
Child's health care, age 6-8	yr	680	1999	60r
Child's health care, age 9-11	yr	720	1999	60r
Child's health care, age 12-14	yr	730	1999	60r
Child's health care, age 15-17	yr	760	1999	60r
Child's housing, age 0-2	yr	3070	1999	60r
Child's housing, age 3-5	yr	3050	1999	60r
Child's housing, age 6-8	yr	3010	1999	60r
Child's housing, age 9-11	yr	2850	1999	60r
Child's housing, age 12-14	yr	3040	1999	60r
Child's housing, age 15-17	yr	2650	1999	60r
Child's personal care, reading, age 0-2	yr	910	1999	60r
Child's personal care, reading, age 3-5	yr	930	1999	60r
Child's personal care, reading, age 6-8	yr	960	1999	60r
Child's personal care, reading, age 9-11	yr	1000	1999	60r
Child's personal care, reading, age 12-14	yr	1170	1999	60r
Child's personal care, reading, age 15-17	yr	950	1999	60r

Values are in dollars or fractions of dollars. In the column headed *Ref*, references are shown to sources. Each reference is followed by a letter. These refer to the geographical level for which data were reported: s=State, r=Region, and c=City or metro. The abbreviation *ex* is used to mean *except* or *excluding*; *exp* stands for *expenditures*. For other abbreviations and further explanations, please see the Introduction.

Birmingham, AL - continued

Item	Per	Value	Date	Ref.
Clothing				
Apparel and services purchases	yr	1610	1999	30r
Boys' brief, cotton	3	5.83	3/01	4c
Boys, 2 to 15, expenditures on	yr	89	1999	30r
Children under 2, expenditures on	yr	79	1999	30r
Footwear, expenditures on	yr	283	1999	30r
Girls, 2 to 15, expenditures on	yr	103	1999	30r
Men and boys, expenditures on	yr	351	1999	30r
Men, 16 and over, expenditures on	yr	262	1999	30r
Shirt, man's dress shirt		24.99	3/01	4c
Slacks, man's "No Wrinkles" khaki		39.19	3/01	4c
Women, 16 and over, expenditures on	yr	538	1999	30r
Communications				
Newspaper subscription, daily and Sunday delivery	mos	11.90	3/01	4c
Phone line, single, business, field visit	inst.	69.00	12/97	17s
Phone line, single, business, no field visit	inst.	69.00	12/97	17s
Phone line, single, residence, field visit	inst.	40.00	12/97	17s
Phone line, single, residence, no field visit	inst.	40.00	12/97	17s
Postage and stationery, expenditures on	yr	104	1999	30r
Postal rate, express mail, up to half-pound		12.45	7/01	108r
Postal rate, letter, first class, first ounce		0.34	7/01	108r
Postal rate, letter, two ounces		0.57	7/01	108r
Postal rate, post card		0.21	7/01	108r
Postal rate, priority mail, two pounds		3.95	7/01	108r
Postal rate, priority mail, up to one pound		3.50	7/01	108r
Telephone bill, business, basic rate	mos	40.71	12/97	18c
Telephone bill, family of three	mos	23.64	3/01	4c
Telephone bill, residential, basic rate	mos	16.30	12/97	18c
Telephone services, expenditures on	yr	860	1999	30r
Education				
Board, 4-year private college/university	yr	2256	1996	38s
Board, 4-year public college/university	yr	1739	1996	38s
Education expenditures	yr	431	1999	30r
Room, 4-year private college/university	yr	1799	1996	38s
Room, 4-year public college/university	yr	1757	1996	38s
Total cost, 4-year private college/university	yr	11635	1996	38s
Total cost, 4-year public college/university	yr	5737	1996	38s
Tuition, 2-year public college/university, in state	yr	1317	1996	38s
Tuition, 4-year private college/university, in state	yr	7580	1996	38s
Tuition, 4-year public college/university	yr	2240	1996	38s
Energy and Fuels				
Electricity	500 KWhs	47.29	7/01	11r
Electricity	KWh	0.09	7/01	11r
Energy, combined forms, 2400 sq ft	mos	135.72	3/01	4c
Energy, exc. electricity, 2400 sq ft	mos	67.92	3/01	4c
Fuel oil #2	gal	1.43	7/01	11r
Fuel oil and other fuels, expenditures on	yr	45	1999	30r
Gas, cooking, winter, 10 therms	mos	14.36	2/96	98c
Gas, cooking, winter, 30 therms	mos	27.10	2/96	98c
Gas, cooking, winter, 50 therms	mos	39.84	2/96	98c
Gas, heating, winter, average use	mos	100.50	2/96	98c
Gas, natural, commercial rate	1000 cf	9.50	11/00	88s
Gas, regular unleaded, cash, self-service	gal	1.33	3/01	4c
Gasoline, all types	gal	1.60	7/01	11r
Gasoline, unleaded midgrade	gal	1.65	7/01	11r
Gasoline, unleaded premium	gal	1.74	7/01	11r
Natural gas, expenditures on	yr	164	1999	30r
Utility (piped) gas, therm		1.01	7/01	11r
Utility (piped) gas, 40 therms		44.29	7/01	11r
Utility (piped) gas, 100 therms		97.44	7/01	11r
Entertainment				
Bowling, Saturday evening rate	line	3.52	3/01	4c
Entertainment purchases	yr	1574	1999	30r
Fees and admissions paid	yr	371	1999	30r
Monopoly game, Parker Brothers', No. 9	game	11.43	3/01	4c
Movie, first-run, Saturday, evening	adm.	7.25	3/01	4c
Reading purchases	yr	121	1999	30r

Birmingham, AL - continued

Item	Per	Value	Date	Ref.
Entertainment - continued				
Television, radios, sound equipment, expenditures on	yr	561	1999	30r
Tennis balls, yellow, Wilson or Penn, 3	can	2.75	3/01	4c
Groceries				
Groceries, ACCRA Index		93.60	3/01	4c
American processed cheese	lb	3.50	7/01	11r
Antibiotic ointment, Polysporin	0.5 oz	4.65	3/01	4c
Baby food, strained vegetables or fruit, lowest price	4-4.5 oz	0.34	3/01	4c
Bakery products, expenditures on	yr	261	1999	30r
Bananas	lb	0.50	3/01	4c
Bananas	lb	0.47	7/01	11r
Beans, dried, any type, all sizes	lb	0.63	7/01	11r
Beef for stew, boneless	lb	2.86	7/01	11r
Beef or hamburger, ground	lb	1.63	3/01	4c
Beef, expenditures on	yr	210	1999	30r
Bologna, all beef or mixed	lb	2.29	7/01	11r
Bread, French	lb	1.66	7/01	11r
Bread, white	loaf	0.88	3/01	4c
Bread, white, pan	lb	0.87	7/01	11r
Bread, whole wheat, pan	lb	1.38	7/01	11r
Broccoli	lb	1.04	7/01	11r
Butter, salted, grade AA, stick	lb	2.26	7/01	11r
Butter, yoghurt, cheese, etc, expenditures on	yr	170	1999	30r
Cabbage	lb	0.42	7/01	11r
Cereals and cereal products, expenditures on	yr	140	1999	30r
Cheddar cheese, natural	lb	3.75	7/01	11r
Cheese, Kraft grated Parmesan	8 oz	3.15	3/01	4c
Chicken breast, bone-in	lb	1.85	7/01	11r
Chicken legs, bone-in	lb	1.34	7/01	11r
Chicken, fresh, whole	lb	1.05	7/01	11r
Chicken, whole fryer	lb	0.93	3/01	4c
Chops, boneless,	lb	4.13	7/01	11r
Chuck roast, graded and ungraded, excl U.S. prime and choice	lb	2.35	7/01	11r
Chuck roast, U.S. choice, boneless	lb	2.67	7/01	11r
Cigarettes, Winston, Kings	carton	28.26	3/01	4c
Coffee, 100%, ground roast, all sizes	lb	2.88	7/01	11r
Coffee, instant, plain, regular, all sizes	16 oz	9.25	7/01	11r
Coffee, vacuum-packed	13 oz	2.29	3/01	4c
Cola, non diet,	2 liter	1.11	7/01	11r
Corn Flakes, Kellogg's or Post Toasties	18 oz	2.93	3/01	4c
Corn, frozen, whole kernel, lowest price	16 oz	1.24	3/01	4c
Crackers, soda, salted	lb	1.70	7/01	11r
Dairy product purchases	yr	282	1999	30r
Eggs, expenditures on	yr	32	1999	30r
Eggs, Grade A or AA	dozen	1.04	3/01	4c
Fats and oils, expenditures on	yr	79	1999	30r
Fish and seafood, expenditures on	yr	99	1999	30r
Flour, white, all purpose	lb	0.32	7/01	11r
Food (excl fruit and vegetables), eaten at home, purchases	yr	815	1999	30r
Food cooked on trips, expenditures on	yr	36	1999	30r
Food purchases	yr	4533	1999	30r
Food purchases, eaten away from home	yr	1873	1999	30r
Food purchases, food eaten at home	yr	2660	1999	30r
Fresh fruits, expenditures on	yr	128	1999	30r
Fresh milk and cream, expenditures on	yr	112	1999	30r
Fresh vegetables, expenditures on	yr	131	1999	30r
Fruit and vegetable purchases	yr	438	1999	30r
Grapefruit	lb	0.59	7/01	11r
Grapes, Thompson, seedless	lb	2.12	7/01	11r
Ground beef, 100% beef	lb	1.76	7/01	11r
Ground beef, lean and extra lean	lb	2.60	7/01	11r
Ground chuck, 100% beef	lb	2.08	7/01	11r
Ham, boneless, excl canned	lb	2.71	7/01	11r
Ham, rump or shank half, bone-in, smoked	lb	2.19	7/01	11r
Ice cream, prepackaged, bulk, regular	1/2 gal	3.93	7/01	11r
Lemons	lb	1.32	7/01	11r
Lettuce, iceberg	head	0.97	3/01	4c
Lettuce, iceberg	lb	0.76	7/01	11r

Values are in dollars or fractions of dollars. In the column headed *Ref*, references are shown to sources. Each reference is followed by a letter. These refer to the geographical level for which data were reported: s=State, r=Region, and c=City or metro. The abbreviation *ex* is used to mean *except* or *excluding; exp* stands for *expenditures*. For other abbreviations and further explanations, please see the Introduction.

Birmingham, AL - continued

Item	Per	Value	Date	Ref.
Groceries				
Margarine, Blue Bonnet or Parkay, stick	lb	0.62	3/01	4c
Milk, fresh, low fat,	gal	2.75	7/01	11r
Milk, fresh, whole, fortified	gal	2.97	7/01	11r
Milk, whole	1/2 gal	1.78	3/01	4c
Nonalcoholic beverages, expenditures on	yr	228	1999	30r
Orange juice, frozen concentrate	16 oz	1.95	7/01	11r
Orange juice, Minute Maid frozen	12 oz	1.70	3/01	4c
Oranges, Navel	lb	0.73	7/01	11r
Oranges, Valencia	lb	0.55	7/01	11r
Peaches, halves or slices, Hunt's, Del Monte, or Libby's	29 oz	1.54	3/01	4c
Peanut butter, creamy, all sizes	lb	1.83	7/01	11r
Pears, Anjou	lb	0.98	7/01	11r
Peas, green, Del Monte or Green Giant	15 oz	0.68	3/01	4c
Pork chops, center cut, bone-in	lb	3.33	7/01	11r
Pork sausage, fresh, loose	lb	2.59	7/01	11r
Pork shoulder picnic, bone-in, smoked	lb	1.12	7/01	11r
Pork, expenditures on	yr	162	1999	30r
Potato chips	16 oz	3.59	7/01	11r
Potatoes, frozen, french fried	lb	1.00	7/01	11r
Potatoes, white or red	10 lb	2.62	3/01	4c
Potatoes, white, all types	lb	0.44	7/01	11r
Poultry, expenditures on	yr	137	1999	30r
Processed fruits, expenditures on	yr	97	1999	30r
Processed vegetables, expenditures on	yr	82	1999	30r
Rice, white, long grain, uncooked	lb	0.51	7/01	11r
Round roast, graded and ungraded, excl U.S. prime and choice	lb	2.96	7/01	11r
Round steak, graded and ungraded, excl U.S. prime and choice	lb	3.11	7/01	11r
Sausage, Jimmy Dean/Owens pork	lb	2.27	3/01	4c
Shortening, vegetable, Crisco	3 lb	3.15	3/01	4c
Sirloin steak, graded and ungraded, excl U.S. prime and choice	lb	4.23	7/01	11r
Soft drink, Coca Cola, ex deposit	2 liter	1.17	3/01	4c
Spaghetti and macaroni	lb	0.78	7/01	11r
Steak, round, U.S. choice, boneless	lb	3.56	7/01	11r
Steak, sirloin, U.S. choice, boneless	lb	5.65	7/01	11r
Steak, T-bone	lb	6.62	3/01	4c
Strawberries, dry pint	12 oz	1.50	7/01	11r
Sugar and other sweets, expenditures on	yr	99	1999	30r
Sugar, cane or beet	4 lbs	1.40	3/01	4c
Sugar, white, 33-80 ounce package	lb	0.39	7/01	11r
Sugar, white, all sizes	lb	0.42	7/01	11r
Tobacco products and smoking supplies purchases	yr	288	1999	30r
Tomatoes, field grown	lb	1.43	7/01	11r
Tomatoes, Hunt's or Del Monte	14.5 oz	0.78	3/01	4c
Tuna, chunk, light	6 oz	0.47	3/01	4c
Tuna, light, chunk	lb	1.77	7/01	11r
Turkey, frozen, whole	lb	1.05	7/01	11r
Goods and Services				
Miscellaneous goods and services, ACCRA Index		103.00	3/01	4c
Hunting license	yr	16.00	4/01	34s
Health Care				
Health care, ACCRA Index		90.70	3/01	4c
Cardiac catheterization, ave hospital/ physician charges		15260	1998	77s
Childbirth, Cesarean delivery		11587	1997	13r
Childbirth, vaginal delivery		6725	1997	13r
Dentist's fee, adult teeth cleaning and periodic oral exam	visit	58.40	3/01	4c
Doctor's fee, routine exam, established patient	visit	51.90	3/01	4c
Drugs, expenditures on	yr	399	1999	30r
Health care purchases	yr	1971	1999	30r
Health insurance expenditures	yr	933	1999	30r
Home health care aide cost, licensed agency	hour	14	2000	82c
Hospital care, private room	day	562.00	3/01	4c

Birmingham, AL - continued

Item	Per	Value	Date	Ref.
Health Care - continued				
Hysterectomy, laproscopically-assisted, ave hospital/physician charges		16780	1998	76s
Hysterectomy, vaginal, ave hospital and physician charges		10990	1998	76s
Medicaid dispensing fee		5.40	1999	87s
Medical services expenditures	yr	547	1999	30r
Medical supplies, expenditures on	yr	91	1999	30r
Nursing home costs, private room	day	105	2000	82c
Nursing home stay, private room	day	105	2000	83c
Household Goods				
Dishwashing powder, Cascade	50 oz	2.97	3/01	4c
Floor coverings, expenditures on	yr	44	1999	30r
Furniture, expenditures on	yr	335	1999	30r
Household furnishings and equipment purchases	yr	1328	1999	30r
Household textiles, expenditures on	yr	89	1999	30r
Laundry and cleaning supplies, expenditures on	yr	113	1999	30r
Tissues, facial, Kleenex brand	175	1.32	3/01	4c
Housing				
Housing, ACCRA Index		86.70	3/01	4c
Home price, existing, ave		160100	10/00	90r
Home value, median		115000	2001	53s
House, 2400 sq ft, 8000 sq ft lot, new, urban, utilities	total	180310	3/01	4c
House payment, principal and interest, 25% down payment	mos	886	3/01	4c
Household operation expenditures	yr	553	1999	30r
Housekeeping supplies purchases	yr	473	1999	30r
Housing, expenditures on	yr	10303	1999	30r
Maintenance, repairs, insurance expenditures	yr	699	1999	30r
Monthly rental value of owned home	mos	505	1999	30r
Owned dwellings, expenditures own	yr	3465	1999	30r
Rent expenditures	yr	1641	1999	30r
Rent, apartment, 2 br, 1 1/2-2 baths, unfurn, 950 sq ft, water	mos	624	3/01	4c
Rental unit, 1 bedroom, with utilities	mos	454	4/01	41c
Rental unit, 2 bedroom, with utilities	mos	528	4/01	41c
Rental unit, 3 bedroom, with utilities	mos	717	4/01	41c
Rental unit, 4 bedroom, with utilities	mos	794	4/01	41c
Shelter, expenditures on	yr	5467	1999	30r
Insurance and Pensions				
Life and other personal insurance purchases	yr	414	1999	30r
Pensions and Social Security, expenditures on	yr	2635	1999	30r
Personal insurance and pensions, expenditures on	yr	3048	1999	30r
Legal Fees				
Divorce, filing fee		146.00-193.00	4/01	35s
Driver's license fee	renew	18.50	1999	48s
Driver's license fee	orig	18.50	1999	48s
Personal Goods				
Personal care products and services purchases	yr	393	1999	30r
Shampoo, Alberto VO5	15 oz	1.08	3/01	4c
Toothpaste, Crest or Colgate	6-7 oz	2.54	3/01	4c
Personal Services				
Dry cleaning, man's 2-pc suit		7.64	3/01	4c
Man's haircut, barbershop, no styling		11.60	3/01	4c
Personal services, household, expenditures on	yr	258	1999	30r
Woman's shampoo, trim, blow-dry, no style-change		25.39	3/01	4c
Pets				
Pets, toys, and playground equipment, expenditures on	yr	306	1999	30r

Values are in dollars or fractions of dollars. In the column headed *Ref*, references are shown to sources. Each reference is followed by a letter. These refer to the geographical level for which data were reported: s=State, r=Region, and c=City or metro. The abbreviation *ex* is used to mean *except* or *excluding*; *exp* stands for *expenditures*. For other abbreviations and further explanations, please see the Introduction.

Birmingham, AL - continued

Item	Per	Value	Date	Ref.
Restaurant Food				
Chicken, fried, thigh and drumstick, KFC/ Church's		2.09	3/01	4c
Hamburger with cheese, McDonald's	1/4 lb	2.23	3/01	4c
Pizza, Pizza Hut or Pizza Inn	11-12 in	9.49	3/01	4c
Taxes				
Federal income taxes paid	yr	2047	1999	30r
Personal taxes, expenditures on	yr	2554	1999	30r
Property taxes paid	yr	726	1999	30r
State and local income taxes paid	yr	363	1999	30r
Transportation				
Transportation, ACCRA Index		96.50	3/01	4c
Bus fare, one-way	trip	1.00	2000	1c
Bus fare, to central business district	1-way	1.00	3/01	4c
Cars and trucks, new, expenditures on	yr	1648	1999	30r
Cars and trucks, used, expenditures on	yr	1651	1999	30r
Diesel at the pump	gal	1.19	10/99	73s
Gasoline and motor oil purchases	yr	1052	1999	30r
Gasoline before-tax price (cents)	gal	104.10	10/00	43s
Maintenance and repair expenditures	yr	621	1999	30r
Public transportation, expenditures on	yr	298	1999	30r
Tire balance, computer or spin balance, front	wheel	7.95	3/01	4c
Transportation purchases	yr	6738	1999	30r
Vehicle expenses, miscellaneous, purchases	yr	2033	1999	30r
Vehicle insurance payments	yr	696	1999	30r
Vehicle purchases (net outlay)	yr	3354	1999	30r
Vehicle rental, lease expenditures	yr	352	1999	30r
Utilities				
Utilities, ACCRA Index		110.90	3/01	4c
Electrical bill, average	mos	83.42	9/00	9s
Electricity, expenditures on	yr	1115	1999	30r
Electricity, summer, 250 KWh	mos	24.63	2/96	97c
Electricity, summer, 500 KWh	mos	41.39	2/96	97c
Electricity, summer, 750 KWh	mos	58.15	2/96	97c
Electricity, summer, 1000 KWh	mos	71.81	2/96	97c
Electricity and other, mixed, 2400 sq ft, new home	mos	67.80	3/01	4c
Electricity cost, average	KWh	5.60	9/00	9s
Water and other public services, expenditures on	yr	298	1999	30r
Weddings				
Wedding (national average cost)		19936	2000	33r
Attendants' gifts		321	1998	33r
Bridal attendants' apparel (5 persons)		824	2000	33r
Bride's headpiece/veil		173	1998	33r
Bride's wedding dress		859	1998	33r
Clergy, religious facility fee		242	1998	33r
Engagement ring		3177	1998	33r
Flowers		789	1998	33r
Groom's formalwear rental		99	2000	33r
Limousine		410	1998	33r
Marriage license cost		25.00	4/01	35s
Men's formalwear (ushers, best man)		469	2000	33r
Mother of bride apparel		241	2000	33r
Music		866	1998	33r
Photography and videography		1368	1998	33r
Rehearsal dinner		728	1998	33r
Wedding invitations and announcements		341	1998	33r
Wedding reception		7968	2000	33r
Wedding rings (bride and groom)		1060	1998	33r

Bismarck, ND

Item	Per	Value	Date	Ref.
Average annual expenditures	yr	35369	1999	30r
Alcoholic Beverages				
Alcoholic beverage purchases	yr	304	1999	30r
Malt beverages, all types, all sizes, any origin	16 oz	0.93	7/01	11r
Wine, red and white table, all sizes, any origin	liter	7.04	7/01	11r

Bismarck, ND - continued

Item	Per	Value	Date	Ref.
Appliances				
Major appliances, expenditures on	yr	165	1999	30r
Small appliances, housewares, expenditures on	yr	90	1999	30r
Banking and Money				
Mortgage interest and charges paid	yr	2277	1999	30r
Mortgage principal paid on owned property	yr	1230	1999	30r
Vehicle finance charges paid	yr	328	1999	30r
Charity				
Cash contributions, expenditures	yr	1126	1999	30r
Child Care				
Child raising cost, total, age 0-2	yr	7890	1999	60r
Child raising cost, total, age 3-5	yr	8130	1999	60r
Child raising cost, total, age 6-8	yr	8170	1999	60r
Child raising cost, total, age 9-11	yr	8190	1999	60r
Child raising cost, total, age 12-14	yr	8890	1999	60r
Child raising cost, total, age 15-17	yr	9050	1999	60r
Child's child care and education, age 0-2	yr	1240	1999	60r
Child's child care and education, age 3-5	yr	1370	1999	60r
Child's child care and education, age 6-8	yr	880	1999	60r
Child's child care and education, age 9-11	yr	570	1999	60r
Child's child care and education, age 12-14	yr	420	1999	60r
Child's child care and education, age 15-17	yr	720	1999	60r
Child's clothing, age 0-2	yr	410	1999	60r
Child's clothing, age 3-5	yr	400	1999	60r
Child's clothing, age 6-8	yr	450	1999	60r
Child's clothing, age 9-11	yr	500	1999	60r
Child's clothing, age 12-14	yr	840	1999	60r
Child's clothing, age 15-17	yr	740	1999	60r
Child's food, age 0-2	yr	960	1999	60r
Child's food, age 3-5	yr	1120	1999	60r
Child's food, age 6-8	yr	1430	1999	60r
Child's food, age 9-11	yr	1710	1999	60r
Child's food, age 12-14	yr	1710	1999	60r
Child's food, age 15-17	yr	1920	1999	60r
Child's health care, age 0-2	yr	520	1999	60r
Child's health care, age 3-5	yr	500	1999	60r
Child's health care, age 6-8	yr	570	1999	60r
Child's health care, age 9-11	yr	610	1999	60r
Child's health care, age 12-14	yr	630	1999	60r
Child's health care, age 15-17	yr	650	1999	60r
Child's housing, age 0-2	yr	2860	1999	60r
Child's housing, age 3-5	yr	2840	1999	60r
Child's housing, age 6-8	yr	2800	1999	60r
Child's housing, age 9-11	yr	2650	1999	60r
Child's housing, age 12-14	yr	2840	1999	60r
Child's housing, age 15-17	yr	2440	1999	60r
Child's personal care, reading, age 0-2	yr	880	1999	60r
Child's personal care, reading, age 3-5	yr	900	1999	60r
Child's personal care, reading, age 6-8	yr	930	1999	60r
Child's personal care, reading, age 9-11	yr	970	1999	60r
Child's personal care, reading, age 12-14	yr	1150	1999	60r
Child's personal care, reading, age 15-17	yr	920	1999	60r
Clothing				
Apparel and services purchases	yr	1607	1999	30r
Boys, 2 to 15, expenditures on	yr	91	1999	30r
Children under 2, expenditures on	yr	59	1999	30r
Footwear, expenditures on	yr	285	1999	30r
Girls, 2 to 15, expenditures on	yr	116	1999	30r
Men and boys, expenditures on	yr	433	1999	30r
Men, 16 and over, expenditures on	yr	341	1999	30r
Women, 16 and over, expenditures on	yr	490	1999	30r
Communications				
Phone line, single, business, field visit	inst.	52.67	12/97	17s
Phone line, single, business, no field visit	inst.	52.67	12/97	17s
Phone line, single, residence, field visit	inst.	31.79	12/97	17s
Phone line, single, residence, no field visit	inst.	31.79	12/97	17s
Postage and stationery, expenditures on	yr	140	1999	30r
Postal rate, express mail, up to half-pound		12.45	7/01	108r
Postal rate, letter, first class, first ounce		0.34	7/01	108r

Values are in dollars or fractions of dollars. In the column headed *Ref*, references are shown to sources. Each reference is followed by a letter. These refer to the geographical level for which data were reported: s=State, r=Region, and c=City or metro. The abbreviation *ex* is used to mean *except* or *excluding*; *exp* stands for *expenditures*. For other abbreviations and further explanations, please see the Introduction.

Bismarck, ND - continued

Item	Per	Value	Date	Ref.
Communications				
Postal rate, letter, two ounces		0.57	7/01	108r
Postal rate, post card		0.21	7/01	108r
Postal rate, priority mail, two pounds		3.95	7/01	108r
Postal rate, priority mail, up to one pound		3.50	7/01	108r
Telephone bill, business, basic rate	mos	29.35	12/97	18c
Telephone bill, residential, basic rate	mos	11.95	12/97	18c
Telephone services, expenditures on	yr	830	1999	30r
Education				
Board, 4-year private college/university	yr	1649	1996	38s
Board, 4-year public college/university	yr	2378	1996	38s
Education expenditures	yr	583	1999	30r
Room, 4-year private college/university	yr	1260	1996	38s
Room, 4-year public college/university	yr	1016	1996	38s
Total cost, 4-year private college/university	yr	9907	1996	38s
Total cost, 4-year public college/university	yr	5642	1996	38s
Tuition, 2-year public college/university, in state	yr	1698	1996	38s
Tuition, 4-year private college/university, in state	yr	6998	1996	38s
Tuition, 4-year public college/university	yr	2248	1996	38s
Energy and Fuels				
Electricity	500 KWhs	46.59	7/01	11r
Fuel oil #2	gal	1.27	7/01	11r
Fuel oil and other fuels, expenditures on	yr	68	1999	30r
Gas, cooking, winter, 10 therms	mos	10.38	2/96	98c
Gas, cooking, winter, 30 therms	mos	18.15	2/96	98c
Gas, cooking, winter, 50 therms	mos	25.91	2/96	98c
Gas, heating, winter, average use	mos	87.67	2/96	98c
Gas, natural, commercial rate	1000 cf	6.91	11/00	88s
Gasoline, unleaded midgrade	gal	1.79	7/01	11r
Gasoline, unleaded premium	gal	1.86	7/01	11r
Gasoline, unleaded regular	gal	1.58	7/01	11r
Natural gas, expenditures on	yr	389	1999	30r
Utility (piped) gas, therm		0.81	7/01	11r
Utility (piped) gas, 40 therms		38.01	7/01	11r
Utility (piped) gas, 100 therms		81.75	7/01	11r
Entertainment				
Entertainment purchases	yr	1984	1999	30r
Fees and admissions paid	yr	444	1999	30r
Television, radios, sound equipment, expenditures on	yr	580	1999	30r
Funerals				
Cosmetology, hair, other preparation		178.32	1/99	78r
Embalming		408.19	1/99	78r
Funeral at funeral home		362.13	1/99	78r
Professional service charges		1375.51	1/99	78r
Transfer of remains to funeral home		155.92	1/99	78r
Visitation/viewing		294.38	1/99	78r
Groceries				
Bacon, sliced	lb	3.15	7/01	11r
Bakery products, expenditures on	yr	281	1999	30r
Bananas	lb	0.48	7/01	11r
Beans, dried, any type, all sizes	lb	0.61	7/01	11r
Beef for stew, boneless	lb	3.08	7/01	11r
Beef, expenditures on	yr	217	1999	30r
Bologna, all beef or mixed	lb	2.52	7/01	11r
Bread, white, pan	lb	1.06	7/01	11r
Broccoli	lb	0.91	7/01	11r
Butter, salted, grade AA, stick	lb	3.04	7/01	11r
Butter, yoghurt, cheese, etc, expenditures on	yr	183	1999	30r
Cereals and bakery product purchases	yr	430	1999	30r
Cereals and cereal products, expenditures on	yr	149	1999	30r
Chicken, fresh, whole	lb	1.07	7/01	11r
Chops, boneless,	lb	3.64	7/01	11r
Chuck roast, U.S. choice, boneless	lb	2.47	7/01	11r
Coffee, 100%, ground roast, all sizes	lb	2.69	7/01	11r
Cookies, chocolate chip	lb	2.87	7/01	11r

Bismarck, ND - continued

Item	Per	Value	Date	Ref.
Groceries - continued				
Dairy product purchases	yr	304	1999	30r
Eggs, expenditures on	yr	26	1999	30r
Eggs, grade A, large	dozen	0.88	7/01	11r
Fats and oils, expenditures on	yr	75	1999	30r
Fish and seafood, expenditures on	yr	72	1999	30r
Food (excl fruit and vegetables), eaten at home, purchases	yr	887	1999	30r
Food cooked on trips, expenditures on	yr	44	1999	30r
Food purchases	yr	4802	1999	30r
Food purchases, eaten away from home	yr	2069	1999	30r
Food purchases, food eaten at home	yr	2733	1999	30r
Fresh fruits, expenditures on	yr	138	1999	30r
Fresh milk and cream, expenditures on	yr	120	1999	30r
Fresh vegetables, expenditures on	yr	126	1999	30r
Grapefruit	lb	0.66	7/01	11r
Grapes, Thompson, seedless	lb	1.64	7/01	11r
Ground beef, 100% beef	lb	1.64	7/01	11r
Ground beef, lean and extra lean	lb	2.16	7/01	11r
Ground chuck, 100% beef	lb	2.13	7/01	11r
Ham, boneless, excl canned	lb	2.62	7/01	11r
Ice cream, prepackaged, bulk, regular	1/2 gal	3.35	7/01	11r
Lemons	lb	1.19	7/01	11r
Lettuce, iceberg	lb	0.73	7/01	11r
Margarine, soft, tubs	lb	0.89	7/01	11r
Meats, poultry, fish, and egg purchases	yr	671	1999	30r
Milk, fresh, whole, fortified	gal	2.71	7/01	11r
Nonalcoholic beverages, expenditures on	yr	239	1999	30r
Oranges, Navel	lb	0.80	7/01	11r
Oranges, Valencia	lb	0.66	7/01	11r
Pears, Anjou	lb	0.93	7/01	11r
Pork chops, center cut, bone-in	lb	3.63	7/01	11r
Pork, expenditures on	yr	150	1999	30r
Potato chips	16 oz	3.52	7/01	11r
Potatoes, frozen, french fried	lb	1.08	7/01	11r
Potatoes, white, all types	lb	0.33	7/01	11r
Poultry, expenditures on	yr	108	1999	30r
Processed fruits, expenditures on	yr	98	1999	30r
Processed vegetables, expenditures on	yr	80	1999	30r
Round roast, U.S. choice, boneless	lb	3.07	7/01	11r
Round steak, graded and ungraded, excl U.S. prime and choice	lb	3.41	7/01	11r
Shortening, vegetable oil blends	lb	1.13	7/01	11r
Spaghetti and macaroni	lb	0.80	7/01	11r
Steak, round, U.S. choice, boneless	lb	3.23	7/01	11r
Steak, T-bone, U.S. choice, bone-in	lb	6.68	7/01	11r
Strawberries, dry pint	12 oz	1.32	7/01	11r
Sugar and other sweets, expenditures on	yr	114	1999	30r
Sugar, white, 33-80 ounce package	lb	0.42	7/01	11r
Sugar, white, all sizes	lb	0.43	7/01	11r
Tobacco products and smoking supplies purchases	yr	331	1999	30r
Tomatoes, field grown	lb	1.46	7/01	11r
Tuna, light, chunk	lb	1.80	7/01	11r
Turkey, frozen, whole	lb	1.15	7/01	11r
Goods and Services				
B&B Japanese maple (acer japonicum)	gal	29.99-169.99	4/00	93r
Boxwood (buxus)	2 gal	18.99-39.99	4/00	93r
Daylily (hemerocallis)	gal	4.99-25.00	4/00	93r
Flat of annuals		11.98-24.99	4/00	93r
Fountain grass (pennisetum)	gal	5.98-12.98	4/00	93r
Hanging basket (10 in)		12.99-27.99	4/00	93r
Hardy geranium (geranium)	gal	7.99-9.99	4/00	93r
Hosta (hosta)	gal	6.00-25.00	4/00	93r

Values are in dollars or fractions of dollars. In the column headed *Ref*, references are shown to sources. Each reference is followed by a letter. These refer to the geographical level for which data were reported: s=State, r=Region, and c=City or metro. The abbreviation *ex* is used to mean *except* or *excluding*; *exp* stands for *expenditures*. For other abbreviations and further explanations, please see the Introduction.

Bismarck, ND - continued

Item	Per	Value	Date	Ref.
Goods and Services				
Lilac (syrubga vulgaris)	2 gal	14.99-24.99	4/00	93r
Miscellaneous purchases	yr	865	1999	30r
Rhododendron (rhododendron)	2 gal	23.98-42.99	4/00	93r
Sage (salvia)	gal	6.00-9.99	4/00	93r
Wintercreeper euonymus (euonymus fortunei)	2 gal	16.00-169.99	4/00	93r
Hunting license	yr	8.00	4/01	34s
Health Care				
Cardiac catheterization, ave hospital/ physician charges		10040	1998	77s
Childbirth, Cesarean delivery		10722	1997	13r
Childbirth, vaginal delivery		6223	1997	13r
Drugs, expenditures on	yr	394	1999	30r
Health care purchases	yr	2048	1999	30r
Health insurance expenditures	yr	978	1999	30r
Hysterectomy, laproscopically-assisted, ave hospital/physician charges		11070	1998	76s
Hysterectomy, vaginal, ave hospital and physician charges		7310	1998	76s
Medicaid dispensing fee		4.60	1999	87s
Medical services expenditures	yr	554	1999	30r
Medical supplies, expenditures on	yr	122	1999	30r
Plastic surgery, breast augmentation		3184	2000	7r
Plastic surgery, breast lift		3585	2000	7r
Plastic surgery, facelift		4999	2000	7r
Plastic surgery, hair transplantation		3105	2000	7r
Plastic surgery, lip augmentation		1290	2000	7r
Plastic surgery, lower body lift		8135	2000	7r
Plastic surgery, thigh lift		3839	2000	7r
Household Goods				
Floor coverings, expenditures on	yr	52	1999	30r
Furniture, expenditures on	yr	344	1999	30r
Household furnishings and equipment purchases	yr	1475	1999	30r
Household textiles, expenditures on	yr	109	1999	30r
Laundry and cleaning supplies, expenditures on	yr	134	1999	30r
Housing				
Home price, existing, ave		144400	10/00	90r
Home value, median		99000	2001	53s
Household operation expenditures	yr	542	1999	30r
Housekeeping supplies purchases	yr	508	1999	30r
Lodging expenditures	yr	430	1999	30r
Maintenance, repairs, insurance expenditures	yr	853	1999	30r
Monthly rental value of owned home	mos	547	1999	30r
Owned dwellings, expenditures own	yr	4282	1999	30r
Rent expenditures	yr	1558	1999	30r
Rental unit, 1 bedroom, with utilities	mos	392	4/01	41c
Rental unit, 2 bedroom, with utilities	mos	522	4/01	41c
Rental unit, 3 bedroom, with utilities	mos	727	4/01	41c
Rental unit, 4 bedroom, with utilities	mos	860	4/01	41c
Shelter, expenditures on	yr	6270	1999	30r
Insurance and Pensions				
Auto insurance premium	yr	545.50	1999	57s
Life and other personal insurance purchases	yr	387	1999	30r
Pensions and Social Security, expenditures on	yr	2968	1999	30r
Legal Fees				
Combination hunting and fishing license	yr	27.00	4/01	34s
Driver's license fee	orig	10.00	1999	48s
Driver's license fee	renew	10.00	1999	48s
Fishing license	yr	10.00	4/01	34s
Personal Goods				
Personal care products and services purchases	yr	385	1999	30r

Bismarck, ND - continued

Item	Per	Value	Date	Ref.
Personal Services				
Personal services, household, expenditures on	yr	300	1999	30r
Pets				
Pets, toys, and playground equipment, expenditures on	yr	375	1999	30r
Taxes				
Federal income taxes paid	yr	2326	1999	30r
Personal taxes, expenditures on	yr	3223	1999	30r
Property taxes paid	yr	1152	1999	30r
State and local income taxes paid	yr	753	1999	30r
Transportation				
Auto operation, annual cost		6236	2000	27c
Cars and trucks, new, expenditures on	yr	1280	1999	30r
Cars and trucks, used, expenditures on	yr	1763	1999	30r
Diesel at the pump	gal	1.27	10/99	73s
Gasoline and motor oil purchases	yr	1036	1999	30r
Gasoline before-tax price (cents)	gal	120.80	10/00	43s
Maintenance and repair expenditures	yr	594	1999	30r
Public transportation, expenditures on	yr	341	1999	30r
Transportation purchases	yr	6617	1999	30r
Vehicle expenses, miscellaneous, purchases	yr	2159	1999	30r
Vehicle insurance payments	yr	701	1999	30r
Vehicle purchases (net outlay)	yr	3081	1999	30r
Vehicle rental, lease expenditures	yr	536	1999	30r
Travel				
Hotel room	night	48.95	2/01	94s
Utilities				
Electrical bill, average	mos	62.50	9/00	9s
Electricity, expenditures on	yr	841	1999	30r
Electricity, summer, 250 KWh	mos	20.11	2/96	96c
Electricity, summer, 500 KWh	mos	36.53	2/96	96c
Electricity, summer, 750 KWh	mos	52.14	2/96	96c
Electricity, summer, 1000 KWh	mos	66.26	2/96	96c
Electricity cost, average	KWh	5.90	9/00	9s
Utilities, fuels, and public services purchased	yr	2401	1999	30r
Water and other public services, expenditures on	yr	273	1999	30r
Weddings				
Wedding (national average cost)		19936	2000	33r
Wedding (regional average total cost)		16195	1997	110r
Attendants' gifts		321	1998	33r
Bridal attendants' apparel (5 persons)		824	2000	33r
Bride's headpiece/veil		173	1998	33r
Bride's wedding dress		859	1998	33r
Clergy, religious facility fee		242	1998	33r
Engagement ring		3177	1998	33r
Flowers		789	1998	33r
Groom's formalwear rental		99	2000	33r
Limousine		410	1998	33r
Marriage license cost		30.00	4/01	35s
Men's formalwear (ushers, best man)		469	2000	33r
Mother of bride apparel		241	2000	33r
Music		866	1998	33r
Photography and videography		1368	1998	33r
Rehearsal dinner		728	1998	33r
Wedding invitations and announcements		341	1998	33r
Wedding reception		7968	2000	33r
Wedding rings (bride and groom)		1060	1998	33r

Bloomington, IN

Item	Per	Value	Date	Ref.
Average annual expenditures	yr	35369	1999	30r
Composite, ACCRA index		100.00	12/00	5c
Alcoholic Beverages				
Alcoholic beverage purchases	yr	304	1999	30r
Beer, Heineken, 12-oz, ex deposit	6	6.32	12/00	5c
J & B Scotch	750-ml	19.66	12/00	5c
Malt beverages, all types, all sizes, any origin	16 oz	0.93	7/01	11r

Values are in dollars or fractions of dollars. In the column headed *Ref*, references are shown to sources. Each reference is followed by a letter. These refer to the geographical level for which data were reported: s=State, r=Region, and c=City or metro. The abbreviation *ex* is used to mean *except* or *excluding*; *exp* stands for *expenditures*. For other abbreviations and further explanations, please see the Introduction.

Bloomington, IN - continued

Item	Per	Value	Date	Ref.
Alcoholic Beverages				
Wine, Livingston or Gallo, Chablis blanc	1.5 liter	3.83	12/00	5c
Wine, red and white table, all sizes, any origin	liter	7.04	7/01	11r
Appliances				
Appliance repair, service call, washing machine	min lab chg	50.65	12/00	5c
Major appliances, expenditures on	yr	165	1999	30r
Small appliances, housewares, expenditures on	yr	90	1999	30r
Banking and Money				
Mortgage interest and charges paid	yr	2277	1999	30r
Mortgage principal paid on owned property	yr	1230	1999	30r
Mortgage rate, incl. points and orig. fee, 30-yr. conv. fixed or ARM	mos	8.08	12/00	5c
Vehicle finance charges paid	yr	328	1999	30r
Charity				
Cash contributions, expenditures	yr	1126	1999	30r
Child Care				
Child raising cost, total, age 0-2	yr	7890	1999	60r
Child raising cost, total, age 3-5	yr	8130	1999	60r
Child raising cost, total, age 6-8	yr	8170	1999	60r
Child raising cost, total, age 9-11	yr	8190	1999	60r
Child raising cost, total, age 12-14	yr	8890	1999	60r
Child raising cost, total, age 15-17	yr	9050	1999	60r
Child's child care and education, age 0-2	yr	1240	1999	60r
Child's child care and education, age 3-5	yr	1370	1999	60r
Child's child care and education, age 6-8	yr	880	1999	60r
Child's child care and education, age 9-11	yr	570	1999	60r
Child's child care and education, age 12-14	yr	420	1999	60r
Child's child care and education, age 15-17	yr	720	1999	60r
Child's clothing, age 0-2	yr	410	1999	60r
Child's clothing, age 3-5	yr	400	1999	60r
Child's clothing, age 6-8	yr	450	1999	60r
Child's clothing, age 9-11	yr	500	1999	60r
Child's clothing, age 12-14	yr	840	1999	60r
Child's clothing, age 15-17	yr	740	1999	60r
Child's food, age 0-2	yr	960	1999	60r
Child's food, age 3-5	yr	1120	1999	60r
Child's food, age 6-8	yr	1430	1999	60r
Child's food, age 9-11	yr	1710	1999	60r
Child's food, age 12-14	yr	1710	1999	60r
Child's food, age 15-17	yr	1920	1999	60r
Child's health care, age 0-2	yr	520	1999	60r
Child's health care, age 3-5	yr	500	1999	60r
Child's health care, age 6-8	yr	570	1999	60r
Child's health care, age 9-11	yr	610	1999	60r
Child's health care, age 12-14	yr	630	1999	60r
Child's health care, age 15-17	yr	650	1999	60r
Child's housing, age 0-2	yr	2860	1999	60r
Child's housing, age 3-5	yr	2840	1999	60r
Child's housing, age 6-8	yr	2800	1999	60r
Child's housing, age 9-11	yr	2650	1999	60r
Child's housing, age 12-14	yr	2840	1999	60r
Child's housing, age 15-17	yr	2440	1999	60r
Child's personal care, reading, age 0-2	yr	880	1999	60r
Child's personal care, reading, age 3-5	yr	900	1999	60r
Child's personal care, reading, age 6-8	yr	930	1999	60r
Child's personal care, reading, age 9-11	yr	970	1999	60r
Child's personal care, reading, age 12-14	yr	1150	1999	60r
Child's personal care, reading, age 15-17	yr	920	1999	60r
Clothing				
Apparel and services purchases	yr	1607	1999	30r
Boys' brief, cotton	3	7.66	12/00	5c
Boys, 2 to 15, expenditures on	yr	91	1999	30r
Children under 2, expenditures on	yr	59	1999	30r
Footwear, expenditures on	yr	285	1999	30r
Girls, 2 to 15, expenditures on	yr	116	1999	30r
Men and boys, expenditures on	yr	433	1999	30r
Men, 16 and over, expenditures on	yr	341	1999	30r

Bloomington, IN - continued

Item	Per	Value	Date	Ref.
Clothing - continued				
Shirt, man's dress shirt		19.99	12/00	5c
Slacks, man's "No Wrinkles" khaki		47.66	12/00	5c
Women, 16 and over, expenditures on	yr	490	1999	30r
Communications				
Newspaper subscription, daily and Sunday delivery	mos	12.95	12/00	5c
Phone line, single, business, field visit	inst.	59.00	12/97	17s
Phone line, single, business, no field visit	inst.	59.00	12/97	17s
Phone line, single, residence, field visit	inst.	47.00	12/97	17s
Phone line, single, residence, no field visit	inst.	47.00	12/97	17s
Postage and stationery, expenditures on	yr	140	1999	30r
Postal rate, express mail, up to half-pound		12.45	7/01	108r
Postal rate, letter, first class, first ounce		0.34	7/01	108r
Postal rate, letter, two ounces		0.57	7/01	108r
Postal rate, post card		0.21	7/01	108r
Postal rate, priority mail, two pounds		3.95	7/01	108r
Postal rate, priority mail, up to one pound		3.50	7/01	108r
Telephone bill, family of three	mos	23.56	12/00	5c
Telephone services, expenditures on	yr	830	1999	30r
Education				
Board, 4-year private college/university	yr	2250	1996	38s
Board, 4-year public college/university	yr	2425	1996	38s
Education expenditures	yr	583	1999	30r
Room, 4-year private college/university	yr	1987	1996	38s
Room, 4-year public college/university	yr	1931	1996	38s
Total cost, 4-year private college/university	yr	16829	1996	38s
Total cost, 4-year public college/university	yr	7392	1996	38s
Tuition, 2-year public college/university, in state	yr	1937	1996	38s
Tuition, 4-year private college/university, in state	yr	12592	1996	38s
Tuition, 4-year public college/university	yr	3037	1996	38s
Energy and Fuels				
Electricity	500 KWhs	46.59	7/01	11r
Energy, combined forms, 2400 sq ft	mos	103.39	12/00	5c
Energy, exc. electricity, 2400 sq ft	mos	47.61	12/00	5c
Fuel oil #2	gal	1.27	7/01	11r
Fuel oil and other fuels, expenditures on	yr	68	1999	30r
Gas, natural, commercial rate	1000 cf	6.24	11/00	88s
Gas, regular unleaded, cash, self-service	gal	1.44	12/00	5c
Gasoline, unleaded midgrade	gal	1.79	7/01	11r
Gasoline, unleaded premium	gal	1.86	7/01	11r
Gasoline, unleaded regular	gal	1.58	7/01	11r
Natural gas, expenditures on	yr	389	1999	30r
Utility (piped) gas, therm		0.81	7/01	11r
Utility (piped) gas, 40 therms		38.01	7/01	11r
Utility (piped) gas, 100 therms		81.75	7/01	11r
Entertainment				
Bowling, Saturday evening rate	line	2.70	12/00	5c
Entertainment purchases	yr	1984	1999	30r
Fees and admissions paid	yr	444	1999	30r
Monopoly game, Parker Brothers', No. 9	game	14.99	12/00	5c
Movie, first-run, Saturday, evening	adm.	7.00	12/00	5c
Television, radios, sound equipment, expenditures on	yr	580	1999	30r
Tennis balls, yellow, Wilson or Penn, 3	can	3.09	12/00	5c
Funerals				
Cosmetology, hair, other preparation		178.32	1/99	78r
Embalming		408.19	1/99	78r
Funeral at funeral home		362.13	1/99	78r
Professional service charges		1375.51	1/99	78r
Transfer of remains to funeral home		155.92	1/99	78r
Visitation/viewing		294.38	1/99	78r
Groceries				
Groceries, ACCRA Index		106.00	12/00	5c
Antibiotic ointment, Polysporin	0.5 oz	4.44	12/00	5c
Baby food, strained vegetables or fruit, lowest price	4-4.5 oz	0.39	12/00	5c

Values are in dollars or fractions of dollars. In the column headed *Ref*, references are shown to sources. Each reference is followed by a letter. These refer to the geographical level for which data were reported: s=State, r=Region, and c=City or metro. The abbreviation *ex* is used to mean *except* or *excluding*; *exp* stands for *expenditures*. For other abbreviations and further explanations, please see the Introduction.

Bloomington, IN - continued

Item	Per	Value	Date	Ref.
Groceries				
Bacon, sliced	lb	3.15	7/01	11r
Bakery products, expenditures on	yr	281	1999	30r
Bananas	lb	0.48	7/01	11r
Bananas	lb	0.48	12/00	5c
Beans, dried, any type, all sizes	lb	0.61	7/01	11r
Beef for stew, boneless	lb	3.08	7/01	11r
Beef or hamburger, ground	lb	1.89	12/00	5c
Beef, expenditures on	yr	217	1999	30r
Bologna, all beef or mixed	lb	2.52	7/01	11r
Bread, white	loaf	1.13	12/00	5c
Bread, white, pan	lb	1.06	7/01	11r
Broccoli	lb	0.91	7/01	11r
Butter, salted, grade AA, stick	lb	3.04	7/01	11r
Butter, yoghurt, cheese, etc, expenditures on	yr	183	1999	30r
Cereals and bakery product purchases	yr	430	1999	30r
Cereals and cereal products, expenditures on	yr	149	1999	30r
Cheese, Kraft grated Parmesan	8 oz	3.92	12/00	5c
Chicken, fresh, whole	lb	1.07	7/01	11r
Chicken, whole fryer	lb	0.89	12/00	5c
Chops, boneless,	lb	3.64	7/01	11r
Chuck roast, U.S. choice, boneless	lb	2.47	7/01	11r
Cigarettes, Winston, Kings	carton	26.62	12/00	5c
Coffee, 100%, ground roast, all sizes	lb	2.69	7/01	11r
Coffee, vacuum-packed	13 oz	2.90	12/00	5c
Cookies, chocolate chip	lb	2.87	7/01	11r
Corn Flakes, Kellogg's or Post Toasties	18 oz	2.22	12/00	5c
Corn, frozen, whole kernel, lowest price	16 oz	1.42	12/00	5c
Dairy product purchases	yr	304	1999	30r
Eggs, expenditures on	yr	26	1999	30r
Eggs, Grade A or AA	dozen	0.91	12/00	5c
Eggs, grade A, large	dozen	0.88	7/01	11r
Fats and oils, expenditures on	yr	75	1999	30r
Fish and seafood, expenditures on	yr	72	1999	30r
Food (excl fruit and vegetables), eaten at home, purchases	yr	887	1999	30r
Food cooked on trips, expenditures on	yr	44	1999	30r
Food purchases	yr	4802	1999	30r
Food purchases, eaten away from home	yr	2069	1999	30r
Food purchases, food eaten at home	yr	2733	1999	30r
Fresh fruits, expenditures on	yr	138	1999	30r
Fresh milk and cream, expenditures on	yr	120	1999	30r
Fresh vegetables, expenditures on	yr	126	1999	30r
Grapefruit	lb	0.66	7/01	11r
Grapes, Thompson, seedless	lb	1.64	7/01	11r
Ground beef, 100% beef	lb	1.64	7/01	11r
Ground beef, lean and extra lean	lb	2.16	7/01	11r
Ground chuck, 100% beef	lb	2.13	7/01	11r
Ham, boneless, excl canned	lb	2.62	7/01	11r
Ice cream, prepackaged, bulk, regular	1/2 gal	3.35	7/01	11r
Lemons	lb	1.19	7/01	11r
Lettuce, iceberg	lb	0.73	7/01	11r
Lettuce, iceberg	head	1.39	12/00	5c
Margarine, Blue Bonnet or Parkay, stick	lb	0.70	12/00	5c
Margarine, soft, tubs	lb	0.89	7/01	11r
Meats, poultry, fish, and egg purchases	yr	671	1999	30r
Milk, fresh, whole, fortified	gal	2.71	7/01	11r
Milk, whole	1/2 gal	1.89	12/00	5c
Nonalcoholic beverages, expenditures on	yr	239	1999	30r
Orange juice, Minute Maid frozen	12 oz	1.81	12/00	5c
Oranges, Navel	lb	0.80	7/01	11r
Oranges, Valencia	lb	0.66	7/01	11r
Peaches, halves or slices, Hunt's, Del Monte, or Libby's	29 oz	1.69	12/00	5c
Pears, Anjou	lb	0.93	7/01	11r
Peas, green, Del Monte or Green Giant	15 oz	0.76	12/00	5c
Pork chops, center cut, bone-in	lb	3.63	7/01	11r
Pork, expenditures on	yr	150	1999	30r
Potato chips	16 oz	3.52	7/01	11r
Potatoes, frozen, french fried	lb	1.08	7/01	11r
Potatoes, white or red	10 lb	3.49	12/00	5c
Potatoes, white, all types	lb	0.33	7/01	11r

Bloomington, IN - continued

Item	Per	Value	Date	Ref.
Groceries - continued				
Poultry, expenditures on	yr	108	1999	30r
Processed fruits, expenditures on	yr	98	1999	30r
Processed vegetables, expenditures on	yr	80	1999	30r
Round roast, U.S. choice, boneless	lb	3.07	7/01	11r
Round steak, graded and ungraded, excl U.S. prime and choice	lb	3.41	7/01	11r
Sausage, Jimmy Dean/Owens pork	lb	2.52	12/00	5c
Shortening, vegetable oil blends	lb	1.13	7/01	11r
Shortening, vegetable, Crisco	3 lb	3.02	12/00	5c
Soft drink, Coca Cola, ex deposit	2 liter	1.32	12/00	5c
Spaghetti and macaroni	lb	0.80	7/01	11r
Steak, round, U.S. choice, boneless	lb	3.23	7/01	11r
Steak, T-bone	lb	7.56	12/00	5c
Steak, T-bone, U.S. choice, bone-in	lb	6.68	7/01	11r
Strawberries, dry pint	12 oz	1.32	7/01	11r
Sugar and other sweets, expenditures on	yr	114	1999	30r
Sugar, cane or beet	4 lbs	1.66	12/00	5c
Sugar, white, 33-80 ounce package	lb	0.42	7/01	11r
Sugar, white, all sizes	lb	0.43	7/01	11r
Tobacco products and smoking supplies purchases	yr	331	1999	30r
Tomatoes, field grown	lb	1.46	7/01	11r
Tomatoes, Hunt's or Del Monte	14.5 oz	0.99	12/00	5c
Tuna, chunk, light	6 oz	0.77	12/00	5c
Tuna, light, chunk	lb	1.80	7/01	11r
Turkey, frozen, whole	lb	1.15	7/01	11r
Goods and Services				
Miscellaneous goods and services, ACCRA Index		106.80	12/00	5c
B&B Japanese maple (acer japonicum)	gal	29.99-169.99	4/00	93r
Boxwood (buxus)	2 gal	18.99-39.99	4/00	93r
Daylilly (hemerocallis)	gal	4.99-25.00	4/00	93r
Flat of annuals		11.98-24.99	4/00	93r
Fountain grass (pennisetum)	gal	5.98-12.98	4/00	93r
Hanging basket (10 in)		12.99-27.99	4/00	93r
Hardy geranium (geranium)	gal	7.99-9.99	4/00	93r
Hosta (hosta)	gal	6.00-25.00	4/00	93r
Lilac (syrubga vulgaris)	2 gal	14.99-24.99	4/00	93r
Miscellaneous purchases	yr	865	1999	30r
Rhododendron (rhododendron)	2 gal	23.98-42.99	4/00	93r
Sage (salvia)	gal	6.00-9.99	4/00	93r
Wintercreeper euonymus (euonymus fortunei)	2 gal	16.00-169.99	4/00	93r
Hunting license	yr	8.75	4/01	34s
Health Care				
Health care, ACCRA Index		102.60	12/00	5c
Cardiac catheterization, ave hospital/ physician charges		13380	1998	77s
Childbirth, Cesarean delivery		10722	1997	13r
Childbirth, vaginal delivery		6223	1997	13r
Dentist's fee, adult teeth cleaning and periodic oral exam	visit	70.00	12/00	5c
Doctor's fee, routine exam, established patient	visit	56.33	12/00	5c
Drugs, expenditures on	yr	394	1999	30r
Health care purchases	yr	2048	1999	30r
Health insurance expenditures	yr	978	1999	30r
Hospital care, private room	day	609.00	12/00	5c
Hysterectomy, laproscopically-assisted, ave hospital/physician charges		11310	1998	76s

Values are in dollars or fractions of dollars. In the column headed *Ref*, references are shown to sources. Each reference is followed by a letter. These refer to the geographical level for which data were reported: s=State, r=Region, and c=City or metro. The abbreviation *ex* is used to mean *except* or *excluding*; *exp* stands for expenditures. For other abbreviations and further explanations, please see the Introduction.

Bloomington, IN - continued

Item	Per	Value	Date	Ref.
Health Care				
Hysterectomy, vaginal, ave hospital and physician charges		9160	1998	76s
Medicaid dispensing fee		4.00	1999	87s
Medical services expenditures	yr	554	1999	30r
Medical supplies, expenditures on	yr	122	1999	30r
Plastic surgery, breast augmentation		3184	2000	7r
Plastic surgery, breast lift		3585	2000	7r
Plastic surgery, facelift		4999	2000	7r
Plastic surgery, hair transplantation		3105	2000	7r
Plastic surgery, lip augmentation		1290	2000	7r
Plastic surgery, lower body lift		8135	2000	7r
Plastic surgery, thigh lift		3839	2000	7r
Household Goods				
Dishwashing powder, Cascade	50 oz	3.26	12/00	5c
Floor coverings, expenditures on	yr	52	1999	30r
Furniture, expenditures on	yr	344	1999	30r
Household furnishings and equipment purchases	yr	1475	1999	30r
Household textiles, expenditures on	yr	109	1999	30r
Laundry and cleaning supplies, expenditures on	yr	134	1999	30r
Tissues, facial, Kleenex brand	175	1.41	12/00	5c
Housing				
Housing, ACCRA Index		91.90	12/00	5c
Home price, existing, ave		144400	10/00	90r
Home value, median		102000	2001	53s
House, 2400 sq ft, 8000 sq ft lot, new, urban, utilities	total	185900	12/00	5c
House payment, principal and interest, 25% down payment	mos	1031	12/00	5c
Household operation expenditures	yr	542	1999	30r
Housekeeping supplies purchases	yr	508	1999	30r
Lodging expenditures	yr	430	1999	30r
Maintenance, repairs, insurance expenditures	yr	853	1999	30r
Monthly rental value of owned home	mos	547	1999	30r
Owned dwellings, expenditures own	yr	4282	1999	30r
Rent expenditures	yr	1558	1999	30r
Rent, apartment, 2 br, 1 1/2-2 baths, unfurn, 950 sq ft, water	mos	642	12/00	5c
Rental unit, 1 bedroom, with utilities	mos	486	4/01	41c
Rental unit, 2 bedroom, with utilities	mos	647	4/01	41c
Rental unit, 3 bedroom, with utilities	mos	900	4/01	41c
Rental unit, 4 bedroom, with utilities	mos	1063	4/01	41c
Shelter, expenditures on	yr	6270	1999	30r
Insurance and Pensions				
Life and other personal insurance purchases	yr	387	1999	30r
Pensions and Social Security, expenditures on	yr	2968	1999	30r
Legal Fees				
Divorce, filing fee		100.00	4/01	35s
Driver's license fee	orig	6.00	1999	48s
Driver's license fee	renew	6.00	1999	48s
Personal Goods				
Personal care products and services purchases	yr	385	1999	30r
Shampoo, Alberto VO5	15 oz	1.29	12/00	5c
Toothpaste, Crest or Colgate	6-7 oz	2.49	12/00	5c
Personal Services				
Dry cleaning, man's 2-pc suit		7.85	12/00	5c
Man's haircut, barbershop, no styling		10.65	12/00	5c
Personal services, household, expenditures on	yr	300	1999	30r
Woman's shampoo, trim, blow-dry, no style-change		20.33	12/00	5c
Pets				
Pets, toys, and playground equipment, expenditures on	yr	375	1999	30r

Bloomington, IN - continued

Item	Per	Value	Date	Ref.
Restaurant Food				
Chicken, fried, thigh and drumstick, KFC/Church's		2.69	12/00	5c
Hamburger with cheese, McDonald's	1/4 lb	1.99	12/00	5c
Pizza, Pizza Hut or Pizza Inn	11-12 in	8.99	12/00	5c
Taxes				
Federal income taxes paid	yr	2326	1999	30r
Personal taxes, expenditures on	yr	3223	1999	30r
Property taxes paid	yr	1152	1999	30r
State and local income taxes paid	yr	753	1999	30r
Transportation				
Transportation, ACCRA Index		93.90	12/00	5c
Bus fare, one-way	trip	0.75	2000	1c
Bus fare, to central business district	1-way	0.75	12/00	5c
Cars and trucks, new, expenditures on	yr	1280	1999	30r
Cars and trucks, used, expenditures on	yr	1763	1999	30r
Diesel at the pump	gal	1.17	10/99	73s
Gasoline and motor oil purchases	yr	1036	1999	30r
Gasoline before-tax price (cents)	gal	110.00	10/00	43s
Maintenance and repair expenditures	yr	594	1999	30r
Public transportation, expenditures on	yr	341	1999	30r
Tire balance, computer or spin balance, front	wheel	7.63	12/00	5c
Transportation purchases	yr	6617	1999	30r
Vehicle expenses, miscellaneous, purchases	yr	2159	1999	30r
Vehicle insurance payments	yr	701	1999	30r
Vehicle purchases (net outlay)	yr	3081	1999	30r
Vehicle rental, lease expenditures	yr	536	1999	30r
Utilities				
Utilities, ACCRA Index		94.50	12/00	5c
Electrical bill, average	mos	66.66	9/00	9s
Electricity, expenditures on	yr	841	1999	30r
Electricity and other, mixed, 2400 sq ft, new home	mos	55.78	12/00	5c
Electricity cost, average	KWh	5.00	9/00	9s
Utilities, fuels, and public services purchased	yr	2401	1999	30r
Water and other public services, expenditures on	yr	273	1999	30r
Weddings				
Wedding (national average cost)		19936	2000	33r
Wedding (regional average total cost)		16195	1997	110r
Attendants' gifts		321	1998	33r
Bridal attendants' apparel (5 persons)		824	2000	33r
Bride's headpiece/veil		173	1998	33r
Bride's wedding dress		859	1998	33r
Clergy, religious facility fee		242	1998	33r
Engagement ring		3177	1998	33r
Flowers		789	1998	33r
Groom's formalwear rental		99	2000	33r
Limousine		410	1998	33r
Marriage license cost		18.00	4/01	35s
Men's formalwear (ushers, best man)		469	2000	33r
Mother of bride apparel		241	2000	33r
Music		866	1998	33r
Photography and videography		1368	1998	33r
Rehearsal dinner		728	1998	33r
Wedding invitations and announcements		341	1998	33r
Wedding reception		7968	2000	33r
Wedding rings (bride and groom)		1060	1998	33r

Bloomington-Normal, IL

Item	Per	Value	Date	Ref.
Average annual expenditures	yr	35369	1999	30r
Composite, ACCRA index		105.30	12/00	5c
Alcoholic Beverages				
Alcoholic beverage purchases	yr	304	1999	30r
Beer, Heineken, 12-oz, ex deposit	6	7.29	12/00	5c
J & B Scotch	750-ml	20.19	12/00	5c
Malt beverages, all types, all sizes, any origin	16 oz	0.93	7/01	11r
Wine, Livingston or Gallo, Chablis blanc	1.5 liter	4.79	12/00	5c

Values are in dollars or fractions of dollars. In the column headed *Ref*, references are shown to sources. Each reference is followed by a letter. These refer to the geographical level for which data were reported: s=State, r=Region, and c=City or metro. The abbreviation *ex* is used to mean *except* or *excluding*; *exp* stands for expenditures. For other abbreviations and further explanations, please see the Introduction.

Bloomington-Normal, IL - continued

Item	Per	Value	Date	Ref.
Alcoholic Beverages				
Wine, red and white table, all sizes, any origin	liter	7.04	7/01	11r
Appliances				
Appliance repair, service call, washing machine	min lab chg	49.38	12/00	5c
Major appliances, expenditures on	yr	165	1999	30r
Small appliances, housewares, expenditures on	yr	90	1999	30r
Banking and Money				
Mortgage interest and charges paid	yr	2277	1999	30r
Mortgage principal paid on owned property	yr	1230	1999	30r
Mortgage rate, incl. points and orig. fee, 30-yr. conv. fixed or ARM	mos	7.60	12/00	5c
Vehicle finance charges paid	yr	328	1999	30r
Charity				
Cash contributions, expenditures	yr	1126	1999	30r
Child Care				
Child raising cost, total, age 0-2	yr	7890	1999	60r
Child raising cost, total, age 3-5	yr	8130	1999	60r
Child raising cost, total, age 6-8	yr	8170	1999	60r
Child raising cost, total, age 9-11	yr	8190	1999	60r
Child raising cost, total, age 12-14	yr	8890	1999	60r
Child raising cost, total, age 15-17	yr	9050	1999	60r
Child's child care and education, age 0-2	yr	1240	1999	60r
Child's child care and education, age 3-5	yr	1370	1999	60r
Child's child care and education, age 6-8	yr	880	1999	60r
Child's child care and education, age 9-11	yr	570	1999	60r
Child's child care and education, age 12-14	yr	420	1999	60r
Child's child care and education, age 15-17	yr	720	1999	60r
Child's clothing, age 0-2	yr	410	1999	60r
Child's clothing, age 3-5	yr	400	1999	60r
Child's clothing, age 6-8	yr	450	1999	60r
Child's clothing, age 9-11	yr	500	1999	60r
Child's clothing, age 12-14	yr	840	1999	60r
Child's clothing, age 15-17	yr	740	1999	60r
Child's food, age 0-2	yr	960	1999	60r
Child's food, age 3-5	yr	1120	1999	60r
Child's food, age 6-8	yr	1430	1999	60r
Child's food, age 9-11	yr	1710	1999	60r
Child's food, age 12-14	yr	1710	1999	60r
Child's food, age 15-17	yr	1920	1999	60r
Child's health care, age 0-2	yr	520	1999	60r
Child's health care, age 3-5	yr	500	1999	60r
Child's health care, age 6-8	yr	570	1999	60r
Child's health care, age 9-11	yr	610	1999	60r
Child's health care, age 12-14	yr	630	1999	60r
Child's health care, age 15-17	yr	650	1999	60r
Child's housing, age 0-2	yr	2860	1999	60r
Child's housing, age 3-5	yr	2840	1999	60r
Child's housing, age 6-8	yr	2800	1999	60r
Child's housing, age 9-11	yr	2650	1999	60r
Child's housing, age 12-14	yr	2840	1999	60r
Child's housing, age 15-17	yr	2440	1999	60r
Child's personal care, reading, age 0-2	yr	880	1999	60r
Child's personal care, reading, age 3-5	yr	900	1999	60r
Child's personal care, reading, age 6-8	yr	930	1999	60r
Child's personal care, reading, age 9-11	yr	970	1999	60r
Child's personal care, reading, age 12-14	yr	1150	1999	60r
Child's personal care, reading, age 15-17	yr	920	1999	60r
Clothing				
Apparel and services purchases	yr	1607	1999	30r
Boys' brief, cotton	3	7.00	12/00	5c
Boys, 2 to 15, expenditures on	yr	91	1999	30r
Children under 2, expenditures on	yr	59	1999	30r
Footwear, expenditures on	yr	285	1999	30r
Girls, 2 to 15, expenditures on	yr	116	1999	30r
Men and boys, expenditures on	yr	433	1999	30r
Men, 16 and over, expenditures on	yr	341	1999	30r
Shirt, man's dress shirt		27.90	12/00	5c

Bloomington-Normal, IL - continued

Item	Per	Value	Date	Ref.
Clothing - continued				
Slacks, man's "No Wrinkles" khaki		43.60	12/00	5c
Women, 16 and over, expenditures on	yr	490	1999	30r
Communications				
Cable modem installation, Adelphi		54.90	6/99	103s
Cable modem installation, AT&T-BIS		150.00	6/99	103s
Cable modem installation, Media One		100.00	6/99	103s
Cable modem rate, cable subscriber, Adelphi	mos	34.95	6/99	103s
Cable modem rate, cable subscriber, AT&T-BIS	mos	39.95	6/99	103s
Cable modem rate, cable subscriber, Media One	mos	34.95-39.95	6/99	103s
Cable modem rate, non-cable subscriber, Adelphi	mos	44.95	6/99	103s
Cable modem rate, non-cable subscriber, Media One	mos	49.95	6/99	103s
Newspaper subscription, daily and Sunday delivery	mos	15.48	12/00	5c
Phone line, single, business, field visit	inst.	52.35	12/97	17s
Phone line, single, business, no field visit	inst.	52.35	12/97	17s
Phone line, single, residence, field visit	inst.	55.00	12/97	17s
Phone line, single, residence, no field visit	inst.	55.00	12/97	17s
Postage and stationery, expenditures on	yr	140	1999	30r
Postal rate, express mail, up to half-pound		12.45	7/01	108r
Postal rate, letter, first class, first ounce		0.34	7/01	108r
Postal rate, letter, two ounces		0.57	7/01	108r
Postal rate, post card		0.21	7/01	108r
Postal rate, priority mail, two pounds		3.95	7/01	108r
Postal rate, priority mail, up to one pound		3.50	7/01	108r
Telephone bill, family of three	mos	29.16	12/00	5c
Telephone services, expenditures on	yr	830	1999	30r
Education				
Board, 4-year private college/university	yr	2306	1996	38s
Board, 4-year public college/university	yr	2405	1996	38s
Education expenditures	yr	583	1999	30r
Room, 4-year private college/university	yr	2718	1996	38s
Room, 4-year public college/university	yr	2072	1996	38s
Total cost, 4-year private college/university	yr	16678	1996	38s
Total cost, 4-year public college/university	yr	7829	1996	38s
Tuition, 2-year public college/university, in state	yr	1232	1996	38s
Tuition, 4-year private college/university, in state	yr	11653	1996	38s
Tuition, 4-year public college/university	yr	3352	1996	38s
Energy and Fuels				
Electricity	500 KWhs	46.59	7/01	11r
Energy, combined forms, 2400 sq ft	mos	130.05	12/00	5c
Energy, exc. electricity, 2400 sq ft	mos	65.29	12/00	5c
Fuel oil #2	gal	1.27	7/01	11r
Fuel oil and other fuels, expenditures on	yr	68	1999	30r
Gas, natural, commercial rate	1000 cf	8.47	11/00	88s
Gas, regular unleaded, cash, self-service	gal	1.60	12/00	5c
Gasoline, unleaded midgrade	gal	1.79	7/01	11r
Gasoline, unleaded premium	gal	1.86	7/01	11r
Gasoline, unleaded regular	gal	1.58	7/01	11r
Natural gas, expenditures on	yr	389	1999	30r
Utility (piped) gas, therm		0.81	7/01	11r
Utility (piped) gas, 40 therms		38.01	7/01	11r
Utility (piped) gas, 100 therms		81.75	7/01	11r
Entertainment				
Bowling, Saturday evening rate	line	2.75	12/00	5c
Entertainment purchases	yr	1984	1999	30r
Fees and admissions paid	yr	444	1999	30r
Monopoly game, Parker Brothers', No. 9	game	12.89	12/00	5c
Movie, first-run, Saturday, evening	adm.	7.00	12/00	5c
Television, radios, sound equipment, expenditures on	yr	580	1999	30r
Tennis balls, yellow, Wilson or Penn, 3	can	3.00	12/00	5c

Values are in dollars or fractions of dollars. In the column headed *Ref*, references are shown to sources. Each reference is followed by a letter. These refer to the geographical level for which data were reported: s=State, r=Region, and c=City or metro. The abbreviation *ex* is used to mean *except* or *excluding*; *exp* stands for expenditures. For other abbreviations and further explanations, please see the Introduction.

Bloomington-Normal, IL - continued

Item	Per	Value	Date	Ref.
Funerals				
Cosmetology, hair, other preparation		178.32	1/99	78r
Embalming		408.19	1/99	78r
Funeral at funeral home		362.13	1/99	78r
Professional service charges		1375.51	1/99	78r
Transfer of remains to funeral home		155.92	1/99	78r
Visitation/viewing		294.38	1/99	78r
Groceries				
Groceries, ACCRA Index		100.00	12/00	5c
Antibiotic ointment, Polysporin	0.5 oz	4.73	12/00	5c
Baby food, strained vegetables or fruit, lowest price	4-4.5 oz	0.45	12/00	5c
Bacon, sliced	lb	3.15	7/01	11r
Bakery products, expenditures on	yr	281	1999	30r
Bananas	lb	0.48	7/01	11r
Bananas	lb	0.53	12/00	5c
Beans, dried, any type, all sizes	lb	0.61	7/01	11r
Beef for stew, boneless	lb	3.08	7/01	11r
Beef or hamburger, ground	lb	1.33	12/00	5c
Beef, expenditures on	yr	217	1999	30r
Bologna, all beef or mixed	lb	2.52	7/01	11r
Bread, white	loaf	0.52	12/00	5c
Bread, white, pan	lb	1.06	7/01	11r
Broccoli	lb	0.91	7/01	11r
Butter, salted, grade AA, stick	lb	3.04	7/01	11r
Butter, yoghurt, cheese, etc, expenditures on	yr	183	1999	30r
Cereals and bakery product purchases	yr	430	1999	30r
Cereals and cereal products, expenditures on	yr	149	1999	30r
Cheese, Kraft grated Parmesan	8 oz	4.00	12/00	5c
Chicken, fresh, whole	lb	1.07	7/01	11r
Chicken, whole fryer	lb	1.11	12/00	5c
Chops, boneless,	lb	3.64	7/01	11r
Chuck roast, U.S. choice, boneless	lb	2.47	7/01	11r
Cigarettes, Winston, Kings	carton	32.07	12/00	5c
Coffee, 100%, ground roast, all sizes	lb	2.69	7/01	11r
Coffee, vacuum-packed	13 oz	2.99	12/00	5c
Cookies, chocolate chip	lb	2.87	7/01	11r
Corn Flakes, Kellogg's or Post Toasties	18 oz	2.15	12/00	5c
Corn, frozen, whole kernel, lowest price	16 oz	1.35	12/00	5c
Dairy product purchases	yr	304	1999	30r
Eggs, expenditures on	yr	26	1999	30r
Eggs, Grade A or AA	dozen	0.89	12/00	5c
Eggs, grade A, large	dozen	0.88	7/01	11r
Fats and oils, expenditures on	yr	75	1999	30r
Fish and seafood, expenditures on	yr	72	1999	30r
Food (excl fruit and vegetables), eaten at home, purchases	yr	887	1999	30r
Food cooked on trips, expenditures on	yr	44	1999	30r
Food purchases	yr	4802	1999	30r
Food purchases, eaten away from home	yr	2069	1999	30r
Food purchases, food eaten at home	yr	2733	1999	30r
Fresh fruits, expenditures on	yr	138	1999	30r
Fresh milk and cream, expenditures on	yr	120	1999	30r
Fresh vegetables, expenditures on	yr	126	1999	30r
Grapefruit	lb	0.66	7/01	11r
Grapes, Thompson, seedless	lb	1.64	7/01	11r
Ground beef, 100% beef	lb	1.64	7/01	11r
Ground beef, lean and extra lean	lb	2.16	7/01	11r
Ground chuck, 100% beef	lb	2.13	7/01	11r
Ham, boneless, excl canned	lb	2.62	7/01	11r
Ice cream, prepackaged, bulk, regular	1/2 gal	3.35	7/01	11r
Lemons	lb	1.19	7/01	11r
Lettuce, iceberg	lb	0.73	7/01	11r
Lettuce, iceberg	head	1.13	12/00	5c
Margarine, Blue Bonnet or Parkay, stick	lb	1.00	12/00	5c
Margarine, soft, tubs	lb	0.89	7/01	11r
Meats, poultry, fish, and egg purchases	yr	671	1999	30r
Milk, fresh, whole, fortified	gal	2.71	7/01	11r
Milk, whole	1/2 gal	1.82	12/00	5c
Nonalcoholic beverages, expenditures on	yr	239	1999	30r
Orange juice, Minute Maid frozen	12 oz	1.64	12/00	5c
Oranges, Navel	lb	0.80	7/01	11r

Bloomington-Normal, IL - continued

Item	Per	Value	Date	Ref.
Groceries - continued				
Oranges, Valencia	lb	0.66	7/01	11r
Peaches, halves or slices, Hunt's, Del Monte, or Libby's	29 oz	1.53	12/00	5c
Pears, Anjou	lb	0.93	7/01	11r
Peas, green, Del Monte or Green Giant	15 oz	0.56	12/00	5c
Pork chops, center cut, bone-in	lb	3.63	7/01	11r
Pork, expenditures on	yr	150	1999	30r
Potato chips	16 oz	3.52	7/01	11r
Potatoes, frozen, french fried	lb	1.08	7/01	11r
Potatoes, white or red	10 lb	3.01	12/00	5c
Potatoes, white, all types	lb	0.33	7/01	11r
Poultry, expenditures on	yr	108	1999	30r
Processed fruits, expenditures on	yr	98	1999	30r
Processed vegetables, expenditures on	yr	80	1999	30r
Round roast, U.S. choice, boneless	lb	3.07	7/01	11r
Round steak, graded and ungraded, excl U.S. prime and choice	lb	3.41	7/01	11r
Sausage, Jimmy Dean/Owens pork	lb	3.17	12/00	5c
Shortening, vegetable oil blends	lb	1.13	7/01	11r
Shortening, vegetable, Crisco	3 lb	2.61	12/00	5c
Soft drink, Coca Cola, ex deposit	2 liter	1.15	12/00	5c
Spaghetti and macaroni	lb	0.80	7/01	11r
Steak, round, U.S. choice, boneless	lb	3.23	7/01	11r
Steak, T-bone	lb	6.47	12/00	5c
Steak, T-bone, U.S. choice, bone-in	lb	6.68	7/01	11r
Strawberries, dry pint	12 oz	1.32	7/01	11r
Sugar and other sweets, expenditures on	yr	114	1999	30r
Sugar, cane or beet	4 lbs	1.75	12/00	5c
Sugar, white, 33-80 ounce package	lb	0.42	7/01	11r
Sugar, white, all sizes	lb	0.43	7/01	11r
Tobacco products and smoking supplies purchases	yr	331	1999	30r
Tomatoes, field grown	lb	1.46	7/01	11r
Tomatoes, Hunt's or Del Monte	14.5 oz	0.95	12/00	5c
Tuna, chunk, light	6 oz	0.79	12/00	5c
Tuna, light, chunk	lb	1.80	7/01	11r
Turkey, frozen, whole	lb	1.15	7/01	11r
Goods and Services				
Miscellaneous goods and services, ACCRA Index		109.70	12/00	5c
B&B Japanese maple (acer japonicum)	gal	29.99-169.99	4/00	93r
Boxwood (buxus)	2 gal	18.99-39.99	4/00	93r
Daylilly (hemerocallis)	gal	4.99-25.00	4/00	93r
Flat of annuals		11.98-24.99	4/00	93r
Fountain grass (pennisetum)	gal	5.98-12.98	4/00	93r
Hanging basket (10 in)		12.99-27.99	4/00	93r
Hardy geranium (geranium)	gal	7.99-9.99	4/00	93r
Hosta (hosta)	gal	6.00-25.00	4/00	93r
Lilac (syrubga vulgaris)	2 gal	14.99-24.99	4/00	93r
Miscellaneous purchases	yr	865	1999	30r
Rhododendron (rhododendron)	2 gal	23.98-42.99	4/00	93r
Sage (salvia)	gal	6.00-9.99	4/00	93r
Wintercreeper euonymus (euonymus fortunei)	2 gal	16.00-169.99	4/00	93r
Hunting license	yr	7.50	4/01	34s
Health Care				
Health care, ACCRA Index		103.80	12/00	5c
Cardiac catheterization, ave hospital/ physician charges		17690	1998	77s
Childbirth, Cesarean delivery		10722	1997	13r

Values are in dollars or fractions of dollars. In the column headed *Ref*, references are shown to sources. Each reference is followed by a letter. These refer to the geographical level for which data were reported: s=State, r=Region, and c=City or metro. The abbreviation *ex* is used to mean *except* or *excluding*; *exp* stands for *expenditures*. For other abbreviations and further explanations, please see the Introduction.

Bloomington-Normal, IL - continued

Item	Per	Value	Date	Ref.
Health Care				
Childbirth, vaginal delivery		6223	1997	13r
Dentist's fee, adult teeth cleaning and periodic oral exam	visit	72.80	12/00	5c
Doctor's fee, routine exam, established patient	visit	58.00	12/00	5c
Drugs, expenditures on	yr	394	1999	30r
Health care purchases	yr	2048	1999	30r
Health insurance expenditures	yr	978	1999	30r
Hospital care, private room	day	555.40	12/00	5c
Hysterectomy, laproscopically-assisted, ave hospital/physician charges		15850	1998	76s
Hysterectomy, vaginal, ave hospital and physician charges		11810	1998	76s
Medicaid dispensing fee		3.69-15.45	1999	87s
Medical services expenditures	yr	554	1999	30r
Medical supplies, expenditures on	yr	122	1999	30r
Plastic surgery, breast augmentation		3184	2000	7r
Plastic surgery, breast lift		3585	2000	7r
Plastic surgery, facelift		4999	2000	7r
Plastic surgery, hair transplantation		3105	2000	7r
Plastic surgery, lip augmentation		1290	2000	7r
Plastic surgery, lower body lift		8135	2000	7r
Plastic surgery, thigh lift		3839	2000	7r
Household Goods				
Dishwashing powder, Cascade	50 oz	2.53	12/00	5c
Floor coverings, expenditures on	yr	52	1999	30r
Furniture, expenditures on	yr	344	1999	30r
Household furnishings and equipment purchases	yr	1475	1999	30r
Household textiles, expenditures on	yr	109	1999	30r
Laundry and cleaning supplies, expenditures on	yr	134	1999	30r
Tissues, facial, Kleenex brand	175	1.27	12/00	5c
Housing				
Housing, ACCRA Index		99.90	12/00	5c
Home price, existing, ave		144400	10/00	90r
Home value, median		183000	2001	53s
House, 2400 sq ft, 8000 sq ft lot, new, urban, utilities	total	207787	12/00	5c
House payment, principal and interest, 25% down payment	mos	1101	12/00	5c
Household operation expenditures	yr	542	1999	30r
Housekeeping supplies purchases	yr	508	1999	30r
Lodging expenditures	yr	430	1999	30r
Maintenance, repairs, insurance expenditures	yr	853	1999	30r
Monthly rental value of owned home	mos	547	1999	30r
Owned dwellings, expenditures own	yr	4282	1999	30r
Rent expenditures	yr	1558	1999	30r
Rent, apartment, 2 br, 1 1/2-2 baths, unfurn, 950 sq ft, water	mos	748	12/00	5c
Rental unit, 1 bedroom, with utilities	mos	422	4/01	41c
Rental unit, 2 bedroom, with utilities	mos	565	4/01	41c
Rental unit, 3 bedroom, with utilities	mos	785	4/01	41c
Rental unit, 4 bedroom, with utilities	mos	829	4/01	41c
Shelter, expenditures on	yr	6270	1999	30r
Insurance and Pensions				
Life and other personal insurance purchases	yr	387	1999	30r
Pensions and Social Security, expenditures on	yr	2968	1999	30r
Legal Fees				
Divorce, filing fee		100.00-150.00	4/01	35s
Driver's license fee	orig	10.00	1999	48s
Driver's license fee	renew	20.00	1999	48s
Personal Goods				
Personal care products and services purchases	yr	385	1999	30r

Bloomington-Normal, IL - continued

Item	Per	Value	Date	Ref.
Personal Goods - continued				
Shampoo, Alberto VO5	15 oz	1.45	12/00	5c
Toothpaste, Crest or Colgate	6-7 oz	2.67	12/00	5c
Personal Services				
Dry cleaning, man's 2-pc suit		7.59	12/00	5c
Man's haircut, barbershop, no styling		12.60	12/00	5c
Personal services, household, expenditures on	yr	300	1999	30r
Woman's shampoo, trim, blow-dry, no style-change		23.00	12/00	5c
Pets				
Pets, toys, and playground equipment, expenditures on	yr	375	1999	30r
Restaurant Food				
Chicken, fried, thigh and drumstick, KFC/Church's		2.38	12/00	5c
Hamburger with cheese, McDonald's	1/4 lb	2.33	12/00	5c
Pizza, Pizza Hut or Pizza Inn	11-12 in	8.99	12/00	5c
Taxes				
Federal income taxes paid	yr	2326	1999	30r
Personal taxes, expenditures on	yr	3223	1999	30r
Property taxes paid	yr	1152	1999	30r
State and local income taxes paid	yr	753	1999	30r
Transportation				
Transportation, ACCRA Index		104.10	12/00	5c
Cars and trucks, new, expenditures on	yr	1280	1999	30r
Cars and trucks, used, expenditures on	yr	1763	1999	30r
Diesel at the pump	gal	1.33	10/99	73s
Gasoline and motor oil purchases	yr	1036	1999	30r
Gasoline before-tax price (cents)	gal	112.70	10/00	43s
Maintenance and repair expenditures	yr	594	1999	30r
Public transportation, expenditures on	yr	341	1999	30r
Tire balance, computer or spin balance, front	wheel	7.80	12/00	5c
Transportation purchases	yr	6617	1999	30r
Vehicle expenses, miscellaneous, purchases	yr	2159	1999	30r
Vehicle insurance payments	yr	701	1999	30r
Vehicle purchases (net outlay)	yr	3081	1999	30r
Vehicle rental, lease expenditures	yr	536	1999	30r
Utilities				
Utilities, ACCRA Index		118.60	12/00	5c
Electrical bill, average	mos	63.08	9/00	9s
Electricity, expenditures on	yr	841	1999	30r
Electricity and other, mixed, 2400 sq ft, new home	mos	64.76	12/00	5c
Electricity cost, average	KWh	6.49	9/00	9s
Utilities, fuels, and public services purchased	yr	2401	1999	30r
Water and other public services, expenditures on	yr	273	1999	30r
Weddings				
Wedding (national average cost)		19936	2000	33r
Wedding (regional average total cost)		16195	1997	110r
Attendants' gifts		321	1998	33r
Bridal attendants' apparel (5 persons)		824	2000	33r
Bride's headpiece/veil		173	1998	33r
Bride's wedding dress		859	1998	33r
Clergy, religious facility fee		242	1998	33r
Engagement ring		3177	1998	33r
Flowers		789	1998	33r
Groom's formalwear rental		99	2000	33r
Limousine		410	1998	33r
Marriage license cost		15.00-20.00	4/01	35s
Men's formalwear (ushers, best man)		469	2000	33r
Mother of bride apparel		241	2000	33r
Music		866	1998	33r
Photography and videography		1368	1998	33r
Rehearsal dinner		728	1998	33r
Wedding invitations and announcements		341	1998	33r
Wedding reception		7968	2000	33r

Values are in dollars or fractions of dollars. In the column headed *Ref*, references are shown to sources. Each reference is followed by a letter. These refer to the geographical level for which data were reported: s=State, r=Region, and c=City or metro. The abbreviation *ex* is used to mean *except* or *excluding*; *exp* stands for expenditures. For other abbreviations and further explanations, please see the Introduction.

Bloomington-Normal, IL - continued

Item	Per	Value	Date	Ref.
Weddings				
Wedding rings (bride and groom)		1060	1998	33r

Boise, ID

Item	Per	Value	Date	Ref.
Composite, ACCRA index		100.40	3/01	4c
Alcoholic Beverages				
Beer, Heineken, 12-oz, ex deposit	6	7.61	3/01	4c
J & B Scotch	750-ml	21.95	3/01	4c
Wine, Livingston or Gallo, Chablis blanc	1.5 liter	5.56	3/01	4c
Appliances				
Appliance repair, service call, washing machine	min lab chg	40.56	3/01	4c
Banking and Money				
Mortgage rate, incl. points and orig. fee, 30-yr. conv. fixed or ARM	mos	7.08	3/01	4c
Clothing				
Boys' brief, cotton	3	4.79	3/01	4c
Shirt, man's dress shirt		24.99	3/01	4c
Slacks, man's "No Wrinkles" khaki		34.99	3/01	4c
Communications				
Newspaper subscription, daily and Sunday delivery	mos	14.13	3/01	4c
Phone line, single, business, field visit	inst.	47.50	12/97	17s
Phone line, single, business, no field visit	inst.	47.50	12/97	17s
Phone line, single, residence, field visit	inst.	28.50	12/97	17s
Phone line, single, residence, no field visit	inst.	28.50	12/97	17s
Postal rate, express mail, up to half-pound		12.45	7/01	108r
Postal rate, letter, first class, first ounce		0.34	7/01	108r
Postal rate, letter, two ounces		0.57	7/01	108r
Postal rate, post card		0.21	7/01	108r
Postal rate, priority mail, two pounds		3.95	7/01	108r
Postal rate, priority mail, up to one pound		3.50	7/01	108r
Telephone bill, business, basic rate	mos	31.10	12/97	18c
Telephone bill, family of three	mos	24.20	3/01	4c
Telephone bill, residential, basic rate	mos	12.00	12/97	18c
Education				
Board, 4-year private college/university	yr	2035	1996	38s
Board, 4-year public college/university	yr	2098	1996	38s
Room, 4-year private college/university	yr	1430	1996	38s
Room, 4-year public college/university	yr	1541	1996	38s
Total cost, 4-year private college/university	yr	15307	1996	38s
Total cost, 4-year public college/university	yr	5321	1996	38s
Tuition, 2-year public college/university, in state	yr	991	1996	38s
Tuition, 4-year private college/university, in state	yr	11843	1996	38s
Tuition, 4-year public college/university	yr	1682	1996	38s
Energy and Fuels				
Energy, combined forms, 2400 sq ft	mos	84.18	3/01	4c
Energy, exc. electricity, 2400 sq ft	mos	47.40	3/01	4c
Gas, cooking, winter, 10 therms	mos	8.68	2/96	98c
Gas, cooking, winter, 30 therms	mos	21.04	2/96	98c
Gas, cooking, winter, 50 therms	mos	33.41	2/96	98c
Gas, heating, winter, average use	mos	69.64	2/96	98c
Gas, natural, commercial rate	1000 cf	6.71	11/00	88s
Gas, regular unleaded, cash, self-service	gal	1.55	3/01	4c
Entertainment				
Bowling, Saturday evening rate	line	2.65	3/01	4c
Monopoly game, Parker Brothers', No. 9	game	11.17	3/01	4c
Movie, first-run, Saturday, evening	adm.	6.75	3/01	4c
Tennis balls, yellow, Wilson or Penn, 3	can	2.37	3/01	4c
Funerals				
Total cost of funeral		5401.08	1/99	78r
Acknowledgement cards		33.64	1/99	78r
Casket		2170.43	1/99	78r
Cosmetology, hair, other preparation		136.32	1/99	78r
Embalming		319.13	1/99	78r

Boise, ID - continued

Item	Per	Value	Date	Ref.
Funerals - continued				
Funeral at funeral home		370.21	1/99	78r
Hearse (local)		161.04	1/99	78r
Professional service charges		963.15	1/99	78r
Service car/van		133.99	1/99	78r
Transfer of remains to funeral home		159.82	1/99	78r
Vault		778.07	1/99	78r
Visitation/viewing		175.28	1/99	78r
Groceries				
Groceries, ACCRA Index		96.50	3/01	4c
Antibiotic ointment, Polysporin	0.5 oz	4.62	3/01	4c
Baby food, strained vegetables or fruit, lowest price	4-4.5 oz	0.33	3/01	4c
Bananas	lb	0.46	3/01	4c
Beef or hamburger, ground	lb	1.62	3/01	4c
Bread, white	loaf	0.90	3/01	4c
Cheese, Kraft grated Parmesan	8 oz	3.81	3/01	4c
Chicken, whole fryer	lb	1.09	3/01	4c
Cigarettes, Winston, Kings	carton	25.95	3/01	4c
Coffee, vacuum-packed	13 oz	2.75	3/01	4c
Corn Flakes, Kellogg's or Post Toasties	18 oz	2.66	3/01	4c
Corn, frozen, whole kernel, lowest price	16 oz	0.95	3/01	4c
Eggs, Grade A or AA	dozen	1.13	3/01	4c
Lettuce, iceberg	head	0.94	3/01	4c
Margarine, Blue Bonnet or Parkay, stick	lb	0.65	3/01	4c
Milk, whole	1/2 gal	1.46	3/01	4c
Orange juice, Minute Maid frozen	12 oz	1.24	3/01	4c
Peaches, halves or slices, Hunt's, Del Monte, or Libby's	29 oz	1.50	3/01	4c
Peas, green, Del Monte or Green Giant	15 oz	0.77	3/01	4c
Potatoes, white or red	10 lb	1.95	3/01	4c
Sausage, Jimmy Dean/Owens pork	lb	4.24	3/01	4c
Shortening, vegetable, Crisco	3 lb	2.81	3/01	4c
Soft drink, Coca Cola, ex deposit	2 liter	1.22	3/01	4c
Steak, T-bone	lb	5.98	3/01	4c
Sugar, cane or beet	4 lbs	1.71	3/01	4c
Tomatoes, Hunt's or Del Monte	14.5 oz	0.89	3/01	4c
Tuna, chunk, light	6 oz	0.55	3/01	4c
Goods and Services				
Miscellaneous goods and services, ACCRA Index		99.20	3/01	4c
Hunting license	yr	11.50	4/01	34s
Health Care				
Health care, ACCRA Index		110.70	3/01	4c
Cardiac catheterization, ave hospital/ physician charges		14550	1998	77s
Childbirth, Cesarean delivery		11587	1997	13r
Childbirth, vaginal delivery		6725	1997	13r
Dentist's fee, adult teeth cleaning and periodic oral exam	visit	83.88	3/01	4c
Doctor's fee, routine exam, established patient	visit	63.38	3/01	4c
Hospital care, private room	day	581.25	3/01	4c
Hysterectomy, laproscopically-assisted, ave hospital/physician charges		10640	1998	76s
Hysterectomy, vaginal, ave hospital and physician charges		8560	1998	76s
Medicaid dispensing fee		4.94	1999	87s
Household Goods				
Dishwashing powder, Cascade	50 oz	3.60	3/01	4c
Tissues, facial, Kleenex brand	175	1.38	3/01	4c
Housing				
Housing, ACCRA Index		109.20	3/01	4c
Home, 2200 sq ft, 4-br, 2-bath, 2-car garage, average		193000	2000	47c
Home value, median		112000	2001	53s
House, 2400 sq ft, 8000 sq ft lot, new, urban, utilities	total	224950	3/01	4c
House payment, principal and interest, 25% down payment	mos	1132	3/01	4c

Values are in dollars or fractions of dollars. In the column headed *Ref*, references are shown to sources. Each reference is followed by a letter. These refer to the geographical level for which data were reported: s=State, r=Region, and c=City or metro. The abbreviation *ex* is used to mean *except* or *excluding*; *exp* stands for *expenditures*. For other abbreviations and further explanations, please see the Introduction.

Boise, ID - continued

Item	Per	Value	Date	Ref.
Housing				
Rent, apartment, 2 br, 1 1/2-2 baths, unfurn, 950 sq ft, water	mos	741	3/01	4c
Rental unit, 1 bedroom, with utilities	mos	451	4/01	41c
Rental unit, 2 bedroom, with utilities	mos	548	4/01	41c
Rental unit, 3 bedroom, with utilities	mos	761	4/01	41c
Rental unit, 4 bedroom, with utilities	mos	900	4/01	41c
Insurance and Pensions				
Auto insurance premium	yr	577.07	1999	57s
Legal Fees				
Driver's license fee	orig	20.50	1999	48s
Driver's license fee	renew	20.50	1999	48s
Personal Goods				
Shampoo, Alberto VO5	15 oz	1.01	3/01	4c
Toothpaste, Crest or Colgate	6-7 oz	2.71	3/01	4c
Personal Services				
Dry cleaning, man's 2-pc suit		7.74	3/01	4c
Man's haircut, barbershop, no styling		10.19	3/01	4c
Woman's shampoo, trim, blow-dry, no style-change		22.89	3/01	4c
Restaurant Food				
Chicken, fried, thigh and drumstick, KFC/Church's		2.59	3/01	4c
Hamburger with cheese, McDonald's	1/4 lb	2.19	3/01	4c
Pizza, Pizza Hut or Pizza Inn	11-12 in	9.59	3/01	4c
Transportation				
Transportation, ACCRA Index		101.10	3/01	4c
Bus fare, one-way	trip	0.75	2000	1c
Bus fare, to central business district	1-way	0.75	3/01	4c
Diesel at the pump	gal	1.33	10/99	73s
Gasoline before-tax price (cents)	gal	123.50	10/00	43s
Tire balance, computer or spin balance, front	wheel	7.75	3/01	4c
Utilities				
Utilities, ACCRA Index		74.80	3/01	4c
Electrical bill, average	mos	57.75	9/00	9s
Electricity and other, mixed, 2400 sq ft, new home	mos	36.78	3/01	4c
Electricity cost, average	KWh	4.10	9/00	9s
Weddings				
Wedding (national average cost)		19936	2000	33r
Attendants' gifts		321	1998	33r
Bridal attendants' apparel (5 persons)		824	2000	33r
Bride's headpiece/veil		173	1998	33r
Bride's wedding dress		859	1998	33r
Clergy, religious facility fee		242	1998	33r
Engagement ring		3177	1998	33r
Flowers		789	1998	33r
Groom's formalwear rental		99	2000	33r
Limousine		410	1998	33r
Marriage license cost		28.00	4/01	35s
Men's formalwear (ushers, best man)		469	2000	33r
Mother of bride apparel		241	2000	33r
Music		866	1998	33r
Photography and videography		1368	1998	33r
Rehearsal dinner		728	1998	33r
Wedding invitations and announcements		341	1998	33r
Wedding reception		7968	2000	33r
Wedding rings (bride and groom)		1060	1998	33r

Boston, MA

Item	Per	Value	Date	Ref.
Average annual expenditures	yr	39286	1999	30c
Composite, ACCRA index		132.40	3/01	4c
Alcoholic Beverages				
Alcoholic beverage purchases	yr	519	1999	30c
Beer, Heineken, 12-oz, ex deposit	6	7.05	3/01	4c
J & B Scotch	750-ml	18.79	3/01	4c
Wine, Livingston or Gallo, Chablis blanc	1.5 liter	6.75	3/01	4c

Boston, MA - continued

Item	Per	Value	Date	Ref.
Alcoholic Beverages - continued				
Wine, red and white table, all sizes, any origin	liter	9.64	7/01	11r
Appliances				
Appliance repair, service call, washing machine	min lab chg	54.78	3/01	4c
Major appliances, expenditures on	yr	194	1999	30r
Small appliances, housewares, expenditures on	yr	93	1999	30r
Banking and Money				
Mortgage interest and charges paid	yr	2622	1999	30r
Mortgage principal paid on owned property	yr	1262	1999	30r
Mortgage rate, incl. points and orig. fee, 30-yr. conv. fixed or ARM	mos	7.25	3/01	4c
Vehicle finance charges paid	yr	240	1999	30r
Business Expenses				
Business travel, car rental	day	59	2001	3c
Business travel, food	day	62	2001	3c
Business travel, hotel	day	220	2001	3c
Medical office space cost	sq ft	137.83	2001	31c
Office space, 2-4 storey building	sq ft	120.75	2001	31c
Office space, 5-10 storey building	sq ft	106.66	2001	31c
Office space, 11-20 storey building	sq ft	102.52	2001	31c
Office space, central business district, Class A	sq ft	47.93	3/99	74c
Charity				
Cash contributions, expenditures	yr	1191	1999	30c
Child Care				
Child care fee, one year old	week	238	5/99	26c
Child care fee, six year old	week	72	5/99	26c
Child care fee, three year old	week	156	5/99	26c
Child raising cost, total, age 0-2	yr	8670	1999	60r
Child raising cost, total, age 3-5	yr	8910	1999	60r
Child raising cost, total, age 6-8	yr	9040	1999	60r
Child raising cost, total, age 9-11	yr	9100	1999	60r
Child raising cost, total, age 12-14	yr	9890	1999	60r
Child raising cost, total, age 15-17	yr	10010	1999	60r
Child's child care and education, age 0-2	yr	1070	1999	60r
Child's child care and education, age 3-5	yr	1190	1999	60r
Child's child care and education, age 6-8	yr	740	1999	60r
Child's child care and education, age 9-11	yr	470	1999	60r
Child's child care and education, age 12-14	yr	350	1999	60r
Child's child care and education, age 15-17	yr	590	1999	60r
Child's clothing, age 0-2	yr	480	1999	60r
Child's clothing, age 3-5	yr	470	1999	60r
Child's clothing, age 6-8	yr	520	1999	60r
Child's clothing, age 9-11	yr	570	1999	60r
Child's clothing, age 12-14	yr	970	1999	60r
Child's clothing, age 15-17	yr	870	1999	60r
Child's food, age 0-2	yr	1130	1999	60r
Child's food, age 3-5	yr	1290	1999	60r
Child's food, age 6-8	yr	1640	1999	60r
Child's food, age 9-11	yr	1930	1999	60r
Child's food, age 12-14	yr	1940	1999	60r
Child's food, age 15-17	yr	2150	1999	60r
Child's health care, age 0-2	yr	550	1999	60r
Child's health care, age 3-5	yr	530	1999	60r
Child's health care, age 6-8	yr	610	1999	60r
Child's health care, age 9-11	yr	650	1999	60r
Child's health care, age 12-14	yr	660	1999	60r
Child's health care, age 15-17	yr	690	1999	60r
Child's housing, age 0-2	yr	3555	1999	60r
Child's housing, age 3-5	yr	3530	1999	60r
Child's housing, age 6-8	yr	3490	1999	60r
Child's housing, age 9-11	yr	3340	1999	60r
Child's housing, age 12-14	yr	3530	1999	60r
Child's housing, age 15-17	yr	3140	1999	60r
Child's personal care, reading, age 0-2	yr	920	1999	60r
Child's personal care, reading, age 3-5	yr	950	1999	60r
Child's personal care, reading, age 6-8	yr	980	1999	60r

Values are in dollars or fractions of dollars. In the column headed *Ref*, references are shown to sources. Each reference is followed by a letter. These refer to the geographical level for which data were reported: s=State, r=Region, and c=City or metro. The abbreviation *ex* is used to mean *except* or *excluding*; *exp* stands for expenditures. For other abbreviations and further explanations, please see the Introduction.

Boston, MA - continued

Item	Per	Value	Date	Ref.
Child Care				
Child's personal care, reading, age 9-11	yr	1020	1999	60r
Child's personal care, reading, age 12-14	yr	1190	1999	60r
Child's personal care, reading, age 15-17	yr	970	1999	60r
Daycare	mos	718	1998	37c
Daycare, 3-year old, 5 days, 8 hrs/day	mos	718	1998	85c
Clothing				
Apparel and services purchases	yr	1671	1999	30c
Boys' brief, cotton	3	5.89	3/01	4c
Boys, 2 to 15, expenditures on	yr	92	1999	30r
Children under 2, expenditures on	yr	63	1999	30r
Footwear, expenditures on	yr	300	1999	30r
Girls, 2 to 15, expenditures on	yr	101	1999	30r
Men and boys, expenditures on	yr	446	1999	30r
Men, 16 and over, expenditures on	yr	354	1999	30r
Shirt, man's dress shirt		26.20	3/01	4c
Slacks, man's "No Wrinkles" khaki		38.80	3/01	4c
Women, 16 and over, expenditures on	yr	584	1999	30r
Communications				
Cable modem installation, Adelphi		54.90	6/99	103s
Cable modem installation, Media One		100.00	6/99	103s
Cable modem rate, cable subscriber, Adelphi	mos	34.95	6/99	103s
Cable modem rate, cable subscriber, Media One	mos	34.95-39.95	6/99	103s
Cable modem rate, non-cable subscriber, Adelphi	mos	44.95	6/99	103s
Cable modem rate, non-cable subscriber, Media One	mos	49.95	6/99	103s
Cellular phone service	mos	40.92	2/01	55c
Newspaper subscription, daily and Sunday delivery	mos	22.75	3/01	4c
Phone line, single, business, field visit	inst.	120.52	12/97	17s
Phone line, single, business, no field visit	inst.	93.02	12/97	17s
Phone line, single, residence, field visit	inst.	64.57	12/97	17s
Phone line, single, residence, no field visit	inst.	37.07	12/97	17s
Postage and stationery, expenditures on	yr	138	1999	30r
Postal rate, express mail, up to half-pound		12.45	7/01	108r
Postal rate, letter, first class, first ounce		0.34	7/01	108r
Postal rate, letter, two ounces		0.57	7/01	108r
Postal rate, post card		0.21	7/01	108r
Postal rate, priority mail, two pounds		3.95	7/01	108r
Postal rate, priority mail, up to one pound		3.50	7/01	108r
Telephone bill, business, basic rate	mos	39.77	12/97	18c
Telephone bill, family of three	mos	23.00	3/01	4c
Telephone bill, residential, basic rate	mos	16.85	12/97	18c
Telephone services, expenditures on	yr	830	1999	30r
Education				
Board, 4-year private college/university	yr	3244	1996	38s
Board, 4-year public college/university	yr	2042	1996	38s
Education expenditures	yr	1252	1999	30c
Room, 4-year private college/university	yr	3688	1996	38s
Room, 4-year public college/university	yr	2462	1996	38s
Total cost, 4-year private college/university	yr	23335	1996	38s
Total cost, 4-year public college/university	yr	8757	1996	38s
Tuition, 2-year public college/university, in state	yr	2359	1996	38s
Tuition, 4-year private college/university, in state	yr	16403	1996	38s
Tuition, 4-year public college/university	yr	4253	1996	38s
Energy and Fuels				
Electricity	KWh	0.12	7/01	11c
Electricity	500 KWhs	67.70	7/01	11c
Energy, combined forms, 2400 sq ft	mos	165.27	3/01	4c
Energy, exc. electricity, 2400 sq ft	mos	89.93	3/01	4c
Fuel oil #2	gal	1.31	7/01	11r
Fuel oil and other fuels, expenditures on	yr	207	1999	30r
Gas, cooking, winter, 10 therms	mos	18.73	2/96	98c
Gas, cooking, winter, 30 therms	mos	37.92	2/96	98c
Gas, cooking, winter, 50 therms	mos	52.99	2/96	98c
Gas, heating, winter, average use	mos	211.55	2/96	98c

Boston, MA - continued

Item	Per	Value	Date	Ref.
Energy and Fuels - continued				
Gas, natural, commercial rate	1000 cf	10.82	11/00	88s
Gas, regular unleaded, cash, self-service	gal	1.57	3/01	4c
Gasoline, all types	gal	1.80	7/01	11c
Gasoline, unleaded midgrade	gal	1.84	7/01	11c
Gasoline, unleaded premium	gal	1.91	7/01	11r
Gasoline, unleaded regular	gal	1.74	7/01	11c
Natural gas, expenditures on	yr	368	1999	30r
Utility (piped) gas, therm		1.07	7/01	11c
Utility (piped) gas, 40 therms		50.87	7/01	11r
Utility (piped) gas, 100 therms		112.87	7/01	11c
Entertainment				
Biking: bicycle		300	1998	36c
Biking: helmet		40	1998	36c
Biking: pump		20	1998	36c
Biking: repair kit		2	1998	36c
Biking: spare inner tube		4	1998	36c
Bowling, Saturday evening rate	line	2.83	3/01	4c
Entertainment purchases	yr	1937	1999	30c
Fees and admissions paid	yr	511	1999	30r
Major League baseball ticket		28.83	2000	16c
Monopoly game, Parker Brothers', No. 9	game	13.39	3/01	4c
Movie ticket, evening	person	8.00	1999	104c
Movie, first-run, Saturday, evening	adm.	8.15	3/01	4c
Television, radios, sound equipment, expenditures on	yr	650	1999	30r
Tennis balls, yellow, Wilson or Penn, 3	can	2.64	3/01	4c
Funerals				
Total cost of funeral		5776.91	1/99	78r
Acknowledgement cards		14.47	1/99	78r
Casket		2090.19	1/99	78r
Cosmetology, hair, other preparation		132.92	1/99	78r
Embalming		377.33	1/99	78r
Funeral at funeral home		352.43	1/99	78r
Hearse (local)		185.55	1/99	78r
Professional service charges		1289.95	1/99	78r
Service car/van		87.42	1/99	78r
Transfer of remains to funeral home		175.48	1/99	78r
Vault		729.40	1/99	78r
Visitation/viewing		341.76	1/99	78r
Groceries				
Groceries, ACCRA Index		110.60	3/01	4c
Antibiotic ointment, Polysporin	0.5 oz	5.23	3/01	4c
Apples	pound	1.22		29c
Apples, red delicious	lb	0.95	7/01	11r
Baby food, strained vegetables or fruit, lowest price	4-4.5 oz	0.49	3/01	4c
Bacon, sliced	lb	3.44	7/01	11r
Bakery products, expenditures on	yr	310	1999	30r
Bananas	lb	0.58	3/01	4c
Bananas	lb	0.55	7/01	11r
Beef or hamburger, ground	lb	1.87	3/01	4c
Beef, expenditures on	yr	236	1999	30r
Bread, white	loaf	1.21	3/01	4c
Bread, white, pan	lb	1.09	7/01	11r
Butter, yoghurt, cheese, etc, expenditures on	yr	214	1999	30r
Cereals and bakery product purchases	yr	382	1999	30c
Cereals and cereal products, expenditures on	yr	164	1999	30r
Cheese, Kraft grated Parmesan	8 oz	3.02	3/01	4c
Chicken legs, bone-in	lb	1.23	7/01	11r
Chicken, fresh, whole	lb	1.13	7/01	11r
Chicken, whole fryer	lb	1.23	3/01	4c
Chuck roast, U.S. choice, boneless	lb	2.79	7/01	11r
Cigarettes, Winston, Kings	carton	44.34	3/01	4c
Coffee, 100%, ground roast, all sizes	lb	3.40	7/01	11r
Coffee, vacuum-packed	13 oz	2.59	3/01	4c
Corn Flakes, Kellogg's or Post Toasties	18 oz	2.45	3/01	4c
Corn, frozen, whole kernel, lowest price	16 oz	1.11	3/01	4c
Dairy product purchases	yr	285	1999	30c
Eggs, expenditures on	yr	34	1999	30r
Eggs, Grade A or AA	dozen	1.33	3/01	4c

Values are in dollars or fractions of dollars. In the column headed *Ref*, references are shown to sources. Each reference is followed by a letter. These refer to the geographical level for which data were reported: s=State, r=Region, and c=City or metro. The abbreviation *ex* is used to mean *except* or *excluding*; *exp* stands for expenditures. For other abbreviations and further explanations, please see the Introduction.

Boston, MA - continued

Item	Per	Value	Date	Ref.
Groceries				
Eggs, grade A, large	dozen	0.82	7/01	11r
Fats and oils, expenditures on	yr	80	1999	30r
Fish and seafood, expenditures on	yr	123	1999	30r
Food (excl fruit and vegetables), eaten at home, purchases	yr	653	1999	30c
Food cooked on trips, expenditures on	yr	48	1999	30r
Food purchases	yr	4904	1999	30c
Food purchases, eaten away from home	yr	2417	1999	30c
Food purchases, food eaten at home	yr	2486	1999	30c
Fresh fruits, expenditures on	yr	169	1999	30r
Fresh milk and cream, expenditures on	yr	128	1999	30r
Fresh vegetables, expenditures on	yr	164	1999	30r
Grapefruit	lb	0.67	7/01	11r
Grapes, Thompson, seedless	lb	2.18	7/01	11r
Ground beef, lean and extra lean	lb	2.66	7/01	11r
Ground chuck, 100% beef	lb	2.04	7/01	11r
Lettuce, iceberg	head	1.31	3/01	4c
Lettuce, iceberg	lb	0.76	7/01	11r
Margarine, Blue Bonnet or Parkay, stick	lb	0.77	3/01	4c
Meats, poultry, fish, and egg purchases	yr	659	1999	30c
Milk, whole	1/2 gal	1.78	3/01	4c
Nonalcoholic beverages, expenditures on	yr	225	1999	30r
Orange juice, frozen concentrate	16 oz	1.88	7/01	11r
Orange juice, Minute Maid frozen	12 oz	1.43	3/01	4c
Oranges, Navel	lb	0.79	7/01	11r
Oranges, Valencia	lb	0.56	7/01	11r
Peaches	lb	1.16	7/01	11r
Peaches, halves or slices, Hunt's, Del Monte, or Libby's	29 oz	1.66	3/01	4c
Peanut butter, creamy, all sizes	lb	2.01	7/01	11r
Pears, Anjou	lb	1.16	7/01	11r
Peas, green, Del Monte or Green Giant	15 oz	0.78	3/01	4c
Pork chops, center cut, bone-in	lb	3.57	7/01	11r
Pork, expenditures on	yr	146	1999	30r
Potato chips	16 oz	3.37	7/01	11r
Potatoes, white or red	10 lb	1.47	3/01	4c
Potatoes, white, all types	lb	0.42	7/01	11r
Poultry, expenditures on	yr	158	1999	30r
Processed fruits, expenditures on	yr	124	1999	30r
Processed vegetables, expenditures on	yr	82	1999	30r
Round roast, U.S. choice, boneless	lb	3.04	7/01	11r
Sausage, Jimmy Dean/Owens pork	lb	3.99	3/01	4c
Shortening, vegetable, Crisco	3 lb	3.33	3/01	4c
Soft drink, Coca Cola, ex deposit	2 liter	1.31	3/01	4c
Spaghetti and macaroni	lb	1.04	7/01	11r
Steak, sirloin, U.S. choice, boneless	lb	5.39	7/01	11r
Steak, T-bone	lb	5.59	3/01	4c
Strawberries, dry pint	12 oz	1.51	7/01	11r
Sugar and other sweets, expenditures on	yr	110	1999	30r
Sugar, cane or beet	4 lbs	1.61	3/01	4c
Sugar, white, 33-80 ounce package	lb	0.46	7/01	11r
Sugar, white, all sizes	lb	0.47	7/01	11r
Tobacco products and smoking supplies purchases	yr	292	1999	30c
Tomatoes, Hunt's or Del Monte	14.5 oz	0.91	3/01	4c
Tuna, chunk, light	6 oz	0.73	7/01	11r
Yogurt, natural, fruit flavored	8 oz	0.79	7/01	11r
Goods and Services				
Miscellaneous goods and services, ACCRA Index		112.60	3/01	4c
B&B Japanese maple (acer japonicum)	gal	38.99-125.00	4/00	93r
Boxwood (buxus)	2 gal	15.99-49.95	4/00	93r
Daylily (hemerocallis)	gal	4.95	4/00	93r
Flat of annuals		8.00-14.99	4/00	93r
Fountain grass (pennisetum)	gal	6.99-9.99	4/00	93r
Hanging basket (10 in)		12.95-19.99	4/00	93r

Boston, MA - continued

Item	Per	Value	Date	Ref.
Goods and Services - continued				
Hardy geranium (geranium)	gal	6.95-7.99	4/00	93r
Hosta (hosta)	gal	4.95	4/00	93r
Lilac (syrubga vulgaris)	2 gal	17.99-74.95	4/00	93r
Miscellaneous purchases	yr	711	1999	30c
Rhododendron (rhododendron)	2 gal	23.99-54.95	4/00	93r
Sage (salvia)	gal	6.95-7.99	4/00	93r
Wintercreeper euonymus (euonymus fortunei)	2 gal	14.99-23.95	4/00	93r
Hunting license	yr	27.50	4/01	34s
Health Care				
Health care, ACCRA Index		128.90	3/01	4c
Cardiac catheterization, ave hospital/physician charges		17080	1998	77s
Childbirth, Cesarean delivery		14716	1997	13r
Childbirth, vaginal delivery		8541	1997	13r
Dentist's fee, adult teeth cleaning and periodic oral exam	visit	88.20	3/01	4c
Doctor's fee, routine exam, established patient	visit	79.80	3/01	4c
Drugs, expenditures on	yr	296	1999	30r
Health care purchases	yr	1686	1999	30c
Health insurance expenditures	yr	875	1999	30r
Home health care aide cost, licensed agency	hour	19	2000	82c
Hospital care, private room	day	713.00	3/01	4c
Hysterectomy, laproscopically-assisted, ave hospital/physician charges		13100	1998	76s
Hysterectomy, vaginal, ave hospital and physician charges		8780	1998	76s
Medicaid dispensing fee		3.00	1999	87s
Medical services expenditures	yr	516	1999	30r
Medical supplies, expenditures on	yr	102	1999	30r
Nursing home costs, private room	day	278	2000	82c
Nursing home stay, private room	day	278	2000	83c
Plastic surgery, breast augmentation		4232	2000	7r
Plastic surgery, breast lift		4605	2000	7r
Plastic surgery, facelift		6964	2000	7r
Plastic surgery, hair transplantation		4193	2000	7r
Plastic surgery, lip augmentation		1675	2000	7r
Plastic surgery, lower body lift		6611	2000	7r
Plastic surgery, thigh lift		4751	2000	7r
Household Goods				
Dishwashing powder, Cascade	50 oz	3.54	3/01	4c
Floor coverings, expenditures on	yr	59	1999	30r
Furniture, expenditures on	yr	388	1999	30r
Household furnishings and equipment purchases	yr	1684	1999	30c
Household textiles, expenditures on	yr	112	1999	30r
Laundry and cleaning supplies, expenditures on	yr	104	1999	30r
Tissues, facial, Kleenex brand	175	1.35	3/01	4c
Housing				
Housing, ACCRA Index		174.40	3/01	4c
Home, 2200 sq ft, 4-br, 2-bath, 2-car garage, average		319500	2000	47c
Home, suburban, 2,200 square feet		324500	2000	23c
Home price, existing, ave		180800	10/00	90r
Home purchase, 2,000 sq ft		560000	11/00	111c
Home value, median		261000	2001	53s
House, 2-story, 2,400 sq ft, 2-car garage, new		195500	2000	54c
House, 2400 sq ft, 8000 sq ft lot, new, urban, utilities	total	339250	3/01	4c
House payment, principal and interest, 25% down payment	mos	1736	3/01	4c
Household operation expenditures	yr	667	1999	30c
Housekeeping supplies purchases	yr	363	1999	30c
Lodging expenditures	yr	973	1999	30c

Values are in dollars or fractions of dollars. In the column headed *Ref*, references are shown to sources. Each reference is followed by a letter. These refer to the geographical level for which data were reported: s=State, r=Region, and c=City or metro. The abbreviation *ex* is used to mean *except* or *excluding*; *exp* stands for expenditures. For other abbreviations and further explanations, please see the Introduction.

Boston, MA - continued

Item	Per	Value	Date	Ref.
Housing				
Maintenance, repairs, insurance expenditures	yr	835	1999	30r
Monthly rental value of owned home	mos	663	1999	30r
Owned dwellings, expenditures own	yr	6110	1999	30c
Rent expenditures	yr	2396	1999	30c
Rent, apartment, 2 br, 1 1/2-2 baths, unfurn, 950 sq ft, water	mos	1374	3/01	4c
Rental unit, 1 bedroom, with utilities	mos	782	4/01	41c
Rental unit, 2 bedroom, with utilities	mos	979	4/01	41c
Rental unit, 3 bedroom, with utilities	mos	1223	4/01	41c
Rental unit, 4 bedroom, with utilities	mos	1437	4/01	41c
Shelter, expenditures on	yr	9478	1999	30c
Single-family home, purchase price		255000	2000	19c
Insurance and Pensions				
Auto insurance, no teens	yr	1030	1999	68c
Life and other personal insurance purchases	yr	396	1999	30c
Pensions and Social Security, expenditures on	yr	3235	1999	30c
Legal Fees				
Divorce, filing fee		100.00	4/01	35s
Driver's license fee	renew	33.75	1999	48s
Driver's license fee	orig	33.75	1999	48s
Fishing license	yr	27.50	4/01	34s
Parking in front of hydrant, fine		50	1998	20c
Parking in loading zone, fine		25	1998	20c
Parking meter violation, fine		20	1998	20c
Personal Goods				
Personal care products and services purchases	yr	344	1999	30c
Shampoo, Alberto VO5	15 oz	1.23	3/01	4c
Toothpaste, Crest or Colgate	6-7 oz	2.43	3/01	4c
Personal Services				
Dry cleaning, man's 2-pc suit		9.07	3/01	4c
Man's haircut, barbershop, no styling		10.40	3/01	4c
Personal services, household, expenditures on	yr	271	1999	30r
Woman's shampoo, trim, blow-dry, no style-change		40.60	3/01	4c
Pets				
Pets, toys, and playground equipment, expenditures on	yr	325	1999	30r
Restaurant Food				
Chicken, fried, thigh and drumstick, KFC/Church's		3.00	3/01	4c
Hamburger with cheese, McDonald's	1/4 lb	2.51	3/01	4c
Pizza, Pizza Hut or Pizza Inn	11-12 in	8.99	3/01	4c
Starbucks latte		1.95	1999	68c
Taxes				
Federal income taxes paid	yr	2606	1999	30r
Personal taxes, expenditures on	yr	3567	1999	30r
Property taxes paid	yr	1752	1999	30r
State and local income taxes paid	yr	694	1999	30r
Transportation				
Transportation, ACCRA Index		117.20	3/01	4c
Bus fare, one-way	trip	0.60	2000	1c
Bus fare, to central business district	1-way	2.00	3/01	4c
Cars and trucks, new, expenditures on	yr	1496	1999	30r
Cars and trucks, used, expenditures on	yr	1251	1999	30r
Commuter rail, one-way	trip	0.85	2000	2c
Diesel at the pump	gal	1.32	10/99	73s
Ferry boat transit fare, one-way	trip	4.00	2000	2c
Gasoline and motor oil purchases	yr	923	1999	30c
Gasoline before-tax price (cents)	gal	118.70	10/00	43s
Heavy rail transit fare, one-way	trip	0.85	2000	2c
Light rail transit fare, one-way	trip	0.85	2000	2c
Maintenance and repair expenditures	yr	618	1999	30r
Public transportation, expenditures on	yr	600	1999	30c
Tire balance, computer or spin balance, front	wheel	8.38	3/01	4c

Boston, MA - continued

Item	Per	Value	Date	Ref.
Transportation - continued				
Transportation purchases	yr	6312	1999	30c
Trolley bus transit fare, one-way	trip	0.60	2000	2c
Vehicle expenses, miscellaneous, purchases	yr	2143	1999	30c
Vehicle insurance payments	yr	824	1999	30r
Vehicle purchases (net outlay)	yr	2761	1999	30r
Vehicle rental, lease expenditures	yr	584	1999	30r
Travel				
Hotel rate, ave	day	191.00	1999	45c
Hotel room	night	111.15	2/01	95s
Hotel room, ave	night	199.54	2000	70c
Utilities				
Utilities, ACCRA Index		131.30	3/01	4c
Electrical bill, average	mos	58.58	9/00	9s
Electricity, expenditures on	yr	837	1999	30r
Electricity, summer, 250 KWh	mos	35.62	2/96	97c
Electricity, summer, 500 KWh	mos	64.08	2/96	97c
Electricity, summer, 750 KWh	mos	92.53	2/96	97c
Electricity, summer, 1000 KWh	mos	120.98	2/96	97c
Electricity and other, mixed, 2400 sq ft, new home	mos	75.34	3/01	4c
Electricity cost, average	KWh	8.90	9/00	9s
Utilities, fuels, and public services purchased	yr	2419	1999	30c
Water and other public services, expenditures on	yr	215	1999	30r
Weddings				
Wedding (national average cost)		19936	2000	33r
Wedding (regional average total cost)		29454	1997	110r
Attendants' gifts		321	1998	33r
Bridal attendants' apparel (5 persons)		824	2000	33r
Bride's headpiece/veil		173	1998	33r
Bride's wedding dress		859	1998	33r
Clergy, religious facility fee		242	1998	33r
Engagement ring		3177	1998	33r
Flowers		789	1998	33r
Groom's formalwear rental		99	2000	33r
Limousine		410	1998	33r
Marriage license cost		25.00	4/01	35s
Men's formalwear (ushers, best man)		469	2000	33r
Mother of bride apparel		241	2000	33r
Music		866	1998	33r
Photography and videography		1368	1998	33r
Rehearsal dinner		728	1998	33r
Wedding invitations and announcements		341	1998	33r
Wedding reception		7968	2000	33r
Wedding rings (bride and groom)		1060	1998	33r

Boulder, CO

Item	Per	Value	Date	Ref.
Child Care				
Child care fee, one year old	week	186	5/99	26c
Child care fee, six year old	week	68	5/99	26c
Child care fee, three year old	week	143	5/99	26c
Communications				
Cable modem installation, AT&T-BIS		150.00	6/99	103s
Cable modem rate, cable subscriber, AT&T-BIS	mos	39.95	6/99	103s
Phone line, single, business, field visit	inst.	70.00	12/97	17s
Phone line, single, business, no field visit	inst.	70.00	12/97	17s
Phone line, single, residence, field visit	inst.	35.00	12/97	17s
Phone line, single, residence, no field visit	inst.	35.00	12/97	17s
Postal rate, express mail, up to half-pound		12.45	7/01	108r
Postal rate, letter, first class, first ounce		0.34	7/01	108r
Postal rate, letter, two ounces		0.57	7/01	108r
Postal rate, post card		0.21	7/01	108r
Postal rate, priority mail, two pounds		3.95	7/01	108r
Postal rate, priority mail, up to one pound		3.50	7/01	108r
Telephone bill, business, basic rate	mos	37.31	12/97	18c
Telephone bill, residential, basic rate	mos	14.87	12/97	18c

Values are in dollars or fractions of dollars. In the column headed *Ref*, references are shown to sources. Each reference is followed by a letter. These refer to the geographical level for which data were reported: s=State, r=Region, and c=City or metro. The abbreviation *ex* is used to mean *except* or *excluding*; *exp* stands for *expenditures*. For other abbreviations and further explanations, please see the Introduction.

Boulder, CO - continued

Item	Per	Value	Date	Ref.
Education				
Board, 4-year private college/university	yr	2750	1996	38s
Board, 4-year public college/university	yr	2564	1996	38s
Room, 4-year private college/university	yr	2574	1996	38s
Room, 4-year public college/university	yr	2000	1996	38s
Total cost, 4-year private college/university	yr	17120	1996	38s
Total cost, 4-year public college/university	yr	7037	1996	38s
Tuition, 2-year public college/university, in state	yr	1340	1996	38s
Tuition, 4-year private college/university, in state	yr	11796	1996	38s
Tuition, 4-year public college/university	yr	2473	1996	38s
Energy and Fuels				
Gas, natural, commercial rate	1000 cf	6.42	11/00	88s
Funerals				
Total cost of funeral		5401.08	1/99	78r
Acknowledgement cards		33.64	1/99	78r
Casket		2170.43	1/99	78r
Cosmetology, hair, other preparation		136.32	1/99	78r
Embalming		319.13	1/99	78r
Funeral at funeral home		370.21	1/99	78r
Hearse (local)		161.04	1/99	78r
Professional service charges		963.15	1/99	78r
Service car/van		133.99	1/99	78r
Transfer of remains to funeral home		159.82	1/99	78r
Vault		778.07	1/99	78r
Visitation/viewing		175.28	1/99	78r
Groceries				
Bacon	lb	3.99	5/99	8s
Bread, white, 20 oz loaf		0.64	5/99	8s
Cheddar cheese, mild	lb	3.59	5/99	8s
Cheerios, 10 oz box		2.99	5/99	8s
Corn oil, Mazola, 32 oz		2.75	5/99	8s
Flour, all purpose	5 lb	1.69	5/99	8s
Grade A large eggs	doz	1.59	5/99	8s
Ground chuck	lb	1.99	5/99	8s
Mayonnaise, Kraft, 32 oz		2.50	5/99	8s
Potatoes, russet	5 lb	1.79	5/99	8s
Red Delicious apples	lb	1.39	5/99	8s
Sirloin tip roast	lb	3.99	5/99	8s
Vegetable oil, Crisco, 32 oz		1.89	5/99	8s
Whole fryer	lb	1.99	5/99	8s
Whole milk	gal	0.89	5/99	8s
Goods and Services				
Hunting license	yr	15.25	4/01	34s
Health Care				
Cardiac catheterization, ave hospital/ physician charges		17910	1998	77s
Childbirth, Cesarean delivery		11587	1997	13r
Childbirth, vaginal delivery		6725	1997	13r
Hysterectomy, laproscopically-assisted, ave hospital/physician charges		16210	1998	76s
Hysterectomy, vaginal, ave hospital and physician charges		11690	1998	76s
Medicaid dispensing fee		4.08	1999	87s
Housing				
Home value, median		173000	2001	53s
Legal Fees				
Divorce, filing fee		65.00	4/01	35s
Driver's license fee	orig	15.00	1999	48s
Driver's license fee	renew	15.00	1999	48s
Transportation				
Bus fare, one-way	trip	0.75	2000	1c
Diesel at the pump	gal	1.28	10/99	73s
Gasoline before-tax price (cents)	gal	117.00	10/00	43s
Travel				
Hotel room	night	118.98	2/01	95s

Boulder, CO - continued

Item	Per	Value	Date	Ref.
Utilities				
Electrical bill, average	mos	47.17	9/00	9s
Electricity cost, average	KWh	5.90	9/00	9s
Weddings				
Wedding (national average cost)		19936	2000	33r
Attendants' gifts		321	1998	33r
Bridal attendants' apparel (5 persons)		824	2000	33r
Bride's headpiece/veil		173	1998	33r
Bride's wedding dress		859	1998	33r
Clergy, religious facility fee		242	1998	33r
Engagement ring		3177	1998	33r
Flowers		789	1998	33r
Groom's formalwear rental		99	2000	33r
Limousine		410	1998	33r
Marriage license cost		20.00	4/01	35s
Men's formalwear (ushers, best man)		469	2000	33r
Mother of bride apparel		241	2000	33r
Music		866	1998	33r
Photography and videography		1368	1998	33r
Rehearsal dinner		728	1998	33r
Wedding invitations and announcements		341	1998	33r
Wedding reception		7968	2000	33r
Wedding rings (bride and groom)		1060	1998	33r

Boulder-Longmont, CO

Item	Per	Value	Date	Ref.
Communications				
Cable modem installation, AT&T-BIS		150.00	6/99	103s
Cable modem rate, cable subscriber, AT&T-BIS	mos	39.95	6/99	103s
Phone line, single, business, field visit	inst.	70.00	12/97	17s
Phone line, single, business, no field visit	inst.	70.00	12/97	17s
Phone line, single, residence, field visit	inst.	35.00	12/97	17s
Phone line, single, residence, no field visit	inst.	35.00	12/97	17s
Postal rate, express mail, up to half-pound		12.45	7/01	108r
Postal rate, letter, first class, first ounce		0.34	7/01	108r
Postal rate, letter, two ounces		0.57	7/01	108r
Postal rate, post card		0.21	7/01	108r
Postal rate, priority mail, two pounds		3.95	7/01	108r
Postal rate, priority mail, up to one pound		3.50	7/01	108r
Education				
Board, 4-year private college/university	yr	2750	1996	38s
Board, 4-year public college/university	yr	2564	1996	38s
Room, 4-year private college/university	yr	2574	1996	38s
Room, 4-year public college/university	yr	2000	1996	38s
Total cost, 4-year private college/university	yr	17120	1996	38s
Total cost, 4-year public college/university	yr	7037	1996	38s
Tuition, 2-year public college/university, in state	yr	1340	1996	38s
Tuition, 4-year private college/university, in state	yr	11796	1996	38s
Tuition, 4-year public college/university	yr	2473	1996	38s
Energy and Fuels				
Gas, natural, commercial rate	1000 cf	6.42	11/00	88s
Funerals				
Total cost of funeral		5401.08	1/99	78r
Acknowledgement cards		33.64	1/99	78r
Casket		2170.43	1/99	78r
Cosmetology, hair, other preparation		136.32	1/99	78r
Embalming		319.13	1/99	78r
Funeral at funeral home		370.21	1/99	78r
Hearse (local)		161.04	1/99	78r
Professional service charges		963.15	1/99	78r
Service car/van		133.99	1/99	78r
Transfer of remains to funeral home		159.82	1/99	78r
Vault		778.07	1/99	78r
Visitation/viewing		175.28	1/99	78r
Groceries				
Bacon	lb	3.99	5/99	8s

Values are in dollars or fractions of dollars. In the column headed *Ref*, references are shown to sources. Each reference is followed by a letter. These refer to the geographical level for which data were reported: s=State, r=Region, and c=City or metro. The abbreviation *ex* is used to mean *except* or *excluding*; *exp* stands for expenditures. For other abbreviations and further explanations, please see the Introduction.

Boulder-Longmont, CO - continued

Item	Per	Value	Date	Ref.
Groceries				
Bread, white, 20 oz loaf		0.64	5/99	8s
Cheddar cheese, mild	lb	3.59	5/99	8s
Cheerios, 10 oz box		2.99	5/99	8s
Corn oil, Mazola, 32 oz		2.75	5/99	8s
Flour, all purpose	5 lb	1.69	5/99	8s
Grade A large eggs	doz	1.59	5/99	8s
Ground chuck	lb	1.99	5/99	8s
Mayonnaise, Kraft, 32 oz		2.50	5/99	8s
Potatoes, russet	5 lb	1.79	5/99	8s
Red Delicious apples	lb	1.39	5/99	8s
Sirloin tip roast	lb	3.99	5/99	8s
Vegetable oil, Crisco, 32 oz		1.89	5/99	8s
Whole fryer	lb	1.99	5/99	8s
Whole milk	gal	0.89	5/99	8s
Goods and Services				
Hunting license	yr	15.25	4/01	34s
Health Care				
Cardiac catheterization, ave hospital/ physician charges		17910	1998	77s
Childbirth, Cesarean delivery		11587	1997	13r
Childbirth, vaginal delivery		6725	1997	13r
Hysterectomy, laproscopically-assisted, ave hospital/physician charges		16210	1998	76s
Hysterectomy, vaginal, ave hospital and physician charges		11690	1998	76s
Medicaid dispensing fee		4.08	1999	87s
Housing				
Home value, median		173000	2001	53s
Rental unit, 1 bedroom, with utilities	mos	661	4/01	41c
Rental unit, 2 bedroom, with utilities	mos	848	4/01	41c
Rental unit, 3 bedroom, with utilities	mos	1181	4/01	41c
Rental unit, 4 bedroom, with utilities	mos	1392	4/01	41c
Legal Fees				
Divorce, filing fee		65.00	4/01	35s
Driver's license fee	orig	15.00	1999	48s
Driver's license fee	renew	15.00	1999	48s
Transportation				
Diesel at the pump	gal	1.28	10/99	73s
Gasoline before-tax price (cents)	gal	117.00	10/00	43s
Travel				
Hotel room	night	118.98	2/01	95s
Utilities				
Electrical bill, average	mos	47.17	9/00	9s
Electricity cost, average	KWh	5.90	9/00	9s
Weddings				
Wedding (national average cost)		19936	2000	33r
Attendants' gifts		321	1998	33r
Bridal attendants' apparel (5 persons)		824	2000	33r
Bride's headpiece/veil		173	1998	33r
Bride's wedding dress		859	1998	33r
Clergy, religious facility fee		242	1998	33r
Engagement ring		3177	1998	33r
Flowers		789	1998	33r
Groom's formalwear rental		99	2000	33r
Limousine		410	1998	33r
Marriage license cost		20.00	4/01	35s
Men's formalwear (ushers, best man)		469	2000	33r
Mother of bride apparel		241	2000	33r
Music		866	1998	33r
Photography and videography		1368	1998	33r
Rehearsal dinner		728	1998	33r
Wedding invitations and announcements		341	1998	33r
Wedding reception		7968	2000	33r
Wedding rings (bride and groom)		1060	1998	33r

Brazoria, TX

Item	Per	Value	Date	Ref.
Alcoholic Beverages				
Alcoholic beverage purchases	yr	253	1999	30r
Malt beverages, all types, all sizes, any origin	16 oz	0.96	7/01	11r
Appliances				
Major appliances, expenditures on	yr	172	1999	30r
Small appliances, housewares, expenditures on	yr	81	1999	30r
Banking and Money				
Mortgage interest and charges paid	yr	2039	1999	30r
Mortgage principal paid on owned property	yr	1026	1999	30r
Vehicle finance charges paid	yr	365	1999	30r
Charity				
Cash contributions, expenditures	yr	1127	1999	30r
Child Care				
Child raising cost, total, age 0-2	yr	8540	1999	60r
Child raising cost, total, age 3-5	yr	8780	1999	60r
Child raising cost, total, age 6-8	yr	8820	1999	60r
Child raising cost, total, age 9-11	yr	8800	1999	60r
Child raising cost, total, age 12-14	yr	9510	1999	60r
Child raising cost, total, age 15-17	yr	9740	1999	60r
Child's child care and education, age 0-2	yr	1380	1999	60r
Child's child care and education, age 3-5	yr	1520	1999	60r
Child's child care and education, age 6-8	yr	990	1999	60r
Child's child care and education, age 9-11	yr	650	1999	60r
Child's child care and education, age 12-14	yr	490	1999	60r
Child's child care and education, age 15-17	yr	840	1999	60r
Child's clothing, age 0-2	yr	480	1999	60r
Child's clothing, age 3-5	yr	470	1999	60r
Child's clothing, age 6-8	yr	520	1999	60r
Child's clothing, age 9-11	yr	570	1999	60r
Child's clothing, age 12-14	yr	950	1999	60r
Child's clothing, age 15-17	yr	850	1999	60r
Child's food, age 0-2	yr	1000	1999	60r
Child's food, age 3-5	yr	1160	1999	60r
Child's food, age 6-8	yr	1490	1999	60r
Child's food, age 9-11	yr	1770	1999	60r
Child's food, age 12-14	yr	1770	1999	60r
Child's food, age 15-17	yr	1980	1999	60r
Child's health care, age 0-2	yr	620	1999	60r
Child's health care, age 3-5	yr	590	1999	60r
Child's health care, age 6-8	yr	680	1999	60r
Child's health care, age 9-11	yr	720	1999	60r
Child's health care, age 12-14	yr	730	1999	60r
Child's health care, age 15-17	yr	760	1999	60r
Child's housing, age 0-2	yr	3070	1999	60r
Child's housing, age 3-5	yr	3050	1999	60r
Child's housing, age 6-8	yr	3010	1999	60r
Child's housing, age 9-11	yr	2850	1999	60r
Child's housing, age 12-14	yr	3040	1999	60r
Child's housing, age 15-17	yr	2650	1999	60r
Child's personal care, reading, age 0-2	yr	910	1999	60r
Child's personal care, reading, age 3-5	yr	930	1999	60r
Child's personal care, reading, age 6-8	yr	960	1999	60r
Child's personal care, reading, age 9-11	yr	1000	1999	60r
Child's personal care, reading, age 12-14	yr	1170	1999	60r
Child's personal care, reading, age 15-17	yr	950	1999	60r
Clothing				
Apparel and services purchases	yr	1610	1999	30r
Boys, 2 to 15, expenditures on	yr	89	1999	30r
Children under 2, expenditures on	yr	79	1999	30r
Footwear, expenditures on	yr	283	1999	30r
Girls, 2 to 15, expenditures on	yr	103	1999	30r
Men and boys, expenditures on	yr	351	1999	30r
Men, 16 and over, expenditures on	yr	262	1999	30r
Women, 16 and over, expenditures on	yr	538	1999	30r
Communications				
Cable modem installation, AT&T-BIS		150.00	6/99	103s
Cable modem installation, Marcus		499.00	6/99	103s

Values are in dollars or fractions of dollars. In the column headed *Ref*, references are shown to sources. Each reference is followed by a letter. These refer to the geographical level for which data were reported: s=State, r=Region, and c=City or metro. The abbreviation *ex* is used to mean *except* or *excluding*; *exp* stands for *expenditures*. For other abbreviations and further explanations, please see the Introduction.

Brazoria, TX - continued

Item	Per	Value	Date	Ref.
Communications				
Cable modem installation, Time Warner		75.00-225.00	6/99	103s
Cable modem rate, cable subscriber, AT&T-BIS	mos	39.95	6/99	103s
Cable modem rate, cable subscriber, Marcus	mos	14.95-49.95	6/99	103s
Cable modem rate, cable subscriber, Time Warner	mos	39.95-49.95	6/99	103s
Cable modem rate, non-cable subscriber, Marcus	mos	60.95	6/99	103s
Cable modem rate, non-cable subscriber, Time Warner	mos	39.95-54.95	6/99	103s
Phone line, single, business, field visit	inst.	71.90	12/97	17s
Phone line, single, business, no field visit	inst.	57.30	12/97	17s
Phone line, single, residence, field visit	inst.	52.95	12/97	17s
Phone line, single, residence, no field visit	inst.	38.35	12/97	17s
Postage and stationery, expenditures on	yr	104	1999	30r
Postal rate, express mail, up to half-pound		12.45	7/01	108r
Postal rate, letter, first class, first ounce		0.34	7/01	108r
Postal rate, letter, two ounces		0.57	7/01	108r
Postal rate, post card		0.21	7/01	108r
Postal rate, priority mail, two pounds		3.95	7/01	108r
Postal rate, priority mail, up to one pound		3.50	7/01	108r
Telephone services, expenditures on	yr	860	1999	30r
Education				
Board, 4-year private college/university	yr	2198	1996	38s
Board, 4-year public college/university	yr	1759	1996	38s
Education expenditures	yr	431	1999	30r
Room, 4-year private college/university	yr	2000	1996	38s
Room, 4-year public college/university	yr	1885	1996	38s
Total cost, 4-year private college/university	yr	13156	1996	38s
Total cost, 4-year public college/university	yr	5464	1996	38s
Tuition, 2-year public college/university, in state	yr	771	1996	38s
Tuition, 4-year private college/university, in state	yr	8959	1996	38s
Tuition, 4-year public college/university	yr	1820	1996	38s
Energy and Fuels				
Electricity	KWh	0.09	7/01	11r
Electricity	500 KWhs	47.29	7/01	11r
Fuel oil #2	gal	1.43	7/01	11r
Fuel oil and other fuels, expenditures on	yr	45	1999	30r
Gas, natural, commercial rate	1000 cf	6.94	11/00	88s
Gasoline, all types	gal	1.60	7/01	11r
Gasoline, unleaded midgrade	gal	1.65	7/01	11r
Gasoline, unleaded premium	gal	1.74	7/01	11r
Natural gas, expenditures on	yr	164	1999	30r
Utility (piped) gas, therm		1.01	7/01	11r
Utility (piped) gas, 40 therms		44.29	7/01	11r
Utility (piped) gas, 100 therms		97.44	7/01	11r
Entertainment				
Entertainment purchases	yr	1574	1999	30r
Fees and admissions paid	yr	371	1999	30r
Reading purchases	yr	121	1999	30r
Television, radios, sound equipment, expenditures on	yr	561	1999	30r
Funerals				
Total cost of funeral		5842.28	1/99	78r
Acknowledgement cards		28.35	1/99	78r
Casket		2494.29	1/99	78r
Cosmetology, hair, other preparation		109.22	1/99	78r
Embalming		361.42	1/99	78r
Funeral at funeral home		349.20	1/99	78r
Hearse (local)		161.91	1/99	78r
Professional service charges		1116.50	1/99	78r
Service car/van		65.56	1/99	78r
Transfer of remains to funeral home		143.56	1/99	78r
Vault		785.25	1/99	78r
Visitation/viewing		227.02	1/99	78r

Brazoria, TX - continued

Item	Per	Value	Date	Ref.
Groceries				
American processed cheese	lb	3.50	7/01	11r
Bakery products, expenditures on	yr	261	1999	30r
Bananas	lb	0.47	7/01	11r
Beans, dried, any type, all sizes	lb	0.63	7/01	11r
Beef for stew, boneless	lb	2.86	7/01	11r
Beef, expenditures on	yr	210	1999	30r
Bologna, all beef or mixed	lb	2.29	7/01	11r
Bread, French	lb	1.66	7/01	11r
Bread, white, pan	lb	0.87	7/01	11r
Bread, whole wheat, pan	lb	1.38	7/01	11r
Broccoli	lb	1.04	7/01	11r
Butter, salted, grade AA, stick	lb	2.26	7/01	11r
Butter, yoghurt, cheese, etc, expenditures on	yr	170	1999	30r
Cabbage	lb	0.42	7/01	11r
Cereals and cereal products, expenditures on	yr	140	1999	30r
Cheddar cheese, natural	lb	3.75	7/01	11r
Chicken breast, bone-in	lb	1.85	7/01	11r
Chicken legs, bone-in	lb	1.34	7/01	11r
Chicken, fresh, whole	lb	1.05	7/01	11r
Chops, boneless,	lb	4.13	7/01	11r
Chuck roast, graded and ungraded, excl U.S. prime and choice	lb	2.35	7/01	11r
Chuck roast, U.S. choice, boneless	lb	2.67	7/01	11r
Coffee, 100%, ground roast, all sizes	lb	2.88	7/01	11r
Coffee, instant, plain, regular, all sizes	16 oz	9.25	7/01	11r
Cola, non diet,	2 liter	1.11	7/01	11r
Crackers, soda, salted	lb	1.70	7/01	11r
Dairy product purchases	yr	282	1999	30r
Eggs, expenditures on	yr	32	1999	30r
Fats and oils, expenditures on	yr	79	1999	30r
Fish and seafood, expenditures on	yr	99	1999	30r
Flour, white, all purpose	lb	0.32	7/01	11r
Food (excl fruit and vegetables), eaten at home, purchases	yr	815	1999	30r
Food cooked on trips, expenditures on	yr	36	1999	30r
Food purchases	yr	4533	1999	30r
Food purchases, eaten away from home	yr	1873	1999	30r
Food purchases, food eaten at home	yr	2660	1999	30r
Fresh fruits, expenditures on	yr	128	1999	30r
Fresh milk and cream, expenditures on	yr	112	1999	30r
Fresh vegetables, expenditures on	yr	131	1999	30r
Fruit and vegetable purchases	yr	438	1999	30r
Grapefruit	lb	0.59	7/01	11r
Grapes, Thompson, seedless	lb	2.12	7/01	11r
Ground beef, 100% beef	lb	1.76	7/01	11r
Ground beef, lean and extra lean	lb	2.60	7/01	11r
Ground chuck, 100% beef	lb	2.08	7/01	11r
Ham, boneless, excl canned	lb	2.71	7/01	11r
Ham, rump or shank half, bone-in, smoked	lb	2.19	7/01	11r
Ice cream, prepackaged, bulk, regular	1/2 gal	3.93	7/01	11r
Lemons	lb	1.32	7/01	11r
Lettuce, iceberg	lb	0.76	7/01	11r
Milk, fresh, low fat	gal	2.75	7/01	11r
Milk, fresh, whole, fortified	gal	2.97	7/01	11r
Nonalcoholic beverages, expenditures on	yr	228	1999	30r
Orange juice, frozen concentrate	16 oz	1.95	7/01	11r
Oranges, Navel	lb	0.73	7/01	11r
Oranges, Valencia	lb	0.55	7/01	11r
Peanut butter, creamy, all sizes	lb	1.83	7/01	11r
Pears, Anjou	lb	0.98	7/01	11r
Pork chops, center cut, bone-in	lb	3.33	7/01	11r
Pork sausage, fresh, loose	lb	2.59	7/01	11r
Pork shoulder picnic, bone-in, smoked	lb	1.12	7/01	11r
Pork, expenditures on	yr	162	1999	30r
Potato chips	16 oz	3.59	7/01	11r
Potatoes, frozen, french fried	lb	1.00	7/01	11r
Potatoes, white, all types	lb	0.44	7/01	11r
Poultry, expenditures on	yr	137	1999	30r
Processed fruits, expenditures on	yr	97	1999	30r
Processed vegetables, expenditures on	yr	82	1999	30r
Rice, white, long grain, uncooked	lb	0.51	7/01	11r

Values are in dollars or fractions of dollars. In the column headed *Ref*, references are shown to sources. Each reference is followed by a letter. These refer to the geographical level for which data were reported: s=State, r=Region, and c=City or metro. The abbreviation *ex* is used to mean *except* or *excluding*; *exp* stands for *expenditures*. For other abbreviations and further explanations, please see the Introduction.

Brazoria, TX - continued

Item	Per	Value	Date	Ref.
Groceries				
Round roast, graded and ungraded, excl U.S. prime and choice	lb	2.96	7/01	11r
Round steak, graded and ungraded, excl U.S. prime and choice	lb	3.11	7/01	11r
Sirloin steak, graded and ungraded, excl U.S. prime and choice	lb	4.23	7/01	11r
Spaghetti and macaroni	lb	0.78	7/01	11r
Steak, round, U.S. choice, boneless	lb	3.56	7/01	11r
Steak, sirloin, U.S. choice, boneless	lb	5.65	7/01	11r
Strawberries, dry pint	12 oz	1.50	7/01	11r
Sugar and other sweets, expenditures on	yr	99	1999	30r
Sugar, white, 33-80 ounce package	lb	0.39	7/01	11r
Sugar, white, all sizes	lb	0.42	7/01	11r
Tobacco products and smoking supplies purchases	yr	288	1999	30r
Tomatoes, field grown	lb	1.43	7/01	11r
Tuna, light, chunk	lb	1.77	7/01	11r
Turkey, frozen, whole	lb	1.05	7/01	11r
Goods and Services				
B&B Japanese maple (acer japonicum)	gal	79.98-99.00	4/00	93r
Boxwood (buxus)	2 gal	12.98-18.99	4/00	93r
Christmas tree, noble fir		40-60	2000	65s
Daylily (hemerocallis)	gal	7.96-11.00	4/00	93r
Flat of annuals		13.99-27.99	4/00	93r
Fountain grass (pennisetum)	gal	6.96-9.00	4/00	93r
Hanging basket (10 in)		9.99-24.99	4/00	93r
Hardy geranium (geranium)	gal	5.96-8.00	4/00	93r
Hosta (hosta)	gal	8.96-12.99	4/00	93r
Lilac (syrubga vulgaris)	2 gal	13.00-19.99	4/00	93r
Rhododendron (rhododendron)	2 gal	12.98-29.99	4/00	93r
Sage (salvia)	gal	5.96-8.00	4/00	93r
Wintercreeper euonymus (euonymus fortunei)	2 gal	13.00-18.99	4/00	93r
Hunting license	yr	19.00	4/01	34s
Health Care				
Cardiac catheterization, ave hospital/ physician charges		20140	1998	77s
Childbirth, Cesarean delivery		11587	1997	13r
Childbirth, vaginal delivery		6725	1997	13r
Drugs, expenditures on	yr	399	1999	30r
Health care purchases	yr	1971	1999	30r
Health insurance expenditures	yr	933	1999	30r
Hysterectomy, laproscopically-assisted, ave hospital/physician charges		15700	1998	76s
Hysterectomy, vaginal, ave hospital and physician charges		12180	1998	76s
Medicaid dispensing fee		5.27	1999	87s
Medical services expenditures	yr	547	1999	30r
Medical supplies, expenditures on	yr	91	1999	30r
Household Goods				
Floor coverings, expenditures on	yr	44	1999	30r
Furniture, expenditures on	yr	335	1999	30r
Household furnishings and equipment purchases	yr	1328	1999	30r
Household textiles, expenditures on	yr	89	1999	30r
Laundry and cleaning supplies, expenditures on	yr	113	1999	30r

Brazoria, TX - continued

Item	Per	Value	Date	Ref.
Housing				
Home price, existing, ave		160100	10/00	90r
Home value, median		112000	2001	53s
Household operation expenditures	yr	553	1999	30r
Housekeeping supplies purchases	yr	473	1999	30r
Housing, expenditures on	yr	10303	1999	30r
Maintenance, repairs, insurance expenditures	yr	699	1999	30r
Monthly rental value of owned home	mos	505	1999	30r
Owned dwellings, expenditures own	yr	3465	1999	30r
Rent expenditures	yr	1641	1999	30r
Rental unit, 1 bedroom, with utilities	mos	527	4/01	41c
Rental unit, 2 bedroom, with utilities	mos	658	4/01	41c
Rental unit, 3 bedroom, with utilities	mos	917	4/01	41c
Rental unit, 4 bedroom, with utilities	mos	1079	4/01	41c
Shelter, expenditures on	yr	5467	1999	30r
Insurance and Pensions				
Life and other personal insurance purchases	yr	414	1999	30r
Pensions and Social Security, expenditures on	yr	2635	1999	30r
Personal insurance and pensions, expenditures on	yr	3048	1999	30r
Legal Fees				
Divorce, filing fee		150.00-200.00	4/01	35s
Driver's license fee	orig	24.00	1999	48s
Driver's license fee	renew	20.00	1999	48s
Fishing license	yr	19.00	4/01	34s
Personal Goods				
Personal care products and services purchases	yr	393	1999	30r
Personal Services				
Personal services, household, expenditures on	yr	258	1999	30r
Pets				
Pets, toys, and playground equipment, expenditures on	yr	306	1999	30r
Taxes				
Federal income taxes paid	yr	2047	1999	30r
Personal taxes, expenditures on	yr	2554	1999	30r
Property taxes paid	yr	726	1999	30r
State and local income taxes paid	yr	363	1999	30r
Transportation				
Cars and trucks, new, expenditures on	yr	1648	1999	30r
Cars and trucks, used, expenditures on	yr	1651	1999	30r
Diesel at the pump	gal	1.18	10/99	73s
Gasoline and motor oil purchases	yr	1052	1999	30r
Gasoline before-tax price (cents)	gal	101.30	10/00	43s
Maintenance and repair expenditures	yr	621	1999	30r
Public transportation, expenditures on	yr	298	1999	30r
Transportation purchases	yr	6738	1999	30r
Vehicle expenses, miscellaneous, purchases	yr	2033	1999	30r
Vehicle insurance payments	yr	696	1999	30r
Vehicle purchases (net outlay)	yr	3354	1999	30r
Vehicle rental, lease expenditures	yr	352	1999	30r
Utilities				
Electrical bill, average	mos	87.17	9/00	9s
Electricity, expenditures on	yr	1115	1999	30r
Electricity cost, average	KWh	6.48	9/00	9s
Water and other public services, expenditures on	yr	298	1999	30r
Weddings				
Wedding (national average cost)		19936	2000	33r
Attendants' gifts		321	1998	33r
Bridal attendants' apparel (5 persons)		824	2000	33r
Bride's headpiece/veil		173	1998	33r
Bride's wedding dress		859	1998	33r
Clergy, religious facility fee		242	1998	33r

Values are in dollars or fractions of dollars. In the column headed *Ref*, references are shown to sources. Each reference is followed by a letter. These refer to the geographical level for which data were reported: s=State, r=Region, and c=City or metro. The abbreviation *ex* is used to mean *except* or *excluding*; *exp* stands for expenditures. For other abbreviations and further explanations, please see the Introduction.

Brazoria, TX - continued

Item	Per	Value	Date	Ref.
Weddings				
Engagement ring		3177	1998	33r
Flowers		789	1998	33r
Groom's formalwear rental		99	2000	33r
Limousine		410	1998	33r
Marriage license cost		36.00	4/01	35s
Men's formalwear (ushers, best man)		469	2000	33r
Mother of bride apparel		241	2000	33r
Music		866	1998	33r
Photography and videography		1368	1998	33r
Rehearsal dinner		728	1998	33r
Wedding invitations and announcements		341	1998	33r
Wedding reception		7968	2000	33r
Wedding rings (bride and groom)		1060	1998	33r

Bremerton, WA

Item	Per	Value	Date	Ref.
Average annual expenditures	yr	40662	1999	30r
Alcoholic Beverages				
Alcoholic beverage purchases	yr	372	1999	30r
Malt beverages, all types, all sizes, any origin	16 oz	0.94	7/01	11r
Wine, red and white table, all sizes, any origin	liter	6.00	7/01	11r
Appliances				
Major appliances, expenditures on	yr	167	1999	30r
Small appliances, housewares, expenditures on	yr	105	1999	30r
Banking and Money				
Mortgage interest and charges paid	yr	3368	1999	30r
Mortgage principal paid on owned property	yr	1677	1999	30r
Vehicle finance charges paid	yr	311	1999	30r
Charity				
Cash contributions, expenditures	yr	1344	1999	30r
Child Care				
Child raising cost, total, age 0-2	yr	9140	1999	60r
Child raising cost, total, age 3-5	yr	9370	1999	60r
Child raising cost, total, age 6-8	yr	9450	1999	60r
Child raising cost, total, age 9-11	yr	9470	1999	60r
Child raising cost, total, age 12-14	yr	10170	1999	60r
Child raising cost, total, age 15-17	yr	10360	1999	60r
Child's child care and education, age 0-2	yr	1250	1999	60r
Child's child care and education, age 3-5	yr	1380	1999	60r
Child's child care and education, age 6-8	yr	890	1999	60r
Child's child care and education, age 9-11	yr	580	1999	60r
Child's child care and education, age 12-14	yr	430	1999	60r
Child's child care and education, age 15-17	yr	730	1999	60r
Child's clothing, age 0-2	yr	430	1999	60r
Child's clothing, age 3-5	yr	420	1999	60r
Child's clothing, age 6-8	yr	470	1999	60r
Child's clothing, age 9-11	yr	520	1999	60r
Child's clothing, age 12-14	yr	870	1999	60r
Child's clothing, age 15-17	yr	770	1999	60r
Child's food, age 0-2	yr	1120	1999	60r
Child's food, age 3-5	yr	1280	1999	60r
Child's food, age 6-8	yr	1640	1999	60r
Child's food, age 9-11	yr	1930	1999	60r
Child's food, age 12-14	yr	1940	1999	60r
Child's food, age 15-17	yr	2150	1999	60r
Child's health care, age 0-2	yr	490	1999	60r
Child's health care, age 3-5	yr	470	1999	60r
Child's health care, age 6-8	yr	530	1999	60r
Child's health care, age 9-11	yr	570	1999	60r
Child's health care, age 12-14	yr	580	1999	60r
Child's health care, age 15-17	yr	610	1999	60r
Child's housing, age 0-2	yr	3630	1999	60r
Child's housing, age 3-5	yr	3610	1999	60r
Child's housing, age 6-8	yr	3570	1999	60r
Child's housing, age 9-11	yr	3410	1999	60r
Child's housing, age 12-14	yr	3600	1999	60r
Child's housing, age 15-17	yr	3210	1999	60r

Item	Per	Value	Date	Ref.
Child Care - continued				
Child's personal care, reading, age 0-2	yr	1040	1999	60r
Child's personal care, reading, age 3-5	yr	1060	1999	60r
Child's personal care, reading, age 6-8	yr	1090	1999	60r
Child's personal care, reading, age 9-11	yr	1130	1999	60r
Child's personal care, reading, age 12-14	yr	1300	1999	60r
Child's personal care, reading, age 15-17	yr	1080	1999	60r
Clothing				
Apparel and services purchases	yr	1863	1999	30r
Boys, 2 to 15, expenditures on	yr	80	1999	30r
Children under 2, expenditures on	yr	74	1999	30r
Footwear, expenditures on	yr	307	1999	30r
Girls, 2 to 15, expenditures on	yr	101	1999	30r
Men and boys, expenditures on	yr	443	1999	30r
Men, 16 and over, expenditures on	yr	363	1999	30r
Women, 16 and over, expenditures on	yr	594	1999	30r
Communications				
Cable modem installation, AT&T-BIS		150.00	6/99	103s
Cable modem rate, cable subscriber, AT&T-BIS	mos	39.95	6/99	103s
Phone line, single, business, field visit	inst.	48.00	12/97	17s
Phone line, single, business, no field visit	inst.	48.00	12/97	17s
Phone line, single, residence, field visit	inst.	31.00	12/97	17s
Phone line, single, residence, no field visit	inst.	31.00	12/97	17s
Postage and stationery, expenditures on	yr	150	1999	30r
Postal rate, express mail, up to half-pound		12.45	7/01	108r
Postal rate, letter, first class, first ounce		0.34	7/01	108r
Postal rate, letter, two ounces		0.57	7/01	108r
Postal rate, post card		0.21	7/01	108r
Postal rate, priority mail, two pounds		3.95	7/01	108r
Postal rate, priority mail, up to one pound		3.50	7/01	108r
Telephone services, expenditures on	yr	825	1999	30r
Education				
Board, 4-year private college/university	yr	2329	1996	38s
Board, 4-year public college/university	yr	2158	1996	38s
Education expenditures	yr	676	1999	30r
Room, 4-year private college/university	yr	2487	1996	38s
Room, 4-year public college/university	yr	2187	1996	38s
Total cost, 4-year private college/university	yr	18092	1996	38s
Total cost, 4-year public college/university	yr	7136	1996	38s
Tuition, 2-year public college/university, in state	yr	1369	1996	38s
Tuition, 4-year private college/university, in state	yr	13276	1996	38s
Tuition, 4-year public college/university	yr	2791	1996	38s
Energy and Fuels				
Electricity	500 KWhs	48.23	7/01	11r
Electricity	KWh	0.11	7/01	11r
Fuel oil and other fuels, expenditures on	yr	35	1999	30r
Gas, natural, commercial rate	1000 cf	6.89	11/00	88s
Gasoline, all types	gal	1.91	7/01	11r
Gasoline, unleaded premium	gal	2.05	7/01	11r
Gasoline, unleaded regular	gal	1.83	7/01	11r
Natural gas, expenditures on	yr	255	1999	30r
Utility (piped) gas, therm		0.98	7/01	11r
Utility (piped) gas, 40 therms		40.74	7/01	11r
Utility (piped) gas, 100 therms		96.80	7/01	11r
Entertainment				
Entertainment purchases	yr	2139	1999	30r
Fees and admissions paid	yr	545	1999	30r
Television, radios, sound equipment, expenditures on	yr	624	1999	30r
Funerals				
Total cost of funeral		5401.08	1/99	78r
Acknowledgement cards		33.64	1/99	78r
Casket		2170.43	1/99	78r
Cosmetology, hair, other preparation		136.32	1/99	78r
Embalming		319.13	1/99	78r
Funeral at funeral home		370.21	1/99	78r

Values are in dollars or fractions of dollars. In the column headed *Ref*, references are shown to sources. Each reference is followed by a letter. These refer to the geographical level for which data were reported: s=State, r=Region, and c=City or metro. The abbreviation *ex* is used to mean *except* or *excluding*; *exp* stands for *expenditures*. For other abbreviations and further explanations, please see the Introduction.

Bremerton, WA - continued

Item	Per	Value	Date	Ref.
Funerals				
Hearse (local)		161.04	1/99	78r
Professional service charges		963.15	1/99	78r
Service car/van		133.99	1/99	78r
Transfer of remains to funeral home		159.82	1/99	78r
Vault		778.07	1/99	78r
Visitation/viewing		175.28	1/99	78r
Groceries				
Apples, red delicious	lb	0.84	7/01	11r
Bacon, sliced	lb	3.38	7/01	11r
Bakery products, expenditures on	yr	299	1999	30r
Bananas	lb	0.54	7/01	11r
Beans, dried, any type, all sizes	lb	0.76	7/01	11r
Beef, expenditures on	yr	222	1999	30r
Bread, white, pan	lb	0.99	7/01	11r
Butter, yoghurt, cheese, etc, expenditures on	yr	211	1999	30r
Cereals and bakery product purchases	yr	466	1999	30r
Cereals and cereal products, expenditures on	yr	168	1999	30r
Chicken breast, bone-in	lb	2.45	7/01	11r
Chicken, fresh, whole	lb	1.19	7/01	11r
Chops, boneless,	lb	4.00	7/01	11r
Chuck roast, graded and ungraded, excl U.S. prime and choice	lb	2.55	7/01	11r
Coffee, 100%, ground roast, all sizes	lb	3.80	7/01	11r
Cookies, chocolate chip	lb	2.83	7/01	11r
Dairy product purchases	yr	341	1999	30r
Eggs, expenditures on	yr	39	1999	30r
Eggs, grade AA, large	dozen	1.23	7/01	11r
Fats and oils, expenditures on	yr	88	1999	30r
Fish and seafood, expenditures on	yr	121	1999	30r
Food (excl fruit and vegetables), eaten at home, purchases	yr	1001	1999	30r
Food cooked on trips, expenditures on	yr	64	1999	30r
Food purchases	yr	5312	1999	30r
Food purchases, eaten away from home	yr	2180	1999	30r
Food purchases, food eaten at home	yr	3132	1999	30r
Fresh fruits, expenditures on	yr	186	1999	30r
Fresh milk and cream, expenditures on	yr	130	1999	30r
Fresh vegetables, expenditures on	yr	177	1999	30r
Grapefruit	lb	0.68	7/01	11r
Grapes, Thompson, seedless	lb	2.42	7/01	11r
Ground beef, lean and extra lean	lb	2.46	7/01	11r
Ice cream, prepackaged, bulk, regular	1/2 gal	3.62	7/01	11r
Lettuce, iceberg	lb	0.63	7/01	11r
Meats, poultry, fish, and egg purchases	yr	761	1999	30r
Milk, fresh, low fat,	gal	2.80	7/01	11r
Milk, fresh, whole, fortified	gal	2.88	7/01	11r
Nonalcoholic beverages, expenditures on	yr	258	1999	30r
Oranges, Navel	lb	0.97	7/01	11r
Oranges, Valencia	lb	0.43	7/01	11r
Peaches	lb	1.38	7/01	11r
Peanut butter, creamy, all sizes	lb	2.14	7/01	11r
Pork chops, center cut, bone-in	lb	3.83	7/01	11r
Pork, expenditures on	yr	141	1999	30r
Potatoes, white, all types	lb	0.37	7/01	11r
Poultry, expenditures on	yr	146	1999	30r
Processed fruits, expenditures on	yr	118	1999	30r
Processed vegetables, expenditures on	yr	81	1999	30r
Round roast, graded and ungraded, excl U.S. prime and choice	lb	3.07	7/01	11r
Round roast, U.S. choice, boneless	lb	3.37	7/01	11r
Round steak, graded and ungraded, excl U.S. prime and choice	lb	3.51	7/01	11r
Sirloin steak, graded and ungraded, excl U.S. prime and choice	lb	4.67	7/01	11r
Steak, sirloin, U.S. choice, boneless	lb	6.20	7/01	11r
Strawberries, dry pint	12 oz	1.79	7/01	11r
Sugar and other sweets, expenditures on	yr	124	1999	30r
Sugar, white, all sizes	lb	0.46	7/01	11r
Tobacco products and smoking supplies purchases	yr	217	1999	30r
Tomatoes, field grown	lb	1.17	7/01	11r

Bremerton, WA - continued

Item	Per	Value	Date	Ref.
Groceries - continued				
Tuna, light, chunk	lb	2.05	7/01	11r
Goods and Services				
B&B Japanese maple (acer japonicum)	gal	39.99	4/00	93r
Boxwood (buxus)	2 gal	14.99-24.99	4/00	93r
Daylily (hemerocallis)	gal	6.99-8.99	4/00	93r
Flat of annuals		16.68	4/00	93r
Fountain grass (pennisetum)	gal	7.99-11.99	4/00	93r
Hanging basket (10 in)		29.99	4/00	93r
Hardy geranium (geranium)	gal	6.99-11.99	4/00	93r
Hosta (hosta)	gal	6.99-18.99	4/00	93r
Lilac (syrubga vulgaris)	2 gal	14.99-17.99	4/00	93r
Miscellaneous purchases	yr	1070	1999	30r
Rhododendron (rhododendron)	2 gal	14.99	4/00	93r
Sage (salvia)	gal	6.99	4/00	93r
Wintercreeper euonymus (euonymus fortunei)	2 gal	14.99-22.99	4/00	93r
Hunting license	yr	30.00	4/01	34s
Health Care				
Cardiac catheterization, ave hospital/physician charges		13290	1998	77s
Childbirth, Cesarean delivery		11587	1997	13r
Childbirth, vaginal delivery		6725	1997	13r
Drugs, expenditures on	yr	309	1999	30r
Health care purchases	yr	1869	1999	30r
Health insurance expenditures	yr	868	1999	30r
Hysterectomy, laproscopically-assisted, ave hospital/physician charges		10960	1998	76s
Hysterectomy, vaginal, ave hospital and physician charges		9000	1998	76s
Medicaid dispensing fee		3.98-4.92	1999	87s
Medical services expenditures	yr	580	1999	30r
Medical supplies, expenditures on	yr	112	1999	30r
Household Goods				
Floor coverings, expenditures on	yr	49	1999	30r
Furniture, expenditures on	yr	444	1999	30r
Household furnishings and equipment purchases	yr	1768	1999	30r
Household textiles, expenditures on	yr	141	1999	30r
Laundry and cleaning supplies, expenditures on	yr	128	1999	30r
Housing				
Home price, existing, ave		239400	10/00	90r
Home value, median		195000	2001	53s
Household operation expenditures	yr	781	1999	30r
Housekeeping supplies purchases	yr	513	1999	30r
Lodging expenditures	yr	575	1999	30r
Maintenance, repairs, insurance expenditures	yr	939	1999	30r
Monthly rental value of owned home	mos	662	1999	30r
Owned dwellings, expenditures own	yr	5231	1999	30r
Rent expenditures	yr	2709	1999	30r
Rental unit, 1 bedroom, with utilities	mos	524	4/01	41c
Rental unit, 2 bedroom, with utilities	mos	679	4/01	41c
Rental unit, 3 bedroom, with utilities	mos	917	4/01	41c
Rental unit, 4 bedroom, with utilities	mos	1115	4/01	41c
Shelter, expenditures on	yr	8516	1999	30r
Insurance and Pensions				
Life and other personal insurance purchases	yr	355	1999	30r
Pensions and Social Security, expenditures on	yr	3636	1999	30r

Values are in dollars or fractions of dollars. In the column headed *Ref*, references are shown to sources. Each reference is followed by a letter. These refer to the geographical level for which data were reported: s=State, r=Region, and c=City or metro. The abbreviation *ex* is used to mean *except* or *excluding*; *exp* stands for expenditures. For other abbreviations and further explanations, please see the Introduction.

Bremerton, WA - continued

Item	Per	Value	Date	Ref.
Legal Fees				
Divorce, filing fee		100.00	4/01	35s
Driver's license fee	renew	14.00	1999	48s
Driver's license fee	orig	14.00	1999	48s
Fishing license	yr	20.00	4/01	34s
Personal Goods				
Personal care products and services purchases	yr	449	1999	30r
Personal Services				
Personal services, household, expenditures on	yr	353	1999	30r
Pets				
Pets, toys, and playground equipment, expenditures on	yr	358	1999	30r
Taxes				
Federal income taxes paid	yr	3200	1999	30r
Personal taxes, expenditures on	yr	4153	1999	30r
Property taxes paid	yr	923	1999	30r
State and local income taxes paid	yr	812	1999	30r
Transportation				
Bus fare, one-way	trip	1.00	2000	1c
Cars and trucks, new, expenditures on	yr	1534	1999	30r
Cars and trucks, used, expenditures on	yr	1593	1999	30r
Diesel at the pump	gal	1.37	10/99	73s
Ferry boat transit fare, one-way	trip	1.25	2000	2c
Gasoline and motor oil purchases	yr	1129	1999	30r
Gasoline before-tax price (cents)	gal	127.10	10/00	43s
Maintenance and repair expenditures	yr	797	1999	30r
Public transportation, expenditures on	yr	530	1999	30r
Transportation purchases	yr	7423	1999	30r
Vehicle expenses, miscellaneous, purchases	yr	2585	1999	30r
Vehicle insurance payments	yr	811	1999	30r
Vehicle purchases (net outlay)	yr	3180	1999	30r
Vehicle rental, lease expenditures	yr	666	1999	30r
Utilities				
Electrical bill, average	mos	58.33	9/00	9s
Electricity, expenditures on	yr	725	1999	30r
Electricity cost, average	KWh	4.47	9/00	9s
Utilities, fuels, and public services purchased	yr	2179	1999	30r
Water and other public services, expenditures on	yr	339	1999	30r
Weddings				
Wedding (national average cost)		19936	2000	33r
Wedding (regional average total cost)		18918	1997	110r
Attendants' gifts		321	1998	33r
Bridal attendants' apparel (5 persons)		824	2000	33r
Bride's headpiece/veil		173	1998	33r
Bride's wedding dress		859	1998	33r
Clergy, religious facility fee		242	1998	33r
Engagement ring		3177	1998	33r
Flowers		789	1998	33r
Groom's formalwear rental		99	2000	33r
Limousine		410	1998	33r
Marriage license cost		52.00	4/01	35s
Men's formalwear (ushers, best man)		469	2000	33r
Mother of bride apparel		241	2000	33r
Music		866	1998	33r
Photography and videography		1368	1998	33r
Rehearsal dinner		728	1998	33r
Wedding invitations and announcements		341	1998	33r
Wedding reception		7968	2000	33r
Wedding rings (bride and groom)		1060	1998	33r

Bridgeport, CT

Item	Per	Value	Date	Ref.
Average annual expenditures	yr	37971	1999	30r
Alcoholic Beverages				
Alcoholic beverage purchases	yr	368	1999	30r
Wine, red and white table, all sizes, any origin	liter	9.64	7/01	11r
Appliances				
Major appliances, expenditures on	yr	194	1999	30r
Small appliances, housewares, expenditures on	yr	93	1999	30r
Banking and Money				
Mortgage interest and charges paid	yr	2622	1999	30r
Mortgage principal paid on owned property	yr	1262	1999	30r
Vehicle finance charges paid	yr	240	1999	30r
Charity				
Cash contributions, expenditures	yr	1001	1999	30r
Child Care				
Child raising cost, total, age 0-2	yr	8670	1999	60r
Child raising cost, total, age 3-5	yr	8910	1999	60r
Child raising cost, total, age 6-8	yr	9040	1999	60r
Child raising cost, total, age 9-11	yr	9100	1999	60r
Child raising cost, total, age 12-14	yr	9890	1999	60r
Child raising cost, total, age 15-17	yr	10010	1999	60r
Child's child care and education, age 0-2	yr	1070	1999	60r
Child's child care and education, age 3-5	yr	1190	1999	60r
Child's child care and education, age 6-8	yr	740	1999	60r
Child's child care and education, age 9-11	yr	470	1999	60r
Child's child care and education, age 12-14	yr	350	1999	60r
Child's child care and education, age 15-17	yr	590	1999	60r
Child's clothing, age 0-2	yr	480	1999	60r
Child's clothing, age 3-5	yr	470	1999	60r
Child's clothing, age 6-8	yr	520	1999	60r
Child's clothing, age 9-11	yr	570	1999	60r
Child's clothing, age 12-14	yr	970	1999	60r
Child's clothing, age 15-17	yr	870	1999	60r
Child's food, age 0-2	yr	1130	1999	60r
Child's food, age 3-5	yr	1290	1999	60r
Child's food, age 6-8	yr	1640	1999	60r
Child's food, age 9-11	yr	1930	1999	60r
Child's food, age 12-14	yr	1940	1999	60r
Child's food, age 15-17	yr	2150	1999	60r
Child's health care, age 0-2	yr	550	1999	60r
Child's health care, age 3-5	yr	530	1999	60r
Child's health care, age 6-8	yr	610	1999	60r
Child's health care, age 9-11	yr	650	1999	60r
Child's health care, age 12-14	yr	660	1999	60r
Child's health care, age 15-17	yr	690	1999	60r
Child's housing, age 0-2	yr	3555	1999	60r
Child's housing, age 3-5	yr	3530	1999	60r
Child's housing, age 6-8	yr	3490	1999	60r
Child's housing, age 9-11	yr	3340	1999	60r
Child's housing, age 12-14	yr	3530	1999	60r
Child's housing, age 15-17	yr	3140	1999	60r
Child's personal care, reading, age 0-2	yr	920	1999	60r
Child's personal care, reading, age 3-5	yr	950	1999	60r
Child's personal care, reading, age 6-8	yr	980	1999	60r
Child's personal care, reading, age 9-11	yr	1020	1999	60r
Child's personal care, reading, age 12-14	yr	1190	1999	60r
Child's personal care, reading, age 15-17	yr	970	1999	60r
Clothing				
Apparel and services purchases	yr	1831	1999	30r
Boys, 2 to 15, expenditures on	yr	92	1999	30r
Children under 2, expenditures on	yr	63	1999	30r
Footwear, expenditures on	yr	300	1999	30r
Girls, 2 to 15, expenditures on	yr	101	1999	30r
Men and boys, expenditures on	yr	446	1999	30r
Men, 16 and over, expenditures on	yr	354	1999	30r
Women, 16 and over, expenditures on	yr	584	1999	30r
Communications				
Cable modem installation, AT&T-BIS		150.00	6/99	103s

Values are in dollars or fractions of dollars. In the column headed *Ref*, references are shown to sources. Each reference is followed by a letter. These refer to the geographical level for which data were reported: s=State, r=Region, and c=City or metro. The abbreviation *ex* is used to mean *except* or *excluding*; *exp* stands for *expenditures*. For other abbreviations and further explanations, please see the Introduction.

Bridgeport, CT - continued

Item	Per	Value	Date	Ref.
Communications				
Cable modem installation, Cablevision Systems		150.00	6/99	103s
Cable modem installation, Cox		99.00-174.95	6/99	103s
Cable modem installation, Media One		100.00	6/99	103s
Cable modem rate, cable subscriber, AT&T-BIS	mos	39.95	6/99	103s
Cable modem rate, cable subscriber, Cablevision Systems	mos	44.95	6/99	103s
Cable modem rate, cable subscriber, Cox	mos	29.95-44.95	6/99	103s
Cable modem rate, cable subscriber, Media One	mos	34.95-39.95	6/99	103s
Cable modem rate, non-cable subscriber, Cablevision Systems	mos	54.95	6/99	103s
Cable modem rate, non-cable subscriber, Cox	mos	42.95-54.95	6/99	103s
Cable modem rate, non-cable subscriber, Media One	mos	49.95	6/99	103s
Phone line, single, business, field visit	inst.	65.00	12/97	17s
Phone line, single, business, no field visit	inst.	65.00	12/97	17s
Phone line, single, residence, field visit	inst.	45.00	12/97	17s
Phone line, single, residence, no field visit	inst.	45.00	12/97	17s
Postage and stationery, expenditures on	yr	138	1999	30r
Postal rate, express mail, up to half-pound		12.45	7/01	108r
Postal rate, letter, first class, first ounce		0.34	7/01	108r
Postal rate, letter, two ounces		0.57	7/01	108r
Postal rate, post card		0.21	7/01	108r
Postal rate, priority mail, two pounds		3.95	7/01	108r
Postal rate, priority mail, up to one pound		3.50	7/01	108r
Telephone bill, business, basic rate	mos	33.73	12/97	18c
Telephone bill, residential, basic rate	mos	12.53	12/97	18c
Telephone services, expenditures on	yr	830	1999	30r
Education				
Board, 4-year private college/university	yr	2744	1996	38s
Board, 4-year public college/university	yr	2299	1996	38s
Education expenditures	yr	877	1999	30r
Room, 4-year private college/university	yr	3621	1996	38s
Room, 4-year public college/university	yr	2609	1996	38s
Total cost, 4-year private college/university	yr	23011	1996	38s
Total cost, 4-year public college/university	yr	8753	1996	38s
Tuition, 2-year public college/university, in state	yr	1646	1996	38s
Tuition, 4-year private college/university, in state	yr	16646	1996	38s
Tuition, 4-year public college/university	yr	3845	1996	38s
Energy and Fuels				
Electricity	KWh	0.12	7/01	11r
Fuel oil #2	gal	1.31	7/01	11r
Fuel oil and other fuels, expenditures on	yr	207	1999	30r
Gas, natural, commercial rate	1000 cf	7.08	11/00	88s
Gasoline, all types	gal	1.80	7/01	11r
Gasoline, unleaded midgrade	gal	1.85	7/01	11r
Gasoline, unleaded premium	gal	1.91	7/01	11r
Gasoline, unleaded regular	gal	1.71	7/01	11r
Natural gas, expenditures on	yr	368	1999	30r
Utility (piped) gas, therm		1.08	7/01	11r
Utility (piped) gas, 40 therms		50.87	7/01	11r
Utility (piped) gas, 100 therms		111.06	7/01	11r
Entertainment				
Entertainment purchases	yr	1821	1999	30r
Fees and admissions paid	yr	511	1999	30r
Hockey equipment, girls' hockey		800	2001	101s
Television, radios, sound equipment, expenditures on	yr	650	1999	30r
Funerals				
Total cost of funeral		5776.91	1/99	78r
Acknowledgement cards		14.47	1/99	78r
Casket		2090.19	1/99	78r
Cosmetology, hair, other preparation		132.92	1/99	78r

Bridgeport, CT - continued

Item	Per	Value	Date	Ref.
Funerals - continued				
Embalming		377.33	1/99	78r
Funeral at funeral home		352.43	1/99	78r
Hearse (local)		185.55	1/99	78r
Professional service charges		1289.95	1/99	78r
Service car/van		87.42	1/99	78r
Transfer of remains to funeral home		175.48	1/99	78r
Vault		729.40	1/99	78r
Visitation/viewing		341.76	1/99	78r
Groceries				
Apples, red delicious	lb	0.95	7/01	11r
Bacon, sliced	lb	3.44	7/01	11r
Bakery products, expenditures on	yr	310	1999	30r
Bananas	lb	0.55	7/01	11r
Beef, expenditures on	yr	236	1999	30r
Bread, white, pan	lb	1.09	7/01	11r
Butter, yoghurt, cheese, etc, expenditures on	yr	214	1999	30r
Cereals and bakery product purchases	yr	474	1999	30r
Cereals and cereal products, expenditures on	yr	164	1999	30r
Chicken legs, bone-in	lb	1.23	7/01	11r
Chicken, fresh, whole	lb	1.13	7/01	11r
Chuck roast, U.S. choice, boneless	lb	2.79	7/01	11r
Coffee, 100%, ground roast, all sizes	lb	3.40	7/01	11r
Dairy product purchases	yr	342	1999	30r
Eggs, expenditures on	yr	34	1999	30r
Eggs, grade A, large	dozen	0.82	7/01	11r
Fats and oils, expenditures on	yr	80	1999	30r
Fish and seafood, expenditures on	yr	123	1999	30r
Food (excl fruit and vegetables), eaten at home, purchases	yr	838	1999	30r
Food cooked on trips, expenditures on	yr	48	1999	30r
Food purchases	yr	5314	1999	30r
Food purchases, eaten away from home	yr	2313	1999	30r
Food purchases, food eaten at home	yr	3001	1999	30r
Fresh fruits, expenditures on	yr	169	1999	30r
Fresh milk and cream, expenditures on	yr	128	1999	30r
Fresh vegetables, expenditures on	yr	164	1999	30r
Grapefruit	lb	0.67	7/01	11r
Grapes, Thompson, seedless	lb	2.18	7/01	11r
Ground beef, lean and extra lean	lb	2.66	7/01	11r
Ground chuck, 100% beef	lb	2.04	7/01	11r
Lettuce, iceberg	lb	0.76	7/01	11r
Meats, poultry, fish, and egg purchases	yr	808	1999	30r
Nonalcoholic beverages, expenditures on	yr	225	1999	30r
Orange juice, frozen concentrate	16 oz	1.88	7/01	11r
Oranges, Navel	lb	0.79	7/01	11r
Oranges, Valencia	lb	0.56	7/01	11r
Peaches	lb	1.16	7/01	11r
Peanut butter, creamy, all sizes	lb	2.01	7/01	11r
Pears, Anjou	lb	1.16	7/01	11r
Pork chops, center cut, bone-in	lb	3.57	7/01	11r
Pork, expenditures on	yr	146	1999	30r
Potato chips	16 oz	3.37	7/01	11r
Potatoes, white, all types	lb	0.42	7/01	11r
Poultry, expenditures on	yr	158	1999	30r
Processed fruits, expenditures on	yr	124	1999	30r
Processed vegetables, expenditures on	yr	82	1999	30r
Round roast, U.S. choice, boneless	lb	3.04	7/01	11r
Spaghetti and macaroni	lb	1.04	7/01	11r
Steak, sirloin, U.S. choice, boneless	lb	5.39	7/01	11r
Strawberries, dry pint	12 oz	1.51	7/01	11r
Sugar and other sweets, expenditures on	yr	110	1999	30r
Sugar, white, 33-80 ounce package	lb	0.46	7/01	11r
Sugar, white, all sizes	lb	0.47	7/01	11r
Tobacco products and smoking supplies purchases	yr	309	1999	30r
Yogurt, natural, fruit flavored	8 oz	0.79	7/01	11r
Goods and Services				
B&B Japanese maple (acer japonicum)	gal	38.99-125.00	4/00	93r

Values are in dollars or fractions of dollars. In the column headed *Ref*, references are shown to sources. Each reference is followed by a letter. These refer to the geographical level for which data were reported: s=State, r=Region, and c=City or metro. The abbreviation *ex* is used to mean *except* or *excluding*; *exp* stands for *expenditures*. For other abbreviations and further explanations, please see the Introduction.

Bridgeport, CT - continued

Item	Per	Value	Date	Ref.
Goods and Services				
Boxwood (buxus)	2 gal	15.99-49.95	4/00	93r
Daylily (hemerocallis)	gal	4.95	4/00	93r
Flat of annuals		8.00-14.99	4/00	93r
Fountain grass (pennisetum)	gal	6.99-9.99	4/00	93r
Hanging basket (10 in)		12.95-19.99	4/00	93r
Hardy geranium (geranium)	gal	6.95-7.99	4/00	93r
Hosta (hosta)	gal	4.95	4/00	93r
Lilac (syrubga vulgaris)	2 gal	17.99-74.95	4/00	93r
Miscellaneous purchases	yr	872	1999	30r
Rhododendron (rhododendron)	2 gal	23.99-54.95	4/00	93r
Sage (salvia)	gal	6.95-7.99	4/00	93r
Wintercreeper euonymus (euonymus fortunei)	2 gal	14.99-23.95	4/00	93r
Hunting license	yr	10.00	4/01	34s
Health Care				
Cardiac catheterization, ave hospital/physician charges		14090	1998	77s
Childbirth, Cesarean delivery		14716	1997	13r
Childbirth, vaginal delivery		8541	1997	13r
Drugs, expenditures on	yr	296	1999	30r
Health care purchases	yr	1788	1999	30r
Health insurance expenditures	yr	875	1999	30r
Hysterectomy, laproscopically-assisted, ave hospital/physician charges		11610	1998	76s
Hysterectomy, vaginal, ave hospital and physician charges		12780	1998	76s
Medicaid dispensing fee		4.10	1999	87s
Medical services expenditures	yr	516	1999	30r
Medical supplies, expenditures on	yr	102	1999	30r
Plastic surgery, breast augmentation		4232	2000	7r
Plastic surgery, breast lift		4605	2000	7r
Plastic surgery, facelift		6964	2000	7r
Plastic surgery, hair transplantation		4193	2000	7r
Plastic surgery, lip augmentation		1675	2000	7r
Plastic surgery, lower body lift		6611	2000	7r
Plastic surgery, thigh lift		4751	2000	7r
Household Goods				
Floor coverings, expenditures on	yr	59	1999	30r
Furniture, expenditures on	yr	388	1999	30r
Household furnishings and equipment purchases	yr	1567	1999	30r
Household textiles, expenditures on	yr	112	1999	30r
Laundry and cleaning supplies, expenditures on	yr	104	1999	30r
Housing				
Home price, existing, ave		180800	10/00	90r
Home value, median		157000	2001	53s
Household operation expenditures	yr	581	1999	30r
Housekeeping supplies purchases	yr	474	1999	30r
Lodging expenditures	yr	550	1999	30r
Maintenance, repairs, insurance expenditures	yr	835	1999	30r
Monthly rental value of owned home	mos	663	1999	30r
Owned dwellings, expenditures own	yr	5209	1999	30r
Rent expenditures	yr	2390	1999	30r
Rental unit, 1 bedroom, with utilities	mos	619	4/01	41c
Rental unit, 2 bedroom, with utilities	mos	745	4/01	41c
Rental unit, 3 bedroom, with utilities	mos	932	4/01	41c
Rental unit, 4 bedroom, with utilities	mos	1162	4/01	41c
Shelter, expenditures on	yr	8149	1999	30r

Item	Per	Value	Date	Ref.
Insurance and Pensions				
Auto insurance premium	yr	982.00	1999	57s
Life and other personal insurance purchases	yr	424	1999	30r
Pensions and Social Security, expenditures on	yr	3037	1999	30r
Legal Fees				
Divorce, filing fee		150.00	4/01	35s
Driver's license fee	renew	28.50	1999	48s
Driver's license fee	orig	43.50	1999	48s
Personal Goods				
Personal care products and services purchases	yr	399	1999	30r
Personal Services				
Personal services, household, expenditures on	yr	271	1999	30r
Pets				
Pets, toys, and playground equipment, expenditures on	yr	325	1999	30r
Taxes				
Federal income taxes paid	yr	2606	1999	30r
Personal taxes, expenditures on	yr	3567	1999	30r
Property taxes paid	yr	1752	1999	30r
State and local income taxes paid	yr	694	1999	30r
Transportation				
Auto operation, annual cost		8543	2000	27c
Bus fare, one-way	trip	1.10	2000	1c
Cars and trucks, new, expenditures on	yr	1496	1999	30r
Cars and trucks, used, expenditures on	yr	1251	1999	30r
Diesel at the pump	gal	1.36	10/99	73s
Gasoline and motor oil purchases	yr	901	1999	30r
Gasoline before-tax price (cents)	gal	117.10	10/00	43s
Maintenance and repair expenditures	yr	618	1999	30r
Public transportation, expenditures on	yr	575	1999	30r
Transportation purchases	yr	6503	1999	30r
Vehicle expenses, miscellaneous, purchases	yr	2266	1999	30r
Vehicle insurance payments	yr	824	1999	30r
Vehicle purchases (net outlay)	yr	2761	1999	30r
Vehicle rental, lease expenditures	yr	584	1999	30r
Utilities				
Electrical bill, average	mos	81.50	9/00	9s
Electricity, expenditures on	yr	837	1999	30r
Electricity, summer, 250 KWh	mos	38.96	2/96	97c
Electricity, summer, 500 KWh	mos	68.42	2/96	97c
Electricity, summer, 750 KWh	mos	97.88	2/96	97c
Electricity, summer, 1000 KWh	mos	127.34	2/96	97c
Electricity cost, average	KWh	9.47	9/00	9s
Utilities, fuels, and public services purchased	yr	2457	1999	30r
Water and other public services, expenditures on	yr	215	1999	30r
Weddings				
Wedding (national average cost)		19936	2000	33r
Wedding (regional average total cost)		29454	1997	110r
Attendants' gifts		321	1998	33r
Bridal attendants' apparel (5 persons)		824	2000	33r
Bride's headpiece/veil		173	1998	33r
Bride's wedding dress		859	1998	33r
Clergy, religious facility fee		242	1998	33r
Engagement ring		3177	1998	33r
Flowers		789	1998	33r
Groom's formalwear rental		99	2000	33r
Limousine		410	1998	33r
Marriage license cost		30.00	4/01	35s
Men's formalwear (ushers, best man)		469	2000	33r
Mother of bride apparel		241	2000	33r
Music		866	1998	33r
Photography and videography		1368	1998	33r
Rehearsal dinner		728	1998	33r
Wedding invitations and announcements		341	1998	33r
Wedding reception		7968	2000	33r

Values are in dollars or fractions of dollars. In the column headed *Ref*, references are shown to sources. Each reference is followed by a letter. These refer to the geographical level for which data were reported: s=State, r=Region, and c=City or metro. The abbreviation *ex* is used to mean *except* or *excluding*; *exp* stands for *expenditures*. For other abbreviations and further explanations, please see the Introduction.

Bridgeport, CT - continued

Item	Per	Value	Date	Ref.
Weddings				
Wedding rings (bride and groom)		1060	1998	33r

Brockton, MA

Item	Per	Value	Date	Ref.
Average annual expenditures	yr	37971	1999	30r
Alcoholic Beverages				
Alcoholic beverage purchases	yr	368	1999	30r
Wine, red and white table, all sizes, any origin	liter	9.64	7/01	11r
Appliances				
Major appliances, expenditures on	yr	194	1999	30r
Small appliances, housewares, expenditures on	yr	93	1999	30r
Banking and Money				
Mortgage interest and charges paid	yr	2622	1999	30r
Mortgage principal paid on owned property	yr	1262	1999	30r
Vehicle finance charges paid	yr	240	1999	30r
Charity				
Cash contributions, expenditures	yr	1001	1999	30r
Child Care				
Child raising cost, total, age 0-2	yr	8670	1999	60r
Child raising cost, total, age 3-5	yr	8910	1999	60r
Child raising cost, total, age 6-8	yr	9040	1999	60r
Child raising cost, total, age 9-11	yr	9100	1999	60r
Child raising cost, total, age 12-14	yr	9890	1999	60r
Child raising cost, total, age 15-17	yr	10010	1999	60r
Child's child care and education, age 0-2	yr	1070	1999	60r
Child's child care and education, age 3-5	yr	1190	1999	60r
Child's child care and education, age 6-8	yr	740	1999	60r
Child's child care and education, age 9-11	yr	470	1999	60r
Child's child care and education, age 12-14	yr	350	1999	60r
Child's child care and education, age 15-17	yr	590	1999	60r
Child's clothing, age 0-2	yr	480	1999	60r
Child's clothing, age 3-5	yr	470	1999	60r
Child's clothing, age 6-8	yr	520	1999	60r
Child's clothing, age 9-11	yr	570	1999	60r
Child's clothing, age 12-14	yr	970	1999	60r
Child's clothing, age 15-17	yr	870	1999	60r
Child's food, age 0-2	yr	1130	1999	60r
Child's food, age 3-5	yr	1290	1999	60r
Child's food, age 6-8	yr	1640	1999	60r
Child's food, age 9-11	yr	1930	1999	60r
Child's food, age 12-14	yr	1940	1999	60r
Child's food, age 15-17	yr	2150	1999	60r
Child's health care, age 0-2	yr	550	1999	60r
Child's health care, age 3-5	yr	530	1999	60r
Child's health care, age 6-8	yr	610	1999	60r
Child's health care, age 9-11	yr	650	1999	60r
Child's health care, age 12-14	yr	660	1999	60r
Child's health care, age 15-17	yr	690	1999	60r
Child's housing, age 0-2	yr	3555	1999	60r
Child's housing, age 3-5	yr	3530	1999	60r
Child's housing, age 6-8	yr	3490	1999	60r
Child's housing, age 9-11	yr	3340	1999	60r
Child's housing, age 12-14	yr	3530	1999	60r
Child's housing, age 15-17	yr	3140	1999	60r
Child's personal care, reading, age 0-2	yr	920	1999	60r
Child's personal care, reading, age 3-5	yr	950	1999	60r
Child's personal care, reading, age 6-8	yr	980	1999	60r
Child's personal care, reading, age 9-11	yr	1020	1999	60r
Child's personal care, reading, age 12-14	yr	1190	1999	60r
Child's personal care, reading, age 15-17	yr	970	1999	60r
Clothing				
Apparel and services purchases	yr	1831	1999	30r
Boys, 2 to 15, expenditures on	yr	92	1999	30r
Children under 2, expenditures on	yr	63	1999	30r
Footwear, expenditures on	yr	300	1999	30r
Girls, 2 to 15, expenditures on	yr	101	1999	30r

Brockton, MA - continued

Item	Per	Value	Date	Ref.
Clothing - continued				
Men and boys, expenditures on	yr	446	1999	30r
Men, 16 and over, expenditures on	yr	354	1999	30r
Women, 16 and over, expenditures on	yr	584	1999	30r
Communications				
Cable modem installation, Adelphi		54.90	6/99	103s
Cable modem installation, Media One		100.00	6/99	103s
Cable modem rate, cable subscriber, Adelphi	mos	34.95	6/99	103s
Cable modem rate, cable subscriber, Media One	mos	34.95-39.95	6/99	103s
Cable modem rate, non-cable subscriber, Adelphi	mos	44.95	6/99	103s
Cable modem rate, non-cable subscriber, Media One	mos	49.95	6/99	103s
Phone line, single, business, field visit	inst.	120.52	12/97	17s
Phone line, single, business, no field visit	inst.	93.02	12/97	17s
Phone line, single, residence, field visit	inst.	64.57	12/97	17s
Phone line, single, residence, no field visit	inst.	37.07	12/97	17s
Postage and stationery, expenditures on	yr	138	1999	30r
Postal rate, express mail, up to half-pound		12.45	7/01	108r
Postal rate, letter, first class, first ounce		0.34	7/01	108r
Postal rate, letter, two ounces		0.57	7/01	108r
Postal rate, post card		0.21	7/01	108r
Postal rate, priority mail, two pounds		3.95	7/01	108r
Postal rate, priority mail, up to one pound		3.50	7/01	108r
Telephone services, expenditures on	yr	830	1999	30r
Education				
Board, 4-year private college/university	yr	3244	1996	38s
Board, 4-year public college/university	yr	2042	1996	38s
Education expenditures	yr	877	1999	30r
Room, 4-year private college/university	yr	3688	1996	38s
Room, 4-year public college/university	yr	2462	1996	38s
Total cost, 4-year private college/university	yr	23335	1996	38s
Total cost, 4-year public college/university	yr	8757	1996	38s
Tuition, 2-year public college/university, in state	yr	2359	1996	38s
Tuition, 4-year private college/university, in state	yr	16403	1996	38s
Tuition, 4-year public college/university	yr	4253	1996	38s
Energy and Fuels				
Electricity	KWh	0.12	7/01	11r
Fuel oil #2	gal	1.31	7/01	11r
Fuel oil and other fuels, expenditures on	yr	207	1999	30r
Gas, natural, commercial rate	1000 cf	10.82	11/00	88s
Gasoline, all types	gal	1.80	7/01	11r
Gasoline, unleaded midgrade	gal	1.85	7/01	11r
Gasoline, unleaded premium	gal	1.91	7/01	11r
Gasoline, unleaded regular	gal	1.71	7/01	11r
Natural gas, expenditures on	yr	368	1999	30r
Utility (piped) gas, therm		1.08	7/01	11r
Utility (piped) gas, 40 therms		50.87	7/01	11r
Utility (piped) gas, 100 therms		111.06	7/01	11r
Entertainment				
Entertainment purchases	yr	1821	1999	30r
Fees and admissions paid	yr	511	1999	30r
Television, radios, sound equipment, expenditures on	yr	650	1999	30r
Funerals				
Total cost of funeral		5776.91	1/99	78r
Acknowledgement cards		14.47	1/99	78r
Casket		2090.19	1/99	78r
Cosmetology, hair, other preparation		132.92	1/99	78r
Embalming		377.33	1/99	78r
Funeral at funeral home		352.43	1/99	78r
Hearse (local)		185.55	1/99	78r
Professional service charges		1289.95	1/99	78r
Service car/van		87.42	1/99	78r
Transfer of remains to funeral home		175.48	1/99	78r
Vault		729.40	1/99	78r
Visitation/viewing		341.76	1/99	78r

Values are in dollars or fractions of dollars. In the column headed *Ref*, references are shown to sources. Each reference is followed by a letter. These refer to the geographical level for which data were reported: s=State, r=Region, and c=City or metro. The abbreviation *ex* is used to mean *except* or *excluding*; *exp* stands for *expenditures*. For other abbreviations and further explanations, please see the Introduction.

Brockton, MA - continued

Item	Per	Value	Date	Ref.
Groceries				
Apples, red delicious	lb	0.95	7/01	11r
Bacon, sliced	lb	3.44	7/01	11r
Bakery products, expenditures on	yr	310	1999	30r
Bananas	lb	0.55	7/01	11r
Beef, expenditures on	yr	236	1999	30r
Bread, white, pan	lb	1.09	7/01	11r
Butter, yoghurt, cheese, etc, expenditures on	yr	214	1999	30r
Cereals and bakery product purchases	yr	474	1999	30r
Cereals and cereal products, expenditures on	yr	164	1999	30r
Chicken legs, bone-in	lb	1.23	7/01	11r
Chicken, fresh, whole	lb	1.13	7/01	11r
Chuck roast, U.S. choice, boneless	lb	2.79	7/01	11r
Coffee, 100%, ground roast, all sizes	lb	3.40	7/01	11r
Dairy product purchases	yr	342	1999	30r
Eggs, expenditures on	yr	34	1999	30r
Eggs, grade A, large	dozen	0.82	7/01	11r
Fats and oils, expenditures on	yr	80	1999	30r
Fish and seafood, expenditures on	yr	123	1999	30r
Food (excl fruit and vegetables), eaten at home, purchases	yr	838	1999	30r
Food cooked on trips, expenditures on	yr	48	1999	30r
Food purchases	yr	5314	1999	30r
Food purchases, eaten away from home	yr	2313	1999	30r
Food purchases, food eaten at home	yr	3001	1999	30r
Fresh fruits, expenditures on	yr	169	1999	30r
Fresh milk and cream, expenditures on	yr	128	1999	30r
Fresh vegetables, expenditures on	yr	164	1999	30r
Grapefruit	lb	0.67	7/01	11r
Grapes, Thompson, seedless	lb	2.18	7/01	11r
Ground beef, lean and extra lean	lb	2.66	7/01	11r
Ground chuck, 100% beef	lb	2.04	7/01	11r
Lettuce, iceberg	lb	0.76	7/01	11r
Meats, poultry, fish, and egg purchases	yr	808	1999	30r
Nonalcoholic beverages, expenditures on	yr	225	1999	30r
Orange juice, frozen concentrate	16 oz	1.88	7/01	11r
Oranges, Navel	lb	0.79	7/01	11r
Oranges, Valencia	lb	0.56	7/01	11r
Peaches	lb	1.16	7/01	11r
Peanut butter, creamy, all sizes	lb	2.01	7/01	11r
Pears, Anjou	lb	1.16	7/01	11r
Pork chops, center cut, bone-in	lb	3.57	7/01	11r
Pork, expenditures on	yr	146	1999	30r
Potato chips	16 oz	3.37	7/01	11r
Potatoes, white, all types	lb	0.42	7/01	11r
Poultry, expenditures on	yr	158	1999	30r
Processed fruits, expenditures on	yr	124	1999	30r
Processed vegetables, expenditures on	yr	82	1999	30r
Round roast, U.S. choice, boneless	lb	3.04	7/01	11r
Spaghetti and macaroni	lb	1.04	7/01	11r
Steak, sirloin, U.S. choice, boneless	lb	5.39	7/01	11r
Strawberries, dry pint	12 oz	1.51	7/01	11r
Sugar and other sweets, expenditures on	yr	110	1999	30r
Sugar, white, 33-80 ounce package	lb	0.46	7/01	11r
Sugar, white, all sizes	lb	0.47	7/01	11r
Tobacco products and smoking supplies purchases	yr	309	1999	30r
Yogurt, natural, fruit flavored	8 oz	0.79	7/01	11r
Goods and Services				
B&B Japanese maple (acer japonicum)	gal	38.99-125.00	4/00	93r
Boxwood (buxus)	2 gal	15.99-49.95	4/00	93r
Daylilly (hemerocallis)	gal	4.95	4/00	93r
Flat of annuals		8.00-14.99	4/00	93r
Fountain grass (pennisetum)	gal	6.99-9.99	4/00	93r
Hanging basket (10 in)		12.95-19.99	4/00	93r
Hardy geranium (geranium)	gal	6.95-7.99	4/00	93r

Brockton, MA - continued

Item	Per	Value	Date	Ref.
Goods and Services - continued				
Hosta (hosta)	gal	4.95	4/00	93r
Lilac (syrubga vulgaris)	2 gal	17.99-74.95	4/00	93r
Miscellaneous purchases	yr	872	1999	30r
Rhododendron (rhododendron)	2 gal	23.99-54.95	4/00	93r
Sage (salvia)	gal	6.95-7.99	4/00	93r
Wintercreeper euonymus (euonymus fortunei)	2 gal	14.99-23.95	4/00	93r
Hunting license	yr	27.50	4/01	34s
Health Care				
Cardiac catheterization, ave hospital/physician charges		17080	1998	77s
Childbirth, Cesarean delivery		14716	1997	13r
Childbirth, vaginal delivery		8541	1997	13r
Drugs, expenditures on	yr	296	1999	30r
Health care purchases	yr	1788	1999	30r
Health insurance expenditures	yr	875	1999	30r
Hysterectomy, laproscopically-assisted, ave hospital/physician charges		13100	1998	76s
Hysterectomy, vaginal, ave hospital and physician charges		8780	1998	76s
Medicaid dispensing fee		3.00	1999	87s
Medical services expenditures	yr	516	1999	30r
Medical supplies, expenditures on	yr	102	1999	30r
Plastic surgery, breast augmentation		4232	2000	7r
Plastic surgery, breast lift		4605	2000	7r
Plastic surgery, facelift		6964	2000	7r
Plastic surgery, hair transplantation		4193	2000	7r
Plastic surgery, lip augmentation		1675	2000	7r
Plastic surgery, lower body lift		6611	2000	7r
Plastic surgery, thigh lift		4751	2000	7r
Household Goods				
Floor coverings, expenditures on	yr	59	1999	30r
Furniture, expenditures on	yr	388	1999	30r
Household furnishings and equipment purchases	yr	1567	1999	30r
Household textiles, expenditures on	yr	112	1999	30r
Laundry and cleaning supplies, expenditures on	yr	104	1999	30r
Housing				
Home price, existing, ave		180800	10/00	90r
Home value, median		261000	2001	53s
Household operation expenditures	yr	581	1999	30r
Housekeeping supplies purchases	yr	474	1999	30r
Lodging expenditures	yr	550	1999	30r
Maintenance, repairs, insurance expenditures	yr	835	1999	30r
Monthly rental value of owned home	mos	663	1999	30r
Owned dwellings, expenditures own	yr	5209	1999	30r
Rent expenditures	yr	2390	1999	30r
Rental unit, 1 bedroom, with utilities	mos	611	4/01	41c
Rental unit, 2 bedroom, with utilities	mos	750	4/01	41c
Rental unit, 3 bedroom, with utilities	mos	932	4/01	41c
Rental unit, 4 bedroom, with utilities	mos	1063	4/01	41c
Shelter, expenditures on	yr	8149	1999	30r
Insurance and Pensions				
Life and other personal insurance purchases	yr	424	1999	30r
Pensions and Social Security, expenditures on	yr	3037	1999	30r
Legal Fees				
Divorce, filing fee		100.00	4/01	35s
Driver's license fee	renew	33.75	1999	48s
Driver's license fee	orig	33.75	1999	48s
Fishing license	yr	27.50	4/01	34s
Personal Goods				
Personal care products and services purchases	yr	399	1999	30r

Values are in dollars or fractions of dollars. In the column headed *Ref*, references are shown to sources. Each reference is followed by a letter. These refer to the geographical level for which data were reported: s=State, r=Region, and c=City or metro. The abbreviation *ex* is used to mean *except* or *excluding*; *exp* stands for *expenditures*. For other abbreviations and further explanations, please see the Introduction.

Brockton, MA - continued

Item	Per	Value	Date	Ref.
Personal Services				
Personal services, household, expenditures on	yr	271	1999	30r
Pets				
Pets, toys, and playground equipment, expenditures on	yr	325	1999	30r
Taxes				
Federal income taxes paid	yr	2606	1999	30r
Personal taxes, expenditures on	yr	3567	1999	30r
Property taxes paid	yr	1752	1999	30r
State and local income taxes paid	yr	694	1999	30r
Transportation				
Cars and trucks, new, expenditures on	yr	1496	1999	30r
Cars and trucks, used, expenditures on	yr	1251	1999	30r
Diesel at the pump	gal	1.32	10/99	73s
Gasoline and motor oil purchases	yr	901	1999	30r
Gasoline before-tax price (cents)	gal	118.70	10/00	43s
Maintenance and repair expenditures	yr	618	1999	30r
Public transportation, expenditures on	yr	575	1999	30r
Transportation purchases	yr	6503	1999	30r
Vehicle expenses, miscellaneous, purchases	yr	2266	1999	30r
Vehicle insurance payments	yr	824	1999	30r
Vehicle purchases (net outlay)	yr	2761	1999	30r
Vehicle rental, lease expenditures	yr	584	1999	30r
Travel				
Hotel room	night	111.15	2/01	95s
Utilities				
Electrical bill, average	mos	58.58	9/00	9s
Electricity, expenditures on	yr	837	1999	30r
Electricity, summer, 250 KWh	mos	28.35	2/96	97c
Electricity, summer, 500 KWh	mos	55.06	2/96	97c
Electricity, summer, 750 KWh	mos	81.76	2/96	97c
Electricity, summer, 1000 KWh	mos	108.46	2/96	97c
Electricity cost, average	KWh	8.90	9/00	9s
Utilities, fuels, and public services purchased	yr	2457	1999	30r
Water and other public services, expenditures on	yr	215	1999	30r
Weddings				
Wedding (national average cost)		19936	2000	33r
Wedding (regional average total cost)		29454	1997	110r
Attendants' gifts		321	1998	33r
Bridal attendants' apparel (5 persons)		824	2000	33r
Bride's headpiece/veil		173	1998	33r
Bride's wedding dress		859	1998	33r
Clergy, religious facility fee		242	1998	33r
Engagement ring		3177	1998	33r
Flowers		789	1998	33r
Groom's formalwear rental		99	2000	33r
Limousine		410	1998	33r
Marriage license cost		25.00	4/01	35s
Men's formalwear (ushers, best man)		469	2000	33r
Mother of bride apparel		241	2000	33r
Music		866	1998	33r
Photography and videography		1368	1998	33r
Rehearsal dinner		728	1998	33r
Wedding invitations and announcements		341	1998	33r
Wedding reception		7968	2000	33r
Wedding rings (bride and groom)		1060	1998	33r

Brownsville-Harlingen-San Benito, TX

Item	Per	Value	Date	Ref.
Alcoholic Beverages				
Alcoholic beverage purchases	yr	253	1999	30r
Malt beverages, all types, all sizes, any origin	16 oz	0.96	7/01	11r
Appliances				
Major appliances, expenditures on	yr	172	1999	30r
Small appliances, housewares, expenditures on	yr	81	1999	30r

Brownsville-Harlingen-San Benito, TX - continued

Item	Per	Value	Date	Ref.
Banking and Money				
Mortgage interest and charges paid	yr	2039	1999	30r
Mortgage principal paid on owned property	yr	1026	1999	30r
Vehicle finance charges paid	yr	365	1999	30r
Charity				
Cash contributions, expenditures	yr	1127	1999	30r
Child Care				
Child raising cost, total, age 0-2	yr	8540	1999	60r
Child raising cost, total, age 3-5	yr	8780	1999	60r
Child raising cost, total, age 6-8	yr	8820	1999	60r
Child raising cost, total, age 9-11	yr	8800	1999	60r
Child raising cost, total, age 12-14	yr	9510	1999	60r
Child raising cost, total, age 15-17	yr	9740	1999	60r
Child's child care and education, age 0-2	yr	1380	1999	60r
Child's child care and education, age 3-5	yr	1520	1999	60r
Child's child care and education, age 6-8	yr	990	1999	60r
Child's child care and education, age 9-11	yr	650	1999	60r
Child's child care and education, age 12-14	yr	490	1999	60r
Child's child care and education, age 15-17	yr	840	1999	60r
Child's clothing, age 0-2	yr	480	1999	60r
Child's clothing, age 3-5	yr	470	1999	60r
Child's clothing, age 6-8	yr	520	1999	60r
Child's clothing, age 9-11	yr	570	1999	60r
Child's clothing, age 12-14	yr	950	1999	60r
Child's clothing, age 15-17	yr	850	1999	60r
Child's food, age 0-2	yr	1000	1999	60r
Child's food, age 3-5	yr	1160	1999	60r
Child's food, age 6-8	yr	1490	1999	60r
Child's food, age 9-11	yr	1770	1999	60r
Child's food, age 12-14	yr	1770	1999	60r
Child's food, age 15-17	yr	1980	1999	60r
Child's health care, age 0-2	yr	620	1999	60r
Child's health care, age 3-5	yr	590	1999	60r
Child's health care, age 6-8	yr	680	1999	60r
Child's health care, age 9-11	yr	720	1999	60r
Child's health care, age 12-14	yr	730	1999	60r
Child's health care, age 15-17	yr	760	1999	60r
Child's housing, age 0-2	yr	3070	1999	60r
Child's housing, age 3-5	yr	3050	1999	60r
Child's housing, age 6-8	yr	3010	1999	60r
Child's housing, age 9-11	yr	2850	1999	60r
Child's housing, age 12-14	yr	3040	1999	60r
Child's housing, age 15-17	yr	2650	1999	60r
Child's personal care, reading, age 0-2	yr	910	1999	60r
Child's personal care, reading, age 3-5	yr	930	1999	60r
Child's personal care, reading, age 6-8	yr	960	1999	60r
Child's personal care, reading, age 9-11	yr	1000	1999	60r
Child's personal care, reading, age 12-14	yr	1170	1999	60r
Child's personal care, reading, age 15-17	yr	950	1999	60r
Clothing				
Apparel and services purchases	yr	1610	1999	30r
Boys, 2 to 15, expenditures on	yr	89	1999	30r
Children under 2, expenditures on	yr	79	1999	30r
Footwear, expenditures on	yr	283	1999	30r
Girls, 2 to 15, expenditures on	yr	103	1999	30r
Men and boys, expenditures on	yr	351	1999	30r
Men, 16 and over, expenditures on	yr	262	1999	30r
Women, 16 and over, expenditures on	yr	538	1999	30r
Communications				
Cable modem installation, AT&T-BIS		150.00	6/99	103s
Cable modem installation, Marcus		499.00	6/99	103s
Cable modem installation, Time Warner		75.00-225.00	6/99	103s
Cable modem rate, cable subscriber, AT&T-BIS	mos	39.95	6/99	103s
Cable modem rate, cable subscriber, Marcus	mos	14.95-49.95	6/99	103s
Cable modem rate, cable subscriber, Time Warner	mos	39.95-49.95	6/99	103s
Cable modem rate, non-cable subscriber, Marcus	mos	60.95	6/99	103s

Values are in dollars or fractions of dollars. In the column headed *Ref*, references are shown to sources. Each reference is followed by a letter. These refer to the geographical level for which data were reported: s=State, r=Region, and c=City or metro. The abbreviation *ex* is used to mean *except* or *excluding*; *exp* stands for *expenditures*. For other abbreviations and further explanations, please see the Introduction.

Brownsville-Harlingen-San Benito, TX - continued

Item	Per	Value	Date	Ref.
Communications				
Cable modem rate, non-cable subscriber, Time Warner	mos	39.95–	6/99	103s
		54.95		
Phone line, single, business, field visit	inst.	71.90	12/97	17s
Phone line, single, business, no field visit	inst.	57.30	12/97	17s
Phone line, single, residence, field visit	inst.	52.95	12/97	17s
Phone line, single, residence, no field visit	inst.	38.35	12/97	17s
Postage and stationery, expenditures on	yr	104	1999	30r
Postal rate, express mail, up to half-pound		12.45	7/01	108r
Postal rate, letter, first class, first ounce		0.34	7/01	108r
Postal rate, letter, two ounces		0.57	7/01	108r
Postal rate, post card		0.21	7/01	108r
Postal rate, priority mail, two pounds		3.95	7/01	108r
Postal rate, priority mail, up to one pound		3.50	7/01	108r
Telephone services, expenditures on	yr	860	1999	30r
Education				
Board, 4-year private college/university	yr	2198	1996	38s
Board, 4-year public college/university	yr	1759	1996	38s
Education expenditures	yr	431	1999	30r
Room, 4-year private college/university	yr	2000	1996	38s
Room, 4-year public college/university	yr	1885	1996	38s
Total cost, 4-year private college/university	yr	13156	1996	38s
Total cost, 4-year public college/university	yr	5464	1996	38s
Tuition, 2-year public college/university, in state	yr	771	1996	38s
Tuition, 4-year private college/university, in state	yr	8959	1996	38s
Tuition, 4-year public college/university	yr	1820	1996	38s
Energy and Fuels				
Electricity	KWh	0.09	7/01	11r
Electricity	500 KWhs	47.29	7/01	11r
Fuel oil #2	gal	1.43	7/01	11r
Fuel oil and other fuels, expenditures on	yr	45	1999	30r
Gas, natural, commercial rate	1000 cf	6.94	11/00	88s
Gasoline, all types	gal	1.60	7/01	11r
Gasoline, unleaded midgrade	gal	1.65	7/01	11r
Gasoline, unleaded premium	gal	1.74	7/01	11r
Natural gas, expenditures on	yr	164	1999	30r
Utility (piped) gas, therm		1.01	7/01	11r
Utility (piped) gas, 40 therms		44.29	7/01	11r
Utility (piped) gas, 100 therms		97.44	7/01	11r
Entertainment				
Entertainment purchases	yr	1574	1999	30r
Fees and admissions paid	yr	371	1999	30r
Reading purchases	yr	121	1999	30r
Television, radios, sound equipment, expenditures on	yr	561	1999	30r
Funerals				
Total cost of funeral		5842.28	1/99	78r
Acknowledgement cards		28.35	1/99	78r
Casket		2494.29	1/99	78r
Cosmetology, hair, other preparation		109.22	1/99	78r
Embalming		361.42	1/99	78r
Funeral at funeral home		349.20	1/99	78r
Hearse (local)		161.91	1/99	78r
Professional service charges		1116.50	1/99	78r
Service car/van		65.56	1/99	78r
Transfer of remains to funeral home		143.56	1/99	78r
Vault		785.25	1/99	78r
Visitation/viewing		227.02	1/99	78r
Groceries				
American processed cheese	lb	3.50	7/01	11r
Bakery products, expenditures on	yr	261	1999	30r
Bananas	lb	0.47	7/01	11r
Beans, dried, any type, all sizes	lb	0.63	7/01	11r
Beef for stew, boneless	lb	2.86	7/01	11r
Beef, expenditures on	yr	210	1999	30r
Bologna, all beef or mixed	lb	2.29	7/01	11r
Bread, French	lb	1.66	7/01	11r

Brownsville-Harlingen-San Benito, TX - continued

Item	Per	Value	Date	Ref.
Groceries - continued				
Bread, white, pan	lb	0.87	7/01	11r
Bread, whole wheat, pan	lb	1.38	7/01	11r
Broccoli	lb	1.04	7/01	11r
Butter, salted, grade AA, stick	lb	2.26	7/01	11r
Butter, yoghurt, cheese, etc, expenditures on	yr	170	1999	30r
Cabbage	lb	0.42	7/01	11r
Cereals and cereal products, expenditures on	yr	140	1999	30r
Cheddar cheese, natural	lb	3.75	7/01	11r
Chicken breast, bone-in	lb	1.85	7/01	11r
Chicken legs, bone-in	lb	1.34	7/01	11r
Chicken, fresh, whole	lb	1.05	7/01	11r
Chops, boneless,	lb	4.13	7/01	11r
Chuck roast, graded and ungraded, excl U.S. prime and choice	lb	2.35	7/01	11r
Chuck roast, U.S. choice, boneless	lb	2.67	7/01	11r
Coffee, 100%, ground roast, all sizes	lb	2.88	7/01	11r
Coffee, instant, plain, regular, all sizes	16 oz	9.25	7/01	11r
Cola, non diet,	2 liter	1.11	7/01	11r
Crackers, soda, salted	lb	1.70	7/01	11r
Dairy product purchases	yr	282	1999	30r
Eggs, expenditures on	yr	32	1999	30r
Fats and oils, expenditures on	yr	79	1999	30r
Fish and seafood, expenditures on	yr	99	1999	30r
Flour, white, all purpose	lb	0.32	7/01	11r
Food (excl fruit and vegetables), eaten at home, purchases	yr	815	1999	30r
Food cooked on trips, expenditures on	yr	36	1999	30r
Food purchases	yr	4533	1999	30r
Food purchases, eaten away from home	yr	1873	1999	30r
Food purchases, food eaten at home	yr	2660	1999	30r
Fresh fruits, expenditures on	yr	128	1999	30r
Fresh milk and cream, expenditures on	yr	112	1999	30r
Fresh vegetables, expenditures on	yr	131	1999	30r
Fruit and vegetable purchases	yr	438	1999	30r
Grapefruit	lb	0.59	7/01	11r
Grapes, Thompson, seedless	lb	2.12	7/01	11r
Ground beef, 100% beef	lb	1.76	7/01	11r
Ground beef, lean and extra lean	lb	2.60	7/01	11r
Ground chuck, 100% beef	lb	2.08	7/01	11r
Ham, boneless, excl canned	lb	2.71	7/01	11r
Ham, rump or shank half, bone-in, smoked	lb	2.19	7/01	11r
Ice cream, prepackaged, bulk, regular	1/2 gal	3.93	7/01	11r
Lemons	lb	1.32	7/01	11r
Lettuce, iceberg	lb	0.76	7/01	11r
Milk, fresh, low fat,	gal	2.75	7/01	11r
Milk, fresh, whole, fortified	gal	2.97	7/01	11r
Nonalcoholic beverages, expenditures on	yr	228	1999	30r
Orange juice, frozen concentrate	16 oz	1.95	7/01	11r
Oranges, Navel	lb	0.73	7/01	11r
Oranges, Valencia	lb	0.55	7/01	11r
Peanut butter, creamy, all sizes	lb	1.83	7/01	11r
Pears, Anjou	lb	0.98	7/01	11r
Pork chops, center cut, bone-in	lb	3.33	7/01	11r
Pork sausage, fresh, loose	lb	2.59	7/01	11r
Pork shoulder picnic, bone-in, smoked	lb	1.12	7/01	11r
Pork, expenditures on	yr	162	1999	30r
Potato chips	16 oz	3.59	7/01	11r
Potatoes, frozen, french fried	lb	1.00	7/01	11r
Potatoes, white, all types	lb	0.44	7/01	11r
Poultry, expenditures on	yr	137	1999	30r
Processed fruits, expenditures on	yr	97	1999	30r
Processed vegetables, expenditures on	yr	82	1999	30r
Rice, white, long grain, uncooked	lb	0.51	7/01	11r
Round roast, graded and ungraded, excl U.S. prime and choice	lb	2.96	7/01	11r
Round steak, graded and ungraded, excl U.S. prime and choice	lb	3.11	7/01	11r
Sirloin steak, graded and ungraded, excl U.S. prime and choice	lb	4.23	7/01	11r
Spaghetti and macaroni	lb	0.78	7/01	11r
Steak, round, U.S. choice, boneless	lb	3.56	7/01	11r

Values are in dollars or fractions of dollars. In the column headed *Ref*, references are shown to sources. Each reference is followed by a letter. These refer to the geographical level for which data were reported: s=State, r=Region, and c=City or metro. The abbreviation *ex* is used to mean *except* or *excluding*; *exp* stands for *expenditures*. For other abbreviations and further explanations, please see the Introduction.

Brownsville-Harlingen-San Benito, TX - continued

Item	Per	Value	Date	Ref.
Groceries				
Steak, sirloin, U.S. choice, boneless	lb	5.65	7/01	11r
Strawberries, dry pint	12 oz	1.50	7/01	11r
Sugar and other sweets, expenditures on	yr	99	1999	30r
Sugar, white, 33-80 ounce package	lb	0.39	7/01	11r
Sugar, white, all sizes	lb	0.42	7/01	11r
Tobacco products and smoking supplies purchases	yr	288	1999	30r
Tomatoes, field grown	lb	1.43	7/01	11r
Tuna, light, chunk	lb	1.77	7/01	11r
Turkey, frozen, whole	lb	1.05	7/01	11r
Goods and Services				
B&B Japanese maple (acer japonicum)	gal	79.98-99.00	4/00	93r
Boxwood (buxus)	2 gal	12.98-18.99	4/00	93r
Christmas tree, noble fir		40-60	2000	65s
Daylilly (hemerocallis)	gal	7.96-11.00	4/00	93r
Flat of annuals		13.99-27.99	4/00	93r
Fountain grass (pennisetum)	gal	6.96-9.00	4/00	93r
Hanging basket (10 in)		9.99-24.99	4/00	93r
Hardy geranium (geranium)	gal	5.96-8.00	4/00	93r
Hosta (hosta)	gal	8.96-12.99	4/00	93r
Lilac (syrubga vulgaris)	2 gal	13.00-19.99	4/00	93r
Rhododendron (rhododendron)	2 gal	12.98-29.99	4/00	93r
Sage (salvia)	gal	5.96-8.00	4/00	93r
Wintercreeper euonymus (euonymus fortunei)	2 gal	13.00-18.99	4/00	93r
Hunting license	yr	19.00	4/01	34s
Health Care				
Cardiac catheterization, ave hospital/ physician charges		20140	1998	77s
Childbirth, Cesarean delivery		11587	1997	13r
Childbirth, vaginal delivery		6725	1997	13r
Drugs, expenditures on	yr	399	1999	30r
Health care purchases	yr	1971	1999	30r
Health insurance expenditures	yr	933	1999	30r
Hysterectomy, laproscopically-assisted, ave hospital/physician charges		15700	1998	76s
Hysterectomy, vaginal, ave hospital and physician charges		12180	1998	76s
Medicaid dispensing fee		5.27	1999	87s
Medical services expenditures	yr	547	1999	30r
Medical supplies, expenditures on	yr	91	1999	30r
Household Goods				
Floor coverings, expenditures on	yr	44	1999	30r
Furniture, expenditures on	yr	335	1999	30r
Household furnishings and equipment purchases	yr	1328	1999	30r
Household textiles, expenditures on	yr	89	1999	30r
Laundry and cleaning supplies, expenditures on	yr	113	1999	30r
Housing				
Home price, existing, ave		160100	10/00	90r
Home value, median		112000	2001	53s
Household operation expenditures	yr	553	1999	30r
Housekeeping supplies purchases	yr	473	1999	30r
Housing, expenditures on	yr	10303	1999	30r
Maintenance, repairs, insurance expenditures	yr	699	1999	30r
Monthly rental value of owned home	mos	505	1999	30r
Owned dwellings, expenditures own	yr	3465	1999	30r

Brownsville-Harlingen-San Benito, TX - continued

Item	Per	Value	Date	Ref.
Housing - continued				
Rent expenditures	yr	1641	1999	30r
Rental unit, 1 bedroom, with utilities	mos	378	4/01	41c
Rental unit, 2 bedroom, with utilities	mos	472	4/01	41c
Rental unit, 3 bedroom, with utilities	mos	591	4/01	41c
Rental unit, 4 bedroom, with utilities	mos	738	4/01	41c
Shelter, expenditures on	yr	5467	1999	30r
Insurance and Pensions				
Life and other personal insurance purchases	yr	414	1999	30r
Pensions and Social Security, expenditures on	yr	2635	1999	30r
Personal insurance and pensions, expenditures on	yr	3048	1999	30r
Legal Fees				
Divorce, filing fee		150.00-200.00	4/01	35s
Driver's license fee	orig	24.00	1999	48s
Driver's license fee	renew	20.00	1999	48s
Fishing license	yr	19.00	4/01	34s
Personal Goods				
Personal care products and services purchases	yr	393	1999	30r
Personal Services				
Personal services, household, expenditures on	yr	258	1999	30r
Pets				
Pets, toys, and playground equipment, expenditures on	yr	306	1999	30r
Taxes				
Federal income taxes paid	yr	2047	1999	30r
Personal taxes, expenditures on	yr	2554	1999	30r
Property taxes paid	yr	726	1999	30r
State and local income taxes paid	yr	363	1999	30r
Transportation				
Cars and trucks, new, expenditures on	yr	1648	1999	30r
Cars and trucks, used, expenditures on	yr	1651	1999	30r
Diesel at the pump	gal	1.18	10/99	73s
Gasoline and motor oil purchases	yr	1052	1999	30r
Gasoline before-tax price (cents)	gal	101.30	10/00	43s
Maintenance and repair expenditures	yr	621	1999	30r
Public transportation, expenditures on	yr	298	1999	30r
Transportation purchases	yr	6738	1999	30r
Vehicle expenses, miscellaneous, purchases	yr	2033	1999	30r
Vehicle insurance payments	yr	696	1999	30r
Vehicle purchases (net outlay)	yr	3354	1999	30r
Vehicle rental, lease expenditures	yr	352	1999	30r
Utilities				
Electrical bill, average	mos	87.17	9/00	9s
Electricity, expenditures on	yr	1115	1999	30r
Electricity cost, average	KWh	6.48	9/00	9s
Water and other public services, expenditures on	yr	298	1999	30r
Weddings				
Wedding (national average cost)		19936	2000	33r
Attendants' gifts		321	1998	33r
Bridal attendants' apparel (5 persons)		824	2000	33r
Bride's headpiece/veil		173	1998	33r
Bride's wedding dress		859	1998	33r
Clergy, religious facility fee		242	1998	33r
Engagement ring		3177	1998	33r
Flowers		789	1998	33r
Groom's formalwear rental		99	2000	33r
Limousine		410	1998	33r
Marriage license cost		36.00	4/01	35s
Men's formalwear (ushers, best man)		469	2000	33r
Mother of bride apparel		241	2000	33r
Music		866	1998	33r
Photography and videography		1368	1998	33r

Values are in dollars or fractions of dollars. In the column headed *Ref*, references are shown to sources. Each reference is followed by a letter. These refer to the geographical level for which data were reported: s=State, r=Region, and c=City or metro. The abbreviation *ex* is used to mean *except* or *excluding*; *exp* stands for expenditures. For other abbreviations and further explanations, please see the Introduction.

Brownsville-Harlingen-San Benito, TX - continued

Item	Per	Value	Date	Ref.
Weddings				
Rehearsal dinner		728	1998	33r
Wedding invitations and announcements		341	1998	33r
Wedding reception		7968	2000	33r
Wedding rings (bride and groom)		1060	1998	33r

Bryan-College Station, TX

Item	Per	Value	Date	Ref.
Composite, ACCRA index		86.90	3/01	4c
Alcoholic Beverages				
Alcoholic beverage purchases	yr	253	1999	30r
Beer, Heineken, 12-oz, ex deposit	6	6.75	3/01	4c
J & B Scotch	750-ml	20.29	3/01	4c
Malt beverages, all types, all sizes, any origin	16 oz	0.96	7/01	11r
Wine, Livingston or Gallo, Chablis blanc	1.5 liter	5.03	3/01	4c
Appliances				
Appliance repair, service call, washing machine	min lab chg	41.83	3/01	4c
Major appliances, expenditures on	yr	172	1999	30r
Small appliances, housewares, expenditures on	yr	81	1999	30r
Banking and Money				
Mortgage interest and charges paid	yr	2039	1999	30r
Mortgage principal paid on owned property	yr	1026	1999	30r
Mortgage rate, incl. points and orig. fee, 30-yr. conv. fixed or ARM	mos	6.93	3/01	4c
Vehicle finance charges paid	yr	365	1999	30r
Charity				
Cash contributions, expenditures	yr	1127	1999	30r
Child Care				
Child raising cost, total, age 0-2	yr	8540	1999	60r
Child raising cost, total, age 3-5	yr	8780	1999	60r
Child raising cost, total, age 6-8	yr	8820	1999	60r
Child raising cost, total, age 9-11	yr	8800	1999	60r
Child raising cost, total, age 12-14	yr	9510	1999	60r
Child raising cost, total, age 15-17	yr	9740	1999	60r
Child's child care and education, age 0-2	yr	1380	1999	60r
Child's child care and education, age 3-5	yr	1520	1999	60r
Child's child care and education, age 6-8	yr	990	1999	60r
Child's child care and education, age 9-11	yr	650	1999	60r
Child's child care and education, age 12-14	yr	490	1999	60r
Child's child care and education, age 15-17	yr	840	1999	60r
Child's clothing, age 0-2	yr	480	1999	60r
Child's clothing, age 3-5	yr	470	1999	60r
Child's clothing, age 6-8	yr	520	1999	60r
Child's clothing, age 9-11	yr	570	1999	60r
Child's clothing, age 12-14	yr	950	1999	60r
Child's clothing, age 15-17	yr	850	1999	60r
Child's food, age 0-2	yr	1000	1999	60r
Child's food, age 3-5	yr	1160	1999	60r
Child's food, age 6-8	yr	1490	1999	60r
Child's food, age 9-11	yr	1770	1999	60r
Child's food, age 12-14	yr	1770	1999	60r
Child's food, age 15-17	yr	1980	1999	60r
Child's health care, age 0-2	yr	620	1999	60r
Child's health care, age 3-5	yr	590	1999	60r
Child's health care, age 6-8	yr	680	1999	60r
Child's health care, age 9-11	yr	720	1999	60r
Child's health care, age 12-14	yr	730	1999	60r
Child's health care, age 15-17	yr	760	1999	60r
Child's housing, age 0-2	yr	3070	1999	60r
Child's housing, age 3-5	yr	3050	1999	60r
Child's housing, age 6-8	yr	3010	1999	60r
Child's housing, age 9-11	yr	2850	1999	60r
Child's housing, age 12-14	yr	3040	1999	60r
Child's housing, age 15-17	yr	2650	1999	60r
Child's personal care, reading, age 0-2	yr	910	1999	60r
Child's personal care, reading, age 3-5	yr	930	1999	60r
Child's personal care, reading, age 6-8	yr	960	1999	60r
Child's personal care, reading, age 9-11	yr	1000	1999	60r

Bryan-College Station, TX - continued

Item	Per	Value	Date	Ref.
Child Care - continued				
Child's personal care, reading, age 12-14	yr	1170	1999	60r
Child's personal care, reading, age 15-17	yr	950	1999	60r
Clothing				
Apparel and services purchases	yr	1610	1999	30r
Boys' brief, cotton	3	3.41	3/01	4c
Boys, 2 to 15, expenditures on	yr	89	1999	30r
Children under 2, expenditures on	yr	79	1999	30r
Footwear, expenditures on	yr	283	1999	30r
Girls, 2 to 15, expenditures on	yr	103	1999	30r
Men and boys, expenditures on	yr	351	1999	30r
Men, 16 and over, expenditures on	yr	262	1999	30r
Shirt, man's dress shirt		28.00	3/01	4c
Slacks, man's "No Wrinkles" khaki		29.99	3/01	4c
Women, 16 and over, expenditures on	yr	538	1999	30r
Communications				
Cable modem installation, AT&T-BIS		150.00	6/99	103s
Cable modem installation, Marcus		499.00	6/99	103s
Cable modem installation, Time Warner		75.00-225.00	6/99	103s
Cable modem rate, cable subscriber, AT&T-BIS	mos	39.95	6/99	103s
Cable modem rate, cable subscriber, Marcus	mos	14.95-49.95	6/99	103s
Cable modem rate, cable subscriber, Time Warner	mos	39.95-49.95	6/99	103s
Cable modem rate, non-cable subscriber, Marcus	mos	60.95	6/99	103s
Cable modem rate, non-cable subscriber, Time Warner	mos	39.95-54.95	6/99	103s
Newspaper subscription, daily and Sunday delivery	mos	9.72	3/01	4c
Phone line, single, business, field visit	inst.	71.90	12/97	17s
Phone line, single, business, no field visit	inst.	57.30	12/97	17s
Phone line, single, residence, field visit	inst.	52.95	12/97	17s
Phone line, single, residence, no field visit	inst.	38.35	12/97	17s
Postage and stationery, expenditures on	yr	104	1999	30r
Postal rate, express mail, up to half-pound		12.45	7/01	108r
Postal rate, letter, first class, first ounce		0.34	7/01	108r
Postal rate, letter, two ounces		0.57	7/01	108r
Postal rate, post card		0.21	7/01	108r
Postal rate, priority mail, two pounds		3.95	7/01	108r
Postal rate, priority mail, up to one pound		3.50	7/01	108r
Telephone bill, family of three	mos	20.09	3/01	4c
Telephone services, expenditures on	yr	860	1999	30r
Education				
Board, 4-year private college/university	yr	2198	1996	38s
Board, 4-year public college/university	yr	1759	1996	38s
Education expenditures	yr	431	1999	30r
Room, 4-year private college/university	yr	2000	1996	38s
Room, 4-year public college/university	yr	1885	1996	38s
Total cost, 4-year private college/university	yr	13156	1996	38s
Total cost, 4-year public college/university	yr	5464	1996	38s
Tuition, 2-year public college/university, in state	yr	771	1996	38s
Tuition, 4-year private college/university, in state	yr	8959	1996	38s
Tuition, 4-year public college/university	yr	1820	1996	38s
Energy and Fuels				
Electricity	KWh	0.09	7/01	11r
Electricity	500 KWhs	47.29	7/01	11r
Energy, combined forms, 2400 sq ft	mos	105.55	3/01	4c
Energy, exc. electricity, 2400 sq ft	mos	23.48	3/01	4c
Fuel oil #2	gal	1.43	7/01	11r
Fuel oil and other fuels, expenditures on	yr	45	1999	30r
Gas, natural, commercial rate	1000 cf	6.94	11/00	88s
Gas, regular unleaded, cash, self-service	gal	1.28	3/01	4c
Gasoline, all types	gal	1.60	7/01	11r
Gasoline, unleaded midgrade	gal	1.65	7/01	11r
Gasoline, unleaded premium	gal	1.74	7/01	11r

Values are in dollars or fractions of dollars. In the column headed *Ref*, references are shown to sources. Each reference is followed by a letter. These refer to the geographical level for which data were reported: s=State, r=Region, and c=City or metro. The abbreviation *ex* is used to mean *except* or *excluding*; *exp* stands for *expenditures*. For other abbreviations and further explanations, please see the Introduction.

Bryan-College Station, TX - continued

Item	Per	Value	Date	Ref.
Energy and Fuels				
Natural gas, expenditures on	yr	164	1999	30r
Utility (piped) gas, therm		1.01	7/01	11r
Utility (piped) gas, 40 therms		44.29	7/01	11r
Utility (piped) gas, 100 therms		97.44	7/01	11r
Entertainment				
Bowling, Saturday evening rate	line	3.00	3/01	4c
Entertainment purchases	yr	1574	1999	30r
Fees and admissions paid	yr	371	1999	30r
Monopoly game, Parker Brothers', No. 9	game	9.57	3/01	4c
Movie, first-run, Saturday, evening	adm.	6.13	3/01	4c
Reading purchases	yr	121	1999	30r
Television, radios, sound equipment, expenditures on	yr	561	1999	30r
Tennis balls, yellow, Wilson or Penn, 3	can	2.09	3/01	4c
Funerals				
Total cost of funeral		5842.28	1/99	78r
Acknowledgement cards		28.35	1/99	78r
Casket		2494.29	1/99	78r
Cosmetology, hair, other preparation		109.22	1/99	78r
Embalming		361.42	1/99	78r
Funeral at funeral home		349.20	1/99	78r
Hearse (local)		161.91	1/99	78r
Professional service charges		1116.50	1/99	78r
Service car/van		65.56	1/99	78r
Transfer of remains to funeral home		143.56	1/99	78r
Vault		785.25	1/99	78r
Visitation/viewing		227.02	1/99	78r
Groceries				
Groceries, ACCRA Index		83.70	3/01	4c
American processed cheese	lb	3.50	7/01	11r
Antibiotic ointment, Polysporin	0.5 oz	4.47	3/01	4c
Baby food, strained vegetables or fruit, lowest price	4-4.5 oz	0.28	3/01	4c
Bakery products, expenditures on	yr	261	1999	30r
Bananas	lb	0.40	3/01	4c
Bananas	lb	0.47	7/01	11r
Beans, dried, any type, all sizes	lb	0.63	7/01	11r
Beef for stew, boneless	lb	2.86	7/01	11r
Beef or hamburger, ground	lb	1.12	3/01	4c
Beef, expenditures on	yr	210	1999	30r
Bologna, all beef or mixed	lb	2.29	7/01	11r
Bread, French	lb	1.66	7/01	11r
Bread, white	loaf	0.68	3/01	4c
Bread, white, pan	lb	0.87	7/01	11r
Bread, whole wheat, pan	lb	1.38	7/01	11r
Broccoli	lb	1.04	7/01	11r
Butter, salted, grade AA, stick	lb	2.26	7/01	11r
Butter, yoghurt, cheese, etc, expenditures on	yr	170	1999	30r
Cabbage	lb	0.42	7/01	11r
Cereals and cereal products, expenditures on	yr	140	1999	30r
Cheddar cheese, natural	lb	3.75	7/01	11r
Cheese, Kraft grated Parmesan	8 oz	3.57	3/01	4c
Chicken breast, bone-in	lb	1.85	7/01	11r
Chicken legs, bone-in	lb	1.34	7/01	11r
Chicken, fresh, whole	lb	1.05	7/01	11r
Chicken, whole fryer	lb	0.70	3/01	4c
Chops, boneless,	lb	4.13	7/01	11r
Chuck roast, graded and ungraded, excl U.S. prime and choice	lb	2.35	7/01	11r
Chuck roast, U.S. choice, boneless	lb	2.67	7/01	11r
Cigarettes, Winston, Kings	carton	31.09	3/01	4c
Coffee, 100%, ground roast, all sizes	lb	2.88	7/01	11r
Coffee, instant, plain, regular, all sizes	16 oz	9.25	7/01	11r
Coffee, vacuum-packed	13 oz	2.13	3/01	4c
Cola, non diet,	2 liter	1.11	7/01	11r
Corn Flakes, Kellogg's or Post Toasties	18 oz	1.83	3/01	4c
Corn, frozen, whole kernel, lowest price	16 oz	1.12	3/01	4c
Crackers, soda, salted	lb	1.70	7/01	11r
Dairy product purchases	yr	282	1999	30r
Eggs, expenditures on	yr	32	1999	30r

Bryan-College Station, TX - continued

Item	Per	Value	Date	Ref.
Groceries - continued				
Eggs, Grade A or AA	dozen	1.15	3/01	4c
Fats and oils, expenditures on	yr	79	1999	30r
Fish and seafood, expenditures on	yr	99	1999	30r
Flour, white, all purpose	lb	0.32	7/01	11r
Food (excl fruit and vegetables), eaten at home, purchases	yr	815	1999	30r
Food cooked on trips, expenditures on	yr	36	1999	30r
Food purchases	yr	4533	1999	30r
Food purchases, eaten away from home	yr	1873	1999	30r
Food purchases, food eaten at home	yr	2660	1999	30r
Fresh fruits, expenditures on	yr	128	1999	30r
Fresh milk and cream, expenditures on	yr	112	1999	30r
Fresh vegetables, expenditures on	yr	131	1999	30r
Fruit and vegetable purchases	yr	438	1999	30r
Grapefruit	lb	0.59	7/01	11r
Grapes, Thompson, seedless	lb	2.12	7/01	11r
Ground beef, 100% beef	lb	1.76	7/01	11r
Ground beef, lean and extra lean	lb	2.60	7/01	11r
Ground chuck, 100% beef	lb	2.08	7/01	11r
Ham, boneless, excl canned	lb	2.71	7/01	11r
Ham, rump or shank half, bone-in, smoked	lb	2.19	7/01	11r
Ice cream, prepackaged, bulk, regular	1/2 gal	3.93	7/01	11r
Lemons	lb	1.32	7/01	11r
Lettuce, iceberg	head	1.00	3/01	4c
Lettuce, iceberg	lb	0.76	7/01	11r
Margarine, Blue Bonnet or Parkay, stick	lb	0.65	3/01	4c
Milk, fresh, low fat,	gal	2.75	7/01	11r
Milk, fresh, whole, fortified	gal	2.97	7/01	11r
Milk, whole	1/2 gal	1.66	3/01	4c
Nonalcoholic beverages, expenditures on	yr	228	1999	30r
Orange juice, frozen concentrate	16 oz	1.95	7/01	11r
Orange juice, Minute Maid frozen	12 oz	1.57	3/01	4c
Oranges, Navel	lb	0.73	7/01	11r
Oranges, Valencia	lb	0.55	7/01	11r
Peaches, halves or slices, Hunt's, Del Monte, or Libby's	29 oz	1.48	3/01	4c
Peanut butter, creamy, all sizes	lb	1.83	7/01	11r
Pears, Anjou	lb	0.98	7/01	11r
Peas, green, Del Monte or Green Giant	15 oz	0.58	3/01	4c
Pork chops, center cut, bone-in	lb	3.33	7/01	11r
Pork sausage, fresh, loose	lb	2.59	7/01	11r
Pork shoulder picnic, bone-in, smoked	lb	1.12	7/01	11r
Pork, expenditures on	yr	162	1999	30r
Potato chips	16 oz	3.59	7/01	11r
Potatoes, frozen, french fried	lb	1.00	7/01	11r
Potatoes, white or red	10 lb	2.31	3/01	4c
Potatoes, white, all types	lb	0.44	7/01	11r
Poultry, expenditures on	yr	137	1999	30r
Processed fruits, expenditures on	yr	97	1999	30r
Processed vegetables, expenditures on	yr	82	1999	30r
Rice, white, long grain, uncooked	lb	0.51	7/01	11r
Round roast, graded and ungraded, excl U.S. prime and choice	lb	2.96	7/01	11r
Round steak, graded and ungraded, excl U.S. prime and choice	lb	3.11	7/01	11r
Sausage, Jimmy Dean/Owens pork	lb	2.35	3/01	4c
Shortening, vegetable, Crisco	3 lb	2.72	3/01	4c
Sirloin steak, graded and ungraded, excl U.S. prime and choice	lb	4.23	7/01	11r
Soft drink, Coca Cola, ex deposit	2 liter	1.00	3/01	4c
Spaghetti and macaroni	lb	0.78	7/01	11r
Steak, round, U.S. choice, boneless	lb	3.56	7/01	11r
Steak, sirloin, U.S. choice, boneless	lb	5.65	7/01	11r
Steak, T-bone	lb	5.85	3/01	4c
Strawberries, dry pint	12 oz	1.50	7/01	11r
Sugar and other sweets, expenditures on	yr	99	1999	30r
Sugar, cane or beet	4 lbs	1.45	3/01	4c
Sugar, white, 33-80 ounce package	lb	0.39	7/01	11r
Sugar, white, all sizes	lb	0.42	7/01	11r
Tobacco products and smoking supplies purchases	yr	288	1999	30r
Tomatoes, field grown	lb	1.43	7/01	11r

Values are in dollars or fractions of dollars. In the column headed *Ref*, references are shown to sources. Each reference is followed by a letter. These refer to the geographical level for which data were reported: s=State, r=Region, and c=City or metro. The abbreviation *ex* is used to mean *except* or *excluding*; *exp* stands for expenditures. For other abbreviations and further explanations, please see the Introduction.

Bryan-College Station, TX - continued

Item	Per	Value	Date	Ref.
Groceries				
Tomatoes, Hunt's or Del Monte	14.5 oz	0.75	3/01	4c
Tuna, chunk, light	6 oz	0.43	3/01	4c
Tuna, light, chunk	lb	1.77	7/01	11r
Turkey, frozen, whole	lb	1.05	7/01	11r
Goods and Services				
Miscellaneous goods and services, ACCRA Index		91.50	3/01	4c
B&B Japanese maple (acer japonicum)	gal	79.98-99.00	4/00	93r
Boxwood (buxus)	2 gal	12.98-18.99	4/00	93r
Christmas tree, noble fir		40-60	2000	65s
Daylilly (hemerocallis)	gal	7.96-11.00	4/00	93r
Flat of annuals		13.99-27.99	4/00	93r
Fountain grass (pennisetum)	gal	6.96-9.00	4/00	93r
Hanging basket (10 in)		9.99-24.99	4/00	93r
Hardy geranium (geranium)	gal	5.96-8.00	4/00	93r
Hosta (hosta)	gal	8.96-12.99	4/00	93r
Lilac (syrubga vulgaris)	2 gal	13.00-19.99	4/00	93r
Rhododendron (rhododendron)	2 gal	12.98-29.99	4/00	93r
Sage (salvia)	gal	5.96-8.00	4/00	93r
Wintercreeper euonymus (euonymus fortunei)	2 gal	13.00-18.99	4/00	93r
Hunting license	yr	19.00	4/01	34s
Health Care				
Health care, ACCRA Index		92.60	3/01	4c
Cardiac catheterization, ave hospital/physician charges		20140	1998	77s
Childbirth, Cesarean delivery		11587	1997	13r
Childbirth, vaginal delivery		6725	1997	13r
Dentist's fee, adult teeth cleaning and periodic oral exam	visit	62.00	3/01	4c
Doctor's fee, routine exam, established patient	visit	59.20	3/01	4c
Drugs, expenditures on	yr	399	1999	30r
Health care purchases	yr	1971	1999	30r
Health insurance expenditures	yr	933	1999	30r
Hospital care, private room	day	450.00	3/01	4c
Hysterectomy, laproscopically-assisted, ave hospital/physician charges		15700	1998	76s
Hysterectomy, vaginal, ave hospital and physician charges		12180	1998	76s
Medicaid dispensing fee		5.27	1999	87s
Medical services expenditures	yr	547	1999	30r
Medical supplies, expenditures on	yr	91	1999	30r
Household Goods				
Dishwashing powder, Cascade	50 oz	3.16	3/01	4c
Floor coverings, expenditures on	yr	44	1999	30r
Furniture, expenditures on	yr	335	1999	30r
Household furnishings and equipment purchases	yr	1328	1999	30r
Household textiles, expenditures on	yr	89	1999	30r
Laundry and cleaning supplies, expenditures on	yr	113	1999	30r
Tissues, facial, Kleenex brand	175	1.17	3/01	4c
Housing				
Housing, ACCRA Index		80.40	3/01	4c
Home, 2200 sq ft, 4-br, 2-bath, 2-car garage, average		144200	2000	47c
Home price, existing, ave		160100	10/00	90r
Home value, median		112000	2001	53s

Bryan-College Station, TX - continued

Item	Per	Value	Date	Ref.
Housing - continued				
House, 2400 sq ft, 8000 sq ft lot, new, urban, utilities	total	168471	3/01	4c
House payment, principal and interest, 25% down payment	mos	834	3/01	4c
Household operation expenditures	yr	553	1999	30r
Housekeeping supplies purchases	yr	473	1999	30r
Housing, expenditures on	yr	10303	1999	30r
Maintenance, repairs, insurance expenditures	yr	699	1999	30r
Monthly rental value of owned home	mos	505	1999	30r
Owned dwellings, expenditures own	yr	3465	1999	30r
Rent expenditures	yr	1641	1999	30r
Rent, apartment, 2 br, 1 1/2-2 baths, unfurn, 950 sq ft, water	mos	545	3/01	4c
Rental unit, 1 bedroom, with utilities	mos	443	4/01	41c
Rental unit, 2 bedroom, with utilities	mos	560	4/01	41c
Rental unit, 3 bedroom, with utilities	mos	781	4/01	41c
Rental unit, 4 bedroom, with utilities	mos	921	4/01	41c
Shelter, expenditures on	yr	5467	1999	30r
Insurance and Pensions				
Life and other personal insurance purchases	yr	414	1999	30r
Pensions and Social Security, expenditures on	yr	2635	1999	30r
Personal insurance and pensions, expenditures on	yr	3048	1999	30r
Legal Fees				
Divorce, filing fee		150.00-200.00	4/01	35s
Driver's license fee	orig	24.00	1999	48s
Driver's license fee	renew	20.00	1999	48s
Fishing license	yr	19.00	4/01	34s
Personal Goods				
Personal care products and services purchases	yr	393	1999	30r
Shampoo, Alberto VO5	15 oz	0.86	3/01	4c
Toothpaste, Crest or Colgate	6-7 oz	2.36	3/01	4c
Personal Services				
Dry cleaning, man's 2-pc suit		6.36	3/01	4c
Man's haircut, barbershop, no styling		8.80	3/01	4c
Personal services, household, expenditures on	yr	258	1999	30r
Woman's shampoo, trim, blow-dry, no style-change		25.00	3/01	4c
Pets				
Pets, toys, and playground equipment, expenditures on	yr	306	1999	30r
Restaurant Food				
Chicken, fried, thigh and drumstick, KFC/Church's		2.30	3/01	4c
Hamburger with cheese, McDonald's	1/4 lb	1.99	3/01	4c
Pizza, Pizza Hut or Pizza Inn	11-12 in	8.99	3/01	4c
Taxes				
Federal income taxes paid	yr	2047	1999	30r
Personal taxes, expenditures on	yr	2554	1999	30r
Property taxes paid	yr	726	1999	30r
State and local income taxes paid	yr	363	1999	30r
Transportation				
Transportation, ACCRA Index		92.00	3/01	4c
Cars and trucks, new, expenditures on	yr	1648	1999	30r
Cars and trucks, used, expenditures on	yr	1651	1999	30r
Diesel at the pump	gal	1.18	10/99	73s
Gasoline and motor oil purchases	yr	1052	1999	30r
Gasoline before-tax price (cents)	gal	101.30	10/00	43s
Maintenance and repair expenditures	yr	621	1999	30r
Public transportation, expenditures on	yr	298	1999	30r
Tire balance, computer or spin balance, front	wheel	7.40	3/01	4c
Transportation purchases	yr	6738	1999	30r
Vehicle expenses, miscellaneous, purchases	yr	2033	1999	30r

Values are in dollars or fractions of dollars. In the column headed *Ref*, references are shown to sources. Each reference is followed by a letter. These refer to the geographical level for which data were reported: s=State, r=Region, and c=City or metro. The abbreviation *ex* is used to mean *except* or *excluding*; *exp* stands for expenditures. For other abbreviations and further explanations, please see the Introduction.

Bryan-College Station, TX - continued

Item	Per	Value	Date	Ref.
Transportation				
Vehicle insurance payments	yr	696	1999	30r
Vehicle purchases (net outlay)	yr	3354	1999	30r
Vehicle rental, lease expenditures	yr	352	1999	30r
Utilities				
Utilities, ACCRA Index		87.30	3/01	4c
Electrical bill, average	mos	87.17	9/00	9s
Electricity, expenditures on	yr	1115	1999	30r
Electricity and other, mixed, 2400 sq ft, new home	mos	82.07	3/01	4c
Electricity cost, average	KWh	6.48	9/00	9s
Water and other public services, expenditures on	yr	298	1999	30r
Weddings				
Wedding (national average cost)		19936	2000	33r
Attendants' gifts		321	1998	33r
Bridal attendants' apparel (5 persons)		824	2000	33r
Bride's headpiece/veil		173	1998	33r
Bride's wedding dress		859	1998	33r
Clergy, religious facility fee		242	1998	33r
Engagement ring		3177	1998	33r
Flowers		789	1998	33r
Groom's formalwear rental		99	2000	33r
Limousine		410	1998	33r
Marriage license cost		36.00	4/01	35s
Men's formalwear (ushers, best man)		469	2000	33r
Mother of bride apparel		241	2000	33r
Music		866	1998	33r
Photography and videography		1368	1998	33r
Rehearsal dinner		728	1998	33r
Wedding invitations and announcements		341	1998	33r
Wedding reception		7968	2000	33r
Wedding rings (bride and groom)		1060	1998	33r

Buffalo-Niagra Falls, NY

Item	Per	Value	Date	Ref.
Average annual expenditures	yr	37971	1999	30r
Alcoholic Beverages				
Alcoholic beverage purchases	yr	368	1999	30r
Wine, red and white table, all sizes, any origin	liter	9.64	7/01	11r
Appliances				
Major appliances, expenditures on	yr	194	1999	30r
Small appliances, housewares, expenditures on	yr	93	1999	30r
Banking and Money				
Mortgage interest and charges paid	yr	2622	1999	30r
Mortgage principal paid on owned property	yr	1262	1999	30r
Vehicle finance charges paid	yr	240	1999	30r
Charity				
Cash contributions, expenditures	yr	1001	1999	30r
Child Care				
Child raising cost, total, age 0-2	yr	8670	1999	60r
Child raising cost, total, age 3-5	yr	8910	1999	60r
Child raising cost, total, age 6-8	yr	9040	1999	60r
Child raising cost, total, age 9-11	yr	9100	1999	60r
Child raising cost, total, age 12-14	yr	9890	1999	60r
Child raising cost, total, age 15-17	yr	10010	1999	60r
Child's child care and education, age 0-2	yr	1070	1999	60r
Child's child care and education, age 3-5	yr	1190	1999	60r
Child's child care and education, age 6-8	yr	740	1999	60r
Child's child care and education, age 9-11	yr	470	1999	60r
Child's child care and education, age 12-14	yr	350	1999	60r
Child's child care and education, age 15-17	yr	590	1999	60r
Child's clothing, age 0-2	yr	480	1999	60r
Child's clothing, age 3-5	yr	470	1999	60r
Child's clothing, age 6-8	yr	520	1999	60r
Child's clothing, age 9-11	yr	570	1999	60r
Child's clothing, age 12-14	yr	970	1999	60r

Buffalo-Niagra Falls, NY - continued

Item	Per	Value	Date	Ref.
Child Care - continued				
Child's clothing, age 15-17	yr	870	1999	60r
Child's food, age 0-2	yr	1130	1999	60r
Child's food, age 3-5	yr	1290	1999	60r
Child's food, age 6-8	yr	1640	1999	60r
Child's food, age 9-11	yr	1930	1999	60r
Child's food, age 12-14	yr	1940	1999	60r
Child's food, age 15-17	yr	2150	1999	60r
Child's health care, age 0-2	yr	550	1999	60r
Child's health care, age 3-5	yr	530	1999	60r
Child's health care, age 6-8	yr	610	1999	60r
Child's health care, age 9-11	yr	650	1999	60r
Child's health care, age 12-14	yr	660	1999	60r
Child's health care, age 15-17	yr	690	1999	60r
Child's housing, age 0-2	yr	3555	1999	60r
Child's housing, age 3-5	yr	3530	1999	60r
Child's housing, age 6-8	yr	3490	1999	60r
Child's housing, age 9-11	yr	3340	1999	60r
Child's housing, age 12-14	yr	3530	1999	60r
Child's housing, age 15-17	yr	3140	1999	60r
Child's personal care, reading, age 0-2	yr	920	1999	60r
Child's personal care, reading, age 3-5	yr	950	1999	60r
Child's personal care, reading, age 6-8	yr	980	1999	60r
Child's personal care, reading, age 9-11	yr	1020	1999	60r
Child's personal care, reading, age 12-14	yr	1190	1999	60r
Child's personal care, reading, age 15-17	yr	970	1999	60r
Nannies: criminal background check		74	1998	84s
Clothing				
Apparel and services purchases	yr	1831	1999	30r
Boys, 2 to 15, expenditures on	yr	92	1999	30r
Children under 2, expenditures on	yr	63	1999	30r
Footwear, expenditures on	yr	300	1999	30r
Girls, 2 to 15, expenditures on	yr	101	1999	30r
Men and boys, expenditures on	yr	446	1999	30r
Men, 16 and over, expenditures on	yr	354	1999	30r
Women, 16 and over, expenditures on	yr	584	1999	30r
Communications				
Cable modem installation, Adelphi		54.90	6/99	103s
Cable modem installation, Cablevision Systems		150.00	6/99	103s
Cable modem installation, Time Warner		75.00-225.00	6/99	103s
Cable modem rate, cable subscriber, Adelphi	mos	34.95	6/99	103s
Cable modem rate, cable subscriber, Cablevision Systems	mos	44.95	6/99	103s
Cable modem rate, cable subscriber, Century	mos	39.95	6/99	103s
Cable modem rate, cable subscriber, Time Warner	mos	39.95-49.95	6/99	103s
Cable modem rate, non-cable subscriber, Adelphi	mos	44.95	6/99	103s
Cable modem rate, non-cable subscriber, Cablevision Systems	mos	54.95	6/99	103s
Cable modem rate, non-cable subscriber, Time Warner	mos	39.95-54.95	6/99	103s
Phone line, single, business, field visit	inst.	142.76	12/97	17s
Phone line, single, business, no field visit	inst.	106.05	12/97	17s
Phone line, single, residence, field visit	inst.	102.78	12/97	17s
Phone line, single, residence, no field visit	inst.	55.00	12/97	17s
Postage and stationery, expenditures on	yr	138	1999	30r
Postal rate, express mail, up to half-pound		12.45	7/01	108r
Postal rate, letter, first class, first ounce		0.34	7/01	108r
Postal rate, letter, two ounces		0.57	7/01	108r
Postal rate, post card		0.21	7/01	108r
Postal rate, priority mail, two pounds		3.95	7/01	108r
Postal rate, priority mail, up to one pound		3.50	7/01	108r
Telephone services, expenditures on	yr	830	1999	30r
Education				
Board, 4-year private college/university	yr	3255	1996	38s
Board, 4-year public college/university	yr	2310	1996	38s
Education expenditures	yr	877	1999	30r
Room, 4-year private college/university	yr	3724	1996	38s
Room, 4-year public college/university	yr	2937	1996	38s

Values are in dollars or fractions of dollars. In the column headed *Ref*, references are shown to sources. Each reference is followed by a letter. These refer to the geographical level for which data were reported: s=State, r=Region, and c=City or metro. The abbreviation *ex* is used to mean *except* or *excluding*; *exp* stands for *expenditures*. For other abbreviations and further explanations, please see the Introduction.

Buffalo-Niagra Falls, NY - continued

Item	Per	Value	Date	Ref.
Education				
Total cost, 4-year private college/university	yr	20831	1996	38s
Total cost, 4-year public college/university	yr	8960	1996	38s
Tuition, 2-year public college/university, in state	yr	2427	1996	38s
Tuition, 4-year private college/university, in state	yr	13852	1996	38s
Tuition, 4-year public college/university	yr	3714	1996	38s
Energy and Fuels				
Electricity	KWh	0.12	7/01	11r
Fuel oil #2	gal	1.31	7/01	11r
Fuel oil and other fuels, expenditures on	yr	207	1999	30r
Gasoline, all types	gal	1.80	7/01	11r
Gasoline, unleaded midgrade	gal	1.85	7/01	11r
Gasoline, unleaded premium	gal	1.91	7/01	11r
Gasoline, unleaded regular	gal	1.71	7/01	11r
Natural gas, expenditures on	yr	368	1999	30r
Utility (piped) gas, therm		1.08	7/01	11r
Utility (piped) gas, 40 therms		50.87	7/01	11r
Utility (piped) gas, 100 therms		111.06	7/01	11r
Entertainment				
Entertainment purchases	yr	1821	1999	30r
Fees and admissions paid	yr	511	1999	30r
Television, radios, sound equipment, expenditures on	yr	650	1999	30r
Funerals				
Total cost of funeral		5813.50	1/99	78r
Acknowledgement cards		28.32	1/99	78r
Casket		2082.20	1/99	78r
Cosmetology, hair, other preparation		169.59	1/99	78r
Embalming		465.60	1/99	78r
Funeral at funeral home		339.56	1/99	78r
Hearse (local)		183.96	1/99	78r
Professional service charges		1157.85	1/99	78r
Service car/van		100.41	1/99	78r
Transfer of remains to funeral home		158.66	1/99	78r
Vault		766.31	1/99	78r
Visitation/viewing		361.04	1/99	78r
Groceries				
Apples, red delicious	lb	0.95	7/01	11r
Bacon, sliced	lb	3.44	7/01	11r
Bakery products, expenditures on	yr	310	1999	30r
Bananas	lb	0.55	7/01	11r
Beef, expenditures on	yr	236	1999	30r
Bread, white, pan	lb	1.09	7/01	11r
Butter, yoghurt, cheese, etc, expenditures on	yr	214	1999	30r
Cereals and bakery product purchases	yr	474	1999	30r
Cereals and cereal products, expenditures on	yr	164	1999	30r
Chicken legs, bone-in	lb	1.23	7/01	11r
Chicken, fresh, whole	lb	1.13	7/01	11r
Chuck roast, U.S. choice, boneless	lb	2.79	7/01	11r
Coffee, 100%, ground roast, all sizes	lb	3.40	7/01	11r
Dairy product purchases	yr	342	1999	30r
Eggs, expenditures on	yr	34	1999	30r
Eggs, grade A, large	dozen	0.82	7/01	11r
Fats and oils, expenditures on	yr	80	1999	30r
Fish and seafood, expenditures on	yr	123	1999	30r
Food (excl fruit and vegetables), eaten at home, purchases	yr	838	1999	30r
Food cooked on trips, expenditures on	yr	48	1999	30r
Food purchases	yr	5314	1999	30r
Food purchases, eaten away from home	yr	2313	1999	30r
Food purchases, food eaten at home	yr	3001	1999	30r
Fresh fruits, expenditures on	yr	169	1999	30r
Fresh milk and cream, expenditures on	yr	128	1999	30r
Fresh vegetables, expenditures on	yr	164	1999	30r
Grapefruit	lb	0.67	7/01	11r
Grapes, Thompson, seedless	lb	2.18	7/01	11r
Ground beef, lean and extra lean	lb	2.66	7/01	11r
Ground chuck, 100% beef	lb	2.04	7/01	11r

Buffalo-Niagra Falls, NY - continued

Item	Per	Value	Date	Ref.
Groceries - continued				
Lettuce, iceberg	lb	0.76	7/01	11r
Meats, poultry, fish, and egg purchases	yr	808	1999	30r
Nonalcoholic beverages, expenditures on	yr	225	1999	30r
Orange juice, frozen concentrate	16 oz	1.88	7/01	11r
Oranges, Navel	lb	0.79	7/01	11r
Oranges, Valencia	lb	0.56	7/01	11r
Peaches	lb	1.16	7/01	11r
Peanut butter, creamy, all sizes	lb	2.01	7/01	11r
Pears, Anjou	lb	1.16	7/01	11r
Pork chops, center cut, bone-in	lb	3.57	7/01	11r
Pork, expenditures on	yr	146	1999	30r
Potato chips	16 oz	3.37	7/01	11r
Potatoes, white, all types	lb	0.42	7/01	11r
Poultry, expenditures on	yr	158	1999	30r
Processed fruits, expenditures on	yr	124	1999	30r
Processed vegetables, expenditures on	yr	82	1999	30r
Round roast, U.S. choice, boneless	lb	3.04	7/01	11r
Spaghetti and macaroni	lb	1.04	7/01	11r
Steak, sirloin, U.S. choice, boneless	lb	5.39	7/01	11r
Strawberries, dry pint	12 oz	1.51	7/01	11r
Sugar and other sweets, expenditures on	yr	110	1999	30r
Sugar, white, 33-80 ounce package	lb	0.46	7/01	11r
Sugar, white, all sizes	lb	0.47	7/01	11r
Tobacco products and smoking supplies purchases	yr	309	1999	30r
Yogurt, natural, fruit flavored	8 oz	0.79	7/01	11r
Goods and Services				
B&B Japanese maple (acer japonicum)	gal	38.99-125.00	4/00	93r
Boxwood (buxus)	2 gal	15.99-49.95	4/00	93r
Daylily (hemerocallis)	gal	4.95	4/00	93r
Flat of annuals		8.00-14.99	4/00	93r
Fountain grass (pennisetum)	gal	6.99-9.99	4/00	93r
Hanging basket (10 in)		12.95-19.99	4/00	93r
Hardy geranium (geranium)	gal	6.95-7.99	4/00	93r
Hosta (hosta)	gal	4.95	4/00	93r
Lilac (syrubga vulgaris)	2 gal	17.99-74.95	4/00	93r
Miscellaneous purchases	yr	872	1999	30r
Rhododendron (rhododendron)	2 gal	23.99-54.95	4/00	93r
Sage (salvia)	gal	6.95-7.99	4/00	93r
Wintercreeper euonymus (euonymus fortunei)	2 gal	14.99-23.95	4/00	93r
Hunting license	yr	11.00	4/01	34s
Health Care				
Cardiac catheterization, ave hospital/ physician charges		12750	1998	77s
Childbirth, Cesarean delivery		14716	1997	13r
Childbirth, vaginal delivery		8541	1997	13r
Drugs, expenditures on	yr	296	1999	30r
Health care purchases	yr	1788	1999	30r
Health insurance expenditures	yr	875	1999	30r
Hysterectomy, laproscopically-assisted, ave hospital/physician charges		13460	1998	76s
Hysterectomy, vaginal, ave hospital and physician charges		10310	1998	76s
Medicaid dispensing fee		3.50-4.50	1999	87s
Medical services expenditures	yr	516	1999	30r
Medical supplies, expenditures on	yr	102	1999	30r
Plastic surgery, breast augmentation		4232	2000	7r
Plastic surgery, breast lift		4605	2000	7r
Plastic surgery, facelift		6964	2000	7r
Plastic surgery, hair transplantation		4193	2000	7r

Values are in dollars or fractions of dollars. In the column headed *Ref*, references are shown to sources. Each reference is followed by a letter. These refer to the geographical level for which data were reported: s=State, r=Region, and c=City or metro. The abbreviation *ex* is used to mean *except* or *excluding*; *exp* stands for *expenditures*. For other abbreviations and further explanations, please see the Introduction.

Buffalo-Niagra Falls, NY - continued

Item	Per	Value	Date	Ref.
Health Care				
Plastic surgery, lip augmentation		1675	2000	7r
Plastic surgery, lower body lift		6611	2000	7r
Plastic surgery, thigh lift		4751	2000	7r
Household Goods				
Floor coverings, expenditures on	yr	59	1999	30r
Furniture, expenditures on	yr	388	1999	30r
Household furnishings and equipment purchases	yr	1567	1999	30r
Household textiles, expenditures on	yr	112	1999	30r
Laundry and cleaning supplies, expenditures on	yr	104	1999	30r
Housing				
Home price, existing, ave		180800	10/00	90r
Home value, median		179000	2001	53s
Household operation expenditures	yr	581	1999	30r
Housekeeping supplies purchases	yr	474	1999	30r
Lodging expenditures	yr	550	1999	30r
Maintenance, repairs, insurance expenditures	yr	835	1999	30r
Monthly rental value of owned home	mos	663	1999	30r
Owned dwellings, expenditures own	yr	5209	1999	30r
Rent expenditures	yr	2390	1999	30r
Rental unit, 1 bedroom, with utilities	mos	425	4/01	41c
Rental unit, 2 bedroom, with utilities	mos	513	4/01	41c
Rental unit, 3 bedroom, with utilities	mos	640	4/01	41c
Rental unit, 4 bedroom, with utilities	mos	718	4/01	41c
Shelter, expenditures on	yr	8149	1999	30r
Insurance and Pensions				
Auto insurance premium	yr	1113.55	1999	57s
Life and other personal insurance purchases	yr	424	1999	30r
Pensions and Social Security, expenditures on	yr	3037	1999	30r
Legal Fees				
Divorce, filing fee		270.00	4/01	35s
Driver's license fee	renew	25.00	1999	48s
Driver's license fee	orig	25.00	1999	48s
Fishing license	yr	14.00	4/01	34s
Personal Goods				
Personal care products and services purchases	yr	399	1999	30r
Personal Services				
Personal services, household, expenditures on	yr	271	1999	30r
Pets				
Pets, toys, and playground equipment, expenditures on	yr	325	1999	30r
Taxes				
Federal income taxes paid	yr	2606	1999	30r
Personal taxes, expenditures on	yr	3567	1999	30r
Property taxes paid	yr	1752	1999	30r
State and local income taxes paid	yr	694	1999	30r
Transportation				
Cars and trucks, new, expenditures on	yr	1496	1999	30r
Cars and trucks, used, expenditures on	yr	1251	1999	30r
Diesel at the pump	gal	1.33	10/99	73s
Gasoline and motor oil purchases	yr	901	1999	30r
Gasoline before-tax price (cents)	gal	110.70	10/00	43s
Maintenance and repair expenditures	yr	618	1999	30r
Public transportation, expenditures on	yr	575	1999	30r
Transportation purchases	yr	6503	1999	30r
Vehicle expenses, miscellaneous, purchases	yr	2266	1999	30r
Vehicle insurance payments	yr	824	1999	30r
Vehicle purchases (net outlay)	yr	2761	1999	30r
Vehicle rental, lease expenditures	yr	584	1999	30r
Travel				
Hotel room	night	139.88	2/01	95s

Buffalo-Niagra Falls, NY - continued

Item	Per	Value	Date	Ref.
Utilities				
Electrical bill, average	mos	71.50	9/00	9s
Electricity, expenditures on	yr	837	1999	30r
Electricity cost, average	KWh	11.34	9/00	9s
Utilities, fuels, and public services purchased	yr	2457	1999	30r
Water and other public services, expenditures on	yr	215	1999	30r
Weddings				
Wedding (national average cost)		19936	2000	33r
Wedding (regional average total cost)		29454	1997	110r
Attendants' gifts		321	1998	33r
Bridal attendants' apparel (5 persons)		824	2000	33r
Bride's headpiece/veil		173	1998	33r
Bride's wedding dress		859	1998	33r
Clergy, religious facility fee		242	1998	33r
Engagement ring		3177	1998	33r
Flowers		789	1998	33r
Groom's formalwear rental		99	2000	33r
Limousine		410	1998	33r
Marriage license cost		25.00	4/01	35s
Men's formalwear (ushers, best man)		469	2000	33r
Mother of bride apparel		241	2000	33r
Music		866	1998	33r
Photography and videography		1368	1998	33r
Rehearsal dinner		728	1998	33r
Wedding invitations and announcements		341	1998	33r
Wedding reception		7968	2000	33r
Wedding rings (bride and groom)		1060	1998	33r

Burlington, VT

Item	Per	Value	Date	Ref.
Average annual expenditures	yr	37971	1999	30r
Alcoholic Beverages				
Alcoholic beverage purchases	yr	368	1999	30r
Wine, red and white table, all sizes, any origin	liter	9.64	7/01	11r
Appliances				
Major appliances, expenditures on	yr	194	1999	30r
Small appliances, housewares, expenditures on	yr	93	1999	30r
Banking and Money				
Mortgage interest and charges paid	yr	2622	1999	30r
Mortgage principal paid on owned property	yr	1262	1999	30r
Vehicle finance charges paid	yr	240	1999	30r
Charity				
Cash contributions, expenditures	yr	1001	1999	30r
Child Care				
Child raising cost, total, age 0-2	yr	8670	1999	60r
Child raising cost, total, age 3-5	yr	8910	1999	60r
Child raising cost, total, age 6-8	yr	9040	1999	60r
Child raising cost, total, age 9-11	yr	9100	1999	60r
Child raising cost, total, age 12-14	yr	9890	1999	60r
Child raising cost, total, age 15-17	yr	10010	1999	60r
Child's child care and education, age 0-2	yr	1070	1999	60r
Child's child care and education, age 3-5	yr	1190	1999	60r
Child's child care and education, age 6-8	yr	740	1999	60r
Child's child care and education, age 9-11	yr	470	1999	60r
Child's child care and education, age 12-14	yr	350	1999	60r
Child's child care and education, age 15-17	yr	590	1999	60r
Child's clothing, age 0-2	yr	480	1999	60r
Child's clothing, age 3-5	yr	470	1999	60r
Child's clothing, age 6-8	yr	520	1999	60r
Child's clothing, age 9-11	yr	570	1999	60r
Child's clothing, age 12-14	yr	970	1999	60r
Child's clothing, age 15-17	yr	870	1999	60r
Child's food, age 0-2	yr	1130	1999	60r
Child's food, age 3-5	yr	1290	1999	60r
Child's food, age 6-8	yr	1640	1999	60r
Child's food, age 9-11	yr	1930	1999	60r

Values are in dollars or fractions of dollars. In the column headed *Ref*, references are shown to sources. Each reference is followed by a letter. These refer to the geographical level for which data were reported: s=State, r=Region, and c=City or metro. The abbreviation *ex* is used to mean *except* or *excluding*; *exp* stands for *expenditures*. For other abbreviations and further explanations, please see the Introduction.

Burlington, VT - continued

Item	Per	Value	Date	Ref.
Child Care				
Child's food, age 12-14	yr	1940	1999	60r
Child's food, age 15-17	yr	2150	1999	60r
Child's health care, age 0-2	yr	550	1999	60r
Child's health care, age 3-5	yr	530	1999	60r
Child's health care, age 6-8	yr	610	1999	60r
Child's health care, age 9-11	yr	650	1999	60r
Child's health care, age 12-14	yr	660	1999	60r
Child's health care, age 15-17	yr	690	1999	60r
Child's housing, age 0-2	yr	3555	1999	60r
Child's housing, age 3-5	yr	3530	1999	60r
Child's housing, age 6-8	yr	3490	1999	60r
Child's housing, age 9-11	yr	3340	1999	60r
Child's housing, age 12-14	yr	3530	1999	60r
Child's housing, age 15-17	yr	3140	1999	60r
Child's personal care, reading, age 0-2	yr	920	1999	60r
Child's personal care, reading, age 3-5	yr	950	1999	60r
Child's personal care, reading, age 6-8	yr	980	1999	60r
Child's personal care, reading, age 9-11	yr	1020	1999	60r
Child's personal care, reading, age 12-14	yr	1190	1999	60r
Child's personal care, reading, age 15-17	yr	970	1999	60r
Clothing				
Apparel and services purchases	yr	1831	1999	30r
Boys, 2 to 15, expenditures on	yr	92	1999	30r
Children under 2, expenditures on	yr	63	1999	30r
Footwear, expenditures on	yr	300	1999	30r
Girls, 2 to 15, expenditures on	yr	101	1999	30r
Men and boys, expenditures on	yr	446	1999	30r
Men, 16 and over, expenditures on	yr	354	1999	30r
Women, 16 and over, expenditures on	yr	584	1999	30r
Communications				
Cable modem installation, Adelphi		54.90	6/99	103s
Cable modem rate, cable subscriber, Adelphi	mos	34.95	6/99	103s
Cable modem rate, non-cable subscriber, Adelphi	mos	44.95	6/99	103s
Phone line, single, business, field visit	inst.	76.00	12/97	17s
Phone line, single, business, no field visit	inst.	46.00	12/97	17s
Phone line, single, residence, field visit	inst.	53.00	12/97	17s
Phone line, single, residence, no field visit	inst.	33.00	12/97	17s
Postage and stationery, expenditures on	yr	138	1999	30r
Postal rate, express mail, up to half-pound		12.45	7/01	108r
Postal rate, letter, first class, first ounce		0.34	7/01	108r
Postal rate, letter, two ounces		0.57	7/01	108r
Postal rate, post card		0.21	7/01	108r
Postal rate, priority mail, two pounds		3.95	7/01	108r
Postal rate, priority mail, up to one pound		3.50	7/01	108r
Telephone bill, business, basic rate	mos	43.05	12/97	18c
Telephone bill, residential, basic rate	mos	17.50	12/97	18c
Telephone services, expenditures on	yr	830	1999	30r
Education				
Board, 4-year private college/university	yr	2567	1996	38s
Board, 4-year public college/university	yr	1670	1996	38s
Education expenditures	yr	877	1999	30r
Room, 4-year private college/university	yr	3375	1996	38s
Room, 4-year public college/university	yr	3072	1996	38s
Total cost, 4-year private college/university	yr	21612	1996	38s
Total cost, 4-year public college/university	yr	10640	1996	38s
Tuition, 2-year public college/university, in state	yr	2370	1996	38s
Tuition, 4-year private college/university, in state	yr	15670	1996	38s
Tuition, 4-year public college/university	yr	5898	1996	38s
Energy and Fuels				
Electricity	KWh	0.12	7/01	11r
Fuel oil #2	gal	1.31	7/01	11r
Fuel oil and other fuels, expenditures on	yr	207	1999	30r
Gas, cooking, winter, 10 therms	mos	12.00	2/96	98c
Gas, cooking, winter, 30 therms	mos	23.12	2/96	98c
Gas, cooking, winter, 50 therms	mos	34.24	2/96	98c
Gas, heating, winter, average use	mos	108.73	2/96	98c
Gas, natural, commercial rate	1000 cf	7.20	11/00	88s

Burlington, VT - continued

Item	Per	Value	Date	Ref.
Energy and Fuels - continued				
Gasoline, all types	gal	1.80	7/01	11r
Gasoline, unleaded midgrade	gal	1.85	7/01	11r
Gasoline, unleaded premium	gal	1.91	7/01	11r
Gasoline, unleaded regular	gal	1.71	7/01	11r
Natural gas, expenditures on	yr	368	1999	30r
Utility (piped) gas, therm		1.08	7/01	11r
Utility (piped) gas, 40 therms		50.87	7/01	11r
Utility (piped) gas, 100 therms		111.06	7/01	11r
Entertainment				
Entertainment purchases	yr	1821	1999	30r
Fees and admissions paid	yr	511	1999	30r
Television, radios, sound equipment, expenditures on	yr	650	1999	30r
Funerals				
Total cost of funeral		5776.91	1/99	78r
Acknowledgement cards		14.47	1/99	78r
Casket		2090.19	1/99	78r
Cosmetology, hair, other preparation		132.92	1/99	78r
Embalming		377.33	1/99	78r
Funeral at funeral home		352.43	1/99	78r
Hearse (local)		185.55	1/99	78r
Professional service charges		1289.95	1/99	78r
Service car/van		87.42	1/99	78r
Transfer of remains to funeral home		175.48	1/99	78r
Vault		729.40	1/99	78r
Visitation/viewing		341.76	1/99	78r
Groceries				
Apples, red delicious	lb	0.95	7/01	11r
Bacon, sliced	lb	3.44	7/01	11r
Bakery products, expenditures on	yr	310	1999	30r
Bananas	lb	0.55	7/01	11r
Beef, expenditures on	yr	236	1999	30r
Bread, white, pan	lb	1.09	7/01	11r
Butter, yoghurt, cheese, etc, expenditures on	yr	214	1999	30r
Cereals and bakery product purchases	yr	474	1999	30r
Cereals and cereal products, expenditures on	yr	164	1999	30r
Chicken legs, bone-in	lb	1.23	7/01	11r
Chicken, fresh, whole	lb	1.13	7/01	11r
Chuck roast, U.S. choice, boneless	lb	2.79	7/01	11r
Coffee, 100%, ground roast, all sizes	lb	3.40	7/01	11r
Dairy product purchases	yr	342	1999	30r
Eggs, expenditures on	yr	34	1999	30r
Eggs, grade A, large	dozen	0.82	7/01	11r
Fats and oils, expenditures on	yr	80	1999	30r
Fish and seafood, expenditures on	yr	123	1999	30r
Food (excl fruit and vegetables), eaten at home, purchases	yr	838	1999	30r
Food cooked on trips, expenditures on	yr	48	1999	30r
Food purchases	yr	5314	1999	30r
Food purchases, eaten away from home	yr	2313	1999	30r
Food purchases, food eaten at home	yr	3001	1999	30r
Fresh fruits, expenditures on	yr	169	1999	30r
Fresh milk and cream, expenditures on	yr	128	1999	30r
Fresh vegetables, expenditures on	yr	164	1999	30r
Grapefruit	lb	0.67	7/01	11r
Grapes, Thompson, seedless	lb	2.18	7/01	11r
Ground beef, lean and extra lean	lb	2.66	7/01	11r
Ground chuck, 100% beef	lb	2.04	7/01	11r
Lettuce, iceberg	lb	0.76	7/01	11r
Meats, poultry, fish, and egg purchases	yr	808	1999	30r
Nonalcoholic beverages, expenditures on	yr	225	1999	30r
Orange juice, frozen concentrate	16 oz	1.88	7/01	11r
Oranges, Navel	lb	0.79	7/01	11r
Oranges, Valencia	lb	0.56	7/01	11r
Peaches	lb	1.16	7/01	11r
Peanut butter, creamy, all sizes	lb	2.01	7/01	11r
Pears, Anjou	lb	1.16	7/01	11r
Pork chops, center cut, bone-in	lb	3.57	7/01	11r
Pork, expenditures on	yr	146	1999	30r
Potato chips	16 oz	3.37	7/01	11r

Values are in dollars or fractions of dollars. In the column headed *Ref*, references are shown to sources. Each reference is followed by a letter. These refer to the geographical level for which data were reported: s=State, r=Region, and c=City or metro. The abbreviation *ex* is used to mean *except* or *excluding*; *exp* stands for *expenditures*. For other abbreviations and further explanations, please see the Introduction.

Burlington, VT - continued

Item	Per	Value	Date	Ref.
Groceries				
Potatoes, white, all types	lb	0.42	7/01	11r
Poultry, expenditures on	yr	158	1999	30r
Processed fruits, expenditures on	yr	124	1999	30r
Processed vegetables, expenditures on	yr	82	1999	30r
Round roast, U.S. choice, boneless	lb	3.04	7/01	11r
Spaghetti and macaroni	lb	1.04	7/01	11r
Steak, sirloin, U.S. choice, boneless	lb	5.39	7/01	11r
Strawberries, dry pint	12 oz	1.51	7/01	11r
Sugar and other sweets, expenditures on	yr	110	1999	30r
Sugar, white, 33-80 ounce package	lb	0.46	7/01	11r
Sugar, white, all sizes	lb	0.47	7/01	11r
Tobacco products and smoking supplies purchases	yr	309	1999	30r
Yogurt, natural, fruit flavored	8 oz	0.79	7/01	11r
Goods and Services				
B&B Japanese maple (acer japonicum)	gal	38.99-125.00	4/00	93r
Boxwood (buxus)	2 gal	15.99-49.95	4/00	93r
Daylilly (hemerocallis)	gal	4.95	4/00	93r
Flat of annuals		8.00-14.99	4/00	93r
Fountain grass (pennisetum)	gal	6.99-9.99	4/00	93r
Hanging basket (10 in)		12.95-19.99	4/00	93r
Hardy geranium (geranium)	gal	6.95-7.99	4/00	93r
Hosta (hosta)	gal	4.95	4/00	93r
Lilac (syrubga vulgaris)	2 gal	17.99-74.95	4/00	93r
Miscellaneous purchases	yr	872	1999	30r
Rhododendron (rhododendron)	2 gal	23.99-54.95	4/00	93r
Sage (salvia)	gal	6.95-7.99	4/00	93r
Wintercreeper euonymus (euonymus fortunei)	2 gal	14.99-23.95	4/00	93r
Hunting license	yr	14.00	4/01	34s
Health Care				
Cardiac catheterization, ave hospital/ physician charges		17090	1998	77s
Childbirth, Cesarean delivery		14716	1997	13r
Childbirth, vaginal delivery		8541	1997	13r
Drugs, expenditures on	yr	296	1999	30r
Health care purchases	yr	1788	1999	30r
Health insurance expenditures	yr	875	1999	30r
Hysterectomy, laproscopically-assisted, ave hospital/physician charges		11240	1998	76s
Hysterectomy, vaginal, ave hospital and physician charges		7480	1998	76s
Medicaid dispensing fee		4.25	1999	87s
Medical services expenditures	yr	516	1999	30r
Medical supplies, expenditures on	yr	102	1999	30r
Plastic surgery, breast augmentation		4232	2000	7r
Plastic surgery, breast lift		4605	2000	7r
Plastic surgery, facelift		6964	2000	7r
Plastic surgery, hair transplantation		4193	2000	7r
Plastic surgery, lip augmentation		1675	2000	7r
Plastic surgery, lower body lift		6611	2000	7r
Plastic surgery, thigh lift		4751	2000	7r
Household Goods				
Floor coverings, expenditures on	yr	59	1999	30r
Furniture, expenditures on	yr	388	1999	30r
Household furnishings and equipment purchases	yr	1567	1999	30r
Household textiles, expenditures on	yr	112	1999	30r
Laundry and cleaning supplies, expenditures on	yr	104	1999	30r

Burlington, VT - continued

Item	Per	Value	Date	Ref.
Housing				
Home, 2200 sq ft, 4-br, 2-bath, 2-car garage, average		226125	2000	47c
Home price, existing, ave		180800	10/00	90r
Home value, median		145000	2001	53s
Household operation expenditures	yr	581	1999	30r
Housekeeping supplies purchases	yr	474	1999	30r
Lodging expenditures	yr	550	1999	30r
Maintenance, repairs, insurance expenditures	yr	835	1999	30r
Monthly rental value of owned home	mos	663	1999	30r
Owned dwellings, expenditures own	yr	5209	1999	30r
Rent expenditures	yr	2390	1999	30r
Rental unit, 1 bedroom, with utilities	mos	529	4/01	41c
Rental unit, 2 bedroom, with utilities	mos	706	4/01	41c
Rental unit, 3 bedroom, with utilities	mos	962	4/01	41c
Rental unit, 4 bedroom, with utilities	mos	1161	4/01	41c
Shelter, expenditures on	yr	8149	1999	30r
Insurance and Pensions				
Auto insurance premium	yr	592.97	1999	57s
Life and other personal insurance purchases	yr	424	1999	30r
Pensions and Social Security, expenditures on	yr	3037	1999	30r
Legal Fees				
Combination hunting and fishing license	yr	26.00	4/01	34s
Divorce, filing fee		125.00	4/01	35s
Driver's license fee	orig	35.00	1999	48s
Driver's license fee	renew	20.00	1999	48s
Fishing license	yr	20.00	4/01	34s
Personal Goods				
Personal care products and services purchases	yr	399	1999	30r
Personal Services				
Personal services, household, expenditures on	yr	271	1999	30r
Pets				
Pets, toys, and playground equipment, expenditures on	yr	325	1999	30r
Taxes				
Federal income taxes paid	yr	2606	1999	30r
Personal taxes, expenditures on	yr	3567	1999	30r
Property taxes paid	yr	1752	1999	30r
State and local income taxes paid	yr	694	1999	30r
Transportation				
Auto operation, annual cost		6257	2000	27c
Bus fare, one-way	trip	1.00	2000	1c
Cars and trucks, new, expenditures on	yr	1496	1999	30r
Cars and trucks, used, expenditures on	yr	1251	1999	30r
Diesel at the pump	gal	1.26	10/99	73s
Gasoline and motor oil purchases	yr	901	1999	30r
Gasoline before-tax price (cents)	gal	117.50	10/00	43s
Maintenance and repair expenditures	yr	618	1999	30r
Public transportation, expenditures on	yr	575	1999	30r
Transportation purchases	yr	6503	1999	30r
Vehicle expenses, miscellaneous, purchases	yr	2266	1999	30r
Vehicle insurance payments	yr	824	1999	30r
Vehicle purchases (net outlay)	yr	2761	1999	30r
Vehicle rental, lease expenditures	yr	584	1999	30r
Utilities				
Electrical bill, average	mos	72.25	9/00	9s
Electricity, expenditures on	yr	837	1999	30r
Electricity, summer, 250 KWh	mos	31.94	2/96	96s
Electricity, summer, 500 KWh	mos	60.97	2/96	96s
Electricity, summer, 750 KWh	mos	90.46	2/96	96s
Electricity, summer, 1000 KWh	mos	119.95	2/96	96s
Electricity cost, average	KWh	10.30	9/00	9s
Utilities, fuels, and public services purchased	yr	2457	1999	30r
Water and other public services, expenditures on	yr	215	1999	30r

Values are in dollars or fractions of dollars. In the column headed *Ref*, references are shown to sources. Each reference is followed by a letter. These refer to the geographical level for which data were reported: s=State, r=Region, and c=City or metro. The abbreviation *ex* is used to mean *except* or *excluding*; *exp* stands for *expenditures*. For other abbreviations and further explanations, please see the Introduction.

Burlington, VT - continued

Item	Per	Value	Date	Ref.
Weddings				
Wedding (national average cost)		19936	2000	33r
Wedding (regional average total cost)		29454	1997	110r
Attendants' gifts		321	1998	33r
Bridal attendants' apparel (5 persons)		824	2000	33r
Bride's headpiece/veil		173	1998	33r
Bride's wedding dress		859	1998	33r
Clergy, religious facility fee		242	1998	33r
Engagement ring		3177	1998	33r
Flowers		789	1998	33r
Groom's formalwear rental		99	2000	33r
Limousine		410	1998	33r
Marriage license cost		20.00	4/01	35s
Men's formalwear (ushers, best man)		469	2000	33r
Mother of bride apparel		241	2000	33r
Music		866	1998	33r
Photography and videography		1368	1998	33r
Rehearsal dinner		728	1998	33r
Wedding invitations and announcements		341	1998	33r
Wedding reception		7968	2000	33r
Wedding rings (bride and groom)		1060	1998	33r

Canton-Massillon, OH

Item	Per	Value	Date	Ref.
Average annual expenditures	yr	35369	1999	30r
Alcoholic Beverages				
Alcoholic beverage purchases	yr	304	1999	30r
Malt beverages, all types, all sizes, any origin	16 oz	0.93	7/01	11r
Wine, red and white table, all sizes, any origin	liter	7.04	7/01	11r
Appliances				
Major appliances, expenditures on	yr	165	1999	30r
Small appliances, housewares, expenditures on	yr	90	1999	30r
Banking and Money				
Mortgage interest and charges paid	yr	2277	1999	30r
Mortgage principal paid on owned property	yr	1230	1999	30r
Vehicle finance charges paid	yr	328	1999	30r
Charity				
Cash contributions, expenditures	yr	1126	1999	30r
Child Care				
Child raising cost, total, age 0-2	yr	7890	1999	60r
Child raising cost, total, age 3-5	yr	8130	1999	60r
Child raising cost, total, age 6-8	yr	8170	1999	60r
Child raising cost, total, age 9-11	yr	8190	1999	60r
Child raising cost, total, age 12-14	yr	8890	1999	60r
Child raising cost, total, age 15-17	yr	9050	1999	60r
Child's child care and education, age 0-2	yr	1240	1999	60r
Child's child care and education, age 3-5	yr	1370	1999	60r
Child's child care and education, age 6-8	yr	880	1999	60r
Child's child care and education, age 9-11	yr	570	1999	60r
Child's child care and education, age 12-14	yr	420	1999	60r
Child's child care and education, age 15-17	yr	720	1999	60r
Child's clothing, age 0-2	yr	410	1999	60r
Child's clothing, age 3-5	yr	400	1999	60r
Child's clothing, age 6-8	yr	450	1999	60r
Child's clothing, age 9-11	yr	500	1999	60r
Child's clothing, age 12-14	yr	840	1999	60r
Child's clothing, age 15-17	yr	740	1999	60r
Child's food, age 0-2	yr	960	1999	60r
Child's food, age 3-5	yr	1120	1999	60r
Child's food, age 6-8	yr	1430	1999	60r
Child's food, age 9-11	yr	1710	1999	60r
Child's food, age 12-14	yr	1710	1999	60r
Child's food, age 15-17	yr	1920	1999	60r
Child's health care, age 0-2	yr	520	1999	60r
Child's health care, age 3-5	yr	500	1999	60r
Child's health care, age 6-8	yr	570	1999	60r
Child's health care, age 9-11	yr	610	1999	60r
Child's health care, age 12-14	yr	630	1999	60r

Canton-Massillon, OH - continued

Item	Per	Value	Date	Ref.
Child Care - continued				
Child's health care, age 15-17	yr	650	1999	60r
Child's housing, age 0-2	yr	2860	1999	60r
Child's housing, age 3-5	yr	2840	1999	60r
Child's housing, age 6-8	yr	2800	1999	60r
Child's housing, age 9-11	yr	2650	1999	60r
Child's housing, age 12-14	yr	2840	1999	60r
Child's housing, age 15-17	yr	2440	1999	60r
Child's personal care, reading, age 0-2	yr	880	1999	60r
Child's personal care, reading, age 3-5	yr	900	1999	60r
Child's personal care, reading, age 6-8	yr	930	1999	60r
Child's personal care, reading, age 9-11	yr	970	1999	60r
Child's personal care, reading, age 12-14	yr	1150	1999	60r
Child's personal care, reading, age 15-17	yr	920	1999	60r
Clothing				
Apparel and services purchases	yr	1607	1999	30r
Boys, 2 to 15, expenditures on	yr	91	1999	30r
Children under 2, expenditures on	yr	59	1999	30r
Footwear, expenditures on	yr	285	1999	30r
Girls, 2 to 15, expenditures on	yr	116	1999	30r
Men and boys, expenditures on	yr	433	1999	30r
Men, 16 and over, expenditures on	yr	341	1999	30r
Women, 16 and over, expenditures on	yr	490	1999	30r
Communications				
Cable modem installation, Adelphi		54.90	6/99	103s
Cable modem installation, Media One		100.00	6/99	103s
Cable modem installation, Time Warner		75.00-225.00	6/99	103s
Cable modem rate, cable subscriber, Adelphi	mos	34.95	6/99	103s
Cable modem rate, cable subscriber, Media One	mos	34.95-39.95	6/99	103s
Cable modem rate, cable subscriber, Time Warner	mos	39.95-49.95	6/99	103s
Cable modem rate, non-cable subscriber, Adelphi	mos	44.95	6/99	103s
Cable modem rate, non-cable subscriber, Media One	mos	49.95	6/99	103s
Cable modem rate, non-cable subscriber, Time Warner	mos	39.95-54.95	6/99	103s
Phone line, single, business, field visit	inst.	56.32	12/97	17s
Phone line, single, business, no field visit	inst.	56.32	12/97	17s
Phone line, single, residence, field visit	inst.	31.10	12/97	17s
Phone line, single, residence, no field visit	inst.	31.10	12/97	17s
Postage and stationery, expenditures on	yr	140	1999	30r
Postal rate, express mail, up to half-pound		12.45	7/01	108r
Postal rate, letter, first class, first ounce		0.34	7/01	108r
Postal rate, letter, two ounces		0.57	7/01	108r
Postal rate, post card		0.21	7/01	108r
Postal rate, priority mail, two pounds		3.95	7/01	108r
Postal rate, priority mail, up to one pound		3.50	7/01	108r
Telephone services, expenditures on	yr	830	1999	30r
Education				
Board, 4-year private college/university	yr	2414	1996	38s
Board, 4-year public college/university	yr	2181	1996	38s
Education expenditures	yr	583	1999	30r
Room, 4-year private college/university	yr	2349	1996	38s
Room, 4-year public college/university	yr	2386	1996	38s
Total cost, 4-year private college/university	yr	17139	1996	38s
Total cost, 4-year public college/university	yr	8169	1996	38s
Tuition, 2-year public college/university, in state	yr	2261	1996	38s
Tuition, 4-year private college/university, in state	yr	12377	1996	38s
Tuition, 4-year public college/university	yr	3603	1996	38s
Energy and Fuels				
Electricity	500 KWhs	46.59	7/01	11r
Fuel oil #2	gal	1.27	7/01	11r
Fuel oil and other fuels, expenditures on	yr	68	1999	30r
Gas, natural, commercial rate	1000 cf	8.65	11/00	88s
Gasoline, unleaded midgrade	gal	1.79	7/01	11r

Values are in dollars or fractions of dollars. In the column headed *Ref*, references are shown to sources. Each reference is followed by a letter. These refer to the geographical level for which data were reported: s=State, r=Region, and c=City or metro. The abbreviation *ex* is used to mean *except* or *excluding*; *exp* stands for *expenditures*. For other abbreviations and further explanations, please see the Introduction.

Canton-Massillon, OH - continued

Item	Per	Value	Date	Ref.
Energy and Fuels				
Gasoline, unleaded premium	gal	1.86	7/01	11r
Gasoline, unleaded regular	gal	1.58	7/01	11r
Natural gas, expenditures on	yr	389	1999	30r
Utility (piped) gas, therm		0.81	7/01	11r
Utility (piped) gas, 40 therms		38.01	7/01	11r
Utility (piped) gas, 100 therms		81.75	7/01	11r
Entertainment				
Entertainment purchases	yr	1984	1999	30r
Fees and admissions paid	yr	444	1999	30r
Television, radios, sound equipment, expenditures on	yr	580	1999	30r
Funerals				
Cosmetology, hair, other preparation		178.32	1/99	78r
Embalming		408.19	1/99	78r
Funeral at funeral home		362.13	1/99	78r
Professional service charges		1375.51	1/99	78r
Transfer of remains to funeral home		155.92	1/99	78r
Visitation/viewing		294.38	1/99	78r
Groceries				
Bacon, sliced	lb	3.15	7/01	11r
Bakery products, expenditures on	yr	281	1999	30r
Bananas	lb	0.48	7/01	11r
Beans, dried, any type, all sizes	lb	0.61	7/01	11r
Beef for stew, boneless	lb	3.08	7/01	11r
Beef, expenditures on	yr	217	1999	30r
Bologna, all beef or mixed	lb	2.52	7/01	11r
Bread, white, pan	lb	1.06	7/01	11r
Broccoli	lb	0.91	7/01	11r
Butter, salted, grade AA, stick	lb	3.04	7/01	11r
Butter, yoghurt, cheese, etc, expenditures on	yr	183	1999	30r
Cereals and bakery product purchases	yr	430	1999	30r
Cereals and cereal products, expenditures on	yr	149	1999	30r
Chicken, fresh, whole	lb	1.07	7/01	11r
Chops, boneless,	lb	3.64	7/01	11r
Chuck roast, U.S. choice, boneless	lb	2.47	7/01	11r
Coffee, 100%, ground roast, all sizes	lb	2.69	7/01	11r
Cookies, chocolate chip	lb	2.87	7/01	11r
Dairy product purchases	yr	304	1999	30r
Eggs, expenditures on	yr	26	1999	30r
Eggs, grade A, large	dozen	0.88	7/01	11r
Fats and oils, expenditures on	yr	75	1999	30r
Fish and seafood, expenditures on	yr	72	1999	30r
Food (excl fruit and vegetables), eaten at home, purchases	yr	887	1999	30r
Food cooked on trips, expenditures on	yr	44	1999	30r
Food purchases	yr	4802	1999	30r
Food purchases, eaten away from home	yr	2069	1999	30r
Food purchases, food eaten at home	yr	2733	1999	30r
Fresh fruits, expenditures on	yr	138	1999	30r
Fresh milk and cream, expenditures on	yr	120	1999	30r
Fresh vegetables, expenditures on	yr	126	1999	30r
Grapefruit	lb	0.66	7/01	11r
Grapes, Thompson, seedless	lb	1.64	7/01	11r
Ground beef, 100% beef	lb	1.64	7/01	11r
Ground beef, lean and extra lean	lb	2.16	7/01	11r
Ground chuck, 100% beef	lb	2.13	7/01	11r
Ham, boneless, excl canned	lb	2.62	7/01	11r
Ice cream, prepackaged, bulk, regular	1/2 gal	3.35	7/01	11r
Lemons	lb	1.19	7/01	11r
Lettuce, iceberg	lb	0.73	7/01	11r
Margarine, soft, tubs	lb	0.89	7/01	11r
Meats, poultry, fish, and egg purchases	yr	671	1999	30r
Milk, fresh, whole, fortified	gal	2.71	7/01	11r
Nonalcoholic beverages, expenditures on	yr	239	1999	30r
Oranges, Navel	lb	0.80	7/01	11r
Oranges, Valencia	lb	0.66	7/01	11r
Pears, Anjou	lb	0.93	7/01	11r
Pork chops, center cut, bone-in	lb	3.63	7/01	11r
Pork, expenditures on	yr	150	1999	30r
Potato chips	16 oz	3.52	7/01	11r

Canton-Massillon, OH - continued

Item	Per	Value	Date	Ref.
Groceries - continued				
Potatoes, frozen, french fried	lb	1.08	7/01	11r
Potatoes, white, all types	lb	0.33	7/01	11r
Poultry, expenditures on	yr	108	1999	30r
Processed fruits, expenditures on	yr	98	1999	30r
Processed vegetables, expenditures on	yr	80	1999	30r
Round roast, U.S. choice, boneless	lb	3.07	7/01	11r
Round steak, graded and ungraded, excl U.S. prime and choice	lb	3.41	7/01	11r
Shortening, vegetable oil blends	lb	1.13	7/01	11r
Spaghetti and macaroni	lb	0.80	7/01	11r
Steak, round, U.S. choice, boneless	lb	3.23	7/01	11r
Steak, T-bone, U.S. choice, bone-in	lb	6.68	7/01	11r
Strawberries, dry pint	12 oz	1.32	7/01	11r
Sugar and other sweets, expenditures on	yr	114	1999	30r
Sugar, white, 33-80 ounce package	lb	0.42	7/01	11r
Sugar, white, all sizes	lb	0.43	7/01	11r
Tobacco products and smoking supplies purchases	yr	331	1999	30r
Tomatoes, field grown	lb	1.46	7/01	11r
Tuna, light, chunk	lb	1.80	7/01	11r
Turkey, frozen, whole	lb	1.15	7/01	11r
Goods and Services				
B&B Japanese maple (acer japonicum)	gal	29.99-169.99	4/00	93r
Boxwood (buxus)	2 gal	18.99-39.99	4/00	93r
Daylily (hemerocallis)	gal	4.99-25.00	4/00	93r
Flat of annuals		11.98-24.99	4/00	93r
Fountain grass (pennisetum)	gal	5.98-12.98	4/00	93r
Hanging basket (10 in)		12.99-27.99	4/00	93r
Hardy geranium (geranium)	gal	7.99-9.99	4/00	93r
Hosta (hosta)	gal	6.00-25.00	4/00	93r
Lilac (syrubga vulgaris)	2 gal	14.99-24.99	4/00	93r
Miscellaneous purchases	yr	865	1999	30r
Rhododendron (rhododendron)	2 gal	23.98-42.99	4/00	93r
Sage (salvia)	gal	6.00-9.99	4/00	93r
Wintercreeper euonymus (euonymus fortunei)	2 gal	16.00-169.99	4/00	93r
Hunting license	yr	15.00	4/01	34s
Health Care				
Cardiac catheterization, ave hospital/ physician charges		11760	1998	77s
Childbirth, Cesarean delivery		10722	1997	13r
Childbirth, vaginal delivery		6223	1997	13r
Drugs, expenditures on	yr	394	1999	30r
Health care purchases	yr	2048	1999	30r
Health insurance expenditures	yr	978	1999	30r
Hysterectomy, laproscopically-assisted, ave hospital/physician charges		11730	1998	76s
Hysterectomy, vaginal, ave hospital and physician charges		9640	1998	76s
Medicaid dispensing fee		3.70	1999	87s
Medical services expenditures	yr	554	1999	30r
Medical supplies, expenditures on	yr	122	1999	30r
Plastic surgery, breast augmentation		3184	2000	7r
Plastic surgery, breast lift		3585	2000	7r
Plastic surgery, facelift		4999	2000	7r
Plastic surgery, hair transplantation		3105	2000	7r
Plastic surgery, lip augmentation		1290	2000	7r
Plastic surgery, lower body lift		8135	2000	7r
Plastic surgery, thigh lift		3839	2000	7r

Values are in dollars or fractions of dollars. In the column headed *Ref*, references are shown to sources. Each reference is followed by a letter. These refer to the geographical level for which data were reported: s=State, r=Region, and c=City or metro. The abbreviation *ex* is used to mean *except* or *excluding*; *exp* stands for *expenditures*. For other abbreviations and further explanations, please see the Introduction.

Canton-Massillon, OH - continued

Item	Per	Value	Date	Ref.
Household Goods				
Floor coverings, expenditures on	yr	52	1999	30r
Furniture, expenditures on	yr	344	1999	30r
Household furnishings and equipment purchases	yr	1475	1999	30r
Household textiles, expenditures on	yr	109	1999	30r
Laundry and cleaning supplies, expenditures on	yr	134	1999	30r
Housing				
Home price, existing, ave		144400	10/00	90r
Home value, median		96000	2001	53s
Household operation expenditures	yr	542	1999	30r
Housekeeping supplies purchases	yr	508	1999	30r
Lodging expenditures	yr	430	1999	30r
Maintenance, repairs, insurance expenditures	yr	853	1999	30r
Monthly rental value of owned home	mos	547	1999	30r
Owned dwellings, expenditures own	yr	4282	1999	30r
Rent expenditures	yr	1558	1999	30r
Rental unit, 1 bedroom, with utilities	mos	380	4/01	41c
Rental unit, 2 bedroom, with utilities	mos	484	4/01	41c
Rental unit, 3 bedroom, with utilities	mos	606	4/01	41c
Rental unit, 4 bedroom, with utilities	mos	681	4/01	41c
Shelter, expenditures on	yr	6270	1999	30r
Insurance and Pensions				
Life and other personal insurance purchases	yr	387	1999	30r
Pensions and Social Security, expenditures on	yr	2968	1999	30r
Legal Fees				
Divorce, filing fee		100.00	4/01	35s
Driver's license fee	orig	14.50	1999	48s
Driver's license fee	renew	14.50	1999	48s
Fishing license	yr	15.00	4/01	34s
Personal Goods				
Personal care products and services purchases	yr	385	1999	30r
Personal Services				
Personal services, household, expenditures on	yr	300	1999	30r
Pets				
Pets, toys, and playground equipment, expenditures on	yr	375	1999	30r
Taxes				
Federal income taxes paid	yr	2326	1999	30r
Personal taxes, expenditures on	yr	3223	1999	30r
Property taxes paid	yr	1152	1999	30r
State and local income taxes paid	yr	753	1999	30r
Transportation				
Cars and trucks, new, expenditures on	yr	1280	1999	30r
Cars and trucks, used, expenditures on	yr	1763	1999	30r
Diesel at the pump	gal	1.25	10/99	73s
Gasoline and motor oil purchases	yr	1036	1999	30r
Gasoline before-tax price (cents)	gal	109.50	10/00	43s
Maintenance and repair expenditures	yr	594	1999	30r
Public transportation, expenditures on	yr	341	1999	30r
Transportation purchases	yr	6617	1999	30r
Vehicle expenses, miscellaneous, purchases	yr	2159	1999	30r
Vehicle insurance payments	yr	701	1999	30r
Vehicle purchases (net outlay)	yr	3081	1999	30r
Vehicle rental, lease expenditures	yr	536	1999	30r
Utilities				
Electrical bill, average	mos	72.83	9/00	9s
Electricity, expenditures on	yr	841	1999	30r
Electricity cost, average	KWh	6.59	9/00	9s
Utilities, fuels, and public services purchased	yr	2401	1999	30r
Water and other public services, expenditures on	yr	273	1999	30r

Canton-Massillon, OH - continued

Item	Per	Value	Date	Ref.
Weddings				
Wedding (national average cost)		19936	2000	33r
Wedding (regional average total cost)		16195	1997	110r
Attendants' gifts		321	1998	33r
Bridal attendants' apparel (5 persons)		824	2000	33r
Bride's headpiece/veil		173	1998	33r
Bride's wedding dress		859	1998	33r
Clergy, religious facility fee		242	1998	33r
Engagement ring		3177	1998	33r
Flowers		789	1998	33r
Groom's formalwear rental		99	2000	33r
Limousine		410	1998	33r
Marriage license cost		45.00	4/01	35s
Men's formalwear (ushers, best man)		469	2000	33r
Mother of bride apparel		241	2000	33r
Music		866	1998	33r
Photography and videography		1368	1998	33r
Rehearsal dinner		728	1998	33r
Wedding invitations and announcements		341	1998	33r
Wedding reception		7968	2000	33r
Wedding rings (bride and groom)		1060	1998	33r

Casper, WY

Item	Per	Value	Date	Ref.
Child Care				
Daycare	mos	312	1998	37c
Daycare, 3-year old, 5 days, 8 hrs/day	mos	312	1998	85c
Communications				
Phone line, single, business, field visit	inst.	66.00	12/97	17s
Phone line, single, business, no field visit	inst.	66.00	12/97	17s
Phone line, single, residence, field visit	inst.	36.25	12/97	17s
Phone line, single, residence, no field visit	inst.	36.25	12/97	17s
Postal rate, express mail, up to half-pound		12.45	7/01	108r
Postal rate, letter, first class, first ounce		0.34	7/01	108r
Postal rate, letter, two ounces		0.57	7/01	108r
Postal rate, post card		0.21	7/01	108r
Postal rate, priority mail, two pounds		3.95	7/01	108r
Postal rate, priority mail, up to one pound		3.50	7/01	108r
Telephone bill, business, basic rate	mos	18.63	12/97	18c
Telephone bill, residential, basic rate	mos	14.00	12/97	18c
Education				
Board, 4-year public college/university	yr	1912	1996	38s
Room, 4-year public college/university	yr	1512	1996	38s
Total cost, 4-year public college/university	yr	5429	1996	38s
Tuition, 2-year public college/university, in state	yr	948	1996	38s
Tuition, 4-year public college/university	yr	2005	1996	38s
Energy and Fuels				
Gas, heating, winter, average use	mos	83.28	2/96	98c
Funerals				
Total cost of funeral		5401.08	1/99	78r
Acknowledgement cards		33.64	1/99	78r
Casket		2170.43	1/99	78r
Cosmetology, hair, other preparation		136.32	1/99	78r
Embalming		319.13	1/99	78r
Funeral at funeral home		370.21	1/99	78r
Hearse (local)		161.04	1/99	78r
Professional service charges		963.15	1/99	78r
Service car/van		133.99	1/99	78r
Transfer of remains to funeral home		159.82	1/99	78r
Vault		778.07	1/99	78r
Visitation/viewing		175.28	1/99	78r
Goods and Services				
Hunting license	yr	15.00	4/01	34s
Health Care				
Cardiac catheterization, ave hospital/ physician charges		24500	1998	77s
Childbirth, Cesarean delivery		11587	1997	13r
Childbirth, vaginal delivery		6725	1997	13r

Values are in dollars or fractions of dollars. In the column headed *Ref*, references are shown to sources. Each reference is followed by a letter. These refer to the geographical level for which data were reported: s=State, r=Region, and c=City or metro. The abbreviation *ex* is used to mean *except* or *excluding*; *exp* stands for *expenditures*. For other abbreviations and further explanations, please see the Introduction.

Casper, WY - continued

Item	Per	Value	Date	Ref.
Health Care				
Hysterectomy, laproscopically-assisted, ave hospital/physician charges		14380	1998	76s
Hysterectomy, vaginal, ave hospital and physician charges		9360	1998	76s
Medicaid dispensing fee		4.70	1999	87s
Housing				
Home value, median		99000	2001	53s
Rental unit, 1 bedroom, with utilities	mos	381	4/01	41c
Rental unit, 2 bedroom, with utilities	mos	487	4/01	41c
Rental unit, 3 bedroom, with utilities	mos	667	4/01	41c
Rental unit, 4 bedroom, with utilities	mos	788	4/01	41c
Insurance and Pensions				
Auto insurance premium	yr	620.11	1999	57s
Legal Fees				
Driver's license fee	orig	20.00	1999	48s
Driver's license fee	renew	15.00	1999	48s
Fishing license	yr	15.00	4/01	34s
Transportation				
Diesel at the pump	gal	1.20	10/99	73s
Gasoline before-tax price (cents)	gal	119.10	10/00	43s
Travel				
Hotel room	night	53.09	2/01	94s
Utilities				
Electrical bill, average	mos	48.91	9/00	9s
Electricity, summer, 250 KWh	mos	15.02	2/96	96c
Electricity, summer, 500 KWh	mos	30.03	2/96	96c
Electricity, summer, 750 KWh	mos	42.30	2/96	96c
Electricity, summer, 1000 KWh	mos	54.56	2/96	96c
Electricity cost, average	KWh	4.40	9/00	9s
Weddings				
Wedding (national average cost)		19936	2000	33r
Attendants' gifts		321	1998	33r
Bridal attendants' apparel (5 persons)		824	2000	33r
Bride's headpiece/veil		173	1998	33r
Bride's wedding dress		859	1998	33r
Clergy, religious facility fee		242	1998	33r
Engagement ring		3177	1998	33r
Flowers		789	1998	33r
Groom's formalwear rental		99	2000	33r
Limousine		410	1998	33r
Marriage license cost		25.00	4/01	35s
Men's formalwear (ushers, best man)		469	2000	33r
Mother of bride apparel		241	2000	33r
Music		866	1998	33r
Photography and videography		1368	1998	33r
Rehearsal dinner		728	1998	33r
Wedding invitations and announcements		341	1998	33r
Wedding reception		7968	2000	33r
Wedding rings (bride and groom)		1060	1998	33r

Cedar Rapids, IA

Item	Per	Value	Date	Ref.
Average annual expenditures	yr	35369	1999	30r
Composite, ACCRA index		97.20	3/01	4c
Alcoholic Beverages				
Alcoholic beverage purchases	yr	304	1999	30r
Beer, Heineken, 12-oz, ex deposit	6	6.89	3/01	4c
J & B Scotch	750-ml	23.07	3/01	4c
Malt beverages, all types, all sizes, any origin	16 oz	0.93	7/01	11r
Wine, Livingston or Gallo, Chablis blanc	1.5 liter	6.05	3/01	4c
Wine, red and white table, all sizes, any origin	liter	7.04	7/01	11r
Appliances				
Appliance repair, service call, washing machine	min lab chg	42.17	3/01	4c
Major appliances, expenditures on	yr	165	1999	30r

Cedar Rapids, IA - continued

Item	Per	Value	Date	Ref.
Appliances - continued				
Small appliances, housewares, expenditures on	yr	90	1999	30r
Banking and Money				
Mortgage interest and charges paid	yr	2277	1999	30r
Mortgage principal paid on owned property	yr	1230	1999	30r
Mortgage rate, incl. points and orig. fee, 30-yr. conv. fixed or ARM	mos	6.97	3/01	4c
Vehicle finance charges paid	yr	328	1999	30r
Charity				
Cash contributions, expenditures	yr	1126	1999	30r
Child Care				
Child raising cost, total, age 0-2	yr	7890	1999	60r
Child raising cost, total, age 3-5	yr	8130	1999	60r
Child raising cost, total, age 6-8	yr	8170	1999	60r
Child raising cost, total, age 9-11	yr	8190	1999	60r
Child raising cost, total, age 12-14	yr	8890	1999	60r
Child raising cost, total, age 15-17	yr	9050	1999	60r
Child's child care and education, age 0-2	yr	1240	1999	60r
Child's child care and education, age 3-5	yr	1370	1999	60r
Child's child care and education, age 6-8	yr	880	1999	60r
Child's child care and education, age 9-11	yr	570	1999	60r
Child's child care and education, age 12-14	yr	420	1999	60r
Child's child care and education, age 15-17	yr	720	1999	60r
Child's clothing, age 0-2	yr	410	1999	60r
Child's clothing, age 3-5	yr	400	1999	60r
Child's clothing, age 6-8	yr	450	1999	60r
Child's clothing, age 9-11	yr	500	1999	60r
Child's clothing, age 12-14	yr	840	1999	60r
Child's clothing, age 15-17	yr	740	1999	60r
Child's food, age 0-2	yr	960	1999	60r
Child's food, age 3-5	yr	1120	1999	60r
Child's food, age 6-8	yr	1430	1999	60r
Child's food, age 9-11	yr	1710	1999	60r
Child's food, age 12-14	yr	1710	1999	60r
Child's food, age 15-17	yr	1920	1999	60r
Child's health care, age 0-2	yr	520	1999	60r
Child's health care, age 3-5	yr	500	1999	60r
Child's health care, age 6-8	yr	570	1999	60r
Child's health care, age 9-11	yr	610	1999	60r
Child's health care, age 12-14	yr	630	1999	60r
Child's health care, age 15-17	yr	650	1999	60r
Child's housing, age 0-2	yr	2860	1999	60r
Child's housing, age 3-5	yr	2840	1999	60r
Child's housing, age 6-8	yr	2800	1999	60r
Child's housing, age 9-11	yr	2650	1999	60r
Child's housing, age 12-14	yr	2840	1999	60r
Child's housing, age 15-17	yr	2440	1999	60r
Child's personal care, reading, age 0-2	yr	880	1999	60r
Child's personal care, reading, age 3-5	yr	900	1999	60r
Child's personal care, reading, age 6-8	yr	930	1999	60r
Child's personal care, reading, age 9-11	yr	970	1999	60r
Child's personal care, reading, age 12-14	yr	1150	1999	60r
Child's personal care, reading, age 15-17	yr	920	1999	60r
Clothing				
Apparel and services purchases	yr	1607	1999	30r
Boys' brief, cotton	3	3.41	3/01	4c
Boys, 2 to 15, expenditures on	yr	91	1999	30r
Children under 2, expenditures on	yr	59	1999	30r
Footwear, expenditures on	yr	285	1999	30r
Girls, 2 to 15, expenditures on	yr	116	1999	30r
Men and boys, expenditures on	yr	433	1999	30r
Men, 16 and over, expenditures on	yr	341	1999	30r
Shirt, man's dress shirt		28.37	3/01	4c
Slacks, man's "No Wrinkles" khaki		41.00	3/01	4c
Women, 16 and over, expenditures on	yr	490	1999	30r
Communications				
Newspaper subscription, daily and Sunday delivery	mos	18.21	3/01	4c
Phone line, single, business, field visit	inst.	50.00	12/97	17s

Values are in dollars or fractions of dollars. In the column headed *Ref*, references are shown to sources. Each reference is followed by a letter. These refer to the geographical level for which data were reported: s=State, r=Region, and c=City or metro. The abbreviation *ex* is used to mean *except* or *excluding*; *exp* stands for expenditures. For other abbreviations and further explanations, please see the Introduction.

Cedar Rapids, IA - continued

Item	Per	Value	Date	Ref.
Communications				
Phone line, single, business, no field visit	inst.	50.00	12/97	17s
Phone line, single, residence, field visit	inst.	35.00	12/97	17s
Phone line, single, residence, no field visit	inst.	35.00	12/97	17s
Postage and stationery, expenditures on	yr	140	1999	30r
Postal rate, express mail, up to half-pound		12.45	7/01	108r
Postal rate, letter, first class, first ounce		0.34	7/01	108r
Postal rate, letter, two ounces		0.57	7/01	108r
Postal rate, post card		0.21	7/01	108r
Postal rate, priority mail, two pounds		3.95	7/01	108r
Postal rate, priority mail, up to one pound		3.50	7/01	108r
Telephone bill, business, basic rate	mos	32.15	12/97	18c
Telephone bill, family of three	mos	17.41	3/01	4c
Telephone bill, residential, basic rate	mos	13.05	12/97	18c
Telephone services, expenditures on	yr	830	1999	30r
Education				
Board, 4-year private college/university	yr	2138	1996	38s
Board, 4-year public college/university	yr	1688	1996	38s
Education expenditures	yr	583	1999	30r
Room, 4-year private college/university	yr	1864	1996	38s
Room, 4-year public college/university	yr	1693	1996	38s
Total cost, 4-year private college/university	yr	15934	1996	38s
Total cost, 4-year public college/university	yr	5945	1996	38s
Tuition, 2-year public college/university, in state	yr	1782	1996	38s
Tuition, 4-year private college/university, in state	yr	11932	1996	38s
Tuition, 4-year public college/university	yr	2565	1996	38s
Energy and Fuels				
Electricity	500 KWhs	46.59	7/01	11r
Energy, combined forms, 2400 sq ft	mos	186.33	3/01	4c
Energy, exc. electricity, 2400 sq ft	mos	101.62	3/01	4c
Fuel oil #2	gal	1.27	7/01	11r
Fuel oil and other fuels, expenditures on	yr	68	1999	30r
Gas, cooking, winter, 10 therms	mos	11.49	2/96	98c
Gas, cooking, winter, 30 therms	mos	21.46	2/96	98c
Gas, cooking, winter, 50 therms	mos	31.43	2/96	98c
Gas, heating, winter, average use	mos	107.22	2/96	98c
Gas, natural, commercial rate	1000 cf	7.18	11/00	88s
Gas, regular unleaded, cash, self-service	gal	1.40	3/01	4c
Gasoline, unleaded midgrade	gal	1.79	7/01	11r
Gasoline, unleaded premium	gal	1.86	7/01	11r
Gasoline, unleaded regular	gal	1.58	7/01	11r
Natural gas, expenditures on	yr	389	1999	30r
Utility (piped) gas, therm		0.81	7/01	11r
Utility (piped) gas, 40 therms		38.01	7/01	11r
Utility (piped) gas, 100 therms		81.75	7/01	11r
Entertainment				
Bowling, Saturday evening rate	line	2.82	3/01	4c
Entertainment purchases	yr	1984	1999	30r
Fees and admissions paid	yr	444	1999	30r
Monopoly game, Parker Brothers', No. 9	game	9.80	3/01	4c
Movie, first-run, Saturday, evening	adm.	6.67	3/01	4c
Television, radios, sound equipment, expenditures on	yr	580	1999	30r
Tennis balls, yellow, Wilson or Penn, 3	can	2.17	3/01	4c
Funerals				
Cosmetology, hair, other preparation		178.32	1/99	78r
Embalming		408.19	1/99	78r
Funeral at funeral home		362.13	1/99	78r
Professional service charges		1375.51	1/99	78r
Transfer of remains to funeral home		155.92	1/99	78r
Visitation/viewing		294.38	1/99	78r
Groceries				
Groceries, ACCRA Index		89.50	3/01	4c
Antibiotic ointment, Polysporin	0.5 oz	4.57	3/01	4c
Baby food, strained vegetables or fruit, lowest price	4-4.5 oz	0.45	3/01	4c
Bacon, sliced	lb	3.15	7/01	11r

Cedar Rapids, IA - continued

Item	Per	Value	Date	Ref.
Groceries - continued				
Bakery products, expenditures on	yr	281	1999	30r
Bananas	lb	0.37	3/01	4c
Bananas	lb	0.48	7/01	11r
Beans, dried, any type, all sizes	lb	0.61	7/01	11r
Beef for stew, boneless	lb	3.08	7/01	11r
Beef or hamburger, ground	lb	1.62	3/01	4c
Beef, expenditures on	yr	217	1999	30r
Bologna, all beef or mixed	lb	2.52	7/01	11r
Bread, white	loaf	0.80	3/01	4c
Bread, white, pan	lb	1.06	7/01	11r
Broccoli	lb	0.91	7/01	11r
Butter, salted, grade AA, stick	lb	3.04	7/01	11r
Butter, yoghurt, cheese, etc, expenditures on	yr	183	1999	30r
Cereals and bakery product purchases	yr	430	1999	30r
Cereals and cereal products, expenditures on	yr	149	1999	30r
Cheese, Kraft grated Parmesan	8 oz	3.66	3/01	4c
Chicken, fresh, whole	lb	1.07	7/01	11r
Chicken, whole fryer	lb	0.82	3/01	4c
Chops, boneless,	lb	3.64	7/01	11r
Chuck roast, U.S. choice, boneless	lb	2.47	7/01	11r
Cigarettes, Winston, Kings	carton	27.31	3/01	4c
Coffee, 100%, ground roast, all sizes	lb	2.69	7/01	11r
Coffee, vacuum-packed	13 oz	2.35	3/01	4c
Cookies, chocolate chip	lb	2.87	7/01	11r
Corn Flakes, Kellogg's or Post Toasties	18 oz	1.79	3/01	4c
Corn, frozen, whole kernel, lowest price	16 oz	0.99	3/01	4c
Dairy product purchases	yr	304	1999	30r
Eggs, expenditures on	yr	26	1999	30r
Eggs, Grade A or AA	dozen	1.06	3/01	4c
Eggs, grade A, large	dozen	0.88	7/01	11r
Fats and oils, expenditures on	yr	75	1999	30r
Fish and seafood, expenditures on	yr	72	1999	30r
Food (excl fruit and vegetables), eaten at home, purchases	yr	887	1999	30r
Food cooked on trips, expenditures on	yr	44	1999	30r
Food purchases	yr	4802	1999	30r
Food purchases, eaten away from home	yr	2069	1999	30r
Food purchases, food eaten at home	yr	2733	1999	30r
Fresh fruits, expenditures on	yr	138	1999	30r
Fresh milk and cream, expenditures on	yr	120	1999	30r
Fresh vegetables, expenditures on	yr	126	1999	30r
Grapefruit	lb	0.66	7/01	11r
Grapes, Thompson, seedless	lb	1.64	7/01	11r
Ground beef, 100% beef	lb	1.64	7/01	11r
Ground beef, lean and extra lean	lb	2.16	7/01	11r
Ground chuck, 100% beef	lb	2.13	7/01	11r
Ham, boneless, excl canned	lb	2.62	7/01	11r
Ice cream, prepackaged, bulk, regular	1/2 gal	3.35	7/01	11r
Lemons	lb	1.19	7/01	11r
Lettuce, iceberg	head	0.95	3/01	4c
Lettuce, iceberg	lb	0.73	7/01	11r
Margarine, Blue Bonnet or Parkay, stick	lb	0.54	3/01	4c
Margarine, soft, tubs	lb	0.89	7/01	11r
Meats, poultry, fish, and egg purchases	yr	671	1999	30r
Milk, fresh, whole, fortified	gal	2.71	7/01	11r
Milk, whole	1/2 gal	1.48	3/01	4c
Nonalcoholic beverages, expenditures on	yr	239	1999	30r
Orange juice, Minute Maid frozen	12 oz	1.59	3/01	4c
Oranges, Navel	lb	0.80	7/01	11r
Oranges, Valencia	lb	0.66	7/01	11r
Peaches, halves or slices, Hunt's, Del Monte, or Libby's	29 oz	1.55	3/01	4c
Pears, Anjou	lb	0.93	7/01	11r
Peas, green, Del Monte or Green Giant	15 oz	0.65	3/01	4c
Pork chops, center cut, bone-in	lb	3.63	7/01	11r
Pork, expenditures on	yr	150	1999	30r
Potato chips	16 oz	3.52	7/01	11r
Potatoes, frozen, french fried	lb	1.08	7/01	11r
Potatoes, white or red	10 lb	2.33	3/01	4c
Potatoes, white, all types	lb	0.33	7/01	11r
Poultry, expenditures on	yr	108	1999	30r

Values are in dollars or fractions of dollars. In the column headed *Ref*, references are shown to sources. Each reference is followed by a letter. These refer to the geographical level for which data were reported: s=State, r=Region, and c=City or metro. The abbreviation *ex* is used to mean *except* or *excluding*; *exp* stands for *expenditures*. For other abbreviations and further explanations, please see the Introduction.

Cedar Rapids, IA - continued

Item	Per	Value	Date	Ref.
Groceries				
Processed fruits, expenditures on	yr	98	1999	30r
Processed vegetables, expenditures on	yr	80	1999	30r
Round roast, U.S. choice, boneless	lb	3.07	7/01	11r
Round steak, graded and ungraded, excl U.S. prime and choice	lb	3.41	7/01	11r
Sausage, Jimmy Dean/Owens pork	lb	3.05	3/01	4c
Shortening, vegetable oil blends	lb	1.13	7/01	11r
Shortening, vegetable, Crisco	3 lb	2.77	3/01	4c
Soft drink, Coca Cola, ex deposit	2 liter	1.10	3/01	4c
Spaghetti and macaroni	lb	0.80	7/01	11r
Steak, round, U.S. choice, boneless	lb	3.23	7/01	11r
Steak, T-bone	lb	6.37	3/01	4c
Steak, T-bone, U.S. choice, bone-in	lb	6.68	7/01	11r
Strawberries, dry pint	12 oz	1.32	7/01	11r
Sugar and other sweets, expenditures on	yr	114	1999	30r
Sugar, cane or beet	4 lbs	1.55	3/01	4c
Sugar, white, 33-80 ounce package	lb	0.42	7/01	11r
Sugar, white, all sizes	lb	0.43	7/01	11r
Tobacco products and smoking supplies purchases	yr	331	1999	30r
Tomatoes, field grown	lb	1.46	7/01	11r
Tomatoes, Hunt's or Del Monte	14.5 oz	0.84	3/01	4c
Tuna, chunk, light	6 oz	0.55	3/01	4c
Tuna, light, chunk	lb	1.80	7/01	11r
Turkey, frozen, whole	lb	1.15	7/01	11r
Goods and Services				
Miscellaneous goods and services, ACCRA Index		100.10	3/01	4c
B&B Japanese maple (acer japonicum)	gal	29.99-169.99	4/00	93r
Boxwood (buxus)	2 gal	18.99-39.99	4/00	93r
Daylilly (hemerocallis)	gal	4.99-25.00	4/00	93r
Flat of annuals		11.98-24.99	4/00	93r
Fountain grass (pennisetum)	gal	5.98-12.98	4/00	93r
Hanging basket (10 in)		12.99-27.99	4/00	93r
Hardy geranium (geranium)	gal	7.99-9.99	4/00	93r
Hosta (hosta)	gal	6.00-25.00	4/00	93r
Lilac (syrubga vulgaris)	2 gal	14.99-24.99	4/00	93r
Miscellaneous purchases	yr	865	1999	30r
Rhododendron (rhododendron)	2 gal	23.98-42.99	4/00	93r
Sage (salvia)	gal	6.00-9.99	4/00	93r
Wintercreeper euonymus (euonymus fortunei)	2 gal	16.00-169.99	4/00	93r
Hunting license	yr	16.00	4/01	34s
Health Care				
Health care, ACCRA Index		92.60	3/01	4c
Cardiac catheterization, ave hospital/ physician charges		8810	1998	77s
Childbirth, Cesarean delivery		10722	1997	13r
Childbirth, vaginal delivery		6223	1997	13r
Dentist's fee, adult teeth cleaning and periodic oral exam	visit	67.48	3/01	4c
Doctor's fee, routine exam, established patient	visit	57.60	3/01	4c
Drugs, expenditures on	yr	394	1999	30r
Health care purchases	yr	2048	1999	30r
Health insurance expenditures	yr	978	1999	30r
Hospital care, private room	day	395.33	3/01	4c
Hysterectomy, laproscopically-assisted, ave hospital/physician charges		8620	1998	76s

Cedar Rapids, IA - continued

Item	Per	Value	Date	Ref.
Health Care - continued				
Hysterectomy, vaginal, ave hospital and physician charges		6630	1998	76s
Medicaid dispensing fee		4.10-6.38	1999	87s
Medical services expenditures	yr	554	1999	30r
Medical supplies, expenditures on	yr	122	1999	30r
Plastic surgery, breast augmentation		3184	2000	7r
Plastic surgery, breast lift		3585	2000	7r
Plastic surgery, facelift		4999	2000	7r
Plastic surgery, hair transplantation		3105	2000	7r
Plastic surgery, lip augmentation		1290	2000	7r
Plastic surgery, lower body lift		8135	2000	7r
Plastic surgery, thigh lift		3839	2000	7r
Household Goods				
Dishwashing powder, Cascade	50 oz	2.51	3/01	4c
Floor coverings, expenditures on	yr	52	1999	30r
Furniture, expenditures on	yr	344	1999	30r
Household furnishings and equipment purchases	yr	1475	1999	30r
Household textiles, expenditures on	yr	109	1999	30r
Laundry and cleaning supplies, expenditures on	yr	134	1999	30r
Tissues, facial, Kleenex brand	175	1.05	3/01	4c
Housing				
Housing, ACCRA Index		86.20	3/01	4c
Home, 2200 sq ft, 4-br, 2-bath, 2-car garage, average		181497	2000	47c
Home price, existing, ave		144400	10/00	90r
Home value, median		100000	2001	53s
House, 2400 sq ft, 8000 sq ft lot, new, urban, utilities	total	179983	3/01	4c
House payment, principal and interest, 25% down payment	mos	896	3/01	4c
Household operation expenditures	yr	542	1999	30r
Housekeeping supplies purchases	yr	508	1999	30r
Lodging expenditures	yr	430	1999	30r
Maintenance, repairs, insurance expenditures	yr	853	1999	30r
Monthly rental value of owned home	mos	547	1999	30r
Owned dwellings, expenditures own	yr	4282	1999	30r
Rent expenditures	yr	1558	1999	30r
Rent, apartment, 2 br, 1 1/2-2 baths, unfurn, 950 sq ft, water	mos	581	3/01	4c
Rental unit, 1 bedroom, with utilities	mos	394	4/01	41c
Rental unit, 2 bedroom, with utilities	mos	507	4/01	41c
Rental unit, 3 bedroom, with utilities	mos	705	4/01	41c
Rental unit, 4 bedroom, with utilities	mos	757	4/01	41c
Shelter, expenditures on	yr	6270	1999	30r
Insurance and Pensions				
Auto insurance premium	yr	520.76	1999	57s
Life and other personal insurance purchases	yr	387	1999	30r
Pensions and Social Security, expenditures on	yr	2968	1999	30r
Legal Fees				
Divorce, filing fee		110.00	4/01	35s
Driver's license fee	renew	16.00	1999	48s
Driver's license fee	orig	16.00	1999	48s
Personal Goods				
Personal care products and services purchases	yr	385	1999	30r
Shampoo, Alberto VO5	15 oz	0.94	3/01	4c
Toothpaste, Crest or Colgate	6-7 oz	1.92	3/01	4c
Personal Services				
Dry cleaning, man's 2-pc suit		8.02	3/01	4c
Man's haircut, barbershop, no styling		9.00	3/01	4c
Personal services, household, expenditures on	yr	300	1999	30r
Woman's shampoo, trim, blow-dry, no style-change		20.06	3/01	4c

Values are in dollars or fractions of dollars. In the column headed *Ref*, references are shown to sources. Each reference is followed by a letter. These refer to the geographical level for which data were reported: s=State, r=Region, and c=City or metro. The abbreviation *ex* is used to mean *except* or *excluding*; *exp* stands for *expenditures*. For other abbreviations and further explanations, please see the Introduction.

Cedar Rapids, IA - continued

Item	Per	Value	Date	Ref.
Pets				
Pets, toys, and playground equipment, expenditures on	yr	375	1999	30r
Restaurant Food				
Chicken, fried, thigh and drumstick, KFC/ Church's		2.59	3/01	4c
Hamburger with cheese, McDonald's	1/4 lb	2.19	3/01	4c
Pizza, Pizza Hut or Pizza Inn	11-12 in	8.99	3/01	4c
Taxes				
Federal income taxes paid	yr	2326	1999	30r
Personal taxes, expenditures on	yr	3223	1999	30r
Property taxes paid	yr	1152	1999	30r
State and local income taxes paid	yr	753	1999	30r
Transportation				
Transportation, ACCRA Index		96.90	3/01	4c
Cars and trucks, new, expenditures on	yr	1280	1999	30r
Cars and trucks, used, expenditures on	yr	1763	1999	30r
Diesel at the pump	gal	1.25	10/99	73s
Gasoline and motor oil purchases	yr	1036	1999	30r
Gasoline before-tax price (cents)	gal	112.30	10/00	43s
Maintenance and repair expenditures	yr	594	1999	30r
Public transportation, expenditures on	yr	341	1999	30r
Tire balance, computer or spin balance, front	wheel	7.39	3/01	4c
Transportation purchases	yr	6617	1999	30r
Vehicle expenses, miscellaneous, purchases	yr	2159	1999	30r
Vehicle insurance payments	yr	701	1999	30r
Vehicle purchases (net outlay)	yr	3081	1999	30r
Vehicle rental, lease expenditures	yr	536	1999	30r
Utilities				
Utilities, ACCRA Index		142.70	3/01	4c
Electrical bill, average	mos	67.25	9/00	9s
Electricity, expenditures on	yr	841	1999	30r
Electricity, summer, 250 KWh	mos	29.30	2/96	97c
Electricity, summer, 500 KWh	mos	49.60	2/96	97c
Electricity, summer, 750 KWh	mos	66.23	2/96	97c
Electricity, summer, 1000 KWh	mos	82.85	2/96	97c
Electricity and other, mixed, 2400 sq ft, new home	mos	84.71	3/01	4c
Electricity cost, average	KWh	5.90	9/00	9s
Utilities, fuels, and public services purchased	yr	2401	1999	30r
Water and other public services, expenditures on	yr	273	1999	30r
Weddings				
Wedding (national average cost)		19936	2000	33r
Wedding (regional average total cost)		16195	1997	110r
Attendants' gifts		321	1998	33r
Bridal attendants' apparel (5 persons)		824	2000	33r
Bride's headpiece/veil		173	1998	33r
Bride's wedding dress		859	1998	33r
Clergy, religious facility fee		242	1998	33r
Engagement ring		3177	1998	33r
Flowers		789	1998	33r
Groom's formalwear rental		99	2000	33r
Limousine		410	1998	33r
Marriage license cost		30.00	4/01	35s
Men's formalwear (ushers, best man)		469	2000	33r
Mother of bride apparel		241	2000	33r
Music		866	1998	33r
Photography and videography		1368	1998	33r
Rehearsal dinner		728	1998	33r
Wedding invitations and announcements		341	1998	33r
Wedding reception		7968	2000	33r
Wedding rings (bride and groom)		1060	1998	33r

Champaign-Urbana, IL

Item	Per	Value	Date	Ref.
Average annual expenditures	yr	35369	1999	30r
Composite, ACCRA index		103.20	3/01	4c
Alcoholic Beverages				
Alcoholic beverage purchases	yr	304	1999	30r
Beer, Heineken, 12-oz, ex deposit	6	7.31	3/01	4c
J & B Scotch	750-ml	19.39	3/01	4c
Malt beverages, all types, all sizes, any origin	16 oz	0.93	7/01	11r
Wine, Livingston or Gallo, Chablis blanc	1.5 liter	5.19	3/01	4c
Wine, red and white table, all sizes, any origin	liter	7.04	7/01	11r
Appliances				
Appliance repair, service call, washing machine	min lab chg	43.50	3/01	4c
Major appliances, expenditures on	yr	165	1999	30r
Small appliances, housewares, expenditures on	yr	90	1999	30r
Banking and Money				
Mortgage interest and charges paid	yr	2277	1999	30r
Mortgage principal paid on owned property	yr	1230	1999	30r
Mortgage rate, incl. points and orig. fee, 30-yr. conv. fixed or ARM	mos	7.10	3/01	4c
Vehicle finance charges paid	yr	328	1999	30r
Charity				
Cash contributions, expenditures	yr	1126	1999	30r
Child Care				
Child raising cost, total, age 0-2	yr	7890	1999	60r
Child raising cost, total, age 3-5	yr	8130	1999	60r
Child raising cost, total, age 6-8	yr	8170	1999	60r
Child raising cost, total, age 9-11	yr	8190	1999	60r
Child raising cost, total, age 12-14	yr	8890	1999	60r
Child raising cost, total, age 15-17	yr	9050	1999	60r
Child's child care and education, age 0-2	yr	1240	1999	60r
Child's child care and education, age 3-5	yr	1370	1999	60r
Child's child care and education, age 6-8	yr	880	1999	60r
Child's child care and education, age 9-11	yr	570	1999	60r
Child's child care and education, age 12-14	yr	420	1999	60r
Child's child care and education, age 15-17	yr	720	1999	60r
Child's clothing, age 0-2	yr	410	1999	60r
Child's clothing, age 3-5	yr	400	1999	60r
Child's clothing, age 6-8	yr	450	1999	60r
Child's clothing, age 9-11	yr	500	1999	60r
Child's clothing, age 12-14	yr	840	1999	60r
Child's clothing, age 15-17	yr	740	1999	60r
Child's food, age 0-2	yr	960	1999	60r
Child's food, age 3-5	yr	1120	1999	60r
Child's food, age 6-8	yr	1430	1999	60r
Child's food, age 9-11	yr	1710	1999	60r
Child's food, age 12-14	yr	1710	1999	60r
Child's food, age 15-17	yr	1920	1999	60r
Child's health care, age 0-2	yr	520	1999	60r
Child's health care, age 3-5	yr	500	1999	60r
Child's health care, age 6-8	yr	570	1999	60r
Child's health care, age 9-11	yr	610	1999	60r
Child's health care, age 12-14	yr	630	1999	60r
Child's health care, age 15-17	yr	650	1999	60r
Child's housing, age 0-2	yr	2860	1999	60r
Child's housing, age 3-5	yr	2840	1999	60r
Child's housing, age 6-8	yr	2800	1999	60r
Child's housing, age 9-11	yr	2650	1999	60r
Child's housing, age 12-14	yr	2840	1999	60r
Child's housing, age 15-17	yr	2440	1999	60r
Child's personal care, reading, age 0-2	yr	880	1999	60r
Child's personal care, reading, age 3-5	yr	900	1999	60r
Child's personal care, reading, age 6-8	yr	930	1999	60r
Child's personal care, reading, age 9-11	yr	970	1999	60r
Child's personal care, reading, age 12-14	yr	1150	1999	60r
Child's personal care, reading, age 15-17	yr	920	1999	60r
Clothing				
Apparel and services purchases	yr	1607	1999	30r
Boys' brief, cotton	3	4.90	3/01	4c

Values are in dollars or fractions of dollars. In the column headed *Ref*, references are shown to sources. Each reference is followed by a letter. These refer to the geographical level for which data were reported: s=State, r=Region, and c=City or metro. The abbreviation *ex* is used to mean *except* or *excluding*; *exp* stands for expenditures. For other abbreviations and further explanations, please see the Introduction.

Champaign-Urbana, IL - continued

Item	Per	Value	Date	Ref.
Clothing				
Boys, 2 to 15, expenditures on	yr	91	1999	30r
Children under 2, expenditures on	yr	59	1999	30r
Footwear, expenditures on	yr	285	1999	30r
Girls, 2 to 15, expenditures on	yr	116	1999	30r
Men and boys, expenditures on	yr	433	1999	30r
Men, 16 and over, expenditures on	yr	341	1999	30r
Shirt, man's dress shirt		33.33	3/01	4c
Slacks, man's "No Wrinkles" khaki		46.00	3/01	4c
Women, 16 and over, expenditures on	yr	490	1999	30r
Communications				
Cable modem installation, Adelphi		54.90	6/99	103s
Cable modem installation, AT&T-BIS		150.00	6/99	103s
Cable modem installation, Media One		100.00	6/99	103s
Cable modem rate, cable subscriber, Adelphi	mos	34.95	6/99	103s
Cable modem rate, cable subscriber, AT&T-BIS	mos	39.95	6/99	103s
Cable modem rate, cable subscriber, Media One	mos	34.95-39.95	6/99	103s
Cable modem rate, non-cable subscriber, Adelphi	mos	44.95	6/99	103s
Cable modem rate, non-cable subscriber, Media One	mos	49.95	6/99	103s
Newspaper subscription, daily and Sunday delivery	mos	13.65	3/01	4c
Phone line, single, business, field visit	inst.	52.35	12/97	17s
Phone line, single, business, no field visit	inst.	52.35	12/97	17s
Phone line, single, residence, field visit	inst.	55.00	12/97	17s
Phone line, single, residence, no field visit	inst.	55.00	12/97	17s
Postage and stationery, expenditures on	yr	140	1999	30r
Postal rate, express mail, up to half-pound		12.45	7/01	108r
Postal rate, letter, first class, first ounce		0.34	7/01	108r
Postal rate, letter, two ounces		0.57	7/01	108r
Postal rate, post card		0.21	7/01	108r
Postal rate, priority mail, two pounds		3.95	7/01	108r
Postal rate, priority mail, up to one pound		3.50	7/01	108r
Telephone bill, family of three	mos	26.74	3/01	4c
Telephone services, expenditures on	yr	830	1999	30r
Education				
Board, 4-year private college/university	yr	2306	1996	38s
Board, 4-year public college/university	yr	2405	1996	38s
Education expenditures	yr	583	1999	30r
Room, 4-year private college/university	yr	2718	1996	38s
Room, 4-year public college/university	yr	2072	1996	38s
Total cost, 4-year private college/university	yr	16678	1996	38s
Total cost, 4-year public college/university	yr	7829	1996	38s
Tuition, 2-year public college/university, in state	yr	1232	1996	38s
Tuition, 4-year private college/university, in state	yr	11653	1996	38s
Tuition, 4-year public college/university	yr	3352	1996	38s
Energy and Fuels				
Electricity	500 KWhs	46.59	7/01	11r
Energy, combined forms, 2400 sq ft	mos	133.57	3/01	4c
Energy, exc. electricity, 2400 sq ft	mos	67.45	3/01	4c
Fuel oil #2	gal	1.27	7/01	11r
Fuel oil and other fuels, expenditures on	yr	68	1999	30r
Gas, natural, commercial rate	1000 cf	8.47	11/00	88s
Gas, regular unleaded, cash, self-service	gal	1.51	3/01	4c
Gasoline, unleaded midgrade	gal	1.79	7/01	11r
Gasoline, unleaded premium	gal	1.86	7/01	11r
Gasoline, unleaded regular	gal	1.58	7/01	11r
Natural gas, expenditures on	yr	389	1999	30r
Utility (piped) gas, therm		0.81	7/01	11r
Utility (piped) gas, 40 therms		38.01	7/01	11r
Utility (piped) gas, 100 therms		81.75	7/01	11r
Entertainment				
Bowling, Saturday evening rate	line	3.03	3/01	4c
Entertainment purchases	yr	1984	1999	30r
Fees and admissions paid	yr	444	1999	30r

Champaign-Urbana, IL - continued

Item	Per	Value	Date	Ref.
Entertainment - continued				
Monopoly game, Parker Brothers', No. 9	game	11.37	3/01	4c
Movie, first-run, Saturday, evening	adm.	6.67	3/01	4c
Television, radios, sound equipment, expenditures on	yr	580	1999	30r
Tennis balls, yellow, Wilson or Penn, 3	can	2.55	3/01	4c
Funerals				
Cosmetology, hair, other preparation		178.32	1/99	78r
Embalming		408.19	1/99	78r
Funeral at funeral home		362.13	1/99	78r
Professional service charges		1375.51	1/99	78r
Transfer of remains to funeral home		155.92	1/99	78r
Visitation/viewing		294.38	1/99	78r
Groceries				
Groceries, ACCRA Index		99.80	3/01	4c
Antibiotic ointment, Polysporin	0.5 oz	4.48	3/01	4c
Baby food, strained vegetables or fruit, lowest price	4-4.5 oz	0.41	3/01	4c
Bacon, sliced	lb	3.15	7/01	11r
Bakery products, expenditures on	yr	281	1999	30r
Bananas	lb	0.53	3/01	4c
Bananas	lb	0.48	7/01	11r
Beans, dried, any type, all sizes	lb	0.61	7/01	11r
Beef for stew, boneless	lb	3.08	7/01	11r
Beef or hamburger, ground	lb	1.61	3/01	4c
Beef, expenditures on	yr	217	1999	30r
Bologna, all beef or mixed	lb	2.52	7/01	11r
Bread, white	loaf	0.82	3/01	4c
Bread, white, pan	lb	1.06	7/01	11r
Broccoli	lb	0.91	7/01	11r
Butter, salted, grade AA, stick	lb	3.04	7/01	11r
Butter, yoghurt, cheese, etc, expenditures on	yr	183	1999	30r
Cereals and bakery product purchases	yr	430	1999	30r
Cereals and cereal products, expenditures on	yr	149	1999	30r
Cheese, Kraft grated Parmesan	8 oz	3.65	3/01	4c
Chicken, fresh, whole	lb	1.07	7/01	11r
Chicken, whole fryer	lb	0.95	7/01	4c
Chops, boneless,	lb	3.64	7/01	11r
Chuck roast, U.S. choice, boneless	lb	2.47	7/01	11r
Cigarettes, Winston, Kings	carton	31.87	3/01	4c
Coffee, 100%, ground roast, all sizes	lb	2.69	7/01	11r
Coffee, vacuum-packed	13 oz	2.67	3/01	4c
Cookies, chocolate chip	lb	2.87	7/01	11r
Corn Flakes, Kellogg's or Post Toasties	18 oz	2.66	3/01	4c
Corn, frozen, whole kernel, lowest price	16 oz	1.11	3/01	4c
Dairy product purchases	yr	304	1999	30r
Eggs, expenditures on	yr	26	1999	30r
Eggs, Grade A or AA	dozen	1.17	3/01	4c
Eggs, grade A, large	dozen	0.88	7/01	11r
Fats and oils, expenditures on	yr	75	1999	30r
Fish and seafood, expenditures on	yr	72	1999	30r
Food (excl fruit and vegetables), eaten at home, purchases	yr	887	1999	30r
Food cooked on trips, expenditures on	yr	44	1999	30r
Food purchases	yr	4802	1999	30r
Food purchases, eaten away from home	yr	2069	1999	30r
Food purchases, food eaten at home	yr	2733	1999	30r
Fresh fruits, expenditures on	yr	138	1999	30r
Fresh milk and cream, expenditures on	yr	120	1999	30r
Fresh vegetables, expenditures on	yr	126	1999	30r
Grapefruit	lb	0.66	7/01	11r
Grapes, Thompson, seedless	lb	1.64	7/01	11r
Ground beef, 100% beef	lb	1.64	7/01	11r
Ground beef, lean and extra lean	lb	2.16	7/01	11r
Ground chuck, 100% beef	lb	2.13	7/01	11r
Ham, boneless, excl canned	lb	2.62	7/01	11r
Ice cream, prepackaged, bulk, regular	1/2 gal	3.35	7/01	11r
Lemons	lb	1.19	7/01	11r
Lettuce, iceberg	head	1.11	3/01	4c
Lettuce, iceberg	lb	0.73	7/01	11r
Margarine, Blue Bonnet or Parkay, stick	lb	0.85	3/01	4c

Values are in dollars or fractions of dollars. In the column headed *Ref*, references are shown to sources. Each reference is followed by a letter. These refer to the geographical level for which data were reported: s=State, r=Region, and c=City or metro. The abbreviation *ex* is used to mean *except* or *excluding*; *exp* stands for *expenditures*. For other abbreviations and further explanations, please see the Introduction.

Champaign-Urbana, IL - continued

Item	Per	Value	Date	Ref.
Groceries				
Margarine, soft, tubs	lb	0.89	7/01	11r
Meats, poultry, fish, and egg purchases	yr	671	1999	30r
Milk, fresh, whole, fortified	gal	2.71	7/01	11r
Milk, whole	1/2 gal	1.70	3/01	4c
Nonalcoholic beverages, expenditures on	yr	239	1999	30r
Orange juice, Minute Maid frozen	12 oz	1.60	3/01	4c
Oranges, Navel	lb	0.80	7/01	11r
Oranges, Valencia	lb	0.66	7/01	11r
Peaches, halves or slices, Hunt's, Del Monte, or Libby's	29 oz	1.55	3/01	4c
Pears, Anjou	lb	0.93	7/01	11r
Peas, green, Del Monte or Green Giant	15 oz	0.72	3/01	4c
Pork chops, center cut, bone-in	lb	3.63	7/01	11r
Pork, expenditures on	yr	150	1999	30r
Potato chips	16 oz	3.52	7/01	11r
Potatoes, frozen, french fried	lb	1.08	7/01	11r
Potatoes, white or red	10 lb	2.80	3/01	4c
Potatoes, white, all types	lb	0.33	7/01	11r
Poultry, expenditures on	yr	108	1999	30r
Processed fruits, expenditures on	yr	98	1999	30r
Processed vegetables, expenditures on	yr	80	1999	30r
Round roast, U.S. choice, boneless	lb	3.07	7/01	11r
Round steak, graded and ungraded, excl U.S. prime and choice	lb	3.41	7/01	11r
Sausage, Jimmy Dean/Owens pork	lb	3.35	3/01	4c
Shortening, vegetable oil blends	lb	1.13	7/01	11r
Shortening, vegetable, Crisco	3 lb	2.50	3/01	4c
Soft drink, Coca Cola, ex deposit	2 liter	1.39	3/01	4c
Spaghetti and macaroni	lb	0.80	7/01	11r
Steak, round, U.S. choice, boneless	lb	3.23	7/01	11r
Steak, T-bone	lb	6.87	3/01	4c
Steak, T-bone, U.S. choice, bone-in	lb	6.68	7/01	11r
Strawberries, dry pint	12 oz	1.32	7/01	11r
Sugar and other sweets, expenditures on	yr	114	1999	30r
Sugar, cane or beet	4 lbs	1.46	3/01	4c
Sugar, white, 33-80 ounce package	lb	0.42	7/01	11r
Sugar, white, all sizes	lb	0.43	7/01	11r
Tobacco products and smoking supplies purchases	yr	331	1999	30r
Tomatoes, field grown	lb	1.46	7/01	11r
Tomatoes, Hunt's or Del Monte	14.5 oz	0.87	3/01	4c
Tuna, chunk, light	6 oz	0.67	3/01	4c
Tuna, light, chunk	lb	1.80	7/01	11r
Turkey, frozen, whole	lb	1.15	7/01	11r
Goods and Services				
Miscellaneous goods and services, ACCRA Index		108.90	3/01	4c
B&B Japanese maple (acer japonicum)	gal	29.99-169.99	4/00	93r
Boxwood (buxus)	2 gal	18.99-39.99	4/00	93r
Daylilly (hemerocallis)	gal	4.99-25.00	4/00	93r
Flat of annuals		11.98-24.99	4/00	93r
Fountain grass (pennisetum)	gal	5.98-12.98	4/00	93r
Hanging basket (10 in)		12.99-27.99	4/00	93r
Hardy geranium (geranium)	gal	7.99-9.99	4/00	93r
Hosta (hosta)	gal	6.00-25.00	4/00	93r
Lilac (syrubga vulgaris)	2 gal	14.99-24.99	4/00	93r
Miscellaneous purchases	yr	865	1999	30r
Rhododendron (rhododendron)	2 gal	23.98-42.99	4/00	93r
Sage (salvia)	gal	6.00-9.99	4/00	93r
Wintercreeper euonymus (euonymus fortunei)	2 gal	16.00-169.99	4/00	93r

Champaign-Urbana, IL - continued

Item	Per	Value	Date	Ref.
Goods and Services - continued				
Hunting license	yr	7.50	4/01	34s
Health Care				
Health care, ACCRA Index		104.20	3/01	4c
Cardiac catheterization, ave hospital/ physician charges		17690	1998	77s
Childbirth, Cesarean delivery		10722	1997	13r
Childbirth, vaginal delivery		6223	1997	13r
Dentist's fee, adult teeth cleaning and periodic oral exam	visit	74.85	3/01	4c
Doctor's fee, routine exam, established patient	visit	58.05	3/01	4c
Drugs, expenditures on	yr	394	1999	30r
Health care purchases	yr	2048	1999	30r
Health insurance expenditures	yr	978	1999	30r
Hospital care, private room	day	625.00	3/01	4c
Hysterectomy, laproscopically-assisted, ave hospital/physician charges		15850	1998	76s
Hysterectomy, vaginal, ave hospital and physician charges		11810	1998	76s
Medicaid dispensing fee		3.69-15.45	1999	87s
Medical services expenditures	yr	554	1999	30r
Medical supplies, expenditures on	yr	122	1999	30r
Plastic surgery, breast augmentation		3184	2000	7r
Plastic surgery, breast lift		3585	2000	7r
Plastic surgery, facelift		4999	2000	7r
Plastic surgery, hair transplantation		3105	2000	7r
Plastic surgery, lip augmentation		1290	2000	7r
Plastic surgery, lower body lift		8135	2000	7r
Plastic surgery, thigh lift		3839	2000	7r
Household Goods				
Dishwashing powder, Cascade	50 oz	2.93	3/01	4c
Floor coverings, expenditures on	yr	52	1999	30r
Furniture, expenditures on	yr	344	1999	30r
Household furnishings and equipment purchases	yr	1475	1999	30r
Household textiles, expenditures on	yr	109	1999	30r
Laundry and cleaning supplies, expenditures on	yr	134	1999	30r
Tissues, facial, Kleenex brand	175	1.11	3/01	4c
Housing				
Housing, ACCRA Index		95.50	3/01	4c
Home price, existing, ave		144400	10/00	90r
Home value, median		183000	2001	53s
House, 2400 sq ft, 8000 sq ft lot, new, urban, utilities	total	186112	3/01	4c
House payment, principal and interest, 25% down payment	mos	939	3/01	4c
Household operation expenditures	yr	542	1999	30r
Housekeeping supplies purchases	yr	508	1999	30r
Lodging expenditures	yr	430	1999	30r
Maintenance, repairs, insurance expenditures	yr	853	1999	30r
Monthly rental value of owned home	mos	547	1999	30r
Owned dwellings, expenditures own	yr	4282	1999	30r
Rent expenditures	yr	1558	1999	30r
Rent, apartment, 2 br, 1 1/2-2 baths, unfurn, 950 sq ft, water	mos	783	3/01	4c
Rental unit, 1 bedroom, with utilities	mos	467	4/01	41c
Rental unit, 2 bedroom, with utilities	mos	605	4/01	41c
Rental unit, 3 bedroom, with utilities	mos	830	4/01	41c
Rental unit, 4 bedroom, with utilities	mos	994	4/01	41c
Shelter, expenditures on	yr	6270	1999	30r
Insurance and Pensions				
Life and other personal insurance purchases	yr	387	1999	30r
Pensions and Social Security, expenditures on	yr	2968	1999	30r

Values are in dollars or fractions of dollars. In the column headed *Ref*, references are shown to sources. Each reference is followed by a letter. These refer to the geographical level for which data were reported: s=State, r=Region, and c=City or metro. The abbreviation *ex* is used to mean *except* or *excluding*; *exp* stands for *expenditures*. For other abbreviations and further explanations, please see the Introduction.

Champaign-Urbana, IL - continued

Item	Per	Value	Date	Ref.
Legal Fees				
Divorce, filing fee		100.00-150.00	4/01	35s
Driver's license fee	orig	10.00	1999	48s
Driver's license fee	renew	20.00	1999	48s
Personal Goods				
Personal care products and services purchases	yr	385	1999	30r
Shampoo, Alberto VO5	15 oz	1.21	3/01	4c
Toothpaste, Crest or Colgate	6-7 oz	2.52	3/01	4c
Personal Services				
Dry cleaning, man's 2-pc suit		8.31	3/01	4c
Man's haircut, barbershop, no styling		11.50	3/01	4c
Personal services, household, expenditures on	yr	300	1999	30r
Woman's shampoo, trim, blow-dry, no style-change		27.38	3/01	4c
Pets				
Pets, toys, and playground equipment, expenditures on	yr	375	1999	30r
Restaurant Food				
Chicken, fried, thigh and drumstick, KFC/Church's		2.58	3/01	4c
Hamburger with cheese, McDonald's	1/4 lb	2.20	3/01	4c
Pizza, Pizza Hut or Pizza Inn	11-12 in	9.49	3/01	4c
Taxes				
Federal income taxes paid	yr	2326	1999	30r
Personal taxes, expenditures on	yr	3223	1999	30r
Property taxes paid	yr	1152	1999	30r
State and local income taxes paid	yr	753	1999	30r
Transportation				
Transportation, ACCRA Index		104.30	3/01	4c
Bus fare, one-way	trip	0.75	2000	1c
Bus fare, to central business district	1-way	0.75	3/01	4c
Cars and trucks, new, expenditures on	yr	1280	1999	30r
Cars and trucks, used, expenditures on	yr	1763	1999	30r
Diesel at the pump	gal	1.33	10/99	73s
Gasoline and motor oil purchases	yr	1036	1999	30r
Gasoline before-tax price (cents)	gal	112.70	10/00	43s
Maintenance and repair expenditures	yr	594	1999	30r
Public transportation, expenditures on	yr	341	1999	30r
Tire balance, computer or spin balance, front	wheel	8.70	3/01	4c
Transportation purchases	yr	6617	1999	30r
Vehicle expenses, miscellaneous, purchases	yr	2159	1999	30r
Vehicle insurance payments	yr	701	1999	30r
Vehicle purchases (net outlay)	yr	3081	1999	30r
Vehicle rental, lease expenditures	yr	536	1999	30r
Utilities				
Utilities, ACCRA Index		111.30	3/01	4c
Electrical bill, average	mos	63.08	9/00	9s
Electricity, expenditures on	yr	841	1999	30r
Electricity and other, mixed, 2400 sq ft, new home	mos	66.12	3/01	4c
Electricity cost, average	KWh	6.49	9/00	9s
Utilities, fuels, and public services purchased	yr	2401	1999	30r
Water and other public services, expenditures on	yr	273	1999	30r
Weddings				
Wedding (national average cost)		19936	2000	33r
Wedding (regional average total cost)		16195	1997	110r
Attendants' gifts		321	1998	33r
Bridal attendants' apparel (5 persons)		824	2000	33r
Bride's headpiece/veil		173	1998	33r
Bride's wedding dress		859	1998	33r
Clergy, religious facility fee		242	1998	33r
Engagement ring		3177	1998	33r
Flowers		789	1998	33r
Groom's formalwear rental		99	2000	33r
Limousine		410	1998	33r

Item	Per	Value	Date	Ref.
Weddings - continued				
Marriage license cost		15.00-20.00	4/01	35s
Men's formalwear (ushers, best man)		469	2000	33r
Mother of bride apparel		241	2000	33r
Music		866	1998	33r
Photography and videography		1368	1998	33r
Rehearsal dinner		728	1998	33r
Wedding invitations and announcements		341	1998	33r
Wedding reception		7968	2000	33r
Wedding rings (bride and groom)		1060	1998	33r

Charleston, SC

Item	Per	Value	Date	Ref.
Alcoholic Beverages				
Alcoholic beverage purchases	yr	253	1999	30r
Malt beverages, all types, all sizes, any origin	16 oz	0.96	7/01	11r
Appliances				
Major appliances, expenditures on	yr	172	1999	30r
Small appliances, housewares, expenditures on	yr	81	1999	30r
Banking and Money				
Mortgage interest and charges paid	yr	2039	1999	30r
Mortgage principal paid on owned property	yr	1026	1999	30r
Vehicle finance charges paid	yr	365	1999	30r
Business Expenses				
Business travel, car rental	day	51	2001	3c
Business travel, food	day	54	2001	3c
Business travel, hotel	day	107	2001	3c
Charity				
Cash contributions, expenditures	yr	1127	1999	30r
Child Care				
Child raising cost, total, age 0-2	yr	8540	1999	60r
Child raising cost, total, age 3-5	yr	8780	1999	60r
Child raising cost, total, age 6-8	yr	8820	1999	60r
Child raising cost, total, age 9-11	yr	8800	1999	60r
Child raising cost, total, age 12-14	yr	9510	1999	60r
Child raising cost, total, age 15-17	yr	9740	1999	60r
Child's child care and education, age 0-2	yr	1380	1999	60r
Child's child care and education, age 3-5	yr	1520	1999	60r
Child's child care and education, age 6-8	yr	990	1999	60r
Child's child care and education, age 9-11	yr	650	1999	60r
Child's child care and education, age 12-14	yr	490	1999	60r
Child's child care and education, age 15-17	yr	840	1999	60r
Child's clothing, age 0-2	yr	480	1999	60r
Child's clothing, age 3-5	yr	470	1999	60r
Child's clothing, age 6-8	yr	520	1999	60r
Child's clothing, age 9-11	yr	570	1999	60r
Child's clothing, age 12-14	yr	950	1999	60r
Child's clothing, age 15-17	yr	850	1999	60r
Child's food, age 0-2	yr	1000	1999	60r
Child's food, age 3-5	yr	1160	1999	60r
Child's food, age 6-8	yr	1490	1999	60r
Child's food, age 9-11	yr	1770	1999	60r
Child's food, age 12-14	yr	1770	1999	60r
Child's food, age 15-17	yr	1980	1999	60r
Child's health care, age 0-2	yr	620	1999	60r
Child's health care, age 3-5	yr	590	1999	60r
Child's health care, age 6-8	yr	680	1999	60r
Child's health care, age 9-11	yr	720	1999	60r
Child's health care, age 12-14	yr	730	1999	60r
Child's health care, age 15-17	yr	760	1999	60r
Child's housing, age 0-2	yr	3070	1999	60r
Child's housing, age 3-5	yr	3050	1999	60r
Child's housing, age 6-8	yr	3010	1999	60r
Child's housing, age 9-11	yr	2850	1999	60r
Child's housing, age 12-14	yr	3040	1999	60r
Child's housing, age 15-17	yr	2650	1999	60r
Child's personal care, reading, age 0-2	yr	910	1999	60r

Values are in dollars or fractions of dollars. In the column headed *Ref*, references are shown to sources. Each reference is followed by a letter. These refer to the geographical level for which data were reported: s=State, r=Region, and c=City or metro. The abbreviation *ex* is used to mean *except* or *excluding*; *exp* stands for expenditures. For other abbreviations and further explanations, please see the Introduction.

Charleston, SC - continued

Item	Per	Value	Date	Ref.
Child Care				
Child's personal care, reading, age 3-5	yr	930	1999	60r
Child's personal care, reading, age 6-8	yr	960	1999	60r
Child's personal care, reading, age 9-11	yr	1000	1999	60r
Child's personal care, reading, age 12-14	yr	1170	1999	60r
Child's personal care, reading, age 15-17	yr	950	1999	60r
Clothing				
Apparel and services purchases	yr	1610	1999	30r
Boys, 2 to 15, expenditures on	yr	89	1999	30r
Children under 2, expenditures on	yr	79	1999	30r
Footwear, expenditures on	yr	283	1999	30r
Girls, 2 to 15, expenditures on	yr	103	1999	30r
Men and boys, expenditures on	yr	351	1999	30r
Men, 16 and over, expenditures on	yr	262	1999	30r
Women, 16 and over, expenditures on	yr	538	1999	30r
Communications				
Cable modem installation, Adelphi		54.90	6/99	103s
Cable modem installation, Comcast		95.00	6/99	103s
Cable modem installation, Intermedia		149.95	6/99	103s
Cable modem rate, cable subscriber, Adelphi	mos	34.95	6/99	103s
Cable modem rate, cable subscriber, Comcast	mos	39.95	6/99	103s
Cable modem rate, cable subscriber, Intermedia	mos	49.95	6/99	103s
Cable modem rate, non-cable subscriber, Adelphi	mos	44.95	6/99	103s
Cable modem rate, non-cable subscriber, Comcast	mos	49.95	6/99	103s
Cable modem rate, non-cable subscriber, Intermedia	mos	54.95	6/99	103s
Phone line, single, business, field visit	inst.	64.00	12/97	17s
Phone line, single, business, no field visit	inst.	64.00	12/97	17s
Phone line, single, residence, field visit	inst.	40.00	12/97	17s
Phone line, single, residence, no field visit	inst.	40.00	12/97	17s
Postage and stationery, expenditures on	yr	104	1999	30r
Postal rate, express mail, up to half-pound		12.45	7/01	108r
Postal rate, letter, first class, first ounce		0.34	7/01	108r
Postal rate, letter, two ounces		0.57	7/01	108r
Postal rate, post card		0.21	7/01	108r
Postal rate, priority mail, two pounds		3.95	7/01	108r
Postal rate, priority mail, up to one pound		3.50	7/01	108r
Telephone services, expenditures on	yr	860	1999	30r
Education				
Board, 4-year private college/university	yr	1990	1996	38s
Board, 4-year public college/university	yr	1872	1996	38s
Education expenditures	yr	431	1999	30r
Room, 4-year private college/university	yr	1786	1996	38s
Room, 4-year public college/university	yr	1998	1996	38s
Total cost, 4-year private college/university	yr	13517	1996	38s
Total cost, 4-year public college/university	yr	6964	1996	38s
Tuition, 2-year public college/university, in state	yr	1071	1996	38s
Tuition, 4-year private college/university, in state	yr	9741	1996	38s
Tuition, 4-year public college/university	yr	3094	1996	38s
Energy and Fuels				
Electricity	KWh	0.09	7/01	11r
Electricity	500 KWhs	47.29	7/01	11r
Fuel oil #2	gal	1.43	7/01	11r
Fuel oil and other fuels, expenditures on	yr	45	1999	30r
Gas, natural, commercial rate	1000 cf	9.50	11/00	88s
Gasoline, all types	gal	1.60	7/01	11r
Gasoline, unleaded midgrade	gal	1.65	7/01	11r
Gasoline, unleaded premium	gal	1.74	7/01	11r
Natural gas, expenditures on	yr	164	1999	30r
Utility (piped) gas, therm		1.01	7/01	11r
Utility (piped) gas, 40 therms		44.29	7/01	11r
Utility (piped) gas, 100 therms		97.44	7/01	11r

Charleston, SC - continued

Item	Per	Value	Date	Ref.
Entertainment				
Entertainment purchases	yr	1574	1999	30r
Fees and admissions paid	yr	371	1999	30r
Reading purchases	yr	121	1999	30r
Television, radios, sound equipment, expenditures on	yr	561	1999	30r
Funerals				
Total cost of funeral		5922.53	1/99	78r
Acknowledgement cards		63.43	1/99	78r
Casket		2258.77	1/99	78r
Cosmetology, hair, other preparation		127.09	1/99	78r
Embalming		393.49	1/99	78r
Funeral at funeral home		367.50	1/99	78r
Hearse (local)		169.66	1/99	78r
Professional service charges		1211.32	1/99	78r
Service car/van		80.69	1/99	78r
Transfer of remains to funeral home		144.25	1/99	78r
Vault		803.50	1/99	78r
Visitation/viewing		302.83	1/99	78r
Groceries				
American processed cheese	lb	3.50	7/01	11r
Bakery products, expenditures on	yr	261	1999	30r
Bananas	lb	0.47	7/01	11r
Beans, dried, any type, all sizes	lb	0.63	7/01	11r
Beef for stew, boneless	lb	2.86	7/01	11r
Beef, expenditures on	yr	210	1999	30r
Bologna, all beef or mixed	lb	2.29	7/01	11r
Bread, French	lb	1.66	7/01	11r
Bread, white, pan	lb	0.87	7/01	11r
Bread, whole wheat, pan	lb	1.38	7/01	11r
Broccoli	lb	1.04	7/01	11r
Butter, salted, grade AA, stick	lb	2.26	7/01	11r
Butter, yoghurt, cheese, etc, expenditures on	yr	170	1999	30r
Cabbage	lb	0.42	7/01	11r
Cereals and cereal products, expenditures on	yr	140	1999	30r
Cheddar cheese, natural	lb	3.75	7/01	11r
Chicken breast, bone-in	lb	1.85	7/01	11r
Chicken legs, bone-in	lb	1.34	7/01	11r
Chicken, fresh, whole	lb	1.05	7/01	11r
Chops, boneless,	lb	4.13	7/01	11r
Chuck roast, graded and ungraded, excl U.S. prime and choice	lb	2.35	7/01	11r
Chuck roast, U.S. choice, boneless	lb	2.67	7/01	11r
Coffee, 100%, ground roast, all sizes	lb	2.88	7/01	11r
Coffee, instant, plain, regular, all sizes	16 oz	9.25	7/01	11r
Cola, non diet,	2 liter	1.11	7/01	11r
Crackers, soda, salted	lb	1.70	7/01	11r
Dairy product purchases	yr	282	1999	30r
Eggs, expenditures on	yr	32	1999	30r
Fats and oils, expenditures on	yr	79	1999	30r
Fish and seafood, expenditures on	yr	99	1999	30r
Flour, white, all purpose	lb	0.32	7/01	11r
Food (excl fruit and vegetables), eaten at home, purchases	yr	815	1999	30r
Food cooked on trips, expenditures on	yr	36	1999	30r
Food purchases	yr	4533	1999	30r
Food purchases, eaten away from home	yr	1873	1999	30r
Food purchases, food eaten at home	yr	2660	1999	30r
Fresh fruits, expenditures on	yr	128	1999	30r
Fresh milk and cream, expenditures on	yr	112	1999	30r
Fresh vegetables, expenditures on	yr	131	1999	30r
Fruit and vegetable purchases	yr	438	1999	30r
Grapefruit	lb	0.59	7/01	11r
Grapes, Thompson, seedless	lb	2.12	7/01	11r
Ground beef, 100% beef	lb	1.76	7/01	11r
Ground beef, lean and extra lean	lb	2.60	7/01	11r
Ground chuck, 100% beef	lb	2.08	7/01	11r
Ham, boneless, excl canned	lb	2.71	7/01	11r
Ham, rump or shank half, bone-in, smoked	lb	2.19	7/01	11r
Ice cream, prepackaged, bulk, regular	1/2 gal	3.93	7/01	11r
Lemons	lb	1.32	7/01	11r

Values are in dollars or fractions of dollars. In the column headed *Ref*, references are shown to sources. Each reference is followed by a letter. These refer to the geographical level for which data were reported: s=State, r=Region, and c=City or metro. The abbreviation *ex* is used to mean *except* or *excluding*; *exp* stands for *expenditures*. For other abbreviations and further explanations, please see the Introduction.

Charleston, SC - continued

Item	Per	Value	Date	Ref.
Groceries				
Lettuce, iceberg	lb	0.76	7/01	11r
Milk, fresh, low fat,	gal	2.75	7/01	11r
Milk, fresh, whole, fortified	gal	2.97	7/01	11r
Nonalcoholic beverages, expenditures on	yr	228	1999	30r
Orange juice, frozen concentrate	16 oz	1.95	7/01	11r
Oranges, Navel	lb	0.73	7/01	11r
Oranges, Valencia	lb	0.55	7/01	11r
Peanut butter, creamy, all sizes	lb	1.83	7/01	11r
Pears, Anjou	lb	0.98	7/01	11r
Pork chops, center cut, bone-in	lb	3.33	7/01	11r
Pork sausage, fresh, loose	lb	2.59	7/01	11r
Pork shoulder picnic, bone-in, smoked	lb	1.12	7/01	11r
Pork, expenditures on	yr	162	1999	30r
Potato chips	16 oz	3.59	7/01	11r
Potatoes, frozen, french fried	lb	1.00	7/01	11r
Potatoes, white, all types	lb	0.44	7/01	11r
Poultry, expenditures on	yr	137	1999	30r
Processed fruits, expenditures on	yr	97	1999	30r
Processed vegetables, expenditures on	yr	82	1999	30r
Rice, white, long grain, uncooked	lb	0.51	7/01	11r
Round roast, graded and ungraded, excl U.S. prime and choice	lb	2.96	7/01	11r
Round steak, graded and ungraded, excl U.S. prime and choice	lb	3.11	7/01	11r
Sirloin steak, graded and ungraded, excl U.S. prime and choice	lb	4.23	7/01	11r
Spaghetti and macaroni	lb	0.78	7/01	11r
Steak, round, U.S. choice, boneless	lb	3.56	7/01	11r
Steak, sirloin, U.S. choice, boneless	lb	5.65	7/01	11r
Strawberries, dry pint	12 oz	1.50	7/01	11r
Sugar and other sweets, expenditures on	yr	99	1999	30r
Sugar, white, 33-80 ounce package	lb	0.39	7/01	11r
Sugar, white, all sizes	lb	0.42	7/01	11r
Tobacco products and smoking supplies purchases	yr	288	1999	30r
Tomatoes, field grown	lb	1.43	7/01	11r
Tuna, light, chunk	lb	1.77	7/01	11r
Turkey, frozen, whole	lb	1.05	7/01	11r
Goods and Services				
B&B Japanese maple (acer japonicum)	gal	49.98-129.00	4/00	93r
Boxwood (buxus)	2 gal	12.99-16.99	4/00	93r
Daylily (hemerocallis)	gal	4.99-8.99	4/00	93r
Flat of annuals		11.00-13.92	4/00	93r
Fountain grass (pennisetum)	gal	5.98-7.98	4/00	93r
Hanging basket (10 in)		7.99-14.98	4/00	93r
Hardy geranium (geranium)	gal	5.98-8.00	4/00	93r
Hosta (hosta)	gal	4.99-10.98	4/00	93r
Lilac (syrubga vulgaris)	2 gal	12.99-21.99	4/00	93r
Rhododendron (rhododendron)	2 gal	14.99-24.99	4/00	93r
Sage (salvia)	gal	5.98-6.99	4/00	93r
Wintercreeper euonymus (euonymus fortunei)	2 gal	7.99-89.99	4/00	93r
Hunting license	yr	12.00	4/01	34s
Health Care				
Cardiac catheterization, ave hospital/ physician charges		12360	1998	77s
Childbirth, Cesarean delivery		11587	1997	13r
Childbirth, vaginal delivery		6725	1997	13r
Drugs, expenditures on	yr	399	1999	30r
Health care purchases	yr	1971	1999	30r

Charleston, SC - continued

Item	Per	Value	Date	Ref.
Health Care - continued				
Health insurance expenditures	yr	933	1999	30r
Hysterectomy, laproscopically-assisted, ave hospital/physician charges		11920	1998	76s
Hysterectomy, vaginal, ave hospital and physician charges		4890	1998	76s
Medicaid dispensing fee		4.05	1999	87s
Medical services expenditures	yr	547	1999	30r
Medical supplies, expenditures on	yr	91	1999	30r
Nursing home costs, private room	day	108	2000	82c
Nursing home stay, private room	day	108	2000	81c
Plastic surgery, breast augmentation		2870	2000	7r
Plastic surgery, breast lift		3649	2000	7r
Plastic surgery, facelift		5008	2000	7r
Plastic surgery, hair transplantation		3425	2000	7r
Plastic surgery, lip augmentation		1227	2000	7r
Plastic surgery, lower body lift		4793	2000	7r
Plastic surgery, thigh lift		3862	2000	7r
Household Goods				
Floor coverings, expenditures on	yr	44	1999	30r
Furniture, expenditures on	yr	335	1999	30r
Household furnishings and equipment purchases	yr	1328	1999	30r
Household textiles, expenditures on	yr	89	1999	30r
Laundry and cleaning supplies, expenditures on	yr	113	1999	30r
Housing				
Home price, existing, ave		160100	10/00	90r
Home value, median		119000	2001	53s
Household operation expenditures	yr	553	1999	30r
Housekeeping supplies purchases	yr	473	1999	30r
Housing, expenditures on	yr	10303	1999	30r
Maintenance, repairs, insurance expenditures	yr	699	1999	30r
Monthly rental value of owned home	mos	505	1999	30r
Owned dwellings, expenditures own	yr	3465	1999	30r
Rent expenditures	yr	1641	1999	30r
Rental unit, 1 bedroom, with utilities	mos	476	4/01	41c
Rental unit, 2 bedroom, with utilities	mos	546	4/01	41c
Rental unit, 3 bedroom, with utilities	mos	726	4/01	41c
Rental unit, 4 bedroom, with utilities	mos	846	4/01	41c
Shelter, expenditures on	yr	5467	1999	30r
Insurance and Pensions				
Auto insurance	yr	655.33	1998	86s
Life and other personal insurance purchases	yr	414	1999	30r
Pensions and Social Security, expenditures on	yr	2635	1999	30r
Personal insurance and pensions, expenditures on	yr	3048	1999	30r
Legal Fees				
Combination hunting and fishing license	yr	20.00	4/01	34s
Driver's license fee	renew	12.50	1999	48s
Driver's license fee	orig	12.50	1999	48s
Fishing license	yr	10.00	4/01	34s
Personal Goods				
Personal care products and services purchases	yr	393	1999	30r
Personal Services				
Personal services, household, expenditures on	yr	258	1999	30r
Pets				
Pets, toys, and playground equipment, expenditures on	yr	306	1999	30r
Taxes				
Federal income taxes paid	yr	2047	1999	30r
Personal taxes, expenditures on	yr	2554	1999	30r
Property taxes paid	yr	726	1999	30r
State and local income taxes paid	yr	363	1999	30r

Values are in dollars or fractions of dollars. In the column headed *Ref*, references are shown to sources. Each reference is followed by a letter. These refer to the geographical level for which data were reported: s=State, r=Region, and c=City or metro. The abbreviation *ex* is used to mean *except* or *excluding*; *exp* stands for *expenditures*. For other abbreviations and further explanations, please see the Introduction.

Charleston, SC - continued

Item	Per	Value	Date	Ref.
Transportation				
Bus fare, one-way	trip	0.75	2000	1c
Cars and trucks, new, expenditures on	yr	1648	1999	30r
Cars and trucks, used, expenditures on	yr	1651	1999	30r
Diesel at the pump	gal	1.13	10/99	73s
Gasoline and motor oil purchases	yr	1052	1999	30r
Gasoline before-tax price (cents)	gal	101.70	10/00	43s
Maintenance and repair expenditures	yr	621	1999	30r
Public transportation, expenditures on	yr	298	1999	30r
Transportation purchases	yr	6738	1999	30r
Vehicle expenses, miscellaneous, purchases	yr	2033	1999	30r
Vehicle insurance payments	yr	696	1999	30r
Vehicle purchases (net outlay)	yr	3354	1999	30r
Vehicle rental, lease expenditures	yr	352	1999	30r
Utilities				
Electrical bill, average	mos	86.42	9/00	9s
Electricity, expenditures on	yr	1115	1999	30r
Electricity cost, average	KWh	5.40	9/00	9s
Water and other public services, expenditures on	yr	298	1999	30r
Weddings				
Wedding (national average cost)		19936	2000	33r
Wedding (regional average total cost)		16293	1997	110r
Attendants' gifts		321	1998	33r
Bridal attendants' apparel (5 persons)		824	2000	33r
Bride's headpiece/veil		173	1998	33r
Bride's wedding dress		859	1998	33r
Clergy, religious facility fee		242	1998	33r
Engagement ring		3177	1998	33r
Flowers		789	1998	33r
Groom's formalwear rental		99	2000	33r
Limousine		410	1998	33r
Marriage license cost		25.00	4/01	35s
Men's formalwear (ushers, best man)		469	2000	33r
Mother of bride apparel		241	2000	33r
Music		866	1998	33r
Photography and videography		1368	1998	33r
Rehearsal dinner		728	1998	33r
Wedding invitations and announcements		341	1998	33r
Wedding reception		7968	2000	33r
Wedding rings (bride and groom)		1060	1998	33r

Charleston, WV

Item	Per	Value	Date	Ref.
Composite, ACCRA index		91.90	3/01	4c
Alcoholic Beverages				
Alcoholic beverage purchases	yr	253	1999	30r
Beer, Heineken, 12-oz, ex deposit	6	6.93	3/01	4c
J & B Scotch	750-ml	18.53	3/01	4c
Malt beverages, all types, all sizes, any origin	16 oz	0.96	7/01	11r
Wine, Livingston or Gallo, Chablis blanc	1.5 liter	6.68	3/01	4c
Appliances				
Appliance repair, service call, washing machine	min lab chg	40.98	3/01	4c
Major appliances, expenditures on	yr	172	1999	30r
Small appliances, housewares, expenditures on	yr	81	1999	30r
Banking and Money				
Mortgage interest and charges paid	yr	2039	1999	30r
Mortgage principal paid on owned property	yr	1026	1999	30r
Mortgage rate, incl. points and orig. fee, 30-yr. conv. fixed or ARM	mos	7.01	3/01	4c
Vehicle finance charges paid	yr	365	1999	30r
Business Expenses				
Business travel, car rental	day	59	2001	3c
Business travel, food	day	40	2001	3c
Business travel, hotel	day	95	2001	3c

Charleston, WV - continued

Item	Per	Value	Date	Ref.
Charity				
Cash contributions, expenditures	yr	1127	1999	30r
Child Care				
Child raising cost, total, age 0-2	yr	8540	1999	60r
Child raising cost, total, age 3-5	yr	8780	1999	60r
Child raising cost, total, age 6-8	yr	8820	1999	60r
Child raising cost, total, age 9-11	yr	8800	1999	60r
Child raising cost, total, age 12-14	yr	9510	1999	60r
Child raising cost, total, age 15-17	yr	9740	1999	60r
Child's child care and education, age 0-2	yr	1380	1999	60r
Child's child care and education, age 3-5	yr	1520	1999	60r
Child's child care and education, age 6-8	yr	990	1999	60r
Child's child care and education, age 9-11	yr	650	1999	60r
Child's child care and education, age 12-14	yr	490	1999	60r
Child's child care and education, age 15-17	yr	840	1999	60r
Child's clothing, age 0-2	yr	480	1999	60r
Child's clothing, age 3-5	yr	470	1999	60r
Child's clothing, age 6-8	yr	520	1999	60r
Child's clothing, age 9-11	yr	570	1999	60r
Child's clothing, age 12-14	yr	950	1999	60r
Child's clothing, age 15-17	yr	850	1999	60r
Child's food, age 0-2	yr	1000	1999	60r
Child's food, age 3-5	yr	1160	1999	60r
Child's food, age 6-8	yr	1490	1999	60r
Child's food, age 9-11	yr	1770	1999	60r
Child's food, age 12-14	yr	1770	1999	60r
Child's food, age 15-17	yr	1980	1999	60r
Child's health care, age 0-2	yr	620	1999	60r
Child's health care, age 3-5	yr	590	1999	60r
Child's health care, age 6-8	yr	680	1999	60r
Child's health care, age 9-11	yr	720	1999	60r
Child's health care, age 12-14	yr	730	1999	60r
Child's health care, age 15-17	yr	760	1999	60r
Child's housing, age 0-2	yr	3070	1999	60r
Child's housing, age 3-5	yr	3050	1999	60r
Child's housing, age 6-8	yr	3010	1999	60r
Child's housing, age 9-11	yr	2850	1999	60r
Child's housing, age 12-14	yr	3040	1999	60r
Child's housing, age 15-17	yr	2650	1999	60r
Child's personal care, reading, age 0-2	yr	910	1999	60r
Child's personal care, reading, age 3-5	yr	930	1999	60r
Child's personal care, reading, age 6-8	yr	960	1999	60r
Child's personal care, reading, age 9-11	yr	1000	1999	60r
Child's personal care, reading, age 12-14	yr	1170	1999	60r
Child's personal care, reading, age 15-17	yr	950	1999	60r
Clothing				
Apparel and services purchases	yr	1610	1999	30r
Boys' brief, cotton	3	5.38	3/01	4c
Boys, 2 to 15, expenditures on	yr	89	1999	30r
Children under 2, expenditures on	yr	79	1999	30r
Footwear, expenditures on	yr	283	1999	30r
Girls, 2 to 15, expenditures on	yr	103	1999	30r
Men and boys, expenditures on	yr	351	1999	30r
Men, 16 and over, expenditures on	yr	262	1999	30r
Shirt, man's dress shirt		25.41	3/01	4c
Slacks, man's "No Wrinkles" khaki		35.29	3/01	4c
Women, 16 and over, expenditures on	yr	538	1999	30r
Communications				
Newspaper subscription, daily and Sunday delivery	mos	12.25	3/01	4c
Phone line, single, business, field visit	inst.	96.90	12/97	17s
Phone line, single, business, no field visit	inst.	96.90	12/97	17s
Phone line, single, residence, field visit	inst.	42.00	12/97	17s
Phone line, single, residence, no field visit	inst.	42.00	12/97	17s
Postage and stationery, expenditures on	yr	104	1999	30r
Postal rate, express mail, up to half-pound		12.45	7/01	108r
Postal rate, letter, first class, first ounce		0.34	7/01	108r
Postal rate, letter, two ounces		0.57	7/01	108r
Postal rate, post card		0.21	7/01	108r
Postal rate, priority mail, two pounds		3.95	7/01	108r
Postal rate, priority mail, up to one pound		3.50	7/01	108r
Telephone bill, business, basic rate	mos	24.50	12/97	18c

Values are in dollars or fractions of dollars. In the column headed *Ref*, references are shown to sources. Each reference is followed by a letter. These refer to the geographical level for which data were reported: s=State, r=Region, and c=City or metro. The abbreviation *ex* is used to mean *except* or *excluding*; *exp* stands for *expenditures*. For other abbreviations and further explanations, please see the Introduction.

Charleston, WV - continued

Item	Per	Value	Date	Ref.
Communications				
Telephone bill, family of three	mos	26.26	3/01	4c
Telephone bill, residential, basic rate	mos	36.15	12/97	18c
Telephone services, expenditures on	yr	860	1999	30r
Education				
Board, 4-year private college/university	yr	2370	1996	38s
Board, 4-year public college/university	yr	2133	1996	38s
Education expenditures	yr	431	1999	30r
Room, 4-year private college/university	yr	1853	1996	38s
Room, 4-year public college/university	yr	1970	1996	38s
Total cost, 4-year private college/university	yr	14231	1996	38s
Total cost, 4-year public college/university	yr	6128	1996	38s
Tuition, 2-year public college/university, in state	yr	1312	1996	38s
Tuition, 4-year private college/university, in state	yr	10008	1996	38s
Tuition, 4-year public college/university	yr	2024	1996	38s
Energy and Fuels				
Electricity	KWh	0.09	7/01	11r
Electricity	500 KWhs	47.29	7/01	11r
Energy, combined forms, 2400 sq ft	mos	87.16	3/01	4c
Energy, exc. electricity, 2400 sq ft	mos	45.19	3/01	4c
Fuel oil #2	gal	1.43	7/01	11r
Fuel oil and other fuels, expenditures on	yr	45	1999	30r
Gas, cooking, winter, 10 therms	mos	10.87	2/96	98c
Gas, cooking, winter, 30 therms	mos	22.61	2/96	98c
Gas, cooking, winter, 50 therms	mos	34.35	2/96	98c
Gas, heating, winter, average use	mos	117.06	2/96	98c
Gas, natural, commercial rate	1000 cf	6.75	11/00	88s
Gas, regular unleaded, cash, self-service	gal	1.49	3/01	4c
Gasoline, all types	gal	1.60	7/01	11r
Gasoline, unleaded midgrade	gal	1.65	7/01	11r
Gasoline, unleaded premium	gal	1.74	7/01	11r
Natural gas, expenditures on	yr	164	1999	30r
Utility (piped) gas, therm		1.01	7/01	11r
Utility (piped) gas, 40 therms		44.29	7/01	11r
Utility (piped) gas, 100 therms		97.44	7/01	11r
Entertainment				
Bowling, Saturday evening rate	line	2.17	3/01	4c
Entertainment purchases	yr	1574	1999	30r
Fees and admissions paid	yr	371	1999	30r
Monopoly game, Parker Brothers', No. 9	game	11.34	3/01	4c
Movie, first-run, Saturday, evening	adm.	6.81	3/01	4c
Reading purchases	yr	121	1999	30r
Television, radios, sound equipment, expenditures on	yr	561	1999	30r
Tennis balls, yellow, Wilson or Penn, 3	can	2.17	3/01	4c
Funerals				
Total cost of funeral		5922.53	1/99	78r
Acknowledgement cards		63.43	1/99	78r
Casket		2258.77	1/99	78r
Cosmetology, hair, other preparation		127.09	1/99	78r
Embalming		393.49	1/99	78r
Funeral at funeral home		367.50	1/99	78r
Hearse (local)		169.66	1/99	78r
Professional service charges		1211.32	1/99	78r
Service car/van		80.69	1/99	78r
Transfer of remains to funeral home		144.25	1/99	78r
Vault		803.50	1/99	78r
Visitation/viewing		302.83	1/99	78r
Groceries				
Groceries, ACCRA Index		98.40	3/01	4c
American processed cheese	lb	3.50	7/01	11r
Antibiotic ointment, Polysporin	0.5 oz	4.71	3/01	4c
Baby food, strained vegetables or fruit, lowest price	4-4.5 oz	0.42	3/01	4c
Bakery products, expenditures on	yr	261	1999	30r
Bananas	lb	0.47	3/01	4c
Bananas	lb	0.47	7/01	11r

Charleston, WV - continued

Item	Per	Value	Date	Ref.
Groceries - continued				
Beans, dried, any type, all sizes	lb	0.63	7/01	11r
Beef for stew, boneless	lb	2.86	7/01	11r
Beef or hamburger, ground	lb	2.31	3/01	4c
Beef, expenditures on	yr	210	1999	30r
Bologna, all beef or mixed	lb	2.29	7/01	11r
Bread, French	lb	1.66	7/01	11r
Bread, white	loaf	0.98	3/01	4c
Bread, white, pan	lb	0.87	7/01	11r
Bread, whole wheat, pan	lb	1.38	7/01	11r
Broccoli	lb	1.04	7/01	11r
Butter, salted, grade AA, stick	lb	2.26	7/01	11r
Butter, yoghurt, cheese, etc, expenditures on	yr	170	1999	30r
Cabbage	lb	0.42	7/01	11r
Cereals and cereal products, expenditures on	yr	140	1999	30r
Cheddar cheese, natural	lb	3.75	7/01	11r
Cheese, Kraft grated Parmesan	8 oz	3.73	3/01	4c
Chicken breast, bone-in	lb	1.85	7/01	11r
Chicken legs, bone-in	lb	1.34	7/01	11r
Chicken, fresh, whole	lb	1.05	7/01	11r
Chicken, whole fryer	lb	1.09	3/01	4c
Chops, boneless,	lb	4.13	7/01	11r
Chuck roast, graded and ungraded, excl U.S. prime and choice	lb	2.35	7/01	11r
Chuck roast, U.S. choice, boneless	lb	2.67	7/01	11r
Cigarettes, Winston, Kings	carton	25.23	3/01	4c
Coffee, 100%, ground roast, all sizes	lb	2.88	7/01	11r
Coffee, instant, plain, regular, all sizes	16 oz	9.25	7/01	11r
Coffee, vacuum-packed	13 oz	2.33	3/01	4c
Cola, non diet,	2 liter	1.11	7/01	11r
Corn Flakes, Kellogg's or Post Toasties	18 oz	2.40	3/01	4c
Corn, frozen, whole kernel, lowest price	16 oz	1.12	3/01	4c
Crackers, soda, salted	lb	1.70	7/01	11r
Dairy product purchases	yr	282	1999	30r
Eggs, expenditures on	yr	32	1999	30r
Eggs, Grade A or AA	dozen	0.94	3/01	4c
Fats and oils, expenditures on	yr	79	1999	30r
Fish and seafood, expenditures on	yr	99	1999	30r
Flour, white, all purpose	lb	0.32	7/01	11r
Food (excl fruit and vegetables), eaten at home, purchases	yr	815	1999	30r
Food cooked on trips, expenditures on	yr	36	1999	30r
Food purchases	yr	4533	1999	30r
Food purchases, eaten away from home	yr	1873	1999	30r
Food purchases, food eaten at home	yr	2660	1999	30r
Fresh fruits, expenditures on	yr	128	1999	30r
Fresh milk and cream, expenditures on	yr	112	1999	30r
Fresh vegetables, expenditures on	yr	131	1999	30r
Fruit and vegetable purchases	yr	438	1999	30r
Grapefruit	lb	0.59	7/01	11r
Grapes, Thompson, seedless	lb	2.12	7/01	11r
Ground beef, 100% beef	lb	1.76	7/01	11r
Ground beef, lean and extra lean	lb	2.60	7/01	11r
Ground chuck, 100% beef	lb	2.08	7/01	11r
Ham, boneless, excl canned	lb	2.71	7/01	11r
Ham, rump or shank half, bone-in, smoked	lb	2.19	7/01	11r
Ice cream, prepackaged, bulk, regular	1/2 gal	3.93	7/01	11r
Lemons	lb	1.32	7/01	11r
Lettuce, iceberg	head	1.17	3/01	4c
Lettuce, iceberg	lb	0.76	7/01	11r
Margarine, Blue Bonnet or Parkay, stick	lb	0.70	3/01	4c
Milk, fresh, low fat,	gal	2.75	7/01	11r
Milk, fresh, whole, fortified	gal	2.97	7/01	11r
Milk, whole	1/2 gal	1.64	3/01	4c
Nonalcoholic beverages, expenditures on	yr	228	1999	30r
Orange juice, frozen concentrate	16 oz	1.95	7/01	11r
Orange juice, Minute Maid frozen	12 oz	1.56	3/01	4c
Oranges, Navel	lb	0.73	7/01	11r
Oranges, Valencia	lb	0.55	7/01	11r
Peaches, halves or slices, Hunt's, Del Monte, or Libby's	29 oz	1.68	3/01	4c
Peanut butter, creamy, all sizes	lb	1.83	7/01	11r

Values are in dollars or fractions of dollars. In the column headed *Ref*, references are shown to sources. Each reference is followed by a letter. These refer to the geographical level for which data were reported: s=State, r=Region, and c=City or metro. The abbreviation *ex* is used to mean *except* or *excluding; exp* stands for *expenditures*. For other abbreviations and further explanations, please see the Introduction.

Charleston, WV - continued

Item	Per	Value	Date	Ref.
Groceries				
Pears, Anjou	lb	0.98	7/01	11r
Peas, green, Del Monte or Green Giant	15 oz	0.61	3/01	4c
Pork chops, center cut, bone-in	lb	3.33	7/01	11r
Pork sausage, fresh, loose	lb	2.59	7/01	11r
Pork shoulder picnic, bone-in, smoked	lb	1.12	7/01	11r
Pork, expenditures on	yr	162	1999	30r
Potato chips	16 oz	3.59	7/01	11r
Potatoes, frozen, french fried	lb	1.00	7/01	11r
Potatoes, white or red	10 lb	2.80	3/01	4c
Potatoes, white, all types	lb	0.44	7/01	11r
Poultry, expenditures on	yr	137	1999	30r
Processed fruits, expenditures on	yr	97	1999	30r
Processed vegetables, expenditures on	yr	82	1999	30r
Rice, white, long grain, uncooked	lb	0.51	7/01	11r
Round roast, graded and ungraded, excl U.S. prime and choice	lb	2.96	7/01	11r
Round steak, graded and ungraded, excl U.S. prime and choice	lb	3.11	7/01	11r
Sausage, Jimmy Dean/Owens pork	lb	3.05	3/01	4c
Shortening, vegetable, Crisco	3 lb	2.97	3/01	4c
Sirloin steak, graded and ungraded, excl U.S. prime and choice	lb	4.23	7/01	11r
Soft drink, Coca Cola, ex deposit	2 liter	1.05	3/01	4c
Spaghetti and macaroni	lb	0.78	7/01	11r
Steak, round, U.S. choice, boneless	lb	3.56	7/01	11r
Steak, sirloin, U.S. choice, boneless	lb	5.65	7/01	11r
Steak, T-bone	lb	6.23	3/01	4c
Strawberries, dry pint	12 oz	1.50	7/01	11r
Sugar and other sweets, expenditures on	yr	99	1999	30r
Sugar, cane or beet	4 lbs	1.57	3/01	4c
Sugar, white, 33-80 ounce package	lb	0.39	7/01	11r
Sugar, white, all sizes	lb	0.42	7/01	11r
Tobacco products and smoking supplies purchases	yr	288	1999	30r
Tomatoes, field grown	lb	1.43	7/01	11r
Tomatoes, Hunt's or Del Monte	14.5 oz	0.97	3/01	4c
Tuna, chunk, light	6 oz	0.59	3/01	4c
Tuna, light, chunk	lb	1.77	7/01	11r
Turkey, frozen, whole	lb	1.05	7/01	11r
Goods and Services				
Miscellaneous goods and services, ACCRA Index		94.90	3/01	4c
B&B Japanese maple (acer japonicum)	gal	49.98-129.00	4/00	93r
Boxwood (buxus)	2 gal	12.99-16.99	4/00	93r
Daylily (hemerocallis)	gal	4.99-8.99	4/00	93r
Flat of annuals		11.00-13.92	4/00	93r
Fountain grass (pennisetum)	gal	5.98-7.98	4/00	93r
Hanging basket (10 in)		7.99-14.98	4/00	93r
Hardy geranium (geranium)	gal	5.98-8.00	4/00	93r
Hosta (hosta)	gal	4.99-10.98	4/00	93r
Lilac (syrubga vulgaris)	2 gal	12.99-21.99	4/00	93r
Rhododendron (rhododendron)	2 gal	14.99-24.99	4/00	93r
Sage (salvia)	gal	5.98-6.99	4/00	93r
Wintercreeper euonymus (euonymus fortunei)	2 gal	7.99-89.99	4/00	93r
Hunting license	yr	11.00	4/01	34s
Health Care				
Health care, ACCRA Index		87.80	3/01	4c
Cardiac catheterization, ave hospital/ physician charges		10540	1998	77s

Charleston, WV - continued

Item	Per	Value	Date	Ref.
Health Care - continued				
Childbirth, Cesarean delivery		11587	1997	13r
Childbirth, vaginal delivery		6725	1997	13r
Dentist's fee, adult teeth cleaning and periodic oral exam	visit	65.71	3/01	4c
Doctor's fee, routine exam, established patient	visit	55.29	3/01	4c
Drugs, expenditures on	yr	399	1999	30r
Health care purchases	yr	1971	1999	30r
Health insurance expenditures	yr	933	1999	30r
Hospital care, private room	day	314.67	3/01	4c
Hysterectomy, laproscopically-assisted, ave hospital/physician charges		11620	1998	76s
Hysterectomy, vaginal, ave hospital and physician charges		8550	1998	76s
Medicaid dispensing fee		3.90-4.90	1999	87s
Medical services expenditures	yr	547	1999	30r
Medical supplies, expenditures on	yr	91	1999	30r
Plastic surgery, breast augmentation		2870	2000	7r
Plastic surgery, breast lift		3649	2000	7r
Plastic surgery, facelift		5008	2000	7r
Plastic surgery, hair transplantation		3425	2000	7r
Plastic surgery, lip augmentation		1227	2000	7r
Plastic surgery, lower body lift		4793	2000	7r
Plastic surgery, thigh lift		3862	2000	7r
Household Goods				
Dishwashing powder, Cascade	50 oz	3.11	3/01	4c
Floor coverings, expenditures on	yr	44	1999	30r
Furniture, expenditures on	yr	335	1999	30r
Household furnishings and equipment purchases	yr	1328	1999	30r
Household textiles, expenditures on	yr	89	1999	30r
Laundry and cleaning supplies, expenditures on	yr	113	1999	30r
Tissues, facial, Kleenex brand	175	1.15	3/01	4c
Housing				
Housing, ACCRA Index		86.30	3/01	4c
Home, 2200 sq ft, 4-br, 2-bath, 2-car garage, average		189000	2000	47c
Home price, existing, ave		160100	10/00	90r
Home value, median		93000	2001	53s
House, 2400 sq ft, 8000 sq ft lot, new, urban, utilities	total	180000	3/01	4c
House payment, principal and interest, 25% down payment	mos	899	3/01	4c
Household operation expenditures	yr	553	1999	30r
Housekeeping supplies purchases	yr	473	1999	30r
Housing, expenditures on	yr	10303	1999	30r
Maintenance, repairs, insurance expenditures	yr	699	1999	30r
Monthly rental value of owned home	mos	505	1999	30r
Owned dwellings, expenditures own	yr	3465	1999	30r
Rent expenditures	yr	1641	1999	30r
Rent, apartment, 2 br, 1 1/2-2 baths, unfurn, 950 sq ft, water	mos	573	3/01	4c
Rental unit, 1 bedroom, with utilities	mos	393	4/01	41c
Rental unit, 2 bedroom, with utilities	mos	499	4/01	41c
Rental unit, 3 bedroom, with utilities	mos	685	4/01	41c
Rental unit, 4 bedroom, with utilities	mos	749	4/01	41c
Shelter, expenditures on	yr	5467	1999	30r
Insurance and Pensions				
Life and other personal insurance purchases	yr	414	1999	30r
Pensions and Social Security, expenditures on	yr	2635	1999	30r
Personal insurance and pensions, expenditures on	yr	3048	1999	30r
Legal Fees				
Combination hunting and fishing license	yr	17.00	4/01	34s
Driver's license fee	renew	12.50	1999	48s
Driver's license fee	orig	12.50	1999	48s

Values are in dollars or fractions of dollars. In the column headed *Ref*, references are shown to sources. Each reference is followed by a letter. These refer to the geographical level for which data were reported: s=State, r=Region, and c=City or metro. The abbreviation *ex* is used to mean *except* or *excluding*; *exp* stands for *expenditures*. For other abbreviations and further explanations, please see the Introduction.

Charleston, WV - continued

Item	Per	Value	Date	Ref.
Legal Fees				
Fishing license	yr	11.00	4/01	34s
Personal Goods				
Personal care products and services purchases	yr	393	1999	30r
Shampoo, Alberto VO5	15 oz	1.15	3/01	4c
Toothpaste, Crest or Colgate	6-7 oz	2.45	3/01	4c
Personal Services				
Dry cleaning, man's 2-pc suit		7.58	3/01	4c
Man's haircut, barbershop, no styling		8.20	3/01	4c
Personal services, household, expenditures on	yr	258	1999	30r
Woman's shampoo, trim, blow-dry, no style-change		23.90	3/01	4c
Pets				
Pets, toys, and playground equipment, expenditures on	yr	306	1999	30r
Restaurant Food				
Chicken, fried, thigh and drumstick, KFC/Church's		2.18	3/01	4c
Hamburger with cheese, McDonald's	1/4 lb	2.17	3/01	4c
Pizza, Pizza Hut or Pizza Inn	11-12 in	7.99	3/01	4c
Taxes				
Federal income taxes paid	yr	2047	1999	30r
Personal taxes, expenditures on	yr	2554	1999	30r
Property taxes paid	yr	726	1999	30r
State and local income taxes paid	yr	363	1999	30r
Transportation				
Transportation, ACCRA Index		100.00	3/01	4c
Cars and trucks, new, expenditures on	yr	1648	1999	30r
Cars and trucks, used, expenditures on	yr	1651	1999	30r
Diesel at the pump	gal	1.30	10/99	73s
Gasoline and motor oil purchases	yr	1052	1999	30r
Gasoline before-tax price (cents)	gal	108.80	10/00	43s
Maintenance and repair expenditures	yr	621	1999	30r
Public transportation, expenditures on	yr	298	1999	30r
Tire balance, computer or spin balance, front	wheel	7.30	3/01	4c
Transportation purchases	yr	6738	1999	30r
Vehicle expenses, miscellaneous, purchases	yr	2033	1999	30r
Vehicle insurance payments	yr	696	1999	30r
Vehicle purchases (net outlay)	yr	3354	1999	30r
Vehicle rental, lease expenditures	yr	352	1999	30r
Utilities				
Utilities, ACCRA Index		78.20	3/01	4c
Electrical bill, average	mos	60.66	9/00	9s
Electricity, expenditures on	yr	1115	1999	30r
Electricity, summer, 250 KWh	mos	21.62	2/96	96s
Electricity, summer, 500 KWh	mos	38.93	2/96	96s
Electricity, summer, 750 KWh	mos	55.12	2/96	96s
Electricity, summer, 1000 KWh	mos	71.41	2/96	96s
Electricity and other, mixed, 2400 sq ft, new home	mos	41.97	3/01	4c
Electricity cost, average	KWh	5.20	9/00	9s
Water and other public services, expenditures on	yr	298	1999	30r
Weddings				
Wedding (national average cost)		19936	2000	33r
Wedding (regional average total cost)		16293	1997	110r
Attendants' gifts		321	1998	33r
Bridal attendants' apparel (5 persons)		824	2000	33r
Bride's headpiece/veil		173	1998	33r
Bride's wedding dress		859	1998	33r
Clergy, religious facility fee		242	1998	33r
Engagement ring		3177	1998	33r
Flowers		789	1998	33r
Groom's formalwear rental		99	2000	33r
Limousine		410	1998	33r
Marriage license cost		23.00	4/01	35s
Men's formalwear (ushers, best man)		469	2000	33r

Charleston, WV - continued

Item	Per	Value	Date	Ref.
Weddings - continued				
Mother of bride apparel		241	2000	33r
Music		866	1998	33r
Photography and videography		1368	1998	33r
Rehearsal dinner		728	1998	33r
Wedding invitations and announcements		341	1998	33r
Wedding reception		7968	2000	33r
Wedding rings (bride and groom)		1060	1998	33r

Charleston-North Charleston, SC

Item	Per	Value	Date	Ref.
Composite, ACCRA index		101.80	3/01	4c
Alcoholic Beverages				
Alcoholic beverage purchases	yr	253	1999	30r
Beer, Heineken, 12-oz, ex deposit	6	7.49	3/01	4c
J & B Scotch	750-ml	19.26	3/01	4c
Malt beverages, all types, all sizes, any origin	16 oz	0.96	7/01	11r
Wine, Livingston or Gallo, Chablis blanc	1.5 liter	5.85	3/01	4c
Appliances				
Appliance repair, service call, washing machine	min lab chg	46.24	3/01	4c
Major appliances, expenditures on	yr	172	1999	30r
Small appliances, housewares, expenditures on	yr	81	1999	30r
Banking and Money				
Mortgage interest and charges paid	yr	2039	1999	30r
Mortgage principal paid on owned property	yr	1026	1999	30r
Mortgage rate, incl. points and orig. fee, 30-yr. conv. fixed or ARM	mos	6.95	3/01	4c
Vehicle finance charges paid	yr	365	1999	30r
Charity				
Cash contributions, expenditures	yr	1127	1999	30r
Child Care				
Child raising cost, total, age 0-2	yr	8540	1999	60r
Child raising cost, total, age 3-5	yr	8780	1999	60r
Child raising cost, total, age 6-8	yr	8820	1999	60r
Child raising cost, total, age 9-11	yr	8800	1999	60r
Child raising cost, total, age 12-14	yr	9510	1999	60r
Child raising cost, total, age 15-17	yr	9740	1999	60r
Child's child care and education, age 0-2	yr	1380	1999	60r
Child's child care and education, age 3-5	yr	1520	1999	60r
Child's child care and education, age 6-8	yr	990	1999	60r
Child's child care and education, age 9-11	yr	650	1999	60r
Child's child care and education, age 12-14	yr	490	1999	60r
Child's child care and education, age 15-17	yr	840	1999	60r
Child's clothing, age 0-2	yr	480	1999	60r
Child's clothing, age 3-5	yr	470	1999	60r
Child's clothing, age 6-8	yr	520	1999	60r
Child's clothing, age 9-11	yr	570	1999	60r
Child's clothing, age 12-14	yr	950	1999	60r
Child's clothing, age 15-17	yr	850	1999	60r
Child's food, age 0-2	yr	1000	1999	60r
Child's food, age 3-5	yr	1160	1999	60r
Child's food, age 6-8	yr	1490	1999	60r
Child's food, age 9-11	yr	1770	1999	60r
Child's food, age 12-14	yr	1770	1999	60r
Child's food, age 15-17	yr	1980	1999	60r
Child's health care, age 0-2	yr	620	1999	60r
Child's health care, age 3-5	yr	590	1999	60r
Child's health care, age 6-8	yr	680	1999	60r
Child's health care, age 9-11	yr	720	1999	60r
Child's health care, age 12-14	yr	730	1999	60r
Child's health care, age 15-17	yr	760	1999	60r
Child's housing, age 0-2	yr	3070	1999	60r
Child's housing, age 3-5	yr	3050	1999	60r
Child's housing, age 6-8	yr	3010	1999	60r
Child's housing, age 9-11	yr	2850	1999	60r
Child's housing, age 12-14	yr	3040	1999	60r
Child's housing, age 15-17	yr	2650	1999	60r
Child's personal care, reading, age 0-2	yr	910	1999	60r

Values are in dollars or fractions of dollars. In the column headed *Ref*, references are shown to sources. Each reference is followed by a letter. These refer to the geographical level for which data were reported: s=State, r=Region, and c=City or metro. The abbreviation *ex* is used to mean *except* or *excluding*; *exp* stands for expenditures. For other abbreviations and further explanations, please see the Introduction.

Charleston-North Charleston, SC - continued

Item	Per	Value	Date	Ref.
Child Care				
Child's personal care, reading, age 3-5	yr	930	1999	60r
Child's personal care, reading, age 6-8	yr	960	1999	60r
Child's personal care, reading, age 9-11	yr	1000	1999	60r
Child's personal care, reading, age 12-14	yr	1170	1999	60r
Child's personal care, reading, age 15-17	yr	950	1999	60r
Clothing				
Apparel and services purchases	yr	1610	1999	30r
Boys' brief, cotton	3	6.87	3/01	4c
Boys, 2 to 15, expenditures on	yr	89	1999	30r
Children under 2, expenditures on	yr	79	1999	30r
Footwear, expenditures on	yr	283	1999	30r
Girls, 2 to 15, expenditures on	yr	103	1999	30r
Men and boys, expenditures on	yr	351	1999	30r
Men, 16 and over, expenditures on	yr	262	1999	30r
Shirt, man's dress shirt		29.83	3/01	4c
Slacks, man's "No Wrinkles" khaki		42.00	3/01	4c
Women, 16 and over, expenditures on	yr	538	1999	30r
Communications				
Cable modem installation, Adelphi		54.90	6/99	103s
Cable modem installation, Comcast		95.00	6/99	103s
Cable modem installation, Intermedia		149.95	6/99	103s
Cable modem rate, cable subscriber, Adelphi	mos	34.95	6/99	103s
Cable modem rate, cable subscriber, Comcast	mos	39.95	6/99	103s
Cable modem rate, cable subscriber, Intermedia	mos	49.95	6/99	103s
Cable modem rate, non-cable subscriber, Adelphi	mos	44.95	6/99	103s
Cable modem rate, non-cable subscriber, Comcast	mos	49.95	6/99	103s
Cable modem rate, non-cable subscriber, Intermedia	mos	54.95	6/99	103s
Newspaper subscription, daily and Sunday delivery	mos	11.95	3/01	4c
Phone line, single, business, field visit	inst.	64.00	12/97	17s
Phone line, single, business, no field visit	inst.	64.00	12/97	17s
Phone line, single, residence, field visit	inst.	40.00	12/97	17s
Phone line, single, residence, no field visit	inst.	40.00	12/97	17s
Postage and stationery, expenditures on	yr	104	1999	30r
Postal rate, express mail, up to half-pound		12.45	7/01	108r
Postal rate, letter, first class, first ounce		0.34	7/01	108r
Postal rate, letter, two ounces		0.57	7/01	108r
Postal rate, post card		0.21	7/01	108r
Postal rate, priority mail, two pounds		3.95	7/01	108r
Postal rate, priority mail, up to one pound		3.50	7/01	108r
Telephone bill, family of three	mos	22.77	3/01	4c
Telephone services, expenditures on	yr	860	1999	30r
Education				
Board, 4-year private college/university	yr	1990	1996	38s
Board, 4-year public college/university	yr	1872	1996	38s
Education expenditures	yr	431	1999	30r
Room, 4-year private college/university	yr	1786	1996	38s
Room, 4-year public college/university	yr	1998	1996	38s
Total cost, 4-year private college/university	yr	13517	1996	38s
Total cost, 4-year public college/university	yr	6964	1996	38s
Tuition, 2-year public college/university, in state	yr	1071	1996	38s
Tuition, 4-year private college/university, in state	yr	9741	1996	38s
Tuition, 4-year public college/university	yr	3094	1996	38s
Energy and Fuels				
Electricity	KWh	0.09	7/01	11r
Electricity	500 KWhs	47.29	7/01	11r
Energy, combined forms, 2400 sq ft	mos	110.91	3/01	4c
Fuel oil #2	gal	1.43	7/01	11r
Fuel oil and other fuels, expenditures on	yr	45	1999	30r
Gas, natural, commercial rate	1000 cf	9.50	11/00	88s
Gas, regular unleaded, cash, self-service	gal	1.33	3/01	4c
Gasoline, all types	gal	1.60	7/01	11r

Charleston-North Charleston, SC - continued

Item	Per	Value	Date	Ref.
Energy and Fuels - continued				
Gasoline, unleaded midgrade	gal	1.65	7/01	11r
Gasoline, unleaded premium	gal	1.74	7/01	11r
Natural gas, expenditures on	yr	164	1999	30r
Utility (piped) gas, therm		1.01	7/01	11r
Utility (piped) gas, 40 therms		44.29	7/01	11r
Utility (piped) gas, 100 therms		97.44	7/01	11r
Entertainment				
Bowling, Saturday evening rate	line	3.02	3/01	4c
Entertainment purchases	yr	1574	1999	30r
Fees and admissions paid	yr	371	1999	30r
Monopoly game, Parker Brothers', No. 9	game	11.39	3/01	4c
Movie, first-run, Saturday, evening	adm.	6.75	3/01	4c
Reading purchases	yr	121	1999	30r
Television, radios, sound equipment, expenditures on	yr	561	1999	30r
Tennis balls, yellow, Wilson or Penn, 3	can	2.28	3/01	4c
Funerals				
Total cost of funeral		5922.53	1/99	78r
Acknowledgement cards		63.43	1/99	78r
Casket		2258.77	1/99	78r
Cosmetology, hair, other preparation		127.09	1/99	78r
Embalming		393.49	1/99	78r
Funeral at funeral home		367.50	1/99	78r
Hearse (local)		169.66	1/99	78r
Professional service charges		1211.32	1/99	78r
Service car/van		80.69	1/99	78r
Transfer of remains to funeral home		144.25	1/99	78r
Vault		803.50	1/99	78r
Visitation/viewing		302.83	1/99	78r
Groceries				
Groceries, ACCRA Index		102.10	3/01	4c
American processed cheese	lb	3.50	7/01	11r
Antibiotic ointment, Polysporin	0.5 oz	4.28	3/01	4c
Baby food, strained vegetables or fruit, lowest price	4-4.5 oz	0.40	3/01	4c
Bakery products, expenditures on	yr	261	1999	30r
Bananas	lb	0.57	3/01	4c
Bananas	lb	0.47	7/01	11r
Beans, dried, any type, all sizes	lb	0.63	7/01	11r
Beef for stew, boneless	lb	2.86	7/01	11r
Beef or hamburger, ground	lb	1.59	3/01	4c
Beef, expenditures on	yr	210	1999	30r
Bologna, all beef or mixed	lb	2.29	7/01	11r
Bread, French	lb	1.66	7/01	11r
Bread, white	loaf	1.12	3/01	4c
Bread, white, pan	lb	0.87	7/01	11r
Bread, whole wheat, pan	lb	1.38	7/01	11r
Broccoli	lb	1.04	7/01	11r
Butter, salted, grade AA, stick	lb	2.26	7/01	11r
Butter, yoghurt, cheese, etc, expenditures on	yr	170	1999	30r
Cabbage	lb	0.42	7/01	11r
Cereals and cereal products, expenditures on	yr	140	1999	30r
Cheddar cheese, natural	lb	3.75	7/01	11r
Cheese, Kraft grated Parmesan	8 oz	3.24	3/01	4c
Chicken breast, bone-in	lb	1.85	7/01	11r
Chicken legs, bone-in	lb	1.34	7/01	11r
Chicken, fresh, whole	lb	1.05	7/01	11r
Chicken, whole fryer	lb	0.97	3/01	4c
Chops, boneless,	lb	4.13	7/01	11r
Chuck roast, graded and ungraded, excl U.S. prime and choice	lb	2.35	7/01	11r
Chuck roast, U.S. choice, boneless	lb	2.67	7/01	11r
Cigarettes, Winston, Kings	carton	25.79	3/01	4c
Coffee, 100%, ground roast, all sizes	lb	2.88	7/01	11r
Coffee, instant, plain, regular, all sizes	16 oz	9.25	7/01	11r
Coffee, vacuum-packed	13 oz	2.87	3/01	4c
Cola, non diet,	2 liter	1.11	7/01	11r
Corn Flakes, Kellogg's or Post Toasties	18 oz	2.95	3/01	4c
Corn, frozen, whole kernel, lowest price	16 oz	1.23	3/01	4c
Crackers, soda, salted	lb	1.70	7/01	11r

Values are in dollars or fractions of dollars. In the column headed *Ref*, references are shown to sources. Each reference is followed by a letter. These refer to the geographical level for which data were reported: s=State, r=Region, and c=City or metro. The abbreviation *ex* is used to mean *except* or *excluding*; *exp* stands for *expenditures*. For other abbreviations and further explanations, please see the Introduction.

Charleston-North Charleston, SC - continued

Item	Per	Value	Date	Ref.
Groceries				
Dairy product purchases	yr	282	1999	30r
Eggs, expenditures on	yr	32	1999	30r
Eggs, Grade A or AA	dozen	1.11	3/01	4c
Fats and oils, expenditures on	yr	79	1999	30r
Fish and seafood, expenditures on	yr	99	1999	30r
Flour, white, all purpose	lb	0.32	7/01	11r
Food (excl fruit and vegetables), eaten at home, purchases	yr	815	1999	30r
Food cooked on trips, expenditures on	yr	36	1999	30r
Food purchases	yr	4533	1999	30r
Food purchases, eaten away from home	yr	1873	1999	30r
Food purchases, food eaten at home	yr	2660	1999	30r
Fresh fruits, expenditures on	yr	128	1999	30r
Fresh milk and cream, expenditures on	yr	112	1999	30r
Fresh vegetables, expenditures on	yr	131	1999	30r
Fruit and vegetable purchases	yr	438	1999	30r
Grapefruit	lb	0.59	7/01	11r
Grapes, Thompson, seedless	lb	2.12	7/01	11r
Ground beef, 100% beef	lb	1.76	7/01	11r
Ground beef, lean and extra lean	lb	2.60	7/01	11r
Ground chuck, 100% beef	lb	2.08	7/01	11r
Ham, boneless, excl canned	lb	2.71	7/01	11r
Ham, rump or shank half, bone-in, smoked	lb	2.19	7/01	11r
Ice cream, prepackaged, bulk, regular	1/2 gal	3.93	7/01	11r
Lemons	lb	1.32	7/01	11r
Lettuce, iceberg	head	1.19	3/01	4c
Lettuce, iceberg	lb	0.76	7/01	11r
Margarine, Blue Bonnet or Parkay, stick	lb	0.65	3/01	4c
Milk, fresh, low fat,	gal	2.75	7/01	11r
Milk, fresh, whole, fortified	gal	2.97	7/01	11r
Milk, whole	1/2 gal	1.97	3/01	4c
Nonalcoholic beverages, expenditures on	yr	228	1999	30r
Orange juice, frozen concentrate	16 oz	1.95	7/01	11r
Orange juice, Minute Maid frozen	12 oz	1.28	3/01	4c
Oranges, Navel	lb	0.73	7/01	11r
Oranges, Valencia	lb	0.55	7/01	11r
Peaches, halves or slices, Hunt's, Del Monte, or Libby's	29 oz	1.65	3/01	4c
Peanut butter, creamy, all sizes	lb	1.83	7/01	11r
Pears, Anjou	lb	0.98	7/01	11r
Peas, green, Del Monte or Green Giant	15 oz	0.67	3/01	4c
Pork chops, center cut, bone-in	lb	3.33	7/01	11r
Pork sausage, fresh, loose	lb	2.59	7/01	11r
Pork shoulder picnic, bone-in, smoked	lb	1.12	7/01	11r
Pork, expenditures on	yr	162	1999	30r
Potato chips	16 oz	3.59	7/01	11r
Potatoes, frozen, french fried	lb	1.00	7/01	11r
Potatoes, white or red	10 lb	2.89	3/01	4c
Potatoes, white, all types	lb	0.44	7/01	11r
Poultry, expenditures on	yr	137	1999	30r
Processed fruits, expenditures on	yr	97	1999	30r
Processed vegetables, expenditures on	yr	82	1999	30r
Rice, white, long grain, uncooked	lb	0.51	7/01	11r
Round roast, graded and ungraded, excl U.S. prime and choice	lb	2.96	7/01	11r
Round steak, graded and ungraded, excl U.S. prime and choice	lb	3.11	7/01	11r
Sausage, Jimmy Dean/Owens pork	lb	3.11	3/01	4c
Shortening, vegetable, Crisco	3 lb	3.27	3/01	4c
Sirloin steak, graded and ungraded, excl U.S. prime and choice	lb	4.23	7/01	11r
Soft drink, Coca Cola, ex deposit	2 liter	1.21	3/01	4c
Spaghetti and macaroni	lb	0.78	7/01	11r
Steak, round, U.S. choice, boneless	lb	3.56	7/01	11r
Steak, sirloin, U.S. choice, boneless	lb	5.65	7/01	11r
Steak, T-bone	lb	6.79	3/01	4c
Strawberries, dry pint	12 oz	1.50	7/01	11r
Sugar and other sweets, expenditures on	yr	99	1999	30r
Sugar, cane or beet	4 lbs	1.40	3/01	4c
Sugar, white, 33-80 ounce package	lb	0.39	7/01	11r
Sugar, white, all sizes	lb	0.42	7/01	11r

Charleston-North Charleston, SC - continued

Item	Per	Value	Date	Ref.
Groceries - continued				
Tobacco products and smoking supplies purchases	yr	288	1999	30r
Tomatoes, field grown	lb	1.43	7/01	11r
Tomatoes, Hunt's or Del Monte	14.5 oz	0.77	3/01	4c
Tuna, chunk, light	6 oz	0.73	3/01	4c
Tuna, light, chunk	lb	1.77	7/01	11r
Turkey, frozen, whole	lb	1.05	7/01	11r
Goods and Services				
Miscellaneous goods and services, ACCRA Index		104.20	3/01	4c
B&B Japanese maple (acer japonicum)	gal	49.98-129.00	4/00	93r
Boxwood (buxus)	2 gal	12.99-16.99	4/00	93r
Daylilly (hemerocallis)	gal	4.99-8.99	4/00	93r
Flat of annuals		11.00-13.92	4/00	93r
Fountain grass (pennisetum)	gal	5.98-7.98	4/00	93r
Hanging basket (10 in)		7.99-14.98	4/00	93r
Hardy geranium (geranium)	gal	5.98-8.00	4/00	93r
Hosta (hosta)	gal	4.99-10.98	4/00	93r
Lilac (syrubga vulgaris)	2 gal	12.99-21.99	4/00	93r
Rhododendron (rhododendron)	2 gal	14.99-24.99	4/00	93r
Sage (salvia)	gal	5.98-6.99	4/00	93r
Wintercreeper euonymus (euonymus fortunei)	2 gal	7.99-89.99	4/00	93r
Hunting license	yr	12.00	4/01	34s
Health Care				
Health care, ACCRA Index		101.10	3/01	4c
Cardiac catheterization, ave hospital/ physician charges		12360	1998	77s
Childbirth, Cesarean delivery		11587	1997	13r
Childbirth, vaginal delivery		6725	1997	13r
Dentist's fee, adult teeth cleaning and periodic oral exam	visit	74.80	3/01	4c
Doctor's fee, routine exam, established patient	visit	62.40	3/01	4c
Drugs, expenditures on	yr	399	1999	30r
Health care purchases	yr	1971	1999	30r
Health insurance expenditures	yr	933	1999	30r
Hospital care, private room	day	472.00	3/01	4c
Hysterectomy, laproscopically-assisted, ave hospital/physician charges		11920	1998	76s
Hysterectomy, vaginal, ave hospital and physician charges		4890	1998	76s
Medicaid dispensing fee		4.05	1999	87s
Medical services expenditures	yr	547	1999	30r
Medical supplies, expenditures on	yr	91	1999	30r
Plastic surgery, breast augmentation		2870	2000	7r
Plastic surgery, breast lift		3649	2000	7r
Plastic surgery, facelift		5008	2000	7r
Plastic surgery, hair transplantation		3425	2000	7r
Plastic surgery, lip augmentation		1227	2000	7r
Plastic surgery, lower body lift		4793	2000	7r
Plastic surgery, thigh lift		3862	2000	7r
Household Goods				
Dishwashing powder, Cascade	50 oz	3.17	3/01	4c
Floor coverings, expenditures on	yr	44	1999	30r
Furniture, expenditures on	yr	335	1999	30r
Household furnishings and equipment purchases	yr	1328	1999	30r
Household textiles, expenditures on	yr	89	1999	30r

Values are in dollars or fractions of dollars. In the column headed *Ref*, references are shown to sources. Each reference is followed by a letter. These refer to the geographical level for which data were reported: s=State, r=Region, and c=City or metro. The abbreviation *ex* is used to mean *except* or *excluding*; *exp* stands for expenditures. For other abbreviations and further explanations, please see the Introduction.

Charleston-North Charleston, SC - continued

Household Goods

Item	Per	Value	Date	Ref.
Laundry and cleaning supplies, expenditures on	yr	113	1999	30r
Tissues, facial, Kleenex brand	175	1.32	3/01	4c

Housing

Item	Per	Value	Date	Ref.
Housing, ACCRA Index		104.30	3/01	4c
Home price, existing, ave		160100	10/00	90r
Home value, median		119000	2001	53s
House, 2400 sq ft, 8000 sq ft lot, new, urban, utilities	total	217117	3/01	4c
House payment, principal and interest, 25% down payment	mos	1078	3/01	4c
Household operation expenditures	yr	553	1999	30r
Housekeeping supplies purchases	yr	473	1999	30r
Housing, expenditures on	yr	10303	1999	30r
Maintenance, repairs, insurance expenditures	yr	699	1999	30r
Monthly rental value of owned home	mos	505	1999	30r
Owned dwellings, expenditures own	yr	3465	1999	30r
Rent expenditures	yr	1641	1999	30r
Rent, apartment, 2 br, 1 1/2-2 baths, unfurn, 950 sq ft, water	mos	718	3/01	4c
Shelter, expenditures on	yr	5467	1999	30r

Insurance and Pensions

Item	Per	Value	Date	Ref.
Auto insurance	yr	655.33	1998	86s
Life and other personal insurance purchases	yr	414	1999	30r
Pensions and Social Security, expenditures on	yr	2635	1999	30r
Personal insurance and pensions, expenditures on	yr	3048	1999	30r

Legal Fees

Item	Per	Value	Date	Ref.
Combination hunting and fishing license	yr	20.00	4/01	34s
Driver's license fee	renew	12.50	1999	48s
Driver's license fee	orig	12.50	1999	48s
Fishing license	yr	10.00	4/01	34s

Personal Goods

Item	Per	Value	Date	Ref.
Personal care products and services purchases	yr	393	1999	30r
Shampoo, Alberto VO5	15 oz	1.05	3/01	4c
Toothpaste, Crest or Colgate	6-7 oz	2.31	3/01	4c

Personal Services

Item	Per	Value	Date	Ref.
Dry cleaning, man's 2-pc suit		7.70	3/01	4c
Man's haircut, barbershop, no styling		9.60	3/01	4c
Personal services, household, expenditures on	yr	258	1999	30r
Woman's shampoo, trim, blow-dry, no style-change		32.17	3/01	4c

Pets

Item	Per	Value	Date	Ref.
Pets, toys, and playground equipment, expenditures on	yr	306	1999	30r

Restaurant Food

Item	Per	Value	Date	Ref.
Chicken, fried, thigh and drumstick, KFC/Church's		2.36	3/01	4c
Hamburger with cheese, McDonald's	1/4 lb	2.01	3/01	4c
Pizza, Pizza Hut or Pizza Inn	11-12 in	8.79	3/01	4c

Taxes

Item	Per	Value	Date	Ref.
Federal income taxes paid	yr	2047	1999	30r
Personal taxes, expenditures on	yr	2554	1999	30r
Property taxes paid	yr	726	1999	30r
State and local income taxes paid	yr	363	1999	30r

Transportation

Item	Per	Value	Date	Ref.
Transportation, ACCRA Index		94.20	3/01	4c
Bus fare, to central business district	1-way	0.75	3/01	4c
Cars and trucks, new, expenditures on	yr	1648	1999	30r
Cars and trucks, used, expenditures on	yr	1651	1999	30r
Diesel at the pump	gal	1.13	10/99	73s
Gasoline and motor oil purchases	yr	1052	1999	30r
Gasoline before-tax price (cents)	gal	101.70	10/00	43s

Charleston-North Charleston, SC - continued

Transportation - continued

Item	Per	Value	Date	Ref.
Maintenance and repair expenditures	yr	621	1999	30r
Public transportation, expenditures on	yr	298	1999	30r
Tire balance, computer or spin balance, front	wheel	7.98	3/01	4c
Transportation purchases	yr	6738	1999	30r
Vehicle expenses, miscellaneous, purchases	yr	2033	1999	30r
Vehicle insurance payments	yr	696	1999	30r
Vehicle purchases (net outlay)	yr	3354	1999	30r
Vehicle rental, lease expenditures	yr	352	1999	30r

Utilities

Item	Per	Value	Date	Ref.
Utilities, ACCRA Index		92.80	3/01	4c
Electrical bill, average	mos	86.42	9/00	9s
Electricity, 2400 sq ft, new home	mos	110.91	3/01	4c
Electricity, expenditures on	yr	1115	1999	30r
Electricity cost, average	KWh	5.40	9/00	9s
Water and other public services, expenditures on	yr	298	1999	30r

Weddings

Item	Per	Value	Date	Ref.
Wedding (national average cost)		19936	2000	33r
Wedding (regional average total cost)		16293	1997	110r
Attendants' gifts		321	1998	33r
Bridal attendants' apparel (5 persons)		824	2000	33r
Bride's headpiece/veil		173	1998	33r
Bride's wedding dress		859	1998	33r
Clergy, religious facility fee		242	1998	33r
Engagement ring		3177	1998	33r
Flowers		789	1998	33r
Groom's formalwear rental		99	2000	33r
Limousine		410	1998	33r
Marriage license cost		25.00	4/01	35s
Men's formalwear (ushers, best man)		469	2000	33r
Mother of bride apparel		241	2000	33r
Music		866	1998	33r
Photography and videography		1368	1998	33r
Rehearsal dinner		728	1998	33r
Wedding invitations and announcements		341	1998	33r
Wedding reception		7968	2000	33r
Wedding rings (bride and groom)		1060	1998	33r

Charlotte-Gastonia-Rock Hill, NC

Alcoholic Beverages

Item	Per	Value	Date	Ref.
Alcoholic beverage purchases	yr	253	1999	30r
Malt beverages, all types, all sizes, any origin	16 oz	0.96	7/01	11r

Appliances

Item	Per	Value	Date	Ref.
Major appliances, expenditures on	yr	172	1999	30r
Small appliances, housewares, expenditures on	yr	81	1999	30r

Banking and Money

Item	Per	Value	Date	Ref.
Mortgage interest and charges paid	yr	2039	1999	30r
Mortgage principal paid on owned property	yr	1026	1999	30r
Vehicle finance charges paid	yr	365	1999	30r

Charity

Item	Per	Value	Date	Ref.
Cash contributions, expenditures	yr	1127	1999	30r

Child Care

Item	Per	Value	Date	Ref.
Child raising cost, total, age 0-2	yr	8540	1999	60r
Child raising cost, total, age 3-5	yr	8780	1999	60r
Child raising cost, total, age 6-8	yr	8820	1999	60r
Child raising cost, total, age 9-11	yr	8800	1999	60r
Child raising cost, total, age 12-14	yr	9510	1999	60r
Child raising cost, total, age 15-17	yr	9740	1999	60r
Child's child care and education, age 0-2	yr	1380	1999	60r
Child's child care and education, age 3-5	yr	1520	1999	60r
Child's child care and education, age 6-8	yr	990	1999	60r
Child's child care and education, age 9-11	yr	650	1999	60r
Child's child care and education, age 12-14	yr	490	1999	60r
Child's child care and education, age 15-17	yr	840	1999	60r
Child's clothing, age 0-2	yr	480	1999	60r
Child's clothing, age 3-5	yr	470	1999	60r

Values are in dollars or fractions of dollars. In the column headed *Ref*, references are shown to sources. Each reference is followed by a letter. These refer to the geographical level for which data were reported: s=State, r=Region, and c=City or metro. The abbreviation *ex* is used to mean *except* or *excluding*; *exp* stands for *expenditures*. For other abbreviations and further explanations, please see the Introduction.

Charlotte-Gastonia-Rock Hill, NC - continued

Item	Per	Value	Date	Ref.
Child Care				
Child's clothing, age 6-8	yr	520	1999	60r
Child's clothing, age 9-11	yr	570	1999	60r
Child's clothing, age 12-14	yr	950	1999	60r
Child's clothing, age 15-17	yr	850	1999	60r
Child's food, age 0-2	yr	1000	1999	60r
Child's food, age 3-5	yr	1160	1999	60r
Child's food, age 6-8	yr	1490	1999	60r
Child's food, age 9-11	yr	1770	1999	60r
Child's food, age 12-14	yr	1770	1999	60r
Child's food, age 15-17	yr	1980	1999	60r
Child's health care, age 0-2	yr	620	1999	60r
Child's health care, age 3-5	yr	590	1999	60r
Child's health care, age 6-8	yr	680	1999	60r
Child's health care, age 9-11	yr	720	1999	60r
Child's health care, age 12-14	yr	730	1999	60r
Child's health care, age 15-17	yr	760	1999	60r
Child's housing, age 0-2	yr	3070	1999	60r
Child's housing, age 3-5	yr	3050	1999	60r
Child's housing, age 6-8	yr	3010	1999	60r
Child's housing, age 9-11	yr	2850	1999	60r
Child's housing, age 12-14	yr	3040	1999	60r
Child's housing, age 15-17	yr	2650	1999	60r
Child's personal care, reading, age 0-2	yr	910	1999	60r
Child's personal care, reading, age 3-5	yr	930	1999	60r
Child's personal care, reading, age 6-8	yr	960	1999	60r
Child's personal care, reading, age 9-11	yr	1000	1999	60r
Child's personal care, reading, age 12-14	yr	1170	1999	60r
Child's personal care, reading, age 15-17	yr	950	1999	60r
Clothing				
Apparel and services purchases	yr	1610	1999	30r
Boys, 2 to 15, expenditures on	yr	89	1999	30r
Children under 2, expenditures on	yr	79	1999	30r
Footwear, expenditures on	yr	283	1999	30r
Girls, 2 to 15, expenditures on	yr	103	1999	30r
Men and boys, expenditures on	yr	351	1999	30r
Men, 16 and over, expenditures on	yr	262	1999	30r
Women, 16 and over, expenditures on	yr	538	1999	30r
Communications				
Cable modem installation, Intermedia		149.95	6/99	103s
Cable modem installation, Time Warner		75.00-225.00	6/99	103s
Cable modem rate, cable subscriber, Intermedia	mos	49.95	6/99	103s
Cable modem rate, cable subscriber, Time Warner	mos	39.95-49.95	6/99	103s
Cable modem rate, non-cable subscriber, Intermedia	mos	54.95	6/99	103s
Cable modem rate, non-cable subscriber, Time Warner	mos	39.95-54.95	6/99	103s
Phone line, single, business, field visit	inst.	65.00	12/97	17s
Phone line, single, business, no field visit	inst.	65.00	12/97	17s
Phone line, single, residence, field visit	inst.	42.75	12/97	17s
Phone line, single, residence, no field visit	inst.	42.75	12/97	17s
Postage and stationery, expenditures on	yr	104	1999	30r
Postal rate, express mail, up to half-pound		12.45	7/01	108r
Postal rate, letter, first class, first ounce		0.34	7/01	108r
Postal rate, letter, two ounces		0.57	7/01	108r
Postal rate, post card		0.21	7/01	108r
Postal rate, priority mail, two pounds		3.95	7/01	108r
Postal rate, priority mail, up to one pound		3.50	7/01	108r
Telephone services, expenditures on	yr	860	1999	30r
Education				
Board, 4-year private college/university	yr	2316	1996	38s
Board, 4-year public college/university	yr	1737	1996	38s
Education expenditures	yr	431	1999	30r
Room, 4-year private college/university	yr	2128	1996	38s
Room, 4-year public college/university	yr	1742	1996	38s
Total cost, 4-year private college/university	yr	15428	1996	38s
Total cost, 4-year public college/university	yr	5119	1996	38s
Tuition, 4-year private college/university, in state	yr	10984	1996	38s

Charlotte-Gastonia-Rock Hill, NC - continued

Item	Per	Value	Date	Ref.
Education - continued				
Tuition, 4-year public college/university	yr	1639	1996	38s
Energy and Fuels				
Electricity	500 KWhs	47.29	7/01	11r
Electricity	KWh	0.09	7/01	11r
Fuel oil #2	gal	1.43	7/01	11r
Fuel oil and other fuels, expenditures on	yr	45	1999	30r
Gas, natural, commercial rate	1000 cf	9.25	11/00	88s
Gasoline, all types	gal	1.60	7/01	11r
Gasoline, unleaded midgrade	gal	1.65	7/01	11r
Gasoline, unleaded premium	gal	1.74	7/01	11r
Natural gas, expenditures on	yr	164	1999	30r
Utility (piped) gas, therm		1.01	7/01	11r
Utility (piped) gas, 40 therms		44.29	7/01	11r
Utility (piped) gas, 100 therms		97.44	7/01	11r
Entertainment				
Entertainment purchases	yr	1574	1999	30r
Fees and admissions paid	yr	371	1999	30r
Reading purchases	yr	121	1999	30r
Television, radios, sound equipment, expenditures on	yr	561	1999	30r
Funerals				
Total cost of funeral		5922.53	1/99	78r
Acknowledgement cards		63.43	1/99	78r
Casket		2258.77	1/99	78r
Cosmetology, hair, other preparation		127.09	1/99	78r
Embalming		393.49	1/99	78r
Funeral at funeral home		367.50	1/99	78r
Hearse (local)		169.66	1/99	78r
Professional service charges		1211.32	1/99	78r
Service car/van		80.69	1/99	78r
Transfer of remains to funeral home		144.25	1/99	78r
Vault		803.50	1/99	78r
Visitation/viewing		302.83	1/99	78r
Groceries				
American processed cheese	lb	3.50	7/01	11r
Bakery products, expenditures on	yr	261	1999	30r
Bananas	lb	0.47	7/01	11r
Beans, dried, any type, all sizes	lb	0.63	7/01	11r
Beef for stew, boneless	lb	2.86	7/01	11r
Beef, expenditures on	yr	210	1999	30r
Bologna, all beef or mixed	lb	2.29	7/01	11r
Bread, French	lb	1.66	7/01	11r
Bread, white, pan	lb	0.87	7/01	11r
Bread, whole wheat, pan	lb	1.38	7/01	11r
Broccoli	lb	1.04	7/01	11r
Butter, salted, grade AA, stick	lb	2.26	7/01	11r
Butter, yoghurt, cheese, etc, expenditures on	yr	170	1999	30r
Cabbage	lb	0.42	7/01	11r
Cereals and cereal products, expenditures on	yr	140	1999	30r
Cheddar cheese, natural	lb	3.75	7/01	11r
Chicken breast, bone-in	lb	1.85	7/01	11r
Chicken legs, bone-in	lb	1.34	7/01	11r
Chicken, fresh, whole	lb	1.05	7/01	11r
Chops, boneless,	lb	4.13	7/01	11r
Chuck roast, graded and ungraded, excl U.S. prime and choice	lb	2.35	7/01	11r
Chuck roast, U.S. choice, boneless	lb	2.67	7/01	11r
Coffee, 100%, ground roast, all sizes	lb	2.88	7/01	11r
Coffee, instant, plain, regular, all sizes	16 oz	9.25	7/01	11r
Cola, non diet	2 liter	1.11	7/01	11r
Crackers, soda, salted	lb	1.70	7/01	11r
Dairy product purchases	yr	282	1999	30r
Eggs, expenditures on	yr	32	1999	30r
Fats and oils, expenditures on	yr	79	1999	30r
Fish and seafood, expenditures on	yr	99	1999	30r
Flour, white, all purpose	lb	0.32	7/01	11r
Food (excl fruit and vegetables), eaten at home, purchases	yr	815	1999	30r

Values are in dollars or fractions of dollars. In the column headed *Ref*, references are shown to sources. Each reference is followed by a letter. These refer to the geographical level for which data were reported: s=State, r=Region, and c=City or metro. The abbreviation *ex* is used to mean *except* or *excluding*; *exp* stands for *expenditures*. For other abbreviations and further explanations, please see the Introduction.

Charlotte-Gastonia-Rock Hill, NC - continued

Item	Per	Value	Date	Ref.
Groceries				
Food cooked on trips, expenditures on	yr	36	1999	30r
Food purchases	yr	4533	1999	30r
Food purchases, eaten away from home	yr	1873	1999	30r
Food purchases, food eaten at home	yr	2660	1999	30r
Fresh fruits, expenditures on	yr	128	1999	30r
Fresh milk and cream, expenditures on	yr	112	1999	30r
Fresh vegetables, expenditures on	yr	131	1999	30r
Fruit and vegetable purchases	yr	438	1999	30r
Grapefruit	lb	0.59	7/01	11r
Grapes, Thompson, seedless	lb	2.12	7/01	11r
Ground beef, 100% beef	lb	1.76	7/01	11r
Ground beef, lean and extra lean	lb	2.60	7/01	11r
Ground chuck, 100% beef	lb	2.08	7/01	11r
Ham, boneless, excl canned	lb	2.71	7/01	11r
Ham, rump or shank half, bone-in, smoked	lb	2.19	7/01	11r
Ice cream, prepackaged, bulk, regular	1/2 gal	3.93	7/01	11r
Lemons	lb	1.32	7/01	11r
Lettuce, iceberg	lb	0.76	7/01	11r
Milk, fresh, low fat,	gal	2.75	7/01	11r
Milk, fresh, whole, fortified	gal	2.97	7/01	11r
Nonalcoholic beverages, expenditures on	yr	228	1999	30r
Orange juice, frozen concentrate	16 oz	1.95	7/01	11r
Oranges, Navel	lb	0.73	7/01	11r
Oranges, Valencia	lb	0.55	7/01	11r
Peanut butter, creamy, all sizes	lb	1.83	7/01	11r
Pears, Anjou	lb	0.98	7/01	11r
Pork chops, center cut, bone-in	lb	3.33	7/01	11r
Pork sausage, fresh, loose	lb	2.59	7/01	11r
Pork shoulder picnic, bone-in, smoked	lb	1.12	7/01	11r
Pork, expenditures on	yr	162	1999	30r
Potato chips	16 oz	3.59	7/01	11r
Potatoes, frozen, french fried	lb	1.00	7/01	11r
Potatoes, white, all types	lb	0.44	7/01	11r
Poultry, expenditures on	yr	137	1999	30r
Processed fruits, expenditures on	yr	97	1999	30r
Processed vegetables, expenditures on	yr	82	1999	30r
Rice, white, long grain, uncooked	lb	0.51	7/01	11r
Round roast, graded and ungraded, excl U.S. prime and choice	lb	2.96	7/01	11r
Round steak, graded and ungraded, excl U.S. prime and choice	lb	3.11	7/01	11r
Sirloin steak, graded and ungraded, excl U.S. prime and choice	lb	4.23	7/01	11r
Spaghetti and macaroni	lb	0.78	7/01	11r
Steak, round, U.S. choice, boneless	lb	3.56	7/01	11r
Steak, sirloin, U.S. choice, boneless	lb	5.65	7/01	11r
Strawberries, dry pint	12 oz	1.50	7/01	11r
Sugar and other sweets, expenditures on	yr	99	1999	30r
Sugar, white, 33-80 ounce package	lb	0.39	7/01	11r
Sugar, white, all sizes	lb	0.42	7/01	11r
Tobacco products and smoking supplies purchases	yr	288	1999	30r
Tomatoes, field grown	lb	1.43	7/01	11r
Tuna, light, chunk	lb	1.77	7/01	11r
Turkey, frozen, whole	lb	1.05	7/01	11r
Goods and Services				
B&B Japanese maple (acer japonicum)	gal	49.98-129.00	4/00	93r
Boxwood (buxus)	2 gal	12.99-16.99	4/00	93r
Daylilly (hemerocallis)	gal	4.99-8.99	4/00	93r
Flat of annuals		11.00-13.92	4/00	93r
Fountain grass (pennisetum)	gal	5.98-7.98	4/00	93r
Hanging basket (10 in)		7.99-14.98	4/00	93r
Hardy geranium (geranium)	gal	5.98-8.00	4/00	93r
Hosta (hosta)	gal	4.99-10.98	4/00	93r

Charlotte-Gastonia-Rock Hill, NC - continued

Item	Per	Value	Date	Ref.
Goods and Services - continued				
Lilac (syrubga vulgaris)	2 gal	12.99-21.99	4/00	93r
Rhododendron (rhododendron)	2 gal	14.99-24.99	4/00	93r
Sage (salvia)	gal	5.98-6.99	4/00	93r
Wintercreeper euonymus (euonymus fortunei)	2 gal	7.99-89.99	4/00	93r
Hunting license	yr	15.00	4/01	34s
Health Care				
Cardiac catheterization, ave hospital/ physician charges		12500	1998	77s
Childbirth, Cesarean delivery		11587	1997	13r
Childbirth, vaginal delivery		6725	1997	13r
Drugs, expenditures on	yr	399	1999	30r
Health care purchases	yr	1971	1999	30r
Health insurance expenditures	yr	933	1999	30r
Hysterectomy, laproscopically-assisted, ave hospital/physician charges		12260	1998	76s
Hysterectomy, vaginal, ave hospital and physician charges		8440	1998	76s
Medicaid dispensing fee		5.60	1999	87s
Medical services expenditures	yr	547	1999	30r
Medical supplies, expenditures on	yr	91	1999	30r
Plastic surgery, breast augmentation		2870	2000	7r
Plastic surgery, breast lift		3649	2000	7r
Plastic surgery, facelift		5008	2000	7r
Plastic surgery, hair transplantation		3425	2000	7r
Plastic surgery, lip augmentation		1227	2000	7r
Plastic surgery, lower body lift		4793	2000	7r
Plastic surgery, thigh lift		3862	2000	7r
Household Goods				
Floor coverings, expenditures on	yr	44	1999	30r
Furniture, expenditures on	yr	335	1999	30r
Household furnishings and equipment purchases	yr	1328	1999	30r
Household textiles, expenditures on	yr	89	1999	30r
Laundry and cleaning supplies, expenditures on	yr	113	1999	30r
Housing				
Home price, existing, ave		160100	10/00	90r
Home value, median		146000	2001	53s
Household operation expenditures	yr	553	1999	30r
Housekeeping supplies purchases	yr	473	1999	30r
Housing, expenditures on	yr	10303	1999	30r
Maintenance, repairs, insurance expenditures	yr	699	1999	30r
Monthly rental value of owned home	mos	505	1999	30r
Owned dwellings, expenditures own	yr	3465	1999	30r
Rent expenditures	yr	1641	1999	30r
Rental unit, 1 bedroom, with utilities	mos	585	4/01	41c
Rental unit, 2 bedroom, with utilities	mos	659	4/01	41c
Rental unit, 3 bedroom, with utilities	mos	869	4/01	41c
Rental unit, 4 bedroom, with utilities	mos	1040	4/01	41c
Shelter, expenditures on	yr	5467	1999	30r
Insurance and Pensions				
Life and other personal insurance purchases	yr	414	1999	30r
Pensions and Social Security, expenditures on	yr	2635	1999	30r
Personal insurance and pensions, expenditures on	yr	3048	1999	30r
Legal Fees				
Combination hunting and fishing license	yr	20.00	4/01	34s
Divorce, filing fee		80.00	4/01	35s
Driver's license fee	orig	10.00	1999	48s
Driver's license fee	renew	10.00	1999	48s
Fishing license	yr	15.00	4/01	34s

Values are in dollars or fractions of dollars. In the column headed *Ref*, references are shown to sources. Each reference is followed by a letter. These refer to the geographical level for which data were reported: s=State, r=Region, and c=City or metro. The abbreviation *ex* is used to mean *except* or *excluding*; *exp* stands for *expenditures*. For other abbreviations and further explanations, please see the Introduction.

Charlotte-Gastonia-Rock Hill, NC - continued

Item	Per	Value	Date	Ref.
Personal Goods				
Personal care products and services purchases	yr	393	1999	30r
Personal Services				
Personal services, household, expenditures on	yr	258	1999	30r
Pets				
Pets, toys, and playground equipment, expenditures on	yr	306	1999	30r
Taxes				
Federal income taxes paid	yr	2047	1999	30r
Personal taxes, expenditures on	yr	2554	1999	30r
Property taxes paid	yr	726	1999	30r
State and local income taxes paid	yr	363	1999	30r
Transportation				
Cars and trucks, new, expenditures on	yr	1648	1999	30r
Cars and trucks, used, expenditures on	yr	1651	1999	30r
Diesel at the pump	gal	1.19	10/99	73s
Gasoline and motor oil purchases	yr	1052	1999	30r
Gasoline before-tax price (cents)	gal	103.20	10/00	43s
Maintenance and repair expenditures	yr	621	1999	30r
Motorcycle license fee	orig	1.50	1999	49s
Motorcycle license fee	renew	1.50	1999	49s
Public transportation, expenditures on	yr	298	1999	30r
Transportation purchases	yr	6738	1999	30r
Vehicle expenses, miscellaneous, purchases	yr	2033	1999	30r
Vehicle insurance payments	yr	696	1999	30r
Vehicle purchases (net outlay)	yr	3354	1999	30r
Vehicle rental, lease expenditures	yr	352	1999	30r
Utilities				
Electrical bill, average	mos	83.66	9/00	9s
Electricity, expenditures on	yr	1115	1999	30r
Electricity cost, average	KWh	6.40	9/00	9s
Water and other public services, expenditures on	yr	298	1999	30r
Weddings				
Wedding (national average cost)		19936	2000	33r
Wedding (regional average total cost)		16293	1997	110r
Attendants' gifts		321	1998	33r
Bridal attendants' apparel (5 persons)		824	2000	33r
Bride's headpiece/veil		173	1998	33r
Bride's wedding dress		859	1998	33r
Clergy, religious facility fee		242	1998	33r
Engagement ring		3177	1998	33r
Flowers		789	1998	33r
Groom's formalwear rental		99	2000	33r
Limousine		410	1998	33r
Marriage license cost		40.00	4/01	35s
Men's formalwear (ushers, best man)		469	2000	33r
Mother of bride apparel		241	2000	33r
Music		866	1998	33r
Photography and videography		1368	1998	33r
Rehearsal dinner		728	1998	33r
Wedding invitations and announcements		341	1998	33r
Wedding reception		7968	2000	33r
Wedding rings (bride and groom)		1060	1998	33r

Charlottesville, VA

Item	Per	Value	Date	Ref.
Alcoholic Beverages				
Alcoholic beverage purchases	yr	253	1999	30r
Malt beverages, all types, all sizes, any origin	16 oz	0.96	7/01	11r
Appliances				
Major appliances, expenditures on	yr	172	1999	30r
Small appliances, housewares, expenditures on	yr	81	1999	30r

Charlottesville, VA - continued

Item	Per	Value	Date	Ref.
Banking and Money				
Mortgage interest and charges paid	yr	2039	1999	30r
Mortgage principal paid on owned property	yr	1026	1999	30r
Vehicle finance charges paid	yr	365	1999	30r
Charity				
Cash contributions, expenditures	yr	1127	1999	30r
Child Care				
Child raising cost, total, age 0-2	yr	8540	1999	60r
Child raising cost, total, age 3-5	yr	8780	1999	60r
Child raising cost, total, age 6-8	yr	8820	1999	60r
Child raising cost, total, age 9-11	yr	8800	1999	60r
Child raising cost, total, age 12-14	yr	9510	1999	60r
Child raising cost, total, age 15-17	yr	9740	1999	60r
Child's child care and education, age 0-2	yr	1380	1999	60r
Child's child care and education, age 3-5	yr	1520	1999	60r
Child's child care and education, age 6-8	yr	990	1999	60r
Child's child care and education, age 9-11	yr	650	1999	60r
Child's child care and education, age 12-14	yr	490	1999	60r
Child's child care and education, age 15-17	yr	840	1999	60r
Child's clothing, age 0-2	yr	480	1999	60r
Child's clothing, age 3-5	yr	470	1999	60r
Child's clothing, age 6-8	yr	520	1999	60r
Child's clothing, age 9-11	yr	570	1999	60r
Child's clothing, age 12-14	yr	950	1999	60r
Child's clothing, age 15-17	yr	850	1999	60r
Child's food, age 0-2	yr	1000	1999	60r
Child's food, age 3-5	yr	1160	1999	60r
Child's food, age 6-8	yr	1490	1999	60r
Child's food, age 9-11	yr	1770	1999	60r
Child's food, age 12-14	yr	1770	1999	60r
Child's food, age 15-17	yr	1980	1999	60r
Child's health care, age 0-2	yr	620	1999	60r
Child's health care, age 3-5	yr	590	1999	60r
Child's health care, age 6-8	yr	680	1999	60r
Child's health care, age 9-11	yr	720	1999	60r
Child's health care, age 12-14	yr	730	1999	60r
Child's health care, age 15-17	yr	760	1999	60r
Child's housing, age 0-2	yr	3070	1999	60r
Child's housing, age 3-5	yr	3050	1999	60r
Child's housing, age 6-8	yr	3010	1999	60r
Child's housing, age 9-11	yr	2850	1999	60r
Child's housing, age 12-14	yr	3040	1999	60r
Child's housing, age 15-17	yr	2650	1999	60r
Child's personal care, reading, age 0-2	yr	910	1999	60r
Child's personal care, reading, age 3-5	yr	930	1999	60r
Child's personal care, reading, age 6-8	yr	960	1999	60r
Child's personal care, reading, age 9-11	yr	1000	1999	60r
Child's personal care, reading, age 12-14	yr	1170	1999	60r
Child's personal care, reading, age 15-17	yr	950	1999	60r
Clothing				
Apparel and services purchases	yr	1610	1999	30r
Boys, 2 to 15, expenditures on	yr	89	1999	30r
Children under 2, expenditures on	yr	79	1999	30r
Footwear, expenditures on	yr	283	1999	30r
Girls, 2 to 15, expenditures on	yr	103	1999	30r
Men and boys, expenditures on	yr	351	1999	30r
Men, 16 and over, expenditures on	yr	262	1999	30r
Women, 16 and over, expenditures on	yr	538	1999	30r
Communications				
Cable modem installation, Adelphi		54.90	6/99	103s
Cable modem installation, Comcast		95.00	6/99	103s
Cable modem installation, Cox		99.00-174.95	6/99	103s
Cable modem installation, Jones Intercable		100.00	6/99	103s
Cable modem rate, cable subscriber, Adelphi	mos	34.95	6/99	103s
Cable modem rate, cable subscriber, Comcast	mos	39.95	6/99	103s
Cable modem rate, cable subscriber, Cox	mos	29.95-44.95	6/99	103s
Cable modem rate, cable subscriber, Jones Intercable	mos	29.95-39.95	6/99	103s

Values are in dollars or fractions of dollars. In the column headed *Ref*, references are shown to sources. Each reference is followed by a letter. These refer to the geographical level for which data were reported: s=State, r=Region, and c=City or metro. The abbreviation *ex* is used to mean *except* or *excluding*; *exp* stands for *expenditures*. For other abbreviations and further explanations, please see the Introduction.

Charlottesville, VA - continued

Item	Per	Value	Date	Ref.
Communications				
Cable modem rate, non-cable subscriber, Adelphi	mos	44.95	6/99	103s
Cable modem rate, non-cable subscriber, Comcast	mos	49.95	6/99	103s
Cable modem rate, non-cable subscriber, Cox	mos	42.95-54.95	6/99	103s
Phone line, single, business, field visit	inst.	64.00	12/97	17s
Phone line, single, business, no field visit	inst.	64.00	12/97	17s
Phone line, single, residence, field visit	inst.	38.50	12/97	17s
Phone line, single, residence, no field visit	inst.	38.50	12/97	17s
Postage and stationery, expenditures on	yr	104	1999	30r
Postal rate, express mail, up to half-pound		12.45	7/01	108r
Postal rate, letter, first class, first ounce		0.34	7/01	108r
Postal rate, letter, two ounces		0.57	7/01	108r
Postal rate, post card		0.21	7/01	108r
Postal rate, priority mail, two pounds		3.95	7/01	108r
Postal rate, priority mail, up to one pound		3.50	7/01	108r
Telephone services, expenditures on	yr	860	1999	30r
Education				
Board, 4-year private college/university	yr	2363	1996	38s
Board, 4-year public college/university	yr	2033	1996	38s
Education expenditures	yr	431	1999	30r
Room, 4-year private college/university	yr	2062	1996	38s
Room, 4-year public college/university	yr	2261	1996	38s
Total cost, 4-year private college/university	yr	15021	1996	38s
Total cost, 4-year public college/university	yr	8202	1996	38s
Tuition, 2-year public college/university, in state	yr	1433	1996	38s
Tuition, 4-year private college/university, in state	yr	10596	1996	38s
Tuition, 4-year public college/university	yr	3907	1996	38s
Energy and Fuels				
Electricity	500 KWhs	47.29	7/01	11r
Electricity	KWh	0.09	7/01	11r
Fuel oil #2	gal	1.43	7/01	11r
Fuel oil and other fuels, expenditures on	yr	45	1999	30r
Gas, natural, commercial rate	1000 cf	9.01	11/00	88s
Gasoline, all types	gal	1.60	7/01	11r
Gasoline, unleaded midgrade	gal	1.65	7/01	11r
Gasoline, unleaded premium	gal	1.74	7/01	11r
Natural gas, expenditures on	yr	164	1999	30r
Utility (piped) gas, therm		1.01	7/01	11r
Utility (piped) gas, 40 therms		44.29	7/01	11r
Utility (piped) gas, 100 therms		97.44	7/01	11r
Entertainment				
Entertainment purchases	yr	1574	1999	30r
Fees and admissions paid	yr	371	1999	30r
Reading purchases	yr	121	1999	30r
Television, radios, sound equipment, expenditures on	yr	561	1999	30r
Funerals				
Total cost of funeral		5922.53	1/99	78r
Acknowledgement cards		63.43	1/99	78r
Casket		2258.77	1/99	78r
Cosmetology, hair, other preparation		127.09	1/99	78r
Embalming		393.49	1/99	78r
Funeral at funeral home		367.50	1/99	78r
Hearse (local)		169.66	1/99	78r
Professional service charges		1211.32	1/99	78r
Service car/van		80.69	1/99	78r
Transfer of remains to funeral home		144.25	1/99	78r
Vault		803.50	1/99	78r
Visitation/viewing		302.83	1/99	78r
Groceries				
American processed cheese	lb	3.50	7/01	11r
Bakery products, expenditures on	yr	261	1999	30r
Bananas	lb	0.47	7/01	11r
Beans, dried, any type, all sizes	lb	0.63	7/01	11r

Charlottesville, VA - continued

Item	Per	Value	Date	Ref.
Groceries - continued				
Beef for stew, boneless	lb	2.86	7/01	11r
Beef, expenditures on	yr	210	1999	30r
Bologna, all beef or mixed	lb	2.29	7/01	11r
Bread, French	lb	1.66	7/01	11r
Bread, white, pan	lb	0.87	7/01	11r
Bread, whole wheat, pan	lb	1.38	7/01	11r
Broccoli	lb	1.04	7/01	11r
Butter, salted, grade AA, stick	lb	2.26	7/01	11r
Butter, yoghurt, cheese, etc, expenditures on	yr	170	1999	30r
Cabbage	lb	0.42	7/01	11r
Cereals and cereal products, expenditures on	yr	140	1999	30r
Cheddar cheese, natural	lb	3.75	7/01	11r
Chicken breast, bone-in	lb	1.85	7/01	11r
Chicken legs, bone-in	lb	1.34	7/01	11r
Chicken, fresh, whole	lb	1.05	7/01	11r
Chops, boneless,	lb	4.13	7/01	11r
Chuck roast, graded and ungraded, excl U.S. prime and choice	lb	2.35	7/01	11r
Chuck roast, U.S. choice, boneless	lb	2.67	7/01	11r
Coffee, 100%, ground roast, all sizes	lb	2.88	7/01	11r
Coffee, instant, plain, regular, all sizes	16 oz	9.25	7/01	11r
Cola, non diet,	2 liter	1.11	7/01	11r
Crackers, soda, salted	lb	1.70	7/01	11r
Dairy product purchases	yr	282	1999	30r
Eggs, expenditures on	yr	32	1999	30r
Fats and oils, expenditures on	yr	79	1999	30r
Fish and seafood, expenditures on	yr	99	1999	30r
Flour, white, all purpose	lb	0.32	7/01	11r
Food (excl fruit and vegetables), eaten at home, purchases	yr	815	1999	30r
Food cooked on trips, expenditures on	yr	36	1999	30r
Food purchases	yr	4533	1999	30r
Food purchases, eaten away from home	yr	1873	1999	30r
Food purchases, food eaten at home	yr	2660	1999	30r
Fresh fruits, expenditures on	yr	128	1999	30r
Fresh milk and cream, expenditures on	yr	112	1999	30r
Fresh vegetables, expenditures on	yr	131	1999	30r
Fruit and vegetable purchases	yr	438	1999	30r
Grapefruit	lb	0.59	7/01	11r
Grapes, Thompson, seedless	lb	2.12	7/01	11r
Ground beef, 100% beef	lb	1.76	7/01	11r
Ground beef, lean and extra lean	lb	2.60	7/01	11r
Ground chuck, 100% beef	lb	2.08	7/01	11r
Ham, boneless, excl canned	lb	2.71	7/01	11r
Ham, rump or shank half, bone-in, smoked	lb	2.19	7/01	11r
Ice cream, prepackaged, bulk, regular	1/2 gal	3.93	7/01	11r
Lemons	lb	1.32	7/01	11r
Lettuce, iceberg	lb	0.76	7/01	11r
Milk, fresh, low fat,	gal	2.75	7/01	11r
Milk, fresh, whole, fortified	gal	2.97	7/01	11r
Nonalcoholic beverages, expenditures on	yr	228	1999	30r
Orange juice, frozen concentrate	16 oz	1.95	7/01	11r
Oranges, Navel	lb	0.73	7/01	11r
Oranges, Valencia	lb	0.55	7/01	11r
Peanut butter, creamy, all sizes	lb	1.83	7/01	11r
Pears, Anjou	lb	0.98	7/01	11r
Pork chops, center cut, bone-in	lb	3.33	7/01	11r
Pork sausage, fresh, loose	lb	2.59	7/01	11r
Pork shoulder picnic, bone-in, smoked	lb	1.12	7/01	11r
Pork, expenditures on	yr	162	1999	30r
Potato chips	16 oz	3.59	7/01	11r
Potatoes, frozen, french fried	lb	1.00	7/01	11r
Potatoes, white, all types	lb	0.44	7/01	11r
Poultry, expenditures on	yr	137	1999	30r
Processed fruits, expenditures on	yr	97	1999	30r
Processed vegetables, expenditures on	yr	82	1999	30r
Rice, white, long grain, uncooked	lb	0.51	7/01	11r
Round roast, graded and ungraded, excl U.S. prime and choice	lb	2.96	7/01	11r
Round steak, graded and ungraded, excl U.S. prime and choice	lb	3.11	7/01	11r

Values are in dollars or fractions of dollars. In the column headed *Ref*, references are shown to sources. Each reference is followed by a letter. These refer to the geographical level for which data were reported: s=State, r=Region, and c=City or metro. The abbreviation *ex* is used to mean *except* or *excluding*; *exp* stands for expenditures. For other abbreviations and further explanations, please see the Introduction.

Charlottesville, VA - continued

Item	Per	Value	Date	Ref.
Groceries				
Sirloin steak, graded and ungraded, excl U.S. prime and choice	lb	4.23	7/01	11r
Spaghetti and macaroni	lb	0.78	7/01	11r
Steak, round, U.S. choice, boneless	lb	3.56	7/01	11r
Steak, sirloin, U.S. choice, boneless	lb	5.65	7/01	11r
Strawberries, dry pint	12 oz	1.50	7/01	11r
Sugar and other sweets, expenditures on	yr	99	1999	30r
Sugar, white, 33-80 ounce package	lb	0.39	7/01	11r
Sugar, white, all sizes	lb	0.42	7/01	11r
Tobacco products and smoking supplies purchases	yr	288	1999	30r
Tomatoes, field grown	lb	1.43	7/01	11r
Tuna, light, chunk	lb	1.77	7/01	11r
Turkey, frozen, whole	lb	1.05	7/01	11r
Goods and Services				
B&B Japanese maple (acer japonicum)	gal	49.98-129.00	4/00	93r
Boxwood (buxus)	2 gal	12.99-16.99	4/00	93r
Daylilly (hemerocallis)	gal	4.99-8.99	4/00	93r
Flat of annuals		11.00-13.92	4/00	93r
Fountain grass (pennisetum)	gal	5.98-7.98	4/00	93r
Hanging basket (10 in)		7.99-14.98	4/00	93r
Hardy geranium (geranium)	gal	5.98-8.00	4/00	93r
Hosta (hosta)	gal	4.99-10.98	4/00	93r
Lilac (syrubga vulgaris)	2 gal	12.99-21.99	4/00	93r
Rhododendron (rhododendron)	2 gal	14.99-24.99	4/00	93r
Sage (salvia)	gal	5.98-6.99	4/00	93r
Wintercreeper euonymus (euonymus fortunei)	2 gal	7.99-89.99	4/00	93r
Hunting license	yr	12.00	4/01	34s
Health Care				
Cardiac catheterization, ave hospital/physician charges		15370	1998	77s
Childbirth, Cesarean delivery		11587	1997	13r
Childbirth, vaginal delivery		6725	1997	13r
Drugs, expenditures on	yr	399	1999	30r
Health care purchases	yr	1971	1999	30r
Health insurance expenditures	yr	933	1999	30r
Hysterectomy, laproscopically-assisted, ave hospital/physician charges		15660	1998	76s
Hysterectomy, vaginal, ave hospital and physician charges		10260	1998	76s
Medicaid dispensing fee		4.25	1999	87s
Medical services expenditures	yr	547	1999	30r
Medical supplies, expenditures on	yr	91	1999	30r
Plastic surgery, breast augmentation		2870	2000	7r
Plastic surgery, breast lift		3649	2000	7r
Plastic surgery, facelift		5008	2000	7r
Plastic surgery, hair transplantation		3425	2000	7r
Plastic surgery, lip augmentation		1227	2000	7r
Plastic surgery, lower body lift		4793	2000	7r
Plastic surgery, thigh lift		3862	2000	7r
Household Goods				
Floor coverings, expenditures on	yr	44	1999	30r
Furniture, expenditures on	yr	335	1999	30r
Household furnishings and equipment purchases	yr	1328	1999	30r
Household textiles, expenditures on	yr	89	1999	30r
Laundry and cleaning supplies, expenditures on	yr	113	1999	30r

Charlottesville, VA - continued

Item	Per	Value	Date	Ref.
Housing				
Home price, existing, ave		160100	10/00	90r
Home value, median		141000	2001	53s
Household operation expenditures	yr	553	1999	30r
Housekeeping supplies purchases	yr	473	1999	30r
Housing, expenditures on	yr	10303	1999	30r
Maintenance, repairs, insurance expenditures	yr	699	1999	30r
Monthly rental value of owned home	mos	505	1999	30r
Owned dwellings, expenditures own	yr	3465	1999	30r
Rent expenditures	yr	1641	1999	30r
Rental unit, 1 bedroom, with utilities	mos	513	4/01	41c
Rental unit, 2 bedroom, with utilities	mos	656	4/01	41c
Rental unit, 3 bedroom, with utilities	mos	872	4/01	41c
Rental unit, 4 bedroom, with utilities	mos	977	4/01	41c
Shelter, expenditures on	yr	5467	1999	30r
Insurance and Pensions				
Auto insurance premium	yr	628.58	1999	57s
Life and other personal insurance purchases	yr	414	1999	30r
Pensions and Social Security, expenditures on	yr	2635	1999	30r
Personal insurance and pensions, expenditures on	yr	3048	1999	30r
Legal Fees				
Divorce, filing fee		64.00	4/01	35s
Driver's license fee	orig	7.20	1999	48s
Driver's license fee	renew	7.20	1999	48s
Fishing license	yr	12.50	4/01	34s
Personal Goods				
Personal care products and services purchases	yr	393	1999	30r
Personal Services				
Personal services, household, expenditures on	yr	258	1999	30r
Pets				
Pets, toys, and playground equipment, expenditures on	yr	306	1999	30r
Taxes				
Federal income taxes paid	yr	2047	1999	30r
Personal taxes, expenditures on	yr	2554	1999	30r
Property taxes paid	yr	726	1999	30r
State and local income taxes paid	yr	363	1999	30r
Transportation				
Cars and trucks, new, expenditures on	yr	1648	1999	30r
Cars and trucks, used, expenditures on	yr	1651	1999	30r
Diesel at the pump	gal	1.14	10/99	73s
Gasoline and motor oil purchases	yr	1052	1999	30r
Gasoline before-tax price (cents)	gal	107.30	10/00	43s
Maintenance and repair expenditures	yr	621	1999	30r
Public transportation, expenditures on	yr	298	1999	30r
Transportation purchases	yr	6738	1999	30r
Vehicle expenses, miscellaneous, purchases	yr	2033	1999	30r
Vehicle insurance payments	yr	696	1999	30r
Vehicle purchases (net outlay)	yr	3354	1999	30r
Vehicle rental, lease expenditures	yr	352	1999	30r
Utilities				
Electrical bill, average	mos	82.17	9/00	9s
Electricity, expenditures on	yr	1115	1999	30r
Electricity cost, average	KWh	5.90	9/00	9s
Water and other public services, expenditures on	yr	298	1999	30r
Weddings				
Wedding (national average cost)		19936	2000	33r
Wedding (regional average total cost)		16293	1997	110r
Attendants' gifts		321	1998	33r
Bridal attendants' apparel (5 persons)		824	2000	33r
Bride's headpiece/veil		173	1998	33r
Bride's wedding dress		859	1998	33r

Values are in dollars or fractions of dollars. In the column headed *Ref*, references are shown to sources. Each reference is followed by a letter. These refer to the geographical level for which data were reported: s=State, r=Region, and c=City or metro. The abbreviation *ex* is used to mean *except* or *excluding*; *exp* stands for *expenditures*. For other abbreviations and further explanations, please see the Introduction.

Charlottesville, VA - continued

Item	Per	Value	Date	Ref.
Weddings				
Clergy, religious facility fee		242	1998	33r
Engagement ring		3177	1998	33r
Flowers		789	1998	33r
Groom's formalwear rental		99	2000	33r
Limousine		410	1998	33r
Marriage license cost		30.00	4/01	35s
Men's formalwear (ushers, best man)		469	2000	33r
Mother of bride apparel		241	2000	33r
Music		866	1998	33r
Photography and videography		1368	1998	33r
Rehearsal dinner		728	1998	33r
Wedding invitations and announcements		341	1998	33r
Wedding reception		7968	2000	33r
Wedding rings (bride and groom)		1060	1998	33r

Chattanooga, TN

Item	Per	Value	Date	Ref.
Composite, ACCRA index		99.10	3/01	4c
Alcoholic Beverages				
Alcoholic beverage purchases	yr	253	1999	30r
Beer, Heineken, 12-oz, ex deposit	6	7.29	3/01	4c
J & B Scotch	750-ml	21.17	3/01	4c
Malt beverages, all types, all sizes, any origin	16 oz	0.96	7/01	11r
Wine, Livingston or Gallo, Chablis blanc	1.5 liter	5.73	3/01	4c
Appliances				
Appliance repair, service call, washing machine	min lab chg	34.49	3/01	4c
Major appliances, expenditures on	yr	172	1999	30r
Small appliances, housewares, expenditures on	yr	81	1999	30r
Banking and Money				
Mortgage interest and charges paid	yr	2039	1999	30r
Mortgage principal paid on owned property	yr	1026	1999	30r
Mortgage rate, incl. points and orig. fee, 30-yr. conv. fixed or ARM	mos	6.89	3/01	4c
Vehicle finance charges paid	yr	365	1999	30r
Business Expenses				
Business travel, car rental	day	40	2001	3c
Business travel, food	day	40	2001	3c
Business travel, hotel	day	77	2001	3c
Charity				
Cash contributions, expenditures	yr	1127	1999	30r
Child Care				
Child raising cost, total, age 0-2	yr	8540	1999	60r
Child raising cost, total, age 3-5	yr	8780	1999	60r
Child raising cost, total, age 6-8	yr	8820	1999	60r
Child raising cost, total, age 9-11	yr	8800	1999	60r
Child raising cost, total, age 12-14	yr	9510	1999	60r
Child raising cost, total, age 15-17	yr	9740	1999	60r
Child's child care and education, age 0-2	yr	1380	1999	60r
Child's child care and education, age 3-5	yr	1520	1999	60r
Child's child care and education, age 6-8	yr	990	1999	60r
Child's child care and education, age 9-11	yr	650	1999	60r
Child's child care and education, age 12-14	yr	490	1999	60r
Child's child care and education, age 15-17	yr	840	1999	60r
Child's clothing, age 0-2	yr	480	1999	60r
Child's clothing, age 3-5	yr	470	1999	60r
Child's clothing, age 6-8	yr	520	1999	60r
Child's clothing, age 9-11	yr	570	1999	60r
Child's clothing, age 12-14	yr	950	1999	60r
Child's clothing, age 15-17	yr	850	1999	60r
Child's food, age 0-2	yr	1000	1999	60r
Child's food, age 3-5	yr	1160	1999	60r
Child's food, age 6-8	yr	1490	1999	60r
Child's food, age 9-11	yr	1770	1999	60r
Child's food, age 12-14	yr	1770	1999	60r
Child's food, age 15-17	yr	1980	1999	60r
Child's health care, age 0-2	yr	620	1999	60r

Chattanooga, TN - continued

Item	Per	Value	Date	Ref.
Child Care - continued				
Child's health care, age 3-5	yr	590	1999	60r
Child's health care, age 6-8	yr	680	1999	60r
Child's health care, age 9-11	yr	720	1999	60r
Child's health care, age 12-14	yr	730	1999	60r
Child's health care, age 15-17	yr	760	1999	60r
Child's housing, age 0-2	yr	3070	1999	60r
Child's housing, age 3-5	yr	3050	1999	60r
Child's housing, age 6-8	yr	3010	1999	60r
Child's housing, age 9-11	yr	2850	1999	60r
Child's housing, age 12-14	yr	3040	1999	60r
Child's housing, age 15-17	yr	2650	1999	60r
Child's personal care, reading, age 0-2	yr	910	1999	60r
Child's personal care, reading, age 3-5	yr	930	1999	60r
Child's personal care, reading, age 6-8	yr	960	1999	60r
Child's personal care, reading, age 9-11	yr	1000	1999	60r
Child's personal care, reading, age 12-14	yr	1170	1999	60r
Child's personal care, reading, age 15-17	yr	950	1999	60r
Clothing				
Apparel and services purchases	yr	1610	1999	30r
Boys' brief, cotton	3	4.15	3/01	4c
Boys, 2 to 15, expenditures on	yr	89	1999	30r
Children under 2, expenditures on	yr	79	1999	30r
Footwear, expenditures on	yr	283	1999	30r
Girls, 2 to 15, expenditures on	yr	103	1999	30r
Men and boys, expenditures on	yr	351	1999	30r
Men, 16 and over, expenditures on	yr	262	1999	30r
Shirt, man's dress shirt		29.40	3/01	4c
Slacks, man's "No Wrinkles" khaki		41.80	3/01	4c
Women, 16 and over, expenditures on	yr	538	1999	30r
Communications				
Cable modem installation, Intermedia		149.95	6/99	103s
Cable modem installation, Time Warner		75.00-225.00	6/99	103s
Cable modem rate, cable subscriber, Intermedia	mos	49.95	6/99	103s
Cable modem rate, cable subscriber, Time Warner	mos	39.95-49.95	6/99	103s
Cable modem rate, non-cable subscriber, Intermedia	mos	54.95	6/99	103s
Cable modem rate, non-cable subscriber, Time Warner	mos	39.95-54.95	6/99	103s
Newspaper subscription, daily and Sunday delivery	mos	11.30	3/01	4c
Phone line, single, business, field visit	inst.	58.50	12/97	17s
Phone line, single, business, no field visit	inst.	58.50	12/97	17s
Phone line, single, residence, field visit	inst.	41.50	12/97	17s
Phone line, single, residence, no field visit	inst.	41.50	12/97	17s
Postage and stationery, expenditures on	yr	104	1999	30r
Postal rate, express mail, up to half-pound		12.45	7/01	108r
Postal rate, letter, first class, first ounce		0.34	7/01	108r
Postal rate, letter, two ounces		0.57	7/01	108r
Postal rate, post card		0.21	7/01	108r
Postal rate, priority mail, two pounds		3.95	7/01	108r
Postal rate, priority mail, up to one pound		3.50	7/01	108r
Telephone bill, business, basic rate	mos	39.05	12/97	18c
Telephone bill, family of three	mos	20.37	3/01	4c
Telephone bill, residential, basic rate	mos	11.85	12/97	18c
Telephone services, expenditures on	yr	860	1999	30r
Education				
Board, 4-year private college/university	yr	2085	1996	38s
Board, 4-year public college/university	yr	1737	1996	38s
Education expenditures	yr	431	1999	30r
Room, 4-year private college/university	yr	2153	1996	38s
Room, 4-year public college/university	yr	1644	1996	38s
Total cost, 4-year private college/university	yr	14068	1996	38s
Total cost, 4-year public college/university	yr	5372	1996	38s
Tuition, 2-year public college/university, in state	yr	1022	1996	38s
Tuition, 4-year private college/university, in state	yr	9830	1996	38s
Tuition, 4-year public college/university	yr	1990	1996	38s

Values are in dollars or fractions of dollars. In the column headed *Ref*, references are shown to sources. Each reference is followed by a letter. These refer to the geographical level for which data were reported: s=State, r=Region, and c=City or metro. The abbreviation *ex* is used to mean *except* or *excluding*; *exp* stands for expenditures. For other abbreviations and further explanations, please see the Introduction.

Chattanooga, TN - continued

Item	Per	Value	Date	Ref.
Energy and Fuels				
Electricity	500 KWhs	47.29	7/01	11r
Electricity	KWh	0.09	7/01	11r
Energy, combined forms, 2400 sq ft	mos	115.04	3/01	4c
Energy, exc. electricity, 2400 sq ft	mos	66.72	3/01	4c
Fuel oil #2	gal	1.43	7/01	11r
Fuel oil and other fuels, expenditures on	yr	45	1999	30r
Gas, cooking, winter, 10 therms	mos	14.87	2/96	98c
Gas, cooking, winter, 30 therms	mos	29.08	2/96	98c
Gas, cooking, winter, 50 therms	mos	41.61	2/96	98c
Gas, heating, winter, average use	mos	121.31	2/96	98c
Gas, natural, commercial rate	1000 cf	8.61	11/00	88s
Gas, regular unleaded, cash, self-service	gal	1.33	3/01	4c
Gasoline, all types	gal	1.60	7/01	11r
Gasoline, unleaded midgrade	gal	1.65	7/01	11r
Gasoline, unleaded premium	gal	1.74	7/01	11r
Natural gas, expenditures on	yr	164	1999	30r
Utility (piped) gas, therm		1.01	7/01	11r
Utility (piped) gas, 40 therms		44.29	7/01	11r
Utility (piped) gas, 100 therms		97.44	7/01	11r
Entertainment				
Bowling, Saturday evening rate	line	3.17	3/01	4c
Entertainment purchases	yr	1574	1999	30r
Fees and admissions paid	yr	371	1999	30r
Monopoly game, Parker Brothers', No. 9	game	12.39	3/01	4c
Movie, first-run, Saturday, evening	adm.	6.95	3/01	4c
Reading purchases	yr	121	1999	30r
Television, radios, sound equipment, expenditures on	yr	561	1999	30r
Tennis balls, yellow, Wilson or Penn, 3	can	1.99	3/01	4c
Groceries				
Groceries, ACCRA Index		97.50	3/01	4c
American processed cheese	lb	3.50	7/01	11r
Antibiotic ointment, Polysporin	0.5 oz	4.25	3/01	4c
Baby food, strained vegetables or fruit, lowest price	4-4.5 oz	0.51	3/01	4c
Bakery products, expenditures on	yr	261	1999	30r
Bananas	lb	0.55	3/01	4c
Bananas	lb	0.47	7/01	11r
Beans, dried, any type, all sizes	lb	0.63	7/01	11r
Beef for stew, boneless	lb	2.86	7/01	11r
Beef or hamburger, ground	lb	1.52	3/01	4c
Beef, expenditures on	yr	210	1999	30r
Bologna, all beef or mixed	lb	2.29	7/01	11r
Bread, French	lb	1.66	7/01	11r
Bread, white	loaf	1.04	3/01	4c
Bread, white, pan	lb	0.87	7/01	11r
Bread, whole wheat, pan	lb	1.38	7/01	11r
Broccoli	lb	1.04	7/01	11r
Butter, salted, grade AA, stick	lb	2.26	7/01	11r
Butter, yoghurt, cheese, etc, expenditures on	yr	170	1999	30r
Cabbage	lb	0.42	7/01	11r
Cereals and cereal products, expenditures on	yr	140	1999	30r
Cheddar cheese, natural	lb	3.75	7/01	11r
Cheese, Kraft grated Parmesan	8 oz	3.22	3/01	4c
Chicken breast, bone-in	lb	1.85	7/01	11r
Chicken legs, bone-in	lb	1.34	7/01	11r
Chicken, fresh, whole	lb	1.05	7/01	11r
Chicken, whole fryer	lb	0.99	3/01	4c
Chops, boneless	lb	4.13	7/01	11r
Chuck roast, graded and ungraded, excl U.S. prime and choice	lb	2.35	7/01	11r
Chuck roast, U.S. choice, boneless	lb	2.67	7/01	11r
Cigarettes, Winston, Kings	carton	24.26	3/01	4c
Coffee, 100%, ground roast, all sizes	lb	2.88	7/01	11r
Coffee, instant, plain, regular, all sizes	16 oz	9.25	7/01	11r
Coffee, vacuum-packed	13 oz	2.32	3/01	4c
Cola, non diet	2 liter	1.11	7/01	11r
Corn Flakes, Kellogg's or Post Toasties	18 oz	2.79	3/01	4c
Corn, frozen, whole kernel, lowest price	16 oz	1.15	3/01	4c

Chattanooga, TN - continued

Item	Per	Value	Date	Ref.
Groceries - continued				
Crackers, soda, salted	lb	1.70	7/01	11r
Dairy product purchases	yr	282	1999	30r
Eggs, expenditures on	yr	32	1999	30r
Eggs, Grade A or AA	dozen	1.16	3/01	4c
Fats and oils, expenditures on	yr	79	1999	30r
Fish and seafood, expenditures on	yr	99	1999	30r
Flour, white, all purpose	lb	0.32	7/01	11r
Food (excl fruit and vegetables), eaten at home, purchases	yr	815	1999	30r
Food cooked on trips, expenditures on	yr	36	1999	30r
Food purchases	yr	4533	1999	30r
Food purchases, eaten away from home	yr	1873	1999	30r
Food purchases, food eaten at home	yr	2660	1999	30r
Fresh fruits, expenditures on	yr	128	1999	30r
Fresh milk and cream, expenditures on	yr	112	1999	30r
Fresh vegetables, expenditures on	yr	131	1999	30r
Fruit and vegetable purchases	yr	438	1999	30r
Grapefruit	lb	0.59	7/01	11r
Grapes, Thompson, seedless	lb	2.12	7/01	11r
Ground beef, 100% beef	lb	1.76	7/01	11r
Ground beef, lean and extra lean	lb	2.60	7/01	11r
Ground chuck, 100% beef	lb	2.08	7/01	11r
Ham, boneless, excl canned	lb	2.71	7/01	11r
Ham, rump or shank half, bone-in, smoked	lb	2.19	7/01	11r
Ice cream, prepackaged, bulk, regular	1/2 gal	3.93	7/01	11r
Lemons	lb	1.32	7/01	11r
Lettuce, iceberg	head	1.16	3/01	4c
Lettuce, iceberg	lb	0.76	7/01	11r
Margarine, Blue Bonnet or Parkay, stick	lb	0.58	3/01	4c
Milk, fresh, low fat	gal	2.75	7/01	11r
Milk, fresh, whole, fortified	gal	2.97	7/01	11r
Milk, whole	1/2 gal	1.82	3/01	4c
Nonalcoholic beverages, expenditures on	yr	228	1999	30r
Orange juice, frozen concentrate	16 oz	1.95	7/01	11r
Orange juice, Minute Maid frozen	12 oz	1.59	3/01	4c
Oranges, Navel	lb	0.73	7/01	11r
Oranges, Valencia	lb	0.55	7/01	11r
Peaches, halves or slices, Hunt's, Del Monte, or Libby's	29 oz	1.59	3/01	4c
Peanut butter, creamy, all sizes	lb	1.83	7/01	11r
Pears, Anjou	lb	0.98	7/01	11r
Peas, green, Del Monte or Green Giant	15 oz	0.66	3/01	4c
Pork chops, center cut, bone-in	lb	3.33	7/01	11r
Pork sausage, fresh, loose	lb	2.59	7/01	11r
Pork shoulder picnic, bone-in, smoked	lb	1.12	7/01	11r
Pork, expenditures on	yr	162	1999	30r
Potato chips	16 oz	3.59	7/01	11r
Potatoes, frozen, french fried	lb	1.00	7/01	11r
Potatoes, white or red	10 lb	2.27	3/01	4c
Potatoes, white, all types	lb	0.44	7/01	11r
Poultry, expenditures on	yr	137	1999	30r
Processed fruits, expenditures on	yr	97	1999	30r
Processed vegetables, expenditures on	yr	82	1999	30r
Rice, white, long grain, uncooked	lb	0.51	7/01	11r
Round roast, graded and ungraded, excl U.S. prime and choice	lb	2.96	7/01	11r
Round steak, graded and ungraded, excl U.S. prime and choice	lb	3.11	7/01	11r
Sausage, Jimmy Dean/Owens pork	lb	2.76	3/01	4c
Shortening, vegetable, Crisco	3 lb	2.99	3/01	4c
Sirloin steak, graded and ungraded, excl U.S. prime and choice	lb	4.23	7/01	11r
Soft drink, Coca Cola, ex deposit	2 liter	1.12	3/01	4c
Spaghetti and macaroni	lb	0.78	7/01	11r
Steak, round, U.S. choice, boneless	lb	3.56	7/01	11r
Steak, sirloin, U.S. choice, boneless	lb	5.65	7/01	11r
Steak, T-bone	lb	7.32	3/01	4c
Strawberries, dry pint	12 oz	1.50	7/01	11r
Sugar and other sweets, expenditures on	yr	99	1999	30r
Sugar, cane or beet	4 lbs	1.27	3/01	4c
Sugar, white, 33-80 ounce package	lb	0.39	7/01	11r
Sugar, white, all sizes	lb	0.42	7/01	11r

Values are in dollars or fractions of dollars. In the column headed *Ref*, references are shown to sources. Each reference is followed by a letter. These refer to the geographical level for which data were reported: s=State, r=Region, and c=City or metro. The abbreviation *ex* is used to mean *except* or *excluding*; *exp* stands for expenditures. For other abbreviations and further explanations, please see the Introduction.

Chattanooga, TN - continued

Item	Per	Value	Date	Ref.
Groceries				
Tobacco products and smoking supplies purchases	yr	288	1999	30r
Tomatoes, field grown	lb	1.43	7/01	11r
Tomatoes, Hunt's or Del Monte	14.5 oz	0.89	3/01	4c
Tuna, chunk, light	6 oz	0.43	3/01	4c
Tuna, light, chunk	lb	1.77	7/01	11r
Turkey, frozen, whole	lb	1.05	7/01	11r
Goods and Services				
Miscellaneous goods and services, ACCRA Index		102.30	3/01	4c
Health Care				
Health care, ACCRA Index		86.50	3/01	4c
Cardiac catheterization, ave hospital/physician charges		12170	1998	77s
Childbirth, Cesarean delivery		11587	1997	13r
Childbirth, vaginal delivery		6725	1997	13r
Dentist's fee, adult teeth cleaning and periodic oral exam	visit	59.20	3/01	4c
Doctor's fee, routine exam, established patient	visit	53.80	3/01	4c
Drugs, expenditures on	yr	399	1999	30r
Health care purchases	yr	1971	1999	30r
Health insurance expenditures	yr	933	1999	30r
Home health care aide cost, licensed agency	hour	15	2000	82c
Hospital care, private room	day	423.00	3/01	4c
Hysterectomy, laproscopically-assisted, ave hospital/physician charges		13470	1998	76s
Hysterectomy, vaginal, ave hospital and physician charges		9530	1998	76s
Medical services expenditures	yr	547	1999	30r
Medical supplies, expenditures on	yr	91	1999	30r
Nursing home costs, private room	day	136	2000	82c
Nursing home stay, private room	day	136	2000	81c
Household Goods				
Dishwashing powder, Cascade	50 oz	3.02	3/01	4c
Floor coverings, expenditures on	yr	44	1999	30r
Furniture, expenditures on	yr	335	1999	30r
Household furnishings and equipment purchases	yr	1328	1999	30r
Household textiles, expenditures on	yr	89	1999	30r
Laundry and cleaning supplies, expenditures on	yr	113	1999	30r
Tissues, facial, Kleenex brand	175	1.20	3/01	4c
Housing				
Housing, ACCRA Index		101.10	3/01	4c
Home, 2200 sq ft, 4-br, 2-bath, 2-car garage, average		132000	2000	47c
Home price, existing, ave		160100	10/00	90r
Home value, median		112000	2001	53s
House, 2400 sq ft, 8000 sq ft lot, new, urban, utilities	total	217901	3/01	4c
House payment, principal and interest, 25% down payment	mos	1075	3/01	4c
Household operation expenditures	yr	553	1999	30r
Housekeeping supplies purchases	yr	473	1999	30r
Housing, expenditures on	yr	10303	1999	30r
Maintenance, repairs, insurance expenditures	yr	699	1999	30r
Monthly rental value of owned home	mos	505	1999	30r
Owned dwellings, expenditures own	yr	3465	1999	30r
Rent expenditures	yr	1641	1999	30r
Rent, apartment, 2 br, 1 1/2-2 baths, unfurn, 950 sq ft, water	mos	616	3/01	4c
Rental unit, 1 bedroom, with utilities	mos	434	4/01	41c
Rental unit, 2 bedroom, with utilities	mos	522	4/01	41c
Rental unit, 3 bedroom, with utilities	mos	674	4/01	41c
Rental unit, 4 bedroom, with utilities	mos	768	4/01	41c
Shelter, expenditures on	yr	5467	1999	30r

Chattanooga, TN - continued

Item	Per	Value	Date	Ref.
Insurance and Pensions				
Life and other personal insurance purchases	yr	414	1999	30r
Pensions and Social Security, expenditures on	yr	2635	1999	30r
Personal insurance and pensions, expenditures on	yr	3048	1999	30r
Legal Fees				
Combination hunting and fishing license	yr	21.00	4/01	34s
Divorce, filing fee		64.00	4/01	35s
Driver's license fee	renew	17.50	1999	48s
Driver's license fee	orig	17.50	1999	48s
Personal Goods				
Personal care products and services purchases	yr	393	1999	30r
Shampoo, Alberto VO5	15 oz	1.02	3/01	4c
Toothpaste, Crest or Colgate	6-7 oz	2.29	3/01	4c
Personal Services				
Dry cleaning, man's 2-pc suit		6.35	3/01	4c
Man's haircut, barbershop, no styling		9.60	3/01	4c
Personal services, household, expenditures on	yr	258	1999	30r
Woman's shampoo, trim, blow-dry, no style-change		32.40	3/01	4c
Pets				
Pets, toys, and playground equipment, expenditures on	yr	306	1999	30r
Restaurant Food				
Chicken, fried, thigh and drumstick, KFC/Church's		2.91	3/01	4c
Hamburger with cheese, McDonald's	1/4 lb	2.13	3/01	4c
Pizza, Pizza Hut or Pizza Inn	11-12 in	8.99	3/01	4c
Taxes				
Federal income taxes paid	yr	2047	1999	30r
Personal taxes, expenditures on	yr	2554	1999	30r
Property taxes paid	yr	726	1999	30r
State and local income taxes paid	yr	363	1999	30r
Transportation				
Transportation, ACCRA Index		95.50	3/01	4c
Bus fare, to central business district	1-way	1.00	3/01	4c
Cars and trucks, new, expenditures on	yr	1648	1999	30r
Cars and trucks, used, expenditures on	yr	1651	1999	30r
Diesel at the pump	gal	1.18	10/99	73s
Gasoline and motor oil purchases	yr	1052	1999	30r
Gasoline before-tax price	gal	102.50	10/00	43s
Maintenance and repair expenditures	yr	621	1999	30r
Public transportation, expenditures on	yr	298	1999	30r
Tire balance, computer or spin balance, front	wheel	7.70	3/01	4c
Transportation purchases	yr	6738	1999	30r
Vehicle expenses, miscellaneous, purchases	yr	2033	1999	30r
Vehicle insurance payments	yr	696	1999	30r
Vehicle purchases (net outlay)	yr	3354	1999	30r
Vehicle rental, lease expenditures	yr	352	1999	30r
Utilities				
Utilities, ACCRA Index		94.20	3/01	4c
Electrical bill, average	mos	79.16	9/00	9s
Electricity, expenditures on	yr	1115	1999	30r
Electricity and other, mixed, 2400 sq ft, new home	mos	48.32	3/01	4c
Electricity cost, average	KWh	5.60	9/00	9s
Water and other public services, expenditures on	yr	298	1999	30r
Weddings				
Wedding (national average cost)		19936	2000	33r
Attendants' gifts		321	1998	33r
Bridal attendants' apparel (5 persons)		824	2000	33r
Bride's headpiece/veil		173	1998	33r
Bride's wedding dress		859	1998	33r
Clergy, religious facility fee		242	1998	33r

Values are in dollars or fractions of dollars. In the column headed *Ref*, references are shown to sources. Each reference is followed by a letter. These refer to the geographical level for which data were reported: s=State, r=Region, and c=City or metro. The abbreviation *ex* is used to mean *except* or *excluding*; *exp* stands for expenditures. For other abbreviations and further explanations, please see the Introduction.

Chattanooga, TN - continued

Item	Per	Value	Date	Ref.
Weddings				
Engagement ring		3177	1998	33r
Flowers		789	1998	33r
Groom's formalwear rental		99	2000	33r
Limousine		410	1998	33r
Marriage license cost		31.00	4/01	35s
Men's formalwear (ushers, best man)		469	2000	33r
Mother of bride apparel		241	2000	33r
Music		866	1998	33r
Photography and videography		1368	1998	33r
Rehearsal dinner		728	1998	33r
Wedding invitations and announcements		341	1998	33r
Wedding reception		7968	2000	33r
Wedding rings (bride and groom)		1060	1998	33r

Cheyenne, WY

Item	Per	Value	Date	Ref.
Composite, ACCRA index		96.70	3/01	4c
Alcoholic Beverages				
Beer, Heineken, 12-oz, ex deposit	6	6.86	3/01	4c
J & B Scotch	750-ml	19.82	3/01	4c
Wine, Livingston or Gallo, Chablis blanc	1.5 liter	6.01	3/01	4c
Appliances				
Appliance repair, service call, washing machine	min lab chg	43.00	3/01	4c
Banking and Money				
Mortgage rate, incl. points and orig. fee, 30-yr. conv. fixed or ARM	mos	7.11	3/01	4c
Clothing				
Boys' brief, cotton	3	5.09	3/01	4c
Shirt, man's dress shirt		30.00	3/01	4c
Slacks, man's "No Wrinkles" khaki		40.99	3/01	4c
Communications				
Newspaper subscription, daily and Sunday delivery	mos	9.45	3/01	4c
Phone line, single, business, field visit	inst.	66.00	12/97	17s
Phone line, single, business, no field visit	inst.	66.00	12/97	17s
Phone line, single, residence, field visit	inst.	36.25	12/97	17s
Phone line, single, residence, no field visit	inst.	36.25	12/97	17s
Postal rate, express mail, up to half-pound		12.45	7/01	108r
Postal rate, letter, first class, first ounce		0.34	7/01	108r
Postal rate, letter, two ounces		0.57	7/01	108r
Postal rate, post card		0.21	7/01	108r
Postal rate, priority mail, two pounds		3.95	7/01	108r
Postal rate, priority mail, up to one pound		3.50	7/01	108r
Telephone bill, business, basic rate	mos	18.63	12/97	18c
Telephone bill, family of three	mos	27.88	3/01	4c
Telephone bill, residential, basic rate	mos	14.00	12/97	18c
Education				
Board, 4-year public college/university	yr	1912	1996	38s
Room, 4-year public college/university	yr	1512	1996	38s
Total cost, 4-year public college/university	yr	5429	1996	38s
Tuition, 2-year public college/university, in state	yr	948	1996	38s
Tuition, 4-year public college/university	yr	2005	1996	38s
Energy and Fuels				
Energy, combined forms, 2400 sq ft	mos	101.85	3/01	4c
Energy, exc. electricity, 2400 sq ft	mos	58.61	3/01	4c
Gas, heating, winter, average use	mos	53.35	2/96	98c
Gas, regular unleaded, cash, self-service	gal	1.22	3/01	4c
Entertainment				
Bowling, Saturday evening rate	line	2.62	3/01	4c
Monopoly game, Parker Brothers', No. 9	game	10.78	3/01	4c
Movie, first-run, Saturday, evening	adm.	6.50	3/01	4c
Tennis balls, yellow, Wilson or Penn, 3	can	2.05	3/01	4c
Funerals				
Total cost of funeral		5401.08	1/99	78r
Acknowledgement cards		33.64	1/99	78r

Cheyenne, WY - continued

Item	Per	Value	Date	Ref.
Funerals - continued				
Casket		2170.43	1/99	78r
Cosmetology, hair, other preparation		136.32	1/99	78r
Embalming		319.13	1/99	78r
Funeral at funeral home		370.21	1/99	78r
Hearse (local)		161.04	1/99	78r
Professional service charges		963.15	1/99	78r
Service car/van		133.99	1/99	78r
Transfer of remains to funeral home		159.82	1/99	78r
Vault		778.07	1/99	78r
Visitation/viewing		175.28	1/99	78r
Groceries				
Groceries, ACCRA Index		110.60	3/01	4c
Antibiotic ointment, Polysporin	0.5 oz	5.38	3/01	4c
Baby food, strained vegetables or fruit, lowest price	4-4.5 oz	0.40	3/01	4c
Bananas	lb	0.52	3/01	4c
Beef or hamburger, ground	lb	1.45	3/01	4c
Bread, white	loaf	0.98	3/01	4c
Cheese, Kraft grated Parmesan	8 oz	3.79	3/01	4c
Chicken, whole fryer	lb	1.08	3/01	4c
Cigarettes, Winston, Kings	carton	30.47	3/01	4c
Coffee, vacuum-packed	13 oz	3.35	3/01	4c
Corn Flakes, Kellogg's or Post Toasties	18 oz	3.14	3/01	4c
Corn, frozen, whole kernel, lowest price	16 oz	1.42	3/01	4c
Eggs, Grade A or AA	dozen	1.09	3/01	4c
Lettuce, iceberg	head	1.26	3/01	4c
Margarine, Blue Bonnet or Parkay, stick	lb	0.88	3/01	4c
Milk, whole	1/2 gal	1.90	3/01	4c
Orange juice, Minute Maid frozen	12 oz	1.84	3/01	4c
Peaches, halves or slices, Hunt's, Del Monte, or Libby's	29 oz	2.19	3/01	4c
Peas, green, Del Monte or Green Giant	15 oz	0.88	3/01	4c
Potatoes, white or red	10 lb	2.26	3/01	4c
Sausage, Jimmy Dean/Owens pork	lb	4.58	3/01	4c
Shortening, vegetable, Crisco	3 lb	3.11	3/01	4c
Soft drink, Coca Cola, ex deposit	2 liter	1.24	3/01	4c
Steak, T-bone	lb	6.09	3/01	4c
Sugar, cane or beet	4 lbs	1.60	3/01	4c
Tomatoes, Hunt's or Del Monte	14.5 oz	1.00	3/01	4c
Tuna, chunk, light	6 oz	0.87	3/01	4c
Goods and Services				
Miscellaneous goods and services, ACCRA Index		97.70	3/01	4c
Hunting license	yr	15.00	4/01	34s
Health Care				
Health care, ACCRA Index		104.90	3/01	4c
Cardiac catheterization, ave hospital/physician charges		24500	1998	77s
Childbirth, Cesarean delivery		11587	1997	13r
Childbirth, vaginal delivery		6725	1997	13r
Dentist's fee, adult teeth cleaning and periodic oral exam	visit	75.20	3/01	4c
Doctor's fee, routine exam, established patient	visit	58.02	3/01	4c
Hospital care, private room	day	578.00	3/01	4c
Hysterectomy, laproscopically-assisted, ave hospital/physician charges		14380	1998	76s
Hysterectomy, vaginal, ave hospital and physician charges		9360	1998	76s
Medicaid dispensing fee		4.70	1999	87s
Household Goods				
Dishwashing powder, Cascade	50 oz	3.74	3/01	4c
Tissues, facial, Kleenex brand	175	1.34	3/01	4c
Housing				
Housing, ACCRA Index		89.80	3/01	4c
Home, 2200 sq ft, 4-br, 2-bath, 2-car garage, average		175250	2000	47c
Home value, median		99000	2001	53s

Values are in dollars or fractions of dollars. In the column headed *Ref*, references are shown to sources. Each reference is followed by a letter. These refer to the geographical level for which data were reported: s=State, r=Region, and c=City or metro. The abbreviation *ex* is used to mean *except* or *excluding*; *exp* stands for *expenditures*. For other abbreviations and further explanations, please see the Introduction.

Cheyenne, WY - continued

Item	Per	Value	Date	Ref.
Housing				
House, 2400 sq ft, 8000 sq ft lot, new, urban, utilities	total	186225	3/01	4c
House payment, principal and interest, 25% down payment	mos	939	3/01	4c
Rent, apartment, 2 br, 1 1/2-2 baths, unfurn, 950 sq ft, water	mos	587	3/01	4c
Rental unit, 1 bedroom, with utilities	mos	465	4/01	41c
Rental unit, 2 bedroom, with utilities	mos	621	4/01	41c
Rental unit, 3 bedroom, with utilities	mos	794	4/01	41c
Rental unit, 4 bedroom, with utilities	mos	964	4/01	41c
Insurance and Pensions				
Auto insurance premium	yr	620.11	1999	57s
Legal Fees				
Driver's license fee	renew	15.00	1999	48s
Driver's license fee	orig	20.00	1999	48s
Fishing license	yr	15.00	4/01	34s
Personal Goods				
Shampoo, Alberto VO5	15 oz	1.35	3/01	4c
Toothpaste, Crest or Colgate	6-7 oz	2.47	3/01	4c
Personal Services				
Dry cleaning, man's 2-pc suit		7.66	3/01	4c
Man's haircut, barbershop, no styling		10.80	3/01	4c
Woman's shampoo, trim, blow-dry, no style-change		24.40	3/01	4c
Restaurant Food				
Chicken, fried, thigh and drumstick, KFC/Church's		2.65	3/01	4c
Hamburger with cheese, McDonald's	1/4 lb	1.00	3/01	4c
Pizza, Pizza Hut or Pizza Inn	11-12 in	9.99	3/01	4c
Transportation				
Transportation, ACCRA Index		91.60	3/01	4c
Bus fare, to central business district	1-way	1.00	3/01	4c
Diesel at the pump	gal	1.20	10/99	73s
Gasoline before-tax price (cents)	gal	119.10	10/00	43s
Tire balance, computer or spin balance, front	wheel	7.78	3/01	4c
Travel				
Car rental	day	45.00	2000	52c
Hotel room	night	53.09	2/01	94s
Utilities				
Utilities, ACCRA Index		89.60	3/01	4c
Electrical bill, average	mos	48.91	9/00	9s
Electricity, summer, 250 KWh	mos	15.63	2/96	96c
Electricity, summer, 500 KWh	mos	31.26	2/96	96c
Electricity, summer, 750 KWh	mos	43.63	2/96	96c
Electricity, summer, 1000 KWh	mos	56.01	2/96	96c
Electricity and other, mixed, 2400 sq ft, new home	mos	43.24	3/01	4c
Electricity cost, average	KWh	4.40	9/00	9s
Weddings				
Wedding (national average cost)		19936	2000	33r
Attendants' gifts		321	1998	33r
Bridal attendants' apparel (5 persons)		824	2000	33r
Bride's headpiece/veil		173	1998	33r
Bride's wedding dress		859	1998	33r
Clergy, religious facility fee		242	1998	33r
Engagement ring		3177	1998	33r
Flowers		789	1998	33r
Groom's formalwear rental		99	2000	33r
Limousine		410	1998	33r
Marriage license cost		25.00	4/01	35s
Men's formalwear (ushers, best man)		469	2000	33r
Mother of bride apparel		241	2000	33r
Music		866	1998	33r
Photography and videography		1368	1998	33r
Rehearsal dinner		728	1998	33r
Wedding invitations and announcements		341	1998	33r
Wedding reception		7968	2000	33r

Cheyenne, WY - continued

Item	Per	Value	Date	Ref.
Weddings - continued				
Wedding rings (bride and groom)		1060	1998	33r

Chicago, IL

Item	Per	Value	Date	Ref.
Average annual expenditures	yr	35369	1999	30r
Alcoholic Beverages				
Alcoholic beverage purchases	yr	411	1999	30c
Malt beverages, all types, all sizes, any origin	16 oz	0.93	7/01	11r
Wine, red and white table, all sizes, any origin	liter	7.04	7/01	11r
Appliances				
Major appliances, expenditures on	yr	165	1999	30r
Small appliances, housewares, expenditures on	yr	90	1999	30r
Banking and Money				
Mortgage interest and charges paid	yr	2277	1999	30r
Mortgage principal paid on owned property	yr	1230	1999	30r
Vehicle finance charges paid	yr	328	1999	30r
Business Expenses				
Business travel, car rental	day	60	2001	3c
Business travel, food	day	62	2001	3c
Business travel, hotel	day	190	2001	3c
Medical office space cost	sq ft	133.51	2001	31c
Office space, 2-4 storey building	sq ft	116.97	2001	31c
Office space, 5-10 storey building	sq ft	103.32	2001	31c
Office space, 11-20 storey building	sq ft	99.31	2001	31c
Office space, central business district, Class A	sq ft	31.71	3/99	74c
Charity				
Cash contributions, expenditures	yr	1249	1999	30c
Child Care				
Child raising cost, total, age 0-2	yr	7890	1999	60r
Child raising cost, total, age 3-5	yr	8130	1999	60r
Child raising cost, total, age 6-8	yr	8170	1999	60r
Child raising cost, total, age 9-11	yr	8190	1999	60r
Child raising cost, total, age 12-14	yr	8890	1999	60r
Child raising cost, total, age 15-17	yr	9050	1999	60r
Child's child care and education, age 0-2	yr	1240	1999	60r
Child's child care and education, age 3-5	yr	1370	1999	60r
Child's child care and education, age 6-8	yr	880	1999	60r
Child's child care and education, age 9-11	yr	570	1999	60r
Child's child care and education, age 12-14	yr	420	1999	60r
Child's child care and education, age 15-17	yr	720	1999	60r
Child's clothing, age 0-2	yr	410	1999	60r
Child's clothing, age 3-5	yr	400	1999	60r
Child's clothing, age 6-8	yr	450	1999	60r
Child's clothing, age 9-11	yr	500	1999	60r
Child's clothing, age 12-14	yr	840	1999	60r
Child's clothing, age 15-17	yr	740	1999	60r
Child's food, age 0-2	yr	960	1999	60r
Child's food, age 3-5	yr	1120	1999	60r
Child's food, age 6-8	yr	1430	1999	60r
Child's food, age 9-11	yr	1710	1999	60r
Child's food, age 12-14	yr	1710	1999	60r
Child's food, age 15-17	yr	1920	1999	60r
Child's health care, age 0-2	yr	520	1999	60r
Child's health care, age 3-5	yr	500	1999	60r
Child's health care, age 6-8	yr	570	1999	60r
Child's health care, age 9-11	yr	610	1999	60r
Child's health care, age 12-14	yr	630	1999	60r
Child's health care, age 15-17	yr	650	1999	60r
Child's housing, age 0-2	yr	2860	1999	60r
Child's housing, age 3-5	yr	2840	1999	60r
Child's housing, age 6-8	yr	2800	1999	60r
Child's housing, age 9-11	yr	2650	1999	60r
Child's housing, age 12-14	yr	2840	1999	60r
Child's housing, age 15-17	yr	2440	1999	60r
Child's personal care, reading, age 0-2	yr	880	1999	60r

Values are in dollars or fractions of dollars. In the column headed *Ref*, references are shown to sources. Each reference is followed by a letter. These refer to the geographical level for which data were reported: s=State, r=Region, and c=City or metro. The abbreviation *ex* is used to mean *except* or *excluding*; *exp* stands for expenditures. For other abbreviations and further explanations, please see the Introduction.

Chicago, IL - continued

Item	Per	Value	Date	Ref.
Child Care				
Child's personal care, reading, age 3-5	yr	900	1999	60r
Child's personal care, reading, age 6-8	yr	930	1999	60r
Child's personal care, reading, age 9-11	yr	970	1999	60r
Child's personal care, reading, age 12-14	yr	1150	1999	60r
Child's personal care, reading, age 15-17	yr	920	1999	60r
Daycare	mos	545	1998	37c
Daycare, 3-year old, 5 days, 8 hrs/day	mos	545	1998	85c
Clothing				
Apparel and services purchases	yr	1888	1999	30c
Boys, 2 to 15, expenditures on	yr	91	1999	30r
Children under 2, expenditures on	yr	59	1999	30r
Footwear, expenditures on	yr	285	1999	30r
Girls, 2 to 15, expenditures on	yr	116	1999	30r
Men and boys, expenditures on	yr	433	1999	30r
Men, 16 and over, expenditures on	yr	341	1999	30r
Women, 16 and over, expenditures on	yr	490	1999	30r
Communications				
Cable modem installation, Adelphi		54.90	6/99	103s
Cable modem installation, AT&T-BIS		150.00	6/99	103s
Cable modem installation, Media One		100.00	6/99	103s
Cable modem rate, cable subscriber, Adelphi	mos	34.95	6/99	103s
Cable modem rate, cable subscriber, AT&T-BIS	mos	39.95	6/99	103s
Cable modem rate, cable subscriber, Media One	mos	34.95-39.95	6/99	103s
Cable modem rate, non-cable subscriber, Adelphi	mos	44.95	6/99	103s
Cable modem rate, non-cable subscriber, Media One	mos	49.95	6/99	103s
Phone line, single, business, field visit	inst.	52.35	12/97	17s
Phone line, single, business, no field visit	inst.	52.35	12/97	17s
Phone line, single, residence, field visit	inst.	55.00	12/97	17s
Phone line, single, residence, no field visit	inst.	55.00	12/97	17s
Postage and stationery, expenditures on	yr	140	1999	30r
Postal rate, express mail, up to half-pound		12.45	7/01	108r
Postal rate, letter, first class, first ounce		0.34	7/01	108r
Postal rate, letter, two ounces		0.57	7/01	108r
Postal rate, post card		0.21	7/01	108r
Postal rate, priority mail, two pounds		3.95	7/01	108r
Postal rate, priority mail, up to one pound		3.50	7/01	108r
Telephone bill, business, basic rate	mos	6.61	12/97	18c
Telephone bill, residential, basic rate	mos	4.04	12/97	18c
Telephone services, expenditures on	yr	830	1999	30r
Education				
Board, 4-year private college/university	yr	2306	1996	38s
Board, 4-year public college/university	yr	2405	1996	38s
Education expenditures	yr	938	1999	30c
Room, 4-year private college/university	yr	2718	1996	38s
Room, 4-year public college/university	yr	2072	1996	38s
Total cost, 4-year private college/university	yr	16678	1996	38s
Total cost, 4-year public college/university	yr	7829	1996	38s
Tuition, 2-year public college/university, in state	yr	1232	1996	38s
Tuition, 4-year private college/university, in state	yr	11653	1996	38s
Tuition, 4-year public college/university	yr	3352	1996	38s
Energy and Fuels				
Electricity	500 KWhs	46.59	7/01	11r
Fuel oil #2	gal	1.27	7/01	11r
Fuel oil and other fuels, expenditures on	yr	68	1999	30r
Gas, natural, commercial rate	1000 cf	8.47	11/00	88s
Gasoline, unleaded midgrade	gal	1.79	7/01	11r
Gasoline, unleaded premium	gal	1.86	7/01	11r
Gasoline, unleaded regular	gal	1.58	7/01	11r
Natural gas, expenditures on	yr	389	1999	30r
Utility (piped) gas, therm		0.81	7/01	11r
Utility (piped) gas, 40 therms		38.01	7/01	11r
Utility (piped) gas, 100 therms		81.75	7/01	11r

Chicago, IL - continued

Item	Per	Value	Date	Ref.
Entertainment				
Entertainment purchases	yr	1771	1999	30c
Fees and admissions paid	yr	444	1999	30r
Reading purchases	yr	151	1999	30c
Television, radios, sound equipment, expenditures on	yr	580	1999	30r
Funerals				
Cosmetology, hair, other preparation		178.32	1/99	78r
Embalming		408.19	1/99	78r
Funeral at funeral home		362.13	1/99	78r
Professional service charges		1375.51	1/99	78r
Transfer of remains to funeral home		155.92	1/99	78r
Visitation/viewing		294.38	1/99	78r
Groceries				
Apples	pound	1.10		29c
Bacon, sliced	lb	3.15	7/01	11r
Bakery products, expenditures on	yr	281	1999	30r
Bananas	lb	0.48	7/01	11r
Beans, dried, any type, all sizes	lb	0.61	7/01	11r
Beef for stew, boneless	lb	3.08	7/01	11r
Beef, expenditures on	yr	217	1999	30r
Bologna, all beef or mixed	lb	2.52	7/01	11r
Bread, white, pan	lb	1.06	7/01	11r
Broccoli	lb	0.91	7/01	11r
Butter, salted, grade AA, stick	lb	3.04	7/01	11r
Butter, yoghurt, cheese, etc, expenditures on	yr	183	1999	30r
Cereals and bakery product purchases	yr	430	1999	30r
Cereals and cereal products, expenditures on	yr	149	1999	30r
Chicken, fresh, whole	lb	1.07	7/01	11r
Chops, boneless,	lb	3.64	7/01	11r
Chuck roast, U.S. choice, boneless	lb	2.47	7/01	11r
Coffee, 100%, ground roast, all sizes	lb	2.69	7/01	11r
Cookies, chocolate chip	lb	2.87	7/01	11r
Dairy product purchases	yr	285	1999	30c
Eggs, expenditures on	yr	26	1999	30r
Eggs, grade A, large	dozen	0.88	7/01	11r
Fats and oils, expenditures on	yr	75	1999	30r
Fish and seafood, expenditures on	yr	72	1999	30r
Food (excl fruit and vegetables), eaten at home, purchases	yr	849	1999	30c
Food cooked on trips, expenditures on	yr	44	1999	30r
Food purchases	yr	5092	1999	30c
Food purchases, eaten away from home	yr	2290	1999	30c
Food purchases, food eaten at home	yr	2802	1999	30c
Fresh fruits, expenditures on	yr	138	1999	30r
Fresh milk and cream, expenditures on	yr	120	1999	30r
Fresh vegetables, expenditures on	yr	126	1999	30r
Fruit and vegetable purchases	yr	514	1999	30c
Grapefruit	lb	0.66	7/01	11r
Grapes, Thompson, seedless	lb	1.64	7/01	11r
Ground beef, 100% beef	lb	1.64	7/01	11r
Ground beef, lean and extra lean	lb	2.16	7/01	11r
Ground chuck, 100% beef	lb	2.13	7/01	11r
Ham, boneless, excl canned	lb	2.62	7/01	11r
Ice cream, prepackaged, bulk, regular	1/2 gal	3.35	7/01	11r
Lemons	lb	1.19	7/01	11r
Lettuce, iceberg	lb	0.73	7/01	11r
Margarine, soft, tubs	lb	0.89	7/01	11r
Meats, poultry, fish, and egg purchases	yr	671	1999	30r
Milk, fresh, whole, fortified	gal	2.71	7/01	11r
Nonalcoholic beverages, expenditures on	yr	239	1999	30r
Oranges, Navel	lb	0.80	7/01	11r
Oranges, Valencia	lb	0.66	7/01	11r
Pears, Anjou	lb	0.93	7/01	11r
Pork chops, center cut, bone-in	lb	3.63	7/01	11r
Pork, expenditures on	yr	150	1999	30r
Potato chips	16 oz	3.52	7/01	11r
Potatoes, frozen, french fried	lb	1.08	7/01	11r
Potatoes, white, all types	lb	0.33	7/01	11r
Poultry, expenditures on	yr	108	1999	30r
Processed fruits, expenditures on	yr	98	1999	30r

Values are in dollars or fractions of dollars. In the column headed *Ref*, references are shown to sources. Each reference is followed by a letter. These refer to the geographical level for which data were reported: s=State, r=Region, and c=City or metro. The abbreviation *ex* is used to mean *except* or *excluding*; *exp* stands for expenditures. For other abbreviations and further explanations, please see the Introduction.

Chicago, IL - continued

Item	Per	Value	Date	Ref.
Groceries				
Processed vegetables, expenditures on	yr	80	1999	30r
Round roast, U.S. choice, boneless	lb	3.07	7/01	11r
Round steak, graded and ungraded, excl U.S. prime and choice	lb	3.41	7/01	11r
Shortening, vegetable oil blends	lb	1.13	7/01	11r
Spaghetti and macaroni	lb	0.80	7/01	11r
Steak, round, U.S. choice, boneless	lb	3.23	7/01	11r
Steak, T-bone, U.S. choice, bone-in	lb	6.68	7/01	11r
Strawberries, dry pint	12 oz	1.32	7/01	11r
Sugar and other sweets, expenditures on	yr	114	1999	30r
Sugar, white, 33-80 ounce package	lb	0.42	7/01	11r
Sugar, white, all sizes	lb	0.43	7/01	11r
Tobacco products and smoking supplies purchases	yr	266	1999	30c
Tomatoes, field grown	lb	1.46	7/01	11r
Tuna, light, chunk	lb	1.80	7/01	11r
Turkey, frozen, whole	lb	1.15	7/01	11r
Goods and Services				
B&B Japanese maple (acer japonicum)	gal	29.99-169.99	4/00	93r
Boxwood (buxus)	2 gal	18.99-39.99	4/00	93r
Daylilly (hemerocallis)	gal	4.99-25.00	4/00	93r
Flat of annuals		11.98-24.99	4/00	93r
Fountain grass (pennisetum)	gal	5.98-12.98	4/00	93r
Hanging basket (10 in)		12.99-27.99	4/00	93r
Hardy geranium (geranium)	gal	7.99-9.99	4/00	93r
Hosta (hosta)	gal	6.00-25.00	4/00	93r
Lilac (syrubga vulgaris)	2 gal	14.99-24.99	4/00	93r
Miscellaneous purchases	yr	865	1999	30r
Rhododendron (rhododendron)	2 gal	23.98-42.99	4/00	93r
Sage (salvia)	gal	6.00-9.99	4/00	93r
Wintercreeper euonymus (euonymus fortunei)	2 gal	16.00-169.99	4/00	93r
Hunting license	yr	7.50	4/01	34s
Health Care				
Cardiac catheterization, ave hospital/ physician charges		17690	1998	77s
Childbirth, Cesarean delivery		10722	1997	13r
Childbirth, vaginal delivery		6223	1997	13r
Drugs, expenditures on	yr	394	1999	30r
Health care purchases	yr	1951	1999	30c
Health insurance expenditures	yr	978	1999	30r
Home health care aide cost, licensed agency	hour	17	2000	82c
Hysterectomy, laproscopically-assisted, ave hospital/physician charges		15850	1998	76s
Hysterectomy, vaginal, ave hospital and physician charges		11810	1998	76s
Medicaid dispensing fee		3.69-15.45	1999	87s
Medical services expenditures	yr	554	1999	30r
Medical supplies, expenditures on	yr	122	1999	30r
Nursing home costs, private room	day	120	2000	82c
Nursing home stay, private room	day	120	2000	83c
Plastic surgery, breast augmentation		3184	2000	7r
Plastic surgery, breast lift		3585	2000	7r
Plastic surgery, facelift		4999	2000	7r
Plastic surgery, hair transplantation		3105	2000	7r
Plastic surgery, lip augmentation		1290	2000	7r
Plastic surgery, lower body lift		8135	2000	7r
Plastic surgery, thigh lift		3839	2000	7r

Chicago, IL - continued

Item	Per	Value	Date	Ref.
Household Goods				
Floor coverings, expenditures on	yr	52	1999	30r
Furniture, expenditures on	yr	344	1999	30r
Household furnishings and equipment purchases	yr	1590	1999	30c
Household textiles, expenditures on	yr	109	1999	30r
Laundry and cleaning supplies, expenditures on	yr	134	1999	30r
Housing				
Home price, existing, ave		144400	10/00	90r
Home value, median		183000	2001	53s
House, 2-story, 2,400 sq ft, 2-car garage, new		200200	2000	54c
Household operation expenditures	yr	520	1999	30c
Housekeeping supplies purchases	yr	567	1999	30c
Housing, expenditures on	yr	13732	1999	30c
Lodging expenditures	yr	430	1999	30r
Maintenance, repairs, insurance expenditures	yr	853	1999	30r
Monthly rental value of owned home	mos	547	1999	30r
Owned dwellings, expenditures own	yr	5625	1999	30c
Rent expenditures	yr	2238	1999	30c
Rental unit, 1 bedroom, with utilities	mos	661	4/01	41c
Rental unit, 2 bedroom, with utilities	mos	788	4/01	41c
Rental unit, 3 bedroom, with utilities	mos	985	4/01	41c
Rental unit, 4 bedroom, with utilities	mos	1102	4/01	41c
Shelter, expenditures on	yr	8408	1999	30c
Insurance and Pensions				
Life and other personal insurance purchases	yr	392	1999	30c
Pensions and Social Security, expenditures on	yr	2875	1999	30c
Personal insurance and pensions, expenditures on	yr	3267	1999	30c
Legal Fees				
Divorce, filing fee		100.00-150.00	4/01	35s
Driver's license fee	orig	10.00	1999	48s
Driver's license fee	renew	20.00	1999	48s
Personal Goods				
Personal care products and services purchases	yr	429	1999	30c
Personal Services				
Personal services, household, expenditures on	yr	300	1999	30r
Pets				
Pets, toys, and playground equipment, expenditures on	yr	375	1999	30r
Restaurant Food				
Cheeseburger, 1/4-lb, large fries, medium soft drink, excl tax		4.36	1999	40c
Taxes				
Federal income taxes paid	yr	2326	1999	30r
Personal taxes, expenditures on	yr	3223	1999	30r
Property taxes paid	yr	1152	1999	30r
State and local income taxes paid	yr	753	1999	30r
Transportation				
Bus fare, one-way	trip	1.33	2000	1c
Cars and trucks, new, expenditures on	yr	1280	1999	30r
Cars and trucks, used, expenditures on	yr	1763	1999	30r
Commuter rail, one-way	trip	1.75-3.15	2000	2c
Diesel at the pump	gal	1.33	10/99	73s
Gasoline and motor oil purchases	yr	928	1999	30c
Gasoline before-tax price (cents)	gal	112.70	10/00	43s
Heavy rail transit fare, one-way	trip	1.50	2000	2c
Maintenance and repair expenditures	yr	594	1999	30r
Parking at airport, lowest rate	day	8.00	2000	46c
Public transportation, expenditures on	yr	568	1999	30c

Values are in dollars or fractions of dollars. In the column headed *Ref*, references are shown to sources. Each reference is followed by a letter. These refer to the geographical level for which data were reported: s=State, r=Region, and c=City or metro. The abbreviation *ex* is used to mean *except* or *excluding*; *exp* stands for expenditures. For other abbreviations and further explanations, please see the Introduction.

Chicago, IL - continued

Item	Per	Value	Date	Ref.
Transportation				
Transportation purchases	yr	6233	1999	30c
Vehicle expenses, miscellaneous, purchases	yr	1958	1999	30c
Vehicle insurance payments	yr	701	1999	30r
Vehicle purchases (net outlay)	yr	2779	1999	30c
Vehicle rental, lease expenditures	yr	536	1999	30r
Travel				
Car rental	day	79.00	2000	24c
Hotel rate, ave	day	140.48	1999	45c
Hotel room, ave	night	142.05	2000	70c
Utilities				
Electrical bill, average	mos	63.08	9/00	9s
Electricity, expenditures on	yr	841	1999	30r
Electricity, summer, 250 KWh	mos	34.89	2/96	97c
Electricity, summer, 500 KWh	mos	58.29	2/96	97c
Electricity, summer, 750 KWh	mos	77.81	2/96	97c
Electricity, summer, 1000 KWh	mos	97.33	2/96	97c
Electricity cost, average	KWh	6.49	9/00	9s
Utilities, fuels, and public services purchased	yr	2401	1999	30r
Water and other public services, expenditures on	yr	273	1999	30r
Water price	100 cf	0.80	2000	109c
Water price, dwelling unit	mos	15.74	2000	109c
Weddings				
Wedding (national average cost)		19936	2000	33r
Wedding (regional average total cost)		16195	1997	110r
Attendants' gifts		321	1998	33r
Bridal attendants' apparel (5 persons)		824	2000	33r
Bride's headpiece/veil		173	1998	33r
Bride's wedding dress		859	1998	33r
Clergy, religious facility fee		242	1998	33r
Engagement ring		3177	1998	33r
Flowers		789	1998	33r
Groom's formalwear rental		99	2000	33r
Limousine		410	1998	33r
Marriage license cost		15.00-20.00	4/01	35s
Men's formalwear (ushers, best man)		469	2000	33r
Mother of bride apparel		241	2000	33r
Music		866	1998	33r
Photography and videography		1368	1998	33r
Rehearsal dinner		728	1998	33r
Wedding invitations and announcements		341	1998	33r
Wedding reception		7968	2000	33r
Wedding rings (bride and groom)		1060	1998	33r

Chicago-Gary-Kenosha, IL-IN-WI

Item	Per	Value	Date	Ref.
Average annual expenditures	yr	35369	1999	30r
Alcoholic Beverages				
Alcoholic beverage purchases	yr	304	1999	30r
Malt beverages, all types, all sizes, any origin	16 oz	0.93	7/01	11r
Wine, red and white table, all sizes, any origin	liter	7.04	7/01	11r
Appliances				
Major appliances, expenditures on	yr	165	1999	30r
Small appliances, housewares, expenditures on	yr	90	1999	30r
Banking and Money				
Mortgage interest and charges paid	yr	2277	1999	30r
Mortgage principal paid on owned property	yr	1230	1999	30r
Vehicle finance charges paid	yr	328	1999	30r
Charity				
Cash contributions, expenditures	yr	1126	1999	30r
Child Care				
Child raising cost, total, age 0-2	yr	7890	1999	60r
Child raising cost, total, age 3-5	yr	8130	1999	60r
Child raising cost, total, age 6-8	yr	8170	1999	60r

Chicago-Gary-Kenosha, IL-IN-WI - continued

Item	Per	Value	Date	Ref.
Child Care - continued				
Child raising cost, total, age 9-11	yr	8190	1999	60r
Child raising cost, total, age 12-14	yr	8890	1999	60r
Child raising cost, total, age 15-17	yr	9050	1999	60r
Child's child care and education, age 0-2	yr	1240	1999	60r
Child's child care and education, age 3-5	yr	1370	1999	60r
Child's child care and education, age 6-8	yr	880	1999	60r
Child's child care and education, age 9-11	yr	570	1999	60r
Child's child care and education, age 12-14	yr	420	1999	60r
Child's child care and education, age 15-17	yr	720	1999	60r
Child's clothing, age 0-2	yr	410	1999	60r
Child's clothing, age 3-5	yr	400	1999	60r
Child's clothing, age 6-8	yr	450	1999	60r
Child's clothing, age 9-11	yr	500	1999	60r
Child's clothing, age 12-14	yr	840	1999	60r
Child's clothing, age 15-17	yr	740	1999	60r
Child's food, age 0-2	yr	960	1999	60r
Child's food, age 3-5	yr	1120	1999	60r
Child's food, age 6-8	yr	1430	1999	60r
Child's food, age 9-11	yr	1710	1999	60r
Child's food, age 12-14	yr	1710	1999	60r
Child's food, age 15-17	yr	1920	1999	60r
Child's health care, age 0-2	yr	520	1999	60r
Child's health care, age 3-5	yr	500	1999	60r
Child's health care, age 6-8	yr	570	1999	60r
Child's health care, age 9-11	yr	610	1999	60r
Child's health care, age 12-14	yr	630	1999	60r
Child's health care, age 15-17	yr	650	1999	60r
Child's housing, age 0-2	yr	2860	1999	60r
Child's housing, age 3-5	yr	2840	1999	60r
Child's housing, age 6-8	yr	2800	1999	60r
Child's housing, age 9-11	yr	2650	1999	60r
Child's housing, age 12-14	yr	2840	1999	60r
Child's housing, age 15-17	yr	2440	1999	60r
Child's personal care, reading, age 0-2	yr	880	1999	60r
Child's personal care, reading, age 3-5	yr	900	1999	60r
Child's personal care, reading, age 6-8	yr	930	1999	60r
Child's personal care, reading, age 9-11	yr	970	1999	60r
Child's personal care, reading, age 12-14	yr	1150	1999	60r
Child's personal care, reading, age 15-17	yr	920	1999	60r
Clothing				
Apparel and services purchases	yr	1607	1999	30r
Boys, 2 to 15, expenditures on	yr	91	1999	30r
Children under 2, expenditures on	yr	59	1999	30r
Footwear, expenditures on	yr	285	1999	30r
Girls, 2 to 15, expenditures on	yr	116	1999	30r
Men and boys, expenditures on	yr	433	1999	30r
Men, 16 and over, expenditures on	yr	341	1999	30r
Women, 16 and over, expenditures on	yr	490	1999	30r
Communications				
Cable modem installation, Adelphi		54.90	6/99	103s
Cable modem installation, AT&T-BIS		150.00	6/99	103s
Cable modem installation, Media One		100.00	6/99	103s
Cable modem rate, cable subscriber, Adelphi	mos	34.95	6/99	103s
Cable modem rate, cable subscriber, AT&T-BIS	mos	39.95	6/99	103s
Cable modem rate, cable subscriber, Media One	mos	34.95-39.95	6/99	103s
Cable modem rate, non-cable subscriber, Adelphi	mos	44.95	6/99	103s
Cable modem rate, non-cable subscriber, Media One	mos	49.95	6/99	103s
Phone line, single, business, field visit	inst.	52.35	12/97	17s
Phone line, single, business, no field visit	inst.	52.35	12/97	17s
Phone line, single, residence, field visit	inst.	55.00	12/97	17s
Phone line, single, residence, no field visit	inst.	55.00	12/97	17s
Postage and stationery, expenditures on	yr	140	1999	30r
Postal rate, express mail, up to half-pound		12.45	7/01	108r
Postal rate, letter, first class, first ounce		0.34	7/01	108r
Postal rate, letter, two ounces		0.57	7/01	108r
Postal rate, post card		0.21	7/01	108r
Postal rate, priority mail, two pounds		3.95	7/01	108r

Values are in dollars or fractions of dollars. In the column headed *Ref*, references are shown to sources. Each reference is followed by a letter. These refer to the geographical level for which data were reported: s=State, r=Region, and c=City or metro. The abbreviation *ex* is used to mean *except* or *excluding*; *exp* stands for expenditures. For other abbreviations and further explanations, please see the Introduction.

Chicago-Gary-Kenosha, IL-IN-WI - continued

Item	Per	Value	Date	Ref.
Communications				
Postal rate, priority mail, up to one pound		3.50	7/01	108r
Telephone services, expenditures on	yr	830	1999	30r
Education				
Board, 4-year private college/university	yr	2306	1996	38s
Board, 4-year public college/university	yr	2405	1996	38s
Education expenditures	yr	583	1999	30r
Room, 4-year private college/university	yr	2718	1996	38s
Room, 4-year public college/university	yr	2072	1996	38s
Total cost, 4-year private college/university	yr	16678	1996	38s
Total cost, 4-year public college/university	yr	7829	1996	38s
Tuition, 2-year public college/university, in state	yr	1232	1996	38s
Tuition, 4-year private college/university, in state	yr	11653	1996	38s
Tuition, 4-year public college/university	yr	3352	1996	38s
Energy and Fuels				
Electricity	500 KWhs	54.14	7/01	11c
Electricity	KWh	0.11	7/01	11c
Fuel oil #2	gal	1.27	7/01	11r
Fuel oil and other fuels, expenditures on	yr	68	1999	30r
Gas, natural, commercial rate	1000 cf	8.47	11/00	88s
Gasoline, all types	gal	1.88	7/01	11c
Gasoline, unleaded midgrade	gal	1.89	7/01	11c
Gasoline, unleaded premium	gal	1.86	7/01	11r
Gasoline, unleaded regular	gal	1.80	7/01	11c
Natural gas, expenditures on	yr	389	1999	30r
Utility (piped) gas, therm		0.80	7/01	11c
Utility (piped) gas, 40 therms		38.01	7/01	11r
Utility (piped) gas, 100 therms		80.45	7/01	11c
Entertainment				
Entertainment purchases	yr	1984	1999	30r
Fees and admissions paid	yr	444	1999	30r
Television, radios, sound equipment, expenditures on	yr	580	1999	30r
Funerals				
Cosmetology, hair, other preparation		178.32	1/99	78r
Embalming		408.19	1/99	78r
Funeral at funeral home		362.13	1/99	78r
Professional service charges		1375.51	1/99	78r
Transfer of remains to funeral home		155.92	1/99	78r
Visitation/viewing		294.38	1/99	78r
Groceries				
Bacon, sliced	lb	3.15	7/01	11r
Bakery products, expenditures on	yr	281	1999	30r
Bananas	lb	0.48	7/01	11r
Beans, dried, any type, all sizes	lb	0.61	7/01	11r
Beef for stew, boneless	lb	3.08	7/01	11r
Beef, expenditures on	yr	217	1999	30r
Bologna, all beef or mixed	lb	2.52	7/01	11r
Bread, white, pan	lb	1.06	7/01	11r
Broccoli	lb	0.91	7/01	11r
Butter, salted, grade AA, stick	lb	3.04	7/01	11r
Butter, yoghurt, cheese, etc, expenditures on	yr	183	1999	30r
Cereals and bakery product purchases	yr	430	1999	30r
Cereals and cereal products, expenditures on	yr	149	1999	30r
Chicken, fresh, whole	lb	1.07	7/01	11r
Chops, boneless,	lb	3.64	7/01	11r
Chuck roast, U.S. choice, boneless	lb	2.47	7/01	11r
Coffee, 100%, ground roast, all sizes	lb	2.69	7/01	11r
Cookies, chocolate chip	lb	2.87	7/01	11r
Dairy product purchases	yr	304	1999	30r
Eggs, expenditures on	yr	26	1999	30r
Eggs, grade A, large	dozen	0.88	7/01	11r
Fats and oils, expenditures on	yr	75	1999	30r
Fish and seafood, expenditures on	yr	72	1999	30r
Food (excl fruit and vegetables), eaten at home, purchases	yr	887	1999	30r

Chicago-Gary-Kenosha, IL-IN-WI - continued

Item	Per	Value	Date	Ref.
Groceries - continued				
Food cooked on trips, expenditures on	yr	44	1999	30r
Food purchases	yr	4802	1999	30r
Food purchases, eaten away from home	yr	2069	1999	30r
Food purchases, food eaten at home	yr	2733	1999	30r
Fresh fruits, expenditures on	yr	138	1999	30r
Fresh milk and cream, expenditures on	yr	120	1999	30r
Fresh vegetables, expenditures on	yr	126	1999	30r
Grapefruit	lb	0.66	7/01	11r
Grapes, Thompson, seedless	lb	1.64	7/01	11r
Ground beef, 100% beef	lb	1.64	7/01	11r
Ground beef, lean and extra lean	lb	2.16	7/01	11r
Ground chuck, 100% beef	lb	2.13	7/01	11r
Ham, boneless, excl canned	lb	2.62	7/01	11r
Ice cream, prepackaged, bulk, regular	1/2 gal	3.35	7/01	11r
Lemons	lb	1.19	7/01	11r
Lettuce, iceberg	lb	0.73	7/01	11r
Margarine, soft, tubs	lb	0.89	7/01	11r
Meats, poultry, fish, and egg purchases	yr	671	1999	30r
Milk, fresh, whole, fortified	gal	2.71	7/01	11r
Nonalcoholic beverages, expenditures on	yr	239	1999	30r
Oranges, Navel	lb	0.80	7/01	11r
Oranges, Valencia	lb	0.66	7/01	11r
Pears, Anjou	lb	0.93	7/01	11r
Pork chops, center cut, bone-in	lb	3.63	7/01	11r
Pork, expenditures on	yr	150	1999	30r
Potato chips	16 oz	3.52	7/01	11r
Potatoes, frozen, french fried	lb	1.08	7/01	11r
Potatoes, white, all types	lb	0.33	7/01	11r
Poultry, expenditures on	yr	108	1999	30r
Processed fruits, expenditures on	yr	98	1999	30r
Processed vegetables, expenditures on	yr	80	1999	30r
Round roast, U.S. choice, boneless	lb	3.07	7/01	11r
Round steak, graded and ungraded, excl U.S. prime and choice	lb	3.41	7/01	11r
Shortening, vegetable oil blends	lb	1.13	7/01	11r
Spaghetti and macaroni	lb	0.80	7/01	11r
Steak, round, U.S. choice, boneless	lb	3.23	7/01	11r
Steak, T-bone, U.S. choice, bone-in	lb	6.68	7/01	11r
Strawberries, dry pint	12 oz	1.32	7/01	11r
Sugar and other sweets, expenditures on	yr	114	1999	30r
Sugar, white, 33-80 ounce package	lb	0.42	7/01	11r
Sugar, white, all sizes	lb	0.43	7/01	11r
Tobacco products and smoking supplies purchases	yr	331	1999	30r
Tomatoes, field grown	lb	1.46	7/01	11r
Tuna, light, chunk	lb	1.80	7/01	11r
Turkey, frozen, whole	lb	1.15	7/01	11r
Goods and Services				
B&B Japanese maple (acer japonicum)	gal	29.99-169.99	4/00	93r
Boxwood (buxus)	2 gal	18.99-39.99	4/00	93r
Daylilly (hemerocallis)	gal	4.99-25.00	4/00	93r
Flat of annuals		11.98-24.99	4/00	93r
Fountain grass (pennisetum)	gal	5.98-12.98	4/00	93r
Hanging basket (10 in)		12.99-27.99	4/00	93r
Hardy geranium (geranium)	gal	7.99-9.99	4/00	93r
Hosta (hosta)	gal	6.00-25.00	4/00	93r
Lilac (syrubga vulgaris)	2 gal	14.99-24.99	4/00	93r
Miscellaneous purchases	yr	865	1999	30r
Rhododendron (rhododendron)	2 gal	23.98-42.99	4/00	93r
Sage (salvia)	gal	6.00-9.99	4/00	93r

Values are in dollars or fractions of dollars. In the column headed *Ref*, references are shown to sources. Each reference is followed by a letter. These refer to the geographical level for which data were reported: s=State, r=Region, and c=City or metro. The abbreviation *ex* is used to mean *except* or *excluding*; *exp* stands for *expenditures*. For other abbreviations and further explanations, please see the Introduction.

Chicago-Gary-Kenosha, IL-IN-WI - continued

Item	Per	Value	Date	Ref.
Goods and Services				
Wintercreeper euonymus (euonymus fortunei)	2 gal	16.00-169.99	4/00	93r
Hunting license	yr	7.50	4/01	34s
Health Care				
Cardiac catheterization, ave hospital/ physician charges		17690	1998	77s
Childbirth, Cesarean delivery		10722	1997	13r
Childbirth, vaginal delivery		6223	1997	13r
Drugs, expenditures on	yr	394	1999	30r
Health care purchases	yr	2048	1999	30r
Health insurance expenditures	yr	978	1999	30r
Hysterectomy, laproscopically-assisted, ave hospital/physician charges		15850	1998	76s
Hysterectomy, vaginal, ave hospital and physician charges		11810	1998	76s
Medicaid dispensing fee		3.69-15.45	1999	87s
Medical services expenditures	yr	554	1999	30r
Medical supplies, expenditures on	yr	122	1999	30r
Plastic surgery, breast augmentation		3184	2000	7r
Plastic surgery, breast lift		3585	2000	7r
Plastic surgery, facelift		4999	2000	7r
Plastic surgery, hair transplantation		3105	2000	7r
Plastic surgery, lip augmentation		1290	2000	7r
Plastic surgery, lower body lift		8135	2000	7r
Plastic surgery, thigh lift		3839	2000	7r
Household Goods				
Floor coverings, expenditures on	yr	52	1999	30r
Furniture, expenditures on	yr	344	1999	30r
Household furnishings and equipment purchases	yr	1475	1999	30r
Household textiles, expenditures on	yr	109	1999	30r
Laundry and cleaning supplies, expenditures on	yr	134	1999	30r
Housing				
Home price, existing, ave		144400	10/00	90r
Home value, median		183000	2001	53s
Household operation expenditures	yr	542	1999	30r
Housekeeping supplies purchases	yr	508	1999	30r
Lodging expenditures	yr	430	1999	30r
Maintenance, repairs, insurance expenditures	yr	853	1999	30r
Monthly rental value of owned home	mos	547	1999	30r
Owned dwellings, expenditures own	yr	4282	1999	30r
Rent expenditures	yr	1558	1999	30r
Shelter, expenditures on	yr	6270	1999	30r
Insurance and Pensions				
Life and other personal insurance purchases	yr	387	1999	30r
Pensions and Social Security, expenditures on	yr	2968	1999	30r
Legal Fees				
Divorce, filing fee		100.00-150.00	4/01	35s
Driver's license fee	renew	20.00	1999	48s
Driver's license fee	orig	10.00	1999	48s
Personal Goods				
Personal care products and services purchases	yr	385	1999	30r
Personal Services				
Personal services, household, expenditures on	yr	300	1999	30r
Pets				
Pets, toys, and playground equipment, expenditures on	yr	375	1999	30r
Taxes				
Federal income taxes paid	yr	2326	1999	30r
Personal taxes, expenditures on	yr	3223	1999	30r

Chicago-Gary-Kenosha, IL-IN-WI - continued

Item	Per	Value	Date	Ref.
Taxes - continued				
Property taxes paid	yr	1152	1999	30r
State and local income taxes paid	yr	753	1999	30r
Transportation				
Cars and trucks, new, expenditures on	yr	1280	1999	30r
Cars and trucks, used, expenditures on	yr	1763	1999	30r
Diesel at the pump	gal	1.33	10/99	73s
Gasoline and motor oil purchases	yr	1036	1999	30r
Gasoline before-tax price (cents)	gal	112.70	10/00	43s
Maintenance and repair expenditures	yr	594	1999	30r
Public transportation, expenditures on	yr	341	1999	30r
Transportation purchases	yr	6617	1999	30r
Vehicle expenses, miscellaneous, purchases	yr	2159	1999	30r
Vehicle insurance payments	yr	701	1999	30r
Vehicle purchases (net outlay)	yr	3081	1999	30r
Vehicle rental, lease expenditures	yr	536	1999	30r
Utilities				
Electrical bill, average	mos	63.08	9/00	9s
Electricity, expenditures on	yr	841	1999	30r
Electricity cost, average	KWh	6.49	9/00	9s
Utilities, fuels, and public services purchased	yr	2401	1999	30r
Water and other public services, expenditures on	yr	273	1999	30r
Weddings				
Wedding (national average cost)		19936	2000	33r
Wedding (regional average total cost)		16195	1997	110r
Attendants' gifts		321	1998	33r
Bridal attendants' apparel (5 persons)		824	2000	33r
Bride's headpiece/veil		173	1998	33r
Bride's wedding dress		859	1998	33r
Clergy, religious facility fee		242	1998	33r
Engagement ring		3177	1998	33r
Flowers		789	1998	33r
Groom's formalwear rental		99	2000	33r
Limousine		410	1998	33r
Marriage license cost		15.00-20.00	4/01	35s
Men's formalwear (ushers, best man)		469	2000	33r
Mother of bride apparel		241	2000	33r
Music		866	1998	33r
Photography and videography		1368	1998	33r
Rehearsal dinner		728	1998	33r
Wedding invitations and announcements		341	1998	33r
Wedding reception		7968	2000	33r
Wedding rings (bride and groom)		1060	1998	33r

Chico-Paradise, CA

Item	Per	Value	Date	Ref.
Average annual expenditures	yr	40662	1999	30r
Alcoholic Beverages				
Alcoholic beverage purchases	yr	372	1999	30r
Malt beverages, all types, all sizes, any origin	16 oz	0.94	7/01	11r
Wine, red and white table, all sizes, any origin	liter	6.00	7/01	11r
Appliances				
Major appliances, expenditures on	yr	167	1999	30r
Small appliances, housewares, expenditures on	yr	105	1999	30r
Banking and Money				
Mortgage interest and charges paid	yr	3368	1999	30r
Mortgage principal paid on owned property	yr	1677	1999	30r
Vehicle finance charges paid	yr	311	1999	30r
Charity				
Cash contributions, expenditures	yr	1344	1999	30r
Child Care				
Child raising cost, total, age 0-2	yr	9140	1999	60r
Child raising cost, total, age 3-5	yr	9370	1999	60r
Child raising cost, total, age 6-8	yr	9450	1999	60r

Values are in dollars or fractions of dollars. In the column headed *Ref*, references are shown to sources. Each reference is followed by a letter. These refer to the geographical level for which data were reported: s=State, r=Region, and c=City or metro. The abbreviation *ex* is used to mean *except* or *excluding; exp* stands for expenditures. For other abbreviations and further explanations, please see the Introduction.

Chico-Paradise, CA - continued

Item	Per	Value	Date	Ref.
Child Care				
Child raising cost, total, age 9-11	yr	9470	1999	60r
Child raising cost, total, age 12-14	yr	10170	1999	60r
Child raising cost, total, age 15-17	yr	10360	1999	60r
Child's child care and education, age 0-2	yr	1250	1999	60r
Child's child care and education, age 3-5	yr	1380	1999	60r
Child's child care and education, age 6-8	yr	890	1999	60r
Child's child care and education, age 9-11	yr	580	1999	60r
Child's child care and education, age 12-14	yr	430	1999	60r
Child's child care and education, age 15-17	yr	730	1999	60r
Child's clothing, age 0-2	yr	430	1999	60r
Child's clothing, age 3-5	yr	420	1999	60r
Child's clothing, age 6-8	yr	470	1999	60r
Child's clothing, age 9-11	yr	520	1999	60r
Child's clothing, age 12-14	yr	870	1999	60r
Child's clothing, age 15-17	yr	770	1999	60r
Child's food, age 0-2	yr	1120	1999	60r
Child's food, age 3-5	yr	1280	1999	60r
Child's food, age 6-8	yr	1640	1999	60r
Child's food, age 9-11	yr	1930	1999	60r
Child's food, age 12-14	yr	1940	1999	60r
Child's food, age 15-17	yr	2150	1999	60r
Child's health care, age 0-2	yr	490	1999	60r
Child's health care, age 3-5	yr	470	1999	60r
Child's health care, age 6-8	yr	530	1999	60r
Child's health care, age 9-11	yr	570	1999	60r
Child's health care, age 12-14	yr	580	1999	60r
Child's health care, age 15-17	yr	610	1999	60r
Child's housing, age 0-2	yr	3630	1999	60r
Child's housing, age 3-5	yr	3610	1999	60r
Child's housing, age 6-8	yr	3570	1999	60r
Child's housing, age 9-11	yr	3410	1999	60r
Child's housing, age 12-14	yr	3600	1999	60r
Child's housing, age 15-17	yr	3210	1999	60r
Child's personal care, reading, age 0-2	yr	1040	1999	60r
Child's personal care, reading, age 3-5	yr	1060	1999	60r
Child's personal care, reading, age 6-8	yr	1090	1999	60r
Child's personal care, reading, age 9-11	yr	1130	1999	60r
Child's personal care, reading, age 12-14	yr	1300	1999	60r
Child's personal care, reading, age 15-17	yr	1080	1999	60r
Clothing				
Apparel and services purchases	yr	1863	1999	30r
Boys, 2 to 15, expenditures on	yr	80	1999	30r
Children under 2, expenditures on	yr	74	1999	30r
Footwear, expenditures on	yr	307	1999	30r
Girls, 2 to 15, expenditures on	yr	101	1999	30r
Men and boys, expenditures on	yr	443	1999	30r
Men, 16 and over, expenditures on	yr	363	1999	30r
Women, 16 and over, expenditures on	yr	594	1999	30r
Communications				
Cable modem installation, AT&T-BIS		150.00	6/99	103s
Cable modem installation, Charter		99.00-169.00	6/99	103s
Cable modem installation, Comcast		95.00	6/99	103s
Cable modem installation, Cox		99.00-174.95	6/99	103s
Cable modem installation, Media One		100.00	6/99	103s
Cable modem installation, Time Warner		75.00-225.00	6/99	103s
Cable modem rate, cable subscriber, AT&T-BIS	mos	39.95	6/99	103s
Cable modem rate, cable subscriber, Charter	mos	49.95-79.95	6/99	103s
Cable modem rate, cable subscriber, Comcast	mos	39.95	6/99	103s
Cable modem rate, cable subscriber, Cox	mos	29.95-44.95	6/99	103s
Cable modem rate, cable subscriber, Media One	mos	34.95-39.95	6/99	103s
Cable modem rate, cable subscriber, Time Warner	mos	39.95-49.95	6/99	103s

Chico-Paradise, CA - continued

Item	Per	Value	Date	Ref.
Communications - continued				
Cable modem rate, non-cable subscriber, Charter	mos	59.95-89.95	6/99	103s
Cable modem rate, non-cable subscriber, Comcast	mos	49.95	6/99	103s
Cable modem rate, non-cable subscriber, Cox	mos	42.95-54.95	6/99	103s
Cable modem rate, non-cable subscriber, Media One	mos	49.95	6/99	103s
Cable modem rate, non-cable subscriber, Time Warner	mos	39.95-54.95	6/99	103s
Phone line, single, business, field visit	inst.	70.75	12/97	17s
Phone line, single, business, no field visit	inst.	70.75	12/97	17s
Phone line, single, residence, field visit	inst.	34.75	12/97	17s
Phone line, single, residence, no field visit	inst.	34.75	12/97	17s
Postage and stationery, expenditures on	yr	150	1999	30r
Postal rate, express mail, up to half-pound		12.45	7/01	108r
Postal rate, letter, first class, first ounce		0.34	7/01	108r
Postal rate, letter, two ounces		0.57	7/01	108r
Postal rate, post card		0.21	7/01	108r
Postal rate, priority mail, two pounds		3.95	7/01	108r
Postal rate, priority mail, up to one pound		3.50	7/01	108r
Telephone services, expenditures on	yr	825	1999	30r
Education				
Board, 4-year private college/university	yr	2970	1996	38s
Board, 4-year public college/university	yr	2516	1996	38s
Education expenditures	yr	676	1999	30r
Room, 4-year private college/university	yr	3196	1996	38s
Room, 4-year public college/university	yr	3031	1996	38s
Total cost, 4-year private college/university	yr	20143	1996	38s
Total cost, 4-year public college/university	yr	8213	1996	38s
Tuition, 2-year public college/university, in state	yr	362	1996	38s
Tuition, 4-year private college/university, in state	yr	13977	1996	38s
Tuition, 4-year public college/university	yr	2666	1996	38s
Energy and Fuels				
Electricity	500 KWhs	48.23	7/01	11r
Electricity	KWh	0.11	7/01	11r
Fuel oil and other fuels, expenditures on	yr	35	1999	30r
Gas, natural, commercial rate	1000 cf	8.74	11/00	88s
Gasoline, all types	gal	1.91	7/01	11r
Gasoline, unleaded premium	gal	2.05	7/01	11r
Gasoline, unleaded regular	gal	1.83	7/01	11r
Natural gas, expenditures on	yr	255	1999	30r
Utility (piped) gas, therm		0.98	7/01	11r
Utility (piped) gas, 40 therms		40.74	7/01	11r
Utility (piped) gas, 100 therms		96.80	7/01	11r
Entertainment				
Entertainment purchases	yr	2139	1999	30r
Fees and admissions paid	yr	545	1999	30r
Television, radios, sound equipment, expenditures on	yr	624	1999	30r
Funerals				
Total cost of funeral		5401.08	1/99	78r
Acknowledgement cards		33.64	1/99	78r
Casket		2170.43	1/99	78r
Cosmetology, hair, other preparation		136.32	1/99	78r
Embalming		319.13	1/99	78r
Funeral at funeral home		370.21	1/99	78r
Hearse (local)		161.04	1/99	78r
Professional service charges		963.15	1/99	78r
Service car/van		133.99	1/99	78r
Transfer of remains to funeral home		159.82	1/99	78r
Vault		778.07	1/99	78r
Visitation/viewing		175.28	1/99	78r
Groceries				
Apples, red delicious	lb	0.84	7/01	11r
Bacon, sliced	lb	3.38	7/01	11r

Values are in dollars or fractions of dollars. In the column headed *Ref*, references are shown to sources. Each reference is followed by a letter. These refer to the geographical level for which data were reported: s=State, r=Region, and c=City or metro. The abbreviation *ex* is used to mean *except* or *excluding*; *exp* stands for expenditures. For other abbreviations and further explanations, please see the Introduction.

Chico-Paradise, CA - continued

Item	Per	Value	Date	Ref.
Groceries				
Bakery products, expenditures on	yr	299	1999	30r
Bananas	lb	0.54	7/01	11r
Beans, dried, any type, all sizes	lb	0.76	7/01	11r
Beef, expenditures on	yr	222	1999	30r
Bread, white, pan	lb	0.99	7/01	11r
Butter, yoghurt, cheese, etc, expenditures on	yr	211	1999	30r
Cereals and bakery product purchases	yr	466	1999	30r
Cereals and cereal products, expenditures on	yr	168	1999	30r
Chicken breast, bone-in	lb	2.45	7/01	11r
Chicken, fresh, whole	lb	1.19	7/01	11r
Chops, boneless,	lb	4.00	7/01	11r
Chuck roast, graded and ungraded, excl U.S. prime and choice	lb	2.55	7/01	11r
Coffee, 100%, ground roast, all sizes	lb	3.80	7/01	11r
Cookies, chocolate chip	lb	2.83	7/01	11r
Dairy product purchases	yr	341	1999	30r
Eggs, expenditures on	yr	39	1999	30r
Eggs, grade AA, large	dozen	1.23	7/01	11r
Fats and oils, expenditures on	yr	88	1999	30r
Fish and seafood, expenditures on	yr	121	1999	30r
Food (excl fruit and vegetables), eaten at home, purchases	yr	1001	1999	30r
Food cooked on trips, expenditures on	yr	64	1999	30r
Food purchases	yr	5312	1999	30r
Food purchases, eaten away from home	yr	2180	1999	30r
Food purchases, food eaten at home	yr	3132	1999	30r
Fresh fruits, expenditures on	yr	186	1999	30r
Fresh milk and cream, expenditures on	yr	130	1999	30r
Fresh vegetables, expenditures on	yr	177	1999	30r
Grapefruit	lb	0.68	7/01	11r
Grapes, Thompson, seedless	lb	2.42	7/01	11r
Ground beef, lean and extra lean	lb	2.46	7/01	11r
Ice cream, prepackaged, bulk, regular	1/2 gal	3.62	7/01	11r
Lettuce, iceberg	lb	0.63	7/01	11r
Meats, poultry, fish, and egg purchases	yr	761	1999	30r
Milk, fresh, low fat,	gal	2.80	7/01	11r
Milk, fresh, whole, fortified	gal	2.88	7/01	11r
Nonalcoholic beverages, expenditures on	yr	258	1999	30r
Oranges, Navel	lb	0.97	7/01	11r
Oranges, Valencia	lb	0.43	7/01	11r
Peaches	lb	1.38	7/01	11r
Peanut butter, creamy, all sizes	lb	2.14	7/01	11r
Pork chops, center cut, bone-in	lb	3.83	7/01	11r
Pork, expenditures on	yr	141	1999	30r
Potatoes, white, all types	lb	0.37	7/01	11r
Poultry, expenditures on	yr	146	1999	30r
Processed fruits, expenditures on	yr	118	1999	30r
Processed vegetables, expenditures on	yr	81	1999	30r
Round roast, graded and ungraded, excl U.S. prime and choice	lb	3.07	7/01	11r
Round roast, U.S. choice, boneless	lb	3.37	7/01	11r
Round steak, graded and ungraded, excl U.S. prime and choice	lb	3.51	7/01	11r
Sirloin steak, graded and ungraded, excl U.S. prime and choice	lb	4.67	7/01	11r
Steak, sirloin, U.S. choice, boneless	lb	6.20	7/01	11r
Strawberries, dry pint	12 oz	1.79	7/01	11r
Sugar and other sweets, expenditures on	yr	124	1999	30r
Sugar, white, all sizes	lb	0.46	7/01	11r
Tobacco products and smoking supplies purchases	yr	217	1999	30r
Tomatoes, field grown	lb	1.17	7/01	11r
Tuna, light, chunk	lb	2.05	7/01	11r
Goods and Services				
B&B Japanese maple (acer japonicum)	gal	39.99	4/00	93r
Boxwood (buxus)	2 gal	14.99-24.99	4/00	93r
Christmas tree, noble fir		40-60	2000	65s
Daylilly (hemerocallis)	gal	6.99-8.99	4/00	93r
Flat of annuals		16.68	4/00	93r

Chico-Paradise, CA - continued

Item	Per	Value	Date	Ref.
Goods and Services - continued				
Fountain grass (pennisetum)	gal	7.99-11.99	4/00	93r
Hanging basket (10 in)		29.99	4/00	93r
Hardy geranium (geranium)	gal	6.99-11.99	4/00	93r
Hosta (hosta)	gal	6.99-18.99	4/00	93r
Lilac (syrubga vulgaris)	2 gal	14.99-17.99	4/00	93r
Miscellaneous purchases	yr	1070	1999	30r
Rhododendron (rhododendron)	2 gal	14.99	4/00	93r
Sage (salvia)	gal	6.99	4/00	93r
Wintercreeper euonymus (euonymus fortunei)	2 gal	14.99-22.99	4/00	93r
Hunting license	yr	29.95	4/01	34s
Health Care				
Cardiac catheterization, ave hospital/physician charges		24000	1998	77s
Childbirth, Cesarean delivery		11587	1997	13r
Childbirth, vaginal delivery		6725	1997	13r
Drugs, expenditures on	yr	309	1999	30r
Health care purchases	yr	1869	1999	30r
Health insurance expenditures	yr	868	1999	30r
Hysterectomy, laproscopically-assisted, ave hospital/physician charges		20760	1998	76s
Hysterectomy, vaginal, ave hospital and physician charges		14570	1998	76s
Medicaid dispensing fee		4.05	1999	87s
Medical services expenditures	yr	580	1999	30r
Medical supplies, expenditures on	yr	112	1999	30r
Household Goods				
Floor coverings, expenditures on	yr	49	1999	30r
Furniture, expenditures on	yr	444	1999	30r
Household furnishings and equipment purchases	yr	1768	1999	30r
Household textiles, expenditures on	yr	141	1999	30r
Laundry and cleaning supplies, expenditures on	yr	128	1999	30r
Housing				
Home price, existing, ave		239400	10/00	90r
Home value, median		215000	2001	53s
Household operation expenditures	yr	781	1999	30r
Housekeeping supplies purchases	yr	513	1999	30r
Lodging expenditures	yr	575	1999	30r
Maintenance, repairs, insurance expenditures	yr	939	1999	30r
Monthly rental value of owned home	mos	662	1999	30r
Owned dwellings, expenditures own	yr	5231	1999	30r
Rent expenditures	yr	2709	1999	30r
Rental unit, 1 bedroom, with utilities	mos	439	4/01	41c
Rental unit, 2 bedroom, with utilities	mos	584	4/01	41c
Rental unit, 3 bedroom, with utilities	mos	800	4/01	41c
Rental unit, 4 bedroom, with utilities	mos	957	4/01	41c
Shelter, expenditures on	yr	8516	1999	30r
Insurance and Pensions				
Life and other personal insurance purchases	yr	355	1999	30r
Pensions and Social Security, expenditures on	yr	3636	1999	30r
Legal Fees				
Divorce, filing fee		182.00	4/01	35s
Driver's license fee	orig	12.00	1999	48s
Driver's license fee	renew	15.00	1999	48s
Personal Goods				
Personal care products and services purchases	yr	449	1999	30r
Personal Services				
Personal services, household, expenditures on	yr	353	1999	30r

Values are in dollars or fractions of dollars. In the column headed *Ref*, references are shown to sources. Each reference is followed by a letter. These refer to the geographical level for which data were reported: s=State, r=Region, and c=City or metro. The abbreviation *ex* is used to mean *except* or *excluding*; *exp* stands for *expenditures*. For other abbreviations and further explanations, please see the Introduction.

Chico-Paradise, CA - continued

Item	Per	Value	Date	Ref.
Pets				
Pets, toys, and playground equipment, expenditures on	yr	358	1999	30r
Taxes				
Federal income taxes paid	yr	3200	1999	30r
Personal taxes, expenditures on	yr	4153	1999	30r
Property taxes paid	yr	923	1999	30r
State and local income taxes paid	yr	812	1999	30r
Transportation				
Cars and trucks, new, expenditures on	yr	1534	1999	30r
Cars and trucks, used, expenditures on	yr	1593	1999	30r
Diesel at the pump	gal	1.37	10/99	73s
Gasoline and motor oil purchases	yr	1129	1999	30r
Gasoline before-tax price (cents)	gal	128.80	10/00	43s
Maintenance and repair expenditures	yr	797	1999	30r
Public transportation, expenditures on	yr	530	1999	30r
Transportation purchases	yr	7423	1999	30r
Vehicle expenses, miscellaneous, purchases	yr	2585	1999	30r
Vehicle insurance payments	yr	811	1999	30r
Vehicle purchases (net outlay)	yr	3180	1999	30r
Vehicle rental, lease expenditures	yr	666	1999	30r
Utilities				
Electrical bill, average	mos	58.66	9/00	9s
Electricity, expenditures on	yr	725	1999	30r
Electricity cost, average	KWh	7.75	9/00	9s
Utilities, fuels, and public services purchased	yr	2179	1999	30r
Water and other public services, expenditures on	yr	339	1999	30r
Weddings				
Wedding (national average cost)		19936	2000	33r
Wedding (regional average total cost)		18918	1997	110r
Attendants' gifts		321	1998	33r
Bridal attendants' apparel (5 persons)		824	2000	33r
Bride's headpiece/veil		173	1998	33r
Bride's wedding dress		859	1998	33r
Clergy, religious facility fee		242	1998	33r
Engagement ring		3177	1998	33r
Flowers		789	1998	33r
Groom's formalwear rental		99	2000	33r
Limousine		410	1998	33r
Marriage license cost		50.00-80.00	4/01	35s
Men's formalwear (ushers, best man)		469	2000	33r
Mother of bride apparel		241	2000	33r
Music		866	1998	33r
Photography and videography		1368	1998	33r
Rehearsal dinner		728	1998	33r
Wedding invitations and announcements		341	1998	33r
Wedding reception		7968	2000	33r
Wedding rings (bride and groom)		1060	1998	33r

Cincinnati, OH

Item	Per	Value	Date	Ref.
Average annual expenditures	yr	37392	1999	30c
Composite, ACCRA index		98.30	3/01	4c
Alcoholic Beverages				
Alcoholic beverage purchases	yr	356	1999	30c
Beer, Heineken, 12-oz, ex deposit	6	7.49	3/01	4c
J & B Scotch	750-ml	21.35	3/01	4c
Malt beverages, all types, all sizes, any origin	16 oz	0.93	7/01	11r
Wine, Livingston or Gallo, Chablis blanc	1.5 liter	6.24	3/01	4c
Wine, red and white table, all sizes, any origin	liter	7.04	7/01	11r
Appliances				
Appliance repair, service call, washing machine	min lab chg	46.67	3/01	4c
Major appliances, expenditures on	yr	165	1999	30r
Small appliances, housewares, expenditures on	yr	90	1999	30r

Cincinnati, OH - continued

Item	Per	Value	Date	Ref.
Banking and Money				
Mortgage interest and charges paid	yr	2277	1999	30r
Mortgage principal paid on owned property	yr	1230	1999	30r
Mortgage rate, incl. points and orig. fee, 30-yr. conv. fixed or ARM	mos	6.94	3/01	4c
Vehicle finance charges paid	yr	328	1999	30r
Business Expenses				
Business travel, car rental	day	56	2001	3c
Business travel, food	day	48	2001	3c
Business travel, hotel	day	122	2001	3c
Charity				
Cash contributions, expenditures	yr	1760	1999	30c
Child Care				
Child raising cost, total, age 0-2	yr	7890	1999	60r
Child raising cost, total, age 3-5	yr	8130	1999	60r
Child raising cost, total, age 6-8	yr	8170	1999	60r
Child raising cost, total, age 9-11	yr	8190	1999	60r
Child raising cost, total, age 12-14	yr	8890	1999	60r
Child raising cost, total, age 15-17	yr	9050	1999	60r
Child's child care and education, age 0-2	yr	1240	1999	60r
Child's child care and education, age 3-5	yr	1370	1999	60r
Child's child care and education, age 6-8	yr	880	1999	60r
Child's child care and education, age 9-11	yr	570	1999	60r
Child's child care and education, age 12-14	yr	420	1999	60r
Child's child care and education, age 15-17	yr	720	1999	60r
Child's clothing, age 0-2	yr	410	1999	60r
Child's clothing, age 3-5	yr	400	1999	60r
Child's clothing, age 6-8	yr	450	1999	60r
Child's clothing, age 9-11	yr	500	1999	60r
Child's clothing, age 12-14	yr	840	1999	60r
Child's clothing, age 15-17	yr	740	1999	60r
Child's food, age 0-2	yr	960	1999	60r
Child's food, age 3-5	yr	1120	1999	60r
Child's food, age 6-8	yr	1430	1999	60r
Child's food, age 9-11	yr	1710	1999	60r
Child's food, age 12-14	yr	1710	1999	60r
Child's food, age 15-17	yr	1920	1999	60r
Child's health care, age 0-2	yr	520	1999	60r
Child's health care, age 3-5	yr	500	1999	60r
Child's health care, age 6-8	yr	570	1999	60r
Child's health care, age 9-11	yr	610	1999	60r
Child's health care, age 12-14	yr	630	1999	60r
Child's health care, age 15-17	yr	650	1999	60r
Child's housing, age 0-2	yr	2860	1999	60r
Child's housing, age 3-5	yr	2840	1999	60r
Child's housing, age 6-8	yr	2800	1999	60r
Child's housing, age 9-11	yr	2650	1999	60r
Child's housing, age 12-14	yr	2840	1999	60r
Child's housing, age 15-17	yr	2440	1999	60r
Child's personal care, reading, age 0-2	yr	880	1999	60r
Child's personal care, reading, age 3-5	yr	900	1999	60r
Child's personal care, reading, age 6-8	yr	930	1999	60r
Child's personal care, reading, age 9-11	yr	970	1999	60r
Child's personal care, reading, age 12-14	yr	1150	1999	60r
Child's personal care, reading, age 15-17	yr	920	1999	60r
Clothing				
Apparel and services purchases	yr	1595	1999	30c
Boys' brief, cotton	3	6.59	3/01	4c
Boys, 2 to 15, expenditures on	yr	91	1999	30r
Children under 2, expenditures on	yr	59	1999	30r
Footwear, expenditures on	yr	285	1999	30r
Girls, 2 to 15, expenditures on	yr	116	1999	30r
Men and boys, expenditures on	yr	433	1999	30r
Men, 16 and over, expenditures on	yr	341	1999	30r
Shirt, man's dress shirt		25.59	3/01	4c
Slacks, man's "No Wrinkles" khaki		34.19	3/01	4c
Women, 16 and over, expenditures on	yr	490	1999	30r
Communications				
Cable modem installation, Adelphi		54.90	6/99	103s
Cable modem installation, Media One		100.00	6/99	103s

Values are in dollars or fractions of dollars. In the column headed *Ref*, references are shown to sources. Each reference is followed by a letter. These refer to the geographical level for which data were reported: s=State, r=Region, and c=City or metro. The abbreviation *ex* is used to mean *except* or *excluding*; *exp* stands for expenditures. For other abbreviations and further explanations, please see the Introduction.

Cincinnati, OH - continued

Item	Per	Value	Date	Ref.
Communications				
Cable modem installation, Time Warner		75.00- 225.00	6/99	103s
Cable modem rate, cable subscriber, Adelphi	mos	34.95	6/99	103s
Cable modem rate, cable subscriber, Media One	mos	34.95- 39.95	6/99	103s
Cable modem rate, cable subscriber, Time Warner	mos	39.95- 49.95	6/99	103s
Cable modem rate, non-cable subscriber, Adelphi	mos	44.95	6/99	103s
Cable modem rate, non-cable subscriber, Media One	mos	49.95	6/99	103s
Cable modem rate, non-cable subscriber, Time Warner	mos	39.95- 54.95	6/99	103s
Cellular phone service	mos	41.47	2/01	55c
Newspaper subscription, daily and Sunday delivery	mos	17.29	3/01	4c
Phone line, single, business, field visit	inst.	56.32	12/97	17s
Phone line, single, business, no field visit	inst.	56.32	12/97	17s
Phone line, single, residence, field visit	inst.	31.10	12/97	17s
Phone line, single, residence, no field visit	inst.	31.10	12/97	17s
Postage and stationery, expenditures on	yr	140	1999	30r
Postal rate, express mail, up to half-pound		12.45	7/01	108r
Postal rate, letter, first class, first ounce		0.34	7/01	108r
Postal rate, letter, two ounces		0.57	7/01	108r
Postal rate, post card		0.21	7/01	108r
Postal rate, priority mail, two pounds		3.95	7/01	108r
Postal rate, priority mail, up to one pound		3.50	7/01	108r
Telephone bill, business, basic rate	mos	46.27	12/97	18c
Telephone bill, family of three	mos	23.00	3/01	4c
Telephone bill, residential, basic rate	mos	16.20	12/97	18c
Telephone services, expenditures on	yr	830	1999	30r
Education				
Board, 4-year private college/university	yr	2414	1996	38s
Board, 4-year public college/university	yr	2181	1996	38s
Education expenditures	yr	691	1999	30c
Room, 4-year private college/university	yr	2349	1996	38s
Room, 4-year public college/university	yr	2386	1996	38s
Total cost, 4-year private college/university	yr	17139	1996	38s
Total cost, 4-year public college/university	yr	8169	1996	38s
Tuition, 2-year public college/university, in state	yr	2261	1996	38s
Tuition, 4-year private college/university, in state	yr	12377	1996	38s
Tuition, 4-year public college/university	yr	3603	1996	38s
Energy and Fuels				
Electricity	500 KWhs	46.59	7/01	11r
Energy, combined forms, 2400 sq ft	mos	124.86	3/01	4c
Energy, exc. electricity, 2400 sq ft	mos	9.64	3/01	4c
Fuel oil #2	gal	1.27	7/01	11r
Fuel oil and other fuels, expenditures on	yr	68	1999	30r
Gas, cooking, winter, 10 therms	mos	10.23	2/96	98c
Gas, cooking, winter, 30 therms	mos	19.70	2/96	98c
Gas, cooking, winter, 50 therms	mos	29.17	2/96	98c
Gas, heating, winter, average use	mos	114.82	2/96	98c
Gas, natural, commercial rate	1000 cf	8.65	11/00	88s
Gas, regular unleaded, cash, self-service	gal	1.56	3/01	4c
Gasoline, unleaded midgrade	gal	1.79	7/01	11r
Gasoline, unleaded premium	gal	1.86	7/01	11r
Gasoline, unleaded regular	gal	1.58	7/01	11r
Natural gas, expenditures on	yr	389	1999	30r
Utility (piped) gas, therm		0.81	7/01	11r
Utility (piped) gas, 40 therms		38.01	7/01	11r
Utility (piped) gas, 100 therms		81.75	7/01	11r
Entertainment				
Bowling, Saturday evening rate	line	3.10	3/01	4c
Entertainment purchases	yr	1851	1999	30c
Fees and admissions paid	yr	444	1999	30r
Monopoly game, Parker Brothers', No. 9	game	11.34	3/01	4c
Movie, first-run, Saturday, evening	adm.	8.25	3/01	4c

Cincinnati, OH - continued

Item	Per	Value	Date	Ref.
Entertainment - continued				
Television, radios, sound equipment, expenditures on	yr	580	1999	30r
Tennis balls, yellow, Wilson or Penn, 3	can	2.34	3/01	4c
Funerals				
Cosmetology, hair, other preparation		178.32	1/99	78r
Embalming		408.19	1/99	78r
Funeral at funeral home		362.13	1/99	78r
Professional service charges		1375.51	1/99	78r
Transfer of remains to funeral home		155.92	1/99	78r
Visitation/viewing		294.38	1/99	78r
Groceries				
Groceries, ACCRA Index		98.90	3/01	4c
Antibiotic ointment, Polysporin	0.5 oz	4.36	3/01	4c
Baby food, strained vegetables or fruit, lowest price	4-4.5 oz	0.37	3/01	4c
Bacon, sliced	lb	3.15	7/01	11r
Bakery products, expenditures on	yr	281	1999	30r
Bananas	lb	0.49	3/01	4c
Bananas	lb	0.48	7/01	11r
Beans, dried, any type, all sizes	lb	0.61	7/01	11r
Beef for stew, boneless	lb	3.08	7/01	11r
Beef or hamburger, ground	lb	1.61	3/01	4c
Beef, expenditures on	yr	217	1999	30r
Bologna, all beef or mixed	lb	2.52	7/01	11r
Bread, white	loaf	1.05	3/01	4c
Bread, white, pan	lb	1.06	7/01	11r
Broccoli	lb	0.91	7/01	11r
Butter, salted, grade AA, stick	lb	3.04	7/01	11r
Butter, yoghurt, cheese, etc, expenditures on	yr	183	1999	30r
Cereals and bakery product purchases	yr	397	1999	30c
Cereals and cereal products, expenditures on	yr	149	1999	30r
Cheese, Kraft grated Parmesan	8 oz	3.51	3/01	4c
Chicken, fresh, whole	lb	1.07	7/01	11r
Chicken, whole fryer	lb	0.97	3/01	4c
Chops, boneless,	lb	3.64	7/01	11r
Chuck roast, U.S. choice, boneless	lb	2.47	7/01	11r
Cigarettes, Winston, Kings	carton	27.61	3/01	4c
Coffee, 100%, ground roast, all sizes	lb	2.69	7/01	11r
Coffee, vacuum-packed	13 oz	2.29	3/01	4c
Cookies, chocolate chip	lb	2.87	7/01	11r
Corn Flakes, Kellogg's or Post Toasties	18 oz	2.53	3/01	4c
Corn, frozen, whole kernel, lowest price	16 oz	1.14	3/01	4c
Dairy product purchases	yr	312	1999	30c
Eggs, expenditures on	yr	26	1999	30r
Eggs, Grade A or AA	dozen	1.07	3/01	4c
Eggs, grade A, large	dozen	0.88	7/01	11r
Fats and oils, expenditures on	yr	75	1999	30r
Fish and seafood, expenditures on	yr	72	1999	30r
Food (excl fruit and vegetables), eaten at home, purchases	yr	912	1999	30c
Food cooked on trips, expenditures on	yr	44	1999	30r
Food purchases	yr	4994	1999	30c
Food purchases, eaten away from home	yr	2389	1999	30c
Food purchases, food eaten at home	yr	2605	1999	30c
Fresh fruits, expenditures on	yr	138	1999	30r
Fresh milk and cream, expenditures on	yr	120	1999	30r
Fresh vegetables, expenditures on	yr	126	1999	30r
Grapefruit	lb	0.66	7/01	11r
Grapes, Thompson, seedless	lb	1.64	7/01	11r
Ground beef, 100% beef	lb	1.64	7/01	11r
Ground beef, lean and extra lean	lb	2.16	7/01	11r
Ground chuck, 100% beef	lb	2.13	7/01	11r
Ham, boneless, excl canned	lb	2.62	7/01	11r
Ice cream, prepackaged, bulk, regular	1/2 gal	3.35	7/01	11r
Lemons	lb	1.19	7/01	11r
Lettuce, iceberg	head	0.99	3/01	4c
Lettuce, iceberg	lb	0.73	7/01	11r
Margarine, Blue Bonnet or Parkay, stick	lb	0.87	3/01	4c
Margarine, soft, tubs	lb	0.89	7/01	11r
Meats, poultry, fish, and egg purchases	yr	600	1999	30c

Values are in dollars or fractions of dollars. In the column headed *Ref*, references are shown to sources. Each reference is followed by a letter. These refer to the geographical level for which data were reported: s=State, r=Region, and c=City or metro. The abbreviation *ex* is used to mean *except* or *excluding*; *exp* stands for *expenditures*. For other abbreviations and further explanations, please see the Introduction.

Cincinnati, OH - continued

Item	Per	Value	Date	Ref.
Groceries				
Milk, fresh, whole, fortified	gal	2.71	7/01	11r
Milk, whole	1/2 gal	1.82	3/01	4c
Nonalcoholic beverages, expenditures on	yr	239	1999	30r
Orange juice, Minute Maid frozen	12 oz	1.59	3/01	4c
Oranges, Navel	lb	0.80	7/01	11r
Oranges, Valencia	lb	0.66	7/01	11r
Peaches, halves or slices, Hunt's, Del Monte, or Libby's	29 oz	1.65	3/01	4c
Pears, Anjou	lb	0.93	7/01	11r
Peas, green, Del Monte or Green Giant	15 oz	0.74	3/01	4c
Pork chops, center cut, bone-in	lb	3.63	7/01	11r
Pork, expenditures on	yr	150	1999	30r
Potato chips	16 oz	3.52	7/01	11r
Potatoes, frozen, french fried	lb	1.08	7/01	11r
Potatoes, white or red	10 lb	2.92	3/01	4c
Potatoes, white, all types	lb	0.33	7/01	11r
Poultry, expenditures on	yr	108	1999	30r
Processed fruits, expenditures on	yr	98	1999	30r
Processed vegetables, expenditures on	yr	80	1999	30r
Round roast, U.S. choice, boneless	lb	3.07	7/01	11r
Round steak, graded and ungraded, excl U.S. prime and choice	lb	3.41	7/01	11r
Sausage, Jimmy Dean/Owens pork	lb	3.12	3/01	4c
Shortening, vegetable oil blends	lb	1.13	7/01	11r
Shortening, vegetable, Crisco	3 lb	3.12	3/01	4c
Soft drink, Coca Cola, ex deposit	2 liter	1.17	3/01	4c
Spaghetti and macaroni	lb	0.80	7/01	11r
Steak, round, U.S. choice, boneless	lb	3.23	7/01	11r
Steak, T-bone	lb	5.62	3/01	4c
Steak, T-bone, U.S. choice, bone-in	lb	6.68	7/01	11r
Strawberries, dry pint	12 oz	1.32	7/01	11r
Sugar and other sweets, expenditures on	yr	114	1999	30r
Sugar, cane or beet	4 lbs	1.79	3/01	4c
Sugar, white, 33-80 ounce package	lb	0.42	7/01	11r
Sugar, white, all sizes	lb	0.43	7/01	11r
Tobacco products and smoking supplies purchases	yr	402	1999	30c
Tomatoes, field grown	lb	1.46	7/01	11r
Tomatoes, Hunt's or Del Monte	14.5 oz	0.83	3/01	4c
Tuna, chunk, light	6 oz	0.60	3/01	4c
Tuna, light, chunk	lb	1.80	7/01	11r
Turkey, frozen, whole	lb	1.15	7/01	11r
Goods and Services				
Miscellaneous goods and services, ACCRA Index		101.40	3/01	4c
B&B Japanese maple (acer japonicum)	gal	29.99-169.99	4/00	93r
Boxwood (buxus)	2 gal	18.99-39.99	4/00	93r
Daylilly (hemerocallis)	gal	4.99-25.00	4/00	93r
Flat of annuals		11.98-24.99	4/00	93r
Fountain grass (pennisetum)	gal	5.98-12.98	4/00	93r
Hanging basket (10 in)		12.99-27.99	4/00	93r
Hardy geranium (geranium)	gal	7.99-9.99	4/00	93r
Hosta (hosta)	gal	6.00-25.00	4/00	93r
Lilac (syrubga vulgaris)	2 gal	14.99-24.99	4/00	93r
Miscellaneous purchases	yr	955	1999	30c
Rhododendron (rhododendron)	2 gal	23.98-42.99	4/00	93r
Sage (salvia)	gal	6.00-9.99	4/00	93r
Wintercreeper euonymus (euonymus fortunei)	2 gal	16.00-169.99	4/00	93r
Hunting license	yr	15.00	4/01	34s

Item	Per	Value	Date	Ref.
Health Care				
Health care, ACCRA Index		94.30	3/01	4c
Cardiac catheterization, ave hospital/ physician charges		11760	1998	77s
Childbirth, Cesarean delivery		10722	1997	13r
Childbirth, vaginal delivery		6223	1997	13r
Dentist's fee, adult teeth cleaning and periodic oral exam	visit	71.60	3/01	4c
Doctor's fee, routine exam, established patient	visit	52.75	3/01	4c
Drugs, expenditures on	yr	394	1999	30r
Health care purchases	yr	2280	1999	30c
Health insurance expenditures	yr	978	1999	30r
Hospital care, private room	day	487.10	3/01	4c
Hysterectomy, laproscopically-assisted, ave hospital/physician charges		11730	1998	76s
Hysterectomy, vaginal, ave hospital and physician charges		9640	1998	76s
Medicaid dispensing fee		3.70	1999	87s
Medical services expenditures	yr	554	1999	30r
Medical supplies, expenditures on	yr	122	1999	30r
Nursing home costs, private room	day	127	2000	82c
Nursing home stay, private room	day	127	2000	81c
Plastic surgery, breast augmentation		3184	2000	7r
Plastic surgery, breast lift		3585	2000	7r
Plastic surgery, facelift		4999	2000	7r
Plastic surgery, hair transplantation		3105	2000	7r
Plastic surgery, lip augmentation		1290	2000	7r
Plastic surgery, lower body lift		8135	2000	7r
Plastic surgery, thigh lift		3839	2000	7r
Household Goods				
Dishwashing powder, Cascade	50 oz	3.47	3/01	4c
Floor coverings, expenditures on	yr	52	1999	30r
Furniture, expenditures on	yr	344	1999	30r
Household furnishings and equipment purchases	yr	1568	1999	30c
Household textiles, expenditures on	yr	109	1999	30r
Laundry and cleaning supplies, expenditures on	yr	134	1999	30r
Tissues, facial, Kleenex brand	175	1.17	3/01	4c
Housing				
Housing, ACCRA Index		92.60	3/01	4c
Home, 2200 sq ft, 4-br, 2-bath, 2-car garage, average		214411	2000	47c
Home price, existing, ave		144400	10/00	90r
Home value, median		96000	2001	53s
House, 2400 sq ft, 8000 sq ft lot, new, urban, utilities	total	188537	3/01	4c
House payment, principal and interest, 25% down payment	mos	935	3/01	4c
Household operation expenditures	yr	797	1999	30c
Housekeeping supplies purchases	yr	433	1999	30c
Lodging expenditures	yr	449	1999	30c
Maintenance, repairs, insurance expenditures	yr	853	1999	30r
Monthly rental value of owned home	mos	547	1999	30r
Owned dwellings, expenditures own	yr	4331	1999	30c
Rent expenditures	yr	2153	1999	30c
Rent, apartment, 2 br, 1 1/2-2 baths, unfurn, 950 sq ft, water	mos	695	3/01	4c
Rental unit, 1 bedroom, with utilities	mos	416	4/01	41c
Rental unit, 2 bedroom, with utilities	mos	557	4/01	41c
Rental unit, 3 bedroom, with utilities	mos	746	4/01	41c
Rental unit, 4 bedroom, with utilities	mos	806	4/01	41c
Shelter, expenditures on	yr	6933	1999	30c
Insurance and Pensions				
Life and other personal insurance purchases	yr	371	1999	30c
Pensions and Social Security, expenditures on	yr	2658	1999	30c

Values are in dollars or fractions of dollars. In the column headed *Ref*, references are shown to sources. Each reference is followed by a letter. These refer to the geographical level for which data were reported: s=State, r=Region, and c=City or metro. The abbreviation *ex* is used to mean *except* or *excluding*; *exp* stands for expenditures. For other abbreviations and further explanations, please see the Introduction.

Cincinnati, OH - continued

Item	Per	Value	Date	Ref.
Legal Fees				
Divorce, filing fee		100.00	4/01	35s
Driver's license fee	renew	14.50	1999	48s
Driver's license fee	orig	14.50	1999	48s
Fishing license	yr	15.00	4/01	34s
Personal Goods				
Personal care products and services purchases	yr	369	1999	30c
Shampoo, Alberto VO5	15 oz	0.93	3/01	4c
Toothpaste, Crest or Colgate	6-7 oz	2.25	3/01	4c
Personal Services				
Dry cleaning, man's 2-pc suit		7.93	3/01	4c
Man's haircut, barbershop, no styling		9.40	3/01	4c
Personal services, household, expenditures on	yr	300	1999	30r
Woman's shampoo, trim, blow-dry, no style-change		24.80	3/01	4c
Pets				
Pets, toys, and playground equipment, expenditures on	yr	375	1999	30r
Restaurant Food				
Chicken, fried, thigh and drumstick, KFC/Church's		2.30	3/01	4c
Hamburger with cheese, McDonald's	1/4 lb	2.09	3/01	4c
Pizza, Pizza Hut or Pizza Inn	11-12 in	8.99	3/01	4c
Taxes				
Federal income taxes paid	yr	2326	1999	30r
Personal taxes, expenditures on	yr	3223	1999	30r
Property taxes paid	yr	1152	1999	30r
State and local income taxes paid	yr	753	1999	30r
Transportation				
Transportation, ACCRA Index		101.20	3/01	4c
Bus fare, one-way	trip	0.70	2000	1c
Bus fare, to central business district	1-way	0.80	3/01	4c
Cars and trucks, new, expenditures on	yr	1280	1999	30r
Cars and trucks, used, expenditures on	yr	1763	1999	30r
Diesel at the pump	gal	1.25	10/99	73s
Gasoline and motor oil purchases	yr	1029	1999	30c
Gasoline before-tax price (cents)	gal	109.50	10/00	43s
Maintenance and repair expenditures	yr	594	1999	30r
Public transportation, expenditures on	yr	332	1999	30c
Tire balance, computer or spin balance, front	wheel	7.56	3/01	4c
Transportation purchases	yr	6857	1999	30c
Vehicle expenses, miscellaneous, purchases	yr	2388	1999	30c
Vehicle insurance payments	yr	701	1999	30r
Vehicle purchases (net outlay)	yr	3081	1999	30r
Vehicle rental, lease expenditures	yr	536	1999	30r
Utilities				
Utilities, ACCRA Index		102.80	3/01	4c
Electrical bill, average	mos	72.83	9/00	9s
Electricity, expenditures on	yr	841	1999	30r
Electricity, summer, 250 KWh	mos	23.51	2/96	96c
Electricity, summer, 500 KWh	mos	43.02	2/96	96c
Electricity, summer, 750 KWh	mos	62.53	2/96	96c
Electricity, summer, 1000 KWh	mos	82.03	2/96	96c
Electricity and other, mixed, 2400 sq ft, new home	mos	115.22	3/01	4c
Electricity cost, average	KWh	6.59	9/00	9s
Utilities, fuels, and public services purchased	yr	2341	1999	30c
Water and other public services, expenditures on	yr	273	1999	30r
Weddings				
Wedding (national average cost)		19936	2000	33r
Wedding (regional average total cost)		16195	1997	110r
Attendants' gifts		321	1998	33r
Bridal attendants' apparel (5 persons)		824	2000	33r
Bride's headpiece/veil		173	1998	33r
Bride's wedding dress		859	1998	33r
Clergy, religious facility fee		242	1998	33r

Cincinnati, OH - continued

Item	Per	Value	Date	Ref.
Weddings - continued				
Engagement ring		3177	1998	33r
Flowers		789	1998	33r
Groom's formalwear rental		99	2000	33r
Limousine		410	1998	33r
Marriage license cost		45.00	4/01	35s
Men's formalwear (ushers, best man)		469	2000	33r
Mother of bride apparel		241	2000	33r
Music		866	1998	33r
Photography and videography		1368	1998	33r
Rehearsal dinner		728	1998	33r
Wedding invitations and announcements		341	1998	33r
Wedding reception		7968	2000	33r
Wedding rings (bride and groom)		1060	1998	33r

Clarksville-Hopkinsville, TN-KY

Item	Per	Value	Date	Ref.
Alcoholic Beverages				
Alcoholic beverage purchases	yr	253	1999	30r
Malt beverages, all types, all sizes, any origin	16 oz	0.96	7/01	11r
Appliances				
Major appliances, expenditures on	yr	172	1999	30r
Small appliances, housewares, expenditures on	yr	81	1999	30r
Banking and Money				
Mortgage interest and charges paid	yr	2039	1999	30r
Mortgage principal paid on owned property	yr	1026	1999	30r
Vehicle finance charges paid	yr	365	1999	30r
Charity				
Cash contributions, expenditures	yr	1127	1999	30r
Child Care				
Child raising cost, total, age 0-2	yr	8540	1999	60r
Child raising cost, total, age 3-5	yr	8780	1999	60r
Child raising cost, total, age 6-8	yr	8820	1999	60r
Child raising cost, total, age 9-11	yr	8800	1999	60r
Child raising cost, total, age 12-14	yr	9510	1999	60r
Child raising cost, total, age 15-17	yr	9740	1999	60r
Child's child care and education, age 0-2	yr	1380	1999	60r
Child's child care and education, age 3-5	yr	1520	1999	60r
Child's child care and education, age 6-8	yr	990	1999	60r
Child's child care and education, age 9-11	yr	650	1999	60r
Child's child care and education, age 12-14	yr	490	1999	60r
Child's child care and education, age 15-17	yr	840	1999	60r
Child's clothing, age 0-2	yr	480	1999	60r
Child's clothing, age 3-5	yr	470	1999	60r
Child's clothing, age 6-8	yr	520	1999	60r
Child's clothing, age 9-11	yr	570	1999	60r
Child's clothing, age 12-14	yr	950	1999	60r
Child's clothing, age 15-17	yr	850	1999	60r
Child's food, age 0-2	yr	1000	1999	60r
Child's food, age 3-5	yr	1160	1999	60r
Child's food, age 6-8	yr	1490	1999	60r
Child's food, age 9-11	yr	1770	1999	60r
Child's food, age 12-14	yr	1770	1999	60r
Child's food, age 15-17	yr	1980	1999	60r
Child's health care, age 0-2	yr	620	1999	60r
Child's health care, age 3-5	yr	590	1999	60r
Child's health care, age 6-8	yr	680	1999	60r
Child's health care, age 9-11	yr	720	1999	60r
Child's health care, age 12-14	yr	730	1999	60r
Child's health care, age 15-17	yr	760	1999	60r
Child's housing, age 0-2	yr	3070	1999	60r
Child's housing, age 3-5	yr	3050	1999	60r
Child's housing, age 6-8	yr	3010	1999	60r
Child's housing, age 9-11	yr	2850	1999	60r
Child's housing, age 12-14	yr	3040	1999	60r
Child's housing, age 15-17	yr	2650	1999	60r
Child's personal care, reading, age 0-2	yr	910	1999	60r
Child's personal care, reading, age 3-5	yr	930	1999	60r
Child's personal care, reading, age 6-8	yr	960	1999	60r

Values are in dollars or fractions of dollars. In the column headed *Ref*, references are shown to sources. Each reference is followed by a letter. These refer to the geographical level for which data were reported: s=State, r=Region, and c=City or metro. The abbreviation *ex* is used to mean *except* or *excluding*; *exp* stands for expenditures. For other abbreviations and further explanations, please see the Introduction.

Clarksville-Hopkinsville, TN-KY - continued

Item	Per	Value	Date	Ref.
Child Care				
Child's personal care, reading, age 9-11	yr	1000	1999	60r
Child's personal care, reading, age 12-14	yr	1170	1999	60r
Child's personal care, reading, age 15-17	yr	950	1999	60r
Clothing				
Apparel and services purchases	yr	1610	1999	30r
Boys, 2 to 15, expenditures on	yr	89	1999	30r
Children under 2, expenditures on	yr	79	1999	30r
Footwear, expenditures on	yr	283	1999	30r
Girls, 2 to 15, expenditures on	yr	103	1999	30r
Men and boys, expenditures on	yr	351	1999	30r
Men, 16 and over, expenditures on	yr	262	1999	30r
Women, 16 and over, expenditures on	yr	538	1999	30r
Communications				
Cable modem installation, Intermedia		149.95	6/99	103s
Cable modem installation, Time Warner		75.00-225.00	6/99	103s
Cable modem rate, cable subscriber, Intermedia	mos	49.95	6/99	103s
Cable modem rate, cable subscriber, Time Warner	mos	39.95-49.95	6/99	103s
Cable modem rate, non-cable subscriber, Intermedia	mos	54.95	6/99	103s
Cable modem rate, non-cable subscriber, Time Warner	mos	39.95-54.95	6/99	103s
Phone line, single, business, field visit	inst.	58.50	12/97	17s
Phone line, single, business, no field visit	inst.	58.50	12/97	17s
Phone line, single, residence, field visit	inst.	41.50	12/97	17s
Phone line, single, residence, no field visit	inst.	41.50	12/97	17s
Postage and stationery, expenditures on	yr	104	1999	30r
Postal rate, express mail, up to half-pound		12.45	7/01	108r
Postal rate, letter, first class, first ounce		0.34	7/01	108r
Postal rate, letter, two ounces		0.57	7/01	108r
Postal rate, post card		0.21	7/01	108r
Postal rate, priority mail, two pounds		3.95	7/01	108r
Postal rate, priority mail, up to one pound		3.50	7/01	108r
Telephone services, expenditures on	yr	860	1999	30r
Education				
Board, 4-year private college/university	yr	2085	1996	38s
Board, 4-year public college/university	yr	1737	1996	38s
Education expenditures	yr	431	1999	30r
Room, 4-year private college/university	yr	2153	1996	38s
Room, 4-year public college/university	yr	1644	1996	38s
Total cost, 4-year private college/university	yr	14068	1996	38s
Total cost, 4-year public college/university	yr	5372	1996	38s
Tuition, 2-year public college/university, in state	yr	1022	1996	38s
Tuition, 4-year private college/university, in state	yr	9830	1996	38s
Tuition, 4-year public college/university	yr	1990	1996	38s
Energy and Fuels				
Electricity	500 KWhs	47.29	7/01	11r
Electricity	KWh	0.09	7/01	11r
Fuel oil #2	gal	1.43	7/01	11r
Fuel oil and other fuels, expenditures on	yr	45	1999	30r
Gas, natural, commercial rate	1000 cf	8.61	11/00	88s
Gasoline, all types	gal	1.60	7/01	11r
Gasoline, unleaded midgrade	gal	1.65	7/01	11r
Gasoline, unleaded premium	gal	1.74	7/01	11r
Natural gas, expenditures on	yr	164	1999	30r
Utility (piped) gas, therm		1.01	7/01	11r
Utility (piped) gas, 40 therms		44.29	7/01	11r
Utility (piped) gas, 100 therms		97.44	7/01	11r
Entertainment				
Entertainment purchases	yr	1574	1999	30r
Fees and admissions paid	yr	371	1999	30r
Reading purchases	yr	121	1999	30r
Television, radios, sound equipment, expenditures on	yr	561	1999	30r

Clarksville-Hopkinsville, TN-KY - continued

Item	Per	Value	Date	Ref.
Groceries				
American processed cheese	lb	3.50	7/01	11r
Bakery products, expenditures on	yr	261	1999	30r
Bananas	lb	0.47	7/01	11r
Beans, dried, any type, all sizes	lb	0.63	7/01	11r
Beef for stew, boneless	lb	2.86	7/01	11r
Beef, expenditures on	yr	210	1999	30r
Bologna, all beef or mixed	lb	2.29	7/01	11r
Bread, French	lb	1.66	7/01	11r
Bread, white, pan	lb	0.87	7/01	11r
Bread, whole wheat, pan	lb	1.38	7/01	11r
Broccoli	lb	1.04	7/01	11r
Butter, salted, grade AA, stick	lb	2.26	7/01	11r
Butter, yoghurt, cheese, etc, expenditures on	yr	170	1999	30r
Cabbage	lb	0.42	7/01	11r
Cereals and cereal products, expenditures on	yr	140	1999	30r
Cheddar cheese, natural	lb	3.75	7/01	11r
Chicken breast, bone-in	lb	1.85	7/01	11r
Chicken legs, bone-in	lb	1.34	7/01	11r
Chicken, fresh, whole	lb	1.05	7/01	11r
Chops, boneless,	lb	4.13	7/01	11r
Chuck roast, graded and ungraded, excl U.S. prime and choice	lb	2.35	7/01	11r
Chuck roast, U.S. choice, boneless	lb	2.67	7/01	11r
Coffee, 100%, ground roast, all sizes	lb	2.88	7/01	11r
Coffee, instant, plain, regular, all sizes	16 oz	9.25	7/01	11r
Cola, non diet,	2 liter	1.11	7/01	11r
Crackers, soda, salted	lb	1.70	7/01	11r
Dairy product purchases	yr	282	1999	30r
Eggs, expenditures on	yr	32	1999	30r
Fats and oils, expenditures on	yr	79	1999	30r
Fish and seafood, expenditures on	yr	99	1999	30r
Flour, white, all purpose	lb	0.32	7/01	11r
Food (excl fruit and vegetables), eaten at home, purchases	yr	815	1999	30r
Food cooked on trips, expenditures on	yr	36	1999	30r
Food purchases	yr	4533	1999	30r
Food purchases, eaten away from home	yr	1873	1999	30r
Food purchases, food eaten at home	yr	2660	1999	30r
Fresh fruits, expenditures on	yr	128	1999	30r
Fresh milk and cream, expenditures on	yr	112	1999	30r
Fresh vegetables, expenditures on	yr	131	1999	30r
Fruit and vegetable purchases	yr	438	1999	30r
Grapefruit	lb	0.59	7/01	11r
Grapes, Thompson, seedless	lb	2.12	7/01	11r
Ground beef, 100% beef	lb	1.76	7/01	11r
Ground beef, lean and extra lean	lb	2.60	7/01	11r
Ground chuck, 100% beef	lb	2.08	7/01	11r
Ham, boneless, excl canned	lb	2.71	7/01	11r
Ham, rump or shank half, bone-in, smoked	lb	2.19	7/01	11r
Ice cream, prepackaged, bulk, regular	1/2 gal	3.93	7/01	11r
Lemons	lb	1.32	7/01	11r
Lettuce, iceberg	lb	0.76	7/01	11r
Milk, fresh, low fat,	gal	2.75	7/01	11r
Milk, fresh, whole, fortified	gal	2.97	7/01	11r
Nonalcoholic beverages, expenditures on	yr	228	1999	30r
Orange juice, frozen concentrate	16 oz	1.95	7/01	11r
Oranges, Navel	lb	0.73	7/01	11r
Oranges, Valencia	lb	0.55	7/01	11r
Peanut butter, creamy, all sizes	lb	1.83	7/01	11r
Pears, Anjou	lb	0.98	7/01	11r
Pork chops, center cut, bone-in	lb	3.33	7/01	11r
Pork sausage, fresh, loose	lb	2.59	7/01	11r
Pork shoulder picnic, bone-in, smoked	lb	1.12	7/01	11r
Pork, expenditures on	yr	162	1999	30r
Potato chips	16 oz	3.59	7/01	11r
Potatoes, frozen, french fried	lb	1.00	7/01	11r
Potatoes, white, all types	lb	0.44	7/01	11r
Poultry, expenditures on	yr	137	1999	30r
Processed fruits, expenditures on	yr	97	1999	30r
Processed vegetables, expenditures on	yr	82	1999	30r
Rice, white, long grain, uncooked	lb	0.51	7/01	11r

Values are in dollars or fractions of dollars. In the column headed *Ref*, references are shown to sources. Each reference is followed by a letter. These refer to the geographical level for which data were reported: s=State, r=Region, and c=City or metro. The abbreviation *ex* is used to mean *except* or *excluding*; *exp* stands for expenditures. For other abbreviations and further explanations, please see the Introduction.

Clarksville-Hopkinsville, TN-KY - continued

Item	Per	Value	Date	Ref.
Groceries				
Round roast, graded and ungraded, excl U.S. prime and choice	lb	2.96	7/01	11r
Round steak, graded and ungraded, excl U.S. prime and choice	lb	3.11	7/01	11r
Sirloin steak, graded and ungraded, excl U.S. prime and choice	lb	4.23	7/01	11r
Spaghetti and macaroni	lb	0.78	7/01	11r
Steak, round, U.S. choice, boneless	lb	3.56	7/01	11r
Steak, sirloin, U.S. choice, boneless	lb	5.65	7/01	11r
Strawberries, dry pint	12 oz	1.50	7/01	11r
Sugar and other sweets, expenditures on	yr	99	1999	30r
Sugar, white, 33-80 ounce package	lb	0.39	7/01	11r
Sugar, white, all sizes	lb	0.42	7/01	11r
Tobacco products and smoking supplies purchases	yr	288	1999	30r
Tomatoes, field grown	lb	1.43	7/01	11r
Tuna, light, chunk	lb	1.77	7/01	11r
Turkey, frozen, whole	lb	1.05	7/01	11r
Health Care				
Cardiac catheterization, ave hospital/ physician charges		12170	1998	77s
Childbirth, Cesarean delivery		11587	1997	13r
Childbirth, vaginal delivery		6725	1997	13r
Drugs, expenditures on	yr	399	1999	30r
Health care purchases	yr	1971	1999	30r
Health insurance expenditures	yr	933	1999	30r
Hysterectomy, laproscopically-assisted, ave hospital/physician charges		13470	1998	76s
Hysterectomy, vaginal, ave hospital and physician charges		9530	1998	76s
Medical services expenditures	yr	547	1999	30r
Medical supplies, expenditures on	yr	91	1999	30r
Household Goods				
Floor coverings, expenditures on	yr	44	1999	30r
Furniture, expenditures on	yr	335	1999	30r
Household furnishings and equipment purchases	yr	1328	1999	30r
Household textiles, expenditures on	yr	89	1999	30r
Laundry and cleaning supplies, expenditures on	yr	113	1999	30r
Housing				
Home price, existing, ave		160100	10/00	90r
Home value, median		112000	2001	53s
Household operation expenditures	yr	553	1999	30r
Housekeeping supplies purchases	yr	473	1999	30r
Housing, expenditures on	yr	10303	1999	30r
Maintenance, repairs, insurance expenditures	yr	699	1999	30r
Monthly rental value of owned home	mos	505	1999	30r
Owned dwellings, expenditures own	yr	3465	1999	30r
Rent expenditures	yr	1641	1999	30r
Rental unit, 1 bedroom, with utilities	mos	386	4/01	41c
Rental unit, 2 bedroom, with utilities	mos	454	4/01	41c
Rental unit, 3 bedroom, with utilities	mos	618	4/01	41c
Rental unit, 4 bedroom, with utilities	mos	636	4/01	41c
Shelter, expenditures on	yr	5467	1999	30r
Insurance and Pensions				
Life and other personal insurance purchases	yr	414	1999	30r
Pensions and Social Security, expenditures on	yr	2635	1999	30r
Personal insurance and pensions, expenditures on	yr	3048	1999	30r
Legal Fees				
Combination hunting and fishing license	yr	21.00	4/01	34s
Divorce, filing fee		64.00	4/01	35s
Driver's license fee	renew	17.50	1999	48s
Driver's license fee	orig	17.50	1999	48s

Clarksville-Hopkinsville, TN-KY - continued

Item	Per	Value	Date	Ref.
Personal Goods				
Personal care products and services purchases	yr	393	1999	30r
Personal Services				
Personal services, household, expenditures on	yr	258	1999	30r
Pets				
Pets, toys, and playground equipment, expenditures on	yr	306	1999	30r
Taxes				
Federal income taxes paid	yr	2047	1999	30r
Personal taxes, expenditures on	yr	2554	1999	30r
Property taxes paid	yr	726	1999	30r
State and local income taxes paid	yr	363	1999	30r
Transportation				
Cars and trucks, new, expenditures on	yr	1648	1999	30r
Cars and trucks, used, expenditures on	yr	1651	1999	30r
Diesel at the pump	gal	1.18	10/99	73s
Gasoline and motor oil purchases	yr	1052	1999	30r
Gasoline before-tax price (cents)	gal	102.50	10/00	43s
Maintenance and repair expenditures	yr	621	1999	30r
Public transportation, expenditures on	yr	298	1999	30r
Transportation purchases	yr	6738	1999	30r
Vehicle expenses, miscellaneous, purchases	yr	2033	1999	30r
Vehicle insurance payments	yr	696	1999	30r
Vehicle purchases (net outlay)	yr	3354	1999	30r
Vehicle rental, lease expenditures	yr	352	1999	30r
Utilities				
Electrical bill, average	mos	79.16	9/00	9s
Electricity, expenditures on	yr	1115	1999	30r
Electricity cost, average	KWh	5.60	9/00	9s
Water and other public services, expenditures on	yr	298	1999	30r
Weddings				
Wedding (national average cost)		19936	2000	33r
Attendants' gifts		321	1998	33r
Bridal attendants' apparel (5 persons)		824	2000	33r
Bride's headpiece/veil		173	1998	33r
Bride's wedding dress		859	1998	33r
Clergy, religious facility fee		242	1998	33r
Engagement ring		3177	1998	33r
Flowers		789	1998	33r
Groom's formalwear rental		99	2000	33r
Limousine		410	1998	33r
Marriage license cost		31.00	4/01	35s
Men's formalwear (ushers, best man)		469	2000	33r
Mother of bride apparel		241	2000	33r
Music		866	1998	33r
Photography and videography		1368	1998	33r
Rehearsal dinner		728	1998	33r
Wedding invitations and announcements		341	1998	33r
Wedding reception		7968	2000	33r
Wedding rings (bride and groom)		1060	1998	33r

Cleveland, OH

Item	Per	Value	Date	Ref.
Average annual expenditures	yr	35369	1999	30r
Composite, ACCRA index		108.30	3/01	4c
Alcoholic Beverages				
Alcoholic beverage purchases	yr	295	1999	30c
Beer, Heineken, 12-oz, ex deposit	6	7.46	3/01	4c
J & B Scotch	750-ml	22.15	3/01	4c
Malt beverages, all types, all sizes, any origin	16 oz	0.93	7/01	11r
Wine, Livingston or Gallo, Chablis blanc	1.5 liter	6.44	3/01	4c
Wine, red and white table, all sizes, any origin	liter	7.04	7/01	11r

Values are in dollars or fractions of dollars. In the column headed *Ref*, references are shown to sources. Each reference is followed by a letter. These refer to the geographical level for which data were reported: s=State, r=Region, and c=City or metro. The abbreviation *ex* is used to mean *except* or *excluding*; *exp* stands for expenditures. For other abbreviations and further explanations, please see the Introduction.

Cleveland, OH - continued

Item	Per	Value	Date	Ref.
Appliances				
Appliance repair, service call, washing machine	min lab chg	40.35	3/01	4c
Major appliances, expenditures on	yr	165	1999	30r
Small appliances, housewares, expenditures on	yr	90	1999	30r
Banking and Money				
Mortgage interest and charges paid	yr	2277	1999	30r
Mortgage principal paid on owned property	yr	1230	1999	30r
Mortgage rate, incl. points and orig. fee, 30-yr. conv. fixed or ARM	mos	7.16	3/01	4c
Vehicle finance charges paid	yr	328	1999	30r
Business Expenses				
Business travel, car rental	day	55	2001	3c
Business travel, food	day	54	2001	3c
Business travel, hotel	day	105	2001	3c
Medical office space cost	sq ft	123.33	2001	31c
Office space, 2-4 storey building	sq ft	108.05	2001	31c
Office space, 5-10 storey building	sq ft	95.44	2001	31c
Office space, 11-20 storey building	sq ft	91.74	2001	31c
Charity				
Cash contributions, expenditures	yr	939	1999	30c
Child Care				
Child raising cost, total, age 0-2	yr	7890	1999	60r
Child raising cost, total, age 3-5	yr	8130	1999	60r
Child raising cost, total, age 6-8	yr	8170	1999	60r
Child raising cost, total, age 9-11	yr	8190	1999	60r
Child raising cost, total, age 12-14	yr	8890	1999	60r
Child raising cost, total, age 15-17	yr	9050	1999	60r
Child's child care and education, age 0-2	yr	1240	1999	60r
Child's child care and education, age 3-5	yr	1370	1999	60r
Child's child care and education, age 6-8	yr	880	1999	60r
Child's child care and education, age 9-11	yr	570	1999	60r
Child's child care and education, age 12-14	yr	420	1999	60r
Child's child care and education, age 15-17	yr	720	1999	60r
Child's clothing, age 0-2	yr	410	1999	60r
Child's clothing, age 3-5	yr	400	1999	60r
Child's clothing, age 6-8	yr	450	1999	60r
Child's clothing, age 9-11	yr	500	1999	60r
Child's clothing, age 12-14	yr	840	1999	60r
Child's clothing, age 15-17	yr	740	1999	60r
Child's food, age 0-2	yr	960	1999	60r
Child's food, age 3-5	yr	1120	1999	60r
Child's food, age 6-8	yr	1430	1999	60r
Child's food, age 9-11	yr	1710	1999	60r
Child's food, age 12-14	yr	1710	1999	60r
Child's food, age 15-17	yr	1920	1999	60r
Child's health care, age 0-2	yr	520	1999	60r
Child's health care, age 3-5	yr	500	1999	60r
Child's health care, age 6-8	yr	570	1999	60r
Child's health care, age 9-11	yr	610	1999	60r
Child's health care, age 12-14	yr	630	1999	60r
Child's health care, age 15-17	yr	650	1999	60r
Child's housing, age 0-2	yr	2860	1999	60r
Child's housing, age 3-5	yr	2840	1999	60r
Child's housing, age 6-8	yr	2800	1999	60r
Child's housing, age 9-11	yr	2650	1999	60r
Child's housing, age 12-14	yr	2840	1999	60r
Child's housing, age 15-17	yr	2440	1999	60r
Child's personal care, reading, age 0-2	yr	880	1999	60r
Child's personal care, reading, age 3-5	yr	900	1999	60r
Child's personal care, reading, age 6-8	yr	930	1999	60r
Child's personal care, reading, age 9-11	yr	970	1999	60r
Child's personal care, reading, age 12-14	yr	1150	1999	60r
Child's personal care, reading, age 15-17	yr	920	1999	60r
Clothing				
Apparel and services purchases	yr	1777	1999	30c
Boys' brief, cotton	3	5.83	3/01	4c
Boys, 2 to 15, expenditures on	yr	91	1999	30r
Children under 2, expenditures on	yr	59	1999	30r

Cleveland, OH - continued

Item	Per	Value	Date	Ref.
Clothing - continued				
Footwear, expenditures on	yr	285	1999	30r
Girls, 2 to 15, expenditures on	yr	116	1999	30r
Men and boys, expenditures on	yr	433	1999	30r
Men, 16 and over, expenditures on	yr	341	1999	30r
Shirt, man's dress shirt		27.42	3/01	4c
Slacks, man's "No Wrinkles" khaki		34.59	3/01	4c
Women, 16 and over, expenditures on	yr	490	1999	30r
Communications				
Cable modem installation, Adelphi		54.90	6/99	103s
Cable modem installation, Media One		100.00	6/99	103s
Cable modem installation, Time Warner		75.00-225.00	6/99	103s
Cable modem rate, cable subscriber, Adelphi	mos	34.95	6/99	103s
Cable modem rate, cable subscriber, Media One	mos	34.95-39.95	6/99	103s
Cable modem rate, cable subscriber, Time Warner	mos	39.95-49.95	6/99	103s
Cable modem rate, non-cable subscriber, Adelphi	mos	44.95	6/99	103s
Cable modem rate, non-cable subscriber, Media One	mos	49.95	6/99	103s
Cable modem rate, non-cable subscriber, Time Warner	mos	39.95-54.95	6/99	103s
Newspaper subscription, daily and Sunday delivery	mos	15.68	3/01	4c
Phone line, single, business, field visit	inst.	56.32	12/97	17s
Phone line, single, business, no field visit	inst.	56.32	12/97	17s
Phone line, single, residence, field visit	inst.	31.10	12/97	17s
Phone line, single, residence, no field visit	inst.	31.10	12/97	17s
Postage and stationery, expenditures on	yr	140	1999	30r
Postal rate, express mail, up to half-pound		12.45	7/01	108r
Postal rate, letter, first class, first ounce		0.34	7/01	108r
Postal rate, letter, two ounces		0.57	7/01	108r
Postal rate, post card		0.21	7/01	108r
Postal rate, priority mail, two pounds		3.95	7/01	108r
Postal rate, priority mail, up to one pound		3.50	7/01	108r
Telephone bill, business, basic rate	mos	26.15	12/97	18c
Telephone bill, family of three	mos	19.50	3/01	4c
Telephone bill, residential, basic rate	mos	14.70	12/97	18c
Telephone services, expenditures on	yr	830	1999	30r
Education				
Board, 4-year private college/university	yr	2414	1996	38s
Board, 4-year public college/university	yr	2181	1996	38s
Education expenditures	yr	632	1999	30c
Room, 4-year private college/university	yr	2349	1996	38s
Room, 4-year public college/university	yr	2386	1996	38s
Total cost, 4-year private college/university	yr	17139	1996	38s
Total cost, 4-year public college/university	yr	8169	1996	38s
Tuition, 2-year public college/university, in state	yr	2261	1996	38s
Tuition, 4-year private college/university, in state	yr	12377	1996	38s
Tuition, 4-year public college/university	yr	3603	1996	38s
Energy and Fuels				
Electricity	500 KWhs	62.76	7/01	11c
Electricity	KWh	0.10	7/01	11c
Energy, combined forms, 2400 sq ft	mos	161.77	3/01	4c
Energy, exc. electricity, 2400 sq ft	mos	76.80	3/01	4c
Fuel oil #2	gal	1.27	7/01	11r
Fuel oil and other fuels, expenditures on	yr	68	1999	30r
Gas, cooking, winter, 10 therms	mos	10.15	2/96	98c
Gas, cooking, winter, 30 therms	mos	19.05	2/96	98c
Gas, cooking, winter, 50 therms	mos	27.63	2/96	98c
Gas, heating, winter, average use	mos	110.25	2/96	98c
Gas, natural, commercial rate	1000 cf	8.65	11/00	88s
Gas, regular unleaded, cash, self-service	gal	1.50	3/01	4c
Gasoline, all types	gal	1.61	7/01	11c
Gasoline, unleaded midgrade	gal	1.65	7/01	11c
Gasoline, unleaded premium	gal	1.86	7/01	11r
Gasoline, unleaded regular	gal	1.56	7/01	11c

Values are in dollars or fractions of dollars. In the column headed *Ref*, references are shown to sources. Each reference is followed by a letter. These refer to the geographical level for which data were reported: s=State, r=Region, and c=City or metro. The abbreviation *ex* is used to mean *except* or *excluding*; *exp* stands for *expenditures*. For other abbreviations and further explanations, please see the Introduction.

Cleveland, OH - continued

Item	Per	Value	Date	Ref.
Energy and Fuels				
Natural gas, expenditures on	yr	389	1999	30r
Utility (piped) gas, therm		1.06	7/01	11c
Utility (piped) gas, 40 therms		38.01	7/01	11r
Utility (piped) gas, 100 therms		106.92	7/01	11c
Entertainment				
Bowling, Saturday evening rate	line	2.62	3/01	4c
Entertainment purchases	yr	2294	1999	30c
Fees and admissions paid	yr	444	1999	30r
Major League baseball ticket		20.58	2000	16c
Monopoly game, Parker Brothers', No. 9	game	11.51	3/01	4c
Movie, first-run, Saturday, evening	adm.	7.50	3/01	4c
Reading purchases	yr	201	1999	30c
Television, radios, sound equipment, expenditures on	yr	580	1999	30r
Tennis balls, yellow, Wilson or Penn, 3	can	2.68	3/01	4c
Funerals				
Cosmetology, hair, other preparation		178.32	1/99	78r
Embalming		408.19	1/99	78r
Funeral at funeral home		362.13	1/99	78r
Professional service charges		1375.51	1/99	78r
Transfer of remains to funeral home		155.92	1/99	78r
Visitation/viewing		294.38	1/99	78r
Groceries				
Groceries, ACCRA Index		105.40	3/01	4c
Antibiotic ointment, Polysporin	0.5 oz	4.54	3/01	4c
Baby food, strained vegetables or fruit, lowest price	4-4.5 oz	0.48	3/01	4c
Bacon, sliced	lb	3.15	7/01	11r
Bakery products, expenditures on	yr	281	1999	30r
Bananas	lb	0.49	3/01	4c
Bananas	lb	0.48	7/01	11r
Beans, dried, any type, all sizes	lb	0.61	7/01	11r
Beef for stew, boneless	lb	3.08	7/01	11r
Beef or hamburger, ground	lb	1.51	3/01	4c
Beef, expenditures on	yr	217	1999	30r
Bologna, all beef or mixed	lb	2.52	7/01	11r
Bread, white	loaf	0.95	3/01	4c
Bread, white, pan	lb	1.06	7/01	11r
Broccoli	lb	0.91	7/01	11r
Butter, salted, grade AA, stick	lb	3.04	7/01	11r
Butter, yoghurt, cheese, etc, expenditures on	yr	183	1999	30r
Cereals and bakery product purchases	yr	430	1999	30r
Cereals and cereal products, expenditures on	yr	149	1999	30r
Cheese, Kraft grated Parmesan	8 oz	3.33	3/01	4c
Chicken, fresh, whole	lb	1.07	7/01	11r
Chicken, whole fryer	lb	1.33	3/01	4c
Chops, boneless,	lb	3.64	7/01	11r
Chuck roast, U.S. choice, boneless	lb	2.47	7/01	11r
Cigarettes, Winston, Kings	carton	27.12	3/01	4c
Coffee, 100%, ground roast, all sizes	lb	2.69	7/01	11r
Coffee, vacuum-packed	13 oz	2.59	3/01	4c
Cookies, chocolate chip	lb	2.87	7/01	11r
Corn Flakes, Kellogg's or Post Toasties	18 oz	2.85	3/01	4c
Corn, frozen, whole kernel, lowest price	16 oz	1.23	3/01	4c
Dairy product purchases	yr	302	1999	30c
Eggs, expenditures on	yr	26	1999	30r
Eggs, Grade A or AA	dozen	1.18	3/01	4c
Eggs, grade A, large	dozen	0.88	7/01	11r
Fats and oils, expenditures on	yr	75	1999	30r
Fish and seafood, expenditures on	yr	72	1999	30r
Food (excl fruit and vegetables), eaten at home, purchases	yr	854	1999	30c
Food cooked on trips, expenditures on	yr	44	1999	30r
Food purchases	yr	4940	1999	30c
Food purchases, eaten away from home	yr	2048	1999	30c
Food purchases, food eaten at home	yr	2892	1999	30c
Fresh fruits, expenditures on	yr	138	1999	30r
Fresh milk and cream, expenditures on	yr	120	1999	30r
Fresh vegetables, expenditures on	yr	126	1999	30r
Fruit and vegetable purchases	yr	465	1999	30c

Cleveland, OH - continued

Item	Per	Value	Date	Ref.
Groceries - continued				
Grapefruit	lb	0.66	7/01	11r
Grapes, Thompson, seedless	lb	1.64	7/01	11r
Ground beef, 100% beef	lb	1.64	7/01	11r
Ground beef, lean and extra lean	lb	2.16	7/01	11r
Ground chuck, 100% beef	lb	2.13	7/01	11r
Ham, boneless, excl canned	lb	2.62	7/01	11r
Ice cream, prepackaged, bulk, regular	1/2 gal	3.35	7/01	11r
Lemons	lb	1.19	7/01	11r
Lettuce, iceberg	head	1.15	3/01	4c
Lettuce, iceberg	lb	0.73	7/01	11r
Margarine, Blue Bonnet or Parkay, stick	lb	0.87	3/01	4c
Margarine, soft, tubs	lb	0.89	7/01	11r
Meats, poultry, fish, and egg purchases	yr	671	1999	30r
Milk, fresh, whole, fortified	gal	2.71	7/01	11r
Milk, whole	1/2 gal	1.62	3/01	4c
Nonalcoholic beverages, expenditures on	yr	239	1999	30r
Orange juice, Minute Maid frozen	12 oz	1.67	3/01	4c
Oranges, Navel	lb	0.80	7/01	11r
Oranges, Valencia	lb	0.66	7/01	11r
Peaches, halves or slices, Hunt's, Del Monte, or Libby's	29 oz	1.59	3/01	4c
Pears, Anjou	lb	0.93	7/01	11r
Peas, green, Del Monte or Green Giant	15 oz	0.79	3/01	4c
Pork chops, center cut, bone-in	lb	3.63	7/01	11r
Pork, expenditures on	yr	150	1999	30r
Potato chips	16 oz	3.52	7/01	11r
Potatoes, frozen, french fried	lb	1.08	7/01	11r
Potatoes, white or red	10 lb	3.19	3/01	4c
Potatoes, white, all types	lb	0.33	7/01	11r
Poultry, expenditures on	yr	108	1999	30r
Processed fruits, expenditures on	yr	98	1999	30r
Processed vegetables, expenditures on	yr	80	1999	30r
Round roast, U.S. choice, boneless	lb	3.07	7/01	11r
Round steak, graded and ungraded, excl U.S. prime and choice	lb	3.41	7/01	11r
Sausage, Jimmy Dean/Owens pork	lb	3.32	3/01	4c
Shortening, vegetable oil blends	lb	1.13	7/01	11r
Shortening, vegetable, Crisco	3 lb	2.99	3/01	4c
Soft drink, Coca Cola, ex deposit	2 liter	1.22	3/01	4c
Spaghetti and macaroni	lb	0.80	7/01	11r
Steak, round, U.S. choice, boneless	lb	3.23	7/01	11r
Steak, T-bone	lb	8.69	3/01	4c
Steak, T-bone, U.S. choice, bone-in	lb	6.68	7/01	11r
Strawberries, dry pint	12 oz	1.32	7/01	11r
Sugar and other sweets, expenditures on	yr	114	1999	30r
Sugar, cane or beet	4 lbs	1.59	3/01	4c
Sugar, white, 33-80 ounce package	lb	0.42	7/01	11r
Sugar, white, all sizes	lb	0.43	7/01	11r
Tobacco products and smoking supplies purchases	yr	321	1999	30c
Tomatoes, field grown	lb	1.46	7/01	11r
Tomatoes, Hunt's or Del Monte	14.5 oz	0.89	3/01	4c
Tuna, chunk, light	6 oz	0.70	3/01	4c
Tuna, light, chunk	lb	1.80	7/01	11r
Turkey, frozen, whole	lb	1.15	7/01	11r
Goods and Services				
Miscellaneous goods and services, ACCRA Index		103.40	3/01	4c
B&B Japanese maple (acer japonicum)	gal	29.99-169.99	4/00	93r
Boxwood (buxus)	2 gal	18.99-39.99	4/00	93r
Daylily (hemerocallis)	gal	4.99-25.00	4/00	93r
Flat of annuals		11.98-24.99	4/00	93r
Fountain grass (pennisetum)	gal	5.98-12.98	4/00	93r
Hanging basket (10 in)		12.99-27.99	4/00	93r
Hardy geranium (geranium)	gal	7.99-9.99	4/00	93r

Values are in dollars or fractions of dollars. In the column headed *Ref*, references are shown to sources. Each reference is followed by a letter. These refer to the geographical level for which data were reported: s=State, r=Region, and c=City or metro. The abbreviation *ex* is used to mean *except* or *excluding*; *exp* stands for expenditures. For other abbreviations and further explanations, please see the Introduction.

Cleveland, OH - continued

Item	Per	Value	Date	Ref.
Goods and Services				
Hosta (hosta)	gal	6.00-25.00	4/00	93r
Lilac (syrubga vulgaris)	2 gal	14.99-24.99	4/00	93r
Miscellaneous purchases	yr	865	1999	30r
Rhododendron (rhododendron)	2 gal	23.98-42.99	4/00	93r
Sage (salvia)	gal	6.00-9.99	4/00	93r
Wintercreeper euonymus (euonymus fortunei)	2 gal	16.00-169.99	4/00	93r
Hunting license	yr	15.00	4/01	34s
Health Care				
Health care, ACCRA Index		115.40	3/01	4c
Cardiac catheterization, ave hospital/ physician charges		11760	1998	77s
Childbirth, Cesarean delivery		10722	1997	13r
Childbirth, vaginal delivery		6223	1997	13r
Dentist's fee, adult teeth cleaning and periodic oral exam	visit	79.80	3/01	4c
Doctor's fee, routine exam, established patient	visit	66.00	3/01	4c
Drugs, expenditures on	yr	394	1999	30r
Health care purchases	yr	1661	1999	30c
Health insurance expenditures	yr	978	1999	30r
Home health care aide cost, licensed agency	hour	17	2000	82c
Hospital care, private room	day	732.20	3/01	4c
Hysterectomy, laproscopically-assisted, ave hospital/physician charges		11730	1998	76s
Hysterectomy, vaginal, ave hospital and physician charges		9640	1998	76s
Medicaid dispensing fee		3.70	1999	87s
Medical services expenditures	yr	554	1999	30r
Medical supplies, expenditures on	yr	122	1999	30r
Nursing home costs, private room	day	200	2000	82c
Nursing home stay, private room	day	200	2000	83c
Plastic surgery, breast augmentation		3184	2000	7r
Plastic surgery, breast lift		3585	2000	7r
Plastic surgery, facelift		4999	2000	7r
Plastic surgery, hair transplantation		3105	2000	7r
Plastic surgery, lip augmentation		1290	2000	7r
Plastic surgery, lower body lift		8135	2000	7r
Plastic surgery, thigh lift		3839	2000	7r
Household Goods				
Dishwashing powder, Cascade	50 oz	3.51	3/01	4c
Floor coverings, expenditures on	yr	52	1999	30r
Furniture, expenditures on	yr	344	1999	30r
Household furnishings and equipment purchases	yr	1515	1999	30c
Household textiles, expenditures on	yr	109	1999	30r
Laundry and cleaning supplies, expenditures on	yr	134	1999	30r
Tissues, facial, Kleenex brand	175	1.22	3/01	4c
Housing				
Housing, ACCRA Index		108.30	3/01	4c
Home, 2200 sq ft, 4-br, 2-bath, 2-car garage, average		170500	2000	47c
Home price, existing, ave		144400	10/00	90r
Home value, median		96000	2001	53s
House, 2400 sq ft, 8000 sq ft lot, new, urban, utilities	total	213767	3/01	4c
House payment, principal and interest, 25% down payment	mos	1084	3/01	4c
Household operation expenditures	yr	410	1999	30c
Housekeeping supplies purchases	yr	554	1999	30c
Housing, expenditures on	yr	11944	1999	30c
Lodging expenditures	yr	430	1999	30r
Maintenance, repairs, insurance expenditures	yr	853	1999	30r
Monthly rental value of owned home	mos	547	1999	30r
Owned dwellings, expenditures own	yr	4925	1999	30c

Cleveland, OH - continued

Item	Per	Value	Date	Ref.
Housing - continued				
Rent expenditures	yr	1469	1999	30c
Rent, apartment, 2 br, 1 1/2-2 baths, unfurn, 950 sq ft, water	mos	835	3/01	4c
Shelter, expenditures on	yr	6942	1999	30c
Insurance and Pensions				
Life and other personal insurance purchases	yr	416	1999	30c
Pensions and Social Security, expenditures on	yr	3307	1999	30c
Personal insurance and pensions, expenditures on	yr	3723	1999	30c
Legal Fees				
Divorce, filing fee		100.00	4/01	35s
Driver's license fee	renew	14.50	1999	48s
Driver's license fee	orig	14.50	1999	48s
Fishing license	yr	15.00	4/01	34s
Personal Goods				
Personal care products and services purchases	yr	481	1999	30c
Shampoo, Alberto VO5	15 oz	1.09	3/01	4c
Toothpaste, Crest or Colgate	6-7 oz	2.19	3/01	4c
Personal Services				
Dry cleaning, man's 2-pc suit		8.19	3/01	4c
Man's haircut, barbershop, no styling		11.75	3/01	4c
Personal services, household, expenditures on	yr	300	1999	30r
Woman's shampoo, trim, blow-dry, no style-change		23.50	3/01	4c
Pets				
Pets, toys, and playground equipment, expenditures on	yr	375	1999	30r
Restaurant Food				
Chicken, fried, thigh and drumstick, KFC/ Church's		2.69	3/01	4c
Hamburger with cheese, McDonald's	1/4 lb	2.21	3/01	4c
Pizza, Pizza Hut or Pizza Inn	11-12 in	9.09	3/01	4c
Taxes				
Federal income taxes paid	yr	2326	1999	30r
Personal taxes, expenditures on	yr	3223	1999	30r
Property taxes paid	yr	1152	1999	30r
State and local income taxes paid	yr	753	1999	30r
Transportation				
Transportation, ACCRA Index		110.60	3/01	4c
Bus fare, one-way	trip	1.00	2000	1c
Bus fare, to central business district	1-way	1.50	3/01	4c
Cars and trucks, new, expenditures on	yr	1280	1999	30r
Cars and trucks, used, expenditures on	yr	1763	1999	30r
Diesel at the pump	gal	1.25	10/99	73s
Gasoline and motor oil purchases	yr	916	1999	30c
Gasoline before-tax price (cents)	gal	109.50	10/00	43s
Heavy rail transit fare, one-way	trip	1.50	2000	2c
Light rail transit fare, one-way	trip	1.50	2000	2c
Maintenance and repair expenditures	yr	594	1999	30r
Public transportation, expenditures on	yr	442	1999	30c
Tire balance, computer or spin balance, front	wheel	8.59	3/01	4c
Transportation purchases	yr	7133	1999	30c
Vehicle expenses, miscellaneous, purchases	yr	2304	1999	30c
Vehicle insurance payments	yr	701	1999	30r
Vehicle purchases (net outlay)	yr	3471	1999	30c
Vehicle rental, lease expenditures	yr	536	1999	30r
Travel				
Car rental	day	86.50	2000	24c
Utilities				
Utilities, ACCRA Index		126.60	3/01	4c
Electrical bill, average	mos	72.83	9/00	9s
Electricity, expenditures on	yr	841	1999	30r
Electricity, summer, 250 KWh	mos	28.13	2/96	96c
Electricity, summer, 500 KWh	mos	56.27	2/96	96c

Values are in dollars or fractions of dollars. In the column headed *Ref*, references are shown to sources. Each reference is followed by a letter. These refer to the geographical level for which data were reported: s=State, r=Region, and c=City or metro. The abbreviation *ex* is used to mean *except* or *excluding*; *exp* stands for expenditures. For other abbreviations and further explanations, please see the Introduction.

Cleveland, OH - continued

Item	Per	Value	Date	Ref.
Utilities				
Electricity, summer, 750 KWh	mos	82.86	2/96	96c
Electricity, summer, 1000 KWh	mos	109.45	2/96	96c
Electricity and other, mixed, 2400 sq ft, new home	mos	84.97	3/01	4c
Electricity cost, average	KWh	6.59	9/00	9s
Utilities, fuels, and public services purchased	yr	2401	1999	30r
Water and other public services, expenditures on	yr	273	1999	30r
Weddings				
Wedding (national average cost)		19936	2000	33r
Wedding (regional average total cost)		16195	1997	110r
Attendants' gifts		321	1998	33r
Bridal attendants' apparel (5 persons)		824	2000	33r
Bride's headpiece/veil		173	1998	33r
Bride's wedding dress		859	1998	33r
Clergy, religious facility fee		242	1998	33r
Engagement ring		3177	1998	33r
Flowers		789	1998	33r
Groom's formalwear rental		99	2000	33r
Limousine		410	1998	33r
Marriage license cost		45.00	4/01	35s
Men's formalwear (ushers, best man)		469	2000	33r
Mother of bride apparel		241	2000	33r
Music		866	1998	33r
Photography and videography		1368	1998	33r
Rehearsal dinner		728	1998	33r
Wedding invitations and announcements		341	1998	33r
Wedding reception		7968	2000	33r
Wedding rings (bride and groom)		1060	1998	33r

Cleveland-Lorain-Elyria, OH

Item	Per	Value	Date	Ref.
Average annual expenditures	yr	35369	1999	30r
Alcoholic Beverages				
Alcoholic beverage purchases	yr	304	1999	30r
Malt beverages, all types, all sizes, any origin	16 oz	0.93	7/01	11r
Wine, red and white table, all sizes, any origin	liter	7.04	7/01	11r
Appliances				
Major appliances, expenditures on	yr	165	1999	30r
Small appliances, housewares, expenditures on	yr	90	1999	30r
Banking and Money				
Mortgage interest and charges paid	yr	2277	1999	30r
Mortgage principal paid on owned property	yr	1230	1999	30r
Vehicle finance charges paid	yr	328	1999	30r
Charity				
Cash contributions, expenditures	yr	1126	1999	30r
Child Care				
Child raising cost, total, age 0-2	yr	7890	1999	60r
Child raising cost, total, age 3-5	yr	8130	1999	60r
Child raising cost, total, age 6-8	yr	8170	1999	60r
Child raising cost, total, age 9-11	yr	8190	1999	60r
Child raising cost, total, age 12-14	yr	8890	1999	60r
Child raising cost, total, age 15-17	yr	9050	1999	60r
Child's child care and education, age 0-2	yr	1240	1999	60r
Child's child care and education, age 3-5	yr	1370	1999	60r
Child's child care and education, age 6-8	yr	880	1999	60r
Child's child care and education, age 9-11	yr	570	1999	60r
Child's child care and education, age 12-14	yr	420	1999	60r
Child's child care and education, age 15-17	yr	720	1999	60r
Child's clothing, age 0-2	yr	410	1999	60r
Child's clothing, age 3-5	yr	400	1999	60r
Child's clothing, age 6-8	yr	450	1999	60r
Child's clothing, age 9-11	yr	500	1999	60r
Child's clothing, age 12-14	yr	840	1999	60r
Child's clothing, age 15-17	yr	740	1999	60r
Child's food, age 0-2	yr	960	1999	60r

Cleveland-Lorain-Elyria, OH - continued

Item	Per	Value	Date	Ref.
Child Care - continued				
Child's food, age 3-5	yr	1120	1999	60r
Child's food, age 6-8	yr	1430	1999	60r
Child's food, age 9-11	yr	1710	1999	60r
Child's food, age 12-14	yr	1710	1999	60r
Child's food, age 15-17	yr	1920	1999	60r
Child's health care, age 0-2	yr	520	1999	60r
Child's health care, age 3-5	yr	500	1999	60r
Child's health care, age 6-8	yr	570	1999	60r
Child's health care, age 9-11	yr	610	1999	60r
Child's health care, age 12-14	yr	630	1999	60r
Child's health care, age 15-17	yr	650	1999	60r
Child's housing, age 0-2	yr	2860	1999	60r
Child's housing, age 3-5	yr	2840	1999	60r
Child's housing, age 6-8	yr	2800	1999	60r
Child's housing, age 9-11	yr	2650	1999	60r
Child's housing, age 12-14	yr	2840	1999	60r
Child's housing, age 15-17	yr	2440	1999	60r
Child's personal care, reading, age 0-2	yr	880	1999	60r
Child's personal care, reading, age 3-5	yr	900	1999	60r
Child's personal care, reading, age 6-8	yr	930	1999	60r
Child's personal care, reading, age 9-11	yr	970	1999	60r
Child's personal care, reading, age 12-14	yr	1150	1999	60r
Child's personal care, reading, age 15-17	yr	920	1999	60r
Clothing				
Apparel and services purchases	yr	1607	1999	30r
Boys, 2 to 15, expenditures on	yr	91	1999	30r
Children under 2, expenditures on	yr	59	1999	30r
Footwear, expenditures on	yr	285	1999	30r
Girls, 2 to 15, expenditures on	yr	116	1999	30r
Men and boys, expenditures on	yr	433	1999	30r
Men, 16 and over, expenditures on	yr	341	1999	30r
Women, 16 and over, expenditures on	yr	490	1999	30r
Communications				
Cable modem installation, Adelphi		54.90	6/99	103s
Cable modem installation, Media One		100.00	6/99	103s
Cable modem installation, Time Warner		75.00-225.00	6/99	103s
Cable modem rate, cable subscriber, Adelphi	mos	34.95	6/99	103s
Cable modem rate, cable subscriber, Media One	mos	34.95-39.95	6/99	103s
Cable modem rate, cable subscriber, Time Warner	mos	39.95-49.95	6/99	103s
Cable modem rate, non-cable subscriber, Adelphi	mos	44.95	6/99	103s
Cable modem rate, non-cable subscriber, Media One	mos	49.95	6/99	103s
Cable modem rate, non-cable subscriber, Time Warner	mos	39.95-54.95	6/99	103s
Phone line, single, business, field visit	inst.	56.32	12/97	17s
Phone line, single, business, no field visit	inst.	56.32	12/97	17s
Phone line, single, residence, field visit	inst.	31.10	12/97	17s
Phone line, single, residence, no field visit	inst.	31.10	12/97	17s
Postage and stationery, expenditures on	yr	140	1999	30r
Postal rate, express mail, up to half-pound		12.45	7/01	108r
Postal rate, letter, first class, first ounce		0.34	7/01	108r
Postal rate, letter, two ounces		0.57	7/01	108r
Postal rate, post card		0.21	7/01	108r
Postal rate, priority mail, two pounds		3.95	7/01	108r
Postal rate, priority mail, up to one pound		3.50	7/01	108r
Telephone services, expenditures on	yr	830	1999	30r
Education				
Board, 4-year private college/university	yr	2414	1996	38s
Board, 4-year public college/university	yr	2181	1996	38s
Education expenditures	yr	583	1999	30r
Room, 4-year private college/university	yr	2349	1996	38s
Room, 4-year public college/university	yr	2386	1996	38s
Total cost, 4-year private college/university	yr	17139	1996	38s
Total cost, 4-year public college/university	yr	8169	1996	38s
Tuition, 2-year public college/university, in state	yr	2261	1996	38s

Values are in dollars or fractions of dollars. In the column headed *Ref*, references are shown to sources. Each reference is followed by a letter. These refer to the geographical level for which data were reported: s=State, r=Region, and c=City or metro. The abbreviation *ex* is used to mean *except* or *excluding*; *exp* stands for expenditures. For other abbreviations and further explanations, please see the Introduction.

Cleveland-Lorain-Elyria, OH - continued

Item	Per	Value	Date	Ref.
Education				
Tuition, 4-year private college/university, in state	yr	12377	1996	38s
Tuition, 4-year public college/university	yr	3603	1996	38s
Energy and Fuels				
Electricity	500 KWhs	46.59	7/01	11r
Fuel oil #2	gal	1.27	7/01	11r
Fuel oil and other fuels, expenditures on	yr	68	1999	30r
Gas, natural, commercial rate	1000 cf	8.65	11/00	88s
Gasoline, unleaded midgrade	gal	1.79	7/01	11r
Gasoline, unleaded premium	gal	1.86	7/01	11r
Gasoline, unleaded regular	gal	1.58	7/01	11r
Natural gas, expenditures on	yr	389	1999	30r
Utility (piped) gas, therm		0.81	7/01	11r
Utility (piped) gas, 40 therms		38.01	7/01	11r
Utility (piped) gas, 100 therms		81.75	7/01	11r
Entertainment				
Entertainment purchases	yr	1984	1999	30r
Fees and admissions paid	yr	444	1999	30r
Television, radios, sound equipment, expenditures on	yr	580	1999	30r
Funerals				
Cosmetology, hair, other preparation		178.32	1/99	78r
Embalming		408.19	1/99	78r
Funeral at funeral home		362.13	1/99	78r
Professional service charges		1375.51	1/99	78r
Transfer of remains to funeral home		155.92	1/99	78r
Visitation/viewing		294.38	1/99	78r
Groceries				
Bacon, sliced	lb	3.15	7/01	11r
Bakery products, expenditures on	yr	281	1999	30r
Bananas	lb	0.48	7/01	11r
Beans, dried, any type, all sizes	lb	0.61	7/01	11r
Beef for stew, boneless	lb	3.08	7/01	11r
Beef, expenditures on	yr	217	1999	30r
Bologna, all beef or mixed	lb	2.52	7/01	11r
Bread, white, pan	lb	1.06	7/01	11r
Broccoli	lb	0.91	7/01	11r
Butter, salted, grade AA, stick	lb	3.04	7/01	11r
Butter, yoghurt, cheese, etc, expenditures on	yr	183	1999	30r
Cereals and bakery product purchases	yr	430	1999	30r
Cereals and cereal products, expenditures on	yr	149	1999	30r
Chicken, fresh, whole	lb	1.07	7/01	11r
Chops, boneless	lb	3.64	7/01	11r
Chuck roast, U.S. choice, boneless	lb	2.47	7/01	11r
Coffee, 100%, ground roast, all sizes	lb	2.69	7/01	11r
Cookies, chocolate chip	lb	2.87	7/01	11r
Dairy product purchases	yr	304	1999	30r
Eggs, expenditures on	yr	26	1999	30r
Eggs, grade A, large	dozen	0.88	7/01	11r
Fats and oils, expenditures on	yr	75	1999	30r
Fish and seafood, expenditures on	yr	72	1999	30r
Food (excl fruit and vegetables), eaten at home, purchases	yr	887	1999	30r
Food cooked on trips, expenditures on	yr	44	1999	30r
Food purchases	yr	4802	1999	30r
Food purchases, eaten away from home	yr	2069	1999	30r
Food purchases, food eaten at home	yr	2733	1999	30r
Fresh fruits, expenditures on	yr	138	1999	30r
Fresh milk and cream, expenditures on	yr	120	1999	30r
Fresh vegetables, expenditures on	yr	126	1999	30r
Grapefruit	lb	0.66	7/01	11r
Grapes, Thompson, seedless	lb	1.64	7/01	11r
Ground beef, 100% beef	lb	1.64	7/01	11r
Ground beef, lean and extra lean	lb	2.16	7/01	11r
Ground chuck, 100% beef	lb	2.13	7/01	11r
Ham, boneless, excl canned	lb	2.62	7/01	11r
Ice cream, prepackaged, bulk, regular	1/2 gal	3.35	7/01	11r
Lemons	lb	1.19	7/01	11r

Item	Per	Value	Date	Ref.
Groceries - continued				
Lettuce, iceberg	lb	0.73	7/01	11r
Margarine, soft, tubs	lb	0.89	7/01	11r
Meats, poultry, fish, and egg purchases	yr	671	1999	30r
Milk, fresh, whole, fortified	gal	2.71	7/01	11r
Nonalcoholic beverages, expenditures on	yr	239	1999	30r
Oranges, Navel	lb	0.80	7/01	11r
Oranges, Valencia	lb	0.66	7/01	11r
Pears, Anjou	lb	0.93	7/01	11r
Pork chops, center cut, bone-in	lb	3.63	7/01	11r
Pork, expenditures on	yr	150	1999	30r
Potato chips	16 oz	3.52	7/01	11r
Potatoes, frozen, french fried	lb	1.08	7/01	11r
Potatoes, white, all types	lb	0.33	7/01	11r
Poultry, expenditures on	yr	108	1999	30r
Processed fruits, expenditures on	yr	98	1999	30r
Processed vegetables, expenditures on	yr	80	1999	30r
Round roast, U.S. choice, boneless	lb	3.07	7/01	11r
Round steak, graded and ungraded, excl U.S. prime and choice	lb	3.41	7/01	11r
Shortening, vegetable oil blends	lb	1.13	7/01	11r
Spaghetti and macaroni	lb	0.80	7/01	11r
Steak, round, U.S. choice, boneless	lb	3.23	7/01	11r
Steak, T-bone, U.S. choice, bone-in	lb	6.68	7/01	11r
Strawberries, dry pint	12 oz	1.32	7/01	11r
Sugar and other sweets, expenditures on	yr	114	1999	30r
Sugar, white, 33-80 ounce package	lb	0.42	7/01	11r
Sugar, white, all sizes	lb	0.43	7/01	11r
Tobacco products and smoking supplies purchases	yr	331	1999	30r
Tomatoes, field grown	lb	1.46	7/01	11r
Tuna, light, chunk	lb	1.80	7/01	11r
Turkey, frozen, whole	lb	1.15	7/01	11r
Goods and Services				
B&B Japanese maple (acer japonicum)	gal	29.99-169.99	4/00	93r
Boxwood (buxus)	2 gal	18.99-39.99	4/00	93r
Daylilly (hemerocallis)	gal	4.99-25.00	4/00	93r
Flat of annuals		11.98-24.99	4/00	93r
Fountain grass (pennisetum)	gal	5.98-12.98	4/00	93r
Hanging basket (10 in)		12.99-27.99	4/00	93r
Hardy geranium (geranium)	gal	7.99-9.99	4/00	93r
Hosta (hosta)	gal	6.00-25.00	4/00	93r
Lilac (syrubga vulgaris)	2 gal	14.99-24.99	4/00	93r
Miscellaneous purchases	yr	865	1999	30r
Rhododendron (rhododendron)	2 gal	23.98-42.99	4/00	93r
Sage (salvia)	gal	6.00-9.99	4/00	93r
Wintercreeper euonymus (euonymus fortunei)	2 gal	16.00-169.99	4/00	93r
Hunting license	yr	15.00	4/01	34s
Health Care				
Cardiac catheterization, ave hospital/ physician charges		11760	1998	77s
Childbirth, Cesarean delivery		10722	1997	13r
Childbirth, vaginal delivery		6223	1997	13r
Drugs, expenditures on	yr	394	1999	30r
Health care purchases	yr	2048	1999	30r
Health insurance expenditures	yr	978	1999	30r
Hysterectomy, laproscopically-assisted, ave hospital/physician charges		11730	1998	76s
Hysterectomy, vaginal, ave hospital and physician charges		9640	1998	76s

Values are in dollars or fractions of dollars. In the column headed *Ref*, references are shown to sources. Each reference is followed by a letter. These refer to the geographical level for which data were reported: s=State, r=Region, and c=City or metro. The abbreviation *ex* is used to mean *except* or *excluding*; *exp* stands for expenditures. For other abbreviations and further explanations, please see the Introduction.

Cleveland-Lorain-Elyria, OH - continued

Item	Per	Value	Date	Ref.
Health Care				
Medicaid dispensing fee		3.70	1999	87s
Medical services expenditures	yr	554	1999	30r
Medical supplies, expenditures on	yr	122	1999	30r
Plastic surgery, breast augmentation		3184	2000	7r
Plastic surgery, breast lift		3585	2000	7r
Plastic surgery, facelift		4999	2000	7r
Plastic surgery, hair transplantation		3105	2000	7r
Plastic surgery, lip augmentation		1290	2000	7r
Plastic surgery, lower body lift		8135	2000	7r
Plastic surgery, thigh lift		3839	2000	7r
Household Goods				
Floor coverings, expenditures on	yr	52	1999	30r
Furniture, expenditures on	yr	344	1999	30r
Household furnishings and equipment purchases	yr	1475	1999	30r
Household textiles, expenditures on	yr	109	1999	30r
Laundry and cleaning supplies, expenditures on	yr	134	1999	30r
Housing				
Home price, existing, ave		144400	10/00	90r
Home value, median		96000	2001	53s
Household operation expenditures	yr	542	1999	30r
Housekeeping supplies purchases	yr	508	1999	30r
Lodging expenditures	yr	430	1999	30r
Maintenance, repairs, insurance expenditures	yr	853	1999	30r
Monthly rental value of owned home	mos	547	1999	30r
Owned dwellings, expenditures own	yr	4282	1999	30r
Rent expenditures	yr	1558	1999	30r
Rental unit, 1 bedroom, with utilities	mos	521	4/01	41c
Rental unit, 2 bedroom, with utilities	mos	645	4/01	41c
Rental unit, 3 bedroom, with utilities	mos	820	4/01	41c
Rental unit, 4 bedroom, with utilities	mos	924	4/01	41c
Shelter, expenditures on	yr	6270	1999	30r
Insurance and Pensions				
Life and other personal insurance purchases	yr	387	1999	30r
Pensions and Social Security, expenditures on	yr	2968	1999	30r
Legal Fees				
Divorce, filing fee		100.00	4/01	35s
Driver's license fee	orig	14.50	1999	48s
Driver's license fee	renew	14.50	1999	48s
Fishing license	yr	15.00	4/01	34s
Personal Goods				
Personal care products and services purchases	yr	385	1999	30r
Personal Services				
Personal services, household, expenditures on	yr	300	1999	30r
Pets				
Pets, toys, and playground equipment, expenditures on	yr	375	1999	30r
Taxes				
Federal income taxes paid	yr	2326	1999	30r
Personal taxes, expenditures on	yr	3223	1999	30r
Property taxes paid	yr	1152	1999	30r
State and local income taxes paid	yr	753	1999	30r
Transportation				
Cars and trucks, new, expenditures on	yr	1280	1999	30r
Cars and trucks, used, expenditures on	yr	1763	1999	30r
Diesel at the pump	gal	1.25	10/99	73s
Gasoline and motor oil purchases	yr	1036	1999	30r
Gasoline before-tax price (cents)	gal	109.50	10/00	43s
Maintenance and repair expenditures	yr	594	1999	30r
Public transportation, expenditures on	yr	341	1999	30r
Transportation purchases	yr	6617	1999	30r
Vehicle expenses, miscellaneous, purchases	yr	2159	1999	30r

Cleveland-Lorain-Elyria, OH - continued

Item	Per	Value	Date	Ref.
Transportation - continued				
Vehicle insurance payments	yr	701	1999	30r
Vehicle purchases (net outlay)	yr	3081	1999	30r
Vehicle rental, lease expenditures	yr	536	1999	30r
Utilities				
Electrical bill, average	mos	72.83	9/00	9s
Electricity, expenditures on	yr	841	1999	30r
Electricity cost, average	KWh	6.59	9/00	9s
Utilities, fuels, and public services purchased	yr	2401	1999	30r
Water and other public services, expenditures on	yr	273	1999	30r
Weddings				
Wedding (national average cost)		19936	2000	33r
Wedding (regional average total cost)		16195	1997	110r
Attendants' gifts		321	1998	33r
Bridal attendants' apparel (5 persons)		824	2000	33r
Bride's headpiece/veil		173	1998	33r
Bride's wedding dress		859	1998	33r
Clergy, religious facility fee		242	1998	33r
Engagement ring		3177	1998	33r
Flowers		789	1998	33r
Groom's formalwear rental		99	2000	33r
Limousine		410	1998	33r
Marriage license cost		45.00	4/01	35s
Men's formalwear (ushers, best man)		469	2000	33r
Mother of bride apparel		241	2000	33r
Music		866	1998	33r
Photography and videography		1368	1998	33r
Rehearsal dinner		728	1998	33r
Wedding invitations and announcements		341	1998	33r
Wedding reception		7968	2000	33r
Wedding rings (bride and groom)		1060	1998	33r

Colorado Springs, CO

Item	Per	Value	Date	Ref.
Composite, ACCRA index		98.50	3/01	4c
Alcoholic Beverages				
Beer, Heineken, 12-oz, ex deposit	6	6.74	3/01	4c
J & B Scotch	750-ml	20.91	3/01	4c
Wine, Livingston or Gallo, Chablis blanc	1.5 liter	4.59	3/01	4c
Appliances				
Appliance repair, service call, washing machine	min lab chg	31.21	3/01	4c
Banking and Money				
Mortgage rate, incl. points and orig. fee, 30-yr. conv. fixed or ARM	mos	6.92	3/01	4c
Clothing				
Boys' brief, cotton	3	3.78	3/01	4c
Shirt, man's dress shirt		31.30	3/01	4c
Slacks, man's "No Wrinkles" khaki		37.19	3/01	4c
Communications				
Cable modem installation, AT&T-BIS		150.00	6/99	103s
Cable modem rate, cable subscriber, AT&T-BIS	mos	39.95	6/99	103s
Newspaper subscription, daily and Sunday delivery	mos	9.95	3/01	4c
Phone line, single, business, field visit	inst.	70.00	12/97	17s
Phone line, single, business, no field visit	inst.	70.00	12/97	17s
Phone line, single, residence, field visit	inst.	35.00	12/97	17s
Phone line, single, residence, no field visit	inst.	35.00	12/97	17s
Postal rate, express mail, up to half-pound		12.45	7/01	108r
Postal rate, letter, first class, first ounce		0.34	7/01	108r
Postal rate, letter, two ounces		0.57	7/01	108r
Postal rate, post card		0.21	7/01	108r
Postal rate, priority mail, two pounds		3.95	7/01	108r
Postal rate, priority mail, up to one pound		3.50	7/01	108r
Telephone bill, business, basic rate	mos	37.31	12/97	18c
Telephone bill, family of three	mos	21.60	3/01	4c
Telephone bill, residential, basic rate	mos	14.87	12/97	18c

Values are in dollars or fractions of dollars. In the column headed *Ref*, references are shown to sources. Each reference is followed by a letter. These refer to the geographic level for which data were reported: s=State, r=Region, and c=City or metro. The abbreviation *ex* is used to mean *except* or *excluding*; *exp* stands for expenditures. For other abbreviations and further explanations, please see the Introduction.

Colorado Springs, CO - continued

Item	Per	Value	Date	Ref.
Education				
Board, 4-year private college/university	yr	2750	1996	38s
Board, 4-year public college/university	yr	2564	1996	38s
Room, 4-year private college/university	yr	2574	1996	38s
Room, 4-year public college/university	yr	2000	1996	38s
Total cost, 4-year private college/university	yr	17120	1996	38s
Total cost, 4-year public college/university	yr	7037	1996	38s
Tuition, 2-year public college/university, in state	yr	1340	1996	38s
Tuition, 4-year private college/university, in state	yr	11796	1996	38s
Tuition, 4-year public college/university	yr	2473	1996	38s
Energy and Fuels				
Energy, combined forms, 2400 sq ft	mos	91.24	3/01	4c
Energy, exc. electricity, 2400 sq ft	mos	49.23	3/01	4c
Gas, natural, commercial rate	1000 cf	6.42	11/00	88s
Gas, regular unleaded, cash, self-service	gal	1.37	3/01	4c
Entertainment				
Bowling, Saturday evening rate	line	2.77	3/01	4c
Monopoly game, Parker Brothers', No. 9	game	9.75	3/01	4c
Movie, first-run, Saturday, evening	adm.	6.75	3/01	4c
Tennis balls, yellow, Wilson or Penn, 3	can	2.01	3/01	4c
Funerals				
Total cost of funeral		5401.08	1/99	78r
Acknowledgement cards		33.64	1/99	78r
Casket		2170.43	1/99	78r
Cosmetology, hair, other preparation		136.32	1/99	78r
Embalming		319.13	1/99	78r
Funeral at funeral home		370.21	1/99	78r
Hearse (local)		161.04	1/99	78r
Professional service charges		963.15	1/99	78r
Service car/van		133.99	1/99	78r
Transfer of remains to funeral home		159.82	1/99	78r
Vault		778.07	1/99	78r
Visitation/viewing		175.28	1/99	78r
Groceries				
Groceries, ACCRA Index		102.00	3/01	4c
Antibiotic ointment, Polysporin	0.5 oz	4.73	3/01	4c
Baby food, strained vegetables or fruit, lowest price	4-4.5 oz	0.42	3/01	4c
Bacon	lb	3.99	5/99	8s
Bananas	lb	0.51	3/01	4c
Beef or hamburger, ground	lb	1.55	3/01	4c
Bread, white	loaf	1.00	3/01	4c
Bread, white, 20 oz loaf		0.64	5/99	8s
Cheddar cheese, mild	lb	3.59	5/99	8s
Cheerios, 10 oz box		2.99	5/99	8s
Cheese, Kraft grated Parmesan	8 oz	3.90	3/01	4c
Chicken, whole fryer	lb	1.06	3/01	4c
Cigarettes, Winston, Kings	carton	27.97	3/01	4c
Coffee, vacuum-packed	13 oz	3.45	3/01	4c
Corn Flakes, Kellogg's or Post Toasties	18 oz	2.41	3/01	4c
Corn oil, Mazola, 32 oz		2.75	5/99	8s
Corn, frozen, whole kernel, lowest price	16 oz	1.11	3/01	4c
Eggs, Grade A or AA	dozen	0.97	3/01	4c
Flour, all purpose	5 lb	1.69	5/99	8s
Grade A large eggs	doz	1.59	5/99	8s
Ground chuck	lb	1.99	5/99	8s
Lettuce, iceberg	head	1.16	3/01	4c
Margarine, Blue Bonnet or Parkay, stick	lb	0.72	5/99	8s
Mayonnaise, Kraft, 32 oz		2.50	5/99	8s
Milk, whole	1/2 gal	1.93	3/01	4c
Orange juice, Minute Maid frozen	12 oz	1.47	3/01	4c
Peaches, halves or slices, Hunt's, Del Monte, or Libby's	29 oz	2.10	3/01	4c
Peas, green, Del Monte or Green Giant	15 oz	0.76	3/01	4c
Potatoes, russet	5 lb	1.79	5/99	8s
Potatoes, white or red	10 lb	1.95	3/01	4c
Red Delicious apples	lb	1.39	5/99	8s
Sausage, Jimmy Dean/Owens pork	lb	3.71	3/01	4c
Shortening, vegetable, Crisco	3 lb	3.05	3/01	4c

Colorado Springs, CO - continued

Item	Per	Value	Date	Ref.
Groceries - continued				
Sirloin tip roast	lb	3.99	5/99	8s
Soft drink, Coca Cola, ex deposit	2 liter	1.08	3/01	4c
Steak, T-bone	lb	6.35	3/01	4c
Sugar, cane or beet	4 lbs	1.51	3/01	4c
Tomatoes, Hunt's or Del Monte	14.5 oz	1.03	3/01	4c
Tuna, chunk, light	6 oz	0.38	3/01	4c
Vegetable oil, Crisco, 32 oz		1.89	5/99	8s
Whole fryer	lb	1.99	5/99	8s
Whole milk	gal	0.89	5/99	8s
Goods and Services				
Miscellaneous goods and services, ACCRA Index		91.50	3/01	4c
Hunting license	yr	15.25	4/01	34s
Health Care				
Health care, ACCRA Index		118.80	3/01	4c
Cardiac catheterization, ave hospital/ physician charges		17910	1998	77s
Childbirth, Cesarean delivery		11587	1997	13r
Childbirth, vaginal delivery		6725	1997	13r
Dentist's fee, adult teeth cleaning and periodic oral exam	visit	83.12	3/01	4c
Doctor's fee, routine exam, established patient	visit	72.59	3/01	4c
Hospital care, private room	day	654.50	3/01	4c
Hysterectomy, laproscopically-assisted, ave hospital/physician charges		16210	1998	76s
Hysterectomy, vaginal, ave hospital and physician charges		11690	1998	76s
Medicaid dispensing fee		4.08	1999	87s
Household Goods				
Dishwashing powder, Cascade	50 oz	3.37	3/01	4c
Tissues, facial, Kleenex brand	175	1.43	3/01	4c
Housing				
Housing, ACCRA Index		105.90	3/01	4c
Home, 2200 sq ft, 4-br, 2-bath, 2-car garage, average		157900	2000	47c
Home value, median		173000	2001	53s
House, 2400 sq ft, 8000 sq ft lot, new, urban, utilities	total	214189	3/01	4c
House payment, principal and interest, 25% down payment	mos	1061	3/01	4c
Rent, apartment, 2 br, 1 1/2-2 baths, unfurn, 950 sq ft, water	mos	817	3/01	4c
Rental unit, 1 bedroom, with utilities	mos	486	4/01	41c
Rental unit, 2 bedroom, with utilities	mos	647	4/01	41c
Rental unit, 3 bedroom, with utilities	mos	902	4/01	41c
Rental unit, 4 bedroom, with utilities	mos	1065	4/01	41c
Legal Fees				
Divorce, filing fee		65.00	4/01	35s
Driver's license fee	renew	15.00	1999	48s
Driver's license fee	orig	15.00	1999	48s
Personal Goods				
Shampoo, Alberto VO5	15 oz	1.03	3/01	4c
Toothpaste, Crest or Colgate	6-7 oz	2.09	3/01	4c
Personal Services				
Dry cleaning, man's 2-pc suit		6.07	3/01	4c
Man's haircut, barbershop, no styling		11.08	3/01	4c
Woman's shampoo, trim, blow-dry, no style-change		25.20	3/01	4c
Restaurant Food				
Chicken, fried, thigh and drumstick, KFC/ Church's		2.52	3/01	4c
Hamburger with cheese, McDonald's	1/4 lb	1.00	3/01	4c
Pizza, Pizza Hut or Pizza Inn	11-12 in	8.99	3/01	4c
Transportation				
Transportation, ACCRA Index		101.50	3/01	4c
Bus fare, one-way	trip	1.00	2000	1c

Values are in dollars or fractions of dollars. In the column headed *Ref*, references are shown to sources. Each reference is followed by a letter. These refer to the geographical level for which data were reported: s=State, r=Region, and c=City or metro. The abbreviation *ex* is used to mean *except* or *excluding*; *exp* stands for *expenditures*. For other abbreviations and further explanations, please see the Introduction.

Colorado Springs, CO - continued

Item	Per	Value	Date	Ref.
Transportation				
Diesel at the pump	gal	1.28	10/99	73s
Gasoline before-tax price (cents)	gal	117.00	10/00	43s
Tire balance, computer or spin balance, front	wheel	8.50	3/01	4c
Travel				
Hotel room	night	118.98	2/01	95s
Hotel room, ave	night	79.78	2000	70c
Utilities				
Utilities, ACCRA Index		78.10	3/01	4c
Electrical bill, average	mos	47.17	9/00	9s
Electricity and other, mixed, 2400 sq ft, new home	mos	42.01	3/01	4c
Electricity cost, average	KWh	5.90	9/00	9s
Weddings				
Wedding (national average cost)		19936	2000	33r
Attendants' gifts		321	1998	33r
Bridal attendants' apparel (5 persons)		824	2000	33r
Bride's headpiece/veil		173	1998	33r
Bride's wedding dress		859	1998	33r
Clergy, religious facility fee		242	1998	33r
Engagement ring		3177	1998	33r
Flowers		789	1998	33r
Groom's formalwear rental		99	2000	33r
Limousine		410	1998	33r
Marriage license cost		20.00	4/01	35s
Men's formalwear (ushers, best man)		469	2000	33r
Mother of bride apparel		241	2000	33r
Music		866	1998	33r
Photography and videography		1368	1998	33r
Rehearsal dinner		728	1998	33r
Wedding invitations and announcements		341	1998	33r
Wedding reception		7968	2000	33r
Wedding rings (bride and groom)		1060	1998	33r

Columbia, MD

Item	Per	Value	Date	Ref.
Alcoholic Beverages				
Alcoholic beverage purchases	yr	253	1999	30r
Malt beverages, all types, all sizes, any origin	16 oz	0.96	7/01	11r
Appliances				
Major appliances, expenditures on	yr	172	1999	30r
Small appliances, housewares, expenditures on	yr	81	1999	30r
Banking and Money				
Mortgage interest and charges paid	yr	2039	1999	30r
Mortgage principal paid on owned property	yr	1026	1999	30r
Vehicle finance charges paid	yr	365	1999	30r
Charity				
Cash contributions, expenditures	yr	1127	1999	30r
Child Care				
Child raising cost, total, age 0-2	yr	8540	1999	60r
Child raising cost, total, age 3-5	yr	8780	1999	60r
Child raising cost, total, age 6-8	yr	8820	1999	60r
Child raising cost, total, age 9-11	yr	8800	1999	60r
Child raising cost, total, age 12-14	yr	9510	1999	60r
Child raising cost, total, age 15-17	yr	9740	1999	60r
Child's child care and education, age 0-2	yr	1380	1999	60r
Child's child care and education, age 3-5	yr	1520	1999	60r
Child's child care and education, age 6-8	yr	990	1999	60r
Child's child care and education, age 9-11	yr	650	1999	60r
Child's child care and education, age 12-14	yr	490	1999	60r
Child's child care and education, age 15-17	yr	840	1999	60r
Child's clothing, age 0-2	yr	480	1999	60r
Child's clothing, age 3-5	yr	470	1999	60r
Child's clothing, age 6-8	yr	520	1999	60r
Child's clothing, age 9-11	yr	570	1999	60r
Child's clothing, age 12-14	yr	950	1999	60r
Child's clothing, age 15-17	yr	850	1999	60r

Columbia, MD - continued

Item	Per	Value	Date	Ref.
Child Care - continued				
Child's food, age 0-2	yr	1000	1999	60r
Child's food, age 3-5	yr	1160	1999	60r
Child's food, age 6-8	yr	1490	1999	60r
Child's food, age 9-11	yr	1770	1999	60r
Child's food, age 12-14	yr	1770	1999	60r
Child's food, age 15-17	yr	1980	1999	60r
Child's health care, age 0-2	yr	620	1999	60r
Child's health care, age 3-5	yr	590	1999	60r
Child's health care, age 6-8	yr	680	1999	60r
Child's health care, age 9-11	yr	720	1999	60r
Child's health care, age 12-14	yr	730	1999	60r
Child's health care, age 15-17	yr	760	1999	60r
Child's housing, age 0-2	yr	3070	1999	60r
Child's housing, age 3-5	yr	3050	1999	60r
Child's housing, age 6-8	yr	3010	1999	60r
Child's housing, age 9-11	yr	2850	1999	60r
Child's housing, age 12-14	yr	3040	1999	60r
Child's housing, age 15-17	yr	2650	1999	60r
Child's personal care, reading, age 0-2	yr	910	1999	60r
Child's personal care, reading, age 3-5	yr	930	1999	60r
Child's personal care, reading, age 6-8	yr	960	1999	60r
Child's personal care, reading, age 9-11	yr	1000	1999	60r
Child's personal care, reading, age 12-14	yr	1170	1999	60r
Child's personal care, reading, age 15-17	yr	950	1999	60r
Clothing				
Apparel and services purchases	yr	1610	1999	30r
Boys, 2 to 15, expenditures on	yr	89	1999	30r
Children under 2, expenditures on	yr	79	1999	30r
Footwear, expenditures on	yr	283	1999	30r
Girls, 2 to 15, expenditures on	yr	103	1999	30r
Men and boys, expenditures on	yr	351	1999	30r
Men, 16 and over, expenditures on	yr	262	1999	30r
Women, 16 and over, expenditures on	yr	538	1999	30r
Communications				
Cable modem installation, Comcast		95.00	6/99	103s
Cable modem rate, cable subscriber, Comcast	mos	39.95	6/99	103s
Cable modem rate, non-cable subscriber, Comcast	mos	49.95	6/99	103s
Phone line, single, business, field visit	inst.	98.50	12/97	17s
Phone line, single, business, no field visit	inst.	98.50	12/97	17s
Phone line, single, residence, field visit	inst.	48.00	12/97	17s
Phone line, single, residence, no field visit	inst.	48.00	12/97	17s
Postage and stationery, expenditures on	yr	104	1999	30r
Postal rate, express mail, up to half-pound		12.45	7/01	108r
Postal rate, letter, first class, first ounce		0.34	7/01	108r
Postal rate, letter, two ounces		0.57	7/01	108r
Postal rate, post card		0.21	7/01	108r
Postal rate, priority mail, two pounds		3.95	7/01	108r
Postal rate, priority mail, up to one pound		3.50	7/01	108r
Telephone services, expenditures on	yr	860	1999	30r
Education				
Board, 4-year private college/university	yr	3022	1996	38s
Board, 4-year public college/university	yr	2435	1996	38s
Education expenditures	yr	431	1999	30r
Room, 4-year private college/university	yr	3524	1996	38s
Room, 4-year public college/university	yr	2722	1996	38s
Total cost, 4-year private college/university	yr	21245	1996	38s
Total cost, 4-year public college/university	yr	8728	1996	38s
Tuition, 2-year public college/university, in state	yr	1967	1996	38s
Tuition, 4-year private college/university, in state	yr	14700	1996	38s
Tuition, 4-year public college/university	yr	3572	1996	38s
Energy and Fuels				
Electricity	KWh	0.09	7/01	11r
Electricity	500 KWhs	47.29	7/01	11r
Fuel oil #2	gal	1.43	7/01	11r
Fuel oil and other fuels, expenditures on	yr	45	1999	30r

Values are in dollars or fractions of dollars. In the column headed *Ref*, references are shown to sources. Each reference is followed by a letter. These refer to the geographical level for which data were reported: s=State, r=Region, and c=City or metro. The abbreviation *ex* is used to mean *except* or *excluding*; *exp* stands for *expenditures*. For other abbreviations and further explanations, please see the Introduction.

Columbia, MD - continued

Item	Per	Value	Date	Ref.
Energy and Fuels				
Gas, natural, commercial rate	1000 cf	8.64	11/00	88s
Gasoline, all types	gal	1.60	7/01	11r
Gasoline, unleaded midgrade	gal	1.65	7/01	11r
Gasoline, unleaded premium	gal	1.74	7/01	11r
Natural gas, expenditures on	yr	164	1999	30r
Utility (piped) gas, therm		1.01	7/01	11r
Utility (piped) gas, 40 therms		44.29	7/01	11r
Utility (piped) gas, 100 therms		97.44	7/01	11r
Entertainment				
Entertainment purchases	yr	1574	1999	30r
Fees and admissions paid	yr	371	1999	30r
Reading purchases	yr	121	1999	30r
Television, radios, sound equipment, expenditures on	yr	561	1999	30r
Funerals				
Total cost of funeral		5922.53	1/99	78r
Acknowledgement cards		63.43	1/99	78r
Casket		2258.77	1/99	78r
Cosmetology, hair, other preparation		127.09	1/99	78r
Embalming		393.49	1/99	78r
Funeral at funeral home		367.50	1/99	78r
Hearse (local)		169.66	1/99	78r
Professional service charges		1211.32	1/99	78r
Service car/van		80.69	1/99	78r
Transfer of remains to funeral home		144.25	1/99	78r
Vault		803.50	1/99	78r
Visitation/viewing		302.83	1/99	78r
Groceries				
American processed cheese	lb	3.50	7/01	11r
Bakery products, expenditures on	yr	261	1999	30r
Bananas	lb	0.47	7/01	11r
Beans, dried, any type, all sizes	lb	0.63	7/01	11r
Beef for stew, boneless	lb	2.86	7/01	11r
Beef, expenditures on	yr	210	1999	30r
Bologna, all beef or mixed	lb	2.29	7/01	11r
Bread, French	lb	1.66	7/01	11r
Bread, white, pan	lb	0.87	7/01	11r
Bread, whole wheat, pan	lb	1.38	7/01	11r
Broccoli	lb	1.04	7/01	11r
Butter, salted, grade AA, stick	lb	2.26	7/01	11r
Butter, yoghurt, cheese, etc, expenditures on	yr	170	1999	30r
Cabbage	lb	0.42	7/01	11r
Cereals and cereal products, expenditures on	yr	140	1999	30r
Cheddar cheese, natural	lb	3.75	7/01	11r
Chicken breast, bone-in	lb	1.85	7/01	11r
Chicken legs, bone-in	lb	1.34	7/01	11r
Chicken, fresh, whole	lb	1.05	7/01	11r
Chops, boneless,	lb	4.13	7/01	11r
Chuck roast, graded and ungraded, excl U.S. prime and choice	lb	2.35	7/01	11r
Chuck roast, U.S. choice, boneless	lb	2.67	7/01	11r
Coffee, 100%, ground roast, all sizes	lb	2.88	7/01	11r
Coffee, instant, plain, regular, all sizes	16 oz	9.25	7/01	11r
Cola, non diet,	2 liter	1.11	7/01	11r
Crackers, soda, salted	lb	1.70	7/01	11r
Dairy product purchases	yr	282	1999	30r
Eggs, expenditures on	yr	32	1999	30r
Fats and oils, expenditures on	yr	79	1999	30r
Fish and seafood, expenditures on	yr	99	1999	30r
Flour, white, all purpose	lb	0.32	7/01	11r
Food (excl fruit and vegetables), eaten at home, purchases	yr	815	1999	30r
Food cooked on trips, expenditures on	yr	36	1999	30r
Food purchases	yr	4533	1999	30r
Food purchases, eaten away from home	yr	1873	1999	30r
Food purchases, food eaten at home	yr	2660	1999	30r
Fresh fruits, expenditures on	yr	128	1999	30r
Fresh milk and cream, expenditures on	yr	112	1999	30r
Fresh vegetables, expenditures on	yr	131	1999	30r
Fruit and vegetable purchases	yr	438	1999	30r

Columbia, MD - continued

Item	Per	Value	Date	Ref.
Groceries - continued				
Grapefruit	lb	0.59	7/01	11r
Grapes, Thompson, seedless	lb	2.12	7/01	11r
Ground beef, 100% beef	lb	1.76	7/01	11r
Ground beef, lean and extra lean	lb	2.60	7/01	11r
Ground chuck, 100% beef	lb	2.08	7/01	11r
Ham, boneless, excl canned	lb	2.71	7/01	11r
Ham, rump or shank half, bone-in, smoked	lb	2.19	7/01	11r
Ice cream, prepackaged, bulk, regular	1/2 gal	3.93	7/01	11r
Lemons	lb	1.32	7/01	11r
Lettuce, iceberg	lb	0.76	7/01	11r
Milk, fresh, low fat,	gal	2.75	7/01	11r
Milk, fresh, whole, fortified	gal	2.97	7/01	11r
Nonalcoholic beverages, expenditures on	yr	228	1999	30r
Orange juice, frozen concentrate	16 oz	1.95	7/01	11r
Oranges, Navel	lb	0.73	7/01	11r
Oranges, Valencia	lb	0.55	7/01	11r
Peanut butter, creamy, all sizes	lb	1.83	7/01	11r
Pears, Anjou	lb	0.98	7/01	11r
Pork chops, center cut, bone-in	lb	3.33	7/01	11r
Pork sausage, fresh, loose	lb	2.59	7/01	11r
Pork shoulder picnic, bone-in, smoked	lb	1.12	7/01	11r
Pork, expenditures on	yr	162	1999	30r
Potato chips	16 oz	3.59	7/01	11r
Potatoes, frozen, french fried	lb	1.00	7/01	11r
Potatoes, white, all types	lb	0.44	7/01	11r
Poultry, expenditures on	yr	137	1999	30r
Processed fruits, expenditures on	yr	97	1999	30r
Processed vegetables, expenditures on	yr	82	1999	30r
Rice, white, long grain, uncooked	lb	0.51	7/01	11r
Round roast, graded and ungraded, excl U.S. prime and choice	lb	2.96	7/01	11r
Round steak, graded and ungraded, excl U.S. prime and choice	lb	3.11	7/01	11r
Sirloin steak, graded and ungraded, excl U.S. prime and choice	lb	4.23	7/01	11r
Spaghetti and macaroni	lb	0.78	7/01	11r
Steak, round, U.S. choice, boneless	lb	3.56	7/01	11r
Steak, sirloin, U.S. choice, boneless	lb	5.65	7/01	11r
Strawberries, dry pint	12 oz	1.50	7/01	11r
Sugar and other sweets, expenditures on	yr	99	1999	30r
Sugar, white, 33-80 ounce package	lb	0.39	7/01	11r
Sugar, white, all sizes	lb	0.42	7/01	11r
Tobacco products and smoking supplies purchases	yr	288	1999	30r
Tomatoes, field grown	lb	1.43	7/01	11r
Tuna, light, chunk	lb	1.77	7/01	11r
Turkey, frozen, whole	lb	1.05	7/01	11r
Goods and Services				
B&B Japanese maple (acer japonicum)	gal	49.98- 129.00	4/00	93r
Boxwood (buxus)	2 gal	12.99- 16.99	4/00	93r
Daylilly (hemerocallis)	gal	4.99- 8.99	4/00	93r
Flat of annuals		11.00- 13.92	4/00	93r
Fountain grass (pennisetum)	gal	5.98- 7.98	4/00	93r
Hanging basket (10 in)		7.99- 14.98	4/00	93r
Hardy geranium (geranium)	gal	5.98- 8.00	4/00	93r
Hosta (hosta)	gal	4.99- 10.98	4/00	93r
Lilac (syrubga vulgaris)	2 gal	12.99- 21.99	4/00	93r
Rhododendron (rhododendron)	2 gal	14.99- 24.99	4/00	93r
Sage (salvia)	gal	5.98- 6.99	4/00	93r
Wintercreeper euonymus (euonymus fortunei)	2 gal	7.99- 89.99	4/00	93r

Values are in dollars or fractions of dollars. In the column headed *Ref*, references are shown to sources. Each reference is followed by a letter. These refer to the geographical level for which data were reported: s=State, r=Region, and c=City or metro. The abbreviation *ex* is used to mean *except* or *excluding*; *exp* stands for *expenditures*. For other abbreviations and further explanations, please see the Introduction.

Columbia, MD - continued

Item	Per	Value	Date	Ref.
Goods and Services				
Hunting license	yr	15.50	4/01	34s
Health Care				
Cardiac catheterization, ave hospital/ physician charges		11420	1998	77s
Childbirth, Cesarean delivery		11587	1997	13r
Childbirth, vaginal delivery		6725	1997	13r
Drugs, expenditures on	yr	399	1999	30r
Health care purchases	yr	1971	1999	30r
Health insurance expenditures	yr	933	1999	30r
Hysterectomy, laproscopically-assisted, ave hospital/physician charges		11890	1998	76s
Hysterectomy, vaginal, ave hospital and physician charges		8120	1998	76s
Medicaid dispensing fee		4.21	1999	87s
Medical services expenditures	yr	547	1999	30r
Medical supplies, expenditures on	yr	91	1999	30r
Plastic surgery, breast augmentation		2870	2000	7r
Plastic surgery, breast lift		3649	2000	7r
Plastic surgery, facelift		5008	2000	7r
Plastic surgery, hair transplantation		3425	2000	7r
Plastic surgery, lip augmentation		1227	2000	7r
Plastic surgery, lower body lift		4793	2000	7r
Plastic surgery, thigh lift		3862	2000	7r
Household Goods				
Floor coverings, expenditures on	yr	44	1999	30r
Furniture, expenditures on	yr	335	1999	30r
Household furnishings and equipment purchases	yr	1328	1999	30r
Household textiles, expenditures on	yr	89	1999	30r
Laundry and cleaning supplies, expenditures on	yr	113	1999	30r
Housing				
Home price, existing, ave		160100	10/00	90r
Home value, median		146000	2001	53s
Household operation expenditures	yr	553	1999	30r
Housekeeping supplies purchases	yr	473	1999	30r
Housing, expenditures on	yr	10303	1999	30r
Maintenance, repairs, insurance expenditures	yr	699	1999	30r
Monthly rental value of owned home	mos	505	1999	30r
Owned dwellings, expenditures own	yr	3465	1999	30r
Rent expenditures	yr	1641	1999	30r
Rental unit, 1 bedroom, with utilities	mos	773	4/01	41c
Rental unit, 2 bedroom, with utilities	mos	901	4/01	41c
Rental unit, 3 bedroom, with utilities	mos	1190	4/01	41c
Rental unit, 4 bedroom, with utilities	mos	1487	4/01	41c
Shelter, expenditures on	yr	5467	1999	30r
Insurance and Pensions				
Life and other personal insurance purchases	yr	414	1999	30r
Pensions and Social Security, expenditures on	yr	2635	1999	30r
Personal insurance and pensions, expenditures on	yr	3048	1999	30r
Legal Fees				
Driver's license fee	renew	20.00	1999	48s
Driver's license fee	orig	30.00	1999	48s
Fishing license	yr	9.00	4/01	34s
Personal Goods				
Personal care products and services purchases	yr	393	1999	30r
Personal Services				
Personal services, household, expenditures on	yr	258	1999	30r
Pets				
Pets, toys, and playground equipment, expenditures on	yr	306	1999	30r

Columbia, MD - continued

Item	Per	Value	Date	Ref.
Taxes				
Federal income taxes paid	yr	2047	1999	30r
Personal taxes, expenditures on	yr	2554	1999	30r
Property taxes paid	yr	726	1999	30r
State and local income taxes paid	yr	363	1999	30r
Transportation				
Cars and trucks, new, expenditures on	yr	1648	1999	30r
Cars and trucks, used, expenditures on	yr	1651	1999	30r
Diesel at the pump	gal	1.29	10/99	73s
Gasoline and motor oil purchases	yr	1052	1999	30r
Gasoline before-tax price (cents)	gal	106.80	10/00	43s
Maintenance and repair expenditures	yr	621	1999	30r
Public transportation, expenditures on	yr	298	1999	30r
Transportation purchases	yr	6738	1999	30r
Vehicle expenses, miscellaneous, purchases	yr	2033	1999	30r
Vehicle insurance payments	yr	696	1999	30r
Vehicle purchases (net outlay)	yr	3354	1999	30r
Vehicle rental, lease expenditures	yr	352	1999	30r
Utilities				
Electrical bill, average	mos	83.58	9/00	9s
Electricity, expenditures on	yr	1115	1999	30r
Electricity cost, average	KWh	6.90	9/00	9s
Water and other public services, expenditures on	yr	298	1999	30r
Weddings				
Wedding (national average cost)		19936	2000	33r
Wedding (regional average total cost)		16293	1997	110r
Attendants' gifts		321	1998	33r
Bridal attendants' apparel (5 persons)		824	2000	33r
Bride's headpiece/veil		173	1998	33r
Bride's wedding dress		859	1998	33r
Clergy, religious facility fee		242	1998	33r
Engagement ring		3177	1998	33r
Flowers		789	1998	33r
Groom's formalwear rental		99	2000	33r
Limousine		410	1998	33r
Marriage license cost		55.00	4/01	35s
Men's formalwear (ushers, best man)		469	2000	33r
Mother of bride apparel		241	2000	33r
Music		866	1998	33r
Photography and videography		1368	1998	33r
Rehearsal dinner		728	1998	33r
Wedding invitations and announcements		341	1998	33r
Wedding reception		7968	2000	33r
Wedding rings (bride and groom)		1060	1998	33r

Columbia, MO

Item	Per	Value	Date	Ref.
Average annual expenditures	yr	35369	1999	30r
Composite, ACCRA index		98.60	3/01	4c
Alcoholic Beverages				
Alcoholic beverage purchases	yr	304	1999	30r
Beer, Heineken, 12-oz, ex deposit	6	7.35	3/01	4c
J & B Scotch	750-ml	20.84	3/01	4c
Malt beverages, all types, all sizes, any origin	16 oz	0.93	7/01	11r
Wine, Livingston or Gallo, Chablis blanc	1.5 liter	6.25	3/01	4c
Wine, red and white table, all sizes, any origin	liter	7.04	7/01	11r
Appliances				
Appliance repair, service call, washing machine	min lab chg	47.88	3/01	4c
Major appliances, expenditures on	yr	165	1999	30r
Small appliances, housewares, expenditures on	yr	90	1999	30r
Banking and Money				
Mortgage interest and charges paid	yr	2277	1999	30r
Mortgage principal paid on owned property	yr	1230	1999	30r
Mortgage rate, incl. points and orig. fee, 30-yr. conv. fixed or ARM	mos	7.14	3/01	4c

Values are in dollars or fractions of dollars. In the column headed *Ref*, references are shown to sources. Each reference is followed by a letter. These refer to the geographical level for which data were reported: s=State, r=Region, and c=City or metro. The abbreviation *ex* is used to mean *except* or *excluding*; *exp* stands for expenditures. For other abbreviations and further explanations, please see the Introduction.

Columbia, MO - continued

Item	Per	Value	Date	Ref.
Banking and Money				
Vehicle finance charges paid	yr	328	1999	30r
Charity				
Cash contributions, expenditures	yr	1126	1999	30r
Child Care				
Child raising cost, total, age 0-2	yr	7890	1999	60r
Child raising cost, total, age 3-5	yr	8130	1999	60r
Child raising cost, total, age 6-8	yr	8170	1999	60r
Child raising cost, total, age 9-11	yr	8190	1999	60r
Child raising cost, total, age 12-14	yr	8890	1999	60r
Child raising cost, total, age 15-17	yr	9050	1999	60r
Child's child care and education, age 0-2	yr	1240	1999	60r
Child's child care and education, age 3-5	yr	1370	1999	60r
Child's child care and education, age 6-8	yr	880	1999	60r
Child's child care and education, age 9-11	yr	570	1999	60r
Child's child care and education, age 12-14	yr	420	1999	60r
Child's child care and education, age 15-17	yr	720	1999	60r
Child's clothing, age 0-2	yr	410	1999	60r
Child's clothing, age 3-5	yr	400	1999	60r
Child's clothing, age 6-8	yr	450	1999	60r
Child's clothing, age 9-11	yr	500	1999	60r
Child's clothing, age 12-14	yr	840	1999	60r
Child's clothing, age 15-17	yr	740	1999	60r
Child's food, age 0-2	yr	960	1999	60r
Child's food, age 3-5	yr	1120	1999	60r
Child's food, age 6-8	yr	1430	1999	60r
Child's food, age 9-11	yr	1710	1999	60r
Child's food, age 12-14	yr	1710	1999	60r
Child's food, age 15-17	yr	1920	1999	60r
Child's health care, age 0-2	yr	520	1999	60r
Child's health care, age 3-5	yr	500	1999	60r
Child's health care, age 6-8	yr	570	1999	60r
Child's health care, age 9-11	yr	610	1999	60r
Child's health care, age 12-14	yr	630	1999	60r
Child's health care, age 15-17	yr	650	1999	60r
Child's housing, age 0-2	yr	2860	1999	60r
Child's housing, age 3-5	yr	2840	1999	60r
Child's housing, age 6-8	yr	2800	1999	60r
Child's housing, age 9-11	yr	2650	1999	60r
Child's housing, age 12-14	yr	2840	1999	60r
Child's housing, age 15-17	yr	2440	1999	60r
Child's personal care, reading, age 0-2	yr	880	1999	60r
Child's personal care, reading, age 3-5	yr	900	1999	60r
Child's personal care, reading, age 6-8	yr	930	1999	60r
Child's personal care, reading, age 9-11	yr	970	1999	60r
Child's personal care, reading, age 12-14	yr	1150	1999	60r
Child's personal care, reading, age 15-17	yr	920	1999	60r
Clothing				
Apparel and services purchases	yr	1607	1999	30r
Boys' brief, cotton	3	5.84	3/01	4c
Boys, 2 to 15, expenditures on	yr	91	1999	30r
Children under 2, expenditures on	yr	59	1999	30r
Footwear, expenditures on	yr	285	1999	30r
Girls, 2 to 15, expenditures on	yr	116	1999	30r
Men and boys, expenditures on	yr	433	1999	30r
Men, 16 and over, expenditures on	yr	341	1999	30r
Shirt, man's dress shirt		25.50	3/01	4c
Slacks, man's "No Wrinkles" khaki		36.00	3/01	4c
Women, 16 and over, expenditures on	yr	490	1999	30r
Communications				
Newspaper subscription, daily and Sunday delivery	mos	10.28	3/01	4c
Phone line, single, business, field visit	inst.	52.25	12/97	17s
Phone line, single, business, no field visit	inst.	52.25	12/97	17s
Phone line, single, residence, field visit	inst.	36.50	12/97	17s
Phone line, single, residence, no field visit	inst.	36.50	12/97	17s
Postage and stationery, expenditures on	yr	140	1999	30r
Postal rate, express mail, up to half-pound		12.45	7/01	108r
Postal rate, letter, first class, first ounce		0.34	7/01	108r
Postal rate, letter, two ounces		0.57	7/01	108r
Postal rate, post card		0.21	7/01	108r

Columbia, MO - continued

Item	Per	Value	Date	Ref.
Communications - continued				
Postal rate, priority mail, two pounds		3.95	7/01	108r
Postal rate, priority mail, up to one pound		3.50	7/01	108r
Telephone bill, family of three	mos	14.60	3/01	4c
Telephone services, expenditures on	yr	830	1999	30r
Education				
Board, 4-year private college/university	yr	2387	1996	38s
Board, 4-year public college/university	yr	1713	1996	38s
Education expenditures	yr	583	1999	30r
Room, 4-year private college/university	yr	2162	1996	38s
Room, 4-year public college/university	yr	2022	1996	38s
Total cost, 4-year private college/university	yr	14116	1996	38s
Total cost, 4-year public college/university	yr	6750	1996	38s
Tuition, 2-year public college/university, in state	yr	1255	1996	38s
Tuition, 4-year private college/university, in state	yr	9566	1996	38s
Tuition, 4-year public college/university	yr	3015	1996	38s
Energy and Fuels				
Electricity	500 KWhs	46.59	7/01	11r
Energy, combined forms, 2400 sq ft	mos	118.59	3/01	4c
Energy, exc. electricity, 2400 sq ft	mos	63.79	3/01	4c
Fuel oil #2	gal	1.27	7/01	11r
Fuel oil and other fuels, expenditures on	yr	68	1999	30r
Gas, cooking, winter, 10 therms	mos	10.66	2/96	98c
Gas, cooking, winter, 30 therms	mos	19.77	2/96	98c
Gas, cooking, winter, 50 therms	mos	28.89	2/96	98c
Gas, heating, winter, average use	mos	77.48	2/96	98c
Gas, natural, commercial rate	1000 cf	8.38	11/00	88s
Gas, regular unleaded, cash, self-service	gal	1.36	3/01	4c
Gasoline, unleaded midgrade	gal	1.79	7/01	11r
Gasoline, unleaded premium	gal	1.86	7/01	11r
Gasoline, unleaded regular	gal	1.58	7/01	11r
Natural gas, expenditures on	yr	389	1999	30r
Utility (piped) gas, therm		0.81	7/01	11r
Utility (piped) gas, 40 therms		38.01	7/01	11r
Utility (piped) gas, 100 therms		81.75	7/01	11r
Entertainment				
Bowling, Saturday evening rate	line	2.88	3/01	4c
Entertainment purchases	yr	1984	1999	30r
Fees and admissions paid	yr	444	1999	30r
Monopoly game, Parker Brothers', No. 9	game	10.44	3/01	4c
Movie, first-run, Saturday, evening	adm.	6.75	3/01	4c
Television, radios, sound equipment, expenditures on	yr	580	1999	30r
Tennis balls, yellow, Wilson or Penn, 3	can	2.28	3/01	4c
Funerals				
Cosmetology, hair, other preparation		178.32	1/99	78r
Embalming		408.19	1/99	78r
Funeral at funeral home		362.13	1/99	78r
Professional service charges		1375.51	1/99	78r
Transfer of remains to funeral home		155.92	1/99	78r
Visitation/viewing		294.38	1/99	78r
Groceries				
Groceries, ACCRA Index		96.20	3/01	4c
Antibiotic ointment, Polysporin	0.5 oz	4.53	3/01	4c
Baby food, strained vegetables or fruit, lowest price	4-4.5 oz	0.33	3/01	4c
Bacon, sliced	lb	3.15	7/01	11r
Bakery products, expenditures on	yr	281	1999	30r
Bananas	lb	0.52	3/01	4c
Bananas	lb	0.48	7/01	11r
Beans, dried, any type, all sizes	lb	0.61	7/01	11r
Beef for stew, boneless	lb	3.08	7/01	11r
Beef or hamburger, ground	lb	1.29	3/01	4c
Beef, expenditures on	yr	217	1999	30r
Bologna, all beef or mixed	lb	2.52	7/01	11r
Bread, white	loaf	0.88	3/01	4c
Bread, white, pan	lb	1.06	7/01	11r

Values are in dollars or fractions of dollars. In the column headed *Ref*, references are shown to sources. Each reference is followed by a letter. These refer to the geographical level for which data were reported: s=State, r=Region, and c=City or metro. The abbreviation *ex* is used to mean *except* or *excluding*; *exp* stands for *expenditures*. For other abbreviations and further explanations, please see the Introduction.

Columbia, MO - continued

Item	Per	Value	Date	Ref.
Groceries				
Broccoli	lb	0.91	7/01	11r
Butter, salted, grade AA, stick	lb	3.04	7/01	11r
Butter, yoghurt, cheese, etc, expenditures on	yr	183	1999	30r
Cereals and bakery product purchases	yr	430	1999	30r
Cereals and cereal products, expenditures on	yr	149	1999	30r
Cheese, Kraft grated Parmesan	8 oz	3.70	3/01	4c
Chicken, fresh, whole	lb	1.07	7/01	11r
Chicken, whole fryer	lb	0.74	3/01	4c
Chops, boneless,	lb	3.64	7/01	11r
Chuck roast, U.S. choice, boneless	lb	2.47	7/01	11r
Cigarettes, Winston, Kings	carton	31.28	3/01	4c
Coffee, 100%, ground roast, all sizes	lb	2.69	7/01	11r
Coffee, vacuum-packed	13 oz	2.63	3/01	4c
Cookies, chocolate chip	lb	2.87	7/01	11r
Corn Flakes, Kellogg's or Post Toasties	18 oz	2.55	3/01	4c
Corn, frozen, whole kernel, lowest price	16 oz	1.12	3/01	4c
Dairy product purchases	yr	304	1999	30r
Eggs, expenditures on	yr	26	1999	30r
Eggs, Grade A or AA	dozen	1.13	3/01	4c
Eggs, grade A, large	dozen	0.88	7/01	11r
Fats and oils, expenditures on	yr	75	1999	30r
Fish and seafood, expenditures on	yr	72	1999	30r
Food (excl fruit and vegetables), eaten at home, purchases	yr	887	1999	30r
Food cooked on trips, expenditures on	yr	44	1999	30r
Food purchases	yr	4802	1999	30r
Food purchases, eaten away from home	yr	2069	1999	30r
Food purchases, food eaten at home	yr	2733	1999	30r
Fresh fruits, expenditures on	yr	138	1999	30r
Fresh milk and cream, expenditures on	yr	120	1999	30r
Fresh vegetables, expenditures on	yr	126	1999	30r
Grapefruit	lb	0.66	7/01	11r
Grapes, Thompson, seedless	lb	1.64	7/01	11r
Ground beef, 100% beef	lb	1.64	7/01	11r
Ground beef, lean and extra lean	lb	2.16	7/01	11r
Ground chuck, 100% beef	lb	2.13	7/01	11r
Ham, boneless, excl canned	lb	2.62	7/01	11r
Ice cream, prepackaged, bulk, regular	1/2 gal	3.35	7/01	11r
Lemons	lb	1.19	7/01	11r
Lettuce, iceberg	head	0.98	3/01	4c
Lettuce, iceberg	lb	0.73	7/01	11r
Margarine, Blue Bonnet or Parkay, stick	lb	0.73	3/01	4c
Margarine, soft, tubs	lb	0.89	7/01	11r
Meats, poultry, fish, and egg purchases	yr	671	1999	30r
Milk, fresh, whole, fortified	gal	2.71	7/01	11r
Milk, whole	1/2 gal	1.65	3/01	4c
Nonalcoholic beverages, expenditures on	yr	239	1999	30r
Orange juice, Minute Maid frozen	12 oz	1.99	3/01	4c
Oranges, Navel	lb	0.80	7/01	11r
Oranges, Valencia	lb	0.66	7/01	11r
Peaches, halves or slices, Hunt's, Del Monte, or Libby's	29 oz	1.49	3/01	4c
Pears, Anjou	lb	0.93	7/01	11r
Peas, green, Del Monte or Green Giant	15 oz	0.72	3/01	4c
Pork chops, center cut, bone-in	lb	3.63	7/01	11r
Pork, expenditures on	yr	150	1999	30r
Potato chips	16 oz	3.52	7/01	11r
Potatoes, frozen, french fried	lb	1.08	7/01	11r
Potatoes, white or red	10 lb	2.47	3/01	4c
Potatoes, white, all types	lb	0.33	7/01	11r
Poultry, expenditures on	yr	108	1999	30r
Processed fruits, expenditures on	yr	98	1999	30r
Processed vegetables, expenditures on	yr	80	1999	30r
Round roast, U.S. choice, boneless	lb	3.07	7/01	11r
Round steak, graded and ungraded, excl U.S. prime and choice	lb	3.41	7/01	11r
Sausage, Jimmy Dean/Owens pork	lb	3.05	3/01	4c
Shortening, vegetable oil blends	lb	1.13	7/01	11r
Shortening, vegetable, Crisco	3 lb	2.78	3/01	4c
Soft drink, Coca Cola, ex deposit	2 liter	1.15	3/01	4c
Spaghetti and macaroni	lb	0.80	7/01	11r

Columbia, MO - continued

Item	Per	Value	Date	Ref.
Groceries - continued				
Steak, round, U.S. choice, boneless	lb	3.23	7/01	11r
Steak, T-bone	lb	6.34	3/01	4c
Steak, T-bone, U.S. choice, bone-in	lb	6.68	7/01	11r
Strawberries, dry pint	12 oz	1.32	7/01	11r
Sugar and other sweets, expenditures on	yr	114	1999	30r
Sugar, cane or beet	4 lbs	1.44	3/01	4c
Sugar, white, 33-80 ounce package	lb	0.42	7/01	11r
Sugar, white, all sizes	lb	0.43	7/01	11r
Tobacco products and smoking supplies purchases	yr	331	1999	30r
Tomatoes, field grown	lb	1.46	7/01	11r
Tomatoes, Hunt's or Del Monte	14.5 oz	0.93	3/01	4c
Tuna, chunk, light	6 oz	0.65	3/01	4c
Tuna, light, chunk	lb	1.80	7/01	11r
Turkey, frozen, whole	lb	1.15	7/01	11r
Goods and Services				
Miscellaneous goods and services, ACCRA Index		102.10	3/01	4c
B&B Japanese maple (acer japonicum)	gal	29.99-169.99	4/00	93r
Boxwood (buxus)	2 gal	18.99-39.99	4/00	93r
Daylilly (hemerocallis)	gal	4.99-25.00	4/00	93r
Flat of annuals		11.98-24.99	4/00	93r
Fountain grass (pennisetum)	gal	5.98-12.98	4/00	93r
Hanging basket (10 in)		12.99-27.99	4/00	93r
Hardy geranium (geranium)	gal	7.99-9.99	4/00	93r
Hosta (hosta)	gal	6.00-25.00	4/00	93r
Lilac (syrubga vulgaris)	2 gal	14.99-24.99	4/00	93r
Miscellaneous purchases	yr	865	1999	30r
Rhododendron (rhododendron)	2 gal	23.98-42.99	4/00	93r
Sage (salvia)	gal	6.00-9.99	4/00	93r
Wintercreeper euonymus (euonymus fortunei)	2 gal	16.00-169.99	4/00	93r
Hunting license	yr	9.00	4/01	34s
Health Care				
Health care, ACCRA Index		96.50	3/01	4c
Cardiac catheterization, ave hospital/ physician charges		13930	1998	77s
Childbirth, Cesarean delivery		10722	1997	13r
Childbirth, vaginal delivery		6223	1997	13r
Dentist's fee, adult teeth cleaning and periodic oral exam	visit	74.71	3/01	4c
Doctor's fee, routine exam, established patient	visit	49.00	3/01	4c
Drugs, expenditures on	yr	394	1999	30r
Health care purchases	yr	2048	1999	30r
Health insurance expenditures	yr	978	1999	30r
Hospital care, private room	day	561.67	3/01	4c
Hysterectomy, laproscopically-assisted, ave hospital/physician charges		11300	1998	76s
Hysterectomy, vaginal, ave hospital and physician charges		9200	1998	76s
Medicaid dispensing fee		4.09	1999	87s
Medical services expenditures	yr	554	1999	30r
Medical supplies, expenditures on	yr	122	1999	30r
Plastic surgery, breast augmentation		3184	2000	7r
Plastic surgery, breast lift		3585	2000	7r
Plastic surgery, facelift		4999	2000	7r
Plastic surgery, hair transplantation		3105	2000	7r
Plastic surgery, lip augmentation		1290	2000	7r
Plastic surgery, lower body lift		8135	2000	7r

Values are in dollars or fractions of dollars. In the column headed *Ref*, references are shown to sources. Each reference is followed by a letter. These refer to the geographical level for which data were reported: s=State, r=Region, and c=City or metro. The abbreviation *ex* is used to mean *except* or *excluding*; *exp* stands for *expenditures*. For other abbreviations and further explanations, please see the Introduction.

Columbia, MO - continued

Item	Per	Value	Date	Ref.
Health Care				
Plastic surgery, thigh lift		3839	2000	7r
Household Goods				
Dishwashing powder, Cascade	50 oz	3.14	3/01	4c
Floor coverings, expenditures on	yr	52	1999	30r
Furniture, expenditures on	yr	344	1999	30r
Household furnishings and equipment purchases	yr	1475	1999	30r
Household textiles, expenditures on	yr	109	1999	30r
Laundry and cleaning supplies, expenditures on	yr	134	1999	30r
Tissues, facial, Kleenex brand	175	1.27	3/01	4c
Housing				
Housing, ACCRA Index		97.00	3/01	4c
Home price, existing, ave		144400	10/00	90r
Home value, median		89000	2001	53s
House, 2400 sq ft, 8000 sq ft lot, new, urban, utilities	total	206100	3/01	4c
House payment, principal and interest, 25% down payment	mos	1043	3/01	4c
Household operation expenditures	yr	542	1999	30r
Housekeeping supplies purchases	yr	508	1999	30r
Lodging expenditures	yr	430	1999	30r
Maintenance, repairs, insurance expenditures	yr	853	1999	30r
Monthly rental value of owned home	mos	547	1999	30r
Owned dwellings, expenditures own	yr	4282	1999	30r
Rent expenditures	yr	1558	1999	30r
Rent, apartment, 2 br, 1 1/2-2 baths, unfurn, 950 sq ft, water	mos	562	3/01	4c
Rental unit, 1 bedroom, with utilities	mos	374	4/01	41c
Rental unit, 2 bedroom, with utilities	mos	487	4/01	41c
Rental unit, 3 bedroom, with utilities	mos	677	4/01	41c
Rental unit, 4 bedroom, with utilities	mos	798	4/01	41c
Shelter, expenditures on	yr	6270	1999	30r
Insurance and Pensions				
Life and other personal insurance purchases	yr	387	1999	30r
Pensions and Social Security, expenditures on	yr	2968	1999	30r
Legal Fees				
Driver's license fee	orig	15.00	1999	48s
Driver's license fee	renew	15.00	1999	48s
Fishing license	yr	11.00	4/01	34s
Personal Goods				
Personal care products and services purchases	yr	385	1999	30r
Shampoo, Alberto VO5	15 oz	1.25	3/01	4c
Toothpaste, Crest or Colgate	6-7 oz	2.35	3/01	4c
Personal Services				
Dry cleaning, man's 2-pc suit		7.24	3/01	4c
Man's haircut, barbershop, no styling		10.29	3/01	4c
Personal services, household, expenditures on	yr	300	1999	30r
Woman's shampoo, trim, blow-dry, no style-change		27.30	3/01	4c
Pets				
Pets, toys, and playground equipment, expenditures on	yr	375	1999	30r
Restaurant Food				
Chicken, fried, thigh and drumstick, KFC/Church's		2.79	3/01	4c
Hamburger with cheese, McDonald's	1/4 lb	2.19	3/01	4c
Pizza, Pizza Hut or Pizza Inn	11-12 in	9.99	3/01	4c
Taxes				
Federal income taxes paid	yr	2326	1999	30r
Personal taxes, expenditures on	yr	3223	1999	30r
Property taxes paid	yr	1152	1999	30r
State and local income taxes paid	yr	753	1999	30r

Columbia, MO - continued

Item	Per	Value	Date	Ref.
Transportation				
Transportation, ACCRA Index		100.60	3/01	4c
Cars and trucks, new, expenditures on	yr	1280	1999	30r
Cars and trucks, used, expenditures on	yr	1763	1999	30r
Diesel at the pump	gal	1.16	10/99	73s
Gasoline and motor oil purchases	yr	1036	1999	30r
Gasoline before-tax price (cents)	gal	108.50	10/00	43s
Maintenance and repair expenditures	yr	594	1999	30r
Public transportation, expenditures on	yr	341	1999	30r
Tire balance, computer or spin balance, front	wheel	8.37	3/01	4c
Transportation purchases	yr	6617	1999	30r
Vehicle expenses, miscellaneous, purchases	yr	2159	1999	30r
Vehicle insurance payments	yr	701	1999	30r
Vehicle purchases (net outlay)	yr	3081	1999	30r
Vehicle rental, lease expenditures	yr	536	1999	30r
Utilities				
Utilities, ACCRA Index		93.00	3/01	4c
Electrical bill, average	mos	68.50	9/00	9s
Electricity, expenditures on	yr	841	1999	30r
Electricity and other, mixed, 2400 sq ft, new home	mos	54.80	3/01	4c
Electricity cost, average	KWh	6.00	9/00	9s
Utilities, fuels, and public services purchased	yr	2401	1999	30r
Water and other public services, expenditures on	yr	273	1999	30r
Weddings				
Wedding (national average cost)		19936	2000	33r
Wedding (regional average total cost)		16195	1997	110r
Attendants' gifts		321	1998	33r
Bridal attendants' apparel (5 persons)		824	2000	33r
Bride's headpiece/veil		173	1998	33r
Bride's wedding dress		859	1998	33r
Clergy, religious facility fee		242	1998	33r
Engagement ring		3177	1998	33r
Flowers		789	1998	33r
Groom's formalwear rental		99	2000	33r
Limousine		410	1998	33r
Marriage license cost		50.00	4/01	35s
Men's formalwear (ushers, best man)		469	2000	33r
Mother of bride apparel		241	2000	33r
Music		866	1998	33r
Photography and videography		1368	1998	33r
Rehearsal dinner		728	1998	33r
Wedding invitations and announcements		341	1998	33r
Wedding reception		7968	2000	33r
Wedding rings (bride and groom)		1060	1998	33r

Columbia, SC

Item	Per	Value	Date	Ref.
Composite, ACCRA index		93.30	3/01	4c
Alcoholic Beverages				
Alcoholic beverage purchases	yr	253	1999	30r
Beer, Heineken, 12-oz, ex deposit	6	6.95	3/01	4c
J & B Scotch	750-ml	19.73	3/01	4c
Malt beverages, all types, all sizes, any origin	16 oz	0.96	7/01	11r
Wine, Livingston or Gallo, Chablis blanc	1.5 liter	6.29	3/01	4c
Appliances				
Appliance repair, service call, washing machine	min lab chg	42.40	3/01	4c
Major appliances, expenditures on	yr	172	1999	30r
Small appliances, housewares, expenditures on	yr	81	1999	30r
Banking and Money				
Mortgage interest and charges paid	yr	2039	1999	30r
Mortgage principal paid on owned property	yr	1026	1999	30r
Mortgage rate, incl. points and orig. fee, 30-yr. conv. fixed or ARM	mos	6.82	3/01	4c
Vehicle finance charges paid	yr	365	1999	30r

Values are in dollars or fractions of dollars. In the column headed *Ref*, references are shown to sources. Each reference is followed by a letter. These refer to the geographical level for which data were reported: s=State, r=Region, and c=City or metro. The abbreviation *ex* is used to mean *except* or *excluding; exp* stands for *expenditures*. For other abbreviations and further explanations, please see the Introduction.

Columbia, SC - continued

Item	Per	Value	Date	Ref.
Business Expenses				
Business travel, car rental	day	57	2001	3c
Business travel, food	day	41	2001	3c
Business travel, hotel	day	95	2001	3c
Charity				
Cash contributions, expenditures	yr	1127	1999	30r
Child Care				
Child raising cost, total, age 0-2	yr	8540	1999	60r
Child raising cost, total, age 3-5	yr	8780	1999	60r
Child raising cost, total, age 6-8	yr	8820	1999	60r
Child raising cost, total, age 9-11	yr	8800	1999	60r
Child raising cost, total, age 12-14	yr	9510	1999	60r
Child raising cost, total, age 15-17	yr	9740	1999	60r
Child's child care and education, age 0-2	yr	1380	1999	60r
Child's child care and education, age 3-5	yr	1520	1999	60r
Child's child care and education, age 6-8	yr	990	1999	60r
Child's child care and education, age 9-11	yr	650	1999	60r
Child's child care and education, age 12-14	yr	490	1999	60r
Child's child care and education, age 15-17	yr	840	1999	60r
Child's clothing, age 0-2	yr	480	1999	60r
Child's clothing, age 3-5	yr	470	1999	60r
Child's clothing, age 6-8	yr	520	1999	60r
Child's clothing, age 9-11	yr	570	1999	60r
Child's clothing, age 12-14	yr	950	1999	60r
Child's clothing, age 15-17	yr	850	1999	60r
Child's food, age 0-2	yr	1000	1999	60r
Child's food, age 3-5	yr	1160	1999	60r
Child's food, age 6-8	yr	1490	1999	60r
Child's food, age 9-11	yr	1770	1999	60r
Child's food, age 12-14	yr	1770	1999	60r
Child's food, age 15-17	yr	1980	1999	60r
Child's health care, age 0-2	yr	620	1999	60r
Child's health care, age 3-5	yr	590	1999	60r
Child's health care, age 6-8	yr	680	1999	60r
Child's health care, age 9-11	yr	720	1999	60r
Child's health care, age 12-14	yr	730	1999	60r
Child's health care, age 15-17	yr	760	1999	60r
Child's housing, age 0-2	yr	3070	1999	60r
Child's housing, age 3-5	yr	3050	1999	60r
Child's housing, age 6-8	yr	3010	1999	60r
Child's housing, age 9-11	yr	2850	1999	60r
Child's housing, age 12-14	yr	3040	1999	60r
Child's housing, age 15-17	yr	2650	1999	60r
Child's personal care, reading, age 0-2	yr	910	1999	60r
Child's personal care, reading, age 3-5	yr	930	1999	60r
Child's personal care, reading, age 6-8	yr	960	1999	60r
Child's personal care, reading, age 9-11	yr	1000	1999	60r
Child's personal care, reading, age 12-14	yr	1170	1999	60r
Child's personal care, reading, age 15-17	yr	950	1999	60r
Daycare	mos	338	1998	37c
Daycare, 3-year old, 5 days, 8 hrs/day	mos	338	1998	85c
Clothing				
Apparel and services purchases	yr	1610	1999	30r
Boys' brief, cotton	3	3.64	3/01	4c
Boys, 2 to 15, expenditures on	yr	89	1999	30r
Children under 2, expenditures on	yr	79	1999	30r
Footwear, expenditures on	yr	283	1999	30r
Girls, 2 to 15, expenditures on	yr	103	1999	30r
Men and boys, expenditures on	yr	351	1999	30r
Men, 16 and over, expenditures on	yr	262	1999	30r
Shirt, man's dress shirt		23.60	3/01	4c
Slacks, man's "No Wrinkles" khaki		30.99	3/01	4c
Women, 16 and over, expenditures on	yr	538	1999	30r
Communications				
Cable modem installation, Adelphi		54.90	6/99	103s
Cable modem installation, Comcast		95.00	6/99	103s
Cable modem installation, Intermedia		149.95	6/99	103s
Cable modem rate, cable subscriber, Adelphi	mos	34.95	6/99	103s
Cable modem rate, cable subscriber, Comcast	mos	39.95	6/99	103s

Columbia, SC - continued

Item	Per	Value	Date	Ref.
Communications - continued				
Cable modem rate, cable subscriber, Intermedia	mos	49.95	6/99	103s
Cable modem rate, non-cable subscriber, Adelphi	mos	44.95	6/99	103s
Cable modem rate, non-cable subscriber, Comcast	mos	49.95	6/99	103s
Cable modem rate, non-cable subscriber, Intermedia	mos	54.95	6/99	103s
Newspaper subscription, daily and Sunday delivery	mos	14.32	3/01	4c
Phone line, single, business, field visit	inst.	64.00	12/97	17s
Phone line, single, business, no field visit	inst.	64.00	12/97	17s
Phone line, single, residence, field visit	inst.	40.00	12/97	17s
Phone line, single, residence, no field visit	inst.	40.00	12/97	17s
Postage and stationery, expenditures on	yr	104	1999	30r
Postal rate, express mail, up to half-pound		12.45	7/01	108r
Postal rate, letter, first class, first ounce		0.34	7/01	108r
Postal rate, letter, two ounces		0.57	7/01	108r
Postal rate, post card		0.21	7/01	108r
Postal rate, priority mail, two pounds		3.95	7/01	108r
Postal rate, priority mail, up to one pound		3.50	7/01	108r
Telephone bill, business, basic rate	mos	43.75	12/97	18c
Telephone bill, family of three	mos	23.89	3/01	4c
Telephone bill, residential, basic rate	mos	16.40	12/97	18c
Telephone services, expenditures on	yr	860	1999	30r
Education				
Board, 4-year private college/university	yr	1990	1996	38s
Board, 4-year public college/university	yr	1872	1996	38s
Education expenditures	yr	431	1999	30r
Room, 4-year private college/university	yr	1786	1996	38s
Room, 4-year public college/university	yr	1998	1996	38s
Total cost, 4-year private college/university	yr	13517	1996	38s
Total cost, 4-year public college/university	yr	6964	1996	38s
Tuition, 2-year public college/university, in state	yr	1071	1996	38s
Tuition, 4-year private college/university, in state	yr	9741	1996	38s
Tuition, 4-year public college/university	yr	3094	1996	38s
Energy and Fuels				
Electricity	500 KWhs	47.29	7/01	11r
Electricity	KWh	0.09	7/01	11r
Energy, combined forms, 2400 sq ft	mos	117.47	3/01	4c
Fuel oil #2	gal	1.43	7/01	11r
Fuel oil and other fuels, expenditures on	yr	45	1999	30r
Gas, cooking, winter, 10 therms	mos	9.55	2/96	98c
Gas, cooking, winter, 30 therms	mos	22.99	2/96	98c
Gas, cooking, winter, 50 therms	mos	37.41	2/96	98c
Gas, heating, winter, average use	mos	95.06	2/96	98c
Gas, natural, commercial rate	1000 cf	9.50	11/00	88s
Gas, regular unleaded, cash, self-service	gal	1.30	3/01	4c
Gasoline, all types	gal	1.60	7/01	11r
Gasoline, unleaded midgrade	gal	1.65	7/01	11r
Gasoline, unleaded premium	gal	1.74	7/01	11r
Natural gas, expenditures on	yr	164	1999	30r
Utility (piped) gas, therm		1.01	7/01	11r
Utility (piped) gas, 40 therms		44.29	7/01	11r
Utility (piped) gas, 100 therms		97.44	7/01	11r
Entertainment				
Bowling, Saturday evening rate	line	3.10	3/01	4c
Entertainment purchases	yr	1574	1999	30r
Fees and admissions paid	yr	371	1999	30r
Monopoly game, Parker Brothers', No. 9	game	9.67	3/01	4c
Movie, first-run, Saturday, evening	adm.	6.90	3/01	4c
Reading purchases	yr	121	1999	30r
Television, radios, sound equipment, expenditures on	yr	561	1999	30r
Tennis balls, yellow, Wilson or Penn, 3	can	2.75	3/01	4c

Values are in dollars or fractions of dollars. In the column headed *Ref*, references are shown as sources. Each reference is followed by a letter. These refer to the geographical level for which data were reported: s=State, r=Region, and c=City or metro. The abbreviation *ex* is used to mean *except* or *excluding*; *exp* stands for expenditures. For other abbreviations and further explanations, please see the Introduction.

Columbia, SC - continued

Item	Per	Value	Date	Ref.
Funerals				
Total cost of funeral		5922.53	1/99	78r
Acknowledgement cards		63.43	1/99	78r
Casket		2258.77	1/99	78r
Cosmetology, hair, other preparation		127.09	1/99	78r
Embalming		393.49	1/99	78r
Funeral at funeral home		367.50	1/99	78r
Hearse (local)		169.66	1/99	78r
Professional service charges		1211.32	1/99	78r
Service car/van		80.69	1/99	78r
Transfer of remains to funeral home		144.25	1/99	78r
Vault		803.50	1/99	78r
Visitation/viewing		302.83	1/99	78r
Groceries				
Groceries, ACCRA Index		100.50	3/01	4c
American processed cheese	lb	3.50	7/01	11r
Antibiotic ointment, Polysporin	0.5 oz	4.56	3/01	4c
Baby food, strained vegetables or fruit, lowest price	4-4.5 oz	0.46	3/01	4c
Bakery products, expenditures on	yr	261	1999	30r
Bananas	lb	0.52	3/01	4c
Bananas	lb	0.47	7/01	11r
Beans, dried, any type, all sizes	lb	0.63	7/01	11r
Beef for stew, boneless	lb	2.86	7/01	11r
Beef or hamburger, ground	lb	1.61	3/01	4c
Beef, expenditures on	yr	210	1999	30r
Bologna, all beef or mixed	lb	2.29	7/01	11r
Bread, French	lb	1.66	7/01	11r
Bread, white	loaf	0.99	3/01	4c
Bread, white, pan	lb	0.87	7/01	11r
Bread, whole wheat, pan	lb	1.38	7/01	11r
Broccoli	lb	1.04	7/01	11r
Butter, salted, grade AA, stick	lb	2.26	7/01	11r
Butter, yoghurt, cheese, etc, expenditures on	yr	170	1999	30r
Cabbage	lb	0.42	7/01	11r
Cereals and cereal products, expenditures on	yr	140	1999	30r
Cheddar cheese, natural	lb	3.75	7/01	11r
Cheese, Kraft grated Parmesan	8 oz	3.45	3/01	4c
Chicken breast, bone-in	lb	1.85	7/01	11r
Chicken legs, bone-in	lb	1.34	7/01	11r
Chicken, fresh, whole	lb	1.05	7/01	11r
Chicken, whole fryer	lb	0.99	3/01	4c
Chops, boneless,	lb	4.13	7/01	11r
Chuck roast, graded and ungraded, excl U.S. prime and choice	lb	2.35	7/01	11r
Chuck roast, U.S. choice, boneless	lb	2.67	7/01	11r
Cigarettes, Winston, Kings	carton	25.67	3/01	4c
Coffee, 100%, ground roast, all sizes	lb	2.88	7/01	11r
Coffee, instant, plain, regular, all sizes	16 oz	9.25	7/01	11r
Coffee, vacuum-packed	13 oz	2.27	3/01	4c
Cola, non diet,	2 liter	1.11	7/01	11r
Corn Flakes, Kellogg's or Post Toasties	18 oz	2.73	3/01	4c
Corn, frozen, whole kernel, lowest price	16 oz	1.17	3/01	4c
Crackers, soda, salted	lb	1.70	7/01	11r
Dairy product purchases	yr	282	1999	30r
Eggs, expenditures on	yr	32	1999	30r
Eggs, Grade A or AA	dozen	1.33	3/01	4c
Fats and oils, expenditures on	yr	79	1999	30r
Fish and seafood, expenditures on	yr	99	1999	30r
Flour, white, all purpose	lb	0.32	7/01	11r
Food (excl fruit and vegetables), eaten at home, purchases	yr	815	1999	30r
Food cooked on trips, expenditures on	yr	36	1999	30r
Food purchases	yr	4533	1999	30r
Food purchases, eaten away from home	yr	1873	1999	30r
Food purchases, food eaten at home	yr	2660	1999	30r
Fresh fruits, expenditures on	yr	128	1999	30r
Fresh milk and cream, expenditures on	yr	112	1999	30r
Fresh vegetables, expenditures on	yr	131	1999	30r
Fruit and vegetable purchases	yr	438	1999	30r
Grapefruit	lb	0.59	7/01	11r
Grapes, Thompson, seedless	lb	2.12	7/01	11r

Columbia, SC - continued

Item	Per	Value	Date	Ref.
Groceries - continued				
Ground beef, 100% beef	lb	1.76	7/01	11r
Ground beef, lean and extra lean	lb	2.60	7/01	11r
Ground chuck, 100% beef	lb	2.08	7/01	11r
Ham, boneless, excl canned	lb	2.71	7/01	11r
Ham, rump or shank half, bone-in, smoked	lb	2.19	7/01	11r
Ice cream, prepackaged, bulk, regular	1/2 gal	3.93	7/01	11r
Lemons	lb	1.32	7/01	11r
Lettuce, iceberg	head	1.13	3/01	4c
Lettuce, iceberg	lb	0.76	7/01	11r
Margarine, Blue Bonnet or Parkay, stick	lb	0.67	3/01	4c
Milk, fresh, low fat,	gal	2.75	7/01	11r
Milk, fresh, whole, fortified	gal	2.97	7/01	11r
Milk, whole	1/2 gal	1.93	3/01	4c
Nonalcoholic beverages, expenditures on	yr	228	1999	30r
Orange juice, frozen concentrate	16 oz	1.95	7/01	11r
Orange juice, Minute Maid frozen	12 oz	1.39	3/01	4c
Oranges, Navel	lb	0.73	7/01	11r
Oranges, Valencia	lb	0.55	7/01	11r
Peaches, halves or slices, Hunt's, Del Monte, or Libby's	29 oz	1.64	3/01	4c
Peanut butter, creamy, all sizes	lb	1.83	7/01	11r
Pears, Anjou	lb	0.98	7/01	11r
Peas, green, Del Monte or Green Giant	15 oz	0.67	3/01	4c
Pork chops, center cut, bone-in	lb	3.33	7/01	11r
Pork sausage, fresh, loose	lb	2.59	7/01	11r
Pork shoulder picnic, bone-in, smoked	lb	1.12	7/01	11r
Pork, expenditures on	yr	162	1999	30r
Potato chips	16 oz	3.59	7/01	11r
Potatoes, frozen, french fried	lb	1.00	7/01	11r
Potatoes, white or red	10 lb	3.27	3/01	4c
Potatoes, white, all types	lb	0.44	7/01	11r
Poultry, expenditures on	yr	137	1999	30r
Processed fruits, expenditures on	yr	97	1999	30r
Processed vegetables, expenditures on	yr	82	1999	30r
Rice, white, long grain, uncooked	lb	0.51	7/01	11r
Round roast, graded and ungraded, excl U.S. prime and choice	lb	2.96	7/01	11r
Round steak, graded and ungraded, excl U.S. prime and choice	lb	3.11	7/01	11r
Sausage, Jimmy Dean/Owens pork	lb	3.31	3/01	4c
Shortening, vegetable, Crisco	3 lb	3.01	3/01	4c
Sirloin steak, graded and ungraded, excl U.S. prime and choice	lb	4.23	7/01	11r
Soft drink, Coca Cola, ex deposit	2 liter	1.11	3/01	4c
Spaghetti and macaroni	lb	0.78	7/01	11r
Steak, round, U.S. choice, boneless	lb	3.56	7/01	11r
Steak, sirloin, U.S. choice, boneless	lb	5.65	7/01	11r
Steak, T-bone	lb	6.99	3/01	4c
Strawberries, dry pint	12 oz	1.50	7/01	11r
Sugar and other sweets, expenditures on	yr	99	1999	30r
Sugar, cane or beet	4 lbs	1.59	3/01	4c
Sugar, white, 33-80 ounce package	lb	0.39	7/01	11r
Sugar, white, all sizes	lb	0.42	7/01	11r
Tobacco products and smoking supplies purchases	yr	288	1999	30r
Tomatoes, field grown	lb	1.43	7/01	11r
Tomatoes, Hunt's or Del Monte	14.5 oz	0.77	3/01	4c
Tuna, chunk, light	6 oz	0.64	3/01	4c
Tuna, light, chunk	lb	1.77	7/01	11r
Turkey, frozen, whole	lb	1.05	7/01	11r
Goods and Services				
Miscellaneous goods and services, ACCRA Index		93.40	3/01	4c
B&B Japanese maple (acer japonicum)	gal	49.98-129.00	4/00	93r
Boxwood (buxus)	2 gal	12.99-16.99	4/00	93r
Daylilly (hemerocallis)	gal	4.99-8.99	4/00	93r
Flat of annuals		11.00-13.92	4/00	93r

Values are in dollars or fractions of dollars. In the column headed *Ref*, references are shown to sources. Each reference is followed by a letter. These refer to the geographical level for which data were reported: s=State, r=Region, and c=City or metro. The abbreviation *ex* is used to mean *except* or *excluding*; *exp* stands for *expenditures*. For other abbreviations and further explanations, please see the Introduction.

Columbia, SC - continued

Item	Per	Value	Date	Ref.
Goods and Services				
Fountain grass (pennisetum)	gal	5.98-7.98	4/00	93r
Hanging basket (10 in)		7.99-14.98	4/00	93r
Hardy geranium (geranium)	gal	5.98-8.00	4/00	93r
Hosta (hosta)	gal	4.99-10.98	4/00	93r
Lilac (syrubga vulgaris)	2 gal	12.99-21.99	4/00	93r
Rhododendron (rhododendron)	2 gal	14.99-24.99	4/00	93r
Sage (salvia)	gal	5.98-6.99	4/00	93r
Wintercreeper euonymus (euonymus fortunei)	2 gal	7.99-89.99	4/00	93r
Hunting license	yr	12.00	4/01	34s
Health Care				
Health care, ACCRA Index		89.70	3/01	4c
Cardiac catheterization, ave hospital/physician charges		12360	1998	77s
Childbirth, Cesarean delivery		11587	1997	13r
Childbirth, vaginal delivery		6725	1997	13r
Dentist's fee, adult teeth cleaning and periodic oral exam	visit	71.92	3/01	4c
Doctor's fee, routine exam, established patient	visit	50.00	3/01	4c
Drugs, expenditures on	yr	399	1999	30r
Health care purchases	yr	1971	1999	30r
Health insurance expenditures	yr	933	1999	30r
Hospital care, private room	day	383.75	3/01	4c
Hysterectomy, laproscopically-assisted, ave hospital/physician charges		11920	1998	76s
Hysterectomy, vaginal, ave hospital and physician charges		4890	1998	76s
Medicaid dispensing fee		4.05	1999	87s
Medical services expenditures	yr	547	1999	30r
Medical supplies, expenditures on	yr	91	1999	30r
Nursing home costs, private room	day	120	2000	82c
Nursing home stay, private room	day	120	2000	83c
Plastic surgery, breast augmentation		2870	2000	7r
Plastic surgery, breast lift		3649	2000	7r
Plastic surgery, facelift		5008	2000	7r
Plastic surgery, hair transplantation		3425	2000	7r
Plastic surgery, lip augmentation		1227	2000	7r
Plastic surgery, lower body lift		4793	2000	7r
Plastic surgery, thigh lift		3862	2000	7r
Household Goods				
Dishwashing powder, Cascade	50 oz	3.45	3/01	4c
Floor coverings, expenditures on	yr	44	1999	30r
Furniture, expenditures on	yr	335	1999	30r
Household furnishings and equipment purchases	yr	1328	1999	30r
Household textiles, expenditures on	yr	89	1999	30r
Laundry and cleaning supplies, expenditures on	yr	113	1999	30r
Tissues, facial, Kleenex brand	175	1.28	3/01	4c
Housing				
Housing, ACCRA Index		90.50	3/01	4c
Home, 2200 sq ft, 4-br, 2-bath, 2-car garage, average		159725	2000	47c
Home price, existing, ave		160100	10/00	90r
Home value, median		119000	2001	53s
House, 2400 sq ft, 8000 sq ft lot, new, urban, utilities	total	189352	3/01	4c
House payment, principal and interest, 25% down payment	mos	928	3/01	4c
Household operation expenditures	yr	553	1999	30r
Housekeeping supplies purchases	yr	473	1999	30r
Housing, expenditures on	yr	10303	1999	30r

Columbia, SC - continued

Item	Per	Value	Date	Ref.
Housing - continued				
Maintenance, repairs, insurance expenditures	yr	699	1999	30r
Monthly rental value of owned home	mos	505	1999	30r
Owned dwellings, expenditures own	yr	3465	1999	30r
Rent expenditures	yr	1641	1999	30r
Rent, apartment, 2 br, 1 1/2-2 baths, unfurn, 950 sq ft, water	mos	642	3/01	4c
Rental unit, 1 bedroom, with utilities	mos	484	4/01	41c
Rental unit, 2 bedroom, with utilities	mos	556	4/01	41c
Rental unit, 3 bedroom, with utilities	mos	735	4/01	41c
Rental unit, 4 bedroom, with utilities	mos	846	4/01	41c
Shelter, expenditures on	yr	5467	1999	30r
Insurance and Pensions				
Auto insurance	yr	655.33	1998	86s
Life and other personal insurance purchases	yr	414	1999	30r
Pensions and Social Security, expenditures on	yr	2635	1999	30r
Personal insurance and pensions, expenditures on	yr	3048	1999	30r
Legal Fees				
Combination hunting and fishing license	yr	20.00	4/01	34s
Driver's license fee	orig	12.50	1999	48s
Driver's license fee	renew	12.50	1999	48s
Fishing license	yr	10.00	4/01	34s
Personal Goods				
Personal care products and services purchases	yr	393	1999	30r
Shampoo, Alberto VO5	15 oz	1.05	3/01	4c
Toothpaste, Crest or Colgate	6-7 oz	2.29	3/01	4c
Personal Services				
Dry cleaning, man's 2-pc suit		8.15	3/01	4c
Man's haircut, barbershop, no styling		11.00	3/01	4c
Personal services, household, expenditures on	yr	258	1999	30r
Woman's shampoo, trim, blow-dry, no style-change		17.80	3/01	4c
Pets				
Pets, toys, and playground equipment, expenditures on	yr	306	1999	30r
Restaurant Food				
Chicken, fried, thigh and drumstick, KFC/Church's		1.99	3/01	4c
Hamburger with cheese, McDonald's	1/4 lb	1.99	3/01	4c
Pizza, Pizza Hut or Pizza Inn	11-12 in	8.99	3/01	4c
Taxes				
Federal income taxes paid	yr	2047	1999	30r
Personal taxes, expenditures on	yr	2554	1999	30r
Property taxes paid	yr	726	1999	30r
State and local income taxes paid	yr	363	1999	30r
Transportation				
Transportation, ACCRA Index		87.50	3/01	4c
Cars and trucks, new, expenditures on	yr	1648	1999	30r
Cars and trucks, used, expenditures on	yr	1651	1999	30r
Diesel at the pump	gal	1.13	10/99	73s
Gasoline and motor oil purchases	yr	1052	1999	30r
Gasoline before-tax price (cents)	gal	101.70	10/00	43s
Maintenance and repair expenditures	yr	621	1999	30r
Public transportation, expenditures on	yr	298	1999	30r
Tire balance, computer or spin balance, front	wheel	6.39	3/01	4c
Transportation purchases	yr	6738	1999	30r
Vehicle expenses, miscellaneous, purchases	yr	2033	1999	30r
Vehicle insurance payments	yr	696	1999	30r
Vehicle purchases (net outlay)	yr	3354	1999	30r
Vehicle rental, lease expenditures	yr	352	1999	30r
Utilities				
Utilities, ACCRA Index		98.10	3/01	4c
Electrical bill, average	mos	86.42	9/00	9s

Values are in dollars or fractions of dollars. In the column headed *Ref*, references are shown to sources. Each reference is followed by a letter. These refer to the geographical level for which data were reported: s=State, r=Region, and c=City or metro. The abbreviation *ex* is used to mean *except* or *excluding*; *exp* stands for expenditures. For other abbreviations and further explanations, please see the Introduction.

Columbia, SC - continued

Item	Per	Value	Date	Ref.
Utilities				
Electricity, 2400 sq ft, new home	mos	117.47	3/01	4c
Electricity, expenditures on	yr	1115	1999	30r
Electricity, summer, 250 KWh	mos	24.75	2/96	96c
Electricity, summer, 500 KWh	mos	42.99	2/96	96c
Electricity, summer, 750 KWh	mos	61.24	2/96	96c
Electricity, summer, 1000 KWh	mos	78.60	2/96	96c
Electricity cost, average	KWh	5.40	9/00	9s
Water and other public services, expenditures on	yr	298	1999	30r
Weddings				
Wedding (national average cost)		19936	2000	33r
Wedding (regional average total cost)		16293	1997	110r
Attendants' gifts		321	1998	33r
Bridal attendants' apparel (5 persons)		824	2000	33r
Bride's headpiece/veil		173	1998	33r
Bride's wedding dress		859	1998	33r
Clergy, religious facility fee		242	1998	33r
Engagement ring		3177	1998	33r
Flowers		789	1998	33r
Groom's formalwear rental		99	2000	33r
Limousine		410	1998	33r
Marriage license cost		25.00	4/01	35s
Men's formalwear (ushers, best man)		469	2000	33r
Mother of bride apparel		241	2000	33r
Music		866	1998	33r
Photography and videography		1368	1998	33r
Rehearsal dinner		728	1998	33r
Wedding invitations and announcements		341	1998	33r
Wedding reception		7968	2000	33r
Wedding rings (bride and groom)		1060	1998	33r

Columbus, GA

Item	Per	Value	Date	Ref.
Alcoholic Beverages				
Alcoholic beverage purchases	yr	253	1999	30r
Malt beverages, all types, all sizes, any origin	16 oz	0.96	7/01	11r
Appliances				
Major appliances, expenditures on	yr	172	1999	30r
Small appliances, housewares, expenditures on	yr	81	1999	30r
Banking and Money				
Mortgage interest and charges paid	yr	2039	1999	30r
Mortgage principal paid on owned property	yr	1026	1999	30r
Vehicle finance charges paid	yr	365	1999	30r
Charity				
Cash contributions, expenditures	yr	1127	1999	30r
Child Care				
Child raising cost, total, age 0-2	yr	8540	1999	60r
Child raising cost, total, age 3-5	yr	8780	1999	60r
Child raising cost, total, age 6-8	yr	8820	1999	60r
Child raising cost, total, age 9-11	yr	8800	1999	60r
Child raising cost, total, age 12-14	yr	9510	1999	60r
Child raising cost, total, age 15-17	yr	9740	1999	60r
Child's child care and education, age 0-2	yr	1380	1999	60r
Child's child care and education, age 3-5	yr	1520	1999	60r
Child's child care and education, age 6-8	yr	990	1999	60r
Child's child care and education, age 9-11	yr	650	1999	60r
Child's child care and education, age 12-14	yr	490	1999	60r
Child's child care and education, age 15-17	yr	840	1999	60r
Child's clothing, age 0-2	yr	480	1999	60r
Child's clothing, age 3-5	yr	470	1999	60r
Child's clothing, age 6-8	yr	520	1999	60r
Child's clothing, age 9-11	yr	570	1999	60r
Child's clothing, age 12-14	yr	950	1999	60r
Child's clothing, age 15-17	yr	850	1999	60r
Child's food, age 0-2	yr	1000	1999	60r
Child's food, age 3-5	yr	1160	1999	60r
Child's food, age 6-8	yr	1490	1999	60r

Columbus, GA - continued

Item	Per	Value	Date	Ref.
Child Care - continued				
Child's food, age 9-11	yr	1770	1999	60r
Child's food, age 12-14	yr	1770	1999	60r
Child's food, age 15-17	yr	1980	1999	60r
Child's health care, age 0-2	yr	620	1999	60r
Child's health care, age 3-5	yr	590	1999	60r
Child's health care, age 6-8	yr	680	1999	60r
Child's health care, age 9-11	yr	720	1999	60r
Child's health care, age 12-14	yr	730	1999	60r
Child's health care, age 15-17	yr	760	1999	60r
Child's housing, age 0-2	yr	3070	1999	60r
Child's housing, age 3-5	yr	3050	1999	60r
Child's housing, age 6-8	yr	3010	1999	60r
Child's housing, age 9-11	yr	2850	1999	60r
Child's housing, age 12-14	yr	3040	1999	60r
Child's housing, age 15-17	yr	2650	1999	60r
Child's personal care, reading, age 0-2	yr	910	1999	60r
Child's personal care, reading, age 3-5	yr	930	1999	60r
Child's personal care, reading, age 6-8	yr	960	1999	60r
Child's personal care, reading, age 9-11	yr	1000	1999	60r
Child's personal care, reading, age 12-14	yr	1170	1999	60r
Child's personal care, reading, age 15-17	yr	950	1999	60r
Clothing				
Apparel and services purchases	yr	1610	1999	30r
Boys, 2 to 15, expenditures on	yr	89	1999	30r
Children under 2, expenditures on	yr	79	1999	30r
Footwear, expenditures on	yr	283	1999	30r
Girls, 2 to 15, expenditures on	yr	103	1999	30r
Men and boys, expenditures on	yr	351	1999	30r
Men, 16 and over, expenditures on	yr	262	1999	30r
Women, 16 and over, expenditures on	yr	538	1999	30r
Communications				
Cable modem installation, Charter		99.00-169.00	6/99	103s
Cable modem installation, Comcast		95.00	6/99	103s
Cable modem installation, Intermedia		149.95	6/99	103s
Cable modem installation, Media One		100.00	6/99	103s
Cable modem rate, cable subscriber, Charter	mos	49.95-79.95	6/99	103s
Cable modem rate, cable subscriber, Comcast	mos	39.95	6/99	103s
Cable modem rate, cable subscriber, Intermedia	mos	49.95	6/99	103s
Cable modem rate, cable subscriber, Media One	mos	34.95-39.95	6/99	103s
Cable modem rate, non-cable subscriber, Charter	mos	59.95-89.95	6/99	103s
Cable modem rate, non-cable subscriber, Comcast	mos	49.95	6/99	103s
Cable modem rate, non-cable subscriber, Intermedia	mos	54.95	6/99	103s
Cable modem rate, non-cable subscriber, Media One	mos	49.95	6/99	103s
Phone line, single, business, field visit	inst.	58.25	12/97	17s
Phone line, single, business, no field visit	inst.	58.25	12/97	17s
Phone line, single, residence, field visit	inst.	42.50	12/97	17s
Phone line, single, residence, no field visit	inst.	42.50	12/97	17s
Postage and stationery, expenditures on	yr	104	1999	30r
Postal rate, express mail, up to half-pound		12.45	7/01	108r
Postal rate, letter, first class, first ounce		0.34	7/01	108r
Postal rate, letter, two ounces		0.57	7/01	108r
Postal rate, post card		0.21	7/01	108r
Postal rate, priority mail, two pounds		3.95	7/01	108r
Postal rate, priority mail, up to one pound		3.50	7/01	108r
Telephone bill, business, basic rate	mos	37.30	12/97	18c
Telephone bill, residential, basic rate	mos	13.55	12/97	18c
Telephone services, expenditures on	yr	860	1999	30r
Education				
Board, 4-year private college/university	yr	2267	1996	38s
Board, 4-year public college/university	yr	1877	1996	38s
Education expenditures	yr	431	1999	30r
Room, 4-year private college/university	yr	2719	1996	38s

Values are in dollars or fractions of dollars. In the column headed *Ref*, references are shown to sources. Each reference is followed by a letter. These refer to the geographical level for which data were reported: s=State, r=Region, and c=City or metro. The abbreviation *ex* is used to mean *except* or *excluding*; *exp* stands for expenditures. For other abbreviations and further explanations, please see the Introduction.

Columbus, GA - continued

Item	Per	Value	Date	Ref.
Education				
Room, 4-year public college/university	yr	1712	1996	38s
Total cost, 4-year private college/university	yr	15194	1996	38s
Total cost, 4-year public college/university	yr	5691	1996	38s
Tuition, 2-year public college/university, in state	yr	1062	1996	38s
Tuition, 4-year private college/university, in state	yr	10208	1996	38s
Tuition, 4-year public college/university	yr	2103	1996	38s
Energy and Fuels				
Electricity	500 KWhs	47.29	7/01	11r
Electricity	KWh	0.09	7/01	11r
Fuel oil #2	gal	1.43	7/01	11r
Fuel oil and other fuels, expenditures on	yr	45	1999	30r
Gasoline, all types	gal	1.60	7/01	11r
Gasoline, unleaded midgrade	gal	1.65	7/01	11r
Gasoline, unleaded premium	gal	1.74	7/01	11r
Natural gas, expenditures on	yr	164	1999	30r
Utility (piped) gas, therm		1.01	7/01	11r
Utility (piped) gas, 40 therms		44.29	7/01	11r
Utility (piped) gas, 100 therms		97.44	7/01	11r
Entertainment				
Entertainment purchases	yr	1574	1999	30r
Fees and admissions paid	yr	371	1999	30r
Reading purchases	yr	121	1999	30r
Television, radios, sound equipment, expenditures on	yr	561	1999	30r
Funerals				
Total cost of funeral		5922.53	1/99	78r
Acknowledgement cards		63.43	1/99	78r
Casket		2258.77	1/99	78r
Cosmetology, hair, other preparation		127.09	1/99	78r
Embalming		393.49	1/99	78r
Funeral at funeral home		367.50	1/99	78r
Hearse (local)		169.66	1/99	78r
Professional service charges		1211.32	1/99	78r
Service car/van		80.69	1/99	78r
Transfer of remains to funeral home		144.25	1/99	78r
Vault		803.50	1/99	78r
Visitation/viewing		302.83	1/99	78r
Groceries				
American processed cheese	lb	3.50	7/01	11r
Bakery products, expenditures on	yr	261	1999	30r
Bananas	lb	0.47	7/01	11r
Beans, dried, any type, all sizes	lb	0.63	7/01	11r
Beef for stew, boneless	lb	2.86	7/01	11r
Beef, expenditures on	yr	210	1999	30r
Bologna, all beef or mixed	lb	2.29	7/01	11r
Bread, French	lb	1.66	7/01	11r
Bread, white, pan	lb	0.87	7/01	11r
Bread, whole wheat, pan	lb	1.38	7/01	11r
Broccoli	lb	1.04	7/01	11r
Butter, salted, grade AA, stick	lb	2.26	7/01	11r
Butter, yoghurt, cheese, etc, expenditures on	yr	170	1999	30r
Cabbage	lb	0.42	7/01	11r
Cereals and cereal products, expenditures on	yr	140	1999	30r
Cheddar cheese, natural	lb	3.75	7/01	11r
Chicken breast, bone-in	lb	1.85	7/01	11r
Chicken legs, bone-in	lb	1.34	7/01	11r
Chicken, fresh, whole	lb	1.05	7/01	11r
Chops, boneless,	lb	4.13	7/01	11r
Chuck roast, graded and ungraded, excl U.S. prime and choice	lb	2.35	7/01	11r
Chuck roast, U.S. choice, boneless	lb	2.67	7/01	11r
Coffee, 100%, ground roast, all sizes	lb	2.88	7/01	11r
Coffee, instant, plain, regular, all sizes	16 oz	9.25	7/01	11r
Cola, non diet	2 liter	1.11	7/01	11r
Crackers, soda, salted	lb	1.70	7/01	11r
Dairy product purchases	yr	282	1999	30r

Columbus, GA - continued

Item	Per	Value	Date	Ref.
Groceries - continued				
Eggs, expenditures on	yr	32	1999	30r
Fats and oils, expenditures on	yr	79	1999	30r
Fish and seafood, expenditures on	yr	99	1999	30r
Flour, white, all purpose	lb	0.32	7/01	11r
Food (excl fruit and vegetables), eaten at home, purchases	yr	815	1999	30r
Food cooked on trips, expenditures on	yr	36	1999	30r
Food purchases	yr	4533	1999	30r
Food purchases, eaten away from home	yr	1873	1999	30r
Food purchases, food eaten at home	yr	2660	1999	30r
Fresh fruits, expenditures on	yr	128	1999	30r
Fresh milk and cream, expenditures on	yr	112	1999	30r
Fresh vegetables, expenditures on	yr	131	1999	30r
Fruit and vegetable purchases	yr	438	1999	30r
Grapefruit	lb	0.59	7/01	11r
Grapes, Thompson, seedless	lb	2.12	7/01	11r
Ground beef, 100% beef	lb	1.76	7/01	11r
Ground beef, lean and extra lean	lb	2.60	7/01	11r
Ground chuck, 100% beef	lb	2.08	7/01	11r
Ham, boneless, excl canned	lb	2.71	7/01	11r
Ham, rump or shank half, bone-in, smoked	lb	2.19	7/01	11r
Ice cream, prepackaged, bulk, regular	1/2 gal	3.93	7/01	11r
Lemons	lb	1.32	7/01	11r
Lettuce, iceberg	lb	0.76	7/01	11r
Milk, fresh, low fat,	gal	2.75	7/01	11r
Milk, fresh, whole, fortified	gal	2.97	7/01	11r
Nonalcoholic beverages, expenditures on	yr	228	1999	30r
Orange juice, frozen concentrate	16 oz	1.95	7/01	11r
Oranges, Navel	lb	0.73	7/01	11r
Oranges, Valencia	lb	0.55	7/01	11r
Peanut butter, creamy, all sizes	lb	1.83	7/01	11r
Pears, Anjou	lb	0.98	7/01	11r
Pork chops, center cut, bone-in	lb	3.33	7/01	11r
Pork sausage, fresh, loose	lb	2.59	7/01	11r
Pork shoulder picnic, bone-in, smoked	lb	1.12	7/01	11r
Pork, expenditures on	yr	162	1999	30r
Potato chips	16 oz	3.59	7/01	11r
Potatoes, frozen, french fried	lb	1.00	7/01	11r
Potatoes, white, all types	lb	0.44	7/01	11r
Poultry, expenditures on	yr	137	1999	30r
Processed fruits, expenditures on	yr	97	1999	30r
Processed vegetables, expenditures on	yr	82	1999	30r
Rice, white, long grain, uncooked	lb	0.51	7/01	11r
Round roast, graded and ungraded, excl U.S. prime and choice	lb	2.96	7/01	11r
Round steak, graded and ungraded, excl U.S. prime and choice	lb	3.11	7/01	11r
Sirloin steak, graded and ungraded, excl U.S. prime and choice	lb	4.23	7/01	11r
Spaghetti and macaroni	lb	0.78	7/01	11r
Steak, round, U.S. choice, boneless	lb	3.56	7/01	11r
Steak, sirloin, U.S. choice, boneless	lb	5.65	7/01	11r
Strawberries, dry pint	12 oz	1.50	7/01	11r
Sugar and other sweets, expenditures on	yr	99	1999	30r
Sugar, white, 33-80 ounce package	lb	0.39	7/01	11r
Sugar, white, all sizes	lb	0.42	7/01	11r
Tobacco products and smoking supplies purchases	yr	288	1999	30r
Tomatoes, field grown	lb	1.43	7/01	11r
Tuna, light, chunk	lb	1.77	7/01	11r
Turkey, frozen, whole	lb	1.05	7/01	11r
Goods and Services				
B&B Japanese maple (acer japonicum)	gal	49.98-129.00	4/00	93r
Boxwood (buxus)	2 gal	12.99-16.99	4/00	93r
Daylilly (hemerocallis)	gal	4.99-8.99	4/00	93r
Flat of annuals		11.00-13.92	4/00	93r
Fountain grass (pennisetum)	gal	5.98-7.98	4/00	93r

Values are in dollars or fractions of dollars. In the column headed *Ref*, references are shown to sources. Each reference is followed by a letter. These refer to the geographical level for which data were reported: s=State, r=Region, and c=City or metro. The abbreviation *ex* is used to mean *except* or *excluding*; *exp* stands for *expenditures*. For other abbreviations and further explanations, please see the Introduction.

Columbus, GA - continued

Item	Per	Value	Date	Ref.
Goods and Services				
Hanging basket (10 in)		7.99-14.98	4/00	93r
Hardy geranium (geranium)	gal	5.98-8.00	4/00	93r
Hosta (hosta)	gal	4.99-10.98	4/00	93r
Lilac (syrubga vulgaris)	2 gal	12.99-21.99	4/00	93r
Rhododendron (rhododendron)	2 gal	14.99-24.99	4/00	93r
Sage (salvia)	gal	5.98-6.99	4/00	93r
Wintercreeper euonymus (euonymus fortunei)	2 gal	7.99-89.99	4/00	93r
Hunting license	yr	10.00	4/01	34s
Health Care				
Cardiac catheterization, ave hospital/physician charges		14190	1998	77s
Childbirth, Cesarean delivery		11587	1997	13r
Childbirth, vaginal delivery		6725	1997	13r
Drugs, expenditures on	yr	399	1999	30r
Health care purchases	yr	1971	1999	30r
Health insurance expenditures	yr	933	1999	30r
Hysterectomy, laproscopically-assisted, ave hospital/physician charges		16760	1998	76s
Hysterectomy, vaginal, ave hospital and physician charges		11160	1998	76s
Medicaid dispensing fee		4.63	1999	87s
Medical services expenditures	yr	547	1999	30r
Medical supplies, expenditures on	yr	91	1999	30r
Plastic surgery, breast augmentation		2870	2000	7r
Plastic surgery, breast lift		3649	2000	7r
Plastic surgery, facelift		5008	2000	7r
Plastic surgery, hair transplantation		3425	2000	7r
Plastic surgery, lip augmentation		1227	2000	7r
Plastic surgery, lower body lift		4793	2000	7r
Plastic surgery, thigh lift		3862	2000	7r
Household Goods				
Floor coverings, expenditures on	yr	44	1999	30r
Furniture, expenditures on	yr	335	1999	30r
Household furnishings and equipment purchases	yr	1328	1999	30r
Household textiles, expenditures on	yr	89	1999	30r
Laundry and cleaning supplies, expenditures on	yr	113	1999	30r
Housing				
Home, 2200 sq ft, 4-br, 2-bath, 2-car garage, average		141425	2000	47c
Home price, existing, ave		160100	10/00	90r
Home value, median		131000	2001	53s
Household operation expenditures	yr	553	1999	30r
Housekeeping supplies purchases	yr	473	1999	30r
Housing, expenditures on	yr	10303	1999	30r
Maintenance, repairs, insurance expenditures	yr	699	1999	30r
Monthly rental value of owned home	mos	505	1999	30r
Owned dwellings, expenditures own	yr	3465	1999	30r
Rent expenditures	yr	1641	1999	30r
Rental unit, 1 bedroom, with utilities	mos	396	4/01	41c
Rental unit, 2 bedroom, with utilities	mos	475	4/01	41c
Rental unit, 3 bedroom, with utilities	mos	620	4/01	41c
Rental unit, 4 bedroom, with utilities	mos	673	4/01	41c
Shelter, expenditures on	yr	5467	1999	30r
Insurance and Pensions				
Life and other personal insurance purchases	yr	414	1999	30r
Pensions and Social Security, expenditures on	yr	2635	1999	30r
Personal insurance and pensions, expenditures on	yr	3048	1999	30r

Columbus, GA - continued

Item	Per	Value	Date	Ref.
Legal Fees				
Divorce, filing fee		65.00-85.00	4/01	35s
Driver's license fee	orig	16.50	1999	48s
Driver's license fee	renew	15.00	1999	48s
Personal Goods				
Personal care products and services purchases	yr	393	1999	30r
Personal Services				
Personal services, household, expenditures on	yr	258	1999	30r
Pets				
Pets, toys, and playground equipment, expenditures on	yr	306	1999	30r
Taxes				
Federal income taxes paid	yr	2047	1999	30r
Personal taxes, expenditures on	yr	2554	1999	30r
Property taxes paid	yr	726	1999	30r
State and local income taxes paid	yr	363	1999	30r
Transportation				
Cars and trucks, new, expenditures on	yr	1648	1999	30r
Cars and trucks, used, expenditures on	yr	1651	1999	30r
Diesel at the pump	gal	1.10	10/99	73s
Gasoline and motor oil purchases	yr	1052	1999	30r
Gasoline before-tax price (cents)	gal	102.00	10/00	43s
Maintenance and repair expenditures	yr	621	1999	30r
Public transportation, expenditures on	yr	298	1999	30r
Transportation purchases	yr	6738	1999	30r
Vehicle expenses, miscellaneous, purchases	yr	2033	1999	30r
Vehicle insurance payments	yr	696	1999	30r
Vehicle purchases (net outlay)	yr	3354	1999	30r
Vehicle rental, lease expenditures	yr	352	1999	30r
Utilities				
Electrical bill, average	mos	79.83	9/00	9s
Electricity, expenditures on	yr	1115	1999	30r
Electricity cost, average	KWh	6.10	9/00	9s
Water and other public services, expenditures on	yr	298	1999	30r
Weddings				
Wedding (national average cost)		19936	2000	33r
Wedding (regional average total cost)		16293	1997	110r
Attendants' gifts		321	1998	33r
Bridal attendants' apparel (5 persons)		824	2000	33r
Bride's headpiece/veil		173	1998	33r
Bride's wedding dress		859	1998	33r
Clergy, religious facility fee		242	1998	33r
Engagement ring		3177	1998	33r
Flowers		789	1998	33r
Groom's formalwear rental		99	2000	33r
Limousine		410	1998	33r
Marriage license cost		40.00	4/01	35s
Men's formalwear (ushers, best man)		469	2000	33r
Mother of bride apparel		241	2000	33r
Music		866	1998	33r
Photography and videography		1368	1998	33r
Rehearsal dinner		728	1998	33r
Wedding invitations and announcements		341	1998	33r
Wedding reception		7968	2000	33r
Wedding rings (bride and groom)		1060	1998	33r

Columbus, OH

Item	Per	Value	Date	Ref.
Average annual expenditures	yr	35369	1999	30r
Composite, ACCRA index		106.90	3/01	4c
Alcoholic Beverages				
Alcoholic beverage purchases	yr	304	1999	30r
Beer, Heineken, 12-oz, ex deposit	6	7.49	3/01	4c
J & B Scotch	750-ml	21.30	3/01	4c

Values are in dollars or fractions of dollars. In the column headed *Ref*, references are shown to sources. Each reference is followed by a letter. These refer to the geographical level for which data were reported: s=State, r=Region, and c=City or metro. The abbreviation *ex* is used to mean *except* or *excluding*; *exp* stands for *expenditures*. For other abbreviations and further explanations, please see the Introduction.

Columbus, OH - continued

Item	Per	Value	Date	Ref.
Alcoholic Beverages				
Malt beverages, all types, all sizes, any origin	16 oz	0.93	7/01	11r
Wine, Livingston or Gallo, Chablis blanc	1.5 liter	5.82	3/01	4c
Wine, red and white table, all sizes, any origin	liter	7.04	7/01	11r
Appliances				
Appliance repair, service call, washing machine	min lab chg	35.39	3/01	4c
Major appliances, expenditures on	yr	165	1999	30r
Small appliances, housewares, expenditures on	yr	90	1999	30r
Banking and Money				
Mortgage interest and charges paid	yr	2277	1999	30r
Mortgage principal paid on owned property	yr	1230	1999	30r
Mortgage rate, incl. points and orig. fee, 30-yr. conv. fixed or ARM	mos	6.97	3/01	4c
Vehicle finance charges paid	yr	328	1999	30r
Business Expenses				
Business travel, car rental	day	64	2001	3c
Business travel, food	day	43	2001	3c
Business travel, hotel	day	130	2001	3c
Charity				
Cash contributions, expenditures	yr	1126	1999	30r
Child Care				
Child raising cost, total, age 0-2	yr	7890	1999	60r
Child raising cost, total, age 3-5	yr	8130	1999	60r
Child raising cost, total, age 6-8	yr	8170	1999	60r
Child raising cost, total, age 9-11	yr	8190	1999	60r
Child raising cost, total, age 12-14	yr	8890	1999	60r
Child raising cost, total, age 15-17	yr	9050	1999	60r
Child's child care and education, age 0-2	yr	1240	1999	60r
Child's child care and education, age 3-5	yr	1370	1999	60r
Child's child care and education, age 6-8	yr	880	1999	60r
Child's child care and education, age 9-11	yr	570	1999	60r
Child's child care and education, age 12-14	yr	420	1999	60r
Child's child care and education, age 15-17	yr	720	1999	60r
Child's clothing, age 0-2	yr	410	1999	60r
Child's clothing, age 3-5	yr	400	1999	60r
Child's clothing, age 6-8	yr	450	1999	60r
Child's clothing, age 9-11	yr	500	1999	60r
Child's clothing, age 12-14	yr	840	1999	60r
Child's clothing, age 15-17	yr	740	1999	60r
Child's food, age 0-2	yr	960	1999	60r
Child's food, age 3-5	yr	1120	1999	60r
Child's food, age 6-8	yr	1430	1999	60r
Child's food, age 9-11	yr	1710	1999	60r
Child's food, age 12-14	yr	1710	1999	60r
Child's food, age 15-17	yr	1920	1999	60r
Child's health care, age 0-2	yr	520	1999	60r
Child's health care, age 3-5	yr	500	1999	60r
Child's health care, age 6-8	yr	570	1999	60r
Child's health care, age 9-11	yr	610	1999	60r
Child's health care, age 12-14	yr	630	1999	60r
Child's health care, age 15-17	yr	650	1999	60r
Child's housing, age 0-2	yr	2860	1999	60r
Child's housing, age 3-5	yr	2840	1999	60r
Child's housing, age 6-8	yr	2800	1999	60r
Child's housing, age 9-11	yr	2650	1999	60r
Child's housing, age 12-14	yr	2840	1999	60r
Child's housing, age 15-17	yr	2440	1999	60r
Child's personal care, reading, age 0-2	yr	880	1999	60r
Child's personal care, reading, age 3-5	yr	900	1999	60r
Child's personal care, reading, age 6-8	yr	930	1999	60r
Child's personal care, reading, age 9-11	yr	970	1999	60r
Child's personal care, reading, age 12-14	yr	1150	1999	60r
Child's personal care, reading, age 15-17	yr	920	1999	60r
Clothing				
Apparel and services purchases	yr	1607	1999	30r
Boys' brief, cotton	3	3.77	3/01	4c
Boys, 2 to 15, expenditures on	yr	91	1999	30r

Columbus, OH - continued

Item	Per	Value	Date	Ref.
Clothing - continued				
Children under 2, expenditures on	yr	59	1999	30r
Footwear, expenditures on	yr	285	1999	30r
Girls, 2 to 15, expenditures on	yr	116	1999	30r
Men and boys, expenditures on	yr	433	1999	30r
Men, 16 and over, expenditures on	yr	341	1999	30r
Shirt, man's dress shirt		26.89	3/01	4c
Slacks, man's "No Wrinkles" khaki		46.40	3/01	4c
Women, 16 and over, expenditures on	yr	490	1999	30r
Communications				
Cable modem installation, Adelphi		54.90	6/99	103s
Cable modem installation, Media One		100.00	6/99	103s
Cable modem installation, Time Warner		75.00-225.00	6/99	103s
Cable modem rate, cable subscriber, Adelphi	mos	34.95	6/99	103s
Cable modem rate, cable subscriber, Media One	mos	34.95-39.95	6/99	103s
Cable modem rate, cable subscriber, Time Warner	mos	39.95-49.95	6/99	103s
Cable modem rate, non-cable subscriber, Adelphi	mos	44.95	6/99	103s
Cable modem rate, non-cable subscriber, Media One	mos	49.95	6/99	103s
Cable modem rate, non-cable subscriber, Time Warner	mos	39.95-54.95	6/99	103s
Newspaper subscription, daily and Sunday delivery	mos	13.91	3/01	4c
Phone line, single, business, field visit	inst.	56.32	12/97	17s
Phone line, single, business, no field visit	inst.	56.32	12/97	17s
Phone line, single, residence, field visit	inst.	31.10	12/97	17s
Phone line, single, residence, no field visit	inst.	31.10	12/97	17s
Postage and stationery, expenditures on	yr	140	1999	30r
Postal rate, express mail, up to half-pound		12.45	7/01	108r
Postal rate, letter, first class, first ounce		0.34	7/01	108r
Postal rate, letter, two ounces		0.57	7/01	108r
Postal rate, post card		0.21	7/01	108r
Postal rate, priority mail, two pounds		3.95	7/01	108r
Postal rate, priority mail, up to one pound		3.50	7/01	108r
Telephone bill, business, basic rate	mos	26.15	12/97	18c
Telephone bill, family of three	mos	18.74	3/01	4c
Telephone bill, residential, basic rate	mos	14.70	12/97	18c
Telephone services, expenditures on	yr	830	1999	30r
Education				
Board, 4-year private college/university	yr	2414	1996	38s
Board, 4-year public college/university	yr	2181	1996	38s
Education expenditures	yr	583	1999	30r
Room, 4-year private college/university	yr	2349	1996	38s
Room, 4-year public college/university	yr	2386	1996	38s
Total cost, 4-year private college/university	yr	17139	1996	38s
Total cost, 4-year public college/university	yr	8169	1996	38s
Tuition, 2-year public college/university, in state	yr	2261	1996	38s
Tuition, 4-year private college/university, in state	yr	12377	1996	38s
Tuition, 4-year public college/university	yr	3603	1996	38s
Energy and Fuels				
Electricity	500 KWhs	46.59	7/01	11r
Energy, combined forms, 2400 sq ft	mos	139.51	3/01	4c
Energy, exc. electricity, 2400 sq ft	mos	74.03	3/01	4c
Fuel oil #2	gal	1.27	7/01	11r
Fuel oil and other fuels, expenditures on	yr	68	1999	30r
Gas, cooking, winter, 10 therms	mos	11.32	2/96	98c
Gas, cooking, winter, 30 therms	mos	20.95	2/96	98c
Gas, cooking, winter, 50 therms	mos	30.60	2/96	98c
Gas, heating, winter, average use	mos	104.32	2/96	98c
Gas, natural, commercial rate	1000 cf	8.65	11/00	88s
Gas, regular unleaded, cash, self-service	gal	1.49	3/01	4c
Gasoline, unleaded midgrade	gal	1.79	7/01	11r
Gasoline, unleaded premium	gal	1.86	7/01	11r
Gasoline, unleaded regular	gal	1.58	7/01	11r
Natural gas, expenditures on	yr	389	1999	30r

Values are in dollars or fractions of dollars. In the column headed *Ref*, references are shown to sources. Each reference is followed by a letter. These refer to the geographical level for which data were reported: s=State, r=Region, and c=City or metro. The abbreviation *ex* is used to mean *except* or *excluding*; *exp* stands for *expenditures*. For other abbreviations and further explanations, please see the Introduction.

Columbus, OH - continued

Item	Per	Value	Date	Ref.
Energy and Fuels				
Utility (piped) gas, therm		0.81	7/01	11r
Utility (piped) gas, 40 therms		38.01	7/01	11r
Utility (piped) gas, 100 therms		81.75	7/01	11r
Entertainment				
Bowling, Saturday evening rate	line	2.91	3/01	4c
Entertainment purchases	yr	1984	1999	30r
Fees and admissions paid	yr	444	1999	30r
Monopoly game, Parker Brothers', No. 9	game	10.52	3/01	4c
Movie, first-run, Saturday, evening	adm.	6.58	3/01	4c
Television, radios, sound equipment, expenditures on	yr	580	1999	30r
Tennis balls, yellow, Wilson or Penn, 3	can	2.28	3/01	4c
Funerals				
Cosmetology, hair, other preparation		178.32	1/99	78r
Embalming		408.19	1/99	78r
Funeral at funeral home		362.13	1/99	78r
Professional service charges		1375.51	1/99	78r
Transfer of remains to funeral home		155.92	1/99	78r
Visitation/viewing		294.38	1/99	78r
Groceries				
Groceries, ACCRA Index		103.40	3/01	4c
Antibiotic ointment, Polysporin	0.5 oz	4.37	3/01	4c
Baby food, strained vegetables or fruit, lowest price	4-4.5 oz	0.37	3/01	4c
Bacon, sliced	lb	3.15	7/01	11r
Bakery products, expenditures on	yr	281	1999	30r
Bananas	lb	0.49	3/01	4c
Bananas	lb	0.48	7/01	11r
Beans, dried, any type, all sizes	lb	0.61	7/01	11r
Beef for stew, boneless	lb	3.08	7/01	11r
Beef or hamburger, ground	lb	1.72	3/01	4c
Beef, expenditures on	yr	217	1999	30r
Bologna, all beef or mixed	lb	2.52	7/01	11r
Bread, white	loaf	0.96	3/01	4c
Bread, white, pan	lb	1.06	7/01	11r
Broccoli	lb	0.91	7/01	11r
Butter, salted, grade AA, stick	lb	3.04	7/01	11r
Butter, yoghurt, cheese, etc, expenditures on	yr	183	1999	30r
Cereals and bakery product purchases	yr	430	1999	30r
Cereals and cereal products, expenditures on	yr	149	1999	30r
Cheese, Kraft grated Parmesan	8 oz	4.31	3/01	4c
Chicken, fresh, whole	lb	1.07	7/01	11r
Chicken, whole fryer	lb	1.09	3/01	4c
Chops, boneless,	lb	3.64	7/01	11r
Chuck roast, U.S. choice, boneless	lb	2.47	7/01	11r
Cigarettes, Winston, Kings	carton	29.35	3/01	4c
Coffee, 100%, ground roast, all sizes	lb	2.69	7/01	11r
Coffee, vacuum-packed	13 oz	2.77	3/01	4c
Cookies, chocolate chip	lb	2.87	7/01	11r
Corn Flakes, Kellogg's or Post Toasties	18 oz	2.59	3/01	4c
Corn, frozen, whole kernel, lowest price	16 oz	1.14	3/01	4c
Dairy product purchases	yr	304	1999	30r
Eggs, expenditures on	yr	26	1999	30r
Eggs, Grade A or AA	dozen	1.14	3/01	4c
Eggs, grade A, large	dozen	0.88	7/01	11r
Fats and oils, expenditures on	yr	75	1999	30r
Fish and seafood, expenditures on	yr	72	1999	30r
Food (excl fruit and vegetables), eaten at home, purchases	yr	887	1999	30r
Food cooked on trips, expenditures on	yr	44	1999	30r
Food purchases	yr	4802	1999	30r
Food purchases, eaten away from home	yr	2069	1999	30r
Food purchases, food eaten at home	yr	2733	1999	30r
Fresh fruits, expenditures on	yr	138	1999	30r
Fresh milk and cream, expenditures on	yr	120	1999	30r
Fresh vegetables, expenditures on	yr	126	1999	30r
Grapefruit	lb	0.66	7/01	11r
Grapes, Thompson, seedless	lb	1.64	7/01	11r
Ground beef, 100% beef	lb	1.64	7/01	11r
Ground beef, lean and extra lean	lb	2.16	7/01	11r

Columbus, OH - continued

Item	Per	Value	Date	Ref.
Groceries - continued				
Ground chuck, 100% beef	lb	2.13	7/01	11r
Ham, boneless, excl canned	lb	2.62	7/01	11r
Ice cream, prepackaged, bulk, regular	1/2 gal	3.35	7/01	11r
Lemons	lb	1.19	7/01	11r
Lettuce, iceberg	head	0.91	3/01	4c
Lettuce, iceberg	lb	0.73	7/01	11r
Margarine, Blue Bonnet or Parkay, stick	lb	1.12	3/01	4c
Margarine, soft, tubs	lb	0.89	7/01	11r
Meats, poultry, fish, and egg purchases	yr	671	1999	30r
Milk, fresh, whole, fortified	gal	2.71	7/01	11r
Milk, whole	1/2 gal	1.56	3/01	4c
Nonalcoholic beverages, expenditures on	yr	239	1999	30r
Orange juice, Minute Maid frozen	12 oz	1.72	3/01	4c
Oranges, Navel	lb	0.80	7/01	11r
Oranges, Valencia	lb	0.66	7/01	11r
Peaches, halves or slices, Hunt's, Del Monte, or Libby's	29 oz	1.92	3/01	4c
Pears, Anjou	lb	0.93	7/01	11r
Peas, green, Del Monte or Green Giant	15 oz	0.86	3/01	4c
Pork chops, center cut, bone-in	lb	3.63	7/01	11r
Pork, expenditures on	yr	150	1999	30r
Potato chips	16 oz	3.52	7/01	11r
Potatoes, frozen, french fried	lb	1.08	7/01	11r
Potatoes, white or red	10 lb	1.99	3/01	4c
Potatoes, white, all types	lb	0.33	7/01	11r
Poultry, expenditures on	yr	108	1999	30r
Processed fruits, expenditures on	yr	98	1999	30r
Processed vegetables, expenditures on	yr	80	1999	30r
Round roast, U.S. choice, boneless	lb	3.07	7/01	11r
Round steak, graded and ungraded, excl U.S. prime and choice	lb	3.41	7/01	11r
Sausage, Jimmy Dean/Owens pork	lb	2.86	3/01	4c
Shortening, vegetable oil blends	lb	1.13	7/01	11r
Shortening, vegetable, Crisco	3 lb	3.81	3/01	4c
Soft drink, Coca Cola, ex deposit	2 liter	1.24	3/01	4c
Spaghetti and macaroni	lb	0.80	7/01	11r
Steak, round, U.S. choice, boneless	lb	3.23	7/01	11r
Steak, T-bone	lb	6.43	3/01	4c
Steak, T-bone, U.S. choice, bone-in	lb	6.68	7/01	11r
Strawberries, dry pint	12 oz	1.32	7/01	11r
Sugar and other sweets, expenditures on	yr	114	1999	30r
Sugar, cane or beet	4 lbs	1.77	3/01	4c
Sugar, white, 33-80 ounce package	lb	0.42	7/01	11r
Sugar, white, all sizes	lb	0.43	7/01	11r
Tobacco products and smoking supplies purchases	yr	331	1999	30r
Tomatoes, field grown	lb	1.46	7/01	11r
Tomatoes, Hunt's or Del Monte	14.5 oz	0.96	3/01	4c
Tuna, chunk, light	6 oz	0.59	3/01	4c
Tuna, light, chunk	lb	1.80	7/01	11r
Turkey, frozen, whole	lb	1.15	7/01	11r
Goods and Services				
Miscellaneous goods and services, ACCRA Index		101.30	3/01	4c
B&B Japanese maple (acer japonicum)	gal	29.99-169.99	4/00	93r
Boxwood (buxus)	2 gal	18.99-39.99	4/00	93r
Daylily (hemerocallis)	gal	4.99-25.00	4/00	93r
Flat of annuals		11.98-24.99	4/00	93r
Fountain grass (pennisetum)	gal	5.98-12.98	4/00	93r
Hanging basket (10 in)		12.99-27.99	4/00	93r
Hardy geranium (geranium)	gal	7.99-9.99	4/00	93r
Hosta (hosta)	gal	6.00-25.00	4/00	93r
Lilac (syrubga vulgaris)	2 gal	14.99-24.99	4/00	93r

Values are in dollars or fractions of dollars. In the column headed *Ref*, references are shown to sources. Each reference is followed by a letter. These refer to the geographical level for which data were reported: s=State, r=Region, and c=City or metro. The abbreviation *ex* is used to mean *except* or *excluding*; *exp* stands for expenditures. For other abbreviations and further explanations, please see the Introduction.

Columbus, OH - continued

Item	Per	Value	Date	Ref.
Goods and Services				
Miscellaneous purchases	yr	865	1999	30r
Rhododendron (rhododendron)	2 gal	23.98-42.99	4/00	93r
Sage (salvia)	gal	6.00-9.99	4/00	93r
Wintercreeper euonymus (euonymus fortunei)	2 gal	16.00-169.99	4/00	93r
Hunting license	yr	15.00	4/01	34s
Health Care				
Health care, ACCRA Index		95.00	3/01	4c
Cardiac catheterization, ave hospital/physician charges		11760	1998	77s
Childbirth, Cesarean delivery		10722	1997	13r
Childbirth, vaginal delivery		6223	1997	13r
Dentist's fee, adult teeth cleaning and periodic oral exam	visit	72.11	3/01	4c
Doctor's fee, routine exam, established patient	visit	56.40	3/01	4c
Drugs, expenditures on	yr	394	1999	30r
Health care purchases	yr	2048	1999	30r
Health insurance expenditures	yr	978	1999	30r
Hospital care, private room	day	436.11	3/01	4c
Hysterectomy, laproscopically-assisted, ave hospital/physician charges		11730	1998	76s
Hysterectomy, vaginal, ave hospital and physician charges		9640	1998	76s
Medicaid dispensing fee		3.70	1999	87s
Medical services expenditures	yr	554	1999	30r
Medical supplies, expenditures on	yr	122	1999	30r
Nursing home costs, private room	day	162	2000	82c
Nursing home stay, private room	day	162	2000	81c
Plastic surgery, breast augmentation		3184	2000	7r
Plastic surgery, breast lift		3585	2000	7r
Plastic surgery, facelift		4999	2000	7r
Plastic surgery, hair transplantation		3105	2000	7r
Plastic surgery, lip augmentation		1290	2000	7r
Plastic surgery, lower body lift		8135	2000	7r
Plastic surgery, thigh lift		3839	2000	7r
Household Goods				
Dishwashing powder, Cascade	50 oz	3.68	3/01	4c
Floor coverings, expenditures on	yr	52	1999	30r
Furniture, expenditures on	yr	344	1999	30r
Household furnishings and equipment purchases	yr	1475	1999	30r
Household textiles, expenditures on	yr	109	1999	30r
Laundry and cleaning supplies, expenditures on	yr	134	1999	30r
Tissues, facial, Kleenex brand	175	1.47	3/01	4c
Housing				
Housing, ACCRA Index		116.70	3/01	4c
Home, 2200 sq ft, 4-br, 2-bath, 2-car garage, average		193278	2000	47c
Home price, existing, ave		144400	10/00	90r
Home value, median		96000	2001	53s
House, 2400 sq ft, 8000 sq ft lot, new, urban, utilities	total	252565	3/01	4c
House payment, principal and interest, 25% down payment	mos	1257	3/01	4c
Household operation expenditures	yr	542	1999	30r
Housekeeping supplies purchases	yr	508	1999	30r
Lodging expenditures	yr	430	1999	30r
Maintenance, repairs, insurance expenditures	yr	853	1999	30r
Monthly rental value of owned home	mos	547	1999	30r
Owned dwellings, expenditures own	yr	4282	1999	30r
Rent expenditures	yr	1558	1999	30r
Rent, apartment, 2 br, 1 1/2-2 baths, unfurn, 950 sq ft, water	mos	668	3/01	4c
Rental unit, 1 bedroom, with utilities	mos	471	4/01	41c
Rental unit, 2 bedroom, with utilities	mos	605	4/01	41c
Rental unit, 3 bedroom, with utilities	mos	768	4/01	41c

Columbus, OH - continued

Item	Per	Value	Date	Ref.
Housing - continued				
Rental unit, 4 bedroom, with utilities	mos	883	4/01	41c
Shelter, expenditures on	yr	6270	1999	30r
Insurance and Pensions				
Life and other personal insurance purchases	yr	387	1999	30r
Pensions and Social Security, expenditures on	yr	2968	1999	30r
Legal Fees				
Divorce, filing fee		100.00	4/01	35s
Driver's license fee	renew	14.50	1999	48s
Driver's license fee	orig	14.50	1999	48s
Fishing license	yr	15.00	4/01	34s
Personal Goods				
Personal care products and services purchases	yr	385	1999	30r
Shampoo, Alberto VO5	15 oz	1.15	3/01	4c
Toothpaste, Crest or Colgate	6-7 oz	2.26	3/01	4c
Personal Services				
Dry cleaning, man's 2-pc suit		8.51	3/01	4c
Man's haircut, barbershop, no styling		11.22	3/01	4c
Personal services, household, expenditures on	yr	300	1999	30r
Woman's shampoo, trim, blow-dry, no style-change		26.00	3/01	4c
Pets				
Pets, toys, and playground equipment, expenditures on	yr	375	1999	30r
Restaurant Food				
Chicken, fried, thigh and drumstick, KFC/Church's		2.33	3/01	4c
Hamburger with cheese, McDonald's	1/4 lb	2.22	3/01	4c
Pizza, Pizza Hut or Pizza Inn	11-12 in	8.99	3/01	4c
Taxes				
Federal income taxes paid	yr	2326	1999	30r
Personal taxes, expenditures on	yr	3223	1999	30r
Property taxes paid	yr	1152	1999	30r
State and local income taxes paid	yr	753	1999	30r
Transportation				
Transportation, ACCRA Index		106.60	3/01	4c
Bus fare, one-way	trip	1.10	2000	1c
Bus fare, to central business district	1-way	1.10	3/01	4c
Cars and trucks, new, expenditures on	yr	1280	1999	30r
Cars and trucks, used, expenditures on	yr	1763	1999	30r
Diesel at the pump	gal	1.25	10/99	73s
Gasoline and motor oil purchases	yr	1036	1999	30r
Gasoline before-tax price (cents)	gal	109.50	10/00	43s
Maintenance and repair expenditures	yr	594	1999	30r
Public transportation, expenditures on	yr	341	1999	30r
Tire balance, computer or spin balance, front	wheel	8.65	3/01	4c
Transportation purchases	yr	6617	1999	30r
Vehicle expenses, miscellaneous, purchases	yr	2159	1999	30r
Vehicle insurance payments	yr	701	1999	30r
Vehicle purchases (net outlay)	yr	3081	1999	30r
Vehicle rental, lease expenditures	yr	536	1999	30r
Utilities				
Utilities, ACCRA Index		110.40	3/01	4c
Electrical bill, average	mos	72.83	9/00	9s
Electricity, expenditures on	yr	841	1999	30r
Electricity, summer, 250 KWh	mos	25.93	2/96	96c
Electricity, summer, 500 KWh	mos	46.95	2/96	96c
Electricity, summer, 750 KWh	mos	67.94	2/96	96c
Electricity, summer, 1000 KWh	mos	79.88	2/96	96c
Electricity and other, mixed, 2400 sq ft, new home	mos	65.48	3/01	4c
Electricity cost, average	KWh	6.59	9/00	9s
Utilities, fuels, and public services purchased	yr	2401	1999	30r
Water and other public services, expenditures on	yr	273	1999	30r

Values are in dollars or fractions of dollars. In the column headed *Ref*, references are shown to sources. Each reference is followed by a letter. These refer to the geographical level for which data were reported: s=State, r=Region, and c=City or metro. The abbreviation *ex* is used to mean *except* or *excluding*; *exp* stands for expenditures. For other abbreviations and further explanations, please see the Introduction.

Columbus, OH - continued

Item	Per	Value	Date	Ref.
Weddings				
Wedding (national average cost)		19936	2000	33r
Wedding (regional average total cost)		16195	1997	110r
Attendants' gifts		321	1998	33r
Bridal attendants' apparel (5 persons)		824	2000	33r
Bride's headpiece/veil		173	1998	33r
Bride's wedding dress		859	1998	33r
Clergy, religious facility fee		242	1998	33r
Engagement ring		3177	1998	33r
Flowers		789	1998	33r
Groom's formalwear rental		99	2000	33r
Limousine		410	1998	33r
Marriage license cost		45.00	4/01	35s
Men's formalwear (ushers, best man)		469	2000	33r
Mother of bride apparel		241	2000	33r
Music		866	1998	33r
Photography and videography		1368	1998	33r
Rehearsal dinner		728	1998	33r
Wedding invitations and announcements		341	1998	33r
Wedding reception		7968	2000	33r
Wedding rings (bride and groom)		1060	1998	33r

Corpus Christi, TX

Item	Per	Value	Date	Ref.
Alcoholic Beverages				
Alcoholic beverage purchases	yr	253	1999	30r
Malt beverages, all types, all sizes, any origin	16 oz	0.96	7/01	11r
Appliances				
Major appliances, expenditures on	yr	172	1999	30r
Small appliances, housewares, expenditures on	yr	81	1999	30r
Banking and Money				
Mortgage interest and charges paid	yr	2039	1999	30r
Mortgage principal paid on owned property	yr	1026	1999	30r
Vehicle finance charges paid	yr	365	1999	30r
Business Expenses				
Business travel, car rental	day	48	2001	3c
Business travel, food	day	40	2001	3c
Business travel, hotel	day	94	2001	3c
Charity				
Cash contributions, expenditures	yr	1127	1999	30r
Child Care				
Child raising cost, total, age 0-2	yr	8540	1999	60r
Child raising cost, total, age 3-5	yr	8780	1999	60r
Child raising cost, total, age 6-8	yr	8820	1999	60r
Child raising cost, total, age 9-11	yr	8800	1999	60r
Child raising cost, total, age 12-14	yr	9510	1999	60r
Child raising cost, total, age 15-17	yr	9740	1999	60r
Child's child care and education, age 0-2	yr	1380	1999	60r
Child's child care and education, age 3-5	yr	1520	1999	60r
Child's child care and education, age 6-8	yr	990	1999	60r
Child's child care and education, age 9-11	yr	650	1999	60r
Child's child care and education, age 12-14	yr	490	1999	60r
Child's child care and education, age 15-17	yr	840	1999	60r
Child's clothing, age 0-2	yr	480	1999	60r
Child's clothing, age 3-5	yr	470	1999	60r
Child's clothing, age 6-8	yr	520	1999	60r
Child's clothing, age 9-11	yr	570	1999	60r
Child's clothing, age 12-14	yr	950	1999	60r
Child's clothing, age 15-17	yr	850	1999	60r
Child's food, age 0-2	yr	1000	1999	60r
Child's food, age 3-5	yr	1160	1999	60r
Child's food, age 6-8	yr	1490	1999	60r
Child's food, age 9-11	yr	1770	1999	60r
Child's food, age 12-14	yr	1770	1999	60r
Child's food, age 15-17	yr	1980	1999	60r
Child's health care, age 0-2	yr	620	1999	60r
Child's health care, age 3-5	yr	590	1999	60r
Child's health care, age 6-8	yr	680	1999	60r

Corpus Christi, TX - continued

Item	Per	Value	Date	Ref.
Child Care - continued				
Child's health care, age 9-11	yr	720	1999	60r
Child's health care, age 12-14	yr	730	1999	60r
Child's health care, age 15-17	yr	760	1999	60r
Child's housing, age 0-2	yr	3070	1999	60r
Child's housing, age 3-5	yr	3050	1999	60r
Child's housing, age 6-8	yr	3010	1999	60r
Child's housing, age 9-11	yr	2850	1999	60r
Child's housing, age 12-14	yr	3040	1999	60r
Child's housing, age 15-17	yr	2650	1999	60r
Child's personal care, reading, age 0-2	yr	910	1999	60r
Child's personal care, reading, age 3-5	yr	930	1999	60r
Child's personal care, reading, age 6-8	yr	960	1999	60r
Child's personal care, reading, age 9-11	yr	1000	1999	60r
Child's personal care, reading, age 12-14	yr	1170	1999	60r
Child's personal care, reading, age 15-17	yr	950	1999	60r
Clothing				
Apparel and services purchases	yr	1610	1999	30r
Boys, 2 to 15, expenditures on	yr	89	1999	30r
Children under 2, expenditures on	yr	79	1999	30r
Footwear, expenditures on	yr	283	1999	30r
Girls, 2 to 15, expenditures on	yr	103	1999	30r
Men and boys, expenditures on	yr	351	1999	30r
Men, 16 and over, expenditures on	yr	262	1999	30r
Women, 16 and over, expenditures on	yr	538	1999	30r
Communications				
Cable modem installation, AT&T-BIS		150.00	6/99	103s
Cable modem installation, Marcus		499.00	6/99	103s
Cable modem installation, Time Warner		75.00-225.00	6/99	103s
Cable modem rate, cable subscriber, AT&T-BIS	mos	39.95	6/99	103s
Cable modem rate, cable subscriber, Marcus	mos	14.95-49.95	6/99	103s
Cable modem rate, cable subscriber, Time Warner	mos	39.95-49.95	6/99	103s
Cable modem rate, non-cable subscriber, Marcus	mos	60.95	6/99	103s
Cable modem rate, non-cable subscriber, Time Warner	mos	39.95-54.95	6/99	103s
Phone line, single, business, field visit	inst.	71.90	12/97	17s
Phone line, single, business, no field visit	inst.	57.30	12/97	17s
Phone line, single, residence, field visit	inst.	52.95	12/97	17s
Phone line, single, residence, no field visit	inst.	38.35	12/97	17s
Postage and stationery, expenditures on	yr	104	1999	30r
Postal rate, express mail, up to half-pound		12.45	7/01	108r
Postal rate, letter, first class, first ounce		0.34	7/01	108r
Postal rate, letter, two ounces		0.57	7/01	108r
Postal rate, post card		0.21	7/01	108r
Postal rate, priority mail, two pounds		3.95	7/01	108r
Postal rate, priority mail, up to one pound		3.50	7/01	108r
Telephone bill, business, basic rate	mos	21.30	12/97	18c
Telephone bill, residential, basic rate	mos	9.10	12/97	18c
Telephone services, expenditures on	yr	860	1999	30r
Education				
Board, 4-year private college/university	yr	2198	1996	38s
Board, 4-year public college/university	yr	1759	1996	38s
Education expenditures	yr	431	1999	30r
Room, 4-year private college/university	yr	2000	1996	38s
Room, 4-year public college/university	yr	1885	1996	38s
Total cost, 4-year private college/university	yr	13156	1996	38s
Total cost, 4-year public college/university	yr	5464	1996	38s
Tuition, 2-year public college/university, in state	yr	771	1996	38s
Tuition, 4-year private college/university, in state	yr	8959	1996	38s
Tuition, 4-year public college/university	yr	1820	1996	38s
Energy and Fuels				
Electricity	KWh	0.09	7/01	11r
Electricity	500 KWhs	47.29	7/01	11r

Values are in dollars or fractions of dollars. In the column headed *Ref*, references are shown to sources. Each reference is followed by a letter. These refer to the geographical level for which data were reported: s=State, r=Region, and c=City or metro. The abbreviation *ex* is used to mean *except* or *excluding*; *exp* stands for *expenditures*. For other abbreviations and further explanations, please see the Introduction.

Corpus Christi, TX - continued

Item	Per	Value	Date	Ref.
Energy and Fuels				
Fuel oil #2	gal	1.43	7/01	11r
Fuel oil and other fuels, expenditures on	yr	45	1999	30r
Gas, natural, commercial rate	1000 cf	6.94	11/00	88s
Gasoline, all types	gal	1.60	7/01	11r
Gasoline, unleaded midgrade	gal	1.65	7/01	11r
Gasoline, unleaded premium	gal	1.74	7/01	11r
Natural gas, expenditures on	yr	164	1999	30r
Utility (piped) gas, therm		1.01	7/01	11r
Utility (piped) gas, 40 therms		44.29	7/01	11r
Utility (piped) gas, 100 therms		97.44	7/01	11r
Entertainment				
Entertainment purchases	yr	1574	1999	30r
Fees and admissions paid	yr	371	1999	30r
Reading purchases	yr	121	1999	30r
Television, radios, sound equipment, expenditures on	yr	561	1999	30r
Funerals				
Total cost of funeral		5842.28	1/99	78r
Acknowledgement cards		28.35	1/99	78r
Casket		2494.29	1/99	78r
Cosmetology, hair, other preparation		109.22	1/99	78r
Embalming		361.42	1/99	78r
Funeral at funeral home		349.20	1/99	78r
Hearse (local)		161.91	1/99	78r
Professional service charges		1116.50	1/99	78r
Service car/van		65.56	1/99	78r
Transfer of remains to funeral home		143.56	1/99	78r
Vault		785.25	1/99	78r
Visitation/viewing		227.02	1/99	78r
Groceries				
American processed cheese	lb	3.50	7/01	11r
Bakery products, expenditures on	yr	261	1999	30r
Bananas	lb	0.47	7/01	11r
Beans, dried, any type, all sizes	lb	0.63	7/01	11r
Beef for stew, boneless	lb	2.86	7/01	11r
Beef, expenditures on	yr	210	1999	30r
Bologna, all beef or mixed	lb	2.29	7/01	11r
Bread, French	lb	1.66	7/01	11r
Bread, white, pan	lb	0.87	7/01	11r
Bread, whole wheat, pan	lb	1.38	7/01	11r
Broccoli	lb	1.04	7/01	11r
Butter, salted, grade AA, stick	lb	2.26	7/01	11r
Butter, yoghurt, cheese, etc, expenditures on	yr	170	1999	30r
Cabbage	lb	0.42	7/01	11r
Cereals and cereal products, expenditures on	yr	140	1999	30r
Cheddar cheese, natural	lb	3.75	7/01	11r
Chicken breast, bone-in	lb	1.85	7/01	11r
Chicken legs, bone-in	lb	1.34	7/01	11r
Chicken, fresh, whole	lb	1.05	7/01	11r
Chops, boneless,	lb	4.13	7/01	11r
Chuck roast, graded and ungraded, excl U.S. prime and choice	lb	2.35	7/01	11r
Chuck roast, U.S. choice, boneless	lb	2.67	7/01	11r
Coffee, 100%, ground roast, all sizes	lb	2.88	7/01	11r
Coffee, instant, plain, regular, all sizes	16 oz	9.25	7/01	11r
Cola, non diet,	2 liter	1.11	7/01	11r
Crackers, soda, salted	lb	1.70	7/01	11r
Dairy product purchases	yr	282	1999	30r
Eggs, expenditures on	yr	32	1999	30r
Fats and oils, expenditures on	yr	79	1999	30r
Fish and seafood, expenditures on	yr	99	1999	30r
Flour, white, all purpose	lb	0.32	7/01	11r
Food (excl fruit and vegetables), eaten at home, purchases	yr	815	1999	30r
Food cooked on trips, expenditures on	yr	36	1999	30r
Food purchases	yr	4533	1999	30r
Food purchases, eaten away from home	yr	1873	1999	30r
Food purchases, food eaten at home	yr	2660	1999	30r
Fresh fruits, expenditures on	yr	128	1999	30r
Fresh milk and cream, expenditures on	yr	112	1999	30r

Corpus Christi, TX - continued

Item	Per	Value	Date	Ref.
Groceries - continued				
Fresh vegetables, expenditures on	yr	131	1999	30r
Fruit and vegetable purchases	yr	438	1999	30r
Grapefruit	lb	0.59	7/01	11r
Grapes, Thompson, seedless	lb	2.12	7/01	11r
Ground beef, 100% beef	lb	1.76	7/01	11r
Ground beef, lean and extra lean	lb	2.60	7/01	11r
Ground chuck, 100% beef	lb	2.08	7/01	11r
Ham, boneless, excl canned	lb	2.71	7/01	11r
Ham, rump or shank half, bone-in, smoked	lb	2.19	7/01	11r
Ice cream, prepackaged, bulk, regular	1/2 gal	3.93	7/01	11r
Lemons	lb	1.32	7/01	11r
Lettuce, iceberg	lb	0.76	7/01	11r
Milk, fresh, low fat,	gal	2.75	7/01	11r
Milk, fresh, whole, fortified	gal	2.97	7/01	11r
Nonalcoholic beverages, expenditures on	yr	228	1999	30r
Orange juice, frozen concentrate	16 oz	1.95	7/01	11r
Oranges, Navel	lb	0.73	7/01	11r
Oranges, Valencia	lb	0.55	7/01	11r
Peanut butter, creamy, all sizes	lb	1.83	7/01	11r
Pears, Anjou	lb	0.98	7/01	11r
Pork chops, center cut, bone-in	lb	3.33	7/01	11r
Pork sausage, fresh, loose	lb	2.59	7/01	11r
Pork shoulder picnic, bone-in, smoked	lb	1.12	7/01	11r
Pork, expenditures on	yr	162	1999	30r
Potato chips	16 oz	3.59	7/01	11r
Potatoes, frozen, french fried	lb	1.00	7/01	11r
Potatoes, white, all types	lb	0.44	7/01	11r
Poultry, expenditures on	yr	137	1999	30r
Processed fruits, expenditures on	yr	97	1999	30r
Processed vegetables, expenditures on	yr	82	1999	30r
Rice, white, long grain, uncooked	lb	0.51	7/01	11r
Round roast, graded and ungraded, excl U.S. prime and choice	lb	2.96	7/01	11r
Round steak, graded and ungraded, excl U.S. prime and choice	lb	3.11	7/01	11r
Sirloin steak, graded and ungraded, excl U.S. prime and choice	lb	4.23	7/01	11r
Spaghetti and macaroni	lb	0.78	7/01	11r
Steak, round, U.S. choice, boneless	lb	3.56	7/01	11r
Steak, sirloin, U.S. choice, boneless	lb	5.65	7/01	11r
Strawberries, dry pint	12 oz	1.50	7/01	11r
Sugar and other sweets, expenditures on	yr	99	1999	30r
Sugar, white, 33-80 ounce package	lb	0.39	7/01	11r
Sugar, white, all sizes	lb	0.42	7/01	11r
Tobacco products and smoking supplies purchases	yr	288	1999	30r
Tomatoes, field grown	lb	1.43	7/01	11r
Tuna, light, chunk	lb	1.77	7/01	11r
Turkey, frozen, whole	lb	1.05	7/01	11r
Goods and Services				
B&B Japanese maple (acer japonicum)	gal	79.98-99.00	4/00	93r
Boxwood (buxus)	2 gal	12.98-18.99	4/00	93r
Christmas tree, noble fir		40-60	2000	65s
Daylily (hemerocallis)	gal	7.96-11.00	4/00	93r
Flat of annuals		13.99-27.99	4/00	93r
Fountain grass (pennisetum)	gal	6.96-9.00	4/00	93r
Hanging basket (10 in)		9.99-24.99	4/00	93r
Hardy geranium (geranium)	gal	5.96-8.00	4/00	93r
Hosta (hosta)	gal	8.96-12.99	4/00	93r
Lilac (syrubga vulgaris)	2 gal	13.00-19.99	4/00	93r
Rhododendron (rhododendron)	2 gal	12.98-29.99	4/00	93r

Values are in dollars or fractions of dollars. In the column headed *Ref*, references are shown to sources. Each reference is followed by a letter. These refer to the geographical level for which data were reported: s=State, r=Region, and c=City or metro. The abbreviation *ex* is used to mean *except* or *excluding*; *exp* stands for *expenditures*. For other abbreviations and further explanations, please see the Introduction.

Corpus Christi, TX - continued

Item	Per	Value	Date	Ref.
Goods and Services				
Sage (salvia)	gal	5.96-8.00	4/00	93r
Wintercreeper euonymus (euonymus fortunei)	2 gal	13.00-18.99	4/00	93r
Hunting license	yr	19.00	4/01	34s
Health Care				
Cardiac catheterization, ave hospital/physician charges		20140	1998	77s
Childbirth, Cesarean delivery		11587	1997	13r
Childbirth, vaginal delivery		6725	1997	13r
Drugs, expenditures on	yr	399	1999	30r
Health care purchases	yr	1971	1999	30r
Health insurance expenditures	yr	933	1999	30r
Hysterectomy, laproscopically-assisted, ave hospital/physician charges		15700	1998	76s
Hysterectomy, vaginal, ave hospital and physician charges		12180	1998	76s
Medicaid dispensing fee		5.27	1999	87s
Medical services expenditures	yr	547	1999	30r
Medical supplies, expenditures on	yr	91	1999	30r
Household Goods				
Floor coverings, expenditures on	yr	44	1999	30r
Furniture, expenditures on	yr	335	1999	30r
Household furnishings and equipment purchases	yr	1328	1999	30r
Household textiles, expenditures on	yr	89	1999	30r
Laundry and cleaning supplies, expenditures on	yr	113	1999	30r
Housing				
Home, 2200 sq ft, 4-br, 2-bath, 2-car garage, average		145667	2000	47c
Home price, existing, ave		160100	10/00	90r
Home value, median		112000	2001	53s
Household operation expenditures	yr	553	1999	30r
Housekeeping supplies purchases	yr	473	1999	30r
Housing, expenditures on	yr	10303	1999	30r
Maintenance, repairs, insurance expenditures	yr	699	1999	30r
Monthly rental value of owned home	mos	505	1999	30r
Owned dwellings, expenditures own	yr	3465	1999	30r
Rent expenditures	yr	1641	1999	30r
Rental unit, 1 bedroom, with utilities	mos	438	4/01	41c
Rental unit, 2 bedroom, with utilities	mos	559	4/01	41c
Rental unit, 3 bedroom, with utilities	mos	761	4/01	41c
Rental unit, 4 bedroom, with utilities	mos	900	4/01	41c
Shelter, expenditures on	yr	5467	1999	30r
Insurance and Pensions				
Life and other personal insurance purchases	yr	414	1999	30r
Pensions and Social Security, expenditures on	yr	2635	1999	30r
Personal insurance and pensions, expenditures on	yr	3048	1999	30r
Legal Fees				
Divorce, filing fee		150.00-200.00	4/01	35s
Driver's license fee	renew	20.00	1999	48s
Driver's license fee	orig	24.00	1999	48s
Fishing license	yr	19.00	4/01	34s
Personal Goods				
Personal care products and services purchases	yr	393	1999	30r
Personal Services				
Personal services, household, expenditures on	yr	258	1999	30r
Pets				
Pets, toys, and playground equipment, expenditures on	yr	306	1999	30r

Corpus Christi, TX - continued

Item	Per	Value	Date	Ref.
Taxes				
Federal income taxes paid	yr	2047	1999	30r
Personal taxes, expenditures on	yr	2554	1999	30r
Property taxes paid	yr	726	1999	30r
State and local income taxes paid	yr	363	1999	30r
Transportation				
Bus fare, one-way	trip	0.50	2000	1c
Cars and trucks, new, expenditures on	yr	1648	1999	30r
Cars and trucks, used, expenditures on	yr	1651	1999	30r
Diesel at the pump	gal	1.18	10/99	73s
Gasoline and motor oil purchases	yr	1052	1999	30r
Gasoline before-tax price (cents)	gal	101.30	10/00	43s
Maintenance and repair expenditures	yr	621	1999	30r
Public transportation, expenditures on	yr	298	1999	30r
Transportation purchases	yr	6738	1999	30r
Vehicle expenses, miscellaneous, purchases	yr	2033	1999	30r
Vehicle insurance payments	yr	696	1999	30r
Vehicle purchases (net outlay)	yr	3354	1999	30r
Vehicle rental, lease expenditures	yr	352	1999	30r
Utilities				
Electrical bill, average	mos	87.17	9/00	9s
Electricity, expenditures on	yr	1115	1999	30r
Electricity, summer, 250 KWh	mos	24.22	2/96	96c
Electricity, summer, 500 KWh	mos	41.16	2/96	96c
Electricity, summer, 750 KWh	mos	58.11	2/96	96c
Electricity, summer, 1000 KWh	mos	75.05	2/96	96c
Electricity cost, average	KWh	6.48	9/00	9s
Water and other public services, expenditures on	yr	298	1999	30r
Weddings				
Wedding (national average cost)		19936	2000	33r
Attendants' gifts		321	1998	33r
Bridal attendants' apparel (5 persons)		824	2000	33r
Bride's headpiece/veil		173	1998	33r
Bride's wedding dress		859	1998	33r
Clergy, religious facility fee		242	1998	33r
Engagement ring		3177	1998	33r
Flowers		789	1998	33r
Groom's formalwear rental		99	2000	33r
Limousine		410	1998	33r
Marriage license cost		36.00	4/01	35s
Men's formalwear (ushers, best man)		469	2000	33r
Mother of bride apparel		241	2000	33r
Music		866	1998	33r
Photography and videography		1368	1998	33r
Rehearsal dinner		728	1998	33r
Wedding invitations and announcements		341	1998	33r
Wedding reception		7968	2000	33r
Wedding rings (bride and groom)		1060	1998	33r

Corvallis, OR

Item	Per	Value	Date	Ref.
Average annual expenditures	yr	40662	1999	30r
Composite, ACCRA index		112.40	3/01	4c
Alcoholic Beverages				
Alcoholic beverage purchases	yr	372	1999	30r
Beer, Heineken, 12-oz, ex deposit	6	6.87	3/01	4c
J & B Scotch	750-ml	22.95	3/01	4c
Malt beverages, all types, all sizes, any origin	16 oz	0.94	7/01	11r
Wine, Livingston or Gallo, Chablis blanc	1.5 liter	5.67	3/01	4c
Wine, red and white table, all sizes, any origin	liter	6.00	7/01	11r
Appliances				
Appliance repair, service call, washing machine	min lab chg	47.23	3/01	4c
Major appliances, expenditures on	yr	167	1999	30r
Small appliances, housewares, expenditures on	yr	105	1999	30r

Values are in dollars or fractions of dollars. In the column headed *Ref*, references are shown to sources. Each reference is followed by a letter. These refer to the geographical level for which data were reported: s=State, r=Region, and c=City or metro. The abbreviation *ex* is used to mean *except* or *excluding*; *exp* stands for expenditures. For other abbreviations and further explanations, please see the Introduction.

Corvallis, OR - continued

Item	Per	Value	Date	Ref.
Banking and Money				
Mortgage interest and charges paid	yr	3368	1999	30r
Mortgage principal paid on owned property	yr	1677	1999	30r
Mortgage rate, incl. points and orig. fee, 30-yr. conv. fixed or ARM	mos	6.87	3/01	4c
Vehicle finance charges paid	yr	311	1999	30r
Charity				
Cash contributions, expenditures	yr	1344	1999	30r
Child Care				
Child raising cost, total, age 0-2	yr	9140	1999	60r
Child raising cost, total, age 3-5	yr	9370	1999	60r
Child raising cost, total, age 6-8	yr	9450	1999	60r
Child raising cost, total, age 9-11	yr	9470	1999	60r
Child raising cost, total, age 12-14	yr	10170	1999	60r
Child raising cost, total, age 15-17	yr	10360	1999	60r
Child's child care and education, age 0-2	yr	1250	1999	60r
Child's child care and education, age 3-5	yr	1380	1999	60r
Child's child care and education, age 6-8	yr	890	1999	60r
Child's child care and education, age 9-11	yr	580	1999	60r
Child's child care and education, age 12-14	yr	430	1999	60r
Child's child care and education, age 15-17	yr	730	1999	60r
Child's clothing, age 0-2	yr	430	1999	60r
Child's clothing, age 3-5	yr	420	1999	60r
Child's clothing, age 6-8	yr	470	1999	60r
Child's clothing, age 9-11	yr	520	1999	60r
Child's clothing, age 12-14	yr	870	1999	60r
Child's clothing, age 15-17	yr	770	1999	60r
Child's food, age 0-2	yr	1120	1999	60r
Child's food, age 3-5	yr	1280	1999	60r
Child's food, age 6-8	yr	1640	1999	60r
Child's food, age 9-11	yr	1930	1999	60r
Child's food, age 12-14	yr	1940	1999	60r
Child's food, age 15-17	yr	2150	1999	60r
Child's health care, age 0-2	yr	490	1999	60r
Child's health care, age 3-5	yr	470	1999	60r
Child's health care, age 6-8	yr	530	1999	60r
Child's health care, age 9-11	yr	570	1999	60r
Child's health care, age 12-14	yr	580	1999	60r
Child's health care, age 15-17	yr	610	1999	60r
Child's housing, age 0-2	yr	3630	1999	60r
Child's housing, age 3-5	yr	3610	1999	60r
Child's housing, age 6-8	yr	3570	1999	60r
Child's housing, age 9-11	yr	3410	1999	60r
Child's housing, age 12-14	yr	3600	1999	60r
Child's housing, age 15-17	yr	3210	1999	60r
Child's personal care, reading, age 0-2	yr	1040	1999	60r
Child's personal care, reading, age 3-5	yr	1060	1999	60r
Child's personal care, reading, age 6-8	yr	1090	1999	60r
Child's personal care, reading, age 9-11	yr	1130	1999	60r
Child's personal care, reading, age 12-14	yr	1300	1999	60r
Child's personal care, reading, age 15-17	yr	1080	1999	60r
Clothing				
Apparel and services purchases	yr	1863	1999	30r
Boys' brief, cotton	3	5.38	3/01	4c
Boys, 2 to 15, expenditures on	yr	80	1999	30r
Children under 2, expenditures on	yr	74	1999	30r
Footwear, expenditures on	yr	307	1999	30r
Girls, 2 to 15, expenditures on	yr	101	1999	30r
Men and boys, expenditures on	yr	443	1999	30r
Men, 16 and over, expenditures on	yr	363	1999	30r
Shirt, man's dress shirt		24.47	3/01	4c
Slacks, man's "No Wrinkles" khaki		46.00	3/01	4c
Women, 16 and over, expenditures on	yr	594	1999	30r
Communications				
Newspaper subscription, daily and Sunday delivery	mos	11.41	3/01	4c
Phone line, single, business, field visit	inst.	31.00	12/97	17s
Phone line, single, business, no field visit	inst.	31.00	12/97	17s
Phone line, single, residence, field visit	inst.	12.00	12/97	17s
Phone line, single, residence, no field visit	inst.	12.00	12/97	17s
Postage and stationery, expenditures on	yr	150	1999	30r

Corvallis, OR - continued

Item	Per	Value	Date	Ref.
Communications - continued				
Postal rate, express mail, up to half-pound		12.45	7/01	108r
Postal rate, letter, first class, first ounce		0.34	7/01	108r
Postal rate, letter, two ounces		0.57	7/01	108r
Postal rate, post card		0.21	7/01	108r
Postal rate, priority mail, two pounds		3.95	7/01	108r
Postal rate, priority mail, up to one pound		3.50	7/01	108r
Telephone bill, family of three	mos	24.00	3/01	4c
Telephone services, expenditures on	yr	825	1999	30r
Education				
Board, 4-year private college/university	yr	2750	1996	38s
Board, 4-year public college/university	yr	2474	1996	38s
Education expenditures	yr	676	1999	30r
Room, 4-year private college/university	yr	2257	1996	38s
Room, 4-year public college/university	yr	1647	1996	38s
Total cost, 4-year private college/university	yr	18899	1996	38s
Total cost, 4-year public college/university	yr	7354	1996	38s
Tuition, 2-year public college/university, in state	yr	1338	1996	38s
Tuition, 4-year private college/university, in state	yr	13892	1996	38s
Tuition, 4-year public college/university	yr	3233	1996	38s
Energy and Fuels				
Electricity	500 KWhs	48.23	7/01	11r
Electricity	KWh	0.11	7/01	11r
Energy, combined forms, 2400 sq ft	mos	121.04	3/01	4c
Energy, exc. electricity, 2400 sq ft	mos	76.87	3/01	4c
Fuel oil and other fuels, expenditures on	yr	35	1999	30r
Gas, natural, commercial rate	1000 cf	7.55	11/00	88s
Gas, regular unleaded, cash, self-service	gal	1.55	3/01	4c
Gasoline, all types	gal	1.91	7/01	11r
Gasoline, unleaded premium	gal	2.05	7/01	11r
Gasoline, unleaded regular	gal	1.83	7/01	11r
Natural gas, expenditures on	yr	255	1999	30r
Utility (piped) gas, therm		0.98	7/01	11r
Utility (piped) gas, 40 therms		40.74	7/01	11r
Utility (piped) gas, 100 therms		96.80	7/01	11r
Entertainment				
Bowling, Saturday evening rate	line	2.50	3/01	4c
Entertainment purchases	yr	2139	1999	30r
Fees and admissions paid	yr	545	1999	30r
Monopoly game, Parker Brothers', No. 9	game	12.49	3/01	4c
Movie, first-run, Saturday, evening	adm.	6.75	3/01	4c
Television, radios, sound equipment, expenditures on	yr	624	1999	30r
Tennis balls, yellow, Wilson or Penn, 3	can	2.24	3/01	4c
Funerals				
Total cost of funeral		5401.08	1/99	78r
Acknowledgement cards		33.64	1/99	78r
Casket		2170.43	1/99	78r
Cosmetology, hair, other preparation		136.32	1/99	78r
Embalming		319.13	1/99	78r
Funeral at funeral home		370.21	1/99	78r
Hearse (local)		161.04	1/99	78r
Professional service charges		963.15	1/99	78r
Service car/van		133.99	1/99	78r
Transfer of remains to funeral home		159.82	1/99	78r
Vault		778.07	1/99	78r
Visitation/viewing		175.28	1/99	78r
Groceries				
Groceries, ACCRA Index		101.60	3/01	4c
Antibiotic ointment, Polysporin	0.5 oz	4.63	3/01	4c
Apples, red delicious	lb	0.84	7/01	11r
Baby food, strained vegetables or fruit, lowest price	4-4.5 oz	0.36	3/01	4c
Bacon, sliced	lb	3.38	7/01	11r
Bakery products, expenditures on	yr	299	1999	30r
Bananas	lb	0.61	3/01	4c
Bananas	lb	0.54	7/01	11r

Values are in dollars or fractions of dollars. In the column headed *Ref*, references are shown to sources. Each reference is followed by a letter. These refer to the geographical level for which data were reported: s=State, r=Region, and c=City or metro. The abbreviation *ex* is used to mean *except* or *excluding*; *exp* stands for *expenditures*. For other abbreviations and further explanations, please see the Introduction.

Corvallis, OR - continued

Item	Per	Value	Date	Ref.
Groceries				
Beans, dried, any type, all sizes	lb	0.76	7/01	11r
Beef or hamburger, ground	lb	1.75	3/01	4c
Beef, expenditures on	yr	222	1999	30r
Bread, white	loaf	0.72	3/01	4c
Bread, white, pan	lb	0.99	7/01	11r
Butter, yoghurt, cheese, etc, expenditures on	yr	211	1999	30r
Cereals and bakery product purchases	yr	466	1999	30r
Cereals and cereal products, expenditures on	yr	168	1999	30r
Cheese, Kraft grated Parmesan	8 oz	3.84	3/01	4c
Chicken breast, bone-in	lb	2.45	7/01	11r
Chicken, fresh, whole	lb	1.19	7/01	11r
Chicken, whole fryer	lb	1.11	3/01	4c
Chops, boneless,	lb	4.00	7/01	11r
Chuck roast, graded and ungraded, excl U.S. prime and choice	lb	2.55	7/01	11r
Cigarettes, Winston, Kings	carton	33.05	3/01	4c
Coffee, 100%, ground roast, all sizes	lb	3.80	7/01	11r
Coffee, vacuum-packed	13 oz	3.52	3/01	4c
Cookies, chocolate chip	lb	2.83	7/01	11r
Corn Flakes, Kellogg's or Post Toasties	18 oz	2.79	3/01	4c
Corn, frozen, whole kernel, lowest price	16 oz	1.02	3/01	4c
Dairy product purchases	yr	341	1999	30r
Eggs, expenditures on	yr	39	1999	30r
Eggs, Grade A or AA	dozen	1.38	3/01	4c
Eggs, grade AA, large	dozen	1.23	7/01	11r
Fats and oils, expenditures on	yr	88	1999	30r
Fish and seafood, expenditures on	yr	121	1999	30r
Food (excl fruit and vegetables), eaten at home, purchases	yr	1001	1999	30r
Food cooked on trips, expenditures on	yr	64	1999	30r
Food purchases	yr	5312	1999	30r
Food purchases, eaten away from home	yr	2180	1999	30r
Food purchases, food eaten at home	yr	3132	1999	30r
Fresh fruits, expenditures on	yr	186	1999	30r
Fresh milk and cream, expenditures on	yr	130	1999	30r
Fresh vegetables, expenditures on	yr	177	1999	30r
Grapefruit	lb	0.68	7/01	11r
Grapes, Thompson, seedless	lb	2.42	7/01	11r
Ground beef, lean and extra lean	lb	2.46	7/01	11r
Ice cream, prepackaged, bulk, regular	1/2 gal	3.62	7/01	11r
Lettuce, iceberg	head	0.81	3/01	4c
Lettuce, iceberg	lb	0.63	7/01	11r
Margarine, Blue Bonnet or Parkay, stick	lb	0.64	3/01	4c
Meats, poultry, fish, and egg purchases	yr	761	1999	30r
Milk, fresh, low fat,	gal	2.80	7/01	11r
Milk, fresh, whole, fortified	gal	2.88	7/01	11r
Milk, whole	1/2 gal	1.79	3/01	4c
Nonalcoholic beverages, expenditures on	yr	258	1999	30r
Orange juice, Minute Maid frozen	12 oz	1.27	3/01	4c
Oranges, Navel	lb	0.97	7/01	11r
Oranges, Valencia	lb	0.43	7/01	11r
Peaches	lb	1.38	7/01	11r
Peaches, halves or slices, Hunt's, Del Monte, or Libby's	29 oz	1.70	3/01	4c
Peanut butter, creamy, all sizes	lb	2.14	7/01	11r
Peas, green, Del Monte or Green Giant	15 oz	0.84	3/01	4c
Pork chops, center cut, bone-in	lb	3.83	7/01	11r
Pork, expenditures on	yr	141	1999	30r
Potatoes, white or red	10 lb	1.65	3/01	4c
Potatoes, white, all types	lb	0.37	7/01	11r
Poultry, expenditures on	yr	146	1999	30r
Processed fruits, expenditures on	yr	118	1999	30r
Processed vegetables, expenditures on	yr	81	1999	30r
Round roast, graded and ungraded, excl U.S. prime and choice	lb	3.07	7/01	11r
Round roast, U.S. choice, boneless	lb	3.37	7/01	11r
Round steak, graded and ungraded, excl U.S. prime and choice	lb	3.51	7/01	11r
Sausage, Jimmy Dean/Owens pork	lb	3.47	3/01	4c
Shortening, vegetable, Crisco	3 lb	2.78	3/01	4c

Corvallis, OR - continued

Item	Per	Value	Date	Ref.
Groceries - continued				
Sirloin steak, graded and ungraded, excl U.S. prime and choice	lb	4.67	7/01	11r
Soft drink, Coca Cola, ex deposit	2 liter	1.29	3/01	4c
Steak, sirloin, U.S. choice, boneless	lb	6.20	7/01	11r
Steak, T-bone	lb	6.05	3/01	4c
Strawberries, dry pint	12 oz	1.79	7/01	11r
Sugar and other sweets, expenditures on	yr	124	1999	30r
Sugar, cane or beet	4 lbs	1.69	3/01	4c
Sugar, white, all sizes	lb	0.46	7/01	11r
Tobacco products and smoking supplies purchases	yr	217	1999	30r
Tomatoes, field grown	lb	1.17	7/01	11r
Tomatoes, Hunt's or Del Monte	14.5 oz	0.92	3/01	4c
Tuna, chunk, light	6 oz	0.60	3/01	4c
Tuna, light, chunk	lb	2.05	7/01	11r
Goods and Services				
Miscellaneous goods and services, ACCRA Index		106.50	3/01	4c
B&B Japanese maple (acer japonicum)	gal	39.99	4/00	93r
Boxwood (buxus)	2 gal	14.99-24.99	4/00	93r
Christmas tree, noble fir		20-25	2000	65s
Daylily (hemerocallis)	gal	6.99-8.99	4/00	93r
Flat of annuals		16.68	4/00	93r
Fountain grass (pennisetum)	gal	7.99-11.99	4/00	93r
Hanging basket (10 in)		29.99	4/00	93r
Hardy geranium (geranium)	gal	6.99-11.99	4/00	93r
Hosta (hosta)	gal	6.99-18.99	4/00	93r
Lilac (syrubga vulgaris)	2 gal	14.99-17.99	4/00	93r
Miscellaneous purchases	yr	1070	1999	30r
Rhododendron (rhododendron)	2 gal	14.99	4/00	93r
Sage (salvia)	gal	6.99	4/00	93r
Wintercreeper euonymus (euonymus fortunei)	2 gal	14.99-22.99	4/00	93r
Hunting license	yr	17.50	4/01	34s
Health Care				
Health care, ACCRA Index		128.00	3/01	4c
Cardiac catheterization, ave hospital/ physician charges		10940	1998	77s
Childbirth, Cesarean delivery		11587	1997	13r
Childbirth, vaginal delivery		6725	1997	13r
Dentist's fee, adult teeth cleaning and periodic oral exam	visit	107.60	3/01	4c
Doctor's fee, routine exam, established patient	visit	73.33	3/01	4c
Drugs, expenditures on	yr	309	1999	30r
Health care purchases	yr	1869	1999	30r
Health insurance expenditures	yr	868	1999	30r
Hospital care, private room	day	575.00	3/01	4c
Hysterectomy, laproscopically-assisted, ave hospital/physician charges		11660	1998	76s
Hysterectomy, vaginal, ave hospital and physician charges		6680	1998	76s
Medicaid dispensing fee		3.80-4.16	1999	87s
Medical services expenditures	yr	580	1999	30r
Medical supplies, expenditures on	yr	112	1999	30r
Household Goods				
Dishwashing powder, Cascade	50 oz	3.79	3/01	4c
Floor coverings, expenditures on	yr	49	1999	30r
Furniture, expenditures on	yr	444	1999	30r
Household furnishings and equipment purchases	yr	1768	1999	30r
Household textiles, expenditures on	yr	141	1999	30r
Laundry and cleaning supplies, expenditures on	yr	128	1999	30r

Values are in dollars or fractions of dollars. In the column headed *Ref*, references are shown to sources. Each reference is followed by a letter. These refer to the geographical level for which data were reported: s=State, r=Region, and c=City or metro. The abbreviation *ex* is used to mean *except* or *excluding*; *exp* stands for expenditures. For other abbreviations and further explanations, please see the Introduction.

Corvallis, OR - continued

Item	Per	Value	Date	Ref.
Household Goods				
Tissues, facial, Kleenex brand	175	1.54	3/01	4c
Housing				
Housing, ACCRA Index		127.30	3/01	4c
Home price, existing, ave		239400	10/00	90r
Home value, median		149000	2001	53s
House, 2400 sq ft, 8000 sq ft lot, new, urban, utilities	total	281000	3/01	4c
House payment, principal and interest, 25% down payment	mos	1384	3/01	4c
Household operation expenditures	yr	781	1999	30r
Housekeeping supplies purchases	yr	513	1999	30r
Lodging expenditures	yr	575	1999	30r
Maintenance, repairs, insurance expenditures	yr	939	1999	30r
Monthly rental value of owned home	mos	662	1999	30r
Owned dwellings, expenditures own	yr	5231	1999	30r
Rent expenditures	yr	2709	1999	30r
Rent, apartment, 2 br, 1 1/2-2 baths, unfurn, 950 sq ft, water	mos	695	3/01	4c
Rental unit, 1 bedroom, with utilities	mos	499	4/01	41c
Rental unit, 2 bedroom, with utilities	mos	633	4/01	41c
Rental unit, 3 bedroom, with utilities	mos	952	4/01	41c
Rental unit, 4 bedroom, with utilities	mos	1011	4/01	41c
Shelter, expenditures on	yr	8516	1999	30r
Insurance and Pensions				
Life and other personal insurance purchases	yr	355	1999	30r
Pensions and Social Security, expenditures on	yr	3636	1999	30r
Legal Fees				
Combination hunting and fishing license	yr	33.75	4/01	34s
Divorce, filing fee		100.00-250.00	4/01	35s
Driver's license fee	renew	16.25	1999	48s
Driver's license fee	orig	26.25	1999	48s
Fishing license	yr	19.75	4/01	34s
Personal Goods				
Personal care products and services purchases	yr	449	1999	30r
Shampoo, Alberto VO5	15 oz	1.02	3/01	4c
Toothpaste, Crest or Colgate	6-7 oz	2.50	3/01	4c
Personal Services				
Dry cleaning, man's 2-pc suit		9.44	3/01	4c
Man's haircut, barbershop, no styling		13.00	3/01	4c
Personal services, household, expenditures on	yr	353	1999	30r
Woman's shampoo, trim, blow-dry, no style-change		23.99	3/01	4c
Pets				
Pets, toys, and playground equipment, expenditures on	yr	358	1999	30r
Restaurant Food				
Chicken, fried, thigh and drumstick, KFC/Church's		3.14	3/01	4c
Hamburger with cheese, McDonald's	1/4 lb	2.15	3/01	4c
Pizza, Pizza Hut or Pizza Inn	11-12 in	9.99	3/01	4c
Taxes				
Federal income taxes paid	yr	3200	1999	30r
Personal taxes, expenditures on	yr	4153	1999	30r
Property taxes paid	yr	923	1999	30r
State and local income taxes paid	yr	812	1999	30r
Transportation				
Transportation, ACCRA Index		109.30	3/01	4c
Cars and trucks, new, expenditures on	yr	1534	1999	30r
Cars and trucks, used, expenditures on	yr	1593	1999	30r
Diesel at the pump	gal	1.16	10/99	73s
Gasoline and motor oil purchases	yr	1129	1999	30r
Gasoline before-tax price (cents)	gal	128.30	10/00	43s

Corvallis, OR - continued

Item	Per	Value	Date	Ref.
Transportation - continued				
Maintenance and repair expenditures	yr	797	1999	30r
Public transportation, expenditures on	yr	530	1999	30r
Tire balance, computer or spin balance, front	wheel	8.55	3/01	4c
Transportation purchases	yr	7423	1999	30r
Vehicle expenses, miscellaneous, purchases	yr	2585	1999	30r
Vehicle insurance payments	yr	811	1999	30r
Vehicle purchases (net outlay)	yr	3180	1999	30r
Vehicle rental, lease expenditures	yr	666	1999	30r
Utilities				
Utilities, ACCRA Index		100.70	3/01	4c
Electrical bill, average	mos	61.42	9/00	9s
Electricity, expenditures on	yr	725	1999	30r
Electricity and other, mixed, 2400 sq ft, new home	mos	44.17	3/01	4c
Electricity cost, average	KWh	4.70	9/00	9s
Utilities, fuels, and public services purchased	yr	2179	1999	30r
Water and other public services, expenditures on	yr	339	1999	30r
Weddings				
Wedding (national average cost)		19936	2000	33r
Wedding (regional average total cost)		18918	1997	110r
Attendants' gifts		321	1998	33r
Bridal attendants' apparel (5 persons)		824	2000	33r
Bride's headpiece/veil		173	1998	33r
Bride's wedding dress		859	1998	33r
Clergy, religious facility fee		242	1998	33r
Engagement ring		3177	1998	33r
Flowers		789	1998	33r
Groom's formalwear rental		99	2000	33r
Limousine		410	1998	33r
Marriage license cost		60.00	4/01	35s
Men's formalwear (ushers, best man)		469	2000	33r
Mother of bride apparel		241	2000	33r
Music		866	1998	33r
Photography and videography		1368	1998	33r
Rehearsal dinner		728	1998	33r
Wedding invitations and announcements		341	1998	33r
Wedding reception		7968	2000	33r
Wedding rings (bride and groom)		1060	1998	33r

Cumberland, MD

Item	Per	Value	Date	Ref.
Composite, ACCRA index		97.90	12/00	5c
Alcoholic Beverages				
Alcoholic beverage purchases	yr	253	1999	30r
Beer, Heineken, 12-oz, ex deposit	6	6.63	12/00	5c
J & B Scotch	750-ml	19.74	12/00	5c
Malt beverages, all types, all sizes, any origin	16 oz	0.96	7/01	11r
Wine, Livingston or Gallo, Chablis blanc	1.5 liter	6.66	12/00	5c
Appliances				
Appliance repair, service call, washing machine	min lab chg	38.00	12/00	5c
Major appliances, expenditures on	yr	172	1999	30r
Small appliances, housewares, expenditures on	yr	81	1999	30r
Banking and Money				
Mortgage interest and charges paid	yr	2039	1999	30r
Mortgage principal paid on owned property	yr	1026	1999	30r
Mortgage rate, incl. points and orig. fee, 30-yr. conv. fixed or ARM	mos	8.08	12/00	5c
Vehicle finance charges paid	yr	365	1999	30r
Charity				
Cash contributions, expenditures	yr	1127	1999	30r
Child Care				
Child raising cost, total, age 0-2	yr	8540	1999	60r
Child raising cost, total, age 3-5	yr	8780	1999	60r
Child raising cost, total, age 6-8	yr	8820	1999	60r
Child raising cost, total, age 9-11	yr	8800	1999	60r

Values are in dollars or fractions of dollars. In the column headed *Ref*, references are shown to sources. Each reference is followed by a letter. These refer to the geographical level for which data were reported: s=State, r=Region, and c=City or metro. The abbreviation *ex* is used to mean *except* or *excluding*; *exp* stands for expenditures. For other abbreviations and further explanations, please see the Introduction.

Cumberland, MD - continued

Item	Per	Value	Date	Ref.
Child Care				
Child raising cost, total, age 12-14	yr	9510	1999	60r
Child raising cost, total, age 15-17	yr	9740	1999	60r
Child's child care and education, age 0-2	yr	1380	1999	60r
Child's child care and education, age 3-5	yr	1520	1999	60r
Child's child care and education, age 6-8	yr	990	1999	60r
Child's child care and education, age 9-11	yr	650	1999	60r
Child's child care and education, age 12-14	yr	490	1999	60r
Child's child care and education, age 15-17	yr	840	1999	60r
Child's clothing, age 0-2	yr	480	1999	60r
Child's clothing, age 3-5	yr	470	1999	60r
Child's clothing, age 6-8	yr	520	1999	60r
Child's clothing, age 9-11	yr	570	1999	60r
Child's clothing, age 12-14	yr	950	1999	60r
Child's clothing, age 15-17	yr	850	1999	60r
Child's food, age 0-2	yr	1000	1999	60r
Child's food, age 3-5	yr	1160	1999	60r
Child's food, age 6-8	yr	1490	1999	60r
Child's food, age 9-11	yr	1770	1999	60r
Child's food, age 12-14	yr	1770	1999	60r
Child's food, age 15-17	yr	1980	1999	60r
Child's health care, age 0-2	yr	620	1999	60r
Child's health care, age 3-5	yr	590	1999	60r
Child's health care, age 6-8	yr	680	1999	60r
Child's health care, age 9-11	yr	720	1999	60r
Child's health care, age 12-14	yr	730	1999	60r
Child's health care, age 15-17	yr	760	1999	60r
Child's housing, age 0-2	yr	3070	1999	60r
Child's housing, age 3-5	yr	3050	1999	60r
Child's housing, age 6-8	yr	3010	1999	60r
Child's housing, age 9-11	yr	2850	1999	60r
Child's housing, age 12-14	yr	3040	1999	60r
Child's housing, age 15-17	yr	2650	1999	60r
Child's personal care, reading, age 0-2	yr	910	1999	60r
Child's personal care, reading, age 3-5	yr	930	1999	60r
Child's personal care, reading, age 6-8	yr	960	1999	60r
Child's personal care, reading, age 9-11	yr	1000	1999	60r
Child's personal care, reading, age 12-14	yr	1170	1999	60r
Child's personal care, reading, age 15-17	yr	950	1999	60r
Clothing				
Apparel and services purchases	yr	1610	1999	30r
Boys' brief, cotton	3	3.74	12/00	5c
Boys, 2 to 15, expenditures on	yr	89	1999	30r
Children under 2, expenditures on	yr	79	1999	30r
Footwear, expenditures on	yr	283	1999	30r
Girls, 2 to 15, expenditures on	yr	103	1999	30r
Men and boys, expenditures on	yr	351	1999	30r
Men, 16 and over, expenditures on	yr	262	1999	30r
Shirt, man's dress shirt		31.00	12/00	5c
Slacks, man's "No Wrinkles" khaki		49.00	12/00	5c
Women, 16 and over, expenditures on	yr	538	1999	30r
Communications				
Cable modem installation, Comcast		95.00	6/99	103s
Cable modem rate, cable subscriber, Comcast	mos	39.95	6/99	103s
Cable modem rate, non-cable subscriber, Comcast	mos	49.95	6/99	103s
Newspaper subscription, daily and Sunday delivery	mos	12.34	12/00	5c
Phone line, single, business, field visit	inst.	98.50	12/97	17s
Phone line, single, business, no field visit	inst.	98.50	12/97	17s
Phone line, single, residence, field visit	inst.	48.00	12/97	17s
Phone line, single, residence, no field visit	inst.	48.00	12/97	17s
Postage and stationery, expenditures on	yr	104	1999	30r
Postal rate, express mail, up to half-pound		12.45	7/01	108r
Postal rate, letter, first class, first ounce		0.34	7/01	108r
Postal rate, letter, two ounces		0.57	7/01	108r
Postal rate, post card		0.21	7/01	108r
Postal rate, priority mail, two pounds		3.95	7/01	108r
Postal rate, priority mail, up to one pound		3.50	7/01	108r
Telephone bill, family of three	mos	17.51	12/00	5c
Telephone services, expenditures on	yr	860	1999	30r

Cumberland, MD - continued

Item	Per	Value	Date	Ref.
Education				
Board, 4-year private college/university	yr	3022	1996	38s
Board, 4-year public college/university	yr	2435	1996	38s
Education expenditures	yr	431	1999	30r
Room, 4-year private college/university	yr	3524	1996	38s
Room, 4-year public college/university	yr	2722	1996	38s
Total cost, 4-year private college/university	yr	21245	1996	38s
Total cost, 4-year public college/university	yr	8728	1996	38s
Tuition, 2-year public college/university, in state	yr	1967	1996	38s
Tuition, 4-year private college/university, in state	yr	14700	1996	38s
Tuition, 4-year public college/university	yr	3572	1996	38s
Energy and Fuels				
Electricity	500 KWhs	47.29	7/01	11r
Electricity	KWh	0.09	7/01	11r
Energy, combined forms, 2400 sq ft	mos	112.89	12/00	5c
Fuel oil #2	gal	1.43	7/01	11r
Fuel oil and other fuels, expenditures on	yr	45	1999	30r
Gas, cooking, winter, 10 therms	mos	15.74	2/96	98c
Gas, cooking, winter, 30 therms	mos	28.73	2/96	98c
Gas, cooking, winter, 50 therms	mos	41.71	2/96	98c
Gas, heating, winter, average use	mos	143.01	2/96	98c
Gas, natural, commercial rate	1000 cf	8.64	11/00	88s
Gas, regular unleaded, cash, self-service	gal	1.46	12/00	5c
Gasoline, all types	gal	1.60	7/01	11r
Gasoline, unleaded midgrade	gal	1.65	7/01	11r
Gasoline, unleaded premium	gal	1.74	7/01	11r
Natural gas, expenditures on	yr	164	1999	30r
Utility (piped) gas, therm		1.01	7/01	11r
Utility (piped) gas, 40 therms		44.29	7/01	11r
Utility (piped) gas, 100 therms		97.44	7/01	11r
Entertainment				
Bowling, Saturday evening rate	line	2.80	12/00	5c
Entertainment purchases	yr	1574	1999	30r
Fees and admissions paid	yr	371	1999	30r
Monopoly game, Parker Brothers', No. 9	game	12.74	12/00	5c
Movie, first-run, Saturday, evening	adm.	5.67	12/00	5c
Reading purchases	yr	121	1999	30r
Television, radios, sound equipment, expenditures on	yr	561	1999	30r
Tennis balls, yellow, Wilson or Penn, 3	can	2.42	12/00	5c
Funerals				
Total cost of funeral		5922.53	1/99	78r
Acknowledgement cards		63.43	1/99	78r
Casket		2258.77	1/99	78r
Cosmetology, hair, other preparation		127.09	1/99	78r
Embalming		393.49	1/99	78r
Funeral at funeral home		367.50	1/99	78r
Hearse (local)		169.66	1/99	78r
Professional service charges		1211.32	1/99	78r
Service car/van		80.69	1/99	78r
Transfer of remains to funeral home		144.25	1/99	78r
Vault		803.50	1/99	78r
Visitation/viewing		302.83	1/99	78r
Groceries				
Groceries, ACCRA Index		89.10	12/00	5c
American processed cheese	lb	3.50	7/01	11r
Antibiotic ointment, Polysporin	0.5 oz	3.74	12/00	5c
Baby food, strained vegetables or fruit, lowest price	4-4.5 oz	0.43	12/00	5c
Bakery products, expenditures on	yr	261	1999	30r
Bananas	lb	0.47	7/01	11r
Bananas	lb	0.45	12/00	5c
Beans, dried, any type, all sizes	lb	0.63	7/01	11r
Beef for stew, boneless	lb	2.86	7/01	11r
Beef or hamburger, ground	lb	1.31	12/00	5c
Beef, expenditures on	yr	210	1999	30r
Bologna, all beef or mixed	lb	2.29	7/01	11r
Bread, French	lb	1.66	7/01	11r

Values are in dollars or fractions of dollars. In the column headed *Ref*, references are shown to sources. Each reference is followed by a letter. These refer to the geographical level for which data were reported: s=State, r=Region, and c=City or metro. The abbreviation *ex* is used to mean *except* or *excluding*; *exp* stands for expenditures. For other abbreviations and further explanations, please see the Introduction.

Cumberland, MD - continued

Item	Per	Value	Date	Ref.
Groceries				
Bread, white	loaf	0.81	12/00	5c
Bread, white, pan	lb	0.87	7/01	11r
Bread, whole wheat, pan	lb	1.38	7/01	11r
Broccoli	lb	1.04	7/01	11r
Butter, salted, grade AA, stick	lb	2.26	7/01	11r
Butter, yoghurt, cheese, etc, expenditures on	yr	170	1999	30r
Cabbage	lb	0.42	7/01	11r
Cereals and cereal products, expenditures on	yr	140	1999	30r
Cheddar cheese, natural	lb	3.75	7/01	11r
Cheese, Kraft grated Parmesan	8 oz	3.31	12/00	5c
Chicken breast, bone-in	lb	1.85	7/01	11r
Chicken legs, bone-in	lb	1.34	7/01	11r
Chicken, fresh, whole	lb	1.05	7/01	11r
Chicken, whole fryer	lb	0.90	12/00	5c
Chops, boneless,	lb	4.13	7/01	11r
Chuck roast, graded and ungraded, excl U.S. prime and choice	lb	2.35	7/01	11r
Chuck roast, U.S. choice, boneless	lb	2.67	7/01	11r
Cigarettes, Winston, Kings	carton	27.63	12/00	5c
Coffee, 100%, ground roast, all sizes	lb	2.88	7/01	11r
Coffee, instant, plain, regular, all sizes	16 oz	9.25	7/01	11r
Coffee, vacuum-packed	13 oz	2.30	12/00	5c
Cola, non diet,	2 liter	1.11	7/01	11r
Corn Flakes, Kellogg's or Post Toasties	18 oz	2.43	12/00	5c
Corn, frozen, whole kernel, lowest price	16 oz	1.03	12/00	5c
Crackers, soda, salted	lb	1.70	7/01	11r
Dairy product purchases	yr	282	1999	30r
Eggs, expenditures on	yr	32	1999	30r
Eggs, Grade A or AA	dozen	0.91	12/00	5c
Fats and oils, expenditures on	yr	79	1999	30r
Fish and seafood, expenditures on	yr	99	1999	30r
Flour, white, all purpose	lb	0.32	7/01	11r
Food (excl fruit and vegetables), eaten at home, purchases	yr	815	1999	30r
Food cooked on trips, expenditures on	yr	36	1999	30r
Food purchases	yr	4533	1999	30r
Food purchases, eaten away from home	yr	1873	1999	30r
Food purchases, food eaten at home	yr	2660	1999	30r
Fresh fruits, expenditures on	yr	128	1999	30r
Fresh milk and cream, expenditures on	yr	112	1999	30r
Fresh vegetables, expenditures on	yr	131	1999	30r
Fruit and vegetable purchases	yr	438	1999	30r
Grapefruit	lb	0.59	7/01	11r
Grapes, Thompson, seedless	lb	2.12	7/01	11r
Ground beef, 100% beef	lb	1.76	7/01	11r
Ground beef, lean and extra lean	lb	2.60	7/01	11r
Ground chuck, 100% beef	lb	2.08	7/01	11r
Ham, boneless, excl canned	lb	2.71	7/01	11r
Ham, rump or shank half, bone-in, smoked	lb	2.19	7/01	11r
Ice cream, prepackaged, bulk, regular	1/2 gal	3.93	7/01	11r
Lemons	lb	1.32	7/01	11r
Lettuce, iceberg	lb	0.76	7/01	11r
Lettuce, iceberg	head	0.91	12/00	5c
Margarine, Blue Bonnet or Parkay, stick	lb	0.92	12/00	5c
Milk, fresh, low fat,	gal	2.75	7/01	11r
Milk, fresh, whole, fortified	gal	2.97	7/01	11r
Milk, whole	1/2 gal	1.26	12/00	5c
Nonalcoholic beverages, expenditures on	yr	228	1999	30r
Orange juice, frozen concentrate	16 oz	1.95	7/01	11r
Orange juice, Minute Maid frozen	12 oz	1.19	12/00	5c
Oranges, Navel	lb	0.73	7/01	11r
Oranges, Valencia	lb	0.55	7/01	11r
Peaches, halves or slices, Hunt's, Del Monte, or Libby's	29 oz	1.38	12/00	5c
Peanut butter, creamy, all sizes	lb	1.83	7/01	11r
Pears, Anjou	lb	0.98	7/01	11r
Peas, green, Del Monte or Green Giant	15 oz	0.42	12/00	5c
Pork chops, center cut, bone-in	lb	3.33	7/01	11r
Pork sausage, fresh, loose	lb	2.59	7/01	11r
Pork shoulder picnic, bone-in, smoked	lb	1.12	7/01	11r
Pork, expenditures on	yr	162	1999	30r

Cumberland, MD - continued

Item	Per	Value	Date	Ref.
Groceries - continued				
Potato chips	16 oz	3.59	7/01	11r
Potatoes, frozen, french fried	lb	1.00	7/01	11r
Potatoes, white or red	10 lb	1.75	12/00	5c
Potatoes, white, all types	lb	0.44	7/01	11r
Poultry, expenditures on	yr	137	1999	30r
Processed fruits, expenditures on	yr	97	1999	30r
Processed vegetables, expenditures on	yr	82	1999	30r
Rice, white, long grain, uncooked	lb	0.51	7/01	11r
Round roast, graded and ungraded, excl U.S. prime and choice	lb	2.96	7/01	11r
Round steak, graded and ungraded, excl U.S. prime and choice	lb	3.11	7/01	11r
Sausage, Jimmy Dean/Owens pork	lb	3.02	12/00	5c
Shortening, vegetable, Crisco	3 lb	2.79	12/00	5c
Sirloin steak, graded and ungraded, excl U.S. prime and choice	lb	4.23	7/01	11r
Soft drink, Coca Cola, ex deposit	2 liter	1.01	12/00	5c
Spaghetti and macaroni	lb	0.78	7/01	11r
Steak, round, U.S. choice, boneless	lb	3.56	7/01	11r
Steak, sirloin, U.S. choice, boneless	lb	5.65	7/01	11r
Steak, T-bone	lb	6.25	12/00	5c
Strawberries, dry pint	12 oz	1.50	7/01	11r
Sugar and other sweets, expenditures on	yr	99	1999	30r
Sugar, cane or beet	4 lbs	1.51	12/00	5c
Sugar, white, 33-80 ounce package	lb	0.39	7/01	11r
Sugar, white, all sizes	lb	0.42	7/01	11r
Tobacco products and smoking supplies purchases	yr	288	1999	30r
Tomatoes, field grown	lb	1.43	7/01	11r
Tomatoes, Hunt's or Del Monte	14.5 oz	0.71	12/00	5c
Tuna, chunk, light	6 oz	0.54	12/00	5c
Tuna, light, chunk	lb	1.77	7/01	11r
Turkey, frozen, whole	lb	1.05	7/01	11r
Goods and Services				
Miscellaneous goods and services, ACCRA Index		104.70	12/00	5c
B&B Japanese maple (acer japonicum)	gal	49.98-129.00	4/00	93r
Boxwood (buxus)	2 gal	12.99-16.99	4/00	93r
Daylilly (hemerocallis)	gal	4.99-8.99	4/00	93r
Flat of annuals		11.00-13.92	4/00	93r
Fountain grass (pennisetum)	gal	5.98-7.98	4/00	93r
Hanging basket (10 in)		7.99-14.98	4/00	93r
Hardy geranium (geranium)	gal	5.98-8.00	4/00	93r
Hosta (hosta)	gal	4.99-10.98	4/00	93r
Lilac (syrubga vulgaris)	2 gal	12.99-21.99	4/00	93r
Rhododendron (rhododendron)	2 gal	14.99-24.99	4/00	93r
Sage (salvia)	gal	5.98-6.99	4/00	93r
Wintercreeper euonymus (euonymus fortunei)	2 gal	7.99-89.99	4/00	93r
Hunting license	yr	15.50	4/01	34s
Health Care				
Health care, ACCRA Index		90.10	12/00	5c
Cardiac catheterization, ave hospital/ physician charges		11420	1998	77s
Childbirth, Cesarean delivery		11587	1997	13r
Childbirth, vaginal delivery		6725	1997	13r
Dentist's fee, adult teeth cleaning and periodic oral exam	visit	58.00	12/00	5c
Doctor's fee, routine exam, established patient	visit	58.00	12/00	5c

Values are in dollars or fractions of dollars. In the column headed *Ref*, references are shown to sources. Each reference is followed by a letter. These refer to the geographical level for which data were reported: s=State, r=Region, and c=City or metro. The abbreviation *ex* is used to mean *except* or *excluding*; *exp* stands for *expenditures*. For other abbreviations and further explanations, please see the Introduction.

Cumberland, MD - continued

Item	Per	Value	Date	Ref.
Health Care				
Drugs, expenditures on	yr	399	1999	30r
Health care purchases	yr	1971	1999	30r
Health insurance expenditures	yr	933	1999	30r
Hospital care, private room	day	444.33	12/00	5c
Hysterectomy, laproscopically-assisted, ave hospital/physician charges		11890	1998	76s
Hysterectomy, vaginal, ave hospital and physician charges		8120	1998	76s
Medicaid dispensing fee		4.21	1999	87s
Medical services expenditures	yr	547	1999	30r
Medical supplies, expenditures on	yr	91	1999	30r
Plastic surgery, breast augmentation		2870	2000	7r
Plastic surgery, breast lift		3649	2000	7r
Plastic surgery, facelift		5008	2000	7r
Plastic surgery, hair transplantation		3425	2000	7r
Plastic surgery, lip augmentation		1227	2000	7r
Plastic surgery, lower body lift		4793	2000	7r
Plastic surgery, thigh lift		3862	2000	7r
Household Goods				
Dishwashing powder, Cascade	50 oz	2.32	12/00	5c
Floor coverings, expenditures on	yr	44	1999	30r
Furniture, expenditures on	yr	335	1999	30r
Household furnishings and equipment purchases	yr	1328	1999	30r
Household textiles, expenditures on	yr	89	1999	30r
Laundry and cleaning supplies, expenditures on	yr	113	1999	30r
Tissues, facial, Kleenex brand	175	1.01	12/00	5c
Housing				
Housing, ACCRA Index		99.90	12/00	5c
Home price, existing, ave		160100	10/00	90r
Home value, median		146000	2001	53s
House, 2400 sq ft, 8000 sq ft lot, new, urban, utilities	total	210200	12/00	5c
House payment, principal and interest, 25% down payment	mos	1165	12/00	5c
Household operation expenditures	yr	553	1999	30r
Housekeeping supplies purchases	yr	473	1999	30r
Housing, expenditures on	yr	10303	1999	30r
Maintenance, repairs, insurance expenditures	yr	699	1999	30r
Monthly rental value of owned home	mos	505	1999	30r
Owned dwellings, expenditures own	yr	3465	1999	30r
Rent expenditures	yr	1641	1999	30r
Rent, apartment, 2 br, 1 1/2-2 baths, unfurn, 950 sq ft, water	mos	593	12/00	5c
Rental unit, 1 bedroom, with utilities	mos	409	4/01	41c
Rental unit, 2 bedroom, with utilities	mos	506	4/01	41c
Rental unit, 3 bedroom, with utilities	mos	668	4/01	41c
Rental unit, 4 bedroom, with utilities	mos	763	4/01	41c
Shelter, expenditures on	yr	5467	1999	30r
Insurance and Pensions				
Life and other personal insurance purchases	yr	414	1999	30r
Pensions and Social Security, expenditures on	yr	2635	1999	30r
Personal insurance and pensions, expenditures on	yr	3048	1999	30r
Legal Fees				
Driver's license fee	orig	30.00	1999	48s
Driver's license fee	renew	20.00	1999	48s
Fishing license	yr	9.00	4/01	34s
Personal Goods				
Personal care products and services purchases	yr	393	1999	30r
Shampoo, Alberto VO5	15 oz	1.09	12/00	5c
Toothpaste, Crest or Colgate	6-7 oz	1.97	12/00	5c
Personal Services				
Dry cleaning, man's 2-pc suit		6.10	12/00	5c
Man's haircut, barbershop, no styling		7.20	12/00	5c

Cumberland, MD - continued

Item	Per	Value	Date	Ref.
Personal Services - continued				
Personal services, household, expenditures on	yr	258	1999	30r
Woman's shampoo, trim, blow-dry, no style-change		16.80	12/00	5c
Pets				
Pets, toys, and playground equipment, expenditures on	yr	306	1999	30r
Restaurant Food				
Chicken, fried, thigh and drumstick, KFC/Church's		2.99	12/00	5c
Hamburger with cheese, McDonald's	1/4 lb	1.99	12/00	5c
Pizza, Pizza Hut or Pizza Inn	11-12 in	9.99	12/00	5c
Taxes				
Federal income taxes paid	yr	2047	1999	30r
Personal taxes, expenditures on	yr	2554	1999	30r
Property taxes paid	yr	726	1999	30r
State and local income taxes paid	yr	363	1999	30r
Transportation				
Transportation, ACCRA Index		87.80	12/00	5c
Cars and trucks, new, expenditures on	yr	1648	1999	30r
Cars and trucks, used, expenditures on	yr	1651	1999	30r
Diesel at the pump	gal	1.29	10/99	73s
Gasoline and motor oil purchases	yr	1052	1999	30r
Gasoline before-tax price (cents)	gal	106.80	10/00	43s
Maintenance and repair expenditures	yr	621	1999	30r
Public transportation, expenditures on	yr	298	1999	30r
Tire balance, computer or spin balance, front	wheel	5.80	12/00	5c
Transportation purchases	yr	6738	1999	30r
Vehicle expenses, miscellaneous, purchases	yr	2033	1999	30r
Vehicle insurance payments	yr	696	1999	30r
Vehicle purchases (net outlay)	yr	3354	1999	30r
Vehicle rental, lease expenditures	yr	352	1999	30r
Utilities				
Utilities, ACCRA Index		97.90	12/00	5c
Electrical bill, average	mos	83.58	9/00	9s
Electricity, 2400 sq ft, new home	mos	112.89	12/00	5c
Electricity, expenditures on	yr	1115	1999	30r
Electricity cost, average	KWh	6.90	9/00	9s
Water and other public services, expenditures on	yr	298	1999	30r
Weddings				
Wedding (national average cost)		19936	2000	33r
Wedding (regional average total cost)		16293	1997	110r
Attendants' gifts		321	1998	33r
Bridal attendants' apparel (5 persons)		824	2000	33r
Bride's headpiece/veil		173	1998	33r
Bride's wedding dress		859	1998	33r
Clergy, religious facility fee		242	1998	33r
Engagement ring		3177	1998	33r
Flowers		789	1998	33r
Groom's formalwear rental		99	2000	33r
Limousine		410	1998	33r
Marriage license cost		55.00	4/01	35s
Men's formalwear (ushers, best man)		469	2000	33r
Mother of bride apparel		241	2000	33r
Music		866	1998	33r
Photography and videography		1368	1998	33r
Rehearsal dinner		728	1998	33r
Wedding invitations and announcements		341	1998	33r
Wedding reception		7968	2000	33r
Wedding rings (bride and groom)		1060	1998	33r

Dallas, TX

Item	Per	Value	Date	Ref.
Composite, ACCRA index		97.00	3/01	4c

Values are in dollars or fractions of dollars. In the column headed *Ref*, references are shown to sources. Each reference is followed by a letter. These refer to the geographical level for which data were reported: s=State, r=Region, and c=City or metro. The abbreviation *ex* is used to mean *except* or *excluding*; *exp* stands for expenditures. For other abbreviations and further explanations, please see the Introduction.

Dallas, TX - continued

Item	Per	Value	Date	Ref.
Alcoholic Beverages				
Alcoholic beverage purchases	yr	253	1999	30r
Beer, Heineken, 12-oz, ex deposit	6	7.37	3/01	4c
J & B Scotch	750-ml	22.49	3/01	4c
Malt beverages, all types, all sizes, any origin	16 oz	0.96	7/01	11r
Wine, Livingston or Gallo, Chablis blanc	1.5 liter	5.53	3/01	4c
Appliances				
Appliance repair, service call, washing machine	min lab chg	39.81	3/01	4c
Major appliances, expenditures on	yr	172	1999	30r
Small appliances, housewares, expenditures on	yr	81	1999	30r
Banking and Money				
Mortgage interest and charges paid	yr	2039	1999	30r
Mortgage principal paid on owned property	yr	1026	1999	30r
Mortgage rate, incl. points and orig. fee, 30-yr. conv. fixed or ARM	mos	6.78	3/01	4c
Vehicle finance charges paid	yr	365	1999	30r
Business Expenses				
Business travel, car rental	day	51	2001	3c
Business travel, food	day	55	2001	3c
Business travel, hotel	day	188	2001	3c
Medical office space cost	sq ft	102.61	2001	31c
Office space, 2-4 storey building	sq ft	89.25	2001	31c
Office space, 5-10 storey building	sq ft	78.84	2001	31c
Office space, 11-20 storey building	sq ft	75.78	2001	31c
Office space, central business district, Class A	sq ft	22.42	3/99	74c
Charity				
Cash contributions, expenditures	yr	1127	1999	30r
Child Care				
Child care fee, one year old	week	103	5/99	26c
Child care fee, six year old	week	51	5/99	26c
Child care fee, three year old	week	82	5/99	26c
Child raising cost, total, age 0-2	yr	8540	1999	60r
Child raising cost, total, age 3-5	yr	8780	1999	60r
Child raising cost, total, age 6-8	yr	8820	1999	60r
Child raising cost, total, age 9-11	yr	8800	1999	60r
Child raising cost, total, age 12-14	yr	9510	1999	60r
Child raising cost, total, age 15-17	yr	9740	1999	60r
Child's child care and education, age 0-2	yr	1380	1999	60r
Child's child care and education, age 3-5	yr	1520	1999	60r
Child's child care and education, age 6-8	yr	990	1999	60r
Child's child care and education, age 9-11	yr	650	1999	60r
Child's child care and education, age 12-14	yr	490	1999	60r
Child's child care and education, age 15-17	yr	840	1999	60r
Child's clothing, age 0-2	yr	480	1999	60r
Child's clothing, age 3-5	yr	470	1999	60r
Child's clothing, age 6-8	yr	520	1999	60r
Child's clothing, age 9-11	yr	570	1999	60r
Child's clothing, age 12-14	yr	950	1999	60r
Child's clothing, age 15-17	yr	850	1999	60r
Child's food, age 0-2	yr	1000	1999	60r
Child's food, age 3-5	yr	1160	1999	60r
Child's food, age 6-8	yr	1490	1999	60r
Child's food, age 9-11	yr	1770	1999	60r
Child's food, age 12-14	yr	1770	1999	60r
Child's food, age 15-17	yr	1980	1999	60r
Child's health care, age 0-2	yr	620	1999	60r
Child's health care, age 3-5	yr	590	1999	60r
Child's health care, age 6-8	yr	680	1999	60r
Child's health care, age 9-11	yr	720	1999	60r
Child's health care, age 12-14	yr	730	1999	60r
Child's health care, age 15-17	yr	760	1999	60r
Child's housing, age 0-2	yr	3070	1999	60r
Child's housing, age 3-5	yr	3050	1999	60r
Child's housing, age 6-8	yr	3010	1999	60r
Child's housing, age 9-11	yr	2850	1999	60r
Child's housing, age 12-14	yr	3040	1999	60r
Child's housing, age 15-17	yr	2650	1999	60r

Dallas, TX - continued

Item	Per	Value	Date	Ref.
Child Care - continued				
Child's personal care, reading, age 0-2	yr	910	1999	60r
Child's personal care, reading, age 3-5	yr	930	1999	60r
Child's personal care, reading, age 6-8	yr	960	1999	60r
Child's personal care, reading, age 9-11	yr	1000	1999	60r
Child's personal care, reading, age 12-14	yr	1170	1999	60r
Child's personal care, reading, age 15-17	yr	950	1999	60r
Clothing				
Apparel and services purchases	yr	1610	1999	30r
Boys' brief, cotton	3	6.07	3/01	4c
Boys, 2 to 15, expenditures on	yr	89	1999	30r
Children under 2, expenditures on	yr	79	1999	30r
Footwear, expenditures on	yr	283	1999	30r
Girls, 2 to 15, expenditures on	yr	103	1999	30r
Men and boys, expenditures on	yr	351	1999	30r
Men, 16 and over, expenditures on	yr	262	1999	30r
Shirt, man's dress shirt		29.33	3/01	4c
Slacks, man's "No Wrinkles" khaki		30.49	3/01	4c
Women, 16 and over, expenditures on	yr	538	1999	30r
Communications				
Cable modem installation, AT&T-BIS		150.00	6/99	103s
Cable modem installation, Marcus		499.00	6/99	103s
Cable modem installation, Time Warner		75.00-225.00	6/99	103s
Cable modem rate, cable subscriber, AT&T-BIS	mos	39.95	6/99	103s
Cable modem rate, cable subscriber, Marcus	mos	14.95-49.95	6/99	103s
Cable modem rate, cable subscriber, Time Warner	mos	39.95-49.95	6/99	103s
Cable modem rate, non-cable subscriber, Marcus	mos	60.95	6/99	103s
Cable modem rate, non-cable subscriber, Time Warner	mos	39.95-54.95	6/99	103s
Newspaper subscription, daily and Sunday delivery	mos	13.00	3/01	4c
Phone line, single, business, field visit	inst.	71.90	12/97	17s
Phone line, single, business, no field visit	inst.	57.30	12/97	17s
Phone line, single, residence, field visit	inst.	52.95	12/97	17s
Phone line, single, residence, no field visit	inst.	38.35	12/97	17s
Postage and stationery, expenditures on	yr	104	1999	30r
Postal rate, express mail, up to half-pound		12.45	7/01	108r
Postal rate, letter, first class, first ounce		0.34	7/01	108r
Postal rate, letter, two ounces		0.57	7/01	108r
Postal rate, post card		0.21	7/01	108r
Postal rate, priority mail, two pounds		3.95	7/01	108r
Postal rate, priority mail, up to one pound		3.50	7/01	108r
Telephone bill, business, basic rate	mos	25.25	12/97	18c
Telephone bill, family of three	mos	16.33	3/01	4c
Telephone bill, residential, basic rate	mos	10.40	12/97	18c
Telephone services, expenditures on	yr	860	1999	30r
Wireless services	mos	45.38	1/00	42c
Education				
Board, 4-year private college/university	yr	2198	1996	38s
Board, 4-year public college/university	yr	1759	1996	38s
Education expenditures	yr	431	1999	30r
Room, 4-year private college/university	yr	2000	1996	38s
Room, 4-year public college/university	yr	1885	1996	38s
Total cost, 4-year private college/university	yr	13156	1996	38s
Total cost, 4-year public college/university	yr	5464	1996	38s
Tuition, 2-year public college/university, in state	yr	771	1996	38s
Tuition, 4-year private college/university, in state	yr	8959	1996	38s
Tuition, 4-year public college/university	yr	1820	1996	38s
Energy and Fuels				
Electricity	KWh	0.09	7/01	11r
Electricity	500 KWhs	47.29	7/01	11r
Energy, combined forms, 2400 sq ft	mos	113.21	3/01	4c
Energy, exc. electricity, 2400 sq ft	mos	32.57	3/01	4c

Values are in dollars or fractions of dollars. In the column headed *Ref*, references are shown to sources. Each reference is followed by a letter. These refer to the geographical level for which data were reported: s=State, r=Region, and c=City or metro. The abbreviation *ex* is used to mean *except* or *excluding*; *exp* stands for expenditures. For other abbreviations and further explanations, please see the Introduction.

Dallas, TX - continued

Item	Per	Value	Date	Ref.
Energy and Fuels				
Fuel oil #2	gal	1.43	7/01	11r
Fuel oil and other fuels, expenditures on	yr	45	1999	30r
Gas, cooking, winter, 10 therms	mos	10.30	2/96	98c
Gas, cooking, winter, 30 therms	mos	19.91	2/96	98c
Gas, cooking, winter, 50 therms	mos	29.50	2/96	98c
Gas, heating, winter, average use	mos	83.86	2/96	98c
Gas, natural, commercial rate	1000 cf	6.94	11/00	88s
Gas, regular unleaded, cash, self-service	gal	1.32	3/01	4c
Gasoline, all types	gal	1.60	7/01	11r
Gasoline, unleaded midgrade	gal	1.65	7/01	11r
Gasoline, unleaded premium	gal	1.74	7/01	11r
Natural gas, expenditures on	yr	164	1999	30r
Utility (piped) gas, therm		1.01	7/01	11r
Utility (piped) gas, 40 therms		44.29	7/01	11r
Utility (piped) gas, 100 therms		97.44	7/01	11r
Entertainment				
Bowling, Saturday evening rate	line	3.21	3/01	4c
Entertainment purchases	yr	1574	1999	30r
Fees and admissions paid	yr	371	1999	30r
Monopoly game, Parker Brothers', No. 9	game	9.24	3/01	4c
Movie, first-run, Saturday, evening	adm.	6.88	3/01	4c
Reading purchases	yr	121	1999	30r
Television, radios, sound equipment, expenditures on	yr	561	1999	30r
Tennis balls, yellow, Wilson or Penn, 3	can	2.46	3/01	4c
Funerals				
Total cost of funeral		5842.28	1/99	78r
Acknowledgement cards		28.35	1/99	78r
Casket		2494.29	1/99	78r
Cosmetology, hair, other preparation		109.22	1/99	78r
Embalming		361.42	1/99	78r
Funeral at funeral home		349.20	1/99	78r
Hearse (local)		161.91	1/99	78r
Professional service charges		1116.50	1/99	78r
Service car/van		65.56	1/99	78r
Transfer of remains to funeral home		143.56	1/99	78r
Vault		785.25	1/99	78r
Visitation/viewing		227.02	1/99	78r
Groceries				
Groceries, ACCRA Index		97.20	3/01	4c
American processed cheese	lb	3.50	7/01	11r
Antibiotic ointment, Polysporin	0.5 oz	4.91	3/01	4c
Apples	pound	1.37		29c
Baby food, strained vegetables or fruit, lowest price	4-4.5 oz	0.30	3/01	4c
Bakery products, expenditures on	yr	261	1999	30r
Bananas	lb	0.49	3/01	4c
Bananas	lb	0.47	7/01	11r
Beans, dried, any type, all sizes	lb	0.63	7/01	11r
Beef for stew, boneless	lb	2.86	7/01	11r
Beef or hamburger, ground	lb	1.61	3/01	4c
Beef, expenditures on	yr	210	1999	30r
Bologna, all beef or mixed	lb	2.29	7/01	11r
Bread, French	lb	1.66	7/01	11r
Bread, white	loaf	0.83	3/01	4c
Bread, white, pan	lb	0.87	7/01	11r
Bread, whole wheat, pan	lb	1.38	7/01	11r
Broccoli	lb	1.04	7/01	11r
Butter, salted, grade AA, stick	lb	2.26	7/01	11r
Butter, yoghurt, cheese, etc, expenditures on	yr	170	1999	30r
Cabbage	lb	0.42	7/01	11r
Cereals and cereal products, expenditures on	yr	140	1999	30r
Cheddar cheese, natural	lb	3.75	7/01	11r
Cheese, Kraft grated Parmesan	8 oz	3.58	3/01	4c
Chicken breast, bone-in	lb	1.85	7/01	11r
Chicken legs, bone-in	lb	1.34	7/01	11r
Chicken, fresh, whole	lb	1.05	7/01	11r
Chicken, whole fryer	lb	0.78	3/01	4c
Chops, boneless,	lb	4.13	7/01	11r

Dallas, TX - continued

Item	Per	Value	Date	Ref.
Groceries - continued				
Chuck roast, graded and ungraded, excl U.S. prime and choice	lb	2.35	7/01	11r
Chuck roast, U.S. choice, boneless	lb	2.67	7/01	11r
Cigarettes, Winston, Kings	carton	31.17	3/01	4c
Coffee, 100%, ground roast, all sizes	lb	2.88	7/01	11r
Coffee, instant, plain, regular, all sizes	16 oz	9.25	7/01	11r
Coffee, vacuum-packed	13 oz	2.45	3/01	4c
Cola, non diet	2 liter	1.11	7/01	11r
Corn Flakes, Kellogg's or Post Toasties	18 oz	2.27	3/01	4c
Corn, frozen, whole kernel, lowest price	16 oz	1.33	3/01	4c
Crackers, soda, salted	lb	1.70	7/01	11r
Dairy product purchases	yr	282	1999	30r
Eggs, expenditures on	yr	32	1999	30r
Eggs, Grade A or AA	dozen	1.00	3/01	4c
Fats and oils, expenditures on	yr	79	1999	30r
Fish and seafood, expenditures on	yr	99	1999	30r
Flour, white, all purpose	lb	0.32	7/01	11r
Food (excl fruit and vegetables), eaten at home, purchases	yr	815	1999	30r
Food cooked on trips, expenditures on	yr	36	1999	30r
Food purchases	yr	4533	1999	30r
Food purchases, eaten away from home	yr	1873	1999	30r
Food purchases, food eaten at home	yr	2660	1999	30r
Fresh fruits, expenditures on	yr	128	1999	30r
Fresh milk and cream, expenditures on	yr	112	1999	30r
Fresh vegetables, expenditures on	yr	131	1999	30r
Fruit and vegetable purchases	yr	438	1999	30r
Grapefruit	lb	0.59	7/01	11r
Grapes, Thompson, seedless	lb	2.12	7/01	11r
Ground beef, 100% beef	lb	1.76	7/01	11r
Ground beef, lean and extra lean	lb	2.60	7/01	11r
Ground chuck, 100% beef	lb	2.08	7/01	11r
Ham, boneless, excl canned	lb	2.71	7/01	11r
Ham, rump or shank half, bone-in, smoked	lb	2.19	7/01	11r
Ice cream, prepackaged, bulk, regular	1/2 gal	3.93	7/01	11r
Lemons	lb	1.32	7/01	11r
Lettuce, iceberg	head	1.29	3/01	4c
Lettuce, iceberg	lb	0.76	7/01	11r
Margarine, Blue Bonnet or Parkay, stick	lb	0.77	3/01	4c
Milk, fresh, low fat,	gal	2.75	7/01	11r
Milk, fresh, whole, fortified	gal	2.97	7/01	11r
Milk, whole	1/2 gal	1.60	3/01	4c
Nonalcoholic beverages, expenditures on	yr	228	1999	30r
Orange juice, frozen concentrate	16 oz	1.95	7/01	11r
Orange juice, Minute Maid frozen	12 oz	1.66	3/01	4c
Oranges, Navel	lb	0.73	7/01	11r
Oranges, Valencia	lb	0.55	7/01	11r
Peaches, halves or slices, Hunt's, Del Monte, or Libby's	29 oz	1.67	3/01	4c
Peanut butter, creamy, all sizes	lb	1.83	7/01	11r
Pears, Anjou	lb	0.98	7/01	11r
Peas, green, Del Monte or Green Giant	15 oz	0.73	3/01	4c
Pork chops, center cut, bone-in	lb	3.33	7/01	11r
Pork sausage, fresh, loose	lb	2.59	7/01	11r
Pork shoulder picnic, bone-in, smoked	lb	1.12	7/01	11r
Pork, expenditures on	yr	162	1999	30r
Potato chips	16 oz	3.59	7/01	11r
Potatoes, frozen, french fried	lb	1.00	7/01	11r
Potatoes, white or red	10 lb	3.00	3/01	4c
Potatoes, white, all types	lb	0.44	7/01	11r
Poultry, expenditures on	yr	137	1999	30r
Processed fruits, expenditures on	yr	97	1999	30r
Processed vegetables, expenditures on	yr	82	1999	30r
Rice, white, long grain, uncooked	lb	0.51	7/01	11r
Round roast, graded and ungraded, excl U.S. prime and choice	lb	2.96	7/01	11r
Round steak, graded and ungraded, excl U.S. prime and choice	lb	3.11	7/01	11r
Sausage, Jimmy Dean/Owens pork	lb	3.10	3/01	4c
Shortening, vegetable, Crisco	3 lb	2.86	3/01	4c
Sirloin steak, graded and ungraded, excl U.S. prime and choice	lb	4.23	7/01	11r

Values are in dollars or fractions of dollars. In the column headed *Ref*, references are shown to sources. Each reference is followed by a letter. These refer to the geographical level for which data were reported: s=State, r=Region, and c=City or metro. The abbreviation *ex* is used to mean *except* or *excluding*; *exp* stands for expenditures. For other abbreviations and further explanations, please see the Introduction.

Dallas, TX - continued

Item	Per	Value	Date	Ref.
Groceries				
Soft drink, Coca Cola, ex deposit	2 liter	1.32	3/01	4c
Spaghetti and macaroni	lb	0.78	7/01	11r
Steak, round, U.S. choice, boneless	lb	3.56	7/01	11r
Steak, sirloin, U.S. choice, boneless	lb	5.65	7/01	11r
Steak, T-bone	lb	6.79	3/01	4c
Strawberries, dry pint	12 oz	1.50	7/01	11r
Sugar and other sweets, expenditures on	yr	99	1999	30r
Sugar, cane or beet	4 lbs	1.68	3/01	4c
Sugar, white, 33-80 ounce package	lb	0.39	7/01	11r
Sugar, white, all sizes	lb	0.42	7/01	11r
Tobacco products and smoking supplies purchases	yr	288	1999	30r
Tomatoes, field grown	lb	1.43	7/01	11r
Tomatoes, Hunt's or Del Monte	14.5 oz	0.82	3/01	4c
Tuna, chunk, light	6 oz	0.66	3/01	4c
Tuna, light, chunk	lb	1.77	7/01	11r
Turkey, frozen, whole	lb	1.05	7/01	11r
Goods and Services				
Miscellaneous goods and services, ACCRA Index		100.00	3/01	4c
B&B Japanese maple (acer japonicum)	gal	79.98-99.00	4/00	93r
Boxwood (buxus)	2 gal	12.98-18.99	4/00	93r
Christmas tree, noble fir		40-60	2000	65s
Daylilly (hemerocallis)	gal	7.96-11.00	4/00	93r
Flat of annuals		13.99-27.99	4/00	93r
Fountain grass (pennisetum)	gal	6.96-9.00	4/00	93r
Hanging basket (10 in)		9.99-24.99	4/00	93r
Hardy geranium (geranium)	gal	5.96-8.00	4/00	93r
Hosta (hosta)	gal	8.96-12.99	4/00	93r
Lilac (syrubga vulgaris)	2 gal	13.00-19.99	4/00	93r
Rhododendron (rhododendron)	2 gal	12.98-29.99	4/00	93r
Sage (salvia)	gal	5.96-8.00	4/00	93r
Wintercreeper euonymus (euonymus fortunei)	2 gal	13.00-18.99	4/00	93r
Hunting license	yr	19.00	4/01	34s
Health Care				
Health care, ACCRA Index		93.80	3/01	4c
Cardiac catheterization, ave hospital/ physician charges		20140	1998	77s
Childbirth, Cesarean delivery		11587	1997	13r
Childbirth, vaginal delivery		6725	1997	13r
Dentist's fee, adult teeth cleaning and periodic oral exam	visit	66.10	3/01	4c
Doctor's fee, routine exam, established patient	visit	50.33	3/01	4c
Drugs, expenditures on	yr	399	1999	30r
Health care purchases	yr	1971	1999	30r
Health insurance expenditures	yr	933	1999	30r
Home health care aide cost, licensed agency	hour	15	2000	82c
Hospital care, private room	day	552.89	3/01	4c
Hysterectomy, laproscopically-assisted, ave hospital/physician charges		15700	1998	76s
Hysterectomy, vaginal, ave hospital and physician charges		12180	1998	76s
Medicaid dispensing fee		5.27	1999	87s
Medical services expenditures	yr	547	1999	30r
Medical supplies, expenditures on	yr	91	1999	30r
Nursing home costs, private room	day	149	2000	82c
Nursing home stay, private room	day	149	2000	83c

Dallas, TX - continued

Item	Per	Value	Date	Ref.
Household Goods				
Dishwashing powder, Cascade	50 oz	3.50	3/01	4c
Floor coverings, expenditures on	yr	44	1999	30r
Furniture, expenditures on	yr	335	1999	30r
Household furnishings and equipment purchases	yr	1328	1999	30r
Household textiles, expenditures on	yr	89	1999	30r
Laundry and cleaning supplies, expenditures on	yr	113	1999	30r
Tissues, facial, Kleenex brand	175	1.36	3/01	4c
Housing				
Housing, ACCRA Index		95.80	3/01	4c
Home, 2200 sq ft, 4-br, 2-bath, 2-car garage, average		179500	2000	47c
Home price, existing, ave		160100	10/00	90r
Home value, median		112000	2001	53s
House, 2400 sq ft, 8000 sq ft lot, new, urban, utilities	total	188000	3/01	4c
House payment, principal and interest, 25% down payment	mos	917	3/01	4c
Household operation expenditures	yr	553	1999	30r
Housekeeping supplies purchases	yr	473	1999	30r
Housing, expenditures on	yr	10303	1999	30r
Maintenance, repairs, insurance expenditures	yr	699	1999	30r
Monthly rental value of owned home	mos	505	1999	30r
Owned dwellings, expenditures own	yr	3465	1999	30r
Rent expenditures	yr	1641	1999	30r
Rent, apartment, 2 br, 1 1/2-2 baths, unfurn, 950 sq ft, water	mos	852	3/01	4c
Rental unit, 1 bedroom, with utilities	mos	609	4/01	41c
Rental unit, 2 bedroom, with utilities	mos	781	4/01	41c
Rental unit, 3 bedroom, with utilities	mos	1080	4/01	41c
Rental unit, 4 bedroom, with utilities	mos	1277	4/01	41c
Shelter, expenditures on	yr	5467	1999	30r
Insurance and Pensions				
Life and other personal insurance purchases	yr	414	1999	30r
Pensions and Social Security, expenditures on	yr	2635	1999	30r
Personal insurance and pensions, expenditures on	yr	3048	1999	30r
Legal Fees				
Divorce, filing fee		150.00-200.00	4/01	35s
Driver's license fee	renew	20.00	1999	48s
Driver's license fee	orig	24.00	1999	48s
Fishing license	yr	19.00	4/01	34s
Personal Goods				
Personal care products and services purchases	yr	393	1999	30r
Shampoo, Alberto VO5	15 oz	1.27	3/01	4c
Toothpaste, Crest or Colgate	6-7 oz	2.11	3/01	4c
Personal Services				
Dry cleaning, man's 2-pc suit		7.20	3/01	4c
Man's haircut, barbershop, no styling		11.29	3/01	4c
Personal services, household, expenditures on	yr	258	1999	30r
Woman's shampoo, trim, blow-dry, no style-change		34.78	3/01	4c
Pets				
Pets, toys, and playground equipment, expenditures on	yr	306	1999	30r
Restaurant Food				
Cheeseburger, 1/4-lb, large fries, medium soft drink, excl tax		4.27	1999	40c
Chicken, fried, thigh and drumstick, KFC/ Church's		2.28	3/01	4c
Hamburger with cheese, McDonald's	1/4 lb	2.22	3/01	4c
Pizza, Pizza Hut or Pizza Inn	11-12 in	8.66	3/01	4c

Values are in dollars or fractions of dollars. In the column headed *Ref*, references are shown to sources. Each reference is followed by a letter. These refer to the geographical level for which data were reported: s=State, r=Region, and c=City or metro. The abbreviation *ex* is used to mean *except* or *excluding*; *exp* stands for expenditures. For other abbreviations and further explanations, please see the Introduction.

Dallas, TX - continued

Item	Per	Value	Date	Ref.
Taxes				
Federal income taxes paid	yr	2047	1999	30r
Personal taxes, expenditures on	yr	2554	1999	30r
Property taxes paid	yr	726	1999	30r
State and local income taxes paid	yr	363	1999	30r
Transportation				
Transportation, ACCRA Index		97.00	3/01	4c
Bus fare, to central business district	1-way	1.00	3/01	4c
Cars and trucks, new, expenditures on	yr	1648	1999	30r
Cars and trucks, used, expenditures on	yr	1651	1999	30r
Commuter rail, one-way	trip	1.00	2000	2c
Diesel at the pump	gal	1.18	10/99	73s
Gasoline and motor oil purchases	yr	1052	1999	30r
Gasoline before-tax price (cents)	gal	101.30	10/00	43s
Light rail transit fare, one-way	trip	1.00	2000	2c
Maintenance and repair expenditures	yr	621	1999	30r
Public transportation, expenditures on	yr	298	1999	30r
Tire balance, computer or spin balance, front	wheel	8.12	3/01	4c
Transportation purchases	yr	6738	1999	30r
Vehicle expenses, miscellaneous, purchases	yr	2033	1999	30r
Vehicle insurance payments	yr	696	1999	30r
Vehicle purchases (net outlay)	yr	3354	1999	30r
Vehicle rental, lease expenditures	yr	352	1999	30r
Utilities				
Utilities, ACCRA Index		90.30	3/01	4c
Electrical bill, average	mos	87.17	9/00	9s
Electricity, expenditures on	yr	1115	1999	30r
Electricity and other, mixed, 2400 sq ft, new home	mos	80.64	3/01	4c
Electricity cost, average	KWh	6.48	9/00	9s
Water and other public services, expenditures on	yr	298	1999	30r
Weddings				
Wedding (national average cost)		19936	2000	33r
Attendants' gifts		321	1998	33r
Bridal attendants' apparel (5 persons)		824	2000	33r
Bride's headpiece/veil		173	1998	33r
Bride's wedding dress		859	1998	33r
Clergy, religious facility fee		242	1998	33r
Engagement ring		3177	1998	33r
Flowers		789	1998	33r
Groom's formalwear rental		99	2000	33r
Limousine		410	1998	33r
Marriage license cost		36.00	4/01	35s
Men's formalwear (ushers, best man)		469	2000	33r
Mother of bride apparel		241	2000	33r
Music		866	1998	33r
Photography and videography		1368	1998	33r
Rehearsal dinner		728	1998	33r
Wedding invitations and announcements		341	1998	33r
Wedding reception		7968	2000	33r
Wedding rings (bride and groom)		1060	1998	33r

Dallas-Fort Worth, TX

Item	Per	Value	Date	Ref.
Average annual expenditures	yr	44225	1999	30c
Alcoholic Beverages				
Alcoholic beverage purchases	yr	329	1999	30c
Malt beverages, all types, all sizes, any origin	16 oz	0.96	7/01	11r
Appliances				
Major appliances, expenditures on	yr	172	1999	30r
Small appliances, housewares, expenditures on	yr	81	1999	30r
Banking and Money				
Mortgage interest and charges paid	yr	2039	1999	30r
Mortgage principal paid on owned property	yr	1026	1999	30r
Vehicle finance charges paid	yr	365	1999	30r

Dallas-Fort Worth, TX - continued

Item	Per	Value	Date	Ref.
Charity				
Cash contributions, expenditures	yr	2251	1999	30c
Child Care				
Child raising cost, total, age 0-2	yr	8540	1999	60r
Child raising cost, total, age 3-5	yr	8780	1999	60r
Child raising cost, total, age 6-8	yr	8820	1999	60r
Child raising cost, total, age 9-11	yr	8800	1999	60r
Child raising cost, total, age 12-14	yr	9510	1999	60r
Child raising cost, total, age 15-17	yr	9740	1999	60r
Child's child care and education, age 0-2	yr	1380	1999	60r
Child's child care and education, age 3-5	yr	1520	1999	60r
Child's child care and education, age 6-8	yr	990	1999	60r
Child's child care and education, age 9-11	yr	650	1999	60r
Child's child care and education, age 12-14	yr	490	1999	60r
Child's child care and education, age 15-17	yr	840	1999	60r
Child's clothing, age 0-2	yr	480	1999	60r
Child's clothing, age 3-5	yr	470	1999	60r
Child's clothing, age 6-8	yr	520	1999	60r
Child's clothing, age 9-11	yr	570	1999	60r
Child's clothing, age 12-14	yr	950	1999	60r
Child's clothing, age 15-17	yr	850	1999	60r
Child's food, age 0-2	yr	1000	1999	60r
Child's food, age 3-5	yr	1160	1999	60r
Child's food, age 6-8	yr	1490	1999	60r
Child's food, age 9-11	yr	1770	1999	60r
Child's food, age 12-14	yr	1770	1999	60r
Child's food, age 15-17	yr	1980	1999	60r
Child's health care, age 0-2	yr	620	1999	60r
Child's health care, age 3-5	yr	590	1999	60r
Child's health care, age 6-8	yr	680	1999	60r
Child's health care, age 9-11	yr	720	1999	60r
Child's health care, age 12-14	yr	730	1999	60r
Child's health care, age 15-17	yr	760	1999	60r
Child's housing, age 0-2	yr	3070	1999	60r
Child's housing, age 3-5	yr	3050	1999	60r
Child's housing, age 6-8	yr	3010	1999	60r
Child's housing, age 9-11	yr	2850	1999	60r
Child's housing, age 12-14	yr	3040	1999	60r
Child's housing, age 15-17	yr	2650	1999	60r
Child's personal care, reading, age 0-2	yr	910	1999	60r
Child's personal care, reading, age 3-5	yr	930	1999	60r
Child's personal care, reading, age 6-8	yr	960	1999	60r
Child's personal care, reading, age 9-11	yr	1000	1999	60r
Child's personal care, reading, age 12-14	yr	1170	1999	60r
Child's personal care, reading, age 15-17	yr	950	1999	60r
Clothing				
Apparel and services purchases	yr	2492	1999	30c
Boys, 2 to 15, expenditures on	yr	89	1999	30r
Children under 2, expenditures on	yr	79	1999	30r
Footwear, expenditures on	yr	283	1999	30r
Girls, 2 to 15, expenditures on	yr	103	1999	30r
Men and boys, expenditures on	yr	351	1999	30r
Men, 16 and over, expenditures on	yr	262	1999	30r
Women, 16 and over, expenditures on	yr	538	1999	30r
Communications				
Cable modem installation, AT&T-BIS		150.00	6/99	103s
Cable modem installation, Marcus		499.00	6/99	103s
Cable modem installation, Time Warner		75.00-225.00	6/99	103s
Cable modem rate, cable subscriber, AT&T-BIS	mos	39.95	6/99	103s
Cable modem rate, cable subscriber, Marcus	mos	14.95-49.95	6/99	103s
Cable modem rate, cable subscriber, Time Warner	mos	39.95-49.95	6/99	103s
Cable modem rate, non-cable subscriber, Marcus	mos	60.95	6/99	103s
Cable modem rate, non-cable subscriber, Time Warner	mos	39.95-54.95	6/99	103s
Phone line, single, business, field visit	inst.	71.90	12/97	17s
Phone line, single, business, no field visit	inst.	57.30	12/97	17s
Phone line, single, residence, field visit	inst.	52.95	12/97	17s

Values are in dollars or fractions of dollars. In the column headed *Ref*, references are shown to sources. Each reference is followed by a letter. These refer to the geographical level for which data were reported: s=State, r=Region, and c=City or metro. The abbreviation *ex* is used to mean *except* or *excluding*; *exp* stands for expenditures. For other abbreviations and further explanations, please see the Introduction.

Dallas-Fort Worth, TX - continued

Item	Per	Value	Date	Ref.
Communications				
Phone line, single, residence, no field visit	inst.	38.35	12/97	17s
Postage and stationery, expenditures on	yr	104	1999	30r
Postal rate, express mail, up to half-pound		12.45	7/01	108r
Postal rate, letter, first class, first ounce		0.34	7/01	108r
Postal rate, letter, two ounces		0.57	7/01	108r
Postal rate, post card		0.21	7/01	108r
Postal rate, priority mail, two pounds		3.95	7/01	108r
Postal rate, priority mail, up to one pound		3.50	7/01	108r
Telephone services, expenditures on	yr	860	1999	30r
Education				
Board, 4-year private college/university	yr	2198	1996	38s
Board, 4-year public college/university	yr	1759	1996	38s
Education expenditures	yr	535	1999	30c
Room, 4-year private college/university	yr	2000	1996	38s
Room, 4-year public college/university	yr	1885	1996	38s
Total cost, 4-year private college/university	yr	13156	1996	38s
Total cost, 4-year public college/university	yr	5464	1996	38s
Tuition, 2-year public college/university, in state	yr	771	1996	38s
Tuition, 4-year private college/university, in state	yr	8959	1996	38s
Tuition, 4-year public college/university	yr	1820	1996	38s
Energy and Fuels				
Electricity	KWh	0.09	7/01	11r
Electricity	500 KWhs	53.90	7/01	11c
Electricity	KWh	0.10	7/01	11c
Fuel oil #2	gal	1.43	7/01	11r
Fuel oil and other fuels, expenditures on	yr	45	1999	30r
Gas, natural, commercial rate	1000 cf	6.94	11/00	88s
Gasoline, all types	gal	1.66	7/01	11c
Gasoline, unleaded midgrade	gal	1.69	7/01	11c
Gasoline, unleaded premium	gal	1.74	7/01	11r
Gasoline, unleaded regular	gal	1.60	7/01	11c
Natural gas, expenditures on	yr	164	1999	30r
Utility (piped) gas, therm		0.84	7/01	11c
Utility (piped) gas, 40 therms		44.29	7/01	11r
Utility (piped) gas, 100 therms		87.52	7/01	11c
Entertainment				
Entertainment purchases	yr	2011	1999	30c
Equipment, high school hockey player		500	2000	67c
Fees and admissions paid	yr	371	1999	30r
Ice time, high school hockey team	hour	250	2000	67c
Reading purchases	yr	121	1999	30r
Television, radios, sound equipment, expenditures on	yr	561	1999	30r
Funerals				
Total cost of funeral		5842.28	1/99	78r
Acknowledgement cards		28.35	1/99	78r
Casket		2494.29	1/99	78r
Cosmetology, hair, other preparation		109.22	1/99	78r
Embalming		361.42	1/99	78r
Funeral at funeral home		349.20	1/99	78r
Hearse (local)		161.91	1/99	78r
Professional service charges		1116.50	1/99	78r
Service car/van		65.56	1/99	78r
Transfer of remains to funeral home		143.56	1/99	78r
Vault		785.25	1/99	78r
Visitation/viewing		227.02	1/99	78r
Groceries				
American processed cheese	lb	3.50	7/01	11r
Bakery products, expenditures on	yr	261	1999	30r
Bananas	lb	0.47	7/01	11r
Beans, dried, any type, all sizes	lb	0.63	7/01	11r
Beef for stew, boneless	lb	2.86	7/01	11r
Beef, expenditures on	yr	210	1999	30r
Bologna, all beef or mixed	lb	2.29	7/01	11r
Bread, French	lb	1.66	7/01	11r
Bread, white, pan	lb	0.87	7/01	11r

Dallas-Fort Worth, TX - continued

Item	Per	Value	Date	Ref.
Groceries - continued				
Bread, whole wheat, pan	lb	1.38	7/01	11r
Broccoli	lb	1.04	7/01	11r
Butter, salted, grade AA, stick	lb	2.26	7/01	11r
Butter, yoghurt, cheese, etc, expenditures on	yr	170	1999	30r
Cabbage	lb	0.42	7/01	11r
Cereals and bakery product purchases	yr	535	1999	30c
Cereals and cereal products, expenditures on	yr	140	1999	30r
Cheddar cheese, natural	lb	3.75	7/01	11r
Chicken breast, bone-in	lb	1.85	7/01	11r
Chicken legs, bone-in	lb	1.34	7/01	11r
Chicken, fresh, whole	lb	1.05	7/01	11r
Chops, boneless,	lb	4.13	7/01	11r
Chuck roast, graded and ungraded, excl U.S. prime and choice	lb	2.35	7/01	11r
Chuck roast, U.S. choice, boneless	lb	2.67	7/01	11r
Coffee, 100%, ground roast, all sizes	lb	2.88	7/01	11r
Coffee, instant, plain, regular, all sizes	16 oz	9.25	7/01	11r
Cola, non diet	2 liter	1.11	7/01	11r
Crackers, soda, salted	lb	1.70	7/01	11r
Dairy product purchases	yr	384	1999	30c
Eggs, expenditures on	yr	32	1999	30r
Fats and oils, expenditures on	yr	79	1999	30r
Fish and seafood, expenditures on	yr	99	1999	30r
Flour, white, all purpose	lb	0.32	7/01	11r
Food (excl fruit and vegetables), eaten at home, purchases	yr	1082	1999	30c
Food cooked on trips, expenditures on	yr	36	1999	30r
Food purchases	yr	6490	1999	30c
Food purchases, eaten away from home	yr	2979	1999	30c
Food purchases, food eaten at home	yr	3512	1999	30c
Fresh fruits, expenditures on	yr	128	1999	30r
Fresh milk and cream, expenditures on	yr	112	1999	30r
Fresh vegetables, expenditures on	yr	131	1999	30r
Fruit and vegetable purchases	yr	438	1999	30r
Grapefruit	lb	0.59	7/01	11r
Grapes, Thompson, seedless	lb	2.12	7/01	11r
Ground beef, 100% beef	lb	1.76	7/01	11r
Ground beef, lean and extra lean	lb	2.60	7/01	11r
Ground chuck, 100% beef	lb	2.08	7/01	11r
Ham, boneless, excl canned	lb	2.71	7/01	11r
Ham, rump or shank half, bone-in, smoked	lb	2.19	7/01	11r
Ice cream, prepackaged, bulk, regular	1/2 gal	3.93	7/01	11r
Lemons	lb	1.32	7/01	11r
Lettuce, iceberg	lb	0.76	7/01	11r
Meats, poultry, fish, and egg purchases	yr	910	1999	30c
Milk, fresh, low fat,	gal	2.75	7/01	11r
Milk, fresh, whole, fortified	gal	2.97	7/01	11r
Nonalcoholic beverages, expenditures on	yr	228	1999	30r
Orange juice, frozen concentrate	16 oz	1.95	7/01	11r
Oranges, Navel	lb	0.73	7/01	11r
Oranges, Valencia	lb	0.55	7/01	11r
Peanut butter, creamy, all sizes	lb	1.83	7/01	11r
Pears, Anjou	lb	0.98	7/01	11r
Pork chops, center cut, bone-in	lb	3.33	7/01	11r
Pork sausage, fresh, loose	lb	2.59	7/01	11r
Pork shoulder picnic, bone-in, smoked	lb	1.12	7/01	11r
Pork, expenditures on	yr	162	1999	30r
Potato chips	16 oz	3.59	7/01	11r
Potatoes, frozen, french fried	lb	1.00	7/01	11r
Potatoes, white, all types	lb	0.44	7/01	11r
Poultry, expenditures on	yr	137	1999	30r
Processed fruits, expenditures on	yr	97	1999	30r
Processed vegetables, expenditures on	yr	82	1999	30r
Rice, white, long grain, uncooked	lb	0.51	7/01	11r
Round roast, graded and ungraded, excl U.S. prime and choice	lb	2.96	7/01	11r
Round steak, graded and ungraded, excl U.S. prime and choice	lb	3.11	7/01	11r
Sirloin steak, graded and ungraded, excl U.S. prime and choice	lb	4.23	7/01	11r
Spaghetti and macaroni	lb	0.78	7/01	11r

Values are in dollars or fractions of dollars. In the column headed *Ref*, references are shown to sources. Each reference is followed by a letter. These refer to the geographical level for which data were reported: s=State, r=Region, and c=City or metro. The abbreviation *ex* is used to mean *except* or *excluding*; *exp* stands for *expenditures*. For other abbreviations and further explanations, please see the Introduction.

Dallas-Fort Worth, TX - continued

Item	Per	Value	Date	Ref.
Groceries				
Steak, round, U.S. choice, boneless	lb	3.56	7/01	11r
Steak, sirloin, U.S. choice, boneless	lb	5.65	7/01	11r
Strawberries, dry pint	12 oz	1.50	7/01	11r
Sugar and other sweets, expenditures on	yr	99	1999	30r
Sugar, white, 33-80 ounce package	lb	0.39	7/01	11r
Sugar, white, all sizes	lb	0.42	7/01	11r
Tobacco products and smoking supplies purchases	yr	301	1999	30c
Tomatoes, field grown	lb	1.43	7/01	11r
Tuna, light, chunk	lb	1.77	7/01	11r
Turkey, frozen, whole	lb	1.05	7/01	11r
Goods and Services				
B&B Japanese maple (acer japonicum)	gal	79.98-99.00	4/00	93r
Boxwood (buxus)	2 gal	12.98-18.99	4/00	93r
Christmas tree, noble fir		40-60	2000	65s
Daylily (hemerocallis)	gal	7.96-11.00	4/00	93r
Flat of annuals		13.99-27.99	4/00	93r
Fountain grass (pennisetum)	gal	6.96-9.00	4/00	93r
Hanging basket (10 in)		9.99-24.99	4/00	93r
Hardy geranium (geranium)	gal	5.96-8.00	4/00	93r
Hosta (hosta)	gal	8.96-12.99	4/00	93r
Lilac (syrubga vulgaris)	2 gal	13.00-19.99	4/00	93r
Miscellaneous purchases	yr	794	1999	30c
Rhododendron (rhododendron)	2 gal	12.98-29.99	4/00	93r
Sage (salvia)	gal	5.96-8.00	4/00	93r
Wintercreeper euonymus (euonymus fortunei)	2 gal	13.00-18.99	4/00	93r
Hunting license	yr	19.00	4/01	34s
Health Care				
Cardiac catheterization, ave hospital/physician charges		20140	1998	77s
Childbirth, Cesarean delivery		11587	1997	13r
Childbirth, vaginal delivery		6725	1997	13r
Drugs, expenditures on	yr	399	1999	30r
Health care purchases	yr	2148	1999	30c
Health insurance expenditures	yr	933	1999	30r
Hysterectomy, laproscopically-assisted, ave hospital/physician charges		15700	1998	76s
Hysterectomy, vaginal, ave hospital and physician charges		12180	1998	76s
Medicaid dispensing fee		5.27	1999	87s
Medical services expenditures	yr	547	1999	30r
Medical supplies, expenditures on	yr	91	1999	30r
Household Goods				
Floor coverings, expenditures on	yr	44	1999	30r
Furniture, expenditures on	yr	335	1999	30r
Household furnishings and equipment purchases	yr	1624	1999	30c
Household textiles, expenditures on	yr	89	1999	30r
Laundry and cleaning supplies, expenditures on	yr	113	1999	30r
Housing				
Home price, existing, ave		160100	10/00	90r
Home value, median		112000	2001	53s
Household operation expenditures	yr	798	1999	30c
Housekeeping supplies purchases	yr	538	1999	30c
Housing, expenditures on	yr	10303	1999	30r
Lodging expenditures	yr	302	1999	30c

Dallas-Fort Worth, TX - continued

Item	Per	Value	Date	Ref.
Housing - continued				
Maintenance, repairs, insurance expenditures	yr	699	1999	30r
Monthly rental value of owned home	mos	505	1999	30r
Owned dwellings, expenditures own	yr	4394	1999	30c
Rent expenditures	yr	2662	1999	30c
Shelter, expenditures on	yr	7358	1999	30c
Insurance and Pensions				
Life and other personal insurance purchases	yr	545	1999	30c
Pensions and Social Security, expenditures on	yr	4575	1999	30c
Personal insurance and pensions, expenditures on	yr	3048	1999	30r
Legal Fees				
Divorce, filing fee		150.00-200.00	4/01	35s
Driver's license fee	orig	24.00	1999	48s
Driver's license fee	renew	20.00	1999	48s
Fishing license	yr	19.00	4/01	34s
Personal Goods				
Personal care products and services purchases	yr	528	1999	30c
Personal Services				
Personal services, household, expenditures on	yr	258	1999	30r
Pets				
Pets, toys, and playground equipment, expenditures on	yr	306	1999	30r
Taxes				
Federal income taxes paid	yr	2047	1999	30r
Personal taxes, expenditures on	yr	2554	1999	30r
Property taxes paid	yr	726	1999	30r
State and local income taxes paid	yr	363	1999	30r
Transportation				
Bus fare, one-way	trip	0.90	2000	1c
Cars and trucks, new, expenditures on	yr	1648	1999	30r
Cars and trucks, used, expenditures on	yr	1651	1999	30r
Diesel at the pump	gal	1.18	10/99	73s
Gasoline and motor oil purchases	yr	1272	1999	30c
Gasoline before-tax price (cents)	gal	101.30	10/00	43s
Household transportation expenditures	yr	8717	97-1998	102c
Maintenance and repair expenditures	yr	621	1999	30r
Parking at airport, lowest rate	day	5.00	2000	46c
Public transportation, expenditures on	yr	407	1999	30c
Transportation purchases	yr	7835	1999	30c
Vehicle expenses, miscellaneous, purchases	yr	2468	1999	30c
Vehicle insurance payments	yr	696	1999	30r
Vehicle purchases (net outlay)	yr	3354	1999	30r
Vehicle rental, lease expenditures	yr	352	1999	30r
Utilities				
Electrical bill, average	mos	87.17	9/00	9s
Electricity, expenditures on	yr	1115	1999	30r
Electricity, summer, 250 KWh	mos	22.82	2/96	96c
Electricity, summer, 500 KWh	mos	39.64	2/96	96c
Electricity, summer, 750 KWh	mos	53.80	2/96	96c
Electricity, summer, 1000 KWh	mos	66.21	2/96	96c
Electricity cost, average	KWh	6.48	9/00	9s
Utilities, fuels, and public services purchased	yr	2909	1999	30c
Water and other public services, expenditures on	yr	298	1999	30r
Weddings				
Wedding (national average cost)		19936	2000	33r
Attendants' gifts		321	1998	33r
Bridal attendants' apparel (5 persons)		824	2000	33r
Bride's headpiece/veil		173	1998	33r
Bride's wedding dress		859	1998	33r
Clergy, religious facility fee		242	1998	33r
Engagement ring		3177	1998	33r

Values are in dollars or fractions of dollars. In the column headed *Ref*, references are shown to sources. Each reference is followed by a letter. These refer to the geographical level for which data were reported: s=State, r=Region, and c=City or metro. The abbreviation *ex* is used to mean *except* or *excluding*; *exp* stands for *expenditures*. For other abbreviations and further explanations, please see the Introduction.

Dallas-Fort Worth, TX - continued

Item	Per	Value	Date	Ref.
Weddings				
Flowers		789	1998	33r
Groom's formalwear rental		99	2000	33r
Limousine		410	1998	33r
Marriage license cost		36.00	4/01	35s
Men's formalwear (ushers, best man)		469	2000	33r
Mother of bride apparel		241	2000	33r
Music		866	1998	33r
Photography and videography		1368	1998	33r
Rehearsal dinner		728	1998	33r
Wedding invitations and announcements		341	1998	33r
Wedding reception		7968	2000	33r
Wedding rings (bride and groom)		1060	1998	33r

Danbury, CT

Item	Per	Value	Date	Ref.
Average annual expenditures	yr	37971	1999	30r
Alcoholic Beverages				
Alcoholic beverage purchases	yr	368	1999	30r
Wine, red and white table, all sizes, any origin	liter	9.64	7/01	11r
Appliances				
Major appliances, expenditures on	yr	194	1999	30r
Small appliances, housewares, expenditures on	yr	93	1999	30r
Banking and Money				
Mortgage interest and charges paid	yr	2622	1999	30r
Mortgage principal paid on owned property	yr	1262	1999	30r
Vehicle finance charges paid	yr	240	1999	30r
Charity				
Cash contributions, expenditures	yr	1001	1999	30r
Child Care				
Child raising cost, total, age 0-2	yr	8670	1999	60r
Child raising cost, total, age 3-5	yr	8910	1999	60r
Child raising cost, total, age 6-8	yr	9040	1999	60r
Child raising cost, total, age 9-11	yr	9100	1999	60r
Child raising cost, total, age 12-14	yr	9890	1999	60r
Child raising cost, total, age 15-17	yr	10010	1999	60r
Child's child care and education, age 0-2	yr	1070	1999	60r
Child's child care and education, age 3-5	yr	1190	1999	60r
Child's child care and education, age 6-8	yr	740	1999	60r
Child's child care and education, age 9-11	yr	470	1999	60r
Child's child care and education, age 12-14	yr	350	1999	60r
Child's child care and education, age 15-17	yr	590	1999	60r
Child's clothing, age 0-2	yr	480	1999	60r
Child's clothing, age 3-5	yr	470	1999	60r
Child's clothing, age 6-8	yr	520	1999	60r
Child's clothing, age 9-11	yr	570	1999	60r
Child's clothing, age 12-14	yr	970	1999	60r
Child's clothing, age 15-17	yr	870	1999	60r
Child's food, age 0-2	yr	1130	1999	60r
Child's food, age 3-5	yr	1290	1999	60r
Child's food, age 6-8	yr	1640	1999	60r
Child's food, age 9-11	yr	1930	1999	60r
Child's food, age 12-14	yr	1940	1999	60r
Child's food, age 15-17	yr	2150	1999	60r
Child's health care, age 0-2	yr	550	1999	60r
Child's health care, age 3-5	yr	530	1999	60r
Child's health care, age 6-8	yr	610	1999	60r
Child's health care, age 9-11	yr	650	1999	60r
Child's health care, age 12-14	yr	660	1999	60r
Child's health care, age 15-17	yr	690	1999	60r
Child's housing, age 0-2	yr	3555	1999	60r
Child's housing, age 3-5	yr	3530	1999	60r
Child's housing, age 6-8	yr	3490	1999	60r
Child's housing, age 9-11	yr	3340	1999	60r
Child's housing, age 12-14	yr	3530	1999	60r
Child's housing, age 15-17	yr	3140	1999	60r
Child's personal care, reading, age 0-2	yr	920	1999	60r
Child's personal care, reading, age 3-5	yr	950	1999	60r

Danbury, CT - continued

Item	Per	Value	Date	Ref.
Child Care - continued				
Child's personal care, reading, age 6-8	yr	980	1999	60r
Child's personal care, reading, age 9-11	yr	1020	1999	60r
Child's personal care, reading, age 12-14	yr	1190	1999	60r
Child's personal care, reading, age 15-17	yr	970	1999	60r
Clothing				
Apparel and services purchases	yr	1831	1999	30r
Boys, 2 to 15, expenditures on	yr	92	1999	30r
Children under 2, expenditures on	yr	63	1999	30r
Footwear, expenditures on	yr	300	1999	30r
Girls, 2 to 15, expenditures on	yr	101	1999	30r
Men and boys, expenditures on	yr	446	1999	30r
Men, 16 and over, expenditures on	yr	354	1999	30r
Women, 16 and over, expenditures on	yr	584	1999	30r
Communications				
Cable modem installation, AT&T-BIS		150.00	6/99	103s
Cable modem installation, Cablevision Systems		150.00	6/99	103s
Cable modem installation, Cox		99.00-174.95	6/99	103s
Cable modem installation, Media One		100.00	6/99	103s
Cable modem rate, cable subscriber, AT&T-BIS	mos	39.95	6/99	103s
Cable modem rate, cable subscriber, Cablevision Systems	mos	44.95	6/99	103s
Cable modem rate, cable subscriber, Cox	mos	29.95-44.95	6/99	103s
Cable modem rate, cable subscriber, Media One	mos	34.95-39.95	6/99	103s
Cable modem rate, non-cable subscriber, Cablevision Systems	mos	54.95	6/99	103s
Cable modem rate, non-cable subscriber, Cox	mos	42.95-54.95	6/99	103s
Cable modem rate, non-cable subscriber, Media One	mos	49.95	6/99	103s
Phone line, single, business, field visit	inst.	65.00	12/97	17s
Phone line, single, business, no field visit	inst.	65.00	12/97	17s
Phone line, single, residence, field visit	inst.	45.00	12/97	17s
Phone line, single, residence, no field visit	inst.	45.00	12/97	17s
Postage and stationery, expenditures on	yr	138	1999	30r
Postal rate, express mail, up to half-pound		12.45	7/01	108r
Postal rate, letter, first class, first ounce		0.34	7/01	108r
Postal rate, letter, two ounces		0.57	7/01	108r
Postal rate, post card		0.21	7/01	108r
Postal rate, priority mail, two pounds		3.95	7/01	108r
Postal rate, priority mail, up to one pound		3.50	7/01	108r
Telephone services, expenditures on	yr	830	1999	30r
Education				
Board, 4-year private college/university	yr	2744	1996	38s
Board, 4-year public college/university	yr	2299	1996	38s
Education expenditures	yr	877	1999	30r
Room, 4-year private college/university	yr	3621	1996	38s
Room, 4-year public college/university	yr	2609	1996	38s
Total cost, 4-year private college/university	yr	23011	1996	38s
Total cost, 4-year public college/university	yr	8753	1996	38s
Tuition, 2-year public college/university, in state	yr	1646	1996	38s
Tuition, 4-year private college/university, in state	yr	16646	1996	38s
Tuition, 4-year public college/university	yr	3845	1996	38s
Energy and Fuels				
Electricity	KWh	0.12	7/01	11r
Fuel oil #2	gal	1.31	7/01	11r
Fuel oil and other fuels, expenditures on	yr	207	1999	30r
Gas, natural, commercial rate	1000 cf	7.08	11/00	88s
Gasoline, all types	gal	1.80	7/01	11r
Gasoline, unleaded midgrade	gal	1.85	7/01	11r
Gasoline, unleaded premium	gal	1.91	7/01	11r
Gasoline, unleaded regular	gal	1.71	7/01	11r
Natural gas, expenditures on	yr	368	1999	30r
Utility (piped) gas, therm		1.08	7/01	11r

Values are in dollars or fractions of dollars. In the column headed *Ref*, references are shown to sources. Each reference is followed by a letter. These refer to the geographical level for which data were reported: s=State, r=Region, and c=City or metro. The abbreviation *ex* is used to mean *except* or *excluding*; *exp* stands for *expenditures*. For other abbreviations and further explanations, please see the Introduction.

Danbury, CT - continued

Item	Per	Value	Date	Ref.
Energy and Fuels				
Utility (piped) gas, 40 therms		50.87	7/01	11r
Utility (piped) gas, 100 therms		111.06	7/01	11r
Entertainment				
Entertainment purchases	yr	1821	1999	30r
Fees and admissions paid	yr	511	1999	30r
Hockey equipment, girls' hockey		800	2001	101s
Television, radios, sound equipment, expenditures on	yr	650	1999	30r
Funerals				
Total cost of funeral		5776.91	1/99	78r
Acknowledgement cards		14.47	1/99	78r
Casket		2090.19	1/99	78r
Cosmetology, hair, other preparation		132.92	1/99	78r
Embalming		377.33	1/99	78r
Funeral at funeral home		352.43	1/99	78r
Hearse (local)		185.55	1/99	78r
Professional service charges		1289.95	1/99	78r
Service car/van		87.42	1/99	78r
Transfer of remains to funeral home		175.48	1/99	78r
Vault		729.40	1/99	78r
Visitation/viewing		341.76	1/99	78r
Groceries				
Apples, red delicious	lb	0.95	7/01	11r
Bacon, sliced	lb	3.44	7/01	11r
Bakery products, expenditures on	yr	310	1999	30r
Bananas	lb	0.55	7/01	11r
Beef, expenditures on	yr	236	1999	30r
Bread, white, pan	lb	1.09	7/01	11r
Butter, yoghurt, cheese, etc, expenditures on	yr	214	1999	30r
Cereals and bakery product purchases	yr	474	1999	30r
Cereals and cereal products, expenditures on	yr	164	1999	30r
Chicken legs, bone-in	lb	1.23	7/01	11r
Chicken, fresh, whole	lb	1.13	7/01	11r
Chuck roast, U.S. choice, boneless	lb	2.79	7/01	11r
Coffee, 100%, ground roast, all sizes	lb	3.40	7/01	11r
Dairy product purchases	yr	342	1999	30r
Eggs, expenditures on	yr	34	1999	30r
Eggs, grade A, large	dozen	0.82	7/01	11r
Fats and oils, expenditures on	yr	80	1999	30r
Fish and seafood, expenditures on	yr	123	1999	30r
Food (excl fruit and vegetables), eaten at home, purchases	yr	838	1999	30r
Food cooked on trips, expenditures on	yr	48	1999	30r
Food purchases	yr	5314	1999	30r
Food purchases, eaten away from home	yr	2313	1999	30r
Food purchases, food eaten at home	yr	3001	1999	30r
Fresh fruits, expenditures on	yr	169	1999	30r
Fresh milk and cream, expenditures on	yr	128	1999	30r
Fresh vegetables, expenditures on	yr	164	1999	30r
Grapefruit	lb	0.67	7/01	11r
Grapes, Thompson, seedless	lb	2.18	7/01	11r
Ground beef, lean and extra lean	lb	2.66	7/01	11r
Ground chuck, 100% beef	lb	2.04	7/01	11r
Lettuce, iceberg	lb	0.76	7/01	11r
Meats, poultry, fish, and egg purchases	yr	808	1999	30r
Nonalcoholic beverages, expenditures on	yr	225	1999	30r
Orange juice, frozen concentrate	16 oz	1.88	7/01	11r
Oranges, Navel	lb	0.79	7/01	11r
Oranges, Valencia	lb	0.56	7/01	11r
Peaches	lb	1.16	7/01	11r
Peanut butter, creamy, all sizes	lb	2.01	7/01	11r
Pears, Anjou	lb	1.16	7/01	11r
Pork chops, center cut, bone-in	lb	3.57	7/01	11r
Pork, expenditures on	yr	146	1999	30r
Potato chips	16 oz	3.37	7/01	11r
Potatoes, white, all types	lb	0.42	7/01	11r
Poultry, expenditures on	yr	158	1999	30r
Processed fruits, expenditures on	yr	124	1999	30r
Processed vegetables, expenditures on	yr	82	1999	30r
Round roast, U.S. choice, boneless	lb	3.04	7/01	11r

Danbury, CT - continued

Item	Per	Value	Date	Ref.
Groceries - continued				
Spaghetti and macaroni	lb	1.04	7/01	11r
Steak, sirloin, U.S. choice, boneless	lb	5.39	7/01	11r
Strawberries, dry pint	12 oz	1.51	7/01	11r
Sugar and other sweets, expenditures on	yr	110	1999	30r
Sugar, white, 33-80 ounce package	lb	0.46	7/01	11r
Sugar, white, all sizes	lb	0.47	7/01	11r
Tobacco products and smoking supplies purchases	yr	309	1999	30r
Yogurt, natural, fruit flavored	8 oz	0.79	7/01	11r
Goods and Services				
B&B Japanese maple (acer japonicum)	gal	38.99-125.00	4/00	93r
Boxwood (buxus)	2 gal	15.99-49.95	4/00	93r
Daylilly (hemerocallis)	gal	4.95	4/00	93r
Flat of annuals		8.00-14.99	4/00	93r
Fountain grass (pennisetum)	gal	6.99-9.99	4/00	93r
Hanging basket (10 in)		12.95-19.99	4/00	93r
Hardy geranium (geranium)	gal	6.95-7.99	4/00	93r
Hosta (hosta)	gal	4.95	4/00	93r
Lilac (syrubga vulgaris)	2 gal	17.99-74.95	4/00	93r
Miscellaneous purchases	yr	872	1999	30r
Rhododendron (rhododendron)	2 gal	23.99-54.95	4/00	93r
Sage (salvia)	gal	6.95-7.99	4/00	93r
Wintercreeper euonymus (euonymus fortunei)	2 gal	14.99-23.95	4/00	93r
Hunting license	yr	10.00	4/01	34s
Health Care				
Cardiac catheterization, ave hospital/physician charges		14090	1998	77s
Childbirth, Cesarean delivery		14716	1997	13r
Childbirth, vaginal delivery		8541	1997	13r
Drugs, expenditures on	yr	296	1999	30r
Health care purchases	yr	1788	1999	30r
Health insurance expenditures	yr	875	1999	30r
Home health care aide cost, licensed agency	hour	21	2000	82c
Hysterectomy, laproscopically-assisted, ave hospital/physician charges		11610	1998	76s
Hysterectomy, vaginal, ave hospital and physician charges		12780	1998	76s
Medicaid dispensing fee		4.10	1999	87s
Medical services expenditures	yr	516	1999	30r
Medical supplies, expenditures on	yr	102	1999	30r
Plastic surgery, breast augmentation		4232	2000	7r
Plastic surgery, breast lift		4605	2000	7r
Plastic surgery, facelift		6964	2000	7r
Plastic surgery, hair transplantation		4193	2000	7r
Plastic surgery, lip augmentation		1675	2000	7r
Plastic surgery, lower body lift		6611	2000	7r
Plastic surgery, thigh lift		4751	2000	7r
Household Goods				
Floor coverings, expenditures on	yr	59	1999	30r
Furniture, expenditures on	yr	388	1999	30r
Household furnishings and equipment purchases	yr	1567	1999	30r
Household textiles, expenditures on	yr	112	1999	30r
Laundry and cleaning supplies, expenditures on	yr	104	1999	30r
Housing				
Home, 2200 sq ft, 4-br, 2-bath, 2-car garage, average		252125	2000	47c
Home price, existing, ave		180800	10/00	90r
Home value, median		157000	2001	53s

Values are in dollars or fractions of dollars. In the column headed *Ref*, references are shown to sources. Each reference is followed by a letter. These refer to the geographical level for which data were reported: s=State, r=Region, and c=City or metro. The abbreviation *ex* is used to mean *except* or *excluding*; *exp* stands for *expenditures*. For other abbreviations and further explanations, please see the Introduction.

Danbury, CT - continued

Item	Per	Value	Date	Ref.
Housing				
Household operation expenditures	yr	581	1999	30r
Housekeeping supplies purchases	yr	474	1999	30r
Lodging expenditures	yr	550	1999	30r
Maintenance, repairs, insurance				
expenditures	yr	835	1999	30r
Monthly rental value of owned home	mos	663	1999	30r
Owned dwellings, expenditures own	yr	5209	1999	30r
Rent expenditures	yr	2390	1999	30r
Rental unit, 1 bedroom, with utilities	mos	769	4/01	41c
Rental unit, 2 bedroom, with utilities	mos	961	4/01	41c
Rental unit, 3 bedroom, with utilities	mos	1268	4/01	41c
Rental unit, 4 bedroom, with utilities	mos	1462	4/01	41c
Shelter, expenditures on	yr	8149	1999	30r
Insurance and Pensions				
Auto insurance premium	yr	982.00	1999	57s
Life and other personal insurance purchases	yr	424	1999	30r
Pensions and Social Security, expenditures				
on	yr	3037	1999	30r
Legal Fees				
Divorce, filing fee		150.00	4/01	35s
Driver's license fee	renew	28.50	1999	48s
Driver's license fee	orig	43.50	1999	48s
Personal Goods				
Personal care products and services				
purchases	yr	399	1999	30r
Personal Services				
Personal services, household, expenditures				
on	yr	271	1999	30r
Pets				
Pets, toys, and playground equipment,				
expenditures on	yr	325	1999	30r
Taxes				
Federal income taxes paid	yr	2606	1999	30r
Personal taxes, expenditures on	yr	3567	1999	30r
Property taxes paid	yr	1752	1999	30r
State and local income taxes paid	yr	694	1999	30r
Transportation				
Cars and trucks, new, expenditures on	yr	1496	1999	30r
Cars and trucks, used, expenditures on	yr	1251	1999	30r
Diesel at the pump	gal	1.36	10/99	73s
Gasoline and motor oil purchases	yr	901	1999	30r
Gasoline before-tax price (cents)	gal	117.10	10/00	43s
Maintenance and repair expenditures	yr	618	1999	30r
Public transportation, expenditures on	yr	575	1999	30r
Transportation purchases	yr	6503	1999	30r
Vehicle expenses, miscellaneous, purchases	yr	2266	1999	30r
Vehicle insurance payments	yr	824	1999	30r
Vehicle purchases (net outlay)	yr	2761	1999	30r
Vehicle rental, lease expenditures	yr	584	1999	30r
Utilities				
Electrical bill, average	mos	81.50	9/00	9s
Electricity, expenditures on	yr	837	1999	30r
Electricity cost, average	KWh	9.47	9/00	9s
Utilities, fuels, and public services purchased	yr	2457	1999	30r
Water and other public services,				
expenditures on	yr	215	1999	30r
Weddings				
Wedding (national average cost)		19936	2000	33r
Wedding (regional average total cost)		29454	1997	110r
Attendants' gifts		321	1998	33r
Bridal attendants' apparel (5 persons)		824	2000	33r
Bride's headpiece/veil		173	1998	33r
Bride's wedding dress		859	1998	33r
Clergy, religious facility fee		242	1998	33r
Engagement ring		3177	1998	33r
Flowers		789	1998	33r
Groom's formalwear rental		99	2000	33r

Danbury, CT - continued

Item	Per	Value	Date	Ref.
Weddings - continued				
Limousine		410	1998	33r
Marriage license cost		30.00	4/01	35s
Men's formalwear (ushers, best man)		469	2000	33r
Mother of bride apparel		241	2000	33r
Music		866	1998	33r
Photography and videography		1368	1998	33r
Rehearsal dinner		728	1998	33r
Wedding invitations and announcements		341	1998	33r
Wedding reception		7968	2000	33r
Wedding rings (bride and groom)		1060	1998	33r

Danville, VA

Item	Per	Value	Date	Ref.
Alcoholic Beverages				
Alcoholic beverage purchases	yr	253	1999	30r
Malt beverages, all types, all sizes, any origin	16 oz	0.96	7/01	11r
Appliances				
Major appliances, expenditures on	yr	172	1999	30r
Small appliances, housewares, expenditures				
on	yr	81	1999	30r
Banking and Money				
Mortgage interest and charges paid	yr	2039	1999	30r
Mortgage principal paid on owned property	yr	1026	1999	30r
Vehicle finance charges paid	yr	365	1999	30r
Charity				
Cash contributions, expenditures	yr	1127	1999	30r
Child Care				
Child raising cost, total, age 0-2	yr	8540	1999	60r
Child raising cost, total, age 3-5	yr	8780	1999	60r
Child raising cost, total, age 6-8	yr	8820	1999	60r
Child raising cost, total, age 9-11	yr	8800	1999	60r
Child raising cost, total, age 12-14	yr	9510	1999	60r
Child raising cost, total, age 15-17	yr	9740	1999	60r
Child's child care and education, age 0-2	yr	1380	1999	60r
Child's child care and education, age 3-5	yr	1520	1999	60r
Child's child care and education, age 6-8	yr	990	1999	60r
Child's child care and education, age 9-11	yr	650	1999	60r
Child's child care and education, age 12-14	yr	490	1999	60r
Child's child care and education, age 15-17	yr	840	1999	60r
Child's clothing, age 0-2	yr	480	1999	60r
Child's clothing, age 3-5	yr	470	1999	60r
Child's clothing, age 6-8	yr	520	1999	60r
Child's clothing, age 9-11	yr	570	1999	60r
Child's clothing, age 12-14	yr	950	1999	60r
Child's clothing, age 15-17	yr	850	1999	60r
Child's food, age 0-2	yr	1000	1999	60r
Child's food, age 3-5	yr	1160	1999	60r
Child's food, age 6-8	yr	1490	1999	60r
Child's food, age 9-11	yr	1770	1999	60r
Child's food, age 12-14	yr	1770	1999	60r
Child's food, age 15-17	yr	1980	1999	60r
Child's health care, age 0-2	yr	620	1999	60r
Child's health care, age 3-5	yr	590	1999	60r
Child's health care, age 6-8	yr	680	1999	60r
Child's health care, age 9-11	yr	720	1999	60r
Child's health care, age 12-14	yr	730	1999	60r
Child's health care, age 15-17	yr	760	1999	60r
Child's housing, age 0-2	yr	3070	1999	60r
Child's housing, age 3-5	yr	3050	1999	60r
Child's housing, age 6-8	yr	3010	1999	60r
Child's housing, age 9-11	yr	2850	1999	60r
Child's housing, age 12-14	yr	3040	1999	60r
Child's housing, age 15-17	yr	2650	1999	60r
Child's personal care, reading, age 0-2	yr	910	1999	60r
Child's personal care, reading, age 3-5	yr	930	1999	60r
Child's personal care, reading, age 6-8	yr	960	1999	60r
Child's personal care, reading, age 9-11	yr	1000	1999	60r
Child's personal care, reading, age 12-14	yr	1170	1999	60r
Child's personal care, reading, age 15-17	yr	950	1999	60r

Values are in dollars or fractions of dollars. In the column headed *Ref*, references are shown to sources. Each reference is followed by a letter. These refer to the geographical level for which data were reported: s=State, r=Region, and c=City or metro. The abbreviation *ex* is used to mean *except* or *excluding*; *exp* stands for expenditures. For other abbreviations and further explanations, please see the Introduction.

Danville, VA - continued

Item	Per	Value	Date	Ref.
Clothing				
Apparel and services purchases	yr	1610	1999	30r
Boys, 2 to 15, expenditures on	yr	89	1999	30r
Children under 2, expenditures on	yr	79	1999	30r
Footwear, expenditures on	yr	283	1999	30r
Girls, 2 to 15, expenditures on	yr	103	1999	30r
Men and boys, expenditures on	yr	351	1999	30r
Men, 16 and over, expenditures on	yr	262	1999	30r
Women, 16 and over, expenditures on	yr	538	1999	30r
Communications				
Cable modem installation, Adelphi		54.90	6/99	103s
Cable modem installation, Comcast		95.00	6/99	103s
Cable modem installation, Cox		99.00-174.95	6/99	103s
Cable modem installation, Jones Intercable		100.00	6/99	103s
Cable modem rate, cable subscriber, Adelphi	mos	34.95	6/99	103s
Cable modem rate, cable subscriber, Comcast	mos	39.95	6/99	103s
Cable modem rate, cable subscriber, Cox	mos	29.95-44.95	6/99	103s
Cable modem rate, cable subscriber, Jones Intercable	mos	29.95-39.95	6/99	103s
Cable modem rate, non-cable subscriber, Adelphi	mos	44.95	6/99	103s
Cable modem rate, non-cable subscriber, Comcast	mos	49.95	6/99	103s
Cable modem rate, non-cable subscriber, Cox	mos	42.95-54.95	6/99	103s
Phone line, single, business, field visit	inst.	64.00	12/97	17s
Phone line, single, business, no field visit	inst.	64.00	12/97	17s
Phone line, single, residence, field visit	inst.	38.50	12/97	17s
Phone line, single, residence, no field visit	inst.	38.50	12/97	17s
Postage and stationery, expenditures on	yr	104	1999	30r
Postal rate, express mail, up to half-pound		12.45	7/01	108r
Postal rate, letter, first class, first ounce		0.34	7/01	108r
Postal rate, letter, two ounces		0.57	7/01	108r
Postal rate, post card		0.21	7/01	108r
Postal rate, priority mail, two pounds		3.95	7/01	108r
Postal rate, priority mail, up to one pound		3.50	7/01	108r
Telephone services, expenditures on	yr	860	1999	30r
Education				
Board, 4-year private college/university	yr	2363	1996	38s
Board, 4-year public college/university	yr	2033	1996	38s
Education expenditures	yr	431	1999	30r
Room, 4-year private college/university	yr	2062	1996	38s
Room, 4-year public college/university	yr	2261	1996	38s
Total cost, 4-year private college/university	yr	15021	1996	38s
Total cost, 4-year public college/university	yr	8202	1996	38s
Tuition, 2-year public college/university, in state	yr	1433	1996	38s
Tuition, 4-year private college/university, in state	yr	10596	1996	38s
Tuition, 4-year public college/university	yr	3907	1996	38s
Energy and Fuels				
Electricity	KWh	0.09	7/01	11r
Electricity	500 KWhs	47.29	7/01	11r
Fuel oil #2	gal	1.43	7/01	11r
Fuel oil and other fuels, expenditures on	yr	45	1999	30r
Gas, natural, commercial rate	1000 cf	9.01	11/00	88s
Gasoline, all types	gal	1.60	7/01	11r
Gasoline, unleaded midgrade	gal	1.65	7/01	11r
Gasoline, unleaded premium	gal	1.74	7/01	11r
Natural gas, expenditures on	yr	164	1999	30r
Utility (piped) gas, therm		1.01	7/01	11r
Utility (piped) gas, 40 therms		44.29	7/01	11r
Utility (piped) gas, 100 therms		97.44	7/01	11r
Entertainment				
Entertainment purchases	yr	1574	1999	30r
Fees and admissions paid	yr	371	1999	30r
Reading purchases	yr	121	1999	30r

Danville, VA - continued

Item	Per	Value	Date	Ref.
Entertainment - continued				
Television, radios, sound equipment, expenditures on	yr	561	1999	30r
Funerals				
Total cost of funeral		5922.53	1/99	78r
Acknowledgement cards		63.43	1/99	78r
Casket		2258.77	1/99	78r
Cosmetology, hair, other preparation		127.09	1/99	78r
Embalming		393.49	1/99	78r
Funeral at funeral home		367.50	1/99	78r
Hearse (local)		169.66	1/99	78r
Professional service charges		1211.32	1/99	78r
Service car/van		80.69	1/99	78r
Transfer of remains to funeral home		144.25	1/99	78r
Vault		803.50	1/99	78r
Visitation/viewing		302.83	1/99	78r
Groceries				
American processed cheese	lb	3.50	7/01	11r
Bakery products, expenditures on	yr	261	1999	30r
Bananas	lb	0.47	7/01	11r
Beans, dried, any type, all sizes	lb	0.63	7/01	11r
Beef for stew, boneless	lb	2.86	7/01	11r
Beef, expenditures on	yr	210	1999	30r
Bologna, all beef or mixed	lb	2.29	7/01	11r
Bread, French	lb	1.66	7/01	11r
Bread, white, pan	lb	0.87	7/01	11r
Bread, whole wheat, pan	lb	1.38	7/01	11r
Broccoli	lb	1.04	7/01	11r
Butter, salted, grade AA, stick	lb	2.26	7/01	11r
Butter, yoghurt, cheese, etc, expenditures on	yr	170	1999	30r
Cabbage	lb	0.42	7/01	11r
Cereals and cereal products, expenditures on	yr	140	1999	30r
Cheddar cheese, natural	lb	3.75	7/01	11r
Chicken breast, bone-in	lb	1.85	7/01	11r
Chicken legs, bone-in	lb	1.34	7/01	11r
Chicken, fresh, whole	lb	1.05	7/01	11r
Chops, boneless,	lb	4.13	7/01	11r
Chuck roast, graded and ungraded, excl U.S. prime and choice	lb	2.35	7/01	11r
Chuck roast, U.S. choice, boneless	lb	2.67	7/01	11r
Coffee, 100%, ground roast, all sizes	lb	2.88	7/01	11r
Coffee, instant, plain, regular, all sizes	16 oz	9.25	7/01	11r
Cola, non diet	2 liter	1.11	7/01	11r
Crackers, soda, salted	lb	1.70	7/01	11r
Dairy product purchases	yr	282	1999	30r
Eggs, expenditures on	yr	32	1999	30r
Fats and oils, expenditures on	yr	79	1999	30r
Fish and seafood, expenditures on	yr	99	1999	30r
Flour, white, all purpose	lb	0.32	7/01	11r
Food (excl fruit and vegetables), eaten at home, purchases	yr	815	1999	30r
Food cooked on trips, expenditures on	yr	36	1999	30r
Food purchases	yr	4533	1999	30r
Food purchases, eaten away from home	yr	1873	1999	30r
Food purchases, food eaten at home	yr	2660	1999	30r
Fresh fruits, expenditures on	yr	128	1999	30r
Fresh milk and cream, expenditures on	yr	112	1999	30r
Fresh vegetables, expenditures on	yr	131	1999	30r
Fruit and vegetable purchases	yr	438	1999	30r
Grapefruit	lb	0.59	7/01	11r
Grapes, Thompson, seedless	lb	2.12	7/01	11r
Ground beef, 100% beef	lb	1.76	7/01	11r
Ground beef, lean and extra lean	lb	2.60	7/01	11r
Ground chuck, 100% beef	lb	2.08	7/01	11r
Ham, boneless, excl canned	lb	2.71	7/01	11r
Ham, rump or shank half, bone-in, smoked	lb	2.19	7/01	11r
Ice cream, prepackaged, bulk, regular	1/2 gal	3.93	7/01	11r
Lemons	lb	1.32	7/01	11r
Lettuce, iceberg	lb	0.76	7/01	11r
Milk, fresh, low fat,	gal	2.75	7/01	11r
Milk, fresh, whole, fortified	gal	2.97	7/01	11r

Values are in dollars or fractions of dollars. In the column headed *Ref*, references are shown to sources. Each reference is followed by a letter. These refer to the geographical level for which data were reported: s=State, r=Region, and c=City or metro. The abbreviation *ex* is used to mean *except* or *excluding*; *exp* stands for expenditures. For other abbreviations and further explanations, please see the Introduction.

Danville, VA - continued

Item	Per	Value	Date	Ref.
Groceries				
Nonalcoholic beverages, expenditures on	yr	228	1999	30r
Orange juice, frozen concentrate	16 oz	1.95	7/01	11r
Oranges, Navel	lb	0.73	7/01	11r
Oranges, Valencia	lb	0.55	7/01	11r
Peanut butter, creamy, all sizes	lb	1.83	7/01	11r
Pears, Anjou	lb	0.98	7/01	11r
Pork chops, center cut, bone-in	lb	3.33	7/01	11r
Pork sausage, fresh, loose	lb	2.59	7/01	11r
Pork shoulder picnic, bone-in, smoked	lb	1.12	7/01	11r
Pork, expenditures on	yr	162	1999	30r
Potato chips	16 oz	3.59	7/01	11r
Potatoes, frozen, french fried	lb	1.00	7/01	11r
Potatoes, white, all types	lb	0.44	7/01	11r
Poultry, expenditures on	yr	137	1999	30r
Processed fruits, expenditures on	yr	97	1999	30r
Processed vegetables, expenditures on	yr	82	1999	30r
Rice, white, long grain, uncooked	lb	0.51	7/01	11r
Round roast, graded and ungraded, excl U.S. prime and choice	lb	2.96	7/01	11r
Round steak, graded and ungraded, excl U.S. prime and choice	lb	3.11	7/01	11r
Sirloin steak, graded and ungraded, excl U.S. prime and choice	lb	4.23	7/01	11r
Spaghetti and macaroni	lb	0.78	7/01	11r
Steak, round, U.S. choice, boneless	lb	3.56	7/01	11r
Steak, sirloin, U.S. choice, boneless	lb	5.65	7/01	11r
Strawberries, dry pint	12 oz	1.50	7/01	11r
Sugar and other sweets, expenditures on	yr	99	1999	30r
Sugar, white, 33-80 ounce package	lb	0.39	7/01	11r
Sugar, white, all sizes	lb	0.42	7/01	11r
Tobacco products and smoking supplies purchases	yr	288	1999	30r
Tomatoes, field grown	lb	1.43	7/01	11r
Tuna, light, chunk	lb	1.77	7/01	11r
Turkey, frozen, whole	lb	1.05	7/01	11r
Goods and Services				
B&B Japanese maple (acer japonicum)	gal	49.98-129.00	4/00	93r
Boxwood (buxus)	2 gal	12.99-16.99	4/00	93r
Daylily (hemerocallis)	gal	4.99-8.99	4/00	93r
Flat of annuals		11.00-13.92	4/00	93r
Fountain grass (pennisetum)	gal	5.98-7.98	4/00	93r
Hanging basket (10 in)		7.99-14.98	4/00	93r
Hardy geranium (geranium)	gal	5.98-8.00	4/00	93r
Hosta (hosta)	gal	4.99-10.98	4/00	93r
Lilac (syrubga vulgaris)	2 gal	12.99-21.99	4/00	93r
Rhododendron (rhododendron)	2 gal	14.99-24.99	4/00	93r
Sage (salvia)	gal	5.98-6.99	4/00	93r
Wintercreeper euonymus (euonymus fortunei)	2 gal	7.99-89.99	4/00	93r
Hunting license	yr	12.00	4/01	34s
Health Care				
Cardiac catheterization, ave hospital/ physician charges		15370	1998	77s
Childbirth, Cesarean delivery		11587	1997	13r
Childbirth, vaginal delivery		6725	1997	13r
Drugs, expenditures on	yr	399	1999	30r
Health care purchases	yr	1971	1999	30r
Health insurance expenditures	yr	933	1999	30r
Hysterectomy, laproscopically-assisted, ave hospital/physician charges		15660	1998	76s

Danville, VA - continued

Item	Per	Value	Date	Ref.
Health Care - continued				
Hysterectomy, vaginal, ave hospital and physician charges		10260	1998	76s
Medicaid dispensing fee		4.25	1999	87s
Medical services expenditures	yr	547	1999	30r
Medical supplies, expenditures on	yr	91	1999	30r
Plastic surgery, breast augmentation		2870	2000	7r
Plastic surgery, breast lift		3649	2000	7r
Plastic surgery, facelift		5008	2000	7r
Plastic surgery, hair transplantation		3425	2000	7r
Plastic surgery, lip augmentation		1227	2000	7r
Plastic surgery, lower body lift		4793	2000	7r
Plastic surgery, thigh lift		3862	2000	7r
Household Goods				
Floor coverings, expenditures on	yr	44	1999	30r
Furniture, expenditures on	yr	335	1999	30r
Household furnishings and equipment purchases	yr	1328	1999	30r
Household textiles, expenditures on	yr	89	1999	30r
Laundry and cleaning supplies, expenditures on	yr	113	1999	30r
Housing				
Home price, existing, ave		160100	10/00	90r
Home value, median		141000	2001	53s
Household operation expenditures	yr	553	1999	30r
Housekeeping supplies purchases	yr	473	1999	30r
Housing, expenditures on	yr	10303	1999	30r
Maintenance, repairs, insurance expenditures	yr	699	1999	30r
Monthly rental value of owned home	mos	505	1999	30r
Owned dwellings, expenditures own	yr	3465	1999	30r
Rent expenditures	yr	1641	1999	30r
Rental unit, 1 bedroom, with utilities	mos	373	4/01	41c
Rental unit, 2 bedroom, with utilities	mos	438	4/01	41c
Rental unit, 3 bedroom, with utilities	mos	588	4/01	41c
Rental unit, 4 bedroom, with utilities	mos	709	4/01	41c
Shelter, expenditures on	yr	5467	1999	30r
Insurance and Pensions				
Auto insurance premium	yr	628.58	1999	57s
Life and other personal insurance purchases	yr	414	1999	30r
Pensions and Social Security, expenditures on	yr	2635	1999	30r
Personal insurance and pensions, expenditures on	yr	3048	1999	30r
Legal Fees				
Divorce, filing fee		64.00	4/01	35s
Driver's license fee	renew	7.20	1999	48s
Driver's license fee	orig	7.20	1999	48s
Fishing license	yr	12.50	4/01	34s
Personal Goods				
Personal care products and services purchases	yr	393	1999	30r
Personal Services				
Personal services, household, expenditures on	yr	258	1999	30r
Pets				
Pets, toys, and playground equipment, expenditures on	yr	306	1999	30r
Taxes				
Federal income taxes paid	yr	2047	1999	30r
Personal taxes, expenditures on	yr	2554	1999	30r
Property taxes paid	yr	726	1999	30r
State and local income taxes paid	yr	363	1999	30r
Transportation				
Cars and trucks, new, expenditures on	yr	1648	1999	30r
Cars and trucks, used, expenditures on	yr	1651	1999	30r
Diesel at the pump	gal	1.14	10/99	73s
Gasoline and motor oil purchases	yr	1052	1999	30r

Values are in dollars or fractions of dollars. In the column headed *Ref*, references are shown to sources. Each reference is followed by a letter. These refer to the geographical level for which data were reported: s=State, r=Region, and c=City or metro. The abbreviation *ex* is used to mean *except* or *excluding*; *exp* stands for *expenditures*. For other abbreviations and further explanations, please see the Introduction.

Danville, VA - continued

Item	Per	Value	Date	Ref.
Transportation				
Gasoline before-tax price (cents)	gal	107.30	10/00	43s
Maintenance and repair expenditures	yr	621	1999	30r
Public transportation, expenditures on	yr	298	1999	30r
Transportation purchases	yr	6738	1999	30r
Vehicle expenses, miscellaneous, purchases	yr	2033	1999	30r
Vehicle insurance payments	yr	696	1999	30r
Vehicle purchases (net outlay)	yr	3354	1999	30r
Vehicle rental, lease expenditures	yr	352	1999	30r
Utilities				
Electrical bill, average	mos	82.17	9/00	9s
Electricity, expenditures on	yr	1115	1999	30r
Electricity cost, average	KWh	5.90	9/00	9s
Water and other public services, expenditures on	yr	298	1999	30r
Weddings				
Wedding (national average cost)		19936	2000	33r
Wedding (regional average total cost)		16293	1997	110r
Attendants' gifts		321	1998	33r
Bridal attendants' apparel (5 persons)		824	2000	33r
Bride's headpiece/veil		173	1998	33r
Bride's wedding dress		859	1998	33r
Clergy, religious facility fee		242	1998	33r
Engagement ring		3177	1998	33r
Flowers		789	1998	33r
Groom's formalwear rental		99	2000	33r
Limousine		410	1998	33r
Marriage license cost		30.00	4/01	35s
Men's formalwear (ushers, best man)		469	2000	33r
Mother of bride apparel		241	2000	33r
Music		866	1998	33r
Photography and videography		1368	1998	33r
Rehearsal dinner		728	1998	33r
Wedding invitations and announcements		341	1998	33r
Wedding reception		7968	2000	33r
Wedding rings (bride and groom)		1060	1998	33r

Davenport-Moline-Rock Island, IA-IL

Item	Per	Value	Date	Ref.
Average annual expenditures	yr	35369	1999	30r
Composite, ACCRA index		100.30	3/01	4c
Alcoholic Beverages				
Alcoholic beverage purchases	yr	304	1999	30r
Beer, Heineken, 12-oz, ex deposit	6	7.68	3/01	4c
J & B Scotch	750-ml	19.15	3/01	4c
Malt beverages, all types, all sizes, any origin	16 oz	0.93	7/01	11r
Wine, Livingston or Gallo, Chablis blanc	1.5 liter	5.43	3/01	4c
Wine, red and white table, all sizes, any origin	liter	7.04	7/01	11r
Appliances				
Appliance repair, service call, washing machine	min lab chg	43.14	3/01	4c
Major appliances, expenditures on	yr	165	1999	30r
Small appliances, housewares, expenditures on	yr	90	1999	30r
Banking and Money				
Mortgage interest and charges paid	yr	2277	1999	30r
Mortgage principal paid on owned property	yr	1230	1999	30r
Mortgage rate, incl. points and orig. fee, 30-yr. conv. fixed or ARM	mos	7.16	3/01	4c
Vehicle finance charges paid	yr	328	1999	30r
Charity				
Cash contributions, expenditures	yr	1126	1999	30r
Child Care				
Child raising cost, total, age 0-2	yr	7890	1999	60r
Child raising cost, total, age 3-5	yr	8130	1999	60r
Child raising cost, total, age 6-8	yr	8170	1999	60r
Child raising cost, total, age 9-11	yr	8190	1999	60r
Child raising cost, total, age 12-14	yr	8890	1999	60r

Item	Per	Value	Date	Ref.
Child Care - continued				
Child raising cost, total, age 15-17	yr	9050	1999	60r
Child's child care and education, age 0-2	yr	1240	1999	60r
Child's child care and education, age 3-5	yr	1370	1999	60r
Child's child care and education, age 6-8	yr	880	1999	60r
Child's child care and education, age 9-11	yr	570	1999	60r
Child's child care and education, age 12-14	yr	420	1999	60r
Child's child care and education, age 15-17	yr	720	1999	60r
Child's clothing, age 0-2	yr	410	1999	60r
Child's clothing, age 3-5	yr	400	1999	60r
Child's clothing, age 6-8	yr	450	1999	60r
Child's clothing, age 9-11	yr	500	1999	60r
Child's clothing, age 12-14	yr	840	1999	60r
Child's clothing, age 15-17	yr	740	1999	60r
Child's food, age 0-2	yr	960	1999	60r
Child's food, age 3-5	yr	1120	1999	60r
Child's food, age 6-8	yr	1430	1999	60r
Child's food, age 9-11	yr	1710	1999	60r
Child's food, age 12-14	yr	1710	1999	60r
Child's food, age 15-17	yr	1920	1999	60r
Child's health care, age 0-2	yr	520	1999	60r
Child's health care, age 3-5	yr	500	1999	60r
Child's health care, age 6-8	yr	570	1999	60r
Child's health care, age 9-11	yr	610	1999	60r
Child's health care, age 12-14	yr	630	1999	60r
Child's health care, age 15-17	yr	650	1999	60r
Child's housing, age 0-2	yr	2860	1999	60r
Child's housing, age 3-5	yr	2840	1999	60r
Child's housing, age 6-8	yr	2800	1999	60r
Child's housing, age 9-11	yr	2650	1999	60r
Child's housing, age 12-14	yr	2840	1999	60r
Child's housing, age 15-17	yr	2440	1999	60r
Child's personal care, reading, age 0-2	yr	880	1999	60r
Child's personal care, reading, age 3-5	yr	900	1999	60r
Child's personal care, reading, age 6-8	yr	930	1999	60r
Child's personal care, reading, age 9-11	yr	970	1999	60r
Child's personal care, reading, age 12-14	yr	1150	1999	60r
Child's personal care, reading, age 15-17	yr	920	1999	60r
Clothing				
Apparel and services purchases	yr	1607	1999	30r
Boys' brief, cotton	3	4.10	3/01	4c
Boys, 2 to 15, expenditures on	yr	91	1999	30r
Children under 2, expenditures on	yr	59	1999	30r
Footwear, expenditures on	yr	285	1999	30r
Girls, 2 to 15, expenditures on	yr	116	1999	30r
Men and boys, expenditures on	yr	433	1999	30r
Men, 16 and over, expenditures on	yr	341	1999	30r
Shirt, man's dress shirt		25.63	3/01	4c
Slacks, man's "No Wrinkles" khaki		34.14	3/01	4c
Women, 16 and over, expenditures on	yr	490	1999	30r
Communications				
Newspaper subscription, daily and Sunday delivery	mos	15.62	3/01	4c
Phone line, single, business, field visit	inst.	50.00	12/97	17s
Phone line, single, business, no field visit	inst.	50.00	12/97	17s
Phone line, single, residence, field visit	inst.	35.00	12/97	17s
Phone line, single, residence, no field visit	inst.	35.00	12/97	17s
Postage and stationery, expenditures on	yr	140	1999	30r
Postal rate, express mail, up to half-pound		12.45	7/01	108r
Postal rate, letter, first class, first ounce		0.34	7/01	108r
Postal rate, letter, two ounces		0.57	7/01	108r
Postal rate, post card		0.21	7/01	108r
Postal rate, priority mail, two pounds		3.95	7/01	108r
Postal rate, priority mail, up to one pound		3.50	7/01	108r
Telephone bill, family of three	mos	20.12	3/01	4c
Telephone services, expenditures on	yr	830	1999	30r
Education				
Board, 4-year private college/university	yr	2138	1996	38s
Board, 4-year public college/university	yr	1688	1996	38s
Education expenditures	yr	583	1999	30r
Room, 4-year private college/university	yr	1864	1996	38s
Room, 4-year public college/university	yr	1693	1996	38s

Values are in dollars or fractions of dollars. In the column headed *Ref*, references are shown to sources. Each reference is followed by a letter. These refer to the geographical level for which data were reported: s=State, r=Region, and c=City or metro. The abbreviation *ex* is used to mean *except* or *excluding*; *exp* stands for expenditures. For other abbreviations and further explanations, please see the Introduction.

Davenport-Moline-Rock Island, IA-IL - continued

Item	Per	Value	Date	Ref.
Education				
Total cost, 4-year private college/university	yr	15934	1996	38s
Total cost, 4-year public college/university	yr	5945	1996	38s
Tuition, 2-year public college/university, in state	yr	1782	1996	38s
Tuition, 4-year private college/university, in state	yr	11932	1996	38s
Tuition, 4-year public college/university	yr	2565	1996	38s
Energy and Fuels				
Electricity	500 KWhs	46.59	7/01	11r
Energy, combined forms, 2400 sq ft	mos	162.75	3/01	4c
Energy, exc. electricity, 2400 sq ft	mos	102.89	3/01	4c
Fuel oil #2	gal	1.27	7/01	11r
Fuel oil and other fuels, expenditures on	yr	68	1999	30r
Gas, natural, commercial rate	1000 cf	7.18	11/00	88s
Gas, regular unleaded, cash, self-service	gal	1.36	3/01	4c
Gasoline, unleaded midgrade	gal	1.79	7/01	11r
Gasoline, unleaded premium	gal	1.86	7/01	11r
Gasoline, unleaded regular	gal	1.58	7/01	11r
Natural gas, expenditures on	yr	389	1999	30r
Utility (piped) gas, therm		0.81	7/01	11r
Utility (piped) gas, 40 therms		38.01	7/01	11r
Utility (piped) gas, 100 therms		81.75	7/01	11r
Entertainment				
Bowling, Saturday evening rate	line	2.13	3/01	4c
Entertainment purchases	yr	1984	1999	30r
Fees and admissions paid	yr	444	1999	30r
Monopoly game, Parker Brothers', No. 9	game	11.21	3/01	4c
Movie, first-run, Saturday, evening	adm.	7.75	3/01	4c
Television, radios, sound equipment, expenditures on	yr	580	1999	30r
Tennis balls, yellow, Wilson or Penn, 3	can	2.04	3/01	4c
Funerals				
Cosmetology, hair, other preparation		178.32	1/99	78r
Embalming		408.19	1/99	78r
Funeral at funeral home		362.13	1/99	78r
Professional service charges		1375.51	1/99	78r
Transfer of remains to funeral home		155.92	1/99	78r
Visitation/viewing		294.38	1/99	78r
Groceries				
Groceries, ACCRA Index		98.10	3/01	4c
Antibiotic ointment, Polysporin	0.5 oz	4.57	3/01	4c
Baby food, strained vegetables or fruit, lowest price	4-4.5 oz	0.41	3/01	4c
Bacon, sliced	lb	3.15	7/01	11r
Bakery products, expenditures on	yr	281	1999	30r
Bananas	lb	0.35	3/01	4c
Bananas	lb	0.48	7/01	11r
Beans, dried, any type, all sizes	lb	0.61	7/01	11r
Beef for stew, boneless	lb	3.08	7/01	11r
Beef or hamburger, ground	lb	1.68	3/01	4c
Beef, expenditures on	yr	217	1999	30r
Bologna, all beef or mixed	lb	2.52	7/01	11r
Bread, white	loaf	1.00	3/01	4c
Bread, white, pan	lb	1.06	7/01	11r
Broccoli	lb	0.91	7/01	11r
Butter, salted, grade AA, stick	lb	3.04	7/01	11r
Butter, yoghurt, cheese, etc, expenditures on	yr	183	1999	30r
Cereals and bakery product purchases	yr	430	1999	30r
Cereals and cereal products, expenditures on	yr	149	1999	30r
Cheese, Kraft grated Parmesan	8 oz	3.44	3/01	4c
Chicken, fresh, whole	lb	1.07	7/01	11r
Chicken, whole fryer	lb	1.07	3/01	4c
Chops, boneless	lb	3.64	7/01	11r
Chuck roast, U.S. choice, boneless	lb	2.47	7/01	11r
Cigarettes, Winston, Kings	carton	34.89	3/01	4c
Coffee, 100%, ground roast, all sizes	lb	2.69	7/01	11r
Coffee, vacuum-packed	13 oz	2.66	3/01	4c
Cookies, chocolate chip	lb	2.87	7/01	11r

Davenport-Moline-Rock Island, IA-IL - continued

Item	Per	Value	Date	Ref.
Groceries - continued				
Corn Flakes, Kellogg's or Post Toasties	18 oz	2.50	3/01	4c
Corn, frozen, whole kernel, lowest price	16 oz	1.10	3/01	4c
Dairy product purchases	yr	304	1999	30r
Eggs, expenditures on	yr	26	1999	30r
Eggs, Grade A or AA	dozen	0.88	3/01	4c
Eggs, grade A, large	dozen	0.88	7/01	11r
Fats and oils, expenditures on	yr	75	1999	30r
Fish and seafood, expenditures on	yr	72	1999	30r
Food (excl fruit and vegetables), eaten at home, purchases	yr	887	1999	30r
Food cooked on trips, expenditures on	yr	44	1999	30r
Food purchases	yr	4802	1999	30r
Food purchases, eaten away from home	yr	2069	1999	30r
Food purchases, food eaten at home	yr	2733	1999	30r
Fresh fruits, expenditures on	yr	138	1999	30r
Fresh milk and cream, expenditures on	yr	120	1999	30r
Fresh vegetables, expenditures on	yr	126	1999	30r
Grapefruit	lb	0.66	7/01	11r
Grapes, Thompson, seedless	lb	1.64	7/01	11r
Ground beef, 100% beef	lb	1.64	7/01	11r
Ground beef, lean and extra lean	lb	2.16	7/01	11r
Ground chuck, 100% beef	lb	2.13	7/01	11r
Ham, boneless, excl canned	lb	2.62	7/01	11r
Ice cream, prepackaged, bulk, regular	1/2 gal	3.35	7/01	11r
Lemons	lb	1.19	7/01	11r
Lettuce, iceberg	head	0.96	3/01	4c
Lettuce, iceberg	lb	0.73	7/01	11r
Margarine, Blue Bonnet or Parkay, stick	lb	0.74	3/01	4c
Margarine, soft, tubs	lb	0.89	7/01	11r
Meats, poultry, fish, and egg purchases	yr	671	1999	30r
Milk, fresh, whole, fortified	gal	2.71	7/01	11r
Milk, whole	1/2 gal	1.43	3/01	4c
Nonalcoholic beverages, expenditures on	yr	239	1999	30r
Orange juice, Minute Maid frozen	12 oz	1.18	3/01	4c
Oranges, Navel	lb	0.80	7/01	11r
Oranges, Valencia	lb	0.66	7/01	11r
Peaches, halves or slices, Hunt's, Del Monte, or Libby's	29 oz	1.46	3/01	4c
Pears, Anjou	lb	0.93	7/01	11r
Peas, green, Del Monte or Green Giant	15 oz	0.55	3/01	4c
Pork chops, center cut, bone-in	lb	3.63	7/01	11r
Pork, expenditures on	yr	150	1999	30r
Potato chips	16 oz	3.52	7/01	11r
Potatoes, frozen, french fried	lb	1.08	7/01	11r
Potatoes, white or red	10 lb	2.86	3/01	4c
Potatoes, white, all types	lb	0.33	7/01	11r
Poultry, expenditures on	yr	108	1999	30r
Processed fruits, expenditures on	yr	98	1999	30r
Processed vegetables, expenditures on	yr	80	1999	30r
Round roast, U.S. choice, boneless	lb	3.07	7/01	11r
Round steak, graded and ungraded, excl U.S. prime and choice	lb	3.41	7/01	11r
Sausage, Jimmy Dean/Owens pork	lb	3.15	3/01	4c
Shortening, vegetable oil blends	lb	1.13	7/01	11r
Shortening, vegetable, Crisco	3 lb	2.53	3/01	4c
Soft drink, Coca Cola, ex deposit	2 liter	1.21	3/01	4c
Spaghetti and macaroni	lb	0.80	7/01	11r
Steak, round, U.S. choice, boneless	lb	3.23	7/01	11r
Steak, T-bone	lb	5.88	3/01	4c
Steak, T-bone, U.S. choice, bone-in	lb	6.68	7/01	11r
Strawberries, dry pint	12 oz	1.32	7/01	11r
Sugar and other sweets, expenditures on	yr	114	1999	30r
Sugar, cane or beet	4 lbs	1.85	3/01	4c
Sugar, white, 33-80 ounce package	lb	0.42	7/01	11r
Sugar, white, all sizes	lb	0.43	7/01	11r
Tobacco products and smoking supplies purchases	yr	331	1999	30r
Tomatoes, field grown	lb	1.46	7/01	11r
Tomatoes, Hunt's or Del Monte	14.5 oz	0.68	3/01	4c
Tuna, chunk, light	6 oz	0.71	3/01	4c
Tuna, light, chunk	lb	1.80	7/01	11r
Turkey, frozen, whole	lb	1.15	7/01	11r

Values are in dollars or fractions of dollars. In the column headed *Ref*, references are shown to sources. Each reference is followed by a letter. These refer to the geographical level for which data were reported: s=State, r=Region, and c=City or metro. The abbreviation *ex* is used to mean *except* or *excluding*; *exp* stands for expenditures. For other abbreviations and further explanations, please see the Introduction.

Davenport-Moline-Rock Island, IA-IL - continued

Item	Per	Value	Date	Ref.
Goods and Services				
Miscellaneous goods and services, ACCRA Index		97.20	3/01	4c
B&B Japanese maple (acer japonicum)	gal	29.99-169.99	4/00	93r
Boxwood (buxus)	2 gal	18.99-39.99	4/00	93r
Daylilly (hemerocallis)	gal	4.99-25.00	4/00	93r
Flat of annuals		11.98-24.99	4/00	93r
Fountain grass (pennisetum)	gal	5.98-12.98	4/00	93r
Hanging basket (10 in)		12.99-27.99	4/00	93r
Hardy geranium (geranium)	gal	7.99-9.99	4/00	93r
Hosta (hosta)	gal	6.00-25.00	4/00	93r
Lilac (syrubga vulgaris)	2 gal	14.99-24.99	4/00	93r
Miscellaneous purchases	yr	865	1999	30r
Rhododendron (rhododendron)	2 gal	23.98-42.99	4/00	93r
Sage (salvia)	gal	6.00-9.99	4/00	93r
Wintercreeper euonymus (euonymus fortunei)	2 gal	16.00-169.99	4/00	93r
Hunting license	yr	16.00	4/01	34s
Health Care				
Health care, ACCRA Index		100.50	3/01	4c
Cardiac catheterization, ave hospital/ physician charges		8810	1998	77s
Childbirth, Cesarean delivery		10722	1997	13r
Childbirth, vaginal delivery		6223	1997	13r
Dentist's fee, adult teeth cleaning and periodic oral exam	visit	73.90	3/01	4c
Doctor's fee, routine exam, established patient	visit	64.07	3/01	4c
Drugs, expenditures on	yr	394	1999	30r
Health care purchases	yr	2048	1999	30r
Health insurance expenditures	yr	978	1999	30r
Hospital care, private room	day	418.33	3/01	4c
Hysterectomy, laproscopically-assisted, ave hospital/physician charges		8620	1998	76s
Hysterectomy, vaginal, ave hospital and physician charges		6630	1998	76s
Medicaid dispensing fee		4.10-6.38	1999	87s
Medical services expenditures	yr	554	1999	30r
Medical supplies, expenditures on	yr	122	1999	30r
Plastic surgery, breast augmentation		3184	2000	7r
Plastic surgery, breast lift		3585	2000	7r
Plastic surgery, facelift		4999	2000	7r
Plastic surgery, hair transplantation		3105	2000	7r
Plastic surgery, lip augmentation		1290	2000	7r
Plastic surgery, lower body lift		8135	2000	7r
Plastic surgery, thigh lift		3839	2000	7r
Household Goods				
Dishwashing powder, Cascade	50 oz	3.29	3/01	4c
Floor coverings, expenditures on	yr	52	1999	30r
Furniture, expenditures on	yr	344	1999	30r
Household furnishings and equipment purchases	yr	1475	1999	30r
Household textiles, expenditures on	yr	109	1999	30r
Laundry and cleaning supplies, expenditures on	yr	134	1999	30r
Tissues, facial, Kleenex brand	175	1.26	3/01	4c
Housing				
Housing, ACCRA Index		97.60	3/01	4c
Home price, existing, ave		144400	10/00	90r
Home value, median		100000	2001	53s

Davenport-Moline-Rock Island, IA-IL - continued

Item	Per	Value	Date	Ref.
Housing - continued				
House, 2400 sq ft, 8000 sq ft lot, new, urban, utilities	total	208878	3/01	4c
House payment, principal and interest, 25% down payment	mos	1059	3/01	4c
Household operation expenditures	yr	542	1999	30r
Housekeeping supplies purchases	yr	508	1999	30r
Lodging expenditures	yr	430	1999	30r
Maintenance, repairs, insurance expenditures	yr	853	1999	30r
Monthly rental value of owned home	mos	547	1999	30r
Owned dwellings, expenditures own	yr	4282	1999	30r
Rent expenditures	yr	1558	1999	30r
Rent, apartment, 2 br, 1 1/2-2 baths, unfurn, 950 sq ft, water	mos	538	3/01	4c
Rental unit, 1 bedroom, with utilities	mos	395	4/01	41c
Rental unit, 2 bedroom, with utilities	mos	489	4/01	41c
Rental unit, 3 bedroom, with utilities	mos	632	4/01	41c
Rental unit, 4 bedroom, with utilities	mos	685	4/01	41c
Shelter, expenditures on	yr	6270	1999	30r
Insurance and Pensions				
Auto insurance premium	yr	520.76	1999	57s
Life and other personal insurance purchases	yr	387	1999	30r
Pensions and Social Security, expenditures on	yr	2968	1999	30r
Legal Fees				
Divorce, filing fee		110.00	4/01	35s
Driver's license fee	orig	16.00	1999	48s
Driver's license fee	renew	16.00	1999	48s
Personal Goods				
Personal care products and services purchases	yr	385	1999	30r
Shampoo, Alberto VO5	15 oz	1.13	3/01	4c
Toothpaste, Crest or Colgate	6-7 oz	2.45	3/01	4c
Personal Services				
Dry cleaning, man's 2-pc suit		8.64	3/01	4c
Man's haircut, barbershop, no styling		10.08	3/01	4c
Personal services, household, expenditures on	yr	300	1999	30r
Woman's shampoo, trim, blow-dry, no style-change		21.06	3/01	4c
Pets				
Pets, toys, and playground equipment, expenditures on	yr	375	1999	30r
Restaurant Food				
Chicken, fried, thigh and drumstick, KFC/ Church's		2.62	3/01	4c
Hamburger with cheese, McDonald's	1/4 lb	2.13	3/01	4c
Pizza, Pizza Hut or Pizza Inn	11-12 in	8.99	3/01	4c
Taxes				
Federal income taxes paid	yr	2326	1999	30r
Personal taxes, expenditures on	yr	3223	1999	30r
Property taxes paid	yr	1152	1999	30r
State and local income taxes paid	yr	753	1999	30r
Transportation				
Transportation, ACCRA Index		99.10	3/01	4c
Cars and trucks, new, expenditures on	yr	1280	1999	30r
Cars and trucks, used, expenditures on	yr	1763	1999	30r
Diesel at the pump	gal	1.25	10/99	73s
Gasoline and motor oil purchases	yr	1036	1999	30r
Gasoline before-tax price (cents)	gal	112.30	10/00	43s
Maintenance and repair expenditures	yr	594	1999	30r
Public transportation, expenditures on	yr	341	1999	30r
Tire balance, computer or spin balance, front	wheel	8.10	3/01	4c
Transportation purchases	yr	6617	1999	30r
Vehicle expenses, miscellaneous, purchases	yr	2159	1999	30r
Vehicle insurance payments	yr	701	1999	30r
Vehicle purchases (net outlay)	yr	3081	1999	30r
Vehicle rental, lease expenditures	yr	536	1999	30r

Values are in dollars or fractions of dollars. In the column headed *Ref*, references are shown to sources. Each reference is followed by a letter. These refer to the geographical level for which data were reported: s=State, r=Region, and c=City or metro. The abbreviation *ex* is used to mean *except* or *excluding*; *exp* stands for expenditures. For other abbreviations and further explanations, please see the Introduction.

Davenport-Moline-Rock Island, IA-IL - continued

Item	Per	Value	Date	Ref.
Utilities				
Utilities, ACCRA Index		127.70	3/01	4c
Electrical bill, average	mos	67.25	9/00	9s
Electricity, expenditures on	yr	841	1999	30r
Electricity and other, mixed, 2400 sq ft, new home	mos	59.86	3/01	4c
Electricity cost, average	KWh	5.90	9/00	9s
Utilities, fuels, and public services purchased	yr	2401	1999	30r
Water and other public services, expenditures on	yr	273	1999	30r
Weddings				
Wedding (national average cost)		19936	2000	33r
Wedding (regional average total cost)		16195	1997	110r
Attendants' gifts		321	1998	33r
Bridal attendants' apparel (5 persons)		824	2000	33r
Bride's headpiece/veil		173	1998	33r
Bride's wedding dress		859	1998	33r
Clergy, religious facility fee		242	1998	33r
Engagement ring		3177	1998	33r
Flowers		789	1998	33r
Groom's formalwear rental		99	2000	33r
Limousine		410	1998	33r
Marriage license cost		30.00	4/01	35s
Men's formalwear (ushers, best man)		469	2000	33r
Mother of bride apparel		241	2000	33r
Music		866	1998	33r
Photography and videography		1368	1998	33r
Rehearsal dinner		728	1998	33r
Wedding invitations and announcements		341	1998	33r
Wedding reception		7968	2000	33r
Wedding rings (bride and groom)		1060	1998	33r

Dayton-Springfield, OH

Item	Per	Value	Date	Ref.
Average annual expenditures	yr	35369	1999	30r
Composite, ACCRA index		96.30	3/01	4c
Alcoholic Beverages				
Alcoholic beverage purchases	yr	304	1999	30r
Beer, Heineken, 12-oz, ex deposit	6	7.49	3/01	4c
J & B Scotch	750-ml	21.35	3/01	4c
Malt beverages, all types, all sizes, any origin	16 oz	0.93	7/01	11r
Wine, Livingston or Gallo, Chablis blanc	1.5 liter	6.19	3/01	4c
Wine, red and white table, all sizes, any origin	liter	7.04	7/01	11r
Appliances				
Appliance repair, service call, washing machine	min lab chg	39.50	3/01	4c
Major appliances, expenditures on	yr	165	1999	30r
Small appliances, housewares, expenditures on	yr	90	1999	30r
Banking and Money				
Mortgage interest and charges paid	yr	2277	1999	30r
Mortgage principal paid on owned property	yr	1230	1999	30r
Mortgage rate, incl. points and orig. fee, 30-yr. conv. fixed or ARM	mos	7.15	3/01	4c
Vehicle finance charges paid	yr	328	1999	30r
Charity				
Cash contributions, expenditures	yr	1126	1999	30r
Child Care				
Child raising cost, total, age 0-2	yr	7890	1999	60r
Child raising cost, total, age 3-5	yr	8130	1999	60r
Child raising cost, total, age 6-8	yr	8170	1999	60r
Child raising cost, total, age 9-11	yr	8190	1999	60r
Child raising cost, total, age 12-14	yr	8890	1999	60r
Child raising cost, total, age 15-17	yr	9050	1999	60r
Child's child care and education, age 0-2	yr	1240	1999	60r
Child's child care and education, age 3-5	yr	1370	1999	60r
Child's child care and education, age 6-8	yr	880	1999	60r
Child's child care and education, age 9-11	yr	570	1999	60r

Item	Per	Value	Date	Ref.
Child Care - continued				
Child's child care and education, age 12-14	yr	420	1999	60r
Child's child care and education, age 15-17	yr	720	1999	60r
Child's clothing, age 0-2	yr	410	1999	60r
Child's clothing, age 3-5	yr	400	1999	60r
Child's clothing, age 6-8	yr	450	1999	60r
Child's clothing, age 9-11	yr	500	1999	60r
Child's clothing, age 12-14	yr	840	1999	60r
Child's clothing, age 15-17	yr	740	1999	60r
Child's food, age 0-2	yr	960	1999	60r
Child's food, age 3-5	yr	1120	1999	60r
Child's food, age 6-8	yr	1430	1999	60r
Child's food, age 9-11	yr	1710	1999	60r
Child's food, age 12-14	yr	1710	1999	60r
Child's food, age 15-17	yr	1920	1999	60r
Child's health care, age 0-2	yr	520	1999	60r
Child's health care, age 3-5	yr	500	1999	60r
Child's health care, age 6-8	yr	570	1999	60r
Child's health care, age 9-11	yr	610	1999	60r
Child's health care, age 12-14	yr	630	1999	60r
Child's health care, age 15-17	yr	650	1999	60r
Child's housing, age 0-2	yr	2860	1999	60r
Child's housing, age 3-5	yr	2840	1999	60r
Child's housing, age 6-8	yr	2800	1999	60r
Child's housing, age 9-11	yr	2650	1999	60r
Child's housing, age 12-14	yr	2840	1999	60r
Child's housing, age 15-17	yr	2440	1999	60r
Child's personal care, reading, age 0-2	yr	880	1999	60r
Child's personal care, reading, age 3-5	yr	900	1999	60r
Child's personal care, reading, age 6-8	yr	930	1999	60r
Child's personal care, reading, age 9-11	yr	970	1999	60r
Child's personal care, reading, age 12-14	yr	1150	1999	60r
Child's personal care, reading, age 15-17	yr	920	1999	60r
Clothing				
Apparel and services purchases	yr	1607	1999	30r
Boys' brief, cotton	3	3.76	3/01	4c
Boys, 2 to 15, expenditures on	yr	91	1999	30r
Children under 2, expenditures on	yr	59	1999	30r
Footwear, expenditures on	yr	285	1999	30r
Girls, 2 to 15, expenditures on	yr	116	1999	30r
Men and boys, expenditures on	yr	433	1999	30r
Men, 16 and over, expenditures on	yr	341	1999	30r
Shirt, man's dress shirt		28.74	3/01	4c
Slacks, man's "No Wrinkles" khaki		32.99	3/01	4c
Women, 16 and over, expenditures on	yr	490	1999	30r
Communications				
Cable modem installation, Adelphi		54.90	6/99	103s
Cable modem installation, Media One		100.00	6/99	103s
Cable modem installation, Time Warner		75.00-225.00	6/99	103s
Cable modem rate, cable subscriber, Adelphi	mos	34.95	6/99	103s
Cable modem rate, cable subscriber, Media One	mos	34.95-39.95	6/99	103s
Cable modem rate, cable subscriber, Time Warner	mos	39.95-49.95	6/99	103s
Cable modem rate, non-cable subscriber, Adelphi	mos	44.95	6/99	103s
Cable modem rate, non-cable subscriber, Media One	mos	49.95	6/99	103s
Cable modem rate, non-cable subscriber, Time Warner	mos	39.95-54.95	6/99	103s
Newspaper subscription, daily and Sunday delivery	mos	16.04	3/01	4c
Phone line, single, business, field visit	inst.	56.32	12/97	17s
Phone line, single, business, no field visit	inst.	56.32	12/97	17s
Phone line, single, residence, field visit	inst.	31.10	12/97	17s
Phone line, single, residence, no field visit	inst.	31.10	12/97	17s
Postage and stationery, expenditures on	yr	140	1999	30r
Postal rate, express mail, up to half-pound		12.45	7/01	108r
Postal rate, letter, first class, first ounce		0.34	7/01	108r
Postal rate, letter, two ounces		0.57	7/01	108r
Postal rate, post card		0.21	7/01	108r

Values are in dollars or fractions of dollars. In the column headed *Ref*, references are shown to sources. Each reference is followed by a letter. These refer to the geographical level for which data were reported: s=State, r=Region, and c=City or metro. The abbreviation *ex* is used to mean *except* or *excluding*; *exp* stands for *expenditures*. For other abbreviations and further explanations, please see the Introduction.

Dayton-Springfield, OH - continued

Item	Per	Value	Date	Ref.
Communications				
Postal rate, priority mail, two pounds		3.95	7/01	108r
Postal rate, priority mail, up to one pound		3.50	7/01	108r
Telephone bill, family of three	mos	20.71	3/01	4c
Telephone services, expenditures on	yr	830	1999	30r
Education				
Board, 4-year private college/university	yr	2414	1996	38s
Board, 4-year public college/university	yr	2181	1996	38s
Education expenditures	yr	583	1999	30r
Room, 4-year private college/university	yr	2349	1996	38s
Room, 4-year public college/university	yr	2386	1996	38s
Total cost, 4-year private college/university	yr	17139	1996	38s
Total cost, 4-year public college/university	yr	8169	1996	38s
Tuition, 2-year public college/university, in state	yr	2261	1996	38s
Tuition, 4-year private college/university, in state	yr	12377	1996	38s
Tuition, 4-year public college/university	yr	3603	1996	38s
Energy and Fuels				
Electricity	500 KWhs	46.59	7/01	11r
Energy, combined forms, 2400 sq ft	mos	123.76	3/01	4c
Energy, exc. electricity, 2400 sq ft	mos	60.35	3/01	4c
Fuel oil #2	gal	1.27	7/01	11r
Fuel oil and other fuels, expenditures on	yr	68	1999	30r
Gas, natural, commercial rate	1000 cf	8.65	11/00	88s
Gas, regular unleaded, cash, self-service	gal	1.48	3/01	4c
Gasoline, unleaded midgrade	gal	1.79	7/01	11r
Gasoline, unleaded premium	gal	1.86	7/01	11r
Gasoline, unleaded regular	gal	1.58	7/01	11r
Natural gas, expenditures on	yr	389	1999	30r
Utility (piped) gas, therm		0.81	7/01	11r
Utility (piped) gas, 40 therms		38.01	7/01	11r
Utility (piped) gas, 100 therms		81.75	7/01	11r
Entertainment				
Bowling, Saturday evening rate	line	2.63	3/01	4c
Entertainment purchases	yr	1984	1999	30r
Fees and admissions paid	yr	444	1999	30r
Monopoly game, Parker Brothers', No. 9	game	10.57	3/01	4c
Movie, first-run, Saturday, evening	adm.	8.10	3/01	4c
Television, radios, sound equipment, expenditures on	yr	580	1999	30r
Tennis balls, yellow, Wilson or Penn, 3	can	1.51	3/01	4c
Funerals				
Cosmetology, hair, other preparation		178.32	1/99	78r
Embalming		408.19	1/99	78r
Funeral at funeral home		362.13	1/99	78r
Professional service charges		1375.51	1/99	78r
Transfer of remains to funeral home		155.92	1/99	78r
Visitation/viewing		294.38	1/99	78r
Groceries				
Groceries, ACCRA Index		96.70	3/01	4c
Antibiotic ointment, Polysporin	0.5 oz	4.35	3/01	4c
Baby food, strained vegetables or fruit, lowest price	4-4.5 oz	0.30	3/01	4c
Bacon, sliced	lb	3.15	7/01	11r
Bakery products, expenditures on	yr	281	1999	30r
Bananas	lb	0.43	3/01	4c
Bananas	lb	0.48	7/01	11r
Beans, dried, any type, all sizes	lb	0.61	7/01	11r
Beef for stew, boneless	lb	3.08	7/01	11r
Beef or hamburger, ground	lb	1.84	3/01	4c
Beef, expenditures on	yr	217	1999	30r
Bologna, all beef or mixed	lb	2.52	7/01	11r
Bread, white	loaf	0.92	3/01	4c
Bread, white, pan	lb	1.06	7/01	11r
Broccoli	lb	0.91	7/01	11r
Butter, salted, grade AA, stick	lb	3.04	7/01	11r
Butter, yoghurt, cheese, etc, expenditures on	yr	183	1999	30r
Cereals and bakery product purchases	yr	430	1999	30r

Dayton-Springfield, OH - continued

Item	Per	Value	Date	Ref.
Groceries - continued				
Cereals and cereal products, expenditures on	yr	149	1999	30r
Cheese, Kraft grated Parmesan	8 oz	3.17	3/01	4c
Chicken, fresh, whole	lb	1.07	7/01	11r
Chicken, whole fryer	lb	0.93	3/01	4c
Chops, boneless,	lb	3.64	7/01	11r
Chuck roast, U.S. choice, boneless	lb	2.47	7/01	11r
Cigarettes, Winston, Kings	carton	27.27	3/01	4c
Coffee, 100%, ground roast, all sizes	lb	2.69	7/01	11r
Coffee, vacuum-packed	13 oz	2.55	3/01	4c
Cookies, chocolate chip	lb	2.87	7/01	11r
Corn Flakes, Kellogg's or Post Toasties	18 oz	2.41	3/01	4c
Corn, frozen, whole kernel, lowest price	16 oz	1.14	3/01	4c
Dairy product purchases	yr	304	1999	30r
Eggs, expenditures on	yr	26	1999	30r
Eggs, Grade A or AA	dozen	1.14	3/01	4c
Eggs, grade A, large	dozen	0.88	7/01	11r
Fats and oils, expenditures on	yr	75	1999	30r
Fish and seafood, expenditures on	yr	72	1999	30r
Food (excl fruit and vegetables), eaten at home, purchases	yr	887	1999	30r
Food cooked on trips, expenditures on	yr	44	1999	30r
Food purchases	yr	4802	1999	30r
Food purchases, eaten away from home	yr	2069	1999	30r
Food purchases, food eaten at home	yr	2733	1999	30r
Fresh fruits, expenditures on	yr	138	1999	30r
Fresh milk and cream, expenditures on	yr	120	1999	30r
Fresh vegetables, expenditures on	yr	126	1999	30r
Grapefruit	lb	0.66	7/01	11r
Grapes, Thompson, seedless	lb	1.64	7/01	11r
Ground beef, 100% beef	lb	1.64	7/01	11r
Ground beef, lean and extra lean	lb	2.16	7/01	11r
Ground chuck, 100% beef	lb	2.13	7/01	11r
Ham, boneless, excl canned	lb	2.62	7/01	11r
Ice cream, prepackaged, bulk, regular	1/2 gal	3.35	7/01	11r
Lemons	lb	1.19	7/01	11r
Lettuce, iceberg	head	0.88	3/01	4c
Lettuce, iceberg	lb	0.73	7/01	11r
Margarine, Blue Bonnet or Parkay, stick	lb	0.95	3/01	4c
Margarine, soft, tubs	lb	0.89	7/01	11r
Meats, poultry, fish, and egg purchases	yr	671	1999	30r
Milk, fresh, whole, fortified	gal	2.71	7/01	11r
Milk, whole	1/2 gal	1.74	3/01	4c
Nonalcoholic beverages, expenditures on	yr	239	1999	30r
Orange juice, Minute Maid frozen	12 oz	1.62	3/01	4c
Oranges, Navel	lb	0.80	7/01	11r
Oranges, Valencia	lb	0.66	7/01	11r
Peaches, halves or slices, Hunt's, Del Monte, or Libby's	29 oz	1.64	3/01	4c
Pears, Anjou	lb	0.93	7/01	11r
Peas, green, Del Monte or Green Giant	15 oz	0.70	3/01	4c
Pork chops, center cut, bone-in	lb	3.63	7/01	11r
Pork, expenditures on	yr	150	1999	30r
Potato chips	16 oz	3.52	7/01	11r
Potatoes, frozen, french fried	lb	1.08	7/01	11r
Potatoes, white or red	10 lb	2.19	3/01	4c
Potatoes, white, all types	lb	0.33	7/01	11r
Poultry, expenditures on	yr	108	1999	30r
Processed fruits, expenditures on	yr	98	1999	30r
Processed vegetables, expenditures on	yr	80	1999	30r
Round roast, U.S. choice, boneless	lb	3.07	7/01	11r
Round steak, graded and ungraded, excl U.S. prime and choice	lb	3.41	7/01	11r
Sausage, Jimmy Dean/Owens pork	lb	2.69	3/01	4c
Shortening, vegetable oil blends	lb	1.13	7/01	11r
Shortening, vegetable, Crisco	3 lb	3.17	3/01	4c
Soft drink, Coca Cola, ex deposit	2 liter	1.17	3/01	4c
Spaghetti and macaroni	lb	0.80	7/01	11r
Steak, round, U.S. choice, boneless	lb	3.23	7/01	11r
Steak, T-bone	lb	6.87	3/01	4c
Steak, T-bone, U.S. choice, bone-in	lb	6.68	7/01	11r
Strawberries, dry pint	12 oz	1.32	7/01	11r

Values are in dollars or fractions of dollars. In the column headed *Ref*, references are shown to sources. Each reference is followed by a letter. These refer to the geographical level for which data were reported: s=State, r=Region, and c=City or metro. The abbreviation *ex* is used to mean *except* or *excluding*; *exp* stands for *expenditures*. For other abbreviations and further explanations, please see the Introduction.

Dayton-Springfield, OH - continued

Item	Per	Value	Date	Ref.
Groceries				
Sugar and other sweets, expenditures on	yr	114	1999	30r
Sugar, cane or beet	4 lbs	1.92	3/01	4c
Sugar, white, 33-80 ounce package	lb	0.42	7/01	11r
Sugar, white, all sizes	lb	0.43	7/01	11r
Tobacco products and smoking supplies purchases	yr	331	1999	30r
Tomatoes, field grown	lb	1.46	7/01	11r
Tomatoes, Hunt's or Del Monte	14.5 oz	0.86	3/01	4c
Tuna, chunk, light	6 oz	0.63	3/01	4c
Tuna, light, chunk	lb	1.80	7/01	11r
Turkey, frozen, whole	lb	1.15	7/01	11r
Goods and Services				
Miscellaneous goods and services, ACCRA Index		97.10	3/01	4c
B&B Japanese maple (acer japonicum)	gal	29.99-169.99	4/00	93r
Boxwood (buxus)	2 gal	18.99-39.99	4/00	93r
Daylily (hemerocallis)	gal	4.99-25.00	4/00	93r
Flat of annuals		11.98-24.99	4/00	93r
Fountain grass (pennisetum)	gal	5.98-12.98	4/00	93r
Hanging basket (10 in)		12.99-27.99	4/00	93r
Hardy geranium (geranium)	gal	7.99-9.99	4/00	93r
Hosta (hosta)	gal	6.00-25.00	4/00	93r
Lilac (syrubga vulgaris)	2 gal	14.99-24.99	4/00	93r
Miscellaneous purchases	yr	865	1999	30r
Rhododendron (rhododendron)	2 gal	23.99-42.99	4/00	93r
Sage (salvia)	gal	6.00-9.99	4/00	93r
Wintercreeper euonymus (euonymus fortunei)	2 gal	16.00-169.99	4/00	93r
Hunting license	yr	15.00	4/01	34s
Health Care				
Health care, ACCRA Index		99.60	3/01	4c
Cardiac catheterization, ave hospital/physician charges		11760	1998	77s
Childbirth, Cesarean delivery		10722	1997	13r
Childbirth, vaginal delivery		6223	1997	13r
Dentist's fee, adult teeth cleaning and periodic oral exam	visit	73.00	3/01	4c
Doctor's fee, routine exam, established patient	visit	56.57	3/01	4c
Drugs, expenditures on	yr	394	1999	30r
Health care purchases	yr	2048	1999	30r
Health insurance expenditures	yr	978	1999	30r
Hospital care, private room	day	553.80	3/01	4c
Hysterectomy, laproscopically-assisted, ave hospital/physician charges		11730	1998	76s
Hysterectomy, vaginal, ave hospital and physician charges		9640	1998	76s
Medicaid dispensing fee		3.70	1999	87s
Medical services expenditures	yr	554	1999	30r
Medical supplies, expenditures on	yr	122	1999	30r
Plastic surgery, breast augmentation		3184	2000	7r
Plastic surgery, breast lift		3585	2000	7r
Plastic surgery, facelift		4999	2000	7r
Plastic surgery, hair transplantation		3105	2000	7r
Plastic surgery, lip augmentation		1290	2000	7r
Plastic surgery, lower body lift		8135	2000	7r
Plastic surgery, thigh lift		3839	2000	7r
Household Goods				
Dishwashing powder, Cascade	50 oz	3.35	3/01	4c
Floor coverings, expenditures on	yr	52	1999	30r

Dayton-Springfield, OH - continued

Item	Per	Value	Date	Ref.
Household Goods - continued				
Furniture, expenditures on	yr	344	1999	30r
Household furnishings and equipment purchases	yr	1475	1999	30r
Household textiles, expenditures on	yr	109	1999	30r
Laundry and cleaning supplies, expenditures on	yr	134	1999	30r
Tissues, facial, Kleenex brand	175	1.34	3/01	4c
Housing				
Housing, ACCRA Index		91.10	3/01	4c
Home price, existing, ave		144400	10/00	90r
Home value, median		96000	2001	53s
House, 2400 sq ft, 8000 sq ft lot, new, urban, utilities	total	188217	3/01	4c
House payment, principal and interest, 25% down payment	mos	953	3/01	4c
Household operation expenditures	yr	542	1999	30r
Housekeeping supplies purchases	yr	508	1999	30r
Lodging expenditures	yr	430	1999	30r
Maintenance, repairs, insurance expenditures	yr	853	1999	30r
Monthly rental value of owned home	mos	547	1999	30r
Owned dwellings, expenditures own	yr	4282	1999	30r
Rent expenditures	yr	1558	1999	30r
Rent, apartment, 2 br, 1 1/2-2 baths, unfurn, 950 sq ft, water	mos	593	3/01	4c
Rental unit, 1 bedroom, with utilities	mos	436	4/01	41c
Rental unit, 2 bedroom, with utilities	mos	556	4/01	41c
Rental unit, 3 bedroom, with utilities	mos	718	4/01	41c
Rental unit, 4 bedroom, with utilities	mos	806	4/01	41c
Shelter, expenditures on	yr	6270	1999	30r
Insurance and Pensions				
Life and other personal insurance purchases	yr	387	1999	30r
Pensions and Social Security, expenditures on	yr	2968	1999	30r
Legal Fees				
Divorce, filing fee		100.00	4/01	35s
Driver's license fee	renew	14.50	1999	48s
Driver's license fee	orig	14.50	1999	48s
Fishing license	yr	15.00	4/01	34s
Personal Goods				
Personal care products and services purchases	yr	385	1999	30r
Shampoo, Alberto VO5	15 oz	1.05	3/01	4c
Toothpaste, Crest or Colgate	6-7 oz	1.85	3/01	4c
Personal Services				
Dry cleaning, man's 2-pc suit		8.67	3/01	4c
Man's haircut, barbershop, no styling		11.20	3/01	4c
Personal services, household, expenditures on	yr	300	1999	30r
Woman's shampoo, trim, blow-dry, no style-change		24.67	3/01	4c
Pets				
Pets, toys, and playground equipment, expenditures on	yr	375	1999	30r
Restaurant Food				
Chicken, fried, thigh and drumstick, KFC/Church's		2.59	3/01	4c
Hamburger with cheese, McDonald's	1/4 lb	2.19	3/01	4c
Pizza, Pizza Hut or Pizza Inn	11-12 in	8.99	3/01	4c
Taxes				
Federal income taxes paid	yr	2326	1999	30r
Personal taxes, expenditures on	yr	3223	1999	30r
Property taxes paid	yr	1152	1999	30r
State and local income taxes paid	yr	753	1999	30r
Transportation				
Transportation, ACCRA Index		102.60	3/01	4c
Bus fare, to central business district	1-way	1.00	3/01	4c

Values are in dollars or fractions of dollars. In the column headed *Ref*, references are shown to sources. Each reference is followed by a letter. These refer to the geographical level for which data were reported: s=State, r=Region, and c=City or metro. The abbreviation *ex* is used to mean *except* or *excluding*; *exp* stands for expenditures. For other abbreviations and further explanations, please see the Introduction.

Dayton-Springfield, OH - continued

Item	Per	Value	Date	Ref.
Transportation				
Cars and trucks, new, expenditures on	yr	1280	1999	30r
Cars and trucks, used, expenditures on	yr	1763	1999	30r
Diesel at the pump	gal	1.25	10/99	73s
Gasoline and motor oil purchases	yr	1036	1999	30r
Gasoline before-tax price (cents)	gal	109.50	10/00	43s
Maintenance and repair expenditures	yr	594	1999	30r
Public transportation, expenditures on	yr	341	1999	30r
Tire balance, computer or spin balance, front	wheel	8.04	3/01	4c
Transportation purchases	yr	6617	1999	30r
Vehicle expenses, miscellaneous, purchases	yr	2159	1999	30r
Vehicle insurance payments	yr	701	1999	30r
Vehicle purchases (net outlay)	yr	3081	1999	30r
Vehicle rental, lease expenditures	yr	536	1999	30r
Utilities				
Utilities, ACCRA Index		100.50	3/01	4c
Electrical bill, average	mos	72.83	9/00	9s
Electricity, expenditures on	yr	841	1999	30r
Electricity and other, mixed, 2400 sq ft, new home	mos	63.41	3/01	4c
Electricity cost, average	KWh	6.59	9/00	9s
Utilities, fuels, and public services purchased	yr	2401	1999	30r
Water and other public services, expenditures on	yr	273	1999	30r
Weddings				
Wedding (national average cost)		19936	2000	33r
Wedding (regional average total cost)		16195	1997	110r
Attendants' gifts		321	1998	33r
Bridal attendants' apparel (5 persons)		824	2000	33r
Bride's headpiece/veil		173	1998	33r
Bride's wedding dress		859	1998	33r
Clergy, religious facility fee		242	1998	33r
Engagement ring		3177	1998	33r
Flowers		789	1998	33r
Groom's formalwear rental		99	2000	33r
Limousine		410	1998	33r
Marriage license cost		45.00	4/01	35s
Men's formalwear (ushers, best man)		469	2000	33r
Mother of bride apparel		241	2000	33r
Music		866	1998	33r
Photography and videography		1368	1998	33r
Rehearsal dinner		728	1998	33r
Wedding invitations and announcements		341	1998	33r
Wedding reception		7968	2000	33r
Wedding rings (bride and groom)		1060	1998	33r

Daytona Beach, FL

Item	Per	Value	Date	Ref.
Alcoholic Beverages				
Alcoholic beverage purchases	yr	253	1999	30r
Malt beverages, all types, all sizes, any origin	16 oz	0.96	7/01	11r
Appliances				
Major appliances, expenditures on	yr	172	1999	30r
Small appliances, housewares, expenditures on	yr	81	1999	30r
Banking and Money				
Mortgage interest and charges paid	yr	2039	1999	30r
Mortgage principal paid on owned property	yr	1026	1999	30r
Vehicle finance charges paid	yr	365	1999	30r
Charity				
Cash contributions, expenditures	yr	1127	1999	30r
Child Care				
Child raising cost, total, age 0-2	yr	8540	1999	60r
Child raising cost, total, age 3-5	yr	8780	1999	60r
Child raising cost, total, age 6-8	yr	8820	1999	60r
Child raising cost, total, age 9-11	yr	8800	1999	60r
Child raising cost, total, age 12-14	yr	9510	1999	60r
Child raising cost, total, age 15-17	yr	9740	1999	60r
Child's child care and education, age 0-2	yr	1380	1999	60r

Daytona Beach, FL - continued

Item	Per	Value	Date	Ref.
Child Care - continued				
Child's child care and education, age 3-5	yr	1520	1999	60r
Child's child care and education, age 6-8	yr	990	1999	60r
Child's child care and education, age 9-11	yr	650	1999	60r
Child's child care and education, age 12-14	yr	490	1999	60r
Child's child care and education, age 15-17	yr	840	1999	60r
Child's clothing, age 0-2	yr	480	1999	60r
Child's clothing, age 3-5	yr	470	1999	60r
Child's clothing, age 6-8	yr	520	1999	60r
Child's clothing, age 9-11	yr	570	1999	60r
Child's clothing, age 12-14	yr	950	1999	60r
Child's clothing, age 15-17	yr	850	1999	60r
Child's food, age 0-2	yr	1000	1999	60r
Child's food, age 3-5	yr	1160	1999	60r
Child's food, age 6-8	yr	1490	1999	60r
Child's food, age 9-11	yr	1770	1999	60r
Child's food, age 12-14	yr	1770	1999	60r
Child's food, age 15-17	yr	1980	1999	60r
Child's health care, age 0-2	yr	620	1999	60r
Child's health care, age 3-5	yr	590	1999	60r
Child's health care, age 6-8	yr	680	1999	60r
Child's health care, age 9-11	yr	720	1999	60r
Child's health care, age 12-14	yr	730	1999	60r
Child's health care, age 15-17	yr	760	1999	60r
Child's housing, age 0-2	yr	3070	1999	60r
Child's housing, age 3-5	yr	3050	1999	60r
Child's housing, age 6-8	yr	3010	1999	60r
Child's housing, age 9-11	yr	2850	1999	60r
Child's housing, age 12-14	yr	3040	1999	60r
Child's housing, age 15-17	yr	2650	1999	60r
Child's personal care, reading, age 0-2	yr	910	1999	60r
Child's personal care, reading, age 3-5	yr	930	1999	60r
Child's personal care, reading, age 6-8	yr	960	1999	60r
Child's personal care, reading, age 9-11	yr	1000	1999	60r
Child's personal care, reading, age 12-14	yr	1170	1999	60r
Child's personal care, reading, age 15-17	yr	950	1999	60r
Clothing				
Apparel and services purchases	yr	1610	1999	30r
Boys, 2 to 15, expenditures on	yr	89	1999	30r
Children under 2, expenditures on	yr	79	1999	30r
Footwear, expenditures on	yr	283	1999	30r
Girls, 2 to 15, expenditures on	yr	103	1999	30r
Men and boys, expenditures on	yr	351	1999	30r
Men, 16 and over, expenditures on	yr	262	1999	30r
Women, 16 and over, expenditures on	yr	538	1999	30r
Communications				
Cable modem installation, Adelphi		54.90	6/99	103s
Cable modem installation, Comcast		95.00	6/99	103s
Cable modem installation, Media One		100.00	6/99	103s
Cable modem installation, Time Warner		75.00-225.00	6/99	103s
Cable modem rate, cable subscriber, Adelphi	mos	34.95	6/99	103s
Cable modem rate, cable subscriber, Comcast	mos	39.95	6/99	103s
Cable modem rate, cable subscriber, Media One	mos	34.95-39.95	6/99	103s
Cable modem rate, cable subscriber, Time Warner	mos	39.95-49.95	6/99	103s
Cable modem rate, non-cable subscriber, Adelphi	mos	44.95	6/99	103s
Cable modem rate, non-cable subscriber, Comcast	mos	49.95	6/99	103s
Cable modem rate, non-cable subscriber, Media One	mos	49.95	6/99	103s
Cable modem rate, non-cable subscriber, Time Warner	mos	39.95-54.95	6/99	103s
Phone line, single, business, field visit	inst.	56.00	12/97	17s
Phone line, single, business, no field visit	inst.	56.00	12/97	17s
Phone line, single, residence, field visit	inst.	40.00	12/97	17s
Phone line, single, residence, no field visit	inst.	40.00	12/97	17s
Postage and stationery, expenditures on	yr	104	1999	30r
Postal rate, express mail, up to half-pound		12.45	7/01	108r

Values are in dollars or fractions of dollars. In the column headed *Ref*, references are shown to sources. Each reference is followed by a letter. These refer to the geographical level for which data were reported: s=State, r=Region, and c=City or metro. The abbreviation *ex* is used to mean *except* or *excluding*; *exp* stands for *expenditures*. For other abbreviations and further explanations, please see the Introduction.

Daytona Beach, FL - continued

Item	Per	Value	Date	Ref.
Communications				
Postal rate, letter, first class, first ounce		0.34	7/01	108r
Postal rate, letter, two ounces		0.57	7/01	108r
Postal rate, post card		0.21	7/01	108r
Postal rate, priority mail, two pounds		3.95	7/01	108r
Postal rate, priority mail, up to one pound		3.50	7/01	108r
Telephone services, expenditures on	yr	860	1999	30r
Education				
Board, 4-year private college/university	yr	2236	1996	38s
Board, 4-year public college/university	yr	2295	1996	38s
Education expenditures	yr	431	1999	30r
Room, 4-year private college/university	yr	2428	1996	38s
Room, 4-year public college/university	yr	2193	1996	38s
Total cost, 4-year private college/university	yr	15028	1996	38s
Total cost, 4-year public college/university	yr	6254	1996	38s
Tuition, 2-year public college/university, in state	yr	1103	1996	38s
Tuition, 4-year private college/university, in state	yr	10364	1996	38s
Tuition, 4-year public college/university	yr	1767	1996	38s
Energy and Fuels				
Electricity	KWh	0.09	7/01	11r
Electricity	500 KWhs	47.29	7/01	11r
Fuel oil #2	gal	1.43	7/01	11r
Fuel oil and other fuels, expenditures on	yr	45	1999	30r
Gas, natural, commercial rate	1000 cf	8.44	11/00	88s
Gasoline, all types	gal	1.60	7/01	11r
Gasoline, unleaded midgrade	gal	1.65	7/01	11r
Gasoline, unleaded premium	gal	1.74	7/01	11r
Natural gas, expenditures on	yr	164	1999	30r
Utility (piped) gas, therm		1.01	7/01	11r
Utility (piped) gas, 40 therms		44.29	7/01	11r
Utility (piped) gas, 100 therms		97.44	7/01	11r
Entertainment				
Entertainment purchases	yr	1574	1999	30r
Fees and admissions paid	yr	371	1999	30r
Reading purchases	yr	121	1999	30r
Television, radios, sound equipment, expenditures on	yr	561	1999	30r
Funerals				
Total cost of funeral		5922.53	1/99	78r
Acknowledgement cards		63.43	1/99	78r
Casket		2258.77	1/99	78r
Cosmetology, hair, other preparation		127.09	1/99	78r
Embalming		393.49	1/99	78r
Funeral at funeral home		367.50	1/99	78r
Hearse (local)		169.66	1/99	78r
Professional service charges		1211.32	1/99	78r
Service car/van		80.69	1/99	78r
Transfer of remains to funeral home		144.25	1/99	78r
Vault		803.50	1/99	78r
Visitation/viewing		302.83	1/99	78r
Groceries				
American processed cheese	lb	3.50	7/01	11r
Bakery products, expenditures on	yr	261	1999	30r
Bananas	lb	0.47	7/01	11r
Beans, dried, any type, all sizes	lb	0.63	7/01	11r
Beef for stew, boneless	lb	2.86	7/01	11r
Beef, expenditures on	yr	210	1999	30r
Bologna, all beef or mixed	lb	2.29	7/01	11r
Bread, French	lb	1.66	7/01	11r
Bread, white, pan	lb	0.87	7/01	11r
Bread, whole wheat, pan	lb	1.38	7/01	11r
Broccoli	lb	1.04	7/01	11r
Butter, salted, grade AA, stick	lb	2.26	7/01	11r
Butter, yoghurt, cheese, etc, expenditures on	yr	170	1999	30r
Cabbage	lb	0.42	7/01	11r
Cereals and cereal products, expenditures on	yr	140	1999	30r

Daytona Beach, FL - continued

Item	Per	Value	Date	Ref.
Groceries - continued				
Cheddar cheese, natural	lb	3.75	7/01	11r
Chicken breast, bone-in	lb	1.85	7/01	11r
Chicken legs, bone-in	lb	1.34	7/01	11r
Chicken, fresh, whole	lb	1.05	7/01	11r
Chops, boneless,	lb	4.13	7/01	11r
Chuck roast, graded and ungraded, excl U.S. prime and choice	lb	2.35	7/01	11r
Chuck roast, U.S. choice, boneless	lb	2.67	7/01	11r
Coffee, 100%, ground roast, all sizes	lb	2.88	7/01	11r
Coffee, instant, plain, regular, all sizes	16 oz	9.25	7/01	11r
Cola, non diet	2 liter	1.11	7/01	11r
Crackers, soda, salted	lb	1.70	7/01	11r
Dairy product purchases	yr	282	1999	30r
Eggs, expenditures on	yr	32	1999	30r
Fats and oils, expenditures on	yr	79	1999	30r
Fish and seafood, expenditures on	yr	99	1999	30r
Flour, white, all purpose	lb	0.32	7/01	11r
Food (excl fruit and vegetables), eaten at home, purchases	yr	815	1999	30r
Food cooked on trips, expenditures on	yr	36	1999	30r
Food purchases	yr	4533	1999	30r
Food purchases, eaten away from home	yr	1873	1999	30r
Food purchases, food eaten at home	yr	2660	1999	30r
Fresh fruits, expenditures on	yr	128	1999	30r
Fresh milk and cream, expenditures on	yr	112	1999	30r
Fresh vegetables, expenditures on	yr	131	1999	30r
Fruit and vegetable purchases	yr	438	1999	30r
Grapefruit	lb	0.59	7/01	11r
Grapes, Thompson, seedless	lb	2.12	7/01	11r
Ground beef, 100% beef	lb	1.76	7/01	11r
Ground beef, lean and extra lean	lb	2.60	7/01	11r
Ground chuck, 100% beef	lb	2.08	7/01	11r
Ham, boneless, excl canned	lb	2.71	7/01	11r
Ham, rump or shank half, bone-in, smoked	lb	2.19	7/01	11r
Ice cream, prepackaged, bulk, regular	1/2 gal	3.93	7/01	11r
Lemons	lb	1.32	7/01	11r
Lettuce, iceberg	lb	0.76	7/01	11r
Milk, fresh, low fat,	gal	2.75	7/01	11r
Milk, fresh, whole, fortified	gal	2.97	7/01	11r
Nonalcoholic beverages, expenditures on	yr	228	1999	30r
Orange juice, frozen concentrate	16 oz	1.95	7/01	11r
Oranges, Navel	lb	0.73	7/01	11r
Oranges, Valencia	lb	0.55	7/01	11r
Peanut butter, creamy, all sizes	lb	1.83	7/01	11r
Pears, Anjou	lb	0.98	7/01	11r
Pork chops, center cut, bone-in	lb	3.33	7/01	11r
Pork sausage, fresh, loose	lb	2.59	7/01	11r
Pork shoulder picnic, bone-in, smoked	lb	1.12	7/01	11r
Pork, expenditures on	yr	162	1999	30r
Potato chips	16 oz	3.59	7/01	11r
Potatoes, frozen, french fried	lb	1.00	7/01	11r
Potatoes, white, all types	lb	0.44	7/01	11r
Poultry, expenditures on	yr	137	1999	30r
Processed fruits, expenditures on	yr	97	1999	30r
Processed vegetables, expenditures on	yr	82	1999	30r
Rice, white, long grain, uncooked	lb	0.51	7/01	11r
Round roast, graded and ungraded, excl U.S. prime and choice	lb	2.96	7/01	11r
Round steak, graded and ungraded, excl U.S. prime and choice	lb	3.11	7/01	11r
Sirloin steak, graded and ungraded, excl U.S. prime and choice	lb	4.23	7/01	11r
Spaghetti and macaroni	lb	0.78	7/01	11r
Steak, round, U.S. choice, boneless	lb	3.56	7/01	11r
Steak, sirloin, U.S. choice, boneless	lb	5.65	7/01	11r
Strawberries, dry pint	12 oz	1.50	7/01	11r
Sugar and other sweets, expenditures on	yr	99	1999	30r
Sugar, white, 33-80 ounce package	lb	0.39	7/01	11r
Sugar, white, all sizes	lb	0.42	7/01	11r
Tobacco products and smoking supplies purchases	yr	288	1999	30r
Tomatoes, field grown	lb	1.43	7/01	11r

Values are in dollars or fractions of dollars. In the column headed *Ref*, references are shown to sources. Each reference is followed by a letter. These refer to the geographical level for which data were reported: s=State, r=Region, and c=City or metro. The abbreviation *ex* is used to mean *except* or *excluding*; *exp* stands for *expenditures*. For other abbreviations and further explanations, please see the Introduction.

Daytona Beach, FL - continued

Item	Per	Value	Date	Ref.
Groceries				
Tuna, light, chunk	lb	1.77	7/01	11r
Turkey, frozen, whole	lb	1.05	7/01	11r
Goods and Services				
B&B Japanese maple (acer japonicum)	gal	49.98-129.00	4/00	93r
Boxwood (buxus)	2 gal	12.99-16.99	4/00	93r
Daylilly (hemerocallis)	gal	4.99-8.99	4/00	93r
Flat of annuals		11.00-13.92	4/00	93r
Fountain grass (pennisetum)	gal	5.98-7.98	4/00	93r
Hanging basket (10 in)		7.99-14.98	4/00	93r
Hardy geranium (geranium)	gal	5.98-8.00	4/00	93r
Hosta (hosta)	gal	4.99-10.98	4/00	93r
Lilac (syrubga vulgaris)	2 gal	12.99-21.99	4/00	93r
Rhododendron (rhododendron)	2 gal	14.99-24.99	4/00	93r
Sage (salvia)	gal	5.98-6.99	4/00	93r
Wintercreeper euonymus (euonymus fortunei)	2 gal	7.99-89.99	4/00	93r
Hunting license	yr	12.50	4/01	34s
Health Care				
Cardiac catheterization, ave hospital/ physician charges		15060	1998	77s
Childbirth, Cesarean delivery		11587	1997	13r
Childbirth, vaginal delivery		6725	1997	13r
Drugs, expenditures on	yr	399	1999	30r
Health care purchases	yr	1971	1999	30r
Health insurance expenditures	yr	933	1999	30r
Hysterectomy, laproscopically-assisted, ave hospital/physician charges		14760	1998	76s
Hysterectomy, vaginal, ave hospital and physician charges		11320	1998	76s
Medicaid dispensing fee		4.23	1999	87s
Medical services expenditures	yr	547	1999	30r
Medical supplies, expenditures on	yr	91	1999	30r
Plastic surgery, breast augmentation		2870	2000	7r
Plastic surgery, breast lift		3649	2000	7r
Plastic surgery, facelift		5008	2000	7r
Plastic surgery, hair transplantation		3425	2000	7r
Plastic surgery, lip augmentation		1227	2000	7r
Plastic surgery, lower body lift		4793	2000	7r
Plastic surgery, thigh lift		3862	2000	7r
Household Goods				
Floor coverings, expenditures on	yr	44	1999	30r
Furniture, expenditures on	yr	335	1999	30r
Household furnishings and equipment purchases	yr	1328	1999	30r
Household textiles, expenditures on	yr	89	1999	30r
Laundry and cleaning supplies, expenditures on	yr	113	1999	30r
Housing				
Home price, existing, ave		160100	10/00	90r
Home value, median		104000	2001	53s
Household operation expenditures	yr	553	1999	30r
Housekeeping supplies purchases	yr	473	1999	30r
Housing, expenditures on	yr	10303	1999	30r
Maintenance, repairs, insurance expenditures	yr	699	1999	30r
Monthly rental value of owned home	mos	505	1999	30r
Owned dwellings, expenditures own	yr	3465	1999	30r
Rent expenditures	yr	1641	1999	30r
Rental unit, 1 bedroom, with utilities	mos	464	4/01	41c

Daytona Beach, FL - continued

Item	Per	Value	Date	Ref.
Housing - continued				
Rental unit, 2 bedroom, with utilities	mos	593	4/01	41c
Rental unit, 3 bedroom, with utilities	mos	787	4/01	41c
Rental unit, 4 bedroom, with utilities	mos	836	4/01	41c
Shelter, expenditures on	yr	5467	1999	30r
Insurance and Pensions				
Life and other personal insurance purchases	yr	414	1999	30r
Medigap health insurance, Plan H	yr	2887	2000	69s
Medigap health insurance, Plan I	yr	3302	2000	69s
Medigap health insurance, Plan J	yr	3889	2000	69s
Pensions and Social Security, expenditures on	yr	2635	1999	30r
Personal insurance and pensions, expenditures on	yr	3048	1999	30r
Legal Fees				
Divorce, filing fee		65.00-85.00	4/01	35s
Driver's license fee	renew	15.00	1999	48s
Driver's license fee	orig	20.00	1999	48s
Personal Goods				
Personal care products and services purchases	yr	393	1999	30r
Personal Services				
Personal services, household, expenditures on	yr	258	1999	30r
Pets				
Pets, toys, and playground equipment, expenditures on	yr	306	1999	30r
Taxes				
Federal income taxes paid	yr	2047	1999	30r
Personal taxes, expenditures on	yr	2554	1999	30r
Property taxes paid	yr	726	1999	30r
State and local income taxes paid	yr	363	1999	30r
Transportation				
Bus fare, one-way	trip	1.00	2000	1c
Cars and trucks, new, expenditures on	yr	1648	1999	30r
Cars and trucks, used, expenditures on	yr	1651	1999	30r
Diesel at the pump	gal	1.26	10/99	73s
Gasoline and motor oil purchases	yr	1052	1999	30r
Gasoline before-tax price (cents)	gal	101.90	10/00	43s
Maintenance and repair expenditures	yr	621	1999	30r
Public transportation, expenditures on	yr	298	1999	30r
Transportation purchases	yr	6738	1999	30r
Vehicle expenses, miscellaneous, purchases	yr	2033	1999	30r
Vehicle insurance payments	yr	696	1999	30r
Vehicle purchases (net outlay)	yr	3354	1999	30r
Vehicle rental, lease expenditures	yr	352	1999	30r
Travel				
Hotel room	night	110.57	2/01	95s
Utilities				
Electrical bill, average	mos	86.33	9/00	9s
Electricity, expenditures on	yr	1115	1999	30r
Electricity cost, average	KWh	6.80	9/00	9s
Water and other public services, expenditures on	yr	298	1999	30r
Weddings				
Wedding (national average cost)		19936	2000	33r
Wedding (regional average total cost)		16293	1997	110r
Attendants' gifts		321	1998	33r
Bridal attendants' apparel (5 persons)		824	2000	33r
Bride's headpiece/veil		173	1998	33r
Bride's wedding dress		859	1998	33r
Clergy, religious facility fee		242	1998	33r
Engagement ring		3177	1998	33r
Flowers		789	1998	33r
Groom's formalwear rental		99	2000	33r
Limousine		410	1998	33r

Values are in dollars or fractions of dollars. In the column headed *Ref*, references are shown to sources. Each reference is followed by a letter. These refer to the geographical level for which data were reported: s=State, r=Region, and c=City or metro. The abbreviation *ex* is used to mean *except* or *excluding*; *exp* stands for expenditures. For other abbreviations and further explanations, please see the Introduction.

Daytona Beach, FL - continued

Item	Per	Value	Date	Ref.
Weddings				
Marriage license cost		56.00- 88.50	4/01	35s
Men's formalwear (ushers, best man)		469	2000	33r
Mother of bride apparel		241	2000	33r
Music		866	1998	33r
Photography and videography		1368	1998	33r
Rehearsal dinner		728	1998	33r
Wedding invitations and announcements		341	1998	33r
Wedding reception		7968	2000	33r
Wedding rings (bride and groom)		1060	1998	33r

Decatur, AL

Item	Per	Value	Date	Ref.
Alcoholic Beverages				
Alcoholic beverage purchases	yr	253	1999	30r
Malt beverages, all types, all sizes, any origin	16 oz	0.96	7/01	11r
Appliances				
Major appliances, expenditures on	yr	172	1999	30r
Small appliances, housewares, expenditures on	yr	81	1999	30r
Banking and Money				
Mortgage interest and charges paid	yr	2039	1999	30r
Mortgage principal paid on owned property	yr	1026	1999	30r
Vehicle finance charges paid	yr	365	1999	30r
Charity				
Cash contributions, expenditures	yr	1127	1999	30r
Child Care				
Child raising cost, total, age 0-2	yr	8540	1999	60r
Child raising cost, total, age 3-5	yr	8780	1999	60r
Child raising cost, total, age 6-8	yr	8820	1999	60r
Child raising cost, total, age 9-11	yr	8800	1999	60r
Child raising cost, total, age 12-14	yr	9510	1999	60r
Child raising cost, total, age 15-17	yr	9740	1999	60r
Child's child care and education, age 0-2	yr	1380	1999	60r
Child's child care and education, age 3-5	yr	1520	1999	60r
Child's child care and education, age 6-8	yr	990	1999	60r
Child's child care and education, age 9-11	yr	650	1999	60r
Child's child care and education, age 12-14	yr	490	1999	60r
Child's child care and education, age 15-17	yr	840	1999	60r
Child's clothing, age 0-2	yr	480	1999	60r
Child's clothing, age 3-5	yr	470	1999	60r
Child's clothing, age 6-8	yr	520	1999	60r
Child's clothing, age 9-11	yr	570	1999	60r
Child's clothing, age 12-14	yr	950	1999	60r
Child's clothing, age 15-17	yr	850	1999	60r
Child's food, age 0-2	yr	1000	1999	60r
Child's food, age 3-5	yr	1160	1999	60r
Child's food, age 6-8	yr	1490	1999	60r
Child's food, age 9-11	yr	1770	1999	60r
Child's food, age 12-14	yr	1770	1999	60r
Child's food, age 15-17	yr	1980	1999	60r
Child's health care, age 0-2	yr	620	1999	60r
Child's health care, age 3-5	yr	590	1999	60r
Child's health care, age 6-8	yr	680	1999	60r
Child's health care, age 9-11	yr	720	1999	60r
Child's health care, age 12-14	yr	730	1999	60r
Child's health care, age 15-17	yr	760	1999	60r
Child's housing, age 0-2	yr	3070	1999	60r
Child's housing, age 3-5	yr	3050	1999	60r
Child's housing, age 6-8	yr	3010	1999	60r
Child's housing, age 9-11	yr	2850	1999	60r
Child's housing, age 12-14	yr	3040	1999	60r
Child's housing, age 15-17	yr	2650	1999	60r
Child's personal care, reading, age 0-2	yr	910	1999	60r
Child's personal care, reading, age 3-5	yr	930	1999	60r
Child's personal care, reading, age 6-8	yr	960	1999	60r
Child's personal care, reading, age 9-11	yr	1000	1999	60r
Child's personal care, reading, age 12-14	yr	1170	1999	60r
Child's personal care, reading, age 15-17	yr	950	1999	60r

Decatur, AL - continued

Item	Per	Value	Date	Ref.
Clothing				
Apparel and services purchases	yr	1610	1999	30r
Boys, 2 to 15, expenditures on	yr	89	1999	30r
Children under 2, expenditures on	yr	79	1999	30r
Footwear, expenditures on	yr	283	1999	30r
Girls, 2 to 15, expenditures on	yr	103	1999	30r
Men and boys, expenditures on	yr	351	1999	30r
Men, 16 and over, expenditures on	yr	262	1999	30r
Women, 16 and over, expenditures on	yr	538	1999	30r
Communications				
Phone line, single, business, field visit	inst.	69.00	12/97	17s
Phone line, single, business, no field visit	inst.	69.00	12/97	17s
Phone line, single, residence, field visit	inst.	40.00	12/97	17s
Phone line, single, residence, no field visit	inst.	40.00	12/97	17s
Postage and stationery, expenditures on	yr	104	1999	30r
Postal rate, express mail, up to half-pound		12.45	7/01	108r
Postal rate, letter, first class, first ounce		0.34	7/01	108r
Postal rate, letter, two ounces		0.57	7/01	108r
Postal rate, post card		0.21	7/01	108r
Postal rate, priority mail, two pounds		3.95	7/01	108r
Postal rate, priority mail, up to one pound		3.50	7/01	108r
Telephone services, expenditures on	yr	860	1999	30r
Education				
Board, 4-year private college/university	yr	2256	1996	38s
Board, 4-year public college/university	yr	1739	1996	38s
Education expenditures	yr	431	1999	30r
Room, 4-year private college/university	yr	1799	1996	38s
Room, 4-year public college/university	yr	1757	1996	38s
Total cost, 4-year private college/university	yr	11635	1996	38s
Total cost, 4-year public college/university	yr	5737	1996	38s
Tuition, 2-year public college/university, in state	yr	1317	1996	38s
Tuition, 4-year private college/university, in state	yr	7580	1996	38s
Tuition, 4-year public college/university	yr	2240	1996	38s
Energy and Fuels				
Electricity	KWh	0.09	7/01	11r
Electricity	500 KWhs	47.29	7/01	11r
Fuel oil #2	gal	1.43	7/01	11r
Fuel oil and other fuels, expenditures on	yr	45	1999	30r
Gas, natural, commercial rate	1000 cf	9.50	11/00	88s
Gasoline, all types	gal	1.60	7/01	11r
Gasoline, unleaded midgrade	gal	1.65	7/01	11r
Gasoline, unleaded premium	gal	1.74	7/01	11r
Natural gas, expenditures on	yr	164	1999	30r
Utility (piped) gas, therm		1.01	7/01	11r
Utility (piped) gas, 40 therms		44.29	7/01	11r
Utility (piped) gas, 100 therms		97.44	7/01	11r
Entertainment				
Entertainment purchases	yr	1574	1999	30r
Fees and admissions paid	yr	371	1999	30r
Reading purchases	yr	121	1999	30r
Television, radios, sound equipment, expenditures on	yr	561	1999	30r
Groceries				
American processed cheese	lb	3.50	7/01	11r
Bakery products, expenditures on	yr	261	1999	30r
Bananas	lb	0.47	7/01	11r
Beans, dried, any type, all sizes	lb	0.63	7/01	11r
Beef for stew, boneless	lb	2.86	7/01	11r
Beef, expenditures on	yr	210	1999	30r
Bologna, all beef or mixed	lb	2.29	7/01	11r
Bread, French	lb	1.66	7/01	11r
Bread, white, pan	lb	0.87	7/01	11r
Bread, whole wheat, pan	lb	1.38	7/01	11r
Broccoli	lb	1.04	7/01	11r
Butter, salted, grade AA, stick	lb	2.26	7/01	11r
Butter, yoghurt, cheese, etc, expenditures on	yr	170	1999	30r
Cabbage	lb	0.42	7/01	11r

Values are in dollars or fractions of dollars. In the column headed *Ref*, references are shown to sources. Each reference is followed by a letter. These refer to the geographical level for which data were reported: s=State, r=Region, and c=City or metro. The abbreviation *ex* is used to mean *except* or *excluding*; *exp* stands for expenditures. For other abbreviations and further explanations, please see the Introduction.

Decatur, AL - continued

Item	Per	Value	Date	Ref.
Groceries				
Cereals and cereal products, expenditures on	yr	140	1999	30r
Cheddar cheese, natural	lb	3.75	7/01	11r
Chicken breast, bone-in	lb	1.85	7/01	11r
Chicken legs, bone-in	lb	1.34	7/01	11r
Chicken, fresh, whole	lb	1.05	7/01	11r
Chops, boneless	lb	4.13	7/01	11r
Chuck roast, graded and ungraded, excl U.S. prime and choice	lb	2.35	7/01	11r
Chuck roast, U.S. choice, boneless	lb	2.67	7/01	11r
Coffee, 100%, ground roast, all sizes	lb	2.88	7/01	11r
Coffee, instant, plain, regular, all sizes	16 oz	9.25	7/01	11r
Cola, non diet,	2 liter	1.11	7/01	11r
Crackers, soda, salted	lb	1.70	7/01	11r
Dairy product purchases	yr	282	1999	30r
Eggs, expenditures on	yr	32	1999	30r
Fats and oils, expenditures on	yr	79	1999	30r
Fish and seafood, expenditures on	yr	99	1999	30r
Flour, white, all purpose	lb	0.32	7/01	11r
Food (excl fruit and vegetables), eaten at home, purchases	yr	815	1999	30r
Food cooked on trips, expenditures on	yr	36	1999	30r
Food purchases	yr	4533	1999	30r
Food purchases, eaten away from home	yr	1873	1999	30r
Food purchases, food eaten at home	yr	2660	1999	30r
Fresh fruits, expenditures on	yr	128	1999	30r
Fresh milk and cream, expenditures on	yr	112	1999	30r
Fresh vegetables, expenditures on	yr	131	1999	30r
Fruit and vegetable purchases	yr	438	1999	30r
Grapefruit	lb	0.59	7/01	11r
Grapes, Thompson, seedless	lb	2.12	7/01	11r
Ground beef, 100% beef	lb	1.76	7/01	11r
Ground beef, lean and extra lean	lb	2.60	7/01	11r
Ground chuck, 100% beef	lb	2.08	7/01	11r
Ham, boneless, excl canned	lb	2.71	7/01	11r
Ham, rump or shank half, bone-in, smoked	lb	2.19	7/01	11r
Ice cream, prepackaged, bulk, regular	1/2 gal	3.93	7/01	11r
Lemons	lb	1.32	7/01	11r
Lettuce, iceberg	lb	0.76	7/01	11r
Milk, fresh, low fat,	gal	2.75	7/01	11r
Milk, fresh, whole, fortified	gal	2.97	7/01	11r
Nonalcoholic beverages, expenditures on	yr	228	1999	30r
Orange juice, frozen concentrate	16 oz	1.95	7/01	11r
Oranges, Navel	lb	0.73	7/01	11r
Oranges, Valencia	lb	0.55	7/01	11r
Peanut butter, creamy, all sizes	lb	1.83	7/01	11r
Pears, Anjou	lb	0.98	7/01	11r
Pork chops, center cut, bone-in	lb	3.33	7/01	11r
Pork sausage, fresh, loose	lb	2.59	7/01	11r
Pork shoulder picnic, bone-in, smoked	lb	1.12	7/01	11r
Pork, expenditures on	yr	162	1999	30r
Potato chips	16 oz	3.59	7/01	11r
Potatoes, frozen, french fried	lb	1.00	7/01	11r
Potatoes, white, all types	lb	0.44	7/01	11r
Poultry, expenditures on	yr	137	1999	30r
Processed fruits, expenditures on	yr	97	1999	30r
Processed vegetables, expenditures on	yr	82	1999	30r
Rice, white, long grain, uncooked	lb	0.51	7/01	11r
Round roast, graded and ungraded, excl U.S. prime and choice	lb	2.96	7/01	11r
Round steak, graded and ungraded, excl U.S. prime and choice	lb	3.11	7/01	11r
Sirloin steak, graded and ungraded, excl U.S. prime and choice	lb	4.23	7/01	11r
Spaghetti and macaroni	lb	0.78	7/01	11r
Steak, round, U.S. choice, boneless	lb	3.56	7/01	11r
Steak, sirloin, U.S. choice, boneless	lb	5.65	7/01	11r
Strawberries, dry pint	12 oz	1.50	7/01	11r
Sugar and other sweets, expenditures on	yr	99	1999	30r
Sugar, white, 33-80 ounce package	lb	0.39	7/01	11r
Sugar, white, all sizes	lb	0.42	7/01	11r

Decatur, AL - continued

Item	Per	Value	Date	Ref.
Groceries - continued				
Tobacco products and smoking supplies purchases	yr	288	1999	30r
Tomatoes, field grown	lb	1.43	7/01	11r
Tuna, light, chunk	lb	1.77	7/01	11r
Turkey, frozen, whole	lb	1.05	7/01	11r
Goods and Services				
Hunting license	yr	16.00	4/01	34s
Health Care				
Cardiac catheterization, ave hospital/ physician charges		15260	1998	77s
Childbirth, Cesarean delivery		11587	1997	13r
Childbirth, vaginal delivery		6725	1997	13r
Drugs, expenditures on	yr	399	1999	30r
Health care purchases	yr	1971	1999	30r
Health insurance expenditures	yr	933	1999	30r
Hysterectomy, laproscopically-assisted, ave hospital/physician charges		16780	1998	76s
Hysterectomy, vaginal, ave hospital and physician charges		10990	1998	76s
Medicaid dispensing fee		5.40	1999	87s
Medical services expenditures	yr	547	1999	30r
Medical supplies, expenditures on	yr	91	1999	30r
Household Goods				
Floor coverings, expenditures on	yr	44	1999	30r
Furniture, expenditures on	yr	335	1999	30r
Household furnishings and equipment purchases	yr	1328	1999	30r
Household textiles, expenditures on	yr	89	1999	30r
Laundry and cleaning supplies, expenditures on	yr	113	1999	30r
Housing				
Home price, existing, ave		160100	10/00	90r
Home value, median		115000	2001	53s
Household operation expenditures	yr	553	1999	30r
Housekeeping supplies purchases	yr	473	1999	30r
Housing, expenditures on	yr	10303	1999	30r
Maintenance, repairs, insurance expenditures	yr	699	1999	30r
Monthly rental value of owned home	mos	505	1999	30r
Owned dwellings, expenditures own	yr	3465	1999	30r
Rent expenditures	yr	1641	1999	30r
Rental unit, 1 bedroom, with utilities	mos	354	4/01	41c
Rental unit, 2 bedroom, with utilities	mos	445	4/01	41c
Rental unit, 3 bedroom, with utilities	mos	677	4/01	41c
Rental unit, 4 bedroom, with utilities	mos	690	4/01	41c
Shelter, expenditures on	yr	5467	1999	30r
Insurance and Pensions				
Life and other personal insurance purchases	yr	414	1999	30r
Pensions and Social Security, expenditures on	yr	2635	1999	30r
Personal insurance and pensions, expenditures on	yr	3048	1999	30r
Legal Fees				
Divorce, filing fee		146.00-193.00	4/01	35s
Driver's license fee	renew	18.50	1999	48s
Driver's license fee	orig	18.50	1999	48s
Personal Goods				
Personal care products and services purchases	yr	393	1999	30r
Personal Services				
Personal services, household, expenditures on	yr	258	1999	30r
Pets				
Pets, toys, and playground equipment, expenditures on	yr	306	1999	30r

Values are in dollars or fractions of dollars. In the column headed *Ref*, references are shown to sources. Each reference is followed by a letter. These refer to the geographical level for which data were reported: s=State, r=Region, and c=City or metro. The abbreviation *ex* is used to mean *except* or *excluding*; *exp* stands for *expenditures*. For other abbreviations and further explanations, please see the Introduction.

Decatur, AL - continued

Item	Per	Value	Date	Ref.
Taxes				
Federal income taxes paid	yr	2047	1999	30r
Personal taxes, expenditures on	yr	2554	1999	30r
Property taxes paid	yr	726	1999	30r
State and local income taxes paid	yr	363	1999	30r
Transportation				
Cars and trucks, new, expenditures on	yr	1648	1999	30r
Cars and trucks, used, expenditures on	yr	1651	1999	30r
Diesel at the pump	gal	1.19	10/99	73s
Gasoline and motor oil purchases	yr	1052	1999	30r
Gasoline before-tax price (cents)	gal	104.10	10/00	43s
Maintenance and repair expenditures	yr	621	1999	30r
Public transportation, expenditures on	yr	298	1999	30r
Transportation purchases	yr	6738	1999	30r
Vehicle expenses, miscellaneous, purchases	yr	2033	1999	30r
Vehicle insurance payments	yr	696	1999	30r
Vehicle purchases (net outlay)	yr	3354	1999	30r
Vehicle rental, lease expenditures	yr	352	1999	30r
Utilities				
Electrical bill, average	mos	83.42	9/00	9s
Electricity, expenditures on	yr	1115	1999	30r
Electricity cost, average	KWh	5.60	9/00	9s
Water and other public services, expenditures on	yr	298	1999	30r
Weddings				
Wedding (national average cost)		19936	2000	33r
Attendants' gifts		321	1998	33r
Bridal attendants' apparel (5 persons)		824	2000	33r
Bride's headpiece/veil		173	1998	33r
Bride's wedding dress		859	1998	33r
Clergy, religious facility fee		242	1998	33r
Engagement ring		3177	1998	33r
Flowers		789	1998	33r
Groom's formalwear rental		99	2000	33r
Limousine		410	1998	33r
Marriage license cost		25.00	4/01	35s
Men's formalwear (ushers, best man)		469	2000	33r
Mother of bride apparel		241	2000	33r
Music		866	1998	33r
Photography and videography		1368	1998	33r
Rehearsal dinner		728	1998	33r
Wedding invitations and announcements		341	1998	33r
Wedding reception		7968	2000	33r
Wedding rings (bride and groom)		1060	1998	33r

Decatur, IL

Item	Per	Value	Date	Ref.
Average annual expenditures	yr	35369	1999	30r
Composite, ACCRA index		93.80	3/01	4c
Alcoholic Beverages				
Alcoholic beverage purchases	yr	304	1999	30r
Beer, Heineken, 12-oz, ex deposit	6	6.66	3/01	4c
J & B Scotch	750-ml	18.44	3/01	4c
Malt beverages, all types, all sizes, any origin	16 oz	0.93	7/01	11r
Wine, Livingston or Gallo, Chablis blanc	1.5 liter	5.40	3/01	4c
Wine, red and white table, all sizes, any origin	liter	7.04	7/01	11r
Appliances				
Appliance repair, service call, washing machine	min lab chg	36.00	3/01	4c
Major appliances, expenditures on	yr	165	1999	30r
Small appliances, housewares, expenditures on	yr	90	1999	30r
Banking and Money				
Mortgage interest and charges paid	yr	2277	1999	30r
Mortgage principal paid on owned property	yr	1230	1999	30r
Mortgage rate, incl. points and orig. fee, 30-yr. conv. fixed or ARM	mos	7.15	3/01	4c
Vehicle finance charges paid	yr	328	1999	30r

Decatur, IL - continued

Item	Per	Value	Date	Ref.
Charity				
Cash contributions, expenditures	yr	1126	1999	30r
Child Care				
Child raising cost, total, age 0-2	yr	7890	1999	60r
Child raising cost, total, age 3-5	yr	8130	1999	60r
Child raising cost, total, age 6-8	yr	8170	1999	60r
Child raising cost, total, age 9-11	yr	8190	1999	60r
Child raising cost, total, age 12-14	yr	8890	1999	60r
Child raising cost, total, age 15-17	yr	9050	1999	60r
Child's child care and education, age 0-2	yr	1240	1999	60r
Child's child care and education, age 3-5	yr	1370	1999	60r
Child's child care and education, age 6-8	yr	880	1999	60r
Child's child care and education, age 9-11	yr	570	1999	60r
Child's child care and education, age 12-14	yr	420	1999	60r
Child's child care and education, age 15-17	yr	720	1999	60r
Child's clothing, age 0-2	yr	410	1999	60r
Child's clothing, age 3-5	yr	400	1999	60r
Child's clothing, age 6-8	yr	450	1999	60r
Child's clothing, age 9-11	yr	500	1999	60r
Child's clothing, age 12-14	yr	840	1999	60r
Child's clothing, age 15-17	yr	740	1999	60r
Child's food, age 0-2	yr	960	1999	60r
Child's food, age 3-5	yr	1120	1999	60r
Child's food, age 6-8	yr	1430	1999	60r
Child's food, age 9-11	yr	1710	1999	60r
Child's food, age 12-14	yr	1710	1999	60r
Child's food, age 15-17	yr	1920	1999	60r
Child's health care, age 0-2	yr	520	1999	60r
Child's health care, age 3-5	yr	500	1999	60r
Child's health care, age 6-8	yr	570	1999	60r
Child's health care, age 9-11	yr	610	1999	60r
Child's health care, age 12-14	yr	630	1999	60r
Child's health care, age 15-17	yr	650	1999	60r
Child's housing, age 0-2	yr	2860	1999	60r
Child's housing, age 3-5	yr	2840	1999	60r
Child's housing, age 6-8	yr	2800	1999	60r
Child's housing, age 9-11	yr	2650	1999	60r
Child's housing, age 12-14	yr	2840	1999	60r
Child's housing, age 15-17	yr	2440	1999	60r
Child's personal care, reading, age 0-2	yr	880	1999	60r
Child's personal care, reading, age 3-5	yr	900	1999	60r
Child's personal care, reading, age 6-8	yr	930	1999	60r
Child's personal care, reading, age 9-11	yr	970	1999	60r
Child's personal care, reading, age 12-14	yr	1150	1999	60r
Child's personal care, reading, age 15-17	yr	920	1999	60r
Clothing				
Apparel and services purchases	yr	1607	1999	30r
Boys' brief, cotton	3	3.18	3/01	4c
Boys, 2 to 15, expenditures on	yr	91	1999	30r
Children under 2, expenditures on	yr	59	1999	30r
Footwear, expenditures on	yr	285	1999	30r
Girls, 2 to 15, expenditures on	yr	116	1999	30r
Men and boys, expenditures on	yr	433	1999	30r
Men, 16 and over, expenditures on	yr	341	1999	30r
Shirt, man's dress shirt		25.12	3/01	4c
Slacks, man's "No Wrinkles" khaki		42.25	3/01	4c
Women, 16 and over, expenditures on	yr	490	1999	30r
Communications				
Cable modem installation, Adelphi		54.90	6/99	103s
Cable modem installation, AT&T-BIS		150.00	6/99	103s
Cable modem installation, Media One		100.00	6/99	103s
Cable modem rate, cable subscriber, Adelphi	mos	34.95	6/99	103s
Cable modem rate, cable subscriber, AT&T-BIS	mos	39.95	6/99	103s
Cable modem rate, cable subscriber, Media One	mos	34.95-39.95	6/99	103s
Cable modem rate, non-cable subscriber, Adelphi	mos	44.95	6/99	103s
Cable modem rate, non-cable subscriber, Media One	mos	49.95	6/99	103s
Newspaper subscription, daily and Sunday delivery	mos	16.52	3/01	4c

Values are in dollars or fractions of dollars. In the column headed *Ref*, references are shown to sources. Each reference is followed by a letter. These refer to the geographical level for which data were reported: s=State, r=Region, and c=City or metro. The abbreviation *ex* is used to mean *except* or *excluding*; *exp* stands for expenditures. For other abbreviations and further explanations, please see the Introduction.

Decatur, IL - continued

Item	Per	Value	Date	Ref.
Communications				
Phone line, single, business, field visit	inst.	52.35	12/97	17s
Phone line, single, business, no field visit	inst.	52.35	12/97	17s
Phone line, single, residence, field visit	inst.	55.00	12/97	17s
Phone line, single, residence, no field visit	inst.	55.00	12/97	17s
Postage and stationery, expenditures on	yr	140	1999	30r
Postal rate, express mail, up to half-pound		12.45	7/01	108r
Postal rate, letter, first class, first ounce		0.34	7/01	108r
Postal rate, letter, two ounces		0.57	7/01	108r
Postal rate, post card		0.21	7/01	108r
Postal rate, priority mail, two pounds		3.95	7/01	108r
Postal rate, priority mail, up to one pound		3.50	7/01	108r
Telephone bill, business, basic rate	mos	11.87	12/97	18c
Telephone bill, family of three	mos	18.00	3/01	4c
Telephone bill, residential, basic rate	mos	9.00	12/97	18c
Telephone services, expenditures on	yr	830	1999	30r
Education				
Board, 4-year private college/university	yr	2306	1996	38s
Board, 4-year public college/university	yr	2405	1996	38s
Education expenditures	yr	583	1999	30r
Room, 4-year private college/university	yr	2718	1996	38s
Room, 4-year public college/university	yr	2072	1996	38s
Total cost, 4-year private college/university	yr	16678	1996	38s
Total cost, 4-year public college/university	yr	7829	1996	38s
Tuition, 2-year public college/university, in state	yr	1232	1996	38s
Tuition, 4-year private college/university, in state	yr	11653	1996	38s
Tuition, 4-year public college/university	yr	3352	1996	38s
Energy and Fuels				
Electricity	500 KWhs	46.59	7/01	11r
Energy, combined forms, 2400 sq ft	mos	116.60	3/01	4c
Energy, exc. electricity, 2400 sq ft	mos	51.14	3/01	4c
Fuel oil #2	gal	1.27	7/01	11r
Fuel oil and other fuels, expenditures on	yr	68	1999	30r
Gas, natural, commercial rate	1000 cf	8.47	11/00	88s
Gas, regular unleaded, cash, self-service	gal	1.54	3/01	4c
Gasoline, unleaded midgrade	gal	1.79	7/01	11r
Gasoline, unleaded premium	gal	1.86	7/01	11r
Gasoline, unleaded regular	gal	1.58	7/01	11r
Natural gas, expenditures on	yr	389	1999	30r
Utility (piped) gas, therm		0.81	7/01	11r
Utility (piped) gas, 40 therms		38.01	7/01	11r
Utility (piped) gas, 100 therms		81.75	7/01	11r
Entertainment				
Bowling, Saturday evening rate	line	1.95	3/01	4c
Entertainment purchases	yr	1984	1999	30r
Fees and admissions paid	yr	444	1999	30r
Monopoly game, Parker Brothers', No. 9	game	9.94	3/01	4c
Movie, first-run, Saturday, evening	adm.	6.75	3/01	4c
Television, radios, sound equipment, expenditures on	yr	580	1999	30r
Tennis balls, yellow, Wilson or Penn, 3	can	1.93	3/01	4c
Funerals				
Cosmetology, hair, other preparation		178.32	1/99	78r
Embalming		408.19	1/99	78r
Funeral at funeral home		362.13	1/99	78r
Professional service charges		1375.51	1/99	78r
Transfer of remains to funeral home		155.92	1/99	78r
Visitation/viewing		294.38	1/99	78r
Groceries				
Groceries, ACCRA Index		93.30	3/01	4c
Antibiotic ointment, Polysporin	0.5 oz	4.26	3/01	4c
Baby food, strained vegetables or fruit, lowest price	4-4.5 oz	0.37	3/01	4c
Bacon, sliced	lb	3.15	7/01	11r
Bakery products, expenditures on	yr	281	1999	30r
Bananas	lb	0.49	3/01	4c
Bananas	lb	0.48	7/01	11r

Decatur, IL - continued

Item	Per	Value	Date	Ref.
Groceries - continued				
Beans, dried, any type, all sizes	lb	0.61	7/01	11r
Beef for stew, boneless	lb	3.08	7/01	11r
Beef or hamburger, ground	lb	1.56	3/01	4c
Beef, expenditures on	yr	217	1999	30r
Bologna, all beef or mixed	lb	2.52	7/01	11r
Bread, white	loaf	0.98	3/01	4c
Bread, white, pan	lb	1.06	7/01	11r
Broccoli	lb	0.91	7/01	11r
Butter, salted, grade AA, stick	lb	3.04	7/01	11r
Butter, yoghurt, cheese, etc, expenditures on	yr	183	1999	30r
Cereals and bakery product purchases	yr	430	1999	30r
Cereals and cereal products, expenditures on	yr	149	1999	30r
Cheese, Kraft grated Parmesan	8 oz	3.81	3/01	4c
Chicken, fresh, whole	lb	1.07	7/01	11r
Chicken, whole fryer	lb	0.66	3/01	4c
Chops, boneless,	lb	3.64	7/01	11r
Chuck roast, U.S. choice, boneless	lb	2.47	7/01	11r
Cigarettes, Winston, Kings	carton	31.90	3/01	4c
Coffee, 100%, ground roast, all sizes	lb	2.69	7/01	11r
Coffee, vacuum-packed	13 oz	2.61	3/01	4c
Cookies, chocolate chip	lb	2.87	7/01	11r
Corn Flakes, Kellogg's or Post Toasties	18 oz	2.26	3/01	4c
Corn, frozen, whole kernel, lowest price	16 oz	1.13	3/01	4c
Dairy product purchases	yr	304	1999	30r
Eggs, expenditures on	yr	26	1999	30r
Eggs, Grade A or AA	dozen	0.90	3/01	4c
Eggs, grade A, large	dozen	0.88	7/01	11r
Fats and oils, expenditures on	yr	75	1999	30r
Fish and seafood, expenditures on	yr	72	1999	30r
Food (excl fruit and vegetables), eaten at home, purchases	yr	887	1999	30r
Food cooked on trips, expenditures on	yr	44	1999	30r
Food purchases	yr	4802	1999	30r
Food purchases, eaten away from home	yr	2069	1999	30r
Food purchases, food eaten at home	yr	2733	1999	30r
Fresh fruits, expenditures on	yr	138	1999	30r
Fresh milk and cream, expenditures on	yr	120	1999	30r
Fresh vegetables, expenditures on	yr	126	1999	30r
Grapefruit	lb	0.66	7/01	11r
Grapes, Thompson, seedless	lb	1.64	7/01	11r
Ground beef, 100% beef	lb	1.64	7/01	11r
Ground beef, lean and extra lean	lb	2.16	7/01	11r
Ground chuck, 100% beef	lb	2.13	7/01	11r
Ham, boneless, excl canned	lb	2.62	7/01	11r
Ice cream, prepackaged, bulk, regular	1/2 gal	3.35	7/01	11r
Lemons	lb	1.19	7/01	11r
Lettuce, iceberg	head	0.99	3/01	4c
Lettuce, iceberg	lb	0.73	7/01	11r
Margarine, Blue Bonnet or Parkay, stick	lb	0.82	3/01	4c
Margarine, soft, tubs	lb	0.89	7/01	11r
Meats, poultry, fish, and egg purchases	yr	671	1999	30r
Milk, fresh, whole, fortified	gal	2.71	7/01	11r
Milk, whole	1/2 gal	1.64	3/01	4c
Nonalcoholic beverages, expenditures on	yr	239	1999	30r
Orange juice, Minute Maid frozen	12 oz	1.45	3/01	4c
Oranges, Navel	lb	0.80	7/01	11r
Oranges, Valencia	lb	0.66	7/01	11r
Peaches, halves or slices, Hunt's, Del Monte, or Libby's	29 oz	1.56	3/01	4c
Pears, Anjou	lb	0.93	7/01	11r
Peas, green, Del Monte or Green Giant	15 oz	0.73	3/01	4c
Pork chops, center cut, bone-in	lb	3.63	7/01	11r
Pork, expenditures on	yr	150	1999	30r
Potato chips	16 oz	3.52	7/01	11r
Potatoes, frozen, french fried	lb	1.08	7/01	11r
Potatoes, white or red	10 lb	2.14	3/01	4c
Potatoes, white, all types	lb	0.33	7/01	11r
Poultry, expenditures on	yr	108	1999	30r
Processed fruits, expenditures on	yr	98	1999	30r
Processed vegetables, expenditures on	yr	80	1999	30r
Round roast, U.S. choice, boneless	lb	3.07	7/01	11r

Values are in dollars or fractions of dollars. In the column headed *Ref*, references are shown to sources. Each reference is followed by a letter. These refer to the geographical level for which data were reported: s=State, r=Region, and c=City or metro. The abbreviation *ex* is used to mean *except* or *excluding*; *exp* stands for *expenditures*. For other abbreviations and further explanations, please see the Introduction.

Decatur, IL - continued

Item	Per	Value	Date	Ref.
Groceries				
Round steak, graded and ungraded, excl U.S. prime and choice	lb	3.41	7/01	11r
Sausage, Jimmy Dean/Owens pork	lb	2.69	3/01	4c
Shortening, vegetable oil blends	lb	1.13	7/01	11r
Shortening, vegetable, Crisco	3 lb	2.81	3/01	4c
Soft drink, Coca Cola, ex deposit	2 liter	1.10	3/01	4c
Spaghetti and macaroni	lb	0.80	7/01	11r
Steak, round, U.S. choice, boneless	lb	3.23	7/01	11r
Steak, T-bone	lb	5.31	3/01	4c
Steak, T-bone, U.S. choice, bone-in	lb	6.68	7/01	11r
Strawberries, dry pint	12 oz	1.32	7/01	11r
Sugar and other sweets, expenditures on	yr	114	1999	30r
Sugar, cane or beet	4 lbs	1.57	3/01	4c
Sugar, white, 33-80 ounce package	lb	0.42	7/01	11r
Sugar, white, all sizes	lb	0.43	7/01	11r
Tobacco products and smoking supplies purchases	yr	331	1999	30r
Tomatoes, field grown	lb	1.46	7/01	11r
Tomatoes, Hunt's or Del Monte	14.5 oz	0.99	3/01	4c
Tuna, chunk, light	6 oz	0.60	3/01	4c
Tuna, light, chunk	lb	1.80	7/01	11r
Turkey, frozen, whole	lb	1.15	7/01	11r
Goods and Services				
Miscellaneous goods and services, ACCRA Index		95.50	3/01	4c
B&B Japanese maple (acer japonicum)	gal	29.99-169.99	4/00	93r
Boxwood (buxus)	2 gal	18.99-39.99	4/00	93r
Daylily (hemerocallis)	gal	4.99-25.00	4/00	93r
Flat of annuals		11.98-24.99	4/00	93r
Fountain grass (pennisetum)	gal	5.98-12.98	4/00	93r
Hanging basket (10 in)		12.99-27.99	4/00	93r
Hardy geranium (geranium)	gal	7.99-9.99	4/00	93r
Hosta (hosta)	gal	6.00-25.00	4/00	93r
Lilac (syrubga vulgaris)	2 gal	14.99-24.99	4/00	93r
Miscellaneous purchases	yr	865	1999	30r
Rhododendron (rhododendron)	2 gal	23.98-42.99	4/00	93r
Sage (salvia)	gal	6.00-9.99	4/00	93r
Wintercreeper euonymus (euonymus fortunei)	2 gal	16.00-169.99	4/00	93r
Hunting license	yr	7.50	4/01	34s
Health Care				
Health care, ACCRA Index		87.30	3/01	4c
Cardiac catheterization, ave hospital/ physician charges		17690	1998	77s
Childbirth, Cesarean delivery		10722	1997	13r
Childbirth, vaginal delivery		6223	1997	13r
Dentist's fee, adult teeth cleaning and periodic oral exam	visit	64.80	3/01	4c
Doctor's fee, routine exam, established patient	visit	54.60	3/01	4c
Drugs, expenditures on	yr	394	1999	30r
Health care purchases	yr	2048	1999	30r
Health insurance expenditures	yr	978	1999	30r
Hospital care, private room	day	355.00	3/01	4c
Hysterectomy, laproscopically-assisted, ave hospital/physician charges		15850	1998	76s
Hysterectomy, vaginal, ave hospital and physician charges		11810	1998	76s
Medicaid dispensing fee		3.69-15.45	1999	87s

Decatur, IL - continued

Item	Per	Value	Date	Ref.
Health Care - continued				
Medical services expenditures	yr	554	1999	30r
Medical supplies, expenditures on	yr	122	1999	30r
Plastic surgery, breast augmentation		3184	2000	7r
Plastic surgery, breast lift		3585	2000	7r
Plastic surgery, facelift		4999	2000	7r
Plastic surgery, hair transplantation		3105	2000	7r
Plastic surgery, lip augmentation		1290	2000	7r
Plastic surgery, lower body lift		8135	2000	7r
Plastic surgery, thigh lift		3839	2000	7r
Household Goods				
Dishwashing powder, Cascade	50 oz	2.47	3/01	4c
Floor coverings, expenditures on	yr	52	1999	30r
Furniture, expenditures on	yr	344	1999	30r
Household furnishings and equipment purchases	yr	1475	1999	30r
Household textiles, expenditures on	yr	109	1999	30r
Laundry and cleaning supplies, expenditures on	yr	134	1999	30r
Tissues, facial, Kleenex brand	175	1.14	3/01	4c
Housing				
Housing, ACCRA Index		90.20	3/01	4c
Home price, existing, ave		144400	10/00	90r
Home value, median		183000	2001	53s
House, 2400 sq ft, 8000 sq ft lot, new, urban,	total	191000	3/01	4c
House payment, principal and interest, 25% down payment	mos	968	3/01	4c
Household operation expenditures	yr	542	1999	30r
Housekeeping supplies purchases	yr	508	1999	30r
Lodging expenditures	yr	430	1999	30r
Maintenance, repairs, insurance expenditures	yr	853	1999	30r
Monthly rental value of owned home	mos	547	1999	30r
Owned dwellings, expenditures own	yr	4282	1999	30r
Rent expenditures	yr	1558	1999	30r
Rent, apartment, 2 br, 1 1/2-2 baths, unfurn, 950 sq ft, water	mos	525	3/01	4c
Rental unit, 1 bedroom, with utilities	mos	357	4/01	41c
Rental unit, 2 bedroom, with utilities	mos	459	4/01	41c
Rental unit, 3 bedroom, with utilities	mos	620	4/01	41c
Rental unit, 4 bedroom, with utilities	mos	642	4/01	41c
Shelter, expenditures on	yr	6270	1999	30r
Insurance and Pensions				
Life and other personal insurance purchases	yr	387	1999	30r
Pensions and Social Security, expenditures on	yr	2968	1999	30r
Legal Fees				
Divorce, filing fee		100.00-150.00	4/01	35s
Driver's license fee	renew	20.00	1999	48s
Driver's license fee	orig	10.00	1999	48s
Personal Goods				
Personal care products and services purchases	yr	385	1999	30r
Shampoo, Alberto VO5	15 oz	0.95	3/01	4c
Toothpaste, Crest or Colgate	6-7 oz	2.11	3/01	4c
Personal Services				
Dry cleaning, man's 2-pc suit		8.81	3/01	4c
Man's haircut, barbershop, no styling		9.30	3/01	4c
Personal services, household, expenditures on	yr	300	1999	30r
Woman's shampoo, trim, blow-dry, no style-change		22.80	3/01	4c
Pets				
Pets, toys, and playground equipment, expenditures on	yr	375	1999	30r

Values are in dollars or fractions of dollars. In the column headed *Ref*, references are shown to sources. Each reference is followed by a letter. These refer to the geographical level for which data were reported: s=State, r=Region, and c=City or metro. The abbreviation *ex* is used to mean *except* or *excluding*; *exp* stands for expenditures. For other abbreviations and further explanations, please see the Introduction.

Decatur, IL - continued

Item	Per	Value	Date	Ref.
Restaurant Food				
Chicken, fried, thigh and drumstick, KFC/ Church's		2.59	3/01	4c
Hamburger with cheese, McDonald's	1/4 lb	1.90	3/01	4c
Pizza, Pizza Hut or Pizza Inn	11-12 in	9.99	3/01	4c
Taxes				
Federal income taxes paid	yr	2326	1999	30r
Personal taxes, expenditures on	yr	3223	1999	30r
Property taxes paid	yr	1152	1999	30r
State and local income taxes paid	yr	753	1999	30r
Transportation				
Transportation, ACCRA Index		102.70	3/01	4c
Cars and trucks, new, expenditures on	yr	1280	1999	30r
Cars and trucks, used, expenditures on	yr	1763	1999	30r
Diesel at the pump	gal	1.33	10/99	73s
Gasoline and motor oil purchases	yr	1036	1999	30r
Gasoline before-tax price (cents)	gal	112.70	10/00	43s
Maintenance and repair expenditures	yr	594	1999	30r
Public transportation, expenditures on	yr	341	1999	30r
Tire balance, computer or spin balance, front	wheel	7.40	3/01	4c
Transportation purchases	yr	6617	1999	30r
Vehicle expenses, miscellaneous, purchases	yr	2159	1999	30r
Vehicle insurance payments	yr	701	1999	30r
Vehicle purchases (net outlay)	yr	3081	1999	30r
Vehicle rental, lease expenditures	yr	536	1999	30r
Utilities				
Utilities, ACCRA Index		93.80	3/01	4c
Electrical bill, average	mos	63.08	9/00	9s
Electricity, expenditures on	yr	841	1999	30r
Electricity, summer, 250 KWh	mos	33.85	2/96	97c
Electricity, summer, 500 KWh	mos	53.35	2/96	97c
Electricity, summer, 750 KWh	mos	71.74	2/96	97c
Electricity, summer, 1000 KWh	mos	90.14	2/96	97c
Electricity and other, mixed, 2400 sq ft, new home	mos	65.46	3/01	4c
Electricity cost, average	KWh	6.49	9/00	9s
Utilities, fuels, and public services purchased	yr	2401	1999	30r
Water and other public services, expenditures on	yr	273	1999	30r
Weddings				
Wedding (national average cost)		19936	2000	33r
Wedding (regional average total cost)		16195	1997	110r
Attendants' gifts		321	1998	33r
Bridal attendants' apparel (5 persons)		824	2000	33r
Bride's headpiece/veil		173	1998	33r
Bride's wedding dress		859	1998	33r
Clergy, religious facility fee		242	1998	33r
Engagement ring		3177	1998	33r
Flowers		789	1998	33r
Groom's formalwear rental		99	2000	33r
Limousine		410	1998	33r
Marriage license cost		15.00-20.00	4/01	35s
Men's formalwear (ushers, best man)		469	2000	33r
Mother of bride apparel		241	2000	33r
Music		866	1998	33r
Photography and videography		1368	1998	33r
Rehearsal dinner		728	1998	33r
Wedding invitations and announcements		341	1998	33r
Wedding reception		7968	2000	33r
Wedding rings (bride and groom)		1060	1998	33r

Denver, CO

Item	Per	Value	Date	Ref.
Composite, ACCRA index		109.60	3/01	4c
Alcoholic Beverages				
Alcoholic beverage purchases	yr	490	1999	30c
Beer, Heineken, 12-oz, ex deposit	6	6.96	3/01	4c
J & B Scotch	750-ml	20.13	3/01	4c
Wine, Livingston or Gallo, Chablis blanc	1.5 liter	5.79	3/01	4c

Denver, CO - continued

Item	Per	Value	Date	Ref.
Appliances				
Appliance repair, service call, washing machine	min lab chg	42.15	3/01	4c
Banking and Money				
Mortgage rate, incl. points and orig. fee, 30-yr. conv. fixed or ARM	mos	6.71	3/01	4c
Business Expenses				
Business travel, car rental	day	61	2001	3c
Business travel, food	day	54	2001	3c
Business travel, hotel	day	112	2001	3c
Medical office space cost	sq ft	114.10	2001	31c
Office space, 2-4 storey building	sq ft	99.96	2001	31c
Office space, 5-10 storey building	sq ft	88.30	2001	31c
Office space, 11-20 storey building	sq ft	84.87	2001	31c
Office space, central business district, Class A	sq ft	23.15	3/99	74c
Charity				
Cash contributions, expenditures	yr	970	1999	30c
Clothing				
Apparel and services purchases	yr	1958	1999	30c
Boys' brief, cotton	3	4.41	3/01	4c
Shirt, man's dress shirt		25.24	3/01	4c
Slacks, man's "No Wrinkles" khaki		36.19	3/01	4c
Communications				
Cable modem installation, AT&T-BIS		150.00	6/99	103s
Cable modem rate, cable subscriber, AT&T-BIS	mos	39.95	6/99	103s
Newspaper subscription, daily and Sunday delivery	mos	10.67	3/01	4c
Phone line, single, business, field visit	inst.	70.00	12/97	17s
Phone line, single, business, no field visit	inst.	70.00	12/97	17s
Phone line, single, residence, field visit	inst.	35.00	12/97	17s
Phone line, single, residence, no field visit	inst.	35.00	12/97	17s
Postal rate, express mail, up to half-pound		12.45	7/01	108r
Postal rate, letter, first class, first ounce		0.34	7/01	108r
Postal rate, letter, two ounces		0.57	7/01	108r
Postal rate, post card		0.21	7/01	108r
Postal rate, priority mail, two pounds		3.95	7/01	108r
Postal rate, priority mail, up to one pound		3.50	7/01	108r
Telephone bill, business, basic rate	mos	37.31	18c	
Telephone bill, family of three	mos	22.08	3/01	4c
Telephone bill, residential, basic rate	mos	14.87	12/97	18c
Education				
Board, 4-year private college/university	yr	2750	1996	38s
Board, 4-year public college/university	yr	2564	1996	38s
Education expenditures	yr	632	1999	30c
Room, 4-year private college/university	yr	2574	1996	38s
Room, 4-year public college/university	yr	2000	1996	38s
Total cost, 4-year private college/university	yr	17120	1996	38s
Total cost, 4-year public college/university	yr	7037	1996	38s
Tuition, 2-year public college/university, in state	yr	1340	1996	38s
Tuition, 4-year private college/university, in state	yr	11796	1996	38s
Tuition, 4-year public college/university	yr	2473	1996	38s
Energy and Fuels				
Energy, combined forms, 2400 sq ft	mos	126.85	3/01	4c
Energy, exc. electricity, 2400 sq ft	mos	80.43	3/01	4c
Gas, cooking, winter, 10 therms	mos	10.66	2/96	98c
Gas, cooking, winter, 30 therms	mos	17.91	2/96	98c
Gas, cooking, winter, 50 therms	mos	25.28	2/96	98c
Gas, heating, winter, average use	mos	57.85	2/96	98c
Gas, natural, commercial rate	1000 cf	6.42	11/00	88s
Gas, regular unleaded, cash, self-service	gal	1.46	3/01	4c
Entertainment				
Bowling, Saturday evening rate	line	3.72	3/01	4c
Entertainment purchases	yr	2570	1999	30c
Monopoly game, Parker Brothers', No. 9	game	9.55	3/01	4c
Movie, first-run, Saturday, evening	adm.	7.64	3/01	4c

Values are in dollars or fractions of dollars. In the column headed *Ref*, references are shown to sources. Each reference is followed by a letter. These refer to the geographical level for which data were reported: s=State, r=Region, and c=City or metro. The abbreviation *ex* is used to mean *except* or *excluding*; *exp* stands for *expenditures*. For other abbreviations and further explanations, please see the Introduction.

Denver, CO - continued

Item	Per	Value	Date	Ref.
Entertainment				
Reading purchases	yr	234	1999	30c
Tennis balls, yellow, Wilson or Penn, 3	can	2.26	3/01	4c
Funerals				
Total cost of funeral		5401.08	1/99	78r
Acknowledgement cards		33.64	1/99	78r
Casket		2170.43	1/99	78r
Cosmetology, hair, other preparation		136.32	1/99	78r
Embalming		319.13	1/99	78r
Funeral at funeral home		370.21	1/99	78r
Hearse (local)		161.04	1/99	78r
Professional service charges		963.15	1/99	78r
Service car/van		133.99	1/99	78r
Transfer of remains to funeral home		159.82	1/99	78r
Vault		778.07	1/99	78r
Visitation/viewing		175.28	1/99	78r
Groceries				
Groceries, ACCRA Index		114.90	3/01	4c
Antibiotic ointment, Polysporin	0.5 oz	5.49	3/01	4c
Baby food, strained vegetables or fruit, lowest price	4-4.5 oz	0.49	3/01	4c
Bacon	lb	3.99	5/99	8s
Bananas	lb	0.54	3/01	4c
Beef or hamburger, ground	lb	2.00	3/01	4c
Bread, white	loaf	1.08	3/01	4c
Bread, white, 20 oz loaf		0.64	5/99	8s
Cheddar cheese, mild	lb	3.59	5/99	8s
Cheerios, 10 oz box		2.99	5/99	8s
Cheese, Kraft grated Parmesan	8 oz	4.04	3/01	4c
Chicken, whole fryer	lb	0.89	3/01	4c
Cigarettes, Winston, Kings	carton	28.96	3/01	4c
Coffee, vacuum-packed	13 oz	3.75	3/01	4c
Corn Flakes, Kellogg's or Post Toasties	18 oz	2.91	3/01	4c
Corn oil, Mazola, 32 oz		2.75	5/99	8s
Corn, frozen, whole kernel, lowest price	16 oz	1.40	3/01	4c
Dairy product purchases	yr	318	1999	30c
Eggs, Grade A or AA	dozen	1.29	3/01	4c
Flour, all purpose	5 lb	1.69	5/99	8s
Food (excl fruit and vegetables), eaten at home, purchases	yr	1012	1999	30c
Food purchases	yr	5172	1999	30c
Food purchases, eaten away from home	yr	2378	1999	30c
Food purchases, food eaten at home	yr	2793	1999	30c
Fruit and vegetable purchases	yr	439	1999	30c
Grade A large eggs	doz	1.59	5/99	8s
Ground chuck	lb	1.99	5/99	8s
Lettuce, iceberg	head	1.27	3/01	4c
Margarine, Blue Bonnet or Parkay, stick	lb	0.72	3/01	4c
Mayonnaise, Kraft, 32 oz		2.50	5/99	8s
Milk, whole	1/2 gal	1.96	3/01	4c
Orange juice, Minute Maid frozen	12 oz	1.90	3/01	4c
Peaches, halves or slices, Hunt's, Del Monte, or Libby's	29 oz	2.19	3/01	4c
Peas, green, Del Monte or Green Giant	15 oz	0.90	3/01	4c
Potatoes, russet	5 lb	1.79	5/99	8s
Potatoes, white or red	10 lb	2.76	3/01	4c
Red Delicious apples	lb	1.39	5/99	8s
Sausage, Jimmy Dean/Owens pork	lb	4.35	3/01	4c
Shortening, vegetable, Crisco	3 lb	3.14	3/01	4c
Sirloin tip roast	lb	3.99	5/99	8s
Soft drink, Coca Cola, ex deposit	2 liter	1.22	3/01	4c
Steak, T-bone	lb	6.91	3/01	4c
Sugar, cane or beet	4 lbs	1.58	3/01	4c
Tobacco products and smoking supplies purchases	yr	288	1999	30c
Tomatoes, Hunt's or Del Monte	14.5 oz	1.00	3/01	4c
Tuna, chunk, light	6 oz	0.87	3/01	4c
Vegetable oil, Crisco, 32 oz		1.89	5/99	8s
Whole fryer	lb	1.99	5/99	8s
Whole milk	gal	0.89	5/99	8s

Denver, CO - continued

Item	Per	Value	Date	Ref.
Goods and Services				
Miscellaneous goods and services, ACCRA Index		98.80	3/01	4c
Hunting license	yr	15.25	4/01	34s
Health Care				
Health care, ACCRA Index		127.10	3/01	4c
Cardiac catheterization, ave hospital/ physician charges		17910	1998	77s
Childbirth, Cesarean delivery		11587	1997	13r
Childbirth, vaginal delivery		6725	1997	13r
Dentist's fee, adult teeth cleaning and periodic oral exam	visit	94.67	3/01	4c
Doctor's fee, routine exam, established patient	visit	71.20	3/01	4c
Health care purchases	yr	1915	1999	30c
Home health care aide cost, licensed agency	hour	22	2000	82c
Hospital care, private room	day	705.00	3/01	4c
Hysterectomy, laproscopically-assisted, ave hospital/physician charges		16210	1998	76s
Hysterectomy, vaginal, ave hospital and physician charges		11690	1998	76s
Medicaid dispensing fee		4.08	1999	87s
Nursing home costs, private room	day	141	2000	82c
Nursing home stay, private room	day	141	2000	83c
Household Goods				
Dishwashing powder, Cascade	50 oz	3.89	3/01	4c
Household furnishings and equipment purchases	yr	2147	1999	30c
Tissues, facial, Kleenex brand	175	1.40	3/01	4c
Housing				
Housing, ACCRA Index		118.00	3/01	4c
Condominium ave price		137716	3/01	50c
Home, 2200 sq ft, 4-br, 2-bath, 2-car garage, average		244675	2000	47c
Home price, single family, ave		250210	9/00	92c
Home value, median		173000	2001	53s
House, 2400 sq ft, 8000 sq ft lot, new, urban, utilities	total	245924	3/01	4c
House payment, principal and interest, 25% down payment	mos	1191	3/01	4c
Household operation expenditures	yr	860	1999	30c
Housekeeping supplies purchases	yr	482	1999	30c
Housing, expenditures on	yr	15415	1999	30c
Owned dwellings, expenditures own	yr	6118	1999	30c
Rent expenditures	yr	2296	1999	30c
Rent, apartment, 2 br, 1 1/2-2 baths, unfurn, 950 sq ft, water	mos	886	3/01	4c
Rental unit, 1 bedroom, with utilities	mos	575	4/01	41c
Rental unit, 2 bedroom, with utilities	mos	765	4/01	41c
Rental unit, 3 bedroom, with utilities	mos	1062	4/01	41c
Rental unit, 4 bedroom, with utilities	mos	1254	4/01	41c
Shelter, expenditures on	yr	9726	1999	30c
Single-family home ave price		228887	3/01	50c
Insurance and Pensions				
Life and other personal insurance purchases	yr	427	1999	30c
Pensions and Social Security, expenditures on	yr	4363	1999	30c
Personal insurance and pensions, expenditures on	yr	4791	1999	30c
Legal Fees				
Divorce, filing fee		65.00	4/01	35s
Driver's license fee	orig	15.00	1999	48s
Driver's license fee	renew	15.00	1999	48s
Personal Goods				
Personal care products and services purchases	yr	419	1999	30c
Shampoo, Alberto VO5	15 oz	1.24	3/01	4c
Toothpaste, Crest or Colgate	6-7 oz	2.47	3/01	4c

Values are in dollars or fractions of dollars. In the column headed *Ref*, references are shown to sources. Each reference is followed by a letter. These refer to the geographical level for which data were reported: s=State, r=Region, and c=City or metro. The abbreviation *ex* is used to mean *except* or *excluding*; *exp* stands for *expenditures*. For other abbreviations and further explanations, please see the Introduction.

Denver, CO - continued

Item	Per	Value	Date	Ref.
Personal Services				
Dry cleaning, man's 2-pc suit		8.34	3/01	4c
Man's haircut, barbershop, no styling		10.74	3/01	4c
Woman's shampoo, trim, blow-dry, no style-change		27.29	3/01	4c
Restaurant Food				
Chicken, fried, thigh and drumstick, KFC/Church's		2.34	3/01	4c
Hamburger with cheese, McDonald's	1/4 lb	2.15	3/01	4c
Pizza, Pizza Hut or Pizza Inn	11-12 in	8.99	3/01	4c
Transportation				
Transportation, ACCRA Index		109.70	3/01	4c
Bus fare, one-way	trip	0.75	2000	1c
Bus fare, to central business district	1-way	1.62	3/01	4c
Diesel at the pump	gal	1.28	10/99	73s
Gasoline and motor oil purchases	yr	1107	1999	30c
Gasoline before-tax price (cents)	gal	117.00	10/00	43s
Light rail transit fare, one-way	trip	0.75	2000	2c
Parking at airport, lowest rate	day	4.00	2000	46c
Public transportation, expenditures on	yr	631	1999	30c
Tire balance, computer or spin balance, front	wheel	8.43	3/01	4c
Transportation purchases	yr	8233	1999	30c
Vehicle expenses, miscellaneous, purchases	yr	3380	1999	30c
Vehicle purchases (net outlay)	yr	3116	1999	30c
Travel				
Hotel room	night	118.98	2/01	95s
Utilities				
Utilities, ACCRA Index		103.60	3/01	4c
Electrical bill, average	mos	47.17	9/00	9s
Electricity, summer, 250 KWh	mos	21.72	2/96	97c
Electricity, summer, 500 KWh	mos	38.37	2/96	97c
Electricity, summer, 750 KWh	mos	55.03	2/96	97c
Electricity, summer, 1000 KWh	mos	71.68	2/96	97c
Electricity and other, mixed, 2400 sq ft, new home	mos	46.42	3/01	4c
Electricity cost, average	KWh	5.90	9/00	9s
Water price	100 cf	1.03	2000	109c
Water price, dwelling unit	mos	20.19	2000	109c
Weddings				
Wedding (national average cost)		19936	2000	33r
Attendants' gifts		321	1998	33r
Bridal attendants' apparel (5 persons)		824	2000	33r
Bride's headpiece/veil		173	1998	33r
Bride's wedding dress		859	1998	33r
Clergy, religious facility fee		242	1998	33r
Engagement ring		3177	1998	33r
Flowers		789	1998	33r
Groom's formalwear rental		99	2000	33r
Limousine		410	1998	33r
Marriage license cost		20.00	4/01	35s
Men's formalwear (ushers, best man)		469	2000	33r
Mother of bride apparel		241	2000	33r
Music		866	1998	33r
Photography and videography		1368	1998	33r
Rehearsal dinner		728	1998	33r
Wedding invitations and announcements		341	1998	33r
Wedding reception		7968	2000	33r
Wedding rings (bride and groom)		1060	1998	33r

Des Moines, IA

Item	Per	Value	Date	Ref.
Average annual expenditures	yr	35369	1999	30r
Composite, ACCRA index		99.40	3/01	4c
Alcoholic Beverages				
Alcoholic beverage purchases	yr	304	1999	30r
Beer, Heineken, 12-oz, ex deposit	6	6.49	3/01	4c
J & B Scotch	750-ml	24.22	3/01	4c
Malt beverages, all types, all sizes, any origin	16 oz	0.93	7/01	11r
Wine, Livingston or Gallo, Chablis blanc	1.5 liter	6.02	3/01	4c

Des Moines, IA - continued

Item	Per	Value	Date	Ref.
Alcoholic Beverages - continued				
Wine, red and white table, all sizes, any origin	liter	7.04	7/01	11r
Appliances				
Appliance repair, service call, washing machine	min lab chg	39.20	3/01	4c
Major appliances, expenditures on	yr	165	1999	30r
Small appliances, housewares, expenditures on	yr	90	1999	30r
Banking and Money				
Mortgage interest and charges paid	yr	2277	1999	30r
Mortgage principal paid on owned property	yr	1230	1999	30r
Mortgage rate, incl. points and orig. fee, 30-yr. conv. fixed or ARM	mos	7.00	3/01	4c
Vehicle finance charges paid	yr	328	1999	30r
Business Expenses				
Business travel, car rental	day	55	2001	3c
Business travel, food	day	36	2001	3c
Business travel, hotel	day	83	2001	3c
Charity				
Cash contributions, expenditures	yr	1126	1999	30r
Child Care				
Child raising cost, total, age 0-2	yr	7890	1999	60r
Child raising cost, total, age 3-5	yr	8130	1999	60r
Child raising cost, total, age 6-8	yr	8170	1999	60r
Child raising cost, total, age 9-11	yr	8190	1999	60r
Child raising cost, total, age 12-14	yr	8890	1999	60r
Child raising cost, total, age 15-17	yr	9050	1999	60r
Child's child care and education, age 0-2	yr	1240	1999	60r
Child's child care and education, age 3-5	yr	1370	1999	60r
Child's child care and education, age 6-8	yr	880	1999	60r
Child's child care and education, age 9-11	yr	570	1999	60r
Child's child care and education, age 12-14	yr	420	1999	60r
Child's child care and education, age 15-17	yr	720	1999	60r
Child's clothing, age 0-2	yr	410	1999	60r
Child's clothing, age 3-5	yr	400	1999	60r
Child's clothing, age 6-8	yr	450	1999	60r
Child's clothing, age 9-11	yr	500	1999	60r
Child's clothing, age 12-14	yr	840	1999	60r
Child's clothing, age 15-17	yr	740	1999	60r
Child's food, age 0-2	yr	960	1999	60r
Child's food, age 3-5	yr	1120	1999	60r
Child's food, age 6-8	yr	1430	1999	60r
Child's food, age 9-11	yr	1710	1999	60r
Child's food, age 12-14	yr	1710	1999	60r
Child's food, age 15-17	yr	1920	1999	60r
Child's health care, age 0-2	yr	520	1999	60r
Child's health care, age 3-5	yr	500	1999	60r
Child's health care, age 6-8	yr	570	1999	60r
Child's health care, age 9-11	yr	610	1999	60r
Child's health care, age 12-14	yr	630	1999	60r
Child's health care, age 15-17	yr	650	1999	60r
Child's housing, age 0-2	yr	2860	1999	60r
Child's housing, age 3-5	yr	2840	1999	60r
Child's housing, age 6-8	yr	2800	1999	60r
Child's housing, age 9-11	yr	2650	1999	60r
Child's housing, age 12-14	yr	2840	1999	60r
Child's housing, age 15-17	yr	2440	1999	60r
Child's personal care, reading, age 0-2	yr	880	1999	60r
Child's personal care, reading, age 3-5	yr	900	1999	60r
Child's personal care, reading, age 6-8	yr	930	1999	60r
Child's personal care, reading, age 9-11	yr	970	1999	60r
Child's personal care, reading, age 12-14	yr	1150	1999	60r
Child's personal care, reading, age 15-17	yr	920	1999	60r
Clothing				
Apparel and services purchases	yr	1607	1999	30r
Boys' brief, cotton	3	3.52	3/01	4c
Boys, 2 to 15, expenditures on	yr	91	1999	30r
Children under 2, expenditures on	yr	59	1999	30r
Footwear, expenditures on	yr	285	1999	30r

Values are in dollars or fractions of dollars. In the column headed *Ref*, references are shown to sources. Each reference is followed by a letter. These refer to the geographical level for which data were reported: s=State, r=Region, and c=City or metro. The abbreviation *ex* is used to mean *except* or *excluding*; *exp* stands for expenditures. For other abbreviations and further explanations, please see the Introduction.

Des Moines, IA - continued

Item	Per	Value	Date	Ref.
Clothing				
Girls, 2 to 15, expenditures on	yr	116	1999	30r
Men and boys, expenditures on	yr	433	1999	30r
Men, 16 and over, expenditures on	yr	341	1999	30r
Shirt, man's dress shirt		27.08	3/01	4c
Slacks, man's "No Wrinkles" khaki		41.71	3/01	4c
Women, 16 and over, expenditures on	yr	490	1999	30r
Communications				
Newspaper subscription, daily and Sunday delivery	mos	15.22	3/01	4c
Phone line, single, business, field visit	inst.	50.00	12/97	17s
Phone line, single, business, no field visit	inst.	50.00	12/97	17s
Phone line, single, residence, field visit	inst.	35.00	12/97	17s
Phone line, single, residence, no field visit	inst.	35.00	12/97	17s
Postage and stationery, expenditures on	yr	140	1999	30r
Postal rate, express mail, up to half-pound		12.45	7/01	108r
Postal rate, letter, first class, first ounce		0.34	7/01	108r
Postal rate, letter, two ounces		0.57	7/01	108r
Postal rate, post card		0.21	7/01	108r
Postal rate, priority mail, two pounds		3.95	7/01	108r
Postal rate, priority mail, up to one pound		3.50	7/01	108r
Telephone bill, business, basic rate	mos	32.15	12/97	18c
Telephone bill, family of three	mos	18.66	3/01	4c
Telephone bill, residential, basic rate	mos	13.05	12/97	18c
Telephone services, expenditures on	yr	830	1999	30r
Education				
Board, 4-year private college/university	yr	2138	1996	38s
Board, 4-year public college/university	yr	1688	1996	38s
Education expenditures	yr	583	1999	30r
Room, 4-year private college/university	yr	1864	1996	38s
Room, 4-year public college/university	yr	1693	1996	38s
Total cost, 4-year private college/university	yr	15934	1996	38s
Total cost, 4-year public college/university	yr	5945	1996	38s
Tuition, 2-year public college/university, in state	yr	1782	1996	38s
Tuition, 4-year private college/university, in state	yr	11932	1996	38s
Tuition, 4-year public college/university	yr	2565	1996	38s
Energy and Fuels				
Electricity	500 KWhs	46.59	7/01	11r
Energy, combined forms, 2400 sq ft	mos	175.05	3/01	4c
Energy, exc. electricity, 2400 sq ft	mos	112.14	3/01	4c
Fuel oil #2	gal	1.27	7/01	11r
Fuel oil and other fuels, expenditures on	yr	68	1999	30r
Gas, cooking, winter, 10 therms	mos	14.18	2/96	98c
Gas, cooking, winter, 30 therms	mos	25.05	2/96	98c
Gas, cooking, winter, 50 therms	mos	35.92	2/96	98c
Gas, heating, winter, average use	mos	128.31	2/96	98c
Gas, natural, commercial rate	1000 cf	7.18	11/00	88s
Gas, regular unleaded, cash, self-service	gal	1.33	3/01	4c
Gasoline, unleaded midgrade	gal	1.79	7/01	11r
Gasoline, unleaded premium	gal	1.86	7/01	11r
Gasoline, unleaded regular	gal	1.58	7/01	11r
Natural gas, expenditures on	yr	389	1999	30r
Utility (piped) gas, therm		0.81	7/01	11r
Utility (piped) gas, 40 therms		38.01	7/01	11r
Utility (piped) gas, 100 therms		81.75	7/01	11r
Entertainment				
Bowling, Saturday evening rate	line	3.02	3/01	4c
Entertainment purchases	yr	1984	1999	30r
Fees and admissions paid	yr	444	1999	30r
Monopoly game, Parker Brothers', No. 9	game	9.77	3/01	4c
Movie, first-run, Saturday, evening	adm.	6.40	3/01	4c
Television, radios, sound equipment, expenditures on	yr	580	1999	30r
Tennis balls, yellow, Wilson or Penn, 3	can	2.29	3/01	4c
Funerals				
Cosmetology, hair, other preparation		178.32	1/99	78r
Embalming		408.19	1/99	78r

Des Moines, IA - continued

Item	Per	Value	Date	Ref.
Funerals - continued				
Funeral at funeral home		362.13	1/99	78r
Professional service charges		1375.51	1/99	78r
Transfer of remains to funeral home		155.92	1/99	78r
Visitation/viewing		294.38	1/99	78r
Groceries				
Groceries, ACCRA Index		93.20	3/01	4c
Antibiotic ointment, Polysporin	0.5 oz	5.44	3/01	4c
Baby food, strained vegetables or fruit, lowest price	4-4.5 oz	0.43	3/01	4c
Bacon, sliced	lb	3.15	7/01	11r
Bakery products, expenditures on	yr	281	1999	30r
Bananas	lb	0.45	3/01	4c
Bananas	lb	0.48	7/01	11r
Beans, dried, any type, all sizes	lb	0.61	7/01	11r
Beef for stew, boneless	lb	3.08	7/01	11r
Beef or hamburger, ground	lb	1.61	3/01	4c
Beef, expenditures on	yr	217	1999	30r
Bologna, all beef or mixed	lb	2.52	7/01	11r
Bread, white	loaf	0.73	3/01	4c
Bread, white, pan	lb	1.06	7/01	11r
Broccoli	lb	0.91	7/01	11r
Butter, salted, grade AA, stick	lb	3.04	7/01	11r
Butter, yoghurt, cheese, etc, expenditures on	yr	183	1999	30r
Cereals and bakery product purchases	yr	430	1999	30r
Cereals and cereal products, expenditures on	yr	149	1999	30r
Cheese, Kraft grated Parmesan	8 oz	3.85	3/01	4c
Chicken, fresh, whole	lb	1.07	7/01	11r
Chicken, whole fryer	lb	0.83	3/01	4c
Chops, boneless,	lb	3.64	7/01	11r
Chuck roast, U.S. choice, boneless	lb	2.47	7/01	11r
Cigarettes, Winston, Kings	carton	28.72	3/01	4c
Coffee, 100%, ground roast, all sizes	lb	2.69	7/01	11r
Coffee, vacuum-packed	13 oz	2.65	3/01	4c
Cookies, chocolate chip	lb	2.87	7/01	11r
Corn Flakes, Kellogg's or Post Toasties	18 oz	2.01	3/01	4c
Corn, frozen, whole kernel, lowest price	16 oz	1.06	3/01	4c
Dairy product purchases	yr	304	1999	30r
Eggs, expenditures on	yr	26	1999	30r
Eggs, Grade A or AA	dozen	1.11	3/01	4c
Eggs, grade A, large	dozen	0.88	7/01	11r
Fats and oils, expenditures on	yr	75	1999	30r
Fish and seafood, expenditures on	yr	72	1999	30r
Food (excl fruit and vegetables), eaten at home, purchases	yr	887	1999	30r
Food cooked on trips, expenditures on	yr	44	1999	30r
Food purchases	yr	4802	1999	30r
Food purchases, eaten away from home	yr	2069	1999	30r
Food purchases, food eaten at home	yr	2733	1999	30r
Fresh fruits, expenditures on	yr	138	1999	30r
Fresh milk and cream, expenditures on	yr	120	1999	30r
Fresh vegetables, expenditures on	yr	126	1999	30r
Grapefruit	lb	0.66	7/01	11r
Grapes, Thompson, seedless	lb	1.64	7/01	11r
Ground beef, 100% beef	lb	1.64	7/01	11r
Ground beef, lean and extra lean	lb	2.16	7/01	11r
Ground chuck, 100% beef	lb	2.13	7/01	11r
Ham, boneless, excl canned	lb	2.62	7/01	11r
Ice cream, prepackaged, bulk, regular	1/2 gal	3.35	7/01	11r
Lemons	lb	1.19	7/01	11r
Lettuce, iceberg	head	1.09	3/01	4c
Lettuce, iceberg	lb	0.73	7/01	11r
Margarine, Blue Bonnet or Parkay, stick	lb	0.49	3/01	4c
Margarine, soft, tubs	lb	0.89	7/01	11r
Meats, poultry, fish, and egg purchases	yr	671	1999	30r
Milk, fresh, whole, fortified	gal	2.71	7/01	11r
Milk, whole	1/2 gal	1.43	3/01	4c
Nonalcoholic beverages, expenditures on	yr	239	1999	30r
Orange juice, Minute Maid frozen	12 oz	1.72	3/01	4c
Oranges, Navel	lb	0.80	7/01	11r
Oranges, Valencia	lb	0.66	7/01	11r

Values are in dollars or fractions of dollars. In the column headed *Ref*, references are shown to sources. Each reference is followed by a letter. These refer to the geographical level for which data were reported: s=State, r=Region, and c=City or metro. The abbreviation *ex* is used to mean *except* or *excluding*; *exp* stands for *expenditures*. For other abbreviations and further explanations, please see the Introduction.

Des Moines, IA - continued

Item	Per	Value	Date	Ref.
Groceries				
Peaches, halves or slices, Hunt's, Del Monte, or Libby's	29 oz	1.73	3/01	4c
Pears, Anjou	lb	0.93	7/01	11r
Peas, green, Del Monte or Green Giant	15 oz	0.75	3/01	4c
Pork chops, center cut, bone-in	lb	3.63	7/01	11r
Pork, expenditures on	yr	150	1999	30r
Potato chips	16 oz	3.52	7/01	11r
Potatoes, frozen, french fried	lb	1.08	7/01	11r
Potatoes, white or red	10 lb	2.39	3/01	4c
Potatoes, white, all types	lb	0.33	7/01	11r
Poultry, expenditures on	yr	108	1999	30r
Processed fruits, expenditures on	yr	98	1999	30r
Processed vegetables, expenditures on	yr	80	1999	30r
Round roast, U.S. choice, boneless	lb	3.07	7/01	11r
Round steak, graded and ungraded, excl U.S. prime and choice	lb	3.41	7/01	11r
Sausage, Jimmy Dean/Owens pork	lb	3.80	3/01	4c
Shortening, vegetable oil blends	lb	1.13	7/01	11r
Shortening, vegetable, Crisco	3 lb	2.83	3/01	4c
Soft drink, Coca Cola, ex deposit	2 liter	1.03	3/01	4c
Spaghetti and macaroni	lb	0.80	7/01	11r
Steak, round, U.S. choice, boneless	lb	3.23	7/01	11r
Steak, T-bone	lb	6.24	3/01	4c
Steak, T-bone, U.S. choice, bone-in	lb	6.68	7/01	11r
Strawberries, dry pint	12 oz	1.32	7/01	11r
Sugar and other sweets, expenditures on	yr	114	1999	30r
Sugar, cane or beet	4 lbs	1.47	3/01	4c
Sugar, white, 33-80 ounce package	lb	0.42	7/01	11r
Sugar, white, all sizes	lb	0.43	7/01	11r
Tobacco products and smoking supplies purchases	yr	331	1999	30r
Tomatoes, field grown	lb	1.46	7/01	11r
Tomatoes, Hunt's or Del Monte	14.5 oz	0.88	3/01	4c
Tuna, chunk, light	6 oz	0.38	3/01	4c
Tuna, light, chunk	lb	1.80	7/01	11r
Turkey, frozen, whole	lb	1.15	7/01	11r
Goods and Services				
Miscellaneous goods and services, ACCRA Index		101.10	3/01	4c
B&B Japanese maple (acer japonicum)	gal	29.99-169.99	4/00	93r
Boxwood (buxus)	2 gal	18.99-39.99	4/00	93r
Daylilly (hemerocallis)	gal	4.99-25.00	4/00	93r
Flat of annuals		11.98-24.99	4/00	93r
Fountain grass (pennisetum)	gal	5.98-12.98	4/00	93r
Hanging basket (10 in)		12.99-27.99	4/00	93r
Hardy geranium (geranium)	gal	7.99-9.99	4/00	93r
Hosta (hosta)	gal	6.00-25.00	4/00	93r
Lilac (syrubga vulgaris)	2 gal	14.99-24.99	4/00	93r
Miscellaneous purchases	yr	865	1999	30r
Rhododendron (rhododendron)	2 gal	23.98-42.99	4/00	93r
Sage (salvia)	gal	6.00-9.99	4/00	93r
Wintercreeper euonymus (euonymus fortunei)	2 gal	16.00-169.99	4/00	93r
Hunting license	yr	16.00	4/01	34s
Health Care				
Health care, ACCRA Index		106.10	3/01	4c
Cardiac catheterization, ave hospital/ physician charges		8810	1998	77s
Childbirth, Cesarean delivery		10722	1997	13r
Childbirth, vaginal delivery		6223	1997	13r

Des Moines, IA - continued

Item	Per	Value	Date	Ref.
Health Care - continued				
Dentist's fee, adult teeth cleaning and periodic oral exam	visit	70.40	3/01	4c
Doctor's fee, routine exam, established patient	visit	65.50	3/01	4c
Drugs, expenditures on	yr	394	1999	30r
Health care purchases	yr	2048	1999	30r
Health insurance expenditures	yr	978	1999	30r
Home health care aide cost, licensed agency	hour	18	2000	82c
Hospital care, private room	day	544.20	3/01	4c
Hysterectomy, laproscopically-assisted, ave hospital/physician charges		8620	1998	76s
Hysterectomy, vaginal, ave hospital and physician charges		6630	1998	76s
Medicaid dispensing fee		4.10-6.38	1999	87s
Medical services expenditures	yr	554	1999	30r
Medical supplies, expenditures on	yr	122	1999	30r
Nursing home costs, private room	day	102	2000	82c
Nursing home stay, private room	day	102	2000	83c
Plastic surgery, breast augmentation		3184	2000	7r
Plastic surgery, breast lift		3585	2000	7r
Plastic surgery, facelift		4999	2000	7r
Plastic surgery, hair transplantation		3105	2000	7r
Plastic surgery, lip augmentation		1290	2000	7r
Plastic surgery, lower body lift		8135	2000	7r
Plastic surgery, thigh lift		3839	2000	7r
Household Goods				
Dishwashing powder, Cascade	50 oz	3.53	3/01	4c
Floor coverings, expenditures on	yr	52	1999	30r
Furniture, expenditures on	yr	344	1999	30r
Household furnishings and equipment purchases	yr	1475	1999	30r
Household textiles, expenditures on	yr	109	1999	30r
Laundry and cleaning supplies, expenditures on	yr	134	1999	30r
Tissues, facial, Kleenex brand	175	1.19	3/01	4c
Housing				
Housing, ACCRA Index		91.10	3/01	4c
Home, 2200 sq ft, 4-br, 2-bath, 2-car garage, average		182075	2000	47c
Home price, existing, ave		144400	10/00	90r
Home value, median		100000	2001	53s
House, 2400 sq ft, 8000 sq ft lot, new, urban, utilities	total	187400	3/01	4c
House payment, principal and interest, 25% down payment	mos	935	3/01	4c
Household operation expenditures	yr	542	1999	30r
Housekeeping supplies purchases	yr	508	1999	30r
Lodging expenditures	yr	430	1999	30r
Maintenance, repairs, insurance expenditures	yr	853	1999	30r
Monthly rental value of owned home	mos	547	1999	30r
Owned dwellings, expenditures own	yr	4282	1999	30r
Rent expenditures	yr	1558	1999	30r
Rent, apartment, 2 br, 1 1/2-2 baths, unfurn, 950 sq ft, water	mos	641	3/01	4c
Rental unit, 1 bedroom, with utilities	mos	458	4/01	41c
Rental unit, 2 bedroom, with utilities	mos	565	4/01	41c
Rental unit, 3 bedroom, with utilities	mos	733	4/01	41c
Rental unit, 4 bedroom, with utilities	mos	770	4/01	41c
Shelter, expenditures on	yr	6270	1999	30r
Insurance and Pensions				
Auto insurance premium	yr	520.76	1999	57s
Life and other personal insurance purchases	yr	387	1999	30r
Pensions and Social Security, expenditures on	yr	2968	1999	30r
Legal Fees				
Divorce, filing fee		110.00	4/01	35s
Driver's license fee	renew	16.00	1999	48s
Driver's license fee	orig	16.00	1999	48s

Values are in dollars or fractions of dollars. In the column headed *Ref*, references are shown to sources. Each reference is followed by a letter. These refer to the geographical level for which data were reported: s=State, r=Region, and c=City or metro. The abbreviation *ex* is used to mean *except* or *excluding*; *exp* stands for *expenditures*. For other abbreviations and further explanations, please see the Introduction.

Des Moines, IA - continued

Item	Per	Value	Date	Ref.
Personal Goods				
Personal care products and services purchases	yr	385	1999	30r
Shampoo, Alberto VO5	15 oz	1.18	3/01	4c
Toothpaste, Crest or Colgate	6-7 oz	2.12	3/01	4c
Personal Services				
Dry cleaning, man's 2-pc suit		8.61	3/01	4c
Man's haircut, barbershop, no styling		10.49	3/01	4c
Personal services, household, expenditures on	yr	300	1999	30r
Woman's shampoo, trim, blow-dry, no style-change		25.38	3/01	4c
Pets				
Pets, toys, and playground equipment, expenditures on	yr	375	1999	30r
Restaurant Food				
Chicken, fried, thigh and drumstick, KFC/Church's		2.69	3/01	4c
Hamburger with cheese, McDonald's	1/4 lb	2.21	3/01	4c
Pizza, Pizza Hut or Pizza Inn	11-12 in	8.99	3/01	4c
Taxes				
Federal income taxes paid	yr	2326	1999	30r
Personal taxes, expenditures on	yr	3223	1999	30r
Property taxes paid	yr	1152	1999	30r
State and local income taxes paid	yr	753	1999	30r
Transportation				
Transportation, ACCRA Index		95.10	3/01	4c
Auto operation, annual cost		6197	2000	27c
Bus fare, one-way	trip	1.00	2000	1c
Bus fare, to central business district	1-way	1.00	3/01	4c
Cars and trucks, new, expenditures on	yr	1280	1999	30r
Cars and trucks, used, expenditures on	yr	1763	1999	30r
Diesel at the pump	gal	1.25	10/99	73s
Gasoline and motor oil purchases	yr	1036	1999	30r
Gasoline before-tax price (cents)	gal	112.30	10/00	43s
Maintenance and repair expenditures	yr	594	1999	30r
Public transportation, expenditures on	yr	341	1999	30r
Tire balance, computer or spin balance, front	wheel	7.66	3/01	4c
Transportation purchases	yr	6617	1999	30r
Vehicle expenses, miscellaneous, purchases	yr	2159	1999	30r
Vehicle insurance payments	yr	701	1999	30r
Vehicle purchases (net outlay)	yr	3081	1999	30r
Vehicle rental, lease expenditures	yr	536	1999	30r
Utilities				
Utilities, ACCRA Index		135.50	3/01	4c
Electrical bill, average	mos	67.25	9/00	9s
Electricity, expenditures on	yr	841	1999	30r
Electricity, summer, 250 KWh	mos	30.65	2/96	97c
Electricity, summer, 500 KWh	mos	52.72	2/96	97c
Electricity, summer, 750 KWh	mos	74.79	2/96	97c
Electricity, summer, 1000 KWh	mos	96.86	2/96	97c
Electricity and other, mixed, 2400 sq ft, new home	mos	62.91	3/01	4c
Electricity cost, average	KWh	5.90	9/00	9s
Utilities, fuels, and public services purchased	yr	2401	1999	30r
Water and other public services, expenditures on	yr	273	1999	30r
Water price	100 cf	1.45	2000	109c
Water price, dwelling unit	mos	28.38	2000	109c
Weddings				
Wedding (national average cost)		19936	2000	33r
Wedding (regional average total cost)		16195	1997	110r
Attendants' gifts		321	1998	33r
Bridal attendants' apparel (5 persons)		824	2000	33r
Bride's headpiece/veil		173	1998	33r
Bride's wedding dress		859	1998	33r
Clergy, religious facility fee		242	1998	33r
Engagement ring		3177	1998	33r
Flowers		789	1998	33r

Des Moines, IA - continued

Item	Per	Value	Date	Ref.
Weddings - continued				
Groom's formalwear rental		99	2000	33r
Limousine		410	1998	33r
Marriage license cost		30.00	4/01	35s
Men's formalwear (ushers, best man)		469	2000	33r
Mother of bride apparel		241	2000	33r
Music		866	1998	33r
Photography and videography		1368	1998	33r
Rehearsal dinner		728	1998	33r
Wedding invitations and announcements		341	1998	33r
Wedding reception		7968	2000	33r
Wedding rings (bride and groom)		1060	1998	33r

Detroit, MI

Item	Per	Value	Date	Ref.
Average annual expenditures	yr	38120	1999	30c
Composite, ACCRA index		107.10	3/01	4c
Alcoholic Beverages				
Alcoholic beverage purchases	yr	346	1999	30c
Beer, Heineken, 12-oz, ex deposit	6	7.78	3/01	4c
J & B Scotch	750-ml	21.40	3/01	4c
Malt beverages, all types, all sizes, any origin	16 oz	0.93	7/01	11r
Wine, Livingston or Gallo, Chablis blanc	1.5 liter	5.35	3/01	4c
Wine, red and white table, all sizes, any origin	liter	7.04	7/01	11r
Appliances				
Appliance repair, service call, washing machine	min lab chg	37.29	3/01	4c
Major appliances, expenditures on	yr	165	1999	30r
Small appliances, housewares, expenditures on	yr	90	1999	30r
Banking and Money				
Mortgage interest and charges paid	yr	2277	1999	30r
Mortgage principal paid on owned property	yr	1230	1999	30r
Mortgage rate, incl. points and orig. fee, 30-yr. conv. fixed or ARM	mos	6.86	3/01	4c
Vehicle finance charges paid	yr	328	1999	30r
Business Expenses				
Business travel, car rental	day	56	2001	3c
Business travel, food	day	49	2001	3c
Business travel, hotel	day	99	2001	3c
Medical office space cost	sq ft	127.28	2001	31c
Office space, 2-4 storey building	sq ft	111.51	2001	31c
Office space, 5-10 storey building	sq ft	98.50	2001	31c
Office space, 11-20 storey building	sq ft	94.68	2001	31c
Office space, central business district, Class A	sq ft	23.68	3/99	74c
Charity				
Cash contributions, expenditures	yr	685	1999	30c
Child Care				
Child raising cost, total, age 0-2	yr	7890	1999	60r
Child raising cost, total, age 3-5	yr	8130	1999	60r
Child raising cost, total, age 6-8	yr	8170	1999	60r
Child raising cost, total, age 9-11	yr	8190	1999	60r
Child raising cost, total, age 12-14	yr	8890	1999	60r
Child raising cost, total, age 15-17	yr	9050	1999	60r
Child's child care and education, age 0-2	yr	1240	1999	60r
Child's child care and education, age 3-5	yr	1370	1999	60r
Child's child care and education, age 6-8	yr	880	1999	60r
Child's child care and education, age 9-11	yr	570	1999	60r
Child's child care and education, age 12-14	yr	420	1999	60r
Child's child care and education, age 15-17	yr	720	1999	60r
Child's clothing, age 0-2	yr	410	1999	60r
Child's clothing, age 3-5	yr	400	1999	60r
Child's clothing, age 6-8	yr	450	1999	60r
Child's clothing, age 9-11	yr	500	1999	60r
Child's clothing, age 12-14	yr	840	1999	60r
Child's clothing, age 15-17	yr	740	1999	60r
Child's food, age 0-2	yr	960	1999	60r

Values are in dollars or fractions of dollars. In the column headed *Ref*, references are shown to sources. Each reference is followed by a letter. These refer to the geographical level for which data were reported: s=State, r=Region, and c=City or metro. The abbreviation *ex* is used to mean *except* or *excluding*; *exp* stands for expenditures. For other abbreviations and further explanations, please see the Introduction.

Detroit, MI - continued

Item	Per	Value	Date	Ref.
Child Care				
Child's food, age 3-5	yr	1120	1999	60r
Child's food, age 6-8	yr	1430	1999	60r
Child's food, age 9-11	yr	1710	1999	60r
Child's food, age 12-14	yr	1710	1999	60r
Child's food, age 15-17	yr	1920	1999	60r
Child's health care, age 0-2	yr	520	1999	60r
Child's health care, age 3-5	yr	500	1999	60r
Child's health care, age 6-8	yr	570	1999	60r
Child's health care, age 9-11	yr	610	1999	60r
Child's health care, age 12-14	yr	630	1999	60r
Child's health care, age 15-17	yr	650	1999	60r
Child's housing, age 0-2	yr	2860	1999	60r
Child's housing, age 3-5	yr	2840	1999	60r
Child's housing, age 6-8	yr	2800	1999	60r
Child's housing, age 9-11	yr	2650	1999	60r
Child's housing, age 12-14	yr	2840	1999	60r
Child's housing, age 15-17	yr	2440	1999	60r
Child's personal care, reading, age 0-2	yr	880	1999	60r
Child's personal care, reading, age 3-5	yr	900	1999	60r
Child's personal care, reading, age 6-8	yr	930	1999	60r
Child's personal care, reading, age 9-11	yr	970	1999	60r
Child's personal care, reading, age 12-14	yr	1150	1999	60r
Child's personal care, reading, age 15-17	yr	920	1999	60r
Clothing				
Apparel and services purchases	yr	2056	1999	30c
Boys' brief, cotton	3	3.35	3/01	4c
Boys, 2 to 15, expenditures on	yr	91	1999	30r
Children under 2, expenditures on	yr	59	1999	30r
Footwear, expenditures on	yr	285	1999	30r
Girls, 2 to 15, expenditures on	yr	116	1999	30r
Men and boys, expenditures on	yr	433	1999	30r
Men, 16 and over, expenditures on	yr	341	1999	30r
Shirt, man's dress shirt		23.89	3/01	4c
Slacks, man's "No Wrinkles" khaki		29.19	3/01	4c
Women, 16 and over, expenditures on	yr	490	1999	30r
Communications				
Cable modem installation, Bresnan		99.95	6/99	103s
Cable modem installation, Comcast		95.00	6/99	103s
Cable modem installation, Media One		100.00	6/99	103s
Cable modem rate, cable subscriber, Bresnan	mos	39.95	6/99	103s
Cable modem rate, cable subscriber, Comcast	mos	39.95	6/99	103s
Cable modem rate, cable subscriber, Media One	mos	34.95-39.95	6/99	103s
Cable modem rate, non-cable subscriber, Bresnan	mos	49.95	6/99	103s
Cable modem rate, non-cable subscriber, Comcast	mos	49.95	6/99	103s
Cable modem rate, non-cable subscriber, Media One	mos	49.95	6/99	103s
Cellular phone service	mos	39.23	2001	25c
Newspaper subscription, daily and Sunday delivery	mos	11.96	3/01	4c
Phone line, single, business, field visit	inst.	42.00	12/97	17s
Phone line, single, business, no field visit	inst.	42.00	12/97	17s
Phone line, single, residence, field visit	inst.	42.00	12/97	17s
Phone line, single, residence, no field visit	inst.	42.00	12/97	17s
Postage and stationery, expenditures on	yr	140	1999	30r
Postal rate, express mail, up to half-pound		12.45	7/01	108r
Postal rate, letter, first class, first ounce		0.34	7/01	108r
Postal rate, letter, two ounces		0.57	7/01	108r
Postal rate, post card		0.21	7/01	108r
Postal rate, priority mail, two pounds		3.95	7/01	108r
Postal rate, priority mail, up to one pound		3.50	7/01	108r
Telephone bill, business, basic rate	mos	12.78	12/97	18c
Telephone bill, family of three	mos	24.74	3/01	4c
Telephone bill, residential, basic rate	mos	10.00	12/97	18c
Telephone services, expenditures on	yr	830	1999	30r

Detroit, MI - continued

Item	Per	Value	Date	Ref.
Education				
Board, 4-year private college/university	yr	2182	1996	38s
Board, 4-year public college/university	yr	2276	1996	38s
Education expenditures	yr	399	1999	30c
Room, 4-year private college/university	yr	1974	1996	38s
Room, 4-year public college/university	yr	2024	1996	38s
Total cost, 4-year private college/university	yr	13331	1996	38s
Total cost, 4-year public college/university	yr	8195	1996	38s
Tuition, 2-year public college/university, in state	yr	1529	1996	38s
Tuition, 4-year private college/university, in state	yr	9176	1996	38s
Tuition, 4-year public college/university	yr	3895	1996	38s
Energy and Fuels				
Electricity	500 KWhs	43.92	7/01	11c
Electricity	KWh	0.10	7/01	11c
Energy, combined forms, 2400 sq ft	mos	106.24	3/01	4c
Energy, exc. electricity, 2400 sq ft	mos	41.82	3/01	4c
Fuel oil #2	gal	1.27	7/01	11r
Fuel oil and other fuels, expenditures on	yr	68	1999	30r
Gas, cooking, winter, 10 therms	mos	11.48	2/96	98c
Gas, cooking, winter, 30 therms	mos	19.44	2/96	98c
Gas, cooking, winter, 50 therms	mos	27.41	2/96	98c
Gas, heating, winter, average use	mos	101.42	2/96	98c
Gas, natural, commercial rate	1000 cf	4.91	11/00	88s
Gas, regular unleaded, cash, self-service	gal	1.47	3/01	4c
Gasoline, all types	gal	1.78	7/01	11c
Gasoline, unleaded midgrade	gal	1.83	7/01	11c
Gasoline, unleaded premium	gal	1.86	7/01	11r
Gasoline, unleaded regular	gal	1.73	7/01	11c
Natural gas, expenditures on	yr	389	1999	30r
Utility (piped) gas, therm		0.56	7/01	11c
Utility (piped) gas, 40 therms		38.01	7/01	11r
Utility (piped) gas, 100 therms		57.19	7/01	11c
Entertainment				
Bowling, Saturday evening rate	line	2.88	3/01	4c
Entertainment purchases	yr	2123	1999	30c
Fees and admissions paid	yr	444	1999	30r
Major League baseball ticket		24.83	2000	16c
Monopoly game, Parker Brothers', No. 9	game	10.31	3/01	4c
Movie, first-run, Saturday, evening	adm.	7.38	3/01	4c
Television, radios, sound equipment, expenditures on	yr	580	1999	30r
Tennis balls, yellow, Wilson or Penn, 3	can	2.29	3/01	4c
Funerals				
Cosmetology, hair, other preparation		178.32	1/99	78r
Embalming		408.19	1/99	78r
Funeral at funeral home		362.13	1/99	78r
Professional service charges		1375.51	1/99	78r
Transfer of remains to funeral home		155.92	1/99	78r
Visitation/viewing		294.38	1/99	78r
Groceries				
Groceries, ACCRA Index		108.10	3/01	4c
Antibiotic ointment, Polysporin	0.5 oz	4.88	3/01	4c
Baby food, strained vegetables or fruit, lowest price	4-4.5 oz	0.44	3/01	4c
Bacon, sliced	lb	3.15	7/01	11r
Bakery products, expenditures on	yr	281	1999	30r
Bananas	lb	0.50	3/01	4c
Bananas	lb	0.48	7/01	11r
Beans, dried, any type, all sizes	lb	0.61	7/01	11r
Beef for stew, boneless	lb	3.08	7/01	11r
Beef or hamburger, ground	lb	1.32	3/01	4c
Beef, expenditures on	yr	217	1999	30r
Bologna, all beef or mixed	lb	2.52	7/01	11r
Bread, white	loaf	1.25	3/01	4c
Bread, white, pan	lb	1.06	7/01	11r
Broccoli	lb	0.91	7/01	11r
Butter, salted, grade AA, stick	lb	3.04	7/01	11r
Butter, yoghurt, cheese, etc, expenditures on	yr	183	1999	30r

Values are in dollars or fractions of dollars. In the column headed *Ref*, references are shown to sources. Each reference is followed by a letter. These refer to the geographical level for which data were reported: s=State, r=Region, and c=City or metro. The abbreviation *ex* is used to mean *except* or *excluding*; *exp* stands for *expenditures*. For other abbreviations and further explanations, please see the Introduction.

Detroit, MI - continued

Item	Per	Value	Date	Ref.
Groceries				
Cereals and bakery product purchases	yr	504	1999	30c
Cereals and cereal products, expenditures on	yr	149	1999	30r
Cheese, Kraft grated Parmesan	8 oz	3.91	3/01	4c
Chicken, fresh, whole	lb	1.07	7/01	11r
Chicken, whole fryer	lb	0.96	3/01	4c
Chops, boneless,	lb	3.64	7/01	11r
Chuck roast, U.S. choice, boneless	lb	2.47	7/01	11r
Cigarettes, Winston, Kings	carton	36.85	3/01	4c
Coffee, 100%, ground roast, all sizes	lb	2.69	7/01	11r
Coffee, vacuum-packed	13 oz	2.74	3/01	4c
Cookies, chocolate chip	lb	2.87	7/01	11r
Corn Flakes, Kellogg's or Post Toasties	18 oz	3.06	3/01	4c
Corn, frozen, whole kernel, lowest price	16 oz	1.11	3/01	4c
Dairy product purchases	yr	329	1999	30c
Eggs, expenditures on	yr	26	1999	30r
Eggs, Grade A or AA	dozen	1.24	3/01	4c
Eggs, grade A, large	dozen	0.88	7/01	11r
Fats and oils, expenditures on	yr	75	1999	30r
Fish and seafood, expenditures on	yr	72	1999	30r
Food (excl fruit and vegetables), eaten at home, purchases	yr	939	1999	30c
Food cooked on trips, expenditures on	yr	44	1999	30r
Food purchases	yr	5580	1999	30c
Food purchases, eaten away from home	yr	2454	1999	30c
Food purchases, food eaten at home	yr	3126	1999	30c
Fresh fruits, expenditures on	yr	138	1999	30r
Fresh milk and cream, expenditures on	yr	120	1999	30r
Fresh vegetables, expenditures on	yr	126	1999	30r
Grapefruit	lb	0.66	7/01	11r
Grapes, Thompson, seedless	lb	1.64	7/01	11r
Ground beef, 100% beef	lb	1.64	7/01	11r
Ground beef, lean and extra lean	lb	2.16	7/01	11r
Ground chuck, 100% beef	lb	2.13	7/01	11r
Ham, boneless, excl canned	lb	2.62	7/01	11r
Ice cream, prepackaged, bulk, regular	1/2 gal	3.35	7/01	11r
Lemons	lb	1.19	7/01	11r
Lettuce, iceberg	head	0.99	3/01	4c
Lettuce, iceberg	lb	0.73	7/01	11r
Margarine, Blue Bonnet or Parkay, stick	lb	0.83	3/01	4c
Margarine, soft, tubs	lb	0.89	7/01	11r
Meats, poultry, fish, and egg purchases	yr	845	1999	30c
Milk, fresh, whole, fortified	gal	2.71	7/01	11r
Milk, whole	1/2 gal	1.92	3/01	4c
Nonalcoholic beverages, expenditures on	yr	239	1999	30r
Orange juice, Minute Maid frozen	12 oz	1.66	3/01	4c
Oranges, Navel	lb	0.80	7/01	11r
Oranges, Valencia	lb	0.66	7/01	11r
Peaches, halves or slices, Hunt's, Del Monte, or Libby's	29 oz	1.73	3/01	4c
Pears, Anjou	lb	0.93	7/01	11r
Peas, green, Del Monte or Green Giant	15 oz	0.74	3/01	4c
Pork chops, center cut, bone-in	lb	3.63	7/01	11r
Pork, expenditures on	yr	150	1999	30r
Potato chips	16 oz	3.52	7/01	11r
Potatoes, frozen, french fried	lb	1.08	7/01	11r
Potatoes, white or red	10 lb	2.64	3/01	4c
Potatoes, white, all types	lb	0.33	7/01	11r
Poultry, expenditures on	yr	108	1999	30r
Processed fruits, expenditures on	yr	98	1999	30r
Processed vegetables, expenditures on	yr	80	1999	30r
Round roast, U.S. choice, boneless	lb	3.07	7/01	11r
Round steak, graded and ungraded, excl U.S. prime and choice	lb	3.41	7/01	11r
Sausage, Jimmy Dean/Owens pork	lb	3.51	3/01	4c
Shortening, vegetable oil blends	lb	1.13	7/01	11r
Shortening, vegetable, Crisco	3 lb	3.22	3/01	4c
Soft drink, Coca Cola, ex deposit	2 liter	1.36	3/01	4c
Spaghetti and macaroni	lb	0.80	7/01	11r
Steak, round, U.S. choice, boneless	lb	3.23	7/01	11r
Steak, T-bone	lb	6.52	3/01	4c
Steak, T-bone, U.S. choice, bone-in	lb	6.68	7/01	11r

Detroit, MI - continued

Item	Per	Value	Date	Ref.
Groceries - continued				
Strawberries, dry pint	12 oz	1.32	7/01	11r
Sugar and other sweets, expenditures on	yr	114	1999	30r
Sugar, cane or beet	4 lbs	1.73	3/01	4c
Sugar, white, 33-80 ounce package	lb	0.42	7/01	11r
Sugar, white, all sizes	lb	0.43	7/01	11r
Tobacco products and smoking supplies purchases	yr	403	1999	30c
Tomatoes, field grown	lb	1.46	7/01	11r
Tomatoes, Hunt's or Del Monte	14.5 oz	1.01	3/01	4c
Tuna, chunk, light	6 oz	0.61	3/01	4c
Tuna, light, chunk	lb	1.80	7/01	11r
Turkey, frozen, whole	lb	1.15	7/01	11r
Goods and Services				
Miscellaneous goods and services, ACCRA Index		96.60	3/01	4c
B&B Japanese maple (acer japonicum)	gal	29.99-169.99	4/00	93r
Boxwood (buxus)	2 gal	18.99-39.99	4/00	93r
Daylilly (hemerocallis)	gal	4.99-25.00	4/00	93r
Flat of annuals		11.98-24.99	4/00	93r
Fountain grass (pennisetum)	gal	5.98-12.98	4/00	93r
Hanging basket (10 in)		12.99-27.99	4/00	93r
Hardy geranium (geranium)	gal	7.99-9.99	4/00	93r
Hosta (hosta)	gal	6.00-25.00	4/00	93r
Lilac (syrubga vulgaris)	2 gal	14.99-24.99	4/00	93r
Miscellaneous purchases	yr	831	1999	30c
Rhododendron (rhododendron)	2 gal	23.98-42.99	4/00	93r
Sage (salvia)	gal	6.00-9.99	4/00	93r
Snowblower, single stage		400-600	12/00	99s
Wintercreeper euonymus (euonymus fortunei)	2 gal	16.00-169.99	4/00	93r
Hunting license	yr	14.00	4/01	34s
Health Care				
Health care, ACCRA Index		114.10	3/01	4c
Cardiac catheterization, ave hospital/ physician charges		11830	1998	77s
Childbirth, Cesarean delivery		10722	1997	13r
Childbirth, vaginal delivery		6223	1997	13r
Dentist's fee, adult teeth cleaning and periodic oral exam	visit	87.10	3/01	4c
Doctor's fee, routine exam, established patient	visit	59.00	3/01	4c
Drugs, expenditures on	yr	394	1999	30r
Health care purchases	yr	1701	1999	30c
Health insurance expenditures	yr	978	1999	30r
Home health care aide cost, licensed agency	hour	17	2000	82c
Hospital care, private room	day	693.60	3/01	4c
Hysterectomy, laproscopically-assisted, ave hospital/physician charges		13820	1998	76s
Hysterectomy, vaginal, ave hospital and physician charges		8780	1998	76s
Medicaid dispensing fee		3.72	1999	87s
Medical services expenditures	yr	554	1999	30r
Medical supplies, expenditures on	yr	122	1999	30r
Nursing home costs, private room	day	113	2000	82c
Nursing home stay, private room	day	113	2000	83c
Plastic surgery, breast augmentation		3184	2000	7r
Plastic surgery, breast lift		3585	2000	7r
Plastic surgery, facelift		4999	2000	7r
Plastic surgery, hair transplantation		3105	2000	7r
Plastic surgery, lip augmentation		1290	2000	7r

Values are in dollars or fractions of dollars. In the column headed *Ref*, references are shown to sources. Each reference is followed by a letter. These refer to the geographical level for which data were reported: s=State, r=Region, and c=City or metro. The abbreviation *ex* is used to mean *except* or *excluding*; *exp* stands for *expenditures*. For other abbreviations and further explanations, please see the Introduction.

Detroit, MI - continued

Item	Per	Value	Date	Ref.
Health Care				
Plastic surgery, lower body lift		8135	2000	7r
Plastic surgery, thigh lift		3839	2000	7r
Household Goods				
Dishwashing powder, Cascade	50 oz	3.29	3/01	4c
Floor coverings, expenditures on	yr	52	1999	30r
Furniture, expenditures on	yr	344	1999	30r
Household furnishings and equipment purchases	yr	1582	1999	30c
Household textiles, expenditures on	yr	109	1999	30r
Laundry and cleaning supplies, expenditures on	yr	134	1999	30r
Tissues, facial, Kleenex brand	175	1.33	3/01	4c
Housing				
Housing, ACCRA Index		123.60	3/01	4c
Home, 2200 sq ft, 4-br, 2-bath, 2-car garage, average		243867	2000	47c
Home price, existing, ave		144400	10/00	90r
Home value, median		135000	2001	53s
House, 2400 sq ft, 8000 sq ft lot, new, urban, utilities	total	265600	3/01	4c
House payment, principal and interest, 25% down payment	mos	1306	3/01	4c
Household operation expenditures	yr	673	1999	30c
Housekeeping supplies purchases	yr	558	1999	30c
Lodging expenditures	yr	457	1999	30c
Maintenance, repairs, insurance expenditures	yr	853	1999	30r
Monthly rental value of owned home	mos	547	1999	30r
Owned dwellings, expenditures own	yr	5474	1999	30c
Rent expenditures	yr	1668	1999	30c
Rent, apartment, 2 br, 1 1/2-2 baths, unfurn, 950 sq ft, water	mos	773	3/01	4c
Rental unit, 1 bedroom, with utilities	mos	551	4/01	41c
Rental unit, 2 bedroom, with utilities	mos	666	4/01	41c
Rental unit, 3 bedroom, with utilities	mos	833	4/01	41c
Rental unit, 4 bedroom, with utilities	mos	933	4/01	41c
Shelter, expenditures on	yr	7599	1999	30c
Insurance and Pensions				
Life and other personal insurance purchases	yr	394	1999	30c
Pensions and Social Security, expenditures on	yr	2712	1999	30c
Legal Fees				
Divorce, filing fee		65.00	4/01	35s
Driver's license fee	orig	20.00	1999	48s
Driver's license fee	renew	5.00	1999	48s
Fishing license	yr	14.00	4/01	34s
Personal Goods				
Personal care products and services purchases	yr	532	1999	30c
Shampoo, Alberto VO5	15 oz	1.09	3/01	4c
Toothpaste, Crest or Colgate	6-7 oz	2.17	3/01	4c
Personal Services				
Dry cleaning, man's 2-pc suit		8.35	3/01	4c
Man's haircut, barbershop, no styling		12.55	3/01	4c
Personal services, household, expenditures on	yr	300	1999	30r
Woman's shampoo, trim, blow-dry, no style-change		34.40	3/01	4c
Pets				
Pets, toys, and playground equipment, expenditures on	yr	375	1999	30r
Restaurant Food				
Chicken, fried, thigh and drumstick, KFC/Church's		2.67	3/01	4c
Hamburger with cheese, McDonald's	1/4 lb	2.23	3/01	4c
Pizza, Pizza Hut or Pizza Inn	11-12 in	9.94	3/01	4c

Detroit, MI - continued

Item	Per	Value	Date	Ref.
Taxes				
Federal income taxes paid	yr	2326	1999	30r
Personal taxes, expenditures on	yr	3223	1999	30r
Property taxes paid	yr	1152	1999	30r
State and local income taxes paid	yr	753	1999	30r
Transportation				
Transportation, ACCRA Index		103.10	3/01	4c
Auto operation, annual cost		8455	2000	27c
Bus fare, one-way	trip	1.25	2000	1c
Bus fare, to central business district	1-way	1.50	3/01	4c
Cars and trucks, new, expenditures on	yr	1280	1999	30r
Cars and trucks, used, expenditures on	yr	1763	1999	30r
Diesel at the pump	gal	1.19	10/99	73s
Gasoline and motor oil purchases	yr	1054	1999	30c
Gasoline before-tax price (cents)	gal	111.50	10/00	43s
Maintenance and repair expenditures	yr	594	1999	30r
Parking at airport, lowest rate	day	7.00	2000	46c
Public transportation, expenditures on	yr	419	1999	30c
Tire balance, computer or spin balance, front	wheel	7.25	3/01	4c
Transportation purchases	yr	7162	1999	30c
Vehicle expenses, miscellaneous, purchases	yr	2835	1999	30c
Vehicle insurance payments	yr	701	1999	30r
Vehicle purchases (net outlay)	yr	3081	1999	30r
Vehicle rental, lease expenditures	yr	536	1999	30r
Utilities				
Utilities, ACCRA Index		90.70	3/01	4c
Electrical bill, average	mos	55.00	9/00	9s
Electricity, expenditures on	yr	841	1999	30r
Electricity and other, mixed, 2400 sq ft, new home	mos	64.42	3/01	4c
Electricity cost, average	KWh	7.00	9/00	9s
Utilities, fuels, and public services purchased	yr	2607	1999	30c
Water and other public services, expenditures on	yr	273	1999	30r
Weddings				
Wedding (national average cost)		19936	2000	33r
Wedding (regional average total cost)		16195	1997	110r
Attendants' gifts		321	1998	33r
Bridal attendants' apparel (5 persons)		824	2000	33r
Bride's headpiece/veil		173	1998	33r
Bride's wedding dress		859	1998	33r
Clergy, religious facility fee		242	1998	33r
Engagement ring		3177	1998	33r
Flowers		789	1998	33r
Groom's formalwear rental		99	2000	33r
Limousine		410	1998	33r
Marriage license cost		20.00	4/01	35s
Men's formalwear (ushers, best man)		469	2000	33r
Mother of bride apparel		241	2000	33r
Music		866	1998	33r
Photography and videography		1368	1998	33r
Rehearsal dinner		728	1998	33r
Wedding invitations and announcements		341	1998	33r
Wedding reception		7968	2000	33r
Wedding rings (bride and groom)		1060	1998	33r

Detroit-Ann Arbor-Flint, MI

Item	Per	Value	Date	Ref.
Average annual expenditures	yr	35369	1999	30r
Alcoholic Beverages				
Alcoholic beverage purchases	yr	304	1999	30r
Malt beverages, all types, all sizes, any origin	16 oz	0.93	7/01	11r
Wine, red and white table, all sizes, any origin	liter	7.04	7/01	11r
Appliances				
Major appliances, expenditures on	yr	165	1999	30r
Small appliances, housewares, expenditures on	yr	90	1999	30r

Values are in dollars or fractions of dollars. In the column headed *Ref*, references are shown to sources. Each reference is followed by a letter. These refer to the geographical level for which data were reported: s=State, r=Region, and c=City or metro. The abbreviation *ex* is used to mean *except* or *excluding*; *exp* stands for *expenditures*. For other abbreviations and further explanations, please see the Introduction.

Detroit-Ann Arbor-Flint, MI - continued

Item	Per	Value	Date	Ref.
Banking and Money				
Mortgage interest and charges paid	yr	2277	1999	30r
Mortgage principal paid on owned property	yr	1230	1999	30r
Vehicle finance charges paid	yr	328	1999	30r
Charity				
Cash contributions, expenditures	yr	1126	1999	30r
Child Care				
Child raising cost, total, age 0-2	yr	7890	1999	60r
Child raising cost, total, age 3-5	yr	8130	1999	60r
Child raising cost, total, age 6-8	yr	8170	1999	60r
Child raising cost, total, age 9-11	yr	8190	1999	60r
Child raising cost, total, age 12-14	yr	8890	1999	60r
Child raising cost, total, age 15-17	yr	9050	1999	60r
Child's child care and education, age 0-2	yr	1240	1999	60r
Child's child care and education, age 3-5	yr	1370	1999	60r
Child's child care and education, age 6-8	yr	880	1999	60r
Child's child care and education, age 9-11	yr	570	1999	60r
Child's child care and education, age 12-14	yr	420	1999	60r
Child's child care and education, age 15-17	yr	720	1999	60r
Child's clothing, age 0-2	yr	410	1999	60r
Child's clothing, age 3-5	yr	400	1999	60r
Child's clothing, age 6-8	yr	450	1999	60r
Child's clothing, age 9-11	yr	500	1999	60r
Child's clothing, age 12-14	yr	840	1999	60r
Child's clothing, age 15-17	yr	740	1999	60r
Child's food, age 0-2	yr	960	1999	60r
Child's food, age 3-5	yr	1120	1999	60r
Child's food, age 6-8	yr	1430	1999	60r
Child's food, age 9-11	yr	1710	1999	60r
Child's food, age 12-14	yr	1710	1999	60r
Child's food, age 15-17	yr	1920	1999	60r
Child's health care, age 0-2	yr	520	1999	60r
Child's health care, age 3-5	yr	500	1999	60r
Child's health care, age 6-8	yr	570	1999	60r
Child's health care, age 9-11	yr	610	1999	60r
Child's health care, age 12-14	yr	630	1999	60r
Child's health care, age 15-17	yr	650	1999	60r
Child's housing, age 0-2	yr	2860	1999	60r
Child's housing, age 3-5	yr	2840	1999	60r
Child's housing, age 6-8	yr	2800	1999	60r
Child's housing, age 9-11	yr	2650	1999	60r
Child's housing, age 12-14	yr	2840	1999	60r
Child's housing, age 15-17	yr	2440	1999	60r
Child's personal care, reading, age 0-2	yr	880	1999	60r
Child's personal care, reading, age 3-5	yr	900	1999	60r
Child's personal care, reading, age 6-8	yr	930	1999	60r
Child's personal care, reading, age 9-11	yr	970	1999	60r
Child's personal care, reading, age 12-14	yr	1150	1999	60r
Child's personal care, reading, age 15-17	yr	920	1999	60r
Clothing				
Apparel and services purchases	yr	1607	1999	30r
Boys, 2 to 15, expenditures on	yr	91	1999	30r
Children under 2, expenditures on	yr	59	1999	30r
Footwear, expenditures on	yr	285	1999	30r
Girls, 2 to 15, expenditures on	yr	116	1999	30r
Men and boys, expenditures on	yr	433	1999	30r
Men, 16 and over, expenditures on	yr	341	1999	30r
Women, 16 and over, expenditures on	yr	490	1999	30r
Communications				
Cable modem installation, Bresnan		99.95	6/99	103s
Cable modem installation, Comcast		95.00	6/99	103s
Cable modem installation, Media One		100.00	6/99	103s
Cable modem rate, cable subscriber, Bresnan	mos	39.95	6/99	103s
Cable modem rate, cable subscriber, Comcast	mos	39.95	6/99	103s
Cable modem rate, cable subscriber, Media One	mos	34.95-39.95	6/99	103s
Cable modem rate, non-cable subscriber, Bresnan	mos	49.95	6/99	103s

Detroit-Ann Arbor-Flint, MI - continued

Item	Per	Value	Date	Ref.
Communications - continued				
Cable modem rate, non-cable subscriber, Comcast	mos	49.95	6/99	103s
Cable modem rate, non-cable subscriber, Media One	mos	49.95	6/99	103s
Phone line, single, business, field visit	inst.	42.00	12/97	17s
Phone line, single, business, no field visit	inst.	42.00	12/97	17s
Phone line, single, residence, field visit	inst.	42.00	12/97	17s
Phone line, single, residence, no field visit	inst.	42.00	12/97	17s
Postage and stationery, expenditures on	yr	140	1999	30r
Postal rate, express mail, up to half-pound		12.45	7/01	108r
Postal rate, letter, first class, first ounce		0.34	7/01	108r
Postal rate, letter, two ounces		0.57	7/01	108r
Postal rate, post card		0.21	7/01	108r
Postal rate, priority mail, two pounds		3.95	7/01	108r
Postal rate, priority mail, up to one pound		3.50	7/01	108r
Telephone services, expenditures on	yr	830	1999	30r
Education				
Board, 4-year private college/university	yr	2182	1996	38s
Board, 4-year public college/university	yr	2276	1996	38s
Education expenditures	yr	583	1999	30r
Room, 4-year private college/university	yr	1974	1996	38s
Room, 4-year public college/university	yr	2024	1996	38s
Total cost, 4-year private college/university	yr	13331	1996	38s
Total cost, 4-year public college/university	yr	8195	1996	38s
Tuition, 2-year public college/university, in state	yr	1529	1996	38s
Tuition, 4-year private college/university, in state	yr	9176	1996	38s
Tuition, 4-year public college/university	yr	3895	1996	38s
Energy and Fuels				
Electricity	500 KWhs	46.59	7/01	11r
Fuel oil #2	gal	1.27	7/01	11r
Fuel oil and other fuels, expenditures on	yr	68	1999	30r
Gas, natural, commercial rate	1000 cf	4.91	11/00	88s
Gasoline, unleaded midgrade	gal	1.79	7/01	11r
Gasoline, unleaded premium	gal	1.86	7/01	11r
Gasoline, unleaded regular	gal	1.58	7/01	11r
Natural gas, expenditures on	yr	389	1999	30r
Utility (piped) gas, therm		0.81	7/01	11r
Utility (piped) gas, 40 therms		38.01	7/01	11r
Utility (piped) gas, 100 therms		81.75	7/01	11r
Entertainment				
Entertainment purchases	yr	1984	1999	30r
Fees and admissions paid	yr	444	1999	30r
Television, radios, sound equipment, expenditures on	yr	580	1999	30r
Funerals				
Cosmetology, hair, other preparation		178.32	1/99	78r
Embalming		408.19	1/99	78r
Funeral at funeral home		362.13	1/99	78r
Professional service charges		1375.51	1/99	78r
Transfer of remains to funeral home		155.92	1/99	78r
Visitation/viewing		294.38	1/99	78r
Groceries				
Bacon, sliced	lb	3.15	7/01	11r
Bakery products, expenditures on	yr	281	1999	30r
Bananas	lb	0.48	7/01	11r
Beans, dried, any type, all sizes	lb	0.61	7/01	11r
Beef for stew, boneless	lb	3.08	7/01	11r
Beef, expenditures on	yr	217	1999	30r
Bologna, all beef or mixed	lb	2.52	7/01	11r
Bread, white, pan	lb	1.06	7/01	11r
Broccoli	lb	0.91	7/01	11r
Butter, salted, grade AA, stick	lb	3.04	7/01	11r
Butter, yoghurt, cheese, etc, expenditures on	yr	183	1999	30r
Cereals and bakery product purchases	yr	430	1999	30r
Cereals and cereal products, expenditures on	yr	149	1999	30r

Values are in dollars or fractions of dollars. In the column headed *Ref*, references are shown to sources. Each reference is followed by a letter. These refer to the geographical level for which data were reported: s=State, r=Region, and c=City or metro. The abbreviation *ex* is used to mean *except* or *excluding*; *exp* stands for expenditures. For other abbreviations and further explanations, please see the Introduction.

Detroit-Ann Arbor-Flint, MI - continued

Item	Per	Value	Date	Ref.
Groceries				
Chicken, fresh, whole	lb	1.07	7/01	11r
Chops, boneless,	lb	3.64	7/01	11r
Chuck roast, U.S. choice, boneless	lb	2.47	7/01	11r
Coffee, 100%, ground roast, all sizes	lb	2.69	7/01	11r
Cookies, chocolate chip	lb	2.87	7/01	11r
Dairy product purchases	yr	304	1999	30r
Eggs, expenditures on	yr	26	1999	30r
Eggs, grade A, large	dozen	0.88	7/01	11r
Fats and oils, expenditures on	yr	75	1999	30r
Fish and seafood, expenditures on	yr	72	1999	30r
Food (excl fruit and vegetables), eaten at home, purchases	yr	887	1999	30r
Food cooked on trips, expenditures on	yr	44	1999	30r
Food purchases	yr	4802	1999	30r
Food purchases, eaten away from home	yr	2069	1999	30r
Food purchases, food eaten at home	yr	2733	1999	30r
Fresh fruits, expenditures on	yr	138	1999	30r
Fresh milk and cream, expenditures on	yr	120	1999	30r
Fresh vegetables, expenditures on	yr	126	1999	30r
Grapefruit	lb	0.66	7/01	11r
Grapes, Thompson, seedless	lb	1.64	7/01	11r
Ground beef, 100% beef	lb	1.64	7/01	11r
Ground beef, lean and extra lean	lb	2.16	7/01	11r
Ground chuck, 100% beef	lb	2.13	7/01	11r
Ham, boneless, excl canned	lb	2.62	7/01	11r
Ice cream, prepackaged, bulk, regular	1/2 gal	3.35	7/01	11r
Lemons	lb	1.19	7/01	11r
Lettuce, iceberg	lb	0.73	7/01	11r
Margarine, soft, tubs	lb	0.89	7/01	11r
Meats, poultry, fish, and egg purchases	yr	671	1999	30r
Milk, fresh, whole, fortified	gal	2.71	7/01	11r
Nonalcoholic beverages, expenditures on	yr	239	1999	30r
Oranges, Navel	lb	0.80	7/01	11r
Oranges, Valencia	lb	0.66	7/01	11r
Pears, Anjou	lb	0.93	7/01	11r
Pork chops, center cut, bone-in	lb	3.63	7/01	11r
Pork, expenditures on	yr	150	1999	30r
Potato chips	16 oz	3.52	7/01	11r
Potatoes, frozen, french fried	lb	1.08	7/01	11r
Potatoes, white, all types	lb	0.33	7/01	11r
Poultry, expenditures on	yr	108	1999	30r
Processed fruits, expenditures on	yr	98	1999	30r
Processed vegetables, expenditures on	yr	80	1999	30r
Round roast, U.S. choice, boneless	lb	3.07	7/01	11r
Round steak, graded and ungraded, excl U.S. prime and choice	lb	3.41	7/01	11r
Shortening, vegetable oil blends	lb	1.13	7/01	11r
Spaghetti and macaroni	lb	0.80	7/01	11r
Steak, round, U.S. choice, boneless	lb	3.23	7/01	11r
Steak, T-bone, U.S. choice, bone-in	lb	6.68	7/01	11r
Strawberries, dry pint	12 oz	1.32	7/01	11r
Sugar and other sweets, expenditures on	yr	114	1999	30r
Sugar, white, 33-80 ounce package	lb	0.42	7/01	11r
Sugar, white, all sizes	lb	0.43	7/01	11r
Tobacco products and smoking supplies purchases	yr	331	1999	30r
Tomatoes, field grown	lb	1.46	7/01	11r
Tuna, light, chunk	lb	1.80	7/01	11r
Turkey, frozen, whole	lb	1.15	7/01	11r
Goods and Services				
B&B Japanese maple (acer japonicum)	gal	29.99-169.99	4/00	93r
Boxwood (buxus)	2 gal	18.99-39.99	4/00	93r
Daylily (hemerocallis)	gal	4.99-25.00	4/00	93r
Flat of annuals		11.98-24.99	4/00	93r
Fountain grass (pennisetum)	gal	5.98-12.98	4/00	93r
Hanging basket (10 in)		12.99-27.99	4/00	93r

Detroit-Ann Arbor-Flint, MI - continued

Item	Per	Value	Date	Ref.
Goods and Services - continued				
Hardy geranium (geranium)	gal	7.99-9.99	4/00	93r
Hosta (hosta)	gal	6.00-25.00	4/00	93r
Lilac (syrubga vulgaris)	2 gal	14.99-24.99	4/00	93r
Miscellaneous purchases	yr	865	1999	30r
Rhododendron (rhododendron)	2 gal	23.98-42.99	4/00	93r
Sage (salvia)	gal	6.00-9.99	4/00	93r
Snowblower, single stage		400-600	12/00	99s
Wintercreeper euonymus (euonymus fortunei)	2 gal	16.00-169.99	4/00	93r
Hunting license	yr	14.00	4/01	34s
Health Care				
Cardiac catheterization, ave hospital/ physician charges		11830	1998	77s
Childbirth, Cesarean delivery		10722	1997	13r
Childbirth, vaginal delivery		6223	1997	13r
Drugs, expenditures on	yr	394	1999	30r
Health care purchases	yr	2048	1999	30r
Health insurance expenditures	yr	978	1999	30r
Hysterectomy, laproscopically-assisted, ave hospital/physician charges		13820	1998	76s
Hysterectomy, vaginal, ave hospital and physician charges		8780	1998	76s
Medicaid dispensing fee		3.72	1999	87s
Medical services expenditures	yr	554	1999	30r
Medical supplies, expenditures on	yr	122	1999	30r
Plastic surgery, breast augmentation		3184	2000	7r
Plastic surgery, breast lift		3585	2000	7r
Plastic surgery, facelift		4999	2000	7r
Plastic surgery, hair transplantation		3105	2000	7r
Plastic surgery, lip augmentation		1290	2000	7r
Plastic surgery, lower body lift		8135	2000	7r
Plastic surgery, thigh lift		3839	2000	7r
Household Goods				
Floor coverings, expenditures on	yr	52	1999	30r
Furniture, expenditures on	yr	344	1999	30r
Household furnishings and equipment purchases	yr	1475	1999	30r
Household textiles, expenditures on	yr	109	1999	30r
Laundry and cleaning supplies, expenditures on	yr	134	1999	30r
Housing				
Home price, existing, ave		144400	10/00	90r
Home value, median		135000	2001	53s
Household operation expenditures	yr	542	1999	30r
Housekeeping supplies purchases	yr	508	1999	30r
Lodging expenditures	yr	430	1999	30r
Maintenance, repairs, insurance expenditures	yr	853	1999	30r
Monthly rental value of owned home	mos	547	1999	30r
Owned dwellings, expenditures own	yr	4282	1999	30r
Rent expenditures	yr	1558	1999	30r
Shelter, expenditures on	yr	6270	1999	30r
Insurance and Pensions				
Life and other personal insurance purchases	yr	387	1999	30r
Pensions and Social Security, expenditures on	yr	2968	1999	30r
Legal Fees				
Divorce, filing fee		65.00	4/01	35s
Driver's license fee	orig	20.00	1999	48s
Driver's license fee	renew	5.00	1999	48s
Fishing license	yr	14.00	4/01	34s
Personal Goods				
Personal care products and services purchases	yr	385	1999	30r

Values are in dollars or fractions of dollars. In the column headed *Ref*, references are shown to sources. Each reference is followed by a letter. These refer to the geographical level for which data were reported: s=State, r=Region, and c=City or metro. The abbreviation *ex* is used to mean *except* or *excluding*; *exp* stands for expenditures. For other abbreviations and further explanations, please see the Introduction.

Detroit-Ann Arbor-Flint, MI - continued

Item	Per	Value	Date	Ref.
Personal Services				
Personal services, household, expenditures on	yr	300	1999	30r
Pets				
Pets, toys, and playground equipment, expenditures on	yr	375	1999	30r
Taxes				
Federal income taxes paid	yr	2326	1999	30r
Personal taxes, expenditures on	yr	3223	1999	30r
Property taxes paid	yr	1152	1999	30r
State and local income taxes paid	yr	753	1999	30r
Transportation				
Cars and trucks, new, expenditures on	yr	1280	1999	30r
Cars and trucks, used, expenditures on	yr	1763	1999	30r
Diesel at the pump	gal	1.19	10/99	73s
Gasoline and motor oil purchases	yr	1036	1999	30r
Gasoline before-tax price (cents)	gal	111.50	10/00	43s
Household transportation expenditures	yr	6710	97-1998	102c
Maintenance and repair expenditures	yr	594	1999	30r
Public transportation, expenditures on	yr	341	1999	30r
Transportation purchases	yr	6617	1999	30r
Vehicle expenses, miscellaneous, purchases	yr	2159	1999	30r
Vehicle insurance payments	yr	701	1999	30r
Vehicle purchases (net outlay)	yr	3081	1999	30r
Vehicle rental, lease expenditures	yr	536	1999	30r
Utilities				
Electrical bill, average	mos	55.00	9/00	9s
Electricity, expenditures on	yr	841	1999	30r
Electricity, summer, 250 KWh	mos	23.01	2/96	97c
Electricity, summer, 500 KWh	mos	46.02	2/96	97c
Electricity, summer, 750 KWh	mos	72.59	2/96	97c
Electricity, summer, 1000 KWh	mos	99.30	2/96	97c
Electricity cost, average	KWh	7.00	9/00	9s
Utilities, fuels, and public services purchased	yr	2401	1999	30r
Water and other public services, expenditures on	yr	273	1999	30r
Weddings				
Wedding (national average cost)		19936	2000	33r
Wedding (regional average total cost)		16195	1997	110r
Attendants' gifts		321	1998	33r
Bridal attendants' apparel (5 persons)		824	2000	33r
Bride's headpiece/veil		173	1998	33r
Bride's wedding dress		859	1998	33r
Clergy, religious facility fee		242	1998	33r
Engagement ring		3177	1998	33r
Flowers		789	1998	33r
Groom's formalwear rental		99	2000	33r
Limousine		410	1998	33r
Marriage license cost		20.00	4/01	35s
Men's formalwear (ushers, best man)		469	2000	33r
Mother of bride apparel		241	2000	33r
Music		866	1998	33r
Photography and videography		1368	1998	33r
Rehearsal dinner		728	1998	33r
Wedding invitations and announcements		341	1998	33r
Wedding reception		7968	2000	33r
Wedding rings (bride and groom)		1060	1998	33r

Dothan, AL

Item	Per	Value	Date	Ref.
Composite, ACCRA index		91.50	3/01	4c
Alcoholic Beverages				
Alcoholic beverage purchases	yr	253	1999	30r
Beer, Heineken, 12-oz, ex deposit	6	7.00	3/01	4c
J & B Scotch	750-ml	23.99	3/01	4c
Malt beverages, all types, all sizes, any origin	16 oz	0.96	7/01	11r
Wine, Livingston or Gallo, Chablis blanc	1.5 liter	6.32	3/01	4c

Dothan, AL - continued

Item	Per	Value	Date	Ref.
Appliances				
Appliance repair, service call, washing machine	min lab chg	29.00	3/01	4c
Major appliances, expenditures on	yr	172	1999	30r
Small appliances, housewares, expenditures on	yr	81	1999	30r
Banking and Money				
Mortgage interest and charges paid	yr	2039	1999	30r
Mortgage principal paid on owned property	yr	1026	1999	30r
Mortgage rate, incl. points and orig. fee, 30-yr. conv. fixed or ARM	mos	6.81	3/01	4c
Vehicle finance charges paid	yr	365	1999	30r
Charity				
Cash contributions, expenditures	yr	1127	1999	30r
Child Care				
Child raising cost, total, age 0-2	yr	8540	1999	60r
Child raising cost, total, age 3-5	yr	8780	1999	60r
Child raising cost, total, age 6-8	yr	8820	1999	60r
Child raising cost, total, age 9-11	yr	8800	1999	60r
Child raising cost, total, age 12-14	yr	9510	1999	60r
Child raising cost, total, age 15-17	yr	9740	1999	60r
Child's child care and education, age 0-2	yr	1380	1999	60r
Child's child care and education, age 3-5	yr	1520	1999	60r
Child's child care and education, age 6-8	yr	990	1999	60r
Child's child care and education, age 9-11	yr	650	1999	60r
Child's child care and education, age 12-14	yr	490	1999	60r
Child's child care and education, age 15-17	yr	840	1999	60r
Child's clothing, age 0-2	yr	480	1999	60r
Child's clothing, age 3-5	yr	470	1999	60r
Child's clothing, age 6-8	yr	520	1999	60r
Child's clothing, age 9-11	yr	570	1999	60r
Child's clothing, age 12-14	yr	950	1999	60r
Child's clothing, age 15-17	yr	850	1999	60r
Child's food, age 0-2	yr	1000	1999	60r
Child's food, age 3-5	yr	1160	1999	60r
Child's food, age 6-8	yr	1490	1999	60r
Child's food, age 9-11	yr	1770	1999	60r
Child's food, age 12-14	yr	1770	1999	60r
Child's food, age 15-17	yr	1980	1999	60r
Child's health care, age 0-2	yr	620	1999	60r
Child's health care, age 3-5	yr	590	1999	60r
Child's health care, age 6-8	yr	680	1999	60r
Child's health care, age 9-11	yr	720	1999	60r
Child's health care, age 12-14	yr	730	1999	60r
Child's health care, age 15-17	yr	760	1999	60r
Child's housing, age 0-2	yr	3070	1999	60r
Child's housing, age 3-5	yr	3050	1999	60r
Child's housing, age 6-8	yr	3010	1999	60r
Child's housing, age 9-11	yr	2850	1999	60r
Child's housing, age 12-14	yr	3040	1999	60r
Child's housing, age 15-17	yr	2650	1999	60r
Child's personal care, reading, age 0-2	yr	910	1999	60r
Child's personal care, reading, age 3-5	yr	930	1999	60r
Child's personal care, reading, age 6-8	yr	960	1999	60r
Child's personal care, reading, age 9-11	yr	1000	1999	60r
Child's personal care, reading, age 12-14	yr	1170	1999	60r
Child's personal care, reading, age 15-17	yr	950	1999	60r
Clothing				
Apparel and services purchases	yr	1610	1999	30r
Boys' brief, cotton	3	5.69	3/01	4c
Boys, 2 to 15, expenditures on	yr	89	1999	30r
Children under 2, expenditures on	yr	79	1999	30r
Footwear, expenditures on	yr	283	1999	30r
Girls, 2 to 15, expenditures on	yr	103	1999	30r
Men and boys, expenditures on	yr	351	1999	30r
Men, 16 and over, expenditures on	yr	262	1999	30r
Shirt, man's dress shirt		30.39	3/01	4c
Slacks, man's "No Wrinkles" khaki		38.59	3/01	4c
Women, 16 and over, expenditures on	yr	538	1999	30r

Values are in dollars or fractions of dollars. In the column headed *Ref*, references are shown to sources. Each reference is followed by a letter. These refer to the geographical level for which data were reported: s=State, r=Region, and c=City or metro. The abbreviation *ex* is used to mean *except* or *excluding*; *exp* stands for expenditures. For other abbreviations and further explanations, please see the Introduction.

Dothan, AL - continued

Item	Per	Value	Date	Ref.
Communications				
Newspaper subscription, daily and Sunday delivery	mos	11.90	3/01	4c
Phone line, single, business, field visit	inst.	69.00	12/97	17s
Phone line, single, business, no field visit	inst.	69.00	12/97	17s
Phone line, single, residence, field visit	inst.	40.00	12/97	17s
Phone line, single, residence, no field visit	inst.	40.00	12/97	17s
Postage and stationery, expenditures on	yr	104	1999	30r
Postal rate, express mail, up to half-pound		12.45	7/01	108r
Postal rate, letter, first class, first ounce		0.34	7/01	108r
Postal rate, letter, two ounces		0.57	7/01	108r
Postal rate, post card		0.21	7/01	108r
Postal rate, priority mail, two pounds		3.95	7/01	108r
Postal rate, priority mail, up to one pound		3.50	7/01	108r
Telephone bill, family of three	mos	22.66	3/01	4c
Telephone services, expenditures on	yr	860	1999	30r
Education				
Board, 4-year private college/university	yr	2256	1996	38s
Board, 4-year public college/university	yr	1739	1996	38s
Education expenditures	yr	431	1999	30r
Room, 4-year private college/university	yr	1799	1996	38s
Room, 4-year public college/university	yr	1757	1996	38s
Total cost, 4-year private college/university	yr	11635	1996	38s
Total cost, 4-year public college/university	yr	5737	1996	38s
Tuition, 2-year public college/university, in state	yr	1317	1996	38s
Tuition, 4-year private college/university, in state	yr	7580	1996	38s
Tuition, 4-year public college/university	yr	2240	1996	38s
Energy and Fuels				
Electricity	KWh	0.09	7/01	11r
Electricity	500 KWhs	47.29	7/01	11r
Energy, combined forms, 2400 sq ft	mos	89.15	3/01	4c
Fuel oil #2	gal	1.43	7/01	11r
Fuel oil and other fuels, expenditures on	yr	45	1999	30r
Gas, natural, commercial rate	1000 cf	9.50	11/00	88s
Gas, regular unleaded, cash, self-service	gal	1.31	3/01	4c
Gasoline, all types	gal	1.60	7/01	11r
Gasoline, unleaded midgrade	gal	1.65	7/01	11r
Gasoline, unleaded premium	gal	1.74	7/01	11r
Natural gas, expenditures on	yr	164	1999	30r
Utility (piped) gas, therm		1.01	7/01	11r
Utility (piped) gas, 40 therms		44.29	7/01	11r
Utility (piped) gas, 100 therms		97.44	7/01	11r
Entertainment				
Bowling, Saturday evening rate	line	2.57	3/01	4c
Entertainment purchases	yr	1574	1999	30r
Fees and admissions paid	yr	371	1999	30r
Monopoly game, Parker Brothers', No. 9	game	9.99	3/01	4c
Movie, first-run, Saturday, evening	adm.	6.50	3/01	4c
Reading purchases	yr	121	1999	30r
Television, radios, sound equipment, expenditures on	yr	561	1999	30r
Tennis balls, yellow, Wilson or Penn, 3	can	2.18	3/01	4c
Groceries				
Groceries, ACCRA Index		98.30	3/01	4c
American processed cheese	lb	3.50	7/01	11r
Antibiotic ointment, Polysporin	0.5 oz	4.65	3/01	4c
Baby food, strained vegetables or fruit, lowest price	4-4.5 oz	0.39	3/01	4c
Bakery products, expenditures on	yr	261	1999	30r
Bananas	lb	0.53	3/01	4c
Bananas	lb	0.47	7/01	11r
Beans, dried, any type, all sizes	lb	0.63	7/01	11r
Beef for stew, boneless	lb	2.86	7/01	11r
Beef or hamburger, ground	lb	1.59	3/01	4c
Beef, expenditures on	yr	210	1999	30r
Bologna, all beef or mixed	lb	2.29	7/01	11r
Bread, French	lb	1.66	7/01	11r
Bread, white	loaf	0.95	3/01	4c

Dothan, AL - continued

Item	Per	Value	Date	Ref.
Groceries - continued				
Bread, white, pan	lb	0.87	7/01	11r
Bread, whole wheat, pan	lb	1.38	7/01	11r
Broccoli	lb	1.04	7/01	11r
Butter, salted, grade AA, stick	lb	2.26	7/01	11r
Butter, yoghurt, cheese, etc, expenditures on	yr	170	1999	30r
Cabbage	lb	0.42	7/01	11r
Cereals and cereal products, expenditures on	yr	140	1999	30r
Cheddar cheese, natural	lb	3.75	7/01	11r
Cheese, Kraft grated Parmesan	8 oz	3.31	3/01	4c
Chicken breast, bone-in	lb	1.85	7/01	11r
Chicken legs, bone-in	lb	1.34	7/01	11r
Chicken, fresh, whole	lb	1.05	7/01	11r
Chicken, whole fryer	lb	0.91	3/01	4c
Chops, boneless,	lb	4.13	7/01	11r
Chuck roast, graded and ungraded, excl U.S. prime and choice	lb	2.35	7/01	11r
Chuck roast, U.S. choice, boneless	lb	2.67	7/01	11r
Cigarettes, Winston, Kings	carton	28.71	3/01	4c
Coffee, 100%, ground roast, all sizes	lb	2.88	7/01	11r
Coffee, instant, plain, regular, all sizes	16 oz	9.25	7/01	11r
Coffee, vacuum-packed	13 oz	2.74	3/01	4c
Cola, non diet	2 liter	1.11	7/01	11r
Corn Flakes, Kellogg's or Post Toasties	18 oz	2.96	3/01	4c
Corn, frozen, whole kernel, lowest price	16 oz	1.11	3/01	4c
Crackers, soda, salted	lb	1.70	7/01	11r
Dairy product purchases	yr	282	1999	30r
Eggs, expenditures on	yr	32	1999	30r
Eggs, Grade A or AA	dozen	1.02	3/01	4c
Fats and oils, expenditures on	yr	79	1999	30r
Fish and seafood, expenditures on	yr	99	1999	30r
Flour, white, all purpose	lb	0.32	7/01	11r
Food (excl fruit and vegetables), eaten at home, purchases	yr	815	1999	30r
Food cooked on trips, expenditures on	yr	36	1999	30r
Food purchases	yr	4533	1999	30r
Food purchases, eaten away from home	yr	1873	1999	30r
Food purchases, food eaten at home	yr	2660	1999	30r
Fresh fruits, expenditures on	yr	128	1999	30r
Fresh milk and cream, expenditures on	yr	112	1999	30r
Fresh vegetables, expenditures on	yr	131	1999	30r
Fruit and vegetable purchases	yr	438	1999	30r
Grapefruit	lb	0.59	7/01	11r
Grapes, Thompson, seedless	lb	2.12	7/01	11r
Ground beef, 100% beef	lb	1.76	7/01	11r
Ground beef, lean and extra lean	lb	2.60	7/01	11r
Ground chuck, 100% beef	lb	2.08	7/01	11r
Ham, boneless, excl canned	lb	2.71	7/01	11r
Ham, rump or shank half, bone-in, smoked	lb	2.19	7/01	11r
Ice cream, prepackaged, bulk, regular	1/2 gal	3.93	7/01	11r
Lemons	lb	1.32	7/01	11r
Lettuce, iceberg	head	0.97	3/01	4c
Lettuce, iceberg	lb	0.76	7/01	11r
Margarine, Blue Bonnet or Parkay, stick	lb	0.78	3/01	4c
Milk, fresh, low fat	gal	2.75	7/01	11r
Milk, fresh, whole, fortified	gal	2.97	7/01	11r
Milk, whole	1/2 gal	1.75	3/01	4c
Nonalcoholic beverages, expenditures on	yr	228	1999	30r
Orange juice, frozen concentrate	16 oz	1.95	7/01	11r
Orange juice, Minute Maid frozen	12 oz	1.46	3/01	4c
Oranges, Navel	lb	0.73	7/01	11r
Oranges, Valencia	lb	0.55	7/01	11r
Peaches, halves or slices, Hunt's, Del Monte, or Libby's	29 oz	1.55	3/01	4c
Peanut butter, creamy, all sizes	lb	1.83	7/01	11r
Pears, Anjou	lb	0.98	7/01	11r
Peas, green, Del Monte or Green Giant	15 oz	0.68	3/01	4c
Pork chops, center cut, bone-in	lb	3.33	7/01	11r
Pork sausage, fresh, loose	lb	2.59	7/01	11r
Pork shoulder picnic, bone-in, smoked	lb	1.12	7/01	11r
Pork, expenditures on	yr	162	1999	30r
Potato chips	16 oz	3.59	7/01	11r

Values are in dollars or fractions of dollars. In the column headed *Ref*, references are shown to sources. Each reference is followed by a letter. These refer to the geographical level for which data were reported: s=State, r=Region, and c=City or metro. The abbreviation *ex* is used to mean *except* or *excluding*; *exp* stands for expenditures. For other abbreviations and further explanations, please see the Introduction.

Dothan, AL - continued

Item	Per	Value	Date	Ref.
Groceries				
Potatoes, frozen, french fried	lb	1.00	7/01	11r
Potatoes, white or red	10 lb	2.83	3/01	4c
Potatoes, white, all types	lb	0.44	7/01	11r
Poultry, expenditures on	yr	137	1999	30r
Processed fruits, expenditures on	yr	97	1999	30r
Processed vegetables, expenditures on	yr	82	1999	30r
Rice, white, long grain, uncooked	lb	0.51	7/01	11r
Round roast, graded and ungraded, excl U.S. prime and choice	lb	2.96	7/01	11r
Round steak, graded and ungraded, excl U.S. prime and choice	lb	3.11	7/01	11r
Sausage, Jimmy Dean/Owens pork	lb	2.79	3/01	4c
Shortening, vegetable, Crisco	3 lb	2.99	3/01	4c
Sirloin steak, graded and ungraded, excl U.S. prime and choice	lb	4.23	7/01	11r
Soft drink, Coca Cola, ex deposit	2 liter	1.03	3/01	4c
Spaghetti and macaroni	lb	0.78	7/01	11r
Steak, round, U.S. choice, boneless	lb	3.56	7/01	11r
Steak, sirloin, U.S. choice, boneless	lb	5.65	7/01	11r
Steak, T-bone	lb	7.11	3/01	4c
Strawberries, dry pint	12 oz	1.50	7/01	11r
Sugar and other sweets, expenditures on	yr	99	1999	30r
Sugar, cane or beet	4 lbs	1.60	3/01	4c
Sugar, white, 33-80 ounce package	lb	0.39	7/01	11r
Sugar, white, all sizes	lb	0.42	7/01	11r
Tobacco products and smoking supplies purchases	yr	288	1999	30r
Tomatoes, field grown	lb	1.43	7/01	11r
Tomatoes, Hunt's or Del Monte	14.5 oz	0.62	3/01	4c
Tuna, chunk, light	6 oz	0.55	3/01	4c
Tuna, light, chunk	lb	1.77	7/01	11r
Turkey, frozen, whole	lb	1.05	7/01	11r
Goods and Services				
Miscellaneous goods and services, ACCRA Index		101.40	3/01	4c
Hunting license	yr	16.00	4/01	34s
Health Care				
Health care, ACCRA Index		88.80	3/01	4c
Cardiac catheterization, ave hospital/ physician charges		15260	1998	77s
Childbirth, Cesarean delivery		11587	1997	13r
Childbirth, vaginal delivery		6725	1997	13r
Dentist's fee, adult teeth cleaning and periodic oral exam	visit	58.80	3/01	4c
Doctor's fee, routine exam, established patient	visit	50.00	3/01	4c
Drugs, expenditures on	yr	399	1999	30r
Health care purchases	yr	1971	1999	30r
Health insurance expenditures	yr	933	1999	30r
Hospital care, private room	day	535.50	3/01	4c
Hysterectomy, laproscopically-assisted, ave hospital/physician charges		16780	1998	76s
Hysterectomy, vaginal, ave hospital and physician charges		10990	1998	76s
Medicaid dispensing fee		5.40	1999	87s
Medical services expenditures	yr	547	1999	30r
Medical supplies, expenditures on	yr	91	1999	30r
Household Goods				
Dishwashing powder, Cascade	50 oz	3.31	3/01	4c
Floor coverings, expenditures on	yr	44	1999	30r
Furniture, expenditures on	yr	335	1999	30r
Household furnishings and equipment purchases	yr	1328	1999	30r
Household textiles, expenditures on	yr	89	1999	30r
Laundry and cleaning supplies, expenditures on	yr	113	1999	30r
Tissues, facial, Kleenex brand	175	1.31	3/01	4c
Housing				
Housing, ACCRA Index		80.80	3/01	4c
Home price, existing, ave		160100	10/00	90r

Dothan, AL - continued

Item	Per	Value	Date	Ref.
Housing - continued				
Home value, median		115000	2001	53s
House, 2400 sq ft, 8000 sq ft lot, new, urban, utilities	total	172500	3/01	4c
House payment, principal and interest, 25% down payment	mos	844	3/01	4c
Household operation expenditures	yr	553	1999	30r
Housekeeping supplies purchases	yr	473	1999	30r
Housing, expenditures on	yr	10303	1999	30r
Maintenance, repairs, insurance expenditures	yr	699	1999	30r
Monthly rental value of owned home	mos	505	1999	30r
Owned dwellings, expenditures own	yr	3465	1999	30r
Rent expenditures	yr	1641	1999	30r
Rent, apartment, 2 br, 1 1/2-2 baths, unfurn, 950 sq ft, water	mos	530	3/01	4c
Rental unit, 1 bedroom, with utilities	mos	324	4/01	41c
Rental unit, 2 bedroom, with utilities	mos	403	4/01	41c
Rental unit, 3 bedroom, with utilities	mos	554	4/01	41c
Rental unit, 4 bedroom, with utilities	mos	562	4/01	41c
Shelter, expenditures on	yr	5467	1999	30r
Insurance and Pensions				
Life and other personal insurance purchases	yr	414	1999	30r
Pensions and Social Security, expenditures on	yr	2635	1999	30r
Personal insurance and pensions, expenditures on	yr	3048	1999	30r
Legal Fees				
Divorce, filing fee		146.00-193.00	4/01	35s
Driver's license fee	renew	18.50	1999	48s
Driver's license fee	orig	18.50	1999	48s
Personal Goods				
Personal care products and services purchases	yr	393	1999	30r
Shampoo, Alberto VO5	15 oz	1.17	3/01	4c
Toothpaste, Crest or Colgate	6-7 oz	2.60	3/01	4c
Personal Services				
Dry cleaning, man's 2-pc suit		6.09	3/01	4c
Man's haircut, barbershop, no styling		8.80	3/01	4c
Personal services, household, expenditures on	yr	258	1999	30r
Woman's shampoo, trim, blow-dry, no style-change		20.00	3/01	4c
Pets				
Pets, toys, and playground equipment, expenditures on	yr	306	1999	30r
Restaurant Food				
Chicken, fried, thigh and drumstick, KFC/ Church's		2.07	3/01	4c
Hamburger with cheese, McDonald's	1/4 lb	2.29	3/01	4c
Pizza, Pizza Hut or Pizza Inn	11-12 in	12.19	3/01	4c
Taxes				
Federal income taxes paid	yr	2047	1999	30r
Personal taxes, expenditures on	yr	2554	1999	30r
Property taxes paid	yr	726	1999	30r
State and local income taxes paid	yr	363	1999	30r
Transportation				
Transportation, ACCRA Index		90.70	3/01	4c
Cars and trucks, new, expenditures on	yr	1648	1999	30r
Cars and trucks, used, expenditures on	yr	1651	1999	30r
Diesel at the pump	gal	1.19	10/99	73s
Gasoline and motor oil purchases	yr	1052	1999	30r
Gasoline before-tax price (cents)	gal	104.10	10/00	43s
Maintenance and repair expenditures	yr	621	1999	30r
Public transportation, expenditures on	yr	298	1999	30r
Tire balance, computer or spin balance, front	wheel	6.90	3/01	4c
Transportation purchases	yr	6738	1999	30r
Vehicle expenses, miscellaneous, purchases	yr	2033	1999	30r

Values are in dollars or fractions of dollars. In the column headed *Ref*, references are shown to sources. Each reference is followed by a letter. These refer to the geographical level for which data were reported: s=State, r=Region, and c=City or metro. The abbreviation *ex* is used to mean *except* or *excluding*; *exp* stands for *expenditures*. For other abbreviations and further explanations, please see the Introduction.

Dothan, AL - continued

Item	Per	Value	Date	Ref.
Transportation				
Vehicle insurance payments	yr	696	1999	30r
Vehicle purchases (net outlay)	yr	3354	1999	30r
Vehicle rental, lease expenditures	yr	352	1999	30r
Utilities				
Utilities, ACCRA Index		77.30	3/01	4c
Electrical bill, average	mos	83.42	9/00	9s
Electricity, 2400 sq ft, new home	mos	89.15	3/01	4c
Electricity, expenditures on	yr	1115	1999	30r
Electricity cost, average	KWh	5.60	9/00	9s
Water and other public services, expenditures on	yr	298	1999	30r
Weddings				
Wedding (national average cost)		19936	2000	33r
Attendants' gifts		321	1998	33r
Bridal attendants' apparel (5 persons)		824	2000	33r
Bride's headpiece/veil		173	1998	33r
Bride's wedding dress		859	1998	33r
Clergy, religious facility fee		242	1998	33r
Engagement ring		3177	1998	33r
Flowers		789	1998	33r
Groom's formalwear rental		99	2000	33r
Limousine		410	1998	33r
Marriage license cost		25.00	4/01	35s
Men's formalwear (ushers, best man)		469	2000	33r
Mother of bride apparel		241	2000	33r
Music		866	1998	33r
Photography and videography		1368	1998	33r
Rehearsal dinner		728	1998	33r
Wedding invitations and announcements		341	1998	33r
Wedding reception		7968	2000	33r
Wedding rings (bride and groom)		1060	1998	33r

Dover, DE

Item	Per	Value	Date	Ref.
Composite, ACCRA index		101.00	3/01	4c
Alcoholic Beverages				
Alcoholic beverage purchases	yr	253	1999	30r
Beer, Heineken, 12-oz, ex deposit	6	6.88	3/01	4c
J & B Scotch	750-ml	18.24	3/01	4c
Malt beverages, all types, all sizes, any origin	16 oz	0.96	7/01	11r
Wine, Livingston or Gallo, Chablis blanc	1.5 liter	6.23	3/01	4c
Appliances				
Appliance repair, service call, washing machine	min lab chg	54.67	3/01	4c
Major appliances, expenditures on	yr	172	1999	30r
Small appliances, housewares, expenditures on	yr	81	1999	30r
Banking and Money				
Mortgage interest and charges paid	yr	2039	1999	30r
Mortgage principal paid on owned property	yr	1026	1999	30r
Mortgage rate, incl. points and orig. fee, 30-yr. conv. fixed or ARM	mos	7.21	3/01	4c
Vehicle finance charges paid	yr	365	1999	30r
Charity				
Cash contributions, expenditures	yr	1127	1999	30r
Child Care				
Child raising cost, total, age 0-2	yr	8540	1999	60r
Child raising cost, total, age 3-5	yr	8780	1999	60r
Child raising cost, total, age 6-8	yr	8820	1999	60r
Child raising cost, total, age 9-11	yr	8800	1999	60r
Child raising cost, total, age 12-14	yr	9510	1999	60r
Child raising cost, total, age 15-17	yr	9740	1999	60r
Child's child care and education, age 0-2	yr	1380	1999	60r
Child's child care and education, age 3-5	yr	1520	1999	60r
Child's child care and education, age 6-8	yr	990	1999	60r
Child's child care and education, age 9-11	yr	650	1999	60r
Child's child care and education, age 12-14	yr	490	1999	60r
Child's child care and education, age 15-17	yr	840	1999	60r

Item	Per	Value	Date	Ref.
Child Care - continued				
Child's clothing, age 0-2	yr	480	1999	60r
Child's clothing, age 3-5	yr	470	1999	60r
Child's clothing, age 6-8	yr	520	1999	60r
Child's clothing, age 9-11	yr	570	1999	60r
Child's clothing, age 12-14	yr	950	1999	60r
Child's clothing, age 15-17	yr	850	1999	60r
Child's food, age 0-2	yr	1000	1999	60r
Child's food, age 3-5	yr	1160	1999	60r
Child's food, age 6-8	yr	1490	1999	60r
Child's food, age 9-11	yr	1770	1999	60r
Child's food, age 12-14	yr	1770	1999	60r
Child's food, age 15-17	yr	1980	1999	60r
Child's health care, age 0-2	yr	620	1999	60r
Child's health care, age 3-5	yr	590	1999	60r
Child's health care, age 6-8	yr	680	1999	60r
Child's health care, age 9-11	yr	720	1999	60r
Child's health care, age 12-14	yr	730	1999	60r
Child's health care, age 15-17	yr	760	1999	60r
Child's housing, age 0-2	yr	3070	1999	60r
Child's housing, age 3-5	yr	3050	1999	60r
Child's housing, age 6-8	yr	3010	1999	60r
Child's housing, age 9-11	yr	2850	1999	60r
Child's housing, age 12-14	yr	3040	1999	60r
Child's housing, age 15-17	yr	2650	1999	60r
Child's personal care, reading, age 0-2	yr	910	1999	60r
Child's personal care, reading, age 3-5	yr	930	1999	60r
Child's personal care, reading, age 6-8	yr	960	1999	60r
Child's personal care, reading, age 9-11	yr	1000	1999	60r
Child's personal care, reading, age 12-14	yr	1170	1999	60r
Child's personal care, reading, age 15-17	yr	950	1999	60r
Clothing				
Apparel and services purchases	yr	1610	1999	30r
Boys' brief, cotton	3	4.19	3/01	4c
Boys, 2 to 15, expenditures on	yr	89	1999	30r
Children under 2, expenditures on	yr	79	1999	30r
Footwear, expenditures on	yr	283	1999	30r
Girls, 2 to 15, expenditures on	yr	103	1999	30r
Men and boys, expenditures on	yr	351	1999	30r
Men, 16 and over, expenditures on	yr	262	1999	30r
Shirt, man's dress shirt		22.62	3/01	4c
Slacks, man's "No Wrinkles" khaki		30.24	3/01	4c
Women, 16 and over, expenditures on	yr	538	1999	30r
Communications				
Newspaper subscription, daily and Sunday delivery	mos	10.87	3/01	4c
Phone line, single, business, field visit	inst.	60.94	12/97	17s
Phone line, single, business, no field visit	inst.	60.94	12/97	17s
Phone line, single, residence, field visit	inst.	35.96	12/97	17s
Phone line, single, residence, no field visit	inst.	35.96	12/97	17s
Postage and stationery, expenditures on	yr	104	1999	30r
Postal rate, express mail, up to half-pound		12.45	7/01	108r
Postal rate, letter, first class, first ounce		0.34	7/01	108r
Postal rate, letter, two ounces		0.57	7/01	108r
Postal rate, post card		0.21	7/01	108r
Postal rate, priority mail, two pounds		3.95	7/01	108r
Postal rate, priority mail, up to one pound		3.50	7/01	108r
Telephone bill, business, basic rate	mos	4.35	12/97	18c
Telephone bill, family of three	mos	16.86	3/01	4c
Telephone bill, residential, basic rate	mos	1.60	12/97	18c
Telephone services, expenditures on	yr	860	1999	30r
Education				
Board, 4-year private college/university	yr	1443	1996	38s
Board, 4-year public college/university	yr	2101	1996	38s
Education expenditures	yr	431	1999	30r
Room, 4-year private college/university	yr	2701	1996	38s
Room, 4-year public college/university	yr	2407	1996	38s
Total cost, 4-year private college/university	yr	11518	1996	38s
Total cost, 4-year public college/university	yr	8489	1996	38s
Tuition, 2-year public college/university, in state	yr	1266	1996	38s

Values are in dollars or fractions of dollars. In the column headed *Ref*, references are shown to sources. Each reference is followed by a letter. These refer to the geographical level for which data were reported: s=State, r=Region, and c=City or metro. The abbreviation *ex* is used to mean *except* or *excluding*; *exp* stands for *expenditures*. For other abbreviations and further explanations, please see the Introduction.

Dover, DE - continued

Item	Per	Value	Date	Ref.
Education				
Tuition, 4-year private college/university, in state	yr	7373	1996	38s
Tuition, 4-year public college/university	yr	3981	1996	38s
Energy and Fuels				
Electricity	KWh	0.09	7/01	11r
Electricity	500 KWhs	47.29	7/01	11r
Energy, combined forms, 2400 sq ft	mos	155.32	3/01	4c
Energy, exc. electricity, 2400 sq ft	mos	85.35	3/01	4c
Fuel oil #2	gal	1.43	7/01	11r
Fuel oil and other fuels, expenditures on	yr	45	1999	30r
Gas, cooking, winter, 10 therms	mos	13.93	2/96	98c
Gas, cooking, winter, 30 therms	mos	30.56	2/96	98c
Gas, cooking, winter, 50 therms	mos	46.07	2/96	98c
Gas, heating, winter, average use	mos	127.82	2/96	98c
Gas, natural, commercial rate	1000 cf	7.37	11/00	88s
Gas, regular unleaded, cash, self-service	gal	1.43	3/01	4c
Gasoline, all types	gal	1.60	7/01	11r
Gasoline, unleaded midgrade	gal	1.65	7/01	11r
Gasoline, unleaded premium	gal	1.74	7/01	11r
Natural gas, expenditures on	yr	164	1999	30r
Utility (piped) gas, therm		1.01	7/01	11r
Utility (piped) gas, 40 therms		44.29	7/01	11r
Utility (piped) gas, 100 therms		97.44	7/01	11r
Entertainment				
Bowling, Saturday evening rate	line	3.05	3/01	4c
Entertainment purchases	yr	1574	1999	30r
Fees and admissions paid	yr	371	1999	30r
Monopoly game, Parker Brothers', No. 9	game	11.69	3/01	4c
Movie, first-run, Saturday, evening	adm.	7.00	3/01	4c
Reading purchases	yr	121	1999	30r
Television, radios, sound equipment, expenditures on	yr	561	1999	30r
Tennis balls, yellow, Wilson or Penn, 3	can	2.03	3/01	4c
Funerals				
Total cost of funeral		5922.53	1/99	78r
Acknowledgement cards		63.43	1/99	78r
Casket		2258.77	1/99	78r
Cosmetology, hair, other preparation		127.09	1/99	78r
Embalming		393.49	1/99	78r
Funeral at funeral home		367.50	1/99	78r
Hearse (local)		169.66	1/99	78r
Professional service charges		1211.32	1/99	78r
Service car/van		80.69	1/99	78r
Transfer of remains to funeral home		144.25	1/99	78r
Vault		803.50	1/99	78r
Visitation/viewing		302.83	1/99	78r
Groceries				
Groceries, ACCRA Index		104.70	3/01	4c
American processed cheese	lb	3.50	7/01	11r
Antibiotic ointment, Polysporin	0.5 oz	4.78	3/01	4c
Baby food, strained vegetables or fruit, lowest price	4-4.5 oz	0.48	3/01	4c
Bakery products, expenditures on	yr	261	1999	30r
Bananas	lb	0.54	3/01	4c
Bananas	lb	0.47	7/01	11r
Beans, dried, any type, all sizes	lb	0.63	7/01	11r
Beef for stew, boneless	lb	2.86	7/01	11r
Beef or hamburger, ground	lb	1.43	3/01	4c
Beef, expenditures on	yr	210	1999	30r
Bologna, all beef or mixed	lb	2.29	7/01	11r
Bread, French	lb	1.66	7/01	11r
Bread, white	loaf	0.89	3/01	4c
Bread, white, pan	lb	0.87	7/01	11r
Bread, whole wheat, pan	lb	1.38	7/01	11r
Broccoli	lb	1.04	7/01	11r
Butter, salted, grade AA, stick	lb	2.26	7/01	11r
Butter, yoghurt, cheese, etc, expenditures on	yr	170	1999	30r
Cabbage	lb	0.42	7/01	11r

Dover, DE - continued

Item	Per	Value	Date	Ref.
Groceries - continued				
Cereals and cereal products, expenditures on	yr	140	1999	30r
Cheddar cheese, natural	lb	3.75	7/01	11r
Cheese, Kraft grated Parmesan	8 oz	4.35	3/01	4c
Chicken breast, bone-in	lb	1.85	7/01	11r
Chicken legs, bone-in	lb	1.34	7/01	11r
Chicken, fresh, whole	lb	1.05	7/01	11r
Chicken, whole fryer	lb	1.27	3/01	4c
Chops, boneless,	lb	4.13	7/01	11r
Chuck roast, graded and ungraded, excl U.S. prime and choice	lb	2.35	7/01	11r
Chuck roast, U.S. choice, boneless	lb	2.67	7/01	11r
Cigarettes, Winston, Kings	carton	30.10	3/01	4c
Coffee, 100%, ground roast, all sizes	lb	2.88	7/01	11r
Coffee, instant, plain, regular, all sizes	16 oz	9.25	7/01	11r
Coffee, vacuum-packed	13 oz	2.29	3/01	4c
Cola, non diet,	2 liter	1.11	7/01	11r
Corn Flakes, Kellogg's or Post Toasties	18 oz	2.99	3/01	4c
Corn, frozen, whole kernel, lowest price	16 oz	0.89	3/01	4c
Crackers, soda, salted	lb	1.70	7/01	11r
Dairy product purchases	yr	282	1999	30r
Eggs, expenditures on	yr	32	1999	30r
Eggs, Grade A or AA	dozen	1.27	3/01	4c
Fats and oils, expenditures on	yr	79	1999	30r
Fish and seafood, expenditures on	yr	99	1999	30r
Flour, white, all purpose	lb	0.32	7/01	11r
Food (excl fruit and vegetables), eaten at home, purchases	yr	815	1999	30r
Food cooked on trips, expenditures on	yr	36	1999	30r
Food purchases	yr	4533	1999	30r
Food purchases, eaten away from home	yr	1873	1999	30r
Food purchases, food eaten at home	yr	2660	1999	30r
Fresh fruits, expenditures on	yr	128	1999	30r
Fresh milk and cream, expenditures on	yr	112	1999	30r
Fresh vegetables, expenditures on	yr	131	1999	30r
Fruit and vegetable purchases	yr	438	1999	30r
Grapefruit	lb	0.59	7/01	11r
Grapes, Thompson, seedless	lb	2.12	7/01	11r
Ground beef, 100% beef	lb	1.76	7/01	11r
Ground beef, lean and extra lean	lb	2.60	7/01	11r
Ground chuck, 100% beef	lb	2.08	7/01	11r
Ham, boneless, excl canned	lb	2.71	7/01	11r
Ham, rump or shank half, bone-in, smoked	lb	2.19	7/01	11r
Ice cream, prepackaged, bulk, regular	1/2 gal	3.93	7/01	11r
Lemons	lb	1.32	7/01	11r
Lettuce, iceberg	head	1.27	3/01	4c
Lettuce, iceberg	lb	0.76	7/01	11r
Margarine, Blue Bonnet or Parkay, stick	lb	0.91	3/01	4c
Milk, fresh, low fat,	gal	2.75	7/01	11r
Milk, fresh, whole, fortified	gal	2.97	7/01	11r
Milk, whole	1/2 gal	1.66	3/01	4c
Nonalcoholic beverages, expenditures on	yr	228	1999	30r
Orange juice, frozen concentrate	16 oz	1.95	7/01	11r
Orange juice, Minute Maid frozen	12 oz	1.67	3/01	4c
Oranges, Navel	lb	0.73	7/01	11r
Oranges, Valencia	lb	0.55	7/01	11r
Peaches, halves or slices, Hunt's, Del Monte, or Libby's	29 oz	1.63	3/01	4c
Peanut butter, creamy, all sizes	lb	1.83	7/01	11r
Pears, Anjou	lb	0.98	7/01	11r
Peas, green, Del Monte or Green Giant	15 oz	0.70	3/01	4c
Pork chops, center cut, bone-in	lb	3.33	7/01	11r
Pork sausage, fresh, loose	lb	2.59	7/01	11r
Pork shoulder picnic, bone-in, smoked	lb	1.12	7/01	11r
Pork, expenditures on	yr	162	1999	30r
Potato chips	16 oz	3.59	7/01	11r
Potatoes, frozen, french fried	lb	1.00	7/01	11r
Potatoes, white or red	10 lb	2.75	3/01	4c
Potatoes, white, all types	lb	0.44	7/01	11r
Poultry, expenditures on	yr	137	1999	30r
Processed fruits, expenditures on	yr	97	1999	30r
Processed vegetables, expenditures on	yr	82	1999	30r

Values are in dollars or fractions of dollars. In the column headed *Ref*, references are shown to sources. Each reference is followed by a letter. These refer to the geographical level for which data were reported: s=State, r=Region, and c=City or metro. The abbreviation *ex* is used to mean *except* or *excluding*; *exp* stands for expenditures. For other abbreviations and further explanations, please see the Introduction.

Dover, DE - continued

Item	Per	Value	Date	Ref.
Groceries				
Rice, white, long grain, uncooked	lb	0.51	7/01	11r
Round roast, graded and ungraded, excl U.S. prime and choice	lb	2.96	7/01	11r
Round steak, graded and ungraded, excl U.S. prime and choice	lb	3.11	7/01	11r
Sausage, Jimmy Dean/Owens pork	lb	2.96	3/01	4c
Shortening, vegetable, Crisco	3 lb	3.51	3/01	4c
Sirloin steak, graded and ungraded, excl U.S. prime and choice	lb	4.23	7/01	11r
Soft drink, Coca Cola, ex deposit	2 liter	1.14	3/01	4c
Spaghetti and macaroni	lb	0.78	7/01	11r
Steak, round, U.S. choice, boneless	lb	3.56	7/01	11r
Steak, sirloin, U.S. choice, boneless	lb	5.65	7/01	11r
Steak, T-bone	lb	7.75	3/01	4c
Strawberries, dry pint	12 oz	1.50	7/01	11r
Sugar and other sweets, expenditures on	yr	99	1999	30r
Sugar, cane or beet	4 lbs	1.82	3/01	4c
Sugar, white, 33-80 ounce package	lb	0.39	7/01	11r
Sugar, white, all sizes	lb	0.42	7/01	11r
Tobacco products and smoking supplies purchases	yr	288	1999	30r
Tomatoes, field grown	lb	1.43	7/01	11r
Tomatoes, Hunt's or Del Monte	14.5 oz	0.93	3/01	4c
Tuna, chunk, light	6 oz	0.66	3/01	4c
Tuna, light, chunk	lb	1.77	7/01	11r
Turkey, frozen, whole	lb	1.05	7/01	11r
Goods and Services				
Miscellaneous goods and services, ACCRA Index		98.10	3/01	4c
B&B Japanese maple (acer japonicum)	gal	49.98-129.00	4/00	93r
Boxwood (buxus)	2 gal	12.99-16.99	4/00	93r
Daylilly (hemerocallis)	gal	4.99-8.99	4/00	93r
Flat of annuals		11.00-13.92	4/00	93r
Fountain grass (pennisetum)	gal	5.98-7.98	4/00	93r
Hanging basket (10 in)		7.99-14.98	4/00	93r
Hardy geranium (geranium)	gal	5.98-8.00	4/00	93r
Hosta (hosta)	gal	4.99-10.98	4/00	93r
Lilac (syrubga vulgaris)	2 gal	12.99-21.99	4/00	93r
Rhododendron (rhododendron)	2 gal	14.99-24.99	4/00	93r
Sage (salvia)	gal	5.98-6.99	4/00	93r
Wintercreeper euonymus (euonymus fortunei)	2 gal	7.99-89.99	4/00	93r
Hunting license	yr	12.50	4/01	34s
Health Care				
Health care, ACCRA Index		94.90	3/01	4c
Cardiac catheterization, ave hospital/physician charges		14610	1998	77s
Childbirth, Cesarean delivery		11587	1997	13r
Childbirth, vaginal delivery		6725	1997	13r
Dentist's fee, adult teeth cleaning and periodic oral exam	visit	80.00	3/01	4c
Doctor's fee, routine exam, established patient	visit	46.75	3/01	4c
Drugs, expenditures on	yr	399	1999	30r
Health care purchases	yr	1971	1999	30r
Health insurance expenditures	yr	933	1999	30r
Hospital care, private room	day	464.00	3/01	4c
Hysterectomy, laproscopically-assisted, ave hospital/physician charges		12750	1998	76s

Dover, DE - continued

Item	Per	Value	Date	Ref.
Health Care - continued				
Hysterectomy, vaginal, ave hospital and physician charges		7150	1998	76s
Medicaid dispensing fee		3.65	1999	87s
Medical services expenditures	yr	547	1999	30r
Medical supplies, expenditures on	yr	91	1999	30r
Plastic surgery, breast augmentation		2870	2000	7r
Plastic surgery, breast lift		3649	2000	7r
Plastic surgery, facelift		5008	2000	7r
Plastic surgery, hair transplantation		3425	2000	7r
Plastic surgery, lip augmentation		1227	2000	7r
Plastic surgery, lower body lift		4793	2000	7r
Plastic surgery, thigh lift		3862	2000	7r
Household Goods				
Dishwashing powder, Cascade	50 oz	2.67	3/01	4c
Floor coverings, expenditures on	yr	44	1999	30r
Furniture, expenditures on	yr	335	1999	30r
Household furnishings and equipment purchases	yr	1328	1999	30r
Household textiles, expenditures on	yr	89	1999	30r
Laundry and cleaning supplies, expenditures on	yr	113	1999	30r
Tissues, facial, Kleenex brand	175	1.54	3/01	4c
Housing				
Housing, ACCRA Index		100.00	3/01	4c
Home price, existing, ave		160100	10/00	90r
Home value, median		181000	2001	53s
House, 2400 sq ft, 8000 sq ft lot, new, urban, utilities	total	210196	3/01	4c
House payment, principal and interest, 25% down payment	mos	1071	3/01	4c
Household operation expenditures	yr	553	1999	30r
Housekeeping supplies purchases	yr	473	1999	30r
Housing, expenditures on	yr	10303	1999	30r
Maintenance, repairs, insurance expenditures	yr	699	1999	30r
Monthly rental value of owned home	mos	505	1999	30r
Owned dwellings, expenditures own	yr	3465	1999	30r
Rent expenditures	yr	1641	1999	30r
Rent, apartment, 2 br, 1 1/2-2 baths, unfurn, 950 sq ft, water	mos	590	3/01	4c
Rental unit, 1 bedroom, with utilities	mos	547	4/01	41c
Rental unit, 2 bedroom, with utilities	mos	624	4/01	41c
Rental unit, 3 bedroom, with utilities	mos	809	4/01	41c
Rental unit, 4 bedroom, with utilities	mos	920	4/01	41c
Shelter, expenditures on	yr	5467	1999	30r
Insurance and Pensions				
Life and other personal insurance purchases	yr	414	1999	30r
Pensions and Social Security, expenditures on	yr	2635	1999	30r
Personal insurance and pensions, expenditures on	yr	3048	1999	30r
Legal Fees				
Divorce, filing fee		75.00	4/01	35s
Driver's license fee	orig	12.50	1999	48s
Driver's license fee	renew	12.50	1999	48s
Personal Goods				
Personal care products and services purchases	yr	393	1999	30r
Shampoo, Alberto VO5	15 oz	1.12	3/01	4c
Toothpaste, Crest or Colgate	6-7 oz	1.97	3/01	4c
Personal Services				
Dry cleaning, man's 2-pc suit		7.92	3/01	4c
Man's haircut, barbershop, no styling		8.20	3/01	4c
Personal services, household, expenditures on	yr	258	1999	30r
Woman's shampoo, trim, blow-dry, no style-change		22.60	3/01	4c

Values are in dollars or fractions of dollars. In the column headed *Ref*, references are shown to sources. Each reference is followed by a letter. These refer to the geographical level for which data were reported: s=State, r=Region, and c=City or metro. The abbreviation *ex* is used to mean *except* or *excluding*; *exp* stands for *expenditures*. For other abbreviations and further explanations, please see the Introduction.

Dover, DE - continued

Item	Per	Value	Date	Ref.
Pets				
Pets, toys, and playground equipment, expenditures on	yr	306	1999	30r
Restaurant Food				
Chicken, fried, thigh and drumstick, KFC/ Church's		2.79	3/01	4c
Hamburger with cheese, McDonald's	1/4 lb	2.29	3/01	4c
Pizza, Pizza Hut or Pizza Inn	11-12 in	10.79	3/01	4c
Taxes				
Federal income taxes paid	yr	2047	1999	30r
Personal taxes, expenditures on	yr	2554	1999	30r
Property taxes paid	yr	726	1999	30r
State and local income taxes paid	yr	363	1999	30r
Transportation				
Transportation, ACCRA Index		95.40	3/01	4c
Cars and trucks, new, expenditures on	yr	1648	1999	30r
Cars and trucks, used, expenditures on	yr	1651	1999	30r
Diesel at the pump	gal	1.26	10/99	73s
Gasoline and motor oil purchases	yr	1052	1999	30r
Gasoline before-tax price (cents)	gal	112.60	10/00	43s
Maintenance and repair expenditures	yr	621	1999	30r
Motorcycle license fee	orig	5.00	1999	49s
Motorcycle license fee	renew	5.00	1999	49s
Public transportation, expenditures on	yr	298	1999	30r
Tire balance, computer or spin balance, front	wheel	6.83	3/01	4c
Transportation purchases	yr	6738	1999	30r
Vehicle expenses, miscellaneous, purchases	yr	2033	1999	30r
Vehicle insurance payments	yr	696	1999	30r
Vehicle purchases (net outlay)	yr	3354	1999	30r
Vehicle rental, lease expenditures	yr	352	1999	30r
Utilities				
Utilities, ACCRA Index		120.40	3/01	4c
Electrical bill, average	mos	81.50	9/00	9s
Electricity, expenditures on	yr	1115	1999	30r
Electricity and other, mixed, 2400 sq ft, new home	mos	69.97	3/01	4c
Electricity cost, average	KWh	6.60	9/00	9s
Water and other public services, expenditures on	yr	298	1999	30r
Weddings				
Wedding (national average cost)		19936	2000	33r
Wedding (regional average total cost)		16293	1997	110r
Attendants' gifts		321	1998	33r
Bridal attendants' apparel (5 persons)		824	2000	33r
Bride's headpiece/veil		173	1998	33r
Bride's wedding dress		859	1998	33r
Clergy, religious facility fee		242	1998	33r
Engagement ring		3177	1998	33r
Flowers		789	1998	33r
Groom's formalwear rental		99	2000	33r
Limousine		410	1998	33r
Marriage license cost		35.00	4/01	35s
Men's formalwear (ushers, best man)		469	2000	33r
Mother of bride apparel		241	2000	33r
Music		866	1998	33r
Photography and videography		1368	1998	33r
Rehearsal dinner		728	1998	33r
Wedding invitations and announcements		341	1998	33r
Wedding reception		7968	2000	33r
Wedding rings (bride and groom)		1060	1998	33r

Dubuque, IA

Item	Per	Value	Date	Ref.
Average annual expenditures	yr	35369	1999	30r
Alcoholic Beverages				
Alcoholic beverage purchases	yr	304	1999	30r
Malt beverages, all types, all sizes, any origin	16 oz	0.93	7/01	11r
Wine, red and white table, all sizes, any origin	liter	7.04	7/01	11r

Dubuque, IA - continued

Item	Per	Value	Date	Ref.
Appliances				
Major appliances, expenditures on	yr	165	1999	30r
Small appliances, housewares, expenditures on	yr	90	1999	30r
Banking and Money				
Mortgage interest and charges paid	yr	2277	1999	30r
Mortgage principal paid on owned property	yr	1230	1999	30r
Vehicle finance charges paid	yr	328	1999	30r
Charity				
Cash contributions, expenditures	yr	1126	1999	30r
Child Care				
Child raising cost, total, age 0-2	yr	7890	1999	60r
Child raising cost, total, age 3-5	yr	8130	1999	60r
Child raising cost, total, age 6-8	yr	8170	1999	60r
Child raising cost, total, age 9-11	yr	8190	1999	60r
Child raising cost, total, age 12-14	yr	8890	1999	60r
Child raising cost, total, age 15-17	yr	9050	1999	60r
Child's child care and education, age 0-2	yr	1240	1999	60r
Child's child care and education, age 3-5	yr	1370	1999	60r
Child's child care and education, age 6-8	yr	880	1999	60r
Child's child care and education, age 9-11	yr	570	1999	60r
Child's child care and education, age 12-14	yr	420	1999	60r
Child's child care and education, age 15-17	yr	720	1999	60r
Child's clothing, age 0-2	yr	410	1999	60r
Child's clothing, age 3-5	yr	400	1999	60r
Child's clothing, age 6-8	yr	450	1999	60r
Child's clothing, age 9-11	yr	500	1999	60r
Child's clothing, age 12-14	yr	840	1999	60r
Child's clothing, age 15-17	yr	740	1999	60r
Child's food, age 0-2	yr	960	1999	60r
Child's food, age 3-5	yr	1120	1999	60r
Child's food, age 6-8	yr	1430	1999	60r
Child's food, age 9-11	yr	1710	1999	60r
Child's food, age 12-14	yr	1710	1999	60r
Child's food, age 15-17	yr	1920	1999	60r
Child's health care, age 0-2	yr	520	1999	60r
Child's health care, age 3-5	yr	500	1999	60r
Child's health care, age 6-8	yr	570	1999	60r
Child's health care, age 9-11	yr	610	1999	60r
Child's health care, age 12-14	yr	630	1999	60r
Child's health care, age 15-17	yr	650	1999	60r
Child's housing, age 0-2	yr	2860	1999	60r
Child's housing, age 3-5	yr	2840	1999	60r
Child's housing, age 6-8	yr	2800	1999	60r
Child's housing, age 9-11	yr	2650	1999	60r
Child's housing, age 12-14	yr	2840	1999	60r
Child's housing, age 15-17	yr	2440	1999	60r
Child's personal care, reading, age 0-2	yr	880	1999	60r
Child's personal care, reading, age 3-5	yr	900	1999	60r
Child's personal care, reading, age 6-8	yr	930	1999	60r
Child's personal care, reading, age 9-11	yr	970	1999	60r
Child's personal care, reading, age 12-14	yr	1150	1999	60r
Child's personal care, reading, age 15-17	yr	920	1999	60r
Clothing				
Apparel and services purchases	yr	1607	1999	30r
Boys, 2 to 15, expenditures on	yr	91	1999	30r
Children under 2, expenditures on	yr	59	1999	30r
Footwear, expenditures on	yr	285	1999	30r
Girls, 2 to 15, expenditures on	yr	116	1999	30r
Men and boys, expenditures on	yr	433	1999	30r
Men, 16 and over, expenditures on	yr	341	1999	30r
Women, 16 and over, expenditures on	yr	490	1999	30r
Communications				
Phone line, single, business, field visit	inst.	50.00	12/97	17s
Phone line, single, business, no field visit	inst.	50.00	12/97	17s
Phone line, single, residence, field visit	inst.	35.00	12/97	17s
Phone line, single, residence, no field visit	inst.	35.00	12/97	17s
Postage and stationery, expenditures on	yr	140	1999	30r
Postal rate, express mail, up to half-pound		12.45	7/01	108r
Postal rate, letter, first class, first ounce		0.34	7/01	108r

Values are in dollars or fractions of dollars. In the column headed *Ref*, references are shown to sources. Each reference is followed by a letter. These refer to the geographical level for which data were reported: s=State, r=Region, and c=City or metro. The abbreviation *ex* is used to mean *except* or *excluding*; *exp* stands for *expenditures*. For other abbreviations and further explanations, please see the Introduction.

Dubuque, IA - continued

Item	Per	Value	Date	Ref.
Communications				
Postal rate, letter, two ounces		0.57	7/01	108r
Postal rate, post card		0.21	7/01	108r
Postal rate, priority mail, two pounds		3.95	7/01	108r
Postal rate, priority mail, up to one pound		3.50	7/01	108r
Telephone bill, business, basic rate	mos	30.15	12/97	18c
Telephone bill, residential, basic rate	mos	12.05	12/97	18c
Telephone services, expenditures on	yr	830	1999	30r
Education				
Board, 4-year private college/university	yr	2138	1996	38s
Board, 4-year public college/university	yr .	1688	1996	38s
Education expenditures	yr	583	1999	30r
Room, 4-year private college/university	yr	1864	1996	38s
Room, 4-year public college/university	yr	1693	1996	38s
Total cost, 4-year private college/university	yr	15934	1996	38s
Total cost, 4-year public college/university	yr	5945	1996	38s
Tuition, 2-year public college/university, in state	yr	1782	1996	38s
Tuition, 4-year private college/university, in state	yr	11932	1996	38s
Tuition, 4-year public college/university	yr	2565	1996	38s
Energy and Fuels				
Electricity	500 KWhs	46.59	7/01	11r
Fuel oil #2	gal	1.27	7/01	11r
Fuel oil and other fuels, expenditures on	yr	68	1999	30r
Gas, natural, commercial rate	1000 cf	7.18	11/00	88s
Gasoline, unleaded midgrade	gal	1.79	7/01	11r
Gasoline, unleaded premium	gal	1.86	7/01	11r
Gasoline, unleaded regular	gal	1.58	7/01	11r
Natural gas, expenditures on	yr	389	1999	30r
Utility (piped) gas, therm		0.81	7/01	11r
Utility (piped) gas, 40 therms		38.01	7/01	11r
Utility (piped) gas, 100 therms		81.75	7/01	11r
Entertainment				
Entertainment purchases	yr	1984	1999	30r
Fees and admissions paid	yr	444	1999	30r
Television, radios, sound equipment, expenditures on	yr	580	1999	30r
Funerals				
Cosmetology, hair, other preparation		178.32	1/99	78r
Embalming		408.19	1/99	78r
Funeral at funeral home		362.13	1/99	78r
Professional service charges		1375.51	1/99	78r
Transfer of remains to funeral home		155.92	1/99	78r
Visitation/viewing		294.38	1/99	78r
Groceries				
Bacon, sliced	lb	3.15	7/01	11r
Bakery products, expenditures on	yr	281	1999	30r
Bananas	lb	0.48	7/01	11r
Beans, dried, any type, all sizes	lb	0.61	7/01	11r
Beef for stew, boneless	lb	3.08	7/01	11r
Beef, expenditures on	yr	217	1999	30r
Bologna, all beef or mixed	lb	2.52	7/01	11r
Bread, white, pan	lb	1.06	7/01	11r
Broccoli	lb	0.91	7/01	11r
Butter, salted, grade AA, stick	lb	3.04	7/01	11r
Butter, yoghurt, cheese, etc, expenditures on	yr	183	1999	30r
Cereals and bakery product purchases	yr	430	1999	30r
Cereals and cereal products, expenditures on	yr	149	1999	30r
Chicken, fresh, whole	lb	1.07	7/01	11r
Chops, boneless,	lb	3.64	7/01	11r
Chuck roast, U.S. choice, boneless	lb	2.47	7/01	11r
Coffee, 100%, ground roast, all sizes	lb	2.69	7/01	11r
Cookies, chocolate chip	lb	2.87	7/01	11r
Dairy product purchases	yr	304	1999	30r
Eggs, expenditures on	yr	26	1999	30r
Eggs, grade A, large	dozen	0.88	7/01	11r
Fats and oils, expenditures on	yr	75	1999	30r

Dubuque, IA - continued

Item	Per	Value	Date	Ref.
Groceries - continued				
Fish and seafood, expenditures on	yr	72	1999	30r
Food (excl fruit and vegetables), eaten at home, purchases	yr	887	1999	30r
Food cooked on trips, expenditures on	yr	44	1999	30r
Food purchases	yr	4802	1999	30r
Food purchases, eaten away from home	yr	2069	1999	30r
Food purchases, food eaten at home	yr	2733	1999	30r
Fresh fruits, expenditures on	yr	138	1999	30r
Fresh milk and cream, expenditures on	yr	120	1999	30r
Fresh vegetables, expenditures on	yr	126	1999	30r
Grapefruit	lb	0.66	7/01	11r
Grapes, Thompson, seedless	lb	1.64	7/01	11r
Ground beef, 100% beef	lb	1.64	7/01	11r
Ground beef, lean and extra lean	lb	2.16	7/01	11r
Ground chuck, 100% beef	lb	2.13	7/01	11r
Ham, boneless, excl canned	lb	2.62	7/01	11r
Ice cream, prepackaged, bulk, regular	1/2 gal	3.35	7/01	11r
Lemons	lb	1.19	7/01	11r
Lettuce, iceberg	lb	0.73	7/01	11r
Margarine, soft, tubs	lb	0.89	7/01	11r
Meats, poultry, fish, and egg purchases	yr	671	1999	30r
Milk, fresh, whole, fortified	gal	2.71	7/01	11r
Nonalcoholic beverages, expenditures on	yr	239	1999	30r
Oranges, Navel	lb	0.80	7/01	11r
Oranges, Valencia	lb	0.66	7/01	11r
Pears, Anjou	lb	0.93	7/01	11r
Pork chops, center cut, bone-in	lb	3.63	7/01	11r
Pork, expenditures on	yr	150	1999	30r
Potato chips	16 oz	3.52	7/01	11r
Potatoes, frozen, french fried	lb	1.08	7/01	11r
Potatoes, white, all types	lb	0.33	7/01	11r
Poultry, expenditures on	yr	108	1999	30r
Processed fruits, expenditures on	yr	98	1999	30r
Processed vegetables, expenditures on	yr	80	1999	30r
Round roast, U.S. choice, boneless	lb	3.07	7/01	11r
Round steak, graded and ungraded, excl U.S. prime and choice	lb	3.41	7/01	11r
Shortening, vegetable oil blends	lb	1.13	7/01	11r
Spaghetti and macaroni	lb	0.80	7/01	11r
Steak, round, U.S. choice, boneless	lb	3.23	7/01	11r
Steak, T-bone, U.S. choice, bone-in	lb	6.68	7/01	11r
Strawberries, dry pint	12 oz	1.32	7/01	11r
Sugar and other sweets, expenditures on	yr	114	1999	30r
Sugar, white, 33-80 ounce package	lb	0.42	7/01	11r
Sugar, white, all sizes	lb	0.43	7/01	11r
Tobacco products and smoking supplies purchases	yr	331	1999	30r
Tomatoes, field grown	lb	1.46	7/01	11r
Tuna, light, chunk	lb	1.80	7/01	11r
Turkey, frozen, whole	lb	1.15	7/01	11r
Goods and Services				
B&B Japanese maple (acer japonicum)	gal	29.99- 169.99	4/00	93r
Boxwood (buxus)	2 gal	18.99- 39.99	4/00	93r
Daylily (hemerocallis)	gal	4.99- 25.00	4/00	93r
Flat of annuals		11.98- 24.99	4/00	93r
Fountain grass (pennisetum)	gal	5.98- 12.98	4/00	93r
Hanging basket (10 in)		12.99- 27.99	4/00	93r
Hardy geranium (geranium)	gal	7.99- 9.99	4/00	93r
Hosta (hosta)	gal	6.00- 25.00	4/00	93r
Lilac (syrubga vulgaris)	2 gal	14.99- 24.99	4/00	93r
Miscellaneous purchases	yr	865	1999	30r
Rhododendron (rhododendron)	2 gal	23.98- 42.99	4/00	93r

Values are in dollars or fractions of dollars. In the column headed *Ref*, references are shown to sources. Each reference is followed by a letter. These refer to the geographical level for which data were reported: s=State, r=Region, and c=City or metro. The abbreviation *ex* is used to mean *except* or *excluding*; *exp* stands for expenditures. For other abbreviations and further explanations, please see the Introduction.

Dubuque, IA - continued

Item	Per	Value	Date	Ref.
Goods and Services				
Sage (salvia)	gal	6.00-9.99	4/00	93r
Wintercreeper euonymus (euonymus fortunei)	2 gal	16.00-169.99	4/00	93r
Hunting license	yr	16.00	4/01	34s
Health Care				
Cardiac catheterization, ave hospital/physician charges		8810	1998	77s
Childbirth, Cesarean delivery		10722	1997	13r
Childbirth, vaginal delivery		6223	1997	13r
Drugs, expenditures on	yr	394	1999	30r
Health care purchases	yr	2048	1999	30r
Health insurance expenditures	yr	978	1999	30r
Hysterectomy, laproscopically-assisted, ave hospital/physician charges		8620	1998	76s
Hysterectomy, vaginal, ave hospital and physician charges		6630	1998	76s
Medicaid dispensing fee		4.10-6.38	1999	87s
Medical services expenditures	yr	554	1999	30r
Medical supplies, expenditures on	yr	122	1999	30r
Plastic surgery, breast augmentation		3184	2000	7r
Plastic surgery, breast lift		3585	2000	7r
Plastic surgery, facelift		4999	2000	7r
Plastic surgery, hair transplantation		3105	2000	7r
Plastic surgery, lip augmentation		1290	2000	7r
Plastic surgery, lower body lift		8135	2000	7r
Plastic surgery, thigh lift		3839	2000	7r
Household Goods				
Floor coverings, expenditures on	yr	52	1999	30r
Furniture, expenditures on	yr	344	1999	30r
Household furnishings and equipment purchases	yr	1475	1999	30r
Household textiles, expenditures on	yr	109	1999	30r
Laundry and cleaning supplies, expenditures on	yr	134	1999	30r
Housing				
Home, 2200 sq ft, 4-br, 2-bath, 2-car garage, average		156575	2000	47c
Home price, existing, ave		144400	10/00	90r
Home value, median		100000	2001	53s
Household operation expenditures	yr	542	1999	30r
Housekeeping supplies purchases	yr	508	1999	30r
Lodging expenditures	yr	430	1999	30r
Maintenance, repairs, insurance expenditures	yr	853	1999	30r
Monthly rental value of owned home	mos	547	1999	30r
Owned dwellings, expenditures own	yr	4282	1999	30r
Rent expenditures	yr	1558	1999	30r
Rental unit, 1 bedroom, with utilities	mos	363	4/01	41c
Rental unit, 2 bedroom, with utilities	mos	466	4/01	41c
Rental unit, 3 bedroom, with utilities	mos	596	4/01	41c
Rental unit, 4 bedroom, with utilities	mos	727	4/01	41c
Shelter, expenditures on	yr	6270	1999	30r
Insurance and Pensions				
Auto insurance premium	yr	520.76	1999	57s
Life and other personal insurance purchases	yr	387	1999	30r
Pensions and Social Security, expenditures on	yr	2968	1999	30r
Legal Fees				
Divorce, filing fee		110.00	4/01	35s
Driver's license fee	renew	16.00	1999	48s
Driver's license fee	orig	16.00	1999	48s
Personal Goods				
Personal care products and services purchases	yr	385	1999	30r

Dubuque, IA - continued

Item	Per	Value	Date	Ref.
Personal Services				
Personal services, household, expenditures on	yr	300	1999	30r
Pets				
Pets, toys, and playground equipment, expenditures on	yr	375	1999	30r
Taxes				
Federal income taxes paid	yr	2326	1999	30r
Personal taxes, expenditures on	yr	3223	1999	30r
Property taxes paid	yr	1152	1999	30r
State and local income taxes paid	yr	753	1999	30r
Transportation				
Cars and trucks, new, expenditures on	yr	1280	1999	30r
Cars and trucks, used, expenditures on	yr	1763	1999	30r
Diesel at the pump	gal	1.25	10/99	73s
Gasoline and motor oil purchases	yr	1036	1999	30r
Gasoline before-tax price (cents)	gal	112.30	10/00	43s
Maintenance and repair expenses	yr	594	1999	30r
Public transportation, expenditures on	yr	341	1999	30r
Transportation purchases	yr	6617	1999	30r
Vehicle expenses, miscellaneous, purchases	yr	2159	1999	30r
Vehicle insurance payments	yr	701	1999	30r
Vehicle purchases (net outlay)	yr	3081	1999	30r
Vehicle rental, lease expenditures	yr	536	1999	30r
Utilities				
Electrical bill, average	mos	67.25	9/00	9s
Electricity, expenditures on	yr	841	1999	30r
Electricity, summer, 250 KWh	mos	22.89	2/96	97c
Electricity, summer, 500 KWh	mos	40.09	2/96	97c
Electricity, summer, 750 KWh	mos	57.29	2/96	97c
Electricity, summer, 1000 KWh	mos	74.50	2/96	97c
Electricity cost, average	KWh	5.90	9/00	9s
Utilities, fuels, and public services purchased	yr	2401	1999	30r
Water and other public services, expenditures on	yr	273	1999	30r
Weddings				
Wedding (national average cost)		19936	2000	33r
Wedding (regional average total cost)		16195	1997	110r
Attendants' gifts		321	1998	33r
Bridal attendants' apparel (5 persons)		824	2000	33r
Bride's headpiece/veil		173	1998	33r
Bride's wedding dress		859	1998	33r
Clergy, religious facility fee		242	1998	33r
Engagement ring		3177	1998	33r
Flowers		789	1998	33r
Groom's formalwear rental		99	2000	33r
Limousine		410	1998	33r
Marriage license cost		30.00	4/01	35s
Men's formalwear (ushers, best man)		469	2000	33r
Mother of bride apparel		241	2000	33r
Music		866	1998	33r
Photography and videography		1368	1998	33r
Rehearsal dinner		728	1998	33r
Wedding invitations and announcements		341	1998	33r
Wedding reception		7968	2000	33r
Wedding rings (bride and groom)		1060	1998	33r

Duluth-Superior, MN-WI

Item	Per	Value	Date	Ref.
Average annual expenditures	yr	35369	1999	30r
Alcoholic Beverages				
Alcoholic beverage purchases	yr	304	1999	30r
Malt beverages, all types, all sizes, any origin	16 oz	0.93	7/01	11r
Wine, red and white table, all sizes, any origin	liter	7.04	7/01	11r
Appliances				
Major appliances, expenditures on	yr	165	1999	30r
Small appliances, housewares, expenditures on	yr	90	1999	30r

Values are in dollars or fractions of dollars. In the column headed *Ref*, references are shown to sources. Each reference is followed by a letter. These refer to the geographical level for which data were reported: s=State, r=Region, and c=City or metro. The abbreviation *ex* is used to mean *except* or *excluding*; *exp* stands for *expenditures*. For other abbreviations and further explanations, please see the Introduction.

Duluth-Superior, MN-WI - continued

Item	Per	Value	Date	Ref.
Banking and Money				
Mortgage interest and charges paid	yr	2277	1999	30r
Mortgage principal paid on owned property	yr	1230	1999	30r
Vehicle finance charges paid	yr	328	1999	30r
Charity				
Cash contributions, expenditures	yr	1126	1999	30r
Child Care				
Child raising cost, total, age 0-2	yr	7890	1999	60r
Child raising cost, total, age 3-5	yr	8130	1999	60r
Child raising cost, total, age 6-8	yr	8170	1999	60r
Child raising cost, total, age 9-11	yr	8190	1999	60r
Child raising cost, total, age 12-14	yr	8890	1999	60r
Child raising cost, total, age 15-17	yr	9050	1999	60r
Child's child care and education, age 0-2	yr	1240	1999	60r
Child's child care and education, age 3-5	yr	1370	1999	60r
Child's child care and education, age 6-8	yr	880	1999	60r
Child's child care and education, age 9-11	yr	570	1999	60r
Child's child care and education, age 12-14	yr	420	1999	60r
Child's child care and education, age 15-17	yr	720	1999	60r
Child's clothing, age 0-2	yr	410	1999	60r
Child's clothing, age 3-5	yr	400	1999	60r
Child's clothing, age 6-8	yr	450	1999	60r
Child's clothing, age 9-11	yr	500	1999	60r
Child's clothing, age 12-14	yr	840	1999	60r
Child's clothing, age 15-17	yr	740	1999	60r
Child's food, age 0-2	yr	960	1999	60r
Child's food, age 3-5	yr	1120	1999	60r
Child's food, age 6-8	yr	1430	1999	60r
Child's food, age 9-11	yr	1710	1999	60r
Child's food, age 12-14	yr	1710	1999	60r
Child's food, age 15-17	yr	1920	1999	60r
Child's health care, age 0-2	yr	520	1999	60r
Child's health care, age 3-5	yr	500	1999	60r
Child's health care, age 6-8	yr	570	1999	60r
Child's health care, age 9-11	yr	610	1999	60r
Child's health care, age 12-14	yr	630	1999	60r
Child's health care, age 15-17	yr	650	1999	60r
Child's housing, age 0-2	yr	2860	1999	60r
Child's housing, age 3-5	yr	2840	1999	60r
Child's housing, age 6-8	yr	2800	1999	60r
Child's housing, age 9-11	yr	2650	1999	60r
Child's housing, age 12-14	yr	2840	1999	60r
Child's housing, age 15-17	yr	2440	1999	60r
Child's personal care, reading, age 0-2	yr	880	1999	60r
Child's personal care, reading, age 3-5	yr	900	1999	60r
Child's personal care, reading, age 6-8	yr	930	1999	60r
Child's personal care, reading, age 9-11	yr	970	1999	60r
Child's personal care, reading, age 12-14	yr	1150	1999	60r
Child's personal care, reading, age 15-17	yr	920	1999	60r
Clothing				
Apparel and services purchases	yr	1607	1999	30r
Boys, 2 to 15, expenditures on	yr	91	1999	30r
Children under 2, expenditures on	yr	59	1999	30r
Footwear, expenditures on	yr	285	1999	30r
Girls, 2 to 15, expenditures on	yr	116	1999	30r
Men and boys, expenditures on	yr	433	1999	30r
Men, 16 and over, expenditures on	yr	341	1999	30r
Women, 16 and over, expenditures on	yr	490	1999	30r
Communications				
Cable modem installation, Media One		100.00	6/99	103s
Cable modem rate, cable subscriber, Media One	mos	34.95-39.95	6/99	103s
Cable modem rate, non-cable subscriber, Media One	mos	49.95	6/99	103s
Phone line, single, business, field visit	inst.	45.00	12/97	17s
Phone line, single, business, no field visit	inst.	45.00	12/97	17s
Phone line, single, residence, field visit	inst.	16.25	12/97	17s
Phone line, single, residence, no field visit	inst.	16.25	12/97	17s
Postage and stationery, expenditures on	yr	140	1999	30r
Postal rate, express mail, up to half-pound		12.45	7/01	108r
Postal rate, letter, first class, first ounce		0.34	7/01	108r

Duluth-Superior, MN-WI - continued

Item	Per	Value	Date	Ref.
Communications - continued				
Postal rate, letter, two ounces		0.57	7/01	108r
Postal rate, post card		0.21	7/01	108r
Postal rate, priority mail, two pounds		3.95	7/01	108r
Postal rate, priority mail, up to one pound		3.50	7/01	108r
Telephone services, expenditures on	yr	830	1999	30r
Education				
Board, 4-year private college/university	yr	2267	1996	38s
Board, 4-year public college/university	yr	1474	1996	38s
Education expenditures	yr	583	1999	30r
Room, 4-year private college/university	yr	2058	1996	38s
Room, 4-year public college/university	yr	2022	1996	38s
Total cost, 4-year private college/university	yr	17222	1996	38s
Total cost, 4-year public college/university	yr	6712	1996	38s
Tuition, 2-year public college/university, in state	yr	2065	1996	38s
Tuition, 4-year private college/university, in state	yr	12897	1996	38s
Tuition, 4-year public college/university	yr	3216	1996	38s
Energy and Fuels				
Electricity	500 KWhs	46.59	7/01	11r
Fuel oil #2	gal	1.27	7/01	11r
Fuel oil and other fuels, expenditures on	yr	68	1999	30r
Gas, natural, commercial rate	1000 cf	6.86	11/00	88s
Gasoline, unleaded midgrade	gal	1.79	7/01	11r
Gasoline, unleaded premium	gal	1.86	7/01	11r
Gasoline, unleaded regular	gal	1.58	7/01	11r
Natural gas, expenditures on	yr	389	1999	30r
Utility (piped) gas, therm		0.81	7/01	11r
Utility (piped) gas, 40 therms		38.01	7/01	11r
Utility (piped) gas, 100 therms		81.75	7/01	11r
Entertainment				
Entertainment purchases	yr	1984	1999	30r
Fees and admissions paid	yr	444	1999	30r
Television, radios, sound equipment, expenditures on	yr	580	1999	30r
Funerals				
Cosmetology, hair, other preparation		178.32	1/99	78r
Embalming		408.19	1/99	78r
Funeral at funeral home		362.13	1/99	78r
Professional service charges		1375.51	1/99	78r
Transfer of remains to funeral home		155.92	1/99	78r
Visitation/viewing		294.38	1/99	78r
Groceries				
Bacon, sliced	lb	3.15	7/01	11r
Bakery products, expenditures on	yr	281	1999	30r
Bananas	lb	0.48	7/01	11r
Beans, dried, any type, all sizes	lb	0.61	7/01	11r
Beef for stew, boneless	lb	3.08	7/01	11r
Beef, expenditures on	yr	217	1999	30r
Bologna, all beef or mixed	lb	2.52	7/01	11r
Bread, white, pan	lb	1.06	7/01	11r
Broccoli	lb	0.91	7/01	11r
Butter, salted, grade AA, stick	lb	3.04	7/01	11r
Butter, yoghurt, cheese, etc, expenditures on	yr	183	1999	30r
Cereals and bakery product purchases	yr	430	1999	30r
Cereals and cereal products, expenditures on	yr	149	1999	30r
Chicken, fresh, whole	lb	1.07	7/01	11r
Chops, boneless,	lb	3.64	7/01	11r
Chuck roast, U.S. choice, boneless	lb	2.47	7/01	11r
Coffee, 100%, ground roast, all sizes	lb	2.69	7/01	11r
Cookies, chocolate chip	lb	2.87	7/01	11r
Dairy product purchases	yr	304	1999	30r
Eggs, expenditures on	yr	26	1999	30r
Eggs, grade A, large	dozen	0.88	7/01	11r
Fats and oils, expenditures on	yr	75	1999	30r
Fish and seafood, expenditures on	yr	72	1999	30r

Values are in dollars or fractions of dollars. In the column headed *Ref*, references are shown to sources. Each reference is followed by a letter. These refer to the geographical level for which data were reported: s=State, r=Region, and c=City or metro. The abbreviation *ex* is used to mean *except* or *excluding*; *exp* stands for expenditures. For other abbreviations and further explanations, please see the Introduction.

Duluth-Superior, MN-WI - continued

Item	Per	Value	Date	Ref.
Groceries				
Food (excl fruit and vegetables), eaten at home, purchases	yr	887	1999	30r
Food cooked on trips, expenditures on	yr	44	1999	30r
Food purchases	yr	4802	1999	30r
Food purchases, eaten away from home	yr	2069	1999	30r
Food purchases, food eaten at home	yr	2733	1999	30r
Fresh fruits, expenditures on	yr	138	1999	30r
Fresh milk and cream, expenditures on	yr	120	1999	30r
Fresh vegetables, expenditures on	yr	126	1999	30r
Grapefruit	lb	0.66	7/01	11r
Grapes, Thompson, seedless	lb	1.64	7/01	11r
Ground beef, 100% beef	lb	1.64	7/01	11r
Ground beef, lean and extra lean	lb	2.16	7/01	11r
Ground chuck, 100% beef	lb	2.13	7/01	11r
Ham, boneless, excl canned	lb	2.62	7/01	11r
Ice cream, prepackaged, bulk, regular	1/2 gal	3.35	7/01	11r
Lemons	lb	1.19	7/01	11r
Lettuce, iceberg	lb	0.73	7/01	11r
Margarine, soft, tubs	lb	0.89	7/01	11r
Meats, poultry, fish, and egg purchases	yr	671	1999	30r
Milk, fresh, whole, fortified	gal	2.71	7/01	11r
Nonalcoholic beverages, expenditures on	yr	239	1999	30r
Oranges, Navel	lb	0.80	7/01	11r
Oranges, Valencia	lb	0.66	7/01	11r
Pears, Anjou	lb	0.93	7/01	11r
Pork chops, center cut, bone-in	lb	3.63	7/01	11r
Pork, expenditures on	yr	150	1999	30r
Potato chips	16 oz	3.52	7/01	11r
Potatoes, frozen, french fried	lb	1.08	7/01	11r
Potatoes, white, all types	lb	0.33	7/01	11r
Poultry, expenditures on	yr	108	1999	30r
Processed fruits, expenditures on	yr	98	1999	30r
Processed vegetables, expenditures on	yr	80	1999	30r
Round roast, U.S. choice, boneless	lb	3.07	7/01	11r
Round steak, graded and ungraded, excl U.S. prime and choice	lb	3.41	7/01	11r
Shortening, vegetable oil blends	lb	1.13	7/01	11r
Spaghetti and macaroni	lb	0.80	7/01	11r
Steak, round, U.S. choice, boneless	lb	3.23	7/01	11r
Steak, T-bone, U.S. choice, bone-in	lb	6.68	7/01	11r
Strawberries, dry pint	12 oz	1.32	7/01	11r
Sugar and other sweets, expenditures on	yr	114	1999	30r
Sugar, white, 33-80 ounce package	lb	0.42	7/01	11r
Sugar, white, all sizes	lb	0.43	7/01	11r
Tobacco products and smoking supplies purchases	yr	331	1999	30r
Tomatoes, field grown	lb	1.46	7/01	11r
Tuna, light, chunk	lb	1.80	7/01	11r
Turkey, frozen, whole	lb	1.15	7/01	11r
Goods and Services				
B&B Japanese maple (acer japonicum)	gal	29.99-169.99	4/00	93r
Boxwood (buxus)	2 gal	18.99-39.99	4/00	93r
Daylily (hemerocallis)	gal	4.99-25.00	4/00	93r
Flat of annuals		11.98-24.99	4/00	93r
Fountain grass (pennisetum)	gal	5.98-12.98	4/00	93r
Hanging basket (10 in)		12.99-27.99	4/00	93r
Hardy geranium (geranium)	gal	7.99-9.99	4/00	93r
Hosta (hosta)	gal	6.00-25.00	4/00	93r
Lilac (syrubga vulgaris)	2 gal	14.99-24.99	4/00	93r
Miscellaneous purchases	yr	865	1999	30r
Rhododendron (rhododendron)	2 gal	23.98-42.99	4/00	93r

Duluth-Superior, MN-WI - continued

Item	Per	Value	Date	Ref.
Goods and Services - continued				
Sage (salvia)	gal	6.00-9.99	4/00	93r
Wintercreeper euonymus (euonymus fortunei)	2 gal	16.00-169.99	4/00	93r
Hunting license	yr	17.00	4/01	34s
Health Care				
Cardiac catheterization, ave hospital/physician charges		19020	1998	77s
Childbirth, Cesarean delivery		10722	1997	13r
Childbirth, vaginal delivery		6223	1997	13r
Drugs, expenditures on	yr	394	1999	30r
Health care purchases	yr	2048	1999	30r
Health insurance expenditures	yr	978	1999	30r
Hysterectomy, laproscopically-assisted, ave hospital/physician charges		15580	1998	76s
Hysterectomy, vaginal, ave hospital and physician charges		10690	1998	76s
Medicaid dispensing fee		3.65	1999	87s
Medical services expenditures	yr	554	1999	30r
Medical supplies, expenditures on	yr	122	1999	30r
Plastic surgery, breast augmentation		3184	2000	7r
Plastic surgery, breast lift		3585	2000	7r
Plastic surgery, facelift		4999	2000	7r
Plastic surgery, hair transplantation		3105	2000	7r
Plastic surgery, lip augmentation		1290	2000	7r
Plastic surgery, lower body lift		8135	2000	7r
Plastic surgery, thigh lift		3839	2000	7r
Household Goods				
Floor coverings, expenditures on	yr	52	1999	30r
Furniture, expenditures on	yr	344	1999	30r
Household furnishings and equipment purchases	yr	1475	1999	30r
Household textiles, expenditures on	yr	109	1999	30r
Laundry and cleaning supplies, expenditures on	yr	134	1999	30r
Housing				
Home price, existing, ave		144400	10/00	90r
Home value, median		135000	2001	53s
Household operation expenditures	yr	542	1999	30r
Housekeeping supplies purchases	yr	508	1999	30r
Lodging expenditures	yr	430	1999	30r
Maintenance, repairs, insurance expenditures	yr	853	1999	30r
Monthly rental value of owned home	mos	547	1999	30r
Owned dwellings, expenditures own	yr	4282	1999	30r
Rent expenditures	yr	1558	1999	30r
Rental unit, 1 bedroom, with utilities	mos	367	4/01	41c
Rental unit, 2 bedroom, with utilities	mos	471	4/01	41c
Rental unit, 3 bedroom, with utilities	mos	629	4/01	41c
Rental unit, 4 bedroom, with utilities	mos	733	4/01	41c
Shelter, expenditures on	yr	6270	1999	30r
Insurance and Pensions				
Life and other personal insurance purchases	yr	387	1999	30r
Pensions and Social Security, expenditures on	yr	2968	1999	30r
Legal Fees				
Divorce, filing fee		122.00	4/01	35s
Driver's license fee	orig	16.00	1999	48s
Driver's license fee	renew	13.00	1999	48s
Fishing license	yr	18.00	4/01	34s
Personal Goods				
Personal care products and services purchases	yr	385	1999	30r
Personal Services				
Personal services, household, expenditures on	yr	300	1999	30r

Values are in dollars or fractions of dollars. In the column headed *Ref*, references are shown to sources. Each reference is followed by a letter. These refer to the geographical level for which data were reported: s=State, r=Region, and c=City or metro. The abbreviation *ex* is used to mean *except* or *excluding*; *exp* stands for *expenditures*. For other abbreviations and further explanations, please see the Introduction.

Duluth-Superior, MN-WI - continued

Item	Per	Value	Date	Ref.
Pets				
Pets, toys, and playground equipment, expenditures on	yr	375	1999	30r
Taxes				
Federal income taxes paid	yr	2326	1999	30r
Personal taxes, expenditures on	yr	3223	1999	30r
Property taxes paid	yr	1152	1999	30r
State and local income taxes paid	yr	753	1999	30r
Transportation				
Cars and trucks, new, expenditures on	yr	1280	1999	30r
Cars and trucks, used, expenditures on	yr	1763	1999	30r
Diesel at the pump	gal	1.28	10/99	73s
Gasoline and motor oil purchases	yr	1036	1999	30r
Gasoline before-tax price (cents)	gal	117.20	10/00	43s
Maintenance and repair expenditures	yr	594	1999	30r
Motorcycle license fee	orig	16.00	1999	49s
Motorcycle license fee	renew	13.00	1999	49s
Public transportation, expenditures on	yr	341	1999	30r
Transportation purchases	yr	6617	1999	30r
Vehicle expenses, miscellaneous, purchases	yr	2159	1999	30r
Vehicle insurance payments	yr	701	1999	30r
Vehicle purchases (net outlay)	yr	3081	1999	30r
Vehicle rental, lease expenditures	yr	536	1999	30r
Utilities				
Electrical bill, average	mos	55.08	9/00	9s
Electricity, expenditures on	yr	841	1999	30r
Electricity cost, average	KWh	5.80	9/00	9s
Utilities, fuels, and public services purchased	yr	2401	1999	30r
Water and other public services, expenditures on	yr	273	1999	30r
Weddings				
Wedding (national average cost)		19936	2000	33r
Wedding (regional average total cost)		16195	1997	110r
Attendants' gifts		321	1998	33r
Bridal attendants' apparel (5 persons)		824	2000	33r
Bride's headpiece/veil		173	1998	33r
Bride's wedding dress		859	1998	33r
Clergy, religious facility fee		242	1998	33r
Engagement ring		3177	1998	33r
Flowers		789	1998	33r
Groom's formalwear rental		99	2000	33r
Limousine		410	1998	33r
Marriage license cost		70.00	4/01	35s
Men's formalwear (ushers, best man)		469	2000	33r
Mother of bride apparel		241	2000	33r
Music		866	1998	33r
Photography and videography		1368	1998	33r
Rehearsal dinner		728	1998	33r
Wedding invitations and announcements		341	1998	33r
Wedding reception		7968	2000	33r
Wedding rings (bride and groom)		1060	1998	33r

Eau Claire, WI

Item	Per	Value	Date	Ref.
Average annual expenditures	yr	35369	1999	30r
Composite, ACCRA index		99.70	3/01	4c
Alcoholic Beverages				
Alcoholic beverage purchases	yr	304	1999	30r
Beer, Heineken, 12-oz, ex deposit	6	6.91	3/01	4c
J & B Scotch	750-ml	20.74	3/01	4c
Malt beverages, all types, all sizes, any origin	16 oz	0.93	7/01	11r
Wine, Livingston or Gallo, Chablis blanc	1.5 liter	4.83	3/01	4c
Wine, red and white table, all sizes, any origin	liter	7.04	7/01	11r
Appliances				
Appliance repair, service call, washing machine	min lab chg	41.46	3/01	4c
Major appliances, expenditures on	yr	165	1999	30r

Eau Claire, WI - continued

Item	Per	Value	Date	Ref.
Appliances - continued				
Small appliances, housewares, expenditures on	yr	90	1999	30r
Banking and Money				
Mortgage interest and charges paid	yr	2277	1999	30r
Mortgage principal paid on owned property	yr	1230	1999	30r
Mortgage rate, incl. points and orig. fee, 30-yr. conv. fixed or ARM	mos	7.21	3/01	4c
Vehicle finance charges paid	yr	328	1999	30r
Charity				
Cash contributions, expenditures	yr	1126	1999	30r
Child Care				
Child raising cost, total, age 0-2	yr	7890	1999	60r
Child raising cost, total, age 3-5	yr	8130	1999	60r
Child raising cost, total, age 6-8	yr	8170	1999	60r
Child raising cost, total, age 9-11	yr	8190	1999	60r
Child raising cost, total, age 12-14	yr	8890	1999	60r
Child raising cost, total, age 15-17	yr	9050	1999	60r
Child's child care and education, age 0-2	yr	1240	1999	60r
Child's child care and education, age 3-5	yr	1370	1999	60r
Child's child care and education, age 6-8	yr	880	1999	60r
Child's child care and education, age 9-11	yr	570	1999	60r
Child's child care and education, age 12-14	yr	420	1999	60r
Child's child care and education, age 15-17	yr	720	1999	60r
Child's clothing, age 0-2	yr	410	1999	60r
Child's clothing, age 3-5	yr	400	1999	60r
Child's clothing, age 6-8	yr	450	1999	60r
Child's clothing, age 9-11	yr	500	1999	60r
Child's clothing, age 12-14	yr	840	1999	60r
Child's clothing, age 15-17	yr	740	1999	60r
Child's food, age 0-2	yr	960	1999	60r
Child's food, age 3-5	yr	1120	1999	60r
Child's food, age 6-8	yr	1430	1999	60r
Child's food, age 9-11	yr	1710	1999	60r
Child's food, age 12-14	yr	1710	1999	60r
Child's food, age 15-17	yr	1920	1999	60r
Child's health care, age 0-2	yr	520	1999	60r
Child's health care, age 3-5	yr	500	1999	60r
Child's health care, age 6-8	yr	570	1999	60r
Child's health care, age 9-11	yr	610	1999	60r
Child's health care, age 12-14	yr	630	1999	60r
Child's health care, age 15-17	yr	650	1999	60r
Child's housing, age 0-2	yr	2860	1999	60r
Child's housing, age 3-5	yr	2840	1999	60r
Child's housing, age 6-8	yr	2800	1999	60r
Child's housing, age 9-11	yr	2650	1999	60r
Child's housing, age 12-14	yr	2840	1999	60r
Child's housing, age 15-17	yr	2440	1999	60r
Child's personal care, reading, age 0-2	yr	880	1999	60r
Child's personal care, reading, age 3-5	yr	900	1999	60r
Child's personal care, reading, age 6-8	yr	930	1999	60r
Child's personal care, reading, age 9-11	yr	970	1999	60r
Child's personal care, reading, age 12-14	yr	1150	1999	60r
Child's personal care, reading, age 15-17	yr	920	1999	60r
Clothing				
Apparel and services purchases	yr	1607	1999	30r
Boys' brief, cotton	3	4.15	3/01	4c
Boys, 2 to 15, expenditures on	yr	91	1999	30r
Children under 2, expenditures on	yr	59	1999	30r
Footwear, expenditures on	yr	285	1999	30r
Girls, 2 to 15, expenditures on	yr	116	1999	30r
Men and boys, expenditures on	yr	433	1999	30r
Men, 16 and over, expenditures on	yr	341	1999	30r
Shirt, man's dress shirt		24.33	3/01	4c
Slacks, man's "No Wrinkles" khaki		37.66	3/01	4c
Women, 16 and over, expenditures on	yr	490	1999	30r
Communications				
Cable modem installation, Bresnan		99.95	6/99	103s
Cable modem installation, Marcus		499.00	6/99	103s

Values are in dollars or fractions of dollars. In the column headed *Ref*, references are shown to sources. Each reference is followed by a letter. These refer to the geographical level for which data were reported: s=State, r=Region, and c=City or metro. The abbreviation *ex* is used to mean *except* or *excluding*; *exp* stands for *expenditures*. For other abbreviations and further explanations, please see the Introduction.

Eau Claire, WI - continued

Item	Per	Value	Date	Ref.
Communications				
Cable modem rate, cable subscriber, Bresnan	mos	39.95	6/99	103s
Cable modem rate, cable subscriber, Marcus	mos	14.95-49.95	6/99	103s
Cable modem rate, non-cable subscriber, Bresnan	mos	49.95	6/99	103s
Cable modem rate, non-cable subscriber, Marcus	mos	60.95	6/99	103s
Newspaper subscription, daily and Sunday delivery	mos	16.70	3/01	4c
Phone line, single, business, field visit	inst.	64.65	12/97	17s
Phone line, single, business, no field visit	inst.	64.65	12/97	17s
Phone line, single, residence, field visit	inst.	33.05	12/97	17s
Phone line, single, residence, no field visit	inst.	33.05	12/97	17s
Postage and stationery, expenditures on	yr	140	1999	30r
Postal rate, express mail, up to half-pound		12.45	7/01	108r
Postal rate, letter, first class, first ounce		0.34	7/01	108r
Postal rate, letter, two ounces		0.57	7/01	108r
Postal rate, post card		0.21	7/01	108r
Postal rate, priority mail, two pounds		3.95	7/01	108r
Postal rate, priority mail, up to one pound		3.50	7/01	108r
Telephone bill, business, basic rate	mos	20.85	12/97	18c
Telephone bill, family of three	mos	17.12	3/01	4c
Telephone bill, residential, basic rate	mos	5.40	12/97	18c
Telephone services, expenditures on	yr	830	1999	30r
Education				
Board, 4-year private college/university	yr	2271	1996	38s
Board, 4-year public college/university	yr	1527	1996	38s
Education expenditures	yr	583	1999	30r
Room, 4-year private college/university	yr	1812	1996	38s
Room, 4-year public college/university	yr	1706	1996	38s
Total cost, 4-year private college/university	yr	15652	1996	38s
Total cost, 4-year public college/university	yr	5847	1996	38s
Tuition, 2-year public college/university, in state	yr	1840	1996	38s
Tuition, 4-year private college/university, in state	yr	11569	1996	38s
Tuition, 4-year public college/university	yr	2614	1996	38s
Energy and Fuels				
Electricity	500 KWhs	46.59	7/01	11r
Energy, combined forms, 2400 sq ft	mos	174.29	3/01	4c
Energy, exc. electricity, 2400 sq ft	mos	123.69	3/01	4c
Fuel oil #2	gal	1.27	7/01	11r
Fuel oil and other fuels, expenditures on	yr	68	1999	30r
Gas, cooking, winter, 10 therms	mos	11.19	2/96	98c
Gas, cooking, winter, 30 therms	mos	23.56	2/96	98c
Gas, cooking, winter, 50 therms	mos	35.93	2/96	98c
Gas, heating, winter, average use	mos	116.97	2/96	98c
Gas, natural, commercial rate	1000 cf	7.32	11/00	88s
Gas, regular unleaded, cash, self-service	gal	1.51	3/01	4c
Gasoline, unleaded midgrade	gal	1.79	7/01	11r
Gasoline, unleaded premium	gal	1.86	7/01	11r
Gasoline, unleaded regular	gal	1.58	7/01	11r
Natural gas, expenditures on	yr	389	1999	30r
Utility (piped) gas, therm		0.81	7/01	11r
Utility (piped) gas, 40 therms		38.01	7/01	11r
Utility (piped) gas, 100 therms		81.75	7/01	11r
Entertainment				
Bowling, Saturday evening rate	line	2.25	3/01	4c
Entertainment purchases	yr	1984	1999	30r
Fees and admissions paid	yr	444	1999	30r
Monopoly game, Parker Brothers', No. 9	game	10.99	3/01	4c
Movie, first-run, Saturday, evening	adm.	7.00	3/01	4c
Television, radios, sound equipment, expenditures on	yr	580	1999	30r
Tennis balls, yellow, Wilson or Penn, 3	can	2.35	3/01	4c
Funerals				
Cosmetology, hair, other preparation		178.32	1/99	78r
Embalming		408.19	1/99	78r

Eau Claire, WI - continued

Item	Per	Value	Date	Ref.
Funerals - continued				
Funeral at funeral home		362.13	1/99	78r
Professional service charges		1375.51	1/99	78r
Transfer of remains to funeral home		155.92	1/99	78r
Visitation/viewing		294.38	1/99	78r
Groceries				
Groceries, ACCRA Index		101.30	3/01	4c
Antibiotic ointment, Polysporin	0.5 oz	4.55	3/01	4c
Baby food, strained vegetables or fruit, lowest price	4-4.5 oz	0.53	3/01	4c
Bacon, sliced	lb	3.15	7/01	11r
Bakery products, expenditures on	yr	281	1999	30r
Bananas	lb	0.47	3/01	4c
Bananas	lb	0.48	7/01	11r
Beans, dried, any type, all sizes	lb	0.61	7/01	11r
Beef for stew, boneless	lb	3.08	7/01	11r
Beef or hamburger, ground	lb	1.45	3/01	4c
Beef, expenditures on	yr	217	1999	30r
Bologna, all beef or mixed	lb	2.52	7/01	11r
Bread, white	loaf	0.94	3/01	4c
Bread, white, pan	lb	1.06	7/01	11r
Broccoli	lb	0.91	7/01	11r
Butter, salted, grade AA, stick	lb	3.04	7/01	11r
Butter, yoghurt, cheese, etc, expenditures on	yr	183	1999	30r
Cereals and bakery product purchases	yr	430	1999	30r
Cereals and cereal products, expenditures on	yr	149	1999	30r
Cheese, Kraft grated Parmesan	8 oz	3.04	3/01	4c
Chicken, fresh, whole	lb	1.07	7/01	11r
Chicken, whole fryer	lb	1.13	3/01	4c
Chops, boneless,	lb	3.64	7/01	11r
Chuck roast, U.S. choice, boneless	lb	2.47	7/01	11r
Cigarettes, Winston, Kings	carton	33.60	3/01	4c
Coffee, 100%, ground roast, all sizes	lb	2.69	7/01	11r
Coffee, vacuum-packed	13 oz	2.23	3/01	4c
Cookies, chocolate chip	lb	2.87	7/01	11r
Corn Flakes, Kellogg's or Post Toasties	18 oz	1.88	3/01	4c
Corn, frozen, whole kernel, lowest price	16 oz	1.02	3/01	4c
Dairy product purchases	yr	304	1999	30r
Eggs, expenditures on	yr	26	1999	30r
Eggs, Grade A or AA	dozen	1.15	3/01	4c
Eggs, grade A, large	dozen	0.88	7/01	11r
Fats and oils, expenditures on	yr	75	1999	30r
Fish and seafood, expenditures on	yr	72	1999	30r
Food (excl fruit and vegetables), eaten at home, purchases	yr	887	1999	30r
Food cooked on trips, expenditures on	yr	44	1999	30r
Food purchases	yr	4802	1999	30r
Food purchases, eaten away from home	yr	2069	1999	30r
Food purchases, food eaten at home	yr	2733	1999	30r
Fresh fruits, expenditures on	yr	138	1999	30r
Fresh milk and cream, expenditures on	yr	120	1999	30r
Fresh vegetables, expenditures on	yr	126	1999	30r
Grapefruit	lb	0.66	7/01	11r
Grapes, Thompson, seedless	lb	1.64	7/01	11r
Ground beef, 100% beef	lb	1.64	7/01	11r
Ground beef, lean and extra lean	lb	2.16	7/01	11r
Ground chuck, 100% beef	lb	2.13	7/01	11r
Ham, boneless, excl canned	lb	2.62	7/01	11r
Ice cream, prepackaged, bulk, regular	1/2 gal	3.35	7/01	11r
Lemons	lb	1.19	7/01	11r
Lettuce, iceberg	head	0.95	3/01	4c
Lettuce, iceberg	lb	0.73	7/01	11r
Margarine, Blue Bonnet or Parkay, stick	lb	1.01	3/01	4c
Margarine, soft, tubs	lb	0.89	7/01	11r
Meats, poultry, fish, and egg purchases	yr	671	1999	30r
Milk, fresh, whole, fortified	gal	2.71	7/01	11r
Milk, whole	1/2 gal	1.59	3/01	4c
Nonalcoholic beverages, expenditures on	yr	239	1999	30r
Orange juice, Minute Maid frozen	12 oz	1.43	3/01	4c
Oranges, Navel	lb	0.80	7/01	11r
Oranges, Valencia	lb	0.66	7/01	11r

Values are in dollars or fractions of dollars. In the column headed *Ref*, references are shown to sources. Each reference is followed by a letter. These refer to the geographical level for which data were reported: s=State, r=Region, and c=City or metro. The abbreviation *ex* is used to mean *except* or *excluding*; *exp* stands for *expenditures*. For other abbreviations and further explanations, please see the Introduction.

Eau Claire, WI - continued

Item	Per	Value	Date	Ref.
Groceries				
Peaches, halves or slices, Hunt's, Del Monte, or Libby's	29 oz	1.58	3/01	4c
Pears, Anjou	lb	0.93	7/01	11r
Peas, green, Del Monte or Green Giant	15 oz	0.66	3/01	4c
Pork chops, center cut, bone-in	lb	3.63	7/01	11r
Pork, expenditures on	yr	150	1999	30r
Potato chips	16 oz	3.52	7/01	11r
Potatoes, frozen, french fried	lb	1.08	7/01	11r
Potatoes, white or red	10 lb	3.38	3/01	4c
Potatoes, white, all types	lb	0.33	7/01	11r
Poultry, expenditures on	yr	108	1999	30r
Processed fruits, expenditures on	yr	98	1999	30r
Processed vegetables, expenditures on	yr	80	1999	30r
Round roast, U.S. choice, boneless	lb	3.07	7/01	11r
Round steak, graded and ungraded, excl U.S. prime and choice	lb	3.41	7/01	11r
Sausage, Jimmy Dean/Owens pork	lb	3.77	3/01	4c
Shortening, vegetable oil blends	lb	1.13	7/01	11r
Shortening, vegetable, Crisco	3 lb	2.98	3/01	4c
Soft drink, Coca Cola, ex deposit	2 liter	1.21	3/01	4c
Spaghetti and macaroni	lb	0.80	7/01	11r
Steak, round, U.S. choice, boneless	ib	3.23	7/01	11r
Steak, T-bone	lb	7.15	3/01	4c
Steak, T-bone, U.S. choice, bone-in	lb	6.68	7/01	11r
Strawberries, dry pint	12 oz	1.32	7/01	11r
Sugar and other sweets, expenditures on	yr	114	1999	30r
Sugar, cane or beet	4 lbs	1.49	3/01	4c
Sugar, white, 33-80 ounce package	lb	0.42	7/01	11r
Sugar, white, all sizes	lb	0.43	7/01	11r
Tobacco products and smoking supplies purchases	yr	331	1999	30r
Tomatoes, field grown	lb	1.46	7/01	11r
Tomatoes, Hunt's or Del Monte	14.5 oz	0.83	3/01	4c
Tuna, chunk, light	6 oz	0.57	3/01	4c
Tuna, light, chunk	lb	1.80	7/01	11r
Turkey, frozen, whole	lb	1.15	7/01	11r
Goods and Services				
Miscellaneous goods and services, ACCRA Index		98.20	3/01	4c
B&B Japanese maple (acer japonicum)	gal	29.99-169.99	4/00	93r
Boxwood (buxus)	2 gal	18.99-39.99	4/00	93r
Daylilly (hemerocallis)	gal	4.99-25.00	4/00	93r
Flat of annuals		11.98-24.99	4/00	93r
Fountain grass (pennisetum)	gal	5.98-12.98	4/00	93r
Hanging basket (10 in)		12.99-27.99	4/00	93r
Hardy geranium (geranium)	gal	7.99-9.99	4/00	93r
Hosta (hosta)	gal	6.00-25.00	4/00	93r
Lilac (syrubga vulgaris)	2 gal	14.99-24.99	4/00	93r
Miscellaneous purchases	yr	865	1999	30r
Rhododendron (rhododendron)	2 gal	23.98-42.99	4/00	93r
Sage (salvia)	gal	6.00-9.99	4/00	93r
Wintercreeper euonymus (euonymus fortunei)	2 gal	16.00-169.99	4/00	93r
Hunting license	yr	14.00	4/01	34s
Health Care				
Health care, ACCRA Index		110.10	3/01	4c
Cardiac catheterization, ave hospital/physician charges		13240	1998	77s
Childbirth, Cesarean delivery		10722	1997	13r
Childbirth, vaginal delivery		6223	1997	13r

Eau Claire, WI - continued

Item	Per	Value	Date	Ref.
Health Care - continued				
Dentist's fee, adult teeth cleaning and periodic oral exam	visit	79.60	3/01	4c
Doctor's fee, routine exam, established patient	visit	79.08	3/01	4c
Drugs, expenditures on	yr	394	1999	30r
Health care purchases	yr	2048	1999	30r
Health insurance expenditures	yr	978	1999	30r
Hospital care, private room	day	352.50	3/01	4c
Hysterectomy, laproscopically-assisted, ave hospital/physician charges		13270	1998	76s
Hysterectomy, vaginal, ave hospital and physician charges		9170	1998	76s
Laser eye surgery	eye	1950-2400	2000	63s
Medicaid dispensing fee		4.88-40.11	1999	87s
Medical services expenditures	yr	554	1999	30r
Medical supplies, expenditures on	yr	122	1999	30r
Plastic surgery, breast augmentation		3184	2000	7r
Plastic surgery, breast lift		3585	2000	7r
Plastic surgery, facelift		4999	2000	7r
Plastic surgery, hair transplantation		3105	2000	7r
Plastic surgery, lip augmentation		1290	2000	7r
Plastic surgery, lower body lift		8135	2000	7r
Plastic surgery, thigh lift		3839	2000	7r
Household Goods				
Dishwashing powder, Cascade	50 oz	3.56	3/01	4c
Floor coverings, expenditures on	yr	52	1999	30r
Furniture, expenditures on	yr	344	1999	30r
Household furnishings and equipment purchases	yr	1475	1999	30r
Household textiles, expenditures on	yr	109	1999	30r
Laundry and cleaning supplies, expenditures on	yr	134	1999	30r
Tissues, facial, Kleenex brand	175	1.23	3/01	4c
Housing				
Housing, ACCRA Index		86.40	3/01	4c
Home, 2200 sq ft, 4-br, 2-bath, 2-car garage, average		109654	2000	47c
Home price, existing, ave		144400	10/00	90r
Home value, median		117000	2001	53s
House, 2400 sq ft, 8000 sq ft lot, new, urban, utilities	total	173500	3/01	4c
House payment, principal and interest, 25% down payment	mos	884	3/01	4c
Household operation expenditures	yr	542	1999	30r
Housekeeping supplies purchases	yr	508	1999	30r
Lodging expenditures	yr	430	1999	30r
Maintenance, repairs, insurance expenditures	yr	853	1999	30r
Monthly rental value of owned home	mos	547	1999	30r
Owned dwellings, expenditures own	yr	4282	1999	30r
Rent expenditures	yr	1558	1999	30r
Rent, apartment, 2 br, 1 1/2-2 baths, unfurn, 950 sq ft, water	mos	617	3/01	4c
Rental unit, 1 bedroom, with utilities	mos	382	4/01	41c
Rental unit, 2 bedroom, with utilities	mos	501	4/01	41c
Rental unit, 3 bedroom, with utilities	mos	642	4/01	41c
Rental unit, 4 bedroom, with utilities	mos	723	4/01	41c
Shelter, expenditures on	yr	6270	1999	30r
Insurance and Pensions				
Auto insurance premium	yr	603.84	1999	57s
Life and other personal insurance purchases	yr	387	1999	30r
Pensions and Social Security, expenditures on	yr	2968	1999	30r
Legal Fees				
Divorce, filing fee		142.00-150.00	4/01	35s
Driver's license fee	renew	12.00	1999	48s
Driver's license fee	orig	18.00	1999	48s

Values are in dollars or fractions of dollars. In the column headed *Ref*, references are shown to sources. Each reference is followed by a letter. These refer to the geographical level for which data were reported: s=State, r=Region, and c=City or metro. The abbreviation *ex* is used to mean *except* or *excluding*; *exp* stands for *expenditures*. For other abbreviations and further explanations, please see the Introduction.

Eau Claire, WI - continued

Item	Per	Value	Date	Ref.
Legal Fees				
Fishing license	yr	14.00	4/01	34s
Personal Goods				
Personal care products and services purchases	yr	385	1999	30r
Shampoo, Alberto VO5	15 oz	1.16	3/01	4c
Toothpaste, Crest or Colgate	6-7 oz	2.24	3/01	4c
Personal Services				
Dry cleaning, man's 2-pc suit		7.98	3/01	4c
Man's haircut, barbershop, no styling		11.40	3/01	4c
Personal services, household, expenditures on	yr	300	1999	30r
Woman's shampoo, trim, blow-dry, no style-change		20.80	3/01	4c
Pets				
Pets, toys, and playground equipment, expenditures on	yr	375	1999	30r
Restaurant Food				
Chicken, fried, thigh and drumstick, KFC/Church's		2.70	3/01	4c
Hamburger with cheese, McDonald's	1/4 lb	2.09	3/01	4c
Pizza, Pizza Hut or Pizza Inn	11-12 in	8.99	3/01	4c
Taxes				
Federal income taxes paid	yr	2326	1999	30r
Personal taxes, expenditures on	yr	3223	1999	30r
Property taxes paid	yr	1152	1999	30r
State and local income taxes paid	yr	753	1999	30r
Transportation				
Transportation, ACCRA Index		106.20	3/01	4c
Auto operation, annual cost		6210	2000	27c
Cars and trucks, new, expenditures on	yr	1280	1999	30r
Cars and trucks, used, expenditures on	yr	1763	1999	30r
Diesel at the pump	gal	1.34	10/99	73s
Gasoline and motor oil purchases	yr	1036	1999	30r
Gasoline before-tax price (cents)	gal	113.40	10/00	43s
Maintenance and repair expenditures	yr	594	1999	30r
Public transportation, expenditures on	yr	341	1999	30r
Tire balance, computer or spin balance, front	wheel	8.30	3/01	4c
Transportation purchases	yr	6617	1999	30r
Vehicle expenses, miscellaneous, purchases	yr	2159	1999	30r
Vehicle insurance payments	yr	701	1999	30r
Vehicle purchases (net outlay)	yr	3081	1999	30r
Vehicle rental, lease expenditures	yr	536	1999	30r
Utilities				
Utilities, ACCRA Index		134.00	3/01	4c
Electrical bill, average	mos	52.08	9/00	9s
Electricity, expenditures on	yr	841	1999	30r
Electricity, summer, 250 KWh	mos	20.17	2/96	96c
Electricity, summer, 500 KWh	mos	36.84	2/96	96c
Electricity, summer, 750 KWh	mos	53.50	2/96	96c
Electricity, summer, 1000 KWh	mos	70.17	2/96	96c
Electricity and other, mixed, 2400 sq ft, new home	mos	50.60	3/01	4c
Electricity cost, average	KWh	5.69	9/00	9s
Utilities, fuels, and public services purchased	yr	2401	1999	30r
Water and other public services, expenditures on	yr	273	1999	30r
Weddings				
Wedding (national average cost)		19936	2000	33r
Wedding (regional average total cost)		16195	1997	110r
Attendants' gifts		321	1998	33r
Bridal attendants' apparel (5 persons)		824	2000	33r
Bride's headpiece/veil		173	1998	33r
Bride's wedding dress		859	1998	33r
Clergy, religious facility fee		242	1998	33r
Engagement ring		3177	1998	33r
Flowers		789	1998	33r
Groom's formalwear rental		99	2000	33r
Limousine		410	1998	33r

Eau Claire, WI - continued

Item	Per	Value	Date	Ref.
Weddings - continued				
Marriage license cost		50.00-60.00	4/01	35s
Men's formalwear (ushers, best man)		469	2000	33r
Mother of bride apparel		241	2000	33r
Music		866	1998	33r
Photography and videography		1368	1998	33r
Rehearsal dinner		728	1998	33r
Wedding invitations and announcements		341	1998	33r
Wedding reception		7968	2000	33r
Wedding rings (bride and groom)		1060	1998	33r

El Paso, TX

Item	Per	Value	Date	Ref.
Composite, ACCRA index		93.90	12/00	5c
Alcoholic Beverages				
Alcoholic beverage purchases	yr	253	1999	30r
Beer, Heineken, 12-oz, ex deposit	6	6.74	12/00	5c
J & B Scotch	750-ml	20.41	12/00	5c
Malt beverages, all types, all sizes, any origin	16 oz	0.96	7/01	11r
Wine, Livingston or Gallo, Chablis blanc	1.5 liter	7.09	12/00	5c
Appliances				
Appliance repair, service call, washing machine	min lab chg	27.34	12/00	5c
Major appliances, expenditures on	yr	172	1999	30r
Small appliances, housewares, expenditures on	yr	81	1999	30r
Banking and Money				
Mortgage interest and charges paid	yr	2039	1999	30r
Mortgage principal paid on owned property	yr	1026	1999	30r
Mortgage rate, incl. points and orig. fee, 30-yr. conv. fixed or ARM	mos	7.91	12/00	5c
Vehicle finance charges paid	yr	365	1999	30r
Business Expenses				
Business travel, car rental	day	50	2001	3c
Business travel, food	day	41	2001	3c
Business travel, hotel	day	91	2001	3c
Charity				
Cash contributions, expenditures	yr	1127	1999	30r
Child Care				
Child raising cost, total, age 0-2	yr	8540	1999	60r
Child raising cost, total, age 3-5	yr	8780	1999	60r
Child raising cost, total, age 6-8	yr	8820	1999	60r
Child raising cost, total, age 9-11	yr	8800	1999	60r
Child raising cost, total, age 12-14	yr	9510	1999	60r
Child raising cost, total, age 15-17	yr	9740	1999	60r
Child's child care and education, age 0-2	yr	1380	1999	60r
Child's child care and education, age 3-5	yr	1520	1999	60r
Child's child care and education, age 6-8	yr	990	1999	60r
Child's child care and education, age 9-11	yr	650	1999	60r
Child's child care and education, age 12-14	yr	490	1999	60r
Child's child care and education, age 15-17	yr	840	1999	60r
Child's clothing, age 0-2	yr	480	1999	60r
Child's clothing, age 3-5	yr	470	1999	60r
Child's clothing, age 6-8	yr	520	1999	60r
Child's clothing, age 9-11	yr	570	1999	60r
Child's clothing, age 12-14	yr	950	1999	60r
Child's clothing, age 15-17	yr	850	1999	60r
Child's food, age 0-2	yr	1000	1999	60r
Child's food, age 3-5	yr	1160	1999	60r
Child's food, age 6-8	yr	1490	1999	60r
Child's food, age 9-11	yr	1770	1999	60r
Child's food, age 12-14	yr	1770	1999	60r
Child's food, age 15-17	yr	1980	1999	60r
Child's health care, age 0-2	yr	620	1999	60r
Child's health care, age 3-5	yr	590	1999	60r
Child's health care, age 6-8	yr	680	1999	60r
Child's health care, age 9-11	yr	720	1999	60r
Child's health care, age 12-14	yr	730	1999	60r

Values are in dollars or fractions of dollars. In the column headed *Ref*, references are shown to sources. Each reference is followed by a letter. These refer to the geographical level for which data were reported: s=State, r=Region, and c=City or metro. The abbreviation *ex* is used to mean *except* or *excluding*; *exp* stands for expenditures. For other abbreviations and further explanations, please see the Introduction.

El Paso, TX - continued

Item	Per	Value	Date	Ref.
Child Care				
Child's health care, age 15-17	yr	760	1999	60r
Child's housing, age 0-2	yr	3070	1999	60r
Child's housing, age 3-5	yr	3050	1999	60r
Child's housing, age 6-8	yr	3010	1999	60r
Child's housing, age 9-11	yr	2850	1999	60r
Child's housing, age 12-14	yr	3040	1999	60r
Child's housing, age 15-17	yr	2650	1999	60r
Child's personal care, reading, age 0-2	yr	910	1999	60r
Child's personal care, reading, age 3-5	yr	930	1999	60r
Child's personal care, reading, age 6-8	yr	960	1999	60r
Child's personal care, reading, age 9-11	yr	1000	1999	60r
Child's personal care, reading, age 12-14	yr	1170	1999	60r
Child's personal care, reading, age 15-17	yr	950	1999	60r
Clothing				
Apparel and services purchases	yr	1610	1999	30r
Boys' brief, cotton	3	4.49	12/00	5c
Boys, 2 to 15, expenditures on	yr	89	1999	30r
Children under 2, expenditures on	yr	79	1999	30r
Footwear, expenditures on	yr	283	1999	30r
Girls, 2 to 15, expenditures on	yr	103	1999	30r
Men and boys, expenditures on	yr	351	1999	30r
Men, 16 and over, expenditures on	yr	262	1999	30r
Shirt, man's dress shirt		24.83	12/00	5c
Slacks, man's "No Wrinkles" khaki		35.99	12/00	5c
Women, 16 and over, expenditures on	yr	538	1999	30r
Communications				
Cable modem installation, AT&T-BIS		150.00	6/99	103s
Cable modem installation, Marcus		499.00	6/99	103s
Cable modem installation, Time Warner		75.00-225.00	6/99	103s
Cable modem rate, cable subscriber, AT&T-BIS	mos	39.95	6/99	103s
Cable modem rate, cable subscriber, Marcus	mos	14.95-49.95	6/99	103s
Cable modem rate, cable subscriber, Time Warner	mos	39.95-49.95	6/99	103s
Cable modem rate, non-cable subscriber, Marcus	mos	60.95	6/99	103s
Cable modem rate, non-cable subscriber, Time Warner	mos	39.95-54.95	6/99	103s
Newspaper subscription, daily and Sunday delivery	mos	11.50	12/00	5c
Phone line, single, business, field visit	inst.	71.90	12/97	17s
Phone line, single, business, no field visit	inst.	57.30	12/97	17s
Phone line, single, residence, field visit	inst.	52.95	12/97	17s
Phone line, single, residence, no field visit	inst.	38.35	12/97	17s
Postage and stationery, expenditures on	yr	104	1999	30r
Postal rate, express mail, up to half-pound		12.45	7/01	108r
Postal rate, letter, first class, first ounce		0.34	7/01	108r
Postal rate, letter, two ounces		0.57	7/01	108r
Postal rate, post card		0.21	7/01	108r
Postal rate, priority mail, two pounds		3.95	7/01	108r
Postal rate, priority mail, up to one pound		3.50	7/01	108r
Telephone bill, business, basic rate	mos	22.00	12/97	18c
Telephone bill, family of three	mos	15.50	12/00	5c
Telephone bill, residential, basic rate	mos	9.35	12/97	18c
Telephone services, expenditures on	yr	860	1999	30r
Education				
Board, 4-year private college/university	yr	2198	1996	38s
Board, 4-year public college/university	yr	1759	1996	38s
Education expenditures	yr	431	1999	30r
Room, 4-year private college/university	yr	2000	1996	38s
Room, 4-year public college/university	yr	1885	1996	38s
Total cost, 4-year private college/university	yr	13156	1996	38s
Total cost, 4-year public college/university	yr	5464	1996	38s
Tuition, 2-year public college/university, in state	yr	771	1996	38s
Tuition, 4-year private college/university, in state	yr	8959	1996	38s
Tuition, 4-year public college/university	yr	1820	1996	38s

El Paso, TX - continued

Item	Per	Value	Date	Ref.
Energy and Fuels				
Electricity	KWh	0.09	7/01	11r
Electricity	500 KWhs	47.29	7/01	11r
Energy, combined forms, 2400 sq ft	mos	129.35	12/00	5c
Energy, exc. electricity, 2400 sq ft	mos	37.53	12/00	5c
Fuel oil #2	gal	1.43	7/01	11r
Fuel oil and other fuels, expenditures on	yr	45	1999	30r
Gas, cooking, winter, 10 therms	mos	7.96	2/96	98c
Gas, cooking, winter, 30 therms	mos	13.36	2/96	98c
Gas, cooking, winter, 50 therms	mos	18.77	2/96	98c
Gas, heating, winter, average use	mos	30.39	2/96	98c
Gas, natural, commercial rate	1000 cf	6.94	11/00	88s
Gas, regular unleaded, cash, self-service	gal	1.39	12/00	5c
Gasoline, all types	gal	1.60	7/01	11r
Gasoline, unleaded midgrade	gal	1.65	7/01	11r
Gasoline, unleaded premium	gal	1.74	7/01	11r
Natural gas, expenditures on	yr	164	1999	30r
Utility (piped) gas, therm		1.01	7/01	11r
Utility (piped) gas, 40 therms		44.29	7/01	11r
Utility (piped) gas, 100 therms		97.44	7/01	11r
Entertainment				
Bowling, Saturday evening rate	line	2.78	12/00	5c
Entertainment purchases	yr	1574	1999	30r
Fees and admissions paid	yr	371	1999	30r
Monopoly game, Parker Brothers', No. 9	game	8.88	12/00	5c
Movie, first-run, Saturday, evening	adm.	7.12	12/00	5c
Reading purchases	yr	121	1999	30r
Television, radios, sound equipment, expenditures on	yr	561	1999	30r
Tennis balls, yellow, Wilson or Penn, 3	can	1.98	12/00	5c
Funerals				
Total cost of funeral		5842.28	1/99	78r
Acknowledgement cards		28.35	1/99	78r
Casket		2494.29	1/99	78r
Cosmetology, hair, other preparation		109.22	1/99	78r
Embalming		361.42	1/99	78r
Funeral at funeral home		349.20	1/99	78r
Hearse (local)		161.91	1/99	78r
Professional service charges		1116.50	1/99	78r
Service car/van		65.56	1/99	78r
Transfer of remains to funeral home		143.56	1/99	78r
Vault		785.25	1/99	78r
Visitation/viewing		227.02	1/99	78r
Groceries				
Groceries, ACCRA Index		102.80	12/00	5c
American processed cheese	lb	3.50	7/01	11r
Antibiotic ointment, Polysporin	0.5 oz	4.47	12/00	5c
Baby food, strained vegetables or fruit, lowest price	4-4.5 oz	0.41	12/00	5c
Bakery products, expenditures on	yr	261	1999	30r
Bananas	lb	0.47	7/01	11r
Bananas	lb	0.45	12/00	5c
Beans, dried, any type, all sizes	lb	0.63	7/01	11r
Beef for stew, boneless	lb	2.86	7/01	11r
Beef or hamburger, ground	lb	1.33	12/00	5c
Beef, expenditures on	yr	210	1999	30r
Bologna, all beef or mixed	lb	2.29	7/01	11r
Bread, French	lb	1.66	7/01	11r
Bread, white	loaf	0.75	12/00	5c
Bread, white, pan	lb	0.87	7/01	11r
Bread, whole wheat, pan	lb	1.38	7/01	11r
Broccoli	lb	1.04	7/01	11r
Butter, salted, grade AA, stick	lb	2.26	7/01	11r
Butter, yoghurt, cheese, etc, expenditures on	yr	170	1999	30r
Cabbage	lb	0.42	7/01	11r
Cereals and cereal products, expenditures on	yr	140	1999	30r
Cheddar cheese, natural	lb	3.75	7/01	11r
Cheese, Kraft grated Parmesan	8 oz	4.08	12/00	5c
Chicken breast, bone-in	lb	1.85	7/01	11r
Chicken legs, bone-in	lb	1.34	7/01	11r

Values are in dollars or fractions of dollars. In the column headed *Ref*, references are shown to sources. Each reference is followed by a letter. These refer to the geographical level for which data were reported: s=State, r=Region, and c=City or metro. The abbreviation *ex* is used to mean *except* or *excluding*; *exp* stands for expenditures. For other abbreviations and further explanations, please see the Introduction.

El Paso, TX - continued

Item	Per	Value	Date	Ref.
Groceries				
Chicken, fresh, whole	lb	1.05	7/01	11r
Chicken, whole fryer	lb	1.08	12/00	5c
Chops, boneless,	lb	4.13	7/01	11r
Chuck roast, graded and ungraded, excl U.S. prime and choice	lb	2.35	7/01	11r
Chuck roast, U.S. choice, boneless	lb	2.67	7/01	11r
Cigarettes, Winston, Kings	carton	29.48	12/00	5c
Coffee, 100%, ground roast, all sizes	lb	2.88	7/01	11r
Coffee, instant, plain, regular, all sizes	16 oz	9.25	7/01	11r
Coffee, vacuum-packed	13 oz	3.19	12/00	5c
Cola, non diet,	2 liter	1.11	7/01	11r
Corn Flakes, Kellogg's or Post Toasties	18 oz	3.07	12/00	5c
Corn, frozen, whole kernel, lowest price	16 oz	1.08	12/00	5c
Crackers, soda, salted	lb	1.70	7/01	11r
Dairy product purchases	yr	282	1999	30r
Eggs, expenditures on	yr	32	1999	30r
Eggs, Grade A or AA	dozen	0.98	12/00	5c
Fats and oils, expenditures on	yr	79	1999	30r
Fish and seafood, expenditures on	yr	99	1999	30r
Flour, white, all purpose	lb	0.32	7/01	11r
Food (excl fruit and vegetables), eaten at home, purchases	yr	815	1999	30r
Food cooked on trips, expenditures on	yr	36	1999	30r
Food purchases	yr	4533	1999	30r
Food purchases, eaten away from home	yr	1873	1999	30r
Food purchases, food eaten at home	yr	2660	1999	30r
Fresh fruits, expenditures on	yr	128	1999	30r
Fresh milk and cream, expenditures on	yr	112	1999	30r
Fresh vegetables, expenditures on	yr	131	1999	30r
Fruit and vegetable purchases	yr	438	1999	30r
Grapefruit	lb	0.59	7/01	11r
Grapes, Thompson, seedless	lb	2.12	7/01	11r
Ground beef, 100% beef	lb	1.76	7/01	11r
Ground beef, lean and extra lean	lb	2.60	7/01	11r
Ground chuck, 100% beef	lb	2.08	7/01	11r
Ham, boneless, excl canned	lb	2.71	7/01	11r
Ham, rump or shank half, bone-in, smoked	lb	2.19	7/01	11r
Ice cream, prepackaged, bulk, regular	1/2 gal	3.93	7/01	11r
Lemons	lb	1.32	7/01	11r
Lettuce, iceberg	lb	0.76	7/01	11r
Lettuce, iceberg	head	1.22	12/00	5c
Margarine, Blue Bonnet or Parkay, stick	lb	0.83	12/00	5c
Milk, fresh, low fat,	gal	2.75	7/01	11r
Milk, fresh, whole, fortified	gal	2.97	7/01	11r
Milk, whole	1/2 gal	1.68	12/00	5c
Nonalcoholic beverages, expenditures on	yr	228	1999	30r
Orange juice, frozen concentrate	16 oz	1.95	7/01	11r
Orange juice, Minute Maid frozen	12 oz	1.76	12/00	5c
Oranges, Navel	lb	0.73	7/01	11r
Oranges, Valencia	lb	0.55	7/01	11r
Peaches, halves or slices, Hunt's, Del Monte, or Libby's	29 oz	1.82	12/00	5c
Peanut butter, creamy, all sizes	lb	1.83	7/01	11r
Pears, Anjou	lb	0.98	7/01	11r
Peas, green, Del Monte or Green Giant	15 oz	0.73	12/00	5c
Pork chops, center cut, bone-in	lb	3.33	7/01	11r
Pork sausage, fresh, loose	lb	2.59	7/01	11r
Pork shoulder picnic, bone-in, smoked	lb	1.12	7/01	11r
Pork, expenditures on	yr	162	1999	30r
Potato chips	16 oz	3.59	7/01	11r
Potatoes, frozen, french fried	lb	1.00	7/01	11r
Potatoes, white or red	10 lb	2.37	12/00	5c
Potatoes, white, all types	lb	0.44	7/01	11r
Poultry, expenditures on	yr	137	1999	30r
Processed fruits, expenditures on	yr	97	1999	30r
Processed vegetables, expenditures on	yr	82	1999	30r
Rice, white, long grain, uncooked	lb	0.51	7/01	11r
Round roast, graded and ungraded, excl U.S. prime and choice	lb	2.96	7/01	11r
Round steak, graded and ungraded, excl U.S. prime and choice	lb	3.11	7/01	11r
Sausage, Jimmy Dean/Owens pork	lb	2.87	12/00	5c

El Paso, TX - continued

Item	Per	Value	Date	Ref.
Groceries - continued				
Shortening, vegetable, Crisco	3 lb	3.44	12/00	5c
Sirloin steak, graded and ungraded, excl U.S. prime and choice	lb	4.23	7/01	11r
Soft drink, Coca Cola, ex deposit	2 liter	1.26	12/00	5c
Spaghetti and macaroni	lb	0.78	7/01	11r
Steak, round, U.S. choice, boneless	lb	3.56	7/01	11r
Steak, sirloin, U.S. choice, boneless	lb	5.65	7/01	11r
Steak, T-bone	lb	6.34	12/00	5c
Strawberries, dry pint	12 oz	1.50	7/01	11r
Sugar and other sweets, expenditures on	yr	99	1999	30r
Sugar, cane or beet	4 lbs	1.62	12/00	5c
Sugar, white, 33-80 ounce package	lb	0.39	7/01	11r
Sugar, white, all sizes	lb	0.42	7/01	11r
Tobacco products and smoking supplies purchases	yr	288	1999	30r
Tomatoes, field grown	lb	1.43	7/01	11r
Tomatoes, Hunt's or Del Monte	14.5 oz	0.87	12/00	5c
Tuna, chunk, light	6 oz	0.59	12/00	5c
Tuna, light, chunk	lb	1.77	7/01	11r
Turkey, frozen, whole	lb	1.05	7/01	11r
Goods and Services				
Miscellaneous goods and services, ACCRA Index		95.20	12/00	5c
B&B Japanese maple (acer japonicum)	gal	79.98-99.00	4/00	93r
Boxwood (buxus)	2 gal	12.98-18.99	4/00	93r
Christmas tree, noble fir		40-60	2000	65s
Daylilly (hemerocallis)	gal	7.96-11.00	4/00	93r
Flat of annuals		13.99-27.99	4/00	93r
Fountain grass (pennisetum)	gal	6.96-9.00	4/00	93r
Hanging basket (10 in)		9.99-24.99	4/00	93r
Hardy geranium (geranium)	gal	5.96-8.00	4/00	93r
Hosta (hosta)	gal	8.96-12.99	4/00	93r
Lilac (syrubga vulgaris)	2 gal	13.00-19.99	4/00	93r
Rhododendron (rhododendron)	2 gal	12.98-29.99	4/00	93r
Sage (salvia)	gal	5.96-8.00	4/00	93r
Wintercreeper euonymus (euonymus fortunei)	2 gal	13.00-18.99	4/00	93r
Hunting license	yr	19.00	4/01	34s
Health Care				
Health care, ACCRA Index		90.10	12/00	5c
Cardiac catheterization, ave hospital/ physician charges		20140	1998	77s
Childbirth, Cesarean delivery		11587	1997	13r
Childbirth, vaginal delivery		6725	1997	13r
Dentist's fee, adult teeth cleaning and periodic oral exam	visit	61.25	12/00	5c
Doctor's fee, routine exam, established patient	visit	53.00	12/00	5c
Drugs, expenditures on	yr	399	1999	30r
Health care purchases	yr	1971	1999	30r
Health insurance expenditures	yr	933	1999	30r
Hospital care, private room	day	437.50	12/00	5c
Hysterectomy, laproscopically-assisted, ave hospital/physician charges		15700	1998	76s
Hysterectomy, vaginal, ave hospital and physician charges		12180	1998	76s
Medicaid dispensing fee		5.27	1999	87s
Medical services expenditures	yr	547	1999	30r
Medical supplies, expenditures on	yr	91	1999	30r

Values are in dollars or fractions of dollars. In the column headed *Ref*, references are shown to sources. Each reference is followed by a letter. These refer to the geographical level for which data were reported: s=State, r=Region, and c=City or metro. The abbreviation *ex* is used to mean *except* or *excluding*; *exp* stands for expenditures. For other abbreviations and further explanations, please see the Introduction.

El Paso, TX - continued

Item	Per	Value	Date	Ref.
Household Goods				
Dishwashing powder, Cascade	50 oz	3.21	12/00	5c
Floor coverings, expenditures on	yr	44	1999	30r
Furniture, expenditures on	yr	335	1999	30r
Household furnishings and equipment purchases	yr	1328	1999	30r
Household textiles, expenditures on	yr	89	1999	30r
Laundry and cleaning supplies, expenditures on	yr	113	1999	30r
Tissues, facial, Kleenex brand	175	1.64	12/00	5c
Housing				
Housing, ACCRA Index		80.20	12/00	5c
Home, 2200 sq ft, 4-br, 2-bath, 2-car garage, average		147250	2000	47c
Home price, existing, ave		160100	10/00	90r
Home value, median		112000	2001	53s
House, 2400 sq ft, 8000 sq ft lot, new, urban, utilities	total	164667	12/00	5c
House payment, principal and interest, 25% down payment	mos	899	12/00	5c
Household operation expenditures	yr	553	1999	30r
Housekeeping supplies purchases	yr	473	1999	30r
Housing, expenditures on	yr	10303	1999	30r
Maintenance, repairs, insurance expenditures	yr	699	1999	30r
Monthly rental value of owned home	mos	505	1999	30r
Owned dwellings, expenditures own	yr	3465	1999	30r
Rent expenditures	yr	1641	1999	30r
Rent, apartment, 2 br, 1 1/2-2 baths, unfurn, 950 sq ft, water	mos	561	12/00	5c
Rental unit, 1 bedroom, with utilities	mos	451	4/01	41c
Rental unit, 2 bedroom, with utilities	mos	534	4/01	41c
Rental unit, 3 bedroom, with utilities	mos	739	4/01	41c
Rental unit, 4 bedroom, with utilities	mos	877	4/01	41c
Shelter, expenditures on	yr	5467	1999	30r
Insurance and Pensions				
Life and other personal insurance purchases	yr	414	1999	30r
Pensions and Social Security, expenditures on	yr	2635	1999	30r
Personal insurance and pensions, expenditures on	yr	3048	1999	30r
Legal Fees				
Divorce, filing fee		150.00-200.00	4/01	35s
Driver's license fee	renew	20.00	1999	48s
Driver's license fee	orig	24.00	1999	48s
Fishing license	yr	19.00	4/01	34s
Personal Goods				
Personal care products and services purchases	yr	393	1999	30r
Shampoo, Alberto VO5	15 oz	0.97	12/00	5c
Toothpaste, Crest or Colgate	6-7 oz	2.49	12/00	5c
Personal Services				
Dry cleaning, man's 2-pc suit		7.02	12/00	5c
Man's haircut, barbershop, no styling		7.40	12/00	5c
Personal services, household, expenditures on	yr	258	1999	30r
Woman's shampoo, trim, blow-dry, no style-change		36.60	12/00	5c
Pets				
Pets, toys, and playground equipment, expenditures on	yr	306	1999	30r
Restaurant Food				
Chicken, fried, thigh and drumstick, KFC/Church's		2.69	12/00	5c
Hamburger with cheese, McDonald's	1/4 lb	2.00	12/00	5c
Pizza, Pizza Hut or Pizza Inn	11-12 in	9.48	12/00	5c

El Paso, TX - continued

Item	Per	Value	Date	Ref.
Taxes				
Federal income taxes paid	yr	2047	1999	30r
Personal taxes, expenditures on	yr	2554	1999	30r
Property taxes paid	yr	726	1999	30r
State and local income taxes paid	yr	363	1999	30r
Transportation				
Transportation, ACCRA Index		103.30	12/00	5c
Bus fare, one-way	trip	1.00	2000	1c
Bus fare, to central business district	1-way	1.00	12/00	5c
Cars and trucks, new, expenditures on	yr	1648	1999	30r
Cars and trucks, used, expenditures on	yr	1651	1999	30r
Diesel at the pump	gal	1.18	10/99	73s
Gasoline and motor oil purchases	yr	1052	1999	30r
Gasoline before-tax price (cents)	gal	101.30	10/00	43s
Maintenance and repair expenditures	yr	621	1999	30r
Public transportation, expenditures on	yr	298	1999	30r
Tire balance, computer or spin balance, front	wheel	9.37	12/00	5c
Transportation purchases	yr	6738	1999	30r
Vehicle expenses, miscellaneous, purchases	yr	2033	1999	30r
Vehicle insurance payments	yr	696	1999	30r
Vehicle purchases (net outlay)	yr	3354	1999	30r
Vehicle rental, lease expenditures	yr	352	1999	30r
Utilities				
Utilities, ACCRA Index		109.30	12/00	5c
Electrical bill, average	mos	87.17	9/00	9s
Electricity, expenditures on	yr	1115	1999	30r
Electricity, summer, 250 KWh	mos	28.07	2/96	96c
Electricity, summer, 500 KWh	mos	51.64	2/96	96c
Electricity, summer, 750 KWh	mos	75.21	2/96	96c
Electricity, summer, 1000 KWh	mos	98.78	2/96	96c
Electricity and other, mixed, 2400 sq ft, new home	mos	91.82	12/00	5c
Electricity cost, average	KWh	6.48	9/00	9s
Water and other public services, expenditures on	yr	298	1999	30r
Weddings				
Wedding (national average cost)		19936	2000	33r
Attendants' gifts		321	1998	33r
Bridal attendants' apparel (5 persons)		824	2000	33r
Bride's headpiece/veil		173	1998	33r
Bride's wedding dress		859	1998	33r
Clergy, religious facility fee		242	1998	33r
Engagement ring		3177	1998	33r
Flowers		789	1998	33r
Groom's formalwear rental		99	2000	33r
Limousine		410	1998	33r
Marriage license cost		36.00	4/01	35s
Men's formalwear (ushers, best man)		469	2000	33r
Mother of bride apparel		241	2000	33r
Music		866	1998	33r
Photography and videography		1368	1998	33r
Rehearsal dinner		728	1998	33r
Wedding invitations and announcements		341	1998	33r
Wedding reception		7968	2000	33r
Wedding rings (bride and groom)		1060	1998	33r

Elkhart-Goshen, IN

Item	Per	Value	Date	Ref.
Average annual expenditures	yr	35369	1999	30r
Composite, ACCRA index		97.60	3/01	4c
Alcoholic Beverages				
Alcoholic beverage purchases	yr	304	1999	30r
Beer, Heineken, 12-oz, ex deposit	6	7.55	3/01	4c
J & B Scotch	750-ml	19.51	3/01	4c
Malt beverages, all types, all sizes, any origin	16 oz	0.93	7/01	11r
Wine, Livingston or Gallo, Chablis blanc	1.5 liter	4.57	3/01	4c
Wine, red and white table, all sizes, any origin	liter	7.04	7/01	11r

Values are in dollars or fractions of dollars. In the column headed *Ref*, references are shown to sources. Each reference is followed by a letter. These refer to the geographical level for which data were reported: s=State, r=Region, and c=City or metro. The abbreviation *ex* is used to mean *except* or *excluding*; *exp* stands for *expenditures*. For other abbreviations and further explanations, please see the Introduction.

Elkhart-Goshen, IN - continued

Item	Per	Value	Date	Ref.
Appliances				
Appliance repair, service call, washing machine	min lab chg	45.39	3/01	4c
Major appliances, expenditures on	yr	165	1999	30r
Small appliances, housewares, expenditures on	yr	90	1999	30r
Banking and Money				
Mortgage interest and charges paid	yr	2277	1999	30r
Mortgage principal paid on owned property	yr	1230	1999	30r
Mortgage rate, incl. points and orig. fee, 30-yr. conv. fixed or ARM	mos	7.33	3/01	4c
Vehicle finance charges paid	yr	328	1999	30r
Charity				
Cash contributions, expenditures	yr	1126	1999	30r
Child Care				
Child raising cost, total, age 0-2	yr	7890	1999	60r
Child raising cost, total, age 3-5	yr	8130	1999	60r
Child raising cost, total, age 6-8	yr	8170	1999	60r
Child raising cost, total, age 9-11	yr	8190	1999	60r
Child raising cost, total, age 12-14	yr	8890	1999	60r
Child raising cost, total, age 15-17	yr	9050	1999	60r
Child's child care and education, age 0-2	yr	1240	1999	60r
Child's child care and education, age 3-5	yr	1370	1999	60r
Child's child care and education, age 6-8	yr	880	1999	60r
Child's child care and education, age 9-11	yr	570	1999	60r
Child's child care and education, age 12-14	yr	420	1999	60r
Child's child care and education, age 15-17	yr	720	1999	60r
Child's clothing, age 0-2	yr	410	1999	60r
Child's clothing, age 3-5	yr	400	1999	60r
Child's clothing, age 6-8	yr	450	1999	60r
Child's clothing, age 9-11	yr	500	1999	60r
Child's clothing, age 12-14	yr	840	1999	60r
Child's clothing, age 15-17	yr	740	1999	60r
Child's food, age 0-2	yr	960	1999	60r
Child's food, age 3-5	yr	1120	1999	60r
Child's food, age 6-8	yr	1430	1999	60r
Child's food, age 9-11	yr	1710	1999	60r
Child's food, age 12-14	yr	1710	1999	60r
Child's food, age 15-17	yr	1920	1999	60r
Child's health care, age 0-2	yr	520	1999	60r
Child's health care, age 3-5	yr	500	1999	60r
Child's health care, age 6-8	yr	570	1999	60r
Child's health care, age 9-11	yr	610	1999	60r
Child's health care, age 12-14	yr	630	1999	60r
Child's health care, age 15-17	yr	650	1999	60r
Child's housing, age 0-2	yr	2860	1999	60r
Child's housing, age 3-5	yr	2840	1999	60r
Child's housing, age 6-8	yr	2800	1999	60r
Child's housing, age 9-11	yr	2650	1999	60r
Child's housing, age 12-14	yr	2840	1999	60r
Child's housing, age 15-17	yr	2440	1999	60r
Child's personal care, reading, age 0-2	yr	880	1999	60r
Child's personal care, reading, age 3-5	yr	900	1999	60r
Child's personal care, reading, age 6-8	yr	930	1999	60r
Child's personal care, reading, age 9-11	yr	970	1999	60r
Child's personal care, reading, age 12-14	yr	1150	1999	60r
Child's personal care, reading, age 15-17	yr	920	1999	60r
Clothing				
Apparel and services purchases	yr	1607	1999	30r
Boys' brief, cotton	3	3.84	3/01	4c
Boys, 2 to 15, expenditures on	yr	91	1999	30r
Children under 2, expenditures on	yr	59	1999	30r
Footwear, expenditures on	yr	285	1999	30r
Girls, 2 to 15, expenditures on	yr	116	1999	30r
Men and boys, expenditures on	yr	433	1999	30r
Men, 16 and over, expenditures on	yr	341	1999	30r
Shirt, man's dress shirt		27.10	3/01	4c
Slacks, man's "No Wrinkles" khaki		42.99	3/01	4c
Women, 16 and over, expenditures on	yr	490	1999	30r

Elkhart-Goshen, IN - continued

Item	Per	Value	Date	Ref.
Communications				
Newspaper subscription, daily and Sunday delivery	mos	10.58	3/01	4c
Phone line, single, business, field visit	inst.	59.00	12/97	17s
Phone line, single, business, no field visit	inst.	59.00	12/97	17s
Phone line, single, residence, field visit	inst.	47.00	12/97	17s
Phone line, single, residence, no field visit	inst.	47.00	12/97	17s
Postage and stationery, expenditures on	yr	140	1999	30r
Postal rate, express mail, up to half-pound		12.45	7/01	108r
Postal rate, letter, first class, first ounce		0.34	7/01	108r
Postal rate, letter, two ounces		0.57	7/01	108r
Postal rate, post card		0.21	7/01	108r
Postal rate, priority mail, two pounds		3.95	7/01	108r
Postal rate, priority mail, up to one pound		3.50	7/01	108r
Telephone bill, family of three	mos	21.99	3/01	4c
Telephone services, expenditures on	yr	830	1999	30r
Education				
Board, 4-year private college/university	yr	2250	1996	38s
Board, 4-year public college/university	yr	2425	1996	38s
Education expenditures	yr	583	1999	30r
Room, 4-year private college/university	yr	1987	1996	38s
Room, 4-year public college/university	yr	1931	1996	38s
Total cost, 4-year private college/university	yr	16829	1996	38s
Total cost, 4-year public college/university	yr	7392	1996	38s
Tuition, 2-year public college/university, in state	yr	1937	1996	38s
Tuition, 4-year private college/university, in state	yr	12592	1996	38s
Tuition, 4-year public college/university	yr	3037	1996	38s
Energy and Fuels				
Electricity	500 KWhs	46.59	7/01	11r
Energy, combined forms, 2400 sq ft	mos	135.54	3/01	4c
Energy, exc. electricity, 2400 sq ft	mos	86.11	3/01	4c
Fuel oil #2	gal	1.27	7/01	11r
Fuel oil and other fuels, expenditures on	yr	68	1999	30r
Gas, natural, commercial rate	1000 cf	6.24	11/00	88s
Gas, regular unleaded, cash, self-service	gal	1.36	3/01	4c
Gasoline, unleaded midgrade	gal	1.79	7/01	11r
Gasoline, unleaded premium	gal	1.86	7/01	11r
Gasoline, unleaded regular	gal	1.58	7/01	11r
Natural gas, expenditures on	yr	389	1999	30r
Utility (piped) gas, therm		0.81	7/01	11r
Utility (piped) gas, 40 therms		38.01	7/01	11r
Utility (piped) gas, 100 therms		81.75	7/01	11r
Entertainment				
Bowling, Saturday evening rate	line	2.54	3/01	4c
Entertainment purchases	yr	1984	1999	30r
Fees and admissions paid	yr	444	1999	30r
Monopoly game, Parker Brothers', No. 9	game	10.74	3/01	4c
Movie, first-run, Saturday, evening	adm.	6.50	3/01	4c
Television, radios, sound equipment, expenditures on	yr	580	1999	30r
Tennis balls, yellow, Wilson or Penn, 3	can	2.34	3/01	4c
Funerals				
Cosmetology, hair, other preparation		178.32	1/99	78r
Embalming		408.19	1/99	78r
Funeral at funeral home		362.13	1/99	78r
Professional service charges		1375.51	1/99	78r
Transfer of remains to funeral home		155.92	1/99	78r
Visitation/viewing		294.38	1/99	78r
Groceries				
Groceries, ACCRA Index		95.90	3/01	4c
Antibiotic ointment, Polysporin	0.5 oz	4.52	3/01	4c
Baby food, strained vegetables or fruit, lowest price	4-4.5 oz	0.45	3/01	4c
Bacon, sliced	lb	3.15	7/01	11r
Bakery products, expenditures on	yr	281	1999	30r
Bananas	lb	0.45	3/01	4c
Bananas	lb	0.48	7/01	11r

Values are in dollars or fractions of dollars. In the column headed *Ref*, references are shown to sources. Each reference is followed by a letter. These refer to the geographical level for which data were reported: s=State, r=Region, and c=City or metro. The abbreviation *ex* is used to mean *except* or *excluding*; *exp* stands for expenditures. For other abbreviations and further explanations, please see the Introduction.

Elkhart-Goshen, IN - continued

Item	Per	Value	Date	Ref.
Groceries				
Beans, dried, any type, all sizes	lb	0.61	7/01	11r
Beef for stew, boneless	lb	3.08	7/01	11r
Beef or hamburger, ground	lb	1.51	3/01	4c
Beef, expenditures on	yr	217	1999	30r
Bologna, all beef or mixed	lb	2.52	7/01	11r
Bread, white	loaf	0.91	3/01	4c
Bread, white, pan	lb	1.06	7/01	11r
Broccoli	lb	0.91	7/01	11r
Butter, salted, grade AA, stick	lb	3.04	7/01	11r
Butter, yoghurt, cheese, etc, expenditures on	yr	183	1999	30r
Cereals and bakery product purchases	yr	430	1999	30r
Cereals and cereal products, expenditures on	yr	149	1999	30r
Cheese, Kraft grated Parmesan	8 oz	3.70	3/01	4c
Chicken, fresh, whole	lb	1.07	7/01	11r
Chicken, whole fryer	lb	0.79	3/01	4c
Chops, boneless,	lb	3.64	7/01	11r
Chuck roast, U.S. choice, boneless	lb	2.47	7/01	11r
Cigarettes, Winston, Kings	carton	27.36	3/01	4c
Coffee, 100%, ground roast, all sizes	lb	2.69	7/01	11r
Coffee, vacuum-packed	13 oz	2.80	3/01	4c
Cookies, chocolate chip	lb	2.87	7/01	11r
Corn Flakes, Kellogg's or Post Toasties	18 oz	2.80	3/01	4c
Corn, frozen, whole kernel, lowest price	16 oz	1.14	3/01	4c
Dairy product purchases	yr	304	1999	30r
Eggs, expenditures on	yr	26	1999	30r
Eggs, Grade A or AA	dozen	1.18	3/01	4c
Eggs, grade A, large	dozen	0.88	7/01	11r
Fats and oils, expenditures on	yr	75	1999	30r
Fish and seafood, expenditures on	yr	72	1999	30r
Food (excl fruit and vegetables), eaten at home, purchases	yr	887	1999	30r
Food cooked on trips, expenditures on	yr	44	1999	30r
Food purchases	yr	4802	1999	30r
Food purchases, eaten away from home	yr	2069	1999	30r
Food purchases, food eaten at home	yr	2733	1999	30r
Fresh fruits, expenditures on	yr	138	1999	30r
Fresh milk and cream, expenditures on	yr	120	1999	30r
Fresh vegetables, expenditures on	yr	126	1999	30r
Grapefruit	lb	0.66	7/01	11r
Grapes, Thompson, seedless	lb	1.64	7/01	11r
Ground beef, 100% beef	lb	1.64	7/01	11r
Ground beef, lean and extra lean	lb	2.16	7/01	11r
Ground chuck, 100% beef	lb	2.13	7/01	11r
Ham, boneless, excl canned	lb	2.62	7/01	11r
Ice cream, prepackaged, bulk, regular	1/2 gal	3.35	7/01	11r
Lemons	lb	1.19	7/01	11r
Lettuce, iceberg	head	0.93	3/01	4c
Lettuce, iceberg	lb	0.73	7/01	11r
Margarine, Blue Bonnet or Parkay, stick	lb	0.72	3/01	4c
Margarine, soft, tubs	lb	0.89	7/01	11r
Meats, poultry, fish, and egg purchases	yr	671	1999	30r
Milk, fresh, whole, fortified	gal	2.71	7/01	11r
Milk, whole	1/2 gal	1.64	3/01	4c
Nonalcoholic beverages, expenditures on	yr	239	1999	30r
Orange juice, Minute Maid frozen	12 oz	1.53	3/01	4c
Oranges, Navel	lb	0.80	7/01	11r
Oranges, Valencia	lb	0.66	7/01	11r
Peaches, halves or slices, Hunt's, Del Monte, or Libby's	29 oz	1.63	3/01	4c
Pears, Anjou	lb	0.93	7/01	11r
Peas, green, Del Monte or Green Giant	15 oz	0.72	3/01	4c
Pork chops, center cut, bone-in	lb	3.63	7/01	11r
Pork, expenditures on	yr	150	1999	30r
Potato chips	16 oz	3.52	7/01	11r
Potatoes, frozen, french fried	lb	1.08	7/01	11r
Potatoes, white or red	10 lb	2.03	3/01	4c
Potatoes, white, all types	lb	0.33	7/01	11r
Poultry, expenditures on	yr	108	1999	30r
Processed fruits, expenditures on	yr	98	1999	30r
Processed vegetables, expenditures on	yr	80	1999	30r
Round roast, U.S. choice, boneless	lb	3.07	7/01	11r

Elkhart-Goshen, IN - continued

Item	Per	Value	Date	Ref.
Groceries - continued				
Round steak, graded and ungraded, excl U.S. prime and choice	lb	3.41	7/01	11r
Sausage, Jimmy Dean/Owens pork	lb	2.89	3/01	4c
Shortening, vegetable oil blends	lb	1.13	7/01	11r
Shortening, vegetable, Crisco	3 lb	2.47	3/01	4c
Soft drink, Coca Cola, ex deposit	2 liter	1.19	3/01	4c
Spaghetti and macaroni	lb	0.80	7/01	11r
Steak, round, U.S. choice, boneless	lb	3.23	7/01	11r
Steak, T-bone	lb	6.28	3/01	4c
Steak, T-bone, U.S. choice, bone-in	lb	6.68	7/01	11r
Strawberries, dry pint	12 oz	1.32	7/01	11r
Sugar and other sweets, expenditures on	yr	114	1999	30r
Sugar, cane or beet	4 lbs	1.47	3/01	4c
Sugar, white, 33-80 ounce package	lb	0.42	7/01	11r
Sugar, white, all sizes	lb	0.43	7/01	11r
Tobacco products and smoking supplies purchases	yr	331	1999	30r
Tomatoes, field grown	lb	1.46	7/01	11r
Tomatoes, Hunt's or Del Monte	14.5 oz	0.95	3/01	4c
Tuna, chunk, light	6 oz	0.62	3/01	4c
Tuna, light, chunk	lb	1.80	7/01	11r
Turkey, frozen, whole	lb	1.15	7/01	11r
Goods and Services				
Miscellaneous goods and services, ACCRA Index		98.60	3/01	4c
B&B Japanese maple (acer japonicum)	gal	29.99-169.99	4/00	93r
Boxwood (buxus)	2 gal	18.99-39.99	4/00	93r
Daylilly (hemerocallis)	gal	4.99-25.00	4/00	93r
Flat of annuals		11.98-24.99	4/00	93r
Fountain grass (pennisetum)	gal	5.98-12.98	4/00	93r
Hanging basket (10 in)		12.99-27.99	4/00	93r
Hardy geranium (geranium)	gal	7.99-9.99	4/00	93r
Hosta (hosta)	gal	6.00-25.00	4/00	93r
Lilac (syrubga vulgaris)	2 gal	14.99-24.99	4/00	93r
Miscellaneous purchases	yr	865	1999	30r
Rhododendron (rhododendron)	2 gal	23.98-42.99	4/00	93r
Sage (salvia)	gal	6.00-9.99	4/00	93r
Wintercreeper euonymus (euonymus fortunei)	2 gal	16.00-169.99	4/00	93r
Hunting license	yr	8.75	4/01	34s
Health Care				
Health care, ACCRA Index		94.90	3/01	4c
Cardiac catheterization, ave hospital/physician charges		13380	1998	77s
Childbirth, Cesarean delivery		10722	1997	13r
Childbirth, vaginal delivery		6223	1997	13r
Dentist's fee, adult teeth cleaning and periodic oral exam	visit	61.60	3/01	4c
Doctor's fee, routine exam, established patient	visit	52.40	3/01	4c
Drugs, expenditures on	yr	394	1999	30r
Health care purchases	yr	2048	1999	30r
Health insurance expenditures	yr	978	1999	30r
Hospital care, private room	day	636.00	3/01	4c
Hysterectomy, laproscopically-assisted, ave hospital/physician charges		11310	1998	76s
Hysterectomy, vaginal, ave hospital and physician charges		9160	1998	76s
Medicaid dispensing fee		4.00	1999	87s
Medical services expenditures	yr	554	1999	30r

Values are in dollars or fractions of dollars. In the column headed *Ref*, references are shown to sources. Each reference is followed by a letter. These refer to the geographical level for which data were reported: s=State, r=Region, and c=City or metro. The abbreviation *ex* is used to mean *except* or *excluding*; *exp* stands for *expenditures*. For other abbreviations and further explanations, please see the Introduction.

Elkhart-Goshen, IN - continued

Item	Per	Value	Date	Ref.
Health Care				
Medical supplies, expenditures on	yr	122	1999	30r
Plastic surgery, breast augmentation		3184	2000	7r
Plastic surgery, breast lift		3585	2000	7r
Plastic surgery, facelift		4999	2000	7r
Plastic surgery, hair transplantation		3105	2000	7r
Plastic surgery, lip augmentation		1290	2000	7r
Plastic surgery, lower body lift		8135	2000	7r
Plastic surgery, thigh lift		3839	2000	7r
Household Goods				
Dishwashing powder, Cascade	50 oz	2.90	3/01	4c
Floor coverings, expenditures on	yr	52	1999	30r
Furniture, expenditures on	yr	344	1999	30r
Household furnishings and equipment purchases	yr	1475	1999	30r
Household textiles, expenditures on	yr	109	1999	30r
Laundry and cleaning supplies, expenditures on	yr	134	1999	30r
Tissues, facial, Kleenex brand	175	1.22	3/01	4c
Housing				
Housing, ACCRA Index		93.90	3/01	4c
Home price, existing, ave		144400	10/00	90r
Home value, median		102000	2001	53s
House, 2400 sq ft, 8000 sq ft lot, new, urban, utilities	total	190860	3/01	4c
House payment, principal and interest, 25% down payment	mos	984	3/01	4c
Household operation expenditures	yr	542	1999	30r
Housekeeping supplies purchases	yr	508	1999	30r
Lodging expenditures	yr	430	1999	30r
Maintenance, repairs, insurance expenditures	yr	853	1999	30r
Monthly rental value of owned home	mos	547	1999	30r
Owned dwellings, expenditures own	yr	4282	1999	30r
Rent expenditures	yr	1558	1999	30r
Rent, apartment, 2 br, 1 1/2-2 baths, unfurn, 950 sq ft, water	mos	610	3/01	4c
Rental unit, 1 bedroom, with utilities	mos	433	4/01	41c
Rental unit, 2 bedroom, with utilities	mos	547	4/01	41c
Rental unit, 3 bedroom, with utilities	mos	700	4/01	41c
Rental unit, 4 bedroom, with utilities	mos	804	4/01	41c
Shelter, expenditures on	yr	6270	1999	30r
Insurance and Pensions				
Life and other personal insurance purchases	yr	387	1999	30r
Pensions and Social Security, expenditures on	yr	2968	1999	30r
Legal Fees				
Divorce, filing fee		100.00	4/01	35s
Driver's license fee	renew	6.00	1999	48s
Driver's license fee	orig	6.00	1999	48s
Personal Goods				
Personal care products and services purchases	yr	385	1999	30r
Shampoo, Alberto VO5	15 oz	1.23	3/01	4c
Toothpaste, Crest or Colgate	6-7 oz	2.15	3/01	4c
Personal Services				
Dry cleaning, man's 2-pc suit		8.39	3/01	4c
Man's haircut, barbershop, no styling		10.35	3/01	4c
Personal services, household, expenditures on	yr	300	1999	30r
Woman's shampoo, trim, blow-dry, no style-change		18.30	3/01	4c
Pets				
Pets, toys, and playground equipment, expenditures on	yr	375	1999	30r
Restaurant Food				
Chicken, fried, thigh and drumstick, KFC/Church's		2.49	3/01	4c
Hamburger with cheese, McDonald's	1/4 lb	1.97	3/01	4c

Elkhart-Goshen, IN - continued

Item	Per	Value	Date	Ref.
Restaurant Food - continued				
Pizza, Pizza Hut or Pizza Inn	11-12 in	8.99	3/01	4c
Taxes				
Federal income taxes paid	yr	2326	1999	30r
Personal taxes, expenditures on	yr	3223	1999	30r
Property taxes paid	yr	1152	1999	30r
State and local income taxes paid	yr	753	1999	30r
Transportation				
Transportation, ACCRA Index		98.80	3/01	4c
Cars and trucks, new, expenditures on	yr	1280	1999	30r
Cars and trucks, used, expenditures on	yr	1763	1999	30r
Diesel at the pump	gal	1.17	10/99	73s
Gasoline and motor oil purchases	yr	1036	1999	30r
Gasoline before-tax price (cents)	gal	110.00	10/00	43s
Maintenance and repair expenditures	yr	594	1999	30r
Public transportation, expenditures on	yr	341	1999	30r
Tire balance, computer or spin balance, front	wheel	8.03	3/01	4c
Transportation purchases	yr	6617	1999	30r
Vehicle expenses, miscellaneous, purchases	yr	2159	1999	30r
Vehicle insurance payments	yr	701	1999	30r
Vehicle purchases (net outlay)	yr	3081	1999	30r
Vehicle rental, lease expenditures	yr	536	1999	30r
Utilities				
Utilities, ACCRA Index		109.70	3/01	4c
Electrical bill, average	mos	66.66	9/00	9s
Electricity, expenditures on	yr	841	1999	30r
Electricity and other, mixed, 2400 sq ft, new home	mos	49.43	3/01	4c
Electricity cost, average	KWh	5.00	9/00	9s
Utilities, fuels, and public services purchased	yr	2401	1999	30r
Water and other public services, expenditures on	yr	273	1999	30r
Weddings				
Wedding (national average cost)		19936	2000	33r
Wedding (regional average total cost)		16195	1997	110r
Attendants' gifts		321	1998	33r
Bridal attendants' apparel (5 persons)		824	2000	33r
Bride's headpiece/veil		173	1998	33r
Bride's wedding dress		859	1998	33r
Clergy, religious facility fee		242	1998	33r
Engagement ring		3177	1998	33r
Flowers		789	1998	33r
Groom's formalwear rental		99	2000	33r
Limousine		410	1998	33r
Marriage license cost		18.00	4/01	35s
Men's formalwear (ushers, best man)		469	2000	33r
Mother of bride apparel		241	2000	33r
Music		866	1998	33r
Photography and videography		1368	1998	33r
Rehearsal dinner		728	1998	33r
Wedding invitations and announcements		341	1998	33r
Wedding reception		7968	2000	33r
Wedding rings (bride and groom)		1060	1998	33r

Elmira, NY

Item	Per	Value	Date	Ref.
Average annual expenditures	yr	37971	1999	30r
Alcoholic Beverages				
Alcoholic beverage purchases	yr	368	1999	30r
Wine, red and white table, all sizes, any origin	liter	9.64	7/01	11r
Appliances				
Major appliances, expenditures on	yr	194	1999	30r
Small appliances, housewares, expenditures on	yr	93	1999	30r
Banking and Money				
Mortgage interest and charges paid	yr	2622	1999	30r
Mortgage principal paid on owned property	yr	1262	1999	30r
Vehicle finance charges paid	yr	240	1999	30r

Values are in dollars or fractions of dollars. In the column headed *Ref*, references are shown to sources. Each reference is followed by a letter. These refer to the geographical level for which data were reported: s=State, r=Region, and c=City or metro. The abbreviation *ex* is used to mean *except* or *excluding*; *exp* stands for expenditures. For other abbreviations and further explanations, please see the Introduction.

Elmira, NY - continued

Item	Per	Value	Date	Ref.
Charity				
Cash contributions, expenditures	yr	1001	1999	30r
Child Care				
Child raising cost, total, age 0-2	yr	8670	1999	60r
Child raising cost, total, age 3-5	yr	8910	1999	60r
Child raising cost, total, age 6-8	yr	9040	1999	60r
Child raising cost, total, age 9-11	yr	9100	1999	60r
Child raising cost, total, age 12-14	yr	9890	1999	60r
Child raising cost, total, age 15-17	yr	10010	1999	60r
Child's child care and education, age 0-2	yr	1070	1999	60r
Child's child care and education, age 3-5	yr	1190	1999	60r
Child's child care and education, age 6-8	yr	740	1999	60r
Child's child care and education, age 9-11	yr	470	1999	60r
Child's child care and education, age 12-14	yr	350	1999	60r
Child's child care and education, age 15-17	yr	590	1999	60r
Child's clothing, age 0-2	yr	480	1999	60r
Child's clothing, age 3-5	yr	470	1999	60r
Child's clothing, age 6-8	yr	520	1999	60r
Child's clothing, age 9-11	yr	570	1999	60r
Child's clothing, age 12-14	yr	970	1999	60r
Child's clothing, age 15-17	yr	870	1999	60r
Child's food, age 0-2	yr	1130	1999	60r
Child's food, age 3-5	yr	1290	1999	60r
Child's food, age 6-8	yr	1640	1999	60r
Child's food, age 9-11	yr	1930	1999	60r
Child's food, age 12-14	yr	1940	1999	60r
Child's food, age 15-17	yr	2150	1999	60r
Child's health care, age 0-2	yr	550	1999	60r
Child's health care, age 3-5	yr	530	1999	60r
Child's health care, age 6-8	yr	610	1999	60r
Child's health care, age 9-11	yr	650	1999	60r
Child's health care, age 12-14	yr	660	1999	60r
Child's health care, age 15-17	yr	690	1999	60r
Child's housing, age 0-2	yr	3555	1999	60r
Child's housing, age 3-5	yr	3530	1999	60r
Child's housing, age 6-8	yr	3490	1999	60r
Child's housing, age 9-11	yr	3340	1999	60r
Child's housing, age 12-14	yr	3530	1999	60r
Child's housing, age 15-17	yr	3140	1999	60r
Child's personal care, reading, age 0-2	yr	920	1999	60r
Child's personal care, reading, age 3-5	yr	950	1999	60r
Child's personal care, reading, age 6-8	yr	980	1999	60r
Child's personal care, reading, age 9-11	yr	1020	1999	60r
Child's personal care, reading, age 12-14	yr	1190	1999	60r
Child's personal care, reading, age 15-17	yr	970	1999	60r
Nannies: criminal background check		74	1998	84s
Clothing				
Apparel and services purchases	yr	1831	1999	30r
Boys, 2 to 15, expenditures on	yr	92	1999	30r
Children under 2, expenditures on	yr	63	1999	30r
Footwear, expenditures on	yr	300	1999	30r
Girls, 2 to 15, expenditures on	yr	101	1999	30r
Men and boys, expenditures on	yr	446	1999	30r
Men, 16 and over, expenditures on	yr	354	1999	30r
Women, 16 and over, expenditures on	yr	584	1999	30r
Communications				
Cable modem installation, Adelphi		54.90	6/99	103s
Cable modem installation, Cablevision Systems		150.00	6/99	103s
Cable modem installation, Time Warner		75.00-225.00	6/99	103s
Cable modem rate, cable subscriber, Adelphi	mos	34.95	6/99	103s
Cable modem rate, cable subscriber, Cablevision Systems	mos	44.95	6/99	103s
Cable modem rate, cable subscriber, Century	mos	39.95	6/99	103s
Cable modem rate, cable subscriber, Time Warner	mos	39.95-49.95	6/99	103s
Cable modem rate, non-cable subscriber, Adelphi	mos	44.95	6/99	103s
Cable modem rate, non-cable subscriber, Cablevision Systems	mos	54.95	6/99	103s

Elmira, NY - continued

Item	Per	Value	Date	Ref.
Communications - continued				
Cable modem rate, non-cable subscriber, Time Warner	mos	39.95-54.95	6/99	103s
Phone line, single, business, field visit	inst.	142.76	12/97	17s
Phone line, single, business, no field visit	inst.	106.05	12/97	17s
Phone line, single, residence, field visit	inst.	102.78	12/97	17s
Phone line, single, residence, no field visit	inst.	55.00	12/97	17s
Postage and stationery, expenditures on	yr	138	1999	30r
Postal rate, express mail, up to half-pound		12.45	7/01	108r
Postal rate, letter, first class, first ounce		0.34	7/01	108r
Postal rate, letter, two ounces		0.57	7/01	108r
Postal rate, post card		0.21	7/01	108r
Postal rate, priority mail, two pounds		3.95	7/01	108r
Postal rate, priority mail, up to one pound		3.50	7/01	108r
Telephone services, expenditures on	yr	830	1999	30r
Education				
Board, 4-year private college/university	yr	3255	1996	38s
Board, 4-year public college/university	yr	2310	1996	38s
Education expenditures	yr	877	1999	30r
Room, 4-year private college/university	yr	3724	1996	38s
Room, 4-year public college/university	yr	2937	1996	38s
Total cost, 4-year private college/university	yr	20831	1996	38s
Total cost, 4-year public college/university	yr	8960	1996	38s
Tuition, 2-year public college/university, in state	yr	2427	1996	38s
Tuition, 4-year private college/university, in state	yr	13852	1996	38s
Tuition, 4-year public college/university	yr	3714	1996	38s
Energy and Fuels				
Electricity	KWh	0.12	7/01	11r
Fuel oil #2	gal	1.31	7/01	11r
Fuel oil and other fuels, expenditures on	yr	207	1999	30r
Gasoline, all types	gal	1.80	7/01	11r
Gasoline, unleaded midgrade	gal	1.85	7/01	11r
Gasoline, unleaded premium	gal	1.91	7/01	11r
Gasoline, unleaded regular	gal	1.71	7/01	11r
Natural gas, expenditures on	yr	368	1999	30r
Utility (piped) gas, therm		1.08	7/01	11r
Utility (piped) gas, 40 therms		50.87	7/01	11r
Utility (piped) gas, 100 therms		111.06	7/01	11r
Entertainment				
Entertainment purchases	yr	1821	1999	30r
Fees and admissions paid	yr	511	1999	30r
Television, radios, sound equipment, expenditures on	yr	650	1999	30r
Funerals				
Total cost of funeral		5813.50	1/99	78r
Acknowledgement cards		28.32	1/99	78r
Casket		2082.20	1/99	78r
Cosmetology, hair, other preparation		169.59	1/99	78r
Embalming		465.60	1/99	78r
Funeral at funeral home		339.56	1/99	78r
Hearse (local)		183.96	1/99	78r
Professional service charges		1157.85	1/99	78r
Service car/van		100.41	1/99	78r
Transfer of remains to funeral home		158.66	1/99	78r
Vault		766.31	1/99	78r
Visitation/viewing		361.04	1/99	78r
Groceries				
Apples, red delicious	lb	0.95	7/01	11r
Bacon, sliced	lb	3.44	7/01	11r
Bakery products, expenditures on	yr	310	1999	30r
Bananas	lb	0.55	7/01	11r
Beef, expenditures on	yr	236	1999	30r
Bread, white, pan	lb	1.09	7/01	11r
Butter, yoghurt, cheese, etc, expenditures on	yr	214	1999	30r
Cereals and bakery product purchases	yr	474	1999	30r
Cereals and cereal products, expenditures on	yr	164	1999	30r
Chicken legs, bone-in	lb	1.23	7/01	11r

Values are in dollars or fractions of dollars. In the column headed *Ref*, references are shown to sources. Each reference is followed by a letter. These refer to the geographical level for which data were reported: s=State, r=Region, and c=City or metro. The abbreviation *ex* is used to mean *except* or *excluding*; *exp* stands for expenditures. For other abbreviations and further explanations, please see the Introduction.

Elmira, NY - continued

Item	Per	Value	Date	Ref.
Groceries				
Chicken, fresh, whole	lb	1.13	7/01	11r
Chuck roast, U.S. choice, boneless	lb	2.79	7/01	11r
Coffee, 100%, ground roast, all sizes	lb	3.40	7/01	11r
Dairy product purchases	yr	342	1999	30r
Eggs, expenditures on	yr	34	1999	30r
Eggs, grade A, large	dozen	0.82	7/01	11r
Fats and oils, expenditures on	yr	80	1999	30r
Fish and seafood, expenditures on	yr	123	1999	30r
Food (excl fruit and vegetables), eaten at home, purchases	yr	838	1999	30r
Food cooked on trips, expenditures on	yr	48	1999	30r
Food purchases	yr	5314	1999	30r
Food purchases, eaten away from home	yr	2313	1999	30r
Food purchases, food eaten at home	yr	3001	1999	30r
Fresh fruits, expenditures on	yr	169	1999	30r
Fresh milk and cream, expenditures on	yr	128	1999	30r
Fresh vegetables, expenditures on	yr	164	1999	30r
Grapefruit	lb	0.67	7/01	11r
Grapes, Thompson, seedless	lb	2.18	7/01	11r
Ground beef, lean and extra lean	lb	2.66	7/01	11r
Ground chuck, 100% beef	lb	2.04	7/01	11r
Lettuce, iceberg	lb	0.76	7/01	11r
Meats, poultry, fish, and egg purchases	yr	808	1999	30r
Nonalcoholic beverages, expenditures on	yr	225	1999	30r
Orange juice, frozen concentrate	16 oz	1.88	7/01	11r
Oranges, Navel	lb	0.79	7/01	11r
Oranges, Valencia	lb	0.56	7/01	11r
Peaches	lb	1.16	7/01	11r
Peanut butter, creamy, all sizes	lb	2.01	7/01	11r
Pears, Anjou	lb	1.16	7/01	11r
Pork chops, center cut, bone-in	lb	3.57	7/01	11r
Pork, expenditures on	yr	146	1999	30r
Potato chips	16 oz	3.37	7/01	11r
Potatoes, white, all types	lb	0.42	7/01	11r
Poultry, expenditures on	yr	158	1999	30r
Processed fruits, expenditures on	yr	124	1999	30r
Processed vegetables, expenditures on	yr	82	1999	30r
Round roast, U.S. choice, boneless	lb	3.04	7/01	11r
Spaghetti and macaroni	lb	1.04	7/01	11r
Steak, sirloin, U.S. choice, boneless	lb	5.39	7/01	11r
Strawberries, dry pint	12 oz	1.51	7/01	11r
Sugar and other sweets, expenditures on	yr	110	1999	30r
Sugar, white, 33-80 ounce package	lb	0.46	7/01	11r
Sugar, white, all sizes	lb	0.47	7/01	11r
Tobacco products and smoking supplies purchases	yr	309	1999	30r
Yogurt, natural, fruit flavored	8 oz	0.79	7/01	11r
Goods and Services				
B&B Japanese maple (acer japonicum)	gal	38.99-125.00	4/00	93r
Boxwood (buxus)	2 gal	15.99-49.95	4/00	93r
Daylily (hemerocallis)	gal	4.95	4/00	93r
Flat of annuals		8.00-14.99	4/00	93r
Fountain grass (pennisetum)	gal	6.99-9.99	4/00	93r
Hanging basket (10 in)		12.95-19.99	4/00	93r
Hardy geranium (geranium)	gal	6.95-7.99	4/00	93r
Hosta (hosta)	gal	4.95	4/00	93r
Lilac (syrubga vulgaris)	2 gal	17.99-74.95	4/00	93r
Miscellaneous purchases	yr	872	1999	30r
Rhododendron (rhododendron)	2 gal	23.99-54.95	4/00	93r
Sage (salvia)	gal	6.95-7.99	4/00	93r
Wintercreeper euonymus (euonymus fortunei)	2 gal	14.99-23.95	4/00	93r
Hunting license	yr	11.00	4/01	34s

Elmira, NY - continued

Item	Per	Value	Date	Ref.
Health Care				
Cardiac catheterization, ave hospital/physician charges		12750	1998	77s
Childbirth, Cesarean delivery		14716	1997	13r
Childbirth, vaginal delivery		8541	1997	13r
Drugs, expenditures on	yr	296	1999	30r
Health care purchases	yr	1788	1999	30r
Health insurance expenditures	yr	875	1999	30r
Hysterectomy, laproscopically-assisted, ave hospital/physician charges		13460	1998	76s
Hysterectomy, vaginal, ave hospital and physician charges		10310	1998	76s
Medicaid dispensing fee		3.50-4.50	1999	87s
Medical services expenditures	yr	516	1999	30r
Medical supplies, expenditures on	yr	102	1999	30r
Plastic surgery, breast augmentation		4232	2000	7r
Plastic surgery, breast lift		4605	2000	7r
Plastic surgery, facelift		6964	2000	7r
Plastic surgery, hair transplantation		4193	2000	7r
Plastic surgery, lip augmentation		1675	2000	7r
Plastic surgery, lower body lift		6611	2000	7r
Plastic surgery, thigh lift		4751	2000	7r
Household Goods				
Floor coverings, expenditures on	yr	59	1999	30r
Furniture, expenditures on	yr	388	1999	30r
Household furnishings and equipment purchases	yr	1567	1999	30r
Household textiles, expenditures on	yr	112	1999	30r
Laundry and cleaning supplies, expenditures on	yr	104	1999	30r
Housing				
Home price, existing, ave		180800	10/00	90r
Home value, median		179000	2001	53s
Household operation expenditures	yr	581	1999	30r
Housekeeping supplies purchases	yr	474	1999	30r
Lodging expenditures	yr	550	1999	30r
Maintenance, repairs, insurance expenditures	yr	835	1999	30r
Monthly rental value of owned home	mos	663	1999	30r
Owned dwellings, expenditures own	yr	5209	1999	30r
Rent expenditures	yr	2390	1999	30r
Rental unit, 1 bedroom, with utilities	mos	404	4/01	41c
Rental unit, 2 bedroom, with utilities	mos	496	4/01	41c
Rental unit, 3 bedroom, with utilities	mos	627	4/01	41c
Rental unit, 4 bedroom, with utilities	mos	748	4/01	41c
Shelter, expenditures on	yr	8149	1999	30r
Insurance and Pensions				
Auto insurance premium	yr	1113.55	1999	57s
Life and other personal insurance purchases	yr	424	1999	30r
Pensions and Social Security, expenditures on	yr	3037	1999	30r
Legal Fees				
Divorce, filing fee		270.00	4/01	35s
Driver's license fee	orig	25.00	1999	48s
Driver's license fee	renew	25.00	1999	48s
Fishing license	yr	14.00	4/01	34s
Personal Goods				
Personal care products and services purchases	yr	399	1999	30r
Personal Services				
Personal services, household, expenditures on	yr	271	1999	30r
Pets				
Pets, toys, and playground equipment, expenditures on	yr	325	1999	30r
Taxes				
Federal income taxes paid	yr	2606	1999	30r
Personal taxes, expenditures on	yr	3567	1999	30r

Values are in dollars or fractions of dollars. In the column headed *Ref*, references are shown to sources. Each reference is followed by a letter. These refer to the geographical level for which data were reported: s=State, r=Region, and c=City or metro. The abbreviation *ex* is used to mean *except* or *excluding*; *exp* stands for expenditures. For other abbreviations and further explanations, please see the Introduction.

Elmira, NY - continued

Item	Per	Value	Date	Ref.
Taxes				
Property taxes paid	yr	1752	1999	30r
State and local income taxes paid	yr	694	1999	30r
Transportation				
Cars and trucks, new, expenditures on	yr	1496	1999	30r
Cars and trucks, used, expenditures on	yr	1251	1999	30r
Diesel at the pump	gal	1.33	10/99	73s
Gasoline and motor oil purchases	yr	901	1999	30r
Gasoline before-tax price (cents)	gal	110.70	10/00	43s
Maintenance and repair expenditures	yr	618	1999	30r
Public transportation, expenditures on	yr	575	1999	30r
Transportation purchases	yr	6503	1999	30r
Vehicle expenses, miscellaneous, purchases	yr	2266	1999	30r
Vehicle insurance payments	yr	824	1999	30r
Vehicle purchases (net outlay)	yr	2761	1999	30r
Vehicle rental, lease expenditures	yr	584	1999	30r
Travel				
Hotel room	night	139.88	2/01	95s
Utilities				
Electrical bill, average	mos	71.50	9/00	9s
Electricity, expenditures on	yr	837	1999	30r
Electricity cost, average	KWh	11.34	9/00	9s
Utilities, fuels, and public services purchased	yr	2457	1999	30r
Water and other public services, expenditures on	yr	215	1999	30r
Weddings				
Wedding (national average cost)		19936	2000	33r
Wedding (regional average total cost)		29454	1997	110r
Attendants' gifts		321	1998	33r
Bridal attendants' apparel (5 persons)		824	2000	33r
Bride's headpiece/veil		173	1998	33r
Bride's wedding dress		859	1998	33r
Clergy, religious facility fee		242	1998	33r
Engagement ring		3177	1998	33r
Flowers		789	1998	33r
Groom's formalwear rental		99	2000	33r
Limousine		410	1998	33r
Marriage license cost		25.00	4/01	35s
Men's formalwear (ushers, best man)		469	2000	33r
Mother of bride apparel		241	2000	33r
Music		866	1998	33r
Photography and videography		1368	1998	33r
Rehearsal dinner		728	1998	33r
Wedding invitations and announcements		341	1998	33r
Wedding reception		7968	2000	33r
Wedding rings (bride and groom)		1060	1998	33r

Enid, OK

Item	Per	Value	Date	Ref.
Composite, ACCRA index		94.80	3/01	4c
Alcoholic Beverages				
Alcoholic beverage purchases	yr	253	1999	30r
Beer, Heineken, 12-oz, ex deposit	6	8.14	3/01	4c
J & B Scotch	750-ml	18.92	3/01	4c
Malt beverages, all types, all sizes, any origin	16 oz	0.96	7/01	11r
Wine, Livingston or Gallo, Chablis blanc	1.5 liter	6.71	3/01	4c
Appliances				
Appliance repair, service call, washing machine	min lab chg	38.00	3/01	4c
Major appliances, expenditures on	yr	172	1999	30r
Small appliances, housewares, expenditures on	yr	81	1999	30r
Banking and Money				
Mortgage interest and charges paid	yr	2039	1999	30r
Mortgage principal paid on owned property	yr	1026	1999	30r
Mortgage rate, incl. points and orig. fee, 30-yr. conv. fixed or ARM	mos	7.00	3/01	4c
Vehicle finance charges paid	yr	365	1999	30r

Enid, OK - continued

Item	Per	Value	Date	Ref.
Charity				
Cash contributions, expenditures	yr	1127	1999	30r
Child Care				
Child raising cost, total, age 0-2	yr	8540	1999	60r
Child raising cost, total, age 3-5	yr	8780	1999	60r
Child raising cost, total, age 6-8	yr	8820	1999	60r
Child raising cost, total, age 9-11	yr	8800	1999	60r
Child raising cost, total, age 12-14	yr	9510	1999	60r
Child raising cost, total, age 15-17	yr	9740	1999	60r
Child's child care and education, age 0-2	yr	1380	1999	60r
Child's child care and education, age 3-5	yr	1520	1999	60r
Child's child care and education, age 6-8	yr	990	1999	60r
Child's child care and education, age 9-11	yr	650	1999	60r
Child's child care and education, age 12-14	yr	490	1999	60r
Child's child care and education, age 15-17	yr	840	1999	60r
Child's clothing, age 0-2	yr	480	1999	60r
Child's clothing, age 3-5	yr	470	1999	60r
Child's clothing, age 6-8	yr	520	1999	60r
Child's clothing, age 9-11	yr	570	1999	60r
Child's clothing, age 12-14	yr	950	1999	60r
Child's clothing, age 15-17	yr	850	1999	60r
Child's food, age 0-2	yr	1000	1999	60r
Child's food, age 3-5	yr	1160	1999	60r
Child's food, age 6-8	yr	1490	1999	60r
Child's food, age 9-11	yr	1770	1999	60r
Child's food, age 12-14	yr	1770	1999	60r
Child's food, age 15-17	yr	1980	1999	60r
Child's health care, age 0-2	yr	620	1999	60r
Child's health care, age 3-5	yr	590	1999	60r
Child's health care, age 6-8	yr	680	1999	60r
Child's health care, age 9-11	yr	720	1999	60r
Child's health care, age 12-14	yr	730	1999	60r
Child's health care, age 15-17	yr	760	1999	60r
Child's housing, age 0-2	yr	3070	1999	60r
Child's housing, age 3-5	yr	3050	1999	60r
Child's housing, age 6-8	yr	3010	1999	60r
Child's housing, age 9-11	yr	2850	1999	60r
Child's housing, age 12-14	yr	3040	1999	60r
Child's housing, age 15-17	yr	2650	1999	60r
Child's personal care, reading, age 0-2	yr	910	1999	60r
Child's personal care, reading, age 3-5	yr	930	1999	60r
Child's personal care, reading, age 6-8	yr	960	1999	60r
Child's personal care, reading, age 9-11	yr	1000	1999	60r
Child's personal care, reading, age 12-14	yr	1170	1999	60r
Child's personal care, reading, age 15-17	yr	950	1999	60r
Clothing				
Apparel and services purchases	yr	1610	1999	30r
Boys' brief, cotton	3	6.99	3/01	4c
Boys, 2 to 15, expenditures on	yr	89	1999	30r
Children under 2, expenditures on	yr	79	1999	30r
Footwear, expenditures on	yr	283	1999	30r
Girls, 2 to 15, expenditures on	yr	103	1999	30r
Men and boys, expenditures on	yr	351	1999	30r
Men, 16 and over, expenditures on	yr	262	1999	30r
Shirt, man's dress shirt		28.75	3/01	4c
Slacks, man's "No Wrinkles" khaki		36.00	3/01	4c
Women, 16 and over, expenditures on	yr	538	1999	30r
Communications				
Cable modem installation, Cox		99.00-174.95	6/99	103s
Cable modem rate, cable subscriber, Cox	mos	29.95-44.95	6/99	103s
Cable modem rate, non-cable subscriber, Cox	mos	42.95-54.95	6/99	103s
Newspaper subscription, daily and Sunday delivery	mos	12.60	3/01	4c
Phone line, single, business, field visit	inst.	82.75	12/97	17s
Phone line, single, business, no field visit	inst.	82.75	12/97	17s
Phone line, single, residence, field visit	inst.	44.45	12/97	17s
Phone line, single, residence, no field visit	inst.	44.45	12/97	17s
Postage and stationery, expenditures on	yr	104	1999	30r
Postal rate, express mail, up to half-pound		12.45	7/01	108r

Values are in dollars or fractions of dollars. In the column headed *Ref*, references are shown to sources. Each reference is followed by a letter. These refer to the geographical level for which data were reported: s=State, r=Region, and c=City or metro. The abbreviation *ex* is used to mean *except* or *excluding*; *exp* stands for expenditures. For other abbreviations and further explanations, please see the Introduction.

Enid, OK - continued

Item	Per	Value	Date	Ref.
Communications				
Postal rate, letter, first class, first ounce		0.34	7/01	108r
Postal rate, letter, two ounces		0.57	7/01	108r
Postal rate, post card		0.21	7/01	108r
Postal rate, priority mail, two pounds		3.95	7/01	108r
Postal rate, priority mail, up to one pound		3.50	7/01	108r
Telephone bill, family of three	mos	18.93	3/01	4c
Telephone services, expenditures on	yr	860	1999	30r
Education				
Board, 4-year private college/university	yr	1401	1996	38s
Board, 4-year public college/university	yr	61111	1996	38s
Education expenditures	yr	431	1999	30r
Room, 4-year private college/university	yr	8032	1996	38s
Room, 4-year public college/university	yr	8371	1996	38s
Total cost, 4-year private college/university	yr	7737	1996	38s
Total cost, 4-year public college/university	yr	4287	1996	38s
Tuition, 2-year public college/university, in state	yr	260	1996	38s
Tuition, 4-year private college/university, in state	yr	8311	1996	38s
Tuition, 4-year public college/university	yr	1839	1996	38s
Energy and Fuels				
Electricity	KWh	0.09	7/01	11r
Electricity	500 KWhs	47.29	7/01	11r
Energy, combined forms, 2400 sq ft	mos	122.66	3/01	4c
Energy, exc. electricity, 2400 sq ft	mos	52.05	3/01	4c
Fuel oil #2	gal	1.43	7/01	11r
Fuel oil and other fuels, expenditures on	yr	45	1999	30r
Gas, natural, commercial rate	1000 cf	7.50	11/00	88s
Gas, regular unleaded, cash, self-service	gal	1.33	3/01	4c
Gasoline, all types	gal	1.60	7/01	11r
Gasoline, unleaded midgrade	gal	1.65	7/01	11r
Gasoline, unleaded premium	gal	1.74	7/01	11r
Natural gas, expenditures on	yr	164	1999	30r
Utility (piped) gas, therm		1.01	7/01	11r
Utility (piped) gas, 40 therms		44.29	7/01	11r
Utility (piped) gas, 100 therms		97.44	7/01	11r
Entertainment				
Bowling, Saturday evening rate	line	2.75	3/01	4c
Entertainment purchases	yr	1574	1999	30r
Fees and admissions paid	yr	371	1999	30r
Monopoly game, Parker Brothers', No. 9	game	11.60	3/01	4c
Movie, first-run, Saturday, evening	adm.	6.25	3/01	4c
Reading purchases	yr	121	1999	30r
Television, radios, sound equipment, expenditures on	yr	561	1999	30r
Tennis balls, yellow, Wilson or Penn, 3	can	2.90	3/01	4c
Funerals				
Total cost of funeral		5842.28	1/99	78r
Acknowledgement cards		28.35	1/99	78r
Casket		2494.29	1/99	78r
Cosmetology, hair, other preparation		109.22	1/99	78r
Embalming		361.42	1/99	78r
Funeral at funeral home		349.20	1/99	78r
Hearse (local)		161.91	1/99	78r
Professional service charges		1116.50	1/99	78r
Service car/van		65.56	1/99	78r
Transfer of remains to funeral home		143.56	1/99	78r
Vault		785.25	1/99	78r
Visitation/viewing		227.02	1/99	78r
Groceries				
Groceries, ACCRA Index		96.80	3/01	4c
American processed cheese	lb	3.50	7/01	11r
Antibiotic ointment, Polysporin	0.5 oz	4.59	3/01	4c
Baby food, strained vegetables or fruit, lowest price	4-4.5 oz	0.45	3/01	4c
Bakery products, expenditures on	yr	261	1999	30r
Bananas	lb	0.49	3/01	4c
Bananas	lb	0.47	7/01	11r

Enid, OK - continued

Item	Per	Value	Date	Ref.
Groceries - continued		•		
Beans, dried, any type, all sizes	lb	0.63	7/01	11r
Beef for stew, boneless	lb	2.86	7/01	11r
Beef or hamburger, ground	lb	1.52	3/01	4c
Beef, expenditures on	yr	210	1999	30r
Bologna, all beef or mixed	lb	2.29	7/01	11r
Bread, French	lb	1.66	7/01	11r
Bread, white	loaf	1.02	3/01	4c
Bread, white, pan	lb	0.87	7/01	11r
Bread, whole wheat, pan	lb	1.38	7/01	11r
Broccoli	lb	1.04	7/01	11r
Butter, salted, grade AA, stick	lb	2.26	7/01	11r
Butter, yoghurt, cheese, etc, expenditures on	yr	170	1999	30r
Cabbage	lb	0.42	7/01	11r
Cereals and cereal products, expenditures on	yr	140	1999	30r
Cheddar cheese, natural	lb	3.75	7/01	11r
Cheese, Kraft grated Parmesan	8 oz	3.31	3/01	4c
Chicken breast, bone-in	lb	1.85	7/01	11r
Chicken legs, bone-in	lb	1.34	7/01	11r
Chicken, fresh, whole	lb	1.05	7/01	11r
Chicken, whole fryer	lb	0.86	3/01	4c
Chops, boneless,	lb	4.13	7/01	11r
Chuck roast, graded and ungraded, excl U.S. prime and choice	lb	2.35	7/01	11r
Chuck roast, U.S. choice, boneless	lb	2.67	7/01	11r
Cigarettes, Winston, Kings	carton	28.61	3/01	4c
Coffee, 100%, ground roast, all sizes	lb	2.88	7/01	11r
Coffee, instant, plain, regular, all sizes	16 oz	9.25	7/01	11r
Coffee, vacuum-packed	13 oz	2.39	3/01	4c
Cola, non diet	2 liter	1.11	7/01	11r
Corn Flakes, Kellogg's or Post Toasties	18 oz	1.71	3/01	4c
Corn, frozen, whole kernel, lowest price	16 oz	1.19	3/01	4c
Crackers, soda, salted	lb	1.70	7/01	11r
Dairy product purchases	yr	282	1999	30r
Eggs, expenditures on	yr	32	1999	30r
Eggs, Grade A or AA	dozen	1.00	3/01	4c
Fats and oils, expenditures on	yr	79	1999	30r
Fish and seafood, expenditures on	yr	99	1999	30r
Flour, white, all purpose	lb	0.32	7/01	11r
Food (excl fruit and vegetables), eaten at home, purchases	yr	815	1999	30r
Food cooked on trips, expenditures on	yr	36	1999	30r
Food purchases	yr	4533	1999	30r
Food purchases, eaten away from home	yr	1873	1999	30r
Food purchases, food eaten at home	yr	2660	1999	30r
Fresh fruits, expenditures on	yr	128	1999	30r
Fresh milk and cream, expenditures on	yr	112	1999	30r
Fresh vegetables, expenditures on	yr	131	1999	30r
Fruit and vegetable purchases	yr	438	1999	30r
Grapefruit	lb	0.59	7/01	11r
Grapes, Thompson, seedless	lb	2.12	7/01	11r
Ground beef, 100% beef	lb	1.76	7/01	11r
Ground beef, lean and extra lean	lb	2.60	7/01	11r
Ground chuck, 100% beef	lb	2.08	7/01	11r
Ham, boneless, excl canned	lb	2.71	7/01	11r
Ham, rump or shank half, bone-in, smoked	lb	2.19	7/01	11r
Ice cream, prepackaged, bulk, regular	1/2 gal	3.93	7/01	11r
Lemons	lb	1.32	7/01	11r
Lettuce, iceberg	head	0.89	3/01	4c
Lettuce, iceberg	lb	0.76	7/01	11r
Margarine, Blue Bonnet or Parkay, stick	lb	0.86	3/01	4c
Milk, fresh, low fat,	gal	2.75	7/01	11r
Milk, fresh, whole, fortified	gal	2.97	7/01	11r
Milk, whole	1/2 gal	1.74	3/01	4c
Nonalcoholic beverages, expenditures on	yr	228	1999	30r
Orange juice, frozen concentrate	16 oz	1.95	7/01	11r
Orange juice, Minute Maid frozen	12 oz	1.54	3/01	4c
Oranges, Navel	lb	0.73	7/01	11r
Oranges, Valencia	lb	0.55	7/01	11r
Peaches, halves or slices, Hunt's, Del Monte, or Libby's	29 oz	1.61	3/01	4c
Peanut butter, creamy, all sizes	lb	1.83	7/01	11r

Values are in dollars or fractions of dollars. In the column headed *Ref*, references are shown to sources. Each reference is followed by a letter. These refer to the geographical level for which data were reported: s=State, r=Region, and c=City or metro. The abbreviation *ex* is used to mean *except* or *excluding*; *exp* stands for expenditures. For other abbreviations and further explanations, please see the Introduction.

Enid, OK - continued

Item	Per	Value	Date	Ref.
Groceries				
Pears, Anjou	lb	0.98	7/01	11r
Peas, green, Del Monte or Green Giant	15 oz	0.65	3/01	4c
Pork chops, center cut, bone-in	lb	3.33	7/01	11r
Pork sausage, fresh, loose	lb	2.59	7/01	11r
Pork shoulder picnic, bone-in, smoked	lb	1.12	7/01	11r
Pork, expenditures on	yr	162	1999	30r
Potato chips	16 oz	3.59	7/01	11r
Potatoes, frozen, french fried	lb	1.00	7/01	11r
Potatoes, white or red	10 lb	1.79	3/01	4c
Potatoes, white, all types	lb	0.44	7/01	11r
Poultry, expenditures on	yr	137	1999	30r
Processed fruits, expenditures on	yr	97	1999	30r
Processed vegetables, expenditures on	yr	82	1999	30r
Rice, white, long grain, uncooked	lb	0.51	7/01	11r
Round roast, graded and ungraded, excl U.S. prime and choice	lb	2.96	7/01	11r
Round steak, graded and ungraded, excl U.S. prime and choice	lb	3.11	7/01	11r
Sausage, Jimmy Dean/Owens pork	lb	3.05	3/01	4c
Shortening, vegetable, Crisco	3 lb	2.86	3/01	4c
Sirloin steak, graded and ungraded, excl U.S. prime and choice	lb	4.23	7/01	11r
Soft drink, Coca Cola, ex deposit	2 liter	1.06	3/01	4c
Spaghetti and macaroni	lb	0.78	7/01	11r
Steak, round, U.S. choice, boneless	lb	3.56	7/01	11r
Steak, sirloin, U.S. choice, boneless	lb	5.65	7/01	11r
Steak, T-bone	lb	5.81	3/01	4c
Strawberries, dry pint	12 oz	1.50	7/01	11r
Sugar and other sweets, expenditures on	yr	99	1999	30r
Sugar, cane or beet	4 lbs	1.65	3/01	4c
Sugar, white, 33-80 ounce package	lb	0.39	7/01	11r
Sugar, white, all sizes	lb	0.42	7/01	11r
Tobacco products and smoking supplies purchases	yr	288	1999	30r
Tomatoes, field grown	lb	1.43	7/01	11r
Tomatoes, Hunt's or Del Monte	14.5 oz	0.95	3/01	4c
Tuna, chunk, light	6 oz	0.67	3/01	4c
Tuna, light, chunk	lb	1.77	7/01	11r
Turkey, frozen, whole	lb	1.05	7/01	11r
Goods and Services				
Miscellaneous goods and services, ACCRA Index		104.70	3/01	4c
B&B Japanese maple (acer japonicum)	gal	79.98-99.00	4/00	93r
Boxwood (buxus)	2 gal	12.98-18.99	4/00	93r
Daylilly (hemerocallis)	gal	7.96-11.00	4/00	93r
Flat of annuals		13.99-27.99	4/00	93r
Fountain grass (pennisetum)	gal	6.96-9.00	4/00	93r
Hanging basket (10 in)		9.99-24.99	4/00	93r
Hardy geranium (geranium)	gal	5.96-8.00	4/00	93r
Hosta (hosta)	gal	8.96-12.99	4/00	93r
Lilac (syrubga vulgaris)	2 gal	13.00-19.99	4/00	93r
Rhododendron (rhododendron)	2 gal	12.98-29.99	4/00	93r
Sage (salvia)	gal	5.96-8.00	4/00	93r
Wintercreeper euonymus (euonymus fortunei)	2 gal	13.00-18.99	4/00	93r
Hunting license	yr	12.50	4/01	34s
Health Care				
Health care, ACCRA Index		92.90	3/01	4c
Cardiac catheterization, ave hospital/ physician charges		15750	1998	77s

Enid, OK - continued

Item	Per	Value	Date	Ref.
Health Care - continued				
Childbirth, Cesarean delivery		11587	1997	13r
Childbirth, vaginal delivery		6725	1997	13r
Dentist's fee, adult teeth cleaning and periodic oral exam	visit	67.50	3/01	4c
Doctor's fee, routine exam, established patient	visit	52.20	3/01	4c
Drugs, expenditures on	yr	399	1999	30r
Health care purchases	yr	1971	1999	30r
Health insurance expenditures	yr	933	1999	30r
Hospital care, private room	day	497.50	3/01	4c
Hysterectomy, laproscopically-assisted, ave hospital/physician charges		16080	1998	76s
Hysterectomy, vaginal, ave hospital and physician charges		8140	1998	76s
Medicaid dispensing fee		4.15	1999	87s
Medical services expenditures	yr	547	1999	30r
Medical supplies, expenditures on	yr	91	1999	30r
Household Goods				
Dishwashing powder, Cascade	50 oz	3.29	3/01	4c
Floor coverings, expenditures on	yr	44	1999	30r
Furniture, expenditures on	yr	335	1999	30r
Household furnishings and equipment purchases	yr	1328	1999	30r
Household textiles, expenditures on	yr	89	1999	30r
Laundry and cleaning supplies, expenditures on	yr	113	1999	30r
Tissues, facial, Kleenex brand	175	1.51	3/01	4c
Housing				
Housing, ACCRA Index		82.60	3/01	4c
Home price, existing, ave		160100	10/00	90r
Home value, median		88000	2001	53s
House, 2400 sq ft, 8000 sq ft lot, new, urban, utilities	total	177833	3/01	4c
House payment, principal and interest, 25% down payment	mos	887	3/01	4c
Household operation expenditures	yr	553	1999	30r
Housekeeping supplies purchases	yr	473	1999	30r
Housing, expenditures on	yr	10303	1999	30r
Maintenance, repairs, insurance expenditures	yr	699	1999	30r
Monthly rental value of owned home	mos	505	1999	30r
Owned dwellings, expenditures own	yr	3465	1999	30r
Rent expenditures	yr	1641	1999	30r
Rent, apartment, 2 br, 1 1/2-2 baths, unfurn, 950 sq ft, water	mos	482	3/01	4c
Rental unit, 1 bedroom, with utilities	mos	304	4/01	41c
Rental unit, 2 bedroom, with utilities	mos	403	4/01	41c
Rental unit, 3 bedroom, with utilities	mos	561	4/01	41c
Rental unit, 4 bedroom, with utilities	mos	642	4/01	41c
Shelter, expenditures on	yr	5467	1999	30r
Insurance and Pensions				
Life and other personal insurance purchases	yr	414	1999	30r
Pensions and Social Security, expenditures on	yr	2635	1999	30r
Personal insurance and pensions, expenditures on	yr	3048	1999	30r
Legal Fees				
Combination hunting and fishing license	yr	21.00	4/01	34s
Divorce, filing fee		84.00	4/01	35s
Driver's license fee	orig	15.00	1999	48s
Driver's license fee	renew	15.00	1999	48s
Fishing license	yr	12.50	4/01	34s
Personal Goods				
Personal care products and services purchases	yr	393	1999	30r
Shampoo, Alberto VO5	15 oz	1.19	3/01	4c
Toothpaste, Crest or Colgate	6-7 oz	2.36	3/01	4c

Values are in dollars or fractions of dollars. In the column headed *Ref*, references are shown to sources. Each reference is followed by a letter. These refer to the geographical level for which data were reported: s=State, r=Region, and c=City or metro. The abbreviation *ex* is used to mean *except* or *excluding*; *exp* stands for expenditures. For other abbreviations and further explanations, please see the Introduction.

Enid, OK - continued

Item	Per	Value	Date	Ref.
Personal Services				
Dry cleaning, man's 2-pc suit		6.64	3/01	4c
Man's haircut, barbershop, no styling		10.75	3/01	4c
Personal services, household, expenditures on	yr	258	1999	30r
Woman's shampoo, trim, blow-dry, no style-change		22.59	3/01	4c
Pets				
Pets, toys, and playground equipment, expenditures on	yr	306	1999	30r
Restaurant Food				
Chicken, fried, thigh and drumstick, KFC/Church's		2.79	3/01	4c
Hamburger with cheese, McDonald's	1/4 lb	1.99	3/01	4c
Pizza, Pizza Hut or Pizza Inn	11-12 in	9.98	3/01	4c
Taxes				
Federal income taxes paid	yr	2047	1999	30r
Personal taxes, expenditures on	yr	2554	1999	30r
Property taxes paid	yr	726	1999	30r
State and local income taxes paid	yr	363	1999	30r
Transportation				
Transportation, ACCRA Index		90.70	3/01	4c
Cars and trucks, new, expenditures on	yr	1648	1999	30r
Cars and trucks, used, expenditures on	yr	1651	1999	30r
Diesel at the pump	gal	1.13	10/99	73s
Gasoline and motor oil purchases	yr	1052	1999	30r
Gasoline before-tax price (cents)	gal	103.70	10/00	43s
Maintenance and repair expenditures	yr	621	1999	30r
Public transportation, expenditures on	yr	298	1999	30r
Tire balance, computer or spin balance, front	wheel	6.75	3/01	4c
Transportation purchases	yr	6738	1999	30r
Vehicle expenses, miscellaneous, purchases	yr	2033	1999	30r
Vehicle insurance payments	yr	696	1999	30r
Vehicle purchases (net outlay)	yr	3354	1999	30r
Vehicle rental, lease expenditures	yr	352	1999	30r
Travel				
Hotel room	night	55.28	2/01	94s
Utilities				
Utilities, ACCRA Index		98.60	3/01	4c
Electrical bill, average	mos	67.33	9/00	9s
Electricity, expenditures on	yr	1115	1999	30r
Electricity and other, mixed, 2400 sq ft, new home	mos	70.61	3/01	4c
Electricity cost, average	KWh	5.66	9/00	9s
Water and other public services, expenditures on	yr	298	1999	30r
Weddings				
Wedding (national average cost)		19936	2000	33r
Attendants' gifts		321	1998	33r
Bridal attendants' apparel (5 persons)		824	2000	33r
Bride's headpiece/veil		173	1998	33r
Bride's wedding dress		859	1998	33r
Clergy, religious facility fee		242	1998	33r
Engagement ring		3177	1998	33r
Flowers		789	1998	33r
Groom's formalwear rental		99	2000	33r
Limousine		410	1998	33r
Marriage license cost		25.00	4/01	35s
Men's formalwear (ushers, best man)		469	2000	33r
Mother of bride apparel		241	2000	33r
Music		866	1998	33r
Photography and videography		1368	1998	33r
Rehearsal dinner		728	1998	33r
Wedding invitations and announcements		341	1998	33r
Wedding reception		7968	2000	33r
Wedding rings (bride and groom)		1060	1998	33r

Erie, PA

Item	Per	Value	Date	Ref.
Average annual expenditures	yr	37971	1999	30r
Alcoholic Beverages				
Alcoholic beverage purchases	yr	368	1999	30r
Wine, red and white table, all sizes, any origin	liter	9.64	7/01	11r
Appliances				
Major appliances, expenditures on	yr	194	1999	30r
Small appliances, housewares, expenditures on	yr	93	1999	30r
Banking and Money				
Mortgage interest and charges paid	yr	2622	1999	30r
Mortgage principal paid on owned property	yr	1262	1999	30r
Vehicle finance charges paid	yr	240	1999	30r
Charity				
Cash contributions, expenditures	yr	1001	1999	30r
Child Care				
Child raising cost, total, age 0-2	yr	8670	1999	60r
Child raising cost, total, age 3-5	yr	8910	1999	60r
Child raising cost, total, age 6-8	yr	9040	1999	60r
Child raising cost, total, age 9-11	yr	9100	1999	60r
Child raising cost, total, age 12-14	yr	9890	1999	60r
Child raising cost, total, age 15-17	yr	10010	1999	60r
Child's child care and education, age 0-2	yr	1070	1999	60r
Child's child care and education, age 3-5	yr	1190	1999	60r
Child's child care and education, age 6-8	yr	740	1999	60r
Child's child care and education, age 9-11	yr	470	1999	60r
Child's child care and education, age 12-14	yr	350	1999	60r
Child's child care and education, age 15-17	yr	590	1999	60r
Child's clothing, age 0-2	yr	480	1999	60r
Child's clothing, age 3-5	yr	470	1999	60r
Child's clothing, age 6-8	yr	520	1999	60r
Child's clothing, age 9-11	yr	570	1999	60r
Child's clothing, age 12-14	yr	970	1999	60r
Child's clothing, age 15-17	yr	870	1999	60r
Child's food, age 0-2	yr	1130	1999	60r
Child's food, age 3-5	yr	1290	1999	60r
Child's food, age 6-8	yr	1640	1999	60r
Child's food, age 9-11	yr	1930	1999	60r
Child's food, age 12-14	yr	1940	1999	60r
Child's food, age 15-17	yr	2150	1999	60r
Child's health care, age 0-2	yr	550	1999	60r
Child's health care, age 3-5	yr	530	1999	60r
Child's health care, age 6-8	yr	610	1999	60r
Child's health care, age 9-11	yr	650	1999	60r
Child's health care, age 12-14	yr	660	1999	60r
Child's health care, age 15-17	yr	690	1999	60r
Child's housing, age 0-2	yr	3555	1999	60r
Child's housing, age 3-5	yr	3530	1999	60r
Child's housing, age 6-8	yr	3490	1999	60r
Child's housing, age 9-11	yr	3340	1999	60r
Child's housing, age 12-14	yr	3530	1999	60r
Child's housing, age 15-17	yr	3140	1999	60r
Child's personal care, reading, age 0-2	yr	920	1999	60r
Child's personal care, reading, age 3-5	yr	950	1999	60r
Child's personal care, reading, age 6-8	yr	980	1999	60r
Child's personal care, reading, age 9-11	yr	1020	1999	60r
Child's personal care, reading, age 12-14	yr	1190	1999	60r
Child's personal care, reading, age 15-17	yr	970	1999	60r
Clothing				
Apparel and services purchases	yr	1831	1999	30r
Boys, 2 to 15, expenditures on	yr	92	1999	30r
Children under 2, expenditures on	yr	63	1999	30r
Footwear, expenditures on	yr	300	1999	30r
Girls, 2 to 15, expenditures on	yr	101	1999	30r
Men and boys, expenditures on	yr	446	1999	30r
Men, 16 and over, expenditures on	yr	354	1999	30r
Women, 16 and over, expenditures on	yr	584	1999	30r
Communications				
Cable modem installation, Adelphi		54.90	6/99	103s

Values are in dollars or fractions of dollars. In the column headed *Ref*, references are shown as sources. Each reference is followed by a letter. These refer to the geographical level for which data were reported: s=State, r=Region, and c=City or metro. The abbreviation *ex* is used to mean *except* or *excluding*; *exp* stands for expenditures. For other abbreviations and further explanations, please see the Introduction.

Erie, PA - continued

Item	Per	Value	Date	Ref.
Communications				
Cable modem installation, Comcast		95.00	6/99	103s
Cable modem rate, cable subscriber, Adelphi	mos	34.95	6/99	103s
Cable modem rate, cable subscriber, Comcast	mos	39.95	6/99	103s
Cable modem rate, non-cable subscriber, Adelphi	mos	44.95	6/99	103s
Cable modem rate, non-cable subscriber, Comcast	mos	49.95	6/99	103s
Phone line, single, business, field visit	inst.	75.00	12/97	17s
Phone line, single, business, no field visit	inst.	75.00	12/97	17s
Phone line, single, residence, field visit	inst.	40.00	12/97	17s
Phone line, single, residence, no field visit	inst.	40.00	12/97	17s
Postage and stationery, expenditures on	yr	138	1999	30r
Postal rate, express mail, up to half-pound		12.45	7/01	108r
Postal rate, letter, first class, first ounce		0.34	7/01	108r
Postal rate, letter, two ounces		0.57	7/01	108r
Postal rate, post card		0.21	7/01	108r
Postal rate, priority mail, two pounds		3.95	7/01	108r
Postal rate, priority mail, up to one pound		3.50	7/01	108r
Telephone bill, business, basic rate	mos	19.20	12/97	18c
Telephone bill, residential, basic rate	mos	6.85	12/97	18c
Telephone services, expenditures on	yr	830	1999	30r
Education				
Board, 4-year private college/university	yr	2822	1996	38s
Board, 4-year public college/university	yr	2174	1996	38s
Education expenditures	yr	877	1999	30r
Room, 4-year private college/university	yr	2943	1996	38s
Room, 4-year public college/university	yr	2227	1996	38s
Total cost, 4-year private college/university	yr	19876	1996	38s
Total cost, 4-year public college/university	yr	9124	1996	38s
Tuition, 2-year public college/university, in state	yr	1909	1996	38s
Tuition, 4-year private college/university, in state	yr	14111	1996	38s
Tuition, 4-year public college/university	yr	4723	1996	38s
Energy and Fuels				
Electricity	KWh	0.12	7/01	11r
Fuel oil #2	gal	1.31	7/01	11r
Fuel oil and other fuels, expenditures on	yr	207	1999	30r
Gas, cooking, winter, 10 therms	mos	17.71	2/96	98c
Gas, cooking, winter, 30 therms	mos	29.77	2/96	98c
Gas, cooking, winter, 50 therms	mos	41.83	2/96	98c
Gas, heating, winter, average use	mos	139.02	2/96	98c
Gas, natural, commercial rate	1000 cf	5.96	11/00	88s
Gasoline, all types	gal	1.80	7/01	11r
Gasoline, unleaded midgrade	gal	1.85	7/01	11r
Gasoline, unleaded premium	gal	1.91	7/01	11r
Gasoline, unleaded regular	gal	1.71	7/01	11r
Natural gas, expenditures on	yr	368	1999	30r
Utility (piped) gas, therm		1.08	7/01	11r
Utility (piped) gas, 40 therms		50.87	7/01	11r
Utility (piped) gas, 100 therms		111.06	7/01	11r
Entertainment				
Entertainment purchases	yr	1821	1999	30r
Fees and admissions paid	yr	511	1999	30r
Television, radios, sound equipment, expenditures on	yr	650	1999	30r
Funerals				
Total cost of funeral		5813.50	1/99	78r
Acknowledgement cards		28.32	1/99	78r
Casket		2082.20	1/99	78r
Cosmetology, hair, other preparation		169.59	1/99	78r
Embalming		465.60	1/99	78r
Funeral at funeral home		339.56	1/99	78r
Hearse (local)		183.96	1/99	78r
Professional service charges		1157.85	1/99	78r
Service car/van		100.41	1/99	78r
Transfer of remains to funeral home		158.66	1/99	78r
Vault		766.31	1/99	78r
Visitation/viewing		361.04	1/99	78r

Erie, PA - continued

Item	Per	Value	Date	Ref.
Groceries				
Apples, red delicious	lb	0.95	7/01	11r
Bacon, sliced	lb	3.44	7/01	11r
Bakery products, expenditures on	yr	310	1999	30r
Bananas	lb	0.55	7/01	11r
Beef, expenditures on	yr	236	1999	30r
Bread, white, pan	lb	1.09	7/01	11r
Butter, yoghurt, cheese, etc, expenditures on	yr	214	1999	30r
Cereals and bakery product purchases	yr	474	1999	30r
Cereals and cereal products, expenditures on	yr	164	1999	30r
Chicken legs, bone-in	lb	1.23	7/01	11r
Chicken, fresh, whole	lb	1.13	7/01	11r
Chuck roast, U.S. choice, boneless	lb	2.79	7/01	11r
Coffee, 100%, ground roast, all sizes	lb	3.40	7/01	11r
Dairy product purchases	yr	342	1999	30r
Eggs, expenditures on	yr	34	1999	30r
Eggs, grade A, large	dozen	0.82	7/01	11r
Fats and oils, expenditures on	yr	80	1999	30r
Fish and seafood, expenditures on	yr	123	1999	30r
Food (excl fruit and vegetables), eaten at home, purchases	yr	838	1999	30r
Food cooked on trips, expenditures on	yr	48	1999	30r
Food purchases	yr	5314	1999	30r
Food purchases, eaten away from home	yr	2313	1999	30r
Food purchases, food eaten at home	yr	3001	1999	30r
Fresh fruits, expenditures on	yr	169	1999	30r
Fresh milk and cream, expenditures on	yr	128	1999	30r
Fresh vegetables, expenditures on	yr	164	1999	30r
Grapefruit	lb	0.67	7/01	11r
Grapes, Thompson, seedless	lb	2.18	7/01	11r
Ground beef, lean and extra lean	lb	2.66	7/01	11r
Ground chuck, 100% beef	lb	2.04	7/01	11r
Lettuce, iceberg	lb	0.76	7/01	11r
Meats, poultry, fish, and egg purchases	yr	808	1999	30r
Nonalcoholic beverages, expenditures on	yr	225	1999	30r
Orange juice, frozen concentrate	16 oz	1.88	7/01	11r
Oranges, Navel	lb	0.79	7/01	11r
Oranges, Valencia	lb	0.56	7/01	11r
Peaches	lb	1.16	7/01	11r
Peanut butter, creamy, all sizes	lb	2.01	7/01	11r
Pears, Anjou	lb	1.16	7/01	11r
Pork chops, center cut, bone-in	lb	3.57	7/01	11r
Pork, expenditures on	yr	146	1999	30r
Potato chips	16 oz	3.37	7/01	11r
Potatoes, white, all types	lb	0.42	7/01	11r
Poultry, expenditures on	yr	158	1999	30r
Processed fruits, expenditures on	yr	124	1999	30r
Processed vegetables, expenditures on	yr	82	1999	30r
Round roast, U.S. choice, boneless	lb	3.04	7/01	11r
Spaghetti and macaroni	lb	1.04	7/01	11r
Steak, sirloin, U.S. choice, boneless	lb	5.39	7/01	11r
Strawberries, dry pint	12 oz	1.51	7/01	11r
Sugar and other sweets, expenditures on	yr	110	1999	30r
Sugar, white, 33-80 ounce package	lb	0.46	7/01	11r
Sugar, white, all sizes	lb	0.47	7/01	11r
Tobacco products and smoking supplies purchases	yr	309	1999	30r
Yogurt, natural, fruit flavored	8 oz	0.79	7/01	11r
Goods and Services				
B&B Japanese maple (acer japonicum)	gal	38.99- 125.00	4/00	93r
Boxwood (buxus)	2 gal	15.99- 49.95	4/00	93r
Daylily (hemerocallis)	gal	4.95	4/00	93r
Flat of annuals		8.00- 14.99	4/00	93r
Fountain grass (pennisetum)	gal	6.99- 9.99	4/00	93r
Hanging basket (10 in)		12.95- 19.99	4/00	93r
Hardy geranium (geranium)	gal	6.95- 7.99	4/00	93r

Values are in dollars or fractions of dollars. In the column headed *Ref*, references are shown to sources. Each reference is followed by a letter. These refer to the geographical level for which data were reported: s=State, r=Region, and c=City or metro. The abbreviation *ex* is used to mean *except* or *excluding*; *exp* stands for *expenditures*. For other abbreviations and further explanations, please see the Introduction.

Erie, PA - continued

Item	Per	Value	Date	Ref.
Goods and Services				
Hosta (hosta)	gal	4.95	4/00	93r
Lilac (syrubga vulgaris)	2 gal	17.99-74.95	4/00	93r
Miscellaneous purchases	yr	872	1999	30r
Rhododendron (rhododendron)	2 gal	23.99-54.95	4/00	93r
Sage (salvia)	gal	6.95-7.99	4/00	93r
Wintercreeper euonymus (euonymus fortunei)	2 gal	14.99-23.95	4/00	93r
Hunting license	yr	20.00	4/01	34s
Health Care				
Cardiac catheterization, ave hospital/ physician charges		13870	1998	77s
Childbirth, Cesarean delivery		14716	1997	13r
Childbirth, vaginal delivery		8541	1997	13r
Drugs, expenditures on	yr	296	1999	30r
Health care purchases	yr	1788	1999	30r
Health insurance expenditures	yr	875	1999	30r
Hysterectomy, laproscopically-assisted, ave hospital/physician charges		14760	1998	76s
Hysterectomy, vaginal, ave hospital and physician charges		9270	1998	76s
Medicaid dispensing fee		4.00	1999	87s
Medical services expenditures	yr	516	1999	30r
Medical supplies, expenditures on	yr	102	1999	30r
Plastic surgery, breast augmentation		4232	2000	7r
Plastic surgery, breast lift		4605	2000	7r
Plastic surgery, facelift		6964	2000	7r
Plastic surgery, hair transplantation		4193	2000	7r
Plastic surgery, lip augmentation		1675	2000	7r
Plastic surgery, lower body lift		6611	2000	7r
Plastic surgery, thigh lift		4751	2000	7r
Household Goods				
Floor coverings, expenditures on	yr	59	1999	30r
Furniture, expenditures on	yr	388	1999	30r
Household furnishings and equipment purchases	yr	1567	1999	30r
Household textiles, expenditures on	yr	112	1999	30r
Laundry and cleaning supplies, expenditures on	yr	104	1999	30r
Housing				
Home price, existing, ave		180800	10/00	90r
Home value, median		115000	2001	53s
Household operation expenditures	yr	581	1999	30r
Housekeeping supplies purchases	yr	474	1999	30r
Lodging expenditures	yr	550	1999	30r
Maintenance, repairs, insurance expenditures	yr	835	1999	30r
Monthly rental value of owned home	mos	663	1999	30r
Owned dwellings, expenditures own	yr	5209	1999	30r
Rent expenditures	yr	2390	1999	30r
Rental unit, 1 bedroom, with utilities	mos	381	4/01	41c
Rental unit, 2 bedroom, with utilities	mos	448	4/01	41c
Rental unit, 3 bedroom, with utilities	mos	579	4/01	41c
Rental unit, 4 bedroom, with utilities	mos	647	4/01	41c
Shelter, expenditures on	yr	8149	1999	30r
Insurance and Pensions				
Life and other personal insurance purchases	yr	424	1999	30r
Pensions and Social Security, expenditures on	yr	3037	1999	30r
Legal Fees				
Divorce, filing fee		65.00	4/01	35s
Driver's license fee	renew	24.00	1999	48s
Driver's license fee	orig	29.00	1999	48s
Fishing license	yr	17.00	4/01	34s
Personal Goods				
Personal care products and services purchases	yr	399	1999	30r

Erie, PA - continued

Item	Per	Value	Date	Ref.
Personal Services				
Personal services, household, expenditures on	yr	271	1999	30r
Pets				
Pets, toys, and playground equipment, expenditures on	yr	325	1999	30r
Taxes				
Federal income taxes paid	yr	2606	1999	30r
Personal taxes, expenditures on	yr	3567	1999	30r
Property taxes paid	yr	1752	1999	30r
State and local income taxes paid	yr	694	1999	30r
Transportation				
Cars and trucks, new, expenditures on	yr	1496	1999	30r
Cars and trucks, used, expenditures on	yr	1251	1999	30r
Diesel at the pump	gal	1.31	10/99	73s
Gasoline and motor oil purchases	yr	901	1999	30r
Gasoline before-tax price (cents)	gal	106.60	10/00	43s
Maintenance and repair expenditures	yr	618	1999	30r
Public transportation, expenditures on	yr	575	1999	30r
Transportation purchases	yr	6503	1999	30r
Vehicle expenses, miscellaneous, purchases	yr	2266	1999	30r
Vehicle insurance payments	yr	824	1999	30r
Vehicle purchases (net outlay)	yr	2761	1999	30r
Vehicle rental, lease expenditures	yr	584	1999	30r
Utilities				
Electrical bill, average	mos	69.16	9/00	9s
Electricity, expenditures on	yr	837	1999	30r
Electricity, summer, 250 KWh	mos	25.67	2/96	96c
Electricity, summer, 500 KWh	mos	44.53	2/96	96c
Electricity, summer, 750 KWh	mos	63.39	2/96	96c
Electricity, summer, 1000 KWh	mos	82.25	2/96	96c
Electricity cost, average	KWh	5.08	9/00	9s
Utilities, fuels, and public services purchased	yr	2457	1999	30r
Water and other public services, expenditures on	yr	215	1999	30r
Weddings				
Wedding (national average cost)		19936	2000	33r
Wedding (regional average total cost)		29454	1997	110r
Attendants' gifts		321	1998	33r
Bridal attendants' apparel (5 persons)		824	2000	33r
Bride's headpiece/veil		173	1998	33r
Bride's wedding dress		859	1998	33r
Clergy, religious facility fee		242	1998	33r
Engagement ring		3177	1998	33r
Flowers		789	1998	33r
Groom's formalwear rental		99	2000	33r
Limousine		410	1998	33r
Marriage license cost		25.00-40.00	4/01	35s
Men's formalwear (ushers, best man)		469	2000	33r
Mother of bride apparel		241	2000	33r
Music		866	1998	33r
Photography and videography		1368	1998	33r
Rehearsal dinner		728	1998	33r
Wedding invitations and announcements		341	1998	33r
Wedding reception		7968	2000	33r
Wedding rings (bride and groom)		1060	1998	33r

Eugene-Springfield, OR

Item	Per	Value	Date	Ref.
Average annual expenditures	yr	40662	1999	30r
Alcoholic Beverages				
Alcoholic beverage purchases	yr	372	1999	30r
Malt beverages, all types, all sizes, any origin	16 oz	0.94	7/01	11r
Wine, red and white table, all sizes, any origin	liter	6.00	7/01	11r
Appliances				
Major appliances, expenditures on	yr	167	1999	30r

Values are in dollars or fractions of dollars. In the column headed *Ref*, references are shown to sources. Each reference is followed by a letter. These refer to the geographical level for which data were reported: s=State, r=Region, and c=City or metro. The abbreviation *ex* is used to mean *except* or *excluding*; *exp* stands for expenditures. For other abbreviations and further explanations, please see the Introduction.

Eugene-Springfield, OR - continued

Item	Per	Value	Date	Ref.
Appliances				
Small appliances, housewares, expenditures on	yr	105	1999	30r
Banking and Money				
Mortgage interest and charges paid	yr	3368	1999	30r
Mortgage principal paid on owned property	yr	1677	1999	30r
Vehicle finance charges paid	yr	311	1999	30r
Charity				
Cash contributions, expenditures	yr	1344	1999	30r
Child Care				
Child raising cost, total, age 0-2	yr	9140	1999	60r
Child raising cost, total, age 3-5	yr	9370	1999	60r
Child raising cost, total, age 6-8	yr	9450	1999	60r
Child raising cost, total, age 9-11	yr	9470	1999	60r
Child raising cost, total, age 12-14	yr	10170	1999	60r
Child raising cost, total, age 15-17	yr	10360	1999	60r
Child's child care and education, age 0-2	yr	1250	1999	60r
Child's child care and education, age 3-5	yr	1380	1999	60r
Child's child care and education, age 6-8	yr	890	1999	60r
Child's child care and education, age 9-11	yr	580	1999	60r
Child's child care and education, age 12-14	yr	430	1999	60r
Child's child care and education, age 15-17	yr	730	1999	60r
Child's clothing, age 0-2	yr	430	1999	60r
Child's clothing, age 3-5	yr	420	1999	60r
Child's clothing, age 6-8	yr	470	1999	60r
Child's clothing, age 9-11	yr	520	1999	60r
Child's clothing, age 12-14	yr	870	1999	60r
Child's clothing, age 15-17	yr	770	1999	60r
Child's food, age 0-2	yr	1120	1999	60r
Child's food, age 3-5	yr	1280	1999	60r
Child's food, age 6-8	yr	1640	1999	60r
Child's food, age 9-11	yr	1930	1999	60r
Child's food, age 12-14	yr	1940	1999	60r
Child's food, age 15-17	yr	2150	1999	60r
Child's health care, age 0-2	yr	490	1999	60r
Child's health care, age 3-5	yr	470	1999	60r
Child's health care, age 6-8	yr	530	1999	60r
Child's health care, age 9-11	yr	570	1999	60r
Child's health care, age 12-14	yr	580	1999	60r
Child's health care, age 15-17	yr	610	1999	60r
Child's housing, age 0-2	yr	3630	1999	60r
Child's housing, age 3-5	yr	3610	1999	60r
Child's housing, age 6-8	yr	3570	1999	60r
Child's housing, age 9-11	yr	3410	1999	60r
Child's housing, age 12-14	yr	3600	1999	60r
Child's housing, age 15-17	yr	3210	1999	60r
Child's personal care, reading, age 0-2	yr	1040	1999	60r
Child's personal care, reading, age 3-5	yr	1060	1999	60r
Child's personal care, reading, age 6-8	yr	1090	1999	60r
Child's personal care, reading, age 9-11	yr	1130	1999	60r
Child's personal care, reading, age 12-14	yr	1300	1999	60r
Child's personal care, reading, age 15-17	yr	1080	1999	60r
Clothing				
Apparel and services purchases	yr	1863	1999	30r
Boys, 2 to 15, expenditures on	yr	80	1999	30r
Children under 2, expenditures on	yr	74	1999	30r
Footwear, expenditures on	yr	307	1999	30r
Girls, 2 to 15, expenditures on	yr	101	1999	30r
Men and boys, expenditures on	yr	443	1999	30r
Men, 16 and over, expenditures on	yr	363	1999	30r
Women, 16 and over, expenditures on	yr	594	1999	30r
Communications				
Phone line, single, business, field visit	inst.	31.00	12/97	17s
Phone line, single, business, no field visit	inst.	31.00	12/97	17s
Phone line, single, residence, field visit	inst.	12.00	12/97	17s
Phone line, single, residence, no field visit	inst.	12.00	12/97	17s
Postage and stationery, expenditures on	yr	150	1999	30r
Postal rate, express mail, up to half-pound		12.45	7/01	108r
Postal rate, letter, first class, first ounce		0.34	7/01	108r
Postal rate, letter, two ounces		0.57	7/01	108r

Eugene-Springfield, OR - continued

Item	Per	Value	Date	Ref.
Communications - continued				
Postal rate, post card		0.21	7/01	108r
Postal rate, priority mail, two pounds		3.95	7/01	108r
Postal rate, priority mail, up to one pound		3.50	7/01	108r
Telephone bill, business, basic rate	mos	18.00	12/97	18c
Telephone bill, residential, basic rate	mos	6.37	12/97	18c
Telephone services, expenditures on	yr	825	1999	30r
Education				
Board, 4-year private college/university	yr	2750	1996	38s
Board, 4-year public college/university	yr	2474	1996	38s
Education expenditures	yr	676	1999	30r
Room, 4-year private college/university	yr	2257	1996	38s
Room, 4-year public college/university	yr	1647	1996	38s
Total cost, 4-year private college/university	yr	18899	1996	38s
Total cost, 4-year public college/university	yr	7354	1996	38s
Tuition, 2-year public college/university, in state	yr	1338	1996	38s
Tuition, 4-year private college/university, in state	yr	13892	1996	38s
Tuition, 4-year public college/university	yr	3233	1996	38s
Energy and Fuels				
Electricity	KWh	0.11	7/01	11r
Electricity	500 KWhs	48.23	7/01	11r
Fuel oil and other fuels, expenditures on	yr	35	1999	30r
Gas, natural, commercial rate	1000 cf	7.55	11/00	88s
Gasoline, all types	gal	1.91	7/01	11r
Gasoline, unleaded premium	gal	2.05	7/01	11r
Gasoline, unleaded regular	gal	1.83	7/01	11r
Natural gas, expenditures on	yr	255	1999	30r
Utility (piped) gas, therm		0.98	7/01	11r
Utility (piped) gas, 40 therms		40.74	7/01	11r
Utility (piped) gas, 100 therms		96.80	7/01	11r
Entertainment				
Entertainment purchases	yr	2139	1999	30r
Fees and admissions paid	yr	545	1999	30r
Television, radios, sound equipment, expenditures on	yr	624	1999	30r
Funerals				
Total cost of funeral		5401.08	1/99	78r
Acknowledgement cards		33.64	1/99	78r
Casket		2170.43	1/99	78r
Cosmetology, hair, other preparation		136.32	1/99	78r
Embalming		319.13	1/99	78r
Funeral at funeral home		370.21	1/99	78r
Hearse (local)		161.04	1/99	78r
Professional service charges		963.15	1/99	78r
Service car/van		133.99	1/99	78r
Transfer of remains to funeral home		159.82	1/99	78r
Vault		778.07	1/99	78r
Visitation/viewing		175.28	1/99	78r
Groceries				
Apples, red delicious	lb	0.84	7/01	11r
Bacon, sliced	lb	3.38	7/01	11r
Bakery products, expenditures on	yr	299	1999	30r
Bananas	lb	0.54	7/01	11r
Beans, dried, any type, all sizes	lb	0.76	7/01	11r
Beef, expenditures on	yr	222	1999	30r
Bread, white, pan	lb	0.99	7/01	11r
Butter, yoghurt, cheese, etc, expenditures on	yr	211	1999	30r
Cereals and bakery product purchases	yr	466	1999	30r
Cereals and cereal products, expenditures on	yr	168	1999	30r
Chicken breast, bone-in	lb	2.45	7/01	11r
Chicken, fresh, whole	lb	1.19	7/01	11r
Chops, boneless,	lb	4.00	7/01	11r
Chuck roast, graded and ungraded, excl U.S. prime and choice	lb	2.55	7/01	11r
Coffee, 100%, ground roast, all sizes	lb	3.80	7/01	11r
Cookies, chocolate chip	lb	2.83	7/01	11r

Values are in dollars or fractions of dollars. In the column headed *Ref*, references are shown to sources. Each reference is followed by a letter. These refer to the geographical level for which data were reported: s=State, r=Region, and c=City or metro. The abbreviation *ex* is used to mean *except* or *excluding*; *exp* stands for *expenditures*. For other abbreviations and further explanations, please see the Introduction.

Eugene-Springfield, OR - continued

Item	Per	Value	Date	Ref.
Groceries				
Dairy product purchases	yr	341	1999	30r
Eggs, expenditures on	yr	39	1999	30r
Eggs, grade AA, large	dozen	1.23	7/01	11r
Fats and oils, expenditures on	yr	88	1999	30r
Fish and seafood, expenditures on	yr	121	1999	30r
Food (excl fruit and vegetables), eaten at home, purchases	yr	1001	1999	30r
Food cooked on trips, expenditures on	yr	64	1999	30r
Food purchases	yr	5312	1999	30r
Food purchases, eaten away from home	yr	2180	1999	30r
Food purchases, food eaten at home	yr	3132	1999	30r
Fresh fruits, expenditures on	yr	186	1999	30r
Fresh milk and cream, expenditures on	yr	130	1999	30r
Fresh vegetables, expenditures on	yr	177	1999	30r
Grapefruit	lb	0.68	7/01	11r
Grapes, Thompson, seedless	lb	2.42	7/01	11r
Ground beef, lean and extra lean	lb	2.46	7/01	11r
Ice cream, prepackaged, bulk, regular	1/2 gal	3.62	7/01	11r
Lettuce, iceberg	lb	0.63	7/01	11r
Meats, poultry, fish, and egg purchases	yr	761	1999	30r
Milk, fresh, low fat	gal	2.80	7/01	11r
Milk, fresh, whole, fortified	gal	2.88	7/01	11r
Nonalcoholic beverages, expenditures on	yr	258	1999	30r
Oranges, Navel	lb	0.97	7/01	11r
Oranges, Valencia	lb	0.43	7/01	11r
Peaches	lb	1.38	7/01	11r
Peanut butter, creamy, all sizes	lb	2.14	7/01	11r
Pork chops, center cut, bone-in	lb	3.83	7/01	11r
Pork, expenditures on	yr	141	1999	30r
Potatoes, white, all types	lb	0.37	7/01	11r
Poultry, expenditures on	yr	146	1999	30r
Processed fruits, expenditures on	yr	118	1999	30r
Processed vegetables, expenditures on	yr	81	1999	30r
Round roast, graded and ungraded, excl U.S. prime and choice	lb	3.07	7/01	11r
Round roast, U.S. choice, boneless	lb	3.37	7/01	11r
Round steak, graded and ungraded, excl U.S. prime and choice	lb	3.51	7/01	11r
Sirloin steak, graded and ungraded, excl U.S. prime and choice	lb	4.67	7/01	11r
Steak, sirloin, U.S. choice, boneless	lb	6.20	7/01	11r
Strawberries, dry pint	12 oz	1.79	7/01	11r
Sugar and other sweets, expenditures on	yr	124	1999	30r
Sugar, white, all sizes	lb	0.46	7/01	11r
Tobacco products and smoking supplies purchases	yr	217	1999	30r
Tomatoes, field grown	lb	1.17	7/01	11r
Tuna, light, chunk	lb	2.05	7/01	11r
Goods and Services				
B&B Japanese maple (acer japonicum)	gal	39.99	4/00	93r
Boxwood (buxus)	2 gal	14.99-24.99	4/00	93r
Christmas tree, noble fir		20-25	2000	65s
Daylily (hemerocallis)	gal	6.99-8.99	4/00	93r
Flat of annuals		16.68	4/00	93r
Fountain grass (pennisetum)	gal	7.99-11.99	4/00	93r
Hanging basket (10 in)		29.99	4/00	93r
Hardy geranium (geranium)	gal	6.99-11.99	4/00	93r
Hosta (hosta)	gal	6.99-18.99	4/00	93r
Lilac (syrubga vulgaris)	2 gal	14.99-17.99	4/00	93r
Miscellaneous purchases	yr	1070	1999	30r
Rhododendron (rhododendron)	2 gal	14.99	4/00	93r
Sage (salvia)	gal	6.99	4/00	93r
Wintercreeper euonymus (euonymus fortunei)	2 gal	14.99-22.99	4/00	93r
Hunting license	yr	17.50	4/01	34s

Eugene-Springfield, OR - continued

Item	Per	Value	Date	Ref.
Health Care				
Cardiac catheterization, ave hospital/ physician charges		10940	1998	77s
Childbirth, Cesarean delivery		11587	1997	13r
Childbirth, vaginal delivery		6725	1997	13r
Drugs, expenditures on	yr	309	1999	30r
Health care purchases	yr	1869	1999	30r
Health insurance expenditures	yr	868	1999	30r
Hysterectomy, laproscopically-assisted, ave hospital/physician charges		11660	1998	76s
Hysterectomy, vaginal, ave hospital and physician charges		6680	1998	76s
Medicaid dispensing fee		3.80-4.16	1999	87s
Medical services expenditures	yr	580	1999	30r
Medical supplies, expenditures on	yr	112	1999	30r
Household Goods				
Floor coverings, expenditures on	yr	49	1999	30r
Furniture, expenditures on	yr	444	1999	30r
Household furnishings and equipment purchases	yr	1768	1999	30r
Household textiles, expenditures on	yr	141	1999	30r
Laundry and cleaning supplies, expenditures on	yr	128	1999	30r
Housing				
Home price, existing, ave		239400	10/00	90r
Home value, median		149000	2001	53s
Household operation expenditures	yr	781	1999	30r
Housekeeping supplies purchases	yr	513	1999	30r
Lodging expenditures	yr	575	1999	30r
Maintenance, repairs, insurance expenditures	yr	939	1999	30r
Monthly rental value of owned home	mos	662	1999	30r
Owned dwellings, expenditures own	yr	5231	1999	30r
Rent expenditures	yr	2709	1999	30r
Rental unit, 1 bedroom, with utilities	mos	465	4/01	41c
Rental unit, 2 bedroom, with utilities	mos	606	4/01	41c
Rental unit, 3 bedroom, with utilities	mos	846	4/01	41c
Rental unit, 4 bedroom, with utilities	mos	977	4/01	41c
Shelter, expenditures on	yr	8516	1999	30r
Insurance and Pensions				
Life and other personal insurance purchases	yr	355	1999	30r
Pensions and Social Security, expenditures on	yr	3636	1999	30r
Legal Fees				
Combination hunting and fishing license	yr	33.75	4/01	34s
Divorce, filing fee		100.00-250.00	4/01	35s
Driver's license fee	orig	26.25	1999	48s
Driver's license fee	renew	16.25	1999	48s
Fishing license	yr	19.75	4/01	34s
Personal Goods				
Personal care products and services purchases	yr	449	1999	30r
Personal Services				
Personal services, household, expenditures on	yr	353	1999	30r
Pets				
Pets, toys, and playground equipment, expenditures on	yr	358	1999	30r
Taxes				
Federal income taxes paid	yr	3200	1999	30r
Personal taxes, expenditures on	yr	4153	1999	30r
Property taxes paid	yr	923	1999	30r
State and local income taxes paid	yr	812	1999	30r
Transportation				
Cars and trucks, new, expenditures on	yr	1534	1999	30r
Cars and trucks, used, expenditures on	yr	1593	1999	30r

Values are in dollars or fractions of dollars. In the column headed *Ref*, references are shown to sources. Each reference is followed by a letter. These refer to the geographical level for which data were reported: s=State, r=Region, and c=City or metro. The abbreviation *ex* is used to mean *except* or *excluding*; *exp* stands for expenditures. For other abbreviations and further explanations, please see the Introduction.

Eugene-Springfield, OR - continued

Item	Per	Value	Date	Ref.
Transportation				
Diesel at the pump	gal	1.16	10/99	73s
Gasoline and motor oil purchases	yr	1129	1999	30r
Gasoline before-tax price (cents)	gal	128.30	10/00	43s
Maintenance and repair expenditures	yr	797	1999	30r
Public transportation, expenditures on	yr	530	1999	30r
Transportation purchases	yr	7423	1999	30r
Vehicle expenses, miscellaneous, purchases	yr	2585	1999	30r
Vehicle insurance payments	yr	811	1999	30r
Vehicle purchases (net outlay)	yr	3180	1999	30r
Vehicle rental, lease expenditures	yr	666	1999	30r
Utilities				
Electrical bill, average	mos	61.42	9/00	9s
Electricity, expenditures on	yr	725	1999	30r
Electricity cost, average	KWh	4.70	9/00	9s
Utilities, fuels, and public services purchased	yr	2179	1999	30r
Water and other public services, expenditures on	yr	339	1999	30r
Weddings				
Wedding (national average cost)		19936	2000	33r
Wedding (regional average total cost)		18918	1997	110r
Attendants' gifts		321	1998	33r
Bridal attendants' apparel (5 persons)		824	2000	33r
Bride's headpiece/veil		173	1998	33r
Bride's wedding dress		859	1998	33r
Clergy, religious facility fee		242	1998	33r
Engagement ring		3177	1998	33r
Flowers		789	1998	33r
Groom's formalwear rental		99	2000	33r
Limousine		410	1998	33r
Marriage license cost		60.00	4/01	35s
Men's formalwear (ushers, best man)		469	2000	33r
Mother of bride apparel		241	2000	33r
Music		866	1998	33r
Photography and videography		1368	1998	33r
Rehearsal dinner		728	1998	33r
Wedding invitations and announcements		341	1998	33r
Wedding reception		7968	2000	33r
Wedding rings (bride and groom)		1060	1998	33r

Evansville-Henderson, IN-KY

Item	Per	Value	Date	Ref.
Average annual expenditures	yr	35369	1999	30r
Alcoholic Beverages				
Alcoholic beverage purchases	yr	304	1999	30r
Malt beverages, all types, all sizes, any origin	16 oz	0.93	7/01	11r
Wine, red and white table, all sizes, any origin	liter	7.04	7/01	11r
Appliances				
Major appliances, expenditures on	yr	165	1999	30r
Small appliances, housewares, expenditures on	yr	90	1999	30r
Banking and Money				
Mortgage interest and charges paid	yr	2277	1999	30r
Mortgage principal paid on owned property	yr	1230	1999	30r
Vehicle finance charges paid	yr	328	1999	30r
Charity				
Cash contributions, expenditures	yr	1126	1999	30r
Child Care				
Child raising cost, total, age 0-2	yr	7890	1999	60r
Child raising cost, total, age 3-5	yr	8130	1999	60r
Child raising cost, total, age 6-8	yr	8170	1999	60r
Child raising cost, total, age 9-11	yr	8190	1999	60r
Child raising cost, total, age 12-14	yr	8890	1999	60r
Child raising cost, total, age 15-17	yr	9050	1999	60r
Child's child care and education, age 0-2	yr	1240	1999	60r
Child's child care and education, age 3-5	yr	1370	1999	60r
Child's child care and education, age 6-8	yr	880	1999	60r
Child's child care and education, age 9-11	yr	570	1999	60r

Evansville-Henderson, IN-KY - continued

Item	Per	Value	Date	Ref.
Child Care - continued				
Child's child care and education, age 12-14	yr	420	1999	60r
Child's child care and education, age 15-17	yr	720	1999	60r
Child's clothing, age 0-2	yr	410	1999	60r
Child's clothing, age 3-5	yr	400	1999	60r
Child's clothing, age 6-8	yr	450	1999	60r
Child's clothing, age 9-11	yr	500	1999	60r
Child's clothing, age 12-14	yr	840	1999	60r
Child's clothing, age 15-17	yr	740	1999	60r
Child's food, age 0-2	yr	960	1999	60r
Child's food, age 3-5	yr	1120	1999	60r
Child's food, age 6-8	yr	1430	1999	60r
Child's food, age 9-11	yr	1710	1999	60r
Child's food, age 12-14	yr	1710	1999	60r
Child's food, age 15-17	yr	1920	1999	60r
Child's health care, age 0-2	yr	520	1999	60r
Child's health care, age 3-5	yr	500	1999	60r
Child's health care, age 6-8	yr	570	1999	60r
Child's health care, age 9-11	yr	610	1999	60r
Child's health care, age 12-14	yr	630	1999	60r
Child's health care, age 15-17	yr	650	1999	60r
Child's housing, age 0-2	yr	2860	1999	60r
Child's housing, age 3-5	yr	2840	1999	60r
Child's housing, age 6-8	yr	2800	1999	60r
Child's housing, age 9-11	yr	2650	1999	60r
Child's housing, age 12-14	yr	2840	1999	60r
Child's housing, age 15-17	yr	2440	1999	60r
Child's personal care, reading, age 0-2	yr	880	1999	60r
Child's personal care, reading, age 3-5	yr	900	1999	60r
Child's personal care, reading, age 6-8	yr	930	1999	60r
Child's personal care, reading, age 9-11	yr	970	1999	60r
Child's personal care, reading, age 12-14	yr	1150	1999	60r
Child's personal care, reading, age 15-17	yr	920	1999	60r
Clothing				
Apparel and services purchases	yr	1607	1999	30r
Boys, 2 to 15, expenditures on	yr	91	1999	30r
Children under 2, expenditures on	yr	59	1999	30r
Footwear, expenditures on	yr	285	1999	30r
Girls, 2 to 15, expenditures on	yr	116	1999	30r
Men and boys, expenditures on	yr	433	1999	30r
Men, 16 and over, expenditures on	yr	341	1999	30r
Women, 16 and over, expenditures on	yr	490	1999	30r
Communications				
Phone line, single, business, field visit	inst.	59.00	12/97	17s
Phone line, single, business, no field visit	inst.	59.00	12/97	17s
Phone line, single, residence, field visit	inst.	47.00	12/97	17s
Phone line, single, residence, no field visit	inst.	47.00	12/97	17s
Postage and stationery, expenditures on	yr	140	1999	30r
Postal rate, express mail, up to half-pound		12.45	7/01	108r
Postal rate, letter, first class, first ounce		0.34	7/01	108r
Postal rate, letter, two ounces		0.57	7/01	108r
Postal rate, post card		0.21	7/01	108r
Postal rate, priority mail, two pounds		3.95	7/01	108r
Postal rate, priority mail, up to one pound		3.50	7/01	108r
Telephone services, expenditures on	yr	830	1999	30r
Education				
Board, 4-year private college/university	yr	2250	1996	38s
Board, 4-year public college/university	yr	2425	1996	38s
Education expenditures	yr	583	1999	30r
Room, 4-year private college/university	yr	1987	1996	38s
Room, 4-year public college/university	yr	1931	1996	38s
Total cost, 4-year private college/university	yr	16829	1996	38s
Total cost, 4-year public college/university	yr	7392	1996	38s
Tuition, 2-year public college/university, in state	yr	1937	1996	38s
Tuition, 4-year private college/university, in state	yr	12592	1996	38s
Tuition, 4-year public college/university	yr	3037	1996	38s
Energy and Fuels				
Electricity	500 KWhs	46.59	7/01	11r

Values are in dollars or fractions of dollars. In the column headed *Ref*, references are shown to sources. Each reference is followed by a letter. These refer to the geographical level for which data were reported: s=State, r=Region, and c=City or metro. The abbreviation *ex* is used to mean *except* or *excluding; exp* stands for expenditures. For other abbreviations and further explanations, please see the Introduction.

Evansville-Henderson, IN-KY - continued

Item	Per	Value	Date	Ref.
Energy and Fuels				
Fuel oil #2	gal	1.27	7/01	11r
Fuel oil and other fuels, expenditures on	yr	68	1999	30r
Gas, natural, commercial rate	1000 cf	6.24	11/00	88s
Gasoline, unleaded midgrade	gal	1.79	7/01	11r
Gasoline, unleaded premium	gal	1.86	7/01	11r
Gasoline, unleaded regular	gal	1.58	7/01	11r
Natural gas, expenditures on	yr	389	1999	30r
Utility (piped) gas, therm		0.81	7/01	11r
Utility (piped) gas, 40 therms		38.01	7/01	11r
Utility (piped) gas, 100 therms		81.75	7/01	11r
Entertainment				
Entertainment purchases	yr	1984	1999	30r
Fees and admissions paid	yr	444	1999	30r
Television, radios, sound equipment, expenditures on	yr	580	1999	30r
Funerals				
Cosmetology, hair, other preparation		178.32	1/99	78r
Embalming		408.19	1/99	78r
Funeral at funeral home		362.13	1/99	78r
Professional service charges		1375.51	1/99	78r
Transfer of remains to funeral home		155.92	1/99	78r
Visitation/viewing		294.38	1/99	78r
Groceries				
Bacon, sliced	lb	3.15	7/01	11r
Bakery products, expenditures on	yr	281	1999	30r
Bananas	lb	0.48	7/01	11r
Beans, dried, any type, all sizes	lb	0.61	7/01	11r
Beef for stew, boneless	lb	3.08	7/01	11r
Beef, expenditures on	yr	217	1999	30r
Bologna, all beef or mixed	lb	2.52	7/01	11r
Bread, white, pan	lb	1.06	7/01	11r
Broccoli	lb	0.91	7/01	11r
Butter, salted, grade AA, stick	lb	3.04	7/01	11r
Butter, yoghurt, cheese, etc, expenditures on	yr	183	1999	30r
Cereals and bakery product purchases	yr	430	1999	30r
Cereals and cereal products, expenditures on	yr	149	1999	30r
Chicken, fresh, whole	lb	1.07	7/01	11r
Chops, boneless,	lb	3.64	7/01	11r
Chuck roast, U.S. choice, boneless	lb	2.47	7/01	11r
Coffee, 100%, ground roast, all sizes	lb	2.69	7/01	11r
Cookies, chocolate chip	lb	2.87	7/01	11r
Dairy product purchases	yr	304	1999	30r
Eggs, expenditures on	yr	26	1999	30r
Eggs, grade A, large	dozen	0.88	7/01	11r
Fats and oils, expenditures on	yr	75	1999	30r
Fish and seafood, expenditures on	yr	72	1999	30r
Food (excl fruit and vegetables), eaten at home, purchases	yr	887	1999	30r
Food cooked on trips, expenditures on	yr	44	1999	30r
Food purchases	yr	4802	1999	30r
Food purchases, eaten away from home	yr	2069	1999	30r
Food purchases, food eaten at home	yr	2733	1999	30r
Fresh fruits, expenditures on	yr	138	1999	30r
Fresh milk and cream, expenditures on	yr	120	1999	30r
Fresh vegetables, expenditures on	yr	126	1999	30r
Grapefruit	lb	0.66	7/01	11r
Grapes, Thompson, seedless	lb	1.64	7/01	11r
Ground beef, 100% beef	lb	1.64	7/01	11r
Ground beef, lean and extra lean	lb	2.16	7/01	11r
Ground chuck, 100% beef	lb	2.13	7/01	11r
Ham, boneless, excl canned	lb	2.62	7/01	11r
Ice cream, prepackaged, bulk, regular	1/2 gal	3.35	7/01	11r
Lemons	lb	1.19	7/01	11r
Lettuce, iceberg	lb	0.73	7/01	11r
Margarine, soft, tubs	lb	0.89	7/01	11r
Meats, poultry, fish, and egg purchases	yr	671	1999	30r
Milk, fresh, whole, fortified	gal	2.71	7/01	11r
Nonalcoholic beverages, expenditures on	yr	239	1999	30r
Oranges, Navel	lb	0.80	7/01	11r
Oranges, Valencia	lb	0.66	7/01	11r

Evansville-Henderson, IN-KY - continued

Item	Per	Value	Date	Ref.
Groceries - continued				
Pears, Anjou	lb	0.93	7/01	11r
Pork chops, center cut, bone-in	lb	3.63	7/01	11r
Pork, expenditures on	yr	150	1999	30r
Potato chips	16 oz	3.52	7/01	11r
Potatoes, frozen, french fried	lb	1.08	7/01	11r
Potatoes, white, all types	lb	0.33	7/01	11r
Poultry, expenditures on	yr	108	1999	30r
Processed fruits, expenditures on	yr	98	1999	30r
Processed vegetables, expenditures on	yr	80	1999	30r
Round roast, U.S. choice, boneless	lb	3.07	7/01	11r
Round steak, graded and ungraded, excl U.S. prime and choice	lb	3.41	7/01	11r
Shortening, vegetable oil blends	lb	1.13	7/01	11r
Spaghetti and macaroni	lb	0.80	7/01	11r
Steak, round, U.S. choice, boneless	lb	3.23	7/01	11r
Steak, T-bone, U.S. choice, bone-in	lb	6.68	7/01	11r
Strawberries, dry pint	12 oz	1.32	7/01	11r
Sugar and other sweets, expenditures on	yr	114	1999	30r
Sugar, white, 33-80 ounce package	lb	0.42	7/01	11r
Sugar, white, all sizes	lb	0.43	7/01	11r
Tobacco products and smoking supplies purchases	yr	331	1999	30r
Tomatoes, field grown	lb	1.46	7/01	11r
Tuna, light, chunk	lb	1.80	7/01	11r
Turkey, frozen, whole	lb	1.15	7/01	11r
Goods and Services				
B&B Japanese maple (acer japonicum)	gal	29.99-169.99	4/00	93r
Boxwood (buxus)	2 gal	18.99-39.99	4/00	93r
Daylilly (hemerocallis)	gal	4.99-25.00	4/00	93r
Flat of annuals		11.98-24.99	4/00	93r
Fountain grass (pennisetum)	gal	5.98-12.98	4/00	93r
Hanging basket (10 in)		12.99-27.99	4/00	93r
Hardy geranium (geranium)	gal	7.99-9.99	4/00	93r
Hosta (hosta)	gal	6.00-25.00	4/00	93r
Lilac (syrubga vulgaris)	2 gal	14.99-24.99	4/00	93r
Miscellaneous purchases	yr	865	1999	30r
Rhododendron (rhododendron)	2 gal	23.98-42.99	4/00	93r
Sage (salvia)	gal	6.00-9.99	4/00	93r
Wintercreeper euonymus (euonymus fortunei)	2 gal	16.00-169.99	4/00	93r
Hunting license	yr	8.75	4/01	34s
Health Care				
Cardiac catheterization, ave hospital/ physician charges		13380	1998	77s
Childbirth, Cesarean delivery		10722	1997	13r
Childbirth, vaginal delivery		6223	1997	13r
Drugs, expenditures on	yr	394	1999	30r
Health care purchases	yr	2048	1999	30r
Health insurance expenditures	yr	978	1999	30r
Hysterectomy, laproscopically-assisted, ave hospital/physician charges		11310	1998	76s
Hysterectomy, vaginal, ave hospital and physician charges		9160	1998	76s
Medicaid dispensing fee		4.00	1999	87s
Medical services expenditures	yr	554	1999	30r
Medical supplies, expenditures on	yr	122	1999	30r
Plastic surgery, breast augmentation		3184	2000	7r
Plastic surgery, breast lift		3585	2000	7r
Plastic surgery, facelift		4999	2000	7r
Plastic surgery, hair transplantation		3105	2000	7r

Values are in dollars or fractions of dollars. In the column headed *Ref*, references are shown to sources. Each reference is followed by a letter. These refer to the geographical level for which data were reported: s=State, r=Region, and c=City or metro. The abbreviation *ex* is used to mean *except* or *excluding*; *exp* stands for expenditures. For other abbreviations and further explanations, please see the Introduction.

Evansville-Henderson, IN-KY - continued

Item	Per	Value	Date	Ref.
Health Care				
Plastic surgery, lip augmentation		1290	2000	7r
Plastic surgery, lower body lift		8135	2000	7r
Plastic surgery, thigh lift		3839	2000	7r
Household Goods				
Floor coverings, expenditures on	yr	52	1999	30r
Furniture, expenditures on	yr	344	1999	30r
Household furnishings and equipment purchases	yr	1475	1999	30r
Household textiles, expenditures on	yr	109	1999	30r
Laundry and cleaning supplies, expenditures on	yr	134	1999	30r
Housing				
Home price, existing, ave		144400	10/00	90r
Home value, median		102000	2001	53s
Household operation expenditures	yr	542	1999	30r
Housekeeping supplies purchases	yr	508	1999	30r
Lodging expenditures	yr	430	1999	30r
Maintenance, repairs, insurance expenditures	yr	853	1999	30r
Monthly rental value of owned home	mos	547	1999	30r
Owned dwellings, expenditures own	yr	4282	1999	30r
Rent expenditures	yr	1558	1999	30r
Rental unit, 1 bedroom, with utilities	mos	387	4/01	41c
Rental unit, 2 bedroom, with utilities	mos	503	4/01	41c
Rental unit, 3 bedroom, with utilities	mos	628	4/01	41c
Rental unit, 4 bedroom, with utilities	mos	703	4/01	41c
Shelter, expenditures on	yr	6270	1999	30r
Insurance and Pensions				
Life and other personal insurance purchases	yr	387	1999	30r
Pensions and Social Security, expenditures on	yr	2968	1999	30r
Legal Fees				
Divorce, filing fee		100.00	4/01	35s
Driver's license fee	renew	6.00	1999	48s
Driver's license fee	orig	6.00	1999	48s
Personal Goods				
Personal care products and services purchases	yr	385	1999	30r
Personal Services				
Personal services, household, expenditures on	yr	300	1999	30r
Pets				
Pets, toys, and playground equipment, expenditures on	yr	375	1999	30r
Taxes				
Federal income taxes paid	yr	2326	1999	30r
Personal taxes, expenditures on	yr	3223	1999	30r
Property taxes paid	yr	1152	1999	30r
State and local income taxes paid	yr	753	1999	30r
Transportation				
Cars and trucks, new, expenditures on	yr	1280	1999	30r
Cars and trucks, used, expenditures on	yr	1763	1999	30r
Diesel at the pump	gal	1.17	10/99	73s
Gasoline and motor oil purchases	yr	1036	1999	30r
Gasoline before-tax price (cents)	gal	110.00	10/00	43s
Maintenance and repair expenditures	yr	594	1999	30r
Public transportation, expenditures on	yr	341	1999	30r
Transportation purchases	yr	6617	1999	30r
Vehicle expenses, miscellaneous, purchases	yr	2159	1999	30r
Vehicle insurance payments	yr	701	1999	30r
Vehicle purchases (net outlay)	yr	3081	1999	30r
Vehicle rental, lease expenditures	yr	536	1999	30r
Utilities				
Electrical bill, average	mos	66.66	9/00	9s
Electricity, expenditures on	yr	841	1999	30r
Electricity cost, average	KWh	5.00	9/00	9s
Utilities, fuels, and public services purchased	yr	2401	1999	30r

Evansville-Henderson, IN-KY - continued

Item	Per	Value	Date	Ref.
Utilities - continued				
Water and other public services, expenditures on	yr	273	1999	30r
Weddings				
Wedding (national average cost)		19936	2000	33r
Wedding (regional average total cost)		16195	1997	110r
Attendants' gifts		321	1998	33r
Bridal attendants' apparel (5 persons)		824	2000	33r
Bride's headpiece/veil		173	1998	33r
Bride's wedding dress		859	1998	33r
Clergy, religious facility fee		242	1998	33r
Engagement ring		3177	1998	33r
Flowers		789	1998	33r
Groom's formalwear rental		99	2000	33r
Limousine		410	1998	33r
Marriage license cost		18.00	4/01	35s
Men's formalwear (ushers, best man)		469	2000	33r
Mother of bride apparel		241	2000	33r
Music		866	1998	33r
Photography and videography		1368	1998	33r
Rehearsal dinner		728	1998	33r
Wedding invitations and announcements		341	1998	33r
Wedding reception		7968	2000	33r
Wedding rings (bride and groom)		1060	1998	33r

Fargo-Moorhead, ND-MN

Item	Per	Value	Date	Ref.
Average annual expenditures	yr	35369	1999	30r
Composite, ACCRA index		99.60	3/01	4c
Alcoholic Beverages				
Alcoholic beverage purchases	yr	304	1999	30r
Beer, Heineken, 12-oz, ex deposit	6	7.05	3/01	4c
J & B Scotch	750-ml	20.39	3/01	4c
Malt beverages, all types, all sizes, any origin	16 oz	0.93	7/01	11r
Wine, Livingston or Gallo, Chablis blanc	1.5 liter	5.37	3/01	4c
Wine, red and white table, all sizes, any origin	liter	7.04	7/01	11r
Appliances				
Appliance repair, service call, washing machine	min lab chg	44.89	3/01	4c
Major appliances, expenditures on	yr	165	1999	30r
Small appliances, housewares, expenditures on	yr	90	1999	30r
Banking and Money				
Mortgage interest and charges paid	yr	2277	1999	30r
Mortgage principal paid on owned property	yr	1230	1999	30r
Mortgage rate, incl. points and orig. fee, 30-yr. conv. fixed or ARM	mos	7.15	3/01	4c
Vehicle finance charges paid	yr	328	1999	30r
Charity				
Cash contributions, expenditures	yr	1126	1999	30r
Child Care				
Child raising cost, total, age 0-2	yr	7890	1999	60r
Child raising cost, total, age 3-5	yr	8130	1999	60r
Child raising cost, total, age 6-8	yr	8170	1999	60r
Child raising cost, total, age 9-11	yr	8190	1999	60r
Child raising cost, total, age 12-14	yr	8890	1999	60r
Child raising cost, total, age 15-17	yr	9050	1999	60r
Child's child care and education, age 0-2	yr	1240	1999	60r
Child's child care and education, age 3-5	yr	1370	1999	60r
Child's child care and education, age 6-8	yr	880	1999	60r
Child's child care and education, age 9-11	yr	570	1999	60r
Child's child care and education, age 12-14	yr	420	1999	60r
Child's child care and education, age 15-17	yr	720	1999	60r
Child's clothing, age 0-2	yr	410	1999	60r
Child's clothing, age 3-5	yr	400	1999	60r
Child's clothing, age 6-8	yr	450	1999	60r
Child's clothing, age 9-11	yr	500	1999	60r
Child's clothing, age 12-14	yr	840	1999	60r

Values are in dollars or fractions of dollars. In the column headed *Ref*, references are shown to sources. Each reference is followed by a letter. These refer to the geographical level for which data were reported: s=State, r=Region, and c=City or metro. The abbreviation *ex* is used to mean *except* or *excluding*; *exp* stands for expenditures. For other abbreviations and further explanations, please see the Introduction.

Fargo-Moorhead, ND-MN - continued

Item	Per	Value	Date	Ref.
Child Care				
Child's clothing, age 15-17	yr	740	1999	60r
Child's food, age 0-2	yr	960	1999	60r
Child's food, age 3-5	yr	1120	1999	60r
Child's food, age 6-8	yr	1430	1999	60r
Child's food, age 9-11	yr	1710	1999	60r
Child's food, age 12-14	yr	1710	1999	60r
Child's food, age 15-17	yr	1920	1999	60r
Child's health care, age 0-2	yr	520	1999	60r
Child's health care, age 3-5	yr	500	1999	60r
Child's health care, age 6-8	yr	570	1999	60r
Child's health care, age 9-11	yr	610	1999	60r
Child's health care, age 12-14	yr	630	1999	60r
Child's health care, age 15-17	yr	650	1999	60r
Child's housing, age 0-2	yr	2860	1999	60r
Child's housing, age 3-5	yr	2840	1999	60r
Child's housing, age 6-8	yr	2800	1999	60r
Child's housing, age 9-11	yr	2650	1999	60r
Child's housing, age 12-14	yr	2840	1999	60r
Child's housing, age 15-17	yr	2440	1999	60r
Child's personal care, reading, age 0-2	yr	880	1999	60r
Child's personal care, reading, age 3-5	yr	900	1999	60r
Child's personal care, reading, age 6-8	yr	930	1999	60r
Child's personal care, reading, age 9-11	yr	970	1999	60r
Child's personal care, reading, age 12-14	yr	1150	1999	60r
Child's personal care, reading, age 15-17	yr	920	1999	60r
Clothing				
Apparel and services purchases	yr	1607	1999	30r
Boys' brief, cotton	3	3.50	3/01	4c
Boys, 2 to 15, expenditures on	yr	91	1999	30r
Children under 2, expenditures on	yr	59	1999	30r
Footwear, expenditures on	yr	285	1999	30r
Girls, 2 to 15, expenditures on	yr	116	1999	30r
Men and boys, expenditures on	yr	433	1999	30r
Men, 16 and over, expenditures on	yr	341	1999	30r
Shirt, man's dress shirt		29.90	3/01	4c
Slacks, man's "No Wrinkles" khaki		46.40	3/01	4c
Women, 16 and over, expenditures on	yr	490	1999	30r
Communications				
Newspaper subscription, daily and Sunday delivery	mos	15.20	3/01	4c
Phone line, single, business, field visit	inst.	52.67	12/97	17s
Phone line, single, business, no field visit	inst.	52.67	12/97	17s
Phone line, single, residence, field visit	inst.	31.79	12/97	17s
Phone line, single, residence, no field visit	inst.	31.79	12/97	17s
Postage and stationery, expenditures on	yr	140	1999	30r
Postal rate, express mail, up to half-pound		12.45	7/01	108r
Postal rate, letter, first class, first ounce		0.34	7/01	108r
Postal rate, letter, two ounces		0.57	7/01	108r
Postal rate, post card		0.21	7/01	108r
Postal rate, priority mail, two pounds		3.95	7/01	108r
Postal rate, priority mail, up to one pound		3.50	7/01	108r
Telephone bill, family of three	mos	26.80	3/01	4c
Telephone services, expenditures on	yr	830	1999	30r
Education				
Board, 4-year private college/university	yr	1649	1996	38s
Board, 4-year public college/university	yr	2378	1996	38s
Education expenditures	yr	583	1999	30r
Room, 4-year private college/university	yr	1260	1996	38s
Room, 4-year public college/university	yr	1016	1996	38s
Total cost, 4-year private college/university	yr	9907	1996	38s
Total cost, 4-year public college/university	yr	5642	1996	38s
Tuition, 2-year public college/university, in state	yr	1698	1996	38s
Tuition, 4-year private college/university, in state	yr	6998	1996	38s
Tuition, 4-year public college/university	yr	2248	1996	38s
Energy and Fuels				
Electricity	500 KWhs	46.59	7/01	11r
Energy, combined forms, 2400 sq ft	mos	115.33	3/01	4c

Fargo-Moorhead, ND-MN - continued

Item	Per	Value	Date	Ref.
Energy and Fuels - continued				
Energy, exc. electricity, 2400 sq ft	mos	71.17	3/01	4c
Fuel oil #2	gal	1.27	7/01	11r
Fuel oil and other fuels, expenditures on	yr	68	1999	30r
Gas, natural, commercial rate	1000 cf	6.91	11/00	88s
Gas, regular unleaded, cash, self-service	gal	1.50	3/01	4c
Gasoline, unleaded midgrade	gal	1.79	7/01	11r
Gasoline, unleaded premium	gal	1.86	7/01	11r
Gasoline, unleaded regular	gal	1.58	7/01	11r
Natural gas, expenditures on	yr	389	1999	30r
Utility (piped) gas, therm		0.81	7/01	11r
Utility (piped) gas, 40 therms		38.01	7/01	11r
Utility (piped) gas, 100 therms		81.75	7/01	11r
Entertainment				
Bowling, Saturday evening rate	line	2.44	3/01	4c
Entertainment purchases	yr	1984	1999	30r
Fees and admissions paid	yr	444	1999	30r
Monopoly game, Parker Brothers', No. 9	game	7.89	3/01	4c
Movie, first-run, Saturday, evening	adm.	6.50	3/01	4c
Television, radios, sound equipment, expenditures on	yr	580	1999	30r
Tennis balls, yellow, Wilson or Penn, 3	can	1.97	3/01	4c
Funerals				
Cosmetology, hair, other preparation		178.32	1/99	78r
Embalming		408.19	1/99	78r
Funeral at funeral home		362.13	1/99	78r
Professional service charges		1375.51	1/99	78r
Transfer of remains to funeral home		155.92	1/99	78r
Visitation/viewing		294.38	1/99	78r
Groceries				
Groceries, ACCRA Index		99.80	3/01	4c
Antibiotic ointment, Polysporin	0.5 oz	4.70	3/01	4c
Baby food, strained vegetables or fruit, lowest price	4-4.5 oz	0.47	3/01	4c
Bacon, sliced	lb	3.15	7/01	11r
Bakery products, expenditures on	yr	281	1999	30r
Bananas	lb	0.47	3/01	4c
Bananas	lb	0.48	7/01	11r
Beans, dried, any type, all sizes	lb	0.61	7/01	11r
Beef for stew, boneless	lb	3.08	7/01	11r
Beef or hamburger, ground	lb	1.61	3/01	4c
Beef, expenditures on	yr	217	1999	30r
Bologna, all beef or mixed	lb	2.52	7/01	11r
Bread, white	loaf	1.01	3/01	4c
Bread, white, pan	lb	1.06	7/01	11r
Broccoli	lb	0.91	7/01	11r
Butter, salted, grade AA, stick	lb	3.04	7/01	11r
Butter, yoghurt, cheese, etc, expenditures on	yr	183	1999	30r
Cereals and bakery product purchases	yr	430	1999	30r
Cereals and cereal products, expenditures on	yr	149	1999	30r
Cheese, Kraft grated Parmesan	8 oz	3.54	3/01	4c
Chicken, fresh, whole	lb	1.07	7/01	11r
Chicken, whole fryer	lb	1.11	3/01	4c
Chops, boneless,	lb	3.64	7/01	11r
Chuck roast, U.S. choice, boneless	lb	2.47	7/01	11r
Cigarettes, Winston, Kings	carton	30.66	3/01	4c
Coffee, 100%, ground roast, all sizes	lb	2.69	7/01	11r
Coffee, vacuum-packed	13 oz	2.27	3/01	4c
Cookies, chocolate chip	lb	2.87	7/01	11r
Corn Flakes, Kellogg's or Post Toasties	18 oz	2.22	3/01	4c
Corn, frozen, whole kernel, lowest price	16 oz	1.07	3/01	4c
Dairy product purchases	yr	304	1999	30r
Eggs, expenditures on	yr	26	1999	30r
Eggs, Grade A or AA	dozen	1.14	3/01	4c
Eggs, grade A, large	dozen	0.88	7/01	11r
Fats and oils, expenditures on	yr	75	1999	30r
Fish and seafood, expenditures on	yr	72	1999	30r
Food (excl fruit and vegetables), eaten at home, purchases	yr	887	1999	30r
Food cooked on trips, expenditures on	yr	44	1999	30r
Food purchases	yr	4802	1999	30r

Values are in dollars or fractions of dollars. In the column headed *Ref*, references are shown to sources. Each reference is followed by a letter. These refer to the geographical level for which data were reported: s=State, r=Region, and c=City or metro. The abbreviation *ex* is used to mean *except* or *excluding*; *exp* stands for *expenditures*. For other abbreviations and further explanations, please see the Introduction.

Fargo-Moorhead, ND-MN - continued

Item	Per	Value	Date	Ref.
Groceries				
Food purchases, eaten away from home	yr	2069	1999	30r
Food purchases, food eaten at home	yr	2733	1999	30r
Fresh fruits, expenditures on	yr	138	1999	30r
Fresh milk and cream, expenditures on	yr	120	1999	30r
Fresh vegetables, expenditures on	yr	126	1999	30r
Grapefruit	lb	0.66	7/01	11r
Grapes, Thompson, seedless	lb	1.64	7/01	11r
Ground beef, 100% beef	lb	1.64	7/01	11r
Ground beef, lean and extra lean	lb	2.16	7/01	11r
Ground chuck, 100% beef	lb	2.13	7/01	11r
Ham, boneless, excl canned	lb	2.62	7/01	11r
Ice cream, prepackaged, bulk, regular	1/2 gal	3.35	7/01	11r
Lemons	lb	1.19	7/01	11r
Lettuce, iceberg	head	0.93	3/01	4c
Lettuce, iceberg	lb	0.73	7/01	11r
Margarine, Blue Bonnet or Parkay, stick	lb	0.65	3/01	4c
Margarine, soft, tubs	lb	0.89	7/01	11r
Meats, poultry, fish, and egg purchases	yr	671	1999	30r
Milk, fresh, whole, fortified	gal	2.71	7/01	11r
Milk, whole	1/2 gal	1.62	3/01	4c
Nonalcoholic beverages, expenditures on	yr	239	1999	30r
Orange juice, Minute Maid frozen	12 oz	1.66	3/01	4c
Oranges, Navel	lb	0.80	7/01	11r
Oranges, Valencia	lb	0.66	7/01	11r
Peaches, halves or slices, Hunt's, Del Monte, or Libby's	29 oz	1.60	3/01	4c
Pears, Anjou	lb	0.93	7/01	11r
Peas, green, Del Monte or Green Giant	15 oz	0.74	3/01	4c
Pork chops, center cut, bone-in	lb	3.63	7/01	11r
Pork, expenditures on	yr	150	1999	30r
Potato chips	16 oz	3.52	7/01	11r
Potatoes, frozen, french fried	lb	1.08	7/01	11r
Potatoes, white or red	10 lb	1.63	3/01	4c
Potatoes, white, all types	lb	0.33	7/01	11r
Poultry, expenditures on	yr	108	1999	30r
Processed fruits, expenditures on	yr	98	1999	30r
Processed vegetables, expenditures on	yr	80	1999	30r
Round roast, U.S. choice, boneless	lb	3.07	7/01	11r
Round steak, graded and ungraded, excl U.S. prime and choice	lb	3.41	7/01	11r
Sausage, Jimmy Dean/Owens pork	lb	3.88	3/01	4c
Shortening, vegetable oil blends	lb	1.13	7/01	11r
Shortening, vegetable, Crisco	3 lb	2.69	3/01	4c
Soft drink, Coca Cola, ex deposit	2 liter	1.05	3/01	4c
Spaghetti and macaroni	lb	0.80	7/01	11r
Steak, round, U.S. choice, boneless	lb	3.23	7/01	11r
Steak, T-bone	lb	7.47	3/01	4c
Steak, T-bone, U.S. choice, bone-in	lb	6.68	7/01	11r
Strawberries, dry pint	12 oz	1.32	7/01	11r
Sugar and other sweets, expenditures on	yr	114	1999	30r
Sugar, cane or beet	4 lbs	1.45	3/01	4c
Sugar, white, 33-80 ounce package	lb	0.42	7/01	11r
Sugar, white, all sizes	lb	0.43	7/01	11r
Tobacco products and smoking supplies purchases	yr	331	1999	30r
Tomatoes, field grown	lb	1.46	7/01	11r
Tomatoes, Hunt's or Del Monte	14.5 oz	0.90	3/01	4c
Tuna, chunk, light	6 oz	0.70	3/01	4c
Tuna, light, chunk	lb	1.80	7/01	11r
Turkey, frozen, whole	lb	1.15	7/01	11r
Goods and Services				
Miscellaneous goods and services, ACCRA Index		101.30	3/01	4c
B&B Japanese maple (acer japonicum)	gal	29.99-169.99	4/00	93r
Boxwood (buxus)	2 gal	18.99-39.99	4/00	93r
Daylily (hemerocallis)	gal	4.99-25.00	4/00	93r
Flat of annuals		11.98-24.99	4/00	93r

Fargo-Moorhead, ND-MN - continued

Item	Per	Value	Date	Ref.
Goods and Services - continued				
Fountain grass (pennisetum)	gal	5.98-12.98	4/00	93r
Hanging basket (10 in)		12.99-27.99	4/00	93r
Hardy geranium (geranium)	gal	7.99-9.99	4/00	93r
Hosta (hosta)	gal	6.00-25.00	4/00	93r
Lilac (syrubga vulgaris)	2 gal	14.99-24.99	4/00	93r
Miscellaneous purchases	yr	865	1999	30r
Rhododendron (rhododendron)	2 gal	23.98-42.99	4/00	93r
Sage (salvia)	gal	6.00-9.99	4/00	93r
Wintercreeper euonymus (euonymus fortunei)	2 gal	16.00-169.99	4/00	93r
Hunting license	yr	8.00	4/01	34s
Health Care				
Health care, ACCRA Index		101.50	3/01	4c
Cardiac catheterization, ave hospital/physician charges		10040	1998	77s
Childbirth, Cesarean delivery		10722	1997	13r
Childbirth, vaginal delivery		6223	1997	13r
Dentist's fee, adult teeth cleaning and periodic oral exam	visit	73.00	3/01	4c
Doctor's fee, routine exam, established patient	visit	63.25	3/01	4c
Drugs, expenditures on	yr	394	1999	30r
Health care purchases	yr	2048	1999	30r
Health insurance expenditures	yr	978	1999	30r
Hospital care, private room	day	465.00	3/01	4c
Hysterectomy, laproscopically-assisted, ave hospital/physician charges		11070	1998	76s
Hysterectomy, vaginal, ave hospital and physician charges		7310	1998	76s
Medicaid dispensing fee		4.60	1999	87s
Medical services expenditures	yr	554	1999	30r
Medical supplies, expenditures on	yr	122	1999	30r
Plastic surgery, breast augmentation		3184	2000	7r
Plastic surgery, breast lift		3585	2000	7r
Plastic surgery, facelift		4999	2000	7r
Plastic surgery, hair transplantation		3105	2000	7r
Plastic surgery, lip augmentation		1290	2000	7r
Plastic surgery, lower body lift		8135	2000	7r
Plastic surgery, thigh lift		3839	2000	7r
Household Goods				
Dishwashing powder, Cascade	50 oz	3.31	3/01	4c
Floor coverings, expenditures on	yr	52	1999	30r
Furniture, expenditures on	yr	344	1999	30r
Household furnishings and equipment purchases	yr	1475	1999	30r
Household textiles, expenditures on	yr	109	1999	30r
Laundry and cleaning supplies, expenditures on	yr	134	1999	30r
Tissues, facial, Kleenex brand	175	1.24	3/01	4c
Housing				
Housing, ACCRA Index		97.60	3/01	4c
Home price, existing, ave		144400	10/00	90r
Home value, median		99000	2001	53s
House, 2400 sq ft, 8000 sq ft lot, new, urban, utilities	total	202400	3/01	4c
House payment, principal and interest, 25% down payment	mos	1025	3/01	4c
Household operation expenditures	yr	542	1999	30r
Housekeeping supplies purchases	yr	508	1999	30r
Lodging expenditures	yr	430	1999	30r
Maintenance, repairs, insurance expenditures	yr	853	1999	30r
Monthly rental value of owned home	mos	547	1999	30r
Owned dwellings, expenditures own	yr	4282	1999	30r

Values are in dollars or fractions of dollars. In the column headed *Ref*, references are shown to sources. Each reference is followed by a letter. These refer to the geographical level for which data were reported: s=State, r=Region, and c=City or metro. The abbreviation *ex* is used to mean *except* or *excluding*; *exp* stands for expenditures. For other abbreviations and further explanations, please see the Introduction.

Fargo-Moorhead, ND-MN - continued

Item	Per	Value	Date	Ref.
Housing				
Rent expenditures	yr	1558	1999	30r
Rent, apartment, 2 br, 1 1/2-2 baths, unfurn, 950 sq ft, water	mos	628	3/01	4c
Rental unit, 1 bedroom, with utilities	mos	473	4/01	41c
Rental unit, 2 bedroom, with utilities	mos	571	4/01	41c
Rental unit, 3 bedroom, with utilities	mos	793	4/01	41c
Rental unit, 4 bedroom, with utilities	mos	849	4/01	41c
Shelter, expenditures on	yr	6270	1999	30r
Insurance and Pensions				
Auto insurance premium	yr	545.50	1999	57s
Life and other personal insurance purchases	yr	387	1999	30r
Pensions and Social Security, expenditures on	yr	2968	1999	30r
Legal Fees				
Combination hunting and fishing license	yr	27.00	4/01	34s
Driver's license fee	orig	10.00	1999	48s
Driver's license fee	renew	10.00	1999	48s
Fishing license	yr	10.00	4/01	34s
Personal Goods				
Personal care products and services purchases	yr	385	1999	30r
Shampoo, Alberto VO5	15 oz	1.05	3/01	4c
Toothpaste, Crest or Colgate	6-7 oz	2.12	3/01	4c
Personal Services				
Dry cleaning, man's 2-pc suit		8.20	3/01	4c
Man's haircut, barbershop, no styling		12.20	3/01	4c
Personal services, household, expenditures on	yr	300	1999	30r
Woman's shampoo, trim, blow-dry, no style-change		23.40	3/01	4c
Pets				
Pets, toys, and playground equipment, expenditures on	yr	375	1999	30r
Restaurant Food				
Chicken, fried, thigh and drumstick, KFC/ Church's		2.58	3/01	4c
Hamburger with cheese, McDonald's	1/4 lb	2.09	3/01	4c
Pizza, Pizza Hut or Pizza Inn	11-12 in	9.49	3/01	4c
Taxes				
Federal income taxes paid	yr	2326	1999	30r
Personal taxes, expenditures on	yr	3223	1999	30r
Property taxes paid	yr	1152	1999	30r
State and local income taxes paid	yr	753	1999	30r
Transportation				
Transportation, ACCRA Index		99.20	3/01	4c
Bus fare, one-way	trip	1.00	2000	1c
Bus fare, to central business district	1-way	1.00	3/01	4c
Cars and trucks, new, expenditures on	yr	1280	1999	30r
Cars and trucks, used, expenditures on	yr	1763	1999	30r
Diesel at the pump	gal	1.27	10/99	73s
Gasoline and motor oil purchases	yr	1036	1999	30r
Gasoline before-tax price (cents)	gal	120.80	10/00	43s
Maintenance and repair expenditures	yr	594	1999	30r
Public transportation, expenditures on	yr	341	1999	30r
Tire balance, computer or spin balance, front	wheel	7.20	3/01	4c
Transportation purchases	yr	6617	1999	30r
Vehicle expenses, miscellaneous, purchases	yr	2159	1999	30r
Vehicle insurance payments	yr	701	1999	30r
Vehicle purchases (net outlay)	yr	3081	1999	30r
Vehicle rental, lease expenditures	yr	536	1999	30r
Travel				
Hotel room	night	48.95	2/01	94s
Utilities				
Utilities, ACCRA Index		98.40	3/01	4c
Electrical bill, average	mos	62.50	9/00	9s
Electricity, expenditures on	yr	841	1999	30r
Electricity, summer, 250 KWh	mos	17.64	2/96	96c

Fargo-Moorhead, ND-MN - continued

Item	Per	Value	Date	Ref.
Utilities - continued				
Electricity, summer, 500 KWh	mos	31.19	2/96	96c
Electricity, summer, 750 KWh	mos	44.75	2/96	96c
Electricity, summer, 1000 KWh	mos	58.30	2/96	96c
Electricity and other, mixed, 2400 sq ft, new home	mos	44.16	3/01	4c
Electricity cost, average	KWh	5.90	9/00	9s
Utilities, fuels, and public services purchased	yr	2401	1999	30r
Water and other public services, expenditures on	yr	273	1999	30r
Weddings				
Wedding (national average cost)		19936	2000	33r
Wedding (regional average total cost)		16195	1997	110r
Attendants' gifts		321	1998	33r
Bridal attendants' apparel (5 persons)		824	2000	33r
Bride's headpiece/veil		173	1998	33r
Bride's wedding dress		859	1998	33r
Clergy, religious facility fee		242	1998	33r
Engagement ring		3177	1998	33r
Flowers		789	1998	33r
Groom's formalwear rental		99	2000	33r
Limousine		410	1998	33r
Marriage license cost		30.00	4/01	35s
Men's formalwear (ushers, best man)		469	2000	33r
Mother of bride apparel		241	2000	33r
Music		866	1998	33r
Photography and videography		1368	1998	33r
Rehearsal dinner		728	1998	33r
Wedding invitations and announcements		341	1998	33r
Wedding reception		7968	2000	33r
Wedding rings (bride and groom)		1060	1998	33r

Fayetteville, NC

Item	Per	Value	Date	Ref.
Composite, ACCRA index		100.10	12/00	5c
Alcoholic Beverages				
Alcoholic beverage purchases	yr	253	1999	30r
Beer, Heineken, 12-oz, ex deposit	6	6.61	12/00	5c
J & B Scotch	750-ml	20.75	12/00	5c
Malt beverages, all types, all sizes, any origin	16 oz	0.96	7/01	11r
Wine, Livingston or Gallo, Chablis blanc	1.5 liter	5.49	12/00	5c
Appliances				
Appliance repair, service call, washing machine	min lab chg	44.60	12/00	5c
Major appliances, expenditures on	yr	172	1999	30r
Small appliances, housewares, expenditures on	yr	81	1999	30r
Banking and Money				
Mortgage interest and charges paid	yr	2039	1999	30r
Mortgage principal paid on owned property	yr	1026	1999	30r
Mortgage rate, incl. points and orig. fee, 30-yr. conv. fixed or ARM	mos	8.05	12/00	5c
Vehicle finance charges paid	yr	365	1999	30r
Charity				
Cash contributions, expenditures	yr	1127	1999	30r
Child Care				
Child raising cost, total, age 0-2	yr	8540	1999	60r
Child raising cost, total, age 3-5	yr	8780	1999	60r
Child raising cost, total, age 6-8	yr	8820	1999	60r
Child raising cost, total, age 9-11	yr	8800	1999	60r
Child raising cost, total, age 12-14	yr	9510	1999	60r
Child raising cost, total, age 15-17	yr	9740	1999	60r
Child's child care and education, age 0-2	yr	1380	1999	60r
Child's child care and education, age 3-5	yr	1520	1999	60r
Child's child care and education, age 6-8	yr	990	1999	60r
Child's child care and education, age 9-11	yr	650	1999	60r
Child's child care and education, age 12-14	yr	490	1999	60r
Child's child care and education, age 15-17	yr	840	1999	60r
Child's clothing, age 0-2	yr	480	1999	60r

Values are in dollars or fractions of dollars. In the column headed *Ref*, references are shown to sources. Each reference is followed by a letter. These refer to the geographical level for which data were reported: s=State, r=Region, and c=City or metro. The abbreviation *ex* is used to mean *except* or *excluding*; *exp* stands for expenditures. For other abbreviations and further explanations, please see the Introduction.

Fayetteville, NC - continued

Item	Per	Value	Date	Ref.
Child Care				
Child's clothing, age 3-5	yr	470	1999	60r
Child's clothing, age 6-8	yr	520	1999	60r
Child's clothing, age 9-11	yr	570	1999	60r
Child's clothing, age 12-14	yr	950	1999	60r
Child's clothing, age 15-17	yr	850	1999	60r
Child's food, age 0-2	yr	1000	1999	60r
Child's food, age 3-5	yr	1160	1999	60r
Child's food, age 6-8	yr	1490	1999	60r
Child's food, age 9-11	yr	1770	1999	60r
Child's food, age 12-14	yr	1770	1999	60r
Child's food, age 15-17	yr	1980	1999	60r
Child's health care, age 0-2	yr	620	1999	60r
Child's health care, age 3-5	yr	590	1999	60r
Child's health care, age 6-8	yr	680	1999	60r
Child's health care, age 9-11	yr	720	1999	60r
Child's health care, age 12-14	yr	730	1999	60r
Child's health care, age 15-17	yr	760	1999	60r
Child's housing, age 0-2	yr	3070	1999	60r
Child's housing, age 3-5	yr	3050	1999	60r
Child's housing, age 6-8	yr	3010	1999	60r
Child's housing, age 9-11	yr	2850	1999	60r
Child's housing, age 12-14	yr	3040	1999	60r
Child's housing, age 15-17	yr	2650	1999	60r
Child's personal care, reading, age 0-2	yr	910	1999	60r
Child's personal care, reading, age 3-5	yr	930	1999	60r
Child's personal care, reading, age 6-8	yr	960	1999	60r
Child's personal care, reading, age 9-11	yr	1000	1999	60r
Child's personal care, reading, age 12-14	yr	1170	1999	60r
Child's personal care, reading, age 15-17	yr	950	1999	60r
Clothing				
Apparel and services purchases	yr	1610	1999	30r
Boys' brief, cotton	3	7.24	12/00	5c
Boys, 2 to 15, expenditures on	yr	89	1999	30r
Children under 2, expenditures on	yr	79	1999	30r
Footwear, expenditures on	yr	283	1999	30r
Girls, 2 to 15, expenditures on	yr	103	1999	30r
Men and boys, expenditures on	yr	351	1999	30r
Men, 16 and over, expenditures on	yr	262	1999	30r
Shirt, man's dress shirt		31.11	12/00	5c
Slacks, man's "No Wrinkles" khaki		49.00	12/00	5c
Women, 16 and over, expenditures on	yr	538	1999	30r
Communications				
Cable modem installation, Intermedia		149.95	6/99	103s
Cable modem installation, Time Warner		75.00-225.00	6/99	103s
Cable modem rate, cable subscriber, Intermedia	mos	49.95	6/99	103s
Cable modem rate, cable subscriber, Time Warner	mos	39.95-49.95	6/99	103s
Cable modem rate, non-cable subscriber, Intermedia	mos	54.95	6/99	103s
Cable modem rate, non-cable subscriber, Time Warner	mos	39.95-54.95	6/99	103s
Newspaper subscription, daily and Sunday delivery	mos	11.12	12/00	5c
Phone line, single, business, field visit	inst.	65.00	12/97	17s
Phone line, single, business, no field visit	inst.	65.00	12/97	17s
Phone line, single, residence, field visit	inst.	42.75	12/97	17s
Phone line, single, residence, no field visit	inst.	42.75	12/97	17s
Postage and stationery, expenditures on	yr	104	1999	30r
Postal rate, express mail, up to half-pound		12.45	7/01	108r
Postal rate, letter, first class, first ounce		0.34	7/01	108r
Postal rate, letter, two ounces		0.57	7/01	108r
Postal rate, post card		0.21	7/01	108r
Postal rate, priority mail, two pounds		3.95	7/01	108r
Postal rate, priority mail, up to one pound		3.50	7/01	108r
Telephone bill, family of three	mos	18.59	12/00	5c
Telephone services, expenditures on	yr	860	1999	30r
Education				
Board, 4-year private college/university	yr	2316	1996	38s
Board, 4-year public college/university	yr	1737	1996	38s

Fayetteville, NC - continued

Item	Per	Value	Date	Ref.
Education - continued				
Education expenditures	yr	431	1999	30r
Room, 4-year private college/university	yr	2128	1996	38s
Room, 4-year public college/university	yr	1742	1996	38s
Total cost, 4-year private college/university	yr	15428	1996	38s
Total cost, 4-year public college/university	yr	5119	1996	38s
Tuition, 4-year private college/university, in state	yr	10984	1996	38s
Tuition, 4-year public college/university	yr	1639	1996	38s
Energy and Fuels				
Electricity	KWh	0.09	7/01	11r
Electricity	500 KWhs	47.29	7/01	11r
Energy, combined forms, 2400 sq ft	mos	118.53	12/00	5c
Fuel oil #2	gal	1.43	7/01	11r
Fuel oil and other fuels, expenditures on	yr	45	1999	30r
Gas, cooking, winter, 10 therms	mos	14.05	2/96	98c
Gas, cooking, winter, 30 therms	mos	25.95	2/96	98c
Gas, cooking, winter, 50 therms	mos	37.85	2/96	98c
Gas, heating, winter, average use	mos	79.24	2/96	98c
Gas, natural, commercial rate	1000 cf	9.25	11/00	88s
Gas, regular unleaded, cash, self-service	gal	1.40	12/00	5c
Gasoline, all types	gal	1.60	7/01	11r
Gasoline, unleaded midgrade	gal	1.65	7/01	11r
Gasoline, unleaded premium	gal	1.74	7/01	11r
Natural gas, expenditures on	yr	164	1999	30r
Utility (piped) gas, therm		1.01	7/01	11r
Utility (piped) gas, 40 therms		44.29	7/01	11r
Utility (piped) gas, 100 therms		97.44	7/01	11r
Entertainment				
Bowling, Saturday evening rate	line	2.67	12/00	5c
Entertainment purchases	yr	1574	1999	30r
Fees and admissions paid	yr	371	1999	30r
Monopoly game, Parker Brothers', No. 9	game	9.99	12/00	5c
Movie, first-run, Saturday, evening	adm.	6.90	12/00	5c
Reading purchases	yr	121	1999	30r
Television, radios, sound equipment, expenditures on	yr	561	1999	30r
Tennis balls, yellow, Wilson or Penn, 3	can	2.36	12/00	5c
Funerals				
Total cost of funeral		5922.53	1/99	78r
Acknowledgement cards		63.43	1/99	78r
Casket		2258.77	1/99	78r
Cosmetology, hair, other preparation		127.09	1/99	78r
Embalming		393.49	1/99	78r
Funeral at funeral home		367.50	1/99	78r
Hearse (local)		169.66	1/99	78r
Professional service charges		1211.32	1/99	78r
Service car/van		80.69	1/99	78r
Transfer of remains to funeral home		144.25	1/99	78r
Vault		803.50	1/99	78r
Visitation/viewing		302.83	1/99	78r
Groceries				
Groceries, ACCRA Index		108.10	12/00	5c
American processed cheese	lb	3.50	7/01	11r
Antibiotic ointment, Polysporin	0.5 oz	4.28	12/00	5c
Baby food, strained vegetables or fruit, lowest price	4-4.5 oz	0.48	12/00	5c
Bakery products, expenditures on	yr	261	1999	30r
Bananas	lb	0.47	7/01	11r
Bananas	lb	0.58	12/00	5c
Beans, dried, any type, all sizes	lb	0.63	7/01	11r
Beef for stew, boneless	lb	2.86	7/01	11r
Beef or hamburger, ground	lb	1.86	12/00	5c
Beef, expenditures on	yr	210	1999	30r
Bologna, all beef or mixed	lb	2.29	7/01	11r
Bread, French	lb	1.66	7/01	11r
Bread, white	loaf	1.38	12/00	5c
Bread, white, pan	lb	0.87	7/01	11r
Bread, whole wheat, pan	lb	1.38	7/01	11r
Broccoli	lb	1.04	7/01	11r

Values are in dollars or fractions of dollars. In the column headed *Ref*, references are shown to sources. Each reference is followed by a letter. These refer to the geographical level for which data were reported: s=State, r=Region, and c=City or metro. The abbreviation *ex* is used to mean *except* or *excluding*; *exp* stands for expenditures. For other abbreviations and further explanations, please see the Introduction.

Fayetteville, NC - continued

Item	Per	Value	Date	Ref.
Groceries				
Butter, salted, grade AA, stick	lb	2.26	7/01	11r
Butter, yoghurt, cheese, etc, expenditures on	yr	170	1999	30r
Cabbage	lb	0.42	7/01	11r
Cereals and cereal products, expenditures on	yr	140	1999	30r
Cheddar cheese, natural	lb	3.75	7/01	11r
Cheese, Kraft grated Parmesan	8 oz	2.92	12/00	5c
Chicken breast, bone-in	lb	1.85	7/01	11r
Chicken legs, bone-in	lb	1.34	7/01	11r
Chicken, fresh, whole	lb	1.05	7/01	11r
Chicken, whole fryer	lb	1.06	12/00	5c
Chops, boneless	lb	4.13	7/01	11r
Chuck roast, graded and ungraded, excl U.S. prime and choice	lb	2.35	7/01	11r
Chuck roast, U.S. choice, boneless	lb	2.67	7/01	11r
Cigarettes, Winston, Kings	carton	30.07	12/00	5c
Coffee, 100%, ground roast, all sizes	lb	2.88	7/01	11r
Coffee, instant, plain, regular, all sizes	16 oz	9.25	7/01	11r
Coffee, vacuum-packed	13 oz	1.99	12/00	5c
Cola, non diet,	2 liter	1.11	7/01	11r
Corn Flakes, Kellogg's or Post Toasties	18 oz	2.86	12/00	5c
Corn, frozen, whole kernel, lowest price	16 oz	1.46	12/00	5c
Crackers, soda, salted	lb	1.70	7/01	11r
Dairy product purchases	yr	282	1999	30r
Eggs, expenditures on	yr	32	1999	30r
Eggs, Grade A or AA	dozen	0.96	12/00	5c
Fats and oils, expenditures on	yr	79	1999	30r
Fish and seafood, expenditures on	yr	99	1999	30r
Flour, white, all purpose	lb	0.32	7/01	11r
Food (excl fruit and vegetables), eaten at home, purchases	yr	815	1999	30r
Food cooked on trips, expenditures on	yr	36	1999	30r
Food purchases	yr	4533	1999	30r
Food purchases, eaten away from home	yr	1873	1999	30r
Food purchases, food eaten at home	yr	2660	1999	30r
Fresh fruits, expenditures on	yr	128	1999	30r
Fresh milk and cream, expenditures on	yr	112	1999	30r
Fresh vegetables, expenditures on	yr	131	1999	30r
Fruit and vegetable purchases	yr	438	1999	30r
Grapefruit	lb	0.59	7/01	11r
Grapes, Thompson, seedless	lb	2.12	7/01	11r
Ground beef, 100% beef	lb	1.76	7/01	11r
Ground beef, lean and extra lean	lb	2.60	7/01	11r
Ground chuck, 100% beef	lb	2.08	7/01	11r
Ham, boneless, excl canned	lb	2.71	7/01	11r
Ham, rump or shank half, bone-in, smoked	lb	2.19	7/01	11r
Ice cream, prepackaged, bulk, regular	1/2 gal	3.93	7/01	11r
Lemons	lb	1.32	7/01	11r
Lettuce, iceberg	lb	0.76	7/01	11r
Lettuce, iceberg	head	1.36	12/00	5c
Margarine, Blue Bonnet or Parkay, stick	lb	0.66	12/00	5c
Milk, fresh, low fat	gal	2.75	7/01	11r
Milk, fresh, whole, fortified	gal	2.97	7/01	11r
Milk, whole	1/2 gal	1.89	12/00	5c
Nonalcoholic beverages, expenditures on	yr	228	1999	30r
Orange juice, frozen concentrate	16 oz	1.95	7/01	11r
Orange juice, Minute Maid frozen	12 oz	1.61	12/00	5c
Oranges, Navel	lb	0.73	7/01	11r
Oranges, Valencia	lb	0.55	7/01	11r
Peaches, halves or slices, Hunt's, Del Monte, or Libby's	29 oz	1.53	12/00	5c
Peanut butter, creamy, all sizes	lb	1.83	7/01	11r
Pears, Anjou	lb	0.98	7/01	11r
Peas, green, Del Monte or Green Giant	15 oz	0.68	12/00	5c
Pork chops, center cut, bone-in	lb	3.33	7/01	11r
Pork sausage, fresh, loose	lb	2.59	7/01	11r
Pork shoulder picnic, bone-in, smoked	lb	1.12	7/01	11r
Pork, expenditures on	yr	162	1999	30r
Potato chips	16 oz	3.59	7/01	11r
Potatoes, frozen, french fried	lb	1.00	7/01	11r
Potatoes, white or red	10 lb	3.09	12/00	5c
Potatoes, white, all types	lb	0.44	7/01	11r

Fayetteville, NC - continued

Item	Per	Value	Date	Ref.
Groceries - continued				
Poultry, expenditures on	yr	137	1999	30r
Processed fruits, expenditures on	yr	97	1999	30r
Processed vegetables, expenditures on	yr	82	1999	30r
Rice, white, long grain, uncooked	lb	0.51	7/01	11r
Round roast, graded and ungraded, excl U.S. prime and choice	lb	2.96	7/01	11r
Round steak, graded and ungraded, excl U.S. prime and choice	lb	3.11	7/01	11r
Sausage, Jimmy Dean/Owens pork	lb	3.49	12/00	5c
Shortening, vegetable, Crisco	3 lb	3.09	12/00	5c
Sirloin steak, graded and ungraded, excl U.S. prime and choice	lb	4.23	7/01	11r
Soft drink, Coca Cola, ex deposit	2 liter	1.22	12/00	5c
Spaghetti and macaroni	lb	0.78	7/01	11r
Steak, round, U.S. choice, boneless	lb	3.56	7/01	11r
Steak, sirloin, U.S. choice, boneless	lb	5.65	7/01	11r
Steak, T-bone	lb	7.16	12/00	5c
Strawberries, dry pint	12 oz	1.50	7/01	11r
Sugar and other sweets, expenditures on	yr	99	1999	30r
Sugar, cane or beet	4 lbs	1.59	12/00	5c
Sugar, white, 33-80 ounce package	lb	0.39	7/01	11r
Sugar, white, all sizes	lb	0.42	7/01	11r
Tobacco products and smoking supplies purchases	yr	288	1999	30r
Tomatoes, field grown	lb	1.43	7/01	11r
Tomatoes, Hunt's or Del Monte	14.5 oz	0.94	12/00	5c
Tuna, chunk, light	6 oz	0.63	12/00	5c
Tuna, light, chunk	lb	1.77	7/01	11r
Turkey, frozen, whole	lb	1.05	7/01	11r
Goods and Services				
Miscellaneous goods and services, ACCRA Index		108.40	12/00	5c
B&B Japanese maple (acer japonicum)	gal	49.98-129.00	4/00	93r
Boxwood (buxus)	2 gal	12.99-16.99	4/00	93r
Daylilly (hemerocallis)	gal	4.99-8.99	4/00	93r
Flat of annuals		11.00-13.92	4/00	93r
Fountain grass (pennisetum)	gal	5.98-7.98	4/00	93r
Hanging basket (10 in)		7.99-14.98	4/00	93r
Hardy geranium (geranium)	gal	5.98-8.00	4/00	93r
Hosta (hosta)	gal	4.99-10.98	4/00	93r
Lilac (syrubga vulgaris)	2 gal	12.99-21.99	4/00	93r
Rhododendron (rhododendron)	2 gal	14.99-24.99	4/00	93r
Sage (salvia)	gal	5.98-6.99	4/00	93r
Wintercreeper euonymus (euonymus fortunei)	2 gal	7.99-89.99	4/00	93r
Hunting license	yr	15.00	4/01	34s
Health Care				
Health care, ACCRA Index		100.20	12/00	5c
Cardiac catheterization, ave hospital/ physician charges		12500	1998	77s
Childbirth, Cesarean delivery		11587	1997	13r
Childbirth, vaginal delivery		6725	1997	13r
Dentist's fee, adult teeth cleaning and periodic oral exam	visit	68.33	12/00	5c
Doctor's fee, routine exam, established patient	visit	59.50	12/00	5c
Drugs, expenditures on	yr	399	1999	30r
Health care purchases	yr	1971	1999	30r
Health insurance expenditures	yr	933	1999	30r
Hospital care, private room	day	520.00	12/00	5c

Values are in dollars or fractions of dollars. In the column headed *Ref*, references are shown to sources. Each reference is followed by a letter. These refer to the geographical level for which data were reported: s=State, r=Region, and c=City or metro. The abbreviation *ex* is used to mean *except* or *excluding*; *exp* stands for expenditures. For other abbreviations and further explanations, please see the Introduction.

Fayetteville, NC - continued

Item	Per	Value	Date	Ref.
Health Care				
Hysterectomy, laproscopically-assisted, ave hospital/physician charges		12260	1998	76s
Hysterectomy, vaginal, ave hospital and physician charges		8440	1998	76s
Medicaid dispensing fee		5.60	1999	87s
Medical services expenditures	yr	547	1999	30r
Medical supplies, expenditures on	yr	91	1999	30r
Plastic surgery, breast augmentation		2870	2000	7r
Plastic surgery, breast lift		3649	2000	7r
Plastic surgery, facelift		5008	2000	7r
Plastic surgery, hair transplantation		3425	2000	7r
Plastic surgery, lip augmentation		1227	2000	7r
Plastic surgery, lower body lift		4793	2000	7r
Plastic surgery, thigh lift		3862	2000	7r
Household Goods				
Dishwashing powder, Cascade	50 oz	2.77	12/00	5c
Floor coverings, expenditures on	yr	44	1999	30r
Furniture, expenditures on	yr	335	1999	30r
Household furnishings and equipment purchases	yr	1328	1999	30r
Household textiles, expenditures on	yr	89	1999	30r
Laundry and cleaning supplies, expenditures on	yr	113	1999	30r
Tissues, facial, Kleenex brand	175	1.29	12/00	5c
Housing				
Housing, ACCRA Index		85.70	12/00	5c
Home, 2200 sq ft, 4-br, 2-bath, 2-car garage, average		138000	2000	47c
Home price, existing, ave		160100	10/00	90r
Home value, median		146000	2001	53s
House, 2400 sq ft, 8000 sq ft lot, new, urban, utilities	total	176225	12/00	5c
House payment, principal and interest, 25% down payment	mos	975	12/00	5c
Household operation expenditures	yr	553	1999	30r
Housekeeping supplies purchases	yr	473	1999	30r
Housing, expenditures on	yr	10303	1999	30r
Maintenance, repairs, insurance expenditures	yr	699	1999	30r
Monthly rental value of owned home	mos	505	1999	30r
Owned dwellings, expenditures own	yr	3465	1999	30r
Rent expenditures	yr	1641	1999	30r
Rent, apartment, 2 br, 1 1/2-2 baths, unfurn, 950 sq ft, water	mos	568	12/00	5c
Rental unit, 1 bedroom, with utilities	mos	434	4/01	41c
Rental unit, 2 bedroom, with utilities	mos	487	4/01	41c
Rental unit, 3 bedroom, with utilities	mos	674	4/01	41c
Rental unit, 4 bedroom, with utilities	mos	801	4/01	41c
Shelter, expenditures on	yr	5467	1999	30r
Insurance and Pensions				
Life and other personal insurance purchases	yr	414	1999	30r
Pensions and Social Security, expenditures on	yr	2635	1999	30r
Personal insurance and pensions, expenditures on	yr	3048	1999	30r
Legal Fees				
Combination hunting and fishing license	yr	20.00	4/01	34s
Divorce, filing fee		80.00	4/01	35s
Driver's license fee	orig	10.00	1999	48s
Driver's license fee	renew	10.00	1999	48s
Fishing license	yr	15.00	4/01	34s
Personal Goods				
Personal care products and services purchases	yr	393	1999	30r
Shampoo, Alberto VO5	15 oz	1.05	12/00	5c
Toothpaste, Crest or Colgate	6-7 oz	2.52	12/00	5c
Personal Services				
Dry cleaning, man's 2-pc suit		6.87	12/00	5c
Man's haircut, barbershop, no styling		7.75	12/00	5c

Fayetteville, NC - continued

Item	Per	Value	Date	Ref.
Personal Services - continued				
Personal services, household, expenditures on	yr	258	1999	30r
Woman's shampoo, trim, blow-dry, no style-change		24.00	12/00	5c
Pets				
Pets, toys, and playground equipment, expenditures on	yr	306	1999	30r
Restaurant Food				
Chicken, fried, thigh and drumstick, KFC/ Church's		2.75	12/00	5c
Hamburger with cheese, McDonald's	1/4 lb	2.13	12/00	5c
Pizza, Pizza Hut or Pizza Inn	11-12 in	9.99	12/00	5c
Taxes				
Federal income taxes paid	yr	2047	1999	30r
Personal taxes, expenditures on	yr	2554	1999	30r
Property taxes paid	yr	726	1999	30r
State and local income taxes paid	yr	363	1999	30r
Transportation				
Transportation, ACCRA Index		98.20	12/00	5c
Bus fare, to central business district	1-way	0.75	12/00	5c
Cars and trucks, new, expenditures on	yr	1648	1999	30r
Cars and trucks, used, expenditures on	yr	1651	1999	30r
Diesel at the pump	gal	1.19	10/99	73s
Gasoline and motor oil purchases	yr	1052	1999	30r
Gasoline before-tax price (cents)	gal	103.20	10/00	43s
Maintenance and repair expenditures	yr	621	1999	30r
Motorcycle license fee	orig	1.50	1999	49s
Motorcycle license fee	renew	1.50	1999	49s
Public transportation, expenditures on	yr	298	1999	30r
Tire balance, computer or spin balance, front	wheel	8.75	12/00	5c
Transportation purchases	yr	6738	1999	30r
Vehicle expenses, miscellaneous, purchases	yr	2033	1999	30r
Vehicle insurance payments	yr	696	1999	30r
Vehicle purchases (net outlay)	yr	3354	1999	30r
Vehicle rental, lease expenditures	yr	352	1999	30r
Utilities				
Utilities, ACCRA Index		103.00	12/00	5c
Electrical bill, average	mos	83.66	9/00	9s
Electricity, 2400 sq ft, new home	mos	118.53	12/00	5c
Electricity, expenditures on	yr	1115	1999	30r
Electricity cost, average	KWh	6.40	9/00	9s
Water and other public services, expenditures on	yr	298	1999	30r
Weddings				
Wedding (national average cost)		19936	2000	33r
Wedding (regional average total cost)		16293	1997	110r
Attendants' gifts		321	1998	33r
Bridal attendants' apparel (5 persons)		824	2000	33r
Bride's headpiece/veil		173	1998	33r
Bride's wedding dress		859	1998	33r
Clergy, religious facility fee		242	1998	33r
Engagement ring		3177	1998	33r
Flowers		789	1998	33r
Groom's formalwear rental		99	2000	33r
Limousine		410	1998	33r
Marriage license cost		40.00	4/01	35s
Men's formalwear (ushers, best man)		469	2000	33r
Mother of bride apparel		241	2000	33r
Music		866	1998	33r
Photography and videography		1368	1998	33r
Rehearsal dinner		728	1998	33r
Wedding invitations and announcements		341	1998	33r
Wedding reception		7968	2000	33r
Wedding rings (bride and groom)		1060	1998	33r

Values are in dollars or fractions of dollars. In the column headed *Ref*, references are shown to sources. Each reference is followed by a letter. These refer to the geographical level for which data were reported: s=State, r=Region, and c=City or metro. The abbreviation *ex* is used to mean *except* or *excluding*; *exp* stands for *expenditures*. For other abbreviations and further explanations, please see the Introduction.

Fayetteville-Springdale-Rogers, AR

Item	Per	Value	Date	Ref.
Alcoholic Beverages				
Alcoholic beverage purchases	yr	253	1999	30r
Malt beverages, all types, all sizes, any origin	16 oz	0.96	7/01	11r
Appliances				
Major appliances, expenditures on	yr	172	1999	30r
Small appliances, housewares, expenditures on	yr	81	1999	30r
Banking and Money				
Mortgage interest and charges paid	yr	2039	1999	30r
Mortgage principal paid on owned property	yr	1026	1999	30r
Vehicle finance charges paid	yr	365	1999	30r
Charity				
Cash contributions, expenditures	yr	1127	1999	30r
Child Care				
Child raising cost, total, age 0-2	yr	8540	1999	60r
Child raising cost, total, age 3-5	yr	8780	1999	60r
Child raising cost, total, age 6-8	yr	8820	1999	60r
Child raising cost, total, age 9-11	yr	8800	1999	60r
Child raising cost, total, age 12-14	yr	9510	1999	60r
Child raising cost, total, age 15-17	yr	9740	1999	60r
Child's child care and education, age 0-2	yr	1380	1999	60r
Child's child care and education, age 3-5	yr	1520	1999	60r
Child's child care and education, age 6-8	yr	990	1999	60r
Child's child care and education, age 9-11	yr	650	1999	60r
Child's child care and education, age 12-14	yr	490	1999	60r
Child's child care and education, age 15-17	yr	840	1999	60r
Child's clothing, age 0-2	yr	480	1999	60r
Child's clothing, age 3-5	yr	470	1999	60r
Child's clothing, age 6-8	yr	520	1999	60r
Child's clothing, age 9-11	yr	570	1999	60r
Child's clothing, age 12-14	yr	950	1999	60r
Child's clothing, age 15-17	yr	850	1999	60r
Child's food, age 0-2	yr	1000	1999	60r
Child's food, age 3-5	yr	1160	1999	60r
Child's food, age 6-8	yr	1490	1999	60r
Child's food, age 9-11	yr	1770	1999	60r
Child's food, age 12-14	yr	1770	1999	60r
Child's food, age 15-17	yr	1980	1999	60r
Child's health care, age 0-2	yr	620	1999	60r
Child's health care, age 3-5	yr	590	1999	60r
Child's health care, age 6-8	yr	680	1999	60r
Child's health care, age 9-11	yr	720	1999	60r
Child's health care, age 12-14	yr	730	1999	60r
Child's health care, age 15-17	yr	760	1999	60r
Child's housing, age 0-2	yr	3070	1999	60r
Child's housing, age 3-5	yr	3050	1999	60r
Child's housing, age 6-8	yr	3010	1999	60r
Child's housing, age 9-11	yr	2850	1999	60r
Child's housing, age 12-14	yr	3040	1999	60r
Child's housing, age 15-17	yr	2650	1999	60r
Child's personal care, reading, age 0-2	yr	910	1999	60r
Child's personal care, reading, age 3-5	yr	930	1999	60r
Child's personal care, reading, age 6-8	yr	960	1999	60r
Child's personal care, reading, age 9-11	yr	1000	1999	60r
Child's personal care, reading, age 12-14	yr	1170	1999	60r
Child's personal care, reading, age 15-17	yr	950	1999	60r
Clothing				
Apparel and services purchases	yr	1610	1999	30r
Boys, 2 to 15, expenditures on	yr	89	1999	30r
Children under 2, expenditures on	yr	79	1999	30r
Footwear, expenditures on	yr	283	1999	30r
Girls, 2 to 15, expenditures on	yr	103	1999	30r
Men and boys, expenditures on	yr	351	1999	30r
Men, 16 and over, expenditures on	yr	262	1999	30r
Women, 16 and over, expenditures on	yr	538	1999	30r
Communications				
Phone line, single, business, field visit	inst.	84.00	12/97	17s
Phone line, single, business, no field visit	inst.	84.00	12/97	17s
Phone line, single, residence, field visit	inst.	39.70	12/97	17s

Fayetteville-Springdale-Rogers, AR - continued

Item	Per	Value	Date	Ref.
Communications - continued				
Phone line, single, residence, no field visit	inst.	39.70	12/97	17s
Postage and stationery, expenditures on	yr	104	1999	30r
Postal rate, express mail, up to half-pound		12.45	7/01	108r
Postal rate, letter, first class, first ounce		0.34	7/01	108r
Postal rate, letter, two ounces		0.57	7/01	108r
Postal rate, post card		0.21	7/01	108r
Postal rate, priority mail, two pounds		3.95	7/01	108r
Postal rate, priority mail, up to one pound		3.50	7/01	108r
Telephone services, expenditures on	yr	860	1999	30r
Education				
Board, 4-year private college/university	yr	2121	1996	38s
Board, 4-year public college/university	yr	1423	1996	38s
Education expenditures	yr	431	1999	30r
Room, 4-year private college/university	yr	1488	1996	38s
Room, 4-year public college/university	yr	1613	1996	38s
Total cost, 4-year private college/university	yr	10183	1996	38s
Total cost, 4-year public college/university	yr	5064	1996	38s
Tuition, 2-year public college/university, in state	yr	903	1996	38s
Tuition, 4-year private college/university, in state	yr	6574	1996	38s
Tuition, 4-year public college/university	yr	2028	1996	38s
Energy and Fuels				
Electricity	KWh	0.09	7/01	11r
Electricity	500 KWhs	47.29	7/01	11r
Fuel oil #2	gal	1.43	7/01	11r
Fuel oil and other fuels, expenditures on	yr	45	1999	30r
Gasoline, all types	gal	1.60	7/01	11r
Gasoline, unleaded midgrade	gal	1.65	7/01	11r
Gasoline, unleaded premium	gal	1.74	7/01	11r
Natural gas, expenditures on	yr	164	1999	30r
Utility (piped) gas, therm		1.01	7/01	11r
Utility (piped) gas, 40 therms		44.29	7/01	11r
Utility (piped) gas, 100 therms		97.44	7/01	11r
Entertainment				
Entertainment purchases	yr	1574	1999	30r
Fees and admissions paid	yr	371	1999	30r
Reading purchases	yr	121	1999	30r
Television, radios, sound equipment, expenditures on	yr	561	1999	30r
Funerals				
Total cost of funeral		5842.28	1/99	78r
Acknowledgement cards		28.35	1/99	78r
Casket		2494.29	1/99	78r
Cosmetology, hair, other preparation		109.22	1/99	78r
Embalming		361.42	1/99	78r
Funeral at funeral home		349.20	1/99	78r
Hearse (local)		161.91	1/99	78r
Professional service charges		1116.50	1/99	78r
Service car/van		65.56	1/99	78r
Transfer of remains to funeral home		143.56	1/99	78r
Vault		785.25	1/99	78r
Visitation/viewing		227.02	1/99	78r
Groceries				
American processed cheese	lb	3.50	7/01	11r
Bakery products, expenditures on	yr	261	1999	30r
Bananas	lb	0.47	7/01	11r
Beans, dried, any type, all sizes	lb	0.63	7/01	11r
Beef for stew, boneless	lb	2.86	7/01	11r
Beef, expenditures on	yr	210	1999	30r
Bologna, all beef or mixed	lb	2.29	7/01	11r
Bread, French	lb	1.66	7/01	11r
Bread, white, pan	lb	0.87	7/01	11r
Bread, whole wheat, pan	lb	1.38	7/01	11r
Broccoli	lb	1.04	7/01	11r
Butter, salted, grade AA, stick	lb	2.26	7/01	11r
Butter, yoghurt, cheese, etc, expenditures on	yr	170	1999	30r
Cabbage	lb	0.42	7/01	11r

Values are in dollars or fractions of dollars. In the column headed *Ref*, references are shown to sources. Each reference is followed by a letter. These refer to the geographical level for which data were reported: s=State, r=Region, and c=City or metro. The abbreviation *ex* is used to mean *except* or *excluding*; *exp* stands for *expenditures*. For other abbreviations and further explanations, please see the Introduction.

Fayetteville-Springdale-Rogers, AR - continued

Item	Per	Value	Date	Ref.
Groceries				
Cereals and cereal products, expenditures on	yr	140	1999	30r
Cheddar cheese, natural	lb	3.75	7/01	11r
Chicken breast, bone-in	lb	1.85	7/01	11r
Chicken legs, bone-in	lb	1.34	7/01	11r
Chicken, fresh, whole	lb	1.05	7/01	11r
Chops, boneless,	lb	4.13	7/01	11r
Chuck roast, graded and ungraded, excl U.S. prime and choice	lb	2.35	7/01	11r
Chuck roast, U.S. choice, boneless	lb	2.67	7/01	11r
Coffee, 100%, ground roast, all sizes	lb	2.88	7/01	11r
Coffee, instant, plain, regular, all sizes	16 oz	9.25	7/01	11r
Cola, non diet,	2 liter	1.11	7/01	11r
Crackers, soda, salted	lb	1.70	7/01	11r
Dairy product purchases	yr	282	1999	30r
Eggs, expenditures on	yr	32	1999	30r
Fats and oils, expenditures on	yr	79	1999	30r
Fish and seafood, expenditures on	yr	99	1999	30r
Flour, white, all purpose	lb	0.32	7/01	11r
Food (excl fruit and vegetables), eaten at home, purchases	yr	815	1999	30r
Food cooked on trips, expenditures on	yr	36	1999	30r
Food purchases	yr	4533	1999	30r
Food purchases, eaten away from home	yr	1873	1999	30r
Food purchases, food eaten at home	yr	2660	1999	30r
Fresh fruits, expenditures on	yr	128	1999	30r
Fresh milk and cream, expenditures on	yr	112	1999	30r
Fresh vegetables, expenditures on	yr	131	1999	30r
Fruit and vegetable purchases	yr	438	1999	30r
Grapefruit	lb	0.59	7/01	11r
Grapes, Thompson, seedless	lb	2.12	7/01	11r
Ground beef, 100% beef	lb	1.76	7/01	11r
Ground beef, lean and extra lean	lb	2.60	7/01	11r
Ground chuck, 100% beef	lb	2.08	7/01	11r
Ham, boneless, excl canned	lb	2.71	7/01	11r
Ham, rump or shank half, bone-in, smoked	lb	2.19	7/01	11r
Ice cream, prepackaged, bulk, regular	1/2 gal	3.93	7/01	11r
Lemons	lb	1.32	7/01	11r
Lettuce, iceberg	lb	0.76	7/01	11r
Milk, fresh, low fat,	gal	2.75	7/01	11r
Milk, fresh, whole, fortified	gal	2.97	7/01	11r
Nonalcoholic beverages, expenditures on	yr	228	1999	30r
Orange juice, frozen concentrate	16 oz	1.95	7/01	11r
Oranges, Navel	lb	0.73	7/01	11r
Oranges, Valencia	lb	0.55	7/01	11r
Peanut butter, creamy, all sizes	lb	1.83	7/01	11r
Pears, Anjou	lb	0.98	7/01	11r
Pork chops, center cut, bone-in	lb	3.33	7/01	11r
Pork sausage, fresh, loose	lb	2.59	7/01	11r
Pork shoulder picnic, bone-in, smoked	lb	1.12	7/01	11r
Pork, expenditures on	yr	162	1999	30r
Potato chips	16 oz	3.59	7/01	11r
Potatoes, frozen, french fried	lb	1.00	7/01	11r
Potatoes, white, all types	lb	0.44	7/01	11r
Poultry, expenditures on	yr	137	1999	30r
Processed fruits, expenditures on	yr	97	1999	30r
Processed vegetables, expenditures on	yr	82	1999	30r
Rice, white, long grain, uncooked	lb	0.51	7/01	11r
Round roast, graded and ungraded, excl U.S. prime and choice	lb	2.96	7/01	11r
Round steak, graded and ungraded, excl U.S. prime and choice	lb	3.11	7/01	11r
Sirloin steak, graded and ungraded, excl U.S. prime and choice	lb	4.23	7/01	11r
Spaghetti and macaroni	lb	0.78	7/01	11r
Steak, round, U.S. choice, boneless	lb	3.56	7/01	11r
Steak, sirloin, U.S. choice, boneless	lb	5.65	7/01	11r
Strawberries, dry pint	12 oz	1.50	7/01	11r
Sugar and other sweets, expenditures on	yr	99	1999	30r
Sugar, white, 33-80 ounce package	lb	0.39	7/01	11r
Sugar, white, all sizes	lb	0.42	7/01	11r

Fayetteville-Springdale-Rogers, AR - continued

Item	Per	Value	Date	Ref.
Groceries - continued				
Tobacco products and smoking supplies purchases	yr	288	1999	30r
Tomatoes, field grown	lb	1.43	7/01	11r
Tuna, light, chunk	lb	1.77	7/01	11r
Turkey, frozen, whole	lb	1.05	7/01	11r
Goods and Services				
B&B Japanese maple (acer japonicum)	gal	79.98-99.00	4/00	93r
Boxwood (buxus)	2 gal	12.98-18.99	4/00	93r
Daylilly (hemerocallis)	gal	7.96-11.00	4/00	93r
Flat of annuals		13.99-27.99	4/00	93r
Fountain grass (pennisetum)	gal	6.96-9.00	4/00	93r
Hanging basket (10 in)		9.99-24.99	4/00	93r
Hardy geranium (geranium)	gal	5.96-8.00	4/00	93r
Hosta (hosta)	gal	8.96-12.99	4/00	93r
Lilac (syrubga vulgaris)	2 gal	13.00-19.99	4/00	93r
Rhododendron (rhododendron)	2 gal	12.98-29.99	4/00	93r
Sage (salvia)	gal	5.96-8.00	4/00	93r
Wintercreeper euonymus (euonymus fortunei)	2 gal	13.00-18.99	4/00	93r
Hunting license	yr	25.00	4/01	34s
Health Care				
Cardiac catheterization, ave hospital/physician charges		12240	1998	77s
Childbirth, Cesarean delivery		11587	1997	13r
Childbirth, vaginal delivery		6725	1997	13r
Drugs, expenditures on	yr	399	1999	30r
Health care purchases	yr	1971	1999	30r
Health insurance expenditures	yr	933	1999	30r
Hysterectomy, laproscopically-assisted, ave hospital/physician charges		10580	1998	76s
Hysterectomy, vaginal, ave hospital and physician charges		8270	1998	76s
Medicaid dispensing fee		5.51	1999	87s
Medical services expenditures	yr	547	1999	30r
Medical supplies, expenditures on	yr	91	1999	30r
Household Goods				
Floor coverings, expenditures on	yr	44	1999	30r
Furniture, expenditures on	yr	335	1999	30r
Household furnishings and equipment purchases	yr	1328	1999	30r
Household textiles, expenditures on	yr	89	1999	30r
Laundry and cleaning supplies, expenditures on	yr	113	1999	30r
Housing				
Home price, existing, ave		160100	10/00	90r
Home value, median		94000	2001	53s
Household operation expenditures	yr	553	1999	30r
Housekeeping supplies purchases	yr	473	1999	30r
Housing, expenditures on	yr	10303	1999	30r
Maintenance, repairs, insurance expenditures	yr	699	1999	30r
Monthly rental value of owned home	mos	505	1999	30r
Owned dwellings, expenditures own	yr	3465	1999	30r
Rent expenditures	yr	1641	1999	30r
Rental unit, 1 bedroom, with utilities	mos	390	4/01	41c
Rental unit, 2 bedroom, with utilities	mos	513	4/01	41c
Rental unit, 3 bedroom, with utilities	mos	693	4/01	41c
Rental unit, 4 bedroom, with utilities	mos	717	4/01	41c
Shelter, expenditures on	yr	5467	1999	30r

Values are in dollars or fractions of dollars. In the column headed *Ref*, references are shown to sources. Each reference is followed by a letter. These refer to the geographical level for which data were reported: s=State, r=Region, and c=City or metro. The abbreviation *ex* is used to mean *except* or *excluding*; *exp* stands for *expenditures*. For other abbreviations and further explanations, please see the Introduction.

Fayetteville-Springdale-Rogers, AR - continued

Item	Per	Value	Date	Ref.
Insurance and Pensions				
Life and other personal insurance purchases	yr	414	1999	30r
Pensions and Social Security, expenditures on	yr	2635	1999	30r
Personal insurance and pensions, expenditures on	yr	3048	1999	30r
Legal Fees				
Divorce, filing fee		100.00	4/01	35s
Driver's license fee	renew	14.00	1999	48s
Driver's license fee	orig	14.00	1999	48s
Personal Goods				
Personal care products and services purchases	yr	393	1999	30r
Personal Services				
Personal services, household, expenditures on	yr	258	1999	30r
Pets				
Pets, toys, and playground equipment, expenditures on	yr	306	1999	30r
Taxes				
Federal income taxes paid	yr	2047	1999	30r
Personal taxes, expenditures on	yr	2554	1999	30r
Property taxes paid	yr	726	1999	30r
State and local income taxes paid	yr	363	1999	30r
Transportation				
Cars and trucks, new, expenditures on	yr	1648	1999	30r
Cars and trucks, used, expenditures on	yr	1651	1999	30r
Diesel at the pump	gal	1.17	10/99	73s
Gasoline and motor oil purchases	yr	1052	1999	30r
Gasoline before-tax price (cents)	gal	102.60	10/00	43s
Maintenance and repair expenditures	yr	621	1999	30r
Public transportation, expenditures on	yr	298	1999	30r
Transportation purchases	yr	6738	1999	30r
Vehicle expenses, miscellaneous, purchases	yr	2033	1999	30r
Vehicle insurance payments	yr	696	1999	30r
Vehicle purchases (net outlay)	yr	3354	1999	30r
Vehicle rental, lease expenditures	yr	352	1999	30r
Utilities				
Electrical bill, average	mos	75.00	9/00	9s
Electricity, expenditures on	yr	1115	1999	30r
Electricity cost, average	KWh	5.70	9/00	9s
Water and other public services, expenditures on	yr	298	1999	30r
Weddings				
Wedding (national average cost)		19936	2000	33r
Attendants' gifts		321	1998	33r
Bridal attendants' apparel (5 persons)		824	2000	33r
Bride's headpiece/veil		173	1998	33r
Bride's wedding dress		859	1998	33r
Clergy, religious facility fee		242	1998	33r
Engagement ring		3177	1998	33r
Flowers		789	1998	33r
Groom's formalwear rental		99	2000	33r
Limousine		410	1998	33r
Marriage license cost		30.00	4/01	35s
Men's formalwear (ushers, best man)		469	2000	33r
Mother of bride apparel		241	2000	33r
Music		866	1998	33r
Photography and videography		1368	1998	33r
Rehearsal dinner		728	1998	33r
Wedding invitations and announcements		341	1998	33r
Wedding reception		7968	2000	33r
Wedding rings (bride and groom)		1060	1998	33r

Fitchburg-Leominster, MA

Item	Per	Value	Date	Ref.
Average annual expenditures	yr	37971	1999	30r
Composite, ACCRA index		106.20	3/01	4c
Alcoholic Beverages				
Alcoholic beverage purchases	yr	368	1999	30r
Beer, Heineken, 12-oz, ex deposit	6	7.24	3/01	4c
J & B Scotch	750-ml	21.85	3/01	4c
Wine, Livingston or Gallo, Chablis blanc	1.5 liter	6.53	3/01	4c
Wine, red and white table, all sizes, any origin	liter	9.64	7/01	11r
Appliances				
Appliance repair, service call, washing machine	min lab chg	47.75	3/01	4c
Major appliances, expenditures on	yr	194	1999	30r
Small appliances, housewares, expenditures on	yr	93	1999	30r
Banking and Money				
Mortgage interest and charges paid	yr	2622	1999	30r
Mortgage principal paid on owned property	yr	1262	1999	30r
Mortgage rate, incl. points and orig. fee, 30-yr. conv. fixed or ARM	mos	7.27	3/01	4c
Vehicle finance charges paid	yr	240	1999	30r
Charity				
Cash contributions, expenditures	yr	1001	1999	30r
Child Care				
Child raising cost, total, age 0-2	yr	8670	1999	60r
Child raising cost, total, age 3-5	yr	8910	1999	60r
Child raising cost, total, age 6-8	yr	9040	1999	60r
Child raising cost, total, age 9-11	yr	9100	1999	60r
Child raising cost, total, age 12-14	yr	9890	1999	60r
Child raising cost, total, age 15-17	yr	10010	1999	60r
Child's child care and education, age 0-2	yr	1070	1999	60r
Child's child care and education, age 3-5	yr	1190	1999	60r
Child's child care and education, age 6-8	yr	740	1999	60r
Child's child care and education, age 9-11	yr	470	1999	60r
Child's child care and education, age 12-14	yr	350	1999	60r
Child's child care and education, age 15-17	yr	590	1999	60r
Child's clothing, age 0-2	yr	480	1999	60r
Child's clothing, age 3-5	yr	470	1999	60r
Child's clothing, age 6-8	yr	520	1999	60r
Child's clothing, age 9-11	yr	570	1999	60r
Child's clothing, age 12-14	yr	970	1999	60r
Child's clothing, age 15-17	yr	870	1999	60r
Child's food, age 0-2	yr	1130	1999	60r
Child's food, age 3-5	yr	1290	1999	60r
Child's food, age 6-8	yr	1640	1999	60r
Child's food, age 9-11	yr	1930	1999	60r
Child's food, age 12-14	yr	1940	1999	60r
Child's food, age 15-17	yr	2150	1999	60r
Child's health care, age 0-2	yr	550	1999	60r
Child's health care, age 3-5	yr	530	1999	60r
Child's health care, age 6-8	yr	610	1999	60r
Child's health care, age 9-11	yr	650	1999	60r
Child's health care, age 12-14	yr	660	1999	60r
Child's health care, age 15-17	yr	690	1999	60r
Child's housing, age 0-2	yr	3555	1999	60r
Child's housing, age 3-5	yr	3530	1999	60r
Child's housing, age 6-8	yr	3490	1999	60r
Child's housing, age 9-11	yr	3340	1999	60r
Child's housing, age 12-14	yr	3530	1999	60r
Child's housing, age 15-17	yr	3140	1999	60r
Child's personal care, reading, age 0-2	yr	920	1999	60r
Child's personal care, reading, age 3-5	yr	950	1999	60r
Child's personal care, reading, age 6-8	yr	980	1999	60r
Child's personal care, reading, age 9-11	yr	1020	1999	60r
Child's personal care, reading, age 12-14	yr	1190	1999	60r
Child's personal care, reading, age 15-17	yr	970	1999	60r
Clothing				
Apparel and services purchases	yr	1831	1999	30r
Boys' brief, cotton	3	4.25	3/01	4c
Boys, 2 to 15, expenditures on	yr	92	1999	30r

Values are in dollars or fractions of dollars. In the column headed *Ref*, references are shown to sources. Each reference is followed by a letter. These refer to the geographical level for which data were reported: s=State, r=Region, and c=City or metro. The abbreviation *ex* is used to mean *except* or *excluding*; *exp* stands for *expenditures*. For other abbreviations and further explanations, please see the Introduction.

Fitchburg-Leominster, MA - continued

Item	Per	Value	Date	Ref.
Clothing				
Children under 2, expenditures on	yr	63	1999	30r
Footwear, expenditures on	yr	300	1999	30r
Girls, 2 to 15, expenditures on	yr	101	1999	30r
Men and boys, expenditures on	yr	446	1999	30r
Men, 16 and over, expenditures on	yr	354	1999	30r
Shirt, man's dress shirt		31.87	3/01	4c
Slacks, man's "No Wrinkles" khaki		46.87	3/01	4c
Women, 16 and over, expenditures on	yr	584	1999	30r
Communications				
Cable modem installation, Adelphi		54.90	6/99	103s
Cable modem installation, Media One		100.00	6/99	103s
Cable modem rate, cable subscriber, Adelphi	mos	34.95	6/99	103s
Cable modem rate, cable subscriber, Media One	mos	34.95-39.95	6/99	103s
Cable modem rate, non-cable subscriber, Adelphi	mos	44.95	6/99	103s
Cable modem rate, non-cable subscriber, Media One	mos	49.95	6/99	103s
Newspaper subscription, daily and Sunday delivery	mos	20.00	3/01	4c
Phone line, single, business, field visit	inst.	120.52	12/97	17s
Phone line, single, business, no field visit	inst.	93.02	12/97	17s
Phone line, single, residence, field visit	inst.	64.57	12/97	17s
Phone line, single, residence, no field visit	inst.	37.07	12/97	17s
Postage and stationery, expenditures on	yr	138	1999	30r
Postal rate, express mail, up to half-pound		12.45	7/01	108r
Postal rate, letter, first class, first ounce		0.34	7/01	108r
Postal rate, letter, two ounces		0.57	7/01	108r
Postal rate, post card		0.21	7/01	108r
Postal rate, priority mail, two pounds		3.95	7/01	108r
Postal rate, priority mail, up to one pound		3.50	7/01	108r
Telephone bill, family of three	mos	25.86	3/01	4c
Telephone services, expenditures on	yr	830	1999	30r
Education				
Board, 4-year private college/university	yr	3244	1996	38s
Board, 4-year public college/university	yr	2042	1996	38s
Education expenditures	yr	877	1999	30r
Room, 4-year private college/university	yr	3688	1996	38s
Room, 4-year public college/university	yr	2462	1996	38s
Total cost, 4-year private college/university	yr	23335	1996	38s
Total cost, 4-year public college/university	yr	8757	1996	38s
Tuition, 2-year public college/university, in state	yr	2359	1996	38s
Tuition, 4-year private college/university, in state	yr	16403	1996	38s
Tuition, 4-year public college/university	yr	4253	1996	38s
Energy and Fuels				
Electricity	KWh	0.12	7/01	11r
Energy, combined forms, 2400 sq ft	mos	130.01	3/01	4c
Energy, exc. electricity, 2400 sq ft	mos	54.11	3/01	4c
Fuel oil #2	gal	1.31	7/01	11r
Fuel oil and other fuels, expenditures on	yr	207	1999	30r
Gas, natural, commercial rate	1000 cf	10.82	11/00	88s
Gas, regular unleaded, cash, self-service	gal	1.59	3/01	4c
Gasoline, all types	gal	1.80	7/01	11r
Gasoline, unleaded midgrade	gal	1.85	7/01	11r
Gasoline, unleaded premium	gal	1.91	7/01	11r
Gasoline, unleaded regular	gal	1.71	7/01	11r
Natural gas, expenditures on	yr	368	1999	30r
Utility (piped) gas, therm		1.08	7/01	11r
Utility (piped) gas, 40 therms		50.87	7/01	11r
Utility (piped) gas, 100 therms		111.06	7/01	11r
Entertainment				
Bowling, Saturday evening rate	line	1.91	3/01	4c
Entertainment purchases	yr	1821	1999	30r
Fees and admissions paid	yr	511	1999	30r
Monopoly game, Parker Brothers', No. 9	game	10.88	3/01	4c
Movie, first-run, Saturday, evening	adm.	6.50	3/01	4c
Television, radios, sound equipment, expenditures on	yr	650	1999	30r

Fitchburg-Leominster, MA - continued

Item	Per	Value	Date	Ref.
Entertainment - continued				
Tennis balls, yellow, Wilson or Penn, 3	can	2.84	3/01	4c
Funerals				
Total cost of funeral		5776.91	1/99	78r
Acknowledgement cards		14.47	1/99	78r
Casket		2090.19	1/99	78r
Cosmetology, hair, other preparation		132.92	1/99	78r
Embalming		377.33	1/99	78r
Funeral at funeral home		352.43	1/99	78r
Hearse (local)		185.55	1/99	78r
Professional service charges		1289.95	1/99	78r
Service car/van		87.42	1/99	78r
Transfer of remains to funeral home		175.48	1/99	78r
Vault		729.40	1/99	78r
Visitation/viewing		341.76	1/99	78r
Groceries				
Groceries, ACCRA Index		102.80	3/01	4c
Antibiotic ointment, Polysporin	0.5 oz	5.15	3/01	4c
Apples, red delicious	lb	0.95	7/01	11r
Baby food, strained vegetables or fruit, lowest price	4-4.5 oz	0.47	3/01	4c
Bacon, sliced	lb	3.44	7/01	11r
Bakery products, expenditures on	yr	310	1999	30r
Bananas	lb	0.52	3/01	4c
Bananas	lb	0.55	7/01	11r
Beef or hamburger, ground	lb	1.57	3/01	4c
Beef, expenditures on	yr	236	1999	30r
Bread, white	loaf	0.98	3/01	4c
Bread, white, pan	lb	1.09	7/01	11r
Butter, yoghurt, cheese, etc, expenditures on	yr	214	1999	30r
Cereals and bakery product purchases	yr	474	1999	30r
Cereals and cereal products, expenditures on	yr	164	1999	30r
Cheese, Kraft grated Parmesan	8 oz	3.24	3/01	4c
Chicken legs, bone-in	lb	1.23	7/01	11r
Chicken, fresh, whole	lb	1.13	7/01	11r
Chicken, whole fryer	lb	1.19	3/01	4c
Chuck roast, U.S. choice, boneless	lb	2.79	7/01	11r
Cigarettes, Winston, Kings	carton	40.85	3/01	4c
Coffee, 100%, ground roast, all sizes	lb	3.40	7/01	11r
Coffee, vacuum-packed	13 oz	2.72	3/01	4c
Corn Flakes, Kellogg's or Post Toasties	18 oz	3.06	3/01	4c
Corn, frozen, whole kernel, lowest price	16 oz	0.86	3/01	4c
Dairy product purchases	yr	342	1999	30r
Eggs, expenditures on	yr	34	1999	30r
Eggs, Grade A or AA	dozen	1.24	3/01	4c
Eggs, grade A, large	dozen	0.82	7/01	11r
Fats and oils, expenditures on	yr	80	1999	30r
Fish and seafood, expenditures on	yr	123	1999	30r
Food (excl fruit and vegetables), eaten at home, purchases	yr	838	1999	30r
Food cooked on trips, expenditures on	yr	48	1999	30r
Food purchases	yr	5314	1999	30r
Food purchases, eaten away from home	yr	2313	1999	30r
Food purchases, food eaten at home	yr	3001	1999	30r
Fresh fruits, expenditures on	yr	169	1999	30r
Fresh milk and cream, expenditures on	yr	128	1999	30r
Fresh vegetables, expenditures on	yr	164	1999	30r
Grapefruit	lb	0.67	7/01	11r
Grapes, Thompson, seedless	lb	2.18	7/01	11r
Ground beef, lean and extra lean	lb	2.66	7/01	11r
Ground chuck, 100% beef	lb	2.04	7/01	11r
Lettuce, iceberg	head	1.02	3/01	4c
Lettuce, iceberg	lb	0.76	7/01	11r
Margarine, Blue Bonnet or Parkay, stick	lb	0.56	3/01	4c
Meats, poultry, fish, and egg purchases	yr	808	1999	30r
Milk, whole	1/2 gal	1.57	3/01	4c
Nonalcoholic beverages, expenditures on	yr	225	1999	30r
Orange juice, frozen concentrate	16 oz	1.88	7/01	11r
Orange juice, Minute Maid frozen	12 oz	1.24	3/01	4c
Oranges, Navel	lb	0.79	7/01	11r
Oranges, Valencia	lb	0.56	7/01	11r

Values are in dollars or fractions of dollars. In the column headed *Ref*, references are shown to sources. Each reference is followed by a letter. These refer to the geographical level for which data were reported: s=State, r=Region, and c=City or metro. The abbreviation *ex* is used to mean *except* or *excluding*; *exp* stands for *expenditures*. For other abbreviations and further explanations, please see the Introduction.

Fitchburg-Leominster, MA - continued

Item	Per	Value	Date	Ref.
Groceries				
Peaches	lb	1.16	7/01	11r
Peaches, halves or slices, Hunt's, Del Monte, or Libby's	29 oz	1.59	3/01	4c
Peanut butter, creamy, all sizes	lb	2.01	7/01	11r
Pears, Anjou	lb	1.16	7/01	11r
Peas, green, Del Monte or Green Giant	15 oz	0.66	3/01	4c
Pork chops, center cut, bone-in	lb	3.57	7/01	11r
Pork, expenditures on	yr	146	1999	30r
Potato chips	16 oz	3.37	7/01	11r
Potatoes, white or red	10 lb	2.79	3/01	4c
Potatoes, white, all types	lb	0.42	7/01	11r
Poultry, expenditures on	yr	158	1999	30r
Processed fruits, expenditures on	yr	124	1999	30r
Processed vegetables, expenditures on	yr	82	1999	30r
Round roast, U.S. choice, boneless	lb	3.04	7/01	11r
Sausage, Jimmy Dean/Owens pork	lb	2.69	3/01	4c
Shortening, vegetable, Crisco	3 lb	3.02	3/01	4c
Soft drink, Coca Cola, ex deposit	2 liter	1.24	3/01	4c
Spaghetti and macaroni	lb	1.04	7/01	11r
Steak, sirloin, U.S. choice, boneless	lb	5.39	7/01	11r
Steak, T-bone	lb	6.84	3/01	4c
Strawberries, dry pint	12 oz	1.51	7/01	11r
Sugar and other sweets, expenditures on	yr	110	1999	30r
Sugar, cane or beet	4 lbs	1.59	3/01	4c
Sugar, white, 33-80 ounce package	lb	0.46	7/01	11r
Sugar, white, all sizes	lb	0.47	7/01	11r
Tobacco products and smoking supplies purchases	yr	309	1999	30r
Tomatoes, Hunt's or Del Monte	14.5 oz	0.82	3/01	4c
Tuna, chunk, light	6 oz	0.71	3/01	4c
Yogurt, natural, fruit flavored	8 oz	0.79	7/01	11r
Goods and Services				
Miscellaneous goods and services, ACCRA Index		109.90	3/01	4c
B&B Japanese maple (acer japonicum)	gal	38.99-125.00	4/00	93r
Boxwood (buxus)	2 gal	15.99-49.95	4/00	93r
Daylily (hemerocallis)	gal	4.95	4/00	93r
Flat of annuals		8.00-14.99	4/00	93r
Fountain grass (pennisetum)	gal	6.99-9.99	4/00	93r
Hanging basket (10 in)		12.95-19.99	4/00	93r
Hardy geranium (geranium)	gal	6.95-7.99	4/00	93r
Hosta (hosta)	gal	4.95	4/00	93r
Lilac (syrubga vulgaris)	2 gal	17.99-74.95	4/00	93r
Miscellaneous purchases	yr	872	1999	30r
Rhododendron (rhododendron)	2 gal	23.99-54.95	4/00	93r
Sage (salvia)	gal	6.95-7.99	4/00	93r
Wintercreeper euonymus (euonymus fortunei)	2 gal	14.99-23.95	4/00	93r
Hunting license	yr	27.50	4/01	34s
Health Care				
Health care, ACCRA Index		124.20	3/01	4c
Cardiac catheterization, ave hospital/ physician charges		17080	1998	77s
Childbirth, Cesarean delivery		14716	1997	13r
Childbirth, vaginal delivery		8541	1997	13r
Dentist's fee, adult teeth cleaning and periodic oral exam	visit	102.00	3/01	4c
Doctor's fee, routine exam, established patient	visit	69.50	3/01	4c
Drugs, expenditures on	yr	296	1999	30r
Health care purchases	yr	1788	1999	30r
Health insurance expenditures	yr	875	1999	30r

Fitchburg-Leominster, MA - continued

Item	Per	Value	Date	Ref.
Health Care - continued				
Hospital care, private room	day	574.40	3/01	4c
Hysterectomy, laproscopically-assisted, ave hospital/physician charges		13100	1998	76s
Hysterectomy, vaginal, ave hospital and physician charges		8780	1998	76s
Medicaid dispensing fee		3.00	1999	87s
Medical services expenditures	yr	516	1999	30r
Medical supplies, expenditures on	yr	102	1999	30r
Plastic surgery, breast augmentation		4232	2000	7r
Plastic surgery, breast lift		4605	2000	7r
Plastic surgery, facelift		6964	2000	7r
Plastic surgery, hair transplantation		4193	2000	7r
Plastic surgery, lip augmentation		1675	2000	7r
Plastic surgery, lower body lift		6611	2000	7r
Plastic surgery, thigh lift		4751	2000	7r
Household Goods				
Dishwashing powder, Cascade	50 oz	2.79	3/01	4c
Floor coverings, expenditures on	yr	59	1999	30r
Furniture, expenditures on	yr	388	1999	30r
Household furnishings and equipment purchases	yr	1567	1999	30r
Household textiles, expenditures on	yr	112	1999	30r
Laundry and cleaning supplies, expenditures on	yr	104	1999	30r
Tissues, facial, Kleenex brand	175	1.36	3/01	4c
Housing				
Housing, ACCRA Index		100.40	3/01	4c
Home price, existing, ave		180800	10/00	90r
Home value, median		261000	2001	53s
House, 2400 sq ft, 8000 sq ft lot, new, urban, utilities	total	204900	3/01	4c
House payment, principal and interest, 25% down payment	mos	1050	3/01	4c
Household operation expenditures	yr	581	1999	30r
Housekeeping supplies purchases	yr	474	1999	30r
Lodging expenditures	yr	550	1999	30r
Maintenance, repairs, insurance expenditures	yr	835	1999	30r
Monthly rental value of owned home	mos	663	1999	30r
Owned dwellings, expenditures own	yr	5209	1999	30r
Rent expenditures	yr	2390	1999	30r
Rent, apartment, 2 br, 1 1/2-2 baths, unfurn, 950 sq ft, water	mos	656	3/01	4c
Rental unit, 1 bedroom, with utilities	mos	510	4/01	41c
Rental unit, 2 bedroom, with utilities	mos	662	4/01	41c
Rental unit, 3 bedroom, with utilities	mos	851	4/01	41c
Rental unit, 4 bedroom, with utilities	mos	925	4/01	41c
Shelter, expenditures on	yr	8149	1999	30r
Insurance and Pensions				
Life and other personal insurance purchases	yr	424	1999	30r
Pensions and Social Security, expenditures on	yr	3037	1999	30r
Legal Fees				
Divorce, filing fee		100.00	4/01	35s
Driver's license fee	orig	33.75	1999	48s
Driver's license fee	renew	33.75	1999	48s
Fishing license	yr	27.50	4/01	34s
Personal Goods				
Personal care products and services purchases	yr	399	1999	30r
Shampoo, Alberto VO5	15 oz	1.41	3/01	4c
Toothpaste, Crest or Colgate	6-7 oz	2.87	3/01	4c
Personal Services				
Dry cleaning, man's 2-pc suit		7.61	3/01	4c
Man's haircut, barbershop, no styling		8.65	3/01	4c
Personal services, household, expenditures on	yr	271	1999	30r
Woman's shampoo, trim, blow-dry, no style-change		25.00	3/01	4c

Values are in dollars or fractions of dollars. In the column headed *Ref*, references are shown to sources. Each reference is followed by a letter. These refer to the geographical level for which data were reported: s=State, r=Region, and c=City or metro. The abbreviation *ex* is used to mean *except* or *excluding*; *exp* stands for *expenditures*. For other abbreviations and further explanations, please see the Introduction.

Fitchburg-Leominster, MA - continued

Item	Per	Value	Date	Ref.
Pets				
Pets, toys, and playground equipment, expenditures on	yr	325	1999	30r
Restaurant Food				
Chicken, fried, thigh and drumstick, KFC/ Church's		2.63	3/01	4c
Hamburger with cheese, McDonald's	1/4 lb	2.49	3/01	4c
Pizza, Pizza Hut or Pizza Inn	11-12 in	8.99	3/01	4c
Taxes				
Federal income taxes paid	yr	2606	1999	30r
Personal taxes, expenditures on	yr	3567	1999	30r
Property taxes paid	yr	1752	1999	30r
State and local income taxes paid	yr	694	1999	30r
Transportation				
Transportation, ACCRA Index		105.10	3/01	4c
Bus fare, to central business district	1-way	1.00	3/01	4c
Cars and trucks, new, expenditures on	yr	1496	1999	30r
Cars and trucks, used, expenditures on	yr	1251	1999	30r
Diesel at the pump	gal	1.32	10/99	73s
Gasoline and motor oil purchases	yr	901	1999	30r
Gasoline before-tax price (cents)	gal	118.70	10/00	43s
Maintenance and repair expenditures	yr	618	1999	30r
Public transportation, expenditures on	yr	575	1999	30r
Tire balance, computer or spin balance, front	wheel	7.74	3/01	4c
Transportation purchases	yr	6503	1999	30r
Vehicle expenses, miscellaneous, purchases	yr	2266	1999	30r
Vehicle insurance payments	yr	824	1999	30r
Vehicle purchases (net outlay)	yr	2761	1999	30r
Vehicle rental, lease expenditures	yr	584	1999	30r
Travel				
Hotel room	night	111.15	2/01	95s
Utilities				
Utilities, ACCRA Index		108.20	3/01	4c
Electrical bill, average	mos	58.58	9/00	9s
Electricity, expenditures on	yr	837	1999	30r
Electricity, summer, 250 KWh	mos	30.83	2/96	97c
Electricity, summer, 500 KWh	mos	58.51	2/96	97c
Electricity, summer, 750 KWh	mos	86.19	2/96	97c
Electricity, summer, 1000 KWh	mos	113.87	2/96	97c
Electricity and other, mixed, 2400 sq ft, new home	mos	75.90	3/01	4c
Electricity cost, average	KWh	8.90	9/00	9s
Utilities, fuels, and public services purchased	yr	2457	1999	30r
Water and other public services, expenditures on	yr	215	1999	30r
Weddings				
Wedding (national average cost)		19936	2000	33r
Wedding (regional average total cost)		29454	1997	110r
Attendants' gifts		321	1998	33r
Bridal attendants' apparel (5 persons)		824	2000	33r
Bride's headpiece/veil		173	1998	33r
Bride's wedding dress		859	1998	33r
Clergy, religious facility fee		242	1998	33r
Engagement ring		3177	1998	33r
Flowers		789	1998	33r
Groom's formalwear rental		99	2000	33r
Limousine		410	1998	33r
Marriage license cost		25.00	4/01	35s
Men's formalwear (ushers, best man)		469	2000	33r
Mother of bride apparel		241	2000	33r
Music		866	1998	33r
Photography and videography		1368	1998	33r
Rehearsal dinner		728	1998	33r
Wedding invitations and announcements		341	1998	33r
Wedding reception		7968	2000	33r
Wedding rings (bride and groom)		1060	1998	33r

Flint, MI

Item	Per	Value	Date	Ref.
Average annual expenditures	yr	35369	1999	30r
Alcoholic Beverages				
Alcoholic beverage purchases	yr	304	1999	30r
Malt beverages, all types, all sizes, any origin	16 oz	0.93	7/01	11r
Wine, red and white table, all sizes, any origin	liter	7.04	7/01	11r
Appliances				
Major appliances, expenditures on	yr	165	1999	30r
Small appliances, housewares, expenditures on	yr	90	1999	30r
Banking and Money				
Mortgage interest and charges paid	yr	2277	1999	30r
Mortgage principal paid on owned property	yr	1230	1999	30r
Vehicle finance charges paid	yr	328	1999	30r
Charity				
Cash contributions, expenditures	yr	1126	1999	30r
Child Care				
Child raising cost, total, age 0-2	yr	7890	1999	60r
Child raising cost, total, age 3-5	yr	8130	1999	60r
Child raising cost, total, age 6-8	yr	8170	1999	60r
Child raising cost, total, age 9-11	yr	8190	1999	60r
Child raising cost, total, age 12-14	yr	8890	1999	60r
Child raising cost, total, age 15-17	yr	9050	1999	60r
Child's child care and education, age 0-2	yr	1240	1999	60r
Child's child care and education, age 3-5	yr	1370	1999	60r
Child's child care and education, age 6-8	yr	880	1999	60r
Child's child care and education, age 9-11	yr	570	1999	60r
Child's child care and education, age 12-14	yr	420	1999	60r
Child's child care and education, age 15-17	yr	720	1999	60r
Child's clothing, age 0-2	yr	410	1999	60r
Child's clothing, age 3-5	yr	400	1999	60r
Child's clothing, age 6-8	yr	450	1999	60r
Child's clothing, age 9-11	yr	500	1999	60r
Child's clothing, age 12-14	yr	840	1999	60r
Child's clothing, age 15-17	yr	740	1999	60r
Child's food, age 0-2	yr	960	1999	60r
Child's food, age 3-5	yr	1120	1999	60r
Child's food, age 6-8	yr	1430	1999	60r
Child's food, age 9-11	yr	1710	1999	60r
Child's food, age 12-14	yr	1710	1999	60r
Child's food, age 15-17	yr	1920	1999	60r
Child's health care, age 0-2	yr	520	1999	60r
Child's health care, age 3-5	yr	500	1999	60r
Child's health care, age 6-8	yr	570	1999	60r
Child's health care, age 9-11	yr	610	1999	60r
Child's health care, age 12-14	yr	630	1999	60r
Child's health care, age 15-17	yr	650	1999	60r
Child's housing, age 0-2	yr	2860	1999	60r
Child's housing, age 3-5	yr	2840	1999	60r
Child's housing, age 6-8	yr	2800	1999	60r
Child's housing, age 9-11	yr	2650	1999	60r
Child's housing, age 12-14	yr	2840	1999	60r
Child's housing, age 15-17	yr	2440	1999	60r
Child's personal care, reading, age 0-2	yr	880	1999	60r
Child's personal care, reading, age 3-5	yr	900	1999	60r
Child's personal care, reading, age 6-8	yr	930	1999	60r
Child's personal care, reading, age 9-11	yr	970	1999	60r
Child's personal care, reading, age 12-14	yr	1150	1999	60r
Child's personal care, reading, age 15-17	yr	920	1999	60r
Clothing				
Apparel and services purchases	yr	1607	1999	30r
Boys, 2 to 15, expenditures on	yr	91	1999	30r
Children under 2, expenditures on	yr	59	1999	30r
Footwear, expenditures on	yr	285	1999	30r
Girls, 2 to 15, expenditures on	yr	116	1999	30r
Men and boys, expenditures on	yr	433	1999	30r
Men, 16 and over, expenditures on	yr	341	1999	30r
Women, 16 and over, expenditures on	yr	490	1999	30r

Values are in dollars or fractions of dollars. In the column headed *Ref*, references are shown to sources. Each reference is followed by a letter. These refer to the geographical level for which data were reported: s=State, r=Region, and c=City or metro. The abbreviation *ex* is used to mean *except* or *excluding*; *exp* stands for *expenditures*. For other abbreviations and further explanations, please see the Introduction.

Item	Per	Value	Date	Ref.
Communications				
Cable modem installation, Bresnan		99.95	6/99	103s
Cable modem installation, Comcast		95.00	6/99	103s
Cable modem installation, Media One		100.00	6/99	103s
Cable modem rate, cable subscriber, Bresnan	mos	39.95	6/99	103s
Cable modem rate, cable subscriber, Comcast	mos	39.95	6/99	103s
Cable modem rate, cable subscriber, Media One	mos	34.95-39.95	6/99	103s
Cable modem rate, non-cable subscriber, Bresnan	mos	49.95	6/99	103s
Cable modem rate, non-cable subscriber, Comcast	mos	49.95	6/99	103s
Cable modem rate, non-cable subscriber, Media One	mos	49.95	6/99	103s
Phone line, single, business, field visit	inst.	42.00	12/97	17s
Phone line, single, business, no field visit	inst.	42.00	12/97	17s
Phone line, single, residence, field visit	inst.	42.00	12/97	17s
Phone line, single, residence, no field visit	inst.	42.00	12/97	17s
Postage and stationery, expenditures on	yr	140	1999	30r
Postal rate, express mail, up to half-pound		12.45	7/01	108r
Postal rate, letter, first class, first ounce		0.34	7/01	108r
Postal rate, letter, two ounces		0.57	7/01	108r
Postal rate, post card		0.21	7/01	108r
Postal rate, priority mail, two pounds		3.95	7/01	108r
Postal rate, priority mail, up to one pound		3.50	7/01	108r
Telephone bill, business, basic rate	mos	13.04	12/97	18c
Telephone bill, residential, basic rate	mos	10.40	12/97	18c
Telephone services, expenditures on	yr	830	1999	30r
Education				
Board, 4-year private college/university	yr	2182	1996	38s
Board, 4-year public college/university	yr	2276	1996	38s
Education expenditures	yr	583	1999	30r
Room, 4-year private college/university	yr	1974	1996	38s
Room, 4-year public college/university	yr	2024	1996	38s
Total cost, 4-year private college/university	yr	13331	1996	38s
Total cost, 4-year public college/university	yr	8195	1996	38s
Tuition, 2-year public college/university, in state	yr	1529	1996	38s
Tuition, 4-year private college/university, in state	yr	9176	1996	38s
Tuition, 4-year public college/university	yr	3895	1996	38s
Energy and Fuels				
Electricity	500 KWhs	46.59	7/01	11r
Fuel oil #2	gal	1.27	7/01	11r
Fuel oil and other fuels, expenditures on	yr	68	1999	30r
Gas, cooking, winter, 10 therms	mos	10.43	2/96	98c
Gas, cooking, winter, 30 therms	mos	18.29	2/96	98c
Gas, cooking, winter, 50 therms	mos	26.15	2/96	98c
Gas, heating, winter, average use	mos	94.62	2/96	98c
Gas, natural, commercial rate	1000 cf	4.91	11/00	88s
Gasoline, unleaded midgrade	gal	1.79	7/01	11r
Gasoline, unleaded premium	gal	1.86	7/01	11r
Gasoline, unleaded regular	gal	1.58	7/01	11r
Natural gas, expenditures on	yr	389	1999	30r
Utility (piped) gas, therm		0.81	7/01	11r
Utility (piped) gas, 40 therms		38.01	7/01	11r
Utility (piped) gas, 100 therms		81.75	7/01	11r
Entertainment				
Entertainment purchases	yr	1984	1999	30r
Fees and admissions paid	yr	444	1999	30r
Television, radios, sound equipment, expenditures on	yr	580	1999	30r
Funerals				
Cosmetology, hair, other preparation		178.32	1/99	78r
Embalming		408.19	1/99	78r
Funeral at funeral home		362.13	1/99	78r
Professional service charges		1375.51	1/99	78r
Transfer of remains to funeral home		155.92	1/99	78r

Item	Per	Value	Date	Ref.
Funerals - continued				
Visitation/viewing		294.38	1/99	78r
Groceries				
Bacon, sliced	lb	3.15	7/01	11r
Bakery products, expenditures on	yr	281	1999	30r
Bananas	lb	0.48	7/01	11r
Beans, dried, any type, all sizes	lb	0.61	7/01	11r
Beef for stew, boneless	lb	3.08	7/01	11r
Beef, expenditures on	yr	217	1999	30r
Bologna, all beef or mixed	lb	2.52	7/01	11r
Bread, white, pan	lb	1.06	7/01	11r
Broccoli	lb	0.91	7/01	11r
Butter, salted, grade AA, stick	lb	3.04	7/01	11r
Butter, yoghurt, cheese, etc, expenditures on	yr	183	1999	30r
Cereals and bakery product purchases	yr	430	1999	30r
Cereals and cereal products, expenditures on	yr	149	1999	30r
Chicken, fresh, whole	lb	1.07	7/01	11r
Chops, boneless,	lb	3.64	7/01	11r
Chuck roast, U.S. choice, boneless	lb	2.47	7/01	11r
Coffee, 100%, ground roast, all sizes	lb	2.69	7/01	11r
Cookies, chocolate chip	lb	2.87	7/01	11r
Dairy product purchases	yr	304	1999	30r
Eggs, expenditures on	yr	26	1999	30r
Eggs, grade A, large	dozen	0.88	7/01	11r
Fats and oils, expenditures on	yr	75	1999	30r
Fish and seafood, expenditures on	yr	72	1999	30r
Food (excl fruit and vegetables), eaten at home, purchases	yr	887	1999	30r
Food cooked on trips, expenditures on	yr	44	1999	30r
Food purchases	yr	4802	1999	30r
Food purchases, eaten away from home	yr	2069	1999	30r
Food purchases, food eaten at home	yr	2733	1999	30r
Fresh fruits, expenditures on	yr	138	1999	30r
Fresh milk and cream, expenditures on	yr	120	1999	30r
Fresh vegetables, expenditures on	yr	126	1999	30r
Grapefruit	lb	0.66	7/01	11r
Grapes, Thompson, seedless	lb	1.64	7/01	11r
Ground beef, 100% beef	lb	1.64	7/01	11r
Ground beef, lean and extra lean	lb	2.16	7/01	11r
Ground chuck, 100% beef	lb	2.13	7/01	11r
Ham, boneless, excl canned	lb	2.62	7/01	11r
Ice cream, prepackaged, bulk, regular	1/2 gal	3.35	7/01	11r
Lemons	lb	1.19	7/01	11r
Lettuce, iceberg	lb	0.73	7/01	11r
Margarine, soft, tubs	lb	0.89	7/01	11r
Meats, poultry, fish, and egg purchases	yr	671	1999	30r
Milk, fresh, whole, fortified	gal	2.71	7/01	11r
Nonalcoholic beverages, expenditures on	yr	239	1999	30r
Oranges, Navel	lb	0.80	7/01	11r
Oranges, Valencia	lb	0.66	7/01	11r
Pears, Anjou	lb	0.93	7/01	11r
Pork chops, center cut, bone-in	lb	3.63	7/01	11r
Pork, expenditures on	yr	150	1999	30r
Potato chips	16 oz	3.52	7/01	11r
Potatoes, frozen, french fried	lb	1.08	7/01	11r
Potatoes, white, all types	lb	0.33	7/01	11r
Poultry, expenditures on	yr	108	1999	30r
Processed fruits, expenditures on	yr	98	1999	30r
Processed vegetables, expenditures on	yr	80	1999	30r
Round roast, U.S. choice, boneless	lb	3.07	7/01	11r
Round steak, graded and ungraded, excl U.S. prime and choice	lb	3.41	7/01	11r
Shortening, vegetable oil blends	lb	1.13	7/01	11r
Spaghetti and macaroni	lb	0.80	7/01	11r
Steak, round, U.S. choice, boneless	lb	3.23	7/01	11r
Steak, T-bone, U.S. choice, bone-in	lb	6.68	7/01	11r
Strawberries, dry pint	12 oz	1.32	7/01	11r
Sugar and other sweets, expenditures on	yr	114	1999	30r
Sugar, white, 33-80 ounce package	lb	0.42	7/01	11r
Sugar, white, all sizes	lb	0.43	7/01	11r
Tobacco products and smoking supplies purchases	yr	331	1999	30r

Values are in dollars or fractions of dollars. In the column headed *Ref*, references are shown to sources. Each reference is followed by a letter. These refer to the geographical level for which data were reported: s=State, r=Region, and c=City or metro. The abbreviation *ex* is used to mean *except* or *excluding*; *exp* stands for expenditures. For other abbreviations and further explanations, please see the Introduction.

Flint, MI - continued

Item	Per	Value	Date	Ref.
Groceries				
Tomatoes, field grown	lb	1.46	7/01	11r
Tuna, light, chunk	lb	1.80	7/01	11r
Turkey, frozen, whole	lb	1.15	7/01	11r
Goods and Services				
B&B Japanese maple (acer japonicum)	gal	29.99-169.99	4/00	93r
Boxwood (buxus)	2 gal	18.99-39.99	4/00	93r
Daylilly (hemerocallis)	gal	4.99-25.00	4/00	93r
Flat of annuals		11.98-24.99	4/00	93r
Fountain grass (pennisetum)	gal	5.98-12.98	4/00	93r
Hanging basket (10 in)		12.99-27.99	4/00	93r
Hardy geranium (geranium)	gal	7.99-9.99	4/00	93r
Hosta (hosta)	gal	6.00-25.00	4/00	93r
Lilac (syrubga vulgaris)	2 gal	14.99-24.99	4/00	93r
Miscellaneous purchases	yr	865	1999	30r
Rhododendron (rhododendron)	2 gal	23.98-42.99	4/00	93r
Sage (salvia)	gal	6.00-9.99	4/00	93r
Snowblower, single stage		400-600	12/00	99s
Wintercreeper euonymus (euonymus fortunei)	2 gal	16.00-169.99	4/00	93r
Hunting license	yr	14.00	4/01	34s
Health Care				
Cardiac catheterization, ave hospital/physician charges		11830	1998	77s
Childbirth, Cesarean delivery		10722	1997	13r
Childbirth, vaginal delivery		6223	1997	13r
Drugs, expenditures on	yr	394	1999	30r
Health care purchases	yr	2048	1999	30r
Health insurance expenditures	yr	978	1999	30r
Hysterectomy, laproscopically-assisted, ave hospital/physician charges		13820	1998	76s
Hysterectomy, vaginal, ave hospital and physician charges		8780	1998	76s
Medicaid dispensing fee		3.72	1999	87s
Medical services expenditures	yr	554	1999	30r
Medical supplies, expenditures on	yr	122	1999	30r
Nursing home costs, private room	day	134	2000	82c
Nursing home stay, private room	day	134	2000	81c
Plastic surgery, breast augmentation		3184	2000	7r
Plastic surgery, breast lift		3585	2000	7r
Plastic surgery, facelift		4999	2000	7r
Plastic surgery, hair transplantation		3105	2000	7r
Plastic surgery, lip augmentation		1290	2000	7r
Plastic surgery, lower body lift		8135	2000	7r
Plastic surgery, thigh lift		3839	2000	7r
Household Goods				
Floor coverings, expenditures on	yr	52	1999	30r
Furniture, expenditures on	yr	344	1999	30r
Household furnishings and equipment purchases	yr	1475	1999	30r
Household textiles, expenditures on	yr	109	1999	30r
Laundry and cleaning supplies, expenditures on	yr	134	1999	30r
Housing				
Home price, existing, ave		144400	10/00	90r
Home value, median		135000	2001	53s
Household operation expenditures	yr	542	1999	30r
Housekeeping supplies purchases	yr	508	1999	30r
Lodging expenditures	yr	430	1999	30r

Flint, MI - continued

Item	Per	Value	Date	Ref.
Housing - continued				
Maintenance, repairs, insurance expenditures	yr	853	1999	30r
Monthly rental value of owned home	mos	547	1999	30r
Owned dwellings, expenditures own	yr	4282	1999	30r
Rent expenditures	yr	1558	1999	30r
Rental unit, 1 bedroom, with utilities	mos	436	4/01	41c
Rental unit, 2 bedroom, with utilities	mos	547	4/01	41c
Rental unit, 3 bedroom, with utilities	mos	698	4/01	41c
Rental unit, 4 bedroom, with utilities	mos	765	4/01	41c
Shelter, expenditures on	yr	6270	1999	30r
Insurance and Pensions				
Life and other personal insurance purchases	yr	387	1999	30r
Pensions and Social Security, expenditures on	yr	2968	1999	30r
Legal Fees				
Divorce, filing fee		65.00	4/01	35s
Driver's license fee	orig	20.00	1999	48s
Driver's license fee	renew	5.00	1999	48s
Fishing license	yr	14.00	4/01	34s
Personal Goods				
Personal care products and services purchases	yr	385	1999	30r
Personal Services				
Personal services, household, expenditures on	yr	300	1999	30r
Pets				
Pets, toys, and playground equipment, expenditures on	yr	375	1999	30r
Taxes				
Federal income taxes paid	yr	2326	1999	30r
Personal taxes, expenditures on	yr	3223	1999	30r
Property taxes paid	yr	1152	1999	30r
State and local income taxes paid	yr	753	1999	30r
Transportation				
Bus fare, one-way	trip	1.00	2000	1c
Cars and trucks, new, expenditures on	yr	1280	1999	30r
Cars and trucks, used, expenditures on	yr	1763	1999	30r
Diesel at the pump	gal	1.19	10/99	73s
Gasoline and motor oil purchases	yr	1036	1999	30r
Gasoline before-tax price (cents)	gal	111.50	10/00	43s
Maintenance and repair expenditures	yr	594	1999	30r
Public transportation, expenditures on	yr	341	1999	30r
Transportation purchases	yr	6617	1999	30r
Vehicle expenses, miscellaneous, purchases	yr	2159	1999	30r
Vehicle insurance payments	yr	701	1999	30r
Vehicle purchases (net outlay)	yr	3081	1999	30r
Vehicle rental, lease expenditures	yr	536	1999	30r
Utilities				
Electrical bill, average	mos	55.00	9/00	9s
Electricity, expenditures on	yr	841	1999	30r
Electricity cost, average	KWh	7.00	9/00	9s
Utilities, fuels, and public services purchased	yr	2401	1999	30r
Water and other public services, expenditures on	yr	273	1999	30r
Weddings				
Wedding (national average cost)		19936	2000	33r
Wedding (regional average total cost)		16195	1997	110r
Attendants' gifts		321	1998	33r
Bridal attendants' apparel (5 persons)		824	2000	33r
Bride's headpiece/veil		173	1998	33r
Bride's wedding dress		859	1998	33r
Clergy, religious facility fee		242	1998	33r
Engagement ring		3177	1998	33r
Flowers		789	1998	33r
Groom's formalwear rental		99	2000	33r
Limousine		410	1998	33r
Marriage license cost		20.00	4/01	35s

Values are in dollars or fractions of dollars. In the column headed *Ref*, references are shown to sources. Each reference is followed by a letter. These refer to the geographical level for which data were reported: s=State, r=Region, and c=City or metro. The abbreviation *ex* is used to mean *except* or *excluding*; *exp* stands for *expenditures*. For other abbreviations and further explanations, please see the Introduction.

Flint, MI - continued

Item	Per	Value	Date	Ref.
Weddings				
Men's formalwear (ushers, best man)		469	2000	33r
Mother of bride apparel		241	2000	33r
Music		866	1998	33r
Photography and videography		1368	1998	33r
Rehearsal dinner		728	1998	33r
Wedding invitations and announcements		341	1998	33r
Wedding reception		7968	2000	33r
Wedding rings (bride and groom)		1060	1998	33r

Florence, AL

Item	Per	Value	Date	Ref.
Composite, ACCRA index		89.40	3/01	4c
Alcoholic Beverages				
Alcoholic beverage purchases	yr	253	1999	30r
Beer, Heineken, 12-oz, ex deposit	6	7.11	3/01	4c
J & B Scotch	750-ml	23.99	3/01	4c
Malt beverages, all types, all sizes, any origin	16 oz	0.96	7/01	11r
Wine, Livingston or Gallo, Chablis blanc	1.5 liter	5.90	3/01	4c
Appliances				
Appliance repair, service call, washing machine	min lab chg	44.37	3/01	4c
Major appliances, expenditures on	yr	172	1999	30r
Small appliances, housewares, expenditures on	yr	81	1999	30r
Banking and Money				
Mortgage interest and charges paid	yr	2039	1999	30r
Mortgage principal paid on owned property	yr	1026	1999	30r
Mortgage rate, incl. points and orig. fee, 30-yr. conv. fixed or ARM	mos	6.90	3/01	4c
Vehicle finance charges paid	yr	365	1999	30r
Charity				
Cash contributions, expenditures	yr	1127	1999	30r
Child Care				
Child raising cost, total, age 0-2	yr	8540	1999	60r
Child raising cost, total, age 3-5	yr	8780	1999	60r
Child raising cost, total, age 6-8	yr	8820	1999	60r
Child raising cost, total, age 9-11	yr	8800	1999	60r
Child raising cost, total, age 12-14	yr	9510	1999	60r
Child raising cost, total, age 15-17	yr	9740	1999	60r
Child's child care and education, age 0-2	yr	1380	1999	60r
Child's child care and education, age 3-5	yr	1520	1999	60r
Child's child care and education, age 6-8	yr	990	1999	60r
Child's child care and education, age 9-11	yr	650	1999	60r
Child's child care and education, age 12-14	yr	490	1999	60r
Child's child care and education, age 15-17	yr	840	1999	60r
Child's clothing, age 0-2	yr	480	1999	60r
Child's clothing, age 3-5	yr	470	1999	60r
Child's clothing, age 6-8	yr	520	1999	60r
Child's clothing, age 9-11	yr	570	1999	60r
Child's clothing, age 12-14	yr	950	1999	60r
Child's clothing, age 15-17	yr	850	1999	60r
Child's food, age 0-2	yr	1000	1999	60r
Child's food, age 3-5	yr	1160	1999	60r
Child's food, age 6-8	yr	1490	1999	60r
Child's food, age 9-11	yr	1770	1999	60r
Child's food, age 12-14	yr	1770	1999	60r
Child's food, age 15-17	yr	1980	1999	60r
Child's health care, age 0-2	yr	620	1999	60r
Child's health care, age 3-5	yr	590	1999	60r
Child's health care, age 6-8	yr	680	1999	60r
Child's health care, age 9-11	yr	720	1999	60r
Child's health care, age 12-14	yr	730	1999	60r
Child's health care, age 15-17	yr	760	1999	60r
Child's housing, age 0-2	yr	3070	1999	60r
Child's housing, age 3-5	yr	3050	1999	60r
Child's housing, age 6-8	yr	3010	1999	60r
Child's housing, age 9-11	yr	2850	1999	60r
Child's housing, age 12-14	yr	3040	1999	60r
Child's housing, age 15-17	yr	2650	1999	60r

Florence, AL - continued

Item	Per	Value	Date	Ref.
Child Care - continued				
Child's personal care, reading, age 0-2	yr	910	1999	60r
Child's personal care, reading, age 3-5	yr	930	1999	60r
Child's personal care, reading, age 6-8	yr	960	1999	60r
Child's personal care, reading, age 9-11	yr	1000	1999	60r
Child's personal care, reading, age 12-14	yr	1170	1999	60r
Child's personal care, reading, age 15-17	yr	950	1999	60r
Clothing				
Apparel and services purchases	yr	1610	1999	30r
Boys' brief, cotton	3	4.18	3/01	4c
Boys, 2 to 15, expenditures on	yr	89	1999	30r
Children under 2, expenditures on	yr	79	1999	30r
Footwear, expenditures on	yr	283	1999	30r
Girls, 2 to 15, expenditures on	yr	103	1999	30r
Men and boys, expenditures on	yr	351	1999	30r
Men, 16 and over, expenditures on	yr	262	1999	30r
Shirt, man's dress shirt		24.12	3/01	4c
Slacks, man's "No Wrinkles" khaki		34.19	3/01	4c
Women, 16 and over, expenditures on	yr	538	1999	30r
Communications				
Newspaper subscription, daily and Sunday delivery	mos	11.25	3/01	4c
Phone line, single, business, field visit	inst.	69.00	12/97	17s
Phone line, single, business, no field visit	inst.	69.00	12/97	17s
Phone line, single, residence, field visit	inst.	40.00	12/97	17s
Phone line, single, residence, no field visit	inst.	40.00	12/97	17s
Postage and stationery, expenditures on	yr	104	1999	30r
Postal rate, express mail, up to half-pound		12.45	7/01	108r
Postal rate, letter, first class, first ounce		0.34	7/01	108r
Postal rate, letter, two ounces		0.57	7/01	108r
Postal rate, post card		0.21	7/01	108r
Postal rate, priority mail, two pounds		3.95	7/01	108r
Postal rate, priority mail, up to one pound		3.50	7/01	108r
Telephone bill, family of three	mos	24.37	3/01	4c
Telephone services, expenditures on	yr	860	1999	30r
Education				
Board, 4-year private college/university	yr	2256	1996	38s
Board, 4-year public college/university	yr	1739	1996	38s
Education expenditures	yr	431	1999	30r
Room, 4-year private college/university	yr	1799	1996	38s
Room, 4-year public college/university	yr	1757	1996	38s
Total cost, 4-year private college/university	yr	11635	1996	38s
Total cost, 4-year public college/university	yr	5737	1996	38s
Tuition, 2-year public college/university, in state	yr	1317	1996	38s
Tuition, 4-year private college/university, in state	yr	7580	1996	38s
Tuition, 4-year public college/university	yr	2240	1996	38s
Energy and Fuels				
Electricity	KWh	0.09	7/01	11r
Electricity	500 KWhs	47.29	7/01	11r
Energy, combined forms, 2400 sq ft	mos	100.60	3/01	4c
Fuel oil #2	gal	1.43	7/01	11r
Fuel oil and other fuels, expenditures on	yr	45	1999	30r
Gas, natural, commercial rate	1000 cf	9.50	11/00	88s
Gas, regular unleaded, cash, self-service	gal	1.35	3/01	4c
Gasoline, all types	gal	1.60	7/01	11r
Gasoline, unleaded midgrade	gal	1.65	7/01	11r
Gasoline, unleaded premium	gal	1.74	7/01	11r
Natural gas, expenditures on	yr	164	1999	30r
Utility (piped) gas, therm		1.01	7/01	11r
Utility (piped) gas, 40 therms		44.29	7/01	11r
Utility (piped) gas, 100 therms		97.44	7/01	11r
Entertainment				
Bowling, Saturday evening rate	line	2.97	3/01	4c
Entertainment purchases	yr	1574	1999	30r
Fees and admissions paid	yr	371	1999	30r
Monopoly game, Parker Brothers', No. 9	game	10.07	3/01	4c
Movie, first-run, Saturday, evening	adm.	6.50	3/01	4c

Values are in dollars or fractions of dollars. In the column headed *Ref*, references are shown to sources. Each reference is followed by a letter. These refer to the geographical level for which data were reported: s=State, r=Region, and c=City or metro. The abbreviation *ex* is used to mean *except* or *excluding*; *exp* stands for *expenditures*. For other abbreviations and further explanations, please see the Introduction.

Florence, AL - continued

Item	Per	Value	Date	Ref.
Entertainment				
Reading purchases	yr	121	1999	30r
Television, radios, sound equipment, expenditures on	yr	561	1999	30r
Tennis balls, yellow, Wilson or Penn, 3	can	2.05	3/01	4c
Groceries				
Groceries, ACCRA Index		91.90	3/01	4c
American processed cheese	lb	3.50	7/01	11r
Antibiotic ointment, Polysporin	0.5 oz	4.76	3/01	4c
Baby food, strained vegetables or fruit, lowest price	4-4.5 oz	0.40	3/01	4c
Bakery products, expenditures on	yr	261	1999	30r
Bananas	lb	0.51	3/01	4c
Bananas	lb	0.47	7/01	11r
Beans, dried, any type, all sizes	lb	0.63	7/01	11r
Beef for stew, boneless	lb	2.86	7/01	11r
Beef or hamburger, ground	lb	1.48	3/01	4c
Beef, expenditures on	yr	210	1999	30r
Bologna, all beef or mixed	lb	2.29	7/01	11r
Bread, French	lb	1.66	7/01	11r
Bread, white	loaf	0.94	3/01	4c
Bread, white, pan	lb	0.87	7/01	11r
Bread, whole wheat, pan	lb	1.38	7/01	11r
Broccoli	lb	1.04	7/01	11r
Butter, salted, grade AA, stick	lb	2.26	7/01	11r
Butter, yoghurt, cheese, etc, expenditures on	yr	170	1999	30r
Cabbage	lb	0.42	7/01	11r
Cereals and cereal products, expenditures on	yr	140	1999	30r
Cheddar cheese, natural	lb	3.75	7/01	11r
Cheese, Kraft grated Parmesan	8 oz	3.16	3/01	4c
Chicken breast, bone-in	lb	1.85	7/01	11r
Chicken legs, bone-in	lb	1.34	7/01	11r
Chicken, fresh, whole	lb	1.05	7/01	11r
Chicken, whole fryer	lb	0.91	3/01	4c
Chops, boneless,	lb	4.13	7/01	11r
Chuck roast, graded and ungraded, excl U.S. prime and choice	lb	2.35	7/01	11r
Chuck roast, U.S. choice, boneless	lb	2.67	7/01	11r
Cigarettes, Winston, Kings	carton	27.63	3/01	4c
Coffee, 100%, ground roast, all sizes	lb	2.88	7/01	11r
Coffee, instant, plain, regular, all sizes	16 oz	9.25	7/01	11r
Coffee, vacuum-packed	13 oz	2.04	3/01	4c
Cola, non diet,	2 liter	1.11	7/01	11r
Corn Flakes, Kellogg's or Post Toasties	18 oz	2.42	3/01	4c
Corn, frozen, whole kernel, lowest price	16 oz	1.03	3/01	4c
Crackers, soda, salted	lb	1.70	7/01	11r
Dairy product purchases	yr	282	1999	30r
Eggs, expenditures on	yr	32	1999	30r
Eggs, Grade A or AA	dozen	1.05	3/01	4c
Fats and oils, expenditures on	yr	79	1999	30r
Fish and seafood, expenditures on	yr	99	1999	30r
Flour, white, all purpose	lb	0.32	7/01	11r
Food (excl fruit and vegetables), eaten at home, purchases	yr	815	1999	30r
Food cooked on trips, expenditures on	yr	36	1999	30r
Food purchases	yr	4533	1999	30r
Food purchases, eaten away from home	yr	1873	1999	30r
Food purchases, food eaten at home	yr	2660	1999	30r
Fresh fruits, expenditures on	yr	128	1999	30r
Fresh milk and cream, expenditures on	yr	112	1999	30r
Fresh vegetables, expenditures on	yr	131	1999	30r
Fruit and vegetable purchases	yr	438	1999	30r
Grapefruit	lb	0.59	7/01	11r
Grapes, Thompson, seedless	lb	2.12	7/01	11r
Ground beef, 100% beef	lb	1.76	7/01	11r
Ground beef, lean and extra lean	lb	2.60	7/01	11r
Ground chuck, 100% beef	lb	2.08	7/01	11r
Ham, boneless, excl canned	lb	2.71	7/01	11r
Ham, rump or shank half, bone-in, smoked	lb	2.19	7/01	11r
Ice cream, prepackaged, bulk, regular	1/2 gal	3.93	7/01	11r
Lemons	lb	1.32	7/01	11r
Lettuce, iceberg	head	0.84	3/01	4c

Florence, AL - continued

Item	Per	Value	Date	Ref.
Groceries - continued				
Lettuce, iceberg	lb	0.76	7/01	11r
Margarine, Blue Bonnet or Parkay, stick	lb	0.55	3/01	4c
Milk, fresh, low fat,	gal	2.75	7/01	11r
Milk, fresh, whole, fortified	gal	2.97	7/01	11r
Milk, whole	1/2 gal	1.62	3/01	4c
Nonalcoholic beverages, expenditures on	yr	228	1999	30r
Orange juice, frozen concentrate	16 oz	1.95	7/01	11r
Orange juice, Minute Maid frozen	12 oz	1.56	3/01	4c
Oranges, Navel	lb	0.73	7/01	11r
Oranges, Valencia	lb	0.55	7/01	11r
Peaches, halves or slices, Hunt's, Del Monte, or Libby's	29 oz	1.51	3/01	4c
Peanut butter, creamy, all sizes	lb	1.83	7/01	11r
Pears, Anjou	lb	0.98	7/01	11r
Peas, green, Del Monte or Green Giant	15 oz	0.61	3/01	4c
Pork chops, center cut, bone-in	lb	3.33	7/01	11r
Pork sausage, fresh, loose	lb	2.59	7/01	11r
Pork shoulder picnic, bone-in, smoked	lb	1.12	7/01	11r
Pork, expenditures on	yr	162	1999	30r
Potato chips	16 oz	3.59	7/01	11r
Potatoes, frozen, french fried	lb	1.00	7/01	11r
Potatoes, white or red	10 lb	2.51	3/01	4c
Potatoes, white, all types	lb	0.44	7/01	11r
Poultry, expenditures on	yr	137	1999	30r
Processed fruits, expenditures on	yr	97	1999	30r
Processed vegetables, expenditures on	yr	82	1999	30r
Rice, white, long grain, uncooked	lb	0.51	7/01	11r
Round roast, graded and ungraded, excl U.S. prime and choice	lb	2.96	7/01	11r
Round steak, graded and ungraded, excl U.S. prime and choice	lb	3.11	7/01	11r
Sausage, Jimmy Dean/Owens pork	lb	2.54	3/01	4c
Shortening, vegetable, Crisco	3 lb	3.00	3/01	4c
Sirloin steak, graded and ungraded, excl U.S. prime and choice	lb	4.23	7/01	11r
Soft drink, Coca Cola, ex deposit	2 liter	1.09	3/01	4c
Spaghetti and macaroni	lb	0.78	7/01	11r
Steak, round, U.S. choice, boneless	lb	3.56	7/01	11r
Steak, sirloin, U.S. choice, boneless	lb	5.65	7/01	11r
Steak, T-bone	lb	6.71	3/01	4c
Strawberries, dry pint	12 oz	1.50	7/01	11r
Sugar and other sweets, expenditures on	yr	99	1999	30r
Sugar, cane or beet	4 lbs	1.42	3/01	4c
Sugar, white, 33-80 ounce package	lb	0.39	7/01	11r
Sugar, white, all sizes	lb	0.42	7/01	11r
Tobacco products and smoking supplies purchases	yr	288	1999	30r
Tomatoes, field grown	lb	1.43	7/01	11r
Tomatoes, Hunt's or Del Monte	14.5 oz	0.76	3/01	4c
Tuna, chunk, light	6 oz	0.45	3/01	4c
Tuna, light, chunk	lb	1.77	7/01	11r
Turkey, frozen, whole	lb	1.05	7/01	11r
Goods and Services				
Miscellaneous goods and services, ACCRA Index		95.50	3/01	4c
Hunting license	yr	16.00	4/01	34s
Health Care				
Health care, ACCRA Index		87.50	3/01	4c
Cardiac catheterization, ave hospital/ physician charges		15260	1998	77s
Childbirth, Cesarean delivery		11587	1997	13r
Childbirth, vaginal delivery		6725	1997	13r
Dentist's fee, adult teeth cleaning and periodic oral exam	visit	57.67	3/01	4c
Doctor's fee, routine exam, established patient	visit	55.67	3/01	4c
Drugs, expenditures on	yr	399	1999	30r
Health care purchases	yr	1971	1999	30r
Health insurance expenditures	yr	933	1999	30r
Hospital care, private room	day	406.67	3/01	4c

Values are in dollars or fractions of dollars. In the column headed *Ref*, references are shown to sources. Each reference is followed by a letter. These refer to the geographical level for which data were reported: s=State, r=Region, and c=City or metro. The abbreviation *ex* is used to mean *except* or *excluding*; *exp* stands for expenditures. For other abbreviations and further explanations, please see the Introduction.

Florence, AL - continued

Item	Per	Value	Date	Ref.
Health Care				
Hysterectomy, laproscopically-assisted, ave hospital/physician charges		16780	1998	76s
Hysterectomy, vaginal, ave hospital and physician charges		10990	1998	76s
Medicaid dispensing fee		5.40	1999	87s
Medical services expenditures	yr	547	1999	30r
Medical supplies, expenditures on	yr	91	1999	30r
Household Goods				
Dishwashing powder, Cascade	50 oz	3.28	3/01	4c
Floor coverings, expenditures on	yr	44	1999	30r
Furniture, expenditures on	yr	335	1999	30r
Household furnishings and equipment purchases	yr	1328	1999	30r
Household textiles, expenditures on	yr	89	1999	30r
Laundry and cleaning supplies, expenditures on	yr	113	1999	30r
Tissues, facial, Kleenex brand	175	1.27	3/01	4c
Housing				
Housing, ACCRA Index		82.60	3/01	4c
Home price, existing, ave		160100	10/00	90r
Home value, median		115000	2001	53s
House, 2400 sq ft, 8000 sq ft lot, new, urban, utilities	total	180000	3/01	4c
House payment, principal and interest, 25% down payment	mos	889	3/01	4c
Household operation expenditures	yr	553	1999	30r
Housekeeping supplies purchases	yr	473	1999	30r
Housing, expenditures on	yr	10303	1999	30r
Maintenance, repairs, insurance expenditures	yr	699	1999	30r
Monthly rental value of owned home	mos	505	1999	30r
Owned dwellings, expenditures own	yr	3465	1999	30r
Rent expenditures	yr	1641	1999	30r
Rent, apartment, 2 br, 1 1/2-2 baths, unfurn, 950 sq ft, water	mos	473	3/01	4c
Rental unit, 1 bedroom, with utilities	mos	341	4/01	41c
Rental unit, 2 bedroom, with utilities	mos	438	4/01	41c
Rental unit, 3 bedroom, with utilities	mos	547	4/01	41c
Rental unit, 4 bedroom, with utilities	mos	613	4/01	41c
Shelter, expenditures on	yr	5467	1999	30r
Insurance and Pensions				
Life and other personal insurance purchases	yr	414	1999	30r
Pensions and Social Security, expenditures on	yr	2635	1999	30r
Personal insurance and pensions, expenditures on	yr	3048	1999	30r
Legal Fees				
Divorce, filing fee		146.00-193.00	4/01	35s
Driver's license fee	renew	18.50	1999	48s
Driver's license fee	orig	18.50	1999	48s
Personal Goods				
Personal care products and services purchases	yr	393	1999	30r
Shampoo, Alberto VO5	15 oz	1.08	3/01	4c
Toothpaste, Crest or Colgate	6-7 oz	2.20	3/01	4c
Personal Services				
Dry cleaning, man's 2-pc suit		7.54	3/01	4c
Man's haircut, barbershop, no styling		7.75	3/01	4c
Personal services, household, expenditures on	yr	258	1999	30r
Woman's shampoo, trim, blow-dry, no style-change		27.50	3/01	4c
Pets				
Pets, toys, and playground equipment, expenditures on	yr	306	1999	30r

Florence, AL - continued

Item	Per	Value	Date	Ref.
Restaurant Food				
Chicken, fried, thigh and drumstick, KFC/ Church's		2.49	3/01	4c
Hamburger with cheese, McDonald's	1/4 lb	2.09	3/01	4c
Pizza, Pizza Hut or Pizza Inn	11-12 in	9.49	3/01	4c
Taxes				
Federal income taxes paid	yr	2047	1999	30r
Personal taxes, expenditures on	yr	2554	1999	30r
Property taxes paid	yr	726	1999	30r
State and local income taxes paid	yr	363	1999	30r
Transportation				
Transportation, ACCRA Index		87.40	3/01	4c
Cars and trucks, new, expenditures on	yr	1648	1999	30r
Cars and trucks, used, expenditures on	yr	1651	1999	30r
Diesel at the pump	gal	1.19	10/99	73s
Gasoline and motor oil purchases	yr	1052	1999	30r
Gasoline before-tax price (cents)	gal	104.10	10/00	43s
Maintenance and repair expenditures	yr	621	1999	30r
Public transportation, expenditures on	yr	298	1999	30r
Tire balance, computer or spin balance, front	wheel	6.00	3/01	4c
Transportation purchases	yr	6738	1999	30r
Vehicle expenses, miscellaneous, purchases	yr	2033	1999	30r
Vehicle insurance payments	yr	696	1999	30r
Vehicle purchases (net outlay)	yr	3354	1999	30r
Vehicle rental, lease expenditures	yr	352	1999	30r
Utilities				
Utilities, ACCRA Index		86.50	3/01	4c
Electrical bill, average	mos	83.42	9/00	9s
Electricity, 2400 sq ft, new home	mos	100.60	3/01	4c
Electricity, expenditures on	yr	1115	1999	30r
Electricity cost, average	KWh	5.60	9/00	9s
Water and other public services, expenditures on	yr	298	1999	30r
Weddings				
Wedding (national average cost)		19936	2000	33r
Attendants' gifts		321	1998	33r
Bridal attendants' apparel (5 persons)		824	2000	33r
Bride's headpiece/veil		173	1998	33r
Bride's wedding dress		859	1998	33r
Clergy, religious facility fee		242	1998	33r
Engagement ring		3177	1998	33r
Flowers		789	1998	33r
Groom's formalwear rental		99	2000	33r
Limousine		410	1998	33r
Marriage license cost		25.00	4/01	35s
Men's formalwear (ushers, best man)		469	2000	33r
Mother of bride apparel		241	2000	33r
Music		866	1998	33r
Photography and videography		1368	1998	33r
Rehearsal dinner		728	1998	33r
Wedding invitations and announcements		341	1998	33r
Wedding reception		7968	2000	33r
Wedding rings (bride and groom)		1060	1998	33r

Florence, SC

Item	Per	Value	Date	Ref.
Alcoholic Beverages				
Alcoholic beverage purchases	yr	253	1999	30r
Malt beverages, all types, all sizes, any origin	16 oz	0.96	7/01	11r
Appliances				
Major appliances, expenditures on	yr	172	1999	30r
Small appliances, housewares, expenditures on	yr	81	1999	30r
Banking and Money				
Mortgage interest and charges paid	yr	2039	1999	30r
Mortgage principal paid on owned property	yr	1026	1999	30r
Vehicle finance charges paid	yr	365	1999	30r

Values are in dollars or fractions of dollars. In the column headed *Ref*, references are shown to sources. Each reference is followed by a letter. These refer to the geographical level for which data were reported: s=State, r=Region, and c=City or metro. The abbreviation *ex* is used to mean *except* or *excluding*; *exp* stands for *expenditures*. For other abbreviations and further explanations, please see the Introduction.

Florence, SC - continued

Item	Per	Value	Date	Ref.
Charity				
Cash contributions, expenditures	yr	1127	1999	30r
Child Care				
Child raising cost, total, age 0-2	yr	8540	1999	60r
Child raising cost, total, age 3-5	yr	8780	1999	60r
Child raising cost, total, age 6-8	yr	8820	1999	60r
Child raising cost, total, age 9-11	yr	8800	1999	60r
Child raising cost, total, age 12-14	yr	9510	1999	60r
Child raising cost, total, age 15-17	yr	9740	1999	60r
Child's child care and education, age 0-2	yr	1380	1999	60r
Child's child care and education, age 3-5	yr	1520	1999	60r
Child's child care and education, age 6-8	yr	990	1999	60r
Child's child care and education, age 9-11	yr	650	1999	60r
Child's child care and education, age 12-14	yr	490	1999	60r
Child's child care and education, age 15-17	yr	840	1999	60r
Child's clothing, age 0-2	yr	480	1999	60r
Child's clothing, age 3-5	yr	470	1999	60r
Child's clothing, age 6-8	yr	520	1999	60r
Child's clothing, age 9-11	yr	570	1999	60r
Child's clothing, age 12-14	yr	950	1999	60r
Child's clothing, age 15-17	yr	850	1999	60r
Child's food, age 0-2	yr	1000	1999	60r
Child's food, age 3-5	yr	1160	1999	60r
Child's food, age 6-8	yr	1490	1999	60r
Child's food, age 9-11	yr	1770	1999	60r
Child's food, age 12-14	yr	1770	1999	60r
Child's food, age 15-17	yr	1980	1999	60r
Child's health care, age 0-2	yr	620	1999	60r
Child's health care, age 3-5	yr	590	1999	60r
Child's health care, age 6-8	yr	680	1999	60r
Child's health care, age 9-11	yr	720	1999	60r
Child's health care, age 12-14	yr	730	1999	60r
Child's health care, age 15-17	yr	760	1999	60r
Child's housing, age 0-2	yr	3070	1999	60r
Child's housing, age 3-5	yr	3050	1999	60r
Child's housing, age 6-8	yr	3010	1999	60r
Child's housing, age 9-11	yr	2850	1999	60r
Child's housing, age 12-14	yr	3040	1999	60r
Child's housing, age 15-17	yr	2650	1999	60r
Child's personal care, reading, age 0-2	yr	910	1999	60r
Child's personal care, reading, age 3-5	yr	930	1999	60r
Child's personal care, reading, age 6-8	yr	960	1999	60r
Child's personal care, reading, age 9-11	yr	1000	1999	60r
Child's personal care, reading, age 12-14	yr	1170	1999	60r
Child's personal care, reading, age 15-17	yr	950	1999	60r
Clothing				
Apparel and services purchases	yr	1610	1999	30r
Boys, 2 to 15, expenditures on	yr	89	1999	30r
Children under 2, expenditures on	yr	79	1999	30r
Footwear, expenditures on	yr	283	1999	30r
Girls, 2 to 15, expenditures on	yr	103	1999	30r
Men and boys, expenditures on	yr	351	1999	30r
Men, 16 and over, expenditures on	yr	262	1999	30r
Women, 16 and over, expenditures on	yr	538	1999	30r
Communications				
Cable modem installation, Adelphi		54.90	6/99	103s
Cable modem installation, Comcast		95.00	6/99	103s
Cable modem installation, Intermedia		149.95	6/99	103s
Cable modem rate, cable subscriber, Adelphi	mos	34.95	6/99	103s
Cable modem rate, cable subscriber, Comcast	mos	39.95	6/99	103s
Cable modem rate, cable subscriber, Intermedia	mos	49.95	6/99	103s
Cable modem rate, non-cable subscriber, Adelphi	mos	44.95	6/99	103s
Cable modem rate, non-cable subscriber, Comcast	mos	49.95	6/99	103s
Cable modem rate, non-cable subscriber, Intermedia	mos	54.95	6/99	103s
Phone line, single, business, field visit	inst.	64.00	12/97	17s
Phone line, single, business, no field visit	inst.	64.00	12/97	17s
Phone line, single, residence, field visit	inst.	40.00	12/97	17s

Florence, SC - continued

Item	Per	Value	Date	Ref.
Communications - continued				
Phone line, single, residence, no field visit	inst.	40.00	12/97	17s
Postage and stationery, expenditures on	yr	104	1999	30r
Postal rate, express mail, up to half-pound		12.45	7/01	108r
Postal rate, letter, first class, first ounce		0.34	7/01	108r
Postal rate, letter, two ounces		0.57	7/01	108r
Postal rate, post card		0.21	7/01	108r
Postal rate, priority mail, two pounds		3.95	7/01	108r
Postal rate, priority mail, up to one pound		3.50	7/01	108r
Telephone services, expenditures on	yr	860	1999	30r
Education				
Board, 4-year private college/university	yr	1990	1996	38s
Board, 4-year public college/university	yr	1872	1996	38s
Education expenditures	yr	431	1999	30r
Room, 4-year private college/university	yr	1786	1996	38s
Room, 4-year public college/university	yr	1998	1996	38s
Total cost, 4-year private college/university	yr	13517	1996	38s
Total cost, 4-year public college/university	yr	6964	1996	38s
Tuition, 2-year public college/university, in state	yr	1071	1996	38s
Tuition, 4-year private college/university, in state	yr	9741	1996	38s
Tuition, 4-year public college/university	yr	3094	1996	38s
Energy and Fuels				
Electricity	KWh	0.09	7/01	11r
Electricity	500 KWhs	47.29	7/01	11r
Fuel oil #2	gal	1.43	7/01	11r
Fuel oil and other fuels, expenditures on	yr	45	1999	30r
Gas, natural, commercial rate	1000 cf	9.50	11/00	88s
Gasoline, all types	gal	1.60	7/01	11r
Gasoline, unleaded midgrade	gal	1.65	7/01	11r
Gasoline, unleaded premium	gal	1.74	7/01	11r
Natural gas, expenditures on	yr	164	1999	30r
Utility (piped) gas, therm		1.01	7/01	11r
Utility (piped) gas, 40 therms		44.29	7/01	11r
Utility (piped) gas, 100 therms		97.44	7/01	11r
Entertainment				
Entertainment purchases	yr	1574	1999	30r
Fees and admissions paid	yr	371	1999	30r
Reading purchases	yr	121	1999	30r
Television, radios, sound equipment, expenditures on	yr	561	1999	30r
Funerals				
Total cost of funeral		5922.53	1/99	78r
Acknowledgement cards		63.43	1/99	78r
Casket		2258.77	1/99	78r
Cosmetology, hair, other preparation		127.09	1/99	78r
Embalming		393.49	1/99	78r
Funeral at funeral home		367.50	1/99	78r
Hearse (local)		169.66	1/99	78r
Professional service charges		1211.32	1/99	78r
Service car/van		80.69	1/99	78r
Transfer of remains to funeral home		144.25	1/99	78r
Vault		803.50	1/99	78r
Visitation/viewing		302.83	1/99	78r
Groceries				
American processed cheese	lb	3.50	7/01	11r
Bakery products, expenditures on	yr	261	1999	30r
Bananas	lb	0.47	7/01	11r
Beans, dried, any type, all sizes	lb	0.63	7/01	11r
Beef for stew, boneless	lb	2.86	7/01	11r
Beef, expenditures on	yr	210	1999	30r
Bologna, all beef or mixed	lb	2.29	7/01	11r
Bread, French	lb	1.66	7/01	11r
Bread, white, pan	lb	0.87	7/01	11r
Bread, whole wheat, pan	lb	1.38	7/01	11r
Broccoli	lb	1.04	7/01	11r
Butter, salted, grade AA, stick	lb	2.26	7/01	11r
Butter, yoghurt, cheese, etc, expenditures on	yr	170	1999	30r

Values are in dollars or fractions of dollars. In the column headed *Ref*, references are shown to sources. Each reference is followed by a letter. These refer to the geographical level for which data were reported: s=State, r=Region, and c=City or metro. The abbreviation *ex* is used to mean *except* or *excluding; exp* stands for expenditures. For other abbreviations and further explanations, please see the Introduction.

Florence, SC - continued

Item	Per	Value	Date	Ref.
Groceries				
Cabbage	lb	0.42	7/01	11r
Cereals and cereal products, expenditures on	yr	140	1999	30r
Cheddar cheese, natural	lb	3.75	7/01	11r
Chicken breast, bone-in	lb	1.85	7/01	11r
Chicken legs, bone-in	lb	1.34	7/01	11r
Chicken, fresh, whole	lb	1.05	7/01	11r
Chops, boneless	lb	4.13	7/01	11r
Chuck roast, graded and ungraded, excl U.S. prime and choice	lb	2.35	7/01	11r
Chuck roast, U.S. choice, boneless	lb	2.67	7/01	11r
Coffee, 100%, ground roast, all sizes	lb	2.88	7/01	11r
Coffee, instant, plain, regular, all sizes	16 oz	9.25	7/01	11r
Cola, non diet,	2 liter	1.11	7/01	11r
Crackers, soda, salted	lb	1.70	7/01	11r
Dairy product purchases	yr	282	1999	30r
Eggs, expenditures on	yr	32	1999	30r
Fats and oils, expenditures on	yr	79	1999	30r
Fish and seafood, expenditures on	yr	99	1999	30r
Flour, white, all purpose	lb	0.32	7/01	11r
Food (excl fruit and vegetables), eaten at home, purchases	yr	815	1999	30r
Food cooked on trips, expenditures on	yr	36	1999	30r
Food purchases	yr	4533	1999	30r
Food purchases, eaten away from home	yr	1873	1999	30r
Food purchases, food eaten at home	yr	2660	1999	30r
Fresh fruits, expenditures on	yr	128	1999	30r
Fresh milk and cream, expenditures on	yr	112	1999	30r
Fresh vegetables, expenditures on	yr	131	1999	30r
Fruit and vegetable purchases	yr	438	1999	30r
Grapefruit	lb	0.59	7/01	11r
Grapes, Thompson, seedless	lb	2.12	7/01	11r
Ground beef, 100% beef	lb	1.76	7/01	11r
Ground beef, lean and extra lean	lb	2.60	7/01	11r
Ground chuck, 100% beef	lb	2.08	7/01	11r
Ham, boneless, excl canned	lb	2.71	7/01	11r
Ham, rump or shank half, bone-in, smoked	lb	2.19	7/01	11r
Ice cream, prepackaged, bulk, regular	1/2 gal	3.93	7/01	11r
Lemons	lb	1.32	7/01	11r
Lettuce, iceberg	lb	0.76	7/01	11r
Milk, fresh, low fat,	gal	2.75	7/01	11r
Milk, fresh, whole, fortified	gal	2.97	7/01	11r
Nonalcoholic beverages, expenditures on	yr	228	1999	30r
Orange juice, frozen concentrate	16 oz	1.95	7/01	11r
Oranges, Navel	lb	0.73	7/01	11r
Oranges, Valencia	lb	0.55	7/01	11r
Peanut butter, creamy, all sizes	lb	1.83	7/01	11r
Pears, Anjou	lb	0.98	7/01	11r
Pork chops, center cut, bone-in	lb	3.33	7/01	11r
Pork sausage, fresh, loose	lb	2.59	7/01	11r
Pork shoulder picnic, bone-in, smoked	lb	1.12	7/01	11r
Pork, expenditures on	yr	162	1999	30r
Potato chips	16 oz	3.59	7/01	11r
Potatoes, frozen, french fried	lb	1.00	7/01	11r
Potatoes, white, all types	lb	0.44	7/01	11r
Poultry, expenditures on	yr	137	1999	30r
Processed fruits, expenditures on	yr	97	1999	30r
Processed vegetables, expenditures on	yr	82	1999	30r
Rice, white, long grain, uncooked	lb	0.51	7/01	11r
Round roast, graded and ungraded, excl U.S. prime and choice	lb	2.96	7/01	11r
Round steak, graded and ungraded, excl U.S. prime and choice	lb	3.11	7/01	11r
Sirloin steak, graded and ungraded, excl U.S. prime and choice	lb	4.23	7/01	11r
Spaghetti and macaroni	lb	0.78	7/01	11r
Steak, round, U.S. choice, boneless	lb	3.56	7/01	11r
Steak, sirloin, U.S. choice, boneless	lb	5.65	7/01	11r
Strawberries, dry pint	12 oz	1.50	7/01	11r
Sugar and other sweets, expenditures on	yr	99	1999	30r
Sugar, white, 33-80 ounce package	lb	0.39	7/01	11r
Sugar, white, all sizes	lb	0.42	7/01	11r

Florence, SC - continued

Item	Per	Value	Date	Ref.
Groceries - continued				
Tobacco products and smoking supplies purchases	yr	288	1999	30r
Tomatoes, field grown	lb	1.43	7/01	11r
Tuna, light, chunk	lb	1.77	7/01	11r
Turkey, frozen, whole	lb	1.05	7/01	11r
Goods and Services				
B&B Japanese maple (acer japonicum)	gal	49.98- 129.00	4/00	93r
Boxwood (buxus)	2 gal	12.99- 16.99	4/00	93r
Daylilly (hemerocallis)	gal	4.99- 8.99	4/00	93r
Flat of annuals		11.00- 13.92	4/00	93r
Fountain grass (pennisetum)	gal	5.98- 7.98	4/00	93r
Hanging basket (10 in)		7.99- 14.98	4/00	93r
Hardy geranium (geranium)	gal	5.98- 8.00	4/00	93r
Hosta (hosta)	gal	4.99- 10.98	4/00	93r
Lilac (syrubga vulgaris)	2 gal	12.99- 21.99	4/00	93r
Rhododendron (rhododendron)	2 gal	14.99- 24.99	4/00	93r
Sage (salvia)	gal	5.98- 6.99	4/00	93r
Wintercreeper euonymus (euonymus fortunei)	2 gal	7.99- 89.99	4/00	93r
Hunting license	yr	12.00	4/01	34s
Health Care				
Cardiac catheterization, ave hospital/ physician charges		12360	1998	77s
Childbirth, Cesarean delivery		11587	1997	13r
Childbirth, vaginal delivery		6725	1997	13r
Drugs, expenditures on	yr	399	1999	30r
Health care purchases	yr	1971	1999	30r
Health insurance expenditures	yr	933	1999	30r
Hysterectomy, laproscopically-assisted, ave hospital/physician charges		11920	1998	76s
Hysterectomy, vaginal, ave hospital and physician charges		4890	1998	76s
Medicaid dispensing fee		4.05	1999	87s
Medical services expenditures	yr	547	1999	30r
Medical supplies, expenditures on	yr	91	1999	30r
Plastic surgery, breast augmentation		2870	2000	7r
Plastic surgery, breast lift		3649	2000	7r
Plastic surgery, facelift		5008	2000	7r
Plastic surgery, hair transplantation		3425	2000	7r
Plastic surgery, lip augmentation		1227	2000	7r
Plastic surgery, lower body lift		4793	2000	7r
Plastic surgery, thigh lift		3862	2000	7r
Household Goods				
Floor coverings, expenditures on	yr	44	1999	30r
Furniture, expenditures on	yr	335	1999	30r
Household furnishings and equipment purchases	yr	1328	1999	30r
Household textiles, expenditures on	yr	89	1999	30r
Laundry and cleaning supplies, expenditures on	yr	113	1999	30r
Housing				
Home price, existing, ave		160100	10/00	90r
Home value, median		119000	2001	53s
Household operation expenditures	yr	553	1999	30r
Housekeeping supplies purchases	yr	473	1999	30r
Housing, expenditures on	yr	10303	1999	30r
Maintenance, repairs, insurance expenditures	yr	699	1999	30r
Monthly rental value of owned home	mos	505	1999	30r

Values are in dollars or fractions of dollars. In the column headed *Ref*, references are shown to sources. Each reference is followed by a letter. These refer to the geographical level for which data were reported: s=State, r=Region, and c=City or metro. The abbreviation *ex* is used to mean *except* or *excluding*; *exp* stands for *expenditures*. For other abbreviations and further explanations, please see the Introduction.

Florence, SC - continued

Item	Per	Value	Date	Ref.
Housing				
Owned dwellings, expenditures own	yr	3465	1999	30r
Rent expenditures	yr	1641	1999	30r
Rental unit, 1 bedroom, with utilities	mos	370	4/01	41c
Rental unit, 2 bedroom, with utilities	mos	481	4/01	41c
Rental unit, 3 bedroom, with utilities	mos	600	4/01	41c
Rental unit, 4 bedroom, with utilities	mos	673	4/01	41c
Shelter, expenditures on	yr	5467	1999	30r
Insurance and Pensions				
Auto insurance	yr	655.33	1998	86s
Life and other personal insurance purchases	yr	414	1999	30r
Pensions and Social Security, expenditures on	yr	2635	1999	30r
Personal insurance and pensions, expenditures on	yr	3048	1999	30r
Legal Fees				
Combination hunting and fishing license	yr	20.00	4/01	34s
Driver's license fee	renew	12.50	1999	48s
Driver's license fee	orig	12.50	1999	48s
Fishing license	yr	10.00	4/01	34s
Personal Goods				
Personal care products and services purchases	yr	393	1999	30r
Personal Services				
Personal services, household, expenditures on	yr	258	1999	30r
Pets				
Pets, toys, and playground equipment, expenditures on	yr	306	1999	30r
Taxes				
Federal income taxes paid	yr	2047	1999	30r
Personal taxes, expenditures on	yr	2554	1999	30r
Property taxes paid	yr	726	1999	30r
State and local income taxes paid	yr	363	1999	30r
Transportation				
Bus fare, one-way	trip	1.00	2000	1c
Cars and trucks, new, expenditures on	yr	1648	1999	30r
Cars and trucks, used, expenditures on	yr	1651	1999	30r
Diesel at the pump	gal	1.13	10/99	73s
Gasoline and motor oil purchases	yr	1052	1999	30r
Gasoline before-tax price (cents)	gal	101.70	10/00	43s
Maintenance and repair expenditures	yr	621	1999	30r
Public transportation, expenditures on	yr	298	1999	30r
Transportation purchases	yr	6738	1999	30r
Vehicle expenses, miscellaneous, purchases	yr	2033	1999	30r
Vehicle insurance payments	yr	696	1999	30r
Vehicle purchases (net outlay)	yr	3354	1999	30r
Vehicle rental, lease expenditures	yr	352	1999	30r
Utilities				
Electrical bill, average	mos	86.42	9/00	9s
Electricity, expenditures on	yr	1115	1999	30r
Electricity, summer, 250 KWh	mos	25.97	2/96	96c
Electricity, summer, 500 KWh	mos	45.45	2/96	96c
Electricity, summer, 750 KWh	mos	64.92	2/96	96c
Electricity, summer, 1000 KWh	mos	82.39	2/96	96c
Electricity cost, average	KWh	5.40	9/00	9s
Water and other public services, expenditures on	yr	298	1999	30r
Weddings				
Wedding (national average cost)		19936	2000	33r
Wedding (regional average total cost)		16293	1997	110r
Attendants' gifts		321	1998	33r
Bridal attendants' apparel (5 persons)		824	2000	33r
Bride's headpiece/veil		173	1998	33r
Bride's wedding dress		859	1998	33r
Clergy, religious facility fee		242	1998	33r
Engagement ring		3177	1998	33r
Flowers		789	1998	33r

Florence, SC - continued

Item	Per	Value	Date	Ref.
Weddings - continued				
Groom's formalwear rental		99	2000	33r
Limousine		410	1998	33r
Marriage license cost		25.00	4/01	35s
Men's formalwear (ushers, best man)		469	2000	33r
Mother of bride apparel		241	2000	33r
Music		866	1998	33r
Photography and videography		1368	1998	33r
Rehearsal dinner		728	1998	33r
Wedding invitations and announcements		341	1998	33r
Wedding reception		7968	2000	33r
Wedding rings (bride and groom)		1060	1998	33r

Fort Collins-Loveland, CO

Item	Per	Value	Date	Ref.
Communications				
Cable modem installation, AT&T-BIS		150.00	6/99	103s
Cable modem rate, cable subscriber, AT&T-BIS	mos	39.95	6/99	103s
Phone line, single, business, field visit	inst.	70.00	12/97	17s
Phone line, single, business, no field visit	inst.	70.00	12/97	17s
Phone line, single, residence, field visit	inst.	35.00	12/97	17s
Phone line, single, residence, no field visit	inst.	35.00	12/97	17s
Postal rate, express mail, up to half-pound		12.45	7/01	108r
Postal rate, letter, first class, first ounce		0.34	7/01	108r
Postal rate, letter, two ounces		0.57	7/01	108r
Postal rate, post card		0.21	7/01	108r
Postal rate, priority mail, two pounds		3.95	7/01	108r
Postal rate, priority mail, up to one pound		3.50	7/01	108r
Education				
Board, 4-year private college/university	yr	2750	1996	38s
Board, 4-year public college/university	yr	2564	1996	38s
Room, 4-year private college/university	yr	2574	1996	38s
Room, 4-year public college/university	yr	2000	1996	38s
Total cost, 4-year private college/university	yr	17120	1996	38s
Total cost, 4-year public college/university	yr	7037	1996	38s
Tuition, 2-year public college/university, in state	yr	1340	1996	38s
Tuition, 4-year private college/university, in state	yr	11796	1996	38s
Tuition, 4-year public college/university	yr	2473	1996	38s
Energy and Fuels				
Gas, natural, commercial rate	1000 cf	6.42	11/00	88s
Funerals				
Total cost of funeral		5401.08	1/99	78r
Acknowledgement cards		33.64	1/99	78r
Casket		2170.43	1/99	78r
Cosmetology, hair, other preparation		136.32	1/99	78r
Embalming		319.13	1/99	78r
Funeral at funeral home		370.21	1/99	78r
Hearse (local)		161.04	1/99	78r
Professional service charges		963.15	1/99	78r
Service car/van		133.99	1/99	78r
Transfer of remains to funeral home		159.82	1/99	78r
Vault		778.07	1/99	78r
Visitation/viewing		175.28	1/99	78r
Groceries				
Bacon	lb	3.99	5/99	8s
Bread, white, 20 oz loaf		0.64	5/99	8s
Cheddar cheese, mild	lb	3.59	5/99	8s
Cheerios, 10 oz box		2.99	5/99	8s
Corn oil, Mazola, 32 oz		2.75	5/99	8s
Flour, all purpose	5 lb	1.69	5/99	8s
Grade A large eggs	doz	1.59	5/99	8s
Ground chuck	lb	1.99	5/99	8s
Mayonnaise, Kraft, 32 oz		2.50	5/99	8s
Potatoes, russet	5 lb	1.79	5/99	8s
Red Delicious apples	lb	1.39	5/99	8s
Sirloin tip roast	lb	3.99	5/99	8s
Vegetable oil, Crisco, 32 oz		1.89	5/99	8s

Values are in dollars or fractions of dollars. In the column headed *Ref*, references are shown to sources. Each reference is followed by a letter. These refer to the geographical level for which data were reported: s=State, r=Region, and c=City or metro. The abbreviation *ex* is used to mean *except* or *excluding*; *exp* stands for expenditures. For other abbreviations and further explanations, please see the Introduction.

Fort Collins-Loveland, CO - continued

Item	Per	Value	Date	Ref.
Groceries				
Whole fryer	lb	1.99	5/99	8s
Whole milk	gal	0.89	5/99	8s
Goods and Services				
Hunting license	yr	15.25	4/01	34s
Health Care				
Cardiac catheterization, ave hospital/ physician charges		17910	1998	77s
Childbirth, Cesarean delivery		11587	1997	13r
Childbirth, vaginal delivery		6725	1997	13r
Hysterectomy, laproscopically-assisted, ave hospital/physician charges		16210	1998	76s
Hysterectomy, vaginal, ave hospital and physician charges		11690	1998	76s
Medicaid dispensing fee		4.08	1999	87s
Housing				
Home value, median		173000	2001	53s
Rental unit, 1 bedroom, with utilities	mos	522	4/01	41c
Rental unit, 2 bedroom, with utilities	mos	681	4/01	41c
Rental unit, 3 bedroom, with utilities	mos	947	4/01	41c
Rental unit, 4 bedroom, with utilities	mos	1118	4/01	41c
Legal Fees				
Divorce, filing fee		65.00	4/01	35s
Driver's license fee	orig	15.00	1999	48s
Driver's license fee	renew	15.00	1999	48s
Transportation				
Diesel at the pump	gal	1.28	10/99	73s
Gasoline before-tax price (cents)	gal	117.00	10/00	43s
Travel				
Hotel room	night	118.98	2/01	95s
Utilities				
Electrical bill, average	mos	47.17	9/00	9s
Electricity cost, average	KWh	5.90	9/00	9s
Weddings				
Wedding (national average cost)		19936	2000	33r
Attendants' gifts		321	1998	33r
Bridal attendants' apparel (5 persons)		824	2000	33r
Bride's headpiece/veil		173	1998	33r
Bride's wedding dress		859	1998	33r
Clergy, religious facility fee		242	1998	33r
Engagement ring		3177	1998	33r
Flowers		789	1998	33r
Groom's formalwear rental		99	2000	33r
Limousine		410	1998	33r
Marriage license cost		20.00	4/01	35s
Men's formalwear (ushers, best man)		469	2000	33r
Mother of bride apparel		241	2000	33r
Music		866	1998	33r
Photography and videography		1368	1998	33r
Rehearsal dinner		728	1998	33r
Wedding invitations and announcements		341	1998	33r
Wedding reception		7968	2000	33r
Wedding rings (bride and groom)		1060	1998	33r

Fort Lauderdale, FL

Item	Per	Value	Date	Ref.
Alcoholic Beverages				
Alcoholic beverage purchases	yr	253	1999	30r
Malt beverages, all types, all sizes, any origin	16 oz	0.96	7/01	11r
Appliances				
Major appliances, expenditures on	yr	172	1999	30r
Small appliances, housewares, expenditures on	yr	81	1999	30r
Banking and Money				
Mortgage interest and charges paid	yr	2039	1999	30r
Mortgage principal paid on owned property	yr	1026	1999	30r
Vehicle finance charges paid	yr	365	1999	30r

Fort Lauderdale, FL - continued

Item	Per	Value	Date	Ref.
Business Expenses				
Business travel, car rental	day	51	2001	3c
Business travel, food	day	49	2001	3c
Business travel, hotel	day	129	2001	3c
Charity				
Cash contributions, expenditures	yr	1127	1999	30r
Child Care				
Child raising cost, total, age 0-2	yr	8540	1999	60r
Child raising cost, total, age 3-5	yr	8780	1999	60r
Child raising cost, total, age 6-8	yr	8820	1999	60r
Child raising cost, total, age 9-11	yr	8800	1999	60r
Child raising cost, total, age 12-14	yr	9510	1999	60r
Child raising cost, total, age 15-17	yr	9740	1999	60r
Child's child care and education, age 0-2	yr	1380	1999	60r
Child's child care and education, age 3-5	yr	1520	1999	60r
Child's child care and education, age 6-8	yr	990	1999	60r
Child's child care and education, age 9-11	yr	650	1999	60r
Child's child care and education, age 12-14	yr	490	1999	60r
Child's child care and education, age 15-17	yr	840	1999	60r
Child's clothing, age 0-2	yr	480	1999	60r
Child's clothing, age 3-5	yr	470	1999	60r
Child's clothing, age 6-8	yr	520	1999	60r
Child's clothing, age 9-11	yr	570	1999	60r
Child's clothing, age 12-14	yr	950	1999	60r
Child's clothing, age 15-17	yr	850	1999	60r
Child's food, age 0-2	yr	1000	1999	60r
Child's food, age 3-5	yr	1160	1999	60r
Child's food, age 6-8	yr	1490	1999	60r
Child's food, age 9-11	yr	1770	1999	60r
Child's food, age 12-14	yr	1770	1999	60r
Child's food, age 15-17	yr	1980	1999	60r
Child's health care, age 0-2	yr	620	1999	60r
Child's health care, age 3-5	yr	590	1999	60r
Child's health care, age 6-8	yr	680	1999	60r
Child's health care, age 9-11	yr	720	1999	60r
Child's health care, age 12-14	yr	730	1999	60r
Child's health care, age 15-17	yr	760	1999	60r
Child's housing, age 0-2	yr	3070	1999	60r
Child's housing, age 3-5	yr	3050	1999	60r
Child's housing, age 6-8	yr	3010	1999	60r
Child's housing, age 9-11	yr	2850	1999	60r
Child's housing, age 12-14	yr	3040	1999	60r
Child's housing, age 15-17	yr	2650	1999	60r
Child's personal care, reading, age 0-2	yr	910	1999	60r
Child's personal care, reading, age 3-5	yr	930	1999	60r
Child's personal care, reading, age 6-8	yr	960	1999	60r
Child's personal care, reading, age 9-11	yr	1000	1999	60r
Child's personal care, reading, age 12-14	yr	1170	1999	60r
Child's personal care, reading, age 15-17	yr	950	1999	60r
Clothing				
Apparel and services purchases	yr	1610	1999	30r
Boys, 2 to 15, expenditures on	yr	89	1999	30r
Children under 2, expenditures on	yr	79	1999	30r
Footwear, expenditures on	yr	283	1999	30r
Girls, 2 to 15, expenditures on	yr	103	1999	30r
Men and boys, expenditures on	yr	351	1999	30r
Men, 16 and over, expenditures on	yr	262	1999	30r
Women, 16 and over, expenditures on	yr	538	1999	30r
Communications				
Cable modem installation, Adelphi		54.90	6/99	103s
Cable modem installation, Comcast		95.00	6/99	103s
Cable modem installation, Media One		100.00	6/99	103s
Cable modem installation, Time Warner		75.00-225.00	6/99	103s
Cable modem rate, cable subscriber, Adelphi	mos	34.95	6/99	103s
Cable modem rate, cable subscriber, Comcast	mos	39.95	6/99	103s
Cable modem rate, cable subscriber, Media One	mos	34.95-39.95	6/99	103s
Cable modem rate, cable subscriber, Time Warner	mos	39.95-49.95	6/99	103s

Values are in dollars or fractions of dollars. In the column headed *Ref*, references are shown to sources. Each reference is followed by a letter. These refer to the geographical level for which data were reported: s=State, r=Region, and c=City or metro. The abbreviation *ex* is used to mean *except* or *excluding*; *exp* stands for expenditures. For other abbreviations and further explanations, please see the Introduction.

Fort Lauderdale, FL - continued

Item	Per	Value	Date	Ref.
Communications				
Cable modem rate, non-cable subscriber, Adelphi	mos	44.95	6/99	103s
Cable modem rate, non-cable subscriber, Comcast	mos	49.95	6/99	103s
Cable modem rate, non-cable subscriber, Media One	mos	49.95	6/99	103s
Cable modem rate, non-cable subscriber, Time Warner	mos	39.95-54.95	6/99	103s
Phone line, single, business, field visit	inst.	56.00	12/97	17s
Phone line, single, business, no field visit	inst.	56.00	12/97	17s
Phone line, single, residence, field visit	inst.	40.00	12/97	17s
Phone line, single, residence, no field visit	inst.	40.00	12/97	17s
Postage and stationery, expenditures on	yr	104	1999	30r
Postal rate, express mail, up to half-pound		12.45	7/01	108r
Postal rate, letter, first class, first ounce		0.34	7/01	108r
Postal rate, letter, two ounces		0.57	7/01	108r
Postal rate, post card		0.21	7/01	108r
Postal rate, priority mail, two pounds		3.95	7/01	108r
Postal rate, priority mail, up to one pound		3.50	7/01	108r
Telephone bill, business, basic rate	mos	29.10	12/97	18c
Telephone bill, residential, basic rate	mos	10.65	12/97	18c
Telephone services, expenditures on	yr	860	1999	30r
Education				
Board, 4-year private college/university	yr	2236	1996	38s
Board, 4-year public college/university	yr	2295	1996	38s
Education expenditures	yr	431	1999	30r
Room, 4-year private college/university	yr	2428	1996	38s
Room, 4-year public college/university	yr	2193	1996	38s
Total cost, 4-year private college/university	yr	15028	1996	38s
Total cost, 4-year public college/university	yr	6254	1996	38s
Tuition, 2-year public college/university, in state	yr	1103	1996	38s
Tuition, 4-year private college/university, in state	yr	10364	1996	38s
Tuition, 4-year public college/university	yr	1767	1996	38s
Energy and Fuels				
Electricity	500 KWhs	47.29	7/01	11r
Electricity	KWh	0.09	7/01	11r
Fuel oil #2	gal	1.43	7/01	11r
Fuel oil and other fuels, expenditures on	yr	45	1999	30r
Gas, natural, commercial rate	1000 cf	8.44	11/00	88s
Gasoline, all types	gal	1.60	7/01	11r
Gasoline, unleaded midgrade	gal	1.65	7/01	11r
Gasoline, unleaded premium	gal	1.74	7/01	11r
Natural gas, expenditures on	yr	164	1999	30r
Utility (piped) gas, therm		1.01	7/01	11r
Utility (piped) gas, 40 therms		44.29	7/01	11r
Utility (piped) gas, 100 therms		97.44	7/01	11r
Entertainment				
Entertainment purchases	yr	1574	1999	30r
Fees and admissions paid	yr	371	1999	30r
Reading purchases	yr	121	1999	30r
Television, radios, sound equipment, expenditures on	yr	561	1999	30r
Funerals				
Total cost of funeral		5922.53	1/99	78r
Acknowledgement cards		63.43	1/99	78r
Casket		2258.77	1/99	78r
Cosmetology, hair, other preparation		127.09	1/99	78r
Embalming		393.49	1/99	78r
Funeral at funeral home		367.50	1/99	78r
Hearse (local)		169.66	1/99	78r
Professional service charges		1211.32	1/99	78r
Service car/van		80.69	1/99	78r
Transfer of remains to funeral home		144.25	1/99	78r
Vault		803.50	1/99	78r
Visitation/viewing		302.83	1/99	78r

Fort Lauderdale, FL - continued

Item	Per	Value	Date	Ref.
Groceries				
American processed cheese	lb	3.50	7/01	11r
Bakery products, expenditures on	yr	261	1999	30r
Bananas	lb	0.47	7/01	11r
Beans, dried, any type, all sizes	lb	0.63	7/01	11r
Beef for stew, boneless	lb	2.86	7/01	11r
Beef, expenditures on	yr	210	1999	30r
Bologna, all beef or mixed	lb	2.29	7/01	11r
Bread, French	lb	1.66	7/01	11r
Bread, white, pan	lb	0.87	7/01	11r
Bread, whole wheat, pan	lb	1.38	7/01	11r
Broccoli	lb	1.04	7/01	11r
Butter, salted, grade AA, stick	lb	2.26	7/01	11r
Butter, yoghurt, cheese, etc, expenditures on	yr	170	1999	30r
Cabbage	lb	0.42	7/01	11r
Cereals and cereal products, expenditures on	yr	140	1999	30r
Cheddar cheese, natural	lb	3.75	7/01	11r
Chicken breast, bone-in	lb	1.85	7/01	11r
Chicken legs, bone-in	lb	1.34	7/01	11r
Chicken, fresh, whole	lb	1.05	7/01	11r
Chops, boneless	lb	4.13	7/01	11r
Chuck roast, graded and ungraded, excl U.S. prime and choice	lb	2.35	7/01	11r
Chuck roast, U.S. choice, boneless	lb	2.67	7/01	11r
Coffee, 100%, ground roast, all sizes	lb	2.88	7/01	11r
Coffee, instant, plain, regular, all sizes	16 oz	9.25	7/01	11r
Cola, non diet	2 liter	1.11	7/01	11r
Crackers, soda, salted	lb	1.70	7/01	11r
Dairy product purchases	yr	282	1999	30r
Eggs, expenditures on	yr	32	1999	30r
Fats and oils, expenditures on	yr	79	1999	30r
Fish and seafood, expenditures on	yr	99	1999	30r
Flour, white, all purpose	lb	0.32	7/01	11r
Food (excl fruit and vegetables), eaten at home, purchases	yr	815	1999	30r
Food cooked on trips, expenditures on	yr	36	1999	30r
Food purchases	yr	4533	1999	30r
Food purchases, eaten away from home	yr	1873	1999	30r
Food purchases, food eaten at home	yr	2660	1999	30r
Fresh fruits, expenditures on	yr	128	1999	30r
Fresh milk and cream, expenditures on	yr	112	1999	30r
Fresh vegetables, expenditures on	yr	131	1999	30r
Fruit and vegetable purchases	yr	438	1999	30r
Grapefruit	lb	0.59	7/01	11r
Grapes, Thompson, seedless	lb	2.12	7/01	11r
Ground beef, 100% beef	lb	1.76	7/01	11r
Ground beef, lean and extra lean	lb	2.60	7/01	11r
Ground chuck, 100% beef	lb	2.08	7/01	11r
Ham, boneless, excl canned	lb	2.71	7/01	11r
Ham, rump or shank half, bone-in, smoked	lb	2.19	7/01	11r
Ice cream, prepackaged, bulk, regular	1/2 gal	3.93	7/01	11r
Lemons	lb	1.32	7/01	11r
Lettuce, iceberg	lb	0.76	7/01	11r
Milk, fresh, low fat,	gal	2.75	7/01	11r
Milk, fresh, whole, fortified	gal	2.97	7/01	11r
Nonalcoholic beverages, expenditures on	yr	228	1999	30r
Orange juice, frozen concentrate	16 oz	1.95	7/01	11r
Oranges, Navel	lb	0.73	7/01	11r
Oranges, Valencia	lb	0.55	7/01	11r
Peanut butter, creamy, all sizes	lb	1.83	7/01	11r
Pears, Anjou	lb	0.98	7/01	11r
Pork chops, center cut, bone-in	lb	3.33	7/01	11r
Pork sausage, fresh, loose	lb	2.59	7/01	11r
Pork shoulder picnic, bone-in, smoked	lb	1.12	7/01	11r
Pork, expenditures on	yr	162	1999	30r
Potato chips	16 oz	3.59	7/01	11r
Potatoes, frozen, french fried	lb	1.00	7/01	11r
Potatoes, white, all types	lb	0.44	7/01	11r
Poultry, expenditures on	yr	137	1999	30r
Processed fruits, expenditures on	yr	97	1999	30r
Processed vegetables, expenditures on	yr	82	1999	30r
Rice, white, long grain, uncooked	lb	0.51	7/01	11r

Values are in dollars or fractions of dollars. In the column headed *Ref*, references are shown to sources. Each reference is followed by a letter. These refer to the geographical level for which data were reported: s=State, r=Region, and c=City or metro. The abbreviation *ex* is used to mean *except* or *excluding*; *exp* stands for expenditures. For other abbreviations and further explanations, please see the Introduction.

Fort Lauderdale, FL - continued

Item	Per	Value	Date	Ref.
Groceries				
Round roast, graded and ungraded, excl U.S. prime and choice	lb	2.96	7/01	11r
Round steak, graded and ungraded, excl U.S. prime and choice	lb	3.11	7/01	11r
Sirloin steak, graded and ungraded, excl U.S. prime and choice	lb	4.23	7/01	11r
Spaghetti and macaroni	lb	0.78	7/01	11r
Steak, round, U.S. choice, boneless	lb	3.56	7/01	11r
Steak, sirloin, U.S. choice, boneless	lb	5.65	7/01	11r
Strawberries, dry pint	12 oz	1.50	7/01	11r
Sugar and other sweets, expenditures on	yr	99	1999	30r
Sugar, white, 33-80 ounce package	lb	0.39	7/01	11r
Sugar, white, all sizes	lb	0.42	7/01	11r
Tobacco products and smoking supplies purchases	yr	288	1999	30r
Tomatoes, field grown	lb	1.43	7/01	11r
Tuna, light, chunk	lb	1.77	7/01	11r
Turkey, frozen, whole	lb	1.05	7/01	11r
Goods and Services				
B&B Japanese maple (acer japonicum)	gal	49.98-129.00	4/00	93r
Boxwood (buxus)	2 gal	12.99-16.99	4/00	93r
Daylily (hemerocallis)	gal	4.99-8.99	4/00	93r
Flat of annuals		11.00-13.92	4/00	93r
Fountain grass (pennisetum)	gal	5.98-7.98	4/00	93r
Hanging basket (10 in)		7.99-14.98	4/00	93r
Hardy geranium (geranium)	gal	5.98-8.00	4/00	93r
Hosta (hosta)	gal	4.99-10.98	4/00	93r
Lilac (syrubga vulgaris)	2 gal	12.99-21.99	4/00	93r
Rhododendron (rhododendron)	2 gal	14.99-24.99	4/00	93r
Sage (salvia)	gal	5.98-6.99	4/00	93r
Wintercreeper euonymus (euonymus fortunei)	2 gal	7.99-89.99	4/00	93r
Hunting license	yr	12.50	4/01	34s
Health Care				
Cardiac catheterization, ave hospital/ physician charges		15060	1998	77s
Childbirth, Cesarean delivery		11587	1997	13r
Childbirth, vaginal delivery		6725	1997	13r
Drugs, expenditures on	yr	399	1999	30r
Health care purchases	yr	1971	1999	30r
Health insurance expenditures	yr	933	1999	30r
Hysterectomy, laproscopically-assisted, ave hospital/physician charges		14760	1998	76s
Hysterectomy, vaginal, ave hospital and physician charges		11320	1998	76s
Medicaid dispensing fee		4.23	1999	87s
Medical services expenditures	yr	547	1999	30r
Medical supplies, expenditures on	yr	91	1999	30r
Plastic surgery, breast augmentation		2870	2000	7r
Plastic surgery, breast lift		3649	2000	7r
Plastic surgery, facelift		5008	2000	7r
Plastic surgery, hair transplantation		3425	2000	7r
Plastic surgery, lip augmentation		1227	2000	7r
Plastic surgery, lower body lift		4793	2000	7r
Plastic surgery, thigh lift		3862	2000	7r
Household Goods				
Floor coverings, expenditures on	yr	44	1999	30r
Furniture, expenditures on	yr	335	1999	30r
Household furnishings and equipment purchases	yr	1328	1999	30r

Fort Lauderdale, FL - continued

Item	Per	Value	Date	Ref.
Household Goods - continued				
Household textiles, expenditures on	yr	89	1999	30r
Laundry and cleaning supplies, expenditures on	yr	113	1999	30r
Housing				
Home, 2200 sq ft, 4-br, 2-bath, 2-car garage, average		204666	2000	47c
Home price, existing, ave		160100	10/00	90r
Home value, median		104000	2001	53s
Household operation expenditures	yr	553	1999	30r
Housekeeping supplies purchases	yr	473	1999	30r
Housing, expenditures on	yr	10303	1999	30r
Maintenance, repairs, insurance expenditures	yr	699	1999	30r
Monthly rental value of owned home	mos	505	1999	30r
Owned dwellings, expenditures own	yr	3465	1999	30r
Rent expenditures	yr	1641	1999	30r
Rental unit, 1 bedroom, with utilities	mos	580	4/01	41c
Rental unit, 2 bedroom, with utilities	mos	718	4/01	41c
Rental unit, 3 bedroom, with utilities	mos	999	4/01	41c
Rental unit, 4 bedroom, with utilities	mos	1175	4/01	41c
Shelter, expenditures on	yr	5467	1999	30r
Insurance and Pensions				
Life and other personal insurance purchases	yr	414	1999	30r
Medigap health insurance, Plan H	yr	2887	2000	69s
Medigap health insurance, Plan I	yr	3302	2000	69s
Medigap health insurance, Plan J	yr	3889	2000	69s
Pensions and Social Security, expenditures on	yr	2635	1999	30r
Personal insurance and pensions, expenditures on	yr	3048	1999	30r
Legal Fees				
Divorce, filing fee		65.00-85.00	4/01	35s
Driver's license fee	renew	15.00	1999	48s
Driver's license fee	orig	20.00	1999	48s
Personal Goods				
Personal care products and services purchases	yr	393	1999	30r
Personal Services				
Personal services, household, expenditures on	yr	258	1999	30r
Pets				
Pets, toys, and playground equipment, expenditures on	yr	306	1999	30r
Taxes				
Federal income taxes paid	yr	2047	1999	30r
Personal taxes, expenditures on	yr	2554	1999	30r
Property taxes paid	yr	726	1999	30r
State and local income taxes paid	yr	363	1999	30r
Transportation				
Bus fare, one-way	trip	1.00	2000	1c
Cars and trucks, new, expenditures on	yr	1648	1999	30r
Cars and trucks, used, expenditures on	yr	1651	1999	30r
Diesel at the pump	gal	1.26	10/99	73s
Gasoline and motor oil purchases	yr	1052	1999	30r
Gasoline before-tax price (cents)	gal	101.90	10/00	43s
Maintenance and repair expenditures	yr	621	1999	30r
Public transportation, expenditures on	yr	298	1999	30r
Transportation purchases	yr	6738	1999	30r
Vehicle expenses, miscellaneous, purchases	yr	2033	1999	30r
Vehicle insurance payments	yr	696	1999	30r
Vehicle purchases (net outlay)	yr	3354	1999	30r
Vehicle rental, lease expenditures	yr	352	1999	30r
Travel				
Car rental	day	42.50	2000	52c
Hotel room	night	110.57	2/01	95s

Values are in dollars or fractions of dollars. In the column headed *Ref*, references are shown to sources. Each reference is followed by a letter. These refer to the geographical level for which data were reported: s=State, r=Region, and c=City or metro. The abbreviation *ex* is used to mean *except* or *excluding*; *exp* stands for *expenditures*. For other abbreviations and further explanations, please see the Introduction.

Fort Lauderdale, FL - continued

Item	Per	Value	Date	Ref.
Utilities				
Electrical bill, average	mos	86.33	9/00	9s
Electricity, expenditures on	yr	1115	1999	30r
Electricity cost, average	KWh	6.80	9/00	9s
Water and other public services, expenditures on	yr	298	1999	30r
Weddings				
Wedding (national average cost)		19936	2000	33r
Wedding (regional average total cost)		16293	1997	110r
Attendants' gifts		321	1998	33r
Bridal attendants' apparel (5 persons)		824	2000	33r
Bride's headpiece/veil		173	1998	33r
Bride's wedding dress		859	1998	33r
Clergy, religious facility fee		242	1998	33r
Engagement ring		3177	1998	33r
Flowers		789	1998	33r
Groom's formalwear rental		99	2000	33r
Limousine		410	1998	33r
Marriage license cost		56.00-88.50	4/01	35s
Men's formalwear (ushers, best man)		469	2000	33r
Mother of bride apparel		241	2000	33r
Music		866	1998	33r
Photography and videography		1368	1998	33r
Rehearsal dinner		728	1998	33r
Wedding invitations and announcements		341	1998	33r
Wedding reception		7968	2000	33r
Wedding rings (bride and groom)		1060	1998	33r

Fort Myers-Cape Coral, FL

Item	Per	Value	Date	Ref.
Composite, ACCRA index		99.30	3/01	4c
Alcoholic Beverages				
Alcoholic beverage purchases	yr	253	1999	30r
Beer, Heineken, 12-oz, ex deposit	6	6.76	3/01	4c
J & B Scotch	750-ml	20.59	3/01	4c
Malt beverages, all types, all sizes, any origin	16 oz	0.96	7/01	11r
Wine, Livingston or Gallo, Chablis blanc	1.5 liter	5.81	3/01	4c
Appliances				
Appliance repair, service call, washing machine	min lab chg	42.82	3/01	4c
Major appliances, expenditures on	yr	172	1999	30r
Small appliances, housewares, expenditures on	yr	81	1999	30r
Banking and Money				
Mortgage interest and charges paid	yr	2039	1999	30r
Mortgage principal paid on owned property	yr	1026	1999	30r
Mortgage rate, incl. points and orig. fee, 30-yr. conv. fixed or ARM	mos	6.98	3/01	4c
Vehicle finance charges paid	yr	365	1999	30r
Charity				
Cash contributions, expenditures	yr	1127	1999	30r
Child Care				
Child raising cost, total, age 0-2	yr	8540	1999	60r
Child raising cost, total, age 3-5	yr	8780	1999	60r
Child raising cost, total, age 6-8	yr	8820	1999	60r
Child raising cost, total, age 9-11	yr	8800	1999	60r
Child raising cost, total, age 12-14	yr	9510	1999	60r
Child raising cost, total, age 15-17	yr	9740	1999	60r
Child's child care and education, age 0-2	yr	1380	1999	60r
Child's child care and education, age 3-5	yr	1520	1999	60r
Child's child care and education, age 6-8	yr	990	1999	60r
Child's child care and education, age 9-11	yr	650	1999	60r
Child's child care and education, age 12-14	yr	490	1999	60r
Child's child care and education, age 15-17	yr	840	1999	60r
Child's clothing, age 0-2	yr	480	1999	60r
Child's clothing, age 3-5	yr	470	1999	60r
Child's clothing, age 6-8	yr	520	1999	60r
Child's clothing, age 9-11	yr	570	1999	60r

Fort Myers-Cape Coral, FL - continued

Item	Per	Value	Date	Ref.
Child Care - continued				
Child's clothing, age 12-14	yr	950	1999	60r
Child's clothing, age 15-17	yr	850	1999	60r
Child's food, age 0-2	yr	1000	1999	60r
Child's food, age 3-5	yr	1160	1999	60r
Child's food, age 6-8	yr	1490	1999	60r
Child's food, age 9-11	yr	1770	1999	60r
Child's food, age 12-14	yr	1770	1999	60r
Child's food, age 15-17	yr	1980	1999	60r
Child's health care, age 0-2	yr	620	1999	60r
Child's health care, age 3-5	yr	590	1999	60r
Child's health care, age 6-8	yr	680	1999	60r
Child's health care, age 9-11	yr	720	1999	60r
Child's health care, age 12-14	yr	730	1999	60r
Child's health care, age 15-17	yr	760	1999	60r
Child's housing, age 0-2	yr	3070	1999	60r
Child's housing, age 3-5	yr	3050	1999	60r
Child's housing, age 6-8	yr	3010	1999	60r
Child's housing, age 9-11	yr	2850	1999	60r
Child's housing, age 12-14	yr	3040	1999	60r
Child's housing, age 15-17	yr	2650	1999	60r
Child's personal care, reading, age 0-2	yr	910	1999	60r
Child's personal care, reading, age 3-5	yr	930	1999	60r
Child's personal care, reading, age 6-8	yr	960	1999	60r
Child's personal care, reading, age 9-11	yr	1000	1999	60r
Child's personal care, reading, age 12-14	yr	1170	1999	60r
Child's personal care, reading, age 15-17	yr	950	1999	60r
Clothing				
Apparel and services purchases	yr	1610	1999	30r
Boys' brief, cotton	3	4.52	3/01	4c
Boys, 2 to 15, expenditures on	yr	89	1999	30r
Children under 2, expenditures on	yr	79	1999	30r
Footwear, expenditures on	yr	283	1999	30r
Girls, 2 to 15, expenditures on	yr	103	1999	30r
Men and boys, expenditures on	yr	351	1999	30r
Men, 16 and over, expenditures on	yr	262	1999	30r
Shirt, man's dress shirt		23.49	3/01	4c
Slacks, man's "No Wrinkles" khaki		38.74	3/01	4c
Women, 16 and over, expenditures on	yr	538	1999	30r
Communications				
Cable modem installation, Adelphi		54.90	6/99	103s
Cable modem installation, Comcast		95.00	6/99	103s
Cable modem installation, Media One		100.00	6/99	103s
Cable modem installation, Time Warner		75.00-225.00	6/99	103s
Cable modem rate, cable subscriber, Adelphi	mos	34.95	6/99	103s
Cable modem rate, cable subscriber, Comcast	mos	39.95	6/99	103s
Cable modem rate, cable subscriber, Media One	mos	34.95-39.95	6/99	103s
Cable modem rate, cable subscriber, Time Warner	mos	39.95-49.95	6/99	103s
Cable modem rate, non-cable subscriber, Adelphi	mos	44.95	6/99	103s
Cable modem rate, non-cable subscriber, Comcast	mos	49.95	6/99	103s
Cable modem rate, non-cable subscriber, Media One	mos	49.95	6/99	103s
Cable modem rate, non-cable subscriber, Time Warner	mos	39.95-54.95	6/99	103s
Newspaper subscription, daily and Sunday delivery	mos	16.08	3/01	4c
Phone line, single, business, field visit	inst.	56.00	12/97	17s
Phone line, single, business, no field visit	inst.	56.00	12/97	17s
Phone line, single, residence, field visit	inst.	40.00	12/97	17s
Phone line, single, residence, no field visit	inst.	40.00	12/97	17s
Postage and stationery, expenditures on	yr	104	1999	30r
Postal rate, express mail, up to half-pound		12.45	7/01	108r
Postal rate, letter, first class, first ounce		0.34	7/01	108r
Postal rate, letter, two ounces		0.57	7/01	108r
Postal rate, post card		0.21	7/01	108r
Postal rate, priority mail, two pounds		3.95	7/01	108r

Values are in dollars or fractions of dollars. In the column headed *Ref*, references are shown to sources. Each reference is followed by a letter. These refer to the geographical level for which data were reported: s=State, r=Region, and c=City or metro. The abbreviation *ex* is used to mean *except* or *excluding*; *exp* stands for expenditures. For other abbreviations and further explanations, please see the Introduction.

Fort Myers-Cape Coral, FL - continued

Item	Per	Value	Date	Ref.
Communications				
Postal rate, priority mail, up to one pound		3.50	7/01	108r
Telephone bill, family of three	mos	16.81	3/01	4c
Telephone services, expenditures on	yr	860	1999	30r
Education				
Board, 4-year private college/university	yr	2236	1996	38s
Board, 4-year public college/university	yr	2295	1996	38s
Education expenditures	yr	431	1999	30r
Room, 4-year private college/university	yr	2428	1996	38s
Room, 4-year public college/university	yr	2193	1996	38s
Total cost, 4-year private college/university	yr	15028	1996	38s
Total cost, 4-year public college/university	yr	6254	1996	38s
Tuition, 2-year public college/university, in state	yr	1103	1996	38s
Tuition, 4-year private college/university, in state	yr	10364	1996	38s
Tuition, 4-year public college/university	yr	1767	1996	38s
Energy and Fuels				
Electricity	KWh	0.09	7/01	11r
Electricity	500 KWhs	47.29	7/01	11r
Energy, combined forms, 2400 sq ft	mos	125.26	3/01	4c
Fuel oil #2	gal	1.43	7/01	11r
Fuel oil and other fuels, expenditures on	yr	45	1999	30r
Gas, natural, commercial rate	1000 cf	8.44	11/00	88s
Gas, regular unleaded, cash, self-service	gal	1.42	3/01	4c
Gasoline, all types	gal	1.60	7/01	11r
Gasoline, unleaded midgrade	gal	1.65	7/01	11r
Gasoline, unleaded premium	gal	1.74	7/01	11r
Natural gas, expenditures on	yr	164	1999	30r
Utility (piped) gas, therm		1.01	7/01	11r
Utility (piped) gas, 40 therms		44.29	7/01	11r
Utility (piped) gas, 100 therms		97.44	7/01	11r
Entertainment				
Bowling, Saturday evening rate	line	3.01	3/01	4c
Entertainment purchases	yr	1574	1999	30r
Fees and admissions paid	yr	371	1999	30r
Monopoly game, Parker Brothers', No. 9	game	11.91	3/01	4c
Movie, first-run, Saturday, evening	adm.	6.00	3/01	4c
Reading purchases	yr	121	1999	30r
Television, radios, sound equipment, expenditures on	yr	561	1999	30r
Tennis balls, yellow, Wilson or Penn, 3	can	2.60	3/01	4c
Funerals				
Total cost of funeral		5922.53	1/99	78r
Acknowledgement cards		63.43	1/99	78r
Casket		2258.77	1/99	78r
Cosmetology, hair, other preparation		127.09	1/99	78r
Embalming		393.49	1/99	78r
Funeral at funeral home		367.50	1/99	78r
Hearse (local)		169.66	1/99	78r
Professional service charges		1211.32	1/99	78r
Service car/van		80.69	1/99	78r
Transfer of remains to funeral home		144.25	1/99	78r
Vault		803.50	1/99	78r
Visitation/viewing		302.83	1/99	78r
Groceries				
Groceries, ACCRA Index		101.30	3/01	4c
American processed cheese	lb	3.50	7/01	11r
Antibiotic ointment, Polysporin	0.5 oz	5.07	3/01	4c
Baby food, strained vegetables or fruit, lowest price	4-4.5 oz	0.45	3/01	4c
Bakery products, expenditures on	yr	261	1999	30r
Bananas	lb	0.49	3/01	4c
Bananas	lb	0.47	7/01	11r
Beans, dried, any type, all sizes	lb	0.63	7/01	11r
Beef for stew, boneless	lb	2.86	7/01	11r
Beef or hamburger, ground	lb	1.50	3/01	4c
Beef, expenditures on	yr	210	1999	30r
Bologna, all beef or mixed	lb	2.29	7/01	11r

Item	Per	Value	Date	Ref.
Groceries - continued				
Bread, French	lb	1.66	7/01	11r
Bread, white	loaf	1.04	3/01	4c
Bread, white, pan	lb	0.87	7/01	11r
Bread, whole wheat, pan	lb	1.38	7/01	11r
Broccoli	lb	1.04	7/01	11r
Butter, salted, grade AA, stick	lb	2.26	7/01	11r
Butter, yoghurt, cheese, etc, expenditures on	yr	170	1999	30r
Cabbage	lb	0.42	7/01	11r
Cereals and cereal products, expenditures on	yr	140	1999	30r
Cheddar cheese, natural	lb	3.75	7/01	11r
Cheese, Kraft grated Parmesan	8 oz	3.37	3/01	4c
Chicken breast, bone-in	lb	1.85	7/01	11r
Chicken legs, bone-in	lb	1.34	7/01	11r
Chicken, fresh, whole	lb	1.05	7/01	11r
Chicken, whole fryer	lb	0.96	3/01	4c
Chops, boneless	lb	4.13	7/01	11r
Chuck roast, graded and ungraded, excl U.S. prime and choice	lb	2.35	7/01	11r
Chuck roast, U.S. choice, boneless	lb	2.67	7/01	11r
Cigarettes, Winston, Kings	carton	27.42	3/01	4c
Coffee, 100%, ground roast, all sizes	lb	2.88	7/01	11r
Coffee, instant, plain, regular, all sizes	16 oz	9.25	7/01	11r
Coffee, vacuum-packed	13 oz	2.62	3/01	4c
Cola, non diet,	2 liter	1.11	7/01	11r
Corn Flakes, Kellogg's or Post Toasties	18 oz	3.03	3/01	4c
Corn, frozen, whole kernel, lowest price	16 oz	1.03	3/01	4c
Crackers, soda, salted	lb	1.70	7/01	11r
Dairy product purchases	yr	282	1999	30r
Eggs, expenditures on	yr	32	1999	30r
Eggs, Grade A or AA	dozen	1.27	3/01	4c
Fats and oils, expenditures on	yr	79	1999	30r
Fish and seafood, expenditures on	yr	99	1999	30r
Flour, white, all purpose	lb	0.32	7/01	11r
Food (excl fruit and vegetables), eaten at home, purchases	yr	815	1999	30r
Food cooked on trips, expenditures on	yr	36	1999	30r
Food purchases	yr	4533	1999	30r
Food purchases, eaten away from home	yr	1873	1999	30r
Food purchases, food eaten at home	yr	2660	1999	30r
Fresh fruits, expenditures on	yr	128	1999	30r
Fresh milk and cream, expenditures on	yr	112	1999	30r
Fresh vegetables, expenditures on	yr	131	1999	30r
Fruit and vegetable purchases	yr	438	1999	30r
Grapefruit	lb	0.59	7/01	11r
Grapes, Thompson, seedless	lb	2.12	7/01	11r
Ground beef, 100% beef	lb	1.76	7/01	11r
Ground beef, lean and extra lean	lb	2.60	7/01	11r
Ground chuck, 100% beef	lb	2.08	7/01	11r
Ham, boneless, excl canned	lb	2.71	7/01	11r
Ham, rump or shank half, bone-in, smoked	lb	2.19	7/01	11r
Ice cream, prepackaged, bulk, regular	1/2 gal	3.93	7/01	11r
Lemons	lb	1.32	7/01	11r
Lettuce, iceberg	head	0.81	3/01	4c
Lettuce, iceberg	lb	0.76	7/01	11r
Margarine, Blue Bonnet or Parkay, stick	lb	0.81	3/01	4c
Milk, fresh, low fat,	gal	2.75	7/01	11r
Milk, fresh, whole, fortified	gal	2.97	7/01	11r
Milk, whole	1/2 gal	1.83	3/01	4c
Nonalcoholic beverages, expenditures on	yr	228	1999	30r
Orange juice, frozen concentrate	16 oz	1.95	7/01	11r
Orange juice, Minute Maid frozen	12 oz	1.44	3/01	4c
Oranges, Navel	lb	0.73	7/01	11r
Oranges, Valencia	lb	0.55	7/01	11r
Peaches, halves or slices, Hunt's, Del Monte, or Libby's	29 oz	1.52	3/01	4c
Peanut butter, creamy, all sizes	lb	1.83	7/01	11r
Pears, Anjou	lb	0.98	7/01	11r
Peas, green, Del Monte or Green Giant	15 oz	0.62	3/01	4c
Pork chops, center cut, bone-in	lb	3.33	7/01	11r
Pork sausage, fresh, loose	lb	2.59	7/01	11r
Pork shoulder picnic, bone-in, smoked	lb	1.12	7/01	11r

Values are in dollars or fractions of dollars. In the column headed *Ref*, references are shown to sources. Each reference is followed by a letter. These refer to the geographical level for which data were reported: s=State, r=Region, and c=City or metro. The abbreviation *ex* is used to mean *except* or *excluding*; *exp* stands for *expenditures*. For other abbreviations and further explanations, please see the Introduction.

Fort Myers-Cape Coral, FL - continued

Fort Myers-Cape Coral, FL - continued

Item	Per	Value	Date	Ref.
Groceries				
Pork, expenditures on	yr	162	1999	30r
Potato chips	16 oz	3.59	7/01	11r
Potatoes, frozen, french fried	lb	1.00	7/01	11r
Potatoes, white or red	10 lb	3.38	3/01	4c
Potatoes, white, all types	lb	0.44	7/01	11r
Poultry, expenditures on	yr	137	1999	30r
Processed fruits, expenditures on	yr	97	1999	30r
Processed vegetables, expenditures on	yr	82	1999	30r
Rice, white, long grain, uncooked	lb	0.51	7/01	11r
Round roast, graded and ungraded, excl U.S. prime and choice	lb	2.96	7/01	11r
Round steak, graded and ungraded, excl U.S. prime and choice	lb	3.11	7/01	11r
Sausage, Jimmy Dean/Owens pork	lb	3.09	3/01	4c
Shortening, vegetable, Crisco	3 lb	3.21	3/01	4c
Sirloin steak, graded and ungraded, excl U.S. prime and choice	lb	4.23	7/01	11r
Soft drink, Coca Cola, ex deposit	2 liter	1.20	3/01	4c
Spaghetti and macaroni	lb	0.78	7/01	11r
Steak, round, U.S. choice, boneless	lb	3.56	7/01	11r
Steak, sirloin, U.S. choice, boneless	lb	5.65	7/01	11r
Steak, T-bone	lb	6.91	3/01	4c
Strawberries, dry pint	12 oz	1.50	7/01	11r
Sugar and other sweets, expenditures on	yr	99	1999	30r
Sugar, cane or beet	4 lbs	1.49	3/01	4c
Sugar, white, 33-80 ounce package	lb	0.39	7/01	11r
Sugar, white, all sizes	lb	0.42	7/01	11r
Tobacco products and smoking supplies purchases	yr	288	1999	30r
Tomatoes, field grown	lb	1.43	7/01	11r
Tomatoes, Hunt's or Del Monte	14.5 oz	0.86	3/01	4c
Tuna, chunk, light	6 oz	0.56	3/01	4c
Tuna, light, chunk	lb	1.77	7/01	11r
Turkey, frozen, whole	lb	1.05	7/01	11r
Goods and Services				
Miscellaneous goods and services, ACCRA Index		98.10	3/01	4c
B&B Japanese maple (acer japonicum)	gal	49.98-129.00	4/00	93r
Boxwood (buxus)	2 gal	12.99-16.99	4/00	93r
Daylilly (hemerocallis)	gal	4.99-8.99	4/00	93r
Flat of annuals		11.00-13.92	4/00	93r
Fountain grass (pennisetum)	gal	5.98-7.98	4/00	93r
Hanging basket (10 in)		7.99-14.98	4/00	93r
Hardy geranium (geranium)	gal	5.98-8.00	4/00	93r
Hosta (hosta)	gal	4.99-10.98	4/00	93r
Lilac (syrubga vulgaris)	2 gal	12.99-21.99	4/00	93r
Rhododendron (rhododendron)	2 gal	14.99-24.99	4/00	93r
Sage (salvia)	gal	5.98-6.99	4/00	93r
Wintercreeper euonymus (euonymus fortunei)	2 gal	7.99-89.99	4/00	93r
Hunting license	yr	12.50	4/01	34s
Health Care				
Health care, ACCRA Index		95.00	3/01	4c
Cardiac catheterization, ave hospital/physician charges		15060	1998	77s
Childbirth, Cesarean delivery		11587	1997	13r
Childbirth, vaginal delivery		6725	1997	13r
Dentist's fee, adult teeth cleaning and periodic oral exam	visit	61.60	3/01	4c

Fort Myers-Cape Coral, FL - continued

Item	Per	Value	Date	Ref.
Health Care - continued				
Doctor's fee, routine exam, established patient	visit	59.83	3/01	4c
Drugs, expenditures on	yr	399	1999	30r
Health care purchases	yr	1971	1999	30r
Health insurance expenditures	yr	933	1999	30r
Hospital care, private room	day	473.58	3/01	4c
Hysterectomy, laproscopically-assisted, ave hospital/physician charges		14760	1998	76s
Hysterectomy, vaginal, ave hospital and physician charges		11320	1998	76s
Medicaid dispensing fee		4.23	1999	87s
Medical services expenditures	yr	547	1999	30r
Medical supplies, expenditures on	yr	91	1999	30r
Plastic surgery, breast augmentation		2870	2000	7r
Plastic surgery, breast lift		3649	2000	7r
Plastic surgery, facelift		5008	2000	7r
Plastic surgery, hair transplantation		3425	2000	7r
Plastic surgery, lip augmentation		1227	2000	7r
Plastic surgery, lower body lift		4793	2000	7r
Plastic surgery, thigh lift		3862	2000	7r
Household Goods				
Dishwashing powder, Cascade	50 oz	3.59	3/01	4c
Floor coverings, expenditures on	yr	44	1999	30r
Furniture, expenditures on	yr	335	1999	30r
Household furnishings and equipment purchases	yr	1328	1999	30r
Household textiles, expenditures on	yr	89	1999	30r
Laundry and cleaning supplies, expenditures on	yr	113	1999	30r
Tissues, facial, Kleenex brand	175	1.37	3/01	4c
Housing				
Housing, ACCRA Index		97.30	3/01	4c
Home price, existing, ave		160100	10/00	90r
Home value, median		104000	2001	53s
House, 2400 sq ft, 8000 sq ft lot, new, urban, utilities	total	206733	3/01	4c
House payment, principal and interest, 25% down payment	mos	1029	3/01	4c
Household operation expenditures	yr	553	1999	30r
Housekeeping supplies purchases	yr	473	1999	30r
Housing, expenditures on	yr	10303	1999	30r
Maintenance, repairs, insurance expenditures	yr	699	1999	30r
Monthly rental value of owned home	mos	505	1999	30r
Owned dwellings, expenditures own	yr	3465	1999	30r
Rent expenditures	yr	1641	1999	30r
Rent, apartment, 2 br, 1 1/2-2 baths, unfurn, 950 sq ft, water	mos	607	3/01	4c
Rental unit, 1 bedroom, with utilities	mos	490	4/01	41c
Rental unit, 2 bedroom, with utilities	mos	591	4/01	41c
Rental unit, 3 bedroom, with utilities	mos	826	4/01	41c
Rental unit, 4 bedroom, with utilities	mos	861	4/01	41c
Shelter, expenditures on	yr	5467	1999	30r
Insurance and Pensions				
Life and other personal insurance purchases	yr	414	1999	30r
Medigap health insurance, Plan H	yr	2887	2000	69s
Medigap health insurance, Plan I	yr	3302	2000	69s
Medigap health insurance, Plan J	yr	3889	2000	69s
Pensions and Social Security, expenditures on	yr	2635	1999	30r
Personal insurance and pensions, expenditures on	yr	3048	1999	30r
Legal Fees				
Divorce, filing fee		65.00-85.00	4/01	35s
Driver's license fee	renew	15.00	1999	48s
Driver's license fee	orig	20.00	1999	48s

Values are in dollars or fractions of dollars. In the column headed *Ref*, references are shown to sources. Each reference is followed by a letter. These refer to the geographical level for which data were reported: s=State, r=Region, and c=City or metro. The abbreviation *ex* is used to mean *except* or *excluding*; *exp* stands for expenditures. For other abbreviations and further explanations, please see the Introduction.

Fort Myers-Cape Coral, FL - continued

Item	Per	Value	Date	Ref.
Personal Goods				
Personal care products and services purchases	yr	393	1999	30r
Shampoo, Alberto VO5	15 oz	0.99	3/01	4c
Toothpaste, Crest or Colgate	6-7 oz	2.25	3/01	4c
Personal Services				
Dry cleaning, man's 2-pc suit		8.53	3/01	4c
Man's haircut, barbershop, no styling		9.00	3/01	4c
Personal services, household, expenditures on	yr	258	1999	30r
Woman's shampoo, trim, blow-dry, no style-change		25.80	3/01	4c
Pets				
Pets, toys, and playground equipment, expenditures on	yr	306	1999	30r
Restaurant Food				
Chicken, fried, thigh and drumstick, KFC/ Church's		2.25	3/01	4c
Hamburger with cheese, McDonald's	1/4 lb	2.14	3/01	4c
Pizza, Pizza Hut or Pizza Inn	11-12 in	8.25	3/01	4c
Taxes				
Federal income taxes paid	yr	2047	1999	30r
Personal taxes, expenditures on	yr	2554	1999	30r
Property taxes paid	yr	726	1999	30r
State and local income taxes paid	yr	363	1999	30r
Transportation				
Transportation, ACCRA Index		108.40	3/01	4c
Cars and trucks, new, expenditures on	yr	1648	1999	30r
Cars and trucks, used, expenditures on	yr	1651	1999	30r
Diesel at the pump	gal	1.26	10/99	73s
Gasoline and motor oil purchases	yr	1052	1999	30r
Gasoline before-tax price (cents)	gal	101.90	10/00	43s
Maintenance and repair expenditures	yr	621	1999	30r
Public transportation, expenditures on	yr	298	1999	30r
Tire balance, computer or spin balance, front	wheel	9.39	3/01	4c
Transportation purchases	yr	6738	1999	30r
Vehicle expenses, miscellaneous, purchases	yr	2033	1999	30r
Vehicle insurance payments	yr	696	1999	30r
Vehicle purchases (net outlay)	yr	3354	1999	30r
Vehicle rental, lease expenditures	yr	352	1999	30r
Travel				
Hotel room	night	110.57	2/01	95s
Utilities				
Utilities, ACCRA Index		99.10	3/01	4c
Electrical bill, average	mos	86.33	9/00	9s
Electricity, 2400 sq ft, new home	mos	125.26	3/01	4c
Electricity, expenditures on	yr	1115	1999	30r
Electricity cost, average	KWh	6.80	9/00	9s
Water and other public services, expenditures on	yr	298	1999	30r
Weddings				
Wedding (national average cost)		19936	2000	33r
Wedding (regional average total cost)		16293	1997	110r
Attendants' gifts		321	1998	33r
Bridal attendants' apparel (5 persons)		824	2000	33r
Bride's headpiece/veil		173	1998	33r
Bride's wedding dress		859	1998	33r
Clergy, religious facility fee		242	1998	33r
Engagement ring		3177	1998	33r
Flowers		789	1998	33r
Groom's formalwear rental		99	2000	33r
Limousine		410	1998	33r
Marriage license cost		56.00-88.50	4/01	35s
Men's formalwear (ushers, best man)		469	2000	33r
Mother of bride apparel		241	2000	33r
Music		866	1998	33r
Photography and videography		1368	1998	33r
Rehearsal dinner		728	1998	33r

Fort Myers-Cape Coral, FL - continued

Item	Per	Value	Date	Ref.
Weddings - continued				
Wedding invitations and announcements		341	1998	33r
Wedding reception		7968	2000	33r
Wedding rings (bride and groom)		1060	1998	33r

Fort Pierce-Port St. Lucie, FL

Item	Per	Value	Date	Ref.
Alcoholic Beverages				
Alcoholic beverage purchases	yr	253	1999	30r
Malt beverages, all types, all sizes, any origin	16 oz	0.96	7/01	11r
Appliances				
Major appliances, expenditures on	yr	172	1999	30r
Small appliances, housewares, expenditures on	yr	81	1999	30r
Banking and Money				
Mortgage interest and charges paid	yr	2039	1999	30r
Mortgage principal paid on owned property	yr	1026	1999	30r
Vehicle finance charges paid	yr	365	1999	30r
Charity				
Cash contributions, expenditures	yr	1127	1999	30r
Child Care				
Child raising cost, total, age 0-2	yr	8540	1999	60r
Child raising cost, total, age 3-5	yr	8780	1999	60r
Child raising cost, total, age 6-8	yr	8820	1999	60r
Child raising cost, total, age 9-11	yr	8800	1999	60r
Child raising cost, total, age 12-14	yr	9510	1999	60r
Child raising cost, total, age 15-17	yr	9740	1999	60r
Child's child care and education, age 0-2	yr	1380	1999	60r
Child's child care and education, age 3-5	yr	1520	1999	60r
Child's child care and education, age 6-8	yr	990	1999	60r
Child's child care and education, age 9-11	yr	650	1999	60r
Child's child care and education, age 12-14	yr	490	1999	60r
Child's child care and education, age 15-17	yr	840	1999	60r
Child's clothing, age 0-2	yr	480	1999	60r
Child's clothing, age 3-5	yr	470	1999	60r
Child's clothing, age 6-8	yr	520	1999	60r
Child's clothing, age 9-11	yr	570	1999	60r
Child's clothing, age 12-14	yr	950	1999	60r
Child's clothing, age 15-17	yr	850	1999	60r
Child's food, age 0-2	yr	1000	1999	60r
Child's food, age 3-5	yr	1160	1999	60r
Child's food, age 6-8	yr	1490	1999	60r
Child's food, age 9-11	yr	1770	1999	60r
Child's food, age 12-14	yr	1770	1999	60r
Child's food, age 15-17	yr	1980	1999	60r
Child's health care, age 0-2	yr	620	1999	60r
Child's health care, age 3-5	yr	590	1999	60r
Child's health care, age 6-8	yr	680	1999	60r
Child's health care, age 9-11	yr	720	1999	60r
Child's health care, age 12-14	yr	730	1999	60r
Child's health care, age 15-17	yr	760	1999	60r
Child's housing, age 0-2	yr	3070	1999	60r
Child's housing, age 3-5	yr	3050	1999	60r
Child's housing, age 6-8	yr	3010	1999	60r
Child's housing, age 9-11	yr	2850	1999	60r
Child's housing, age 12-14	yr	3040	1999	60r
Child's housing, age 15-17	yr	2650	1999	60r
Child's personal care, reading, age 0-2	yr	910	1999	60r
Child's personal care, reading, age 3-5	yr	930	1999	60r
Child's personal care, reading, age 6-8	yr	960	1999	60r
Child's personal care, reading, age 9-11	yr	1000	1999	60r
Child's personal care, reading, age 12-14	yr	1170	1999	60r
Child's personal care, reading, age 15-17	yr	950	1999	60r
Clothing				
Apparel and services purchases	yr	1610	1999	30r
Boys, 2 to 15, expenditures on	yr	89	1999	30r
Children under 2, expenditures on	yr	79	1999	30r
Footwear, expenditures on	yr	283	1999	30r
Girls, 2 to 15, expenditures on	yr	103	1999	30r

Values are in dollars or fractions of dollars. In the column headed *Ref,* references are shown to sources. Each reference is followed by a letter. These refer to the geographical level for which data were reported: s=State, r=Region, and c=City or metro. The abbreviation *ex* is used to mean *except* or *excluding*; *exp* stands for expenditures. For other abbreviations and further explanations, please see the Introduction.

Fort Pierce-Port St. Lucie, FL - continued

Item	Per	Value	Date	Ref.
Clothing				
Men and boys, expenditures on	yr	351	1999	30r
Men, 16 and over, expenditures on	yr	262	1999	30r
Women, 16 and over, expenditures on	yr	538	1999	30r
Communications				
Cable modem installation, Adelphi		54.90	6/99	103s
Cable modem installation, Comcast		95.00	6/99	103s
Cable modem installation, Media One		100.00	6/99	103s
Cable modem installation, Time Warner		75.00-225.00	6/99	103s
Cable modem rate, cable subscriber, Adelphi	mos	34.95	6/99	103s
Cable modem rate, cable subscriber, Comcast	mos	39.95	6/99	103s
Cable modem rate, cable subscriber, Media One	mos	34.95-39.95	6/99	103s
Cable modem rate, cable subscriber, Time Warner	mos	39.95-49.95	6/99	103s
Cable modem rate, non-cable subscriber, Adelphi	mos	44.95	6/99	103s
Cable modem rate, non-cable subscriber, Comcast	mos	49.95	6/99	103s
Cable modem rate, non-cable subscriber, Media One	mos	49.95	6/99	103s
Cable modem rate, non-cable subscriber, Time Warner	mos	39.95-54.95	6/99	103s
Phone line, single, business, field visit	inst.	56.00	12/97	17s
Phone line, single, business, no field visit	inst.	56.00	12/97	17s
Phone line, single, residence, field visit	inst.	40.00	12/97	17s
Phone line, single, residence, no field visit	inst.	40.00	12/97	17s
Postage and stationery, expenditures on	yr	104	1999	30r
Postal rate, express mail, up to half-pound		12.45	7/01	108r
Postal rate, letter, first class, first ounce		0.34	7/01	108r
Postal rate, letter, two ounces		0.57	7/01	108r
Postal rate, post card		0.21	7/01	108r
Postal rate, priority mail, two pounds		3.95	7/01	108r
Postal rate, priority mail, up to one pound		3.50	7/01	108r
Telephone services, expenditures on	yr	860	1999	30r
Education				
Board, 4-year private college/university	yr	2236	1996	38s
Board, 4-year public college/university	yr	2295	1996	38s
Education expenditures	yr	431	1999	30r
Room, 4-year private college/university	yr	2428	1996	38s
Room, 4-year public college/university	yr	2193	1996	38s
Total cost, 4-year private college/university	yr	15028	1996	38s
Total cost, 4-year public college/university	yr	6254	1996	38s
Tuition, 2-year public college/university, in state	yr	1103	1996	38s
Tuition, 4-year private college/university, in state	yr	10364	1996	38s
Tuition, 4-year public college/university	yr	1767	1996	38s
Energy and Fuels				
Electricity	500 KWhs	47.29	7/01	11r
Electricity	KWh	0.09	7/01	11r
Fuel oil #2	gal	1.43	7/01	11r
Fuel oil and other fuels, expenditures on	yr	45	1999	30r
Gas, natural, commercial rate	1000 cf	8.44	11/00	88s
Gasoline, all types	gal	1.60	7/01	11r
Gasoline, unleaded midgrade	gal	1.65	7/01	11r
Gasoline, unleaded premium	gal	1.74	7/01	11r
Natural gas, expenditures on	yr	164	1999	30r
Utility (piped) gas, therm		1.01	7/01	11r
Utility (piped) gas, 40 therms		44.29	7/01	11r
Utility (piped) gas, 100 therms		97.44	7/01	11r
Entertainment				
Entertainment purchases	yr	1574	1999	30r
Fees and admissions paid	yr	371	1999	30r
Reading purchases	yr	121	1999	30r
Television, radios, sound equipment, expenditures on	yr	561	1999	30r

Fort Pierce-Port St. Lucie, FL - continued

Item	Per	Value	Date	Ref.
Funerals				
Total cost of funeral		5922.53	1/99	78r
Acknowledgement cards		63.43	1/99	78r
Casket		2258.77	1/99	78r
Cosmetology, hair, other preparation		127.09	1/99	78r
Embalming		393.49	1/99	78r
Funeral at funeral home		367.50	1/99	78r
Hearse (local)		169.66	1/99	78r
Professional service charges		1211.32	1/99	78r
Service car/van		80.69	1/99	78r
Transfer of remains to funeral home		144.25	1/99	78r
Vault		803.50	1/99	78r
Visitation/viewing		302.83	1/99	78r
Groceries				
American processed cheese	lb	3.50	7/01	11r
Bakery products, expenditures on	yr	261	1999	30r
Bananas	lb	0.47	7/01	11r
Beans, dried, any type, all sizes	lb	0.63	7/01	11r
Beef for stew, boneless	lb	2.86	7/01	11r
Beef, expenditures on	yr	210	1999	30r
Bologna, all beef or mixed	lb	2.29	7/01	11r
Bread, French	lb	1.66	7/01	11r
Bread, white, pan	lb	0.87	7/01	11r
Bread, whole wheat, pan	lb	1.38	7/01	11r
Broccoli	lb	1.04	7/01	11r
Butter, salted, grade AA, stick	lb	2.26	7/01	11r
Butter, yoghurt, cheese, etc, expenditures on	yr	170	1999	30r
Cabbage	lb	0.42	7/01	11r
Cereals and cereal products, expenditures on	yr	140	1999	30r
Cheddar cheese, natural	lb	3.75	7/01	11r
Chicken breast, bone-in	lb	1.85	7/01	11r
Chicken legs, bone-in	lb	1.34	7/01	11r
Chicken, fresh, whole	lb	1.05	7/01	11r
Chops, boneless,	lb	4.13	7/01	11r
Chuck roast, graded and ungraded, excl U.S. prime and choice	lb	2.35	7/01	11r
Chuck roast, U.S. choice, boneless	lb	2.67	7/01	11r
Coffee, 100%, ground roast, all sizes	lb	2.88	7/01	11r
Coffee, instant, plain, regular, all sizes	16 oz	9.25	7/01	11r
Cola, non diet	2 liter	1.11	7/01	11r
Crackers, soda, salted	lb	1.70	7/01	11r
Dairy product purchases	yr	282	1999	30r
Eggs, expenditures on	yr	32	1999	30r
Fats and oils, expenditures on	yr	79	1999	30r
Fish and seafood, expenditures on	yr	99	1999	30r
Flour, white, all purpose	lb	0.32	7/01	11r
Food (excl fruit and vegetables), eaten at home, purchases	yr	815	1999	30r
Food cooked on trips, expenditures on	yr	36	1999	30r
Food purchases	yr	4533	1999	30r
Food purchases, eaten away from home	yr	1873	1999	30r
Food purchases, food eaten at home	yr	2660	1999	30r
Fresh fruits, expenditures on	yr	128	1999	30r
Fresh milk and cream, expenditures on	yr	112	1999	30r
Fresh vegetables, expenditures on	yr	131	1999	30r
Fruit and vegetable purchases	yr	438	1999	30r
Grapefruit	lb	0.59	7/01	11r
Grapes, Thompson, seedless	lb	2.12	7/01	11r
Ground beef, 100% beef	lb	1.76	7/01	11r
Ground beef, lean and extra lean	lb	2.60	7/01	11r
Ground chuck, 100% beef	lb	2.08	7/01	11r
Ham, boneless, excl canned	lb	2.71	7/01	11r
Ham, rump or shank half, bone-in, smoked	lb	2.19	7/01	11r
Ice cream, prepackaged, bulk, regular	1/2 gal	3.93	7/01	11r
Lemons	lb	1.32	7/01	11r
Lettuce, iceberg	lb	0.76	7/01	11r
Milk, fresh, low fat	gal	2.75	7/01	11r
Milk, fresh, whole, fortified	gal	2.97	7/01	11r
Nonalcoholic beverages, expenditures on	yr	228	1999	30r
Orange juice, frozen concentrate	16 oz	1.95	7/01	11r
Oranges, Navel	lb	0.73	7/01	11r
Oranges, Valencia	lb	0.55	7/01	11r

Values are in dollars or fractions of dollars. In the column headed *Ref*, references are shown to sources. Each reference is followed by a letter. These refer to the geographical level for which data were reported: s=State, r=Region, and c=City or metro. The abbreviation *ex* is used to mean *except* or *excluding; exp* stands for *expenditures*. For other abbreviations and further explanations, please see the Introduction.

Fort Pierce-Port St. Lucie, FL - continued

Item	Per	Value	Date	Ref.
Groceries				
Peanut butter, creamy, all sizes	lb	1.83	7/01	11r
Pears, Anjou	lb	0.98	7/01	11r
Pork chops, center cut, bone-in	lb	3.33	7/01	11r
Pork sausage, fresh, loose	lb	2.59	7/01	11r
Pork shoulder picnic, bone-in, smoked	lb	1.12	7/01	11r
Pork, expenditures on	yr	162	1999	30r
Potato chips	16 oz	3.59	7/01	11r
Potatoes, frozen, french fried	lb	1.00	7/01	11r
Potatoes, white, all types	lb	0.44	7/01	11r
Poultry, expenditures on	yr	137	1999	30r
Processed fruits, expenditures on	yr	97	1999	30r
Processed vegetables, expenditures on	yr	82	1999	30r
Rice, white, long grain, uncooked	lb	0.51	7/01	11r
Round roast, graded and ungraded, excl U.S. prime and choice	lb	2.96	7/01	11r
Round steak, graded and ungraded, excl U.S. prime and choice	lb	3.11	7/01	11r
Sirloin steak, graded and ungraded, excl U.S. prime and choice	lb	4.23	7/01	11r
Spaghetti and macaroni	lb	0.78	7/01	11r
Steak, round, U.S. choice, boneless	lb	3.56	7/01	11r
Steak, sirloin, U.S. choice, boneless	lb	5.65	7/01	11r
Strawberries, dry pint	12 oz	1.50	7/01	11r
Sugar and other sweets, expenditures on	yr	99	1999	30r
Sugar, white, 33-80 ounce package	lb	0.39	7/01	11r
Sugar, white, all sizes	lb	0.42	7/01	11r
Tobacco products and smoking supplies purchases	yr	288	1999	30r
Tomatoes, field grown	lb	1.43	7/01	11r
Tuna, light, chunk	lb	1.77	7/01	11r
Turkey, frozen, whole	lb	1.05	7/01	11r
Goods and Services				
B&B Japanese maple (acer japonicum)	gal	49.98-129.00	4/00	93r
Boxwood (buxus)	2 gal	12.99-16.99	4/00	93r
Daylily (hemerocallis)	gal	4.99-8.99	4/00	93r
Flat of annuals		11.00-13.92	4/00	93r
Fountain grass (pennisetum)	gal	5.98-7.98	4/00	93r
Hanging basket (10 in)		7.99-14.98	4/00	93r
Hardy geranium (geranium)	gal	5.98-8.00	4/00	93r
Hosta (hosta)	gal	4.99-10.98	4/00	93r
Lilac (syrubga vulgaris)	2 gal	12.99-21.99	4/00	93r
Rhododendron (rhododendron)	2 gal	14.99-24.99	4/00	93r
Sage (salvia)	gal	5.98-6.99	4/00	93r
Wintercreeper euonymus (euonymus fortunei)	2 gal	7.99-89.99	4/00	93r
Hunting license	yr	12.50	4/01	34s
Health Care				
Cardiac catheterization, ave hospital/ physician charges		15060	1998	77s
Childbirth, Cesarean delivery		11587	1997	13r
Childbirth, vaginal delivery		6725	1997	13r
Drugs, expenditures on	yr	399	1999	30r
Health care purchases	yr	1971	1999	30r
Health insurance expenditures	yr	933	1999	30r
Hysterectomy, laproscopically-assisted, ave hospital/physician charges		14760	1998	76s
Hysterectomy, vaginal, ave hospital and physician charges		11320	1998	76s
Medicaid dispensing fee		4.23	1999	87s
Medical services expenditures	yr	547	1999	30r

Fort Pierce-Port St. Lucie, FL - continued

Item	Per	Value	Date	Ref.
Health Care - continued				
Medical supplies, expenditures on	yr	91	1999	30r
Plastic surgery, breast augmentation		2870	2000	7r
Plastic surgery, breast lift		3649	2000	7r
Plastic surgery, facelift		5008	2000	7r
Plastic surgery, hair transplantation		3425	2000	7r
Plastic surgery, lip augmentation		1227	2000	7r
Plastic surgery, lower body lift		4793	2000	7r
Plastic surgery, thigh lift		3862	2000	7r
Household Goods				
Floor coverings, expenditures on	yr	44	1999	30r
Furniture, expenditures on	yr	335	1999	30r
Household furnishings and equipment purchases	yr	1328	1999	30r
Household textiles, expenditures on	yr	89	1999	30r
Laundry and cleaning supplies, expenditures on	yr	113	1999	30r
Housing				
Home price, existing, ave		160100	10/00	90r
Home value, median		104000	2001	53s
Household operation expenditures	yr	553	1999	30r
Housekeeping supplies purchases	yr	473	1999	30r
Housing, expenditures on	yr	10303	1999	30r
Maintenance, repairs, insurance expenditures	yr	699	1999	30r
Monthly rental value of owned home	mos	505	1999	30r
Owned dwellings, expenditures own	yr	3465	1999	30r
Rent expenditures	yr	1641	1999	30r
Rental unit, 1 bedroom, with utilities	mos	519	4/01	41c
Rental unit, 2 bedroom, with utilities	mos	672	4/01	41c
Rental unit, 3 bedroom, with utilities	mos	874	4/01	41c
Rental unit, 4 bedroom, with utilities	mos	942	4/01	41c
Shelter, expenditures on	yr	5467	1999	30r
Insurance and Pensions				
Life and other personal insurance purchases	yr	414	1999	30r
Medigap health insurance, Plan H	yr	2887	2000	69s
Medigap health insurance, Plan I	yr	3302	2000	69s
Medigap health insurance, Plan J	yr	3889	2000	69s
Pensions and Social Security, expenditures on	yr	2635	1999	30r
Personal insurance and pensions, expenditures on	yr	3048	1999	30r
Legal Fees				
Divorce, filing fee		65.00-85.00	4/01	35s
Driver's license fee	renew	15.00	1999	48s
Driver's license fee	orig	20.00	1999	48s
Personal Goods				
Personal care products and services purchases	yr	393	1999	30r
Personal Services				
Personal services, household, expenditures on	yr	258	1999	30r
Pets				
Pets, toys, and playground equipment, expenditures on	yr	306	1999	30r
Taxes				
Federal income taxes paid	yr	2047	1999	30r
Personal taxes, expenditures on	yr	2554	1999	30r
Property taxes paid	yr	726	1999	30r
State and local income taxes paid	yr	363	1999	30r
Transportation				
Cars and trucks, new, expenditures on	yr	1648	1999	30r
Cars and trucks, used, expenditures on	yr	1651	1999	30r
Diesel at the pump	gal	1.26	10/99	73s
Gasoline and motor oil purchases	yr	1052	1999	30r
Gasoline before-tax price (cents)	gal	101.90	10/00	43s
Maintenance and repair expenditures	yr	621	1999	30r

Values are in dollars or fractions of dollars. In the column headed *Ref*, references are shown to sources. Each reference is followed by a letter. These refer to the geographical level for which data were reported: s=State, r=Region, and c=City or metro. The abbreviation *ex* is used to mean *except* or *excluding*; *exp* stands for *expenditures*. For other abbreviations and further explanations, please see the Introduction.

Fort Pierce-Port St. Lucie, FL - continued

Item	Per	Value	Date	Ref.
Transportation				
Public transportation, expenditures on	yr	298	1999	30r
Transportation purchases	yr	6738	1999	30r
Vehicle expenses, miscellaneous, purchases	yr	2033	1999	30r
Vehicle insurance payments	yr	696	1999	30r
Vehicle purchases (net outlay)	yr	3354	1999	30r
Vehicle rental, lease expenditures	yr	352	1999	30r
Travel				
Hotel room	night	110.57	2/01	95s
Utilities				
Electrical bill, average	mos	86.33	9/00	9s
Electricity, expenditures on	yr	1115	1999	30r
Electricity cost, average	KWh	6.80	9/00	9s
Water and other public services, expenditures on	yr	298	1999	30r
Weddings				
Wedding (national average cost)		19936	2000	33r
Wedding (regional average total cost)		16293	1997	110r
Attendants' gifts		321	1998	33r
Bridal attendants' apparel (5 persons)		824	2000	33r
Bride's headpiece/veil		173	1998	33r
Bride's wedding dress		859	1998	33r
Clergy, religious facility fee		242	1998	33r
Engagement ring		3177	1998	33r
Flowers		789	1998	33r
Groom's formalwear rental		99	2000	33r
Limousine		410	1998	33r
Marriage license cost		56.00-88.50	4/01	35s
Men's formalwear (ushers, best man)		469	2000	33r
Mother of bride apparel		241	2000	33r
Music		866	1998	33r
Photography and videography		1368	1998	33r
Rehearsal dinner		728	1998	33r
Wedding invitations and announcements		341	1998	33r
Wedding reception		7968	2000	33r
Wedding rings (bride and groom)		1060	1998	33r

Fort Smith, AR

Item	Per	Value	Date	Ref.
Composite, ACCRA index		88.50	3/01	4c
Alcoholic Beverages				
Alcoholic beverage purchases	yr	253	1999	30r
Beer, Heineken, 12-oz, ex deposit	6	7.19	3/01	4c
J & B Scotch	750-ml	18.81	3/01	4c
Malt beverages, all types, all sizes, any origin	16 oz	0.96	7/01	11r
Wine, Livingston or Gallo, Chablis blanc	1.5 liter	6.53	3/01	4c
Appliances				
Appliance repair, service call, washing machine	min lab chg	49.95	3/01	4c
Major appliances, expenditures on	yr	172	1999	30r
Small appliances, housewares, expenditures on	yr	81	1999	30r
Banking and Money				
Mortgage interest and charges paid	yr	2039	1999	30r
Mortgage principal paid on owned property	yr	1026	1999	30r
Mortgage rate, incl. points and orig. fee, 30-yr. conv. fixed or ARM	mos	7.14	3/01	4c
Vehicle finance charges paid	yr	365	1999	30r
Charity				
Cash contributions, expenditures	yr	1127	1999	30r
Child Care				
Child raising cost, total, age 0-2	yr	8540	1999	60r
Child raising cost, total, age 3-5	yr	8780	1999	60r
Child raising cost, total, age 6-8	yr	8820	1999	60r
Child raising cost, total, age 9-11	yr	8800	1999	60r
Child raising cost, total, age 12-14	yr	9510	1999	60r
Child raising cost, total, age 15-17	yr	9740	1999	60r

Fort Smith, AR - continued

Item	Per	Value	Date	Ref.
Child Care - continued				
Child's child care and education, age 0-2	yr	1380	1999	60r
Child's child care and education, age 3-5	yr	1520	1999	60r
Child's child care and education, age 6-8	yr	990	1999	60r
Child's child care and education, age 9-11	yr	650	1999	60r
Child's child care and education, age 12-14	yr	490	1999	60r
Child's child care and education, age 15-17	yr	840	1999	60r
Child's clothing, age 0-2	yr	480	1999	60r
Child's clothing, age 3-5	yr	470	1999	60r
Child's clothing, age 6-8	yr	520	1999	60r
Child's clothing, age 9-11	yr	570	1999	60r
Child's clothing, age 12-14	yr	950	1999	60r
Child's clothing, age 15-17	yr	850	1999	60r
Child's food, age 0-2	yr	1000	1999	60r
Child's food, age 3-5	yr	1160	1999	60r
Child's food, age 6-8	yr	1490	1999	60r
Child's food, age 9-11	yr	1770	1999	60r
Child's food, age 12-14	yr	1770	1999	60r
Child's food, age 15-17	yr	1980	1999	60r
Child's health care, age 0-2	yr	620	1999	60r
Child's health care, age 3-5	yr	590	1999	60r
Child's health care, age 6-8	yr	680	1999	60r
Child's health care, age 9-11	yr	720	1999	60r
Child's health care, age 12-14	yr	730	1999	60r
Child's health care, age 15-17	yr	760	1999	60r
Child's housing, age 0-2	yr	3070	1999	60r
Child's housing, age 3-5	yr	3050	1999	60r
Child's housing, age 6-8	yr	3010	1999	60r
Child's housing, age 9-11	yr	2850	1999	60r
Child's housing, age 12-14	yr	3040	1999	60r
Child's housing, age 15-17	yr	2650	1999	60r
Child's personal care, reading, age 0-2	yr	910	1999	60r
Child's personal care, reading, age 3-5	yr	930	1999	60r
Child's personal care, reading, age 6-8	yr	960	1999	60r
Child's personal care, reading, age 9-11	yr	1000	1999	60r
Child's personal care, reading, age 12-14	yr	1170	1999	60r
Child's personal care, reading, age 15-17	yr	950	1999	60r
Clothing				
Apparel and services purchases	yr	1610	1999	30r
Boys' brief, cotton	3	4.19	3/01	4c
Boys, 2 to 15, expenditures on	yr	89	1999	30r
Children under 2, expenditures on	yr	79	1999	30r
Footwear, expenditures on	yr	283	1999	30r
Girls, 2 to 15, expenditures on	yr	103	1999	30r
Men and boys, expenditures on	yr	351	1999	30r
Men, 16 and over, expenditures on	yr	262	1999	30r
Shirt, man's dress shirt		29.95	3/01	4c
Slacks, man's "No Wrinkles" khaki		31.95	3/01	4c
Women, 16 and over, expenditures on	yr	538	1999	30r
Communications				
Newspaper subscription, daily and Sunday delivery	mos	9.30	3/01	4c
Phone line, single, business, field visit	inst.	84.00	12/97	17s
Phone line, single, business, no field visit	inst.	84.00	12/97	17s
Phone line, single, residence, field visit	inst.	39.70	12/97	17s
Phone line, single, residence, no field visit	inst.	39.70	12/97	17s
Postage and stationery, expenditures on	yr	104	1999	30r
Postal rate, express mail, up to half-pound		12.45	7/01	108r
Postal rate, letter, first class, first ounce		0.34	7/01	108r
Postal rate, letter, two ounces		0.57	7/01	108r
Postal rate, post card		0.21	7/01	108r
Postal rate, priority mail, two pounds		3.95	7/01	108r
Postal rate, priority mail, up to one pound		3.50	7/01	108r
Telephone bill, business, basic rate	mos	17.18-18.78	12/97	18c
Telephone bill, family of three	mos	22.30	3/01	4c
Telephone bill, residential, basic rate	mos	7.67-8.67	12/97	18c
Telephone services, expenditures on	yr	860	1999	30r
Education				
Board, 4-year private college/university	yr	2121	1996	38s
Board, 4-year public college/university	yr	1423	1996	38s

Values are in dollars or fractions of dollars. In the column headed *Ref*, references are shown to sources. Each reference is followed by a letter. These refer to the geographical level for which data were reported: s=State, r=Region, and c=City or metro. The abbreviation *ex* is used to mean *except* or *excluding*; *exp* stands for expenditures. For other abbreviations and further explanations, please see the Introduction.

Fort Smith, AR - continued

Item	Per	Value	Date	Ref.
Education				
Education expenditures	yr	431	1999	30r
Room, 4-year private college/university	yr	1488	1996	38s
Room, 4-year public college/university	yr	1613	1996	38s
Total cost, 4-year private college/university	yr	10183	1996	38s
Total cost, 4-year public college/university	yr	5064	1996	38s
Tuition, 2-year public college/university, in state	yr	903	1996	38s
Tuition, 4-year private college/university, in state	yr	6574	1996	38s
Tuition, 4-year public college/university	yr	2028	1996	38s
Energy and Fuels				
Electricity	KWh	0.09	7/01	11r
Electricity	500 KWhs	47.29	7/01	11r
Energy, combined forms, 2400 sq ft	mos	103.96	3/01	4c
Energy, exc. electricity, 2400 sq ft	mos	43.10	3/01	4c
Fuel oil #2	gal	1.43	7/01	11r
Fuel oil and other fuels, expenditures on	yr	45	1999	30r
Gas, heating, winter, average use	mos	66.67	2/96	98c
Gas, regular unleaded, cash, self-service	gal	1.43	3/01	4c
Gasoline, all types	gal	1.60	7/01	11r
Gasoline, unleaded midgrade	gal	1.65	7/01	11r
Gasoline, unleaded premium	gal	1.74	7/01	11r
Natural gas, expenditures on	yr	164	1999	30r
Utility (piped) gas, therm		1.01	7/01	11r
Utility (piped) gas, 40 therms		44.29	7/01	11r
Utility (piped) gas, 100 therms		97.44	7/01	11r
Entertainment				
Bowling, Saturday evening rate	line	2.50	3/01	4c
Entertainment purchases	yr	1574	1999	30r
Fees and admissions paid	yr	371	1999	30r
Monopoly game, Parker Brothers', No. 9	game	10.97	3/01	4c
Movie, first-run, Saturday, evening	adm.	6.50	3/01	4c
Reading purchases	yr	121	1999	30r
Television, radios, sound equipment, expenditures on	yr	561	1999	30r
Tennis balls, yellow, Wilson or Penn, 3	can	2.99	3/01	4c
Funerals				
Total cost of funeral		5842.28	1/99	78r
Acknowledgement cards		28.35	1/99	78r
Casket		2494.29	1/99	78r
Cosmetology, hair, other preparation		109.22	1/99	78r
Embalming		361.42	1/99	78r
Funeral at funeral home		349.20	1/99	78r
Hearse (local)		161.91	1/99	78r
Professional service charges		1116.50	1/99	78r
Service car/van		65.56	1/99	78r
Transfer of remains to funeral home		143.56	1/99	78r
Vault		785.25	1/99	78r
Visitation/viewing		227.02	1/99	78r
Groceries				
Groceries, ACCRA Index		89.10	3/01	4c
American processed cheese	lb	3.50	7/01	11r
Antibiotic ointment, Polysporin	0.5 oz	3.99	3/01	4c
Baby food, strained vegetables or fruit, lowest price	4-4.5 oz	0.49	3/01	4c
Bakery products, expenditures on	yr	261	1999	30r
Bananas	lb	0.48	3/01	4c
Bananas	lb	0.47	7/01	11r
Beans, dried, any type, all sizes	lb	0.63	7/01	11r
Beef for stew, boneless	lb	2.86	7/01	11r
Beef or hamburger, ground	lb	1.69	3/01	4c
Beef, expenditures on	yr	210	1999	30r
Bologna, all beef or mixed	lb	2.29	7/01	11r
Bread, French	lb	1.66	7/01	11r
Bread, white	loaf	0.74	3/01	4c
Bread, white, pan	lb	0.87	7/01	11r
Bread, whole wheat, pan	lb	1.38	7/01	11r
Broccoli	lb	1.04	7/01	11r
Butter, salted, grade AA, stick	lb	2.26	7/01	11r

Fort Smith, AR - continued

Item	Per	Value	Date	Ref.
Groceries - continued				
Butter, yoghurt, cheese, etc, expenditures on	yr	170	1999	30r
Cabbage	lb	0.42	7/01	11r
Cereals and cereal products, expenditures on	yr	140	1999	30r
Cheddar cheese, natural	lb	3.75	7/01	11r
Cheese, Kraft grated Parmesan	8 oz	2.99	3/01	4c
Chicken breast, bone-in	lb	1.85	7/01	11r
Chicken legs, bone-in	lb	1.34	7/01	11r
Chicken, fresh, whole	lb	1.05	7/01	11r
Chicken, whole fryer	lb	0.67	3/01	4c
Chops, boneless,	lb	4.13	7/01	11r
Chuck roast, graded and ungraded, excl U.S. prime and choice	lb	2.35	7/01	11r
Chuck roast, U.S. choice, boneless	lb	2.67	7/01	11r
Cigarettes, Winston, Kings	carton	29.63	3/01	4c
Coffee, 100%, ground roast, all sizes	lb	2.88	7/01	11r
Coffee, instant, plain, regular, all sizes	16 oz	9.25	7/01	11r
Coffee, vacuum-packed	13 oz	2.10	3/01	4c
Cola, non diet,	2 liter	1.11	7/01	11r
Corn Flakes, Kellogg's or Post Toasties	18 oz	1.27	3/01	4c
Corn, frozen, whole kernel, lowest price	16 oz	1.08	3/01	4c
Crackers, soda, salted	lb	1.70	7/01	11r
Dairy product purchases	yr	282	1999	30r
Eggs, expenditures on	yr	32	1999	30r
Eggs, Grade A or AA	dozen	0.98	3/01	4c
Fats and oils, expenditures on	yr	79	1999	30r
Fish and seafood, expenditures on	yr	99	1999	30r
Flour, white, all purpose	lb	0.32	7/01	11r
Food (excl fruit and vegetables), eaten at home, purchases	yr	815	1999	30r
Food cooked on trips, expenditures on	yr	36	1999	30r
Food purchases	yr	4533	1999	30r
Food purchases, eaten away from home	yr	1873	1999	30r
Food purchases, food eaten at home	yr	2660	1999	30r
Fresh fruits, expenditures on	yr	128	1999	30r
Fresh milk and cream, expenditures on	yr	112	1999	30r
Fresh vegetables, expenditures on	yr	131	1999	30r
Fruit and vegetable purchases	yr	438	1999	30r
Grapefruit	lb	0.59	7/01	11r
Grapes, Thompson, seedless	lb	2.12	7/01	11r
Ground beef, 100% beef	lb	1.76	7/01	11r
Ground beef, lean and extra lean	lb	2.60	7/01	11r
Ground chuck, 100% beef	lb	2.08	7/01	11r
Ham, boneless, excl canned	lb	2.71	7/01	11r
Ham, rump or shank half, bone-in, smoked	lb	2.19	7/01	11r
Ice cream, prepackaged, bulk, regular	1/2 gal	3.93	7/01	11r
Lemons	lb	1.32	7/01	11r
Lettuce, iceberg	head	1.06	3/01	4c
Lettuce, iceberg	lb	0.76	7/01	11r
Margarine, Blue Bonnet or Parkay, stick	lb	0.50	3/01	4c
Milk, fresh, low fat,	gal	2.75	7/01	11r
Milk, fresh, whole, fortified	gal	2.97	7/01	11r
Milk, whole	1/2 gal	1.42	3/01	4c
Nonalcoholic beverages, expenditures on	yr	228	1999	30r
Orange juice, frozen concentrate	16 oz	1.95	7/01	11r
Orange juice, Minute Maid frozen	12 oz	1.45	3/01	4c
Oranges, Navel	lb	0.73	7/01	11r
Oranges, Valencia	lb	0.55	7/01	11r
Peaches, halves or slices, Hunt's, Del Monte, or Libby's	29 oz	1.56	3/01	4c
Peanut butter, creamy, all sizes	lb	1.83	7/01	11r
Pears, Anjou	lb	0.98	7/01	11r
Peas, green, Del Monte or Green Giant	15 oz	0.66	3/01	4c
Pork chops, center cut, bone-in	lb	3.33	7/01	11r
Pork sausage, fresh, loose	lb	2.59	7/01	11r
Pork shoulder picnic, bone-in, smoked	lb	1.12	7/01	11r
Pork, expenditures on	yr	162	1999	30r
Potato chips	16 oz	3.59	7/01	11r
Potatoes, frozen, french fried	lb	1.00	7/01	11r
Potatoes, white or red	10 lb	2.29	3/01	4c
Potatoes, white, all types	lb	0.44	7/01	11r
Poultry, expenditures on	yr	137	1999	30r

Values are in dollars or fractions of dollars. In the column headed *Ref*, references are shown to sources. Each reference is followed by a letter. These refer to the geographical level for which data were reported: s=State, r=Region, and c=City or metro. The abbreviation *ex* is used to mean *except* or *excluding*; *exp* stands for expenditures. For other abbreviations and further explanations, please see the Introduction.

Fort Smith, AR - continued

Item	Per	Value	Date	Ref.
Groceries				
Processed fruits, expenditures on	yr	97	1999	30r
Processed vegetables, expenditures on	yr	82	1999	30r
Rice, white, long grain, uncooked	lb	0.51	7/01	11r
Round roast, graded and ungraded, excl U.S. prime and choice	lb	2.96	7/01	11r
Round steak, graded and ungraded, excl U.S. prime and choice	lb	3.11	7/01	11r
Sausage, Jimmy Dean/Owens pork	lb	2.42	3/01	4c
Shortening, vegetable, Crisco	3 lb	2.88	3/01	4c
Sirloin steak, graded and ungraded, excl U.S. prime and choice	lb	4.23	7/01	11r
Soft drink, Coca Cola, ex deposit	2 liter	1.23	3/01	4c
Spaghetti and macaroni	lb	0.78	7/01	11r
Steak, round, U.S. choice, boneless	lb	3.56	7/01	11r
Steak, sirloin, U.S. choice, boneless	lb	5.65	7/01	11r
Steak, T-bone	lb	7.14	3/01	4c
Strawberries, dry pint	12 oz	1.50	7/01	11r
Sugar and other sweets, expenditures on	yr	99	1999	30r
Sugar, cane or beet	4 lbs	1.44	3/01	4c
Sugar, white, 33-80 ounce package	lb	0.39	7/01	11r
Sugar, white, all sizes	lb	0.42	7/01	11r
Tobacco products and smoking supplies purchases	yr	288	1999	30r
Tomatoes, field grown	lb	1.43	7/01	11r
Tomatoes, Hunt's or Del Monte	14.5 oz	0.97	3/01	4c
Tuna, chunk, light	6 oz	0.53	3/01	4c
Tuna, light, chunk	lb	1.77	7/01	11r
Turkey, frozen, whole	lb	1.05	7/01	11r
Goods and Services				
Miscellaneous goods and services, ACCRA Index		96.30	3/01	4c
B&B Japanese maple (acer japonicum)	gal	79.98-99.00	4/00	93r
Boxwood (buxus)	2 gal	12.98-18.99	4/00	93r
Daylilly (hemerocallis)	gal	7.96-11.00	4/00	93r
Flat of annuals		13.99-27.99	4/00	93r
Fountain grass (pennisetum)	gal	6.96-9.00	4/00	93r
Hanging basket (10 in)		9.99-24.99	4/00	93r
Hardy geranium (geranium)	gal	5.96-8.00	4/00	93r
Hosta (hosta)	gal	8.96-12.99	4/00	93r
Lilac (syrubga vulgaris)	2 gal	13.00-19.99	4/00	93r
Rhododendron (rhododendron)	2 gal	12.98-29.99	4/00	93r
Sage (salvia)	gal	5.96-8.00	4/00	93r
Wintercreeper euonymus (euonymus fortunei)	2 gal	13.00-18.99	4/00	93r
Hunting license	yr	25.00	4/01	34s
Health Care				
Health care, ACCRA Index		85.50	3/01	4c
Cardiac catheterization, ave hospital/ physician charges		12240	1998	77s
Childbirth, Cesarean delivery		11587	1997	13r
Childbirth, vaginal delivery		6725	1997	13r
Dentist's fee, adult teeth cleaning and periodic oral exam	visit	65.00	3/01	4c
Doctor's fee, routine exam, established patient	visit	55.67	3/01	4c
Drugs, expenditures on	yr	399	1999	30r
Health care purchases	yr	1971	1999	30r
Health insurance expenditures	yr	933	1999	30r
Hospital care, private room	day	300.00	3/01	4c

Fort Smith, AR - continued

Item	Per	Value	Date	Ref.
Health Care - continued				
Hysterectomy, laproscopically-assisted, ave hospital/physician charges		10580	1998	76s
Hysterectomy, vaginal, ave hospital and physician charges		8270	1998	76s
Medicaid dispensing fee		5.51	1999	87s
Medical services expenditures	yr	547	1999	30r
Medical supplies, expenditures on	yr	91	1999	30r
Household Goods				
Dishwashing powder, Cascade	50 oz	3.26	3/01	4c
Floor coverings, expenditures on	yr	44	1999	30r
Furniture, expenditures on	yr	335	1999	30r
Household furnishings and equipment purchases	yr	1328	1999	30r
Household textiles, expenditures on	yr	89	1999	30r
Laundry and cleaning supplies, expenditures on	yr	113	1999	30r
Tissues, facial, Kleenex brand	175	1.17	3/01	4c
Housing				
Housing, ACCRA Index		77.70	3/01	4c
Home, 2200 sq ft, 4-br, 2-bath, 2-car garage, average		136750	2000	47c
Home price, existing, ave		160100	10/00	90r
Home value, median		94000	2001	53s
House, 2400 sq ft, 8000 sq ft lot, new, urban, utilities	total	162000	3/01	4c
House payment, principal and interest, 25% down payment	mos	820	3/01	4c
Household operation expenditures	yr	553	1999	30r
Housekeeping supplies purchases	yr	473	1999	30r
Housing, expenditures on	yr	10303	1999	30r
Maintenance, repairs, insurance expenditures	yr	699	1999	30r
Monthly rental value of owned home	mos	505	1999	30r
Owned dwellings, expenditures own	yr	3465	1999	30r
Rent expenditures	yr	1641	1999	30r
Rent, apartment, 2 br, 1 1/2-2 baths, unfurn, 950 sq ft, water	mos	490	3/01	4c
Rental unit, 1 bedroom, with utilities	mos	341	4/01	41c
Rental unit, 2 bedroom, with utilities	mos	449	4/01	41c
Rental unit, 3 bedroom, with utilities	mos	600	4/01	41c
Rental unit, 4 bedroom, with utilities	mos	630	4/01	41c
Shelter, expenditures on	yr	5467	1999	30r
Insurance and Pensions				
Life and other personal insurance purchases	yr	414	1999	30r
Pensions and Social Security, expenditures on	yr	2635	1999	30r
Personal insurance and pensions, expenditures on	yr	3048	1999	30r
Legal Fees				
Divorce, filing fee		100.00	4/01	35s
Driver's license fee	orig	14.00	1999	48s
Driver's license fee	renew	14.00	1999	48s
Personal Goods				
Personal care products and services purchases	yr	393	1999	30r
Shampoo, Alberto VO5	15 oz	1.00	3/01	4c
Toothpaste, Crest or Colgate	6-7 oz	2.16	3/01	4c
Personal Services				
Dry cleaning, man's 2-pc suit		6.12	3/01	4c
Man's haircut, barbershop, no styling		10.63	3/01	4c
Personal services, household, expenditures on	yr	258	1999	30r
Woman's shampoo, trim, blow-dry, no style-change		14.83	3/01	4c
Pets				
Pets, toys, and playground equipment, expenditures on	yr	306	1999	30r

Values are in dollars or fractions of dollars. In the column headed *Ref*, references are shown to sources. Each reference is followed by a letter. These refer to the geographical level for which data were reported: s=State, r=Region, and c=City or metro. The abbreviation *ex* is used to mean *except* or *excluding*; *exp* stands for expenditures. For other abbreviations and further explanations, please see the Introduction.

Fort Smith, AR - continued

Item	Per	Value	Date	Ref.
Restaurant Food				
Chicken, fried, thigh and drumstick, KFC/ Church's		2.29	3/01	4c
Hamburger with cheese, McDonald's	1/4 lb	1.97	3/01	4c
Pizza, Pizza Hut or Pizza Inn	11-12 in	7.99	3/01	4c
Taxes				
Federal income taxes paid	yr	2047	1999	30r
Personal taxes, expenditures on	yr	2554	1999	30r
Property taxes paid	yr	726	1999	30r
State and local income taxes paid	yr	363	1999	30r
Transportation				
Transportation, ACCRA Index		94.50	3/01	4c
Bus fare, to central business district	1-way	1.00	3/01	4c
Cars and trucks, new, expenditures on	yr	1648	1999	30r
Cars and trucks, used, expenditures on	yr	1651	1999	30r
Diesel at the pump	gal	1.17	10/99	73s
Gasoline and motor oil purchases	yr	1052	1999	30r
Gasoline before-tax price (cents)	gal	102.60	10/00	43s
Maintenance and repair expenditures	yr	621	1999	30r
Public transportation, expenditures on	yr	298	1999	30r
Tire balance, computer or spin balance, front	wheel	6.74	3/01	4c
Transportation purchases	yr	6738	1999	30r
Vehicle expenses, miscellaneous, purchases	yr	2033	1999	30r
Vehicle insurance payments	yr	696	1999	30r
Vehicle purchases (net outlay)	yr	3354	1999	30r
Vehicle rental, lease expenditures	yr	352	1999	30r
Utilities				
Utilities, ACCRA Index		87.60	3/01	4c
Electrical bill, average	mos	75.00	9/00	9s
Electricity, expenditures on	yr	1115	1999	30r
Electricity, summer, 250 KWh	mos	17.71	2/96	97c
Electricity, summer, 500 KWh	mos	29.46	2/96	97c
Electricity, summer, 750 KWh	mos	41.23	2/96	97c
Electricity, summer, 1000 KWh	mos	52.98	2/96	97c
Electricity and other, mixed, 2400 sq ft, new home	mos	60.86	3/01	4c
Electricity cost, average	KWh	5.70	9/00	9s
Water and other public services, expenditures on	yr	298	1999	30r
Weddings				
Wedding (national average cost)		19936	2000	33r
Attendants' gifts		321	1998	33r
Bridal attendants' apparel (5 persons)		824	2000	33r
Bride's headpiece/veil		173	1998	33r
Bride's wedding dress		859	1998	33r
Clergy, religious facility fee		242	1998	33r
Engagement ring		3177	1998	33r
Flowers		789	1998	33r
Groom's formalwear rental		99	2000	33r
Limousine		410	1998	33r
Marriage license cost		30.00	4/01	35s
Men's formalwear (ushers, best man)		469	2000	33r
Mother of bride apparel		241	2000	33r
Music		866	1998	33r
Photography and videography		1368	1998	33r
Rehearsal dinner		728	1998	33r
Wedding invitations and announcements		341	1998	33r
Wedding reception		7968	2000	33r
Wedding rings (bride and groom)		1060	1998	33r

Fort Walton Beach, FL

Item	Per	Value	Date	Ref.
Composite, ACCRA index		99.10	3/01	4c
Alcoholic Beverages				
Alcoholic beverage purchases	yr	253	1999	30r
Beer, Heineken, 12-oz, ex deposit	6	6.98	3/01	4c
J & B Scotch	750-ml	20.62	3/01	4c
Malt beverages, all types, all sizes, any origin	16 oz	0.96	7/01	11r
Wine, Livingston or Gallo, Chablis blanc	1.5 liter	5.65	3/01	4c

Fort Walton Beach, FL - continued

Item	Per	Value	Date	Ref.
Appliances				
Appliance repair, service call, washing machine	min lab chg	50.00	3/01	4c
Major appliances, expenditures on	yr	172	1999	30r
Small appliances, housewares, expenditures on	yr	81	1999	30r
Banking and Money				
Mortgage interest and charges paid	yr	2039	1999	30r
Mortgage principal paid on owned property	yr	1026	1999	30r
Mortgage rate, incl. points and orig. fee, 30-yr. conv. fixed or ARM	mos	6.94	3/01	4c
Vehicle finance charges paid	yr	365	1999	30r
Charity				
Cash contributions, expenditures	yr	1127	1999	30r
Child Care				
Child raising cost, total, age 0-2	yr	8540	1999	60r
Child raising cost, total, age 3-5	yr	8780	1999	60r
Child raising cost, total, age 6-8	yr	8820	1999	60r
Child raising cost, total, age 9-11	yr	8800	1999	60r
Child raising cost, total, age 12-14	yr	9510	1999	60r
Child raising cost, total, age 15-17	yr	9740	1999	60r
Child's child care and education, age 0-2	yr	1380	1999	60r
Child's child care and education, age 3-5	yr	1520	1999	60r
Child's child care and education, age 6-8	yr	990	1999	60r
Child's child care and education, age 9-11	yr	650	1999	60r
Child's child care and education, age 12-14	yr	490	1999	60r
Child's child care and education, age 15-17	yr	840	1999	60r
Child's clothing, age 0-2	yr	480	1999	60r
Child's clothing, age 3-5	yr	470	1999	60r
Child's clothing, age 6-8	yr	520	1999	60r
Child's clothing, age 9-11	yr	570	1999	60r
Child's clothing, age 12-14	yr	950	1999	60r
Child's clothing, age 15-17	yr	850	1999	60r
Child's food, age 0-2	yr	1000	1999	60r
Child's food, age 3-5	yr	1160	1999	60r
Child's food, age 6-8	yr	1490	1999	60r
Child's food, age 9-11	yr	1770	1999	60r
Child's food, age 12-14	yr	1770	1999	60r
Child's food, age 15-17	yr	1980	1999	60r
Child's health care, age 0-2	yr	620	1999	60r
Child's health care, age 3-5	yr	590	1999	60r
Child's health care, age 6-8	yr	680	1999	60r
Child's health care, age 9-11	yr	720	1999	60r
Child's health care, age 12-14	yr	730	1999	60r
Child's health care, age 15-17	yr	760	1999	60r
Child's housing, age 0-2	yr	3070	1999	60r
Child's housing, age 3-5	yr	3050	1999	60r
Child's housing, age 6-8	yr	3010	1999	60r
Child's housing, age 9-11	yr	2850	1999	60r
Child's housing, age 12-14	yr	3040	1999	60r
Child's housing, age 15-17	yr	2650	1999	60r
Child's personal care, reading, age 0-2	yr	910	1999	60r
Child's personal care, reading, age 3-5	yr	930	1999	60r
Child's personal care, reading, age 6-8	yr	960	1999	60r
Child's personal care, reading, age 9-11	yr	1000	1999	60r
Child's personal care, reading, age 12-14	yr	1170	1999	60r
Child's personal care, reading, age 15-17	yr	950	1999	60r
Clothing				
Apparel and services purchases	yr	1610	1999	30r
Boys' brief, cotton	3	7.24	3/01	4c
Boys, 2 to 15, expenditures on	yr	89	1999	30r
Children under 2, expenditures on	yr	79	1999	30r
Footwear, expenditures on	yr	283	1999	30r
Girls, 2 to 15, expenditures on	yr	103	1999	30r
Men and boys, expenditures on	yr	351	1999	30r
Men, 16 and over, expenditures on	yr	262	1999	30r
Shirt, man's dress shirt		25.99	3/01	4c
Slacks, man's "No Wrinkles" khaki		29.99	3/01	4c
Women, 16 and over, expenditures on	yr	538	1999	30r

Values are in dollars or fractions of dollars. In the column headed *Ref*, references are shown to sources. Each reference is followed by a letter. These refer to the geographical level for which data were reported: s=State, r=Region, and c=City or metro. The abbreviation *ex* is used to mean *except* or *excluding*; *exp* stands for expenditures. For other abbreviations and further explanations, please see the Introduction.

Fort Walton Beach, FL - continued

Item	Per	Value	Date	Ref.
Communications				
Cable modem installation, Adelphi		54.90	6/99	103s
Cable modem installation, Comcast		95.00	6/99	103s
Cable modem installation, Media One		100.00	6/99	103s
Cable modem installation, Time Warner		75.00-225.00	6/99	103s
Cable modem rate, cable subscriber, Adelphi	mos	34.95	6/99	103s
Cable modem rate, cable subscriber, Comcast	mos	39.95	6/99	103s
Cable modem rate, cable subscriber, Media One	mos	34.95-39.95	6/99	103s
Cable modem rate, cable subscriber, Time Warner	mos	39.95-49.95	6/99	103s
Cable modem rate, non-cable subscriber, Adelphi	mos	44.95	6/99	103s
Cable modem rate, non-cable subscriber, Comcast	mos	49.95	6/99	103s
Cable modem rate, non-cable subscriber, Media One	mos	49.95	6/99	103s
Cable modem rate, non-cable subscriber, Time Warner	mos	39.95-54.95	6/99	103s
Newspaper subscription, daily and Sunday delivery	mos	12.33	3/01	4c
Phone line, single, business, field visit	inst.	56.00	12/97	17s
Phone line, single, business, no field visit	inst.	56.00	12/97	17s
Phone line, single, residence, field visit	inst.	40.00	12/97	17s
Phone line, single, residence, no field visit	inst.	40.00	12/97	17s
Postage and stationery, expenditures on	yr	104	1999	30r
Postal rate, express mail, up to half-pound		12.45	7/01	108r
Postal rate, letter, first class, first ounce		0.34	7/01	108r
Postal rate, letter, two ounces		0.57	7/01	108r
Postal rate, post card		0.21	7/01	108r
Postal rate, priority mail, two pounds		3.95	7/01	108r
Postal rate, priority mail, up to one pound		3.50	7/01	108r
Telephone bill, family of three	mos	17.69	3/01	4c
Telephone services, expenditures on	yr	860	1999	30r
Education				
Board, 4-year private college/university	yr	2236	1996	38s
Board, 4-year public college/university	yr	2295	1996	38s
Education expenditures	yr	431	1999	30r
Room, 4-year private college/university	yr	2428	1996	38s
Room, 4-year public college/university	yr	2193	1996	38s
Total cost, 4-year private college/university	yr	15028	1996	38s
Total cost, 4-year public college/university	yr	6254	1996	38s
Tuition, 2-year public college/university, in state	yr	1103	1996	38s
Tuition, 4-year private college/university, in state	yr	10364	1996	38s
Tuition, 4-year public college/university	yr	1767	1996	38s
Energy and Fuels				
Electricity	KWh	0.09	7/01	11r
Electricity	500 KWhs	47.29	7/01	11r
Energy, combined forms, 2400 sq ft	mos	101.31	3/01	4c
Energy, exc. electricity, 2400 sq ft	mos	40.49	3/01	4c
Fuel oil #2	gal	1.43	7/01	11r
Fuel oil and other fuels, expenditures on	yr	45	1999	30r
Gas, natural, commercial rate	1000 cf	8.44	11/00	88s
Gas, regular unleaded, cash, self-service	gal	1.29	3/01	4c
Gasoline, all types	gal	1.60	7/01	11r
Gasoline, unleaded midgrade	gal	1.65	7/01	11r
Gasoline, unleaded premium	gal	1.74	7/01	11r
Natural gas, expenditures on	yr	164	1999	30r
Utility (piped) gas, therm		1.01	7/01	11r
Utility (piped) gas, 40 therms		44.29	7/01	11r
Utility (piped) gas, 100 therms		97.44	7/01	11r
Entertainment				
Bowling, Saturday evening rate	line	2.90	3/01	4c
Entertainment purchases	yr	1574	1999	30r
Fees and admissions paid	yr	371	1999	30r
Monopoly game, Parker Brothers', No. 9	game	14.09	3/01	4c
Movie, first-run, Saturday evening	adm.	6.75	3/01	4c

Fort Walton Beach, FL - continued

Item	Per	Value	Date	Ref.
Entertainment - continued				
Reading purchases	yr	121	1999	30r
Television, radios, sound equipment, expenditures on	yr	561	1999	30r
Tennis balls, yellow, Wilson or Penn, 3	can	2.93	3/01	4c
Funerals				
Total cost of funeral		5922.53	1/99	78r
Acknowledgement cards		63.43	1/99	78r
Casket		2258.77	1/99	78r
Cosmetology, hair, other preparation		127.09	1/99	78r
Embalming		393.49	1/99	78r
Funeral at funeral home		367.50	1/99	78r
Hearse (local)		169.66	1/99	78r
Professional service charges		1211.32	1/99	78r
Service car/van		80.69	1/99	78r
Transfer of remains to funeral home		144.25	1/99	78r
Vault		803.50	1/99	78r
Visitation/viewing		302.83	1/99	78r
Groceries				
Groceries, ACCRA Index		96.00	3/01	4c
American processed cheese	lb	3.50	7/01	11r
Antibiotic ointment, Polysporin	0.5 oz	4.76	3/01	4c
Baby food, strained vegetables or fruit, lowest price	4-4.5 oz	0.41	3/01	4c
Bakery products, expenditures on	yr	261	1999	30r
Bananas	lb	0.48	3/01	4c
Bananas	lb	0.47	7/01	11r
Beans, dried, any type, all sizes	lb	0.63	7/01	11r
Beef for stew, boneless	lb	2.86	7/01	11r
Beef or hamburger, ground	lb	1.64	3/01	4c
Beef, expenditures on	yr	210	1999	30r
Bologna, all beef or mixed	lb	2.29	7/01	11r
Bread, French	lb	1.66	7/01	11r
Bread, white	loaf	0.89	3/01	4c
Bread, white, pan	lb	0.87	7/01	11r
Bread, whole wheat, pan	lb	1.38	7/01	11r
Broccoli	lb	1.04	7/01	11r
Butter, salted, grade AA, stick	lb	2.26	7/01	11r
Butter, yoghurt, cheese, etc, expenditures on	yr	170	1999	30r
Cabbage	lb	0.42	7/01	11r
Cereals and cereal products, expenditures on	yr	140	1999	30r
Cheddar cheese, natural	lb	3.75	7/01	11r
Cheese, Kraft grated Parmesan	8 oz	3.71	3/01	4c
Chicken breast, bone-in	lb	1.85	7/01	11r
Chicken legs, bone-in	lb	1.34	7/01	11r
Chicken, fresh, whole	lb	1.05	7/01	11r
Chicken, whole fryer	lb	0.91	3/01	4c
Chops, boneless	lb	4.13	7/01	11r
Chuck roast, graded and ungraded, excl U.S. prime and choice	lb	2.35	7/01	11r
Chuck roast, U.S. choice, boneless	lb	2.67	7/01	11r
Cigarettes, Winston, Kings	carton	27.47	3/01	4c
Coffee, 100%, ground roast, all sizes	lb	2.88	7/01	11r
Coffee, instant, plain, regular, all sizes	16 oz	9.25	7/01	11r
Coffee, vacuum-packed	13 oz	2.29	3/01	4c
Cola, non diet	2 liter	1.11	7/01	11r
Corn Flakes, Kellogg's or Post Toasties	18 oz	2.89	3/01	4c
Corn, frozen, whole kernel, lowest price	16 oz	1.38	3/01	4c
Crackers, soda, salted	lb	1.70	7/01	11r
Dairy product purchases	yr	282	1999	30r
Eggs, expenditures on	yr	32	1999	30r
Eggs, Grade A or AA	dozen	0.99	3/01	4c
Fats and oils, expenditures on	yr	79	1999	30r
Fish and seafood, expenditures on	yr	99	1999	30r
Flour, white, all purpose	lb	0.32	7/01	11r
Food (excl fruit and vegetables), eaten at home, purchases	yr	815	1999	30r
Food cooked on trips, expenditures on	yr	36	1999	30r
Food purchases	yr	4533	1999	30r
Food purchases, eaten away from home	yr	1873	1999	30r
Food purchases, food eaten at home	yr	2660	1999	30r

Values are in dollars or fractions of dollars. In the column headed *Ref*, references are shown to sources. Each reference is followed by a letter. These refer to the geographical level for which data were reported: s=State, r=Region, and c=City or metro. The abbreviation *ex* is used to mean *except* or *excluding*; *exp* stands for *expenditures*. For other abbreviations and further explanations, please see the Introduction.

Fort Walton Beach, FL - continued

Item	Per	Value	Date	Ref.
Groceries				
Fresh fruits, expenditures on	yr	128	1999	30r
Fresh milk and cream, expenditures on	yr	112	1999	30r
Fresh vegetables, expenditures on	yr	131	1999	30r
Fruit and vegetable purchases	yr	438	1999	30r
Grapefruit	lb	0.59	7/01	11r
Grapes, Thompson, seedless	lb	2.12	7/01	11r
Ground beef, 100% beef	lb	1.76	7/01	11r
Ground beef, lean and extra lean	lb	2.60	7/01	11r
Ground chuck, 100% beef	lb	2.08	7/01	11r
Ham, boneless, excl canned	lb	2.71	7/01	11r
Ham, rump or shank half, bone-in, smoked	lb	2.19	7/01	11r
Ice cream, prepackaged, bulk, regular	1/2 gal	3.93	7/01	11r
Lemons	lb	1.32	7/01	11r
Lettuce, iceberg	head	1.03	3/01	4c
Lettuce, iceberg	lb	0.76	7/01	11r
Margarine, Blue Bonnet or Parkay, stick	lb	0.48	3/01	4c
Milk, fresh, low fat,	gal	2.75	7/01	11r
Milk, fresh, whole, fortified	gal	2.97	7/01	11r
Milk, whole	1/2 gal	1.80	3/01	4c
Nonalcoholic beverages, expenditures on	yr	228	1999	30r
Orange juice, frozen concentrate	16 oz	1.95	7/01	11r
Orange juice, Minute Maid frozen	12 oz	1.80	3/01	4c
Oranges, Navel	lb	0.73	7/01	11r
Oranges, Valencia	lb	0.55	7/01	11r
Peaches, halves or slices, Hunt's, Del Monte, or Libby's	29 oz	1.54	3/01	4c
Peanut butter, creamy, all sizes	lb	1.83	7/01	11r
Pears, Anjou	lb	0.98	7/01	11r
Peas, green, Del Monte or Green Giant	15 oz	0.61	3/01	4c
Pork chops, center cut, bone-in	lb	3.33	7/01	11r
Pork sausage, fresh, loose	lb	2.59	7/01	11r
Pork shoulder picnic, bone-in, smoked	lb	1.12	7/01	11r
Pork, expenditures on	yr	162	1999	30r
Potato chips	16 oz	3.59	7/01	11r
Potatoes, frozen, french fried	lb	1.00	7/01	11r
Potatoes, white or red	10 lb	2.06	3/01	4c
Potatoes, white, all types	lb	0.44	7/01	11r
Poultry, expenditures on	yr	137	1999	30r
Processed fruits, expenditures on	yr	97	1999	30r
Processed vegetables, expenditures on	yr	82	1999	30r
Rice, white, long grain, uncooked	lb	0.51	7/01	11r
Round roast, graded and ungraded, excl U.S. prime and choice	lb	2.96	7/01	11r
Round steak, graded and ungraded, excl U.S. prime and choice	lb	3.11	7/01	11r
Sausage, Jimmy Dean/Owens pork	lb	2.69	3/01	4c
Shortening, vegetable, Crisco	3 lb	3.06	3/01	4c
Sirloin steak, graded and ungraded, excl U.S. prime and choice	lb	4.23	7/01	11r
Soft drink, Coca Cola, ex deposit	2 liter	1.04	3/01	4c
Spaghetti and macaroni	lb	0.78	7/01	11r
Steak, round, U.S. choice, boneless	lb	3.56	7/01	11r
Steak, sirloin, U.S. choice, boneless	lb	5.65	7/01	11r
Steak, T-bone	lb	6.89	3/01	4c
Strawberries, dry pint	12 oz	1.50	7/01	11r
Sugar and other sweets, expenditures on	yr	99	1999	30r
Sugar, cane or beet	4 lbs	1.45	3/01	4c
Sugar, white, 33-80 ounce package	lb	0.39	7/01	11r
Sugar, white, all sizes	lb	0.42	7/01	11r
Tobacco products and smoking supplies purchases	yr	288	1999	30r
Tomatoes, field grown	lb	1.43	7/01	11r
Tomatoes, Hunt's or Del Monte	14.5 oz	0.79	3/01	4c
Tuna, chunk, light	6 oz	0.51	3/01	4c
Tuna, light, chunk	lb	1.77	7/01	11r
Turkey, frozen, whole	lb	1.05	7/01	11r
Goods and Services				
Miscellaneous goods and services, ACCRA Index		102.90	3/01	4c
B&B Japanese maple (acer japonicum)	gal	49.98-129.00	4/00	93r

Fort Walton Beach, FL - continued

Item	Per	Value	Date	Ref.
Goods and Services - continued				
Boxwood (buxus)	2 gal	12.99-16.99	4/00	93r
Daylilly (hemerocalis)	gal	4.99-8.99	4/00	93r
Flat of annuals		11.00-13.92	4/00	93r
Fountain grass (pennisetum)	gal	5.98-7.98	4/00	93r
Hanging basket (10 in)		7.99-14.98	4/00	93r
Hardy geranium (geranium)	gal	5.98-8.00	4/00	93r
Hosta (hosta)	gal	4.99-10.98	4/00	93r
Lilac (syrubga vulgaris)	2 gal	12.99-21.99	4/00	93r
Rhododendron (rhododendron)	2 gal	14.99-24.99	4/00	93r
Sage (salvia)	gal	5.98-6.99	4/00	93r
Wintercreeper euonymus (euonymus fortunei)	2 gal	7.99-89.99	4/00	93r
Hunting license	yr	12.50	4/01	34s
Health Care				
Health care, ACCRA Index		106.20	3/01	4c
Cardiac catheterization, ave hospital/physician charges		15060	1998	77s
Childbirth, Cesarean delivery		11587	1997	13r
Childbirth, vaginal delivery		6725	1997	13r
Dentist's fee, adult teeth cleaning and periodic oral exam	visit	71.80	3/01	4c
Doctor's fee, routine exam, established patient	visit	64.40	3/01	4c
Drugs, expenditures on	yr	399	1999	30r
Health care purchases	yr	1971	1999	30r
Health insurance expenditures	yr	933	1999	30r
Hospital care, private room	day	594.00	3/01	4c
Hysterectomy, laproscopically-assisted, ave hospital/physician charges		14760	1998	76s
Hysterectomy, vaginal, ave hospital and physician charges		11320	1998	76s
Medicaid dispensing fee		4.23	1999	87s
Medical services expenditures	yr	547	1999	30r
Medical supplies, expenditures on	yr	91	1999	30r
Plastic surgery, breast augmentation		2870	2000	7r
Plastic surgery, breast lift		3649	2000	7r
Plastic surgery, facelift		5008	2000	7r
Plastic surgery, hair transplantation		3425	2000	7r
Plastic surgery, lip augmentation		1227	2000	7r
Plastic surgery, lower body lift		4793	2000	7r
Plastic surgery, thigh lift		3862	2000	7r
Household Goods				
Dishwashing powder, Cascade	50 oz	3.36	3/01	4c
Floor coverings, expenditures on	yr	44	1999	30r
Furniture, expenditures on	yr	335	1999	30r
Household furnishings and equipment purchases	yr	1328	1999	30r
Household textiles, expenditures on	yr	89	1999	30r
Laundry and cleaning supplies, expenditures on	yr	113	1999	30r
Tissues, facial, Kleenex brand	175	1.43	3/01	4c
Housing				
Housing, ACCRA Index		98.60	3/01	4c
Home price, existing, ave		160100	10/00	90r
Home value, median		104000	2001	53s
House, 2400 sq ft, 8000 sq ft lot, new, urban, utilities	total	207865	3/01	4c
House payment, principal and interest, 25% down payment	mos	1031	3/01	4c
Household operation expenditures	yr	553	1999	30r
Housekeeping supplies purchases	yr	473	1999	30r

Values are in dollars or fractions of dollars. In the column headed *Ref*, references are shown to sources. Each reference is followed by a letter. These refer to the geographical level for which data were reported: s=State, r=Region, and c=City or metro. The abbreviation *ex* is used to mean *except* or *excluding*; *exp* stands for *expenditures*. For other abbreviations and further explanations, please see the Introduction.

Fort Walton Beach, FL - continued

Item	Per	Value	Date	Ref.
Housing				
Housing, expenditures on	yr	10303	1999	30r
Maintenance, repairs, insurance expenditures	yr	699	1999	30r
Monthly rental value of owned home	mos	505	1999	30r
Owned dwellings, expenditures own	yr	3465	1999	30r
Rent expenditures	yr	1641	1999	30r
Rent, apartment, 2 br, 1 1/2-2 baths, unfurn, 950 sq ft, water	mos	646	3/01	4c
Rental unit, 1 bedroom, with utilities	mos	451	4/01	41c
Rental unit, 2 bedroom, with utilities	mos	512	4/01	41c
Rental unit, 3 bedroom, with utilities	mos	694	4/01	41c
Rental unit, 4 bedroom, with utilities	mos	818	4/01	41c
Shelter, expenditures on	yr	5467	1999	30r
Insurance and Pensions				
Life and other personal insurance purchases	yr	414	1999	30r
Medigap health insurance, Plan H	yr	2887	2000	69s
Medigap health insurance, Plan I	yr	3302	2000	69s
Medigap health insurance, Plan J	yr	3889	2000	69s
Pensions and Social Security, expenditures on	yr	2635	1999	30r
Personal insurance and pensions, expenditures on	yr	3048	1999	30r
Legal Fees				
Divorce, filing fee		65.00-85.00	4/01	35s
Driver's license fee	renew	15.00	1999	48s
Driver's license fee	orig	20.00	1999	48s
Personal Goods				
Personal care products and services purchases	yr	393	1999	30r
Shampoo, Alberto VO5	15 oz	1.11	3/01	4c
Toothpaste, Crest or Colgate	6-7 oz	2.53	3/01	4c
Personal Services				
Dry cleaning, man's 2-pc suit		7.58	3/01	4c
Man's haircut, barbershop, no styling		10.92	3/01	4c
Personal services, household, expenditures on	yr	258	1999	30r
Woman's shampoo, trim, blow-dry, no style-change		18.80	3/01	4c
Pets				
Pets, toys, and playground equipment, expenditures on	yr	306	1999	30r
Restaurant Food				
Chicken, fried, thigh and drumstick, KFC/Church's		2.49	3/01	4c
Hamburger with cheese, McDonald's	1/4 lb	2.19	3/01	4c
Pizza, Pizza Hut or Pizza Inn	11-12 in	8.99	3/01	4c
Taxes				
Federal income taxes paid	yr	2047	1999	30r
Personal taxes, expenditures on	yr	2554	1999	30r
Property taxes paid	yr	726	1999	30r
State and local income taxes paid	yr	363	1999	30r
Transportation				
Transportation, ACCRA Index		102.20	3/01	4c
Cars and trucks, new, expenditures on	yr	1648	1999	30r
Cars and trucks, used, expenditures on	yr	1651	1999	30r
Diesel at the pump	gal	1.26	10/99	73s
Gasoline and motor oil purchases	yr	1052	1999	30r
Gasoline before-tax price (cents)	gal	101.90	10/00	43s
Maintenance and repair expenditures	yr	621	1999	30r
Public transportation, expenditures on	yr	298	1999	30r
Tire balance, computer or spin balance, front	wheel	9.21	3/01	4c
Transportation purchases	yr	6738	1999	30r
Vehicle expenses, miscellaneous, purchases	yr	2033	1999	30r
Vehicle insurance payments	yr	696	1999	30r
Vehicle purchases (net outlay)	yr	3354	1999	30r
Vehicle rental, lease expenditures	yr	352	1999	30r

Fort Walton Beach, FL - continued

Item	Per	Value	Date	Ref.
Travel				
Hotel room	night	110.57	2/01	95s
Utilities				
Utilities, ACCRA Index		82.80	3/01	4c
Electrical bill, average	mos	86.33	9/00	9s
Electricity, expenditures on	yr	1115	1999	30r
Electricity and other, mixed, 2400 sq ft, new home	mos	60.82	3/01	4c
Electricity cost, average	KWh	6.80	9/00	9s
Water and other public services, expenditures on	yr	298	1999	30r
Weddings				
Wedding (national average cost)		19936	2000	33r
Wedding (regional average total cost)		16293	1997	110r
Attendants' gifts		321	1998	33r
Bridal attendants' apparel (5 persons)		824	2000	33r
Bride's headpiece/veil		173	1998	33r
Bride's wedding dress		859	1998	33r
Clergy, religious facility fee		242	1998	33r
Engagement ring		3177	1998	33r
Flowers		789	1998	33r
Groom's formalwear rental		99	2000	33r
Limousine		410	1998	33r
Marriage license cost		56.00-88.50	4/01	35s
Men's formalwear (ushers, best man)		469	2000	33r
Mother of bride apparel		241	2000	33r
Music		866	1998	33r
Photography and videography		1368	1998	33r
Rehearsal dinner		728	1998	33r
Wedding invitations and announcements		341	1998	33r
Wedding reception		7968	2000	33r
Wedding rings (bride and groom)		1060	1998	33r

Fort Wayne, IN

Item	Per	Value	Date	Ref.
Average annual expenditures	yr	35369	1999	30r
Alcoholic Beverages				
Alcoholic beverage purchases	yr	304	1999	30r
Malt beverages, all types, all sizes, any origin	16 oz	0.93	7/01	11r
Wine, red and white table, all sizes, any origin	liter	7.04	7/01	11r
Appliances				
Major appliances, expenditures on	yr	165	1999	30r
Small appliances, housewares, expenditures on	yr	90	1999	30r
Banking and Money				
Mortgage interest and charges paid	yr	2277	1999	30r
Mortgage principal paid on owned property	yr	1230	1999	30r
Vehicle finance charges paid	yr	328	1999	30r
Business Expenses				
Business travel, car rental	day	54	2001	3c
Business travel, food	day	37	2001	3c
Business travel, hotel	day	88	2001	3c
Charity				
Cash contributions, expenditures	yr	1126	1999	30r
Child Care				
Child raising cost, total, age 0-2	yr	7890	1999	60r
Child raising cost, total, age 3-5	yr	8130	1999	60r
Child raising cost, total, age 6-8	yr	8170	1999	60r
Child raising cost, total, age 9-11	yr	8190	1999	60r
Child raising cost, total, age 12-14	yr	8890	1999	60r
Child raising cost, total, age 15-17	yr	9050	1999	60r
Child's child care and education, age 0-2	yr	1240	1999	60r
Child's child care and education, age 3-5	yr	1370	1999	60r
Child's child care and education, age 6-8	yr	880	1999	60r
Child's child care and education, age 9-11	yr	570	1999	60r
Child's child care and education, age 12-14	yr	420	1999	60r

Values are in dollars or fractions of dollars. In the column headed *Ref*, references are shown to sources. Each reference is followed by a letter. These refer to the geographical level for which data were reported: s=State, r=Region, and c=City or metro. The abbreviation *ex* is used to mean *except* or *excluding*; *exp* stands for expenditures. For other abbreviations and further explanations, please see the Introduction.

Fort Wayne, IN - continued

Item	Per	Value	Date	Ref.
Child Care				
Child's child care and education, age 15-17	yr	720	1999	60r
Child's clothing, age 0-2	yr	410	1999	60r
Child's clothing, age 3-5	yr	400	1999	60r
Child's clothing, age 6-8	yr	450	1999	60r
Child's clothing, age 9-11	yr	500	1999	60r
Child's clothing, age 12-14	yr	840	1999	60r
Child's clothing, age 15-17	yr	740	1999	60r
Child's food, age 0-2	yr	960	1999	60r
Child's food, age 3-5	yr	1120	1999	60r
Child's food, age 6-8	yr	1430	1999	60r
Child's food, age 9-11	yr	1710	1999	60r
Child's food, age 12-14	yr	1710	1999	60r
Child's food, age 15-17	yr	1920	1999	60r
Child's health care, age 0-2	yr	520	1999	60r
Child's health care, age 3-5	yr	500	1999	60r
Child's health care, age 6-8	yr	570	1999	60r
Child's health care, age 9-11	yr	610	1999	60r
Child's health care, age 12-14	yr	630	1999	60r
Child's health care, age 15-17	yr	650	1999	60r
Child's housing, age 0-2	yr	2860	1999	60r
Child's housing, age 3-5	yr	2840	1999	60r
Child's housing, age 6-8	yr	2800	1999	60r
Child's housing, age 9-11	yr	2650	1999	60r
Child's housing, age 12-14	yr	2840	1999	60r
Child's housing, age 15-17	yr	2440	1999	60r
Child's personal care, reading, age 0-2	yr	880	1999	60r
Child's personal care, reading, age 3-5	yr	900	1999	60r
Child's personal care, reading, age 6-8	yr	930	1999	60r
Child's personal care, reading, age 9-11	yr	970	1999	60r
Child's personal care, reading, age 12-14	yr	1150	1999	60r
Child's personal care, reading, age 15-17	yr	920	1999	60r
Clothing				
Apparel and services purchases	yr	1607	1999	30r
Boys, 2 to 15, expenditures on	yr	91	1999	30r
Children under 2, expenditures on	yr	59	1999	30r
Footwear, expenditures on	yr	285	1999	30r
Girls, 2 to 15, expenditures on	yr	116	1999	30r
Men and boys, expenditures on	yr	433	1999	30r
Men, 16 and over, expenditures on	yr	341	1999	30r
Women, 16 and over, expenditures on	yr	490	1999	30r
Communications				
Phone line, single, business, field visit	inst.	59.00	12/97	17s
Phone line, single, business, no field visit	inst.	59.00	12/97	17s
Phone line, single, residence, field visit	inst.	47.00	12/97	17s
Phone line, single, residence, no field visit	inst.	47.00	12/97	17s
Postage and stationery, expenditures on	yr	140	1999	30r
Postal rate, express mail, up to half-pound		12.45	7/01	108r
Postal rate, letter, first class, first ounce		0.34	7/01	108r
Postal rate, letter, two ounces		0.57	7/01	108r
Postal rate, post card		0.21	7/01	108r
Postal rate, priority mail, two pounds		3.95	7/01	108r
Postal rate, priority mail, up to one pound		3.50	7/01	108r
Telephone services, expenditures on	yr	830	1999	30r
Education				
Board, 4-year private college/university	yr	2250	1996	38s
Board, 4-year public college/university	yr	2425	1996	38s
Education expenditures	yr	583	1999	30r
Room, 4-year private college/university	yr	1987	1996	38s
Room, 4-year public college/university	yr	1931	1996	38s
Total cost, 4-year private college/university	yr	16829	1996	38s
Total cost, 4-year public college/university	yr	7392	1996	38s
Tuition, 2-year public college/university, in state	yr	1937	1996	38s
Tuition, 4-year private college/university, in state	yr	12592	1996	38s
Tuition, 4-year public college/university	yr	3037	1996	38s
Energy and Fuels				
Electricity	500 KWhs	46.59	7/01	11r
Fuel oil #2	gal	1.27	7/01	11r

Fort Wayne, IN - continued

Item	Per	Value	Date	Ref.
Energy and Fuels - continued				
Fuel oil and other fuels, expenditures on	yr	68	1999	30r
Gas, natural, commercial rate	1000 cf	6.24	11/00	88s
Gasoline, unleaded midgrade	gal	1.79	7/01	11r
Gasoline, unleaded premium	gal	1.86	7/01	11r
Gasoline, unleaded regular	gal	1.58	7/01	11r
Natural gas, expenditures on	yr	389	1999	30r
Utility (piped) gas, therm		0.81	7/01	11r
Utility (piped) gas, 40 therms		38.01	7/01	11r
Utility (piped) gas, 100 therms		81.75	7/01	11r
Entertainment				
Entertainment purchases	yr	1984	1999	30r
Fees and admissions paid	yr	444	1999	30r
Television, radios, sound equipment, expenditures on	yr	580	1999	30r
Funerals				
Cosmetology, hair, other preparation		178.32	1/99	78r
Embalming		408.19	1/99	78r
Funeral at funeral home		362.13	1/99	78r
Professional service charges		1375.51	1/99	78r
Transfer of remains to funeral home		155.92	1/99	78r
Visitation/viewing		294.38	1/99	78r
Groceries				
Bacon, sliced	lb	3.15	7/01	11r
Bakery products, expenditures on	yr	281	1999	30r
Bananas	lb	0.48	7/01	11r
Beans, dried, any type, all sizes	lb	0.61	7/01	11r
Beef for stew, boneless	lb	3.08	7/01	11r
Beef, expenditures on	yr	217	1999	30r
Bologna, all beef or mixed	lb	2.52	7/01	11r
Bread, white, pan	lb	1.06	7/01	11r
Broccoli	lb	0.91	7/01	11r
Butter, salted, grade AA, stick	lb	3.04	7/01	11r
Butter, yoghurt, cheese, etc, expenditures on	yr	183	1999	30r
Cereals and bakery product purchases	yr	430	1999	30r
Cereals and cereal products, expenditures on	yr	149	1999	30r
Chicken, fresh, whole	lb	1.07	7/01	11r
Chops, boneless,	lb	3.64	7/01	11r
Chuck roast, U.S. choice, boneless	lb	2.47	7/01	11r
Coffee, 100%, ground roast, all sizes	lb	2.69	7/01	11r
Cookies, chocolate chip	lb	2.87	7/01	11r
Dairy product purchases	yr	304	1999	30r
Eggs, expenditures on	yr	26	1999	30r
Eggs, grade A, large	dozen	0.88	7/01	11r
Fats and oils, expenditures on	yr	75	1999	30r
Fish and seafood, expenditures on	yr	72	1999	30r
Food (excl fruit and vegetables), eaten at home, purchases	yr	887	1999	30r
Food cooked on trips, expenditures on	yr	44	1999	30r
Food purchases	yr	4802	1999	30r
Food purchases, eaten away from home	yr	2069	1999	30r
Food purchases, food eaten at home	yr	2733	1999	30r
Fresh fruits, expenditures on	yr	138	1999	30r
Fresh milk and cream, expenditures on	yr	120	1999	30r
Fresh vegetables, expenditures on	yr	126	1999	30r
Grapefruit	lb	0.66	7/01	11r
Grapes, Thompson, seedless	lb	1.64	7/01	11r
Ground beef, 100% beef	lb	1.64	7/01	11r
Ground beef, lean and extra lean	lb	2.16	7/01	11r
Ground chuck, 100% beef	lb	2.13	7/01	11r
Ham, boneless, excl canned	lb	2.62	7/01	11r
Ice cream, prepackaged, bulk, regular	1/2 gal	3.35	7/01	11r
Lemons	lb	1.19	7/01	11r
Lettuce, iceberg	lb	0.73	7/01	11r
Margarine, soft, tubs	lb	0.89	7/01	11r
Meats, poultry, fish, and egg purchases	yr	671	1999	30r
Milk, fresh, whole, fortified	gal	2.71	7/01	11r
Nonalcoholic beverages, expenditures on	yr	239	1999	30r
Oranges, Navel	lb	0.80	7/01	11r
Oranges, Valencia	lb	0.66	7/01	11r
Pears, Anjou	lb	0.93	7/01	11r

Values are in dollars or fractions of dollars. In the column headed *Ref*, references are shown to sources. Each reference is followed by a letter. These refer to the geographical level for which data were reported: s=State, r=Region, and c=City or metro. The abbreviation *ex* is used to mean *except* or *excluding*; *exp* stands for expenditures. For other abbreviations and further explanations, please see the Introduction.

Fort Wayne, IN - continued

Item	Per	Value	Date	Ref.
Groceries				
Pork chops, center cut, bone-in	lb	3.63	7/01	11r
Pork, expenditures on	yr	150	1999	30r
Potato chips	16 oz	3.52	7/01	11r
Potatoes, frozen, french fried	lb	1.08	7/01	11r
Potatoes, white, all types	lb	0.33	7/01	11r
Poultry, expenditures on	yr	108	1999	30r
Processed fruits, expenditures on	yr	98	1999	30r
Processed vegetables, expenditures on	yr	80	1999	30r
Round roast, U.S. choice, boneless	lb	3.07	7/01	11r
Round steak, graded and ungraded, excl U.S. prime and choice	lb	3.41	7/01	11r
Shortening, vegetable oil blends	lb	1.13	7/01	11r
Spaghetti and macaroni	lb	0.80	7/01	11r
Steak, round, U.S. choice, boneless	lb	3.23	7/01	11r
Steak, T-bone, U.S. choice, bone-in	lb	6.68	7/01	11r
Strawberries, dry pint	12 oz	1.32	7/01	11r
Sugar and other sweets, expenditures on	yr	114	1999	30r
Sugar, white, 33-80 ounce package	lb	0.42	7/01	11r
Sugar, white, all sizes	lb	0.43	7/01	11r
Tobacco products and smoking supplies purchases	yr	331	1999	30r
Tomatoes, field grown	lb	1.46	7/01	11r
Tuna, light, chunk	lb	1.80	7/01	11r
Turkey, frozen, whole	lb	1.15	7/01	11r
Goods and Services				
B&B Japanese maple (acer japonicum)	gal	29.99-169.99	4/00	93r
Boxwood (buxus)	2 gal	18.99-39.99	4/00	93r
Daylilly (hemerocallis)	gal	4.99-25.00	4/00	93r
Flat of annuals		11.98-24.99	4/00	93r
Fountain grass (pennisetum)	gal	5.98-12.98	4/00	93r
Hanging basket (10 in)		12.99-27.99	4/00	93r
Hardy geranium (geranium)	gal	7.99-9.99	4/00	93r
Hosta (hosta)	gal	6.00-25.00	4/00	93r
Lilac (syrubga vulgaris)	2 gal	14.99-24.99	4/00	93r
Miscellaneous purchases	yr	865	1999	30r
Rhododendron (rhododendron)	2 gal	23.98-42.99	4/00	93r
Sage (salvia)	gal	6.00-9.99	4/00	93r
Wintercreeper euonymus (euonymus fortunei)	2 gal	16.00-169.99	4/00	93r
Hunting license	yr	8.75	4/01	34s
Health Care				
Cardiac catheterization, ave hospital/ physician charges		13380	1998	77s
Childbirth, Cesarean delivery		10722	1997	13r
Childbirth, vaginal delivery		6223	1997	13r
Drugs, expenditures on	yr	394	1999	30r
Health care purchases	yr	2048	1999	30r
Health insurance expenditures	yr	978	1999	30r
Home health care aide cost, licensed agency	hour	17	2000	82c
Hysterectomy, laproscopically-assisted, ave hospital/physician charges		11310	1998	76s
Hysterectomy, vaginal, ave hospital and physician charges		9160	1998	76s
Medicaid dispensing fee		4.00	1999	87s
Medical services expenditures	yr	554	1999	30r
Medical supplies, expenditures on	yr	122	1999	30r
Nursing home costs, private room	day	137	2000	82c
Nursing home stay, private room	day	137	2000	81c
Plastic surgery, breast augmentation		3184	2000	7r
Plastic surgery, breast lift		3585	2000	7r

Fort Wayne, IN - continued

Item	Per	Value	Date	Ref.
Health Care - continued				
Plastic surgery, facelift		4999	2000	7r
Plastic surgery, hair transplantation		3105	2000	7r
Plastic surgery, lip augmentation		1290	2000	7r
Plastic surgery, lower body lift		8135	2000	7r
Plastic surgery, thigh lift		3839	2000	7r
Household Goods				
Floor coverings, expenditures on	yr	52	1999	30r
Furniture, expenditures on	yr	344	1999	30r
Household furnishings and equipment purchases	yr	1475	1999	30r
Household textiles, expenditures on	yr	109	1999	30r
Laundry and cleaning supplies, expenditures on	yr	134	1999	30r
Housing				
Home, 2200 sq ft, 4-br, 2-bath, 2-car garage, average		126725	2000	47c
Home price, existing, ave		144400	10/00	90r
Home price, median		92900	2000	59c
Home value, median		102000	2001	53s
Household operation expenditures	yr	542	1999	30r
Housekeeping supplies purchases	yr	508	1999	30r
Lodging expenditures	yr	430	1999	30r
Maintenance, repairs, insurance expenditures	yr	853	1999	30r
Monthly rental value of owned home	mos	547	1999	30r
Owned dwellings, expenditures own	yr	4282	1999	30r
Rent expenditures	yr	1558	1999	30r
Rental unit, 1 bedroom, with utilities	mos	414	4/01	41c
Rental unit, 2 bedroom, with utilities	mos	515	4/01	41c
Rental unit, 3 bedroom, with utilities	mos	664	4/01	41c
Rental unit, 4 bedroom, with utilities	mos	720	4/01	41c
Shelter, expenditures on	yr	6270	1999	30r
Insurance and Pensions				
Life and other personal insurance purchases	yr	387	1999	30r
Pensions and Social Security, expenditures on	yr	2968	1999	30r
Legal Fees				
Divorce, filing fee		100.00	4/01	35s
Driver's license fee	renew	6.00	1999	48s
Driver's license fee	orig	6.00	1999	48s
Personal Goods				
Personal care products and services purchases	yr	385	1999	30r
Personal Services				
Personal services, household, expenditures on	yr	300	1999	30r
Pets				
Pets, toys, and playground equipment, expenditures on	yr	375	1999	30r
Taxes				
Federal income taxes paid	yr	2326	1999	30r
Personal taxes, expenditures on	yr	3223	1999	30r
Property taxes paid	yr	1152	1999	30r
State and local income taxes paid	yr	753	1999	30r
Transportation				
Bus fare, one-way	trip	1.00	2000	1c
Cars and trucks, new, expenditures on	yr	1280	1999	30r
Cars and trucks, used, expenditures on	yr	1763	1999	30r
Diesel at the pump	gal	1.17	10/99	73s
Gasoline and motor oil purchases	yr	1036	1999	30r
Gasoline before-tax price (cents)	gal	110.00	10/00	43s
Maintenance and repair expenditures	yr	594	1999	30r
Public transportation, expenditures on	yr	341	1999	30r
Transportation purchases	yr	6617	1999	30r
Vehicle expenses, miscellaneous, purchases	yr	2159	1999	30r
Vehicle insurance payments	yr	701	1999	30r
Vehicle purchases (net outlay)	yr	3081	1999	30r

Values are in dollars or fractions of dollars. In the column headed *Ref*, references are shown to sources. Each reference is followed by a letter. These refer to the geographical level for which data were reported: s=State, r=Region, and c=City or metro. The abbreviation *ex* is used to mean *except* or *excluding*; *exp* stands for *expenditures*. For other abbreviations and further explanations, please see the Introduction.

Fort Wayne, IN - continued

Item	Per	Value	Date	Ref.
Transportation				
Vehicle rental, lease expenditures	yr	536	1999	30r
Utilities				
Electrical bill, average	mos	66.66	9/00	9s
Electricity, expenditures on	yr	841	1999	30r
Electricity, summer, 250 KWh	mos	24.89	2/96	97c
Electricity, summer, 500 KWh	mos	40.63	2/96	97c
Electricity, summer, 750 KWh	mos	55.23	2/96	97c
Electricity, summer, 1000 KWh	mos	69.83	2/96	97c
Electricity cost, average	KWh	5.00	9/00	9s
Utilities, fuels, and public services purchased	yr	2401	1999	30r
Water and other public services, expenditures on	yr	273	1999	30r
Weddings				
Wedding (national average cost)		19936	2000	33r
Wedding (regional average total cost)		16195	1997	110r
Attendants' gifts		321	1998	33r
Bridal attendants' apparel (5 persons)		824	2000	33r
Bride's headpiece/veil		173	1998	33r
Bride's wedding dress		859	1998	33r
Clergy, religious facility fee		242	1998	33r
Engagement ring		3177	1998	33r
Flowers		789	1998	33r
Groom's formalwear rental		99	2000	33r
Limousine		410	1998	33r
Marriage license cost		18.00	4/01	35s
Men's formalwear (ushers, best man)		469	2000	33r
Mother of bride apparel		241	2000	33r
Music		866	1998	33r
Photography and videography		1368	1998	33r
Rehearsal dinner		728	1998	33r
Wedding invitations and announcements		341	1998	33r
Wedding reception		7968	2000	33r
Wedding rings (bride and groom)		1060	1998	33r

Fort Worth-Arlington, TX

Item	Per	Value	Date	Ref.
Alcoholic Beverages				
Alcoholic beverage purchases	yr	253	1999	30r
Malt beverages, all types, all sizes, any origin	16 oz	0.96	7/01	11r
Appliances				
Major appliances, expenditures on	yr	172	1999	30r
Small appliances, housewares, expenditures on	yr	81	1999	30r
Banking and Money				
Mortgage interest and charges paid	yr	2039	1999	30r
Mortgage principal paid on owned property	yr	1026	1999	30r
Vehicle finance charges paid	yr	365	1999	30r
Charity				
Cash contributions, expenditures	yr	1127	1999	30r
Child Care				
Child raising cost, total, age 0-2	yr	8540	1999	60r
Child raising cost, total, age 3-5	yr	8780	1999	60r
Child raising cost, total, age 6-8	yr	8820	1999	60r
Child raising cost, total, age 9-11	yr	8800	1999	60r
Child raising cost, total, age 12-14	yr	9510	1999	60r
Child raising cost, total, age 15-17	yr	9740	1999	60r
Child's child care and education, age 0-2	yr	1380	1999	60r
Child's child care and education, age 3-5	yr	1520	1999	60r
Child's child care and education, age 6-8	yr	990	1999	60r
Child's child care and education, age 9-11	yr	650	1999	60r
Child's child care and education, age 12-14	yr	490	1999	60r
Child's child care and education, age 15-17	yr	840	1999	60r
Child's clothing, age 0-2	yr	480	1999	60r
Child's clothing, age 3-5	yr	470	1999	60r
Child's clothing, age 6-8	yr	520	1999	60r
Child's clothing, age 9-11	yr	570	1999	60r
Child's clothing, age 12-14	yr	950	1999	60r
Child's clothing, age 15-17	yr	850	1999	60r

Fort Worth-Arlington, TX - continued

Item	Per	Value	Date	Ref.
Child Care - continued				
Child's food, age 0-2	yr	1000	1999	60r
Child's food, age 3-5	yr	1160	1999	60r
Child's food, age 6-8	yr	1490	1999	60r
Child's food, age 9-11	yr	1770	1999	60r
Child's food, age 12-14	yr	1770	1999	60r
Child's food, age 15-17	yr	1980	1999	60r
Child's health care, age 0-2	yr	620	1999	60r
Child's health care, age 3-5	yr	590	1999	60r
Child's health care, age 6-8	yr	680	1999	60r
Child's health care, age 9-11	yr	720	1999	60r
Child's health care, age 12-14	yr	730	1999	60r
Child's health care, age 15-17	yr	760	1999	60r
Child's housing, age 0-2	yr	3070	1999	60r
Child's housing, age 3-5	yr	3050	1999	60r
Child's housing, age 6-8	yr	3010	1999	60r
Child's housing, age 9-11	yr	2850	1999	60r
Child's housing, age 12-14	yr	3040	1999	60r
Child's housing, age 15-17	yr	2650	1999	60r
Child's personal care, reading, age 0-2	yr	910	1999	60r
Child's personal care, reading, age 3-5	yr	930	1999	60r
Child's personal care, reading, age 6-8	yr	960	1999	60r
Child's personal care, reading, age 9-11	yr	1000	1999	60r
Child's personal care, reading, age 12-14	yr	1170	1999	60r
Child's personal care, reading, age 15-17	yr	950	1999	60r
Clothing				
Apparel and services purchases	yr	1610	1999	30r
Boys, 2 to 15, expenditures on	yr	89	1999	30r
Children under 2, expenditures on	yr	79	1999	30r
Footwear, expenditures on	yr	283	1999	30r
Girls, 2 to 15, expenditures on	yr	103	1999	30r
Men and boys, expenditures on	yr	351	1999	30r
Men, 16 and over, expenditures on	yr	262	1999	30r
Women, 16 and over, expenditures on	yr	538	1999	30r
Communications				
Cable modem installation, AT&T-BIS		150.00	6/99	103s
Cable modem installation, Marcus		499.00	6/99	103s
Cable modem installation, Time Warner		75.00-225.00	6/99	103s
Cable modem rate, cable subscriber, AT&T-BIS	mos	39.95	6/99	103s
Cable modem rate, cable subscriber, Marcus	mos	14.95-49.95	6/99	103s
Cable modem rate, cable subscriber, Time Warner	mos	39.95-49.95	6/99	103s
Cable modem rate, non-cable subscriber, Marcus	mos	60.95	6/99	103s
Cable modem rate, non-cable subscriber, Time Warner	mos	39.95-54.95	6/99	103s
Phone line, single, business, field visit	inst.	71.90	12/97	17s
Phone line, single, business, no field visit	inst.	57.30	12/97	17s
Phone line, single, residence, field visit	inst.	52.95	12/97	17s
Phone line, single, residence, no field visit	inst.	38.35	12/97	17s
Postage and stationery, expenditures on	yr	104	1999	30r
Postal rate, express mail, up to half-pound		12.45	7/01	108r
Postal rate, letter, first class, first ounce		0.34	7/01	108r
Postal rate, letter, two ounces		0.57	7/01	108r
Postal rate, post card		0.21	7/01	108r
Postal rate, priority mail, two pounds		3.95	7/01	108r
Postal rate, priority mail, up to one pound		3.50	7/01	108r
Telephone services, expenditures on	yr	860	1999	30r
Education				
Board, 4-year private college/university	yr	2198	1996	38s
Board, 4-year public college/university	yr	1759	1996	38s
Education expenditures	yr	431	1999	30r
Room, 4-year private college/university	yr	2000	1996	38s
Room, 4-year public college/university	yr	1885	1996	38s
Total cost, 4-year private college/university	yr	13156	1996	38s
Total cost, 4-year public college/university	yr	5464	1996	38s
Tuition, 2-year public college/university, in state	yr	771	1996	38s

Values are in dollars or fractions of dollars. In the column headed *Ref*, references are shown to sources. Each reference is followed by a letter. These refer to the geographical level for which data were reported: s=State, r=Region, and c=City or metro. The abbreviation *ex* is used to mean *except* or *excluding*; *exp* stands for *expenditures*. For other abbreviations and further explanations, please see the Introduction.

Fort Worth-Arlington, TX - continued

Item	Per	Value	Date	Ref.
Education				
Tuition, 4-year private college/university, in state	yr	8959	1996	38s
Tuition, 4-year public college/university	yr	1820	1996	38s
Energy and Fuels				
Electricity	KWh	0.09	7/01	11r
Electricity	500 KWhs	47.29	7/01	11r
Fuel oil #2	gal	1.43	7/01	11r
Fuel oil and other fuels, expenditures on	yr	45	1999	30r
Gas, natural, commercial rate	1000 cf	6.94	11/00	88s
Gasoline, all types	gal	1.60	7/01	11r
Gasoline, unleaded midgrade	gal	1.65	7/01	11r
Gasoline, unleaded premium	gal	1.74	7/01	11r
Natural gas, expenditures on	yr	164	1999	30r
Utility (piped) gas, therm		1.01	7/01	11r
Utility (piped) gas, 40 therms		44.29	7/01	11r
Utility (piped) gas, 100 therms		97.44	7/01	11r
Entertainment				
Entertainment purchases	yr	1574	1999	30r
Fees and admissions paid	yr	371	1999	30r
Reading purchases	yr	121	1999	30r
Television, radios, sound equipment, expenditures on	yr	561	1999	30r
Funerals				
Total cost of funeral		5842.28	1/99	78r
Acknowledgement cards		28.35	1/99	78r
Casket		2494.29	1/99	78r
Cosmetology, hair, other preparation		109.22	1/99	78r
Embalming		361.42	1/99	78r
Funeral at funeral home		349.20	1/99	78r
Hearse (local)		161.91	1/99	78r
Professional service charges		1116.50	1/99	78r
Service car/van		65.56	1/99	78r
Transfer of remains to funeral home		143.56	1/99	78r
Vault		785.25	1/99	78r
Visitation/viewing		227.02	1/99	78r
Groceries				
American processed cheese	lb	3.50	7/01	11r
Bakery products, expenditures on	yr	261	1999	30r
Bananas	lb	0.47	7/01	11r
Beans, dried, any type, all sizes	lb	0.63	7/01	11r
Beef for stew, boneless	lb	2.86	7/01	11r
Beef, expenditures on	yr	210	1999	30r
Bologna, all beef or mixed	lb	2.29	7/01	11r
Bread, French	lb	1.66	7/01	11r
Bread, white, pan	lb	0.87	7/01	11r
Bread, whole wheat, pan	lb	1.38	7/01	11r
Broccoli	lb	1.04	7/01	11r
Butter, salted, grade AA, stick	lb	2.26	7/01	11r
Butter, yoghurt, cheese, etc, expenditures on	yr	170	1999	30r
Cabbage	lb	0.42	7/01	11r
Cereals and cereal products, expenditures on	yr	140	1999	30r
Cheddar cheese, natural	lb	3.75	7/01	11r
Chicken breast, bone-in	lb	1.85	7/01	11r
Chicken legs, bone-in	lb	1.34	7/01	11r
Chicken, fresh, whole	lb	1.05	7/01	11r
Chops, boneless,	lb	4.13	7/01	11r
Chuck roast, graded and ungraded, excl U.S. prime and choice	lb	2.35	7/01	11r
Chuck roast, U.S. choice, boneless	lb	2.67	7/01	11r
Coffee, 100%, ground roast, all sizes	lb	2.88	7/01	11r
Coffee, instant, plain, regular, all sizes	16 oz	9.25	7/01	11r
Cola, non diet,	2 liter	1.11	7/01	11r
Crackers, soda, salted	lb	1.70	7/01	11r
Dairy product purchases	yr	282	1999	30r
Eggs, expenditures on	yr	32	1999	30r
Fats and oils, expenditures on	yr	79	1999	30r
Fish and seafood, expenditures on	yr	99	1999	30r
Flour, white, all purpose	lb	0.32	7/01	11r

Fort Worth-Arlington, TX - continued

Item	Per	Value	Date	Ref.
Groceries - continued				
Food (excl fruit and vegetables), eaten at home, purchases	yr	815	1999	30r
Food cooked on trips, expenditures on	yr	36	1999	30r
Food purchases	yr	4533	1999	30r
Food purchases, eaten away from home	yr	1873	1999	30r
Food purchases, food eaten at home	yr	2660	1999	30r
Fresh fruits, expenditures on	yr	128	1999	30r
Fresh milk and cream, expenditures on	yr	112	1999	30r
Fresh vegetables, expenditures on	yr	131	1999	30r
Fruit and vegetable purchases	yr	438	1999	30r
Grapefruit	lb	0.59	7/01	11r
Grapes, Thompson, seedless	lb	2.12	7/01	11r
Ground beef, 100% beef	lb	1.76	7/01	11r
Ground beef, lean and extra lean	lb	2.60	7/01	11r
Ground chuck, 100% beef	lb	2.08	7/01	11r
Ham, boneless, excl canned	lb	2.71	7/01	11r
Ham, rump or shank half, bone-in, smoked	lb	2.19	7/01	11r
Ice cream, prepackaged, bulk, regular	1/2 gal	3.93	7/01	11r
Lemons	lb	1.32	7/01	11r
Lettuce, iceberg	lb	0.76	7/01	11r
Milk, fresh, low fat,	gal	2.75	7/01	11r
Milk, fresh, whole, fortified	gal	2.97	7/01	11r
Nonalcoholic beverages, expenditures on	yr	228	1999	30r
Orange juice, frozen concentrate	16 oz	1.95	7/01	11r
Oranges, Navel	lb	0.73	7/01	11r
Oranges, Valencia	lb	0.55	7/01	11r
Peanut butter, creamy, all sizes	lb	1.83	7/01	11r
Pears, Anjou	lb	0.98	7/01	11r
Pork chops, center cut, bone-in	lb	3.33	7/01	11r
Pork sausage, fresh, loose	lb	2.59	7/01	11r
Pork shoulder picnic, bone-in, smoked	lb	1.12	7/01	11r
Pork, expenditures on	yr	162	1999	30r
Potato chips	16 oz	3.59	7/01	11r
Potatoes, frozen, french fried	lb	1.00	7/01	11r
Potatoes, white, all types	lb	0.44	7/01	11r
Poultry, expenditures on	yr	137	1999	30r
Processed fruits, expenditures on	yr	97	1999	30r
Processed vegetables, expenditures on	yr	82	1999	30r
Rice, white, long grain, uncooked	lb	0.51	7/01	11r
Round roast, graded and ungraded, excl U.S. prime and choice	lb	2.96	7/01	11r
Round steak, graded and ungraded, excl U.S. prime and choice	lb	3.11	7/01	11r
Sirloin steak, graded and ungraded, excl U.S. prime and choice	lb	4.23	7/01	11r
Spaghetti and macaroni	lb	0.78	7/01	11r
Steak, round, U.S. choice, boneless	lb	3.56	7/01	11r
Steak, sirloin, U.S. choice, boneless	lb	5.65	7/01	11r
Strawberries, dry pint	12 oz	1.50	7/01	11r
Sugar and other sweets, expenditures on	yr	99	1999	30r
Sugar, white, 33-80 ounce package	lb	0.39	7/01	11r
Sugar, white, all sizes	lb	0.42	7/01	11r
Tobacco products and smoking supplies purchases	yr	288	1999	30r
Tomatoes, field grown	lb	1.43	7/01	11r
Tuna, light, chunk	lb	1.77	7/01	11r
Turkey, frozen, whole	lb	1.05	7/01	11r
Goods and Services				
B&B Japanese maple (acer japonicum)	gal	79.98-99.00	4/00	93r
Boxwood (buxus)	2 gal	12.98-18.99	4/00	93r
Christmas tree, noble fir		40-60	2000	65s
Daylilly (hemerocallis)	gal	7.96-11.00	4/00	93r
Flat of annuals		13.99-27.99	4/00	93r
Fountain grass (pennisetum)	gal	6.96-9.00	4/00	93r
Hanging basket (10 in)		9.99-24.99	4/00	93r

Values are in dollars or fractions of dollars. In the column headed *Ref*, references are shown to sources. Each reference is followed by a letter. These refer to the geographical level for which data were reported: s=State, r=Region, and c=City or metro. The abbreviation *ex* is used to mean *except* or *excluding*; *exp* stands for *expenditures*. For other abbreviations and further explanations, please see the Introduction.

Fort Worth-Arlington, TX - continued

Item	Per	Value	Date	Ref.
Goods and Services				
Hardy geranium (geranium)	gal	5.96-8.00	4/00	93r
Hosta (hosta)	gal	8.96-12.99	4/00	93r
Lilac (syrubga vulgaris)	2 gal	13.00-19.99	4/00	93r
Rhododendron (rhododendron)	2 gal	12.98-29.99	4/00	93r
Sage (salvia)	gal	5.96-8.00	4/00	93r
Wintercreeper euonymus (euonymus fortunei)	2 gal	13.00-18.99	4/00	93r
Hunting license	yr	19.00	4/01	34s
Health Care				
Cardiac catheterization, ave hospital/physician charges		20140	1998	77s
Childbirth, Cesarean delivery		11587	1997	13r
Childbirth, vaginal delivery		6725	1997	13r
Drugs, expenditures on	yr	399	1999	30r
Health care purchases	yr	1971	1999	30r
Health insurance expenditures	yr	933	1999	30r
Hysterectomy, laproscopically-assisted, ave hospital/physician charges		15700	1998	76s
Hysterectomy, vaginal, ave hospital and physician charges		12180	1998	76s
Medicaid dispensing fee		5.27	1999	87s
Medical services expenditures	yr	547	1999	30r
Medical supplies, expenditures on	yr	91	1999	30r
Household Goods				
Floor coverings, expenditures on	yr	44	1999	30r
Furniture, expenditures on	yr	335	1999	30r
Household furnishings and equipment purchases	yr	1328	1999	30r
Household textiles, expenditures on	yr	89	1999	30r
Laundry and cleaning supplies, expenditures on	yr	113	1999	30r
Housing				
Home price, existing, ave		160100	10/00	90r
Home value, median		112000	2001	53s
Household operation expenditures	yr	553	1999	30r
Housekeeping supplies purchases	yr	473	1999	30r
Housing, expenditures on	yr	10303	1999	30r
Maintenance, repairs, insurance expenditures	yr	699	1999	30r
Monthly rental value of owned home	mos	505	1999	30r
Owned dwellings, expenditures own	yr	3465	1999	30r
Rent expenditures	yr	1641	1999	30r
Rental unit, 1 bedroom, with utilities	mos	491	4/01	41c
Rental unit, 2 bedroom, with utilities	mos	637	4/01	41c
Rental unit, 3 bedroom, with utilities	mos	889	4/01	41c
Rental unit, 4 bedroom, with utilities	mos	1048	4/01	41c
Shelter, expenditures on	yr	5467	1999	30r
Insurance and Pensions				
Life and other personal insurance purchases	yr	414	1999	30r
Pensions and Social Security, expenditures on	yr	2635	1999	30r
Personal insurance and pensions, expenditures on	yr	3048	1999	30r
Legal Fees				
Divorce, filing fee		150.00-200.00	4/01	35s
Driver's license fee	orig	24.00	1999	48s
Driver's license fee	renew	20.00	1999	48s
Fishing license	yr	19.00	4/01	34s
Personal Goods				
Personal care products and services purchases	yr	393	1999	30r

Item	Per	Value	Date	Ref.
Personal Services				
Personal services, household, expenditures on	yr	258	1999	30r
Pets				
Pets, toys, and playground equipment, expenditures on	yr	306	1999	30r
Taxes				
Federal income taxes paid	yr	2047	1999	30r
Personal taxes, expenditures on	yr	2554	1999	30r
Property taxes paid	yr	726	1999	30r
State and local income taxes paid	yr	363	1999	30r
Transportation				
Cars and trucks, new, expenditures on	yr	1648	1999	30r
Cars and trucks, used, expenditures on	yr	1651	1999	30r
Diesel at the pump	gal	1.18	10/99	73s
Gasoline and motor oil purchases	yr	1052	1999	30r
Gasoline before-tax price (cents)	gal	101.30	10/00	43s
Maintenance and repair expenditures	yr	621	1999	30r
Public transportation, expenditures on	yr	298	1999	30r
Transportation purchases	yr	6738	1999	30r
Vehicle expenses, miscellaneous, purchases	yr	2033	1999	30r
Vehicle insurance payments	yr	696	1999	30r
Vehicle purchases (net outlay)	yr	3354	1999	30r
Vehicle rental, lease expenditures	yr	352	1999	30r
Utilities				
Electrical bill, average	mos	87.17	9/00	9s
Electricity, expenditures on	yr	1115	1999	30r
Electricity cost, average	KWh	6.48	9/00	9s
Water and other public services, expenditures on	yr	298	1999	30r
Weddings				
Wedding (national average cost)		19936	2000	33r
Attendants' gifts		321	1998	33r
Bridal attendants' apparel (5 persons)		824	2000	33r
Bride's headpiece/veil		173	1998	33r
Bride's wedding dress		859	1998	33r
Clergy, religious facility fee		242	1998	33r
Engagement ring		3177	1998	33r
Flowers		789	1998	33r
Groom's formalwear rental		99	2000	33r
Limousine		410	1998	33r
Marriage license cost		36.00	4/01	35s
Men's formalwear (ushers, best man)		469	2000	33r
Mother of bride apparel		241	2000	33r
Music		866	1998	33r
Photography and videography		1368	1998	33r
Rehearsal dinner		728	1998	33r
Wedding invitations and announcements		341	1998	33r
Wedding reception		7968	2000	33r
Wedding rings (bride and groom)		1060	1998	33r

Fresno, CA

Item	Per	Value	Date	Ref.
Average annual expenditures	yr	40662	1999	30r
Composite, ACCRA index		106.00	12/00	5c
Alcoholic Beverages				
Alcoholic beverage purchases	yr	372	1999	30r
Beer, Heineken, 12-oz, ex deposit	6	7.35	12/00	5c
J & B Scotch	750-ml	21.19	12/00	5c
Malt beverages, all types, all sizes, any origin	16 oz	0.94	7/01	11r
Wine, Livingston or Gallo, Chablis blanc	1.5 liter	5.07	12/00	5c
Wine, red and white table, all sizes, any origin	liter	6.00	7/01	11r
Appliances				
Appliance repair, service call, washing machine	min lab chg	53.29	12/00	5c
Major appliances, expenditures on	yr	167	1999	30r
Small appliances, housewares, expenditures on	yr	105	1999	30r

Values are in dollars or fractions of dollars. In the column headed *Ref*, references are shown to sources. Each reference is followed by a letter. These refer to the geographical level for which data were reported: s=State, r=Region, and c=City or metro. The abbreviation *ex* is used to mean *except* or *excluding*; *exp* stands for expenditures. For other abbreviations and further explanations, please see the Introduction.

Fresno, CA - continued

Item	Per	Value	Date	Ref.
Banking and Money				
Mortgage interest and charges paid	yr	3368	1999	30r
Mortgage principal paid on owned property	yr	1677	1999	30r
Mortgage rate, incl. points and orig. fee, 30-yr. conv. fixed or ARM	mos	7.68	12/00	5c
Vehicle finance charges paid	yr	311	1999	30r
Business Expenses				
Business travel, car rental	day	41	2001	3c
Business travel, food	day	44	2001	3c
Business travel, hotel	day	83	2001	3c
Charity				
Cash contributions, expenditures	yr	1344	1999	30r
Child Care				
Child raising cost, total, age 0-2	yr	9140	1999	60r
Child raising cost, total, age 3-5	yr	9370	1999	60r
Child raising cost, total, age 6-8	yr	9450	1999	60r
Child raising cost, total, age 9-11	yr	9470	1999	60r
Child raising cost, total, age 12-14	yr	10170	1999	60r
Child raising cost, total, age 15-17	yr	10360	1999	60r
Child's child care and education, age 0-2	yr	1250	1999	60r
Child's child care and education, age 3-5	yr	1380	1999	60r
Child's child care and education, age 6-8	yr	890	1999	60r
Child's child care and education, age 9-11	yr	580	1999	60r
Child's child care and education, age 12-14	yr	430	1999	60r
Child's child care and education, age 15-17	yr	730	1999	60r
Child's clothing, age 0-2	yr	430	1999	60r
Child's clothing, age 3-5	yr	420	1999	60r
Child's clothing, age 6-8	yr	470	1999	60r
Child's clothing, age 9-11	yr	520	1999	60r
Child's clothing, age 12-14	yr	870	1999	60r
Child's clothing, age 15-17	yr	770	1999	60r
Child's food, age 0-2	yr	1120	1999	60r
Child's food, age 3-5	yr	1280	1999	60r
Child's food, age 6-8	yr	1640	1999	60r
Child's food, age 9-11	yr	1930	1999	60r
Child's food, age 12-14	yr	1940	1999	60r
Child's food, age 15-17	yr	2150	1999	60r
Child's health care, age 0-2	yr	490	1999	60r
Child's health care, age 3-5	yr	470	1999	60r
Child's health care, age 6-8	yr	530	1999	60r
Child's health care, age 9-11	yr	570	1999	60r
Child's health care, age 12-14	yr	580	1999	60r
Child's health care, age 15-17	yr	610	1999	60r
Child's housing, age 0-2	yr	3630	1999	60r
Child's housing, age 3-5	yr	3610	1999	60r
Child's housing, age 6-8	yr	3570	1999	60r
Child's housing, age 9-11	yr	3410	1999	60r
Child's housing, age 12-14	yr	3600	1999	60r
Child's housing, age 15-17	yr	3210	1999	60r
Child's personal care, reading, age 0-2	yr	1040	1999	60r
Child's personal care, reading, age 3-5	yr	1060	1999	60r
Child's personal care, reading, age 6-8	yr	1090	1999	60r
Child's personal care, reading, age 9-11	yr	1130	1999	60r
Child's personal care, reading, age 12-14	yr	1300	1999	60r
Child's personal care, reading, age 15-17	yr	1080	1999	60r
Clothing				
Apparel and services purchases	yr	1863	1999	30r
Boys' brief, cotton	3	3.98	12/00	5c
Boys, 2 to 15, expenditures on	yr	80	1999	30r
Children under 2, expenditures on	yr	74	1999	30r
Footwear, expenditures on	yr	307	1999	30r
Girls, 2 to 15, expenditures on	yr	101	1999	30r
Men and boys, expenditures on	yr	443	1999	30r
Men, 16 and over, expenditures on	yr	363	1999	30r
Shirt, man's dress shirt		30.12	12/00	5c
Slacks, man's "No Wrinkles" khaki		39.50	12/00	5c
Women, 16 and over, expenditures on	yr	594	1999	30r
Communications				
Cable modem installation, AT&T-BIS		150.00	6/99	103s

Fresno, CA - continued

Item	Per	Value	Date	Ref.
Communications - continued				
Cable modem installation, Charter		99.00-169.00	6/99	103s
Cable modem installation, Comcast		95.00	6/99	103s
Cable modem installation, Cox		99.00-174.95	6/99	103s
Cable modem installation, Media One		100.00	6/99	103s
Cable modem installation, Time Warner		75.00-225.00	6/99	103s
Cable modem rate, cable subscriber, AT&T-BIS	mos	39.95	6/99	103s
Cable modem rate, cable subscriber, Charter	mos	49.95-79.95	6/99	103s
Cable modem rate, cable subscriber, Comcast	mos	39.95	6/99	103s
Cable modem rate, cable subscriber, Cox	mos	29.95-44.95	6/99	103s
Cable modem rate, cable subscriber, Media One	mos	34.95-39.95	6/99	103s
Cable modem rate, cable subscriber, Time Warner	mos	39.95-49.95	6/99	103s
Cable modem rate, non-cable subscriber, Charter	mos	59.95-89.95	6/99	103s
Cable modem rate, non-cable subscriber, Comcast	mos	49.95	6/99	103s
Cable modem rate, non-cable subscriber, Cox	mos	42.95-54.95	6/99	103s
Cable modem rate, non-cable subscriber, Media One	mos	49.95	6/99	103s
Cable modem rate, non-cable subscriber, Time Warner	mos	39.95-54.95	6/99	103s
Newspaper subscription, daily and Sunday delivery	mos	11.45	12/00	5c
Phone line, single, business, field visit	inst.	70.75	12/97	17s
Phone line, single, business, no field visit	inst.	70.75	12/97	17s
Phone line, single, residence, field visit	inst.	34.75	12/97	17s
Phone line, single, residence, no field visit	inst.	34.75	12/97	17s
Postage and stationery, expenditures on	yr	150	1999	30r
Postal rate, express mail, up to half-pound		12.45	7/01	108r
Postal rate, letter, first class, first ounce		0.34	7/01	108r
Postal rate, letter, two ounces		0.57	7/01	108r
Postal rate, post card		0.21	7/01	108r
Postal rate, priority mail, two pounds		3.95	7/01	108r
Postal rate, priority mail, up to one pound		3.50	7/01	108r
Telephone bill, family of three	mos	16.27	12/00	5c
Telephone services, expenditures on	yr	825	1999	30r
Education				
Board, 4-year private college/university	yr	2970	1996	38s
Board, 4-year public college/university	yr	2516	1996	38s
Education expenditures	yr	676	1999	30r
Room, 4-year private college/university	yr	3196	1996	38s
Room, 4-year public college/university	yr	3031	1996	38s
Total cost, 4-year private college/university	yr	20143	1996	38s
Total cost, 4-year public college/university	yr	8213	1996	38s
Tuition, 2-year public college/university, in state	yr	362	1996	38s
Tuition, 4-year private college/university, in state	yr	13977	1996	38s
Tuition, 4-year public college/university	yr	2666	1996	38s
Energy and Fuels				
Electricity	500 KWhs	48.23	7/01	11r
Electricity	KWh	0.11	7/01	11r
Energy, combined forms, 2400 sq ft	mos	149.16	12/00	5c
Energy, exc. electricity, 2400 sq ft	mos	57.24	12/00	5c
Fuel oil and other fuels, expenditures on	yr	35	1999	30r
Gas, natural, commercial rate	1000 cf	8.74	11/00	88s
Gas, regular unleaded, cash, self-service	gal	1.88	12/00	5c
Gasoline, all types	gal	1.91	7/01	11r
Gasoline, unleaded premium	gal	2.05	7/01	11r
Gasoline, unleaded regular	gal	1.83	7/01	11r
Natural gas, expenditures on	yr	255	1999	30r

Values are in dollars or fractions of dollars. In the column headed *Ref*, references are shown to sources. Each reference is followed by a letter. These refer to the geographical level for which data were reported: s=State, r=Region, and c=City or metro. The abbreviation *ex* is used to mean *except* or *excluding*; *exp* stands for expenditures. For other abbreviations and further explanations, please see the Introduction.

Fresno, CA - continued

Item	Per	Value	Date	Ref.
Energy and Fuels				
Utility (piped) gas, therm		0.98	7/01	11r
Utility (piped) gas, 40 therms		40.74	7/01	11r
Utility (piped) gas, 100 therms		96.80	7/01	11r
Entertainment				
Bowling, Saturday evening rate	line	3.19	12/00	5c
Entertainment purchases	yr	2139	1999	30r
Fees and admissions paid	yr	545	1999	30r
Monopoly game, Parker Brothers', No. 9	game	11.39	12/00	5c
Movie, first-run, Saturday, evening	adm.	7.70	12/00	5c
Television, radios, sound equipment, expenditures on	yr	624	1999	30r
Tennis balls, yellow, Wilson or Penn, 3	can	2.27	12/00	5c
Funerals				
Total cost of funeral		5401.08	1/99	78r
Acknowledgement cards		33.64	1/99	78r
Casket		2170.43	1/99	78r
Cosmetology, hair, other preparation		136.32	1/99	78r
Embalming		319.13	1/99	78r
Funeral at funeral home		370.21	1/99	78r
Hearse (local)		161.04	1/99	78r
Professional service charges		963.15	1/99	78r
Service car/van		133.99	1/99	78r
Transfer of remains to funeral home		159.82	1/99	78r
Vault		778.07	1/99	78r
Visitation/viewing		175.28	1/99	78r
Groceries				
Groceries, ACCRA Index		107.30	12/00	5c
Antibiotic ointment, Polysporin	0.5 oz	4.93	12/00	5c
Apples, red delicious	lb	0.84	7/01	11r
Baby food, strained vegetables or fruit, lowest price	4-4.5 oz	0.50	12/00	5c
Bacon, sliced	lb	3.38	7/01	11r
Bakery products, expenditures on	yr	299	1999	30r
Bananas	lb	0.54	7/01	11r
Bananas	lb	0.46	12/00	5c
Beans, dried, any type, all sizes	lb	0.76	7/01	11r
Beef or hamburger, ground	lb	1.66	12/00	5c
Beef, expenditures on	yr	222	1999	30r
Bread, white	loaf	1.03	12/00	5c
Bread, white, pan	lb	0.99	7/01	11r
Butter, yoghurt, cheese, etc, expenditures on	yr	211	1999	30r
Cereals and bakery product purchases	yr	466	1999	30r
Cereals and cereal products, expenditures on	yr	168	1999	30r
Cheese, Kraft grated Parmesan	8 oz	4.10	12/00	5c
Chicken breast, bone-in	lb	2.45	7/01	11r
Chicken, fresh, whole	lb	1.19	7/01	11r
Chicken, whole fryer	lb	0.86	12/00	5c
Chops, boneless,	lb	4.00	7/01	11r
Chuck roast, graded and ungraded, excl U.S. prime and choice	lb	2.55	7/01	11r
Cigarettes, Winston, Kings	carton	37.36	12/00	5c
Coffee, 100%, ground roast, all sizes	lb	3.80	7/01	11r
Coffee, vacuum-packed	13 oz	3.00	12/00	5c
Cookies, chocolate chip	lb	2.83	7/01	11r
Corn Flakes, Kellogg's or Post Toasties	18 oz	3.09	12/00	5c
Corn, frozen, whole kernel, lowest price	16 oz	1.38	12/00	5c
Dairy product purchases	yr	341	1999	30r
Eggs, expenditures on	yr	39	1999	30r
Eggs, Grade A or AA	dozen	1.47	12/00	5c
Eggs, grade AA, large	dozen	1.23	7/01	11r
Fats and oils, expenditures on	yr	88	1999	30r
Fish and seafood, expenditures on	yr	121	1999	30r
Food (excl fruit and vegetables), eaten at home, purchases	yr	1001	1999	30r
Food cooked on trips, expenditures on	yr	64	1999	30r
Food purchases	yr	5312	1999	30r
Food purchases, eaten away from home	yr	2180	1999	30r
Food purchases, food eaten at home	yr	3132	1999	30r
Fresh fruits, expenditures on	yr	186	1999	30r
Fresh milk and cream, expenditures on	yr	130	1999	30r

Fresno, CA - continued

Item	Per	Value	Date	Ref.
Groceries - continued				
Fresh vegetables, expenditures on	yr	177	1999	30r
Grapefruit	lb	0.68	7/01	11r
Grapes, Thompson, seedless	lb	2.42	7/01	11r
Ground beef, lean and extra lean	lb	2.46	7/01	11r
Ice cream, prepackaged, bulk, regular	1/2 gal	3.62	7/01	11r
Lettuce, iceberg	lb	0.63	7/01	11r
Lettuce, iceberg	head	0.93	12/00	5c
Margarine, Blue Bonnet or Parkay, stick	lb	0.78	12/00	5c
Meats, poultry, fish, and egg purchases	yr	761	1999	30r
Milk, fresh, low fat,	gal	2.80	7/01	11r
Milk, fresh, whole, fortified	gal	2.88	7/01	11r
Milk, whole	1/2 gal	1.98	12/00	5c
Nonalcoholic beverages, expenditures on	yr	258	1999	30r
Orange juice, Minute Maid frozen	12 oz	1.56	12/00	5c
Oranges, Navel	lb	0.97	7/01	11r
Oranges, Valencia	lb	0.43	7/01	11r
Peaches	lb	1.38	7/01	11r
Peaches, halves or slices, Hunt's, Del Monte, or Libby's	29 oz	1.79	12/00	5c
Peanut butter, creamy, all sizes	lb	2.14	7/01	11r
Peas, green, Del Monte or Green Giant	15 oz	0.44	12/00	5c
Pork chops, center cut, bone-in	lb	3.83	7/01	11r
Pork, expenditures on	yr	141	1999	30r
Potatoes, white or red	10 lb	1.79	12/00	5c
Potatoes, white, all types	lb	0.37	7/01	11r
Poultry, expenditures on	yr	146	1999	30r
Processed fruits, expenditures on	yr	118	1999	30r
Processed vegetables, expenditures on	yr	81	1999	30r
Round roast, graded and ungraded, excl U.S. prime and choice	lb	3.07	7/01	11r
Round roast, U.S. choice, boneless	lb	3.37	7/01	11r
Round steak, graded and ungraded, excl U.S. prime and choice	lb	3.51	7/01	11r
Sausage, Jimmy Dean/Owens pork	lb	2.64	12/00	5c
Shortening, vegetable, Crisco	3 lb	3.64	12/00	5c
Sirloin steak, graded and ungraded, excl U.S. prime and choice	lb	4.67	7/01	11r
Soft drink, Coca Cola, ex deposit	2 liter	1.32	12/00	5c
Steak, sirloin, U.S. choice, boneless	lb	6.20	7/01	11r
Steak, T-bone	lb	6.51	12/00	5c
Strawberries, dry pint	12 oz	1.79	7/01	11r
Sugar and other sweets, expenditures on	yr	124	1999	30r
Sugar, cane or beet	4 lbs	1.76	12/00	5c
Sugar, white, all sizes	lb	0.46	7/01	11r
Tobacco products and smoking supplies purchases	yr	217	1999	30r
Tomatoes, field grown	lb	1.17	7/01	11r
Tomatoes, Hunt's or Del Monte	14.5 oz	0.99	12/00	5c
Tuna, chunk, light	6 oz	0.69	12/00	5c
Tuna, light, chunk	lb	2.05	7/01	11r
Goods and Services				
Miscellaneous goods and services, ACCRA Index		105.70	12/00	5c
B&B Japanese maple (acer japonicum)	gal	39.99	4/00	93r
Boxwood (buxus)	2 gal	14.99-24.99	4/00	93r
Christmas tree, noble fir		40-60	2000	65s
Daylily (hemerocallis)	gal	6.99-8.99	4/00	93r
Flat of annuals		16.68	4/00	93r
Fountain grass (pennisetum)	gal	7.99-11.99	4/00	93r
Hanging basket (10 in)		29.99	4/00	93r
Hardy geranium (geranium)	gal	6.99-11.99	4/00	93r
Hosta (hosta)	gal	6.99-18.99	4/00	93r
Lilac (syrubga vulgaris)	2 gal	14.99-17.99	4/00	93r
Miscellaneous purchases	yr	1070	1999	30r
Rhododendron (rhododendron)	2 gal	14.99	4/00	93r
Sage (salvia)	gal	6.99	4/00	93r

Values are in dollars or fractions of dollars. In the column headed *Ref*, references are shown to sources. Each reference is followed by a letter. These refer to the geographical level for which data were reported: s=State, r=Region, and c=City or metro. The abbreviation *ex* is used to mean *except* or *excluding*; *exp* stands for *expenditures*. For other abbreviations and further explanations, please see the Introduction.

Fresno, CA - continued

Item	Per	Value	Date	Ref.
Goods and Services				
Wintercreeper euonymus (euonymus fortunei)	2 gal	14.99-22.99	4/00	93r
Hunting license	yr	29.95	4/01	34s
Health Care				
Health care, ACCRA Index		115.50	12/00	5c
Cardiac catheterization, ave hospital/physician charges		24000	1998	77s
Childbirth, Cesarean delivery		11587	1997	13r
Childbirth, vaginal delivery		6725	1997	13r
Dentist's fee, adult teeth cleaning and periodic oral exam	visit	87.78	12/00	5c
Doctor's fee, routine exam, established patient	visit	56.75	12/00	5c
Drugs, expenditures on	yr	309	1999	30r
Health care purchases	yr	1869	1999	30r
Health insurance expenditures	yr	868	1999	30r
Hospital care, private room	day	683.50	12/00	5c
Hysterectomy, laproscopically-assisted, ave hospital/physician charges		20760	1998	76s
Hysterectomy, vaginal, ave hospital and physician charges		14570	1998	76s
Medicaid dispensing fee		4.05	1999	87s
Medical services expenditures	yr	580	1999	30r
Medical supplies, expenditures on	yr	112	1999	30r
Household Goods				
Dishwashing powder, Cascade	50 oz	2.96	12/00	5c
Floor coverings, expenditures on	yr	49	1999	30r
Furniture, expenditures on	yr	444	1999	30r
Household furnishings and equipment purchases	yr	1768	1999	30r
Household textiles, expenditures on	yr	141	1999	30r
Laundry and cleaning supplies, expenditures on	yr	128	1999	30r
Tissues, facial, Kleenex brand	175	1.36	12/00	5c
Housing				
Housing, ACCRA Index		95.60	12/00	5c
Home, 2200 sq ft, 4-br, 2-bath, 2-car garage, average		188000	2000	47c
Home price, existing, ave		239400	10/00	90r
Home value, median		215000	2001	53s
House, 2400 sq ft, 8000 sq ft lot, new, urban, utilities	total	199704	12/00	5c
House payment, principal and interest, 25% down payment	mos	1066	12/00	5c
Household operation expenditures	yr	781	1999	30r
Housekeeping supplies purchases	yr	513	1999	30r
Lodging expenditures	yr	575	1999	30r
Maintenance, repairs, insurance expenditures	yr	939	1999	30r
Monthly rental value of owned home	mos	662	1999	30r
Owned dwellings, expenditures own	yr	5231	1999	30r
Rent expenditures	yr	2709	1999	30r
Rent, apartment, 2 br, 1 1/2-2 baths, unfurn, 950 sq ft, water	mos	685	12/00	5c
Rental unit, 1 bedroom, with utilities	mos	433	4/01	41c
Rental unit, 2 bedroom, with utilities	mos	517	4/01	41c
Rental unit, 3 bedroom, with utilities	mos	720	4/01	41c
Rental unit, 4 bedroom, with utilities	mos	830	4/01	41c
Shelter, expenditures on	yr	8516	1999	30r
Insurance and Pensions				
Life and other personal insurance purchases	yr	355	1999	30r
Pensions and Social Security, expenditures on	yr	3636	1999	30r
Legal Fees				
Divorce, filing fee		182.00	4/01	35s
Driver's license fee	orig	12.00	1999	48s
Driver's license fee	renew	15.00	1999	48s

Fresno, CA - continued

Item	Per	Value	Date	Ref.
Personal Goods				
Personal care products and services purchases	yr	449	1999	30r
Shampoo, Alberto VO5	15 oz	1.35	12/00	5c
Toothpaste, Crest or Colgate	6-7 oz	2.41	12/00	5c
Personal Services				
Dry cleaning, man's 2-pc suit		6.60	12/00	5c
Man's haircut, barbershop, no styling		9.67	12/00	5c
Personal services, household, expenditures on	yr	353	1999	30r
Woman's shampoo, trim, blow-dry, no style-change		30.29	12/00	5c
Pets				
Pets, toys, and playground equipment, expenditures on	yr	358	1999	30r
Restaurant Food				
Chicken, fried, thigh and drumstick, KFC/Church's		2.58	12/00	5c
Hamburger with cheese, McDonald's	1/4 lb	2.07	12/00	5c
Pizza, Pizza Hut or Pizza Inn	11-12 in	10.99	12/00	5c
Taxes				
Federal income taxes paid	yr	3200	1999	30r
Personal taxes, expenditures on	yr	4153	1999	30r
Property taxes paid	yr	923	1999	30r
State and local income taxes paid	yr	812	1999	30r
Transportation				
Transportation, ACCRA Index		113.80	12/00	5c
Bus fare, one-way	trip	0.75	2000	1c
Bus fare, to central business district	1-way	0.75	12/00	5c
Cars and trucks, new, expenditures on	yr	1534	1999	30r
Cars and trucks, used, expenditures on	yr	1593	1999	30r
Diesel at the pump	gal	1.37	10/99	73s
Gasoline and motor oil purchases	yr	1129	1999	30r
Gasoline before-tax price (cents)	gal	128.80	10/00	43s
Maintenance and repair expenditures	yr	797	1999	30r
Public transportation, expenditures on	yr	530	1999	30r
Tire balance, computer or spin balance, front	wheel	8.59	12/00	5c
Transportation purchases	yr	7423	1999	30r
Vehicle expenses, miscellaneous, purchases	yr	2585	1999	30r
Vehicle insurance payments	yr	811	1999	30r
Vehicle purchases (net outlay)	yr	3180	1999	30r
Vehicle rental, lease expenditures	yr	666	1999	30r
Utilities				
Utilities, ACCRA Index		125.00	12/00	5c
Electrical bill, average	mos	58.66	9/00	9s
Electricity, expenditures on	yr	725	1999	30r
Electricity and other, mixed, 2400 sq ft, new home	mos	91.92	12/00	5c
Electricity cost, average	KWh	7.75	9/00	9s
Utilities, fuels, and public services purchased	yr	2179	1999	30r
Water and other public services, expenditures on	yr	339	1999	30r
Weddings				
Wedding (national average cost)		19936	2000	33r
Wedding (regional average total cost)		18918	1997	110r
Attendants' gifts		321	1998	33r
Bridal attendants' apparel (5 persons)		824	2000	33r
Bride's headpiece/veil		173	1998	33r
Bride's wedding dress		859	1998	33r
Clergy, religious facility fee		242	1998	33r
Engagement ring		3177	1998	33r
Flowers		789	1998	33r
Groom's formalwear rental		99	2000	33r
Limousine		410	1998	33r
Marriage license cost		50.00-80.00	4/01	35s
Men's formalwear (ushers, best man)		469	2000	33r
Mother of bride apparel		241	2000	33r
Music		866	1998	33r

Values are in dollars or fractions of dollars. In the column headed *Ref*, references are shown to sources. Each reference is followed by a letter. These refer to the geographical level for which data were reported: s=State, r=Region, and c=City or metro. The abbreviation *ex* is used to mean *except* or *excluding*; *exp* stands for *expenditures*. For other abbreviations and further explanations, please see the Introduction.

Fresno, CA - continued

Item	Per	Value	Date	Ref.
Weddings				
Photography and videography		1368	1998	33r
Rehearsal dinner		728	1998	33r
Wedding invitations and announcements		341	1998	33r
Wedding reception		7968	2000	33r
Wedding rings (bride and groom)		1060	1998	33r

Gadsden, AL

Item	Per	Value	Date	Ref.
Alcoholic Beverages				
Alcoholic beverage purchases	yr	253	1999	30r
Malt beverages, all types, all sizes, any origin	16 oz	0.96	7/01	11r
Appliances				
Major appliances, expenditures on	yr	172	1999	30r
Small appliances, housewares, expenditures on	yr	81	1999	30r
Banking and Money				
Mortgage interest and charges paid	yr	2039	1999	30r
Mortgage principal paid on owned property	yr	1026	1999	30r
Vehicle finance charges paid	yr	365	1999	30r
Charity				
Cash contributions, expenditures	yr	1127	1999	30r
Child Care				
Child raising cost, total, age 0-2	yr	8540	1999	60r
Child raising cost, total, age 3-5	yr	8780	1999	60r
Child raising cost, total, age 6-8	yr	8820	1999	60r
Child raising cost, total, age 9-11	yr	8800	1999	60r
Child raising cost, total, age 12-14	yr	9510	1999	60r
Child raising cost, total, age 15-17	yr	9740	1999	60r
Child's child care and education, age 0-2	yr	1380	1999	60r
Child's child care and education, age 3-5	yr	1520	1999	60r
Child's child care and education, age 6-8	yr	990	1999	60r
Child's child care and education, age 9-11	yr	650	1999	60r
Child's child care and education, age 12-14	yr	490	1999	60r
Child's child care and education, age 15-17	yr	840	1999	60r
Child's clothing, age 0-2	yr	480	1999	60r
Child's clothing, age 3-5	yr	470	1999	60r
Child's clothing, age 6-8	yr	520	1999	60r
Child's clothing, age 9-11	yr	570	1999	60r
Child's clothing, age 12-14	yr	950	1999	60r
Child's clothing, age 15-17	yr	850	1999	60r
Child's food, age 0-2	yr	1000	1999	60r
Child's food, age 3-5	yr	1160	1999	60r
Child's food, age 6-8	yr	1490	1999	60r
Child's food, age 9-11	yr	1770	1999	60r
Child's food, age 12-14	yr	1770	1999	60r
Child's food, age 15-17	yr	1980	1999	60r
Child's health care, age 0-2	yr	620	1999	60r
Child's health care, age 3-5	yr	590	1999	60r
Child's health care, age 6-8	yr	680	1999	60r
Child's health care, age 9-11	yr	720	1999	60r
Child's health care, age 12-14	yr	730	1999	60r
Child's health care, age 15-17	yr	760	1999	60r
Child's housing, age 0-2	yr	3070	1999	60r
Child's housing, age 3-5	yr	3050	1999	60r
Child's housing, age 6-8	yr	3010	1999	60r
Child's housing, age 9-11	yr	2850	1999	60r
Child's housing, age 12-14	yr	3040	1999	60r
Child's housing, age 15-17	yr	2650	1999	60r
Child's personal care, reading, age 0-2	yr	910	1999	60r
Child's personal care, reading, age 3-5	yr	930	1999	60r
Child's personal care, reading, age 6-8	yr	960	1999	60r
Child's personal care, reading, age 9-11	yr	1000	1999	60r
Child's personal care, reading, age 12-14	yr	1170	1999	60r
Child's personal care, reading, age 15-17	yr	950	1999	60r
Clothing				
Apparel and services purchases	yr	1610	1999	30r
Boys, 2 to 15, expenditures on	yr	89	1999	30r
Children under 2, expenditures on	yr	79	1999	30r

Gadsden, AL - continued

Item	Per	Value	Date	Ref.
Clothing - continued				
Footwear, expenditures on	yr	283	1999	30r
Girls, 2 to 15, expenditures on	yr	103	1999	30r
Men and boys, expenditures on	yr	351	1999	30r
Men, 16 and over, expenditures on	yr	262	1999	30r
Women, 16 and over, expenditures on	yr	538	1999	30r
Communications				
Phone line, single, business, field visit	inst.	69.00	12/97	17s
Phone line, single, business, no field visit	inst.	69.00	12/97	17s
Phone line, single, residence, field visit	inst.	40.00	12/97	17s
Phone line, single, residence, no field visit	inst.	40.00	12/97	17s
Postage and stationery, expenditures on	yr	104	1999	30r
Postal rate, express mail, up to half-pound		12.45	7/01	108r
Postal rate, letter, first class, first ounce		0.34	7/01	108r
Postal rate, letter, two ounces		0.57	7/01	108r
Postal rate, post card		0.21	7/01	108r
Postal rate, priority mail, two pounds		3.95	7/01	108r
Postal rate, priority mail, up to one pound		3.50	7/01	108r
Telephone services, expenditures on	yr	860	1999	30r
Education				
Board, 4-year private college/university	yr	2256	1996	38s
Board, 4-year public college/university	yr	1739	1996	38s
Education expenditures	yr	431	1999	30r
Room, 4-year private college/university	yr	1799	1996	38s
Room, 4-year public college/university	yr	1757	1996	38s
Total cost, 4-year private college/university	yr	11635	1996	38s
Total cost, 4-year public college/university	yr	5737	1996	38s
Tuition, 2-year public college/university, in state	yr	1317	1996	38s
Tuition, 4-year private college/university, in state	yr	7580	1996	38s
Tuition, 4-year public college/university	yr	2240	1996	38s
Energy and Fuels				
Electricity	500 KWhs	47.29	7/01	11r
Electricity	KWh	0.09	7/01	11r
Fuel oil #2	gal	1.43	7/01	11r
Fuel oil and other fuels, expenditures on	yr	45	1999	30r
Gas, natural, commercial rate	1000 cf	9.50	11/00	88s
Gasoline, all types	gal	1.60	7/01	11r
Gasoline, unleaded midgrade	gal	1.65	7/01	11r
Gasoline, unleaded premium	gal	1.74	7/01	11r
Natural gas, expenditures on	yr	164	1999	30r
Utility (piped) gas, therm		1.01	7/01	11r
Utility (piped) gas, 40 therms		44.29	7/01	11r
Utility (piped) gas, 100 therms		97.44	7/01	11r
Entertainment				
Entertainment purchases	yr	1574	1999	30r
Fees and admissions paid	yr	371	1999	30r
Reading purchases	yr	121	1999	30r
Television, radios, sound equipment, expenditures on	yr	561	1999	30r
Groceries				
American processed cheese	lb	3.50	7/01	11r
Bakery products, expenditures on	yr	261	1999	30r
Bananas	lb	0.47	7/01	11r
Beans, dried, any type, all sizes	lb	0.63	7/01	11r
Beef for stew, boneless	lb	2.86	7/01	11r
Beef, expenditures on	yr	210	1999	30r
Bologna, all beef or mixed	lb	2.29	7/01	11r
Bread, French	lb	1.66	7/01	11r
Bread, white, pan	lb	0.87	7/01	11r
Bread, whole wheat, pan	lb	1.38	7/01	11r
Broccoli	lb	1.04	7/01	11r
Butter, salted, grade AA, stick	lb	2.26	7/01	11r
Butter, yoghurt, cheese, etc, expenditures on	yr	170	1999	30r
Cabbage	lb	0.42	7/01	11r
Cereals and cereal products, expenditures on	yr	140	1999	30r
Cheddar cheese, natural	lb	3.75	7/01	11r

Values are in dollars or fractions of dollars. In the column headed *Ref*, references are shown to sources. Each reference is followed by a letter. These refer to the geographical level for which data were reported: s=State, r=Region, and c=City or metro. The abbreviation *ex* is used to mean *except* or *excluding*; *exp* stands for *expenditures*. For other abbreviations and further explanations, please see the Introduction.

Gadsden, AL - continued

Item	Per	Value	Date	Ref.
Groceries				
Chicken breast, bone-in	lb	1.85	7/01	11r
Chicken legs, bone-in	lb	1.34	7/01	11r
Chicken, fresh, whole	lb	1.05	7/01	11r
Chops, boneless,	lb	4.13	7/01	11r
Chuck roast, graded and ungraded, excl U.S. prime and choice	lb	2.35	7/01	11r
Chuck roast, U.S. choice, boneless	lb	2.67	7/01	11r
Coffee, 100%, ground roast, all sizes	lb	2.88	7/01	11r
Coffee, instant, plain, regular, all sizes	16 oz	9.25	7/01	11r
Cola, non diet,	2 liter	1.11	7/01	11r
Crackers, soda, salted	lb	1.70	7/01	11r
Dairy product purchases	yr	282	1999	30r
Eggs, expenditures on	yr	32	1999	30r
Fats and oils, expenditures on	yr	79	1999	30r
Fish and seafood, expenditures on	yr	99	1999	30r
Flour, white, all purpose	lb	0.32	7/01	11r
Food (excl fruit and vegetables), eaten at home, purchases	yr	815	1999	30r
Food cooked on trips, expenditures on	yr	36	1999	30r
Food purchases	yr	4533	1999	30r
Food purchases, eaten away from home	yr	1873	1999	30r
Food purchases, food eaten at home	yr	2660	1999	30r
Fresh fruits, expenditures on	yr	128	1999	30r
Fresh milk and cream, expenditures on	yr	112	1999	30r
Fresh vegetables, expenditures on	yr	131	1999	30r
Fruit and vegetable purchases	yr	438	1999	30r
Grapefruit	lb	0.59	7/01	11r
Grapes, Thompson, seedless	lb	2.12	7/01	11r
Ground beef, 100% beef	lb	1.76	7/01	11r
Ground beef, lean and extra lean	lb	2.60	7/01	11r
Ground chuck, 100% beef	lb	2.08	7/01	11r
Ham, boneless, excl canned	lb	2.71	7/01	11r
Ham, rump or shank half, bone-in, smoked	lb	2.19	7/01	11r
Ice cream, prepackaged, bulk, regular	1/2 gal	3.93	7/01	11r
Lemons	lb	1.32	7/01	11r
Lettuce, iceberg	lb	0.76	7/01	11r
Milk, fresh, low fat,	gal	2.75	7/01	11r
Milk, fresh, whole, fortified	gal	2.97	7/01	11r
Nonalcoholic beverages, expenditures on	yr	228	1999	30r
Orange juice, frozen concentrate	16 oz	1.95	7/01	11r
Oranges, Navel	lb	0.73	7/01	11r
Oranges, Valencia	lb	0.55	7/01	11r
Peanut butter, creamy, all sizes	lb	1.83	7/01	11r
Pears, Anjou	lb	0.98	7/01	11r
Pork chops, center cut, bone-in	lb	3.33	7/01	11r
Pork sausage, fresh, loose	lb	2.59	7/01	11r
Pork shoulder picnic, bone-in, smoked	lb	1.12	7/01	11r
Pork, expenditures on	yr	162	1999	30r
Potato chips	16 oz	3.59	7/01	11r
Potatoes, frozen, french fried	lb	1.00	7/01	11r
Potatoes, white, all types	lb	0.44	7/01	11r
Poultry, expenditures on	yr	137	1999	30r
Processed fruits, expenditures on	yr	97	1999	30r
Processed vegetables, expenditures on	yr	82	1999	30r
Rice, white, long grain, uncooked	lb	0.51	7/01	11r
Round roast, graded and ungraded, excl U.S. prime and choice	lb	2.96	7/01	11r
Round steak, graded and ungraded, excl U.S. prime and choice	lb	3.11	7/01	11r
Sirloin steak, graded and ungraded, excl U.S. prime and choice	lb	4.23	7/01	11r
Spaghetti and macaroni	lb	0.78	7/01	11r
Steak, round, U.S. choice, boneless	lb	3.56	7/01	11r
Steak, sirloin, U.S. choice, boneless	lb	5.65	7/01	11r
Strawberries, dry pint	12 oz	1.50	7/01	11r
Sugar and other sweets, expenditures on	yr	99	1999	30r
Sugar, white, 33-80 ounce package	lb	0.39	7/01	11r
Sugar, white, all sizes	lb	0.42	7/01	11r
Tobacco products and smoking supplies purchases	yr	288	1999	30r
Tomatoes, field grown	lb	1.43	7/01	11r
Tuna, light, chunk	lb	1.77	7/01	11r

Gadsden, AL - continued

Item	Per	Value	Date	Ref.
Groceries - continued				
Turkey, frozen, whole	lb	1.05	7/01	11r
Goods and Services				
Hunting license	yr	16.00	4/01	34s
Health Care				
Cardiac catheterization, ave hospital/ physician charges		15260	1998	77s
Childbirth, Cesarean delivery		11587	1997	13r
Childbirth, vaginal delivery		6725	1997	13r
Drugs, expenditures on	yr	399	1999	30r
Health care purchases	yr	1971	1999	30r
Health insurance expenditures	yr	933	1999	30r
Hysterectomy, laproscopically-assisted, ave hospital/physician charges		16780	1998	76s
Hysterectomy, vaginal, ave hospital and physician charges		10990	1998	76s
Medicaid dispensing fee		5.40	1999	87s
Medical services expenditures	yr	547	1999	30r
Medical supplies, expenditures on	yr	91	1999	30r
Household Goods				
Floor coverings, expenditures on	yr	44	1999	30r
Furniture, expenditures on	yr	335	1999	30r
Household furnishings and equipment purchases	yr	1328	1999	30r
Household textiles, expenditures on	yr	89	1999	30r
Laundry and cleaning supplies, expenditures on	yr	113	1999	30r
Housing				
Home price, existing, ave		160100	10/00	90r
Home value, median		115000	2001	53s
Household operation expenditures	yr	553	1999	30r
Housekeeping supplies purchases	yr	473	1999	30r
Housing, expenditures on	yr	10303	1999	30r
Maintenance, repairs, insurance expenditures	yr	699	1999	30r
Monthly rental value of owned home	mos	505	1999	30r
Owned dwellings, expenditures own	yr	3465	1999	30r
Rent expenditures	yr	1641	1999	30r
Rental unit, 1 bedroom, with utilities	mos	322	4/01	41c
Rental unit, 2 bedroom, with utilities	mos	372	4/01	41c
Rental unit, 3 bedroom, with utilities	mos	483	4/01	41c
Rental unit, 4 bedroom, with utilities	mos	594	4/01	41c
Shelter, expenditures on	yr	5467	1999	30r
Insurance and Pensions				
Life and other personal insurance purchases	yr	414	1999	30r
Pensions and Social Security, expenditures on	yr	2635	1999	30r
Personal insurance and pensions, expenditures on	yr	3048	1999	30r
Legal Fees				
Divorce, filing fee		146.00- 193.00	4/01	35s
Driver's license fee	orig	18.50	1999	48s
Driver's license fee	renew	18.50	1999	48s
Personal Goods				
Personal care products and services purchases	yr	393	1999	30r
Personal Services				
Personal services, household, expenditures on	yr	258	1999	30r
Pets				
Pets, toys, and playground equipment, expenditures on	yr	306	1999	30r
Taxes				
Federal income taxes paid	yr	2047	1999	30r
Personal taxes, expenditures on	yr	2554	1999	30r
Property taxes paid	yr	726	1999	30r
State and local income taxes paid	yr	363	1999	30r

Values are in dollars or fractions of dollars. In the column headed *Ref*, references are shown to sources. Each reference is followed by a letter. These refer to the geographical level for which data were reported: s=State, r=Region, and c=City or metro. The abbreviation *ex* is used to mean *except* or *excluding*; *exp* stands for *expenditures*. For other abbreviations and further explanations, please see the Introduction.

Gadsden, AL - continued

Item	Per	Value	Date	Ref.
Transportation				
Cars and trucks, new, expenditures on	yr	1648	1999	30r
Cars and trucks, used, expenditures on	yr	1651	1999	30r
Diesel at the pump	gal	1.19	10/99	73s
Gasoline and motor oil purchases	yr	1052	1999	30r
Gasoline before-tax price (cents)	gal	104.10	10/00	43s
Maintenance and repair expenditures	yr	621	1999	30r
Public transportation, expenditures on	yr	298	1999	30r
Transportation purchases	yr	6738	1999	30r
Vehicle expenses, miscellaneous, purchases	yr	2033	1999	30r
Vehicle insurance payments	yr	696	1999	30r
Vehicle purchases (net outlay)	yr	3354	1999	30r
Vehicle rental, lease expenditures	yr	352	1999	30r
Utilities				
Electrical bill, average	mos	83.42	9/00	9s
Electricity, expenditures on	yr	1115	1999	30r
Electricity cost, average	KWh	5.60	9/00	9s
Water and other public services, expenditures on	yr	298	1999	30r
Weddings				
Wedding (national average cost)		19936	2000	33r
Attendants' gifts		321	1998	33r
Bridal attendants' apparel (5 persons)		824	2000	33r
Bride's headpiece/veil		173	1998	33r
Bride's wedding dress		859	1998	33r
Clergy, religious facility fee		242	1998	33r
Engagement ring		3177	1998	33r
Flowers		789	1998	33r
Groom's formalwear rental		99	2000	33r
Limousine		410	1998	33r
Marriage license cost		25.00	4/01	35s
Men's formalwear (ushers, best man)		469	2000	33r
Mother of bride apparel		241	2000	33r
Music		866	1998	33r
Photography and videography		1368	1998	33r
Rehearsal dinner		728	1998	33r
Wedding invitations and announcements		341	1998	33r
Wedding reception		7968	2000	33r
Wedding rings (bride and groom)		1060	1998	33r

Gainseville, FL

Item	Per	Value	Date	Ref.
Alcoholic Beverages				
Alcoholic beverage purchases	yr	253	1999	30r
Malt beverages, all types, all sizes, any origin	16 oz	0.96	7/01	11r
Appliances				
Major appliances, expenditures on	yr	172	1999	30r
Small appliances, housewares, expenditures on	yr	81	1999	30r
Banking and Money				
Mortgage interest and charges paid	yr	2039	1999	30r
Mortgage principal paid on owned property	yr	1026	1999	30r
Vehicle finance charges paid	yr	365	1999	30r
Charity				
Cash contributions, expenditures	yr	1127	1999	30r
Child Care				
Child raising cost, total, age 0-2	yr	8540	1999	60r
Child raising cost, total, age 3-5	yr	8780	1999	60r
Child raising cost, total, age 6-8	yr	8820	1999	60r
Child raising cost, total, age 9-11	yr	8800	1999	60r
Child raising cost, total, age 12-14	yr	9510	1999	60r
Child raising cost, total, age 15-17	yr	9740	1999	60r
Child's child care and education, age 0-2	yr	1380	1999	60r
Child's child care and education, age 3-5	yr	1520	1999	60r
Child's child care and education, age 6-8	yr	990	1999	60r
Child's child care and education, age 9-11	yr	650	1999	60r
Child's child care and education, age 12-14	yr	490	1999	60r
Child's child care and education, age 15-17	yr	840	1999	60r
Child's clothing, age 0-2	yr	480	1999	60r

Gainseville, FL - continued

Item	Per	Value	Date	Ref.
Child Care - continued				
Child's clothing, age 3-5	yr	470	1999	60r
Child's clothing, age 6-8	yr	520	1999	60r
Child's clothing, age 9-11	yr	570	1999	60r
Child's clothing, age 12-14	yr	950	1999	60r
Child's clothing, age 15-17	yr	850	1999	60r
Child's food, age 0-2	yr	1000	1999	60r
Child's food, age 3-5	yr	1160	1999	60r
Child's food, age 6-8	yr	1490	1999	60r
Child's food, age 9-11	yr	1770	1999	60r
Child's food, age 12-14	yr	1770	1999	60r
Child's food, age 15-17	yr	1980	1999	60r
Child's health care, age 0-2	yr	620	1999	60r
Child's health care, age 3-5	yr	590	1999	60r
Child's health care, age 6-8	yr	680	1999	60r
Child's health care, age 9-11	yr	720	1999	60r
Child's health care, age 12-14	yr	730	1999	60r
Child's health care, age 15-17	yr	760	1999	60r
Child's housing, age 0-2	yr	3070	1999	60r
Child's housing, age 3-5	yr	3050	1999	60r
Child's housing, age 6-8	yr	3010	1999	60r
Child's housing, age 9-11	yr	2850	1999	60r
Child's housing, age 12-14	yr	3040	1999	60r
Child's housing, age 15-17	yr	2650	1999	60r
Child's personal care, reading, age 0-2	yr	910	1999	60r
Child's personal care, reading, age 3-5	yr	930	1999	60r
Child's personal care, reading, age 6-8	yr	960	1999	60r
Child's personal care, reading, age 9-11	yr	1000	1999	60r
Child's personal care, reading, age 12-14	yr	1170	1999	60r
Child's personal care, reading, age 15-17	yr	950	1999	60r
Clothing				
Apparel and services purchases	yr	1610	1999	30r
Boys, 2 to 15, expenditures on	yr	89	1999	30r
Children under 2, expenditures on	yr	79	1999	30r
Footwear, expenditures on	yr	283	1999	30r
Girls, 2 to 15, expenditures on	yr	103	1999	30r
Men and boys, expenditures on	yr	351	1999	30r
Men, 16 and over, expenditures on	yr	262	1999	30r
Women, 16 and over, expenditures on	yr	538	1999	30r
Communications				
Cable modem installation, Adelphi		54.90	6/99	103s
Cable modem installation, Comcast		95.00	6/99	103s
Cable modem installation, Media One		100.00	6/99	103s
Cable modem installation, Time Warner		75.00-225.00	6/99	103s
Cable modem rate, cable subscriber, Adelphi	mos	34.95	6/99	103s
Cable modem rate, cable subscriber, Comcast	mos	39.95	6/99	103s
Cable modem rate, cable subscriber, Media One	mos	34.95-39.95	6/99	103s
Cable modem rate, cable subscriber, Time Warner	mos	39.95-49.95	6/99	103s
Cable modem rate, non-cable subscriber, Adelphi	mos	44.95	6/99	103s
Cable modem rate, non-cable subscriber, Comcast	mos	49.95	6/99	103s
Cable modem rate, non-cable subscriber, Media One	mos	49.95	6/99	103s
Cable modem rate, non-cable subscriber, Time Warner	mos	39.95-54.95	6/99	103s
Phone line, single, business, field visit	inst.	56.00	12/97	17s
Phone line, single, business, no field visit	inst.	56.00	12/97	17s
Phone line, single, residence, field visit	inst.	40.00	12/97	17s
Phone line, single, residence, no field visit	inst.	40.00	12/97	17s
Postage and stationery, expenditures on	yr	104	1999	30r
Postal rate, express mail, up to half-pound		12.45	7/01	108r
Postal rate, letter, first class, first ounce		0.34	7/01	108r
Postal rate, letter, two ounces		0.57	7/01	108r
Postal rate, post card		0.21	7/01	108r
Postal rate, priority mail, two pounds		3.95	7/01	108r
Postal rate, priority mail, up to one pound		3.50	7/01	108r
Telephone services, expenditures on	yr	860	1999	30r

Values are in dollars or fractions of dollars. In the column headed *Ref*, references are shown to sources. Each reference is followed by a letter. These refer to the geographical level for which data were reported: s=State, r=Region, and c=City or metro. The abbreviation *ex* is used to mean *except* or *excluding*; *exp* stands for expenditures. For other abbreviations and further explanations, please see the Introduction.

Gainseville, FL - continued

Item	Per	Value	Date	Ref.
Education				
Board, 4-year private college/university	yr	2236	1996	38s
Board, 4-year public college/university	yr	2295	1996	38s
Education expenditures	yr	431	1999	30r
Room, 4-year private college/university	yr	2428	1996	38s
Room, 4-year public college/university	yr	2193	1996	38s
Total cost, 4-year private college/university	yr	15028	1996	38s
Total cost, 4-year public college/university	yr	6254	1996	38s
Tuition, 2-year public college/university, in state	yr	1103	1996	38s
Tuition, 4-year private college/university, in state	yr	10364	1996	38s
Tuition, 4-year public college/university	yr	1767	1996	38s
Energy and Fuels				
Electricity	KWh	0.09	7/01	11r
Electricity	500 KWhs	47.29	7/01	11r
Fuel oil #2	gal	1.43	7/01	11r
Fuel oil and other fuels, expenditures on	yr	45	1999	30r
Gas, natural, commercial rate	1000 cf	8.44	11/00	88s
Gasoline, all types	gal	1.60	7/01	11r
Gasoline, unleaded midgrade	gal	1.65	7/01	11r
Gasoline, unleaded premium	gal	1.74	7/01	11r
Natural gas, expenditures on	yr	164	1999	30r
Utility (piped) gas, therm		1.01	7/01	11r
Utility (piped) gas, 40 therms		44.29	7/01	11r
Utility (piped) gas, 100 therms		97.44	7/01	11r
Entertainment				
Entertainment purchases	yr	1574	1999	30r
Fees and admissions paid	yr	371	1999	30r
Reading purchases	yr	121	1999	30r
Television, radios, sound equipment, expenditures on	yr	561	1999	30r
Funerals				
Total cost of funeral		5922.53	1/99	78r
Acknowledgement cards		63.43	1/99	78r
Casket		2258.77	1/99	78r
Cosmetology, hair, other preparation		127.09	1/99	78r
Embalming		393.49	1/99	78r
Funeral at funeral home		367.50	1/99	78r
Hearse (local)		169.66	1/99	78r
Professional service charges		1211.32	1/99	78r
Service car/van		80.69	1/99	78r
Transfer of remains to funeral home		144.25	1/99	78r
Vault		803.50	1/99	78r
Visitation/viewing		302.83	1/99	78r
Groceries				
American processed cheese	lb	3.50	7/01	11r
Bakery products, expenditures on	yr	261	1999	30r
Bananas	lb	0.47	7/01	11r
Beans, dried, any type, all sizes	lb	0.63	7/01	11r
Beef for stew, boneless	lb	2.86	7/01	11r
Beef, expenditures on	yr	210	1999	30r
Bologna, all beef or mixed	lb	2.29	7/01	11r
Bread, French	lb	1.66	7/01	11r
Bread, white, pan	lb	0.87	7/01	11r
Bread, whole wheat, pan	lb	1.38	7/01	11r
Broccoli	lb	1.04	7/01	11r
Butter, salted, grade AA, stick	lb	2.26	7/01	11r
Butter, yoghurt, cheese, etc, expenditures on	yr	170	1999	30r
Cabbage	lb	0.42	7/01	11r
Cereals and cereal products, expenditures on	yr	140	1999	30r
Cheddar cheese, natural	lb	3.75	7/01	11r
Chicken breast, bone-in	lb	1.85	7/01	11r
Chicken legs, bone-in	lb	1.34	7/01	11r
Chicken, fresh, whole	lb	1.05	7/01	11r
Chops, boneless,	lb	4.13	7/01	11r
Chuck roast, graded and ungraded, excl U.S. prime and choice	lb	2.35	7/01	11r
Chuck roast, U.S. choice, boneless	lb	2.67	7/01	11r

Gainseville, FL - continued

Item	Per	Value	Date	Ref.
Groceries - continued				
Coffee, 100%, ground roast, all sizes	lb	2.88	7/01	11r
Coffee, instant, plain, regular, all sizes	16 oz	9.25	7/01	11r
Cola, non diet,	2 liter	1.11	7/01	11r
Crackers, soda, salted	lb	1.70	7/01	11r
Dairy product purchases	yr	282	1999	30r
Eggs, expenditures on	yr	32	1999	30r
Fats and oils, expenditures on	yr	79	1999	30r
Fish and seafood, expenditures on	yr	99	1999	30r
Flour, white, all purpose	lb	0.32	7/01	11r
Food (excl fruit and vegetables), eaten at home, purchases	yr	815	1999	30r
Food cooked on trips, expenditures on	yr	36	1999	30r
Food purchases	yr	4533	1999	30r
Food purchases, eaten away from home	yr	1873	1999	30r
Food purchases, food eaten at home	yr	2660	1999	30r
Fresh fruits, expenditures on	yr	128	1999	30r
Fresh milk and cream, expenditures on	yr	112	1999	30r
Fresh vegetables, expenditures on	yr	131	1999	30r
Fruit and vegetable purchases	yr	438	1999	30r
Grapefruit	lb	0.59	7/01	11r
Grapes, Thompson, seedless	lb	2.12	7/01	11r
Ground beef, 100% beef	lb	1.76	7/01	11r
Ground beef, lean and extra lean	lb	2.60	7/01	11r
Ground chuck, 100% beef	lb	2.08	7/01	11r
Ham, boneless, excl canned	lb	2.71	7/01	11r
Ham, rump or shank half, bone-in, smoked	lb	2.19	7/01	11r
Ice cream, prepackaged, bulk, regular	1/2 gal	3.93	7/01	11r
Lemons	lb	1.32	7/01	11r
Lettuce, iceberg	lb	0.76	7/01	11r
Milk, fresh, low fat,	gal	2.75	7/01	11r
Milk, fresh, whole, fortified	gal	2.97	7/01	11r
Nonalcoholic beverages, expenditures on	yr	228	1999	30r
Orange juice, frozen concentrate	16 oz	1.95	7/01	11r
Oranges, Navel	lb	0.73	7/01	11r
Oranges, Valencia	lb	0.55	7/01	11r
Peanut butter, creamy, all sizes	lb	1.83	7/01	11r
Pears, Anjou	lb	0.98	7/01	11r
Pork chops, center cut, bone-in	lb	3.33	7/01	11r
Pork sausage, fresh, loose	lb	2.59	7/01	11r
Pork shoulder picnic, bone-in, smoked	lb	1.12	7/01	11r
Pork, expenditures on	yr	162	1999	30r
Potato chips	16 oz	3.59	7/01	11r
Potatoes, frozen, french fried	lb	1.00	7/01	11r
Potatoes, white, all types	lb	0.44	7/01	11r
Poultry, expenditures on	yr	137	1999	30r
Processed fruits, expenditures on	yr	97	1999	30r
Processed vegetables, expenditures on	yr	82	1999	30r
Rice, white, long grain, uncooked	lb	0.51	7/01	11r
Round roast, graded and ungraded, excl U.S. prime and choice	lb	2.96	7/01	11r
Round steak, graded and ungraded, excl U.S. prime and choice	lb	3.11	7/01	11r
Sirloin steak, graded and ungraded, excl U.S. prime and choice	lb	4.23	7/01	11r
Spaghetti and macaroni	lb	0.78	7/01	11r
Steak, round, U.S. choice, boneless	lb	3.56	7/01	11r
Steak, sirloin, U.S. choice, boneless	lb	5.65	7/01	11r
Strawberries, dry pint	12 oz	1.50	7/01	11r
Sugar and other sweets, expenditures on	yr	99	1999	30r
Sugar, white, 33-80 ounce package	lb	0.39	7/01	11r
Sugar, white, all sizes	lb	0.42	7/01	11r
Tobacco products and smoking supplies purchases	yr	288	1999	30r
Tomatoes, field grown	lb	1.43	7/01	11r
Tuna, light, chunk	lb	1.77	7/01	11r
Turkey, frozen, whole	lb	1.05	7/01	11r
Goods and Services				
B&B Japanese maple (acer japonicum)	gal	49.98- 129.00	4/00	93r
Boxwood (buxus)	2 gal	12.99- 16.99	4/00	93r

Values are in dollars or fractions of dollars. In the column headed *Ref*, references are shown to sources. Each reference is followed by a letter. These refer to the geographical level for which data were reported: s=State, r=Region, and c=City or metro. The abbreviation *ex* is used to mean *except* or *excluding*; *exp* stands for *expenditures*. For other abbreviations and further explanations, please see the Introduction.

Gainseville, FL - continued

Item	Per	Value	Date	Ref.
Goods and Services				
Daylilly (hemerocallis)	gal	4.99-8.99	4/00	93r
Flat of annuals		11.00-13.92	4/00	93r
Fountain grass (pennisetum)	gal	5.98-7.98	4/00	93r
Hanging basket (10 in)		7.99-14.98	4/00	93r
Hardy geranium (geranium)	gal	5.98-8.00	4/00	93r
Hosta (hosta)	gal	4.99-10.98	4/00	93r
Lilac (syrubga vulgaris)	2 gal	12.99-21.99	4/00	93r
Rhododendron (rhododendron)	2 gal	14.99-24.99	4/00	93r
Sage (salvia)	gal	5.98-6.99	4/00	93r
Wintercreeper euonymus (euonymus fortunei)	2 gal	7.99-89.99	4/00	93r
Hunting license	yr	12.50	4/01	34s
Health Care				
Cardiac catheterization, ave hospital/ physician charges		15060	1998	77s
Childbirth, Cesarean delivery		11587	1997	13r
Childbirth, vaginal delivery		6725	1997	13r
Drugs, expenditures on	yr	399	1999	30r
Health care purchases	yr	1971	1999	30r
Health insurance expenditures	yr	933	1999	30r
Hysterectomy, laproscopically-assisted, ave hospital/physician charges		14760	1998	76s
Hysterectomy, vaginal, ave hospital and physician charges		11320	1998	76s
Medicaid dispensing fee		4.23	1999	87s
Medical services expenditures	yr	547	1999	30r
Medical supplies, expenditures on	yr	91	1999	30r
Plastic surgery, breast augmentation		2870	2000	7r
Plastic surgery, breast lift		3649	2000	7r
Plastic surgery, facelift		5008	2000	7r
Plastic surgery, hair transplantation		3425	2000	7r
Plastic surgery, lip augmentation		1227	2000	7r
Plastic surgery, lower body lift		4793	2000	7r
Plastic surgery, thigh lift		3862	2000	7r
Household Goods				
Floor coverings, expenditures on	yr	44	1999	30r
Furniture, expenditures on	yr	335	1999	30r
Household furnishings and equipment purchases	yr	1328	1999	30r
Household textiles, expenditures on	yr	89	1999	30r
Laundry and cleaning supplies, expenditures on	yr	113	1999	30r
Housing				
Home price, existing, ave		160100	10/00	90r
Home value, median		104000	2001	53s
Household operation expenditures	yr	553	1999	30r
Housekeeping supplies purchases	yr	473	1999	30r
Housing, expenditures on	yr	10303	1999	30r
Maintenance, repairs, insurance expenditures	yr	699	1999	30r
Monthly rental value of owned home	mos	505	1999	30r
Owned dwellings, expenditures own	yr	3465	1999	30r
Rent expenditures	yr	1641	1999	30r
Rental unit, 1 bedroom, with utilities	mos	451	4/01	41c
Rental unit, 2 bedroom, with utilities	mos	548	4/01	41c
Rental unit, 3 bedroom, with utilities	mos	751	4/01	41c
Rental unit, 4 bedroom, with utilities	mos	887	4/01	41c
Shelter, expenditures on	yr	5467	1999	30r
Insurance and Pensions				
Life and other personal insurance purchases	yr	414	1999	30r
Medigap health insurance, Plan H	yr	2887	2000	69s

Gainseville, FL - continued

Item	Per	Value	Date	Ref.
Insurance and Pensions - continued				
Medigap health insurance, Plan I	yr	3302	2000	69s
Medigap health insurance, Plan J	yr	3889	2000	69s
Pensions and Social Security, expenditures on	yr	2635	1999	30r
Personal insurance and pensions, expenditures on	yr	3048	1999	30r
Legal Fees				
Divorce, filing fee		65.00-85.00	4/01	35s
Driver's license fee	orig	20.00	1999	48s
Driver's license fee	renew	15.00	1999	48s
Personal Goods				
Personal care products and services purchases	yr	393	1999	30r
Personal Services				
Personal services, household, expenditures on	yr	258	1999	30r
Pets				
Pets, toys, and playground equipment, expenditures on	yr	306	1999	30r
Taxes				
Federal income taxes paid	yr	2047	1999	30r
Personal taxes, expenditures on	yr	2554	1999	30r
Property taxes paid	yr	726	1999	30r
State and local income taxes paid	yr	363	1999	30r
Transportation				
Cars and trucks, new, expenditures on	yr	1648	1999	30r
Cars and trucks, used, expenditures on	yr	1651	1999	30r
Diesel at the pump	gal	1.26	10/99	73s
Gasoline and motor oil purchases	yr	1052	1999	30r
Gasoline before-tax price (cents)	gal	101.90	10/00	43s
Maintenance and repair expenditures	yr	621	1999	30r
Public transportation, expenditures on	yr	298	1999	30r
Transportation purchases	yr	6738	1999	30r
Vehicle expenses, miscellaneous, purchases	yr	2033	1999	30r
Vehicle insurance payments	yr	696	1999	30r
Vehicle purchases (net outlay)	yr	3354	1999	30r
Vehicle rental, lease expenditures	yr	352	1999	30r
Travel				
Hotel room	night	110.57	2/01	95s
Utilities				
Electrical bill, average	mos	86.33	9/00	9s
Electricity, expenditures on	yr	1115	1999	30r
Electricity cost, average	KWh	6.80	9/00	9s
Water and other public services, expenditures on	yr	298	1999	30r
Weddings				
Wedding (national average cost)		19936	2000	33r
Wedding (regional average total cost)		16293	1997	110r
Attendants' gifts		321	1998	33r
Bridal attendants' apparel (5 persons)		824	2000	33r
Bride's headpiece/veil		173	1998	33r
Bride's wedding dress		859	1998	33r
Clergy, religious facility fee		242	1998	33r
Engagement ring		3177	1998	33r
Flowers		789	1998	33r
Groom's formalwear rental		99	2000	33r
Limousine		410	1998	33r
Marriage license cost		56.00-88.50	4/01	35s
Men's formalwear (ushers, best man)		469	2000	33r
Mother of bride apparel		241	2000	33r
Music		866	1998	33r
Photography and videography		1368	1998	33r
Rehearsal dinner		728	1998	33r
Wedding invitations and announcements		341	1998	33r
Wedding reception		7968	2000	33r

Values are in dollars or fractions of dollars. In the column headed *Ref*, references are shown to sources. Each reference is followed by a letter. These refer to the geographical level for which data were reported: s=State, r=Region, and c=City or metro. The abbreviation *ex* is used to mean *except* or *excluding*; *exp* stands for expenditures. For other abbreviations and further explanations, please see the Introduction.

Gainseville, FL - continued

Item	Per	Value	Date	Ref.
Weddings				
Wedding rings (bride and groom)		1060	1998	33r

Galveston-Texas City, TX

Item	Per	Value	Date	Ref.
Alcoholic Beverages				
Alcoholic beverage purchases	yr	253	1999	30r
Malt beverages, all types, all sizes, any origin	16 oz	0.96	7/01	11r
Appliances				
Major appliances, expenditures on	yr	172	1999	30r
Small appliances, housewares, expenditures on	yr	81	1999	30r
Banking and Money				
Mortgage interest and charges paid	yr	2039	1999	30r
Mortgage principal paid on owned property	yr	1026	1999	30r
Vehicle finance charges paid	yr	365	1999	30r
Charity				
Cash contributions, expenditures	yr	1127	1999	30r
Child Care				
Child raising cost, total, age 0-2	yr	8540	1999	60r
Child raising cost, total, age 3-5	yr	8780	1999	60r
Child raising cost, total, age 6-8	yr	8820	1999	60r
Child raising cost, total, age 9-11	yr	8800	1999	60r
Child raising cost, total, age 12-14	yr	9510	1999	60r
Child raising cost, total, age 15-17	yr	9740	1999	60r
Child's child care and education, age 0-2	yr	1380	1999	60r
Child's child care and education, age 3-5	yr	1520	1999	60r
Child's child care and education, age 6-8	yr	990	1999	60r
Child's child care and education, age 9-11	yr	650	1999	60r
Child's child care and education, age 12-14	yr	490	1999	60r
Child's child care and education, age 15-17	yr	840	1999	60r
Child's clothing, age 0-2	yr	480	1999	60r
Child's clothing, age 3-5	yr	470	1999	60r
Child's clothing, age 6-8	yr	520	1999	60r
Child's clothing, age 9-11	yr	570	1999	60r
Child's clothing, age 12-14	yr	950	1999	60r
Child's clothing, age 15-17	yr	850	1999	60r
Child's food, age 0-2	yr	1000	1999	60r
Child's food, age 3-5	yr	1160	1999	60r
Child's food, age 6-8	yr	1490	1999	60r
Child's food, age 9-11	yr	1770	1999	60r
Child's food, age 12-14	yr	1770	1999	60r
Child's food, age 15-17	yr	1980	1999	60r
Child's health care, age 0-2	yr	620	1999	60r
Child's health care, age 3-5	yr	590	1999	60r
Child's health care, age 6-8	yr	680	1999	60r
Child's health care, age 9-11	yr	720	1999	60r
Child's health care, age 12-14	yr	730	1999	60r
Child's health care, age 15-17	yr	760	1999	60r
Child's housing, age 0-2	yr	3070	1999	60r
Child's housing, age 3-5	yr	3050	1999	60r
Child's housing, age 6-8	yr	3010	1999	60r
Child's housing, age 9-11	yr	2850	1999	60r
Child's housing, age 12-14	yr	3040	1999	60r
Child's housing, age 15-17	yr	2650	1999	60r
Child's personal care, reading, age 0-2	yr	910	1999	60r
Child's personal care, reading, age 3-5	yr	930	1999	60r
Child's personal care, reading, age 6-8	yr	960	1999	60r
Child's personal care, reading, age 9-11	yr	1000	1999	60r
Child's personal care, reading, age 12-14	yr	1170	1999	60r
Child's personal care, reading, age 15-17	yr	950	1999	60r
Clothing				
Apparel and services purchases	yr	1610	1999	30r
Boys, 2 to 15, expenditures on	yr	89	1999	30r
Children under 2, expenditures on	yr	79	1999	30r
Footwear, expenditures on	yr	283	1999	30r
Girls, 2 to 15, expenditures on	yr	103	1999	30r
Men and boys, expenditures on	yr	351	1999	30r
Men, 16 and over, expenditures on	yr	262	1999	30r

Galveston-Texas City, TX - continued

Item	Per	Value	Date	Ref.
Clothing - continued				
Women, 16 and over, expenditures on	yr	538	1999	30r
Communications				
Cable modem installation, AT&T-BIS		150.00	6/99	103s
Cable modem installation, Marcus		499.00	6/99	103s
Cable modem installation, Time Warner		75.00-225.00	6/99	103s
Cable modem rate, cable subscriber, AT&T-BIS	mos	39.95	6/99	103s
Cable modem rate, cable subscriber, Marcus	mos	14.95-49.95	6/99	103s
Cable modem rate, cable subscriber, Time Warner	mos	39.95-49.95	6/99	103s
Cable modem rate, non-cable subscriber, Marcus	mos	60.95	6/99	103s
Cable modem rate, non-cable subscriber, Time Warner	mos	39.95-54.95	6/99	103s
Phone line, single, business, field visit	inst.	71.90	12/97	17s
Phone line, single, business, no field visit	inst.	57.30	12/97	17s
Phone line, single, residence, field visit	inst.	52.95	12/97	17s
Phone line, single, residence, no field visit	inst.	38.35	12/97	17s
Postage and stationery, expenditures on	yr	104	1999	30r
Postal rate, express mail, up to half-pound		12.45	7/01	108r
Postal rate, letter, first class, first ounce		0.34	7/01	108r
Postal rate, letter, two ounces		0.57	7/01	108r
Postal rate, post card		0.21	7/01	108r
Postal rate, priority mail, two pounds		3.95	7/01	108r
Postal rate, priority mail, up to one pound		3.50	7/01	108r
Telephone services, expenditures on	yr	860	1999	30r
Education				
Board, 4-year private college/university	yr	2198	1996	38s
Board, 4-year public college/university	yr	1759	1996	38s
Education expenditures	yr	431	1999	30r
Room, 4-year private college/university	yr	2000	1996	38s
Room, 4-year public college/university	yr	1885	1996	38s
Total cost, 4-year private college/university	yr	13156	1996	38s
Total cost, 4-year public college/university	yr	5464	1996	38s
Tuition, 2-year public college/university, in state	yr	771	1996	38s
Tuition, 4-year private college/university, in state	yr	8959	1996	38s
Tuition, 4-year public college/university	yr	1820	1996	38s
Energy and Fuels				
Electricity	KWh	0.09	7/01	11r
Electricity	500 KWhs	47.29	7/01	11r
Fuel oil #2	gal	1.43	7/01	11r
Fuel oil and other fuels, expenditures on	yr	45	1999	30r
Gas, natural, commercial rate	1000 cf	6.94	11/00	88s
Gasoline, all types	gal	1.60	7/01	11r
Gasoline, unleaded midgrade	gal	1.65	7/01	11r
Gasoline, unleaded premium	gal	1.74	7/01	11r
Natural gas, expenditures on	yr	164	1999	30r
Utility (piped) gas, therm		1.01	7/01	11r
Utility (piped) gas, 40 therms		44.29	7/01	11r
Utility (piped) gas, 100 therms		97.44	7/01	11r
Entertainment				
Entertainment purchases	yr	1574	1999	30r
Fees and admissions paid	yr	371	1999	30r
Reading purchases	yr	121	1999	30r
Television, radios, sound equipment, expenditures on	yr	561	1999	30r
Funerals				
Total cost of funeral		5842.28	1/99	78r
Acknowledgement cards		28.35	1/99	78r
Casket		2494.29	1/99	78r
Cosmetology, hair, other preparation		109.22	1/99	78r
Embalming		361.42	1/99	78r
Funeral at funeral home		349.20	1/99	78r
Hearse (local)		161.91	1/99	78r

Values are in dollars or fractions of dollars. In the column headed *Ref*, references are shown to sources. Each reference is followed by a letter. These refer to the geographical level for which data were reported: s=State, r=Region, and c=City or metro. The abbreviation *ex* is used to mean *except* or *excluding*; *exp* stands for expenditures. For other abbreviations and further explanations, please see the Introduction.

Galveston-Texas City, TX - continued

Item	Per	Value	Date	Ref.
Funerals				
Professional service charges		1116.50	1/99	78r
Service car/van		65.56	1/99	78r
Transfer of remains to funeral home		143.56	1/99	78r
Vault		785.25	1/99	78r
Visitation/viewing		227.02	1/99	78r
Groceries				
American processed cheese	lb	3.50	7/01	11r
Bakery products, expenditures on	yr	261	1999	30r
Bananas	lb	0.47	7/01	11r
Beans, dried, any type, all sizes	lb	0.63	7/01	11r
Beef for stew, boneless	lb	2.86	7/01	11r
Beef, expenditures on	yr	210	1999	30r
Bologna, all beef or mixed	lb	2.29	7/01	11r
Bread, French	lb	1.66	7/01	11r
Bread, white, pan	lb	0.87	7/01	11r
Bread, whole wheat, pan	lb	1.38	7/01	11r
Broccoli	lb	1.04	7/01	11r
Butter, salted, grade AA, stick	lb	2.26	7/01	11r
Butter, yoghurt, cheese, etc, expenditures on	yr	170	1999	30r
Cabbage	lb	0.42	7/01	11r
Cereals and cereal products, expenditures on	yr	140	1999	30r
Cheddar cheese, natural	lb	3.75	7/01	11r
Chicken breast, bone-in	lb	1.85	7/01	11r
Chicken legs, bone-in	lb	1.34	7/01	11r
Chicken, fresh, whole	lb	1.05	7/01	11r
Chops, boneless,	lb	4.13	7/01	11r
Chuck roast, graded and ungraded, excl U.S. prime and choice	lb	2.35	7/01	11r
Chuck roast, U.S. choice, boneless	lb	2.67	7/01	11r
Coffee, 100%, ground roast, all sizes	lb	2.88	7/01	11r
Coffee, instant, plain, regular, all sizes	16 oz	9.25	7/01	11r
Cola, non diet	2 liter	1.11	7/01	11r
Crackers, soda, salted	lb	1.70	7/01	11r
Dairy product purchases	yr	282	1999	30r
Eggs, expenditures on	yr	32	1999	30r
Fats and oils, expenditures on	yr	79	1999	30r
Fish and seafood, expenditures on	yr	99	1999	30r
Flour, white, all purpose	lb	0.32	7/01	11r
Food (excl fruit and vegetables), eaten at home, purchases	yr	815	1999	30r
Food cooked on trips, expenditures on	yr	36	1999	30r
Food purchases	yr	4533	1999	30r
Food purchases, eaten away from home	yr	1873	1999	30r
Food purchases, food eaten at home	yr	2660	1999	30r
Fresh fruits, expenditures on	yr	128	1999	30r
Fresh milk and cream, expenditures on	yr	112	1999	30r
Fresh vegetables, expenditures on	yr	131	1999	30r
Fruit and vegetable purchases	yr	438	1999	30r
Grapefruit	lb	0.59	7/01	11r
Grapes, Thompson, seedless	lb	2.12	7/01	11r
Ground beef, 100% beef	lb	1.76	7/01	11r
Ground beef, lean and extra lean	lb	2.60	7/01	11r
Ground chuck, 100% beef	lb	2.08	7/01	11r
Ham, boneless, excl canned	lb	2.71	7/01	11r
Ham, rump or shank half, bone-in, smoked	lb	2.19	7/01	11r
Ice cream, prepackaged, bulk, regular	1/2 gal	3.93	7/01	11r
Lemons	lb	1.32	7/01	11r
Lettuce, iceberg	lb	0.76	7/01	11r
Milk, fresh, low fat	gal	2.75	7/01	11r
Milk, fresh, whole, fortified	gal	2.97	7/01	11r
Nonalcoholic beverages, expenditures on	yr	228	1999	30r
Orange juice, frozen concentrate	16 oz	1.95	7/01	11r
Oranges, Navel	lb	0.73	7/01	11r
Oranges, Valencia	lb	0.55	7/01	11r
Peanut butter, creamy, all sizes	lb	1.83	7/01	11r
Pears, Anjou	lb	0.98	7/01	11r
Pork chops, center cut, bone-in	lb	3.33	7/01	11r
Pork sausage, fresh, loose	lb	2.59	7/01	11r
Pork shoulder picnic, bone-in, smoked	lb	1.12	7/01	11r
Pork, expenditures on	yr	162	1999	30r
Potato chips	16 oz	3.59	7/01	11r

Item	Per	Value	Date	Ref.
Groceries - continued				
Potatoes, frozen, french fried	lb	1.00	7/01	11r
Potatoes, white, all types	lb	0.44	7/01	11r
Poultry, expenditures on	yr	137	1999	30r
Processed fruits, expenditures on	yr	97	1999	30r
Processed vegetables, expenditures on	yr	82	1999	30r
Rice, white, long grain, uncooked	lb	0.51	7/01	11r
Round roast, graded and ungraded, excl U.S. prime and choice	lb	2.96	7/01	11r
Round steak, graded and ungraded, excl U.S. prime and choice	lb	3.11	7/01	11r
Sirloin steak, graded and ungraded, excl U.S. prime and choice	lb	4.23	7/01	11r
Spaghetti and macaroni	lb	0.78	7/01	11r
Steak, round, U.S. choice, boneless	lb	3.56	7/01	11r
Steak, sirloin, U.S. choice, boneless	lb	5.65	7/01	11r
Strawberries, dry pint	12 oz	1.50	7/01	11r
Sugar and other sweets, expenditures on	yr	99	1999	30r
Sugar, white, 33-80 ounce package	lb	0.39	7/01	11r
Sugar, white, all sizes	lb	0.42	7/01	11r
Tobacco products and smoking supplies purchases	yr	288	1999	30r
Tomatoes, field grown	lb	1.43	7/01	11r
Tuna, light, chunk	lb	1.77	7/01	11r
Turkey, frozen, whole	lb	1.05	7/01	11r
Goods and Services				
B&B Japanese maple (acer japonicum)	gal	79.98-99.00	4/00	93r
Boxwood (buxus)	2 gal	12.98-18.99	4/00	93r
Christmas tree, noble fir		40-60	2000	65s
Daylilly (hemerocallis)	gal	7.96-11.00	4/00	93r
Flat of annuals		13.99-27.99	4/00	93r
Fountain grass (pennisetum)	gal	6.96-9.00	4/00	93r
Hanging basket (10 in)		9.99-24.99	4/00	93r
Hardy geranium (geranium)	gal	5.96-8.00	4/00	93r
Hosta (hosta)	gal	8.96-12.99	4/00	93r
Lilac (syrubga vulgaris)	2 gal	13.00-19.99	4/00	93r
Rhododendron (rhododendron)	2 gal	12.98-29.99	4/00	93r
Sage (salvia)	gal	5.96-8.00	4/00	93r
Wintercreeper euonymus (euonymus fortunei)	2 gal	13.00-18.99	4/00	93r
Hunting license	yr	19.00	4/01	34s
Health Care				
Cardiac catheterization, ave hospital/ physician charges		20140	1998	77s
Childbirth, Cesarean delivery		11587	1997	13r
Childbirth, vaginal delivery		6725	1997	13r
Drugs, expenditures on	yr	399	1999	30r
Health care purchases	yr	1971	1999	30r
Health insurance expenditures	yr	933	1999	30r
Hysterectomy, laproscopically-assisted, ave hospital/physician charges		15700	1998	76s
Hysterectomy, vaginal, ave hospital and physician charges		12180	1998	76s
Medicaid dispensing fee		5.27	1999	87s
Medical services expenditures	yr	547	1999	30r
Medical supplies, expenditures on	yr	91	1999	30r
Household Goods				
Floor coverings, expenditures on	yr	44	1999	30r
Furniture, expenditures on	yr	335	1999	30r
Household furnishings and equipment purchases	yr	1328	1999	30r

Values are in dollars or fractions of dollars. In the column headed *Ref*, references are shown to sources. Each reference is followed by a letter. These refer to the geographical level for which data were reported: s=State, r=Region, and c=City or metro. The abbreviation *ex* is used to mean *except* or *excluding*; *exp* stands for *expenditures*. For other abbreviations and further explanations, please see the Introduction.

Galveston-Texas City, TX - continued

Item	Per	Value	Date	Ref.
Household Goods				
Household textiles, expenditures on	yr	89	1999	30r
Laundry and cleaning supplies, expenditures on	yr	113	1999	30r
Housing				
Home price, existing, ave		160100	10/00	90v
Home value, median		112000	2001	53s
Household operation expenditures	yr	553	1999	30r
Housekeeping supplies purchases	yr	473	1999	30r
Housing, expenditures on	yr	10303	1999	30r
Maintenance, repairs, insurance expenditures	yr	699	1999	30r
Monthly rental value of owned home	mos	505	1999	30r
Owned dwellings, expenditures own	yr	3465	1999	30r
Rent expenditures	yr	1641	1999	30r
Rental unit, 1 bedroom, with utilities	mos	477	4/01	41c
Rental unit, 2 bedroom, with utilities	mos	597	4/01	41c
Rental unit, 3 bedroom, with utilities	mos	829	4/01	41c
Rental unit, 4 bedroom, with utilities	mos	979	4/01	41c
Shelter, expenditures on	yr	5467	1999	30r
Insurance and Pensions				
Life and other personal insurance purchases	yr	414	1999	30r
Pensions and Social Security, expenditures on	yr	2635	1999	30r
Personal insurance and pensions, expenditures on	yr	3048	1999	30r
Legal Fees				
Divorce, filing fee		150.00-200.00	4/01	35s
Driver's license fee	orig	24.00	1999	48s
Driver's license fee	renew	20.00	1999	48s
Fishing license	yr	19.00	4/01	34s
Personal Goods				
Personal care products and services purchases	yr	393	1999	30r
Personal Services				
Personal services, household, expenditures on	yr	258	1999	30r
Pets				
Pets, toys, and playground equipment, expenditures on	yr	306	1999	30r
Taxes				
Federal income taxes paid	yr	2047	1999	30r
Personal taxes, expenditures on	yr	2554	1999	30r
Property taxes paid	yr	726	1999	30r
State and local income taxes paid	yr	363	1999	30r
Transportation				
Cars and trucks, new, expenditures on	yr	1648	1999	30r
Cars and trucks, used, expenditures on	yr	1651	1999	30r
Diesel at the pump	gal	1.18	10/99	73s
Gasoline and motor oil purchases	yr	1052	1999	30r
Gasoline before-tax price (cents)	gal	101.30	10/00	43s
Maintenance and repair expenditures	yr	621	1999	30r
Public transportation, expenditures on	yr	298	1999	30r
Transportation purchases	yr	6738	1999	30r
Vehicle expenses, miscellaneous, purchases	yr	2033	1999	30r
Vehicle insurance payments	yr	696	1999	30r
Vehicle purchases (net outlay)	yr	3354	1999	30r
Vehicle rental, lease expenditures	yr	352	1999	30r
Utilities				
Electrical bill, average	mos	87.17	9/00	9s
Electricity, expenditures on	yr	1115	1999	30r
Electricity cost, average	KWh	6.48	9/00	9s
Water and other public services, expenditures on	yr	298	1999	30r
Weddings				
Wedding (national average cost)		19936	2000	33r
Attendants' gifts		321	1998	33r

Galveston-Texas City, TX - continued

Item	Per	Value	Date	Ref.
Weddings - continued				
Bridal attendants' apparel (5 persons)		824	2000	33r
Bride's headpiece/veil		173	1998	33r
Bride's wedding dress		859	1998	33r
Clergy, religious facility fee		242	1998	33r
Engagement ring		3177	1998	33r
Flowers		789	1998	33r
Groom's formalwear rental		99	2000	33r
Limousine		410	1998	33r
Marriage license cost		36.00	4/01	35s
Men's formalwear (ushers, best man)		469	2000	33r
Mother of bride apparel		241	2000	33r
Music		866	1998	33r
Photography and videography		1368	1998	33r
Rehearsal dinner		728	1998	33r
Wedding invitations and announcements		341	1998	33r
Wedding reception		7968	2000	33r
Wedding rings (bride and groom)		1060	1998	33r

Gary, IN

Item	Per	Value	Date	Ref.
Average annual expenditures	yr	35369	1999	30r
Alcoholic Beverages				
Alcoholic beverage purchases	yr	304	1999	30r
Malt beverages, all types, all sizes, any origin	16 oz	0.93	7/01	11r
Wine, red and white table, all sizes, any origin	liter	7.04	7/01	11r
Appliances				
Major appliances, expenditures on	yr	165	1999	30r
Small appliances, housewares, expenditures on	yr	90	1999	30r
Banking and Money				
Mortgage interest and charges paid	yr	2277	1999	30r
Mortgage principal paid on owned property	yr	1230	1999	30r
Vehicle finance charges paid	yr	328	1999	30r
Charity				
Cash contributions, expenditures	yr	1126	1999	30r
Child Care				
Child raising cost, total, age 0-2	yr	7890	1999	60r
Child raising cost, total, age 3-5	yr	8130	1999	60r
Child raising cost, total, age 6-8	yr	8170	1999	60r
Child raising cost, total, age 9-11	yr	8190	1999	60r
Child raising cost, total, age 12-14	yr	8890	1999	60r
Child raising cost, total, age 15-17	yr	9050	1999	60r
Child's child care and education, age 0-2	yr	1240	1999	60r
Child's child care and education, age 3-5	yr	1370	1999	60r
Child's child care and education, age 6-8	yr	880	1999	60r
Child's child care and education, age 9-11	yr	570	1999	60r
Child's child care and education, age 12-14	yr	420	1999	60r
Child's child care and education, age 15-17	yr	720	1999	60r
Child's clothing, age 0-2	yr	410	1999	60r
Child's clothing, age 3-5	yr	400	1999	60r
Child's clothing, age 6-8	yr	450	1999	60r
Child's clothing, age 9-11	yr	500	1999	60r
Child's clothing, age 12-14	yr	840	1999	60r
Child's clothing, age 15-17	yr	740	1999	60r
Child's food, age 0-2	yr	960	1999	60r
Child's food, age 3-5	yr	1120	1999	60r
Child's food, age 6-8	yr	1430	1999	60r
Child's food, age 9-11	yr	1710	1999	60r
Child's food, age 12-14	yr	1710	1999	60r
Child's food, age 15-17	yr	1920	1999	60r
Child's health care, age 0-2	yr	520	1999	60r
Child's health care, age 3-5	yr	500	1999	60r
Child's health care, age 6-8	yr	570	1999	60r
Child's health care, age 9-11	yr	610	1999	60r
Child's health care, age 12-14	yr	630	1999	60r
Child's health care, age 15-17	yr	650	1999	60r
Child's housing, age 0-2	yr	2860	1999	60r
Child's housing, age 3-5	yr	2840	1999	60r

Values are in dollars or fractions of dollars. In the column headed *Ref*, references are shown to sources. Each reference is followed by a letter. These refer to the geographical level for which data were reported: s=State, r=Region, and c=City or metro. The abbreviation *ex* is used to mean *except* or *excluding*; *exp* stands for expenditures. For other abbreviations and further explanations, please see the Introduction.

Gary, IN - continued

Item	Per	Value	Date	Ref.
Child Care				
Child's housing, age 6-8	yr	2800	1999	60r
Child's housing, age 9-11	yr	2650	1999	60r
Child's housing, age 12-14	yr	2840	1999	60r
Child's housing, age 15-17	yr	2440	1999	60r
Child's personal care, reading, age 0-2	yr	880	1999	60r
Child's personal care, reading, age 3-5	yr	900	1999	60r
Child's personal care, reading, age 6-8	yr	930	1999	60r
Child's personal care, reading, age 9-11	yr	970	1999	60r
Child's personal care, reading, age 12-14	yr	1150	1999	60r
Child's personal care, reading, age 15-17	yr	920	1999	60r
Clothing				
Apparel and services purchases	yr	1607	1999	30r
Boys, 2 to 15, expenditures on	yr	91	1999	30r
Children under 2, expenditures on	yr	59	1999	30r
Footwear, expenditures on	yr	285	1999	30r
Girls, 2 to 15, expenditures on	yr	116	1999	30r
Men and boys, expenditures on	yr	433	1999	30r
Men, 16 and over, expenditures on	yr	341	1999	30r
Women, 16 and over, expenditures on	yr	490	1999	30r
Communications				
Phone line, single, business, field visit	inst.	59.00	12/97	17s
Phone line, single, business, no field visit	inst.	59.00	12/97	17s
Phone line, single, residence, field visit	inst.	47.00	12/97	17s
Phone line, single, residence, no field visit	inst.	47.00	12/97	17s
Postage and stationery, expenditures on	yr	140	1999	30r
Postal rate, express mail, up to half-pound		12.45	7/01	108r
Postal rate, letter, first class, first ounce		0.34	7/01	108r
Postal rate, letter, two ounces		0.57	7/01	108r
Postal rate, post card		0.21	7/01	108r
Postal rate, priority mail, two pounds		3.95	7/01	108r
Postal rate, priority mail, up to one pound		3.50	7/01	108r
Telephone bill, business, basic rate	mos	37.75	12/97	18c
Telephone bill, residential, basic rate	mos	11.11	12/97	18c
Telephone services, expenditures on	yr	830	1999	30r
Education				
Board, 4-year private college/university	yr	2250	1996	38s
Board, 4-year public college/university	yr	2425	1996	38s
Education expenditures	yr	583	1999	30r
Room, 4-year private college/university	yr	1987	1996	38s
Room, 4-year public college/university	yr	1931	1996	38s
Total cost, 4-year private college/university	yr	16829	1996	38s
Total cost, 4-year public college/university	yr	7392	1996	38s
Tuition, 2-year public college/university, in state	yr	1937	1996	38s
Tuition, 4-year private college/university, in state	yr	12592	1996	38s
Tuition, 4-year public college/university	yr	3037	1996	38s
Energy and Fuels				
Electricity	500 KWhs	46.59	7/01	11r
Fuel oil #2	gal	1.27	7/01	11r
Fuel oil and other fuels, expenditures on	yr	68	1999	30r
Gas, cooking, winter, 10 therms	mos	10.25	2/96	98c
Gas, cooking, winter, 30 therms	mos	23.63	2/96	98c
Gas, cooking, winter, 50 therms	mos	36.99	2/96	98c
Gas, heating, winter, average use	mos	141.43	2/96	98c
Gas, natural, commercial rate	1000 cf	6.24	11/00	88s
Gasoline, unleaded midgrade	gal	1.79	7/01	11r
Gasoline, unleaded premium	gal	1.86	7/01	11r
Gasoline, unleaded regular	gal	1.58	7/01	11r
Natural gas, expenditures on	yr	389	1999	30r
Utility (piped) gas, therm		0.81	7/01	11r
Utility (piped) gas, 40 therms		38.01	7/01	11r
Utility (piped) gas, 100 therms		81.75	7/01	11r
Entertainment				
Entertainment purchases	yr	1984	1999	30r
Fees and admissions paid	yr	444	1999	30r
Television, radios, sound equipment, expenditures on	yr	580	1999	30r

Gary, IN - continued

Item	Per	Value	Date	Ref.
Funerals				
Cosmetology, hair, other preparation		178.32	1/99	78r
Embalming		408.19	1/99	78r
Funeral at funeral home		362.13	1/99	78r
Professional service charges		1375.51	1/99	78r
Transfer of remains to funeral home		155.92	1/99	78r
Visitation/viewing		294.38	1/99	78r
Groceries				
Bacon, sliced	lb	3.15	7/01	11r
Bakery products, expenditures on	yr	281	1999	30r
Bananas	lb	0.48	7/01	11r
Beans, dried, any type, all sizes	lb	0.61	7/01	11r
Beef for stew, boneless	lb	3.08	7/01	11r
Beef, expenditures on	yr	217	1999	30r
Bologna, all beef or mixed	lb	2.52	7/01	11r
Bread, white, pan	lb	1.06	7/01	11r
Broccoli	lb	0.91	7/01	11r
Butter, salted, grade AA, stick	lb	3.04	7/01	11r
Butter, yoghurt, cheese, etc, expenditures on	yr	183	1999	30r
Cereals and bakery product purchases	yr	430	1999	30r
Cereals and cereal products, expenditures on	yr	149	1999	30r
Chicken, fresh, whole	lb	1.07	7/01	11r
Chops, boneless,	lb	3.64	7/01	11r
Chuck roast, U.S. choice, boneless	lb	2.47	7/01	11r
Coffee, 100%, ground roast, all sizes	lb	2.69	7/01	11r
Cookies, chocolate chip	lb	2.87	7/01	11r
Dairy product purchases	yr	304	1999	30r
Eggs, expenditures on	yr	26	1999	30r
Eggs, grade A, large	dozen	0.88	7/01	11r
Fats and oils, expenditures on	yr	75	1999	30r
Fish and seafood, expenditures on	yr	72	1999	30r
Food (excl fruit and vegetables), eaten at home, purchases	yr	887	1999	30r
Food cooked on trips, expenditures on	yr	44	1999	30r
Food purchases	yr	4802	1999	30r
Food purchases, eaten away from home	yr	2069	1999	30r
Food purchases, food eaten at home	yr	2733	1999	30r
Fresh fruits, expenditures on	yr	138	1999	30r
Fresh milk and cream, expenditures on	yr	120	1999	30r
Fresh vegetables, expenditures on	yr	126	1999	30r
Grapefruit	lb	0.66	7/01	11r
Grapes, Thompson, seedless	lb	1.64	7/01	11r
Ground beef, 100% beef	lb	1.64	7/01	11r
Ground beef, lean and extra lean	lb	2.16	7/01	11r
Ground chuck, 100% beef	lb	2.13	7/01	11r
Ham, boneless, excl canned	lb	2.62	7/01	11r
Ice cream, prepackaged, bulk, regular	1/2 gal	3.35	7/01	11r
Lemons	lb	1.19	7/01	11r
Lettuce, iceberg	lb	0.73	7/01	11r
Margarine, soft, tubs	lb	0.89	7/01	11r
Meats, poultry, fish, and egg purchases	yr	671	1999	30r
Milk, fresh, whole, fortified	gal	2.71	7/01	11r
Nonalcoholic beverages, expenditures on	yr	239	1999	30r
Oranges, Navel	lb	0.80	7/01	11r
Oranges, Valencia	lb	0.66	7/01	11r
Pears, Anjou	lb	0.93	7/01	11r
Pork chops, center cut, bone-in	lb	3.63	7/01	11r
Pork, expenditures on	yr	150	1999	30r
Potato chips	16 oz	3.52	7/01	11r
Potatoes, frozen, french fried	lb	1.08	7/01	11r
Potatoes, white, all types	lb	0.33	7/01	11r
Poultry, expenditures on	yr	108	1999	30r
Processed fruits, expenditures on	yr	98	1999	30r
Processed vegetables, expenditures on	yr	80	1999	30r
Round roast, U.S. choice, boneless	lb	3.07	7/01	11r
Round steak, graded and ungraded, excl U.S. prime and choice	lb	3.41	7/01	11r
Shortening, vegetable oil blends	lb	1.13	7/01	11r
Spaghetti and macaroni	lb	0.80	7/01	11r
Steak, round, U.S. choice, boneless	lb	3.23	7/01	11r
Steak, T-bone, U.S. choice, bone-in	lb	6.68	7/01	11r
Strawberries, dry pint	12 oz	1.32	7/01	11r

Values are in dollars or fractions of dollars. In the column headed *Ref*, references are shown to sources. Each reference is followed by a letter. These refer to the geographical level for which data were reported: s=State, r=Region, and c=City or metro. The abbreviation *ex* is used to mean *except* or *excluding*; *exp* stands for expenditures. For other abbreviations and further explanations, please see the Introduction.

Gary, IN - continued

Item	Per	Value	Date	Ref.
Groceries				
Sugar and other sweets, expenditures on	yr	114	1999	30r
Sugar, white, 33-80 ounce package	lb	0.42	7/01	11r
Sugar, white, all sizes	lb	0.43	7/01	11r
Tobacco products and smoking supplies purchases	yr	331	1999	30r
Tomatoes, field grown	lb	1.46	7/01	11r
Tuna, light, chunk	lb	1.80	7/01	11r
Turkey, frozen, whole	lb	1.15	7/01	11r
Goods and Services				
B&B Japanese maple (acer japonicum)	gal	29.99-169.99	4/00	93r
Boxwood (buxus)	2 gal	18.99-39.99	4/00	93r
Daylilly (hemerocallis)	gal	4.99-25.00	4/00	93r
Flat of annuals		11.98-24.99	4/00	93r
Fountain grass (pennisetum)	gal	5.98-12.98	4/00	93r
Hanging basket (10 in)		12.99-27.99	4/00	93r
Hardy geranium (geranium)	gal	7.99-9.99	4/00	93r
Hosta (hosta)	gal	6.00-25.00	4/00	93r
Lilac (syrubga vulgaris)	2 gal	14.99-24.99	4/00	93r
Miscellaneous purchases	yr	865	1999	30r
Rhododendron (rhododendron)	2 gal	23.98-42.99	4/00	93r
Sage (salvia)	gal	6.00-9.99	4/00	93r
Wintercreeper euonymus (euonymus fortunei)	2 gal	16.00-169.99	4/00	93r
Hunting license	yr	8.75	4/01	34s
Health Care				
Cardiac catheterization, ave hospital/ physician charges		13380	1998	77s
Childbirth, Cesarean delivery		10722	1997	13r
Childbirth, vaginal delivery		6223	1997	13r
Drugs, expenditures on	yr	394	1999	30r
Health care purchases	yr	2048	1999	30r
Health insurance expenditures	yr	978	1999	30r
Home health care aide cost, licensed agency	hour	16	2000	82c
Hysterectomy, laproscopically-assisted, ave hospital/physician charges		11310	1998	76s
Hysterectomy, vaginal, ave hospital and physician charges		9160	1998	76s
Medicaid dispensing fee		4.00	1999	87s
Medical services expenditures	yr	554	1999	30r
Medical supplies, expenditures on	yr	122	1999	30r
Nursing home costs, private room	day	98	2000	82c
Nursing home stay, private room	day	98	2000	81c
Plastic surgery, breast augmentation		3184	2000	7r
Plastic surgery, breast lift		3585	2000	7r
Plastic surgery, facelift		4999	2000	7r
Plastic surgery, hair transplantation		3105	2000	7r
Plastic surgery, lip augmentation		1290	2000	7r
Plastic surgery, lower body lift		8135	2000	7r
Plastic surgery, thigh lift		3839	2000	7r
Household Goods				
Floor coverings, expenditures on	yr	52	1999	30r
Furniture, expenditures on	yr	344	1999	30r
Household furnishings and equipment purchases	yr	1475	1999	30r
Household textiles, expenditures on	yr	109	1999	30r
Laundry and cleaning supplies, expenditures on	yr	134	1999	30r

Gary, IN - continued

Item	Per	Value	Date	Ref.
Housing				
Home price, existing, ave		144400	10/00	90r
Home value, median		102000	2001	53s
Household operation expenditures	yr	542	1999	30r
Housekeeping supplies purchases	yr	508	1999	30r
Lodging expenditures	yr	430	1999	30r
Maintenance, repairs, insurance expenditures	yr	853	1999	30r
Monthly rental value of owned home	mos	547	1999	30r
Owned dwellings, expenditures own	yr	4282	1999	30r
Rent expenditures	yr	1558	1999	30r
Rental unit, 1 bedroom, with utilities	mos	526	4/01	41c
Rental unit, 2 bedroom, with utilities	mos	656	4/01	41c
Rental unit, 3 bedroom, with utilities	mos	824	4/01	41c
Rental unit, 4 bedroom, with utilities	mos	920	4/01	41c
Shelter, expenditures on	yr	6270	1999	30r
Insurance and Pensions				
Life and other personal insurance purchases	yr	387	1999	30r
Pensions and Social Security, expenditures on	yr	2968	1999	30r
Legal Fees				
Divorce, filing fee		100.00	4/01	35s
Driver's license fee	orig	6.00	1999	48s
Driver's license fee	renew	6.00	1999	48s
Personal Goods				
Personal care products and services purchases	yr	385	1999	30r
Personal Services				
Personal services, household, expenditures on	yr	300	1999	30r
Pets				
Pets, toys, and playground equipment, expenditures on	yr	375	1999	30r
Taxes				
Federal income taxes paid	yr	2326	1999	30r
Personal taxes, expenditures on	yr	3223	1999	30r
Property taxes paid	yr	1152	1999	30r
State and local income taxes paid	yr	753	1999	30r
Transportation				
Cars and trucks, new, expenditures on	yr	1280	1999	30r
Cars and trucks, used, expenditures on	yr	1763	1999	30r
Diesel at the pump	gal	1.17	10/99	73s
Gasoline and motor oil purchases	yr	1036	1999	30r
Gasoline before-tax price (cents)	gal	110.00	10/00	43s
Maintenance and repair expenditures	yr	594	1999	30r
Public transportation, expenditures on	yr	341	1999	30r
Transportation purchases	yr	6617	1999	30r
Vehicle expenses, miscellaneous, purchases	yr	2159	1999	30r
Vehicle insurance payments	yr	701	1999	30r
Vehicle purchases (net outlay)	yr	3081	1999	30r
Vehicle rental, lease expenditures	yr	536	1999	30r
Utilities				
Electrical bill, average	mos	66.66	9/00	9s
Electricity, expenditures on	yr	841	1999	30r
Electricity, summer, 250 KWh	mos	29.62	2/96	97c
Electricity, summer, 500 KWh	mos	52.18	2/96	97c
Electricity, summer, 750 KWh	mos	74.75	2/96	97c
Electricity, summer, 1000 KWh	mos	97.31	2/96	97c
Electricity cost, average	KWh	5.00	9/00	9s
Utilities, fuels, and public services purchased	yr	2401	1999	30r
Water and other public services, expenditures on	yr	273	1999	30r
Weddings				
Wedding (national average cost)		19936	2000	33r
Wedding (regional average total cost)		16195	1997	110r
Attendants' gifts		321	1998	33r
Bridal attendants' apparel (5 persons)		824	2000	33r
Bride's headpiece/veil		173	1998	33r

Values are in dollars or fractions of dollars. In the column headed *Ref*, references are shown to sources. Each reference is followed by a letter. These refer to the geographical level for which data were reported: s=State, r=Region, and c=City or metro. The abbreviation *ex* is used to mean *except* or *excluding*; *exp* stands for *expenditures*. For other abbreviations and further explanations, please see the Introduction.

Gary, IN - continued

Item	Per	Value	Date	Ref.
Weddings				
Bride's wedding dress		859	1998	33r
Clergy, religious facility fee		242	1998	33r
Engagement ring		3177	1998	33r
Flowers		789	1998	33r
Groom's formalwear rental		99	2000	33r
Limousine		410	1998	33r
Marriage license cost		18.00	4/01	35s
Men's formalwear (ushers, best man)		469	2000	33r
Mother of bride apparel		241	2000	33r
Music		866	1998	33r
Photography and videography		1368	1998	33r
Rehearsal dinner		728	1998	33r
Wedding invitations and announcements		341	1998	33r
Wedding reception		7968	2000	33r
Wedding rings (bride and groom)		1060	1998	33r

Glens Falls, NY

Item	Per	Value	Date	Ref.
Average annual expenditures	yr	37971	1999	30r
Composite, ACCRA index		103.70	3/01	4c
Alcoholic Beverages				
Alcoholic beverage purchases	yr	368	1999	30r
Beer, Heineken, 12-oz, ex deposit	6	7.17	3/01	4c
J & B Scotch	750-ml	22.66	3/01	4c
Wine, Livingston or Gallo, Chablis blanc	1.5 liter	5.99	3/01	4c
Wine, red and white table, all sizes, any origin	liter	9.64	7/01	11r
Appliances				
Appliance repair, service call, washing machine	min lab chg	40.97	3/01	4c
Major appliances, expenditures on	yr	194	1999	30r
Small appliances, housewares, expenditures on	yr	93	1999	30r
Banking and Money				
Mortgage interest and charges paid	yr	2622	1999	30r
Mortgage principal paid on owned property	yr	1262	1999	30r
Mortgage rate, incl. points and orig. fee, 30-yr. conv. fixed or ARM	mos	7.28	3/01	4c
Vehicle finance charges paid	yr	240	1999	30r
Charity				
Cash contributions, expenditures	yr	1001	1999	30r
Child Care				
Child raising cost, total, age 0-2	yr	8670	1999	60r
Child raising cost, total, age 3-5	yr	8910	1999	60r
Child raising cost, total, age 6-8	yr	9040	1999	60r
Child raising cost, total, age 9-11	yr	9100	1999	60r
Child raising cost, total, age 12-14	yr	9890	1999	60r
Child raising cost, total, age 15-17	yr	10010	1999	60r
Child's child care and education, age 0-2	yr	1070	1999	60r
Child's child care and education, age 3-5	yr	1190	1999	60r
Child's child care and education, age 6-8	yr	740	1999	60r
Child's child care and education, age 9-11	yr	470	1999	60r
Child's child care and education, age 12-14	yr	350	1999	60r
Child's child care and education, age 15-17	yr	590	1999	60r
Child's clothing, age 0-2	yr	480	1999	60r
Child's clothing, age 3-5	yr	470	1999	60r
Child's clothing, age 6-8	yr	520	1999	60r
Child's clothing, age 9-11	yr	570	1999	60r
Child's clothing, age 12-14	yr	970	1999	60r
Child's clothing, age 15-17	yr	870	1999	60r
Child's food, age 0-2	yr	1130	1999	60r
Child's food, age 3-5	yr	1290	1999	60r
Child's food, age 6-8	yr	1640	1999	60r
Child's food, age 9-11	yr	1930	1999	60r
Child's food, age 12-14	yr	1940	1999	60r
Child's food, age 15-17	yr	2150	1999	60r
Child's health care, age 0-2	yr	550	1999	60r
Child's health care, age 3-5	yr	530	1999	60r
Child's health care, age 6-8	yr	610	1999	60r

Item	Per	Value	Date	Ref.
Child Care - continued				
Child's health care, age 9-11	yr	650	1999	60r
Child's health care, age 12-14	yr	660	1999	60r
Child's health care, age 15-17	yr	690	1999	60r
Child's housing, age 0-2	yr	3555	1999	60r
Child's housing, age 3-5	yr	3530	1999	60r
Child's housing, age 6-8	yr	3490	1999	60r
Child's housing, age 9-11	yr	3340	1999	60r
Child's housing, age 12-14	yr	3530	1999	60r
Child's housing, age 15-17	yr	3140	1999	60r
Child's personal care, reading, age 0-2	yr	920	1999	60r
Child's personal care, reading, age 3-5	yr	950	1999	60r
Child's personal care, reading, age 6-8	yr	980	1999	60r
Child's personal care, reading, age 9-11	yr	1020	1999	60r
Child's personal care, reading, age 12-14	yr	1190	1999	60r
Child's personal care, reading, age 15-17	yr	970	1999	60r
Nannies: criminal background check		74	1998	84s
Clothing				
Apparel and services purchases	yr	1831	1999	30r
Boys' brief, cotton	3	4.34	3/01	4c
Boys, 2 to 15, expenditures on	yr	92	1999	30r
Children under 2, expenditures on	yr	63	1999	30r
Footwear, expenditures on	yr	300	1999	30r
Girls, 2 to 15, expenditures on	yr	101	1999	30r
Men and boys, expenditures on	yr	446	1999	30r
Men, 16 and over, expenditures on	yr	354	1999	30r
Shirt, man's dress shirt		28.83	3/01	4c
Slacks, man's "No Wrinkles" khaki		35.99	3/01	4c
Women, 16 and over, expenditures on	yr	584	1999	30r
Communications				
Cable modem installation, Adelphi		54.90	6/99	103s
Cable modem installation, Cablevision Systems		150.00	6/99	103s
Cable modem installation, Time Warner		75.00-225.00	6/99	103s
Cable modem rate, cable subscriber, Adelphi	mos	34.95	6/99	103s
Cable modem rate, cable subscriber, Cablevision Systems	mos	44.95	6/99	103s
Cable modem rate, cable subscriber, Century	mos	39.95	6/99	103s
Cable modem rate, cable subscriber, Time Warner	mos	39.95-49.95	6/99	103s
Cable modem rate, non-cable subscriber, Adelphi	mos	44.95	6/99	103s
Cable modem rate, non-cable subscriber, Cablevision Systems	mos	54.95	6/99	103s
Cable modem rate, non-cable subscriber, Time Warner	mos	39.95-54.95	6/99	103s
Newspaper subscription, daily and Sunday delivery	mos	14.13	3/01	4c
Phone line, single, business, field visit	inst.	142.76	12/97	17s
Phone line, single, business, no field visit	inst.	106.05	12/97	17s
Phone line, single, residence, field visit	inst.	102.78	12/97	17s
Phone line, single, residence, no field visit	inst.	55.00	12/97	17s
Postage and stationery, expenditures on	yr	138	1999	30r
Postal rate, express mail, up to half-pound		12.45	7/01	108r
Postal rate, letter, first class, first ounce		0.34	7/01	108r
Postal rate, letter, two ounces		0.57	7/01	108r
Postal rate, post card		0.21	7/01	108r
Postal rate, priority mail, two pounds		3.95	7/01	108r
Postal rate, priority mail, up to one pound		3.50	7/01	108r
Telephone bill, family of three	mos	27.20	3/01	4c
Telephone services, expenditures on	yr	830	1999	30r
Education				
Board, 4-year private college/university	yr	3255	1996	38s
Board, 4-year public college/university	yr	2310	1996	38s
Education expenditures	yr	877	1999	30r
Room, 4-year private college/university	yr	3724	1996	38s
Room, 4-year public college/university	yr	2937	1996	38s
Total cost, 4-year private college/university	yr	20831	1996	38s
Total cost, 4-year public college/university	yr	8960	1996	38s
Tuition, 2-year public college/university, in state	yr	2427	1996	38s

Values are in dollars or fractions of dollars. In the column headed *Ref*, references are shown to sources. Each reference is followed by a letter. These refer to the geographical level for which data were reported: s=State, r=Region, and c=City or metro. The abbreviation *ex* is used to mean *except* or *excluding*; *exp* stands for expenditures. For other abbreviations and further explanations, please see the Introduction.

Glens Falls, NY - continued

Item	Per	Value	Date	Ref.
Education				
Tuition, 4-year private college/university, in state	yr	13852	1996	38s
Tuition, 4-year public college/university	yr	3714	1996	38s
Energy and Fuels				
Electricity	KWh	0.12	7/01	11r
Energy, combined forms, 2400 sq ft	mos	173.81	3/01	4c
Energy, exc. electricity, 2400 sq ft	mos	101.61	3/01	4c
Fuel oil #2	gal	1.31	7/01	11r
Fuel oil and other fuels, expenditures on	yr	207	1999	30r
Gas, regular unleaded, cash, self-service	gal	1.52	3/01	4c
Gasoline, all types	gal	1.80	7/01	11r
Gasoline, unleaded midgrade	gal	1.85	7/01	11r
Gasoline, unleaded premium	gal	1.91	7/01	11r
Gasoline, unleaded regular	gal	1.71	7/01	11r
Natural gas, expenditures on	yr	368	1999	30r
Utility (piped) gas, therm		1.08	7/01	11r
Utility (piped) gas, 40 therms		50.87	7/01	11r
Utility (piped) gas, 100 therms		111.06	7/01	11r
Entertainment				
Bowling, Saturday evening rate	line	3.17	3/01	4c
Entertainment purchases	yr	1821	1999	30r
Fees and admissions paid	yr	511	1999	30r
Monopoly game, Parker Brothers', No. 9	game	11.91	3/01	4c
Movie, first-run, Saturday, evening	adm.	8.00	3/01	4c
Television, radios, sound equipment, expenditures on	yr	650	1999	30r
Tennis balls, yellow, Wilson or Penn, 3	can	2.76	3/01	4c
Funerals				
Total cost of funeral		5813.50	1/99	78r
Acknowledgement cards		28.32	1/99	78r
Casket		2082.20	1/99	78r
Cosmetology, hair, other preparation		169.59	1/99	78r
Embalming		465.60	1/99	78r
Funeral at funeral home		339.56	1/99	78r
Hearse (local)		183.96	1/99	78r
Professional service charges		1157.85	1/99	78r
Service car/van		100.41	1/99	78r
Transfer of remains to funeral home		158.66	1/99	78r
Vault		766.31	1/99	78r
Visitation/viewing		361.04	1/99	78r
Groceries				
Groceries, ACCRA Index		102.00	3/01	4c
Antibiotic ointment, Polysporin	0.5 oz	4.88	3/01	4c
Apples, red delicious	lb	0.95	7/01	11r
Baby food, strained vegetables or fruit, lowest price	4-4.5 oz	0.40	3/01	4c
Bacon, sliced	lb	3.44	7/01	11r
Bakery products, expenditures on	yr	310	1999	30r
Bananas	lb	0.63	3/01	4c
Bananas	lb	0.55	7/01	11r
Beef or hamburger, ground	lb	0.92	3/01	4c
Beef, expenditures on	yr	236	1999	30r
Bread, white	loaf	0.86	3/01	4c
Bread, white, pan	lb	1.09	7/01	11r
Butter, yoghurt, cheese, etc, expenditures on	yr	214	1999	30r
Cereals and bakery product purchases	yr	474	1999	30r
Cereals and cereal products, expenditures on	yr	164	1999	30r
Cheese, Kraft grated Parmesan	8 oz	3.05	3/01	4c
Chicken legs, bone-in	lb	1.23	7/01	11r
Chicken, fresh, whole	lb	1.13	7/01	11r
Chicken, whole fryer	lb	0.92	3/01	4c
Chuck roast, U.S. choice, boneless	lb	2.79	7/01	11r
Cigarettes, Winston, Kings	carton	43.01	3/01	4c
Coffee, 100%, ground roast, all sizes	lb	3.40	7/01	11r
Coffee, vacuum-packed	13 oz	2.39	3/01	4c
Corn Flakes, Kellogg's or Post Toasties	18 oz	2.79	3/01	4c
Corn, frozen, whole kernel, lowest price	16 oz	0.91	3/01	4c
Dairy product purchases	yr	342	1999	30r
Eggs, expenditures on	yr	34	1999	30r

Glens Falls, NY - continued

Item	Per	Value	Date	Ref.
Groceries - continued				
Eggs, Grade A or AA	dozen	1.21	3/01	4c
Eggs, grade A, large	dozen	0.82	7/01	11r
Fats and oils, expenditures on	yr	80	1999	30r
Fish and seafood, expenditures on	yr	123	1999	30r
Food (excl fruit and vegetables), eaten at home, purchases	yr	838	1999	30r
Food cooked on trips, expenditures on	yr	48	1999	30r
Food purchases	yr	5314	1999	30r
Food purchases, eaten away from home	yr	2313	1999	30r
Food purchases, food eaten at home	yr	3001	1999	30r
Fresh fruits, expenditures on	yr	169	1999	30r
Fresh milk and cream, expenditures on	yr	128	1999	30r
Fresh vegetables, expenditures on	yr	164	1999	30r
Grapefruit	lb	0.67	7/01	11r
Grapes, Thompson, seedless	lb	2.18	7/01	11r
Ground beef, lean and extra lean	lb	2.66	7/01	11r
Ground chuck, 100% beef	lb	2.04	7/01	11r
Lettuce, iceberg	head	1.31	3/01	4c
Lettuce, iceberg	lb	0.76	7/01	11r
Margarine, Blue Bonnet or Parkay, stick	lb	0.69	3/01	4c
Meats, poultry, fish, and egg purchases	yr	808	1999	30r
Milk, whole	1/2 gal	1.34	3/01	4c
Nonalcoholic beverages, expenditures on	yr	225	1999	30r
Orange juice, frozen concentrate	16 oz	1.88	7/01	11r
Orange juice, Minute Maid frozen	12 oz	1.44	3/01	4c
Oranges, Navel	lb	0.79	7/01	11r
Oranges, Valencia	lb	0.56	7/01	11r
Peaches	lb	1.16	7/01	11r
Peaches, halves or slices, Hunt's, Del Monte, or Libby's	29 oz	1.61	3/01	4c
Peanut butter, creamy, all sizes	lb	2.01	7/01	11r
Pears, Anjou	lb	1.16	7/01	11r
Peas, green, Del Monte or Green Giant	15 oz	0.65	3/01	4c
Pork chops, center cut, bone-in	lb	3.57	7/01	11r
Pork, expenditures on	yr	146	1999	30r
Potato chips	16 oz	3.37	7/01	11r
Potatoes, white or red	10 lb	3.05	3/01	4c
Potatoes, white, all types	lb	0.42	7/01	11r
Poultry, expenditures on	yr	158	1999	30r
Processed fruits, expenditures on	yr	124	1999	30r
Processed vegetables, expenditures on	yr	82	1999	30r
Round roast, U.S. choice, boneless	lb	3.04	7/01	11r
Sausage, Jimmy Dean/Owens pork	lb	3.62	3/01	4c
Shortening, vegetable, Crisco	3 lb	3.11	3/01	4c
Soft drink, Coca Cola, ex deposit	2 liter	1.22	3/01	4c
Spaghetti and macaroni	lb	1.04	7/01	11r
Steak, sirloin, U.S. choice, boneless	lb	5.39	7/01	11r
Steak, T-bone	lb	7.23	3/01	4c
Strawberries, dry pint	12 oz	1.51	7/01	11r
Sugar and other sweets, expenditures on	yr	110	1999	30r
Sugar, cane or beet	4 lbs	1.52	3/01	4c
Sugar, white, 33-80 ounce package	lb	0.46	7/01	11r
Sugar, white, all sizes	lb	0.47	7/01	11r
Tobacco products and smoking supplies purchases	yr	309	1999	30r
Tomatoes, Hunt's or Del Monte	14.5 oz	0.79	3/01	4c
Tuna, chunk, light	6 oz	0.81	3/01	4c
Yogurt, natural, fruit flavored	8 oz	0.79	7/01	11r
Goods and Services				
Miscellaneous goods and services, ACCRA Index		107.20	3/01	4c
B&B Japanese maple (acer japonicum)	gal	38.99-125.00	4/00	93r
Boxwood (buxus)	2 gal	15.99-49.95	4/00	93r
Daylilly (hemerocallis)	gal	4.95	4/00	93r
Flat of annuals		8.00-14.99	4/00	93r
Fountain grass (pennisetum)	gal	6.99-9.99	4/00	93r
Hanging basket (10 in)		12.95-19.99	4/00	93r

Values are in dollars or fractions of dollars. In the column headed *Ref*, references are shown to sources. Each reference is followed by a letter. These refer to the geographical level for which data were reported: s=State, r=Region, and c=City or metro. The abbreviation *ex* is used to mean *except* or *excluding*; *exp* stands for *expenditures*. For other abbreviations and further explanations, please see the Introduction.

Glens Falls, NY - continued

Item	Per	Value	Date	Ref.
Goods and Services				
Hardy geranium (geranium)	gal	6.95-7.99	4/00	93r
Hosta (hosta)	gal	4.95	4/00	93r
Lilac (syrubga vulgaris)	2 gal	17.99-74.95	4/00	93r
Miscellaneous purchases	yr	872	1999	30r
Rhododendron (rhododendron)	2 gal	23.99-54.95	4/00	93r
Sage (salvia)	gal	6.95-7.99	4/00	93r
Wintercreeper euonymus (euonymus fortunei)	2 gal	14.99-23.95	4/00	93r
Hunting license	yr	11.00	4/01	34s
Health Care				
Health care, ACCRA Index		100.60	3/01	4c
Cardiac catheterization, ave hospital/ physician charges		12750	1998	77s
Childbirth, Cesarean delivery		14716	1997	13r
Childbirth, vaginal delivery		8541	1997	13r
Dentist's fee, adult teeth cleaning and periodic oral exam	visit	71.50	3/01	4c
Doctor's fee, routine exam, established patient	visit	60.50	3/01	4c
Drugs, expenditures on	yr	296	1999	30r
Health care purchases	yr	1788	1999	30r
Health insurance expenditures	yr	875	1999	30r
Hospital care, private room	day	496.00	3/01	4c
Hysterectomy, laproscopically-assisted, ave hospital/physician charges		13460	1998	76s
Hysterectomy, vaginal, ave hospital and physician charges		10310	1998	76s
Medicaid dispensing fee		3.50-4.50	1999	87s
Medical services expenditures	yr	516	1999	30r
Medical supplies, expenditures on	yr	102	1999	30r
Plastic surgery, breast augmentation		4232	2000	7r
Plastic surgery, breast lift		4605	2000	7r
Plastic surgery, facelift		6964	2000	7r
Plastic surgery, hair transplantation		4193	2000	7r
Plastic surgery, lip augmentation		1675	2000	7r
Plastic surgery, lower body lift		6611	2000	7r
Plastic surgery, thigh lift		4751	2000	7r
Household Goods				
Dishwashing powder, Cascade	50 oz	3.64	3/01	4c
Floor coverings, expenditures on	yr	59	1999	30r
Furniture, expenditures on	yr	388	1999	30r
Household furnishings and equipment purchases	yr	1567	1999	30r
Household textiles, expenditures on	yr	112	1999	30r
Laundry and cleaning supplies, expenditures on	yr	104	1999	30r
Tissues, facial, Kleenex brand	175	1.34	3/01	4c
Housing				
Housing, ACCRA Index		90.00	3/01	4c
Home price, existing, ave		180800	10/00	90r
Home value, median		179000	2001	53s
House, 2400 sq ft, 8000 sq ft lot, new, urban, utilities	total	181794	3/01	4c
House payment, principal and interest, 25% down payment	mos	932	3/01	4c
Household operation expenditures	yr	581	1999	30r
Housekeeping supplies purchases	yr	474	1999	30r
Lodging expenditures	yr	550	1999	30r
Maintenance, repairs, insurance expenditures	yr	835	1999	30r
Monthly rental value of owned home	mos	663	1999	30r
Owned dwellings, expenditures own	yr	5209	1999	30r
Rent expenditures	yr	2390	1999	30r
Rent, apartment, 2 br, 1 1/2-2 baths, unfurn, 950 sq ft, water	mos	613	3/01	4c
Rental unit, 1 bedroom, with utilities	mos	468	4/01	41c

Glens Falls, NY - continued

Item	Per	Value	Date	Ref.
Housing - continued				
Rental unit, 2 bedroom, with utilities	mos	571	4/01	41c
Rental unit, 3 bedroom, with utilities	mos	715	4/01	41c
Rental unit, 4 bedroom, with utilities	mos	799	4/01	41c
Shelter, expenditures on	yr	8149	1999	30r
Insurance and Pensions				
Auto insurance premium	yr	1113.55	1999	57s
Life and other personal insurance purchases	yr	424	1999	30r
Pensions and Social Security, expenditures on	yr	3037	1999	30r
Legal Fees				
Divorce, filing fee		270.00	4/01	35s
Driver's license fee	renew	25.00	1999	48s
Driver's license fee	orig	25.00	1999	48s
Fishing license	yr	14.00	4/01	34s
Personal Goods				
Personal care products and services purchases	yr	399	1999	30r
Shampoo, Alberto VO5	15 oz	1.19	3/01	4c
Toothpaste, Crest or Colgate	6-7 oz	2.33	3/01	4c
Personal Services				
Dry cleaning, man's 2-pc suit		8.00	3/01	4c
Man's haircut, barbershop, no styling		11.24	3/01	4c
Personal services, household, expenditures on	yr	271	1999	30r
Woman's shampoo, trim, blow-dry, no style-change		20.25	3/01	4c
Pets				
Pets, toys, and playground equipment, expenditures on	yr	325	1999	30r
Restaurant Food				
Chicken, fried, thigh and drumstick, KFC/ Church's		2.99	3/01	4c
Hamburger with cheese, McDonald's	1/4 lb	2.29	3/01	4c
Pizza, Pizza Hut or Pizza Inn	11-12 in	10.75	3/01	4c
Taxes				
Federal income taxes paid	yr	2606	1999	30r
Personal taxes, expenditures on	yr	3567	1999	30r
Property taxes paid	yr	1752	1999	30r
State and local income taxes paid	yr	694	1999	30r
Transportation				
Transportation, ACCRA Index		105.30	3/01	4c
Cars and trucks, new, expenditures on	yr	1496	1999	30r
Cars and trucks, used, expenditures on	yr	1251	1999	30r
Diesel at the pump	gal	1.33	10/99	73s
Gasoline and motor oil purchases	yr	901	1999	30r
Gasoline before-tax price (cents)	gal	110.70	10/00	43s
Maintenance and repair expenditures	yr	618	1999	30r
Public transportation, expenditures on	yr	575	1999	30r
Tire balance, computer or spin balance, front	wheel	8.00	3/01	4c
Transportation purchases	yr	6503	1999	30r
Vehicle expenses, miscellaneous, purchases	yr	2266	1999	30r
Vehicle insurance payments	yr	824	1999	30r
Vehicle purchases (net outlay)	yr	2761	1999	30r
Vehicle rental, lease expenditures	yr	584	1999	30r
Travel				
Hotel room	night	139.88	2/01	95s
Utilities				
Utilities, ACCRA Index		140.00	3/01	4c
Electrical bill, average	mos	71.50	9/00	9s
Electricity, expenditures on	yr	837	1999	30r
Electricity and other, mixed, 2400 sq ft, new home	mos	72.20	3/01	4c
Electricity cost, average	KWh	11.34	9/00	9s
Utilities, fuels, and public services purchased	yr	2457	1999	30r
Water and other public services, expenditures on	yr	215	1999	30r

Values are in dollars or fractions of dollars. In the column headed *Ref*, references are shown to sources. Each reference is followed by a letter. These refer to the geographical level for which data were reported: s=State, r=Region, and c=City or metro. The abbreviation *ex* is used to mean *except* or *excluding*; *exp* stands for expenditures. For other abbreviations and further explanations, please see the Introduction.

Glens Falls, NY - continued

Item	Per	Value	Date	Ref.
Weddings				
Wedding (national average cost)		19936	2000	33r
Wedding (regional average total cost)		29454	1997	110r
Attendants' gifts		321	1998	33r
Bridal attendants' apparel (5 persons)		824	2000	33r
Bride's headpiece/veil		173	1998	33r
Bride's wedding dress		859	1998	33r
Clergy, religious facility fee		242	1998	33r
Engagement ring		3177	1998	33r
Flowers		789	1998	33r
Groom's formalwear rental		99	2000	33r
Limousine		410	1998	33r
Marriage license cost		25.00	4/01	35s
Men's formalwear (ushers, best man)		469	2000	33r
Mother of bride apparel		241	2000	33r
Music		866	1998	33r
Photography and videography		1368	1998	33r
Rehearsal dinner		728	1998	33r
Wedding invitations and announcements		341	1998	33r
Wedding reception		7968	2000	33r
Wedding rings (bride and groom)		1060	1998	33r

Goldsboro, NC

Item	Per	Value	Date	Ref.
Composite, ACCRA index		94.00	3/01	4c
Alcoholic Beverages				
Alcoholic beverage purchases	yr	253	1999	30r
Beer, Heineken, 12-oz, ex deposit	6	6.62	3/01	4c
J & B Scotch	750-ml	20.75	3/01	4c
Malt beverages, all types, all sizes, any origin	16 oz	0.96	7/01	11r
Wine, Livingston or Gallo, Chablis blanc	1.5 liter	4.50	3/01	4c
Appliances				
Appliance repair, service call, washing machine	min lab chg	43.25	3/01	4c
Major appliances, expenditures on	yr	172	1999	30r
Small appliances, housewares, expenditures on	yr	81	1999	30r
Banking and Money				
Mortgage interest and charges paid	yr	2039	1999	30r
Mortgage principal paid on owned property	yr	1026	1999	30r
Mortgage rate, incl. points and orig. fee, 30-yr. conv. fixed or ARM	mos	6.95	3/01	4c
Vehicle finance charges paid	yr	365	1999	30r
Charity				
Cash contributions, expenditures	yr	1127	1999	30r
Child Care				
Child raising cost, total, age 0-2	yr	8540	1999	60r
Child raising cost, total, age 3-5	yr	8780	1999	60r
Child raising cost, total, age 6-8	yr	8820	1999	60r
Child raising cost, total, age 9-11	yr	8800	1999	60r
Child raising cost, total, age 12-14	yr	9510	1999	60r
Child raising cost, total, age 15-17	yr	9740	1999	60r
Child's child care and education, age 0-2	yr	1380	1999	60r
Child's child care and education, age 3-5	yr	1520	1999	60r
Child's child care and education, age 6-8	yr	990	1999	60r
Child's child care and education, age 9-11	yr	650	1999	60r
Child's child care and education, age 12-14	yr	490	1999	60r
Child's child care and education, age 15-17	yr	840	1999	60r
Child's clothing, age 0-2	yr	480	1999	60r
Child's clothing, age 3-5	yr	470	1999	60r
Child's clothing, age 6-8	yr	520	1999	60r
Child's clothing, age 9-11	yr	570	1999	60r
Child's clothing, age 12-14	yr	950	1999	60r
Child's clothing, age 15-17	yr	850	1999	60r
Child's food, age 0-2	yr	1000	1999	60r
Child's food, age 3-5	yr	1160	1999	60r
Child's food, age 6-8	yr	1490	1999	60r
Child's food, age 9-11	yr	1770	1999	60r
Child's food, age 12-14	yr	1770	1999	60r
Child's food, age 15-17	yr	1980	1999	60r

Goldsboro, NC - continued

Item	Per	Value	Date	Ref.
Child Care - continued				
Child's health care, age 0-2	yr	620	1999	60r
Child's health care, age 3-5	yr	590	1999	60r
Child's health care, age 6-8	yr	680	1999	60r
Child's health care, age 9-11	yr	720	1999	60r
Child's health care, age 12-14	yr	730	1999	60r
Child's health care, age 15-17	yr	760	1999	60r
Child's housing, age 0-2	yr	3070	1999	60r
Child's housing, age 3-5	yr	3050	1999	60r
Child's housing, age 6-8	yr	3010	1999	60r
Child's housing, age 9-11	yr	2850	1999	60r
Child's housing, age 12-14	yr	3040	1999	60r
Child's housing, age 15-17	yr	2650	1999	60r
Child's personal care, reading, age 0-2	yr	910	1999	60r
Child's personal care, reading, age 3-5	yr	930	1999	60r
Child's personal care, reading, age 6-8	yr	960	1999	60r
Child's personal care, reading, age 9-11	yr	1000	1999	60r
Child's personal care, reading, age 12-14	yr	1170	1999	60r
Child's personal care, reading, age 15-17	yr	950	1999	60r
Clothing				
Apparel and services purchases	yr	1610	1999	30r
Boys' brief, cotton	3	4.07	3/01	4c
Boys, 2 to 15, expenditures on	yr	89	1999	30r
Children under 2, expenditures on	yr	79	1999	30r
Footwear, expenditures on	yr	283	1999	30r
Girls, 2 to 15, expenditures on	yr	103	1999	30r
Men and boys, expenditures on	yr	351	1999	30r
Men, 16 and over, expenditures on	yr	262	1999	30r
Shirt, man's dress shirt		26.66	3/01	4c
Slacks, man's "No Wrinkles" khaki		35.66	3/01	4c
Women, 16 and over, expenditures on	yr	538	1999	30r
Communications				
Cable modem installation, Intermedia		149.95	6/99	103s
Cable modem installation, Time Warner		75.00-225.00	6/99	103s
Cable modem rate, cable subscriber, Intermedia	mos	49.95	6/99	103s
Cable modem rate, cable subscriber, Time Warner	mos	39.95-49.95	6/99	103s
Cable modem rate, non-cable subscriber, Intermedia	mos	54.95	6/99	103s
Cable modem rate, non-cable subscriber, Time Warner	mos	39.95-54.95	6/99	103s
Newspaper subscription, daily and Sunday delivery	mos	8.75	3/01	4c
Phone line, single, business, field visit	inst.	65.00	12/97	17s
Phone line, single, business, no field visit	inst.	65.00	12/97	17s
Phone line, single, residence, field visit	inst.	42.75	12/97	17s
Phone line, single, residence, no field visit	inst.	42.75	12/97	17s
Postage and stationery, expenditures on	yr	104	1999	30r
Postal rate, express mail, up to half-pound		12.45	7/01	108r
Postal rate, letter, first class, first ounce		0.34	7/01	108r
Postal rate, letter, two ounces		0.57	7/01	108r
Postal rate, post card		0.21	7/01	108r
Postal rate, priority mail, two pounds		3.95	7/01	108r
Postal rate, priority mail, up to one pound		3.50	7/01	108r
Telephone bill, family of three	mos	17.04	3/01	4c
Telephone services, expenditures on	yr	860	1999	30r
Education				
Board, 4-year private college/university	yr	2316	1996	38s
Board, 4-year public college/university	yr	1737	1996	38s
Education expenditures	yr	431	1999	30r
Room, 4-year private college/university	yr	2128	1996	38s
Room, 4-year public college/university	yr	1742	1996	38s
Total cost, 4-year private college/university	yr	15428	1996	38s
Total cost, 4-year public college/university	yr	5119	1996	38s
Tuition, 4-year private college/university, in state	yr	10984	1996	38s
Tuition, 4-year public college/university	yr	1639	1996	38s

Values are in dollars or fractions of dollars. In the column headed *Ref*, references are shown to sources. Each reference is followed by a letter. These refer to the geographical level for which data were reported: s=State, r=Region, and c=City or metro. The abbreviation *ex* is used to mean *except* or *excluding*; *exp* stands for expenditures. For other abbreviations and further explanations, please see the Introduction.

Goldsboro, NC - continued

Item	Per	Value	Date	Ref.
Energy and Fuels				
Electricity	500 KWhs	47.29	7/01	11r
Electricity	KWh	0.09	7/01	11r
Energy, combined forms, 2400 sq ft	mos	115.60	3/01	4c
Fuel oil #2	gal	1.43	7/01	11r
Fuel oil and other fuels, expenditures on	yr	45	1999	30r
Gas, natural, commercial rate	1000 cf	9.25	11/00	88s
Gas, regular unleaded, cash, self-service	gal	1.35	7/01	4c
Gasoline, all types	gal	1.60	7/01	11r
Gasoline, unleaded midgrade	gal	1.65	7/01	11r
Gasoline, unleaded premium	gal	1.74	7/01	11r
Natural gas, expenditures on	yr	164	1999	30r
Utility (piped) gas, therm		1.01	7/01	11r
Utility (piped) gas, 40 therms		44.29	7/01	11r
Utility (piped) gas, 100 therms		97.44	7/01	11r
Entertainment				
Bowling, Saturday evening rate	line	3.50	3/01	4c
Entertainment purchases	yr	1574	1999	30r
Fees and admissions paid	yr	371	1999	30r
Monopoly game, Parker Brothers', No. 9	game	10.87	3/01	4c
Movie, first-run, Saturday, evening	adm.	6.37	3/01	4c
Reading purchases	yr	121	1999	30r
Television, radios, sound equipment, expenditures on	yr	561	1999	30r
Tennis balls, yellow, Wilson or Penn, 3	can	2.31	3/01	4c
Funerals				
Total cost of funeral		5922.53	1/99	78r
Acknowledgement cards		63.43	1/99	78r
Casket		2258.77	1/99	78r
Cosmetology, hair, other preparation		127.09	1/99	78r
Embalming		393.49	1/99	78r
Funeral at funeral home		367.50	1/99	78r
Hearse (local)		169.66	1/99	78r
Professional service charges		1211.32	1/99	78r
Service car/van		80.69	1/99	78r
Transfer of remains to funeral home		144.25	1/99	78r
Vault		803.50	1/99	78r
Visitation/viewing		302.83	1/99	78r
Groceries				
Groceries, ACCRA Index		94.20	3/01	4c
American processed cheese	lb	3.50	7/01	11r
Antibiotic ointment, Polysporin	0.5 oz	4.38	3/01	4c
Baby food, strained vegetables or fruit, lowest price	4-4.5 oz	0.45	3/01	4c
Bakery products, expenditures on	yr	261	1999	30r
Bananas	lb	0.52	3/01	4c
Bananas	lb	0.47	7/01	11r
Beans, dried, any type, all sizes	lb	0.63	7/01	11r
Beef for stew, boneless	lb	2.86	7/01	11r
Beef or hamburger, ground	lb	1.21	3/01	4c
Beef, expenditures on	yr	210	1999	30r
Bologna, all beef or mixed	lb	2.29	7/01	11r
Bread, French	lb	1.66	7/01	11r
Bread, white	loaf	0.93	3/01	4c
Bread, white, pan	lb	0.87	7/01	11r
Bread, whole wheat, pan	lb	1.38	7/01	11r
Broccoli	lb	1.04	7/01	11r
Butter, salted, grade AA, stick	lb	2.26	7/01	11r
Butter, yoghurt, cheese, etc, expenditures on	yr	170	1999	30r
Cabbage	lb	0.42	7/01	11r
Cereals and cereal products, expenditures on	yr	140	1999	30r
Cheddar cheese, natural	lb	3.75	7/01	11r
Cheese, Kraft grated Parmesan	8 oz	3.58	3/01	4c
Chicken breast, bone-in	lb	1.85	7/01	11r
Chicken legs, bone-in	lb	1.34	7/01	11r
Chicken, fresh, whole	lb	1.05	7/01	11r
Chicken, whole fryer	lb	0.85	3/01	4c
Chops, boneless,	lb	4.13	7/01	11r
Chuck roast, graded and ungraded, excl U.S. prime and choice	lb	2.35	7/01	11r

Goldsboro, NC - continued

Item	Per	Value	Date	Ref.
Groceries - continued				
Chuck roast, U.S. choice, boneless	lb	2.67	7/01	11r
Cigarettes, Winston, Kings	carton	23.73	3/01	4c
Coffee, 100%, ground roast, all sizes	lb	2.88	7/01	11r
Coffee, instant, plain, regular, all sizes	16 oz	9.25	7/01	11r
Coffee, vacuum-packed	13 oz	2.15	3/01	4c
Cola, non diet,	2 liter	1.11	7/01	11r
Corn Flakes, Kellogg's or Post Toasties	18 oz	2.57	3/01	4c
Corn, frozen, whole kernel, lowest price	16 oz	0.99	3/01	4c
Crackers, soda, salted	lb	1.70	7/01	11r
Dairy product purchases	yr	282	1999	30r
Eggs, expenditures on	yr	32	1999	30r
Eggs, Grade A or AA	dozen	1.27	3/01	4c
Fats and oils, expenditures on	yr	79	1999	30r
Fish and seafood, expenditures on	yr	99	1999	30r
Flour, white, all purpose	lb	0.32	7/01	11r
Food (excl fruit and vegetables), eaten at home, purchases	yr	815	1999	30r
Food cooked on trips, expenditures on	yr	36	1999	30r
Food purchases	yr	4533	1999	30r
Food purchases, eaten away from home	yr	1873	1999	30r
Food purchases, food eaten at home	yr	2660	1999	30r
Fresh fruits, expenditures on	yr	128	1999	30r
Fresh milk and cream, expenditures on	yr	112	1999	30r
Fresh vegetables, expenditures on	yr	131	1999	30r
Fruit and vegetable purchases	yr	438	1999	30r
Grapefruit	lb	0.59	7/01	11r
Grapes, Thompson, seedless	lb	2.12	7/01	11r
Ground beef, 100% beef	lb	1.76	7/01	11r
Ground beef, lean and extra lean	lb	2.60	7/01	11r
Ground chuck, 100% beef	lb	2.08	7/01	11r
Ham, boneless, excl canned	lb	2.71	7/01	11r
Ham, rump or shank half, bone-in, smoked	lb	2.19	7/01	11r
Ice cream, prepackaged, bulk, regular	1/2 gal	3.93	7/01	11r
Lemons	lb	1.32	7/01	11r
Lettuce, iceberg	head	1.06	3/01	4c
Lettuce, iceberg	lb	0.76	7/01	11r
Margarine, Blue Bonnet or Parkay, stick	lb	0.99	3/01	4c
Milk, fresh, low fat,	gal	2.75	7/01	11r
Milk, fresh, whole, fortified	gal	2.97	7/01	11r
Milk, whole	1/2 gal	1.98	3/01	4c
Nonalcoholic beverages, expenditures on	yr	228	1999	30r
Orange juice, frozen concentrate	16 oz	1.95	7/01	11r
Orange juice, Minute Maid frozen	12 oz	1.31	3/01	4c
Oranges, Navel	lb	0.73	7/01	11r
Oranges, Valencia	lb	0.55	7/01	11r
Peaches, halves or slices, Hunt's, Del Monte, or Libby's	29 oz	1.51	3/01	4c
Peanut butter, creamy, all sizes	lb	1.83	7/01	11r
Pears, Anjou	lb	0.98	7/01	11r
Peas, green, Del Monte or Green Giant	15 oz	0.64	3/01	4c
Pork chops, center cut, bone-in	lb	3.33	7/01	11r
Pork sausage, fresh, loose	lb	2.59	7/01	11r
Pork shoulder picnic, bone-in, smoked	lb	1.12	7/01	11r
Pork, expenditures on	yr	162	1999	30r
Potato chips	16 oz	3.59	7/01	11r
Potatoes, frozen, french fried	lb	1.00	7/01	11r
Potatoes, white or red	10 lb	2.37	3/01	4c
Potatoes, white, all types	lb	0.44	7/01	11r
Poultry, expenditures on	yr	137	1999	30r
Processed fruits, expenditures on	yr	97	1999	30r
Processed vegetables, expenditures on	yr	82	1999	30r
Rice, white, long grain, uncooked	lb	0.51	7/01	11r
Round roast, graded and ungraded, excl U.S. prime and choice	lb	2.96	7/01	11r
Round steak, graded and ungraded, excl U.S. prime and choice	lb	3.11	7/01	11r
Sausage, Jimmy Dean/Owens pork	lb	3.01	3/01	4c
Shortening, vegetable, Crisco	3 lb	2.91	3/01	4c
Sirloin steak, graded and ungraded, excl U.S. prime and choice	lb	4.23	7/01	11r
Soft drink, Coca Cola, ex deposit	2 liter	1.06	3/01	4c
Spaghetti and macaroni	lb	0.78	7/01	11r

Values are in dollars or fractions of dollars. In the column headed *Ref*, references are shown to sources. Each reference is followed by a letter. These refer to the geographical level for which data were reported: s=State, r=Region, and c=City or metro. The abbreviation *ex* is used to mean *except* or *excluding*; *exp* stands for *expenditures*. For other abbreviations and further explanations, please see the Introduction.

Goldsboro, NC - continued

Groceries

Item	Per	Value	Date	Ref.
Steak, round, U.S. choice, boneless	lb	3.56	7/01	11r
Steak, sirloin, U.S. choice, boneless	lb	5.65	7/01	11r
Steak, T-bone	lb	6.54	3/01	4c
Strawberries, dry pint	12 oz	1.50	7/01	11r
Sugar and other sweets, expenditures on	yr	99	1999	30r
Sugar, cane or beet	4 lbs	1.42	3/01	4c
Sugar, white, 33-80 ounce package	lb	0.39	7/01	11r
Sugar, white, all sizes	lb	0.42	7/01	11r
Tobacco products and smoking supplies purchases	yr	288	1999	30r
Tomatoes, field grown	lb	1.43	7/01	11r
Tomatoes, Hunt's or Del Monte	14.5 oz	0.78	3/01	4c
Tuna, chunk, light	6 oz	0.45	3/01	4c
Tuna, light, chunk	lb	1.77	7/01	11r
Turkey, frozen, whole	lb	1.05	7/01	11r

Goods and Services

Item	Per	Value	Date	Ref.
Miscellaneous goods and services, ACCRA Index		98.40	3/01	4c
B&B Japanese maple (acer japonicum)	gal	49.98-129.00	4/00	93r
Boxwood (buxus)	2 gal	12.99-16.99	4/00	93r
Daylilly (hemerocallis)	gal	4.99-8.99	4/00	93r
Flat of annuals		11.00-13.92	4/00	93r
Fountain grass (pennisetum)	gal	5.98-7.98	4/00	93r
Hanging basket (10 in)		7.99-14.98	4/00	93r
Hardy geranium (geranium)	gal	5.98-8.00	4/00	93r
Hosta (hosta)	gal	4.99-10.98	4/00	93r
Lilac (syrubga vulgaris)	2 gal	12.99-21.99	4/00	93r
Rhododendron (rhododendron)	2 gal	14.99-24.99	4/00	93r
Sage (salvia)	gal	5.98-6.99	4/00	93r
Wintercreeper euonymus (euonymus fortunei)	2 gal	7.99-89.99	4/00	93r
Hunting license	yr	15.00	4/01	34s

Health Care

Item	Per	Value	Date	Ref.
Health care, ACCRA Index		88.00	3/01	4c
Cardiac catheterization, ave hospital/physician charges		12500	1998	77s
Childbirth, Cesarean delivery		11587	1997	13r
Childbirth, vaginal delivery		6725	1997	13r
Dentist's fee, adult teeth cleaning and periodic oral exam	visit	63.50	3/01	4c
Doctor's fee, routine exam, established patient	visit	55.00	3/01	4c
Drugs, expenditures on	yr	399	1999	30r
Health care purchases	yr	1971	1999	30r
Health insurance expenditures	yr	933	1999	30r
Hospital care, private room	day	378.00	3/01	4c
Hysterectomy, laproscopically-assisted, ave hospital/physician charges		12260	1998	76s
Hysterectomy, vaginal, ave hospital and physician charges		8440	1998	76s
Medicaid dispensing fee		5.60	1999	87s
Medical services expenditures	yr	547	1999	30r
Medical supplies, expenditures on	yr	91	1999	30r
Plastic surgery, breast augmentation		2870	2000	7r
Plastic surgery, breast lift		3649	2000	7r
Plastic surgery, facelift		5008	2000	7r
Plastic surgery, hair transplantation		3425	2000	7r
Plastic surgery, lip augmentation		1227	2000	7r
Plastic surgery, lower body lift		4793	2000	7r
Plastic surgery, thigh lift		3862	2000	7r

Goldsboro, NC - continued

Household Goods

Item	Per	Value	Date	Ref.
Dishwashing powder, Cascade	50 oz	3.21	3/01	4c
Floor coverings, expenditures on	yr	44	1999	30r
Furniture, expenditures on	yr	335	1999	30r
Household furnishings and equipment purchases	yr	1328	1999	30r
Household textiles, expenditures on	yr	89	1999	30r
Laundry and cleaning supplies, expenditures on	yr	113	1999	30r
Tissues, facial, Kleenex brand	175	1.21	3/01	4c

Housing

Item	Per	Value	Date	Ref.
Housing, ACCRA Index		91.80	3/01	4c
Home price, existing, ave		160100	10/00	90r
Home value, median		146000	2001	53s
House, 2400 sq ft, 8000 sq ft lot, new, urban, utilities	total	194667	3/01	4c
House payment, principal and interest, 25% down payment	mos	966	3/01	4c
Household operation expenditures	yr	553	1999	30r
Housekeeping supplies purchases	yr	473	1999	30r
Housing, expenditures on	yr	10303	1999	30r
Maintenance, repairs, insurance expenditures	yr	699	1999	30r
Monthly rental value of owned home	mos	505	1999	30r
Owned dwellings, expenditures own	yr	3465	1999	30r
Rent expenditures	yr	1641	1999	30r
Rent, apartment, 2 br, 1 1/2-2 baths, unfurn, 950 sq ft, water	mos	585	3/01	4c
Rental unit, 1 bedroom, with utilities	mos	361	4/01	41c
Rental unit, 2 bedroom, with utilities	mos	438	4/01	41c
Rental unit, 3 bedroom, with utilities	mos	564	4/01	41c
Rental unit, 4 bedroom, with utilities	mos	659	4/01	41c
Shelter, expenditures on	yr	5467	1999	30r

Insurance and Pensions

Item	Per	Value	Date	Ref.
Life and other personal insurance purchases	yr	414	1999	30r
Pensions and Social Security, expenditures on	yr	2635	1999	30r
Personal insurance and pensions, expenditures on	yr	3048	1999	30r

Legal Fees

Item	Per	Value	Date	Ref.
Combination hunting and fishing license	yr	20.00	4/01	34s
Divorce, filing fee		80.00	4/01	35s
Driver's license fee	orig	10.00	1999	48s
Driver's license fee	renew	10.00	1999	48s
Fishing license	yr	15.00	4/01	34s

Personal Goods

Item	Per	Value	Date	Ref.
Personal care products and services purchases	yr	393	1999	30r
Shampoo, Alberto VO5	15 oz	1.01	3/01	4c
Toothpaste, Crest or Colgate	6-7 oz	2.18	3/01	4c

Personal Services

Item	Per	Value	Date	Ref.
Dry cleaning, man's 2-pc suit		7.66	3/01	4c
Man's haircut, barbershop, no styling		7.50	3/01	4c
Personal services, household, expenditures on	yr	258	1999	30r
Woman's shampoo, trim, blow-dry, no style-change		18.59	3/01	4c

Pets

Item	Per	Value	Date	Ref.
Pets, toys, and playground equipment, expenditures on	yr	306	1999	30r

Restaurant Food

Item	Per	Value	Date	Ref.
Chicken, fried, thigh and drumstick, KFC/Church's		2.83	3/01	4c
Hamburger with cheese, McDonald's	1/4 lb	2.17	3/01	4c
Pizza, Pizza Hut or Pizza Inn	11-12 in	9.67	3/01	4c

Taxes

Item	Per	Value	Date	Ref.
Federal income taxes paid	yr	2047	1999	30r
Personal taxes, expenditures on	yr	2554	1999	30r
Property taxes paid	yr	726	1999	30r

Values are in dollars or fractions of dollars. In the column headed *Ref*, references are shown to sources. Each reference is followed by a letter. These refer to the geographical level for which data were reported: s=State, r=Region, and c=City or metro. The abbreviation *ex* is used to mean *except* or *excluding*; *exp* stands for *expenditures*. For other abbreviations and further explanations, please see the Introduction.

Goldsboro, NC - continued

Item	Per	Value	Date	Ref.
Taxes				
State and local income taxes paid	yr	363	1999	30r
Transportation				
Transportation, ACCRA Index		89.10	3/01	4c
Bus fare, to central business district	1-way	1.00	3/01	4c
Cars and trucks, new, expenditures on	yr	1648	1999	30r
Cars and trucks, used, expenditures on	yr	1651	1999	30r
Diesel at the pump	gal	1.19	10/99	73s
Gasoline and motor oil purchases	yr	1052	1999	30r
Gasoline before-tax price (cents)	gal	103.20	10/00	43s
Maintenance and repair expenditures	yr	621	1999	30r
Motorcycle license fee	renew	1.50	1999	49s
Motorcycle license fee	orig	1.50	1999	49s
Public transportation, expenditures on	yr	298	1999	30r
Tire balance, computer or spin balance, front	wheel	6.25	3/01	4c
Transportation purchases	yr	6738	1999	30r
Vehicle expenses, miscellaneous, purchases	yr	2033	1999	30r
Vehicle insurance payments	yr	696	1999	30r
Vehicle purchases (net outlay)	yr	3354	1999	30r
Vehicle rental, lease expenditures	yr	352	1999	30r
Utilities				
Utilities, ACCRA Index		92.50	3/01	4c
Electrical bill, average	mos	83.66	9/00	9s
Electricity, 2400 sq ft, new home	mos	115.60	3/01	4c
Electricity, expenditures on	yr	1115	1999	30r
Electricity cost, average	KWh	6.40	9/00	9s
Water and other public services, expenditures on	yr	298	1999	30r
Weddings				
Wedding (national average cost)		19936	2000	33r
Wedding (regional average total cost)		16293	1997	110r
Attendants' gifts		321	1998	33r
Bridal attendants' apparel (5 persons)		824	2000	33r
Bride's headpiece/veil		173	1998	33r
Bride's wedding dress		859	1998	33r
Clergy, religious facility fee		242	1998	33r
Engagement ring		3177	1998	33r
Flowers		789	1998	33r
Groom's formalwear rental		99	2000	33r
Limousine		410	1998	33r
Marriage license cost		40.00	4/01	35s
Men's formalwear (ushers, best man)		469	2000	33r
Mother of bride apparel		241	2000	33r
Music		866	1998	33r
Photography and videography		1368	1998	33r
Rehearsal dinner		728	1998	33r
Wedding invitations and announcements		341	1998	33r
Wedding reception		7968	2000	33r
Wedding rings (bride and groom)		1060	1998	33r

Grand Forks, ND

Item	Per	Value	Date	Ref.
Average annual expenditures	yr	35369	1999	30r
Alcoholic Beverages				
Alcoholic beverage purchases	yr	304	1999	30r
Malt beverages, all types, all sizes, any origin	16 oz	0.93	7/01	11r
Wine, red and white table, all sizes, any origin	liter	7.04	7/01	11r
Appliances				
Major appliances, expenditures on	yr	165	1999	30r
Small appliances, housewares, expenditures on	yr	90	1999	30r
Banking and Money				
Mortgage interest and charges paid	yr	2277	1999	30r
Mortgage principal paid on owned property	yr	1230	1999	30r
Vehicle finance charges paid	yr	328	1999	30r
Charity				
Cash contributions, expenditures	yr	1126	1999	30r

Grand Forks, ND - continued

Item	Per	Value	Date	Ref.
Child Care				
Child raising cost, total, age 0-2	yr	7890	1999	60r
Child raising cost, total, age 3-5	yr	8130	1999	60r
Child raising cost, total, age 6-8	yr	8170	1999	60r
Child raising cost, total, age 9-11	yr	8190	1999	60r
Child raising cost, total, age 12-14	yr	8890	1999	60r
Child raising cost, total, age 15-17	yr	9050	1999	60r
Child's child care and education, age 0-2	yr	1240	1999	60r
Child's child care and education, age 3-5	yr	1370	1999	60r
Child's child care and education, age 6-8	yr	880	1999	60r
Child's child care and education, age 9-11	yr	570	1999	60r
Child's child care and education, age 12-14	yr	420	1999	60r
Child's child care and education, age 15-17	yr	720	1999	60r
Child's clothing, age 0-2	yr	410	1999	60r
Child's clothing, age 3-5	yr	400	1999	60r
Child's clothing, age 6-8	yr	450	1999	60r
Child's clothing, age 9-11	yr	500	1999	60r
Child's clothing, age 12-14	yr	840	1999	60r
Child's clothing, age 15-17	yr	740	1999	60r
Child's food, age 0-2	yr	960	1999	60r
Child's food, age 3-5	yr	1120	1999	60r
Child's food, age 6-8	yr	1430	1999	60r
Child's food, age 9-11	yr	1710	1999	60r
Child's food, age 12-14	yr	1710	1999	60r
Child's food, age 15-17	yr	1920	1999	60r
Child's health care, age 0-2	yr	520	1999	60r
Child's health care, age 3-5	yr	500	1999	60r
Child's health care, age 6-8	yr	570	1999	60r
Child's health care, age 9-11	yr	610	1999	60r
Child's health care, age 12-14	yr	630	1999	60r
Child's health care, age 15-17	yr	650	1999	60r
Child's housing, age 0-2	yr	2860	1999	60r
Child's housing, age 3-5	yr	2840	1999	60r
Child's housing, age 6-8	yr	2800	1999	60r
Child's housing, age 9-11	yr	2650	1999	60r
Child's housing, age 12-14	yr	2840	1999	60r
Child's housing, age 15-17	yr	2440	1999	60r
Child's personal care, reading, age 0-2	yr	880	1999	60r
Child's personal care, reading, age 3-5	yr	900	1999	60r
Child's personal care, reading, age 6-8	yr	930	1999	60r
Child's personal care, reading, age 9-11	yr	970	1999	60r
Child's personal care, reading, age 12-14	yr	1150	1999	60r
Child's personal care, reading, age 15-17	yr	920	1999	60r
Clothing				
Apparel and services purchases	yr	1607	1999	30r
Boys, 2 to 15, expenditures on	yr	91	1999	30r
Children under 2, expenditures on	yr	59	1999	30r
Footwear, expenditures on	yr	285	1999	30r
Girls, 2 to 15, expenditures on	yr	116	1999	30r
Men and boys, expenditures on	yr	433	1999	30r
Men, 16 and over, expenditures on	yr	341	1999	30r
Women, 16 and over, expenditures on	yr	490	1999	30r
Communications				
Phone line, single, business, field visit	inst.	52.67	12/97	17s
Phone line, single, business, no field visit	inst.	52.67	12/97	17s
Phone line, single, residence, field visit	inst.	31.79	12/97	17s
Phone line, single, residence, no field visit	inst.	31.79	12/97	17s
Postage and stationery, expenditures on	yr	140	1999	30r
Postal rate, express mail, up to half-pound		12.45	7/01	108r
Postal rate, letter, first class, first ounce		0.34	7/01	108r
Postal rate, letter, two ounces		0.57	7/01	108r
Postal rate, post card		0.21	7/01	108r
Postal rate, priority mail, two pounds		3.95	7/01	108r
Postal rate, priority mail, up to one pound		3.50	7/01	108r
Telephone services, expenditures on	yr	830	1999	30r
Education				
Board, 4-year private college/university	yr	1649	1996	38s
Board, 4-year public college/university	yr	2378	1996	38s
Education expenditures	yr	583	1999	30r
Room, 4-year private college/university	yr	1260	1996	38s
Room, 4-year public college/university	yr	1016	1996	38s
Total cost, 4-year private college/university	yr	9907	1996	38s

Values are in dollars or fractions of dollars. In the column headed *Ref*, references are shown to sources. Each reference is followed by a letter. These refer to the geographical level for which data were reported: s=State, r=Region, and c=City or metro. The abbreviation *ex* is used to mean *except* or *excluding*; *exp* stands for expenditures. For other abbreviations and further explanations, please see the Introduction.

Grand Forks, ND - continued

Item	Per	Value	Date	Ref.
Education				
Total cost, 4-year public college/university	yr	5642	1996	38s
Tuition, 2-year public college/university, in state	yr	1698	1996	38s
Tuition, 4-year private college/university, in state	yr	6998	1996	38s
Tuition, 4-year public college/university	yr	2248	1996	38s
Energy and Fuels				
Electricity	500 KWhs	46.59	7/01	11r
Fuel oil #2	gal	1.27	7/01	11r
Fuel oil and other fuels, expenditures on	yr	68	1999	30r
Gas, natural, commercial rate	1000 cf	6.91	11/00	88s
Gasoline, unleaded midgrade	gal	1.79	7/01	11r
Gasoline, unleaded premium	gal	1.86	7/01	11r
Gasoline, unleaded regular	gal	1.58	7/01	11r
Natural gas, expenditures on	yr	389	1999	30r
Utility (piped) gas, therm		0.81	7/01	11r
Utility (piped) gas, 40 therms		38.01	7/01	11r
Utility (piped) gas, 100 therms		81.75	7/01	11r
Entertainment				
Entertainment purchases	yr	1984	1999	30r
Fees and admissions paid	yr	444	1999	30r
Television, radios, sound equipment, expenditures on	yr	580	1999	30r
Funerals				
Cosmetology, hair, other preparation		178.32	1/99	78r
Embalming		408.19	1/99	78r
Funeral at funeral home		362.13	1/99	78r
Professional service charges		1375.51	1/99	78r
Transfer of remains to funeral home		155.92	1/99	78r
Visitation/viewing		294.38	1/99	78r
Groceries				
Bacon, sliced	lb	3.15	7/01	11r
Bakery products, expenditures on	yr	281	1999	30r
Bananas	lb	0.48	7/01	11r
Beans, dried, any type, all sizes	lb	0.61	7/01	11r
Beef for stew, boneless	lb	3.08	7/01	11r
Beef, expenditures on	yr	217	1999	30r
Bologna, all beef or mixed	lb	2.52	7/01	11r
Bread, white, pan	lb	1.06	7/01	11r
Broccoli	lb	0.91	7/01	11r
Butter, salted, grade AA, stick	lb	3.04	7/01	11r
Butter, yoghurt, cheese, etc, expenditures on	yr	183	1999	30r
Cereals and bakery product purchases	yr	430	1999	30r
Cereals and cereal products, expenditures on	yr	149	1999	30r
Chicken, fresh, whole	lb	1.07	7/01	11r
Chops, boneless	lb	3.64	7/01	11r
Chuck roast, U.S. choice, boneless	lb	2.47	7/01	11r
Coffee, 100%, ground roast, all sizes	lb	2.69	7/01	11r
Cookies, chocolate chip	lb	2.87	7/01	11r
Dairy product purchases	yr	304	1999	30r
Eggs, expenditures on	yr	26	1999	30r
Eggs, grade A, large	dozen	0.88	7/01	11r
Fats and oils, expenditures on	yr	75	1999	30r
Fish and seafood, expenditures on	yr	72	1999	30r
Food (excl fruit and vegetables), eaten at home, purchases	yr	887	1999	30r
Food cooked on trips, expenditures on	yr	44	1999	30r
Food purchases	yr	4802	1999	30r
Food purchases, eaten away from home	yr	2069	1999	30r
Food purchases, food eaten at home	yr	2733	1999	30r
Fresh fruits, expenditures on	yr	138	1999	30r
Fresh milk and cream, expenditures on	yr	120	1999	30r
Fresh vegetables, expenditures on	yr	126	1999	30r
Grapefruit	lb	0.66	7/01	11r
Grapes, Thompson, seedless	lb	1.64	7/01	11r
Ground beef, 100% beef	lb	1.64	7/01	11r
Ground beef, lean and extra lean	lb	2.16	7/01	11r
Ground chuck, 100% beef	lb	2.13	7/01	11r

Grand Forks, ND - continued

Item	Per	Value	Date	Ref.
Groceries - continued				
Ham, boneless, excl canned	lb	2.62	7/01	11r
Ice cream, prepackaged, bulk, regular	1/2 gal	3.35	7/01	11r
Lemons	lb	1.19	7/01	11r
Lettuce, iceberg	lb	0.73	7/01	11r
Margarine, soft, tubs	lb	0.89	7/01	11r
Meats, poultry, fish, and egg purchases	yr	671	1999	30r
Milk, fresh, whole, fortified	gal	2.71	7/01	11r
Nonalcoholic beverages, expenditures on	yr	239	1999	30r
Oranges, Navel	lb	0.80	7/01	11r
Oranges, Valencia	lb	0.66	7/01	11r
Pears, Anjou	lb	0.93	7/01	11r
Pork chops, center cut, bone-in	lb	3.63	7/01	11r
Pork, expenditures on	yr	150	1999	30r
Potato chips	16 oz	3.52	7/01	11r
Potatoes, frozen, french fried	lb	1.08	7/01	11r
Potatoes, white, all types	lb	0.33	7/01	11r
Poultry, expenditures on	yr	108	1999	30r
Processed fruits, expenditures on	yr	98	1999	30r
Processed vegetables, expenditures on	yr	80	1999	30r
Round roast, U.S. choice, boneless	lb	3.07	7/01	11r
Round steak, graded and ungraded, excl U.S. prime and choice	lb	3.41	7/01	11r
Shortening, vegetable oil blends	lb	1.13	7/01	11r
Spaghetti and macaroni	lb	0.80	7/01	11r
Steak, round, U.S. choice, boneless	lb	3.23	7/01	11r
Steak, T-bone, U.S. choice, bone-in	lb	6.68	7/01	11r
Strawberries, dry pint	12 oz	1.32	7/01	11r
Sugar and other sweets, expenditures on	yr	114	1999	30r
Sugar, white, 33-80 ounce package	lb	0.42	7/01	11r
Sugar, white, all sizes	lb	0.43	7/01	11r
Tobacco products and smoking supplies purchases	yr	331	1999	30r
Tomatoes, field grown	lb	1.46	7/01	11r
Tuna, light, chunk	lb	1.80	7/01	11r
Turkey, frozen, whole	lb	1.15	7/01	11r
Goods and Services				
B&B Japanese maple (acer japonicum)	gal	29.99-169.99	4/00	93r
Boxwood (buxus)	2 gal	18.99-39.99	4/00	93r
Daylilly (hemerocallis)	gal	4.99-25.00	4/00	93r
Flat of annuals		11.98-24.99	4/00	93r
Fountain grass (pennisetum)	gal	5.98-12.98	4/00	93r
Hanging basket (10 in)		12.99-27.99	4/00	93r
Hardy geranium (geranium)	gal	7.99-9.99	4/00	93r
Hosta (hosta)	gal	6.00-25.00	4/00	93r
Lilac (syrubga vulgaris)	2 gal	14.99-24.99	4/00	93r
Miscellaneous purchases	yr	865	1999	30r
Rhododendron (rhododendron)	2 gal	23.98-42.99	4/00	93r
Sage (salvia)	gal	6.00-9.99	4/00	93r
Wintercreeper euonymus (euonymus fortunei)	2 gal	16.00-169.99	4/00	93r
Hunting license	yr	8.00	4/01	34s
Health Care				
Cardiac catheterization, ave hospital/ physician charges		10040	1998	77s
Childbirth, Cesarean delivery		10722	1997	13r
Childbirth, vaginal delivery		6223	1997	13r
Drugs, expenditures on	yr	394	1999	30r
Health care purchases	yr	2048	1999	30r
Health insurance expenditures	yr	978	1999	30r

Values are in dollars or fractions of dollars. In the column headed *Ref*, references are shown to sources. Each reference is followed by a letter. These refer to the geographical level for which data were reported: s=State, r=Region, and c=City or metro. The abbreviation *ex* is used to mean *except* or *excluding*; *exp* stands for expenditures. For other abbreviations and further explanations, please see the Introduction.

Grand Forks, ND - continued

Item	Per	Value	Date	Ref.
Health Care				
Hysterectomy, laproscopically-assisted, ave hospital/physician charges		11070	1998	76s
Hysterectomy, vaginal, ave hospital and physician charges		7310	1998	76s
Medicaid dispensing fee		4.60	1999	87s
Medical services expenditures	yr	554	1999	30r
Medical supplies, expenditures on	yr	122	1999	30r
Plastic surgery, breast augmentation		3184	2000	7r
Plastic surgery, breast lift		3585	2000	7r
Plastic surgery, facelift		4999	2000	7r
Plastic surgery, hair transplantation		3105	2000	7r
Plastic surgery, lip augmentation		1290	2000	7r
Plastic surgery, lower body lift		8135	2000	7r
Plastic surgery, thigh lift		3839	2000	7r
Household Goods				
Floor coverings, expenditures on	yr	52	1999	30r
Furniture, expenditures on	yr	344	1999	30r
Household furnishings and equipment purchases	yr	1475	1999	30r
Household textiles, expenditures on	yr	109	1999	30r
Laundry and cleaning supplies, expenditures on	yr	134	1999	30r
Housing				
Home price, existing, ave		144400	10/00	90r
Home value, median		99000	2001	53s
Household operation expenditures	yr	542	1999	30r
Housekeeping supplies purchases	yr	508	1999	30r
Lodging expenditures	yr	430	1999	30r
Maintenance, repairs, insurance expenditures	yr	853	1999	30r
Monthly rental value of owned home	mos	547	1999	30r
Owned dwellings, expenditures own	yr	4282	1999	30r
Rent expenditures	yr	1558	1999	30r
Rental unit, 1 bedroom, with utilities	mos	423	4/01	41c
Rental unit, 2 bedroom, with utilities	mos	557	4/01	41c
Rental unit, 3 bedroom, with utilities	mos	768	4/01	41c
Rental unit, 4 bedroom, with utilities	mos	857	4/01	41c
Shelter, expenditures on	yr	6270	1999	30r
Insurance and Pensions				
Auto insurance premium	yr	545.50	1999	57s
Life and other personal insurance purchases	yr	387	1999	30r
Pensions and Social Security, expenditures on	yr	2968	1999	30r
Legal Fees				
Combination hunting and fishing license	yr	27.00	4/01	34s
Driver's license fee	orig	10.00	1999	48s
Driver's license fee	renew	10.00	1999	48s
Fishing license	yr	10.00	4/01	34s
Personal Goods				
Personal care products and services purchases	yr	385	1999	30r
Personal Services				
Personal services, household, expenditures on	yr	300	1999	30r
Pets				
Pets, toys, and playground equipment, expenditures on	yr	375	1999	30r
Taxes				
Federal income taxes paid	yr	2326	1999	30r
Personal taxes, expenditures on	yr	3223	1999	30r
Property taxes paid	yr	1152	1999	30r
State and local income taxes paid	yr	753	1999	30r
Transportation				
Cars and trucks, new, expenditures on	yr	1280	1999	30r
Cars and trucks, used, expenditures on	yr	1763	1999	30r
Diesel at the pump	gal	1.27	10/99	73s
Gasoline and motor oil purchases	yr	1036	1999	30r

Grand Forks, ND - continued

Item	Per	Value	Date	Ref.
Transportation - continued				
Gasoline before-tax price (cents)	gal	120.80	10/00	43s
Maintenance and repair expenditures	yr	594	1999	30r
Public transportation, expenditures on	yr	341	1999	30r
Transportation purchases	yr	6617	1999	30r
Vehicle expenses, miscellaneous, purchases	yr	2159	1999	30r
Vehicle insurance payments	yr	701	1999	30r
Vehicle purchases (net outlay)	yr	3081	1999	30r
Vehicle rental, lease expenditures	yr	536	1999	30r
Travel				
Hotel room	night	48.95	2/01	94s
Utilities				
Electrical bill, average	mos	62.50	9/00	9s
Electricity, expenditures on	yr	841	1999	30r
Electricity cost, average	KWh	5.90	9/00	9s
Utilities, fuels, and public services purchased	yr	2401	1999	30r
Water and other public services, expenditures on	yr	273	1999	30r
Water price	100 cf	1.78	2000	109c
Water price, dwelling unit	mos	34.97	2000	109c
Weddings				
Wedding (national average cost)		19936	2000	33r
Wedding (regional average total cost)		16195	1997	110r
Attendants' gifts		321	1998	33r
Bridal attendants' apparel (5 persons)		824	2000	33r
Bride's headpiece/veil		173	1998	33r
Bride's wedding dress		859	1998	33r
Clergy, religious facility fee		242	1998	33r
Engagement ring		3177	1998	33r
Flowers		789	1998	33r
Groom's formalwear rental		99	2000	33r
Limousine		410	1998	33r
Marriage license cost		30.00	4/01	35s
Men's formalwear (ushers, best man)		469	2000	33r
Mother of bride apparel		241	2000	33r
Music		866	1998	33r
Photography and videography		1368	1998	33r
Rehearsal dinner		728	1998	33r
Wedding invitations and announcements		341	1998	33r
Wedding reception		7968	2000	33r
Wedding rings (bride and groom)		1060	1998	33r

Grand Junction, CO

Item	Per	Value	Date	Ref.
Composite, ACCRA index		96.60	3/01	4c
Alcoholic Beverages				
Beer, Heineken, 12-oz, ex deposit	6	7.18	3/01	4c
J & B Scotch	750-ml	21.99	3/01	4c
Wine, Livingston or Gallo, Chablis blanc	1.5 liter	4.82	3/01	4c
Appliances				
Appliance repair, service call, washing machine	min lab chg	45.00	3/01	4c
Banking and Money				
Mortgage rate, incl. points and orig. fee, 30-yr. conv. fixed or ARM	mos	7.04	3/01	4c
Clothing				
Boys' brief, cotton	3	3.97	3/01	4c
Shirt, man's dress shirt		27.66	3/01	4c
Slacks, man's "No Wrinkles" khaki		41.99	3/01	4c
Communications				
Cable modem installation, AT&T-BIS		150.00	6/99	103s
Cable modem rate, cable subscriber, AT&T-BIS	mos	39.95	6/99	103s
Newspaper subscription, daily and Sunday delivery	mos	9.78	3/01	4c
Phone line, single, business, field visit	inst.	70.00	12/97	17s
Phone line, single, business, no field visit	inst.	70.00	12/97	17s
Phone line, single, residence, field visit	inst.	35.00	12/97	17s

Values are in dollars or fractions of dollars. In the column headed *Ref*, references are shown to sources. Each reference is followed by a letter. These refer to the geographical level for which data were reported: s=State, r=Region, and c=City or metro. The abbreviation *ex* is used to mean *except* or *excluding*; *exp* stands for *expenditures*. For other abbreviations and further explanations, please see the Introduction.

Grand Junction, CO - continued

Item	Per	Value	Date	Ref.
Communications				
Phone line, single, residence, no field visit	inst.	35.00	12/97	17s
Postal rate, express mail, up to half-pound		12.45	7/01	108r
Postal rate, letter, first class, first ounce		0.34	7/01	108r
Postal rate, letter, two ounces		0.57	7/01	108r
Postal rate, post card		0.21	7/01	108r
Postal rate, priority mail, two pounds		3.95	7/01	108r
Postal rate, priority mail, up to one pound		3.50	7/01	108r
Telephone bill, family of three	mos	22.45	3/01	4c
Education				
Board, 4-year private college/university	yr	2750	1996	38s
Board, 4-year public college/university	yr	2564	1996	38s
Room, 4-year private college/university	yr	2574	1996	38s
Room, 4-year public college/university	yr	2000	1996	38s
Total cost, 4-year private college/university	yr	17120	1996	38s
Total cost, 4-year public college/university	yr	7037	1996	38s
Tuition, 2-year public college/university, in state	yr	1340	1996	38s
Tuition, 4-year private college/university, in state	yr	11796	1996	38s
Tuition, 4-year public college/university	yr	2473	1996	38s
Energy and Fuels				
Energy, combined forms, 2400 sq ft	mos	123.04	3/01	4c
Energy, exc. electricity, 2400 sq ft	mos	73.61	3/01	4c
Gas, natural, commercial rate	1000 cf	6.42	11/00	88s
Gas, regular unleaded, cash, self-service	gal	1.43	3/01	4c
Entertainment				
Bowling, Saturday evening rate	line	2.77	3/01	4c
Monopoly game, Parker Brothers', No. 9	game	10.31	3/01	4c
Movie, first-run, Saturday, evening	adm.	6.75	3/01	4c
Tennis balls, yellow, Wilson or Penn, 3	can	2.19	3/01	4c
Funerals				
Total cost of funeral		5401.08	1/99	78r
Acknowledgement cards		33.64	1/99	78r
Casket		2170.43	1/99	78r
Cosmetology, hair, other preparation		136.32	1/99	78r
Embalming		319.13	1/99	78r
Funeral at funeral home		370.21	1/99	78r
Hearse (local)		161.04	1/99	78r
Professional service charges		963.15	1/99	78r
Service car/van		133.99	1/99	78r
Transfer of remains to funeral home		159.82	1/99	78r
Vault		778.07	1/99	78r
Visitation/viewing		175.28	1/99	78r
Groceries				
Groceries, ACCRA Index		102.10	3/01	4c
Antibiotic ointment, Polysporin	0.5 oz	4.49	3/01	4c
Baby food, strained vegetables or fruit, lowest price	4-4.5 oz	0.35	3/01	4c
Bacon	lb	3.99	5/99	8s
Bananas	lb	0.54	3/01	4c
Beef or hamburger, ground	lb	1.91	3/01	4c
Bread, white	loaf	0.91	3/01	4c
Bread, white, 20 oz loaf		0.64	5/99	8s
Cheddar cheese, mild	lb	3.59	5/99	8s
Cheerios, 10 oz box		2.99	5/99	8s
Cheese, Kraft grated Parmesan	8 oz	3.78	3/01	4c
Chicken, whole fryer	lb	0.89	3/01	4c
Cigarettes, Winston, Kings	carton	26.07	3/01	4c
Coffee, vacuum-packed	13 oz	3.44	3/01	4c
Corn Flakes, Kellogg's or Post Toasties	18 oz	2.32	3/01	4c
Corn oil, Mazola, 32 oz		2.75	5/99	8s
Corn, frozen, whole kernel, lowest price	16 oz	1.05	3/01	4c
Eggs, Grade A or AA	dozen	0.95	3/01	4c
Flour, all purpose	5 lb	1.69	5/99	8s
Grade A large eggs	doz	1.59	5/99	8s
Ground chuck	lb	1.99	5/99	8s
Lettuce, iceberg	head	0.99	3/01	4c
Margarine, Blue Bonnet or Parkay, stick	lb	0.75	3/01	4c
Mayonnaise, Kraft, 32 oz		2.50	5/99	8s

Grand Junction, CO - continued

Item	Per	Value	Date	Ref.
Groceries - continued				
Milk, whole	1/2 gal	1.88	3/01	4c
Orange juice, Minute Maid frozen	12 oz	1.49	3/01	4c
Peaches, halves or slices, Hunt's, Del Monte, or Libby's	29 oz	1.96	3/01	4c
Peas, green, Del Monte or Green Giant	15 oz	0.79	3/01	4c
Potatoes, russet	5 lb	1.79	5/99	8s
Potatoes, white or red	10 lb	2.69	3/01	4c
Red Delicious apples	lb	1.39	5/99	8s
Sausage, Jimmy Dean/Owens pork	lb	4.15	3/01	4c
Shortening, vegetable, Crisco	3 lb	3.67	3/01	4c
Sirloin tip roast	lb	3.99	5/99	8s
Soft drink, Coca Cola, ex deposit	2 liter	1.43	3/01	4c
Steak, T-bone	lb	6.61	3/01	4c
Sugar, cane or beet	4 lbs	1.55	3/01	4c
Tomatoes, Hunt's or Del Monte	14.5 oz	1.11	3/01	4c
Tuna, chunk, light	6 oz	0.41	3/01	4c
Vegetable oil, Crisco, 32 oz		1.89	5/99	8s
Whole fryer	lb	1.99	5/99	8s
Whole milk	gal	0.89	5/99	8s
Goods and Services				
Miscellaneous goods and services, ACCRA Index		93.30	3/01	4c
Hunting license	yr	15.25	4/01	34s
Health Care				
Health care, ACCRA Index		102.70	3/01	4c
Cardiac catheterization, ave hospital/ physician charges		17910	1998	77s
Childbirth, Cesarean delivery		11587	1997	13r
Childbirth, vaginal delivery		6725	1997	13r
Dentist's fee, adult teeth cleaning and periodic oral exam	visit	76.71	3/01	4c
Doctor's fee, routine exam, established patient	visit	56.79	3/01	4c
Hospital care, private room	day	575.32	3/01	4c
Hysterectomy, laproscopically-assisted, ave hospital/physician charges		16210	1998	76s
Hysterectomy, vaginal, ave hospital and physician charges		11690	1998	76s
Medicaid dispensing fee		4.08	1999	87s
Household Goods				
Dishwashing powder, Cascade	50 oz	3.24	3/01	4c
Tissues, facial, Kleenex brand	175	1.37	3/01	4c
Housing				
Housing, ACCRA Index		92.80	3/01	4c
Home value, median		173000	2001	53s
House, 2400 sq ft, 8000 sq ft lot, new, urban, utilities	total	192756		4c
House payment, principal and interest, 25% down payment	mos	966	3/01	4c
Rent, apartment, 2 br, 1 1/2-2 baths, unfurn, 950 sq ft, water	mos	621	3/01	4c
Rental unit, 1 bedroom, with utilities	mos	427	4/01	41c
Rental unit, 2 bedroom, with utilities	mos	534	4/01	41c
Rental unit, 3 bedroom, with utilities	mos	720	4/01	41c
Rental unit, 4 bedroom, with utilities	mos	857	4/01	41c
Legal Fees				
Divorce, filing fee		65.00	4/01	35s
Driver's license fee	orig	15.00	1999	48s
Driver's license fee	renew	15.00	1999	48s
Personal Goods				
Shampoo, Alberto VO5	15 oz	1.05	3/01	4c
Toothpaste, Crest or Colgate	6-7 oz	2.00	3/01	4c
Personal Services				
Dry cleaning, man's 2-pc suit		7.37	3/01	4c
Man's haircut, barbershop, no styling		10.00	3/01	4c
Woman's shampoo, trim, blow-dry, no style-change		21.50	3/01	4c

Values are in dollars or fractions of dollars. In the column headed *Ref*, references are shown to sources. Each reference is followed by a letter. These refer to the geographical level for which data were reported: s=State, r=Region, and c=City or metro. The abbreviation *ex* is used to mean *except* or *excluding*; *exp* stands for expenditures. For other abbreviations and further explanations, please see the Introduction.

Grand Junction, CO - continued

Item	Per	Value	Date	Ref.
Restaurant Food				
Chicken, fried, thigh and drumstick, KFC/ Church's		2.49	3/01	4c
Hamburger with cheese, McDonald's	1/4 lb	1.00	3/01	4c
Pizza, Pizza Hut or Pizza Inn	11-12 in	8.49	3/01	4c
Transportation				
Transportation, ACCRA Index		102.90	3/01	4c
Diesel at the pump	gal	1.28	10/99	73s
Gasoline before-tax price (cents)	gal	117.00	10/00	43s
Tire balance, computer or spin balance, front	wheel	8.28	3/01	4c
Travel				
Hotel room	night	118.98	2/01	95s
Utilities				
Utilities, ACCRA Index		101.10	3/01	4c
Electrical bill, average	mos	47.17	9/00	9s
Electricity and other, mixed, 2400 sq ft, new home	mos	49.43	3/01	4c
Electricity cost, average	KWh	5.90	9/00	9s
Weddings				
Wedding (national average cost)		19936	2000	33r
Attendants' gifts		321	1998	33r
Bridal attendants' apparel (5 persons)		824	2000	33r
Bride's headpiece/veil		173	1998	33r
Bride's wedding dress		859	1998	33r
Clergy, religious facility fee		242	1998	33r
Engagement ring		3177	1998	33r
Flowers		789	1998	33r
Groom's formalwear rental		99	2000	33r
Limousine		410	1998	33r
Marriage license cost		20.00	4/01	35s
Men's formalwear (ushers, best man)		469	2000	33r
Mother of bride apparel		241	2000	33r
Music		866	1998	33r
Photography and videography		1368	1998	33r
Rehearsal dinner		728	1998	33r
Wedding invitations and announcements		341	1998	33r
Wedding reception		7968	2000	33r
Wedding rings (bride and groom)		1060	1998	33r

Grand Rapids-Muskegon-Holland, MI

Item	Per	Value	Date	Ref.
Average annual expenditures	yr	35369	1999	30r
Alcoholic Beverages				
Alcoholic beverage purchases	yr	304	1999	30r
Malt beverages, all types, all sizes, any origin	16 oz	0.93	7/01	11r
Wine, red and white table, all sizes, any origin	liter	7.04	7/01	11r
Appliances				
Major appliances, expenditures on	yr	165	1999	30r
Small appliances, housewares, expenditures on	yr	90	1999	30r
Banking and Money				
Mortgage interest and charges paid	yr	2277	1999	30r
Mortgage principal paid on owned property	yr	1230	1999	30r
Vehicle finance charges paid	yr	328	1999	30r
Charity				
Cash contributions, expenditures	yr	1126	1999	30r
Child Care				
Child raising cost, total, age 0-2	yr	7890	1999	60r
Child raising cost, total, age 3-5	yr	8130	1999	60r
Child raising cost, total, age 6-8	yr	8170	1999	60r
Child raising cost, total, age 9-11	yr	8190	1999	60r
Child raising cost, total, age 12-14	yr	8890	1999	60r
Child raising cost, total, age 15-17	yr	9050	1999	60r
Child's child care and education, age 0-2	yr	1240	1999	60r
Child's child care and education, age 3-5	yr	1370	1999	60r
Child's child care and education, age 6-8	yr	880	1999	60r
Child's child care and education, age 9-11	yr	570	1999	60r

Grand Rapids-Muskegon-Holland, MI - continued

Item	Per	Value	Date	Ref.
Child Care - continued				
Child's child care and education, age 12-14	yr	420	1999	60r
Child's child care and education, age 15-17	yr	720	1999	60r
Child's clothing, age 0-2	yr	410	1999	60r
Child's clothing, age 3-5	yr	400	1999	60r
Child's clothing, age 6-8	yr	450	1999	60r
Child's clothing, age 9-11	yr	500	1999	60r
Child's clothing, age 12-14	yr	840	1999	60r
Child's clothing, age 15-17	yr	740	1999	60r
Child's food, age 0-2	yr	960	1999	60r
Child's food, age 3-5	yr	1120	1999	60r
Child's food, age 6-8	yr	1430	1999	60r
Child's food, age 9-11	yr	1710	1999	60r
Child's food, age 12-14	yr	1710	1999	60r
Child's food, age 15-17	yr	1920	1999	60r
Child's health care, age 0-2	yr	520	1999	60r
Child's health care, age 3-5	yr	500	1999	60r
Child's health care, age 6-8	yr	570	1999	60r
Child's health care, age 9-11	yr	610	1999	60r
Child's health care, age 12-14	yr	630	1999	60r
Child's health care, age 15-17	yr	650	1999	60r
Child's housing, age 0-2	yr	2860	1999	60r
Child's housing, age 3-5	yr	2840	1999	60r
Child's housing, age 6-8	yr	2800	1999	60r
Child's housing, age 9-11	yr	2650	1999	60r
Child's housing, age 12-14	yr	2840	1999	60r
Child's housing, age 15-17	yr	2440	1999	60r
Child's personal care, reading, age 0-2	yr	880	1999	60r
Child's personal care, reading, age 3-5	yr	900	1999	60r
Child's personal care, reading, age 6-8	yr	930	1999	60r
Child's personal care, reading, age 9-11	yr	970	1999	60r
Child's personal care, reading, age 12-14	yr	1150	1999	60r
Child's personal care, reading, age 15-17	yr	920	1999	60r
Clothing				
Apparel and services purchases	yr	1607	1999	30r
Boys, 2 to 15, expenditures on	yr	91	1999	30r
Children under 2, expenditures on	yr	59	1999	30r
Footwear, expenditures on	yr	285	1999	30r
Girls, 2 to 15, expenditures on	yr	116	1999	30r
Men and boys, expenditures on	yr	433	1999	30r
Men, 16 and over, expenditures on	yr	341	1999	30r
Women, 16 and over, expenditures on	yr	490	1999	30r
Communications				
Cable modem installation, Bresnan		99.95	6/99	103s
Cable modem installation, Comcast		95.00	6/99	103s
Cable modem installation, Media One		100.00	6/99	103s
Cable modem rate, cable subscriber, Bresnan	mos	39.95	6/99	103s
Cable modem rate, cable subscriber, Comcast	mos	39.95	6/99	103s
Cable modem rate, cable subscriber, Media One	mos	34.95- 39.95	6/99	103s
Cable modem rate, non-cable subscriber, Bresnan	mos	49.95	6/99	103s
Cable modem rate, non-cable subscriber, Comcast	mos	49.95	6/99	103s
Cable modem rate, non-cable subscriber, Media One	mos	49.95	6/99	103s
Phone line, single, business, field visit	inst.	42.00	12/97	17s
Phone line, single, business, no field visit	inst.	42.00	12/97	17s
Phone line, single, residence, field visit	inst.	42.00	12/97	17s
Phone line, single, residence, no field visit	inst.	42.00	12/97	17s
Postage and stationery, expenditures on	yr	140	1999	30r
Postal rate, express mail, up to half-pound		12.45	7/01	108r
Postal rate, letter, first class, first ounce		0.34	7/01	108r
Postal rate, letter, two ounces		0.57	7/01	108r
Postal rate, post card		0.21	7/01	108r
Postal rate, priority mail, two pounds		3.95	7/01	108r
Postal rate, priority mail, up to one pound		3.50	7/01	108r
Telephone services, expenditures on	yr	830	1999	30r

Values are in dollars or fractions of dollars. In the column headed *Ref*, references are shown to sources. Each reference is followed by a letter. These refer to the geographical level for which data were reported: s=State, r=Region, and c=City or metro. The abbreviation *ex* is used to mean *except* or *excluding*; *exp* stands for expenditures. For other abbreviations and further explanations, please see the Introduction.

Grand Rapids-Muskegon-Holland, MI - continued

Item	Per	Value	Date	Ref.
Education				
Board, 4-year private college/university	yr	2182	1996	38s
Board, 4-year public college/university	yr	2276	1996	38s
Education expenditures	yr	583	1999	30r
Room, 4-year private college/university	yr	1974	1996	38s
Room, 4-year public college/university	yr	2024	1996	38s
Total cost, 4-year private college/university	yr	13331	1996	38s
Total cost, 4-year public college/university	yr	8195	1996	38s
Tuition, 2-year public college/university, in state	yr	1529	1996	38s
Tuition, 4-year private college/university, in state	yr	9176	1996	38s
Tuition, 4-year public college/university	yr	3895	1996	38s
Energy and Fuels				
Electricity	500 KWhs	46.59	7/01	11r
Fuel oil #2	gal	1.27	7/01	11r
Fuel oil and other fuels, expenditures on	yr	68	1999	30r
Gas, natural, commercial rate	1000 cf	4.91	11/00	88s
Gasoline, unleaded midgrade	gal	1.79	7/01	11r
Gasoline, unleaded premium	gal	1.86	7/01	11r
Gasoline, unleaded regular	gal	1.58	7/01	11r
Natural gas, expenditures on	yr	389	1999	30r
Utility (piped) gas, therm		0.81	7/01	11r
Utility (piped) gas, 40 therms		38.01	7/01	11r
Utility (piped) gas, 100 therms		81.75	7/01	11r
Entertainment				
Entertainment purchases	yr	1984	1999	30r
Fees and admissions paid	yr	444	1999	30r
Television, radios, sound equipment, expenditures on	yr	580	1999	30r
Funerals				
Cosmetology, hair, other preparation		178.32	1/99	78r
Embalming		408.19	1/99	78r
Funeral at funeral home		362.13	1/99	78r
Professional service charges		1375.51	1/99	78r
Transfer of remains to funeral home		155.92	1/99	78r
Visitation/viewing		294.38	1/99	78r
Groceries				
Bacon, sliced	lb	3.15	7/01	11r
Bakery products, expenditures on	yr	281	1999	30r
Bananas	lb	0.48	7/01	11r
Beans, dried, any type, all sizes	lb	0.61	7/01	11r
Beef for stew, boneless	lb	3.08	7/01	11r
Beef, expenditures on	yr	217	1999	30r
Bologna, all beef or mixed	lb	2.52	7/01	11r
Bread, white, pan	lb	1.06	7/01	11r
Broccoli	lb	0.91	7/01	11r
Butter, salted, grade AA, stick	lb	3.04	7/01	11r
Butter, yoghurt, cheese, etc, expenditures on	yr	183	1999	30r
Cereals and bakery product purchases	yr	430	1999	30r
Cereals and cereal products, expenditures on	yr	149	1999	30r
Chicken, fresh, whole	lb	1.07	7/01	11r
Chops, boneless,	lb	3.64	7/01	11r
Chuck roast, U.S. choice, boneless	lb	2.47	7/01	11r
Coffee, 100%, ground roast, all sizes	lb	2.69	7/01	11r
Cookies, chocolate chip	lb	2.87	7/01	11r
Dairy product purchases	yr	304	1999	30r
Eggs, expenditures on	yr	26	1999	30r
Eggs, grade A, large	dozen	0.88	7/01	11r
Fats and oils, expenditures on	yr	75	1999	30r
Fish and seafood, expenditures on	yr	72	1999	30r
Food (excl fruit and vegetables), eaten at home, purchases	yr	887	1999	30r
Food cooked on trips, expenditures on	yr	44	1999	30r
Food purchases	yr	4802	1999	30r
Food purchases, eaten away from home	yr	2069	1999	30r
Food purchases, food eaten at home	yr	2733	1999	30r
Fresh fruits, expenditures on	yr	138	1999	30r
Fresh milk and cream, expenditures on	yr	120	1999	30r

Grand Rapids-Muskegon-Holland, MI - continued

Item	Per	Value	Date	Ref.
Groceries - continued				
Fresh vegetables, expenditures on	yr	126	1999	30r
Grapefruit	lb	0.66	7/01	11r
Grapes, Thompson, seedless	lb	1.64	7/01	11r
Ground beef, 100% beef	lb	1.64	7/01	11r
Ground beef, lean and extra lean	lb	2.16	7/01	11r
Ground chuck, 100% beef	lb	2.13	7/01	11r
Ham, boneless, excl canned	lb	2.62	7/01	11r
Ice cream, prepackaged, bulk, regular	1/2 gal	3.35	7/01	11r
Lemons	lb	1.19	7/01	11r
Lettuce, iceberg	lb	0.73	7/01	11r
Margarine, soft, tubs	lb	0.89	7/01	11r
Meats, poultry, fish, and egg purchases	yr	671	1999	30r
Milk, fresh, whole, fortified	gal	2.71	7/01	11r
Nonalcoholic beverages, expenditures on	yr	239	1999	30r
Oranges, Navel	lb	0.80	7/01	11r
Oranges, Valencia	lb	0.66	7/01	11r
Pears, Anjou	lb	0.93	7/01	11r
Pork chops, center cut, bone-in	lb	3.63	7/01	11r
Pork, expenditures on	yr	150	1999	30r
Potato chips	16 oz	3.52	7/01	11r
Potatoes, frozen, french fried	lb	1.08	7/01	11r
Potatoes, white, all types	lb	0.33	7/01	11r
Poultry, expenditures on	yr	108	1999	30r
Processed fruits, expenditures on	yr	98	1999	30r
Processed vegetables, expenditures on	yr	80	1999	30r
Round roast, U.S. choice, boneless	lb	3.07	7/01	11r
Round steak, graded and ungraded, excl U.S. prime and choice	lb	3.41	7/01	11r
Shortening, vegetable oil blends	lb	1.13	7/01	11r
Spaghetti and macaroni	lb	0.80	7/01	11r
Steak, round, U.S. choice, boneless	lb	3.23	7/01	11r
Steak, T-bone, U.S. choice, bone-in	lb	6.68	7/01	11r
Strawberries, dry pint	12 oz	1.32	7/01	11r
Sugar and other sweets, expenditures on	yr	114	1999	30r
Sugar, white, 33-80 ounce package	lb	0.42	7/01	11r
Sugar, white, all sizes	lb	0.43	7/01	11r
Tobacco products and smoking supplies purchases	yr	331	1999	30r
Tomatoes, field grown	lb	1.46	7/01	11r
Tuna, light, chunk	lb	1.80	7/01	11r
Turkey, frozen, whole	lb	1.15	7/01	11r
Goods and Services				
B&B Japanese maple (acer japonicum)	gal	29.99-169.99	4/00	93r
Boxwood (buxus)	2 gal	18.99-39.99	4/00	93r
Daylilly (hemerocallis)	gal	4.99-25.00	4/00	93r
Flat of annuals		11.98-24.99	4/00	93r
Fountain grass (pennisetum)	gal	5.98-12.98	4/00	93r
Hanging basket (10 in)		12.99-27.99	4/00	93r
Hardy geranium (geranium)	gal	7.99-9.99	4/00	93r
Hosta (hosta)	gal	6.00-25.00	4/00	93r
Lilac (syrubga vulgaris)	2 gal	14.99-24.99	4/00	93r
Miscellaneous purchases	yr	865	1999	30r
Rhododendron (rhododendron)	2 gal	23.98-42.99	4/00	93r
Sage (salvia)	gal	6.00-9.99	4/00	93r
Snowblower, single stage		400-600	12/00	99s
Wintercreeper euonymus (euonymus fortunei)	2 gal	16.00-169.99	4/00	93r
Hunting license	yr	14.00	4/01	34s

Values are in dollars or fractions of dollars. In the column headed *Ref*, references are shown to sources. Each reference is followed by a letter. These refer to the geographical level for which data were reported: s=State, r=Region, and c=City or metro. The abbreviation *ex* is used to mean *except* or *excluding*; *exp* stands for *expenditures*. For other abbreviations and further explanations, please see the Introduction.

Grand Rapids-Muskegon-Holland, MI - continued

Item	Per	Value	Date	Ref.
Health Care				
Cardiac catheterization, ave hospital/ physician charges		11830	1998	77s
Childbirth, Cesarean delivery		10722	1997	13r
Childbirth, vaginal delivery		6223	1997	13r
Drugs, expenditures on	yr	394	1999	30r
Health care purchases	yr	2048	1999	30r
Health insurance expenditures	yr	978	1999	30r
Hysterectomy, laproscopically-assisted, ave hospital/physician charges		13820	1998	76s
Hysterectomy, vaginal, ave hospital and physician charges		8780	1998	76s
Medicaid dispensing fee		3.72	1999	87s
Medical services expenditures	yr	554	1999	30r
Medical supplies, expenditures on	yr	122	1999	30r
Plastic surgery, breast augmentation		3184	2000	7r
Plastic surgery, breast lift		3585	2000	7r
Plastic surgery, facelift		4999	2000	7r
Plastic surgery, hair transplantation		3105	2000	7r
Plastic surgery, lip augmentation		1290	2000	7r
Plastic surgery, lower body lift		8135	2000	7r
Plastic surgery, thigh lift		3839	2000	7r
Household Goods				
Floor coverings, expenditures on	yr	52	1999	30r
Furniture, expenditures on	yr	344	1999	30r
Household furnishings and equipment purchases	yr	1475	1999	30r
Household textiles, expenditures on	yr	109	1999	30r
Laundry and cleaning supplies, expenditures on	yr	134	1999	30r
Housing				
Home price, existing, ave		144400	10/00	90r
Home value, median		135000	2001	53s
Household operation expenditures	yr	542	1999	30r
Housekeeping supplies purchases	yr	508	1999	30r
Lodging expenditures	yr	430	1999	30r
Maintenance, repairs, insurance expenditures	yr	853	1999	30r
Monthly rental value of owned home	mos	547	1999	30r
Owned dwellings, expenditures own	yr	4282	1999	30r
Rent expenditures	yr	1558	1999	30r
Rental unit, 1 bedroom, with utilities	mos	470	4/01	41c
Rental unit, 2 bedroom, with utilities	mos	574	4/01	41c
Rental unit, 3 bedroom, with utilities	mos	719	4/01	41c
Rental unit, 4 bedroom, with utilities	mos	805	4/01	41c
Shelter, expenditures on	yr	6270	1999	30r
Insurance and Pensions				
Life and other personal insurance purchases	yr	387	1999	30r
Pensions and Social Security, expenditures on	yr	2968	1999	30r
Legal Fees				
Divorce, filing fee		65.00	4/01	35s
Driver's license fee	orig	20.00	1999	48s
Driver's license fee	renew	5.00	1999	48s
Fishing license	yr	14.00	4/01	34s
Personal Goods				
Personal care products and services purchases	yr	385	1999	30r
Personal Services				
Personal services, household, expenditures on	yr	300	1999	30r
Pets				
Pets, toys, and playground equipment, expenditures on	yr	375	1999	30r
Taxes				
Federal income taxes paid	yr	2326	1999	30r
Personal taxes, expenditures on	yr	3223	1999	30r
Property taxes paid	yr	1152	1999	30r
State and local income taxes paid	yr	753	1999	30r

Grand Rapids-Muskegon-Holland, MI - continued

Item	Per	Value	Date	Ref.
Transportation				
Cars and trucks, new, expenditures on	yr	1280	1999	30r
Cars and trucks, used, expenditures on	yr	1763	1999	30r
Diesel at the pump	gal	1.19	10/99	73s
Gasoline and motor oil purchases	yr	1036	1999	30r
Gasoline before-tax price (cents)	gal	111.50	10/00	43s
Maintenance and repair expenditures	yr	594	1999	30r
Public transportation, expenditures on	yr	341	1999	30r
Transportation purchases	yr	6617	1999	30r
Vehicle expenses, miscellaneous, purchases	yr	2159	1999	30r
Vehicle insurance payments	yr	701	1999	30r
Vehicle purchases (net outlay)	yr	3081	1999	30r
Vehicle rental, lease expenditures	yr	536	1999	30r
Utilities				
Electrical bill, average	mos	55.00	9/00	9s
Electricity, expenditures on	yr	841	1999	30r
Electricity cost, average	KWh	7.00	9/00	9s
Utilities, fuels, and public services purchased	yr	2401	1999	30r
Water and other public services, expenditures on	yr	273	1999	30r
Weddings				
Wedding (national average cost)		19936	2000	33r
Wedding (regional average total cost)		16195	1997	110r
Attendants' gifts		321	1998	33r
Bridal attendants' apparel (5 persons)		824	2000	33r
Bride's headpiece/veil		173	1998	33r
Bride's wedding dress		859	1998	33r
Clergy, religious facility fee		242	1998	33r
Engagement ring		3177	1998	33r
Flowers		789	1998	33r
Groom's formalwear rental		99	2000	33r
Limousine		410	1998	33r
Marriage license cost		20.00	4/01	35s
Men's formalwear (ushers, best man)		469	2000	33r
Mother of bride apparel		241	2000	33r
Music		866	1998	33r
Photography and videography		1368	1998	33r
Rehearsal dinner		728	1998	33r
Wedding invitations and announcements		341	1998	33r
Wedding reception		7968	2000	33r
Wedding rings (bride and groom)		1060	1998	33r

Great Falls, MT

Item	Per	Value	Date	Ref.
Composite, ACCRA index		102.40	3/01	4c
Alcoholic Beverages				
Beer, Heineken, 12-oz, ex deposit	6	7.23	3/01	4c
J & B Scotch	750-ml	22.07	3/01	4c
Wine, Livingston or Gallo, Chablis blanc	1.5 liter	5.99	3/01	4c
Appliances				
Appliance repair, service call, washing machine	min lab chg	39.60	3/01	4c
Banking and Money				
Mortgage rate, incl. points and orig. fee, 30-yr. conv. fixed or ARM	mos	7.06	3/01	4c
Clothing				
Boys' brief, cotton	3	5.36	3/01	4c
Shirt, man's dress shirt		24.50	3/01	4c
Slacks, man's "No Wrinkles" khaki		36.66	3/01	4c
Communications				
Newspaper subscription, daily and Sunday delivery	mos	15.65	3/01	4c
Phone line, single, business, field visit	inst.	61.40	12/97	17s
Phone line, single, business, no field visit	inst.	61.40	12/97	17s
Phone line, single, residence, field visit	inst.	25.00	12/97	17s
Phone line, single, residence, no field visit	inst.	25.00	12/97	17s
Postal rate, express mail, up to half-pound		12.45	7/01	108r
Postal rate, letter, first class, first ounce		0.34	7/01	108r
Postal rate, letter, two ounces		0.57	7/01	108r

Values are in dollars or fractions of dollars. In the column headed *Ref*, references are shown to sources. Each reference is followed by a letter. These refer to the geographical level for which data were reported: s=State, r=Region, and c=City or metro. The abbreviation *ex* is used to mean *except* or *excluding*; *exp* stands for expenditures. For other abbreviations and further explanations, please see the Introduction.

Great Falls, MT - continued

Item	Per	Value	Date	Ref.
Communications				
Postal rate, post card		0.21	7/01	108r
Postal rate, priority mail, two pounds		3.95	7/01	108r
Postal rate, priority mail, up to one pound		3.50	7/01	108r
Telephone bill, business, basic rate	mos	38.69	12/97	18c
Telephone bill, family of three	mos	26.29	3/01	4c
Telephone bill, residential, basic rate	mos	13.84	12/97	18c
Education				
Board, 4-year private college/university	yr	2128	1996	38s
Board, 4-year public college/university	yr	3609	1996	38s
Room, 4-year private college/university	yr	1388	1996	38s
Room, 4-year public college/university	yr	1778	1996	38s
Total cost, 4-year private college/university	yr	11062	1996	38s
Total cost, 4-year public college/university	yr	7754	1996	38s
Tuition, 2-year public college/university, in state	yr	1382	1996	38s
Tuition, 4-year private college/university, in state	yr	7545	1996	38s
Tuition, 4-year public college/university	yr	2367	1996	38s
Energy and Fuels				
Energy, combined forms, 2400 sq ft	mos	109.67	3/01	4c
Energy, exc. electricity, 2400 sq ft	mos	67.22	3/01	4c
Gas, cooking, winter, 10 therms	mos	7.36	2/96	98c
Gas, cooking, winter, 30 therms	mos	14.07	2/96	98c
Gas, cooking, winter, 50 therms	mos	20.79	2/96	98c
Gas, heating, winter, average use	mos	37.45	2/96	98c
Gas, natural, commercial rate	1000 cf	5.54	11/00	88s
Gas, regular unleaded, cash, self-service	gal	1.49	3/01	4c
Entertainment				
Bowling, Saturday evening rate	line	1.95	3/01	4c
Monopoly game, Parker Brothers', No. 9	game	9.90	3/01	4c
Movie, first-run, Saturday, evening	adm.	6.50	3/01	4c
Tennis balls, yellow, Wilson or Penn, 3	can	2.01	3/01	4c
Funerals				
Total cost of funeral		5401.08	1/99	78r
Acknowledgement cards		33.64	1/99	78r
Casket		2170.43	1/99	78r
Cosmetology, hair, other preparation		136.32	1/99	78r
Embalming		319.13	1/99	78r
Funeral at funeral home		370.21	1/99	78r
Hearse (local)		161.04	1/99	78r
Professional service charges		963.15	1/99	78r
Service car/van		133.99	1/99	78r
Transfer of remains to funeral home		159.82	1/99	78r
Vault		778.07	1/99	78r
Visitation/viewing		175.28	1/99	78r
Groceries				
Groceries, ACCRA Index		102.60	3/01	4c
Antibiotic ointment, Polysporin	0.5 oz	4.93	3/01	4c
Baby food, strained vegetables or fruit, lowest price	4-4.5 oz	0.31	3/01	4c
Bananas	lb	0.46	3/01	4c
Beef or hamburger, ground	lb	1.67	3/01	4c
Bread, white	loaf	0.90	3/01	4c
Cheese, Kraft grated Parmesan	8 oz	4.49	3/01	4c
Chicken, whole fryer	lb	0.99	3/01	4c
Cigarettes, Winston, Kings	carton	30.78	3/01	4c
Coffee, vacuum-packed	13 oz	2.85	3/01	4c
Corn Flakes, Kellogg's or Post Toasties	18 oz	3.31	3/01	4c
Corn, frozen, whole kernel, lowest price	16 oz	1.18	3/01	4c
Eggs, Grade A or AA	dozen	1.00	3/01	4c
Lettuce, iceberg	head	0.92	3/01	4c
Margarine, Blue Bonnet or Parkay, stick	lb	0.79	3/01	4c
Milk, whole	1/2 gal	1.60	3/01	4c
Orange juice, Minute Maid frozen	12 oz	1.67	3/01	4c
Peaches, halves or slices, Hunt's, Del Monte, or Libby's	29 oz	1.68	3/01	4c
Peas, green, Del Monte or Green Giant	15 oz	0.84	3/01	4c
Potatoes, white or red	10 lb	1.97	3/01	4c
Sausage, Jimmy Dean/Owens pork	lb	4.11	3/01	4c

Great Falls, MT

Great Falls, MT - continued

Item	Per	Value	Date	Ref.
Groceries - continued				
Shortening, vegetable, Crisco	3 lb	3.29	3/01	4c
Soft drink, Coca Cola, ex deposit	2 liter	1.08	3/01	4c
Steak, T-bone	lb	5.33	3/01	4c
Sugar, cane or beet	4 lbs	2.05	3/01	4c
Tomatoes, Hunt's or Del Monte	14.5 oz	0.99	3/01	4c
Tuna, chunk, light	6 oz	0.80	3/01	4c
Goods and Services				
Miscellaneous goods and services, ACCRA Index		97.70	3/01	4c
Hunting license	yr	10.00	4/01	34s
Health Care				
Health care, ACCRA Index		91.20	3/01	4c
Cardiac catheterization, ave hospital/physician charges		13700	1998	77s
Childbirth, Cesarean delivery		11587	1997	13r
Childbirth, vaginal delivery		6725	1997	13r
Dentist's fee, adult teeth cleaning and periodic oral exam	visit	69.20	3/01	4c
Doctor's fee, routine exam, established patient	visit	54.50	3/01	4c
Hospital care, private room	day	361.00	3/01	4c
Hysterectomy, laproscopically-assisted, ave hospital/physician charges		11400	1998	76s
Hysterectomy, vaginal, ave hospital and physician charges		8290	1998	76s
Medicaid dispensing fee		2.00-4.20	1999	87s
Household Goods				
Dishwashing powder, Cascade	50 oz	3.83	3/01	4c
Tissues, facial, Kleenex brand	175	1.20	3/01	4c
Housing				
Housing, ACCRA Index		115.50	3/01	4c
Home value, median		108000	2001	53s
House, 2400 sq ft, 8000 sq ft lot, new, urban, utilities	total	260000	3/01	4c
House payment, principal and interest, 25% down payment	mos	1305	3/01	4c
Rent, apartment, 2 br, 1 1/2-2 baths, unfurn, 950 sq ft, water	mos	502	3/01	4c
Rental unit, 1 bedroom, with utilities	mos	387	4/01	41c
Rental unit, 2 bedroom, with utilities	mos	510	4/01	41c
Rental unit, 3 bedroom, with utilities	mos	664	4/01	41c
Rental unit, 4 bedroom, with utilities	mos	790	4/01	41c
Legal Fees				
Divorce, filing fee		230.00	4/01	35s
Driver's license fee	orig	16.00	1999	48s
Driver's license fee	renew	16.00	1999	48s
Fishing license	yr	17.00	4/01	34s
Personal Goods				
Shampoo, Alberto VO5	15 oz	1.02	3/01	4c
Toothpaste, Crest or Colgate	6-7 oz	2.32	3/01	4c
Personal Services				
Dry cleaning, man's 2-pc suit		7.65	3/01	4c
Man's haircut, barbershop, no styling		7.80	3/01	4c
Woman's shampoo, trim, blow-dry, no style-change		22.60	3/01	4c
Restaurant Food				
Chicken, fried, thigh and drumstick, KFC/Church's		2.60	3/01	4c
Hamburger with cheese, McDonald's	1/4 lb	2.19	3/01	4c
Pizza, Pizza Hut or Pizza Inn	11-12 in	10.49	3/01	4c
Transportation				
Transportation, ACCRA Index		93.60	3/01	4c
Bus fare, one-way	trip	0.50	2000	1c
Bus fare, to central business district	1-way	0.50	3/01	4c
Diesel at the pump	gal	1.35	10/99	73s
Gasoline before-tax price (cents)	gal	126.00	10/00	43s

Values are in dollars or fractions of dollars. In the column headed *Ref*, references are shown to sources. Each reference is followed by a letter. These refer to the geographical level for which data were reported: s=State, r=Region, and c=City or metro. The abbreviation *ex* is used to mean *except* or *excluding*; *exp* stands for *expenditures*. For other abbreviations and further explanations, please see the Introduction.

Great Falls, MT - continued

Item	Per	Value	Date	Ref.
Transportation				
Tire balance, computer or spin balance, front	wheel	7.10	3/01	4c
Travel				
Hotel room	night	54.24	2/01	94s
Utilities				
Utilities, ACCRA Index		94.10	3/01	4c
Electrical bill, average	mos	52.58	9/00	9s
Electricity and other, mixed, 2400 sq ft, new home	mos	42.45	3/01	4c
Electricity cost, average	KWh	5.92	9/00	9s
Weddings				
Wedding (national average cost)		19936	2000	33r
Attendants' gifts		321	1998	33r
Bridal attendants' apparel (5 persons)		824	2000	33r
Bride's headpiece/veil		173	1998	33r
Bride's wedding dress		859	1998	33r
Clergy, religious facility fee		242	1998	33r
Engagement ring		3177	1998	33r
Flowers		789	1998	33r
Groom's formalwear rental		99	2000	33r
Limousine		410	1998	33r
Marriage license cost		30.25	4/01	35s
Men's formalwear (ushers, best man)		469	2000	33r
Mother of bride apparel		241	2000	33r
Music		866	1998	33r
Photography and videography		1368	1998	33r
Rehearsal dinner		728	1998	33r
Wedding invitations and announcements		341	1998	33r
Wedding reception		7968	2000	33r
Wedding rings (bride and groom)		1060	1998	33r

Greeley, CO

Item	Per	Value	Date	Ref.
Composite, ACCRA index		102.40	3/01	4c
Alcoholic Beverages				
Beer, Heineken, 12-oz, ex deposit	6	6.91	3/01	4c
J & B Scotch	750-ml	21.74	3/01	4c
Wine, Livingston or Gallo, Chablis blanc	1.5 liter	4.86	3/01	4c
Appliances				
Appliance repair, service call, washing machine	min lab chg	48.38	3/01	4c
Banking and Money				
Mortgage rate, incl. points and orig. fee, 30-yr. conv. fixed or ARM	mos	6.75	3/01	4c
Clothing				
Boys' brief, cotton	3	4.15	3/01	4c
Shirt, man's dress shirt		21.46	3/01	4c
Slacks, man's "No Wrinkles" khaki		36.67	3/01	4c
Communications				
Cable modem installation, AT&T-BIS		150.00	6/99	103s
Cable modem rate, cable subscriber, AT&T-BIS	mos	39.95	6/99	103s
Newspaper subscription, daily and Sunday delivery	mos	9.50	3/01	4c
Phone line, single, business, field visit	inst.	70.00	12/97	17s
Phone line, single, business, no field visit	inst.	70.00	12/97	17s
Phone line, single, residence, field visit	inst.	35.00	12/97	17s
Phone line, single, residence, no field visit	inst.	35.00	12/97	17s
Postal rate, express mail, up to half-pound		12.45	7/01	108r
Postal rate, letter, first class, first ounce		0.34	7/01	108r
Postal rate, letter, two ounces		0.57	7/01	108r
Postal rate, post card		0.21	7/01	108r
Postal rate, priority mail, two pounds		3.95	7/01	108r
Postal rate, priority mail, up to one pound		3.50	7/01	108r
Telephone bill, family of three	mos	22.29	3/01	4c
Education				
Board, 4-year private college/university	yr	2750	1996	38s
Board, 4-year public college/university	yr	2564	1996	38s

Greeley, CO - continued

Item	Per	Value	Date	Ref.
Education - continued				
Room, 4-year private college/university	yr	2574	1996	38s
Room, 4-year public college/university	yr	2000	1996	38s
Total cost, 4-year private college/university	yr	17120	1996	38s
Total cost, 4-year public college/university	yr	7037	1996	38s
Tuition, 2-year public college/university, in state	yr	1340	1996	38s
Tuition, 4-year private college/university, in state	yr	11796	1996	38s
Tuition, 4-year public college/university	yr	2473	1996	38s
Energy and Fuels				
Energy, combined forms, 2400 sq ft	mos	124.29	3/01	4c
Energy, exc. electricity, 2400 sq ft	mos	79.37	3/01	4c
Gas, cooking, winter, 10 therms	mos	11.58	2/96	98c
Gas, cooking, winter, 30 therms	mos	21.25	2/96	98c
Gas, cooking, winter, 50 therms	mos	30.44	2/96	98c
Gas, heating, winter, average use	mos	85.06	2/96	98c
Gas, natural, commercial rate	1000 cf	6.42	11/00	88s
Gas, regular unleaded, cash, self-service	gal	1.49	3/01	4c
Entertainment				
Bowling, Saturday evening rate	line	2.65	3/01	4c
Monopoly game, Parker Brothers', No. 9	game	7.89	3/01	4c
Movie, first-run, Saturday, evening	adm.	6.75	3/01	4c
Tennis balls, yellow, Wilson or Penn, 3	can	2.77	3/01	4c
Funerals				
Total cost of funeral		5401.08	1/99	78r
Acknowledgement cards		33.64	1/99	78r
Casket		2170.43	1/99	78r
Cosmetology, hair, other preparation		136.32	1/99	78r
Embalming		319.13	1/99	78r
Funeral at funeral home		370.21	1/99	78r
Hearse (local)		161.04	1/99	78r
Professional service charges		963.15	1/99	78r
Service car/van		133.99	1/99	78r
Transfer of remains to funeral home		159.82	1/99	78r
Vault		778.07	1/99	78r
Visitation/viewing		175.28	1/99	78r
Groceries				
Groceries, ACCRA Index		108.70	3/01	4c
Antibiotic ointment, Polysporin	0.5 oz	5.69	3/01	4c
Baby food, strained vegetables or fruit, lowest price	4-4.5 oz	0.44	3/01	4c
Bacon	lb	3.99	5/99	8s
Bananas	lb	0.54	3/01	4c
Beef or hamburger, ground	lb	1.39	3/01	4c
Bread, white	loaf	1.08	3/01	4c
Bread, white, 20 oz loaf		0.64	5/99	8s
Cheddar cheese, mild	lb	3.59	5/99	8s
Cheerios, 10 oz box		2.99	5/99	8s
Cheese, Kraft grated Parmesan	8 oz	3.96	3/01	4c
Chicken, whole fryer	lb	1.04	3/01	4c
Cigarettes, Winston, Kings	carton	27.85	3/01	4c
Coffee, vacuum-packed	13 oz	3.84	3/01	4c
Corn Flakes, Kellogg's or Post Toasties	18 oz	2.49	3/01	4c
Corn oil, Mazola, 32 oz		2.75	5/99	8s
Corn, frozen, whole kernel, lowest price	16 oz	1.34	3/01	4c
Eggs, Grade A or AA	dozen	1.56	3/01	4c
Flour, all purpose	5 lb	1.69	5/99	8s
Grade A large eggs	doz	1.59	5/99	8s
Ground chuck	lb	1.99	5/99	8s
Lettuce, iceberg	head	0.99	3/01	4c
Margarine, Blue Bonnet or Parkay, stick	lb	0.71	3/01	4c
Mayonnaise, Kraft, 32 oz		2.50	5/99	8s
Milk, whole	1/2 gal	1.96	3/01	4c
Orange juice, Minute Maid frozen	12 oz	1.62	3/01	4c
Peaches, halves or slices, Hunt's, Del Monte, or Libby's	29 oz	2.44	3/01	4c
Peas, green, Del Monte or Green Giant	15 oz	0.91	3/01	4c
Potatoes, russet	5 lb	1.79	5/99	8s
Potatoes, white or red	10 lb	2.39	3/01	4c
Red Delicious apples	lb	1.39	5/99	8s

Values are in dollars or fractions of dollars. In the column headed *Ref*, references are shown to sources. Each reference is followed by a letter. These refer to the geographical level for which data were reported: s=State, r=Region, and c=City or metro. The abbreviation *ex* is used to mean *except* or *excluding*; *exp* stands for *expenditures*. For other abbreviations and further explanations, please see the Introduction.

Greeley, CO - continued

Item	Per	Value	Date	Ref.
Groceries				
Sausage, Jimmy Dean/Owens pork	lb	4.23	3/01	4c
Shortening, vegetable, Crisco	3 lb	3.19	3/01	4c
Sirloin tip roast	lb	3.99	5/99	8s
Soft drink, Coca Cola, ex deposit	2 liter	1.24	3/01	4c
Steak, T-bone	lb	7.19	3/01	4c
Sugar, cane or beet	4 lbs	1.62	3/01	4c
Tomatoes, Hunt's or Del Monte	14.5 oz	1.14	3/01	4c
Tuna, chunk, light	6 oz	0.37	3/01	4c
Vegetable oil, Crisco, 32 oz		1.89	5/99	8s
Whole fryer	lb	1.99	5/99	8s
Whole milk	gal	0.89	5/99	8s
Goods and Services				
Miscellaneous goods and services, ACCRA Index		95.50	3/01	4c
Hunting license	yr	15.25	4/01	34s
Health Care				
Health care, ACCRA Index		113.10	3/01	4c
Cardiac catheterization, ave hospital/ physician charges		17910	1998	77s
Childbirth, Cesarean delivery		11587	1997	13r
Childbirth, vaginal delivery		6725	1997	13r
Dentist's fee, adult teeth cleaning and periodic oral exam	visit	75.67	3/01	4c
Doctor's fee, routine exam, established patient	visit	63.80	3/01	4c
Hospital care, private room	day	685.00	3/01	4c
Hysterectomy, laproscopically-assisted, ave hospital/physician charges		16210	1998	76s
Hysterectomy, vaginal, ave hospital and physician charges		11690	1998	76s
Medicaid dispensing fee		4.08	1999	87s
Household Goods				
Dishwashing powder, Cascade	50 oz	3.37	3/01	4c
Tissues, facial, Kleenex brand	175	1.71	3/01	4c
Housing				
Housing, ACCRA Index		108.00	3/01	4c
Home value, median		173000	2001	53s
House, 2400 sq ft, 8000 sq ft lot, new, urban, utilities	total	235852	3/01	4c
House payment, principal and interest, 25% down payment	mos	1148	3/01	4c
Rent, apartment, 2 br, 1 1/2-2 baths, unfurn, 950 sq ft, water	mos	658	3/01	4c
Rental unit, 1 bedroom, with utilities	mos	511	4/01	41c
Rental unit, 2 bedroom, with utilities	mos	643	4/01	41c
Rental unit, 3 bedroom, with utilities	mos	892	4/01	41c
Rental unit, 4 bedroom, with utilities	mos	1055	4/01	41c
Legal Fees				
Divorce, filing fee		65.00	4/01	35s
Driver's license fee	renew	15.00	1999	48s
Driver's license fee	orig	15.00	1999	48s
Personal Goods				
Shampoo, Alberto VO5	15 oz	1.14	3/01	4c
Toothpaste, Crest or Colgate	6-7 oz	2.36	3/01	4c
Personal Services				
Dry cleaning, man's 2-pc suit		9.01	3/01	4c
Man's haircut, barbershop, no styling		9.80	3/01	4c
Woman's shampoo, trim, blow-dry, no style-change		21.00	3/01	4c
Restaurant Food				
Chicken, fried, thigh and drumstick, KFC/ Church's		2.30	3/01	4c
Hamburger with cheese, McDonald's	1/4 lb	2.26	3/01	4c
Pizza, Pizza Hut or Pizza Inn	11-12 in	8.99	3/01	4c
Transportation				
Transportation, ACCRA Index		94.80	3/01	4c
Bus fare, to central business district	1-way	0.85	3/01	4c

Greeley, CO - continued

Item	Per	Value	Date	Ref.
Transportation - continued				
Diesel at the pump	gal	1.28	10/99	73s
Gasoline before-tax price (cents)	gal	117.00	10/00	43s
Tire balance, computer or spin balance, front	wheel	6.70	3/01	4c
Travel				
Hotel room	night	118.98	2/01	95s
Utilities				
Utilities, ACCRA Index		101.90	3/01	4c
Electrical bill, average	mos	47.17	9/00	9s
Electricity and other, mixed, 2400 sq ft, new home	mos	44.92	3/01	4c
Electricity cost, average	KWh	5.90	9/00	9s
Weddings				
Wedding (national average cost)		19936	2000	33r
Attendants' gifts		321	1998	33r
Bridal attendants' apparel (5 persons)		824	2000	33r
Bride's headpiece/veil		173	1998	33r
Bride's wedding dress		859	1998	33r
Clergy, religious facility fee		242	1998	33r
Engagement ring		3177	1998	33r
Flowers		789	1998	33r
Groom's formalwear rental		99	2000	33r
Limousine		410	1998	33r
Marriage license cost		20.00	4/01	35s
Men's formalwear (ushers, best man)		469	2000	33r
Mother of bride apparel		241	2000	33r
Music		866	1998	33r
Photography and videography		1368	1998	33r
Rehearsal dinner		728	1998	33r
Wedding invitations and announcements		341	1998	33r
Wedding reception		7968	2000	33r
Wedding rings (bride and groom)		1060	1998	33r

Green Bay, WI

Item	Per	Value	Date	Ref.
Average annual expenditures	yr	35369	1999	30r
Composite, ACCRA index		97.00	12/00	5c
Alcoholic Beverages				
Alcoholic beverage purchases	yr	304	1999	30r
Beer, Heineken, 12-oz, ex deposit	6	6.49	12/00	5c
J & B Scotch	750-ml	19.22	12/00	5c
Malt beverages, all types, all sizes, any origin	16 oz	0.93	7/01	11r
Wine, Livingston or Gallo, Chablis blanc	1.5 liter	4.91	12/00	5c
Wine, red and white table, all sizes, any origin	liter	7.04	7/01	11r
Appliances				
Appliance repair, service call, washing machine	min lab chg	42.45	12/00	5c
Major appliances, expenditures on	yr	165	1999	30r
Small appliances, housewares, expenditures on	yr	90	1999	30r
Banking and Money				
Mortgage interest and charges paid	yr	2277	1999	30r
Mortgage principal paid on owned property	yr	1230	1999	30r
Mortgage rate, incl. points and orig. fee, 30-yr. conv. fixed or ARM	mos	8.13	12/00	5c
Vehicle finance charges paid	yr	328	1999	30r
Charity				
Cash contributions, expenditures	yr	1126	1999	30r
Child Care				
Child raising cost, total, age 0-2	yr	7890	1999	60r
Child raising cost, total, age 3-5	yr	8130	1999	60r
Child raising cost, total, age 6-8	yr	8170	1999	60r
Child raising cost, total, age 9-11	yr	8190	1999	60r
Child raising cost, total, age 12-14	yr	8890	1999	60r
Child raising cost, total, age 15-17	yr	9050	1999	60r
Child's child care and education, age 0-2	yr	1240	1999	60r
Child's child care and education, age 3-5	yr	1370	1999	60r

Values are in dollars or fractions of dollars. In the column headed *Ref*, references are shown to sources. Each reference is followed by a letter. These refer to the geographical level for which data were reported: s=State, r=Region, and c=City or metro. The abbreviation *ex* is used to mean *except* or *excluding*; *exp* stands for expenditures. For other abbreviations and further explanations, please see the Introduction.

Green Bay, WI - continued

Item	Per	Value	Date	Ref.
Child Care				
Child's child care and education, age 6-8	yr	880	1999	60r
Child's child care and education, age 9-11	yr	570	1999	60r
Child's child care and education, age 12-14	yr	420	1999	60r
Child's child care and education, age 15-17	yr	720	1999	60r
Child's clothing, age 0-2	yr	410	1999	60r
Child's clothing, age 3-5	yr	400	1999	60r
Child's clothing, age 6-8	yr	450	1999	60r
Child's clothing, age 9-11	yr	500	1999	60r
Child's clothing, age 12-14	yr	840	1999	60r
Child's clothing, age 15-17	yr	740	1999	60r
Child's food, age 0-2	yr	960	1999	60r
Child's food, age 3-5	yr	1120	1999	60r
Child's food, age 6-8	yr	1430	1999	60r
Child's food, age 9-11	yr	1710	1999	60r
Child's food, age 12-14	yr	1710	1999	60r
Child's food, age 15-17	yr	1920	1999	60r
Child's health care, age 0-2	yr	520	1999	60r
Child's health care, age 3-5	yr	500	1999	60r
Child's health care, age 6-8	yr	570	1999	60r
Child's health care, age 9-11	yr	610	1999	60r
Child's health care, age 12-14	yr	630	1999	60r
Child's health care, age 15-17	yr	650	1999	60r
Child's housing, age 0-2	yr	2860	1999	60r
Child's housing, age 3-5	yr	2840	1999	60r
Child's housing, age 6-8	yr	2800	1999	60r
Child's housing, age 9-11	yr	2650	1999	60r
Child's housing, age 12-14	yr	2840	1999	60r
Child's housing, age 15-17	yr	2440	1999	60r
Child's personal care, reading, age 0-2	yr	880	1999	60r
Child's personal care, reading, age 3-5	yr	900	1999	60r
Child's personal care, reading, age 6-8	yr	930	1999	60r
Child's personal care, reading, age 9-11	yr	970	1999	60r
Child's personal care, reading, age 12-14	yr	1150	1999	60r
Child's personal care, reading, age 15-17	yr	920	1999	60r
Clothing				
Apparel and services purchases	yr	1607	1999	30r
Boys' brief, cotton	3	3.24	12/00	5c
Boys, 2 to 15, expenditures on	yr	91	1999	30r
Children under 2, expenditures on	yr	59	1999	30r
Footwear, expenditures on	yr	285	1999	30r
Girls, 2 to 15, expenditures on	yr	116	1999	30r
Men and boys, expenditures on	yr	433	1999	30r
Men, 16 and over, expenditures on	yr	341	1999	30r
Shirt, man's dress shirt		34.29	12/00	5c
Slacks, man's "No Wrinkles" khaki		29.99	12/00	5c
Women, 16 and over, expenditures on	yr	490	1999	30r
Communications				
Cable modem installation, Bresnan		99.95	6/99	103s
Cable modem installation, Marcus		499.00	6/99	103s
Cable modem rate, cable subscriber, Bresnan	mos	39.95	6/99	103s
Cable modem rate, cable subscriber, Marcus	mos	14.95-49.95	6/99	103s
Cable modem rate, non-cable subscriber, Bresnan	mos	49.95	6/99	103s
Cable modem rate, non-cable subscriber, Marcus	mos	60.95	6/99	103s
Newspaper subscription, daily and Sunday delivery	mos	15.22	12/00	5c
Phone line, single, business, field visit	inst.	64.65	12/97	17s
Phone line, single, business, no field visit	inst.	64.65	12/97	17s
Phone line, single, residence, field visit	inst.	33.05	12/97	17s
Phone line, single, residence, no field visit	inst.	33.05	12/97	17s
Postage and stationery, expenditures on	yr	140	1999	30r
Postal rate, express mail, up to half-pound		12.45	7/01	108r
Postal rate, letter, first class, first ounce		0.34	7/01	108r
Postal rate, letter, two ounces		0.57	7/01	108r
Postal rate, post card		0.21	7/01	108r
Postal rate, priority mail, two pounds		3.95	7/01	108r
Postal rate, priority mail, up to one pound		3.50	7/01	108r
Telephone bill, business, basic rate	mos	20.85	12/97	18c

Green Bay, WI - continued

Item	Per	Value	Date	Ref.
Communications - continued				
Telephone bill, family of three	mos	18.38	12/00	5c
Telephone bill, residential, basic rate	mos	5.40	12/97	18c
Telephone services, expenditures on	yr	830	1999	30r
Education				
Board, 4-year private college/university	yr	2271	1996	38s
Board, 4-year public college/university	yr	1527	1996	38s
Education expenditures	yr	583	1999	30r
Room, 4-year private college/university	yr	1812	1996	38s
Room, 4-year public college/university	yr	1706	1996	38s
Total cost, 4-year private college/university	yr	15652	1996	38s
Total cost, 4-year public college/university	yr	5847	1996	38s
Tuition, 2-year public college/university, in state	yr	1840	1996	38s
Tuition, 4-year private college/university, in state	yr	11569	1996	38s
Tuition, 4-year public college/university	yr	2614	1996	38s
Energy and Fuels				
Electricity	500 KWhs	46.59	7/01	11r
Energy, combined forms, 2400 sq ft	mos	119.96	12/00	5c
Energy, exc. electricity, 2400 sq ft	mos	77.30	12/00	5c
Fuel oil #2	gal	1.27	7/01	11r
Fuel oil and other fuels, expenditures on	yr	68	1999	30r
Gas, cooking, winter, 10 therms	mos	9.13	2/96	98c
Gas, cooking, winter, 30 therms	mos	19.38	2/96	98c
Gas, cooking, winter, 50 therms	mos	29.64	2/96	98c
Gas, heating, winter, average use	mos	101.41	2/96	98c
Gas, natural, commercial rate	1000 cf	7.32	11/00	88s
Gas, regular unleaded, cash, self-service	gal	1.49	12/00	5c
Gasoline, unleaded midgrade	gal	1.79	7/01	11r
Gasoline, unleaded premium	gal	1.86	7/01	11r
Gasoline, unleaded regular	gal	1.58	7/01	11r
Natural gas, expenditures on	yr	389	1999	30r
Utility (piped) gas, therm		0.81	7/01	11r
Utility (piped) gas, 40 therms		38.01	7/01	11r
Utility (piped) gas, 100 therms		81.75	7/01	11r
Entertainment				
Bowling, Saturday evening rate	line	2.11	12/00	5c
Entertainment purchases	yr	1984	1999	30r
Fees and admissions paid	yr	444	1999	30r
Monopoly game, Parker Brothers', No. 9	game	10.62	12/00	5c
Movie, first-run, Saturday, evening	adm.	7.25	12/00	5c
Television, radios, sound equipment, expenditures on	yr	580	1999	30r
Tennis balls, yellow, Wilson or Penn, 3	can	2.05	12/00	5c
Funerals				
Cosmetology, hair, other preparation		178.32	1/99	78r
Embalming		408.19	1/99	78r
Funeral at funeral home		362.13	1/99	78r
Professional service charges		1375.51	1/99	78r
Transfer of remains to funeral home		155.92	1/99	78r
Visitation/viewing		294.38	1/99	78r
Groceries				
Groceries, ACCRA Index		89.10	12/00	5c
Antibiotic ointment, Polysporin	0.5 oz	4.23	12/00	5c
Baby food, strained vegetables or fruit, lowest price	4-4.5 oz	0.46	12/00	5c
Bacon, sliced	lb	3.15	7/01	11r
Bakery products, expenditures on	yr	281	1999	30r
Bananas	lb	0.48	7/01	11r
Bananas	lb	0.38	12/00	5c
Beans, dried, any type, all sizes	lb	0.61	7/01	11r
Beef for stew, boneless	lb	3.08	7/01	11r
Beef or hamburger, ground	lb	1.11	12/00	5c
Beef, expenditures on	yr	217	1999	30r
Bologna, all beef or mixed	lb	2.52	7/01	11r
Bread, white	loaf	0.70	12/00	5c
Bread, white, pan	lb	1.06	7/01	11r
Broccoli	lb	0.91	7/01	11r

Values are in dollars or fractions of dollars. In the column headed *Ref*, references are shown to sources. Each reference is followed by a letter. These refer to the geographical level for which data were reported: s=State, r=Region, and c=City or metro. The abbreviation *ex* is used to mean *except* or *excluding*; *exp* stands for *expenditures*. For other abbreviations and further explanations, please see the Introduction.

Green Bay, WI - continued

Item	Per	Value	Date	Ref.
Groceries				
Butter, salted, grade AA, stick	lb	3.04	7/01	11r
Butter, yoghurt, cheese, etc, expenditures on	yr	183	1999	30r
Cereals and bakery product purchases	yr	430	1999	30r
Cereals and cereal products, expenditures on	yr	149	1999	30r
Cheese, Kraft grated Parmesan	8 oz	3.58	12/00	5c
Chicken, fresh, whole	lb	1.07	7/01	11r
Chicken, whole fryer	lb	0.69	12/00	5c
Chops, boneless,	lb	3.64	7/01	11r
Chuck roast, U.S. choice, boneless	lb	2.47	7/01	11r
Cigarettes, Winston, Kings	carton	32.52	12/00	5c
Coffee, 100%, ground roast, all sizes	lb	2.69	7/01	11r
Coffee, vacuum-packed	13 oz	2.19	12/00	5c
Cookies, chocolate chip	lb	2.87	7/01	11r
Corn Flakes, Kellogg's or Post Toasties	18 oz	1.61	12/00	5c
Corn, frozen, whole kernel, lowest price	16 oz	0.97	12/00	5c
Dairy product purchases	yr	304	1999	30r
Eggs, expenditures on	yr	26	1999	30r
Eggs, Grade A or AA	dozen	0.78	12/00	5c
Eggs, grade A, large	dozen	0.88	7/01	11r
Fats and oils, expenditures on	yr	75	1999	30r
Fish and seafood, expenditures on	yr	72	1999	30r
Food (excl fruit and vegetables), eaten at home, purchases	yr	887	1999	30r
Food cooked on trips, expenditures on	yr	44	1999	30r
Food purchases	yr	4802	1999	30r
Food purchases, eaten away from home	yr	2069	1999	30r
Food purchases, food eaten at home	yr	2733	1999	30r
Fresh fruits, expenditures on	yr	138	1999	30r
Fresh milk and cream, expenditures on	yr	120	1999	30r
Fresh vegetables, expenditures on	yr	126	1999	30r
Grapefruit	lb	0.66	7/01	11r
Grapes, Thompson, seedless	lb	1.64	7/01	11r
Ground beef, 100% beef	lb	1.64	7/01	11r
Ground beef, lean and extra lean	lb	2.16	7/01	11r
Ground chuck, 100% beef	lb	2.13	7/01	11r
Ham, boneless, excl canned	lb	2.62	7/01	11r
Ice cream, prepackaged, bulk, regular	1/2 gal	3.35	7/01	11r
Lemons	lb	1.19	7/01	11r
Lettuce, iceberg	lb	0.73	7/01	11r
Lettuce, iceberg	head	0.97	12/00	5c
Margarine, Blue Bonnet or Parkay, stick	lb	0.77	12/00	5c
Margarine, soft, tubs	lb	0.89	7/01	11r
Meats, poultry, fish, and egg purchases	yr	671	1999	30r
Milk, fresh, whole, fortified	gal	2.71	7/01	11r
Milk, whole	1/2 gal	1.41	12/00	5c
Nonalcoholic beverages, expenditures on	yr	239	1999	30r
Orange juice, Minute Maid frozen	12 oz	1.28	12/00	5c
Oranges, Navel	lb	0.80	7/01	11r
Oranges, Valencia	lb	0.66	7/01	11r
Peaches, halves or slices, Hunt's, Del Monte, or Libby's	29 oz	1.51	12/00	5c
Pears, Anjou	lb	0.93	7/01	11r
Peas, green, Del Monte or Green Giant	15 oz	0.55	12/00	5c
Pork chops, center cut, bone-in	lb	3.63	7/01	11r
Pork, expenditures on	yr	150	1999	30r
Potato chips	16 oz	3.52	7/01	11r
Potatoes, frozen, french fried	lb	1.08	7/01	11r
Potatoes, white or red	10 lb	2.44	12/00	5c
Potatoes, white, all types	lb	0.33	7/01	11r
Poultry, expenditures on	yr	108	1999	30r
Processed fruits, expenditures on	yr	98	1999	30r
Processed vegetables, expenditures on	yr	80	1999	30r
Round roast, U.S. choice, boneless	lb	3.07	7/01	11r
Round steak, graded and ungraded, excl U.S. prime and choice	lb	3.41	7/01	11r
Sausage, Jimmy Dean/Owens pork	lb	3.49	12/00	5c
Shortening, vegetable oil blends	lb	1.13	7/01	11r
Shortening, vegetable, Crisco	3 lb	2.77	12/00	5c
Soft drink, Coca Cola, ex deposit	2 liter	1.09	12/00	5c
Spaghetti and macaroni	lb	0.80	7/01	11r
Steak, round, U.S. choice, boneless	lb	3.23	7/01	11r

Green Bay, WI - continued

Item	Per	Value	Date	Ref.
Groceries - continued				
Steak, T-bone	lb	5.55	12/00	5c
Steak, T-bone, U.S. choice, bone-in	lb	6.68	7/01	11r
Strawberries, dry pint	12 oz	1.32	7/01	11r
Sugar and other sweets, expenditures on	yr	114	1999	30r
Sugar, cane or beet	4 lbs	1.46	12/00	5c
Sugar, white, 33-80 ounce package	lb	0.42	7/01	11r
Sugar, white, all sizes	lb	0.43	7/01	11r
Tobacco products and smoking supplies purchases	yr	331	1999	30r
Tomatoes, field grown	lb	1.46	7/01	11r
Tomatoes, Hunt's or Del Monte	14.5 oz	0.81	12/00	5c
Tuna, chunk, light	6 oz	0.54	12/00	5c
Tuna, light, chunk	lb	1.80	7/01	11r
Turkey, frozen, whole	lb	1.15	7/01	11r
Goods and Services				
Miscellaneous goods and services, ACCRA Index		96.80	12/00	5c
B&B Japanese maple (acer japonicum)	gal	29.99-169.99	4/00	93r
Boxwood (buxus)	2 gal	18.99-39.99	4/00	93r
Daylilly (hemerocallis)	gal	4.99-25.00	4/00	93r
Flat of annuals		11.98-24.99	4/00	93r
Fountain grass (pennisetum)	gal	5.98-12.98	4/00	93r
Hanging basket (10 in)		12.99-27.99	4/00	93r
Hardy geranium (geranium)	gal	7.99-9.99	4/00	93r
Hosta (hosta)	gal	6.00-25.00	4/00	93r
Lilac (syrubga vulgaris)	2 gal	14.99-24.99	4/00	93r
Miscellaneous purchases	yr	865	1999	30r
Rhododendron (rhododendron)	2 gal	23.98-42.99	4/00	93r
Sage (salvia)	gal	6.00-9.99	4/00	93r
Wintercreeper euonymus (euonymus fortunei)	2 gal	16.00-169.99	4/00	93r
Hunting license	yr	14.00	4/01	34s
Health Care				
Health care, ACCRA Index		105.50	12/00	5c
Cardiac catheterization, ave hospital/ physician charges		13240	1998	77s
Childbirth, Cesarean delivery		10722	1997	13r
Childbirth, vaginal delivery		6223	1997	13r
Dentist's fee, adult teeth cleaning and periodic oral exam	visit	75.60	12/00	5c
Doctor's fee, routine exam, established patient	visit	67.95	12/00	5c
Drugs, expenditures on	yr	394	1999	30r
Health care purchases	yr	2048	1999	30r
Health insurance expenditures	yr	978	1999	30r
Hospital care, private room	day	424.67	12/00	5c
Hysterectomy, laproscopically-assisted, ave hospital/physician charges		13270	1998	76s
Hysterectomy, vaginal, ave hospital and physician charges		9170	1998	76s
Laser eye surgery	eye	1950-2400	2000	63s
Medicaid dispensing fee		4.88-40.11	1999	87s
Medical services expenditures	yr	554	1999	30r
Medical supplies, expenditures on	yr	122	1999	30r
Plastic surgery, breast augmentation		3184	2000	7r
Plastic surgery, breast lift		3585	2000	7r
Plastic surgery, facelift		4999	2000	7r
Plastic surgery, hair transplantation		3105	2000	7r

Values are in dollars or fractions of dollars. In the column headed *Ref*, references are shown to sources. Each reference is followed by a letter. These refer to the geographical level for which data were reported: s=State, r=Region, and c=City or metro. The abbreviation *ex* is used to mean *except* or *excluding*; *exp* stands for *expenditures*. For other abbreviations and further explanations, please see the Introduction.

Green Bay, WI - continued

Item	Per	Value	Date	Ref.
Health Care				
Plastic surgery, lip augmentation		1290	2000	7r
Plastic surgery, lower body lift		8135	2000	7r
Plastic surgery, thigh lift		3839	2000	7r
Household Goods				
Dishwashing powder, Cascade	50 oz	3.08	12/00	5c
Floor coverings, expenditures on	yr	52	1999	30r
Furniture, expenditures on	yr	344	1999	30r
Household furnishings and equipment purchases	yr	1475	1999	30r
Household textiles, expenditures on	yr	109	1999	30r
Laundry and cleaning supplies, expenditures on	yr	134	1999	30r
Tissues, facial, Kleenex brand	175	1.25	12/00	5c
Housing				
Housing, ACCRA Index		97.70	12/00	5c
Home, 2200 sq ft, 4-br, 2-bath, 2-car garage, average		175562	2000	47c
Home price, existing, ave		144400	10/00	90r
Home value, median		117000	2001	53s
House, 2400 sq ft, 8000 sq ft lot, new, urban, utilities	total	204850	12/00	5c
House payment, principal and interest, 25% down payment	mos	1141	12/00	5c
Household operation expenditures	yr	542	1999	30r
Housekeeping supplies purchases	yr	508	1999	30r
Lodging expenditures	yr	430	1999	30r
Maintenance, repairs, insurance expenditures	yr	853	1999	30r
Monthly rental value of owned home	mos	547	1999	30r
Owned dwellings, expenditures own	yr	4282	1999	30r
Rent expenditures	yr	1558	1999	30r
Rent, apartment, 2 br, 1 1/2-2 baths, unfurn, 950 sq ft, water	mos	575	12/00	5c
Rental unit, 1 bedroom, with utilities	mos	424	4/01	41c
Rental unit, 2 bedroom, with utilities	mos	544	4/01	41c
Rental unit, 3 bedroom, with utilities	mos	756	4/01	41c
Rental unit, 4 bedroom, with utilities	mos	760	4/01	41c
Shelter, expenditures on	yr	6270	1999	30r
Insurance and Pensions				
Auto insurance premium	yr	603.84	1999	57s
Life and other personal insurance purchases	yr	387	1999	30r
Pensions and Social Security, expenditures on	yr	2968	1999	30r
Legal Fees				
Divorce, filing fee		142.00-150.00	4/01	35s
Driver's license fee	renew	12.00	1999	48s
Driver's license fee	orig	18.00	1999	48s
Fishing license	yr	14.00	4/01	34s
Personal Goods				
Personal care products and services purchases	yr	385	1999	30r
Shampoo, Alberto VO5	15 oz	0.94	12/00	5c
Toothpaste, Crest or Colgate	6-7 oz	1.98	12/00	5c
Personal Services				
Dry cleaning, man's 2-pc suit		8.63	12/00	5c
Man's haircut, barbershop, no styling		7.80	12/00	5c
Personal services, household, expenditures on	yr	300	1999	30r
Woman's shampoo, trim, blow-dry, no style-change		19.79	12/00	5c
Pets				
Pets, toys, and playground equipment, expenditures on	yr	375	1999	30r
Restaurant Food				
Chicken, fried, thigh and drumstick, KFC/Church's		2.89	12/00	5c
Hamburger with cheese, McDonald's	1/4 lb	1.91	12/00	5c

Green Bay, WI - continued

Item	Per	Value	Date	Ref.
Restaurant Food - continued				
Pizza, Pizza Hut or Pizza Inn	11-12 in	8.99	12/00	5c
Taxes				
Federal income taxes paid	yr	2326	1999	30r
Personal taxes, expenditures on	yr	3223	1999	30r
Property taxes paid	yr	1152	1999	30r
State and local income taxes paid	yr	753	1999	30r
Transportation				
Transportation, ACCRA Index		98.50	12/00	5c
Bus fare, to central business district	1-way	1.00	12/00	5c
Cars and trucks, new, expenditures on	yr	1280	1999	30r
Cars and trucks, used, expenditures on	yr	1763	1999	30r
Diesel at the pump	gal	1.34	10/99	73s
Gasoline and motor oil purchases	yr	1036	1999	30r
Gasoline before-tax price (cents)	gal	113.40	10/00	43s
Maintenance and repair expenditures	yr	594	1999	30r
Public transportation, expenditures on	yr	341	1999	30r
Tire balance, computer or spin balance, front	wheel	7.69	12/00	5c
Transportation purchases	yr	6617	1999	30r
Vehicle expenses, miscellaneous, purchases	yr	2159	1999	30r
Vehicle insurance payments	yr	701	1999	30r
Vehicle purchases (net outlay)	yr	3081	1999	30r
Vehicle rental, lease expenditures	yr	536	1999	30r
Utilities				
Utilities, ACCRA Index		103.90	12/00	5c
Electrical bill, average	mos	52.08	9/00	9s
Electricity, expenditures on	yr	841	1999	30r
Electricity, summer, 250 KWh	mos	18.58	2/96	96c
Electricity, summer, 500 KWh	mos	33.57	2/96	96c
Electricity, summer, 750 KWh	mos	48.55	2/96	96c
Electricity, summer, 1000 KWh	mos	63.53	2/96	96c
Electricity and other, mixed, 2400 sq ft, new home	mos	42.66	12/00	5c
Electricity cost, average	KWh	5.69	9/00	9s
Utilities, fuels, and public services purchased	yr	2401	1999	30r
Water and other public services, expenditures on	yr	273	1999	30r
Weddings				
Wedding (national average cost)		19936	2000	33r
Wedding (regional average total cost)		16195	1997	110r
Attendants' gifts		321	1998	33r
Bridal attendants' apparel (5 persons)		824	2000	33r
Bride's headpiece/veil		173	1998	33r
Bride's wedding dress		859	1998	33r
Clergy, religious facility fee		242	1998	33r
Engagement ring		3177	1998	33r
Flowers		789	1998	33r
Groom's formalwear rental		99	2000	33r
Limousine		410	1998	33r
Marriage license cost		50.00-60.00	4/01	35s
Men's formalwear (ushers, best man)		469	2000	33r
Mother of bride apparel		241	2000	33r
Music		866	1998	33r
Photography and videography		1368	1998	33r
Rehearsal dinner		728	1998	33r
Wedding invitations and announcements		341	1998	33r
Wedding reception		7968	2000	33r
Wedding rings (bride and groom)		1060	1998	33r

Greensboro-Winston-Salem-High Point, NC

Item	Per	Value	Date	Ref.
Alcoholic Beverages				
Alcoholic beverage purchases	yr	253	1999	30r
Malt beverages, all types, all sizes, any origin	16 oz	0.96	7/01	11r
Appliances				
Major appliances, expenditures on	yr	172	1999	30r
Small appliances, housewares, expenditures on	yr	81	1999	30r

Values are in dollars or fractions of dollars. In the column headed *Ref*, references are shown to sources. Each reference is followed by a letter. These refer to the geographical level for which data were reported: s=State, r=Region, and c=City or metro. The abbreviation *ex* is used to mean *except* or *excluding*; *exp* stands for *expenditures*. For other abbreviations and further explanations, please see the Introduction.

Greensboro-Winston-Salem-High Point, NC - continued

Item	Per	Value	Date	Ref.
Banking and Money				
Mortgage interest and charges paid	yr	2039	1999	30r
Mortgage principal paid on owned property	yr	1026	1999	30r
Vehicle finance charges paid	yr	365	1999	30r
Charity				
Cash contributions, expenditures	yr	1127	1999	30r
Child Care				
Child raising cost, total, age 0-2	yr	8540	1999	60r
Child raising cost, total, age 3-5	yr	8780	1999	60r
Child raising cost, total, age 6-8	yr	8820	1999	60r
Child raising cost, total, age 9-11	yr	8800	1999	60r
Child raising cost, total, age 12-14	yr	9510	1999	60r
Child raising cost, total, age 15-17	yr	9740	1999	60r
Child's child care and education, age 0-2	yr	1380	1999	60r
Child's child care and education, age 3-5	yr	1520	1999	60r
Child's child care and education, age 6-8	yr	990	1999	60r
Child's child care and education, age 9-11	yr	650	1999	60r
Child's child care and education, age 12-14	yr	490	1999	60r
Child's child care and education, age 15-17	yr	840	1999	60r
Child's clothing, age 0-2	yr	480	1999	60r
Child's clothing, age 3-5	yr	470	1999	60r
Child's clothing, age 6-8	yr	520	1999	60r
Child's clothing, age 9-11	yr	570	1999	60r
Child's clothing, age 12-14	yr	950	1999	60r
Child's clothing, age 15-17	yr	850	1999	60r
Child's food, age 0-2	yr	1000	1999	60r
Child's food, age 3-5	yr	1160	1999	60r
Child's food, age 6-8	yr	1490	1999	60r
Child's food, age 9-11	yr	1770	1999	60r
Child's food, age 12-14	yr	1770	1999	60r
Child's food, age 15-17	yr	1980	1999	60r
Child's health care, age 0-2	yr	620	1999	60r
Child's health care, age 3-5	yr	590	1999	60r
Child's health care, age 6-8	yr	680	1999	60r
Child's health care, age 9-11	yr	720	1999	60r
Child's health care, age 12-14	yr	730	1999	60r
Child's health care, age 15-17	yr	760	1999	60r
Child's housing, age 0-2	yr	3070	1999	60r
Child's housing, age 3-5	yr	3050	1999	60r
Child's housing, age 6-8	yr	3010	1999	60r
Child's housing, age 9-11	yr	2850	1999	60r
Child's housing, age 12-14	yr	3040	1999	60r
Child's housing, age 15-17	yr	2650	1999	60r
Child's personal care, reading, age 0-2	yr	910	1999	60r
Child's personal care, reading, age 3-5	yr	930	1999	60r
Child's personal care, reading, age 6-8	yr	960	1999	60r
Child's personal care, reading, age 9-11	yr	1000	1999	60r
Child's personal care, reading, age 12-14	yr	1170	1999	60r
Child's personal care, reading, age 15-17	yr	950	1999	60r
Clothing				
Apparel and services purchases	yr	1610	1999	30r
Boys, 2 to 15, expenditures on	yr	89	1999	30r
Children under 2, expenditures on	yr	79	1999	30r
Footwear, expenditures on	yr	283	1999	30r
Girls, 2 to 15, expenditures on	yr	103	1999	30r
Men and boys, expenditures on	yr	351	1999	30r
Men, 16 and over, expenditures on	yr	262	1999	30r
Women, 16 and over, expenditures on	yr	538	1999	30r
Communications				
Cable modem installation, Intermedia		149.95	6/99	103s
Cable modem installation, Time Warner		75.00-225.00	6/99	103s
Cable modem rate, cable subscriber, Intermedia	mos	49.95	6/99	103s
Cable modem rate, cable subscriber, Time Warner	mos	39.95-49.95	6/99	103s
Cable modem rate, non-cable subscriber, Intermedia	mos	54.95	6/99	103s
Cable modem rate, non-cable subscriber, Time Warner	mos	39.95-54.95	6/99	103s
Phone line, single, business, field visit	inst.	65.00	12/97	17s

Greensboro-Winston-Salem-High Point, NC - continued

Item	Per	Value	Date	Ref.
Communications - continued				
Phone line, single, business, no field visit	inst.	65.00	12/97	17s
Phone line, single, residence, field visit	inst.	42.75	12/97	17s
Phone line, single, residence, no field visit	inst.	42.75	12/97	17s
Postage and stationery, expenditures on	yr	104	1999	30r
Postal rate, express mail, up to half-pound		12.45	7/01	108r
Postal rate, letter, first class, first ounce		0.34	7/01	108r
Postal rate, letter, two ounces		0.57	7/01	108r
Postal rate, post card		0.21	7/01	108r
Postal rate, priority mail, two pounds		3.95	7/01	108r
Postal rate, priority mail, up to one pound		3.50	7/01	108r
Telephone services, expenditures on	yr	860	1999	30r
Education				
Board, 4-year private college/university	yr	2316	1996	38s
Board, 4-year public college/university	yr	1737	1996	38s
Education expenditures	yr	431	1999	30r
Room, 4-year private college/university	yr	2128	1996	38s
Room, 4-year public college/university	yr	1742	1996	38s
Total cost, 4-year private college/university	yr	15428	1996	38s
Total cost, 4-year public college/university	yr	5119	1996	38s
Tuition, 4-year private college/university, in state	yr	10984	1996	38s
Tuition, 4-year public college/university	yr	1639	1996	38s
Energy and Fuels				
Electricity	KWh	0.09	7/01	11r
Electricity	500 KWhs	47.29	7/01	11r
Fuel oil #2	gal	1.43	7/01	11r
Fuel oil and other fuels, expenditures on	yr	45	1999	30r
Gas, natural, commercial rate	1000 cf	9.25	11/00	88s
Gasoline, all types	gal	1.60	7/01	11r
Gasoline, unleaded midgrade	gal	1.65	7/01	11r
Gasoline, unleaded premium	gal	1.74	7/01	11r
Natural gas, expenditures on	yr	164	1999	30r
Utility (piped) gas, therm		1.01	7/01	11r
Utility (piped) gas, 40 therms		44.29	7/01	11r
Utility (piped) gas, 100 therms		97.44	7/01	11r
Entertainment				
Entertainment purchases	yr	1574	1999	30r
Fees and admissions paid	yr	371	1999	30r
Reading purchases	yr	121	1999	30r
Television, radios, sound equipment, expenditures on	yr	561	1999	30r
Funerals				
Total cost of funeral		5922.53	1/99	78r
Acknowledgement cards		63.43	1/99	78r
Casket		2258.77	1/99	78r
Cosmetology, hair, other preparation		127.09	1/99	78r
Embalming		393.49	1/99	78r
Funeral at funeral home		367.50	1/99	78r
Hearse (local)		169.66	1/99	78r
Professional service charges		1211.32	1/99	78r
Service car/van		80.69	1/99	78r
Transfer of remains to funeral home		144.25	1/99	78r
Vault		803.50	1/99	78r
Visitation/viewing		302.83	1/99	78r
Groceries				
American processed cheese	lb	3.50	7/01	11r
Bakery products, expenditures on	yr	261	1999	30r
Bananas	lb	0.47	7/01	11r
Beans, dried, any type, all sizes	lb	0.63	7/01	11r
Beef for stew, boneless	lb	2.86	7/01	11r
Beef, expenditures on	yr	210	1999	30r
Bologna, all beef or mixed	lb	2.29	7/01	11r
Bread, French	lb	1.66	7/01	11r
Bread, white, pan	lb	0.87	7/01	11r
Bread, whole wheat, pan	lb	1.38	7/01	11r
Broccoli	lb	1.04	7/01	11r
Butter, salted, grade AA, stick	lb	2.26	7/01	11r
Butter, yoghurt, cheese, etc, expenditures on	yr	170	1999	30r

Values are in dollars or fractions of dollars. In the column headed *Ref*, references are shown to sources. Each reference is followed by a letter. These refer to the geographical level for which data were reported: s=State, r=Region, and c=City or metro. The abbreviation *ex* is used to mean *except* or *excluding*; *exp* stands for expenditures. For other abbreviations and further explanations, please see the Introduction.

Greensboro-Winston-Salem-High Point, NC - continued

Item	Per	Value	Date	Ref.
Groceries				
Cabbage	lb	0.42	7/01	11r
Cereals and cereal products, expenditures on	yr	140	1999	30r
Cheddar cheese, natural	lb	3.75	7/01	11r
Chicken breast, bone-in	lb	1.85	7/01	11r
Chicken legs, bone-in	lb	1.34	7/01	11r
Chicken, fresh, whole	lb	1.05	7/01	11r
Chops, boneless,	lb	4.13	7/01	11r
Chuck roast, graded and ungraded, excl U.S. prime and choice	lb	2.35	7/01	11r
Chuck roast, U.S. choice, boneless	lb	2.67	7/01	11r
Coffee, 100%, ground roast, all sizes	lb	2.88	7/01	11r
Coffee, instant, plain, regular, all sizes	16 oz	9.25	7/01	11r
Cola, non diet,	2 liter	1.11	7/01	11r
Crackers, soda, salted	lb	1.70	7/01	11r
Dairy product purchases	yr	282	1999	30r
Eggs, expenditures on	yr	32	1999	30r
Fats and oils, expenditures on	yr	79	1999	30r
Fish and seafood, expenditures on	yr	99	1999	30r
Flour, white, all purpose	lb	0.32	7/01	11r
Food (excl fruit and vegetables), eaten at home, purchases	yr	815	1999	30r
Food cooked on trips, expenditures on	yr	36	1999	30r
Food purchases	yr	4533	1999	30r
Food purchases, eaten away from home	yr	1873	1999	30r
Food purchases, food eaten at home	yr	2660	1999	30r
Fresh fruits, expenditures on	yr	128	1999	30r
Fresh milk and cream, expenditures on	yr	112	1999	30r
Fresh vegetables, expenditures on	yr	131	1999	30r
Fruit and vegetable purchases	yr	438	1999	30r
Grapefruit	lb	0.59	7/01	11r
Grapes, Thompson, seedless	lb	2.12	7/01	11r
Ground beef, 100% beef	lb	1.76	7/01	11r
Ground beef, lean and extra lean	lb	2.60	7/01	11r
Ground chuck, 100% beef	lb	2.08	7/01	11r
Ham, boneless, excl canned	lb	2.71	7/01	11r
Ham, rump or shank half, bone-in, smoked	lb	2.19	7/01	11r
Ice cream, prepackaged, bulk, regular	1/2 gal	3.93	7/01	11r
Lemons	lb	1.32	7/01	11r
Lettuce, iceberg	lb	0.76	7/01	11r
Milk, fresh, low fat,	gal	2.75	7/01	11r
Milk, fresh, whole, fortified	gal	2.97	7/01	11r
Nonalcoholic beverages, expenditures on	yr	228	1999	30r
Orange juice, frozen concentrate	16 oz	1.95	7/01	11r
Oranges, Navel	lb	0.73	7/01	11r
Oranges, Valencia	lb	0.55	7/01	11r
Peanut butter, creamy, all sizes	lb	1.83	7/01	11r
Pears, Anjou	lb	0.98	7/01	11r
Pork chops, center cut, bone-in	lb	3.33	7/01	11r
Pork sausage, fresh, loose	lb	2.59	7/01	11r
Pork shoulder picnic, bone-in, smoked	lb	1.12	7/01	11r
Pork, expenditures on	yr	162	1999	30r
Potato chips	16 oz	3.59	7/01	11r
Potatoes, frozen, french fried	lb	1.00	7/01	11r
Potatoes, white, all types	lb	0.44	7/01	11r
Poultry, expenditures on	yr	137	1999	30r
Processed fruits, expenditures on	yr	97	1999	30r
Processed vegetables, expenditures on	yr	82	1999	30r
Rice, white, long grain, uncooked	lb	0.51	7/01	11r
Round roast, graded and ungraded, excl U.S. prime and choice	lb	2.96	7/01	11r
Round steak, graded and ungraded, excl U.S. prime and choice	lb	3.11	7/01	11r
Sirloin steak, graded and ungraded, excl U.S. prime and choice	lb	4.23	7/01	11r
Spaghetti and macaroni	lb	0.78	7/01	11r
Steak, round, U.S. choice, boneless	lb	3.56	7/01	11r
Steak, sirloin, U.S. choice, boneless	lb	5.65	7/01	11r
Strawberries, dry pint	12 oz	1.50	7/01	11r
Sugar and other sweets, expenditures on	yr	99	1999	30r
Sugar, white, 33-80 ounce package	lb	0.39	7/01	11r
Sugar, white, all sizes	lb	0.42	7/01	11r

Greensboro-Winston-Salem-High Point, NC - continued

Item	Per	Value	Date	Ref.
Groceries - continued				
Tobacco products and smoking supplies purchases	yr	288	1999	30r
Tomatoes, field grown	lb	1.43	7/01	11r
Tuna, light, chunk	lb	1.77	7/01	11r
Turkey, frozen, whole	lb	1.05	7/01	11r
Goods and Services				
B&B Japanese maple (acer japonicum)	gal	49.98-129.00	4/00	93r
Boxwood (buxus)	2 gal	12.99-16.99	4/00	93r
Daylily (hemerocallis)	gal	4.99-8.99	4/00	93r
Flat of annuals		11.00-13.92	4/00	93r
Fountain grass (pennisetum)	gal	5.98-7.98	4/00	93r
Hanging basket (10 in)		7.99-14.98	4/00	93r
Hardy geranium (geranium)	gal	5.98-8.00	4/00	93r
Hosta (hosta)	gal	4.99-10.98	4/00	93r
Lilac (syrubga vulgaris)	2 gal	12.99-21.99	4/00	93r
Rhododendron (rhododendron)	2 gal	14.99-24.99	4/00	93r
Sage (salvia)	gal	5.98-6.99	4/00	93r
Wintercreeper euonymus (euonymus fortunei)	2 gal	7.99-89.99	4/00	93r
Hunting license	yr	15.00	4/01	34s
Health Care				
Cardiac catheterization, ave hospital/ physician charges		12500	1998	77s
Childbirth, Cesarean delivery		11587	1997	13r
Childbirth, vaginal delivery		6725	1997	13r
Drugs, expenditures on	yr	399	1999	30r
Health care purchases	yr	1971	1999	30r
Health insurance expenditures	yr	933	1999	30r
Hysterectomy, laproscopically-assisted, ave hospital/physician charges		12260	1998	76s
Hysterectomy, vaginal, ave hospital and physician charges		8440	1998	76s
Medicaid dispensing fee		5.60	1999	87s
Medical services expenditures	yr	547	1999	30r
Medical supplies, expenditures on	yr	91	1999	30r
Plastic surgery, breast augmentation		2870	2000	7r
Plastic surgery, breast lift		3649	2000	7r
Plastic surgery, facelift		5008	2000	7r
Plastic surgery, hair transplantation		3425	2000	7r
Plastic surgery, lip augmentation		1227	2000	7r
Plastic surgery, lower body lift		4793	2000	7r
Plastic surgery, thigh lift		3862	2000	7r
Household Goods				
Floor coverings, expenditures on	yr	44	1999	30r
Furniture, expenditures on	yr	335	1999	30r
Household furnishings and equipment purchases	yr	1328	1999	30r
Household textiles, expenditures on	yr	89	1999	30r
Laundry and cleaning supplies, expenditures on	yr	113	1999	30r
Housing				
Home price, existing, ave		160100	10/00	90r
Home value, median		146000	2001	53s
Household operation expenditures	yr	553	1999	30r
Housekeeping supplies purchases	yr	473	1999	30r
Housing, expenditures on	yr	10303	1999	30r
Maintenance, repairs, insurance expenditures	yr	699	1999	30r
Monthly rental value of owned home	mos	505	1999	30r

Values are in dollars or fractions of dollars. In the column headed *Ref*, references are shown to sources. Each reference is followed by a letter. These refer to the geographical level for which data were reported: s=State, r=Region, and c=City or metro. The abbreviation *ex* is used to mean *except* or *excluding*; *exp* stands for *expenditures*. For other abbreviations and further explanations, please see the Introduction.

Greensboro-Winston-Salem-High Point, NC - continued

Item	Per	Value	Date	Ref.
Housing				
Owned dwellings, expenditures own	yr	3465	1999	30r
Rent expenditures	yr	1641	1999	30r
Rental unit, 1 bedroom, with utilities	mos	472	4/01	41c
Rental unit, 2 bedroom, with utilities	mos	562	4/01	41c
Rental unit, 3 bedroom, with utilities	mos	775	4/01	41c
Rental unit, 4 bedroom, with utilities	mos	788	4/01	41c
Shelter, expenditures on	yr	5467	1999	30r
Insurance and Pensions				
Life and other personal insurance purchases	yr	414	1999	30r
Pensions and Social Security, expenditures on	yr	2635	1999	30r
Personal insurance and pensions, expenditures on	yr	3048	1999	30r
Legal Fees				
Combination hunting and fishing license	yr	20.00	4/01	34s
Divorce, filing fee		80.00	4/01	35s
Driver's license fee	renew	10.00	1999	48s
Driver's license fee	orig	10.00	1999	48s
Fishing license	yr	15.00	4/01	34s
Personal Goods				
Personal care products and services purchases	yr	393	1999	30r
Personal Services				
Personal services, household, expenditures on	yr	258	1999	30r
Pets				
Pets, toys, and playground equipment, expenditures on	yr	306	1999	30r
Taxes				
Federal income taxes paid	yr	2047	1999	30r
Personal taxes, expenditures on	yr	2554	1999	30r
Property taxes paid	yr	726	1999	30r
State and local income taxes paid	yr	363	1999	30r
Transportation				
Cars and trucks, new, expenditures on	yr	1648	1999	30r
Cars and trucks, used, expenditures on	yr	1651	1999	30r
Diesel at the pump	gal	1.19	10/99	73s
Gasoline and motor oil purchases	yr	1052	1999	30r
Gasoline before-tax price (cents)	gal	103.20	10/00	43s
Maintenance and repair expenditures	yr	621	1999	30r
Motorcycle license fee	orig	1.50	1999	49s
Motorcycle license fee	renew	1.50	1999	49s
Public transportation, expenditures on	yr	298	1999	30r
Transportation purchases	yr	6738	1999	30r
Vehicle expenses, miscellaneous, purchases	yr	2033	1999	30r
Vehicle insurance payments	yr	696	1999	30r
Vehicle purchases (net outlay)	yr	3354	1999	30r
Vehicle rental, lease expenditures	yr	352	1999	30r
Utilities				
Electrical bill, average	mos	83.66	9/00	9s
Electricity, expenditures on	yr	1115	1999	30r
Electricity cost, average	KWh	6.40	9/00	9s
Water and other public services, expenditures on	yr	298	1999	30r
Weddings				
Wedding (national average cost)		19936	2000	33r
Wedding (regional average total cost)		16293	1997	110r
Attendants' gifts		321	1998	33r
Bridal attendants' apparel (5 persons)		824	2000	33r
Bride's headpiece/veil		173	1998	33r
Bride's wedding dress		859	1998	33r
Clergy, religious facility fee		242	1998	33r
Engagement ring		3177	1998	33r
Flowers		789	1998	33r
Groom's formalwear rental		99	2000	33r
Limousine		410	1998	33r
Marriage license cost		40.00	4/01	35s

Greensboro-Winston-Salem-High Point, NC - continued

Item	Per	Value	Date	Ref.
Weddings - continued				
Men's formalwear (ushers, best man)		469	2000	33r
Mother of bride apparel		241	2000	33r
Music		866	1998	33r
Photography and videography		1368	1998	33r
Rehearsal dinner		728	1998	33r
Wedding invitations and announcements		341	1998	33r
Wedding reception		7968	2000	33r
Wedding rings (bride and groom)		1060	1998	33r

Greenville, NC

Item	Per	Value	Date	Ref.
Composite, ACCRA index		100.00	12/00	5c
Alcoholic Beverages				
Alcoholic beverage purchases	yr	253	1999	30r
Beer, Heineken, 12-oz, ex deposit	6	7.02	12/00	5c
J & B Scotch	750-ml	20.75	12/00	5c
Malt beverages, all types, all sizes, any origin	16 oz	0.96	7/01	11r
Wine, Livingston or Gallo, Chablis blanc	1.5 liter	5.81	12/00	5c
Appliances				
Appliance repair, service call, washing machine	min lab chg	47.25	12/00	5c
Major appliances, expenditures on	yr	172	1999	30r
Small appliances, housewares, expenditures on	yr	81	1999	30r
Banking and Money				
Mortgage interest and charges paid	yr	2039	1999	30r
Mortgage principal paid on owned property	yr	1026	1999	30r
Mortgage rate, incl. points and orig. fee, 30-yr. conv. fixed or ARM	mos	7.98	12/00	5c
Vehicle finance charges paid	yr	365	1999	30r
Charity				
Cash contributions, expenditures	yr	1127	1999	30r
Child Care				
Child raising cost, total, age 0-2	yr	8540	1999	60r
Child raising cost, total, age 3-5	yr	8780	1999	60r
Child raising cost, total, age 6-8	yr	8820	1999	60r
Child raising cost, total, age 9-11	yr	8800	1999	60r
Child raising cost, total, age 12-14	yr	9510	1999	60r
Child raising cost, total, age 15-17	yr	9740	1999	60r
Child's child care and education, age 0-2	yr	1380	1999	60r
Child's child care and education, age 3-5	yr	1520	1999	60r
Child's child care and education, age 6-8	yr	990	1999	60r
Child's child care and education, age 9-11	yr	650	1999	60r
Child's child care and education, age 12-14	yr	490	1999	60r
Child's child care and education, age 15-17	yr	840	1999	60r
Child's clothing, age 0-2	yr	480	1999	60r
Child's clothing, age 3-5	yr	470	1999	60r
Child's clothing, age 6-8	yr	520	1999	60r
Child's clothing, age 9-11	yr	570	1999	60r
Child's clothing, age 12-14	yr	950	1999	60r
Child's clothing, age 15-17	yr	850	1999	60r
Child's food, age 0-2	yr	1000	1999	60r
Child's food, age 3-5	yr	1160	1999	60r
Child's food, age 6-8	yr	1490	1999	60r
Child's food, age 9-11	yr	1770	1999	60r
Child's food, age 12-14	yr	1770	1999	60r
Child's food, age 15-17	yr	1980	1999	60r
Child's health care, age 0-2	yr	620	1999	60r
Child's health care, age 3-5	yr	590	1999	60r
Child's health care, age 6-8	yr	680	1999	60r
Child's health care, age 9-11	yr	720	1999	60r
Child's health care, age 12-14	yr	730	1999	60r
Child's health care, age 15-17	yr	760	1999	60r
Child's housing, age 0-2	yr	3070	1999	60r
Child's housing, age 3-5	yr	3050	1999	60r
Child's housing, age 6-8	yr	3010	1999	60r
Child's housing, age 9-11	yr	2850	1999	60r
Child's housing, age 12-14	yr	3040	1999	60r
Child's housing, age 15-17	yr	2650	1999	60r

Values are in dollars or fractions of dollars. In the column headed *Ref*, references are shown to sources. Each reference is followed by a letter. These refer to the geographical level for which data were reported: s=State, r=Region, and c=City or metro. The abbreviation *ex* is used to mean *except* or *excluding*; *exp* stands for expenditures. For other abbreviations and further explanations, please see the Introduction.

Greenville, NC - continued

Item	Per	Value	Date	Ref.
Child Care				
Child's personal care, reading, age 0-2	yr	910	1999	60r
Child's personal care, reading, age 3-5	yr	930	1999	60r
Child's personal care, reading, age 6-8	yr	960	1999	60r
Child's personal care, reading, age 9-11	yr	1000	1999	60r
Child's personal care, reading, age 12-14	yr	1170	1999	60r
Child's personal care, reading, age 15-17	yr	950	1999	60r
Clothing				
Apparel and services purchases	yr	1610	1999	30r
Boys' brief, cotton	3	3.28	12/00	5c
Boys, 2 to 15, expenditures on	yr	89	1999	30r
Children under 2, expenditures on	yr	79	1999	30r
Footwear, expenditures on	yr	283	1999	30r
Girls, 2 to 15, expenditures on	yr	103	1999	30r
Men and boys, expenditures on	yr	351	1999	30r
Men, 16 and over, expenditures on	yr	262	1999	30r
Shirt, man's dress shirt		22.66	12/00	5c
Slacks, man's "No Wrinkles" khaki		33.32	12/00	5c
Women, 16 and over, expenditures on	yr	538	1999	30r
Communications				
Cable modem installation, Intermedia		149.95	6/99	103s
Cable modem installation, Time Warner		75.00-225.00	6/99	103s
Cable modem rate, cable subscriber, Intermedia	mos	49.95	6/99	103s
Cable modem rate, cable subscriber, Time Warner	mos	39.95-49.95	6/99	103s
Cable modem rate, non-cable subscriber, Intermedia	mos	54.95	6/99	103s
Cable modem rate, non-cable subscriber, Time Warner	mos	39.95-54.95	6/99	103s
Newspaper subscription, daily and Sunday delivery	mos	10.17	12/00	5c
Phone line, single, business, field visit	inst.	65.00	12/97	17s
Phone line, single, business, no field visit	inst.	65.00	12/97	17s
Phone line, single, residence, field visit	inst.	42.75	12/97	17s
Phone line, single, residence, no field visit	inst.	42.75	12/97	17s
Postage and stationery, expenditures on	yr	104	1999	30r
Postal rate, express mail, up to half-pound		12.45	7/01	108r
Postal rate, letter, first class, first ounce		0.34	7/01	108r
Postal rate, letter, two ounces		0.57	7/01	108r
Postal rate, post card		0.21	7/01	108r
Postal rate, priority mail, two pounds		3.95	7/01	108r
Postal rate, priority mail, up to one pound		3.50	7/01	108r
Telephone bill, family of three	mos	22.41	12/00	5c
Telephone services, expenditures on	yr	860	1999	30r
Education				
Board, 4-year private college/university	yr	2316	1996	38s
Board, 4-year public college/university	yr	1737	1996	38s
Education expenditures	yr	431	1999	30r
Room, 4-year private college/university	yr	2128	1996	38s
Room, 4-year public college/university	yr	1742	1996	38s
Total cost, 4-year private college/university	yr	15428	1996	38s
Total cost, 4-year public college/university	yr	5119	1996	38s
Tuition, 4-year private college/university, in state	yr	10984	1996	38s
Tuition, 4-year public college/university	yr	1639	1996	38s
Energy and Fuels				
Electricity	500 KWhs	47.29	7/01	11r
Electricity	KWh	0.09	7/01	11r
Energy, combined forms, 2400 sq ft	mos	144.49	12/00	5c
Fuel oil #2	gal	1.43	7/01	11r
Fuel oil and other fuels, expenditures on	yr	45	1999	30r
Gas, natural, commercial rate	1000 cf	9.25	11/00	88s
Gas, regular unleaded, cash, self-service	gal	1.43	12/00	5c
Gasoline, all types	gal	1.60	7/01	11r
Gasoline, unleaded midgrade	gal	1.65	7/01	11r
Gasoline, unleaded premium	gal	1.74	7/01	11r
Natural gas, expenditures on	yr	164	1999	30r
Utility (piped) gas, therm		1.01	7/01	11r

Greenville, NC - continued

Item	Per	Value	Date	Ref.
Energy and Fuels - continued				
Utility (piped) gas, 40 therms		44.29	7/01	11r
Utility (piped) gas, 100 therms		97.44	7/01	11r
Entertainment				
Bowling, Saturday evening rate	line	3.50	12/00	5c
Entertainment purchases	yr	1574	1999	30r
Fees and admissions paid	yr	371	1999	30r
Monopoly game, Parker Brothers', No. 9	game	10.98	12/00	5c
Movie, first-run, Saturday, evening	adm.	6.50	12/00	5c
Reading purchases	yr	121	1999	30r
Television, radios, sound equipment, expenditures on	yr	561	1999	30r
Tennis balls, yellow, Wilson or Penn, 3	can	1.94	12/00	5c
Funerals				
Total cost of funeral		5922.53	1/99	78r
Acknowledgement cards		63.43	1/99	78r
Casket		2258.77	1/99	78r
Cosmetology, hair, other preparation		127.09	1/99	78r
Embalming		393.49	1/99	78r
Funeral at funeral home		367.50	1/99	78r
Hearse (local)		169.66	1/99	78r
Professional service charges		1211.32	1/99	78r
Service car/van		80.69	1/99	78r
Transfer of remains to funeral home		144.25	1/99	78r
Vault		803.50	1/99	78r
Visitation/viewing		302.83	1/99	78r
Groceries				
Groceries, ACCRA Index		94.70	12/00	5c
American processed cheese	lb	3.50	7/01	11r
Antibiotic ointment, Polysporin	0.5 oz	4.48	12/00	5c
Baby food, strained vegetables or fruit, lowest price	4-4.5 oz	0.43	12/00	5c
Bakery products, expenditures on	yr	261	1999	30r
Bananas	lb	0.47	7/01	11r
Bananas	lb	0.52	12/00	5c
Beans, dried, any type, all sizes	lb	0.63	7/01	11r
Beef for stew, boneless	lb	2.86	7/01	11r
Beef or hamburger, ground	lb	1.21	12/00	5c
Beef, expenditures on	yr	210	1999	30r
Bologna, all beef or mixed	lb	2.29	7/01	11r
Bread, French	lb	1.66	7/01	11r
Bread, white	loaf	0.88	12/00	5c
Bread, white, pan	lb	0.87	7/01	11r
Bread, whole wheat, pan	lb	1.38	7/01	11r
Broccoli	lb	1.04	7/01	11r
Butter, salted, grade AA, stick	lb	2.26	7/01	11r
Butter, yoghurt, cheese, etc, expenditures on	yr	170	1999	30r
Cabbage	lb	0.42	7/01	11r
Cereals and cereal products, expenditures on	yr	140	1999	30r
Cheddar cheese, natural	lb	3.75	7/01	11r
Cheese, Kraft grated Parmesan	8 oz	3.27	12/00	5c
Chicken breast, bone-in	lb	1.85	7/01	11r
Chicken legs, bone-in	lb	1.34	7/01	11r
Chicken, fresh, whole	lb	1.05	7/01	11r
Chicken, whole fryer	lb	1.06	12/00	5c
Chops, boneless,	lb	4.13	7/01	11r
Chuck roast, graded and ungraded, excl U.S. prime and choice	lb	2.35	7/01	11r
Chuck roast, U.S. choice, boneless	lb	2.67	7/01	11r
Cigarettes, Winston, Kings	carton	24.31	12/00	5c
Coffee, 100%, ground roast, all sizes	lb	2.88	7/01	11r
Coffee, instant, plain, regular, all sizes	16 oz	9.25	7/01	11r
Coffee, vacuum-packed	13 oz	2.10	12/00	5c
Cola, non diet,	2 liter	1.11	7/01	11r
Corn Flakes, Kellogg's or Post Toasties	18 oz	2.10	12/00	5c
Corn, frozen, whole kernel, lowest price	16 oz	0.99	12/00	5c
Crackers, soda, salted	lb	1.70	7/01	11r
Dairy product purchases	yr	282	1999	30r
Eggs, expenditures on	yr	32	1999	30r
Eggs, Grade A or AA	dozen	0.94	12/00	5c
Fats and oils, expenditures on	yr	79	1999	30r

Values are in dollars or fractions of dollars. In the column headed *Ref*, references are shown to sources. Each reference is followed by a letter. These refer to the geographical level for which data were reported: s=State, r=Region, and c=City or metro. The abbreviation *ex* is used to mean *except* or *excluding*; *exp* stands for *expenditures*. For other abbreviations and further explanations, please see the Introduction.

Greenville, NC - continued

Groceries

Item	Per	Value	Date	Ref.
Fish and seafood, expenditures on	yr	99	1999	30r
Flour, white, all purpose	lb	0.32	7/01	11r
Food (excl fruit and vegetables), eaten at home, purchases	yr	815	1999	30r
Food cooked on trips, expenditures on	yr	36	1999	30r
Food purchases	yr	4533	1999	30r
Food purchases, eaten away from home	yr	1873	1999	30r
Food purchases, food eaten at home	yr	2660	1999	30r
Fresh fruits, expenditures on	yr	128	1999	30r
Fresh milk and cream, expenditures on	yr	112	1999	30r
Fresh vegetables, expenditures on	yr	131	1999	30r
Fruit and vegetable purchases	yr	438	1999	30r
Grapefruit	lb	0.59	7/01	11r
Grapes, Thompson, seedless	lb	2.12	7/01	11r
Ground beef, 100% beef	lb	1.76	7/01	11r
Ground beef, lean and extra lean	lb	2.60	7/01	11r
Ground chuck, 100% beef	lb	2.08	7/01	11r
Ham, boneless, excl canned	lb	2.71	7/01	11r
Ham, rump or shank half, bone-in, smoked	lb	2.19	7/01	11r
Ice cream, prepackaged, bulk, regular	1/2 gal	3.93	7/01	11r
Lemons	lb	1.32	7/01	11r
Lettuce, iceberg	lb	0.76	7/01	11r
Lettuce, iceberg	head	1.25	12/00	5c
Margarine, Blue Bonnet or Parkay, stick	lb	0.71	12/00	5c
Milk, fresh, low fat,	gal	2.75	7/01	11r
Milk, fresh, whole, fortified	gal	2.97	7/01	11r
Milk, whole	1/2 gal	1.82	12/00	5c
Nonalcoholic beverages, expenditures on	yr	228	1999	30r
Orange juice, frozen concentrate	16 oz	1.95	7/01	11r
Orange juice, Minute Maid frozen	12 oz	1.56	12/00	5c
Oranges, Navel	lb	0.73	7/01	11r
Oranges, Valencia	lb	0.55	7/01	11r
Peaches, halves or slices, Hunt's, Del Monte, or Libby's	29 oz	1.43	12/00	5c
Peanut butter, creamy, all sizes	lb	1.83	7/01	11r
Pears, Anjou	lb	0.98	7/01	11r
Peas, green, Del Monte or Green Giant	15 oz	0.58	12/00	5c
Pork chops, center cut, bone-in	lb	3.33	7/01	11r
Pork sausage, fresh, loose	lb	2.59	7/01	11r
Pork shoulder picnic, bone-in, smoked	lb	1.12	7/01	11r
Pork, expenditures on	yr	162	1999	30r
Potato chips	16 oz	3.59	7/01	11r
Potatoes, frozen, french fried	lb	1.00	7/01	11r
Potatoes, white or red	10 lb	2.91	12/00	5c
Potatoes, white, all types	lb	0.44	7/01	11r
Poultry, expenditures on	yr	137	1999	30r
Processed fruits, expenditures on	yr	97	1999	30r
Processed vegetables, expenditures on	yr	82	1999	30r
Rice, white, long grain, uncooked	lb	0.51	7/01	11r
Round roast, graded and ungraded, excl U.S. prime and choice	lb	2.96	7/01	11r
Round steak, graded and ungraded, excl U.S. prime and choice	lb	3.11	7/01	11r
Sausage, Jimmy Dean/Owens pork	lb	2.86	12/00	5c
Shortening, vegetable, Crisco	3 lb	3.05	12/00	5c
Sirloin steak, graded and ungraded, excl U.S. prime and choice	lb	4.23	7/01	11r
Soft drink, Coca Cola, ex deposit	2 liter	1.06	12/00	5c
Spaghetti and macaroni	lb	0.78	7/01	11r
Steak, round, U.S. choice, boneless	lb	3.56	7/01	11r
Steak, sirloin, U.S. choice, boneless	lb	5.65	7/01	11r
Steak, T-bone	lb	6.63	12/00	5c
Strawberries, dry pint	12 oz	1.50	7/01	11r
Sugar and other sweets, expenditures on	yr	99	1999	30r
Sugar, cane or beet	4 lbs	1.46	12/00	5c
Sugar, white, 33-80 ounce package	lb	0.39	7/01	11r
Sugar, white, all sizes	lb	0.42	7/01	11r
Tobacco products and smoking supplies purchases	yr	288	1999	30r
Tomatoes, field grown	lb	1.43	7/01	11r
Tomatoes, Hunt's or Del Monte	14.5 oz	0.75	12/00	5c
Tuna, chunk, light	6 oz	0.61	12/00	5c

Greenville, NC - continued

Groceries - continued

Item	Per	Value	Date	Ref.
Tuna, light, chunk	lb	1.77	7/01	11r
Turkey, frozen, whole	lb	1.05	7/01	11r

Goods and Services

Item	Per	Value	Date	Ref.
Miscellaneous goods and services, ACCRA Index		93.90	12/00	5c
B&B Japanese maple (acer japonicum)	gal	49.98-129.00	4/00	93r
Boxwood (buxus)	2 gal	12.99-16.99	4/00	93r
Daylilly (hemerocallis)	gal	4.99-8.99	4/00	93r
Flat of annuals		11.00-13.92	4/00	93r
Fountain grass (pennisetum)	gal	5.98-7.98	4/00	93r
Hanging basket (10 in)		7.99-14.98	4/00	93r
Hardy geranium (geranium)	gal	5.98-8.00	4/00	93r
Hosta (hosta)	gal	4.99-10.98	4/00	93r
Lilac (syrubga vulgaris)	2 gal	12.99-21.99	4/00	93r
Rhododendron (rhododendron)	2 gal	14.99-24.99	4/00	93r
Sage (salvia)	gal	5.98-6.99	4/00	93r
Wintercreeper euonymus (euonymus fortunei)	2 gal	7.99-89.99	4/00	93r
Hunting license	yr	15.00	4/01	34s

Health Care

Item	Per	Value	Date	Ref.
Health care, ACCRA Index		96.80	12/00	5c
Cardiac catheterization, ave hospital/ physician charges		12500	1998	77s
Childbirth, Cesarean delivery		11587	1997	13r
Childbirth, vaginal delivery		6725	1997	13r
Dentist's fee, adult teeth cleaning and periodic oral exam	visit	77.60	12/00	5c
Doctor's fee, routine exam, established patient	visit	57.60	12/00	5c
Drugs, expenditures on	yr	399	1999	30r
Health care purchases	yr	1971	1999	30r
Health insurance expenditures	yr	933	1999	30r
Hospital care, private room	day	320.00	12/00	5c
Hysterectomy, laproscopically-assisted, ave hospital/physician charges		12260	1998	76s
Hysterectomy, vaginal, ave hospital and physician charges		8440	1998	76s
Medicaid dispensing fee		5.60	1999	87s
Medical services expenditures	yr	547	1999	30r
Medical supplies, expenditures on	yr	91	1999	30r
Plastic surgery, breast augmentation		2870	2000	7r
Plastic surgery, breast lift		3649	2000	7r
Plastic surgery, facelift		5008	2000	7r
Plastic surgery, hair transplantation		3425	2000	7r
Plastic surgery, lip augmentation		1227	2000	7r
Plastic surgery, lower body lift		4793	2000	7r
Plastic surgery, thigh lift		3862	2000	7r

Household Goods

Item	Per	Value	Date	Ref.
Dishwashing powder, Cascade	50 oz	2.84	12/00	5c
Floor coverings, expenditures on	yr	44	1999	30r
Furniture, expenditures on	yr	335	1999	30r
Household furnishings and equipment purchases	yr	1328	1999	30r
Household textiles, expenditures on	yr	89	1999	30r
Laundry and cleaning supplies, expenditures on	yr	113	1999	30r
Tissues, facial, Kleenex brand	175	1.26	12/00	5c

Values are in dollars or fractions of dollars. In the column headed *Ref*, references are shown to sources. Each reference is followed by a letter. These refer to the geographical level for which data were reported: s=State, r=Region, and c=City or metro. The abbreviation *ex* is used to mean *except* or *excluding; exp* stands for *expenditures.* For other abbreviations and further explanations, please see the Introduction.

Greenville, NC - continued

Item	Per	Value	Date	Ref.
Housing				
Housing, ACCRA Index		106.10	12/00	5c
Home price, existing, ave		160100	10/00	90r
Home value, median		146000	2001	53s
House, 2400 sq ft, 8000 sq ft lot, new, urban, utilities	total	230000	12/00	5c
House payment, principal and interest, 25% down payment	mos	1263	12/00	5c
Household operation expenditures	yr	553	1999	30r
Housekeeping supplies purchases	yr	473	1999	30r
Housing, expenditures on	yr	10303	1999	30r
Maintenance, repairs, insurance expenditures	yr	699	1999	30r
Monthly rental value of owned home	mos	505	1999	30r
Owned dwellings, expenditures own	yr	3465	1999	30r
Rent expenditures	yr	1641	1999	30r
Rent, apartment, 2 br, 1 1/2-2 baths, unfurn, 950 sq ft, water	mos	566	12/00	5c
Rental unit, 1 bedroom, with utilities	mos	435	4/01	41c
Rental unit, 2 bedroom, with utilities	mos	564	4/01	41c
Rental unit, 3 bedroom, with utilities	mos	761	4/01	41c
Rental unit, 4 bedroom, with utilities	mos	930	4/01	41c
Shelter, expenditures on	yr	5467	1999	30r
Insurance and Pensions				
Life and other personal insurance purchases	yr	414	1999	30r
Pensions and Social Security, expenditures on	yr	2635	1999	30r
Personal insurance and pensions, expenditures on	yr	3048	1999	30r
Legal Fees				
Combination hunting and fishing license	yr	20.00	4/01	34s
Divorce, filing fee		80.00	4/01	35s
Driver's license fee	orig	10.00	1999	48s
Driver's license fee	renew	10.00	1999	48s
Fishing license	yr	15.00	4/01	34s
Personal Goods				
Personal care products and services purchases	yr	393	1999	30r
Shampoo, Alberto VO5	15 oz	1.02	12/00	5c
Toothpaste, Crest or Colgate	6-7 oz	2.10	12/00	5c
Personal Services				
Dry cleaning, man's 2-pc suit		8.24	12/00	5c
Man's haircut, barbershop, no styling		10.25	12/00	5c
Personal services, household, expenditures on	yr	258	1999	30r
Woman's shampoo, trim, blow-dry, no style-change		22.60	12/00	5c
Pets				
Pets, toys, and playground equipment, expenditures on	yr	306	1999	30r
Restaurant Food				
Chicken, fried, thigh and drumstick, KFC/Church's		2.79	12/00	5c
Hamburger with cheese, McDonald's	1/4 lb	2.04	12/00	5c
Pizza, Pizza Hut or Pizza Inn	11-12 in	8.12	12/00	5c
Taxes				
Federal income taxes paid	yr	2047	1999	30r
Personal taxes, expenditures on	yr	2554	1999	30r
Property taxes paid	yr	726	1999	30r
State and local income taxes paid	yr	363	1999	30r
Transportation				
Transportation, ACCRA Index		92.60	12/00	5c
Cars and trucks, new, expenditures on	yr	1648	1999	30r
Cars and trucks, used, expenditures on	yr	1651	1999	30r
Diesel at the pump	gal	1.19	10/99	73s
Gasoline and motor oil purchases	yr	1052	1999	30r
Gasoline before-tax price (cents)	gal	103.20	10/00	43s
Maintenance and repair expenditures	yr	621	1999	30r
Motorcycle license fee	renew	1.50	1999	49s

Greenville, NC - continued

Item	Per	Value	Date	Ref.
Transportation - continued				
Motorcycle license fee	orig	1.50	1999	49s
Public transportation, expenditures on	yr	298	1999	30r
Tire balance, computer or spin balance, front	wheel	6.90	12/00	5c
Transportation purchases	yr	6738	1999	30r
Vehicle expenses, miscellaneous, purchases	yr	2033	1999	30r
Vehicle insurance payments	yr	696	1999	30r
Vehicle purchases (net outlay)	yr	3354	1999	30r
Vehicle rental, lease expenditures	yr	352	1999	30r
Utilities				
Utilities, ACCRA Index		125.40	12/00	5c
Electrical bill, average	mos	83.66	9/00	9s
Electricity, 2400 sq ft, new home	mos	144.49	12/00	5c
Electricity, expenditures on	yr	1115	1999	30r
Electricity cost, average	KWh	6.40	9/00	9s
Water and other public services, expenditures on	yr	298	1999	30r
Weddings				
Wedding (national average cost)		19936	2000	33r
Wedding (regional average total cost)		16293	1997	110r
Attendants' gifts		321	1998	33r
Bridal attendants' apparel (5 persons)		824	2000	33r
Bride's headpiece/veil		173	1998	33r
Bride's wedding dress		859	1998	33r
Clergy, religious facility fee		242	1998	33r
Engagement ring		3177	1998	33r
Flowers		789	1998	33r
Groom's formalwear rental		99	2000	33r
Limousine		410	1998	33r
Marriage license cost		40.00	4/01	35s
Men's formalwear (ushers, best man)		469	2000	33r
Mother of bride apparel		241	2000	33r
Music		866	1998	33r
Photography and videography		1368	1998	33r
Rehearsal dinner		728	1998	33r
Wedding invitations and announcements		341	1998	33r
Wedding reception		7968	2000	33r
Wedding rings (bride and groom)		1060	1998	33r

Greenville, SC

Item	Per	Value	Date	Ref.
Alcoholic Beverages				
Alcoholic beverage purchases	yr	253	1999	30r
Malt beverages, all types, all sizes, any origin	16 oz	0.96	7/01	11r
Appliances				
Major appliances, expenditures on	yr	172	1999	30r
Small appliances, housewares, expenditures on	yr	81	1999	30r
Banking and Money				
Mortgage interest and charges paid	yr	2039	1999	30r
Mortgage principal paid on owned property	yr	1026	1999	30r
Vehicle finance charges paid	yr	365	1999	30r
Business Expenses				
Business travel, car rental	day	47	2001	3c
Business travel, food	day	46	2001	3c
Business travel, hotel	day	101	2001	3c
Charity				
Cash contributions, expenditures	yr	1127	1999	30r
Child Care				
Child raising cost, total, age 0-2	yr	8540	1999	60r
Child raising cost, total, age 3-5	yr	8780	1999	60r
Child raising cost, total, age 6-8	yr	8820	1999	60r
Child raising cost, total, age 9-11	yr	8800	1999	60r
Child raising cost, total, age 12-14	yr	9510	1999	60r
Child raising cost, total, age 15-17	yr	9740	1999	60r
Child's child care and education, age 0-2	yr	1380	1999	60r
Child's child care and education, age 3-5	yr	1520	1999	60r
Child's child care and education, age 6-8	yr	990	1999	60r

Values are in dollars or fractions of dollars. In the column headed *Ref*, references are shown to sources. Each reference is followed by a letter. These refer to the geographical level for which data were reported: s=State, r=Region, and c=City or metro. The abbreviation *ex* is used to mean *except* or *excluding*; *exp* stands for *expenditures*. For other abbreviations and further explanations, please see the Introduction.

Greenville, SC - continued

Item	Per	Value	Date	Ref.
Child Care				
Child's child care and education, age 9-11	yr	650	1999	60r
Child's child care and education, age 12-14	yr	490	1999	60r
Child's child care and education, age 15-17	yr	840	1999	60r
Child's clothing, age 0-2	yr	480	1999	60r
Child's clothing, age 3-5	yr	470	1999	60r
Child's clothing, age 6-8	yr	520	1999	60r
Child's clothing, age 9-11	yr	570	1999	60r
Child's clothing, age 12-14	yr	950	1999	60r
Child's clothing, age 15-17	yr	850	1999	60r
Child's food, age 0-2	yr	1000	1999	60r
Child's food, age 3-5	yr	1160	1999	60r
Child's food, age 6-8	yr	1490	1999	60r
Child's food, age 9-11	yr	1770	1999	60r
Child's food, age 12-14	yr	1770	1999	60r
Child's food, age 15-17	yr	1980	1999	60r
Child's health care, age 0-2	yr	620	1999	60r
Child's health care, age 3-5	yr	590	1999	60r
Child's health care, age 6-8	yr	680	1999	60r
Child's health care, age 9-11	yr	720	1999	60r
Child's health care, age 12-14	yr	730	1999	60r
Child's health care, age 15-17	yr	760	1999	60r
Child's housing, age 0-2	yr	3070	1999	60r
Child's housing, age 3-5	yr	3050	1999	60r
Child's housing, age 6-8	yr	3010	1999	60r
Child's housing, age 9-11	yr	2850	1999	60r
Child's housing, age 12-14	yr	3040	1999	60r
Child's housing, age 15-17	yr	2650	1999	60r
Child's personal care, reading, age 0-2	yr	910	1999	60r
Child's personal care, reading, age 3-5	yr	930	1999	60r
Child's personal care, reading, age 6-8	yr	960	1999	60r
Child's personal care, reading, age 9-11	yr	1000	1999	60r
Child's personal care, reading, age 12-14	yr	1170	1999	60r
Child's personal care, reading, age 15-17	yr	950	1999	60r
Clothing				
Apparel and services purchases	yr	1610	1999	30r
Boys, 2 to 15, expenditures on	yr	89	1999	30r
Children under 2, expenditures on	yr	79	1999	30r
Footwear, expenditures on	yr	283	1999	30r
Girls, 2 to 15, expenditures on	yr	103	1999	30r
Men and boys, expenditures on	yr	351	1999	30r
Men, 16 and over, expenditures on	yr	262	1999	30r
Women, 16 and over, expenditures on	yr	538	1999	30r
Communications				
Cable modem installation, Adelphi		54.90	6/99	103s
Cable modem installation, Comcast		95.00	6/99	103s
Cable modem installation, Intermedia		149.95	6/99	103s
Cable modem rate, cable subscriber, Adelphi	mos	34.95	6/99	103s
Cable modem rate, cable subscriber, Comcast	mos	39.95	6/99	103s
Cable modem rate, cable subscriber, Intermedia	mos	49.95	6/99	103s
Cable modem rate, non-cable subscriber, Adelphi	mos	44.95	6/99	103s
Cable modem rate, non-cable subscriber, Comcast	mos	49.95	6/99	103s
Cable modem rate, non-cable subscriber, Intermedia	mos	54.95	6/99	103s
Phone line, single, business, field visit	inst.	64.00	12/97	17s
Phone line, single, business, no field visit	inst.	64.00	12/97	17s
Phone line, single, residence, field visit	inst.	40.00	12/97	17s
Phone line, single, residence, no field visit	inst.	40.00	12/97	17s
Postage and stationery, expenditures on	yr	104	1999	30r
Postal rate, express mail, up to half-pound		12.45	7/01	108r
Postal rate, letter, first class, first ounce		0.34	7/01	108r
Postal rate, letter, two ounces		0.57	7/01	108r
Postal rate, post card		0.21	7/01	108r
Postal rate, priority mail, two pounds		3.95	7/01	108r
Postal rate, priority mail, up to one pound		3.50	7/01	108r
Telephone bill, business, basic rate	mos	43.75	12/97	18c
Telephone bill, residential, basic rate	mos	16.40	12/97	18c
Telephone services, expenditures on	yr	860	1999	30r

Greenville, SC - continued

Item	Per	Value	Date	Ref.
Education				
Board, 4-year private college/university	yr	1990	1996	38s
Board, 4-year public college/university	yr	1872	1996	38s
Education expenditures	yr	431	1999	30r
Room, 4-year private college/university	yr	1786	1996	38s
Room, 4-year public college/university	yr	1998	1996	38s
Total cost, 4-year private college/university	yr	13517	1996	38s
Total cost, 4-year public college/university	yr	6964	1996	38s
Tuition, 2-year public college/university, in state	yr	1071	1996	38s
Tuition, 4-year private college/university, in state	yr	9741	1996	38s
Tuition, 4-year public college/university	yr	3094	1996	38s
Energy and Fuels				
Electricity	500 KWhs	47.29	7/01	11r
Electricity	KWh	0.09	7/01	11r
Fuel oil #2	gal	1.43	7/01	11r
Fuel oil and other fuels, expenditures on	yr	45	1999	30r
Gas, cooking, winter, 10 therms	mos	10.60	2/96	98c
Gas, cooking, winter, 30 therms	mos	24.81	2/96	98c
Gas, cooking, winter, 50 therms	mos	39.02	2/96	98c
Gas, heating, winter, average use	mos	117.87	2/96	98c
Gas, natural, commercial rate	1000 cf	9.50	11/00	88s
Gasoline, all types	gal	1.60	7/01	11r
Gasoline, unleaded midgrade	gal	1.65	7/01	11r
Gasoline, unleaded premium	gal	1.74	7/01	11r
Natural gas, expenditures on	yr	164	1999	30r
Utility (piped) gas, therm		1.01	7/01	11r
Utility (piped) gas, 40 therms		44.29	7/01	11r
Utility (piped) gas, 100 therms		97.44	7/01	11r
Entertainment				
Entertainment purchases	yr	1574	1999	30r
Fees and admissions paid	yr	371	1999	30r
Reading purchases	yr	121	1999	30r
Television, radios, sound equipment, expenditures on	yr	561	1999	30r
Funerals				
Total cost of funeral		5922.53	1/99	78r
Acknowledgement cards		63.43	1/99	78r
Casket		2258.77	1/99	78r
Cosmetology, hair, other preparation		127.09	1/99	78r
Embalming		393.49	1/99	78r
Funeral at funeral home		367.50	1/99	78r
Hearse (local)		169.66	1/99	78r
Professional service charges		1211.32	1/99	78r
Service car/van		80.69	1/99	78r
Transfer of remains to funeral home		144.25	1/99	78r
Vault		803.50	1/99	78r
Visitation/viewing		302.83	1/99	78r
Groceries				
American processed cheese	lb	3.50	7/01	11r
Bakery products, expenditures on	yr	261	1999	30r
Bananas	lb	0.47	7/01	11r
Beans, dried, any type, all sizes	lb	0.63	7/01	11r
Beef for stew, boneless	lb	2.86	7/01	11r
Beef, expenditures on	yr	210	1999	30r
Bologna, all beef or mixed	lb	2.29	7/01	11r
Bread, French	lb	1.66	7/01	11r
Bread, white, pan	lb	0.87	7/01	11r
Bread, whole wheat, pan	lb	1.38	7/01	11r
Broccoli	lb	1.04	7/01	11r
Butter, salted, grade AA, stick	lb	2.26	7/01	11r
Butter, yoghurt, cheese, etc, expenditures on	yr	170	1999	30r
Cabbage	lb	0.42	7/01	11r
Cereals and cereal products, expenditures on	yr	140	1999	30r
Cheddar cheese, natural	lb	3.75	7/01	11r
Chicken breast, bone-in	lb	1.85	7/01	11r
Chicken legs, bone-in	lb	1.34	7/01	11r
Chicken, fresh, whole	lb	1.05	7/01	11r

Values are in dollars or fractions of dollars. In the column headed *Ref*, references are shown to sources. Each reference is followed by a letter. These refer to the geographic level for which data were reported: s=State, r=Region, and c=City or metro. The abbreviation *ex* is used to mean *except* or *excluding*; *exp* stands for *expenditures*. For other abbreviations and further explanations, please see the Introduction.

Greenville, SC - continued

Item	Per	Value	Date	Ref.
Groceries				
Chops, boneless,	lb	4.13	7/01	11r
Chuck roast, graded and ungraded, excl U.S. prime and choice	lb	2.35	7/01	11r
Chuck roast, U.S. choice, boneless	lb	2.67	7/01	11r
Coffee, 100%, ground roast, all sizes	lb	2.88	7/01	11r
Coffee, instant, plain, regular, all sizes	16 oz	9.25	7/01	11r
Cola, non diet,	2 liter	1.11	7/01	11r
Crackers, soda, salted	lb	1.70	7/01	11r
Dairy product purchases	yr	282	1999	30r
Eggs, expenditures on	yr	32	1999	30r
Fats and oils, expenditures on	yr	79	1999	30r
Fish and seafood, expenditures on	yr	99	1999	30r
Flour, white, all purpose	lb	0.32	7/01	11r
Food (excl fruit and vegetables), eaten at home, purchases	yr	815	1999	30r
Food cooked on trips, expenditures on	yr	36	1999	30r
Food purchases	yr	4533	1999	30r
Food purchases, eaten away from home	yr	1873	1999	30r
Food purchases, food eaten at home	yr	2660	1999	30r
Fresh fruits, expenditures on	yr	128	1999	30r
Fresh milk and cream, expenditures on	yr	112	1999	30r
Fresh vegetables, expenditures on	yr	131	1999	30r
Fruit and vegetable purchases	yr	438	1999	30r
Grapefruit	lb	0.59	7/01	11r
Grapes, Thompson, seedless	lb	2.12	7/01	11r
Ground beef, 100% beef	lb	1.76	7/01	11r
Ground beef, lean and extra lean	lb	2.60	7/01	11r
Ground chuck, 100% beef	lb	2.08	7/01	11r
Ham, boneless, excl canned	lb	2.71	7/01	11r
Ham, rump or shank half, bone-in, smoked	lb	2.19	7/01	11r
Ice cream, prepackaged, bulk, regular	1/2 gal	3.93	7/01	11r
Lemons	lb	1.32	7/01	11r
Lettuce, iceberg	lb	0.76	7/01	11r
Milk, fresh, low fat,	gal	2.75	7/01	11r
Milk, fresh, whole, fortified	gal	2.97	7/01	11r
Nonalcoholic beverages, expenditures on	yr	228	1999	30r
Orange juice, frozen concentrate	16 oz	1.95	7/01	11r
Oranges, Navel	lb	0.73	7/01	11r
Oranges, Valencia	lb	0.55	7/01	11r
Peanut butter, creamy, all sizes	lb	1.83	7/01	11r
Pears, Anjou	lb	0.98	7/01	11r
Pork chops, center cut, bone-in	lb	3.33	7/01	11r
Pork sausage, fresh, loose	lb	2.59	7/01	11r
Pork shoulder picnic, bone-in, smoked	lb	1.12	7/01	11r
Pork, expenditures on	yr	162	1999	30r
Potato chips	16 oz	3.59	7/01	11r
Potatoes, frozen, french fried	lb	1.00	7/01	11r
Potatoes, white, all types	lb	0.44	7/01	11r
Poultry, expenditures on	yr	137	1999	30r
Processed fruits, expenditures on	yr	97	1999	30r
Processed vegetables, expenditures on	yr	82	1999	30r
Rice, white, long grain, uncooked	lb	0.51	7/01	11r
Round roast, graded and ungraded, excl U.S. prime and choice	lb	2.96	7/01	11r
Round steak, graded and ungraded, excl U.S. prime and choice	lb	3.11	7/01	11r
Sirloin steak, graded and ungraded, excl U.S. prime and choice	lb	4.23	7/01	11r
Spaghetti and macaroni	lb	0.78	7/01	11r
Steak, round, U.S. choice, boneless	lb	3.56	7/01	11r
Steak, sirloin, U.S. choice, boneless	lb	5.65	7/01	11r
Strawberries, dry pint	12 oz	1.50	7/01	11r
Sugar and other sweets, expenditures on	yr	99	1999	30r
Sugar, white, 33-80 ounce package	lb	0.39	7/01	11r
Sugar, white, all sizes	lb	0.42	7/01	11r
Tobacco products and smoking supplies purchases	yr	288	1999	30r
Tomatoes, field grown	lb	1.43	7/01	11r
Tuna, light, chunk	lb	1.77	7/01	11r
Turkey, frozen, whole	lb	1.05	7/01	11r

Greenville, SC - continued

Item	Per	Value	Date	Ref.
Goods and Services				
B&B Japanese maple (acer japonicum)	gal	49.98-129.00	4/00	93r
Boxwood (buxus)	2 gal	12.99-16.99	4/00	93r
Daylilly (hemerocallis)	gal	4.99-8.99	4/00	93r
Flat of annuals		11.00-13.92	4/00	93r
Fountain grass (pennisetum)	gal	5.98-7.98	4/00	93r
Hanging basket (10 in)		7.99-14.98	4/00	93r
Hardy geranium (geranium)	gal	5.98-8.00	4/00	93r
Hosta (hosta)	gal	4.99-10.98	4/00	93r
Lilac (syrubga vulgaris)	2 gal	12.99-21.99	4/00	93r
Rhododendron (rhododendron)	2 gal	14.99-24.99	4/00	93r
Sage (salvia)	gal	5.98-6.99	4/00	93r
Wintercreeper euonymus (euonymus fortunei)	2 gal	7.99-89.99	4/00	93r
Hunting license	yr	12.00	4/01	34s
Health Care				
Cardiac catheterization, ave hospital/physician charges		12360	1998	77s
Childbirth, Cesarean delivery		11587	1997	13r
Childbirth, vaginal delivery		6725	1997	13r
Drugs, expenditures on	yr	399	1999	30r
Health care purchases	yr	1971	1999	30r
Health insurance expenditures	yr	933	1999	30r
Hysterectomy, laproscopically-assisted, ave hospital/physician charges		11920	1998	76s
Hysterectomy, vaginal, ave hospital and physician charges		4890	1998	76s
Medicaid dispensing fee		4.05	1999	87s
Medical services expenditures	yr	547	1999	30r
Medical supplies, expenditures on	yr	91	1999	30r
Plastic surgery, breast augmentation		2870	2000	7r
Plastic surgery, breast lift		3649	2000	7r
Plastic surgery, facelift		5008	2000	7r
Plastic surgery, hair transplantation		3425	2000	7r
Plastic surgery, lip augmentation		1227	2000	7r
Plastic surgery, lower body lift		4793	2000	7r
Plastic surgery, thigh lift		3862	2000	7r
Household Goods				
Floor coverings, expenditures on	yr	44	1999	30r
Furniture, expenditures on	yr	335	1999	30r
Household furnishings and equipment purchases	yr	1328	1999	30r
Household textiles, expenditures on	yr	89	1999	30r
Laundry and cleaning supplies, expenditures on	yr	113	1999	30r
Housing				
Home, 2200 sq ft, 4-br, 2-bath, 2-car garage, average		176500	2000	47c
Home price, existing, ave		160100	10/00	90r
Home value, median		119000	2001	53s
Household operation expenditures	yr	553	1999	30r
Housekeeping supplies purchases	yr	473	1999	30r
Housing, expenditures on	yr	10303	1999	30r
Maintenance, repairs, insurance expenditures	yr	699	1999	30r
Monthly rental value of owned home	mos	505	1999	30r
Owned dwellings, expenditures own	yr	3465	1999	30r
Rent expenditures	yr	1641	1999	30r
Shelter, expenditures on	yr	5467	1999	30r

Values are in dollars or fractions of dollars. In the column headed *Ref*, references are shown to sources. Each reference is followed by a letter. These refer to the geographical level for which data were reported: s=State, r=Region, and c=City or metro. The abbreviation *ex* is used to mean *except* or *excluding*; *exp* stands for expenditures. For other abbreviations and further explanations, please see the Introduction.

Greenville, SC - continued

Item	Per	Value	Date	Ref.
Insurance and Pensions				
Auto insurance	yr	655.33	1998	86s
Life and other personal insurance purchases	yr	414	1999	30r
Pensions and Social Security, expenditures on	yr	2635	1999	30r
Personal insurance and pensions, expenditures on	yr	3048	1999	30r
Legal Fees				
Combination hunting and fishing license	yr	20.00	4/01	34s
Driver's license fee	orig	12.50	1999	48s
Driver's license fee	renew	12.50	1999	48s
Fishing license	yr	10.00	4/01	34s
Personal Goods				
Personal care products and services purchases	yr	393	1999	30r
Personal Services				
Personal services, household, expenditures on	yr	258	1999	30r
Pets				
Pets, toys, and playground equipment, expenditures on	yr	306	1999	30r
Taxes				
Federal income taxes paid	yr	2047	1999	30r
Personal taxes, expenditures on	yr	2554	1999	30r
Property taxes paid	yr	726	1999	30r
State and local income taxes paid	yr	363	1999	30r
Transportation				
Cars and trucks, new, expenditures on	yr	1648	1999	30r
Cars and trucks, used, expenditures on	yr	1651	1999	30r
Diesel at the pump	gal	1.13	10/99	73s
Gasoline and motor oil purchases	yr	1052	1999	30r
Gasoline before-tax price (cents)	gal	101.70	10/00	43s
Maintenance and repair expenditures	yr	621	1999	30r
Public transportation, expenditures on	yr	298	1999	30r
Transportation purchases	yr	6738	1999	30r
Vehicle expenses, miscellaneous, purchases	yr	2033	1999	30r
Vehicle insurance payments	yr	696	1999	30r
Vehicle purchases (net outlay)	yr	3354	1999	30r
Vehicle rental, lease expenditures	yr	352	1999	30r
Utilities				
Electrical bill, average	mos	86.42	9/00	9s
Electricity, expenditures on	yr	1115	1999	30r
Electricity, summer, 250 KWh	mos	25.11	2/96	96c
Electricity, summer, 500 KWh	mos	44.07	2/96	96c
Electricity, summer, 750 KWh	mos	63.02	2/96	96c
Electricity, summer, 1000 KWh	mos	81.97	2/96	96c
Electricity cost, average	KWh	5.40	9/00	9s
Water and other public services, expenditures on	yr	298	1999	30r
Weddings				
Wedding (national average cost)		19936	2000	33r
Wedding (regional average total cost)		16293	1997	110r
Attendants' gifts		321	1998	33r
Bridal attendants' apparel (5 persons)		824	2000	33r
Bride's headpiece/veil		173	1998	33r
Bride's wedding dress		859	1998	33r
Clergy, religious facility fee		242	1998	33r
Engagement ring		3177	1998	33r
Flowers		789	1998	33r
Groom's formalwear rental		99	2000	33r
Limousine		410	1998	33r
Marriage license cost		25.00	4/01	35s
Men's formalwear (ushers, best man)		469	2000	33r
Mother of bride apparel		241	2000	33r
Music		866	1998	33r
Photography and videography		1368	1998	33r
Rehearsal dinner		728	1998	33r
Wedding invitations and announcements		341	1998	33r
Wedding reception		7968	2000	33r

Greenville, SC - continued

Item	Per	Value	Date	Ref.
Weddings - continued				
Wedding rings (bride and groom)		1060	1998	33r

Greenville-Spartanburg-Anderson, SC

Item	Per	Value	Date	Ref.
Alcoholic Beverages				
Alcoholic beverage purchases	yr	253	1999	30r
Malt beverages, all types, all sizes, any origin	16 oz	0.96	7/01	11r
Appliances				
Major appliances, expenditures on	yr	172	1999	30r
Small appliances, housewares, expenditures on	yr	81	1999	30r
Banking and Money				
Mortgage interest and charges paid	yr	2039	1999	30r
Mortgage principal paid on owned property	yr	1026	1999	30r
Vehicle finance charges paid	yr	365	1999	30r
Charity				
Cash contributions, expenditures	yr	1127	1999	30r
Child Care				
Child raising cost, total, age 0-2	yr	8540	1999	60r
Child raising cost, total, age 3-5	yr	8780	1999	60r
Child raising cost, total, age 6-8	yr	8820	1999	60r
Child raising cost, total, age 9-11	yr	8800	1999	60r
Child raising cost, total, age 12-14	yr	9510	1999	60r
Child raising cost, total, age 15-17	yr	9740	1999	60r
Child's child care and education, age 0-2	yr	1380	1999	60r
Child's child care and education, age 3-5	yr	1520	1999	60r
Child's child care and education, age 6-8	yr	990	1999	60r
Child's child care and education, age 9-11	yr	650	1999	60r
Child's child care and education, age 12-14	yr	490	1999	60r
Child's child care and education, age 15-17	yr	840	1999	60r
Child's clothing, age 0-2	yr	480	1999	60r
Child's clothing, age 3-5	yr	470	1999	60r
Child's clothing, age 6-8	yr	520	1999	60r
Child's clothing, age 9-11	yr	570	1999	60r
Child's clothing, age 12-14	yr	950	1999	60r
Child's clothing, age 15-17	yr	850	1999	60r
Child's food, age 0-2	yr	1000	1999	60r
Child's food, age 3-5	yr	1160	1999	60r
Child's food, age 6-8	yr	1490	1999	60r
Child's food, age 9-11	yr	1770	1999	60r
Child's food, age 12-14	yr	1770	1999	60r
Child's food, age 15-17	yr	1980	1999	60r
Child's health care, age 0-2	yr	620	1999	60r
Child's health care, age 3-5	yr	590	1999	60r
Child's health care, age 6-8	yr	680	1999	60r
Child's health care, age 9-11	yr	720	1999	60r
Child's health care, age 12-14	yr	730	1999	60r
Child's health care, age 15-17	yr	760	1999	60r
Child's housing, age 0-2	yr	3070	1999	60r
Child's housing, age 3-5	yr	3050	1999	60r
Child's housing, age 6-8	yr	3010	1999	60r
Child's housing, age 9-11	yr	2850	1999	60r
Child's housing, age 12-14	yr	3040	1999	60r
Child's housing, age 15-17	yr	2650	1999	60r
Child's personal care, reading, age 0-2	yr	910	1999	60r
Child's personal care, reading, age 3-5	yr	930	1999	60r
Child's personal care, reading, age 6-8	yr	960	1999	60r
Child's personal care, reading, age 9-11	yr	1000	1999	60r
Child's personal care, reading, age 12-14	yr	1170	1999	60r
Child's personal care, reading, age 15-17	yr	950	1999	60r
Clothing				
Apparel and services purchases	yr	1610	1999	30r
Boys, 2 to 15, expenditures on	yr	89	1999	30r
Children under 2, expenditures on	yr	79	1999	30r
Footwear, expenditures on	yr	283	1999	30r
Girls, 2 to 15, expenditures on	yr	103	1999	30r
Men and boys, expenditures on	yr	351	1999	30r
Men, 16 and over, expenditures on	yr	262	1999	30r

Values are in dollars or fractions of dollars. In the column headed *Ref*, references are shown to sources. Each reference is followed by a letter. These refer to the geographical level for which data were reported: s=State, r=Region, and c=City or metro. The abbreviation *ex* is used to mean *except* or *excluding*; *exp* stands for expenditures. For other abbreviations and further explanations, please see the Introduction.

Greenville-Spartanburg-Anderson, SC - continued

Item	Per	Value	Date	Ref.
Clothing				
Women, 16 and over, expenditures on	yr	538	1999	30r
Communications				
Cable modem installation, Adelphi		54.90	6/99	103s
Cable modem installation, Comcast		95.00	6/99	103s
Cable modem installation, Intermedia		149.95	6/99	103s
Cable modem rate, cable subscriber, Adelphi	mos	34.95	6/99	103s
Cable modem rate, cable subscriber, Comcast	mos	39.95	6/99	103s
Cable modem rate, cable subscriber, Intermedia	mos	49.95	6/99	103s
Cable modem rate, non-cable subscriber, Adelphi	mos	44.95	6/99	103s
Cable modem rate, non-cable subscriber, Comcast	mos	49.95	6/99	103s
Cable modem rate, non-cable subscriber, Intermedia	mos	54.95	6/99	103s
Phone line, single, business, field visit	inst.	64.00	12/97	17s
Phone line, single, business, no field visit	inst.	64.00	12/97	17s
Phone line, single, residence, field visit	inst.	40.00	12/97	17s
Phone line, single, residence, no field visit	inst.	40.00	12/97	17s
Postage and stationery, expenditures on	yr	104	1999	30r
Postal rate, express mail, up to half-pound		12.45	7/01	108r
Postal rate, letter, first class, first ounce		0.34	7/01	108r
Postal rate, letter, two ounces		0.57	7/01	108r
Postal rate, post card		0.21	7/01	108r
Postal rate, priority mail, two pounds		3.95	7/01	108r
Postal rate, priority mail, up to one pound		3.50	7/01	108r
Telephone services, expenditures on	yr	860	1999	30r
Education				
Board, 4-year private college/university	yr	1990	1996	38s
Board, 4-year public college/university	yr	1872	1996	38s
Education expenditures	yr	431	1999	30r
Room, 4-year private college/university	yr	1786	1996	38s
Room, 4-year public college/university	yr	1998	1996	38s
Total cost, 4-year private college/university	yr	13517	1996	38s
Total cost, 4-year public college/university	yr	6964	1996	38s
Tuition, 2-year public college/university, in state	yr	1071	1996	38s
Tuition, 4-year private college/university, in state	yr	9741	1996	38s
Tuition, 4-year public college/university	yr	3094	1996	38s
Energy and Fuels				
Electricity	500 KWhs	47.29	7/01	11r
Electricity	KWh	0.09	7/01	11r
Fuel oil #2	gal	1.43	7/01	11r
Fuel oil and other fuels, expenditures on	yr	45	1999	30r
Gas, natural, commercial rate	1000 cf	9.50	11/00	88s
Gasoline, all types	gal	1.60	7/01	11r
Gasoline, unleaded midgrade	gal	1.65	7/01	11r
Gasoline, unleaded premium	gal	1.74	7/01	11r
Natural gas, expenditures on	yr	164	1999	30r
Utility (piped) gas, therm		1.01	7/01	11r
Utility (piped) gas, 40 therms		44.29	7/01	11r
Utility (piped) gas, 100 therms		97.44	7/01	11r
Entertainment				
Entertainment purchases	yr	1574	1999	30r
Fees and admissions paid	yr	371	1999	30r
Reading purchases	yr	121	1999	30r
Television, radios, sound equipment, expenditures on	yr	561	1999	30r
Funerals				
Total cost of funeral		5922.53	1/99	78r
Acknowledgement cards		63.43	1/99	78r
Casket		2258.77	1/99	78r
Cosmetology, hair, other preparation		127.09	1/99	78r
Embalming		393.49	1/99	78r
Funeral at funeral home		367.50	1/99	78r
Hearse (local)		169.66	1/99	78r

Greenville-Spartanburg-Anderson, SC - continued

Item	Per	Value	Date	Ref.
Funerals - continued				
Professional service charges		1211.32	1/99	78r
Service car/van		80.69	1/99	78r
Transfer of remains to funeral home		144.25	1/99	78r
Vault		803.50	1/99	78r
Visitation/viewing		302.83	1/99	78r
Groceries				
American processed cheese	lb	3.50	7/01	11r
Bakery products, expenditures on	yr	261	1999	30r
Bananas	lb	0.47	7/01	11r
Beans, dried, any type, all sizes	lb	0.63	7/01	11r
Beef for stew, boneless	lb	2.86	7/01	11r
Beef, expenditures on	yr	210	1999	30r
Bologna, all beef or mixed	lb	2.29	7/01	11r
Bread, French	lb	1.66	7/01	11r
Bread, white, pan	lb	0.87	7/01	11r
Bread, whole wheat, pan	lb	1.38	7/01	11r
Broccoli	lb	1.04	7/01	11r
Butter, salted, grade AA, stick	lb	2.26	7/01	11r
Butter, yoghurt, cheese, etc, expenditures on	yr	170	1999	30r
Cabbage	lb	0.42	7/01	11r
Cereals and cereal products, expenditures on	yr	140	1999	30r
Cheddar cheese, natural	lb	3.75	7/01	11r
Chicken breast, bone-in	lb	1.85	7/01	11r
Chicken legs, bone-in	lb	1.34	7/01	11r
Chicken, fresh, whole	lb	1.05	7/01	11r
Chops, boneless,	lb	4.13	7/01	11r
Chuck roast, graded and ungraded, excl U.S. prime and choice	lb	2.35	7/01	11r
Chuck roast, U.S. choice, boneless	lb	2.67	7/01	11r
Coffee, 100%, ground roast, all sizes	lb	2.88	7/01	11r
Coffee, instant, plain, regular, all sizes	16 oz	9.25	7/01	11r
Cola, non diet,	2 liter	1.11	7/01	11r
Crackers, soda, salted	lb	1.70	7/01	11r
Dairy product purchases	yr	282	1999	30r
Eggs, expenditures on	yr	32	1999	30r
Fats and oils, expenditures on	yr	79	1999	30r
Fish and seafood, expenditures on	yr	99	1999	30r
Flour, white, all purpose	lb	0.32	7/01	11r
Food (excl fruit and vegetables), eaten at home, purchases	yr	815	1999	30r
Food cooked on trips, expenditures on	yr	36	1999	30r
Food purchases	yr	4533	1999	30r
Food purchases, eaten away from home	yr	1873	1999	30r
Food purchases, food eaten at home	yr	2660	1999	30r
Fresh fruits, expenditures on	yr	128	1999	30r
Fresh milk and cream, expenditures on	yr	112	1999	30r
Fresh vegetables, expenditures on	yr	131	1999	30r
Fruit and vegetable purchases	yr	438	1999	30r
Grapefruit	lb	0.59	7/01	11r
Grapes, Thompson, seedless	lb	2.12	7/01	11r
Ground beef, 100% beef	lb	1.76	7/01	11r
Ground beef, lean and extra lean	lb	2.60	7/01	11r
Ground chuck, 100% beef	lb	2.08	7/01	11r
Ham, boneless, excl canned	lb	2.71	7/01	11r
Ham, rump or shank half, bone-in, smoked	lb	2.19	7/01	11r
Ice cream, prepackaged, bulk, regular	1/2 gal	3.93	7/01	11r
Lemons	lb	1.32	7/01	11r
Lettuce, iceberg	lb	0.76	7/01	11r
Milk, fresh, low fat,	gal	2.75	7/01	11r
Milk, fresh, whole, fortified	gal	2.97	7/01	11r
Nonalcoholic beverages, expenditures on	yr	228	1999	30r
Orange juice, frozen concentrate	16 oz	1.95	7/01	11r
Oranges, Navel	lb	0.73	7/01	11r
Oranges, Valencia	lb	0.55	7/01	11r
Peanut butter, creamy, all sizes	lb	1.83	7/01	11r
Pears, Anjou	lb	0.98	7/01	11r
Pork chops, center cut, bone-in	lb	3.33	7/01	11r
Pork sausage, fresh, loose	lb	2.59	7/01	11r
Pork shoulder picnic, bone-in, smoked	lb	1.12	7/01	11r
Pork, expenditures on	yr	162	1999	30r
Potato chips	16 oz	3.59	7/01	11r

Values are in dollars or fractions of dollars. In the column headed *Ref*, references are shown to sources. Each reference is followed by a letter. These refer to the geographical level for which data were reported: s=State, r=Region, and c=City or metro. The abbreviation *ex* is used to mean *except* or *excluding*; *exp* stands for *expenditures*. For other abbreviations and further explanations, please see the Introduction.

Greenville-Spartanburg-Anderson, SC - continued

Item	Per	Value	Date	Ref.
Groceries				
Potatoes, frozen, french fried	lb	1.00	7/01	11r
Potatoes, white, all types	lb	0.44	7/01	11r
Poultry, expenditures on	yr	137	1999	30r
Processed fruits, expenditures on	yr	97	1999	30r
Processed vegetables, expenditures on	yr	82	1999	30r
Rice, white, long grain, uncooked	lb	0.51	7/01	11r
Round roast, graded and ungraded, excl U.S. prime and choice	lb	2.96	7/01	11r
Round steak, graded and ungraded, excl U.S. prime and choice	lb	3.11	7/01	11r
Sirloin steak, graded and ungraded, excl U.S. prime and choice	lb	4.23	7/01	11r
Spaghetti and macaroni	lb	0.78	7/01	11r
Steak, round, U.S. choice, boneless	lb	3.56	7/01	11r
Steak, sirloin, U.S. choice, boneless	lb	5.65	7/01	11r
Strawberries, dry pint	12 oz	1.50	7/01	11r
Sugar and other sweets, expenditures on	yr	99	1999	30r
Sugar, white, 33-80 ounce package	lb	0.39	7/01	11r
Sugar, white, all sizes	lb	0.42	7/01	11r
Tobacco products and smoking supplies purchases	yr	288	1999	30r
Tomatoes, field grown	lb	1.43	7/01	11r
Tuna, light, chunk	lb	1.77	7/01	11r
Turkey, frozen, whole	lb	1.05	7/01	11r
Goods and Services				
B&B Japanese maple (acer japonicum)	gal	49.98-129.00	4/00	93r
Boxwood (buxus)	2 gal	12.99-16.99	4/00	93r
Daylily (hemerocallis)	gal	4.99-8.99	4/00	93r
Flat of annuals		11.00-13.92	4/00	93r
Fountain grass (pennisetum)	gal	5.98-7.98	4/00	93r
Hanging basket (10 in)		7.99-14.98	4/00	93r
Hardy geranium (geranium)	gal	5.98-8.00	4/00	93r
Hosta (hosta)	gal	4.99-10.98	4/00	93r
Lilac (syrubga vulgaris)	2 gal	12.99-21.99	4/00	93r
Rhododendron (rhododendron)	2 gal	14.99-24.99	4/00	93r
Sage (salvia)	gal	5.98-6.99	4/00	93r
Wintercreeper euonymus (euonymus fortunei)	2 gal	7.99-89.99	4/00	93r
Hunting license	yr	12.00	4/01	34s
Health Care				
Cardiac catheterization, ave hospital/ physician charges		12360	1998	77s
Childbirth, Cesarean delivery		11587	1997	13r
Childbirth, vaginal delivery		6725	1997	13r
Drugs, expenditures on	yr	399	1999	30r
Health care purchases	yr	1971	1999	30r
Health insurance expenditures	yr	933	1999	30r
Hysterectomy, laproscopically-assisted, ave hospital/physician charges		11920	1998	76s
Hysterectomy, vaginal, ave hospital and physician charges		4890	1998	76s
Medicaid dispensing fee		4.05	1999	87s
Medical services expenditures	yr	547	1999	30r
Medical supplies, expenditures on	yr	91	1999	30r
Plastic surgery, breast augmentation		2870	2000	7r
Plastic surgery, breast lift		3649	2000	7r
Plastic surgery, facelift		5008	2000	7r
Plastic surgery, hair transplantation		3425	2000	7r
Plastic surgery, lip augmentation		1227	2000	7r
Plastic surgery, lower body lift		4793	2000	7r

Greenville-Spartanburg-Anderson, SC - continued

Item	Per	Value	Date	Ref.
Health Care - continued				
Plastic surgery, thigh lift		3862	2000	7r
Household Goods				
Floor coverings, expenditures on	yr	44	1999	30r
Furniture, expenditures on	yr	335	1999	30r
Household furnishings and equipment purchases	yr	1328	1999	30r
Household textiles, expenditures on	yr	89	1999	30r
Laundry and cleaning supplies, expenditures on	yr	113	1999	30r
Housing				
Home price, existing, ave		160100	10/00	90r
Home value, median		119000	2001	53s
Household operation expenditures	yr	553	1999	30r
Housekeeping supplies purchases	yr	473	1999	30r
Housing, expenditures on	yr	10303	1999	30r
Maintenance, repairs, insurance expenditures	yr	699	1999	30r
Monthly rental value of owned home	mos	505	1999	30r
Owned dwellings, expenditures own	yr	3465	1999	30r
Rent expenditures	yr	1641	1999	30r
Rental unit, 1 bedroom, with utilities	mos	478	4/01	41c
Rental unit, 2 bedroom, with utilities	mos	539	4/01	41c
Rental unit, 3 bedroom, with utilities	mos	679	4/01	41c
Rental unit, 4 bedroom, with utilities	mos	799	4/01	41c
Shelter, expenditures on	yr	5467	1999	30r
Insurance and Pensions				
Auto insurance	yr	655.33	1998	86s
Life and other personal insurance purchases	yr	414	1999	30r
Pensions and Social Security, expenditures on	yr	2635	1999	30r
Personal insurance and pensions, expenditures on	yr	3048	1999	30r
Legal Fees				
Combination hunting and fishing license	yr	20.00	4/01	34s
Driver's license fee	renew	12.50	1999	48s
Driver's license fee	orig	12.50	1999	48s
Fishing license	yr	10.00	4/01	34s
Personal Goods				
Personal care products and services purchases	yr	393	1999	30r
Personal Services				
Personal services, household, expenditures on	yr	258	1999	30r
Pets				
Pets, toys, and playground equipment, expenditures on	yr	306	1999	30r
Taxes				
Federal income taxes paid	yr	2047	1999	30r
Personal taxes, expenditures on	yr	2554	1999	30r
Property taxes paid	yr	726	1999	30r
State and local income taxes paid	yr	363	1999	30r
Transportation				
Cars and trucks, new, expenditures on	yr	1648	1999	30r
Cars and trucks, used, expenditures on	yr	1651	1999	30r
Diesel at the pump	gal	1.13	10/99	73s
Gasoline and motor oil purchases	yr	1052	1999	30r
Gasoline before-tax price (cents)	gal	101.70	10/00	43s
Maintenance and repair expenditures	yr	621	1999	30r
Public transportation, expenditures on	yr	298	1999	30r
Transportation purchases	yr	6738	1999	30r
Vehicle expenses, miscellaneous, purchases	yr	2033	1999	30r
Vehicle insurance payments	yr	696	1999	30r
Vehicle purchases (net outlay)	yr	3354	1999	30r
Vehicle rental, lease expenditures	yr	352	1999	30r
Utilities				
Electrical bill, average	mos	86.42	9/00	9s
Electricity, expenditures on	yr	1115	1999	30r

Values are in dollars or fractions of dollars. In the column headed *Ref*, references are shown to sources. Each reference is followed by a letter. These refer to the geographical level for which data were reported: s=State, r=Region, and c=City or metro. The abbreviation *ex* is used to mean *except* or *excluding*; *exp* stands for expenditures. For other abbreviations and further explanations, please see the Introduction.

Greenville-Spartanburg-Anderson, SC - continued

Item	Per	Value	Date	Ref.
Utilities				
Electricity cost, average	KWh	5.40	9/00	9s
Water and other public services, expenditures on	yr	298	1999	30r
Weddings				
Wedding (national average cost)		19936	2000	33r
Wedding (regional average total cost)		16293	1997	110r
Attendants' gifts		321	1998	33r
Bridal attendants' apparel (5 persons)		824	2000	33r
Bride's headpiece/veil		173	1998	33r
Bride's wedding dress		859	1998	33r
Clergy, religious facility fee		242	1998	33r
Engagement ring		3177	1998	33r
Flowers		789	1998	33r
Groom's formalwear rental		99	2000	33r
Limousine		410	1998	33r
Marriage license cost		25.00	4/01	35s
Men's formalwear (ushers, best man)		469	2000	33r
Mother of bride apparel		241	2000	33r
Music		866	1998	33r
Photography and videography		1368	1998	33r
Rehearsal dinner		728	1998	33r
Wedding invitations and announcements		341	1998	33r
Wedding reception		7968	2000	33r
Wedding rings (bride and groom)		1060	1998	33r

Gulfport-Biloxi, MS

Item	Per	Value	Date	Ref.
Alcoholic Beverages				
Alcoholic beverage purchases	yr	253	1999	30r
Malt beverages, all types, all sizes, any origin	16 oz	0.96	7/01	11r
Appliances				
Major appliances, expenditures on	yr	172	1999	30r
Small appliances, housewares, expenditures on	yr	81	1999	30r
Banking and Money				
Mortgage interest and charges paid	yr	2039	1999	30r
Mortgage principal paid on owned property	yr	1026	1999	30r
Vehicle finance charges paid	yr	365	1999	30r
Charity				
Cash contributions, expenditures	yr	1127	1999	30r
Child Care				
Child raising cost, total, age 0-2	yr	8540	1999	60r
Child raising cost, total, age 3-5	yr	8780	1999	60r
Child raising cost, total, age 6-8	yr	8820	1999	60r
Child raising cost, total, age 9-11	yr	8800	1999	60r
Child raising cost, total, age 12-14	yr	9510	1999	60r
Child raising cost, total, age 15-17	yr	9740	1999	60r
Child's child care and education, age 0-2	yr	1380	1999	60r
Child's child care and education, age 3-5	yr	1520	1999	60r
Child's child care and education, age 6-8	yr	990	1999	60r
Child's child care and education, age 9-11	yr	650	1999	60r
Child's child care and education, age 12-14	yr	490	1999	60r
Child's child care and education, age 15-17	yr	840	1999	60r
Child's clothing, age 0-2	yr	480	1999	60r
Child's clothing, age 3-5	yr	470	1999	60r
Child's clothing, age 6-8	yr	520	1999	60r
Child's clothing, age 9-11	yr	570	1999	60r
Child's clothing, age 12-14	yr	950	1999	60r
Child's clothing, age 15-17	yr	850	1999	60r
Child's food, age 0-2	yr	1000	1999	60r
Child's food, age 3-5	yr	1160	1999	60r
Child's food, age 6-8	yr	1490	1999	60r
Child's food, age 9-11	yr	1770	1999	60r
Child's food, age 12-14	yr	1770	1999	60r
Child's food, age 15-17	yr	1980	1999	60r
Child's health care, age 0-2	yr	620	1999	60r
Child's health care, age 3-5	yr	590	1999	60r
Child's health care, age 6-8	yr	680	1999	60r

Gulfport-Biloxi, MS - continued

Item	Per	Value	Date	Ref.
Child Care - continued				
Child's health care, age 9-11	yr	720	1999	60r
Child's health care, age 12-14	yr	730	1999	60r
Child's health care, age 15-17	yr	760	1999	60r
Child's housing, age 0-2	yr	3070	1999	60r
Child's housing, age 3-5	yr	3050	1999	60r
Child's housing, age 6-8	yr	3010	1999	60r
Child's housing, age 9-11	yr	2850	1999	60r
Child's housing, age 12-14	yr	3040	1999	60r
Child's housing, age 15-17	yr	2650	1999	60r
Child's personal care, reading, age 0-2	yr	910	1999	60r
Child's personal care, reading, age 3-5	yr	930	1999	60r
Child's personal care, reading, age 6-8	yr	960	1999	60r
Child's personal care, reading, age 9-11	yr	1000	1999	60r
Child's personal care, reading, age 12-14	yr	1170	1999	60r
Child's personal care, reading, age 15-17	yr	950	1999	60r
Clothing				
Apparel and services purchases	yr	1610	1999	30r
Boys, 2 to 15, expenditures on	yr	89	1999	30r
Children under 2, expenditures on	yr	79	1999	30r
Footwear, expenditures on	yr	283	1999	30r
Girls, 2 to 15, expenditures on	yr	103	1999	30r
Men and boys, expenditures on	yr	351	1999	30r
Men, 16 and over, expenditures on	yr	262	1999	30r
Women, 16 and over, expenditures on	yr	538	1999	30r
Communications				
Phone line, single, business, field visit	inst.	67.00	12/97	17s
Phone line, single, business, no field visit	inst.	67.00	12/97	17s
Phone line, single, residence, field visit	inst.	46.00	12/97	17s
Phone line, single, residence, no field visit	inst.	46.00	12/97	17s
Postage and stationery, expenditures on	yr	104	1999	30r
Postal rate, express mail, up to half-pound		12.45	7/01	108r
Postal rate, letter, first class, first ounce		0.34	7/01	108r
Postal rate, letter, two ounces		0.57	7/01	108r
Postal rate, post card		0.21	7/01	108r
Postal rate, priority mail, two pounds		3.95	7/01	108r
Postal rate, priority mail, up to one pound		3.50	7/01	108r
Telephone bill, business, basic rate	mos	47.48	12/97	18c
Telephone bill, residential, basic rate	mos	18.66	12/97	18c
Telephone services, expenditures on	yr	860	1999	30r
Education				
Board, 4-year private college/university	yr	1536	1996	38s
Board, 4-year public college/university	yr	1568	1996	38s
Education expenditures	yr	431	1999	30r
Room, 4-year private college/university	yr	1582	1996	38s
Room, 4-year public college/university	yr	1399	1996	38s
Total cost, 4-year private college/university	yr	9901	1996	38s
Total cost, 4-year public college/university	yr	5425	1996	38s
Tuition, 2-year public college/university, in state	yr	941	1996	38s
Tuition, 4-year private college/university, in state	yr	6782	1996	38s
Tuition, 4-year public college/university	yr	2459	1996	38s
Energy and Fuels				
Electricity	500 KWhs	47.29	7/01	11r
Electricity	KWh	0.09	7/01	11r
Fuel oil #2	gal	1.43	7/01	11r
Fuel oil and other fuels, expenditures on	yr	45	1999	30r
Gas, cooking, winter, 10 therms	mos	10.74	2/96	98c
Gas, cooking, winter, 30 therms	mos	20.73	2/96	98c
Gas, cooking, winter, 50 therms	mos	29.42	2/96	98c
Gas, heating, winter, average use	mos	53.57	2/96	98c
Gas, natural, commercial rate	1000 cf	7.01	11/00	88s
Gasoline, all types	gal	1.60	7/01	11r
Gasoline, unleaded midgrade	gal	1.65	7/01	11r
Gasoline, unleaded premium	gal	1.74	7/01	11r
Natural gas, expenditures on	yr	164	1999	30r
Utility (piped) gas, therm		1.01	7/01	11r
Utility (piped) gas, 40 therms		44.29	7/01	11r
Utility (piped) gas, 100 therms		97.44	7/01	11r

Values are in dollars or fractions of dollars. In the column headed *Ref*, references are shown to sources. Each reference is followed by a letter. These refer to the geographical level for which data were reported: s=State, r=Region, and c=City or metro. The abbreviation *ex* is used to mean *except* or *excluding*; *exp* stands for expenditures. For other abbreviations and further explanations, please see the Introduction.

Gulfport-Biloxi, MS - continued

Item	Per	Value	Date	Ref.
Entertainment				
Entertainment purchases	yr	1574	1999	30r
Fees and admissions paid	yr	371	1999	30r
Reading purchases	yr	121	1999	30r
Television, radios, sound equipment, expenditures on	yr	561	1999	30r
Groceries				
American processed cheese	lb	3.50	7/01	11r
Bakery products, expenditures on	yr	261	1999	30r
Bananas	lb	0.47	7/01	11r
Beans, dried, any type, all sizes	lb	0.63	7/01	11r
Beef for stew, boneless	lb	2.86	7/01	11r
Beef, expenditures on	yr	210	1999	30r
Bologna, all beef or mixed	lb	2.29	7/01	11r
Bread, French	lb	1.66	7/01	11r
Bread, white, pan	lb	0.87	7/01	11r
Bread, whole wheat, pan	lb	1.38	7/01	11r
Broccoli	lb	1.04	7/01	11r
Butter, salted, grade AA, stick	lb	2.26	7/01	11r
Butter, yoghurt, cheese, etc, expenditures on	yr	170	1999	30r
Cabbage	lb	0.42	7/01	11r
Cereals and cereal products, expenditures on	yr	140	1999	30r
Cheddar cheese, natural	lb	3.75	7/01	11r
Chicken breast, bone-in	lb	1.85	7/01	11r
Chicken legs, bone-in	lb	1.34	7/01	11r
Chicken, fresh, whole	lb	1.05	7/01	11r
Chops, boneless,	lb	4.13	7/01	11r
Chuck roast, graded and ungraded, excl U.S. prime and choice	lb	2.35	7/01	11r
Chuck roast, U.S. choice, boneless	lb	2.67	7/01	11r
Coffee, 100%, ground roast, all sizes	lb	2.88	7/01	11r
Coffee, instant, plain, regular, all sizes	16 oz	9.25	7/01	11r
Cola, non diet	2 liter	1.11	7/01	11r
Crackers, soda, salted	lb	1.70	7/01	11r
Dairy product purchases	yr	282	1999	30r
Eggs, expenditures on	yr	32	1999	30r
Fats and oils, expenditures on	yr	79	1999	30r
Fish and seafood, expenditures on	yr	99	1999	30r
Flour, white, all purpose	lb	0.32	7/01	11r
Food (excl fruit and vegetables), eaten at home, purchases	yr	815	1999	30r
Food cooked on trips, expenditures on	yr	36	1999	30r
Food purchases	yr	4533	1999	30r
Food purchases, eaten away from home	yr	1873	1999	30r
Food purchases, food eaten at home	yr	2660	1999	30r
Fresh fruits, expenditures on	yr	128	1999	30r
Fresh milk and cream, expenditures on	yr	112	1999	30r
Fresh vegetables, expenditures on	yr	131	1999	30r
Fruit and vegetable purchases	yr	438	1999	30r
Grapefruit	lb	0.59	7/01	11r
Grapes, Thompson, seedless	lb	2.12	7/01	11r
Ground beef, 100% beef	lb	1.76	7/01	11r
Ground beef, lean and extra lean	lb	2.60	7/01	11r
Ground chuck, 100% beef	lb	2.08	7/01	11r
Ham, boneless, excl canned	lb	2.71	7/01	11r
Ham, rump or shank half, bone-in, smoked	lb	2.19	7/01	11r
Ice cream, prepackaged, bulk, regular	1/2 gal	3.93	7/01	11r
Lemons	lb	1.32	7/01	11r
Lettuce, iceberg	lb	0.76	7/01	11r
Milk, fresh, low fat,	gal	2.75	7/01	11r
Milk, fresh, whole, fortified	gal	2.97	7/01	11r
Nonalcoholic beverages, expenditures on	yr	228	1999	30r
Orange juice, frozen concentrate	16 oz	1.95	7/01	11r
Oranges, Navel	lb	0.73	7/01	11r
Oranges, Valencia	lb	0.55	7/01	11r
Peanut butter, creamy, all sizes	lb	1.83	7/01	11r
Pears, Anjou	lb	0.98	7/01	11r
Pork chops, center cut, bone-in	lb	3.33	7/01	11r
Pork sausage, fresh, loose	lb	2.59	7/01	11r
Pork shoulder picnic, bone-in, smoked	lb	1.12	7/01	11r
Pork, expenditures on	yr	162	1999	30r
Potato chips	16 oz	3.59	7/01	11r

Gulfport-Biloxi, MS - continued

Item	Per	Value	Date	Ref.
Groceries - continued				
Potatoes, frozen, french fried	lb	1.00	7/01	11r
Potatoes, white, all types	lb	0.44	7/01	11r
Poultry, expenditures on	yr	137	1999	30r
Processed fruits, expenditures on	yr	97	1999	30r
Processed vegetables, expenditures on	yr	82	1999	30r
Rice, white, long grain, uncooked	lb	0.51	7/01	11r
Round roast, graded and ungraded, excl U.S. prime and choice	lb	2.96	7/01	11r
Round steak, graded and ungraded, excl U.S. prime and choice	lb	3.11	7/01	11r
Sirloin steak, graded and ungraded, excl U.S. prime and choice	lb	4.23	7/01	11r
Spaghetti and macaroni	lb	0.78	7/01	11r
Steak, round, U.S. choice, boneless	lb	3.56	7/01	11r
Steak, sirloin, U.S. choice, boneless	lb	5.65	7/01	11r
Strawberries, dry pint	12 oz	1.50	7/01	11r
Sugar and other sweets, expenditures on	yr	99	1999	30r
Sugar, white, 33-80 ounce package	lb	0.39	7/01	11r
Sugar, white, all sizes	lb	0.42	7/01	11r
Tobacco products and smoking supplies purchases	yr	288	1999	30r
Tomatoes, field grown	lb	1.43	7/01	11r
Tuna, light, chunk	lb	1.77	7/01	11r
Turkey, frozen, whole	lb	1.05	7/01	11r
Goods and Services				
Hunting license	yr	18.00	4/01	34s
Health Care				
Cardiac catheterization, ave hospital/physician charges		10310	1998	77s
Childbirth, Cesarean delivery		11587	1997	13r
Childbirth, vaginal delivery		6725	1997	13r
Drugs, expenditures on	yr	399	1999	30r
Health care purchases	yr	1971	1999	30r
Health insurance expenditures	yr	933	1999	30r
Hysterectomy, laproscopically-assisted, ave hospital/physician charges		14270	1998	76s
Hysterectomy, vaginal, ave hospital and physician charges		10020	1998	76s
Medicaid dispensing fee		4.91	1999	87s
Medical services expenditures	yr	547	1999	30r
Medical supplies, expenditures on	yr	91	1999	30r
Household Goods				
Floor coverings, expenditures on	yr	44	1999	30r
Furniture, expenditures on	yr	335	1999	30r
Household furnishings and equipment purchases	yr	1328	1999	30r
Household textiles, expenditures on	yr	89	1999	30r
Laundry and cleaning supplies, expenditures on	yr	113	1999	30r
Housing				
Home price, existing, ave		160100	10/00	90r
Home value, median		102000	2001	53s
Household operation expenditures	yr	553	1999	30r
Housekeeping supplies purchases	yr	473	1999	30r
Housing, expenditures on	yr	10303	1999	30r
Maintenance, repairs, insurance expenditures	yr	699	1999	30r
Monthly rental value of owned home	mos	505	1999	30r
Owned dwellings, expenditures own	yr	3465	1999	30r
Rent expenditures	yr	1641	1999	30r
Shelter, expenditures on	yr	5467	1999	30r
Insurance and Pensions				
Life and other personal insurance purchases	yr	414	1999	30r
Pensions and Social Security, expenditures on	yr	2635	1999	30r
Personal insurance and pensions, expenditures on	yr	3048	1999	30r

Values are in dollars or fractions of dollars. In the column headed *Ref*, references are shown to sources. Each reference is followed by a letter. These refer to the geographical level for which data were reported: s=State, r=Region, and c=City or metro. The abbreviation *ex* is used to mean *except* or *excluding*; *exp* stands for *expenditures*. For other abbreviations and further explanations, please see the Introduction.

Gulfport-Biloxi, MS - continued

Item	Per	Value	Date	Ref.
Legal Fees				
Combination hunting and fishing license	yr	18.00	4/01	34s
Driver's license fee	renew	5.00	1999	48s
Driver's license fee	orig	20.00	1999	48s
Fishing license	yr	12.00	4/01	34s
Personal Goods				
Personal care products and services purchases	yr	393	1999	30r
Personal Services				
Personal services, household, expenditures on	yr	258	1999	30r
Pets				
Pets, toys, and playground equipment, expenditures on	yr	306	1999	30r
Taxes				
Federal income taxes paid	yr	2047	1999	30r
Personal taxes, expenditures on	yr	2554	1999	30r
Property taxes paid	yr	726	1999	30r
State and local income taxes paid	yr	363	1999	30r
Transportation				
Cars and trucks, new, expenditures on	yr	1648	1999	30r
Cars and trucks, used, expenditures on	yr	1651	1999	30r
Diesel at the pump	gal	1.17	10/99	73s
Gasoline and motor oil purchases	yr	1052	1999	30r
Gasoline before-tax price (cents)	gal	108.40	10/00	43s
Maintenance and repair expenditures	yr	621	1999	30r
Motorcycle license fee	orig	5.00	1999	49s
Motorcycle license fee	renew	5.00	1999	49s
Public transportation, expenditures on	yr	298	1999	30r
Transportation purchases	yr	6738	1999	30r
Vehicle expenses, miscellaneous, purchases	yr	2033	1999	30r
Vehicle insurance payments	yr	696	1999	30r
Vehicle purchases (net outlay)	yr	3354	1999	30r
Vehicle rental, lease expenditures	yr	352	1999	30r
Utilities				
Electrical bill, average	mos	79.66	9/00	9s
Electricity, expenditures on	yr	1115	1999	30r
Electricity cost, average	KWh	5.69	9/00	9s
Water and other public services, expenditures on	yr	298	1999	30r
Weddings				
Wedding (national average cost)		19936	2000	33r
Attendants' gifts		321	1998	33r
Bridal attendants' apparel (5 persons)		824	2000	33r
Bride's headpiece/veil		173	1998	33r
Bride's wedding dress		859	1998	33r
Clergy, religious facility fee		242	1998	33r
Engagement ring		3177	1998	33r
Flowers		789	1998	33r
Groom's formalwear rental		99	2000	33r
Limousine		410	1998	33r
Marriage license cost		21.00	4/01	35s
Men's formalwear (ushers, best man)		469	2000	33r
Mother of bride apparel		241	2000	33r
Music		866	1998	33r
Photography and videography		1368	1998	33r
Rehearsal dinner		728	1998	33r
Wedding invitations and announcements		341	1998	33r
Wedding reception		7968	2000	33r
Wedding rings (bride and groom)		1060	1998	33r

Hagerstown, MD

Item	Per	Value	Date	Ref.
Alcoholic Beverages				
Alcoholic beverage purchases	yr	253	1999	30r
Malt beverages, all types, all sizes, any origin	16 oz	0.96	7/01	11r

Hagerstown, MD - continued

Item	Per	Value	Date	Ref.
Appliances				
Major appliances, expenditures on	yr	172	1999	30r
Small appliances, housewares, expenditures on	yr	81	1999	30r
Banking and Money				
Mortgage interest and charges paid	yr	2039	1999	30r
Mortgage principal paid on owned property	yr	1026	1999	30r
Vehicle finance charges paid	yr	365	1999	30r
Charity				
Cash contributions, expenditures	yr	1127	1999	30r
Child Care				
Child raising cost, total, age 0-2	yr	8540	1999	60r
Child raising cost, total, age 3-5	yr	8780	1999	60r
Child raising cost, total, age 6-8	yr	8820	1999	60r
Child raising cost, total, age 9-11	yr	8800	1999	60r
Child raising cost, total, age 12-14	yr	9510	1999	60r
Child raising cost, total, age 15-17	yr	9740	1999	60r
Child's child care and education, age 0-2	yr	1380	1999	60r
Child's child care and education, age 3-5	yr	1520	1999	60r
Child's child care and education, age 6-8	yr	990	1999	60r
Child's child care and education, age 9-11	yr	650	1999	60r
Child's child care and education, age 12-14	yr	490	1999	60r
Child's child care and education, age 15-17	yr	840	1999	60r
Child's clothing, age 0-2	yr	480	1999	60r
Child's clothing, age 3-5	yr	470	1999	60r
Child's clothing, age 6-8	yr	520	1999	60r
Child's clothing, age 9-11	yr	570	1999	60r
Child's clothing, age 12-14	yr	950	1999	60r
Child's clothing, age 15-17	yr	850	1999	60r
Child's food, age 0-2	yr	1000	1999	60r
Child's food, age 3-5	yr	1160	1999	60r
Child's food, age 6-8	yr	1490	1999	60r
Child's food, age 9-11	yr	1770	1999	60r
Child's food, age 12-14	yr	1770	1999	60r
Child's food, age 15-17	yr	1980	1999	60r
Child's health care, age 0-2	yr	620	1999	60r
Child's health care, age 3-5	yr	590	1999	60r
Child's health care, age 6-8	yr	680	1999	60r
Child's health care, age 9-11	yr	720	1999	60r
Child's health care, age 12-14	yr	730	1999	60r
Child's health care, age 15-17	yr	760	1999	60r
Child's housing, age 0-2	yr	3070	1999	60r
Child's housing, age 3-5	yr	3050	1999	60r
Child's housing, age 6-8	yr	3010	1999	60r
Child's housing, age 9-11	yr	2850	1999	60r
Child's housing, age 12-14	yr	3040	1999	60r
Child's housing, age 15-17	yr	2650	1999	60r
Child's personal care, reading, age 0-2	yr	910	1999	60r
Child's personal care, reading, age 3-5	yr	930	1999	60r
Child's personal care, reading, age 6-8	yr	960	1999	60r
Child's personal care, reading, age 9-11	yr	1000	1999	60r
Child's personal care, reading, age 12-14	yr	1170	1999	60r
Child's personal care, reading, age 15-17	yr	950	1999	60r
Clothing				
Apparel and services purchases	yr	1610	1999	30r
Boys, 2 to 15, expenditures on	yr	89	1999	30r
Children under 2, expenditures on	yr	79	1999	30r
Footwear, expenditures on	yr	283	1999	30r
Girls, 2 to 15, expenditures on	yr	103	1999	30r
Men and boys, expenditures on	yr	351	1999	30r
Men, 16 and over, expenditures on	yr	262	1999	30r
Women, 16 and over, expenditures on	yr	538	1999	30r
Communications				
Cable modem installation, Comcast		95.00	6/99	103s
Cable modem rate, cable subscriber, Comcast	mos	39.95	6/99	103s
Cable modem rate, non-cable subscriber, Comcast	mos	49.95	6/99	103s
Phone line, single, business, field visit	inst.	98.50	12/97	17s
Phone line, single, business, no field visit	inst.	98.50	12/97	17s

Values are in dollars or fractions of dollars. In the column headed *Ref*, references are shown to sources. Each reference is followed by a letter. These refer to the geographical level for which data were reported: s=State, r=Region, and c=City or metro. The abbreviation *ex* is used to mean *except* or *excluding*; *exp* stands for *expenditures*. For other abbreviations and further explanations, please see the Introduction.

Hagerstown, MD - continued

Item	Per	Value	Date	Ref.
Communications				
Phone line, single, residence, field visit	inst.	48.00	12/97	17s
Phone line, single, residence, no field visit	inst.	48.00	12/97	17s
Postage and stationery, expenditures on	yr	104	1999	30r
Postal rate, express mail, up to half-pound		12.45	7/01	108r
Postal rate, letter, first class, first ounce		0.34	7/01	108r
Postal rate, letter, two ounces		0.57	7/01	108r
Postal rate, post card		0.21	7/01	108r
Postal rate, priority mail, two pounds		3.95	7/01	108r
Postal rate, priority mail, up to one pound		3.50	7/01	108r
Telephone services, expenditures on	yr	860	1999	30r
Education				
Board, 4-year private college/university	yr	3022	1996	38s
Board, 4-year public college/university	yr	2435	1996	38s
Education expenditures	yr	431	1999	30r
Room, 4-year private college/university	yr	3524	1996	38s
Room, 4-year public college/university	yr	2722	1996	38s
Total cost, 4-year private college/university	yr	21245	1996	38s
Total cost, 4-year public college/university	yr	8728	1996	38s
Tuition, 2-year public college/university, in state	yr	1967	1996	38s
Tuition, 4-year private college/university, in state	yr	14700	1996	38s
Tuition, 4-year public college/university	yr	3572	1996	38s
Energy and Fuels				
Electricity	KWh	0.09	7/01	11r
Electricity	500 KWhs	47.29	7/01	11r
Fuel oil #2	gal	1.43	7/01	11r
Fuel oil and other fuels, expenditures on	yr	45	1999	30r
Gas, natural, commercial rate	1000 cf	8.64	11/00	88s
Gasoline, all types	gal	1.60	7/01	11r
Gasoline, unleaded midgrade	gal	1.65	7/01	11r
Gasoline, unleaded premium	gal	1.74	7/01	11r
Natural gas, expenditures on	yr	164	1999	30r
Utility (piped) gas, therm		1.01	7/01	11r
Utility (piped) gas, 40 therms		44.29	7/01	11r
Utility (piped) gas, 100 therms		97.44	7/01	11r
Entertainment				
Entertainment purchases	yr	1574	1999	30r
Fees and admissions paid	yr	371	1999	30r
Reading purchases	yr	121	1999	30r
Television, radios, sound equipment, expenditures on	yr	561	1999	30r
Funerals				
Total cost of funeral		5922.53	1/99	78r
Acknowledgement cards		63.43	1/99	78r
Casket		2258.77	1/99	78r
Cosmetology, hair, other preparation		127.09	1/99	78r
Embalming		393.49	1/99	78r
Funeral at funeral home		367.50	1/99	78r
Hearse (local)		169.66	1/99	78r
Professional service charges		1211.32	1/99	78r
Service car/van		80.69	1/99	78r
Transfer of remains to funeral home		144.25	1/99	78r
Vault		803.50	1/99	78r
Visitation/viewing		302.83	1/99	78r
Groceries				
American processed cheese	lb	3.50	7/01	11r
Bakery products, expenditures on	yr	261	1999	30r
Bananas	lb	0.47	7/01	11r
Beans, dried, any type, all sizes	lb	0.63	7/01	11r
Beef for stew, boneless	lb	2.86	7/01	11r
Beef, expenditures on	yr	210	1999	30r
Bologna, all beef or mixed	lb	2.29	7/01	11r
Bread, French	lb	1.66	7/01	11r
Bread, white, pan	lb	0.87	7/01	11r
Bread, whole wheat, pan	lb	1.38	7/01	11r
Broccoli	lb	1.04	7/01	11r
Butter, salted, grade AA, stick	lb	2.26	7/01	11r

Hagerstown, MD - continued

Item	Per	Value	Date	Ref.
Groceries - continued				
Butter, yoghurt, cheese, etc, expenditures on	yr	170	1999	30r
Cabbage	lb	0.42	7/01	11r
Cereals and cereal products, expenditures on	yr	140	1999	30r
Cheddar cheese, natural	lb	3.75	7/01	11r
Chicken breast, bone-in	lb	1.85	7/01	11r
Chicken legs, bone-in	lb	1.34	7/01	11r
Chicken, fresh, whole	lb	1.05	7/01	11r
Chops, boneless,	lb	4.13	7/01	11r
Chuck roast, graded and ungraded, excl U.S. prime and choice	lb	2.35	7/01	11r
Chuck roast, U.S. choice, boneless	lb	2.67	7/01	11r
Coffee, 100%, ground roast, all sizes	lb	2.88	7/01	11r
Coffee, instant, plain, regular, all sizes	16 oz	9.25	7/01	11r
Cola, non diet,	2 liter	1.11	7/01	11r
Crackers, soda, salted	lb	1.70	7/01	11r
Dairy product purchases	yr	282	1999	30r
Eggs, expenditures on	yr	32	1999	30r
Fats and oils, expenditures on	yr	79	1999	30r
Fish and seafood, expenditures on	yr	99	1999	30r
Flour, white, all purpose	lb	0.32	7/01	11r
Food (excl fruit and vegetables), eaten at home, purchases	yr	815	1999	30r
Food cooked on trips, expenditures on	yr	36	1999	30r
Food purchases	yr	4533	1999	30r
Food purchases, eaten away from home	yr	1873	1999	30r
Food purchases, food eaten at home	yr	2660	1999	30r
Fresh fruits, expenditures on	yr	128	1999	30r
Fresh milk and cream, expenditures on	yr	112	1999	30r
Fresh vegetables, expenditures on	yr	131	1999	30r
Fruit and vegetable purchases	yr	438	1999	30r
Grapefruit	lb	0.59	7/01	11r
Grapes, Thompson, seedless	lb	2.12	7/01	11r
Ground beef, 100% beef	lb	1.76	7/01	11r
Ground beef, lean and extra lean	lb	2.60	7/01	11r
Ground chuck, 100% beef	lb	2.08	7/01	11r
Ham, boneless, excl canned	lb	2.71	7/01	11r
Ham, rump or shank half, bone-in, smoked	lb	2.19	7/01	11r
Ice cream, prepackaged, bulk, regular	1/2 gal	3.93	7/01	11r
Lemons	lb	1.32	7/01	11r
Lettuce, iceberg	lb	0.76	7/01	11r
Milk, fresh, low fat,	gal	2.75	7/01	11r
Milk, fresh, whole, fortified	gal	2.97	7/01	11r
Nonalcoholic beverages, expenditures on	yr	228	1999	30r
Orange juice, frozen concentrate	16 oz	1.95	7/01	11r
Oranges, Navel	lb	0.73	7/01	11r
Oranges, Valencia	lb	0.55	7/01	11r
Peanut butter, creamy, all sizes	lb	1.83	7/01	11r
Pears, Anjou	lb	0.98	7/01	11r
Pork chops, center cut, bone-in	lb	3.33	7/01	11r
Pork sausage, fresh, loose	lb	2.59	7/01	11r
Pork shoulder picnic, bone-in, smoked	lb	1.12	7/01	11r
Pork, expenditures on	yr	162	1999	30r
Potato chips	16 oz	3.59	7/01	11r
Potatoes, frozen, french fried	lb	1.00	7/01	11r
Potatoes, white, all types	lb	0.44	7/01	11r
Poultry, expenditures on	yr	137	1999	30r
Processed fruits, expenditures on	yr	97	1999	30r
Processed vegetables, expenditures on	yr	82	1999	30r
Rice, white, long grain, uncooked	lb	0.51	7/01	11r
Round roast, graded and ungraded, excl U.S. prime and choice	lb	2.96	7/01	11r
Round steak, graded and ungraded, excl U.S. prime and choice	lb	3.11	7/01	11r
Sirloin steak, graded and ungraded, excl U.S. prime and choice	lb	4.23	7/01	11r
Spaghetti and macaroni	lb	0.78	7/01	11r
Steak, round, U.S. choice, boneless	lb	3.56	7/01	11r
Steak, sirloin, U.S. choice, boneless	lb	5.65	7/01	11r
Strawberries, dry pint	12 oz	1.50	7/01	11r
Sugar and other sweets, expenditures on	yr	99	1999	30r
Sugar, white, 33-80 ounce package	lb	0.39	7/01	11r

Values are in dollars or fractions of dollars. In the column headed *Ref*, references are shown to sources. Each reference is followed by a letter. These refer to the geographical level for which data were reported: s=State, r=Region, and c=City or metro. The abbreviation *ex* is used to mean *except* or *excluding*; *exp* stands for expenditures. For other abbreviations and further explanations, please see the Introduction.

Hagerstown, MD - continued

Item	Per	Value	Date	Ref.
Groceries				
Sugar, white, all sizes	lb	0.42	7/01	11r
Tobacco products and smoking supplies purchases	yr	288	1999	30r
Tomatoes, field grown	lb	1.43	7/01	11r
Tuna, light, chunk	lb	1.77	7/01	11r
Turkey, frozen, whole	lb	1.05	7/01	11r
Goods and Services				
B&B Japanese maple (acer japonicum)	gal	49.98-129.00	4/00	93r
Boxwood (buxus)	2 gal	12.99-16.99	4/00	93r
Daylilly (hemerocallis)	gal	4.99-8.99	4/00	93r
Flat of annuals		11.00-13.92	4/00	93r
Fountain grass (pennisetum)	gal	5.98-7.98	4/00	93r
Hanging basket (10 in)		7.99-14.98	4/00	93r
Hardy geranium (geranium)	gal	5.98-8.00	4/00	93r
Hosta (hosta)	gal	4.99-10.98	4/00	93r
Lilac (syrubga vulgaris)	2 gal	12.99-21.99	4/00	93r
Rhododendron (rhododendron)	2 gal	14.99-24.99	4/00	93r
Sage (salvia)	gal	5.98-6.99	4/00	93r
Wintercreeper euonymus (euonymus fortunei)	2 gal	7.99-89.99	4/00	93r
Hunting license	yr	15.50	4/01	34s
Health Care				
Cardiac catheterization, ave hospital/ physician charges		11420	1998	77s
Childbirth, Cesarean delivery		11587	1997	13r
Childbirth, vaginal delivery		6725	1997	13r
Drugs, expenditures on	yr	399	1999	30r
Health care purchases	yr	1971	1999	30r
Health insurance expenditures	yr	933	1999	30r
Hysterectomy, laproscopically-assisted, ave hospital/physician charges		11890	1998	76s
Hysterectomy, vaginal, ave hospital and physician charges		8120	1998	76s
Medicaid dispensing fee		4.21	1999	87s
Medical services expenditures	yr	547	1999	30r
Medical supplies, expenditures on	yr	91	1999	30r
Plastic surgery, breast augmentation		2870	2000	7r
Plastic surgery, breast lift		3649	2000	7r
Plastic surgery, facelift		5008	2000	7r
Plastic surgery, hair transplantation		3425	2000	7r
Plastic surgery, lip augmentation		1227	2000	7r
Plastic surgery, lower body lift		4793	2000	7r
Plastic surgery, thigh lift		3862	2000	7r
Household Goods				
Floor coverings, expenditures on	yr	44	1999	30r
Furniture, expenditures on	yr	335	1999	30r
Household furnishings and equipment purchases	yr	1328	1999	30r
Household textiles, expenditures on	yr	89	1999	30r
Laundry and cleaning supplies, expenditures on	yr	113	1999	30r
Housing				
Home, 2200 sq ft, 4-br, 2-bath, 2-car garage, average		181475	2000	47c
Home price, existing, ave		160100	10/00	90r
Home value, median		146000	2001	53s
Household operation expenditures	yr	553	1999	30r
Housekeeping supplies purchases	yr	473	1999	30r
Housing, expenditures on	yr	10303	1999	30r

Hagerstown, MD - continued

Item	Per	Value	Date	Ref.
Housing - continued				
Maintenance, repairs, insurance expenditures	yr	699	1999	30r
Monthly rental value of owned home	mos	505	1999	30r
Owned dwellings, expenditures own	yr	3465	1999	30r
Rent expenditures	yr	1641	1999	30r
Rental unit, 1 bedroom, with utilities	mos	418	4/01	41c
Rental unit, 2 bedroom, with utilities	mos	522	4/01	41c
Rental unit, 3 bedroom, with utilities	mos	683	4/01	41c
Rental unit, 4 bedroom, with utilities	mos	780	4/01	41c
Shelter, expenditures on	yr	5467	1999	30r
Insurance and Pensions				
Life and other personal insurance purchases	yr	414	1999	30r
Pensions and Social Security, expenditures on	yr	2635	1999	30r
Personal insurance and pensions, expenditures on	yr	3048	1999	30r
Legal Fees				
Driver's license fee	renew	20.00	1999	48s
Driver's license fee	orig	30.00	1999	48s
Fishing license	yr	9.00	4/01	34s
Personal Goods				
Personal care products and services purchases	yr	393	1999	30r
Personal Services				
Personal services, household, expenditures on	yr	258	1999	30r
Pets				
Pets, toys, and playground equipment, expenditures on	yr	306	1999	30r
Taxes				
Federal income taxes paid	yr	2047	1999	30r
Personal taxes, expenditures on	yr	2554	1999	30r
Property taxes paid	yr	726	1999	30r
State and local income taxes paid	yr	363	1999	30r
Transportation				
Cars and trucks, new, expenditures on	yr	1648	1999	30r
Cars and trucks, used, expenditures on	yr	1651	1999	30r
Diesel at the pump	gal	1.29	10/99	73s
Gasoline and motor oil purchases	yr	1052	1999	30r
Gasoline before-tax price (cents)	gal	106.80	10/00	43s
Maintenance and repair expenditures	yr	621	1999	30r
Public transportation, expenditures on	yr	298	1999	30r
Transportation purchases	yr	6738	1999	30r
Vehicle expenses, miscellaneous, purchases	yr	2033	1999	30r
Vehicle insurance payments	yr	696	1999	30r
Vehicle purchases (net outlay)	yr	3354	1999	30r
Vehicle rental, lease expenditures	yr	352	1999	30r
Utilities				
Electrical bill, average	mos	83.58	9/00	9s
Electricity, expenditures on	yr	1115	1999	30r
Electricity cost, average	KWh	6.90	9/00	9s
Water and other public services, expenditures on	yr	298	1999	30r
Weddings				
Wedding (national average cost)		19936	2000	33r
Wedding (regional average total cost)		16293	1997	110r
Attendants' gifts		321	1998	33r
Bridal attendants' apparel (5 persons)		824	2000	33r
Bride's headpiece/veil		173	1998	33r
Bride's wedding dress		859	1998	33r
Clergy, religious facility fee		242	1998	33r
Engagement ring		3177	1998	33r
Flowers		789	1998	33r
Groom's formalwear rental		99	2000	33r
Limousine		410	1998	33r
Marriage license cost		55.00	4/01	35s
Men's formalwear (ushers, best man)		469	2000	33r

Values are in dollars or fractions of dollars. In the column headed *Ref*, references are shown to sources. Each reference is followed by a letter. These refer to the geographical level for which data were reported: s=State, r=Region, and c=City or metro. The abbreviation *ex* is used to mean *except* or *excluding*; *exp* stands for expenditures. For other abbreviations and further explanations, please see the Introduction.

Hagerstown, MD - continued

Item	Per	Value	Date	Ref.
Weddings				
Mother of bride apparel		241	2000	33r
Music		866	1998	33r
Photography and videography		1368	1998	33r
Rehearsal dinner		728	1998	33r
Wedding invitations and announcements		341	1998	33r
Wedding reception		7968	2000	33r
Wedding rings (bride and groom)		1060	1998	33r

Hamilton-Middletown, OH

Item	Per	Value	Date	Ref.
Average annual expenditures	yr	35369	1999	30r
Alcoholic Beverages				
Alcoholic beverage purchases	yr	304	1999	30r
Malt beverages, all types, all sizes, any origin	16 oz	0.93	7/01	11r
Wine, red and white table, all sizes, any origin	liter	7.04	7/01	11r
Appliances				
Major appliances, expenditures on	yr	165	1999	30r
Small appliances, housewares, expenditures on	yr	90	1999	30r
Banking and Money				
Mortgage interest and charges paid	yr	2277	1999	30r
Mortgage principal paid on owned property	yr	1230	1999	30r
Vehicle finance charges paid	yr	328	1999	30r
Charity				
Cash contributions, expenditures	yr	1126	1999	30r
Child Care				
Child raising cost, total, age 0-2	yr	7890	1999	60r
Child raising cost, total, age 3-5	yr	8130	1999	60r
Child raising cost, total, age 6-8	yr	8170	1999	60r
Child raising cost, total, age 9-11	yr	8190	1999	60r
Child raising cost, total, age 12-14	yr	8890	1999	60r
Child raising cost, total, age 15-17	yr	9050	1999	60r
Child's child care and education, age 0-2	yr	1240	1999	60r
Child's child care and education, age 3-5	yr	1370	1999	60r
Child's child care and education, age 6-8	yr	880	1999	60r
Child's child care and education, age 9-11	yr	570	1999	60r
Child's child care and education, age 12-14	yr	420	1999	60r
Child's child care and education, age 15-17	yr	720	1999	60r
Child's clothing, age 0-2	yr	410	1999	60r
Child's clothing, age 3-5	yr	400	1999	60r
Child's clothing, age 6-8	yr	450	1999	60r
Child's clothing, age 9-11	yr	500	1999	60r
Child's clothing, age 12-14	yr	840	1999	60r
Child's clothing, age 15-17	yr	740	1999	60r
Child's food, age 0-2	yr	960	1999	60r
Child's food, age 3-5	yr	1120	1999	60r
Child's food, age 6-8	yr	1430	1999	60r
Child's food, age 9-11	yr	1710	1999	60r
Child's food, age 12-14	yr	1710	1999	60r
Child's food, age 15-17	yr	1920	1999	60r
Child's health care, age 0-2	yr	520	1999	60r
Child's health care, age 3-5	yr	500	1999	60r
Child's health care, age 6-8	yr	570	1999	60r
Child's health care, age 9-11	yr	610	1999	60r
Child's health care, age 12-14	yr	630	1999	60r
Child's health care, age 15-17	yr	650	1999	60r
Child's housing, age 0-2	yr	2860	1999	60r
Child's housing, age 3-5	yr	2840	1999	60r
Child's housing, age 6-8	yr	2800	1999	60r
Child's housing, age 9-11	yr	2650	1999	60r
Child's housing, age 12-14	yr	2840	1999	60r
Child's housing, age 15-17	yr	2440	1999	60r
Child's personal care, reading, age 0-2	yr	880	1999	60r
Child's personal care, reading, age 3-5	yr	900	1999	60r
Child's personal care, reading, age 6-8	yr	930	1999	60r
Child's personal care, reading, age 9-11	yr	970	1999	60r
Child's personal care, reading, age 12-14	yr	1150	1999	60r
Child's personal care, reading, age 15-17	yr	920	1999	60r

Hamilton-Middletown, OH - continued

Item	Per	Value	Date	Ref.
Clothing				
Apparel and services purchases	yr	1607	1999	30r
Boys, 2 to 15, expenditures on	yr	91	1999	30r
Children under 2, expenditures on	yr	59	1999	30r
Footwear, expenditures on	yr	285	1999	30r
Girls, 2 to 15, expenditures on	yr	116	1999	30r
Men and boys, expenditures on	yr	433	1999	30r
Men, 16 and over, expenditures on	yr	341	1999	30r
Women, 16 and over, expenditures on	yr	490	1999	30r
Communications				
Cable modem installation, Adelphi		54.90	6/99	103s
Cable modem installation, Media One		100.00	6/99	103s
Cable modem installation, Time Warner		75.00-225.00	6/99	103s
Cable modem rate, cable subscriber, Adelphi	mos	34.95	6/99	103s
Cable modem rate, cable subscriber, Media One	mos	34.95-39.95	6/99	103s
Cable modem rate, cable subscriber, Time Warner	mos	39.95-49.95	6/99	103s
Cable modem rate, non-cable subscriber, Adelphi	mos	44.95	6/99	103s
Cable modem rate, non-cable subscriber, Media One	mos	49.95	6/99	103s
Cable modem rate, non-cable subscriber, Time Warner	mos	39.95-54.95	6/99	103s
Phone line, single, business, field visit	inst.	56.32	12/97	17s
Phone line, single, business, no field visit	inst.	56.32	12/97	17s
Phone line, single, residence, field visit	inst.	31.10	12/97	17s
Phone line, single, residence, no field visit	inst.	31.10	12/97	17s
Postage and stationery, expenditures on	yr	140	1999	30r
Postal rate, express mail, up to half-pound		12.45	7/01	108r
Postal rate, letter, first class, first ounce		0.34	7/01	108r
Postal rate, letter, two ounces		0.57	7/01	108r
Postal rate, post card		0.21	7/01	108r
Postal rate, priority mail, two pounds		3.95	7/01	108r
Postal rate, priority mail, up to one pound		3.50	7/01	108r
Telephone services, expenditures on	yr	830	1999	30r
Education				
Board, 4-year private college/university	yr	2414	1996	38s
Board, 4-year public college/university	yr	2181	1996	38s
Education expenditures	yr	583	1999	30r
Room, 4-year private college/university	yr	2349	1996	38s
Room, 4-year public college/university	yr	2386	1996	38s
Total cost, 4-year private college/university	yr	17139	1996	38s
Total cost, 4-year public college/university	yr	8169	1996	38s
Tuition, 2-year public college/university, in state	yr	2261	1996	38s
Tuition, 4-year private college/university, in state	yr	12377	1996	38s
Tuition, 4-year public college/university	yr	3603	1996	38s
Energy and Fuels				
Electricity	500 KWhs	46.59	7/01	11r
Fuel oil #2	gal	1.27	7/01	11r
Fuel oil and other fuels, expenditures on	yr	68	1999	30r
Gas, natural, commercial rate	1000 cf	8.65	11/00	88s
Gasoline, unleaded midgrade	gal	1.79	7/01	11r
Gasoline, unleaded premium	gal	1.86	7/01	11r
Gasoline, unleaded regular	gal	1.58	7/01	11r
Natural gas, expenditures on	yr	389	1999	30r
Utility (piped) gas, therm		0.81	7/01	11r
Utility (piped) gas, 40 therms		38.01	7/01	11r
Utility (piped) gas, 100 therms		81.75	7/01	11r
Entertainment				
Entertainment purchases	yr	1984	1999	30r
Fees and admissions paid	yr	444	1999	30r
Television, radios, sound equipment, expenditures on	yr	580	1999	30r
Funerals				
Cosmetology, hair, other preparation		178.32	1/99	78r

Values are in dollars or fractions of dollars. In the column headed *Ref*, references are shown to sources. Each reference is followed by a letter. These refer to the geographical level for which data were reported: s=State, r=Region, and c=City or metro. The abbreviation *ex* is used to mean *except* or *excluding*; *exp* stands for expenditures. For other abbreviations and further explanations, please see the Introduction.

Hamilton-Middletown, OH - continued

Item	Per	Value	Date	Ref.
Funerals				
Embalming		408.19	1/99	78r
Funeral at funeral home		362.13	1/99	78r
Professional service charges		1375.51	1/99	78r
Transfer of remains to funeral home		155.92	1/99	78r
Visitation/viewing		294.38	1/99	78r
Groceries				
Bacon, sliced	lb	3.15	7/01	11r
Bakery products, expenditures on	yr	281	1999	30r
Bananas	lb	0.48	7/01	11r
Beans, dried, any type, all sizes	lb	0.61	7/01	11r
Beef for stew, boneless	lb	3.08	7/01	11r
Beef, expenditures on	yr	217	1999	30r
Bologna, all beef or mixed	lb	2.52	7/01	11r
Bread, white, pan	lb	1.06	7/01	11r
Broccoli	lb	0.91	7/01	11r
Butter, salted, grade AA, stick	lb	3.04	7/01	11r
Butter, yoghurt, cheese, etc, expenditures on	yr	183	1999	30r
Cereals and bakery product purchases	yr	430	1999	30r
Cereals and cereal products, expenditures on	yr	149	1999	30r
Chicken, fresh, whole	lb	1.07	7/01	11r
Chops, boneless,	lb	3.64	7/01	11r
Chuck roast, U.S. choice, boneless	lb	2.47	7/01	11r
Coffee, 100%, ground roast, all sizes	lb	2.69	7/01	11r
Cookies, chocolate chip	lb	2.87	7/01	11r
Dairy product purchases	yr	304	1999	30r
Eggs, expenditures on	yr	26	1999	30r
Eggs, grade A, large	dozen	0.88	7/01	11r
Fats and oils, expenditures on	yr	75	1999	30r
Fish and seafood, expenditures on	yr	72	1999	30r
Food (excl fruit and vegetables), eaten at home, purchases	yr	887	1999	30r
Food cooked on trips, expenditures on	yr	44	1999	30r
Food purchases	yr	4802	1999	30r
Food purchases, eaten away from home	yr	2069	1999	30r
Food purchases, food eaten at home	yr	2733	1999	30r
Fresh fruits, expenditures on	yr	138	1999	30r
Fresh milk and cream, expenditures on	yr	120	1999	30r
Fresh vegetables, expenditures on	yr	126	1999	30r
Grapefruit	lb	0.66	7/01	11r
Grapes, Thompson, seedless	lb	1.64	7/01	11r
Ground beef, 100% beef	lb	1.64	7/01	11r
Ground beef, lean and extra lean	lb	2.16	7/01	11r
Ground chuck, 100% beef	lb	2.13	7/01	11r
Ham, boneless, excl canned	lb	2.62	7/01	11r
Ice cream, prepackaged, bulk, regular	1/2 gal	3.35	7/01	11r
Lemons	lb	1.19	7/01	11r
Lettuce, iceberg	lb	0.73	7/01	11r
Margarine, soft, tubs	lb	0.89	7/01	11r
Meats, poultry, fish, and egg purchases	yr	671	1999	30r
Milk, fresh, whole, fortified	gal	2.71	7/01	11r
Nonalcoholic beverages, expenditures on	yr	239	1999	30r
Oranges, Navel	lb	0.80	7/01	11r
Oranges, Valencia	lb	0.66	7/01	11r
Pears, Anjou	lb	0.93	7/01	11r
Pork chops, center cut, bone-in	lb	3.63	7/01	11r
Pork, expenditures on	yr	150	1999	30r
Potato chips	16 oz	3.52	7/01	11r
Potatoes, frozen, french fried	lb	1.08	7/01	11r
Potatoes, white, all types	lb	0.33	7/01	11r
Poultry, expenditures on	yr	108	1999	30r
Processed fruits, expenditures on	yr	98	1999	30r
Processed vegetables, expenditures on	yr	80	1999	30r
Round roast, U.S. choice, boneless	lb	3.07	7/01	11r
Round steak, graded and ungraded, excl U.S. prime and choice	lb	3.41	7/01	11r
Shortening, vegetable oil blends	lb	1.13	7/01	11r
Spaghetti and macaroni	lb	0.80	7/01	11r
Steak, round, U.S. choice, boneless	lb	3.23	7/01	11r
Steak, T-bone, U.S. choice, bone-in	lb	6.68	7/01	11r
Strawberries, dry pint	12 oz	1.32	7/01	11r
Sugar and other sweets, expenditures on	yr	114	1999	30r

Hamilton-Middletown, OH - continued

Item	Per	Value	Date	Ref.
Groceries - continued				
Sugar, white, 33-80 ounce package	lb	0.42	7/01	11r
Sugar, white, all sizes	lb	0.43	7/01	11r
Tobacco products and smoking supplies purchases	yr	331	1999	30r
Tomatoes, field grown	lb	1.46	7/01	11r
Tuna, light, chunk	lb	1.80	7/01	11r
Turkey, frozen, whole	lb	1.15	7/01	11r
Goods and Services				
B&B Japanese maple (acer japonicum)	gal	29.99-169.99	4/00	93r
Boxwood (buxus)	2 gal	18.99-39.99	4/00	93r
Daylilly (hemerocallis)	gal	4.99-25.00	4/00	93r
Flat of annuals		11.98-24.99	4/00	93r
Fountain grass (pennisetum)	gal	5.98-12.98	4/00	93r
Hanging basket (10 in)		12.99-27.99	4/00	93r
Hardy geranium (geranium)	gal	7.99-9.99	4/00	93r
Hosta (hosta)	gal	6.00-25.00	4/00	93r
Lilac (syrubga vulgaris)	2 gal	14.99-24.99	4/00	93r
Miscellaneous purchases	yr	865	1999	30r
Rhododendron (rhododendron)	2 gal	23.98-42.99	4/00	93r
Sage (salvia)	gal	6.00-9.99	4/00	93r
Wintercreeper euonymus (euonymus fortunei)	2 gal	16.00-169.99	4/00	93r
Hunting license	yr	15.00	4/01	34s
Health Care				
Cardiac catheterization, ave hospital/ physician charges		11760	1998	77s
Childbirth, Cesarean delivery		10722	1997	13r
Childbirth, vaginal delivery		6223	1997	13r
Drugs, expenditures on	yr	394	1999	30r
Health care purchases	yr	2048	1999	30r
Health insurance expenditures	yr	978	1999	30r
Hysterectomy, laproscopically-assisted, ave hospital/physician charges		11730	1998	76s
Hysterectomy, vaginal, ave hospital and physician charges		9640	1998	76s
Medicaid dispensing fee		3.70	1999	87s
Medical services expenditures	yr	554	1999	30r
Medical supplies, expenditures on	yr	122	1999	30r
Plastic surgery, breast augmentation		3184	2000	7r
Plastic surgery, breast lift		3585	2000	7r
Plastic surgery, facelift		4999	2000	7r
Plastic surgery, hair transplantation		3105	2000	7r
Plastic surgery, lip augmentation		1290	2000	7r
Plastic surgery, lower body lift		8135	2000	7r
Plastic surgery, thigh lift		3839	2000	7r
Household Goods				
Floor coverings, expenditures on	yr	52	1999	30r
Furniture, expenditures on	yr	344	1999	30r
Household furnishings and equipment purchases	yr	1475	1999	30r
Household textiles, expenditures on	yr	109	1999	30r
Laundry and cleaning supplies, expenditures on	yr	134	1999	30r
Housing				
Home price, existing, ave		144400	10/00	90r
Home value, median		96000	2001	53s
Household operation expenditures	yr	542	1999	30r
Housekeeping supplies purchases	yr	508	1999	30r
Lodging expenditures	yr	430	1999	30r

Values are in dollars or fractions of dollars. In the column headed *Ref*, references are shown to sources. Each reference is followed by a letter. These refer to the geographical level for which data were reported: s=State, r=Region, and c=City or metro. The abbreviation *ex* is used to mean *except* or *excluding*; *exp* stands for expenditures. For other abbreviations and further explanations, please see the Introduction.

Hamilton-Middletown, OH - continued

Item	Per	Value	Date	Ref.
Housing				
Maintenance, repairs, insurance expenditures	yr	853	1999	30r
Monthly rental value of owned home	mos	547	1999	30r
Owned dwellings, expenditures own	yr	4282	1999	30r
Rent expenditures	yr	1558	1999	30r
Rental unit, 1 bedroom, with utilities	mos	464	4/01	41c
Rental unit, 2 bedroom, with utilities	mos	594	4/01	41c
Rental unit, 3 bedroom, with utilities	mos	743	4/01	41c
Rental unit, 4 bedroom, with utilities	mos	832	4/01	41c
Shelter, expenditures on	yr	6270	1999	30r
Insurance and Pensions				
Life and other personal insurance purchases	yr	387	1999	30r
Pensions and Social Security, expenditures on	yr	2968	1999	30r
Legal Fees				
Divorce, filing fee		100.00	4/01	35s
Driver's license fee	orig	14.50	1999	48s
Driver's license fee	renew	14.50	1999	48s
Fishing license	yr	15.00	4/01	34s
Personal Goods				
Personal care products and services purchases	yr	385	1999	30r
Personal Services				
Personal services, household, expenditures on	yr	300	1999	30r
Pets				
Pets, toys, and playground equipment, expenditures on	yr	375	1999	30r
Taxes				
Federal income taxes paid	yr	2326	1999	30r
Personal taxes, expenditures on	yr	3223	1999	30r
Property taxes paid	yr	1152	1999	30r
State and local income taxes paid	yr	753	1999	30r
Transportation				
Cars and trucks, new, expenditures on	yr	1280	1999	30r
Cars and trucks, used, expenditures on	yr	1763	1999	30r
Diesel at the pump	gal	1.25	10/99	73s
Gasoline and motor oil purchases	yr	1036	1999	30r
Gasoline before-tax price (cents)	gal	109.50	10/00	43s
Maintenance and repair expenditures	yr	594	1999	30r
Public transportation, expenditures on	yr	341	1999	30r
Transportation purchases	yr	6617	1999	30r
Vehicle expenses, miscellaneous, purchases	yr	2159	1999	30r
Vehicle insurance payments	yr	701	1999	30r
Vehicle purchases (net outlay)	yr	3081	1999	30r
Vehicle rental, lease expenditures	yr	536	1999	30r
Utilities				
Electrical bill, average	mos	72.83	9/00	9s
Electricity, expenditures on	yr	841	1999	30r
Electricity cost, average	KWh	6.59	9/00	9s
Utilities, fuels, and public services purchased	yr	2401	1999	30r
Water and other public services, expenditures on	yr	273	1999	30r
Weddings				
Wedding (national average cost)		19936	2000	33r
Wedding (regional average total cost)		16195	1997	110r
Attendants' gifts		321	1998	33r
Bridal attendants' apparel (5 persons)		824	2000	33r
Bride's headpiece/veil		173	1998	33r
Bride's wedding dress		859	1998	33r
Clergy, religious facility fee		242	1998	33r
Engagement ring		3177	1998	33r
Flowers		789	1998	33r
Groom's formalwear rental		99	2000	33r
Limousine		410	1998	33r
Marriage license cost		45.00	4/01	35s
Men's formalwear (ushers, best man)		469	2000	33r

Hamilton-Middletown, OH - continued

Item	Per	Value	Date	Ref.
Weddings - continued				
Mother of bride apparel		241	2000	33r
Music		866	1998	33r
Photography and videography		1368	1998	33r
Rehearsal dinner		728	1998	33r
Wedding invitations and announcements		341	1998	33r
Wedding reception		7968	2000	33r
Wedding rings (bride and groom)		1060	1998	33r

Harrisburg-Lebanon-Carlisle, PA

Item	Per	Value	Date	Ref.
Average annual expenditures	yr	37971	1999	30r
Alcoholic Beverages				
Alcoholic beverage purchases	yr	368	1999	30r
Wine, red and white table, all sizes, any origin	liter	9.64	7/01	11r
Appliances				
Major appliances, expenditures on	yr	194	1999	30r
Small appliances, housewares, expenditures on	yr	93	1999	30r
Banking and Money				
Mortgage interest and charges paid	yr	2622	1999	30r
Mortgage principal paid on owned property	yr	1262	1999	30r
Vehicle finance charges paid	yr	240	1999	30r
Charity				
Cash contributions, expenditures	yr	1001	1999	30r
Child Care				
Child raising cost, total, age 0-2	yr	8670	1999	60r
Child raising cost, total, age 3-5	yr	8910	1999	60r
Child raising cost, total, age 6-8	yr	9040	1999	60r
Child raising cost, total, age 9-11	yr	9100	1999	60r
Child raising cost, total, age 12-14	yr	9890	1999	60r
Child raising cost, total, age 15-17	yr	10010	1999	60r
Child's child care and education, age 0-2	yr	1070	1999	60r
Child's child care and education, age 3-5	yr	1190	1999	60r
Child's child care and education, age 6-8	yr	740	1999	60r
Child's child care and education, age 9-11	yr	470	1999	60r
Child's child care and education, age 12-14	yr	350	1999	60r
Child's child care and education, age 15-17	yr	590	1999	60r
Child's clothing, age 0-2	yr	480	1999	60r
Child's clothing, age 3-5	yr	470	1999	60r
Child's clothing, age 6-8	yr	520	1999	60r
Child's clothing, age 9-11	yr	570	1999	60r
Child's clothing, age 12-14	yr	970	1999	60r
Child's clothing, age 15-17	yr	870	1999	60r
Child's food, age 0-2	yr	1130	1999	60r
Child's food, age 3-5	yr	1290	1999	60r
Child's food, age 6-8	yr	1640	1999	60r
Child's food, age 9-11	yr	1930	1999	60r
Child's food, age 12-14	yr	1940	1999	60r
Child's food, age 15-17	yr	2150	1999	60r
Child's health care, age 0-2	yr	550	1999	60r
Child's health care, age 3-5	yr	530	1999	60r
Child's health care, age 6-8	yr	610	1999	60r
Child's health care, age 9-11	yr	650	1999	60r
Child's health care, age 12-14	yr	660	1999	60r
Child's health care, age 15-17	yr	690	1999	60r
Child's housing, age 0-2	yr	3555	1999	60r
Child's housing, age 3-5	yr	3530	1999	60r
Child's housing, age 6-8	yr	3490	1999	60r
Child's housing, age 9-11	yr	3340	1999	60r
Child's housing, age 12-14	yr	3530	1999	60r
Child's housing, age 15-17	yr	3140	1999	60r
Child's personal care, reading, age 0-2	yr	920	1999	60r
Child's personal care, reading, age 3-5	yr	950	1999	60r
Child's personal care, reading, age 6-8	yr	980	1999	60r
Child's personal care, reading, age 9-11	yr	1020	1999	60r
Child's personal care, reading, age 12-14	yr	1190	1999	60r
Child's personal care, reading, age 15-17	yr	970	1999	60r

Values are in dollars or fractions of dollars. In the column headed *Ref*, references are shown to sources. Each reference is followed by a letter. These refer to the geographical level for which data were reported: s=State, r=Region, and c=City or metro. The abbreviation *ex* is used to mean *except* or *excluding*; *exp* stands for expenditures. For other abbreviations and further explanations, please see the Introduction.

Harrisburg-Lebanon-Carlisle, PA - continued

Item	Per	Value	Date	Ref.
Clothing				
Apparel and services purchases	yr	1831	1999	30r
Boys, 2 to 15, expenditures on	yr	92	1999	30r
Children under 2, expenditures on	yr	63	1999	30r
Footwear, expenditures on	yr	300	1999	30r
Girls, 2 to 15, expenditures on	yr	101	1999	30r
Men and boys, expenditures on	yr	446	1999	30r
Men, 16 and over, expenditures on	yr	354	1999	30r
Women, 16 and over, expenditures on	yr	584	1999	30r
Communications				
Cable modem installation, Adelphi		54.90	6/99	103s
Cable modem installation, Comcast		95.00	6/99	103s
Cable modem rate, cable subscriber, Adelphi	mos	34.95	6/99	103s
Cable modem rate, cable subscriber, Comcast	mos	39.95	6/99	103s
Cable modem rate, non-cable subscriber, Adelphi	mos	44.95	6/99	103s
Cable modem rate, non-cable subscriber, Comcast	mos	49.95	6/99	103s
Phone line, single, business, field visit	inst.	75.00	12/97	17s
Phone line, single, business, no field visit	inst.	75.00	12/97	17s
Phone line, single, residence, field visit	inst.	40.00	12/97	17s
Phone line, single, residence, no field visit	inst.	40.00	12/97	17s
Postage and stationery, expenditures on	yr	138	1999	30r
Postal rate, express mail, up to half-pound		12.45	7/01	108r
Postal rate, letter, first class, first ounce		0.34	7/01	108r
Postal rate, letter, two ounces		0.57	7/01	108r
Postal rate, post card		0.21	7/01	108r
Postal rate, priority mail, two pounds		3.95	7/01	108r
Postal rate, priority mail, up to one pound		3.50	7/01	108r
Telephone services, expenditures on	yr	830	1999	30r
Education				
Board, 4-year private college/university	yr	2822	1996	38s
Board, 4-year public college/university	yr	2174	1996	38s
Education expenditures	yr	877	1999	30r
Room, 4-year private college/university	yr	2943	1996	38s
Room, 4-year public college/university	yr	2227	1996	38s
Total cost, 4-year private college/university	yr	19876	1996	38s
Total cost, 4-year public college/university	yr	9124	1996	38s
Tuition, 2-year public college/university, in state	yr	1909	1996	38s
Tuition, 4-year private college/university, in state	yr	14111	1996	38s
Tuition, 4-year public college/university	yr	4723	1996	38s
Energy and Fuels				
Electricity	KWh	0.12	7/01	11r
Fuel oil #2	gal	1.31	7/01	11r
Fuel oil and other fuels, expenditures on	yr	207	1999	30r
Gas, natural, commercial rate	1000 cf	5.96	11/00	88s
Gasoline, all types	gal	1.80	7/01	11r
Gasoline, unleaded midgrade	gal	1.85	7/01	11r
Gasoline, unleaded premium	gal	1.91	7/01	11r
Gasoline, unleaded regular	gal	1.71	7/01	11r
Natural gas, expenditures on	yr	368	1999	30r
Utility (piped) gas, therm		1.08	7/01	11r
Utility (piped) gas, 40 therms		50.87	7/01	11r
Utility (piped) gas, 100 therms		111.06	7/01	11r
Entertainment				
Entertainment purchases	yr	1821	1999	30r
Fees and admissions paid	yr	511	1999	30r
Television, radios, sound equipment, expenditures on	yr	650	1999	30r
Funerals				
Total cost of funeral		5813.50	1/99	78r
Acknowledgement cards		28.32	1/99	78r
Casket		2082.20	1/99	78r
Cosmetology, hair, other preparation		169.59	1/99	78r
Embalming		465.60	1/99	78r
Funeral at funeral home		339.56	1/99	78r
Hearse (local)		183.96	1/99	78r

Harrisburg-Lebanon-Carlisle, PA - continued

Item	Per	Value	Date	Ref.
Funerals - continued				
Professional service charges		1157.85	1/99	78r
Service car/van		100.41	1/99	78r
Transfer of remains to funeral home		158.66	1/99	78r
Vault		766.31	1/99	78r
Visitation/viewing		361.04	1/99	78r
Groceries				
Apples, red delicious	lb	0.95	7/01	11r
Bacon, sliced	lb	3.44	7/01	11r
Bakery products, expenditures on	yr	310	1999	30r
Bananas	lb	0.55	7/01	11r
Beef, expenditures on	yr	236	1999	30r
Bread, white, pan	lb	1.09	7/01	11r
Butter, yoghurt, cheese, etc, expenditures on	yr	214	1999	30r
Cereals and bakery product purchases	yr	474	1999	30r
Cereals and cereal products, expenditures on	yr	164	1999	30r
Chicken legs, bone-in	lb	1.23	7/01	11r
Chicken, fresh, whole	lb	1.13	7/01	11r
Chuck roast, U.S. choice, boneless	lb	2.79	7/01	11r
Coffee, 100%, ground roast, all sizes	lb	3.40	7/01	11r
Dairy product purchases	yr	342	1999	30r
Eggs, expenditures on	yr	34	1999	30r
Eggs, grade A, large	dozen	0.82	7/01	11r
Fats and oils, expenditures on	yr	80	1999	30r
Fish and seafood, expenditures on	yr	123	1999	30r
Food (excl fruit and vegetables), eaten at home, purchases	yr	838	1999	30r
Food cooked on trips, expenditures on	yr	48	1999	30r
Food purchases	yr	5314	1999	30r
Food purchases, eaten away from home	yr	2313	1999	30r
Food purchases, food eaten at home	yr	3001	1999	30r
Fresh fruits, expenditures on	yr	169	1999	30r
Fresh milk and cream, expenditures on	yr	128	1999	30r
Fresh vegetables, expenditures on	yr	164	1999	30r
Grapefruit	lb	0.67	7/01	11r
Grapes, Thompson, seedless	lb	2.18	7/01	11r
Ground beef, lean and extra lean	lb	2.66	7/01	11r
Ground chuck, 100% beef	lb	2.04	7/01	11r
Lettuce, iceberg	lb	0.76	7/01	11r
Meats, poultry, fish, and egg purchases	yr	808	1999	30r
Nonalcoholic beverages, expenditures on	yr	225	1999	30r
Orange juice, frozen concentrate	16 oz	1.88	7/01	11r
Oranges, Navel	lb	0.79	7/01	11r
Oranges, Valencia	lb	0.56	7/01	11r
Peaches	lb	1.16	7/01	11r
Peanut butter, creamy, all sizes	lb	2.01	7/01	11r
Pears, Anjou	lb	1.16	7/01	11r
Pork chops, center cut, bone-in	lb	3.57	7/01	11r
Pork, expenditures on	yr	146	1999	30r
Potato chips	16 oz	3.37	7/01	11r
Potatoes, white, all types	lb	0.42	7/01	11r
Poultry, expenditures on	yr	158	1999	30r
Processed fruits, expenditures on	yr	124	1999	30r
Processed vegetables, expenditures on	yr	82	1999	30r
Round roast, U.S. choice, boneless	lb	3.04	7/01	11r
Spaghetti and macaroni	lb	1.04	7/01	11r
Steak, sirloin, U.S. choice, boneless	lb	5.39	7/01	11r
Strawberries, dry pint	12 oz	1.51	7/01	11r
Sugar and other sweets, expenditures on	yr	110	1999	30r
Sugar, white, 33-80 ounce package	lb	0.46	7/01	11r
Sugar, white, all sizes	lb	0.47	7/01	11r
Tobacco products and smoking supplies purchases	yr	309	1999	30r
Yogurt, natural, fruit flavored	8 oz	0.79	7/01	11r
Goods and Services				
B&B Japanese maple (acer japonicum)	gal	38.99-125.00	4/00	93r
Boxwood (buxus)	2 gal	15.99-49.95	4/00	93r
Daylily (hemerocallis)	gal	4.95	4/00	93r

Values are in dollars or fractions of dollars. In the column headed *Ref*, references are shown to sources. Each reference is followed by a letter. These refer to the geographical level for which data were reported: s=State, r=Region, and c=City or metro. The abbreviation *ex* is used to mean *except* or *excluding*; *exp* stands for expenditures. For other abbreviations and further explanations, please see the Introduction.

Harrisburg-Lebanon-Carlisle, PA - continued

Item	Per	Value	Date	Ref.
Goods and Services				
Flat of annuals		8.00-14.99	4/00	93r
Fountain grass (pennisetum)	gal	6.99-9.99	4/00	93r
Hanging basket (10 in)		12.95-19.99	4/00	93r
Hardy geranium (geranium)	gal	6.95-7.99	4/00	93r
Hosta (hosta)	gal	4.95	4/00	93r
Lilac (syrubga vulgaris)	2 gal	17.99-74.95	4/00	93r
Miscellaneous purchases	yr	872	1999	30r
Rhododendron (rhododendron)	2 gal	23.99-54.95	4/00	93r
Sage (salvia)	gal	6.95-7.99	4/00	93r
Wintercreeper euonymus (euonymus fortunei)	2 gal	14.99-23.95	4/00	93r
Hunting license	yr	20.00	4/01	34s
Health Care				
Cardiac catheterization, ave hospital/physician charges		13870	1998	77s
Childbirth, Cesarean delivery		14716	1997	13r
Childbirth, vaginal delivery		8541	1997	13r
Drugs, expenditures on	yr	296	1999	30r
Health care purchases	yr	1788	1999	30r
Health insurance expenditures	yr	875	1999	30r
Hysterectomy, laproscopically-assisted, ave hospital/physician charges		14760	1998	76s
Hysterectomy, vaginal, ave hospital and physician charges		9270	1998	76s
Medicaid dispensing fee		4.00	1999	87s
Medical services expenditures	yr	516	1999	30r
Medical supplies, expenditures on	yr	102	1999	30r
Plastic surgery, breast augmentation		4232	2000	7r
Plastic surgery, breast lift		4605	2000	7r
Plastic surgery, facelift		6964	2000	7r
Plastic surgery, hair transplantation		4193	2000	7r
Plastic surgery, lip augmentation		1675	2000	7r
Plastic surgery, lower body lift		6611	2000	7r
Plastic surgery, thigh lift		4751	2000	7r
Household Goods				
Floor coverings, expenditures on	yr	59	1999	30r
Furniture, expenditures on	yr	388	1999	30r
Household furnishings and equipment purchases	yr	1567	1999	30r
Household textiles, expenditures on	yr	112	1999	30r
Laundry and cleaning supplies, expenditures on	yr	104	1999	30r
Housing				
Home price, existing, ave		180800	10/00	90r
Home value, median		115000	2001	53s
Household operation expenditures	yr	581	1999	30r
Housekeeping supplies purchases	yr	474	1999	30r
Lodging expenditures	yr	550	1999	30r
Maintenance, repairs, insurance expenditures	yr	835	1999	30r
Monthly rental value of owned home	mos	663	1999	30r
Owned dwellings, expenditures own	yr	5209	1999	30r
Rent expenditures	yr	2390	1999	30r
Rental unit, 1 bedroom, with utilities	mos	443	4/01	41c
Rental unit, 2 bedroom, with utilities	mos	568	4/01	41c
Rental unit, 3 bedroom, with utilities	mos	716	4/01	41c
Rental unit, 4 bedroom, with utilities	mos	798	4/01	41c
Shelter, expenditures on	yr	8149	1999	30r
Insurance and Pensions				
Life and other personal insurance purchases	yr	424	1999	30r
Pensions and Social Security, expenditures on	yr	3037	1999	30r

Harrisburg-Lebanon-Carlisle, PA - continued

Item	Per	Value	Date	Ref.
Legal Fees				
Divorce, filing fee		65.00	4/01	35s
Driver's license fee	renew	24.00	1999	48s
Driver's license fee	orig	29.00	1999	48s
Fishing license	yr	17.00	4/01	34s
Personal Goods				
Personal care products and services purchases	yr	399	1999	30r
Personal Services				
Personal services, household, expenditures on	yr	271	1999	30r
Pets				
Pets, toys, and playground equipment, expenditures on	yr	325	1999	30r
Taxes				
Federal income taxes paid	yr	2606	1999	30r
Personal taxes, expenditures on	yr	3567	1999	30r
Property taxes paid	yr	1752	1999	30r
State and local income taxes paid	yr	694	1999	30r
Transportation				
Cars and trucks, new, expenditures on	yr	1496	1999	30r
Cars and trucks, used, expenditures on	yr	1251	1999	30r
Diesel at the pump	gal	1.31	10/99	73s
Gasoline and motor oil purchases	yr	901	1999	30r
Gasoline before-tax price (cents)	gal	106.60	10/00	43s
Maintenance and repair expenditures	yr	618	1999	30r
Public transportation, expenditures on	yr	575	1999	30r
Transportation purchases	yr	6503	1999	30r
Vehicle expenses, miscellaneous, purchases	yr	2266	1999	30r
Vehicle insurance payments	yr	824	1999	30r
Vehicle purchases (net outlay)	yr	2761	1999	30r
Vehicle rental, lease expenditures	yr	584	1999	30r
Utilities				
Electrical bill, average	mos	69.16	9/00	9s
Electricity, expenditures on	yr	837	1999	30r
Electricity cost, average	KWh	5.08	9/00	9s
Utilities, fuels, and public services purchased	yr	2457	1999	30r
Water and other public services, expenditures on	yr	215	1999	30r
Weddings				
Wedding (national average cost)		19936	2000	33r
Wedding (regional average total cost)		29454	1997	110r
Attendants' gifts		321	1998	33r
Bridal attendants' apparel (5 persons)		824	2000	33r
Bride's headpiece/veil		173	1998	33r
Bride's wedding dress		859	1998	33r
Clergy, religious facility fee		242	1998	33r
Engagement ring		3177	1998	33r
Flowers		789	1998	33r
Groom's formalwear rental		99	2000	33r
Limousine		410	1998	33r
Marriage license cost		25.00-40.00	4/01	35s
Men's formalwear (ushers, best man)		469	2000	33r
Mother of bride apparel		241	2000	33r
Music		866	1998	33r
Photography and videography		1368	1998	33r
Rehearsal dinner		728	1998	33r
Wedding invitations and announcements		341	1998	33r
Wedding reception		7968	2000	33r
Wedding rings (bride and groom)		1060	1998	33r

Hartford, CT

Item	Per	Value	Date	Ref.
Average annual expenditures	yr	37971	1999	30r
Alcoholic Beverages				
Alcoholic beverage purchases	yr	368	1999	30r

Values are in dollars or fractions of dollars. In the column headed *Ref*, references are shown to sources. Each reference is followed by a letter. These refer to the geographical level for which data were reported: s=State, r=Region, and c=City or metro. The abbreviation *ex* is used to mean *except* or *excluding*; *exp* stands for *expenditures*. For other abbreviations and further explanations, please see the Introduction.

Hartford, CT - continued

Item	Per	Value	Date	Ref.
Alcoholic Beverages				
Wine, red and white table, all sizes, any origin	liter	9.64	7/01	11r
Appliances				
Major appliances, expenditures on	yr	194	1999	30r
Small appliances, housewares, expenditures on	yr	93	1999	30r
Banking and Money				
Mortgage interest and charges paid	yr	2622	1999	30r
Mortgage principal paid on owned property	yr	1262	1999	30r
Vehicle finance charges paid	yr	240	1999	30r
Business Expenses				
Business travel, car rental	day	55	2001	3c
Business travel, food	day	52	2001	3c
Business travel, hotel	day	134	2001	3c
Charity				
Cash contributions, expenditures	yr	1001	1999	30r
Child Care				
Child raising cost, total, age 0-2	yr	8670	1999	60r
Child raising cost, total, age 3-5	yr	8910	1999	60r
Child raising cost, total, age 6-8	yr	9040	1999	60r
Child raising cost, total, age 9-11	yr	9100	1999	60r
Child raising cost, total, age 12-14	yr	9890	1999	60r
Child raising cost, total, age 15-17	yr	10010	1999	60r
Child's child care and education, age 0-2	yr	1070	1999	60r
Child's child care and education, age 3-5	yr	1190	1999	60r
Child's child care and education, age 6-8	yr	740	1999	60r
Child's child care and education, age 9-11	yr	470	1999	60r
Child's child care and education, age 12-14	yr	350	1999	60r
Child's child care and education, age 15-17	yr	590	1999	60r
Child's clothing, age 0-2	yr	480	1999	60r
Child's clothing, age 3-5	yr	470	1999	60r
Child's clothing, age 6-8	yr	520	1999	60r
Child's clothing, age 9-11	yr	570	1999	60r
Child's clothing, age 12-14	yr	970	1999	60r
Child's clothing, age 15-17	yr	870	1999	60r
Child's food, age 0-2	yr	1130	1999	60r
Child's food, age 3-5	yr	1290	1999	60r
Child's food, age 6-8	yr	1640	1999	60r
Child's food, age 9-11	yr	1930	1999	60r
Child's food, age 12-14	yr	1940	1999	60r
Child's food, age 15-17	yr	2150	1999	60r
Child's health care, age 0-2	yr	550	1999	60r
Child's health care, age 3-5	yr	530	1999	60r
Child's health care, age 6-8	yr	610	1999	60r
Child's health care, age 9-11	yr	650	1999	60r
Child's health care, age 12-14	yr	660	1999	60r
Child's health care, age 15-17	yr	690	1999	60r
Child's housing, age 0-2	yr	3555	1999	60r
Child's housing, age 3-5	yr	3530	1999	60r
Child's housing, age 6-8	yr	3490	1999	60r
Child's housing, age 9-11	yr	3340	1999	60r
Child's housing, age 12-14	yr	3530	1999	60r
Child's housing, age 15-17	yr	3140	1999	60r
Child's personal care, reading, age 0-2	yr	920	1999	60r
Child's personal care, reading, age 3-5	yr	950	1999	60r
Child's personal care, reading, age 6-8	yr	980	1999	60r
Child's personal care, reading, age 9-11	yr	1020	1999	60r
Child's personal care, reading, age 12-14	yr	1190	1999	60r
Child's personal care, reading, age 15-17	yr	970	1999	60r
Clothing				
Apparel and services purchases	yr	1831	1999	30r
Boys, 2 to 15, expenditures on	yr	92	1999	30r
Children under 2, expenditures on	yr	63	1999	30r
Footwear, expenditures on	yr	300	1999	30r
Girls, 2 to 15, expenditures on	yr	101	1999	30r
Men and boys, expenditures on	yr	446	1999	30r
Men, 16 and over, expenditures on	yr	354	1999	30r
Women, 16 and over, expenditures on	yr	584	1999	30r

Hartford, CT - continued

Item	Per	Value	Date	Ref.
Communications				
Cable modem installation, AT&T-BIS		150.00	6/99	103s
Cable modem installation, Cablevision Systems		150.00	6/99	103s
Cable modem installation, Cox		99.00-174.95	6/99	103s
Cable modem installation, Media One		100.00	6/99	103s
Cable modem rate, cable subscriber, AT&T-BIS	mos	39.95	6/99	103s
Cable modem rate, cable subscriber, Cablevision Systems	mos	44.95	6/99	103s
Cable modem rate, cable subscriber, Cox	mos	29.95-44.95	6/99	103s
Cable modem rate, cable subscriber, Media One	mos	34.95-39.95	6/99	103s
Cable modem rate, non-cable subscriber, Cablevision Systems	mos	54.95	6/99	103s
Cable modem rate, non-cable subscriber, Cox	mos	42.95-54.95	6/99	103s
Cable modem rate, non-cable subscriber, Media One	mos	49.95	6/99	103s
Phone line, single, business, field visit	inst.	65.00	12/97	17s
Phone line, single, business, no field visit	inst.	65.00	12/97	17s
Phone line, single, residence, field visit	inst.	45.00	12/97	17s
Phone line, single, residence, no field visit	inst.	45.00	12/97	17s
Postage and stationery, expenditures on	yr	138	1999	30r
Postal rate, express mail, up to half-pound		12.45	7/01	108r
Postal rate, letter, first class, first ounce		0.34	7/01	108r
Postal rate, letter, two ounces		0.57	7/01	108r
Postal rate, post card		0.21	7/01	108r
Postal rate, priority mail, two pounds		3.95	7/01	108r
Postal rate, priority mail, up to one pound		3.50	7/01	108r
Telephone bill, business, basic rate	mos	39.13	12/97	18c
Telephone bill, residential, basic rate	mos	14.53	12/97	18c
Telephone services, expenditures on	yr	830	1999	30r
Education				
Board, 4-year private college/university	yr	2744	1996	38s
Board, 4-year public college/university	yr	2299	1996	38s
Education expenditures	yr	877	1999	30r
Room, 4-year private college/university	yr	3621	1996	38s
Room, 4-year public college/university	yr	2609	1996	38s
Total cost, 4-year private college/university	yr	23011	1996	38s
Total cost, 4-year public college/university	yr	8753	1996	38s
Tuition, 2-year public college/university, in state	yr	1646	1996	38s
Tuition, 4-year private college/university, in state	yr	16646	1996	38s
Tuition, 4-year public college/university	yr	3845	1996	38s
Energy and Fuels				
Electricity	KWh	0.12	7/01	11r
Fuel oil #2	gal	1.31	7/01	11r
Fuel oil and other fuels, expenditures on	yr	207	1999	30r
Gas, cooking, winter, 10 therms	mos	17.20	2/96	98c
Gas, cooking, winter, 30 therms	mos	35.41	2/96	98c
Gas, cooking, winter, 50 therms	mos	53.62	2/96	98c
Gas, heating, winter, average use	mos	214.17	2/96	98c
Gas, natural, commercial rate	1000 cf	7.08	11/00	88s
Gasoline, all types	gal	1.80	7/01	11r
Gasoline, unleaded midgrade	gal	1.85	7/01	11r
Gasoline, unleaded premium	gal	1.91	7/01	11r
Gasoline, unleaded regular	gal	1.71	7/01	11r
Natural gas, expenditures on	yr	368	1999	30r
Utility (piped) gas, therm		1.08	7/01	11r
Utility (piped) gas, 40 therms		50.87	7/01	11r
Utility (piped) gas, 100 therms		111.06	7/01	11r
Entertainment				
Entertainment purchases	yr	1821	1999	30r
Fees and admissions paid	yr	511	1999	30r
Hockey equipment, girls' hockey		800	2001	101s
Television, radios, sound equipment, expenditures on	yr	650	1999	30r

Values are in dollars or fractions of dollars. In the column headed *Ref*, references are shown to sources. Each reference is followed by a letter. These refer to the geographical level for which data were reported: s=State, r=Region, and c=City or metro. The abbreviation *ex* is used to mean *except* or *excluding*; *exp* stands for *expenditures*. For other abbreviations and further explanations, please see the Introduction.

Hartford, CT - continued

Item	Per	Value	Date	Ref.
Funerals				
Total cost of funeral		5776.91	1/99	78r
Acknowledgement cards		14.47	1/99	78r
Casket		2090.19	1/99	78r
Cosmetology, hair, other preparation		132.92	1/99	78r
Embalming		377.33	1/99	78r
Funeral at funeral home		352.43	1/99	78r
Hearse (local)		185.55	1/99	78r
Professional service charges		1289.95	1/99	78r
Service car/van		87.42	1/99	78r
Transfer of remains to funeral home		175.48	1/99	78r
Vault		729.40	1/99	78r
Visitation/viewing		341.76	1/99	78r
Groceries				
Apples, red delicious	lb	0.95	7/01	11r
Bacon, sliced	lb	3.44	7/01	11r
Bakery products, expenditures on	yr	310	1999	30r
Bananas	lb	0.55	7/01	11r
Beef, expenditures on	yr	236	1999	30r
Bread, white, pan	lb	1.09	7/01	11r
Butter, yoghurt, cheese, etc, expenditures on	yr	214	1999	30r
Cereals and bakery product purchases	yr	474	1999	30r
Cereals and cereal products, expenditures on	yr	164	1999	30r
Chicken legs, bone-in	lb	1.23	7/01	11r
Chicken, fresh, whole	lb	1.13	7/01	11r
Chuck roast, U.S. choice, boneless	lb	2.79	7/01	11r
Coffee, 100%, ground roast, all sizes	lb	3.40	7/01	11r
Dairy product purchases	yr	342	1999	30r
Eggs, expenditures on	yr	34	1999	30r
Eggs, grade A, large	dozen	0.82	7/01	11r
Fats and oils, expenditures on	yr	80	1999	30r
Fish and seafood, expenditures on	yr	123	1999	30r
Food (excl fruit and vegetables), eaten at home, purchases	yr	838	1999	30r
Food cooked on trips, expenditures on	yr	48	1999	30r
Food purchases	yr	5314	1999	30r
Food purchases, eaten away from home	yr	2313	1999	30r
Food purchases, food eaten at home	yr	3001	1999	30r
Fresh fruits, expenditures on	yr	169	1999	30r
Fresh milk and cream, expenditures on	yr	128	1999	30r
Fresh vegetables, expenditures on	yr	164	1999	30r
Grapefruit	lb	0.67	7/01	11r
Grapes, Thompson, seedless	lb	2.18	7/01	11r
Ground beef, lean and extra lean	lb	2.66	7/01	11r
Ground chuck, 100% beef	lb	2.04	7/01	11r
Lettuce, iceberg	lb	0.76	7/01	11r
Meats, poultry, fish, and egg purchases	yr	808	1999	30r
Nonalcoholic beverages, expenditures on	yr	225	1999	30r
Orange juice, frozen concentrate	16 oz	1.88	7/01	11r
Oranges, Navel	lb	0.79	7/01	11r
Oranges, Valencia	lb	0.56	7/01	11r
Peaches	lb	1.16	7/01	11r
Peanut butter, creamy, all sizes	lb	2.01	7/01	11r
Pears, Anjou	lb	1.16	7/01	11r
Pork chops, center cut, bone-in	lb	3.57	7/01	11r
Pork, expenditures on	yr	146	1999	30r
Potato chips	16 oz	3.37	7/01	11r
Potatoes, white, all types	lb	0.42	7/01	11r
Poultry, expenditures on	yr	158	1999	30r
Processed fruits, expenditures on	yr	124	1999	30r
Processed vegetables, expenditures on	yr	82	1999	30r
Round roast, U.S. choice, boneless	lb	3.04	7/01	11r
Spaghetti and macaroni	lb	1.04	7/01	11r
Steak, sirloin, U.S. choice, boneless	lb	5.39	7/01	11r
Strawberries, dry pint	12 oz	1.51	7/01	11r
Sugar and other sweets, expenditures on	yr	110	1999	30r
Sugar, white, 33-80 ounce package	lb	0.46	7/01	11r
Sugar, white, all sizes	lb	0.47	7/01	11r
Tobacco products and smoking supplies purchases	yr	309	1999	30r
Yogurt, natural, fruit flavored	8 oz	0.79	7/01	11r

Hartford, CT - continued

Item	Per	Value	Date	Ref.
Goods and Services				
B&B Japanese maple (acer japonicum)	gal	38.99-125.00	4/00	93r
Boxwood (buxus)	2 gal	15.99-49.95	4/00	93r
Daylilly (hemerocallis)	gal	4.95	4/00	93r
Flat of annuals		8.00-14.99	4/00	93r
Fountain grass (pennisetum)	gal	6.99-9.99	4/00	93r
Hanging basket (10 in)		12.95-19.99	4/00	93r
Hardy geranium (geranium)	gal	6.95-7.99	4/00	93r
Hosta (hosta)	gal	4.95	4/00	93r
Lilac (syrubga vulgaris)	2 gal	17.99-74.95	4/00	93r
Miscellaneous purchases	yr	872	1999	30r
Rhododendron (rhododendron)	2 gal	23.99-54.95	4/00	93r
Sage (salvia)	gal	6.95-7.99	4/00	93r
Wintercreeper euonymus (euonymus fortunei)	2 gal	14.99-23.95	4/00	93r
Hunting license	yr	10.00	4/01	34s
Health Care				
Cardiac catheterization, ave hospital/physician charges		14090	1998	77s
Childbirth, Cesarean delivery		14716	1997	13r
Childbirth, vaginal delivery		8541	1997	13r
Drugs, expenditures on	yr	296	1999	30r
Health care purchases	yr	1788	1999	30r
Health insurance expenditures	yr	875	1999	30r
Home health care aide cost, licensed agency	hour	24	2000	82c
Hysterectomy, laproscopically-assisted, ave hospital/physician charges		11610	1998	76s
Hysterectomy, vaginal, ave hospital and physician charges		12780	1998	76s
Medicaid dispensing fee		4.10	1999	87s
Medical services expenditures	yr	516	1999	30r
Medical supplies, expenditures on	yr	102	1999	30r
Nursing home costs, private room	day	210	2000	82c
Nursing home stay, private room	day	210	2000	83c
Plastic surgery, breast augmentation		4232	2000	7r
Plastic surgery, breast lift		4605	2000	7r
Plastic surgery, facelift		6964	2000	7r
Plastic surgery, hair transplantation		4193	2000	7r
Plastic surgery, lip augmentation		1675	2000	7r
Plastic surgery, lower body lift		6611	2000	7r
Plastic surgery, thigh lift		4751	2000	7r
Household Goods				
Floor coverings, expenditures on	yr	59	1999	30r
Furniture, expenditures on	yr	388	1999	30r
Household furnishings and equipment purchases	yr	1567	1999	30r
Household textiles, expenditures on	yr	112	1999	30r
Laundry and cleaning supplies, expenditures on	yr	104	1999	30r
Housing				
Home price, existing, ave		180800	10/00	90r
Home value, median		157000	2001	53s
Household operation expenditures	yr	581	1999	30r
Housekeeping supplies purchases	yr	474	1999	30r
Lodging expenditures	yr	550	1999	30r
Maintenance, repairs, insurance expenditures	yr	835	1999	30r
Monthly rental value of owned home	mos	663	1999	30r
Owned dwellings, expenditures own	yr	5209	1999	30r
Rent expenditures	yr	2390	1999	30r
Rental unit, 1 bedroom, with utilities	mos	552	4/01	41c
Rental unit, 2 bedroom, with utilities	mos	706	4/01	41c
Rental unit, 3 bedroom, with utilities	mos	886	4/01	41c

Values are in dollars or fractions of dollars. In the column headed *Ref*, references are shown to sources. Each reference is followed by a letter. These refer to the geographical level for which data were reported: s=State, r=Region, and c=City or metro. The abbreviation *ex* is used to mean *except* or *excluding*; *exp* stands for *expenditures*. For other abbreviations and further explanations, please see the Introduction.

Hartford, CT - continued

Item	Per	Value	Date	Ref.
Housing				
Rental unit, 4 bedroom, with utilities	mos	1075	4/01	41c
Shelter, expenditures on	yr	8149	1999	30r
Insurance and Pensions				
Auto insurance premium	yr	982.00	1999	57s
Life and other personal insurance purchases	yr	424	1999	30r
Pensions and Social Security, expenditures on	yr	3037	1999	30r
Legal Fees				
Divorce, filing fee		150.00	4/01	35s
Driver's license fee	orig	43.50	1999	48s
Driver's license fee	renew	28.50	1999	48s
Personal Goods				
Personal care products and services purchases	yr	399	1999	30r
Personal Services				
Personal services, household, expenditures on	yr	271	1999	30r
Pets				
Pets, toys, and playground equipment, expenditures on	yr	325	1999	30r
Taxes				
Federal income taxes paid	yr	2606	1999	30r
Personal taxes, expenditures on	yr	3567	1999	30r
Property taxes paid	yr	1752	1999	30r
State and local income taxes paid	yr	694	1999	30r
Transportation				
Bus fare, one-way	trip	1.00	2000	1c
Cars and trucks, new, expenditures on	yr	1496	1999	30r
Cars and trucks, used, expenditures on	yr	1251	1999	30r
Diesel at the pump	gal	1.36	10/99	73s
Ferry boat transit fare, one-way	trip	0.75	2000	2c
Gasoline and motor oil purchases	yr	901	1999	30r
Gasoline before-tax price (cents)	gal	117.10	10/00	43s
Maintenance and repair expenditures	yr	618	1999	30r
Public transportation, expenditures on	yr	575	1999	30r
Transportation purchases	yr	6503	1999	30r
Vehicle expenses, miscellaneous, purchases	yr	2266	1999	30r
Vehicle insurance payments	yr	824	1999	30r
Vehicle purchases (net outlay)	yr	2761	1999	30r
Vehicle rental, lease expenditures	yr	584	1999	30r
Utilities				
Electrical bill, average	mos	81.50	9/00	9s
Electricity, expenditures on	yr	837	1999	30r
Electricity, summer, 250 KWh	mos	36.92	2/96	97c
Electricity, summer, 500 KWh	mos	64.85	2/96	97c
Electricity, summer, 750 KWh	mos	92.77	2/96	97c
Electricity, summer, 1000 KWh	mos	120.69	2/96	97c
Electricity cost, average	KWh	9.47	9/00	9s
Utilities, fuels, and public services purchased	yr	2457	1999	30r
Water and other public services, expenditures on	yr	215	1999	30r
Water price	100 cf	1.37	2000	109c
Water price, dwelling unit	mos	26.91	2000	109c
Weddings				
Wedding (national average cost)		19936	2000	33r
Wedding (regional average total cost)		29454	1997	110r
Attendants' gifts		321	1998	33r
Bridal attendants' apparel (5 persons)		824	2000	33r
Bride's headpiece/veil		173	1998	33r
Bride's wedding dress		859	1998	33r
Clergy, religious facility fee		242	1998	33r
Engagement ring		3177	1998	33r
Flowers		789	1998	33r
Groom's formalwear rental		99	2000	33r
Limousine		410	1998	33r
Marriage license cost		30.00	4/01	35s
Men's formalwear (ushers, best man)		469	2000	33r

Hartford, CT - continued

Item	Per	Value	Date	Ref.
Weddings - continued				
Mother of bride apparel		241	2000	33r
Music		866	1998	33r
Photography and videography		1368	1998	33r
Rehearsal dinner		728	1998	33r
Wedding invitations and announcements		341	1998	33r
Wedding reception		7968	2000	33r
Wedding rings (bride and groom)		1060	1998	33r

Hattiesburg, MS

Item	Per	Value	Date	Ref.
Composite, ACCRA index		95.00	12/00	5c
Alcoholic Beverages				
Alcoholic beverage purchases	yr	253	1999	30r
Beer, Heineken, 12-oz, ex deposit	6	7.06	12/00	5c
J & B Scotch	750-ml	18.89	12/00	5c
Malt beverages, all types, all sizes, any origin	16 oz	0.96	7/01	11r
Wine, Livingston or Gallo, Chablis blanc	1.5 liter	6.44	12/00	5c
Appliances				
Appliance repair, service call, washing machine	min lab chg	41	12/00	5c
Major appliances, expenditures on	yr	172	1999	30r
Small appliances, housewares, expenditures on	yr	81	1999	30r
Banking and Money				
Mortgage interest and charges paid	yr	2039	1999	30r
Mortgage principal paid on owned property	yr	1026	1999	30r
Mortgage rate, incl. points and orig. fee, 30-yr. conv. fixed or ARM	mos	7.90	12/00	5c
Vehicle finance charges paid	yr	365	1999	30r
Charity				
Cash contributions, expenditures	yr	1127	1999	30r
Child Care				
Child raising cost, total, age 0-2	yr	8540	1999	60r
Child raising cost, total, age 3-5	yr	8780	1999	60r
Child raising cost, total, age 6-8	yr	8820	1999	60r
Child raising cost, total, age 9-11	yr	8800	1999	60r
Child raising cost, total, age 12-14	yr	9510	1999	60r
Child raising cost, total, age 15-17	yr	9740	1999	60r
Child's child care and education, age 0-2	yr	1380	1999	60r
Child's child care and education, age 3-5	yr	1520	1999	60r
Child's child care and education, age 6-8	yr	990	1999	60r
Child's child care and education, age 9-11	yr	650	1999	60r
Child's child care and education, age 12-14	yr	490	1999	60r
Child's child care and education, age 15-17	yr	840	1999	60r
Child's clothing, age 0-2	yr	480	1999	60r
Child's clothing, age 3-5	yr	470	1999	60r
Child's clothing, age 6-8	yr	520	1999	60r
Child's clothing, age 9-11	yr	570	1999	60r
Child's clothing, age 12-14	yr	950	1999	60r
Child's clothing, age 15-17	yr	850	1999	60r
Child's food, age 0-2	yr	1000	1999	60r
Child's food, age 3-5	yr	1160	1999	60r
Child's food, age 6-8	yr	1490	1999	60r
Child's food, age 9-11	yr	1770	1999	60r
Child's food, age 12-14	yr	1770	1999	60r
Child's food, age 15-17	yr	1980	1999	60r
Child's health care, age 0-2	yr	620	1999	60r
Child's health care, age 3-5	yr	590	1999	60r
Child's health care, age 6-8	yr	680	1999	60r
Child's health care, age 9-11	yr	720	1999	60r
Child's health care, age 12-14	yr	730	1999	60r
Child's health care, age 15-17	yr	760	1999	60r
Child's housing, age 0-2	yr	3070	1999	60r
Child's housing, age 3-5	yr	3050	1999	60r
Child's housing, age 6-8	yr	3010	1999	60r
Child's housing, age 9-11	yr	2850	1999	60r
Child's housing, age 12-14	yr	3040	1999	60r
Child's housing, age 15-17	yr	2650	1999	60r
Child's personal care, reading, age 0-2	yr	910	1999	60r

Values are in dollars or fractions of dollars. In the column headed *Ref*, references are shown to sources. Each reference is followed by a letter. These refer to the geographical level for which data were reported: s=State, r=Region, and c=City or metro. The abbreviation *ex* is used to mean *except* or *excluding*; *exp* stands for expenditures. For other abbreviations and further explanations, please see the Introduction.

Hattiesburg, MS - continued

Item	Per	Value	Date	Ref.
Child Care				
Child's personal care, reading, age 3-5	yr	930	1999	60r
Child's personal care, reading, age 6-8	yr	960	1999	60r
Child's personal care, reading, age 9-11	yr	1000	1999	60r
Child's personal care, reading, age 12-14	yr	1170	1999	60r
Child's personal care, reading, age 15-17	yr	950	1999	60r
Clothing				
Apparel and services purchases	yr	1610	1999	30r
Boys' brief, cotton	3	4.22	12/00	5c
Boys, 2 to 15, expenditures on	yr	89	1999	30r
Children under 2, expenditures on	yr	79	1999	30r
Footwear, expenditures on	yr	283	1999	30r
Girls, 2 to 15, expenditures on	yr	103	1999	30r
Men and boys, expenditures on	yr	351	1999	30r
Men, 16 and over, expenditures on	yr	262	1999	30r
Shirt, man's dress shirt		19.99	12/00	5c
Slacks, man's "No Wrinkles" khaki		38.33	12/00	5c
Women, 16 and over, expenditures on	yr	538	1999	30r
Communications				
Newspaper subscription, daily and Sunday delivery	mos	12	12/00	5c
Phone line, single, business, field visit	inst.	67.00	12/97	17s
Phone line, single, business, no field visit	inst.	67.00	12/97	17s
Phone line, single, residence, field visit	inst.	46.00	12/97	17s
Phone line, single, residence, no field visit	inst.	46.00	12/97	17s
Postage and stationery, expenditures on	yr	104	1999	30r
Postal rate, express mail, up to half-pound		12.45	7/01	108r
Postal rate, letter, first class, first ounce		0.34	7/01	108r
Postal rate, letter, two ounces		0.57	7/01	108r
Postal rate, post card		0.21	7/01	108r
Postal rate, priority mail, two pounds		3.95	7/01	108r
Postal rate, priority mail, up to one pound		3.50	7/01	108r
Telephone bill, family of three	mos	24.65	12/00	5c
Telephone services, expenditures on	yr	860	1999	30r
Education				
Board, 4-year private college/university	yr	1536	1996	38s
Board, 4-year public college/university	yr	1568	1996	38s
Education expenditures	yr	431	1999	30r
Room, 4-year private college/university	yr	1582	1996	38s
Room, 4-year public college/university	yr	1399	1996	38s
Total cost, 4-year private college/university	yr	9901	1996	38s
Total cost, 4-year public college/university	yr	5425	1996	38s
Tuition, 2-year public college/university, in state	yr	941	1996	38s
Tuition, 4-year private college/university, in state	yr	6782	1996	38s
Tuition, 4-year public college/university	yr	2459	1996	38s
Energy and Fuels				
Electricity	KWh	0.09	7/01	11r
Electricity	500 KWhs	47.29	7/01	11r
Energy, combined forms, 2400 sq ft	mos	136.63	12/00	5c
Fuel oil #2	gal	1.43	7/01	11r
Fuel oil and other fuels, expenditures on	yr	45	1999	30r
Gas, natural, commercial rate	1000 cf	7.01	11/00	88s
Gas, regular unleaded, cash, self-service	gal	1.39	12/00	5c
Gasoline, all types	gal	1.60	7/01	11r
Gasoline, unleaded midgrade	gal	1.65	7/01	11r
Gasoline, unleaded premium	gal	1.74	7/01	11r
Natural gas, expenditures on	yr	164	1999	30r
Utility (piped) gas, therm		1.01	7/01	11r
Utility (piped) gas, 40 therms		44.29	7/01	11r
Utility (piped) gas, 100 therms		97.44	7/01	11r
Entertainment				
Bowling, Saturday evening rate	line	2.55	12/00	5c
Entertainment purchases	yr	1574	1999	30r
Fees and admissions paid	yr	371	1999	30r
Monopoly game, Parker Brothers', No. 9	game	11.08	12/00	5c
Movie, first-run, Saturday, evening	adm.	6.50	12/00	5c
Reading purchases	yr	121	1999	30r

Hattiesburg, MS - continued

Item	Per	Value	Date	Ref.
Entertainment - continued				
Television, radios, sound equipment, expenditures on	yr	561	1999	30r
Tennis balls, yellow, Wilson or Penn, 3	can	2.24	12/00	5c
Groceries				
Groceries, ACCRA Index		92.50	12/00	5c
American processed cheese	lb	3.50	7/01	11r
Antibiotic ointment, Polysporin	0.5 oz	4.39	12/00	5c
Baby food, strained vegetables or fruit, lowest price	4-4.5 oz	0.29	12/00	5c
Bakery products, expenditures on	yr	261	1999	30r
Bananas	lb	0.47	7/01	11r
Bananas	lb	0.52	12/00	5c
Beans, dried, any type, all sizes	lb	0.63	7/01	11r
Beef for stew, boneless	lb	2.86	7/01	11r
Beef or hamburger, ground	lb	1.45	12/00	5c
Beef, expenditures on	yr	210	1999	30r
Bologna, all beef or mixed	lb	2.29	7/01	11r
Bread, French	lb	1.66	7/01	11r
Bread, white	loaf	1.20	12/00	5c
Bread, white, pan	lb	0.87	7/01	11r
Bread, whole wheat, pan	lb	1.38	7/01	11r
Broccoli	lb	1.04	7/01	11r
Butter, salted, grade AA, stick	lb	2.26	7/01	11r
Butter, yoghurt, cheese, etc, expenditures on	yr	170	1999	30r
Cabbage	lb	0.42	7/01	11r
Cereals and cereal products, expenditures on	yr	140	1999	30r
Cheddar cheese, natural	lb	3.75	7/01	11r
Cheese, Kraft grated Parmesan	8 oz	3.24	12/00	5c
Chicken breast, bone-in	lb	1.85	7/01	11r
Chicken legs, bone-in	lb	1.34	7/01	11r
Chicken, fresh, whole	lb	1.05	7/01	11r
Chicken, whole fryer	lb	0.90	12/00	5c
Chops, boneless,	lb	4.13	7/01	11r
Chuck roast, graded and ungraded, excl U.S. prime and choice	lb	2.35	7/01	11r
Chuck roast, U.S. choice, boneless	lb	2.67	7/01	11r
Cigarettes, Winston, Kings	carton	28.12	12/00	5c
Coffee, 100%, ground roast, all sizes	lb	2.88	7/01	11r
Coffee, instant, plain, regular, all sizes	16 oz	9.25	7/01	11r
Coffee, vacuum-packed	13 oz	2.28	12/00	5c
Cola, non diet,	2 liter	1.11	7/01	11r
Corn Flakes, Kellogg's or Post Toasties	18 oz	1.70	12/00	5c
Corn, frozen, whole kernel, lowest price	16 oz	0.98	12/00	5c
Crackers, soda, salted	lb	1.70	7/01	11r
Dairy product purchases	yr	282	1999	30r
Eggs, expenditures on	yr	32	1999	30r
Eggs, Grade A or AA	dozen	0.93	12/00	5c
Fats and oils, expenditures on	yr	79	1999	30r
Fish and seafood, expenditures on	yr	99	1999	30r
Flour, white, all purpose	lb	0.32	7/01	11r
Food (excl fruit and vegetables), eaten at home, purchases	yr	815	1999	30r
Food cooked on trips, expenditures on	yr	36	1999	30r
Food purchases	yr	4533	1999	30r
Food purchases, eaten away from home	yr	1873	1999	30r
Food purchases, food eaten at home	yr	2660	1999	30r
Fresh fruits, expenditures on	yr	128	1999	30r
Fresh milk and cream, expenditures on	yr	112	1999	30r
Fresh vegetables, expenditures on	yr	131	1999	30r
Fruit and vegetable purchases	yr	438	1999	30r
Grapefruit	lb	0.59	7/01	11r
Grapes, Thompson, seedless	lb	2.12	7/01	11r
Ground beef, 100% beef	lb	1.76	7/01	11r
Ground beef, lean and extra lean	lb	2.60	7/01	11r
Ground chuck, 100% beef	lb	2.08	7/01	11r
Ham, boneless, excl canned	lb	2.71	7/01	11r
Ham, rump or shank half, bone-in, smoked	lb	2.19	7/01	11r
Ice cream, prepackaged, bulk, regular	1/2 gal	3.93	7/01	11r
Lemons	lb	1.32	7/01	11r
Lettuce, iceberg	lb	0.76	7/01	11r
Lettuce, iceberg	head	1.01	12/00	5c

Values are in dollars or fractions of dollars. In the column headed *Ref*, references are shown to sources. Each reference is followed by a letter. These refer to the geographical level for which data were reported: s=State, r=Region, and c=City or metro. The abbreviation *ex* is used to mean *except* or *excluding*; *exp* stands for *expenditures*. For other abbreviations and further explanations, please see the Introduction.

Hattiesburg, MS - continued

Item	Per	Value	Date	Ref.
Groceries				
Margarine, Blue Bonnet or Parkay, stick	lb	0.95	12/00	5c
Milk, fresh, low fat,	gal	2.75	7/01	11r
Milk, fresh, whole, fortified	gal	2.97	7/01	11r
Milk, whole	1/2 gal	1.59	12/00	5c
Nonalcoholic beverages, expenditures on	yr	228	1999	30r
Orange juice, frozen concentrate	16 oz	1.95	7/01	11r
Orange juice, Minute Maid frozen	12 oz	1.33	12/00	5c
Oranges, Navel	lb	0.73	7/01	11r
Oranges, Valencia	lb	0.55	7/01	11r
Peaches, halves or slices, Hunt's, Del Monte, or Libby's	29 oz	1.66	12/00	5c
Peanut butter, creamy, all sizes	lb	1.83	7/01	11r
Pears, Anjou	lb	0.98	7/01	11r
Peas, green, Del Monte or Green Giant	15 oz	0.69	12/00	5c
Pork chops, center cut, bone-in	lb	3.33	7/01	11r
Pork sausage, fresh, loose	lb	2.59	7/01	11r
Pork shoulder picnic, bone-in, smoked	lb	1.12	7/01	11r
Pork, expenditures on	yr	162	1999	30r
Potato chips	16 oz	3.59	7/01	11r
Potatoes, frozen, french fried	lb	1.00	7/01	11r
Potatoes, white or red	10 lb	2.08	12/00	5c
Potatoes, white, all types	lb	0.44	7/01	11r
Poultry, expenditures on	yr	137	1999	30r
Processed fruits, expenditures on	yr	97	1999	30r
Processed vegetables, expenditures on	yr	82	1999	30r
Rice, white, long grain, uncooked	lb	0.51	7/01	11r
Round roast, graded and ungraded, excl U.S. prime and choice	lb	2.96	7/01	11r
Round steak, graded and ungraded, excl U.S. prime and choice	lb	3.11	7/01	11r
Sausage, Jimmy Dean/Owens pork	lb	2.55	12/00	5c
Shortening, vegetable, Crisco	3 lb	2.62	12/00	5c
Sirloin steak, graded and ungraded, excl U.S. prime and choice	lb	4.23	7/01	11r
Soft drink, Coca Cola, ex deposit	2 liter	1.16	12/00	5c
Spaghetti and macaroni	lb	0.78	7/01	11r
Steak, round, U.S. choice, boneless	lb	3.56	7/01	11r
Steak, sirloin, U.S. choice, boneless	lb	5.65	7/01	11r
Steak, T-bone	lb	6.01	12/00	5c
Strawberries, dry pint	12 oz	1.50	7/01	11r
Sugar and other sweets, expenditures on	yr	99	1999	30r
Sugar, cane or beet	4 lbs	1.40	12/00	5c
Sugar, white, 33-80 ounce package	lb	0.39	7/01	11r
Sugar, white, all sizes	lb	0.42	7/01	11r
Tobacco products and smoking supplies purchases	yr	288	1999	30r
Tomatoes, field grown	lb	1.43	7/01	11r
Tomatoes, Hunt's or Del Monte	14.5 oz	0.82	12/00	5c
Tuna, chunk, light	6 oz	0.51	12/00	5c
Tuna, light, chunk	lb	1.77	7/01	11r
Turkey, frozen, whole	lb	1.05	7/01	11r
Goods and Services				
Miscellaneous goods and services, ACCRA Index		95.00	12/00	5c
Hunting license	yr	18.00	4/01	34s
Health Care				
Health care, ACCRA Index		90.40	12/00	5c
Cardiac catheterization, ave hospital/ physician charges		10310	1998	77s
Childbirth, Cesarean delivery		11587	1997	13r
Childbirth, vaginal delivery		6725	1997	13r
Dentist's fee, adult teeth cleaning and periodic oral exam	visit	71.50	12/00	5c
Doctor's fee, routine exam, established patient	visit	50	12/00	5c
Drugs, expenditures on	yr	399	1999	30r
Health care purchases	yr	1971	1999	30r
Health insurance expenditures	yr	933	1999	30r
Hospital care, private room	day	365.00	12/00	5c
Hysterectomy, laproscopically-assisted, ave hospital/physician charges		14270	1998	76s

Hattiesburg, MS - continued

Item	Per	Value	Date	Ref.
Health Care - continued				
Hysterectomy, vaginal, ave hospital and physician charges		10020	1998	76s
Medicaid dispensing fee		4.91	1999	87s
Medical services expenditures	yr	547	1999	30r
Medical supplies, expenditures on	yr	91	1999	30r
Household Goods				
Dishwashing powder, Cascade	50 oz	2.27	12/00	5c
Floor coverings, expenditures on	yr	44	1999	30r
Furniture, expenditures on	yr	335	1999	30r
Household furnishings and equipment purchases	yr	1328	1999	30r
Household textiles, expenditures on	yr	89	1999	30r
Laundry and cleaning supplies, expenditures on	yr	113	1999	30r
Tissues, facial, Kleenex brand	175	1.22	12/00	5c
Housing				
Housing, ACCRA Index		91.30	12/00	5c
Home price, existing, ave		160100	10/00	90r
Home value, median		102000	2001	53s
House, 2400 sq ft, 8000 sq ft lot, new, urban, utilities	total	194157	12/00	5c
House payment, principal and interest, 25% down payment	mos	1059	12/00	5c
Household operation expenditures	yr	553	1999	30r
Housekeeping supplies purchases	yr	473	1999	30r
Housing, expenditures on	yr	10303	1999	30r
Maintenance, repairs, insurance expenditures	yr	699	1999	30r
Monthly rental value of owned home	mos	505	1999	30r
Owned dwellings, expenditures own	yr	3465	1999	30r
Rent expenditures	yr	1641	1999	30r
Rent, apartment, 2 br, 1 1/2-2 baths, unfurn, 950 sq ft, water	mos	556	12/00	5c
Rental unit, 1 bedroom, with utilities	mos	349	4/01	41c
Rental unit, 2 bedroom, with utilities	mos	428	4/01	41c
Rental unit, 3 bedroom, with utilities	mos	574	4/01	41c
Rental unit, 4 bedroom, with utilities	mos	684	4/01	41c
Shelter, expenditures on	yr	5467	1999	30r
Insurance and Pensions				
Life and other personal insurance purchases	yr	414	1999	30r
Pensions and Social Security, expenditures on	yr	2635	1999	30r
Personal insurance and pensions, expenditures on	yr	3048	1999	30r
Legal Fees				
Combination hunting and fishing license	yr	18.00	4/01	34s
Driver's license fee	orig	20.00	1999	48s
Driver's license fee	renew	5.00	1999	48s
Fishing license	yr	12.00	4/01	34s
Personal Goods				
Personal care products and services purchases	yr	393	1999	30r
Shampoo, Alberto VO5	15 oz	1.02	12/00	5c
Toothpaste, Crest or Colgate	6-7 oz	2.23	12/00	5c
Personal Services				
Dry cleaning, man's 2-pc suit		7	12/00	5c
Man's haircut, barbershop, no styling		11.80	12/00	5c
Personal services, household, expenditures on	yr	258	1999	30r
Woman's shampoo, trim, blow-dry, no style-change		27.20	12/00	5c
Pets				
Pets, toys, and playground equipment, expenditures on	yr	306	1999	30r
Restaurant Food				
Chicken, fried, thigh and drumstick, KFC/ Church's		2.39	12/00	5c
Hamburger with cheese, McDonald's	1/4 lb	2.22	12/00	5c

Values are in dollars or fractions of dollars. In the column headed *Ref*, references are shown to sources. Each reference is followed by a letter. These refer to the geographical level for which data were reported: s=State, r=Region, and c=City or metro. The abbreviation *ex* is used to mean *except* or *excluding*; *exp* stands for expenditures. For other abbreviations and further explanations, please see the Introduction.

Hattiesburg, MS - continued

Item	Per	Value	Date	Ref.
Restaurant Food				
Pizza, Pizza Hut or Pizza Inn	11-12 in	8.83	12/00	5c
Taxes				
Federal income taxes paid	yr	2047	1999	30r
Personal taxes, expenditures on	yr	2554	1999	30r
Property taxes paid	yr	726	1999	30r
State and local income taxes paid	yr	363	1999	30r
Transportation				
Transportation, ACCRA Index		91.10	12/00	5c
Cars and trucks, new, expenditures on	yr	1648	1999	30r
Cars and trucks, used, expenditures on	yr	1651	1999	30r
Diesel at the pump	gal	1.17	10/99	73s
Gasoline and motor oil purchases	yr	1052	1999	30r
Gasoline before-tax price (cents)	gal	108.40	10/00	43s
Maintenance and repair expenditures	yr	621	1999	30r
Motorcycle license fee	orig	5.00	1999	49s
Motorcycle license fee	renew	5.00	1999	49s
Public transportation, expenditures on	yr	298	1999	30r
Tire balance, computer or spin balance, front	wheel	6.90	12/00	5c
Transportation purchases	yr	6738	1999	30r
Vehicle expenses, miscellaneous, purchases	yr	2033	1999	30r
Vehicle insurance payments	yr	696	1999	30r
Vehicle purchases (net outlay)	yr	3354	1999	30r
Vehicle rental, lease expenditures	yr	352	1999	30r
Utilities				
Utilities, ACCRA Index		120.70	12/00	5c
Electrical bill, average	mos	79.66	9/00	9s
Electricity, 2400 sq ft, new home	mos	136.63	12/00	5c
Electricity, expenditures on	yr	1115	1999	30r
Electricity cost, average	KWh	5.69	9/00	9s
Water and other public services, expenditures on	yr	298	1999	30r
Weddings				
Wedding (national average cost)		19936	2000	33r
Attendants' gifts		321	1998	33r
Bridal attendants' apparel (5 persons)		824	2000	33r
Bride's headpiece/veil		173	1998	33r
Bride's wedding dress		859	1998	33r
Clergy, religious facility fee		242	1998	33r
Engagement ring		3177	1998	33r
Flowers		789	1998	33r
Groom's formalwear rental		99	2000	33r
Limousine		410	1998	33r
Marriage license cost		21.00	4/01	35s
Men's formalwear (ushers, best man)		469	2000	33r
Mother of bride apparel		241	2000	33r
Music		866	1998	33r
Photography and videography		1368	1998	33r
Rehearsal dinner		728	1998	33r
Wedding invitations and announcements		341	1998	33r
Wedding reception		7968	2000	33r
Wedding rings (bride and groom)		1060	1998	33r

Hickory-Morganton, NC

Item	Per	Value	Date	Ref.
Alcoholic Beverages				
Alcoholic beverage purchases	yr	253	1999	30r
Malt beverages, all types, all sizes, any origin	16 oz	0.96	7/01	11r
Appliances				
Major appliances, expenditures on	yr	172	1999	30r
Small appliances, housewares, expenditures on	yr	81	1999	30r
Banking and Money				
Mortgage interest and charges paid	yr	2039	1999	30r
Mortgage principal paid on owned property	yr	1026	1999	30r
Vehicle finance charges paid	yr	365	1999	30r

Hickory-Morganton, NC - continued

Item	Per	Value	Date	Ref.
Charity				
Cash contributions, expenditures	yr	1127	1999	30r
Child Care				
Child raising cost, total, age 0-2	yr	8540	1999	60r
Child raising cost, total, age 3-5	yr	8780	1999	60r
Child raising cost, total, age 6-8	yr	8820	1999	60r
Child raising cost, total, age 9-11	yr	8800	1999	60r
Child raising cost, total, age 12-14	yr	9510	1999	60r
Child raising cost, total, age 15-17	yr	9740	1999	60r
Child's child care and education, age 0-2	yr	1380	1999	60r
Child's child care and education, age 3-5	yr	1520	1999	60r
Child's child care and education, age 6-8	yr	990	1999	60r
Child's child care and education, age 9-11	yr	650	1999	60r
Child's child care and education, age 12-14	yr	490	1999	60r
Child's child care and education, age 15-17	yr	840	1999	60r
Child's clothing, age 0-2	yr	480	1999	60r
Child's clothing, age 3-5	yr	470	1999	60r
Child's clothing, age 6-8	yr	520	1999	60r
Child's clothing, age 9-11	yr	570	1999	60r
Child's clothing, age 12-14	yr	950	1999	60r
Child's clothing, age 15-17	yr	850	1999	60r
Child's food, age 0-2	yr	1000	1999	60r
Child's food, age 3-5	yr	1160	1999	60r
Child's food, age 6-8	yr	1490	1999	60r
Child's food, age 9-11	yr	1770	1999	60r
Child's food, age 12-14	yr	1770	1999	60r
Child's food, age 15-17	yr	1980	1999	60r
Child's health care, age 0-2	yr	620	1999	60r
Child's health care, age 3-5	yr	590	1999	60r
Child's health care, age 6-8	yr	680	1999	60r
Child's health care, age 9-11	yr	720	1999	60r
Child's health care, age 12-14	yr	730	1999	60r
Child's health care, age 15-17	yr	760	1999	60r
Child's housing, age 0-2	yr	3070	1999	60r
Child's housing, age 3-5	yr	3050	1999	60r
Child's housing, age 6-8	yr	3010	1999	60r
Child's housing, age 9-11	yr	2850	1999	60r
Child's housing, age 12-14	yr	3040	1999	60r
Child's housing, age 15-17	yr	2650	1999	60r
Child's personal care, reading, age 0-2	yr	910	1999	60r
Child's personal care, reading, age 3-5	yr	930	1999	60r
Child's personal care, reading, age 6-8	yr	960	1999	60r
Child's personal care, reading, age 9-11	yr	1000	1999	60r
Child's personal care, reading, age 12-14	yr	1170	1999	60r
Child's personal care, reading, age 15-17	yr	950	1999	60r
Clothing				
Apparel and services purchases	yr	1610	1999	30r
Boys, 2 to 15, expenditures on	yr	89	1999	30r
Children under 2, expenditures on	yr	79	1999	30r
Footwear, expenditures on	yr	283	1999	30r
Girls, 2 to 15, expenditures on	yr	103	1999	30r
Men and boys, expenditures on	yr	351	1999	30r
Men, 16 and over, expenditures on	yr	262	1999	30r
Women, 16 and over, expenditures on	yr	538	1999	30r
Communications				
Cable modem installation, Intermedia		149.95	6/99	103s
Cable modem installation, Time Warner		75.00-225.00	6/99	103s
Cable modem rate, cable subscriber, Intermedia	mos	49.95	6/99	103s
Cable modem rate, cable subscriber, Time Warner	mos	39.95-49.95	6/99	103s
Cable modem rate, non-cable subscriber, Intermedia	mos	54.95	6/99	103s
Cable modem rate, non-cable subscriber, Time Warner	mos	39.95-54.95	6/99	103s
Phone line, single, business, field visit	inst.	65.00	12/97	17s
Phone line, single, business, no field visit	inst.	65.00	12/97	17s
Phone line, single, residence, field visit	inst.	42.75	12/97	17s
Phone line, single, residence, no field visit	inst.	42.75	12/97	17s
Postage and stationery, expenditures on	yr	104	1999	30r
Postal rate, express mail, up to half-pound		12.45	7/01	108r

Values are in dollars or fractions of dollars. In the column headed *Ref*, references are shown to sources. Each reference is followed by a letter. These refer to the geographical level for which data were reported: s=State, r=Region, and c=City or metro. The abbreviation *ex* is used to mean *except* or *excluding*; *exp* stands for expenditures. For other abbreviations and further explanations, please see the Introduction.

Hickory-Morganton, NC - continued

Item	Per	Value	Date	Ref.
Communications				
Postal rate, letter, first class, first ounce		0.34	7/01	108r
Postal rate, letter, two ounces		0.57	7/01	108r
Postal rate, post card		0.21	7/01	108r
Postal rate, priority mail, two pounds		3.95	7/01	108r
Postal rate, priority mail, up to one pound		3.50	7/01	108r
Telephone services, expenditures on	yr	860	1999	30r
Education				
Board, 4-year private college/university	yr	2316	1996	38s
Board, 4-year public college/university	yr	1737	1996	38s
Education expenditures	yr	431	1999	30r
Room, 4-year private college/university	yr	2128	1996	38s
Room, 4-year public college/university	yr	1742	1996	38s
Total cost, 4-year private college/university	yr	15428	1996	38s
Total cost, 4-year public college/university	yr	5119	1996	38s
Tuition, 4-year private college/university, in state	yr	10984	1996	38s
Tuition, 4-year public college/university	yr	1639	1996	38s
Energy and Fuels				
Electricity	KWh	0.09	7/01	11r
Electricity	500 KWhs	47.29	7/01	11r
Fuel oil #2	gal	1.43	7/01	11r
Fuel oil and other fuels, expenditures on	yr	45	1999	30r
Gas, natural, commercial rate	1000 cf	9.25	11/00	88s
Gasoline, all types	gal	1.60	7/01	11r
Gasoline, unleaded midgrade	gal	1.65	7/01	11r
Gasoline, unleaded premium	gal	1.74	7/01	11r
Natural gas, expenditures on	yr	164	1999	30r
Utility (piped) gas, therm		1.01	7/01	11r
Utility (piped) gas, 40 therms		44.29	7/01	11r
Utility (piped) gas, 100 therms		97.44	7/01	11r
Entertainment				
Entertainment purchases	yr	1574	1999	30r
Fees and admissions paid	yr	371	1999	30r
Reading purchases	yr	121	1999	30r
Television, radios, sound equipment, expenditures on	yr	561	1999	30r
Funerals				
Total cost of funeral		5922.53	1/99	78r
Acknowledgement cards		63.43	1/99	78r
Casket		2258.77	1/99	78r
Cosmetology, hair, other preparation		127.09	1/99	78r
Embalming		393.49	1/99	78r
Funeral at funeral home		367.50	1/99	78r
Hearse (local)		169.66	1/99	78r
Professional service charges		1211.32	1/99	78r
Service car/van		80.69	1/99	78r
Transfer of remains to funeral home		144.25	1/99	78r
Vault		803.50	1/99	78r
Visitation/viewing		302.83	1/99	78r
Groceries				
American processed cheese	lb	3.50	7/01	11r
Bakery products, expenditures on	yr	261	1999	30r
Bananas	lb	0.47	7/01	11r
Beans, dried, any type, all sizes	lb	0.63	7/01	11r
Beef for stew, boneless	lb	2.86	7/01	11r
Beef, expenditures on	yr	210	1999	30r
Bologna, all beef or mixed	lb	2.29	7/01	11r
Bread, French	lb	1.66	7/01	11r
Bread, white, pan	lb	0.87	7/01	11r
Bread, whole wheat, pan	lb	1.38	7/01	11r
Broccoli	lb	1.04	7/01	11r
Butter, salted, grade AA, stick	lb	2.26	7/01	11r
Butter, yoghurt, cheese, etc, expenditures on	yr	170	1999	30r
Cabbage	lb	0.42	7/01	11r
Cereals and cereal products, expenditures on	yr	140	1999	30r
Cheddar cheese, natural	lb	3.75	7/01	11r
Chicken breast, bone-in	lb	1.85	7/01	11r

Hickory-Morganton, NC - continued

Item	Per	Value	Date	Ref.
Groceries - continued				
Chicken legs, bone-in	lb	1.34	7/01	11r
Chicken, fresh, whole	lb	1.05	7/01	11r
Chops, boneless,	lb	4.13	7/01	11r
Chuck roast, graded and ungraded, excl U.S. prime and choice	lb	2.35	7/01	11r
Chuck roast, U.S. choice, boneless	lb	2.67	7/01	11r
Coffee, 100%, ground roast, all sizes	lb	2.88	7/01	11r
Coffee, instant, plain, regular, all sizes	16 oz	9.25	7/01	11r
Cola, non diet,	2 liter	1.11	7/01	11r
Crackers, soda, salted	lb	1.70	7/01	11r
Dairy product purchases	yr	282	1999	30r
Eggs, expenditures on	yr	32	1999	30r
Fats and oils, expenditures on	yr	79	1999	30r
Fish and seafood, expenditures on	yr	99	1999	30r
Flour, white, all purpose	lb	0.32	7/01	11r
Food (excl fruit and vegetables), eaten at home, purchases	yr	815	1999	30r
Food cooked on trips, expenditures on	yr	36	1999	30r
Food purchases	yr	4533	1999	30r
Food purchases, eaten away from home	yr	1873	1999	30r
Food purchases, food eaten at home	yr	2660	1999	30r
Fresh fruits, expenditures on	yr	128	1999	30r
Fresh milk and cream, expenditures on	yr	112	1999	30r
Fresh vegetables, expenditures on	yr	131	1999	30r
Fruit and vegetable purchases	yr	438	1999	30r
Grapefruit	lb	0.59	7/01	11r
Grapes, Thompson, seedless	lb	2.12	7/01	11r
Ground beef, 100% beef	lb	1.76	7/01	11r
Ground beef, lean and extra lean	lb	2.60	7/01	11r
Ground chuck, 100% beef	lb	2.08	7/01	11r
Ham, boneless, excl canned	lb	2.71	7/01	11r
Ham, rump or shank half, bone-in, smoked	lb	2.19	7/01	11r
Ice cream, prepackaged, bulk, regular	1/2 gal	3.93	7/01	11r
Lemons	lb	1.32	7/01	11r
Lettuce, iceberg	lb	0.76	7/01	11r
Milk, fresh, low fat,	gal	2.75	7/01	11r
Milk, fresh, whole, fortified	gal	2.97	7/01	11r
Nonalcoholic beverages, expenditures on	yr	228	1999	30r
Orange juice, frozen concentrate	16 oz	1.95	7/01	11r
Oranges, Navel	lb	0.73	7/01	11r
Oranges, Valencia	lb	0.55	7/01	11r
Peanut butter, creamy, all sizes	lb	1.83	7/01	11r
Pears, Anjou	lb	0.98	7/01	11r
Pork chops, center cut, bone-in	lb	3.33	7/01	11r
Pork sausage, fresh, loose	lb	2.59	7/01	11r
Pork shoulder picnic, bone-in, smoked	lb	1.12	7/01	11r
Pork, expenditures on	yr	162	1999	30r
Potato chips	16 oz	3.59	7/01	11r
Potatoes, frozen, french fried	lb	1.00	7/01	11r
Potatoes, white, all types	lb	0.44	7/01	11r
Poultry, expenditures on	yr	137	1999	30r
Processed fruits, expenditures on	yr	97	1999	30r
Processed vegetables, expenditures on	yr	82	1999	30r
Rice, white, long grain, uncooked	lb	0.51	7/01	11r
Round roast, graded and ungraded, excl U.S. prime and choice	lb	2.96	7/01	11r
Round steak, graded and ungraded, excl U.S. prime and choice	lb	3.11	7/01	11r
Sirloin steak, graded and ungraded, excl U.S. prime and choice	lb	4.23	7/01	11r
Spaghetti and macaroni	lb	0.78	7/01	11r
Steak, round, U.S. choice, boneless	lb	3.56	7/01	11r
Steak, sirloin, U.S. choice, boneless	lb	5.65	7/01	11r
Strawberries, dry pint	12 oz	1.50	7/01	11r
Sugar and other sweets, expenditures on	yr	99	1999	30r
Sugar, white, 33-80 ounce package	lb	0.39	7/01	11r
Sugar, white, all sizes	lb	0.42	7/01	11r
Tobacco products and smoking supplies purchases	yr	288	1999	30r
Tomatoes, field grown	lb	1.43	7/01	11r
Tuna, light, chunk	lb	1.77	7/01	11r
Turkey, frozen, whole	lb	1.05	7/01	11r

Values are in dollars or fractions of dollars. In the column headed *Ref*, references are shown to sources. Each reference is followed by a letter. These refer to the geographical level for which data were reported: s=State, r=Region, and c=City or metro. The abbreviation *ex* is used to mean *except* or *excluding*; *exp* stands for *expenditures*. For other abbreviations and further explanations, please see the Introduction.

Hickory-Morganton, NC - continued

Item	Per	Value	Date	Ref.
Goods and Services				
B&B Japanese maple (acer japonicum)	gal	49.98-129.00	4/00	93r
Boxwood (buxus)	2 gal	12.99-16.99	4/00	93r
Daylilly (hemerocallis)	gal	4.99-8.99	4/00	93r
Flat of annuals		11.00-13.92	4/00	93r
Fountain grass (pennisetum)	gal	5.98-7.98	4/00	93r
Hanging basket (10 in)		7.99-14.98	4/00	93r
Hardy geranium (geranium)	gal	5.98-8.00	4/00	93r
Hosta (hosta)	gal	4.99-10.98	4/00	93r
Lilac (syrubga vulgaris)	2 gal	12.99-21.99	4/00	93r
Rhododendron (rhododendron)	2 gal	14.99-24.99	4/00	93r
Sage (salvia)	gal	5.98-6.99	4/00	93r
Wintercreeper euonymus (euonymus fortunei)	2 gal	7.99-89.99	4/00	93r
Hunting license	yr	15.00	4/01	34s
Health Care				
Cardiac catheterization, ave hospital/physician charges		12500	1998	77s
Childbirth, Cesarean delivery		11587	1997	13r
Childbirth, vaginal delivery		6725	1997	13r
Drugs, expenditures on	yr	399	1999	30r
Health care purchases	yr	1971	1999	30r
Health insurance expenditures	yr	933	1999	30r
Hysterectomy, laproscopically-assisted, ave hospital/physician charges		12260	1998	76s
Hysterectomy, vaginal, ave hospital and physician charges		8440	1998	76s
Medicaid dispensing fee		5.60	1999	87s
Medical services expenditures	yr	547	1999	30r
Medical supplies, expenditures on	yr	91	1999	30r
Plastic surgery, breast augmentation		2870	2000	7r
Plastic surgery, breast lift		3649	2000	7r
Plastic surgery, facelift		5008	2000	7r
Plastic surgery, hair transplantation		3425	2000	7r
Plastic surgery, lip augmentation		1227	2000	7r
Plastic surgery, lower body lift		4793	2000	7r
Plastic surgery, thigh lift		3862	2000	7r
Household Goods				
Floor coverings, expenditures on	yr	44	1999	30r
Furniture, expenditures on	yr	335	1999	30r
Household furnishings and equipment purchases	yr	1328	1999	30r
Household textiles, expenditures on	yr	89	1999	30r
Laundry and cleaning supplies, expenditures on	yr	113	1999	30r
Housing				
Home price, existing, ave		160100	10/00	90r
Home value, median		146000	2001	53s
Household operation expenditures	yr	553	1999	30r
Housekeeping supplies purchases	yr	473	1999	30r
Housing, expenditures on	yr	10303	1999	30r
Maintenance, repairs, insurance expenditures	yr	699	1999	30r
Monthly rental value of owned home	mos	505	1999	30r
Owned dwellings, expenditures own	yr	3465	1999	30r
Rent expenditures	yr	1641	1999	30r
Rental unit, 1 bedroom, with utilities	mos	430	4/01	41c
Rental unit, 2 bedroom, with utilities	mos	499	4/01	41c
Rental unit, 3 bedroom, with utilities	mos	630	4/01	41c
Rental unit, 4 bedroom, with utilities	mos	746	4/01	41c
Shelter, expenditures on	yr	5467	1999	30r

Hickory-Morganton, NC - continued

Item	Per	Value	Date	Ref.
Insurance and Pensions				
Life and other personal insurance purchases	yr	414	1999	30r
Pensions and Social Security, expenditures on	yr	2635	1999	30r
Personal insurance and pensions, expenditures on	yr	3048	1999	30r
Legal Fees				
Combination hunting and fishing license	yr	20.00	4/01	34s
Divorce, filing fee		80.00	4/01	35s
Driver's license fee	renew	10.00	1999	48s
Driver's license fee	orig	10.00	1999	48s
Fishing license	yr	15.00	4/01	34s
Personal Goods				
Personal care products and services purchases	yr	393	1999	30r
Personal Services				
Personal services, household, expenditures on	yr	258	1999	30r
Pets				
Pets, toys, and playground equipment, expenditures on	yr	306	1999	30r
Taxes				
Federal income taxes paid	yr	2047	1999	30r
Personal taxes, expenditures on	yr	2554	1999	30r
Property taxes paid	yr	726	1999	30r
State and local income taxes paid	yr	363	1999	30r
Transportation				
Cars and trucks, new, expenditures on	yr	1648	1999	30r
Cars and trucks, used, expenditures on	yr	1651	1999	30r
Diesel at the pump	gal	1.19	10/99	73s
Gasoline and motor oil purchases	yr	1052	1999	30r
Gasoline before-tax price (cents)	gal	103.20	10/00	43s
Maintenance and repair expenditures	yr	621	1999	30r
Motorcycle license fee	orig	1.50	1999	49s
Motorcycle license fee	renew	1.50	1999	49s
Public transportation, expenditures on	yr	298	1999	30r
Transportation purchases	yr	6738	1999	30r
Vehicle expenses, miscellaneous, purchases	yr	2033	1999	30r
Vehicle insurance payments	yr	696	1999	30r
Vehicle purchases (net outlay)	yr	3354	1999	30r
Vehicle rental, lease expenditures	yr	352	1999	30r
Utilities				
Electrical bill, average	mos	83.66	9/00	9s
Electricity, expenditures on	yr	1115	1999	30r
Electricity cost, average	KWh	6.40	9/00	9s
Water and other public services, expenditures on	yr	298	1999	30r
Weddings				
Wedding (national average cost)		19936	2000	33r
Wedding (regional average total cost)		16293	1997	110r
Attendants' gifts		321	1998	33r
Bridal attendants' apparel (5 persons)		824	2000	33r
Bride's headpiece/veil		173	1998	33r
Bride's wedding dress		859	1998	33r
Clergy, religious facility fee		242	1998	33r
Engagement ring		3177	1998	33r
Flowers		789	1998	33r
Groom's formalwear rental		99	2000	33r
Limousine		410	1998	33r
Marriage license cost		40.00	4/01	35s
Men's formalwear (ushers, best man)		469	2000	33r
Mother of bride apparel		241	2000	33r
Music		866	1998	33r
Photography and videography		1368	1998	33r
Rehearsal dinner		728	1998	33r
Wedding invitations and announcements		341	1998	33r
Wedding reception		7968	2000	33r
Wedding rings (bride and groom)		1060	1998	33r

Values are in dollars or fractions of dollars. In the column headed *Ref*, references are shown to sources. Each reference is followed by a letter. These refer to the geographical level for which data were reported: s=State, r=Region, and c=City or metro. The abbreviation *ex* is used to mean *except* or *excluding*; *exp* stands for expenditures. For other abbreviations and further explanations, please see the Introduction.

Honolulu, HI

Item	Per	Value	Date	Ref.
Average annual expenditures	yr	40662	1999	30r
Alcoholic Beverages				
Alcoholic beverage purchases	yr	406	1999	30c
Malt beverages, all types, all sizes, any origin	16 oz	0.94	7/01	11r
Wine, red and white table, all sizes, any origin	liter	6.00	7/01	11r
Appliances				
Major appliances, expenditures on	yr	167	1999	30r
Small appliances, housewares, expenditures on	yr	105	1999	30r
Banking and Money				
Mortgage interest and charges paid	yr	3368	1999	30r
Mortgage principal paid on owned property	yr	1677	1999	30r
Vehicle finance charges paid	yr	311	1999	30r
Business Expenses				
Business travel, car rental	day	36	2001	3c
Business travel, food	day	58	2001	3c
Business travel, hotel	day	166	2001	3c
Charity				
Cash contributions, expenditures	yr	1410	1999	30c
Child Care				
Child raising cost, total, age 0-2	yr	9140	1999	60r
Child raising cost, total, age 3-5	yr	9370	1999	60r
Child raising cost, total, age 6-8	yr	9450	1999	60r
Child raising cost, total, age 9-11	yr	9470	1999	60r
Child raising cost, total, age 12-14	yr	10170	1999	60r
Child raising cost, total, age 15-17	yr	10360	1999	60r
Child's child care and education, age 0-2	yr	1250	1999	60r
Child's child care and education, age 3-5	yr	1380	1999	60r
Child's child care and education, age 6-8	yr	890	1999	60r
Child's child care and education, age 9-11	yr	580	1999	60r
Child's child care and education, age 12-14	yr	430	1999	60r
Child's child care and education, age 15-17	yr	730	1999	60r
Child's clothing, age 0-2	yr	430	1999	60r
Child's clothing, age 3-5	yr	420	1999	60r
Child's clothing, age 6-8	yr	470	1999	60r
Child's clothing, age 9-11	yr	520	1999	60r
Child's clothing, age 12-14	yr	870	1999	60r
Child's clothing, age 15-17	yr	770	1999	60r
Child's food, age 0-2	yr	1120	1999	60r
Child's food, age 3-5	yr	1280	1999	60r
Child's food, age 6-8	yr	1640	1999	60r
Child's food, age 9-11	yr	1930	1999	60r
Child's food, age 12-14	yr	1940	1999	60r
Child's food, age 15-17	yr	2150	1999	60r
Child's health care, age 0-2	yr	490	1999	60r
Child's health care, age 3-5	yr	470	1999	60r
Child's health care, age 6-8	yr	530	1999	60r
Child's health care, age 9-11	yr	570	1999	60r
Child's health care, age 12-14	yr	580	1999	60r
Child's health care, age 15-17	yr	610	1999	60r
Child's housing, age 0-2	yr	3630	1999	60r
Child's housing, age 3-5	yr	3610	1999	60r
Child's housing, age 6-8	yr	3570	1999	60r
Child's housing, age 9-11	yr	3410	1999	60r
Child's housing, age 12-14	yr	3600	1999	60r
Child's housing, age 15-17	yr	3210	1999	60r
Child's personal care, reading, age 0-2	yr	1040	1999	60r
Child's personal care, reading, age 3-5	yr	1060	1999	60r
Child's personal care, reading, age 6-8	yr	1090	1999	60r
Child's personal care, reading, age 9-11	yr	1130	1999	60r
Child's personal care, reading, age 12-14	yr	1300	1999	60r
Child's personal care, reading, age 15-17	yr	1080	1999	60r
Clothing				
Apparel and services purchases	yr	1995	1999	30c
Boys, 2 to 15, expenditures on	yr	80	1999	30r
Children under 2, expenditures on	yr	74	1999	30r
Footwear, expenditures on	yr	307	1999	30r
Girls, 2 to 15, expenditures on	yr	101	1999	30r

Honolulu, HI - continued

Item	Per	Value	Date	Ref.
Clothing - continued				
Men and boys, expenditures on	yr	443	1999	30r
Men, 16 and over, expenditures on	yr	363	1999	30r
Women, 16 and over, expenditures on	yr	594	1999	30r
Communications				
Cable modem installation, Time Warner		75.00-225.00	6/99	103s
Cable modem rate, cable subscriber, Time Warner	mos	39.95-49.95	6/99	103s
Cable modem rate, non-cable subscriber, Time Warner	mos	39.95-54.95	6/99	103s
Postage and stationery, expenditures on	yr	150	1999	30r
Postal rate, express mail, up to half-pound		12.45	7/01	108r
Postal rate, letter, first class, first ounce		0.34	7/01	108r
Postal rate, letter, two ounces		0.57	7/01	108r
Postal rate, post card		0.21	7/01	108r
Postal rate, priority mail, two pounds		3.95	7/01	108r
Postal rate, priority mail, up to one pound		3.50	7/01	108r
Telephone services, expenditures on	yr	825	1999	30r
Education				
Board, 4-year private college/university	yr	2347	1996	38s
Education expenditures	yr	1147	1999	30c
Room, 4-year private college/university	yr	3050	1996	38s
Total cost, 4-year private college/university	yr	11632	1996	38s
Tuition, 2-year public college/university, in state		524	1996	38s
Tuition, 4-year private college/university, in state	yr	6234	1996	38s
Tuition, 4-year public college/university	yr	1576	1996	38s
Energy and Fuels				
Electricity	KWh	0.11	7/01	11r
Electricity	500 KWhs	48.23	7/01	11r
Fuel oil and other fuels, expenditures on	yr	35	1999	30r
Gas, cooking, winter, 10 therms	mos	22.28	2/96	98c
Gas, cooking, winter, 30 therms	mos	54.83	2/96	98c
Gas, cooking, winter, 50 therms	mos	87.39	2/96	98c
Gas, heating, winter, average use	mos	31.55	2/96	98c
Gas, natural, commercial rate	1000 cf	18.11	11/00	88s
Gasoline, all types	gal	1.91	7/01	11r
Gasoline, unleaded premium	gal	2.05	7/01	11r
Gasoline, unleaded regular	gal	1.83	7/01	11r
Natural gas, expenditures on	yr	255	1999	30r
Utility (piped) gas, therm		0.98	7/01	11r
Utility (piped) gas, 40 therms		40.74	7/01	11r
Utility (piped) gas, 100 therms		96.80	7/01	11r
Entertainment				
Entertainment purchases	yr	2083	1999	30c
Fees and admissions paid	yr	545	1999	30r
Reading purchases	yr	193	1999	30c
Television, radios, sound equipment, expenditures on	yr	624	1999	30r
Funerals				
Total cost of funeral		5401.08	1/99	78r
Acknowledgement cards		33.64	1/99	78r
Casket		2170.43	1/99	78r
Cosmetology, hair, other preparation		136.32	1/99	78r
Embalming		319.13	1/99	78r
Funeral at funeral home		370.21	1/99	78r
Hearse (local)		161.04	1/99	78r
Professional service charges		963.15	1/99	78r
Service car/van		133.99	1/99	78r
Transfer of remains to funeral home		159.82	1/99	78r
Vault		778.07	1/99	78r
Visitation/viewing		175.28	1/99	78r
Groceries				
Apples, red delicious	lb	0.84	7/01	11r
Bacon, sliced	lb	3.38	7/01	11r
Bakery products, expenditures on	yr	299	1999	30r
Bananas	lb	0.54	7/01	11r

Values are in dollars or fractions of dollars. In the column headed *Ref*, references are shown to sources. Each reference is followed by a letter. These refer to the geographical level for which data were reported: s=State, r=Region, and c=City or metro. The abbreviation *ex* is used to mean *except* or *excluding*; *exp* stands for expenditures. For other abbreviations and further explanations, please see the Introduction.

Honolulu, HI - continued

Item	Per	Value	Date	Ref.
Groceries				
Beans, dried, any type, all sizes	lb	0.76	7/01	11r
Beef, expenditures on	yr	222	1999	30r
Bread, white, pan	lb	0.99	7/01	11r
Butter, yoghurt, cheese, etc, expenditures on	yr	211	1999	30r
Cereals and bakery product purchases	yr	466	1999	30r
Cereals and cereal products, expenditures on	yr	168	1999	30r
Chicken breast, bone-in	lb	2.45	7/01	11r
Chicken, fresh, whole	lb	1.19	7/01	11r
Chops, boneless,	lb	4.00	7/01	11r
Chuck roast, graded and ungraded, excl U.S. prime and choice	lb	2.55	7/01	11r
Coffee, 100%, ground roast, all sizes	lb	3.80	7/01	11r
Cookies, chocolate chip	lb	2.83	7/01	11r
Dairy product purchases	yr	298	1999	30c
Eggs, expenditures on	yr	39	1999	30r
Eggs, grade AA, large	dozen	1.23	7/01	11r
Fats and oils, expenditures on	yr	88	1999	30r
Fish and seafood, expenditures on	yr	121	1999	30r
Food (excl fruit and vegetables), eaten at home, purchases	yr	999	1999	30c
Food cooked on trips, expenditures on	yr	64	1999	30r
Food purchases	yr	6300	1999	30c
Food purchases, eaten away from home	yr	2877	1999	30c
Food purchases, food eaten at home	yr	3423	1999	30c
Fresh fruits, expenditures on	yr	186	1999	30r
Fresh milk and cream, expenditures on	yr	130	1999	30r
Fresh vegetables, expenditures on	yr	177	1999	30r
Fruit and vegetable purchases	yr	690	1999	30c
Grapefruit	lb	0.68	7/01	11r
Grapes, Thompson, seedless	lb	2.42	7/01	11r
Ground beef, lean and extra lean	lb	2.46	7/01	11r
Ice cream, prepackaged, bulk, regular	1/2 gal	3.62	7/01	11r
Lettuce, iceberg	lb	0.63	7/01	11r
Meats, poultry, fish, and egg purchases	yr	761	1999	30r
Milk, fresh, low fat	gal	2.80	7/01	11r
Milk, fresh, whole, fortified	gal	2.88	7/01	11r
Nonalcoholic beverages, expenditures on	yr	258	1999	30r
Oranges, Navel	lb	0.97	7/01	11r
Oranges, Valencia	lb	0.43	7/01	11r
Peaches	lb	1.38	7/01	11r
Peanut butter, creamy, all sizes	lb	2.14	7/01	11r
Pork chops, center cut, bone-in	lb	3.83	7/01	11r
Pork, expenditures on	yr	141	1999	30r
Potatoes, white, all types	lb	0.37	7/01	11r
Poultry, expenditures on	yr	146	1999	30r
Processed fruits, expenditures on	yr	118	1999	30r
Processed vegetables, expenditures on	yr	81	1999	30r
Round roast, graded and ungraded, excl U.S. prime and choice	lb	3.07	7/01	11r
Round roast, U.S. choice, boneless	lb	3.37	7/01	11r
Round steak, graded and ungraded, excl U.S. prime and choice	lb	3.51	7/01	11r
Sirloin steak, graded and ungraded, excl U.S. prime and choice	lb	4.67	7/01	11r
Steak, sirloin, U.S. choice, boneless	lb	6.20	7/01	11r
Strawberries, dry pint	12 oz	1.79	7/01	11r
Sugar and other sweets, expenditures on	yr	124	1999	30r
Sugar, white, all sizes	lb	0.46	7/01	11r
Tobacco products and smoking supplies purchases	yr	217	1999	30r
Tomatoes, field grown	lb	1.17	7/01	11r
Tuna, light, chunk	lb	2.05	7/01	11r
Goods and Services				
B&B Japanese maple (acer japonicum)	gal	39.99	4/00	93r
Boxwood (buxus)	2 gal	14.99-24.99	4/00	93r
Daylily (hemerocallis)	gal	6.99-8.99	4/00	93r
Flat of annuals		16.68	4/00	93r
Fountain grass (pennisetum)	gal	7.99-11.99	4/00	93r

Honolulu, HI - continued

Item	Per	Value	Date	Ref.
Goods and Services - continued				
Hanging basket (10 in)		29.99	4/00	93r
Hardy geranium (geranium)	gal	6.99-11.99	4/00	93r
Hosta (hosta)	gal	6.99-18.99	4/00	93r
Lilac (syrubga vulgaris)	2 gal	14.99-17.99	4/00	93r
Miscellaneous purchases	yr	1070	1999	30r
Rhododendron (rhododendron)	2 gal	14.99	4/00	93r
Sage (salvia)	gal	6.99	4/00	93r
Wintercreeper euonymus (euonymus fortunei)	2 gal	14.99-22.99	4/00	93r
Hunting license	yr	15.00	4/01	34s
Health Care				
Childbirth, Cesarean delivery		11587	1997	13r
Childbirth, vaginal delivery		6725	1997	13r
Drugs, expenditures on	yr	309	1999	30r
Health care purchases	yr	2188	1999	30c
Health insurance expenditures	yr	868	1999	30r
Medicaid dispensing fee		4.67	1999	87s
Medical services expenditures	yr	580	1999	30r
Medical supplies, expenditures on	yr	112	1999	30r
Household Goods				
Floor coverings, expenditures on	yr	49	1999	30r
Furniture, expenditures on	yr	444	1999	30r
Household furnishings and equipment purchases	yr	1497	1999	30c
Household textiles, expenditures on	yr	141	1999	30r
Laundry and cleaning supplies, expenditures on	yr	128	1999	30r
Housing				
Home, 2200 sq ft, 4-br, 2-bath, 2-car garage, average		380000	2000	47c
Home, suburban, 2,200 square feet		372700	2000	23c
Home price, existing, ave		239400	10/00	90r
Home value, median		249000	2001	53s
Household operation expenditures	yr	513	1999	30c
Housekeeping supplies purchases	yr	554	1999	30c
Housing, expenditures on	yr	14672	1999	30c
Lodging expenditures	yr	575	1999	30r
Maintenance, repairs, insurance expenditures	yr	939	1999	30r
Monthly rental value of owned home	mos	662	1999	30r
Owned dwellings, expenditures own	yr	6152	1999	30c
Rent expenditures	yr	3403	1999	30c
Rental unit, 1 bedroom, with utilities	mos	713	4/01	41c
Rental unit, 2 bedroom, with utilities	mos	839	4/01	41c
Rental unit, 3 bedroom, with utilities	mos	1134	4/01	41c
Rental unit, 4 bedroom, with utilities	mos	1226	4/01	41c
Shelter, expenditures on	yr	10076	1999	30c
Single-family home, purchase price		289000	2000	19c
Insurance and Pensions				
Auto insurance premium	yr	1033.76	1999	57s
Life and other personal insurance purchases	yr	687	1999	30c
Pensions and Social Security, expenditures on	yr	4203	1999	30c
Personal insurance and pensions, expenditures on	yr	4890	1999	30c
Legal Fees				
Divorce, filing fee		100.00-150.00	4/01	35s
Driver's license fee	renew	12.00	1999	48s
Driver's license fee	orig	19.00	1999	48s
Personal Goods				
Personal care products and services purchases	yr	638	1999	30c

Values are in dollars or fractions of dollars. In the column headed *Ref*, references are shown to sources. Each reference is followed by a letter. These refer to the geographical level for which data were reported: s=State, r=Region, and c=City or metro. The abbreviation *ex* is used to mean *except* or *excluding*; *exp* stands for *expenditures*. For other abbreviations and further explanations, please see the Introduction.

Honolulu, HI - continued

Item	Per	Value	Date	Ref.
Personal Services				
Personal services, household, expenditures on	yr	353	1999	30r
Pets				
Pets, toys, and playground equipment, expenditures on	yr	358	1999	30r
Restaurant Food				
Cheeseburger, 1/4-lb, large fries, medium soft drink, excl tax		5.16	1999	40c
Taxes				
Federal income taxes paid	yr	3200	1999	30r
Personal taxes, expenditures on	yr	4153	1999	30r
Property taxes paid	yr	923	1999	30r
State and local income taxes paid	yr	812	1999	30r
Transportation				
Bus fare, one-way	trip	1.00	2000	1c
Cars and trucks, new, expenditures on	yr	1534	1999	30r
Cars and trucks, used, expenditures on	yr	1593	1999	30r
Gasoline and motor oil purchases	yr	1060	1999	30c
Gasoline before-tax price (cents)	gal	139.20	10/00	43s
Maintenance and repair expenditures	yr	797	1999	30r
Public transportation, expenditures on	yr	1033	1999	30c
Transportation purchases	yr	5354	1999	30c
Vehicle expenses, miscellaneous, purchases	yr	2262	1999	30c
Vehicle insurance payments	yr	811	1999	30r
Vehicle purchases (net outlay)	yr	999	1999	30c
Vehicle rental, lease expenditures	yr	666	1999	30r
Travel				
Car rental	day	41.00	2000	52c
Hotel room	night	152.26	2/01	95s
Utilities				
Electrical bill, average	mos	88.03	9/00	9s
Electricity, expenditures on	yr	725	1999	30r
Electricity, summer, 250 KWh	mos	35.89	2/96	97c
Electricity, summer, 500 KWh	mos	64.79	2/96	97c
Electricity, summer, 750 KWh	mos	93.67	2/96	97c
Electricity, summer, 1000 KWh	mos	122.56	2/96	97c
Electricity cost, average	KWh	13.71	9/00	9s
Utilities, fuels, and public services purchased	yr	2179	1999	30r
Water and other public services, expenditures on	yr	339	1999	30r
Weddings				
Wedding (national average cost)		19936	2000	33r
Wedding (regional average total cost)		18918	1997	110r
Attendants' gifts		321	1998	33r
Bridal attendants' apparel (5 persons)		824	2000	33r
Bride's headpiece/veil		173	1998	33r
Bride's wedding dress		859	1998	33r
Clergy, religious facility fee		242	1998	33r
Engagement ring		3177	1998	33r
Flowers		789	1998	33r
Groom's formalwear rental		99	2000	33r
Limousine		410	1998	33r
Marriage license cost		50.00	4/01	35s
Men's formalwear (ushers, best man)		469	2000	33r
Mother of bride apparel		241	2000	33r
Music		866	1998	33r
Photography and videography		1368	1998	33r
Rehearsal dinner		728	1998	33r
Wedding invitations and announcements		341	1998	33r
Wedding reception		7968	2000	33r
Wedding rings (bride and groom)		1060	1998	33r

Houma, LA

Item	Per	Value	Date	Ref.
Alcoholic Beverages				
Alcoholic beverage purchases	yr	253	1999	30r
Malt beverages, all types, all sizes, any origin	16 oz	0.96	7/01	11r
Appliances				
Major appliances, expenditures on	yr	172	1999	30r
Small appliances, housewares, expenditures on	yr	81	1999	30r
Banking and Money				
Mortgage interest and charges paid	yr	2039	1999	30r
Mortgage principal paid on owned property	yr	1026	1999	30r
Vehicle finance charges paid	yr	365	1999	30r
Charity				
Cash contributions, expenditures	yr	1127	1999	30r
Child Care				
Child raising cost, total, age 0-2	yr	8540	1999	60r
Child raising cost, total, age 3-5	yr	8780	1999	60r
Child raising cost, total, age 6-8	yr	8820	1999	60r
Child raising cost, total, age 9-11	yr	8800	1999	60r
Child raising cost, total, age 12-14	yr	9510	1999	60r
Child raising cost, total, age 15-17	yr	9740	1999	60r
Child's child care and education, age 0-2	yr	1380	1999	60r
Child's child care and education, age 3-5	yr	1520	1999	60r
Child's child care and education, age 6-8	yr	990	1999	60r
Child's child care and education, age 9-11	yr	650	1999	60r
Child's child care and education, age 12-14	yr	490	1999	60r
Child's child care and education, age 15-17	yr	840	1999	60r
Child's clothing, age 0-2	yr	480	1999	60r
Child's clothing, age 3-5	yr	470	1999	60r
Child's clothing, age 6-8	yr	520	1999	60r
Child's clothing, age 9-11	yr	570	1999	60r
Child's clothing, age 12-14	yr	950	1999	60r
Child's clothing, age 15-17	yr	850	1999	60r
Child's food, age 0-2	yr	1000	1999	60r
Child's food, age 3-5	yr	1160	1999	60r
Child's food, age 6-8	yr	1490	1999	60r
Child's food, age 9-11	yr	1770	1999	60r
Child's food, age 12-14	yr	1770	1999	60r
Child's food, age 15-17	yr	1980	1999	60r
Child's health care, age 0-2	yr	620	1999	60r
Child's health care, age 3-5	yr	590	1999	60r
Child's health care, age 6-8	yr	680	1999	60r
Child's health care, age 9-11	yr	720	1999	60r
Child's health care, age 12-14	yr	730	1999	60r
Child's health care, age 15-17	yr	760	1999	60r
Child's housing, age 0-2	yr	3070	1999	60r
Child's housing, age 3-5	yr	3050	1999	60r
Child's housing, age 6-8	yr	3010	1999	60r
Child's housing, age 9-11	yr	2850	1999	60r
Child's housing, age 12-14	yr	3040	1999	60r
Child's housing, age 15-17	yr	2650	1999	60r
Child's personal care, reading, age 0-2	yr	910	1999	60r
Child's personal care, reading, age 3-5	yr	930	1999	60r
Child's personal care, reading, age 6-8	yr	960	1999	60r
Child's personal care, reading, age 9-11	yr	1000	1999	60r
Child's personal care, reading, age 12-14	yr	1170	1999	60r
Child's personal care, reading, age 15-17	yr	950	1999	60r
Clothing				
Apparel and services purchases	yr	1610	1999	30r
Boys, 2 to 15, expenditures on	yr	89	1999	30r
Children under 2, expenditures on	yr	79	1999	30r
Footwear, expenditures on	yr	283	1999	30r
Girls, 2 to 15, expenditures on	yr	103	1999	30r
Men and boys, expenditures on	yr	351	1999	30r
Men, 16 and over, expenditures on	yr	262	1999	30r
Women, 16 and over, expenditures on	yr	538	1999	30r
Communications				
Phone line, single, business, field visit	inst.	85.00	12/97	17s
Phone line, single, business, no field visit	inst.	85.00	12/97	17s
Phone line, single, residence, field visit	inst.	41.00	12/97	17s

Values are in dollars or fractions of dollars. In the column headed *Ref*, references are shown to sources. Each reference is followed by a letter. These refer to the geographical level for which data were reported: s=State, r=Region, and c=City or metro. The abbreviation *ex* is used to mean *except* or *excluding*; *exp* stands for expenditures. For other abbreviations and further explanations, please see the Introduction.

Houma, LA - continued

Item	Per	Value	Date	Ref.
Communications				
Phone line, single, residence, no field visit	inst.	41.00	12/97	17s
Postage and stationery, expenditures on	yr	104	1999	30r
Postal rate, express mail, up to half-pound		12.45	7/01	108r
Postal rate, letter, first class, first ounce		0.34	7/01	108r
Postal rate, letter, two ounces		0.57	7/01	108r
Postal rate, post card		0.21	7/01	108r
Postal rate, priority mail, two pounds		3.95	7/01	108r
Postal rate, priority mail, up to one pound		3.50	7/01	108r
Telephone services, expenditures on	yr	860	1999	30r
Education				
Board, 4-year private college/university	yr	2440	1996	38s
Board, 4-year public college/university	yr	1806	1996	38s
Education expenditures	yr	431	1999	30r
Room, 4-year private college/university	yr	2906	1996	38s
Room, 4-year public college/university	yr	1464	1996	38s
Total cost, 4-year private college/university	yr	17796	1996	38s
Total cost, 4-year public college/university	yr	5491	1996	38s
Tuition, 2-year public college/university, in state	yr	1031	1996	38s
Tuition, 4-year private college/university, in state	yr	12449	1996	38s
Tuition, 4-year public college/university	yr	2221	1996	38s
Energy and Fuels				
Electricity	KWh	0.09	7/01	11r
Electricity	500 KWhs	47.29	7/01	11r
Fuel oil #2	gal	1.43	7/01	11r
Fuel oil and other fuels, expenditures on	yr	45	1999	30r
Gas, natural, commercial rate	1000 cf	8.75	11/00	88s
Gasoline, all types	gal	1.60	7/01	11r
Gasoline, unleaded midgrade	gal	1.65	7/01	11r
Gasoline, unleaded premium	gal	1.74	7/01	11r
Natural gas, expenditures on	yr	164	1999	30r
Utility (piped) gas, therm		1.01	7/01	11r
Utility (piped) gas, 40 therms		44.29	7/01	11r
Utility (piped) gas, 100 therms		97.44	7/01	11r
Entertainment				
Entertainment purchases	yr	1574	1999	30r
Fees and admissions paid	yr	371	1999	30r
Reading purchases	yr	121	1999	30r
Television, radios, sound equipment, expenditures on	yr	561	1999	30r
Funerals				
Total cost of funeral		5842.28	1/99	78r
Acknowledgement cards		28.35	1/99	78r
Casket		2494.29	1/99	78r
Cosmetology, hair, other preparation		109.22	1/99	78r
Embalming		361.42	1/99	78r
Funeral at funeral home		349.20	1/99	78r
Hearse (local)		161.91	1/99	78r
Professional service charges		1116.50	1/99	78r
Service car/van		65.56	1/99	78r
Transfer of remains to funeral home		143.56	1/99	78r
Vault		785.25	1/99	78r
Visitation/viewing		227.02	1/99	78r
Groceries				
American processed cheese	lb	3.50	7/01	11r
Bakery products, expenditures on	yr	261	1999	30r
Bananas	lb	0.47	7/01	11r
Beans, dried, any type, all sizes	lb	0.63	7/01	11r
Beef for stew, boneless	lb	2.86	7/01	11r
Beef, expenditures on	yr	210	1999	30r
Bologna, all beef or mixed	lb	2.29	7/01	11r
Bread, French	lb	1.66	7/01	11r
Bread, white, pan	lb	0.87	7/01	11r
Bread, whole wheat, pan	lb	1.38	7/01	11r
Broccoli	lb	1.04	7/01	11r
Butter, salted, grade AA, stick	lb	2.26	7/01	11r
Butter, yoghurt, cheese, etc, expenditures on	yr	170	1999	30r

Houma, LA - continued

Item	Per	Value	Date	Ref.
Groceries - continued				
Cabbage	lb	0.42	7/01	11r
Cereals and cereal products, expenditures on	yr	140	1999	30r
Cheddar cheese, natural	lb	3.75	7/01	11r
Chicken breast, bone-in	lb	1.85	7/01	11r
Chicken legs, bone-in	lb	1.34	7/01	11r
Chicken, fresh, whole	lb	1.05	7/01	11r
Chops, boneless,	lb	4.13	7/01	11r
Chuck roast, graded and ungraded, excl U.S. prime and choice	lb	2.35	7/01	11r
Chuck roast, U.S. choice, boneless	lb	2.67	7/01	11r
Coffee, 100%, ground roast, all sizes	lb	2.88	7/01	11r
Coffee, instant, plain, regular, all sizes	16 oz	9.25	7/01	11r
Cola, non diet,	2 liter	1.11	7/01	11r
Crackers, soda, salted	lb	1.70	7/01	11r
Dairy product purchases	yr	282	1999	30r
Eggs, expenditures on	yr	32	1999	30r
Fats and oils, expenditures on	yr	79	1999	30r
Fish and seafood, expenditures on	yr	99	1999	30r
Flour, white, all purpose	lb	0.32	7/01	11r
Food (excl fruit and vegetables), eaten at home, purchases	yr	815	1999	30r
Food cooked on trips, expenditures on	yr	36	1999	30r
Food purchases	yr	4533	1999	30r
Food purchases, eaten away from home	yr	1873	1999	30r
Food purchases, food eaten at home	yr	2660	1999	30r
Fresh fruits, expenditures on	yr	128	1999	30r
Fresh milk and cream, expenditures on	yr	112	1999	30r
Fresh vegetables, expenditures on	yr	131	1999	30r
Fruit and vegetable purchases	yr	438	1999	30r
Grapefruit	lb	0.59	7/01	11r
Grapes, Thompson, seedless	lb	2.12	7/01	11r
Ground beef, 100% beef	lb	1.76	7/01	11r
Ground beef, lean and extra lean	lb	2.60	7/01	11r
Ground chuck, 100% beef	lb	2.08	7/01	11r
Ham, boneless, excl canned	lb	2.71	7/01	11r
Ham, rump or shank half, bone-in, smoked	lb	2.19	7/01	11r
Ice cream, prepackaged, bulk, regular	1/2 gal	3.93	7/01	11r
Lemons	lb	1.32	7/01	11r
Lettuce, iceberg	lb	0.76	7/01	11r
Milk, fresh, low fat	gal	2.75	7/01	11r
Milk, fresh, whole, fortified	gal	2.97	7/01	11r
Nonalcoholic beverages, expenditures on	yr	228	1999	30r
Orange juice, frozen concentrate	16 oz	1.95	7/01	11r
Oranges, Navel	lb	0.73	7/01	11r
Oranges, Valencia	lb	0.55	7/01	11r
Peanut butter, creamy, all sizes	lb	1.83	7/01	11r
Pears, Anjou	lb	0.98	7/01	11r
Pork chops, center cut, bone-in	lb	3.33	7/01	11r
Pork sausage, fresh, loose	lb	2.59	7/01	11r
Pork shoulder picnic, bone-in, smoked	lb	1.12	7/01	11r
Pork, expenditures on	yr	162	1999	30r
Potato chips	16 oz	3.59	7/01	11r
Potatoes, frozen, french fried	lb	1.00	7/01	11r
Potatoes, white, all types	lb	0.44	7/01	11r
Poultry, expenditures on	yr	137	1999	30r
Processed fruits, expenditures on	yr	97	1999	30r
Processed vegetables, expenditures on	yr	82	1999	30r
Rice, white, long grain, uncooked	lb	0.51	7/01	11r
Round roast, graded and ungraded, excl U.S. prime and choice	lb	2.96	7/01	11r
Round steak, graded and ungraded, excl U.S. prime and choice	lb	3.11	7/01	11r
Sirloin steak, graded and ungraded, excl U.S. prime and choice	lb	4.23	7/01	11r
Spaghetti and macaroni	lb	0.78	7/01	11r
Steak, round, U.S. choice, boneless	lb	3.56	7/01	11r
Steak, sirloin, U.S. choice, boneless	lb	5.65	7/01	11r
Strawberries, dry pint	12 oz	1.50	7/01	11r
Sugar and other sweets, expenditures on	yr	99	1999	30r
Sugar, white, 33-80 ounce package	lb	0.39	7/01	11r
Sugar, white, all sizes	lb	0.42	7/01	11r

Values are in dollars or fractions of dollars. In the column headed *Ref*, references are shown to sources. Each reference is followed by a letter. These refer to the geographical level for which data were reported: s=State, r=Region, and c=City or metro. The abbreviation *ex* is used to mean *except* or *excluding*; *exp* stands for expenditures. For other abbreviations and further explanations, please see the Introduction.

Houma, LA - continued

Item	Per	Value	Date	Ref.
Groceries				
Tobacco products and smoking supplies purchases	yr	288	1999	30r
Tomatoes, field grown	lb	1.43	7/01	11r
Tuna, light, chunk	lb	1.77	7/01	11r
Turkey, frozen, whole	lb	1.05	7/01	11r
Goods and Services				
B&B Japanese maple (acer japonicum)	gal	79.98-99.00	4/00	93r
Boxwood (buxus)	2 gal	12.98-18.99	4/00	93r
Daylilly (hemerocallis)	gal	7.96-11.00	4/00	93r
Flat of annuals		13.99-27.99	4/00	93r
Fountain grass (pennisetum)	gal	6.96-9.00	4/00	93r
Hanging basket (10 in)		9.99-24.99	4/00	93r
Hardy geranium (geranium)	gal	5.96-8.00	4/00	93r
Hosta (hosta)	gal	8.96-12.99	4/00	93r
Lilac (syrubga vulgaris)	2 gal	13.00-19.99	4/00	93r
Rhododendron (rhododendron)	2 gal	12.98-29.99	4/00	93r
Sage (salvia)	gal	5.96-8.00	4/00	93r
Wintercreeper euonymus (euonymus fortunei)	2 gal	13.00-18.99	4/00	93r
Hunting license	yr	15.00	4/01	34s
Health Care				
Cardiac catheterization, ave hospital/ physician charges		15650	1998	77s
Childbirth, Cesarean delivery		11587	1997	13r
Childbirth, vaginal delivery		6725	1997	13r
Drugs, expenditures on	yr	399	1999	30r
Health care purchases	yr	1971	1999	30r
Health insurance expenditures	yr	933	1999	30r
Hysterectomy, laproscopically-assisted, ave hospital/physician charges		14600	1998	76s
Hysterectomy, vaginal, ave hospital and physician charges		10520	1998	76s
Medicaid dispensing fee		5.77	1999	87s
Medical services expenditures	yr	547	1999	30r
Medical supplies, expenditures on	yr	91	1999	30r
Household Goods				
Floor coverings, expenditures on	yr	44	1999	30r
Furniture, expenditures on	yr	335	1999	30r
Household furnishings and equipment purchases	yr	1328	1999	30r
Household textiles, expenditures on	yr	89	1999	30r
Laundry and cleaning supplies, expenditures on	yr	113	1999	30r
Housing				
Home price, existing, ave		160100	10/00	90r
Home value, median		108000	2001	53s
Household operation expenditures	yr	553	1999	30r
Housekeeping supplies purchases	yr	473	1999	30r
Housing, expenditures on	yr	10303	1999	30r
Maintenance, repairs, insurance expenditures	yr	699	1999	30r
Monthly rental value of owned home	mos	505	1999	30r
Owned dwellings, expenditures own	yr	3465	1999	30r
Rent expenditures	yr	1641	1999	30r
Rental unit, 1 bedroom, with utilities	mos	327	4/01	41c
Rental unit, 2 bedroom, with utilities	mos	419	4/01	41c
Rental unit, 3 bedroom, with utilities	mos	581	4/01	41c
Rental unit, 4 bedroom, with utilities	mos	688	4/01	41c
Shelter, expenditures on	yr	5467	1999	30r

Houma, LA - continued

Item	Per	Value	Date	Ref.
Insurance and Pensions				
Auto insurance premium	yr	965.15	1999	57s
Life and other personal insurance purchases	yr	414	1999	30r
Pensions and Social Security, expenditures on	yr	2635	1999	30r
Personal insurance and pensions, expenditures on	yr	3048	1999	30r
Legal Fees				
Divorce, filing fee		162.00	4/01	35s
Driver's license fee	orig	18.00	1999	48s
Driver's license fee	renew	12.50	1999	48s
Fishing license	yr	9.50	4/01	34s
Personal Goods				
Personal care products and services purchases	yr	393	1999	30r
Personal Services				
Personal services, household, expenditures on	yr	258	1999	30r
Pets				
Pets, toys, and playground equipment, expenditures on	yr	306	1999	30r
Taxes				
Federal income taxes paid	yr	2047	1999	30r
Personal taxes, expenditures on	yr	2554	1999	30r
Property taxes paid	yr	726	1999	30r
State and local income taxes paid	yr	363	1999	30r
Transportation				
Cars and trucks, new, expenditures on	yr	1648	1999	30r
Cars and trucks, used, expenditures on	yr	1651	1999	30r
Diesel at the pump	gal	1.19	10/99	73s
Gasoline and motor oil purchases	yr	1052	1999	30r
Gasoline before-tax price (cents)	gal	102.70	10/00	43s
Maintenance and repair expenditures	yr	621	1999	30r
Public transportation, expenditures on	yr	298	1999	30r
Transportation purchases	yr	6738	1999	30r
Vehicle expenses, miscellaneous, purchases	yr	2033	1999	30r
Vehicle insurance payments	yr	696	1999	30r
Vehicle purchases (net outlay)	yr	3354	1999	30r
Vehicle rental, lease expenditures	yr	352	1999	30r
Utilities				
Electrical bill, average	mos	87.50	9/00	9s
Electricity, expenditures on	yr	1115	1999	30r
Electricity cost, average	KWh	6.35	9/00	9s
Water and other public services, expenditures on	yr	298	1999	30r
Weddings				
Wedding (national average cost)		19936	2000	33r
Attendants' gifts		321	1998	33r
Bridal attendants' apparel (5 persons)		824	2000	33r
Bride's headpiece/veil		173	1998	33r
Bride's wedding dress		859	1998	33r
Clergy, religious facility fee		242	1998	33r
Engagement ring		3177	1998	33r
Flowers		789	1998	33r
Groom's formalwear rental		99	2000	33r
Limousine		410	1998	33r
Marriage license cost		25.00	4/01	35s
Men's formalwear (ushers, best man)		469	2000	33r
Mother of bride apparel		241	2000	33r
Music		866	1998	33r
Photography and videography		1368	1998	33r
Rehearsal dinner		728	1998	33r
Wedding invitations and announcements		341	1998	33r
Wedding reception		7968	2000	33r
Wedding rings (bride and groom)		1060	1998	33r

Values are in dollars or fractions of dollars. In the column headed *Ref*, references are shown to sources. Each reference is followed by a letter. These refer to the geographical level for which data were reported: s=State, r=Region, and c=City or metro. The abbreviation *ex* is used to mean *except* or *excluding*; *exp* stands for *expenditures*. For other abbreviations and further explanations, please see the Introduction.

Houston, TX

Item	Per	Value	Date	Ref.
Average annual expenditures	yr	43043	1999	30c
Composite, ACCRA index		95.80	3/01	4c
Alcoholic Beverages				
Alcoholic beverage purchases	yr	412	1999	30c
Beer, Heineken, 12-oz, ex deposit	6	6.65	3/01	4c
J & B Scotch	750-ml	18.02	3/01	4c
Malt beverages, all types, all sizes, any origin	16 oz	0.96	7/01	11r
Wine, Livingston or Gallo, Chablis blanc	1.5 liter	5.53	3/01	4c
Appliances				
Appliance repair, service call, washing machine	min lab chg	39.26	3/01	4c
Major appliances, expenditures on	yr	172	1999	30r
Small appliances, housewares, expenditures on	yr	81	1999	30r
Banking and Money				
Mortgage interest and charges paid	yr	2039	1999	30r
Mortgage principal paid on owned property	yr	1026	1999	30r
Mortgage rate, incl. points and orig. fee, 30-yr. conv. fixed or ARM	mos	6.65	3/01	4c
Vehicle finance charges paid	yr	365	1999	30r
Business Expenses				
Business travel, car rental	day	67	2001	3c
Business travel, food	day	59	2001	3c
Business travel, hotel	day	145	2001	3c
Medical office space cost	sq ft	105.69	2001	31c
Office space, 2-4 storey building	sq ft	92.09	2001	31c
Office space, 5-10 storey building	sq ft	81.34	2001	31c
Office space, 11-20 storey building	sq ft	78.18	2001	31c
Office space, central business district, Class A	sq ft	23.37	3/99	74c
Office space, outside central business district, Class A	sq ft	21.78	3/99	74c
Charity				
Cash contributions, expenditures	yr	1390	1999	30c
Child Care				
Child raising cost, total, age 0-2	yr	8540	1999	60r
Child raising cost, total, age 3-5	yr	8780	1999	60r
Child raising cost, total, age 6-8	yr	8820	1999	60r
Child raising cost, total, age 9-11	yr	8800	1999	60r
Child raising cost, total, age 12-14	yr	9510	1999	60r
Child raising cost, total, age 15-17	yr	9740	1999	60r
Child's child care and education, age 0-2	yr	1380	1999	60r
Child's child care and education, age 3-5	yr	1520	1999	60r
Child's child care and education, age 6-8	yr	990	1999	60r
Child's child care and education, age 9-11	yr	650	1999	60r
Child's child care and education, age 12-14	yr	490	1999	60r
Child's child care and education, age 15-17	yr	840	1999	60r
Child's clothing, age 0-2	yr	480	1999	60r
Child's clothing, age 3-5	yr	470	1999	60r
Child's clothing, age 6-8	yr	520	1999	60r
Child's clothing, age 9-11	yr	570	1999	60r
Child's clothing, age 12-14	yr	950	1999	60r
Child's clothing, age 15-17	yr	850	1999	60r
Child's food, age 0-2	yr	1000	1999	60r
Child's food, age 3-5	yr	1160	1999	60r
Child's food, age 6-8	yr	1490	1999	60r
Child's food, age 9-11	yr	1770	1999	60r
Child's food, age 12-14	yr	1770	1999	60r
Child's food, age 15-17	yr	1980	1999	60r
Child's health care, age 0-2	yr	620	1999	60r
Child's health care, age 3-5	yr	590	1999	60r
Child's health care, age 6-8	yr	680	1999	60r
Child's health care, age 9-11	yr	720	1999	60r
Child's health care, age 12-14	yr	730	1999	60r
Child's health care, age 15-17	yr	760	1999	60r
Child's housing, age 0-2	yr	3070	1999	60r
Child's housing, age 3-5	yr	3050	1999	60r
Child's housing, age 6-8	yr	3010	1999	60r
Child's housing, age 9-11	yr	2850	1999	60r
Child's housing, age 12-14	yr	3040	1999	60r

Houston, TX - continued

Item	Per	Value	Date	Ref.
Child Care - continued				
Child's housing, age 15-17	yr	2650	1999	60r
Child's personal care, reading, age 0-2	yr	910	1999	60r
Child's personal care, reading, age 3-5	yr	930	1999	60r
Child's personal care, reading, age 6-8	yr	960	1999	60r
Child's personal care, reading, age 9-11	yr	1000	1999	60r
Child's personal care, reading, age 12-14	yr	1170	1999	60r
Child's personal care, reading, age 15-17	yr	950	1999	60r
Clothing				
Apparel and services purchases	yr	1950	1999	30c
Boys' brief, cotton	3	5.27	3/01	4c
Boys, 2 to 15, expenditures on	yr	89	1999	30r
Children under 2, expenditures on	yr	79	1999	30r
Footwear, expenditures on	yr	283	1999	30r
Girls, 2 to 15, expenditures on	yr	103	1999	30r
Men and boys, expenditures on	yr	351	1999	30r
Men, 16 and over, expenditures on	yr	262	1999	30r
Shirt, man's dress shirt		28.24	3/01	4c
Slacks, man's "No Wrinkles" khaki		35.27	3/01	4c
Women, 16 and over, expenditures on	yr	538	1999	30r
Communications				
Cable modem installation, AT&T-BIS		150.00	6/99	103s
Cable modem installation, Marcus		499.00	6/99	103s
Cable modem installation, Time Warner		75.00-225.00	6/99	103s
Cable modem rate, cable subscriber, AT&T-BIS	mos	39.95	6/99	103s
Cable modem rate, cable subscriber, Marcus	mos	14.95-49.95	6/99	103s
Cable modem rate, cable subscriber, Time Warner	mos	39.95-49.95	6/99	103s
Cable modem rate, non-cable subscriber, Marcus	mos	60.95	6/99	103s
Cable modem rate, non-cable subscriber, Time Warner	mos	39.95-54.95	6/99	103s
Newspaper subscription, daily and Sunday delivery	mos	15.00	3/01	4c
Phone line, single, business, field visit	inst.	71.90	12/97	17s
Phone line, single, business, no field visit	inst.	57.30	12/97	17s
Phone line, single, residence, field visit	inst.	52.95	12/97	17s
Phone line, single, residence, no field visit	inst.	38.35	12/97	17s
Postage and stationery, expenditures on	yr	104	1999	30r
Postal rate, express mail, up to half-pound		12.45	7/01	108r
Postal rate, letter, first class, first ounce		0.34	7/01	108r
Postal rate, letter, two ounces		0.57	7/01	108r
Postal rate, post card		0.21	7/01	108r
Postal rate, priority mail, two pounds		3.95	7/01	108r
Postal rate, priority mail, up to one pound		3.50	7/01	108r
Telephone bill, business, basic rate	mos	28.25	12/97	18c
Telephone bill, family of three	mos	20.05	3/01	4c
Telephone bill, residential, basic rate	mos	11.05	12/97	18c
Telephone services, expenditures on	yr	860	1999	30r
Education				
Board, 4-year private college/university	yr	2198	1996	38s
Board, 4-year public college/university	yr	1759	1996	38s
Education expenditures	yr	490	1999	30c
Room, 4-year private college/university	yr	2000	1996	38s
Room, 4-year public college/university	yr	1885	1996	38s
Total cost, 4-year private college/university	yr	13156	1996	38s
Total cost, 4-year public college/university	yr	5464	1996	38s
Tuition, 2-year public college/university, in state	yr	771	1996	38s
Tuition, 4-year private college/university, in state	yr	8959	1996	38s
Tuition, 4-year public college/university	yr	1820	1996	38s
Energy and Fuels				
Electricity	KWh	0.09	7/01	11r
Electricity	500 KWhs	52.25	7/01	11c
Electricity	KWh	0.11	7/01	11c
Energy, combined forms, 2400 sq ft	mos	133.68	3/01	4c

Values are in dollars or fractions of dollars. In the column headed *Ref*, references are shown to sources. Each reference is followed by a letter. These refer to the geographical level for which data were reported: s=State, r=Region, and c=City or metro. The abbreviation *ex* is used to mean *except* or *excluding*; *exp* stands for *expenditures*. For other abbreviations and further explanations, please see the Introduction.

Houston, TX - continued

Item	Per	Value	Date	Ref.
Energy and Fuels				
Energy, exc. electricity, 2400 sq ft	mos	32.82	3/01	4c
Fuel oil #2	gal	1.43	7/01	11r
Fuel oil and other fuels, expenditures on	yr	45	1999	30r
Gas, cooking, winter, 10 therms	mos	13.77	2/96	98c
Gas, cooking, winter, 30 therms	mos	22.10	2/96	98c
Gas, cooking, winter, 50 therms	mos	30.45	2/96	98c
Gas, heating, winter, average use	mos	52.54	2/96	98c
Gas, natural, commercial rate	1000 cf	6.94	11/00	88s
Gas, regular unleaded, cash, self-service	gal	1.31	3/01	4c
Gasoline, all types	gal	1.61	7/01	11c
Gasoline, unleaded midgrade	gal	1.66	7/01	11c
Gasoline, unleaded premium	gal	1.74	7/01	11r
Gasoline, unleaded regular	gal	1.56	7/01	11c
Natural gas, expenditures on	yr	164	1999	30r
Utility (piped) gas, therm		0.65	7/01	11c
Utility (piped) gas, 40 therms		44.29	7/01	11r
Utility (piped) gas, 100 therms		61.53	7/01	11c
Entertainment				
Bowling, Saturday evening rate	line	3.34	3/01	4c
Entertainment purchases	yr	1848	1999	30c
Fees and admissions paid	yr	371	1999	30r
Major League baseball ticket		20.01	2000	16c
Monopoly game, Parker Brothers', No. 9	game	12.09	3/01	4c
Movie, first-run, Saturday, evening	adm.	6.92	3/01	4c
Reading purchases	yr	121	1999	30r
Television, radios, sound equipment, expenditures on	yr	561	1999	30r
Tennis balls, yellow, Wilson or Penn, 3	can	2.05	3/01	4c
Funerals				
Total cost of funeral		5842.28	1/99	78r
Acknowledgement cards		28.35	1/99	78r
Casket		2494.29	1/99	78r
Cosmetology, hair, other preparation		109.22	1/99	78r
Embalming		361.42	1/99	78r
Funeral at funeral home		349.20	1/99	78r
Hearse (local)		161.91	1/99	78r
Professional service charges		1116.50	1/99	78r
Service car/van		65.56	1/99	78r
Transfer of remains to funeral home		143.56	1/99	78r
Vault		785.25	1/99	78r
Visitation/viewing		227.02	1/99	78r
Groceries				
Groceries, ACCRA Index		96.20	3/01	4c
American processed cheese	lb	3.50	7/01	11r
Antibiotic ointment, Polysporin	0.5 oz	4.90	3/01	4c
Baby food, strained vegetables or fruit, lowest price	4-4.5 oz	0.32	3/01	4c
Bakery products, expenditures on	yr	261	1999	30r
Bananas	lb	0.43	3/01	4c
Bananas	lb	0.47	7/01	11r
Beans, dried, any type, all sizes	lb	0.63	7/01	11r
Beef for stew, boneless	lb	2.86	7/01	11r
Beef or hamburger, ground	lb	1.54	3/01	4c
Beef, expenditures on	yr	210	1999	30r
Bologna, all beef or mixed	lb	2.29	7/01	11r
Bread, French	lb	1.66	7/01	11r
Bread, white	loaf	0.86	3/01	4c
Bread, white, pan	lb	0.87	7/01	11r
Bread, whole wheat, pan	lb	1.38	7/01	11r
Broccoli	lb	1.04	7/01	11r
Butter, salted, grade AA, stick	lb	2.26	7/01	11r
Butter, yoghurt, cheese, etc, expenditures on	yr	170	1999	30r
Cabbage	lb	0.42	7/01	11r
Cereals and bakery product purchases	yr	409	1999	30c
Cereals and cereal products, expenditures on	yr	140	1999	30r
Cheddar cheese, natural	lb	3.75	7/01	11r
Cheese, Kraft grated Parmesan	8 oz	3.80	3/01	4c
Chicken breast, bone-in	lb	1.85	7/01	11r
Chicken legs, bone-in	lb	1.34	7/01	11r
Chicken, fresh, whole	lb	1.05	7/01	11r

Houston, TX - continued

Item	Per	Value	Date	Ref.
Groceries - continued				
Chicken, whole fryer	lb	0.85	3/01	4c
Chops, boneless,	lb	4.13	7/01	11r
Chuck roast, graded and ungraded, excl U.S. prime and choice	lb	2.35	7/01	11r
Chuck roast, U.S. choice, boneless	lb	2.67	7/01	11r
Cigarettes, Winston, Kings	carton	31.26	3/01	4c
Coffee, 100%, ground roast, all sizes	lb	2.88	7/01	11r
Coffee, instant, plain, regular, all sizes	16 oz	9.25	7/01	11r
Coffee, vacuum-packed	13 oz	2.51	3/01	4c
Cola, non diet,	2 liter	1.11	7/01	11r
Corn Flakes, Kellogg's or Post Toasties	18 oz	2.38	3/01	4c
Corn, frozen, whole kernel, lowest price	16 oz	1.15	3/01	4c
Crackers, soda, salted	lb	1.70	7/01	11r
Dairy product purchases	yr	294	1999	30c
Eggs, expenditures on	yr	32	1999	30r
Eggs, Grade A or AA	dozen	1.08	3/01	4c
Fats and oils, expenditures on	yr	79	1999	30r
Fish and seafood, expenditures on	yr	99	1999	30r
Flour, white, all purpose	lb	0.32	7/01	11r
Food (excl fruit and vegetables), eaten at home, purchases	yr	904	1999	30c
Food cooked on trips, expenditures on	yr	36	1999	30r
Food purchases	yr	5624	1999	30c
Food purchases, eaten away from home	yr	2676	1999	30c
Food purchases, food eaten at home	yr	2948	1999	30c
Fresh fruits, expenditures on	yr	128	1999	30r
Fresh milk and cream, expenditures on	yr	112	1999	30r
Fresh vegetables, expenditures on	yr	131	1999	30r
Fruit and vegetable purchases	yr	438	1999	30r
Grapefruit	lb	0.59	7/01	11r
Grapes, Thompson, seedless	lb	2.12	7/01	11r
Ground beef, 100% beef	lb	1.76	7/01	11r
Ground beef, lean and extra lean	lb	2.60	7/01	11r
Ground chuck, 100% beef	lb	2.08	7/01	11r
Ham, boneless, excl canned	lb	2.71	7/01	11r
Ham, rump or shank half, bone-in, smoked	lb	2.19	7/01	11r
Ice cream, prepackaged, bulk, regular	1/2 gal	3.93	7/01	11r
Lemons	lb	1.32	7/01	11r
Lettuce, iceberg	head	1.26	3/01	4c
Lettuce, iceberg	lb	0.76	7/01	11r
Margarine, Blue Bonnet or Parkay, stick	lb	0.74	3/01	4c
Meats, poultry, fish, and egg purchases	yr	819	1999	30c
Milk, fresh, low fat,	gal	2.75	7/01	11r
Milk, fresh, whole, fortified	gal	2.97	7/01	11r
Milk, whole	1/2 gal	1.77	3/01	4c
Nonalcoholic beverages, expenditures on	yr	228	1999	30r
Orange juice, frozen concentrate	16 oz	1.95	7/01	11r
Orange juice, Minute Maid frozen	12 oz	1.72	3/01	4c
Oranges, Navel	lb	0.73	7/01	11r
Oranges, Valencia	lb	0.55	7/01	11r
Peaches, halves or slices, Hunt's, Del Monte, or Libby's	29 oz	1.56	3/01	4c
Peanut butter, creamy, all sizes	lb	1.83	7/01	11r
Pears, Anjou	lb	0.98	7/01	11r
Peas, green, Del Monte or Green Giant	15 oz	0.71	3/01	4c
Pork chops, center cut, bone-in	lb	3.33	7/01	11r
Pork sausage, fresh, loose	lb	2.59	7/01	11r
Pork shoulder picnic, bone-in, smoked	lb	1.12	7/01	11r
Pork, expenditures on	yr	162	1999	30r
Potato chips	16 oz	3.59	7/01	11r
Potatoes, frozen, french fried	lb	1.00	7/01	11r
Potatoes, white or red	10 lb	3.10	3/01	4c
Potatoes, white, all types	lb	0.44	7/01	11r
Poultry, expenditures on	yr	137	1999	30r
Processed fruits, expenditures on	yr	97	1999	30r
Processed vegetables, expenditures on	yr	82	1999	30r
Rice, white, long grain, uncooked	lb	0.51	7/01	11r
Round roast, graded and ungraded, excl U.S. prime and choice	lb	2.96	7/01	11r
Round steak, graded and ungraded, excl U.S. prime and choice	lb	3.11	7/01	11r
Sausage, Jimmy Dean/Owens pork	lb	3.00	3/01	4c

Values are in dollars or fractions of dollars. In the column headed *Ref*, references are shown to sources. Each reference is followed by a letter. These refer to the geographical level for which data were reported: s=State, r=Region, and c=City or metro. The abbreviation *ex* is used to mean *except* or *excluding*; *exp* stands for expenditures. For other abbreviations and further explanations, please see the Introduction.

Houston, TX - continued

Item	Per	Value	Date	Ref.
Groceries				
Shortening, vegetable, Crisco	3 lb	2.81	3/01	4c
Sirloin steak, graded and ungraded, excl U.S. prime and choice	lb	4.23	7/01	11r
Soft drink, Coca Cola, ex deposit	2 liter	1.16	3/01	4c
Spaghetti and macaroni	lb	0.78	7/01	11r
Steak, round, U.S. choice, boneless	lb	3.56	7/01	11r
Steak, sirloin, U.S. choice, boneless	lb	5.65	7/01	11r
Steak, T-bone	lb	6.28	3/01	4c
Strawberries, dry pint	12 oz	1.50	7/01	11r
Sugar and other sweets, expenditures on	yr	99	1999	30r
Sugar, cane or beet	4 lbs	1.45	3/01	4c
Sugar, white, 33-80 ounce package	lb	0.39	7/01	11r
Sugar, white, all sizes	lb	0.42	7/01	11r
Tobacco products and smoking supplies purchases	yr	346	1999	30c
Tomatoes, field grown	lb	1.43	7/01	11r
Tomatoes, Hunt's or Del Monte	14.5 oz	0.83	3/01	4c
Tuna, chunk, light	6 oz	0.59	3/01	4c
Tuna, light, chunk	lb	1.77	7/01	11r
Turkey, frozen, whole	lb	1.05	7/01	11r
Goods and Services				
Miscellaneous goods and services, ACCRA Index		98.40	3/01	4c
B&B Japanese maple (acer japonicum)	gal	79.98-99.00	4/00	93r
Boxwood (buxus)	2 gal	12.98-18.99	4/00	93r
Christmas tree, noble fir		40-60	2000	65s
Daylilly (hemerocallis)	gal	7.96-11.00	4/00	93r
Flat of annuals		13.99-27.99	4/00	93r
Fountain grass (pennisetum)	gal	6.96-9.00	4/00	93r
Hanging basket (10 in)		9.99-24.99	4/00	93r
Hardy geranium (geranium)	gal	5.96-8.00	4/00	93r
Hosta (hosta)	gal	8.96-12.99	4/00	93r
Lilac (syrubga vulgaris)	2 gal	13.00-19.99	4/00	93r
Miscellaneous purchases	yr	959	1999	30c
Rhododendron (rhododendron)	2 gal	12.98-29.99	4/00	93r
Sage (salvia)	gal	5.96-8.00	4/00	93r
Wintercreeper euonymus (euonymus fortunei)	2 gal	13.00-18.99	4/00	93r
Hunting license	yr	19.00	4/01	34s
Health Care				
Health care, ACCRA Index		110.50	3/01	4c
Cardiac catheterization, ave hospital/ physician charges		20140	1998	77s
Childbirth, Cesarean delivery		11587	1997	13r
Childbirth, vaginal delivery		6725	1997	13r
Dentist's fee, adult teeth cleaning and periodic oral exam	visit	79.45	3/01	4c
Doctor's fee, routine exam, established patient	visit	66.90	3/01	4c
Drugs, expenditures on	yr	399	1999	30r
Health care purchases	yr	1919	1999	30c
Health insurance expenditures	yr	933	1999	30r
Home health care aide cost, licensed agency	hour	16	2000	82c
Hospital care, private room	day	555.23	3/01	4c
Hysterectomy, laproscopically-assisted, ave hospital/physician charges		15700	1998	76s
Hysterectomy, vaginal, ave hospital and physician charges		12180	1998	76s
Medicaid dispensing fee		5.27	1999	87s
Medical services expenditures	yr	547	1999	30r

Houston, TX - continued

Item	Per	Value	Date	Ref.
Health Care - continued				
Medical supplies, expenditures on	yr	91	1999	30r
Nursing home costs, private room	day	111	2000	82c
Nursing home stay, private room	day	111	2000	83c
Household Goods				
Dishwashing powder, Cascade	50 oz	3.13	3/01	4c
Floor coverings, expenditures on	yr	44	1999	30r
Furniture, expenditures on	yr	335	1999	30r
Household furnishings and equipment purchases	yr	1809	1999	30c
Household textiles, expenditures on	yr	89	1999	30r
Laundry and cleaning supplies, expenditures on	yr	113	1999	30r
Tissues, facial, Kleenex brand	175	1.40	3/01	4c
Housing				
Housing, ACCRA Index		84.30	3/01	4c
Home, 2200 sq ft, 4-br, 2-bath, 2-car garage, average		195000	2000	47c
Home price, existing, ave		160100	10/00	90r
Home value, median		112000	2001	53s
House, 2400 sq ft, 8000 sq ft lot, new, urban, utilities	total	170074	3/01	4c
House payment, principal and interest, 25% down payment	mos	819	3/01	4c
Household operation expenditures	yr	762	1999	30c
Housekeeping supplies purchases	yr	489	1999	30c
Housing, expenditures on	yr	10303	1999	30r
Lodging expenditures	yr	471	1999	30c
Maintenance, repairs, insurance expenditures	yr	699	1999	30r
Monthly rental value of owned home	mos	505	1999	30r
Owned dwellings, expenditures own	yr	4123	1999	30c
Rent expenditures	yr	2572	1999	30c
Rent, apartment, 2 br, 1 1/2-2 baths, unfurn, 950 sq ft, water	mos	717	3/01	4c
Rental unit, 1 bedroom, with utilities	mos	495	4/01	41c
Rental unit, 2 bedroom, with utilities	mos	640	4/01	41c
Rental unit, 3 bedroom, with utilities	mos	892	4/01	41c
Rental unit, 4 bedroom, with utilities	mos	1051	4/01	41c
Shelter, expenditures on	yr	7167	1999	30c
Insurance and Pensions				
Life and other personal insurance purchases	yr	478	1999	30c
Pensions and Social Security, expenditures on	yr	4280	1999	30c
Personal insurance and pensions, expenditures on	yr	3048	1999	30r
Legal Fees				
Divorce, filing fee		150.00-200.00	4/01	35s
Driver's license fee	orig	24.00	1999	48s
Driver's license fee	renew	20.00	1999	48s
Fishing license	yr	19.00	4/01	34s
Personal Goods				
Personal care products and services purchases	yr	537	1999	30c
Shampoo, Alberto VO5	15 oz	1.20	3/01	4c
Toothpaste, Crest or Colgate	6-7 oz	2.68	3/01	4c
Personal Services				
Dry cleaning, man's 2-pc suit		5.28	3/01	4c
Man's haircut, barbershop, no styling		10.50	3/01	4c
Personal services, household, expenditures on	yr	258	1999	30r
Woman's shampoo, trim, blow-dry, no style-change		31.00	3/01	4c
Pets				
Pets, toys, and playground equipment, expenditures on	yr	306	1999	30r

Values are in dollars or fractions of dollars. In the column headed *Ref*, references are shown to sources. Each reference is followed by a letter. These refer to the geographical level for which data were reported: s=State, r=Region, and c=City or metro. The abbreviation *ex* is used to mean *except* or *excluding*; *exp* stands for *expenditures*. For other abbreviations and further explanations, please see the Introduction.

Houston, TX - continued

Item	Per	Value	Date	Ref.
Restaurant Food				
Chicken, fried, thigh and drumstick, KFC/ Church's		2.25	3/01	4c
Hamburger with cheese, McDonald's	1/4 lb	1.99	3/01	4c
Pizza, Pizza Hut or Pizza Inn	11-12 in	8.31	3/01	4c
Taxes				
Federal income taxes paid	yr	2047	1999	30r
Personal taxes, expenditures on	yr	2554	1999	30r
Property taxes paid	yr	726	1999	30r
State and local income taxes paid	yr	363	1999	30r
Transportation				
Transportation, ACCRA Index		102.80	3/01	4c
Bus fare, one-way	trip	1.00	2000	1c
Bus fare, to central business district	1-way	1.46	3/01	4c
Cars and trucks, new, expenditures on	yr	1648	1999	30r
Cars and trucks, used, expenditures on	yr	1651	1999	30r
Diesel at the pump	gal	1.18	10/99	73s
Gasoline and motor oil purchases	yr	1243	1999	30c
Gasoline before-tax price (cents)	gal	101.30	10/00	43s
Maintenance and repair expenditures	yr	621	1999	30r
Public transportation, expenditures on	yr	435	1999	30c
Tire balance, computer or spin balance, front	wheel	8.50	3/01	4c
Transportation purchases	yr	9569	1999	30c
Vehicle expenses, miscellaneous, purchases	yr	2853	1999	30c
Vehicle insurance payments	yr	696	1999	30r
Vehicle purchases (net outlay)	yr	3354	1999	30r
Vehicle rental, lease expenditures	yr	352	1999	30r
Travel				
Car rental	day	81.50	2000	24c
Hotel room, ave	night	88.26	2000	70c
Utilities				
Utilities, ACCRA Index		107.10	3/01	4c
Electrical bill, average	mos	87.17	9/00	9s
Electricity, expenditures on	yr	1115	1999	30r
Electricity, summer, 250 KWh	mos	16.28	2/96	96c
Electricity, summer, 500 KWh	mos	39.72	2/96	96c
Electricity, summer, 750 KWh	mos	63.17	2/96	96c
Electricity, summer, 1000 KWh	mos	80.22	2/96	96c
Electricity and other, mixed, 2400 sq ft, new home	mos	100.86	3/01	4c
Electricity cost, average	KWh	6.48	9/00	9s
Utilities, fuels, and public services purchased	yr	2882	1999	30c
Water and other public services, expenditures on	yr	298	1999	30r
Water price	100 cf	1.70	2000	109c
Water price, dwelling unit	mos	33.36	2000	109c
Weddings				
Wedding (national average cost)		19936	2000	33r
Attendants' gifts		321	1998	33r
Bridal attendants' apparel (5 persons)		824	2000	33r
Bride's headpiece/veil		173	1998	33r
Bride's wedding dress		859	1998	33r
Clergy, religious facility fee		242	1998	33r
Engagement ring		3177	1998	33r
Flowers		789	1998	33r
Groom's formalwear rental		99	2000	33r
Limousine		410	1998	33r
Marriage license cost		36.00	4/01	35s
Men's formalwear (ushers, best man)		469	2000	33r
Mother of bride apparel		241	2000	33r
Music		866	1998	33r
Photography and videography		1368	1998	33r
Rehearsal dinner		728	1998	33r
Wedding invitations and announcements		341	1998	33r
Wedding reception		7968	2000	33r
Wedding rings (bride and groom)		1060	1998	33r

Houston-Galveston-Brazoria, TX

Item	Per	Value	Date	Ref.
Alcoholic Beverages				
Alcoholic beverage purchases	yr	253	1999	30r
Malt beverages, all types, all sizes, any origin	16 oz	0.96	7/01	11r
Appliances				
Major appliances, expenditures on	yr	172	1999	30r
Small appliances, housewares, expenditures on	yr	81	1999	30r
Banking and Money				
Mortgage interest and charges paid	yr	2039	1999	30r
Mortgage principal paid on owned property	yr	1026	1999	30r
Vehicle finance charges paid	yr	365	1999	30r
Charity				
Cash contributions, expenditures	yr	1127	1999	30r
Child Care				
Child raising cost, total, age 0-2	yr	8540	1999	60r
Child raising cost, total, age 3-5	yr	8780	1999	60r
Child raising cost, total, age 6-8	yr	8820	1999	60r
Child raising cost, total, age 9-11	yr	8800	1999	60r
Child raising cost, total, age 12-14	yr	9510	1999	60r
Child raising cost, total, age 15-17	yr	9740	1999	60r
Child's child care and education, age 0-2	yr	1380	1999	60r
Child's child care and education, age 3-5	yr	1520	1999	60r
Child's child care and education, age 6-8	yr	990	1999	60r
Child's child care and education, age 9-11	yr	650	1999	60r
Child's child care and education, age 12-14	yr	490	1999	60r
Child's child care and education, age 15-17	yr	840	1999	60r
Child's clothing, age 0-2	yr	480	1999	60r
Child's clothing, age 3-5	yr	470	1999	60r
Child's clothing, age 6-8	yr	520	1999	60r
Child's clothing, age 9-11	yr	570	1999	60r
Child's clothing, age 12-14	yr	950	1999	60r
Child's clothing, age 15-17	yr	850	1999	60r
Child's food, age 0-2	yr	1000	1999	60r
Child's food, age 3-5	yr	1160	1999	60r
Child's food, age 6-8	yr	1490	1999	60r
Child's food, age 9-11	yr	1770	1999	60r
Child's food, age 12-14	yr	1770	1999	60r
Child's food, age 15-17	yr	1980	1999	60r
Child's health care, age 0-2	yr	620	1999	60r
Child's health care, age 3-5	yr	590	1999	60r
Child's health care, age 6-8	yr	680	1999	60r
Child's health care, age 9-11	yr	720	1999	60r
Child's health care, age 12-14	yr	730	1999	60r
Child's health care, age 15-17	yr	760	1999	60r
Child's housing, age 0-2	yr	3070	1999	60r
Child's housing, age 3-5	yr	3050	1999	60r
Child's housing, age 6-8	yr	3010	1999	60r
Child's housing, age 9-11	yr	2850	1999	60r
Child's housing, age 12-14	yr	3040	1999	60r
Child's housing, age 15-17	yr	2650	1999	60r
Child's personal care, reading, age 0-2	yr	910	1999	60r
Child's personal care, reading, age 3-5	yr	930	1999	60r
Child's personal care, reading, age 6-8	yr	960	1999	60r
Child's personal care, reading, age 9-11	yr	1000	1999	60r
Child's personal care, reading, age 12-14	yr	1170	1999	60r
Child's personal care, reading, age 15-17	yr	950	1999	60r
Clothing				
Apparel and services purchases	yr	1610	1999	30r
Boys, 2 to 15, expenditures on	yr	89	1999	30r
Children under 2, expenditures on	yr	79	1999	30r
Footwear, expenditures on	yr	283	1999	30r
Girls, 2 to 15, expenditures on	yr	103	1999	30r
Men and boys, expenditures on	yr	351	1999	30r
Men, 16 and over, expenditures on	yr	262	1999	30r
Women, 16 and over, expenditures on	yr	538	1999	30r
Communications				
Cable modem installation, AT&T-BIS		150.00	6/99	103s
Cable modem installation, Marcus		499.00	6/99	103s

Values are in dollars or fractions of dollars. In the column headed *Ref*, references are shown to sources. Each reference is followed by a letter. These refer to the geographical level for which data were reported: s=State, r=Region, and c=City or metro. The abbreviation *ex* is used to mean *except* or *excluding*; *exp* stands for expenditures. For other abbreviations and further explanations, please see the Introduction.

Houston-Galveston-Brazoria, TX - continued

Item	Per	Value	Date	Ref.
Communications				
Cable modem installation, Time Warner		75.00-225.00	6/99	103s
Cable modem rate, cable subscriber, AT&T-BIS	mos	39.95	6/99	103s
Cable modem rate, cable subscriber, Marcus	mos	14.95-49.95	6/99	103s
Cable modem rate, cable subscriber, Time Warner	mos	39.95-49.95	6/99	103s
Cable modem rate, non-cable subscriber, Marcus	mos	60.95	6/99	103s
Cable modem rate, non-cable subscriber, Time Warner	mos	39.95-54.95	6/99	103s
Phone line, single, business, field visit	inst.	71.90	12/97	17s
Phone line, single, business, no field visit	inst.	57.30	12/97	17s
Phone line, single, residence, field visit	inst.	52.95	12/97	17s
Phone line, single, residence, no field visit	inst.	38.35	12/97	17s
Postage and stationery, expenditures on	yr	104	1999	30r
Postal rate, express mail, up to half-pound		12.45	7/01	108r
Postal rate, letter, first class, first ounce		0.34	7/01	108r
Postal rate, letter, two ounces		0.57	7/01	108r
Postal rate, post card		0.21	7/01	108r
Postal rate, priority mail, two pounds		3.95	7/01	108r
Postal rate, priority mail, up to one pound		3.50	7/01	108r
Telephone services, expenditures on	yr	860	1999	30r
Education				
Board, 4-year private college/university	yr	2198	1996	38s
Board, 4-year public college/university	yr	1759	1996	38s
Education expenditures	yr	431	1999	30r
Room, 4-year private college/university	yr	2000	1996	38s
Room, 4-year public college/university	yr	1885	1996	38s
Total cost, 4-year private college/university	yr	13156	1996	38s
Total cost, 4-year public college/university	yr	5464	1996	38s
Tuition, 2-year public college/university, in state	yr	771	1996	38s
Tuition, 4-year private college/university, in state	yr	8959	1996	38s
Tuition, 4-year public college/university	yr	1820	1996	38s
Energy and Fuels				
Electricity	KWh	0.09	7/01	11r
Electricity	500 KWhs	47.29	7/01	11r
Fuel oil #2	gal	1.43	7/01	11r
Fuel oil and other fuels, expenditures on	yr	45	1999	30r
Gas, natural, commercial rate	1000 cf	6.94	11/00	88s
Gasoline, all types	gal	1.60	7/01	11r
Gasoline, unleaded midgrade	gal	1.65	7/01	11r
Gasoline, unleaded premium	gal	1.74	7/01	11r
Natural gas, expenditures on	yr	164	1999	30r
Utility (piped) gas, therm		1.01	7/01	11r
Utility (piped) gas, 40 therms		44.29	7/01	11r
Utility (piped) gas, 100 therms		97.44	7/01	11r
Entertainment				
Entertainment purchases	yr	1574	1999	30r
Fees and admissions paid	yr	371	1999	30r
Reading purchases	yr	121	1999	30r
Television, radios, sound equipment, expenditures on	yr	561	1999	30r
Funerals				
Total cost of funeral		5842.28	1/99	78r
Acknowledgement cards		28.35	1/99	78r
Casket		2494.29	1/99	78r
Cosmetology, hair, other preparation		109.22	1/99	78r
Embalming		361.42	1/99	78r
Funeral at funeral home		349.20	1/99	78r
Hearse (local)		161.91	1/99	78r
Professional service charges		1116.50	1/99	78r
Service car/van		65.56	1/99	78r
Transfer of remains to funeral home		143.56	1/99	78r
Vault		785.25	1/99	78r
Visitation/viewing		227.02	1/99	78r

Houston-Galveston-Brazoria, TX - continued

Item	Per	Value	Date	Ref.
Groceries				
American processed cheese	lb	3.50	7/01	11r
Bakery products, expenditures on	yr	261	1999	30r
Bananas	lb	0.47	7/01	11r
Beans, dried, any type, all sizes	lb	0.63	7/01	11r
Beef for stew, boneless	lb	2.86	7/01	11r
Beef, expenditures on	yr	210	1999	30r
Bologna, all beef or mixed	lb	2.29	7/01	11r
Bread, French	lb	1.66	7/01	11r
Bread, white, pan	lb	0.87	7/01	11r
Bread, whole wheat, pan	lb	1.38	7/01	11r
Broccoli	lb	1.04	7/01	11r
Butter, salted, grade AA, stick	lb	2.26	7/01	11r
Butter, yoghurt, cheese, etc, expenditures on	yr	170	1999	30r
Cabbage	lb	0.42	7/01	11r
Cereals and cereal products, expenditures on	yr	140	1999	30r
Cheddar cheese, natural	lb	3.75	7/01	11r
Chicken breast, bone-in	lb	1.85	7/01	11r
Chicken legs, bone-in	lb	1.34	7/01	11r
Chicken, fresh, whole	lb	1.05	7/01	11r
Chops, boneless,	lb	4.13	7/01	11r
Chuck roast, graded and ungraded, excl U.S. prime and choice	lb	2.35	7/01	11r
Chuck roast, U.S. choice, boneless	lb	2.67	7/01	11r
Coffee, 100%, ground roast, all sizes	lb	2.88	7/01	11r
Coffee, instant, plain, regular, all sizes	16 oz	9.25	7/01	11r
Cola, non diet,	2 liter	1.11	7/01	11r
Crackers, soda, salted	lb	1.70	7/01	11r
Dairy product purchases	yr	282	1999	30r
Eggs, expenditures on	yr	32	1999	30r
Fats and oils, expenditures on	yr	79	1999	30r
Fish and seafood, expenditures on	yr	99	1999	30r
Flour, white, all purpose	lb	0.32	7/01	11r
Food (excl fruit and vegetables), eaten at home, purchases	yr	815	1999	30r
Food cooked on trips, expenditures on	yr	36	1999	30r
Food purchases	yr	4533	1999	30r
Food purchases, eaten away from home	yr	1873	1999	30r
Food purchases, food eaten at home	yr	2660	1999	30r
Fresh fruits, expenditures on	yr	128	1999	30r
Fresh milk and cream, expenditures on	yr	112	1999	30r
Fresh vegetables, expenditures on	yr	131	1999	30r
Fruit and vegetable purchases	yr	438	1999	30r
Grapefruit	lb	0.59	7/01	11r
Grapes, Thompson, seedless	lb	2.12	7/01	11r
Ground beef, 100% beef	lb	1.76	7/01	11r
Ground beef, lean and extra lean	lb	2.60	7/01	11r
Ground chuck, 100% beef	lb	2.08	7/01	11r
Ham, boneless, excl canned	lb	2.71	7/01	11r
Ham, rump or shank half, bone-in, smoked	lb	2.19	7/01	11r
Ice cream, prepackaged, bulk, regular	1/2 gal	3.93	7/01	11r
Lemons	lb	1.32	7/01	11r
Lettuce, iceberg	lb	0.76	7/01	11r
Milk, fresh, low fat,	gal	2.75	7/01	11r
Milk, fresh, whole, fortified	gal	2.97	7/01	11r
Nonalcoholic beverages, expenditures on	yr	228	1999	30r
Orange juice, frozen concentrate	16 oz	1.95	7/01	11r
Oranges, Navel	lb	0.73	7/01	11r
Oranges, Valencia	lb	0.55	7/01	11r
Peanut butter, creamy, all sizes	lb	1.83	7/01	11r
Pears, Anjou	lb	0.98	7/01	11r
Pork chops, center cut, bone-in	lb	3.33	7/01	11r
Pork sausage, fresh, loose	lb	2.59	7/01	11r
Pork shoulder picnic, bone-in, smoked	lb	1.12	7/01	11r
Pork, expenditures on	yr	162	1999	30r
Potato chips	16 oz	3.59	7/01	11r
Potatoes, frozen, french fried	lb	1.00	7/01	11r
Potatoes, white, all types	lb	0.44	7/01	11r
Poultry, expenditures on	yr	137	1999	30r
Processed fruits, expenditures on	yr	97	1999	30r
Processed vegetables, expenditures on	yr	82	1999	30r
Rice, white, long grain, uncooked	lb	0.51	7/01	11r

Values are in dollars or fractions of dollars. In the column headed *Ref*, references are shown to sources. Each reference is followed by a letter. These refer to the geographical level for which data were reported: s=State, r=Region, and c=City or metro. The abbreviation *ex* is used to mean *except* or *excluding*; *exp* stands for expenditures. For other abbreviations and further explanations, please see the Introduction.

Houston-Galveston-Brazoria, TX - continued

Item	Per	Value	Date	Ref.
Groceries				
Round roast, graded and ungraded, excl U.S. prime and choice	lb	2.96	7/01	11r
Round steak, graded and ungraded, excl U.S. prime and choice	lb	3.11	7/01	11r
Sirloin steak, graded and ungraded, excl U.S. prime and choice	lb	4.23	7/01	11r
Spaghetti and macaroni	lb	0.78	7/01	11r
Steak, round, U.S. choice, boneless	lb	3.56	7/01	11r
Steak, sirloin, U.S. choice, boneless	lb	5.65	7/01	11r
Strawberries, dry pint	12 oz	1.50	7/01	11r
Sugar and other sweets, expenditures on	yr	99	1999	30r
Sugar, white, 33-80 ounce package	lb	0.39	7/01	11r
Sugar, white, all sizes	lb	0.42	7/01	11r
Tobacco products and smoking supplies purchases	yr	288	1999	30r
Tomatoes, field grown	lb	1.43	7/01	11r
Tuna, light, chunk	lb	1.77	7/01	11r
Turkey, frozen, whole	lb	1.05	7/01	11r
Goods and Services				
B&B Japanese maple (acer japonicum)	gal	79.98-99.00	4/00	93r
Boxwood (buxus)	2 gal	12.98-18.99	4/00	93r
Christmas tree, noble fir		40-60	2000	65s
Daylilly (hemerocallis)	gal	7.96-11.00	4/00	93r
Flat of annuals		13.99-27.99	4/00	93r
Fountain grass (pennisetum)	gal	6.96-9.00	4/00	93r
Hanging basket (10 in)		9.99-24.99	4/00	93r
Hardy geranium (geranium)	gal	5.96-8.00	4/00	93r
Hosta (hosta)	gal	8.96-12.99	4/00	93r
Lilac (syrubga vulgaris)	2 gal	13.00-19.99	4/00	93r
Rhododendron (rhododendron)	2 gal	12.98-29.99	4/00	93r
Sage (salvia)	gal	5.96-8.00	4/00	93r
Wintercreeper euonymus (euonymus fortunei)	2 gal	13.00-18.99	4/00	93r
Hunting license	yr	19.00	4/01	34s
Health Care				
Cardiac catheterization, ave hospital/physician charges		20140	1998	77s
Childbirth, Cesarean delivery		11587	1997	13r
Childbirth, vaginal delivery		6725	1997	13r
Drugs, expenditures on	yr	399	1999	30r
Health care purchases	yr	1971	1999	30r
Health insurance expenditures	yr	933	1999	30r
Hysterectomy, laproscopically-assisted, ave hospital/physician charges		15700	1998	76s
Hysterectomy, vaginal, ave hospital and physician charges		12180	1998	76s
Medicaid dispensing fee		5.27	1999	87s
Medical services expenditures	yr	547	1999	30r
Medical supplies, expenditures on	yr	91	1999	30r
Household Goods				
Floor coverings, expenditures on	yr	44	1999	30r
Furniture, expenditures on	yr	335	1999	30r
Household furnishings and equipment purchases	yr	1328	1999	30r
Household textiles, expenditures on	yr	89	1999	30r
Laundry and cleaning supplies, expenditures on	yr	113	1999	30r

Houston-Galveston-Brazoria, TX - continued

Item	Per	Value	Date	Ref.
Housing				
Home price, existing, ave		160100	10/00	90r
Home value, median		112000	2001	53s
Household operation expenditures	yr	553	1999	30r
Housekeeping supplies purchases	yr	473	1999	30r
Housing, expenditures on	yr	10303	1999	30r
Maintenance, repairs, insurance expenditures	yr	699	1999	30r
Monthly rental value of owned home	mos	505	1999	30r
Owned dwellings, expenditures own	yr	3465	1999	30r
Rent expenditures	yr	1641	1999	30r
Shelter, expenditures on	yr	5467	1999	30r
Insurance and Pensions				
Life and other personal insurance purchases	yr	414	1999	30r
Pensions and Social Security, expenditures on	yr	2635	1999	30r
Personal insurance and pensions, expenditures on	yr	3048	1999	30r
Legal Fees				
Divorce, filing fee		150.00-200.00	4/01	35s
Driver's license fee	renew	20.00	1999	48s
Driver's license fee	orig	24.00	1999	48s
Fishing license	yr	19.00	4/01	34s
Personal Goods				
Personal care products and services purchases	yr	393	1999	30r
Personal Services				
Personal services, household, expenditures on	yr	258	1999	30r
Pets				
Pets, toys, and playground equipment, expenditures on	yr	306	1999	30r
Taxes				
Federal income taxes paid	yr	2047	1999	30r
Personal taxes, expenditures on	yr	2554	1999	30r
Property taxes paid	yr	726	1999	30r
State and local income taxes paid	yr	363	1999	30r
Transportation				
Cars and trucks, new, expenditures on	yr	1648	1999	30r
Cars and trucks, used, expenditures on	yr	1651	1999	30r
Diesel at the pump	gal	1.18	10/99	73s
Gasoline and motor oil purchases	yr	1052	1999	30r
Gasoline before-tax price (cents)	gal	101.30	10/00	43s
Household transportation expenditures	yr	8840	97-1998	102c
Maintenance and repair expenditures	yr	621	1999	30r
Public transportation, expenditures on	yr	298	1999	30r
Transportation purchases	yr	6738	1999	30r
Vehicle expenses, miscellaneous, purchases	yr	2033	1999	30r
Vehicle insurance payments	yr	696	1999	30r
Vehicle purchases (net outlay)	yr	3354	1999	30r
Vehicle rental, lease expenditures	yr	352	1999	30r
Utilities				
Electrical bill, average	mos	87.17	9/00	9s
Electricity, expenditures on	yr	1115	1999	30r
Electricity cost, average	KWh	6.48	9/00	9s
Water and other public services, expenditures on	yr	298	1999	30r
Weddings				
Wedding (national average cost)		19936	2000	33r
Attendants' gifts		321	1998	33r
Bridal attendants' apparel (5 persons)		824	2000	33r
Bride's headpiece/veil		173	1998	33r
Bride's wedding dress		859	1998	33r
Clergy, religious facility fee		242	1998	33r
Engagement ring		3177	1998	33r
Flowers		789	1998	33r
Groom's formalwear rental		99	2000	33r

Values are in dollars or fractions of dollars. In the column headed *Ref*, references are shown to sources. Each reference is followed by a letter. These refer to the geographical level for which data were reported: s=State, r=Region, and c=City or metro. The abbreviation *ex* is used to mean *except* or *excluding*; *exp* stands for *expenditures*. For other abbreviations and further explanations, please see the Introduction.

Houston-Galveston-Brazoria, TX - continued

Item	Per	Value	Date	Ref.
Weddings				
Limousine		410	1998	33r
Marriage license cost		36.00	4/01	35s
Men's formalwear (ushers, best man)		469	2000	33r
Mother of bride apparel		241	2000	33r
Music		866	1998	33r
Photography and videography		1368	1998	33r
Rehearsal dinner		728	1998	33r
Wedding invitations and announcements		341	1998	33r
Wedding reception		7968	2000	33r
Wedding rings (bride and groom)		1060	1998	33r

Huntington-Ashland, WV

Item	Per	Value	Date	Ref.
Alcoholic Beverages				
Alcoholic beverage purchases	yr	253	1999	30r
Malt beverages, all types, all sizes, any origin	16 oz	0.96	7/01	11r
Appliances				
Major appliances, expenditures on	yr	172	1999	30r
Small appliances, housewares, expenditures on	yr	81	1999	30r
Banking and Money				
Mortgage interest and charges paid	yr	2039	1999	30r
Mortgage principal paid on owned property	yr	1026	1999	30r
Vehicle finance charges paid	yr	365	1999	30r
Charity				
Cash contributions, expenditures	yr	1127	1999	30r
Child Care				
Child raising cost, total, age 0-2	yr	8540	1999	60r
Child raising cost, total, age 3-5	yr	8780	1999	60r
Child raising cost, total, age 6-8	yr	8820	1999	60r
Child raising cost, total, age 9-11	yr	8800	1999	60r
Child raising cost, total, age 12-14	yr	9510	1999	60r
Child raising cost, total, age 15-17	yr	9740	1999	60r
Child's child care and education, age 0-2	yr	1380	1999	60r
Child's child care and education, age 3-5	yr	1520	1999	60r
Child's child care and education, age 6-8	yr	990	1999	60r
Child's child care and education, age 9-11	yr	650	1999	60r
Child's child care and education, age 12-14	yr	490	1999	60r
Child's child care and education, age 15-17	yr	840	1999	60r
Child's clothing, age 0-2	yr	480	1999	60r
Child's clothing, age 3-5	yr	470	1999	60r
Child's clothing, age 6-8	yr	520	1999	60r
Child's clothing, age 9-11	yr	570	1999	60r
Child's clothing, age 12-14	yr	950	1999	60r
Child's clothing, age 15-17	yr	850	1999	60r
Child's food, age 0-2	yr	1000	1999	60r
Child's food, age 3-5	yr	1160	1999	60r
Child's food, age 6-8	yr	1490	1999	60r
Child's food, age 9-11	yr	1770	1999	60r
Child's food, age 12-14	yr	1770	1999	60r
Child's food, age 15-17	yr	1980	1999	60r
Child's health care, age 0-2	yr	620	1999	60r
Child's health care, age 3-5	yr	590	1999	60r
Child's health care, age 6-8	yr	680	1999	60r
Child's health care, age 9-11	yr	720	1999	60r
Child's health care, age 12-14	yr	730	1999	60r
Child's health care, age 15-17	yr	760	1999	60r
Child's housing, age 0-2	yr	3070	1999	60r
Child's housing, age 3-5	yr	3050	1999	60r
Child's housing, age 6-8	yr	3010	1999	60r
Child's housing, age 9-11	yr	2850	1999	60r
Child's housing, age 12-14	yr	3040	1999	60r
Child's housing, age 15-17	yr	2650	1999	60r
Child's personal care, reading, age 0-2	yr	910	1999	60r
Child's personal care, reading, age 3-5	yr	930	1999	60r
Child's personal care, reading, age 6-8	yr	960	1999	60r
Child's personal care, reading, age 9-11	yr	1000	1999	60r
Child's personal care, reading, age 12-14	yr	1170	1999	60r
Child's personal care, reading, age 15-17	yr	950	1999	60r

Item	Per	Value	Date	Ref.
Clothing				
Apparel and services purchases	yr	1610	1999	30r
Boys, 2 to 15, expenditures on	yr	89	1999	30r
Children under 2, expenditures on	yr	79	1999	30r
Footwear, expenditures on	yr	283	1999	30r
Girls, 2 to 15, expenditures on	yr	103	1999	30r
Men and boys, expenditures on	yr	351	1999	30r
Men, 16 and over, expenditures on	yr	262	1999	30r
Women, 16 and over, expenditures on	yr	538	1999	30r
Communications				
Phone line, single, business, field visit	inst.	96.90	12/97	17s
Phone line, single, business, no field visit	inst.	96.90	12/97	17s
Phone line, single, residence, field visit	inst.	42.00	12/97	17s
Phone line, single, residence, no field visit	inst.	42.00	12/97	17s
Postage and stationery, expenditures on	yr	104	1999	30r
Postal rate, express mail, up to half-pound		12.45	7/01	108r
Postal rate, letter, first class, first ounce		0.34	7/01	108r
Postal rate, letter, two ounces		0.57	7/01	108r
Postal rate, post card		0.21	7/01	108r
Postal rate, priority mail, two pounds		3.95	7/01	108r
Postal rate, priority mail, up to one pound		3.50	7/01	108r
Telephone services, expenditures on	yr	860	1999	30r
Education				
Board, 4-year private college/university	yr	2370	1996	38s
Board, 4-year public college/university	yr	2133	1996	38s
Education expenditures	yr	431	1999	30r
Room, 4-year private college/university	yr	1853	1996	38s
Room, 4-year public college/university	yr	1970	1996	38s
Total cost, 4-year private college/university	yr	14231	1996	38s
Total cost, 4-year public college/university	yr	6128	1996	38s
Tuition, 2-year public college/university, in state	yr	1312	1996	38s
Tuition, 4-year private college/university, in state	yr	10008	1996	38s
Tuition, 4-year public college/university	yr	2024	1996	38s
Energy and Fuels				
Electricity	500 KWhs	47.29	7/01	11r
Electricity	KWh	0.09	7/01	11r
Fuel oil #2	gal	1.43	7/01	11r
Fuel oil and other fuels, expenditures on	yr	45	1999	30r
Gas, natural, commercial rate	1000 cf	6.75	11/00	88s
Gasoline, all types	gal	1.60	7/01	11r
Gasoline, unleaded midgrade	gal	1.65	7/01	11r
Gasoline, unleaded premium	gal	1.74	7/01	11r
Natural gas, expenditures on	yr	164	1999	30r
Utility (piped) gas, therm		1.01	7/01	11r
Utility (piped) gas, 40 therms		44.29	7/01	11r
Utility (piped) gas, 100 therms		97.44	7/01	11r
Entertainment				
Entertainment purchases	yr	1574	1999	30r
Fees and admissions paid	yr	371	1999	30r
Reading purchases	yr	121	1999	30r
Television, radios, sound equipment, expenditures on	yr	561	1999	30r
Funerals				
Total cost of funeral		5922.53	1/99	78r
Acknowledgement cards		63.43	1/99	78r
Casket		2258.77	1/99	78r
Cosmetology, hair, other preparation		127.09	1/99	78r
Embalming		393.49	1/99	78r
Funeral at funeral home		367.50	1/99	78r
Hearse (local)		169.66	1/99	78r
Professional service charges		1211.32	1/99	78r
Service car/van		80.69	1/99	78r
Transfer of remains to funeral home		144.25	1/99	78r
Vault		803.50	1/99	78r
Visitation/viewing		302.83	1/99	78r

Values are in dollars or fractions of dollars. In the column headed *Ref*, references are shown to sources. Each reference is followed by a letter. These refer to the geographical level for which data were reported: s=State, r=Region, and c=City or metro. The abbreviation *ex* is used to mean *except* or *excluding*; *exp* stands for *expenditures*. For other abbreviations and further explanations, please see the Introduction.

Huntington-Ashland, WV - continued

Item	Per	Value	Date	Ref.
Groceries				
American processed cheese	lb	3.50	7/01	11r
Bakery products, expenditures on	yr	261	1999	30r
Bananas	lb	0.47	7/01	11r
Beans, dried, any type, all sizes	lb	0.63	7/01	11r
Beef for stew, boneless	lb	2.86	7/01	11r
Beef, expenditures on	yr	210	1999	30r
Bologna, all beef or mixed	lb	2.29	7/01	11r
Bread, French	lb	1.66	7/01	11r
Bread, white, pan	lb	0.87	7/01	11r
Bread, whole wheat, pan	lb	1.38	7/01	11r
Broccoli	lb	1.04	7/01	11r
Butter, salted, grade AA, stick	lb	2.26	7/01	11r
Butter, yoghurt, cheese, etc, expenditures on	yr	170	1999	30r
Cabbage	lb	0.42	7/01	11r
Cereals and cereal products, expenditures on	yr	140	1999	30r
Cheddar cheese, natural	lb	3.75	7/01	11r
Chicken breast, bone-in	lb	1.85	7/01	11r
Chicken legs, bone-in	lb	1.34	7/01	11r
Chicken, fresh, whole	lb	1.05	7/01	11r
Chops, boneless,	lb	4.13	7/01	11r
Chuck roast, graded and ungraded, excl U.S. prime and choice	lb	2.35	7/01	11r
Chuck roast, U.S. choice, boneless	lb	2.67	7/01	11r
Coffee, 100%, ground roast, all sizes	lb	2.88	7/01	11r
Coffee, instant, plain, regular, all sizes	16 oz	9.25	7/01	11r
Cola, non diet,	2 liter	1.11	7/01	11r
Crackers, soda, salted	lb	1.70	7/01	11r
Dairy product purchases	yr	282	1999	30r
Eggs, expenditures on	yr	32	1999	30r
Fats and oils, expenditures on	yr	79	1999	30r
Fish and seafood, expenditures on	yr	99	1999	30r
Flour, white, all purpose	lb	0.32	7/01	11r
Food (excl fruit and vegetables), eaten at home, purchases	yr	815	1999	30r
Food cooked on trips, expenditures on	yr	36	1999	30r
Food purchases	yr	4533	1999	30r
Food purchases, eaten away from home	yr	1873	1999	30r
Food purchases, food eaten at home	yr	2660	1999	30r
Fresh fruits, expenditures on	yr	128	1999	30r
Fresh milk and cream, expenditures on	yr	112	1999	30r
Fresh vegetables, expenditures on	yr	131	1999	30r
Fruit and vegetable purchases	yr	438	1999	30r
Grapefruit	lb	0.59	7/01	11r
Grapes, Thompson, seedless	lb	2.12	7/01	11r
Ground beef, 100% beef	lb	1.76	7/01	11r
Ground beef, lean and extra lean	lb	2.60	7/01	11r
Ground chuck, 100% beef	lb	2.08	7/01	11r
Ham, boneless, excl canned	lb	2.71	7/01	11r
Ham, rump or shank half, bone-in, smoked	lb	2.19	7/01	11r
Ice cream, prepackaged, bulk, regular	1/2 gal	3.93	7/01	11r
Lemons	lb	1.32	7/01	11r
Lettuce, iceberg	lb	0.76	7/01	11r
Milk, fresh, low fat	gal	2.75	7/01	11r
Milk, fresh, whole, fortified	gal	2.97	7/01	11r
Nonalcoholic beverages, expenditures on	yr	228	1999	30r
Orange juice, frozen concentrate	16 oz	1.95	7/01	11r
Oranges, Navel	lb	0.73	7/01	11r
Oranges, Valencia	lb	0.55	7/01	11r
Peanut butter, creamy, all sizes	lb	1.83	7/01	11r
Pears, Anjou	lb	0.98	7/01	11r
Pork chops, center cut, bone-in	lb	3.33	7/01	11r
Pork sausage, fresh, loose	lb	2.59	7/01	11r
Pork shoulder picnic, bone-in, smoked	lb	1.12	7/01	11r
Pork, expenditures on	yr	162	1999	30r
Potato chips	16 oz	3.59	7/01	11r
Potatoes, frozen, french fried	lb	1.00	7/01	11r
Potatoes, white, all types	lb	0.44	7/01	11r
Poultry, expenditures on	yr	137	1999	30r
Processed fruits, expenditures on	yr	97	1999	30r
Processed vegetables, expenditures on	yr	82	1999	30r
Rice, white, long grain, uncooked	lb	0.51	7/01	11r

Huntington-Ashland, WV - continued

Item	Per	Value	Date	Ref.
Groceries - continued				
Round roast, graded and ungraded, excl U.S. prime and choice	lb	2.96	7/01	11r
Round steak, graded and ungraded, excl U.S. prime and choice	lb	3.11	7/01	11r
Sirloin steak, graded and ungraded, excl U.S. prime and choice	lb	4.23	7/01	11r
Spaghetti and macaroni	lb	0.78	7/01	11r
Steak, round, U.S. choice, boneless	lb	3.56	7/01	11r
Steak, sirloin, U.S. choice, boneless	lb	5.65	7/01	11r
Strawberries, dry pint	12 oz	1.50	7/01	11r
Sugar and other sweets, expenditures on	yr	99	1999	30r
Sugar, white, 33-80 ounce package	lb	0.39	7/01	11r
Sugar, white, all sizes	lb	0.42	7/01	11r
Tobacco products and smoking supplies purchases	yr	288	1999	30r
Tomatoes, field grown	lb	1.43	7/01	11r
Tuna, light, chunk	lb	1.77	7/01	11r
Turkey, frozen, whole	lb	1.05	7/01	11r
Goods and Services				
B&B Japanese maple (acer japonicum)	gal	49.98-129.00	4/00	93r
Boxwood (buxus)	2 gal	12.99-16.99	4/00	93r
Daylilly (hemerocallis)	gal	4.99-8.99	4/00	93r
Flat of annuals		11.00-13.92	4/00	93r
Fountain grass (pennisetum)	gal	5.98-7.98	4/00	93r
Hanging basket (10 in)		7.99-14.98	4/00	93r
Hardy geranium (geranium)	gal	5.98-8.00	4/00	93r
Hosta (hosta)	gal	4.99-10.98	4/00	93r
Lilac (syrubga vulgaris)	2 gal	12.99-21.99	4/00	93r
Rhododendron (rhododendron)	2 gal	14.99-24.99	4/00	93r
Sage (salvia)	gal	5.98-6.99	4/00	93r
Wintercreeper euonymus (euonymus fortunei)	2 gal	7.99-89.99	4/00	93r
Hunting license	yr	11.00	4/01	34s
Health Care				
Cardiac catheterization, ave hospital/physician charges		10540	1998	77s
Childbirth, Cesarean delivery		11587	1997	13r
Childbirth, vaginal delivery		6725	1997	13r
Drugs, expenditures on	yr	399	1999	30r
Health care purchases	yr	1971	1999	30r
Health insurance expenditures	yr	933	1999	30r
Hysterectomy, laproscopically-assisted, ave hospital/physician charges		11620	1998	76s
Hysterectomy, vaginal, ave hospital and physician charges		8550	1998	76s
Medicaid dispensing fee		3.90-4.90	1999	87s
Medical services expenditures	yr	547	1999	30r
Medical supplies, expenditures on	yr	91	1999	30r
Plastic surgery, breast augmentation		2870	2000	7r
Plastic surgery, breast lift		3649	2000	7r
Plastic surgery, facelift		5008	2000	7r
Plastic surgery, hair transplantation		3425	2000	7r
Plastic surgery, lip augmentation		1227	2000	7r
Plastic surgery, lower body lift		4793	2000	7r
Plastic surgery, thigh lift		3862	2000	7r
Household Goods				
Floor coverings, expenditures on	yr	44	1999	30r
Furniture, expenditures on	yr	335	1999	30r

Values are in dollars or fractions of dollars. In the column headed *Ref*, references are shown to sources. Each reference is followed by a letter. These refer to the geographical level for which data were reported: s=State, r=Region, and c=City or metro. The abbreviation *ex* is used to mean *except* or *excluding*; *exp* stands for *expenditures*. For other abbreviations and further explanations, please see the Introduction.

Huntington-Ashland, WV - continued

Item	Per	Value	Date	Ref.
Household Goods				
Household furnishings and equipment purchases	yr	1328	1999	30r
Household textiles, expenditures on	yr	89	1999	30r
Laundry and cleaning supplies, expenditures on	yr	113	1999	30r
Housing				
Home price, existing, ave		160100	10/00	90r
Home value, median		93000	2001	53s
Household operation expenditures	yr	553	1999	30r
Housekeeping supplies purchases	yr	473	1999	30r
Housing, expenditures on	yr	10303	1999	30r
Maintenance, repairs, insurance expenditures	yr	699	1999	30r
Monthly rental value of owned home	mos	505	1999	30r
Owned dwellings, expenditures own	yr	3465	1999	30r
Rent expenditures	yr	1641	1999	30r
Rental unit, 1 bedroom, with utilities	mos	360	4/01	41c
Rental unit, 2 bedroom, with utilities	mos	444	4/01	41c
Rental unit, 3 bedroom, with utilities	mos	566	4/01	41c
Rental unit, 4 bedroom, with utilities	mos	624	4/01	41c
Shelter, expenditures on	yr	5467	1999	30r
Insurance and Pensions				
Life and other personal insurance purchases	yr	414	1999	30r
Pensions and Social Security, expenditures on	yr	2635	1999	30r
Personal insurance and pensions, expenditures on	yr	3048	1999	30r
Legal Fees				
Combination hunting and fishing license	yr	17.00	4/01	34s
Driver's license fee	renew	12.50	1999	48s
Driver's license fee	orig	12.50	1999	48s
Fishing license	yr	11.00	4/01	34s
Personal Goods				
Personal care products and services purchases	yr	393	1999	30r
Personal Services				
Personal services, household, expenditures on	yr	258	1999	30r
Pets				
Pets, toys, and playground equipment, expenditures on	yr	306	1999	30r
Taxes				
Federal income taxes paid	yr	2047	1999	30r
Personal taxes, expenditures on	yr	2554	1999	30r
Property taxes paid	yr	726	1999	30r
State and local income taxes paid	yr	363	1999	30r
Transportation				
Cars and trucks, new, expenditures on	yr	1648	1999	30r
Cars and trucks, used, expenditures on	yr	1651	1999	30r
Diesel at the pump	gal	1.30	10/99	73s
Gasoline and motor oil purchases	yr	1052	1999	30r
Gasoline before-tax price (cents)	gal	108.80	10/00	43s
Maintenance and repair expenditures	yr	621	1999	30r
Public transportation, expenditures on	yr	298	1999	30r
Transportation purchases	yr	6738	1999	30r
Vehicle expenses, miscellaneous, purchases	yr	2033	1999	30r
Vehicle insurance payments	yr	696	1999	30r
Vehicle purchases (net outlay)	yr	3354	1999	30r
Vehicle rental, lease expenditures	yr	352	1999	30r
Utilities				
Electrical bill, average	mos	60.66	9/00	9s
Electricity, expenditures on	yr	1115	1999	30r
Electricity, summer, 250 KWh	mos	21.62	2/96	96s
Electricity, summer, 500 KWh	mos	38.93	2/96	96s
Electricity, summer, 750 KWh	mos	55.12	2/96	96s
Electricity, summer, 1000 KWh	mos	71.41	2/96	96s
Electricity cost, average	KWh	5.20	9/00	9s

Huntington-Ashland, WV - continued

Item	Per	Value	Date	Ref.
Utilities - continued				
Water and other public services, expenditures on	yr	298	1999	30r
Weddings				
Wedding (national average cost)		19936	2000	33r
Wedding (regional average total cost)		16293	1997	110r
Attendants' gifts		321	1998	33r
Bridal attendants' apparel (5 persons)		824	2000	33r
Bride's headpiece/veil		173	1998	33r
Bride's wedding dress		859	1998	33r
Clergy, religious facility fee		242	1998	33r
Engagement ring		3177	1998	33r
Flowers		789	1998	33r
Groom's formalwear rental		99	2000	33r
Limousine		410	1998	33r
Marriage license cost		23.00	4/01	35s
Men's formalwear (ushers, best man)		469	2000	33r
Mother of bride apparel		241	2000	33r
Music		866	1998	33r
Photography and videography		1368	1998	33r
Rehearsal dinner		728	1998	33r
Wedding invitations and announcements		341	1998	33r
Wedding reception		7968	2000	33r
Wedding rings (bride and groom)		1060	1998	33r

Huntsville, AL

Item	Per	Value	Date	Ref.
Composite, ACCRA index		95.10	3/01	4c
Alcoholic Beverages				
Alcoholic beverage purchases	yr	253	1999	30r
Beer, Heineken, 12-oz, ex deposit	6	7.52	3/01	4c
J & B Scotch	750-ml	23.99	3/01	4c
Malt beverages, all types, all sizes, any origin	16 oz	0.96	7/01	11r
Wine, Livingston or Gallo, Chablis blanc	1.5 liter	6.28	3/01	4c
Appliances				
Appliance repair, service call, washing machine	min lab chg	42.80	3/01	4c
Major appliances, expenditures on	yr	172	1999	30r
Small appliances, housewares, expenditures on	yr	81	1999	30r
Banking and Money				
Mortgage interest and charges paid	yr	2039	1999	30r
Mortgage principal paid on owned property	yr	1026	1999	30r
Mortgage rate, incl. points and orig. fee, 30-yr. conv. fixed or ARM	mos	6.75	3/01	4c
Vehicle finance charges paid	yr	365	1999	30r
Charity				
Cash contributions, expenditures	yr	1127	1999	30r
Child Care				
Child raising cost, total, age 0-2	yr	8540	1999	60r
Child raising cost, total, age 3-5	yr	8780	1999	60r
Child raising cost, total, age 6-8	yr	8820	1999	60r
Child raising cost, total, age 9-11	yr	8800	1999	60r
Child raising cost, total, age 12-14	yr	9510	1999	60r
Child raising cost, total, age 15-17	yr	9740	1999	60r
Child's child care and education, age 0-2	yr	1380	1999	60r
Child's child care and education, age 3-5	yr	1520	1999	60r
Child's child care and education, age 6-8	yr	990	1999	60r
Child's child care and education, age 9-11	yr	650	1999	60r
Child's child care and education, age 12-14	yr	490	1999	60r
Child's child care and education, age 15-17	yr	840	1999	60r
Child's clothing, age 0-2	yr	480	1999	60r
Child's clothing, age 3-5	yr	470	1999	60r
Child's clothing, age 6-8	yr	520	1999	60r
Child's clothing, age 9-11	yr	570	1999	60r
Child's clothing, age 12-14	yr	950	1999	60r
Child's clothing, age 15-17	yr	850	1999	60r
Child's food, age 0-2	yr	1000	1999	60r
Child's food, age 3-5	yr	1160	1999	60r

Values are in dollars or fractions of dollars. In the column headed *Ref*, references are shown to sources. Each reference is followed by a letter. These refer to the geographical level for which data were reported: s=State, r=Region, and c=City or metro. The abbreviation *ex* is used to mean *except* or *excluding*; *exp* stands for *expenditures*. For other abbreviations and further explanations, please see the Introduction.

Huntsville, AL - continued

Item	Per	Value	Date	Ref.
Child Care				
Child's food, age 6-8	yr	1490	1999	60r
Child's food, age 9-11	yr	1770	1999	60r
Child's food, age 12-14	yr	1770	1999	60r
Child's food, age 15-17	yr	1980	1999	60r
Child's health care, age 0-2	yr	620	1999	60r
Child's health care, age 3-5	yr	590	1999	60r
Child's health care, age 6-8	yr	680	1999	60r
Child's health care, age 9-11	yr	720	1999	60r
Child's health care, age 12-14	yr	730	1999	60r
Child's health care, age 15-17	yr	760	1999	60r
Child's housing, age 0-2	yr	3070	1999	60r
Child's housing, age 3-5	yr	3050	1999	60r
Child's housing, age 6-8	yr	3010	1999	60r
Child's housing, age 9-11	yr	2850	1999	60r
Child's housing, age 12-14	yr	3040	1999	60r
Child's housing, age 15-17	yr	2650	1999	60r
Child's personal care, reading, age 0-2	yr	910	1999	60r
Child's personal care, reading, age 3-5	yr	930	1999	60r
Child's personal care, reading, age 6-8	yr	960	1999	60r
Child's personal care, reading, age 9-11	yr	1000	1999	60r
Child's personal care, reading, age 12-14	yr	1170	1999	60r
Child's personal care, reading, age 15-17	yr	950	1999	60r
Clothing				
Apparel and services purchases	yr	1610	1999	30r
Boys' brief, cotton	3	5.59	3/01	4c
Boys, 2 to 15, expenditures on	yr	89	1999	30r
Children under 2, expenditures on	yr	79	1999	30r
Footwear, expenditures on	yr	283	1999	30r
Girls, 2 to 15, expenditures on	yr	103	1999	30r
Men and boys, expenditures on	yr	351	1999	30r
Men, 16 and over, expenditures on	yr	262	1999	30r
Shirt, man's dress shirt		26.30	3/01	4c
Slacks, man's "No Wrinkles" khaki		41.60	3/01	4c
Women, 16 and over, expenditures on	yr	538	1999	30r
Communications				
Newspaper subscription, daily and Sunday delivery	mos	10.00	3/01	4c
Phone line, single, business, field visit	inst.	69.00	12/97	17s
Phone line, single, business, no field visit	inst.	69.00	12/97	17s
Phone line, single, residence, field visit	inst.	40.00	12/97	17s
Phone line, single, residence, no field visit	inst.	40.00	12/97	17s
Postage and stationery, expenditures on	yr	104	1999	30r
Postal rate, express mail, up to half-pound		12.45	7/01	108r
Postal rate, letter, first class, first ounce		0.34	7/01	108r
Postal rate, letter, two ounces		0.57	7/01	108r
Postal rate, post card		0.21	7/01	108r
Postal rate, priority mail, two pounds		3.95	7/01	108r
Postal rate, priority mail, up to one pound		3.50	7/01	108r
Telephone bill, family of three	mos	23.90	3/01	4c
Telephone services, expenditures on	yr	860	1999	30r
Education				
Board, 4-year private college/university	yr	2256	1996	38s
Board, 4-year public college/university	yr	1739	1996	38s
Education expenditures	yr	431	1999	30r
Room, 4-year private college/university	yr	1799	1996	38s
Room, 4-year public college/university	yr	1757	1996	38s
Total cost, 4-year private college/university	yr	11635	1996	38s
Total cost, 4-year public college/university	yr	5737	1996	38s
Tuition, 2-year public college/university, in state	yr	1317	1996	38s
Tuition, 4-year private college/university, in state	yr	7580	1996	38s
Tuition, 4-year public college/university	yr	2240	1996	38s
Energy and Fuels				
Electricity	500 KWhs	47.29	7/01	11r
Electricity	KWh	0.09	7/01	11r
Energy, combined forms, 2400 sq ft	mos	89.15	3/01	4c
Fuel oil #2	gal	1.43	7/01	11r
Fuel oil and other fuels, expenditures on		45	1999	30r

Huntsville, AL - continued

Item	Per	Value	Date	Ref.
Energy and Fuels - continued				
Gas, natural, commercial rate	1000 cf	9.50	11/00	88s
Gas, regular unleaded, cash, self-service	gal	1.38	3/01	4c
Gasoline, all types	gal	1.60	7/01	11r
Gasoline, unleaded midgrade	gal	1.65	7/01	11r
Gasoline, unleaded premium	gal	1.74	7/01	11r
Natural gas, expenditures on	yr	164	1999	30r
Utility (piped) gas, therm		1.01	7/01	11r
Utility (piped) gas, 40 therms		44.29	7/01	11r
Utility (piped) gas, 100 therms		97.44	7/01	11r
Entertainment				
Bowling, Saturday evening rate	line	3.31	3/01	4c
Entertainment purchases	yr	1574	1999	30r
Fees and admissions paid	yr	371	1999	30r
Monopoly game, Parker Brothers', No. 9	game	11.91	3/01	4c
Movie, first-run, Saturday, evening	adm.	7.00	3/01	4c
Reading purchases	yr	121	1999	30r
Television, radios, sound equipment, expenditures on	yr	561	1999	30r
Tennis balls, yellow, Wilson or Penn, 3	can	1.93	3/01	4c
Groceries				
Groceries, ACCRA Index		96.90	3/01	4c
American processed cheese	lb	3.50	7/01	11r
Antibiotic ointment, Polysporin	0.5 oz	4.62	3/01	4c
Baby food, strained vegetables or fruit, lowest price	4-4.5 oz	0.38	3/01	4c
Bakery products, expenditures on	yr	261	1999	30r
Bananas	lb	0.50	3/01	4c
Bananas	lb	0.47	7/01	11r
Beans, dried, any type, all sizes	lb	0.63	7/01	11r
Beef for stew, boneless	lb	2.86	7/01	11r
Beef or hamburger, ground	lb	0.95	3/01	4c
Beef, expenditures on	yr	210	1999	30r
Bologna, all beef or mixed	lb	2.29	7/01	11r
Bread, French	lb	1.66	7/01	11r
Bread, white	loaf	0.97	3/01	4c
Bread, white, pan	lb	0.87	7/01	11r
Bread, whole wheat, pan	lb	1.38	7/01	11r
Broccoli	lb	1.04	7/01	11r
Butter, salted, grade AA, stick	lb	2.26	7/01	11r
Butter, yoghurt, cheese, etc, expenditures on	yr	170	1999	30r
Cabbage	lb	0.42	7/01	11r
Cereals and cereal products, expenditures on	yr	140	1999	30r
Cheddar cheese, natural	lb	3.75	7/01	11r
Cheese, Kraft grated Parmesan	8 oz	3.33	3/01	4c
Chicken breast, bone-in	lb	1.85	7/01	11r
Chicken legs, bone-in	lb	1.34	7/01	11r
Chicken, fresh, whole	lb	1.05	7/01	11r
Chicken, whole fryer	lb	0.90	3/01	4c
Chops, boneless,	lb	4.13	7/01	11r
Chuck roast, graded and ungraded, excl U.S. prime and choice	lb	2.35	7/01	11r
Chuck roast, U.S. choice, boneless	lb	2.67	7/01	11r
Cigarettes, Winston, Kings	carton	28.55	3/01	4c
Coffee, 100%, ground roast, all sizes	lb	2.88	7/01	11r
Coffee, instant, plain, regular, all sizes	16 oz	9.25	7/01	11r
Coffee, vacuum-packed	13 oz	2.49	3/01	4c
Cola, non diet,	2 liter	1.11	7/01	11r
Corn Flakes, Kellogg's or Post Toasties	18 oz	2.81	3/01	4c
Corn, frozen, whole kernel, lowest price	16 oz	1.21	3/01	4c
Crackers, soda, salted	lb	1.70	7/01	11r
Dairy product purchases	yr	282	1999	30r
Eggs, expenditures on	yr	32	1999	30r
Eggs, Grade A or AA	dozen	1.18	3/01	4c
Fats and oils, expenditures on	yr	79	1999	30r
Fish and seafood, expenditures on	yr	99	1999	30r
Flour, white, all purpose	lb	0.32	7/01	11r
Food (excl fruit and vegetables), eaten at home, purchases	yr	815	1999	30r
Food cooked on trips, expenditures on	yr	36	1999	30r
Food purchases	yr	4533	1999	30r

Values are in dollars or fractions of dollars. In the column headed *Ref*, references are shown to sources. Each reference is followed by a letter. These refer to the geographical level for which data were reported: s=State, r=Region, and c=City or metro. The abbreviation *ex* is used to mean *except* or *excluding*; *exp* stands for expenditures. For other abbreviations and further explanations, please see the Introduction.

Huntsville, AL - continued

Item	Per	Value	Date	Ref.
Groceries				
Food purchases, eaten away from home	yr	1873	1999	30r
Food purchases, food eaten at home	yr	2660	1999	30r
Fresh fruits, expenditures on	yr	128	1999	30r
Fresh milk and cream, expenditures on	yr	112	1999	30r
Fresh vegetables, expenditures on	yr	131	1999	30r
Fruit and vegetable purchases	yr	438	1999	30r
Grapefruit	lb	0.59	7/01	11r
Grapes, Thompson, seedless	lb	2.12	7/01	11r
Ground beef, 100% beef	lb	1.76	7/01	11r
Ground beef, lean and extra lean	lb	2.60	7/01	11r
Ground chuck, 100% beef	lb	2.08	7/01	11r
Ham, boneless, excl canned	lb	2.71	7/01	11r
Ham, rump or shank half, bone-in, smoked	lb	2.19	7/01	11r
Ice cream, prepackaged, bulk, regular	1/2 gal	3.93	7/01	11r
Lemons	lb	1.32	7/01	11r
Lettuce, iceberg	head	0.91	3/01	4c
Lettuce, iceberg	lb	0.76	7/01	11r
Margarine, Blue Bonnet or Parkay, stick	lb	0.71	3/01	4c
Milk, fresh, low fat	gal	2.75	7/01	11r
Milk, fresh, whole, fortified	gal	2.97	7/01	11r
Milk, whole	1/2 gal	1.72	3/01	4c
Nonalcoholic beverages, expenditures on	yr	228	1999	30r
Orange juice, frozen concentrate	16 oz	1.95	7/01	11r
Orange juice, Minute Maid frozen	12 oz	1.60	3/01	4c
Oranges, Navel	lb	0.73	7/01	11r
Oranges, Valencia	lb	0.55	7/01	11r
Peaches, halves or slices, Hunt's, Del Monte, or Libby's	29 oz	1.59	3/01	4c
Peanut butter, creamy, all sizes	lb	1.83	7/01	11r
Pears, Anjou	lb	0.98	7/01	11r
Peas, green, Del Monte or Green Giant	15 oz	0.69	3/01	4c
Pork chops, center cut, bone-in	lb	3.33	7/01	11r
Pork sausage, fresh, loose	lb	2.59	7/01	11r
Pork shoulder picnic, bone-in, smoked	lb	1.12	7/01	11r
Pork, expenditures on	yr	162	1999	30r
Potato chips	16 oz	3.59	7/01	11r
Potatoes, frozen, french fried	lb	1.00	7/01	11r
Potatoes, white or red	10 lb	3.37	3/01	4c
Potatoes, white, all types	lb	0.44	7/01	11r
Poultry, expenditures on	yr	137	1999	30r
Processed fruits, expenditures on	yr	97	1999	30r
Processed vegetables, expenditures on	yr	82	1999	30r
Rice, white, long grain, uncooked	lb	0.51	7/01	11r
Round roast, graded and ungraded, excl U.S. prime and choice	lb	2.96	7/01	11r
Round steak, graded and ungraded, excl U.S. prime and choice	lb	3.11	7/01	11r
Sausage, Jimmy Dean/Owens pork	lb	2.69	3/01	4c
Shortening, vegetable, Crisco	3 lb	3.17	3/01	4c
Sirloin steak, graded and ungraded, excl U.S. prime and choice	lb	4.23	7/01	11r
Soft drink, Coca Cola, ex deposit	2 liter	1.31	3/01	4c
Spaghetti and macaroni	lb	0.78	7/01	11r
Steak, round, U.S. choice, boneless	lb	3.56	7/01	11r
Steak, sirloin, U.S. choice, boneless	lb	5.65	7/01	11r
Steak, T-bone	lb	6.87	3/01	4c
Strawberries, dry pint	12 oz	1.50	7/01	11r
Sugar and other sweets, expenditures on	yr	99	1999	30r
Sugar, cane or beet	4 lbs	1.41	3/01	4c
Sugar, white, 33-80 ounce package	lb	0.39	7/01	11r
Sugar, white, all sizes	lb	0.42	7/01	11r
Tobacco products and smoking supplies purchases	yr	288	1999	30r
Tomatoes, field grown	lb	1.43	7/01	11r
Tomatoes, Hunt's or Del Monte	14.5 oz	0.75	3/01	4c
Tuna, chunk, light	6 oz	0.61	3/01	4c
Tuna, light, chunk	lb	1.77	7/01	11r
Turkey, frozen, whole	lb	1.05	7/01	11r
Goods and Services				
Miscellaneous goods and services, ACCRA Index		105.20	3/01	4c
Hunting license	yr	16.00	4/01	34s

Huntsville, AL - continued

Item	Per	Value	Date	Ref.
Health Care				
Health care, ACCRA Index		97.40	3/01	4c
Cardiac catheterization, ave hospital/ physician charges		15260	1998	77s
Childbirth, Cesarean delivery		11587	1997	13r
Childbirth, vaginal delivery		6725	1997	13r
Dentist's fee, adult teeth cleaning and periodic oral exam	visit	73.00	3/01	4c
Doctor's fee, routine exam, established patient	visit	55.00	3/01	4c
Drugs, expenditures on	yr	399	1999	30r
Health care purchases	yr	1971	1999	30r
Health insurance expenditures	yr	933	1999	30r
Hospital care, private room	day	499.50	3/01	4c
Hysterectomy, laproscopically-assisted, ave hospital/physician charges		16780	1998	76s
Hysterectomy, vaginal, ave hospital and physician charges		10990	1998	76s
Medicaid dispensing fee		5.40	1999	87s
Medical services expenditures	yr	547	1999	30r
Medical supplies, expenditures on	yr	91	1999	30r
Nursing home costs, private room	day	113	2000	82c
Household Goods				
Dishwashing powder, Cascade	50 oz	3.24	3/01	4c
Floor coverings, expenditures on	yr	44	1999	30r
Furniture, expenditures on	yr	335	1999	30r
Household furnishings and equipment purchases	yr	1328	1999	30r
Household textiles, expenditures on	yr	89	1999	30r
Laundry and cleaning supplies, expenditures on	yr	113	1999	30r
Tissues, facial, Kleenex brand	175	1.34	3/01	4c
Housing				
Housing, ACCRA Index		83.90	3/01	4c
Home, 2200 sq ft, 4-br, 2-bath, 2-car garage, average		161500	2000	47c
Home price, existing, ave		160100	10/00	90r
Home value, median		115000	2001	53s
House, 2400 sq ft, 8000 sq ft lot, new, urban, utilities	total	178495	3/01	4c
House payment, principal and interest, 25% down payment	mos	868	3/01	4c
Household operation expenditures	yr	553	1999	30r
Housekeeping supplies purchases	yr	473	1999	30r
Housing, expenditures on	yr	10303	1999	30r
Maintenance, repairs, insurance expenditures	yr	699	1999	30r
Monthly rental value of owned home	mos	505	1999	30r
Owned dwellings, expenditures own	yr	3465	1999	30r
Rent expenditures	yr	1641	1999	30r
Rent, apartment, 2 br, 1 1/2-2 baths, unfurn, 950 sq ft, water	mos	573	3/01	4c
Rental unit, 1 bedroom, with utilities	mos	430	4/01	41c
Rental unit, 2 bedroom, with utilities	mos	530	4/01	41c
Rental unit, 3 bedroom, with utilities	mos	706	4/01	41c
Rental unit, 4 bedroom, with utilities	mos	841	4/01	41c
Shelter, expenditures on	yr	5467	1999	30r
Insurance and Pensions				
Life and other personal insurance purchases	yr	414	1999	30r
Pensions and Social Security, expenditures on	yr	2635	1999	30r
Personal insurance and pensions, expenditures on	yr	3048	1999	30r
Legal Fees				
Divorce, filing fee		146.00-193.00	4/01	35s
Driver's license fee	renew	18.50	1999	48s
Driver's license fee	orig	18.50	1999	48s

Values are in dollars or fractions of dollars. In the column headed *Ref*, references are shown to sources. Each reference is followed by a letter. These refer to the geographical level for which data were reported: s=State, r=Region, and c=City or metro. The abbreviation *ex* is used to mean *except* or *excluding*; *exp* stands for *expenditures*. For other abbreviations and further explanations, please see the Introduction.

Huntsville, AL - continued

Item	Per	Value	Date	Ref.
Personal Goods				
Personal care products and services purchases	yr	393	1999	30r
Shampoo, Alberto VO5	15 oz	1.12	3/01	4c
Toothpaste, Crest or Colgate	6-7 oz	2.43	3/01	4c
Personal Services				
Dry cleaning, man's 2-pc suit		6.90	3/01	4c
Man's haircut, barbershop, no styling		11.40	3/01	4c
Personal services, household, expenditures on	yr	258	1999	30r
Woman's shampoo, trim, blow-dry, no style-change		23.40	3/01	4c
Pets				
Pets, toys, and playground equipment, expenditures on	yr	306	1999	30r
Restaurant Food				
Chicken, fried, thigh and drumstick, KFC/ Church's		2.61	3/01	4c
Hamburger with cheese, McDonald's	1/4 lb	2.14	3/01	4c
Pizza, Pizza Hut or Pizza Inn	11-12 in	12.19	3/01	4c
Taxes				
Federal income taxes paid	yr	2047	1999	30r
Personal taxes, expenditures on	yr	2554	1999	30r
Property taxes paid	yr	726	1999	30r
State and local income taxes paid	yr	363	1999	30r
Transportation				
Transportation, ACCRA Index		102.90	3/01	4c
Cars and trucks, new, expenditures on	yr	1648	1999	30r
Cars and trucks, used, expenditures on	yr	1651	1999	30r
Diesel at the pump	gal	1.19	10/99	73s
Gasoline and motor oil purchases	yr	1052	1999	30r
Gasoline before-tax price (cents)	gal	104.10	10/00	43s
Maintenance and repair expenditures	yr	621	1999	30r
Public transportation, expenditures on	yr	298	1999	30r
Tire balance, computer or spin balance, front	wheel	8.69	3/01	4c
Transportation purchases	yr	6738	1999	30r
Vehicle expenses, miscellaneous, purchases	yr	2033	1999	30r
Vehicle insurance payments	yr	696	1999	30r
Vehicle purchases (net outlay)	yr	3354	1999	30r
Vehicle rental, lease expenditures	yr	352	1999	30r
Utilities				
Utilities, ACCRA Index		78.10	3/01	4c
Electrical bill, average	mos	83.42	9/00	9s
Electricity, 2400 sq ft, new home	mos	89.15	3/01	4c
Electricity, expenditures on	yr	1115	1999	30r
Electricity cost, average	KWh	5.60	9/00	9s
Water and other public services, expenditures on	yr	298	1999	30r
Weddings				
Wedding (national average cost)		19936	2000	33r
Attendants' gifts		321	1998	33r
Bridal attendants' apparel (5 persons)		824	2000	33r
Bride's headpiece/veil		173	1998	33r
Bride's wedding dress		859	1998	33r
Clergy, religious facility fee		242	1998	33r
Engagement ring		3177	1998	33r
Flowers		789	1998	33r
Groom's formalwear rental		99	2000	33r
Limousine		410	1998	33r
Marriage license cost		25.00	4/01	35s
Men's formalwear (ushers, best man)		469	2000	33r
Mother of bride apparel		241	2000	33r
Music		866	1998	33r
Photography and videography		1368	1998	33r
Rehearsal dinner		728	1998	33r
Wedding invitations and announcements		341	1998	33r
Wedding reception		7968	2000	33r
Wedding rings (bride and groom)		1060	1998	33r

Indianapolis, IN

Item	Per	Value	Date	Ref.
Average annual expenditures	yr	35369	1999	30r
Composite, ACCRA index		96.00	3/01	4c
Alcoholic Beverages				
Alcoholic beverage purchases	yr	304	1999	30r
Beer, Heineken, 12-oz, ex deposit	6	6.75	3/01	4c
J & B Scotch	750-ml	19.31	3/01	4c
Malt beverages, all types, all sizes, any origin	16 oz	0.93	7/01	11r
Wine, Livingston or Gallo, Chablis blanc	1.5 liter	3.90	3/01	4c
Wine, red and white table, all sizes, any origin	liter	7.04	7/01	11r
Appliances				
Appliance repair, service call, washing machine	min lab chg	29.18	3/01	4c
Major appliances, expenditures on	yr	165	1999	30r
Small appliances, housewares, expenditures on	yr	90	1999	30r
Banking and Money				
Mortgage interest and charges paid	yr	2277	1999	30r
Mortgage principal paid on owned property	yr	1230	1999	30r
Mortgage rate, incl. points and orig. fee, 30-yr. conv. fixed or ARM	mos	6.79	3/01	4c
Vehicle finance charges paid	yr	328	1999	30r
Business Expenses				
Business travel, car rental	day	60	2001	3c
Business travel, food	day	42	2001	3c
Business travel, hotel	day	103	2001	3c
Charity				
Cash contributions, expenditures	yr	1126	1999	30r
Child Care				
Child raising cost, total, age 0-2	yr	7890	1999	60r
Child raising cost, total, age 3-5	yr	8130	1999	60r
Child raising cost, total, age 6-8	yr	8170	1999	60r
Child raising cost, total, age 9-11	yr	8190	1999	60r
Child raising cost, total, age 12-14	yr	8890	1999	60r
Child raising cost, total, age 15-17	yr	9050	1999	60r
Child's child care and education, age 0-2	yr	1240	1999	60r
Child's child care and education, age 3-5	yr	1370	1999	60r
Child's child care and education, age 6-8	yr	880	1999	60r
Child's child care and education, age 9-11	yr	570	1999	60r
Child's child care and education, age 12-14	yr	420	1999	60r
Child's child care and education, age 15-17	yr	720	1999	60r
Child's clothing, age 0-2	yr	410	1999	60r
Child's clothing, age 3-5	yr	400	1999	60r
Child's clothing, age 6-8	yr	450	1999	60r
Child's clothing, age 9-11	yr	500	1999	60r
Child's clothing, age 12-14	yr	840	1999	60r
Child's clothing, age 15-17	yr	740	1999	60r
Child's food, age 0-2	yr	960	1999	60r
Child's food, age 3-5	yr	1120	1999	60r
Child's food, age 6-8	yr	1430	1999	60r
Child's food, age 9-11	yr	1710	1999	60r
Child's food, age 12-14	yr	1710	1999	60r
Child's food, age 15-17	yr	1920	1999	60r
Child's health care, age 0-2	yr	520	1999	60r
Child's health care, age 3-5	yr	500	1999	60r
Child's health care, age 6-8	yr	570	1999	60r
Child's health care, age 9-11	yr	610	1999	60r
Child's health care, age 12-14	yr	630	1999	60r
Child's health care, age 15-17	yr	650	1999	60r
Child's housing, age 0-2	yr	2860	1999	60r
Child's housing, age 3-5	yr	2840	1999	60r
Child's housing, age 6-8	yr	2800	1999	60r
Child's housing, age 9-11	yr	2650	1999	60r
Child's housing, age 12-14	yr	2840	1999	60r
Child's housing, age 15-17	yr	2440	1999	60r
Child's personal care, reading, age 0-2	yr	880	1999	60r
Child's personal care, reading, age 3-5	yr	900	1999	60r
Child's personal care, reading, age 6-8	yr	930	1999	60r
Child's personal care, reading, age 9-11	yr	970	1999	60r
Child's personal care, reading, age 12-14	yr	1150	1999	60r

Values are in dollars or fractions of dollars. In the column headed *Ref*, references are shown to sources. Each reference is followed by a letter. These refer to the geographical level for which data were reported: s=State, r=Region, and c=City or metro. The abbreviation *ex* is used to mean *except* or *excluding*; *exp* stands for *expenditures*. For other abbreviations and further explanations, please see the Introduction.

Indianapolis, IN - continued

Item	Per	Value	Date	Ref.
Child Care				
Child's personal care, reading, age 15-17	yr	920	1999	60r
Clothing				
Apparel and services purchases	yr	1607	1999	30r
Boys' brief, cotton	3	3.38	3/01	4c
Boys, 2 to 15, expenditures on	yr	91	1999	30r
Children under 2, expenditures on	yr	59	1999	30r
Footwear, expenditures on	yr	285	1999	30r
Girls, 2 to 15, expenditures on	yr	116	1999	30r
Men and boys, expenditures on	yr	433	1999	30r
Men, 16 and over, expenditures on	yr	341	1999	30r
Shirt, man's dress shirt		23.16	3/01	4c
Slacks, man's "No Wrinkles" khaki		33.59	3/01	4c
Women, 16 and over, expenditures on	yr	490	1999	30r
Communications				
Newspaper subscription, daily and Sunday delivery	mos	15.58	3/01	4c
Phone line, single, business, field visit	inst.	59.00	12/97	17s
Phone line, single, business, no field visit	inst.	59.00	12/97	17s
Phone line, single, residence, field visit	inst.	47.00	12/97	17s
Phone line, single, residence, no field visit	inst.	47.00	12/97	17s
Postage and stationery, expenditures on	yr	140	1999	30r
Postal rate, express mail, up to half-pound		12.45	7/01	108r
Postal rate, letter, first class, first ounce		0.34	7/01	108r
Postal rate, letter, two ounces		0.57	7/01	108r
Postal rate, post card		0.21	7/01	108r
Postal rate, priority mail, two pounds		3.95	7/01	108r
Postal rate, priority mail, up to one pound		3.50	7/01	108r
Telephone bill, business, basic rate	mos	47.40	12/97	18c
Telephone bill, family of three	mos	19.07	3/01	4c
Telephone bill, residential, basic rate	mos	13.17	12/97	18c
Telephone services, expenditures on	yr	830	1999	30r
Education				
Board, 4-year private college/university	yr	2250	1996	38s
Board, 4-year public college/university	yr	2425	1996	38s
Education expenditures	yr	583	1999	30r
Room, 4-year private college/university	yr	1987	1996	38s
Room, 4-year public college/university	yr	1931	1996	38s
Total cost, 4-year private college/university	yr	16829	1996	38s
Total cost, 4-year public college/university	yr	7392	1996	38s
Tuition, 2-year public college/university, in state	yr	1937	1996	38s
Tuition, 4-year private college/university, in state	yr	12592	1996	38s
Tuition, 4-year public college/university	yr	3037	1996	38s
Energy and Fuels				
Electricity	500 KWhs	46.59	7/01	11r
Energy, combined forms, 2400 sq ft	mos	120.33	3/01	4c
Energy, exc. electricity, 2400 sq ft	mos	69.59	3/01	4c
Fuel oil #2	gal	1.27	7/01	11r
Fuel oil and other fuels, expenditures on	yr	68	1999	30r
Gas, cooking, winter, 10 therms	mos	10.22	2/96	98c
Gas, cooking, winter, 30 therms	mos	18.65	2/96	98c
Gas, cooking, winter, 50 therms	mos	27.09	2/96	98c
Gas, heating, winter, average use	mos	91.04	2/96	98c
Gas, natural, commercial rate	1000 cf	6.24	11/00	88s
Gas, regular unleaded, cash, self-service	gal	1.39	3/01	4c
Gasoline, unleaded midgrade	gal	1.79	7/01	11r
Gasoline, unleaded premium	gal	1.86	7/01	11r
Gasoline, unleaded regular	gal	1.58	7/01	11r
Natural gas, expenditures on	yr	389	1999	30r
Utility (piped) gas, therm		0.81	7/01	11r
Utility (piped) gas, 40 therms		38.01	7/01	11r
Utility (piped) gas, 100 therms		81.75	7/01	11r
Entertainment				
Bowling, Saturday evening rate	line	3.21	3/01	4c
Entertainment purchases	yr	1984	1999	30r
Fees and admissions paid	yr	444	1999	30r
Monopoly game, Parker Brothers', No. 9	game	11.44	3/01	4c

Indianapolis, IN - continued

Item	Per	Value	Date	Ref.
Entertainment - continued				
Movie, first-run, Saturday, evening	adm.	7.50	3/01	4c
Television, radios, sound equipment, expenditures on	yr	580	1999	30r
Tennis balls, yellow, Wilson or Penn, 3	can	2.72	3/01	4c
Funerals				
Cosmetology, hair, other preparation		178.32	1/99	78r
Embalming		408.19	1/99	78r
Funeral at funeral home		362.13	1/99	78r
Professional service charges		1375.51	1/99	78r
Transfer of remains to funeral home		155.92	1/99	78r
Visitation/viewing		294.38	1/99	78r
Groceries				
Groceries, ACCRA Index		95.50	3/01	4c
Antibiotic ointment, Polysporin	0.5 oz	4.73	3/01	4c
Baby food, strained vegetables or fruit, lowest price	4-4.5 oz	0.44	3/01	4c
Bacon, sliced	lb	3.15	7/01	11r
Bakery products, expenditures on	yr	281	1999	30r
Bananas	lb	0.49	3/01	4c
Bananas	lb	0.48	7/01	11r
Beans, dried, any type, all sizes	lb	0.61	7/01	11r
Beef for stew, boneless	lb	3.08	7/01	11r
Beef or hamburger, ground	lb	1.67	3/01	4c
Beef, expenditures on	yr	217	1999	30r
Bologna, all beef or mixed	lb	2.52	7/01	11r
Bread, white	loaf	0.77	3/01	4c
Bread, white, pan	lb	1.06	7/01	11r
Broccoli	lb	0.91	7/01	11r
Butter, salted, grade AA, stick	lb	3.04	7/01	11r
Butter, yoghurt, cheese, etc, expenditures on	yr	183	1999	30r
Cereals and bakery product purchases	yr	430	1999	30r
Cereals and cereal products, expenditures on	yr	149	1999	30r
Cheese, Kraft grated Parmesan	8 oz	4.00	3/01	4c
Chicken, fresh, whole	lb	1.07	7/01	11r
Chicken, whole fryer	lb	0.90	7/01	4c
Chops, boneless,	lb	3.64	7/01	11r
Chuck roast, U.S. choice, boneless	lb	2.47	7/01	11r
Cigarettes, Winston, Kings	carton	27.88	3/01	4c
Coffee, 100%, ground roast, all sizes	lb	2.69	7/01	11r
Coffee, vacuum-packed	13 oz	2.52	3/01	4c
Cookies, chocolate chip	lb	2.87	7/01	11r
Corn Flakes, Kellogg's or Post Toasties	18 oz	2.03	3/01	4c
Corn, frozen, whole kernel, lowest price	16 oz	1.12	3/01	4c
Dairy product purchases	yr	304	1999	30r
Eggs, expenditures on	yr	26	1999	30r
Eggs, Grade A or AA	dozen	1.08	3/01	4c
Eggs, grade A, large	dozen	0.88	7/01	11r
Fats and oils, expenditures on	yr	75	1999	30r
Fish and seafood, expenditures on	yr	72	1999	30r
Food (excl fruit and vegetables), eaten at home, purchases	yr	887	1999	30r
Food cooked on trips, expenditures on	yr	44	1999	30r
Food purchases	yr	4802	1999	30r
Food purchases, eaten away from home	yr	2069	1999	30r
Food purchases, food eaten at home	yr	2733	1999	30r
Fresh fruits, expenditures on	yr	138	1999	30r
Fresh milk and cream, expenditures on	yr	120	1999	30r
Fresh vegetables, expenditures on	yr	126	1999	30r
Grapefruit	lb	0.66	7/01	11r
Grapes, Thompson, seedless	lb	1.64	7/01	11r
Ground beef, 100% beef	lb	1.64	7/01	11r
Ground beef, lean and extra lean	lb	2.16	7/01	11r
Ground chuck, 100% beef	lb	2.13	7/01	11r
Ham, boneless, excl canned	lb	2.62	7/01	11r
Ice cream, prepackaged, bulk, regular	1/2 gal	3.35	7/01	11r
Lemons	lb	1.19	7/01	11r
Lettuce, iceberg	head	1.12	3/01	4c
Lettuce, iceberg	lb	0.73	7/01	11r
Margarine, Blue Bonnet or Parkay, stick	lb	0.72	3/01	4c
Margarine, soft, tubs	lb	0.89	7/01	11r

Values are in dollars or fractions of dollars. In the column headed *Ref*, references are shown to sources. Each reference is followed by a letter. These refer to the geographical level for which data were reported: s=State, r=Region, and c=City or metro. The abbreviation *ex* is used to mean *except* or *excluding*; *exp* stands for *expenditures*. For other abbreviations and further explanations, please see the Introduction.

Indianapolis, IN - continued

Item	Per	Value	Date	Ref.
Groceries				
Meats, poultry, fish, and egg purchases	yr	671	1999	30r
Milk, fresh, whole, fortified	gal	2.71	7/01	11r
Milk, whole	1/2 gal	1.73	3/01	4c
Nonalcoholic beverages, expenditures on	yr	239	1999	30r
Orange juice, Minute Maid frozen	12 oz	1.71	3/01	4c
Oranges, Navel	lb	0.80	7/01	11r
Oranges, Valencia	lb	0.66	7/01	11r
Peaches, halves or slices, Hunt's, Del Monte, or Libby's	29 oz	1.58	3/01	4c
Pears, Anjou	lb	0.93	7/01	11r
Peas, green, Del Monte or Green Giant	15 oz	0.71	3/01	4c
Pork chops, center cut, bone-in	lb	3.63	7/01	11r
Pork, expenditures on	yr	150	1999	30r
Potato chips	16 oz	3.52	7/01	11r
Potatoes, frozen, french fried	lb	1.08	7/01	11r
Potatoes, white or red	10 lb	2.52	3/01	4c
Potatoes, white, all types	lb	0.33	7/01	11r
Poultry, expenditures on	yr	108	1999	30r
Processed fruits, expenditures on	yr	98	1999	30r
Processed vegetables, expenditures on	yr	80	1999	30r
Round roast, U.S. choice, boneless	lb	3.07	7/01	11r
Round steak, graded and ungraded, excl U.S. prime and choice	lb	3.41	7/01	11r
Sausage, Jimmy Dean/Owens pork	lb	3.15	3/01	4c
Shortening, vegetable oil blends	lb	1.13	7/01	11r
Shortening, vegetable, Crisco	3 lb	2.57	3/01	4c
Soft drink, Coca Cola, ex deposit	2 liter	1.13	3/01	4c
Spaghetti and macaroni	lb	0.80	7/01	11r
Steak, round, U.S. choice, boneless	lb	3.23	7/01	11r
Steak, T-bone	lb	6.28	3/01	4c
Steak, T-bone, U.S. choice, bone-in	lb	6.68	7/01	11r
Strawberries, dry pint	12 oz	1.32	7/01	11r
Sugar and other sweets, expenditures on	yr	114	1999	30r
Sugar, cane or beet	4 lbs	1.40	3/01	4c
Sugar, white, 33-80 ounce package	lb	0.42	7/01	11r
Sugar, white, all sizes	lb	0.43	7/01	11r
Tobacco products and smoking supplies purchases	yr	331	1999	30r
Tomatoes, field grown	lb	1.46	7/01	11r
Tomatoes, Hunt's or Del Monte	14.5 oz	0.93	3/01	4c
Tuna, chunk, light	6 oz	0.53	3/01	4c
Tuna, light, chunk	lb	1.80	7/01	11r
Turkey, frozen, whole	lb	1.15	7/01	11r
Goods and Services				
Miscellaneous goods and services, ACCRA Index		95.70	3/01	4c
B&B Japanese maple (acer japonicum)	gal	29.99-169.99	4/00	93r
Boxwood (buxus)	2 gal	18.99-39.99	4/00	93r
Daylilly (hemerocallis)	gal	4.99-25.00	4/00	93r
Flat of annuals		11.98-24.99	4/00	93r
Fountain grass (pennisetum)	gal	5.98-12.98	4/00	93r
Hanging basket (10 in)		12.99-27.99	4/00	93r
Hardy geranium (geranium)	gal	7.99-9.99	4/00	93r
Hosta (hosta)	gal	6.00-25.00	4/00	93r
Lilac (syrubga vulgaris)	2 gal	14.99-24.99	4/00	93r
Miscellaneous purchases	yr	865	1999	30r
Rhododendron (rhododendron)	2 gal	23.98-42.99	4/00	93r
Sage (salvia)	gal	6.00-9.99	4/00	93r
Wintercreeper euonymus (euonymus fortunei)	2 gal	16.00-169.99	4/00	93r
Hunting license	yr	8.75	4/01	34s

Indianapolis, IN - continued

Item	Per	Value	Date	Ref.
Health Care				
Health care, ACCRA Index		98.60	3/01	4c
Cardiac catheterization, ave hospital/ physician charges		13380	1998	77s
Childbirth, Cesarean delivery		10722	1997	13r
Childbirth, vaginal delivery		6223	1997	13r
Dentist's fee, adult teeth cleaning and periodic oral exam	visit	69.80	3/01	4c
Doctor's fee, routine exam, established patient	visit	59.60	3/01	4c
Drugs, expenditures on	yr	394	1999	30r
Health care purchases	yr	2048	1999	30r
Health insurance expenditures	yr	978	1999	30r
Home health care aide cost, licensed agency	hour	17	2000	82c
Hospital care, private room	day	489.50	3/01	4c
Hysterectomy, laproscopically-assisted, ave hospital/physician charges		11310	1998	76s
Hysterectomy, vaginal, ave hospital and physician charges		9160	1998	76s
Medicaid dispensing fee		4.00	1999	87s
Medical services expenditures	yr	554	1999	30r
Medical supplies, expenditures on	yr	122	1999	30r
Nursing home costs, private room	day	161	2000	82c
Nursing home stay, private room	day	161	2000	83c
Plastic surgery, breast augmentation		3184	2000	7r
Plastic surgery, breast lift		3585	2000	7r
Plastic surgery, facelift		4999	2000	7r
Plastic surgery, hair transplantation		3105	2000	7r
Plastic surgery, lip augmentation		1290	2000	7r
Plastic surgery, lower body lift		8135	2000	7r
Plastic surgery, thigh lift		3839	2000	7r
Household Goods				
Dishwashing powder, Cascade	50 oz	3.16	3/01	4c
Floor coverings, expenditures on	yr	52	1999	30r
Furniture, expenditures on	yr	344	1999	30r
Household furnishings and equipment purchases	yr	1475	1999	30r
Household textiles, expenditures on	yr	109	1999	30r
Laundry and cleaning supplies, expenditures on	yr	134	1999	30r
Tissues, facial, Kleenex brand	175	1.27	3/01	4c
Housing				
Housing, ACCRA Index		96.90	3/01	4c
Home, 2200 sq ft, 4-br, 2-bath, 2-car garage, average		155222	2000	47c
Home price, existing, ave		144400	10/00	90r
Home value, median		102000	2001	53s
House, 2400 sq ft, 8000 sq ft lot, new, urban, utilities	total	204661	3/01	4c
House payment, principal and interest, 25% down payment	mos	1000	3/01	4c
Household operation expenditures	yr	542	1999	30r
Housekeeping supplies purchases	yr	508	1999	30r
Lodging expenditures	yr	430	1999	30r
Maintenance, repairs, insurance expenditures	yr	853	1999	30r
Monthly rental value of owned home	mos	547	1999	30r
Owned dwellings, expenditures own	yr	4282	1999	30r
Rent expenditures	yr	1558	1999	30r
Rent, apartment, 2 br, 1 1/2-2 baths, unfurn, 950 sq ft, water	mos	670	3/01	4c
Rental unit, 1 bedroom, with utilities	mos	465	4/01	41c
Rental unit, 2 bedroom, with utilities	mos	559	4/01	41c
Rental unit, 3 bedroom, with utilities	mos	700	4/01	41c
Rental unit, 4 bedroom, with utilities	mos	785	4/01	41c
Shelter, expenditures on	yr	6270	1999	30r
Insurance and Pensions				
Life and other personal insurance purchases	yr	387	1999	30r
Pensions and Social Security, expenditures on	yr	2968	1999	30r

Values are in dollars or fractions of dollars. In the column headed *Ref*, references are shown to sources. Each reference is followed by a letter. These refer to the geographical level for which data were reported: s=State, r=Region, and c=City or metro. The abbreviation *ex* is used to mean *except* or *excluding*; *exp* stands for *expenditures*. For other abbreviations and further explanations, please see the Introduction.

Indianapolis, IN - continued

Item	Per	Value	Date	Ref.
Legal Fees				
Divorce, filing fee		100.00	4/01	35s
Driver's license fee	renew	6.00	1999	48s
Driver's license fee	orig	6.00	1999	48s
Personal Goods				
Personal care products and services purchases	yr	385	1999	30r
Shampoo, Alberto VO5	15 oz	0.98	3/01	4c
Toothpaste, Crest or Colgate	6-7 oz	1.90	3/01	4c
Personal Services				
Detective service, finding a missing person	hour	45	1999	22c
Dry cleaning, man's 2-pc suit		8.36	3/01	4c
Man's haircut, barbershop, no styling		11.10	3/01	4c
Personal services, household, expenditures on	yr	300	1999	30r
Woman's shampoo, trim, blow-dry, no style-change		25.90	3/01	4c
Pets				
Pets, toys, and playground equipment, expenditures on	yr	375	1999	30r
Restaurant Food				
Chicken, fried, thigh and drumstick, KFC/Church's		2.39	3/01	4c
Hamburger with cheese, McDonald's	1/4 lb	2.13	3/01	4c
Pizza, Pizza Hut or Pizza Inn	11-12 in	9.29	3/01	4c
Taxes				
Federal income taxes paid	yr	2326	1999	30r
Personal taxes, expenditures on	yr	3223	1999	30r
Property taxes paid	yr	1152	1999	30r
State and local income taxes paid	yr	753	1999	30r
Transportation				
Transportation, ACCRA Index		93.30	3/01	4c
Bus fare, one-way	trip	1.00	2000	1c
Cars and trucks, new, expenditures on	yr	1280	1999	30r
Cars and trucks, used, expenditures on	yr	1763	1999	30r
Diesel at the pump	gal	1.17	10/99	73s
Gasoline and motor oil purchases	yr	1036	1999	30r
Gasoline before-tax price (cents)	gal	110.00	10/00	43s
Maintenance and repair expenditures	yr	594	1999	30r
Public transportation, expenditures on	yr	341	1999	30r
Tire balance, computer or spin balance, front	wheel	6.80	3/01	4c
Transportation purchases	yr	6617	1999	30r
Vehicle expenses, miscellaneous, purchases	yr	2159	1999	30r
Vehicle insurance payments	yr	701	1999	30r
Vehicle purchases (net outlay)	yr	3081	1999	30r
Vehicle rental, lease expenditures	yr	536	1999	30r
Utilities				
Utilities, ACCRA Index		97.10	3/01	4c
Electrical bill, average	mos	66.66	9/00	9s
Electricity, expenditures on	yr	841	1999	30r
Electricity, summer, 250 KWh	mos	22.46	2/96	97c
Electricity, summer, 500 KWh	mos	42.52	2/96	97c
Electricity, summer, 750 KWh	mos	52.68	2/96	97c
Electricity, summer, 1000 KWh	mos	62.84	2/96	97c
Electricity and other, mixed, 2400 sq ft, new home	mos	50.74	3/01	4c
Electricity cost, average	KWh	5.00	9/00	9s
Utilities, fuels, and public services purchased	yr	2401	1999	30r
Water and other public services, expenditures on	yr	273	1999	30r
Weddings				
Wedding (national average cost)		19936	2000	33r
Wedding (regional average total cost)		16195	1997	110r
Attendants' gifts		321	1998	33r
Bridal attendants' apparel (5 persons)		824	2000	33r
Bride's headpiece/veil		173	1998	33r
Bride's wedding dress		859	1998	33r
Clergy, religious facility fee		242	1998	33r
Engagement ring		3177	1998	33r

Indianapolis, IN - continued

Item	Per	Value	Date	Ref.
Weddings - continued				
Flowers		789	1998	33r
Groom's formalwear rental		99	2000	33r
Limousine		410	1998	33r
Marriage license cost		18.00	4/01	35s
Men's formalwear (ushers, best man)		469	2000	33r
Mother of bride apparel		241	2000	33r
Music		866	1998	33r
Photography and videography		1368	1998	33r
Rehearsal dinner		728	1998	33r
Wedding invitations and announcements		341	1998	33r
Wedding reception		7968	2000	33r
Wedding rings (bride and groom)		1060	1998	33r

Iowa City, IA

Item	Per	Value	Date	Ref.
Average annual expenditures	yr	35369	1999	30r
Alcoholic Beverages				
Alcoholic beverage purchases	yr	304	1999	30r
Malt beverages, all types, all sizes, any origin	16 oz	0.93	7/01	11r
Wine, red and white table, all sizes, any origin	liter	7.04	7/01	11r
Appliances				
Major appliances, expenditures on	yr	165	1999	30r
Small appliances, housewares, expenditures on	yr	90	1999	30r
Banking and Money				
Mortgage interest and charges paid	yr	2277	1999	30r
Mortgage principal paid on owned property	yr	1230	1999	30r
Vehicle finance charges paid	yr	328	1999	30r
Charity				
Cash contributions, expenditures	yr	1126	1999	30r
Child Care				
Child raising cost, total, age 0-2	yr	7890	1999	60r
Child raising cost, total, age 3-5	yr	8130	1999	60r
Child raising cost, total, age 6-8	yr	8170	1999	60r
Child raising cost, total, age 9-11	yr	8190	1999	60r
Child raising cost, total, age 12-14	yr	8890	1999	60r
Child raising cost, total, age 15-17	yr	9050	1999	60r
Child's child care and education, age 0-2	yr	1240	1999	60r
Child's child care and education, age 3-5	yr	1370	1999	60r
Child's child care and education, age 6-8	yr	880	1999	60r
Child's child care and education, age 9-11	yr	570	1999	60r
Child's child care and education, age 12-14	yr	420	1999	60r
Child's child care and education, age 15-17	yr	720	1999	60r
Child's clothing, age 0-2	yr	410	1999	60r
Child's clothing, age 3-5	yr	400	1999	60r
Child's clothing, age 6-8	yr	450	1999	60r
Child's clothing, age 9-11	yr	500	1999	60r
Child's clothing, age 12-14	yr	840	1999	60r
Child's clothing, age 15-17	yr	740	1999	60r
Child's food, age 0-2	yr	960	1999	60r
Child's food, age 3-5	yr	1120	1999	60r
Child's food, age 6-8	yr	1430	1999	60r
Child's food, age 9-11	yr	1710	1999	60r
Child's food, age 12-14	yr	1710	1999	60r
Child's food, age 15-17	yr	1920	1999	60r
Child's health care, age 0-2	yr	520	1999	60r
Child's health care, age 3-5	yr	500	1999	60r
Child's health care, age 6-8	yr	570	1999	60r
Child's health care, age 9-11	yr	610	1999	60r
Child's health care, age 12-14	yr	630	1999	60r
Child's health care, age 15-17	yr	650	1999	60r
Child's housing, age 0-2	yr	2860	1999	60r
Child's housing, age 3-5	yr	2840	1999	60r
Child's housing, age 6-8	yr	2800	1999	60r
Child's housing, age 9-11	yr	2650	1999	60r
Child's housing, age 12-14	yr	2840	1999	60r
Child's housing, age 15-17	yr	2440	1999	60r
Child's personal care, reading, age 0-2	yr	880	1999	60r

Values are in dollars or fractions of dollars. In the column headed *Ref*, references are shown to sources. Each reference is followed by a letter. These refer to the geographical level for which data were reported: s=State, r=Region, and c=City or metro. The abbreviation *ex* is used to mean *except* or *excluding*; *exp* stands for *expenditures*. For other abbreviations and further explanations, please see the Introduction.

Iowa City, IA - continued

Item	Per	Value	Date	Ref.
Child Care				
Child's personal care, reading, age 3-5	yr	900	1999	60r
Child's personal care, reading, age 6-8	yr	930	1999	60r
Child's personal care, reading, age 9-11	yr	970	1999	60r
Child's personal care, reading, age 12-14	yr	1150	1999	60r
Child's personal care, reading, age 15-17	yr	920	1999	60r
Clothing				
Apparel and services purchases	yr	1607	1999	30r
Boys, 2 to 15, expenditures on	yr	91	1999	30r
Children under 2, expenditures on	yr	59	1999	30r
Footwear, expenditures on	yr	285	1999	30r
Girls, 2 to 15, expenditures on	yr	116	1999	30r
Men and boys, expenditures on	yr	433	1999	30r
Men, 16 and over, expenditures on	yr	341	1999	30r
Women, 16 and over, expenditures on	yr	490	1999	30r
Communications				
Phone line, single, business, field visit	inst.	50.00	12/97	17s
Phone line, single, business, no field visit	inst.	50.00	12/97	17s
Phone line, single, residence, field visit	inst.	35.00	12/97	17s
Phone line, single, residence, no field visit	inst.	35.00	12/97	17s
Postage and stationery, expenditures on	yr	140	1999	30r
Postal rate, express mail, up to half-pound		12.45	7/01	108r
Postal rate, letter, first class, first ounce		0.34	7/01	108r
Postal rate, letter, two ounces		0.57	7/01	108r
Postal rate, post card		0.21	7/01	108r
Postal rate, priority mail, two pounds		3.95	7/01	108r
Postal rate, priority mail, up to one pound		3.50	7/01	108r
Telephone services, expenditures on	yr	830	1999	30r
Education				
Board, 4-year private college/university	yr	2138	1996	38s
Board, 4-year public college/university	yr	1688	1996	38s
Education expenditures	yr	583	1999	30r
Room, 4-year private college/university	yr	1864	1996	38s
Room, 4-year public college/university	yr	1693	1996	38s
Total cost, 4-year private college/university	yr	15934	1996	38s
Total cost, 4-year public college/university	yr	5945	1996	38s
Tuition, 2-year public college/university, in state	yr	1782	1996	38s
Tuition, 4-year private college/university, in state	yr	11932	1996	38s
Tuition, 4-year public college/university	yr	2565	1996	38s
Energy and Fuels				
Electricity	500 KWhs	46.59	7/01	11r
Fuel oil #2	gal	1.27	7/01	11r
Fuel oil and other fuels, expenditures on	yr	68	1999	30r
Gas, natural, commercial rate	1000 cf	7.18	11/00	88s
Gasoline, unleaded midgrade	gal	1.79	7/01	11r
Gasoline, unleaded premium	gal	1.86	7/01	11r
Gasoline, unleaded regular	gal	1.58	7/01	11r
Natural gas, expenditures on	yr	389	1999	30r
Utility (piped) gas, therm		0.81	7/01	11r
Utility (piped) gas, 40 therms		38.01	7/01	11r
Utility (piped) gas, 100 therms		81.75	7/01	11r
Entertainment				
Entertainment purchases	yr	1984	1999	30r
Fees and admissions paid	yr	444	1999	30r
Television, radios, sound equipment, expenditures on	yr	580	1999	30r
Funerals				
Cosmetology, hair, other preparation		178.32	1/99	78r
Embalming		408.19	1/99	78r
Funeral at funeral home		362.13	1/99	78r
Professional service charges		1375.51	1/99	78r
Transfer of remains to funeral home		155.92	1/99	78r
Visitation/viewing		294.38	1/99	78r
Groceries				
Bacon, sliced	lb	3.15	7/01	11r
Bakery products, expenditures on	yr	281	1999	30r

Iowa City, IA - continued

Item	Per	Value	Date	Ref.
Groceries - continued				
Bananas	lb	0.48	7/01	11r
Beans, dried, any type, all sizes	lb	0.61	7/01	11r
Beef for stew, boneless	lb	3.08	7/01	11r
Beef, expenditures on	yr	217	1999	30r
Bologna, all beef or mixed	lb	2.52	7/01	11r
Bread, white, pan	lb	1.06	7/01	11r
Broccoli	lb	0.91	7/01	11r
Butter, salted, grade AA, stick	lb	3.04	7/01	11r
Butter, yoghurt, cheese, etc, expenditures on	yr	183	1999	30r
Cereals and bakery product purchases	yr	430	1999	30r
Cereals and cereal products, expenditures on	yr	149	1999	30r
Chicken, fresh, whole	lb	1.07	7/01	11r
Chops, boneless,	lb	3.64	7/01	11r
Chuck roast, U.S. choice, boneless	lb	2.47	7/01	11r
Coffee, 100%, ground roast, all sizes	lb	2.69	7/01	11r
Cookies, chocolate chip	lb	2.87	7/01	11r
Dairy product purchases	yr	304	1999	30r
Eggs, expenditures on	yr	26	1999	30r
Eggs, grade A, large	dozen	0.88	7/01	11r
Fats and oils, expenditures on	yr	75	1999	30r
Fish and seafood, expenditures on	yr	72	1999	30r
Food (excl fruit and vegetables), eaten at home, purchases	yr	887	1999	30r
Food cooked on trips, expenditures on	yr	44	1999	30r
Food purchases	yr	4802	1999	30r
Food purchases, eaten away from home	yr	2069	1999	30r
Food purchases, food eaten at home	yr	2733	1999	30r
Fresh fruits, expenditures on	yr	138	1999	30r
Fresh milk and cream, expenditures on	yr	120	1999	30r
Fresh vegetables, expenditures on	yr	126	1999	30r
Grapefruit	lb	0.66	7/01	11r
Grapes, Thompson, seedless	lb	1.64	7/01	11r
Ground beef, 100% beef	lb	1.64	7/01	11r
Ground beef, lean and extra lean	lb	2.16	7/01	11r
Ground chuck, 100% beef	lb	2.13	7/01	11r
Ham, boneless, excl canned	lb	2.62	7/01	11r
Ice cream, prepackaged, bulk, regular	1/2 gal	3.35	7/01	11r
Lemons	lb	1.19	7/01	11r
Lettuce, iceberg	lb	0.73	7/01	11r
Margarine, soft, tubs	lb	0.89	7/01	11r
Meats, poultry, fish, and egg purchases	yr	671	1999	30r
Milk, fresh, whole, fortified	gal	2.71	7/01	11r
Nonalcoholic beverages, expenditures on	yr	239	1999	30r
Oranges, Navel	lb	0.80	7/01	11r
Oranges, Valencia	lb	0.66	7/01	11r
Pears, Anjou	lb	0.93	7/01	11r
Pork chops, center cut, bone-in	lb	3.63	7/01	11r
Pork, expenditures on	yr	150	1999	30r
Potato chips	16 oz	3.52	7/01	11r
Potatoes, frozen, french fried	lb	1.08	7/01	11r
Potatoes, white, all types	lb	0.33	7/01	11r
Poultry, expenditures on	yr	108	1999	30r
Processed fruits, expenditures on	yr	98	1999	30r
Processed vegetables, expenditures on	yr	80	1999	30r
Round roast, U.S. choice, boneless	lb	3.07	7/01	11r
Round steak, graded and ungraded, excl U.S. prime and choice	lb	3.41	7/01	11r
Shortening, vegetable oil blends	lb	1.13	7/01	11r
Spaghetti and macaroni	lb	0.80	7/01	11r
Steak, round, U.S. choice, boneless	lb	3.23	7/01	11r
Steak, T-bone, U.S. choice, bone-in	lb	6.68	7/01	11r
Strawberries, dry pint	12 oz	1.32	7/01	11r
Sugar and other sweets, expenditures on	yr	114	1999	30r
Sugar, white, 33-80 ounce package	lb	0.42	7/01	11r
Sugar, white, all sizes	lb	0.43	7/01	11r
Tobacco products and smoking supplies purchases	yr	331	1999	30r
Tomatoes, field grown	lb	1.46	7/01	11r
Tuna, light, chunk	lb	1.80	7/01	11r
Turkey, frozen, whole	lb	1.15	7/01	11r

Values are in dollars or fractions of dollars. In the column headed *Ref*, references are shown to sources. Each reference is followed by a letter. These refer to the geographical level for which data were reported: s=State, r=Region, and c=City or metro. The abbreviation *ex* is used to mean *except* or *excluding*; *exp* stands for expenditures. For other abbreviations and further explanations, please see the Introduction.

Iowa City, IA - continued

Item	Per	Value	Date	Ref.
Goods and Services				
B&B Japanese maple (acer japonicum)	gal	29.99-169.99	4/00	93r
Boxwood (buxus)	2 gal	18.99-39.99	4/00	93r
Daylilly (hemerocallis)	gal	4.99-25.00	4/00	93r
Flat of annuals		11.98-24.99	4/00	93r
Fountain grass (pennisetum)	gal	5.98-12.98	4/00	93r
Hanging basket (10 in)		12.99-27.99	4/00	93r
Hardy geranium (geranium)	gal	7.99-9.99	4/00	93r
Hosta (hosta)	gal	6.00-25.00	4/00	93r
Lilac (syrubga vulgaris)	2 gal	14.99-24.99	4/00	93r
Miscellaneous purchases	yr	865	1999	30r
Rhododendron (rhododendron)	2 gal	23.98-42.99	4/00	93r
Sage (salvia)	gal	6.00-9.99	4/00	93r
Wintercreeper euonymus (euonymus fortunei)	2 gal	16.00-169.99	4/00	93r
Hunting license	yr	16.00	4/01	34s
Health Care				
Cardiac catheterization, ave hospital/physician charges		8810	1998	77s
Childbirth, Cesarean delivery		10722	1997	13r
Childbirth, vaginal delivery		6223	1997	13r
Drugs, expenditures on	yr	394	1999	30r
Health care purchases	yr	2048	1999	30r
Health insurance expenditures	yr	978	1999	30r
Hysterectomy, laproscopically-assisted, ave hospital/physician charges		8620	1998	76s
Hysterectomy, vaginal, ave hospital and physician charges		6630	1998	76s
Medicaid dispensing fee		4.10-6.38	1999	87s
Medical services expenditures	yr	554	1999	30r
Medical supplies, expenditures on	yr	122	1999	30r
Plastic surgery, breast augmentation		3184	2000	7r
Plastic surgery, breast lift		3585	2000	7r
Plastic surgery, facelift		4999	2000	7r
Plastic surgery, hair transplantation		3105	2000	7r
Plastic surgery, lip augmentation		1290	2000	7r
Plastic surgery, lower body lift		8135	2000	7r
Plastic surgery, thigh lift		3839	2000	7r
Household Goods				
Floor coverings, expenditures on	yr	52	1999	30r
Furniture, expenditures on	yr	344	1999	30r
Household furnishings and equipment purchases	yr	1475	1999	30r
Household textiles, expenditures on	yr	109	1999	30r
Laundry and cleaning supplies, expenditures on	yr	134	1999	30r
Housing				
Home price, existing, ave		144400	10/00	90r
Home value, median		100000	2001	53s
Household operation expenditures	yr	542	1999	30r
Housekeeping supplies purchases	yr	508	1999	30r
Lodging expenditures	yr	430	1999	30r
Maintenance, repairs, insurance expenditures	yr	853	1999	30r
Monthly rental value of owned home	mos	547	1999	30r
Owned dwellings, expenditures own	yr	4282	1999	30r
Rent expenditures	yr	1558	1999	30r
Rental unit, 1 bedroom, with utilities	mos	452	4/01	41c
Rental unit, 2 bedroom, with utilities	mos	582	4/01	41c
Rental unit, 3 bedroom, with utilities	mos	807	4/01	41c

Iowa City, IA - continued

Item	Per	Value	Date	Ref.
Housing - continued				
Rental unit, 4 bedroom, with utilities	mos	954	4/01	41c
Shelter, expenditures on	yr	6270	1999	30r
Insurance and Pensions				
Auto insurance premium	yr	520.76	1999	57s
Life and other personal insurance purchases	yr	387	1999	30r
Pensions and Social Security, expenditures on	yr	2968	1999	30r
Legal Fees				
Divorce, filing fee		110.00	4/01	35s
Driver's license fee	orig	16.00	1999	48s
Driver's license fee	renew	16.00	1999	48s
Personal Goods				
Personal care products and services purchases	yr	385	1999	30r
Personal Services				
Personal services, household, expenditures on	yr	300	1999	30r
Pets				
Pets, toys, and playground equipment, expenditures on	yr	375	1999	30r
Taxes				
Federal income taxes paid	yr	2326	1999	30r
Personal taxes, expenditures on	yr	3223	1999	30r
Property taxes paid	yr	1152	1999	30r
State and local income taxes paid	yr	753	1999	30r
Transportation				
Bus fare, one-way	trip	0.75	2000	1c
Cars and trucks, new, expenditures on	yr	1280	1999	30r
Cars and trucks, used, expenditures on	yr	1763	1999	30r
Diesel at the pump	gal	1.25	10/99	73s
Gasoline and motor oil purchases	yr	1036	1999	30r
Gasoline before-tax price (cents)	gal	112.30	10/00	43s
Maintenance and repair expenditures	yr	594	1999	30r
Public transportation, expenditures on	yr	341	1999	30r
Transportation purchases	yr	6617	1999	30r
Vehicle expenses, miscellaneous, purchases	yr	2159	1999	30r
Vehicle insurance payments	yr	701	1999	30r
Vehicle purchases (net outlay)	yr	3081	1999	30r
Vehicle rental, lease expenditures	yr	536	1999	30r
Utilities				
Electrical bill, average	mos	67.25	9/00	9s
Electricity, expenditures on	yr	841	1999	30r
Electricity cost, average	KWh	5.90	9/00	9s
Utilities, fuels, and public services purchased	yr	2401	1999	30r
Water and other public services, expenditures on	yr	273	1999	30r
Weddings				
Wedding (national average cost)		19936	2000	33r
Wedding (regional average total cost)		16195	1997	110r
Attendants' gifts		321	1998	33r
Bridal attendants' apparel (5 persons)		824	2000	33r
Bride's headpiece/veil		173	1998	33r
Bride's wedding dress		859	1998	33r
Clergy, religious facility fee		242	1998	33r
Engagement ring		3177	1998	33r
Flowers		789	1998	33r
Groom's formalwear rental		99	2000	33r
Limousine		410	1998	33r
Marriage license cost		30.00	4/01	35s
Men's formalwear (ushers, best man)		469	2000	33r
Mother of bride apparel		241	2000	33r
Music		866	1998	33r
Photography and videography		1368	1998	33r
Rehearsal dinner		728	1998	33r
Wedding invitations and announcements		341	1998	33r
Wedding reception		7968	2000	33r
Wedding rings (bride and groom)		1060	1998	33r

Values are in dollars or fractions of dollars. In the column headed *Ref*, references are shown to sources. Each reference is followed by a letter. These refer to the geographical level for which data were reported: s=State, r=Region, and c=City or metro. The abbreviation *ex* is used to mean *except* or *excluding*; *exp* stands for *expenditures*. For other abbreviations and further explanations, please see the Introduction.

Jackson, MI

Item	Per	Value	Date	Ref.
Average annual expenditures	yr	35369	1999	30r
Alcoholic Beverages				
Alcoholic beverage purchases	yr	304	1999	30r
Malt beverages, all types, all sizes, any origin	16 oz	0.93	7/01	11r
Wine, red and white table, all sizes, any origin	liter	7.04	7/01	11r
Appliances				
Major appliances, expenditures on	yr	165	1999	30r
Small appliances, housewares, expenditures on	yr	90	1999	30r
Banking and Money				
Mortgage interest and charges paid	yr	2277	1999	30r
Mortgage principal paid on owned property	yr	1230	1999	30r
Vehicle finance charges paid	yr	328	1999	30r
Charity				
Cash contributions, expenditures	yr	1126	1999	30r
Child Care				
Child raising cost, total, age 0-2	yr	7890	1999	60r
Child raising cost, total, age 3-5	yr	8130	1999	60r
Child raising cost, total, age 6-8	yr	8170	1999	60r
Child raising cost, total, age 9-11	yr	8190	1999	60r
Child raising cost, total, age 12-14	yr	8890	1999	60r
Child raising cost, total, age 15-17	yr	9050	1999	60r
Child's child care and education, age 0-2	yr	1240	1999	60r
Child's child care and education, age 3-5	yr	1370	1999	60r
Child's child care and education, age 6-8	yr	880	1999	60r
Child's child care and education, age 9-11	yr	570	1999	60r
Child's child care and education, age 12-14	yr	420	1999	60r
Child's child care and education, age 15-17	yr	720	1999	60r
Child's clothing, age 0-2	yr	410	1999	60r
Child's clothing, age 3-5	yr	400	1999	60r
Child's clothing, age 6-8	yr	450	1999	60r
Child's clothing, age 9-11	yr	500	1999	60r
Child's clothing, age 12-14	yr	840	1999	60r
Child's clothing, age 15-17	yr	740	1999	60r
Child's food, age 0-2	yr	960	1999	60r
Child's food, age 3-5	yr	1120	1999	60r
Child's food, age 6-8	yr	1430	1999	60r
Child's food, age 9-11	yr	1710	1999	60r
Child's food, age 12-14	yr	1710	1999	60r
Child's food, age 15-17	yr	1920	1999	60r
Child's health care, age 0-2	yr	520	1999	60r
Child's health care, age 3-5	yr	500	1999	60r
Child's health care, age 6-8	yr	570	1999	60r
Child's health care, age 9-11	yr	610	1999	60r
Child's health care, age 12-14	yr	630	1999	60r
Child's health care, age 15-17	yr	650	1999	60r
Child's housing, age 0-2	yr	2860	1999	60r
Child's housing, age 3-5	yr	2840	1999	60r
Child's housing, age 6-8	yr	2800	1999	60r
Child's housing, age 9-11	yr	2650	1999	60r
Child's housing, age 12-14	yr	2840	1999	60r
Child's housing, age 15-17	yr	2440	1999	60r
Child's personal care, reading, age 0-2	yr	880	1999	60r
Child's personal care, reading, age 3-5	yr	900	1999	60r
Child's personal care, reading, age 6-8	yr	930	1999	60r
Child's personal care, reading, age 9-11	yr	970	1999	60r
Child's personal care, reading, age 12-14	yr	1150	1999	60r
Child's personal care, reading, age 15-17	yr	920	1999	60r
Clothing				
Apparel and services purchases	yr	1607	1999	30r
Boys, 2 to 15, expenditures on	yr	91	1999	30r
Children under 2, expenditures on	yr	59	1999	30r
Footwear, expenditures on	yr	285	1999	30r
Girls, 2 to 15, expenditures on	yr	116	1999	30r
Men and boys, expenditures on	yr	433	1999	30r
Men, 16 and over, expenditures on	yr	341	1999	30r
Women, 16 and over, expenditures on	yr	490	1999	30r

Jackson, MI - continued

Item	Per	Value	Date	Ref.
Communications				
Cable modem installation, Bresnan		99.95	6/99	103s
Cable modem installation, Comcast		95.00	6/99	103s
Cable modem installation, Media One		100.00	6/99	103s
Cable modem rate, cable subscriber, Bresnan	mos	39.95	6/99	103s
Cable modem rate, cable subscriber, Comcast	mos	39.95	6/99	103s
Cable modem rate, cable subscriber, Media One	mos	34.95-39.95	6/99	103s
Cable modem rate, non-cable subscriber, Bresnan	mos	49.95	6/99	103s
Cable modem rate, non-cable subscriber, Comcast	mos	49.95	6/99	103s
Cable modem rate, non-cable subscriber, Media One	mos	49.95	6/99	103s
Phone line, single, business, field visit	inst.	42.00	12/97	17s
Phone line, single, business, no field visit	inst.	42.00	12/97	17s
Phone line, single, residence, field visit	inst.	42.00	12/97	17s
Phone line, single, residence, no field visit	inst.	42.00	12/97	17s
Postage and stationery, expenditures on	yr	140	1999	30r
Postal rate, express mail, up to half-pound		12.45	7/01	108r
Postal rate, letter, first class, first ounce		0.34	7/01	108r
Postal rate, letter, two ounces		0.57	7/01	108r
Postal rate, post card		0.21	7/01	108r
Postal rate, priority mail, two pounds		3.95	7/01	108r
Postal rate, priority mail, up to one pound		3.50	7/01	108r
Telephone services, expenditures on	yr	830	1999	30r
Education				
Board, 4-year private college/university	yr	2182	1996	38s
Board, 4-year public college/university	yr	2276	1996	38s
Education expenditures	yr	583	1999	30r
Room, 4-year private college/university	yr	1974	1996	38s
Room, 4-year public college/university	yr	2024	1996	38s
Total cost, 4-year private college/university	yr	13331	1996	38s
Total cost, 4-year public college/university	yr	8195	1996	38s
Tuition, 2-year public college/university, in state	yr	1529	1996	38s
Tuition, 4-year private college/university, in state	yr	9176	1996	38s
Tuition, 4-year public college/university	yr	3895	1996	38s
Energy and Fuels				
Electricity	500 KWhs	46.59	7/01	11r
Fuel oil #2	gal	1.27	7/01	11r
Fuel oil and other fuels, expenditures on	yr	68	1999	30r
Gas, natural, commercial rate	1000 cf	4.91	11/00	88s
Gasoline, unleaded midgrade	gal	1.79	7/01	11r
Gasoline, unleaded premium	gal	1.86	7/01	11r
Gasoline, unleaded regular	gal	1.58	7/01	11r
Natural gas, expenditures on	yr	389	1999	30r
Utility (piped) gas, therm		0.81	7/01	11r
Utility (piped) gas, 40 therms		38.01	7/01	11r
Utility (piped) gas, 100 therms		81.75	7/01	11r
Entertainment				
Entertainment purchases	yr	1984	1999	30r
Fees and admissions paid	yr	444	1999	30r
Television, radios, sound equipment, expenditures on	yr	580	1999	30r
Funerals				
Cosmetology, hair, other preparation		178.32	1/99	78r
Embalming		408.19	1/99	78r
Funeral at funeral home		362.13	1/99	78r
Professional service charges		1375.51	1/99	78r
Transfer of remains to funeral home		155.92	1/99	78r
Visitation/viewing		294.38	1/99	78r
Groceries				
Bacon, sliced	lb	3.15	7/01	11r
Bakery products, expenditures on	yr	281	1999	30r
Bananas	lb	0.48	7/01	11r

Values are in dollars or fractions of dollars. In the column headed *Ref*, references are shown to sources. Each reference is followed by a letter. These refer to the geographical level for which data were reported: s=State, r=Region, and c=City or metro. The abbreviation *ex* is used to mean *except* or *excluding*; *exp* stands for expenditures. For other abbreviations and further explanations, please see the Introduction.

Jackson, MI - continued

Item	Per	Value	Date	Ref.
Groceries				
Beans, dried, any type, all sizes	lb	0.61	7/01	11r
Beef for stew, boneless	lb	3.08	7/01	11r
Beef, expenditures on	yr	217	1999	30r
Bologna, all beef or mixed	lb	2.52	7/01	11r
Bread, white, pan	lb	1.06	7/01	11r
Broccoli	lb	0.91	7/01	11r
Butter, salted, grade AA, stick	lb	3.04	7/01	11r
Butter, yoghurt, cheese, etc, expenditures on	yr	183	1999	30r
Cereals and bakery product purchases	yr	430	1999	30r
Cereals and cereal products, expenditures on	yr	149	1999	30r
Chicken, fresh, whole	lb	1.07	7/01	11r
Chops, boneless,	lb	3.64	7/01	11r
Chuck roast, U.S. choice, boneless	lb	2.47	7/01	11r
Coffee, 100%, ground roast, all sizes	lb	2.69	7/01	11r
Cookies, chocolate chip	lb	2.87	7/01	11r
Dairy product purchases	yr	304	1999	30r
Eggs, expenditures on	yr	26	1999	30r
Eggs, grade A, large	dozen	0.88	7/01	11r
Fats and oils, expenditures on	yr	75	1999	30r
Fish and seafood, expenditures on	yr	72	1999	30r
Food (excl fruit and vegetables), eaten at home, purchases	yr	887	1999	30r
Food cooked on trips, expenditures on	yr	44	1999	30r
Food purchases	yr	4802	1999	30r
Food purchases, eaten away from home	yr	2069	1999	30r
Food purchases, food eaten at home	yr	2733	1999	30r
Fresh fruits, expenditures on	yr	138	1999	30r
Fresh milk and cream, expenditures on	yr	120	1999	30r
Fresh vegetables, expenditures on	yr	126	1999	30r
Grapefruit	lb	0.66	7/01	11r
Grapes, Thompson, seedless	lb	1.64	7/01	11r
Ground beef, 100% beef	lb	1.64	7/01	11r
Ground beef, lean and extra lean	lb	2.16	7/01	11r
Ground chuck, 100% beef	lb	2.13	7/01	11r
Ham, boneless, excl canned	lb	2.62	7/01	11r
Ice cream, prepackaged, bulk, regular	1/2 gal	3.35	7/01	11r
Lemons	lb	1.19	7/01	11r
Lettuce, iceberg	lb	0.73	7/01	11r
Margarine, soft, tubs	lb	0.89	7/01	11r
Meats, poultry, fish, and egg purchases	yr	671	1999	30r
Milk, fresh, whole, fortified	gal	2.71	7/01	11r
Nonalcoholic beverages, expenditures on	yr	239	1999	30r
Oranges, Navel	lb	0.80	7/01	11r
Oranges, Valencia	lb	0.66	7/01	11r
Pears, Anjou	lb	0.93	7/01	11r
Pork chops, center cut, bone-in	lb	3.63	7/01	11r
Pork, expenditures on	yr	150	1999	30r
Potato chips	16 oz	3.52	7/01	11r
Potatoes, frozen, french fried	lb	1.08	7/01	11r
Potatoes, white, all types	lb	0.33	7/01	11r
Poultry, expenditures on	yr	108	1999	30r
Processed fruits, expenditures on	yr	98	1999	30r
Processed vegetables, expenditures on	yr	80	1999	30r
Round roast, U.S. choice, boneless	lb	3.07	7/01	11r
Round steak, graded and ungraded, excl U.S. prime and choice	lb	3.41	7/01	11r
Shortening, vegetable oil blends	lb	1.13	7/01	11r
Spaghetti and macaroni	lb	0.80	7/01	11r
Steak, round, U.S. choice, boneless	lb	3.23	7/01	11r
Steak, T-bone, U.S. choice, bone-in	lb	6.68	7/01	11r
Strawberries, dry pint	12 oz	1.32	7/01	11r
Sugar and other sweets, expenditures on	yr	114	1999	30r
Sugar, white, 33-80 ounce package	lb	0.42	7/01	11r
Sugar, white, all sizes	lb	0.43	7/01	11r
Tobacco products and smoking supplies purchases	yr	331	1999	30r
Tomatoes, field grown	lb	1.46	7/01	11r
Tuna, light, chunk	lb	1.80	7/01	11r
Turkey, frozen, whole	lb	1.15	7/01	11r

Item	Per	Value	Date	Ref.
Goods and Services				
B&B Japanese maple (acer japonicum)	gal	29.99-169.99	4/00	93r
Boxwood (buxus)	2 gal	18.99-39.99	4/00	93r
Daylilly (hemerocallis)	gal	4.99-25.00	4/00	93r
Flat of annuals		11.98-24.99	4/00	93r
Fountain grass (pennisetum)	gal	5.98-12.98	4/00	93r
Hanging basket (10 in)		12.99-27.99	4/00	93r
Hardy geranium (geranium)	gal	7.99-9.99	4/00	93r
Hosta (hosta)	gal	6.00-25.00	4/00	93r
Lilac (syrubga vulgaris)	2 gal	14.99-24.99	4/00	93r
Miscellaneous purchases	yr	865	1999	30r
Rhododendron (rhododendron)	2 gal	23.98-42.99	4/00	93r
Sage (salvia)	gal	6.00-9.99	4/00	93r
Snowblower, single stage		400-600	12/00	99s
Wintercreeper euonymus (euonymus fortunei)	2 gal	16.00-169.99	4/00	93r
Hunting license	yr	14.00	4/01	34s
Health Care				
Cardiac catheterization, ave hospital/ physician charges		11830	1998	77s
Childbirth, Cesarean delivery		10722	1997	13r
Childbirth, vaginal delivery		6223	1997	13r
Drugs, expenditures on	yr	394	1999	30r
Health care purchases	yr	2048	1999	30r
Health insurance expenditures	yr	978	1999	30r
Hysterectomy, laproscopically-assisted, ave hospital/physician charges		13820	1998	76s
Hysterectomy, vaginal, ave hospital and physician charges		8780	1998	76s
Medicaid dispensing fee		3.72	1999	87s
Medical services expenditures	yr	554	1999	30r
Medical supplies, expenditures on	yr	122	1999	30r
Plastic surgery, breast augmentation		3184	2000	7r
Plastic surgery, breast lift		3585	2000	7r
Plastic surgery, facelift		4999	2000	7r
Plastic surgery, hair transplantation		3105	2000	7r
Plastic surgery, lip augmentation		1290	2000	7r
Plastic surgery, lower body lift		8135	2000	7r
Plastic surgery, thigh lift		3839	2000	7r
Household Goods				
Floor coverings, expenditures on	yr	52	1999	30r
Furniture, expenditures on	yr	344	1999	30r
Household furnishings and equipment purchases	yr	1475	1999	30r
Household textiles, expenditures on	yr	109	1999	30r
Laundry and cleaning supplies, expenditures on	yr	134	1999	30r
Housing				
Home, 2200 sq ft, 4-br, 2-bath, 2-car garage, average		156287	2000	47c
Home price, existing, ave		144400	10/00	90r
Home value, median		135000	2001	53s
Household operation expenditures	yr	542	1999	30r
Housekeeping supplies purchases	yr	508	1999	30r
Lodging expenditures	yr	430	1999	30r
Maintenance, repairs, insurance expenditures	yr	853	1999	30r
Monthly rental value of owned home	mos	547	1999	30r
Owned dwellings, expenditures own	yr	4282	1999	30r
Rent expenditures	yr	1558	1999	30r
Rental unit, 1 bedroom, with utilities	mos	407	4/01	41c

Values are in dollars or fractions of dollars. In the column headed *Ref*, references are shown to sources. Each reference is followed by a letter. These refer to the geographical level for which data were reported: s=State, r=Region, and c=City or metro. The abbreviation *ex* is used to mean *except* or *excluding*; *exp* stands for *expenditures*. For other abbreviations and further explanations, please see the Introduction.

Jackson, MI - continued

Item	Per	Value	Date	Ref.
Housing				
Rental unit, 2 bedroom, with utilities	mos	516	4/01	41c
Rental unit, 3 bedroom, with utilities	mos	644	4/01	41c
Rental unit, 4 bedroom, with utilities	mos	722	4/01	41c
Shelter, expenditures on	yr	6270	1999	30r
Insurance and Pensions				
Life and other personal insurance purchases	yr	387	1999	30r
Pensions and Social Security, expenditures on	yr	2968	1999	30r
Legal Fees				
Divorce, filing fee		65.00	4/01	35s
Driver's license fee	orig	20.00	1999	48s
Driver's license fee	renew	5.00	1999	48s
Fishing license	yr	14.00	4/01	34s
Personal Goods				
Personal care products and services purchases	yr	385	1999	30r
Personal Services				
Personal services, household, expenditures on	yr	300	1999	30r
Pets				
Pets, toys, and playground equipment, expenditures on	yr	375	1999	30r
Taxes				
Federal income taxes paid	yr	2326	1999	30r
Personal taxes, expenditures on	yr	3223	1999	30r
Property taxes paid	yr	1152	1999	30r
State and local income taxes paid	yr	753	1999	30r
Transportation				
Cars and trucks, new, expenditures on	yr	1280	1999	30r
Cars and trucks, used, expenditures on	yr	1763	1999	30r
Diesel at the pump	gal	1.19	10/99	73s
Gasoline and motor oil purchases	yr	1036	1999	30r
Gasoline before-tax price (cents)	gal	111.50	10/00	43s
Maintenance and repair expenditures	yr	594	1999	30r
Public transportation, expenditures on	yr	341	1999	30r
Transportation purchases	yr	6617	1999	30r
Vehicle expenses, miscellaneous, purchases	yr	2159	1999	30r
Vehicle insurance payments	yr	701	1999	30r
Vehicle purchases (net outlay)	yr	3081	1999	30r
Vehicle rental, lease expenditures	yr	536	1999	30r
Utilities				
Electrical bill, average	mos	55.00	9/00	9s
Electricity, expenditures on	yr	841	1999	30r
Electricity cost, average	KWh	7.00	9/00	9s
Utilities, fuels, and public services purchased	yr	2401	1999	30r
Water and other public services, expenditures on	yr	273	1999	30r
Weddings				
Wedding (national average cost)		19936	2000	33r
Wedding (regional average total cost)		16195	1997	110r
Attendants' gifts		321	1998	33r
Bridal attendants' apparel (5 persons)		824	2000	33r
Bride's headpiece/veil		173	1998	33r
Bride's wedding dress		859	1998	33r
Clergy, religious facility fee		242	1998	33r
Engagement ring		3177	1998	33r
Flowers		789	1998	33r
Groom's formalwear rental		99	2000	33r
Limousine		410	1998	33r
Marriage license cost		20.00	4/01	35s
Men's formalwear (ushers, best man)		469	2000	33r
Mother of bride apparel		241	2000	33r
Music		866	1998	33r
Photography and videography		1368	1998	33r
Rehearsal dinner		728	1998	33r
Wedding invitations and announcements		341	1998	33r
Wedding reception		7968	2000	33r

Jackson, MI - continued

Item	Per	Value	Date	Ref.
Weddings - continued				
Wedding rings (bride and groom)		1060	1998	33r

Jackson, MS

Item	Per	Value	Date	Ref.
Composite, ACCRA index		88.50	3/01	4c
Alcoholic Beverages				
Alcoholic beverage purchases	yr	253	1999	30r
Beer, Heineken, 12-oz, ex deposit	6	6.73	3/01	4c
J & B Scotch	750-ml	18.60	3/01	4c
Malt beverages, all types, all sizes, any origin	16 oz	0.96	7/01	11r
Wine, Livingston or Gallo, Chablis blanc	1.5 liter	6.03	3/01	4c
Appliances				
Appliance repair, service call, washing machine	min lab chg	44.26	3/01	4c
Major appliances, expenditures on	yr	172	1999	30r
Small appliances, housewares, expenditures on	yr	81	1999	30r
Banking and Money				
Mortgage interest and charges paid	yr	2039	1999	30r
Mortgage principal paid on owned property	yr	1026	1999	30r
Mortgage rate, incl. points and orig. fee, 30-yr. conv. fixed or ARM	mos	6.97	3/01	4c
Vehicle finance charges paid	yr	365	1999	30r
Business Expenses				
Business travel, car rental	day	57	2001	3c
Business travel, food	day	40	2001	3c
Business travel, hotel	day	96	2001	3c
Charity				
Cash contributions, expenditures	yr	1127	1999	30r
Child Care				
Child raising cost, total, age 0-2	yr	8540	1999	60r
Child raising cost, total, age 3-5	yr	8780	1999	60r
Child raising cost, total, age 6-8	yr	8820	1999	60r
Child raising cost, total, age 9-11	yr	8800	1999	60r
Child raising cost, total, age 12-14	yr	9510	1999	60r
Child raising cost, total, age 15-17	yr	9740	1999	60r
Child's child care and education, age 0-2	yr	1380	1999	60r
Child's child care and education, age 3-5	yr	1520	1999	60r
Child's child care and education, age 6-8	yr	990	1999	60r
Child's child care and education, age 9-11	yr	650	1999	60r
Child's child care and education, age 12-14	yr	490	1999	60r
Child's child care and education, age 15-17	yr	840	1999	60r
Child's clothing, age 0-2	yr	480	1999	60r
Child's clothing, age 3-5	yr	470	1999	60r
Child's clothing, age 6-8	yr	520	1999	60r
Child's clothing, age 9-11	yr	570	1999	60r
Child's clothing, age 12-14	yr	950	1999	60r
Child's clothing, age 15-17	yr	850	1999	60r
Child's food, age 0-2	yr	1000	1999	60r
Child's food, age 3-5	yr	1160	1999	60r
Child's food, age 6-8	yr	1490	1999	60r
Child's food, age 9-11	yr	1770	1999	60r
Child's food, age 12-14	yr	1770	1999	60r
Child's food, age 15-17	yr	1980	1999	60r
Child's health care, age 0-2	yr	620	1999	60r
Child's health care, age 3-5	yr	590	1999	60r
Child's health care, age 6-8	yr	680	1999	60r
Child's health care, age 9-11	yr	720	1999	60r
Child's health care, age 12-14	yr	730	1999	60r
Child's health care, age 15-17	yr	760	1999	60r
Child's housing, age 0-2	yr	3070	1999	60r
Child's housing, age 3-5	yr	3050	1999	60r
Child's housing, age 6-8	yr	3010	1999	60r
Child's housing, age 9-11	yr	2850	1999	60r
Child's housing, age 12-14	yr	3040	1999	60r
Child's housing, age 15-17	yr	2650	1999	60r
Child's personal care, reading, age 0-2	yr	910	1999	60r
Child's personal care, reading, age 3-5	yr	930	1999	60r

Values are in dollars or fractions of dollars. In the column headed *Ref*, references are shown to sources. Each reference is followed by a letter. These refer to the geographical level for which data were reported: s=State, r=Region, and c=City or metro. The abbreviation *ex* is used to mean *except* or *excluding*; *exp* stands for *expenditures*. For other abbreviations and further explanations, please see the Introduction.

Jackson, MS - continued

Item	Per	Value	Date	Ref.
Child Care				
Child's personal care, reading, age 6-8	yr	960	1999	60r
Child's personal care, reading, age 9-11	yr	1000	1999	60r
Child's personal care, reading, age 12-14	yr	1170	1999	60r
Child's personal care, reading, age 15-17	yr	950	1999	60r
Daycare	mos	325	1998	37c
Daycare, 3-year old, 5 days, 8 hrs/day	mos	325	1998	85c
Clothing				
Apparel and services purchases	yr	1610	1999	30r
Boys' brief, cotton	3	2.81	3/01	4c
Boys, 2 to 15, expenditures on	yr	89	1999	30r
Children under 2, expenditures on	yr	79	1999	30r
Footwear, expenditures on	yr	283	1999	30r
Girls, 2 to 15, expenditures on	yr	103	1999	30r
Men and boys, expenditures on	yr	351	1999	30r
Men, 16 and over, expenditures on	yr	262	1999	30r
Shirt, man's dress shirt		25.63	3/01	4c
Slacks, man's "No Wrinkles" khaki		41.00	3/01	4c
Women, 16 and over, expenditures on	yr	538	1999	30r
Communications				
Newspaper subscription, daily and Sunday delivery	mos	14.50	3/01	4c
Phone line, single, business, field visit	inst.	67.00	12/97	17s
Phone line, single, business, no field visit	inst.	67.00	12/97	17s
Phone line, single, residence, field visit	inst.	46.00	12/97	17s
Phone line, single, residence, no field visit	inst.	46.00	12/97	17s
Postage and stationery, expenditures on	yr	104	1999	30r
Postal rate, express mail, up to half-pound		12.45	7/01	108r
Postal rate, letter, first class, first ounce		0.34	7/01	108r
Postal rate, letter, two ounces		0.57	7/01	108r
Postal rate, post card		0.21	7/01	108r
Postal rate, priority mail, two pounds		3.95	7/01	108r
Postal rate, priority mail, up to one pound		3.50	7/01	108r
Telephone bill, business, basic rate	mos	48.65	12/97	18c
Telephone bill, family of three	mos	25.71	3/01	4c
Telephone bill, residential, basic rate	mos	19.01	12/97	18c
Telephone services, expenditures on	yr	860	1999	30r
Education				
Board, 4-year private college/university	yr	1536	1996	38s
Board, 4-year public college/university	yr	1568	1996	38s
Education expenditures	yr	431	1999	30r
Room, 4-year private college/university	yr	1582	1996	38s
Room, 4-year public college/university	yr	1399	1996	38s
Total cost, 4-year private college/university	yr	9901	1996	38s
Total cost, 4-year public college/university	yr	5425	1996	38s
Tuition, 2-year public college/university, in state	yr	941	1996	38s
Tuition, 4-year private college/university, in state	yr	6782	1996	38s
Tuition, 4-year public college/university	yr	2459	1996	38s
Energy and Fuels				
Electricity	KWh	0.09	7/01	11r
Electricity	500 KWhs	47.29	7/01	11r
Energy, combined forms, 2400 sq ft	mos	99.54	3/01	4c
Energy, exc. electricity, 2400 sq ft	mos	42.26	3/01	4c
Fuel oil #2	gal	1.43	7/01	11r
Fuel oil and other fuels, expenditures on	yr	45	1999	30r
Gas, cooking, winter, 10 therms	mos	7.97	2/96	98c
Gas, cooking, winter, 30 therms	mos	17.28	2/96	98c
Gas, cooking, winter, 50 therms	mos	26.58	2/96	98c
Gas, heating, winter, average use	mos	62.13	2/96	98c
Gas, natural, commercial rate	1000 cf	7.01	11/00	88s
Gas, regular unleaded, cash, self-service	gal	1.29	3/01	4c
Gasoline, all types	gal	1.60	7/01	11r
Gasoline, unleaded midgrade	gal	1.65	7/01	11r
Gasoline, unleaded premium	gal	1.74	7/01	11r
Natural gas, expenditures on	yr	164	1999	30r
Utility (piped) gas, therm		1.01	7/01	11r
Utility (piped) gas, 40 therms		44.29	7/01	11r
Utility (piped) gas, 100 therms		97.44	7/01	11r

Jackson, MS - continued

Item	Per	Value	Date	Ref.
Entertainment				
Bowling, Saturday evening rate	line	2.81	3/01	4c
Entertainment purchases	yr	1574	1999	30r
Fees and admissions paid	yr	371	1999	30r
Monopoly game, Parker Brothers', No. 9	game	9.50	3/01	4c
Movie, first-run, Saturday, evening	adm.	6.56	3/01	4c
Reading purchases	yr	121	1999	30r
Television, radios, sound equipment, expenditures on	yr	561	1999	30r
Tennis balls, yellow, Wilson or Penn, 3	can	1.91	3/01	4c
Groceries				
Groceries, ACCRA Index		79.90	3/01	4c
American processed cheese	lb	3.50	7/01	11r
Antibiotic ointment, Polysporin	0.5 oz	4.08	3/01	4c
Baby food, strained vegetables or fruit, lowest price	4-4.5 oz	0.24	3/01	4c
Bakery products, expenditures on	yr	261	1999	30r
Bananas	lb	0.35	3/01	4c
Bananas	lb	0.47	7/01	11r
Beans, dried, any type, all sizes	lb	0.63	7/01	11r
Beef for stew, boneless	lb	2.86	7/01	11r
Beef or hamburger, ground	lb	1.46	3/01	4c
Beef, expenditures on	yr	210	1999	30r
Bologna, all beef or mixed	lb	2.29	7/01	11r
Bread, French	lb	1.66	7/01	11r
Bread, white	loaf	0.78	3/01	4c
Bread, white, pan	lb	0.87	7/01	11r
Bread, whole wheat, pan	lb	1.38	7/01	11r
Broccoli	lb	1.04	7/01	11r
Butter, salted, grade AA, stick	lb	2.26	7/01	11r
Butter, yoghurt, cheese, etc, expenditures on	yr	170	1999	30r
Cabbage	lb	0.42	7/01	11r
Cereals and cereal products, expenditures on	yr	140	1999	30r
Cheddar cheese, natural	lb	3.75	7/01	11r
Cheese, Kraft grated Parmesan	8 oz	3.90	3/01	4c
Chicken breast, bone-in	lb	1.85	7/01	11r
Chicken legs, bone-in	lb	1.34	7/01	11r
Chicken, fresh, whole	lb	1.05	7/01	11r
Chicken, whole fryer	lb	0.83	3/01	4c
Chops, boneless	lb	4.13	7/01	11r
Chuck roast, graded and ungraded, excl U.S. prime and choice	lb	2.35	7/01	11r
Chuck roast, U.S. choice, boneless	lb	2.67	7/01	11r
Cigarettes, Winston, Kings	carton	26.22	3/01	4c
Coffee, 100%, ground roast, all sizes	lb	2.88	7/01	11r
Coffee, instant, plain, regular, all sizes	16 oz	9.25	7/01	11r
Coffee, vacuum-packed	13 oz	1.47	3/01	4c
Cola, non-diet	2 liter	1.11	7/01	11r
Corn Flakes, Kellogg's or Post Toasties	18 oz	2.24	3/01	4c
Corn, frozen, whole kernel, lowest price	16 oz	1.05	3/01	4c
Crackers, soda, salted	lb	1.70	7/01	11r
Dairy product purchases	yr	282	1999	30r
Eggs, expenditures on	yr	32	1999	30r
Eggs, Grade A or AA	dozen	0.87	3/01	4c
Fats and oils, expenditures on	yr	79	1999	30r
Fish and seafood, expenditures on	yr	99	1999	30r
Flour, white, all purpose	lb	0.32	7/01	11r
Food (excl fruit and vegetables), eaten at home, purchases	yr	815	1999	30r
Food cooked on trips, expenditures on	yr	36	1999	30r
Food purchases	yr	4533	1999	30r
Food purchases, eaten away from home	yr	1873	1999	30r
Food purchases, food eaten at home	yr	2660	1999	30r
Fresh fruits, expenditures on	yr	128	1999	30r
Fresh milk and cream, expenditures on	yr	112	1999	30r
Fresh vegetables, expenditures on	yr	131	1999	30r
Fruit and vegetable purchases	yr	438	1999	30r
Grapefruit	lb	0.59	7/01	11r
Grapes, Thompson, seedless	lb	2.12	7/01	11r
Ground beef, 100% beef	lb	1.76	7/01	11r
Ground beef, lean and extra lean	lb	2.60	7/01	11r
Ground chuck, 100% beef	lb	2.08	7/01	11r

Values are in dollars or fractions of dollars. In the column headed *Ref*, references are shown to sources. Each reference is followed by a letter. These refer to the geographical level for which data were reported: s=State, r=Region, and c=City or metro. The abbreviation *ex* is used to mean *except* or *excluding*; *exp* stands for *expenditures*. For other abbreviations and further explanations, please see the Introduction.

Jackson, MS - continued

Item	Per	Value	Date	Ref.
Groceries				
Ham, boneless, excl canned	lb	2.71	7/01	11r
Ham, rump or shank half, bone-in, smoked	lb	2.19	7/01	11r
Ice cream, prepackaged, bulk, regular	1/2 gal	3.93	7/01	11r
Lemons	lb	1.32	7/01	11r
Lettuce, iceberg	head	0.92	3/01	4c
Lettuce, iceberg	lb	0.76	7/01	11r
Margarine, Blue Bonnet or Parkay, stick	lb	0.53	3/01	4c
Milk, fresh, low fat,	gal	2.75	7/01	11r
Milk, fresh, whole, fortified	gal	2.97	7/01	11r
Milk, whole	1/2 gal	1.22	3/01	4c
Nonalcoholic beverages, expenditures on	yr	228	1999	30r
Orange juice, frozen concentrate	16 oz	1.95	7/01	11r
Orange juice, Minute Maid frozen	12 oz	1.43	4c	
Oranges, Navel	lb	0.73	7/01	11r
Oranges, Valencia	lb	0.55	7/01	11r
Peaches, halves or slices, Hunt's, Del Monte, or Libby's	29 oz	1.50	3/01	4c
Peanut butter, creamy, all sizes	lb	1.83	7/01	11r
Pears, Anjou	lb	0.98	7/01	11r
Peas, green, Del Monte or Green Giant	15 oz	0.61	3/01	4c
Pork chops, center cut, bone-in	lb	3.33	7/01	11r
Pork sausage, fresh, loose	lb	2.59	7/01	11r
Pork shoulder picnic, bone-in, smoked	lb	1.12	7/01	11r
Pork, expenditures on	yr	162	1999	30r
Potato chips	16 oz	3.59	7/01	11r
Potatoes, frozen, french fried	lb	1.00	7/01	11r
Potatoes, white or red	10 lb	2.88	3/01	4c
Potatoes, white, all types	lb	0.44	7/01	11r
Poultry, expenditures on	yr	137	1999	30r
Processed fruits, expenditures on	yr	97	1999	30r
Processed vegetables, expenditures on	yr	82	1999	30r
Rice, white, long grain, uncooked	lb	0.51	7/01	11r
Round roast, graded and ungraded, excl U.S. prime and choice	lb	2.96	7/01	11r
Round steak, graded and ungraded, excl U.S. prime and choice	lb	3.11	7/01	11r
Sausage, Jimmy Dean/Owens pork	lb	2.33	3/01	4c
Shortening, vegetable, Crisco	3 lb	2.71	3/01	4c
Sirloin steak, graded and ungraded, excl U.S. prime and choice	lb	4.23	7/01	11r
Soft drink, Coca Cola, ex deposit	2 liter	0.67	3/01	4c
Spaghetti and macaroni	lb	0.78	7/01	11r
Steak, round, U.S. choice, boneless	lb	3.56	7/01	11r
Steak, sirloin, U.S. choice, boneless	lb	5.65	7/01	11r
Steak, T-bone	lb	6.26	3/01	4c
Strawberries, dry pint	12 oz	1.50	7/01	11r
Sugar and other sweets, expenditures on	yr	99	1999	30r
Sugar, cane or beet	4 lbs	1.45	3/01	4c
Sugar, white, 33-80 ounce package	lb	0.39	7/01	11r
Sugar, white, all sizes	lb	0.42	7/01	11r
Tobacco products and smoking supplies purchases	yr	288	1999	30r
Tomatoes, field grown	lb	1.43	7/01	11r
Tomatoes, Hunt's or Del Monte	14.5 oz	0.81	3/01	4c
Tuna, chunk, light	6 oz	0.33	3/01	4c
Tuna, light, chunk	lb	1.77	7/01	11r
Turkey, frozen, whole	lb	1.05	7/01	11r
Goods and Services				
Miscellaneous goods and services, ACCRA Index		92.80	3/01	4c
Hunting license	yr	18.00	4/01	34s
Health Care				
Health care, ACCRA Index		78.50	3/01	4c
Cardiac catheterization, ave hospital/ physician charges		10310	1998	77s
Childbirth, Cesarean delivery		11587	1997	13r
Childbirth, vaginal delivery		6725	1997	13r
Dentist's fee, adult teeth cleaning and periodic oral exam	visit	58.13	3/01	4c
Doctor's fee, routine exam, established patient	visit	51.67	3/01	4c

Jackson, MS - continued

Item	Per	Value	Date	Ref.
Health Care - continued				
Drugs, expenditures on	yr	399	1999	30r
Health care purchases	yr	1971	1999	30r
Health insurance expenditures	yr	933	1999	30r
Hospital care, private room	day	258.20	3/01	4c
Hysterectomy, laproscopically-assisted, ave hospital/physician charges		14270	1998	76s
Hysterectomy, vaginal, ave hospital and physician charges		10020	1998	76s
Medicaid dispensing fee		4.91	1999	87s
Medical services expenditures	yr	547	1999	30r
Medical supplies, expenditures on	yr	91	1999	30r
Household Goods				
Dishwashing powder, Cascade	50 oz	2.79	3/01	4c
Floor coverings, expenditures on	yr	44	1999	30r
Furniture, expenditures on	yr	335	1999	30r
Household furnishings and equipment purchases	yr	1328	1999	30r
Household textiles, expenditures on	yr	89	1999	30r
Laundry and cleaning supplies, expenditures on	yr	113	1999	30r
Tissues, facial, Kleenex brand	175	1.26	3/01	4c
Housing				
Housing, ACCRA Index		88.00	3/01	4c
Home, 2200 sq ft, 4-br, 2-bath, 2-car garage, average		161850	2000	47c
Home, suburban, 2,200 square feet		126500	2000	23c
Home price, existing, ave		160100	10/00	90r
Home value, median		102000	2001	53s
House, 2400 sq ft, 8000 sq ft lot, new, urban, utilities	total	180375	3/01	4c
House payment, principal and interest, 25% down payment	mos	898	3/01	4c
Household operation expenditures	yr	553	1999	30r
Housekeeping supplies purchases	yr	473	1999	30r
Housing, expenditures on	yr	10303	1999	30r
Maintenance, repairs, insurance expenditures	yr	699	1999	30r
Monthly rental value of owned home	mos	505	1999	30r
Owned dwellings, expenditures own	yr	3465	1999	30r
Rent expenditures	yr	1641	1999	30r
Rent, apartment, 2 br, 1 1/2-2 baths, unfurn, 950 sq ft, water	mos	635	3/01	4c
Rental unit, 1 bedroom, with utilities	mos	455	4/01	41c
Rental unit, 2 bedroom, with utilities	mos	557	4/01	41c
Rental unit, 3 bedroom, with utilities	mos	740	4/01	41c
Rental unit, 4 bedroom, with utilities	mos	781	4/01	41c
Shelter, expenditures on	yr	5467	1999	30r
Insurance and Pensions				
Life and other personal insurance purchases	yr	414	1999	30r
Pensions and Social Security, expenditures on	yr	2635	1999	30r
Personal insurance and pensions, expenditures on	yr	3048	1999	30r
Legal Fees				
Combination hunting and fishing license	yr	18.00	4/01	34s
Driver's license fee	orig	20.00	1999	48s
Driver's license fee	renew	5.00	1999	48s
Fishing license	yr	12.00	4/01	34s
Personal Goods				
Personal care products and services purchases	yr	393	1999	30r
Shampoo, Alberto VO5	15 oz	0.98	3/01	4c
Toothpaste, Crest or Colgate	6-7 oz	1.89	3/01	4c
Personal Services				
Dry cleaning, man's 2-pc suit		6.36	3/01	4c
Man's haircut, barbershop, no styling		10.38	3/01	4c
Personal services, household, expenditures on	yr	258	1999	30r

Values are in dollars or fractions of dollars. In the column headed *Ref*, references are shown to sources. Each reference is followed by a letter. These refer to the geographical level for which data were reported: s=State, r=Region, and c=City or metro. The abbreviation *ex* is used to mean *except* or *excluding*; *exp* stands for expenditures. For other abbreviations and further explanations, please see the Introduction.

396

Jackson, MS - continued

Item	Per	Value	Date	Ref.
Personal Services				
Woman's shampoo, trim, blow-dry, no style-change		28.14	3/01	4c
Pets				
Pets, toys, and playground equipment, expenditures on	yr	306	1999	30r
Restaurant Food				
Chicken, fried, thigh and drumstick, KFC/Church's		1.97	3/01	4c
Hamburger with cheese, McDonald's	1/4 lb	2.00	3/01	4c
Pizza, Pizza Hut or Pizza Inn	11-12 in	8.10	3/01	4c
Taxes				
Federal income taxes paid	yr	2047	1999	30r
Personal taxes, expenditures on	yr	2554	1999	30r
Property taxes paid	yr	726	1999	30r
State and local income taxes paid	yr	363	1999	30r
Transportation				
Transportation, ACCRA Index		95.60	3/01	4c
Bus fare, one-way	trip	1.00	2000	1c
Bus fare, to central business district	1-way	1.00	3/01	4c
Cars and trucks, new, expenditures on	yr	1648	1999	30r
Cars and trucks, used, expenditures on	yr	1651	1999	30r
Diesel at the pump	gal	1.17	10/99	73s
Gasoline and motor oil purchases	yr	1052	1999	30r
Gasoline before-tax price (cents)	gal	108.40	10/00	43s
Maintenance and repair expenditures	yr	621	1999	30r
Motorcycle license fee	renew	5.00	1999	49s
Motorcycle license fee	orig	5.00	1999	49s
Public transportation, expenditures on	yr	298	1999	30r
Tire balance, computer or spin balance, front	wheel	8.06	3/01	4c
Transportation purchases	yr	6738	1999	30r
Vehicle expenses, miscellaneous, purchases	yr	2033	1999	30r
Vehicle insurance payments	yr	696	1999	30r
Vehicle purchases (net outlay)	yr	3354	1999	30r
Vehicle rental, lease expenditures	yr	352	1999	30r
Utilities				
Utilities, ACCRA Index		86.60	3/01	4c
Electrical bill, average	mos	79.66	9/00	9s
Electricity, expenditures on	yr	1115	1999	30r
Electricity, summer, 250 KWh	mos	29.20	2/96	97c
Electricity, summer, 500 KWh	mos	52.47	2/96	97c
Electricity, summer, 750 KWh	mos	65.92	2/96	97c
Electricity, summer, 1000 KWh	mos	79.38	2/96	97c
Electricity and other, mixed, 2400 sq ft, new home	mos	57.28	3/01	4c
Electricity cost, average	KWh	5.69	9/00	9s
Water and other public services, expenditures on	yr	298	1999	30r
Weddings				
Wedding (national average cost)		19936	2000	33r
Attendants' gifts		321	1998	33r
Bridal attendants' apparel (5 persons)		824	2000	33r
Bride's headpiece/veil		173	1998	33r
Bride's wedding dress		859	1998	33r
Clergy, religious facility fee		242	1998	33r
Engagement ring		3177	1998	33r
Flowers		789	1998	33r
Groom's formalwear rental		99	2000	33r
Limousine		410	1998	33r
Marriage license cost		21.00	4/01	35s
Men's formalwear (ushers, best man)		469	2000	33r
Mother of bride apparel		241	2000	33r
Music		866	1998	33r
Photography and videography		1368	1998	33r
Rehearsal dinner		728	1998	33r
Wedding invitations and announcements		341	1998	33r
Wedding reception		7968	2000	33r
Wedding rings (bride and groom)		1060	1998	33r

Jackson, TN

Item	Per	Value	Date	Ref.
Alcoholic Beverages				
Alcoholic beverage purchases	yr	253	1999	30r
Malt beverages, all types, all sizes, any origin	16 oz	0.96	7/01	11r
Appliances				
Major appliances, expenditures on	yr	172	1999	30r
Small appliances, housewares, expenditures on	yr	81	1999	30r
Banking and Money				
Mortgage interest and charges paid	yr	2039	1999	30r
Mortgage principal paid on owned property	yr	1026	1999	30r
Vehicle finance charges paid	yr	365	1999	30r
Charity				
Cash contributions, expenditures	yr	1127	1999	30r
Child Care				
Child raising cost, total, age 0-2	yr	8540	1999	60r
Child raising cost, total, age 3-5	yr	8780	1999	60r
Child raising cost, total, age 6-8	yr	8820	1999	60r
Child raising cost, total, age 9-11	yr	8800	1999	60r
Child raising cost, total, age 12-14	yr	9510	1999	60r
Child raising cost, total, age 15-17	yr	9740	1999	60r
Child's child care and education, age 0-2	yr	1380	1999	60r
Child's child care and education, age 3-5	yr	1520	1999	60r
Child's child care and education, age 6-8	yr	990	1999	60r
Child's child care and education, age 9-11	yr	650	1999	60r
Child's child care and education, age 12-14	yr	490	1999	60r
Child's child care and education, age 15-17	yr	840	1999	60r
Child's clothing, age 0-2	yr	480	1999	60r
Child's clothing, age 3-5	yr	470	1999	60r
Child's clothing, age 6-8	yr	520	1999	60r
Child's clothing, age 9-11	yr	570	1999	60r
Child's clothing, age 12-14	yr	950	1999	60r
Child's clothing, age 15-17	yr	850	1999	60r
Child's food, age 0-2	yr	1000	1999	60r
Child's food, age 3-5	yr	1160	1999	60r
Child's food, age 6-8	yr	1490	1999	60r
Child's food, age 9-11	yr	1770	1999	60r
Child's food, age 12-14	yr	1770	1999	60r
Child's food, age 15-17	yr	1980	1999	60r
Child's health care, age 0-2	yr	620	1999	60r
Child's health care, age 3-5	yr	590	1999	60r
Child's health care, age 6-8	yr	680	1999	60r
Child's health care, age 9-11	yr	720	1999	60r
Child's health care, age 12-14	yr	730	1999	60r
Child's health care, age 15-17	yr	760	1999	60r
Child's housing, age 0-2	yr	3070	1999	60r
Child's housing, age 3-5	yr	3050	1999	60r
Child's housing, age 6-8	yr	3010	1999	60r
Child's housing, age 9-11	yr	2850	1999	60r
Child's housing, age 12-14	yr	3040	1999	60r
Child's housing, age 15-17	yr	2650	1999	60r
Child's personal care, reading, age 0-2	yr	910	1999	60r
Child's personal care, reading, age 3-5	yr	930	1999	60r
Child's personal care, reading, age 6-8	yr	960	1999	60r
Child's personal care, reading, age 9-11	yr	1000	1999	60r
Child's personal care, reading, age 12-14	yr	1170	1999	60r
Child's personal care, reading, age 15-17	yr	950	1999	60r
Clothing				
Apparel and services purchases	yr	1610	1999	30r
Boys, 2 to 15, expenditures on	yr	89	1999	30r
Children under 2, expenditures on	yr	79	1999	30r
Footwear, expenditures on	yr	283	1999	30r
Girls, 2 to 15, expenditures on	yr	103	1999	30r
Men and boys, expenditures on	yr	351	1999	30r
Men, 16 and over, expenditures on	yr	262	1999	30r
Women, 16 and over, expenditures on	yr	538	1999	30r
Communications				
Cable modem installation, Intermedia		149.95	6/99	103s
Cable modem installation, Time Warner		75.00-225.00	6/99	103s

Values are in dollars or fractions of dollars. In the column headed *Ref*, references are shown to sources. Each reference is followed by a letter. These refer to the geographical level for which data were reported: s=State, r=Region, and c=City or metro. The abbreviation *ex* is used to mean *except* or *excluding*; *exp* stands for *expenditures*. For other abbreviations and further explanations, please see the Introduction.

Jackson, TN - continued

Item	Per	Value	Date	Ref.
Communications				
Cable modem rate, cable subscriber, Intermedia	mos	49.95	6/99	103s
Cable modem rate, cable subscriber, Time Warner	mos	39.95- 49.95	6/99	103s
Cable modem rate, non-cable subscriber, Intermedia	mos	54.95	6/99	103s
Cable modem rate, non-cable subscriber, Time Warner	mos	39.95- 54.95	6/99	103s
Phone line, single, business, field visit	inst.	58.50	12/97	17s
Phone line, single, business, no field visit	inst.	58.50	12/97	17s
Phone line, single, residence, field visit	inst.	41.50	12/97	17s
Phone line, single, residence, no field visit	inst.	41.50	12/97	17s
Postage and stationery, expenditures on	yr	104	1999	30r
Postal rate, express mail, up to half-pound		12.45	7/01	108r
Postal rate, letter, first class, first ounce		0.34	7/01	108r
Postal rate, letter, two ounces		0.57	7/01	108r
Postal rate, post card		0.21	7/01	108r
Postal rate, priority mail, two pounds		3.95	7/01	108r
Postal rate, priority mail, up to one pound		3.50	7/01	108r
Telephone services, expenditures on	yr	860	1999	30r
Education				
Board, 4-year private college/university	yr	2085	1996	38s
Board, 4-year public college/university	yr	1737	1996	38s
Education expenditures	yr	431	1999	30r
Room, 4-year private college/university	yr	2153	1996	38s
Room, 4-year public college/university	yr	1644	1996	38s
Total cost, 4-year private college/university	yr	14068	1996	38s
Total cost, 4-year public college/university	yr	5372	1996	38s
Tuition, 2-year public college/university, in state	yr	1022	1996	38s
Tuition, 4-year private college/university, in state	yr	9830	1996	38s
Tuition, 4-year public college/university	yr	1990	1996	38s
Energy and Fuels				
Electricity	KWh	0.09	7/01	11r
Electricity	500 KWhs	47.29	7/01	11r
Fuel oil #2	gal	1.43	7/01	11r
Fuel oil and other fuels, expenditures on	yr	45	1999	30r
Gas, natural, commercial rate	1000 cf	8.61	11/00	88s
Gasoline, all types	gal	1.60	7/01	11r
Gasoline, unleaded midgrade	gal	1.65	7/01	11r
Gasoline, unleaded premium	gal	1.74	7/01	11r
Natural gas, expenditures on	yr	164	1999	30r
Utility (piped) gas, therm		1.01	7/01	11r
Utility (piped) gas, 40 therms		44.29	7/01	11r
Utility (piped) gas, 100 therms		97.44	7/01	11r
Entertainment				
Entertainment purchases	yr	1574	1999	30r
Fees and admissions paid	yr	371	1999	30r
Reading purchases	yr	121	1999	30r
Television, radios, sound equipment, expenditures on	yr	561	1999	30r
Groceries				
American processed cheese	lb	3.50	7/01	11r
Bakery products, expenditures on	yr	261	1999	30r
Bananas	lb	0.47	7/01	11r
Beans, dried, any type, all sizes	lb	0.63	7/01	11r
Beef for stew, boneless	lb	2.86	7/01	11r
Beef, expenditures on	yr	210	1999	30r
Bologna, all beef or mixed	lb	2.29	7/01	11r
Bread, French	lb	1.66	7/01	11r
Bread, white, pan	lb	0.87	7/01	11r
Bread, whole wheat, pan	lb	1.38	7/01	11r
Broccoli	lb	1.04	7/01	11r
Butter, salted, grade AA, stick	lb	2.26	7/01	11r
Butter, yoghurt, cheese, etc, expenditures on	yr	170	1999	30r
Cabbage	lb	0.42	7/01	11r
Cereals and cereal products, expenditures on	yr	140	1999	30r

Jackson, TN - continued

Item	Per	Value	Date	Ref.
Groceries - continued				
Cheddar cheese, natural	lb	3.75	7/01	11r
Chicken breast, bone-in	lb	1.85	7/01	11r
Chicken legs, bone-in	lb	1.34	7/01	11r
Chicken, fresh, whole	lb	1.05	7/01	11r
Chops, boneless,	lb	4.13	7/01	11r
Chuck roast, graded and ungraded, excl U.S. prime and choice	lb	2.35	7/01	11r
Chuck roast, U.S. choice, boneless	lb	2.67	7/01	11r
Coffee, 100%, ground roast, all sizes	lb	2.88	7/01	11r
Coffee, instant, plain, regular, all sizes	16 oz	9.25	7/01	11r
Cola, non diet	2 liter	1.11	7/01	11r
Crackers, soda, salted	lb	1.70	7/01	11r
Dairy product purchases	yr	282	1999	30r
Eggs, expenditures on	yr	32	1999	30r
Fats and oils, expenditures on	yr	79	1999	30r
Fish and seafood, expenditures on	yr	99	1999	30r
Flour, white, all purpose	lb	0.32	7/01	11r
Food (excl fruit and vegetables), eaten at home, purchases	yr	815	1999	30r
Food cooked on trips, expenditures on	yr	36	1999	30r
Food purchases	yr	4533	1999	30r
Food purchases, eaten away from home	yr	1873	1999	30r
Food purchases, food eaten at home	yr	2660	1999	30r
Fresh fruits, expenditures on	yr	128	1999	30r
Fresh milk and cream, expenditures on	yr	112	1999	30r
Fresh vegetables, expenditures on	yr	131	1999	30r
Fruit and vegetable purchases	yr	438	1999	30r
Grapefruit	lb	0.59	7/01	11r
Grapes, Thompson, seedless	lb	2.12	7/01	11r
Ground beef, 100% beef	lb	1.76	7/01	11r
Ground beef, lean and extra lean	lb	2.60	7/01	11r
Ground chuck, 100% beef	lb	2.08	7/01	11r
Ham, boneless, excl canned	lb	2.71	7/01	11r
Ham, rump or shank half, bone-in, smoked	lb	2.19	7/01	11r
Ice cream, prepackaged, bulk, regular	1/2 gal	3.93	7/01	11r
Lemons	lb	1.32	7/01	11r
Lettuce, iceberg	lb	0.76	7/01	11r
Milk, fresh, low fat,	gal	2.75	7/01	11r
Milk, fresh, whole, fortified	gal	2.97	7/01	11r
Nonalcoholic beverages, expenditures on	yr	228	1999	30r
Orange juice, frozen concentrate	16 oz	1.95	7/01	11r
Oranges, Navel	lb	0.73	7/01	11r
Oranges, Valencia	lb	0.55	7/01	11r
Peanut butter, creamy, all sizes	lb	1.83	7/01	11r
Pears, Anjou	lb	0.98	7/01	11r
Pork chops, center cut, bone-in	lb	3.33	7/01	11r
Pork sausage, fresh, loose	lb	2.59	7/01	11r
Pork shoulder picnic, bone-in, smoked	lb	1.12	7/01	11r
Pork, expenditures on	yr	162	1999	30r
Potato chips	16 oz	3.59	7/01	11r
Potatoes, frozen, french fried	lb	1.00	7/01	11r
Potatoes, white, all types	lb	0.44	7/01	11r
Poultry, expenditures on	yr	137	1999	30r
Processed fruits, expenditures on	yr	97	1999	30r
Processed vegetables, expenditures on	yr	82	1999	30r
Rice, white, long grain, uncooked	lb	0.51	7/01	11r
Round roast, graded and ungraded, excl U.S. prime and choice	lb	2.96	7/01	11r
Round steak, graded and ungraded, excl U.S. prime and choice	lb	3.11	7/01	11r
Sirloin steak, graded and ungraded, excl U.S. prime and choice	lb	4.23	7/01	11r
Spaghetti and macaroni	lb	0.78	7/01	11r
Steak, round, U.S. choice, boneless	lb	3.56	7/01	11r
Steak, sirloin, U.S. choice, boneless	lb	5.65	7/01	11r
Strawberries, dry pint	12 oz	1.50	7/01	11r
Sugar and other sweets, expenditures on	yr	99	1999	30r
Sugar, white, 33-80 ounce package	lb	0.39	7/01	11r
Sugar, white, all sizes	lb	0.42	7/01	11r
Tobacco products and smoking supplies purchases	yr	288	1999	30r
Tomatoes, field grown	lb	1.43	7/01	11r

Values are in dollars or fractions of dollars. In the column headed *Ref*, references are shown to sources. Each reference is followed by a letter. These refer to the geographical level for which data were reported: s=State, r=Region, and c=City or metro. The abbreviation *ex* is used to mean *except* or *excluding*; *exp* stands for expenditures. For other abbreviations and further explanations, please see the Introduction.

Jackson, TN - continued

Item	Per	Value	Date	Ref.
Groceries				
Tuna, light, chunk	lb	1.77	7/01	11r
Turkey, frozen, whole	lb	1.05	7/01	11r
Health Care				
Cardiac catheterization, ave hospital/ physician charges		12170	1998	77s
Childbirth, Cesarean delivery		11587	1997	13r
Childbirth, vaginal delivery		6725	1997	13r
Drugs, expenditures on	yr	399	1999	30r
Health care purchases	yr	1971	1999	30r
Health insurance expenditures	yr	933	1999	30r
Hysterectomy, laproscopically-assisted, ave hospital/physician charges		13470	1998	76s
Hysterectomy, vaginal, ave hospital and physician charges		9530	1998	76s
Medical services expenditures	yr	547	1999	30r
Medical supplies, expenditures on	yr	91	1999	30r
Household Goods				
Floor coverings, expenditures on	yr	44	1999	30r
Furniture, expenditures on	yr	335	1999	30r
Household furnishings and equipment purchases	yr	1328	1999	30r
Household textiles, expenditures on	yr	89	1999	30r
Laundry and cleaning supplies, expenditures on	yr	113	1999	30r
Housing				
Home price, existing, ave		160100	10/00	90r
Home value, median		112000	2001	53s
Household operation expenditures	yr	553	1999	30r
Housekeeping supplies purchases	yr	473	1999	30r
Housing, expenditures on	yr	10303	1999	30r
Maintenance, repairs, insurance expenditures	yr	699	1999	30r
Monthly rental value of owned home	mos	505	1999	30r
Owned dwellings, expenditures own	yr	3465	1999	30r
Rent expenditures	yr	1641	1999	30r
Rental unit, 1 bedroom, with utilities	mos	353	4/01	41c
Rental unit, 2 bedroom, with utilities	mos	473	4/01	41c
Rental unit, 3 bedroom, with utilities	mos	654	4/01	41c
Rental unit, 4 bedroom, with utilities	mos	658	4/01	41c
Shelter, expenditures on	yr	5467	1999	30r
Insurance and Pensions				
Life and other personal insurance purchases	yr	414	1999	30r
Pensions and Social Security, expenditures on	yr	2635	1999	30r
Personal insurance and pensions, expenditures on	yr	3048	1999	30r
Legal Fees				
Combination hunting and fishing license	yr	21.00	4/01	34s
Divorce, filing fee		64.00	4/01	35s
Driver's license fee	renew	17.50	1999	48s
Driver's license fee	orig	17.50	1999	48s
Personal Goods				
Personal care products and services purchases	yr	393	1999	30r
Personal Services				
Personal services, household, expenditures on	yr	258	1999	30r
Pets				
Pets, toys, and playground equipment, expenditures on	yr	306	1999	30r
Taxes				
Federal income taxes paid	yr	2047	1999	30r
Personal taxes, expenditures on	yr	2554	1999	30r
Property taxes paid	yr	726	1999	30r
State and local income taxes paid	yr	363	1999	30r

Jackson, TN - continued

Item	Per	Value	Date	Ref.
Transportation				
Cars and trucks, new, expenditures on	yr	1648	1999	30r
Cars and trucks, used, expenditures on	yr	1651	1999	30r
Diesel at the pump	gal	1.18	10/99	73s
Gasoline and motor oil purchases	yr	1052	1999	30r
Gasoline before-tax price (cents)	gal	102.50	10/00	43s
Maintenance and repair expenditures	yr	621	1999	30r
Public transportation, expenditures on	yr	298	1999	30r
Transportation purchases	yr	6738	1999	30r
Vehicle expenses, miscellaneous, purchases	yr	2033	1999	30r
Vehicle insurance payments	yr	696	1999	30r
Vehicle purchases (net outlay)	yr	3354	1999	30r
Vehicle rental, lease expenditures	yr	352	1999	30r
Utilities				
Electrical bill, average	mos	79.16	9/00	9s
Electricity, expenditures on	yr	1115	1999	30r
Electricity cost, average	KWh	5.60	9/00	9s
Water and other public services, expenditures on	yr	298	1999	30r
Weddings				
Wedding (national average cost)		19936	2000	33r
Attendants' gifts		321	1998	33r
Bridal attendants' apparel (5 persons)		824	2000	33r
Bride's headpiece/veil		173	1998	33r
Bride's wedding dress		859	1998	33r
Clergy, religious facility fee		242	1998	33r
Engagement ring		3177	1998	33r
Flowers		789	1998	33r
Groom's formalwear rental		99	2000	33r
Limousine		410	1998	33r
Marriage license cost		31.00	4/01	35s
Men's formalwear (ushers, best man)		469	2000	33r
Mother of bride apparel		241	2000	33r
Music		866	1998	33r
Photography and videography		1368	1998	33r
Rehearsal dinner		728	1998	33r
Wedding invitations and announcements		341	1998	33r
Wedding reception		7968	2000	33r
Wedding rings (bride and groom)		1060	1998	33r

Jacksonville, FL

Item	Per	Value	Date	Ref.
Composite, ACCRA index		94.70	3/01	4c
Alcoholic Beverages				
Alcoholic beverage purchases	yr	253	1999	30r
Beer, Heineken, 12-oz, ex deposit	6	6.63	3/01	4c
J & B Scotch	750-ml	21.32	3/01	4c
Malt beverages, all types, all sizes, any origin	16 oz	0.96	7/01	11r
Wine, Livingston or Gallo, Chablis blanc	1.5 liter	5.55	3/01	4c
Appliances				
Appliance repair, service call, washing machine	min lab chg	43.07	3/01	4c
Major appliances, expenditures on	yr	172	1999	30r
Small appliances, housewares, expenditures on	yr	81	1999	30r
Banking and Money				
Mortgage interest and charges paid	yr	2039	1999	30r
Mortgage principal paid on owned property	yr	1026	1999	30r
Mortgage rate, incl. points and orig. fee, 30-yr. conv. fixed or ARM	mos	6.97	3/01	4c
Vehicle finance charges paid	yr	365	1999	30r
Charity				
Cash contributions, expenditures	yr	1127	1999	30r
Child Care				
Child raising cost, total, age 0-2	yr	8540	1999	60r
Child raising cost, total, age 3-5	yr	8780	1999	60r
Child raising cost, total, age 6-8	yr	8820	1999	60r
Child raising cost, total, age 9-11	yr	8800	1999	60r
Child raising cost, total, age 12-14	yr	9510	1999	60r

Values are in dollars or fractions of dollars. In the column headed *Ref*, references are shown to sources. Each reference is followed by a letter. These refer to the geographical level for which data were reported: s=State, r=Region, and c=City or metro. The abbreviation *ex* is used to mean *except* or *excluding*; *exp* stands for expenditures. For other abbreviations and further explanations, please see the Introduction.

Jacksonville, FL - continued

Item	Per	Value	Date	Ref.
Child Care				
Child raising cost, total, age 15-17	yr	9740	1999	60r
Child's child care and education, age 0-2	yr	1380	1999	60r
Child's child care and education, age 3-5	yr	1520	1999	60r
Child's child care and education, age 6-8	yr	990	1999	60r
Child's child care and education, age 9-11	yr	650	1999	60r
Child's child care and education, age 12-14	yr	490	1999	60r
Child's child care and education, age 15-17	yr	840	1999	60r
Child's clothing, age 0-2	yr	480	1999	60r
Child's clothing, age 3-5	yr	470	1999	60r
Child's clothing, age 6-8	yr	520	1999	60r
Child's clothing, age 9-11	yr	570	1999	60r
Child's clothing, age 12-14	yr	950	1999	60r
Child's clothing, age 15-17	yr	850	1999	60r
Child's food, age 0-2	yr	1000	1999	60r
Child's food, age 3-5	yr	1160	1999	60r
Child's food, age 6-8	yr	1490	1999	60r
Child's food, age 9-11	yr	1770	1999	60r
Child's food, age 12-14	yr	1770	1999	60r
Child's food, age 15-17	yr	1980	1999	60r
Child's health care, age 0-2	yr	620	1999	60r
Child's health care, age 3-5	yr	590	1999	60r
Child's health care, age 6-8	yr	680	1999	60r
Child's health care, age 9-11	yr	720	1999	60r
Child's health care, age 12-14	yr	730	1999	60r
Child's health care, age 15-17	yr	760	1999	60r
Child's housing, age 0-2	yr	3070	1999	60r
Child's housing, age 3-5	yr	3050	1999	60r
Child's housing, age 6-8	yr	3010	1999	60r
Child's housing, age 9-11	yr	2850	1999	60r
Child's housing, age 12-14	yr	3040	1999	60r
Child's housing, age 15-17	yr	2650	1999	60r
Child's personal care, reading, age 0-2	yr	910	1999	60r
Child's personal care, reading, age 3-5	yr	930	1999	60r
Child's personal care, reading, age 6-8	yr	960	1999	60r
Child's personal care, reading, age 9-11	yr	1000	1999	60r
Child's personal care, reading, age 12-14	yr	1170	1999	60r
Child's personal care, reading, age 15-17	yr	950	1999	60r
Clothing				
Apparel and services purchases	yr	1610	1999	30r
Boys' brief, cotton	3	3.88	3/01	4c
Boys, 2 to 15, expenditures on	yr	89	1999	30r
Children under 2, expenditures on	yr	79	1999	30r
Footwear, expenditures on	yr	283	1999	30r
Girls, 2 to 15, expenditures on	yr	103	1999	30r
Men and boys, expenditures on	yr	351	1999	30r
Men, 16 and over, expenditures on	yr	262	1999	30r
Shirt, man's dress shirt		26.50	3/01	4c
Slacks, man's "No Wrinkles" khaki		42.80	3/01	4c
Women, 16 and over, expenditures on	yr	538	1999	30r
Communications				
Cable modem installation, Adelphi		54.90	6/99	103s
Cable modem installation, Comcast		95.00	6/99	103s
Cable modem installation, Media One		100.00	6/99	103s
Cable modem installation, Time Warner		75.00-225.00	6/99	103s
Cable modem rate, cable subscriber, Adelphi	mos	34.95	6/99	103s
Cable modem rate, cable subscriber, Comcast	mos	39.95	6/99	103s
Cable modem rate, cable subscriber, Media One	mos	34.95-39.95	6/99	103s
Cable modem rate, cable subscriber, Time Warner	mos	39.95-49.95	6/99	103s
Cable modem rate, non-cable subscriber, Adelphi	mos	44.95	6/99	103s
Cable modem rate, non-cable subscriber, Comcast	mos	49.95	6/99	103s
Cable modem rate, non-cable subscriber, Media One	mos	49.95	6/99	103s
Cable modem rate, non-cable subscriber, Time Warner	mos	39.95-54.95	6/99	103s

Jacksonville, FL - continued

Item	Per	Value	Date	Ref.
Communications - continued				
Newspaper subscription, daily and Sunday delivery	mos	14.04	3/01	4c
Phone line, single, business, field visit	inst.	56.00	12/97	17s
Phone line, single, business, no field visit	inst.	56.00	12/97	17s
Phone line, single, residence, field visit	inst.	40.00	12/97	17s
Phone line, single, residence, no field visit	inst.	40.00	12/97	17s
Postage and stationery, expenditures on	yr	104	1999	30r
Postal rate, express mail, up to half-pound		12.45	7/01	108r
Postal rate, letter, first class, first ounce		0.34	7/01	108r
Postal rate, letter, two ounces		0.57	7/01	108r
Postal rate, post card		0.21	7/01	108r
Postal rate, priority mail, two pounds		3.95	7/01	108r
Postal rate, priority mail, up to one pound		3.50	7/01	108r
Telephone bill, business, basic rate	mos	28.00	12/97	18c
Telephone bill, family of three	mos	24.11	3/01	4c
Telephone bill, residential, basic rate	mos	10.30	12/97	18c
Telephone services, expenditures on	yr	860	1999	30r
Education				
Board, 4-year private college/university	yr	2236	1996	38s
Board, 4-year public college/university	yr	2295	1996	38s
Education expenditures	yr	431	1999	30r
Room, 4-year private college/university	yr	2428	1996	38s
Room, 4-year public college/university	yr	2193	1996	38s
Total cost, 4-year private college/university	yr	15028	1996	38s
Total cost, 4-year public college/university	yr	6254	1996	38s
Tuition, 2-year public college/university, in state	yr	1103	1996	38s
Tuition, 4-year private college/university, in state	yr	10364	1996	38s
Tuition, 4-year public college/university	yr	1767	1996	38s
Energy and Fuels				
Electricity	500 KWhs	47.29	7/01	11r
Electricity	KWh	0.09	7/01	11r
Energy, combined forms, 2400 sq ft	mos	98.64	3/01	4c
Fuel oil #2	gal	1.43	7/01	11r
Fuel oil and other fuels, expenditures on	yr	45	1999	30r
Gas, cooking, winter, 10 therms	mos	14.39	2/96	98c
Gas, cooking, winter, 30 therms	mos	29.19	2/96	98c
Gas, cooking, winter, 50 therms	mos	43.98	2/96	98c
Gas, heating, winter, average use	mos	43.98	2/96	98c
Gas, natural, commercial rate	1000 cf	8.44	11/00	88s
Gas, regular unleaded, cash, self-service	gal	1.41	3/01	4c
Gasoline, all types	gal	1.60	7/01	11r
Gasoline, unleaded midgrade	gal	1.65	7/01	11r
Gasoline, unleaded premium	gal	1.74	7/01	11r
Natural gas, expenditures on	yr	164	1999	30r
Utility (piped) gas, therm		1.01	7/01	11r
Utility (piped) gas, 40 therms		44.29	7/01	11r
Utility (piped) gas, 100 therms		97.44	7/01	11r
Entertainment				
Bowling, Saturday evening rate	line	3.20	3/01	4c
Entertainment purchases	yr	1574	1999	30r
Fees and admissions paid	yr	371	1999	30r
Monopoly game, Parker Brothers', No. 9	game	10.59	3/01	4c
Movie, first-run, Saturday, evening	adm.	6.46	3/01	4c
Reading purchases	yr	121	1999	30r
Television, radios, sound equipment, expenditures on	yr	561	1999	30r
Tennis balls, yellow, Wilson or Penn, 3	can	2.16	3/01	4c
Funerals				
Total cost of funeral		5922.53	1/99	78r
Acknowledgement cards		63.43	1/99	78r
Casket		2258.77	1/99	78r
Cosmetology, hair, other preparation		127.09	1/99	78r
Embalming		393.49	1/99	78r
Funeral at funeral home		367.50	1/99	78r
Hearse (local)		169.66	1/99	78r
Professional service charges		1211.32	1/99	78r
Service car/van		80.69	1/99	78r

Values are in dollars or fractions of dollars. In the column headed *Ref*, references are shown to sources. Each reference is followed by a letter. These refer to the geographical level for which data were reported: s=State, r=Region, and c=City or metro. The abbreviation *ex* is used to mean *except* or *excluding*; *exp* stands for *expenditures*. For other abbreviations and further explanations, please see the Introduction.

Jacksonville, FL - continued

Item	Per	Value	Date	Ref.
Funerals				
Transfer of remains to funeral home		144.25	1/99	78r
Vault		803.50	1/99	78r
Visitation/viewing		302.83	1/99	78r
Groceries				
Groceries, ACCRA Index		104.80	3/01	4c
American processed cheese	lb	3.50	7/01	11r
Antibiotic ointment, Polysporin	0.5 oz	4.21	3/01	4c
Baby food, strained vegetables or fruit, lowest price	4-4.5 oz	0.44	3/01	4c
Bakery products, expenditures on	yr	261	1999	30r
Bananas	lb	0.47	3/01	4c
Bananas	lb	0.47	7/01	11r
Beans, dried, any type, all sizes	lb	0.63	7/01	11r
Beef for stew, boneless	lb	2.86	7/01	11r
Beef or hamburger, ground	lb	1.73	3/01	4c
Beef, expenditures on	yr	210	1999	30r
Bologna, all beef or mixed	lb	2.29	7/01	11r
Bread, French	lb	1.66	7/01	11r
Bread, white	loaf	1.04	3/01	4c
Bread, white, pan	lb	0.87	7/01	11r
Bread, whole wheat, pan	lb	1.38	7/01	11r
Broccoli	lb	1.04	7/01	11r
Butter, salted, grade AA, stick	lb	2.26	7/01	11r
Butter, yoghurt, cheese, etc, expenditures on	yr	170	1999	30r
Cabbage	lb	0.42	7/01	11r
Cereals and cereal products, expenditures on	yr	140	1999	30r
Cheddar cheese, natural	lb	3.75	7/01	11r
Cheese, Kraft grated Parmesan	8 oz	3.71	3/01	4c
Chicken breast, bone-in	lb	1.85	7/01	11r
Chicken legs, bone-in	lb	1.34	7/01	11r
Chicken, fresh, whole	lb	1.05	7/01	11r
Chicken, whole fryer	lb	0.99	3/01	4c
Chops, boneless	lb	4.13	7/01	11r
Chuck roast, graded and ungraded, excl U.S. prime and choice	lb	2.35	7/01	11r
Chuck roast, U.S. choice, boneless	lb	2.67	7/01	11r
Cigarettes, Winston, Kings	carton	29.36	3/01	4c
Coffee, 100%, ground roast, all sizes	lb	2.88	7/01	11r
Coffee, instant, plain, regular, all sizes	16 oz	9.25	7/01	11r
Coffee, vacuum-packed	13 oz	2.71	3/01	4c
Cola, non diet	2 liter	1.11	7/01	11r
Corn Flakes, Kellogg's or Post Toasties	18 oz	3.01	3/01	4c
Corn, frozen, whole kernel, lowest price	16 oz	1.20	3/01	4c
Crackers, soda, salted	lb	1.70	7/01	11r
Dairy product purchases	yr	282	1999	30r
Eggs, expenditures on	yr	32	1999	30r
Eggs, Grade A or AA	dozen	1.17	3/01	4c
Fats and oils, expenditures on	yr	79	1999	30r
Fish and seafood, expenditures on	yr	99	1999	30r
Flour, white, all purpose	lb	0.32	7/01	11r
Food (excl fruit and vegetables), eaten at home, purchases	yr	815	1999	30r
Food cooked on trips, expenditures on	yr	36	1999	30r
Food purchases	yr	4533	1999	30r
Food purchases, eaten away from home	yr	1873	1999	30r
Food purchases, food eaten at home	yr	2660	1999	30r
Fresh fruits, expenditures on	yr	128	1999	30r
Fresh milk and cream, expenditures on	yr	112	1999	30r
Fresh vegetables, expenditures on	yr	131	1999	30r
Fruit and vegetable purchases	yr	438	1999	30r
Grapefruit	lb	0.59	7/01	11r
Grapes, Thompson, seedless	lb	2.12	7/01	11r
Ground beef, 100% beef	lb	1.76	7/01	11r
Ground beef, lean and extra lean	lb	2.60	7/01	11r
Ground chuck, 100% beef	lb	2.08	7/01	11r
Ham, boneless, excl canned	lb	2.71	7/01	11r
Ham, rump or shank half, bone-in, smoked	lb	2.19	7/01	11r
Ice cream, prepackaged, bulk, regular	1/2 gal	3.93	7/01	11r
Lemons	lb	1.32	7/01	11r
Lettuce, iceberg	head	0.99	3/01	4c
Lettuce, iceberg	lb	0.76	7/01	11r

Jacksonville, FL - continued

Item	Per	Value	Date	Ref.
Groceries - continued				
Margarine, Blue Bonnet or Parkay, stick	lb	0.72	3/01	4c
Milk, fresh, low fat,	gal	2.75	7/01	11r
Milk, fresh, whole, fortified	gal	2.97	7/01	11r
Milk, whole	1/2 gal	1.93	3/01	4c
Nonalcoholic beverages, expenditures on	yr	228	1999	30r
Orange juice, frozen concentrate	16 oz	1.95	7/01	11r
Orange juice, Minute Maid frozen	12 oz	1.79	3/01	4c
Oranges, Navel	lb	0.73	7/01	11r
Oranges, Valencia	lb	0.55	7/01	11r
Peaches, halves or slices, Hunt's, Del Monte, or Libby's	29 oz	1.57	3/01	4c
Peanut butter, creamy, all sizes	lb	1.83	7/01	11r
Pears, Anjou	lb	0.98	7/01	11r
Peas, green, Del Monte or Green Giant	15 oz	0.67	3/01	4c
Pork chops, center cut, bone-in	lb	3.33	7/01	11r
Pork sausage, fresh, loose	lb	2.59	7/01	11r
Pork shoulder picnic, bone-in, smoked	lb	1.12	7/01	11r
Pork, expenditures on	yr	162	1999	30r
Potato chips	16 oz	3.59	7/01	11r
Potatoes, frozen, french fried	lb	1.00	7/01	11r
Potatoes, white or red	10 lb	3.03	3/01	4c
Potatoes, white, all types	lb	0.44	7/01	11r
Poultry, expenditures on	yr	137	1999	30r
Processed fruits, expenditures on	yr	97	1999	30r
Processed vegetables, expenditures on	yr	82	1999	30r
Rice, white, long grain, uncooked	lb	0.51	7/01	11r
Round roast, graded and ungraded, excl U.S. prime and choice	lb	2.96	7/01	11r
Round steak, graded and ungraded, excl U.S. prime and choice	lb	3.11	7/01	11r
Sausage, Jimmy Dean/Owens pork	lb	2.84	3/01	4c
Shortening, vegetable, Crisco	3 lb	3.25	3/01	4c
Sirloin steak, graded and ungraded, excl U.S. prime and choice	lb	4.23	7/01	11r
Soft drink, Coca Cola, ex deposit	2 liter	1.17	3/01	4c
Spaghetti and macaroni	lb	0.78	7/01	11r
Steak, round, U.S. choice, boneless	lb	3.56	7/01	11r
Steak, sirloin, U.S. choice, boneless	lb	5.65	7/01	11r
Steak, T-bone	lb	7.39	3/01	4c
Strawberries, dry pint	12 oz	1.50	7/01	11r
Sugar and other sweets, expenditures on	yr	99	1999	30r
Sugar, cane or beet	4 lbs	1.57	3/01	4c
Sugar, white, 33-80 ounce package	lb	0.39	7/01	11r
Sugar, white, all sizes	lb	0.42	7/01	11r
Tobacco products and smoking supplies purchases	yr	288	1999	30r
Tomatoes, field grown	lb	1.43	7/01	11r
Tomatoes, Hunt's or Del Monte	14.5 oz	0.79	3/01	4c
Tuna, chunk, light	6 oz	0.74	3/01	4c
Tuna, light, chunk	lb	1.77	7/01	11r
Turkey, frozen, whole	lb	1.05	7/01	11r
Goods and Services				
Miscellaneous goods and services, ACCRA Index		98.80	3/01	4c
B&B Japanese maple (acer japonicum)	gal	49.98-129.00	4/00	93r
Boxwood (buxus)	2 gal	12.99-16.99	4/00	93r
Daylilly (hemerocallis)	gal	4.99-8.99	4/00	93r
Flat of annuals		11.00-13.92	4/00	93r
Fountain grass (pennisetum)	gal	5.98-7.98	4/00	93r
Hanging basket (10 in)		7.99-14.98	4/00	93r
Hardy geranium (geranium)	gal	5.98-8.00	4/00	93r
Hosta (hosta)	gal	4.99-10.98	4/00	93r
Lilac (syrubga vulgaris)	2 gal	12.99-21.99	4/00	93r

Values are in dollars or fractions of dollars. In the column headed *Ref*, references are shown to sources. Each reference is followed by a letter. These refer to the geographical level for which data were reported: s=State, r=Region, and c=City or metro. The abbreviation *ex* is used to mean *except* or *excluding*; *exp* stands for expenditures. For other abbreviations and further explanations, please see the Introduction.

Jacksonville, FL - continued

Item	Per	Value	Date	Ref.
Goods and Services				
Rhododendron (rhododendron)	2 gal	14.99-24.99	4/00	93r
Sage (salvia)	gal	5.98-6.99	4/00	93r
Wintercreeper euonymus (euonymus fortunei)	2 gal	7.99-89.99	4/00	93r
Hunting license	yr	12.50	4/01	34s
Health Care				
Health care, ACCRA Index		87.70	3/01	4c
Cardiac catheterization, ave hospital/physician charges		15060	1998	77s
Childbirth, Cesarean delivery		11587	1997	13r
Childbirth, vaginal delivery		6725	1997	13r
Dentist's fee, adult teeth cleaning and periodic oral exam	visit	59.17	3/01	4c
Doctor's fee, routine exam, established patient	visit	56.33	3/01	4c
Drugs, expenditures on	yr	399	1999	30r
Health care purchases	yr	1971	1999	30r
Health insurance expenditures	yr	933	1999	30r
Home health care aide cost, licensed agency	hour	14	2000	82c
Hospital care, private room	day	417.50	3/01	4c
Hysterectomy, laproscopically-assisted, ave hospital/physician charges		14760	1998	76s
Hysterectomy, vaginal, ave hospital and physician charges		11320	1998	76s
Medicaid dispensing fee		4.23	1999	87s
Medical services expenditures	yr	547	1999	30r
Medical supplies, expenditures on	yr	91	1999	30r
Nursing home costs, private room	day	150	2000	82c
Nursing home stay, private room	day	150	2000	81c
Plastic surgery, breast augmentation		2870	2000	7r
Plastic surgery, breast lift		3649	2000	7r
Plastic surgery, facelift		5008	2000	7r
Plastic surgery, hair transplantation		3425	2000	7r
Plastic surgery, lip augmentation		1227	2000	7r
Plastic surgery, lower body lift		4793	2000	7r
Plastic surgery, thigh lift		3862	2000	7r
Household Goods				
Dishwashing powder, Cascade	50 oz	3.81	3/01	4c
Floor coverings, expenditures on	yr	44	1999	30r
Furniture, expenditures on	yr	335	1999	30r
Household furnishings and equipment purchases	yr	1328	1999	30r
Household textiles, expenditures on	yr	89	1999	30r
Laundry and cleaning supplies, expenditures on	yr	113	1999	30r
Tissues, facial, Kleenex brand	175	1.30	3/01	4c
Housing				
Housing, ACCRA Index		87.00	3/01	4c
Home, 2200 sq ft, 4-br, 2-bath, 2-car garage, average		200225	2000	47c
Home price, existing, ave		160100	10/00	90r
Home value, median		104000	2001	53s
House, 2400 sq ft, 8000 sq ft lot, new, urban, utilities	total	173812	3/01	4c
House payment, principal and interest, 25% down payment	mos	865	3/01	4c
Household operation expenditures	yr	553	1999	30r
Housekeeping supplies purchases	yr	473	1999	30r
Housing, expenditures on	yr	10303	1999	30r
Maintenance, repairs, insurance expenditures	yr	699	1999	30r
Monthly rental value of owned home	mos	505	1999	30r
Owned dwellings, expenditures own	yr	3465	1999	30r
Rent expenditures	yr	1641	1999	30r
Rent, apartment, 2 br, 1 1/2-2 baths, unfurn, 950 sq ft, water	mos	689	3/01	4c
Rental unit, 1 bedroom, with utilities	mos	530	4/01	41c
Rental unit, 2 bedroom, with utilities	mos	638	4/01	41c
Rental unit, 3 bedroom, with utilities	mos	843	4/01	41c

Jacksonville, FL - continued

Item	Per	Value	Date	Ref.
Housing - continued				
Rental unit, 4 bedroom, with utilities	mos	938	4/01	41c
Shelter, expenditures on	yr	5467	1999	30r
Insurance and Pensions				
Life and other personal insurance purchases	yr	414	1999	30r
Medigap health insurance, Plan H	yr	2887	2000	69s
Medigap health insurance, Plan I	yr	3302	2000	69s
Medigap health insurance, Plan J	yr	3889	2000	69s
Pensions and Social Security, expenditures on	yr	2635	1999	30r
Personal insurance and pensions, expenditures on	yr	3048	1999	30r
Legal Fees				
Divorce, filing fee		65.00-85.00	4/01	35s
Driver's license fee	orig	20.00	1999	48s
Driver's license fee	renew	15.00	1999	48s
Personal Goods				
Personal care products and services purchases	yr	393	1999	30r
Shampoo, Alberto VO5	15 oz	1.13	3/01	4c
Toothpaste, Crest or Colgate	6-7 oz	2.47	3/01	4c
Personal Services				
Dry cleaning, man's 2-pc suit		6.54	3/01	4c
Man's haircut, barbershop, no styling		9.17	3/01	4c
Personal services, household, expenditures on	yr	258	1999	30r
Woman's shampoo, trim, blow-dry, no style-change		24.83	3/01	4c
Pets				
Pets, toys, and playground equipment, expenditures on	yr	306	1999	30r
Restaurant Food				
Chicken, fried, thigh and drumstick, KFC/Church's		2.20	3/01	4c
Hamburger with cheese, McDonald's	1/4 lb	2.09	3/01	4c
Pizza, Pizza Hut or Pizza Inn	11-12 in	8.99	3/01	4c
Taxes				
Federal income taxes paid	yr	2047	1999	30r
Personal taxes, expenditures on	yr	2554	1999	30r
Property taxes paid	yr	726	1999	30r
State and local income taxes paid	yr	363	1999	30r
Transportation				
Transportation, ACCRA Index		97.70	3/01	4c
Bus fare, one-way	trip	0.75	2000	1c
Cars and trucks, new, expenditures on	yr	1648	1999	30r
Cars and trucks, used, expenditures on	yr	1651	1999	30r
Diesel at the pump	gal	1.26	10/99	73s
Gasoline and motor oil purchases	yr	1052	1999	30r
Gasoline before-tax price (cents)	gal	101.90	10/00	43s
Maintenance and repair expenditures	yr	621	1999	30r
Public transportation, expenditures on	yr	298	1999	30r
Tire balance, computer or spin balance, front	wheel	7.48	3/01	4c
Transportation purchases	yr	6738	1999	30r
Vehicle expenses, miscellaneous, purchases	yr	2033	1999	30r
Vehicle insurance payments	yr	696	1999	30r
Vehicle purchases (net outlay)	yr	3354	1999	30r
Vehicle rental, lease expenditures	yr	352	1999	30r
Travel				
Hotel room	night	110.57	2/01	95s
Utilities				
Utilities, ACCRA Index		84.90	3/01	4c
Electrical bill, average	mos	86.33	9/00	9s
Electricity, 2400 sq ft, new home	mos	98.64	3/01	4c
Electricity, expenditures on	yr	1115	1999	30r
Electricity cost, average	KWh	6.80	9/00	9s
Water and other public services, expenditures on	yr	298	1999	30r

Values are in dollars or fractions of dollars. In the column headed *Ref*, references are shown to sources. Each reference is followed by a letter. These refer to the geographical level for which data were reported: s=State, r=Region, and c=City or metro. The abbreviation *ex* is used to mean *except* or *excluding*; *exp* stands for *expenditures*. For other abbreviations and further explanations, please see the Introduction.

Jacksonville, FL - continued

Item	Per	Value	Date	Ref.
Weddings				
Wedding (national average cost)		19936	2000	33r
Wedding (regional average total cost)		16293	1997	110r
Attendants' gifts		321	1998	33r
Bridal attendants' apparel (5 persons)		824	2000	33r
Bride's headpiece/veil		173	1998	33r
Bride's wedding dress		859	1998	33r
Clergy, religious facility fee		242	1998	33r
Engagement ring		3177	1998	33r
Flowers		789	1998	33r
Groom's formalwear rental		99	2000	33r
Limousine		410	1998	33r
Marriage license cost		56.00-88.50	4/01	35s
Men's formalwear (ushers, best man)		469	2000	33r
Mother of bride apparel		241	2000	33r
Music		866	1998	33r
Photography and videography		1368	1998	33r
Rehearsal dinner		728	1998	33r
Wedding invitations and announcements		341	1998	33r
Wedding reception		7968	2000	33r
Wedding rings (bride and groom)		1060	1998	33r

Jacksonville, NC

Item	Per	Value	Date	Ref.
Composite, ACCRA index		91.80	3/01	4c
Alcoholic Beverages				
Alcoholic beverage purchases	yr	253	1999	30r
Beer, Heineken, 12-oz, ex deposit	6	6.49	3/01	4c
J & B Scotch	750-ml	20.75	3/01	4c
Malt beverages, all types, all sizes, any origin	16 oz	0.96	7/01	11r
Wine, Livingston or Gallo, Chablis blanc	1.5 liter	5.76	3/01	4c
Appliances				
Appliance repair, service call, washing machine	min lab chg	36.33	3/01	4c
Major appliances, expenditures on	yr	172	1999	30r
Small appliances, housewares, expenditures on	yr	81	1999	30r
Banking and Money				
Mortgage interest and charges paid	yr	2039	1999	30r
Mortgage principal paid on owned property	yr	1026	1999	30r
Mortgage rate, incl. points and orig. fee, 30-yr. conv. fixed or ARM	mos	7.31	3/01	4c
Vehicle finance charges paid	yr	365	1999	30r
Charity				
Cash contributions, expenditures	yr	1127	1999	30r
Child Care				
Child raising cost, total, age 0-2	yr	8540	1999	60r
Child raising cost, total, age 3-5	yr	8780	1999	60r
Child raising cost, total, age 6-8	yr	8820	1999	60r
Child raising cost, total, age 9-11	yr	8800	1999	60r
Child raising cost, total, age 12-14	yr	9510	1999	60r
Child raising cost, total, age 15-17	yr	9740	1999	60r
Child's child care and education, age 0-2	yr	1380	1999	60r
Child's child care and education, age 3-5	yr	1520	1999	60r
Child's child care and education, age 6-8	yr	990	1999	60r
Child's child care and education, age 9-11	yr	650	1999	60r
Child's child care and education, age 12-14	yr	490	1999	60r
Child's child care and education, age 15-17	yr	840	1999	60r
Child's clothing, age 0-2	yr	480	1999	60r
Child's clothing, age 3-5	yr	470	1999	60r
Child's clothing, age 6-8	yr	520	1999	60r
Child's clothing, age 9-11	yr	570	1999	60r
Child's clothing, age 12-14	yr	950	1999	60r
Child's clothing, age 15-17	yr	850	1999	60r
Child's food, age 0-2	yr	1000	1999	60r
Child's food, age 3-5	yr	1160	1999	60r
Child's food, age 6-8	yr	1490	1999	60r
Child's food, age 9-11	yr	1770	1999	60r
Child's food, age 12-14	yr	1770	1999	60r

Jacksonville, NC - continued

Item	Per	Value	Date	Ref.
Child Care - continued				
Child's food, age 15-17	yr	1980	1999	60r
Child's health care, age 0-2	yr	620	1999	60r
Child's health care, age 3-5	yr	590	1999	60r
Child's health care, age 6-8	yr	680	1999	60r
Child's health care, age 9-11	yr	720	1999	60r
Child's health care, age 12-14	yr	730	1999	60r
Child's health care, age 15-17	yr	760	1999	60r
Child's housing, age 0-2	yr	3070	1999	60r
Child's housing, age 3-5	yr	3050	1999	60r
Child's housing, age 6-8	yr	3010	1999	60r
Child's housing, age 9-11	yr	2850	1999	60r
Child's housing, age 12-14	yr	3040	1999	60r
Child's housing, age 15-17	yr	2650	1999	60r
Child's personal care, reading, age 0-2	yr	910	1999	60r
Child's personal care, reading, age 3-5	yr	930	1999	60r
Child's personal care, reading, age 6-8	yr	960	1999	60r
Child's personal care, reading, age 9-11	yr	1000	1999	60r
Child's personal care, reading, age 12-14	yr	1170	1999	60r
Child's personal care, reading, age 15-17	yr	950	1999	60r
Clothing				
Apparel and services purchases	yr	1610	1999	30r
Boys' brief, cotton	3	4.33	3/01	4c
Boys, 2 to 15, expenditures on	yr	89	1999	30r
Children under 2, expenditures on	yr	79	1999	30r
Footwear, expenditures on	yr	283	1999	30r
Girls, 2 to 15, expenditures on	yr	103	1999	30r
Men and boys, expenditures on	yr	351	1999	30r
Men, 16 and over, expenditures on	yr	262	1999	30r
Shirt, man's dress shirt		29.50	3/01	4c
Slacks, man's "No Wrinkles" khaki		43.66	3/01	4c
Women, 16 and over, expenditures on	yr	538	1999	30r
Communications				
Cable modem installation, Intermedia		149.95	6/99	103s
Cable modem installation, Time Warner		75.00-225.00	6/99	103s
Cable modem rate, cable subscriber, Intermedia	mos	49.95	6/99	103s
Cable modem rate, cable subscriber, Time Warner	mos	39.95-49.95	6/99	103s
Cable modem rate, non-cable subscriber, Intermedia	mos	54.95	6/99	103s
Cable modem rate, non-cable subscriber, Time Warner	mos	39.95-54.95	6/99	103s
Newspaper subscription, daily and Sunday delivery	mos	9.00	3/01	4c
Phone line, single, business, field visit	inst.	65.00	12/97	17s
Phone line, single, business, no field visit	inst.	65.00	12/97	17s
Phone line, single, residence, field visit	inst.	42.75	12/97	17s
Phone line, single, residence, no field visit	inst.	42.75	12/97	17s
Postage and stationery, expenditures on	yr	104	1999	30r
Postal rate, express mail, up to half-pound		12.45	7/01	108r
Postal rate, letter, first class, first ounce		0.34	7/01	108r
Postal rate, letter, two ounces		0.57	7/01	108r
Postal rate, post card		0.21	7/01	108r
Postal rate, priority mail, two pounds		3.95	7/01	108r
Postal rate, priority mail, up to one pound		3.50	7/01	108r
Telephone bill, family of three	mos	20.79	3/01	4c
Telephone services, expenditures on	yr	860	1999	30r
Education				
Board, 4-year private college/university	yr	2316	1996	38s
Board, 4-year public college/university	yr	1737	1996	38s
Education expenditures	yr	431	1999	30r
Room, 4-year private college/university	yr	2128	1996	38s
Room, 4-year public college/university	yr	1742	1996	38s
Total cost, 4-year private college/university	yr	15428	1996	38s
Total cost, 4-year public college/university	yr	5119	1996	38s
Tuition, 4-year private college/university, in state	yr	10984	1996	38s
Tuition, 4-year public college/university	yr	1639	1996	38s

Values are in dollars or fractions of dollars. In the column headed *Ref*, references are shown to sources. Each reference is followed by a letter. These refer to the geographical level for which data were reported: s=State, r=Region, and c=City or metro. The abbreviation *ex* is used to mean *except* or *excluding*; *exp* stands for *expenditures*. For other abbreviations and further explanations, please see the Introduction.

Jacksonville, NC - continued

Item	Per	Value	Date	Ref.
Energy and Fuels				
Electricity	KWh	0.09	7/01	11r
Electricity	500 KWhs	47.29	7/01	11r
Energy, combined forms, 2400 sq ft	mos	133.59	3/01	4c
Fuel oil #2	gal	1.43	7/01	11r
Fuel oil and other fuels, expenditures on	yr	45	1999	30r
Gas, natural, commercial rate	1000 cf	9.25	11/00	88s
Gas, regular unleaded, cash, self-service	gal	1.29	3/01	4c
Gasoline, all types	gal	1.60	7/01	11r
Gasoline, unleaded midgrade	gal	1.65	7/01	11r
Gasoline, unleaded premium	gal	1.74	7/01	11r
Natural gas, expenditures on	yr	164	1999	30r
Utility (piped) gas, therm		1.01	7/01	11r
Utility (piped) gas, 40 therms		44.29	7/01	11r
Utility (piped) gas, 100 therms		97.44	7/01	11r
Entertainment				
Bowling, Saturday evening rate	line	2.75	3/01	4c
Entertainment purchases	yr	1574	1999	30r
Fees and admissions paid	yr	371	1999	30r
Monopoly game, Parker Brothers', No. 9	game	9.53	3/01	4c
Movie, first-run, Saturday, evening	adm.	6.75	3/01	4c
Reading purchases	yr	121	1999	30r
Television, radios, sound equipment, expenditures on	yr	561	1999	30r
Tennis balls, yellow, Wilson or Penn, 3	can	1.98	3/01	4c
Funerals				
Total cost of funeral		5922.53	1/99	78r
Acknowledgement cards		63.43	1/99	78r
Casket		2258.77	1/99	78r
Cosmetology, hair, other preparation		127.09	1/99	78r
Embalming		393.49	1/99	78r
Funeral at funeral home		367.50	1/99	78r
Hearse (local)		169.66	1/99	78r
Professional service charges		1211.32	1/99	78r
Service car/van		80.69	1/99	78r
Transfer of remains to funeral home		144.25	1/99	78r
Vault		803.50	1/99	78r
Visitation/viewing		302.83	1/99	78r
Groceries				
Groceries, ACCRA Index		93.50	3/01	4c
American processed cheese	lb	3.50	7/01	11r
Antibiotic ointment, Polysporin	0.5 oz	4.27	3/01	4c
Baby food, strained vegetables or fruit, lowest price	4-4.5 oz	0.49	3/01	4c
Bakery products, expenditures on	yr	261	1999	30r
Bananas	lb	0.54	3/01	4c
Bananas	lb	0.47	7/01	11r
Beans, dried, any type, all sizes	lb	0.63	7/01	11r
Beef for stew, boneless	lb	2.86	7/01	11r
Beef or hamburger, ground	lb	1.46	3/01	4c
Beef, expenditures on	yr	210	1999	30r
Bologna, all beef or mixed	lb	2.29	7/01	11r
Bread, French	lb	1.66	7/01	11r
Bread, white	loaf	0.66	3/01	4c
Bread, white, pan	lb	0.87	7/01	11r
Bread, whole wheat, pan	lb	1.38	7/01	11r
Broccoli	lb	1.04	7/01	11r
Butter, salted, grade AA, stick	lb	2.26	7/01	11r
Butter, yoghurt, cheese, etc, expenditures on	yr	170	1999	30r
Cabbage	lb	0.42	7/01	11r
Cereals and cereal products, expenditures on	yr	140	1999	30r
Cheddar cheese, natural	lb	3.75	7/01	11r
Cheese, Kraft grated Parmesan	8 oz	3.49	3/01	4c
Chicken breast, bone-in	lb	1.85	7/01	11r
Chicken legs, bone-in	lb	1.34	7/01	11r
Chicken, fresh, whole	lb	1.05	7/01	11r
Chicken, whole fryer	lb	0.99	3/01	4c
Chops, boneless,	lb	4.13	7/01	11r
Chuck roast, graded and ungraded, excl U.S. prime and choice	lb	2.35	7/01	11r

Jacksonville, NC - continued

Item	Per	Value	Date	Ref.
Groceries - continued				
Chuck roast, U.S. choice, boneless	lb	2.67	7/01	11r
Cigarettes, Winston, Kings	carton	24.49	3/01	4c
Coffee, 100%, ground roast, all sizes	lb	2.88	7/01	11r
Coffee, instant, plain, regular, all sizes	16 oz	9.25	7/01	11r
Coffee, vacuum-packed	13 oz	1.76	3/01	4c
Cola, non diet,	2 liter	1.11	7/01	11r
Corn Flakes, Kellogg's or Post Toasties	18 oz	2.66	3/01	4c
Corn, frozen, whole kernel, lowest price	16 oz	0.92	3/01	4c
Crackers, soda, salted	lb	1.70	7/01	11r
Dairy product purchases	yr	282	1999	30r
Eggs, expenditures on	yr	32	1999	30r
Eggs, Grade A or AA	dozen	1.40	3/01	4c
Fats and oils, expenditures on	yr	79	1999	30r
Fish and seafood, expenditures on	yr	99	1999	30r
Flour, white, all purpose	lb	0.32	7/01	11r
Food (excl fruit and vegetables), eaten at home, purchases	yr	815	1999	30r
Food cooked on trips, expenditures on	yr	36	1999	30r
Food purchases	yr	4533	1999	30r
Food purchases, eaten away from home	yr	1873	1999	30r
Food purchases, food eaten at home	yr	2660	1999	30r
Fresh fruits, expenditures on	yr	128	1999	30r
Fresh milk and cream, expenditures on	yr	112	1999	30r
Fresh vegetables, expenditures on	yr	131	1999	30r
Fruit and vegetable purchases	yr	438	1999	30r
Grapefruit	lb	0.59	7/01	11r
Grapes, Thompson, seedless	lb	2.12	7/01	11r
Ground beef, 100% beef	lb	1.76	7/01	11r
Ground beef, lean and extra lean	lb	2.60	7/01	11r
Ground chuck, 100% beef	lb	2.08	7/01	11r
Ham, boneless, excl canned	lb	2.71	7/01	11r
Ham, rump or shank half, bone-in, smoked	lb	2.19	7/01	11r
Ice cream, prepackaged, bulk, regular	1/2 gal	3.93	7/01	11r
Lemons	lb	1.32	7/01	11r
Lettuce, iceberg	head	1.02	3/01	4c
Lettuce, iceberg	lb	0.76	7/01	11r
Margarine, Blue Bonnet or Parkay, stick	lb	0.88	3/01	4c
Milk, fresh, low fat,	gal	2.75	7/01	11r
Milk, fresh, whole, fortified	gal	2.97	7/01	11r
Milk, whole	1/2 gal	1.92	3/01	4c
Nonalcoholic beverages, expenditures on	yr	228	1999	30r
Orange juice, frozen concentrate	16 oz	1.95	7/01	11r
Orange juice, Minute Maid frozen	12 oz	1.22	3/01	4c
Oranges, Navel	lb	0.73	7/01	11r
Oranges, Valencia	lb	0.55	7/01	11r
Peaches, halves or slices, Hunt's, Del Monte, or Libby's	29 oz	1.53	3/01	4c
Peanut butter, creamy, all sizes	lb	1.83	7/01	11r
Pears, Anjou	lb	0.98	7/01	11r
Peas, green, Del Monte or Green Giant	15 oz	0.65	3/01	4c
Pork chops, center cut, bone-in	lb	3.33	7/01	11r
Pork sausage, fresh, loose	lb	2.59	7/01	11r
Pork shoulder picnic, bone-in, smoked	lb	1.12	7/01	11r
Pork, expenditures on	yr	162	1999	30r
Potato chips	16 oz	3.59	7/01	11r
Potatoes, frozen, french fried	lb	1.00	7/01	11r
Potatoes, white or red	10 lb	2.56	3/01	4c
Potatoes, white, all types	lb	0.44	7/01	11r
Poultry, expenditures on	yr	137	1999	30r
Processed fruits, expenditures on	yr	97	1999	30r
Processed vegetables, expenditures on	yr	82	1999	30r
Rice, white, long grain, uncooked	lb	0.51	7/01	11r
Round roast, graded and ungraded, excl U.S. prime and choice	lb	2.96	7/01	11r
Round steak, graded and ungraded, excl U.S. prime and choice	lb	3.11	7/01	11r
Sausage, Jimmy Dean/Owens pork	lb	2.99	3/01	4c
Shortening, vegetable, Crisco	3 lb	3.09	3/01	4c
Sirloin steak, graded and ungraded, excl U.S. prime and choice	lb	4.23	7/01	11r
Soft drink, Coca Cola, ex deposit	2 liter	1.19	3/01	4c
Spaghetti and macaroni	lb	0.78	7/01	11r

Values are in dollars or fractions of dollars. In the column headed *Ref*, references are shown to sources. Each reference is followed by a letter. These refer to the geographical level for which data were reported: s=State, r=Region, and c=City or metro. The abbreviation *ex* is used to mean *except* or *excluding*; *exp* stands for expenditures. For other abbreviations and further explanations, please see the Introduction.

Jacksonville, NC - continued

Item	Per	Value	Date	Ref.
Groceries				
Steak, round, U.S. choice, boneless	lb	3.56	7/01	11r
Steak, sirloin, U.S. choice, boneless	lb	5.65	7/01	11r
Steak, T-bone	lb	6.99	3/01	4c
Strawberries, dry pint	12 oz	1.50	7/01	11r
Sugar and other sweets, expenditures on	yr	99	1999	30r
Sugar, cane or beet	4 lbs	1.41	3/01	4c
Sugar, white, 33-80 ounce package	lb	0.39	7/01	11r
Sugar, white, all sizes	lb	0.42	7/01	11r
Tobacco products and smoking supplies purchases	yr	288	1999	30r
Tomatoes, field grown	lb	1.43	7/01	11r
Tomatoes, Hunt's or Del Monte	14.5 oz	0.82	3/01	4c
Tuna, chunk, light	6 oz	0.50	3/01	4c
Tuna, light, chunk	lb	1.77	7/01	11r
Turkey, frozen, whole	lb	1.05	7/01	11r
Goods and Services				
Miscellaneous goods and services, ACCRA Index		97.80	3/01	4c
B&B Japanese maple (acer japonicum)	gal	49.98-129.00	4/00	93r
Boxwood (buxus)	2 gal	12.99-16.99	4/00	93r
Daylilly (hemerocallis)	gal	4.99-8.99	4/00	93r
Flat of annuals		11.00-13.92	4/00	93r
Fountain grass (pennisetum)	gal	5.98-7.98	4/00	93r
Hanging basket (10 in)		7.99-14.98	4/00	93r
Hardy geranium (geranium)	gal	5.98-8.00	4/00	93r
Hosta (hosta)	gal	4.99-10.98	4/00	93r
Lilac (syrubga vulgaris)	2 gal	12.99-21.99	4/00	93r
Rhododendron (rhododendron)	2 gal	14.99-24.99	4/00	93r
Sage (salvia)	gal	5.98-6.99	4/00	93r
Wintercreeper euonymus (euonymus fortunei)	2 gal	7.99-89.99	4/00	93r
Hunting license	yr	15.00	4/01	34s
Health Care				
Health care, ACCRA Index		88.90	3/01	4c
Cardiac catheterization, ave hospital/ physician charges		12500	1998	77s
Childbirth, Cesarean delivery		11587	1997	13r
Childbirth, vaginal delivery		6725	1997	13r
Dentist's fee, adult teeth cleaning and periodic oral exam	visit	79.80	3/01	4c
Doctor's fee, routine exam, established patient	visit	48.40	3/01	4c
Drugs, expenditures on	yr	399	1999	30r
Health care purchases	yr	1971	1999	30r
Health insurance expenditures	yr	933	1999	30r
Hospital care, private room	day	300.00	3/01	4c
Hysterectomy, laproscopically-assisted, ave hospital/physician charges		12260	1998	76s
Hysterectomy, vaginal, ave hospital and physician charges		8440	1998	76s
Medicaid dispensing fee		5.60	1999	87s
Medical services expenditures	yr	547	1999	30r
Medical supplies, expenditures on	yr	91	1999	30r
Plastic surgery, breast augmentation		2870	2000	7r
Plastic surgery, breast lift		3649	2000	7r
Plastic surgery, facelift		5008	2000	7r
Plastic surgery, hair transplantation		3425	2000	7r
Plastic surgery, lip augmentation		1227	2000	7r
Plastic surgery, lower body lift		4793	2000	7r
Plastic surgery, thigh lift		3862	2000	7r

Jacksonville, NC - continued

Item	Per	Value	Date	Ref.
Household Goods				
Dishwashing powder, Cascade	50 oz	3.31	3/01	4c
Floor coverings, expenditures on	yr	44	1999	30r
Furniture, expenditures on	yr	335	1999	30r
Household furnishings and equipment purchases	yr	1328	1999	30r
Household textiles, expenditures on	yr	89	1999	30r
Laundry and cleaning supplies, expenditures on	yr	113	1999	30r
Tissues, facial, Kleenex brand	175	1.32	3/01	4c
Housing				
Housing, ACCRA Index		82.80	3/01	4c
Home price, existing, ave		160100	10/00	90r
Home value, median		146000	2001	53s
House, 2400 sq ft, 8000 sq ft lot, new, urban, utilities	total	168600	3/01	4c
House payment, principal and interest, 25% down payment	mos	868	3/01	4c
Household operation expenditures	yr	553	1999	30r
Housekeeping supplies purchases	yr	473	1999	30r
Housing, expenditures on	yr	10303	1999	30r
Maintenance, repairs, insurance expenditures	yr	699	1999	30r
Monthly rental value of owned home	mos	505	1999	30r
Owned dwellings, expenditures own	yr	3465	1999	30r
Rent expenditures	yr	1641	1999	30r
Rent, apartment, 2 br, 1 1/2-2 baths, unfurn, 950 sq ft, water	mos	537	3/01	4c
Rental unit, 1 bedroom, with utilities	mos	416	4/01	41c
Rental unit, 2 bedroom, with utilities	mos	471	4/01	41c
Rental unit, 3 bedroom, with utilities	mos	653	4/01	41c
Rental unit, 4 bedroom, with utilities	mos	772	4/01	41c
Shelter, expenditures on	yr	5467	1999	30r
Single-family home, ave construction cost		83973	1999	51c
Insurance and Pensions				
Life and other personal insurance purchases	yr	414	1999	30r
Pensions and Social Security, expenditures on	yr	2635	1999	30r
Personal insurance and pensions, expenditures on	yr	3048	1999	30r
Legal Fees				
Combination hunting and fishing license	yr	20.00	4/01	34s
Divorce, filing fee		80.00	4/01	35s
Driver's license fee	renew	10.00	1999	48s
Driver's license fee	orig	10.00	1999	48s
Fishing license	yr	15.00	4/01	34s
Personal Goods				
Personal care products and services purchases	yr	393	1999	30r
Shampoo, Alberto VO5	15 oz	0.92	3/01	4c
Toothpaste, Crest or Colgate	6-7 oz	2.25	3/01	4c
Personal Services				
Dry cleaning, man's 2-pc suit		7.76	3/01	4c
Man's haircut, barbershop, no styling		7.33	3/01	4c
Personal services, household, expenditures on	yr	258	1999	30r
Woman's shampoo, trim, blow-dry, no style-change		26.75	3/01	4c
Pets				
Pets, toys, and playground equipment, expenditures on	yr	306	1999	30r
Restaurant Food				
Chicken, fried, thigh and drumstick, KFC/ Church's		2.29	3/01	4c
Hamburger with cheese, McDonald's	1/4 lb	2.04	3/01	4c
Pizza, Pizza Hut or Pizza Inn	11-12 in	9.55	3/01	4c
Taxes				
Federal income taxes paid	yr	2047	1999	30r
Personal taxes, expenditures on	yr	2554	1999	30r

Values are in dollars or fractions of dollars. In the column headed *Ref*, references are shown to sources. Each reference is followed by a letter. These refer to the geographical level for which data were reported: s=State, r=Region, and c=City or metro. The abbreviation *ex* is used to mean *except* or *excluding*; *exp* stands for *expenditures*. For other abbreviations and further explanations, please see the Introduction.

Jacksonville, NC - continued

Item	Per	Value	Date	Ref.
Taxes				
Property taxes paid	yr	726	1999	30r
State and local income taxes paid	yr	363	1999	30r
Transportation				
Transportation, ACCRA Index		83.20	3/01	4c
Cars and trucks, new, expenditures on	yr	1648	1999	30r
Cars and trucks, used, expenditures on	yr	1651	1999	30r
Diesel at the pump	gal	1.19	10/99	73s
Gasoline and motor oil purchases	yr	1052	1999	30r
Gasoline before-tax price (cents)	gal	103.20	10/00	43s
Maintenance and repair expenditures	yr	621	1999	30r
Motorcycle license fee	orig	1.50	1999	49s
Motorcycle license fee	renew	1.50	1999	49s
Public transportation, expenditures on	yr	298	1999	30r
Tire balance, computer or spin balance, front	wheel	5.67	3/01	4c
Transportation purchases	yr	6738	1999	30r
Vehicle expenses, miscellaneous, purchases	yr	2033	1999	30r
Vehicle insurance payments	yr	696	1999	30r
Vehicle purchases (net outlay)	yr	3354	1999	30r
Vehicle rental, lease expenditures	yr	352	1999	30r
Utilities				
Utilities, ACCRA Index		107.50	3/01	4c
Electrical bill, average	mos	83.66	9/00	9s
Electricity, 2400 sq ft, new home	mos	133.59	3/01	4c
Electricity, expenditures on	yr	1115	1999	30r
Electricity cost, average	KWh	6.40	9/00	9s
Water and other public services, expenditures on	yr	298	1999	30r
Weddings				
Wedding (national average cost)		19936	2000	33r
Wedding (regional average total cost)		16293	1997	110r
Attendants' gifts		321	1998	33r
Bridal attendants' apparel (5 persons)		824	2000	33r
Bride's headpiece/veil		173	1998	33r
Bride's wedding dress		859	1998	33r
Clergy, religious facility fee		242	1998	33r
Engagement ring		3177	1998	33r
Flowers		789	1998	33r
Groom's formalwear rental		99	2000	33r
Limousine		410	1998	33r
Marriage license cost		40.00	4/01	35s
Men's formalwear (ushers, best man)		469	2000	33r
Mother of bride apparel		241	2000	33r
Music		866	1998	33r
Photography and videography		1368	1998	33r
Rehearsal dinner		728	1998	33r
Wedding invitations and announcements		341	1998	33r
Wedding reception		7968	2000	33r
Wedding rings (bride and groom)		1060	1998	33r

Jamestown, NY

Item	Per	Value	Date	Ref.
Average annual expenditures	yr	37971	1999	30r
Alcoholic Beverages				
Alcoholic beverage purchases	yr	368	1999	30r
Wine, red and white table, all sizes, any origin	liter	9.64	7/01	11r
Appliances				
Major appliances, expenditures on	yr	194	1999	30r
Small appliances, housewares, expenditures on	yr	93	1999	30r
Banking and Money				
Mortgage interest and charges paid	yr	2622	1999	30r
Mortgage principal paid on owned property	yr	1262	1999	30r
Vehicle finance charges paid	yr	240	1999	30r
Charity				
Cash contributions, expenditures	yr	1001	1999	30r

Jamestown, NY - continued

Item	Per	Value	Date	Ref.
Child Care				
Child raising cost, total, age 0-2	yr	8670	1999	60r
Child raising cost, total, age 3-5	yr	8910	1999	60r
Child raising cost, total, age 6-8	yr	9040	1999	60r
Child raising cost, total, age 9-11	yr	9100	1999	60r
Child raising cost, total, age 12-14	yr	9890	1999	60r
Child raising cost, total, age 15-17	yr	10010	1999	60r
Child's child care and education, age 0-2	yr	1070	1999	60r
Child's child care and education, age 3-5	yr	1190	1999	60r
Child's child care and education, age 6-8	yr	740	1999	60r
Child's child care and education, age 9-11	yr	470	1999	60r
Child's child care and education, age 12-14	yr	350	1999	60r
Child's child care and education, age 15-17	yr	590	1999	60r
Child's clothing, age 0-2	yr	480	1999	60r
Child's clothing, age 3-5	yr	470	1999	60r
Child's clothing, age 6-8	yr	520	1999	60r
Child's clothing, age 9-11	yr	570	1999	60r
Child's clothing, age 12-14	yr	970	1999	60r
Child's clothing, age 15-17	yr	870	1999	60r
Child's food, age 0-2	yr	1130	1999	60r
Child's food, age 3-5	yr	1290	1999	60r
Child's food, age 6-8	yr	1640	1999	60r
Child's food, age 9-11	yr	1930	1999	60r
Child's food, age 12-14	yr	1940	1999	60r
Child's food, age 15-17	yr	2150	1999	60r
Child's health care, age 0-2	yr	550	1999	60r
Child's health care, age 3-5	yr	530	1999	60r
Child's health care, age 6-8	yr	610	1999	60r
Child's health care, age 9-11	yr	650	1999	60r
Child's health care, age 12-14	yr	660	1999	60r
Child's health care, age 15-17	yr	690	1999	60r
Child's housing, age 0-2	yr	3555	1999	60r
Child's housing, age 3-5	yr	3530	1999	60r
Child's housing, age 6-8	yr	3490	1999	60r
Child's housing, age 9-11	yr	3340	1999	60r
Child's housing, age 12-14	yr	3530	1999	60r
Child's housing, age 15-17	yr	3140	1999	60r
Child's personal care, reading, age 0-2	yr	920	1999	60r
Child's personal care, reading, age 3-5	yr	950	1999	60r
Child's personal care, reading, age 6-8	yr	980	1999	60r
Child's personal care, reading, age 9-11	yr	1020	1999	60r
Child's personal care, reading, age 12-14	yr	1190	1999	60r
Child's personal care, reading, age 15-17	yr	970	1999	60r
Nannies: criminal background check		74	1998	84s
Clothing				
Apparel and services purchases	yr	1831	1999	30r
Boys, 2 to 15, expenditures on	yr	92	1999	30r
Children under 2, expenditures on	yr	63	1999	30r
Footwear, expenditures on	yr	300	1999	30r
Girls, 2 to 15, expenditures on	yr	101	1999	30r
Men and boys, expenditures on	yr	446	1999	30r
Men, 16 and over, expenditures on	yr	354	1999	30r
Women, 16 and over, expenditures on	yr	584	1999	30r
Communications				
Cable modem installation, Adelphi	'	54.90	6/99	103s
Cable modem installation, Cablevision Systems		150.00	6/99	103s
Cable modem installation, Time Warner		75.00-225.00	6/99	103s
Cable modem rate, cable subscriber, Adelphi	mos	34.95	6/99	103s
Cable modem rate, cable subscriber, Cablevision Systems	mos	44.95	6/99	103s
Cable modem rate, cable subscriber, Century	mos	39.95	6/99	103s
Cable modem rate, cable subscriber, Time Warner	mos	39.95-49.95	6/99	103s
Cable modem rate, non-cable subscriber, Adelphi	mos	44.95	6/99	103s
Cable modem rate, non-cable subscriber, Cablevision Systems	mos	54.95	6/99	103s
Cable modem rate, non-cable subscriber, Time Warner	mos	39.95-54.95	6/99	103s
Phone line, single, business, field visit	inst.	142.76	12/97	17s

Values are in dollars or fractions of dollars. In the column headed *Ref*, references are shown to sources. Each reference is followed by a letter. These refer to the geographical level for which data were reported: s=State, r=Region, and c=City or metro. The abbreviation *ex* is used to mean *except* or *excluding*; *exp* stands for expenditures. For other abbreviations and further explanations, please see the Introduction.

Jamestown, NY - continued

Item	Per	Value	Date	Ref.
Communications				
Phone line, single, business, no field visit	inst.	106.05	12/97	17s
Phone line, single, residence, field visit	inst.	102.78	12/97	17s
Phone line, single, residence, no field visit	inst.	55.00	12/97	17s
Postage and stationery, expenditures on	yr	138	1999	30r
Postal rate, express mail, up to half-pound		12.45	7/01	108r
Postal rate, letter, first class, first ounce		0.34	7/01	108r
Postal rate, letter, two ounces		0.57	7/01	108r
Postal rate, post card		0.21	7/01	108r
Postal rate, priority mail, two pounds		3.95	7/01	108r
Postal rate, priority mail, up to one pound		3.50	7/01	108r
Telephone services, expenditures on	yr	830	1999	30r
Education				
Board, 4-year private college/university	yr	3255	1996	38s
Board, 4-year public college/university	yr	2310	1996	38s
Education expenditures	yr	877	1999	30r
Room, 4-year private college/university	yr	3724	1996	38s
Room, 4-year public college/university	yr	2937	1996	38s
Total cost, 4-year private college/university	yr	20831	1996	38s
Total cost, 4-year public college/university	yr	8960	1996	38s
Tuition, 2-year public college/university, in state	yr	2427	1996	38s
Tuition, 4-year private college/university, in state	yr	13852	1996	38s
Tuition, 4-year public college/university	yr	3714	1996	38s
Energy and Fuels				
Electricity	KWh	0.12	7/01	11r
Fuel oil #2	gal	1.31	7/01	11r
Fuel oil and other fuels, expenditures on	yr	207	1999	30r
Gasoline, all types	gal	1.80	7/01	11r
Gasoline, unleaded midgrade	gal	1.85	7/01	11r
Gasoline, unleaded premium	gal	1.91	7/01	11r
Gasoline, unleaded regular	gal	1.71	7/01	11r
Natural gas, expenditures on	yr	368	1999	30r
Utility (piped) gas, therm		1.08	7/01	11r
Utility (piped) gas, 40 therms		50.87	7/01	11r
Utility (piped) gas, 100 therms		111.06	7/01	11r
Entertainment				
Entertainment purchases	yr	1821	1999	30r
Fees and admissions paid	yr	511	1999	30r
Television, radios, sound equipment, expenditures on	yr	650	1999	30r
Funerals				
Total cost of funeral		5813.50	1/99	78r
Acknowledgement cards		28.32	1/99	78r
Casket		2082.20	1/99	78r
Cosmetology, hair, other preparation		169.59	1/99	78r
Embalming		465.60	1/99	78r
Funeral at funeral home		339.56	1/99	78r
Hearse (local)		183.96	1/99	78r
Professional service charges		1157.85	1/99	78r
Service car/van		100.41	1/99	78r
Transfer of remains to funeral home		158.66	1/99	78r
Vault		766.31	1/99	78r
Visitation/viewing		361.04	1/99	78r
Groceries				
Apples, red delicious	lb	0.95	7/01	11r
Bacon, sliced	lb	3.44	7/01	11r
Bakery products, expenditures on	yr	310	1999	30r
Bananas	lb	0.55	7/01	11r
Beef, expenditures on	yr	236	1999	30r
Bread, white, pan	lb	1.09	7/01	11r
Butter, yoghurt, cheese, etc, expenditures on	yr	214	1999	30r
Cereals and bakery product purchases	yr	474	1999	30r
Cereals and cereal products, expenditures on	yr	164	1999	30r
Chicken legs, bone-in	lb	1.23	7/01	11r
Chicken, fresh, whole	lb	1.13	7/01	11r
Chuck roast, U.S. choice, boneless	lb	2.79	7/01	11r
Coffee, 100%, ground roast, all sizes	lb	3.40	7/01	11r

Jamestown, NY - continued

Item	Per	Value	Date	Ref.
Groceries - continued				
Dairy product purchases	yr	342	1999	30r
Eggs, expenditures on	yr	34	1999	30r
Eggs, grade A, large	dozen	0.82	7/01	11r
Fats and oils, expenditures on	yr	80	1999	30r
Fish and seafood, expenditures on	yr	123	1999	30r
Food (excl fruit and vegetables), eaten at home, purchases	yr	838	1999	30r
Food cooked on trips, expenditures on	yr	48	1999	30r
Food purchases	yr	5314	1999	30r
Food purchases, eaten away from home	yr	2313	1999	30r
Food purchases, food eaten at home	yr	3001	1999	30r
Fresh fruits, expenditures on	yr	169	1999	30r
Fresh milk and cream, expenditures on	yr	128	1999	30r
Fresh vegetables, expenditures on	yr	164	1999	30r
Grapefruit	lb	0.67	7/01	11r
Grapes, Thompson, seedless	lb	2.18	7/01	11r
Ground beef, lean and extra lean	lb	2.66	7/01	11r
Ground chuck, 100% beef	lb	2.04	7/01	11r
Lettuce, iceberg	lb	0.76	7/01	11r
Meats, poultry, fish, and egg purchases	yr	808	1999	30r
Nonalcoholic beverages, expenditures on	yr	225	1999	30r
Orange juice, frozen concentrate	16 oz	1.88	7/01	11r
Oranges, Navel	lb	0.79	7/01	11r
Oranges, Valencia	lb	0.56	7/01	11r
Peaches	lb	1.16	7/01	11r
Peanut butter, creamy, all sizes	lb	2.01	7/01	11r
Pears, Anjou	lb	1.16	7/01	11r
Pork chops, center cut, bone-in	lb	3.57	7/01	11r
Pork, expenditures on	yr	146	1999	30r
Potato chips	16 oz	3.37	7/01	11r
Potatoes, white, all types	lb	0.42	7/01	11r
Poultry, expenditures on	yr	158	1999	30r
Processed fruits, expenditures on	yr	124	1999	30r
Processed vegetables, expenditures on	yr	82	1999	30r
Round roast, U.S. choice, boneless	lb	3.04	7/01	11r
Spaghetti and macaroni	lb	1.04	7/01	11r
Steak, sirloin, U.S. choice, boneless	lb	5.39	7/01	11r
Strawberries, dry pint	12 oz	1.51	7/01	11r
Sugar and other sweets, expenditures on	yr	110	1999	30r
Sugar, white, 33-80 ounce package	lb	0.46	7/01	11r
Sugar, white, all sizes	lb	0.47	7/01	11r
Tobacco products and smoking supplies purchases	yr	309	1999	30r
Yogurt, natural, fruit flavored	8 oz	0.79	7/01	11r
Goods and Services				
B&B Japanese maple (acer japonicum)	gal	38.99-125.00	4/00	93r
Boxwood (buxus)	2 gal	15.99-49.95	4/00	93r
Daylilly (hemerocallis)	gal	4.95	4/00	93r
Flat of annuals		8.00-14.99	4/00	93r
Fountain grass (pennisetum)	gal	6.99-9.99	4/00	93r
Hanging basket (10 in)		12.95-19.99	4/00	93r
Hardy geranium (geranium)	gal	6.95-7.99	4/00	93r
Hosta (hosta)	gal	4.95	4/00	93r
Lilac (syrubga vulgaris)	2 gal	17.99-74.95	4/00	93r
Miscellaneous purchases	yr	872	1999	30r
Rhododendron (rhododendron)	2 gal	23.99-54.95	4/00	93r
Sage (salvia)	gal	6.95-7.99	4/00	93r
Wintercreeper euonymus (euonymus fortunei)	2 gal	14.99-23.95	4/00	93r
Hunting license	yr	11.00	4/01	34s

Values are in dollars or fractions of dollars. In the column headed *Ref*, references are shown to sources. Each reference is followed by a letter. These refer to the geographical level for which data were reported: s=State, r=Region, and c=City or metro. The abbreviation *ex* is used to mean *except* or *excluding*; *exp* stands for *expenditures*. For other abbreviations and further explanations, please see the Introduction.

Jamestown, NY - continued

Item	Per	Value	Date	Ref.
Health Care				
Cardiac catheterization, ave hospital/ physician charges		12750	1998	77s
Childbirth, Cesarean delivery		14716	1997	13r
Childbirth, vaginal delivery		8541	1997	13r
Drugs, expenditures on	yr	296	1999	30r
Health care purchases	yr	1788	1999	30r
Health insurance expenditures	yr	875	1999	30r
Hysterectomy, laproscopically-assisted, ave hospital/physician charges		13460	1998	76s
Hysterectomy, vaginal, ave hospital and physician charges		10310	1998	76s
Medicaid dispensing fee		3.50-4.50	1999	87s
Medical services expenditures	yr	516	1999	30r
Medical supplies, expenditures on	yr	102	1999	30r
Plastic surgery, breast augmentation		4232	2000	7r
Plastic surgery, breast lift		4605	2000	7r
Plastic surgery, facelift		6964	2000	7r
Plastic surgery, hair transplantation		4193	2000	7r
Plastic surgery, lip augmentation		1675	2000	7r
Plastic surgery, lower body lift		6611	2000	7r
Plastic surgery, thigh lift		4751	2000	7r
Household Goods				
Floor coverings, expenditures on	yr	59	1999	30r
Furniture, expenditures on	yr	388	1999	30r
Household furnishings and equipment purchases	yr	1567	1999	30r
Household textiles, expenditures on	yr	112	1999	30r
Laundry and cleaning supplies, expenditures on	yr	104	1999	30r
Housing				
Home price, existing, ave		180800	10/00	90r
Home value, median		179000	2001	53s
Household operation expenditures	yr	581	1999	30r
Housekeeping supplies purchases	yr	474	1999	30r
Lodging expenditures	yr	550	1999	30r
Maintenance, repairs, insurance expenditures	yr	835	1999	30r
Monthly rental value of owned home	mos	663	1999	30r
Owned dwellings, expenditures own	yr	5209	1999	30r
Rent expenditures	yr	2390	1999	30r
Rental unit, 1 bedroom, with utilities	mos	404	4/01	41c
Rental unit, 2 bedroom, with utilities	mos	486	4/01	41c
Rental unit, 3 bedroom, with utilities	mos	627	4/01	41c
Rental unit, 4 bedroom, with utilities	mos	718	4/01	41c
Shelter, expenditures on	yr	8149	1999	30r
Insurance and Pensions				
Auto insurance premium	yr	1113.55	1999	57s
Life and other personal insurance purchases	yr	424	1999	30r
Pensions and Social Security, expenditures on	yr	3037	1999	30r
Legal Fees				
Divorce, filing fee		270.00	4/01	35s
Driver's license fee	orig	25.00	1999	48s
Driver's license fee	renew	25.00	1999	48s
Fishing license	yr	14.00	4/01	34s
Personal Goods				
Personal care products and services purchases	yr	399	1999	30r
Personal Services				
Personal services, household, expenditures on	yr	271	1999	30r
Pets				
Pets, toys, and playground equipment, expenditures on	yr	325	1999	30r
Taxes				
Federal income taxes paid	yr	2606	1999	30r
Personal taxes, expenditures on	yr	3567	1999	30r

Jamestown, NY - continued

Item	Per	Value	Date	Ref.
Taxes - continued				
Property taxes paid	yr	1752	1999	30r
State and local income taxes paid	yr	694	1999	30r
Transportation				
Cars and trucks, new, expenditures on	yr	1496	1999	30r
Cars and trucks, used, expenditures on	yr	1251	1999	30r
Diesel at the pump	gal	1.33	10/99	73s
Gasoline and motor oil purchases	yr	901	1999	30r
Gasoline before-tax price (cents)	gal	110.70	10/00	43s
Maintenance and repair expenditures	yr	618	1999	30r
Public transportation, expenditures on	yr	575	1999	30r
Transportation purchases	yr	6503	1999	30r
Vehicle expenses, miscellaneous, purchases	yr	2266	1999	30r
Vehicle insurance payments	yr	824	1999	30r
Vehicle purchases (net outlay)	yr	2761	1999	30r
Vehicle rental, lease expenditures	yr	584	1999	30r
Travel				
Hotel room	night	139.88	2/01	95s
Utilities				
Electrical bill, average	mos	71.50	9/00	9s
Electricity, expenditures on	yr	837	1999	30r
Electricity cost, average	KWh	11.34	9/00	9s
Utilities, fuels, and public services purchased	yr	2457	1999	30r
Water and other public services, expenditures on	yr	215	1999	30r
Weddings				
Wedding (national average cost)		19936	2000	33r
Wedding (regional average total cost)		29454	1997	110r
Attendants' gifts		321	1998	33r
Bridal attendants' apparel (5 persons)		824	2000	33r
Bride's headpiece/veil		173	1998	33r
Bride's wedding dress		859	1998	33r
Clergy, religious facility fee		242	1998	33r
Engagement ring		3177	1998	33r
Flowers		789	1998	33r
Groom's formalwear rental		99	2000	33r
Limousine		410	1998	33r
Marriage license cost		25.00	4/01	35s
Men's formalwear (ushers, best man)		469	2000	33r
Mother of bride apparel		241	2000	33r
Music		866	1998	33r
Photography and videography		1368	1998	33r
Rehearsal dinner		728	1998	33r
Wedding invitations and announcements		341	1998	33r
Wedding reception		7968	2000	33r
Wedding rings (bride and groom)		1060	1998	33r

Janesville-Beloit, WI

Item	Per	Value	Date	Ref.
Average annual expenditures	yr	35369	1999	30r
Alcoholic Beverages				
Alcoholic beverage purchases	yr	304	1999	30r
Malt beverages, all types, all sizes, any origin	16 oz	0.93	7/01	11r
Wine, red and white table, all sizes, any origin	liter	7.04	7/01	11r
Appliances				
Major appliances, expenditures on	yr	165	1999	30r
Small appliances, housewares, expenditures on	yr	90	1999	30r
Banking and Money				
Mortgage interest and charges paid	yr	2277	1999	30r
Mortgage principal paid on owned property	yr	1230	1999	30r
Vehicle finance charges paid	yr	328	1999	30r
Charity				
Cash contributions, expenditures	yr	1126	1999	30r
Child Care				
Child raising cost, total, age 0-2	yr	7890	1999	60r
Child raising cost, total, age 3-5	yr	8130	1999	60r

Values are in dollars or fractions of dollars. In the column headed *Ref*, references are shown to sources. Each reference is followed by a letter. These refer to the geographical level for which data were reported: s=State, r=Region, and c=City or metro. The abbreviation *ex* is used to mean *except* or *excluding*; *exp* stands for *expenditures*. For other abbreviations and further explanations, please see the Introduction.

Janesville-Beloit, WI - continued

Item	Per	Value	Date	Ref.
Child Care				
Child raising cost, total, age 6-8	yr	8170	1999	60r
Child raising cost, total, age 9-11	yr	8190	1999	60r
Child raising cost, total, age 12-14	yr	8890	1999	60r
Child raising cost, total, age 15-17	yr	9050	1999	60r
Child's child care and education, age 0-2	yr	1240	1999	60r
Child's child care and education, age 3-5	yr	1370	1999	60r
Child's child care and education, age 6-8	yr	880	1999	60r
Child's child care and education, age 9-11	yr	570	1999	60r
Child's child care and education, age 12-14	yr	420	1999	60r
Child's child care and education, age 15-17	yr	720	1999	60r
Child's clothing, age 0-2	yr	410	1999	60r
Child's clothing, age 3-5	yr	400	1999	60r
Child's clothing, age 6-8	yr	450	1999	60r
Child's clothing, age 9-11	yr	500	1999	60r
Child's clothing, age 12-14	yr	840	1999	60r
Child's clothing, age 15-17	yr	740	1999	60r
Child's food, age 0-2	yr	960	1999	60r
Child's food, age 3-5	yr	1120	1999	60r
Child's food, age 6-8	yr	1430	1999	60r
Child's food, age 9-11	yr	1710	1999	60r
Child's food, age 12-14	yr	1710	1999	60r
Child's food, age 15-17	yr	1920	1999	60r
Child's health care, age 0-2	yr	520	1999	60r
Child's health care, age 3-5	yr	500	1999	60r
Child's health care, age 6-8	yr	570	1999	60r
Child's health care, age 9-11	yr	610	1999	60r
Child's health care, age 12-14	yr	630	1999	60r
Child's health care, age 15-17	yr	650	1999	60r
Child's housing, age 0-2	yr	2860	1999	60r
Child's housing, age 3-5	yr	2840	1999	60r
Child's housing, age 6-8	yr	2800	1999	60r
Child's housing, age 9-11	yr	2650	1999	60r
Child's housing, age 12-14	yr	2840	1999	60r
Child's housing, age 15-17	yr	2440	1999	60r
Child's personal care, reading, age 0-2	yr	880	1999	60r
Child's personal care, reading, age 3-5	yr	900	1999	60r
Child's personal care, reading, age 6-8	yr	930	1999	60r
Child's personal care, reading, age 9-11	yr	970	1999	60r
Child's personal care, reading, age 12-14	yr	1150	1999	60r
Child's personal care, reading, age 15-17	yr	920	1999	60r
Clothing				
Apparel and services purchases	yr	1607	1999	30r
Boys, 2 to 15, expenditures on	yr	91	1999	30r
Children under 2, expenditures on	yr	59	1999	30r
Footwear, expenditures on	yr	285	1999	30r
Girls, 2 to 15, expenditures on	yr	116	1999	30r
Men and boys, expenditures on	yr	433	1999	30r
Men, 16 and over, expenditures on	yr	341	1999	30r
Women, 16 and over, expenditures on	yr	490	1999	30r
Communications				
Cable modem installation, Bresnan		99.95	6/99	103s
Cable modem installation, Marcus		499.00	6/99	103s
Cable modem rate, cable subscriber, Bresnan	mos	39.95	6/99	103s
Cable modem rate, cable subscriber, Marcus	mos	14.95-49.95	6/99	103s
Cable modem rate, non-cable subscriber, Bresnan	mos	49.95	6/99	103s
Cable modem rate, non-cable subscriber, Marcus	mos	60.95	6/99	103s
Phone line, single, business, field visit	inst.	64.65	12/97	17s
Phone line, single, business, no field visit	inst.	64.65	12/97	17s
Phone line, single, residence, field visit	inst.	33.05	12/97	17s
Phone line, single, residence, no field visit	inst.	33.05	12/97	17s
Postage and stationery, expenditures on	yr	140	1999	30r
Postal rate, express mail, up to half-pound		12.45	7/01	108r
Postal rate, letter, first class, first ounce		0.34	7/01	108r
Postal rate, letter, two ounces		0.57	7/01	108r
Postal rate, post card		0.21	7/01	108r
Postal rate, priority mail, two pounds		3.95	7/01	108r
Postal rate, priority mail, up to one pound		3.50	7/01	108r

Janesville-Beloit, WI - continued

Item	Per	Value	Date	Ref.
Communications - continued				
Telephone services, expenditures on	yr	830	1999	30r
Education				
Board, 4-year private college/university	yr	2271	1996	38s
Board, 4-year public college/university	yr	1527	1996	38s
Education expenditures	yr	583	1999	30r
Room, 4-year private college/university	yr	1812	1996	38s
Room, 4-year public college/university	yr	1706	1996	38s
Total cost, 4-year private college/university	yr	15652	1996	38s
Total cost, 4-year public college/university	yr	5847	1996	38s
Tuition, 2-year public college/university, in state	yr	1840	1996	38s
Tuition, 4-year private college/university, in state	yr	11569	1996	38s
Tuition, 4-year public college/university	yr	2614	1996	38s
Energy and Fuels				
Electricity	500 KWhs	46.59	7/01	11r
Fuel oil #2	gal	1.27	7/01	11r
Fuel oil and other fuels, expenditures on	yr	68	1999	30r
Gas, natural, commercial rate	1000 cf	7.32	11/00	88s
Gasoline, unleaded midgrade	gal	1.79	7/01	11r
Gasoline, unleaded premium	gal	1.86	7/01	11r
Gasoline, unleaded regular	gal	1.58	7/01	11r
Natural gas, expenditures on	yr	389	1999	30r
Utility (piped) gas, therm		0.81	7/01	11r
Utility (piped) gas, 40 therms		38.01	7/01	11r
Utility (piped) gas, 100 therms		81.75	7/01	11r
Entertainment				
Entertainment purchases	yr	1984	1999	30r
Fees and admissions paid	yr	444	1999	30r
Television, radios, sound equipment, expenditures on	yr	580	1999	30r
Funerals				
Cosmetology, hair, other preparation		178.32	1/99	78r
Embalming		408.19	1/99	78r
Funeral at funeral home		362.13	1/99	78r
Professional service charges		1375.51	1/99	78r
Transfer of remains to funeral home		155.92	1/99	78r
Visitation/viewing		294.38	1/99	78r
Groceries				
Bacon, sliced	lb	3.15	7/01	11r
Bakery products, expenditures on	yr	281	1999	30r
Bananas	lb	0.48	7/01	11r
Beans, dried, any type, all sizes	lb	0.61	7/01	11r
Beef for stew, boneless	lb	3.08	7/01	11r
Beef, expenditures on	yr	217	1999	30r
Bologna, all beef or mixed	lb	2.52	7/01	11r
Bread, white, pan	lb	1.06	7/01	11r
Broccoli	lb	0.91	7/01	11r
Butter, salted, grade AA, stick	lb	3.04	7/01	11r
Butter, yoghurt, cheese, etc, expenditures on	yr	183	1999	30r
Cereals and bakery product purchases	yr	430	1999	30r
Cereals and cereal products, expenditures on	yr	149	1999	30r
Chicken, fresh, whole	lb	1.07	7/01	11r
Chops, boneless,	lb	3.64	7/01	11r
Chuck roast, U.S. choice, boneless	lb	2.47	7/01	11r
Coffee, 100%, ground roast, all sizes	lb	2.69	7/01	11r
Cookies, chocolate chip	lb	2.87	7/01	11r
Dairy product purchases	yr	304	1999	30r
Eggs, expenditures on	yr	26	1999	30r
Eggs, grade A, large	dozen	0.88	7/01	11r
Fats and oils, expenditures on	yr	75	1999	30r
Fish and seafood, expenditures on	yr	72	1999	30r
Food (excl fruit and vegetables), eaten at home, purchases	yr	887	1999	30r
Food cooked on trips, expenditures on	yr	44	1999	30r
Food purchases	yr	4802	1999	30r
Food purchases, eaten away from home	yr	2069	1999	30r

Values are in dollars or fractions of dollars. In the column headed *Ref*, references are shown to sources. Each reference is followed by a letter. These refer to the geographical level for which data were reported: s=State, r=Region, and c=City or metro. The abbreviation *ex* is used to mean *except* or *excluding*; *exp* stands for expenditures. For other abbreviations and further explanations, please see the Introduction.

Janesville-Beloit, WI - continued

Item	Per	Value	Date	Ref.
Groceries				
Food purchases, food eaten at home	yr	2733	1999	30r
Fresh fruits, expenditures on	yr	138	1999	30r
Fresh milk and cream, expenditures on	yr	120	1999	30r
Fresh vegetables, expenditures on	yr	126	1999	30r
Grapefruit	lb	0.66	7/01	11r
Grapes, Thompson, seedless	lb	1.64	7/01	11r
Ground beef, 100% beef	lb	1.64	7/01	11r
Ground beef, lean and extra lean	lb	2.16	7/01	11r
Ground chuck, 100% beef	lb	2.13	7/01	11r
Ham, boneless, excl canned	lb	2.62	7/01	11r
Ice cream, prepackaged, bulk, regular	1/2 gal	3.35	7/01	11r
Lemons	lb	1.19	7/01	11r
Lettuce, iceberg	lb	0.73	7/01	11r
Margarine, soft, tubs	lb	0.89	7/01	11r
Meats, poultry, fish, and egg purchases	yr	671	1999	30r
Milk, fresh, whole, fortified	gal	2.71	7/01	11r
Nonalcoholic beverages, expenditures on	yr	239	1999	30r
Oranges, Navel	lb	0.80	7/01	11r
Oranges, Valencia	lb	0.66	7/01	11r
Pears, Anjou	lb	0.93	7/01	11r
Pork chops, center cut, bone-in	lb	3.63	7/01	11r
Pork, expenditures on	yr	150	1999	30r
Potato chips	16 oz	3.52	7/01	11r
Potatoes, frozen, french fried	lb	1.08	7/01	11r
Potatoes, white, all types	lb	0.33	7/01	11r
Poultry, expenditures on	yr	108	1999	30r
Processed fruits, expenditures on	yr	98	1999	30r
Processed vegetables, expenditures on	yr	80	1999	30r
Round roast, U.S. choice, boneless	lb	3.07	7/01	11r
Round steak, graded and ungraded, excl U.S. prime and choice	lb	3.41	7/01	11r
Shortening, vegetable oil blends	lb	1.13	7/01	11r
Spaghetti and macaroni	lb	0.80	7/01	11r
Steak, round, U.S. choice, boneless	lb	3.23	7/01	11r
Steak, T-bone, U.S. choice, bone-in	lb	6.68	7/01	11r
Strawberries, dry pint	12 oz	1.32	7/01	11r
Sugar and other sweets, expenditures on	yr	114	1999	30r
Sugar, white, 33-80 ounce package	lb	0.42	7/01	11r
Sugar, white, all sizes	lb	0.43	7/01	11r
Tobacco products and smoking supplies purchases	yr	331	1999	30r
Tomatoes, field grown	lb	1.46	7/01	11r
Tuna, light, chunk	lb	1.80	7/01	11r
Turkey, frozen, whole	lb	1.15	7/01	11r
Goods and Services				
B&B Japanese maple (acer japonicum)	gal	29.99-169.99	4/00	93r
Boxwood (buxus)	2 gal	18.99-39.99	4/00	93r
Daylily (hemerocallis)	gal	4.99-25.00	4/00	93r
Flat of annuals		11.98-24.99	4/00	93r
Fountain grass (pennisetum)	gal	5.98-12.98	4/00	93r
Hanging basket (10 in)		12.99-27.99	4/00	93r
Hardy geranium (geranium)	gal	7.99-9.99	4/00	93r
Hosta (hosta)	gal	6.00-25.00	4/00	93r
Lilac (syrubga vulgaris)	2 gal	14.99-24.99	4/00	93r
Miscellaneous purchases	yr	865	1999	30r
Rhododendron (rhododendron)	2 gal	23.98-42.99	4/00	93r
Sage (salvia)	gal	6.00-9.99	4/00	93r
Wintercreeper euonymus (euonymus fortunei)	2 gal	16.00-169.99	4/00	93r
Hunting license	yr	14.00	4/01	34s

Janesville-Beloit, WI - continued

Item	Per	Value	Date	Ref.
Health Care				
Cardiac catheterization, ave hospital/ physician charges		13240	1998	77s
Childbirth, Cesarean delivery		10722	1997	13r
Childbirth, vaginal delivery		6223	1997	13r
Drugs, expenditures on	yr	394	1999	30r
Health care purchases	yr	2048	1999	30r
Health insurance expenditures	yr	978	1999	30r
Hysterectomy, laproscopically-assisted, ave hospital/physician charges		13270	1998	76s
Hysterectomy, vaginal, ave hospital and physician charges		9170	1998	76s
Laser eye surgery	eye	1950-2400	2000	63s
Medicaid dispensing fee		4.88-40.11	1999	87s
Medical services expenditures	yr	554	1999	30r
Medical supplies, expenditures on	yr	122	1999	30r
Plastic surgery, breast augmentation		3184	2000	7r
Plastic surgery, breast lift		3585	2000	7r
Plastic surgery, facelift		4999	2000	7r
Plastic surgery, hair transplantation		3105	2000	7r
Plastic surgery, lip augmentation		1290	2000	7r
Plastic surgery, lower body lift		8135	2000	7r
Plastic surgery, thigh lift		3839	2000	7r
Household Goods				
Floor coverings, expenditures on	yr	52	1999	30r
Furniture, expenditures on	yr	344	1999	30r
Household furnishings and equipment purchases	yr	1475	1999	30r
Household textiles, expenditures on	yr	109	1999	30r
Laundry and cleaning supplies, expenditures on	yr	134	1999	30r
Housing				
Home price, existing, ave		144400	10/00	90r
Home value, median		117000	2001	53s
Household operation expenditures	yr	542	1999	30r
Housekeeping supplies purchases	yr	508	1999	30r
Lodging expenditures	yr	430	1999	30r
Maintenance, repairs, insurance expenditures	yr	853	1999	30r
Monthly rental value of owned home	mos	547	1999	30r
Owned dwellings, expenditures own	yr	4282	1999	30r
Rent expenditures	yr	1558	1999	30r
Rental unit, 1 bedroom, with utilities	mos	452	4/01	41c
Rental unit, 2 bedroom, with utilities	mos	559	4/01	41c
Rental unit, 3 bedroom, with utilities	mos	700	4/01	41c
Rental unit, 4 bedroom, with utilities	mos	785	4/01	41c
Shelter, expenditures on	yr	6270	1999	30r
Insurance and Pensions				
Auto insurance premium	yr	603.84	1999	57s
Life and other personal insurance purchases	yr	387	1999	30r
Pensions and Social Security, expenditures on	yr	2968	1999	30r
Legal Fees				
Divorce, filing fee		142.00-150.00	4/01	35s
Driver's license fee	renew	12.00	1999	48s
Driver's license fee	orig	18.00	1999	48s
Fishing license	yr	14.00	4/01	34s
Personal Goods				
Personal care products and services purchases	yr	385	1999	30r
Personal Services				
Personal services, household, expenditures on	yr	300	1999	30r
Pets				
Pets, toys, and playground equipment, expenditures on	yr	375	1999	30r

Values are in dollars or fractions of dollars. In the column headed *Ref*, references are shown to sources. Each reference is followed by a letter. These refer to the geographical level for which data were reported: s=State, r=Region, and c=City or metro. The abbreviation *ex* is used to mean *except* or *excluding*; *exp* stands for expenditures. For other abbreviations and further explanations, please see the Introduction.

Janesville-Beloit, WI - continued

Item	Per	Value	Date	Ref.
Taxes				
Federal income taxes paid	yr	2326	1999	30r
Personal taxes, expenditures on	yr	3223	1999	30r
Property taxes paid	yr	1152	1999	30r
State and local income taxes paid	yr	753	1999	30r
Transportation				
Cars and trucks, new, expenditures on	yr	1280	1999	30r
Cars and trucks, used, expenditures on	yr	1763	1999	30r
Diesel at the pump	gal	1.34	10/99	73s
Gasoline and motor oil purchases	yr	1036	1999	30r
Gasoline before-tax price (cents)	gal	113.40	10/00	43s
Maintenance and repair expenditures	yr	594	1999	30r
Public transportation, expenditures on	yr	341	1999	30r
Transportation purchases	yr	6617	1999	30r
Vehicle expenses, miscellaneous, purchases	yr	2159	1999	30r
Vehicle insurance payments	yr	701	1999	30r
Vehicle purchases (net outlay)	yr	3081	1999	30r
Vehicle rental, lease expenditures	yr	536	1999	30r
Utilities				
Electrical bill, average	mos	52.08	9/00	9s
Electricity, expenditures on	yr	841	1999	30r
Electricity cost, average	KWh	5.69	9/00	9s
Utilities, fuels, and public services purchased	yr	2401	1999	30r
Water and other public services, expenditures on	yr	273	1999	30r
Weddings				
Wedding (national average cost)		19936	2000	33r
Wedding (regional average total cost)		16195	1997	110r
Attendants' gifts		321	1998	33r
Bridal attendants' apparel (5 persons)		824	2000	33r
Bride's headpiece/veil		173	1998	33r
Bride's wedding dress		859	1998	33r
Clergy, religious facility fee		242	1998	33r
Engagement ring		3177	1998	33r
Flowers		789	1998	33r
Groom's formalwear rental		99	2000	33r
Limousine		410	1998	33r
Marriage license cost		50.00-60.00	4/01	35s
Men's formalwear (ushers, best man)		469	2000	33r
Mother of bride apparel		241	2000	33r
Music		866	1998	33r
Photography and videography		1368	1998	33r
Rehearsal dinner		728	1998	33r
Wedding invitations and announcements		341	1998	33r
Wedding reception		7968	2000	33r
Wedding rings (bride and groom)		1060	1998	33r

Jersey City, NJ

Item	Per	Value	Date	Ref.
Average annual expenditures	yr	37971	1999	30r
Alcoholic Beverages				
Alcoholic beverage purchases	yr	368	1999	30r
Wine, red and white table, all sizes, any origin	liter	9.64	7/01	11r
Appliances				
Major appliances, expenditures on	yr	194	1999	30r
Small appliances, housewares, expenditures on	yr	93	1999	30r
Banking and Money				
Mortgage interest and charges paid	yr	2622	1999	30r
Mortgage principal paid on owned property	yr	1262	1999	30r
Vehicle finance charges paid	yr	240	1999	30r
Charity				
Cash contributions, expenditures	yr	1001	1999	30r
Child Care				
Child raising cost, total, age 0-2	yr	8670	1999	60r
Child raising cost, total, age 3-5	yr	8910	1999	60r

Jersey City, NJ - continued

Item	Per	Value	Date	Ref.
Child Care - continued				
Child raising cost, total, age 6-8	yr	9040	1999	60r
Child raising cost, total, age 9-11	yr	9100	1999	60r
Child raising cost, total, age 12-14	yr	9890	1999	60r
Child raising cost, total, age 15-17	yr	10010	1999	60r
Child's child care and education, age 0-2	yr	1070	1999	60r
Child's child care and education, age 3-5	yr	1190	1999	60r
Child's child care and education, age 6-8	yr	740	1999	60r
Child's child care and education, age 9-11	yr	470	1999	60r
Child's child care and education, age 12-14	yr	350	1999	60r
Child's child care and education, age 15-17	yr	590	1999	60r
Child's clothing, age 0-2	yr	480	1999	60r
Child's clothing, age 3-5	yr	470	1999	60r
Child's clothing, age 6-8	yr	520	1999	60r
Child's clothing, age 9-11	yr	570	1999	60r
Child's clothing, age 12-14	yr	970	1999	60r
Child's clothing, age 15-17	yr	870	1999	60r
Child's food, age 0-2	yr	1130	1999	60r
Child's food, age 3-5	yr	1290	1999	60r
Child's food, age 6-8	yr	1640	1999	60r
Child's food, age 9-11	yr	1930	1999	60r
Child's food, age 12-14	yr	1940	1999	60r
Child's food, age 15-17	yr	2150	1999	60r
Child's health care, age 0-2	yr	550	1999	60r
Child's health care, age 3-5	yr	530	1999	60r
Child's health care, age 6-8	yr	610	1999	60r
Child's health care, age 9-11	yr	650	1999	60r
Child's health care, age 12-14	yr	660	1999	60r
Child's health care, age 15-17	yr	690	1999	60r
Child's housing, age 0-2	yr	3555	1999	60r
Child's housing, age 3-5	yr	3530	1999	60r
Child's housing, age 6-8	yr	3490	1999	60r
Child's housing, age 9-11	yr	3340	1999	60r
Child's housing, age 12-14	yr	3530	1999	60r
Child's housing, age 15-17	yr	3140	1999	60r
Child's personal care, reading, age 0-2	yr	920	1999	60r
Child's personal care, reading, age 3-5	yr	950	1999	60r
Child's personal care, reading, age 6-8	yr	980	1999	60r
Child's personal care, reading, age 9-11	yr	1020	1999	60r
Child's personal care, reading, age 12-14	yr	1190	1999	60r
Child's personal care, reading, age 15-17	yr	970	1999	60r
Clothing				
Apparel and services purchases	yr	1831	1999	30r
Boys, 2 to 15, expenditures on	yr	92	1999	30r
Children under 2, expenditures on	yr	63	1999	30r
Footwear, expenditures on	yr	300	1999	30r
Girls, 2 to 15, expenditures on	yr	101	1999	30r
Men and boys, expenditures on	yr	446	1999	30r
Men, 16 and over, expenditures on	yr	354	1999	30r
Women, 16 and over, expenditures on	yr	584	1999	30r
Communications				
Cable modem installation, Adelphi		54.90	6/99	103s
Cable modem installation, Comcast		95.00	6/99	103s
Cable modem rate, cable subscriber, Adelphi	mos	34.95	6/99	103s
Cable modem rate, cable subscriber, Comcast	mos	39.95	6/99	103s
Cable modem rate, non-cable subscriber, Adelphi	mos	44.95	6/99	103s
Cable modem rate, non-cable subscriber, Comcast	mos	49.95	6/99	103s
Phone line, single, business, field visit	inst.	98.50	12/97	17s
Phone line, single, business, no field visit	inst.	79.50	12/97	17s
Phone line, single, residence, field visit	inst.	56.50	12/97	17s
Phone line, single, residence, no field visit	inst.	42.00	12/97	17s
Postage and stationery, expenditures on	yr	138	1999	30r
Postal rate, express mail, up to half-pound		12.45	7/01	108r
Postal rate, letter, first class, first ounce		0.34	7/01	108r
Postal rate, letter, two ounces		0.57	7/01	108r
Postal rate, post card		0.21	7/01	108r
Postal rate, priority mail, two pounds		3.95	7/01	108r
Postal rate, priority mail, up to one pound		3.50	7/01	108r
Telephone services, expenditures on	yr	830	1999	30r

Values are in dollars or fractions of dollars. In the column headed *Ref*, references are shown to sources. Each reference is followed by a letter. These refer to the geographical level for which data were reported: s=State, r=Region, and c=City or metro. The abbreviation *ex* is used to mean *except* or *excluding*; *exp* stands for *expenditures*. For other abbreviations and further explanations, please see the Introduction.

Jersey City, NJ - continued

Item	Per	Value	Date	Ref.
Education				
Board, 4-year private college/university	yr	2959	1996	38s
Board, 4-year public college/university	yr	2052	1996	38s
Education expenditures	yr	877	1999	30r
Room, 4-year private college/university	yr	3226	1996	38s
Room, 4-year public college/university	yr	3101	1996	38s
Total cost, 4-year private college/university	yr	19751	1996	38s
Total cost, 4-year public college/university	yr	9125	1996	38s
Tuition, 2-year public college/university, in state	yr	1878	1996	38s
Tuition, 4-year private college/university, in state	yr	13566	1996	38s
Tuition, 4-year public college/university	yr	3972	1996	38s
Energy and Fuels				
Electricity	KWh	0.12	7/01	11r
Fuel oil #2	gal	1.31	7/01	11r
Fuel oil and other fuels, expenditures on	yr	207	1999	30r
Gas, natural, commercial rate	1000 cf	5.98	11/00	88s
Gasoline, all types	gal	1.80	7/01	11r
Gasoline, unleaded midgrade	gal	1.85	7/01	11r
Gasoline, unleaded premium	gal	1.91	7/01	11r
Gasoline, unleaded regular	gal	1.71	7/01	11r
Natural gas, expenditures on	yr	368	1999	30r
Utility (piped) gas, therm		1.08	7/01	11r
Utility (piped) gas, 40 therms		50.87	7/01	11r
Utility (piped) gas, 100 therms		111.06	7/01	11r
Entertainment				
Entertainment purchases	yr	1821	1999	30r
Fees and admissions paid	yr	511	1999	30r
Television, radios, sound equipment, expenditures on	yr	650	1999	30r
Funerals				
Total cost of funeral		5813.50	1/99	78s
Acknowledgement cards		28.32	1/99	78r
Casket		2082.20	1/99	78r
Cosmetology, hair, other preparation		169.59	1/99	78r
Embalming		465.60	1/99	78r
Funeral at funeral home		339.56	1/99	78r
Hearse (local)		183.96	1/99	78r
Professional service charges		1157.85	1/99	78r
Service car/van		100.41	1/99	78r
Transfer of remains to funeral home		158.66	1/99	78r
Vault		766.31	1/99	78r
Visitation/viewing		361.04	1/99	78r
Groceries				
Apples, red delicious	lb	0.95	7/01	11r
Bacon, sliced	lb	3.44	7/01	11r
Bakery products, expenditures on	yr	310	1999	30r
Bananas	lb	0.55	7/01	11r
Beef, expenditures on	yr	236	1999	30r
Bread, white, pan	lb	1.09	7/01	11r
Butter, yoghurt, cheese, etc, expenditures on	yr	214	1999	30r
Cereals and bakery product purchases	yr	474	1999	30r
Cereals and cereal products, expenditures on	yr	164	1999	30r
Chicken legs, bone-in	lb	1.23	7/01	11r
Chicken, fresh, whole	lb	1.13	7/01	11r
Chuck roast, U.S. choice, boneless	lb	2.79	7/01	11r
Coffee, 100%, ground roast, all sizes	lb	3.40	7/01	11r
Dairy product purchases	yr	342	1999	30r
Eggs, expenditures on	yr	34	1999	30r
Eggs, grade A, large	dozen	0.82	7/01	11r
Fats and oils, expenditures on	yr	80	1999	30r
Fish and seafood, expenditures on	yr	123	1999	30r
Food (excl fruit and vegetables), eaten at home, purchases	yr	838	1999	30r
Food cooked on trips, expenditures on	yr	48	1999	30r
Food purchases	yr	5314	1999	30r
Food purchases, eaten away from home	yr	2313	1999	30r
Food purchases, food eaten at home	yr	3001	1999	30r
Fresh fruits, expenditures on	yr	169	1999	30r

Jersey City, NJ - continued

Item	Per	Value	Date	Ref.
Groceries - continued				
Fresh milk and cream, expenditures on	yr	128	1999	30r
Fresh vegetables, expenditures on	yr	164	1999	30r
Grapefruit	lb	0.67	7/01	11r
Grapes, Thompson, seedless	lb	2.18	7/01	11r
Ground beef, lean and extra lean	lb	2.66	7/01	11r
Ground chuck, 100% beef	lb	2.04	7/01	11r
Lettuce, iceberg	lb	0.76	7/01	11r
Meats, poultry, fish, and egg purchases	yr	808	1999	30r
Nonalcoholic beverages, expenditures on	yr	225	1999	30r
Orange juice, frozen concentrate	16 oz	1.88	7/01	11r
Oranges, Navel	lb	0.79	7/01	11r
Oranges, Valencia	lb	0.56	7/01	11r
Peaches	lb	1.16	7/01	11r
Peanut butter, creamy, all sizes	lb	2.01	7/01	11r
Pears, Anjou	lb	1.16	7/01	11r
Pork chops, center cut, bone-in	lb	3.57	7/01	11r
Pork, expenditures on	yr	146	1999	30r
Potato chips	16 oz	3.37	7/01	11r
Potatoes, white, all types	lb	0.42	7/01	11r
Poultry, expenditures on	yr	158	1999	30r
Processed fruits, expenditures on	yr	124	1999	30r
Processed vegetables, expenditures on	yr	82	1999	30r
Round roast, U.S. choice, boneless	lb	3.04	7/01	11r
Spaghetti and macaroni	lb	1.04	7/01	11r
Steak, sirloin, U.S. choice, boneless	lb	5.39	7/01	11r
Strawberries, dry pint	12 oz	1.51	7/01	11r
Sugar and other sweets, expenditures on	yr	110	1999	30r
Sugar, white, 33-80 ounce package	lb	0.46	7/01	11r
Sugar, white, all sizes	lb	0.47	7/01	11r
Tobacco products and smoking supplies purchases	yr	309	1999	30r
Yogurt, natural, fruit flavored	8 oz	0.79	7/01	11r
Goods and Services				
B&B Japanese maple (acer japonicum)	gal	38.99-125.00	4/00	93r
Boxwood (buxus)	2 gal	15.99-49.95	4/00	93r
Daylilly (hemerocallis)	gal	4.95	4/00	93r
Flat of annuals		8.00-14.99	4/00	93r
Fountain grass (pennisetum)	gal	6.99-9.99	4/00	93r
Hanging basket (10 in)		12.95-19.99	4/00	93r
Hardy geranium (geranium)	gal	6.95-7.99	4/00	93r
Hosta (hosta)	gal	4.95	4/00	93r
Lilac (syrubga vulgaris)	2 gal	17.99-74.95	4/00	93r
Miscellaneous purchases	yr	872	1999	30r
Rhododendron (rhododendron)	2 gal	23.99-54.95	4/00	93r
Sage (salvia)	gal	6.95-7.99	4/00	93r
Wintercreeper euonymus (euonymus fortunei)	2 gal	14.99-23.95	4/00	93r
Hunting license	yr	22.50	4/01	34s
Health Care				
Cardiac catheterization, ave hospital/ physician charges		14680	1998	77s
Childbirth, Cesarean delivery		14716	1997	13r
Childbirth, vaginal delivery		8541	1997	13r
Drugs, expenditures on	yr	296	1999	30r
Health care purchases	yr	1788	1999	30r
Health insurance expenditures	yr	875	1999	30r
Hysterectomy, laproscopically-assisted, ave hospital/physician charges		18330	1998	76s
Hysterectomy, vaginal, ave hospital and physician charges		13620	1998	76s
Medicaid dispensing fee		3.73-4.07	1999	87s

Values are in dollars or fractions of dollars. In the column headed *Ref*, references are shown to sources. Each reference is followed by a letter. These refer to the geographical level for which data were reported: s=State, r=Region, and c=City or metro. The abbreviation *ex* is used to mean *except* or *excluding*; *exp* stands for *expenditures*. For other abbreviations and further explanations, please see the Introduction.

Jersey City, NJ - continued

Item	Per	Value	Date	Ref.
Health Care				
Medical services expenditures	yr	516	1999	30r
Medical supplies, expenditures on	yr	102	1999	30r
Plastic surgery, breast augmentation		4232	2000	7r
Plastic surgery, breast lift		4605	2000	7r
Plastic surgery, facelift		6964	2000	7r
Plastic surgery, hair transplantation		4193	2000	7r
Plastic surgery, lip augmentation		1675	2000	7r
Plastic surgery, lower body lift		6611	2000	7r
Plastic surgery, thigh lift		4751	2000	7r
Household Goods				
Floor coverings, expenditures on	yr	59	1999	30r
Furniture, expenditures on	yr	388	1999	30r
Household furnishings and equipment purchases	yr	1567	1999	30r
Household textiles, expenditures on	yr	112	1999	30r
Laundry and cleaning supplies, expenditures on	yr	104	1999	30r
Housing				
Home price, existing, ave		180800	10/00	90r
Home value, median		213000	2001	53s
Household operation expenditures	yr	581	1999	30r
Housekeeping supplies purchases	yr	474	1999	30r
Lodging expenditures	yr	550	1999	30r
Maintenance, repairs, insurance expenditures	yr	835	1999	30r
Monthly rental value of owned home	mos	663	1999	30r
Owned dwellings, expenditures own	yr	5209	1999	30r
Rent expenditures	yr	2390	1999	30r
Rental unit, 1 bedroom, with utilities	mos	709	4/01	41c
Rental unit, 2 bedroom, with utilities	mos	826	4/01	41c
Rental unit, 3 bedroom, with utilities	mos	1050	4/01	41c
Rental unit, 4 bedroom, with utilities	mos	1155	4/01	41c
Shelter, expenditures on	yr	8149	1999	30r
Insurance and Pensions				
Auto insurance premium	yr	1292.76	1999	57s
Life and other personal insurance purchases	yr	424	1999	30r
Pensions and Social Security, expenditures on	yr	3037	1999	30r
Legal Fees				
Divorce, filing fee		65.00	4/01	35s
Driver's license fee	orig	18.00	1999	48s
Driver's license fee	renew	15.00	1999	48s
Fishing license	yr	22.50	4/01	34s
Personal Goods				
Personal care products and services purchases	yr	399	1999	30r
Personal Services				
Personal services, household, expenditures on	yr	271	1999	30r
Pets				
Pets, toys, and playground equipment, expenditures on	yr	325	1999	30r
Taxes				
Federal income taxes paid	yr	2606	1999	30r
Personal taxes, expenditures on	yr	3567	1999	30r
Property taxes paid	yr	1752	1999	30r
State and local income taxes paid	yr	694	1999	30r
Transportation				
Automobile insurance	yr	975.90	2000	79s
Cars and trucks, new, expenditures on	yr	1496	1999	30r
Cars and trucks, used, expenditures on	yr	1251	1999	30r
Diesel at the pump	gal	1.19	10/99	73s
Gasoline and motor oil purchases	yr	901	1999	30r
Gasoline before-tax price (cents)	gal	114.90	10/00	43s
Maintenance and repair expenditures	yr	618	1999	30r
Motorcycle license fee	orig	15.00	1999	49s
Motorcycle license fee	renew	13.00	1999	49s

Jersey City, NJ - continued

Item	Per	Value	Date	Ref.
Transportation - continued				
Public transportation, expenditures on	yr	575	1999	30r
Transportation purchases	yr	6503	1999	30r
Vehicle expenses, miscellaneous, purchases	yr	2266	1999	30r
Vehicle insurance payments	yr	824	1999	30r
Vehicle purchases (net outlay)	yr	2761	1999	30r
Vehicle rental, lease expenditures	yr	584	1999	30r
Utilities				
Electrical bill, average	mos	74.08	9/00	9s
Electricity, expenditures on	yr	837	1999	30r
Electricity cost, average	KWh	8.91	9/00	9s
Utilities, fuels, and public services purchased	yr	2457	1999	30r
Water and other public services, expenditures on	yr	215	1999	30r
Weddings				
Wedding (national average cost)		19936	2000	33r
Wedding (regional average total cost)		29454	1997	110r
Attendants' gifts		321	1998	33r
Bridal attendants' apparel (5 persons)		824	2000	33r
Bride's headpiece/veil		173	1998	33r
Bride's wedding dress		859	1998	33r
Clergy, religious facility fee		242	1998	33r
Engagement ring		3177	1998	33r
Flowers		789	1998	33r
Groom's formalwear rental		99	2000	33r
Limousine		410	1998	33r
Marriage license cost		28.00	4/01	35s
Men's formalwear (ushers, best man)		469	2000	33r
Mother of bride apparel		241	2000	33r
Music		866	1998	33r
Photography and videography		1368	1998	33r
Rehearsal dinner		728	1998	33r
Wedding invitations and announcements		341	1998	33r
Wedding reception		7968	2000	33r
Wedding rings (bride and groom)		1060	1998	33r

Johnson City-Kingsport-Bristol, TN

Item	Per	Value	Date	Ref.
Alcoholic Beverages				
Alcoholic beverage purchases	yr	253	1999	30r
Malt beverages, all types, all sizes, any origin	16 oz	0.96	7/01	11r
Appliances				
Major appliances, expenditures on	yr	172	1999	30r
Small appliances, housewares, expenditures on	yr	81	1999	30r
Banking and Money				
Mortgage interest and charges paid	yr	2039	1999	30r
Mortgage principal paid on owned property	yr	1026	1999	30r
Vehicle finance charges paid	yr	365	1999	30r
Charity				
Cash contributions, expenditures	yr	1127	1999	30r
Child Care				
Child raising cost, total, age 0-2	yr	8540	1999	60r
Child raising cost, total, age 3-5	yr	8780	1999	60r
Child raising cost, total, age 6-8	yr	8820	1999	60r
Child raising cost, total, age 9-11	yr	8800	1999	60r
Child raising cost, total, age 12-14	yr	9510	1999	60r
Child raising cost, total, age 15-17	yr	9740	1999	60r
Child's child care and education, age 0-2	yr	1380	1999	60r
Child's child care and education, age 3-5	yr	1520	1999	60r
Child's child care and education, age 6-8	yr	990	1999	60r
Child's child care and education, age 9-11	yr	650	1999	60r
Child's child care and education, age 12-14	yr	490	1999	60r
Child's child care and education, age 15-17	yr	840	1999	60r
Child's clothing, age 0-2	yr	480	1999	60r
Child's clothing, age 3-5	yr	470	1999	60r
Child's clothing, age 6-8	yr	520	1999	60r
Child's clothing, age 9-11	yr	570	1999	60r
Child's clothing, age 12-14	yr	950	1999	60r

Values are in dollars or fractions of dollars. In the column headed *Ref*, references are shown to sources. Each reference is followed by a letter. These refer to the geographical level for which data were reported: s=State, r=Region, and c=City or metro. The abbreviation *ex* is used to mean *except* or *excluding; exp* stands for expenditures. For other abbreviations and further explanations, please see the Introduction.

Johnson City-Kingsport-Bristol, TN - continued

Item	Per	Value	Date	Ref.
Child Care				
Child's clothing, age 15-17	yr	850	1999	60r
Child's food, age 0-2	yr	1000	1999	60r
Child's food, age 3-5	yr	1160	1999	60r
Child's food, age 6-8	yr	1490	1999	60r
Child's food, age 9-11	yr	1770	1999	60r
Child's food, age 12-14	yr	1770	1999	60r
Child's food, age 15-17	yr	1980	1999	60r
Child's health care, age 0-2	yr	620	1999	60r
Child's health care, age 3-5	yr	590	1999	60r
Child's health care, age 6-8	yr	680	1999	60r
Child's health care, age 9-11	yr	720	1999	60r
Child's health care, age 12-14	yr	730	1999	60r
Child's health care, age 15-17	yr	760	1999	60r
Child's housing, age 0-2	yr	3070	1999	60r
Child's housing, age 3-5	yr	3050	1999	60r
Child's housing, age 6-8	yr	3010	1999	60r
Child's housing, age 9-11	yr	2850	1999	60r
Child's housing, age 12-14	yr	3040	1999	60r
Child's housing, age 15-17	yr	2650	1999	60r
Child's personal care, reading, age 0-2	yr	910	1999	60r
Child's personal care, reading, age 3-5	yr	930	1999	60r
Child's personal care, reading, age 6-8	yr	960	1999	60r
Child's personal care, reading, age 9-11	yr	1000	1999	60r
Child's personal care, reading, age 12-14	yr	1170	1999	60r
Child's personal care, reading, age 15-17	yr	950	1999	60r
Clothing				
Apparel and services purchases	yr	1610	1999	30r
Boys, 2 to 15, expenditures on	yr	89	1999	30r
Children under 2, expenditures on	yr	79	1999	30r
Footwear, expenditures on	yr	283	1999	30r
Girls, 2 to 15, expenditures on	yr	103	1999	30r
Men and boys, expenditures on	yr	351	1999	30r
Men, 16 and over, expenditures on	yr	262	1999	30r
Women, 16 and over, expenditures on	yr	538	1999	30r
Communications				
Cable modem installation, Intermedia		149.95	6/99	103s
Cable modem installation, Time Warner		75.00-225.00	6/99	103s
Cable modem rate, cable subscriber, Intermedia	mos	49.95	6/99	103s
Cable modem rate, cable subscriber, Time Warner	mos	39.95-49.95	6/99	103s
Cable modem rate, non-cable subscriber, Intermedia	mos	54.95	6/99	103s
Cable modem rate, non-cable subscriber, Time Warner	mos	39.95-54.95	6/99	103s
Phone line, single, business, field visit	inst.	58.50	12/97	17s
Phone line, single, business, no field visit	inst.	58.50	12/97	17s
Phone line, single, residence, field visit	inst.	41.50	12/97	17s
Phone line, single, residence, no field visit	inst.	41.50	12/97	17s
Postage and stationery, expenditures on	yr	104	1999	30r
Postal rate, express mail, up to half-pound		12.45	7/01	108r
Postal rate, letter, first class, first ounce		0.34	7/01	108r
Postal rate, letter, two ounces		0.57	7/01	108r
Postal rate, post card		0.21	7/01	108r
Postal rate, priority mail, two pounds		3.95	7/01	108r
Postal rate, priority mail, up to one pound		3.50	7/01	108r
Telephone services, expenditures on	yr	860	1999	30r
Education				
Board, 4-year private college/university	yr	2085	1996	38s
Board, 4-year public college/university	yr	1737	1996	38s
Education expenditures	yr	431	1999	30r
Room, 4-year private college/university	yr	2153	1996	38s
Room, 4-year public college/university	yr	1644	1996	38s
Total cost, 4-year private college/university	yr	14068	1996	38s
Total cost, 4-year public college/university	yr	5372	1996	38s
Tuition, 2-year public college/university, in state	yr	1022	1996	38s
Tuition, 4-year private college/university, in state	yr	9830	1996	38s
Tuition, 4-year public college/university	yr	1990	1996	38s

Johnson City-Kingsport-Bristol, TN - continued

Item	Per	Value	Date	Ref.
Energy and Fuels				
Electricity	KWh	0.09	7/01	11r
Electricity	500 KWhs	47.29	7/01	11r
Fuel oil #2	gal	1.43	7/01	11r
Fuel oil and other fuels, expenditures on	yr	45	1999	30r
Gas, natural, commercial rate	1000 cf	8.61	11/00	88s
Gasoline, all types	gal	1.60	7/01	11r
Gasoline, unleaded midgrade	gal	1.65	7/01	11r
Gasoline, unleaded premium	gal	1.74	7/01	11r
Natural gas, expenditures on	yr	164	1999	30r
Utility (piped) gas, therm		1.01	7/01	11r
Utility (piped) gas, 40 therms		44.29	7/01	11r
Utility (piped) gas, 100 therms		97.44	7/01	11r
Entertainment				
Entertainment purchases	yr	1574	1999	30r
Fees and admissions paid	yr	371	1999	30r
Reading purchases	yr	121	1999	30r
Television, radios, sound equipment, expenditures on	yr	561	1999	30r
Groceries				
American processed cheese	lb	3.50	7/01	11r
Bakery products, expenditures on	yr	261	1999	30r
Bananas	lb	0.47	7/01	11r
Beans, dried, any type, all sizes	lb	0.63	7/01	11r
Beef for stew, boneless	lb	2.86	7/01	11r
Beef, expenditures on	yr	210	1999	30r
Bologna, all beef or mixed	lb	2.29	7/01	11r
Bread, French	lb	1.66	7/01	11r
Bread, white, pan	lb	0.87	7/01	11r
Bread, whole wheat, pan	lb	1.38	7/01	11r
Broccoli	lb	1.04	7/01	11r
Butter, salted, grade AA, stick	lb	2.26	7/01	11r
Butter, yoghurt, cheese, etc, expenditures on	yr	170	1999	30r
Cabbage	lb	0.42	7/01	11r
Cereals and cereal products, expenditures on	yr	140	1999	30r
Cheddar cheese, natural	lb	3.75	7/01	11r
Chicken breast, bone-in	lb	1.85	7/01	11r
Chicken legs, bone-in	lb	1.34	7/01	11r
Chicken, fresh, whole	lb	1.05	7/01	11r
Chops, boneless	lb	4.13	7/01	11r
Chuck roast, graded and ungraded, excl U.S. prime and choice	lb	2.35	7/01	11r
Chuck roast, U.S. choice, boneless	lb	2.67	7/01	11r
Coffee, 100%, ground roast, all sizes	lb	2.88	7/01	11r
Coffee, instant, plain, regular, all sizes	16 oz	9.25	7/01	11r
Cola, non diet,	2 liter	1.11	7/01	11r
Crackers, soda, salted	lb	1.70	7/01	11r
Dairy product purchases	yr	282	1999	30r
Eggs, expenditures on	yr	32	1999	30r
Fats and oils, expenditures on	yr	79	1999	30r
Fish and seafood, expenditures on	yr	99	1999	30r
Flour, white, all purpose	lb	0.32	7/01	11r
Food (excl fruit and vegetables), eaten at home, purchases	yr	815	1999	30r
Food cooked on trips, expenditures on	yr	36	1999	30r
Food purchases	yr	4533	1999	30r
Food purchases, eaten away from home	yr	1873	1999	30r
Food purchases, food eaten at home	yr	2660	1999	30r
Fresh fruits, expenditures on	yr	128	1999	30r
Fresh milk and cream, expenditures on	yr	112	1999	30r
Fresh vegetables, expenditures on	yr	131	1999	30r
Fruit and vegetable purchases	yr	438	1999	30r
Grapefruit	lb	0.59	7/01	11r
Grapes, Thompson, seedless	lb	2.12	7/01	11r
Ground beef, 100% beef	lb	1.76	7/01	11r
Ground beef, lean and extra lean	lb	2.60	7/01	11r
Ground chuck, 100% beef	lb	2.08	7/01	11r
Ham, boneless, excl canned	lb	2.71	7/01	11r
Ham, rump or shank half, bone-in, smoked	lb	2.19	7/01	11r
Ice cream, prepackaged, bulk, regular	1/2 gal	3.93	7/01	11r

Values are in dollars or fractions of dollars. In the column headed *Ref*, references are shown to sources. Each reference is followed by a letter. These refer to the geographical level for which data were reported: s=State, r=Region, and c=City or metro. The abbreviation *ex* is used to mean *except* or *excluding*; *exp* stands for *expenditures*. For other abbreviations and further explanations, please see the Introduction.

Johnson City-Kingsport-Bristol, TN - continued

Item	Per	Value	Date	Ref.
Groceries				
Lemons	lb	1.32	7/01	11r
Lettuce, iceberg	lb	0.76	7/01	11r
Milk, fresh, low fat,	gal	2.75	7/01	11r
Milk, fresh, whole, fortified	gal	2.97	7/01	11r
Nonalcoholic beverages, expenditures on	yr	228	1999	30r
Orange juice, frozen concentrate	16 oz	1.95	7/01	11r
Oranges, Navel	lb	0.73	7/01	11r
Oranges, Valencia	lb	0.55	7/01	11r
Peanut butter, creamy, all sizes	lb	1.83	7/01	11r
Pears, Anjou	lb	0.98	7/01	11r
Pork chops, center cut, bone-in	lb	3.33	7/01	11r
Pork sausage, fresh, loose	lb	2.59	7/01	11r
Pork shoulder picnic, bone-in, smoked	lb	1.12	7/01	11r
Pork, expenditures on	yr	162	1999	30r
Potato chips	16 oz	3.59	7/01	11r
Potatoes, frozen, french fried	lb	1.00	7/01	11r
Potatoes, white, all types	lb	0.44	7/01	11r
Poultry, expenditures on	yr	137	1999	30r
Processed fruits, expenditures on	yr	97	1999	30r
Processed vegetables, expenditures on	yr	82	1999	30r
Rice, white, long grain, uncooked	lb	0.51	7/01	11r
Round roast, graded and ungraded, excl U.S. prime and choice	lb	2.96	7/01	11r
Round steak, graded and ungraded, excl U.S. prime and choice	lb	3.11	7/01	11r
Sirloin steak, graded and ungraded, excl U.S. prime and choice	lb	4.23	7/01	11r
Spaghetti and macaroni	lb	0.78	7/01	11r
Steak, round, U.S. choice, boneless	lb	3.56	7/01	11r
Steak, sirloin, U.S. choice, boneless	lb	5.65	7/01	11r
Strawberries, dry pint	12 oz	1.50	7/01	11r
Sugar and other sweets, expenditures on	yr	99	1999	30r
Sugar, white, 33-80 ounce package	lb	0.39	7/01	11r
Sugar, white, all sizes	lb	0.42	7/01	11r
Tobacco products and smoking supplies purchases	yr	288	1999	30r
Tomatoes, field grown	lb	1.43	7/01	11r
Tuna, light, chunk	lb	1.77	7/01	11r
Turkey, frozen, whole	lb	1.05	7/01	11r
Health Care				
Cardiac catheterization, ave hospital/ physician charges		12170	1998	77s
Childbirth, Cesarean delivery		11587	1997	13r
Childbirth, vaginal delivery		6725	1997	13r
Drugs, expenditures on	yr	399	1999	30r
Health care purchases	yr	1971	1999	30r
Health insurance expenditures	yr	933	1999	30r
Hysterectomy, laproscopically-assisted, ave hospital/physician charges		13470	1998	76s
Hysterectomy, vaginal, ave hospital and physician charges		9530	1998	76s
Medical services expenditures	yr	547	1999	30r
Medical supplies, expenditures on	yr	91	1999	30r
Household Goods				
Floor coverings, expenditures on	yr	44	1999	30r
Furniture, expenditures on	yr	335	1999	30r
Household furnishings and equipment purchases	yr	1328	1999	30r
Household textiles, expenditures on	yr	89	1999	30r
Laundry and cleaning supplies, expenditures on	yr	113	1999	30r
Housing				
Home price, existing, ave		160100	10/00	90r
Home value, median		112000	2001	53s
Household operation expenditures	yr	553	1999	30r
Housekeeping supplies purchases	yr	473	1999	30r
Housing, expenditures on	yr	10303	1999	30r
Maintenance, repairs, insurance expenditures	yr	699	1999	30r
Monthly rental value of owned home	mos	505	1999	30r
Owned dwellings, expenditures own	yr	3465	1999	30r

Johnson City-Kingsport-Bristol, TN - continued

Item	Per	Value	Date	Ref.
Housing - continued				
Rent expenditures	yr	1641	1999	30r
Rental unit, 1 bedroom, with utilities	mos	370	4/01	41c
Rental unit, 2 bedroom, with utilities	mos	458	4/01	41c
Rental unit, 3 bedroom, with utilities	mos	594	4/01	41c
Rental unit, 4 bedroom, with utilities	mos	704	4/01	41c
Shelter, expenditures on	yr	5467	1999	30r
Insurance and Pensions				
Life and other personal insurance purchases	yr	414	1999	30r
Pensions and Social Security, expenditures on	yr	2635	1999	30r
Personal insurance and pensions, expenditures on	yr	3048	1999	30r
Legal Fees				
Combination hunting and fishing license	yr	21.00	4/01	34s
Divorce, filing fee		64.00	4/01	35s
Driver's license fee	renew	17.50	1999	48s
Driver's license fee	orig	17.50	1999	48s
Personal Goods				
Personal care products and services purchases	yr	393	1999	30r
Personal Services				
Personal services, household, expenditures on	yr	258	1999	30r
Pets				
Pets, toys, and playground equipment, expenditures on	yr	306	1999	30r
Taxes				
Federal income taxes paid	yr	2047	1999	30r
Personal taxes, expenditures on	yr	2554	1999	30r
Property taxes paid	yr	726	1999	30r
State and local income taxes paid	yr	363	1999	30r
Transportation				
Cars and trucks, new, expenditures on	yr	1648	1999	30r
Cars and trucks, used, expenditures on	yr	1651	1999	30r
Diesel at the pump	gal	1.18	10/99	73s
Gasoline and motor oil purchases	yr	1052	1999	30r
Gasoline before-tax price (cents)	gal	102.50	10/00	43s
Maintenance and repair expenditures	yr	621	1999	30r
Public transportation, expenditures on	yr	298	1999	30r
Transportation purchases	yr	6738	1999	30r
Vehicle expenses, miscellaneous, purchases	yr	2033	1999	30r
Vehicle insurance payments	yr	696	1999	30r
Vehicle purchases (net outlay)	yr	3354	1999	30r
Vehicle rental, lease expenditures	yr	352	1999	30r
Utilities				
Electrical bill, average	mos	79.16	9/00	9s
Electricity, expenditures on	yr	1115	1999	30r
Electricity cost, average	KWh	5.60	9/00	9s
Water and other public services, expenditures on	yr	298	1999	30r
Weddings				
Wedding (national average cost)		19936	2000	33r
Attendants' gifts		321	1998	33r
Bridal attendants' apparel (5 persons)		824	2000	33r
Bride's headpiece/veil		173	1998	33r
Bride's wedding dress		859	1998	33r
Clergy, religious facility fee		242	1998	33r
Engagement ring		3177	1998	33r
Flowers		789	1998	33r
Groom's formalwear rental		99	2000	33r
Limousine		410	1998	33r
Marriage license cost		31.00	4/01	35s
Men's formalwear (ushers, best man)		469	2000	33r
Mother of bride apparel		241	2000	33r
Music		866	1998	33r
Photography and videography		1368	1998	33r
Rehearsal dinner		728	1998	33r

Values are in dollars or fractions of dollars. In the column headed *Ref*, references are shown to sources. Each reference is followed by a letter. These refer to the geographical level for which data were reported: s=State, r=Region, and c=City or metro. The abbreviation *ex* is used to mean *except* or *excluding*; *exp* stands for *expenditures*. For other abbreviations and further explanations, please see the Introduction.

Johnson City-Kingsport-Bristol, TN - continued

Item	Per	Value	Date	Ref.
Weddings				
Wedding invitations and announcements		341	1998	33r
Wedding reception		7968	2000	33r
Wedding rings (bride and groom)		1060	1998	33r

Johnstown, PA

Item	Per	Value	Date	Ref.
Average annual expenditures	yr	37971	1999	30r
Alcoholic Beverages				
Alcoholic beverage purchases	yr	368	1999	30r
Wine, red and white table, all sizes, any origin	liter	9.64	7/01	11r
Appliances				
Major appliances, expenditures on	yr	194	1999	30r
Small appliances, housewares, expenditures on	yr	93	1999	30r
Banking and Money				
Mortgage interest and charges paid	yr	2622	1999	30r
Mortgage principal paid on owned property	yr	1262	1999	30r
Vehicle finance charges paid	yr	240	1999	30r
Charity				
Cash contributions, expenditures	yr	1001	1999	30r
Child Care				
Child raising cost, total, age 0-2	yr	8670	1999	60r
Child raising cost, total, age 3-5	yr	8910	1999	60r
Child raising cost, total, age 6-8	yr	9040	1999	60r
Child raising cost, total, age 9-11	yr	9100	1999	60r
Child raising cost, total, age 12-14	yr	9890	1999	60r
Child raising cost, total, age 15-17	yr	10010	1999	60r
Child's child care and education, age 0-2	yr	1070	1999	60r
Child's child care and education, age 3-5	yr	1190	1999	60r
Child's child care and education, age 6-8	yr	740	1999	60r
Child's child care and education, age 9-11	yr	470	1999	60r
Child's child care and education, age 12-14	yr	350	1999	60r
Child's child care and education, age 15-17	yr	590	1999	60r
Child's clothing, age 0-2	yr	480	1999	60r
Child's clothing, age 3-5	yr	470	1999	60r
Child's clothing, age 6-8	yr	520	1999	60r
Child's clothing, age 9-11	yr	570	1999	60r
Child's clothing, age 12-14	yr	970	1999	60r
Child's clothing, age 15-17	yr	870	1999	60r
Child's food, age 0-2	yr	1130	1999	60r
Child's food, age 3-5	yr	1290	1999	60r
Child's food, age 6-8	yr	1640	1999	60r
Child's food, age 9-11	yr	1930	1999	60r
Child's food, age 12-14	yr	1940	1999	60r
Child's food, age 15-17	yr	2150	1999	60r
Child's health care, age 0-2	yr	550	1999	60r
Child's health care, age 3-5	yr	530	1999	60r
Child's health care, age 6-8	yr	610	1999	60r
Child's health care, age 9-11	yr	650	1999	60r
Child's health care, age 12-14	yr	660	1999	60r
Child's health care, age 15-17	yr	690	1999	60r
Child's housing, age 0-2	yr	3555	1999	60r
Child's housing, age 3-5	yr	3530	1999	60r
Child's housing, age 6-8	yr	3490	1999	60r
Child's housing, age 9-11	yr	3340	1999	60r
Child's housing, age 12-14	yr	3530	1999	60r
Child's housing, age 15-17	yr	3140	1999	60r
Child's personal care, reading, age 0-2	yr	920	1999	60r
Child's personal care, reading, age 3-5	yr	950	1999	60r
Child's personal care, reading, age 6-8	yr	980	1999	60r
Child's personal care, reading, age 9-11	yr	1020	1999	60r
Child's personal care, reading, age 12-14	yr	1190	1999	60r
Child's personal care, reading, age 15-17	yr	970	1999	60r
Clothing				
Apparel and services purchases	yr	1831	1999	30r
Boys, 2 to 15, expenditures on	yr	92	1999	30r
Children under 2, expenditures on	yr	63	1999	30r

Johnstown, PA - continued

Item	Per	Value	Date	Ref.
Clothing - continued				
Footwear, expenditures on	yr	300	1999	30r
Girls, 2 to 15, expenditures on	yr	101	1999	30r
Men and boys, expenditures on	yr	446	1999	30r
Men, 16 and over, expenditures on	yr	354	1999	30r
Women, 16 and over, expenditures on	yr	584	1999	30r
Communications				
Cable modem installation, Adelphi		54.90	6/99	103s
Cable modem installation, Comcast		95.00	6/99	103s
Cable modem rate, cable subscriber, Adelphi	mos	34.95	6/99	103s
Cable modem rate, cable subscriber, Comcast	mos	39.95	6/99	103s
Cable modem rate, non-cable subscriber, Adelphi	mos	44.95	6/99	103s
Cable modem rate, non-cable subscriber, Comcast	mos	49.95	6/99	103s
Phone line, single, business, field visit	inst.	75.00	12/97	17s
Phone line, single, business, no field visit	inst.	75.00	12/97	17s
Phone line, single, residence, field visit	inst.	40.00	12/97	17s
Phone line, single, residence, no field visit	inst.	40.00	12/97	17s
Postage and stationery, expenditures on	yr	138	1999	30r
Postal rate, express mail, up to half-pound		12.45	7/01	108r
Postal rate, letter, first class, first ounce		0.34	7/01	108r
Postal rate, letter, two ounces		0.57	7/01	108r
Postal rate, post card		0.21	7/01	108r
Postal rate, priority mail, two pounds		3.95	7/01	108r
Postal rate, priority mail, up to one pound		3.50	7/01	108r
Telephone services, expenditures on	yr	830	1999	30r
Education				
Board, 4-year private college/university	yr	2822	1996	38s
Board, 4-year public college/university	yr	2174	1996	38s
Education expenditures	yr	877	1999	30r
Room, 4-year private college/university	yr	2943	1996	38s
Room, 4-year public college/university	yr	2227	1996	38s
Total cost, 4-year private college/university	yr	19876	1996	38s
Total cost, 4-year public college/university	yr	9124	1996	38s
Tuition, 2-year public college/university, in state	yr	1909	1996	38s
Tuition, 4-year private college/university, in state	yr	14111	1996	38s
Tuition, 4-year public college/university	yr	4723	1996	38s
Energy and Fuels				
Electricity	KWh	0.12	7/01	11r
Fuel oil #2	gal	1.31	7/01	11r
Fuel oil and other fuels, expenditures on	yr	207	1999	30r
Gas, natural, commercial rate	1000 cf	5.96	11/00	88s
Gasoline, all types	gal	1.80	7/01	11r
Gasoline, unleaded midgrade	gal	1.85	7/01	11r
Gasoline, unleaded premium	gal	1.91	7/01	11r
Gasoline, unleaded regular	gal	1.71	7/01	11r
Natural gas, expenditures on	yr	368	1999	30r
Utility (piped) gas, therm		1.08	7/01	11r
Utility (piped) gas, 40 therms		50.87	7/01	11r
Utility (piped) gas, 100 therms		111.06	7/01	11r
Entertainment				
Entertainment purchases	yr	1821	1999	30r
Fees and admissions paid	yr	511	1999	30r
Television, radios, sound equipment, expenditures on	yr	650	1999	30r
Funerals				
Total cost of funeral		5813.50	1/99	78r
Acknowledgement cards		28.32	1/99	78r
Casket		2082.20	1/99	78r
Cosmetology, hair, other preparation		169.59	1/99	78r
Embalming		465.60	1/99	78r
Funeral at funeral home		339.56	1/99	78r
Hearse (local)		183.96	1/99	78r
Professional service charges		1157.85	1/99	78r
Service car/van		100.41	1/99	78r
Transfer of remains to funeral home		158.66	1/99	78r

Values are in dollars or fractions of dollars. In the column headed *Ref*, references are shown to sources. Each reference is followed by a letter. These refer to the geographical level for which data were reported: s=State, r=Region, and c=City or metro. The abbreviation *ex* is used to mean *except* or *excluding*; *exp* stands for *expenditures*. For other abbreviations and further explanations, please see the Introduction.

Johnstown, PA - continued

Item	Per	Value	Date	Ref.
Funerals				
Vault		766.31	1/99	78r
Visitation/viewing		361.04	1/99	78r
Groceries				
Apples, red delicious	lb	0.95	7/01	11r
Bacon, sliced	lb	3.44	7/01	11r
Bakery products, expenditures on	yr	310	1999	30r
Bananas	lb	0.55	7/01	11r
Beef, expenditures on	yr	236	1999	30r
Bread, white, pan	lb	1.09	7/01	11r
Butter, yoghurt, cheese, etc, expenditures on	yr	214	1999	30r
Cereals and bakery product purchases	yr	474	1999	30r
Cereals and cereal products, expenditures on	yr	164	1999	30r
Chicken legs, bone-in	lb	1.23	7/01	11r
Chicken, fresh, whole	lb	1.13	7/01	11r
Chuck roast, U.S. choice, boneless	lb	2.79	7/01	11r
Coffee, 100%, ground roast, all sizes	lb	3.40	7/01	11r
Dairy product purchases	yr	342	1999	30r
Eggs, expenditures on	yr	34	1999	30r
Eggs, grade A, large	dozen	0.82	7/01	11r
Fats and oils, expenditures on	yr	80	1999	30r
Fish and seafood, expenditures on	yr	123	1999	30r
Food (excl fruit and vegetables), eaten at home, purchases	yr	838	1999	30r
Food cooked on trips, expenditures on	yr	48	1999	30r
Food purchases	yr	5314	1999	30r
Food purchases, eaten away from home	yr	2313	1999	30r
Food purchases, food eaten at home	yr	3001	1999	30r
Fresh fruits, expenditures on	yr	169	1999	30r
Fresh milk and cream, expenditures on	yr	128	1999	30r
Fresh vegetables, expenditures on	yr	164	1999	30r
Grapefruit	lb	0.67	7/01	11r
Grapes, Thompson, seedless	lb	2.18	7/01	11r
Ground beef, lean and extra lean	lb	2.66	7/01	11r
Ground chuck, 100% beef	lb	2.04	7/01	11r
Lettuce, iceberg	lb	0.76	7/01	11r
Meats, poultry, fish, and egg purchases	yr	808	1999	30r
Nonalcoholic beverages, expenditures on	yr	225	1999	30r
Orange juice, frozen concentrate	16 oz	1.88	7/01	11r
Oranges, Navel	lb	0.79	7/01	11r
Oranges, Valencia	lb	0.56	7/01	11r
Peaches	lb	1.16	7/01	11r
Peanut butter, creamy, all sizes	lb	2.01	7/01	11r
Pears, Anjou	lb	1.16	7/01	11r
Pork chops, center cut, bone-in	lb	3.57	7/01	11r
Pork, expenditures on	yr	146	1999	30r
Potato chips	16 oz	3.37	7/01	11r
Potatoes, white, all types	lb	0.42	7/01	11r
Poultry, expenditures on	yr	158	1999	30r
Processed fruits, expenditures on	yr	124	1999	30r
Processed vegetables, expenditures on	yr	82	1999	30r
Round roast, U.S. choice, boneless	lb	3.04	7/01	11r
Spaghetti and macaroni	lb	1.04	7/01	11r
Steak, sirloin, U.S. choice, boneless	lb	5.39	7/01	11r
Strawberries, dry pint	12 oz	1.51	7/01	11r
Sugar and other sweets, expenditures on	yr	110	1999	30r
Sugar, white, 33-80 ounce package	lb	0.46	7/01	11r
Sugar, white, all sizes	lb	0.47	7/01	11r
Tobacco products and smoking supplies purchases	yr	309	1999	30r
Yogurt, natural, fruit flavored	8 oz	0.79	7/01	11r
Goods and Services				
B&B Japanese maple (acer japonicum)	gal	38.99-125.00	4/00	93r
Boxwood (buxus)	2 gal	15.99-49.95	4/00	93r
Daylilly (hemerocallis)	gal	4.95	4/00	93r
Flat of annuals		8.00-14.99	4/00	93r
Fountain grass (pennisetum)	gal	6.99-9.99	4/00	93r

Johnstown, PA - continued

Item	Per	Value	Date	Ref.
Goods and Services - continued				
Hanging basket (10 in)		12.95-19.99	4/00	93r
Hardy geranium (geranium)	gal	6.95-7.99	4/00	93r
Hosta (hosta)	gal	4.95	4/00	93r
Lilac (syrubga vulgaris)	2 gal	17.99-74.95	4/00	93r
Miscellaneous purchases	yr	872	1999	30r
Rhododendron (rhododendron)	2 gal	23.99-54.95	4/00	93r
Sage (salvia)	gal	6.95-7.99	4/00	93r
Wintercreeper euonymus (euonymus fortunei)	2 gal	14.99-23.95	4/00	93r
Hunting license	yr	20.00	4/01	34s
Health Care				
Cardiac catheterization, ave hospital/physician charges		13870	1998	77s
Childbirth, Cesarean delivery		14716	1997	13r
Childbirth, vaginal delivery		8541	1997	13r
Drugs, expenditures on	yr	296	1999	30r
Health care purchases	yr	1788	1999	30r
Health insurance expenditures	yr	875	1999	30r
Hysterectomy, laproscopically-assisted, ave hospital/physician charges		14760	1998	76s
Hysterectomy, vaginal, ave hospital and physician charges		9270	1998	76s
Medicaid dispensing fee		4.00	1999	87s
Medical services expenditures	yr	516	1999	30r
Medical supplies, expenditures on	yr	102	1999	30r
Plastic surgery, breast augmentation		4232	2000	7r
Plastic surgery, breast lift		4605	2000	7r
Plastic surgery, facelift		6964	2000	7r
Plastic surgery, hair transplantation		4193	2000	7r
Plastic surgery, lip augmentation		1675	2000	7r
Plastic surgery, lower body lift		6611	2000	7r
Plastic surgery, thigh lift		4751	2000	7r
Household Goods				
Floor coverings, expenditures on	yr	59	1999	30r
Furniture, expenditures on	yr	388	1999	30r
Household furnishings and equipment purchases	yr	1567	1999	30r
Household textiles, expenditures on	yr	112	1999	30r
Laundry and cleaning supplies, expenditures on	yr	104	1999	30r
Housing				
Home price, existing, ave		180800	10/00	90r
Home value, median		115000	2001	53s
Household operation expenditures	yr	581	1999	30r
Housekeeping supplies purchases	yr	474	1999	30r
Lodging expenditures	yr	550	1999	30r
Maintenance, repairs, insurance expenditures	yr	835	1999	30r
Monthly rental value of owned home	mos	663	1999	30r
Owned dwellings, expenditures own	yr	5209	1999	30r
Rent expenditures	yr	2390	1999	30r
Rental unit, 1 bedroom, with utilities	mos	371	4/01	41c
Rental unit, 2 bedroom, with utilities	mos	446	4/01	41c
Rental unit, 3 bedroom, with utilities	mos	579	4/01	41c
Rental unit, 4 bedroom, with utilities	mos	647	4/01	41c
Shelter, expenditures on	yr	8149	1999	30r
Insurance and Pensions				
Life and other personal insurance purchases	yr	424	1999	30r
Pensions and Social Security, expenditures on	yr	3037	1999	30r
Legal Fees				
Divorce, filing fee		65.00	4/01	35s
Driver's license fee	renew	24.00	1999	48s
Driver's license fee	orig	29.00	1999	48s

Values are in dollars or fractions of dollars. In the column headed *Ref*, references are shown to sources. Each reference is followed by a letter. These refer to the geographical level for which data were reported: s=State, r=Region, and c=City or metro. The abbreviation *ex* is used to mean *except* or *excluding*; *exp* stands for expenditures. For other abbreviations and further explanations, please see the Introduction.

Johnstown, PA - continued

Item	Per	Value	Date	Ref.
Legal Fees				
Fishing license	yr	17.00	4/01	34s
Personal Goods				
Personal care products and services purchases	yr	399	1999	30r
Personal Services				
Personal services, household, expenditures on	yr	271	1999	30r
Pets				
Pets, toys, and playground equipment, expenditures on	yr	325	1999	30r
Taxes				
Federal income taxes paid	yr	2606	1999	30r
Personal taxes, expenditures on	yr	3567	1999	30r
Property taxes paid	yr	1752	1999	30r
State and local income taxes paid	yr	694	1999	30r
Transportation				
Bus fare, one-way	trip	1.00	2000	1c
Cars and trucks, new, expenditures on	yr	1496	1999	30r
Cars and trucks, used, expenditures on	yr	1251	1999	30r
Diesel at the pump	gal	1.31	10/99	73s
Gasoline and motor oil purchases	yr	901	1999	30r
Gasoline before-tax price (cents)	gal	106.60	10/00	43s
Maintenance and repair expenditures	yr	618	1999	30r
Public transportation, expenditures on	yr	575	1999	30r
Transportation purchases	yr	6503	1999	30r
Vehicle expenses, miscellaneous, purchases	yr	2266	1999	30r
Vehicle insurance payments	yr	824	1999	30r
Vehicle purchases (net outlay)	yr	2761	1999	30r
Vehicle rental, lease expenditures	yr	584	1999	30r
Utilities				
Electrical bill, average	mos	69.16	9/00	9s
Electricity, expenditures on	yr	837	1999	30r
Electricity cost, average	KWh	5.08	9/00	9s
Utilities, fuels, and public services purchased	yr	2457	1999	30r
Water and other public services, expenditures on	yr	215	1999	30r
Weddings				
Wedding (national average cost)		19936	2000	33r
Wedding (regional average total cost)		29454	1997	110r
Attendants' gifts		321	1998	33r
Bridal attendants' apparel (5 persons)		824	2000	33r
Bride's headpiece/veil		173	1998	33r
Bride's wedding dress		859	1998	33r
Clergy, religious facility fee		242	1998	33r
Engagement ring		3177	1998	33r
Flowers		789	1998	33r
Groom's formalwear rental		99	2000	33r
Limousine		410	1998	33r
Marriage license cost		25.00-40.00	4/01	35s
Men's formalwear (ushers, best man)		469	2000	33r
Mother of bride apparel		241	2000	33r
Music		866	1998	33r
Photography and videography		1368	1998	33r
Rehearsal dinner		728	1998	33r
Wedding invitations and announcements		341	1998	33r
Wedding reception		7968	2000	33r
Wedding rings (bride and groom)		1060	1998	33r

Jonesboro, AR

Item	Per	Value	Date	Ref.
Composite, ACCRA index		87.90	3/01	4c
Alcoholic Beverages				
Alcoholic beverage purchases	yr	253	1999	30r
Beer, Heineken, 12-oz, ex deposit	6	7.40	3/01	4c
J & B Scotch	750-ml	20.95	3/01	4c
Malt beverages, all types, all sizes, any origin	16 oz	0.96	7/01	11r

Jonesboro, AR - continued

Item	Per	Value	Date	Ref.
Alcoholic Beverages - continued				
Wine, Livingston or Gallo, Chablis blanc	1.5 liter	6.78	3/01	4c
Appliances				
Appliance repair, service call, washing machine	min lab chg	36.65	3/01	4c
Major appliances, expenditures on	yr	172	1999	30r
Small appliances, housewares, expenditures on	yr	81	1999	30r
Banking and Money				
Mortgage interest and charges paid	yr	2039	1999	30r
Mortgage principal paid on owned property	yr	1026	1999	30r
Mortgage rate, incl. points and orig. fee, 30-yr. conv. fixed or ARM	mos	6.85	3/01	4c
Vehicle finance charges paid	yr	365	1999	30r
Charity				
Cash contributions, expenditures	yr	1127	1999	30r
Child Care				
Child raising cost, total, age 0-2	yr	8540	1999	60r
Child raising cost, total, age 3-5	yr	8780	1999	60r
Child raising cost, total, age 6-8	yr	8820	1999	60r
Child raising cost, total, age 9-11	yr	8800	1999	60r
Child raising cost, total, age 12-14	yr	9510	1999	60r
Child raising cost, total, age 15-17	yr	9740	1999	60r
Child's child care and education, age 0-2	yr	1380	1999	60r
Child's child care and education, age 3-5	yr	1520	1999	60r
Child's child care and education, age 6-8	yr	990	1999	60r
Child's child care and education, age 9-11	yr	650	1999	60r
Child's child care and education, age 12-14	yr	490	1999	60r
Child's child care and education, age 15-17	yr	840	1999	60r
Child's clothing, age 0-2	yr	480	1999	60r
Child's clothing, age 3-5	yr	470	1999	60r
Child's clothing, age 6-8	yr	520	1999	60r
Child's clothing, age 9-11	yr	570	1999	60r
Child's clothing, age 12-14	yr	950	1999	60r
Child's clothing, age 15-17	yr	850	1999	60r
Child's food, age 0-2	yr	1000	1999	60r
Child's food, age 3-5	yr	1160	1999	60r
Child's food, age 6-8	yr	1490	1999	60r
Child's food, age 9-11	yr	1770	1999	60r
Child's food, age 12-14	yr	1770	1999	60r
Child's food, age 15-17	yr	1980	1999	60r
Child's health care, age 0-2	yr	620	1999	60r
Child's health care, age 3-5	yr	590	1999	60r
Child's health care, age 6-8	yr	680	1999	60r
Child's health care, age 9-11	yr	720	1999	60r
Child's health care, age 12-14	yr	730	1999	60r
Child's health care, age 15-17	yr	760	1999	60r
Child's housing, age 0-2	yr	3070	1999	60r
Child's housing, age 3-5	yr	3050	1999	60r
Child's housing, age 6-8	yr	3010	1999	60r
Child's housing, age 9-11	yr	2850	1999	60r
Child's housing, age 12-14	yr	3040	1999	60r
Child's housing, age 15-17	yr	2650	1999	60r
Child's personal care, reading, age 0-2	yr	910	1999	60r
Child's personal care, reading, age 3-5	yr	930	1999	60r
Child's personal care, reading, age 6-8	yr	960	1999	60r
Child's personal care, reading, age 9-11	yr	1000	1999	60r
Child's personal care, reading, age 12-14	yr	1170	1999	60r
Child's personal care, reading, age 15-17	yr	950	1999	60r
Clothing				
Apparel and services purchases	yr	1610	1999	30r
Boys' brief, cotton	3	3.31	3/01	4c
Boys, 2 to 15, expenditures on	yr	89	1999	30r
Children under 2, expenditures on	yr	79	1999	30r
Footwear, expenditures on	yr	283	1999	30r
Girls, 2 to 15, expenditures on	yr	103	1999	30r
Men and boys, expenditures on	yr	351	1999	30r
Men, 16 and over, expenditures on	yr	262	1999	30r
Shirt, man's dress shirt		28.16	3/01	4c
Slacks, man's "No Wrinkles" khaki		29.66	3/01	4c

Values are in dollars or fractions of dollars. In the column headed *Ref*, references are shown to sources. Each reference is followed by a letter. These refer to the geographical level for which data were reported: s=State, r=Region, and c=City or metro. The abbreviation *ex* is used to mean *except* or *excluding*; *exp* stands for *expenditures*. For other abbreviations and further explanations, please see the Introduction.

Jonesboro, AR - continued

Item	Per	Value	Date	Ref.
Clothing				
Women, 16 and over, expenditures on	yr	538	1999	30r
Communications				
Newspaper subscription, daily and Sunday delivery	mos	9.50	3/01	4c
Phone line, single, business, field visit	inst.	84.00	12/97	17s
Phone line, single, business, no field visit	inst.	84.00	12/97	17s
Phone line, single, residence, field visit	inst.	39.70	12/97	17s
Phone line, single, residence, no field visit	inst.	39.70	12/97	17s
Postage and stationery, expenditures on	yr	104	1999	30r
Postal rate, express mail, up to half-pound		12.45	7/01	108r
Postal rate, letter, first class, first ounce		0.34	7/01	108r
Postal rate, letter, two ounces		0.57	7/01	108r
Postal rate, post card		0.21	7/01	108r
Postal rate, priority mail, two pounds		3.95	7/01	108r
Postal rate, priority mail, up to one pound		3.50	7/01	108r
Telephone bill, family of three	mos	23.48	3/01	4c
Telephone services, expenditures on	yr	860	1999	30r
Education				
Board, 4-year private college/university	yr	2121	1996	38s
Board, 4-year public college/university	yr	1423	1996	38s
Education expenditures	yr	431	1999	30r
Room, 4-year private college/university	yr	1488	1996	38s
Room, 4-year public college/university	yr	1613	1996	38s
Total cost, 4-year private college/university	yr	10183	1996	38s
Total cost, 4-year public college/university	yr	5064	1996	38s
Tuition, 2-year public college/university, in state	yr	903	1996	38s
Tuition, 4-year private college/university, in state	yr	6574	1996	38s
Tuition, 4-year public college/university	yr	2028	1996	38s
Energy and Fuels				
Electricity	KWh	0.09	7/01	11r
Electricity	500 KWhs	47.29	7/01	11r
Energy, combined forms, 2400 sq ft	mos	106.87	3/01	4c
Energy, exc. electricity, 2400 sq ft	mos	57.40	3/01	4c
Fuel oil #2	gal	1.43	7/01	11r
Fuel oil and other fuels, expenditures on	yr	45	1999	30r
Gas, regular unleaded, cash, self-service	gal	1.35	3/01	4c
Gasoline, all types	gal	1.60	7/01	11r
Gasoline, unleaded midgrade	gal	1.65	7/01	11r
Gasoline, unleaded premium	gal	1.74	7/01	11r
Natural gas, expenditures on	yr	164	1999	30r
Utility (piped) gas, therm		1.01	7/01	11r
Utility (piped) gas, 40 therms		44.29	7/01	11r
Utility (piped) gas, 100 therms		97.44	7/01	11r
Entertainment				
Bowling, Saturday evening rate	line	2.34	3/01	4c
Entertainment purchases	yr	1574	1999	30r
Fees and admissions paid	yr	371	1999	30r
Monopoly game, Parker Brothers', No. 9	game	10.36	3/01	4c
Movie, first-run, Saturday, evening	adm.	6.50	3/01	4c
Reading purchases	yr	121	1999	30r
Television, radios, sound equipment, expenditures on	yr	561	1999	30r
Tennis balls, yellow, Wilson or Penn, 3	can	1.88	3/01	4c
Funerals				
Total cost of funeral		5842.28	1/99	78r
Acknowledgement cards		28.35	1/99	78r
Casket		2494.29	1/99	78r
Cosmetology, hair, other preparation		109.22	1/99	78r
Embalming		361.42	1/99	78r
Funeral at funeral home		349.20	1/99	78r
Hearse (local)		161.91	1/99	78r
Professional service charges		1116.50	1/99	78r
Service car/van		65.56	1/99	78r
Transfer of remains to funeral home		143.56	1/99	78r
Vault		785.25	1/99	78r
Visitation/viewing		227.02	1/99	78r

Jonesboro, AR - continued

Item	Per	Value	Date	Ref.
Groceries				
Groceries, ACCRA Index		92.10	3/01	4c
American processed cheese	lb	3.50	7/01	11r
Antibiotic ointment, Polysporin	0.5 oz	4.35	3/01	4c
Baby food, strained vegetables or fruit, lowest price	4-4.5 oz	0.43	3/01	4c
Bakery products, expenditures on	yr	261	1999	30r
Bananas	lb	0.37	3/01	4c
Bananas	lb	0.47	7/01	11r
Beans, dried, any type, all sizes	lb	0.63	7/01	11r
Beef for stew, boneless	lb	2.86	7/01	11r
Beef or hamburger, ground	lb	1.16	3/01	4c
Beef, expenditures on	yr	210	1999	30r
Bologna, all beef or mixed	lb	2.29	7/01	11r
Bread, French	lb	1.66	7/01	11r
Bread, white	loaf	0.91	3/01	4c
Bread, white, pan	lb	0.87	7/01	11r
Bread, whole wheat, pan	lb	1.38	7/01	11r
Broccoli	lb	1.04	7/01	11r
Butter, salted, grade AA, stick	lb	2.26	7/01	11r
Butter, yoghurt, cheese, etc, expenditures on	yr	170	1999	30r
Cabbage	lb	0.42	7/01	11r
Cereals and cereal products, expenditures on	yr	140	1999	30r
Cheddar cheese, natural	lb	3.75	7/01	11r
Cheese, Kraft grated Parmesan	8 oz	3.81	3/01	4c
Chicken breast, bone-in	lb	1.85	7/01	11r
Chicken legs, bone-in	lb	1.34	7/01	11r
Chicken, fresh, whole	lb	1.05	7/01	11r
Chicken, whole fryer	lb	0.75	3/01	4c
Chops, boneless,	lb	4.13	7/01	11r
Chuck roast, graded and ungraded, excl U.S. prime and choice	lb	2.35	7/01	11r
Chuck roast, U.S. choice, boneless	lb	2.67	7/01	11r
Cigarettes, Winston, Kings	carton	27.23	3/01	4c
Coffee, 100%, ground roast, all sizes	lb	2.88	7/01	11r
Coffee, instant, plain, regular, all sizes	16 oz	9.25	7/01	11r
Coffee, vacuum-packed	13 oz	2.42	3/01	4c
Cola, non diet,	2 liter	1.11	7/01	11r
Corn Flakes, Kellogg's or Post Toasties	18 oz	2.12	3/01	4c
Corn, frozen, whole kernel, lowest price	16 oz	1.16	3/01	4c
Crackers, soda, salted	lb	1.70	7/01	11r
Dairy product purchases	yr	282	1999	30r
Eggs, expenditures on	yr	32	1999	30r
Eggs, Grade A or AA	dozen	1.15	3/01	4c
Fats and oils, expenditures on	yr	79	1999	30r
Fish and seafood, expenditures on	yr	99	1999	30r
Flour, white, all purpose	lb	0.32	7/01	11r
Food (excl fruit and vegetables), eaten at home, purchases	yr	815	1999	30r
Food cooked on trips, expenditures on	yr	36	1999	30r
Food purchases	yr	4533	1999	30r
Food purchases, eaten away from home	yr	1873	1999	30r
Food purchases, food eaten at home	yr	2660	1999	30r
Fresh fruits, expenditures on	yr	128	1999	30r
Fresh milk and cream, expenditures on	yr	112	1999	30r
Fresh vegetables, expenditures on	yr	131	1999	30r
Fruit and vegetable purchases	yr	438	1999	30r
Grapefruit	lb	0.59	7/01	11r
Grapes, Thompson, seedless	lb	2.12	7/01	11r
Ground beef, 100% beef	lb	1.76	7/01	11r
Ground beef, lean and extra lean	lb	2.60	7/01	11r
Ground chuck, 100% beef	lb	2.08	7/01	11r
Ham, boneless, excl canned	lb	2.71	7/01	11r
Ham, rump or shank half, bone-in, smoked	lb	2.19	7/01	11r
Ice cream, prepackaged, bulk, regular	1/2 gal	3.93	7/01	11r
Lemons	lb	1.32	7/01	11r
Lettuce, iceberg	head	0.94	3/01	4c
Lettuce, iceberg	lb	0.76	7/01	11r
Margarine, Blue Bonnet or Parkay, stick	lb	0.67	3/01	4c
Milk, fresh, low fat,	gal	2.75	7/01	11r
Milk, fresh, whole, fortified	gal	2.97	7/01	11r
Milk, whole	1/2 gal	1.66	3/01	4c

Values are in dollars or fractions of dollars. In the column headed *Ref*, references are shown to sources. Each reference is followed by a letter. These refer to the geographical level for which data were reported: s=State, r=Region, and c=City or metro. The abbreviation *ex* is used to mean *except* or *excluding*; *exp* stands for *expenditures*. For other abbreviations and further explanations, please see the Introduction.

Jonesboro, AR - continued

Item	Per	Value	Date	Ref.
Groceries				
Nonalcoholic beverages, expenditures on	yr	228	1999	30r
Orange juice, frozen concentrate	16 oz	1.95	7/01	11r
Orange juice, Minute Maid frozen	12 oz	1.63	3/01	4c
Oranges, Navel	lb	0.73	7/01	11r
Oranges, Valencia	lb	0.55	7/01	11r
Peaches, halves or slices, Hunt's, Del Monte, or Libby's	29 oz	1.66	3/01	4c
Peanut butter, creamy, all sizes	lb	1.83	7/01	11r
Pears, Anjou	lb	0.98	7/01	11r
Peas, green, Del Monte or Green Giant	15 oz	0.64	3/01	4c
Pork chops, center cut, bone-in	lb	3.33	7/01	11r
Pork sausage, fresh, loose	lb	2.59	7/01	11r
Pork shoulder picnic, bone-in, smoked	lb	1.12	7/01	11r
Pork, expenditures on	yr	162	1999	30r
Potato chips	16 oz	3.59	7/01	11r
Potatoes, frozen, french fried	lb	1.00	7/01	11r
Potatoes, white or red	10 lb	1.84	3/01	4c
Potatoes, white, all types	lb	0.44	7/01	11r
Poultry, expenditures on	yr	137	1999	30r
Processed fruits, expenditures on	yr	97	1999	30r
Processed vegetables, expenditures on	yr	82	1999	30r
Rice, white, long grain, uncooked	lb	0.51	7/01	11r
Round roast, graded and ungraded, excl U.S. prime and choice	lb	2.96	7/01	11r
Round steak, graded and ungraded, excl U.S. prime and choice	lb	3.11	7/01	11r
Sausage, Jimmy Dean/Owens pork	lb	2.53	3/01	4c
Shortening, vegetable, Crisco	3 lb	2.76	3/01	4c
Sirloin steak, graded and ungraded, excl U.S. prime and choice	lb	4.23	7/01	11r
Soft drink, Coca Cola, ex deposit	2 liter	1.04	3/01	4c
Spaghetti and macaroni	lb	0.78	7/01	11r
Steak, round, U.S. choice, boneless	lb	3.56	7/01	11r
Steak, sirloin, U.S. choice, boneless	lb	5.65	7/01	11r
Steak, T-bone	lb	6.64	3/01	4c
Strawberries, dry pint	12 oz	1.50	7/01	11r
Sugar and other sweets, expenditures on	yr	99	1999	30r
Sugar, cane or beet	4 lbs	1.31	3/01	4c
Sugar, white, 33-80 ounce package	lb	0.39	7/01	11r
Sugar, white, all sizes	lb	0.42	7/01	11r
Tobacco products and smoking supplies purchases	yr	288	1999	30r
Tomatoes, field grown	lb	1.43	7/01	11r
Tomatoes, Hunt's or Del Monte	14.5 oz	0.84	3/01	4c
Tuna, chunk, light	6 oz	0.66	3/01	4c
Tuna, light, chunk	lb	1.77	7/01	11r
Turkey, frozen, whole	lb	1.05	7/01	11r
Goods and Services				
Miscellaneous goods and services, ACCRA Index		90.90	3/01	4c
B&B Japanese maple (acer japonicum)	gal	79.98-99.00	4/00	93r
Boxwood (buxus)	2 gal	12.98-18.99	4/00	93r
Daylilly (hemerocallis)	gal	7.96-11.00	4/00	93r
Flat of annuals		13.99-27.99	4/00	93r
Fountain grass (pennisetum)	gal	6.96-9.00	4/00	93r
Hanging basket (10 in)		9.99-24.99	4/00	93r
Hardy geranium (geranium)	gal	5.96-8.00	4/00	93r
Hosta (hosta)	gal	8.96-12.99	4/00	93r
Lilac (syrubga vulgaris)	2 gal	13.00-19.99	4/00	93r
Rhododendron (rhododendron)	2 gal	12.98-29.99	4/00	93r
Sage (salvia)	gal	5.96-8.00	4/00	93r

Jonesboro, AR - continued

Item	Per	Value	Date	Ref.
Goods and Services - continued				
Wintercreeper euonymus (euonymus fortunei)	2 gal	13.00-18.99	4/00	93r
Hunting license	yr	25.00	4/01	34s
Health Care				
Health care, ACCRA Index		88.80	3/01	4c
Cardiac catheterization, ave hospital/ physician charges		12240	1998	77s
Childbirth, Cesarean delivery		11587	1997	13r
Childbirth, vaginal delivery		6725	1997	13r
Dentist's fee, adult teeth cleaning and periodic oral exam	visit	63.00	3/01	4c
Doctor's fee, routine exam, established patient	visit	60.75	3/01	4c
Drugs, expenditures on	yr	399	1999	30r
Health care purchases	yr	1971	1999	30r
Health insurance expenditures	yr	933	1999	30r
Hospital care, private room	day	307.50	3/01	4c
Hysterectomy, laproscopically-assisted, ave hospital/physician charges		10580	1998	76s
Hysterectomy, vaginal, ave hospital and physician charges		8270	1998	76s
Medicaid dispensing fee		5.51	1999	87s
Medical services expenditures	yr	547	1999	30r
Medical supplies, expenditures on	yr	91	1999	30r
Household Goods				
Dishwashing powder, Cascade	50 oz	3.42	3/01	4c
Floor coverings, expenditures on	yr	44	1999	30r
Furniture, expenditures on	yr	335	1999	30r
Household furnishings and equipment purchases	yr	1328	1999	30r
Household textiles, expenditures on	yr	89	1999	30r
Laundry and cleaning supplies, expenditures on	yr	113	1999	30r
Tissues, facial, Kleenex brand	175	1.34	3/01	4c
Housing				
Housing, ACCRA Index		81.40	3/01	4c
Home price, existing, ave		160100	10/00	90r
Home value, median		94000	2001	53s
House, 2400 sq ft, 8000 sq ft lot, new, urban, utilities	total	176667	3/01	4c
House payment, principal and interest, 25% down payment	mos	868	3/01	4c
Household operation expenditures	yr	553	1999	30r
Housekeeping supplies purchases	yr	473	1999	30r
Housing, expenditures on	yr	10303	1999	30r
Maintenance, repairs, insurance expenditures	yr	699	1999	30r
Monthly rental value of owned home	mos	505	1999	30r
Owned dwellings, expenditures own	yr	3465	1999	30r
Rent expenditures	yr	1641	1999	30r
Rent, apartment, 2 br, 1 1/2-2 baths, unfurn, 950 sq ft, water	mos	490	3/01	4c
Rental unit, 1 bedroom, with utilities	mos	342	4/01	41c
Rental unit, 2 bedroom, with utilities	mos	402	4/01	41c
Rental unit, 3 bedroom, with utilities	mos	554	4/01	41c
Rental unit, 4 bedroom, with utilities	mos	585	4/01	41c
Shelter, expenditures on	yr	5467	1999	30r
Insurance and Pensions				
Life and other personal insurance purchases	yr	414	1999	30r
Pensions and Social Security, expenditures on	yr	2635	1999	30r
Personal insurance and pensions, expenditures on	yr	3048	1999	30r
Legal Fees				
Divorce, filing fee		100.00	4/01	35s
Driver's license fee	orig	14.00	1999	48s
Driver's license fee	renew	14.00	1999	48s

Values are in dollars or fractions of dollars. In the column headed *Ref*, references are shown to sources. Each reference is followed by a letter. These refer to the geographical level for which data were reported: s=State, r=Region, and c=City or metro. The abbreviation *ex* is used to mean *except* or *excluding*; *exp* stands for *expenditures*. For other abbreviations and further explanations, please see the Introduction.

Jonesboro, AR - continued

Item	Per	Value	Date	Ref.
Personal Goods				
Personal care products and services purchases	yr	393	1999	30r
Shampoo, Alberto VO5	15 oz	1.11	3/01	4c
Toothpaste, Crest or Colgate	6-7 oz	1.83	3/01	4c
Personal Services				
Dry cleaning, man's 2-pc suit		7.24	3/01	4c
Man's haircut, barbershop, no styling		8.33	3/01	4c
Personal services, household, expenditures on	yr	258	1999	30r
Woman's shampoo, trim, blow-dry, no style-change		22.00	3/01	4c
Pets				
Pets, toys, and playground equipment, expenditures on	yr	306	1999	30r
Restaurant Food				
Chicken, fried, thigh and drumstick, KFC/Church's		2.34	3/01	4c
Hamburger with cheese, McDonald's	1/4 lb	2.06	3/01	4c
Pizza, Pizza Hut or Pizza Inn	11-12 in	9.12	3/01	4c
Taxes				
Federal income taxes paid	yr	2047	1999	30r
Personal taxes, expenditures on	yr	2554	1999	30r
Property taxes paid	yr	726	1999	30r
State and local income taxes paid	yr	363	1999	30r
Transportation				
Transportation, ACCRA Index		87.40	3/01	4c
Cars and trucks, new, expenditures on	yr	1648	1999	30r
Cars and trucks, used, expenditures on	yr	1651	1999	30r
Diesel at the pump	gal	1.17	10/99	73s
Gasoline and motor oil purchases	yr	1052	1999	30r
Gasoline before-tax price (cents)	gal	102.60	10/00	43s
Maintenance and repair expenditures	yr	621	1999	30r
Public transportation, expenditures on	yr	298	1999	30r
Tire balance, computer or spin balance, front	wheel	6.00	3/01	4c
Transportation purchases	yr	6738	1999	30r
Vehicle expenses, miscellaneous, purchases	yr	2033	1999	30r
Vehicle insurance payments	yr	696	1999	30r
Vehicle purchases (net outlay)	yr	3354	1999	30r
Vehicle rental, lease expenditures	yr	352	1999	30r
Utilities				
Utilities, ACCRA Index		90.40	3/01	4c
Electrical bill, average	mos	75.00	9/00	9s
Electricity, expenditures on	yr	1115	1999	30r
Electricity and other, mixed, 2400 sq ft, new home	mos	49.47	3/01	4c
Electricity cost, average	KWh	5.70	9/00	9s
Water and other public services, expenditures on	yr	298	1999	30r
Weddings				
Wedding (national average cost)		19936	2000	33r
Attendants' gifts		321	1998	33r
Bridal attendants' apparel (5 persons)		824	2000	33r
Bride's headpiece/veil		173	1998	33r
Bride's wedding dress		859	1998	33r
Clergy, religious facility fee		242	1998	33r
Engagement ring		3177	1998	33r
Flowers		789	1998	33r
Groom's formalwear rental		99	2000	33r
Limousine		410	1998	33r
Marriage license cost		30.00	4/01	35s
Men's formalwear (ushers, best man)		469	2000	33r
Mother of bride apparel		241	2000	33r
Music		866	1998	33r
Photography and videography		1368	1998	33r
Rehearsal dinner		728	1998	33r
Wedding invitations and announcements		341	1998	33r
Wedding reception		7968	2000	33r
Wedding rings (bride and groom)		1060	1998	33r

Joplin, MO

Item	Per	Value	Date	Ref.
Average annual expenditures	yr	35369	1999	30r
Composite, ACCRA index		87.90	3/01	4c
Alcoholic Beverages				
Alcoholic beverage purchases	yr	304	1999	30r
Beer, Heineken, 12-oz, ex deposit	6	7.51	3/01	4c
J & B Scotch	750-ml	19.47	3/01	4c
Malt beverages, all types, all sizes, any origin	16 oz	0.93	7/01	11r
Wine, Livingston or Gallo, Chablis blanc	1.5 liter	5.95	3/01	4c
Wine, red and white table, all sizes, any origin	liter	7.04	7/01	11r
Appliances				
Appliance repair, service call, washing machine	min lab chg	31.00	3/01	4c
Major appliances, expenditures on	yr	165	1999	30r
Small appliances, housewares, expenditures on	yr	90	1999	30r
Banking and Money				
Mortgage interest and charges paid	yr	2277	1999	30r
Mortgage principal paid on owned property	yr	1230	1999	30r
Mortgage rate, incl. points and orig. fee, 30-yr. conv. fixed or ARM	mos	7.08	3/01	4c
Vehicle finance charges paid	yr	328	1999	30r
Charity				
Cash contributions, expenditures	yr	1126	1999	30r
Child Care				
Child raising cost, total, age 0-2	yr	7890	1999	60r
Child raising cost, total, age 3-5	yr	8130	1999	60r
Child raising cost, total, age 6-8	yr	8170	1999	60r
Child raising cost, total, age 9-11	yr	8190	1999	60r
Child raising cost, total, age 12-14	yr	8890	1999	60r
Child raising cost, total, age 15-17	yr	9050	1999	60r
Child's child care and education, age 0-2	yr	1240	1999	60r
Child's child care and education, age 3-5	yr	1370	1999	60r
Child's child care and education, age 6-8	yr	880	1999	60r
Child's child care and education, age 9-11	yr	570	1999	60r
Child's child care and education, age 12-14	yr	420	1999	60r
Child's child care and education, age 15-17	yr	720	1999	60r
Child's clothing, age 0-2	yr	410	1999	60r
Child's clothing, age 3-5	yr	400	1999	60r
Child's clothing, age 6-8	yr	450	1999	60r
Child's clothing, age 9-11	yr	500	1999	60r
Child's clothing, age 12-14	yr	840	1999	60r
Child's clothing, age 15-17	yr	740	1999	60r
Child's food, age 0-2	yr	960	1999	60r
Child's food, age 3-5	yr	1120	1999	60r
Child's food, age 6-8	yr	1430	1999	60r
Child's food, age 9-11	yr	1710	1999	60r
Child's food, age 12-14	yr	1710	1999	60r
Child's food, age 15-17	yr	1920	1999	60r
Child's health care, age 0-2	yr	520	1999	60r
Child's health care, age 3-5	yr	500	1999	60r
Child's health care, age 6-8	yr	570	1999	60r
Child's health care, age 9-11	yr	610	1999	60r
Child's health care, age 12-14	yr	630	1999	60r
Child's health care, age 15-17	yr	650	1999	60r
Child's housing, age 0-2	yr	2860	1999	60r
Child's housing, age 3-5	yr	2840	1999	60r
Child's housing, age 6-8	yr	2800	1999	60r
Child's housing, age 9-11	yr	2650	1999	60r
Child's housing, age 12-14	yr	2840	1999	60r
Child's housing, age 15-17	yr	2440	1999	60r
Child's personal care, reading, age 0-2	yr	880	1999	60r
Child's personal care, reading, age 3-5	yr	900	1999	60r
Child's personal care, reading, age 6-8	yr	930	1999	60r
Child's personal care, reading, age 9-11	yr	970	1999	60r
Child's personal care, reading, age 12-14	yr	1150	1999	60r
Child's personal care, reading, age 15-17	yr	920	1999	60r
Clothing				
Apparel and services purchases	yr	1607	1999	30r
Boys' brief, cotton	3	3.66	3/01	4c

Values are in dollars or fractions of dollars. In the column headed *Ref*, references are shown to sources. Each reference is followed by a letter. These refer to the geographical level for which data were reported: s=State, r=Region, and c=City or metro. The abbreviation *ex* is used to mean *except* or *excluding*; *exp* stands for *expenditures*. For other abbreviations and further explanations, please see the Introduction.

Joplin, MO - continued

Item	Per	Value	Date	Ref.
Clothing				
Boys, 2 to 15, expenditures on	yr	91	1999	30r
Children under 2, expenditures on	yr	59	1999	30r
Footwear, expenditures on	yr	285	1999	30r
Girls, 2 to 15, expenditures on	yr	116	1999	30r
Men and boys, expenditures on	yr	433	1999	30r
Men, 16 and over, expenditures on	yr	341	1999	30r
Shirt, man's dress shirt		27.25	3/01	4c
Slacks, man's "No Wrinkles" khaki		29.99	3/01	4c
Women, 16 and over, expenditures on	yr	490	1999	30r
Communications				
Newspaper subscription, daily and Sunday delivery	mos	12.91	3/01	4c
Phone line, single, business, field visit	inst.	52.25	12/97	17s
Phone line, single, business, no field visit	inst.	52.25	12/97	17s
Phone line, single, residence, field visit	inst.	36.50	12/97	17s
Phone line, single, residence, no field visit	inst.	36.50	12/97	17s
Postage and stationery, expenditures on	yr	140	1999	30r
Postal rate, express mail, up to half-pound		12.45	7/01	108r
Postal rate, letter, first class, first ounce		0.34	7/01	108r
Postal rate, letter, two ounces		0.57	7/01	108r
Postal rate, post card		0.21	7/01	108r
Postal rate, priority mail, two pounds		3.95	7/01	108r
Postal rate, priority mail, up to one pound		3.50	7/01	108r
Telephone bill, business, basic rate	mos	23.10	12/97	18c
Telephone bill, family of three	mos	16.39	3/01	4c
Telephone bill, residential, basic rate	mos	9.10	12/97	18c
Telephone services, expenditures on	yr	830	1999	30r
Education				
Board, 4-year private college/university	yr	2387	1996	38s
Board, 4-year public college/university	yr	1713	1996	38s
Education expenditures	yr	583	1999	30r
Room, 4-year private college/university	yr	2162	1996	38s
Room, 4-year public college/university	yr	2022	1996	38s
Total cost, 4-year private college/university	yr	14116	1996	38s
Total cost, 4-year public college/university	yr	6750	1996	38s
Tuition, 2-year public college/university, in state	yr	1255	1996	38s
Tuition, 4-year private college/university, in state	yr	9566	1996	38s
Tuition, 4-year public college/university	yr	3015	1996	38s
Energy and Fuels				
Electricity	500 KWhs	46.59	7/01	11r
Energy, combined forms, 2400 sq ft	mos	96.22	3/01	4c
Fuel oil #2	gal	1.27	7/01	11r
Fuel oil and other fuels, expenditures on	yr	68	1999	30r
Gas, natural, commercial rate	1000 cf	8.38	11/00	88s
Gas, regular unleaded, cash, self-service	gal	1.24	3/01	4c
Gasoline, unleaded midgrade	gal	1.79	7/01	11r
Gasoline, unleaded premium	gal	1.86	7/01	11r
Gasoline, unleaded regular	gal	1.58	7/01	11r
Natural gas, expenditures on	yr	389	1999	30r
Utility (piped) gas, therm		0.81	7/01	11r
Utility (piped) gas, 40 therms		38.01	7/01	11r
Utility (piped) gas, 100 therms		81.75	7/01	11r
Entertainment				
Bowling, Saturday evening rate	line	2.67	3/01	4c
Entertainment purchases	yr	1984	1999	30r
Fees and admissions paid	yr	444	1999	30r
Monopoly game, Parker Brothers', No. 9	game	10.40	3/01	4c
Movie, first-run, Saturday, evening	adm.	7.00	3/01	4c
Television, radios, sound equipment, expenditures on	yr	580	1999	30r
Tennis balls, yellow, Wilson or Penn, 3	can	2.27	3/01	4c
Funerals				
Cosmetology, hair, other preparation		178.32	1/99	78r
Embalming		408.19	1/99	78r
Funeral at funeral home		362.13	1/99	78r
Professional service charges		1375.51	1/99	78r

Joplin, MO - continued

Item	Per	Value	Date	Ref.
Funerals - continued				
Transfer of remains to funeral home		155.92	1/99	78r
Visitation/viewing		294.38	1/99	78r
Groceries				
Groceries, ACCRA Index		92.20	3/01	4c
Antibiotic ointment, Polysporin	0.5 oz	4.81	3/01	4c
Baby food, strained vegetables or fruit, lowest price	4-4.5 oz	0.44	3/01	4c
Bacon, sliced	lb	3.15	7/01	11r
Bakery products, expenditures on	yr	281	1999	30r
Bananas	lb	0.40	3/01	4c
Bananas	lb	0.48	7/01	11r
Beans, dried, any type, all sizes	lb	0.61	7/01	11r
Beef for stew, boneless	lb	3.08	7/01	11r
Beef or hamburger, ground	lb	1.31	3/01	4c
Beef, expenditures on	yr	217	1999	30r
Bologna, all beef or mixed	lb	2.52	7/01	11r
Bread, white	loaf	0.80	3/01	4c
Bread, white, pan	lb	1.06	7/01	11r
Broccoli	lb	0.91	7/01	11r
Butter, salted, grade AA, stick	lb	3.04	7/01	11r
Butter, yoghurt, cheese, etc, expenditures on	yr	183	1999	30r
Cereals and bakery product purchases	yr	430	1999	30r
Cereals and cereal products, expenditures on	yr	149	1999	30r
Cheese, Kraft grated Parmesan	8 oz	4.08	3/01	4c
Chicken, fresh, whole	lb	1.07	7/01	11r
Chicken, whole fryer	lb	0.76	3/01	4c
Chops, boneless,	lb	3.64	7/01	11r
Chuck roast, U.S. choice, boneless	lb	2.47	7/01	11r
Cigarettes, Winston, Kings	carton	29.03	3/01	4c
Coffee, 100%, ground roast, all sizes	lb	2.69	7/01	11r
Coffee, vacuum-packed	13 oz	2.41	3/01	4c
Cookies, chocolate chip	lb	2.87	7/01	11r
Corn Flakes, Kellogg's or Post Toasties	18 oz	2.27	3/01	4c
Corn, frozen, whole kernel, lowest price	16 oz	1.06	3/01	4c
Dairy product purchases	yr	304	1999	30r
Eggs, expenditures on	yr	26	1999	30r
Eggs, Grade A or AA	dozen	1.06	3/01	4c
Eggs, grade A, large	dozen	0.88	7/01	11r
Fats and oils, expenditures on	yr	75	1999	30r
Fish and seafood, expenditures on	yr	72	1999	30r
Food (excl fruit and vegetables), eaten at home, purchases	yr	887	1999	30r
Food cooked on trips, expenditures on	yr	44	1999	30r
Food purchases	yr	4802	1999	30r
Food purchases, eaten away from home	yr	2069	1999	30r
Food purchases, food eaten at home	yr	2733	1999	30r
Fresh fruits, expenditures on	yr	138	1999	30r
Fresh milk and cream, expenditures on	yr	120	1999	30r
Fresh vegetables, expenditures on	yr	126	1999	30r
Grapefruit	lb	0.66	7/01	11r
Grapes, Thompson, seedless	lb	1.64	7/01	11r
Ground beef, 100% beef	lb	1.64	7/01	11r
Ground beef, lean and extra lean	lb	2.16	7/01	11r
Ground chuck, 100% beef	lb	2.13	7/01	11r
Ham, boneless, excl canned	lb	2.62	7/01	11r
Ice cream, prepackaged, bulk, regular	1/2 gal	3.35	7/01	11r
Lemons	lb	1.19	7/01	11r
Lettuce, iceberg	head	0.98	3/01	4c
Lettuce, iceberg	lb	0.73	7/01	11r
Margarine, Blue Bonnet or Parkay, stick	lb	0.78	3/01	4c
Margarine, soft, tubs	lb	0.89	7/01	11r
Meats, poultry, fish, and egg purchases	yr	671	1999	30r
Milk, fresh, whole, fortified	gal	2.71	7/01	11r
Milk, whole	1/2 gal	1.53	3/01	4c
Nonalcoholic beverages, expenditures on	yr	239	1999	30r
Orange juice, Minute Maid frozen	12 oz	1.75	3/01	4c
Oranges, Navel	lb	0.80	7/01	11r
Oranges, Valencia	lb	0.66	7/01	11r
Peaches, halves or slices, Hunt's, Del Monte, or Libby's	29 oz	1.43	3/01	4c
Pears, Anjou	lb	0.93	7/01	11r

Values are in dollars or fractions of dollars. In the column headed *Ref*, references are shown to sources. Each reference is followed by a letter. These refer to the geographical level for which data were reported: s=State, r=Region, and c=City or metro. The abbreviation *ex* is used to mean *except* or *excluding*; *exp* stands for expenditures. For other abbreviations and further explanations, please see the Introduction.

Joplin, MO - continued

Item	Per	Value	Date	Ref.
Groceries				
Peas, green, Del Monte or Green Giant	15 oz	0.62	3/01	4c
Pork chops, center cut, bone-in	lb	3.63	7/01	11r
Pork, expenditures on	yr	150	1999	30r
Potato chips	16 oz	3.52	7/01	11r
Potatoes, frozen, french fried	lb	1.08	7/01	11r
Potatoes, white or red	10 lb	1.99	3/01	4c
Potatoes, white, all types	lb	0.33	7/01	11r
Poultry, expenditures on	yr	108	1999	30r
Processed fruits, expenditures on	yr	98	1999	30r
Processed vegetables, expenditures on	yr	80	1999	30r
Round roast, U.S. choice, boneless	lb	3.07	7/01	11r
Round steak, graded and ungraded, excl U.S. prime and choice	lb	3.41	7/01	11r
Sausage, Jimmy Dean/Owens pork	lb	2.52	3/01	4c
Shortening, vegetable oil blends	lb	1.13	7/01	11r
Shortening, vegetable, Crisco	3 lb	2.91	3/01	4c
Soft drink, Coca Cola, ex deposit	2 liter	1.13	3/01	4c
Spaghetti and macaroni	lb	0.80	7/01	11r
Steak, round, U.S. choice, boneless	lb	3.23	7/01	11r
Steak, T-bone	lb	6.59	3/01	4c
Steak, T-bone, U.S. choice, bone-in	lb	6.68	7/01	11r
Strawberries, dry pint	12 oz	1.32	7/01	11r
Sugar and other sweets, expenditures on	yr	114	1999	30r
Sugar, cane or beet	4 lbs	1.43	3/01	4c
Sugar, white, 33-80 ounce package	lb	0.42	7/01	11r
Sugar, white, all sizes	lb	0.43	7/01	11r
Tobacco products and smoking supplies purchases	yr	331	1999	30r
Tomatoes, field grown	lb	1.46	7/01	11r
Tomatoes, Hunt's or Del Monte	14.5 oz	0.83	3/01	4c
Tuna, chunk, light	6 oz	0.48	3/01	4c
Tuna, light, chunk	lb	1.80	7/01	11r
Turkey, frozen, whole	lb	1.15	7/01	11r
Goods and Services				
Miscellaneous goods and services, ACCRA Index		91.80	3/01	4c
B&B Japanese maple (acer japonicum)	gal	29.99-169.99	4/00	93r
Boxwood (buxus)	2 gal	18.99-39.99	4/00	93r
Daylilly (hemerocallis)	gal	4.99-25.00	4/00	93r
Flat of annuals		11.98-24.99	4/00	93r
Fountain grass (pennisetum)	gal	5.98-12.98	4/00	93r
Hanging basket (10 in)		12.99-27.99	4/00	93r
Hardy geranium (geranium)	gal	7.99-9.99	4/00	93r
Hosta (hosta)	gal	6.00-25.00	4/00	93r
Lilac (syrubga vulgaris)	2 gal	14.99-24.99	4/00	93r
Miscellaneous purchases	yr	865	1999	30r
Rhododendron (rhododendron)	2 gal	23.98-42.99	4/00	93r
Sage (salvia)	gal	6.00-9.99	4/00	93r
Wintercreeper euonymus (euonymus fortunei)	2 gal	16.00-169.99	4/00	93r
Hunting license	yr	9.00	4/01	34s
Health Care				
Health care, ACCRA Index		102.20	3/01	4c
Cardiac catheterization, ave hospital/ physician charges		13930	1998	77s
Childbirth, Cesarean delivery		10722	1997	13r
Childbirth, vaginal delivery		6223	1997	13r
Dentist's fee, adult teeth cleaning and periodic oral exam	visit	69.60	3/01	4c

Joplin, MO - continued

Item	Per	Value	Date	Ref.
Health Care - continued				
Doctor's fee, routine exam, established patient	visit	61.40	3/01	4c
Drugs, expenditures on	yr	394	1999	30r
Health care purchases	yr	2048	1999	30r
Health insurance expenditures	yr	978	1999	30r
Hospital care, private room	day	558.50	3/01	4c
Hysterectomy, laproscopically-assisted, ave hospital/physician charges		11300	1998	76s
Hysterectomy, vaginal, ave hospital and physician charges		9200	1998	76s
Medicaid dispensing fee		4.09	1999	87s
Medical services expenditures	yr	554	1999	30r
Medical supplies, expenditures on	yr	122	1999	30r
Plastic surgery, breast augmentation		3184	2000	7r
Plastic surgery, breast lift		3585	2000	7r
Plastic surgery, facelift		4999	2000	7r
Plastic surgery, hair transplantation		3105	2000	7r
Plastic surgery, lip augmentation		1290	2000	7r
Plastic surgery, lower body lift		8135	2000	7r
Plastic surgery, thigh lift		3839	2000	7r
Household Goods				
Dishwashing powder, Cascade	50 oz	3.70	3/01	4c
Floor coverings, expenditures on	yr	52	1999	30r
Furniture, expenditures on	yr	344	1999	30r
Household furnishings and equipment purchases	yr	1475	1999	30r
Household textiles, expenditures on	yr	109	1999	30r
Laundry and cleaning supplies, expenditures on	yr	134	1999	30r
Tissues, facial, Kleenex brand	175	1.15	3/01	4c
Housing				
Housing, ACCRA Index		84.00	3/01	4c
Home price, existing, ave		144400	10/00	90r
Home value, median		89000	2001	53s
House, 2400 sq ft, 8000 sq ft lot, new, urban, utilities	total	181250	3/01	4c
House payment, principal and interest, 25% down payment	mos	911	3/01	4c
Household operation expenditures	yr	542	1999	30r
Housekeeping supplies purchases	yr	508	1999	30r
Lodging expenditures	yr	430	1999	30r
Maintenance, repairs, insurance expenditures	yr	853	1999	30r
Monthly rental value of owned home	mos	547	1999	30r
Owned dwellings, expenditures own	yr	4282	1999	30r
Rent expenditures	yr	1558	1999	30r
Rent, apartment, 2 br, 1 1/2-2 baths, unfurn, 950 sq ft, water	mos	464	3/01	4c
Rental unit, 1 bedroom, with utilities	mos	300	4/01	41c
Rental unit, 2 bedroom, with utilities	mos	398	4/01	41c
Rental unit, 3 bedroom, with utilities	mos	524	4/01	41c
Rental unit, 4 bedroom, with utilities	mos	563	4/01	41c
Shelter, expenditures on	yr	6270	1999	30r
Insurance and Pensions				
Life and other personal insurance purchases	yr	387	1999	30r
Pensions and Social Security, expenditures on	yr	2968	1999	30r
Legal Fees				
Driver's license fee	orig	15.00	1999	48s
Driver's license fee	renew	15.00	1999	48s
Fishing license	yr	11.00	4/01	34s
Personal Goods				
Personal care products and services purchases	yr	385	1999	30r
Shampoo, Alberto VO5	15 oz	1.12	3/01	4c
Toothpaste, Crest or Colgate	6-7 oz	2.07	3/01	4c
Personal Services				
Dry cleaning, man's 2-pc suit		6.02	3/01	4c
Man's haircut, barbershop, no styling		7.50	3/01	4c

Values are in dollars or fractions of dollars. In the column headed *Ref*, references are shown to sources. Each reference is followed by a letter. These refer to the geographical level for which data were reported: s=State, r=Region, and c=City or metro. The abbreviation *ex* is used to mean *except* or *excluding*; *exp* stands for *expenditures*. For other abbreviations and further explanations, please see the Introduction.

Joplin, MO - continued

Item	Per	Value	Date	Ref.
Personal Services				
Personal services, household, expenditures on	yr	300	1999	30r
Woman's shampoo, trim, blow-dry, no style-change		18.40	3/01	4c
Pets				
Pets, toys, and playground equipment, expenditures on	yr	375	1999	30r
Restaurant Food				
Chicken, fried, thigh and drumstick, KFC/Church's		2.60	3/01	4c
Hamburger with cheese, McDonald's	1/4 lb	2.09	3/01	4c
Pizza, Pizza Hut or Pizza Inn	11-12 in	7.74	3/01	4c
Taxes				
Federal income taxes paid	yr	2326	1999	30r
Personal taxes, expenditures on	yr	3223	1999	30r
Property taxes paid	yr	1152	1999	30r
State and local income taxes paid	yr	753	1999	30r
Transportation				
Transportation, ACCRA Index		79.10	3/01	4c
Cars and trucks, new, expenditures on	yr	1280	1999	30r
Cars and trucks, used, expenditures on	yr	1763	1999	30r
Diesel at the pump	gal	1.16	10/99	73s
Gasoline and motor oil purchases	yr	1036	1999	30r
Gasoline before-tax price (cents)	gal	108.50	10/00	43s
Maintenance and repair expenditures	yr	594	1999	30r
Public transportation, expenditures on	yr	341	1999	30r
Tire balance, computer or spin balance, front	wheel	5.25	3/01	4c
Transportation purchases	yr	6617	1999	30r
Vehicle expenses, miscellaneous, purchases	yr	2159	1999	30r
Vehicle insurance payments	yr	701	1999	30r
Vehicle purchases (net outlay)	yr	3081	1999	30r
Vehicle rental, lease expenditures	yr	536	1999	30r
Utilities				
Utilities, ACCRA Index		78.40	3/01	4c
Electrical bill, average	mos	68.50	9/00	9s
Electricity, 2400 sq ft, new home	mos	96.22	3/01	4c
Electricity, expenditures on	yr	841	1999	30r
Electricity, summer, 250 KWh	mos	23.24	2/96	97c
Electricity, summer, 500 KWh	mos	39.04	2/96	97c
Electricity, summer, 750 KWh	mos	50.95	2/96	97c
Electricity, summer, 1000 KWh	mos	60.26	2/96	97c
Electricity cost, average	KWh	6.00	9/00	9s
Utilities, fuels, and public services purchased	yr	2401	1999	30r
Water and other public services, expenditures on	yr	273	1999	30r
Weddings				
Wedding (national average cost)		19936	2000	33r
Wedding (regional average total cost)		16195	1997	110r
Attendants' gifts		321	1998	33r
Bridal attendants' apparel (5 persons)		824	2000	33r
Bride's headpiece/veil		173	1998	33r
Bride's wedding dress		859	1998	33r
Clergy, religious facility fee		242	1998	33r
Engagement ring		3177	1998	33r
Flowers		789	1998	33r
Groom's formalwear rental		99	2000	33r
Limousine		410	1998	33r
Marriage license cost		50.00	4/01	35s
Men's formalwear (ushers, best man)		469	2000	33r
Mother of bride apparel		241	2000	33r
Music		866	1998	33r
Photography and videography		1368	1998	33r
Rehearsal dinner		728	1998	33r
Wedding invitations and announcements		341	1998	33r
Wedding reception		7968	2000	33r
Wedding rings (bride and groom)		1060	1998	33r

Kalamazoo-Battle Creek, MI

Item	Per	Value	Date	Ref.
Average annual expenditures	yr	35369	1999	30r
Alcoholic Beverages				
Alcoholic beverage purchases	yr	304	1999	30r
Malt beverages, all types, all sizes, any origin	16 oz	0.93	7/01	11r
Wine, red and white table, all sizes, any origin	liter	7.04	7/01	11r
Appliances				
Major appliances, expenditures on	yr	165	1999	30r
Small appliances, housewares, expenditures on	yr	90	1999	30r
Banking and Money				
Mortgage interest and charges paid	yr	2277	1999	30r
Mortgage principal paid on owned property	yr	1230	1999	30r
Vehicle finance charges paid	yr	328	1999	30r
Charity				
Cash contributions, expenditures	yr	1126	1999	30r
Child Care				
Child raising cost, total, age 0-2	yr	7890	1999	60r
Child raising cost, total, age 3-5	yr	8130	1999	60r
Child raising cost, total, age 6-8	yr	8170	1999	60r
Child raising cost, total, age 9-11	yr	8190	1999	60r
Child raising cost, total, age 12-14	yr	8890	1999	60r
Child raising cost, total, age 15-17	yr	9050	1999	60r
Child's child care and education, age 0-2	yr	1240	1999	60r
Child's child care and education, age 3-5	yr	1370	1999	60r
Child's child care and education, age 6-8	yr	880	1999	60r
Child's child care and education, age 9-11	yr	570	1999	60r
Child's child care and education, age 12-14	yr	420	1999	60r
Child's child care and education, age 15-17	yr	720	1999	60r
Child's clothing, age 0-2	yr	410	1999	60r
Child's clothing, age 3-5	yr	400	1999	60r
Child's clothing, age 6-8	yr	450	1999	60r
Child's clothing, age 9-11	yr	500	1999	60r
Child's clothing, age 12-14	yr	840	1999	60r
Child's clothing, age 15-17	yr	740	1999	60r
Child's food, age 0-2	yr	960	1999	60r
Child's food, age 3-5	yr	1120	1999	60r
Child's food, age 6-8	yr	1430	1999	60r
Child's food, age 9-11	yr	1710	1999	60r
Child's food, age 12-14	yr	1710	1999	60r
Child's food, age 15-17	yr	1920	1999	60r
Child's health care, age 0-2	yr	520	1999	60r
Child's health care, age 3-5	yr	500	1999	60r
Child's health care, age 6-8	yr	570	1999	60r
Child's health care, age 9-11	yr	610	1999	60r
Child's health care, age 12-14	yr	630	1999	60r
Child's health care, age 15-17	yr	650	1999	60r
Child's housing, age 0-2	yr	2860	1999	60r
Child's housing, age 3-5	yr	2840	1999	60r
Child's housing, age 6-8	yr	2800	1999	60r
Child's housing, age 9-11	yr	2650	1999	60r
Child's housing, age 12-14	yr	2840	1999	60r
Child's housing, age 15-17	yr	2440	1999	60r
Child's personal care, reading, age 0-2	yr	880	1999	60r
Child's personal care, reading, age 3-5	yr	900	1999	60r
Child's personal care, reading, age 6-8	yr	930	1999	60r
Child's personal care, reading, age 9-11	yr	970	1999	60r
Child's personal care, reading, age 12-14	yr	1150	1999	60r
Child's personal care, reading, age 15-17	yr	920	1999	60r
Clothing				
Apparel and services purchases	yr	1607	1999	30r
Boys, 2 to 15, expenditures on	yr	91	1999	30r
Children under 2, expenditures on	yr	59	1999	30r
Footwear, expenditures on	yr	285	1999	30r
Girls, 2 to 15, expenditures on	yr	116	1999	30r
Men and boys, expenditures on	yr	433	1999	30r
Men, 16 and over, expenditures on	yr	341	1999	30r
Women, 16 and over, expenditures on	yr	490	1999	30r

Values are in dollars or fractions of dollars. In the column headed *Ref*, references are shown to sources. Each reference is followed by a letter. These refer to the geographical level for which data were reported: s=State, r=Region, and c=City or metro. The abbreviation *ex* is used to mean *except* or *excluding*; *exp* stands for *expenditures*. For other abbreviations and further explanations, please see the Introduction.

Kalamazoo-Battle Creek, MI - continued

Item	Per	Value	Date	Ref.
Communications				
Cable modem installation, Bresnan		99.95	6/99	103s
Cable modem installation, Comcast		95.00	6/99	103s
Cable modem installation, Media One		100.00	6/99	103s
Cable modem rate, cable subscriber, Bresnan	mos	39.95	6/99	103s
Cable modem rate, cable subscriber, Comcast	mos	39.95	6/99	103s
Cable modem rate, cable subscriber, Media One	mos	34.95-39.95	6/99	103s
Cable modem rate, non-cable subscriber, Bresnan	mos	49.95	6/99	103s
Cable modem rate, non-cable subscriber, Comcast	mos	49.95	6/99	103s
Cable modem rate, non-cable subscriber, Media One	mos	49.95	6/99	103s
Phone line, single, business, field visit	inst.	42.00	12/97	17s
Phone line, single, business, no field visit	inst.	42.00	12/97	17s
Phone line, single, residence, field visit	inst.	42.00	12/97	17s
Phone line, single, residence, no field visit	inst.	42.00	12/97	17s
Postage and stationery, expenditures on	yr	140	1999	30r
Postal rate, express mail, up to half-pound		12.45	7/01	108r
Postal rate, letter, first class, first ounce		0.34	7/01	108r
Postal rate, letter, two ounces		0.57	7/01	108r
Postal rate, post card		0.21	7/01	108r
Postal rate, priority mail, two pounds		3.95	7/01	108r
Postal rate, priority mail, up to one pound		3.50	7/01	108r
Telephone bill, business, basic rate	mos	13.79	12/97	18c
Telephone bill, residential, basic rate	mos	10.44	12/97	18c
Telephone services, expenditures on	yr	830	1999	30r
Education				
Board, 4-year private college/university	yr	2182	1996	38s
Board, 4-year public college/university	yr	2276	1996	38s
Education expenditures	yr	583	1999	30r
Room, 4-year private college/university	yr	1974	1996	38s
Room, 4-year public college/university	yr	2024	1996	38s
Total cost, 4-year private college/university	yr	13331	1996	38s
Total cost, 4-year public college/university	yr	8195	1996	38s
Tuition, 2-year public college/university, in state	yr	1529	1996	38s
Tuition, 4-year private college/university, in state	yr	9176	1996	38s
Tuition, 4-year public college/university	yr	3895	1996	38s
Energy and Fuels				
Electricity	500 KWhs	46.59	7/01	11r
Fuel oil #2	gal	1.27	7/01	11r
Fuel oil and other fuels, expenditures on	yr	68	1999	30r
Gas, natural, commercial rate	1000 cf	4.91	11/00	88s
Gasoline, unleaded midgrade	gal	1.79	7/01	11r
Gasoline, unleaded premium	gal	1.86	7/01	11r
Gasoline, unleaded regular	gal	1.58	7/01	11r
Natural gas, expenditures on	yr	389	1999	30r
Utility (piped) gas, therm		0.81	7/01	11r
Utility (piped) gas, 40 therms		38.01	7/01	11r
Utility (piped) gas, 100 therms		81.75	7/01	11r
Entertainment				
Entertainment purchases	yr	1984	1999	30r
Fees and admissions paid	yr	444	1999	30r
Television, radios, sound equipment, expenditures on	yr	580	1999	30r
Funerals				
Cosmetology, hair, other preparation		178.32	1/99	78r
Embalming		408.19	1/99	78r
Funeral at funeral home		362.13	1/99	78r
Professional service charges		1375.51	1/99	78r
Transfer of remains to funeral home		155.92	1/99	78r
Visitation/viewing		294.38	1/99	78r
Groceries				
Bacon, sliced	lb	3.15	7/01	11r

Kalamazoo-Battle Creek, MI - continued

Item	Per	Value	Date	Ref.
Groceries - continued				
Bakery products, expenditures on	yr	281	1999	30r
Bananas	lb	0.48	7/01	11r
Beans, dried, any type, all sizes	lb	0.61	7/01	11r
Beef for stew, boneless	lb	3.08	7/01	11r
Beef, expenditures on	yr	217	1999	30r
Bologna, all beef or mixed	lb	2.52	7/01	11r
Bread, white, pan	lb	1.06	7/01	11r
Broccoli	lb	0.91	7/01	11r
Butter, salted, grade AA, stick	lb	3.04	7/01	11r
Butter, yoghurt, cheese, etc, expenditures on	yr	183	1999	30r
Cereals and bakery product purchases	yr	430	1999	30r
Cereals and cereal products, expenditures on	yr	149	1999	30r
Chicken, fresh, whole	lb	1.07	7/01	11r
Chops, boneless,	lb	3.64	7/01	11r
Chuck roast, U.S. choice, boneless	lb	2.47	7/01	11r
Coffee, 100%, ground roast, all sizes	lb	2.69	7/01	11r
Cookies, chocolate chip	lb	2.87	7/01	11r
Dairy product purchases	yr	304	1999	30r
Eggs, expenditures on	yr	26	1999	30r
Eggs, grade A, large	dozen	0.88	7/01	11r
Fats and oils, expenditures on	yr	75	1999	30r
Fish and seafood, expenditures on	yr	72	1999	30r
Food (excl fruit and vegetables), eaten at home, purchases	yr	887	1999	30r
Food cooked on trips, expenditures on	yr	44	1999	30r
Food purchases	yr	4802	1999	30r
Food purchases, eaten away from home	yr	2069	1999	30r
Food purchases, food eaten at home	yr	2733	1999	30r
Fresh fruits, expenditures on	yr	138	1999	30r
Fresh milk and cream, expenditures on	yr	120	1999	30r
Fresh vegetables, expenditures on	yr	126	1999	30r
Grapefruit	lb	0.66	7/01	11r
Grapes, Thompson, seedless	lb	1.64	7/01	11r
Ground beef, 100% beef	lb	1.64	7/01	11r
Ground beef, lean and extra lean	lb	2.16	7/01	11r
Ground chuck, 100% beef	lb	2.13	7/01	11r
Ham, boneless, excl canned	lb	2.62	7/01	11r
Ice cream, prepackaged, bulk, regular	1/2 gal	3.35	7/01	11r
Lemons	lb	1.19	7/01	11r
Lettuce, iceberg	lb	0.73	7/01	11r
Margarine, soft, tubs	lb	0.89	7/01	11r
Meats, poultry, fish, and egg purchases	yr	671	1999	30r
Milk, fresh, whole, fortified	gal	2.71	7/01	11r
Nonalcoholic beverages, expenditures on	yr	239	1999	30r
Oranges, Navel	lb	0.80	7/01	11r
Oranges, Valencia	lb	0.66	7/01	11r
Pears, Anjou	lb	0.93	7/01	11r
Pork chops, center cut, bone-in	lb	3.63	7/01	11r
Pork, expenditures on	yr	150	1999	30r
Potato chips	16 oz	3.52	7/01	11r
Potatoes, frozen, french fried	lb	1.08	7/01	11r
Potatoes, white, all types	lb	0.33	7/01	11r
Poultry, expenditures on	yr	108	1999	30r
Processed fruits, expenditures on	yr	98	1999	30r
Processed vegetables, expenditures on	yr	80	1999	30r
Round roast, U.S. choice, boneless	lb	3.07	7/01	11r
Round steak, graded and ungraded, excl U.S. prime and choice	lb	3.41	7/01	11r
Shortening, vegetable oil blends	lb	1.13	7/01	11r
Spaghetti and macaroni	lb	0.80	7/01	11r
Steak, round, U.S. choice, boneless	lb	3.23	7/01	11r
Steak, T-bone, U.S. choice, bone-in	lb	6.68	7/01	11r
Strawberries, dry pint	12 oz	1.32	7/01	11r
Sugar and other sweets, expenditures on	yr	114	1999	30r
Sugar, white, 33-80 ounce package	lb	0.42	7/01	11r
Sugar, white, all sizes	lb	0.43	7/01	11r
Tobacco products and smoking supplies purchases	yr	331	1999	30r
Tomatoes, field grown	lb	1.46	7/01	11r
Tuna, light, chunk	lb	1.80	7/01	11r
Turkey, frozen, whole	lb	1.15	7/01	11r

Values are in dollars or fractions of dollars. In the column headed *Ref*, references are shown to sources. Each reference is followed by a letter. These refer to the geographical level for which data were reported: s=State, r=Region, and c=City or metro. The abbreviation *ex* is used to mean *except* or *excluding*; *exp* stands for *expenditures*. For other abbreviations and further explanations, please see the Introduction.

Kalamazoo-Battle Creek, MI - continued

Item	Per	Value	Date	Ref.
Goods and Services				
B&B Japanese maple (acer japonicum)	gal	29.99-169.99	4/00	93r
Boxwood (buxus)	2 gal	18.99-39.99	4/00	93r
Daylilly (hemerocallis)	gal	4.99-25.00	4/00	93r
Flat of annuals		11.98-24.99	4/00	93r
Fountain grass (pennisetum)	gal	5.98-12.98	4/00	93r
Hanging basket (10 in)		12.99-27.99	4/00	93r
Hardy geranium (geranium)	gal	7.99-9.99	4/00	93r
Hosta (hosta)	gal	6.00-25.00	4/00	93r
Lilac (syrubga vulgaris)	2 gal	14.99-24.99	4/00	93r
Miscellaneous purchases	yr	865	1999	30r
Rhododendron (rhododendron)	2 gal	23.98-42.99	4/00	93r
Sage (salvia)	gal	6.00-9.99	4/00	93r
Snowblower, single stage		400-600	12/00	99s
Wintercreeper euonymus (euonymus fortunei)	2 gal	16.00-169.99	4/00	93r
Hunting license	yr	14.00	4/01	34s
Health Care				
Cardiac catheterization, ave hospital/physician charges		11830	1998	77s
Childbirth, Cesarean delivery		10722	1997	13r
Childbirth, vaginal delivery		6223	1997	13r
Drugs, expenditures on	yr	394	1999	30r
Health care purchases	yr	2048	1999	30r
Health insurance expenditures	yr	978	1999	30r
Hysterectomy, laproscopically-assisted, ave hospital/physician charges		13820	1998	76s
Hysterectomy, vaginal, ave hospital and physician charges		8780	1998	76s
Medicaid dispensing fee		3.72	1999	87s
Medical services expenditures	yr	554	1999	30r
Medical supplies, expenditures on	yr	122	1999	30r
Plastic surgery, breast augmentation		3184	2000	7r
Plastic surgery, breast lift		3585	2000	7r
Plastic surgery, facelift		4999	2000	7r
Plastic surgery, hair transplantation		3105	2000	7r
Plastic surgery, lip augmentation		1290	2000	7r
Plastic surgery, lower body lift		8135	2000	7r
Plastic surgery, thigh lift		3839	2000	7r
Household Goods				
Floor coverings, expenditures on	yr	52	1999	30r
Furniture, expenditures on	yr	344	1999	30r
Household furnishings and equipment purchases	yr	1475	1999	30r
Household textiles, expenditures on	yr	109	1999	30r
Laundry and cleaning supplies, expenditures on	yr	134	1999	30r
Housing				
Home price, existing, ave		144400	10/00	90r
Home value, median		135000	2001	53s
Household operation expenditures	yr	542	1999	30r
Housekeeping supplies purchases	yr	508	1999	30r
Lodging expenditures	yr	430	1999	30r
Maintenance, repairs, insurance expenditures	yr	853	1999	30r
Monthly rental value of owned home	mos	547	1999	30r
Owned dwellings, expenditures own	yr	4282	1999	30r
Rent expenditures	yr	1558	1999	30r
Rental unit, 1 bedroom, with utilities	mos	432	4/01	41c
Rental unit, 2 bedroom, with utilities	mos	544	4/01	41c
Rental unit, 3 bedroom, with utilities	mos	682	4/01	41c

Kalamazoo-Battle Creek, MI - continued

Item	Per	Value	Date	Ref.
Housing - continued				
Rental unit, 4 bedroom, with utilities	mos	761	4/01	41c
Shelter, expenditures on	yr	6270	1999	30r
Insurance and Pensions				
Life and other personal insurance purchases	yr	387	1999	30r
Pensions and Social Security, expenditures on	yr	2968	1999	30r
Legal Fees				
Divorce, filing fee		65.00	4/01	35s
Driver's license fee	renew	5.00	1999	48s
Driver's license fee	orig	20.00	1999	48s
Fishing license	yr	14.00	4/01	34s
Personal Goods				
Personal care products and services purchases	yr	385	1999	30r
Personal Services				
Personal services, household, expenditures on	yr	300	1999	30r
Pets				
Pets, toys, and playground equipment, expenditures on	yr	375	1999	30r
Taxes				
Federal income taxes paid	yr	2326	1999	30r
Personal taxes, expenditures on	yr	3223	1999	30r
Property taxes paid	yr	1152	1999	30r
State and local income taxes paid	yr	753	1999	30r
Transportation				
Bus fare, one-way	trip	1.00	2000	1c
Cars and trucks, new, expenditures on	yr	1280	1999	30r
Cars and trucks, used, expenditures on	yr	1763	1999	30r
Diesel at the pump	gal	1.19	10/99	73s
Gasoline and motor oil purchases	yr	1036	1999	30r
Gasoline before-tax price (cents)	gal	111.50	10/00	43s
Maintenance and repair expenditures	yr	594	1999	30r
Public transportation, expenditures on	yr	341	1999	30r
Transportation purchases	yr	6617	1999	30r
Vehicle expenses, miscellaneous, purchases	yr	2159	1999	30r
Vehicle insurance payments	yr	701	1999	30r
Vehicle purchases (net outlay)	yr	3081	1999	30r
Vehicle rental, lease expenditures	yr	536	1999	30r
Utilities				
Electrical bill, average	mos	55.00	9/00	9s
Electricity, expenditures on	yr	841	1999	30r
Electricity cost, average	KWh	7.00	9/00	9s
Utilities, fuels, and public services purchased	yr	2401	1999	30r
Water and other public services, expenditures on	yr	273	1999	30r
Weddings				
Wedding (national average cost)		19936	2000	33r
Wedding (regional average total cost)		16195	1997	110r
Attendants' gifts		321	1998	33r
Bridal attendants' apparel (5 persons)		824	2000	33r
Bride's headpiece/veil		173	1998	33r
Bride's wedding dress		859	1998	33r
Clergy, religious facility fee		242	1998	33r
Engagement ring		3177	1998	33r
Flowers		789	1998	33r
Groom's formalwear rental		99	2000	33r
Limousine		410	1998	33r
Marriage license cost		20.00	4/01	35s
Men's formalwear (ushers, best man)		469	2000	33r
Mother of bride apparel		241	2000	33r
Music		866	1998	33r
Photography and videography		1368	1998	33r
Rehearsal dinner		728	1998	33r
Wedding invitations and announcements		341	1998	33r
Wedding reception		7968	2000	33r
Wedding rings (bride and groom)		1060	1998	33r

Values are in dollars or fractions of dollars. In the column headed *Ref*, references are shown to sources. Each reference is followed by a letter. These refer to the geographical level for which data were reported: s=State, r=Region, and c=City or metro. The abbreviation *ex* is used to mean *except* or *excluding*; *exp* stands for expenditures. For other abbreviations and further explanations, please see the Introduction.

Kankakee, IL

Item	Per	Value	Date	Ref.
Average annual expenditures	yr	35369	1999	30r
Alcoholic Beverages				
Alcoholic beverage purchases	yr	304	1999	30r
Malt beverages, all types, all sizes, any origin	16 oz	0.93	7/01	11r
Wine, red and white table, all sizes, any origin	liter	7.04	7/01	11r
Appliances				
Major appliances, expenditures on	yr	165	1999	30r
Small appliances, housewares, expenditures on	yr	90	1999	30r
Banking and Money				
Mortgage interest and charges paid	yr	2277	1999	30r
Mortgage principal paid on owned property	yr	1230	1999	30r
Vehicle finance charges paid	yr	328	1999	30r
Charity				
Cash contributions, expenditures	yr	1126	1999	30r
Child Care				
Child raising cost, total, age 0-2	yr	7890	1999	60r
Child raising cost, total, age 3-5	yr	8130	1999	60r
Child raising cost, total, age 6-8	yr	8170	1999	60r
Child raising cost, total, age 9-11	yr	8190	1999	60r
Child raising cost, total, age 12-14	yr	8890	1999	60r
Child raising cost, total, age 15-17	yr	9050	1999	60r
Child's child care and education, age 0-2	yr	1240	1999	60r
Child's child care and education, age 3-5	yr	1370	1999	60r
Child's child care and education, age 6-8	yr	880	1999	60r
Child's child care and education, age 9-11	yr	570	1999	60r
Child's child care and education, age 12-14	yr	420	1999	60r
Child's child care and education, age 15-17	yr	720	1999	60r
Child's clothing, age 0-2	yr	410	1999	60r
Child's clothing, age 3-5	yr	400	1999	60r
Child's clothing, age 6-8	yr	450	1999	60r
Child's clothing, age 9-11	yr	500	1999	60r
Child's clothing, age 12-14	yr	840	1999	60r
Child's clothing, age 15-17	yr	740	1999	60r
Child's food, age 0-2	yr	960	1999	60r
Child's food, age 3-5	yr	1120	1999	60r
Child's food, age 6-8	yr	1430	1999	60r
Child's food, age 9-11	yr	1710	1999	60r
Child's food, age 12-14	yr	1710	1999	60r
Child's food, age 15-17	yr	1920	1999	60r
Child's health care, age 0-2	yr	520	1999	60r
Child's health care, age 3-5	yr	500	1999	60r
Child's health care, age 6-8	yr	570	1999	60r
Child's health care, age 9-11	yr	610	1999	60r
Child's health care, age 12-14	yr	630	1999	60r
Child's health care, age 15-17	yr	650	1999	60r
Child's housing, age 0-2	yr	2860	1999	60r
Child's housing, age 3-5	yr	2840	1999	60r
Child's housing, age 6-8	yr	2800	1999	60r
Child's housing, age 9-11	yr	2650	1999	60r
Child's housing, age 12-14	yr	2840	1999	60r
Child's housing, age 15-17	yr	2440	1999	60r
Child's personal care, reading, age 0-2	yr	880	1999	60r
Child's personal care, reading, age 3-5	yr	900	1999	60r
Child's personal care, reading, age 6-8	yr	930	1999	60r
Child's personal care, reading, age 9-11	yr	970	1999	60r
Child's personal care, reading, age 12-14	yr	1150	1999	60r
Child's personal care, reading, age 15-17	yr	920	1999	60r
Clothing				
Apparel and services purchases	yr	1607	1999	30r
Boys, 2 to 15, expenditures on	yr	91	1999	30r
Children under 2, expenditures on	yr	59	1999	30r
Footwear, expenditures on	yr	285	1999	30r
Girls, 2 to 15, expenditures on	yr	116	1999	30r
Men and boys, expenditures on	yr	433	1999	30r
Men, 16 and over, expenditures on	yr	341	1999	30r
Women, 16 and over, expenditures on	yr	490	1999	30r

Kankakee, IL - continued

Item	Per	Value	Date	Ref.
Communications				
Cable modem installation, Adelphi		54.90	6/99	103s
Cable modem installation, AT&T-BIS		150.00	6/99	103s
Cable modem installation, Media One		100.00	6/99	103s
Cable modem rate, cable subscriber, Adelphi	mos	34.95	6/99	103s
Cable modem rate, cable subscriber, AT&T-BIS	mos	39.95	6/99	103s
Cable modem rate, cable subscriber, Media One	mos	34.95-39.95	6/99	103s
Cable modem rate, non-cable subscriber, Adelphi	mos	44.95	6/99	103s
Cable modem rate, non-cable subscriber, Media One	mos	49.95	6/99	103s
Phone line, single, business, field visit	inst.	52.35	12/97	17s
Phone line, single, business, no field visit	inst.	52.35	12/97	17s
Phone line, single, residence, field visit	inst.	55.00	12/97	17s
Phone line, single, residence, no field visit	inst.	55.00	12/97	17s
Postage and stationery, expenditures on	yr	140	1999	30r
Postal rate, express mail, up to half-pound		12.45	7/01	108r
Postal rate, letter, first class, first ounce		0.34	7/01	108r
Postal rate, letter, two ounces		0.57	7/01	108r
Postal rate, post card		0.21	7/01	108r
Postal rate, priority mail, two pounds		3.95	7/01	108r
Postal rate, priority mail, up to one pound		3.50	7/01	108r
Telephone services, expenditures on	yr	830	1999	30r
Education				
Board, 4-year private college/university	yr	2306	1996	38s
Board, 4-year public college/university	yr	2405	1996	38s
Education expenditures	yr	583	1999	30r
Room, 4-year private college/university	yr	2718	1996	38s
Room, 4-year public college/university	yr	2072	1996	38s
Total cost, 4-year private college/university	yr	16678	1996	38s
Total cost, 4-year public college/university	yr	7829	1996	38s
Tuition, 2-year public college/university, in state	yr	1232	1996	38s
Tuition, 4-year private college/university, in state	yr	11653	1996	38s
Tuition, 4-year public college/university	yr	3352	1996	38s
Energy and Fuels				
Electricity	500 KWhs	46.59	7/01	11r
Fuel oil #2	gal	1.27	7/01	11r
Fuel oil and other fuels, expenditures on	yr	68	1999	30r
Gas, natural, commercial rate	1000 cf	8.47	11/00	88s
Gasoline, unleaded midgrade	gal	1.79	7/01	11r
Gasoline, unleaded premium	gal	1.86	7/01	11r
Gasoline, unleaded regular	gal	1.58	7/01	11r
Natural gas, expenditures on	yr	389	1999	30r
Utility (piped) gas, therm		0.81	7/01	11r
Utility (piped) gas, 40 therms		38.01	7/01	11r
Utility (piped) gas, 100 therms		81.75	7/01	11r
Entertainment				
Entertainment purchases	yr	1984	1999	30r
Fees and admissions paid	yr	444	1999	30r
Television, radios, sound equipment, expenditures on	yr	580	1999	30r
Funerals				
Cosmetology, hair, other preparation		178.32	1/99	78r
Embalming		408.19	1/99	78r
Funeral at funeral home		362.13	1/99	78r
Professional service charges		1375.51	1/99	78r
Transfer of remains to funeral home		155.92	1/99	78r
Visitation/viewing		294.38	1/99	78r
Groceries				
Bacon, sliced	lb	3.15	7/01	11r
Bakery products, expenditures on	yr	281	1999	30r
Bananas	lb	0.48	7/01	11r
Beans, dried, any type, all sizes	lb	0.61	7/01	11r
Beef for stew, boneless	lb	3.08	7/01	11r
Beef, expenditures on	yr	217	1999	30r

Values are in dollars or fractions of dollars. In the column headed *Ref*, references are shown to sources. Each reference is followed by a letter. These refer to the geographical level for which data were reported: s=State, r=Region, and c=City or metro. The abbreviation *ex* is used to mean *except* or *excluding*; *exp* stands for *expenditures*. For other abbreviations and further explanations, please see the Introduction.

Kankakee, IL - continued

Item	Per	Value	Date	Ref.
Groceries				
Bologna, all beef or mixed	lb	2.52	7/01	11r
Bread, white, pan	lb	1.06	7/01	11r
Broccoli	lb	0.91	7/01	11r
Butter, salted, grade AA, stick	lb	3.04	7/01	11r
Butter, yoghurt, cheese, etc, expenditures on	yr	183	1999	30r
Cereals and bakery product purchases	yr	430	1999	30r
Cereals and cereal products, expenditures on	yr	149	1999	30r
Chicken, fresh, whole	lb	1.07	7/01	11r
Chops, boneless,	lb	3.64	7/01	11r
Chuck roast, U.S. choice, boneless	lb	2.47	7/01	11r
Coffee, 100%, ground roast, all sizes	lb	2.69	7/01	11r
Cookies, chocolate chip	lb	2.87	7/01	11r
Dairy product purchases	yr	304	1999	30r
Eggs, expenditures on	yr	26	1999	30r
Eggs, grade A, large	dozen	0.88	7/01	11r
Fats and oils, expenditures on	yr	75	1999	30r
Fish and seafood, expenditures on	yr	72	1999	30r
Food (excl fruit and vegetables), eaten at home, purchases	yr	887	1999	30r
Food cooked on trips, expenditures on	yr	44	1999	30r
Food purchases	yr	4802	1999	30r
Food purchases, eaten away from home	yr	2069	1999	30r
Food purchases, food eaten at home	yr	2733	1999	30r
Fresh fruits, expenditures on	yr	138	1999	30r
Fresh milk and cream, expenditures on	yr	120	1999	30r
Fresh vegetables, expenditures on	yr	126	1999	30r
Grapefruit	lb	0.66	7/01	11r
Grapes, Thompson, seedless	lb	1.64	7/01	11r
Ground beef, 100% beef	lb	1.64	7/01	11r
Ground beef, lean and extra lean	lb	2.16	7/01	11r
Ground chuck, 100% beef	lb	2.13	7/01	11r
Ham, boneless, excl canned	lb	2.62	7/01	11r
Ice cream, prepackaged, bulk, regular	1/2 gal	3.35	7/01	11r
Lemons	lb	1.19	7/01	11r
Lettuce, iceberg	lb	0.73	7/01	11r
Margarine, soft, tubs	lb	0.89	7/01	11r
Meats, poultry, fish, and egg purchases	yr	671	1999	30r
Milk, fresh, whole, fortified	gal	2.71	7/01	11r
Nonalcoholic beverages, expenditures on	yr	239	1999	30r
Oranges, Navel	lb	0.80	7/01	11r
Oranges, Valencia	lb	0.66	7/01	11r
Pears, Anjou	lb	0.93	7/01	11r
Pork chops, center cut, bone-in	lb	3.63	7/01	11r
Pork, expenditures on	yr	150	1999	30r
Potato chips	16 oz	3.52	7/01	11r
Potatoes, frozen, french fried	lb	1.08	7/01	11r
Potatoes, white, all types	lb	0.33	7/01	11r
Poultry, expenditures on	yr	108	1999	30r
Processed fruits, expenditures on	yr	98	1999	30r
Processed vegetables, expenditures on	yr	80	1999	30r
Round roast, U.S. choice, boneless	lb	3.07	7/01	11r
Round steak, graded and ungraded, excl U.S. prime and choice	lb	3.41	7/01	11r
Shortening, vegetable oil blends	lb	1.13	7/01	11r
Spaghetti and macaroni	lb	0.80	7/01	11r
Steak, round, U.S. choice, boneless	lb	3.23	7/01	11r
Steak, T-bone, U.S. choice, bone-in	lb	6.68	7/01	11r
Strawberries, dry pint	12 oz	1.32	7/01	11r
Sugar and other sweets, expenditures on	yr	114	1999	30r
Sugar, white, 33-80 ounce package	lb	0.42	7/01	11r
Sugar, white, all sizes	lb	0.43	7/01	11r
Tobacco products and smoking supplies purchases	yr	331	1999	30r
Tomatoes, field grown	lb	1.46	7/01	11r
Tuna, light, chunk	lb	1.80	7/01	11r
Turkey, frozen, whole	lb	1.15	7/01	11r
Goods and Services				
B&B Japanese maple (acer japonicum)	gal	29.99-169.99	4/00	93r
Boxwood (buxus)	2 gal	18.99-39.99	4/00	93r

Kankakee, IL - continued

Item	Per	Value	Date	Ref.
Goods and Services - continued				
Daylily (hemerocallis)	gal	4.99-25.00	4/00	93r
Flat of annuals		11.98-24.99	4/00	93r
Fountain grass (pennisetum)	gal	5.98-12.98	4/00	93r
Hanging basket (10 in)		12.99-27.99	4/00	93r
Hardy geranium (geranium)	gal	7.99-9.99	4/00	93r
Hosta (hosta)	gal	6.00-25.00	4/00	93r
Lilac (syrubga vulgaris)	2 gal	14.99-24.99	4/00	93r
Miscellaneous purchases	yr	865	1999	30r
Rhododendron (rhododendron)	2 gal	23.98-42.99	4/00	93r
Sage (salvia)	gal	6.00-9.99	4/00	93r
Wintercreeper euonymus (euonymus fortunei)	2 gal	16.00-169.99	4/00	93r
Hunting license	yr	7.50	4/01	34s
Health Care				
Cardiac catheterization, ave hospital/physician charges		17690	1998	77s
Childbirth, Cesarean delivery		10722	1997	13r
Childbirth, vaginal delivery		6223	1997	13r
Drugs, expenditures on	yr	394	1999	30r
Health care purchases	yr	2048	1999	30r
Health insurance expenditures	yr	978	1999	30r
Hysterectomy, laproscopically-assisted, ave hospital/physician charges		15850	1998	76s
Hysterectomy, vaginal, ave hospital and physician charges		11810	1998	76s
Medicaid dispensing fee		3.69-15.45	1999	87s
Medical services expenditures	yr	554	1999	30r
Medical supplies, expenditures on	yr	122	1999	30r
Plastic surgery, breast augmentation		3184	2000	7r
Plastic surgery, breast lift		3585	2000	7r
Plastic surgery, facelift		4999	2000	7r
Plastic surgery, hair transplantation		3105	2000	7r
Plastic surgery, lip augmentation		1290	2000	7r
Plastic surgery, lower body lift		8135	2000	7r
Plastic surgery, thigh lift		3839	2000	7r
Household Goods				
Floor coverings, expenditures on	yr	52	1999	30r
Furniture, expenditures on	yr	344	1999	30r
Household furnishings and equipment purchases	yr	1475	1999	30r
Household textiles, expenditures on	yr	109	1999	30r
Laundry and cleaning supplies, expenditures on	yr	134	1999	30r
Housing				
Home price, existing, ave		144400	10/00	90r
Home value, median		183000	2001	53s
Household operation expenditures	yr	542	1999	30r
Housekeeping supplies purchases	yr	508	1999	30r
Lodging expenditures	yr	430	1999	30r
Maintenance, repairs, insurance expenditures	yr	853	1999	30r
Monthly rental value of owned home	mos	547	1999	30r
Owned dwellings, expenditures own	yr	4282	1999	30r
Rent expenditures	yr	1558	1999	30r
Rental unit, 1 bedroom, with utilities	mos	433	4/01	41c
Rental unit, 2 bedroom, with utilities	mos	576	4/01	41c
Rental unit, 3 bedroom, with utilities	mos	737	4/01	41c
Rental unit, 4 bedroom, with utilities	mos	809	4/01	41c
Shelter, expenditures on	yr	6270	1999	30r

Values are in dollars or fractions of dollars. In the column headed *Ref*, references are shown to sources. Each reference is followed by a letter. These refer to the geographical level for which data were reported: s=State, r=Region, and c=City or metro. The abbreviation *ex* is used to mean *except* or *excluding*; *exp* stands for *expenditures*. For other abbreviations and further explanations, please see the Introduction.

Kankakee, IL - continued

Item	Per	Value	Date	Ref.
Insurance and Pensions				
Life and other personal insurance purchases	yr	387	1999	30r
Pensions and Social Security, expenditures on	yr	2968	1999	30r
Legal Fees				
Divorce, filing fee		100.00-150.00	4/01	35s
Driver's license fee	renew	20.00	1999	48s
Driver's license fee	orig	10.00	1999	48s
Personal Goods				
Personal care products and services purchases	yr	385	1999	30r
Personal Services				
Personal services, household, expenditures on	yr	300	1999	30r
Pets				
Pets, toys, and playground equipment, expenditures on	yr	375	1999	30r
Taxes				
Federal income taxes paid	yr	2326	1999	30r
Personal taxes, expenditures on	yr	3223	1999	30r
Property taxes paid	yr	1152	1999	30r
State and local income taxes paid	yr	753	1999	30r
Transportation				
Cars and trucks, new, expenditures on	yr	1280	1999	30r
Cars and trucks, used, expenditures on	yr	1763	1999	30r
Diesel at the pump	gal	1.33	10/99	73s
Gasoline and motor oil purchases	yr	1036	1999	30r
Gasoline before-tax price (cents)	gal	112.70	10/00	43s
Maintenance and repair expenses	yr	594	1999	30r
Public transportation, expenditures on	yr	341	1999	30r
Transportation purchases	yr	6617	1999	30r
Vehicle expenses, miscellaneous, purchases	yr	2159	1999	30r
Vehicle insurance payments	yr	701	1999	30r
Vehicle purchases (net outlay)	yr	3081	1999	30r
Vehicle rental, lease expenditures	yr	536	1999	30r
Utilities				
Electrical bill, average	mos	63.08	9/00	9s
Electricity, expenditures on	yr	841	1999	30r
Electricity cost, average	KWh	6.49	9/00	9s
Utilities, fuels, and public services purchased	yr	2401	1999	30r
Water and other public services, expenditures on	yr	273	1999	30r
Weddings				
Wedding (national average cost)		19936	2000	33r
Wedding (regional average total cost)		16195	1997	110r
Attendants' gifts		321	1998	33r
Bridal attendants' apparel (5 persons)		824	2000	33r
Bride's headpiece/veil		173	1998	33r
Bride's wedding dress		859	1998	33r
Clergy, religious facility fee		242	1998	33r
Engagement ring		3177	1998	33r
Flowers		789	1998	33r
Groom's formalwear rental		99	2000	33r
Limousine		410	1998	33r
Marriage license cost		15.00-20.00	4/01	35s
Men's formalwear (ushers, best man)		469	2000	33r
Mother of bride apparel		241	2000	33r
Music		866	1998	33r
Photography and videography		1368	1998	33r
Rehearsal dinner		728	1998	33r
Wedding invitations and announcements		341	1998	33r
Wedding reception		7968	2000	33r
Wedding rings (bride and groom)		1060	1998	33r

Kansas City, MO-KS

Item	Per	Value	Date	Ref.
Average annual expenditures	yr	35369	1999	30r
Composite, ACCRA index		98.70	3/01	4c
Alcoholic Beverages				
Alcoholic beverage purchases	yr	244	1999	30c
Beer, Heineken, 12-oz, ex deposit	6	7.29	3/01	4c
J & B Scotch	750-ml	21.03	3/01	4c
Malt beverages, all types, all sizes, any origin	16 oz	0.93	7/01	11r
Wine, Livingston or Gallo, Chablis blanc	1.5 liter	5.99	3/01	4c
Wine, red and white table, all sizes, any origin	liter	7.04	7/01	11r
Appliances				
Appliance repair, service call, washing machine	min lab chg	41.97	3/01	4c
Major appliances, expenditures on	yr	165	1999	30r
Small appliances, housewares, expenditures on	yr	90	1999	30r
Banking and Money				
Mortgage interest and charges paid	yr	2277	1999	30r
Mortgage principal paid on owned property	yr	1230	1999	30r
Mortgage rate, incl. points and orig. fee, 30-yr. conv. fixed or ARM	mos	7.08	3/01	4c
Vehicle finance charges paid	yr	328	1999	30r
Business Expenses				
Business travel, car rental	day	39	2001	3c
Business travel, food	day	52	2001	3c
Business travel, hotel	day	113	2001	3c
Medical office space cost	sq ft	119.85	2001	31c
Office space, 2-4 storey building	sq ft	105.00	2001	31c
Office space, 5-10 storey building	sq ft	92.75	2001	31c
Office space, 11-20 storey building	sq ft	89.15	2001	31c
Charity				
Cash contributions, expenditures	yr	967	1999	30c
Child Care				
Child raising cost, total, age 0-2	yr	7890	1999	60r
Child raising cost, total, age 3-5	yr	8130	1999	60r
Child raising cost, total, age 6-8	yr	8170	1999	60r
Child raising cost, total, age 9-11	yr	8190	1999	60r
Child raising cost, total, age 12-14	yr	8890	1999	60r
Child raising cost, total, age 15-17	yr	9050	1999	60r
Child's child care and education, age 0-2	yr	1240	1999	60r
Child's child care and education, age 3-5	yr	1370	1999	60r
Child's child care and education, age 6-8	yr	880	1999	60r
Child's child care and education, age 9-11	yr	570	1999	60r
Child's child care and education, age 12-14	yr	420	1999	60r
Child's child care and education, age 15-17	yr	720	1999	60r
Child's clothing, age 0-2	yr	410	1999	60r
Child's clothing, age 3-5	yr	400	1999	60r
Child's clothing, age 6-8	yr	450	1999	60r
Child's clothing, age 9-11	yr	500	1999	60r
Child's clothing, age 12-14	yr	840	1999	60r
Child's clothing, age 15-17	yr	740	1999	60r
Child's food, age 0-2	yr	960	1999	60r
Child's food, age 3-5	yr	1120	1999	60r
Child's food, age 6-8	yr	1430	1999	60r
Child's food, age 9-11	yr	1710	1999	60r
Child's food, age 12-14	yr	1710	1999	60r
Child's food, age 15-17	yr	1920	1999	60r
Child's health care, age 0-2	yr	520	1999	60r
Child's health care, age 3-5	yr	500	1999	60r
Child's health care, age 6-8	yr	570	1999	60r
Child's health care, age 9-11	yr	610	1999	60r
Child's health care, age 12-14	yr	630	1999	60r
Child's health care, age 15-17	yr	650	1999	60r
Child's housing, age 0-2	yr	2860	1999	60r
Child's housing, age 3-5	yr	2840	1999	60r
Child's housing, age 6-8	yr	2800	1999	60r
Child's housing, age 9-11	yr	2650	1999	60r
Child's housing, age 12-14	yr	2840	1999	60r
Child's housing, age 15-17	yr	2440	1999	60r
Child's personal care, reading, age 0-2	yr	880	1999	60r

Values are in dollars or fractions of dollars. In the column headed *Ref*, references are shown to sources. Each reference is followed by a letter. These refer to the geographical level for which data were reported: s=State, r=Region, and c=City or metro. The abbreviation *ex* is used to mean *except* or *excluding*; *exp* stands for *expenditures*. For other abbreviations and further explanations, please see the Introduction.

Kansas City, MO-KS - continued

Item	Per	Value	Date	Ref.
Child Care				
Child's personal care, reading, age 3-5	yr	900	1999	60r
Child's personal care, reading, age 6-8	yr	930	1999	60r
Child's personal care, reading, age 9-11	yr	970	1999	60r
Child's personal care, reading, age 12-14	yr	1150	1999	60r
Child's personal care, reading, age 15-17	yr	920	1999	60r
Clothing				
Apparel and services purchases	yr	1708	1999	30c
Boys' brief, cotton	3	4.47	3/01	4c
Boys, 2 to 15, expenditures on	yr	91	1999	30r
Children under 2, expenditures on	yr	59	1999	30r
Footwear, expenditures on	yr	285	1999	30r
Girls, 2 to 15, expenditures on	yr	116	1999	30r
Men and boys, expenditures on	yr	433	1999	30r
Men, 16 and over, expenditures on	yr	341	1999	30r
Shirt, man's dress shirt		26.97	3/01	4c
Slacks, man's "No Wrinkles" khaki		41.00	3/01	4c
Women, 16 and over, expenditures on	yr	490	1999	30r
Communications				
Newspaper subscription, daily and Sunday delivery	mos	14.95	3/01	4c
Phone line, single, business, field visit	inst.	52.25	12/97	17s
Phone line, single, business, no field visit	inst.	52.25	12/97	17s
Phone line, single, residence, field visit	inst.	36.50	12/97	17s
Phone line, single, residence, no field visit	inst.	36.50	12/97	17s
Postage and stationery, expenditures on	yr	140	1999	30r
Postal rate, express mail, up to half-pound		12.45	7/01	108r
Postal rate, letter, first class, first ounce		0.34	7/01	108r
Postal rate, letter, two ounces		0.57	7/01	108r
Postal rate, post card		0.21	7/01	108r
Postal rate, priority mail, two pounds		3.95	7/01	108r
Postal rate, priority mail, up to one pound		3.50	7/01	108r
Telephone bill, business, basic rate	mos	33.55	12/97	18c
Telephone bill, family of three	mos	31.00	3/01	4c
Telephone bill, residential, basic rate	mos	11.35	12/97	18c
Telephone services, expenditures on	yr	830	1999	30r
Education				
Board, 4-year private college/university	yr	2387	1996	38s
Board, 4-year public college/university	yr	1713	1996	38s
Education expenditures	yr	642	1999	30c
Room, 4-year private college/university	yr	2162	1996	38s
Room, 4-year public college/university	yr	2022	1996	38s
Total cost, 4-year private college/university	yr	14116	1996	38s
Total cost, 4-year public college/university	yr	6750	1996	38s
Tuition, 2-year public college/university, in state	yr	1255	1996	38s
Tuition, 4-year private college/university, in state	yr	9566	1996	38s
Tuition, 4-year public college/university	yr	3015	1996	38s
Energy and Fuels				
Electricity	500 KWhs	46.59	7/01	11r
Energy, combined forms, 2400 sq ft	mos	105.31	3/01	4c
Energy, exc. electricity, 2400 sq ft	mos	50.14	3/01	4c
Fuel oil #2	gal	1.27	7/01	11r
Fuel oil and other fuels, expenditures on	yr	68	1999	30r
Gas, cooking, winter, 10 therms	mos	13.17	2/96	98c
Gas, cooking, winter, 30 therms	mos	21.42	2/96	98c
Gas, cooking, winter, 50 therms	mos	29.66	2/96	98c
Gas, heating, winter, average use	mos	93.22	2/96	98c
Gas, natural, commercial rate	1000 cf	8.38	11/00	88s
Gas, regular unleaded, cash, self-service	gal	1.37	3/01	4c
Gasoline, unleaded midgrade	gal	1.79	7/01	11r
Gasoline, unleaded premium	gal	1.86	7/01	11r
Gasoline, unleaded regular	gal	1.58	7/01	11r
Natural gas, expenditures on	yr	389	1999	30r
Utility (piped) gas, therm		0.81	7/01	11r
Utility (piped) gas, 40 therms		38.01	7/01	11r
Utility (piped) gas, 100 therms		81.75	7/01	11r

Kansas City, MO-KS - continued

Item	Per	Value	Date	Ref.
Entertainment				
Bowling, Saturday evening rate	line	3.25	3/01	4c
Entertainment purchases	yr	1649	1999	30c
Fees and admissions paid	yr	444	1999	30r
Monopoly game, Parker Brothers', No. 9	game	10.65	3/01	4c
Movie, first-run, Saturday, evening	adm.	6.90	3/01	4c
Reading purchases	yr	144	1999	30c
Television, radios, sound equipment, expenditures on	yr	580	1999	30r
Tennis balls, yellow, Wilson or Penn, 3	can	1.99	3/01	4c
Funerals				
Cosmetology, hair, other preparation		178.32	1/99	78r
Embalming		408.19	1/99	78r
Funeral at funeral home		362.13	1/99	78r
Professional service charges		1375.51	1/99	78r
Transfer of remains to funeral home		155.92	1/99	78r
Visitation/viewing		294.38	1/99	78r
Groceries				
Groceries, ACCRA Index		100.50	3/01	4c
Antibiotic ointment, Polysporin	0.5 oz	4.69	3/01	4c
Baby food, strained vegetables or fruit, lowest price	4-4.5 oz	0.40	3/01	4c
Bacon, sliced	lb	3.15	7/01	11r
Bakery products, expenditures on	yr	281	1999	30r
Bananas	lb	0.55	3/01	4c
Bananas	lb	0.48	7/01	11r
Beans, dried, any type, all sizes	lb	0.61	7/01	11r
Beef for stew, boneless	lb	3.08	7/01	11r
Beef or hamburger, ground	lb	1.59	3/01	4c
Beef, expenditures on	yr	217	1999	30r
Bologna, all beef or mixed	lb	2.52	7/01	11r
Bread, white	loaf	1.19	3/01	4c
Bread, white, pan	lb	1.06	7/01	11r
Broccoli	lb	0.91	7/01	11r
Butter, salted, grade AA, stick	lb	3.04	7/01	11r
Butter, yoghurt, cheese, etc, expenditures on	yr	183	1999	30r
Cereals and bakery product purchases	yr	430	1999	30r
Cereals and cereal products, expenditures on	yr	149	1999	30r
Cheese, Kraft grated Parmesan	8 oz	3.19	3/01	4c
Chicken, fresh, whole	lb	1.07	7/01	11r
Chicken, whole fryer	lb	1.13	3/01	4c
Chops, boneless,	lb	3.64	7/01	11r
Chuck roast, U.S. choice, boneless	lb	2.47	7/01	11r
Cigarettes, Winston, Kings	carton	30.79	3/01	4c
Coffee, 100%, ground roast, all sizes	lb	2.69	7/01	11r
Coffee, vacuum-packed	13 oz	2.37	3/01	4c
Cookies, chocolate chip	lb	2.87	7/01	11r
Corn Flakes, Kellogg's or Post Toasties	18 oz	2.96	3/01	4c
Corn, frozen, whole kernel, lowest price	16 oz	1.25	3/01	4c
Dairy product purchases	yr	332	1999	30c
Eggs, expenditures on	yr	26	1999	30r
Eggs, Grade A or AA	dozen	1.20	3/01	4c
Eggs, grade A, large	dozen	0.88	7/01	11r
Fats and oils, expenditures on	yr	75	1999	30r
Fish and seafood, expenditures on	yr	72	1999	30r
Food (excl fruit and vegetables), eaten at home, purchases	yr	1005	1999	30c
Food cooked on trips, expenditures on	yr	44	1999	30r
Food purchases	yr	5115	1999	30c
Food purchases, eaten away from home	yr	1861	1999	30c
Food purchases, food eaten at home	yr	3254	1999	30c
Fresh fruits, expenditures on	yr	138	1999	30r
Fresh milk and cream, expenditures on	yr	120	1999	30r
Fresh vegetables, expenditures on	yr	126	1999	30r
Fruit and vegetable purchases	yr	565	1999	30c
Grapefruit	lb	0.66	7/01	11r
Grapes, Thompson, seedless	lb	1.64	7/01	11r
Ground beef, 100% beef	lb	1.64	7/01	11r
Ground beef, lean and extra lean	lb	2.16	7/01	11r
Ground chuck, 100% beef	lb	2.13	7/01	11r
Ham, boneless, excl canned	lb	2.62	7/01	11r

Values are in dollars or fractions of dollars. In the column headed *Ref*, references are shown to sources. Each reference is followed by a letter. These refer to the geographical level for which data were reported: s=State, r=Region, and c=City or metro. The abbreviation *ex* is used to mean *except* or *excluding*; *exp* stands for *expenditures*. For other abbreviations and further explanations, please see the Introduction.

Kansas City, MO-KS - continued

Item	Per	Value	Date	Ref.
Groceries				
Ice cream, prepackaged, bulk, regular	1/2 gal	3.35	7/01	11r
Lemons	lb	1.19	7/01	11r
Lettuce, iceberg	head	0.95	3/01	4c
Lettuce, iceberg	lb	0.73	7/01	11r
Margarine, Blue Bonnet or Parkay, stick	lb	0.78	3/01	4c
Margarine, soft, tubs	lb	0.89	7/01	11r
Meats, poultry, fish, and egg purchases	yr	671	1999	30r
Milk, fresh, whole, fortified	gal	2.71	7/01	11r
Milk, whole	1/2 gal	1.29	3/01	4c
Nonalcoholic beverages, expenditures on	yr	239	1999	30r
Orange juice, Minute Maid frozen	12 oz	1.65	3/01	4c
Oranges, Navel	lb	0.80	7/01	11r
Oranges, Valencia	lb	0.66	7/01	11r
Peaches, halves or slices, Hunt's, Del Monte, or Libby's	29 oz	1.53	3/01	4c
Pears, Anjou	lb	0.93	7/01	11r
Peas, green, Del Monte or Green Giant	15 oz	0.78	3/01	4c
Pork chops, center cut, bone-in	lb	3.63	7/01	11r
Pork, expenditures on	yr	150	1999	30r
Potato chips	16 oz	3.52	7/01	11r
Potatoes, frozen, french fried	lb	1.08	7/01	11r
Potatoes, white or red	10 lb	2.99	3/01	4c
Potatoes, white, all types	lb	0.33	7/01	11r
Poultry, expenditures on	yr	108	1999	30r
Processed fruits, expenditures on	yr	98	1999	30r
Processed vegetables, expenditures on	yr	80	1999	30r
Round roast, U.S. choice, boneless	lb	3.07	7/01	11r
Round steak, graded and ungraded, excl U.S. prime and choice	lb	3.41	7/01	11r
Sausage, Jimmy Dean/Owens pork	lb	3.18	3/01	4c
Shortening, vegetable oil blends	lb	1.13	7/01	11r
Shortening, vegetable, Crisco	3 lb	2.47	3/01	4c
Soft drink, Coca Cola, ex deposit	2 liter	1.04	3/01	4c
Spaghetti and macaroni	lb	0.80	7/01	11r
Steak, round, U.S. choice, boneless	lb	3.23	7/01	11r
Steak, T-bone	lb	5.85	3/01	4c
Steak, T-bone, U.S. choice, bone-in	lb	6.68	7/01	11r
Strawberries, dry pint	12 oz	1.32	7/01	11r
Sugar and other sweets, expenditures on	yr	114	1999	30r
Sugar, cane or beet	4 lbs	1.47	3/01	4c
Sugar, white, 33-80 ounce package	lb	0.42	7/01	11r
Sugar, white, all sizes	lb	0.43	7/01	11r
Tobacco products and smoking supplies purchases	yr	302	1999	30c
Tomatoes, field grown	lb	1.46	7/01	11r
Tomatoes, Hunt's or Del Monte	14.5 oz	0.89	3/01	4c
Tuna, chunk, light	6 oz	0.70	3/01	4c
Tuna, light, chunk	lb	1.80	7/01	11r
Turkey, frozen, whole	lb	1.15	7/01	11r
Goods and Services				
Miscellaneous goods and services, ACCRA Index		102.40	3/01	4c
B&B Japanese maple (acer japonicum)	gal	29.99-169.99	4/00	93r
Boxwood (buxus)	2 gal	18.99-39.99	4/00	93r
Daylily (hemerocallis)	gal	4.99-25.00	4/00	93r
Flat of annuals		11.98-24.99	4/00	93r
Fountain grass (pennisetum)	gal	5.98-12.98	4/00	93r
Hanging basket (10 in)		12.99-27.99	4/00	93r
Hardy geranium (geranium)	gal	7.99-9.99	4/00	93r
Hosta (hosta)	gal	6.00-25.00	4/00	93r
Lilac (syrubga vulgaris)	2 gal	14.99-24.99	4/00	93r
Miscellaneous purchases	yr	865	1999	30r

Kansas City, MO-KS - continued

Item	Per	Value	Date	Ref.
Goods and Services - continued				
Rhododendron (rhododendron)	2 gal	23.98-42.99	4/00	93r
Sage (salvia)	gal	6.00-9.99	4/00	93r
Wintercreeper euonymus (euonymus fortunei)	2 gal	16.00-169.99	4/00	93r
Hunting license	yr	9.00	4/01	34s
Health Care				
Health care, ACCRA Index		98.00	3/01	4c
Cardiac catheterization, ave hospital/ physician charges		13930	1998	77s
Childbirth, Cesarean delivery		10722	1997	13r
Childbirth, vaginal delivery		6223	1997	13r
Dentist's fee, adult teeth cleaning and periodic oral exam	visit	69.00	3/01	4c
Doctor's fee, routine exam, established patient	visit	54.00	3/01	4c
Drugs, expenditures on	yr	394	1999	30r
Health care purchases	yr	2043	1999	30c
Health insurance expenditures	yr	978	1999	30r
Hospital care, private room	day	583.00	3/01	4c
Hysterectomy, laproscopically-assisted, ave hospital/physician charges		11300	1998	76s
Hysterectomy, vaginal, ave hospital and physician charges		9200	1998	76s
Medicaid dispensing fee		4.09	1999	87s
Medical services expenditures	yr	554	1999	30r
Medical supplies, expenditures on	yr	122	1999	30r
Plastic surgery, breast augmentation		3184	2000	7r
Plastic surgery, breast lift		3585	2000	7r
Plastic surgery, facelift		4999	2000	7r
Plastic surgery, hair transplantation		3105	2000	7r
Plastic surgery, lip augmentation		1290	2000	7r
Plastic surgery, lower body lift		8135	2000	7r
Plastic surgery, thigh lift		3839	2000	7r
Household Goods				
Dishwashing powder, Cascade	50 oz	2.89	3/01	4c
Floor coverings, expenditures on	yr	52	1999	30r
Furniture, expenditures on	yr	344	1999	30r
Household furnishings and equipment purchases	yr	1290	1999	30c
Household textiles, expenditures on	yr	109	1999	30r
Laundry and cleaning supplies, expenditures on	yr	134	1999	30r
Tissues, facial, Kleenex brand	175	1.08	3/01	4c
Housing				
Housing, ACCRA Index		93.50	3/01	4c
Home, 2200 sq ft, 4-br, 2-bath, 2-car garage, average		159000	2000	47c
Home price, existing, ave		144400	10/00	90r
Home value, median		89000	2001	53s
House, 2400 sq ft, 8000 sq ft lot, new, urban, utilities	total	190450	3/01	4c
House payment, principal and interest, 25% down payment	mos	958	3/01	4c
Household operation expenditures	yr	619	1999	30c
Housekeeping supplies purchases	yr	378	1999	30c
Housing, expenditures on	yr	11421	1999	30c
Lodging expenditures	yr	430	1999	30r
Maintenance, repairs, insurance expenditures	yr	853	1999	30r
Monthly rental value of owned home	mos	547	1999	30r
Owned dwellings, expenditures own	yr	4194	1999	30c
Rent expenditures	yr	1979	1999	30c
Rent, apartment, 2 br, 1 1/2-2 baths, unfurn, 950 sq ft, water	mos	665	3/01	4c
Rental unit, 1 bedroom, with utilities	mos	496	4/01	41c
Rental unit, 2 bedroom, with utilities	mos	597	4/01	41c
Rental unit, 3 bedroom, with utilities	mos	826	4/01	41c
Rental unit, 4 bedroom, with utilities	mos	915	4/01	41c
Shelter, expenditures on	yr	6538	1999	30c

Values are in dollars or fractions of dollars. In the column headed *Ref*, references are shown to sources. Each reference is followed by a letter. These refer to the geographical level for which data were reported: s=State, r=Region, and c=City or metro. The abbreviation *ex* is used to mean *except* or *excluding*; *exp* stands for *expenditures*. For other abbreviations and further explanations, please see the Introduction.

Kansas City, MO-KS - continued

Item	Per	Value	Date	Ref.
Insurance and Pensions				
Life and other personal insurance purchases	yr	401	1999	30c
Pensions and Social Security, expenditures on	yr	3270	1999	30c
Personal insurance and pensions, expenditures on	yr	3671	1999	30c
Legal Fees				
Driver's license fee	orig	15.00	1999	48s
Driver's license fee	renew	15.00	1999	48s
Fishing license	yr	11.00	4/01	34s
Personal Goods				
Personal care products and services purchases	yr	307	1999	30c
Shampoo, Alberto VO5	15 oz	1.17	3/01	4c
Toothpaste, Crest or Colgate	6-7 oz	2.09	3/01	4c
Personal Services				
Dry cleaning, man's 2-pc suit		7.16	3/01	4c
Man's haircut, barbershop, no styling		11.80	3/01	4c
Personal services, household, expenditures on	yr	300	1999	30r
Woman's shampoo, trim, blow-dry, no style-change		26.20	3/01	4c
Pets				
Pets, toys, and playground equipment, expenditures on	yr	375	1999	30r
Restaurant Food				
Chicken, fried, thigh and drumstick, KFC/Church's		2.97	3/01	4c
Hamburger with cheese, McDonald's	1/4 lb	2.09	3/01	4c
Pizza, Pizza Hut or Pizza Inn	11-12 in	8.99	3/01	4c
Taxes				
Federal income taxes paid	yr	2326	1999	30r
Personal taxes, expenditures on	yr	3223	1999	30r
Property taxes paid	yr	1152	1999	30r
State and local income taxes paid	yr	753	1999	30r
Transportation				
Transportation, ACCRA Index		102.20	3/01	4c
Bus fare, one-way	trip	0.90	2000	1c
Bus fare, to central business district	1-way	1.00	3/01	4c
Cars and trucks, new, expenditures on	yr	1280	1999	30r
Cars and trucks, used, expenditures on	yr	1763	1999	30r
Diesel at the pump	gal	1.16	10/99	73s
Gasoline and motor oil purchases	yr	1155	1999	30c
Gasoline before-tax price (cents)	gal	108.50	10/00	43s
Household transportation expenditures	yr	6489	97-1998	102c
Maintenance and repair expenditures	yr	594	1999	30r
Public transportation, expenditures on	yr	303	1999	30c
Tire balance, computer or spin balance, front	wheel	8.80	3/01	4c
Transportation purchases	yr	7789	1999	30c
Vehicle expenses, miscellaneous, purchases	yr	2383	1999	30c
Vehicle insurance payments	yr	701	1999	30r
Vehicle purchases (net outlay)	yr	3948	1999	30c
Vehicle rental, lease expenditures	yr	536	1999	30r
Utilities				
Utilities, ACCRA Index		94.00	3/01	4c
Electrical bill, average	mos	68.50	9/00	9s
Electricity, expenditures on	yr	841	1999	30r
Electricity, summer, 250 KWh	mos	24.67	2/96	97c
Electricity, summer, 500 KWh	mos	43.52	2/96	97c
Electricity, summer, 750 KWh	mos	62.37	2/96	97c
Electricity, summer, 1000 KWh	mos	81.22	2/96	97c
Electricity and other, mixed, 2400 sq ft, new home	mos	55.17	3/01	4c
Electricity cost, average	KWh	6.00	9/00	9s
Utilities, fuels, and public services purchased	yr	2401	1999	30r
Water and other public services, expenditures on	yr	273	1999	30r
Water price	100 cf	1.42	2000	109c
Water price, dwelling unit	mos	27.78	2000	109c

Kansas City, MO-KS - continued

Item	Per	Value	Date	Ref.
Weddings				
Wedding (national average cost)		19936	2000	33r
Wedding (regional average total cost)		16195	1997	110r
Attendants' gifts		321	1998	33r
Bridal attendants' apparel (5 persons)		824	2000	33r
Bride's headpiece/veil		173	1998	33r
Bride's wedding dress		859	1998	33r
Clergy, religious facility fee		242	1998	33r
Engagement ring		3177	1998	33r
Flowers		789	1998	33r
Groom's formalwear rental		99	2000	33r
Limousine		410	1998	33r
Marriage license cost		50.00	4/01	35s
Men's formalwear (ushers, best man)		469	2000	33r
Mother of bride apparel		241	2000	33r
Music		866	1998	33r
Photography and videography		1368	1998	33r
Rehearsal dinner		728	1998	33r
Wedding invitations and announcements		341	1998	33r
Wedding reception		7968	2000	33r
Wedding rings (bride and groom)		1060	1998	33r

Kenosha, WI

Item	Per	Value	Date	Ref.
Average annual expenditures	yr	35369	1999	30r
Alcoholic Beverages				
Alcoholic beverage purchases	yr	304	1999	30r
Malt beverages, all types, all sizes, any origin	16 oz	0.93	7/01	11r
Wine, red and white table, all sizes, any origin	liter	7.04	7/01	11r
Appliances				
Major appliances, expenditures on	yr	165	1999	30r
Small appliances, housewares, expenditures on	yr	90	1999	30r
Banking and Money				
Mortgage interest and charges paid	yr	2277	1999	30r
Mortgage principal paid on owned property	yr	1230	1999	30r
Vehicle finance charges paid	yr	328	1999	30r
Charity				
Cash contributions, expenditures	yr	1126	1999	30r
Child Care				
Child raising cost, total, age 0-2	yr	7890	1999	60r
Child raising cost, total, age 3-5	yr	8130	1999	60r
Child raising cost, total, age 6-8	yr	8170	1999	60r
Child raising cost, total, age 9-11	yr	8190	1999	60r
Child raising cost, total, age 12-14	yr	8890	1999	60r
Child raising cost, total, age 15-17	yr	9050	1999	60r
Child's child care and education, age 0-2	yr	1240	1999	60r
Child's child care and education, age 3-5	yr	1370	1999	60r
Child's child care and education, age 6-8	yr	880	1999	60r
Child's child care and education, age 9-11	yr	570	1999	60r
Child's child care and education, age 12-14	yr	420	1999	60r
Child's child care and education, age 15-17	yr	720	1999	60r
Child's clothing, age 0-2	yr	410	1999	60r
Child's clothing, age 3-5	yr	400	1999	60r
Child's clothing, age 6-8	yr	450	1999	60r
Child's clothing, age 9-11	yr	500	1999	60r
Child's clothing, age 12-14	yr	840	1999	60r
Child's clothing, age 15-17	yr	740	1999	60r
Child's food, age 0-2	yr	960	1999	60r
Child's food, age 3-5	yr	1120	1999	60r
Child's food, age 6-8	yr	1430	1999	60r
Child's food, age 9-11	yr	1710	1999	60r
Child's food, age 12-14	yr	1710	1999	60r
Child's food, age 15-17	yr	1920	1999	60r
Child's health care, age 0-2	yr	520	1999	60r
Child's health care, age 3-5	yr	500	1999	60r
Child's health care, age 6-8	yr	570	1999	60r
Child's health care, age 9-11	yr	610	1999	60r
Child's health care, age 12-14	yr	630	1999	60r

Values are in dollars or fractions of dollars. In the column headed *Ref*, references are shown to sources. Each reference is followed by a letter. These refer to the geographical level for which data were reported: s=State, r=Region, and c=City or metro. The abbreviation *ex* is used to mean *except* or *excluding*; *exp* stands for expenditures. For other abbreviations and further explanations, please see the Introduction.

Kenosha, WI - continued

Item	Per	Value	Date	Ref.
Child Care				
Child's health care, age 15-17	yr	650	1999	60r
Child's housing, age 0-2	yr	2860	1999	60r
Child's housing, age 3-5	yr	2840	1999	60r
Child's housing, age 6-8	yr	2800	1999	60r
Child's housing, age 9-11	yr	2650	1999	60r
Child's housing, age 12-14	yr	2840	1999	60r
Child's housing, age 15-17	yr	2440	1999	60r
Child's personal care, reading, age 0-2	yr	880	1999	60r
Child's personal care, reading, age 3-5	yr	900	1999	60r
Child's personal care, reading, age 6-8	yr	930	1999	60r
Child's personal care, reading, age 9-11	yr	970	1999	60r
Child's personal care, reading, age 12-14	yr	1150	1999	60r
Child's personal care, reading, age 15-17	yr	920	1999	60r
Clothing				
Apparel and services purchases	yr	1607	1999	30r
Boys, 2 to 15, expenditures on	yr	91	1999	30r
Children under 2, expenditures on	yr	59	1999	30r
Footwear, expenditures on	yr	285	1999	30r
Girls, 2 to 15, expenditures on	yr	116	1999	30r
Men and boys, expenditures on	yr	433	1999	30r
Men, 16 and over, expenditures on	yr	341	1999	30r
Women, 16 and over, expenditures on	yr	490	1999	30r
Communications				
Cable modem installation, Bresnan		99.95	6/99	103s
Cable modem installation, Marcus		499.00	6/99	103s
Cable modem rate, cable subscriber, Bresnan	mos	39.95	6/99	103s
Cable modem rate, cable subscriber, Marcus	mos	14.95-49.95	6/99	103s
Cable modem rate, non-cable subscriber, Bresnan	mos	49.95	6/99	103s
Cable modem rate, non-cable subscriber, Marcus	mos	60.95	6/99	103s
Phone line, single, business, field visit	inst.	64.65	12/97	17s
Phone line, single, business, no field visit	inst.	64.65	12/97	17s
Phone line, single, residence, field visit	inst.	33.05	12/97	17s
Phone line, single, residence, no field visit	inst.	33.05	12/97	17s
Postage and stationery, expenditures on	yr	140	1999	30r
Postal rate, express mail, up to half-pound		12.45	7/01	108r
Postal rate, letter, first class, first ounce		0.34	7/01	108r
Postal rate, letter, two ounces		0.57	7/01	108r
Postal rate, post card		0.21	7/01	108r
Postal rate, priority mail, two pounds		3.95	7/01	108r
Postal rate, priority mail, up to one pound		3.50	7/01	108r
Telephone services, expenditures on	yr	830	1999	30r
Education				
Board, 4-year private college/university	yr	2271	1996	38s
Board, 4-year public college/university	yr	1527	1996	38s
Education expenditures	yr	583	1999	30r
Room, 4-year private college/university	yr	1812	1996	38s
Room, 4-year public college/university	yr	1706	1996	38s
Total cost, 4-year private college/university	yr	15652	1996	38s
Total cost, 4-year public college/university	yr	5847	1996	38s
Tuition, 2-year public college/university, in state	yr	1840	1996	38s
Tuition, 4-year private college/university, in state	yr	11569	1996	38s
Tuition, 4-year public college/university	yr	2614	1996	38s
Energy and Fuels				
Electricity	500 KWhs	46.59	7/01	11r
Fuel oil #2	gal	1.27	7/01	11r
Fuel oil and other fuels, expenditures on	yr	68	1999	30r
Gas, natural, commercial rate	1000 cf	7.32	11/00	88s
Gasoline, unleaded midgrade	gal	1.79	7/01	11r
Gasoline, unleaded premium	gal	1.86	7/01	11r
Gasoline, unleaded regular	gal	1.58	7/01	11r
Natural gas, expenditures on	yr	389	1999	30r
Utility (piped) gas, therm		0.81	7/01	11r
Utility (piped) gas, 40 therms		38.01	7/01	11r

Kenosha, WI - continued

Item	Per	Value	Date	Ref.
Energy and Fuels - continued				
Utility (piped) gas, 100 therms		81.75	7/01	11r
Entertainment				
Entertainment purchases	yr	1984	1999	30r
Fees and admissions paid	yr	444	1999	30r
Television, radios, sound equipment, expenditures on	yr	580	1999	30r
Funerals				
Cosmetology, hair, other preparation		178.32	1/99	78r
Embalming		408.19	1/99	78r
Funeral at funeral home		362.13	1/99	78r
Professional service charges		1375.51	1/99	78r
Transfer of remains to funeral home		155.92	1/99	78r
Visitation/viewing		294.38	1/99	78r
Groceries				
Bacon, sliced	lb	3.15	7/01	11r
Bakery products, expenditures on	yr	281	1999	30r
Bananas	lb	0.48	7/01	11r
Beans, dried, any type, all sizes	lb	0.61	7/01	11r
Beef for stew, boneless	lb	3.08	7/01	11r
Beef, expenditures on	yr	217	1999	30r
Bologna, all beef or mixed	lb	2.52	7/01	11r
Bread, white, pan	lb	1.06	7/01	11r
Broccoli	lb	0.91	7/01	11r
Butter, salted, grade AA, stick	lb	3.04	7/01	11r
Butter, yoghurt, cheese, etc, expenditures on	yr	183	1999	30r
Cereals and bakery product purchases	yr	430	1999	30r
Cereals and cereal products, expenditures on	yr	149	1999	30r
Chicken, fresh, whole	lb	1.07	7/01	11r
Chops, boneless,	lb	3.64	7/01	11r
Chuck roast, U.S. choice, boneless	lb	2.47	7/01	11r
Coffee, 100%, ground roast, all sizes	lb	2.69	7/01	11r
Cookies, chocolate chip	lb	2.87	7/01	11r
Dairy product purchases	yr	304	1999	30r
Eggs, expenditures on	yr	26	1999	30r
Eggs, grade A, large	dozen	0.88	7/01	11r
Fats and oils, expenditures on	yr	75	1999	30r
Fish and seafood, expenditures on	yr	72	1999	30r
Food (excl fruit and vegetables), eaten at home, purchases	yr	887	1999	30r
Food cooked on trips, expenditures on	yr	44	1999	30r
Food purchases	yr	4802	1999	30r
Food purchases, eaten away from home	yr	2069	1999	30r
Food purchases, food eaten at home	yr	2733	1999	30r
Fresh fruits, expenditures on	yr	138	1999	30r
Fresh milk and cream, expenditures on	yr	120	1999	30r
Fresh vegetables, expenditures on	yr	126	1999	30r
Grapefruit	lb	0.66	7/01	11r
Grapes, Thompson, seedless	lb	1.64	7/01	11r
Ground beef, 100% beef	lb	1.64	7/01	11r
Ground beef, lean and extra lean	lb	2.16	7/01	11r
Ground chuck, 100% beef	lb	2.13	7/01	11r
Ham, boneless, excl canned	lb	2.62	7/01	11r
Ice cream, prepackaged, bulk, regular	1/2 gal	3.35	7/01	11r
Lemons	lb	1.19	7/01	11r
Lettuce, iceberg	lb	0.73	7/01	11r
Margarine, soft, tubs	lb	0.89	7/01	11r
Meats, poultry, fish, and egg purchases	yr	671	1999	30r
Milk, fresh, whole, fortified	gal	2.71	7/01	11r
Nonalcoholic beverages, expenditures on	yr	239	1999	30r
Oranges, Navel	lb	0.80	7/01	11r
Oranges, Valencia	lb	0.66	7/01	11r
Pears, Anjou	lb	0.93	7/01	11r
Pork chops, center cut, bone-in	lb	3.63	7/01	11r
Pork, expenditures on	yr	150	1999	30r
Potato chips	16 oz	3.52	7/01	11r
Potatoes, frozen, french fried	lb	1.08	7/01	11r
Potatoes, white, all types	lb	0.33	7/01	11r
Poultry, expenditures on	yr	108	1999	30r
Processed fruits, expenditures on	yr	98	1999	30r
Processed vegetables, expenditures on	yr	80	1999	30r

Values are in dollars or fractions of dollars. In the column headed *Ref*, references are shown to sources. Each reference is followed by a letter. These refer to the geographical level for which data were reported: s=State, r=Region, and c=City or metro. The abbreviation *ex* is used to mean *except* or *excluding*; *exp* stands for *expenditures*. For other abbreviations and further explanations, please see the Introduction.

Kenosha, WI - continued

Item	Per	Value	Date	Ref.
Groceries				
Round roast, U.S. choice, boneless	lb	3.07	7/01	11r
Round steak, graded and ungraded, excl U.S. prime and choice	lb	3.41	7/01	11r
Shortening, vegetable oil blends	lb	1.13	7/01	11r
Spaghetti and macaroni	lb	0.80	7/01	11r
Steak, round, U.S. choice, boneless	lb	3.23	7/01	11r
Steak, T-bone, U.S. choice, bone-in	lb	6.68	7/01	11r
Strawberries, dry pint	12 oz	1.32	7/01	11r
Sugar and other sweets, expenditures on	yr	114	1999	30r
Sugar, white, 33-80 ounce package	lb	0.42	7/01	11r
Sugar, white, all sizes	lb	0.43	7/01	11r
Tobacco products and smoking supplies purchases	yr	331	1999	30r
Tomatoes, field grown	lb	1.46	7/01	11r
Tuna, light, chunk	lb	1.80	7/01	11r
Turkey, frozen, whole	lb	1.15	7/01	11r
Goods and Services				
B&B Japanese maple (acer japonicum)	gal	29.99-169.99	4/00	93r
Boxwood (buxus)	2 gal	18.99-39.99	4/00	93r
Daylilly (hemerocallis)	gal	4.99-25.00	4/00	93r
Flat of annuals		11.98-24.99	4/00	93r
Fountain grass (pennisetum)	gal	5.98-12.98	4/00	93r
Hanging basket (10 in)		12.99-27.99	4/00	93r
Hardy geranium (geranium)	gal	7.99-9.99	4/00	93r
Hosta (hosta)	gal	6.00-25.00	4/00	93r
Lilac (syrubga vulgaris)	2 gal	14.99-24.99	4/00	93r
Miscellaneous purchases	yr	865	1999	30r
Rhododendron (rhododendron)	2 gal	23.98-42.99	4/00	93r
Sage (salvia)	gal	6.00-9.99	4/00	93r
Wintercreeper euonymus (euonymus fortunei)	2 gal	16.00-169.99	4/00	93r
Hunting license	yr	14.00	4/01	34s
Health Care				
Cardiac catheterization, ave hospital/ physician charges		13240	1998	77s
Childbirth, Cesarean delivery		10722	1997	13r
Childbirth, vaginal delivery		6223	1997	13r
Drugs, expenditures on	yr	394	1999	30r
Health care purchases	yr	2048	1999	30r
Health insurance expenditures	yr	978	1999	30r
Hysterectomy, laproscopically-assisted, ave hospital/physician charges		13270	1998	76s
Hysterectomy, vaginal, ave hospital and physician charges		9170	1998	76s
Laser eye surgery	eye	1950-2400	2000	63s
Medicaid dispensing fee		4.88-40.11	1999	87s
Medical services expenditures	yr	554	1999	30r
Medical supplies, expenditures on	yr	122	1999	30r
Plastic surgery, breast augmentation		3184	2000	7r
Plastic surgery, breast lift		3585	2000	7r
Plastic surgery, facelift		4999	2000	7r
Plastic surgery, hair transplantation		3105	2000	7r
Plastic surgery, lip augmentation		1290	2000	7r
Plastic surgery, lower body lift		8135	2000	7r
Plastic surgery, thigh lift		3839	2000	7r
Household Goods				
Floor coverings, expenditures on	yr	52	1999	30r
Furniture, expenditures on	yr	344	1999	30r

Kenosha, WI - continued

Item	Per	Value	Date	Ref.
Household Goods - continued				
Household furnishings and equipment purchases	yr	1475	1999	30r
Household textiles, expenditures on	yr	109	1999	30r
Laundry and cleaning supplies, expenditures on	yr	134	1999	30r
Housing				
Home price, existing, ave		144400	10/00	90r
Home value, median		117000	2001	53s
Household operation expenditures	yr	542	1999	30r
Housekeeping supplies purchases	yr	508	1999	30r
Lodging expenditures	yr	430	1999	30r
Maintenance, repairs, insurance expenditures	yr	853	1999	30r
Monthly rental value of owned home	mos	547	1999	30r
Owned dwellings, expenditures own	yr	4282	1999	30r
Rent expenditures	yr	1558	1999	30r
Rental unit, 1 bedroom, with utilities	mos	500	4/01	41c
Rental unit, 2 bedroom, with utilities	mos	614	4/01	41c
Rental unit, 3 bedroom, with utilities	mos	844	4/01	41c
Rental unit, 4 bedroom, with utilities	mos	950	4/01	41c
Shelter, expenditures on	yr	6270	1999	30r
Insurance and Pensions				
Auto insurance premium	yr	603.84	1999	57s
Life and other personal insurance purchases	yr	387	1999	30r
Pensions and Social Security, expenditures on	yr	2968	1999	30r
Legal Fees				
Divorce, filing fee		142.00-150.00	4/01	35s
Driver's license fee	renew	12.00	1999	48s
Driver's license fee	orig	18.00	1999	48s
Fishing license	yr	14.00	4/01	34s
Personal Goods				
Personal care products and services purchases	yr	385	1999	30r
Personal Services				
Personal services, household, expenditures on	yr	300	1999	30r
Pets				
Pets, toys, and playground equipment, expenditures on	yr	375	1999	30r
Taxes				
Federal income taxes paid	yr	2326	1999	30r
Personal taxes, expenditures on	yr	3223	1999	30r
Property taxes paid	yr	1152	1999	30r
State and local income taxes paid	yr	753	1999	30r
Transportation				
Bus fare, one-way	trip	1.00	2000	1c
Cars and trucks, new, expenditures on	yr	1280	1999	30r
Cars and trucks, used, expenditures on	yr	1763	1999	30r
Diesel at the pump	gal	1.34	10/99	73s
Gasoline and motor oil purchases	yr	1036	1999	30r
Gasoline before-tax price (cents)	gal	113.40	10/00	43s
Maintenance and repair expenditures	yr	594	1999	30r
Public transportation, expenditures on	yr	341	1999	30r
Transportation purchases	yr	6617	1999	30r
Vehicle expenses, miscellaneous, purchases	yr	2159	1999	30r
Vehicle insurance payments	yr	701	1999	30r
Vehicle purchases (net outlay)	yr	3081	1999	30r
Vehicle rental, lease expenditures	yr	536	1999	30r
Utilities				
Electrical bill, average	mos	52.08	9/00	9s
Electricity, expenditures on	yr	841	1999	30r
Electricity cost, average	KWh	5.69	9/00	9s
Utilities, fuels, and public services purchased	yr	2401	1999	30r
Water and other public services, expenditures on	yr	273	1999	30r

Values are in dollars or fractions of dollars. In the column headed *Ref*, references are shown to sources. Each reference is followed by a letter. These refer to the geographical level for which data were reported: s=State, r=Region, and c=City or metro. The abbreviation *ex* is used to mean *except* or *excluding; exp* stands for expenditures. For other abbreviations and further explanations, please see the Introduction.

Kenosha, WI - continued

Item	Per	Value	Date	Ref.
Weddings				
Wedding (national average cost)		19936	2000	33r
Wedding (regional average total cost)		16195	1997	110r
Attendants' gifts		321	1998	33r
Bridal attendants' apparel (5 persons)		824	2000	33r
Bride's headpiece/veil		173	1998	33r
Bride's wedding dress		859	1998	33r
Clergy, religious facility fee		242	1998	33r
Engagement ring		3177	1998	33r
Flowers		789	1998	33r
Groom's formalwear rental		99	2000	33r
Limousine		410	1998	33r
Marriage license cost		50.00-60.00	4/01	35s
Men's formalwear (ushers, best man)		469	2000	33r
Mother of bride apparel		241	2000	33r
Music		866	1998	33r
Photography and videography		1368	1998	33r
Rehearsal dinner		728	1998	33r
Wedding invitations and announcements		341	1998	33r
Wedding reception		7968	2000	33r
Wedding rings (bride and groom)		1060	1998	33r

Killeen-Temple, TX

Item	Per	Value	Date	Ref.
Alcoholic Beverages				
Alcoholic beverage purchases	yr	253	1999	30r
Malt beverages, all types, all sizes, any origin	16 oz	0.96	7/01	11r
Appliances				
Major appliances, expenditures on	yr	172	1999	30r
Small appliances, housewares, expenditures on	yr	81	1999	30r
Banking and Money				
Mortgage interest and charges paid	yr	2039	1999	30r
Mortgage principal paid on owned property	yr	1026	1999	30r
Vehicle finance charges paid	yr	365	1999	30r
Charity				
Cash contributions, expenditures	yr	1127	1999	30r
Child Care				
Child raising cost, total, age 0-2	yr	8540	1999	60r
Child raising cost, total, age 3-5	yr	8780	1999	60r
Child raising cost, total, age 6-8	yr	8820	1999	60r
Child raising cost, total, age 9-11	yr	8800	1999	60r
Child raising cost, total, age 12-14	yr	9510	1999	60r
Child raising cost, total, age 15-17	yr	9740	1999	60r
Child's child care and education, age 0-2	yr	1380	1999	60r
Child's child care and education, age 3-5	yr	1520	1999	60r
Child's child care and education, age 6-8	yr	990	1999	60r
Child's child care and education, age 9-11	yr	650	1999	60r
Child's child care and education, age 12-14	yr	490	1999	60r
Child's child care and education, age 15-17	yr	840	1999	60r
Child's clothing, age 0-2	yr	480	1999	60r
Child's clothing, age 3-5	yr	470	1999	60r
Child's clothing, age 6-8	yr	520	1999	60r
Child's clothing, age 9-11	yr	570	1999	60r
Child's clothing, age 12-14	yr	950	1999	60r
Child's clothing, age 15-17	yr	850	1999	60r
Child's food, age 0-2	yr	1000	1999	60r
Child's food, age 3-5	yr	1160	1999	60r
Child's food, age 6-8	yr	1490	1999	60r
Child's food, age 9-11	yr	1770	1999	60r
Child's food, age 12-14	yr	1770	1999	60r
Child's food, age 15-17	yr	1980	1999	60r
Child's health care, age 0-2	yr	620	1999	60r
Child's health care, age 3-5	yr	590	1999	60r
Child's health care, age 6-8	yr	680	1999	60r
Child's health care, age 9-11	yr	720	1999	60r
Child's health care, age 12-14	yr	730	1999	60r
Child's health care, age 15-17	yr	760	1999	60r
Child's housing, age 0-2	yr	3070	1999	60r

Item	Per	Value	Date	Ref.
Child Care - continued				
Child's housing, age 3-5	yr	3050	1999	60r
Child's housing, age 6-8	yr	3010	1999	60r
Child's housing, age 9-11	yr	2850	1999	60r
Child's housing, age 12-14	yr	3040	1999	60r
Child's housing, age 15-17	yr	2650	1999	60r
Child's personal care, reading, age 0-2	yr	910	1999	60r
Child's personal care, reading, age 3-5	yr	930	1999	60r
Child's personal care, reading, age 6-8	yr	960	1999	60r
Child's personal care, reading, age 9-11	yr	1000	1999	60r
Child's personal care, reading, age 12-14	yr	1170	1999	60r
Child's personal care, reading, age 15-17	yr	950	1999	60r
Clothing				
Apparel and services purchases	yr	1610	1999	30r
Boys, 2 to 15, expenditures on	yr	89	1999	30r
Children under 2, expenditures on	yr	79	1999	30r
Footwear, expenditures on	yr	283	1999	30r
Girls, 2 to 15, expenditures on	yr	103	1999	30r
Men and boys, expenditures on	yr	351	1999	30r
Men, 16 and over, expenditures on	yr	262	1999	30r
Women, 16 and over, expenditures on	yr	538	1999	30r
Communications				
Cable modem installation, AT&T-BIS		150.00	6/99	103s
Cable modem installation, Marcus		499.00	6/99	103s
Cable modem installation, Time Warner		75.00-225.00	6/99	103s
Cable modem rate, cable subscriber, AT&T-BIS	mos	39.95	6/99	103s
Cable modem rate, cable subscriber, Marcus	mos	14.95-49.95	6/99	103s
Cable modem rate, cable subscriber, Time Warner	mos	39.95-49.95	6/99	103s
Cable modem rate, non-cable subscriber, Marcus	mos	60.95	6/99	103s
Cable modem rate, non-cable subscriber, Time Warner	mos	39.95-54.95	6/99	103s
Phone line, single, business, field visit	inst.	71.90	12/97	17s
Phone line, single, business, no field visit	inst.	57.30	12/97	17s
Phone line, single, residence, field visit	inst.	52.95	12/97	17s
Phone line, single, residence, no field visit	inst.	38.35	12/97	17s
Postage and stationery, expenditures on	yr	104	1999	30r
Postal rate, express mail, up to half-pound		12.45	7/01	108r
Postal rate, letter, first class, first ounce		0.34	7/01	108r
Postal rate, letter, two ounces		0.57	7/01	108r
Postal rate, post card		0.21	7/01	108r
Postal rate, priority mail, two pounds		3.95	7/01	108r
Postal rate, priority mail, up to one pound		3.50	7/01	108r
Telephone services, expenditures on	yr	860	1999	30r
Education				
Board, 4-year private college/university	yr	2198	1996	38s
Board, 4-year public college/university	yr	1759	1996	38s
Education expenditures	yr	431	1999	30r
Room, 4-year private college/university	yr	2000	1996	38s
Room, 4-year public college/university	yr	1885	1996	38s
Total cost, 4-year private college/university	yr	13156	1996	38s
Total cost, 4-year public college/university	yr	5464	1996	38s
Tuition, 2-year public college/university, in state	yr	771	1996	38s
Tuition, 4-year private college/university, in state	yr	8959	1996	38s
Tuition, 4-year public college/university	yr	1820	1996	38s
Energy and Fuels				
Electricity	KWh	0.09	7/01	11r
Electricity	500 KWhs	47.29	7/01	11r
Fuel oil #2	gal	1.43	7/01	11r
Fuel oil and other fuels, expenditures on	yr	45	1999	30r
Gas, natural, commercial rate	1000 cf	6.94	11/00	88s
Gasoline, all types	gal	1.60	7/01	11r
Gasoline, unleaded midgrade	gal	1.65	7/01	11r
Gasoline, unleaded premium	gal	1.74	7/01	11r

Values are in dollars or fractions of dollars. In the column headed *Ref*, references are shown to sources. Each reference is followed by a letter. These refer to the geographical level for which data were reported: s=State, r=Region, and c=City or metro. The abbreviation *ex* is used to mean *except* or *excluding*; *exp* stands for expenditures. For other abbreviations and further explanations, please see the Introduction.

Killeen-Temple, TX - continued

Item	Per	Value	Date	Ref.
Energy and Fuels				
Natural gas, expenditures on	yr	164	1999	30r
Utility (piped) gas, therm		1.01	7/01	11r
Utility (piped) gas, 40 therms		44.29	7/01	11r
Utility (piped) gas, 100 therms		97.44	7/01	11r
Entertainment				
Entertainment purchases	yr	1574	1999	30r
Fees and admissions paid	yr	371	1999	30r
Reading purchases	yr	121	1999	30r
Television, radios, sound equipment, expenditures on	yr	561	1999	30r
Funerals				
Total cost of funeral		5842.28	1/99	78r
Acknowledgement cards		28.35	1/99	78r
Casket		2494.29	1/99	78r
Cosmetology, hair, other preparation		109.22	1/99	78r
Embalming		361.42	1/99	78r
Funeral at funeral home		349.20	1/99	78r
Hearse (local)		161.91	1/99	78r
Professional service charges		1116.50	1/99	78r
Service car/van		65.56	1/99	78r
Transfer of remains to funeral home		143.56	1/99	78r
Vault		785.25	1/99	78r
Visitation/viewing		227.02	1/99	78r
Groceries				
American processed cheese	lb	3.50	7/01	11r
Bakery products, expenditures on	yr	261	1999	30r
Bananas	lb	0.47	7/01	11r
Beans, dried, any type, all sizes	lb	0.63	7/01	11r
Beef for stew, boneless	lb	2.86	7/01	11r
Beef, expenditures on	yr	210	1999	30r
Bologna, all beef or mixed	lb	2.29	7/01	11r
Bread, French	lb	1.66	7/01	11r
Bread, white, pan	lb	0.87	7/01	11r
Bread, whole wheat, pan	lb	1.38	7/01	11r
Broccoli	lb	1.04	7/01	11r
Butter, salted, grade AA, stick	lb	2.26	7/01	11r
Butter, yoghurt, cheese, etc, expenditures on	yr	170	1999	30r
Cabbage	lb	0.42	7/01	11r
Cereals and cereal products, expenditures on	yr	140	1999	30r
Cheddar cheese, natural	lb	3.75	7/01	11r
Chicken breast, bone-in	lb	1.85	7/01	11r
Chicken legs, bone-in	lb	1.34	7/01	11r
Chicken, fresh, whole	lb	1.05	7/01	11r
Chops, boneless,	lb	4.13	7/01	11r
Chuck roast, graded and ungraded, excl U.S. prime and choice	lb	2.35	7/01	11r
Chuck roast, U.S. choice, boneless	lb	2.67	7/01	11r
Coffee, 100%, ground roast, all sizes	lb	2.88	7/01	11r
Coffee, instant, plain, regular, all sizes	16 oz	9.25	7/01	11r
Cola, non diet,	2 liter	1.11	7/01	11r
Crackers, soda, salted	lb	1.70	7/01	11r
Dairy product purchases	yr	282	1999	30r
Eggs, expenditures on	yr	32	1999	30r
Fats and oils, expenditures on	yr	79	1999	30r
Fish and seafood, expenditures on	yr	99	1999	30r
Flour, white, all purpose	lb	0.32	7/01	11r
Food (excl fruit and vegetables), eaten at home, purchases	yr	815	1999	30r
Food cooked on trips, expenditures on	yr	36	1999	30r
Food purchases	yr	4533	1999	30r
Food purchases, eaten away from home	yr	1873	1999	30r
Food purchases, food eaten at home	yr	2660	1999	30r
Fresh fruits, expenditures on	yr	128	1999	30r
Fresh milk and cream, expenditures on	yr	112	1999	30r
Fresh vegetables, expenditures on	yr	131	1999	30r
Fruit and vegetable purchases	yr	438	1999	30r
Grapefruit	lb	0.59	7/01	11r
Grapes, Thompson, seedless	lb	2.12	7/01	11r
Ground beef, 100% beef	lb	1.76	7/01	11r
Ground beef, lean and extra lean	lb	2.60	7/01	11r

Killeen-Temple, TX - continued

Item	Per	Value	Date	Ref.
Groceries - continued				
Ground chuck, 100% beef	lb	2.08	7/01	11r
Ham, boneless, excl canned	lb	2.71	7/01	11r
Ham, rump or shank half, bone-in, smoked	lb	2.19	7/01	11r
Ice cream, prepackaged, bulk, regular	1/2 gal	3.93	7/01	11r
Lemons	lb	1.32	7/01	11r
Lettuce, iceberg	lb	0.76	7/01	11r
Milk, fresh, low fat,	gal	2.75	7/01	11r
Milk, fresh, whole, fortified	gal	2.97	7/01	11r
Nonalcoholic beverages, expenditures on	yr	228	1999	30r
Orange juice, frozen concentrate	16 oz	1.95	7/01	11r
Oranges, Navel	lb	0.73	7/01	11r
Oranges, Valencia	lb	0.55	7/01	11r
Peanut butter, creamy, all sizes	lb	1.83	7/01	11r
Pears, Anjou	lb	0.98	7/01	11r
Pork chops, center cut, bone-in	lb	3.33	7/01	11r
Pork sausage, fresh, loose	lb	2.59	7/01	11r
Pork shoulder picnic, bone-in, smoked	lb	1.12	7/01	11r
Pork, expenditures on	yr	162	1999	30r
Potato chips	16 oz	3.59	7/01	11r
Potatoes, frozen, french fried	lb	1.00	7/01	11r
Potatoes, white, all types	lb	0.44	7/01	11r
Poultry, expenditures on	yr	137	1999	30r
Processed fruits, expenditures on	yr	97	1999	30r
Processed vegetables, expenditures on	yr	82	1999	30r
Rice, white, long grain, uncooked	lb	0.51	7/01	11r
Round roast, graded and ungraded, excl U.S. prime and choice	lb	2.96	7/01	11r
Round steak, graded and ungraded, excl U.S. prime and choice	lb	3.11	7/01	11r
Sirloin steak, graded and ungraded, excl U.S. prime and choice	lb	4.23	7/01	11r
Spaghetti and macaroni	lb	0.78	7/01	11r
Steak, round, U.S. choice, boneless	lb	3.56	7/01	11r
Steak, sirloin, U.S. choice, boneless	lb	5.65	7/01	11r
Strawberries, dry pint	12 oz	1.50	7/01	11r
Sugar and other sweets, expenditures on	yr	99	1999	30r
Sugar, white, 33-80 ounce package	lb	0.39	7/01	11r
Sugar, white, all sizes	lb	0.42	7/01	11r
Tobacco products and smoking supplies purchases	yr	288	1999	30r
Tomatoes, field grown	lb	1.43	7/01	11r
Tuna, light, chunk	lb	1.77	7/01	11r
Turkey, frozen, whole	lb	1.05	7/01	11r
Goods and Services				
B&B Japanese maple (acer japonicum)	gal	79.98-99.00	4/00	93r
Boxwood (buxus)	2 gal	12.98-18.99	4/00	93r
Christmas tree, noble fir		40-60	2000	65s
Daylily (hemerocallis)	gal	7.96-11.00	4/00	93r
Flat of annuals		13.99-27.99	4/00	93r
Fountain grass (pennisetum)	gal	6.96-9.00	4/00	93r
Hanging basket (10 in)		9.99-24.99	4/00	93r
Hardy geranium (geranium)	gal	5.96-8.00	4/00	93r
Hosta (hosta)	gal	8.96-12.99	4/00	93r
Lilac (syrubga vulgaris)	2 gal	13.00-19.99	4/00	93r
Rhododendron (rhododendron)	2 gal	12.98-29.99	4/00	93r
Sage (salvia)	gal	5.96-8.00	4/00	93r
Wintercreeper euonymus (euonymus fortunei)	2 gal	13.00-18.99	4/00	93r
Hunting license	yr	19.00	4/01	34s

Values are in dollars or fractions of dollars. In the column headed *Ref*, references are shown to sources. Each reference is followed by a letter. These refer to the geographical level for which data were reported: s=State, r=Region, and c=City or metro. The abbreviation *ex* is used to mean *except* or *excluding*; *exp* stands for *expenditures*. For other abbreviations and further explanations, please see the Introduction.

Killeen-Temple, TX - continued

Item	Per	Value	Date	Ref.
Health Care				
Cardiac catheterization, ave hospital/ physician charges		20140	1998	77s
Childbirth, Cesarean delivery		11587	1997	13r
Childbirth, vaginal delivery		6725	1997	13r
Drugs, expenditures on	yr	399	1999	30r
Health care purchases	yr	1971	1999	30r
Health insurance expenditures	yr	933	1999	30r
Hysterectomy, laproscopically-assisted, ave hospital/physician charges		15700	1998	76s
Hysterectomy, vaginal, ave hospital and physician charges		12180	1998	76s
Medicaid dispensing fee		5.27	1999	87s
Medical services expenditures	yr	547	1999	30r
Medical supplies, expenditures on	yr	91	1999	30r
Household Goods				
Floor coverings, expenditures on	yr	44	1999	30r
Furniture, expenditures on	yr	335	1999	30r
Household furnishings and equipment purchases	yr	1328	1999	30r
Household textiles, expenditures on	yr	89	1999	30r
Laundry and cleaning supplies, expenditures on	yr	113	1999	30r
Housing				
Home price, existing, ave		160100	10/00	90r
Home value, median		112000	2001	53s
Household operation expenditures	yr	553	1999	30r
Housekeeping supplies purchases	yr	473	1999	30r
Housing, expenditures on	yr	10303	1999	30r
Maintenance, repairs, insurance expenditures	yr	699	1999	30r
Monthly rental value of owned home	mos	505	1999	30r
Owned dwellings, expenditures own	yr	3465	1999	30r
Rent expenditures	yr	1641	1999	30r
Rental unit, 1 bedroom, with utilities	mos	418	4/01	41c
Rental unit, 2 bedroom, with utilities	mos	529	4/01	41c
Rental unit, 3 bedroom, with utilities	mos	735	4/01	41c
Rental unit, 4 bedroom, with utilities	mos	808	4/01	41c
Shelter, expenditures on	yr	5467	1999	30r
Insurance and Pensions				
Life and other personal insurance purchases	yr	414	1999	30r
Pensions and Social Security, expenditures on	yr	2635	1999	30r
Personal insurance and pensions, expenditures on	yr	3048	1999	30r
Legal Fees				
Divorce, filing fee		150.00-200.00	4/01	35s
Driver's license fee	renew	20.00	1999	48s
Driver's license fee	orig	24.00	1999	48s
Fishing license	yr	19.00	4/01	34s
Personal Goods				
Personal care products and services purchases	yr	393	1999	30r
Personal Services				
Personal services, household, expenditures on	yr	258	1999	30r
Pets				
Pets, toys, and playground equipment, expenditures on	yr	306	1999	30r
Taxes				
Federal income taxes paid	yr	2047	1999	30r
Personal taxes, expenditures on	yr	2554	1999	30r
Property taxes paid	yr	726	1999	30r
State and local income taxes paid	yr	363	1999	30r
Transportation				
Cars and trucks, new, expenditures on	yr	1648	1999	30r
Cars and trucks, used, expenditures on	yr	1651	1999	30r

Killeen-Temple, TX - continued

Item	Per	Value	Date	Ref.
Transportation - continued				
Diesel at the pump	gal	1.18	10/99	73s
Gasoline and motor oil purchases	yr	1052	1999	30r
Gasoline before-tax price (cents)	gal	101.30	10/00	43s
Maintenance and repair expenditures	yr	621	1999	30r
Public transportation, expenditures on	yr	298	1999	30r
Transportation purchases	yr	6738	1999	30r
Vehicle expenses, miscellaneous, purchases	yr	2033	1999	30r
Vehicle insurance payments	yr	696	1999	30r
Vehicle purchases (net outlay)	yr	3354	1999	30r
Vehicle rental, lease expenditures	yr	352	1999	30r
Utilities				
Electrical bill, average	mos	87.17	9/00	9s
Electricity, expenditures on	yr	1115	1999	30r
Electricity cost, average	KWh	6.48	9/00	9s
Water and other public services, expenditures on	yr	298	1999	30r
Weddings				
Wedding (national average cost)		19936	2000	33r
Attendants' gifts		321	1998	33r
Bridal attendants' apparel (5 persons)		824	2000	33r
Bride's headpiece/veil		173	1998	33r
Bride's wedding dress		859	1998	33r
Clergy, religious facility fee		242	1998	33r
Engagement ring		3177	1998	33r
Flowers		789	1998	33r
Groom's formalwear rental		99	2000	33r
Limousine		410	1998	33r
Marriage license cost		36.00	4/01	35s
Men's formalwear (ushers, best man)		469	2000	33r
Mother of bride apparel		241	2000	33r
Music		866	1998	33r
Photography and videography		1368	1998	33r
Rehearsal dinner		728	1998	33r
Wedding invitations and announcements		341	1998	33r
Wedding reception		7968	2000	33r
Wedding rings (bride and groom)		1060	1998	33r

Knoxville, TN

Item	Per	Value	Date	Ref.
Composite, ACCRA index		92.50	3/01	4c
Alcoholic Beverages				
Alcoholic beverage purchases	yr	253	1999	30r
Beer, Heineken, 12-oz, ex deposit	6	7.27	3/01	4c
J & B Scotch	750-ml	23.09	3/01	4c
Malt beverages, all types, all sizes, any origin	16 oz	0.96	7/01	11r
Wine, Livingston or Gallo, Chablis blanc	1.5 liter	5.88	3/01	4c
Appliances				
Appliance repair, service call, washing machine	min lab chg	43.74	3/01	4c
Major appliances, expenditures on	yr	172	1999	30r
Small appliances, housewares, expenditures on	yr	81	1999	30r
Banking and Money				
Mortgage interest and charges paid	yr	2039	1999	30r
Mortgage principal paid on owned property	yr	1026	1999	30r
Mortgage rate, incl. points and orig. fee, 30-yr. conv. fixed or ARM	mos	6.87	3/01	4c
Vehicle finance charges paid	yr	365	1999	30r
Business Expenses				
Business travel, car rental	day	55	2001	3c
Business travel, food	day	41	2001	3c
Business travel, hotel	day	109	2001	3c
Charity				
Cash contributions, expenditures	yr	1127	1999	30r
Child Care				
Child raising cost, total, age 0-2	yr	8540	1999	60r
Child raising cost, total, age 3-5	yr	8780	1999	60r

Values are in dollars or fractions of dollars. In the column headed *Ref*, references are shown to sources. Each reference is followed by a letter. These refer to the geographical level for which data were reported: s=State, r=Region, and c=City or metro. The abbreviation *ex* is used to mean *except* or *excluding*; *exp* stands for *expenditures*. For other abbreviations and further explanations, please see the Introduction.

Knoxville, TN - continued

Item	Per	Value	Date	Ref.
Child Care				
Child raising cost, total, age 6-8	yr	8820	1999	60r
Child raising cost, total, age 9-11	yr	8800	1999	60r
Child raising cost, total, age 12-14	yr	9510	1999	60r
Child raising cost, total, age 15-17	yr	9740	1999	60r
Child's child care and education, age 0-2	yr	1380	1999	60r
Child's child care and education, age 3-5	yr	1520	1999	60r
Child's child care and education, age 6-8	yr	990	1999	60r
Child's child care and education, age 9-11	yr	650	1999	60r
Child's child care and education, age 12-14	yr	490	1999	60r
Child's child care and education, age 15-17	yr	840	1999	60r
Child's clothing, age 0-2	yr	480	1999	60r
Child's clothing, age 3-5	yr	470	1999	60r
Child's clothing, age 6-8	yr	520	1999	60r
Child's clothing, age 9-11	yr	570	1999	60r
Child's clothing, age 12-14	yr	950	1999	60r
Child's clothing, age 15-17	yr	850	1999	60r
Child's food, age 0-2	yr	1000	1999	60r
Child's food, age 3-5	yr	1160	1999	60r
Child's food, age 6-8	yr	1490	1999	60r
Child's food, age 9-11	yr	1770	1999	60r
Child's food, age 12-14	yr	1770	1999	60r
Child's food, age 15-17	yr	1980	1999	60r
Child's health care, age 0-2	yr	620	1999	60r
Child's health care, age 3-5	yr	590	1999	60r
Child's health care, age 6-8	yr	680	1999	60r
Child's health care, age 9-11	yr	720	1999	60r
Child's health care, age 12-14	yr	730	1999	60r
Child's health care, age 15-17	yr	760	1999	60r
Child's housing, age 0-2	yr	3070	1999	60r
Child's housing, age 3-5	yr	3050	1999	60r
Child's housing, age 6-8	yr	3010	1999	60r
Child's housing, age 9-11	yr	2850	1999	60r
Child's housing, age 12-14	yr	3040	1999	60r
Child's housing, age 15-17	yr	2650	1999	60r
Child's personal care, reading, age 0-2	yr	910	1999	60r
Child's personal care, reading, age 3-5	yr	930	1999	60r
Child's personal care, reading, age 6-8	yr	960	1999	60r
Child's personal care, reading, age 9-11	yr	1000	1999	60r
Child's personal care, reading, age 12-14	yr	1170	1999	60r
Child's personal care, reading, age 15-17	yr	950	1999	60r
Clothing				
Apparel and services purchases	yr	1610	1999	30r
Boys' brief, cotton	3	3.18	3/01	4c
Boys, 2 to 15, expenditures on	yr	89	1999	30r
Children under 2, expenditures on	yr	79	1999	30r
Footwear, expenditures on	yr	283	1999	30r
Girls, 2 to 15, expenditures on	yr	103	1999	30r
Men and boys, expenditures on	yr	351	1999	30r
Men, 16 and over, expenditures on	yr	262	1999	30r
Shirt, man's dress shirt		25.11	3/01	4c
Slacks, man's "No Wrinkles" khaki		34.59	3/01	4c
Women, 16 and over, expenditures on	yr	538	1999	30r
Communications				
Cable modem installation, Intermedia		149.95	6/99	103s
Cable modem installation, Time Warner		75.00-225.00	6/99	103s
Cable modem rate, cable subscriber, Intermedia	mos	49.95	6/99	103s
Cable modem rate, cable subscriber, Time Warner	mos	39.95-49.95	6/99	103s
Cable modem rate, non-cable subscriber, Intermedia	mos	54.95	6/99	103s
Cable modem rate, non-cable subscriber, Time Warner	mos	39.95-54.95	6/99	103s
Newspaper subscription, daily and Sunday delivery	mos	17.98	3/01	4c
Phone line, single, business, field visit	inst.	58.50	12/97	17s
Phone line, single, business, no field visit	inst.	58.50	12/97	17s
Phone line, single, residence, field visit	inst.	41.50	12/97	17s
Phone line, single, residence, no field visit	inst.	41.50	12/97	17s
Postage and stationery, expenditures on	yr	104	1999	30r

Knoxville, TN - continued

Item	Per	Value	Date	Ref.
Communications - continued				
Postal rate, express mail, up to half-pound		12.45	7/01	108r
Postal rate, letter, first class, first ounce		0.34	7/01	108r
Postal rate, letter, two ounces		0.57	7/01	108r
Postal rate, post card		0.21	7/01	108r
Postal rate, priority mail, two pounds		3.95	7/01	108r
Postal rate, priority mail, up to one pound		3.50	7/01	108r
Telephone bill, family of three	mos	20.34	3/01	4c
Telephone services, expenditures on	yr	860	1999	30r
Education				
Board, 4-year private college/university	yr	2085	1996	38s
Board, 4-year public college/university	yr	1737	1996	38s
Education expenditures	yr	431	1999	30r
Room, 4-year private college/university	yr	2153	1996	38s
Room, 4-year public college/university	yr	1644	1996	38s
Total cost, 4-year private college/university	yr	14068	1996	38s
Total cost, 4-year public college/university	yr	5372	1996	38s
Tuition, 2-year public college/university, in state	yr	1022	1996	38s
Tuition, 4-year private college/university, in state	yr	9830	1996	38s
Tuition, 4-year public college/university	yr	1990	1996	38s
Energy and Fuels				
Electricity	KWh	0.09	7/01	11r
Electricity	500 KWhs	47.29	7/01	11r
Energy, combined forms, 2400 sq ft	mos	115.90	3/01	4c
Energy, exc. electricity, 2400 sq ft	mos	65.86	3/01	4c
Fuel oil #2	gal	1.43	7/01	11r
Fuel oil and other fuels, expenditures on	yr	45	1999	30r
Gas, natural, commercial rate	1000 cf	8.61	11/00	88s
Gas, regular unleaded, cash, self-service	gal	1.27	3/01	4c
Gasoline, all types	gal	1.60	7/01	11r
Gasoline, unleaded midgrade	gal	1.65	7/01	11r
Gasoline, unleaded premium	gal	1.74	7/01	11r
Natural gas, expenditures on	yr	164	1999	30r
Utility (piped) gas, therm		1.01	7/01	11r
Utility (piped) gas, 40 therms		44.29	7/01	11r
Utility (piped) gas, 100 therms		97.44	7/01	11r
Entertainment				
Bowling, Saturday evening rate	line	2.95	3/01	4c
Entertainment purchases	yr	1574	1999	30r
Fees and admissions paid	yr	371	1999	30r
Monopoly game, Parker Brothers', No. 9	game	8.90	3/01	4c
Movie, first-run, Saturday, evening	adm.	6.90	3/01	4c
Reading purchases	yr	121	1999	30r
Television, radios, sound equipment, expenditures on	yr	561	1999	30r
Tennis balls, yellow, Wilson or Penn, 3	can	2.03	3/01	4c
Groceries				
Groceries, ACCRA Index		95.50	3/01	4c
American processed cheese	lb	3.50	7/01	11r
Antibiotic ointment, Polysporin	0.5 oz	4.30	3/01	4c
Baby food, strained vegetables or fruit, lowest price	4-4.5 oz	0.43	3/01	4c
Bakery products, expenditures on	yr	261	1999	30r
Bananas	lb	0.47	3/01	4c
Bananas	lb	0.47	7/01	11r
Beans, dried, any type, all sizes	lb	0.63	7/01	11r
Beef for stew, boneless	lb	2.86	7/01	11r
Beef or hamburger, ground	lb	1.73	3/01	4c
Beef, expenditures on	yr	210	1999	30r
Bologna, all beef or mixed	lb	2.29	7/01	11r
Bread, French	lb	1.66	7/01	11r
Bread, white	loaf	0.95	3/01	4c
Bread, white, pan	lb	0.87	7/01	11r
Bread, whole wheat, pan	lb	1.38	7/01	11r
Broccoli	lb	1.04	7/01	11r
Butter, salted, grade AA, stick	lb	2.26	7/01	11r
Butter, yoghurt, cheese, etc, expenditures on	yr	170	1999	30r
Cabbage	lb	0.42	7/01	11r

Values are in dollars or fractions of dollars. In the column headed *Ref*, references are shown to sources. Each reference is followed by a letter. These refer to the geographical level for which data were reported: s=State, r=Region, and c=City or metro. The abbreviation *ex* is used to mean *except* or *excluding*; *exp* stands for *expenditures*. For other abbreviations and further explanations, please see the Introduction.

Knoxville, TN - continued

Item	Per	Value	Date	Ref.
Groceries				
Cereals and cereal products, expenditures on	yr	140	1999	30r
Cheddar cheese, natural	lb	3.75	7/01	11r
Cheese, Kraft grated Parmesan	8 oz	3.27	3/01	4c
Chicken breast, bone-in	lb	1.85	7/01	11r
Chicken legs, bone-in	lb	1.34	7/01	11r
Chicken, fresh, whole	lb	1.05	7/01	11r
Chicken, whole fryer	lb	0.93	3/01	4c
Chops, boneless,	lb	4.13	7/01	11r
Chuck roast, graded and ungraded, excl U.S. prime and choice	lb	2.35	7/01	11r
Chuck roast, U.S. choice, boneless	lb	2.67	7/01	11r
Cigarettes, Winston, Kings	carton	28.57	3/01	4c
Coffee, 100%, ground roast, all sizes	lb	2.88	7/01	11r
Coffee, instant, plain, regular, all sizes	16 oz	9.25	7/01	11r
Coffee, vacuum-packed	13 oz	2.13	3/01	4c
Cola, non diet,	2 liter	1.11	7/01	11r
Corn Flakes, Kellogg's or Post Toasties	18 oz	2.57	3/01	4c
Corn, frozen, whole kernel, lowest price	16 oz	1.03	3/01	4c
Crackers, soda, salted	lb	1.70	7/01	11r
Dairy product purchases	yr	282	1999	30r
Eggs, expenditures on	yr	32	1999	30r
Eggs, Grade A or AA	dozen	1.26	3/01	4c
Fats and oils, expenditures on	yr	79	1999	30r
Fish and seafood, expenditures on	yr	99	1999	30r
Flour, white, all purpose	lb	0.32	7/01	11r
Food (excl fruit and vegetables), eaten at home, purchases	yr	815	1999	30r
Food cooked on trips, expenditures on	yr	36	1999	30r
Food purchases	yr	4533	1999	30r
Food purchases, eaten away from home	yr	1873	1999	30r
Food purchases, food eaten at home	yr	2660	1999	30r
Fresh fruits, expenditures on	yr	128	1999	30r
Fresh milk and cream, expenditures on	yr	112	1999	30r
Fresh vegetables, expenditures on	yr	131	1999	30r
Fruit and vegetable purchases	yr	438	1999	30r
Grapefruit	lb	0.59	7/01	11r
Grapes, Thompson, seedless	lb	2.12	7/01	11r
Ground beef, 100% beef	lb	1.76	7/01	11r
Ground beef, lean and extra lean	lb	2.60	7/01	11r
Ground chuck, 100% beef	lb	2.08	7/01	11r
Ham, boneless, excl canned	lb	2.71	7/01	11r
Ham, rump or shank half, bone-in, smoked	lb	2.19	7/01	11r
Ice cream, prepackaged, bulk, regular	1/2 gal	3.93	7/01	11r
Lemons	lb	1.32	7/01	11r
Lettuce, iceberg	head	1.21	3/01	4c
Lettuce, iceberg	lb	0.76	7/01	11r
Margarine, Blue Bonnet or Parkay, stick	lb	0.70	3/01	4c
Milk, fresh, low fat,	gal	2.75	7/01	11r
Milk, fresh, whole, fortified	gal	2.97	7/01	11r
Milk, whole	1/2 gal	1.72	3/01	4c
Nonalcoholic beverages, expenditures on	yr	228	1999	30r
Orange juice, frozen concentrate	16 oz	1.95	7/01	11r
Orange juice, Minute Maid frozen	12 oz	1.43	3/01	4c
Oranges, Navel	lb	0.73	7/01	11r
Oranges, Valencia	lb	0.55	7/01	11r
Peaches, halves or slices, Hunt's, Del Monte, or Libby's	29 oz	1.53	3/01	4c
Peanut butter, creamy, all sizes	lb	1.83	7/01	11r
Pears, Anjou	lb	0.98	7/01	11r
Peas, green, Del Monte or Green Giant	15 oz	0.57	3/01	4c
Pork chops, center cut, bone-in	lb	3.33	7/01	11r
Pork sausage, fresh, loose	lb	2.59	7/01	11r
Pork shoulder picnic, bone-in, smoked	lb	1.12	7/01	11r
Pork, expenditures on	yr	162	1999	30r
Potato chips	16 oz	3.59	7/01	11r
Potatoes, frozen, french fried	lb	1.00	7/01	11r
Potatoes, white or red	10 lb	2.65	3/01	4c
Potatoes, white, all types	lb	0.44	7/01	11r
Poultry, expenditures on	yr	137	1999	30r
Processed fruits, expenditures on	yr	97	1999	30r
Processed vegetables, expenditures on	yr	82	1999	30r

Knoxville, TN - continued

Item	Per	Value	Date	Ref.
Groceries - continued				
Rice, white, long grain, uncooked	lb	0.51	7/01	11r
Round roast, graded and ungraded, excl U.S. prime and choice	lb	2.96	7/01	11r
Round steak, graded and ungraded, excl U.S. prime and choice	lb	3.11	7/01	11r
Sausage, Jimmy Dean/Owens pork	lb	3.37	3/01	4c
Shortening, vegetable, Crisco	3 lb	2.95	3/01	4c
Sirloin steak, graded and ungraded, excl U.S. prime and choice	lb	4.23	7/01	11r
Soft drink, Coca Cola, ex deposit	2 liter	1.11	3/01	4c
Spaghetti and macaroni	lb	0.78	7/01	11r
Steak, round, U.S. choice, boneless	lb	3.56	7/01	11r
Steak, sirloin, U.S. choice, boneless	lb	5.65	7/01	11r
Steak, T-bone	lb	6.59	3/01	4c
Strawberries, dry pint	12 oz	1.50	7/01	11r
Sugar and other sweets, expenditures on	yr	99	1999	30r
Sugar, cane or beet	4 lbs	1.69	3/01	4c
Sugar, white, 33-80 ounce package	lb	0.39	7/01	11r
Sugar, white, all sizes	lb	0.42	7/01	11r
Tobacco products and smoking supplies purchases	yr	288	1999	30r
Tomatoes, field grown	lb	1.43	7/01	11r
Tomatoes, Hunt's or Del Monte	14.5 oz	0.81	3/01	4c
Tuna, chunk, light	6 oz	0.48	3/01	4c
Tuna, light, chunk	lb	1.77	7/01	11r
Turkey, frozen, whole	lb	1.05	7/01	11r
Goods and Services				
Miscellaneous goods and services, ACCRA Index		96.90	3/01	4c
Health Care				
Health care, ACCRA Index		90.90	3/01	4c
Cardiac catheterization, ave hospital/ physician charges		12170	1998	77s
Childbirth, Cesarean delivery		11587	1997	13r
Childbirth, vaginal delivery		6725	1997	13r
Dentist's fee, adult teeth cleaning and periodic oral exam	visit	62.20	3/01	4c
Doctor's fee, routine exam, established patient	visit	58.80	3/01	4c
Drugs, expenditures on	yr	399	1999	30r
Health care purchases	yr	1971	1999	30r
Health insurance expenditures	yr	933	1999	30r
Hospital care, private room	day	416.80	3/01	4c
Hysterectomy, laproscopically-assisted, ave hospital/physician charges		13470	1998	76s
Hysterectomy, vaginal, ave hospital and physician charges		9530	1998	76s
Medical services expenditures	yr	547	1999	30r
Medical supplies, expenditures on	yr	91	1999	30r
Household Goods				
Dishwashing powder, Cascade	50 oz	2.61	3/01	4c
Floor coverings, expenditures on	yr	44	1999	30r
Furniture, expenditures on	yr	335	1999	30r
Household furnishings and equipment purchases	yr	1328	1999	30r
Household textiles, expenditures on	yr	89	1999	30r
Laundry and cleaning supplies, expenditures on	yr	113	1999	30r
Tissues, facial, Kleenex brand	175	1.08	3/01	4c
Housing				
Housing, ACCRA Index		86.70	3/01	4c
Home, 2200 sq ft, 4-br, 2-bath, 2-car garage, average		135975	2000	47c
Home price, existing, ave		160100	10/00	90r
Home value, median		112000	2001	53s
House, 2400 sq ft, 8000 sq ft lot, new, urban, utilities	total	183140	3/01	4c
House payment, principal and interest, 25% down payment	mos	902	3/01	4c
Household operation expenditures	yr	553	1999	30r

Values are in dollars or fractions of dollars. In the column headed *Ref*, references are shown to sources. Each reference is followed by a letter. These refer to the geographical level for which data were reported: s=State, r=Region, and c=City or metro. The abbreviation *ex* is used to mean *except* or *excluding*; *exp* stands for *expenditures*. For other abbreviations and further explanations, please see the Introduction.

Knoxville, TN - continued

Item	Per	Value	Date	Ref.
Housing				
Housekeeping supplies purchases	yr	473	1999	30r
Housing, expenditures on	yr	10303	1999	30r
Maintenance, repairs, insurance expenditures	yr	699	1999	30r
Monthly rental value of owned home	mos	505	1999	30r
Owned dwellings, expenditures own	yr	3465	1999	30r
Rent expenditures	yr	1641	1999	30r
Rent, apartment, 2 br, 1 1/2-2 baths, unfurn, 950 sq ft, water	mos	580	3/01	4c
Rental unit, 1 bedroom, with utilities	mos	381	4/01	41c
Rental unit, 2 bedroom, with utilities	mos	479	4/01	41c
Rental unit, 3 bedroom, with utilities	mos	639	4/01	41c
Rental unit, 4 bedroom, with utilities	mos	767	4/01	41c
Shelter, expenditures on	yr	5467	1999	30r
Insurance and Pensions				
Life and other personal insurance purchases	yr	414	1999	30r
Pensions and Social Security, expenditures on	yr	2635	1999	30r
Personal insurance and pensions, expenditures on	yr	3048	1999	30r
Legal Fees				
Combination hunting and fishing license	yr	21.00	4/01	34s
Divorce, filing fee		64.00	4/01	35s
Driver's license fee	orig	17.50	1999	48s
Driver's license fee	renew	17.50	1999	48s
Personal Goods				
Personal care products and services purchases	yr	393	1999	30r
Shampoo, Alberto VO5	15 oz	1.08	3/01	4c
Toothpaste, Crest or Colgate	6-7 oz	2.15	3/01	4c
Personal Services				
Dry cleaning, man's 2-pc suit		7.78	3/01	4c
Man's haircut, barbershop, no styling		8.29	3/01	4c
Personal services, household, expenditures on	yr	258	1999	30r
Woman's shampoo, trim, blow-dry, no style-change		23.80	3/01	4c
Pets				
Pets, toys, and playground equipment, expenditures on	yr	306	1999	30r
Restaurant Food				
Chicken, fried, thigh and drumstick, KFC/ Church's		2.87	3/01	4c
Hamburger with cheese, McDonald's	1/4 lb	2.09	3/01	4c
Pizza, Pizza Hut or Pizza Inn	11-12 in	8.99	3/01	4c
Taxes				
Federal income taxes paid	yr	2047	1999	30r
Personal taxes, expenditures on	yr	2554	1999	30r
Property taxes paid	yr	726	1999	30r
State and local income taxes paid	yr	363	1999	30r
Transportation				
Transportation, ACCRA Index		88.70	3/01	4c
Bus fare, one-way	trip	1.00	2000	1c
Cars and trucks, new, expenditures on	yr	1648	1999	30r
Cars and trucks, used, expenditures on	yr	1651	1999	30r
Diesel at the pump	gal	1.18	10/99	73s
Gasoline and motor oil purchases	yr	1052	1999	30r
Gasoline before-tax price (cents)	gal	102.50	10/00	43s
Maintenance and repair expenditures	yr	621	1999	30r
Public transportation, expenditures on	yr	298	1999	30r
Tire balance, computer or spin balance, front	wheel	6.80	3/01	4c
Transportation purchases	yr	6738	1999	30r
Vehicle expenses, miscellaneous, purchases	yr	2033	1999	30r
Vehicle insurance payments	yr	696	1999	30r
Vehicle purchases (net outlay)	yr	3354	1999	30r
Vehicle rental, lease expenditures	yr	352	1999	30r

Knoxville, TN - continued

Item	Per	Value	Date	Ref.
Utilities				
Utilities, ACCRA Index		94.80	3/01	4c
Electrical bill, average	mos	79.16	9/00	9s
Electricity, expenditures on	yr	1115	1999	30r
Electricity and other, mixed, 2400 sq ft, new home	mos	50.04	3/01	4c
Electricity cost, average	KWh	5.60	9/00	9s
Water and other public services, expenditures on	yr	298	1999	30r
Weddings				
Wedding (national average cost)		19936	2000	33r
Attendants' gifts		321	1998	33r
Bridal attendants' apparel (5 persons)		824	2000	33r
Bride's headpiece/veil		173	1998	33r
Bride's wedding dress		859	1998	33r
Clergy, religious facility fee		242	1998	33r
Engagement ring		3177	1998	33r
Flowers		789	1998	33r
Groom's formalwear rental		99	2000	33r
Limousine		410	1998	33r
Marriage license cost		31.00	4/01	35s
Men's formalwear (ushers, best man)		469	2000	33r
Mother of bride apparel		241	2000	33r
Music		866	1998	33r
Photography and videography		1368	1998	33r
Rehearsal dinner		728	1998	33r
Wedding invitations and announcements		341	1998	33r
Wedding reception		7968	2000	33r
Wedding rings (bride and groom)		1060	1998	33r

La Crosse, WI-MN

Item	Per	Value	Date	Ref.
Average annual expenditures	yr	35369	1999	30r
Alcoholic Beverages				
Alcoholic beverage purchases	yr	304	1999	30r
Malt beverages, all types, all sizes, any origin	16 oz	0.93	7/01	11r
Wine, red and white table, all sizes, any origin	liter	7.04	7/01	11r
Appliances				
Major appliances, expenditures on	yr	165	1999	30r
Small appliances, housewares, expenditures on	yr	90	1999	30r
Banking and Money				
Mortgage interest and charges paid	yr	2277	1999	30r
Mortgage principal paid on owned property	yr	1230	1999	30r
Vehicle finance charges paid	yr	328	1999	30r
Charity				
Cash contributions, expenditures	yr	1126	1999	30r
Child Care				
Child raising cost, total, age 0-2	yr	7890	1999	60r
Child raising cost, total, age 3-5	yr	8130	1999	60r
Child raising cost, total, age 6-8	yr	8170	1999	60r
Child raising cost, total, age 9-11	yr	8190	1999	60r
Child raising cost, total, age 12-14	yr	8890	1999	60r
Child raising cost, total, age 15-17	yr	9050	1999	60r
Child's child care and education, age 0-2	yr	1240	1999	60r
Child's child care and education, age 3-5	yr	1370	1999	60r
Child's child care and education, age 6-8	yr	880	1999	60r
Child's child care and education, age 9-11	yr	570	1999	60r
Child's child care and education, age 12-14	yr	420	1999	60r
Child's child care and education, age 15-17	yr	720	1999	60r
Child's clothing, age 0-2	yr	410	1999	60r
Child's clothing, age 3-5	yr	400	1999	60r
Child's clothing, age 6-8	yr	450	1999	60r
Child's clothing, age 9-11	yr	500	1999	60r
Child's clothing, age 12-14	yr	840	1999	60r
Child's clothing, age 15-17	yr	740	1999	60r
Child's food, age 0-2	yr	960	1999	60r
Child's food, age 3-5	yr	1120	1999	60r

Values are in dollars or fractions of dollars. In the column headed *Ref*, references are shown to sources. Each reference is followed by a letter. These refer to the geographical level for which data were reported: s=State, r=Region, and c=City or metro. The abbreviation *ex* is used to mean *except* or *excluding*; *exp* stands for expenditures. For other abbreviations and further explanations, please see the Introduction.

La Crosse, WI-MN - continued

Item	Per	Value	Date	Ref.
Child Care				
Child's food, age 6-8	yr	1430	1999	60r
Child's food, age 9-11	yr	1710	1999	60r
Child's food, age 12-14	yr	1710	1999	60r
Child's food, age 15-17	yr	1920	1999	60r
Child's health care, age 0-2	yr	520	1999	60r
Child's health care, age 3-5	yr	500	1999	60r
Child's health care, age 6-8	yr	570	1999	60r
Child's health care, age 9-11	yr	610	1999	60r
Child's health care, age 12-14	yr	630	1999	60r
Child's health care, age 15-17	yr	650	1999	60r
Child's housing, age 0-2	yr	2860	1999	60r
Child's housing, age 3-5	yr	2840	1999	60r
Child's housing, age 6-8	yr	2800	1999	60r
Child's housing, age 9-11	yr	2650	1999	60r
Child's housing, age 12-14	yr	2840	1999	60r
Child's housing, age 15-17	yr	2440	1999	60r
Child's personal care, reading, age 0-2	yr	880	1999	60r
Child's personal care, reading, age 3-5	yr	900	1999	60r
Child's personal care, reading, age 6-8	yr	930	1999	60r
Child's personal care, reading, age 9-11	yr	970	1999	60r
Child's personal care, reading, age 12-14	yr	1150	1999	60r
Child's personal care, reading, age 15-17	yr	920	1999	60r
Clothing				
Apparel and services purchases	yr	1607	1999	30r
Boys, 2 to 15, expenditures on	yr	91	1999	30r
Children under 2, expenditures on	yr	59	1999	30r
Footwear, expenditures on	yr	285	1999	30r
Girls, 2 to 15, expenditures on	yr	116	1999	30r
Men and boys, expenditures on	yr	433	1999	30r
Men, 16 and over, expenditures on	yr	341	1999	30r
Women, 16 and over, expenditures on	yr	490	1999	30r
Communications				
Cable modem installation, Bresnan		99.95	6/99	103s
Cable modem installation, Marcus		499.00	6/99	103s
Cable modem rate, cable subscriber, Bresnan	mos	39.95	6/99	103s
Cable modem rate, cable subscriber, Marcus	mos	14.95-49.95	6/99	103s
Cable modem rate, non-cable subscriber, Bresnan	mos	49.95	6/99	103s
Cable modem rate, non-cable subscriber, Marcus	mos	60.95	6/99	103s
Phone line, single, business, field visit	inst.	64.65	12/97	17s
Phone line, single, business, no field visit	inst.	64.65	12/97	17s
Phone line, single, residence, field visit	inst.	33.05	12/97	17s
Phone line, single, residence, no field visit	inst.	33.05	12/97	17s
Postage and stationery, expenditures on	yr	140	1999	30r
Postal rate, express mail, up to half-pound		12.45	7/01	108r
Postal rate, letter, first class, first ounce		0.34	7/01	108r
Postal rate, letter, two ounces		0.57	7/01	108r
Postal rate, post card		0.21	7/01	108r
Postal rate, priority mail, two pounds		3.95	7/01	108r
Postal rate, priority mail, up to one pound		3.50	7/01	108r
Telephone services, expenditures on	yr	830	1999	30r
Education				
Board, 4-year private college/university	yr	2271	1996	38s
Board, 4-year public college/university	yr	1527	1996	38s
Education expenditures	yr	583	1999	30r
Room, 4-year private college/university	yr	1812	1996	38s
Room, 4-year public college/university	yr	1706	1996	38s
Total cost, 4-year private college/university	yr	15652	1996	38s
Total cost, 4-year public college/university	yr	5847	1996	38s
Tuition, 2-year public college/university, in state	yr	1840	1996	38s
Tuition, 4-year private college/university, in state	yr	11569	1996	38s
Tuition, 4-year public college/university	yr	2614	1996	38s
Energy and Fuels				
Electricity	500 KWhs	46.59	7/01	11r

La Crosse, WI-MN - continued

Item	Per	Value	Date	Ref.
Energy and Fuels - continued				
Fuel oil #2	gal	1.27	7/01	11r
Fuel oil and other fuels, expenditures on	yr	68	1999	30r
Gas, natural, commercial rate	1000 cf	7.32	11/00	88s
Gasoline, unleaded midgrade	gal	1.79	7/01	11r
Gasoline, unleaded premium	gal	1.86	7/01	11r
Gasoline, unleaded regular	gal	1.58	7/01	11r
Natural gas, expenditures on	yr	389	1999	30r
Utility (piped) gas, therm		0.81	7/01	11r
Utility (piped) gas, 40 therms		38.01	7/01	11r
Utility (piped) gas, 100 therms		81.75	7/01	11r
Entertainment				
Entertainment purchases	yr	1984	1999	30r
Fees and admissions paid	yr	444	1999	30r
Television, radios, sound equipment, expenditures on	yr	580	1999	30r
Funerals				
Cosmetology, hair, other preparation		178.32	1/99	78r
Embalming		408.19	1/99	78r
Funeral at funeral home		362.13	1/99	78r
Professional service charges		1375.51	1/99	78r
Transfer of remains to funeral home		155.92	1/99	78r
Visitation/viewing		294.38	1/99	78r
Groceries				
Bacon, sliced	lb	3.15	7/01	11r
Bakery products, expenditures on	yr	281	1999	30r
Bananas	lb	0.48	7/01	11r
Beans, dried, any type, all sizes	lb	0.61	7/01	11r
Beef for stew, boneless	lb	3.08	7/01	11r
Beef, expenditures on	yr	217	1999	30r
Bologna, all beef or mixed	lb	2.52	7/01	11r
Bread, white, pan	lb	1.06	7/01	11r
Broccoli	lb	0.91	7/01	11r
Butter, salted, grade AA, stick	lb	3.04	7/01	11r
Butter, yoghurt, cheese, etc, expenditures on	yr	183	1999	30r
Cereals and bakery product purchases	yr	430	1999	30r
Cereals and cereal products, expenditures on	yr	149	1999	30r
Chicken, fresh, whole	lb	1.07	7/01	11r
Chops, boneless,	lb	3.64	7/01	11r
Chuck roast, U.S. choice, boneless	lb	2.47	7/01	11r
Coffee, 100%, ground roast, all sizes	lb	2.69	7/01	11r
Cookies, chocolate chip	lb	2.87	7/01	11r
Dairy product purchases	yr	304	1999	30r
Eggs, expenditures on	yr	26	1999	30r
Eggs, grade A, large	dozen	0.88	7/01	11r
Fats and oils, expenditures on	yr	75	1999	30r
Fish and seafood, expenditures on	yr	72	1999	30r
Food (excl fruit and vegetables), eaten at home, purchases	yr	887	1999	30r
Food cooked on trips, expenditures on	yr	44	1999	30r
Food purchases	yr	4802	1999	30r
Food purchases, eaten away from home	yr	2069	1999	30r
Food purchases, food eaten at home	yr	2733	1999	30r
Fresh fruits, expenditures on	yr	138	1999	30r
Fresh milk and cream, expenditures on	yr	120	1999	30r
Fresh vegetables, expenditures on	yr	126	1999	30r
Grapefruit	lb	0.66	7/01	11r
Grapes, Thompson, seedless	lb	1.64	7/01	11r
Ground beef, 100% beef	lb	1.64	7/01	11r
Ground beef, lean and extra lean	lb	2.16	7/01	11r
Ground chuck, 100% beef	lb	2.13	7/01	11r
Ham, boneless, excl canned	lb	2.62	7/01	11r
Ice cream, prepackaged, bulk, regular	1/2 gal	3.35	7/01	11r
Lemons	lb	1.19	7/01	11r
Lettuce, iceberg	lb	0.73	7/01	11r
Margarine, soft, tubs	lb	0.89	7/01	11r
Meats, poultry, fish, and egg purchases	yr	671	1999	30r
Milk, fresh, whole, fortified	gal	2.71	7/01	11r
Nonalcoholic beverages, expenditures on	yr	239	1999	30r
Oranges, Navel	lb	0.80	7/01	11r
Oranges, Valencia	lb	0.66	7/01	11r

Values are in dollars or fractions of dollars. In the column headed *Ref*, references are shown to sources. Each reference is followed by a letter. These refer to the geographical level for which data were reported: s=State, r=Region, and c=City or metro. The abbreviation *ex* is used to mean *except* or *excluding*; *exp* stands for *expenditures*. For other abbreviations and further explanations, please see the Introduction.

La Crosse, WI-MN - continued

Item	Per	Value	Date	Ref.
Groceries				
Pears, Anjou	lb	0.93	7/01	11r
Pork chops, center cut, bone-in	lb	3.63	7/01	11r
Pork, expenditures on	yr	150	1999	30r
Potato chips	16 oz	3.52	7/01	11r
Potatoes, frozen, french fried	lb	1.08	7/01	11r
Potatoes, white, all types	lb	0.33	7/01	11r
Poultry, expenditures on	yr	108	1999	30r
Processed fruits, expenditures on	yr	98	1999	30r
Processed vegetables, expenditures on	yr	80	1999	30r
Round roast, U.S. choice, boneless	lb	3.07	7/01	11r
Round steak, graded and ungraded, excl U.S. prime and choice	lb	3.41	7/01	11r
Shortening, vegetable oil blends	lb	1.13	7/01	11r
Spaghetti and macaroni	lb	0.80	7/01	11r
Steak, round, U.S. choice, boneless	lb	3.23	7/01	11r
Steak, T-bone, U.S. choice, bone-in	lb	6.68	7/01	11r
Strawberries, dry pint	12 oz	1.32	7/01	11r
Sugar and other sweets, expenditures on	yr	114	1999	30r
Sugar, white, 33-80 ounce package	lb	0.42	7/01	11r
Sugar, white, all sizes	lb	0.43	7/01	11r
Tobacco products and smoking supplies purchases	yr	331	1999	30r
Tomatoes, field grown	lb	1.46	7/01	11r
Tuna, light, chunk	lb	1.80	7/01	11r
Turkey, frozen, whole	lb	1.15	7/01	11r
Goods and Services				
B&B Japanese maple (acer japonicum)	gal	29.99-169.99	4/00	93r
Boxwood (buxus)	2 gal	18.99-39.99	4/00	93r
Daylilly (hemerocallis)	gal	4.99-25.00	4/00	93r
Flat of annuals		11.98-24.99	4/00	93r
Fountain grass (pennisetum)	gal	5.98-12.98	4/00	93r
Hanging basket (10 in)		12.99-27.99	4/00	93r
Hardy geranium (geranium)	gal	7.99-9.99	4/00	93r
Hosta (hosta)	gal	6.00-25.00	4/00	93r
Lilac (syrubga vulgaris)	2 gal	14.99-24.99	4/00	93r
Miscellaneous purchases	yr	865	1999	30r
Rhododendron (rhododendron)	2 gal	23.98-42.99	4/00	93r
Sage (salvia)	gal	6.00-9.99	4/00	93r
Wintercreeper euonymus (euonymus fortunei)	2 gal	16.00-169.99	4/00	93r
Hunting license	yr	14.00	4/01	34s
Health Care				
Cardiac catheterization, ave hospital/physician charges		13240	1998	77s
Childbirth, Cesarean delivery		10722	1997	13r
Childbirth, vaginal delivery		6223	1997	13r
Drugs, expenditures on	yr	394	1999	30r
Health care purchases	yr	2048	1999	30r
Health insurance expenditures	yr	978	1999	30r
Hysterectomy, laproscopically-assisted, ave hospital/physician charges		13270	1998	76s
Hysterectomy, vaginal, ave hospital and physician charges		9170	1998	76s
Laser eye surgery	eye	1950-2400	2000	63s
Medicaid dispensing fee		4.88-40.11	1999	87s
Medical services expenditures	yr	554	1999	30r
Medical supplies, expenditures on	yr	122	1999	30r
Plastic surgery, breast augmentation		3184	2000	7r

La Crosse, WI-MN - continued

Item	Per	Value	Date	Ref.
Health Care - continued				
Plastic surgery, breast lift		3585	2000	7r
Plastic surgery, facelift		4999	2000	7r
Plastic surgery, hair transplantation		3105	2000	7r
Plastic surgery, lip augmentation		1290	2000	7r
Plastic surgery, lower body lift		8135	2000	7r
Plastic surgery, thigh lift		3839	2000	7r
Household Goods				
Floor coverings, expenditures on	yr	52	1999	30r
Furniture, expenditures on	yr	344	1999	30r
Household furnishings and equipment purchases	yr	1475	1999	30r
Household textiles, expenditures on	yr	109	1999	30r
Laundry and cleaning supplies, expenditures on	yr	134	1999	30r
Housing				
Home price, existing, ave		144400	10/00	90r
Home value, median		117000	2001	53s
Household operation expenditures	yr	542	1999	30r
Housekeeping supplies purchases	yr	508	1999	30r
Lodging expenditures	yr	430	1999	30r
Maintenance, repairs, insurance expenditures	yr	853	1999	30r
Monthly rental value of owned home	mos	547	1999	30r
Owned dwellings, expenditures own	yr	4282	1999	30r
Rent expenditures	yr	1558	1999	30r
Rental unit, 1 bedroom, with utilities	mos	372	4/01	41c
Rental unit, 2 bedroom, with utilities	mos	473	4/01	41c
Rental unit, 3 bedroom, with utilities	mos	633	4/01	41c
Rental unit, 4 bedroom, with utilities	mos	767	4/01	41c
Shelter, expenditures on	yr	6270	1999	30r
Insurance and Pensions				
Auto insurance premium	yr	603.84	1999	57s
Life and other personal insurance purchases	yr	387	1999	30r
Pensions and Social Security, expenditures on	yr	2968	1999	30r
Legal Fees				
Divorce, filing fee		142.00-150.00	4/01	35s
Driver's license fee	renew	12.00	1999	48s
Driver's license fee	orig	18.00	1999	48s
Fishing license	yr	14.00	4/01	34s
Personal Goods				
Personal care products and services purchases	yr	385	1999	30r
Personal Services				
Personal services, household, expenditures on	yr	300	1999	30r
Pets				
Pets, toys, and playground equipment, expenditures on	yr	375	1999	30r
Taxes				
Federal income taxes paid	yr	2326	1999	30r
Personal taxes, expenditures on	yr	3223	1999	30r
Property taxes paid	yr	1152	1999	30r
State and local income taxes paid	yr	753	1999	30r
Transportation				
Bus fare, one-way	trip	0.75	2000	1c
Cars and trucks, new, expenditures on	yr	1280	1999	30r
Cars and trucks, used, expenditures on	yr	1763	1999	30r
Diesel at the pump	gal	1.34	10/99	73s
Gasoline and motor oil purchases	yr	1036	1999	30r
Gasoline before-tax price (cents)	gal	113.40	10/00	43s
Maintenance and repair expenditures	yr	594	1999	30r
Public transportation, expenditures on	yr	341	1999	30r
Transportation purchases	yr	6617	1999	30r
Vehicle expenses, miscellaneous, purchases	yr	2159	1999	30r
Vehicle insurance payments	yr	701	1999	30r

Values are in dollars or fractions of dollars. In the column headed *Ref*, references are shown to sources. Each reference is followed by a letter. These refer to the geographical level for which data were reported: s=State, r=Region, and c=City or metro. The abbreviation *ex* is used to mean *except* or *excluding*; *exp* stands for *expenditures*. For other abbreviations and further explanations, please see the Introduction.

La Crosse, WI-MN - continued

Item	Per	Value	Date	Ref.
Transportation				
Vehicle purchases (net outlay)	yr	3081	1999	30r
Vehicle rental, lease expenditures	yr	536	1999	30r
Utilities				
Electrical bill, average	mos	52.08	9/00	9s
Electricity, expenditures on	yr	841	1999	30r
Electricity cost, average	KWh	5.69	9/00	9s
Utilities, fuels, and public services purchased	yr	2401	1999	30r
Water and other public services, expenditures on	yr	273	1999	30r
Weddings				
Wedding (national average cost)		19936	2000	33r
Wedding (regional average total cost)		16195	1997	110r
Attendants' gifts		321	1998	33r
Bridal attendants' apparel (5 persons)		824	2000	33r
Bride's headpiece/veil		173	1998	33r
Bride's wedding dress		859	1998	33r
Clergy, religious facility fee		242	1998	33r
Engagement ring		3177	1998	33r
Flowers		789	1998	33r
Groom's formalwear rental		99	2000	33r
Limousine		410	1998	33r
Marriage license cost		50.00-60.00	4/01	35s
Men's formalwear (ushers, best man)		469	2000	33r
Mother of bride apparel		241	2000	33r
Music		866	1998	33r
Photography and videography		1368	1998	33r
Rehearsal dinner		728	1998	33r
Wedding invitations and announcements		341	1998	33r
Wedding reception		7968	2000	33r
Wedding rings (bride and groom)		1060	1998	33r

Lafayette, IN

Item	Per	Value	Date	Ref.
Average annual expenditures	yr	35369	1999	30r
Composite, ACCRA index		93.80	3/01	4c
Alcoholic Beverages				
Alcoholic beverage purchases	yr	304	1999	30r
Beer, Heineken, 12-oz, ex deposit	6	6.79	3/01	4c
J & B Scotch	750-ml	20.03	3/01	4c
Malt beverages, all types, all sizes, any origin	16 oz	0.93	7/01	11r
Wine, Livingston or Gallo, Chablis blanc	1.5 liter	4.33	3/01	4c
Wine, red and white table, all sizes, any origin	liter	7.04	7/01	11r
Appliances				
Appliance repair, service call, washing machine	min lab chg	43.69	3/01	4c
Major appliances, expenditures on	yr	165	1999	30r
Small appliances, housewares, expenditures on	yr	90	1999	30r
Banking and Money				
Mortgage interest and charges paid	yr	2277	1999	30r
Mortgage principal paid on owned property	yr	1230	1999	30r
Mortgage rate, incl. points and orig. fee, 30-yr. conv. fixed or ARM	mos	7.10	3/01	4c
Vehicle finance charges paid	yr	328	1999	30r
Charity				
Cash contributions, expenditures on	yr	1126	1999	30r
Child Care				
Child raising cost, total, age 0-2	yr	7890	1999	60r
Child raising cost, total, age 3-5	yr	8130	1999	60r
Child raising cost, total, age 6-8	yr	8170	1999	60r
Child raising cost, total, age 9-11	yr	8190	1999	60r
Child raising cost, total, age 12-14	yr	8890	1999	60r
Child raising cost, total, age 15-17	yr	9050	1999	60r
Child's child care and education, age 0-2	yr	1240	1999	60r
Child's child care and education, age 3-5	yr	1370	1999	60r
Child's child care and education, age 6-8	yr	880	1999	60r

Item	Per	Value	Date	Ref.
Child Care - continued				
Child's child care and education, age 9-11	yr	570	1999	60r
Child's child care and education, age 12-14	yr	420	1999	60r
Child's child care and education, age 15-17	yr	720	1999	60r
Child's clothing, age 0-2	yr	410	1999	60r
Child's clothing, age 3-5	yr	400	1999	60r
Child's clothing, age 6-8	yr	450	1999	60r
Child's clothing, age 9-11	yr	500	1999	60r
Child's clothing, age 12-14	yr	840	1999	60r
Child's clothing, age 15-17	yr	740	1999	60r
Child's food, age 0-2	yr	960	1999	60r
Child's food, age 3-5	yr	1120	1999	60r
Child's food, age 6-8	yr	1430	1999	60r
Child's food, age 9-11	yr	1710	1999	60r
Child's food, age 12-14	yr	1710	1999	60r
Child's food, age 15-17	yr	1920	1999	60r
Child's health care, age 0-2	yr	520	1999	60r
Child's health care, age 3-5	yr	500	1999	60r
Child's health care, age 6-8	yr	570	1999	60r
Child's health care, age 9-11	yr	610	1999	60r
Child's health care, age 12-14	yr	630	1999	60r
Child's health care, age 15-17	yr	650	1999	60r
Child's housing, age 0-2	yr	2860	1999	60r
Child's housing, age 3-5	yr	2840	1999	60r
Child's housing, age 6-8	yr	2800	1999	60r
Child's housing, age 9-11	yr	2650	1999	60r
Child's housing, age 12-14	yr	2840	1999	60r
Child's housing, age 15-17	yr	2440	1999	60r
Child's personal care, reading, age 0-2	yr	880	1999	60r
Child's personal care, reading, age 3-5	yr	900	1999	60r
Child's personal care, reading, age 6-8	yr	930	1999	60r
Child's personal care, reading, age 9-11	yr	970	1999	60r
Child's personal care, reading, age 12-14	yr	1150	1999	60r
Child's personal care, reading, age 15-17	yr	920	1999	60r
Clothing				
Apparel and services purchases	yr	1607	1999	30r
Boys' brief, cotton	3	3.22	3/01	4c
Boys, 2 to 15, expenditures on	yr	91	1999	30r
Children under 2, expenditures on	yr	59	1999	30r
Footwear, expenditures on	yr	285	1999	30r
Girls, 2 to 15, expenditures on	yr	116	1999	30r
Men and boys, expenditures on	yr	433	1999	30r
Men, 16 and over, expenditures on	yr	341	1999	30r
Shirt, man's dress shirt		27.59	3/01	4c
Slacks, man's "No Wrinkles" khaki		31.99	3/01	4c
Women, 16 and over, expenditures on	yr	490	1999	30r
Communications				
Newspaper subscription, daily and Sunday delivery	mos	15.22	3/01	4c
Phone line, single, business, field visit	inst.	59.00	12/97	17s
Phone line, single, business, no field visit	inst.	59.00	12/97	17s
Phone line, single, residence, field visit	inst.	47.00	12/97	17s
Phone line, single, residence, no field visit	inst.	47.00	12/97	17s
Postage and stationery, expenditures on	yr	140	1999	30r
Postal rate, express mail, up to half-pound		12.45	7/01	108r
Postal rate, letter, first class, first ounce		0.34	7/01	108r
Postal rate, letter, two ounces		0.57	7/01	108r
Postal rate, post card		0.21	7/01	108r
Postal rate, priority mail, two pounds		3.95	7/01	108r
Postal rate, priority mail, up to one pound		3.50	7/01	108r
Telephone bill, family of three	mos	23.62	3/01	4c
Telephone services, expenditures on	yr	830	1999	30r
Education				
Board, 4-year private college/university	yr	2250	1996	38s
Board, 4-year public college/university	yr	2425	1996	38s
Education expenditures	yr	583	1999	30r
Room, 4-year private college/university	yr	1987	1996	38s
Room, 4-year public college/university	yr	1931	1996	38s
Total cost, 4-year private college/university	yr	16829	1996	38s
Total cost, 4-year public college/university	yr	7392	1996	38s
Tuition, 2-year public college/university, in state	yr	1937	1996	38s

Values are in dollars or fractions of dollars. In the column headed *Ref*, references are shown to sources. Each reference is followed by a letter. These refer to the geographical level for which data were reported: s=State, r=Region, and c=City or metro. The abbreviation *ex* is used to mean *except* or *excluding*; *exp* stands for *expenditures*. For other abbreviations and further explanations, please see the Introduction.

Lafayette, IN - continued

Item	Per	Value	Date	Ref.
Education				
Tuition, 4-year private college/university, in state	yr	12592	1996	38s
Tuition, 4-year public college/university	yr	3037	1996	38s
Energy and Fuels				
Electricity	500 KWhs	46.59	7/01	11r
Energy, combined forms, 2400 sq ft	mos	126.00	3/01	4c
Energy, exc. electricity, 2400 sq ft	mos	77.42	3/01	4c
Fuel oil #2	gal	1.27	7/01	11r
Fuel oil and other fuels, expenditures on	yr	68	1999	30r
Gas, natural, commercial rate	1000 cf	6.24	11/00	88s
Gas, regular unleaded, cash, self-service	gal	1.36	3/01	4c
Gasoline, unleaded midgrade	gal	1.79	7/01	11r
Gasoline, unleaded premium	gal	1.86	7/01	11r
Gasoline, unleaded regular	gal	1.58	7/01	11r
Natural gas, expenditures on	yr	389	1999	30r
Utility (piped) gas, therm		0.81	7/01	11r
Utility (piped) gas, 40 therms		38.01	7/01	11r
Utility (piped) gas, 100 therms		81.75	7/01	11r
Entertainment				
Bowling, Saturday evening rate	line	2.55	3/01	4c
Entertainment purchases	yr	1984	1999	30r
Fees and admissions paid	yr	444	1999	30r
Monopoly game, Parker Brothers', No. 9	game	12.16	3/01	4c
Movie, first-run, Saturday, evening	adm.	7.00	3/01	4c
Television, radios, sound equipment, expenditures on	yr	580	1999	30r
Tennis balls, yellow, Wilson or Penn, 3	can	2.31	3/01	4c
Funerals				
Cosmetology, hair, other preparation		178.32	1/99	78r
Embalming		408.19	1/99	78r
Funeral at funeral home		362.13	1/99	78r
Professional service charges		1375.51	1/99	78r
Transfer of remains to funeral home		155.92	1/99	78r
Visitation/viewing		294.38	1/99	78r
Groceries				
Groceries, ACCRA Index		90.10	3/01	4c
Antibiotic ointment, Polysporin	0.5 oz	4.63	3/01	4c
Baby food, strained vegetables or fruit, lowest price	4-4.5 oz	0.35	3/01	4c
Bacon, sliced	lb	3.15	7/01	11r
Bakery products, expenditures on	yr	281	1999	30r
Bananas	lb	0.45	3/01	4c
Bananas	lb	0.48	7/01	11r
Beans, dried, any type, all sizes	lb	0.61	7/01	11r
Beef for stew, boneless	lb	3.08	7/01	11r
Beef or hamburger, ground	lb	1.65	3/01	4c
Beef, expenditures on	yr	217	1999	30r
Bologna, all beef or mixed	lb	2.52	7/01	11r
Bread, white	loaf	0.99	3/01	4c
Bread, white, pan	lb	1.06	7/01	11r
Broccoli	lb	0.91	7/01	11r
Butter, salted, grade AA, stick	lb	3.04	7/01	11r
Butter, yoghurt, cheese, etc, expenditures on	yr	183	1999	30r
Cereals and bakery product purchases	yr	430	1999	30r
Cereals and cereal products, expenditures on	yr	149	1999	30r
Cheese, Kraft grated Parmesan	8 oz	3.79	3/01	4c
Chicken, fresh, whole	lb	1.07	7/01	11r
Chicken, whole fryer	lb	0.92	3/01	4c
Chops, boneless,	lb	3.64	7/01	11r
Chuck roast, U.S. choice, boneless	lb	2.47	7/01	11r
Cigarettes, Winston, Kings	carton	26.61	3/01	4c
Coffee, 100%, ground roast, all sizes	lb	2.69	7/01	11r
Coffee, vacuum-packed	13 oz	2.31	3/01	4c
Cookies, chocolate chip	lb	2.87	7/01	11r
Corn Flakes, Kellogg's or Post Toasties	18 oz	2.24	3/01	4c
Corn, frozen, whole kernel, lowest price	16 oz	0.97	3/01	4c
Dairy product purchases	yr	304	1999	30r
Eggs, expenditures on	yr	26	1999	30r

Item	Per	Value	Date	Ref.
Groceries - continued				
Eggs, Grade A or AA	dozen	0.92	3/01	4c
Eggs, grade A, large	dozen	0.88	7/01	11r
Fats and oils, expenditures on	yr	75	1999	30r
Fish and seafood, expenditures on	yr	72	1999	30r
Food (excl fruit and vegetables), eaten at home, purchases	yr	887	1999	30r
Food cooked on trips, expenditures on	yr	44	1999	30r
Food purchases	yr	4802	1999	30r
Food purchases, eaten away from home	yr	2069	1999	30r
Food purchases, food eaten at home	yr	2733	1999	30r
Fresh fruits, expenditures on	yr	138	1999	30r
Fresh milk and cream, expenditures on	yr	120	1999	30r
Fresh vegetables, expenditures on	yr	126	1999	30r
Grapefruit	lb	0.66	7/01	11r
Grapes, Thompson, seedless	lb	1.64	7/01	11r
Ground beef, 100% beef	lb	1.64	7/01	11r
Ground beef, lean and extra lean	lb	2.16	7/01	11r
Ground chuck, 100% beef	lb	2.13	7/01	11r
Ham, boneless, excl canned	lb	2.62	7/01	11r
Ice cream, prepackaged, bulk, regular	1/2 gal	3.35	7/01	11r
Lemons	lb	1.19	7/01	11r
Lettuce, iceberg	head	0.97	3/01	4c
Lettuce, iceberg	lb	0.73	7/01	11r
Margarine, Blue Bonnet or Parkay, stick	lb	0.62	3/01	4c
Margarine, soft, tubs	lb	0.89	7/01	11r
Meats, poultry, fish, and egg purchases	yr	671	1999	30r
Milk, fresh, whole, fortified	gal	2.71	7/01	11r
Milk, whole	1/2 gal	1.44	3/01	4c
Nonalcoholic beverages, expenditures on	yr	239	1999	30r
Orange juice, Minute Maid frozen	12 oz	1.42	3/01	4c
Oranges, Navel	lb	0.80	7/01	11r
Oranges, Valencia	lb	0.66	7/01	11r
Peaches, halves or slices, Hunt's, Del Monte, or Libby's	29 oz	1.38	3/01	4c
Pears, Anjou	lb	0.93	7/01	11r
Peas, green, Del Monte or Green Giant	15 oz	0.59	3/01	4c
Pork chops, center cut, bone-in	lb	3.63	7/01	11r
Pork, expenditures on	yr	150	1999	30r
Potato chips	16 oz	3.52	7/01	11r
Potatoes, frozen, french fried	lb	1.08	7/01	11r
Potatoes, white or red	10 lb	2.19	3/01	4c
Potatoes, white, all types	lb	0.33	7/01	11r
Poultry, expenditures on	yr	108	1999	30r
Processed fruits, expenditures on	yr	98	1999	30r
Processed vegetables, expenditures on	yr	80	1999	30r
Round roast, U.S. choice, boneless	lb	3.07	7/01	11r
Round steak, graded and ungraded, excl U.S. prime and choice	lb	3.41	7/01	11r
Sausage, Jimmy Dean/Owens pork	lb	2.69	3/01	4c
Shortening, vegetable oil blends	lb	1.13	7/01	11r
Shortening, vegetable, Crisco	3 lb	2.68	3/01	4c
Soft drink, Coca Cola, ex deposit	2 liter	1.16	3/01	4c
Spaghetti and macaroni	lb	0.80	7/01	11r
Steak, round, U.S. choice, boneless	lb	3.23	7/01	11r
Steak, T-bone	lb	5.35	3/01	4c
Steak, T-bone, U.S. choice, bone-in	lb	6.68	7/01	11r
Strawberries, dry pint	12 oz	1.32	7/01	11r
Sugar and other sweets, expenditures on	yr	114	1999	30r
Sugar, cane or beet	4 lbs	1.31	3/01	4c
Sugar, white, 33-80 ounce package	lb	0.42	7/01	11r
Sugar, white, all sizes	lb	0.43	7/01	11r
Tobacco products and smoking supplies purchases	yr	331	1999	30r
Tomatoes, field grown	lb	1.46	7/01	11r
Tomatoes, Hunt's or Del Monte	14.5 oz	0.81	3/01	4c
Tuna, chunk, light	6 oz	0.57	3/01	4c
Tuna, light, chunk	lb	1.80	7/01	11r
Turkey, frozen, whole	lb	1.15	7/01	11r
Goods and Services				
Miscellaneous goods and services, ACCRA Index		95.50	3/01	4c

Values are in dollars or fractions of dollars. In the column headed *Ref*, references are shown to sources. Each reference is followed by a letter. These refer to the geographical level for which data were reported: s=State, r=Region, and c=City or metro. The abbreviation *ex* is used to mean *except* or *excluding*; *exp* stands for *expenditures*. For other abbreviations and further explanations, please see the Introduction.

Lafayette, IN - continued

Item	Per	Value	Date	Ref.
Goods and Services				
B&B Japanese maple (acer japonicum)	gal	29.99-169.99	4/00	93r
Boxwood (buxus)	2 gal	18.99-39.99	4/00	93r
Daylilly (hemerocallis)	gal	4.99-25.00	4/00	93r
Flat of annuals		11.98-24.99	4/00	93r
Fountain grass (pennisetum)	gal	5.98-12.98	4/00	93r
Hanging basket (10 in)		12.99-27.99	4/00	93r
Hardy geranium (geranium)	gal	7.99-9.99	4/00	93r
Hosta (hosta)	gal	6.00-25.00	4/00	93r
Lilac (syrubga vulgaris)	2 gal	14.99-24.99	4/00	93r
Miscellaneous purchases	yr	865	1999	30r
Rhododendron (rhododendron)	2 gal	23.98-42.99	4/00	93r
Sage (salvia)	gal	6.00-9.99	4/00	93r
Wintercreeper euonymus (euonymus fortunei)	2 gal	16.00-169.99	4/00	93r
Hunting license	yr	8.75	4/01	34s
Health Care				
Health care, ACCRA Index		95.10	3/01	4c
Cardiac catheterization, ave hospital/ physician charges		13380	1998	77s
Childbirth, Cesarean delivery		10722	1997	13r
Childbirth, vaginal delivery		6223	1997	13r
Dentist's fee, adult teeth cleaning and periodic oral exam	visit	76.40	3/01	4c
Doctor's fee, routine exam, established patient	visit	53.40	3/01	4c
Drugs, expenditures on	yr	394	1999	30r
Health care purchases	yr	2048	1999	30r
Health insurance expenditures	yr	978	1999	30r
Hospital care, private room	day	412.50	3/01	4c
Hysterectomy, laproscopically-assisted, ave hospital/physician charges		11310	1998	76s
Hysterectomy, vaginal, ave hospital and physician charges		9160	1998	76s
Medicaid dispensing fee		4.00	1999	87s
Medical services expenditures	yr	554	1999	30r
Medical supplies, expenditures on	yr	122	1999	30r
Plastic surgery, breast augmentation		3184	2000	7r
Plastic surgery, breast lift		3585	2000	7r
Plastic surgery, facelift		4999	2000	7r
Plastic surgery, hair transplantation		3105	2000	7r
Plastic surgery, lip augmentation		1290	2000	7r
Plastic surgery, lower body lift		8135	2000	7r
Plastic surgery, thigh lift		3839	2000	7r
Household Goods				
Dishwashing powder, Cascade	50 oz	2.96	3/01	4c
Floor coverings, expenditures on	yr	52	1999	30r
Furniture, expenditures on	yr	344	1999	30r
Household furnishings and equipment purchases	yr	1475	1999	30r
Household textiles, expenditures on	yr	109	1999	30r
Laundry and cleaning supplies, expenditures on	yr	134	1999	30r
Tissues, facial, Kleenex brand	175	1.07	3/01	4c
Housing				
Housing, ACCRA Index		89.10	3/01	4c
Home price, existing, ave		144400	10/00	90r
Home value, median		102000	2001	53s
House, 2400 sq ft, 8000 sq ft lot, new, urban, utilities	total	178699	3/01	4c

Lafayette, IN - continued

Item	Per	Value	Date	Ref.
Housing - continued				
House payment, principal and interest, 25% down payment	mos	901	3/01	4c
Household operation expenditures	yr	542	1999	30r
Housekeeping supplies purchases	yr	508	1999	30r
Lodging expenditures	yr	430	1999	30r
Maintenance, repairs, insurance expenditures	yr	853	1999	30r
Monthly rental value of owned home	mos	547	1999	30r
Owned dwellings, expenditures own	yr	4282	1999	30r
Rent expenditures	yr	1558	1999	30r
Rent, apartment, 2 br, 1 1/2-2 baths, unfurn, 950 sq ft, water	mos	664	3/01	4c
Rental unit, 1 bedroom, with utilities	mos	450	4/01	41c
Rental unit, 2 bedroom, with utilities	mos	599	4/01	41c
Rental unit, 3 bedroom, with utilities	mos	833	4/01	41c
Rental unit, 4 bedroom, with utilities	mos	984	4/01	41c
Shelter, expenditures on	yr	6270	1999	30r
Insurance and Pensions				
Life and other personal insurance purchases	yr	387	1999	30r
Pensions and Social Security, expenditures on	yr	2968	1999	30r
Legal Fees				
Divorce, filing fee		100.00	4/01	35s
Driver's license fee	renew	6.00	1999	48s
Driver's license fee	orig	6.00	1999	48s
Personal Goods				
Personal care products and services purchases	yr	385	1999	30r
Shampoo, Alberto VO5	15 oz	0.96	3/01	4c
Toothpaste, Crest or Colgate	6-7 oz	2.08	3/01	4c
Personal Services				
Dry cleaning, man's 2-pc suit		9.40	3/01	4c
Man's haircut, barbershop, no styling		8.80	3/01	4c
Personal services, household, expenditures on	yr	300	1999	30r
Woman's shampoo, trim, blow-dry, no style-change		21.40	3/01	4c
Pets				
Pets, toys, and playground equipment, expenditures on	yr	375	1999	30r
Restaurant Food				
Chicken, fried, thigh and drumstick, KFC/ Church's		2.39	3/01	4c
Hamburger with cheese, McDonald's	1/4 lb	2.19	3/01	4c
Pizza, Pizza Hut or Pizza Inn	11-12 in	8.30	3/01	4c
Taxes				
Federal income taxes paid	yr	2326	1999	30r
Personal taxes, expenditures on	yr	3223	1999	30r
Property taxes paid	yr	1152	1999	30r
State and local income taxes paid	yr	753	1999	30r
Transportation				
Transportation, ACCRA Index		98.40	3/01	4c
Bus fare, one-way	trip	0.75	2000	1c
Bus fare, to central business district	1-way	0.75	3/01	4c
Cars and trucks, new, expenditures on	yr	1280	1999	30r
Cars and trucks, used, expenditures on	yr	1763	1999	30r
Diesel at the pump	gal	1.17	10/99	73s
Gasoline and motor oil purchases	yr	1036	1999	30r
Gasoline before-tax price (cents)	gal	110.00	10/00	43s
Maintenance and repair expenditures	yr	594	1999	30r
Public transportation, expenditures on	yr	341	1999	30r
Tire balance, computer or spin balance, front	wheel	8.60	3/01	4c
Transportation purchases	yr	6617	1999	30r
Vehicle expenses, miscellaneous, purchases	yr	2159	1999	30r
Vehicle insurance payments	yr	701	1999	30r
Vehicle purchases (net outlay)	yr	3081	1999	30r
Vehicle rental, lease expenditures	yr	536	1999	30r

Values are in dollars or fractions of dollars. In the column headed *Ref*, references are shown to sources. Each reference is followed by a letter. These refer to the geographical level for which data were reported: s=State, r=Region, and c=City or metro. The abbreviation *ex* is used to mean *except* or *excluding*; *exp* stands for expenditures. For other abbreviations and further explanations, please see the Introduction.

Lafayette, IN - continued

Item	Per	Value	Date	Ref.
Utilities				
Utilities, ACCRA Index		104.00	3/01	4c
Electrical bill, average	mos	66.66	9/00	9s
Electricity, expenditures on	yr	841	1999	30r
Electricity and other, mixed, 2400 sq ft, new home	mos	48.58	3/01	4c
Electricity cost, average	KWh	5.00	9/00	9s
Utilities, fuels, and public services purchased	yr	2401	1999	30r
Water and other public services, expenditures on	yr	273	1999	30r
Weddings				
Wedding (national average cost)		19936	2000	33r
Wedding (regional average total cost)		16195	1997	110r
Attendants' gifts		321	1998	33r
Bridal attendants' apparel (5 persons)		824	2000	33r
Bride's headpiece/veil		173	1998	33r
Bride's wedding dress		859	1998	33r
Clergy, religious facility fee		242	1998	33r
Engagement ring		3177	1998	33r
Flowers		789	1998	33r
Groom's formalwear rental		99	2000	33r
Limousine		410	1998	33r
Marriage license cost		18.00	4/01	35s
Men's formalwear (ushers, best man)		469	2000	33r
Mother of bride apparel		241	2000	33r
Music		866	1998	33r
Photography and videography		1368	1998	33r
Rehearsal dinner		728	1998	33r
Wedding invitations and announcements		341	1998	33r
Wedding reception		7968	2000	33r
Wedding rings (bride and groom)		1060	1998	33r

Lafayette, LA

Item	Per	Value	Date	Ref.
Composite, ACCRA index		96.70	3/01	4c
Alcoholic Beverages				
Alcoholic beverage purchases	yr	253	1999	30r
Beer, Heineken, 12-oz, ex deposit	6	6.40	3/01	4c
J & B Scotch	750-ml	19.06	3/01	4c
Malt beverages, all types, all sizes, any origin	16 oz	0.96	7/01	11r
Wine, Livingston or Gallo, Chablis blanc	1.5 liter	5.59	3/01	4c
Appliances				
Appliance repair, service call, washing machine	min lab chg	45.25	3/01	4c
Major appliances, expenditures on	yr	172	1999	30r
Small appliances, housewares, expenditures on	yr	81	1999	30r
Banking and Money				
Mortgage interest and charges paid	yr	2039	1999	30r
Mortgage principal paid on owned property	yr	1026	1999	30r
Mortgage rate, incl. points and orig. fee, 30-yr. conv. fixed or ARM	mos	6.79	3/01	4c
Vehicle finance charges paid	yr	365	1999	30r
Charity				
Cash contributions, expenditures	yr	1127	1999	30r
Child Care				
Child raising cost, total, age 0-2	yr	8540	1999	60r
Child raising cost, total, age 3-5	yr	8780	1999	60r
Child raising cost, total, age 6-8	yr	8820	1999	60r
Child raising cost, total, age 9-11	yr	8800	1999	60r
Child raising cost, total, age 12-14	yr	9510	1999	60r
Child raising cost, total, age 15-17	yr	9740	1999	60r
Child's child care and education, age 0-2	yr	1380	1999	60r
Child's child care and education, age 3-5	yr	1520	1999	60r
Child's child care and education, age 6-8	yr	990	1999	60r
Child's child care and education, age 9-11	yr	650	1999	60r
Child's child care and education, age 12-14	yr	490	1999	60r
Child's child care and education, age 15-17	yr	840	1999	60r
Child's clothing, age 0-2	yr	480	1999	60r

Lafayette, LA - continued

Item	Per	Value	Date	Ref.
Child Care - continued				
Child's clothing, age 3-5	yr	470	1999	60r
Child's clothing, age 6-8	yr	520	1999	60r
Child's clothing, age 9-11	yr	570	1999	60r
Child's clothing, age 12-14	yr	950	1999	60r
Child's clothing, age 15-17	yr	850	1999	60r
Child's food, age 0-2	yr	1000	1999	60r
Child's food, age 3-5	yr	1160	1999	60r
Child's food, age 6-8	yr	1490	1999	60r
Child's food, age 9-11	yr	1770	1999	60r
Child's food, age 12-14	yr	1770	1999	60r
Child's food, age 15-17	yr	1980	1999	60r
Child's health care, age 0-2	yr	620	1999	60r
Child's health care, age 3-5	yr	590	1999	60r
Child's health care, age 6-8	yr	680	1999	60r
Child's health care, age 9-11	yr	720	1999	60r
Child's health care, age 12-14	yr	730	1999	60r
Child's health care, age 15-17	yr	760	1999	60r
Child's housing, age 0-2	yr	3070	1999	60r
Child's housing, age 3-5	yr	3050	1999	60r
Child's housing, age 6-8	yr	3010	1999	60r
Child's housing, age 9-11	yr	2850	1999	60r
Child's housing, age 12-14	yr	3040	1999	60r
Child's housing, age 15-17	yr	2650	1999	60r
Child's personal care, reading, age 0-2	yr	910	1999	60r
Child's personal care, reading, age 3-5	yr	930	1999	60r
Child's personal care, reading, age 6-8	yr	960	1999	60r
Child's personal care, reading, age 9-11	yr	1000	1999	60r
Child's personal care, reading, age 12-14	yr	1170	1999	60r
Child's personal care, reading, age 15-17	yr	950	1999	60r
Clothing				
Apparel and services purchases	yr	1610	1999	30r
Boys' brief, cotton	3	3.48	3/01	4c
Boys, 2 to 15, expenditures on	yr	89	1999	30r
Children under 2, expenditures on	yr	79	1999	30r
Footwear, expenditures on	yr	283	1999	30r
Girls, 2 to 15, expenditures on	yr	103	1999	30r
Men and boys, expenditures on	yr	351	1999	30r
Men, 16 and over, expenditures on	yr	262	1999	30r
Shirt, man's dress shirt		29.00	3/01	4c
Slacks, man's "No Wrinkles" khaki		39.33	3/01	4c
Women, 16 and over, expenditures on	yr	538	1999	30r
Communications				
Newspaper subscription, daily and Sunday delivery	mos	10.25	3/01	4c
Phone line, single, business, field visit	inst.	85.00	12/97	17s
Phone line, single, business, no field visit	inst.	85.00	12/97	17s
Phone line, single, residence, field visit	inst.	41.00	12/97	17s
Phone line, single, residence, no field visit	inst.	41.00	12/97	17s
Postage and stationery, expenditures on	yr	104	1999	30r
Postal rate, express mail, up to half-pound		12.45	7/01	108r
Postal rate, letter, first class, first ounce		0.34	7/01	108r
Postal rate, letter, two ounces		0.57	7/01	108r
Postal rate, post card		0.21	7/01	108r
Postal rate, priority mail, two pounds		3.95	7/01	108r
Postal rate, priority mail, up to one pound		3.50	7/01	108r
Telephone bill, family of three	mos	20.78	3/01	4c
Telephone services, expenditures on	yr	860	1999	30r
Education				
Board, 4-year private college/university	yr	2440	1996	38s
Board, 4-year public college/university	yr	1806	1996	38s
Education expenditures	yr	431	1999	30r
Room, 4-year private college/university	yr	2906	1996	38s
Room, 4-year public college/university	yr	1464	1996	38s
Total cost, 4-year private college/university	yr	17796	1996	38s
Total cost, 4-year public college/university	yr	5491	1996	38s
Tuition, 2-year public college/university, in state	yr	1031	1996	38s
Tuition, 4-year private college/university, in state	yr	12449	1996	38s
Tuition, 4-year public college/university	yr	2221	1996	38s

Values are in dollars or fractions of dollars. In the column headed *Ref*, references are shown to sources. Each reference is followed by a letter. These refer to the geographical level for which data were reported: s=State, r=Region, and c=City or metro. The abbreviation *ex* is used to mean *except* or *excluding*; *exp* stands for expenditures. For other abbreviations and further explanations, please see the Introduction.

Lafayette, LA - continued

Item	Per	Value	Date	Ref.
Energy and Fuels				
Electricity	KWh	0.09	7/01	11r
Electricity	500 KWhs	47.29	7/01	11r
Energy, combined forms, 2400 sq ft	mos	103.59	3/01	4c
Energy, exc. electricity, 2400 sq ft	mos	44.92	3/01	4c
Fuel oil #2	gal	1.43	7/01	11r
Fuel oil and other fuels, expenditures on	yr	45	1999	30r
Gas, cooking, winter, 10 therms	mos	12.28	2/96	98c
Gas, cooking, winter, 30 therms	mos	24.83	2/96	98c
Gas, cooking, winter, 50 therms	mos	37.38	2/96	98c
Gas, heating, winter, average use	mos	70.68	2/96	98c
Gas, natural, commercial rate	1000 cf	8.75	11/00	88s
Gas, regular unleaded, cash, self-service	gal	1.41	3/01	4c
Gasoline, all types	gal	1.60	7/01	11r
Gasoline, unleaded midgrade	gal	1.65	7/01	11r
Gasoline, unleaded premium	gal	1.74	7/01	11r
Natural gas, expenditures on	yr	164	1999	30r
Utility (piped) gas, therm		1.01	7/01	11r
Utility (piped) gas, 40 therms		44.29	7/01	11r
Utility (piped) gas, 100 therms		97.44	7/01	11r
Entertainment				
Bowling, Saturday evening rate	line	3.25	3/01	4c
Entertainment purchases	yr	1574	1999	30r
Fees and admissions paid	yr	371	1999	30r
Monopoly game, Parker Brothers', No. 9	game	9.43	3/01	4c
Movie, first-run, Saturday, evening	adm.	6.75	3/01	4c
Reading purchases	yr	121	1999	30r
Television, radios, sound equipment, expenditures on	yr	561	1999	30r
Tennis balls, yellow, Wilson or Penn, 3	can	2.31	3/01	4c
Funerals				
Total cost of funeral		5842.28	1/99	78r
Acknowledgement cards		28.35	1/99	78r
Casket		2494.29	1/99	78r
Cosmetology, hair, other preparation		109.22	1/99	78r
Embalming		361.42	1/99	78r
Funeral at funeral home		349.20	1/99	78r
Hearse (local)		161.91	1/99	78r
Professional service charges		1116.50	1/99	78r
Service car/van		65.56	1/99	78r
Transfer of remains to funeral home		143.56	1/99	78r
Vault		785.25	1/99	78r
Visitation/viewing		227.02	1/99	78r
Groceries				
Groceries, ACCRA Index		92.60	3/01	4c
American processed cheese	lb	3.50	7/01	11r
Antibiotic ointment, Polysporin	0.5 oz	4.60	3/01	4c
Baby food, strained vegetables or fruit, lowest price	4-4.5 oz	0.29	3/01	4c
Bakery products, expenditures on	yr	261	1999	30r
Bananas	lb	0.45	3/01	4c
Bananas	lb	0.47	7/01	11r
Beans, dried, any type, all sizes	lb	0.63	7/01	11r
Beef for stew, boneless	lb	2.86	7/01	11r
Beef or hamburger, ground	lb	1.81	3/01	4c
Beef, expenditures on	yr	210	1999	30r
Bologna, all beef or mixed	lb	2.29	7/01	11r
Bread, French	lb	1.66	7/01	11r
Bread, white	loaf	0.96	3/01	4c
Bread, white, pan	lb	0.87	7/01	11r
Bread, whole wheat, pan	lb	1.38	7/01	11r
Broccoli	lb	1.04	7/01	11r
Butter, salted, grade AA, stick	lb	2.26	7/01	11r
Butter, yoghurt, cheese, etc, expenditures on	yr	170	1999	30r
Cabbage	lb	0.42	7/01	11r
Cereals and cereal products, expenditures on	yr	140	1999	30r
Cheddar cheese, natural	lb	3.75	7/01	11r
Cheese, Kraft grated Parmesan	8 oz	3.87	3/01	4c
Chicken breast, bone-in	lb	1.85	7/01	11r
Chicken legs, bone-in	lb	1.34	7/01	11r

Lafayette, LA - continued

Item	Per	Value	Date	Ref.
Groceries - continued				
Chicken, fresh, whole	lb	1.05	7/01	11r
Chicken, whole fryer	lb	0.78	3/01	4c
Chops, boneless,	lb	4.13	7/01	11r
Chuck roast, graded and ungraded, excl U.S. prime and choice	lb	2.35	7/01	11r
Chuck roast, U.S. choice, boneless	lb	2.67	7/01	11r
Cigarettes, Winston, Kings	carton	28.63	3/01	4c
Coffee, 100%, ground roast, all sizes	lb	2.88	7/01	11r
Coffee, instant, plain, regular, all sizes	16 oz	9.25	7/01	11r
Coffee, vacuum-packed	13 oz	2.38	3/01	4c
Cola, non diet,	2 liter	1.11	7/01	11r
Corn Flakes, Kellogg's or Post Toasties	18 oz	2.16	3/01	4c
Corn, frozen, whole kernel, lowest price	16 oz	1.20	3/01	4c
Crackers, soda, salted	lb	1.70	7/01	11r
Dairy product purchases	yr	282	1999	30r
Eggs, expenditures on	yr	32	1999	30r
Eggs, Grade A or AA	dozen	1.10	3/01	4c
Fats and oils, expenditures on	yr	79	1999	30r
Fish and seafood, expenditures on	yr	99	1999	30r
Flour, white, all purpose	lb	0.32	7/01	11r
Food (excl fruit and vegetables), eaten at home, purchases	yr	815	1999	30r
Food cooked on trips, expenditures on	yr	36	1999	30r
Food purchases	yr	4533	1999	30r
Food purchases, eaten away from home	yr	1873	1999	30r
Food purchases, food eaten at home	yr	2660	1999	30r
Fresh fruits, expenditures on	yr	128	1999	30r
Fresh milk and cream, expenditures on	yr	112	1999	30r
Fresh vegetables, expenditures on	yr	131	1999	30r
Fruit and vegetable purchases	yr	438	1999	30r
Grapefruit	lb	0.59	7/01	11r
Grapes, Thompson, seedless	lb	2.12	7/01	11r
Ground beef, 100% beef	lb	1.76	7/01	11r
Ground beef, lean and extra lean	lb	2.60	7/01	11r
Ground chuck, 100% beef	lb	2.08	7/01	11r
Ham, boneless, excl canned	lb	2.71	7/01	11r
Ham, rump or shank half, bone-in, smoked	lb	2.19	7/01	11r
Ice cream, prepackaged, bulk, regular	1/2 gal	3.93	7/01	11r
Lemons	lb	1.32	7/01	11r
Lettuce, iceberg	head	0.96	3/01	4c
Lettuce, iceberg	lb	0.76	7/01	11r
Margarine, Blue Bonnet or Parkay, stick	lb	0.59	3/01	4c
Milk, fresh, low fat,	gal	2.75	7/01	11r
Milk, fresh, whole, fortified	gal	2.97	7/01	11r
Milk, whole	1/2 gal	1.76	3/01	4c
Nonalcoholic beverages, expenditures on	yr	228	1999	30r
Orange juice, frozen concentrate	16 oz	1.95	7/01	11r
Orange juice, Minute Maid frozen	12 oz	1.56	3/01	4c
Oranges, Navel	lb	0.73	7/01	11r
Oranges, Valencia	lb	0.55	7/01	11r
Peaches, halves or slices, Hunt's, Del Monte, or Libby's	29 oz	1.59	3/01	4c
Peanut butter, creamy, all sizes	lb	1.83	7/01	11r
Pears, Anjou	lb	0.98	7/01	11r
Peas, green, Del Monte or Green Giant	15 oz	0.66	3/01	4c
Pork chops, center cut, bone-in	lb	3.33	7/01	11r
Pork sausage, fresh, loose	lb	2.59	7/01	11r
Pork shoulder picnic, bone-in, smoked	lb	1.12	7/01	11r
Pork, expenditures on	yr	162	1999	30r
Potato chips	16 oz	3.59	7/01	11r
Potatoes, frozen, french fried	lb	1.00	7/01	11r
Potatoes, white or red	10 lb	2.29	3/01	4c
Potatoes, white, all types	lb	0.44	7/01	11r
Poultry, expenditures on	yr	137	1999	30r
Processed fruits, expenditures on	yr	97	1999	30r
Processed vegetables, expenditures on	yr	82	1999	30r
Rice, white, long grain, uncooked	lb	0.51	7/01	11r
Round roast, graded and ungraded, excl U.S. prime and choice	lb	2.96	7/01	11r
Round steak, graded and ungraded, excl U.S. prime and choice	lb	3.11	7/01	11r
Sausage, Jimmy Dean/Owens pork	lb	2.96	3/01	4c

Values are in dollars or fractions of dollars. In the column headed *Ref*, references are shown to sources. Each reference is followed by a letter. These refer to the geographical level for which data were reported: s=State, r=Region, and c=City or metro. The abbreviation *ex* is used to mean *except* or *excluding*; *exp* stands for *expenditures*. For other abbreviations and further explanations, please see the Introduction.

Lafayette, LA - continued

Item	Per	Value	Date	Ref.
Groceries				
Shortening, vegetable, Crisco	3 lb	2.82	3/01	4c
Sirloin steak, graded and ungraded, excl U.S. prime and choice	lb	4.23	7/01	11r
Soft drink, Coca Cola, ex deposit	2 liter	1.09	3/01	4c
Spaghetti and macaroni	lb	0.78	7/01	11r
Steak, round, U.S. choice, boneless	lb	3.56	7/01	11r
Steak, sirloin, U.S. choice, boneless	lb	5.65	7/01	11r
Steak, T-bone	lb	6.01	3/01	4c
Strawberries, dry pint	12 oz	1.50	7/01	11r
Sugar and other sweets, expenditures on	yr	99	1999	30r
Sugar, cane or beet	4 lbs	1.58	3/01	4c
Sugar, white, 33-80 ounce package	lb	0.39	7/01	11r
Sugar, white, all sizes	lb	0.42	7/01	11r
Tobacco products and smoking supplies purchases	yr	288	1999	30r
Tomatoes, field grown	lb	1.43	7/01	11r
Tomatoes, Hunt's or Del Monte	14.5 oz	0.85	3/01	4c
Tuna, chunk, light	6 oz	0.46	3/01	4c
Tuna, light, chunk	lb	1.77	7/01	11r
Turkey, frozen, whole	lb	1.05	7/01	11r
Goods and Services				
Miscellaneous goods and services, ACCRA Index		97.10	3/01	4c
B&B Japanese maple (acer japonicum)	gal	79.98-99.00	4/00	93r
Boxwood (buxus)	2 gal	12.98-18.99	4/00	93r
Daylilly (hemerocallis)	gal	7.96-11.00	4/00	93r
Flat of annuals		13.99-27.99	4/00	93r
Fountain grass (pennisetum)	gal	6.96-9.00	4/00	93r
Hanging basket (10 in)		9.99-24.99	4/00	93r
Hardy geranium (geranium)	gal	5.96-8.00	4/00	93r
Hosta (hosta)	gal	8.96-12.99	4/00	93r
Lilac (syrubga vulgaris)	2 gal	13.00-19.99	4/00	93r
Rhododendron (rhododendron)	2 gal	12.98-29.99	4/00	93r
Sage (salvia)	gal	5.96-8.00	4/00	93r
Wintercreeper euonymus (euonymus fortunei)	2 gal	13.00-18.99	4/00	93r
Hunting license	yr	15.00	4/01	34s
Health Care				
Health care, ACCRA Index		90.10	3/01	4c
Cardiac catheterization, ave hospital/physician charges		15650	1998	77s
Childbirth, Cesarean delivery		11587	1997	13r
Childbirth, vaginal delivery		6725	1997	13r
Dentist's fee, adult teeth cleaning and periodic oral exam	visit	68.00	3/01	4c
Doctor's fee, routine exam, established patient	visit	52.00	3/01	4c
Drugs, expenditures on	yr	399	1999	30r
Health care purchases	yr	1971	1999	30r
Health insurance expenditures	yr	933	1999	30r
Hospital care, private room	day	412.50	3/01	4c
Hysterectomy, laproscopically-assisted, ave hospital/physician charges		14600	1998	76s
Hysterectomy, vaginal, ave hospital and physician charges		10520	1998	76s
Medicaid dispensing fee		5.77	1999	87s
Medical services expenditures	yr	547	1999	30r
Medical supplies, expenditures on	yr	91	1999	30r

Lafayette, LA - continued

Item	Per	Value	Date	Ref.
Household Goods				
Dishwashing powder, Cascade	50 oz	3.41	3/01	4c
Floor coverings, expenditures on	yr	44	1999	30r
Furniture, expenditures on	yr	335	1999	30r
Household furnishings and equipment purchases	yr	1328	1999	30r
Household textiles, expenditures on	yr	89	1999	30r
Laundry and cleaning supplies, expenditures on	yr	113	1999	30r
Tissues, facial, Kleenex brand	175	1.24	3/01	4c
Housing				
Housing, ACCRA Index		100.90	3/01	4c
Home, 2200 sq ft, 4-br, 2-bath, 2-car garage, average		188725	2000	47c
Home price, existing, ave		160100	10/00	90r
Home value, median		108000	2001	53s
House, 2400 sq ft, 8000 sq ft lot, new, urban, utilities	total	213168	3/01	4c
House payment, principal and interest, 25% down payment	mos	1041	3/01	4c
Household operation expenditures	yr	553	1999	30r
Housekeeping supplies purchases	yr	473	1999	30r
Housing, expenditures on	yr	10303	1999	30r
Maintenance, repairs, insurance expenditures	yr	699	1999	30r
Monthly rental value of owned home	mos	505	1999	30r
Owned dwellings, expenditures own	yr	3465	1999	30r
Rent expenditures	yr	1641	1999	30r
Rent, apartment, 2 br, 1 1/2-2 baths, unfurn, 950 sq ft, water	mos	699	3/01	4c
Rental unit, 1 bedroom, with utilities	mos	341	4/01	41c
Rental unit, 2 bedroom, with utilities	mos	405	4/01	41c
Rental unit, 3 bedroom, with utilities	mos	558	4/01	41c
Rental unit, 4 bedroom, with utilities	mos	660	4/01	41c
Shelter, expenditures on	yr	5467	1999	30r
Insurance and Pensions				
Auto insurance premium	yr	965.15	1999	57s
Life and other personal insurance purchases	yr	414	1999	30r
Pensions and Social Security, expenditures on	yr	2635	1999	30r
Personal insurance and pensions, expenditures on	yr	3048	1999	30r
Legal Fees				
Divorce, filing fee		162.00	4/01	35s
Driver's license fee	orig	18.00	1999	48s
Driver's license fee	renew	12.50	1999	48s
Fishing license	yr	9.50	4/01	34s
Personal Goods				
Personal care products and services purchases	yr	393	1999	30r
Shampoo, Alberto VO5	15 oz	1.05	3/01	4c
Toothpaste, Crest or Colgate	6-7 oz	2.25	3/01	4c
Personal Services				
Dry cleaning, man's 2-pc suit		8.00	3/01	4c
Man's haircut, barbershop, no styling		11.20	3/01	4c
Personal services, household, expenditures on	yr	258	1999	30r
Woman's shampoo, trim, blow-dry, no style-change		25.60	3/01	4c
Pets				
Pets, toys, and playground equipment, expenditures on	yr	306	1999	30r
Restaurant Food				
Chicken, fried, thigh and drumstick, KFC/Church's		1.99	3/01	4c
Hamburger with cheese, McDonald's	1/4 lb	1.99	3/01	4c
Pizza, Pizza Hut or Pizza Inn	11-12 in	8.99	3/01	4c

Values are in dollars or fractions of dollars. In the column headed *Ref*, references are shown to sources. Each reference is followed by a letter. These refer to the geographical level for which data were reported: s=State, r=Region, and c=City or metro. The abbreviation *ex* is used to mean *except* or *excluding*; *exp* stands for *expenditures*. For other abbreviations and further explanations, please see the Introduction.

Lafayette, LA - continued

Item	Per	Value	Date	Ref.
Taxes				
Federal income taxes paid	yr	2047	1999	30r
Personal taxes, expenditures on	yr	2554	1999	30r
Property taxes paid	yr	726	1999	30r
State and local income taxes paid	yr	363	1999	30r
Transportation				
Transportation, ACCRA Index		101.70	3/01	4c
Cars and trucks, new, expenditures on	yr	1648	1999	30r
Cars and trucks, used, expenditures on	yr	1651	1999	30r
Diesel at the pump	gal	1.19	10/99	73s
Gasoline and motor oil purchases	yr	1052	1999	30r
Gasoline before-tax price (cents)	gal	102.70	10/00	43s
Maintenance and repair expenditures	yr	621	1999	30r
Public transportation, expenditures on	yr	298	1999	30r
Tire balance, computer or spin balance, front	wheel	8.20	3/01	4c
Transportation purchases	yr	6738	1999	30r
Vehicle expenses, miscellaneous, purchases	yr	2033	1999	30r
Vehicle insurance payments	yr	696	1999	30r
Vehicle purchases (net outlay)	yr	3354	1999	30r
Vehicle rental, lease expenditures	yr	352	1999	30r
Utilities				
Utilities, ACCRA Index		86.30	3/01	4c
Electrical bill, average	mos	87.50	9/00	9s
Electricity, expenditures on	yr	1115	1999	30r
Electricity and other, mixed, 2400 sq ft, new home	mos	58.67	3/01	4c
Electricity cost, average	KWh	6.35	9/00	9s
Water and other public services, expenditures on	yr	298	1999	30r
Weddings				
Wedding (national average cost)		19936	2000	33r
Attendants' gifts		321	1998	33r
Bridal attendants' apparel (5 persons)		824	2000	33r
Bride's headpiece/veil		173	1998	33r
Bride's wedding dress		859	1998	33r
Clergy, religious facility fee		242	1998	33r
Engagement ring		3177	1998	33r
Flowers		789	1998	33r
Groom's formalwear rental		99	2000	33r
Limousine		410	1998	33r
Marriage license cost		25.00	4/01	35s
Men's formalwear (ushers, best man)		469	2000	33r
Mother of bride apparel		241	2000	33r
Music		866	1998	33r
Photography and videography		1368	1998	33r
Rehearsal dinner		728	1998	33r
Wedding invitations and announcements		341	1998	33r
Wedding reception		7968	2000	33r
Wedding rings (bride and groom)		1060	1998	33r

Lake Charles, LA

Item	Per	Value	Date	Ref.
Composite, ACCRA index		95.20	3/01	4c
Alcoholic Beverages				
Alcoholic beverage purchases	yr	253	1999	30r
Beer, Heineken, 12-oz, ex deposit	6	6.58	3/01	4c
J & B Scotch	750-ml	19.58	3/01	4c
Malt beverages, all types, all sizes, any origin	16 oz	0.96	7/01	11r
Wine, Livingston or Gallo, Chablis blanc	1.5 liter	5.73	3/01	4c
Appliances				
Appliance repair, service call, washing machine	min lab chg	42.16	3/01	4c
Major appliances, expenditures on	yr	172	1999	30r
Small appliances, housewares, expenditures on	yr	81	1999	30r
Banking and Money				
Mortgage interest and charges paid	yr	2039	1999	30r
Mortgage principal paid on owned property	yr	1026	1999	30r

Lake Charles, LA - continued

Item	Per	Value	Date	Ref.
Banking and Money - continued				
Mortgage rate, incl. points and orig. fee, 30-yr. conv. fixed or ARM	mos	6.89	3/01	4c
Vehicle finance charges paid	yr	365	1999	30r
Charity				
Cash contributions, expenditures	yr	1127	1999	30r
Child Care				
Child raising cost, total, age 0-2	yr	8540	1999	60r
Child raising cost, total, age 3-5	yr	8780	1999	60r
Child raising cost, total, age 6-8	yr	8820	1999	60r
Child raising cost, total, age 9-11	yr	8800	1999	60r
Child raising cost, total, age 12-14	yr	9510	1999	60r
Child raising cost, total, age 15-17	yr	9740	1999	60r
Child's child care and education, age 0-2	yr	1380	1999	60r
Child's child care and education, age 3-5	yr	1520	1999	60r
Child's child care and education, age 6-8	yr	990	1999	60r
Child's child care and education, age 9-11	yr	650	1999	60r
Child's child care and education, age 12-14	yr	490	1999	60r
Child's child care and education, age 15-17	yr	840	1999	60r
Child's clothing, age 0-2	yr	480	1999	60r
Child's clothing, age 3-5	yr	470	1999	60r
Child's clothing, age 6-8	yr	520	1999	60r
Child's clothing, age 9-11	yr	570	1999	60r
Child's clothing, age 12-14	yr	950	1999	60r
Child's clothing, age 15-17	yr	850	1999	60r
Child's food, age 0-2	yr	1000	1999	60r
Child's food, age 3-5	yr	1160	1999	60r
Child's food, age 6-8	yr	1490	1999	60r
Child's food, age 9-11	yr	1770	1999	60r
Child's food, age 12-14	yr	1770	1999	60r
Child's food, age 15-17	yr	1980	1999	60r
Child's health care, age 0-2	yr	620	1999	60r
Child's health care, age 3-5	yr	590	1999	60r
Child's health care, age 6-8	yr	680	1999	60r
Child's health care, age 9-11	yr	720	1999	60r
Child's health care, age 12-14	yr	730	1999	60r
Child's health care, age 15-17	yr	760	1999	60r
Child's housing, age 0-2	yr	3070	1999	60r
Child's housing, age 3-5	yr	3050	1999	60r
Child's housing, age 6-8	yr	3010	1999	60r
Child's housing, age 9-11	yr	2850	1999	60r
Child's housing, age 12-14	yr	3040	1999	60r
Child's housing, age 15-17	yr	2650	1999	60r
Child's personal care, reading, age 0-2	yr	910	1999	60r
Child's personal care, reading, age 3-5	yr	930	1999	60r
Child's personal care, reading, age 6-8	yr	960	1999	60r
Child's personal care, reading, age 9-11	yr	1000	1999	60r
Child's personal care, reading, age 12-14	yr	1170	1999	60r
Child's personal care, reading, age 15-17	yr	950	1999	60r
Clothing				
Apparel and services purchases	yr	1610	1999	30r
Boys' brief, cotton	3	4.42	3/01	4c
Boys, 2 to 15, expenditures on	yr	89	1999	30r
Children under 2, expenditures on	yr	79	1999	30r
Footwear, expenditures on	yr	283	1999	30r
Girls, 2 to 15, expenditures on	yr	103	1999	30r
Men and boys, expenditures on	yr	351	1999	30r
Men, 16 and over, expenditures on	yr	262	1999	30r
Shirt, man's dress shirt		26.41	3/01	4c
Slacks, man's "No Wrinkles" khaki		40.49	3/01	4c
Women, 16 and over, expenditures on	yr	538	1999	30r
Communications				
Newspaper subscription, daily and Sunday delivery	mos	10.08	3/01	4c
Phone line, single, business, field visit	inst.	85.00	12/97	17s
Phone line, single, business, no field visit	inst.	85.00	12/97	17s
Phone line, single, residence, field visit	inst.	41.00	12/97	17s
Phone line, single, residence, no field visit	inst.	41.00	12/97	17s
Postage and stationery, expenditures on	yr	104	1999	30r
Postal rate, express mail, up to half-pound		12.45	7/01	108r
Postal rate, letter, first class, first ounce		0.34	7/01	108r

Values are in dollars or fractions of dollars. In the column headed *Ref*, references are shown to sources. Each reference is followed by a letter. These refer to the geographical level for which data were reported: s=State, r=Region, and c=City or metro. The abbreviation *ex* is used to mean *except* or *excluding*; *exp* stands for *expenditures*. For other abbreviations and further explanations, please see the Introduction.

Lake Charles, LA - continued

Item	Per	Value	Date	Ref.
Communications				
Postal rate, letter, two ounces		0.57	7/01	108r
Postal rate, post card		0.21	7/01	108r
Postal rate, priority mail, two pounds		3.95	7/01	108r
Postal rate, priority mail, up to one pound		3.50	7/01	108r
Telephone bill, business, basic rate	mos	34.51	12/97	18c
Telephone bill, family of three	mos	19.71	3/01	4c
Telephone bill, residential, basic rate	mos	12.64	12/97	18c
Telephone services, expenditures on	yr	860	1999	30r
Education				
Board, 4-year private college/university	yr	2440	1996	38s
Board, 4-year public college/university	yr	1806	1996	38s
Education expenditures	yr	431	1999	30r
Room, 4-year private college/university	yr	2906	1996	38s
Room, 4-year public college/university	yr	1464	1996	38s
Total cost, 4-year private college/university	yr	17796	1996	38s
Total cost, 4-year public college/university	yr	5491	1996	38s
Tuition, 2-year public college/university, in state	yr	1031	1996	38s
Tuition, 4-year private college/university, in state	yr	12449	1996	38s
Tuition, 4-year public college/university	yr	2221	1996	38s
Energy and Fuels				
Electricity	KWh	0.09	7/01	11r
Electricity	500 KWhs	47.29	7/01	11r
Energy, combined forms, 2400 sq ft	mos	97.89	3/01	4c
Fuel oil #2	gal	1.43	7/01	11r
Fuel oil and other fuels, expenditures on	yr	45	1999	30r
Gas, cooking, winter, 10 therms	mos	14.16	2/96	98c
Gas, cooking, winter, 30 therms	mos	23.49	2/96	98c
Gas, cooking, winter, 50 therms	mos	32.80	2/96	98c
Gas, heating, winter, average use	mos	58.89	2/96	98c
Gas, natural, commercial rate	1000 cf	8.75	11/00	88s
Gas, regular unleaded, cash, self-service	gal	1.35	3/01	4c
Gasoline, all types	gal	1.60	7/01	11r
Gasoline, unleaded midgrade	gal	1.65	7/01	11r
Gasoline, unleaded premium	gal	1.74	7/01	11r
Natural gas, expenditures on	yr	164	1999	30r
Utility (piped) gas, therm		1.01	7/01	11r
Utility (piped) gas, 40 therms		44.29	7/01	11r
Utility (piped) gas, 100 therms		97.44	7/01	11r
Entertainment				
Bowling, Saturday evening rate	line	2.70	3/01	4c
Entertainment purchases	yr	1574	1999	30r
Fees and admissions paid	yr	371	1999	30r
Monopoly game, Parker Brothers', No. 9	game	10.41	3/01	4c
Movie, first-run, Saturday, evening	adm.	6.75	3/01	4c
Reading purchases	yr	121	1999	30r
Television, radios, sound equipment, expenditures on	yr	561	1999	30r
Tennis balls, yellow, Wilson or Penn, 3	can	1.99	3/01	4c
Funerals				
Total cost of funeral		5842.28	1/99	78r
Acknowledgement cards		28.35	1/99	78r
Casket		2494.29	1/99	78r
Cosmetology, hair, other preparation		109.22	1/99	78r
Embalming		361.42	1/99	78r
Funeral at funeral home		349.20	1/99	78r
Hearse (local)		161.91	1/99	78r
Professional service charges		1116.50	1/99	78r
Service car/van		65.56	1/99	78r
Transfer of remains to funeral home		143.56	1/99	78r
Vault		785.25	1/99	78r
Visitation/viewing		227.02	1/99	78r
Groceries				
Groceries, ACCRA Index		90.60	3/01	4c
American processed cheese	lb	3.50	7/01	11r
Antibiotic ointment, Polysporin	0.5 oz	4.55	3/01	4c

Lake Charles, LA - continued

Item	Per	Value	Date	Ref.
Groceries - continued				
Baby food, strained vegetables or fruit, lowest price	4-4.5 oz	0.30	3/01	4c
Bakery products, expenditures on	yr	261	1999	30r
Bananas	lb	0.39	3/01	4c
Bananas	lb	0.47	7/01	11r
Beans, dried, any type, all sizes	lb	0.63	7/01	11r
Beef for stew, boneless	lb	2.86	7/01	11r
Beef or hamburger, ground	lb	1.62	3/01	4c
Beef, expenditures on	yr	210	1999	30r
Bologna, all beef or mixed	lb	2.29	7/01	11r
Bread, French	lb	1.66	7/01	11r
Bread, white	loaf	0.85	3/01	4c
Bread, white, pan	lb	0.87	7/01	11r
Bread, whole wheat, pan	lb	1.38	7/01	11r
Broccoli	lb	1.04	7/01	11r
Butter, salted, grade AA, stick	lb	2.26	7/01	11r
Butter, yoghurt, cheese, etc, expenditures on	yr	170	1999	30r
Cabbage	lb	0.42	7/01	11r
Cereals and cereal products, expenditures on	yr	140	1999	30r
Cheddar cheese, natural	lb	3.75	7/01	11r
Cheese, Kraft grated Parmesan	8 oz	4.12	3/01	4c
Chicken breast, bone-in	lb	1.85	7/01	11r
Chicken legs, bone-in	lb	1.34	7/01	11r
Chicken, fresh, whole	lb	1.05	7/01	11r
Chicken, whole fryer	lb	0.73	3/01	4c
Chops, boneless,	lb	4.13	7/01	11r
Chuck roast, graded and ungraded, excl U.S. prime and choice	lb	2.35	7/01	11r
Chuck roast, U.S. choice, boneless	lb	2.67	7/01	11r
Cigarettes, Winston, Kings	carton	29.97	3/01	4c
Coffee, 100%, ground roast, all sizes	lb	2.88	7/01	11r
Coffee, instant, plain, regular, all sizes	16 oz	9.25	7/01	11r
Coffee, vacuum-packed	13 oz	2.40	3/01	4c
Cola, non diet,	2 liter	1.11	7/01	11r
Corn Flakes, Kellogg's or Post Toasties	18 oz	2.04	3/01	4c
Corn, frozen, whole kernel, lowest price	16 oz	1.15	3/01	4c
Crackers, soda, salted	lb	1.70	7/01	11r
Dairy product purchases	yr	282	1999	30r
Eggs, expenditures on	yr	32	1999	30r
Eggs, Grade A or AA	dozen	1.10	3/01	4c
Fats and oils, expenditures on	yr	79	1999	30r
Fish and seafood, expenditures on	yr	99	1999	30r
Flour, white, all purpose	lb	0.32	7/01	11r
Food (excl fruit and vegetables), eaten at home, purchases	yr	815	1999	30r
Food cooked on trips, expenditures on	yr	36	1999	30r
Food purchases	yr	4533	1999	30r
Food purchases, eaten away from home	yr	1873	1999	30r
Food purchases, food eaten at home	yr	2660	1999	30r
Fresh fruits, expenditures on	yr	128	1999	30r
Fresh milk and cream, expenditures on	yr	112	1999	30r
Fresh vegetables, expenditures on	yr	131	1999	30r
Fruit and vegetable purchases	yr	438	1999	30r
Grapefruit	lb	0.59	7/01	11r
Grapes, Thompson, seedless	lb	2.12	7/01	11r
Ground beef, 100% beef	lb	1.76	7/01	11r
Ground beef, lean and extra lean	lb	2.60	7/01	11r
Ground chuck, 100% beef	lb	2.08	7/01	11r
Ham, boneless, excl canned	lb	2.71	7/01	11r
Ham, rump or shank half, bone-in, smoked	lb	2.19	7/01	11r
Ice cream, prepackaged, bulk, regular	1/2 gal	3.93	7/01	11r
Lemons	lb	1.32	7/01	11r
Lettuce, iceberg	head	0.93	3/01	4c
Lettuce, iceberg	lb	0.76	7/01	11r
Margarine, Blue Bonnet or Parkay, stick	lb	0.79	3/01	4c
Milk, fresh, low fat,	gal	2.75	7/01	11r
Milk, fresh, whole, fortified	gal	2.97	7/01	11r
Milk, whole	1/2 gal	1.72	3/01	4c
Nonalcoholic beverages, expenditures on	yr	228	1999	30r
Orange juice, frozen concentrate	16 oz	1.95	7/01	11r
Orange juice, Minute Maid frozen	12 oz	1.51	3/01	4c

Values are in dollars or fractions of dollars. In the column headed *Ref*, references are shown to sources. Each reference is followed by a letter. These refer to the geographical level for which data were reported: s=State, r=Region, and c=City or metro. The abbreviation *ex* is used to mean *except* or *excluding*; *exp* stands for *expenditures*. For other abbreviations and further explanations, please see the Introduction.

Lake Charles, LA - continued

Groceries

Item	Per	Value	Date	Ref.
Oranges, Navel	lb	0.73	7/01	11r
Oranges, Valencia	lb	0.55	7/01	11r
Peaches, halves or slices, Hunt's, Del Monte, or Libby's	29 oz	1.44	3/01	4c
Peanut butter, creamy, all sizes	lb	1.83	7/01	11r
Pears, Anjou	lb	0.98	7/01	11r
Peas, green, Del Monte or Green Giant	15 oz	0.66	3/01	4c
Pork chops, center cut, bone-in	lb	3.33	7/01	11r
Pork sausage, fresh, loose	lb	2.59	7/01	11r
Pork shoulder picnic, bone-in, smoked	lb	1.12	7/01	11r
Pork, expenditures on	yr	162	1999	30r
Potato chips	16 oz	3.59	7/01	11r
Potatoes, frozen, french fried	lb	1.00	7/01	11r
Potatoes, white or red	10 lb	2.38	3/01	4c
Potatoes, white, all types	lb	0.44	7/01	11r
Poultry, expenditures on	yr	137	1999	30r
Processed fruits, expenditures on	yr	97	1999	30r
Processed vegetables, expenditures on	yr	82	1999	30r
Rice, white, long grain, uncooked	lb	0.51	7/01	11r
Round roast, graded and ungraded, excl U.S. prime and choice	lb	2.96	7/01	11r
Round steak, graded and ungraded, excl U.S. prime and choice	lb	3.11	7/01	11r
Sausage, Jimmy Dean/Owens pork	lb	2.55	3/01	4c
Shortening, vegetable, Crisco	3 lb	2.73	3/01	4c
Sirloin steak, graded and ungraded, excl U.S. prime and choice	lb	4.23	7/01	11r
Soft drink, Coca Cola, ex deposit	2 liter	1.07	3/01	4c
Spaghetti and macaroni	lb	0.78	7/01	11r
Steak, round, U.S. choice, boneless	lb	3.56	7/01	11r
Steak, sirloin, U.S. choice, boneless	lb	5.65	7/01	11r
Steak, T-bone	lb	5.75	3/01	4c
Strawberries, dry pint	12 oz	1.50	7/01	11r
Sugar and other sweets, expenditures on	yr	99	1999	30r
Sugar, cane or beet	4 lbs	1.49	3/01	4c
Sugar, white, 33-80 ounce package	lb	0.39	7/01	11r
Sugar, white, all sizes	lb	0.42	7/01	11r
Tobacco products and smoking supplies purchases	yr	288	1999	30r
Tomatoes, field grown	lb	1.43	7/01	11r
Tomatoes, Hunt's or Del Monte	14.5 oz	0.85	3/01	4c
Tuna, chunk, light	6 oz	0.57	3/01	4c
Tuna, light, chunk	lb	1.77	7/01	11r
Turkey, frozen, whole	lb	1.05	7/01	11r

Goods and Services

Item	Per	Value	Date	Ref.
Miscellaneous goods and services, ACCRA Index		94.40	3/01	4c
B&B Japanese maple (acer japonicum)	gal	79.98-99.00	4/00	93r
Boxwood (buxus)	2 gal	12.98-18.99	4/00	93r
Daylily (hemerocallis)	gal	7.96-11.00	4/00	93r
Flat of annuals		13.99-27.99	4/00	93r
Fountain grass (pennisetum)	gal	6.96-9.00	4/00	93r
Hanging basket (10 in)		9.99-24.99	4/00	93r
Hardy geranium (geranium)	gal	5.96-8.00	4/00	93r
Hosta (hosta)	gal	8.96-12.99	4/00	93r
Lilac (syrubga vulgaris)	2 gal	13.00-19.99	4/00	93r
Rhododendron (rhododendron)	2 gal	12.98-29.99	4/00	93r
Sage (salvia)	gal	5.96-8.00	4/00	93r
Wintercreeper euonymus (euonymus fortunei)	2 gal	13.00-18.99	4/00	93r
Hunting license	yr	15.00	4/01	34s

Lake Charles, LA - continued

Health Care

Item	Per	Value	Date	Ref.
Health care, ACCRA Index		93.20	3/01	4c
Cardiac catheterization, ave hospital/ physician charges		15650	1998	77s
Childbirth, Cesarean delivery		11587	1997	13r
Childbirth, vaginal delivery		6725	1997	13r
Dentist's fee, adult teeth cleaning and periodic oral exam	visit	63.29	3/01	4c
Doctor's fee, routine exam, established patient	visit	60.67	3/01	4c
Drugs, expenditures on	yr	399	1999	30r
Health care purchases	yr	1971	1999	30r
Health insurance expenditures	yr	933	1999	30r
Hospital care, private room	day	419.00	3/01	4c
Hysterectomy, laproscopically-assisted, ave hospital/physician charges		14600	1998	76s
Hysterectomy, vaginal, ave hospital and physician charges		10520	1998	76s
Medicaid dispensing fee		5.77	1999	87s
Medical services expenditures	yr	547	1999	30r
Medical supplies, expenditures on	yr	91	1999	30r

Household Goods

Item	Per	Value	Date	Ref.
Dishwashing powder, Cascade	50 oz	3.22	3/01	4c
Floor coverings, expenditures on	yr	44	1999	30r
Furniture, expenditures on	yr	335	1999	30r
Household furnishings and equipment purchases	yr	1328	1999	30r
Household textiles, expenditures on	yr	89	1999	30r
Laundry and cleaning supplies, expenditures on	yr	113	1999	30r
Tissues, facial, Kleenex brand	175	1.36	3/01	4c

Housing

Item	Per	Value	Date	Ref.
Housing, ACCRA Index		100.90	3/01	4c
Home price, existing, ave		160100	10/00	90r
Home value, median		108000	2001	53s
House, 2400 sq ft, 8000 sq ft lot, new, urban, utilities	total	219550	3/01	4c
House payment, principal and interest, 25% down payment	mos	1083	3/01	4c
Household operation expenditures	yr	553	1999	30r
Housekeeping supplies purchases	yr	473	1999	30r
Housing, expenditures on	yr	10303	1999	30r
Maintenance, repairs, insurance expenditures	yr	699	1999	30r
Monthly rental value of owned home	mos	505	1999	30r
Owned dwellings, expenditures own	yr	3465	1999	30r
Rent expenditures	yr	1641	1999	30r
Rent, apartment, 2 br, 1 1/2-2 baths, unfurn, 950 sq ft, water	mos	587	3/01	4c
Rental unit, 1 bedroom, with utilities	mos	379	4/01	41c
Rental unit, 2 bedroom, with utilities	mos	480	4/01	41c
Rental unit, 3 bedroom, with utilities	mos	629	4/01	41c
Rental unit, 4 bedroom, with utilities	mos	788	4/01	41c
Shelter, expenditures on	yr	5467	1999	30r

Insurance and Pensions

Item	Per	Value	Date	Ref.
Auto insurance premium	yr	965.15	1999	57s
Life and other personal insurance purchases	yr	414	1999	30r
Pensions and Social Security, expenditures on	yr	2635	1999	30r
Personal insurance and pensions, expenditures on	yr	3048	1999	30r

Legal Fees

Item	Per	Value	Date	Ref.
Divorce, filing fee		162.00	4/01	35s
Driver's license fee	renew	12.50	1999	48s
Driver's license fee	orig	18.00	1999	48s
Fishing license	yr	9.50	4/01	34s

Personal Goods

Item	Per	Value	Date	Ref.
Personal care products and services purchases	yr	393	1999	30r
Shampoo, Alberto VO5	15 oz	1.15	3/01	4c

Values are in dollars or fractions of dollars. In the column headed *Ref*, references are shown to sources. Each reference is followed by a letter. These refer to the geographical level for which data were reported: s=State, r=Region, and c=City or metro. The abbreviation *ex* is used to mean *except* or *excluding*; *exp* stands for *expenditures*. For other abbreviations and further explanations, please see the Introduction.

Lake Charles, LA - continued

Item	Per	Value	Date	Ref.
Personal Goods				
Toothpaste, Crest or Colgate	6-7 oz	2.46	3/01	4c
Personal Services				
Dry cleaning, man's 2-pc suit		7.66	3/01	4c
Man's haircut, barbershop, no styling		10.33	3/01	4c
Personal services, household, expenditures on	yr	258	1999	30r
Woman's shampoo, trim, blow-dry, no style-change		22.33	3/01	4c
Pets				
Pets, toys, and playground equipment, expenditures on	yr	306	1999	30r
Restaurant Food				
Chicken, fried, thigh and drumstick, KFC/Church's		1.99	3/01	4c
Hamburger with cheese, McDonald's	1/4 lb	1.68	3/01	4c
Pizza, Pizza Hut or Pizza Inn	11-12 in	9.38	3/01	4c
Taxes				
Federal income taxes paid	yr	2047	1999	30r
Personal taxes, expenditures on	yr	2554	1999	30r
Property taxes paid	yr	726	1999	30r
State and local income taxes paid	yr	363	1999	30r
Transportation				
Transportation, ACCRA Index		101.60	3/01	4c
Cars and trucks, new, expenditures on	yr	1648	1999	30r
Cars and trucks, used, expenditures on	yr	1651	1999	30r
Diesel at the pump	gal	1.19	10/99	73s
Gasoline and motor oil purchases	yr	1052	1999	30r
Gasoline before-tax price (cents)	gal	102.70	10/00	43s
Maintenance and repair expenditures	yr	621	1999	30r
Public transportation, expenditures on	yr	298	1999	30r
Tire balance, computer or spin balance, front	wheel	8.66	3/01	4c
Transportation purchases	yr	6738	1999	30r
Vehicle expenses, miscellaneous, purchases	yr	2033	1999	30r
Vehicle insurance payments	yr	696	1999	30r
Vehicle purchases (net outlay)	yr	3354	1999	30r
Vehicle rental, lease expenditures	yr	352	1999	30r
Utilities				
Utilities, ACCRA Index		81.60	3/01	4c
Electrical bill, average	mos	87.50	9/00	9s
Electricity, 2400 sq ft, new home	mos	97.89	3/01	4c
Electricity, expenditures on	yr	1115	1999	30r
Electricity cost, average	KWh	6.35	9/00	9s
Water and other public services, expenditures on	yr	298	1999	30r
Weddings				
Wedding (national average cost)		19936	2000	33r
Attendants' gifts		321	1998	33r
Bridal attendants' apparel (5 persons)		824	2000	33r
Bride's headpiece/veil		173	1998	33r
Bride's wedding dress		859	1998	33r
Clergy, religious facility fee		242	1998	33r
Engagement ring		3177	1998	33r
Flowers		789	1998	33r
Groom's formalwear rental		99	2000	33r
Limousine		410	1998	33r
Marriage license cost		25.00	4/01	35s
Men's formalwear (ushers, best man)		469	2000	33r
Mother of bride apparel		241	2000	33r
Music		866	1998	33r
Photography and videography		1368	1998	33r
Rehearsal dinner		728	1998	33r
Wedding invitations and announcements		341	1998	33r
Wedding reception		7968	2000	33r
Wedding rings (bride and groom)		1060	1998	33r

Lakeland-Winter Haven, FL

Item	Per	Value	Date	Ref.
Alcoholic Beverages				
Alcoholic beverage purchases	yr	253	1999	30r
Malt beverages, all types, all sizes, any origin	16 oz	0.96	7/01	11r
Appliances				
Major appliances, expenditures on	yr	172	1999	30r
Small appliances, housewares, expenditures on	yr	81	1999	30r
Banking and Money				
Mortgage interest and charges paid	yr	2039	1999	30r
Mortgage principal paid on owned property	yr	1026	1999	30r
Vehicle finance charges paid	yr	365	1999	30r
Charity				
Cash contributions, expenditures	yr	1127	1999	30r
Child Care				
Child raising cost, total, age 0-2	yr	8540	1999	60r
Child raising cost, total, age 3-5	yr	8780	1999	60r
Child raising cost, total, age 6-8	yr	8820	1999	60r
Child raising cost, total, age 9-11	yr	8800	1999	60r
Child raising cost, total, age 12-14	yr	9510	1999	60r
Child raising cost, total, age 15-17	yr	9740	1999	60r
Child's child care and education, age 0-2	yr	1380	1999	60r
Child's child care and education, age 3-5	yr	1520	1999	60r
Child's child care and education, age 6-8	yr	990	1999	60r
Child's child care and education, age 9-11	yr	650	1999	60r
Child's child care and education, age 12-14	yr	490	1999	60r
Child's child care and education, age 15-17	yr	840	1999	60r
Child's clothing, age 0-2	yr	480	1999	60r
Child's clothing, age 3-5	yr	470	1999	60r
Child's clothing, age 6-8	yr	520	1999	60r
Child's clothing, age 9-11	yr	570	1999	60r
Child's clothing, age 12-14	yr	950	1999	60r
Child's clothing, age 15-17	yr	850	1999	60r
Child's food, age 0-2	yr	1000	1999	60r
Child's food, age 3-5	yr	1160	1999	60r
Child's food, age 6-8	yr	1490	1999	60r
Child's food, age 9-11	yr	1770	1999	60r
Child's food, age 12-14	yr	1770	1999	60r
Child's food, age 15-17	yr	1980	1999	60r
Child's health care, age 0-2	yr	620	1999	60r
Child's health care, age 3-5	yr	590	1999	60r
Child's health care, age 6-8	yr	680	1999	60r
Child's health care, age 9-11	yr	720	1999	60r
Child's health care, age 12-14	yr	730	1999	60r
Child's health care, age 15-17	yr	760	1999	60r
Child's housing, age 0-2	yr	3070	1999	60r
Child's housing, age 3-5	yr	3050	1999	60r
Child's housing, age 6-8	yr	3010	1999	60r
Child's housing, age 9-11	yr	2850	1999	60r
Child's housing, age 12-14	yr	3040	1999	60r
Child's housing, age 15-17	yr	2650	1999	60r
Child's personal care, reading, age 0-2	yr	910	1999	60r
Child's personal care, reading, age 3-5	yr	930	1999	60r
Child's personal care, reading, age 6-8	yr	960	1999	60r
Child's personal care, reading, age 9-11	yr	1000	1999	60r
Child's personal care, reading, age 12-14	yr	1170	1999	60r
Child's personal care, reading, age 15-17	yr	950	1999	60r
Clothing				
Apparel and services purchases	yr	1610	1999	30r
Boys, 2 to 15, expenditures on	yr	89	1999	30r
Children under 2, expenditures on	yr	79	1999	30r
Footwear, expenditures on	yr	283	1999	30r
Girls, 2 to 15, expenditures on	yr	103	1999	30r
Men and boys, expenditures on	yr	351	1999	30r
Men, 16 and over, expenditures on	yr	262	1999	30r
Women, 16 and over, expenditures on	yr	538	1999	30r
Communications				
Cable modem installation, Adelphi		54.90	6/99	103s
Cable modem installation, Comcast		95.00	6/99	103s
Cable modem installation, Media One		100.00	6/99	103s

Values are in dollars or fractions of dollars. In the column headed *Ref*, references are shown to sources. Each reference is followed by a letter. These refer to the geographical level for which data were reported: s=State, r=Region, and c=City or metro. The abbreviation *ex* is used to mean *except* or *excluding*; *exp* stands for expenditures. For other abbreviations and further explanations, please see the Introduction.

Lakeland-Winter Haven, FL - continued

Item	Per	Value	Date	Ref.
Communications				
Cable modem installation, Time Warner		75.00-225.00	6/99	103s
Cable modem rate, cable subscriber, Adelphi	mos	34.95	6/99	103s
Cable modem rate, cable subscriber, Comcast	mos	39.95	6/99	103s
Cable modem rate, cable subscriber, Media One	mos	34.95-39.95	6/99	103s
Cable modem rate, cable subscriber, Time Warner	mos	39.95-49.95	6/99	103s
Cable modem rate, non-cable subscriber, Adelphi	mos	44.95	6/99	103s
Cable modem rate, non-cable subscriber, Comcast	mos	49.95	6/99	103s
Cable modem rate, non-cable subscriber, Media One	mos	49.95	6/99	103s
Cable modem rate, non-cable subscriber, Time Warner	mos	39.95-54.95	6/99	103s
Phone line, single, business, field visit	inst.	56.00	12/97	17s
Phone line, single, business, no field visit	inst.	56.00	12/97	17s
Phone line, single, residence, field visit	inst.	40.00	12/97	17s
Phone line, single, residence, no field visit	inst.	40.00	12/97	17s
Postage and stationery, expenditures on	yr	104	1999	30r
Postal rate, express mail, up to half-pound		12.45	7/01	108r
Postal rate, letter, first class, first ounce		0.34	7/01	108r
Postal rate, letter, two ounces		0.57	7/01	108r
Postal rate, post card		0.21	7/01	108r
Postal rate, priority mail, two pounds		3.95	7/01	108r
Postal rate, priority mail, up to one pound		3.50	7/01	108r
Telephone services, expenditures on	yr	860	1999	30r
Education				
Board, 4-year private college/university	yr	2236	1996	38s
Board, 4-year public college/university	yr	2295	1996	38s
Education expenditures	yr	431	1999	30r
Room, 4-year private college/university	yr	2428	1996	38s
Room, 4-year public college/university	yr	2193	1996	38s
Total cost, 4-year private college/university	yr	15028	1996	38s
Total cost, 4-year public college/university	yr	6254	1996	38s
Tuition, 2-year public college/university, in state	yr	1103	1996	38s
Tuition, 4-year private college/university, in state	yr	10364	1996	38s
Tuition, 4-year public college/university	yr	1767	1996	38s
Energy and Fuels				
Electricity	KWh	0.09	7/01	11r
Electricity	500 KWhs	47.29	7/01	11r
Fuel oil #2	gal	1.43	7/01	11r
Fuel oil and other fuels, expenditures on	yr	45	1999	30r
Gas, natural, commercial rate	1000 cf	8.44	11/00	88s
Gasoline, all types	gal	1.60	7/01	11r
Gasoline, unleaded midgrade	gal	1.65	7/01	11r
Gasoline, unleaded premium	gal	1.74	7/01	11r
Natural gas, expenditures on	yr	164	1999	30r
Utility (piped) gas, therm		1.01	7/01	11r
Utility (piped) gas, 40 therms		44.29	7/01	11r
Utility (piped) gas, 100 therms		97.44	7/01	11r
Entertainment				
Entertainment purchases	yr	1574	1999	30r
Fees and admissions paid	yr	371	1999	30r
Reading purchases	yr	121	1999	30r
Television, radios, sound equipment, expenditures on	yr	561	1999	30r
Funerals				
Total cost of funeral		5922.53	1/99	78r
Acknowledgement cards		63.43	1/99	78r
Casket		2258.77	1/99	78r
Cosmetology, hair, other preparation		127.09	1/99	78r
Embalming		393.49	1/99	78r
Funeral at funeral home		367.50	1/99	78r
Hearse (local)		169.66	1/99	78r

Lakeland-Winter Haven, FL - continued

Item	Per	Value	Date	Ref.
Funerals - continued				
Professional service charges		1211.32	1/99	78r
Service car/van		80.69	1/99	78r
Transfer of remains to funeral home		144.25	1/99	78r
Vault		803.50	1/99	78r
Visitation/viewing		302.83	1/99	78r
Groceries				
American processed cheese	lb	3.50	7/01	11r
Bakery products, expenditures on	yr	261	1999	30r
Bananas	lb	0.47	7/01	11r
Beans, dried, any type, all sizes	lb	0.63	7/01	11r
Beef for stew, boneless	lb	2.86	7/01	11r
Beef, expenditures on	yr	210	1999	30r
Bologna, all beef or mixed	lb	2.29	7/01	11r
Bread, French	lb	1.66	7/01	11r
Bread, white, pan	lb	0.87	7/01	11r
Bread, whole wheat, pan	lb	1.38	7/01	11r
Broccoli	lb	1.04	7/01	11r
Butter, salted, grade AA, stick	lb	2.26	7/01	11r
Butter, yoghurt, cheese, etc, expenditures on	yr	170	1999	30r
Cabbage	lb	0.42	7/01	11r
Cereals and cereal products, expenditures on	yr	140	1999	30r
Cheddar cheese, natural	lb	3.75	7/01	11r
Chicken breast, bone-in	lb	1.85	7/01	11r
Chicken legs, bone-in	lb	1.34	7/01	11r
Chicken, fresh, whole	lb	1.05	7/01	11r
Chops, boneless	lb	4.13	7/01	11r
Chuck roast, graded and ungraded, excl U.S. prime and choice	lb	2.35	7/01	11r
Chuck roast, U.S. choice, boneless	lb	2.67	7/01	11r
Coffee, 100%, ground roast, all sizes	lb	2.88	7/01	11r
Coffee, instant, plain, regular, all sizes	16 oz	9.25	7/01	11r
Cola, non diet,	2 liter	1.11	7/01	11r
Crackers, soda, salted	lb	1.70	7/01	11r
Dairy product purchases	yr	282	1999	30r
Eggs, expenditures on	yr	32	1999	30r
Fats and oils, expenditures on	yr	79	1999	30r
Fish and seafood, expenditures on	yr	99	1999	30r
Flour, white, all purpose	lb	0.32	7/01	11r
Food (excl fruit and vegetables), eaten at home, purchases	yr	815	1999	30r
Food cooked on trips, expenditures on	yr	36	1999	30r
Food purchases	yr	4533	1999	30r
Food purchases, eaten away from home	yr	1873	1999	30r
Food purchases, food eaten at home	yr	2660	1999	30r
Fresh fruits, expenditures on	yr	128	1999	30r
Fresh milk and cream, expenditures on	yr	112	1999	30r
Fresh vegetables, expenditures on	yr	131	1999	30r
Fruit and vegetable purchases	yr	438	1999	30r
Grapefruit	lb	0.59	7/01	11r
Grapes, Thompson, seedless	lb	2.12	7/01	11r
Ground beef, 100% beef	lb	1.76	7/01	11r
Ground beef, lean and extra lean	lb	2.60	7/01	11r
Ground chuck, 100% beef	lb	2.08	7/01	11r
Ham, boneless, excl canned	lb	2.71	7/01	11r
Ham, rump or shank half, bone-in, smoked	lb	2.19	7/01	11r
Ice cream, prepackaged, bulk, regular	1/2 gal	3.93	7/01	11r
Lemons	lb	1.32	7/01	11r
Lettuce, iceberg	lb	0.76	7/01	11r
Milk, fresh, low fat,	gal	2.75	7/01	11r
Milk, fresh, whole, fortified	gal	2.97	7/01	11r
Nonalcoholic beverages, expenditures on	yr	228	1999	30r
Orange juice, frozen concentrate	16 oz	1.95	7/01	11r
Oranges, Navel	lb	0.73	7/01	11r
Oranges, Valencia	lb	0.55	7/01	11r
Peanut butter, creamy, all sizes	lb	1.83	7/01	11r
Pears, Anjou	lb	0.98	7/01	11r
Pork chops, center cut, bone-in	lb	3.33	7/01	11r
Pork sausage, fresh, loose	lb	2.59	7/01	11r
Pork shoulder picnic, bone-in, smoked	lb	1.12	7/01	11r
Pork, expenditures on	yr	162	1999	30r
Potato chips	16 oz	3.59	7/01	11r

Values are in dollars or fractions of dollars. In the column headed *Ref*, references are shown to sources. Each reference is followed by a letter. These refer to the geographical level for which data were reported: s=State, r=Region, and c=City or metro. The abbreviation *ex* is used to mean *except* or *excluding*; *exp* stands for *expenditures*. For other abbreviations and further explanations, please see the Introduction.

Lakeland-Winter Haven, FL - continued

Item	Per	Value	Date	Ref.
Groceries				
Potatoes, frozen, french fried	lb	1.00	7/01	11r
Potatoes, white, all types	lb	0.44	7/01	11r
Poultry, expenditures on	yr	137	1999	30r
Processed fruits, expenditures on	yr	97	1999	30r
Processed vegetables, expenditures on	yr	82	1999	30r
Rice, white, long grain, uncooked	lb	0.51	7/01	11r
Round roast, graded and ungraded, excl U.S. prime and choice	lb	2.96	7/01	11r
Round steak, graded and ungraded, excl U.S. prime and choice	lb	3.11	7/01	11r
Sirloin steak, graded and ungraded, excl U.S. prime and choice	lb	4.23	7/01	11r
Spaghetti and macaroni	lb	0.78	7/01	11r
Steak, round, U.S. choice, boneless	lb	3.56	7/01	11r
Steak, sirloin, U.S. choice, boneless	lb	5.65	7/01	11r
Strawberries, dry pint	12 oz	1.50	7/01	11r
Sugar and other sweets, expenditures on	yr	99	1999	30r
Sugar, white, 33-80 ounce package	lb	0.39	7/01	11r
Sugar, white, all sizes	lb	0.42	7/01	11r
Tobacco products and smoking supplies purchases	yr	288	1999	30r
Tomatoes, field grown	lb	1.43	7/01	11r
Tuna, light, chunk	lb	1.77	7/01	11r
Turkey, frozen, whole	lb	1.05	7/01	11r
Goods and Services				
B&B Japanese maple (acer japonicum)	gal	49.98-129.00	4/00	93r
Boxwood (buxus)	2 gal	12.99-16.99	4/00	93r
Daylily (hemerocallis)	gal	4.99-8.99	4/00	93r
Flat of annuals		11.00-13.92	4/00	93r
Fountain grass (pennisetum)	gal	5.98-7.98	4/00	93r
Hanging basket (10 in)		7.99-14.98	4/00	93r
Hardy geranium (geranium)	gal	5.98-8.00	4/00	93r
Hosta (hosta)	gal	4.99-10.98	4/00	93r
Lilac (syrubga vulgaris)	2 gal	12.99-21.99	4/00	93r
Rhododendron (rhododendron)	2 gal	14.99-24.99	4/00	93r
Sage (salvia)	gal	5.98-6.99	4/00	93r
Wintercreeper euonymus (euonymus fortunei)	2 gal	7.99-89.99	4/00	93r
Hunting license	yr	12.50	4/01	34s
Health Care				
Cardiac catheterization, ave hospital/physician charges		15060	1998	77s
Childbirth, Cesarean delivery		11587	1997	13r
Childbirth, vaginal delivery		6725	1997	13r
Drugs, expenditures on	yr	399	1999	30r
Health care purchases	yr	1971	1999	30r
Health insurance expenditures	yr	933	1999	30r
Hysterectomy, laproscopically-assisted, ave hospital/physician charges		14760	1998	76s
Hysterectomy, vaginal, ave hospital and physician charges		11320	1998	76s
Medicaid dispensing fee		4.23	1999	87s
Medical services expenditures	yr	547	1999	30r
Medical supplies, expenditures on	yr	91	1999	30r
Plastic surgery, breast augmentation		2870	2000	7r
Plastic surgery, breast lift		3649	2000	7r
Plastic surgery, facelift		5008	2000	7r
Plastic surgery, hair transplantation		3425	2000	7r
Plastic surgery, lip augmentation		1227	2000	7r
Plastic surgery, lower body lift		4793	2000	7r

Lakeland-Winter Haven, FL - continued

Item	Per	Value	Date	Ref.
Health Care - continued				
Plastic surgery, thigh lift		3862	2000	7r
Household Goods				
Floor coverings, expenditures on	yr	44	1999	30r
Furniture, expenditures on	yr	335	1999	30r
Household furnishings and equipment purchases	yr	1328	1999	30r
Household textiles, expenditures on	yr	89	1999	30r
Laundry and cleaning supplies, expenditures on	yr	113	1999	30r
Housing				
Home price, existing, ave		160100	10/00	90r
Home value, median		104000	2001	53s
Household operation expenditures	yr	553	1999	30r
Housekeeping supplies purchases	yr	473	1999	30r
Housing, expenditures on	yr	10303	1999	30r
Maintenance, repairs, insurance expenditures	yr	699	1999	30r
Monthly rental value of owned home	mos	505	1999	30r
Owned dwellings, expenditures own	yr	3465	1999	30r
Rent expenditures	yr	1641	1999	30r
Rental unit, 1 bedroom, with utilities	mos	433	4/01	41c
Rental unit, 2 bedroom, with utilities	mos	490	4/01	41c
Rental unit, 3 bedroom, with utilities	mos	607	4/01	41c
Rental unit, 4 bedroom, with utilities	mos	663	4/01	41c
Shelter, expenditures on	yr	5467	1999	30r
Insurance and Pensions				
Life and other personal insurance purchases	yr	414	1999	30r
Medigap health insurance, Plan H	yr	2887	2000	69s
Medigap health insurance, Plan I	yr	3302	2000	69s
Medigap health insurance, Plan J	yr	3889	2000	69s
Pensions and Social Security, expenditures on	yr	2635	1999	30r
Personal insurance and pensions, expenditures on	yr	3048	1999	30r
Legal Fees				
Divorce, filing fee		65.00-85.00	4/01	35s
Driver's license fee	orig	20.00	1999	48s
Driver's license fee	renew	15.00	1999	48s
Personal Goods				
Personal care products and services purchases	yr	393	1999	30r
Personal Services				
Personal services, household, expenditures on	yr	258	1999	30r
Pets				
Pets, toys, and playground equipment, expenditures on	yr	306	1999	30r
Taxes				
Federal income taxes paid	yr	2047	1999	30r
Personal taxes, expenditures on	yr	2554	1999	30r
Property taxes paid	yr	726	1999	30r
State and local income taxes paid	yr	363	1999	30r
Transportation				
Cars and trucks, new, expenditures on	yr	1648	1999	30r
Cars and trucks, used, expenditures on	yr	1651	1999	30r
Diesel at the pump	gal	1.26	10/99	73s
Gasoline and motor oil purchases	yr	1052	1999	30r
Gasoline before-tax price (cents)	gal	101.90	10/00	43s
Maintenance and repair expenditures	yr	621	1999	30r
Public transportation, expenditures on	yr	298	1999	30r
Transportation purchases	yr	6738	1999	30r
Vehicle expenses, miscellaneous, purchases	yr	2033	1999	30r
Vehicle insurance payments	yr	696	1999	30r
Vehicle purchases (net outlay)	yr	3354	1999	30r
Vehicle rental, lease expenditures	yr	352	1999	30r

Values are in dollars or fractions of dollars. In the column headed *Ref*, references are shown to sources. Each reference is followed by a letter. These refer to the geographical level for which data were reported: s=State, r=Region, and c=City or metro. The abbreviation *ex* is used to mean *except* or *excluding*; *exp* stands for *expenditures*. For other abbreviations and further explanations, please see the Introduction.

Lakeland-Winter Haven, FL - continued

Item	Per	Value	Date	Ref.
Travel				
Hotel room	night	110.57	2/01	95s
Utilities				
Electrical bill, average	mos	86.33	9/00	9s
Electricity, expenditures on	yr	1115	1999	30r
Electricity cost, average	KWh	6.80	9/00	9s
Water and other public services, expenditures on	yr	298	1999	30r
Weddings				
Wedding (national average cost)		19936	2000	33r
Wedding (regional average total cost)		16293	1997	110r
Attendants' gifts		321	1998	33r
Bridal attendants' apparel (5 persons)		824	2000	33r
Bride's headpiece/veil		173	1998	33r
Bride's wedding dress		859	1998	33r
Clergy, religious facility fee		242	1998	33r
Engagement ring		3177	1998	33r
Flowers		789	1998	33r
Groom's formalwear rental		99	2000	33r
Limousine		410	1998	33r
Marriage license cost		56.00-88.50	4/01	35s
Men's formalwear (ushers, best man)		469	2000	33r
Mother of bride apparel		241	2000	33r
Music		866	1998	33r
Photography and videography		1368	1998	33r
Rehearsal dinner		728	1998	33r
Wedding invitations and announcements		341	1998	33r
Wedding reception		7968	2000	33r
Wedding rings (bride and groom)		1060	1998	33r

Lancaster, PA

Item	Per	Value	Date	Ref.
Average annual expenditures	yr	37971	1999	30r
Composite, ACCRA index		95.60	3/01	4c
Alcoholic Beverages				
Alcoholic beverage purchases	yr	368	1999	30r
Beer, Heineken, 12-oz, ex deposit	6	8.23	3/01	4c
J & B Scotch	750-ml	22.99	3/01	4c
Wine, Livingston or Gallo, Chablis blanc	1.5 liter	6.99	3/01	4c
Wine, red and white table, all sizes, any origin	liter	9.64	7/01	11r
Appliances				
Appliance repair, service call, washing machine	min lab chg	33.86	3/01	4c
Major appliances, expenditures on	yr	194	1999	30r
Small appliances, housewares, expenditures on	yr	93	1999	30r
Banking and Money				
Mortgage interest and charges paid	yr	2622	1999	30r
Mortgage principal paid on owned property	yr	1262	1999	30r
Mortgage rate, incl. points and orig. fee, 30-yr. conv. fixed or ARM	mos	7.22	3/01	4c
Vehicle finance charges paid	yr	240	1999	30r
Charity				
Cash contributions, expenditures on	yr	1001	1999	30r
Child Care				
Child raising cost, total, age 0-2	yr	8670	1999	60r
Child raising cost, total, age 3-5	yr	8910	1999	60r
Child raising cost, total, age 6-8	yr	9040	1999	60r
Child raising cost, total, age 9-11	yr	9100	1999	60r
Child raising cost, total, age 12-14	yr	9890	1999	60r
Child raising cost, total, age 15-17	yr	10010	1999	60r
Child's child care and education, age 0-2	yr	1070	1999	60r
Child's child care and education, age 3-5	yr	1190	1999	60r
Child's child care and education, age 6-8	yr	740	1999	60r
Child's child care and education, age 9-11	yr	470	1999	60r
Child's child care and education, age 12-14	yr	350	1999	60r
Child's child care and education, age 15-17	yr	590	1999	60r

Lancaster, PA - continued

Item	Per	Value	Date	Ref.
Child Care - continued				
Child's clothing, age 0-2	yr	480	1999	60r
Child's clothing, age 3-5	yr	470	1999	60r
Child's clothing, age 6-8	yr	520	1999	60r
Child's clothing, age 9-11	yr	570	1999	60r
Child's clothing, age 12-14	yr	970	1999	60r
Child's clothing, age 15-17	yr	870	1999	60r
Child's food, age 0-2	yr	1130	1999	60r
Child's food, age 3-5	yr	1290	1999	60r
Child's food, age 6-8	yr	1640	1999	60r
Child's food, age 9-11	yr	1930	1999	60r
Child's food, age 12-14	yr	1940	1999	60r
Child's food, age 15-17	yr	2150	1999	60r
Child's health care, age 0-2	yr	550	1999	60r
Child's health care, age 3-5	yr	530	1999	60r
Child's health care, age 6-8	yr	610	1999	60r
Child's health care, age 9-11	yr	650	1999	60r
Child's health care, age 12-14	yr	660	1999	60r
Child's health care, age 15-17	yr	690	1999	60r
Child's housing, age 0-2	yr	3555	1999	60r
Child's housing, age 3-5	yr	3530	1999	60r
Child's housing, age 6-8	yr	3490	1999	60r
Child's housing, age 9-11	yr	3340	1999	60r
Child's housing, age 12-14	yr	3530	1999	60r
Child's housing, age 15-17	yr	3140	1999	60r
Child's personal care, reading, age 0-2	yr	920	1999	60r
Child's personal care, reading, age 3-5	yr	950	1999	60r
Child's personal care, reading, age 6-8	yr	980	1999	60r
Child's personal care, reading, age 9-11	yr	1020	1999	60r
Child's personal care, reading, age 12-14	yr	1190	1999	60r
Child's personal care, reading, age 15-17	yr	970	1999	60r
Clothing				
Apparel and services purchases	yr	1831	1999	30r
Boys' brief, cotton	3	4.14	3/01	4c
Boys, 2 to 15, expenditures on	yr	92	1999	30r
Children under 2, expenditures on	yr	63	1999	30r
Footwear, expenditures on	yr	300	1999	30r
Girls, 2 to 15, expenditures on	yr	101	1999	30r
Men and boys, expenditures on	yr	446	1999	30r
Men, 16 and over, expenditures on	yr	354	1999	30r
Shirt, man's dress shirt		23.99	3/01	4c
Slacks, man's "No Wrinkles" khaki		38.59	3/01	4c
Women, 16 and over, expenditures on	yr	584	1999	30r
Communications				
Cable modem installation, Adelphi		54.90	6/99	103s
Cable modem installation, Comcast		95.00	6/99	103s
Cable modem rate, cable subscriber, Adelphi	mos	34.95	6/99	103s
Cable modem rate, cable subscriber, Comcast	mos	39.95	6/99	103s
Cable modem rate, non-cable subscriber, Adelphi	mos	44.95	6/99	103s
Cable modem rate, non-cable subscriber, Comcast	mos	49.95	6/99	103s
Newspaper subscription, daily and Sunday delivery	mos	16.17	3/01	4c
Phone line, single, business, field visit	inst.	75.00	12/97	17s
Phone line, single, business, no field visit	inst.	75.00	12/97	17s
Phone line, single, residence, field visit	inst.	40.00	12/97	17s
Phone line, single, residence, no field visit	inst.	40.00	12/97	17s
Postage and stationery, expenditures on	yr	138	1999	30r
Postal rate, express mail, up to half-pound		12.45	7/01	108r
Postal rate, letter, first class, first ounce		0.34	7/01	108r
Postal rate, letter, two ounces		0.57	7/01	108r
Postal rate, post card		0.21	7/01	108r
Postal rate, priority mail, two pounds		3.95	7/01	108r
Postal rate, priority mail, up to one pound		3.50	7/01	108r
Telephone bill, family of three	mos	18.25	3/01	4c
Telephone services, expenditures on	yr	830	1999	30r
Education				
Board, 4-year private college/university	yr	2822	1996	38s
Board, 4-year public college/university	yr	2174	1996	38s
Education expenditures	yr	877	1999	30r

Values are in dollars or fractions of dollars. In the column headed *Ref*, references are shown to sources. Each reference is followed by a letter. These refer to the geographical level for which data were reported: s=State, r=Region, and c=City or metro. The abbreviation *ex* is used to mean *except* or *excluding*; *exp* stands for *expenditures*. For other abbreviations and further explanations, please see the Introduction.

Lancaster, PA - continued

Item	Per	Value	Date	Ref.
Education				
Room, 4-year private college/university	yr	2943	1996	38s
Room, 4-year public college/university	yr	2227	1996	38s
Total cost, 4-year private college/university	yr	19876	1996	38s
Total cost, 4-year public college/university	yr	9124	1996	38s
Tuition, 2-year public college/university, in state	yr	1909	1996	38s
Tuition, 4-year private college/university, in state	yr	14111	1996	38s
Tuition, 4-year public college/university	yr	4723	1996	38s
Energy and Fuels				
Electricity	KWh	0.12	7/01	11r
Energy, combined forms, 2400 sq ft	mos	119.39	3/01	4c
Energy, exc. electricity, 2400 sq ft	mos	60.66	3/01	4c
Fuel oil #2	gal	1.31	7/01	11r
Fuel oil and other fuels, expenditures on	yr	207	1999	30r
Gas, natural, commercial rate	1000 cf	5.96	11/00	88s
Gas, regular unleaded, cash, self-service	gal	1.37	3/01	4c
Gasoline, all types	gal	1.80	7/01	11r
Gasoline, unleaded midgrade	gal	1.85	7/01	11r
Gasoline, unleaded premium	gal	1.91	7/01	11r
Gasoline, unleaded regular	gal	1.71	7/01	11r
Natural gas, expenditures on	yr	368	1999	30r
Utility (piped) gas, therm		1.08	7/01	11r
Utility (piped) gas, 40 therms		50.87	7/01	11r
Utility (piped) gas, 100 therms		111.06	7/01	11r
Entertainment				
Bowling, Saturday evening rate	line	3.00	3/01	4c
Entertainment purchases	yr	1821	1999	30r
Fees and admissions paid	yr	511	1999	30r
Monopoly game, Parker Brothers', No. 9	game	12.74	3/01	4c
Movie, first-run, Saturday, evening	adm.	6.33	3/01	4c
Television, radios, sound equipment, expenditures on	yr	650	1999	30r
Tennis balls, yellow, Wilson or Penn, 3	can	2.19	3/01	4c
Funerals				
Total cost of funeral		5813.50	1/99	78r
Acknowledgement cards		28.32	1/99	78r
Casket		2082.20	1/99	78r
Cosmetology, hair, other preparation		169.59	1/99	78r
Embalming		465.60	1/99	78r
Funeral at funeral home		339.56	1/99	78r
Hearse (local)		183.96	1/99	78r
Professional service charges		1157.85	1/99	78r
Service car/van		100.41	1/99	78r
Transfer of remains to funeral home		158.66	1/99	78r
Vault		766.31	1/99	78r
Visitation/viewing		361.04	1/99	78r
Groceries				
Groceries, ACCRA Index		91.30	3/01	4c
Antibiotic ointment, Polysporin	0.5 oz	5.24	3/01	4c
Apples, red delicious	lb	0.95	7/01	11r
Baby food, strained vegetables or fruit, lowest price	4-4.5 oz	0.47	3/01	4c
Bacon, sliced	lb	3.44	7/01	11r
Bakery products, expenditures on	yr	310	1999	30r
Bananas	lb	0.47	3/01	4c
Bananas	lb	0.55	7/01	11r
Beef or hamburger, ground	lb	1.11	3/01	4c
Beef, expenditures on	yr	236	1999	30r
Bread, white	loaf	0.73	3/01	4c
Bread, white, pan	lb	1.09	7/01	11r
Butter, yoghurt, cheese, etc, expenditures on	yr	214	1999	30r
Cereals and bakery product purchases	yr	474	1999	30r
Cereals and cereal products, expenditures on	yr	164	1999	30r
Cheese, Kraft grated Parmesan	8 oz	3.32	3/01	4c
Chicken legs, bone-in	lb	1.23	7/01	11r
Chicken, fresh, whole	lb	1.13	7/01	11r
Chicken, whole fryer	lb	0.77	3/01	4c
Chuck roast, U.S. choice, boneless	lb	2.79	7/01	11r

Lancaster, PA - continued

Item	Per	Value	Date	Ref.
Groceries - continued				
Cigarettes, Winston, Kings	carton	27.01	3/01	4c
Coffee, 100%, ground roast, all sizes	lb	3.40	7/01	11r
Coffee, vacuum-packed	13 oz	1.91	3/01	4c
Corn Flakes, Kellogg's or Post Toasties	18 oz	2.69	3/01	4c
Corn, frozen, whole kernel, lowest price	16 oz	0.82	3/01	4c
Dairy product purchases	yr	342	1999	30r
Eggs, expenditures on	yr	34	1999	30r
Eggs, Grade A or AA	dozen	1.10	3/01	4c
Eggs, grade A, large	dozen	0.82	7/01	11r
Fats and oils, expenditures on	yr	80	1999	30r
Fish and seafood, expenditures on	yr	123	1999	30r
Food (excl fruit and vegetables), eaten at home, purchases	yr	838	1999	30r
Food cooked on trips, expenditures on	yr	48	1999	30r
Food purchases	yr	5314	1999	30r
Food purchases, eaten away from home	yr	2313	1999	30r
Food purchases, food eaten at home	yr	3001	1999	30r
Fresh fruits, expenditures on	yr	169	1999	30r
Fresh milk and cream, expenditures on	yr	128	1999	30r
Fresh vegetables, expenditures on	yr	164	1999	30r
Grapefruit	lb	0.67	7/01	11r
Grapes, Thompson, seedless	lb	2.18	7/01	11r
Ground beef, lean and extra lean	lb	2.66	7/01	11r
Ground chuck, 100% beef	lb	2.04	7/01	11r
Lettuce, iceberg	head	0.83	3/01	4c
Lettuce, iceberg	lb	0.76	7/01	11r
Margarine, Blue Bonnet or Parkay, stick	lb	0.73	3/01	4c
Meats, poultry, fish, and egg purchases	yr	808	1999	30r
Milk, whole	1/2 gal	1.50	3/01	4c
Nonalcoholic beverages, expenditures on	yr	225	1999	30r
Orange juice, frozen concentrate	16 oz	1.88	7/01	11r
Orange juice, Minute Maid frozen	12 oz	1.48	3/01	4c
Oranges, Navel	lb	0.79	7/01	11r
Oranges, Valencia	lb	0.56	7/01	11r
Peaches	lb	1.16	7/01	11r
Peaches, halves or slices, Hunt's, Del Monte, or Libby's	29 oz	1.37	3/01	4c
Peanut butter, creamy, all sizes	lb	2.01	7/01	11r
Pears, Anjou	lb	1.16	7/01	11r
Peas, green, Del Monte or Green Giant	15 oz	0.63	3/01	4c
Pork chops, center cut, bone-in	lb	3.57	7/01	11r
Pork, expenditures on	yr	146	1999	30r
Potato chips	16 oz	3.37	7/01	11r
Potatoes, white or red	10 lb	2.99	3/01	4c
Potatoes, white, all types	lb	0.42	7/01	11r
Poultry, expenditures on	yr	158	1999	30r
Processed fruits, expenditures on	yr	124	1999	30r
Processed vegetables, expenditures on	yr	82	1999	30r
Round roast, U.S. choice, boneless	lb	3.04	7/01	11r
Sausage, Jimmy Dean/Owens pork	lb	3.06	3/01	4c
Shortening, vegetable, Crisco	3 lb	2.74	3/01	4c
Soft drink, Coca Cola, ex deposit	2 liter	1.29	3/01	4c
Spaghetti and macaroni	lb	1.04	7/01	11r
Steak, sirloin, U.S. choice, boneless	lb	5.39	7/01	11r
Steak, T-bone	lb	6.39	3/01	4c
Strawberries, dry pint	12 oz	1.51	7/01	11r
Sugar and other sweets, expenditures on	yr	110	1999	30r
Sugar, cane or beet	4 lbs	1.62	3/01	4c
Sugar, white, 33-80 ounce package	lb	0.46	7/01	11r
Sugar, white, all sizes	lb	0.47	7/01	11r
Tobacco products and smoking supplies purchases	yr	309	1999	30r
Tomatoes, Hunt's or Del Monte	14.5 oz	0.84	3/01	4c
Tuna, chunk, light	6 oz	0.58	3/01	4c
Yogurt, natural, fruit flavored	8 oz	0.79	7/01	11r
Goods and Services				
Miscellaneous goods and services, ACCRA Index		100.80	3/01	4c
B&B Japanese maple (acer japonicum)	gal	38.99-125.00	4/00	93r
Boxwood (buxus)	2 gal	15.99-49.95	4/00	93r

Values are in dollars or fractions of dollars. In the column headed *Ref*, references are shown to sources. Each reference is followed by a letter. These refer to the geographical level for which data were reported: s=State, r=Region, and c=City or metro. The abbreviation *ex* is used to mean *except* or *excluding*; *exp* stands for *expenditures*. For other abbreviations and further explanations, please see the Introduction.

Lancaster, PA - continued

Item	Per	Value	Date	Ref.
Goods and Services				
Daylilly (hemerocallis)	gal	4.95	4/00	93r
Flat of annuals		8.00-14.99	4/00	93r
Fountain grass (pennisetum)	gal	6.99-9.99	4/00	93r
Hanging basket (10 in)		12.95-19.99	4/00	93r
Hardy geranium (geranium)	gal	6.95-7.99	4/00	93r
Hosta (hosta)	gal	4.95	4/00	93r
Lilac (syrubga vulgaris)	2 gal	17.99-74.95	4/00	93r
Miscellaneous purchases	yr	872	1999	30r
Rhododendron (rhododendron)	2 gal	23.99-54.95	4/00	93r
Sage (salvia)	gal	6.95-7.99	4/00	93r
Wintercreeper euonymus (euonymus fortunei)	2 gal	14.99-23.95	4/00	93r
Hunting license	yr	20.00	4/01	34s
Health Care				
Health care, ACCRA Index		95.10	3/01	4c
Cardiac catheterization, ave hospital/ physician charges		13870	1998	77s
Childbirth, Cesarean delivery		14716	1997	13r
Childbirth, vaginal delivery		8541	1997	13r
Dentist's fee, adult teeth cleaning and periodic oral exam	visit	68.67	3/01	4c
Doctor's fee, routine exam, established patient	visit	58.50	3/01	4c
Drugs, expenditures on	yr	296	1999	30r
Health care purchases	yr	1788	1999	30r
Health insurance expenditures	yr	875	1999	30r
Hospital care, private room	day	388.67	3/01	4c
Hysterectomy, laproscopically-assisted, ave hospital/physician charges		14760	1998	76s
Hysterectomy, vaginal, ave hospital and physician charges		9270	1998	76s
Medicaid dispensing fee		4.00	1999	87s
Medical services expenditures	yr	516	1999	30r
Medical supplies, expenditures on	yr	102	1999	30r
Plastic surgery, breast augmentation		4232	2000	7r
Plastic surgery, breast lift		4605	2000	7r
Plastic surgery, facelift		6964	2000	7r
Plastic surgery, hair transplantation		4193	2000	7r
Plastic surgery, lip augmentation		1675	2000	7r
Plastic surgery, lower body lift		6611	2000	7r
Plastic surgery, thigh lift		4751	2000	7r
Household Goods				
Dishwashing powder, Cascade	50 oz	3.29	3/01	4c
Floor coverings, expenditures on	yr	59	1999	30r
Furniture, expenditures on	yr	388	1999	30r
Household furnishings and equipment purchases	yr	1567	1999	30r
Household textiles, expenditures on	yr	112	1999	30r
Laundry and cleaning supplies, expenditures on	yr	104	1999	30r
Tissues, facial, Kleenex brand	175	1.19	3/01	4c
Housing				
Housing, ACCRA Index		89.60	3/01	4c
Home, 2200 sq ft, 4-br, 2-bath, 2-car garage, average		183800	2000	47c
Home price, existing, ave		180800	10/00	90r
Home value, median		115000	2001	53s
House, 2400 sq ft, 8000 sq ft lot, new, urban, utilities	total	176300	3/01	4c
House payment, principal and interest, 25% down payment	mos	899	3/01	4c
Household operation expenditures	yr	581	1999	30r
Housekeeping supplies purchases	yr	474	1999	30r
Lodging expenditures	yr	550	1999	30r

Lancaster, PA - continued

Item	Per	Value	Date	Ref.
Housing - continued				
Maintenance, repairs, insurance expenditures	yr	835	1999	30r
Monthly rental value of owned home	mos	663	1999	30r
Owned dwellings, expenditures own	yr	5209	1999	30r
Rent expenditures	yr	2390	1999	30r
Rent, apartment, 2 br, 1 1/2-2 baths, unfurn, 950 sq ft, water	mos	685	3/01	4c
Rental unit, 1 bedroom, with utilities	mos	470	4/01	41c
Rental unit, 2 bedroom, with utilities	mos	586	4/01	41c
Rental unit, 3 bedroom, with utilities	mos	765	4/01	41c
Rental unit, 4 bedroom, with utilities	mos	823	4/01	41c
Shelter, expenditures on	yr	8149	1999	30r
Insurance and Pensions				
Life and other personal insurance purchases	yr	424	1999	30r
Pensions and Social Security, expenditures on	yr	3037	1999	30r
Legal Fees				
Divorce, filing fee		65.00	4/01	35s
Driver's license fee	renew	24.00	1999	48s
Driver's license fee	orig	29.00	1999	48s
Fishing license	yr	17.00	4/01	34s
Personal Goods				
Personal care products and services purchases	yr	399	1999	30r
Shampoo, Alberto VO5	15 oz	1.24	3/01	4c
Toothpaste, Crest or Colgate	6-7 oz	1.97	3/01	4c
Personal Services				
Dry cleaning, man's 2-pc suit		9.21	3/01	4c
Man's haircut, barbershop, no styling		8.40	3/01	4c
Personal services, household, expenditures on	yr	271	1999	30r
Woman's shampoo, trim, blow-dry, no style-change		27.00	3/01	4c
Pets				
Pets, toys, and playground equipment, expenditures on	yr	325	1999	30r
Restaurant Food				
Chicken, fried, thigh and drumstick, KFC/ Church's		2.79	3/01	4c
Hamburger with cheese, McDonald's	1/4 lb	2.29	3/01	4c
Pizza, Pizza Hut or Pizza Inn	11-12 in	8.99	3/01	4c
Taxes				
Federal income taxes paid	yr	2606	1999	30r
Personal taxes, expenditures on	yr	3567	1999	30r
Property taxes paid	yr	1752	1999	30r
State and local income taxes paid	yr	694	1999	30r
Transportation				
Transportation, ACCRA Index		101.80	3/01	4c
Bus fare, one-way	trip	1.10	2000	1c
Cars and trucks, new, expenditures on	yr	1496	1999	30r
Cars and trucks, used, expenditures on	yr	1251	1999	30r
Diesel at the pump	gal	1.31	10/99	73s
Gasoline and motor oil purchases	yr	901	1999	30r
Gasoline before-tax price (cents)	gal	106.60	10/00	43s
Maintenance and repair expenditures	yr	618	1999	30r
Public transportation, expenditures on	yr	575	1999	30r
Tire balance, computer or spin balance, front	wheel	8.49	3/01	4c
Transportation purchases	yr	6503	1999	30r
Vehicle expenses, miscellaneous, purchases	yr	2266	1999	30r
Vehicle insurance payments	yr	824	1999	30r
Vehicle purchases (net outlay)	yr	2761	1999	30r
Vehicle rental, lease expenditures	yr	584	1999	30r
Utilities				
Utilities, ACCRA Index		95.90	3/01	4c
Electrical bill, average	mos	69.16	9/00	9s
Electricity, expenditures on	yr	837	1999	30r

Values are in dollars or fractions of dollars. In the column headed *Ref*, references are shown to sources. Each reference is followed by a letter. These refer to the geographical level for which data were reported: s=State, r=Region, and c=City or metro. The abbreviation *ex* is used to mean *except* or *excluding*; *exp* stands for *expenditures*. For other abbreviations and further explanations, please see the Introduction.

Lancaster, PA - continued

Item	Per	Value	Date	Ref.
Utilities				
Electricity and other, mixed, 2400 sq ft, new home	mos	58.73	3/01	4c
Electricity cost, average	KWh	5.08	9/00	9s
Utilities, fuels, and public services purchased	yr	2457	1999	30r
Water and other public services, expenditures on	yr	215	1999	30r
Weddings				
Wedding (national average cost)		19936	2000	33r
Wedding (regional average total cost)		29454	1997	110r
Attendants' gifts		321	1998	33r
Bridal attendants' apparel (5 persons)		824	2000	33r
Bride's headpiece/veil		173	1998	33r
Bride's wedding dress		859	1998	33r
Clergy, religious facility fee		242	1998	33r
Engagement ring		3177	1998	33r
Flowers		789	1998	33r
Groom's formalwear rental		99	2000	33r
Limousine		410	1998	33r
Marriage license cost		25.00-40.00	4/01	35s
Men's formalwear (ushers, best man)		469	2000	33r
Mother of bride apparel		241	2000	33r
Music		866	1998	33r
Photography and videography		1368	1998	33r
Rehearsal dinner		728	1998	33r
Wedding invitations and announcements		341	1998	33r
Wedding reception		7968	2000	33r
Wedding rings (bride and groom)		1060	1998	33r

Lansing, MI

Item	Per	Value	Date	Ref.
Average annual expenditures	yr	35369	1999	30r
Composite, ACCRA index		97.80	3/01	4c
Alcoholic Beverages				
Alcoholic beverage purchases	yr	304	1999	30r
Beer, Heineken, 12-oz, ex deposit	6	7.87	3/01	4c
J & B Scotch	750-ml	21.40	3/01	4c
Malt beverages, all types, all sizes, any origin	16 oz	0.93	7/01	11r
Wine, Livingston or Gallo, Chablis blanc	1.5 liter	5.62	3/01	4c
Wine, red and white table, all sizes, any origin	liter	7.04	7/01	11r
Appliances				
Appliance repair, service call, washing machine	min lab chg	52.67	3/01	4c
Major appliances, expenditures on	yr	165	1999	30r
Small appliances, housewares, expenditures on	yr	90	1999	30r
Banking and Money				
Mortgage interest and charges paid	yr	2277	1999	30r
Mortgage principal paid on owned property	yr	1230	1999	30r
Mortgage rate, incl. points and orig. fee, 30-yr. conv. fixed or ARM	mos	7.17	3/01	4c
Vehicle finance charges paid	yr	328	1999	30r
Charity				
Cash contributions, expenditures	yr	1126	1999	30r
Child Care				
Child raising cost, total, age 0-2	yr	7890	1999	60r
Child raising cost, total, age 3-5	yr	8130	1999	60r
Child raising cost, total, age 6-8	yr	8170	1999	60r
Child raising cost, total, age 9-11	yr	8190	1999	60r
Child raising cost, total, age 12-14	yr	8890	1999	60r
Child raising cost, total, age 15-17	yr	9050	1999	60r
Child's child care and education, age 0-2	yr	1240	1999	60r
Child's child care and education, age 3-5	yr	1370	1999	60r
Child's child care and education, age 6-8	yr	880	1999	60r
Child's child care and education, age 9-11	yr	570	1999	60r
Child's child care and education, age 12-14	yr	420	1999	60r
Child's child care and education, age 15-17	yr	720	1999	60r

Item	Per	Value	Date	Ref.
Child Care - continued				
Child's clothing, age 0-2	yr	410	1999	60r
Child's clothing, age 3-5	yr	400	1999	60r
Child's clothing, age 6-8	yr	450	1999	60r
Child's clothing, age 9-11	yr	500	1999	60r
Child's clothing, age 12-14	yr	840	1999	60r
Child's clothing, age 15-17	yr	740	1999	60r
Child's food, age 0-2	yr	960	1999	60r
Child's food, age 3-5	yr	1120	1999	60r
Child's food, age 6-8	yr	1430	1999	60r
Child's food, age 9-11	yr	1710	1999	60r
Child's food, age 12-14	yr	1710	1999	60r
Child's food, age 15-17	yr	1920	1999	60r
Child's health care, age 0-2	yr	520	1999	60r
Child's health care, age 3-5	yr	500	1999	60r
Child's health care, age 6-8	yr	570	1999	60r
Child's health care, age 9-11	yr	610	1999	60r
Child's health care, age 12-14	yr	630	1999	60r
Child's health care, age 15-17	yr	650	1999	60r
Child's housing, age 0-2	yr	2860	1999	60r
Child's housing, age 3-5	yr	2840	1999	60r
Child's housing, age 6-8	yr	2800	1999	60r
Child's housing, age 9-11	yr	2650	1999	60r
Child's housing, age 12-14	yr	2840	1999	60r
Child's housing, age 15-17	yr	2440	1999	60r
Child's personal care, reading, age 0-2	yr	880	1999	60r
Child's personal care, reading, age 3-5	yr	900	1999	60r
Child's personal care, reading, age 6-8	yr	930	1999	60r
Child's personal care, reading, age 9-11	yr	970	1999	60r
Child's personal care, reading, age 12-14	yr	1150	1999	60r
Child's personal care, reading, age 15-17	yr	920	1999	60r
Clothing				
Apparel and services purchases	yr	1607	1999	30r
Boys' brief, cotton	3	2.99	3/01	4c
Boys, 2 to 15, expenditures on	yr	91	1999	30r
Children under 2, expenditures on	yr	59	1999	30r
Footwear, expenditures on	yr	285	1999	30r
Girls, 2 to 15, expenditures on	yr	116	1999	30r
Men and boys, expenditures on	yr	433	1999	30r
Men, 16 and over, expenditures on	yr	341	1999	30r
Shirt, man's dress shirt		25.16	3/01	4c
Slacks, man's "No Wrinkles" khaki		41.33	3/01	4c
Women, 16 and over, expenditures on	yr	490	1999	30r
Communications				
Cable modem installation, Bresnan		99.95	6/99	103s
Cable modem installation, Comcast		95.00	6/99	103s
Cable modem installation, Media One		100.00	6/99	103s
Cable modem rate, cable subscriber, Bresnan	mos	39.95	6/99	103s
Cable modem rate, cable subscriber, Comcast	mos	39.95	6/99	103s
Cable modem rate, cable subscriber, Media One	mos	34.95-39.95	6/99	103s
Cable modem rate, non-cable subscriber, Bresnan	mos	49.95	6/99	103s
Cable modem rate, non-cable subscriber, Comcast	mos	49.95	6/99	103s
Cable modem rate, non-cable subscriber, Media One	mos	49.95	6/99	103s
Newspaper subscription, daily and Sunday delivery	mos	15.22	3/01	4c
Phone line, single, business, field visit	inst.	42.00	12/97	17s
Phone line, single, business, no field visit	inst.	42.00	12/97	17s
Phone line, single, residence, field visit	inst.	42.00	12/97	17s
Phone line, single, residence, no field visit	inst.	42.00	12/97	17s
Postage and stationery, expenditures on	yr	140	1999	30r
Postal rate, express mail, up to half-pound		12.45	7/01	108r
Postal rate, letter, first class, first ounce		0.34	7/01	108r
Postal rate, letter, two ounces		0.57	7/01	108r
Postal rate, post card		0.21	7/01	108r
Postal rate, priority mail, two pounds		3.95	7/01	108r
Postal rate, priority mail, up to one pound		3.50	7/01	108r

Values are in dollars or fractions of dollars. In the column headed *Ref*, references are shown by sources. Each reference is followed by a letter. These refer to the geographical level for which data were reported: s=State, r=Region, and c=City or metro. The abbreviation *ex* is used to mean *except* or *excluding*; *exp* stands for expenditures. For other abbreviations and further explanations, please see the Introduction.

Lansing, MI - continued

Item	Per	Value	Date	Ref.
Communications				
Telephone bill, family of three	mos	24.66	3/01	4c
Telephone services, expenditures on	yr	830	1999	30r
Education				
Board, 4-year private college/university	yr	2182	1996	38s
Board, 4-year public college/university	yr	2276	1996	38s
Education expenditures	yr	583	1999	30r
Room, 4-year private college/university	yr	1974	1996	38s
Room, 4-year public college/university	yr	2024	1996	38s
Total cost, 4-year private college/university	yr	13331	1996	38s
Total cost, 4-year public college/university	yr	8195	1996	38s
Tuition, 2-year public college/university, in state	yr	1529	1996	38s
Tuition, 4-year private college/university, in state	yr	9176	1996	38s
Tuition, 4-year public college/university	yr	3895	1996	38s
Energy and Fuels				
Electricity	500 KWhs	46.59	7/01	11r
Energy, combined forms, 2400 sq ft	mos	81.74	3/01	4c
Energy, exc. electricity, 2400 sq ft	mos	41.94	3/01	4c
Fuel oil #2	gal	1.27	7/01	11r
Fuel oil and other fuels, expenditures on	yr	68	1999	30r
Gas, natural, commercial rate	1000 cf	4.91	11/00	88s
Gas, regular unleaded, cash, self-service	gal	1.46	3/01	4c
Gasoline, unleaded midgrade	gal	1.79	7/01	11r
Gasoline, unleaded premium	gal	1.86	7/01	11r
Gasoline, unleaded regular	gal	1.58	7/01	11r
Natural gas, expenditures on	yr	389	1999	30r
Utility (piped) gas, therm		0.81	7/01	11r
Utility (piped) gas, 40 therms		38.01	7/01	11r
Utility (piped) gas, 100 therms		81.75	7/01	11r
Entertainment				
Bowling, Saturday evening rate	line	3.00	3/01	4c
Entertainment purchases	yr	1984	1999	30r
Fees and admissions paid	yr	444	1999	30r
Monopoly game, Parker Brothers', No. 9	game	9.99	3/01	4c
Movie, first-run, Saturday, evening	adm.	6.33	3/01	4c
Television, radios, sound equipment, expenditures on	yr	580	1999	30r
Tennis balls, yellow, Wilson or Penn, 3	can	2.39	3/01	4c
Funerals				
Cosmetology, hair, other preparation		178.32	1/99	78r
Embalming		408.19	1/99	78r
Funeral at funeral home		362.13	1/99	78r
Professional service charges		1375.51	1/99	78r
Transfer of remains to funeral home		155.92	1/99	78r
Visitation/viewing		294.38	1/99	78r
Groceries				
Groceries, ACCRA Index		101.80	3/01	4c
Antibiotic ointment, Polysporin	0.5 oz	4.79	3/01	4c
Baby food, strained vegetables or fruit, lowest price	4-4.5 oz	0.51	3/01	4c
Bacon, sliced	lb	3.15	7/01	11r
Bakery products, expenditures on	yr	281	1999	30r
Bananas	lb	0.51	3/01	4c
Bananas	lb	0.48	7/01	11r
Beans, dried, any type, all sizes	lb	0.61	7/01	11r
Beef for stew, boneless	lb	3.08	7/01	11r
Beef or hamburger, ground	lb	1.73	3/01	4c
Beef, expenditures on	yr	217	1999	30r
Bologna, all beef or mixed	lb	2.52	7/01	11r
Bread, white	loaf	1.09	3/01	4c
Bread, white, pan	lb	1.06	7/01	11r
Broccoli	lb	0.91	7/01	11r
Butter, salted, grade AA, stick	lb	3.04	7/01	11r
Butter, yoghurt, cheese, etc, expenditures on	yr	183	1999	30r
Cereals and bakery product purchases	yr	430	1999	30r
Cereals and cereal products, expenditures on	yr	149	1999	30r

Lansing, MI - continued

Item	Per	Value	Date	Ref.
Groceries - continued				
Cheese, Kraft grated Parmesan	8 oz	3.91	3/01	4c
Chicken, fresh, whole	lb	1.07	7/01	11r
Chicken, whole fryer	lb	0.99	3/01	4c
Chops, boneless,	lb	3.64	7/01	11r
Chuck roast, U.S. choice, boneless	lb	2.47	7/01	11r
Cigarettes, Winston, Kings	carton	35.99	3/01	4c
Coffee, 100%, ground roast, all sizes	lb	2.69	7/01	11r
Coffee, vacuum-packed	13 oz	2.11	3/01	4c
Cookies, chocolate chip	lb	2.87	7/01	11r
Corn Flakes, Kellogg's or Post Toasties	18 oz	2.25	3/01	4c
Corn, frozen, whole kernel, lowest price	16 oz	1.02	3/01	4c
Dairy product purchases	yr	304	1999	30r
Eggs, expenditures on	yr	26	1999	30r
Eggs, Grade A or AA	dozen	1.26	3/01	4c
Eggs, grade A, large	dozen	0.88	7/01	11r
Fats and oils, expenditures on	yr	75	1999	30r
Fish and seafood, expenditures on	yr	72	1999	30r
Food (excl fruit and vegetables), eaten at home, purchases	yr	887	1999	30r
Food cooked on trips, expenditures on	yr	44	1999	30r
Food purchases	yr	4802	1999	30r
Food purchases, eaten away from home	yr	2069	1999	30r
Food purchases, food eaten at home	yr	2733	1999	30r
Fresh fruits, expenditures on	yr	138	1999	30r
Fresh milk and cream, expenditures on	yr	120	1999	30r
Fresh vegetables, expenditures on	yr	126	1999	30r
Grapefruit	lb	0.66	7/01	11r
Grapes, Thompson, seedless	lb	1.64	7/01	11r
Ground beef, 100% beef	lb	1.64	7/01	11r
Ground beef, lean and extra lean	lb	2.16	7/01	11r
Ground chuck, 100% beef	lb	2.13	7/01	11r
Ham, boneless, excl canned	lb	2.62	7/01	11r
Ice cream, prepackaged, bulk, regular	1/2 gal	3.35	7/01	11r
Lemons	lb	1.19	7/01	11r
Lettuce, iceberg	head	0.99	3/01	4c
Lettuce, iceberg	lb	0.73	7/01	11r
Margarine, Blue Bonnet or Parkay, stick	lb	0.81	3/01	4c
Margarine, soft, tubs	lb	0.89	7/01	11r
Meats, poultry, fish, and egg purchases	yr	671	1999	30r
Milk, fresh, whole, fortified	gal	2.71	7/01	11r
Milk, whole	1/2 gal	1.93	3/01	4c
Nonalcoholic beverages, expenditures on	yr	239	1999	30r
Orange juice, Minute Maid frozen	12 oz	1.69	3/01	4c
Oranges, Navel	lb	0.80	7/01	11r
Oranges, Valencia	lb	0.66	7/01	11r
Peaches, halves or slices, Hunt's, Del Monte, or Libby's	29 oz	1.69	3/01	4c
Pears, Anjou	lb	0.93	7/01	11r
Peas, green, Del Monte or Green Giant	15 oz	0.78	3/01	4c
Pork chops, center cut, bone-in	lb	3.63	7/01	11r
Pork, expenditures on	yr	150	1999	30r
Potato chips	16 oz	3.52	7/01	11r
Potatoes, frozen, french fried	lb	1.08	7/01	11r
Potatoes, white or red	10 lb	2.39	3/01	4c
Potatoes, white, all types	lb	0.33	7/01	11r
Poultry, expenditures on	yr	108	1999	30r
Processed fruits, expenditures on	yr	98	1999	30r
Processed vegetables, expenditures on	yr	80	1999	30r
Round roast, U.S. choice, boneless	lb	3.07	7/01	11r
Round steak, graded and ungraded, excl U.S. prime and choice	lb	3.41	7/01	11r
Sausage, Jimmy Dean/Owens pork	lb	2.75	3/01	4c
Shortening, vegetable oil blends	lb	1.13	7/01	11r
Shortening, vegetable, Crisco	3 lb	3.15	3/01	4c
Soft drink, Coca Cola, ex deposit	2 liter	1.15	3/01	4c
Spaghetti and macaroni	lb	0.80	7/01	11r
Steak, round, U.S. choice, boneless	lb	3.23	7/01	11r
Steak, T-bone	lb	5.60	3/01	4c
Steak, T-bone, U.S. choice, bone-in	lb	6.68	7/01	11r
Strawberries, dry pint	12 oz	1.32	7/01	11r
Sugar and other sweets, expenditures on	yr	114	1999	30r
Sugar, cane or beet	4 lbs	1.00	3/01	4c

Values are in dollars or fractions of dollars. In the column headed *Ref*, references are shown to sources. Each reference is followed by a letter. These refer to the geographical level for which data were reported: s=State, r=Region, and c=City or metro. The abbreviation *ex* is used to mean *except* or *excluding*; *exp* stands for expenditures. For other abbreviations and further explanations, please see the Introduction.

Lansing, MI - continued

Item	Per	Value	Date	Ref.
Groceries				
Sugar, white, 33-80 ounce package	lb	0.42	7/01	11r
Sugar, white, all sizes	lb	0.43	7/01	11r
Tobacco products and smoking supplies purchases	yr	331	1999	30r
Tomatoes, field grown	lb	1.46	7/01	11r
Tomatoes, Hunt's or Del Monte	14.5 oz	0.80	3/01	4c
Tuna, chunk, light	6 oz	0.81	3/01	4c
Tuna, light, chunk	lb	1.80	7/01	11r
Turkey, frozen, whole	lb	1.15	7/01	11r
Goods and Services				
Miscellaneous goods and services, ACCRA Index		101.20	3/01	4c
B&B Japanese maple (acer japonicum)	gal	29.99-169.99	4/00	93r
Boxwood (buxus)	2 gal	18.99-39.99	4/00	93r
Daylilly (hemerocallis)	gal	4.99-25.00	4/00	93r
Flat of annuals		11.98-24.99	4/00	93r
Fountain grass (pennisetum)	gal	5.98-12.98	4/00	93r
Hanging basket (10 in)		12.99-27.99	4/00	93r
Hardy geranium (geranium)	gal	7.99-9.99	4/00	93r
Hosta (hosta)	gal	6.00-25.00	4/00	93r
Lilac (syrubga vulgaris)	2 gal	14.99-24.99	4/00	93r
Miscellaneous purchases	yr	865	1999	30r
Rhododendron (rhododendron)	2 gal	23.98-42.99	4/00	93r
Sage (salvia)	gal	6.00-9.99	4/00	93r
Snowblower, single stage		400-600	12/00	99s
Wintercreeper euonymus (euonymus fortunei)	2 gal	16.00-169.99	4/00	93r
Hunting license	yr	14.00	4/01	34s
Health Care				
Health care, ACCRA Index		95.70	3/01	4c
Cardiac catheterization, ave hospital/physician charges		11830	1998	77s
Childbirth, Cesarean delivery		10722	1997	13r
Childbirth, vaginal delivery		6223	1997	13r
Dentist's fee, adult teeth cleaning and periodic oral exam	visit	81.67	3/01	4c
Doctor's fee, routine exam, established patient	visit	41.67	3/01	4c
Drugs, expenditures on	yr	394	1999	30r
Health care purchases	yr	2048	1999	30r
Health insurance expenditures	yr	978	1999	30r
Home health care aide cost, licensed agency	hour	16	2000	82c
Hospital care, private room	day	551.00	3/01	4c
Hysterectomy, laproscopically-assisted, ave hospital/physician charges		13820	1998	76s
Hysterectomy, vaginal, ave hospital and physician charges		8780	1998	76s
Medicaid dispensing fee		3.72	1999	87s
Medical services expenditures	yr	554	1999	30r
Medical supplies, expenditures on	yr	122	1999	30r
Plastic surgery, breast augmentation		3184	2000	7r
Plastic surgery, breast lift		3585	2000	7r
Plastic surgery, facelift		4999	2000	7r
Plastic surgery, hair transplantation		3105	2000	7r
Plastic surgery, lip augmentation		1290	2000	7r
Plastic surgery, lower body lift		8135	2000	7r
Plastic surgery, thigh lift		3839	2000	7r
Household Goods				
Dishwashing powder, Cascade	50 oz	3.64	3/01	4c
Floor coverings, expenditures on	yr	52	1999	30r

Lansing, MI - continued

Item	Per	Value	Date	Ref.
Household Goods - continued				
Furniture, expenditures on	yr	344	1999	30r
Household furnishings and equipment purchases	yr	1475	1999	30r
Household textiles, expenditures on	yr	109	1999	30r
Laundry and cleaning supplies, expenditures on	yr	134	1999	30r
Tissues, facial, Kleenex brand	175	0.95	3/01	4c
Housing				
Housing, ACCRA Index		99.40	3/01	4c
Home, 2200 sq ft, 4-br, 2-bath, 2-car garage, average		178254	2000	47c
Home price, existing, ave		144400	10/00	90r
Home value, median		135000	2001	53s
House, 2400 sq ft, 8000 sq ft lot, new, urban, utilities	total	205500	3/01	4c
House payment, principal and interest, 25% down payment	mos	1043	3/01	4c
Household operation expenditures	yr	542	1999	30r
Housekeeping supplies purchases	yr	508	1999	30r
Lodging expenditures	yr	430	1999	30r
Maintenance, repairs, insurance expenditures	yr	853	1999	30r
Monthly rental value of owned home	mos	547	1999	30r
Owned dwellings, expenditures own	yr	4282	1999	30r
Rent expenditures	yr	1558	1999	30r
Rent, apartment, 2 br, 1 1/2-2 baths, unfurn, 950 sq ft, water	mos	642	3/01	4c
Shelter, expenditures on	yr	6270	1999	30r
Insurance and Pensions				
Life and other personal insurance purchases	yr	387	1999	30r
Pensions and Social Security, expenditures on	yr	2968	1999	30r
Legal Fees				
Divorce, filing fee		65.00	4/01	35s
Driver's license fee	renew	5.00	1999	48s
Driver's license fee	orig	20.00	1999	48s
Fishing license	yr	14.00	4/01	34s
Personal Goods				
Personal care products and services purchases	yr	385	1999	30r
Shampoo, Alberto VO5	15 oz	1.03	3/01	4c
Toothpaste, Crest or Colgate	6-7 oz	2.43	3/01	4c
Personal Services				
Dry cleaning, man's 2-pc suit		7.25	3/01	4c
Man's haircut, barbershop, no styling		9.83	3/01	4c
Personal services, household, expenditures on	yr	300	1999	30r
Woman's shampoo, trim, blow-dry, no style-change		21.33	3/01	4c
Pets				
Pets, toys, and playground equipment, expenditures on	yr	375	1999	30r
Restaurant Food				
Chicken, fried, thigh and drumstick, KFC/Church's		2.75	3/01	4c
Hamburger with cheese, McDonald's	1/4 lb	2.29	3/01	4c
Pizza, Pizza Hut or Pizza Inn	11-12 in	8.99	3/01	4c
Taxes				
Federal income taxes paid	yr	2326	1999	30r
Personal taxes, expenditures on	yr	3223	1999	30r
Property taxes paid	yr	1152	1999	30r
State and local income taxes paid	yr	753	1999	30r
Transportation				
Transportation, ACCRA Index		96.80	3/01	4c
Bus fare, one-way	trip	1.00	2000	1c
Bus fare, to central business district	1-way	1.00	3/01	4c
Cars and trucks, new, expenditures on	yr	1280	1999	30r

Values are in dollars or fractions of dollars. In the column headed *Ref*, references are shown to sources. Each reference is followed by a letter. These refer to the geographical level for which data were reported: s=State, r=Region, and c=City or metro. The abbreviation *ex* is used to mean *except* or *excluding*; *exp* stands for expenditures. For other abbreviations and further explanations, please see the Introduction.

Lansing, MI - continued

Item	Per	Value	Date	Ref.
Transportation				
Cars and trucks, used, expenditures on	yr	1763	1999	30r
Diesel at the pump	gal	1.19	10/99	73s
Gasoline and motor oil purchases	yr	1036	1999	30r
Gasoline before-tax price (cents)	gal	111.50	10/00	43s
Maintenance and repair expenditures	yr	594	1999	30r
Public transportation, expenditures on	yr	341	1999	30r
Tire balance, computer or spin balance, front	wheel	7.00	3/01	4c
Transportation purchases	yr	6617	1999	30r
Vehicle expenses, miscellaneous, purchases	yr	2159	1999	30r
Vehicle insurance payments	yr	701	1999	30r
Vehicle purchases (net outlay)	yr	3081	1999	30r
Vehicle rental, lease expenditures	yr	536	1999	30r
Utilities				
Utilities, ACCRA Index		73.30	3/01	4c
Electrical bill, average	mos	55.00	9/00	9s
Electricity, expenditures on	yr	841	1999	30r
Electricity and other, mixed, 2400 sq ft, new home	mos	39.80	3/01	4c
Electricity cost, average	KWh	7.00	9/00	9s
Utilities, fuels, and public services purchased	yr	2401	1999	30r
Water and other public services, expenditures on	yr	273	1999	30r
Weddings				
Wedding (national average cost)		19936	2000	33r
Wedding (regional average total cost)		16195	1997	110r
Attendants' gifts		321	1998	33r
Bridal attendants' apparel (5 persons)		824	2000	33r
Bride's headpiece/veil		173	1998	33r
Bride's wedding dress		859	1998	33r
Clergy, religious facility fee		242	1998	33r
Engagement ring		3177	1998	33r
Flowers		789	1998	33r
Groom's formalwear rental		99	2000	33r
Limousine		410	1998	33r
Marriage license cost		20.00	4/01	35s
Men's formalwear (ushers, best man)		469	2000	33r
Mother of bride apparel		241	2000	33r
Music		866	1998	33r
Photography and videography		1368	1998	33r
Rehearsal dinner		728	1998	33r
Wedding invitations and announcements		341	1998	33r
Wedding reception		7968	2000	33r
Wedding rings (bride and groom)		1060	1998	33r

Lansing-East Lansing, MI

Item	Per	Value	Date	Ref.
Average annual expenditures	yr	35369	1999	30r
Alcoholic Beverages				
Alcoholic beverage purchases	yr	304	1999	30r
Malt beverages, all types, all sizes, any origin	16 oz	0.93	7/01	11r
Wine, red and white table, all sizes, any origin	liter	7.04	7/01	11r
Appliances				
Major appliances, expenditures on	yr	165	1999	30r
Small appliances, housewares, expenditures on	yr	90	1999	30r
Banking and Money				
Mortgage interest and charges paid	yr	2277	1999	30r
Mortgage principal paid on owned property	yr	1230	1999	30r
Vehicle finance charges paid	yr	328	1999	30r
Charity				
Cash contributions, expenditures	yr	1126	1999	30r
Child Care				
Child raising cost, total, age 0-2	yr	7890	1999	60r
Child raising cost, total, age 3-5	yr	8130	1999	60r
Child raising cost, total, age 6-8	yr	8170	1999	60r
Child raising cost, total, age 9-11	yr	8190	1999	60r
Child raising cost, total, age 12-14	yr	8890	1999	60r

Lansing-East Lansing, MI - continued

Item	Per	Value	Date	Ref.
Child Care - continued				
Child raising cost, total, age 15-17	yr	9050	1999	60r
Child's child care and education, age 0-2	yr	1240	1999	60r
Child's child care and education, age 3-5	yr	1370	1999	60r
Child's child care and education, age 6-8	yr	880	1999	60r
Child's child care and education, age 9-11	yr	570	1999	60r
Child's child care and education, age 12-14	yr	420	1999	60r
Child's child care and education, age 15-17	yr	720	1999	60r
Child's clothing, age 0-2	yr	410	1999	60r
Child's clothing, age 3-5	yr	400	1999	60r
Child's clothing, age 6-8	yr	450	1999	60r
Child's clothing, age 9-11	yr	500	1999	60r
Child's clothing, age 12-14	yr	840	1999	60r
Child's clothing, age 15-17	yr	740	1999	60r
Child's food, age 0-2	yr	960	1999	60r
Child's food, age 3-5	yr	1120	1999	60r
Child's food, age 6-8	yr	1430	1999	60r
Child's food, age 9-11	yr	1710	1999	60r
Child's food, age 12-14	yr	1710	1999	60r
Child's food, age 15-17	yr	1920	1999	60r
Child's health care, age 0-2	yr	520	1999	60r
Child's health care, age 3-5	yr	500	1999	60r
Child's health care, age 6-8	yr	570	1999	60r
Child's health care, age 9-11	yr	610	1999	60r
Child's health care, age 12-14	yr	630	1999	60r
Child's health care, age 15-17	yr	650	1999	60r
Child's housing, age 0-2	yr	2860	1999	60r
Child's housing, age 3-5	yr	2840	1999	60r
Child's housing, age 6-8	yr	2800	1999	60r
Child's housing, age 9-11	yr	2650	1999	60r
Child's housing, age 12-14	yr	2840	1999	60r
Child's housing, age 15-17	yr	2440	1999	60r
Child's personal care, reading, age 0-2	yr	880	1999	60r
Child's personal care, reading, age 3-5	yr	900	1999	60r
Child's personal care, reading, age 6-8	yr	930	1999	60r
Child's personal care, reading, age 9-11	yr	970	1999	60r
Child's personal care, reading, age 12-14	yr	1150	1999	60r
Child's personal care, reading, age 15-17	yr	920	1999	60r
Clothing				
Apparel and services purchases	yr	1607	1999	30r
Boys, 2 to 15, expenditures on	yr	91	1999	30r
Children under 2, expenditures on	yr	59	1999	30r
Footwear, expenditures on	yr	285	1999	30r
Girls, 2 to 15, expenditures on	yr	116	1999	30r
Men and boys, expenditures on	yr	433	1999	30r
Men, 16 and over, expenditures on	yr	341	1999	30r
Women, 16 and over, expenditures on	yr	490	1999	30r
Communications				
Cable modem installation, Bresnan		99.95	6/99	103s
Cable modem installation, Comcast		95.00	6/99	103s
Cable modem installation, Media One		100.00	6/99	103s
Cable modem rate, cable subscriber, Bresnan	mos	39.95	6/99	103s
Cable modem rate, cable subscriber, Comcast	mos	39.95	6/99	103s
Cable modem rate, cable subscriber, Media One	mos	34.95-39.95	6/99	103s
Cable modem rate, non-cable subscriber, Bresnan	mos	49.95	6/99	103s
Cable modem rate, non-cable subscriber, Comcast	mos	49.95	6/99	103s
Cable modem rate, non-cable subscriber, Media One	mos	49.95	6/99	103s
Phone line, single, business, field visit	inst.	42.00	12/97	17s
Phone line, single, business, no field visit	inst.	42.00	12/97	17s
Phone line, single, residence, field visit	inst.	42.00	12/97	17s
Phone line, single, residence, no field visit	inst.	42.00	12/97	17s
Postage and stationery, expenditures on	yr	140	1999	30r
Postal rate, express mail, up to half-pound		12.45	7/01	108r
Postal rate, letter, first class, first ounce		0.34	7/01	108r
Postal rate, letter, two ounces		0.57	7/01	108r
Postal rate, post card		0.21	7/01	108r

Values are in dollars or fractions of dollars. In the column headed *Ref*, references are shown to sources. Each reference is followed by a letter. These refer to the geographical level for which data were reported: s=State, r=Region, and c=City or metro. The abbreviation *ex* is used to mean *except* or *excluding*; *exp* stands for expenditures. For other abbreviations and further explanations, please see the Introduction.

Lansing-East Lansing, MI - continued

Item	Per	Value	Date	Ref.
Communications				
Postal rate, priority mail, two pounds		3.95	7/01	108r
Postal rate, priority mail, up to one pound		3.50	7/01	108r
Telephone services, expenditures on	yr	830	1999	30r
Education				
Board, 4-year private college/university	yr	2182	1996	38s
Board, 4-year public college/university	yr	2276	1996	38s
Education expenditures	yr	583	1999	30r
Room, 4-year private college/university	yr	1974	1996	38s
Room, 4-year public college/university	yr	2024	1996	38s
Total cost, 4-year private college/university	yr	13331	1996	38s
Total cost, 4-year public college/university	yr	8195	1996	38s
Tuition, 2-year public college/university, in state	yr	1529	1996	38s
Tuition, 4-year private college/university, in state	yr	9176	1996	38s
Tuition, 4-year public college/university	yr	3895	1996	38s
Energy and Fuels				
Electricity	500 KWhs	46.59	7/01	11r
Fuel oil #2	gal	1.27	7/01	11r
Fuel oil and other fuels, expenditures on	yr	68	1999	30r
Gas, natural, commercial rate	1000 cf	4.91	11/00	88s
Gasoline, unleaded midgrade	gal	1.79	7/01	11r
Gasoline, unleaded premium	gal	1.86	7/01	11r
Gasoline, unleaded regular	gal	1.58	7/01	11r
Natural gas, expenditures on	yr	389	1999	30r
Utility (piped) gas, therm		0.81	7/01	11r
Utility (piped) gas, 40 therms		38.01	7/01	11r
Utility (piped) gas, 100 therms		81.75	7/01	11r
Entertainment				
Entertainment purchases	yr	1984	1999	30r
Fees and admissions paid	yr	444	1999	30r
Television, radios, sound equipment, expenditures on	yr	580	1999	30r
Funerals				
Cosmetology, hair, other preparation		178.32	1/99	78r
Embalming		408.19	1/99	78r
Funeral at funeral home		362.13	1/99	78r
Professional service charges		1375.51	1/99	78r
Transfer of remains to funeral home		155.92	1/99	78r
Visitation/viewing		294.38	1/99	78r
Groceries				
Bacon, sliced	lb	3.15	7/01	11r
Bakery products, expenditures on	yr	281	1999	30r
Bananas	lb	0.48	7/01	11r
Beans, dried, any type, all sizes	lb	0.61	7/01	11r
Beef for stew, boneless	lb	3.08	7/01	11r
Beef, expenditures on	yr	217	1999	30r
Bologna, all beef or mixed	lb	2.52	7/01	11r
Bread, white, pan	lb	1.06	7/01	11r
Broccoli	lb	0.91	7/01	11r
Butter, salted, grade AA, stick	lb	3.04	7/01	11r
Butter, yoghurt, cheese, etc, expenditures on	yr	183	1999	30r
Cereals and bakery product purchases	yr	430	1999	30r
Cereals and cereal products, expenditures on	yr	149	1999	30r
Chicken, fresh, whole	lb	1.07	7/01	11r
Chops, boneless,	lb	3.64	7/01	11r
Chuck roast, U.S. choice, boneless	lb	2.47	7/01	11r
Coffee, 100%, ground roast, all sizes	lb	2.69	7/01	11r
Cookies, chocolate chip	lb	2.87	7/01	11r
Dairy product purchases	yr	304	1999	30r
Eggs, expenditures on	yr	26	1999	30r
Eggs, grade A, large	dozen	0.88	7/01	11r
Fats and oils, expenditures on	yr	75	1999	30r
Fish and seafood, expenditures on	yr	72	1999	30r
Food (excl fruit and vegetables), eaten at home, purchases	yr	887	1999	30r
Food cooked on trips, expenditures on	yr	44	1999	30r

Lansing-East Lansing, MI - continued

Item	Per	Value	Date	Ref.
Groceries - continued				
Food purchases	yr	4802	1999	30r
Food purchases, eaten away from home	yr	2069	1999	30r
Food purchases, food eaten at home	yr	2733	1999	30r
Fresh fruits, expenditures on	yr	138	1999	30r
Fresh milk and cream, expenditures on	yr	120	1999	30r
Fresh vegetables, expenditures on	yr	126	1999	30r
Grapefruit	lb	0.66	7/01	11r
Grapes, Thompson, seedless	lb	1.64	7/01	11r
Ground beef, 100% beef	lb	1.64	7/01	11r
Ground beef, lean and extra lean	lb	2.16	7/01	11r
Ground chuck, 100% beef	lb	2.13	7/01	11r
Ham, boneless, excl canned	lb	2.62	7/01	11r
Ice cream, prepackaged, bulk, regular	1/2 gal	3.35	7/01	11r
Lemons	lb	1.19	7/01	11r
Lettuce, iceberg	lb	0.73	7/01	11r
Margarine, soft, tubs	lb	0.89	7/01	11r
Meats, poultry, fish, and egg purchases	yr	671	1999	30r
Milk, fresh, whole, fortified	gal	2.71	7/01	11r
Nonalcoholic beverages, expenditures on	yr	239	1999	30r
Oranges, Navel	lb	0.80	7/01	11r
Oranges, Valencia	lb	0.66	7/01	11r
Pears, Anjou	lb	0.93	7/01	11r
Pork chops, center cut, bone-in	lb	3.63	7/01	11r
Pork, expenditures on	yr	150	1999	30r
Potato chips	16 oz	3.52	7/01	11r
Potatoes, frozen, french fried	lb	1.08	7/01	11r
Potatoes, white, all types	lb	0.33	7/01	11r
Poultry, expenditures on	yr	108	1999	30r
Processed fruits, expenditures on	yr	98	1999	30r
Processed vegetables, expenditures on	yr	80	1999	30r
Round roast, U.S. choice, boneless	lb	3.07	7/01	11r
Round steak, graded and ungraded, excl U.S. prime and choice	lb	3.41	7/01	11r
Shortening, vegetable oil blends	lb	1.13	7/01	11r
Spaghetti and macaroni	lb	0.80	7/01	11r
Steak, round, U.S. choice, boneless	lb	3.23	7/01	11r
Steak, T-bone, U.S. choice, bone-in	lb	6.68	7/01	11r
Strawberries, dry pint	12 oz	1.32	7/01	11r
Sugar and other sweets, expenditures on	yr	114	1999	30r
Sugar, white, 33-80 ounce package	lb	0.42	7/01	11r
Sugar, white, all sizes	lb	0.43	7/01	11r
Tobacco products and smoking supplies purchases	yr	331	1999	30r
Tomatoes, field grown	lb	1.46	7/01	11r
Tuna, light, chunk	lb	1.80	7/01	11r
Turkey, frozen, whole	lb	1.15	7/01	11r
Goods and Services				
B&B Japanese maple (acer japonicum)	gal	29.99-169.99	4/00	93r
Boxwood (buxus)	2 gal	18.99-39.99	4/00	93r
Daylily (hemerocallis)	gal	4.99-25.00	4/00	93r
Flat of annuals		11.98-24.99	4/00	93r
Fountain grass (pennisetum)	gal	5.98-12.98	4/00	93r
Hanging basket (10 in)		12.99-27.99	4/00	93r
Hardy geranium (geranium)	gal	7.99-9.99	4/00	93r
Hosta (hosta)	gal	6.00-25.00	4/00	93r
Lilac (syrubga vulgaris)	2 gal	14.99-24.99	4/00	93r
Miscellaneous purchases	yr	865	1999	30r
Rhododendron (rhododendron)	2 gal	23.98-42.99	4/00	93r
Sage (salvia)	gal	6.00-9.99	4/00	93r
Snowblower, single stage		400-600	12/00	99s

Values are in dollars or fractions of dollars. In the column headed *Ref*, references are shown to sources. Each reference is followed by a letter. These refer to the geographical level for which data were reported: s=State, r=Region, and c=City or metro. The abbreviation *ex* is used to mean *except* or *excluding*; *exp* stands for *expenditures*. For other abbreviations and further explanations, please see the Introduction.

Lansing-East Lansing, MI - continued

Item	Per	Value	Date	Ref.
Goods and Services				
Wintercreeper euonymus (euonymus fortunei)	2 gal	16.00-169.99	4/00	93r
Hunting license	yr	14.00	4/01	34s
Health Care				
Cardiac catheterization, ave hospital/ physician charges		11830	1998	77s
Childbirth, Cesarean delivery		10722	1997	13r
Childbirth, vaginal delivery		6223	1997	13r
Drugs, expenditures on	yr	394	1999	30r
Health care purchases	yr	2048	1999	30r
Health insurance expenditures	yr	978	1999	30r
Hysterectomy, laproscopically-assisted, ave hospital/physician charges		13820	1998	76s
Hysterectomy, vaginal, ave hospital and physician charges		8780	1998	76s
Medicaid dispensing fee		3.72	1999	87s
Medical services expenditures	yr	554	1999	30r
Medical supplies, expenditures on	yr	122	1999	30r
Plastic surgery, breast augmentation		3184	2000	7r
Plastic surgery, breast lift		3585	2000	7r
Plastic surgery, facelift		4999	2000	7r
Plastic surgery, hair transplantation		3105	2000	7r
Plastic surgery, lip augmentation		1290	2000	7r
Plastic surgery, lower body lift		8135	2000	7r
Plastic surgery, thigh lift		3839	2000	7r
Household Goods				
Floor coverings, expenditures on	yr	52	1999	30r
Furniture, expenditures on	yr	344	1999	30r
Household furnishings and equipment purchases	yr	1475	1999	30r
Household textiles, expenditures on	yr	109	1999	30r
Laundry and cleaning supplies, expenditures on	yr	134	1999	30r
Housing				
Home price, existing, ave		144400	10/00	90r
Home value, median		135000	2001	53s
Household operation expenditures	yr	542	1999	30r
Housekeeping supplies purchases	yr	508	1999	30r
Lodging expenditures	yr	430	1999	30r
Maintenance, repairs, insurance expenditures	yr	853	1999	30r
Monthly rental value of owned home	mos	547	1999	30r
Owned dwellings, expenditures own	yr	4282	1999	30r
Rent expenditures	yr	1558	1999	30r
Rental unit, 1 bedroom, with utilities	mos	474	4/01	41c
Rental unit, 2 bedroom, with utilities	mos	613	4/01	41c
Rental unit, 3 bedroom, with utilities	mos	801	4/01	41c
Rental unit, 4 bedroom, with utilities	mos	925	4/01	41c
Shelter, expenditures on	yr	6270	1999	30r
Insurance and Pensions				
Life and other personal insurance purchases	yr	387	1999	30r
Pensions and Social Security, expenditures on	yr	2968	1999	30r
Legal Fees				
Divorce, filing fee		65.00	4/01	35s
Driver's license fee	renew	5.00	1999	48s
Driver's license fee	orig	20.00	1999	48s
Fishing license	yr	14.00	4/01	34s
Personal Goods				
Personal care products and services purchases	yr	385	1999	30r
Personal Services				
Personal services, household, expenditures on	yr	300	1999	30r
Pets				
Pets, toys, and playground equipment, expenditures on	yr	375	1999	30r

Lansing-East Lansing, MI - continued

Item	Per	Value	Date	Ref.
Taxes				
Federal income taxes paid	yr	2326	1999	30r
Personal taxes, expenditures on	yr	3223	1999	30r
Property taxes paid	yr	1152	1999	30r
State and local income taxes paid	yr	753	1999	30r
Transportation				
Cars and trucks, new, expenditures on	yr	1280	1999	30r
Cars and trucks, used, expenditures on	yr	1763	1999	30r
Diesel at the pump	gal	1.19	10/99	73s
Gasoline and motor oil purchases	yr	1036	1999	30r
Gasoline before-tax price (cents)	gal	111.50	10/00	43s
Maintenance and repair expenditures	yr	594	1999	30r
Public transportation, expenditures on	yr	341	1999	30r
Transportation purchases	yr	6617	1999	30r
Vehicle expenses, miscellaneous, purchases	yr	2159	1999	30r
Vehicle insurance payments	yr	701	1999	30r
Vehicle purchases (net outlay)	yr	3081	1999	30r
Vehicle rental, lease expenditures	yr	536	1999	30r
Utilities				
Electrical bill, average	mos	55.00	9/00	9s
Electricity, expenditures on	yr	841	1999	30r
Electricity cost, average	KWh	7.00	9/00	9s
Utilities, fuels, and public services purchased	yr	2401	1999	30r
Water and other public services, expenditures on	yr	273	1999	30r
Weddings				
Wedding (national average cost)		19936	2000	33r
Wedding (regional average total cost)		16195	1997	110r
Attendants' gifts		321	1998	33r
Bridal attendants' apparel (5 persons)		824	2000	33r
Bride's headpiece/veil		173	1998	33r
Bride's wedding dress		859	1998	33r
Clergy, religious facility fee		242	1998	33r
Engagement ring		3177	1998	33r
Flowers		789	1998	33r
Groom's formalwear rental		99	2000	33r
Limousine		410	1998	33r
Marriage license cost		20.00	4/01	35s
Men's formalwear (ushers, best man)		469	2000	33r
Mother of bride apparel		241	2000	33r
Music		866	1998	33r
Photography and videography		1368	1998	33r
Rehearsal dinner		728	1998	33r
Wedding invitations and announcements		341	1998	33r
Wedding reception		7968	2000	33r
Wedding rings (bride and groom)		1060	1998	33r

Laredo, TX

Item	Per	Value	Date	Ref.
Alcoholic Beverages				
Alcoholic beverage purchases	yr	253	1999	30r
Malt beverages, all types, all sizes, any origin	16 oz	0.96	7/01	11r
Appliances				
Major appliances, expenditures on	yr	172	1999	30r
Small appliances, housewares, expenditures on	yr	81	1999	30r
Banking and Money				
Mortgage interest and charges paid	yr	2039	1999	30r
Mortgage principal paid on owned property	yr	1026	1999	30r
Vehicle finance charges paid	yr	365	1999	30r
Charity				
Cash contributions, expenditures	yr	1127	1999	30r
Child Care				
Child raising cost, total, age 0-2	yr	8540	1999	60r
Child raising cost, total, age 3-5	yr	8780	1999	60r
Child raising cost, total, age 6-8	yr	8820	1999	60r
Child raising cost, total, age 9-11	yr	8800	1999	60r
Child raising cost, total, age 12-14	yr	9510	1999	60r

Values are in dollars or fractions of dollars. In the column headed *Ref*, references are shown to sources. Each reference is followed by a letter. These refer to the geographical level for which data were reported: s=State, r=Region, and c=City or metro. The abbreviation *ex* is used to mean *except* or *excluding*; *exp* stands for *expenditures*. For other abbreviations and further explanations, please see the Introduction.

Laredo, TX - continued

Item	Per	Value	Date	Ref.
Child Care				
Child raising cost, total, age 15-17	yr	9740	1999	60r
Child's child care and education, age 0-2	yr	1380	1999	60r
Child's child care and education, age 3-5	yr	1520	1999	60r
Child's child care and education, age 6-8	yr	990	1999	60r
Child's child care and education, age 9-11	yr	650	1999	60r
Child's child care and education, age 12-14	yr	490	1999	60r
Child's child care and education, age 15-17	yr	840	1999	60r
Child's clothing, age 0-2	yr	480	1999	60r
Child's clothing, age 3-5	yr	470	1999	60r
Child's clothing, age 6-8	yr	520	1999	60r
Child's clothing, age 9-11	yr	570	1999	60r
Child's clothing, age 12-14	yr	950	1999	60r
Child's clothing, age 15-17	yr	850	1999	60r
Child's food, age 0-2	yr	1000	1999	60r
Child's food, age 3-5	yr	1160	1999	60r
Child's food, age 6-8	yr	1490	1999	60r
Child's food, age 9-11	yr	1770	1999	60r
Child's food, age 12-14	yr	1770	1999	60r
Child's food, age 15-17	yr	1980	1999	60r
Child's health care, age 0-2	yr	620	1999	60r
Child's health care, age 3-5	yr	590	1999	60r
Child's health care, age 6-8	yr	680	1999	60r
Child's health care, age 9-11	yr	720	1999	60r
Child's health care, age 12-14	yr	730	1999	60r
Child's health care, age 15-17	yr	760	1999	60r
Child's housing, age 0-2	yr	3070	1999	60r
Child's housing, age 3-5	yr	3050	1999	60r
Child's housing, age 6-8	yr	3010	1999	60r
Child's housing, age 9-11	yr	2850	1999	60r
Child's housing, age 12-14	yr	3040	1999	60r
Child's housing, age 15-17	yr	2650	1999	60r
Child's personal care, reading, age 0-2	yr	910	1999	60r
Child's personal care, reading, age 3-5	yr	930	1999	60r
Child's personal care, reading, age 6-8	yr	960	1999	60r
Child's personal care, reading, age 9-11	yr	1000	1999	60r
Child's personal care, reading, age 12-14	yr	1170	1999	60r
Child's personal care, reading, age 15-17	yr	950	1999	60r
Clothing				
Apparel and services purchases	yr	1610	1999	30r
Boys, 2 to 15, expenditures on	yr	89	1999	30r
Children under 2, expenditures on	yr	79	1999	30r
Footwear, expenditures on	yr	283	1999	30r
Girls, 2 to 15, expenditures on	yr	103	1999	30r
Men and boys, expenditures on	yr	351	1999	30r
Men, 16 and over, expenditures on	yr	262	1999	30r
Women, 16 and over, expenditures on	yr	538	1999	30r
Communications				
Cable modem installation, AT&T-BIS		150.00	6/99	103s
Cable modem installation, Marcus		499.00	6/99	103s
Cable modem installation, Time Warner		75.00-225.00	6/99	103s
Cable modem rate, cable subscriber, AT&T-BIS	mos	39.95	6/99	103s
Cable modem rate, cable subscriber, Marcus	mos	14.95-49.95	6/99	103s
Cable modem rate, cable subscriber, Time Warner	mos	39.95-49.95	6/99	103s
Cable modem rate, non-cable subscriber, Marcus	mos	60.95	6/99	103s
Cable modem rate, non-cable subscriber, Time Warner	mos	39.95-54.95	6/99	103s
Phone line, single, business, field visit	inst.	71.90	12/97	17s
Phone line, single, business, no field visit	inst.	57.30	12/97	17s
Phone line, single, residence, field visit	inst.	52.95	12/97	17s
Phone line, single, residence, no field visit	inst.	38.35	12/97	17s
Postage and stationery, expenditures on	yr	104	1999	30r
Postal rate, express mail, up to half-pound		12.45	7/01	108r
Postal rate, letter, first class, first ounce		0.34	7/01	108r
Postal rate, letter, two ounces		0.57	7/01	108r
Postal rate, post card		0.21	7/01	108r
Postal rate, priority mail, two pounds		3.95	7/01	108r

Laredo, TX - continued

Item	Per	Value	Date	Ref.
Communications - continued				
Postal rate, priority mail, up to one pound		3.50	7/01	108r
Telephone services, expenditures on	yr	860	1999	30r
Education				
Board, 4-year private college/university	yr	2198	1996	38s
Board, 4-year public college/university	yr	1759	1996	38s
Education expenditures	yr	431	1999	30r
Room, 4-year private college/university	yr	2000	1996	38s
Room, 4-year public college/university	yr	1885	1996	38s
Total cost, 4-year private college/university	yr	13156	1996	38s
Total cost, 4-year public college/university	yr	5464	1996	38s
Tuition, 2-year public college/university, in state	yr	771	1996	38s
Tuition, 4-year private college/university, in state	yr	8959	1996	38s
Tuition, 4-year public college/university	yr	1820	1996	38s
Energy and Fuels				
Electricity	KWh	0.09	7/01	11r
Electricity	500 KWhs	47.29	7/01	11r
Fuel oil #2	gal	1.43	7/01	11r
Fuel oil and other fuels, expenditures on	yr	45	1999	30r
Gas, natural, commercial rate	1000 cf	6.94	11/00	88s
Gasoline, all types	gal	1.60	7/01	11r
Gasoline, unleaded midgrade	gal	1.65	7/01	11r
Gasoline, unleaded premium	gal	1.74	7/01	11r
Natural gas, expenditures on	yr	164	1999	30r
Utility (piped) gas, therm		1.01	7/01	11r
Utility (piped) gas, 40 therms		44.29	7/01	11r
Utility (piped) gas, 100 therms		97.44	7/01	11r
Entertainment				
Entertainment purchases	yr	1574	1999	30r
Fees and admissions paid	yr	371	1999	30r
Reading purchases	yr	121	1999	30r
Television, radios, sound equipment, expenditures on	yr	561	1999	30r
Funerals				
Total cost of funeral		5842.28	1/99	78r
Acknowledgement cards		28.35	1/99	78r
Casket		2494.29	1/99	78r
Cosmetology, hair, other preparation		109.22	1/99	78r
Embalming		361.42	1/99	78r
Funeral at funeral home		349.20	1/99	78r
Hearse (local)		161.91	1/99	78r
Professional service charges		1116.50	1/99	78r
Service car/van		65.56	1/99	78r
Transfer of remains to funeral home		143.56	1/99	78r
Vault		785.25	1/99	78r
Visitation/viewing		227.02	1/99	78r
Groceries				
American processed cheese	lb	3.50	7/01	11r
Bakery products, expenditures on	yr	261	1999	30r
Bananas	lb	0.47	7/01	11r
Beans, dried, any type, all sizes	lb	0.63	7/01	11r
Beef for stew, boneless	lb	2.86	7/01	11r
Beef, expenditures on	yr	210	1999	30r
Bologna, all beef or mixed	lb	2.29	7/01	11r
Bread, French	lb	1.66	7/01	11r
Bread, white, pan	lb	0.87	7/01	11r
Bread, whole wheat, pan	lb	1.38	7/01	11r
Broccoli	lb	1.04	7/01	11r
Butter, salted, grade AA, stick	lb	2.26	7/01	11r
Butter, yoghurt, cheese, etc, expenditures on	yr	170	1999	30r
Cabbage	lb	0.42	7/01	11r
Cereals and cereal products, expenditures on	yr	140	1999	30r
Cheddar cheese, natural	lb	3.75	7/01	11r
Chicken breast, bone-in	lb	1.85	7/01	11r
Chicken legs, bone-in	lb	1.34	7/01	11r
Chicken, fresh, whole	lb	1.05	7/01	11r

Values are in dollars or fractions of dollars. In the column headed *Ref*, references are shown to sources. Each reference is followed by a letter. These refer to the geographical level for which data were reported: s=State, r=Region, and c=City or metro. The abbreviation *ex* is used to mean *except* or *excluding*; *exp* stands for expenditures. For other abbreviations and further explanations, please see the Introduction.

Laredo, TX - continued

Item	Per	Value	Date	Ref.
Groceries				
Chops, boneless,	lb	4.13	7/01	11r
Chuck roast, graded and ungraded, excl U.S. prime and choice	lb	2.35	7/01	11r
Chuck roast, U.S. choice, boneless	lb	2.67	7/01	11r
Coffee, 100%, ground roast, all sizes	lb	2.88	7/01	11r
Coffee, instant, plain, regular, all sizes	16 oz	9.25	7/01	11r
Cola, non diet,	2 liter	1.11	7/01	11r
Crackers, soda, salted	lb	1.70	7/01	11r
Dairy product purchases	yr	282	1999	30r
Eggs, expenditures on	yr	32	1999	30r
Fats and oils, expenditures on	yr	79	1999	30r
Fish and seafood, expenditures on	yr	99	1999	30r
Flour, white, all purpose	lb	0.32	7/01	11r
Food (excl fruit and vegetables), eaten at home, purchases	yr	815	1999	30r
Food cooked on trips, expenditures on	yr	36	1999	30r
Food purchases	yr	4533	1999	30r
Food purchases, eaten away from home	yr	1873	1999	30r
Food purchases, food eaten at home	yr	2660	1999	30r
Fresh fruits, expenditures on	yr	128	1999	30r
Fresh milk and cream, expenditures on	yr	112	1999	30r
Fresh vegetables, expenditures on	yr	131	1999	30r
Fruit and vegetable purchases	yr	438	1999	30r
Grapefruit	lb	0.59	7/01	11r
Grapes, Thompson, seedless	lb	2.12	7/01	11r
Ground beef, 100% beef	lb	1.76	7/01	11r
Ground beef, lean and extra lean	lb	2.60	7/01	11r
Ground chuck, 100% beef	lb	2.08	7/01	11r
Ham, boneless, excl canned	lb	2.71	7/01	11r
Ham, rump or shank half, bone-in, smoked	lb	2.19	7/01	11r
Ice cream, prepackaged, bulk, regular	1/2 gal	3.93	7/01	11r
Lemons	lb	1.32	7/01	11r
Lettuce, iceberg	lb	0.76	7/01	11r
Milk, fresh, low fat,	gal	2.75	7/01	11r
Milk, fresh, whole, fortified	gal	2.97	7/01	11r
Nonalcoholic beverages, expenditures on	yr	228	1999	30r
Orange juice, frozen concentrate	16 oz	1.95	7/01	11r
Oranges, Navel	lb	0.73	7/01	11r
Oranges, Valencia	lb	0.55	7/01	11r
Peanut butter, creamy, all sizes	lb	1.83	7/01	11r
Pears, Anjou	lb	0.98	7/01	11r
Pork chops, center cut, bone-in	lb	3.33	7/01	11r
Pork sausage, fresh, loose	lb	2.59	7/01	11r
Pork shoulder picnic, bone-in, smoked	lb	1.12	7/01	11r
Pork, expenditures on	yr	162	1999	30r
Potato chips	16 oz	3.59	7/01	11r
Potatoes, frozen, french fried	lb	1.00	7/01	11r
Potatoes, white, all types	lb	0.44	7/01	11r
Poultry, expenditures on	yr	137	1999	30r
Processed fruits, expenditures on	yr	97	1999	30r
Processed vegetables, expenditures on	yr	82	1999	30r
Rice, white, long grain, uncooked	lb	0.51	7/01	11r
Round roast, graded and ungraded, excl U.S. prime and choice	lb	2.96	7/01	11r
Round steak, graded and ungraded, excl U.S. prime and choice	lb	3.11	7/01	11r
Sirloin steak, graded and ungraded, excl U.S. prime and choice	lb	4.23	7/01	11r
Spaghetti and macaroni	lb	0.78	7/01	11r
Steak, round, U.S. choice, boneless	lb	3.56	7/01	11r
Steak, sirloin, U.S. choice, boneless	lb	5.65	7/01	11r
Strawberries, dry pint	12 oz	1.50	7/01	11r
Sugar and other sweets, expenditures on	yr	99	1999	30r
Sugar, white, 33-80 ounce package	lb	0.39	7/01	11r
Sugar, white, all sizes	lb	0.42	7/01	11r
Tobacco products and smoking supplies purchases	yr	288	1999	30r
Tomatoes, field grown	lb	1.43	7/01	11r
Tuna, light, chunk	lb	1.77	7/01	11r
Turkey, frozen, whole	lb	1.05	7/01	11r

Laredo, TX - continued

Item	Per	Value	Date	Ref.
Goods and Services				
B&B Japanese maple (acer japonicum)	gal	79.98-99.00	4/00	93r
Boxwood (buxus)	2 gal	12.98-18.99	4/00	93r
Christmas tree, noble fir		40-60	2000	65s
Daylilly (hemerocallis)	gal	7.96-11.00	4/00	93r
Flat of annuals		13.99-27.99	4/00	93r
Fountain grass (pennisetum)	gal	6.96-9.00	4/00	93r
Hanging basket (10 in)		9.99-24.99	4/00	93r
Hardy geranium (geranium)	gal	5.96-8.00	4/00	93r
Hosta (hosta)	gal	8.96-12.99	4/00	93r
Lilac (syrubga vulgaris)	2 gal	13.00-19.99	4/00	93r
Rhododendron (rhododendron)	2 gal	12.98-29.99	4/00	93r
Sage (salvia)	gal	5.96-8.00	4/00	93r
Wintercreeper euonymus (euonymus fortunei)	2 gal	13.00-18.99	4/00	93r
Hunting license	yr	19.00	4/01	34s
Health Care				
Cardiac catheterization, ave hospital/ physician charges		20140	1998	77s
Childbirth, Cesarean delivery		11587	1997	13r
Childbirth, vaginal delivery		6725	1997	13r
Drugs, expenditures on	yr	399	1999	30r
Health care purchases	yr	1971	1999	30r
Health insurance expenditures	yr	933	1999	30r
Hysterectomy, laproscopically-assisted, ave hospital/physician charges		15700	1998	76s
Hysterectomy, vaginal, ave hospital and physician charges		12180	1998	76s
Medicaid dispensing fee		5.27	1999	87s
Medical services expenditures	yr	547	1999	30r
Medical supplies, expenditures on	yr	91	1999	30r
Household Goods				
Floor coverings, expenditures on	yr	44	1999	30r
Furniture, expenditures on	yr	335	1999	30r
Household furnishings and equipment purchases	yr	1328	1999	30r
Household textiles, expenditures on	yr	89	1999	30r
Laundry and cleaning supplies, expenditures on	yr	113	1999	30r
Housing				
Home price, existing, ave		160100	10/00	90r
Home value, median		112000	2001	53s
Household operation expenditures	yr	553	1999	30r
Housekeeping supplies purchases	yr	473	1999	30r
Housing, expenditures on	yr	10303	1999	30r
Maintenance, repairs, insurance expenditures	yr	699	1999	30r
Monthly rental value of owned home	mos	505	1999	30r
Owned dwellings, expenditures own	yr	3465	1999	30r
Rent expenditures	yr	1641	1999	30r
Rental unit, 1 bedroom, with utilities	mos	374	4/01	41c
Rental unit, 2 bedroom, with utilities	mos	491	4/01	41c
Rental unit, 3 bedroom, with utilities	mos	614	4/01	41c
Rental unit, 4 bedroom, with utilities	mos	691	4/01	41c
Shelter, expenditures on	yr	5467	1999	30r
Insurance and Pensions				
Life and other personal insurance purchases	yr	414	1999	30r
Pensions and Social Security, expenditures on	yr	2635	1999	30r

Values are in dollars or fractions of dollars. In the column headed *Ref*, references are shown to sources. Each reference is followed by a letter. These refer to the geographical level for which data were reported: s=State, r=Region, and c=City or metro. The abbreviation *ex* is used to mean *except* or *excluding*; *exp* stands for *expenditures*. For other abbreviations and further explanations, please see the Introduction.

Laredo, TX - continued

Item	Per	Value	Date	Ref.
Insurance and Pensions				
Personal insurance and pensions, expenditures on	yr	3048	1999	30r
Legal Fees				
Divorce, filing fee		150.00-200.00	4/01	35s
Driver's license fee	renew	20.00	1999	48s
Driver's license fee	orig	24.00	1999	48s
Fishing license	yr	19.00	4/01	34s
Personal Goods				
Personal care products and services purchases	yr	393	1999	30r
Personal Services				
Personal services, household, expenditures on	yr	258	1999	30r
Pets				
Pets, toys, and playground equipment, expenditures on	yr	306	1999	30r
Taxes				
Federal income taxes paid	yr	2047	1999	30r
Personal taxes, expenditures on	yr	2554	1999	30r
Property taxes paid	yr	726	1999	30r
State and local income taxes paid	yr	363	1999	30r
Transportation				
Bus fare, one-way	trip	0.75	2000	1c
Cars and trucks, new, expenditures on	yr	1648	1999	30r
Cars and trucks, used, expenditures on	yr	1651	1999	30r
Diesel at the pump	gal	1.18	10/99	73s
Gasoline and motor oil purchases	yr	1052	1999	30r
Gasoline before-tax price (cents)	gal	101.30	10/00	43s
Maintenance and repair expenditures	yr	621	1999	30r
Public transportation, expenditures on	yr	298	1999	30r
Transportation purchases	yr	6738	1999	30r
Vehicle expenses, miscellaneous, purchases	yr	2033	1999	30r
Vehicle insurance payments	yr	696	1999	30r
Vehicle purchases (net outlay)	yr	3354	1999	30r
Vehicle rental, lease expenditures	yr	352	1999	30r
Utilities				
Electrical bill, average	mos	87.17	9/00	9s
Electricity, expenditures on	yr	1115	1999	30r
Electricity cost, average	KWh	6.48	9/00	9s
Water and other public services, expenditures on	yr	298	1999	30r
Weddings				
Wedding (national average cost)		19936	2000	33r
Attendants' gifts		321	1998	33r
Bridal attendants' apparel (5 persons)		824	2000	33r
Bride's headpiece/veil		173	1998	33r
Bride's wedding dress		859	1998	33r
Clergy, religious facility fee		242	1998	33r
Engagement ring		3177	1998	33r
Flowers		789	1998	33r
Groom's formalwear rental		99	2000	33r
Limousine		410	1998	33r
Marriage license cost		36.00	4/01	35s
Men's formalwear (ushers, best man)		469	2000	33r
Mother of bride apparel		241	2000	33r
Music		866	1998	33r
Photography and videography		1368	1998	33r
Rehearsal dinner		728	1998	33r
Wedding invitations and announcements		341	1998	33r
Wedding reception		7968	2000	33r
Wedding rings (bride and groom)		1060	1998	33r

Las Cruces, NM

Item	Per	Value	Date	Ref.
Composite, ACCRA index		98.60	3/01	4c
Alcoholic Beverages				
Beer, Heineken, 12-oz, ex deposit	6	7.27	3/01	4c
J & B Scotch	750-ml	20.13	3/01	4c
Wine, Livingston or Gallo, Chablis blanc	1.5 liter	5.88	3/01	4c
Appliances				
Appliance repair, service call, washing machine	min lab chg	48.12	3/01	4c
Banking and Money				
Mortgage rate, incl. points and orig. fee, 30-yr. conv. fixed or ARM	mos	7.03	3/01	4c
Clothing				
Boys' brief, cotton	3	4.23	3/01	4c
Shirt, man's dress shirt		28.00	3/01	4c
Slacks, man's "No Wrinkles" khaki		35.99	3/01	4c
Communications				
Newspaper subscription, daily and Sunday delivery	mos	11.25	3/01	4c
Phone line, single, business, field visit	inst.	53.95	12/97	17s
Phone line, single, business, no field visit	inst.	53.95	12/97	17s
Phone line, single, residence, field visit	inst.	30.00	12/97	17s
Phone line, single, residence, no field visit	inst.	30.00	12/97	17s
Postal rate, express mail, up to half-pound		12.45	7/01	108r
Postal rate, letter, first class, first ounce		0.34	7/01	108r
Postal rate, letter, two ounces		0.57	7/01	108r
Postal rate, post card		0.21	7/01	108r
Postal rate, priority mail, two pounds		3.95	7/01	108r
Postal rate, priority mail, up to one pound		3.50	7/01	108r
Telephone bill, family of three	mos	18.00	3/01	4c
Education				
Board, 4-year private college/university	yr	2282	1996	38s
Board, 4-year public college/university	yr	1854	1996	38s
Room, 4-year private college/university	yr	2289	1996	38s
Room, 4-year public college/university	yr	1504	1996	38s
Total cost, 4-year private college/university	yr	14355	1996	38s
Total cost, 4-year public college/university	yr	5298	1996	38s
Tuition, 2-year public college/university, in state	yr	690	1996	38s
Tuition, 4-year private college/university, in state	yr	9784	1996	38s
Tuition, 4-year public college/university	yr	1940	1996	38s
Energy and Fuels				
Energy, combined forms, 2400 sq ft	mos	111.48	3/01	4c
Energy, exc. electricity, 2400 sq ft	mos	25.49	3/01	4c
Gas, regular unleaded, cash, self-service	gal	1.30	3/01	4c
Entertainment				
Bowling, Saturday evening rate	line	3.25	3/01	4c
Monopoly game, Parker Brothers', No. 9	game	11.40	3/01	4c
Movie, first-run, Saturday, evening	adm.	6.50	3/01	4c
Tennis balls, yellow, Wilson or Penn, 3	can	2.44	3/01	4c
Funerals				
Total cost of funeral		5401.08	1/99	78r
Acknowledgement cards		33.64	1/99	78r
Casket		2170.43	1/99	78r
Cosmetology, hair, other preparation		136.32	1/99	78r
Embalming		319.13	1/99	78r
Funeral at funeral home		370.21	1/99	78r
Hearse (local)		161.04	1/99	78r
Professional service charges		963.15	1/99	78r
Service car/van		133.99	1/99	78r
Transfer of remains to funeral home		159.82	1/99	78r
Vault		778.07	1/99	78r
Visitation/viewing		175.28	1/99	78r
Groceries				
Groceries, ACCRA Index		104.00	3/01	4c
Antibiotic ointment, Polysporin	0.5 oz	4.70	3/01	4c
Baby food, strained vegetables or fruit, lowest price	4-4.5 oz	0.39	3/01	4c

Values are in dollars or fractions of dollars. In the column headed *Ref*, references are shown to sources. Each reference is followed by a letter. These refer to the geographical level for which data were reported: s=State, r=Region, and c=City or metro. The abbreviation *ex* is used to mean *except* or *excluding*; *exp* stands for *expenditures*. For other abbreviations and further explanations, please see the Introduction.

Las Cruces, NM - continued

Item	Per	Value	Date	Ref.
Groceries				
Bananas	lb	0.51	3/01	4c
Beef or hamburger, ground	lb	1.46	3/01	4c
Bread, white	loaf	0.90	3/01	4c
Cheese, Kraft grated Parmesan	8 oz	4.00	3/01	4c
Chicken, whole fryer	lb	0.92	3/01	4c
Cigarettes, Winston, Kings	carton	27.86	3/01	4c
Coffee, vacuum-packed	13 oz	2.83	3/01	4c
Corn Flakes, Kellogg's or Post Toasties	18 oz	2.67	3/01	4c
Corn, frozen, whole kernel, lowest price	16 oz	1.22	3/01	4c
Eggs, Grade A or AA	dozen	1.30	3/01	4c
Lettuce, iceberg	head	1.07	3/01	4c
Margarine, Blue Bonnet or Parkay, stick	lb	1.09	3/01	4c
Milk, whole	1/2 gal	1.84	3/01	4c
Orange juice, Minute Maid frozen	12 oz	1.83	3/01	4c
Peaches, halves or slices, Hunt's, Del Monte, or Libby's	29 oz	1.81	3/01	4c
Peas, green, Del Monte or Green Giant	15 oz	0.78	3/01	4c
Potatoes, white or red	10 lb	1.84	3/01	4c
Sausage, Jimmy Dean/Owens pork	lb	3.00	3/01	4c
Shortening, vegetable, Crisco	3 lb	3.65	3/01	4c
Soft drink, Coca Cola, ex deposit	2 liter	1.49	3/01	4c
Steak, T-bone	lb	6.04	3/01	4c
Sugar, cane or beet	4 lbs	1.78	3/01	4c
Tomatoes, Hunt's or Del Monte	14.5 oz	0.98	3/01	4c
Tuna, chunk, light	6 oz	0.67	3/01	4c
Goods and Services				
Miscellaneous goods and services, ACCRA Index		99.80	3/01	4c
Hunting license	yr	25.00	4/01	34s
Health Care				
Health care, ACCRA Index		94.50	3/01	4c
Cardiac catheterization, ave hospital/ physician charges		15920	1998	77s
Childbirth, Cesarean delivery		11587	1997	13r
Childbirth, vaginal delivery		6725	1997	13r
Dentist's fee, adult teeth cleaning and periodic oral exam	visit	75.69	3/01	4c
Doctor's fee, routine exam, established patient	visit	50.20	3/01	4c
Hospital care, private room	day	457.00	3/01	4c
Hysterectomy, laproscopically-assisted, ave hospital/physician charges		11750	1998	76s
Hysterectomy, vaginal, ave hospital and physician charges		8980	1998	76s
Medicaid dispensing fee		4.00	1999	87s
Household Goods				
Dishwashing powder, Cascade	50 oz	3.56	3/01	4c
Tissues, facial, Kleenex brand	175	1.62	3/01	4c
Housing				
Housing, ACCRA Index		100.10	3/01	4c
Home, 2200 sq ft, 4-br, 2-bath, 2-car garage, average		165967	2000	47c
Home value, median		119000	2001	53s
House, 2400 sq ft, 8000 sq ft lot, new, urban, utilities	total	216358	3/01	4c
House payment, principal and interest, 25% down payment	mos	1082	3/01	4c
Rent, apartment, 2 br, 1 1/2-2 baths, unfurn, 950 sq ft, water	mos	562	3/01	4c
Rental unit, 1 bedroom, with utilities	mos	372	4/01	41c
Rental unit, 2 bedroom, with utilities	mos	442	4/01	41c
Rental unit, 3 bedroom, with utilities	mos	606	4/01	41c
Rental unit, 4 bedroom, with utilities	mos	714	4/01	41c
Legal Fees				
Combination hunting and fishing license	yr	37.50	4/01	34s
Driver's license fee	orig	10.00	1999	48s
Driver's license fee	renew	10.00	1999	48s
Fishing license	yr	25.00	4/01	34s

Las Cruces, NM - continued

Item	Per	Value	Date	Ref.
Personal Goods				
Shampoo, Alberto VO5	15 oz	1.12	3/01	4c
Toothpaste, Crest or Colgate	6-7 oz	2.30	3/01	4c
Personal Services				
Dry cleaning, man's 2-pc suit		6.70	3/01	4c
Man's haircut, barbershop, no styling		8.50	3/01	4c
Woman's shampoo, trim, blow-dry, no style-change		27.07	3/01	4c
Restaurant Food				
Chicken, fried, thigh and drumstick, KFC/ Church's		2.39	3/01	4c
Hamburger with cheese, McDonald's	1/4 lb	2.16	3/01	4c
Pizza, Pizza Hut or Pizza Inn	11-12 in	8.99	3/01	4c
Transportation				
Transportation, ACCRA Index		90.30	3/01	4c
Bus fare, to central business district	1-way	0.50	3/01	4c
Diesel at the pump	gal	1.22	10/99	73s
Gasoline before-tax price (cents)	gal	115.20	10/00	43s
Tire balance, computer or spin balance, front	wheel	7.91	3/01	4c
Utilities				
Utilities, ACCRA Index		90.20	3/01	4c
Electrical bill, average	mos	46.92	9/00	9s
Electricity, summer, 250 KWh	mos	29.56	2/96	96c
Electricity, summer, 500 KWh	mos	53.11	2/96	96c
Electricity, summer, 750 KWh	mos	76.67	2/96	96c
Electricity, summer, 1000 KWh	mos	100.22	2/96	96c
Electricity and other, mixed, 2400 sq ft, new home	mos	85.99	3/01	4c
Electricity cost, average	KWh	6.30	9/00	9s
Weddings				
Wedding (national average cost)		19936	2000	33r
Attendants' gifts		321	1998	33r
Bridal attendants' apparel (5 persons)		824	2000	33r
Bride's headpiece/veil		173	1998	33r
Bride's wedding dress		859	1998	33r
Clergy, religious facility fee		242	1998	33r
Engagement ring		3177	1998	33r
Flowers		789	1998	33r
Groom's formalwear rental		99	2000	33r
Limousine		410	1998	33r
Marriage license cost		25.00	4/01	35s
Men's formalwear (ushers, best man)		469	2000	33r
Mother of bride apparel		241	2000	33r
Music		866	1998	33r
Photography and videography		1368	1998	33r
Rehearsal dinner		728	1998	33r
Wedding invitations and announcements		341	1998	33r
Wedding reception		7968	2000	33r
Wedding rings (bride and groom)		1060	1998	33r

Las Vegas, NV

Item	Per	Value	Date	Ref.
Composite, ACCRA index		108.90	12/00	5c
Alcoholic Beverages				
Beer, Heineken, 12-oz, ex deposit	6	6.62	12/00	5c
J & B Scotch	750-ml	17.98	12/00	5c
Wine, Livingston or Gallo, Chablis blanc	1.5 liter	5.57	12/00	5c
Appliances				
Appliance repair, service call, washing machine	min lab chg	45.11	12/00	5c
Banking and Money				
Mortgage rate, incl. points and orig. fee, 30-yr. conv. fixed or ARM	mos	7.94	12/00	5c
Business Expenses				
Business travel, car rental	day	43	2001	3c
Business travel, food	day	46	2001	3c
Business travel, hotel	day	97	2001	3c

Values are in dollars or fractions of dollars. In the column headed *Ref*, references are shown to sources. Each reference is followed by a letter. These refer to the geographical level for which data were reported: s=State, r=Region, and c=City or metro. The abbreviation *ex* is used to mean *except* or *excluding*; *exp* stands for *expenditures*. For other abbreviations and further explanations, please see the Introduction.

Las Vegas, NV - continued

Item	Per	Value	Date	Ref.
Clothing				
Boys' brief, cotton	3	5.10	12/00	5c
Shirt, man's dress shirt		29.48	12/00	5c
Slacks, man's "No Wrinkles" khaki		40.19	12/00	5c
Communications				
Cable modem installation, Cox		99.00-174.95	6/99	103s
Cable modem rate, cable subscriber, Cox	mos	29.95-44.95	6/99	103s
Cable modem rate, non-cable subscriber, Cox	mos	42.95-54.95	6/99	103s
Newspaper subscription, daily and Sunday delivery	mos	14.36	12/00	5c
Phone line, single, business, field visit	inst.	91.00	12/97	17s
Phone line, single, business, no field visit	inst.	74.00	12/97	17s
Phone line, single, residence, field visit	inst.	33.50	12/97	17s
Phone line, single, residence, no field visit	inst.	33.50	12/97	17s
Postal rate, express mail, up to half-pound		12.45	7/01	108r
Postal rate, letter, first class, first ounce		0.34	7/01	108r
Postal rate, letter, two ounces		0.57	7/01	108r
Postal rate, post card		0.21	7/01	108r
Postal rate, priority mail, two pounds		3.95	7/01	108r
Postal rate, priority mail, up to one pound		3.50	7/01	108r
Telephone bill, business, basic rate	mos	22.00	12/97	18c
Telephone bill, family of three	mos	13.50	12/00	5c
Telephone bill, residential, basic rate	mos	10.75	12/97	18c
Education				
Board, 4-year public college/university	yr	2614	1996	38s
Room, 4-year private college/university	yr	3050	1996	38s
Room, 4-year public college/university	yr	3090	1996	38s
Total cost, 4-year public college/university	yr	7388	1996	38s
Tuition, 2-year public college/university, in state	yr	970	1996	38s
Tuition, 4-year private college/university, in state	yr	7841	1996	38s
Tuition, 4-year public college/university	yr	1684	1996	38s
Energy and Fuels				
Energy, combined forms, 2400 sq ft	mos	102.49	12/00	5c
Energy, exc. electricity, 2400 sq ft	mos	28.68	12/00	5c
Gas, cooking, winter, 10 therms	mos	10.91	2/96	98c
Gas, cooking, winter, 30 therms	mos	20.92	2/96	98c
Gas, cooking, winter, 50 therms	mos	30.93	2/96	98c
Gas, heating, winter, average use	mos	46.45	2/96	98c
Gas, natural, commercial rate	1000 cf	5.49	11/00	88s
Gas, regular unleaded, cash, self-service	gal	1.79	12/00	5c
Entertainment				
Bowling, Saturday evening rate	line	2.42	12/00	5c
Monopoly game, Parker Brothers', No. 9	game	11.74	12/00	5c
Movie, first-run, Saturday, evening	adm.	8.50	12/00	5c
Tennis balls, yellow, Wilson or Penn, 3	can	2.62	12/00	5c
Funerals				
Total cost of funeral		5401.08	1/99	78r
Acknowledgement cards		33.64	1/99	78r
Casket		2170.43	1/99	78r
Cosmetology, hair, other preparation		136.32	1/99	78r
Embalming		319.13	1/99	78r
Funeral at funeral home		370.21	1/99	78r
Hearse (local)		161.04	1/99	78r
Professional service charges		963.15	1/99	78r
Service car/van		133.99	1/99	78r
Transfer of remains to funeral home		159.82	1/99	78r
Vault		778.07	1/99	78r
Visitation/viewing		175.28	1/99	78r
Groceries				
Groceries, ACCRA Index		113.90	12/00	5c
Antibiotic ointment, Polysporin	0.5 oz	5.47	12/00	5c
Baby food, strained vegetables or fruit, lowest price	4-4.5 oz	0.38	12/00	5c
Bananas	lb	0.56	12/00	5c
Beef or hamburger, ground	lb	1.55	12/00	5c

Las Vegas, NV - continued

Item	Per	Value	Date	Ref.
Groceries - continued				
Bread, white	loaf	1.24	12/00	5c
Cheese, Kraft grated Parmesan	8 oz	3.56	12/00	5c
Chicken, whole fryer	lb	1.19	12/00	5c
Cigarettes, Winston, Kings	carton	29.49	12/00	5c
Coffee, vacuum-packed	13 oz	3.83	12/00	5c
Corn Flakes, Kellogg's or Post Toasties	18 oz	3.51	12/00	5c
Corn, frozen, whole kernel, lowest price	16 oz	1.26	12/00	5c
Eggs, Grade A or AA	dozen	1.76	12/00	5c
Lettuce, iceberg	head	1.16	12/00	5c
Margarine, Blue Bonnet or Parkay, stick	lb	0.82	12/00	5c
Milk, whole	1/2 gal	1.92	12/00	5c
Orange juice, Minute Maid frozen	12 oz	1.71	12/00	5c
Peaches, halves or slices, Hunt's, Del Monte, or Libby's	29 oz	1.82	12/00	5c
Peas, green, Del Monte or Green Giant	15 oz	0.78	12/00	5c
Potatoes, white or red	10 lb	2.16	12/00	5c
Sausage, Jimmy Dean/Owens pork	lb	3.54	12/00	5c
Shortening, vegetable, Crisco	3 lb	3.46	12/00	5c
Soft drink, Coca Cola, ex deposit	2 liter	1.09	12/00	5c
Steak, T-bone	lb	5.99	12/00	5c
Sugar, cane or beet	4 lbs	1.86	12/00	5c
Tomatoes, Hunt's or Del Monte	14.5 oz	0.88	12/00	5c
Tuna, chunk, light	6 oz	0.92	12/00	5c
Goods and Services				
Miscellaneous goods and services, ACCRA Index		104.80	12/00	5c
Hunting license	yr	24.00	4/01	34s
Health Care				
Health care, ACCRA Index		118.30	12/00	5c
Cardiac catheterization, ave hospital/physician charges		26500	1998	77s
Childbirth, Cesarean delivery		11587	1997	13r
Childbirth, vaginal delivery		6725	1997	13r
Dentist's fee, adult teeth cleaning and periodic oral exam	visit	98.25	12/00	5c
Doctor's fee, routine exam, established patient	visit	65.00	12/00	5c
Home health care aide cost, licensed agency	hour	18	2000	82c
Hospital care, private room	day	438.80	12/00	5c
Hysterectomy, laproscopically-assisted, ave hospital/physician charges		19670	1998	76s
Hysterectomy, vaginal, ave hospital and physician charges		15370	1998	76s
Medicaid dispensing fee		4.76	1999	87s
Nursing home costs, private room	day	133	2000	82c
Nursing home stay, private room	day	133	2000	83c
Household Goods				
Dishwashing powder, Cascade	50 oz	3.13	12/00	5c
Tissues, facial, Kleenex brand	175	1.45	12/00	5c
Housing				
Housing, ACCRA Index		112.20	12/00	5c
Home, 2200 sq ft, 4-br, 2-bath, 2-car garage, average		168000	2000	47c
Home value, median		145000	2001	53s
House, 2400 sq ft, 8000 sq ft lot, new, urban, utilities	total	234250	12/00	5c
House payment, principal and interest, 25% down payment	mos	1282	12/00	5c
Rent, apartment, 2 br, 1 1/2-2 baths, unfurn, 950 sq ft, water	mos	730	12/00	5c
Rental unit, 1 bedroom, with utilities	mos	603	4/01	41c
Rental unit, 2 bedroom, with utilities	mos	718	4/01	41c
Rental unit, 3 bedroom, with utilities	mos	999	4/01	41c
Rental unit, 4 bedroom, with utilities	mos	1180	4/01	41c
Insurance and Pensions				
Auto insurance premium	yr	956.06	1999	57s
Legal Fees				
Combination hunting and fishing license	yr	39.00	4/01	34s
Divorce, filing fee		64.00	4/01	35s

Values are in dollars or fractions of dollars. In the column headed *Ref*, references are shown to sources. Each reference is followed by a letter. These refer to the geographical level for which data were reported: s=State, r=Region, and c=City or metro. The abbreviation *ex* is used to mean *except* or *excluding*; *exp* stands for *expenditures*. For other abbreviations and further explanations, please see the Introduction.

Las Vegas, NV - continued

Item	Per	Value	Date	Ref.
Legal Fees				
Driver's license fee	renew	20.50	1999	48s
Driver's license fee	orig	20.50	1999	48s
Fishing license	yr	21.00	4/01	34s
Personal Goods				
Shampoo, Alberto VO5	15 oz	0.99	12/00	5c
Toothpaste, Crest or Colgate	6-7 oz	2.02	12/00	5c
Personal Services				
Detective service, finding a missing person	hour	50	1999	22c
Dry cleaning, man's 2-pc suit		9.02	12/00	5c
Man's haircut, barbershop, no styling		10.63	12/00	5c
Woman's shampoo, trim, blow-dry, no style-change		25.00	12/00	5c
Restaurant Food				
Chicken, fried, thigh and drumstick, KFC/Church's		2.64	12/00	5c
Hamburger with cheese, McDonald's	1/4 lb	2.19	12/00	5c
Pizza, Pizza Hut or Pizza Inn	11-12 in	8.99	12/00	5c
Transportation				
Transportation, ACCRA Index		117.60	12/00	5c
Bus fare, one-way	trip	1.00	2000	1c
Bus fare, to central business district	1-way	1.25	12/00	5c
Diesel at the pump	gal	1.37	10/99	73s
Gasoline before-tax price (cents)	gal	134.20	10/00	43s
Parking at airport, lowest rate	day	6.00	2000	46c
Tire balance, computer or spin balance, front	wheel	8.99	12/00	5c
Travel				
Cost of meals	day	50.30	2000	10c
Hotel cost	day	94.40	2000	10c
Utilities				
Utilities, ACCRA Index		87.40	12/00	5c
Electrical bill, average	mos	65.50	9/00	9s
Electricity, summer, 250 KWh	mos	20.06	2/96	96c
Electricity, summer, 500 KWh	mos	35.10	2/96	96c
Electricity, summer, 750 KWh	mos	50.12	2/96	96c
Electricity, summer, 1000 KWh	mos	65.16	2/96	96c
Electricity and other, mixed, 2400 sq ft, new home	mos	73.81	12/00	5c
Electricity cost, average	KWh	6.10	9/00	9s
Weddings				
Wedding (national average cost)		19936	2000	33r
Attendants' gifts		321	1998	33r
Bridal attendants' apparel (5 persons)		824	2000	33r
Bride's headpiece/veil		173	1998	33r
Bride's wedding dress		859	1998	33r
Clergy, religious facility fee		242	1998	33r
Engagement ring		3177	1998	33r
Flowers		789	1998	33r
Groom's formalwear rental		99	2000	33r
Limousine		410	1998	33r
Marriage license cost		35.00	4/01	35s
Men's formalwear (ushers, best man)		469	2000	33r
Mother of bride apparel		241	2000	33r
Music		866	1998	33r
Photography and videography		1368	1998	33r
Rehearsal dinner		728	1998	33r
Wedding invitations and announcements		341	1998	33r
Wedding reception		7968	2000	33r
Wedding rings (bride and groom)		1060	1998	33r

Lawrence, KS

Item	Per	Value	Date	Ref.
Average annual expenditures	yr	35369	1999	30r
Composite, ACCRA index		103.20	3/01	4c
Alcoholic Beverages				
Alcoholic beverage purchases	yr	304	1999	30r
Beer, Heineken, 12-oz, ex deposit	6	6.86	3/01	4c
J & B Scotch	750-ml	21.31	3/01	4c

Lawrence, KS - continued

Item	Per	Value	Date	Ref.
Alcoholic Beverages - continued				
Malt beverages, all types, all sizes, any origin	16 oz	0.93	7/01	11r
Wine, Livingston or Gallo, Chablis blanc	1.5 liter	5.87	3/01	4c
Wine, red and white table, all sizes, any origin	liter	7.04	7/01	11r
Appliances				
Appliance repair, service call, washing machine	min lab chg	32.32	3/01	4c
Major appliances, expenditures on	yr	165	1999	30r
Small appliances, housewares, expenditures on	yr	90	1999	30r
Banking and Money				
Mortgage interest and charges paid	yr	2277	1999	30r
Mortgage principal paid on owned property	yr	1230	1999	30r
Mortgage rate, incl. points and orig. fee, 30-yr. conv. fixed or ARM	mos	7.03	3/01	4c
Vehicle finance charges paid	yr	328	1999	30r
Charity				
Cash contributions, expenditures	yr	1126	1999	30r
Child Care				
Child raising cost, total, age 0-2	yr	7890	1999	60r
Child raising cost, total, age 3-5	yr	8130	1999	60r
Child raising cost, total, age 6-8	yr	8170	1999	60r
Child raising cost, total, age 9-11	yr	8190	1999	60r
Child raising cost, total, age 12-14	yr	8890	1999	60r
Child raising cost, total, age 15-17	yr	9050	1999	60r
Child's child care and education, age 0-2	yr	1240	1999	60r
Child's child care and education, age 3-5	yr	1370	1999	60r
Child's child care and education, age 6-8	yr	880	1999	60r
Child's child care and education, age 9-11	yr	570	1999	60r
Child's child care and education, age 12-14	yr	420	1999	60r
Child's child care and education, age 15-17	yr	720	1999	60r
Child's clothing, age 0-2	yr	410	1999	60r
Child's clothing, age 3-5	yr	400	1999	60r
Child's clothing, age 6-8	yr	450	1999	60r
Child's clothing, age 9-11	yr	500	1999	60r
Child's clothing, age 12-14	yr	840	1999	60r
Child's clothing, age 15-17	yr	740	1999	60r
Child's food, age 0-2	yr	960	1999	60r
Child's food, age 3-5	yr	1120	1999	60r
Child's food, age 6-8	yr	1430	1999	60r
Child's food, age 9-11	yr	1710	1999	60r
Child's food, age 12-14	yr	1710	1999	60r
Child's food, age 15-17	yr	1920	1999	60r
Child's health care, age 0-2	yr	520	1999	60r
Child's health care, age 3-5	yr	500	1999	60r
Child's health care, age 6-8	yr	570	1999	60r
Child's health care, age 9-11	yr	610	1999	60r
Child's health care, age 12-14	yr	630	1999	60r
Child's health care, age 15-17	yr	650	1999	60r
Child's housing, age 0-2	yr	2860	1999	60r
Child's housing, age 3-5	yr	2840	1999	60r
Child's housing, age 6-8	yr	2800	1999	60r
Child's housing, age 9-11	yr	2650	1999	60r
Child's housing, age 12-14	yr	2840	1999	60r
Child's housing, age 15-17	yr	2440	1999	60r
Child's personal care, reading, age 0-2	yr	880	1999	60r
Child's personal care, reading, age 3-5	yr	900	1999	60r
Child's personal care, reading, age 6-8	yr	930	1999	60r
Child's personal care, reading, age 9-11	yr	970	1999	60r
Child's personal care, reading, age 12-14	yr	1150	1999	60r
Child's personal care, reading, age 15-17	yr	920	1999	60r
Clothing				
Apparel and services purchases	yr	1607	1999	30r
Boys' brief, cotton	3	3.76	3/01	4c
Boys, 2 to 15, expenditures on	yr	91	1999	30r
Children under 2, expenditures on	yr	59	1999	30r
Footwear, expenditures on	yr	285	1999	30r
Girls, 2 to 15, expenditures on	yr	116	1999	30r
Men and boys, expenditures on	yr	433	1999	30r

Lawrence, KS - continued

Item	Per	Value	Date	Ref.
Clothing				
Men, 16 and over, expenditures on	yr	341	1999	30r
Shirt, man's dress shirt		28.50	3/01	4c
Slacks, man's "No Wrinkles" khaki		37.49	3/01	4c
Women, 16 and over, expenditures on	yr	490	1999	30r
Communications				
Newspaper subscription, daily and Sunday delivery	mos	16.50	3/01	4c
Phone line, single, business, field visit	inst.	57.40	12/97	17s
Phone line, single, business, no field visit	inst.	57.40	12/97	17s
Phone line, single, residence, field visit	inst.	39.00	12/97	17s
Phone line, single, residence, no field visit	inst.	39.00	12/97	17s
Postage and stationery, expenditures on	yr	140	1999	30r
Postal rate, express mail, up to half-pound		12.45	7/01	108r
Postal rate, letter, first class, first ounce		0.34	7/01	108r
Postal rate, letter, two ounces		0.57	7/01	108r
Postal rate, post card		0.21	7/01	108r
Postal rate, priority mail, two pounds		3.95	7/01	108r
Postal rate, priority mail, up to one pound		3.50	7/01	108r
Telephone bill, business, basic rate	mos	21.33	12/97	18c
Telephone bill, family of three	mos	23.71	3/01	4c
Telephone bill, residential, basic rate	mos	10.95	12/97	18c
Telephone services, expenditures on	yr	830	1999	30r
Education				
Board, 4-year private college/university	yr	2183	1996	38s
Board, 4-year public college/university	yr	1841	1996	38s
Education expenditures	yr	583	1999	30r
Room, 4-year private college/university	yr	1582	1996	38s
Room, 4-year public college/university	yr	1731	1996	38s
Total cost, 4-year private college/university	yr	12400	1996	38s
Total cost, 4-year public college/university	yr	5691	1996	38s
Tuition, 2-year public college/university, in state	yr	1147	1996	38s
Tuition, 4-year private college/university, in state	yr	8634	1996	38s
Tuition, 4-year public college/university	yr	2120	1996	38s
Energy and Fuels				
Electricity	500 KWhs	46.59	7/01	11r
Energy, combined forms, 2400 sq ft	mos	149.22	3/01	4c
Energy, exc. electricity, 2400 sq ft	mos	103.68	3/01	4c
Fuel oil #2	gal	1.27	7/01	11r
Fuel oil and other fuels, expenditures on	yr	68	1999	30r
Gas, cooking, winter, 10 therms	mos	9.70	2/96	98c
Gas, cooking, winter, 30 therms	mos	20.80	2/96	98c
Gas, cooking, winter, 50 therms	mos	31.90	2/96	98c
Gas, heating, winter, average use	mos	102.38	2/96	98c
Gas, regular unleaded, cash, self-service	gal	1.35	3/01	4c
Gasoline, unleaded midgrade	gal	1.79	7/01	11r
Gasoline, unleaded premium	gal	1.86	7/01	11r
Gasoline, unleaded regular	gal	1.58	7/01	11r
Natural gas, expenditures on	yr	389	1999	30r
Utility (piped) gas, therm		0.81	7/01	11r
Utility (piped) gas, 40 therms		38.01	7/01	11r
Utility (piped) gas, 100 therms		81.75	7/01	11r
Entertainment				
Bowling, Saturday evening rate	line	2.95	3/01	4c
Entertainment purchases	yr	1984	1999	30r
Fees and admissions paid	yr	444	1999	30r
Monopoly game, Parker Brothers', No. 9	game	10.69	3/01	4c
Movie, first-run, Saturday, evening	adm.	6.13	3/01	4c
Television, radios, sound equipment, expenditures on	yr	580	1999	30r
Tennis balls, yellow, Wilson or Penn, 3	can	2.26	3/01	4c
Funerals				
Cosmetology, hair, other preparation		178.32	1/99	78r
Embalming		408.19	1/99	78r
Funeral at funeral home		362.13	1/99	78r
Professional service charges		1375.51	1/99	78r
Transfer of remains to funeral home		155.92	1/99	78r

Lawrence, KS - continued

Item	Per	Value	Date	Ref.
Funerals - continued				
Visitation/viewing		294.38	1/99	78r
Groceries				
Groceries, ACCRA Index		94.10	3/01	4c
Antibiotic ointment, Polysporin	0.5 oz	4.60	3/01	4c
Baby food, strained vegetables or fruit, lowest price	4-4.5 oz	0.36	3/01	4c
Bacon, sliced	lb	3.15	7/01	11r
Bakery products, expenditures on	yr	281	1999	30r
Bananas	lb	0.36	3/01	4c
Bananas	lb	0.48	7/01	11r
Beans, dried, any type, all sizes	lb	0.61	7/01	11r
Beef for stew, boneless	lb	3.08	7/01	11r
Beef or hamburger, ground	lb	1.75	3/01	4c
Beef, expenditures on	yr	217	1999	30r
Bologna, all beef or mixed	lb	2.52	7/01	11r
Bread, white	loaf	0.97	3/01	4c
Bread, white, pan	lb	1.06	7/01	11r
Broccoli	lb	0.91	7/01	11r
Butter, salted, grade AA, stick	lb	3.04	7/01	11r
Butter, yoghurt, cheese, etc, expenditures on	yr	183	1999	30r
Cereals and bakery product purchases	yr	430	1999	30r
Cereals and cereal products, expenditures on	yr	149	1999	30r
Cheese, Kraft grated Parmesan	8 oz	3.69	3/01	4c
Chicken, fresh, whole	lb	1.07	7/01	11r
Chicken, whole fryer	lb	0.84	3/01	4c
Chops, boneless,	lb	3.64	7/01	11r
Chuck roast, U.S. choice, boneless	lb	2.47	7/01	11r
Cigarettes, Winston, Kings	carton	27.71	3/01	4c
Coffee, 100%, ground roast, all sizes	lb	2.69	7/01	11r
Coffee, vacuum-packed	13 oz	2.24	3/01	4c
Cookies, chocolate chip	lb	2.87	7/01	11r
Corn Flakes, Kellogg's or Post Toasties	18 oz	2.71	3/01	4c
Corn, frozen, whole kernel, lowest price	16 oz	1.23	3/01	4c
Dairy product purchases	yr	304	1999	30r
Eggs, expenditures on	yr	26	1999	30r
Eggs, Grade A or AA	dozen	1.01	3/01	4c
Eggs, grade A, large	dozen	0.88	7/01	11r
Fats and oils, expenditures on	yr	75	1999	30r
Fish and seafood, expenditures on	yr	72	1999	30r
Food (excl fruit and vegetables), eaten at home, purchases	yr	887	1999	30r
Food cooked on trips, expenditures on	yr	44	1999	30r
Food purchases	yr	4802	1999	30r
Food purchases, eaten away from home	yr	2069	1999	30r
Food purchases, food eaten at home	yr	2733	1999	30r
Fresh fruits, expenditures on	yr	138	1999	30r
Fresh milk and cream, expenditures on	yr	120	1999	30r
Fresh vegetables, expenditures on	yr	126	1999	30r
Grapefruit	lb	0.66	7/01	11r
Grapes, Thompson, seedless	lb	1.64	7/01	11r
Ground beef, 100% beef	lb	1.64	7/01	11r
Ground beef, lean and extra lean	lb	2.16	7/01	11r
Ground chuck, 100% beef	lb	2.13	7/01	11r
Ham, boneless, excl canned	lb	2.62	7/01	11r
Ice cream, prepackaged, bulk, regular	1/2 gal	3.35	7/01	11r
Lemons	lb	1.19	7/01	11r
Lettuce, iceberg	head	0.82	3/01	4c
Lettuce, iceberg	lb	0.73	7/01	11r
Margarine, Blue Bonnet or Parkay, stick	lb	0.58	3/01	4c
Margarine, soft, tubs	lb	0.89	7/01	11r
Meats, poultry, fish, and egg purchases	yr	671	1999	30r
Milk, fresh, whole, fortified	gal	2.71	7/01	11r
Milk, whole	1/2 gal	1.56	3/01	4c
Nonalcoholic beverages, expenditures on	yr	239	1999	30r
Orange juice, Minute Maid frozen	12 oz	1.75	3/01	4c
Oranges, Navel	lb	0.80	7/01	11r
Oranges, Valencia	lb	0.66	7/01	11r
Peaches, halves or slices, Hunt's, Del Monte, or Libby's	29 oz	1.68	3/01	4c
Pears, Anjou	lb	0.93	7/01	11r
Peas, green, Del Monte or Green Giant	15 oz	0.78	3/01	4c

Values are in dollars or fractions of dollars. In the column headed *Ref*, references are shown to sources. Each reference is followed by a letter. These refer to the geographical level for which data were reported: s=State, r=Region, and c=City or metro. The abbreviation *ex* is used to mean *except* or *excluding*; *exp* stands for *expenditures*. For other abbreviations and further explanations, please see the Introduction.

Lawrence, KS - continued

Item	Per	Value	Date	Ref.
Groceries				
Pork chops, center cut, bone-in	lb	3.63	7/01	11r
Pork, expenditures on	yr	150	1999	30r
Potato chips	16 oz	3.52	7/01	11r
Potatoes, frozen, french fried	lb	1.08	7/01	11r
Potatoes, white or red	10 lb	2.13	3/01	4c
Potatoes, white, all types	lb	0.33	7/01	11r
Poultry, expenditures on	yr	108	1999	30r
Processed fruits, expenditures on	yr	98	1999	30r
Processed vegetables, expenditures on	yr	80	1999	30r
Round roast, U.S. choice, boneless	lb	3.07	7/01	11r
Round steak, graded and ungraded, excl				
U.S. prime and choice	lb	3.41	7/01	11r
Sausage, Jimmy Dean/Owens pork	lb	3.70	3/01	4c
Shortening, vegetable oil blends	lb	1.13	7/01	11r
Shortening, vegetable, Crisco	3 lb	2.79	3/01	4c
Soft drink, Coca Cola, ex deposit	2 liter	1.10	3/01	4c
Spaghetti and macaroni	lb	0.80	7/01	11r
Steak, round, U.S. choice, boneless	lb	3.23	7/01	11r
Steak, T-bone	lb	6.79	3/01	4c
Steak, T-bone, U.S. choice, bone-in	lb	6.68	7/01	11r
Strawberries, dry pint	12 oz	1.32	7/01	11r
Sugar and other sweets, expenditures on	yr	114	1999	30r
Sugar, cane or beet	4 lbs	1.38	3/01	4c
Sugar, white, 33-80 ounce package	lb	0.42	7/01	11r
Sugar, white, all sizes	lb	0.43	7/01	11r
Tobacco products and smoking supplies				
purchases	yr	331	1999	30r
Tomatoes, field grown	lb	1.46	7/01	11r
Tomatoes, Hunt's or Del Monte	14.5 oz	0.88	3/01	4c
Tuna, chunk, light	6 oz	0.46	3/01	4c
Tuna, light, chunk	lb	1.80	7/01	11r
Turkey, frozen, whole	lb	1.15	7/01	11r
Goods and Services				
Miscellaneous goods and services, ACCRA				
Index		99.60	3/01	4c
B&B Japanese maple (acer japonicum)	gal	29.99-169.99	4/00	93r
Boxwood (buxus)	2 gal	18.99-39.99	4/00	93r
Daylilly (hemerocallis)	gal	4.99-25.00	4/00	93r
Flat of annuals		11.98-24.99	4/00	93r
Fountain grass (pennisetum)	gal	5.98-12.98	4/00	93r
Hanging basket (10 in)		12.99-27.99	4/00	93r
Hardy geranium (geranium)	gal	7.99-9.99	4/00	93r
Hosta (hosta)	gal	6.00-25.00	4/00	93r
Lilac (syrubga vulgaris)	2 gal	14.99-24.99	4/00	93r
Miscellaneous purchases	yr	865	1999	30r
Rhododendron (rhododendron)	2 gal	23.98-42.99	4/00	93r
Sage (salvia)	gal	6.00-9.99	4/00	93r
Wintercreeper euonymus (euonymus fortunei)	2 gal	16.00-169.99	4/00	93r
Hunting license	yr	15.50	4/01	34s
Health Care				
Health care, ACCRA Index		90.90	3/01	4c
Cardiac catheterization, ave hospital/physician charges		11230	1998	77s
Childbirth, Cesarean delivery		10722	1997	13r
Childbirth, vaginal delivery		6223	1997	13r
Dentist's fee, adult teeth cleaning and periodic oral exam	visit	71.50	3/01	4c
Doctor's fee, routine exam, established patient	visit	48.50	3/01	4c

Lawrence, KS - continued

Item	Per	Value	Date	Ref.
Health Care - continued				
Drugs, expenditures on	yr	394	1999	30r
Health care purchases	yr	2048	1999	30r
Health insurance expenditures	yr	978	1999	30r
Hospital care, private room	day	450.00	3/01	4c
Hysterectomy, laproscopically-assisted, ave hospital/physician charges		9610	1998	76s
Hysterectomy, vaginal, ave hospital and physician charges		6500	1998	76s
Medicaid dispensing fee		4.94	1999	87s
Medical services expenditures	yr	554	1999	30r
Medical supplies, expenditures on	yr	122	1999	30r
Plastic surgery, breast augmentation		3184	2000	7r
Plastic surgery, breast lift		3585	2000	7r
Plastic surgery, facelift		4999	2000	7r
Plastic surgery, hair transplantation		3105	2000	7r
Plastic surgery, lip augmentation		1290	2000	7r
Plastic surgery, lower body lift		8135	2000	7r
Plastic surgery, thigh lift		3839	2000	7r
Household Goods				
Dishwashing powder, Cascade	50 oz	3.32	3/01	4c
Floor coverings, expenditures on	yr	52	1999	30r
Furniture, expenditures on	yr	344	1999	30r
Household furnishings and equipment purchases	yr	1475	1999	30r
Household textiles, expenditures on	yr	109	1999	30r
Laundry and cleaning supplies, expenditures on	yr	134	1999	30r
Tissues, facial, Kleenex brand	175	1.20	3/01	4c
Housing				
Housing, ACCRA Index		112.20	3/01	4c
Home, 2200 sq ft, 4-br, 2-bath, 2-car garage, average		160686	2000	47c
Home price, existing, ave		144400	10/00	90r
Home value, median		112000	2001	53s
House, 2400 sq ft, 8000 sq ft lot, new, urban, utilities	total	243389	3/01	4c
House payment, principal and interest, 25% down payment	mos	1218	3/01	4c
Household operation expenditures	yr	542	1999	30r
Housekeeping supplies purchases	yr	508	1999	30r
Lodging expenditures	yr	430	1999	30r
Maintenance, repairs, insurance expenditures	yr	853	1999	30r
Monthly rental value of owned home	mos	547	1999	30r
Owned dwellings, expenditures own	yr	4282	1999	30r
Rent expenditures	yr	1558	1999	30r
Rent, apartment, 2 br, 1 1/2-2 baths, unfurn, 950 sq ft, water	mos	619	3/01	4c
Rental unit, 1 bedroom, with utilities	mos	432	4/01	41c
Rental unit, 2 bedroom, with utilities	mos	554	4/01	41c
Rental unit, 3 bedroom, with utilities	mos	771	4/01	41c
Rental unit, 4 bedroom, with utilities	mos	888	4/01	41c
Shelter, expenditures on	yr	6270	1999	30r
Insurance and Pensions				
Life and other personal insurance purchases	yr	387	1999	30r
Pensions and Social Security, expenditures on	yr	2968	1999	30r
Legal Fees				
Combination hunting and fishing license	yr	30.50	4/01	34s
Divorce, filing fee		100.00	4/01	35s
Driver's license fee	orig	18.00	1999	48s
Driver's license fee	renew	18.00	1999	48s
Fishing license	yr	15.50	4/01	34s
Personal Goods				
Personal care products and services purchases	yr	385	1999	30r
Shampoo, Alberto VO5	15 oz	1.11	3/01	4c
Toothpaste, Crest or Colgate	6-7 oz	1.91	3/01	4c

Values are in dollars or fractions of dollars. In the column headed *Ref*, references are shown to sources. Each reference is followed by a letter. These refer to the geographical level for which data were reported: s=State, r=Region, and c=City or metro. The abbreviation *ex* is used to mean *except* or *excluding*; *exp* stands for *expenditures*. For other abbreviations and further explanations, please see the Introduction.

Lawrence, KS - continued

Item	Per	Value	Date	Ref.
Personal Services				
Dry cleaning, man's 2-pc suit		9.23	3/01	4c
Man's haircut, barbershop, no styling		8.83	3/01	4c
Personal services, household, expenditures on	yr	300	1999	30r
Woman's shampoo, trim, blow-dry, no style-change		24.80	3/01	4c
Pets				
Pets, dog day care service	hour	15	2000	14c
Pets, toys, and playground equipment, expenditures on	yr	375	1999	30r
Restaurant Food				
Chicken, fried, thigh and drumstick, KFC/Church's		2.69	3/01	4c
Hamburger with cheese, McDonald's	1/4 lb	2.19	3/01	4c
Pizza, Pizza Hut or Pizza Inn	11-12 in	9.29	3/01	4c
Taxes				
Federal income taxes paid	yr	2326	1999	30r
Personal taxes, expenditures on	yr	3223	1999	30r
Property taxes paid	yr	1152	1999	30r
State and local income taxes paid	yr	753	1999	30r
Transportation				
Transportation, ACCRA Index		96.80	3/01	4c
Cars and trucks, new, expenditures on	yr	1280	1999	30r
Cars and trucks, used, expenditures on	yr	1763	1999	30r
Diesel at the pump	gal	1.24	10/99	73s
Gasoline and motor oil purchases	yr	1036	1999	30r
Gasoline before-tax price (cents)	gal	108.00	10/00	43s
Maintenance and repair expenditures	yr	594	1999	30r
Public transportation, expenditures on	yr	341	1999	30r
Tire balance, computer or spin balance, front	wheel	7.75	3/01	4c
Transportation purchases	yr	6617	1999	30r
Vehicle expenses, miscellaneous, purchases	yr	2159	1999	30r
Vehicle insurance payments	yr	701	1999	30r
Vehicle purchases (net outlay)	yr	3081	1999	30r
Vehicle rental, lease expenditures	yr	536	1999	30r
Utilities				
Utilities, ACCRA Index		120.40	3/01	4c
Electrical bill, average	mos	64.66	9/00	9s
Electricity, expenditures on	yr	841	1999	30r
Electricity and other, mixed, 2400 sq ft, new home	mos	45.54	3/01	4c
Electricity cost, average	KWh	6.30	9/00	9s
Utilities, fuels, and public services purchased	yr	2401	1999	30r
Water and other public services, expenditures on	yr	273	1999	30r
Weddings				
Wedding (national average cost)		19936	2000	33r
Wedding (regional average total cost)		16195	1997	110r
Attendants' gifts		321	1998	33r
Bridal attendants' apparel (5 persons)		824	2000	33r
Bride's headpiece/veil		173	1998	33r
Bride's wedding dress		859	1998	33r
Clergy, religious facility fee		242	1998	33r
Engagement ring		3177	1998	33r
Flowers		789	1998	33r
Groom's formalwear rental		99	2000	33r
Limousine		410	1998	33r
Marriage license cost		50.00	4/01	35s
Men's formalwear (ushers, best man)		469	2000	33r
Mother of bride apparel		241	2000	33r
Music		866	1998	33r
Photography and videography		1368	1998	33r
Rehearsal dinner		728	1998	33r
Wedding invitations and announcements		341	1998	33r
Wedding reception		7968	2000	33r
Wedding rings (bride and groom)		1060	1998	33r

Lawrence, MA

Item	Per	Value	Date	Ref.
Average annual expenditures	yr	37971	1999	30r
Alcoholic Beverages				
Alcoholic beverage purchases	yr	368	1999	30r
Wine, red and white table, all sizes, any origin	liter	9.64	7/01	11r
Appliances				
Major appliances, expenditures on	yr	194	1999	30r
Small appliances, housewares, expenditures on	yr	93	1999	30r
Banking and Money				
Mortgage interest and charges paid	yr	2622	1999	30r
Mortgage principal paid on owned property	yr	1262	1999	30r
Vehicle finance charges paid	yr	240	1999	30r
Charity				
Cash contributions, expenditures	yr	1001	1999	30r
Child Care				
Child raising cost, total, age 0-2	yr	8670	1999	60r
Child raising cost, total, age 3-5	yr	8910	1999	60r
Child raising cost, total, age 6-8	yr	9040	1999	60r
Child raising cost, total, age 9-11	yr	9100	1999	60r
Child raising cost, total, age 12-14	yr	9890	1999	60r
Child raising cost, total, age 15-17	yr	10010	1999	60r
Child's child care and education, age 0-2	yr	1070	1999	60r
Child's child care and education, age 3-5	yr	1190	1999	60r
Child's child care and education, age 6-8	yr	740	1999	60r
Child's child care and education, age 9-11	yr	470	1999	60r
Child's child care and education, age 12-14	yr	350	1999	60r
Child's child care and education, age 15-17	yr	590	1999	60r
Child's clothing, age 0-2	yr	480	1999	60r
Child's clothing, age 3-5	yr	470	1999	60r
Child's clothing, age 6-8	yr	520	1999	60r
Child's clothing, age 9-11	yr	570	1999	60r
Child's clothing, age 12-14	yr	970	1999	60r
Child's clothing, age 15-17	yr	870	1999	60r
Child's food, age 0-2	yr	1130	1999	60r
Child's food, age 3-5	yr	1290	1999	60r
Child's food, age 6-8	yr	1640	1999	60r
Child's food, age 9-11	yr	1930	1999	60r
Child's food, age 12-14	yr	1940	1999	60r
Child's food, age 15-17	yr	2150	1999	60r
Child's health care, age 0-2	yr	550	1999	60r
Child's health care, age 3-5	yr	530	1999	60r
Child's health care, age 6-8	yr	610	1999	60r
Child's health care, age 9-11	yr	650	1999	60r
Child's health care, age 12-14	yr	660	1999	60r
Child's health care, age 15-17	yr	690	1999	60r
Child's housing, age 0-2	yr	3555	1999	60r
Child's housing, age 3-5	yr	3530	1999	60r
Child's housing, age 6-8	yr	3490	1999	60r
Child's housing, age 9-11	yr	3340	1999	60r
Child's housing, age 12-14	yr	3530	1999	60r
Child's housing, age 15-17	yr	3140	1999	60r
Child's personal care, reading, age 0-2	yr	920	1999	60r
Child's personal care, reading, age 3-5	yr	950	1999	60r
Child's personal care, reading, age 6-8	yr	980	1999	60r
Child's personal care, reading, age 9-11	yr	1020	1999	60r
Child's personal care, reading, age 12-14	yr	1190	1999	60r
Child's personal care, reading, age 15-17	yr	970	1999	60r
Clothing				
Apparel and services purchases	yr	1831	1999	30r
Boys, 2 to 15, expenditures on	yr	92	1999	30r
Children under 2, expenditures on	yr	63	1999	30r
Footwear, expenditures on	yr	300	1999	30r
Girls, 2 to 15, expenditures on	yr	101	1999	30r
Men and boys, expenditures on	yr	446	1999	30r
Men, 16 and over, expenditures on	yr	354	1999	30r
Women, 16 and over, expenditures on	yr	584	1999	30r
Communications				
Cable modem installation, Adelphi		54.90	6/99	103s

Values are in dollars or fractions of dollars. In the column headed *Ref*, references are shown to sources. Each reference is followed by a letter. These refer to the geographical level for which data were reported: s=State, r=Region, and c=City or metro. The abbreviation *ex* is used to mean *except* or *excluding*; *exp* stands for expenditures. For other abbreviations and further explanations, please see the Introduction.

Lawrence, MA - continued

Item	Per	Value	Date	Ref.
Communications				
Cable modem installation, Media One		100.00	6/99	103s
Cable modem rate, cable subscriber, Adelphi	mos	34.95	6/99	103s
Cable modem rate, cable subscriber, Media One	mos	34.95-39.95	6/99	103s
Cable modem rate, non-cable subscriber, Adelphi	mos	44.95	6/99	103s
Cable modem rate, non-cable subscriber, Media One	mos	49.95	6/99	103s
Phone line, single, business, field visit	inst.	120.52	12/97	17s
Phone line, single, business, no field visit	inst.	93.02	12/97	17s
Phone line, single, residence, field visit	inst.	64.57	12/97	17s
Phone line, single, residence, no field visit	inst.	37.07	12/97	17s
Postage and stationery, expenditures on	yr	138	1999	30r
Postal rate, express mail, up to half-pound		12.45	7/01	108r
Postal rate, letter, first class, first ounce		0.34	7/01	108r
Postal rate, letter, two ounces		0.57	7/01	108r
Postal rate, post card		0.21	7/01	108r
Postal rate, priority mail, two pounds		3.95	7/01	108r
Postal rate, priority mail, up to one pound		3.50	7/01	108r
Telephone services, expenditures on	yr	830	1999	30r
Education				
Board, 4-year private college/university	yr	3244	1996	38s
Board, 4-year public college/university	yr	2042	1996	38s
Education expenditures	yr	877	1999	30r
Room, 4-year private college/university	yr	3688	1996	38s
Room, 4-year public college/university	yr	2462	1996	38s
Total cost, 4-year private college/university	yr	23335	1996	38s
Total cost, 4-year public college/university	yr	8757	1996	38s
Tuition, 2-year public college/university, in state	yr	2359	1996	38s
Tuition, 4-year private college/university, in state	yr	16403	1996	38s
Tuition, 4-year public college/university	yr	4253	1996	38s
Energy and Fuels				
Electricity	KWh	0.12	7/01	11r
Fuel oil #2	gal	1.31	7/01	11r
Fuel oil and other fuels, expenditures on	yr	207	1999	30r
Gas, natural, commercial rate	1000 cf	10.82	11/00	88s
Gasoline, all types	gal	1.80	7/01	11r
Gasoline, unleaded midgrade	gal	1.85	7/01	11r
Gasoline, unleaded premium	gal	1.91	7/01	11r
Gasoline, unleaded regular	gal	1.71	7/01	11r
Natural gas, expenditures on	yr	368	1999	30r
Utility (piped) gas, therm		1.08	7/01	11r
Utility (piped) gas, 40 therms		50.87	7/01	11r
Utility (piped) gas, 100 therms		111.06	7/01	11r
Entertainment				
Entertainment purchases	yr	1821	1999	30r
Fees and admissions paid	yr	511	1999	30r
Television, radios, sound equipment, expenditures on	yr	650	1999	30r
Funerals				
Total cost of funeral		5776.91	1/99	78r
Acknowledgement cards		14.47	1/99	78r
Casket		2090.19	1/99	78r
Cosmetology, hair, other preparation		132.92	1/99	78r
Embalming		377.33	1/99	78r
Funeral at funeral home		352.43	1/99	78r
Hearse (local)		185.55	1/99	78r
Professional service charges		1289.95	1/99	78r
Service car/van		87.42	1/99	78r
Transfer of remains to funeral home		175.48	1/99	78r
Vault		729.40	1/99	78r
Visitation/viewing		341.76	1/99	78r
Groceries				
Apples, red delicious	lb	0.95	7/01	11r
Bacon, sliced	lb	3.44	7/01	11r
Bakery products, expenditures on	yr	310	1999	30r
Bananas	lb	0.55	7/01	11r

Lawrence, MA - continued

Item	Per	Value	Date	Ref.
Groceries - continued				
Beef, expenditures on	yr	236	1999	30r
Bread, white, pan	lb	1.09	7/01	11r
Butter, yoghurt, cheese, etc, expenditures on	yr	214	1999	30r
Cereals and bakery product purchases	yr	474	1999	30r
Cereals and cereal products, expenditures on	yr	164	1999	30r
Chicken legs, bone-in	lb	1.23	7/01	11r
Chicken, fresh, whole	lb	1.13	7/01	11r
Chuck roast, U.S. choice, boneless	lb	2.79	7/01	11r
Coffee, 100%, ground roast, all sizes	lb	3.40	7/01	11r
Dairy product purchases	yr	342	1999	30r
Eggs, expenditures on	yr	34	1999	30r
Eggs, grade A, large	dozen	0.82	7/01	11r
Fats and oils, expenditures on	yr	80	1999	30r
Fish and seafood, expenditures on	yr	123	1999	30r
Food (excl fruit and vegetables), eaten at home, purchases	yr	838	1999	30r
Food cooked on trips, expenditures on	yr	48	1999	30r
Food purchases	yr	5314	1999	30r
Food purchases, eaten away from home	yr	2313	1999	30r
Food purchases, food eaten at home	yr	3001	1999	30r
Fresh fruits, expenditures on	yr	169	1999	30r
Fresh milk and cream, expenditures on	yr	128	1999	30r
Fresh vegetables, expenditures on	yr	164	1999	30r
Grapefruit	lb	0.67	7/01	11r
Grapes, Thompson, seedless	lb	2.18	7/01	11r
Ground beef, lean and extra lean	lb	2.66	7/01	11r
Ground chuck, 100% beef	lb	2.04	7/01	11r
Lettuce, iceberg	lb	0.76	7/01	11r
Meats, poultry, fish, and egg purchases	yr	808	1999	30r
Nonalcoholic beverages, expenditures on	yr	225	1999	30r
Orange juice, frozen concentrate	16 oz	1.88	7/01	11r
Oranges, Navel	lb	0.79	7/01	11r
Oranges, Valencia	lb	0.56	7/01	11r
Peaches	lb	1.16	7/01	11r
Peanut butter, creamy, all sizes	lb	2.01	7/01	11r
Pears, Anjou	lb	1.16	7/01	11r
Pork chops, center cut, bone-in	lb	3.57	7/01	11r
Pork, expenditures on	yr	146	1999	30r
Potato chips	16 oz	3.37	7/01	11r
Potatoes, white, all types	lb	0.42	7/01	11r
Poultry, expenditures on	yr	158	1999	30r
Processed fruits, expenditures on	yr	124	1999	30r
Processed vegetables, expenditures on	yr	82	1999	30r
Round roast, U.S. choice, boneless	lb	3.04	7/01	11r
Spaghetti and macaroni	lb	1.04	7/01	11r
Steak, sirloin, U.S. choice, boneless	lb	5.39	7/01	11r
Strawberries, dry pint	12 oz	1.51	7/01	11r
Sugar and other sweets, expenditures on	yr	110	1999	30r
Sugar, white, 33-80 ounce package	lb	0.46	7/01	11r
Sugar, white, all sizes	lb	0.47	7/01	11r
Tobacco products and smoking supplies purchases	yr	309	1999	30r
Yogurt, natural, fruit flavored	8 oz	0.79	7/01	11r
Goods and Services				
B&B Japanese maple (acer japonicum)	gal	38.99-125.00	4/00	93r
Boxwood (buxus)	2 gal	15.99-49.95	4/00	93r
Daylily (hemerocallis)	gal	4.95	4/00	93r
Flat of annuals		8.00-14.99	4/00	93r
Fountain grass (pennisetum)	gal	6.99-9.99	4/00	93r
Hanging basket (10 in)		12.95-19.99	4/00	93r
Hardy geranium (geranium)	gal	6.95-7.99	4/00	93r
Hosta (hosta)	gal	4.95	4/00	93r
Lilac (syrubga vulgaris)	2 gal	17.99-74.95	4/00	93r
Miscellaneous purchases	yr	872	1999	30r

Values are in dollars or fractions of dollars. In the column headed *Ref*, references are shown to sources. Each reference is followed by a letter. These refer to the geographical level for which data were reported: s=State, r=Region, and c=City or metro. The abbreviation *ex* is used to mean *except* or *excluding*; *exp* stands for *expenditures*. For other abbreviations and further explanations, please see the Introduction.

Lawrence, MA - continued

Item	Per	Value	Date	Ref.
Goods and Services				
Rhododendron (rhododendron)	2 gal	23.99-54.95	4/00	93r
Sage (salvia)	gal	6.95-7.99	4/00	93r
Wintercreeper euonymus (euonymus fortunei)	2 gal	14.99-23.95	4/00	93r
Hunting license	yr	27.50	4/01	34s
Health Care				
Cardiac catheterization, ave hospital/physician charges		17080	1998	77s
Childbirth, Cesarean delivery		14716	1997	13r
Childbirth, vaginal delivery		8541	1997	13r
Drugs, expenditures on	yr	296	1999	30r
Health care purchases	yr	1788	1999	30r
Health insurance expenditures	yr	875	1999	30r
Hysterectomy, laproscopically-assisted, ave hospital/physician charges		13100	1998	76s
Hysterectomy, vaginal, ave hospital and physician charges		8780	1998	76s
Medicaid dispensing fee		3.00	1999	87s
Medical services expenditures	yr	516	1999	30r
Medical supplies, expenditures on	yr	102	1999	30r
Plastic surgery, breast augmentation		4232	2000	7r
Plastic surgery, breast lift		4605	2000	7r
Plastic surgery, facelift		6964	2000	7r
Plastic surgery, hair transplantation		4193	2000	7r
Plastic surgery, lip augmentation		1675	2000	7r
Plastic surgery, lower body lift		6611	2000	7r
Plastic surgery, thigh lift		4751	2000	7r
Household Goods				
Floor coverings, expenditures on	yr	59	1999	30r
Furniture, expenditures on	yr	388	1999	30r
Household furnishings and equipment purchases	yr	1567	1999	30r
Household textiles, expenditures on	yr	112	1999	30r
Laundry and cleaning supplies, expenditures on	yr	104	1999	30r
Housing				
Home price, existing, ave		180800	10/00	90r
Home value, median		261000	2001	53s
Household operation expenditures	yr	581	1999	30r
Housekeeping supplies purchases	yr	474	1999	30r
Lodging expenditures	yr	550	1999	30r
Maintenance, repairs, insurance expenditures	yr	835	1999	30r
Monthly rental value of owned home	mos	663	1999	30r
Owned dwellings, expenditures own	yr	5209	1999	30r
Rent expenditures	yr	2390	1999	30r
Rental unit, 1 bedroom, with utilities	mos	606	4/01	41c
Rental unit, 2 bedroom, with utilities	mos	763	4/01	41c
Rental unit, 3 bedroom, with utilities	mos	953	4/01	41c
Rental unit, 4 bedroom, with utilities	mos	1172	4/01	41c
Shelter, expenditures on	yr	8149	1999	30r
Insurance and Pensions				
Life and other personal insurance purchases	yr	424	1999	30r
Pensions and Social Security, expenditures on	yr	3037	1999	30r
Legal Fees				
Divorce, filing fee		100.00	4/01	35s
Driver's license fee	orig	33.75	1999	48s
Driver's license fee	renew	33.75	1999	48s
Fishing license	yr	27.50	4/01	34s
Personal Goods				
Personal care products and services purchases	yr	399	1999	30r
Personal Services				
Personal services, household, expenditures on	yr	271	1999	30r

Lawrence, MA - continued

Item	Per	Value	Date	Ref.
Pets				
Pets, toys, and playground equipment, expenditures on	yr	325	1999	30r
Taxes				
Federal income taxes paid	yr	2606	1999	30r
Personal taxes, expenditures on	yr	3567	1999	30r
Property taxes paid	yr	1752	1999	30r
State and local income taxes paid	yr	694	1999	30r
Transportation				
Cars and trucks, new, expenditures on	yr	1496	1999	30r
Cars and trucks, used, expenditures on	yr	1251	1999	30r
Diesel at the pump	gal	1.32	10/99	73s
Gasoline and motor oil purchases	yr	901	1999	30r
Gasoline before-tax price (cents)	gal	118.70	10/00	43s
Maintenance and repair expenditures	yr	618	1999	30r
Public transportation, expenditures on	yr	575	1999	30r
Transportation purchases	yr	6503	1999	30r
Vehicle expenses, miscellaneous, purchases	yr	2266	1999	30r
Vehicle insurance payments	yr	824	1999	30r
Vehicle purchases (net outlay)	yr	2761	1999	30r
Vehicle rental, lease expenditures	yr	584	1999	30r
Travel				
Hotel room	night	111.15	2/01	95s
Utilities				
Electrical bill, average	mos	58.58	9/00	9s
Electricity, expenditures on	yr	837	1999	30r
Electricity cost, average	KWh	8.90	9/00	9s
Utilities, fuels, and public services purchased	yr	2457	1999	30r
Water and other public services, expenditures on	yr	215	1999	30r
Weddings				
Wedding (national average cost)		19936	2000	33r
Wedding (regional average total cost)		29454	1997	110r
Attendants' gifts		321	1998	33r
Bridal attendants' apparel (5 persons)		824	2000	33r
Bride's headpiece/veil		173	1998	33r
Bride's wedding dress		859	1998	33r
Clergy, religious facility fee		242	1998	33r
Engagement ring		3177	1998	33r
Flowers		789	1998	33r
Groom's formalwear rental		99	2000	33r
Limousine		410	1998	33r
Marriage license cost		25.00	4/01	35s
Men's formalwear (ushers, best man)		469	2000	33r
Mother of bride apparel		241	2000	33r
Music		866	1998	33r
Photography and videography		1368	1998	33r
Rehearsal dinner		728	1998	33r
Wedding invitations and announcements		341	1998	33r
Wedding reception		7968	2000	33r
Wedding rings (bride and groom)		1060	1998	33r

Lawton, OK

Item	Per	Value	Date	Ref.
Composite, ACCRA index		95.50	3/01	4c
Alcoholic Beverages				
Alcoholic beverage purchases	yr	253	1999	30r
Beer, Heineken, 12-oz, ex deposit	6	8.12	3/01	4c
J & B Scotch	750-ml	20.01	3/01	4c
Malt beverages, all types, all sizes, any origin	16 oz	0.96	7/01	11r
Wine, Livingston or Gallo, Chablis blanc	1.5 liter	6.63	3/01	4c
Appliances				
Appliance repair, service call, washing machine	min lab chg	42.59	3/01	4c
Major appliances, expenditures on	yr	172	1999	30r
Small appliances, housewares, expenditures on	yr	81	1999	30r

Values are in dollars or fractions of dollars. In the column headed *Ref*, references are shown to sources. Each reference is followed by a letter. These refer to the geographical level for which data were reported: s=State, r=Region, and c=City or metro. The abbreviation *ex* is used to mean *except* or *excluding*; *exp* stands for *expenditures*. For other abbreviations and further explanations, please see the Introduction.

Lawton, OK - continued

Item	Per	Value	Date	Ref.
Banking and Money				
Mortgage interest and charges paid	yr	2039	1999	30r
Mortgage principal paid on owned property	yr	1026	1999	30r
Mortgage rate, incl. points and orig. fee, 30-yr. conv. fixed or ARM	mos	7.13	3/01	4c
Vehicle finance charges paid	yr	365	1999	30r
Charity				
Cash contributions, expenditures	yr	1127	1999	30r
Child Care				
Child raising cost, total, age 0-2	yr	8540	1999	60r
Child raising cost, total, age 3-5	yr	8780	1999	60r
Child raising cost, total, age 6-8	yr	8820	1999	60r
Child raising cost, total, age 9-11	yr	8800	1999	60r
Child raising cost, total, age 12-14	yr	9510	1999	60r
Child raising cost, total, age 15-17	yr	9740	1999	60r
Child's child care and education, age 0-2	yr	1380	1999	60r
Child's child care and education, age 3-5	yr	1520	1999	60r
Child's child care and education, age 6-8	yr	990	1999	60r
Child's child care and education, age 9-11	yr	650	1999	60r
Child's child care and education, age 12-14	yr	490	1999	60r
Child's child care and education, age 15-17	yr	840	1999	60r
Child's clothing, age 0-2	yr	480	1999	60r
Child's clothing, age 3-5	yr	470	1999	60r
Child's clothing, age 6-8	yr	520	1999	60r
Child's clothing, age 9-11	yr	570	1999	60r
Child's clothing, age 12-14	yr	950	1999	60r
Child's clothing, age 15-17	yr	850	1999	60r
Child's food, age 0-2	yr	1000	1999	60r
Child's food, age 3-5	yr	1160	1999	60r
Child's food, age 6-8	yr	1490	1999	60r
Child's food, age 9-11	yr	1770	1999	60r
Child's food, age 12-14	yr	1770	1999	60r
Child's food, age 15-17	yr	1980	1999	60r
Child's health care, age 0-2	yr	620	1999	60r
Child's health care, age 3-5	yr	590	1999	60r
Child's health care, age 6-8	yr	680	1999	60r
Child's health care, age 9-11	yr	720	1999	60r
Child's health care, age 12-14	yr	730	1999	60r
Child's health care, age 15-17	yr	760	1999	60r
Child's housing, age 0-2	yr	3070	1999	60r
Child's housing, age 3-5	yr	3050	1999	60r
Child's housing, age 6-8	yr	3010	1999	60r
Child's housing, age 9-11	yr	2850	1999	60r
Child's housing, age 12-14	yr	3040	1999	60r
Child's housing, age 15-17	yr	2650	1999	60r
Child's personal care, reading, age 0-2	yr	910	1999	60r
Child's personal care, reading, age 3-5	yr	930	1999	60r
Child's personal care, reading, age 6-8	yr	960	1999	60r
Child's personal care, reading, age 9-11	yr	1000	1999	60r
Child's personal care, reading, age 12-14	yr	1170	1999	60r
Child's personal care, reading, age 15-17	yr	950	1999	60r
Clothing				
Apparel and services purchases	yr	1610	1999	30r
Boys' brief, cotton	3	5.48	3/01	4c
Boys, 2 to 15, expenditures on	yr	89	1999	30r
Children under 2, expenditures on	yr	79	1999	30r
Footwear, expenditures on	yr	283	1999	30r
Girls, 2 to 15, expenditures on	yr	103	1999	30r
Men and boys, expenditures on	yr	351	1999	30r
Men, 16 and over, expenditures on	yr	262	1999	30r
Shirt, man's dress shirt		27.50	3/01	4c
Slacks, man's "No Wrinkles" khaki		36.00	3/01	4c
Women, 16 and over, expenditures on	yr	538	1999	30r
Communications				
Cable modem installation, Cox		99.00-174.95	6/99	103s
Cable modem rate, cable subscriber, Cox	mos	29.95-44.95	6/99	103s
Cable modem rate, non-cable subscriber, Cox	mos	42.95-54.95	6/99	103s

Lawton, OK - continued

Item	Per	Value	Date	Ref.
Communications - continued				
Newspaper subscription, daily and Sunday delivery	mos	10.87	3/01	4c
Phone line, single, business, field visit	inst.	82.75	12/97	17s
Phone line, single, business, no field visit	inst.	82.75	12/97	17s
Phone line, single, residence, field visit	inst.	44.45	12/97	17s
Phone line, single, residence, no field visit	inst.	44.45	12/97	17s
Postage and stationery, expenditures on	yr	104	1999	30r
Postal rate, express mail, up to half-pound		12.45	7/01	108r
Postal rate, letter, first class, first ounce		0.34	7/01	108r
Postal rate, letter, two ounces		0.57	7/01	108r
Postal rate, post card		0.21	7/01	108r
Postal rate, priority mail, two pounds		3.95	7/01	108r
Postal rate, priority mail, up to one pound		3.50	7/01	108r
Telephone bill, business, basic rate	mos	32.44	12/97	18c
Telephone bill, family of three	mos	19.08	3/01	4c
Telephone bill, residential, basic rate	mos	12.07	12/97	18c
Telephone services, expenditures on	yr	860	1999	30r
Education				
Board, 4-year private college/university	yr	1401	1996	38s
Board, 4-year public college/university	yr	61111	1996	38s
Education expenditures	yr	431	1999	30r
Room, 4-year private college/university	yr	8032	1996	38s
Room, 4-year public college/university	yr	8371	1996	38s
Total cost, 4-year private college/university	yr	7737	1996	38s
Total cost, 4-year public college/university	yr	4287	1996	38s
Tuition, 2-year public college/university, in state	yr	260	1996	38s
Tuition, 4-year private college/university, in state	yr	8311	1996	38s
Tuition, 4-year public college/university	yr	1839	1996	38s
Energy and Fuels				
Electricity	KWh	0.09	7/01	11r
Electricity	500 KWhs	47.29	7/01	11r
Energy, combined forms, 2400 sq ft	mos	110.41	3/01	4c
Energy, exc. electricity, 2400 sq ft	mos	54.35	3/01	4c
Fuel oil #2	gal	1.43	7/01	11r
Fuel oil and other fuels, expenditures on	yr	45	1999	30r
Gas, cooking, winter, 10 therms	mos	12.21	2/96	98c
Gas, cooking, winter, 30 therms	mos	23.36	2/96	98c
Gas, cooking, winter, 50 therms	mos	34.52	2/96	98c
Gas, heating, winter, average use	mos	94.37	2/96	98c
Gas, natural, commercial rate	1000 cf	7.50	11/00	88s
Gas, regular unleaded, cash, self-service	gal	1.29	3/01	4c
Gasoline, all types	gal	1.60	7/01	11r
Gasoline, unleaded midgrade	gal	1.65	7/01	11r
Gasoline, unleaded premium	gal	1.74	7/01	11r
Natural gas, expenditures on	yr	164	1999	30r
Utility (piped) gas, therm		1.01	7/01	11r
Utility (piped) gas, 40 therms		44.29	7/01	11r
Utility (piped) gas, 100 therms		97.44	7/01	11r
Entertainment				
Bowling, Saturday evening rate	line	2.30	3/01	4c
Entertainment purchases	yr	1574	1999	30r
Fees and admissions paid	yr	371	1999	30r
Monopoly game, Parker Brothers', No. 9	game	13.24	3/01	4c
Movie ticket, evening	person	6.00	1999	104c
Movie, first-run, Saturday, evening	adm.	7.00	3/01	4c
Reading purchases	yr	121	1999	30r
Television, radios, sound equipment, expenditures on	yr	561	1999	30r
Tennis balls, yellow, Wilson or Penn, 3	can	2.99	3/01	4c
Funerals				
Total cost of funeral		5842.28	1/99	78r
Acknowledgement cards		28.35	1/99	78r
Casket		2494.29	1/99	78r
Cosmetology, hair, other preparation		109.22	1/99	78r
Embalming		361.42	1/99	78r
Funeral at funeral home		349.20	1/99	78r
Hearse (local)		161.91	1/99	78r

Values are in dollars or fractions of dollars. In the column headed *Ref*, references are shown to sources. Each reference is followed by a letter. These refer to the geographical level for which data were reported: s=State, r=Region, and c=City or metro. The abbreviation *ex* is used to mean *except* or *excluding*; *exp* stands for expenditures. For other abbreviations and further explanations, please see the Introduction.

Lawton, OK - continued

Item	Per	Value	Date	Ref.
Funerals				
Professional service charges		1116.50	1/99	78r
Service car/van		65.56	1/99	78r
Transfer of remains to funeral home		143.56	1/99	78r
Vault		785.25	1/99	78r
Visitation/viewing		227.02	1/99	78r
Groceries				
Groceries, ACCRA Index		96.10	3/01	4c
American processed cheese	lb	3.50	7/01	11r
Antibiotic ointment, Polysporin	0.5 oz	5.06	3/01	4c
Baby food, strained vegetables or fruit, lowest price	4-4.5 oz	0.42	3/01	4c
Bakery products, expenditures on	yr	261	1999	30r
Bananas	lb	0.52	3/01	4c
Bananas	lb	0.47	7/01	11r
Beans, dried, any type, all sizes	lb	0.63	7/01	11r
Beef for stew, boneless	lb	2.86	7/01	11r
Beef or hamburger, ground	lb	1.67	3/01	4c
Beef, expenditures on	yr	210	1999	30r
Bologna, all beef or mixed	lb	2.29	7/01	11r
Bread, French	lb	1.66	7/01	11r
Bread, white	loaf	0.92	3/01	4c
Bread, white, pan	lb	0.87	7/01	11r
Bread, whole wheat, pan	lb	1.38	7/01	11r
Broccoli	lb	1.04	7/01	11r
Butter, salted, grade AA, stick	lb	2.26	7/01	11r
Butter, yoghurt, cheese, etc, expenditures on	yr	170	1999	30r
Cabbage	lb	0.42	7/01	11r
Cereals and cereal products, expenditures on	yr	140	1999	30r
Cheddar cheese, natural	lb	3.75	7/01	11r
Cheese, Kraft grated Parmesan	8 oz	3.24	3/01	4c
Chicken breast, bone-in	lb	1.85	7/01	11r
Chicken legs, bone-in	lb	1.34	7/01	11r
Chicken, fresh, whole	lb	1.05	7/01	11r
Chicken, whole fryer	lb	0.79	3/01	4c
Chops, boneless	lb	4.13	7/01	11r
Chuck roast, graded and ungraded, excl U.S. prime and choice	lb	2.35	7/01	11r
Chuck roast, U.S. choice, boneless	lb	2.67	7/01	11r
Cigarettes, Winston, Kings	carton	28.04	3/01	4c
Coffee, 100%, ground roast, all sizes	lb	2.88	7/01	11r
Coffee, instant, plain, regular, all sizes	16 oz	9.25	7/01	11r
Coffee, vacuum-packed	13 oz	2.56	3/01	4c
Cola, non diet	2 liter	1.11	7/01	11r
Corn Flakes, Kellogg's or Post Toasties	18 oz	1.60	3/01	4c
Corn, frozen, whole kernel, lowest price	16 oz	1.26	3/01	4c
Crackers, soda, salted	lb	1.70	7/01	11r
Dairy product purchases	yr	282	1999	30r
Eggs, expenditures on	yr	32	1999	30r
Eggs, Grade A or AA	dozen	1.22	3/01	4c
Fats and oils, expenditures on	yr	79	1999	30r
Fish and seafood, expenditures on	yr	99	1999	30r
Flour, white, all purpose	lb	0.32	7/01	11r
Food (excl fruit and vegetables), eaten at home, purchases	yr	815	1999	30r
Food cooked on trips, expenditures on	yr	36	1999	30r
Food purchases	yr	4533	1999	30r
Food purchases, eaten away from home	yr	1873	1999	30r
Food purchases, food eaten at home	yr	2660	1999	30r
Fresh fruits, expenditures on	yr	128	1999	30r
Fresh milk and cream, expenditures on	yr	112	1999	30r
Fresh vegetables, expenditures on	yr	131	1999	30r
Fruit and vegetable purchases	yr	438	1999	30r
Grapefruit	lb	0.59	7/01	11r
Grapes, Thompson, seedless	lb	2.12	7/01	11r
Ground beef, 100% beef	lb	1.76	7/01	11r
Ground beef, lean and extra lean	lb	2.60	7/01	11r
Ground chuck, 100% beef	lb	2.08	7/01	11r
Ham, boneless, excl canned	lb	2.71	7/01	11r
Ham, rump or shank half, bone-in, smoked	lb	2.19	7/01	11r
Ice cream, prepackaged, bulk, regular	1/2 gal	3.93	7/01	11r
Lemons	lb	1.32	7/01	11r

Lawton, OK - continued

Item	Per	Value	Date	Ref.
Groceries - continued				
Lettuce, iceberg	head	1.04	3/01	4c
Lettuce, iceberg	lb	0.76	7/01	11r
Margarine, Blue Bonnet or Parkay, stick	lb	0.93	3/01	4c
Milk, fresh, low fat	gal	2.75	7/01	11r
Milk, fresh, whole, fortified	gal	2.97	7/01	11r
Milk, whole	1/2 gal	1.57	3/01	4c
Nonalcoholic beverages, expenditures on	yr	228	1999	30r
Orange juice, frozen concentrate	16 oz	1.95	7/01	11r
Orange juice, Minute Maid frozen	12 oz	1.39	3/01	4c
Oranges, Navel	lb	0.73	7/01	11r
Oranges, Valencia	lb	0.55	7/01	11r
Peaches, halves or slices, Hunt's, Del Monte, or Libby's	29 oz	1.51	3/01	4c
Peanut butter, creamy, all sizes	lb	1.83	7/01	11r
Pears, Anjou	lb	0.98	7/01	11r
Peas, green, Del Monte or Green Giant	15 oz	0.70	3/01	4c
Pork chops, center cut, bone-in	lb	3.33	7/01	11r
Pork sausage, fresh, loose	lb	2.59	7/01	11r
Pork shoulder picnic, bone-in, smoked	lb	1.12	7/01	11r
Pork, expenditures on	yr	162	1999	30r
Potato chips	16 oz	3.59	7/01	11r
Potatoes, frozen, french fried	lb	1.00	7/01	11r
Potatoes, white or red	10 lb	1.56	3/01	4c
Potatoes, white, all types	lb	0.44	7/01	11r
Poultry, expenditures on	yr	137	1999	30r
Processed fruits, expenditures on	yr	97	1999	30r
Processed vegetables, expenditures on	yr	82	1999	30r
Rice, white, long grain, uncooked	lb	0.51	7/01	11r
Round roast, graded and ungraded, excl U.S. prime and choice	lb	2.96	7/01	11r
Round steak, graded and ungraded, excl U.S. prime and choice	lb	3.11	7/01	11r
Sausage, Jimmy Dean/Owens pork	lb	2.84	3/01	4c
Shortening, vegetable, Crisco	3 lb	2.82	3/01	4c
Sirloin steak, graded and ungraded, excl U.S. prime and choice	lb	4.23	7/01	11r
Soft drink, Coca Cola, ex deposit	2 liter	1.43	3/01	4c
Spaghetti and macaroni	lb	0.78	7/01	11r
Steak, round, U.S. choice, boneless	lb	3.56	7/01	11r
Steak, sirloin, U.S. choice, boneless	lb	5.65	7/01	11r
Steak, T-bone	lb	5.96	3/01	4c
Strawberries, dry pint	12 oz	1.50	7/01	11r
Sugar and other sweets, expenditures on	yr	99	1999	30r
Sugar, cane or beet	4 lbs	1.59	3/01	4c
Sugar, white, 33-80 ounce package	lb	0.39	7/01	11r
Sugar, white, all sizes	lb	0.42	7/01	11r
Tobacco products and smoking supplies purchases	yr	288	1999	30r
Tomatoes, field grown	lb	1.43	7/01	11r
Tomatoes, Hunt's or Del Monte	14.5 oz	0.93	3/01	4c
Tuna, chunk, light	6 oz	0.67	3/01	4c
Tuna, light, chunk	lb	1.77	7/01	11r
Turkey, frozen, whole	lb	1.05	7/01	11r
Goods and Services				
Miscellaneous goods and services, ACCRA Index		103.70	3/01	4c
B&B Japanese maple (acer japonicum)	gal	79.98-99.00	4/00	93r
Boxwood (buxus)	2 gal	12.98-18.99	4/00	93r
Daylilly (hemerocallis)	gal	7.96-11.00	4/00	93r
Flat of annuals		13.99-27.99	4/00	93r
Fountain grass (pennisetum)	gal	6.96-9.00	4/00	93r
Hanging basket (10 in)		9.99-24.99	4/00	93r
Hardy geranium (geranium)	gal	5.96-8.00	4/00	93r
Hosta (hosta)	gal	8.96-12.99	4/00	93r

Values are in dollars or fractions of dollars. In the column headed *Ref*, references are shown to sources. Each reference is followed by a letter. These refer to the geographical level for which data were reported: s=State, r=Region, and c=City or metro. The abbreviation *ex* is used to mean *except* or *excluding*; *exp* stands for *expenditures*. For other abbreviations and further explanations, please see the Introduction.

Lawton, OK - continued

Item	Per	Value	Date	Ref.
Goods and Services				
Lilac (syrubga vulgaris)	2 gal	13.00-19.99	4/00	93r
Rhododendron (rhododendron)	2 gal	12.98-29.99	4/00	93r
Sage (salvia)	gal	5.96-8.00	4/00	93r
Wintercreeper euonymus (euonymus fortunei)	2 gal	13.00-18.99	4/00	93r
Hunting license	yr	12.50	4/01	34s
Health Care				
Health care, ACCRA Index		92.60	3/01	4c
Cardiac catheterization, ave hospital/physician charges		15750	1998	77s
Childbirth, Cesarean delivery		11587	1997	13r
Childbirth, vaginal delivery		6725	1997	13r
Dentist's fee, adult teeth cleaning and periodic oral exam	visit	69.75	3/01	4c
Doctor's fee, routine exam, established patient	visit	56.00	3/01	4c
Drugs, expenditures on	yr	399	1999	30r
Health care purchases	yr	1971	1999	30r
Health insurance expenditures	yr	933	1999	30r
Hospital care, private room	day	358.58	3/01	4c
Hysterectomy, laproscopically-assisted, ave hospital/physician charges		16080	1998	76s
Hysterectomy, vaginal, ave hospital and physician charges		8140	1998	76s
Medicaid dispensing fee		4.15	1999	87s
Medical services expenditures	yr	547	1999	30r
Medical supplies, expenditures on	yr	91	1999	30r
Household Goods				
Dishwashing powder, Cascade	50 oz	3.49	3/01	4c
Floor coverings, expenditures on	yr	44	1999	30r
Furniture, expenditures on	yr	335	1999	30r
Household furnishings and equipment purchases	yr	1328	1999	30r
Household textiles, expenditures on	yr	89	1999	30r
Laundry and cleaning supplies, expenditures on	yr	113	1999	30r
Tissues, facial, Kleenex brand	175	1.46	3/01	4c
Housing				
Housing, ACCRA Index		86.00	3/01	4c
Home price, existing, ave		160100	10/00	90r
Home value, median		88000	2001	53s
House, 2400 sq ft, 8000 sq ft lot, new, urban, utilities	total	180000	3/01	4c
House payment, principal and interest, 25% down payment	mos	910	3/01	4c
Household operation expenditures	yr	553	1999	30r
Housekeeping supplies purchases	yr	473	1999	30r
Housing, expenditures on	yr	10303	1999	30r
Maintenance, repairs, insurance expenditures	yr	699	1999	30r
Monthly rental value of owned home	mos	505	1999	30r
Owned dwellings, expenditures own	yr	3465	1999	30r
Rent expenditures	yr	1641	1999	30r
Rent, apartment, 2 br, 1 1/2-2 baths, unfurn, 950 sq ft, water	mos	536	3/01	4c
Rental unit, 1 bedroom, with utilities	mos	373	4/01	41c
Rental unit, 2 bedroom, with utilities	mos	475	4/01	41c
Rental unit, 3 bedroom, with utilities	mos	659	4/01	41c
Rental unit, 4 bedroom, with utilities	mos	722	4/01	41c
Shelter, expenditures on	yr	5467	1999	30r
Insurance and Pensions				
Life and other personal insurance purchases	yr	414	1999	30r
Pensions and Social Security, expenditures on	yr	2635	1999	30r
Personal insurance and pensions, expenditures on	yr	3048	1999	30r

Lawton, OK - continued

Item	Per	Value	Date	Ref.
Legal Fees				
Combination hunting and fishing license	yr	21.00	4/01	34s
Divorce, filing fee		84.00	4/01	35s
Driver's license fee	renew	15.00	1999	48s
Driver's license fee	orig	15.00	1999	48s
Fishing license	yr	12.50	4/01	34s
Personal Goods				
Personal care products and services purchases	yr	393	1999	30r
Shampoo, Alberto VO5	15 oz	1.15	3/01	4c
Toothpaste, Crest or Colgate	6-7 oz	1.93	3/01	4c
Personal Services				
Dry cleaning, man's 2-pc suit		6.20	3/01	4c
Man's haircut, barbershop, no styling		10.58	3/01	4c
Personal services, household, expenditures on	yr	258	1999	30r
Woman's shampoo, trim, blow-dry, no style-change		23.00	3/01	4c
Pets				
Pets, toys, and playground equipment, expenditures on	yr	306	1999	30r
Restaurant Food				
Chicken, fried, thigh and drumstick, KFC/Church's		2.89	3/01	4c
Hamburger with cheese, McDonald's	1/4 lb	2.04	3/01	4c
Pizza, Pizza Hut or Pizza Inn	11-12 in	9.99	3/01	4c
Taxes				
Federal income taxes paid	yr	2047	1999	30r
Personal taxes, expenditures on	yr	2554	1999	30r
Property taxes paid	yr	726	1999	30r
State and local income taxes paid	yr	363	1999	30r
Transportation				
Transportation, ACCRA Index		100.30	3/01	4c
Cars and trucks, new, expenditures on	yr	1648	1999	30r
Cars and trucks, used, expenditures on	yr	1651	1999	30r
Diesel at the pump	gal	1.13	10/99	73s
Gasoline and motor oil purchases	yr	1052	1999	30r
Gasoline before-tax price (cents)	gal	103.70	10/00	43s
Maintenance and repair expenditures	yr	621	1999	30r
Public transportation, expenditures on	yr	298	1999	30r
Tire balance, computer or spin balance, front	wheel	8.85	3/01	4c
Transportation purchases	yr	6738	1999	30r
Vehicle expenses, miscellaneous, purchases	yr	2033	1999	30r
Vehicle insurance payments	yr	696	1999	30r
Vehicle purchases (net outlay)	yr	3354	1999	30r
Vehicle rental, lease expenditures	yr	352	1999	30r
Travel				
Hotel room	night	55.28	2/01	94s
Utilities				
Utilities, ACCRA Index		90.10	3/01	4c
Electrical bill, average	mos	67.33	9/00	9s
Electricity, expenditures on	yr	1115	1999	30r
Electricity and other, mixed, 2400 sq ft, new home	mos	56.06	3/01	4c
Electricity cost, average	KWh	5.66	9/00	9s
Water and other public services, expenditures on	yr	298	1999	30r
Weddings				
Wedding (national average cost)		19936	2000	33r
Attendants' gifts		321	1998	33r
Bridal attendants' apparel (5 persons)		824	2000	33r
Bride's headpiece/veil		173	1998	33r
Bride's wedding dress		859	1998	33r
Clergy, religious facility fee		242	1998	33r
Engagement ring		3177	1998	33r
Flowers		789	1998	33r
Groom's formalwear rental		99	2000	33r
Limousine		410	1998	33r

Values are in dollars or fractions of dollars. In the column headed *Ref*, references are shown to sources. Each reference is followed by a letter. These refer to the geographical level for which data were reported: s=State, r=Region, and c=City or metro. The abbreviation *ex* is used to mean *except* or *excluding*; *exp* stands for *expenditures*. For other abbreviations and further explanations, please see the Introduction.

Lawton, OK - continued

Item	Per	Value	Date	Ref.
Weddings				
Marriage license cost		25.00	4/01	35s
Men's formalwear (ushers, best man)		469	2000	33r
Mother of bride apparel		241	2000	33r
Music		866	1998	33r
Photography and videography		1368	1998	33r
Rehearsal dinner		728	1998	33r
Wedding invitations and announcements		341	1998	33r
Wedding reception		7968	2000	33r
Wedding rings (bride and groom)		1060	1998	33r

Lewiston-Auburn, ME

Item	Per	Value	Date	Ref.
Average annual expenditures	yr	37971	1999	30r
Alcoholic Beverages				
Alcoholic beverage purchases	yr	368	1999	30r
Wine, red and white table, all sizes, any origin	liter	9.64	7/01	11r
Appliances				
Major appliances, expenditures on	yr	194	1999	30r
Small appliances, housewares, expenditures on	yr	93	1999	30r
Banking and Money				
Mortgage interest and charges paid	yr	2622	1999	30r
Mortgage principal paid on owned property	yr	1262	1999	30r
Vehicle finance charges paid	yr	240	1999	30r
Charity				
Cash contributions, expenditures	yr	1001	1999	30r
Child Care				
Child raising cost, total, age 0-2	yr	8670	1999	60r
Child raising cost, total, age 3-5	yr	8910	1999	60r
Child raising cost, total, age 6-8	yr	9040	1999	60r
Child raising cost, total, age 9-11	yr	9100	1999	60r
Child raising cost, total, age 12-14	yr	9890	1999	60r
Child raising cost, total, age 15-17	yr	10010	1999	60r
Child's child care and education, age 0-2	yr	1070	1999	60r
Child's child care and education, age 3-5	yr	1190	1999	60r
Child's child care and education, age 6-8	yr	740	1999	60r
Child's child care and education, age 9-11	yr	470	1999	60r
Child's child care and education, age 12-14	yr	350	1999	60r
Child's child care and education, age 15-17	yr	590	1999	60r
Child's clothing, age 0-2	yr	480	1999	60r
Child's clothing, age 3-5	yr	470	1999	60r
Child's clothing, age 6-8	yr	520	1999	60r
Child's clothing, age 9-11	yr	570	1999	60r
Child's clothing, age 12-14	yr	970	1999	60r
Child's clothing, age 15-17	yr	870	1999	60r
Child's food, age 0-2	yr	1130	1999	60r
Child's food, age 3-5	yr	1290	1999	60r
Child's food, age 6-8	yr	1640	1999	60r
Child's food, age 9-11	yr	1930	1999	60r
Child's food, age 12-14	yr	1940	1999	60r
Child's food, age 15-17	yr	2150	1999	60r
Child's health care, age 0-2	yr	550	1999	60r
Child's health care, age 3-5	yr	530	1999	60r
Child's health care, age 6-8	yr	610	1999	60r
Child's health care, age 9-11	yr	650	1999	60r
Child's health care, age 12-14	yr	660	1999	60r
Child's health care, age 15-17	yr	690	1999	60r
Child's housing, age 0-2	yr	3555	1999	60r
Child's housing, age 3-5	yr	3530	1999	60r
Child's housing, age 6-8	yr	3490	1999	60r
Child's housing, age 9-11	yr	3340	1999	60r
Child's housing, age 12-14	yr	3530	1999	60r
Child's housing, age 15-17	yr	3140	1999	60r
Child's personal care, reading, age 0-2	yr	920	1999	60r
Child's personal care, reading, age 3-5	yr	950	1999	60r
Child's personal care, reading, age 6-8	yr	980	1999	60r
Child's personal care, reading, age 9-11	yr	1020	1999	60r
Child's personal care, reading, age 12-14	yr	1190	1999	60r

Lewiston-Auburn, ME - continued

Item	Per	Value	Date	Ref.
Child Care - continued				
Child's personal care, reading, age 15-17	yr	970	1999	60r
Clothing				
Apparel and services purchases	yr	1831	1999	30r
Boys, 2 to 15, expenditures on	yr	92	1999	30r
Children under 2, expenditures on	yr	63	1999	30r
Footwear, expenditures on	yr	300	1999	30r
Girls, 2 to 15, expenditures on	yr	101	1999	30r
Men and boys, expenditures on	yr	446	1999	30r
Men, 16 and over, expenditures on	yr	354	1999	30r
Women, 16 and over, expenditures on	yr	584	1999	30r
Communications				
Cable modem installation, Time Warner		75.00-225.00	6/99	103s
Cable modem rate, cable subscriber, Time Warner	mos	39.95-49.95	6/99	103s
Cable modem rate, non-cable subscriber, Time Warner	mos	39.95-54.95	6/99	103s
Phone line, single, business, field visit	inst.	110.00	12/97	17s
Phone line, single, business, no field visit	inst.	75.00	12/97	17s
Phone line, single, residence, field visit	inst.	101.00	12/97	17s
Phone line, single, residence, no field visit	inst.	75.00	12/97	17s
Postage and stationery, expenditures on	yr	138	1999	30r
Postal rate, express mail, up to half-pound		12.45	7/01	108r
Postal rate, letter, first class, first ounce		0.34	7/01	108r
Postal rate, letter, two ounces		0.57	7/01	108r
Postal rate, post card		0.21	7/01	108r
Postal rate, priority mail, two pounds		3.95	7/01	108r
Postal rate, priority mail, up to one pound		3.50	7/01	108r
Telephone services, expenditures on	yr	830	1999	30r
Education				
Board, 4-year private college/university	yr	2910	1996	38s
Board, 4-year public college/university	yr	2257	1996	38s
Education expenditures	yr	877	1999	30r
Room, 4-year private college/university	yr	2758	1996	38s
Room, 4-year public college/university	yr	2235	1996	38s
Total cost, 4-year private college/university	yr	21872	1996	38s
Total cost, 4-year public college/university	yr	7966	1996	38s
Tuition, 2-year public college/university, in state	yr	2381	1996	38s
Tuition, 4-year private college/university, in state	yr	16204	1996	38s
Tuition, 4-year public college/university	yr	3474	1996	38s
Energy and Fuels				
Electricity	KWh	0.12	7/01	11r
Fuel oil #2	gal	1.31	7/01	11r
Fuel oil and other fuels, expenditures on	yr	207	1999	30r
Gasoline, all types	gal	1.80	7/01	11r
Gasoline, unleaded midgrade	gal	1.85	7/01	11r
Gasoline, unleaded premium	gal	1.91	7/01	11r
Gasoline, unleaded regular	gal	1.71	7/01	11r
Natural gas, expenditures on	yr	368	1999	30r
Utility (piped) gas, therm		1.08	7/01	11r
Utility (piped) gas, 40 therms		50.87	7/01	11r
Utility (piped) gas, 100 therms		111.06	7/01	11r
Entertainment				
Entertainment purchases	yr	1821	1999	30r
Fees and admissions paid	yr	511	1999	30r
Television, radios, sound equipment, expenditures on	yr	650	1999	30r
Funerals				
Total cost of funeral		5776.91	1/99	78r
Acknowledgement cards		14.47	1/99	78r
Casket		2090.19	1/99	78r
Cosmetology, hair, other preparation		132.92	1/99	78r
Embalming		377.33	1/99	78r
Funeral at funeral home		352.43	1/99	78r
Hearse (local)		185.55	1/99	78r
Professional service charges		1289.95	1/99	78r
Service car/van		87.42	1/99	78r

Values are in dollars or fractions of dollars. In the column headed *Ref*, references are shown to sources. Each reference is followed by a letter. These refer to the geographical level for which data were reported: s=State, r=Region, and c=City or metro. The abbreviation *ex* is used to mean *except* or *excluding*; *exp* stands for *expenditures*. For other abbreviations and further explanations, please see the Introduction.

Lewiston-Auburn, ME - continued

Item	Per	Value	Date	Ref.
Funerals				
Transfer of remains to funeral home		175.48	1/99	78r
Vault		729.40	1/99	78r
Visitation/viewing		341.76	1/99	78r
Groceries				
Apples, red delicious	lb	0.95	7/01	11r
Bacon, sliced	lb	3.44	7/01	11r
Bakery products, expenditures on	yr	310	1999	30r
Bananas	lb	0.55	7/01	11r
Beef, expenditures on	yr	236	1999	30r
Bread, white, pan	lb	1.09	7/01	11r
Butter, yoghurt, cheese, etc, expenditures on	yr	214	1999	30r
Cereals and bakery product purchases	yr	474	1999	30r
Cereals and cereal products, expenditures on	yr	164	1999	30r
Chicken legs, bone-in	lb	1.23	7/01	11r
Chicken, fresh, whole	lb	1.13	7/01	11r
Chuck roast, U.S. choice, boneless	lb	2.79	7/01	11r
Coffee, 100%, ground roast, all sizes	lb	3.40	7/01	11r
Dairy product purchases	yr	342	1999	30r
Eggs, expenditures on	yr	34	1999	30r
Eggs, grade A, large	dozen	0.82	7/01	11r
Fats and oils, expenditures on	yr	80	1999	30r
Fish and seafood, expenditures on	yr	123	1999	30r
Food (excl fruit and vegetables), eaten at home, purchases	yr	838	1999	30r
Food cooked on trips, expenditures on	yr	48	1999	30r
Food purchases	yr	5314	1999	30r
Food purchases, eaten away from home	yr	2313	1999	30r
Food purchases, food eaten at home	yr	3001	1999	30r
Fresh fruits, expenditures on	yr	169	1999	30r
Fresh milk and cream, expenditures on	yr	128	1999	30r
Fresh vegetables, expenditures on	yr	164	1999	30r
Grapefruit	lb	0.67	7/01	11r
Grapes, Thompson, seedless	lb	2.18	7/01	11r
Ground beef, lean and extra lean	lb	2.66	7/01	11r
Ground chuck, 100% beef	lb	2.04	7/01	11r
Lettuce, iceberg	lb	0.76	7/01	11r
Meats, poultry, fish, and egg purchases	yr	808	1999	30r
Nonalcoholic beverages, expenditures on	yr	225	1999	30r
Orange juice, frozen concentrate	16 oz	1.88	7/01	11r
Oranges, Navel	lb	0.79	7/01	11r
Oranges, Valencia	lb	0.56	7/01	11r
Peaches	lb	1.16	7/01	11r
Peanut butter, creamy, all sizes	lb	2.01	7/01	11r
Pears, Anjou	lb	1.16	7/01	11r
Pork chops, center cut, bone-in	lb	3.57	7/01	11r
Pork, expenditures on	yr	146	1999	30r
Potato chips	16 oz	3.37	7/01	11r
Potatoes, white, all types	lb	0.42	7/01	11r
Poultry, expenditures on	yr	158	1999	30r
Processed fruits, expenditures on	yr	124	1999	30r
Processed vegetables, expenditures on	yr	82	1999	30r
Round roast, U.S. choice, boneless	lb	3.04	7/01	11r
Spaghetti and macaroni	lb	1.04	7/01	11r
Steak, sirloin, U.S. choice, boneless	lb	5.39	7/01	11r
Strawberries, dry pint	12 oz	1.51	7/01	11r
Sugar and other sweets, expenditures on	yr	110	1999	30r
Sugar, white, 33-80 ounce package	lb	0.46	7/01	11r
Sugar, white, all sizes	lb	0.47	7/01	11r
Tobacco products and smoking supplies purchases	yr	309	1999	30r
Yogurt, natural, fruit flavored	8 oz	0.79	7/01	11r
Goods and Services				
B&B Japanese maple (acer japonicum)	gal	38.99-125.00	4/00	93r
Boxwood (buxus)	2 gal	15.99-49.95	4/00	93r
Daylily (hemerocallis)	gal	4.95	4/00	93r
Flat of annuals		8.00-14.99	4/00	93r

Lewiston-Auburn, ME - continued

Item	Per	Value	Date	Ref.
Goods and Services - continued				
Fountain grass (pennisetum)	gal	6.99-9.99	4/00	93r
Hanging basket (10 in)		12.95-19.99	4/00	93r
Hardy geranium (geranium)	gal	6.95-7.99	4/00	93r
Hosta (hosta)	gal	4.95	4/00	93r
Lilac (syrubga vulgaris)	2 gal	17.99-74.95	4/00	93r
Miscellaneous purchases	yr	872	1999	30r
Rhododendron (rhododendron)	2 gal	23.99-54.95	4/00	93r
Sage (salvia)	gal	6.95-7.99	4/00	93r
Wintercreeper euonymus (euonymus fortunei)	2 gal	14.99-23.95	4/00	93r
Hunting license	yr	19.00	4/01	34s
Health Care				
Cardiac catheterization, ave hospital/ physician charges		10740	1998	77s
Childbirth, Cesarean delivery		14716	1997	13r
Childbirth, vaginal delivery		8541	1997	13r
Drugs, expenditures on	yr	296	1999	30r
Health care purchases	yr	1788	1999	30r
Health insurance expenditures	yr	875	1999	30r
Hysterectomy, laproscopically-assisted, ave hospital/physician charges		11180	1998	76s
Hysterectomy, vaginal, ave hospital and physician charges		7810	1998	76s
Medicaid dispensing fee		3.35-5.35	1999	87s
Medical services expenditures	yr	516	1999	30r
Medical supplies, expenditures on	yr	102	1999	30r
Plastic surgery, breast augmentation		4232	2000	7r
Plastic surgery, breast lift		4605	2000	7r
Plastic surgery, facelift		6964	2000	7r
Plastic surgery, hair transplantation		4193	2000	7r
Plastic surgery, lip augmentation		1675	2000	7r
Plastic surgery, lower body lift		6611	2000	7r
Plastic surgery, thigh lift		4751	2000	7r
Household Goods				
Floor coverings, expenditures on	yr	59	1999	30r
Furniture, expenditures on	yr	388	1999	30r
Household furnishings and equipment purchases	yr	1567	1999	30r
Household textiles, expenditures on	yr	112	1999	30r
Laundry and cleaning supplies, expenditures on	yr	104	1999	30r
Housing				
Home price, existing, ave		180800	10/00	90r
Home value, median		112000	2001	53s
Household operation expenditures	yr	581	1999	30r
Housekeeping supplies purchases	yr	474	1999	30r
Lodging expenditures	yr	550	1999	30r
Maintenance, repairs, insurance expenditures	yr	835	1999	30r
Monthly rental value of owned home	mos	663	1999	30r
Owned dwellings, expenditures own	yr	5209	1999	30r
Rent expenditures	yr	2390	1999	30r
Rental unit, 1 bedroom, with utilities	mos	393	4/01	41c
Rental unit, 2 bedroom, with utilities	mos	505	4/01	41c
Rental unit, 3 bedroom, with utilities	mos	633	4/01	41c
Rental unit, 4 bedroom, with utilities	mos	718	4/01	41c
Shelter, expenditures on	yr	8149	1999	30r
Insurance and Pensions				
Auto insurance premium	yr	542.81	1999	57s
Life and other personal insurance purchases	yr	424	1999	30r
Pensions and Social Security, expenditures on	yr	3037	1999	30r

Values are in dollars or fractions of dollars. In the column headed *Ref*, references are shown to sources. Each reference is followed by a letter. These refer to the geographical level for which data were reported: s=State, r=Region, and c=City or metro. The abbreviation *ex* is used to mean *except* or *excluding*; *exp* stands for *expenditures*. For other abbreviations and further explanations, please see the Introduction.

Lewiston-Auburn, ME - continued

Item	Per	Value	Date	Ref.
Legal Fees				
Combination hunting and fishing license	yr	36.00	4/01	34s
Divorce, filing fee		60.00	4/01	35s
Driver's license fee	renew	20.00	1999	48s
Driver's license fee	orig	35.00	1999	48s
Fishing license	yr	19.00	4/01	34s
Personal Goods				
Personal care products and services purchases	yr	399	1999	30r
Personal Services				
Personal services, household, expenditures on	yr	271	1999	30r
Pets				
Pets, toys, and playground equipment, expenditures on	yr	325	1999	30r
Taxes				
Federal income taxes paid	yr	2606	1999	30r
Personal taxes, expenditures on	yr	3567	1999	30r
Property taxes paid	yr	1752	1999	30r
State and local income taxes paid	yr	694	1999	30r
Transportation				
Cars and trucks, new, expenditures on	yr	1496	1999	30r
Cars and trucks, used, expenditures on	yr	1251	1999	30r
Diesel at the pump	gal	1.32	10/99	73s
Gasoline and motor oil purchases	yr	901	1999	30r
Gasoline before-tax price (cents)	gal	117.60	10/00	43s
Maintenance and repair expenditures	yr	618	1999	30r
Public transportation, expenditures on	yr	575	1999	30r
Transportation purchases	yr	6503	1999	30r
Vehicle expenses, miscellaneous, purchases	yr	2266	1999	30r
Vehicle insurance payments	yr	824	1999	30r
Vehicle purchases (net outlay)	yr	2761	1999	30r
Vehicle rental, lease expenditures	yr	584	1999	30r
Utilities				
Electrical bill, average	mos	64.42	9/00	9s
Electricity, expenditures on	yr	837	1999	30r
Electricity cost, average	KWh	10.12	9/00	9s
Utilities, fuels, and public services purchased	yr	2457	1999	30r
Water and other public services, expenditures on	yr	215	1999	30r
Weddings				
Wedding (national average cost)		19936	2000	33r
Wedding (regional average total cost)		29454	1997	110r
Attendants' gifts		321	1998	33r
Bridal attendants' apparel (5 persons)		824	2000	33r
Bride's headpiece/veil		173	1998	33r
Bride's wedding dress		859	1998	33r
Clergy, religious facility fee		242	1998	33r
Engagement ring		3177	1998	33r
Flowers		789	1998	33r
Groom's formalwear rental		99	2000	33r
Limousine		410	1998	33r
Marriage license cost		20.00	4/01	35s
Men's formalwear (ushers, best man)		469	2000	33r
Mother of bride apparel		241	2000	33r
Music		866	1998	33r
Photography and videography		1368	1998	33r
Rehearsal dinner		728	1998	33r
Wedding invitations and announcements		341	1998	33r
Wedding reception		7968	2000	33r
Wedding rings (bride and groom)		1060	1998	33r

Lexington, KY

Item	Per	Value	Date	Ref.
Composite, ACCRA index		98.50	3/01	4c
Alcoholic Beverages				
Alcoholic beverage purchases	yr	253	1999	30r
Beer, Heineken, 12-oz, ex deposit	6	7.36	3/01	4c

Lexington, KY - continued

Item	Per	Value	Date	Ref.
Alcoholic Beverages - continued				
J & B Scotch	750-ml	20.30	3/01	4c
Malt beverages, all types, all sizes, any origin	16 oz	0.96	7/01	11r
Wine, Livingston or Gallo, Chablis blanc	1.5 liter	5.12	3/01	4c
Appliances				
Appliance repair, service call, washing machine	min lab chg	41.15	3/01	4c
Major appliances, expenditures on	yr	172	1999	30r
Small appliances, housewares, expenditures on	yr	81	1999	30r
Banking and Money				
Mortgage interest and charges paid	yr	2039	1999	30r
Mortgage principal paid on owned property	yr	1026	1999	30r
Mortgage rate, incl. points and orig. fee, 30-yr. conv. fixed or ARM	mos	7.07	3/01	4c
Vehicle finance charges paid	yr	365	1999	30r
Business Expenses				
Business travel, car rental	day	49	2001	3c
Business travel, food	day	41	2001	3c
Business travel, hotel	day	89	2001	3c
Charity				
Cash contributions, expenditures	yr	1127	1999	30r
Child Care				
Child raising cost, total, age 0-2	yr	8540	1999	60r
Child raising cost, total, age 3-5	yr	8780	1999	60r
Child raising cost, total, age 6-8	yr	8820	1999	60r
Child raising cost, total, age 9-11	yr	8800	1999	60r
Child raising cost, total, age 12-14	yr	9510	1999	60r
Child raising cost, total, age 15-17	yr	9740	1999	60r
Child's child care and education, age 0-2	yr	1380	1999	60r
Child's child care and education, age 3-5	yr	1520	1999	60r
Child's child care and education, age 6-8	yr	990	1999	60r
Child's child care and education, age 9-11	yr	650	1999	60r
Child's child care and education, age 12-14	yr	490	1999	60r
Child's child care and education, age 15-17	yr	840	1999	60r
Child's clothing, age 0-2	yr	480	1999	60r
Child's clothing, age 3-5	yr	470	1999	60r
Child's clothing, age 6-8	yr	520	1999	60r
Child's clothing, age 9-11	yr	570	1999	60r
Child's clothing, age 12-14	yr	950	1999	60r
Child's clothing, age 15-17	yr	850	1999	60r
Child's food, age 0-2	yr	1000	1999	60r
Child's food, age 3-5	yr	1160	1999	60r
Child's food, age 6-8	yr	1490	1999	60r
Child's food, age 9-11	yr	1770	1999	60r
Child's food, age 12-14	yr	1770	1999	60r
Child's food, age 15-17	yr	1980	1999	60r
Child's health care, age 0-2	yr	620	1999	60r
Child's health care, age 3-5	yr	590	1999	60r
Child's health care, age 6-8	yr	680	1999	60r
Child's health care, age 9-11	yr	720	1999	60r
Child's health care, age 12-14	yr	730	1999	60r
Child's health care, age 15-17	yr	760	1999	60r
Child's housing, age 0-2	yr	3070	1999	60r
Child's housing, age 3-5	yr	3050	1999	60r
Child's housing, age 6-8	yr	3010	1999	60r
Child's housing, age 9-11	yr	2850	1999	60r
Child's housing, age 12-14	yr	3040	1999	60r
Child's housing, age 15-17	yr	2650	1999	60r
Child's personal care, reading, age 0-2	yr	910	1999	60r
Child's personal care, reading, age 3-5	yr	930	1999	60r
Child's personal care, reading, age 6-8	yr	960	1999	60r
Child's personal care, reading, age 9-11	yr	1000	1999	60r
Child's personal care, reading, age 12-14	yr	1170	1999	60r
Child's personal care, reading, age 15-17	yr	950	1999	60r
Clothing				
Apparel and services purchases	yr	1610	1999	30r
Boys' brief, cotton	3	6.24	3/01	4c
Boys, 2 to 15, expenditures on	yr	89	1999	30r
Children under 2, expenditures on	yr	79	1999	30r

Values are in dollars or fractions of dollars. In the column headed *Ref*, references are shown to sources. Each reference is followed by a letter. These refer to the geographical level for which data were reported: s=State, r=Region, and c=City or metro. The abbreviation *ex* is used to mean *except* or *excluding*; *exp* stands for *expenditures*. For other abbreviations and further explanations, please see the Introduction.

Lexington, KY - continued

Item	Per	Value	Date	Ref.
Clothing				
Footwear, expenditures on	yr	283	1999	30r
Girls, 2 to 15, expenditures on	yr	103	1999	30r
Men and boys, expenditures on	yr	351	1999	30r
Men, 16 and over, expenditures on	yr	262	1999	30r
Shirt, man's dress shirt		23.59	3/01	4c
Slacks, man's "No Wrinkles" khaki		28.99	3/01	4c
Women, 16 and over, expenditures on	yr	538	1999	30r
Communications				
Cable modem installation, Intermedia		149.95	6/99	103s
Cable modem rate, cable subscriber, Intermedia	mos	49.95	6/99	103s
Cable modem rate, non-cable subscriber, Intermedia	mos	54.95	6/99	103s
Newspaper subscription, daily and Sunday delivery	mos	18.85	3/01	4c
Phone line, single, business, field visit	inst.	61.39	12/97	17s
Phone line, single, business, no field visit	inst.	61.39	12/97	17s
Phone line, single, residence, field visit	inst.	33.85	12/97	17s
Phone line, single, residence, no field visit	inst.	33.85	12/97	17s
Postage and stationery, expenditures on	yr	104	1999	30r
Postal rate, express mail, up to half-pound		12.45	7/01	108r
Postal rate, letter, first class, first ounce		0.34	7/01	108r
Postal rate, letter, two ounces		0.57	7/01	108r
Postal rate, post card		0.21	7/01	108r
Postal rate, priority mail, two pounds		3.95	7/01	108r
Postal rate, priority mail, up to one pound		3.50	7/01	108r
Telephone bill, family of three	mos	27.66	3/01	4c
Telephone services, expenditures on	yr	860	1999	30r
Education				
Board, 4-year private college/university	yr	1985	1996	38s
Board, 4-year public college/university	yr	1767	1996	38s
Education expenditures	yr	431	1999	30r
Room, 4-year private college/university	yr	1711	1996	38s
Room, 4-year public college/university	yr	1527	1996	38s
Total cost, 4-year private college/university	yr	11192	1996	38s
Total cost, 4-year public college/university	yr	5455	1996	38s
Tuition, 2-year public college/university, in state	yr	1112	1996	38s
Tuition, 4-year private college/university, in state	yr	7497	1996	38s
Tuition, 4-year public college/university	yr	2161	1996	38s
Energy and Fuels				
Electricity	KWh	0.09	7/01	11r
Electricity	500 KWhs	47.29	7/01	11r
Energy, combined forms, 2400 sq ft	mos	113.75	3/01	4c
Energy, exc. electricity, 2400 sq ft	mos	80.94	3/01	4c
Fuel oil #2	gal	1.43	7/01	11r
Fuel oil and other fuels, expenditures on	yr	45	1999	30r
Gas, cooking, winter, 10 therms	mos	11.36	2/96	98c
Gas, cooking, winter, 30 therms	mos	22.06	2/96	98c
Gas, cooking, winter, 50 therms	mos	32.76	2/96	98c
Gas, heating, winter, average use	mos	96.96	2/96	98c
Gas, natural, commercial rate	1000 cf	8.25	11/00	88s
Gas, regular unleaded, cash, self-service	gal	1.45	3/01	4c
Gasoline, all types	gal	1.60	7/01	11r
Gasoline, unleaded midgrade	gal	1.65	7/01	11r
Gasoline, unleaded premium	gal	1.74	7/01	11r
Natural gas, expenditures on	yr	164	1999	30r
Utility (piped) gas, therm		1.01	7/01	11r
Utility (piped) gas, 40 therms		44.29	7/01	11r
Utility (piped) gas, 100 therms		97.44	7/01	11r
Entertainment				
Bowling, Saturday evening rate	line	3.56	3/01	4c
Entertainment purchases	yr	1574	1999	30r
Fees and admissions paid	yr	371	1999	30r
Monopoly game, Parker Brothers', No. 9	game	10.40	3/01	4c
Movie, first-run, Saturday, evening	adm.	6.56	3/01	4c
Reading purchases	yr	121	1999	30r

Item	Per	Value	Date	Ref.
Entertainment - continued				
Television, radios, sound equipment, expenditures on	yr	561	1999	30r
Tennis balls, yellow, Wilson or Penn, 3	can	2.25	3/01	4c
Groceries				
Groceries, ACCRA Index		103.60	3/01	4c
American processed cheese	lb	3.50	7/01	11r
Antibiotic ointment, Polysporin	0.5 oz	5.03	3/01	4c
Baby food, strained vegetables or fruit, lowest price	4-4.5 oz	0.39	3/01	4c
Bakery products, expenditures on	yr	261	1999	30r
Bananas	lb	0.47	3/01	4c
Bananas	lb	0.47	7/01	11r
Beans, dried, any type, all sizes	lb	0.63	7/01	11r
Beef for stew, boneless	lb	2.86	7/01	11r
Beef or hamburger, ground	lb	1.64	3/01	4c
Beef, expenditures on	yr	210	1999	30r
Bologna, all beef or mixed	lb	2.29	7/01	11r
Bread, French	lb	1.66	7/01	11r
Bread, white	loaf	1.18	3/01	4c
Bread, white, pan	lb	0.87	7/01	11r
Bread, whole wheat, pan	lb	1.38	7/01	11r
Broccoli	lb	1.04	7/01	11r
Butter, salted, grade AA, stick	lb	2.26	7/01	11r
Butter, yoghurt, cheese, etc, expenditures on	yr	170	1999	30r
Cabbage	lb	0.42	7/01	11r
Cereals and cereal products, expenditures on	yr	140	1999	30r
Cheddar cheese, natural	lb	3.75	7/01	11r
Cheese, Kraft grated Parmesan	8 oz	3.74	3/01	4c
Chicken breast, bone-in	lb	1.85	7/01	11r
Chicken legs, bone-in	lb	1.34	7/01	11r
Chicken, fresh, whole	lb	1.05	7/01	11r
Chicken, whole fryer	lb	0.92	3/01	4c
Chops, boneless,	lb	4.13	7/01	11r
Chuck roast, graded and ungraded, excl U.S. prime and choice	lb	2.35	7/01	11r
Chuck roast, U.S. choice, boneless	lb	2.67	7/01	11r
Cigarettes, Winston, Kings	carton	27.74	3/01	4c
Coffee, 100%, ground roast, all sizes	lb	2.88	7/01	11r
Coffee, instant, plain, regular, all sizes	16 oz	9.25	7/01	11r
Coffee, vacuum-packed	13 oz	2.71	3/01	4c
Cola, non diet,	2 liter	1.11	7/01	11r
Corn Flakes, Kellogg's or Post Toasties	18 oz	2.18	3/01	4c
Corn, frozen, whole kernel, lowest price	16 oz	1.15	3/01	4c
Crackers, soda, salted	lb	1.70	7/01	11r
Dairy product purchases	yr	282	1999	30r
Eggs, expenditures on	yr	32	1999	30r
Eggs, Grade A or AA	dozen	1.03	3/01	4c
Fats and oils, expenditures on	yr	79	1999	30r
Fish and seafood, expenditures on	yr	99	1999	30r
Flour, white, all purpose	lb	0.32	7/01	11r
Food (excl fruit and vegetables), eaten at home, purchases	yr	815	1999	30r
Food cooked on trips, expenditures on	yr	36	1999	30r
Food purchases	yr	4533	1999	30r
Food purchases, eaten away from home	yr	1873	1999	30r
Food purchases, food eaten at home	yr	2660	1999	30r
Fresh fruits, expenditures on	yr	128	1999	30r
Fresh milk and cream, expenditures on	yr	112	1999	30r
Fresh vegetables, expenditures on	yr	131	1999	30r
Fruit and vegetable purchases	yr	438	1999	30r
Grapefruit	lb	0.59	7/01	11r
Grapes, Thompson, seedless	lb	2.12	7/01	11r
Ground beef, 100% beef	lb	1.76	7/01	11r
Ground beef, lean and extra lean	lb	2.60	7/01	11r
Ground chuck, 100% beef	lb	2.08	7/01	11r
Ham, boneless, excl canned	lb	2.71	7/01	11r
Ham, rump or shank half, bone-in, smoked	lb	2.19	7/01	11r
Ice cream, prepackaged, bulk, regular	1/2 gal	3.93	7/01	11r
Lemons	lb	1.32	7/01	11r
Lettuce, iceberg	head	0.99	3/01	4c
Lettuce, iceberg	lb	0.76	7/01	11r

Values are in dollars or fractions of dollars. In the column headed *Ref*, references are shown to sources. Each reference is followed by a letter. These refer to the geographical level for which data were reported: s=State, r=Region, and c=City or metro. The abbreviation *ex* is used to mean *except* or *excluding*; *exp* stands for *expenditures*. For other abbreviations and further explanations, please see the Introduction.

Lexington, KY - continued

Item	Per	Value	Date	Ref.
Groceries				
Margarine, Blue Bonnet or Parkay, stick	lb	0.62	3/01	4c
Milk, fresh, low fat,	gal	2.75	7/01	11r
Milk, fresh, whole, fortified	gal	2.97	7/01	11r
Milk, whole	1/2 gal	1.68	3/01	4c
Nonalcoholic beverages, expenditures on	yr	228	1999	30r
Orange juice, frozen concentrate	16 oz	1.95	7/01	11r
Orange juice, Minute Maid frozen	12 oz	1.84	3/01	4c
Oranges, Navel	lb	0.73	7/01	11r
Oranges, Valencia	lb	0.55	7/01	11r
Peaches, halves or slices, Hunt's, Del Monte, or Libby's	29 oz	1.71	3/01	4c
Peanut butter, creamy, all sizes	lb	1.83	7/01	11r
Pears, Anjou	lb	0.98	7/01	11r
Peas, green, Del Monte or Green Giant	15 oz	0.71	3/01	4c
Pork chops, center cut, bone-in	lb	3.33	7/01	11r
Pork sausage, fresh, loose	lb	2.59	7/01	11r
Pork shoulder picnic, bone-in, smoked	lb	1.12	7/01	11r
Pork, expenditures on	yr	162	1999	30r
Potato chips	16 oz	3.59	7/01	11r
Potatoes, frozen, french fried	lb	1.00	7/01	11r
Potatoes, white or red	10 lb	2.29	3/01	4c
Potatoes, white, all types	lb	0.44	7/01	11r
Poultry, expenditures on	yr	137	1999	30r
Processed fruits, expenditures on	yr	97	1999	30r
Processed vegetables, expenditures on	yr	82	1999	30r
Rice, white, long grain, uncooked	lb	0.51	7/01	11r
Round roast, graded and ungraded, excl U.S. prime and choice	lb	2.96	7/01	11r
Round steak, graded and ungraded, excl U.S. prime and choice	lb	3.11	7/01	11r
Sausage, Jimmy Dean/Owens pork	lb	3.54	3/01	4c
Shortening, vegetable, Crisco	3 lb	3.49	3/01	4c
Sirloin steak, graded and ungraded, excl U.S. prime and choice	lb	4.23	7/01	11r
Soft drink, Coca Cola, ex deposit	2 liter	1.29	3/01	4c
Spaghetti and macaroni	lb	0.78	7/01	11r
Steak, round, U.S. choice, boneless	lb	3.56	7/01	11r
Steak, sirloin, U.S. choice, boneless	lb	5.65	7/01	11r
Steak, T-bone	lb	7.99	3/01	4c
Strawberries, dry pint	12 oz	1.50	7/01	11r
Sugar and other sweets, expenditures on	yr	99	1999	30r
Sugar, cane or beet	4 lbs	1.63	3/01	4c
Sugar, white, 33-80 ounce package	lb	0.39	7/01	11r
Sugar, white, all sizes	lb	0.42	7/01	11r
Tobacco products and smoking supplies purchases	yr	288	1999	30r
Tomatoes, field grown	lb	1.43	7/01	11r
Tomatoes, Hunt's or Del Monte	14.5 oz	0.99	3/01	4c
Tuna, chunk, light	6 oz	0.61	3/01	4c
Tuna, light, chunk	lb	1.77	7/01	11r
Turkey, frozen, whole	lb	1.05	7/01	11r
Goods and Services				
Miscellaneous goods and services, ACCRA Index		99.00	3/01	4c
Hunting license	yr	15.00	4/01	34s
Health Care				
Health care, ACCRA Index		100.50	3/01	4c
Cardiac catheterization, ave hospital/physician charges		11480	1998	77s
Childbirth, Cesarean delivery		11587	1997	13r
Childbirth, vaginal delivery		6725	1997	13r
Dentist's fee, adult teeth cleaning and periodic oral exam	visit	74.60	3/01	4c
Doctor's fee, routine exam, established patient	visit	61.00	3/01	4c
Drugs, expenditures on	yr	399	1999	30r
Health care purchases	yr	1971	1999	30r
Health insurance expenditures	yr	933	1999	30r
Hospital care, private room	day	432.42	3/01	4c
Hysterectomy, laproscopically-assisted, ave hospital/physician charges		12390	1998	76s

Lexington, KY - continued

Item	Per	Value	Date	Ref.
Health Care - continued				
Hysterectomy, vaginal, ave hospital and physician charges		8440	1998	76s
Medicaid dispensing fee		4.75-5.75	1999	87s
Medical services expenditures	yr	547	1999	30r
Medical supplies, expenditures on	yr	91	1999	30r
Household Goods				
Dishwashing powder, Cascade	50 oz	3.94	3/01	4c
Floor coverings, expenditures on	yr	44	1999	30r
Furniture, expenditures on	yr	335	1999	30r
Household furnishings and equipment purchases	yr	1328	1999	30r
Household textiles, expenditures on	yr	89	1999	30r
Laundry and cleaning supplies, expenditures on	yr	113	1999	30r
Tissues, facial, Kleenex brand	175	1.42	3/01	4c
Housing				
Housing, ACCRA Index		94.70	3/01	4c
Home, 2200 sq ft, 4-br, 2-bath, 2-car garage, average		184000	2000	47c
Home price, existing, ave		160100	10/00	90r
Home value, median		103000	2001	53s
House, 2400 sq ft, 8000 sq ft lot, new, urban, utilities	total	190928	3/01	4c
House payment, principal and interest, 25% down payment	mos	959	3/01	4c
Household operation expenditures	yr	553	1999	30r
Housekeeping supplies purchases	yr	473	1999	30r
Housing, expenditures on	yr	10303	1999	30r
Maintenance, repairs, insurance expenditures	yr	699	1999	30r
Monthly rental value of owned home	mos	505	1999	30r
Owned dwellings, expenditures own	yr	3465	1999	30r
Rent expenditures	yr	1641	1999	30r
Rent, apartment, 2 br, 1 1/2-2 baths, unfurn, 950 sq ft, water	mos	703	3/01	4c
Rental unit, 1 bedroom, with utilities	mos	435	4/01	41c
Rental unit, 2 bedroom, with utilities	mos	533	4/01	41c
Rental unit, 3 bedroom, with utilities	mos	727	4/01	41c
Rental unit, 4 bedroom, with utilities	mos	821	4/01	41c
Shelter, expenditures on	yr	5467	1999	30r
Insurance and Pensions				
Life and other personal insurance purchases	yr	414	1999	30r
Pensions and Social Security, expenditures on	yr	2635	1999	30r
Personal insurance and pensions, expenditures on	yr	3048	1999	30r
Legal Fees				
Combination hunting and fishing license	yr	22.50	4/01	34s
Driver's license fee	orig	16.00	1999	48s
Driver's license fee	renew	10.00	1999	48s
Fishing license	yr	15.00	4/01	34s
Personal Goods				
Personal care products and services purchases	yr	393	1999	30r
Shampoo, Alberto VO5	15 oz	1.06	3/01	4c
Toothpaste, Crest or Colgate	6-7 oz	2.58	3/01	4c
Personal Services				
Dry cleaning, man's 2-pc suit		7.49	3/01	4c
Man's haircut, barbershop, no styling		10.20	3/01	4c
Personal services, household, expenditures on	yr	258	1999	30r
Woman's shampoo, trim, blow-dry, no style-change		29.20	3/01	4c
Pets				
Pets, toys, and playground equipment, expenditures on	yr	306	1999	30r

Values are in dollars or fractions of dollars. In the column headed *Ref*, references are shown to sources. Each reference is followed by a letter. These refer to the geographical level for which data were reported: s=State, r=Region, and c=City or metro. The abbreviation *ex* is used to mean *except* or *excluding*; *exp* stands for expenditures. For other abbreviations and further explanations, please see the Introduction.

Lexington, KY - continued

Item	Per	Value	Date	Ref.
Restaurant Food				
Chicken, fried, thigh and drumstick, KFC/ Church's		2.58	3/01	4c
Hamburger with cheese, McDonald's	1/4 lb	2.07	3/01	4c
Pizza, Pizza Hut or Pizza Inn	11-12 in	9.59	3/01	4c
Taxes				
Federal income taxes paid	yr	2047	1999	30r
Personal taxes, expenditures on	yr	2554	1999	30r
Property taxes paid	yr	726	1999	30r
State and local income taxes paid	yr	363	1999	30r
Transportation				
Transportation, ACCRA Index		98.40	3/01	4c
Bus fare, one-way	trip	0.80	2000	1c
Cars and trucks, new, expenditures on	yr	1648	1999	30r
Cars and trucks, used, expenditures on	yr	1651	1999	30r
Diesel at the pump	gal	1.15	10/99	73s
Gasoline and motor oil purchases	yr	1052	1999	30r
Gasoline before-tax price (cents)	gal	110.40	10/00	43s
Maintenance and repair expenditures	yr	621	1999	30r
Motorcycle license fee	orig	14.00	1999	49s
Motorcycle license fee	renew	3.00	1999	49s
Public transportation, expenditures on	yr	298	1999	30r
Tire balance, computer or spin balance, front	wheel	7.30	3/01	4c
Transportation purchases	yr	6738	1999	30r
Vehicle expenses, miscellaneous, purchases	yr	2033	1999	30r
Vehicle insurance payments	yr	696	1999	30r
Vehicle purchases (net outlay)	yr	3354	1999	30r
Vehicle rental, lease expenditures	yr	352	1999	30r
Utilities				
Utilities, ACCRA Index		97.90	3/01	4c
Electrical bill, average	mos	60.42	9/00	9s
Electricity, expenditures on	yr	1115	1999	30r
Electricity, summer, 250 KWh	mos	14.50	2/96	97c
Electricity, summer, 500 KWh	mos	25.39	2/96	97c
Electricity, summer, 750 KWh	mos	35.65	2/96	97c
Electricity, summer, 1000 KWh	mos	45.91	2/96	97c
Electricity and other, mixed, 2400 sq ft, new home	mos	32.81	3/01	4c
Electricity cost, average	KWh	4.10	9/00	9s
Water and other public services, expenditures on	yr	298	1999	30r
Weddings				
Wedding (national average cost)		19936	2000	33r
Attendants' gifts		321	1998	33r
Bridal attendants' apparel (5 persons)		824	2000	33r
Bride's headpiece/veil		173	1998	33r
Bride's wedding dress		859	1998	33r
Clergy, religious facility fee		242	1998	33r
Engagement ring		3177	1998	33r
Flowers		789	1998	33r
Groom's formalwear rental		99	2000	33r
Limousine		410	1998	33r
Marriage license cost		34.50	4/01	35s
Men's formalwear (ushers, best man)		469	2000	33r
Mother of bride apparel		241	2000	33r
Music		866	1998	33r
Photography and videography		1368	1998	33r
Rehearsal dinner		728	1998	33r
Wedding invitations and announcements		341	1998	33r
Wedding reception		7968	2000	33r
Wedding rings (bride and groom)		1060	1998	33r

Likomo, IN

Item	Per	Value	Date	Ref.
Average annual expenditures	yr	35369	1999	30r
Alcoholic Beverages				
Alcoholic beverage purchases	yr	304	1999	30r
Malt beverages, all types, all sizes, any origin	16 oz	0.93	7/01	11r
Wine, red and white table, all sizes, any origin	liter	7.04	7/01	11r

Likomo, IN - continued

Item	Per	Value	Date	Ref.
Appliances				
Major appliances, expenditures on	yr	165	1999	30r
Small appliances, housewares, expenditures on	yr	90	1999	30r
Banking and Money				
Mortgage interest and charges paid	yr	2277	1999	30r
Mortgage principal paid on owned property	yr	1230	1999	30r
Vehicle finance charges paid	yr	328	1999	30r
Charity				
Cash contributions, expenditures	yr	1126	1999	30r
Child Care				
Child raising cost, total, age 0-2	yr	7890	1999	60r
Child raising cost, total, age 3-5	yr	8130	1999	60r
Child raising cost, total, age 6-8	yr	8170	1999	60r
Child raising cost, total, age 9-11	yr	8190	1999	60r
Child raising cost, total, age 12-14	yr	8890	1999	60r
Child raising cost, total, age 15-17	yr	9050	1999	60r
Child's child care and education, age 0-2	yr	1240	1999	60r
Child's child care and education, age 3-5	yr	1370	1999	60r
Child's child care and education, age 6-8	yr	880	1999	60r
Child's child care and education, age 9-11	yr	570	1999	60r
Child's child care and education, age 12-14	yr	420	1999	60r
Child's child care and education, age 15-17	yr	720	1999	60r
Child's clothing, age 0-2	yr	410	1999	60r
Child's clothing, age 3-5	yr	400	1999	60r
Child's clothing, age 6-8	yr	450	1999	60r
Child's clothing, age 9-11	yr	500	1999	60r
Child's clothing, age 12-14	yr	840	1999	60r
Child's clothing, age 15-17	yr	740	1999	60r
Child's food, age 0-2	yr	960	1999	60r
Child's food, age 3-5	yr	1120	1999	60r
Child's food, age 6-8	yr	1430	1999	60r
Child's food, age 9-11	yr	1710	1999	60r
Child's food, age 12-14	yr	1710	1999	60r
Child's food, age 15-17	yr	1920	1999	60r
Child's health care, age 0-2	yr	520	1999	60r
Child's health care, age 3-5	yr	500	1999	60r
Child's health care, age 6-8	yr	570	1999	60r
Child's health care, age 9-11	yr	610	1999	60r
Child's health care, age 12-14	yr	630	1999	60r
Child's health care, age 15-17	yr	650	1999	60r
Child's housing, age 0-2	yr	2860	1999	60r
Child's housing, age 3-5	yr	2840	1999	60r
Child's housing, age 6-8	yr	2800	1999	60r
Child's housing, age 9-11	yr	2650	1999	60r
Child's housing, age 12-14	yr	2840	1999	60r
Child's housing, age 15-17	yr	2440	1999	60r
Child's personal care, reading, age 0-2	yr	880	1999	60r
Child's personal care, reading, age 3-5	yr	900	1999	60r
Child's personal care, reading, age 6-8	yr	930	1999	60r
Child's personal care, reading, age 9-11	yr	970	1999	60r
Child's personal care, reading, age 12-14	yr	1150	1999	60r
Child's personal care, reading, age 15-17	yr	920	1999	60r
Clothing				
Apparel and services purchases	yr	1607	1999	30r
Boys, 2 to 15, expenditures on	yr	91	1999	30r
Children under 2, expenditures on	yr	59	1999	30r
Footwear, expenditures on	yr	285	1999	30r
Girls, 2 to 15, expenditures on	yr	116	1999	30r
Men and boys, expenditures on	yr	433	1999	30r
Men, 16 and over, expenditures on	yr	341	1999	30r
Women, 16 and over, expenditures on	yr	490	1999	30r
Communications				
Phone line, single, business, field visit	inst.	59.00	12/97	17s
Phone line, single, business, no field visit	inst.	59.00	12/97	17s
Phone line, single, residence, field visit	inst.	47.00	12/97	17s
Phone line, single, residence, no field visit	inst.	47.00	12/97	17s
Postage and stationery, expenditures on	yr	140	1999	30r
Postal rate, express mail, up to half-pound		12.45	7/01	108r
Postal rate, letter, first class, first ounce		0.34	7/01	108r

Values are in dollars or fractions of dollars. In the column headed *Ref*, references are shown to sources. Each reference is followed by a letter. These refer to the geographical level for which data were reported: s=State, r=Region, and c=City or metro. The abbreviation *ex* is used to mean *except* or *excluding*; *exp* stands for expenditures. For other abbreviations and further explanations, please see the Introduction.

Likomo, IN - continued

Item	Per	Value	Date	Ref.
Communications				
Postal rate, letter, two ounces		0.57	7/01	108r
Postal rate, post card		0.21	7/01	108r
Postal rate, priority mail, two pounds		3.95	7/01	108r
Postal rate, priority mail, up to one pound		3.50	7/01	108r
Telephone services, expenditures on	yr	830	1999	30r
Education				
Board, 4-year private college/university	yr	2250	1996	38s
Board, 4-year public college/university	yr	2425	1996	38s
Education expenditures	yr	583	1999	30r
Room, 4-year private college/university	yr	1987	1996	38s
Room, 4-year public college/university	yr	1931	1996	38s
Total cost, 4-year private college/university	yr	16829	1996	38s
Total cost, 4-year public college/university	yr	7392	1996	38s
Tuition, 2-year public college/university, in state	yr	1937	1996	38s
Tuition, 4-year private college/university, in state	yr	12592	1996	38s
Tuition, 4-year public college/university	yr	3037	1996	38s
Energy and Fuels				
Electricity	500 KWhs	46.59	7/01	11r
Fuel oil #2	gal	1.27	7/01	11r
Fuel oil and other fuels, expenditures on	yr	68	1999	30r
Gas, natural, commercial rate	1000 cf	6.24	11/00	88s
Gasoline, unleaded midgrade	gal	1.79	7/01	11r
Gasoline, unleaded premium	gal	1.86	7/01	11r
Gasoline, unleaded regular	gal	1.58	7/01	11r
Natural gas, expenditures on	yr	389	1999	30r
Utility (piped) gas, therm		0.81	7/01	11r
Utility (piped) gas, 40 therms		38.01	7/01	11r
Utility (piped) gas, 100 therms		81.75	7/01	11r
Entertainment				
Entertainment purchases	yr	1984	1999	30r
Fees and admissions paid	yr	444	1999	30r
Television, radios, sound equipment, expenditures on	yr	580	1999	30r
Funerals				
Cosmetology, hair, other preparation		178.32	1/99	78r
Embalming		408.19	1/99	78r
Funeral at funeral home		362.13	1/99	78r
Professional service charges		1375.51	1/99	78r
Transfer of remains to funeral home		155.92	1/99	78r
Visitation/viewing		294.38	1/99	78r
Groceries				
Bacon, sliced	lb	3.15	7/01	11r
Bakery products, expenditures on	yr	281	1999	30r
Bananas	lb	0.48	7/01	11r
Beans, dried, any type, all sizes	lb	0.61	7/01	11r
Beef for stew, boneless	lb	3.08	7/01	11r
Beef, expenditures on	yr	217	1999	30r
Bologna, all beef or mixed	lb	2.52	7/01	11r
Bread, white, pan	lb	1.06	7/01	11r
Broccoli	lb	0.91	7/01	11r
Butter, salted, grade AA, stick	lb	3.04	7/01	11r
Butter, yoghurt, cheese, etc, expenditures on	yr	183	1999	30r
Cereals and bakery product purchases	yr	430	1999	30r
Cereals and cereal products, expenditures on	yr	149	1999	30r
Chicken, fresh, whole	lb	1.07	7/01	11r
Chops, boneless,	lb	3.64	7/01	11r
Chuck roast, U.S. choice, boneless	lb	2.47	7/01	11r
Coffee, 100%, ground roast, all sizes	lb	2.69	7/01	11r
Cookies, chocolate chip	lb	2.87	7/01	11r
Dairy product purchases	yr	304	1999	30r
Eggs, expenditures on	yr	26	1999	30r
Eggs, large grade A, large	dozen	0.88	7/01	11r
Fats and oils, expenditures on	yr	75	1999	30r
Fish and seafood, expenditures on	yr	72	1999	30r

Likomo, IN - continued

Item	Per	Value	Date	Ref.
Groceries - continued				
Food (excl fruit and vegetables), eaten at home, purchases	yr	887	1999	30r
Food cooked on trips, expenditures on	yr	44	1999	30r
Food purchases	yr	4802	1999	30r
Food purchases, eaten away from home	yr	2069	1999	30r
Food purchases, food eaten at home	yr	2733	1999	30r
Fresh fruits, expenditures on	yr	138	1999	30r
Fresh milk and cream, expenditures on	yr	120	1999	30r
Fresh vegetables, expenditures on	yr	126	1999	30r
Grapefruit	lb	0.66	7/01	11r
Grapes, Thompson, seedless	lb	1.64	7/01	11r
Ground beef, 100% beef	lb	1.64	7/01	11r
Ground beef, lean and extra lean	lb	2.16	7/01	11r
Ground chuck, 100% beef	lb	2.13	7/01	11r
Ham, boneless, excl canned	lb	2.62	7/01	11r
Ice cream, prepackaged, bulk, regular	1/2 gal	3.35	7/01	11r
Lemons	lb	1.19	7/01	11r
Lettuce, iceberg	lb	0.73	7/01	11r
Margarine, soft, tubs	lb	0.89	7/01	11r
Meats, poultry, fish, and egg purchases	yr	671	1999	30r
Milk, fresh, whole, fortified	gal	2.71	7/01	11r
Nonalcoholic beverages, expenditures on	yr	239	1999	30r
Oranges, Navel	lb	0.80	7/01	11r
Oranges, Valencia	lb	0.66	7/01	11r
Pears, Anjou	lb	0.93	7/01	11r
Pork chops, center cut, bone-in	lb	3.63	7/01	11r
Pork, expenditures on	yr	150	1999	30r
Potato chips	16 oz	3.52	7/01	11r
Potatoes, frozen, french fried	lb	1.08	7/01	11r
Potatoes, white, all types	lb	0.33	7/01	11r
Poultry, expenditures on	yr	108	1999	30r
Processed fruits, expenditures on	yr	98	1999	30r
Processed vegetables, expenditures on	yr	80	1999	30r
Round roast, U.S. choice, boneless	lb	3.07	7/01	11r
Round steak, graded and ungraded, excl U.S. prime and choice	lb	3.41	7/01	11r
Shortening, vegetable oil blends	lb	1.13	7/01	11r
Spaghetti and macaroni	lb	0.80	7/01	11r
Steak, round, U.S. choice, boneless	lb	3.23	7/01	11r
Steak, T-bone, U.S. choice, bone-in	lb	6.68	7/01	11r
Strawberries, dry pint	12 oz	1.32	7/01	11r
Sugar and other sweets, expenditures on	yr	114	1999	30r
Sugar, white, 33-80 ounce package	lb	0.42	7/01	11r
Sugar, white, all sizes	lb	0.43	7/01	11r
Tobacco products and smoking supplies purchases	yr	331	1999	30r
Tomatoes, field grown	lb	1.46	7/01	11r
Tuna, light, chunk	lb	1.80	7/01	11r
Turkey, frozen, whole	lb	1.15	7/01	11r
Goods and Services				
B&B Japanese maple (acer japonicum)	gal	29.99-169.99	4/00	93r
Boxwood (buxus)	2 gal	18.99-39.99	4/00	93r
Daylilly (hemerocallis)	gal	4.99-25.00	4/00	93r
Flat of annuals		11.98-24.99	4/00	93r
Fountain grass (pennisetum)	gal	5.98-12.98	4/00	93r
Hanging basket (10 in)		12.99-27.99	4/00	93r
Hardy geranium (geranium)	gal	7.99-9.99	4/00	93r
Hosta (hosta)	gal	6.00-25.00	4/00	93r
Lilac (syrubga vulgaris)	2 gal	14.99-24.99	4/00	93r
Miscellaneous purchases	yr	865	1999	30r
Rhododendron (rhododendron)	2 gal	23.98-42.99	4/00	93r

Values are in dollars or fractions of dollars. In the column headed *Ref*, references are shown to sources. Each reference is followed by a letter. These refer to the geographical level for which data were reported: s=State, r=Region, and c=City or metro. The abbreviation *ex* is used to mean *except* or *excluding*; *exp* stands for *expenditures*. For other abbreviations and further explanations, please see the Introduction.

Likomo, IN - continued

Item	Per	Value	Date	Ref.
Goods and Services				
Sage (salvia)	gal	6.00-9.99	4/00	93r
Wintercreeper euonymus (euonymus fortunei)	2 gal	16.00-169.99	4/00	93r
Hunting license	yr	8.75	4/01	34s
Health Care				
Cardiac catheterization, ave hospital/ physician charges		13380	1998	77s
Childbirth, Cesarean delivery		10722	1997	13r
Childbirth, vaginal delivery		6223	1997	13r
Drugs, expenditures on	yr	394	1999	30r
Health care purchases	yr	2048	1999	30r
Health insurance expenditures	yr	978	1999	30r
Hysterectomy, laproscopically-assisted, ave hospital/physician charges		11310	1998	76s
Hysterectomy, vaginal, ave hospital and physician charges		9160	1998	76s
Medicaid dispensing fee		4.00	1999	87s
Medical services expenditures	yr	554	1999	30r
Medical supplies, expenditures on	yr	122	1999	30r
Plastic surgery, breast augmentation		3184	2000	7r
Plastic surgery, breast lift		3585	2000	7r
Plastic surgery, facelift		4999	2000	7r
Plastic surgery, hair transplantation		3105	2000	7r
Plastic surgery, lip augmentation		1290	2000	7r
Plastic surgery, lower body lift		8135	2000	7r
Plastic surgery, thigh lift		3839	2000	7r
Household Goods				
Floor coverings, expenditures on	yr	52	1999	30r
Furniture, expenditures on	yr	344	1999	30r
Household furnishings and equipment purchases	yr	1475	1999	30r
Household textiles, expenditures on	yr	109	1999	30r
Laundry and cleaning supplies, expenditures on	yr	134	1999	30r
Housing				
Home price, existing, ave		144400	10/00	90r
Home value, median		102000	2001	53s
Household operation expenditures	yr	542	1999	30r
Housekeeping supplies purchases	yr	508	1999	30r
Lodging expenditures	yr	430	1999	30r
Maintenance, repairs, insurance expenditures	yr	853	1999	30r
Monthly rental value of owned home	mos	547	1999	30r
Owned dwellings, expenditures own	yr	4282	1999	30r
Rent expenditures	yr	1558	1999	30r
Rental unit, 1 bedroom, with utilities	mos	413	4/01	41c
Rental unit, 2 bedroom, with utilities	mos	539	4/01	41c
Rental unit, 3 bedroom, with utilities	mos	693	4/01	41c
Rental unit, 4 bedroom, with utilities	mos	755	4/01	41c
Shelter, expenditures on	yr	6270	1999	30r
Insurance and Pensions				
Life and other personal insurance purchases	yr	387	1999	30r
Pensions and Social Security, expenditures on	yr	2968	1999	30r
Legal Fees				
Divorce, filing fee		100.00	4/01	35s
Driver's license fee	orig	6.00	1999	48s
Driver's license fee	renew	6.00	1999	48s
Personal Goods				
Personal care products and services purchases	yr	385	1999	30r
Personal Services				
Personal services, household, expenditures on	yr	300	1999	30r
Pets				
Pets, toys, and playground equipment, expenditures on	yr	375	1999	30r

Likomo, IN - continued

Item	Per	Value	Date	Ref.
Taxes				
Federal income taxes paid	yr	2326	1999	30r
Personal taxes, expenditures on	yr	3223	1999	30r
Property taxes paid	yr	1152	1999	30r
State and local income taxes paid	yr	753	1999	30r
Transportation				
Cars and trucks, new, expenditures on	yr	1280	1999	30r
Cars and trucks, used, expenditures on	yr	1763	1999	30r
Diesel at the pump	gal	1.17	10/99	73s
Gasoline and motor oil purchases	yr	1036	1999	30r
Gasoline before-tax price (cents)	gal	110.00	10/00	43s
Maintenance and repair expenditures	yr	594	1999	30r
Public transportation, expenditures on	yr	341	1999	30r
Transportation purchases	yr	6617	1999	30r
Vehicle expenses, miscellaneous, purchases	yr	2159	1999	30r
Vehicle insurance payments	yr	701	1999	30r
Vehicle purchases (net outlay)	yr	3081	1999	30r
Vehicle rental, lease expenditures	yr	536	1999	30r
Utilities				
Electrical bill, average	mos	66.66	9/00	9s
Electricity, expenditures on	yr	841	1999	30r
Electricity cost, average	KWh	5.00	9/00	9s
Utilities, fuels, and public services purchased	yr	2401	1999	30r
Water and other public services, expenditures on	yr	273	1999	30r
Weddings				
Wedding (national average cost)		19936	2000	33r
Wedding (regional average total cost)		16195	1997	110r
Attendants' gifts		321	1998	33r
Bridal attendants' apparel (5 persons)		824	2000	33r
Bride's headpiece/veil		173	1998	33r
Bride's wedding dress		859	1998	33r
Clergy, religious facility fee		242	1998	33r
Engagement ring		3177	1998	33r
Flowers		789	1998	33r
Groom's formalwear rental		99	2000	33r
Limousine		410	1998	33r
Marriage license cost		18.00	4/01	35s
Men's formalwear (ushers, best man)		469	2000	33r
Mother of bride apparel		241	2000	33r
Music		866	1998	33r
Photography and videography		1368	1998	33r
Rehearsal dinner		728	1998	33r
Wedding invitations and announcements		341	1998	33r
Wedding reception		7968	2000	33r
Wedding rings (bride and groom)		1060	1998	33r

Lima, OH

Item	Per	Value	Date	Ref.
Average annual expenditures	yr	35369	1999	30r
Composite, ACCRA index		96.80	3/01	4c
Alcoholic Beverages				
Alcoholic beverage purchases	yr	304	1999	30r
Beer, Heineken, 12-oz, ex deposit	6	7.49	3/01	4c
J & B Scotch	750-ml	21.35	3/01	4c
Malt beverages, all types, all sizes, any origin	16 oz	0.93	7/01	11r
Wine, Livingston or Gallo, Chablis blanc	1.5 liter	6.49	3/01	4c
Wine, red and white table, all sizes, any origin	liter	7.04	7/01	11r
Appliances				
Appliance repair, service call, washing machine	min lab chg	39.67	3/01	4c
Major appliances, expenditures on	yr	165	1999	30r
Small appliances, housewares, expenditures on	yr	90	1999	30r
Banking and Money				
Mortgage interest and charges paid	yr	2277	1999	30r
Mortgage principal paid on owned property	yr	1230	1999	30r

Values are in dollars or fractions of dollars. In the column headed *Ref*, references are shown to sources. Each reference is followed by a letter. These refer to the geographical level for which data were reported: s=State, r=Region, and c=City or metro. The abbreviation *ex* is used to mean *except* or *excluding*; *exp* stands for *expenditures*. For other abbreviations and further explanations, please see the Introduction.

Lima, OH - continued

Item	Per	Value	Date	Ref.
Banking and Money				
Mortgage rate, incl. points and orig. fee, 30-yr. conv. fixed or ARM	mos	7.18	3/01	4c
Vehicle finance charges paid	yr	328	1999	30r
Charity				
Cash contributions, expenditures	yr	1126	1999	30r
Child Care				
Child raising cost, total, age 0-2	yr	7890	1999	60r
Child raising cost, total, age 3-5	yr	8130	1999	60r
Child raising cost, total, age 6-8	yr	8170	1999	60r
Child raising cost, total, age 9-11	yr	8190	1999	60r
Child raising cost, total, age 12-14	yr	8890	1999	60r
Child raising cost, total, age 15-17	yr	9050	1999	60r
Child's child care and education, age 0-2	yr	1240	1999	60r
Child's child care and education, age 3-5	yr	1370	1999	60r
Child's child care and education, age 6-8	yr	880	1999	60r
Child's child care and education, age 9-11	yr	570	1999	60r
Child's child care and education, age 12-14	yr	420	1999	60r
Child's child care and education, age 15-17	yr	720	1999	60r
Child's clothing, age 0-2	yr	410	1999	60r
Child's clothing, age 3-5	yr	400	1999	60r
Child's clothing, age 6-8	yr	450	1999	60r
Child's clothing, age 9-11	yr	500	1999	60r
Child's clothing, age 12-14	yr	840	1999	60r
Child's clothing, age 15-17	yr	740	1999	60r
Child's food, age 0-2	yr	960	1999	60r
Child's food, age 3-5	yr	1120	1999	60r
Child's food, age 6-8	yr	1430	1999	60r
Child's food, age 9-11	yr	1710	1999	60r
Child's food, age 12-14	yr	1710	1999	60r
Child's food, age 15-17	yr	1920	1999	60r
Child's health care, age 0-2	yr	520	1999	60r
Child's health care, age 3-5	yr	500	1999	60r
Child's health care, age 6-8	yr	570	1999	60r
Child's health care, age 9-11	yr	610	1999	60r
Child's health care, age 12-14	yr	630	1999	60r
Child's health care, age 15-17	yr	650	1999	60r
Child's housing, age 0-2	yr	2860	1999	60r
Child's housing, age 3-5	yr	2840	1999	60r
Child's housing, age 6-8	yr	2800	1999	60r
Child's housing, age 9-11	yr	2650	1999	60r
Child's housing, age 12-14	yr	2840	1999	60r
Child's housing, age 15-17	yr	2440	1999	60r
Child's personal care, reading, age 0-2	yr	880	1999	60r
Child's personal care, reading, age 3-5	yr	900	1999	60r
Child's personal care, reading, age 6-8	yr	930	1999	60r
Child's personal care, reading, age 9-11	yr	970	1999	60r
Child's personal care, reading, age 12-14	yr	1150	1999	60r
Child's personal care, reading, age 15-17	yr	920	1999	60r
Clothing				
Apparel and services purchases	yr	1607	1999	30r
Boys' brief, cotton	3	5.18	3/01	4c
Boys, 2 to 15, expenditures on	yr	91	1999	30r
Children under 2, expenditures on	yr	59	1999	30r
Footwear, expenditures on	yr	285	1999	30r
Girls, 2 to 15, expenditures on	yr	116	1999	30r
Men and boys, expenditures on	yr	433	1999	30r
Men, 16 and over, expenditures on	yr	341	1999	30r
Shirt, man's dress shirt		25.87	3/01	4c
Slacks, man's "No Wrinkles" khaki		41.50	3/01	4c
Women, 16 and over, expenditures on	yr	490	1999	30r
Communications				
Cable modem installation, Adelphi		54.90	6/99	103s
Cable modem installation, Media One		100.00	6/99	103s
Cable modem installation, Time Warner		75.00-225.00	6/99	103s
Cable modem rate, cable subscriber, Adelphi	mos	34.95	6/99	103s
Cable modem rate, cable subscriber, Media One	mos	34.95-39.95	6/99	103s
Cable modem rate, cable subscriber, Time Warner	mos	39.95-49.95	6/99	103s

Lima, OH - continued

Item	Per	Value	Date	Ref.
Communications - continued				
Cable modem rate, non-cable subscriber, Adelphi	mos	44.95	6/99	103s
Cable modem rate, non-cable subscriber, Media One	mos	49.95	6/99	103s
Cable modem rate, non-cable subscriber, Time Warner	mos	39.95-54.95	6/99	103s
Newspaper subscription, daily and Sunday delivery	mos	11.64	3/01	4c
Phone line, single, business, field visit	inst.	56.32	12/97	17s
Phone line, single, business, no field visit	inst.	56.32	12/97	17s
Phone line, single, residence, field visit	inst.	31.10	12/97	17s
Phone line, single, residence, no field visit	inst.	31.10	12/97	17s
Postage and stationery, expenditures on	yr	140	1999	30r
Postal rate, express mail, up to half-pound		12.45	7/01	108r
Postal rate, letter, first class, first ounce		0.34	7/01	108r
Postal rate, letter, two ounces		0.57	7/01	108r
Postal rate, post card		0.21	7/01	108r
Postal rate, priority mail, two pounds		3.95	7/01	108r
Postal rate, priority mail, up to one pound		3.50	7/01	108r
Telephone bill, family of three	mos	23.83	3/01	4c
Telephone services, expenditures on	yr	830	1999	30r
Education				
Board, 4-year private college/university	yr	2414	1996	38s
Board, 4-year public college/university	yr	2181	1996	38s
Education expenditures	yr	583	1999	30r
Room, 4-year private college/university	yr	2349	1996	38s
Room, 4-year public college/university	yr	2386	1996	38s
Total cost, 4-year private college/university	yr	17139	1996	38s
Total cost, 4-year public college/university	yr	8169	1996	38s
Tuition, 2-year public college/university, in state	yr	2261	1996	38s
Tuition, 4-year private college/university, in state	yr	12377	1996	38s
Tuition, 4-year public college/university	yr	3603	1996	38s
Energy and Fuels				
Electricity	500 KWhs	46.59	7/01	11r
Energy, combined forms, 2400 sq ft	mos	132.20	3/01	4c
Energy, exc. electricity, 2400 sq ft	mos	83.74	3/01	4c
Fuel oil #2	gal	1.27	7/01	11r
Fuel oil and other fuels, expenditures on	yr	68	1999	30r
Gas, natural, commercial rate	1000 cf	8.65	11/00	88s
Gas, regular unleaded, cash, self-service	gal	1.49	3/01	4c
Gasoline, unleaded midgrade	gal	1.79	7/01	11r
Gasoline, unleaded premium	gal	1.86	7/01	11r
Gasoline, unleaded regular	gal	1.58	7/01	11r
Natural gas, expenditures on	yr	389	1999	30r
Utility (piped) gas, therm		0.81	7/01	11r
Utility (piped) gas, 40 therms		38.01	7/01	11r
Utility (piped) gas, 100 therms		81.75	7/01	11r
Entertainment				
Bowling, Saturday evening rate	line	2.40	3/01	4c
Entertainment purchases	yr	1984	1999	30r
Fees and admissions paid	yr	444	1999	30r
Monopoly game, Parker Brothers', No. 9	game	11.59	3/01	4c
Movie, first-run, Saturday, evening	adm.	6.75	3/01	4c
Television, radios, sound equipment, expenditures on	yr	580	1999	30r
Tennis balls, yellow, Wilson or Penn, 3	can	2.31	3/01	4c
Funerals				
Cosmetology, hair, other preparation		178.32	1/99	78r
Embalming		408.19	1/99	78r
Funeral at funeral home		362.13	1/99	78r
Professional service charges		1375.51	1/99	78r
Transfer of remains to funeral home		155.92	1/99	78r
Visitation/viewing		294.38	1/99	78r
Groceries				
Groceries, ACCRA Index		103.70	3/01	4c
Antibiotic ointment, Polysporin	0.5 oz	5.24	3/01	4c

Values are in dollars or fractions of dollars. In the column headed *Ref*, references are shown to sources. Each reference is followed by a letter. These refer to the geographical level for which data were reported: s=State, r=Region, and c=City or metro. The abbreviation *ex* is used to mean *except* or *excluding*; *exp* stands for expenditures. For other abbreviations and further explanations, please see the Introduction.

Lima, OH - continued

Groceries

Item	Per	Value	Date	Ref.
Baby food, strained vegetables or fruit, lowest price	4-4.5 oz	0.47	3/01	4c
Bacon, sliced	lb	3.15	7/01	11r
Bakery products, expenditures on	yr	281	1999	30r
Bananas	lb	0.49	3/01	4c
Bananas	lb	0.48	7/01	11r
Beans, dried, any type, all sizes	lb	0.61	7/01	11r
Beef for stew, boneless	lb	3.08	7/01	11r
Beef or hamburger, ground	lb	1.67	3/01	4c
Beef, expenditures on	yr	217	1999	30r
Bologna, all beef or mixed	lb	2.52	7/01	11r
Bread, white	loaf	1.10	3/01	4c
Bread, white, pan	lb	1.06	7/01	11r
Broccoli	lb	0.91	7/01	11r
Butter, salted, grade AA, stick	lb	3.04	7/01	11r
Butter, yoghurt, cheese, etc, expenditures on	yr	183	1999	30r
Cereals and bakery product purchases	yr	430	1999	30r
Cereals and cereal products, expenditures on	yr	149	1999	30r
Cheese, Kraft grated Parmesan	8 oz	3.83	3/01	4c
Chicken, fresh, whole	lb	1.07	7/01	11r
Chicken, whole fryer	lb	1.17	3/01	4c
Chops, boneless,	lb	3.64	7/01	11r
Chuck roast, U.S. choice, boneless	lb	2.47	7/01	11r
Cigarettes, Winston, Kings	carton	24.45	3/01	4c
Coffee, 100%, ground roast, all sizes	lb	2.69	7/01	11r
Coffee, vacuum-packed	13 oz	2.44	3/01	4c
Cookies, chocolate chip	lb	2.87	7/01	11r
Corn Flakes, Kellogg's or Post Toasties	18 oz	2.20	3/01	4c
Corn, frozen, whole kernel, lowest price	16 oz	1.21	3/01	4c
Dairy product purchases	yr	304	1999	30r
Eggs, expenditures on	yr	26	1999	30r
Eggs, Grade A or AA	dozen	1.37	3/01	4c
Eggs, grade A, large	dozen	0.88	7/01	11r
Fats and oils, expenditures on	yr	75	1999	30r
Fish and seafood, expenditures on	yr	72	1999	30r
Food (excl fruit and vegetables), eaten at home, purchases	yr	887	1999	30r
Food cooked on trips, expenditures on	yr	44	1999	30r
Food purchases	yr	4802	1999	30r
Food purchases, eaten away from home	yr	2069	1999	30r
Food purchases, food eaten at home	yr	2733	1999	30r
Fresh fruits, expenditures on	yr	138	1999	30r
Fresh milk and cream, expenditures on	yr	120	1999	30r
Fresh vegetables, expenditures on	yr	126	1999	30r
Grapefruit	lb	0.66	7/01	11r
Grapes, Thompson, seedless	lb	1.64	7/01	11r
Ground beef, 100% beef	lb	1.64	7/01	11r
Ground beef, lean and extra lean	lb	2.16	7/01	11r
Ground chuck, 100% beef	lb	2.13	7/01	11r
Ham, boneless, excl canned	lb	2.62	7/01	11r
Ice cream, prepackaged, bulk, regular	1/2 gal	3.35	7/01	11r
Lemons	lb	1.19	7/01	11r
Lettuce, iceberg	head	1.11	3/01	4c
Lettuce, iceberg	lb	0.73	7/01	11r
Margarine, Blue Bonnet or Parkay, stick	lb	0.99	3/01	4c
Margarine, soft, tubs	lb	0.89	7/01	11r
Meats, poultry, fish, and egg purchases	yr	671	1999	30r
Milk, fresh, whole, fortified	gal	2.71	7/01	11r
Milk, whole	1/2 gal	1.69	3/01	4c
Nonalcoholic beverages, expenditures on	yr	239	1999	30r
Orange juice, Minute Maid frozen	12 oz	1.73	3/01	4c
Oranges, Navel	lb	0.80	7/01	11r
Oranges, Valencia	lb	0.66	7/01	11r
Peaches, halves or slices, Hunt's, Del Monte, or Libby's	29 oz	1.69	3/01	4c
Pears, Anjou	lb	0.93	7/01	11r
Peas, green, Del Monte or Green Giant	15 oz	0.68	3/01	4c
Pork chops, center cut, bone-in	lb	3.63	7/01	11r
Pork, expenditures on	yr	150	1999	30r
Potato chips	16 oz	3.52	7/01	11r
Potatoes, frozen, french fried	lb	1.08	7/01	11r

Lima, OH - continued

Lima, OH

Groceries - continued

Item	Per	Value	Date	Ref.
Potatoes, white or red	10 lb	3.05	3/01	4c
Potatoes, white, all types	lb	0.33	7/01	11r
Poultry, expenditures on	yr	108	1999	30r
Processed fruits, expenditures on	yr	98	1999	30r
Processed vegetables, expenditures on	yr	80	1999	30r
Round roast, U.S. choice, boneless	lb	3.07	7/01	11r
Round steak, graded and ungraded, excl U.S. prime and choice	lb	3.41	7/01	11r
Sausage, Jimmy Dean/Owens pork	lb	3.19	3/01	4c
Shortening, vegetable oil blends	lb	1.13	7/01	11r
Shortening, vegetable, Crisco	3 lb	3.01	3/01	4c
Soft drink, Coca Cola, ex deposit	2 liter	1.19	3/01	4c
Spaghetti and macaroni	lb	0.80	7/01	11r
Steak, round, U.S. choice, boneless	lb	3.23	7/01	11r
Steak, T-bone	lb	6.77	3/01	4c
Steak, T-bone, U.S. choice, bone-in	lb	6.68	7/01	11r
Strawberries, dry pint	12 oz	1.32	7/01	11r
Sugar and other sweets, expenditures on	yr	114	1999	30r
Sugar, cane or beet	4 lbs	1.58	3/01	4c
Sugar, white, 33-80 ounce package	lb	0.42	7/01	11r
Sugar, white, all sizes	lb	0.43	7/01	11r
Tobacco products and smoking supplies purchases	yr	331	1999	30r
Tomatoes, field grown	lb	1.46	7/01	11r
Tomatoes, Hunt's or Del Monte	14.5 oz	0.91	3/01	4c
Tuna, chunk, light	6 oz	0.57	3/01	4c
Tuna, light, chunk	lb	1.80	7/01	11r
Turkey, frozen, whole	lb	1.15	7/01	11r

Goods and Services

Item	Per	Value	Date	Ref.
Miscellaneous goods and services, ACCRA Index		98.40	3/01	4c
B&B Japanese maple (acer japonicum)	gal	29.99-169.99	4/00	93r
Boxwood (buxus)	2 gal	18.99-39.99	4/00	93r
Daylilly (hemerocallis)	gal	4.99-25.00	4/00	93r
Flat of annuals		11.98-24.99	4/00	93r
Fountain grass (pennisetum)	gal	5.98-12.98	4/00	93r
Hanging basket (10 in)		12.99-27.99	4/00	93r
Hardy geranium (geranium)	gal	7.99-9.99	4/00	93r
Hosta (hosta)	gal	6.00-25.00	4/00	93r
Lilac (syrubga vulgaris)	2 gal	14.99-24.99	4/00	93r
Miscellaneous purchases	yr	865	1999	30r
Rhododendron (rhododendron)	2 gal	23.98-42.99	4/00	93r
Sage (salvia)	gal	6.00-9.99	4/00	93r
Wintercreeper euonymus (euonymus fortunei)	2 gal	16.00-169.99	4/00	93r
Hunting license	yr	15.00	4/01	34s

Health Care

Item	Per	Value	Date	Ref.
Health care, ACCRA Index		90.50	3/01	4c
Cardiac catheterization, ave hospital/ physician charges		11760	1998	77s
Childbirth, Cesarean delivery		10722	1997	13r
Childbirth, vaginal delivery		6223	1997	13r
Dentist's fee, adult teeth cleaning and periodic oral exam	visit	59.60	3/01	4c
Doctor's fee, routine exam, established patient	visit	55.90	3/01	4c
Drugs, expenditures on	yr	394	1999	30r
Health care purchases	yr	2048	1999	30r
Health insurance expenditures	yr	978	1999	30r
Hospital care, private room	day	430.00	3/01	4c

Values are in dollars or fractions of dollars. In the column headed *Ref*, references are shown to sources. Each reference is followed by a letter. These refer to the geographical level for which data were reported: s=State, r=Region, and c=City or metro. The abbreviation *ex* is used to mean *except* or *excluding*; *exp* stands for *expenditures*. For other abbreviations and further explanations, please see the Introduction.

Lima, OH - continued

Item	Per	Value	Date	Ref.
Health Care				
Hysterectomy, laproscopically-assisted, ave hospital/physician charges		11730	1998	76s
Hysterectomy, vaginal, ave hospital and physician charges		9640	1998	76s
Medicaid dispensing fee		3.70	1999	87s
Medical services expenditures	yr	554	1999	30r
Medical supplies, expenditures on	yr	122	1999	30r
Plastic surgery, breast augmentation		3184	2000	7r
Plastic surgery, breast lift		3585	2000	7r
Plastic surgery, facelift		4999	2000	7r
Plastic surgery, hair transplantation		3105	2000	7r
Plastic surgery, lip augmentation		1290	2000	7r
Plastic surgery, lower body lift		8135	2000	7r
Plastic surgery, thigh lift		3839	2000	7r
Household Goods				
Dishwashing powder, Cascade	50 oz	3.64	3/01	4c
Floor coverings, expenditures on	yr	52	1999	30r
Furniture, expenditures on	yr	344	1999	30r
Household furnishings and equipment purchases	yr	1475	1999	30r
Household textiles, expenditures on	yr	109	1999	30r
Laundry and cleaning supplies, expenditures on	yr	134	1999	30r
Tissues, facial, Kleenex brand	175	1.35	3/01	4c
Housing				
Housing, ACCRA Index		86.20	3/01	4c
Home price, existing, ave		144400	10/00	90r
Home value, median		96000	2001	53s
House, 2400 sq ft, 8000 sq ft lot, new, urban, utilities	total	184109	3/01	4c
House payment, principal and interest, 25% down payment	mos	935	3/01	4c
Household operation expenditures	yr	542	1999	30r
Housekeeping supplies purchases	yr	508	1999	30r
Lodging expenditures	yr	430	1999	30r
Maintenance, repairs, insurance expenditures	yr	853	1999	30r
Monthly rental value of owned home	mos	547	1999	30r
Owned dwellings, expenditures own	yr	4282	1999	30r
Rent expenditures	yr	1558	1999	30r
Rent, apartment, 2 br, 1 1/2-2 baths, unfurn, 950 sq ft, water	mos	477	3/01	4c
Rental unit, 1 bedroom, with utilities	mos	350	4/01	41c
Rental unit, 2 bedroom, with utilities	mos	460	4/01	41c
Rental unit, 3 bedroom, with utilities	mos	587	4/01	41c
Rental unit, 4 bedroom, with utilities	mos	643	4/01	41c
Shelter, expenditures on	yr	6270	1999	30r
Insurance and Pensions				
Life and other personal insurance purchases	yr	387	1999	30r
Pensions and Social Security, expenditures on	yr	2968	1999	30r
Legal Fees				
Divorce, filing fee		100.00	4/01	35s
Driver's license fee	renew	14.50	1999	48s
Driver's license fee	orig	14.50	1999	48s
Fishing license	yr	15.00	4/01	34s
Personal Goods				
Personal care products and services purchases	yr	385	1999	30r
Shampoo, Alberto VO5	15 oz	1.18	3/01	4c
Toothpaste, Crest or Colgate	6-7 oz	2.49	3/01	4c
Personal Services				
Dry cleaning, man's 2-pc suit		6.45	3/01	4c
Man's haircut, barbershop, no styling		9.78	3/01	4c
Personal services, household, expenditures on	yr	300	1999	30r
Woman's shampoo, trim, blow-dry, no style-change		20.44	3/01	4c

Item	Per	Value	Date	Ref.
Pets				
Pets, toys, and playground equipment, expenditures on	yr	375	1999	30r
Restaurant Food				
Chicken, fried, thigh and drumstick, KFC/Church's		2.32	3/01	4c
Hamburger with cheese, McDonald's	1/4 lb	2.15	3/01	4c
Pizza, Pizza Hut or Pizza Inn	11-12 in	8.20	3/01	4c
Taxes				
Federal income taxes paid	yr	2326	1999	30r
Personal taxes, expenditures on	yr	3223	1999	30r
Property taxes paid	yr	1152	1999	30r
State and local income taxes paid	yr	753	1999	30r
Transportation				
Transportation, ACCRA Index		103.70	3/01	4c
Bus fare, to central business district	1-way	0.80	3/01	4c
Cars and trucks, new, expenditures on	yr	1280	1999	30r
Cars and trucks, used, expenditures on	yr	1763	1999	30r
Diesel at the pump	gal	1.25	10/99	73s
Gasoline and motor oil purchases	yr	1036	1999	30r
Gasoline before-tax price (cents)	gal	109.50	10/00	43s
Maintenance and repair expenditures	yr	594	1999	30r
Public transportation, expenditures on	yr	341	1999	30r
Tire balance, computer or spin balance, front	wheel	8.66	3/01	4c
Transportation purchases	yr	6617	1999	30r
Vehicle expenses, miscellaneous, purchases	yr	2159	1999	30r
Vehicle insurance payments	yr	701	1999	30r
Vehicle purchases (net outlay)	yr	3081	1999	30r
Vehicle rental, lease expenditures	yr	536	1999	30r
Utilities				
Utilities, ACCRA Index		108.50	3/01	4c
Electrical bill, average	mos	72.83	9/00	9s
Electricity, expenditures on	yr	841	1999	30r
Electricity and other, mixed, 2400 sq ft, new home	mos	48.46	3/01	4c
Electricity cost, average	KWh	6.59	9/00	9s
Utilities, fuels, and public services purchased	yr	2401	1999	30r
Water and other public services, expenditures on	yr	273	1999	30r
Weddings				
Wedding (national average cost)		19936	2000	33r
Wedding (regional average total cost)		16195	1997	110r
Attendants' gifts		321	1998	33r
Bridal attendants' apparel (5 persons)		824	2000	33r
Bride's headpiece/veil		173	1998	33r
Bride's wedding dress		859	1998	33r
Clergy, religious facility fee		242	1998	33r
Engagement ring		3177	1998	33r
Flowers		789	1998	33r
Groom's formalwear rental		99	2000	33r
Limousine		410	1998	33r
Marriage license cost		45.00	4/01	35s
Men's formalwear (ushers, best man)		469	2000	33r
Mother of bride apparel		241	2000	33r
Music		866	1998	33r
Photography and videography		1368	1998	33r
Rehearsal dinner		728	1998	33r
Wedding invitations and announcements		341	1998	33r
Wedding reception		7968	2000	33r
Wedding rings (bride and groom)		1060	1998	33r

Lincoln, NE

Item	Per	Value	Date	Ref.
Average annual expenditures	yr	35369	1999	30r
Composite, ACCRA index		104.30	3/01	4c
Alcoholic Beverages				
Alcoholic beverage purchases	yr	304	1999	30r
Beer, Heineken, 12-oz, ex deposit	6	7.39	3/01	4c
J & B Scotch	750-ml	19.58	3/01	4c

Values are in dollars or fractions of dollars. In the column headed *Ref*, references are shown to sources. Each reference is followed by a letter. These refer to the geographical level for which data were reported: s=State, r=Region, and c=City or metro. The abbreviation *ex* is used to mean *except* or *excluding*; *exp* stands for *expenditures*. For other abbreviations and further explanations, please see the Introduction.

Lincoln, NE - continued

Item	Per	Value	Date	Ref.
Alcoholic Beverages				
Malt beverages, all types, all sizes, any origin	16 oz	0.93	7/01	11r
Wine, Livingston or Gallo, Chablis blanc	1.5 liter	5.08	3/01	4c
Wine, red and white table, all sizes, any origin	liter	7.04	7/01	11r
Appliances				
Appliance repair, service call, washing machine	min lab chg	32.39	3/01	4c
Major appliances, expenditures on	yr	165	1999	30r
Small appliances, housewares, expenditures on	yr	90	1999	30r
Banking and Money				
Mortgage interest and charges paid	yr	2277	1999	30r
Mortgage principal paid on owned property	yr	1230	1999	30r
Mortgage rate, incl. points and orig. fee, 30-yr. conv. fixed or ARM	mos	7.13	3/01	4c
Vehicle finance charges paid	yr	328	1999	30r
Charity				
Cash contributions, expenditures	yr	1126	1999	30r
Child Care				
Child raising cost, total, age 0-2	yr	7890	1999	60r
Child raising cost, total, age 3-5	yr	8130	1999	60r
Child raising cost, total, age 6-8	yr	8170	1999	60r
Child raising cost, total, age 9-11	yr	8190	1999	60r
Child raising cost, total, age 12-14	yr	8890	1999	60r
Child raising cost, total, age 15-17	yr	9050	1999	60r
Child's child care and education, age 0-2	yr	1240	1999	60r
Child's child care and education, age 3-5	yr	1370	1999	60r
Child's child care and education, age 6-8	yr	880	1999	60r
Child's child care and education, age 9-11	yr	570	1999	60r
Child's child care and education, age 12-14	yr	420	1999	60r
Child's child care and education, age 15-17	yr	720	1999	60r
Child's clothing, age 0-2	yr	410	1999	60r
Child's clothing, age 3-5	yr	400	1999	60r
Child's clothing, age 6-8	yr	450	1999	60r
Child's clothing, age 9-11	yr	500	1999	60r
Child's clothing, age 12-14	yr	840	1999	60r
Child's clothing, age 15-17	yr	740	1999	60r
Child's food, age 0-2	yr	960	1999	60r
Child's food, age 3-5	yr	1120	1999	60r
Child's food, age 6-8	yr	1430	1999	60r
Child's food, age 9-11	yr	1710	1999	60r
Child's food, age 12-14	yr	1710	1999	60r
Child's food, age 15-17	yr	1920	1999	60r
Child's health care, age 0-2	yr	520	1999	60r
Child's health care, age 3-5	yr	500	1999	60r
Child's health care, age 6-8	yr	570	1999	60r
Child's health care, age 9-11	yr	610	1999	60r
Child's health care, age 12-14	yr	630	1999	60r
Child's health care, age 15-17	yr	650	1999	60r
Child's housing, age 0-2	yr	2860	1999	60r
Child's housing, age 3-5	yr	2840	1999	60r
Child's housing, age 6-8	yr	2800	1999	60r
Child's housing, age 9-11	yr	2650	1999	60r
Child's housing, age 12-14	yr	2840	1999	60r
Child's housing, age 15-17	yr	2440	1999	60r
Child's personal care, reading, age 0-2	yr	880	1999	60r
Child's personal care, reading, age 3-5	yr	900	1999	60r
Child's personal care, reading, age 6-8	yr	930	1999	60r
Child's personal care, reading, age 9-11	yr	970	1999	60r
Child's personal care, reading, age 12-14	yr	1150	1999	60r
Child's personal care, reading, age 15-17	yr	920	1999	60r
Clothing				
Apparel and services purchases	yr	1607	1999	30r
Boys' brief, cotton	3	3.79	3/01	4c
Boys, 2 to 15, expenditures on	yr	91	1999	30r
Children under 2, expenditures on	yr	59	1999	30r
Footwear, expenditures on	yr	285	1999	30r
Girls, 2 to 15, expenditures on	yr	116	1999	30r
Men and boys, expenditures on	yr	433	1999	30r

Lincoln, NE - continued

Item	Per	Value	Date	Ref.
Clothing - continued				
Men, 16 and over, expenditures on	yr	341	1999	30r
Shirt, man's dress shirt		28.10	3/01	4c
Slacks, man's "No Wrinkles" khaki		43.99	3/01	4c
Women, 16 and over, expenditures on	yr	490	1999	30r
Communications				
Cable modem installation, Cox		99.00-174.95	6/99	103s
Cable modem rate, cable subscriber, Cox	mos	29.95-44.95	6/99	103s
Cable modem rate, non-cable subscriber, Cox	mos	42.95-54.95	6/99	103s
Newspaper subscription, daily and Sunday delivery	mos	14.30	3/01	4c
Phone line, single, business, field visit	inst.	45.00	12/97	17s
Phone line, single, business, no field visit	inst.	45.00	12/97	17s
Phone line, single, residence, field visit	inst.	33.00	12/97	17s
Phone line, single, residence, no field visit	inst.	33.00	12/97	17s
Postage and stationery, expenditures on	yr	140	1999	30r
Postal rate, express mail, up to half-pound		12.45	7/01	108r
Postal rate, letter, first class, first ounce		0.34	7/01	108r
Postal rate, letter, two ounces		0.57	7/01	108r
Postal rate, post card		0.21	7/01	108r
Postal rate, priority mail, two pounds		3.95	7/01	108r
Postal rate, priority mail, up to one pound		3.50	7/01	108r
Telephone bill, family of three	mos	22.64	3/01	4c
Telephone services, expenditures on	yr	830	1999	30r
Education				
Board, 4-year private college/university	yr	2003	1996	38s
Board, 4-year public college/university	yr	1892	1996	38s
Education expenditures	yr	583	1999	30r
Room, 4-year private college/university	yr	1801	1996	38s
Room, 4-year public college/university	yr	1422	1996	38s
Total cost, 4-year private college/university	yr	13234	1996	38s
Total cost, 4-year public college/university	yr	5497	1996	38s
Tuition, 2-year public college/university, in state	yr	1132	1996	38s
Tuition, 4-year private college/university, in state	yr	9430	1996	38s
Tuition, 4-year public college/university	yr	2182	1996	38s
Energy and Fuels				
Electricity	500 KWhs	46.59	7/01	11r
Energy, combined forms, 2400 sq ft	mos	154.50	3/01	4c
Energy, exc. electricity, 2400 sq ft	mos	108.18	3/01	4c
Fuel oil #2	gal	1.27	7/01	11r
Fuel oil and other fuels, expenditures on	yr	68	1999	30r
Gas, natural, commercial rate	1000 cf	6.59	11/00	88s
Gas, regular unleaded, cash, self-service	gal	1.45	3/01	4c
Gasoline, unleaded midgrade	gal	1.79	7/01	11r
Gasoline, unleaded premium	gal	1.86	7/01	11r
Gasoline, unleaded regular	gal	1.58	7/01	11r
Natural gas, expenditures on	yr	389	1999	30r
Utility (piped) gas, therm		0.81	7/01	11r
Utility (piped) gas, 40 therms		38.01	7/01	11r
Utility (piped) gas, 100 therms		81.75	7/01	11r
Entertainment				
Bowling, Saturday evening rate	line	2.90	3/01	4c
Entertainment purchases	yr	1984	1999	30r
Fees and admissions paid	yr	444	1999	30r
Monopoly game, Parker Brothers', No. 9	game	11.99	3/01	4c
Movie, first-run, Saturday, evening	adm.	6.50	3/01	4c
Television, radios, sound equipment, expenditures on	yr	580	1999	30r
Tennis balls, yellow, Wilson or Penn, 3	can	2.83	3/01	4c
Funerals				
Cosmetology, hair, other preparation		178.32	1/99	78r
Embalming		408.19	1/99	78r
Funeral at funeral home		362.13	1/99	78r
Professional service charges		1375.51	1/99	78r

Values are in dollars or fractions of dollars. In the column headed *Ref*, references are shown to sources. Each reference is followed by a letter. These refer to the geographical level for which data were reported: s=State, r=Region, and c=City or metro. The abbreviation *ex* is used to mean *except* or *excluding*; *exp* stands for *expenditures*. For other abbreviations and further explanations, please see the Introduction.

Lincoln, NE - continued

Item	Per	Value	Date	Ref.
Funerals				
Transfer of remains to funeral home		155.92	1/99	78r
Visitation/viewing		294.38	1/99	78r
Groceries				
Groceries, ACCRA Index		103.30	3/01	4c
Antibiotic ointment, Polysporin	0.5 oz	5.17	3/01	4c
Baby food, strained vegetables or fruit, lowest price	4-4.5 oz	0.48	3/01	4c
Bacon, sliced	lb	3.15	7/01	11r
Bakery products, expenditures on	yr	281	1999	30r
Bananas	lb	0.48	4c	
Bananas	lb	0.48	7/01	11r
Beans, dried, any type, all sizes	lb	0.61	7/01	11r
Beef for stew, boneless	lb	3.08	7/01	11r
Beef or hamburger, ground	lb	1.66	3/01	4c
Beef, expenditures on	yr	217	1999	30r
Bologna, all beef or mixed	lb	2.52	7/01	11r
Bread, white	loaf	1.07	3/01	4c
Bread, white, pan	lb	1.06	7/01	11r
Broccoli	lb	0.91	7/01	11r
Butter, salted, grade AA, stick	lb	3.04	7/01	11r
Butter, yoghurt, cheese, etc, expenditures on	yr	183	1999	30r
Cereals and bakery product purchases	yr	430	1999	30r
Cereals and cereal products, expenditures on	yr	149	1999	30r
Cheese, Kraft grated Parmesan	8 oz	4.01	3/01	4c
Chicken, fresh, whole	lb	1.07	7/01	11r
Chicken, whole fryer	lb	0.97	3/01	4c
Chops, boneless	lb	3.64	7/01	11r
Chuck roast, U.S. choice, boneless	lb	2.47	7/01	11r
Cigarettes, Winston, Kings	carton	28.32	3/01	4c
Coffee, 100%, ground roast, all sizes	lb	2.69	7/01	11r
Coffee, vacuum-packed	13 oz	2.44	3/01	4c
Cookies, chocolate chip	lb	2.87	7/01	11r
Corn Flakes, Kellogg's or Post Toasties	18 oz	2.83	3/01	4c
Corn, frozen, whole kernel, lowest price	16 oz	1.29	3/01	4c
Dairy product purchases	yr	304	1999	30r
Eggs, expenditures on	yr	26	1999	30r
Eggs, Grade A or AA	dozen	1.10	3/01	4c
Eggs, grade A, large	dozen	0.88	7/01	11r
Fats and oils, expenditures on	yr	75	1999	30r
Fish and seafood, expenditures on	yr	72	1999	30r
Food (excl fruit and vegetables), eaten at home, purchases	yr	887	1999	30r
Food cooked on trips, expenditures on	yr	44	1999	30r
Food purchases	yr	4802	1999	30r
Food purchases, eaten away from home	yr	2069	1999	30r
Food purchases, food eaten at home	yr	2733	1999	30r
Fresh fruits, expenditures on	yr	138	1999	30r
Fresh milk and cream, expenditures on	yr	120	1999	30r
Fresh vegetables, expenditures on	yr	126	1999	30r
Grapefruit	lb	0.66	7/01	11r
Grapes, Thompson, seedless	lb	1.64	7/01	11r
Ground beef, 100% beef	lb	1.64	7/01	11r
Ground beef, lean and extra lean	lb	2.16	7/01	11r
Ground chuck, 100% beef	lb	2.13	7/01	11r
Ham, boneless, excl canned	lb	2.62	7/01	11r
Ice cream, prepackaged, bulk, regular	1/2 gal	3.35	7/01	11r
Lemons	lb	1.19	7/01	11r
Lettuce, iceberg	head	1.07	3/01	4c
Lettuce, iceberg	lb	0.73	7/01	11r
Margarine, Blue Bonnet or Parkay, stick	lb	0.67	3/01	4c
Margarine, soft, tubs	lb	0.89	7/01	11r
Meats, poultry, fish, and egg purchases	yr	671	1999	30r
Milk, fresh, whole, fortified	gal	2.71	7/01	11r
Milk, whole	1/2 gal	1.52	3/01	4c
Nonalcoholic beverages, expenditures on	yr	239	1999	30r
Orange juice, Minute Maid frozen	12 oz	1.78	3/01	4c
Oranges, Navel	lb	0.80	7/01	11r
Oranges, Valencia	lb	0.66	7/01	11r
Peaches, halves or slices, Hunt's, Del Monte, or Libby's	29 oz	1.58	3/01	4c
Pears, Anjou	lb	0.93	7/01	11r

Lincoln, NE - continued

Item	Per	Value	Date	Ref.
Groceries - continued				
Peas, green, Del Monte or Green Giant	15 oz	0.75	3/01	4c
Pork chops, center cut, bone-in	lb	3.63	7/01	11r
Pork, expenditures on	yr	150	1999	30r
Potato chips	16 oz	3.52	7/01	11r
Potatoes, frozen, french fried	lb	1.08	7/01	11r
Potatoes, white or red	10 lb	2.79	3/01	4c
Potatoes, white, all types	lb	0.33	7/01	11r
Poultry, expenditures on	yr	108	1999	30r
Processed fruits, expenditures on	yr	98	1999	30r
Processed vegetables, expenditures on	yr	80	1999	30r
Round roast, U.S. choice, boneless	lb	3.07	7/01	11r
Round steak, graded and ungraded, excl U.S. prime and choice	lb	3.41	7/01	11r
Sausage, Jimmy Dean/Owens pork	lb	4.13	3/01	4c
Shortening, vegetable oil blends	lb	1.13	7/01	11r
Shortening, vegetable, Crisco	3 lb	2.90	3/01	4c
Soft drink, Coca Cola, ex deposit	2 liter	1.13	3/01	4c
Spaghetti and macaroni	lb	0.80	7/01	11r
Steak, round, U.S. choice, boneless	lb	3.23	7/01	11r
Steak, T-bone	lb	6.53	3/01	4c
Steak, T-bone, U.S. choice, bone-in	lb	6.68	7/01	11r
Strawberries, dry pint	12 oz	1.32	7/01	11r
Sugar and other sweets, expenditures on	yr	114	1999	30r
Sugar, cane or beet	4 lbs	1.65	3/01	4c
Sugar, white, 33-80 ounce package	lb	0.42	7/01	11r
Sugar, white, all sizes	lb	0.43	7/01	11r
Tobacco products and smoking supplies purchases	yr	331	1999	30r
Tomatoes, field grown	lb	1.46	7/01	11r
Tomatoes, Hunt's or Del Monte	14.5 oz	0.92	3/01	4c
Tuna, chunk, light	6 oz	0.65	3/01	4c
Tuna, light, chunk	lb	1.80	7/01	11r
Turkey, frozen, whole	lb	1.15	7/01	11r
Goods and Services				
Miscellaneous goods and services, ACCRA Index		101.90	3/01	4c
B&B Japanese maple (acer japonicum)	gal	29.99-169.99	4/00	93r
Boxwood (buxus)	2 gal	18.99-39.99	4/00	93r
Daylilly (hemerocallis)	gal	4.99-25.00	4/00	93r
Flat of annuals		11.98-24.99	4/00	93r
Fountain grass (pennisetum)	gal	5.98-12.98	4/00	93r
Hanging basket (10 in)		12.99-27.99	4/00	93r
Hardy geranium (geranium)	gal	7.99-9.99	4/00	93r
Hosta (hosta)	gal	6.00-25.00	4/00	93r
Lilac (syrubga vulgaris)	2 gal	14.99-24.99	4/00	93r
Miscellaneous purchases	yr	865	1999	30r
Rhododendron (rhododendron)	2 gal	23.98-42.99	4/00	93r
Sage (salvia)	gal	6.00-9.99	4/00	93r
Wintercreeper euonymus (euonymus fortunei)	2 gal	16.00-169.99	4/00	93r
Hunting license	yr	9.50	4/01	34s
Health Care				
Health care, ACCRA Index		94.70	3/01	4c
Cardiac catheterization, ave hospital/ physician charges		14740	1998	77s
Childbirth, Cesarean delivery		10722	1997	13r
Childbirth, vaginal delivery		6223	1997	13r
Dentist's fee, adult teeth cleaning and periodic oral exam	visit	58.20	3/01	4c

Values are in dollars or fractions of dollars. In the column headed *Ref*, references are shown to sources. Each reference is followed by a letter. These refer to the geographical level for which data were reported: s=State, r=Region, and c=City or metro. The abbreviation *ex* is used to mean *except* or *excluding*; *exp* stands for expenditures. For other abbreviations and further explanations, please see the Introduction.

Lincoln, NE - continued

Item	Per	Value	Date	Ref.
Health Care				
Doctor's fee, routine exam, established patient	visit	62.40	3/01	4c
Drugs, expenditures on	yr	394	1999	30r
Health care purchases	yr	2048	1999	30r
Health insurance expenditures	yr	978	1999	30r
Hospital care, private room	day	460.00	3/01	4c
Hysterectomy, laproscopically-assisted, ave hospital/physician charges		10690	1998	76s
Hysterectomy, vaginal, ave hospital and physician charges		7730	1998	76s
Medicaid dispensing fee		2.85-5.05	1999	87s
Medical services expenditures	yr	554	1999	30r
Medical supplies, expenditures on	yr	122	1999	30r
Plastic surgery, breast augmentation		3184	2000	7r
Plastic surgery, breast lift		3585	2000	7r
Plastic surgery, facelift		4999	2000	7r
Plastic surgery, hair transplantation		3105	2000	7r
Plastic surgery, lip augmentation		1290	2000	7r
Plastic surgery, lower body lift		8135	2000	7r
Plastic surgery, thigh lift		3839	2000	7r
Household Goods				
Dishwashing powder, Cascade	50 oz	3.26	3/01	4c
Floor coverings, expenditures on	yr	52	1999	30r
Furniture, expenditures on	yr	344	1999	30r
Household furnishings and equipment purchases	yr	1475	1999	30r
Household textiles, expenditures on	yr	109	1999	30r
Laundry and cleaning supplies, expenditures on	yr	134	1999	30r
Tissues, facial, Kleenex brand	175	1.16	3/01	4c
Housing				
Housing, ACCRA Index		105.80	3/01	4c
Home price, existing, ave		144400	10/00	90r
Home value, median		108000	2001	53s
House, 2400 sq ft, 8000 sq ft lot, new, urban, utilities	total	228180	3/01	4c
House payment, principal and interest, 25% down payment	mos	1153	3/01	4c
Household operation expenditures	yr	542	1999	30r
Housekeeping supplies purchases	yr	508	1999	30r
Lodging expenditures	yr	430	1999	30r
Maintenance, repairs, insurance expenditures	yr	853	1999	30r
Monthly rental value of owned home	mos	547	1999	30r
Owned dwellings, expenditures own	yr	4282	1999	30r
Rent expenditures	yr	1558	1999	30r
Rent, apartment, 2 br, 1 1/2-2 baths, unfurn, 950 sq ft, water	mos	570	3/01	4c
Rental unit, 1 bedroom, with utilities	mos	408	4/01	41c
Rental unit, 2 bedroom, with utilities	mos	538	4/01	41c
Rental unit, 3 bedroom, with utilities	mos	714	4/01	41c
Rental unit, 4 bedroom, with utilities	mos	834	4/01	41c
Shelter, expenditures on	yr	6270	1999	30r
Insurance and Pensions				
Auto insurance premium	yr	608.11	1999	57s
Life and other personal insurance purchases	yr	387	1999	30r
Pensions and Social Security, expenditures on	yr	2968	1999	30r
Legal Fees				
Combination hunting and fishing license	yr	21.75	4/01	34s
Divorce, filing fee		83.00	4/01	35s
Driver's license fee	orig	15.00	1999	48s
Driver's license fee	renew	15.00	1999	48s
Fishing license	yr	12.75	4/01	34s
Personal Goods				
Personal care products and services purchases	yr	385	1999	30r
Shampoo, Alberto VO5	15 oz	1.12	3/01	4c

Lincoln, NE - continued

Item	Per	Value	Date	Ref.
Personal Goods - continued				
Toothpaste, Crest or Colgate	6-7 oz	2.41	3/01	4c
Personal Services				
Dry cleaning, man's 2-pc suit		7.70	3/01	4c
Man's haircut, barbershop, no styling		10.80	3/01	4c
Personal services, household, expenditures on	yr	300	1999	30r
Woman's shampoo, trim, blow-dry, no style-change		22.20	3/01	4c
Pets				
Pets, toys, and playground equipment, expenditures on	yr	375	1999	30r
Restaurant Food				
Chicken, fried, thigh and drumstick, KFC/Church's		2.30	3/01	4c
Hamburger with cheese, McDonald's	1/4 lb	2.09	3/01	4c
Pizza, Pizza Hut or Pizza Inn	11-12 in	9.49	3/01	4c
Taxes				
Federal income taxes paid	yr	2326	1999	30r
Personal taxes, expenditures on	yr	3223	1999	30r
Property taxes paid	yr	1152	1999	30r
State and local income taxes paid	yr	753	1999	30r
Transportation				
Transportation, ACCRA Index		99.20	3/01	4c
Bus fare, to central business district	1-way	0.85	3/01	4c
Cars and trucks, new, expenditures on	yr	1280	1999	30r
Cars and trucks, used, expenditures on	yr	1763	1999	30r
Diesel at the pump	gal	1.26	10/99	73s
Gasoline and motor oil purchases	yr	1036	1999	30r
Gasoline before-tax price (cents)	gal	111.50	10/00	43s
Maintenance and repair expenditures	yr	594	1999	30r
Motorcycle license fee	renew	3.75	1999	49s
Motorcycle license fee	orig	15.00	1999	49s
Public transportation, expenditures on	yr	341	1999	30r
Tire balance, computer or spin balance, front	wheel	7.90	3/01	4c
Transportation purchases	yr	6617	1999	30r
Vehicle expenses, miscellaneous, purchases	yr	2159	1999	30r
Vehicle insurance payments	yr	701	1999	30r
Vehicle purchases (net outlay)	yr	3081	1999	30r
Vehicle rental, lease expenditures	yr	536	1999	30r
Utilities				
Utilities, ACCRA Index		123.50	3/01	4c
Electrical bill, average	mos	60.00	9/00	9s
Electricity, expenditures on	yr	841	1999	30r
Electricity and other, mixed, 2400 sq ft, new home	mos	46.32	3/01	4c
Electricity cost, average	KWh	5.30	9/00	9s
Utilities, fuels, and public services purchased	yr	2401	1999	30r
Water and other public services, expenditures on	yr	273	1999	30r
Water price	100 cf	1.09	2000	109c
Water price, dwelling unit	mos	21.31	2000	109c
Weddings				
Wedding (national average cost)		19936	2000	33r
Wedding (regional average total cost)		16195	1997	110r
Attendants' gifts		321	1998	33r
Bridal attendants' apparel (5 persons)		824	2000	33r
Bride's headpiece/veil		173	1998	33r
Bride's wedding dress		859	1998	33r
Clergy, religious facility fee		242	1998	33r
Engagement ring		3177	1998	33r
Flowers		789	1998	33r
Groom's formalwear rental		99	2000	33r
Limousine		410	1998	33r
Marriage license cost		15.00	4/01	35s
Men's formalwear (ushers, best man)		469	2000	33r
Mother of bride apparel		241	2000	33r
Music		866	1998	33r
Photography and videography		1368	1998	33r

Values are in dollars or fractions of dollars. In the column headed *Ref*, references are shown to sources. Each reference is followed by a letter. These refer to the geographical level for which data were reported: s=State, r=Region, and c=City or metro. The abbreviation *ex* is used to mean *except* or *excluding*; *exp* stands for *expenditures*. For other abbreviations and further explanations, please see the Introduction.

Lincoln, NE - continued

Item	Per	Value	Date	Ref.
Weddings				
Rehearsal dinner		728	1998	33r
Wedding invitations and announcements		341	1998	33r
Wedding reception		7968	2000	33r
Wedding rings (bride and groom)		1060	1998	33r

Little Rock-North Little Rock, AR

Item	Per	Value	Date	Ref.
Composite, ACCRA index		95.20	12/00	5c
Alcoholic Beverages				
Alcoholic beverage purchases	yr	253	1999	30r
Beer, Heineken, 12-oz, ex deposit	6	7.47	12/00	5c
J & B Scotch	750-ml	22.20	12/00	5c
Malt beverages, all types, all sizes, any origin	16 oz	0.96	7/01	11r
Wine, Livingston or Gallo, Chablis blanc	1.5 liter	4.99	12/00	5c
Appliances				
Appliance repair, service call, washing machine	min lab chg	66.80	12/00	5c
Major appliances, expenditures on	yr	172	1999	30r
Small appliances, housewares, expenditures on	yr	81	1999	30r
Banking and Money				
Mortgage interest and charges paid	yr	2039	1999	30r
Mortgage principal paid on owned property	yr	1026	1999	30r
Mortgage rate, incl. points and orig. fee, 30-yr. conv. fixed or ARM	mos	7.65	12/00	5c
Vehicle finance charges paid	yr	365	1999	30r
Business Expenses				
Business travel, car rental	day	53	2001	3c
Business travel, food	day	45	2001	3c
Business travel, hotel	day	78	2001	3c
Charity				
Cash contributions, expenditures	yr	1127	1999	30r
Child Care				
Child raising cost, total, age 0-2	yr	8540	1999	60r
Child raising cost, total, age 3-5	yr	8780	1999	60r
Child raising cost, total, age 6-8	yr	8820	1999	60r
Child raising cost, total, age 9-11	yr	8800	1999	60r
Child raising cost, total, age 12-14	yr	9510	1999	60r
Child raising cost, total, age 15-17	yr	9740	1999	60r
Child's child care and education, age 0-2	yr	1380	1999	60r
Child's child care and education, age 3-5	yr	1520	1999	60r
Child's child care and education, age 6-8	yr	990	1999	60r
Child's child care and education, age 9-11	yr	650	1999	60r
Child's child care and education, age 12-14	yr	490	1999	60r
Child's child care and education, age 15-17	yr	840	1999	60r
Child's clothing, age 0-2	yr	480	1999	60r
Child's clothing, age 3-5	yr	470	1999	60r
Child's clothing, age 6-8	yr	520	1999	60r
Child's clothing, age 9-11	yr	570	1999	60r
Child's clothing, age 12-14	yr	950	1999	60r
Child's clothing, age 15-17	yr	850	1999	60r
Child's food, age 0-2	yr	1000	1999	60r
Child's food, age 3-5	yr	1160	1999	60r
Child's food, age 6-8	yr	1490	1999	60r
Child's food, age 9-11	yr	1770	1999	60r
Child's food, age 12-14	yr	1770	1999	60r
Child's food, age 15-17	yr	1980	1999	60r
Child's health care, age 0-2	yr	620	1999	60r
Child's health care, age 3-5	yr	590	1999	60r
Child's health care, age 6-8	yr	680	1999	60r
Child's health care, age 9-11	yr	720	1999	60r
Child's health care, age 12-14	yr	730	1999	60r
Child's health care, age 15-17	yr	760	1999	60r
Child's housing, age 0-2	yr	3070	1999	60r
Child's housing, age 3-5	yr	3050	1999	60r
Child's housing, age 6-8	yr	3010	1999	60r
Child's housing, age 9-11	yr	2850	1999	60r
Child's housing, age 12-14	yr	3040	1999	60r

Little Rock-North Little Rock, AR - continued

Item	Per	Value	Date	Ref.
Child Care - continued				
Child's housing, age 15-17	yr	2650	1999	60r
Child's personal care, reading, age 0-2	yr	910	1999	60r
Child's personal care, reading, age 3-5	yr	930	1999	60r
Child's personal care, reading, age 6-8	yr	960	1999	60r
Child's personal care, reading, age 9-11	yr	1000	1999	60r
Child's personal care, reading, age 12-14	yr	1170	1999	60r
Child's personal care, reading, age 15-17	yr	950	1999	60r
Daycare	mos	319	1998	37c
Daycare, 3-year old, 5 days, 8 hrs/day	mos	319	1998	85c
Clothing				
Apparel and services purchases	yr	1610	1999	30r
Boys' brief, cotton	3	4.11	12/00	5c
Boys, 2 to 15, expenditures on	yr	89	1999	30r
Children under 2, expenditures on	yr	79	1999	30r
Footwear, expenditures on	yr	283	1999	30r
Girls, 2 to 15, expenditures on	yr	103	1999	30r
Men and boys, expenditures on	yr	351	1999	30r
Men, 16 and over, expenditures on	yr	262	1999	30r
Shirt, man's dress shirt		27.70	12/00	5c
Slacks, man's "No Wrinkles" khaki		36.99	12/00	5c
Women, 16 and over, expenditures on	yr	538	1999	30r
Communications				
Newspaper subscription, daily and Sunday delivery	mos	9.95	12/00	5c
Phone line, single, business, field visit	inst.	84.00	12/97	17s
Phone line, single, business, no field visit	inst.	84.00	12/97	17s
Phone line, single, residence, field visit	inst.	39.70	12/97	17s
Phone line, single, residence, no field visit	inst.	39.70	12/97	17s
Postage and stationery, expenditures on	yr	104	1999	30r
Postal rate, express mail, up to half-pound		12.45	7/01	108r
Postal rate, letter, first class, first ounce		0.34	7/01	108r
Postal rate, letter, two ounces		0.57	7/01	108r
Postal rate, post card		0.21	7/01	108r
Postal rate, priority mail, two pounds		3.95	7/01	108r
Postal rate, priority mail, up to one pound		3.50	7/01	108r
Telephone bill, family of three	mos	28.12	12/00	5c
Telephone services, expenditures on	yr	860	1999	30r
Education				
Board, 4-year private college/university	yr	2121	1996	38s
Board, 4-year public college/university	yr	1423	1996	38s
Education expenditures	yr	431	1999	30r
Room, 4-year private college/university	yr	1488	1996	38s
Room, 4-year public college/university	yr	1613	1996	38s
Total cost, 4-year private college/university	yr	10183	1996	38s
Total cost, 4-year public college/university	yr	5064	1996	38s
Tuition, 2-year public college/university, in state	yr	903	1996	38s
Tuition, 4-year private college/university, in state	yr	6574	1996	38s
Tuition, 4-year public college/university	yr	2028	1996	38s
Energy and Fuels				
Electricity	KWh	0.09	7/01	11r
Electricity	500 KWhs	47.29	7/01	11r
Energy, combined forms, 2400 sq ft	mos	120.68	12/00	5c
Energy, exc. electricity, 2400 sq ft	mos	37.87	12/00	5c
Fuel oil #2	gal	1.43	7/01	11r
Fuel oil and other fuels, expenditures on	yr	45	1999	30r
Gas, heating, winter, average use	mos	91.02	2/96	98c
Gas, regular unleaded, cash, self-service	gal	1.53	12/00	5c
Gasoline, all types	gal	1.60	7/01	11r
Gasoline, unleaded midgrade	gal	1.65	7/01	11r
Gasoline, unleaded premium	gal	1.74	7/01	11r
Natural gas, expenditures on	yr	164	1999	30r
Utility (piped) gas, therm		1.01	7/01	11r
Utility (piped) gas, 40 therms		44.29	7/01	11r
Utility (piped) gas, 100 therms		97.44	7/01	11r
Entertainment				
Bowling, Saturday evening rate	line	2.68	12/00	5c

Values are in dollars or fractions of dollars. In the column headed *Ref*, references are shown to sources. Each reference is followed by a letter. These refer to the geographical level for which data were reported: s=State, r=Region, and c=City or metro. The abbreviation *ex* is used to mean *except* or *excluding*; *exp* stands for *expenditures*. For other abbreviations and further explanations, please see the Introduction.

Little Rock-North Little Rock, AR - continued

Item	Per	Value	Date	Ref.
Entertainment				
Entertainment purchases	yr	1574	1999	30r
Fees and admissions paid	yr	371	1999	30r
Monopoly game, Parker Brothers', No. 9	game	9.11	12/00	5c
Movie, first-run, Saturday, evening	adm.	6.60	12/00	5c
Reading purchases	yr	121	1999	30r
Television, radios, sound equipment, expenditures on	yr	561	1999	30r
Tennis balls, yellow, Wilson or Penn, 3	can	2.45	12/00	5c
Funerals				
Total cost of funeral		5842.28	1/99	78r
Acknowledgement cards		28.35	1/99	78r
Casket		2494.29	1/99	78r
Cosmetology, hair, other preparation		109.22	1/99	78r
Embalming		361.42	1/99	78r
Funeral at funeral home		349.20	1/99	78r
Hearse (local)		161.91	1/99	78r
Professional service charges		1116.50	1/99	78r
Service car/van		65.56	1/99	78r
Transfer of remains to funeral home		143.56	1/99	78r
Vault		785.25	1/99	78r
Visitation/viewing		227.02	1/99	78r
Groceries				
Groceries, ACCRA Index		102.00	12/00	5c
American processed cheese	lb	3.50	7/01	11r
Antibiotic ointment, Polysporin	0.5 oz	3.89	12/00	5c
Baby food, strained vegetables or fruit, lowest price	4-4.5 oz	0.32	12/00	5c
Bakery products, expenditures on	yr	261	1999	30r
Bananas	lb	0.47	7/01	11r
Bananas	lb	0.59	12/00	5c
Beans, dried, any type, all sizes	lb	0.63	7/01	11r
Beef for stew, boneless	lb	2.86	7/01	11r
Beef or hamburger, ground	lb	1.54	12/00	5c
Beef, expenditures on	yr	210	1999	30r
Bologna, all beef or mixed	lb	2.29	7/01	11r
Bread, French	lb	1.66	7/01	11r
Bread, white	loaf	1.01	12/00	5c
Bread, white, pan	lb	0.87	7/01	11r
Bread, whole wheat, pan	lb	1.38	7/01	11r
Broccoli	lb	1.04	7/01	11r
Butter, salted, grade AA, stick	lb	2.26	7/01	11r
Butter, yoghurt, cheese, etc, expenditures on	yr	170	1999	30r
Cabbage	lb	0.42	7/01	11r
Cereals and cereal products, expenditures on	yr	140	1999	30r
Cheddar cheese, natural	lb	3.75	7/01	11r
Cheese, Kraft grated Parmesan	8 oz	3.89	12/00	5c
Chicken breast, bone-in	lb	1.85	7/01	11r
Chicken legs, bone-in	lb	1.34	7/01	11r
Chicken, fresh, whole	lb	1.05	7/01	11r
Chicken, whole fryer	lb	0.64	12/00	5c
Chops, boneless,	lb	4.13	7/01	11r
Chuck roast, graded and ungraded, excl U.S. prime and choice	lb	2.35	7/01	11r
Chuck roast, U.S. choice, boneless	lb	2.67	7/01	11r
Cigarettes, Winston, Kings	carton	26.90	12/00	5c
Coffee, 100%, ground roast, all sizes	lb	2.88	7/01	11r
Coffee, instant, plain, regular, all sizes	16 oz	9.25	7/01	11r
Coffee, vacuum-packed	13 oz	3.29	12/00	5c
Cola, non diet,	2 liter	1.11	7/01	11r
Corn Flakes, Kellogg's or Post Toasties	18 oz	3.43	12/00	5c
Corn, frozen, whole kernel, lowest price	16 oz	1.23	12/00	5c
Crackers, soda, salted	lb	1.70	7/01	11r
Dairy product purchases	yr	282	1999	30r
Eggs, expenditures on	yr	32	1999	30r
Eggs, Grade A or AA	dozen	1.09	12/00	5c
Fats and oils, expenditures on	yr	79	1999	30r
Fish and seafood, expenditures on	yr	99	1999	30r
Flour, white, all purpose	lb	0.32	7/01	11r
Food (excl fruit and vegetables), eaten at home, purchases	yr	815	1999	30r

Groceries - continued

Item	Per	Value	Date	Ref.
Food cooked on trips, expenditures on	yr	36	1999	30r
Food purchases	yr	4533	1999	30r
Food purchases, eaten away from home	yr	1873	1999	30r
Food purchases, food eaten at home	yr	2660	1999	30r
Fresh fruits, expenditures on	yr	128	1999	30r
Fresh milk and cream, expenditures on	yr	112	1999	30r
Fresh vegetables, expenditures on	yr	131	1999	30r
Fruit and vegetable purchases	yr	438	1999	30r
Grapefruit	lb	0.59	7/01	11r
Grapes, Thompson, seedless	lb	2.12	7/01	11r
Ground beef, 100% beef	lb	1.76	7/01	11r
Ground beef, lean and extra lean	lb	2.60	7/01	11r
Ground chuck, 100% beef	lb	2.08	7/01	11r
Ham, boneless, excl canned	lb	2.71	7/01	11r
Ham, rump or shank half, bone-in, smoked	lb	2.19	7/01	11r
Ice cream, prepackaged, bulk, regular	1/2 gal	3.93	7/01	11r
Lemons	lb	1.32	7/01	11r
Lettuce, iceberg	lb	0.76	7/01	11r
Lettuce, iceberg	head	0.99	12/00	5c
Margarine, Blue Bonnet or Parkay, stick	lb	0.99	12/00	5c
Milk, fresh, low fat,	gal	2.75	7/01	11r
Milk, fresh, whole, fortified	gal	2.97	7/01	11r
Milk, whole	1/2 gal	1.99	12/00	5c
Nonalcoholic beverages, expenditures on	yr	228	1999	30r
Orange juice, frozen concentrate	16 oz	1.95	7/01	11r
Orange juice, Minute Maid frozen	12 oz	1.69	12/00	5c
Oranges, Navel	lb	0.73	7/01	11r
Oranges, Valencia	lb	0.55	7/01	11r
Peaches, halves or slices, Hunt's, Del Monte, or Libby's	29 oz	1.47	12/00	5c
Peanut butter, creamy, all sizes	lb	1.83	7/01	11r
Pears, Anjou	lb	0.98	7/01	11r
Peas, green, Del Monte or Green Giant	15 oz	0.79	12/00	5c
Pork chops, center cut, bone-in	lb	3.33	7/01	11r
Pork sausage, fresh, loose	lb	2.59	7/01	11r
Pork shoulder picnic, bone-in, smoked	lb	1.12	7/01	11r
Pork, expenditures on	yr	162	1999	30r
Potato chips	16 oz	3.59	7/01	11r
Potatoes, frozen, french fried	lb	1.00	7/01	11r
Potatoes, white or red	10 lb	2.51	12/00	5c
Potatoes, white, all types	lb	0.44	7/01	11r
Poultry, expenditures on	yr	137	1999	30r
Processed fruits, expenditures on	yr	97	1999	30r
Processed vegetables, expenditures on	yr	82	1999	30r
Rice, white, long grain, uncooked	lb	0.51	7/01	11r
Round roast, graded and ungraded, excl U.S. prime and choice	lb	2.96	7/01	11r
Round steak, graded and ungraded, excl U.S. prime and choice	lb	3.11	7/01	11r
Sausage, Jimmy Dean/Owens pork	lb	2.95	12/00	5c
Shortening, vegetable, Crisco	3 lb	2.99	12/00	5c
Sirloin steak, graded and ungraded, excl U.S. prime and choice	lb	4.23	7/01	11r
Soft drink, Coca Cola, ex deposit	2 liter	0.99	12/00	5c
Spaghetti and macaroni	lb	0.78	7/01	11r
Steak, round, U.S. choice, boneless	lb	3.56	7/01	11r
Steak, sirloin, U.S. choice, boneless	lb	5.65	7/01	11r
Steak, T-bone	lb	5.97	12/00	5c
Strawberries, dry pint	12 oz	1.50	7/01	11r
Sugar and other sweets, expenditures on	yr	99	1999	30r
Sugar, cane or beet	4 lbs	1.83	12/00	5c
Sugar, white, 33-80 ounce package	lb	0.39	7/01	11r
Sugar, white, all sizes	lb	0.42	7/01	11r
Tobacco products and smoking supplies purchases	yr	288	1999	30r
Tomatoes, field grown	lb	1.43	7/01	11r
Tomatoes, Hunt's or Del Monte	14.5 oz	0.89	12/00	5c
Tuna, chunk, light	6 oz	0.61	12/00	5c
Tuna, light, chunk	lb	1.77	7/01	11r
Turkey, frozen, whole	lb	1.05	7/01	11r

Values are in dollars or fractions of dollars. In the column headed *Ref*, references are shown to sources. Each reference is followed by a letter. These refer to the geographical level for which data were reported: s=State, r=Region, and c=City or metro. The abbreviation *ex* is used to mean *except* or *excluding*; *exp* stands for *expenditures*. For other abbreviations and further explanations, please see the Introduction.

Little Rock-North Little Rock, AR - continued

Item	Per	Value	Date	Ref.
Goods and Services				
Miscellaneous goods and services, ACCRA Index		98.60	12/00	5c
B&B Japanese maple (acer japonicum)	gal	79.98-99.00	4/00	93r
Boxwood (buxus)	2 gal	12.98-18.99	4/00	93r
Daylilly (hemerocallis)	gal	7.96-11.00	4/00	93r
Flat of annuals		13.99-27.99	4/00	93r
Fountain grass (pennisetum)	gal	6.96-9.00	4/00	93r
Hanging basket (10 in)		9.99-24.99	4/00	93r
Hardy geranium (geranium)	gal	5.96-8.00	4/00	93r
Hosta (hosta)	gal	8.96-12.99	4/00	93r
Lilac (syrubga vulgaris)	2 gal	13.00-19.99	4/00	93r
Rhododendron (rhododendron)	2 gal	12.98-29.99	4/00	93r
Sage (salvia)	gal	5.96-8.00	4/00	93r
Wintercreeper euonymus (euonymus fortunei)	2 gal	13.00-18.99	4/00	93r
Hunting license	yr	25.00	4/01	34s
Health Care				
Health care, ACCRA Index		102.20	12/00	5c
Cardiac catheterization, ave hospital/ physician charges		12240	1998	77s
Childbirth, Cesarean delivery		11587	1997	13r
Childbirth, vaginal delivery		6725	1997	13r
Dentist's fee, adult teeth cleaning and periodic oral exam	visit	69.60	12/00	5c
Doctor's fee, routine exam, established patient	visit	71.80	12/00	5c
Drugs, expenditures on	yr	399	1999	30r
Health care purchases	yr	1971	1999	30r
Health insurance expenditures	yr	933	1999	30r
Hospital care, private room	day	369.60	12/00	5c
Hysterectomy, laproscopically-assisted, ave hospital/physician charges		10580	1998	76s
Hysterectomy, vaginal, ave hospital and physician charges		8270	1998	76s
Medicaid dispensing fee		5.51	1999	87s
Medical services expenditures	yr	547	1999	30r
Medical supplies, expenditures on	yr	91	1999	30r
Household Goods				
Dishwashing powder, Cascade	50 oz	2.89	12/00	5c
Floor coverings, expenditures on	yr	44	1999	30r
Furniture, expenditures on	yr	335	1999	30r
Household furnishings and equipment purchases	yr	1328	1999	30r
Household textiles, expenditures on	yr	89	1999	30r
Laundry and cleaning supplies, expenditures on	yr	113	1999	30r
Tissues, facial, Kleenex brand	175	1.25	12/00	5c
Housing				
Housing, ACCRA Index		79.90	12/00	5c
Home, 2200 sq ft, 4-br, 2-bath, 2-car garage, average		153750	2000	47c
Home price, existing, ave		160100	10/00	90r
Home value, median		94000	2001	53s
House, 2400 sq ft, 8000 sq ft lot, new, urban, utilities	total	167825	12/00	5c
House payment, principal and interest, 25% down payment	mos	893	12/00	5c
Household operation expenditures	yr	553	1999	30r
Housekeeping supplies purchases	yr	473	1999	30r
Housing, expenditures on	yr	10303	1999	30r

Little Rock-North Little Rock, AR - continued

Item	Per	Value	Date	Ref.
Housing - continued				
Maintenance, repairs, insurance expenditures	yr	699	1999	30r
Monthly rental value of owned home	mos	505	1999	30r
Owned dwellings, expenditures own	yr	3465	1999	30r
Rent expenditures	yr	1641	1999	30r
Rent, apartment, 2 br, 1 1/2-2 baths, unfurn, 950 sq ft, water	mos	567	12/00	5c
Rental unit, 1 bedroom, with utilities	mos	424	4/01	41c
Rental unit, 2 bedroom, with utilities	mos	504	4/01	41c
Rental unit, 3 bedroom, with utilities	mos	697	4/01	41c
Rental unit, 4 bedroom, with utilities	mos	814	4/01	41c
Shelter, expenditures on	yr	5467	1999	30r
Insurance and Pensions				
Life and other personal insurance purchases	yr	414	1999	30r
Pensions and Social Security, expenditures on	yr	2635	1999	30r
Personal insurance and pensions, expenditures on	yr	3048	1999	30r
Legal Fees				
Divorce, filing fee		100.00	4/01	35s
Driver's license fee	renew	14.00	1999	48s
Driver's license fee	orig	14.00	1999	48s
Personal Goods				
Personal care products and services purchases	yr	393	1999	30r
Shampoo, Alberto VO5	15 oz	1.29	12/00	5c
Toothpaste, Crest or Colgate	6-7 oz	2.61	12/00	5c
Personal Services				
Dry cleaning, man's 2-pc suit		6.99	12/00	5c
Man's haircut, barbershop, no styling		10.00	12/00	5c
Personal services, household, expenditures on	yr	258	1999	30r
Woman's shampoo, trim, blow-dry, no style-change		22.80	12/00	5c
Pets				
Pets, toys, and playground equipment, expenditures on	yr	306	1999	30r
Restaurant Food				
Chicken, fried, thigh and drumstick, KFC/ Church's		1.99	12/00	5c
Hamburger with cheese, McDonald's	1/4 lb	1.89	12/00	5c
Pizza, Pizza Hut or Pizza Inn	11-12 in	9.59	12/00	5c
Taxes				
Federal income taxes paid	yr	2047	1999	30r
Personal taxes, expenditures on	yr	2554	1999	30r
Property taxes paid	yr	726	1999	30r
State and local income taxes paid	yr	363	1999	30r
Transportation				
Transportation, ACCRA Index		99.60	12/00	5c
Cars and trucks, new, expenditures on	yr	1648	1999	30r
Cars and trucks, used, expenditures on	yr	1651	1999	30r
Diesel at the pump	gal	1.17	10/99	73s
Gasoline and motor oil purchases	yr	1052	1999	30r
Gasoline before-tax price (cents)	gal	102.60	10/00	43s
Maintenance and repair expenditures	yr	621	1999	30r
Public transportation, expenditures on	yr	298	1999	30r
Tire balance, computer or spin balance, front	wheel	7.50	12/00	5c
Transportation purchases	yr	6738	1999	30r
Vehicle expenses, miscellaneous, purchases	yr	2033	1999	30r
Vehicle insurance payments	yr	696	1999	30r
Vehicle purchases (net outlay)	yr	3354	1999	30r
Vehicle rental, lease expenditures	yr	352	1999	30r
Utilities				
Utilities, ACCRA Index		110.70	12/00	5c
Electrical bill, average	mos	75.00	9/00	9s
Electricity, expenditures on	yr	1115	1999	30r
Electricity, summer, 250 KWh	mos	30.52	2/96	97c

Values are in dollars or fractions of dollars. In the column headed *Ref*, references are shown to sources. Each reference is followed by a letter. These refer to the geographical level for which data were reported: s=State, r=Region, and c=City or metro. The abbreviation *ex* is used to mean *except* or *excluding*; *exp* stands for *expenditures*. For other abbreviations and further explanations, please see the Introduction.

Little Rock-North Little Rock, AR - continued

Item	Per	Value	Date	Ref.
Utilities				
Electricity, summer, 500 KWh	mos	53.74	2/96	97c
Electricity, summer, 750 KWh	mos	76.94	2/96	97c
Electricity, summer, 1000 KWh	mos	100.14	2/96	97c
Electricity and other, mixed, 2400 sq ft, new home	mos	82.81	12/00	5c
Electricity cost, average	KWh	5.70	9/00	9s
Water and other public services, expenditures on	yr	298	1999	30r
Weddings				
Wedding (national average cost)		19936	2000	33r
Attendants' gifts		321	1998	33r
Bridal attendants' apparel (5 persons)		824	2000	33r
Bride's headpiece/veil		173	1998	33r
Bride's wedding dress		859	1998	33r
Clergy, religious facility fee		242	1998	33r
Engagement ring		3177	1998	33r
Flowers		789	1998	33r
Groom's formalwear rental		99	2000	33r
Limousine		410	1998	33r
Marriage license cost		30.00	4/01	35s
Men's formalwear (ushers, best man)		469	2000	33r
Mother of bride apparel		241	2000	33r
Music		866	1998	33r
Photography and videography		1368	1998	33r
Rehearsal dinner		728	1998	33r
Wedding invitations and announcements		341	1998	33r
Wedding reception		7968	2000	33r
Wedding rings (bride and groom)		1060	1998	33r

Longview-Marshall, TX

Item	Per	Value	Date	Ref.
Alcoholic Beverages				
Alcoholic beverage purchases	yr	253	1999	30r
Malt beverages, all types, all sizes, any origin	16 oz	0.96	7/01	11r
Appliances				
Major appliances, expenditures on	yr	172	1999	30r
Small appliances, housewares, expenditures on	yr	81	1999	30r
Banking and Money				
Mortgage interest and charges paid	yr	2039	1999	30r
Mortgage principal paid on owned property	yr	1026	1999	30r
Vehicle finance charges paid	yr	365	1999	30r
Charity				
Cash contributions, expenditures on	yr	1127	1999	30r
Child Care				
Child raising cost, total, age 0-2	yr	8540	1999	60r
Child raising cost, total, age 3-5	yr	8780	1999	60r
Child raising cost, total, age 6-8	yr	8820	1999	60r
Child raising cost, total, age 9-11	yr	8800	1999	60r
Child raising cost, total, age 12-14	yr	9510	1999	60r
Child raising cost, total, age 15-17	yr	9740	1999	60r
Child's child care and education, age 0-2	yr	1380	1999	60r
Child's child care and education, age 3-5	yr	1520	1999	60r
Child's child care and education, age 6-8	yr	990	1999	60r
Child's child care and education, age 9-11	yr	650	1999	60r
Child's child care and education, age 12-14	yr	490	1999	60r
Child's child care and education, age 15-17	yr	840	1999	60r
Child's clothing, age 0-2	yr	480	1999	60r
Child's clothing, age 3-5	yr	470	1999	60r
Child's clothing, age 6-8	yr	520	1999	60r
Child's clothing, age 9-11	yr	570	1999	60r
Child's clothing, age 12-14	yr	950	1999	60r
Child's clothing, age 15-17	yr	850	1999	60r
Child's food, age 0-2	yr	1000	1999	60r
Child's food, age 3-5	yr	1160	1999	60r
Child's food, age 6-8	yr	1490	1999	60r
Child's food, age 9-11	yr	1770	1999	60r
Child's food, age 12-14	yr	1770	1999	60r

Longview-Marshall, TX - continued

Item	Per	Value	Date	Ref.
Child Care - continued				
Child's food, age 15-17	yr	1980	1999	60r
Child's health care, age 0-2	yr	620	1999	60r
Child's health care, age 3-5	yr	590	1999	60r
Child's health care, age 6-8	yr	680	1999	60r
Child's health care, age 9-11	yr	720	1999	60r
Child's health care, age 12-14	yr	730	1999	60r
Child's health care, age 15-17	yr	760	1999	60r
Child's housing, age 0-2	yr	3070	1999	60r
Child's housing, age 3-5	yr	3050	1999	60r
Child's housing, age 6-8	yr	3010	1999	60r
Child's housing, age 9-11	yr	2850	1999	60r
Child's housing, age 12-14	yr	3040	1999	60r
Child's housing, age 15-17	yr	2650	1999	60r
Child's personal care, reading, age 0-2	yr	910	1999	60r
Child's personal care, reading, age 3-5	yr	930	1999	60r
Child's personal care, reading, age 6-8	yr	960	1999	60r
Child's personal care, reading, age 9-11	yr	1000	1999	60r
Child's personal care, reading, age 12-14	yr	1170	1999	60r
Child's personal care, reading, age 15-17	yr	950	1999	60r
Clothing				
Apparel and services purchases	yr	1610	1999	30r
Boys, 2 to 15, expenditures on	yr	89	1999	30r
Children under 2, expenditures on	yr	79	1999	30r
Footwear, expenditures on	yr	283	1999	30r
Girls, 2 to 15, expenditures on	yr	103	1999	30r
Men and boys, expenditures on	yr	351	1999	30r
Men, 16 and over, expenditures on	yr	262	1999	30r
Women, 16 and over, expenditures on	yr	538	1999	30r
Communications				
Cable modem installation, AT&T-BIS		150.00	6/99	103s
Cable modem installation, Marcus		499.00	6/99	103s
Cable modem installation, Time Warner		75.00-225.00	6/99	103s
Cable modem rate, cable subscriber, AT&T-BIS	mos	39.95	6/99	103s
Cable modem rate, cable subscriber, Marcus	mos	14.95-49.95	6/99	103s
Cable modem rate, cable subscriber, Time Warner	mos	39.95-49.95	6/99	103s
Cable modem rate, non-cable subscriber, Marcus	mos	60.95	6/99	103s
Cable modem rate, non-cable subscriber, Time Warner	mos	39.95-54.95	6/99	103s
Phone line, single, business, field visit	inst.	71.90	12/97	17s
Phone line, single, business, no field visit	inst.	57.30	12/97	17s
Phone line, single, residence, field visit	inst.	52.95	12/97	17s
Phone line, single, residence, no field visit	inst.	38.35	12/97	17s
Postage and stationery, expenditures on	yr	104	1999	30r
Postal rate, express mail, up to half-pound		12.45	7/01	108r
Postal rate, letter, first class, first ounce		0.34	7/01	108r
Postal rate, letter, two ounces		0.57	7/01	108r
Postal rate, post card		0.21	7/01	108r
Postal rate, priority mail, two pounds		3.95	7/01	108r
Postal rate, priority mail, up to one pound		3.50	7/01	108r
Telephone services, expenditures on	yr	860	1999	30r
Education				
Board, 4-year private college/university	yr	2198	1996	38s
Board, 4-year public college/university	yr	1759	1996	38s
Education expenditures	yr	431	1999	30r
Room, 4-year private college/university	yr	2000	1996	38s
Room, 4-year public college/university	yr	1885	1996	38s
Total cost, 4-year private college/university	yr	13156	1996	38s
Total cost, 4-year public college/university	yr	5464	1996	38s
Tuition, 2-year public college/university, in state	yr	771	1996	38s
Tuition, 4-year private college/university, in state	yr	8959	1996	38s
Tuition, 4-year public college/university	yr	1820	1996	38s

Values are in dollars or fractions of dollars. In the column headed *Ref*, references are shown to sources. Each reference is followed by a letter. These refer to the geographical level for which data were reported: s=State, r=Region, and c=City or metro. The abbreviation *ex* is used to mean *except* or *excluding*; *exp* stands for expenditures. For other abbreviations and further explanations, please see the Introduction.

Longview-Marshall, TX - continued

Item	Per	Value	Date	Ref.
Energy and Fuels				
Electricity	KWh	0.09	7/01	11r
Electricity	500 KWhs	47.29	7/01	11r
Fuel oil #2	gal	1.43	7/01	11r
Fuel oil and other fuels, expenditures on	yr	45	1999	30r
Gas, natural, commercial rate	1000 cf	6.94	11/00	88s
Gasoline, all types	gal	1.60	7/01	11r
Gasoline, unleaded midgrade	gal	1.65	7/01	11r
Gasoline, unleaded premium	gal	1.74	7/01	11r
Natural gas, expenditures on	yr	164	1999	30r
Utility (piped) gas, therm		1.01	7/01	11r
Utility (piped) gas, 40 therms		44.29	7/01	11r
Utility (piped) gas, 100 therms		97.44	7/01	11r
Entertainment				
Entertainment purchases	yr	1574	1999	30r
Fees and admissions paid	yr	371	1999	30r
Reading purchases	yr	121	1999	30r
Television, radios, sound equipment, expenditures on	yr	561	1999	30r
Funerals				
Total cost of funeral		5842.28	1/99	78r
Acknowledgement cards		28.35	1/99	78r
Casket		2494.29	1/99	78r
Cosmetology, hair, other preparation		109.22	1/99	78r
Embalming		361.42	1/99	78r
Funeral at funeral home		349.20	1/99	78r
Hearse (local)		161.91	1/99	78r
Professional service charges		1116.50	1/99	78r
Service car/van		65.56	1/99	78r
Transfer of remains to funeral home		143.56	1/99	78r
Vault		785.25	1/99	78r
Visitation/viewing		227.02	1/99	78r
Groceries				
American processed cheese	lb	3.50	7/01	11r
Bakery products, expenditures on	yr	261	1999	30r
Bananas	lb	0.47	7/01	11r
Beans, dried, any type, all sizes	lb	0.63	7/01	11r
Beef for stew, boneless	lb	2.86	7/01	11r
Beef, expenditures on	yr	210	1999	30r
Bologna, all beef or mixed	lb	2.29	7/01	11r
Bread, French	lb	1.66	7/01	11r
Bread, white, pan	lb	0.87	7/01	11r
Bread, whole wheat, pan	lb	1.38	7/01	11r
Broccoli	lb	1.04	7/01	11r
Butter, salted, grade AA, stick	lb	2.26	7/01	11r
Butter, yoghurt, cheese, etc, expenditures on	yr	170	1999	30r
Cabbage	lb	0.42	7/01	11r
Cereals and cereal products, expenditures on	yr	140	1999	30r
Cheddar cheese, natural	lb	3.75	7/01	11r
Chicken breast, bone-in	lb	1.85	7/01	11r
Chicken legs, bone-in	lb	1.34	7/01	11r
Chicken, fresh, whole	lb	1.05	7/01	11r
Chops, boneless,	lb	4.13	7/01	11r
Chuck roast, graded and ungraded, excl U.S. prime and choice	lb	2.35	7/01	11r
Chuck roast, U.S. choice, boneless	lb	2.67	7/01	11r
Coffee, 100%, ground roast, all sizes	lb	2.88	7/01	11r
Coffee, instant, plain, regular, all sizes	16 oz	9.25	7/01	11r
Cola, non diet,	2 liter	1.11	7/01	11r
Crackers, soda, salted	lb	1.70	7/01	11r
Dairy product purchases	yr	282	1999	30r
Eggs, expenditures on	yr	32	1999	30r
Fats and oils, expenditures on	yr	79	1999	30r
Fish and seafood, expenditures on	yr	99	1999	30r
Flour, white, all purpose	lb	0.32	7/01	11r
Food (excl fruit and vegetables), eaten at home, purchases	yr	815	1999	30r
Food cooked on trips, expenditures on	yr	36	1999	30r
Food purchases	yr	4533	1999	30r
Food purchases, eaten away from home	yr	1873	1999	30r

Longview-Marshall, TX - continued

Item	Per	Value	Date	Ref.
Groceries - continued				
Food purchases, food eaten at home	yr	2660	1999	30r
Fresh fruits, expenditures on	yr	128	1999	30r
Fresh milk and cream, expenditures on	yr	112	1999	30r
Fresh vegetables, expenditures on	yr	131	1999	30r
Fruit and vegetable purchases	yr	438	1999	30r
Grapefruit	lb	0.59	7/01	11r
Grapes, Thompson, seedless	lb	2.12	7/01	11r
Ground beef, 100% beef	lb	1.76	7/01	11r
Ground beef, lean and extra lean	lb	2.60	7/01	11r
Ground chuck, 100% beef	lb	2.08	7/01	11r
Ham, boneless, excl canned	lb	2.71	7/01	11r
Ham, rump or shank half, bone-in, smoked	lb	2.19	7/01	11r
Ice cream, prepackaged, bulk, regular	1/2 gal	3.93	7/01	11r
Lemons	lb	1.32	7/01	11r
Lettuce, iceberg	lb	0.76	7/01	11r
Milk, fresh, low fat,	gal	2.75	7/01	11r
Milk, fresh, whole, fortified	gal	2.97	7/01	11r
Nonalcoholic beverages, expenditures on	yr	228	1999	30r
Orange juice, frozen concentrate	16 oz	1.95	7/01	11r
Oranges, Navel	lb	0.73	7/01	11r
Oranges, Valencia	lb	0.55	7/01	11r
Peanut butter, creamy, all sizes	lb	1.83	7/01	11r
Pears, Anjou	lb	0.98	7/01	11r
Pork chops, center cut, bone-in	lb	3.33	7/01	11r
Pork sausage, fresh, loose	lb	2.59	7/01	11r
Pork shoulder picnic, bone-in, smoked	lb	1.12	7/01	11r
Pork, expenditures on	yr	162	1999	30r
Potato chips	16 oz	3.59	7/01	11r
Potatoes, frozen, french fried	lb	1.00	7/01	11r
Potatoes, white, all types	lb	0.44	7/01	11r
Poultry, expenditures on	yr	137	1999	30r
Processed fruits, expenditures on	yr	97	1999	30r
Processed vegetables, expenditures on	yr	82	1999	30r
Rice, white, long grain, uncooked	lb	0.51	7/01	11r
Round roast, graded and ungraded, excl U.S. prime and choice	lb	2.96	7/01	11r
Round steak, graded and ungraded, excl U.S. prime and choice	lb	3.11	7/01	11r
Sirloin steak, graded and ungraded, excl U.S. prime and choice	lb	4.23	7/01	11r
Spaghetti and macaroni	lb	0.78	7/01	11r
Steak, round, U.S. choice, boneless	lb	3.56	7/01	11r
Steak, sirloin, U.S. choice, boneless	lb	5.65	7/01	11r
Strawberries, dry pint	12 oz	1.50	7/01	11r
Sugar and other sweets, expenditures on	yr	99	1999	30r
Sugar, white, 33-80 ounce package	lb	0.39	7/01	11r
Sugar, white, all sizes	lb	0.42	7/01	11r
Tobacco products and smoking supplies purchases	yr	288	1999	30r
Tomatoes, field grown	lb	1.43	7/01	11r
Tuna, light, chunk	lb	1.77	7/01	11r
Turkey, frozen, whole	lb	1.05	7/01	11r
Goods and Services				
B&B Japanese maple (acer japonicum)	gal	79.98-99.00	4/00	93r
Boxwood (buxus)	2 gal	12.98-18.99	4/00	93r
Christmas tree, noble fir		40-60	2000	65s
Daylily (hemerocallis)	gal	7.96-11.00	4/00	93r
Flat of annuals		13.99-27.99	4/00	93r
Fountain grass (pennisetum)	gal	6.96-9.00	4/00	93r
Hanging basket (10 in)		9.99-24.99	4/00	93r
Hardy geranium (geranium)	gal	5.96-8.00	4/00	93r
Hosta (hosta)	gal	8.96-12.99	4/00	93r
Lilac (syrubga vulgaris)	2 gal	13.00-19.99	4/00	93r

Values are in dollars or fractions of dollars. In the column headed *Ref*, references are shown to sources. Each reference is followed by a letter. These refer to the geographical level for which data were reported: s=State, r=Region, and c=City or metro. The abbreviation *ex* is used to mean *except* or *excluding*; *exp* stands for expenditures. For other abbreviations and further explanations, please see the Introduction.

Longview-Marshall, TX - continued

Item	Per	Value	Date	Ref.
Goods and Services				
Rhododendron (rhododendron)	2 gal	12.98-29.99	4/00	93r
Sage (salvia)	gal	5.96-8.00	4/00	93r
Wintercreeper euonymus (euonymus fortunei)	2 gal	13.00-18.99	4/00	93r
Hunting license	yr	19.00	4/01	34s
Health Care				
Cardiac catheterization, ave hospital/ physician charges		20140	1998	77s
Childbirth, Cesarean delivery		11587	1997	13r
Childbirth, vaginal delivery		6725	1997	13r
Drugs, expenditures on	yr	399	1999	30r
Health care purchases	yr	1971	1999	30r
Health insurance expenditures	yr	933	1999	30r
Hysterectomy, laproscopically-assisted, ave hospital/physician charges		15700	1998	76s
Hysterectomy, vaginal, ave hospital and physician charges		12180	1998	76s
Medicaid dispensing fee		5.27	1999	87s
Medical services expenditures	yr	547	1999	30r
Medical supplies, expenditures on	yr	91	1999	30r
Household Goods				
Floor coverings, expenditures on	yr	44	1999	30r
Furniture, expenditures on	yr	335	1999	30r
Household furnishings and equipment purchases	yr	1328	1999	30r
Household textiles, expenditures on	yr	89	1999	30r
Laundry and cleaning supplies, expenditures on	yr	113	1999	30r
Housing				
Home price, existing, ave		160100	10/00	90r
Home value, median		112000	2001	53s
Household operation expenditures	yr	553	1999	30r
Housekeeping supplies purchases	yr	473	1999	30r
Housing, expenditures on	yr	10303	1999	30r
Maintenance, repairs, insurance expenditures	yr	699	1999	30r
Monthly rental value of owned home	mos	505	1999	30r
Owned dwellings, expenditures own	yr	3465	1999	30r
Rent expenditures	yr	1641	1999	30r
Rental unit, 1 bedroom, with utilities	mos	363	4/01	41c
Rental unit, 2 bedroom, with utilities	mos	445	4/01	41c
Rental unit, 3 bedroom, with utilities	mos	607	4/01	41c
Rental unit, 4 bedroom, with utilities	mos	662	4/01	41c
Shelter, expenditures on	yr	5467	1999	30r
Insurance and Pensions				
Life and other personal insurance purchases	yr	414	1999	30r
Pensions and Social Security, expenditures on	yr	2635	1999	30r
Personal insurance and pensions, expenditures on	yr	3048	1999	30r
Legal Fees				
Divorce, filing fee		150.00-200.00	4/01	35s
Driver's license fee	orig	24.00	1999	48s
Driver's license fee	renew	20.00	1999	48s
Fishing license	yr	19.00	4/01	34s
Personal Goods				
Personal care products and services purchases	yr	393	1999	30r
Personal Services				
Personal services, household, expenditures on	yr	258	1999	30r
Pets				
Pets, toys, and playground equipment, expenditures on	yr	306	1999	30r

Longview-Marshall, TX - continued

Item	Per	Value	Date	Ref.
Taxes				
Federal income taxes paid	yr	2047	1999	30r
Personal taxes, expenditures on	yr	2554	1999	30r
Property taxes paid	yr	726	1999	30r
State and local income taxes paid	yr	363	1999	30r
Transportation				
Cars and trucks, new, expenditures on	yr	1648	1999	30r
Cars and trucks, used, expenditures on	yr	1651	1999	30r
Diesel at the pump	gal	1.18	10/99	73s
Gasoline and motor oil purchases	yr	1052	1999	30r
Gasoline before-tax price (cents)	gal	101.30	10/00	43s
Maintenance and repair expenditures	yr	621	1999	30r
Public transportation, expenditures on	yr	298	1999	30r
Transportation purchases	yr	6738	1999	30r
Vehicle expenses, miscellaneous, purchases	yr	2033	1999	30r
Vehicle insurance payments	yr	696	1999	30r
Vehicle purchases (net outlay)	yr	3354	1999	30r
Vehicle rental, lease expenditures	yr	352	1999	30r
Utilities				
Electrical bill, average	mos	87.17	9/00	9s
Electricity, expenditures on	yr	1115	1999	30r
Electricity cost, average	KWh	6.48	9/00	9s
Water and other public services, expenditures on	yr	298	1999	30r
Weddings				
Wedding (national average cost)		19936	2000	33r
Attendants' gifts		321	1998	33r
Bridal attendants' apparel (5 persons)		824	2000	33r
Bride's headpiece/veil		173	1998	33r
Bride's wedding dress		859	1998	33r
Clergy, religious facility fee		242	1998	33r
Engagement ring		3177	1998	33r
Flowers		789	1998	33r
Groom's formalwear rental		99	2000	33r
Limousine		410	1998	33r
Marriage license cost		36.00	4/01	35s
Men's formalwear (ushers, best man)		469	2000	33r
Mother of bride apparel		241	2000	33r
Music		866	1998	33r
Photography and videography		1368	1998	33r
Rehearsal dinner		728	1998	33r
Wedding invitations and announcements		341	1998	33r
Wedding reception		7968	2000	33r
Wedding rings (bride and groom)		1060	1998	33r

Los Angeles, CA

Item	Per	Value	Date	Ref.
Average annual expenditures	yr	43225	1999	30c
Alcoholic Beverages				
Alcoholic beverage purchases	yr	297	1999	30c
Malt beverages, all types, all sizes, any origin	16 oz	0.94	7/01	11r
Wine, red and white table, all sizes, any origin	liter	6.00	7/01	11r
Appliances				
Major appliances, expenditures on	yr	167	1999	30r
Small appliances, housewares, expenditures on	yr	105	1999	30r
Banking and Money				
Mortgage interest and charges paid	yr	3368	1999	30r
Mortgage principal paid on owned property	yr	1677	1999	30r
Vehicle finance charges paid	yr	311	1999	30r
Business Expenses				
Business travel, car rental	day	56	2001	3c
Business travel, food	day	65	2001	3c
Business travel, hotel	day	178	2001	3c
Medical office space cost	sq ft	130.04	2001	31c
Office space, 2-4 storey building	sq ft	113.93	2001	31c
Office space, 5-10 storey building	sq ft	100.63	2001	31c
Office space, 11-20 storey building	sq ft	96.73	2001	31c

Values are in dollars or fractions of dollars. In the column headed *Ref*, references are shown to sources. Each reference is followed by a letter. These refer to the geographical level for which data were reported: s=State, r=Region, and c=City or metro. The abbreviation *ex* is used to mean *except* or *excluding*; *exp* stands for *expenditures*. For other abbreviations and further explanations, please see the Introduction.

Los Angeles, CA - continued

Item	Per	Value	Date	Ref.
Charity				
Cash contributions, expenditures	yr	1352	1999	30c
Child Care				
Child raising cost, total, age 0-2	yr	9140	1999	60r
Child raising cost, total, age 3-5	yr	9370	1999	60r
Child raising cost, total, age 6-8	yr	9450	1999	60r
Child raising cost, total, age 9-11	yr	9470	1999	60r
Child raising cost, total, age 12-14	yr	10170	1999	60r
Child raising cost, total, age 15-17	yr	10360	1999	60r
Child's child care and education, age 0-2	yr	1250	1999	60r
Child's child care and education, age 3-5	yr	1380	1999	60r
Child's child care and education, age 6-8	yr	890	1999	60r
Child's child care and education, age 9-11	yr	580	1999	60r
Child's child care and education, age 12-14	yr	430	1999	60r
Child's child care and education, age 15-17	yr	730	1999	60r
Child's clothing, age 0-2	yr	430	1999	60r
Child's clothing, age 3-5	yr	420	1999	60r
Child's clothing, age 6-8	yr	470	1999	60r
Child's clothing, age 9-11	yr	520	1999	60r
Child's clothing, age 12-14	yr	870	1999	60r
Child's clothing, age 15-17	yr	770	1999	60r
Child's food, age 0-2	yr	1120	1999	60r
Child's food, age 3-5	yr	1280	1999	60r
Child's food, age 6-8	yr	1640	1999	60r
Child's food, age 9-11	yr	1930	1999	60r
Child's food, age 12-14	yr	1940	1999	60r
Child's food, age 15-17	yr	2150	1999	60r
Child's health care, age 0-2	yr	490	1999	60r
Child's health care, age 3-5	yr	470	1999	60r
Child's health care, age 6-8	yr	530	1999	60r
Child's health care, age 9-11	yr	570	1999	60r
Child's health care, age 12-14	yr	580	1999	60r
Child's health care, age 15-17	yr	610	1999	60r
Child's housing, age 0-2	yr	3630	1999	60r
Child's housing, age 3-5	yr	3610	1999	60r
Child's housing, age 6-8	yr	3570	1999	60r
Child's housing, age 9-11	yr	3410	1999	60r
Child's housing, age 12-14	yr	3600	1999	60r
Child's housing, age 15-17	yr	3210	1999	60r
Child's personal care, reading, age 0-2	yr	1040	1999	60r
Child's personal care, reading, age 3-5	yr	1060	1999	60r
Child's personal care, reading, age 6-8	yr	1090	1999	60r
Child's personal care, reading, age 9-11	yr	1130	1999	60r
Child's personal care, reading, age 12-14	yr	1300	1999	60r
Child's personal care, reading, age 15-17	yr	1080	1999	60r
Clothing				
Apparel and services purchases	yr	2158	1999	30c
Boys, 2 to 15, expenditures on	yr	80	1999	30r
Children under 2, expenditures on	yr	74	1999	30r
Footwear, expenditures on	yr	307	1999	30r
Girls, 2 to 15, expenditures on	yr	101	1999	30r
Men and boys, expenditures on	yr	443	1999	30r
Men, 16 and over, expenditures on	yr	363	1999	30r
Women, 16 and over, expenditures on	yr	594	1999	30r
Communications				
Cable modem installation, AT&T-BIS		150.00	6/99	103s
Cable modem installation, Charter		99.00-169.00	6/99	103s
Cable modem installation, Comcast		95.00	6/99	103s
Cable modem installation, Cox		99.00-174.95	6/99	103s
Cable modem installation, Media One		100.00	6/99	103s
Cable modem installation, Time Warner		75.00-225.00	6/99	103s
Cable modem rate, cable subscriber, AT&T-BIS	mos	39.95	6/99	103s
Cable modem rate, cable subscriber, Charter	mos	49.95-79.95	6/99	103s
Cable modem rate, cable subscriber, Comcast	mos	39.95	6/99	103s
Cable modem rate, cable subscriber, Cox	mos	29.95-44.95	6/99	103s

Los Angeles, CA - continued

Item	Per	Value	Date	Ref.
Communications - continued				
Cable modem rate, cable subscriber, Media One	mos	34.95-39.95	6/99	103s
Cable modem rate, cable subscriber, Time Warner	mos	39.95-49.95	6/99	103s
Cable modem rate, non-cable subscriber, Charter	mos	59.95-89.95	6/99	103s
Cable modem rate, non-cable subscriber, Comcast	mos	49.95	6/99	103s
Cable modem rate, non-cable subscriber, Cox	mos	42.95-54.95	6/99	103s
Cable modem rate, non-cable subscriber, Media One	mos	49.95	6/99	103s
Cable modem rate, non-cable subscriber, Time Warner	mos	39.95-54.95	6/99	103s
Cellular phone service	mos	41.11	2/01	55c
Phone line, single, business, field visit	inst.	70.75	12/97	17s
Phone line, single, business, no field visit	inst.	70.75	12/97	17s
Phone line, single, residence, field visit	inst.	34.75	12/97	17s
Phone line, single, residence, no field visit	inst.	34.75	12/97	17s
Postage and stationery, expenditures on	yr	150	1999	30r
Postal rate, express mail, up to half-pound		12.45	7/01	108r
Postal rate, letter, first class, first ounce		0.34	7/01	108r
Postal rate, letter, two ounces		0.57	7/01	108r
Postal rate, post card		0.21	7/01	108r
Postal rate, priority mail, two pounds		3.95	7/01	108r
Postal rate, priority mail, up to one pound		3.50	7/01	108r
Telephone bill, business, basic rate	mos	10.32	12/97	18c
Telephone bill, residential, basic rate	mos	3.00	12/97	18c
Telephone services, expenditures on	yr	825	1999	30r
Wireless services	mos	46.11	1/00	42c
Education				
Board, 4-year private college/university	yr	2970	1996	38s
Board, 4-year public college/university	yr	2516	1996	38s
Education expenditures	yr	668	1999	30c
Room, 4-year private college/university	yr	3196	1996	38s
Room, 4-year public college/university	yr	3031	1996	38s
Total cost, 4-year private college/university	yr	20143	1996	38s
Total cost, 4-year public college/university	yr	8213	1996	38s
Tuition, 2-year public college/university, in state	yr	362	1996	38s
Tuition, 4-year private college/university, in state	yr	13977	1996	38s
Tuition, 4-year public college/university	yr	2666	1996	38s
Energy and Fuels				
Electricity	KWh	0.11	7/01	11r
Electricity	500 KWhs	48.23	7/01	11r
Fuel oil and other fuels, expenditures on	yr	35	1999	30r
Gas, cooking, winter, 10 therms	mos	9.95	2/96	98c
Gas, cooking, winter, 30 therms	mos	22.94	2/96	98c
Gas, cooking, winter, 50 therms	mos	36.87	2/96	98c
Gas, heating, winter, average use	mos	47.74	2/96	98c
Gas, natural, commercial rate	1000 cf	8.74	11/00	88s
Gasoline, all types	gal	1.91	7/01	11r
Gasoline, unleaded premium	gal	2.05	7/01	11r
Gasoline, unleaded regular	gal	1.83	7/01	11r
Natural gas, expenditures on	yr	255	1999	30r
Utility (piped) gas, therm		0.98	7/01	11r
Utility (piped) gas, 40 therms		40.74	7/01	11r
Utility (piped) gas, 100 therms		96.80	7/01	11r
Entertainment				
Entertainment purchases	yr	1905	1999	30c
Fees and admissions paid	yr	545	1999	30r
Movie ticket, evening	person	8.00	1999	104c
Television, radios, sound equipment, expenditures on	yr	624	1999	30r
Funerals				
Total cost of funeral		5401.08	1/99	78r
Acknowledgement cards		33.64	1/99	78r
Casket		2170.43	1/99	78r

Values are in dollars or fractions of dollars. In the column headed *Ref*, references are shown to sources. Each reference is followed by a letter. These refer to the geographical level for which data were reported: s=State, r=Region, and c=City or metro. The abbreviation *ex* is used to mean *except* or *excluding*; *exp* stands for *expenditures*. For other abbreviations and further explanations, please see the Introduction.

Los Angeles, CA - continued

Item	Per	Value	Date	Ref.
Funerals				
Cosmetology, hair, other preparation		136.32	1/99	78r
Embalming		319.13	1/99	78r
Funeral at funeral home		370.21	1/99	78r
Hearse (local)		161.04	1/99	78r
Professional service charges		963.15	1/99	78r
Service car/van		133.99	1/99	78r
Transfer of remains to funeral home		159.82	1/99	78r
Vault		778.07	1/99	78r
Visitation/viewing		175.28	1/99	78r
Groceries				
Apples	pound	1.03		29c
Apples, red delicious	lb	0.84	7/01	11r
Bacon, sliced	lb	3.38	7/01	11r
Bakery products, expenditures on	yr	299	1999	30r
Bananas	lb	0.54	7/01	11r
Beans, dried, any type, all sizes	lb	0.76	7/01	11r
Beef, expenditures on	yr	222	1999	30r
Bread, white, pan	lb	0.99	7/01	11r
Butter, yoghurt, cheese, etc, expenditures on	yr	211	1999	30r
Cereals and bakery product purchases	yr	435	1999	30c
Cereals and cereal products, expenditures on	yr	168	1999	30r
Chicken breast, bone-in	lb	2.45	7/01	11r
Chicken, fresh, whole	lb	1.19	7/01	11r
Chops, boneless	lb	4.00	7/01	11r
Chuck roast, graded and ungraded, excl U.S. prime and choice	lb	2.55	7/01	11r
Coffee, 100%, ground roast, all sizes	lb	3.80	7/01	11r
Cookies, chocolate chip	lb	2.83	7/01	11r
Dairy product purchases	yr	319	1999	30c
Eggs, expenditures on	yr	39	1999	30r
Eggs, grade AA, large	dozen	1.23	7/01	11r
Fats and oils, expenditures on	yr	88	1999	30r
Fish and seafood, expenditures on	yr	121	1999	30r
Food (excl fruit and vegetables), eaten at home, purchases	yr	881	1999	30c
Food cooked on trips, expenditures on	yr	64	1999	30r
Food purchases	yr	5204	1999	30c
Food purchases, eaten away from home	yr	2192	1999	30c
Food purchases, food eaten at home	yr	3013	1999	30c
Fresh fruits, expenditures on	yr	186	1999	30r
Fresh milk and cream, expenditures on	yr	130	1999	30r
Fresh vegetables, expenditures on	yr	177	1999	30r
Grapefruit	lb	0.68	7/01	11r
Grapes, Thompson, seedless	lb	2.42	7/01	11r
Ground beef, lean and extra lean	lb	2.46	7/01	11r
Ice cream, prepackaged, bulk, regular	1/2 gal	3.62	7/01	11r
Lettuce, iceberg	lb	0.63	7/01	11r
Meats, poultry, fish, and egg purchases	yr	815	1999	30c
Milk, fresh, low fat,	gal	2.80	7/01	11r
Milk, fresh, whole, fortified	gal	2.88	7/01	11r
Nonalcoholic beverages, expenditures on	yr	258	1999	30r
Oranges, Navel	lb	0.97	7/01	11r
Oranges, Valencia	lb	0.43	7/01	11r
Peaches	lb	1.38	7/01	11r
Peanut butter, creamy, all sizes	lb	2.14	7/01	11r
Pork chops, center cut, bone-in	lb	3.83	7/01	11r
Pork, expenditures on	yr	141	1999	30r
Potatoes, white, all types	lb	0.37	7/01	11r
Poultry, expenditures on	yr	146	1999	30r
Processed fruits, expenditures on	yr	118	1999	30r
Processed vegetables, expenditures on	yr	81	1999	30r
Round roast, graded and ungraded, excl U.S. prime and choice	lb	3.07	7/01	11r
Round roast, U.S. choice, boneless	lb	3.37	7/01	11r
Round steak, graded and ungraded, excl U.S. prime and choice	lb	3.51	7/01	11r
Sirloin steak, graded and ungraded, excl U.S. prime and choice	lb	4.67	7/01	11r
Steak, sirloin, U.S. choice, boneless	lb	6.20	7/01	11r
Strawberries, dry pint	12 oz	1.79	7/01	11r
Sugar and other sweets, expenditures on	yr	124	1999	30r

Los Angeles, CA - continued

Item	Per	Value	Date	Ref.
Groceries - continued				
Sugar, white, all sizes	lb	0.46	7/01	11r
Tobacco products and smoking supplies purchases	yr	177	1999	30c
Tomatoes, field grown	lb	1.17	7/01	11r
Tuna, light, chunk	lb	2.05	7/01	11r
Goods and Services				
B&B Japanese maple (acer japonicum)	gal	39.99	4/00	93r
Boxwood (buxus)	2 gal	14.99-24.99	4/00	93r
Christmas tree, noble fir		40-60	2000	65s
Daylilly (hemerocallis)	gal	6.99-8.99	4/00	93r
Flat of annuals		16.68	4/00	93r
Fountain grass (pennisetum)	gal	7.99-11.99	4/00	93r
Hanging basket (10 in)		29.99	4/00	93r
Hardy geranium (geranium)	gal	6.99-11.99	4/00	93r
Hosta (hosta)	gal	6.99-18.99	4/00	93r
Lilac (syrubga vulgaris)	2 gal	14.99-17.99	4/00	93r
Miscellaneous purchases	yr	1338	1999	30c
Rhododendron (rhododendron)	2 gal	14.99	4/00	93r
Sage (salvia)	gal	6.99	4/00	93r
Wintercreeper euonymus (euonymus fortunei)	2 gal	14.99-22.99	4/00	93r
Hunting license	yr	29.95	4/01	34s
Health Care				
Cardiac catheterization, ave hospital/ physician charges		24000	1998	77s
Childbirth, Cesarean delivery		11587	1997	13r
Childbirth, vaginal delivery		6725	1997	13r
Drugs, expenditures on	yr	309	1999	30r
Health care purchases	yr	1757	1999	30c
Health insurance expenditures	yr	868	1999	30r
Home health care aide cost, licensed agency	hour	17	2000	82c
Hysterectomy, laproscopically-assisted, ave hospital/physician charges		20760	1998	76s
Hysterectomy, vaginal, ave hospital and physician charges		14570	1998	76s
Medicaid dispensing fee		4.05	1999	87s
Medical services expenditures	yr	580	1999	30r
Medical supplies, expenditures on	yr	112	1999	30r
Nursing home costs, private room	day	122	2000	82c
Nursing home stay, private room	day	122	2000	83c
Household Goods				
Floor coverings, expenditures on	yr	49	1999	30r
Furniture, expenditures on	yr	444	1999	30r
Household furnishings and equipment purchases	yr	1856	1999	30c
Household textiles, expenditures on	yr	141	1999	30r
Laundry and cleaning supplies, expenditures on	yr	128	1999	30r
Housing				
Home, suburban, 2,200 square feet		326300	2000	23c
Home price, existing, ave		239400	10/00	90r
Home value, median		215000	2001	53s
Household operation expenditures	yr	1256	1999	30c
Housekeeping supplies purchases	yr	469	1999	30c
Lodging expenditures	yr	612	1999	30c
Maintenance, repairs, insurance expenditures	yr	939	1999	30r
Monthly rental value of owned home	mos	662	1999	30r
Owned dwellings, expenditures own	yr	5805	1999	30c
Rent expenditures	yr	3671	1999	30c
Shelter, expenditures on	yr	10087	1999	30c
Insurance and Pensions				
Life and other personal insurance purchases	yr	349	1999	30c

Values are in dollars or fractions of dollars. In the column headed *Ref*, references are shown to sources. Each reference is followed by a letter. These refer to the geographical level for which data were reported: s=State, r=Region, and c=City or metro. The abbreviation *ex* is used to mean *except* or *excluding*; *exp* stands for *expenditures*. For other abbreviations and further explanations, please see the Introduction.

Los Angeles, CA - continued

Item	Per	Value	Date	Ref.
Insurance and Pensions				
Pensions and Social Security, expenditures on	yr	3920	1999	30c
Legal Fees				
Divorce, filing fee		182.00	4/01	35s
Driver's license fee	orig	12.00	1999	48s
Driver's license fee	renew	15.00	1999	48s
Parking in front of hydrant, fine		35	1998	20c
Parking meter violation, fine		30	1998	20c
Personal Goods				
Personal care products and services purchases	yr	472	1999	30c
Personal Services				
Personal services, household, expenditures on	yr	353	1999	30r
Personal trainer	hour	100	1999	64c
Pets				
Pets, toys, and playground equipment, expenditures on	yr	358	1999	30r
Restaurant Food				
Cheeseburger, 1/4-lb, large fries, medium soft drink, excl tax		4.37	1999	40c
Taxes				
Federal income taxes paid	yr	3200	1999	30r
Personal taxes, expenditures on	yr	4153	1999	30r
Property taxes paid	yr	923	1999	30r
State and local income taxes paid	yr	812	1999	30r
Transportation				
Auto operation, annual cost		9254	2000	27c
Bus fare, one-way	trip	0.75	2000	1c
Cars and trucks, new, expenditures on	yr	1534	1999	30r
Cars and trucks, used, expenditures on	yr	1593	1999	30r
Commuter rail, one-way	trip	2.75	2000	2c
Diesel at the pump	gal	1.37	10/99	73s
Gasoline and motor oil purchases	yr	1157	1999	30c
Gasoline before-tax price (cents)	gal	128.80	10/00	43s
Heavy rail transit fare, one-way	trip	1.35	2000	2c
Light rail transit fare, one-way	trip	1.35	2000	2c
Maintenance and repair expenditures	yr	797	1999	30r
Parking at airport, lowest rate	day	5.00	2000	46c
Public transportation, expenditures on	yr	558	1999	30c
Transportation purchases	yr	7551	1999	30c
Vehicle expenses, miscellaneous, purchases	yr	2860	1999	30c
Vehicle insurance payments	yr	811	1999	30r
Vehicle purchases (net outlay)	yr	3180	1999	30r
Vehicle rental, lease expenditures	yr	666	1999	30r
Utilities				
Electrical bill, average	mos	58.66	9/00	9s
Electricity, expenditures on	yr	725	1999	30r
Electricity cost, average	KWh	7.75	9/00	9s
Utilities, fuels, and public services purchased	yr	2267	1999	30c
Water and other public services, expenditures on	yr	339	1999	30r
Water price	100 cf	1.75	2000	109c
Water price, dwelling unit	mos	34.41	2000	109c
Weddings				
Wedding (national average cost)		19936	2000	33r
Wedding (regional average total cost)		18918	1997	110r
Attendants' gifts		321	1998	33r
Bridal attendants' apparel (5 persons)		824	2000	33r
Bride's headpiece/veil		173	1998	33r
Bride's wedding dress		859	1998	33r
Clergy, religious facility fee		242	1998	33r
Engagement ring		3177	1998	33r
Flowers		789	1998	33r
Groom's formalwear rental		99	2000	33r
Limousine		410	1998	33r

Los Angeles, CA - continued

Item	Per	Value	Date	Ref.
Weddings - continued				
Marriage license cost		50.00-80.00	4/01	35s
Men's formalwear (ushers, best man)		469	2000	33r
Mother of bride apparel		241	2000	33r
Music		866	1998	33r
Photography and videography		1368	1998	33r
Rehearsal dinner		728	1998	33r
Wedding invitations and announcements		341	1998	33r
Wedding reception		7968	2000	33r
Wedding rings (bride and groom)		1060	1998	33r

Los Angeles-Long Beach, CA

Item	Per	Value	Date	Ref.
Average annual expenditures	yr	40662	1999	30r
Composite, ACCRA index		143.40	3/01	4c
Alcoholic Beverages				
Alcoholic beverage purchases	yr	372	1999	30r
Beer, Heineken, 12-oz, ex deposit	6	7.64	3/01	4c
J & B Scotch	750-ml	20.16	3/01	4c
Malt beverages, all types, all sizes, any origin	16 oz	0.94	7/01	11r
Wine, Livingston or Gallo, Chablis blanc	1.5 liter	5.32	3/01	4c
Wine, red and white table, all sizes, any origin	liter	6.00	7/01	11r
Appliances				
Appliance repair, service call, washing machine	min lab chg	34.79	3/01	4c
Major appliances, expenditures on	yr	167	1999	30r
Small appliances, housewares, expenditures on	yr	105	1999	30r
Banking and Money				
Mortgage interest and charges paid	yr	3368	1999	30r
Mortgage principal paid on owned property	yr	1677	1999	30r
Mortgage rate, incl. points and orig. fee, 30-yr. conv. fixed or ARM	mos	7.30	3/01	4c
Vehicle finance charges paid	yr	311	1999	30r
Charity				
Cash contributions, expenditures	yr	1344	1999	30r
Child Care				
Child raising cost, total, age 0-2	yr	9140	1999	60r
Child raising cost, total, age 3-5	yr	9370	1999	60r
Child raising cost, total, age 6-8	yr	9450	1999	60r
Child raising cost, total, age 9-11	yr	9470	1999	60r
Child raising cost, total, age 12-14	yr	10170	1999	60r
Child raising cost, total, age 15-17	yr	10360	1999	60r
Child's child care and education, age 0-2	yr	1250	1999	60r
Child's child care and education, age 3-5	yr	1380	1999	60r
Child's child care and education, age 6-8	yr	890	1999	60r
Child's child care and education, age 9-11	yr	580	1999	60r
Child's child care and education, age 12-14	yr	430	1999	60r
Child's child care and education, age 15-17	yr	730	1999	60r
Child's clothing, age 0-2	yr	430	1999	60r
Child's clothing, age 3-5	yr	420	1999	60r
Child's clothing, age 6-8	yr	470	1999	60r
Child's clothing, age 9-11	yr	520	1999	60r
Child's clothing, age 12-14	yr	870	1999	60r
Child's clothing, age 15-17	yr	770	1999	60r
Child's food, age 0-2	yr	1120	1999	60r
Child's food, age 3-5	yr	1280	1999	60r
Child's food, age 6-8	yr	1640	1999	60r
Child's food, age 9-11	yr	1930	1999	60r
Child's food, age 12-14	yr	1940	1999	60r
Child's food, age 15-17	yr	2150	1999	60r
Child's health care, age 0-2	yr	490	1999	60r
Child's health care, age 3-5	yr	470	1999	60r
Child's health care, age 6-8	yr	530	1999	60r
Child's health care, age 9-11	yr	570	1999	60r
Child's health care, age 12-14	yr	580	1999	60r
Child's health care, age 15-17	yr	610	1999	60r
Child's housing, age 0-2	yr	3630	1999	60r

Values are in dollars or fractions of dollars. In the column headed *Ref*, references are shown to sources. Each reference is followed by a letter. These refer to the geographical level for which data were reported: s=State, r=Region, and c=City or metro. The abbreviation *ex* is used to mean *except* or *excluding*; *exp* stands for *expenditures*. For other abbreviations and further explanations, please see the Introduction.

Los Angeles-Long Beach, CA - continued

Item	Per	Value	Date	Ref.
Child Care				
Child's housing, age 3-5	yr	3610	1999	60r
Child's housing, age 6-8	yr	3570	1999	60r
Child's housing, age 9-11	yr	3410	1999	60r
Child's housing, age 12-14	yr	3600	1999	60r
Child's housing, age 15-17	yr	3210	1999	60r
Child's personal care, reading, age 0-2	yr	1040	1999	60r
Child's personal care, reading, age 3-5	yr	1060	1999	60r
Child's personal care, reading, age 6-8	yr	1090	1999	60r
Child's personal care, reading, age 9-11	yr	1130	1999	60r
Child's personal care, reading, age 12-14	yr	1300	1999	60r
Child's personal care, reading, age 15-17	yr	1080	1999	60r
Clothing				
Apparel and services purchases	yr	1863	1999	30r
Boys' brief, cotton	3	5.34	3/01	4c
Boys, 2 to 15, expenditures on	yr	80	1999	30r
Children under 2, expenditures on	yr	74	1999	30r
Footwear, expenditures on	yr	307	1999	30r
Girls, 2 to 15, expenditures on	yr	101	1999	30r
Men and boys, expenditures on	yr	443	1999	30r
Men, 16 and over, expenditures on	yr	363	1999	30r
Shirt, man's dress shirt		28.69	3/01	4c
Slacks, man's "No Wrinkles" khaki		41.83	3/01	4c
Women, 16 and over, expenditures on	yr	594	1999	30r
Communications				
Cable modem installation, AT&T-BIS		150.00	6/99	103s
Cable modem installation, Charter		99.00-169.00	6/99	103s
Cable modem installation, Comcast		95.00	6/99	103s
Cable modem installation, Cox		99.00-174.95	6/99	103s
Cable modem installation, Media One		100.00	6/99	103s
Cable modem installation, Time Warner		75.00-225.00	6/99	103s
Cable modem rate, cable subscriber, AT&T-BIS	mos	39.95	6/99	103s
Cable modem rate, cable subscriber, Charter	mos	49.95-79.95	6/99	103s
Cable modem rate, cable subscriber, Comcast	mos	39.95	6/99	103s
Cable modem rate, cable subscriber, Cox	mos	29.95-44.95	6/99	103s
Cable modem rate, cable subscriber, Media One	mos	34.95-39.95	6/99	103s
Cable modem rate, cable subscriber, Time Warner	mos	39.95-49.95	6/99	103s
Cable modem rate, non-cable subscriber, Charter	mos	59.95-89.95	6/99	103s
Cable modem rate, non-cable subscriber, Comcast	mos	49.95	6/99	103s
Cable modem rate, non-cable subscriber, Cox	mos	42.95-54.95	6/99	103s
Cable modem rate, non-cable subscriber, Media One	mos	49.95	6/99	103s
Cable modem rate, non-cable subscriber, Time Warner	mos	39.95-54.95	6/99	103s
Newspaper subscription, daily and Sunday delivery	mos	18.00	3/01	4c
Phone line, single, business, field visit	inst.	70.75	12/97	17s
Phone line, single, business, no field visit	inst.	70.75	12/97	17s
Phone line, single, residence, field visit	inst.	34.75	12/97	17s
Phone line, single, residence, no field visit	inst.	34.75	12/97	17s
Postage and stationery, expenditures on	yr	150	1999	30r
Postal rate, express mail, up to half-pound		12.45	7/01	108r
Postal rate, letter, first class, first ounce		0.34	7/01	108r
Postal rate, letter, two ounces		0.57	7/01	108r
Postal rate, post card		0.21	7/01	108r
Postal rate, priority mail, two pounds		3.95	7/01	108r
Postal rate, priority mail, up to one pound		3.50	7/01	108r
Telephone bill, family of three	mos	22.17	3/01	4c
Telephone services, expenditures on	yr	825	1999	30r

Los Angeles-Long Beach, CA - continued

Item	Per	Value	Date	Ref.
Education				
Board, 4-year private college/university	yr	2970	1996	38s
Board, 4-year public college/university	yr	2516	1996	38s
Education expenditures	yr	676	1999	30r
Room, 4-year private college/university	yr	3196	1996	38s
Room, 4-year public college/university	yr	3031	1996	38s
Total cost, 4-year private college/university	yr	20143	1996	38s
Total cost, 4-year public college/university	yr	8213	1996	38s
Tuition, 2-year public college/university, in state	yr	362	1996	38s
Tuition, 4-year private college/university, in state	yr	13977	1996	38s
Tuition, 4-year public college/university	yr	2666	1996	38s
Energy and Fuels				
Electricity	500 KWhs	48.23	7/01	11r
Electricity	KWh	0.11	7/01	11r
Electricity	500 KWhs	70.45	7/01	11c
Electricity	KWh	0.17	7/01	11c
Energy, combined forms, 2400 sq ft	mos	121.33	3/01	4c
Energy, exc. electricity, 2400 sq ft	mos	42.73	3/01	4c
Fuel oil and other fuels, expenditures on	yr	35	1999	30r
Gas, natural, commercial rate	1000 cf	8.74	11/00	88s
Gas, regular unleaded, cash, self-service	gal	1.58	3/01	4c
Gasoline, all types	gal	2.05	7/01	11c
Gasoline, unleaded midgrade	gal	2.06	7/01	11c
Gasoline, unleaded premium	gal	2.05	7/01	11r
Gasoline, unleaded regular	gal	1.98	7/01	11c
Natural gas, expenditures on	yr	255	1999	30r
Utility (piped) gas, therm		1.02	7/01	11c
Utility (piped) gas, 40 therms		40.74	7/01	11r
Utility (piped) gas, 100 therms		101.54	7/01	11c
Entertainment				
Bowling, Saturday evening rate	line	3.49	3/01	4c
Entertainment purchases	yr	2139	1999	30r
Fees and admissions paid	yr	545	1999	30r
Monopoly game, Parker Brothers', No. 9	game	11.42	3/01	4c
Movie, first-run, Saturday, evening	adm.	8.75	3/01	4c
Television, radios, sound equipment, expenditures on	yr	624	1999	30r
Tennis balls, yellow, Wilson or Penn, 3	can	2.75	3/01	4c
Funerals				
Total cost of funeral		5401.08	1/99	78r
Acknowledgement cards		33.64	1/99	78r
Casket		2170.43	1/99	78r
Cosmetology, hair, other preparation		136.32	1/99	78r
Embalming		319.13	1/99	78r
Funeral at funeral home		370.21	1/99	78r
Hearse (local)		161.04	1/99	78r
Professional service charges		963.15	1/99	78r
Service car/van		133.99	1/99	78r
Transfer of remains to funeral home		159.82	1/99	78r
Vault		778.07	1/99	78r
Visitation/viewing		175.28	1/99	78r
Groceries				
Groceries, ACCRA Index		112.10	3/01	4c
Antibiotic ointment, Polysporin	0.5 oz	5.65	3/01	4c
Apples, red delicious	lb	0.84	7/01	11r
Baby food, strained vegetables or fruit, lowest price	4-4.5 oz	0.50	3/01	4c
Bacon, sliced	lb	3.38	7/01	11r
Bakery products, expenditures on	yr	299	1999	30r
Bananas	lb	0.58	3/01	4c
Bananas	lb	0.54	7/01	11r
Beans, dried, any type, all sizes	lb	0.76	7/01	11r
Beef or hamburger, ground	lb	1.46	3/01	4c
Beef, expenditures on	yr	222	1999	30r
Bread, white	loaf	0.92	3/01	4c
Bread, white, pan	lb	0.99	7/01	11r
Butter, yoghurt, cheese, etc, expenditures on	yr	211	1999	30r

Values are in dollars or fractions of dollars. In the column headed *Ref*, references are shown to sources. Each reference is followed by a letter. These refer to the geographical level for which data were reported: s=State, r=Region, and c=City or metro. The abbreviation *ex* is used to mean *except* or *excluding*; *exp* stands for *expenditures*. For other abbreviations and further explanations, please see the Introduction.

Los Angeles-Long Beach, CA - continued

Item	Per	Value	Date	Ref.
Groceries				
Cereals and bakery product purchases	yr	466	1999	30r
Cereals and cereal products, expenditures on	yr	168	1999	30r
Cheese, Kraft grated Parmesan	8 oz	4.06	3/01	4c
Chicken breast, bone-in	lb	2.45	7/01	11r
Chicken, fresh, whole	lb	1.19	7/01	11r
Chicken, whole fryer	lb	1.06	3/01	4c
Chops, boneless,	lb	4.00	7/01	11r
Chuck roast, graded and ungraded, excl U.S. prime and choice	lb	2.55	7/01	11r
Cigarettes, Winston, Kings	carton	35.86	3/01	4c
Coffee, 100%, ground roast, all sizes	lb	3.80	7/01	11r
Coffee, vacuum-packed	13 oz	3.41	3/01	4c
Cookies, chocolate chip	lb	2.83	7/01	11r
Corn Flakes, Kellogg's or Post Toasties	18 oz	3.22	3/01	4c
Corn, frozen, whole kernel, lowest price	16 oz	1.36	3/01	4c
Dairy product purchases	yr	341	1999	30r
Eggs, expenditures on	yr	39	1999	30r
Eggs, Grade A or AA	dozen	2.09	3/01	4c
Eggs, grade AA, large	dozen	1.23	7/01	11r
Fats and oils, expenditures on	yr	88	1999	30r
Fish and seafood, expenditures on	yr	121	1999	30r
Food (excl fruit and vegetables), eaten at home, purchases	yr	1001	1999	30r
Food cooked on trips, expenditures on	yr	64	1999	30r
Food purchases	yr	5312	1999	30r
Food purchases, eaten away from home	yr	2180	1999	30r
Food purchases, food eaten at home	yr	3132	1999	30r
Fresh fruits, expenditures on	yr	186	1999	30r
Fresh milk and cream, expenditures on	yr	130	1999	30r
Fresh vegetables, expenditures on	yr	177	1999	30r
Grapefruit	lb	0.68	7/01	11r
Grapes, Thompson, seedless	lb	2.42	7/01	11r
Ground beef, lean and extra lean	lb	2.46	7/01	11r
Ice cream, prepackaged, bulk, regular	1/2 gal	3.62	7/01	11r
Lettuce, iceberg	head	0.99	3/01	4c
Lettuce, iceberg	lb	0.63	7/01	11r
Margarine, Blue Bonnet or Parkay, stick	lb	0.53	3/01	4c
Meats, poultry, fish, and egg purchases	yr	761	1999	30r
Milk, fresh, low fat,	gal	2.80	7/01	11r
Milk, fresh, whole, fortified	gal	2.88	7/01	11r
Milk, whole	1/2 gal	2.07	3/01	4c
Nonalcoholic beverages, expenditures on	yr	258	1999	30r
Orange juice, Minute Maid frozen	12 oz	1.68	3/01	4c
Oranges, Navel	lb	0.97	7/01	11r
Oranges, Valencia	lb	0.43	7/01	11r
Peaches	lb	1.38	7/01	11r
Peaches, halves or slices, Hunt's, Del Monte, or Libby's	29 oz	1.52	3/01	4c
Peanut butter, creamy, all sizes	lb	2.14	7/01	11r
Peas, green, Del Monte or Green Giant	15 oz	0.82	3/01	4c
Pork chops, center cut, bone-in	lb	3.83	7/01	11r
Pork, expenditures on	yr	141	1999	30r
Potatoes, white or red	10 lb	2.39	3/01	4c
Potatoes, white, all types	lb	0.37	7/01	11r
Poultry, expenditures on	yr	146	1999	30r
Processed fruits, expenditures on	yr	118	1999	30r
Processed vegetables, expenditures on	yr	81	1999	30r
Round roast, graded and ungraded, excl U.S. prime and choice	lb	3.07	7/01	11r
Round roast, U.S. choice, boneless	lb	3.37	7/01	11r
Round steak, graded and ungraded, excl U.S. prime and choice	lb	3.51	7/01	11r
Sausage, Jimmy Dean/Owens pork	lb	4.60	3/01	4c
Shortening, vegetable, Crisco	3 lb	3.44	3/01	4c
Sirloin steak, graded and ungraded, excl U.S. prime and choice	lb	4.67	7/01	11r
Soft drink, Coca Cola, ex deposit	2 liter	0.97	3/01	4c
Steak, sirloin, U.S. choice, boneless	lb	6.20	7/01	11r
Steak, T-bone	lb	7.07	3/01	4c
Strawberries, dry pint	12 oz	1.79	7/01	11r
Sugar and other sweets, expenditures on	yr	124	1999	30r

Los Angeles-Long Beach, CA - continued

Item	Per	Value	Date	Ref.
Groceries - continued				
Sugar, cane or beet	4 lbs	1.89	3/01	4c
Sugar, white, all sizes	lb	0.46	7/01	11r
Tobacco products and smoking supplies purchases	yr	217	1999	30r
Tomatoes, field grown	lb	1.17	7/01	11r
Tomatoes, Hunt's or Del Monte	14.5 oz	0.91	3/01	4c
Tuna, chunk, light	6 oz	0.73	3/01	4c
Tuna, light, chunk	lb	2.05	7/01	11r
Goods and Services				
Miscellaneous goods and services, ACCRA Index		110.80	3/01	4c
B&B Japanese maple (acer japonicum)	gal	39.99	4/00	93r
Boxwood (buxus)	2 gal	14.99-24.99	4/00	93r
Christmas tree, noble fir		40-60	2000	65s
Daylily (hemerocallis)	gal	6.99-8.99	4/00	93r
Flat of annuals		16.68	4/00	93r
Fountain grass (pennisetum)	gal	7.99-11.99	4/00	93r
Hanging basket (10 in)		29.99	4/00	93r
Hardy geranium (geranium)	gal	6.99-11.99	4/00	93r
Hosta (hosta)	gal	6.99-18.99	4/00	93r
Lilac (syrubga vulgaris)	2 gal	14.99-17.99	4/00	93r
Miscellaneous purchases	yr	1070	1999	30r
Rhododendron (rhododendron)	2 gal	14.99	4/00	93r
Sage (salvia)	gal	6.99	4/00	93r
Wintercreeper euonymus (euonymus fortunei)	2 gal	14.99-22.99	4/00	93r
Hunting license	yr	29.95	4/01	34s
Health Care				
Health care, ACCRA Index		118.50	3/01	4c
Cardiac catheterization, ave hospital/physician charges		24000	1998	77s
Childbirth, Cesarean delivery		11587	1997	13r
Childbirth, vaginal delivery		6725	1997	13r
Dentist's fee, adult teeth cleaning and periodic oral exam	visit	61.40	3/01	4c
Doctor's fee, routine exam, established patient	visit	64.40	3/01	4c
Drugs, expenditures on	yr	309	1999	30r
Health care purchases	yr	1869	1999	30r
Health insurance expenditures	yr	868	1999	30r
Hospital care, private room	day	1027.60	3/01	4c
Hysterectomy, laproscopically-assisted, ave hospital/physician charges		20760	1998	76s
Hysterectomy, vaginal, ave hospital and physician charges		14570	1998	76s
Medicaid dispensing fee		4.05	1999	87s
Medical services expenditures	yr	580	1999	30r
Medical supplies, expenditures on	yr	112	1999	30r
Household Goods				
Dishwashing powder, Cascade	50 oz	4.14	3/01	4c
Floor coverings, expenditures on	yr	49	1999	30r
Furniture, expenditures on	yr	444	1999	30r
Household furnishings and equipment purchases	yr	1768	1999	30r
Household textiles, expenditures on	yr	141	1999	30r
Laundry and cleaning supplies, expenditures on	yr	128	1999	30r
Tissues, facial, Kleenex brand	175	1.38	3/01	4c
Housing				
Housing, ACCRA Index		228.20	3/01	4c
Home price, existing, ave		239400	10/00	90r
Home value, median		215000	2001	53s
House, 2400 sq ft, 8000 sq ft lot, new, urban, utilities	total	485496	3/01	4c

Values are in dollars or fractions of dollars. In the column headed *Ref*, references are shown to sources. Each reference is followed by a letter. These refer to the geographical level for which data were reported: s=State, r=Region, and c=City or metro. The abbreviation *ex* is used to mean *except* or *excluding*; *exp* stands for *expenditures*. For other abbreviations and further explanations, please see the Introduction.

Los Angeles-Long Beach, CA - continued

Item	Per	Value	Date	Ref.
Housing				
House payment, principal and interest, 25% down payment	mos	2497	3/01	4c
Household operation expenditures	yr	781	1999	30r
Housekeeping supplies purchases	yr	513	1999	30r
Lodging expenditures	yr	575	1999	30r
Maintenance, repairs, insurance expenditures	yr	939	1999	30r
Monthly rental value of owned home	mos	662	1999	30r
Owned dwellings, expenditures own	yr	5231	1999	30r
Rent expenditures	yr	2709	1999	30r
Rent, apartment, 2 br, 1 1/2-2 baths, unfurn, 950 sq ft, water	mos	1202	3/01	4c
Rental unit, 1 bedroom, with utilities	mos	618	4/01	41c
Rental unit, 2 bedroom, with utilities	mos	782	4/01	41c
Rental unit, 3 bedroom, with utilities	mos	1055	4/01	41c
Rental unit, 4 bedroom, with utilities	mos	1260	4/01	41c
Shelter, expenditures on	yr	8516	1999	30r
Insurance and Pensions				
Life and other personal insurance purchases	yr	355	1999	30r
Pensions and Social Security, expenditures on	yr	3636	1999	30r
Legal Fees				
Divorce, filing fee		182.00	4/01	35s
Driver's license fee	renew	15.00	1999	48s
Driver's license fee	orig	12.00	1999	48s
Personal Goods				
Personal care products and services purchases	yr	449	1999	30r
Shampoo, Alberto VO5	15 oz	1.58	3/01	4c
Toothpaste, Crest or Colgate	6-7 oz	2.82	3/01	4c
Personal Services				
Dry cleaning, man's 2-pc suit		6.75	3/01	4c
Man's haircut, barbershop, no styling		11.50	3/01	4c
Personal services, household, expenditures on	yr	353	1999	30r
Woman's shampoo, trim, blow-dry, no style-change		36.80	3/01	4c
Pets				
Pets, toys, and playground equipment, expenditures on	yr	358	1999	30r
Restaurant Food				
Chicken, fried, thigh and drumstick, KFC/Church's		2.76	3/01	4c
Hamburger with cheese, McDonald's	1/4 lb	2.23	3/01	4c
Pizza, Pizza Hut or Pizza Inn	11-12 in	9.99	3/01	4c
Taxes				
Federal income taxes paid	yr	3200	1999	30r
Personal taxes, expenditures on	yr	4153	1999	30r
Property taxes paid	yr	923	1999	30r
State and local income taxes paid	yr	812	1999	30r
Transportation				
Transportation, ACCRA Index		111.40	3/01	4c
Bus fare, to central business district	1-way	1.35	3/01	4c
Cars and trucks, new, expenditures on	yr	1534	1999	30r
Cars and trucks, used, expenditures on	yr	1593	1999	30r
Diesel at the pump	gal	1.37	10/99	73s
Gasoline and motor oil purchases	yr	1129	1999	30r
Gasoline before-tax price (cents)	gal	128.80	10/00	43s
Maintenance and repair expenditures	yr	797	1999	30r
Public transportation, expenditures on	yr	530	1999	30r
Tire balance, computer or spin balance, front	wheel	8.44	3/01	4c
Transportation purchases	yr	7423	1999	30r
Vehicle expenses, miscellaneous, purchases	yr	2585	1999	30r
Vehicle insurance payments	yr	811	1999	30r
Vehicle purchases (net outlay)	yr	3180	1999	30r
Vehicle rental, lease expenditures	yr	666	1999	30r

Los Angeles-Long Beach, CA - continued

Item	Per	Value	Date	Ref.
Utilities				
Utilities, ACCRA Index		99.80	3/01	4c
Electrical bill, average	mos	58.66	9/00	9s
Electricity, expenditures on	yr	725	1999	30r
Electricity and other, mixed, 2400 sq ft, new home	mos	78.60	3/01	4c
Electricity cost, average	KWh	7.75	9/00	9s
Utilities, fuels, and public services purchased	yr	2179	1999	30r
Water and other public services, expenditures on	yr	339	1999	30r
Weddings				
Wedding (national average cost)		19936	2000	33r
Wedding (regional average total cost)		18918	1997	110r
Attendants' gifts		321	1998	33r
Bridal attendants' apparel (5 persons)		824	2000	33r
Bride's headpiece/veil		173	1998	33r
Bride's wedding dress		859	1998	33r
Clergy, religious facility fee		242	1998	33r
Engagement ring		3177	1998	33r
Flowers		789	1998	33r
Groom's formalwear rental		99	2000	33r
Limousine		410	1998	33r
Marriage license cost		50.00-80.00	4/01	35s
Men's formalwear (ushers, best man)		469	2000	33r
Mother of bride apparel		241	2000	33r
Music		866	1998	33r
Photography and videography		1368	1998	33r
Rehearsal dinner		728	1998	33r
Wedding invitations and announcements		341	1998	33r
Wedding reception		7968	2000	33r
Wedding rings (bride and groom)		1060	1998	33r

Louisville, KY

Item	Per	Value	Date	Ref.
Composite, ACCRA index		96.60	3/01	4c
Alcoholic Beverages				
Alcoholic beverage purchases	yr	253	1999	30r
Beer, Heineken, 12-oz, ex deposit	6	7.09	3/01	4c
J & B Scotch	750-ml	18.59	3/01	4c
Malt beverages, all types, all sizes, any origin	16 oz	0.96	7/01	11r
Wine, Livingston or Gallo, Chablis blanc	1.5 liter	7.16	3/01	4c
Appliances				
Appliance repair, service call, washing machine	min lab chg	39.40	3/01	4c
Major appliances, expenditures on	yr	172	1999	30r
Small appliances, housewares, expenditures on	yr	81	1999	30r
Banking and Money				
Mortgage interest and charges paid	yr	2039	1999	30r
Mortgage principal paid on owned property	yr	1026	1999	30r
Mortgage rate, incl. points and orig. fee, 30-yr. conv. fixed or ARM	mos	7.09	3/01	4c
Vehicle finance charges paid	yr	365	1999	30r
Business Expenses				
Business travel, car rental	day	55	2001	3c
Business travel, food	day	50	2001	3c
Business travel, hotel	day	100	2001	3c
Charity				
Cash contributions, expenditures	yr	1127	1999	30r
Child Care				
Child raising cost, total, age 0-2	yr	8540	1999	60r
Child raising cost, total, age 3-5	yr	8780	1999	60r
Child raising cost, total, age 6-8	yr	8820	1999	60r
Child raising cost, total, age 9-11	yr	8800	1999	60r
Child raising cost, total, age 12-14	yr	9510	1999	60r
Child raising cost, total, age 15-17	yr	9740	1999	60r
Child's child care and education, age 0-2	yr	1380	1999	60r
Child's child care and education, age 3-5	yr	1520	1999	60r

Values are in dollars or fractions of dollars. In the column headed *Ref*, references are shown to sources. Each reference is followed by a letter. These refer to the geographical level for which data were reported: s=State, r=Region, and c=City or metro. The abbreviation *ex* is used to mean *except* or *excluding*; *exp* stands for expenditures. For other abbreviations and further explanations, please see the Introduction.

Louisville, KY - continued

Item	Per	Value	Date	Ref.
Child Care				
Child's child care and education, age 6-8	yr	990	1999	60r
Child's child care and education, age 9-11	yr	650	1999	60r
Child's child care and education, age 12-14	yr	490	1999	60r
Child's child care and education, age 15-17	yr	840	1999	60r
Child's clothing, age 0-2	yr	480	1999	60r
Child's clothing, age 3-5	yr	470	1999	60r
Child's clothing, age 6-8	yr	520	1999	60r
Child's clothing, age 9-11	yr	570	1999	60r
Child's clothing, age 12-14	yr	950	1999	60r
Child's clothing, age 15-17	yr	850	1999	60r
Child's food, age 0-2	yr	1000	1999	60r
Child's food, age 3-5	yr	1160	1999	60r
Child's food, age 6-8	yr	1490	1999	60r
Child's food, age 9-11	yr	1770	1999	60r
Child's food, age 12-14	yr	1770	1999	60r
Child's food, age 15-17	yr	1980	1999	60r
Child's health care, age 0-2	yr	620	1999	60r
Child's health care, age 3-5	yr	590	1999	60r
Child's health care, age 6-8	yr	680	1999	60r
Child's health care, age 9-11	yr	720	1999	60r
Child's health care, age 12-14	yr	730	1999	60r
Child's health care, age 15-17	yr	760	1999	60r
Child's housing, age 0-2	yr	3070	1999	60r
Child's housing, age 3-5	yr	3050	1999	60r
Child's housing, age 6-8	yr	3010	1999	60r
Child's housing, age 9-11	yr	2850	1999	60r
Child's housing, age 12-14	yr	3040	1999	60r
Child's housing, age 15-17	yr	2650	1999	60r
Child's personal care, reading, age 0-2	yr	910	1999	60r
Child's personal care, reading, age 3-5	yr	930	1999	60r
Child's personal care, reading, age 6-8	yr	960	1999	60r
Child's personal care, reading, age 9-11	yr	1000	1999	60r
Child's personal care, reading, age 12-14	yr	1170	1999	60r
Child's personal care, reading, age 15-17	yr	950	1999	60r
Clothing				
Apparel and services purchases	yr	1610	1999	30r
Boys' brief, cotton	3	3.91	3/01	4c
Boys, 2 to 15, expenditures on	yr	89	1999	30r
Children under 2, expenditures on	yr	79	1999	30r
Footwear, expenditures on	yr	283	1999	30r
Girls, 2 to 15, expenditures on	yr	103	1999	30r
Men and boys, expenditures on	yr	351	1999	30r
Men, 16 and over, expenditures on	yr	262	1999	30r
Shirt, man's dress shirt		29.59	3/01	4c
Slacks, man's "No Wrinkles" khaki		38.00	3/01	4c
Women, 16 and over, expenditures on	yr	538	1999	30r
Communications				
Cable modem installation, Intermedia		149.95	6/99	103s
Cable modem rate, cable subscriber, Intermedia	mos	49.95	6/99	103s
Cable modem rate, non-cable subscriber, Intermedia	mos	54.95	6/99	103s
Newspaper subscription, daily and Sunday delivery	mos	15.22	3/01	4c
Phone line, single, business, field visit	inst.	61.39	12/97	17s
Phone line, single, business, no field visit	inst.	61.39	12/97	17s
Phone line, single, residence, field visit	inst.	33.85	12/97	17s
Phone line, single, residence, no field visit	inst.	33.85	12/97	17s
Postage and stationery, expenditures on	yr	104	1999	30r
Postal rate, express mail, up to half-pound		12.45	7/01	108r
Postal rate, letter, first class, first ounce		0.34	7/01	108r
Postal rate, letter, two ounces		0.57	7/01	108r
Postal rate, post card		0.21	7/01	108r
Postal rate, priority mail, two pounds		3.95	7/01	108r
Postal rate, priority mail, up to one pound		3.50	7/01	108r
Telephone bill, business, basic rate	mos	43.19	12/97	18c
Telephone bill, family of three	mos	27.67	3/01	4c
Telephone bill, residential, basic rate	mos	17.55	12/97	18c
Telephone services, expenditures on	yr	860	1999	30r

Louisville, KY - continued

Item	Per	Value	Date	Ref.
Education				
Board, 4-year private college/university	yr	1985	1996	38s
Board, 4-year public college/university	yr	1767	1996	38s
Education expenditures	yr	431	1999	30r
Room, 4-year private college/university	yr	1711	1996	38s
Room, 4-year public college/university	yr	1527	1996	38s
Total cost, 4-year private college/university	yr	11192	1996	38s
Total cost, 4-year public college/university	yr	5455	1996	38s
Tuition, 2-year public college/university, in state	yr	1112	1996	38s
Tuition, 4-year private college/university, in state	yr	7497	1996	38s
Tuition, 4-year public college/university	yr	2161	1996	38s
Energy and Fuels				
Electricity	KWh	0.09	7/01	11r
Electricity	500 KWhs	47.29	7/01	11r
Energy, combined forms, 2400 sq ft	mos	118.54	3/01	4c
Energy, exc. electricity, 2400 sq ft	mos	73.10	3/01	4c
Fuel oil #2	gal	1.43	7/01	11r
Fuel oil and other fuels, expenditures on	yr	45	1999	30r
Gas, cooking, winter, 10 therms	mos	8.90	2/96	98c
Gas, cooking, winter, 30 therms	mos	17.74	2/96	98c
Gas, cooking, winter, 50 therms	mos	34.29	2/96	98c
Gas, heating, winter, average use	mos	77.40	2/96	98c
Gas, natural, commercial rate	1000 cf	8.25	11/00	88s
Gas, regular unleaded, cash, self-service	gal	1.31	3/01	4c
Gasoline, all types	gal	1.60	7/01	11r
Gasoline, unleaded midgrade	gal	1.65	7/01	11r
Gasoline, unleaded premium	gal	1.74	7/01	11r
Natural gas, expenditures on	yr	164	1999	30r
Utility (piped) gas, therm		1.01	7/01	11r
Utility (piped) gas, 40 therms		44.29	7/01	11r
Utility (piped) gas, 100 therms		97.44	7/01	11r
Entertainment				
Bowling, Saturday evening rate	line	2.08	3/01	4c
Entertainment purchases	yr	1574	1999	30r
Fees and admissions paid	yr	371	1999	30r
Monopoly game, Parker Brothers', No. 9	game	10.49	3/01	4c
Movie, first-run, Saturday, evening	adm.	7.50	3/01	4c
Reading purchases	yr	121	1999	30r
Television, radios, sound equipment, expenditures on	yr	561	1999	30r
Tennis balls, yellow, Wilson or Penn, 3	can	2.14	3/01	4c
Groceries				
Groceries, ACCRA Index		97.20	3/01	4c
American processed cheese	lb	3.50	7/01	11r
Antibiotic ointment, Polysporin	0.5 oz	4.57	3/01	4c
Baby food, strained vegetables or fruit, lowest price	4-4.5 oz	0.31	3/01	4c
Bakery products, expenditures on	yr	261	1999	30r
Bananas	lb	0.43	3/01	4c
Bananas	lb	0.47	7/01	11r
Beans, dried, any type, all sizes	lb	0.63	7/01	11r
Beef for stew, boneless	lb	2.86	7/01	11r
Beef or hamburger, ground	lb	1.21	3/01	4c
Beef, expenditures on	yr	210	1999	30r
Bologna, all beef or mixed	lb	2.29	7/01	11r
Bread, French	lb	1.66	7/01	11r
Bread, white	loaf	1.00	3/01	4c
Bread, white, pan	lb	0.87	7/01	11r
Bread, whole wheat, pan	lb	1.38	7/01	11r
Broccoli	lb	1.04	7/01	11r
Butter, salted, grade AA, stick	lb	2.26	7/01	11r
Butter, yoghurt, cheese, etc, expenditures on	yr	170	1999	30r
Cabbage	lb	0.42	7/01	11r
Cereals and cereal products, expenditures on	yr	140	1999	30r
Cheddar cheese, natural	lb	3.75	7/01	11r
Cheese, Kraft grated Parmesan	8 oz	3.87	3/01	4c
Chicken breast, bone-in	lb	1.85	7/01	11r
Chicken legs, bone-in	lb	1.34	7/01	11r

Values are in dollars or fractions of dollars. In the column headed *Ref*, references are shown to sources. Each reference is followed by a letter. These refer to the geographical level for which data were reported: s=State, r=Region, and c=City or metro. The abbreviation *ex* is used to mean *except* or *excluding*; *exp* stands for expenditures. For other abbreviations and further explanations, please see the Introduction.

Louisville, KY - continued

Item	Per	Value	Date	Ref.
Groceries				
Chicken, fresh, whole	lb	1.05	7/01	11r
Chicken, whole fryer	lb	0.97	3/01	4c
Chops, boneless,	lb	4.13	7/01	11r
Chuck roast, graded and ungraded, excl U.S. prime and choice	lb	2.35	7/01	11r
Chuck roast, U.S. choice, boneless	lb	2.67	7/01	11r
Cigarettes, Winston, Kings	carton	25.25	3/01	4c
Coffee, 100%, ground roast, all sizes	lb	2.88	7/01	11r
Coffee, instant, plain, regular, all sizes	16 oz	9.25	7/01	11r
Coffee, vacuum-packed	13 oz	3.47	3/01	4c
Cola, non diet,	2 liter	1.11	7/01	11r
Corn Flakes, Kellogg's or Post Toasties	18 oz	3.23	3/01	4c
Corn, frozen, whole kernel, lowest price	16 oz	0.99	3/01	4c
Crackers, soda, salted	lb	1.70	7/01	11r
Dairy product purchases	yr	282	1999	30r
Eggs, expenditures on	yr	32	1999	30r
Eggs, Grade A or AA	dozen	0.95	3/01	4c
Fats and oils, expenditures on	yr	79	1999	30r
Fish and seafood, expenditures on	yr	99	1999	30r
Flour, white, all purpose	lb	0.32	7/01	11r
Food (excl fruit and vegetables), eaten at home, purchases	yr	815	1999	30r
Food cooked on trips, expenditures on	yr	36	1999	30r
Food purchases	yr	4533	1999	30r
Food purchases, eaten away from home	yr	1873	1999	30r
Food purchases, food eaten at home	yr	2660	1999	30r
Fresh fruits, expenditures on	yr	128	1999	30r
Fresh milk and cream, expenditures on	yr	112	1999	30r
Fresh vegetables, expenditures on	yr	131	1999	30r
Fruit and vegetable purchases	yr	438	1999	30r
Grapefruit	lb	0.59	7/01	11r
Grapes, Thompson, seedless	lb	2.12	7/01	11r
Ground beef, 100% beef	lb	1.76	7/01	11r
Ground beef, lean and extra lean	lb	2.60	7/01	11r
Ground chuck, 100% beef	lb	2.08	7/01	11r
Ham, boneless, excl canned	lb	2.71	7/01	11r
Ham, rump or shank half, bone-in, smoked	lb	2.19	7/01	11r
Ice cream, prepackaged, bulk, regular	1/2 gal	3.93	7/01	11r
Lemons	lb	1.32	7/01	11r
Lettuce, iceberg	head	0.95	3/01	4c
Lettuce, iceberg	lb	0.76	7/01	11r
Margarine, Blue Bonnet or Parkay, stick	lb	0.93	3/01	4c
Milk, fresh, low fat,	gal	2.75	7/01	11r
Milk, fresh, whole, fortified	gal	2.97	7/01	11r
Milk, whole	1/2 gal	1.63	3/01	4c
Nonalcoholic beverages, expenditures on	yr	228	1999	30r
Orange juice, frozen concentrate	16 oz	1.95	7/01	11r
Orange juice, Minute Maid frozen	12 oz	1.31	3/01	4c
Oranges, Navel	lb	0.73	7/01	11r
Oranges, Valencia	lb	0.55	7/01	11r
Peaches, halves or slices, Hunt's, Del Monte, or Libby's	29 oz	1.52	3/01	4c
Peanut butter, creamy, all sizes	lb	1.83	7/01	11r
Pears, Anjou	lb	0.98	7/01	11r
Peas, green, Del Monte or Green Giant	15 oz	0.72	3/01	4c
Pork chops, center cut, bone-in	lb	3.33	7/01	11r
Pork sausage, fresh, loose	lb	2.59	7/01	11r
Pork shoulder picnic, bone-in, smoked	lb	1.12	7/01	11r
Pork, expenditures on	yr	162	1999	30r
Potato chips	16 oz	3.59	7/01	11r
Potatoes, frozen, french fried	lb	1.00	7/01	11r
Potatoes, white or red	10 lb	2.13	3/01	4c
Potatoes, white, all types	lb	0.44	7/01	11r
Poultry, expenditures on	yr	137	1999	30r
Processed fruits, expenditures on	yr	97	1999	30r
Processed vegetables, expenditures on	yr	82	1999	30r
Rice, white, long grain, uncooked	lb	0.51	7/01	11r
Round roast, graded and ungraded, excl U.S. prime and choice	lb	2.96	7/01	11r
Round steak, graded and ungraded, excl U.S. prime and choice	lb	3.11	7/01	11r
Sausage, Jimmy Dean/Owens pork	lb	2.77	3/01	4c

Louisville, KY - continued

Item	Per	Value	Date	Ref.
Groceries - continued				
Shortening, vegetable, Crisco	3 lb	3.40	3/01	4c
Sirloin steak, graded and ungraded, excl U.S. prime and choice	lb	4.23	7/01	11r
Soft drink, Coca Cola, ex deposit	2 liter	1.10	3/01	4c
Spaghetti and macaroni	lb	0.78	7/01	11r
Steak, round, U.S. choice, boneless	lb	3.56	7/01	11r
Steak, sirloin, U.S. choice, boneless	lb	5.65	7/01	11r
Steak, T-bone	lb	6.05	3/01	4c
Strawberries, dry pint	12 oz	1.50	7/01	11r
Sugar and other sweets, expenditures on	yr	99	1999	30r
Sugar, cane or beet	4 lbs	1.76	3/01	4c
Sugar, white, 33-80 ounce package	lb	0.39	7/01	11r
Sugar, white, all sizes	lb	0.42	7/01	11r
Tobacco products and smoking supplies purchases	yr	288	1999	30r
Tomatoes, field grown	lb	1.43	7/01	11r
Tomatoes, Hunt's or Del Monte	14.5 oz	1.01	3/01	4c
Tuna, chunk, light	6 oz	0.55	3/01	4c
Tuna, light, chunk	lb	1.77	7/01	11r
Turkey, frozen, whole	lb	1.05	7/01	11r
Goods and Services				
Miscellaneous goods and services, ACCRA Index		98.70	3/01	4c
Hunting license	yr	15.00	4/01	34s
Health Care				
Health care, ACCRA Index		88.70	3/01	4c
Cardiac catheterization, ave hospital/ physician charges		11480	1998	77s
Childbirth, Cesarean delivery		11587	1997	13r
Childbirth, vaginal delivery		6725	1997	13r
Dentist's fee, adult teeth cleaning and periodic oral exam	visit	57.80	3/01	4c
Doctor's fee, routine exam, established patient	visit	57.20	3/01	4c
Drugs, expenditures on	yr	399	1999	30r
Health care purchases	yr	1971	1999	30r
Health insurance expenditures	yr	933	1999	30r
Hospital care, private room	day	425.00	3/01	4c
Hysterectomy, laproscopically-assisted, ave hospital/physician charges		12390	1998	76s
Hysterectomy, vaginal, ave hospital and physician charges		8440	1998	76s
Medicaid dispensing fee		4.75-5.75	1999	87s
Medical services expenditures	yr	547	1999	30r
Medical supplies, expenditures on	yr	91	1999	30r
Household Goods				
Dishwashing powder, Cascade	50 oz	3.57	3/01	4c
Floor coverings, expenditures on	yr	44	1999	30r
Furniture, expenditures on	yr	335	1999	30r
Household furnishings and equipment purchases	yr	1328	1999	30r
Household textiles, expenditures on	yr	89	1999	30r
Laundry and cleaning supplies, expenditures on	yr	113	1999	30r
Tissues, facial, Kleenex brand	175	1.13	3/01	4c
Housing				
Housing, ACCRA Index		91.40	3/01	4c
Home, 2200 sq ft, 4-br, 2-bath, 2-car garage, average		167423	2000	47c
Home price, existing, ave		160100	10/00	90r
Home value, median		103000	2001	53s
House, 2-story, 2,400 sq ft, 2-car garage, new		135700	2000	54c
House, 2400 sq ft, 8000 sq ft lot, new, urban, utilities	total	185890	3/01	4c
House payment, principal and interest, 25% down payment	mos	936	3/01	4c
Household operation expenditures	yr	553	1999	30r
Housekeeping supplies purchases	yr	473	1999	30r

Values are in dollars or fractions of dollars. In the column headed *Ref*, references are shown to sources. Each reference is followed by a letter. These refer to the geographical level for which data were reported: s=State, r=Region, and c=City or metro. The abbreviation *ex* is used to mean *except* or *excluding*; *exp* stands for *expenditures*. For other abbreviations and further explanations, please see the Introduction.

Louisville, KY - continued

Item	Per	Value	Date	Ref.
Housing				
Housing, expenditures on	yr	10303	1999	30r
Maintenance, repairs, insurance expenditures	yr	699	1999	30r
Monthly rental value of owned home	mos	505	1999	30r
Owned dwellings, expenditures own	yr	3465	1999	30r
Rent expenditures	yr	1641	1999	30r
Rent, apartment, 2 br, 1 1/2-2 baths, unfurn, 950 sq ft, water	mos	652	3/01	4c
Rental unit, 1 bedroom, with utilities	mos	415	4/01	41c
Rental unit, 2 bedroom, with utilities	mos	510	4/01	41c
Rental unit, 3 bedroom, with utilities	mos	703	4/01	41c
Rental unit, 4 bedroom, with utilities	mos	741	4/01	41c
Shelter, expenditures on	yr	5467	1999	30r
Insurance and Pensions				
Life and other personal insurance purchases	yr	414	1999	30r
Pensions and Social Security, expenditures on	yr	2635	1999	30r
Personal insurance and pensions, expenditures on	yr	3048	1999	30r
Legal Fees				
Combination hunting and fishing license	yr	22.50	4/01	34s
Driver's license fee	orig	16.00	1999	48s
Driver's license fee	renew	10.00	1999	48s
Fishing license	yr	15.00	4/01	34s
Personal Goods				
Personal care products and services purchases	yr	393	1999	30r
Shampoo, Alberto VO5	15 oz	0.85	3/01	4c
Toothpaste, Crest or Colgate	6-7 oz	2.05	3/01	4c
Personal Services				
Dry cleaning, man's 2-pc suit		8.30	3/01	4c
Man's haircut, barbershop, no styling		9.60	3/01	4c
Personal services, household, expenditures on	yr	258	1999	30r
Woman's shampoo, trim, blow-dry, no style-change		19.60	3/01	4c
Pets				
Pets, toys, and playground equipment, expenditures on	yr	306	1999	30r
Restaurant Food				
Chicken, fried, thigh and drumstick, KFC/Church's		2.39	3/01	4c
Hamburger with cheese, McDonald's	1/4 lb	2.39	3/01	4c
Pizza, Pizza Hut or Pizza Inn	11-12 in	8.69	3/01	4c
Taxes				
Federal income taxes paid	yr	2047	1999	30r
Personal taxes, expenditures on	yr	2554	1999	30r
Property taxes paid	yr	726	1999	30r
State and local income taxes paid	yr	363	1999	30r
Transportation				
Transportation, ACCRA Index		103.70	3/01	4c
Bus fare, one-way	trip	0.75	2000	1c
Bus fare, to central business district	1-way	1.00	3/01	4c
Cars and trucks, new, expenditures on	yr	1648	1999	30r
Cars and trucks, used, expenditures on	yr	1651	1999	30r
Diesel at the pump	gal	1.15	10/99	73s
Gasoline and motor oil purchases	yr	1052	1999	30r
Gasoline before-tax price (cents)	gal	110.40	10/00	43s
Maintenance and repair expenditures	yr	621	1999	30r
Motorcycle license fee	orig	14.00	1999	49s
Motorcycle license fee	renew	3.00	1999	49s
Public transportation, expenditures on	yr	298	1999	30r
Tire balance, computer or spin balance, front	wheel	9.60	3/01	4c
Transportation purchases	yr	6738	1999	30r
Vehicle expenses, miscellaneous, purchases	yr	2033	1999	30r
Vehicle insurance payments	yr	696	1999	30r
Vehicle purchases (net outlay)	yr	3354	1999	30r
Vehicle rental, lease expenditures	yr	352	1999	30r

Louisville, KY - continued

Item	Per	Value	Date	Ref.
Utilities				
Utilities, ACCRA Index		101.30	3/01	4c
Electrical bill, average	mos	60.42	9/00	9s
Electricity, expenditures on	yr	1115	1999	30r
Electricity, summer, 250 KWh	mos	17.35	2/96	97c
Electricity, summer, 500 KWh	mos	31.42	2/96	97c
Electricity, summer, 750 KWh	mos	43.49	2/96	97c
Electricity, summer, 1000 KWh	mos	120.64	2/96	97c
Electricity and other, mixed, 2400 sq ft, new home	mos	45.44	3/01	4c
Electricity cost, average	KWh	4.10	9/00	9s
Water and other public services, expenditures on	yr	298	1999	30r
Weddings				
Wedding (national average cost)		19936	2000	33r
Attendants' gifts		321	1998	33r
Bridal attendants' apparel (5 persons)		824	2000	33r
Bride's headpiece/veil		173	1998	33r
Bride's wedding dress		859	1998	33r
Clergy, religious facility fee		242	1998	33r
Engagement ring		3177	1998	33r
Flowers		789	1998	33r
Groom's formalwear rental		99	2000	33r
Limousine		410	1998	33r
Marriage license cost		34.50	4/01	35s
Men's formalwear (ushers, best man)		469	2000	33r
Mother of bride apparel		241	2000	33r
Music		866	1998	33r
Photography and videography		1368	1998	33r
Rehearsal dinner		728	1998	33r
Wedding invitations and announcements		341	1998	33r
Wedding reception		7968	2000	33r
Wedding rings (bride and groom)		1060	1998	33r

Lowell, MA

Item	Per	Value	Date	Ref.
Average annual expenditures	yr	37971	1999	30r
Alcoholic Beverages				
Alcoholic beverage purchases	yr	368	1999	30r
Wine, red and white table, all sizes, any origin	liter	9.64	7/01	11r
Appliances				
Major appliances, expenditures on	yr	194	1999	30r
Small appliances, housewares, expenditures on	yr	93	1999	30r
Banking and Money				
Mortgage interest and charges paid	yr	2622	1999	30r
Mortgage principal paid on owned property	yr	1262	1999	30r
Vehicle finance charges paid	yr	240	1999	30r
Charity				
Cash contributions, expenditures	yr	1001	1999	30r
Child Care				
Child raising cost, total, age 0-2	yr	8670	1999	60r
Child raising cost, total, age 3-5	yr	8910	1999	60r
Child raising cost, total, age 6-8	yr	9040	1999	60r
Child raising cost, total, age 9-11	yr	9100	1999	60r
Child raising cost, total, age 12-14	yr	9890	1999	60r
Child raising cost, total, age 15-17	yr	10010	1999	60r
Child's child care and education, age 0-2	yr	1070	1999	60r
Child's child care and education, age 3-5	yr	1190	1999	60r
Child's child care and education, age 6-8	yr	740	1999	60r
Child's child care and education, age 9-11	yr	470	1999	60r
Child's child care and education, age 12-14	yr	350	1999	60r
Child's child care and education, age 15-17	yr	590	1999	60r
Child's clothing, age 0-2	yr	480	1999	60r
Child's clothing, age 3-5	yr	470	1999	60r
Child's clothing, age 6-8	yr	520	1999	60r
Child's clothing, age 9-11	yr	570	1999	60r
Child's clothing, age 12-14	yr	970	1999	60r

Values are in dollars or fractions of dollars. In the column headed *Ref*, references are shown to sources. Each reference is followed by a letter. These refer to the geographical level for which data were reported: s=State, r=Region, and c=City or metro. The abbreviation *ex* is used to mean *except* or *excluding*; *exp* stands for expenditures. For other abbreviations and further explanations, please see the Introduction.

Lowell, MA - continued

Item	Per	Value	Date	Ref.
Child Care				
Child's clothing, age 15-17	yr	870	1999	60r
Child's food, age 0-2	yr	1130	1999	60r
Child's food, age 3-5	yr	1290	1999	60r
Child's food, age 6-8	yr	1640	1999	60r
Child's food, age 9-11	yr	1930	1999	60r
Child's food, age 12-14	yr	1940	1999	60r
Child's food, age 15-17	yr	2150	1999	60r
Child's health care, age 0-2	yr	550	1999	60r
Child's health care, age 3-5	yr	530	1999	60r
Child's health care, age 6-8	yr	610	1999	60r
Child's health care, age 9-11	yr	650	1999	60r
Child's health care, age 12-14	yr	660	1999	60r
Child's health care, age 15-17	yr	690	1999	60r
Child's housing, age 0-2	yr	3555	1999	60r
Child's housing, age 3-5	yr	3530	1999	60r
Child's housing, age 6-8	yr	3490	1999	60r
Child's housing, age 9-11	yr	3340	1999	60r
Child's housing, age 12-14	yr	3530	1999	60r
Child's housing, age 15-17	yr	3140	1999	60r
Child's personal care, reading, age 0-2	yr	920	1999	60r
Child's personal care, reading, age 3-5	yr	950	1999	60r
Child's personal care, reading, age 6-8	yr	980	1999	60r
Child's personal care, reading, age 9-11	yr	1020	1999	60r
Child's personal care, reading, age 12-14	yr	1190	1999	60r
Child's personal care, reading, age 15-17	yr	970	1999	60r
Clothing				
Apparel and services purchases	yr	1831	1999	30r
Boys, 2 to 15, expenditures on	yr	92	1999	30r
Children under 2, expenditures on	yr	63	1999	30r
Footwear, expenditures on	yr	300	1999	30r
Girls, 2 to 15, expenditures on	yr	101	1999	30r
Men and boys, expenditures on	yr	446	1999	30r
Men, 16 and over, expenditures on	yr	354	1999	30r
Women, 16 and over, expenditures on	yr	584	1999	30r
Communications				
Cable modem installation, Adelphi		54.90	6/99	103s
Cable modem installation, Media One		100.00	6/99	103s
Cable modem rate, cable subscriber, Adelphi	mos	34.95	6/99	103s
Cable modem rate, cable subscriber, Media One	mos	34.95- 39.95	6/99	103s
Cable modem rate, non-cable subscriber, Adelphi	mos	44.95	6/99	103s
Cable modem rate, non-cable subscriber, Media One	mos	49.95	6/99	103s
Phone line, single, business, field visit	inst.	120.52	12/97	17s
Phone line, single, business, no field visit	inst.	93.02	12/97	17s
Phone line, single, residence, field visit	inst.	64.57	12/97	17s
Phone line, single, residence, no field visit	inst.	37.07	12/97	17s
Postage and stationery, expenditures on	yr	138	1999	30r
Postal rate, express mail, up to half-pound		12.45	7/01	108r
Postal rate, letter, first class, first ounce		0.34	7/01	108r
Postal rate, letter, two ounces		0.57	7/01	108r
Postal rate, post card		0.21	7/01	108r
Postal rate, priority mail, two pounds		3.95	7/01	108r
Postal rate, priority mail, up to one pound		3.50	7/01	108r
Telephone bill, business, basic rate	mos	39.77	12/97	18c
Telephone bill, residential, basic rate	mos	16.85	12/97	18c
Telephone services, expenditures on	yr	830	1999	30r
Education				
Board, 4-year private college/university	yr	3244	1996	38s
Board, 4-year public college/university	yr	2042	1996	38s
Education expenditures	yr	877	1999	30r
Room, 4-year private college/university	yr	3688	1996	38s
Room, 4-year public college/university	yr	2462	1996	38s
Total cost, 4-year private college/university	yr	23335	1996	38s
Total cost, 4-year public college/university	yr	8757	1996	38s
Tuition, 2-year public college/university, in state	yr	2359	1996	38s
Tuition, 4-year private college/university, in state	yr	16403	1996	38s
Tuition, 4-year public college/university	yr	4253	1996	38s

Lowell, MA - continued

Item	Per	Value	Date	Ref.
Energy and Fuels				
Electricity	KWh	0.12	7/01	11r
Fuel oil #2	gal	1.31	7/01	11r
Fuel oil and other fuels, expenditures on	yr	207	1999	30r
Gas, heating, winter, average use	mos	184.29	2/96	98c
Gas, natural, commercial rate	1000 cf	10.82	11/00	88s
Gasoline, all types	gal	1.80	7/01	11r
Gasoline, unleaded midgrade	gal	1.85	7/01	11r
Gasoline, unleaded premium	gal	1.91	7/01	11r
Gasoline, unleaded regular	gal	1.71	7/01	11r
Natural gas, expenditures on	yr	368	1999	30r
Utility (piped) gas, therm		1.08	7/01	11r
Utility (piped) gas, 40 therms		50.87	7/01	11r
Utility (piped) gas, 100 therms		111.06	7/01	11r
Entertainment				
Entertainment purchases	yr	1821	1999	30r
Fees and admissions paid	yr	511	1999	30r
Television, radios, sound equipment, expenditures on	yr	650	1999	30r
Funerals				
Total cost of funeral		5776.91	1/99	78r
Acknowledgement cards		14.47	1/99	78r
Casket		2090.19	1/99	78r
Cosmetology, hair, other preparation		132.92	1/99	78r
Embalming		377.33	1/99	78r
Funeral at funeral home		352.43	1/99	78r
Hearse (local)		185.55	1/99	78r
Professional service charges		1289.95	1/99	78r
Service car/van		87.42	1/99	78r
Transfer of remains to funeral home		175.48	1/99	78r
Vault		729.40	1/99	78r
Visitation/viewing		341.76	1/99	78r
Groceries				
Apples, red delicious	lb	0.95	7/01	11r
Bacon, sliced	lb	3.44	7/01	11r
Bakery products, expenditures on	yr	310	1999	30r
Bananas	lb	0.55	7/01	11r
Beef, expenditures on	yr	236	1999	30r
Bread, white, pan	lb	1.09	7/01	11r
Butter, yoghurt, cheese, etc, expenditures on	yr	214	1999	30r
Cereals and bakery product purchases	yr	474	1999	30r
Cereals and cereal products, expenditures on	yr	164	1999	30r
Chicken legs, bone-in	lb	1.23	7/01	11r
Chicken, fresh, whole	lb	1.13	7/01	11r
Chuck roast, U.S. choice, boneless	lb	2.79	7/01	11r
Coffee, 100%, ground roast, all sizes	lb	3.40	7/01	11r
Dairy product purchases	yr	342	1999	30r
Eggs, expenditures on	yr	34	1999	30r
Eggs, grade A, large	dozen	0.82	7/01	11r
Fats and oils, expenditures on	yr	80	1999	30r
Fish and seafood, expenditures on	yr	123	1999	30r
Food (excl fruit and vegetables), eaten at home, purchases	yr	838	1999	30r
Food cooked on trips, expenditures on	yr	48	1999	30r
Food purchases	yr	5314	1999	30r
Food purchases, eaten away from home	yr	2313	1999	30r
Food purchases, food eaten at home	yr	3001	1999	30r
Fresh fruits, expenditures on	yr	169	1999	30r
Fresh milk and cream, expenditures on	yr	128	1999	30r
Fresh vegetables, expenditures on	yr	164	1999	30r
Grapefruit	lb	0.67	7/01	11r
Grapes, Thompson, seedless	lb	2.18	7/01	11r
Ground beef, lean and extra lean	lb	2.66	7/01	11r
Ground chuck, 100% beef	lb	2.04	7/01	11r
Lettuce, iceberg	lb	0.76	7/01	11r
Meats, poultry, fish, and egg purchases	yr	808	1999	30r
Nonalcoholic beverages, expenditures on	yr	225	1999	30r
Orange juice, frozen concentrate	16 oz	1.88	7/01	11r
Oranges, Navel	lb	0.79	7/01	11r
Oranges, Valencia	lb	0.56	7/01	11r
Peaches	lb	1.16	7/01	11r

Values are in dollars or fractions of dollars. In the column headed *Ref*, references are shown to sources. Each reference is followed by a letter. These refer to the geographical level for which data were reported: s=State, r=Region, and c=City or metro. The abbreviation *ex* is used to mean *except* or *excluding*; *exp* stands for *expenditures*. For other abbreviations and further explanations, please see the Introduction.

Lowell, MA - continued

Item	Per	Value	Date	Ref.
Groceries				
Peanut butter, creamy, all sizes	lb	2.01	7/01	11r
Pears, Anjou	lb	1.16	7/01	11r
Pork chops, center cut, bone-in	lb	3.57	7/01	11r
Pork, expenditures on	yr	146	1999	30r
Potato chips	16 oz	3.37	7/01	11r
Potatoes, white, all types	lb	0.42	7/01	11r
Poultry, expenditures on	yr	158	1999	30r
Processed fruits, expenditures on	yr	124	1999	30r
Processed vegetables, expenditures on	yr	82	1999	30r
Round roast, U.S. choice, boneless	lb	3.04	7/01	11r
Spaghetti and macaroni	lb	1.04	7/01	11r
Steak, sirloin, U.S. choice, boneless	lb	5.39	7/01	11r
Strawberries, dry pint	12 oz	1.51	7/01	11r
Sugar and other sweets, expenditures on	yr	110	1999	30r
Sugar, white, 33-80 ounce package	lb	0.46	7/01	11r
Sugar, white, all sizes	lb	0.47	7/01	11r
Tobacco products and smoking supplies purchases	yr	309	1999	30r
Yogurt, natural, fruit flavored	8 oz	0.79	7/01	11r
Goods and Services				
B&B Japanese maple (acer japonicum)	gal	38.99-125.00	4/00	93r
Boxwood (buxus)	2 gal	15.99-49.95	4/00	93r
Daylily (hemerocallis)	gal	4.95	4/00	93r
Flat of annuals		8.00-14.99	4/00	93r
Fountain grass (pennisetum)	gal	6.99-9.99	4/00	93r
Hanging basket (10 in)		12.95-19.99	4/00	93r
Hardy geranium (geranium)	gal	6.95-7.99	4/00	93r
Hosta (hosta)	gal	4.95	4/00	93r
Lilac (syrubga vulgaris)	2 gal	17.99-74.95	4/00	93r
Miscellaneous purchases	yr	872	1999	30r
Rhododendron (rhododendron)	2 gal	23.99-54.95	4/00	93r
Sage (salvia)	gal	6.95-7.99	4/00	93r
Wintercreeper euonymus (euonymus fortunei)	2 gal	14.99-23.95	4/00	93r
Hunting license	yr	27.50	4/01	34s
Health Care				
Cardiac catheterization, ave hospital/ physician charges		17080	1998	77s
Childbirth, Cesarean delivery		14716	1997	13r
Childbirth, vaginal delivery		8541	1997	13r
Drugs, expenditures on	yr	296	1999	30r
Health care purchases	yr	1788	1999	30r
Health insurance expenditures	yr	875	1999	30r
Hysterectomy, laproscopically-assisted, ave hospital/physician charges		13100	1998	76s
Hysterectomy, vaginal, ave hospital and physician charges		8780	1998	76s
Medicaid dispensing fee		3.00	1999	87s
Medical services expenditures	yr	516	1999	30r
Medical supplies, expenditures on	yr	102	1999	30r
Plastic surgery, breast augmentation		4232	2000	7r
Plastic surgery, breast lift		4605	2000	7r
Plastic surgery, facelift		6964	2000	7r
Plastic surgery, hair transplantation		4193	2000	7r
Plastic surgery, lip augmentation		1675	2000	7r
Plastic surgery, lower body lift		6611	2000	7r
Plastic surgery, thigh lift		4751	2000	7r
Household Goods				
Floor coverings, expenditures on	yr	59	1999	30r
Furniture, expenditures on	yr	388	1999	30r
Household furnishings and equipment purchases	yr	1567	1999	30r

Lowell, MA - continued

Item	Per	Value	Date	Ref.
Household Goods - continued				
Household textiles, expenditures on	yr	112	1999	30r
Laundry and cleaning supplies, expenditures on	yr	104	1999	30r
Housing				
Home price, existing, ave		180800	10/00	90r
Home value, median		261000	2001	53s
Household operation expenditures	yr	581	1999	30r
Housekeeping supplies purchases	yr	474	1999	30r
Lodging expenditures	yr	550	1999	30r
Maintenance, repairs, insurance expenditures	yr	835	1999	30r
Monthly rental value of owned home	mos	663	1999	30r
Owned dwellings, expenditures own	yr	5209	1999	30r
Rent expenditures	yr	2390	1999	30r
Rental unit, 1 bedroom, with utilities	mos	659	4/01	41c
Rental unit, 2 bedroom, with utilities	mos	796	4/01	41c
Rental unit, 3 bedroom, with utilities	mos	997	4/01	41c
Rental unit, 4 bedroom, with utilities	mos	1115	4/01	41c
Shelter, expenditures on	yr	8149	1999	30r
Insurance and Pensions				
Life and other personal insurance purchases	yr	424	1999	30r
Pensions and Social Security, expenditures on	yr	3037	1999	30r
Legal Fees				
Divorce, filing fee		100.00	4/01	35s
Driver's license fee	renew	33.75	1999	48s
Driver's license fee	orig	33.75	1999	48s
Fishing license	yr	27.50	4/01	34s
Personal Goods				
Personal care products and services purchases	yr	399	1999	30r
Personal Services				
Personal services, household, expenditures on	yr	271	1999	30r
Pets				
Pets, toys, and playground equipment, expenditures on	yr	325	1999	30r
Taxes				
Federal income taxes paid	yr	2606	1999	30r
Personal taxes, expenditures on	yr	3567	1999	30r
Property taxes paid	yr	1752	1999	30r
State and local income taxes paid	yr	694	1999	30r
Transportation				
Cars and trucks, new, expenditures on	yr	1496	1999	30r
Cars and trucks, used, expenditures on	yr	1251	1999	30r
Diesel at the pump	gal	1.32	10/99	73s
Gasoline and motor oil purchases	yr	901	1999	30r
Gasoline before-tax price (cents)	gal	118.70	10/00	43s
Maintenance and repair expenditures	yr	618	1999	30r
Public transportation, expenditures on	yr	575	1999	30r
Transportation purchases	yr	6503	1999	30r
Vehicle expenses, miscellaneous, purchases	yr	2266	1999	30r
Vehicle insurance payments	yr	824	1999	30r
Vehicle purchases (net outlay)	yr	2761	1999	30r
Vehicle rental, lease expenditures	yr	584	1999	30r
Travel				
Hotel room	night	111.15	2/01	95s
Utilities				
Electrical bill, average	mos	58.58	9/00	9s
Electricity, expenditures on	yr	837	1999	30r
Electricity cost, average	KWh	8.90	9/00	9s
Utilities, fuels, and public services purchased	yr	2457	1999	30r
Water and other public services, expenditures on	yr	215	1999	30r

Values are in dollars or fractions of dollars. In the column headed *Ref*, references are shown to sources. Each reference is followed by a letter. These refer to the geographical level for which data were reported: s=State, r=Region, and c=City or metro. The abbreviation *ex* is used to mean *except* or *excluding*; *exp* stands for *expenditures*. For other abbreviations and further explanations, please see the Introduction.

Lowell, MA - continued

Item	Per	Value	Date	Ref.
Weddings				
Wedding (national average cost)		19936	2000	33r
Wedding (regional average total cost)		29454	1997	110r
Attendants' gifts		321	1998	33r
Bridal attendants' apparel (5 persons)		824	2000	33r
Bride's headpiece/veil		173	1998	33r
Bride's wedding dress		859	1998	33r
Clergy, religious facility fee		242	1998	33r
Engagement ring		3177	1998	33r
Flowers		789	1998	33r
Groom's formalwear rental		99	2000	33r
Limousine		410	1998	33r
Marriage license cost		25.00	4/01	35s
Men's formalwear (ushers, best man)		469	2000	33r
Mother of bride apparel		241	2000	33r
Music		866	1998	33r
Photography and videography		1368	1998	33r
Rehearsal dinner		728	1998	33r
Wedding invitations and announcements		341	1998	33r
Wedding reception		7968	2000	33r
Wedding rings (bride and groom)		1060	1998	33r

Lubbock, TX

Item	Per	Value	Date	Ref.
Composite, ACCRA index		92.70	3/01	4c
Alcoholic Beverages				
Alcoholic beverage purchases	yr	253	1999	30r
Beer, Heineken, 12-oz, ex deposit	6	8.49	3/01	4c
J & B Scotch	750-ml	22.19	3/01	4c
Malt beverages, all types, all sizes, any origin	16 oz	0.96	7/01	11r
Wine, Livingston or Gallo, Chablis blanc	1.5 liter	6.59	3/01	4c
Appliances				
Appliance repair, service call, washing machine	min lab chg	40.20	3/01	4c
Major appliances, expenditures on	yr	172	1999	30r
Small appliances, housewares, expenditures on	yr	81	1999	30r
Banking and Money				
Mortgage interest and charges paid	yr	2039	1999	30r
Mortgage principal paid on owned property	yr	1026	1999	30r
Mortgage rate, incl. points and orig. fee, 30-yr. conv. fixed or ARM	mos	7.10	3/01	4c
Vehicle finance charges paid	yr	365	1999	30r
Charity				
Cash contributions, expenditures	yr	1127	1999	30r
Child Care				
Child raising cost, total, age 0-2	yr	8540	1999	60r
Child raising cost, total, age 3-5	yr	8780	1999	60r
Child raising cost, total, age 6-8	yr	8820	1999	60r
Child raising cost, total, age 9-11	yr	8800	1999	60r
Child raising cost, total, age 12-14	yr	9510	1999	60r
Child raising cost, total, age 15-17	yr	9740	1999	60r
Child's child care and education, age 0-2	yr	1380	1999	60r
Child's child care and education, age 3-5	yr	1520	1999	60r
Child's child care and education, age 6-8	yr	990	1999	60r
Child's child care and education, age 9-11	yr	650	1999	60r
Child's child care and education, age 12-14	yr	490	1999	60r
Child's child care and education, age 15-17	yr	840	1999	60r
Child's clothing, age 0-2	yr	480	1999	60r
Child's clothing, age 3-5	yr	470	1999	60r
Child's clothing, age 6-8	yr	520	1999	60r
Child's clothing, age 9-11	yr	570	1999	60r
Child's clothing, age 12-14	yr	950	1999	60r
Child's clothing, age 15-17	yr	850	1999	60r
Child's food, age 0-2	yr	1000	1999	60r
Child's food, age 3-5	yr	1160	1999	60r
Child's food, age 6-8	yr	1490	1999	60r
Child's food, age 9-11	yr	1770	1999	60r
Child's food, age 12-14	yr	1770	1999	60r
Child's food, age 15-17	yr	1980	1999	60r

Item	Per	Value	Date	Ref.
Child Care - continued				
Child's health care, age 0-2	yr	620	1999	60r
Child's health care, age 3-5	yr	590	1999	60r
Child's health care, age 6-8	yr	680	1999	60r
Child's health care, age 9-11	yr	720	1999	60r
Child's health care, age 12-14	yr	730	1999	60r
Child's health care, age 15-17	yr	760	1999	60r
Child's housing, age 0-2	yr	3070	1999	60r
Child's housing, age 3-5	yr	3050	1999	60r
Child's housing, age 6-8	yr	3010	1999	60r
Child's housing, age 9-11	yr	2850	1999	60r
Child's housing, age 12-14	yr	3040	1999	60r
Child's housing, age 15-17	yr	2650	1999	60r
Child's personal care, reading, age 0-2	yr	910	1999	60r
Child's personal care, reading, age 3-5	yr	930	1999	60r
Child's personal care, reading, age 6-8	yr	960	1999	60r
Child's personal care, reading, age 9-11	yr	1000	1999	60r
Child's personal care, reading, age 12-14	yr	1170	1999	60r
Child's personal care, reading, age 15-17	yr	950	1999	60r
Clothing				
Apparel and services purchases	yr	1610	1999	30r
Boys' brief, cotton	3	4.01	3/01	4c
Boys, 2 to 15, expenditures on	yr	89	1999	30r
Children under 2, expenditures on	yr	79	1999	30r
Footwear, expenditures on	yr	283	1999	30r
Girls, 2 to 15, expenditures on	yr	103	1999	30r
Men and boys, expenditures on	yr	351	1999	30r
Men, 16 and over, expenditures on	yr	262	1999	30r
Shirt, man's dress shirt		25.80	3/01	4c
Slacks, man's "No Wrinkles" khaki		39.00	3/01	4c
Women, 16 and over, expenditures on	yr	538	1999	30r
Communications				
Cable modem installation, AT&T-BIS		150.00	6/99	103s
Cable modem installation, Marcus		499.00	6/99	103s
Cable modem installation, Time Warner		75.00-225.00	6/99	103s
Cable modem rate, cable subscriber, AT&T-BIS	mos	39.95	6/99	103s
Cable modem rate, cable subscriber, Marcus	mos	14.95-49.95	6/99	103s
Cable modem rate, cable subscriber, Time Warner	mos	39.95-49.95	6/99	103s
Cable modem rate, non-cable subscriber, Marcus	mos	60.95	6/99	103s
Cable modem rate, non-cable subscriber, Time Warner	mos	39.95-54.95	6/99	103s
Newspaper subscription, daily and Sunday delivery	mos	12.15	3/01	4c
Phone line, single, business, field visit	inst.	71.90	12/97	17s
Phone line, single, business, no field visit	inst.	57.30	12/97	17s
Phone line, single, residence, field visit	inst.	52.95	12/97	17s
Phone line, single, residence, no field visit	inst.	38.35	12/97	17s
Postage and stationery, expenditures on	yr	104	1999	30r
Postal rate, express mail, up to half-pound		12.45	7/01	108r
Postal rate, letter, first class, first ounce		0.34	7/01	108r
Postal rate, letter, two ounces		0.57	7/01	108r
Postal rate, post card		0.21	7/01	108r
Postal rate, priority mail, two pounds		3.95	7/01	108r
Postal rate, priority mail, up to one pound		3.50	7/01	108r
Telephone bill, family of three	mos	16.91	3/01	4c
Telephone services, expenditures on	yr	860	1999	30r
Education				
Board, 4-year private college/university	yr	2198	1996	38s
Board, 4-year public college/university	yr	1759	1996	38s
Education expenditures	yr	431	1999	30r
Room, 4-year private college/university	yr	2000	1996	38s
Room, 4-year public college/university	yr	1885	1996	38s
Total cost, 4-year private college/university	yr	13156	1996	38s
Total cost, 4-year public college/university	yr	5464	1996	38s
Tuition, 2-year public college/university, in state	yr	771	1996	38s

Values are in dollars or fractions of dollars. In the column headed *Ref*, references are shown to sources. Each reference is followed by a letter. These refer to the geographical level for which data were reported: s=State, r=Region, and c=City or metro. The abbreviation *ex* is used to mean *except* or *excluding*; *exp* stands for expenditures. For other abbreviations and further explanations, please see the Introduction.

Lubbock, TX - continued

Item	Per	Value	Date	Ref.
Education				
Tuition, 4-year private college/university, in state	yr	8959	1996	38s
Tuition, 4-year public college/university	yr	1820	1996	38s
Energy and Fuels				
Electricity	KWh	0.09	7/01	11r
Electricity	500 KWhs	47.29	7/01	11r
Energy, combined forms, 2400 sq ft	mos	127.06	3/01	4c
Energy, exc. electricity, 2400 sq ft	mos	63.54	3/01	4c
Fuel oil #2	gal	1.43	7/01	11r
Fuel oil and other fuels, expenditures on	yr	45	1999	30r
Gas, natural, commercial rate	1000 cf	6.94	11/00	88s
Gas, regular unleaded, cash, self-service	gal	1.34	3/01	4c
Gasoline, all types	gal	1.60	7/01	11r
Gasoline, unleaded midgrade	gal	1.65	7/01	11r
Gasoline, unleaded premium	gal	1.74	7/01	11r
Natural gas, expenditures on	yr	164	1999	30r
Utility (piped) gas, therm		1.01	7/01	11r
Utility (piped) gas, 40 therms		44.29	7/01	11r
Utility (piped) gas, 100 therms		97.44	7/01	11r
Entertainment				
Bowling, Saturday evening rate	line	3.06	3/01	4c
Entertainment purchases	yr	1574	1999	30r
Fees and admissions paid	yr	371	1999	30r
Monopoly game, Parker Brothers', No. 9	game	10.20	3/01	4c
Movie, first-run, Saturday, evening	adm.	7.00	3/01	4c
Reading purchases	yr	121	1999	30r
Television, radios, sound equipment, expenditures on	yr	561	1999	30r
Tennis balls, yellow, Wilson or Penn, 3	can	1.96	3/01	4c
Funerals				
Total cost of funeral		5842.28	1/99	78r
Acknowledgement cards		28.35	1/99	78r
Casket		2494.29	1/99	78r
Cosmetology, hair, other preparation		109.22	1/99	78r
Embalming		361.42	1/99	78r
Funeral at funeral home		349.20	1/99	78r
Hearse (local)		161.91	1/99	78r
Professional service charges		1116.50	1/99	78r
Service car/van		65.56	1/99	78r
Transfer of remains to funeral home		143.56	1/99	78r
Vault		785.25	1/99	78r
Visitation/viewing		227.02	1/99	78r
Groceries				
Groceries, ACCRA Index		90.90	3/01	4c
American processed cheese	lb	3.50	7/01	11r
Antibiotic ointment, Polysporin	0.5 oz	4.50	3/01	4c
Baby food, strained vegetables or fruit, lowest price	4-4.5 oz	0.33	3/01	4c
Bakery products, expenditures on	yr	261	1999	30r
Bananas	lb	0.49	3/01	4c
Bananas	lb	0.47	7/01	11r
Beans, dried, any type, all sizes	lb	0.63	7/01	11r
Beef for stew, boneless	lb	2.86	7/01	11r
Beef or hamburger, ground	lb	1.74	3/01	4c
Beef, expenditures on	yr	210	1999	30r
Bologna, all beef or mixed	lb	2.29	7/01	11r
Bread, French	lb	1.66	7/01	11r
Bread, white	loaf	0.69	3/01	4c
Bread, white, pan	lb	0.87	7/01	11r
Bread, whole wheat, pan	lb	1.38	7/01	11r
Broccoli	lb	1.04	7/01	11r
Butter, salted, grade AA, stick	lb	2.26	7/01	11r
Butter, yoghurt, cheese, etc, expenditures on	yr	170	1999	30r
Cabbage	lb	0.42	7/01	11r
Cereals and cereal products, expenditures on	yr	140	1999	30r
Cheddar cheese, natural	lb	3.75	7/01	11r
Cheese, Kraft grated Parmesan	8 oz	4.22	3/01	4c
Chicken breast, bone-in	lb	1.85	7/01	11r

Lubbock, TX - continued

Item	Per	Value	Date	Ref.
Groceries - continued				
Chicken legs, bone-in	lb	1.34	7/01	11r
Chicken, fresh, whole	lb	1.05	7/01	11r
Chicken, whole fryer	lb	0.84	3/01	4c
Chops, boneless,	lb	4.13	7/01	11r
Chuck roast, graded and ungraded, excl U.S. prime and choice	lb	2.35	7/01	11r
Chuck roast, U.S. choice, boneless	lb	2.67	7/01	11r
Cigarettes, Winston, Kings	carton	28.57	3/01	4c
Coffee, 100%, ground roast, all sizes	lb	2.88	7/01	11r
Coffee, instant, plain, regular, all sizes	16 oz	9.25	7/01	11r
Coffee, vacuum-packed	13 oz	2.56	3/01	4c
Cola, non diet,	2 liter	1.11	7/01	11r
Corn Flakes, Kellogg's or Post Toasties	18 oz	2.07	3/01	4c
Corn, frozen, whole kernel, lowest price	16 oz	1.04	3/01	4c
Crackers, soda, salted	lb	1.70	7/01	11r
Dairy product purchases	yr	282	1999	30r
Eggs, expenditures on	yr	32	1999	30r
Eggs, Grade A or AA	dozen	1.19	3/01	4c
Fats and oils, expenditures on	yr	79	1999	30r
Fish and seafood, expenditures on	yr	99	1999	30r
Flour, white, all purpose	lb	0.32	7/01	11r
Food (excl fruit and vegetables), eaten at home, purchases	yr	815	1999	30r
Food cooked on trips, expenditures on	yr	36	1999	30r
Food purchases	yr	4533	1999	30r
Food purchases, eaten away from home	yr	1873	1999	30r
Food purchases, food eaten at home	yr	2660	1999	30r
Fresh fruits, expenditures on	yr	128	1999	30r
Fresh milk and cream, expenditures on	yr	112	1999	30r
Fresh vegetables, expenditures on	yr	131	1999	30r
Fruit and vegetable purchases	yr	438	1999	30r
Grapefruit	lb	0.59	7/01	11r
Grapes, Thompson, seedless	lb	2.12	7/01	11r
Ground beef, 100% beef	lb	1.76	7/01	11r
Ground beef, lean and extra lean	lb	2.60	7/01	11r
Ground chuck, 100% beef	lb	2.08	7/01	11r
Ham, boneless, excl canned	lb	2.71	7/01	11r
Ham, rump or shank half, bone-in, smoked	lb	2.19	7/01	11r
Ice cream, prepackaged, bulk, regular	1/2 gal	3.93	7/01	11r
Lemons	lb	1.32	7/01	11r
Lettuce, iceberg	head	1.22	3/01	4c
Lettuce, iceberg	lb	0.76	7/01	11r
Margarine, Blue Bonnet or Parkay, stick	lb	0.78	3/01	4c
Milk, fresh, low fat,	gal	2.75	7/01	11r
Milk, fresh, whole, fortified	gal	2.97	7/01	11r
Milk, whole	1/2 gal	1.37	3/01	4c
Nonalcoholic beverages, expenditures on	yr	228	1999	30r
Orange juice, frozen concentrate	16 oz	1.95	7/01	11r
Orange juice, Minute Maid frozen	12 oz	1.22	3/01	4c
Oranges, Navel	lb	0.73	7/01	11r
Oranges, Valencia	lb	0.55	7/01	11r
Peaches, halves or slices, Hunt's, Del Monte, or Libby's	29 oz	1.64	3/01	4c
Peanut butter, creamy, all sizes	lb	1.83	7/01	11r
Pears, Anjou	lb	0.98	7/01	11r
Peas, green, Del Monte or Green Giant	15 oz	0.67	3/01	4c
Pork chops, center cut, bone-in	lb	3.33	7/01	11r
Pork sausage, fresh, loose	lb	2.59	7/01	11r
Pork shoulder picnic, bone-in, smoked	lb	1.12	7/01	11r
Pork, expenditures on	yr	162	1999	30r
Potato chips	16 oz	3.59	7/01	11r
Potatoes, frozen, french fried	lb	1.00	7/01	11r
Potatoes, white or red	10 lb	2.58	3/01	4c
Potatoes, white, all types	lb	0.44	7/01	11r
Poultry, expenditures on	yr	137	1999	30r
Processed fruits, expenditures on	yr	97	1999	30r
Processed vegetables, expenditures on	yr	82	1999	30r
Rice, white, long grain, uncooked	lb	0.51	7/01	11r
Round roast, graded and ungraded, excl U.S. prime and choice	lb	2.96	7/01	11r
Round steak, graded and ungraded, excl U.S. prime and choice	lb	3.11	7/01	11r

Values are in dollars or fractions of dollars. In the column headed *Ref*, references are shown to sources. Each reference is followed by a letter. These refer to the geographical level for which data were reported: s=State, r=Region, and c=City or metro. The abbreviation *ex* is used to mean *except* or *excluding*; *exp* stands for *expenditures*. For other abbreviations and further explanations, please see the Introduction.

Lubbock, TX - continued

Item	Per	Value	Date	Ref.
Groceries				
Sausage, Jimmy Dean/Owens pork	lb	2.42	3/01	4c
Shortening, vegetable, Crisco	3 lb	2.77	3/01	4c
Sirloin steak, graded and ungraded, excl U.S. prime and choice	lb	4.23	7/01	11r
Soft drink, Coca Cola, ex deposit	2 liter	1.53	3/01	4c
Spaghetti and macaroni	lb	0.78	7/01	11r
Steak, round, U.S. choice, boneless	lb	3.56	7/01	11r
Steak, sirloin, U.S. choice, boneless	lb	5.65	7/01	11r
Steak, T-bone	lb	6.57	3/01	4c
Strawberries, dry pint	12 oz	1.50	7/01	11r
Sugar and other sweets, expenditures on	yr	99	1999	30r
Sugar, cane or beet	4 lbs	1.36	3/01	4c
Sugar, white, 33-80 ounce package	lb	0.39	7/01	11r
Sugar, white, all sizes	lb	0.42	7/01	11r
Tobacco products and smoking supplies purchases	yr	288	1999	30r
Tomatoes, field grown	lb	1.43	7/01	11r
Tomatoes, Hunt's or Del Monte	14.5 oz	0.85	3/01	4c
Tuna, chunk, light	6 oz	0.47	3/01	4c
Tuna, light, chunk	lb	1.77	7/01	11r
Turkey, frozen, whole	lb	1.05	7/01	11r
Goods and Services				
Miscellaneous goods and services, ACCRA Index		96.20	3/01	4c
B&B Japanese maple (acer japonicum)	gal	79.98-99.00	4/00	93r
Boxwood (buxus)	2 gal	12.98-18.99	4/00	93r
Christmas tree, noble fir		40-60	2000	65s
Daylily (hemerocallis)	gal	7.96-11.00	4/00	93r
Flat of annuals		13.99-27.99	4/00	93r
Fountain grass (pennisetum)	gal	6.96-9.00	4/00	93r
Hanging basket (10 in)		9.99-24.99	4/00	93r
Hardy geranium (geranium)	gal	5.96-8.00	4/00	93r
Hosta (hosta)	gal	8.96-12.99	4/00	93r
Lilac (syrubga vulgaris)	2 gal	13.00-19.99	4/00	93r
Rhododendron (rhododendron)	2 gal	12.98-29.99	4/00	93r
Sage (salvia)	gal	5.96-8.00	4/00	93r
Wintercreeper euonymus (euonymus fortunei)	2 gal	13.00-18.99	4/00	93r
Hunting license	yr	19.00	4/01	34s
Health Care				
Health care, ACCRA Index		101.20	3/01	4c
Cardiac catheterization, ave hospital/ physician charges		20140	1998	77s
Childbirth, Cesarean delivery		11587	1997	13r
Childbirth, vaginal delivery		6725	1997	13r
Dentist's fee, adult teeth cleaning and periodic oral exam	visit	70.56	3/01	4c
Doctor's fee, routine exam, established patient	visit	59.44	3/01	4c
Drugs, expenditures on	yr	399	1999	30r
Health care purchases	yr	1971	1999	30r
Health insurance expenditures	yr	933	1999	30r
Hospital care, private room	day	571.00	3/01	4c
Hysterectomy, laproscopically-assisted, ave hospital/physician charges		15700	1998	76s
Hysterectomy, vaginal, ave hospital and physician charges		12180	1998	76s
Medicaid dispensing fee		5.27	1999	87s
Medical services expenditures	yr	547	1999	30r
Medical supplies, expenditures on	yr	91	1999	30r

Lubbock, TX - continued

Item	Per	Value	Date	Ref.
Household Goods				
Dishwashing powder, Cascade	50 oz	3.14	3/01	4c
Floor coverings, expenditures on	yr	44	1999	30r
Furniture, expenditures on	yr	335	1999	30r
Household furnishings and equipment purchases	yr	1328	1999	30r
Household textiles, expenditures on	yr	89	1999	30r
Laundry and cleaning supplies, expenditures on	yr	113	1999	30r
Tissues, facial, Kleenex brand	175	1.19	3/01	4c
Housing				
Housing, ACCRA Index		82.60	3/01	4c
Home, 2200 sq ft, 4-br, 2-bath, 2-car garage, average		131000	2000	47c
Home price, existing, ave		160100	10/00	90r
Home value, median		112000	2001	53s
House, 2400 sq ft, 8000 sq ft lot, new, urban, utilities	total	169589	3/01	4c
House payment, principal and interest, 25% down payment	mos	855	3/01	4c
Household operation expenditures	yr	553	1999	30r
Housekeeping supplies purchases	yr	473	1999	30r
Housing, expenditures on	yr	10303	1999	30r
Maintenance, repairs, insurance expenditures	yr	699	1999	30r
Monthly rental value of owned home	mos	505	1999	30r
Owned dwellings, expenditures own	yr	3465	1999	30r
Rent expenditures	yr	1641	1999	30r
Rent, apartment, 2 br, 1 1/2-2 baths, unfurn, 950 sq ft, water	mos	565	3/01	4c
Rental unit, 1 bedroom, with utilities	mos	390	4/01	41c
Rental unit, 2 bedroom, with utilities	mos	506	4/01	41c
Rental unit, 3 bedroom, with utilities	mos	704	4/01	41c
Rental unit, 4 bedroom, with utilities	mos	780	4/01	41c
Shelter, expenditures on	yr	5467	1999	30r
Insurance and Pensions				
Life and other personal insurance purchases	yr	414	1999	30r
Pensions and Social Security, expenditures on	yr	2635	1999	30r
Personal insurance and pensions, expenditures on	yr	3048	1999	30r
Legal Fees				
Divorce, filing fee		150.00-200.00	4/01	35s
Driver's license fee	renew	20.00	1999	48s
Driver's license fee	orig	24.00	1999	48s
Fishing license	yr	19.00	4/01	34s
Personal Goods				
Personal care products and services purchases	yr	393	1999	30r
Shampoo, Alberto VO5	15 oz	1.02	3/01	4c
Toothpaste, Crest or Colgate	6-7 oz	2.08	3/01	4c
Personal Services				
Dry cleaning, man's 2-pc suit		6.47	3/01	4c
Man's haircut, barbershop, no styling		8.80	3/01	4c
Personal services, household, expenditures on	yr	258	1999	30r
Woman's shampoo, trim, blow-dry, no style-change		22.60	3/01	4c
Pets				
Pets, toys, and playground equipment, expenditures on	yr	306	1999	30r
Restaurant Food				
Chicken, fried, thigh and drumstick, KFC/ Church's		2.40	3/01	4c
Hamburger with cheese, McDonald's	1/4 lb	1.99	3/01	4c
Pizza, Pizza Hut or Pizza Inn	11-12 in	8.99	3/01	4c

Values are in dollars or fractions of dollars. In the column headed *Ref*, references are shown to sources. Each reference is followed by a letter. These refer to the geographical level for which data were reported: s=State, r=Region, and c=City or metro. The abbreviation *ex* is used to mean *except* or *excluding*; *exp* stands for *expenditures*. For other abbreviations and further explanations, please see the Introduction.

Lubbock, TX - continued

Item	Per	Value	Date	Ref.
Taxes				
Federal income taxes paid	yr	2047	1999	30r
Personal taxes, expenditures on	yr	2554	1999	30r
Property taxes paid	yr	726	1999	30r
State and local income taxes paid	yr	363	1999	30r
Transportation				
Transportation, ACCRA Index		102.00	3/01	4c
Bus fare, one-way	trip	1.00	2000	1c
Cars and trucks, new, expenditures on	yr	1648	1999	30r
Cars and trucks, used, expenditures on	yr	1651	1999	30r
Diesel at the pump	gal	1.18	10/99	73s
Gasoline and motor oil purchases	yr	1052	1999	30r
Gasoline before-tax price (cents)	gal	101.30	10/00	43s
Maintenance and repair expenditures	yr	621	1999	30r
Public transportation, expenditures on	yr	298	1999	30r
Tire balance, computer or spin balance, front	wheel	8.80	3/01	4c
Transportation purchases	yr	6738	1999	30r
Vehicle expenses, miscellaneous, purchases	yr	2033	1999	30r
Vehicle insurance payments	yr	696	1999	30r
Vehicle purchases (net outlay)	yr	3354	1999	30r
Vehicle rental, lease expenditures	yr	352	1999	30r
Utilities				
Utilities, ACCRA Index		100.50	3/01	4c
Electrical bill, average	mos	87.17	9/00	9s
Electricity, expenditures on	yr	1115	1999	30r
Electricity and other, mixed, 2400 sq ft, new home	mos	63.52	3/01	4c
Electricity cost, average	KWh	6.48	9/00	9s
Water and other public services, expenditures on	yr	298	1999	30r
Weddings				
Wedding (national average cost)		19936	2000	33r
Attendants' gifts		321	1998	33r
Bridal attendants' apparel (5 persons)		824	2000	33r
Bride's headpiece/veil		173	1998	33r
Bride's wedding dress		859	1998	33r
Clergy, religious facility fee		242	1998	33r
Engagement ring		3177	1998	33r
Flowers		789	1998	33r
Groom's formalwear rental		99	2000	33r
Limousine		410	1998	33r
Marriage license cost		36.00	4/01	35s
Men's formalwear (ushers, best man)		469	2000	33r
Mother of bride apparel		241	2000	33r
Music		866	1998	33r
Photography and videography		1368	1998	33r
Rehearsal dinner		728	1998	33r
Wedding invitations and announcements		341	1998	33r
Wedding reception		7968	2000	33r
Wedding rings (bride and groom)		1060	1998	33r

Lynchburg, VA

Item	Per	Value	Date	Ref.
Composite, ACCRA index		93.10	3/01	4c
Alcoholic Beverages				
Alcoholic beverage purchases	yr	253	1999	30r
Beer, Heineken, 12-oz, ex deposit	6	6.62	3/01	4c
J & B Scotch	750-ml	20.95	3/01	4c
Malt beverages, all types, all sizes, any origin	16 oz	0.96	7/00	11r
Wine, Livingston or Gallo, Chablis blanc	1.5 liter	4.94	3/01	4c
Appliances				
Appliance repair, service call, washing machine	min lab chg	38.00	3/01	4c
Major appliances, expenditures on	yr	172	1999	30r
Small appliances, housewares, expenditures on	yr	81	1999	30r
Banking and Money				
Mortgage interest and charges paid	yr	2039	1999	30r
Mortgage principal paid on owned property	yr	1026	1999	30r

Lynchburg, VA - continued

Item	Per	Value	Date	Ref.
Banking and Money - continued				
Mortgage rate, incl. points and orig. fee, 30-yr. conv. fixed or ARM	mos	7.09	3/01	4c
Vehicle finance charges paid	yr	365	1999	30r
Charity				
Cash contributions, expenditures	yr	1127	1999	30r
Child Care				
Child raising cost, total, age 0-2	yr	8540	1999	60r
Child raising cost, total, age 3-5	yr	8780	1999	60r
Child raising cost, total, age 6-8	yr	8820	1999	60r
Child raising cost, total, age 9-11	yr	8800	1999	60r
Child raising cost, total, age 12-14	yr	9510	1999	60r
Child raising cost, total, age 15-17	yr	9740	1999	60r
Child's child care and education, age 0-2	yr	1380	1999	60r
Child's child care and education, age 3-5	yr	1520	1999	60r
Child's child care and education, age 6-8	yr	990	1999	60r
Child's child care and education, age 9-11	yr	650	1999	60r
Child's child care and education, age 12-14	yr	490	1999	60r
Child's child care and education, age 15-17	yr	840	1999	60r
Child's clothing, age 0-2	yr	480	1999	60r
Child's clothing, age 3-5	yr	470	1999	60r
Child's clothing, age 6-8	yr	520	1999	60r
Child's clothing, age 9-11	yr	570	1999	60r
Child's clothing, age 12-14	yr	950	1999	60r
Child's clothing, age 15-17	yr	850	1999	60r
Child's food, age 0-2	yr	1000	1999	60r
Child's food, age 3-5	yr	1160	1999	60r
Child's food, age 6-8	yr	1490	1999	60r
Child's food, age 9-11	yr	1770	1999	60r
Child's food, age 12-14	yr	1770	1999	60r
Child's food, age 15-17	yr	1980	1999	60r
Child's health care, age 0-2	yr	620	1999	60r
Child's health care, age 3-5	yr	590	1999	60r
Child's health care, age 6-8	yr	680	1999	60r
Child's health care, age 9-11	yr	720	1999	60r
Child's health care, age 12-14	yr	730	1999	60r
Child's health care, age 15-17	yr	760	1999	60r
Child's housing, age 0-2	yr	3070	1999	60r
Child's housing, age 3-5	yr	3050	1999	60r
Child's housing, age 6-8	yr	3010	1999	60r
Child's housing, age 9-11	yr	2850	1999	60r
Child's housing, age 12-14	yr	3040	1999	60r
Child's housing, age 15-17	yr	2650	1999	60r
Child's personal care, reading, age 0-2	yr	910	1999	60r
Child's personal care, reading, age 3-5	yr	930	1999	60r
Child's personal care, reading, age 6-8	yr	960	1999	60r
Child's personal care, reading, age 9-11	yr	1000	1999	60r
Child's personal care, reading, age 12-14	yr	1170	1999	60r
Child's personal care, reading, age 15-17	yr	950	1999	60r
Clothing				
Apparel and services purchases	yr	1610	1999	30r
Boys' brief, cotton	3	3.58	3/01	4c
Boys, 2 to 15, expenditures on	yr	89	1999	30r
Children under 2, expenditures on	yr	79	1999	30r
Footwear, expenditures on	yr	283	1999	30r
Girls, 2 to 15, expenditures on	yr	103	1999	30r
Men and boys, expenditures on	yr	351	1999	30r
Men, 16 and over, expenditures on	yr	262	1999	30r
Shirt, man's dress shirt		25.48	3/01	4c
Slacks, man's "No Wrinkles" khaki		36.33	3/01	4c
Women, 16 and over, expenditures on	yr	538	1999	30r
Communications				
Cable modem installation, Adelphi		54.90	6/99	103s
Cable modem installation, Comcast		95.00	6/99	103s
Cable modem installation, Cox		99.00-174.95	6/99	103s
Cable modem installation, Jones Intercable		100.00	6/99	103s
Cable modem rate, cable subscriber, Adelphi	mos	34.95	6/99	103s
Cable modem rate, cable subscriber, Comcast	mos	39.95	6/99	103s

Values are in dollars or fractions of dollars. In the column headed *Ref*, references are shown to sources. Each reference is followed by a letter. These refer to the geographical level for which data were reported: s=State, r=Region, and c=City or metro. The abbreviation *ex* is used to mean *except* or *excluding*; *exp* stands for expenditures. For other abbreviations and further explanations, please see the Introduction.

Lynchburg, VA - continued

Item	Per	Value	Date	Ref.
Communications				
Cable modem rate, cable subscriber, Cox	mos	29.95- 44.95	6/99	103s
Cable modem rate, cable subscriber, Jones Intercable	mos	29.95- 39.95	6/99	103s
Cable modem rate, non-cable subscriber, Adelphi	mos	44.95	6/99	103s
Cable modem rate, non-cable subscriber, Comcast	mos	49.95	6/99	103s
Cable modem rate, non-cable subscriber, Cox	mos	42.95- 54.95	6/99	103s
Newspaper subscription, daily and Sunday delivery	mos	12.61	3/01	4c
Phone line, single, business, field visit	inst.	64.00	12/97	17s
Phone line, single, business, no field visit	inst.	64.00	12/97	17s
Phone line, single, residence, field visit	inst.	38.50	12/97	17s
Phone line, single, residence, no field visit	inst.	38.50	12/97	17s
Postage and stationery, expenditures on	yr	104	1999	30r
Postal rate, express mail, up to half-pound		12.45	7/01	108r
Postal rate, letter, first class, first ounce		0.34	7/01	108r
Postal rate, letter, two ounces		0.57	7/01	108r
Postal rate, post card		0.21	7/01	108r
Postal rate, priority mail, two pounds		3.95	7/01	108r
Postal rate, priority mail, up to one pound		3.50	7/01	108r
Telephone bill, family of three	mos	24.40	3/01	4c
Telephone services, expenditures on	yr	860	1999	30r
Education				
Board, 4-year private college/university	yr	2363	1996	38s
Board, 4-year public college/university	yr	2033	1996	38s
Education expenditures	yr	431	1999	30r
Room, 4-year private college/university	yr	2062	1996	38s
Room, 4-year public college/university	yr	2261	1996	38s
Total cost, 4-year private college/university	yr	15021	1996	38s
Total cost, 4-year public college/university	yr	8202	1996	38s
Tuition, 2-year public college/university, in state	yr	1433	1996	38s
Tuition, 4-year private college/university, in state	yr	10596	1996	38s
Tuition, 4-year public college/university	yr	3907	1996	38s
Energy and Fuels				
Electricity	KWh	0.09	7/01	11r
Electricity	500 KWhs	47.29	7/01	11r
Energy, combined forms, 2400 sq ft	mos	86.45	3/01	4c
Fuel oil #2	gal	1.43	7/01	11r
Fuel oil and other fuels, expenditures on	yr	45	1999	30r
Gas, natural, commercial rate	1000 cf	9.01	11/00	88s
Gas, regular unleaded, cash, self-service	gal	1.40	3/01	4c
Gasoline, all types	gal	1.60	7/01	11r
Gasoline, unleaded midgrade	gal	1.65	7/01	11r
Gasoline, unleaded premium	gal	1.74	7/01	11r
Natural gas, expenditures on	yr	164	1999	30r
Utility (piped) gas, therm		1.01	7/01	11r
Utility (piped) gas, 40 therms		44.29	7/01	11r
Utility (piped) gas, 100 therms		97.44	7/01	11r
Entertainment				
Bowling, Saturday evening rate	line	3.58	3/01	4c
Entertainment purchases	yr	1574	1999	30r
Fees and admissions paid	yr	371	1999	30r
Monopoly game, Parker Brothers', No. 9	game	10.66	3/01	4c
Movie, first-run, Saturday, evening	adm.	6.75	3/01	4c
Reading purchases	yr	121	1999	30r
Television, radios, sound equipment, expenditures on	yr	561	1999	30r
Tennis balls, yellow, Wilson or Penn, 3	can	2.15	3/01	4c
Funerals				
Total cost of funeral		5922.53	1/99	78r
Acknowledgement cards		63.43	1/99	78r
Casket		2258.77	1/99	78r
Cosmetology, hair, other preparation		127.09	1/99	78r
Embalming		393.49	1/99	78r

Lynchburg, VA - continued

Item	Per	Value	Date	Ref.
Funerals - continued				
Funeral at funeral home		367.50	1/99	78r
Hearse (local)		169.66	1/99	78r
Professional service charges		1211.32	1/99	78r
Service car/van		80.69	1/99	78r
Transfer of remains to funeral home		144.25	1/99	78r
Vault		803.50	1/99	78r
Visitation/viewing		302.83	1/99	78r
Groceries				
Groceries, ACCRA Index		97.30	3/01	4c
American processed cheese	lb	3.50	7/01	11r
Antibiotic ointment, Polysporin	0.5 oz	4.17	3/01	4c
Baby food, strained vegetables or fruit, lowest price	4-4.5 oz	0.46	3/01	4c
Bakery products, expenditures on	yr	261	1999	30r
Bananas	lb	0.48	3/01	4c
Bananas	lb	0.47	7/01	11r
Beans, dried, any type, all sizes	lb	0.63	7/01	11r
Beef for stew, boneless	lb	2.86	7/01	11r
Beef or hamburger, ground	lb	1.29	3/01	4c
Beef, expenditures on	yr	210	1999	30r
Bologna, all beef or mixed	lb	2.29	7/01	11r
Bread, French	lb	1.66	7/01	11r
Bread, white	loaf	0.94	3/01	4c
Bread, white, pan	lb	0.87	7/01	11r
Bread, whole wheat, pan	lb	1.38	7/01	11r
Broccoli	lb	1.04	7/01	11r
Butter, salted, grade AA, stick	lb	2.26	7/01	11r
Butter, yoghurt, cheese, etc, expenditures on	yr	170	1999	30r
Cabbage	lb	0.42	7/01	11r
Cereals and cereal products, expenditures on	yr	140	1999	30r
Cheddar cheese, natural	lb	3.75	7/01	11r
Cheese, Kraft grated Parmesan	8 oz	3.30	3/01	4c
Chicken breast, bone-in	lb	1.85	7/01	11r
Chicken legs, bone-in	lb	1.34	7/01	11r
Chicken, fresh, whole	lb	1.05	7/01	11r
Chicken, whole fryer	lb	0.88	3/01	4c
Chops, boneless,	lb	4.13	7/01	11r
Chuck roast, graded and ungraded, excl U.S. prime and choice	lb	2.35	7/01	11r
Chuck roast, U.S. choice, boneless	lb	2.67	7/01	11r
Cigarettes, Winston, Kings	carton	29.18	3/01	4c
Coffee, 100%, ground roast, all sizes	lb	2.88	7/01	11r
Coffee, instant, plain, regular, all sizes	16 oz	9.25	7/01	11r
Coffee, vacuum-packed	13 oz	2.26	3/01	4c
Cola, non diet	2 liter	1.11	7/01	11r
Corn Flakes, Kellogg's or Post Toasties	18 oz	2.35	3/01	4c
Corn, frozen, whole kernel, lowest price	16 oz	0.95	3/01	4c
Crackers, soda, salted	lb	1.70	7/01	11r
Dairy product purchases	yr	282	1999	30r
Eggs, expenditures on	yr	32	1999	30r
Eggs, Grade A or AA	dozen	1.16	3/01	4c
Fats and oils, expenditures on	yr	79	1999	30r
Fish and seafood, expenditures on	yr	99	1999	30r
Flour, white, all purpose	lb	0.32	7/01	11r
Food (excl fruit and vegetables), eaten at home, purchases	yr	815	1999	30r
Food cooked on trips, expenditures on	yr	36	1999	30r
Food purchases	yr	4533	1999	30r
Food purchases, eaten away from home	yr	1873	1999	30r
Food purchases, food eaten at home	yr	2660	1999	30r
Fresh fruits, expenditures on	yr	128	1999	30r
Fresh milk and cream, expenditures on	yr	112	1999	30r
Fresh vegetables, expenditures on	yr	131	1999	30r
Fruit and vegetable purchases	yr	438	1999	30r
Grapefruit	lb	0.59	7/01	11r
Grapes, Thompson, seedless	lb	2.12	7/01	11r
Ground beef, 100% beef	lb	1.76	7/01	11r
Ground beef, lean and extra lean	lb	2.60	7/01	11r
Ground chuck, 100% beef	lb	2.08	7/01	11r
Ham, boneless, excl canned	lb	2.71	7/01	11r
Ham, rump or shank half, bone-in, smoked	lb	2.19	7/01	11r

Values are in dollars or fractions of dollars. In the column headed *Ref*, references are shown as sources. Each reference is followed by a letter. These refer to the geographical level for which data were reported: s=State, r=Region, and c=City or metro. The abbreviation *ex* is used to mean *except* or *excluding*; *exp* stands for *expenditures*. For other abbreviations and further explanations, please see the Introduction.

Lynchburg, VA - continued

Item	Per	Value	Date	Ref.
Groceries				
Ice cream, prepackaged, bulk, regular	1/2 gal	3.93	7/01	11r
Lemons	lb	1.32	7/01	11r
Lettuce, iceberg	head	1.14	3/01	4c
Lettuce, iceberg	lb	0.76	7/01	11r
Margarine, Blue Bonnet or Parkay, stick	lb	0.78	3/01	4c
Milk, fresh, low fat,	gal	2.75	7/01	11r
Milk, fresh, whole, fortified	gal	2.97	7/01	11r
Milk, whole	1/2 gal	1.77	3/01	4c
Nonalcoholic beverages, expenditures on	yr	228	1999	30r
Orange juice, frozen concentrate	16 oz	1.95	7/01	11r
Orange juice, Minute Maid frozen	12 oz	1.31	3/01	4c
Oranges, Navel	lb	0.73	7/01	11r
Oranges, Valencia	lb	0.55	7/01	11r
Peaches, halves or slices, Hunt's, Del Monte, or Libby's	29 oz	1.46	3/01	4c
Peanut butter, creamy, all sizes	lb	1.83	7/01	11r
Pears, Anjou	lb	0.98	7/01	11r
Peas, green, Del Monte or Green Giant	15 oz	0.63	3/01	4c
Pork chops, center cut, bone-in	lb	3.33	7/01	11r
Pork sausage, fresh, loose	lb	2.59	7/01	11r
Pork shoulder picnic, bone-in, smoked	lb	1.12	7/01	11r
Pork, expenditures on	yr	162	1999	30r
Potato chips	16 oz	3.59	7/01	11r
Potatoes, frozen, french fried	lb	1.00	7/01	11r
Potatoes, white or red	10 lb	3.38	3/01	4c
Potatoes, white, all types	lb	0.44	7/01	11r
Poultry, expenditures on	yr	137	1999	30r
Processed fruits, expenditures on	yr	97	1999	30r
Processed vegetables, expenditures on	yr	82	1999	30r
Rice, white, long grain, uncooked	lb	0.51	7/01	11r
Round roast, graded and ungraded, excl U.S. prime and choice	lb	2.96	7/01	11r
Round steak, graded and ungraded, excl U.S. prime and choice	lb	3.11	7/01	11r
Sausage, Jimmy Dean/Owens pork	lb	3.16	3/01	4c
Shortening, vegetable, Crisco	3 lb	2.89	3/01	4c
Sirloin steak, graded and ungraded, excl U.S. prime and choice	lb	4.23	7/01	11r
Soft drink, Coca Cola, ex deposit	2 liter	1.19	3/01	4c
Spaghetti and macaroni	lb	0.78	7/01	11r
Steak, round, U.S. choice, boneless	lb	3.56	7/01	11r
Steak, sirloin, U.S. choice, boneless	lb	5.65	7/01	11r
Steak, T-bone	lb	6.70	3/01	4c
Strawberries, dry pint	12 oz	1.50	7/01	11r
Sugar and other sweets, expenditures on	yr	99	1999	30r
Sugar, cane or beet	4 lbs	1.62	3/01	4c
Sugar, white, 33-80 ounce package	lb	0.39	7/01	11r
Sugar, white, all sizes	lb	0.42	7/01	11r
Tobacco products and smoking supplies purchases	yr	288	1999	30r
Tomatoes, field grown	lb	1.43	7/01	11r
Tomatoes, Hunt's or Del Monte	14.5 oz	0.78	3/01	4c
Tuna, chunk, light	6 oz	0.68	3/01	4c
Tuna, light, chunk	lb	1.77	7/01	11r
Turkey, frozen, whole	lb	1.05	7/01	11r
Goods and Services				
Miscellaneous goods and services, ACCRA Index		97.50	3/01	4c
B&B Japanese maple (acer japonicum)	gal	49.98-129.00	4/00	93r
Boxwood (buxus)	2 gal	12.99-16.99	4/00	93r
Daylily (hemerocallis)	gal	4.99-8.99	4/00	93r
Flat of annuals		11.00-13.92	4/00	93r
Fountain grass (pennisetum)	gal	5.98-7.98	4/00	93r
Hanging basket (10 in)		7.99-14.98	4/00	93r
Hardy geranium (geranium)	gal	5.98-8.00	4/00	93r

Lynchburg, VA - continued

Item	Per	Value	Date	Ref.
Goods and Services - continued				
Hosta (hosta)	gal	4.99-10.98	4/00	93r
Lilac (syrubga vulgaris)	2 gal	12.99-21.99	4/00	93r
Rhododendron (rhododendron)	2 gal	14.99-24.99	4/00	93r
Sage (salvia)	gal	5.98-6.99	4/00	93r
Wintercreeper euonymus (euonymus fortunei)	2 gal	7.99-89.99	4/00	93r
Hunting license	yr	12.00	4/01	34s
Health Care				
Health care, ACCRA Index		99.00	3/01	4c
Cardiac catheterization, ave hospital/physician charges		15370	1998	77s
Childbirth, Cesarean delivery		11587	1997	13r
Childbirth, vaginal delivery		6725	1997	13r
Dentist's fee, adult teeth cleaning and periodic oral exam	visit	63.20	3/01	4c
Doctor's fee, routine exam, established patient	visit	59.60	3/01	4c
Drugs, expenditures on	yr	399	1999	30r
Health care purchases	yr	1971	1999	30r
Health insurance expenditures	yr	933	1999	30r
Hospital care, private room	day	629.00	3/01	4c
Hysterectomy, laproscopically-assisted, ave hospital/physician charges		15660	1998	76s
Hysterectomy, vaginal, ave hospital and physician charges		10260	1998	76s
Medicaid dispensing fee		4.25	1999	87s
Medical services expenditures	yr	547	1999	30r
Medical supplies, expenditures on	yr	91	1999	30r
Plastic surgery, breast augmentation		2870	2000	7r
Plastic surgery, breast lift		3649	2000	7r
Plastic surgery, facelift		5008	2000	7r
Plastic surgery, hair transplantation		3425	2000	7r
Plastic surgery, lip augmentation		1227	2000	7r
Plastic surgery, lower body lift		4793	2000	7r
Plastic surgery, thigh lift		3862	2000	7r
Household Goods				
Dishwashing powder, Cascade	50 oz	3.18	3/01	4c
Floor coverings, expenditures on	yr	44	1999	30r
Furniture, expenditures on	yr	335	1999	30r
Household furnishings and equipment purchases	yr	1328	1999	30r
Household textiles, expenditures on	yr	89	1999	30r
Laundry and cleaning supplies, expenditures on	yr	113	1999	30r
Tissues, facial, Kleenex brand	175	1.27	3/01	4c
Housing				
Housing, ACCRA Index		91.10	3/01	4c
Home, 2200 sq ft, 4-br, 2-bath, 2-car garage, average		200225	2000	47c
Home price, existing, ave		160100	10/00	90r
Home value, median		141000	2001	53s
House, 2400 sq ft, 8000 sq ft lot, new, urban, utilities	total	192934	3/01	4c
House payment, principal and interest, 25% down payment	mos	972	3/01	4c
Household operation expenditures	yr	553	1999	30r
Housekeeping supplies purchases	yr	473	1999	30r
Housing, expenditures on	yr	10303	1999	30r
Maintenance, repairs, insurance expenditures	yr	699	1999	30r
Monthly rental value of owned home	mos	505	1999	30r
Owned dwellings, expenditures own	yr	3465	1999	30r
Rent expenditures	yr	1641	1999	30r
Rent, apartment, 2 br, 1 1/2-2 baths, unfurn, 950 sq ft, water	mos	547	3/01	4c
Rental unit, 1 bedroom, with utilities	mos	388	4/01	41c
Rental unit, 2 bedroom, with utilities	mos	447	4/01	41c

Values are in dollars or fractions of dollars. In the column headed *Ref*, references are shown to sources. Each reference is followed by a letter. These refer to the geographical level for which data were reported: s=State, r=Region, and c=City or metro. The abbreviation *ex* is used to mean *except* or *excluding*; *exp* stands for *expenditures*. For other abbreviations and further explanations, please see the Introduction.

Lynchburg, VA - continued

Item	Per	Value	Date	Ref.
Housing				
Rental unit, 3 bedroom, with utilities	mos	588	4/01	41c
Rental unit, 4 bedroom, with utilities	mos	709	4/01	41c
Shelter, expenditures on	yr	5467	1999	30r
Insurance and Pensions				
Auto insurance premium	yr	628.58	1999	57s
Life and other personal insurance purchases	yr	414	1999	30r
Pensions and Social Security, expenditures on	yr	2635	1999	30r
Personal insurance and pensions, expenditures on	yr	3048	1999	30r
Legal Fees				
Divorce, filing fee		64.00	4/01	35s
Driver's license fee	orig	7.20	1999	48s
Driver's license fee	renew	7.20	1999	48s
Fishing license	yr	12.50	4/01	34s
Personal Goods				
Personal care products and services purchases	yr	393	1999	30r
Shampoo, Alberto VO5	15 oz	0.95	3/01	4c
Toothpaste, Crest or Colgate	6-7 oz	2.08	3/01	4c
Personal Services				
Dry cleaning, man's 2-pc suit		7.99	3/01	4c
Man's haircut, barbershop, no styling		9.80	3/01	4c
Personal services, household, expenditures on	yr	258	1999	30r
Woman's shampoo, trim, blow-dry, no style-change		24.60	3/01	4c
Pets				
Pets, toys, and playground equipment, expenditures on	yr	306	1999	30r
Restaurant Food				
Chicken, fried, thigh and drumstick, KFC/Church's		2.47	3/01	4c
Hamburger with cheese, McDonald's	1/4 lb	2.23	3/01	4c
Pizza, Pizza Hut or Pizza Inn	11-12 in	9.62	3/01	4c
Taxes				
Federal income taxes paid	yr	2047	1999	30r
Personal taxes, expenditures on	yr	2554	1999	30r
Property taxes paid	yr	726	1999	30r
State and local income taxes paid	yr	363	1999	30r
Transportation				
Transportation, ACCRA Index		87.80	3/01	4c
Bus fare, one-way	trip	1.00	2000	1c
Bus fare, to central business district	1-way	1.00	3/01	4c
Cars and trucks, new, expenditures on	yr	1648	1999	30r
Cars and trucks, used, expenditures on	yr	1651	1999	30r
Diesel at the pump	gal	1.14	10/99	73s
Gasoline and motor oil purchases	yr	1052	1999	30r
Gasoline before-tax price (cents)	gal	107.30	10/00	43s
Maintenance and repair expenditures	yr	621	1999	30r
Public transportation, expenditures on	yr	298	1999	30r
Tire balance, computer or spin balance, front	wheel	5.60	3/01	4c
Transportation purchases	yr	6738	1999	30r
Vehicle expenses, miscellaneous, purchases	yr	2033	1999	30r
Vehicle insurance payments	yr	696	1999	30r
Vehicle purchases (net outlay)	yr	3354	1999	30r
Vehicle rental, lease expenditures	yr	352	1999	30r
Utilities				
Utilities, ACCRA Index		76.50	3/01	4c
Electrical bill, average	mos	82.17	9/00	9s
Electricity, 2400 sq ft, new home	mos	86.45	3/01	4c
Electricity, expenditures on	yr	1115	1999	30r
Electricity cost, average	KWh	5.90	9/00	9s
Water and other public services, expenditures on	yr	298	1999	30r

Lynchburg, VA - continued

Item	Per	Value	Date	Ref.
Weddings				
Wedding (national average cost)		19936	2000	33r
Wedding (regional average total cost)		16293	1997	110r
Attendants' gifts		321	1998	33r
Bridal attendants' apparel (5 persons)		824	2000	33r
Bride's headpiece/veil		173	1998	33r
Bride's wedding dress		859	1998	33r
Clergy, religious facility fee		242	1998	33r
Engagement ring		3177	1998	33r
Flowers		789	1998	33r
Groom's formalwear rental		99	2000	33r
Limousine		410	1998	33r
Marriage license cost		30.00	4/01	35s
Men's formalwear (ushers, best man)		469	2000	33r
Mother of bride apparel		241	2000	33r
Music		866	1998	33r
Photography and videography		1368	1998	33r
Rehearsal dinner		728	1998	33r
Wedding invitations and announcements		341	1998	33r
Wedding reception		7968	2000	33r
Wedding rings (bride and groom)		1060	1998	33r

Macon, GA

Item	Per	Value	Date	Ref.
Alcoholic Beverages				
Alcoholic beverage purchases	yr	253	1999	30r
Malt beverages, all types, all sizes, any origin	16 oz	0.96	7/01	11r
Appliances				
Major appliances, expenditures on	yr	172	1999	30r
Small appliances, housewares, expenditures on	yr	81	1999	30r
Banking and Money				
Mortgage interest and charges paid	yr	2039	1999	30r
Mortgage principal paid on owned property	yr	1026	1999	30r
Vehicle finance charges paid	yr	365	1999	30r
Charity				
Cash contributions, expenditures	yr	1127	1999	30r
Child Care				
Child raising cost, total, age 0-2	yr	8540	1999	60r
Child raising cost, total, age 3-5	yr	8780	1999	60r
Child raising cost, total, age 6-8	yr	8820	1999	60r
Child raising cost, total, age 9-11	yr	8800	1999	60r
Child raising cost, total, age 12-14	yr	9510	1999	60r
Child raising cost, total, age 15-17	yr	9740	1999	60r
Child's child care and education, age 0-2	yr	1380	1999	60r
Child's child care and education, age 3-5	yr	1520	1999	60r
Child's child care and education, age 6-8	yr	990	1999	60r
Child's child care and education, age 9-11	yr	650	1999	60r
Child's child care and education, age 12-14	yr	490	1999	60r
Child's child care and education, age 15-17	yr	840	1999	60r
Child's clothing, age 0-2	yr	480	1999	60r
Child's clothing, age 3-5	yr	470	1999	60r
Child's clothing, age 6-8	yr	520	1999	60r
Child's clothing, age 9-11	yr	570	1999	60r
Child's clothing, age 12-14	yr	950	1999	60r
Child's clothing, age 15-17	yr	850	1999	60r
Child's food, age 0-2	yr	1000	1999	60r
Child's food, age 3-5	yr	1160	1999	60r
Child's food, age 6-8	yr	1490	1999	60r
Child's food, age 9-11	yr	1770	1999	60r
Child's food, age 12-14	yr	1770	1999	60r
Child's food, age 15-17	yr	1980	1999	60r
Child's health care, age 0-2	yr	620	1999	60r
Child's health care, age 3-5	yr	590	1999	60r
Child's health care, age 6-8	yr	680	1999	60r
Child's health care, age 9-11	yr	720	1999	60r
Child's health care, age 12-14	yr	730	1999	60r
Child's health care, age 15-17	yr	760	1999	60r
Child's housing, age 0-2	yr	3070	1999	60r
Child's housing, age 3-5	yr	3050	1999	60r

Values are in dollars or fractions of dollars. In the column headed *Ref*, references are shown to sources. Each reference is followed by a letter. These refer to the geographical level for which data were reported: s=State, r=Region, and c=City or metro. The abbreviation *ex* is used to mean *except* or *excluding*; *exp* stands for *expenditures*. For other abbreviations and further explanations, please see the Introduction.

Macon, GA - continued

Item	Per	Value	Date	Ref.
Child Care				
Child's housing, age 6-8	yr	3010	1999	60r
Child's housing, age 9-11	yr	2850	1999	60r
Child's housing, age 12-14	yr	3040	1999	60r
Child's housing, age 15-17	yr	2650	1999	60r
Child's personal care, reading, age 0-2	yr	910	1999	60r
Child's personal care, reading, age 3-5	yr	930	1999	60r
Child's personal care, reading, age 6-8	yr	960	1999	60r
Child's personal care, reading, age 9-11	yr	1000	1999	60r
Child's personal care, reading, age 12-14	yr	1170	1999	60r
Child's personal care, reading, age 15-17	yr	950	1999	60r
Clothing				
Apparel and services purchases	yr	1610	1999	30r
Boys, 2 to 15, expenditures on	yr	89	1999	30r
Children under 2, expenditures on	yr	79	1999	30r
Footwear, expenditures on	yr	283	1999	30r
Girls, 2 to 15, expenditures on	yr	103	1999	30r
Men and boys, expenditures on	yr	351	1999	30r
Men, 16 and over, expenditures on	yr	262	1999	30r
Women, 16 and over, expenditures on	yr	538	1999	30r
Communications				
Cable modem installation, Charter		99.00-169.00	6/99	103s
Cable modem installation, Comcast		95.00	6/99	103s
Cable modem installation, Intermedia		149.95	6/99	103s
Cable modem installation, Media One		100.00	6/99	103s
Cable modem rate, cable subscriber, Charter	mos	49.95-79.95	6/99	103s
Cable modem rate, cable subscriber, Comcast	mos	39.95	6/99	103s
Cable modem rate, cable subscriber, Intermedia	mos	49.95	6/99	103s
Cable modem rate, cable subscriber, Media One	mos	34.95-39.95	6/99	103s
Cable modem rate, non-cable subscriber, Charter	mos	59.95-89.95	6/99	103s
Cable modem rate, non-cable subscriber, Comcast	mos	49.95	6/99	103s
Cable modem rate, non-cable subscriber, Intermedia	mos	54.95	6/99	103s
Cable modem rate, non-cable subscriber, Media One	mos	49.95	6/99	103s
Phone line, single, business, field visit	inst.	58.25	12/97	17s
Phone line, single, business, no field visit	inst.	58.25	12/97	17s
Phone line, single, residence, field visit	inst.	42.50	12/97	17s
Phone line, single, residence, no field visit	inst.	42.50	12/97	17s
Postage and stationery, expenditures on	yr	104	1999	30r
Postal rate, express mail, up to half-pound		12.45	7/01	108r
Postal rate, letter, first class, first ounce		0.34	7/01	108r
Postal rate, letter, two ounces		0.57	7/01	108r
Postal rate, post card		0.21	7/01	108r
Postal rate, priority mail, two pounds		3.95	7/01	108r
Postal rate, priority mail, up to one pound		3.50	7/01	108r
Telephone services, expenditures on	yr	860	1999	30r
Education				
Board, 4-year private college/university	yr	2267	1996	38s
Board, 4-year public college/university	yr	1877	1996	38s
Education expenditures	yr	431	1999	30r
Room, 4-year private college/university	yr	2719	1996	38s
Room, 4-year public college/university	yr	1712	1996	38s
Total cost, 4-year private college/university	yr	15194	1996	38s
Total cost, 4-year public college/university	yr	5691	1996	38s
Tuition, 2-year public college/university, in state	yr	1062	1996	38s
Tuition, 4-year private college/university, in state	yr	10208	1996	38s
Tuition, 4-year public college/university	yr	2103	1996	38s
Energy and Fuels				
Electricity	KWh	0.09	7/01	11r
Electricity	500 KWhs	47.29	7/01	11r

Macon, GA - continued

Item	Per	Value	Date	Ref.
Energy and Fuels - continued				
Fuel oil #2	gal	1.43	7/01	11r
Fuel oil and other fuels, expenditures on	yr	45	1999	30r
Gasoline, all types	gal	1.60	7/01	11r
Gasoline, unleaded midgrade	gal	1.65	7/01	11r
Gasoline, unleaded premium	gal	1.74	7/01	11r
Natural gas, expenditures on	yr	164	1999	30r
Utility (piped) gas, therm		1.01	7/01	11r
Utility (piped) gas, 40 therms		44.29	7/01	11r
Utility (piped) gas, 100 therms		97.44	7/01	11r
Entertainment				
Entertainment purchases	yr	1574	1999	30r
Fees and admissions paid	yr	371	1999	30r
Reading purchases	yr	121	1999	30r
Television, radios, sound equipment, expenditures on	yr	561	1999	30r
Funerals				
Total cost of funeral		5922.53	1/99	78r
Acknowledgement cards		63.43	1/99	78r
Casket		2258.77	1/99	78r
Cosmetology, hair, other preparation		127.09	1/99	78r
Embalming		393.49	1/99	78r
Funeral at funeral home		367.50	1/99	78r
Hearse (local)		169.66	1/99	78r
Professional service charges		1211.32	1/99	78r
Service car/van		80.69	1/99	78r
Transfer of remains to funeral home		144.25	1/99	78r
Vault		803.50	1/99	78r
Visitation/viewing		302.83	1/99	78r
Groceries				
American processed cheese	lb	3.50	7/01	11r
Bakery products, expenditures on	yr	261	1999	30r
Bananas	lb	0.47	7/01	11r
Beans, dried, any type, all sizes	lb	0.63	7/01	11r
Beef for stew, boneless	lb	2.86	7/01	11r
Beef, expenditures on	yr	210	1999	30r
Bologna, all beef or mixed	lb	2.29	7/01	11r
Bread, French	lb	1.66	7/01	11r
Bread, white, pan	lb	0.87	7/01	11r
Bread, whole wheat, pan	lb	1.38	7/01	11r
Broccoli	lb	1.04	7/01	11r
Butter, salted, grade AA, stick	lb	2.26	7/01	11r
Butter, yoghurt, cheese, etc, expenditures on	yr	170	1999	30r
Cabbage	lb	0.42	7/01	11r
Cereals and cereal products, expenditures on	yr	140	1999	30r
Cheddar cheese, natural	lb	3.75	7/01	11r
Chicken breast, bone-in	lb	1.85	7/01	11r
Chicken legs, bone-in	lb	1.34	7/01	11r
Chicken, fresh, whole	lb	1.05	7/01	11r
Chops, boneless,	lb	4.13	7/01	11r
Chuck roast, graded and ungraded, excl U.S. prime and choice	lb	2.35	7/01	11r
Chuck roast, U.S. choice, boneless	lb	2.67	7/01	11r
Coffee, 100%, ground roast, all sizes	lb	2.88	7/01	11r
Coffee, instant, plain, regular, all sizes	16 oz	9.25	7/01	11r
Cola, non diet	2 liter	1.11	7/01	11r
Crackers, soda, salted	lb	1.70	7/01	11r
Dairy product purchases	yr	282	1999	30r
Eggs, expenditures on	yr	32	1999	30r
Fats and oils, expenditures on	yr	79	1999	30r
Fish and seafood, expenditures on	yr	99	1999	30r
Flour, white, all purpose	lb	0.32	7/01	11r
Food (excl fruit and vegetables), eaten at home, purchases	yr	815	1999	30r
Food cooked on trips, expenditures on	yr	36	1999	30r
Food purchases	yr	4533	1999	30r
Food purchases, eaten away from home	yr	1873	1999	30r
Food purchases, food eaten at home	yr	2660	1999	30r
Fresh fruits, expenditures on	yr	128	1999	30r
Fresh milk and cream, expenditures on	yr	112	1999	30r
Fresh vegetables, expenditures on	yr	131	1999	30r

Values are in dollars or fractions of dollars. In the column headed *Ref*, references are shown to sources. Each reference is followed by a letter. These refer to the geographical level for which data were reported: s=State, r=Region, and c=City or metro. The abbreviation *ex* is used to mean *except* or *excluding*; *exp* stands for *expenditures*. For other abbreviations and further explanations, please see the Introduction.

Macon, GA - continued

Item	Per	Value	Date	Ref.
Groceries				
Fruit and vegetable purchases	yr	438	1999	30r
Grapefruit	lb	0.59	7/01	11r
Grapes, Thompson, seedless	lb	2.12	7/01	11r
Ground beef, 100% beef	lb	1.76	7/01	11r
Ground beef, lean and extra lean	lb	2.60	7/01	11r
Ground chuck, 100% beef	lb	2.08	7/01	11r
Ham, boneless, excl canned	lb	2.71	7/01	11r
Ham, rump or shank half, bone-in, smoked	lb	2.19	7/01	11r
Ice cream, prepackaged, bulk, regular	1/2 gal	3.93	7/01	11r
Lemons	lb	1.32	7/01	11r
Lettuce, iceberg	lb	0.76	7/01	11r
Milk, fresh, low fat,	gal	2.75	7/01	11r
Milk, fresh, whole, fortified	gal	2.97	7/01	11r
Nonalcoholic beverages, expenditures on	yr	228	1999	30r
Orange juice, frozen concentrate	16 oz	1.95	7/01	11r
Oranges, Navel	lb	0.73	7/01	11r
Oranges, Valencia	lb	0.55	7/01	11r
Peanut butter, creamy, all sizes	lb	1.83	7/01	11r
Pears, Anjou	lb	0.98	7/01	11r
Pork chops, center cut, bone-in	lb	3.33	7/01	11r
Pork sausage, fresh, loose	lb	2.59	7/01	11r
Pork shoulder picnic, bone-in, smoked	lb	1.12	7/01	11r
Pork, expenditures on	yr	162	1999	30r
Potato chips	16 oz	3.59	7/01	11r
Potatoes, frozen, french fried	lb	1.00	7/01	11r
Potatoes, white, all types	lb	0.44	7/01	11r
Poultry, expenditures on	yr	137	1999	30r
Processed fruits, expenditures on	yr	97	1999	30r
Processed vegetables, expenditures on	yr	82	1999	30r
Rice, white, long grain, uncooked	lb	0.51	7/01	11r
Round roast, graded and ungraded, excl U.S. prime and choice	lb	2.96	7/01	11r
Round steak, graded and ungraded, excl U.S. prime and choice	lb	3.11	7/01	11r
Sirloin steak, graded and ungraded, excl U.S. prime and choice	lb	4.23	7/01	11r
Spaghetti and macaroni	lb	0.78	7/01	11r
Steak, round, U.S. choice, boneless	lb	3.56	7/01	11r
Steak, sirloin, U.S. choice, boneless	lb	5.65	7/01	11r
Strawberries, dry pint	12 oz	1.50	7/01	11r
Sugar and other sweets, expenditures on	yr	99	1999	30r
Sugar, white, 33-80 ounce package	lb	0.39	7/01	11r
Sugar, white, all sizes	lb	0.42	7/01	11r
Tobacco products and smoking supplies purchases	yr	288	1999	30r
Tomatoes, field grown	lb	1.43	7/01	11r
Tuna, light, chunk	lb	1.77	7/01	11r
Turkey, frozen, whole	lb	1.05	7/01	11r
Goods and Services				
B&B Japanese maple (acer japonicum)	gal	49.98-129.00	4/00	93r
Boxwood (buxus)	2 gal	12.99-16.99	4/00	93r
Daylily (hemerocallis)	gal	4.99-8.99	4/00	93r
Flat of annuals		11.00-13.92	4/00	93r
Fountain grass (pennisetum)	gal	5.98-7.98	4/00	93r
Hanging basket (10 in)		7.99-14.98	4/00	93r
Hardy geranium (geranium)	gal	5.98-8.00	4/00	93r
Hosta (hosta)	gal	4.99-10.98	4/00	93r
Lilac (syrubga vulgaris)	2 gal	12.99-21.99	4/00	93r
Rhododendron (rhododendron)	2 gal	14.99-24.99	4/00	93r
Sage (salvia)	gal	5.98-6.99	4/00	93r

Macon, GA - continued

Item	Per	Value	Date	Ref.
Goods and Services - continued				
Wintercreeper euonymus (euonymus fortunei)	2 gal	7.99-89.99	4/00	93r
Hunting license	yr	10.00	4/01	34s
Health Care				
Cardiac catheterization, ave hospital/ physician charges		14190	1998	77s
Childbirth, Cesarean delivery		11587	1997	13r
Childbirth, vaginal delivery		6725	1997	13r
Drugs, expenditures on	yr	399	1999	30r
Health care purchases	yr	1971	1999	30r
Health insurance expenditures	yr	933	1999	30r
Hysterectomy, laproscopically-assisted, ave hospital/physician charges		16760	1998	76s
Hysterectomy, vaginal, ave hospital and physician charges		11160	1998	76s
Medicaid dispensing fee		4.63	1999	87s
Medical services expenditures	yr	547	1999	30r
Medical supplies, expenditures on	yr	91	1999	30r
Nursing home costs, private room	day	98	2000	82c
Nursing home stay, private room	day	98	2000	81c
Plastic surgery, breast augmentation		2870	2000	7r
Plastic surgery, breast lift		3649	2000	7r
Plastic surgery, facelift		5008	2000	7r
Plastic surgery, hair transplantation		3425	2000	7r
Plastic surgery, lip augmentation		1227	2000	7r
Plastic surgery, lower body lift		4793	2000	7r
Plastic surgery, thigh lift		3862	2000	7r
Household Goods				
Floor coverings, expenditures on	yr	44	1999	30r
Furniture, expenditures on	yr	335	1999	30r
Household furnishings and equipment purchases	yr	1328	1999	30r
Household textiles, expenditures on	yr	89	1999	30r
Laundry and cleaning supplies, expenditures on	yr	113	1999	30r
Housing				
Home, 2200 sq ft, 4-br, 2-bath, 2-car garage, average		171875	2000	47c
Home price, existing, ave		160100	10/00	90r
Home value, median		131000	2001	53s
House, 2-story, 2,400 sq ft, 2-car garage, new		120500	2000	54c
Household operation expenditures	yr	553	1999	30r
Housekeeping supplies purchases	yr	473	1999	30r
Housing, expenditures on	yr	10303	1999	30r
Maintenance, repairs, insurance expenditures	yr	699	1999	30r
Monthly rental value of owned home	mos	505	1999	30r
Owned dwellings, expenditures own	yr	3465	1999	30r
Rent expenditures	yr	1641	1999	30r
Rental unit, 1 bedroom, with utilities	mos	396	4/01	41c
Rental unit, 2 bedroom, with utilities	mos	475	4/01	41c
Rental unit, 3 bedroom, with utilities	mos	620	4/01	41c
Rental unit, 4 bedroom, with utilities	mos	673	4/01	41c
Shelter, expenditures on	yr	5467	1999	30r
Insurance and Pensions				
Life and other personal insurance purchases	yr	414	1999	30r
Pensions and Social Security, expenditures on	yr	2635	1999	30r
Personal insurance and pensions, expenditures on	yr	3048	1999	30r
Legal Fees				
Divorce, filing fee		65.00-85.00	4/01	35s
Driver's license fee	renew	15.00	1999	48s
Driver's license fee	orig	16.50	1999	48s
Personal Goods				
Personal care products and services purchases	yr	393	1999	30r

Values are in dollars or fractions of dollars. In the column headed *Ref*, references are shown to sources. Each reference is followed by a letter. These refer to the geographical level for which data were reported; s=State, r=Region, and c=City or metro. The abbreviation *ex* is used to mean *except* or *excluding*; *exp* stands for expenditures. For other abbreviations and further explanations, please see the Introduction.

Macon, GA - continued

Item	Per	Value	Date	Ref.
Personal Services				
Personal services, household, expenditures on	yr	258	1999	30r
Pets				
Pets, toys, and playground equipment, expenditures on	yr	306	1999	30r
Taxes				
Federal income taxes paid	yr	2047	1999	30r
Personal taxes, expenditures on	yr	2554	1999	30r
Property taxes paid	yr	726	1999	30r
State and local income taxes paid	yr	363	1999	30r
Transportation				
Cars and trucks, new, expenditures on	yr	1648	1999	30r
Cars and trucks, used, expenditures on	yr	1651	1999	30r
Diesel at the pump	gal	1.10	10/99	73s
Gasoline and motor oil purchases	yr	1052	1999	30r
Gasoline before-tax price (cents)	gal	102.00	10/00	43s
Maintenance and repair expenditures	yr	621	1999	30r
Public transportation, expenditures on	yr	298	1999	30r
Transportation purchases	yr	6738	1999	30r
Vehicle expenses, miscellaneous, purchases	yr	2033	1999	30r
Vehicle insurance payments	yr	696	1999	30r
Vehicle purchases (net outlay)	yr	3354	1999	30r
Vehicle rental, lease expenditures	yr	352	1999	30r
Utilities				
Electrical bill, average	mos	79.83	9/00	9s
Electricity, expenditures on	yr	1115	1999	30r
Electricity cost, average	KWh	6.10	9/00	9s
Water and other public services, expenditures on	yr	298	1999	30r
Weddings				
Wedding (national average cost)		19936	2000	33r
Wedding (regional average total cost)		16293	1997	110r
Attendants' gifts		321	1998	33r
Bridal attendants' apparel (5 persons)		824	2000	33r
Bride's headpiece/veil		173	1998	33r
Bride's wedding dress		859	1998	33r
Clergy, religious facility fee		242	1998	33r
Engagement ring		3177	1998	33r
Flowers		789	1998	33r
Groom's formalwear rental		99	2000	33r
Limousine		410	1998	33r
Marriage license cost		40.00	4/01	35s
Men's formalwear (ushers, best man)		469	2000	33r
Mother of bride apparel		241	2000	33r
Music		866	1998	33r
Photography and videography		1368	1998	33r
Rehearsal dinner		728	1998	33r
Wedding invitations and announcements		341	1998	33r
Wedding reception		7968	2000	33r
Wedding rings (bride and groom)		1060	1998	33r

Madison, WI

Item	Per	Value	Date	Ref.
Average annual expenditures	yr	35369	1999	30r
Alcoholic Beverages				
Alcoholic beverage purchases	yr	304	1999	30r
Malt beverages, all types, all sizes, any origin	16 oz	0.93	7/01	11r
Wine, red and white table, all sizes, any origin	liter	7.04	7/01	11r
Appliances				
Major appliances, expenditures on	yr	165	1999	30r
Small appliances, housewares, expenditures on	yr	90	1999	30r
Banking and Money				
Mortgage interest and charges paid	yr	2277	1999	30r
Mortgage principal paid on owned property	yr	1230	1999	30r
Vehicle finance charges paid	yr	328	1999	30r

Madison, WI - continued

Item	Per	Value	Date	Ref.
Business Expenses				
Business travel, car rental	day	59	2001	3c
Business travel, food	day	43	2001	3c
Business travel, hotel	day	92	2001	3c
Charity				
Cash contributions, expenditures	yr	1126	1999	30r
Child Care				
Child raising cost, total, age 0-2	yr	7890	1999	60r
Child raising cost, total, age 3-5	yr	8130	1999	60r
Child raising cost, total, age 6-8	yr	8170	1999	60r
Child raising cost, total, age 9-11	yr	8190	1999	60r
Child raising cost, total, age 12-14	yr	8890	1999	60r
Child raising cost, total, age 15-17	yr	9050	1999	60r
Child's child care and education, age 0-2	yr	1240	1999	60r
Child's child care and education, age 3-5	yr	1370	1999	60r
Child's child care and education, age 6-8	yr	880	1999	60r
Child's child care and education, age 9-11	yr	570	1999	60r
Child's child care and education, age 12-14	yr	420	1999	60r
Child's child care and education, age 15-17	yr	720	1999	60r
Child's clothing, age 0-2	yr	410	1999	60r
Child's clothing, age 3-5	yr	400	1999	60r
Child's clothing, age 6-8	yr	450	1999	60r
Child's clothing, age 9-11	yr	500	1999	60r
Child's clothing, age 12-14	yr	840	1999	60r
Child's clothing, age 15-17	yr	740	1999	60r
Child's food, age 0-2	yr	960	1999	60r
Child's food, age 3-5	yr	1120	1999	60r
Child's food, age 6-8	yr	1430	1999	60r
Child's food, age 9-11	yr	1710	1999	60r
Child's food, age 12-14	yr	1710	1999	60r
Child's food, age 15-17	yr	1920	1999	60r
Child's health care, age 0-2	yr	520	1999	60r
Child's health care, age 3-5	yr	500	1999	60r
Child's health care, age 6-8	yr	570	1999	60r
Child's health care, age 9-11	yr	610	1999	60r
Child's health care, age 12-14	yr	630	1999	60r
Child's health care, age 15-17	yr	650	1999	60r
Child's housing, age 0-2	yr	2860	1999	60r
Child's housing, age 3-5	yr	2840	1999	60r
Child's housing, age 6-8	yr	2800	1999	60r
Child's housing, age 9-11	yr	2650	1999	60r
Child's housing, age 12-14	yr	2840	1999	60r
Child's housing, age 15-17	yr	2440	1999	60r
Child's personal care, reading, age 0-2	yr	880	1999	60r
Child's personal care, reading, age 3-5	yr	900	1999	60r
Child's personal care, reading, age 6-8	yr	930	1999	60r
Child's personal care, reading, age 9-11	yr	970	1999	60r
Child's personal care, reading, age 12-14	yr	1150	1999	60r
Child's personal care, reading, age 15-17	yr	920	1999	60r
Clothing				
Apparel and services purchases	yr	1607	1999	30r
Boys, 2 to 15, expenditures on	yr	91	1999	30r
Children under 2, expenditures on	yr	59	1999	30r
Footwear, expenditures on	yr	285	1999	30r
Girls, 2 to 15, expenditures on	yr	116	1999	30r
Men and boys, expenditures on	yr	433	1999	30r
Men, 16 and over, expenditures on	yr	341	1999	30r
Women, 16 and over, expenditures on	yr	490	1999	30r
Communications				
Cable modem installation, Bresnan		99.95	6/99	103s
Cable modem installation, Marcus		499.00	6/99	103s
Cable modem rate, cable subscriber, Bresnan	mos	39.95	6/99	103s
Cable modem rate, cable subscriber, Marcus	mos	14.95-49.95	6/99	103s
Cable modem rate, non-cable subscriber, Bresnan	mos	49.95	6/99	103s
Cable modem rate, non-cable subscriber, Marcus	mos	60.95	6/99	103s
Phone line, single, business, field visit	inst.	64.65	12/97	17s
Phone line, single, business, no field visit	inst.	64.65	12/97	17s

Values are in dollars or fractions of dollars. In the column headed *Ref*, references are shown to sources. Each reference is followed by a letter. These refer to the geographical level for which data were reported: s=State, r=Region, and c=City or metro. The abbreviation *ex* is used to mean *except* or *excluding*; *exp* stands for *expenditures*. For other abbreviations and further explanations, please see the Introduction.

Madison, WI - continued

Item	Per	Value	Date	Ref.
Communications				
Phone line, single, residence, field visit	inst.	33.05	12/97	17s
Phone line, single, residence, no field visit	inst.	33.05	12/97	17s
Postage and stationery, expenditures on	yr	140	1999	30r
Postal rate, express mail, up to half-pound		12.45	7/01	108r
Postal rate, letter, first class, first ounce		0.34	7/01	108r
Postal rate, letter, two ounces		0.57	7/01	108r
Postal rate, post card		0.21	7/01	108r
Postal rate, priority mail, two pounds		3.95	7/01	108r
Postal rate, priority mail, up to one pound		3.50	7/01	108r
Telephone bill, business, basic rate	mos	20.85	12/97	18c
Telephone bill, residential, basic rate	mos	5.40	12/97	18c
Telephone services, expenditures on	yr	830	1999	30r
Education				
Board, 4-year private college/university	yr	2271	1996	38s
Board, 4-year public college/university	yr	1527	1996	38s
Education expenditures	yr	583	1999	30r
Room, 4-year private college/university	yr	1812	1996	38s
Room, 4-year public college/university	yr	1706	1996	38s
Total cost, 4-year private college/university	yr	15652	1996	38s
Total cost, 4-year public college/university	yr	5847	1996	38s
Tuition, 2-year public college/university, in state	yr	1840	1996	38s
Tuition, 4-year private college/university, in state	yr	11569	1996	38s
Tuition, 4-year public college/university	yr	2614	1996	38s
Energy and Fuels				
Electricity	500 KWhs	46.59	7/01	11r
Fuel oil #2	gal	1.27	7/01	11r
Fuel oil and other fuels, expenditures on	yr	68	1999	30r
Gas, cooking, winter, 10 therms	mos	5.32	2/96	98c
Gas, cooking, winter, 30 therms	mos	15.96	2/96	98c
Gas, cooking, winter, 50 therms	mos	26.61	2/96	98c
Gas, heating, winter, average use	mos	105.36	2/96	98c
Gas, natural, commercial rate	1000 cf	7.32	11/00	88s
Gasoline, unleaded midgrade	gal	1.79	7/01	11r
Gasoline, unleaded premium	gal	1.86	7/01	11r
Gasoline, unleaded regular	gal	1.58	7/01	11r
Natural gas, expenditures on	yr	389	1999	30r
Utility (piped) gas, therm		0.81	7/01	11r
Utility (piped) gas, 40 therms		38.01	7/01	11r
Utility (piped) gas, 100 therms		81.75	7/01	11r
Entertainment				
Entertainment purchases	yr	1984	1999	30r
Fees and admissions paid	yr	444	1999	30r
Television, radios, sound equipment, expenditures on	yr	580	1999	30r
Funerals				
Cosmetology, hair, other preparation		178.32	1/99	78r
Embalming		408.19	1/99	78r
Funeral at funeral home		362.13	1/99	78r
Professional service charges		1375.51	1/99	78r
Transfer of remains to funeral home		155.92	1/99	78r
Visitation/viewing		294.38	1/99	78r
Groceries				
Bacon, sliced	lb	3.15	7/01	11r
Bakery products, expenditures on	yr	281	1999	30r
Bananas	lb	0.48	7/01	11r
Beans, dried, any type, all sizes	lb	0.61	7/01	11r
Beef for stew, boneless	lb	3.08	7/01	11r
Beef, expenditures on	yr	217	1999	30r
Bologna, all beef or mixed	lb	2.52	7/01	11r
Bread, white, pan	lb	1.06	7/01	11r
Broccoli	lb	0.91	7/01	11r
Butter, salted, grade AA, stick	lb	3.04	7/01	11r
Butter, yoghurt, cheese, etc, expenditures on	yr	183	1999	30r
Cereals and bakery product purchases	yr	430	1999	30r
Cereals and cereal products, expenditures on	yr	149	1999	30r

Madison, WI - continued

Item	Per	Value	Date	Ref.
Groceries - continued				
Chicken, fresh, whole	lb	1.07	7/01	11r
Chops, boneless,	lb	3.64	7/01	11r
Chuck roast, U.S. choice, boneless	lb	2.47	7/01	11r
Coffee, 100%, ground roast, all sizes	lb	2.69	7/01	11r
Cookies, chocolate chip	lb	2.87	7/01	11r
Dairy product purchases	yr	304	1999	30r
Eggs, expenditures on	yr	26	1999	30r
Eggs, grade A, large	dozen	0.88	7/01	11r
Fats and oils, expenditures on	yr	75	1999	30r
Fish and seafood, expenditures on	yr	72	1999	30r
Food (excl fruit and vegetables), eaten at home, purchases	yr	887	1999	30r
Food cooked on trips, expenditures on	yr	44	1999	30r
Food purchases	yr	4802	1999	30r
Food purchases, eaten away from home	yr	2069	1999	30r
Food purchases, food eaten at home	yr	2733	1999	30r
Fresh fruits, expenditures on	yr	138	1999	30r
Fresh milk and cream, expenditures on	yr	120	1999	30r
Fresh vegetables, expenditures on	yr	126	1999	30r
Grapefruit	lb	0.66	7/01	11r
Grapes, Thompson, seedless	lb	1.64	7/01	11r
Ground beef, 100% beef	lb	1.64	7/01	11r
Ground beef, lean and extra lean	lb	2.16	7/01	11r
Ground chuck, 100% beef	lb	2.13	7/01	11r
Ham, boneless, excl canned	lb	2.62	7/01	11r
Ice cream, prepackaged, bulk, regular	1/2 gal	3.35	7/01	11r
Lemons	lb	1.19	7/01	11r
Lettuce, iceberg	lb	0.73	7/01	11r
Margarine, soft, tubs	lb	0.89	7/01	11r
Meats, poultry, fish, and egg purchases	yr	671	1999	30r
Milk, fresh, whole, fortified	gal	2.71	7/01	11r
Nonalcoholic beverages, expenditures on	yr	239	1999	30r
Oranges, Navel	lb	0.80	7/01	11r
Oranges, Valencia	lb	0.66	7/01	11r
Pears, Anjou	lb	0.93	7/01	11r
Pork chops, center cut, bone-in	lb	3.63	7/01	11r
Pork, expenditures on	yr	150	1999	30r
Potato chips	16 oz	3.52	7/01	11r
Potatoes, frozen, french fried	lb	1.08	7/01	11r
Potatoes, white, all types	lb	0.33	7/01	11r
Poultry, expenditures on	yr	108	1999	30r
Processed fruits, expenditures on	yr	98	1999	30r
Processed vegetables, expenditures on	yr	80	1999	30r
Round roast, U.S. choice, boneless	lb	3.07	7/01	11r
Round steak, graded and ungraded, excl U.S. prime and choice	lb	3.41	7/01	11r
Shortening, vegetable oil blends	lb	1.13	7/01	11r
Spaghetti and macaroni	lb	0.80	7/01	11r
Steak, round, U.S. choice, boneless	lb	3.23	7/01	11r
Steak, T-bone, U.S. choice, bone-in	lb	6.68	7/01	11r
Strawberries, dry pint	12 oz	1.32	7/01	11r
Sugar and other sweets, expenditures on	yr	114	1999	30r
Sugar, white, 33-80 ounce package	lb	0.42	7/01	11r
Sugar, white, all sizes	lb	0.43	7/01	11r
Tobacco products and smoking supplies purchases	yr	331	1999	30r
Tomatoes, field grown	lb	1.46	7/01	11r
Tuna, light, chunk	lb	1.80	7/01	11r
Turkey, frozen, whole	lb	1.15	7/01	11r
Goods and Services				
B&B Japanese maple (acer japonicum)	gal	29.99-169.99	4/00	93r
Boxwood (buxus)	2 gal	18.99-39.99	4/00	93r
Daylily (hemerocallis)	gal	4.99-25.00	4/00	93r
Flat of annuals		11.98-24.99	4/00	93r
Fountain grass (pennisetum)	gal	5.98-12.98	4/00	93r
Hanging basket (10 in)		12.99-27.99	4/00	93r

Values are in dollars or fractions of dollars. In the column headed *Ref*, references are shown to sources. Each reference is followed by a letter. These refer to the geographical level for which data were reported: s=State, r=Region, and c=City or metro. The abbreviation *ex* is used to mean *except* or *excluding*; *exp* stands for *expenditures*. For other abbreviations and further explanations, please see the Introduction.

Madison, WI - continued

Item	Per	Value	Date	Ref.
Goods and Services				
Hardy geranium (geranium)	gal	7.99-9.99	4/00	93r
Hosta (hosta)	gal	6.00-25.00	4/00	93r
Lilac (syrubga vulgaris)	2 gal	14.99-24.99	4/00	93r
Miscellaneous purchases	yr	865	1999	30r
Rhododendron (rhododendron)	2 gal	23.98-42.99	4/00	93r
Sage (salvia)	gal	6.00-9.99	4/00	93r
Wintercreeper euonymus (euonymus fortunei)	2 gal	16.00-169.99	4/00	93r
Hunting license	yr	14.00	4/01	34s
Health Care				
Cardiac catheterization, ave hospital/ physician charges		13240	1998	77s
Childbirth, Cesarean delivery		10722	1997	13r
Childbirth, vaginal delivery		6223	1997	13r
Drugs, expenditures on	yr	394	1999	30r
Health care purchases	yr	2048	1999	30r
Health insurance expenditures	yr	978	1999	30r
Hysterectomy, laproscopically-assisted, ave hospital/physician charges		13270	1998	76s
Hysterectomy, vaginal, ave hospital and physician charges		9170	1998	76s
Laser eye surgery	eye	1950-2400	2000	63s
Medicaid dispensing fee		4.88-40.11	1999	87s
Medical services expenditures	yr	554	1999	30r
Medical supplies, expenditures on	yr	122	1999	30r
Plastic surgery, breast augmentation		3184	2000	7r
Plastic surgery, breast lift		3585	2000	7r
Plastic surgery, facelift		4999	2000	7r
Plastic surgery, hair transplantation		3105	2000	7r
Plastic surgery, lip augmentation		1290	2000	7r
Plastic surgery, lower body lift		8135	2000	7r
Plastic surgery, thigh lift		3839	2000	7r
Household Goods				
Floor coverings, expenditures on	yr	52	1999	30r
Furniture, expenditures on	yr	344	1999	30r
Household furnishings and equipment purchases	yr	1475	1999	30r
Household textiles, expenditures on	yr	109	1999	30r
Laundry and cleaning supplies, expenditures on	yr	134	1999	30r
Housing				
Home, 2200 sq ft, 4-br, 2-bath, 2-car garage, average		204725	2000	47c
Home price, existing, ave		144400	10/00	90r
Home value, median		117000	2001	53s
Household operation expenditures	yr	542	1999	30r
Housekeeping supplies purchases	yr	508	1999	30r
Lodging expenditures	yr	430	1999	30r
Maintenance, repairs, insurance expenditures	yr	853	1999	30r
Monthly rental value of owned home	mos	547	1999	30r
Owned dwellings, expenditures own	yr	4282	1999	30r
Rent expenditures	yr	1558	1999	30r
Rental unit, 1 bedroom, with utilities	mos	559	4/01	41c
Rental unit, 2 bedroom, with utilities	mos	676	4/01	41c
Rental unit, 3 bedroom, with utilities	mos	938	4/01	41c
Rental unit, 4 bedroom, with utilities	mos	1107	4/01	41c
Shelter, expenditures on	yr	6270	1999	30r
Insurance and Pensions				
Auto insurance premium	yr	603.84	1999	57s
Life and other personal insurance purchases	yr	387	1999	30r
Pensions and Social Security, expenditures on	yr	2968	1999	30r

Madison, WI - continued

Item	Per	Value	Date	Ref.
Legal Fees				
Divorce, filing fee		142.00-150.00	4/01	35s
Driver's license fee	renew	12.00	1999	48s
Driver's license fee	orig	18.00	1999	48s
Fishing license	yr	14.00	4/01	34s
Personal Goods				
Personal care products and services purchases	yr	385	1999	30r
Personal Services				
Personal services, household, expenditures on	yr	300	1999	30r
Pets				
Pets, toys, and playground equipment, expenditures on	yr	375	1999	30r
Taxes				
Federal income taxes paid	yr	2326	1999	30r
Personal taxes, expenditures on	yr	3223	1999	30r
Property taxes paid	yr	1152	1999	30r
State and local income taxes paid	yr	753	1999	30r
Transportation				
Bus fare, one-way	trip	1.25	2000	1c
Cars and trucks, new, expenditures on	yr	1280	1999	30r
Cars and trucks, used, expenditures on	yr	1763	1999	30r
Diesel at the pump	gal	1.34	10/99	73s
Gasoline and motor oil purchases	yr	1036	1999	30r
Gasoline before-tax price (cents)	gal	113.40	10/00	43s
Maintenance and repair expenditures	yr	594	1999	30r
Public transportation, expenditures on	yr	341	1999	30r
Transportation purchases	yr	6617	1999	30r
Vehicle expenses, miscellaneous, purchases	yr	2159	1999	30r
Vehicle insurance payments	yr	701	1999	30r
Vehicle purchases (net outlay)	yr	3081	1999	30r
Vehicle rental, lease expenditures	yr	536	1999	30r
Utilities				
Electrical bill, average	mos	52.08	9/00	9s
Electricity, expenditures on	yr	841	1999	30r
Electricity, summer, 250 KWh	mos	20.00	2/96	96c
Electricity, summer, 500 KWh	mos	36.00	2/96	96c
Electricity, summer, 750 KWh	mos	52.00	2/96	96c
Electricity, summer, 1000 KWh	mos	68.00	2/96	96c
Electricity cost, average	KWh	5.69	9/00	9s
Utilities, fuels, and public services purchased	yr	2401	1999	30r
Water and other public services, expenditures on	yr	273	1999	30r
Weddings				
Wedding (national average cost)		19936	2000	33r
Wedding (regional average total cost)		16195	1997	110r
Attendants' gifts		321	1998	33r
Bridal attendants' apparel (5 persons)		824	2000	33r
Bride's headpiece/veil		173	1998	33r
Bride's wedding dress		859	1998	33r
Clergy, religious facility fee		242	1998	33r
Engagement ring		3177	1998	33r
Flowers		789	1998	33r
Groom's formalwear rental		99	2000	33r
Limousine		410	1998	33r
Marriage license cost		50.00-60.00	4/01	35s
Men's formalwear (ushers, best man)		469	2000	33r
Mother of bride apparel		241	2000	33r
Music		866	1998	33r
Photography and videography		1368	1998	33r
Rehearsal dinner		728	1998	33r
Wedding invitations and announcements		341	1998	33r
Wedding reception		7968	2000	33r
Wedding rings (bride and groom)		1060	1998	33r

Values are in dollars or fractions of dollars. In the column headed *Ref*, references are shown to sources. Each reference is followed by a letter. These refer to the geographical level for which data were reported: s=State, r=Region, and c=City or metro. The abbreviation *ex* is used to mean *except* or *excluding*; *exp* stands for *expenditures*. For other abbreviations and further explanations, please see the Introduction.

Manchester, NH

Item	Per	Value	Date	Ref.
Average annual expenditures	yr	37971	1999	30r
Composite, ACCRA index		105.60	3/01	4c
Alcoholic Beverages				
Alcoholic beverage purchases	yr	368	1999	30r
Beer, Heineken, 12-oz, ex deposit	6	6.76	3/01	4c
J & B Scotch	750-ml	18.99	3/01	4c
Wine, Livingston or Gallo, Chablis blanc	1.5 liter	4.99	3/01	4c
Wine, red and white table, all sizes, any origin	liter	9.64	7/01	11r
Appliances				
Appliance repair, service call, washing machine	min lab chg	62.00	3/01	4c
Major appliances, expenditures on	yr	194	1999	30r
Small appliances, housewares, expenditures on	yr	93	1999	30r
Banking and Money				
Mortgage interest and charges paid	yr	2622	1999	30r
Mortgage principal paid on owned property	yr	1262	1999	30r
Mortgage rate, incl. points and orig. fee, 30-yr. conv. fixed or ARM	mos	6.72	3/01	4c
Vehicle finance charges paid	yr	240	1999	30r
Charity				
Cash contributions, expenditures	yr	1001	1999	30r
Child Care				
Child raising cost, total, age 0-2	yr	8670	1999	60r
Child raising cost, total, age 3-5	yr	8910	1999	60r
Child raising cost, total, age 6-8	yr	9040	1999	60r
Child raising cost, total, age 9-11	yr	9100	1999	60r
Child raising cost, total, age 12-14	yr	9890	1999	60r
Child raising cost, total, age 15-17	yr	10010	1999	60r
Child's child care and education, age 0-2	yr	1070	1999	60r
Child's child care and education, age 3-5	yr	1190	1999	60r
Child's child care and education, age 6-8	yr	740	1999	60r
Child's child care and education, age 9-11	yr	470	1999	60r
Child's child care and education, age 12-14	yr	350	1999	60r
Child's child care and education, age 15-17	yr	590	1999	60r
Child's clothing, age 0-2	yr	480	1999	60r
Child's clothing, age 3-5	yr	470	1999	60r
Child's clothing, age 6-8	yr	520	1999	60r
Child's clothing, age 9-11	yr	570	1999	60r
Child's clothing, age 12-14	yr	970	1999	60r
Child's clothing, age 15-17	yr	870	1999	60r
Child's food, age 0-2	yr	1130	1999	60r
Child's food, age 3-5	yr	1290	1999	60r
Child's food, age 6-8	yr	1640	1999	60r
Child's food, age 9-11	yr	1930	1999	60r
Child's food, age 12-14	yr	1940	1999	60r
Child's food, age 15-17	yr	2150	1999	60r
Child's health care, age 0-2	yr	550	1999	60r
Child's health care, age 3-5	yr	530	1999	60r
Child's health care, age 6-8	yr	610	1999	60r
Child's health care, age 9-11	yr	650	1999	60r
Child's health care, age 12-14	yr	660	1999	60r
Child's health care, age 15-17	yr	690	1999	60r
Child's housing, age 0-2	yr	3555	1999	60r
Child's housing, age 3-5	yr	3530	1999	60r
Child's housing, age 6-8	yr	3490	1999	60r
Child's housing, age 9-11	yr	3340	1999	60r
Child's housing, age 12-14	yr	3530	1999	60r
Child's housing, age 15-17	yr	3140	1999	60r
Child's personal care, reading, age 0-2	yr	920	1999	60r
Child's personal care, reading, age 3-5	yr	950	1999	60r
Child's personal care, reading, age 6-8	yr	980	1999	60r
Child's personal care, reading, age 9-11	yr	1020	1999	60r
Child's personal care, reading, age 12-14	yr	1190	1999	60r
Child's personal care, reading, age 15-17	yr	970	1999	60r
Daycare	mos	584	1998	37c
Clothing				
Apparel and services purchases	yr	1831	1999	30r
Boys' brief, cotton	3	3.22	3/01	4c

Manchester, NH - continued

Item	Per	Value	Date	Ref.
Clothing - continued				
Boys, 2 to 15, expenditures on	yr	92	1999	30r
Children under 2, expenditures on	yr	63	1999	30r
Footwear, expenditures on	yr	300	1999	30r
Girls, 2 to 15, expenditures on	yr	101	1999	30r
Men and boys, expenditures on	yr	446	1999	30r
Men, 16 and over, expenditures on	yr	354	1999	30r
Shirt, man's dress shirt		26.00	3/01	4c
Slacks, man's "No Wrinkles" khaki		34.99	3/01	4c
Women, 16 and over, expenditures on	yr	584	1999	30r
Communications				
Cable modem installation, Media One		100.00	6/99	103s
Cable modem rate, cable subscriber, Media One	mos	34.95-39.95	6/99	103s
Cable modem rate, non-cable subscriber, Media One	mos	49.95	6/99	103s
Newspaper subscription, daily and Sunday delivery	mos	15.83	3/01	4c
Phone line, single, business, field visit	inst.	109.00	12/97	17s
Phone line, single, business, no field visit	inst.	75.00	12/97	17s
Phone line, single, residence, field visit	inst.	81.00	12/97	17s
Phone line, single, residence, no field visit	inst.	49.00	12/97	17s
Postage and stationery, expenditures on	yr	138	1999	30r
Postal rate, express mail, up to half-pound		12.45	7/01	108r
Postal rate, letter, first class, first ounce		0.34	7/01	108r
Postal rate, letter, two ounces		0.57	7/01	108r
Postal rate, post card		0.21	7/01	108r
Postal rate, priority mail, two pounds		3.95	7/01	108r
Postal rate, priority mail, up to one pound		3.50	7/01	108r
Telephone bill, family of three	mos	22.41	3/01	4c
Telephone services, expenditures on	yr	830	1999	30r
Education				
Board, 4-year private college/university	yr	3009	1996	38s
Board, 4-year public college/university	yr	1710	1996	38s
Education expenditures	yr	877	1999	30r
Room, 4-year private college/university	yr	3024	1996	38s
Room, 4-year public college/university	yr	2573	1996	38s
Total cost, 4-year private college/university	yr	21071	1996	38s
Total cost, 4-year public college/university	yr	8729	1996	38s
Tuition, 2-year public college/university, in state	yr	2420	1996	38s
Tuition, 4-year private college/university, in state	yr	15038	1996	38s
Tuition, 4-year public college/university	yr	4446	1996	38s
Energy and Fuels				
Electricity	KWh	0.12	7/01	11r
Energy, combined forms, 2400 sq ft	mos	199.96	3/01	4c
Energy, exc. electricity, 2400 sq ft	mos	114.27	3/01	4c
Fuel oil #2	gal	1.31	7/01	11r
Fuel oil and other fuels, expenditures on	yr	207	1999	30r
Gas, regular unleaded, cash, self-service	gal	1.52	3/01	4c
Gasoline, all types	gal	1.80	7/01	11r
Gasoline, unleaded midgrade	gal	1.85	7/01	11r
Gasoline, unleaded premium	gal	1.91	7/01	11r
Gasoline, unleaded regular	gal	1.71	7/01	11r
Natural gas, expenditures on	yr	368	1999	30r
Utility (piped) gas, therm		1.08	7/01	11r
Utility (piped) gas, 40 therms		50.87	7/01	11r
Utility (piped) gas, 100 therms		111.06	7/01	11r
Entertainment				
Bowling, Saturday evening rate	line	2.50	3/01	4c
Entertainment purchases	yr	1821	1999	30r
Fees and admissions paid	yr	511	1999	30r
Monopoly game, Parker Brothers', No. 9	game	10.99	3/01	4c
Movie, first-run, Saturday, evening	adm.	7.50	3/01	4c
Television, radios, sound equipment, expenditures on	yr	650	1999	30r
Tennis balls, yellow, Wilson or Penn, 3	can	2.39	3/01	4c
Funerals				
Total cost of funeral		5776.91	1/99	78r

Values are in dollars or fractions of dollars. In the column headed *Ref*, references are shown to sources. Each reference is followed by a letter. These refer to the geographical level for which data were reported: s=State, r=Region, and c=City or metro. The abbreviation *ex* is used to mean *except* or *excluding*; *exp* stands for *expenditures*. For other abbreviations and further explanations, please see the Introduction.

Manchester, NH - continued

Item	Per	Value	Date	Ref.
Funerals				
Acknowledgement cards		14.47	1/99	78r
Casket		2090.19	1/99	78r
Cosmetology, hair, other preparation		132.92	1/99	78r
Embalming		377.33	1/99	78r
Funeral at funeral home		352.43	1/99	78r
Hearse (local)		185.55	1/99	78r
Professional service charges		1289.95	1/99	78r
Service car/van		87.42	1/99	78r
Transfer of remains to funeral home		175.48	1/99	78r
Vault		729.40	1/99	78r
Visitation/viewing		341.76	1/99	78r
Groceries				
Groceries, ACCRA Index		101.80	3/01	4c
Antibiotic ointment, Polysporin	0.5 oz	5.49	3/01	4c
Apples, red delicious	lb	0.95	7/01	11r
Baby food, strained vegetables or fruit, lowest price	4-4.5 oz	0.46	3/01	4c
Bacon, sliced	lb	3.44	7/01	11r
Bakery products, expenditures on	yr	310	1999	30r
Bananas	lb	0.46	3/01	4c
Bananas	lb	0.55	7/01	11r
Beef or hamburger, ground	lb	1.56	3/01	4c
Beef, expenditures on	yr	236	1999	30r
Bread, white	loaf	1.11	3/01	4c
Bread, white, pan	lb	1.09	7/01	11r
Butter, yoghurt, cheese, etc, expenditures on	yr	214	1999	30r
Cereals and bakery product purchases	yr	474	1999	30r
Cereals and cereal products, expenditures on	yr	164	1999	30r
Cheese, Kraft grated Parmesan	8 oz	2.99	3/01	4c
Chicken legs, bone-in	lb	1.23	7/01	11r
Chicken, fresh, whole	lb	1.13	7/01	11r
Chicken, whole fryer	lb	0.92	3/01	4c
Chuck roast, U.S. choice, boneless	lb	2.79	7/01	11r
Cigarettes, Winston, Kings	carton	28.14	3/01	4c
Coffee, 100%, ground roast, all sizes	lb	3.40	7/01	11r
Coffee, vacuum-packed	13 oz	2.69	3/01	4c
Corn Flakes, Kellogg's or Post Toasties	18 oz	2.99	3/01	4c
Corn, frozen, whole kernel, lowest price	16 oz	1.26	3/01	4c
Dairy product purchases	yr	342	1999	30r
Eggs, expenditures on	yr	34	1999	30r
Eggs, Grade A or AA	dozen	1.29	3/01	4c
Eggs, grade A, large	dozen	0.82	7/01	11r
Fats and oils, expenditures on	yr	80	1999	30r
Fish and seafood, expenditures on	yr	123	1999	30r
Food (excl fruit and vegetables), eaten at home, purchases	yr	838	1999	30r
Food cooked on trips, expenditures on	yr	48	1999	30r
Food purchases	yr	5314	1999	30r
Food purchases, eaten away from home	yr	2313	1999	30r
Food purchases, food eaten at home	yr	3001	1999	30r
Fresh fruits, expenditures on	yr	169	1999	30r
Fresh milk and cream, expenditures on	yr	128	1999	30r
Fresh vegetables, expenditures on	yr	164	1999	30r
Grapefruit	lb	0.67	7/01	11r
Grapes, Thompson, seedless	lb	2.18	7/01	11r
Ground beef, lean and extra lean	lb	2.66	7/01	11r
Ground chuck, 100% beef	lb	2.04	7/01	11r
Lettuce, iceberg	head	1.19	3/01	4c
Lettuce, iceberg	lb	0.76	7/01	11r
Margarine, Blue Bonnet or Parkay, stick	lb	0.76	3/01	4c
Meats, poultry, fish, and egg purchases	yr	808	1999	30r
Milk, whole	1/2 gal	1.49	3/01	4c
Nonalcoholic beverages, expenditures on	yr	225	1999	30r
Orange juice, frozen concentrate	16 oz	1.88	7/01	11r
Orange juice, Minute Maid frozen	12 oz	1.42	3/01	4c
Oranges, Navel	lb	0.79	7/01	11r
Oranges, Valencia	lb	0.56	7/01	11r
Peaches	lb	1.16	7/01	11r
Peaches, halves or slices, Hunt's, Del Monte, or Libby's	29 oz	1.72	3/01	4c
Peanut butter, creamy, all sizes	lb	2.01	7/01	11r

Manchester, NH - continued

Item	Per	Value	Date	Ref.
Groceries - continued				
Pears, Anjou	lb	1.16	7/01	11r
Peas, green, Del Monte or Green Giant	15 oz	0.72	3/01	4c
Pork chops, center cut, bone-in	lb	3.57	7/01	11r
Pork, expenditures on	yr	146	1999	30r
Potato chips	16 oz	3.37	7/01	11r
Potatoes, white or red	10 lb	3.52	3/01	4c
Potatoes, white, all types	lb	0.42	7/01	11r
Poultry, expenditures on	yr	158	1999	30r
Processed fruits, expenditures on	yr	124	1999	30r
Processed vegetables, expenditures on	yr	82	1999	30r
Round roast, U.S. choice, boneless	lb	3.04	7/01	11r
Sausage, Jimmy Dean/Owens pork	lb	2.92	3/01	4c
Shortening, vegetable, Crisco	3 lb	3.26	3/01	4c
Soft drink, Coca Cola, ex deposit	2 liter	1.09	3/01	4c
Spaghetti and macaroni	lb	1.04	7/01	11r
Steak, sirloin, U.S. choice, boneless	lb	5.39	7/01	11r
Steak, T-bone	lb	6.66	3/01	4c
Strawberries, dry pint	12 oz	1.51	7/01	11r
Sugar and other sweets, expenditures on	yr	110	1999	30r
Sugar, cane or beet	4 lbs	1.30	3/01	4c
Sugar, white, 33-80 ounce package	lb	0.46	7/01	11r
Sugar, white, all sizes	lb	0.47	7/01	11r
Tobacco products and smoking supplies purchases	yr	309	1999	30r
Tomatoes, Hunt's or Del Monte	14.5 oz	0.96	3/01	4c
Tuna, chunk, light	6 oz	0.79	3/01	4c
Yogurt, natural, fruit flavored	8 oz	0.79	7/01	11r
Goods and Services				
Miscellaneous goods and services, ACCRA Index		106.20	3/01	4c
B&B Japanese maple (acer japonicum)	gal	38.99-125.00	4/00	93r
Boxwood (buxus)	2 gal	15.99-49.95	4/00	93r
Daylilly (hemerocallis)	gal	4.95	4/00	93r
Flat of annuals		8.00-14.99	4/00	93r
Fountain grass (pennisetum)	gal	6.99-9.99	4/00	93r
Hanging basket (10 in)		12.95-19.99	4/00	93r
Hardy geranium (geranium)	gal	6.95-7.99	4/00	93r
Hosta (hosta)	gal	4.95	4/00	93r
Lilac (syrubga vulgaris)	2 gal	17.99-74.95	4/00	93r
Miscellaneous purchases	yr	872	1999	30r
Rhododendron (rhododendron)	2 gal	23.99-54.95	4/00	93r
Sage (salvia)	gal	6.95-7.99	4/00	93r
Wintercreeper euonymus (euonymus fortunei)	2 gal	14.99-23.95	4/00	93r
Hunting license	yr	15.50	4/01	34s
Health Care				
Health care, ACCRA Index		105.30	3/01	4c
Cardiac catheterization, ave hospital/physician charges		6880	1998	77s
Childbirth, Cesarean delivery		14716	1997	13r
Childbirth, vaginal delivery		8541	1997	13r
Dentist's fee, adult teeth cleaning and periodic oral exam	visit	73.33	3/01	4c
Doctor's fee, routine exam, established patient	visit	57.33	3/01	4c
Drugs, expenditures on	yr	296	1999	30r
Health care purchases	yr	1788	1999	30r
Health insurance expenditures	yr	875	1999	30r
Hospital care, private room	day	621.00	3/01	4c
Hysterectomy, laproscopically-assisted, ave hospital/physician charges		13100	1998	76s

Values are in dollars or fractions of dollars. In the column headed *Ref*, references are shown to sources. Each reference is followed by a letter. These refer to the geographical level for which data were reported: s=State, r=Region, and c=City or metro. The abbreviation *ex* is used to mean *except* or *excluding*; *exp* stands for *expenditures*. For other abbreviations and further explanations, please see the Introduction.

Manchester, NH - continued

Item	Per	Value	Date	Ref.
Health Care				
Hysterectomy, vaginal, ave hospital and physician charges		7610	1998	76s
Medicaid dispensing fee		2.50	1999	87s
Medical services expenditures	yr	516	1999	30r
Medical supplies, expenditures on	yr	102	1999	30r
Plastic surgery, breast augmentation		4232	2000	7r
Plastic surgery, breast lift		4605	2000	7r
Plastic surgery, facelift		6964	2000	7r
Plastic surgery, hair transplantation		4193	2000	7r
Plastic surgery, lip augmentation		1675	2000	7r
Plastic surgery, lower body lift		6611	2000	7r
Plastic surgery, thigh lift		4751	2000	7r
Household Goods				
Dishwashing powder, Cascade	50 oz	3.19	3/01	4c
Floor coverings, expenditures on	yr	59	1999	30r
Furniture, expenditures on	yr	388	1999	30r
Household furnishings and equipment purchases	yr	1567	1999	30r
Household textiles, expenditures on	yr	112	1999	30r
Laundry and cleaning supplies, expenditures on	yr	104	1999	30r
Tissues, facial, Kleenex brand	175	1.34	3/01	4c
Housing				
Housing, ACCRA Index		94.00	3/01	4c
Home price, existing, ave		180800	10/00	90r
Home value, median		189000	2001	53s
House, 2400 sq ft, 8000 sq ft lot, new, urban, utilities	total	185000	3/01	4c
House payment, principal and interest, 25% down payment	mos	897	3/01	4c
Household operation expenditures	yr	581	1999	30r
Housekeeping supplies purchases	yr	474	1999	30r
Lodging expenditures	yr	550	1999	30r
Maintenance, repairs, insurance expenditures	yr	835	1999	30r
Monthly rental value of owned home	mos	663	1999	30r
Owned dwellings, expenditures own	yr	5209	1999	30r
Rent expenditures	yr	2390	1999	30r
Rent, apartment, 2 br, 1 1/2-2 baths, unfurn, 950 sq ft, water	mos	842	3/01	4c
Rental unit, 1 bedroom, with utilities	mos	585	4/01	41c
Rental unit, 2 bedroom, with utilities	mos	730	4/01	41c
Rental unit, 3 bedroom, with utilities	mos	913	4/01	41c
Rental unit, 4 bedroom, with utilities	mos	1023	4/01	41c
Shelter, expenditures on	yr	8149	1999	30r
Insurance and Pensions				
Life and other personal insurance purchases	yr	424	1999	30r
Pensions and Social Security, expenditures on	yr	3037	1999	30r
Legal Fees				
Combination hunting and fishing license	yr	31.50	4/01	34s
Divorce, filing fee		127.00	4/01	35s
Driver's license fee	orig	32.00	1999	48s
Driver's license fee	renew	32.00	1999	48s
Fishing license	yr	24.25	4/01	34s
Personal Goods				
Personal care products and services purchases	yr	399	1999	30r
Shampoo, Alberto VO5	15 oz	1.14	3/01	4c
Toothpaste, Crest or Colgate	6-7 oz	2.59	3/01	4c
Personal Services				
Dry cleaning, man's 2-pc suit		9.68	3/01	4c
Man's haircut, barbershop, no styling		8.67	3/01	4c
Personal services, household, expenditures on	yr	271	1999	30r
Woman's shampoo, trim, blow-dry, no style-change		28.67	3/01	4c

Item	Per	Value	Date	Ref.
Pets				
Pets, toys, and playground equipment, expenditures on	yr	325	1999	30r
Restaurant Food				
Chicken, fried, thigh and drumstick, KFC/ Church's		3.50	3/01	4c
Hamburger with cheese, McDonald's	1/4 lb	2.66	3/01	4c
Pizza, Pizza Hut or Pizza Inn	11-12 in	8.99	3/01	4c
Taxes				
Federal income taxes paid	yr	2606	1999	30r
Personal taxes, expenditures on	yr	3567	1999	30r
Property taxes paid	yr	1752	1999	30r
State and local income taxes paid	yr	694	1999	30r
Transportation				
Transportation, ACCRA Index		102.80	3/01	4c
Bus fare, to central business district	1-way	0.90	3/01	4c
Cars and trucks, new, expenditures on	yr	1496	1999	30r
Cars and trucks, used, expenditures on	yr	1251	1999	30r
Diesel at the pump	gal	1.26	10/99	73s
Gasoline and motor oil purchases	yr	901	1999	30r
Gasoline before-tax price (cents)	gal	117.80	10/00	43s
Maintenance and repair expenditures	yr	618	1999	30r
Motorcycle license fee	orig	37.00	1999	49s
Motorcycle license fee	renew	37.00	1999	49s
Public transportation, expenditures on	yr	575	1999	30r
Tire balance, computer or spin balance, front	wheel	7.98	3/01	4c
Transportation purchases	yr	6503	1999	30r
Vehicle expenses, miscellaneous, purchases	yr	2266	1999	30r
Vehicle insurance payments	yr	824	1999	30r
Vehicle purchases (net outlay)	yr	2761	1999	30r
Vehicle rental, lease expenditures	yr	584	1999	30r
Travel				
Car rental	day	45.00	2000	52c
Utilities				
Utilities, ACCRA Index		155.50	3/01	4c
Electrical bill, average	mos	77.50	9/00	9s
Electricity, expenditures on	yr	837	1999	30r
Electricity, summer, 250 KWh	mos	36.03	2/96	96c
Electricity, summer, 500 KWh	mos	73.28	2/96	96c
Electricity, summer, 750 KWh	mos	110.54	2/96	96c
Electricity, summer, 1000 KWh	mos	144.66	2/96	96c
Electricity and other, mixed, 2400 sq ft, new home	mos	85.69	3/01	4c
Electricity cost, average	KWh	11.80	9/00	9s
Utilities, fuels, and public services purchased	yr	2457	1999	30r
Water and other public services, expenditures on	yr	215	1999	30r
Weddings				
Wedding (national average cost)		19936	2000	33r
Wedding (regional average total cost)		29454	1997	110r
Attendants' gifts		321	1998	33r
Bridal attendants' apparel (5 persons)		824	2000	33r
Bride's headpiece/veil		173	1998	33r
Bride's wedding dress		859	1998	33r
Clergy, religious facility fee		242	1998	33r
Engagement ring		3177	1998	33r
Flowers		789	1998	33r
Groom's formalwear rental		99	2000	33r
Limousine		410	1998	33r
Marriage license cost		45.00-57.00	4/01	35s
Men's formalwear (ushers, best man)		469	2000	33r
Mother of bride apparel		241	2000	33r
Music		866	1998	33r
Photography and videography		1368	1998	33r
Rehearsal dinner		728	1998	33r
Wedding invitations and announcements		341	1998	33r
Wedding reception		7968	2000	33r
Wedding rings (bride and groom)		1060	1998	33r

Values are in dollars or fractions of dollars. In the column headed *Ref*, references are shown to sources. Each reference is followed by a letter. These refer to the geographical level for which data were reported: s=State, r=Region, and c=City or metro. The abbreviation *ex* is used to mean *except* or *excluding*; *exp* stands for *expenditures*. For other abbreviations and further explanations, please see the Introduction.

Mansfield, OH

Item	Per	Value	Date	Ref.
Average annual expenditures	yr	35369	1999	30r
Composite, ACCRA index		96.10	3/01	4c
Alcoholic Beverages				
Alcoholic beverage purchases	yr	304	1999	30r
Beer, Heineken, 12-oz, ex deposit	6	7.39	3/01	4c
J & B Scotch	750-ml	21.40	3/01	4c
Malt beverages, all types, all sizes, any origin	16 oz	0.93	7/01	11r
Wine, Livingston or Gallo, Chablis blanc	1.5 liter	5.69	3/01	4c
Wine, red and white table, all sizes, any origin	liter	7.04	7/01	11r
Appliances				
Appliance repair, service call, washing machine	min lab chg	42.48	3/01	4c
Major appliances, expenditures on	yr	165	1999	30r
Small appliances, housewares, expenditures on	yr	90	1999	30r
Banking and Money				
Mortgage interest and charges paid	yr	2277	1999	30r
Mortgage principal paid on owned property	yr	1230	1999	30r
Mortgage rate, incl. points and orig. fee, 30-yr. conv. fixed or ARM	mos	7.33	3/01	4c
Vehicle finance charges paid	yr	328	1999	30r
Charity				
Cash contributions, expenditures	yr	1126	1999	30r
Child Care				
Child raising cost, total, age 0-2	yr	7890	1999	60r
Child raising cost, total, age 3-5	yr	8130	1999	60r
Child raising cost, total, age 6-8	yr	8170	1999	60r
Child raising cost, total, age 9-11	yr	8190	1999	60r
Child raising cost, total, age 12-14	yr	8890	1999	60r
Child raising cost, total, age 15-17	yr	9050	1999	60r
Child's child care and education, age 0-2	yr	1240	1999	60r
Child's child care and education, age 3-5	yr	1370	1999	60r
Child's child care and education, age 6-8	yr	880	1999	60r
Child's child care and education, age 9-11	yr	570	1999	60r
Child's child care and education, age 12-14	yr	420	1999	60r
Child's child care and education, age 15-17	yr	720	1999	60r
Child's clothing, age 0-2	yr	410	1999	60r
Child's clothing, age 3-5	yr	400	1999	60r
Child's clothing, age 6-8	yr	450	1999	60r
Child's clothing, age 9-11	yr	500	1999	60r
Child's clothing, age 12-14	yr	840	1999	60r
Child's clothing, age 15-17	yr	740	1999	60r
Child's food, age 0-2	yr	960	1999	60r
Child's food, age 3-5	yr	1120	1999	60r
Child's food, age 6-8	yr	1430	1999	60r
Child's food, age 9-11	yr	1710	1999	60r
Child's food, age 12-14	yr	1710	1999	60r
Child's food, age 15-17	yr	1920	1999	60r
Child's health care, age 0-2	yr	520	1999	60r
Child's health care, age 3-5	yr	500	1999	60r
Child's health care, age 6-8	yr	570	1999	60r
Child's health care, age 9-11	yr	610	1999	60r
Child's health care, age 12-14	yr	630	1999	60r
Child's health care, age 15-17	yr	650	1999	60r
Child's housing, age 0-2	yr	2860	1999	60r
Child's housing, age 3-5	yr	2840	1999	60r
Child's housing, age 6-8	yr	2800	1999	60r
Child's housing, age 9-11	yr	2650	1999	60r
Child's housing, age 12-14	yr	2840	1999	60r
Child's housing, age 15-17	yr	2440	1999	60r
Child's personal care, reading, age 0-2	yr	880	1999	60r
Child's personal care, reading, age 3-5	yr	900	1999	60r
Child's personal care, reading, age 6-8	yr	930	1999	60r
Child's personal care, reading, age 9-11	yr	970	1999	60r
Child's personal care, reading, age 12-14	yr	1150	1999	60r
Child's personal care, reading, age 15-17	yr	920	1999	60r
Clothing				
Apparel and services purchases	yr	1607	1999	30r
Boys' brief, cotton	3	3.52	3/01	4c

Mansfield, OH - continued

Item	Per	Value	Date	Ref.
Clothing - continued				
Boys, 2 to 15, expenditures on	yr	91	1999	30r
Children under 2, expenditures on	yr	59	1999	30r
Footwear, expenditures on	yr	285	1999	30r
Girls, 2 to 15, expenditures on	yr	116	1999	30r
Men and boys, expenditures on	yr	433	1999	30r
Men, 16 and over, expenditures on	yr	341	1999	30r
Shirt, man's dress shirt		22.24	3/01	4c
Slacks, man's "No Wrinkles" khaki		29.99	3/01	4c
Women, 16 and over, expenditures on	yr	490	1999	30r
Communications				
Cable modem installation, Adelphi		54.90	6/99	103s
Cable modem installation, Media One		100.00	6/99	103s
Cable modem installation, Time Warner		75.00-225.00	6/99	103s
Cable modem rate, cable subscriber, Adelphi	mos	34.95	6/99	103s
Cable modem rate, cable subscriber, Media One	mos	34.95-39.95	6/99	103s
Cable modem rate, cable subscriber, Time Warner	mos	39.95-49.95	6/99	103s
Cable modem rate, non-cable subscriber, Adelphi	mos	44.95	6/99	103s
Cable modem rate, non-cable subscriber, Media One	mos	49.95	6/99	103s
Cable modem rate, non-cable subscriber, Time Warner	mos	39.95-54.95	6/99	103s
Newspaper subscription, daily and Sunday delivery	mos	14.15	3/01	4c
Phone line, single, business, field visit	inst.	56.32	12/97	17s
Phone line, single, business, no field visit	inst.	56.32	12/97	17s
Phone line, single, residence, field visit	inst.	31.10	12/97	17s
Phone line, single, residence, no field visit	inst.	31.10	12/97	17s
Postage and stationery, expenditures on	yr	140	1999	30r
Postal rate, express mail, up to half-pound		12.45	7/01	108r
Postal rate, letter, first class, first ounce		0.34	7/01	108r
Postal rate, letter, two ounces		0.57	7/01	108r
Postal rate, post card		0.21	7/01	108r
Postal rate, priority mail, two pounds		3.95	7/01	108r
Postal rate, priority mail, up to one pound		3.50	7/01	108r
Telephone bill, family of three	mos	22.33	3/01	4c
Telephone services, expenditures on	yr	830	1999	30r
Education				
Board, 4-year private college/university	yr	2414	1996	38s
Board, 4-year public college/university	yr	2181	1996	38s
Education expenditures	yr	583	1999	30r
Room, 4-year private college/university	yr	2349	1996	38s
Room, 4-year public college/university	yr	2386	1996	38s
Total cost, 4-year private college/university	yr	17139	1996	38s
Total cost, 4-year public college/university	yr	8169	1996	38s
Tuition, 2-year public college/university, in state	yr	2261	1996	38s
Tuition, 4-year private college/university, in state	yr	12377	1996	38s
Tuition, 4-year public college/university	yr	3603	1996	38s
Energy and Fuels				
Electricity	500 KWhs	46.59	7/01	11r
Energy, combined forms, 2400 sq ft	mos	162.81	3/01	4c
Energy, exc. electricity, 2400 sq ft	mos	81.07	3/01	4c
Fuel oil #2	gal	1.27	7/01	11r
Fuel oil and other fuels, expenditures on	yr	68	1999	30r
Gas, natural, commercial rate	1000 cf	8.65	11/00	88s
Gas, regular unleaded, cash, self-service	gal	1.52	3/01	4c
Gasoline, unleaded midgrade	gal	1.79	7/01	11r
Gasoline, unleaded premium	gal	1.86	7/01	11r
Gasoline, unleaded regular	gal	1.58	7/01	11r
Natural gas, expenditures on	yr	389	1999	30r
Utility (piped) gas, therm		0.81	7/01	11r
Utility (piped) gas, 40 therms		38.01	7/01	11r
Utility (piped) gas, 100 therms		81.75	7/01	11r

Values are in dollars or fractions of dollars. In the column headed *Ref*, references are shown to sources. Each reference is followed by a letter. These refer to the geographical level for which data were reported: s=State, r=Region, and c=City or metro. The abbreviation *ex* is used to mean *except* or *excluding*; *exp* stands for *expenditures*. For other abbreviations and further explanations, please see the Introduction.

Mansfield, OH - continued

Item	Per	Value	Date	Ref.
Entertainment				
Bowling, Saturday evening rate	line	3.08	3/01	4c
Entertainment purchases	yr	1984	1999	30r
Fees and admissions paid	yr	444	1999	30r
Monopoly game, Parker Brothers', No. 9	game	10.54	3/01	4c
Movie, first-run, Saturday, evening	adm.	6.25	3/01	4c
Television, radios, sound equipment, expenditures on	yr	580	1999	30r
Tennis balls, yellow, Wilson or Penn, 3	can	2.22	3/01	4c
Funerals				
Cosmetology, hair, other preparation		178.32	1/99	78r
Embalming		408.19	1/99	78r
Funeral at funeral home		362.13	1/99	78r
Professional service charges		1375.51	1/99	78r
Transfer of remains to funeral home		155.92	1/99	78r
Visitation/viewing		294.38	1/99	78r
Groceries				
Groceries, ACCRA Index		103.30	3/01	4c
Antibiotic ointment, Polysporin	0.5 oz	4.24	3/01	4c
Baby food, strained vegetables or fruit, lowest price	4-4.5 oz	0.42	3/01	4c
Bacon, sliced	lb	3.15	7/01	11r
Bakery products, expenditures on	yr	281	1999	30r
Bananas	lb	0.55	3/01	4c
Bananas	lb	0.48	7/01	11r
Beans, dried, any type, all sizes	lb	0.61	7/01	11r
Beef for stew, boneless	lb	3.08	7/01	11r
Beef or hamburger, ground	lb	1.71	3/01	4c
Beef, expenditures on	yr	217	1999	30r
Bologna, all beef or mixed	lb	2.52	7/01	11r
Bread, white	loaf	0.98	3/01	4c
Bread, white, pan	lb	1.06	7/01	11r
Broccoli	lb	0.91	7/01	11r
Butter, salted, grade AA, stick	lb	3.04	7/01	11r
Butter, yoghurt, cheese, etc, expenditures on	yr	183	1999	30r
Cereals and bakery product purchases	yr	430	1999	30r
Cereals and cereal products, expenditures on	yr	149	1999	30r
Cheese, Kraft grated Parmesan	8 oz	4.25	3/01	4c
Chicken, fresh, whole	lb	1.07	7/01	11r
Chicken, whole fryer	lb	1.13	3/01	4c
Chops, boneless,	lb	3.64	7/01	11r
Chuck roast, U.S. choice, boneless	lb	2.47	7/01	11r
Cigarettes, Winston, Kings	carton	27.62	3/01	4c
Coffee, 100%, ground roast, all sizes	lb	2.69	7/01	11r
Coffee, vacuum-packed	13 oz	3.03	3/01	4c
Cookies, chocolate chip	lb	2.87	7/01	11r
Corn Flakes, Kellogg's or Post Toasties	18 oz	2.07	3/01	4c
Corn, frozen, whole kernel, lowest price	16 oz	1.16	3/01	4c
Dairy product purchases	yr	304	1999	30r
Eggs, expenditures on	yr	26	1999	30r
Eggs, Grade A or AA	dozen	1.27	3/01	4c
Eggs, grade A, large	dozen	0.88	7/01	11r
Fats and oils, expenditures on	yr	75	1999	30r
Fish and seafood, expenditures on	yr	72	1999	30r
Food (excl fruit and vegetables), eaten at home, purchases	yr	887	1999	30r
Food cooked on trips, expenditures on	yr	44	1999	30r
Food purchases	yr	4802	1999	30r
Food purchases, eaten away from home	yr	2069	1999	30r
Food purchases, food eaten at home	yr	2733	1999	30r
Fresh fruits, expenditures on	yr	138	1999	30r
Fresh milk and cream, expenditures on	yr	120	1999	30r
Fresh vegetables, expenditures on	yr	126	1999	30r
Grapefruit	lb	0.66	7/01	11r
Grapes, Thompson, seedless	lb	1.64	7/01	11r
Ground beef, 100% beef	lb	1.64	7/01	11r
Ground beef, lean and extra lean	lb	2.16	7/01	11r
Ground chuck, 100% beef	lb	2.13	7/01	11r
Ham, boneless, excl canned	lb	2.62	7/01	11r
Ice cream, prepackaged, bulk, regular	1/2 gal	3.35	7/01	11r
Lemons	lb	1.19	7/01	11r

Item	Per	Value	Date	Ref.
Groceries - continued				
Lettuce, iceberg	head	0.91	3/01	4c
Lettuce, iceberg	lb	0.73	7/01	11r
Margarine, Blue Bonnet or Parkay, stick	lb	1.01	3/01	4c
Margarine, soft, tubs	lb	0.89	7/01	11r
Meats, poultry, fish, and egg purchases	yr	671	1999	30r
Milk, fresh, whole, fortified	gal	2.71	7/01	11r
Milk, whole	1/2 gal	1.33	3/01	4c
Nonalcoholic beverages, expenditures on	yr	239	1999	30r
Orange juice, Minute Maid frozen	12 oz	1.79	3/01	4c
Oranges, Navel	lb	0.80	7/01	11r
Oranges, Valencia	lb	0.66	7/01	11r
Peaches, halves or slices, Hunt's, Del Monte, or Libby's	29 oz	1.75	3/01	4c
Pears, Anjou	lb	0.93	7/01	11r
Peas, green, Del Monte or Green Giant	15 oz	0.85	3/01	4c
Pork chops, center cut, bone-in	lb	3.63	7/01	11r
Pork, expenditures on	yr	150	1999	30r
Potato chips	16 oz	3.52	7/01	11r
Potatoes, frozen, french fried	lb	1.08	7/01	11r
Potatoes, white or red	10 lb	1.79	3/01	4c
Potatoes, white, all types	lb	0.33	7/01	11r
Poultry, expenditures on	yr	108	1999	30r
Processed fruits, expenditures on	yr	98	1999	30r
Processed vegetables, expenditures on	yr	80	1999	30r
Round roast, U.S. choice, boneless	lb	3.07	7/01	11r
Round steak, graded and ungraded, excl U.S. prime and choice	lb	3.41	7/01	11r
Sausage, Jimmy Dean/Owens pork	lb	3.16	3/01	4c
Shortening, vegetable oil blends	lb	1.13	7/01	11r
Shortening, vegetable, Crisco	3 lb	3.49	3/01	4c
Soft drink, Coca Cola, ex deposit	2 liter	1.27	3/01	4c
Spaghetti and macaroni	lb	0.80	7/01	11r
Steak, round, U.S. choice, boneless	lb	3.23	7/01	11r
Steak, T-bone	lb	6.47	3/01	4c
Steak, T-bone, U.S. choice, bone-in	lb	6.68	7/01	11r
Strawberries, dry pint	12 oz	1.32	7/01	11r
Sugar and other sweets, expenditures on	yr	114	1999	30r
Sugar, cane or beet	4 lbs	1.79	3/01	4c
Sugar, white, 33-80 ounce package	lb	0.42	7/01	11r
Sugar, white, all sizes	lb	0.43	7/01	11r
Tobacco products and smoking supplies purchases	yr	331	1999	30r
Tomatoes, field grown	lb	1.46	7/01	11r
Tomatoes, Hunt's or Del Monte	14.5 oz	0.87	3/01	4c
Tuna, chunk, light	6 oz	0.58	3/01	4c
Tuna, light, chunk	lb	1.80	7/01	11r
Turkey, frozen, whole	lb	1.15	7/01	11r
Goods and Services				
Miscellaneous goods and services, ACCRA Index		92.30	3/01	4c
B&B Japanese maple (acer japonicum)	gal	29.99-169.99	4/00	93r
Boxwood (buxus)	2 gal	18.99-39.99	4/00	93r
Daylily (hemerocallis)	gal	4.99-25.00	4/00	93r
Flat of annuals		11.98-24.99	4/00	93r
Fountain grass (pennisetum)	gal	5.98-12.98	4/00	93r
Hanging basket (10 in)		12.99-27.99	4/00	93r
Hardy geranium (geranium)	gal	7.99-9.99	4/00	93r
Hosta (hosta)	gal	6.00-25.00	4/00	93r
Lilac (syrubga vulgaris)	2 gal	14.99-24.99	4/00	93r
Miscellaneous purchases	yr	865	1999	30r
Rhododendron (rhododendron)	2 gal	23.98-42.99	4/00	93r

Values are in dollars or fractions of dollars. In the column headed *Ref*, references are shown to sources. Each reference is followed by a letter. These refer to the geographical level for which data were reported: s=State, r=Region, and c=City or metro. The abbreviation *ex* is used to mean *except* or *excluding*; *exp* stands for *expenditures*. For other abbreviations and further explanations, please see the Introduction.

Mansfield, OH - continued

Item	Per	Value	Date	Ref.
Goods and Services				
Sage (salvia)	gal	6.00-9.99	4/00	93r
Wintercreeper euonymus (euonymus fortunei)	2 gal	16.00-169.99	4/00	93r
Hunting license	yr	15.00	4/01	34s
Health Care				
Health care, ACCRA Index		88.80	3/01	4c
Cardiac catheterization, ave hospital/physician charges		11760	1998	77s
Childbirth, Cesarean delivery		10722	1997	13r
Childbirth, vaginal delivery		6223	1997	13r
Dentist's fee, adult teeth cleaning and periodic oral exam	visit	59.60	3/01	4c
Doctor's fee, routine exam, established patient	visit	57.20	3/01	4c
Drugs, expenditures on	yr	394	1999	30r
Health care purchases	yr	2048	1999	30r
Health insurance expenditures	yr	978	1999	30r
Hospital care, private room	day	425.00	3/01	4c
Hysterectomy, laproscopically-assisted, ave hospital/physician charges		11730	1998	76s
Hysterectomy, vaginal, ave hospital and physician charges		9640	1998	76s
Medicaid dispensing fee		3.70	1999	87s
Medical services expenditures	yr	554	1999	30r
Medical supplies, expenditures on	yr	122	1999	30r
Plastic surgery, breast augmentation		3184	2000	7r
Plastic surgery, breast lift		3585	2000	7r
Plastic surgery, facelift		4999	2000	7r
Plastic surgery, hair transplantation		3105	2000	7r
Plastic surgery, lip augmentation		1290	2000	7r
Plastic surgery, lower body lift		8135	2000	7r
Plastic surgery, thigh lift		3839	2000	7r
Household Goods				
Dishwashing powder, Cascade	50 oz	3.39	3/01	4c
Floor coverings, expenditures on	yr	52	1999	30r
Furniture, expenditures on	yr	344	1999	30r
Household furnishings and equipment purchases	yr	1475	1999	30r
Household textiles, expenditures on	yr	109	1999	30r
Laundry and cleaning supplies, expenditures on	yr	134	1999	30r
Tissues, facial, Kleenex brand	175	1.45	3/01	4c
Housing				
Housing, ACCRA Index		86.90	3/01	4c
Home price, existing, ave		144400	10/00	90r
Home value, median		96000	2001	53s
House, 2400 sq ft, 8000 sq ft lot, new, urban, utilities	total	182644	3/01	4c
House payment, principal and interest, 25% down payment	mos	942	3/01	4c
Household operation expenditures	yr	542	1999	30r
Housekeeping supplies purchases	yr	508	1999	30r
Lodging expenditures	yr	430	1999	30r
Maintenance, repairs, insurance expenditures	yr	853	1999	30r
Monthly rental value of owned home	mos	547	1999	30r
Owned dwellings, expenditures own	yr	4282	1999	30r
Rent expenditures	yr	1558	1999	30r
Rent, apartment, 2 br, 1 1/2-2 baths, unfurn, 950 sq ft, water	mos	484	3/01	4c
Rental unit, 1 bedroom, with utilities	mos	350	4/01	41c
Rental unit, 2 bedroom, with utilities	mos	445	4/01	41c
Rental unit, 3 bedroom, with utilities	mos	555	4/01	41c
Rental unit, 4 bedroom, with utilities	mos	622	4/01	41c
Shelter, expenditures on	yr	6270	1999	30r
Insurance and Pensions				
Life and other personal insurance purchases	yr	387	1999	30r
Pensions and Social Security, expenditures on	yr	2968	1999	30r

Mansfield, OH - continued

Item	Per	Value	Date	Ref.
Legal Fees				
Divorce, filing fee		100.00	4/01	35s
Driver's license fee	orig	14.50	1999	48s
Driver's license fee	renew	14.50	1999	48s
Fishing license	yr	15.00	4/01	34s
Personal Goods				
Personal care products and services purchases	yr	385	1999	30r
Shampoo, Alberto VO5	15 oz	1.10	3/01	4c
Toothpaste, Crest or Colgate	6-7 oz	1.97	3/01	4c
Personal Services				
Dry cleaning, man's 2-pc suit		7.74	3/01	4c
Man's haircut, barbershop, no styling		8.30	3/01	4c
Personal services, household, expenditures on	yr	300	1999	30r
Woman's shampoo, trim, blow-dry, no style-change		24.80	3/01	4c
Pets				
Pets, toys, and playground equipment, expenditures on	yr	375	1999	30r
Restaurant Food				
Chicken, fried, thigh and drumstick, KFC/Church's		2.45	3/01	4c
Hamburger with cheese, McDonald's	1/4 lb	2.14	3/01	4c
Pizza, Pizza Hut or Pizza Inn	11-12 in	8.50	3/01	4c
Taxes				
Federal income taxes paid	yr	2326	1999	30r
Personal taxes, expenditures on	yr	3223	1999	30r
Property taxes paid	yr	1152	1999	30r
State and local income taxes paid	yr	753	1999	30r
Transportation				
Transportation, ACCRA Index		99.70	3/01	4c
Cars and trucks, new, expenditures on	yr	1280	1999	30r
Cars and trucks, used, expenditures on	yr	1763	1999	30r
Diesel at the pump	gal	1.25	10/99	73s
Gasoline and motor oil purchases	yr	1036	1999	30r
Gasoline before-tax price (cents)	gal	109.50	10/00	43s
Maintenance and repair expenditures	yr	594	1999	30r
Public transportation, expenditures on	yr	341	1999	30r
Tire balance, computer or spin balance, front	wheel	7.00	3/01	4c
Transportation purchases	yr	6617	1999	30r
Vehicle expenses, miscellaneous, purchases	yr	2159	1999	30r
Vehicle insurance payments	yr	701	1999	30r
Vehicle purchases (net outlay)	yr	3081	1999	30r
Vehicle rental, lease expenditures	yr	536	1999	30r
Utilities				
Utilities, ACCRA Index		129.20	3/01	4c
Electrical bill, average	mos	72.83	9/00	9s
Electricity, expenditures on	yr	841	1999	30r
Electricity and other, mixed, 2400 sq ft, new home	mos	81.74	3/01	4c
Electricity cost, average	KWh	6.59	9/00	9s
Utilities, fuels, and public services purchased	yr	2401	1999	30r
Water and other public services, expenditures on	yr	273	1999	30r
Weddings				
Wedding (national average cost)		19936	2000	33r
Wedding (regional average total cost)		16195	1997	110r
Attendants' gifts		321	1998	33r
Bridal attendants' apparel (5 persons)		824	2000	33r
Bride's headpiece/veil		173	1998	33r
Bride's wedding dress		859	1998	33r
Clergy, religious facility fee		242	1998	33r
Engagement ring		3177	1998	33r
Flowers		789	1998	33r
Groom's formalwear rental		99	2000	33r
Limousine		410	1998	33r
Marriage license cost		45.00	4/01	35s
Men's formalwear (ushers, best man)		469	2000	33r

Values are in dollars or fractions of dollars. In the column headed *Ref*, references are shown to sources. Each reference is followed by a letter. These refer to the geographical level for which data were reported: s=State, r=Region, and c=City or metro. The abbreviation *ex* is used to mean *except* or *excluding*; *exp* stands for expenditures. For other abbreviations and further explanations, please see the Introduction.

Mansfield, OH - continued

Item	Per	Value	Date	Ref.
Weddings				
Mother of bride apparel		241	2000	33r
Music		866	1998	33r
Photography and videography		1368	1998	33r
Rehearsal dinner		728	1998	33r
Wedding invitations and announcements		341	1998	33r
Wedding reception		7968	2000	33r
Wedding rings (bride and groom)		1060	1998	33r

McAllen-Edinburg-Mission, TX

Item	Per	Value	Date	Ref.
Alcoholic Beverages				
Alcoholic beverage purchases	yr	253	1999	30r
Malt beverages, all types, all sizes, any origin	16 oz	0.96	7/01	11r
Appliances				
Major appliances, expenditures on	yr	172	1999	30r
Small appliances, housewares, expenditures on	yr	81	1999	30r
Banking and Money				
Mortgage interest and charges paid	yr	2039	1999	30r
Mortgage principal paid on owned property	yr	1026	1999	30r
Vehicle finance charges paid	yr	365	1999	30r
Charity				
Cash contributions, expenditures	yr	1127	1999	30r
Child Care				
Child raising cost, total, age 0-2	yr	8540	1999	60r
Child raising cost, total, age 3-5	yr	8780	1999	60r
Child raising cost, total, age 6-8	yr	8820	1999	60r
Child raising cost, total, age 9-11	yr	8800	1999	60r
Child raising cost, total, age 12-14	yr	9510	1999	60r
Child raising cost, total, age 15-17	yr	9740	1999	60r
Child's child care and education, age 0-2	yr	1380	1999	60r
Child's child care and education, age 3-5	yr	1520	1999	60r
Child's child care and education, age 6-8	yr	990	1999	60r
Child's child care and education, age 9-11	yr	650	1999	60r
Child's child care and education, age 12-14	yr	490	1999	60r
Child's child care and education, age 15-17	yr	840	1999	60r
Child's clothing, age 0-2	yr	480	1999	60r
Child's clothing, age 3-5	yr	470	1999	60r
Child's clothing, age 6-8	yr	520	1999	60r
Child's clothing, age 9-11	yr	570	1999	60r
Child's clothing, age 12-14	yr	950	1999	60r
Child's clothing, age 15-17	yr	850	1999	60r
Child's food, age 0-2	yr	1000	1999	60r
Child's food, age 3-5	yr	1160	1999	60r
Child's food, age 6-8	yr	1490	1999	60r
Child's food, age 9-11	yr	1770	1999	60r
Child's food, age 12-14	yr	1770	1999	60r
Child's food, age 15-17	yr	1980	1999	60r
Child's health care, age 0-2	yr	620	1999	60r
Child's health care, age 3-5	yr	590	1999	60r
Child's health care, age 6-8	yr	680	1999	60r
Child's health care, age 9-11	yr	720	1999	60r
Child's health care, age 12-14	yr	730	1999	60r
Child's health care, age 15-17	yr	760	1999	60r
Child's housing, age 0-2	yr	3070	1999	60r
Child's housing, age 3-5	yr	3050	1999	60r
Child's housing, age 6-8	yr	3010	1999	60r
Child's housing, age 9-11	yr	2850	1999	60r
Child's housing, age 12-14	yr	3040	1999	60r
Child's housing, age 15-17	yr	2650	1999	60r
Child's personal care, reading, age 0-2	yr	910	1999	60r
Child's personal care, reading, age 3-5	yr	930	1999	60r
Child's personal care, reading, age 6-8	yr	960	1999	60r
Child's personal care, reading, age 9-11	yr	1000	1999	60r
Child's personal care, reading, age 12-14	yr	1170	1999	60r
Child's personal care, reading, age 15-17	yr	950	1999	60r
Clothing				
Apparel and services purchases	yr	1610	1999	30r

McAllen-Edinburg-Mission, TX - continued

Item	Per	Value	Date	Ref.
Clothing - continued				
Boys, 2 to 15, expenditures on	yr	89	1999	30r
Children under 2, expenditures on	yr	79	1999	30r
Footwear, expenditures on	yr	283	1999	30r
Girls, 2 to 15, expenditures on	yr	103	1999	30r
Men and boys, expenditures on	yr	351	1999	30r
Men, 16 and over, expenditures on	yr	262	1999	30r
Women, 16 and over, expenditures on	yr	538	1999	30r
Communications				
Cable modem installation, AT&T-BIS		150.00	6/99	103s
Cable modem installation, Marcus		499.00	6/99	103s
Cable modem installation, Time Warner		75.00-225.00	6/99	103s
Cable modem rate, cable subscriber, AT&T-BIS	mos	39.95	6/99	103s
Cable modem rate, cable subscriber, Marcus	mos	14.95-49.95	6/99	103s
Cable modem rate, cable subscriber, Time Warner	mos	39.95-49.95	6/99	103s
Cable modem rate, non-cable subscriber, Marcus	mos	60.95	6/99	103s
Cable modem rate, non-cable subscriber, Time Warner	mos	39.95-54.95	6/99	103s
Phone line, single, business, field visit	inst.	71.90	12/97	17s
Phone line, single, business, no field visit	inst.	57.30	12/97	17s
Phone line, single, residence, field visit	inst.	52.95	12/97	17s
Phone line, single, residence, no field visit	inst.	38.35	12/97	17s
Postage and stationery, expenditures on	yr	104	1999	30r
Postal rate, express mail, up to half-pound		12.45	7/01	108r
Postal rate, letter, first class, first ounce		0.34	7/01	108r
Postal rate, letter, two ounces		0.57	7/01	108r
Postal rate, post card		0.21	7/01	108r
Postal rate, priority mail, two pounds		3.95	7/01	108r
Postal rate, priority mail, up to one pound		3.50	7/01	108r
Telephone services, expenditures on	yr	860	1999	30r
Education				
Board, 4-year private college/university	yr	2198	1996	38s
Board, 4-year public college/university	yr	1759	1996	38s
Education expenditures	yr	431	1999	30r
Room, 4-year private college/university	yr	2000	1996	38s
Room, 4-year public college/university	yr	1885	1996	38s
Total cost, 4-year private college/university	yr	13156	1996	38s
Total cost, 4-year public college/university	yr	5464	1996	38s
Tuition, 2-year public college/university, in state	yr	771	1996	38s
Tuition, 4-year private college/university, in state	yr	8959	1996	38s
Tuition, 4-year public college/university	yr	1820	1996	38s
Energy and Fuels				
Electricity	KWh	0.09	7/01	11r
Electricity	500 KWhs	47.29	7/01	11r
Fuel oil #2	gal	1.43	7/01	11r
Fuel oil and other fuels, expenditures on	yr	45	1999	30r
Gas, natural, commercial rate	1000 cf	6.94	11/00	88s
Gasoline, all types	gal	1.60	7/01	11r
Gasoline, unleaded midgrade	gal	1.65	7/01	11r
Gasoline, unleaded premium	gal	1.74	7/01	11r
Natural gas, expenditures on	yr	164	1999	30r
Utility (piped) gas, therm		1.01	7/01	11r
Utility (piped) gas, 40 therms		44.29	7/01	11r
Utility (piped) gas, 100 therms		97.44	7/01	11r
Entertainment				
Entertainment purchases	yr	1574	1999	30r
Fees and admissions paid	yr	371	1999	30r
Reading purchases	yr	121	1999	30r
Television, radios, sound equipment, expenditures on	yr	561	1999	30r
Funerals				
Total cost of funeral		5842.28	1/99	78r

Values are in dollars or fractions of dollars. In the column headed *Ref*, references are shown to sources. Each reference is followed by a letter. These refer to the geographical level for which data were reported: s=State, r=Region, and c=City or metro. The abbreviation *ex* is used to mean *except* or *excluding*; *exp* stands for *expenditures*. For other abbreviations and further explanations, please see the Introduction.

McAllen-Edinburg-Mission, TX - continued

Item	Per	Value	Date	Ref.
Funerals				
Acknowledgement cards		28.35	1/99	78r
Casket		2494.29	1/99	78r
Cosmetology, hair, other preparation		109.22	1/99	78r
Embalming		361.42	1/99	78r
Funeral at funeral home		349.20	1/99	78r
Hearse (local)		161.91	1/99	78r
Professional service charges		1116.50	1/99	78r
Service car/van		65.56	1/99	78r
Transfer of remains to funeral home		143.56	1/99	78r
Vault		785.25	1/99	78r
Visitation/viewing		227.02	1/99	78r
Groceries				
American processed cheese	lb	3.50	7/01	11r
Bakery products, expenditures on	yr	261	1999	30r
Bananas	lb	0.47	7/01	11r
Beans, dried, any type, all sizes	lb	0.63	7/01	11r
Beef for stew, boneless	lb	2.86	7/01	11r
Beef, expenditures on	yr	210	1999	30r
Bologna, all beef or mixed	lb	2.29	7/01	11r
Bread, French	lb	1.66	7/01	11r
Bread, white, pan	lb	0.87	7/01	11r
Bread, whole wheat, pan	lb	1.38	7/01	11r
Broccoli	lb	1.04	7/01	11r
Butter, salted, grade AA, stick	lb	2.26	7/01	11r
Butter, yoghurt, cheese, etc, expenditures on	yr	170	1999	30r
Cabbage	lb	0.42	7/01	11r
Cereals and cereal products, expenditures on	yr	140	1999	30r
Cheddar cheese, natural	lb	3.75	7/01	11r
Chicken breast, bone-in	lb	1.85	7/01	11r
Chicken legs, bone-in	lb	1.34	7/01	11r
Chicken, fresh, whole	lb	1.05	7/01	11r
Chops, boneless	lb	4.13	7/01	11r
Chuck roast, graded and ungraded, excl U.S. prime and choice	lb	2.35	7/01	11r
Chuck roast, U.S. choice, boneless	lb	2.67	7/01	11r
Coffee, 100%, ground roast, all sizes	lb	2.88	7/01	11r
Coffee, instant, plain, regular, all sizes	16 oz	9.25	7/01	11r
Cola, non diet,	2 liter	1.11	7/01	11r
Crackers, soda, salted	lb	1.70	7/01	11r
Dairy product purchases	yr	282	1999	30r
Eggs, expenditures on	yr	32	1999	30r
Fats and oils, expenditures on	yr	79	1999	30r
Fish and seafood, expenditures on	yr	99	1999	30r
Flour, white, all purpose	lb	0.32	7/01	11r
Food (excl fruit and vegetables), eaten at home, purchases	yr	815	1999	30r
Food cooked on trips, expenditures on	yr	36	1999	30r
Food purchases	yr	4533	1999	30r
Food purchases, eaten away from home	yr	1873	1999	30r
Food purchases, food eaten at home	yr	2660	1999	30r
Fresh fruits, expenditures on	yr	128	1999	30r
Fresh milk and cream, expenditures on	yr	112	1999	30r
Fresh vegetables, expenditures on	yr	131	1999	30r
Fruit and vegetable purchases	yr	438	1999	30r
Grapefruit	lb	0.59	7/01	11r
Grapes, Thompson, seedless	lb	2.12	7/01	11r
Ground beef, 100% beef	lb	1.76	7/01	11r
Ground beef, lean and extra lean	lb	2.60	7/01	11r
Ground chuck, 100% beef	lb	2.08	7/01	11r
Ham, boneless, excl canned	lb	2.71	7/01	11r
Ham, rump or shank half, bone-in, smoked	lb	2.19	7/01	11r
Ice cream, prepackaged, bulk, regular	1/2 gal	3.93	7/01	11r
Lemons	lb	1.32	7/01	11r
Lettuce, iceberg	lb	0.76	7/01	11r
Milk, fresh, low fat,	gal	2.75	7/01	11r
Milk, fresh, whole, fortified	gal	2.97	7/01	11r
Nonalcoholic beverages, expenditures on	yr	228	1999	30r
Orange juice, frozen concentrate	16 oz	1.95	7/01	11r
Oranges, Navel	lb	0.73	7/01	11r
Oranges, Valencia	lb	0.55	7/01	11r
Peanut butter, creamy, all sizes	lb	1.83	7/01	11r

McAllen-Edinburg-Mission, TX - continued

Item	Per	Value	Date	Ref.
Groceries - continued				
Pears, Anjou	lb	0.98	7/01	11r
Pork chops, center cut, bone-in	lb	3.33	7/01	11r
Pork sausage, fresh, loose	lb	2.59	7/01	11r
Pork shoulder picnic, bone-in, smoked	lb	1.12	7/01	11r
Pork, expenditures on	yr	162	1999	30r
Potato chips	16 oz	3.59	7/01	11r
Potatoes, frozen, french fried	lb	1.00	7/01	11r
Potatoes, white, all types	lb	0.44	7/01	11r
Poultry, expenditures on	yr	137	1999	30r
Processed fruits, expenditures on	yr	97	1999	30r
Processed vegetables, expenditures on	yr	82	1999	30r
Rice, white, long grain, uncooked	lb	0.51	7/01	11r
Round roast, graded and ungraded, excl U.S. prime and choice	lb	2.96	7/01	11r
Round steak, graded and ungraded, excl U.S. prime and choice	lb	3.11	7/01	11r
Sirloin steak, graded and ungraded, excl U.S. prime and choice	lb	4.23	7/01	11r
Spaghetti and macaroni	lb	0.78	7/01	11r
Steak, round, U.S. choice, boneless	lb	3.56	7/01	11r
Steak, sirloin, U.S. choice, boneless	lb	5.65	7/01	11r
Strawberries, dry pint	12 oz	1.50	7/01	11r
Sugar and other sweets, expenditures on	yr	99	1999	30r
Sugar, white, 33-80 ounce package	lb	0.39	7/01	11r
Sugar, white, all sizes	lb	0.42	7/01	11r
Tobacco products and smoking supplies purchases	yr	288	1999	30r
Tomatoes, field grown	lb	1.43	7/01	11r
Tuna, light, chunk	lb	1.77	7/01	11r
Turkey, frozen, whole	lb	1.05	7/01	11r
Goods and Services				
B&B Japanese maple (acer japonicum)	gal	79.98-99.00	4/00	93r
Boxwood (buxus)	2 gal	12.98-18.99	4/00	93r
Christmas tree, noble fir		40-60	2000	65s
Daylily (hemerocallis)	gal	7.96-11.00	4/00	93r
Flat of annuals		13.99-27.99	4/00	93r
Fountain grass (pennisetum)	gal	6.96-9.00	4/00	93r
Hanging basket (10 in)		9.99-24.99	4/00	93r
Hardy geranium (geranium)	gal	5.96-8.00	4/00	93r
Hosta (hosta)	gal	8.96-12.99	4/00	93r
Lilac (syrubga vulgaris)	2 gal	13.00-19.99	4/00	93r
Rhododendron (rhododendron)	2 gal	12.98-29.99	4/00	93r
Sage (salvia)	gal	5.96-8.00	4/00	93r
Wintercreeper euonymus (euonymus fortunei)	2 gal	13.00-18.99	4/00	93r
Hunting license	yr	19.00	4/01	34s
Health Care				
Cardiac catheterization, ave hospital/ physician charges		20140	1998	77s
Childbirth, Cesarean delivery		11587	1997	13r
Childbirth, vaginal delivery		6725	1997	13r
Drugs, expenditures on	yr	399	1999	30r
Health care purchases	yr	1971	1999	30r
Health insurance expenditures	yr	933	1999	30r
Hysterectomy, laproscopically-assisted, ave hospital/physician charges		15700	1998	76s
Hysterectomy, vaginal, ave hospital and physician charges		12180	1998	76s
Medicaid dispensing fee		5.27	1999	87s
Medical services expenditures	yr	547	1999	30r

Values are in dollars or fractions of dollars. In the column headed *Ref*, references are shown to sources. Each reference is followed by a letter. These refer to the geographical level for which data were reported: s=State, r=Region, and c=City or metro. The abbreviation *ex* is used to mean *except* or *excluding*; *exp* stands for expenditures. For other abbreviations and further explanations, please see the Introduction.

McAllen-Edinburg-Mission, TX - continued

Item	Per	Value	Date	Ref.
Health Care				
Medical supplies, expenditures on	yr	91	1999	30r
Household Goods				
Floor coverings, expenditures on	yr	44	1999	30r
Furniture, expenditures on	yr	335	1999	30r
Household furnishings and equipment purchases	yr	1328	1999	30r
Household textiles, expenditures on	yr	89	1999	30r
Laundry and cleaning supplies, expenditures on	yr	113	1999	30r
Housing				
Home price, existing, ave		160100	10/00	90r
Home value, median		112000	2001	53s
Household operation expenditures	yr	553	1999	30r
Housekeeping supplies purchases	yr	473	1999	30r
Housing, expenditures on	yr	10303	1999	30r
Maintenance, repairs, insurance expenditures	yr	699	1999	30r
Monthly rental value of owned home	mos	505	1999	30r
Owned dwellings, expenditures own	yr	3465	1999	30r
Rent expenditures	yr	1641	1999	30r
Rental unit, 1 bedroom, with utilities	mos	370	4/01	41c
Rental unit, 2 bedroom, with utilities	mos	424	4/01	41c
Rental unit, 3 bedroom, with utilities	mos	529	4/01	41c
Rental unit, 4 bedroom, with utilities	mos	594	4/01	41c
Shelter, expenditures on	yr	5467	1999	30r
Insurance and Pensions				
Life and other personal insurance purchases	yr	414	1999	30r
Pensions and Social Security, expenditures on	yr	2635	1999	30r
Personal insurance and pensions, expenditures on	yr	3048	1999	30r
Legal Fees				
Divorce, filing fee		150.00-200.00	4/01	35s
Driver's license fee	orig	24.00	1999	48s
Driver's license fee	renew	20.00	1999	48s
Fishing license	yr	19.00	4/01	34s
Personal Goods				
Personal care products and services purchases	yr	393	1999	30r
Personal Services				
Personal services, household, expenditures on	yr	258	1999	30r
Pets				
Pets, toys, and playground equipment, expenditures on	yr	306	1999	30r
Taxes				
Federal income taxes paid	yr	2047	1999	30r
Personal taxes, expenditures on	yr	2554	1999	30r
Property taxes paid	yr	726	1999	30r
State and local income taxes paid	yr	363	1999	30r
Transportation				
Cars and trucks, new, expenditures on	yr	1648	1999	30r
Cars and trucks, used, expenditures on	yr	1651	1999	30r
Diesel at the pump	gal	1.18	10/99	73s
Gasoline and motor oil purchases	yr	1052	1999	30r
Gasoline before-tax price (cents)	gal	101.30	10/00	43s
Maintenance and repair expenditures	yr	621	1999	30r
Public transportation, expenditures on	yr	298	1999	30r
Transportation purchases	yr	6738	1999	30r
Vehicle expenses, miscellaneous, purchases	yr	2033	1999	30r
Vehicle insurance payments	yr	696	1999	30r
Vehicle purchases (net outlay)	yr	3354	1999	30r
Vehicle rental, lease expenditures	yr	352	1999	30r
Utilities				
Electrical bill, average	mos	87.17	9/00	9s
Electricity, expenditures on	yr	1115	1999	30r

McAllen-Edinburg-Mission, TX - continued

Item	Per	Value	Date	Ref.
Utilities - continued				
Electricity cost, average	KWh	6.48	9/00	9s
Water and other public services, expenditures on	yr	298	1999	30r
Weddings				
Wedding (national average cost)		19936	2000	33r
Attendants' gifts		321	1998	33r
Bridal attendants' apparel (5 persons)		824	2000	33r
Bride's headpiece/veil		173	1998	33r
Bride's wedding dress		859	1998	33r
Clergy, religious facility fee		242	1998	33r
Engagement ring		3177	1998	33r
Flowers		789	1998	33r
Groom's formalwear rental		99	2000	33r
Limousine		410	1998	33r
Marriage license cost		36.00	4/01	35s
Men's formalwear (ushers, best man)		469	2000	33r
Mother of bride apparel		241	2000	33r
Music		866	1998	33r
Photography and videography		1368	1998	33r
Rehearsal dinner		728	1998	33r
Wedding invitations and announcements		341	1998	33r
Wedding reception		7968	2000	33r
Wedding rings (bride and groom)		1060	1998	33r

Medford-Ashland, OR

Item	Per	Value	Date	Ref.
Average annual expenditures	yr	40662	1999	30r
Alcoholic Beverages				
Alcoholic beverage purchases	yr	372	1999	30r
Malt beverages, all types, all sizes, any origin	16 oz	0.94	7/01	11r
Wine, red and white table, all sizes, any origin	liter	6.00	7/01	11r
Appliances				
Major appliances, expenditures on	yr	167	1999	30r
Small appliances, housewares, expenditures on	yr	105	1999	30r
Banking and Money				
Mortgage interest and charges paid	yr	3368	1999	30r
Mortgage principal paid on owned property	yr	1677	1999	30r
Vehicle finance charges paid	yr	311	1999	30r
Charity				
Cash contributions, expenditures	yr	1344	1999	30r
Child Care				
Child raising cost, total, age 0-2	yr	9140	1999	60r
Child raising cost, total, age 3-5	yr	9370	1999	60r
Child raising cost, total, age 6-8	yr	9450	1999	60r
Child raising cost, total, age 9-11	yr	9470	1999	60r
Child raising cost, total, age 12-14	yr	10170	1999	60r
Child raising cost, total, age 15-17	yr	10360	1999	60r
Child's child care and education, age 0-2	yr	1250	1999	60r
Child's child care and education, age 3-5	yr	1380	1999	60r
Child's child care and education, age 6-8	yr	890	1999	60r
Child's child care and education, age 9-11	yr	580	1999	60r
Child's child care and education, age 12-14	yr	430	1999	60r
Child's child care and education, age 15-17	yr	730	1999	60r
Child's clothing, age 0-2	yr	430	1999	60r
Child's clothing, age 3-5	yr	420	1999	60r
Child's clothing, age 6-8	yr	470	1999	60r
Child's clothing, age 9-11	yr	520	1999	60r
Child's clothing, age 12-14	yr	870	1999	60r
Child's clothing, age 15-17	yr	770	1999	60r
Child's food, age 0-2	yr	1120	1999	60r
Child's food, age 3-5	yr	1280	1999	60r
Child's food, age 6-8	yr	1640	1999	60r
Child's food, age 9-11	yr	1930	1999	60r
Child's food, age 12-14	yr	1940	1999	60r
Child's food, age 15-17	yr	2150	1999	60r
Child's health care, age 0-2	yr	490	1999	60r

Values are in dollars or fractions of dollars. In the column headed *Ref*, references are shown to sources. Each reference is followed by a letter. These refer to the geographical level for which data were reported: s=State, r=Region, and c=City or metro. The abbreviation *ex* is used to mean *except* or *excluding*; *exp* stands for *expenditures*. For other abbreviations and further explanations, please see the Introduction.

Medford-Ashland, OR - continued

Item	Per	Value	Date	Ref.
Child Care				
Child's health care, age 3-5	yr	470	1999	60r
Child's health care, age 6-8	yr	530	1999	60r
Child's health care, age 9-11	yr	570	1999	60r
Child's health care, age 12-14	yr	580	1999	60r
Child's health care, age 15-17	yr	610	1999	60r
Child's housing, age 0-2	yr	3630	1999	60r
Child's housing, age 3-5	yr	3610	1999	60r
Child's housing, age 6-8	yr	3570	1999	60r
Child's housing, age 9-11	yr	3410	1999	60r
Child's housing, age 12-14	yr	3600	1999	60r
Child's housing, age 15-17	yr	3210	1999	60r
Child's personal care, reading, age 0-2	yr	1040	1999	60r
Child's personal care, reading, age 3-5	yr	1060	1999	60r
Child's personal care, reading, age 6-8	yr	1090	1999	60r
Child's personal care, reading, age 9-11	yr	1130	1999	60r
Child's personal care, reading, age 12-14	yr	1300	1999	60r
Child's personal care, reading, age 15-17	yr	1080	1999	60r
Clothing				
Apparel and services purchases	yr	1863	1999	30r
Boys, 2 to 15, expenditures on	yr	80	1999	30r
Children under 2, expenditures on	yr	74	1999	30r
Footwear, expenditures on	yr	307	1999	30r
Girls, 2 to 15, expenditures on	yr	101	1999	30r
Men and boys, expenditures on	yr	443	1999	30r
Men, 16 and over, expenditures on	yr	363	1999	30r
Women, 16 and over, expenditures on	yr	594	1999	30r
Communications				
Phone line, single, business, field visit	inst.	31.00	12/97	17s
Phone line, single, business, no field visit	inst.	31.00	12/97	17s
Phone line, single, residence, field visit	inst.	12.00	12/97	17s
Phone line, single, residence, no field visit	inst.	12.00	12/97	17s
Postage and stationery, expenditures on	yr	150	1999	30r
Postal rate, express mail, up to half-pound		12.45	7/01	108r
Postal rate, letter, first class, first ounce		0.34	7/01	108r
Postal rate, letter, two ounces		0.57	7/01	108r
Postal rate, post card		0.21	7/01	108r
Postal rate, priority mail, two pounds		3.95	7/01	108r
Postal rate, priority mail, up to one pound		3.50	7/01	108r
Telephone services, expenditures on	yr	825	1999	30r
Education				
Board, 4-year private college/university	yr	2750	1996	38s
Board, 4-year public college/university	yr	2474	1996	38s
Education expenditures	yr	676	1999	30r
Room, 4-year private college/university	yr	2257	1996	38s
Room, 4-year public college/university	yr	1647	1996	38s
Total cost, 4-year private college/university	yr	18899	1996	38s
Total cost, 4-year public college/university	yr	7354	1996	38s
Tuition, 2-year public college/university, in state	yr	1338	1996	38s
Tuition, 4-year private college/university, in state	yr	13892	1996	38s
Tuition, 4-year public college/university	yr	3233	1996	38s
Energy and Fuels				
Electricity	KWh	0.11	7/01	11r
Electricity	500 KWhs	48.23	7/01	11r
Fuel oil and other fuels, expenditures on	yr	35	1999	30r
Gas, natural, commercial rate	1000 cf	7.55	11/00	88s
Gasoline, all types	gal	1.91	7/01	11r
Gasoline, unleaded premium	gal	2.05	7/01	11r
Gasoline, unleaded regular	gal	1.83	7/01	11r
Natural gas, expenditures on	yr	255	1999	30r
Utility (piped) gas, therm		0.98	7/01	11r
Utility (piped) gas, 40 therms		40.74	7/01	11r
Utility (piped) gas, 100 therms		96.80	7/01	11r
Entertainment				
Entertainment purchases	yr	2139	1999	30r
Fees and admissions paid	yr	545	1999	30r

Medford-Ashland, OR - continued

Item	Per	Value	Date	Ref.
Entertainment - continued				
Television, radios, sound equipment, expenditures on	yr	624	1999	30r
Funerals				
Total cost of funeral		5401.08	1/99	78r
Acknowledgement cards		33.64	1/99	78r
Casket		2170.43	1/99	78r
Cosmetology, hair, other preparation		136.32	1/99	78r
Embalming		319.13	1/99	78r
Funeral at funeral home		370.21	1/99	78r
Hearse (local)		161.04	1/99	78r
Professional service charges		963.15	1/99	78r
Service car/van		133.99	1/99	78r
Transfer of remains to funeral home		159.82	1/99	78r
Vault		778.07	1/99	78r
Visitation/viewing		175.28	1/99	78r
Groceries				
Apples, red delicious	lb	0.84	7/01	11r
Bacon, sliced	lb	3.38	7/01	11r
Bakery products, expenditures on	yr	299	1999	30r
Bananas	lb	0.54	7/01	11r
Beans, dried, any type, all sizes	lb	0.76	7/01	11r
Beef, expenditures on	yr	222	1999	30r
Bread, white, pan	lb	0.99	7/01	11r
Butter, yoghurt, cheese, etc, expenditures on	yr	211	1999	30r
Cereals and bakery product purchases	yr	466	1999	30r
Cereals and cereal products, expenditures on	yr	168	1999	30r
Chicken breast, bone-in	lb	2.45	7/01	11r
Chicken, fresh, whole	lb	1.19	7/01	11r
Chops, boneless,	lb	4.00	7/01	11r
Chuck roast, graded and ungraded, excl U.S. prime and choice	lb	2.55	7/01	11r
Coffee, 100%, ground roast, all sizes	lb	3.80	7/01	11r
Cookies, chocolate chip	lb	2.83	7/01	11r
Dairy product purchases	yr	341	1999	30r
Eggs, expenditures on	yr	39	1999	30r
Eggs, grade AA, large	dozen	1.23	7/01	11r
Fats and oils, expenditures on	yr	88	1999	30r
Fish and seafood, expenditures on	yr	121	1999	30r
Food (excl fruit and vegetables), eaten at home, purchases	yr	1001	1999	30r
Food cooked on trips, expenditures on	yr	64	1999	30r
Food purchases	yr	5312	1999	30r
Food purchases, eaten away from home	yr	2180	1999	30r
Food purchases, food eaten at home	yr	3132	1999	30r
Fresh fruits, expenditures on	yr	186	1999	30r
Fresh milk and cream, expenditures on	yr	130	1999	30r
Fresh vegetables, expenditures on	yr	177	1999	30r
Grapefruit	lb	0.68	7/01	11r
Grapes, Thompson, seedless	lb	2.42	7/01	11r
Ground beef, lean and extra lean	lb	2.46	7/01	11r
Ice cream, prepackaged, bulk, regular	1/2 gal	3.62	7/01	11r
Lettuce, iceberg	lb	0.63	7/01	11r
Meats, poultry, fish, and egg purchases	yr	761	1999	30r
Milk, fresh, low fat,	gal	2.80	7/01	11r
Milk, fresh, whole, fortified	gal	2.88	7/01	11r
Nonalcoholic beverages, expenditures on	yr	258	1999	30r
Oranges, Navel	lb	0.97	7/01	11r
Oranges, Valencia	lb	0.43	7/01	11r
Peaches	lb	1.38	7/01	11r
Peanut butter, creamy, all sizes	lb	2.14	7/01	11r
Pork chops, center cut, bone-in	lb	3.83	7/01	11r
Pork, expenditures on	yr	141	1999	30r
Potatoes, white, all types	lb	0.37	7/01	11r
Poultry, expenditures on	yr	146	1999	30r
Processed fruits, expenditures on	yr	118	1999	30r
Processed vegetables, expenditures on	yr	81	1999	30r
Round roast, graded and ungraded, excl U.S. prime and choice	lb	3.07	7/01	11r
Round roast, U.S. choice, boneless	lb	3.37	7/01	11r

Values are in dollars or fractions of dollars. In the column headed *Ref*, references are shown to sources. Each reference is followed by a letter. These refer to the geographical level for which data were reported: s=State, r=Region, and c=City or metro. The abbreviation *ex* is used to mean *except* or *excluding*; *exp* stands for expenditures. For other abbreviations and further explanations, please see the Introduction.

Medford-Ashland, OR - continued

Item	Per	Value	Date	Ref.
Groceries				
Round steak, graded and ungraded, excl U.S. prime and choice	lb	3.51	7/01	11r
Sirloin steak, graded and ungraded, excl U.S. prime and choice	lb	4.67	7/01	11r
Steak, sirloin, U.S. choice, boneless	lb	6.20	7/01	11r
Strawberries, dry pint	12 oz	1.79	7/01	11r
Sugar and other sweets, expenditures on	yr	124	1999	30r
Sugar, white, all sizes	lb	0.46	7/01	11r
Tobacco products and smoking supplies purchases	yr	217	1999	30r
Tomatoes, field grown	lb	1.17	7/01	11r
Tuna, light, chunk	lb	2.05	7/01	11r
Goods and Services				
B&B Japanese maple (acer japonicum)	gal	39.99	4/00	93r
Boxwood (buxus)	2 gal	14.99-24.99	4/00	93r
Christmas tree, noble fir		20-25	2000	65s
Daylily (hemerocallis)	gal	6.99-8.99	4/00	93r
Flat of annuals		16.68	4/00	93r
Fountain grass (pennisetum)	gal	7.99-11.99	4/00	93r
Hanging basket (10 in)		29.99	4/00	93r
Hardy geranium (geranium)	gal	6.99-11.99	4/00	93r
Hosta (hosta)	gal	6.99-18.99	4/00	93r
Lilac (syrubga vulgaris)	2 gal	14.99-17.99	4/00	93r
Miscellaneous purchases	yr	1070	1999	30r
Rhododendron (rhododendron)	2 gal	14.99	4/00	93r
Sage (salvia)	gal	6.99	4/00	93r
Wintercreeper euonymus (euonymus fortunei)	2 gal	14.99-22.99	4/00	93r
Hunting license	yr	17.50	4/01	34s
Health Care				
Cardiac catheterization, ave hospital/physician charges		10940	1998	77s
Childbirth, Cesarean delivery		11587	1997	13r
Childbirth, vaginal delivery		6725	1997	13r
Drugs, expenditures on	yr	309	1999	30r
Health care purchases	yr	1869	1999	30r
Health insurance expenditures	yr	868	1999	30r
Hysterectomy, laproscopically-assisted, ave hospital/physician charges		11660	1998	76s
Hysterectomy, vaginal, ave hospital and physician charges		6680	1998	76s
Medicaid dispensing fee		3.80-4.16	1999	87s
Medical services expenditures	yr	580	1999	30r
Medical supplies, expenditures on	yr	112	1999	30r
Household Goods				
Floor coverings, expenditures on	yr	49	1999	30r
Furniture, expenditures on	yr	444	1999	30r
Household furnishings and equipment purchases	yr	1768	1999	30r
Household textiles, expenditures on	yr	141	1999	30r
Laundry and cleaning supplies, expenditures on	yr	128	1999	30r
Housing				
Home price, existing, ave		239400	10/00	90r
Home value, median		149000	2001	53s
Household operation expenditures	yr	781	1999	30r
Housekeeping supplies purchases	yr	513	1999	30r
Lodging expenditures	yr	575	1999	30r
Maintenance, repairs, insurance expenditures	yr	939	1999	30r
Monthly rental value of owned home	mos	662	1999	30r
Owned dwellings, expenditures own	yr	5231	1999	30r
Rent expenditures	yr	2709	1999	30r

Medford-Ashland, OR - continued

Item	Per	Value	Date	Ref.
Housing - continued				
Rental unit, 1 bedroom, with utilities	mos	456	4/01	41c
Rental unit, 2 bedroom, with utilities	mos	610	4/01	41c
Rental unit, 3 bedroom, with utilities	mos	848	4/01	41c
Rental unit, 4 bedroom, with utilities	mos	945	4/01	41c
Shelter, expenditures on	yr	8516	1999	30r
Insurance and Pensions				
Life and other personal insurance purchases	yr	355	1999	30r
Pensions and Social Security, expenditures on	yr	3636	1999	30r
Legal Fees				
Combination hunting and fishing license	yr	33.75	4/01	34s
Divorce, filing fee		100.00-250.00	4/01	35s
Driver's license fee	orig	26.25	1999	48s
Driver's license fee	renew	16.25	1999	48s
Fishing license	yr	19.75	4/01	34s
Personal Goods				
Personal care products and services purchases	yr	449	1999	30r
Personal Services				
Personal services, household, expenditures on	yr	353	1999	30r
Pets				
Pets, toys, and playground equipment, expenditures on	yr	358	1999	30r
Taxes				
Federal income taxes paid	yr	3200	1999	30r
Personal taxes, expenditures on	yr	4153	1999	30r
Property taxes paid	yr	923	1999	30r
State and local income taxes paid	yr	812	1999	30r
Transportation				
Cars and trucks, new, expenditures on	yr	1534	1999	30r
Cars and trucks, used, expenditures on	yr	1593	1999	30r
Diesel at the pump	gal	1.16	10/99	73s
Gasoline and motor oil purchases	yr	1129	1999	30r
Gasoline before-tax price (cents)	gal	128.30	10/00	43s
Maintenance and repair expenditures	yr	797	1999	30r
Public transportation, expenditures on	yr	530	1999	30r
Transportation purchases	yr	7423	1999	30r
Vehicle expenses, miscellaneous, purchases	yr	2585	1999	30r
Vehicle insurance payments	yr	811	1999	30r
Vehicle purchases (net outlay)	yr	3180	1999	30r
Vehicle rental, lease expenditures	yr	666	1999	30r
Utilities				
Electrical bill, average	mos	61.42	9/00	9s
Electricity, expenditures on	yr	725	1999	30r
Electricity cost, average	KWh	4.70	9/00	9s
Utilities, fuels, and public services purchased	yr	2179	1999	30r
Water and other public services, expenditures on	yr	339	1999	30r
Weddings				
Wedding (national average cost)		19936	2000	33r
Wedding (regional average total cost)		18918	1997	110r
Attendants' gifts		321	1998	33r
Bridal attendants' apparel (5 persons)		824	2000	33r
Bride's headpiece/veil		173	1998	33r
Bride's wedding dress		859	1998	33r
Clergy, religious facility fee		242	1998	33r
Engagement ring		3177	1998	33r
Flowers		789	1998	33r
Groom's formalwear rental		99	2000	33r
Limousine		410	1998	33r
Marriage license cost		60.00	4/01	35s
Men's formalwear (ushers, best man)		469	2000	33r
Mother of bride apparel		241	2000	33r
Music		866	1998	33r
Photography and videography		1368	1998	33r

Values are in dollars or fractions of dollars. In the column headed *Ref*, references are shown to sources. Each reference is followed by a letter. These refer to the geographical level for which data were reported: s=State, r=Region, and c=City or metro. The abbreviation *ex* is used to mean *except* or *excluding*; *exp* stands for expenditures. For other abbreviations and further explanations, please see the Introduction.

Medford-Ashland, OR - continued

Item	Per	Value	Date	Ref.
Weddings				
Rehearsal dinner		728	1998	33r
Wedding invitations and announcements		341	1998	33r
Wedding reception		7968	2000	33r
Wedding rings (bride and groom)		1060	1998	33r

Melbourne-Titusville-Palm Bay, FL

Item	Per	Value	Date	Ref.
Alcoholic Beverages				
Alcoholic beverage purchases	yr	253	1999	30r
Malt beverages, all types, all sizes, any origin	16 oz	0.96	7/01	11r
Appliances				
Major appliances, expenditures on	yr	172	1999	30r
Small appliances, housewares, expenditures on	yr	81	1999	30r
Banking and Money				
Mortgage interest and charges paid	yr	2039	1999	30r
Mortgage principal paid on owned property	yr	1026	1999	30r
Vehicle finance charges paid	yr	365	1999	30r
Charity				
Cash contributions, expenditures	yr	1127	1999	30r
Child Care				
Child raising cost, total, age 0-2	yr	8540	1999	60r
Child raising cost, total, age 3-5	yr	8780	1999	60r
Child raising cost, total, age 6-8	yr	8820	1999	60r
Child raising cost, total, age 9-11	yr	8800	1999	60r
Child raising cost, total, age 12-14	yr	9510	1999	60r
Child raising cost, total, age 15-17	yr	9740	1999	60r
Child's child care and education, age 0-2	yr	1380	1999	60r
Child's child care and education, age 3-5	yr	1520	1999	60r
Child's child care and education, age 6-8	yr	990	1999	60r
Child's child care and education, age 9-11	yr	650	1999	60r
Child's child care and education, age 12-14	yr	490	1999	60r
Child's child care and education, age 15-17	yr	840	1999	60r
Child's clothing, age 0-2	yr	480	1999	60r
Child's clothing, age 3-5	yr	470	1999	60r
Child's clothing, age 6-8	yr	520	1999	60r
Child's clothing, age 9-11	yr	570	1999	60r
Child's clothing, age 12-14	yr	950	1999	60r
Child's clothing, age 15-17	yr	850	1999	60r
Child's food, age 0-2	yr	1000	1999	60r
Child's food, age 3-5	yr	1160	1999	60r
Child's food, age 6-8	yr	1490	1999	60r
Child's food, age 9-11	yr	1770	1999	60r
Child's food, age 12-14	yr	1770	1999	60r
Child's food, age 15-17	yr	1980	1999	60r
Child's health care, age 0-2	yr	620	1999	60r
Child's health care, age 3-5	yr	590	1999	60r
Child's health care, age 6-8	yr	680	1999	60r
Child's health care, age 9-11	yr	720	1999	60r
Child's health care, age 12-14	yr	730	1999	60r
Child's health care, age 15-17	yr	760	1999	60r
Child's housing, age 0-2	yr	3070	1999	60r
Child's housing, age 3-5	yr	3050	1999	60r
Child's housing, age 6-8	yr	3010	1999	60r
Child's housing, age 9-11	yr	2850	1999	60r
Child's housing, age 12-14	yr	3040	1999	60r
Child's housing, age 15-17	yr	2650	1999	60r
Child's personal care, reading, age 0-2	yr	910	1999	60r
Child's personal care, reading, age 3-5	yr	930	1999	60r
Child's personal care, reading, age 6-8	yr	960	1999	60r
Child's personal care, reading, age 9-11	yr	1000	1999	60r
Child's personal care, reading, age 12-14	yr	1170	1999	60r
Child's personal care, reading, age 15-17	yr	950	1999	60r
Clothing				
Apparel and services purchases	yr	1610	1999	30r
Boys, 2 to 15, expenditures on	yr	89	1999	30r
Children under 2, expenditures on	yr	79	1999	30r
Footwear, expenditures on	yr	283	1999	30r

Melbourne-Titusville-Palm Bay, FL - continued

Item	Per	Value	Date	Ref.
Clothing - continued				
Girls, 2 to 15, expenditures on	yr	103	1999	30r
Men and boys, expenditures on	yr	351	1999	30r
Men, 16 and over, expenditures on	yr	262	1999	30r
Women, 16 and over, expenditures on	yr	538	1999	30r
Communications				
Cable modem installation, Adelphi		54.90	6/99	103s
Cable modem installation, Comcast		95.00	6/99	103s
Cable modem installation, Media One		100.00	6/99	103s
Cable modem installation, Time Warner		75.00-225.00	6/99	103s
Cable modem rate, cable subscriber, Adelphi	mos	34.95	6/99	103s
Cable modem rate, cable subscriber, Comcast	mos	39.95	6/99	103s
Cable modem rate, cable subscriber, Media One	mos	34.95-39.95	6/99	103s
Cable modem rate, cable subscriber, Time Warner	mos	39.95-49.95	6/99	103s
Cable modem rate, non-cable subscriber, Adelphi	mos	44.95	6/99	103s
Cable modem rate, non-cable subscriber, Comcast	mos	49.95	6/99	103s
Cable modem rate, non-cable subscriber, Media One	mos	49.95	6/99	103s
Cable modem rate, non-cable subscriber, Time Warner	mos	39.95-54.95	6/99	103s
Phone line, single, business, field visit	inst.	56.00	12/97	17s
Phone line, single, business, no field visit	inst.	56.00	12/97	17s
Phone line, single, residence, field visit	inst.	40.00	12/97	17s
Phone line, single, residence, no field visit	inst.	40.00	12/97	17s
Postage and stationery, expenditures on	yr	104	1999	30r
Postal rate, express mail, up to half-pound		12.45	7/01	108r
Postal rate, letter, first class, first ounce		0.34	7/01	108r
Postal rate, letter, two ounces		0.57	7/01	108r
Postal rate, post card		0.21	7/01	108r
Postal rate, priority mail, two pounds		3.95	7/01	108r
Postal rate, priority mail, up to one pound		3.50	7/01	108r
Telephone services, expenditures on	yr	860	1999	30r
Education				
Board, 4-year private college/university	yr	2236	1996	38s
Board, 4-year public college/university	yr	2295	1996	38s
Education expenditures	yr	431	1999	30r
Room, 4-year private college/university	yr	2428	1996	38s
Room, 4-year public college/university	yr	2193	1996	38s
Total cost, 4-year private college/university	yr	15028	1996	38s
Total cost, 4-year public college/university	yr	6254	1996	38s
Tuition, 2-year public college/university, in state	yr	1103	1996	38s
Tuition, 4-year private college/university, in state	yr	10364	1996	38s
Tuition, 4-year public college/university	yr	1767	1996	38s
Energy and Fuels				
Electricity	500 KWhs	47.29	7/01	11r
Electricity	KWh	0.09	7/01	11r
Fuel oil #2	gal	1.43	7/01	11r
Fuel oil and other fuels, expenditures on	yr	45	1999	30r
Gas, natural, commercial rate	1000 cf	8.44	11/00	88s
Gasoline, all types	gal	1.60	7/01	11r
Gasoline, unleaded midgrade	gal	1.65	7/01	11r
Gasoline, unleaded premium	gal	1.74	7/01	11r
Natural gas, expenditures on	yr	164	1999	30r
Utility (piped) gas, therm		1.01	7/01	11r
Utility (piped) gas, 40 therms		44.29	7/01	11r
Utility (piped) gas, 100 therms		97.44	7/01	11r
Entertainment				
Entertainment purchases	yr	1574	1999	30r
Fees and admissions paid	yr	371	1999	30r
Reading purchases	yr	121	1999	30r
Television, radios, sound equipment, expenditures on	yr	561	1999	30r

Values are in dollars or fractions of dollars. In the column headed *Ref*, references are shown to sources. Each reference is followed by a letter. These refer to the geographical level for which data were reported: s=State, r=Region, and c=City or metro. The abbreviation *ex* is used to mean *except* or *excluding*; *exp* stands for expenditures. For other abbreviations and further explanations, please see the Introduction.

Melbourne-Titusville-Palm Bay, FL - continued

Item	Per	Value	Date	Ref.
Funerals				
Total cost of funeral		5922.53	1/99	78r
Acknowledgement cards		63.43	1/99	78r
Casket		2258.77	1/99	78r
Cosmetology, hair, other preparation		127.09	1/99	78r
Embalming		393.49	1/99	78r
Funeral at funeral home		367.50	1/99	78r
Hearse (local)		169.66	1/99	78r
Professional service charges		1211.32	1/99	78r
Service car/van		80.69	1/99	78r
Transfer of remains to funeral home		144.25	1/99	78r
Vault		803.50	1/99	78r
Visitation/viewing		302.83	1/99	78r
Groceries				
American processed cheese	lb	3.50	7/01	11r
Bakery products, expenditures on	yr	261	1999	30r
Bananas	lb	0.47	7/01	11r
Beans, dried, any type, all sizes	lb	0.63	7/01	11r
Beef for stew, boneless	lb	2.86	7/01	11r
Beef, expenditures on	yr	210	1999	30r
Bologna, all beef or mixed	lb	2.29	7/01	11r
Bread, French	lb	1.66	7/01	11r
Bread, white, pan	lb	0.87	7/01	11r
Bread, whole wheat, pan	lb	1.38	7/01	11r
Broccoli	lb	1.04	7/01	11r
Butter, salted, grade AA, stick	lb	2.26	7/01	11r
Butter, yoghurt, cheese, etc, expenditures on	yr	170	1999	30r
Cabbage	lb	0.42	7/01	11r
Cereals and cereal products, expenditures on	yr	140	1999	30r
Cheddar cheese, natural	lb	3.75	7/01	11r
Chicken breast, bone-in	lb	1.85	7/01	11r
Chicken legs, bone-in	lb	1.34	7/01	11r
Chicken, fresh, whole	lb	1.05	7/01	11r
Chops, boneless,	lb	4.13	7/01	11r
Chuck roast, graded and ungraded, excl U.S. prime and choice	lb	2.35	7/01	11r
Chuck roast, U.S. choice, boneless	lb	2.67	7/01	11r
Coffee, 100%, ground roast, all sizes	lb	2.88	7/01	11r
Coffee, instant, plain, regular, all sizes	16 oz	9.25	7/01	11r
Cola, non diet,	2 liter	1.11	7/01	11r
Crackers, soda, salted	lb	1.70	7/01	11r
Dairy product purchases	yr	282	1999	30r
Eggs, expenditures on	yr	32	1999	30r
Fats and oils, expenditures on	yr	79	1999	30r
Fish and seafood, expenditures on	yr	99	1999	30r
Flour, white, all purpose	lb	0.32	7/01	11r
Food (excl fruit and vegetables), eaten at home, purchases	yr	815	1999	30r
Food cooked on trips, expenditures on	yr	36	1999	30r
Food purchases	yr	4533	1999	30r
Food purchases, eaten away from home	yr	1873	1999	30r
Food purchases, food eaten at home	yr	2660	1999	30r
Fresh fruits, expenditures on	yr	128	1999	30r
Fresh milk and cream, expenditures on	yr	112	1999	30r
Fresh vegetables, expenditures on	yr	131	1999	30r
Fruit and vegetable purchases	yr	438	1999	30r
Grapefruit	lb	0.59	7/01	11r
Grapes, Thompson, seedless	lb	2.12	7/01	11r
Ground beef, 100% beef	lb	1.76	7/01	11r
Ground beef, lean and extra lean	lb	2.60	7/01	11r
Ground chuck, 100% beef	lb	2.08	7/01	11r
Ham, boneless, excl canned	lb	2.71	7/01	11r
Ham, rump or shank half, bone-in, smoked	lb	2.19	7/01	11r
Ice cream, prepackaged, bulk, regular	1/2 gal	3.93	7/01	11r
Lemons	lb	1.32	7/01	11r
Lettuce, iceberg	lb	0.76	7/01	11r
Milk, fresh, low fat,	gal	2.75	7/01	11r
Milk, fresh, whole, fortified	gal	2.97	7/01	11r
Nonalcoholic beverages, expenditures on	yr	228	1999	30r
Orange juice, frozen concentrate	16 oz	1.95	7/01	11r
Oranges, Navel	lb	0.73	7/01	11r
Oranges, Valencia	lb	0.55	7/01	11r

Melbourne-Titusville-Palm Bay, FL - continued

Item	Per	Value	Date	Ref.
Groceries - continued				
Peanut butter, creamy, all sizes	lb	1.83	7/01	11r
Pears, Anjou	lb	0.98	7/01	11r
Pork chops, center cut, bone-in	lb	3.33	7/01	11r
Pork sausage, fresh, loose	lb	2.59	7/01	11r
Pork shoulder picnic, bone-in, smoked	lb	1.12	7/01	11r
Pork, expenditures on	yr	162	1999	30r
Potato chips	16 oz	3.59	7/01	11r
Potatoes, frozen, french fried	lb	1.00	7/01	11r
Potatoes, white, all types	lb	0.44	7/01	11r
Poultry, expenditures on	yr	137	1999	30r
Processed fruits, expenditures on	yr	97	1999	30r
Processed vegetables, expenditures on	yr	82	1999	30r
Rice, white, long grain, uncooked	lb	0.51	7/01	11r
Round roast, graded and ungraded, excl U.S. prime and choice	lb	2.96	7/01	11r
Round steak, graded and ungraded, excl U.S. prime and choice	lb	3.11	7/01	11r
Sirloin steak, graded and ungraded, excl U.S. prime and choice	lb	4.23	7/01	11r
Spaghetti and macaroni	lb	0.78	7/01	11r
Steak, round, U.S. choice, boneless	lb	3.56	7/01	11r
Steak, sirloin, U.S. choice, boneless	lb	5.65	7/01	11r
Strawberries, dry pint	12 oz	1.50	7/01	11r
Sugar and other sweets, expenditures on	yr	99	1999	30r
Sugar, white, 33-80 ounce package	lb	0.39	7/01	11r
Sugar, white, all sizes	lb	0.42	7/01	11r
Tobacco products and smoking supplies purchases	yr	288	1999	30r
Tomatoes, field grown	lb	1.43	7/01	11r
Tuna, light, chunk	lb	1.77	7/01	11r
Turkey, frozen, whole	lb	1.05	7/01	11r
Goods and Services				
B&B Japanese maple (acer japonicum)	gal	49.98-129.00	4/00	93r
Boxwood (buxus)	2 gal	12.99-16.99	4/00	93r
Daylily (hemerocallis)	gal	4.99-8.99	4/00	93r
Flat of annuals		11.00-13.92	4/00	93r
Fountain grass (pennisetum)	gal	5.98-7.98	4/00	93r
Hanging basket (10 in)		7.99-14.98	4/00	93r
Hardy geranium (geranium)	gal	5.98-8.00	4/00	93r
Hosta (hosta)	gal	4.99-10.98	4/00	93r
Lilac (syrubga vulgaris)	2 gal	12.99-21.99	4/00	93r
Rhododendron (rhododendron)	2 gal	14.99-24.99	4/00	93r
Sage (salvia)	gal	5.98-6.99	4/00	93r
Wintercreeper euonymus (euonymus fortunei)	2 gal	7.99-89.99	4/00	93r
Hunting license	yr	12.50	4/01	34s
Health Care				
Cardiac catheterization, ave hospital/ physician charges		15060	1998	77s
Childbirth, Cesarean delivery		11587	1997	13r
Childbirth, vaginal delivery		6725	1997	13r
Drugs, expenditures on	yr	399	1999	30r
Health care purchases	yr	1971	1999	30r
Health insurance expenditures	yr	933	1999	30r
Hysterectomy, laproscopically-assisted, ave hospital/physician charges		14760	1998	76s
Hysterectomy, vaginal, ave hospital and physician charges		11320	1998	76s
Medicaid dispensing fee		4.23	1999	87s
Medical services expenditures	yr	547	1999	30r

Values are in dollars or fractions of dollars. In the column headed *Ref*, references are shown to sources. Each reference is followed by a letter. These refer to the geographical level for which data were reported: s=State, r=Region, and c=City or metro. The abbreviation *ex* is used to mean *except* or *excluding*; *exp* stands for *expenditures*. For other abbreviations and further explanations, please see the Introduction.

Melbourne-Titusville-Palm Bay, FL - continued

Item	Per	Value	Date	Ref.
Health Care				
Medical supplies, expenditures on	yr	91	1999	30r
Plastic surgery, breast augmentation		2870	2000	7r
Plastic surgery, breast lift		3649	2000	7r
Plastic surgery, facelift		5008	2000	7r
Plastic surgery, hair transplantation		3425	2000	7r
Plastic surgery, lip augmentation		1227	2000	7r
Plastic surgery, lower body lift		4793	2000	7r
Plastic surgery, thigh lift		3862	2000	7r
Household Goods				
Floor coverings, expenditures on	yr	44	1999	30r
Furniture, expenditures on	yr	335	1999	30r
Household furnishings and equipment purchases	yr	1328	1999	30r
Household textiles, expenditures on	yr	89	1999	30r
Laundry and cleaning supplies, expenditures on	yr	113	1999	30r
Housing				
Home price, existing, ave		160100	10/00	90r
Home value, median		104000	2001	53s
Household operation expenditures	yr	553	1999	30r
Housekeeping supplies purchases	yr	473	1999	30r
Housing, expenditures on	yr	10303	1999	30r
Maintenance, repairs, insurance expenditures	yr	699	1999	30r
Monthly rental value of owned home	mos	505	1999	30r
Owned dwellings, expenditures own	yr	3465	1999	30r
Rent expenditures	yr	1641	1999	30r
Rental unit, 1 bedroom, with utilities	mos	463	4/01	41c
Rental unit, 2 bedroom, with utilities	mos	579	4/01	41c
Rental unit, 3 bedroom, with utilities	mos	775	4/01	41c
Rental unit, 4 bedroom, with utilities	mos	903	4/01	41c
Shelter, expenditures on	yr	5467	1999	30r
Insurance and Pensions				
Life and other personal insurance purchases	yr	414	1999	30r
Medigap health insurance, Plan H	yr	2887	2000	69s
Medigap health insurance, Plan I	yr	3302	2000	69s
Medigap health insurance, Plan J	yr	3889	2000	69s
Pensions and Social Security, expenditures on	yr	2635	1999	30r
Personal insurance and pensions, expenditures on	yr	3048	1999	30r
Legal Fees				
Divorce, filing fee		65.00-85.00	4/01	35s
Driver's license fee	orig	20.00	1999	48s
Driver's license fee	renew	15.00	1999	48s
Personal Goods				
Personal care products and services purchases	yr	393	1999	30r
Personal Services				
Personal services, household, expenditures on	yr	258	1999	30r
Pets				
Pets, toys, and playground equipment, expenditures on	yr	306	1999	30r
Taxes				
Federal income taxes paid	yr	2047	1999	30r
Personal taxes, expenditures on	yr	2554	1999	30r
Property taxes paid	yr	726	1999	30r
State and local income taxes paid	yr	363	1999	30r
Transportation				
Cars and trucks, new, expenditures on	yr	1648	1999	30r
Cars and trucks, used, expenditures on	yr	1651	1999	30r
Diesel at the pump	gal	1.26	10/99	73s
Gasoline and motor oil purchases	yr	1052	1999	30r
Gasoline before-tax price (cents)	gal	101.90	10/00	43s
Maintenance and repair expenditures	yr	621	1999	30r

Melbourne-Titusville-Palm Bay, FL - continued

Item	Per	Value	Date	Ref.
Transportation - continued				
Public transportation, expenditures on	yr	298	1999	30r
Transportation purchases	yr	6738	1999	30r
Vehicle expenses, miscellaneous, purchases	yr	2033	1999	30r
Vehicle insurance payments	yr	696	1999	30r
Vehicle purchases (net outlay)	yr	3354	1999	30r
Vehicle rental, lease expenditures	yr	352	1999	30r
Travel				
Hotel room	night	110.57	2/01	95s
Utilities				
Electrical bill, average	mos	86.33	9/00	9s
Electricity, expenditures on	yr	1115	1999	30r
Electricity cost, average	KWh	6.80	9/00	9s
Water and other public services, expenditures on	yr	298	1999	30r
Weddings				
Wedding (national average cost)		19936	2000	33r
Wedding (regional average total cost)		16293	1997	110r
Attendants' gifts		321	1998	33r
Bridal attendants' apparel (5 persons)		824	2000	33r
Bride's headpiece/veil		173	1998	33r
Bride's wedding dress		859	1998	33r
Clergy, religious facility fee		242	1998	33r
Engagement ring		3177	1998	33r
Flowers		789	1998	33r
Groom's formalwear rental		99	2000	33r
Limousine		410	1998	33r
Marriage license cost		56.00-88.50	4/01	35s
Men's formalwear (ushers, best man)		469	2000	33r
Mother of bride apparel		241	2000	33r
Music		866	1998	33r
Photography and videography		1368	1998	33r
Rehearsal dinner		728	1998	33r
Wedding invitations and announcements		341	1998	33r
Wedding reception		7968	2000	33r
Wedding rings (bride and groom)		1060	1998	33r

Memphis, TN

Item	Per	Value	Date	Ref.
Composite, ACCRA index		89.20	3/01	4c
Alcoholic Beverages				
Alcoholic beverage purchases	yr	253	1999	30r
Beer, Heineken, 12-oz, ex deposit	6	6.53	3/01	4c
J & B Scotch	750-ml	21.71	3/01	4c
Malt beverages, all types, all sizes, any origin	16 oz	0.96	7/01	11r
Wine, Livingston or Gallo, Chablis blanc	1.5 liter	5.99	3/01	4c
Appliances				
Appliance repair, service call, washing machine	min lab chg	38.59	3/01	4c
Major appliances, expenditures on	yr	172	1999	30r
Small appliances, housewares, expenditures on	yr	81	1999	30r
Banking and Money				
Mortgage interest and charges paid	yr	2039	1999	30r
Mortgage principal paid on owned property	yr	1026	1999	30r
Mortgage rate, incl. points and orig. fee, 30-yr. conv. fixed or ARM	mos	6.88	3/01	4c
Vehicle finance charges paid	yr	365	1999	30r
Business Expenses				
Business travel, car rental	day	70	2001	3c
Business travel, food	day	43	2001	3c
Business travel, hotel	day	114	2001	3c
Charity				
Cash contributions, expenditures	yr	1127	1999	30r
Child Care				
Child raising cost, total, age 0-2	yr	8540	1999	60r
Child raising cost, total, age 3-5	yr	8780	1999	60r

Values are in dollars or fractions of dollars. In the column headed *Ref*, references are shown to sources. Each reference is followed by a letter. These refer to the geographical level for which data were reported: s=State, r=Region, and c=City or metro. The abbreviation *ex* is used to mean *except* or *excluding*; *exp* stands for *expenditures*. For other abbreviations and further explanations, please see the Introduction.

Memphis, TN - continued

Item	Per	Value	Date	Ref.
Child Care				
Child raising cost, total, age 6-8	yr	8820	1999	60r
Child raising cost, total, age 9-11	yr	8800	1999	60r
Child raising cost, total, age 12-14	yr	9510	1999	60r
Child raising cost, total, age 15-17	yr	9740	1999	60r
Child's child care and education, age 0-2	yr	1380	1999	60r
Child's child care and education, age 3-5	yr	1520	1999	60r
Child's child care and education, age 6-8	yr	990	1999	60r
Child's child care and education, age 9-11	yr	650	1999	60r
Child's child care and education, age 12-14	yr	490	1999	60r
Child's child care and education, age 15-17	yr	840	1999	60r
Child's clothing, age 0-2	yr	480	1999	60r
Child's clothing, age 3-5	yr	470	1999	60r
Child's clothing, age 6-8	yr	520	1999	60r
Child's clothing, age 9-11	yr	570	1999	60r
Child's clothing, age 12-14	yr	950	1999	60r
Child's clothing, age 15-17	yr	850	1999	60r
Child's food, age 0-2	yr	1000	1999	60r
Child's food, age 3-5	yr	1160	1999	60r
Child's food, age 6-8	yr	1490	1999	60r
Child's food, age 9-11	yr	1770	1999	60r
Child's food, age 12-14	yr	1770	1999	60r
Child's food, age 15-17	yr	1980	1999	60r
Child's health care, age 0-2	yr	620	1999	60r
Child's health care, age 3-5	yr	590	1999	60r
Child's health care, age 6-8	yr	680	1999	60r
Child's health care, age 9-11	yr	720	1999	60r
Child's health care, age 12-14	yr	730	1999	60r
Child's health care, age 15-17	yr	760	1999	60r
Child's housing, age 0-2	yr	3070	1999	60r
Child's housing, age 3-5	yr	3050	1999	60r
Child's housing, age 6-8	yr	3010	1999	60r
Child's housing, age 9-11	yr	2850	1999	60r
Child's housing, age 12-14	yr	3040	1999	60r
Child's housing, age 15-17	yr	2650	1999	60r
Child's personal care, reading, age 0-2	yr	910	1999	60r
Child's personal care, reading, age 3-5	yr	930	1999	60r
Child's personal care, reading, age 6-8	yr	960	1999	60r
Child's personal care, reading, age 9-11	yr	1000	1999	60r
Child's personal care, reading, age 12-14	yr	1170	1999	60r
Child's personal care, reading, age 15-17	yr	950	1999	60r
Clothing				
Apparel and services purchases	yr	1610	1999	30r
Boys' brief, cotton	3	2.98	3/01	4c
Boys, 2 to 15, expenditures on	yr	89	1999	30r
Children under 2, expenditures on	yr	79	1999	30r
Footwear, expenditures on	yr	283	1999	30r
Girls, 2 to 15, expenditures on	yr	103	1999	30r
Men and boys, expenditures on	yr	351	1999	30r
Men, 16 and over, expenditures on	yr	262	1999	30r
Shirt, man's dress shirt		21.19	3/01	4c
Slacks, man's "No Wrinkles" khaki		29.99	3/01	4c
Women, 16 and over, expenditures on	yr	538	1999	30r
Communications				
Cable modem installation, Intermedia		149.95	6/99	103s
Cable modem installation, Time Warner		75.00-225.00	6/99	103s
Cable modem rate, cable subscriber, Intermedia	mos	49.95	6/99	103s
Cable modem rate, cable subscriber, Time Warner	mos	39.95-49.95	6/99	103s
Cable modem rate, non-cable subscriber, Intermedia	mos	54.95	6/99	103s
Cable modem rate, non-cable subscriber, Time Warner	mos	39.95-54.95	6/99	103s
Newspaper subscription, daily and Sunday delivery	mos	17.50	3/01	4c
Phone line, single, business, field visit	inst.	58.50	12/97	17s
Phone line, single, business, no field visit	inst.	58.50	12/97	17s
Phone line, single, residence, field visit	inst.	41.50	12/97	17s
Phone line, single, residence, no field visit	inst.	41.50	12/97	17s
Postage and stationery, expenditures on	yr	104	1999	30r

Memphis, TN - continued

Item	Per	Value	Date	Ref.
Communications - continued				
Postal rate, express mail, up to half-pound		12.45	7/01	108r
Postal rate, letter, first class, first ounce		0.34	7/01	108r
Postal rate, letter, two ounces		0.57	7/01	108r
Postal rate, post card		0.21	7/01	108r
Postal rate, priority mail, two pounds		3.95	7/01	108r
Postal rate, priority mail, up to one pound		3.50	7/01	108r
Telephone bill, business, basic rate	mos	39.70	12/97	18c
Telephone bill, family of three	mos	20.26	3/01	4c
Telephone bill, residential, basic rate	mos	12.15	12/97	18c
Telephone services, expenditures on	yr	860	1999	30r
Education				
Board, 4-year private college/university	yr	2085	1996	38s
Board, 4-year public college/university	yr	1737	1996	38s
Education expenditures	yr	431	1999	30r
Room, 4-year private college/university	yr	2153	1996	38s
Room, 4-year public college/university	yr	1644	1996	38s
Total cost, 4-year private college/university	yr	14068	1996	38s
Total cost, 4-year public college/university	yr	5372	1996	38s
Tuition, 2-year public college/university, in state	yr	1022	1996	38s
Tuition, 4-year private college/university, in state	yr	9830	1996	38s
Tuition, 4-year public college/university	yr	1990	1996	38s
Energy and Fuels				
Electricity	KWh	0.09	7/01	11r
Electricity	500 KWhs	47.29	7/01	11r
Energy, combined forms, 2400 sq ft	mos	99.60	3/01	4c
Energy, exc. electricity, 2400 sq ft	mos	45.00	3/01	4c
Fuel oil #2	gal	1.43	7/01	11r
Fuel oil and other fuels, expenditures on	yr	45	1999	30r
Gas, natural, commercial rate	1000 cf	8.61	11/00	88s
Gas, regular unleaded, cash, self-service	gal	1.33	3/01	4c
Gasoline, all types	gal	1.60	7/01	11r
Gasoline, unleaded midgrade	gal	1.65	7/01	11r
Gasoline, unleaded premium	gal	1.74	7/01	11r
Natural gas, expenditures on	yr	164	1999	30r
Utility (piped) gas, therm		1.01	7/01	11r
Utility (piped) gas, 40 therms		44.29	7/01	11r
Utility (piped) gas, 100 therms		97.44	7/01	11r
Entertainment				
Bowling, Saturday evening rate	line	2.88	3/01	4c
Entertainment purchases	yr	1574	1999	30r
Fees and admissions paid	yr	371	1999	30r
Monopoly game, Parker Brothers', No. 9	game	8.50	3/01	4c
Movie ticket, evening	person	6.50	1999	104c
Movie, first-run, Saturday, evening	adm.	6.90	3/01	4c
Reading purchases	yr	121	1999	30r
Television, radios, sound equipment, expenditures on	yr	561	1999	30r
Tennis balls, yellow, Wilson or Penn, 3	can	1.90	3/01	4c
Groceries				
Groceries, ACCRA Index		96.00	3/01	4c
American processed cheese	lb	3.50	7/01	11r
Antibiotic ointment, Polysporin	0.5 oz	4.12	3/01	4c
Baby food, strained vegetables or fruit, lowest price	4-4.5 oz	0.36	3/01	4c
Bakery products, expenditures on	yr	261	1999	30r
Bananas	lb	0.51	3/01	4c
Bananas	lb	0.47	7/01	11r
Beans, dried, any type, all sizes	lb	0.63	7/01	11r
Beef for stew, boneless	lb	2.86	7/01	11r
Beef or hamburger, ground	lb	1.59	3/01	4c
Beef, expenditures on	yr	210	1999	30r
Bologna, all beef or mixed	lb	2.29	7/01	11r
Bread, French	lb	1.66	7/01	11r
Bread, white	loaf	0.92	3/01	4c
Bread, white, pan	lb	0.87	7/01	11r
Bread, whole wheat, pan	lb	1.38	7/01	11r
Broccoli	lb	1.04	7/01	11r

Values are in dollars or fractions of dollars. In the column headed *Ref*, references are shown to sources. Each reference is followed by a letter. These refer to the geographical level for which data were reported: s=State, r=Region, and c=City or metro. The abbreviation *ex* is used to mean *except* or *excluding*; *exp* stands for *expenditures*. For other abbreviations and further explanations, please see the Introduction.

Item	Per	Value	Date	Ref.
Groceries				
Butter, salted, grade AA, stick	lb	2.26	7/01	11r
Butter, yoghurt, cheese, etc, expenditures on	yr	170	1999	30r
Cabbage	lb	0.42	7/01	11r
Cereals and cereal products, expenditures on	yr	140	1999	30r
Cheddar cheese, natural	lb	3.75	7/01	11r
Cheese, Kraft grated Parmesan	8 oz	4.05	3/01	4c
Chicken breast, bone-in	lb	1.85	7/01	11r
Chicken legs, bone-in	lb	1.34	7/01	11r
Chicken, fresh, whole	lb	1.05	7/01	11r
Chicken, whole fryer	lb	0.70	3/01	4c
Chops, boneless,	lb	4.13	7/01	11r
Chuck roast, graded and ungraded, excl U.S. prime and choice	lb	2.35	7/01	11r
Chuck roast, U.S. choice, boneless	lb	2.67	7/01	11r
Cigarettes, Winston, Kings	carton	26.87	3/01	4c
Coffee, 100%, ground roast, all sizes	lb	2.88	7/01	11r
Coffee, instant, plain, regular, all sizes	16 oz	9.25	7/01	11r
Coffee, vacuum-packed	13 oz	2.69	3/01	4c
Cola, non diet,	2 liter	1.11	7/01	11r
Corn Flakes, Kellogg's or Post Toasties	18 oz	2.83	3/01	4c
Corn, frozen, whole kernel, lowest price	16 oz	1.27	4/01	4c
Crackers, soda, salted	lb	1.70	7/01	11r
Dairy product purchases	yr	282	1999	30r
Eggs, expenditures on	yr	32	1999	30r
Eggs, Grade A or AA	dozen	1.12	3/01	4c
Fats and oils, expenditures on	yr	79	1999	30r
Fish and seafood, expenditures on	yr	99	1999	30r
Flour, white, all purpose	lb	0.32	7/01	11r
Food (excl fruit and vegetables), eaten at home, purchases	yr	815	1999	30r
Food cooked on trips, expenditures on	yr	36	1999	30r
Food purchases	yr	4533	1999	30r
Food purchases, eaten away from home	yr	1873	1999	30r
Food purchases, food eaten at home	yr	2660	1999	30r
Fresh fruits, expenditures on	yr	128	1999	30r
Fresh milk and cream, expenditures on	yr	112	1999	30r
Fresh vegetables, expenditures on	yr	131	1999	30r
Fruit and vegetable purchases	yr	438	1999	30r
Grapefruit	lb	0.59	7/01	11r
Grapes, Thompson, seedless	lb	2.12	7/01	11r
Ground beef, 100% beef	lb	1.76	7/01	11r
Ground beef, lean and extra lean	lb	2.60	7/01	11r
Ground chuck, 100% beef	lb	2.08	7/01	11r
Ham, boneless, excl canned	lb	2.71	7/01	11r
Ham, rump or shank half, bone-in, smoked	lb	2.19	7/01	11r
Ice cream, prepackaged, bulk, regular	1/2 gal	3.93	7/01	11r
Lemons	lb	1.32	7/01	11r
Lettuce, iceberg	head	0.87	3/01	4c
Lettuce, iceberg	lb	0.76	7/01	11r
Margarine, Blue Bonnet or Parkay, stick	lb	0.73	3/01	4c
Milk, fresh, low fat	gal	2.75	7/01	11r
Milk, fresh, whole, fortified	gal	2.97	7/01	11r
Milk, whole	1/2 gal	1.90	3/01	4c
Nonalcoholic beverages, expenditures on	yr	228	1999	30r
Orange juice, frozen concentrate	16 oz	1.95	7/01	11r
Orange juice, Minute Maid frozen	12 oz	1.69	4/01	4c
Oranges, Navel	lb	0.73	7/01	11r
Oranges, Valencia	lb	0.55	7/01	11r
Peaches, halves or slices, Hunt's, Del Monte, or Libby's	29 oz	1.64	3/01	4c
Peanut butter, creamy, all sizes	lb	1.83	7/01	11r
Pears, Anjou	lb	0.98	7/01	11r
Peas, green, Del Monte or Green Giant	15 oz	0.73	3/01	4c
Pork chops, center cut, bone-in	lb	3.33	7/01	11r
Pork sausage, fresh, loose	lb	2.59	7/01	11r
Pork shoulder picnic, bone-in, smoked	lb	1.12	7/01	11r
Pork, expenditures on	yr	162	1999	30r
Potato chips	16 oz	3.59	7/01	11r
Potatoes, frozen, french fried	lb	1.00	7/01	11r
Potatoes, white or red	10 lb	2.89	3/01	4c
Potatoes, white, all types	lb	0.44	7/01	11r

Item	Per	Value	Date	Ref.
Groceries - continued				
Poultry, expenditures on	yr	137	1999	30r
Processed fruits, expenditures on	yr	97	1999	30r
Processed vegetables, expenditures on	yr	82	1999	30r
Rice, white, long grain, uncooked	lb	0.51	7/01	11r
Round roast, graded and ungraded, excl U.S. prime and choice	lb	2.96	7/01	11r
Round steak, graded and ungraded, excl U.S. prime and choice	lb	3.11	7/01	11r
Sausage, Jimmy Dean/Owens pork	lb	2.54	3/01	4c
Shortening, vegetable, Crisco	3 lb	3.03	3/01	4c
Sirloin steak, graded and ungraded, excl U.S. prime and choice	lb	4.23	7/01	11r
Soft drink, Coca Cola, ex deposit	2 liter	0.96	3/01	4c
Spaghetti and macaroni	lb	0.78	7/01	11r
Steak, round, U.S. choice, boneless	lb	3.56	7/01	11r
Steak, sirloin, U.S. choice, boneless	lb	5.65	7/01	11r
Steak, T-bone	lb	6.53	3/01	4c
Strawberries, dry pint	12 oz	1.50	7/01	11r
Sugar and other sweets, expenditures on	yr	99	1999	30r
Sugar, cane or beet	4 lbs	1.61	3/01	4c
Sugar, white, 33-80 ounce package	lb	0.39	7/01	11r
Sugar, white, all sizes	lb	0.42	7/01	11r
Tobacco products and smoking supplies purchases	yr	288	1999	30r
Tomatoes, field grown	lb	1.43	7/01	11r
Tomatoes, Hunt's or Del Monte	14.5 oz	0.76	3/01	4c
Tuna, chunk, light	6 oz	0.42	3/01	4c
Tuna, light, chunk	lb	1.77	7/01	11r
Turkey, frozen, whole	lb	1.05	7/01	11r
Goods and Services				
Miscellaneous goods and services, ACCRA Index		90.90	3/01	4c
Health Care				
Health care, ACCRA Index		87.70	3/01	4c
Cardiac catheterization, ave hospital/ physician charges		12170	1998	77s
Childbirth, Cesarean delivery		11587	1997	13r
Childbirth, vaginal delivery		6725	1997	13r
Dentist's fee, adult teeth cleaning and periodic oral exam	visit	67.80	3/01	4c
Doctor's fee, routine exam, established patient	visit	56.50	3/01	4c
Drugs, expenditures on	yr	399	1999	30r
Health care purchases	yr	1971	1999	30r
Health insurance expenditures	yr	933	1999	30r
Hospital care, private room	day	300.40	3/01	4c
Hysterectomy, laproscopically-assisted, ave hospital/physician charges		13470	1998	76s
Hysterectomy, vaginal, ave hospital and physician charges		9530	1998	76s
Medical services expenditures	yr	547	1999	30r
Medical supplies, expenditures on	yr	91	1999	30r
Household Goods				
Dishwashing powder, Cascade	50 oz	3.83	3/01	4c
Floor coverings, expenditures on	yr	44	1999	30r
Furniture, expenditures on	yr	335	1999	30r
Household furnishings and equipment purchases	yr	1328	1999	30r
Household textiles, expenditures on	yr	89	1999	30r
Laundry and cleaning supplies, expenditures on	yr	113	1999	30r
Tissues, facial, Kleenex brand	175	1.17	3/01	4c
Housing				
Housing, ACCRA Index		82.20	3/01	4c
Home, 2200 sq ft, 4-br, 2-bath, 2-car garage, average		158000	2000	47c
Home price, existing, ave		160100	10/00	90r
Home value, median		112000	2001	53s
House, 2400 sq ft, 8000 sq ft lot, new, urban, utilities	total	166650	3/01	4c

Values are in dollars or fractions of dollars. In the column headed *Ref*, references are shown to sources. Each reference is followed by a letter. These refer to the geographical level for which data were reported: s=State, r=Region, and c=City or metro. The abbreviation *ex* is used to mean *except* or *excluding*; *exp* stands for expenditures. For other abbreviations and further explanations, please see the Introduction.

Memphis, TN - continued

Item	Per	Value	Date	Ref.
Housing				
House payment, principal and interest, 25% down payment	mos	821	3/01	4c
Household operation expenditures	yr	553	1999	30r
Housekeeping supplies purchases	yr	473	1999	30r
Housing, expenditures on	yr	10303	1999	30r
Maintenance, repairs, insurance expenditures	yr	699	1999	30r
Monthly rental value of owned home	mos	505	1999	30r
Owned dwellings, expenditures own	yr	3465	1999	30r
Rent expenditures	yr	1641	1999	30r
Rent, apartment, 2 br, 1 1/2-2 baths, unfurn, 950 sq ft, water	mos	640	3/01	4c
Rental unit, 1 bedroom, with utilities	mos	462	4/01	41c
Rental unit, 2 bedroom, with utilities	mos	542	4/01	41c
Rental unit, 3 bedroom, with utilities	mos	753	4/01	41c
Rental unit, 4 bedroom, with utilities	mos	791	4/01	41c
Shelter, expenditures on	yr	5467	1999	30r
Insurance and Pensions				
Life and other personal insurance purchases	yr	414	1999	30r
Pensions and Social Security, expenditures on	yr	2635	1999	30r
Personal insurance and pensions, expenditures on	yr	3048	1999	30r
Legal Fees				
Combination hunting and fishing license	yr	21.00	4/01	34s
Divorce, filing fee		64.00	4/01	35s
Driver's license fee	renew	17.50	1999	48s
Driver's license fee	orig	17.50	1999	48s
Personal Goods				
Personal care products and services purchases	yr	393	1999	30r
Shampoo, Alberto VO5	15 oz	0.94	3/01	4c
Toothpaste, Crest or Colgate	6-7 oz	1.86	3/01	4c
Personal Services				
Dry cleaning, man's 2-pc suit		8.58	3/01	4c
Man's haircut, barbershop, no styling		9.60	3/01	4c
Personal services, household, expenditures on	yr	258	1999	30r
Woman's shampoo, trim, blow-dry, no style-change		27.80	3/01	4c
Pets				
Pets, toys, and playground equipment, expenditures on	yr	306	1999	30r
Restaurant Food				
Chicken, fried, thigh and drumstick, KFC/ Church's		2.43	3/01	4c
Hamburger with cheese, McDonald's	1/4 lb	2.12	3/01	4c
Pizza, Pizza Hut or Pizza Inn	11-12 in	9.49	3/01	4c
Taxes				
Federal income taxes paid	yr	2047	1999	30r
Personal taxes, expenditures on	yr	2554	1999	30r
Property taxes paid	yr	726	1999	30r
State and local income taxes paid	yr	363	1999	30r
Transportation				
Transportation, ACCRA Index		98.30	3/01	4c
Bus fare, one-way	trip	1.10	2000	1c
Bus fare, to central business district	1-way	1.25	3/01	4c
Cars and trucks, new, expenditures on	yr	1648	1999	30r
Cars and trucks, used, expenditures on	yr	1651	1999	30r
Diesel at the pump	gal	1.18	10/99	73s
Gasoline and motor oil purchases	yr	1052	1999	30r
Gasoline before-tax price (cents)	gal	102.50	10/00	43s
Light rail transit fare, one-way	trip	0.50	2000	2c
Maintenance and repair expenditures	yr	621	1999	30r
Public transportation, expenditures on	yr	298	1999	30r
Tire balance, computer or spin balance, front	wheel	7.80	3/01	4c
Transportation purchases	yr	6738	1999	30r
Vehicle expenses, miscellaneous, purchases	yr	2033	1999	30r

Memphis, TN - continued

Item	Per	Value	Date	Ref.
Transportation - continued				
Vehicle insurance payments	yr	696	1999	30r
Vehicle purchases (net outlay)	yr	3354	1999	30r
Vehicle rental, lease expenditures	yr	352	1999	30r
Travel				
Hotel room, ave	night	84.28	2000	70c
Utilities				
Utilities, ACCRA Index		83.20	3/01	4c
Electrical bill, average	mos	79.16	9/00	9s
Electricity, expenditures on	yr	1115	1999	30r
Electricity and other, mixed, 2400 sq ft, new home	mos	54.60	3/01	4c
Electricity cost, average	KWh	5.60	9/00	9s
Water and other public services, expenditures on	yr	298	1999	30r
Weddings				
Wedding (national average cost)		19936	2000	33r
Attendants' gifts		321	1998	33r
Bridal attendants' apparel (5 persons)		824	2000	33r
Bride's headpiece/veil		173	1998	33r
Bride's wedding dress		859	1998	33r
Clergy, religious facility fee		242	1998	33r
Engagement ring		3177	1998	33r
Flowers		789	1998	33r
Groom's formalwear rental		99	2000	33r
Limousine		410	1998	33r
Marriage license cost		31.00	4/01	35s
Men's formalwear (ushers, best man)		469	2000	33r
Mother of bride apparel		241	2000	33r
Music		866	1998	33r
Photography and videography		1368	1998	33r
Rehearsal dinner		728	1998	33r
Wedding invitations and announcements		341	1998	33r
Wedding reception		7968	2000	33r
Wedding rings (bride and groom)		1060	1998	33r

Merced, CA

Item	Per	Value	Date	Ref.
Average annual expenditures	yr	40662	1999	30r
Alcoholic Beverages				
Alcoholic beverage purchases	yr	372	1999	30r
Malt beverages, all types, all sizes, any origin	16 oz	0.94	7/01	11r
Wine, red and white table, all sizes, any origin	liter	6.00	7/01	11r
Appliances				
Major appliances, expenditures on	yr	167	1999	30r
Small appliances, housewares, expenditures on	yr	105	1999	30r
Banking and Money				
Mortgage interest and charges paid	yr	3368	1999	30r
Mortgage principal paid on owned property	yr	1677	1999	30r
Vehicle finance charges paid	yr	311	1999	30r
Charity				
Cash contributions, expenditures	yr	1344	1999	30r
Child Care				
Child raising cost, total, age 0-2	yr	9140	1999	60r
Child raising cost, total, age 3-5	yr	9370	1999	60r
Child raising cost, total, age 6-8	yr	9450	1999	60r
Child raising cost, total, age 9-11	yr	9470	1999	60r
Child raising cost, total, age 12-14	yr	10170	1999	60r
Child raising cost, total, age 15-17	yr	10360	1999	60r
Child's child care and education, age 0-2	yr	1250	1999	60r
Child's child care and education, age 3-5	yr	1380	1999	60r
Child's child care and education, age 6-8	yr	890	1999	60r
Child's child care and education, age 9-11	yr	580	1999	60r
Child's child care and education, age 12-14	yr	430	1999	60r
Child's child care and education, age 15-17	yr	730	1999	60r
Child's clothing, age 0-2	yr	430	1999	60r

Values are in dollars or fractions of dollars. In the column headed *Ref*, references are shown to sources. Each reference is followed by a letter. These refer to the geographical level for which data were reported: s=State, r=Region, and c=City or metro. The abbreviation *ex* is used to mean *except* or *excluding*; *exp* stands for expenditures. For other abbreviations and further explanations, please see the Introduction.

Merced, CA - continued

Item	Per	Value	Date	Ref.
Child Care				
Child's clothing, age 3-5	yr	420	1999	60r
Child's clothing, age 6-8	yr	470	1999	60r
Child's clothing, age 9-11	yr	520	1999	60r
Child's clothing, age 12-14	yr	870	1999	60r
Child's clothing, age 15-17	yr	770	1999	60r
Child's food, age 0-2	yr	1120	1999	60r
Child's food, age 3-5	yr	1280	1999	60r
Child's food, age 6-8	yr	1640	1999	60r
Child's food, age 9-11	yr	1930	1999	60r
Child's food, age 12-14	yr	1940	1999	60r
Child's food, age 15-17	yr	2150	1999	60r
Child's health care, age 0-2	yr	490	1999	60r
Child's health care, age 3-5	yr	470	1999	60r
Child's health care, age 6-8	yr	530	1999	60r
Child's health care, age 9-11	yr	570	1999	60r
Child's health care, age 12-14	yr	580	1999	60r
Child's health care, age 15-17	yr	610	1999	60r
Child's housing, age 0-2	yr	3630	1999	60r
Child's housing, age 3-5	yr	3610	1999	60r
Child's housing, age 6-8	yr	3570	1999	60r
Child's housing, age 9-11	yr	3410	1999	60r
Child's housing, age 12-14	yr	3600	1999	60r
Child's housing, age 15-17	yr	3210	1999	60r
Child's personal care, reading, age 0-2	yr	1040	1999	60r
Child's personal care, reading, age 3-5	yr	1060	1999	60r
Child's personal care, reading, age 6-8	yr	1090	1999	60r
Child's personal care, reading, age 9-11	yr	1130	1999	60r
Child's personal care, reading, age 12-14	yr	1300	1999	60r
Child's personal care, reading, age 15-17	yr	1080	1999	60r
Clothing				
Apparel and services purchases	yr	1863	1999	30r
Boys, 2 to 15, expenditures on	yr	80	1999	30r
Children under 2, expenditures on	yr	74	1999	30r
Footwear, expenditures on	yr	307	1999	30r
Girls, 2 to 15, expenditures on	yr	101	1999	30r
Men and boys, expenditures on	yr	443	1999	30r
Men, 16 and over, expenditures on	yr	363	1999	30r
Women, 16 and over, expenditures on	yr	594	1999	30r
Communications				
Cable modem installation, AT&T-BIS		150.00	6/99	103s
Cable modem installation, Charter		99.00-169.00	6/99	103s
Cable modem installation, Comcast		95.00	6/99	103s
Cable modem installation, Cox		99.00-174.95	6/99	103s
Cable modem installation, Media One		100.00	6/99	103s
Cable modem installation, Time Warner		75.00-225.00	6/99	103s
Cable modem rate, cable subscriber, AT&T-BIS	mos	39.95	6/99	103s
Cable modem rate, cable subscriber, Charter	mos	49.95-79.95	6/99	103s
Cable modem rate, cable subscriber, Comcast	mos	39.95	6/99	103s
Cable modem rate, cable subscriber, Cox	mos	29.95-44.95	6/99	103s
Cable modem rate, cable subscriber, Media One	mos	34.95-39.95	6/99	103s
Cable modem rate, cable subscriber, Time Warner	mos	39.95-49.95	6/99	103s
Cable modem rate, non-cable subscriber, Charter	mos	59.95-89.95	6/99	103s
Cable modem rate, non-cable subscriber, Comcast	mos	49.95	6/99	103s
Cable modem rate, non-cable subscriber, Cox	mos	42.95-54.95	6/99	103s
Cable modem rate, non-cable subscriber, Media One	mos	49.95	6/99	103s
Cable modem rate, non-cable subscriber, Time Warner	mos	39.95-54.95	6/99	103s
Phone line, single, business, field visit	inst.	70.75	12/97	17s

Merced, CA - continued

Item	Per	Value	Date	Ref.
Communications - continued				
Phone line, single, business, no field visit	inst.	70.75	12/97	17s
Phone line, single, residence, field visit	inst.	34.75	12/97	17s
Phone line, single, residence, no field visit	inst.	34.75	12/97	17s
Postage and stationery, expenditures on	yr	150	1999	30r
Postal rate, express mail, up to half-pound		12.45	7/01	108r
Postal rate, letter, first class, first ounce		0.34	7/01	108r
Postal rate, letter, two ounces		0.57	7/01	108r
Postal rate, post card		0.21	7/01	108r
Postal rate, priority mail, two pounds		3.95	7/01	108r
Postal rate, priority mail, up to one pound		3.50	7/01	108r
Telephone services, expenditures on	yr	825	1999	30r
Education				
Board, 4-year private college/university	yr	2970	1996	38s
Board, 4-year public college/university	yr	2516	1996	38s
Education expenditures	yr	676	1999	30r
Room, 4-year private college/university	yr	3196	1996	38s
Room, 4-year public college/university	yr	3031	1996	38s
Total cost, 4-year private college/university	yr	20143	1996	38s
Total cost, 4-year public college/university	yr	8213	1996	38s
Tuition, 2-year public college/university, in state	yr	362	1996	38s
Tuition, 4-year private college/university, in state	yr	13977	1996	38s
Tuition, 4-year public college/university	yr	2666	1996	38s
Energy and Fuels				
Electricity	500 KWhs	48.23	7/01	11r
Electricity	KWh	0.11	7/01	11r
Fuel oil and other fuels, expenditures on	yr	35	1999	30r
Gas, natural, commercial rate	1000 cf	8.74	11/00	88s
Gasoline, all types	gal	1.91	7/01	11r
Gasoline, unleaded premium	gal	2.05	7/01	11r
Gasoline, unleaded regular	gal	1.83	7/01	11r
Natural gas, expenditures on	yr	255	1999	30r
Utility (piped) gas, therm		0.98	7/01	11r
Utility (piped) gas, 40 therms		40.74	7/01	11r
Utility (piped) gas, 100 therms		96.80	7/01	11r
Entertainment				
Entertainment purchases	yr	2139	1999	30r
Fees and admissions paid	yr	545	1999	30r
Television, radios, sound equipment, expenditures on	yr	624	1999	30r
Funerals				
Total cost of funeral		5401.08	1/99	78r
Acknowledgement cards		33.64	1/99	78r
Casket		2170.43	1/99	78r
Cosmetology, hair, other preparation		136.32	1/99	78r
Embalming		319.13	1/99	78r
Funeral at funeral home		370.21	1/99	78r
Hearse (local)		161.04	1/99	78r
Professional service charges		963.15	1/99	78r
Service car/van		133.99	1/99	78r
Transfer of remains to funeral home		159.82	1/99	78r
Vault		778.07	1/99	78r
Visitation/viewing		175.28	1/99	78r
Groceries				
Apples, red delicious	lb	0.84	7/01	11r
Bacon, sliced	lb	3.38	7/01	11r
Bakery products, expenditures on	yr	299	1999	30r
Bananas	lb	0.54	7/01	11r
Beans, dried, any type, all sizes	lb	0.76	7/01	11r
Beef, expenditures on	yr	222	1999	30r
Bread, white, pan	lb	0.99	7/01	11r
Butter, yoghurt, cheese, etc, expenditures on	yr	211	1999	30r
Cereals and bakery product purchases	yr	466	1999	30r
Cereals and cereal products, expenditures on	yr	168	1999	30r
Chicken breast, bone-in	lb	2.45	7/01	11r
Chicken, fresh, whole	lb	1.19	7/01	11r

Values are in dollars or fractions of dollars. In the column headed *Ref*, references are shown to sources. Each reference is followed by a letter. These refer to the geographical level for which data were reported: s=State, r=Region, and c=City or metro. The abbreviation *ex* is used to mean *except* or *excluding*; *exp* stands for expenditures. For other abbreviations and further explanations, please see the Introduction.

Merced, CA - continued

Item	Per	Value	Date	Ref.
Groceries				
Chops, boneless,	lb	4.00	7/01	11r
Chuck roast, graded and ungraded, excl U.S. prime and choice	lb	2.55	7/01	11r
Coffee, 100%, ground roast, all sizes	lb	3.80	7/01	11r
Cookies, chocolate chip	lb	2.83	7/01	11r
Dairy product purchases	yr	341	1999	30r
Eggs, expenditures on	yr	39	1999	30r
Eggs, grade AA, large	dozen	1.23	7/01	11r
Fats and oils, expenditures on	yr	88	1999	30r
Fish and seafood, expenditures on	yr	121	1999	30r
Food (excl fruit and vegetables), eaten at home, purchases	yr	1001	1999	30r
Food cooked on trips, expenditures on	yr	64	1999	30r
Food purchases	yr	5312	1999	30r
Food purchases, eaten away from home	yr	2180	1999	30r
Food purchases, food eaten at home	yr	3132	1999	30r
Fresh fruits, expenditures on	yr	186	1999	30r
Fresh milk and cream, expenditures on	yr	130	1999	30r
Fresh vegetables, expenditures on	yr	177	1999	30r
Grapefruit	lb	0.68	7/01	11r
Grapes, Thompson, seedless	lb	2.42	7/01	11r
Ground beef, lean and extra lean	lb	2.46	7/01	11r
Ice cream, prepackaged, bulk, regular	1/2 gal	3.62	7/01	11r
Lettuce, iceberg	lb	0.63	7/01	11r
Meats, poultry, fish, and egg purchases	yr	761	1999	30r
Milk, fresh, low fat,	gal	2.80	7/01	11r
Milk, fresh, whole, fortified	gal	2.88	7/01	11r
Nonalcoholic beverages, expenditures on	yr	258	1999	30r
Oranges, Navel	lb	0.97	7/01	11r
Oranges, Valencia	lb	0.43	7/01	11r
Peaches	lb	1.38	7/01	11r
Peanut butter, creamy, all sizes	lb	2.14	7/01	11r
Pork chops, center cut, bone-in	lb	3.83	7/01	11r
Pork, expenditures on	yr	141	1999	30r
Potatoes, white, all types	lb	0.37	7/01	11r
Poultry, expenditures on	yr	146	1999	30r
Processed fruits, expenditures on	yr	118	1999	30r
Processed vegetables, expenditures on	yr	81	1999	30r
Round roast, graded and ungraded, excl U.S. prime and choice	lb	3.07	7/01	11r
Round roast, U.S. choice, boneless	lb	3.37	7/01	11r
Round steak, graded and ungraded, excl U.S. prime and choice	lb	3.51	7/01	11r
Sirloin steak, graded and ungraded, excl U.S. prime and choice	lb	4.67	7/01	11r
Steak, sirloin, U.S. choice, boneless	lb	6.20	7/01	11r
Strawberries, dry pint	12 oz	1.79	7/01	11r
Sugar and other sweets, expenditures on	yr	124	1999	30r
Sugar, white, all sizes	lb	0.46	7/01	11r
Tobacco products and smoking supplies purchases	yr	217	1999	30r
Tomatoes, field grown	lb	1.17	7/01	11r
Tuna, light, chunk	lb	2.05	7/01	11r
Goods and Services				
B&B Japanese maple (acer japonicum)	gal	39.99	4/00	93r
Boxwood (buxus)	2 gal	14.99- 24.99	4/00	93r
Christmas tree, noble fir		40-60	2000	65s
Daylily (hemerocallis)	gal	6.99- 8.99	4/00	93r
Flat of annuals		16.68	4/00	93r
Fountain grass (pennisetum)	gal	7.99- 11.99	4/00	93r
Hanging basket (10 in)		29.99	4/00	93r
Hardy geranium (geranium)	gal	6.99- 11.99	4/00	93r
Hosta (hosta)	gal	6.99- 18.99	4/00	93r
Lilac (syrubga vulgaris)	2 gal	14.99- 17.99	4/00	93r
Miscellaneous purchases	yr	1070	1999	30r
Rhododendron (rhododendron)	2 gal	14.99	4/00	93r

Merced, CA - continued

Item	Per	Value	Date	Ref.
Goods and Services - continued				
Sage (salvia)	gal	6.99	4/00	93r
Wintercreeper euonymus (euonymus fortunei)	2 gal	14.99- 22.99	4/00	93r
Hunting license	yr	29.95	4/01	34s
Health Care				
Cardiac catheterization, ave hospital/ physician charges		24000	1998	77s
Childbirth, Cesarean delivery		11587	1997	13r
Childbirth, vaginal delivery		6725	1997	13r
Drugs, expenditures on	yr	309	1999	30r
Health care purchases	yr	1869	1999	30r
Health insurance expenditures	yr	868	1999	30r
Hysterectomy, laproscopically-assisted, ave hospital/physician charges		20760	1998	76s
Hysterectomy, vaginal, ave hospital and physician charges		14570	1998	76s
Medicaid dispensing fee		4.05	1999	87s
Medical services expenditures	yr	580	1999	30r
Medical supplies, expenditures on	yr	112	1999	30r
Household Goods				
Floor coverings, expenditures on	yr	49	1999	30r
Furniture, expenditures on	yr	444	1999	30r
Household furnishings and equipment purchases	yr	1768	1999	30r
Household textiles, expenditures on	yr	141	1999	30r
Laundry and cleaning supplies, expenditures on	yr	128	1999	30r
Housing				
Home price, existing, ave		239400	10/00	90r
Home value, median		215000	2001	53s
Household operation expenditures	yr	781	1999	30r
Housekeeping supplies purchases	yr	513	1999	30r
Lodging expenditures	yr	575	1999	30r
Maintenance, repairs, insurance expenditures	yr	939	1999	30r
Monthly rental value of owned home	mos	662	1999	30r
Owned dwellings, expenditures own	yr	5231	1999	30r
Rent expenditures	yr	2709	1999	30r
Rental unit, 1 bedroom, with utilities	mos	459	4/01	41c
Rental unit, 2 bedroom, with utilities	mos	557	4/01	41c
Rental unit, 3 bedroom, with utilities	mos	770	4/01	41c
Rental unit, 4 bedroom, with utilities	mos	909	4/01	41c
Shelter, expenditures on	yr	8516	1999	30r
Insurance and Pensions				
Life and other personal insurance purchases	yr	355	1999	30r
Pensions and Social Security, expenditures on	yr	3636	1999	30r
Legal Fees				
Divorce, filing fee		182.00	4/01	35s
Driver's license fee	renew	15.00	1999	48s
Driver's license fee	orig	12.00	1999	48s
Personal Goods				
Personal care products and services purchases	yr	449	1999	30r
Personal Services				
Personal services, household, expenditures on	yr	353	1999	30r
Pets				
Pets, toys, and playground equipment, expenditures on	yr	358	1999	30r
Taxes				
Federal income taxes paid	yr	3200	1999	30r
Personal taxes, expenditures on	yr	4153	1999	30r
Property taxes paid	yr	923	1999	30r
State and local income taxes paid	yr	812	1999	30r

Values are in dollars or fractions of dollars. In the column headed *Ref*, references are shown to sources. Each reference is followed by a letter. These refer to the geographical level for which data were reported: s=State, r=Region, and c=City or metro. The abbreviation *ex* is used to mean *except* or *excluding*; *exp* stands for *expenditures*. For other abbreviations and further explanations, please see the Introduction.

Merced, CA - continued

Item	Per	Value	Date	Ref.
Transportation				
Cars and trucks, new, expenditures on	yr	1534	1999	30r
Cars and trucks, used, expenditures on	yr	1593	1999	30r
Diesel at the pump	gal	1.37	10/99	73s
Gasoline and motor oil purchases	yr	1129	1999	30r
Gasoline before-tax price (cents)	gal	128.80	10/00	43s
Maintenance and repair expenditures	yr	797	1999	30r
Public transportation, expenditures on	yr	530	1999	30r
Transportation purchases	yr	7423	1999	30r
Vehicle expenses, miscellaneous, purchases	yr	2585	1999	30r
Vehicle insurance payments	yr	811	1999	30r
Vehicle purchases (net outlay)	yr	3180	1999	30r
Vehicle rental, lease expenditures	yr	666	1999	30r
Utilities				
Electrical bill, average	mos	58.66	9/00	9s
Electricity, expenditures on	yr	725	1999	30r
Electricity cost, average	KWh	7.75	9/00	9s
Utilities, fuels, and public services purchased	yr	2179	1999	30r
Water and other public services, expenditures on	yr	339	1999	30r
Weddings				
Wedding (national average cost)		19936	2000	33r
Wedding (regional average total cost)		18918	1997	110r
Attendants' gifts		321	1998	33r
Bridal attendants' apparel (5 persons)		824	2000	33r
Bride's headpiece/veil		173	1998	33r
Bride's wedding dress		859	1998	33r
Clergy, religious facility fee		242	1998	33r
Engagement ring		3177	1998	33r
Flowers		789	1998	33r
Groom's formalwear rental		99	2000	33r
Limousine		410	1998	33r
Marriage license cost		50.00-80.00	4/01	35s
Men's formalwear (ushers, best man)		469	2000	33r
Mother of bride apparel		241	2000	33r
Music		866	1998	33r
Photography and videography		1368	1998	33r
Rehearsal dinner		728	1998	33r
Wedding invitations and announcements		341	1998	33r
Wedding reception		7968	2000	33r
Wedding rings (bride and groom)		1060	1998	33r

Miami, FL

Item	Per	Value	Date	Ref.
Alcoholic Beverages				
Alcoholic beverage purchases	yr	306	1999	30c
Malt beverages, all types, all sizes, any origin	16 oz	0.96	7/01	11r
Appliances				
Major appliances, expenditures on	yr	172	1999	30r
Small appliances, housewares, expenditures on	yr	81	1999	30r
Banking and Money				
Mortgage interest and charges paid	yr	2039	1999	30r
Mortgage principal paid on owned property	yr	1026	1999	30r
Vehicle finance charges paid	yr	365	1999	30r
Business Expenses				
Business travel, car rental	day	47	2001	3c
Business travel, food	day	50	2001	3c
Business travel, hotel	day	128	2001	3c
Medical office space cost	sq ft	103.19	2001	31c
Office space, 2-4 storey building	sq ft	90.41	2001	31c
Office space, 5-10 storey building	sq ft	79.86	2001	31c
Office space, 11-20 storey building	sq ft	76.76	2001	31c
Charity				
Cash contributions, expenditures	yr	1066	1999	30c

Miami, FL - continued

Item	Per	Value	Date	Ref.
Child Care				
Child raising cost, total, age 0-2	yr	8540	1999	60r
Child raising cost, total, age 3-5	yr	8780	1999	60r
Child raising cost, total, age 6-8	yr	8820	1999	60r
Child raising cost, total, age 9-11	yr	8800	1999	60r
Child raising cost, total, age 12-14	yr	9510	1999	60r
Child raising cost, total, age 15-17	yr	9740	1999	60r
Child's child care and education, age 0-2	yr	1380	1999	60r
Child's child care and education, age 3-5	yr	1520	1999	60r
Child's child care and education, age 6-8	yr	990	1999	60r
Child's child care and education, age 9-11	yr	650	1999	60r
Child's child care and education, age 12-14	yr	490	1999	60r
Child's child care and education, age 15-17	yr	840	1999	60r
Child's clothing, age 0-2	yr	480	1999	60r
Child's clothing, age 3-5	yr	470	1999	60r
Child's clothing, age 6-8	yr	520	1999	60r
Child's clothing, age 9-11	yr	570	1999	60r
Child's clothing, age 12-14	yr	950	1999	60r
Child's clothing, age 15-17	yr	850	1999	60r
Child's food, age 0-2	yr	1000	1999	60r
Child's food, age 3-5	yr	1160	1999	60r
Child's food, age 6-8	yr	1490	1999	60r
Child's food, age 9-11	yr	1770	1999	60r
Child's food, age 12-14	yr	1770	1999	60r
Child's food, age 15-17	yr	1980	1999	60r
Child's health care, age 0-2	yr	620	1999	60r
Child's health care, age 3-5	yr	590	1999	60r
Child's health care, age 6-8	yr	680	1999	60r
Child's health care, age 9-11	yr	720	1999	60r
Child's health care, age 12-14	yr	730	1999	60r
Child's health care, age 15-17	yr	760	1999	60r
Child's housing, age 0-2	yr	3070	1999	60r
Child's housing, age 3-5	yr	3050	1999	60r
Child's housing, age 6-8	yr	3010	1999	60r
Child's housing, age 9-11	yr	2850	1999	60r
Child's housing, age 12-14	yr	3040	1999	60r
Child's housing, age 15-17	yr	2650	1999	60r
Child's personal care, reading, age 0-2	yr	910	1999	60r
Child's personal care, reading, age 3-5	yr	930	1999	60r
Child's personal care, reading, age 6-8	yr	960	1999	60r
Child's personal care, reading, age 9-11	yr	1000	1999	60r
Child's personal care, reading, age 12-14	yr	1170	1999	60r
Child's personal care, reading, age 15-17	yr	950	1999	60r
Clothing				
Apparel and services purchases	yr	1734	1999	30c
Boys, 2 to 15, expenditures on	yr	89	1999	30r
Children under 2, expenditures on	yr	79	1999	30r
Footwear, expenditures on	yr	283	1999	30r
Girls, 2 to 15, expenditures on	yr	103	1999	30r
Men and boys, expenditures on	yr	351	1999	30r
Men, 16 and over, expenditures on	yr	262	1999	30r
Women, 16 and over, expenditures on	yr	538	1999	30r
Communications				
Cable modem installation, Adelphi		54.90	6/99	103s
Cable modem installation, Comcast		95.00	6/99	103s
Cable modem installation, Media One		100.00	6/99	103s
Cable modem installation, Time Warner		75.00-225.00	6/99	103s
Cable modem rate, cable subscriber, Adelphi	mos	34.95	6/99	103s
Cable modem rate, cable subscriber, Comcast	mos	39.95	6/99	103s
Cable modem rate, cable subscriber, Media One	mos	34.95-39.95	6/99	103s
Cable modem rate, cable subscriber, Time Warner	mos	39.95-49.95	6/99	103s
Cable modem rate, non-cable subscriber, Adelphi	mos	44.95	6/99	103s
Cable modem rate, non-cable subscriber, Comcast	mos	49.95	6/99	103s
Cable modem rate, non-cable subscriber, Media One	mos	49.95	6/99	103s

Values are in dollars or fractions of dollars. In the column headed *Ref*, references are shown to sources. Each reference is followed by a letter. These refer to the geographical level for which data were reported: s=State, r=Region, and c=City or metro. The abbreviation *ex* is used to mean *except* or *excluding*; *exp* stands for *expenditures*. For other abbreviations and further explanations, please see the Introduction.

Miami, FL - continued

Item	Per	Value	Date	Ref.
Communications				
Cable modem rate, non-cable subscriber, Time Warner	mos	39.95-54.95	6/99	103s
Phone line, single, business, field visit	inst.	56.00	12/97	17s
Phone line, single, business, no field visit	inst.	56.00	12/97	17s
Phone line, single, residence, field visit	inst.	40.00	12/97	17s
Phone line, single, residence, no field visit	inst.	40.00	12/97	17s
Postage and stationery, expenditures on	yr	104	1999	30r
Postal rate, express mail, up to half-pound		12.45	7/01	108r
Postal rate, letter, first class, first ounce		0.34	7/01	108r
Postal rate, letter, two ounces		0.57	7/01	108r
Postal rate, post card		0.21	7/01	108r
Postal rate, priority mail, two pounds		3.95	7/01	108r
Postal rate, priority mail, up to one pound		3.50	7/01	108r
Telephone bill, business, basic rate	mos	29.10	12/97	18c
Telephone bill, residential, basic rate	mos	10.65	12/97	18c
Telephone services, expenditures on	yr	860	1999	30r
Education				
Board, 4-year private college/university	yr	2236	1996	38s
Board, 4-year public college/university	yr	2295	1996	38s
Education expenditures	yr	433	1999	30c
Room, 4-year private college/university	yr	2428	1996	38s
Room, 4-year public college/university	yr	2193	1996	38s
Total cost, 4-year private college/university	yr	15028	1996	38s
Total cost, 4-year public college/university	yr	6254	1996	38s
Tuition, 2-year public college/university, in state	yr	1103	1996	38s
Tuition, 4-year private college/university, in state	yr	10364	1996	38s
Tuition, 4-year public college/university	yr	1767	1996	38s
Energy and Fuels				
Electricity	500 KWhs	47.29	7/01	11r
Electricity	KWh	0.10	7/01	11c
Electricity	500 KWhs	51.31	7/01	11c
Fuel oil #2	gal	1.43	7/01	11r
Fuel oil and other fuels, expenditures on	yr	45	1999	30r
Gas, cooking, winter, 10 therms	mos	13.84	2/96	98c
Gas, cooking, winter, 30 therms	mos	29.53	2/96	98c
Gas, cooking, winter, 50 therms	mos	45.21	2/96	98c
Gas, heating, winter, average use	mos	29.58	2/96	98c
Gas, natural, commercial rate	1000 cf	8.44	11/00	88s
Gasoline, all types	gal	1.74	7/01	11c
Gasoline, unleaded midgrade	gal	1.77	7/01	11c
Gasoline, unleaded premium	gal	1.74	7/01	11r
Gasoline, unleaded regular	gal	1.65	7/01	11c
Natural gas, expenditures on	yr	164	1999	30r
Utility (piped) gas, therm		1.59	7/01	11c
Utility (piped) gas, 40 therms		44.29	7/01	11r
Utility (piped) gas, 100 therms		150.05	7/01	11c
Entertainment				
Entertainment purchases	yr	1779	1999	30c
Fees and admissions paid	yr	371	1999	30r
Reading purchases	yr	88	1999	30c
Television, radios, sound equipment, expenditures on	yr	561	1999	30r
Funerals				
Total cost of funeral		5922.53	1/99	78r
Acknowledgement cards		63.43	1/99	78r
Casket		2258.77	1/99	78r
Cosmetology, hair, other preparation		127.09	1/99	78r
Embalming		393.49	1/99	78r
Funeral at funeral home		367.50	1/99	78r
Hearse (local)		169.66	1/99	78r
Professional service charges		1211.32	1/99	78r
Service car/van		80.69	1/99	78r
Transfer of remains to funeral home		144.25	1/99	78r
Vault		803.50	1/99	78r
Visitation/viewing		302.83	1/99	78r

Miami, FL - continued

Item	Per	Value	Date	Ref.
Groceries				
American processed cheese	lb	3.50	7/01	11r
Bakery products, expenditures on	yr	261	1999	30r
Bananas	lb	0.47	7/01	11r
Beans, dried, any type, all sizes	lb	0.63	7/01	11r
Beef for stew, boneless	lb	2.86	7/01	11r
Beef, expenditures on	yr	210	1999	30r
Bologna, all beef or mixed	lb	2.29	7/01	11r
Bread, French	lb	1.66	7/01	11r
Bread, white, pan	lb	0.87	7/01	11r
Bread, whole wheat, pan	lb	1.38	7/01	11r
Broccoli	lb	1.04	7/01	11r
Butter, salted, grade AA, stick	lb	2.26	7/01	11r
Butter, yoghurt, cheese, etc, expenditures on	yr	170	1999	30r
Cabbage	lb	0.42	7/01	11r
Cereals and cereal products, expenditures on	yr	140	1999	30r
Cheddar cheese, natural	lb	3.75	7/01	11r
Chicken breast, bone-in	lb	1.85	7/01	11r
Chicken legs, bone-in	lb	1.34	7/01	11r
Chicken, fresh, whole	lb	1.05	7/01	11r
Chops, boneless,	lb	4.13	7/01	11r
Chuck roast, graded and ungraded, excl U.S. prime and choice	lb	2.35	7/01	11r
Chuck roast, U.S. choice, boneless	lb	2.67	7/01	11r
Coffee, 100%, ground roast, all sizes	lb	2.88	7/01	11r
Coffee, instant, plain, regular, all sizes	16 oz	9.25	7/01	11r
Cola, non diet	2 liter	1.11	7/01	11r
Crackers, soda, salted	lb	1.70	7/01	11r
Dairy product purchases	yr	326	1999	30c
Eggs, expenditures on	yr	32	1999	30r
Fats and oils, expenditures on	yr	79	1999	30r
Fish and seafood, expenditures on	yr	99	1999	30r
Flour, white, all purpose	lb	0.32	7/01	11r
Food (excl fruit and vegetables), eaten at home, purchases	yr	692	1999	30c
Food cooked on trips, expenditures on	yr	36	1999	30r
Food purchases	yr	4791	1999	30c
Food purchases, eaten away from home	yr	1908	1999	30c
Food purchases, food eaten at home	yr	2884	1999	30c
Fresh fruits, expenditures on	yr	128	1999	30r
Fresh milk and cream, expenditures on	yr	112	1999	30r
Fresh vegetables, expenditures on	yr	131	1999	30r
Fruit and vegetable purchases	yr	497	1999	30c
Grapefruit	lb	0.59	7/01	11r
Grapes, Thompson, seedless	lb	2.12	7/01	11r
Ground beef, 100% beef	lb	1.76	7/01	11r
Ground beef, lean and extra lean	lb	2.60	7/01	11r
Ground chuck, 100% beef	lb	2.08	7/01	11r
Ham, boneless, excl canned	lb	2.71	7/01	11r
Ham, rump or shank half, bone-in, smoked	lb	2.19	7/01	11r
Ice cream, prepackaged, bulk, regular	1/2 gal	3.93	7/01	11r
Lemons	lb	1.32	7/01	11r
Lettuce, iceberg	lb	0.76	7/01	11r
Milk, fresh, low fat,	gal	2.75	7/01	11r
Milk, fresh, whole, fortified	gal	2.97	7/01	11r
Nonalcoholic beverages, expenditures on	yr	228	1999	30r
Orange juice, frozen concentrate	16 oz	1.95	7/01	11r
Oranges, Navel	lb	0.73	7/01	11r
Oranges, Valencia	lb	0.55	7/01	11r
Peanut butter, creamy, all sizes	lb	1.83	7/01	11r
Pears, Anjou	lb	0.98	7/01	11r
Pork chops, center cut, bone-in	lb	3.33	7/01	11r
Pork sausage, fresh, loose	lb	2.59	7/01	11r
Pork shoulder picnic, bone-in, smoked	lb	1.12	7/01	11r
Pork, expenditures on	yr	162	1999	30r
Potato chips	16 oz	3.59	7/01	11r
Potatoes, frozen, french fried	lb	1.00	7/01	11r
Potatoes, white, all types	lb	0.44	7/01	11r
Poultry, expenditures on	yr	137	1999	30r
Processed fruits, expenditures on	yr	97	1999	30r
Processed vegetables, expenditures on	yr	82	1999	30r
Rice, white, long grain, uncooked	lb	0.51	7/01	11r

Values are in dollars or fractions of dollars. In the column headed *Ref*, references are shown to sources. Each reference is followed by a letter. These refer to the geographical level for which data were reported: s=State, r=Region, and c=City or metro. The abbreviation *ex* is used to mean *except* or *excluding*; *exp* stands for *expenditures*. For other abbreviations and further explanations, please see the Introduction.

Miami, FL - continued

Item	Per	Value	Date	Ref.
Groceries				
Round roast, graded and ungraded, excl U.S. prime and choice	lb	2.96	7/01	11r
Round steak, graded and ungraded, excl U.S. prime and choice	lb	3.11	7/01	11r
Sirloin steak, graded and ungraded, excl U.S. prime and choice	lb	4.23	7/01	11r
Spaghetti and macaroni	lb	0.78	7/01	11r
Steak, round, U.S. choice, boneless	lb	3.56	7/01	11r
Steak, sirloin, U.S. choice, boneless	lb	5.65	7/01	11r
Strawberries, dry pint	12 oz	1.50	7/01	11r
Sugar and other sweets, expenditures on	yr	99	1999	30r
Sugar, white, 33-80 ounce package	lb	0.39	7/01	11r
Sugar, white, all sizes	lb	0.42	7/01	11r
Tobacco products and smoking supplies purchases	yr	204	1999	30c
Tomatoes, field grown	lb	1.43	7/01	11r
Tuna, light, chunk	lb	1.77	7/01	11r
Turkey, frozen, whole	lb	1.05	7/01	11r
Goods and Services				
B&B Japanese maple (acer japonicum)	gal	49.98-129.00	4/00	93r
Boxwood (buxus)	2 gal	12.99-16.99	4/00	93r
Daylily (hemerocallis)	gal	4.99-8.99	4/00	93r
Flat of annuals		11.00-13.92	4/00	93r
Fountain grass (pennisetum)	gal	5.98-7.98	4/00	93r
Hanging basket (10 in)		7.99-14.98	4/00	93r
Hardy geranium (geranium)	gal	5.98-8.00	4/00	93r
Hosta (hosta)	gal	4.99-10.98	4/00	93r
Lilac (syrubga vulgaris)	2 gal	12.99-21.99	4/00	93r
Rhododendron (rhododendron)	2 gal	14.99-24.99	4/00	93r
Sage (salvia)	gal	5.98-6.99	4/00	93r
Wintercreeper euonymus (euonymus fortunei)	2 gal	7.99-89.99	4/00	93r
Hunting license	yr	12.50	4/01	34s
Health Care				
Cardiac catheterization, ave hospital/physician charges		15060	1998	77s
Childbirth, Cesarean delivery		11587	1997	13r
Childbirth, vaginal delivery		6725	1997	13r
Drugs, expenditures on	yr	399	1999	30r
Health care purchases	yr	1481	1999	30c
Health insurance expenditures	yr	933	1999	30r
Home health care aide cost, licensed agency	hour	14	2000	82c
Hysterectomy, laproscopically-assisted, ave hospital/physician charges		14760	1998	76s
Hysterectomy, vaginal, ave hospital and physician charges		11320	1998	76s
Medicaid dispensing fee		4.23	1999	87s
Medical services expenditures	yr	547	1999	30r
Medical supplies, expenditures on	yr	91	1999	30r
Nursing home costs, private room	day	123	2000	82c
Nursing home stay, private room	day	123	2000	83c
Plastic surgery, breast augmentation		2870	2000	7r
Plastic surgery, breast lift		3649	2000	7r
Plastic surgery, facelift		5008	2000	7r
Plastic surgery, hair transplantation		3425	2000	7r
Plastic surgery, lip augmentation		1227	2000	7r
Plastic surgery, lower body lift		4793	2000	7r
Plastic surgery, thigh lift		3862	2000	7r

Miami, FL - continued

Item	Per	Value	Date	Ref.
Household Goods				
Floor coverings, expenditures on	yr	44	1999	30r
Furniture, expenditures on	yr	335	1999	30r
Household furnishings and equipment purchases	yr	1372	1999	30c
Household textiles, expenditures on	yr	89	1999	30r
Laundry and cleaning supplies, expenditures on	yr	113	1999	30r
Housing				
Home, 2200 sq ft, 4-br, 2-bath, 2-car garage, average		273626	2000	47c
Home price, existing, ave		160100	10/00	90r
Home value, median		104000	2001	53s
Household operation expenditures	yr	1017	1999	30c
Housekeeping supplies purchases	yr	407	1999	30c
Housing, expenditures on	yr	13963	1999	30c
Maintenance, repairs, insurance expenditures	yr	699	1999	30r
Monthly rental value of owned home	mos	505	1999	30r
Owned dwellings, expenditures own	yr	5380	1999	30c
Rent expenditures	yr	2744	1999	30c
Rental unit, 1 bedroom, with utilities	mos	579	4/01	41c
Rental unit, 2 bedroom, with utilities	mos	722	4/01	41c
Rental unit, 3 bedroom, with utilities	mos	991	4/01	41c
Rental unit, 4 bedroom, with utilities	mos	1149	4/01	41c
Shelter, expenditures on	yr	8443	1999	30c
Insurance and Pensions				
Life and other personal insurance purchases	yr	341	1999	30c
Medigap health insurance, Plan H	yr	2887	2000	69s
Medigap health insurance, Plan I	yr	3302	2000	69s
Medigap health insurance, Plan J	yr	3889	2000	69s
Pensions and Social Security, expenditures on	yr	3474	1999	30c
Personal insurance and pensions, expenditures on	yr	3815	1999	30c
Legal Fees				
Divorce, filing fee		65.00-85.00	4/01	35s
Driver's license fee	renew	15.00	1999	48s
Driver's license fee	orig	20.00	1999	48s
Personal Goods				
Personal care products and services purchases	yr	408	1999	30c
Personal Services				
Personal services, household, expenditures on	yr	258	1999	30r
Pets				
Pets, toys, and playground equipment, expenditures on	yr	306	1999	30r
Restaurant Food				
Cheeseburger, 1/4-lb, large fries, medium soft drink, excl tax		4.30	1999	40c
Taxes				
Federal income taxes paid	yr	2047	1999	30r
Personal taxes, expenditures on	yr	2554	1999	30r
Property taxes paid	yr	726	1999	30r
State and local income taxes paid	yr	363	1999	30r
Transportation				
Bus fare, one-way	trip	1.25	2000	1c
Cars and trucks, new, expenditures on	yr	1648	1999	30r
Cars and trucks, used, expenditures on	yr	1651	1999	30r
Commuter rail, one-way	trip	2.00	2000	2c
Diesel at the pump	gal	1.26	10/99	73s
Gasoline and motor oil purchases	yr	1085	1999	30c
Gasoline before-tax price (cents)	gal	101.90	10/00	43s
Heavy rail transit fare, one-way	trip	1.25	2000	2c
Maintenance and repair expenditures	yr	621	1999	30r
Parking at airport, lowest rate	day	10.00	2000	46c

Values are in dollars or fractions of dollars. In the column headed *Ref*, references are shown to sources. Each reference is followed by a letter. These refer to the geographical level for which data were reported: s=State, r=Region, and c=City or metro. The abbreviation *ex* is used to mean *except* or *excluding*; *exp* stands for expenditures. For other abbreviations and further explanations, please see the Introduction.

Miami, FL - continued

Item	Per	Value	Date	Ref.
Transportation				
Public transportation, expenditures on	yr	446	1999	30c
Transportation purchases	yr	7425	1999	30c
Vehicle expenses, miscellaneous, purchases	yr	3054	1999	30c
Vehicle insurance payments	yr	696	1999	30r
Vehicle purchases (net outlay)	yr	2840	1999	30c
Vehicle purchases (net outlay)	yr	3354	1999	30r
Vehicle rental, lease expenditures	yr	352	1999	30r
Travel				
Hotel room	night	110.57	2/01	95s
Utilities				
Electrical bill, average	mos	86.33	9/00	9s
Electricity, expenditures on	yr	1115	1999	30r
Electricity, summer, 250 KWh	mos	22.56	2/96	97c
Electricity, summer, 500 KWh	mos	39.34	2/96	97c
Electricity, summer, 750 KWh	mos	56.26	2/96	97c
Electricity, summer, 1000 KWh	mos	75.64	2/96	97c
Electricity cost, average	KWh	6.80	9/00	9s
Water and other public services, expenditures on	yr	298	1999	30r
Weddings				
Wedding (national average cost)		19936	2000	33r
Wedding (regional average total cost)		16293	1997	110r
Attendants' gifts		321	1998	33r
Bridal attendants' apparel (5 persons)		824	2000	33r
Bride's headpiece/veil		173	1998	33r
Bride's wedding dress		859	1998	33r
Clergy, religious facility fee		242	1998	33r
Engagement ring		3177	1998	33r
Flowers		789	1998	33r
Groom's formalwear rental		99	2000	33r
Limousine		410	1998	33r
Marriage license cost		56.00-88.50	4/01	35s
Men's formalwear (ushers, best man)		469	2000	33r
Mother of bride apparel		241	2000	33r
Music		866	1998	33r
Photography and videography		1368	1998	33r
Rehearsal dinner		728	1998	33r
Wedding invitations and announcements		341	1998	33r
Wedding reception		7968	2000	33r
Wedding rings (bride and groom)		1060	1998	33r

Miami-Fort Lauderdale, FL

Item	Per	Value	Date	Ref.
Alcoholic Beverages				
Alcoholic beverage purchases	yr	253	1999	30r
Malt beverages, all types, all sizes, any origin	16 oz	0.96	7/01	11r
Appliances				
Major appliances, expenditures on	yr	172	1999	30r
Small appliances, housewares, expenditures on	yr	81	1999	30r
Banking and Money				
Mortgage interest and charges paid	yr	2039	1999	30r
Mortgage principal paid on owned property	yr	1026	1999	30r
Vehicle finance charges paid	yr	365	1999	30r
Charity				
Cash contributions, expenditures	yr	1127	1999	30r
Child Care				
Child raising cost, total, age 0-2	yr	8540	1999	60r
Child raising cost, total, age 3-5	yr	8780	1999	60r
Child raising cost, total, age 6-8	yr	8820	1999	60r
Child raising cost, total, age 9-11	yr	8800	1999	60r
Child raising cost, total, age 12-14	yr	9510	1999	60r
Child raising cost, total, age 15-17	yr	9740	1999	60r
Child's child care and education, age 0-2	yr	1380	1999	60r
Child's child care and education, age 3-5	yr	1520	1999	60r
Child's child care and education, age 6-8	yr	990	1999	60r

Miami-Fort Lauderdale, FL - continued

Item	Per	Value	Date	Ref.
Child Care - continued				
Child's child care and education, age 9-11	yr	650	1999	60r
Child's child care and education, age 12-14	yr	490	1999	60r
Child's child care and education, age 15-17	yr	840	1999	60r
Child's clothing, age 0-2	yr	480	1999	60r
Child's clothing, age 3-5	yr	470	1999	60r
Child's clothing, age 6-8	yr	520	1999	60r
Child's clothing, age 9-11	yr	570	1999	60r
Child's clothing, age 12-14	yr	950	1999	60r
Child's clothing, age 15-17	yr	850	1999	60r
Child's food, age 0-2	yr	1000	1999	60r
Child's food, age 3-5	yr	1160	1999	60r
Child's food, age 6-8	yr	1490	1999	60r
Child's food, age 9-11	yr	1770	1999	60r
Child's food, age 12-14	yr	1770	1999	60r
Child's food, age 15-17	yr	1980	1999	60r
Child's health care, age 0-2	yr	620	1999	60r
Child's health care, age 3-5	yr	590	1999	60r
Child's health care, age 6-8	yr	680	1999	60r
Child's health care, age 9-11	yr	720	1999	60r
Child's health care, age 12-14	yr	730	1999	60r
Child's health care, age 15-17	yr	760	1999	60r
Child's housing, age 0-2	yr	3070	1999	60r
Child's housing, age 3-5	yr	3050	1999	60r
Child's housing, age 6-8	yr	3010	1999	60r
Child's housing, age 9-11	yr	2850	1999	60r
Child's housing, age 12-14	yr	3040	1999	60r
Child's housing, age 15-17	yr	2650	1999	60r
Child's personal care, reading, age 0-2	yr	910	1999	60r
Child's personal care, reading, age 3-5	yr	930	1999	60r
Child's personal care, reading, age 6-8	yr	960	1999	60r
Child's personal care, reading, age 9-11	yr	1000	1999	60r
Child's personal care, reading, age 12-14	yr	1170	1999	60r
Child's personal care, reading, age 15-17	yr	950	1999	60r
Clothing				
Apparel and services purchases	yr	1610	1999	30r
Boys, 2 to 15, expenditures on	yr	89	1999	30r
Children under 2, expenditures on	yr	79	1999	30r
Footwear, expenditures on	yr	283	1999	30r
Girls, 2 to 15, expenditures on	yr	103	1999	30r
Men and boys, expenditures on	yr	351	1999	30r
Men, 16 and over, expenditures on	yr	262	1999	30r
Women, 16 and over, expenditures on	yr	538	1999	30r
Communications				
Cable modem installation, Adelphi		54.90	6/99	103s
Cable modem installation, Comcast		95.00	6/99	103s
Cable modem installation, Media One		100.00	6/99	103s
Cable modem installation, Time Warner		75.00-225.00	6/99	103s
Cable modem rate, cable subscriber, Adelphi	mos	34.95	6/99	103s
Cable modem rate, cable subscriber, Comcast	mos	39.95	6/99	103s
Cable modem rate, cable subscriber, Media One	mos	34.95-39.95	6/99	103s
Cable modem rate, cable subscriber, Time Warner	mos	39.95-49.95	6/99	103s
Cable modem rate, non-cable subscriber, Adelphi	mos	44.95	6/99	103s
Cable modem rate, non-cable subscriber, Comcast	mos	49.95	6/99	103s
Cable modem rate, non-cable subscriber, Media One	mos	49.95	6/99	103s
Cable modem rate, non-cable subscriber, Time Warner	mos	39.95-54.95	6/99	103s
Phone line, single, business, field visit	inst.	56.00	12/97	17s
Phone line, single, business, no field visit	inst.	56.00	12/97	17s
Phone line, single, residence, field visit	inst.	40.00	12/97	17s
Phone line, single, residence, no field visit	inst.	40.00	12/97	17s
Postage and stationery, expenditures on	yr	104	1999	30r
Postal rate, express mail, up to half-pound		12.45	7/01	108r
Postal rate, letter, first class, first ounce		0.34	7/01	108r
Postal rate, letter, two ounces		0.57	7/01	108r

Values are in dollars or fractions of dollars. In the column headed *Ref*, references are shown to sources. Each reference is followed by a letter. These refer to the geographical level for which data were reported: s=State, r=Region, and c=City or metro. The abbreviation *ex* is used to mean *except* or *excluding*; *exp* stands for *expenditures*. For other abbreviations and further explanations, please see the Introduction.

Miami-Fort Lauderdale, FL - continued

Item	Per	Value	Date	Ref.
Communications				
Postal rate, post card		0.21	7/01	108r
Postal rate, priority mail, two pounds		3.95	7/01	108r
Postal rate, priority mail, up to one pound		3.50	7/01	108r
Telephone services, expenditures on	yr	860	1999	30r
Education				
Board, 4-year private college/university	yr	2236	1996	38s
Board, 4-year public college/university	yr	2295	1996	38s
Education expenditures	yr	431	1999	30r
Room, 4-year private college/university	yr	2428	1996	38s
Room, 4-year public college/university	yr	2193	1996	38s
Total cost, 4-year private college/university	yr	15028	1996	38s
Total cost, 4-year public college/university	yr	6254	1996	38s
Tuition, 2-year public college/university, in state	yr	1103	1996	38s
Tuition, 4-year private college/university, in state	yr	10364	1996	38s
Tuition, 4-year public college/university	yr	1767	1996	38s
Energy and Fuels				
Electricity	500 KWhs	47.29	7/01	11r
Electricity	KWh	0.09	7/01	11r
Fuel oil #2	gal	1.43	7/01	11r
Fuel oil and other fuels, expenditures on	yr	45	1999	30r
Gas, natural, commercial rate	1000 cf	8.44	11/00	88s
Gasoline, all types	gal	1.60	7/01	11r
Gasoline, unleaded midgrade	gal	1.65	7/01	11r
Gasoline, unleaded premium	gal	1.74	7/01	11r
Natural gas, expenditures on	yr	164	1999	30r
Utility (piped) gas, therm		1.01	7/01	11r
Utility (piped) gas, 40 therms		44.29	7/01	11r
Utility (piped) gas, 100 therms		97.44	7/01	11r
Entertainment				
Entertainment purchases	yr	1574	1999	30r
Fees and admissions paid	yr	371	1999	30r
Reading purchases	yr	121	1999	30r
Television, radios, sound equipment, expenditures on	yr	561	1999	30r
Funerals				
Total cost of funeral		5922.53	1/99	78r
Acknowledgement cards		63.43	1/99	78r
Casket		2258.77	1/99	78r
Cosmetology, hair, other preparation		127.09	1/99	78r
Embalming		393.49	1/99	78r
Funeral at funeral home		367.50	1/99	78r
Hearse (local)		169.66	1/99	78r
Professional service charges		1211.32	1/99	78r
Service car/van		80.69	1/99	78r
Transfer of remains to funeral home		144.25	1/99	78r
Vault		803.50	1/99	78r
Visitation/viewing		302.83	1/99	78r
Groceries				
American processed cheese	lb	3.50	7/01	11r
Bakery products, expenditures on	yr	261	1999	30r
Bananas	lb	0.47	7/01	11r
Beans, dried, any type, all sizes	lb	0.63	7/01	11r
Beef for stew, boneless	lb	2.86	7/01	11r
Beef, expenditures on	yr	210	1999	30r
Bologna, all beef or mixed	lb	2.29	7/01	11r
Bread, French	lb	1.66	7/01	11r
Bread, white, pan	lb	0.87	7/01	11r
Bread, whole wheat, pan	lb	1.38	7/01	11r
Broccoli	lb	1.04	7/01	11r
Butter, salted, grade AA, stick	lb	2.26	7/01	11r
Butter, yoghurt, cheese, etc, expenditures on	yr	170	1999	30r
Cabbage	lb	0.42	7/01	11r
Cereals and cereal products, expenditures on	yr	140	1999	30r
Cheddar cheese, natural	lb	3.75	7/01	11r
Chicken breast, bone-in	lb	1.85	7/01	11r

Miami-Fort Lauderdale, FL - continued

Item	Per	Value	Date	Ref.
Groceries - continued				
Chicken legs, bone-in	lb	1.34	7/01	11r
Chicken, fresh, whole	lb	1.05	7/01	11r
Chops, boneless,	lb	4.13	7/01	11r
Chuck roast, graded and ungraded, excl U.S. prime and choice	lb	2.35	7/01	11r
Chuck roast, U.S. choice, boneless	lb	2.67	7/01	11r
Coffee, 100%, ground roast, all sizes	lb	2.88	7/01	11r
Coffee, instant, plain, regular, all sizes	16 oz	9.25	7/01	11r
Cola, non diet,	2 liter	1.11	7/01	11r
Crackers, soda, salted	lb	1.70	7/01	11r
Dairy product purchases	yr	282	1999	30r
Eggs, expenditures on	yr	32	1999	30r
Fats and oils, expenditures on	yr	79	1999	30r
Fish and seafood, expenditures on	yr	99	1999	30r
Flour, white, all purpose	lb	0.32	7/01	11r
Food (excl fruit and vegetables), eaten at home, purchases	yr	815	1999	30r
Food cooked on trips, expenditures on	yr	36	1999	30r
Food purchases	yr	4533	1999	30r
Food purchases, eaten away from home	yr	1873	1999	30r
Food purchases, food eaten at home	yr	2660	1999	30r
Fresh fruits, expenditures on	yr	128	1999	30r
Fresh milk and cream, expenditures on	yr	112	1999	30r
Fresh vegetables, expenditures on	yr	131	1999	30r
Fruit and vegetable purchases	yr	438	1999	30r
Grapefruit	lb	0.59	7/01	11r
Grapes, Thompson, seedless	lb	2.12	7/01	11r
Ground beef, 100% beef	lb	1.76	7/01	11r
Ground beef, lean and extra lean	lb	2.60	7/01	11r
Ground chuck, 100% beef	lb	2.08	7/01	11r
Ham, boneless, excl canned	lb	2.71	7/01	11r
Ham, rump or shank half, bone-in, smoked	lb	2.19	7/01	11r
Ice cream, prepackaged, bulk, regular	1/2 gal	3.93	7/01	11r
Lemons	lb	1.32	7/01	11r
Lettuce, iceberg	lb	0.76	7/01	11r
Milk, fresh, low fat,	gal	2.75	7/01	11r
Milk, fresh, whole, fortified	gal	2.97	7/01	11r
Nonalcoholic beverages, expenditures on	yr	228	1999	30r
Orange juice, frozen concentrate	16 oz	1.95	7/01	11r
Oranges, Navel	lb	0.73	7/01	11r
Oranges, Valencia	lb	0.55	7/01	11r
Peanut butter, creamy, all sizes	lb	1.83	7/01	11r
Pears, Anjou	lb	0.98	7/01	11r
Pork chops, center cut, bone-in	lb	3.33	7/01	11r
Pork sausage, fresh, loose	lb	2.59	7/01	11r
Pork shoulder picnic, bone-in, smoked	lb	1.12	7/01	11r
Pork, expenditures on	yr	162	1999	30r
Potato chips	16 oz	3.59	7/01	11r
Potatoes, frozen, french fried	lb	1.00	7/01	11r
Potatoes, white, all types	lb	0.44	7/01	11r
Poultry, expenditures on	yr	137	1999	30r
Processed fruits, expenditures on	yr	97	1999	30r
Processed vegetables, expenditures on	yr	82	1999	30r
Rice, white, long grain, uncooked	lb	0.51	7/01	11r
Round roast, graded and ungraded, excl U.S. prime and choice	lb	2.96	7/01	11r
Round steak, graded and ungraded, excl U.S. prime and choice	lb	3.11	7/01	11r
Sirloin steak, graded and ungraded, excl U.S. prime and choice	lb	4.23	7/01	11r
Spaghetti and macaroni	lb	0.78	7/01	11r
Steak, round, U.S. choice, boneless	lb	3.56	7/01	11r
Steak, sirloin, U.S. choice, boneless	lb	5.65	7/01	11r
Strawberries, dry pint	12 oz	1.50	7/01	11r
Sugar and other sweets, expenditures on	yr	99	1999	30r
Sugar, white, 33-80 ounce package	lb	0.39	7/01	11r
Sugar, white, all sizes	lb	0.42	7/01	11r
Tobacco products and smoking supplies purchases	yr	288	1999	30r
Tomatoes, field grown	lb	1.43	7/01	11r
Tuna, light, chunk	lb	1.77	7/01	11r
Turkey, frozen, whole	lb	1.05	7/01	11r

Values are in dollars or fractions of dollars. In the column headed *Ref*, references are shown to sources. Each reference is followed by a letter. These refer to the geographical level for which data were reported: s=State, r=Region, and c=City or metro. The abbreviation *ex* is used to mean *except* or *excluding*; *exp* stands for expenditures. For other abbreviations and further explanations, please see the Introduction.

Miami-Fort Lauderdale, FL - continued

Item	Per	Value	Date	Ref.
Goods and Services				
B&B Japanese maple (acer japonicum)	gal	49.98-129.00	4/00	93r
Boxwood (buxus)	2 gal	12.99-16.99	4/00	93r
Daylilly (hemerocallis)	gal	4.99-8.99	4/00	93r
Flat of annuals		11.00-13.92	4/00	93r
Fountain grass (pennisetum)	gal	5.98-7.98	4/00	93r
Hanging basket (10 in)		7.99-14.98	4/00	93r
Hardy geranium (geranium)	gal	5.98-8.00	4/00	93r
Hosta (hosta)	gal	4.99-10.98	4/00	93r
Lilac (syrubga vulgaris)	2 gal	12.99-21.99	4/00	93r
Rhododendron (rhododendron)	2 gal	14.99-24.99	4/00	93r
Sage (salvia)	gal	5.98-6.99	4/00	93r
Wintercreeper euonymus (euonymus fortunei)	2 gal	7.99-89.99	4/00	93r
Hunting license	yr	12.50	4/01	34s
Health Care				
Cardiac catheterization, ave hospital/physician charges		15060	1998	77s
Childbirth, Cesarean delivery		11587	1997	13r
Childbirth, vaginal delivery		6725	1997	13r
Drugs, expenditures on	yr	399	1999	30r
Health care purchases	yr	1971	1999	30r
Health insurance expenditures	yr	933	1999	30r
Hysterectomy, laproscopically-assisted, ave hospital/physician charges		14760	1998	76s
Hysterectomy, vaginal, ave hospital and physician charges		11320	1998	76s
Medicaid dispensing fee		4.23	1999	87s
Medical services expenditures	yr	547	1999	30r
Medical supplies, expenditures on	yr	91	1999	30r
Plastic surgery, breast augmentation		2870	2000	7r
Plastic surgery, breast lift		3649	2000	7r
Plastic surgery, facelift		5008	2000	7r
Plastic surgery, hair transplantation		3425	2000	7r
Plastic surgery, lip augmentation		1227	2000	7r
Plastic surgery, lower body lift		4793	2000	7r
Plastic surgery, thigh lift		3862	2000	7r
Household Goods				
Floor coverings, expenditures on	yr	44	1999	30r
Furniture, expenditures on	yr	335	1999	30r
Household furnishings and equipment purchases	yr	1328	1999	30r
Household textiles, expenditures on	yr	89	1999	30r
Laundry and cleaning supplies, expenditures on	yr	113	1999	30r
Housing				
Home price, existing, ave		160100	10/00	90r
Home value, median		104000	2001	53s
Household operation expenditures	yr	553	1999	30r
Housekeeping supplies purchases	yr	473	1999	30r
Housing, expenditures on	yr	10303	1999	30r
Maintenance, repairs, insurance expenditures	yr	699	1999	30r
Monthly rental value of owned home	mos	505	1999	30r
Owned dwellings, expenditures own	yr	3465	1999	30r
Rent expenditures	yr	1641	1999	30r
Shelter, expenditures on	yr	5467	1999	30r
Insurance and Pensions				
Life and other personal insurance purchases	yr	414	1999	30r
Medigap health insurance, Plan H	yr	2887	2000	69s

Miami-Fort Lauderdale, FL - continued

Item	Per	Value	Date	Ref.
Insurance and Pensions - continued				
Medigap health insurance, Plan I	yr	3302	2000	69s
Medigap health insurance, Plan J	yr	3889	2000	69s
Pensions and Social Security, expenditures on	yr	2635	1999	30r
Personal insurance and pensions, expenditures on	yr	3048	1999	30r
Legal Fees				
Divorce, filing fee		65.00-85.00	4/01	35s
Driver's license fee	renew	15.00	1999	48s
Driver's license fee	orig	20.00	1999	48s
Personal Goods				
Personal care products and services purchases	yr	393	1999	30r
Personal Services				
Personal services, household, expenditures on	yr	258	1999	30r
Pets				
Pets, toys, and playground equipment, expenditures on	yr	306	1999	30r
Taxes				
Federal income taxes paid	yr	2047	1999	30r
Personal taxes, expenditures on	yr	2554	1999	30r
Property taxes paid	yr	726	1999	30r
State and local income taxes paid	yr	363	1999	30r
Transportation				
Cars and trucks, new, expenditures on	yr	1648	1999	30r
Cars and trucks, used, expenditures on	yr	1651	1999	30r
Diesel at the pump	gal	1.26	10/99	73s
Gasoline and motor oil purchases	yr	1052	1999	30r
Gasoline before-tax price (cents)	gal	101.90	10/00	43s
Household transportation expenditures	yr	6684	97-1998	102c
Maintenance and repair expenditures	yr	621	1999	30r
Public transportation, expenditures on	yr	298	1999	30r
Transportation purchases	yr	6738	1999	30r
Vehicle expenses, miscellaneous, purchases	yr	2033	1999	30r
Vehicle insurance payments	yr	696	1999	30r
Vehicle purchases (net outlay)	yr	3354	1999	30r
Vehicle rental, lease expenditures	yr	352	1999	30r
Travel				
Hotel room	night	110.57	2/01	95s
Utilities				
Electrical bill, average	mos	86.33	9/00	9s
Electricity, expenditures on	yr	1115	1999	30r
Electricity cost, average	KWh	6.80	9/00	9s
Water and other public services, expenditures on	yr	298	1999	30r
Weddings				
Wedding (national average cost)		19936	2000	33r
Wedding (regional average total cost)		16293	1997	110r
Attendants' gifts		321	1998	33r
Bridal attendants' apparel (5 persons)		824	2000	33r
Bride's headpiece/veil		173	1998	33r
Bride's wedding dress		859	1998	33r
Clergy, religious facility fee		242	1998	33r
Engagement ring		3177	1998	33r
Flowers		789	1998	33r
Groom's formalwear rental		99	2000	33r
Limousine		410	1998	33r
Marriage license cost		56.00-88.50	4/01	35s
Men's formalwear (ushers, best man)		469	2000	33r
Mother of bride apparel		241	2000	33r
Music		866	1998	33r
Photography and videography		1368	1998	33r
Rehearsal dinner		728	1998	33r
Wedding invitations and announcements		341	1998	33r

Values are in dollars or fractions of dollars. In the column headed *Ref*, references are shown to sources. Each reference is followed by a letter. These refer to the geographical level for which data were reported: s=State, r=Region, and c=City or metro. The abbreviation *ex* is used to mean *except* or *excluding*; *exp* stands for *expenditures*. For other abbreviations and further explanations, please see the Introduction.

Miami-Fort Lauderdale, FL - continued

Item	Per	Value	Date	Ref.
Weddings				
Wedding reception		7968	2000	33r
Wedding rings (bride and groom)		1060	1998	33r

Middlesex-Somerset-Hunterdon, NJ

Item	Per	Value	Date	Ref.
Average annual expenditures	yr	37971	1999	30r
Alcoholic Beverages				
Alcoholic beverage purchases	yr	368	1999	30r
Wine, red and white table, all sizes, any origin	liter	9.64	7/01	11r
Appliances				
Major appliances, expenditures on	yr	194	1999	30r
Small appliances, housewares, expenditures on	yr	93	1999	30r
Banking and Money				
Mortgage interest and charges paid	yr	2622	1999	30r
Mortgage principal paid on owned property	yr	1262	1999	30r
Vehicle finance charges paid	yr	240	1999	30r
Charity				
Cash contributions, expenditures	yr	1001	1999	30r
Child Care				
Child raising cost, total, age 0-2	yr	8670	1999	60r
Child raising cost, total, age 3-5	yr	8910	1999	60r
Child raising cost, total, age 6-8	yr	9040	1999	60r
Child raising cost, total, age 9-11	yr	9100	1999	60r
Child raising cost, total, age 12-14	yr	9890	1999	60r
Child raising cost, total, age 15-17	yr	10010	1999	60r
Child's child care and education, age 0-2	yr	1070	1999	60r
Child's child care and education, age 3-5	yr	1190	1999	60r
Child's child care and education, age 6-8	yr	740	1999	60r
Child's child care and education, age 9-11	yr	470	1999	60r
Child's child care and education, age 12-14	yr	350	1999	60r
Child's child care and education, age 15-17	yr	590	1999	60r
Child's clothing, age 0-2	yr	480	1999	60r
Child's clothing, age 3-5	yr	470	1999	60r
Child's clothing, age 6-8	yr	520	1999	60r
Child's clothing, age 9-11	yr	570	1999	60r
Child's clothing, age 12-14	yr	970	1999	60r
Child's clothing, age 15-17	yr	870	1999	60r
Child's food, age 0-2	yr	1130	1999	60r
Child's food, age 3-5	yr	1290	1999	60r
Child's food, age 6-8	yr	1640	1999	60r
Child's food, age 9-11	yr	1930	1999	60r
Child's food, age 12-14	yr	1940	1999	60r
Child's food, age 15-17	yr	2150	1999	60r
Child's health care, age 0-2	yr	550	1999	60r
Child's health care, age 3-5	yr	530	1999	60r
Child's health care, age 6-8	yr	610	1999	60r
Child's health care, age 9-11	yr	650	1999	60r
Child's health care, age 12-14	yr	660	1999	60r
Child's health care, age 15-17	yr	690	1999	60r
Child's housing, age 0-2	yr	3555	1999	60r
Child's housing, age 3-5	yr	3530	1999	60r
Child's housing, age 6-8	yr	3490	1999	60r
Child's housing, age 9-11	yr	3340	1999	60r
Child's housing, age 12-14	yr	3530	1999	60r
Child's housing, age 15-17	yr	3140	1999	60r
Child's personal care, reading, age 0-2	yr	920	1999	60r
Child's personal care, reading, age 3-5	yr	950	1999	60r
Child's personal care, reading, age 6-8	yr	980	1999	60r
Child's personal care, reading, age 9-11	yr	1020	1999	60r
Child's personal care, reading, age 12-14	yr	1190	1999	60r
Child's personal care, reading, age 15-17	yr	970	1999	60r
Clothing				
Apparel and services purchases	yr	1831	1999	30r
Boys, 2 to 15, expenditures on	yr	92	1999	30r
Children under 2, expenditures on	yr	63	1999	30r
Footwear, expenditures on	yr	300	1999	30r

Middlesex-Somerset-Hunterdon, NJ - continued

Item	Per	Value	Date	Ref.
Clothing - continued				
Girls, 2 to 15, expenditures on	yr	101	1999	30r
Men and boys, expenditures on	yr	446	1999	30r
Men, 16 and over, expenditures on	yr	354	1999	30r
Women, 16 and over, expenditures on	yr	584	1999	30r
Communications				
Cable modem installation, Adelphi		54.90	6/99	103s
Cable modem installation, Comcast		95.00	6/99	103s
Cable modem rate, cable subscriber, Adelphi	mos	34.95	6/99	103s
Cable modem rate, cable subscriber, Comcast	mos	39.95	6/99	103s
Cable modem rate, non-cable subscriber, Adelphi	mos	44.95	6/99	103s
Cable modem rate, non-cable subscriber, Comcast	mos	49.95	6/99	103s
Phone line, single, business, field visit	inst.	98.50	12/97	17s
Phone line, single, business, no field visit	inst.	79.50	12/97	17s
Phone line, single, residence, field visit	inst.	56.50	12/97	17s
Phone line, single, residence, no field visit	inst.	42.00	12/97	17s
Postage and stationery, expenditures on	yr	138	1999	30r
Postal rate, express mail, up to half-pound		12.45	7/01	108r
Postal rate, letter, first class, first ounce		0.34	7/01	108r
Postal rate, letter, two ounces		0.57	7/01	108r
Postal rate, post card		0.21	7/01	108r
Postal rate, priority mail, two pounds		3.95	7/01	108r
Postal rate, priority mail, up to one pound		3.50	7/01	108r
Telephone services, expenditures on	yr	830	1999	30r
Education				
Board, 4-year private college/university	yr	2959	1996	38s
Board, 4-year public college/university	yr	2052	1996	38s
Education expenditures	yr	877	1999	30r
Room, 4-year private college/university	yr	3226	1996	38s
Room, 4-year public college/university	yr	3101	1996	38s
Total cost, 4-year private college/university	yr	19751	1996	38s
Total cost, 4-year public college/university	yr	9125	1996	38s
Tuition, 2-year public college/university, in state	yr	1878	1996	38s
Tuition, 4-year private college/university, in state	yr	13566	1996	38s
Tuition, 4-year public college/university	yr	3972	1996	38s
Energy and Fuels				
Electricity	KWh	0.12	7/01	11r
Fuel oil #2	gal	1.31	7/01	11r
Fuel oil and other fuels, expenditures on	yr	207	1999	30r
Gas, natural, commercial rate	1000 cf	5.98	11/00	88s
Gasoline, all types	gal	1.80	7/01	11r
Gasoline, unleaded midgrade	gal	1.85	7/01	11r
Gasoline, unleaded premium	gal	1.91	7/01	11r
Gasoline, unleaded regular	gal	1.71	7/01	11r
Natural gas, expenditures on	yr	368	1999	30r
Utility (piped) gas, therm		1.08	7/01	11r
Utility (piped) gas, 40 therms		50.87	7/01	11r
Utility (piped) gas, 100 therms		111.06	7/01	11r
Entertainment				
Entertainment purchases	yr	1821	1999	30r
Fees and admissions paid	yr	511	1999	30r
Television, radios, sound equipment, expenditures on	yr	650	1999	30r
Funerals				
Total cost of funeral		5813.50	1/99	78r
Acknowledgement cards		28.32	1/99	78r
Casket		2082.20	1/99	78r
Cosmetology, hair, other preparation		169.59	1/99	78r
Embalming		465.60	1/99	78r
Funeral at funeral home		339.56	1/99	78r
Hearse (local)		183.96	1/99	78r
Professional service charges		1157.85	1/99	78r
Service car/van		100.41	1/99	78r
Transfer of remains to funeral home		158.66	1/99	78r
Vault		766.31	1/99	78r

Values are in dollars or fractions of dollars. In the column headed *Ref*, references are shown to sources. Each reference is followed by a letter. These refer to the geographical level for which data were reported: s=State, r=Region, and c=City or metro. The abbreviation *ex* is used to mean *except* or *excluding*; *exp* stands for *expenditures*. For other abbreviations and further explanations, please see the Introduction.

Middlesex-Somerset-Hunterdon, NJ - continued

Item	Per	Value	Date	Ref.
Funerals				
Visitation/viewing		361.04	1/99	78r
Groceries				
Apples, red delicious	lb	0.95	7/01	11r
Bacon, sliced	lb	3.44	7/01	11r
Bakery products, expenditures on	yr	310	1999	30r
Bananas	lb	0.55	7/01	11r
Beef, expenditures on	yr	236	1999	30r
Bread, white, pan	lb	1.09	7/01	11r
Butter, yoghurt, cheese, etc, expenditures on	yr	214	1999	30r
Cereals and bakery product purchases	yr	474	1999	30r
Cereals and cereal products, expenditures on	yr	164	1999	30r
Chicken legs, bone-in	lb	1.23	7/01	11r
Chicken, fresh, whole	lb	1.13	7/01	11r
Chuck roast, U.S. choice, boneless	lb	2.79	7/01	11r
Coffee, 100%, ground roast, all sizes	lb	3.40	7/01	11r
Dairy product purchases	yr	342	1999	30r
Eggs, expenditures on	yr	34	1999	30r
Eggs, grade A, large	dozen	0.82	7/01	11r
Fats and oils, expenditures on	yr	80	1999	30r
Fish and seafood, expenditures on	yr	123	1999	30r
Food (excl fruit and vegetables), eaten at home, purchases	yr	838	1999	30r
Food cooked on trips, expenditures on	yr	48	1999	30r
Food purchases	yr	5314	1999	30r
Food purchases, eaten away from home	yr	2313	1999	30r
Food purchases, food eaten at home	yr	3001	1999	30r
Fresh fruits, expenditures on	yr	169	1999	30r
Fresh milk and cream, expenditures on	yr	128	1999	30r
Fresh vegetables, expenditures on	yr	164	1999	30r
Grapefruit	lb	0.67	7/01	11r
Grapes, Thompson, seedless	lb	2.18	7/01	11r
Ground beef, lean and extra lean	lb	2.66	7/01	11r
Ground chuck, 100% beef	lb	2.04	7/01	11r
Lettuce, iceberg	lb	0.76	7/01	11r
Meats, poultry, fish, and egg purchases	yr	808	1999	30r
Nonalcoholic beverages, expenditures on	yr	225	1999	30r
Orange juice, frozen concentrate	16 oz	1.88	7/01	11r
Oranges, Navel	lb	0.79	7/01	11r
Oranges, Valencia	lb	0.56	7/01	11r
Peaches	lb	1.16	7/01	11r
Peanut butter, creamy, all sizes	lb	2.01	7/01	11r
Pears, Anjou	lb	1.16	7/01	11r
Pork chops, center cut, bone-in	lb	3.57	7/01	11r
Pork, expenditures on	yr	146	1999	30r
Potato chips	16 oz	3.37	7/01	11r
Potatoes, white, all types	lb	0.42	7/01	11r
Poultry, expenditures on	yr	158	1999	30r
Processed fruits, expenditures on	yr	124	1999	30r
Processed vegetables, expenditures on	yr	82	1999	30r
Round roast, U.S. choice, boneless	lb	3.04	7/01	11r
Spaghetti and macaroni	lb	1.04	7/01	11r
Steak, sirloin, U.S. choice, boneless	lb	5.39	7/01	11r
Strawberries, dry pint	12 oz	1.51	7/01	11r
Sugar and other sweets, expenditures on	yr	110	1999	30r
Sugar, white, 33-80 ounce package	lb	0.46	7/01	11r
Sugar, white, all sizes	lb	0.47	7/01	11r
Tobacco products and smoking supplies purchases	yr	309	1999	30r
Yogurt, natural, fruit flavored	8 oz	0.79	7/01	11r
Goods and Services				
B&B Japanese maple (acer japonicum)	gal	38.99-125.00	4/00	93r
Boxwood (buxus)	2 gal	15.99-49.95	4/00	93r
Daylilly (hemerocallis)	gal	4.95	4/00	93r
Flat of annuals		8.00-14.99	4/00	93r
Fountain grass (pennisetum)	gal	6.99-9.99	4/00	93r

Middlesex-Somerset-Hunterdon, NJ - continued

Item	Per	Value	Date	Ref.
Goods and Services - continued				
Hanging basket (10 in)		12.95-19.99	4/00	93r
Hardy geranium (geranium)	gal	6.95-7.99	4/00	93r
Hosta (hosta)	gal	4.95	4/00	93r
Lilac (syrubga vulgaris)	2 gal	17.99-74.95	4/00	93r
Miscellaneous purchases	yr	872	1999	30r
Rhododendron (rhododendron)	2 gal	23.99-54.95	4/00	93r
Sage (salvia)	gal	6.95-7.99	4/00	93r
Wintercreeper euonymus (euonymus fortunei)	2 gal	14.99-23.95	4/00	93r
Hunting license	yr	22.50	4/01	34s
Health Care				
Cardiac catheterization, ave hospital/ physician charges		14680	1998	77s
Childbirth, Cesarean delivery		14716	1997	13r
Childbirth, vaginal delivery		8541	1997	13r
Drugs, expenditures on	yr	296	1999	30r
Health care purchases	yr	1788	1999	30r
Health insurance expenditures	yr	875	1999	30r
Hysterectomy, laproscopically-assisted, ave hospital/physician charges		18330	1998	76s
Hysterectomy, vaginal, ave hospital and physician charges		13620	1998	76s
Medicaid dispensing fee		3.73-4.07	1999	87s
Medical services expenditures	yr	516	1999	30r
Medical supplies, expenditures on	yr	102	1999	30r
Plastic surgery, breast augmentation		4232	2000	7r
Plastic surgery, breast lift		4605	2000	7r
Plastic surgery, facelift		6964	2000	7r
Plastic surgery, hair transplantation		4193	2000	7r
Plastic surgery, lip augmentation		1675	2000	7r
Plastic surgery, lower body lift		6611	2000	7r
Plastic surgery, thigh lift		4751	2000	7r
Household Goods				
Floor coverings, expenditures on	yr	59	1999	30r
Furniture, expenditures on	yr	388	1999	30r
Household furnishings and equipment purchases	yr	1567	1999	30r
Household textiles, expenditures on	yr	112	1999	30r
Laundry and cleaning supplies, expenditures on	yr	104	1999	30r
Housing				
Home price, existing, ave		180800	10/00	90r
Home value, median		213000	2001	53s
Household operation expenditures	yr	581	1999	30r
Housekeeping supplies purchases	yr	474	1999	30r
Lodging expenditures	yr	550	1999	30r
Maintenance, repairs, insurance expenditures	yr	835	1999	30r
Monthly rental value of owned home	mos	663	1999	30r
Owned dwellings, expenditures own	yr	5209	1999	30r
Rent expenditures	yr	2390	1999	30r
Rental unit, 1 bedroom, with utilities	mos	766	4/01	41c
Rental unit, 2 bedroom, with utilities	mos	956	4/01	41c
Rental unit, 3 bedroom, with utilities	mos	1298	4/01	41c
Rental unit, 4 bedroom, with utilities	mos	1499	4/01	41c
Shelter, expenditures on	yr	8149	1999	30r
Insurance and Pensions				
Auto insurance premium	yr	1292.76	1999	57s
Life and other personal insurance purchases	yr	424	1999	30r
Pensions and Social Security, expenditures on	yr	3037	1999	30r
Legal Fees				
Divorce, filing fee		65.00	4/01	35s

Values are in dollars or fractions of dollars. In the column headed *Ref*, references are shown to sources. Each reference is followed by a letter. These refer to the geographical level for which data were reported: s=State, r=Region, and c=City or metro. The abbreviation *ex* is used to mean *except* or *excluding*; *exp* stands for expenditures. For other abbreviations and further explanations, please see the Introduction.

Middlesex-Somerset-Hunterdon, NJ - continued

Item	Per	Value	Date	Ref.
Legal Fees				
Driver's license fee	renew	15.00	1999	48s
Driver's license fee	orig	18.00	1999	48s
Fishing license	yr	22.50	4/01	34s
Personal Goods				
Personal care products and services purchases	yr	399	1999	30r
Personal Services				
Personal services, household, expenditures on	yr	271	1999	30r
Pets				
Pets, toys, and playground equipment, expenditures on	yr	325	1999	30r
Taxes				
Federal income taxes paid	yr	2606	1999	30r
Personal taxes, expenditures on	yr	3567	1999	30r
Property taxes paid	yr	1752	1999	30r
State and local income taxes paid	yr	694	1999	30r
Transportation				
Automobile insurance	yr	975.90	2000	79s
Cars and trucks, new, expenditures on	yr	1496	1999	30r
Cars and trucks, used, expenditures on	yr	1251	1999	30r
Diesel at the pump	gal	1.19	10/99	73s
Gasoline and motor oil purchases	yr	901	1999	30r
Gasoline before-tax price (cents)	gal	114.90	10/00	43s
Maintenance and repair expenditures	yr	618	1999	30r
Motorcycle license fee	renew	13.00	1999	49s
Motorcycle license fee	orig	15.00	1999	49s
Public transportation, expenditures on	yr	575	1999	30r
Transportation purchases	yr	6503	1999	30r
Vehicle expenses, miscellaneous, purchases	yr	2266	1999	30r
Vehicle insurance payments	yr	824	1999	30r
Vehicle purchases (net outlay)	yr	2761	1999	30r
Vehicle rental, lease expenditures	yr	584	1999	30r
Utilities				
Electrical bill, average	mos	74.08	9/00	9s
Electricity, expenditures on	yr	837	1999	30r
Electricity cost, average	KWh	8.91	9/00	9s
Utilities, fuels, and public services purchased	yr	2457	1999	30r
Water and other public services, expenditures on	yr	215	1999	30r
Weddings				
Wedding (national average cost)		19936	2000	33r
Wedding (regional average total cost)		29454	1997	110r
Attendants' gifts		321	1998	33r
Bridal attendants' apparel (5 persons)		824	2000	33r
Bride's headpiece/veil		173	1998	33r
Bride's wedding dress		859	1998	33r
Clergy, religious facility fee		242	1998	33r
Engagement ring		3177	1998	33r
Flowers		789	1998	33r
Groom's formalwear rental		99	2000	33r
Limousine		410	1998	33r
Marriage license cost		28.00	4/01	35s
Men's formalwear (ushers, best man)		469	2000	33r
Mother of bride apparel		241	2000	33r
Music		866	1998	33r
Photography and videography		1368	1998	33r
Rehearsal dinner		728	1998	33r
Wedding invitations and announcements		341	1998	33r
Wedding reception		7968	2000	33r
Wedding rings (bride and groom)		1060	1998	33r

Milwaukee-Waukesha, WI

Item	Per	Value	Date	Ref.
Average annual expenditures	yr	35369	1999	30r
Composite, ACCRA index		105.30	3/01	4c
Alcoholic Beverages				
Alcoholic beverage purchases	yr	356	1999	30c
Beer, Heineken, 12-oz, ex deposit	6	6.69	3/01	4c
J & B Scotch	750-ml	17.83	3/01	4c
Malt beverages, all types, all sizes, any origin	16 oz	0.93	7/01	11r
Wine, Livingston or Gallo, Chablis blanc	1.5 liter	4.69	3/01	4c
Wine, red and white table, all sizes, any origin	liter	7.04	7/01	11r
Appliances				
Appliance repair, service call, washing machine	min lab chg	36.95	3/01	4c
Major appliances, expenditures on	yr	165	1999	30r
Small appliances, housewares, expenditures on	yr	90	1999	30r
Banking and Money				
Mortgage interest and charges paid	yr	2277	1999	30r
Mortgage principal paid on owned property	yr	1230	1999	30r
Mortgage rate, incl. points and orig. fee, 30-yr. conv. fixed or ARM	mos	7.14	3/01	4c
Vehicle finance charges paid	yr	328	1999	30r
Business Expenses				
Business travel, car rental	day	52	2001	3c
Business travel, food	day	48	2001	3c
Business travel, hotel	day	119	2001	3c
Charity				
Cash contributions, expenditures	yr	1085	1999	30c
Child Care				
Child raising cost, total, age 0-2	yr	7890	1999	60r
Child raising cost, total, age 3-5	yr	8130	1999	60r
Child raising cost, total, age 6-8	yr	8170	1999	60r
Child raising cost, total, age 9-11	yr	8190	1999	60r
Child raising cost, total, age 12-14	yr	8890	1999	60r
Child raising cost, total, age 15-17	yr	9050	1999	60r
Child's child care and education, age 0-2	yr	1240	1999	60r
Child's child care and education, age 3-5	yr	1370	1999	60r
Child's child care and education, age 6-8	yr	880	1999	60r
Child's child care and education, age 9-11	yr	570	1999	60r
Child's child care and education, age 12-14	yr	420	1999	60r
Child's child care and education, age 15-17	yr	720	1999	60r
Child's clothing, age 0-2	yr	410	1999	60r
Child's clothing, age 3-5	yr	400	1999	60r
Child's clothing, age 6-8	yr	450	1999	60r
Child's clothing, age 9-11	yr	500	1999	60r
Child's clothing, age 12-14	yr	840	1999	60r
Child's clothing, age 15-17	yr	740	1999	60r
Child's food, age 0-2	yr	960	1999	60r
Child's food, age 3-5	yr	1120	1999	60r
Child's food, age 6-8	yr	1430	1999	60r
Child's food, age 9-11	yr	1710	1999	60r
Child's food, age 12-14	yr	1710	1999	60r
Child's food, age 15-17	yr	1920	1999	60r
Child's health care, age 0-2	yr	520	1999	60r
Child's health care, age 3-5	yr	500	1999	60r
Child's health care, age 6-8	yr	570	1999	60r
Child's health care, age 9-11	yr	610	1999	60r
Child's health care, age 12-14	yr	630	1999	60r
Child's health care, age 15-17	yr	650	1999	60r
Child's housing, age 0-2	yr	2860	1999	60r
Child's housing, age 3-5	yr	2840	1999	60r
Child's housing, age 6-8	yr	2800	1999	60r
Child's housing, age 9-11	yr	2650	1999	60r
Child's housing, age 12-14	yr	2840	1999	60r
Child's housing, age 15-17	yr	2440	1999	60r
Child's personal care, reading, age 0-2	yr	880	1999	60r
Child's personal care, reading, age 3-5	yr	900	1999	60r
Child's personal care, reading, age 6-8	yr	930	1999	60r
Child's personal care, reading, age 9-11	yr	970	1999	60r
Child's personal care, reading, age 12-14	yr	1150	1999	60r

Values are in dollars or fractions of dollars. In the column headed *Ref*, references are shown to sources. Each reference is followed by a letter. These refer to the geographical level for which data were reported: s=State, r=Region, and c=City or metro. The abbreviation *ex* is used to mean *except* or *excluding*; *exp* stands for *expenditures*. For other abbreviations and further explanations, please see the Introduction.

Milwaukee-Waukesha, WI - continued

Item	Per	Value	Date	Ref.
Child Care				
Child's personal care, reading, age 15-17	yr	920	1999	60r
Daycare	mos	533	1998	37c
Daycare, 3-year old, 5 days, 8 hrs/day	mos	533	1998	85c
Clothing				
Apparel and services purchases	yr	1319	1999	30c
Boys' brief, cotton	3	3.72	3/01	4c
Boys, 2 to 15, expenditures on	yr	91	1999	30r
Children under 2, expenditures on	yr	59	1999	30r
Footwear, expenditures on	yr	285	1999	30r
Girls, 2 to 15, expenditures on	yr	116	1999	30r
Men and boys, expenditures on	yr	433	1999	30r
Men, 16 and over, expenditures on	yr	341	1999	30r
Shirt, man's dress shirt		24.39	3/01	4c
Slacks, man's "No Wrinkles" khaki		33.19	3/01	4c
Women, 16 and over, expenditures on	yr	490	1999	30r
Communications				
Cable modem installation, Bresnan		99.95	6/99	103s
Cable modem installation, Marcus		499.00	6/99	103s
Cable modem rate, cable subscriber, Bresnan	mos	39.95	6/99	103s
Cable modem rate, cable subscriber, Marcus	mos	14.95-49.95	6/99	103s
Cable modem rate, non-cable subscriber, Bresnan	mos	49.95	6/99	103s
Cable modem rate, non-cable subscriber, Marcus	mos	60.95	6/99	103s
Newspaper subscription, daily and Sunday delivery	mos	16.74	3/01	4c
Phone line, single, business, field visit	inst.	64.65	12/97	17s
Phone line, single, business, no field visit	inst.	64.65	12/97	17s
Phone line, single, residence, field visit	inst.	33.05	12/97	17s
Phone line, single, residence, no field visit	inst.	33.05	12/97	17s
Postage and stationery, expenditures on	yr	140	1999	30r
Postal rate, express mail, up to half-pound		12.45	7/01	108r
Postal rate, letter, first class, first ounce		0.34	7/01	108r
Postal rate, letter, two ounces		0.57	7/01	108r
Postal rate, post card		0.21	7/01	108r
Postal rate, priority mail, two pounds		3.95	7/01	108r
Postal rate, priority mail, up to one pound		3.50	7/01	108r
Telephone bill, business, basic rate	mos	20.85	12/97	18c
Telephone bill, family of three	mos	16.95	3/01	4c
Telephone bill, residential, basic rate	mos	5.40	12/97	18c
Telephone services, expenditures on	yr	830	1999	30r
Education				
Board, 4-year private college/university	yr	2271	1996	38s
Board, 4-year public college/university	yr	1527	1996	38s
Education expenditures	yr	469	1999	30c
Room, 4-year private college/university	yr	1812	1996	38s
Room, 4-year public college/university	yr	1706	1996	38s
Total cost, 4-year private college/university	yr	15652	1996	38s
Total cost, 4-year public college/university	yr	5847	1996	38s
Tuition, 2-year public college/university, in state	yr	1840	1996	38s
Tuition, 4-year private college/university, in state	yr	11569	1996	38s
Tuition, 4-year public college/university	yr	2614	1996	38s
Energy and Fuels				
Electricity	500 KWhs	46.59	7/01	11r
Energy, combined forms, 2400 sq ft	mos	161.46	3/01	4c
Energy, exc. electricity, 2400 sq ft	mos	107.68	3/01	4c
Fuel oil #2	gal	1.27	7/01	11r
Fuel oil and other fuels, expenditures on	yr	68	1999	30r
Gas, cooking, winter, 10 therms	mos	10.31	2/96	98c
Gas, cooking, winter, 30 therms	mos	21.93	2/96	98c
Gas, cooking, winter, 50 therms	mos	33.56	2/96	98c
Gas, heating, winter, average use	mos	110.84	2/96	98c
Gas, natural, commercial rate	1000 cf	7.32	11/00	88s
Gas, regular unleaded, cash, self-service	gal	1.45	3/01	4c
Gasoline, unleaded midgrade	gal	1.79	7/01	11r

Milwaukee-Waukesha, WI - continued

Item	Per	Value	Date	Ref.
Energy and Fuels - continued				
Gasoline, unleaded premium	gal	1.86	7/01	11r
Gasoline, unleaded regular	gal	1.58	7/01	11r
Natural gas, expenditures on	yr	389	1999	30r
Utility (piped) gas, therm		0.81	7/01	11r
Utility (piped) gas, 40 therms		38.01	7/01	11r
Utility (piped) gas, 100 therms		81.75	7/01	11r
Entertainment				
Bowling, Saturday evening rate	line	2.96	3/01	4c
Entertainment purchases	yr	1676	1999	30c
Fees and admissions paid	yr	444	1999	30r
Monopoly game, Parker Brothers', No. 9	game	9.11	3/01	4c
Movie, first-run, Saturday, evening	adm.	7.55	3/01	4c
Reading purchases	yr	182	1999	30c
Television, radios, sound equipment, expenditures on	yr	580	1999	30r
Tennis balls, yellow, Wilson or Penn, 3	can	2.42	3/01	4c
Funerals				
Cosmetology, hair, other preparation		178.32	1/99	78r
Embalming		408.19	1/99	78r
Funeral at funeral home		362.13	1/99	78r
Professional service charges		1375.51	1/99	78r
Transfer of remains to funeral home		155.92	1/99	78r
Visitation/viewing		294.38	1/99	78r
Groceries				
Groceries, ACCRA Index		100.60	3/01	4c
Antibiotic ointment, Polysporin	0.5 oz	4.26	3/01	4c
Baby food, strained vegetables or fruit, lowest price	4-4.5 oz	0.50	3/01	4c
Bacon, sliced	lb	3.15	7/01	11r
Bakery products, expenditures on	yr	281	1999	30r
Bananas	lb	0.49	3/01	4c
Bananas	lb	0.48	7/01	11r
Beans, dried, any type, all sizes	lb	0.61	7/01	11r
Beef for stew, boneless	lb	3.08	7/01	11r
Beef or hamburger, ground	lb	1.63	3/01	4c
Beef, expenditures on	yr	217	1999	30r
Bologna, all beef or mixed	lb	2.52	7/01	11r
Bread, white	loaf	0.91	3/01	4c
Bread, white, pan	lb	1.06	7/01	11r
Broccoli	lb	0.91	7/01	11r
Butter, salted, grade AA, stick	lb	3.04	7/01	11r
Butter, yoghurt, cheese, etc, expenditures on	yr	183	1999	30r
Cereals and bakery product purchases	yr	430	1999	30r
Cereals and cereal products, expenditures on	yr	149	1999	30r
Cheese, Kraft grated Parmesan	8 oz	3.42	3/01	4c
Chicken, fresh, whole	lb	1.07	7/01	11r
Chicken, whole fryer	lb	0.99	3/01	4c
Chops, boneless,	lb	3.64	7/01	11r
Chuck roast, U.S. choice, boneless	lb	2.47	7/01	11r
Cigarettes, Winston, Kings	carton	33.68	3/01	4c
Coffee, 100%, ground roast, all sizes	lb	2.69	7/01	11r
Coffee, vacuum-packed	13 oz	2.37	3/01	4c
Cookies, chocolate chip	lb	2.87	7/01	11r
Corn Flakes, Kellogg's or Post Toasties	18 oz	1.97	3/01	4c
Corn, frozen, whole kernel, lowest price	16 oz	1.05	3/01	4c
Dairy product purchases	yr	281	1999	30c
Eggs, expenditures on	yr	26	1999	30r
Eggs, Grade A or AA	dozen	1.02	3/01	4c
Eggs, grade A, large	dozen	0.88	7/01	11r
Fats and oils, expenditures on	yr	75	1999	30r
Fish and seafood, expenditures on	yr	72	1999	30r
Food (excl fruit and vegetables), eaten at home, purchases	yr	900	1999	30c
Food cooked on trips, expenditures on	yr	44	1999	30r
Food purchases	yr	4344	1999	30c
Food purchases, eaten away from home	yr	1871	1999	30c
Food purchases, food eaten at home	yr	2473	1999	30c
Fresh fruits, expenditures on	yr	138	1999	30r
Fresh milk and cream, expenditures on	yr	120	1999	30r
Fresh vegetables, expenditures on	yr	126	1999	30r

Values are in dollars or fractions of dollars. In the column headed *Ref*, references are shown to sources. Each reference is followed by a letter. These refer to the geographical level for which data were reported: s=State, r=Region, and c=City or metro. The abbreviation *ex* is used to mean *except* or *excluding*; *exp* stands for *expenditures*. For other abbreviations and further explanations, please see the Introduction.

Milwaukee-Waukesha, WI - continued

Item	Per	Value	Date	Ref.
Groceries				
Fruit and vegetable purchases	yr	391	1999	30c
Grapefruit	lb	0.66	7/01	11r
Grapes, Thompson, seedless	lb	1.64	7/01	11r
Ground beef, 100% beef	lb	1.64	7/01	11r
Ground beef, lean and extra lean	lb	2.16	7/01	11r
Ground chuck, 100% beef	lb	2.13	7/01	11r
Ham, boneless, excl canned	lb	2.62	7/01	11r
Ice cream, prepackaged, bulk, regular	1/2 gal	3.35	7/01	11r
Lemons	lb	1.19	7/01	11r
Lettuce, iceberg	head	1.04	3/01	4c
Lettuce, iceberg	lb	0.73	7/01	11r
Margarine, Blue Bonnet or Parkay, stick	lb	0.65	3/01	4c
Margarine, soft, tubs	lb	0.89	7/01	11r
Meats, poultry, fish, and egg purchases	yr	671	1999	30r
Milk, fresh, whole, fortified	gal	2.71	7/01	11r
Milk, whole	1/2 gal	1.66	3/01	4c
Nonalcoholic beverages, expenditures on	yr	239	1999	30r
Orange juice, Minute Maid frozen	12 oz	1.44	3/01	4c
Oranges, Navel	lb	0.80	7/01	11r
Oranges, Valencia	lb	0.66	7/01	11r
Peaches, halves or slices, Hunt's, Del Monte, or Libby's	29 oz	1.60	3/01	4c
Pears, Anjou	lb	0.93	7/01	11r
Peas, green, Del Monte or Green Giant	15 oz	0.74	3/01	4c
Pork chops, center cut, bone-in	lb	3.63	7/01	11r
Pork, expenditures on	yr	150	1999	30r
Potato chips	16 oz	3.52	7/01	11r
Potatoes, frozen, french fried	lb	1.08	7/01	11r
Potatoes, white or red	10 lb	2.89	3/01	4c
Potatoes, white, all types	lb	0.33	7/01	11r
Poultry, expenditures on	yr	108	1999	30r
Processed fruits, expenditures on	yr	98	1999	30r
Processed vegetables, expenditures on	yr	80	1999	30r
Round roast, U.S. choice, boneless	lb	3.07	7/01	11r
Round steak, graded and ungraded, excl U.S. prime and choice	lb	3.41	7/01	11r
Sausage, Jimmy Dean/Owens pork	lb	3.33	3/01	4c
Shortening, vegetable oil blends	lb	1.13	7/01	11r
Shortening, vegetable, Crisco	3 lb	3.06	3/01	4c
Soft drink, Coca Cola, ex deposit	2 liter	1.23	3/01	4c
Spaghetti and macaroni	lb	0.80	7/01	11r
Steak, round, U.S. choice, boneless	lb	3.23	7/01	11r
Steak, T-bone	lb	8.08	3/01	4c
Steak, T-bone, U.S. choice, bone-in	lb	6.68	7/01	11r
Strawberries, dry pint	12 oz	1.32	7/01	11r
Sugar and other sweets, expenditures on	yr	114	1999	30r
Sugar, cane or beet	4 lbs	1.63	3/01	4c
Sugar, white, 33-80 ounce package	lb	0.42	7/01	11r
Sugar, white, all sizes	lb	0.43	7/01	11r
Tobacco products and smoking supplies purchases	yr	413	1999	30c
Tomatoes, field grown	lb	1.46	7/01	11r
Tomatoes, Hunt's or Del Monte	14.5 oz	0.87	3/01	4c
Tuna, chunk, light	6 oz	0.64	3/01	4c
Tuna, light, chunk	lb	1.80	7/01	11r
Turkey, frozen, whole	lb	1.15	7/01	11r
Goods and Services				
Miscellaneous goods and services, ACCRA Index		96.90	3/01	4c
B&B Japanese maple (acer japonicum)	gal	29.99-169.99	4/00	93r
Boxwood (buxus)	2 gal	18.99-39.99	4/00	93r
Daylilly (hemerocallis)	gal	4.99-25.00	4/00	93r
Flat of annuals		11.98-24.99	4/00	93r
Fountain grass (pennisetum)	gal	5.98-12.98	4/00	93r
Hanging basket (10 in)		12.99-27.99	4/00	93r

Milwaukee-Waukesha, WI - continued

Item	Per	Value	Date	Ref.
Goods and Services - continued				
Hardy geranium (geranium)	gal	7.99-9.99	4/00	93r
Hosta (hosta)	gal	6.00-25.00	4/00	93r
Lilac (syrubga vulgaris)	2 gal	14.99-24.99	4/00	93r
Miscellaneous purchases	yr	865	1999	30r
Rhododendron (rhododendron)	2 gal	23.98-42.99	4/00	93r
Sage (salvia)	gal	6.00-9.99	4/00	93r
Wintercreeper euonymus (euonymus fortunei)	2 gal	16.00-169.99	4/00	93r
Hunting license	yr	14.00	4/01	34s
Health Care				
Health care, ACCRA Index		98.20	3/01	4c
Cardiac catheterization, ave hospital/ physician charges		13240	1998	77s
Childbirth, Cesarean delivery		10722	1997	13r
Childbirth, vaginal delivery		6223	1997	13r
Dentist's fee, adult teeth cleaning and periodic oral exam	visit	71.20	3/01	4c
Doctor's fee, routine exam, established patient	visit	63.40	3/01	4c
Drugs, expenditures on	yr	394	1999	30r
Health care purchases	yr	2050	1999	30c
Health insurance expenditures	yr	978	1999	30r
Home health care aide cost, licensed agency	hour	17	2000	82c
Hospital care, private room	day	424.65	3/01	4c
Hysterectomy, laproscopically-assisted, ave hospital/physician charges		13270	1998	76s
Hysterectomy, vaginal, ave hospital and physician charges		9170	1998	76s
Laser eye surgery	eye	1950-2400	2000	63s
Medicaid dispensing fee		4.88-40.11	1999	87s
Medical services expenditures	yr	554	1999	30r
Medical supplies, expenditures on	yr	122	1999	30r
Nursing home costs, private room	day	179	2000	82c
Nursing home stay, private room	day	179	2000	83c
Plastic surgery, breast augmentation		3184	2000	7r
Plastic surgery, breast lift		3585	2000	7r
Plastic surgery, facelift		4999	2000	7r
Plastic surgery, hair transplantation		3105	2000	7r
Plastic surgery, lip augmentation		1290	2000	7r
Plastic surgery, lower body lift		8135	2000	7r
Plastic surgery, thigh lift		3839	2000	7r
Household Goods				
Dishwashing powder, Cascade	50 oz	3.38	3/01	4c
Floor coverings, expenditures on	yr	52	1999	30r
Furniture, expenditures on	yr	344	1999	30r
Household furnishings and equipment purchases	yr	1531	1999	30c
Household textiles, expenditures on	yr	109	1999	30r
Laundry and cleaning supplies, expenditures on	yr	134	1999	30r
Tissues, facial, Kleenex brand	175	1.30	3/01	4c
Housing				
Housing, ACCRA Index		114.60	3/01	4c
Home, 2200 sq ft, 4-br, 2-bath, 2-car garage, average		201633	2000	47c
Home price, existing, ave		144400	10/00	90r
Home value, median		117000	2001	53s
House, 2400 sq ft, 8000 sq ft lot, new, urban, utilities	total	240375	3/01	4c
House payment, principal and interest, 25% down payment	mos	1216	3/01	4c
Household operation expenditures	yr	590	1999	30c
Housekeeping supplies purchases	yr	500	1999	30c
Housing, expenditures on	yr	13147	1999	30c

Values are in dollars or fractions of dollars. In the column headed *Ref*, references are shown to sources. Each reference is followed by a letter. These refer to the geographical level for which data were reported: s=State, r=Region, and c=City or metro. The abbreviation *ex* is used to mean *except* or *excluding*; *exp* stands for expenditures. For other abbreviations and further explanations, please see the Introduction.

Milwaukee-Waukesha, WI - continued

Item	Per	Value	Date	Ref.
Housing				
Lodging expenditures	yr	430	1999	30r
Maintenance, repairs, insurance expenditures	yr	853	1999	30r
Monthly rental value of owned home	mos	547	1999	30r
Owned dwellings, expenditures own	yr	5540	1999	30c
Rent expenditures	yr	2326	1999	30c
Rent, apartment, 2 br, 1 1/2-2 baths, unfurn, 950 sq ft, water	mos	705	3/01	4c
Rental unit, 1 bedroom, with utilities	mos	504	4/01	41c
Rental unit, 2 bedroom, with utilities	mos	633	4/01	41c
Rental unit, 3 bedroom, with utilities	mos	794	4/01	41c
Rental unit, 4 bedroom, with utilities	mos	887	4/01	41c
Shelter, expenditures on	yr	8249	1999	30c
Insurance and Pensions				
Auto insurance premium	yr	603.84	1999	57s
Life and other personal insurance purchases	yr	359	1999	30c
Pensions and Social Security, expenditures on	yr	2941	1999	30c
Personal insurance and pensions, expenditures on	yr	3300	1999	30c
Legal Fees				
Divorce, filing fee		142.00-150.00	4/01	35s
Driver's license fee	renew	12.00	1999	48s
Driver's license fee	orig	18.00	1999	48s
Fishing license	yr	14.00	4/01	34s
Personal Goods				
Personal care products and services purchases	yr	270	1999	30c
Shampoo, Alberto VO5	15 oz	0.98	3/01	4c
Toothpaste, Crest or Colgate	6-7 oz	2.04	3/01	4c
Personal Services				
Dry cleaning, man's 2-pc suit		8.99	3/01	4c
Man's haircut, barbershop, no styling		10.80	3/01	4c
Personal services, household, expenditures on	yr	300	1999	30r
Woman's shampoo, trim, blow-dry, no style-change		20.79	3/01	4c
Pets				
Pets, toys, and playground equipment, expenditures on	yr	375	1999	30r
Restaurant Food				
Chicken, fried, thigh and drumstick, KFC/Church's		3.09	3/01	4c
Hamburger with cheese, McDonald's	1/4 lb	1.99	3/01	4c
Pizza, Pizza Hut or Pizza Inn	11-12 in	8.99	3/01	4c
Taxes				
Federal income taxes paid	yr	2326	1999	30r
Personal taxes, expenditures on	yr	3223	1999	30r
Property taxes paid	yr	1152	1999	30r
State and local income taxes paid	yr	753	1999	30r
Transportation				
Transportation, ACCRA Index		102.90	3/01	4c
Bus fare, one-way	trip	1.35	2000	1c
Bus fare, to central business district	1-way	1.19	3/01	4c
Cars and trucks, new, expenditures on	yr	1280	1999	30r
Cars and trucks, used, expenditures on	yr	1763	1999	30r
Diesel at the pump	gal	1.34	10/99	73s
Gasoline and motor oil purchases	yr	1022	1999	30c
Gasoline before-tax price (cents)	gal	113.40	10/00	43s
Maintenance and repair expenditures	yr	594	1999	30r
Public transportation, expenditures on	yr	466	1999	30c
Tire balance, computer or spin balance, front	wheel	7.99	3/01	4c
Transportation purchases	yr	7271	1999	30c
Vehicle expenses, miscellaneous, purchases	yr	2140	1999	30c
Vehicle insurance payments	yr	701	1999	30r
Vehicle purchases (net outlay)	yr	3643	1999	30c
Vehicle rental, lease expenditures	yr	536	1999	30r

Milwaukee-Waukesha, WI - continued

Item	Per	Value	Date	Ref.
Utilities				
Utilities, ACCRA Index		124.80	3/01	4c
Electrical bill, average	mos	52.08	9/00	9s
Electricity, expenditures on	yr	841	1999	30r
Electricity, summer, 250 KWh	mos	20.15	2/96	96c
Electricity, summer, 500 KWh	mos	35.80	2/96	96c
Electricity, summer, 750 KWh	mos	53.45	2/96	96c
Electricity, summer, 1000 KWh	mos	57.86	2/96	96c
Electricity and other, mixed, 2400 sq ft, new home	mos	53.78	3/01	4c
Electricity cost, average	KWh	5.69	9/00	9s
Utilities, fuels, and public services purchased	yr	2401	1999	30r
Water and other public services, expenditures on	yr	273	1999	30r
Weddings				
Wedding (national average cost)		19936	2000	33r
Wedding (regional average total cost)		16195	1997	110r
Attendants' gifts		321	1998	33r
Bridal attendants' apparel (5 persons)		824	2000	33r
Bride's headpiece/veil		173	1998	33r
Bride's wedding dress		859	1998	33r
Clergy, religious facility fee		242	1998	33r
Engagement ring		3177	1998	33r
Flowers		789	1998	33r
Groom's formalwear rental		99	2000	33r
Limousine		410	1998	33r
Marriage license cost		50.00-60.00	4/01	35s
Men's formalwear (ushers, best man)		469	2000	33r
Mother of bride apparel		241	2000	33r
Music		866	1998	33r
Photography and videography		1368	1998	33r
Rehearsal dinner		728	1998	33r
Wedding invitations and announcements		341	1998	33r
Wedding reception		7968	2000	33r
Wedding rings (bride and groom)		1060	1998	33r

Minneapolis-St. Paul, MN

Item	Per	Value	Date	Ref.
Average annual expenditures	yr	48444	1999	30c
Alcoholic Beverages				
Alcoholic beverage purchases	yr	507	1999	30c
Malt beverages, all types, all sizes, any origin	16 oz	0.93	7/01	11r
Wine, red and white table, all sizes, any origin	liter	7.04	7/01	11r
Appliances				
Major appliances, expenditures on	yr	165	1999	30r
Small appliances, housewares, expenditures on	yr	90	1999	30r
Banking and Money				
Mortgage interest and charges paid	yr	2277	1999	30r
Mortgage principal paid on owned property	yr	1230	1999	30r
Vehicle finance charges paid	yr	328	1999	30r
Charity				
Cash contributions, expenditures	yr	1454	1999	30c
Child Care				
Child raising cost, total, age 0-2	yr	7890	1999	60r
Child raising cost, total, age 3-5	yr	8130	1999	60r
Child raising cost, total, age 6-8	yr	8170	1999	60r
Child raising cost, total, age 9-11	yr	8190	1999	60r
Child raising cost, total, age 12-14	yr	8890	1999	60r
Child raising cost, total, age 15-17	yr	9050	1999	60r
Child's child care and education, age 0-2	yr	1240	1999	60r
Child's child care and education, age 3-5	yr	1370	1999	60r
Child's child care and education, age 6-8	yr	880	1999	60r
Child's child care and education, age 9-11	yr	570	1999	60r
Child's child care and education, age 12-14	yr	420	1999	60r
Child's child care and education, age 15-17	yr	720	1999	60r
Child's clothing, age 0-2	yr	410	1999	60r

Values are in dollars or fractions of dollars. In the column headed *Ref*, references are shown to sources. Each reference is followed by a letter. These refer to the geographical level for which data were reported: s=State, r=Region, and c=City or metro. The abbreviation *ex* is used to mean *except* or *excluding*; *exp* stands for *expenditures*. For other abbreviations and further explanations, please see the Introduction.

Minneapolis-St. Paul, MN - continued

Item	Per	Value	Date	Ref.
Child Care				
Child's clothing, age 3-5	yr	400	1999	60r
Child's clothing, age 6-8	yr	450	1999	60r
Child's clothing, age 9-11	yr	500	1999	60r
Child's clothing, age 12-14	yr	840	1999	60r
Child's clothing, age 15-17	yr	740	1999	60r
Child's food, age 0-2	yr	960	1999	60r
Child's food, age 3-5	yr	1120	1999	60r
Child's food, age 6-8	yr	1430	1999	60r
Child's food, age 9-11	yr	1710	1999	60r
Child's food, age 12-14	yr	1710	1999	60r
Child's food, age 15-17	yr	1920	1999	60r
Child's health care, age 0-2	yr	520	1999	60r
Child's health care, age 3-5	yr	500	1999	60r
Child's health care, age 6-8	yr	570	1999	60r
Child's health care, age 9-11	yr	610	1999	60r
Child's health care, age 12-14	yr	630	1999	60r
Child's health care, age 15-17	yr	650	1999	60r
Child's housing, age 0-2	yr	2860	1999	60r
Child's housing, age 3-5	yr	2840	1999	60r
Child's housing, age 6-8	yr	2800	1999	60r
Child's housing, age 9-11	yr	2650	1999	60r
Child's housing, age 12-14	yr	2840	1999	60r
Child's housing, age 15-17	yr	2440	1999	60r
Child's personal care, reading, age 0-2	yr	880	1999	60r
Child's personal care, reading, age 3-5	yr	900	1999	60r
Child's personal care, reading, age 6-8	yr	930	1999	60r
Child's personal care, reading, age 9-11	yr	970	1999	60r
Child's personal care, reading, age 12-14	yr	1150	1999	60r
Child's personal care, reading, age 15-17	yr	920	1999	60r
Clothing				
Apparel and services purchases	yr	1979	1999	30c
Boys, 2 to 15, expenditures on	yr	91	1999	30r
Children under 2, expenditures on	yr	59	1999	30r
Footwear, expenditures on	yr	285	1999	30r
Girls, 2 to 15, expenditures on	yr	116	1999	30r
Men and boys, expenditures on	yr	433	1999	30r
Men, 16 and over, expenditures on	yr	341	1999	30r
Women, 16 and over, expenditures on	yr	490	1999	30r
Communications				
Cable modem installation, Media One		100.00	6/99	103s
Cable modem rate, cable subscriber, Media One	mos	34.95-39.95	6/99	103s
Cable modem rate, non-cable subscriber, Media One	mos	49.95	6/99	103s
Phone line, single, business, field visit	inst.	45.00	12/97	17s
Phone line, single, business, no field visit	inst.	45.00	12/97	17s
Phone line, single, residence, field visit	inst.	16.25	12/97	17s
Phone line, single, residence, no field visit	inst.	16.25	12/97	17s
Postage and stationery, expenditures on	yr	140	1999	30r
Postal rate, express mail, up to half-pound		12.45	7/01	108r
Postal rate, letter, first class, first ounce		0.34	7/01	108r
Postal rate, letter, two ounces		0.57	7/01	108r
Postal rate, post card		0.21	7/01	108r
Postal rate, priority mail, two pounds		3.95	7/01	108r
Postal rate, priority mail, up to one pound		3.50	7/01	108r
Telephone bill, business, basic rate	mos	45.83	12/97	18c
Telephone bill, residential, basic rate	mos	15.53	12/97	18c
Telephone services, expenditures on	yr	830	1999	30r
Education				
Board, 4-year private college/university	yr	2267	1996	38s
Board, 4-year public college/university	yr	1474	1996	38s
Education expenditures	yr	767	1999	30c
Room, 4-year private college/university	yr	2058	1996	38s
Room, 4-year public college/university	yr	2022	1996	38s
Total cost, 4-year private college/university	yr	17222	1996	38s
Total cost, 4-year public college/university	yr	6712	1996	38s
Tuition, 2-year public college/university, in state	yr	2065	1996	38s
Tuition, 4-year private college/university, in state	yr	12897	1996	38s
Tuition, 4-year public college/university	yr	3216	1996	38s

Minneapolis-St. Paul, MN - continued

Item	Per	Value	Date	Ref.
Energy and Fuels				
Electricity	500 KWhs	46.59	7/01	11r
Fuel oil #2	gal	1.27	7/01	11r
Fuel oil and other fuels, expenditures on	yr	68	1999	30r
Gas, natural, commercial rate	1000 cf	6.86	11/00	88s
Gasoline, unleaded midgrade	gal	1.79	7/01	11r
Gasoline, unleaded premium	gal	1.86	7/01	11r
Gasoline, unleaded regular	gal	1.58	7/01	11r
Natural gas, expenditures on	yr	389	1999	30r
Utility (piped) gas, therm		0.81	7/01	11r
Utility (piped) gas, 40 therms		38.01	7/01	11r
Utility (piped) gas, 100 therms		81.75	7/01	11r
Entertainment				
Entertainment purchases	yr	2498	1999	30c
Fees and admissions paid	yr	444	1999	30r
Television, radios, sound equipment, expenditures on	yr	580	1999	30r
Funerals				
Cosmetology, hair, other preparation		178.32	1/99	78r
Embalming		408.19	1/99	78r
Funeral at funeral home		362.13	1/99	78r
Professional service charges		1375.51	1/99	78r
Transfer of remains to funeral home		155.92	1/99	78r
Visitation/viewing		294.38	1/99	78r
Groceries				
Bacon, sliced	lb	3.15	7/01	11r
Bakery products, expenditures on	yr	281	1999	30r
Bananas	lb	0.48	7/01	11r
Beans, dried, any type, all sizes	lb	0.61	7/01	11r
Beef for stew, boneless	lb	3.08	7/01	11r
Beef, expenditures on	yr	217	1999	30r
Bologna, all beef or mixed	lb	2.52	7/01	11r
Bread, white, pan	lb	1.06	7/01	11r
Broccoli	lb	0.91	7/01	11r
Butter, salted, grade AA, stick	lb	3.04	7/01	11r
Butter, yoghurt, cheese, etc, expenditures on	yr	183	1999	30r
Cereals and bakery product purchases	yr	435	1999	30c
Cereals and cereal products, expenditures on	yr	149	1999	30r
Chicken, fresh, whole	lb	1.07	7/01	11r
Chops, boneless,	lb	3.64	7/01	11r
Chuck roast, U.S. choice, boneless	lb	2.47	7/01	11r
Coffee, 100%, ground roast, all sizes	lb	2.69	7/01	11r
Cookies, chocolate chip	lb	2.87	7/01	11r
Dairy product purchases	yr	382	1999	30c
Eggs, expenditures on	yr	26	1999	30r
Eggs, grade A, large	dozen	0.88	7/01	11r
Fats and oils, expenditures on	yr	75	1999	30r
Fish and seafood, expenditures on	yr	72	1999	30r
Food (excl fruit and vegetables), eaten at home, purchases	yr	1042	1999	30c
Food cooked on trips, expenditures on	yr	44	1999	30r
Food purchases	yr	5778	1999	30c
Food purchases, eaten away from home	yr	2728	1999	30c
Food purchases, food eaten at home	yr	3050	1999	30c
Fresh fruits, expenditures on	yr	138	1999	30r
Fresh milk and cream, expenditures on	yr	120	1999	30r
Fresh vegetables, expenditures on	yr	126	1999	30r
Grapefruit	lb	0.66	7/01	11r
Grapes, Thompson, seedless	lb	1.64	7/01	11r
Ground beef, 100% beef	lb	1.64	7/01	11r
Ground beef, lean and extra lean	lb	2.16	7/01	11r
Ground chuck, 100% beef	lb	2.13	7/01	11r
Ham, boneless, excl canned	lb	2.62	7/01	11r
Ice cream, prepackaged, bulk, regular	1/2 gal	3.35	7/01	11r
Lemons	lb	1.19	7/01	11r
Lettuce, iceberg	lb	0.73	7/01	11r
Margarine, soft, tubs	lb	0.89	7/01	11r
Meats, poultry, fish, and egg purchases	yr	656	1999	30c
Milk, fresh, whole, fortified	gal	2.71	7/01	11r
Nonalcoholic beverages, expenditures on	yr	239	1999	30r

Values are in dollars or fractions of dollars. In the column headed *Ref*, references are shown to sources. Each reference is followed by a letter. These refer to the geographical level for which data were reported: s=State, r=Region, and c=City or metro. The abbreviation *ex* is used to mean *except* or *excluding*; *exp* stands for expenditures. For other abbreviations and further explanations, please see the Introduction.

Minneapolis-St. Paul, MN - continued

Item	Per	Value	Date	Ref.
Groceries				
Oranges, Navel	lb	0.80	7/01	11r
Oranges, Valencia	lb	0.66	7/01	11r
Pears, Anjou	lb	0.93	7/01	11r
Pork chops, center cut, bone-in	lb	3.63	7/01	11r
Pork, expenditures on	yr	150	1999	30r
Potato chips	16 oz	3.52	7/01	11r
Potatoes, frozen, french fried	lb	1.08	7/01	11r
Potatoes, white, all types	lb	0.33	7/01	11r
Poultry, expenditures on	yr	108	1999	30r
Processed fruits, expenditures on	yr	98	1999	30r
Processed vegetables, expenditures on	yr	80	1999	30r
Round roast, U.S. choice, boneless	lb	3.07	7/01	11r
Round steak, graded and ungraded, excl U.S. prime and choice	lb	3.41	7/01	11r
Shortening, vegetable oil blends	lb	1.13	7/01	11r
Spaghetti and macaroni	lb	0.80	7/01	11r
Steak, round, U.S. choice, boneless	lb	3.23	7/01	11r
Steak, T-bone, U.S. choice, bone-in	lb	6.68	7/01	11r
Strawberries, dry pint	12 oz	1.32	7/01	11r
Sugar and other sweets, expenditures on	yr	114	1999	30r
Sugar, white, 33-80 ounce package	lb	0.42	7/01	11r
Sugar, white, all sizes	lb	0.43	7/01	11r
Tobacco products and smoking supplies purchases	yr	344	1999	30c
Tomatoes, field grown	lb	1.46	7/01	11r
Tuna, light, chunk	lb	1.80	7/01	11r
Turkey, frozen, whole	lb	1.15	7/01	11r
Goods and Services				
B&B Japanese maple (acer japonicum)	gal	29.99-169.99	4/00	93r
Boxwood (buxus)	2 gal	18.99-39.99	4/00	93r
Daylilly (hemerocallis)	gal	4.99-25.00	4/00	93r
Flat of annuals		11.98-24.99	4/00	93r
Fountain grass (pennisetum)	gal	5.98-12.98	4/00	93r
Hanging basket (10 in)		12.99-27.99	4/00	93r
Hardy geranium (geranium)	gal	7.99-9.99	4/00	93r
Hosta (hosta)	gal	6.00-25.00	4/00	93r
Lilac (syrubga vulgaris)	2 gal	14.99-24.99	4/00	93r
Miscellaneous purchases	yr	1402	1999	30c
Rhododendron (rhododendron)	2 gal	23.98-42.99	4/00	93r
Sage (salvia)	gal	6.00-9.99	4/00	93r
Wintercreeper euonymus (euonymus fortunei)	2 gal	16.00-169.99	4/00	93r
Hunting license	yr	17.00	4/01	34s
Health Care				
Cardiac catheterization, ave hospital/ physician charges		19020	1998	77s
Childbirth, Cesarean delivery		10722	1997	13r
Childbirth, vaginal delivery		6223	1997	13r
Drugs, expenditures on	yr	394	1999	30r
Health care purchases	yr	2262	1999	30c
Health insurance expenditures	yr	978	1999	30r
Hysterectomy, laproscopically-assisted, ave hospital/physician charges		15580	1998	76s
Hysterectomy, vaginal, ave hospital and physician charges		10690	1998	76s
Medicaid dispensing fee		3.65	1999	87s
Medical services expenditures	yr	554	1999	30r
Medical supplies, expenditures on	yr	122	1999	30r
Plastic surgery, breast augmentation		3184	2000	7r
Plastic surgery, breast lift		3585	2000	7r

Minneapolis-St. Paul, MN - continued

Item	Per	Value	Date	Ref.
Health Care - continued				
Plastic surgery, facelift		4999	2000	7r
Plastic surgery, hair transplantation		3105	2000	7r
Plastic surgery, lip augmentation		1290	2000	7r
Plastic surgery, lower body lift		8135	2000	7r
Plastic surgery, thigh lift		3839	2000	7r
Household Goods				
Floor coverings, expenditures on	yr	52	1999	30r
Furniture, expenditures on	yr	344	1999	30r
Household furnishings and equipment purchases	yr	2217	1999	30c
Household textiles, expenditures on	yr	109	1999	30r
Laundry and cleaning supplies, expenditures on	yr	134	1999	30r
Housing				
Home price, existing, ave		144400	10/00	90r
Home value, median		135000	2001	53s
Household operation expenditures	yr	1003	1999	30c
Housekeeping supplies purchases	yr	659	1999	30c
Lodging expenditures	yr	719	1999	30c
Maintenance, repairs, insurance expenditures	yr	853	1999	30r
Monthly rental value of owned home	mos	547	1999	30r
Owned dwellings, expenditures own	yr	6063	1999	30c
Rent expenditures	yr	2029	1999	30c
Rental unit, 1 bedroom, with utilities	mos	549	4/01	41c
Rental unit, 2 bedroom, with utilities	mos	702	4/01	41c
Rental unit, 3 bedroom, with utilities	mos	950	4/01	41c
Rental unit, 4 bedroom, with utilities	mos	1076	4/01	41c
Shelter, expenditures on	yr	8811	1999	30c
Insurance and Pensions				
Life and other personal insurance purchases	yr	419	1999	30c
Pensions and Social Security, expenditures on	yr	6440	1999	30c
Legal Fees				
Divorce, filing fee		122.00	4/01	35s
Driver's license fee	renew	13.00	1999	48s
Driver's license fee	orig	16.00	1999	48s
Fishing license	yr	18.00	4/01	34s
Personal Goods				
Personal care products and services purchases	yr	526	1999	30c
Personal Services				
Personal services, household, expenditures on	yr	300	1999	30r
Pets				
Pets, toys, and playground equipment, expenditures on	yr	375	1999	30r
Taxes				
Federal income taxes paid	yr	2326	1999	30r
Personal taxes, expenditures on	yr	3223	1999	30r
Property taxes paid	yr	1152	1999	30r
State and local income taxes paid	yr	753	1999	30r
Transportation				
Bus fare, one-way	trip	1.00	2000	1c
Cars and trucks, new, expenditures on	yr	1280	1999	30r
Cars and trucks, used, expenditures on	yr	1763	1999	30r
Diesel at the pump	gal	1.28	10/99	73s
Gasoline and motor oil purchases	yr	1172	1999	30c
Gasoline before-tax price (cents)	gal	117.20	10/00	43s
Household transportation expenditures	yr	8683	97-1998	102c
Maintenance and repair expenditures	yr	594	1999	30r
Motorcycle license fee	orig	16.00	1999	49s
Motorcycle license fee	renew	13.00	1999	49s
Public transportation, expenditures on	yr	610	1999	30c
Transportation purchases	yr	8847	1999	30c
Vehicle expenses, miscellaneous, purchases	yr	2891	1999	30c
Vehicle insurance payments	yr	701	1999	30r

Values are in dollars or fractions of dollars. In the column headed *Ref*, references are shown to sources. Each reference is followed by a letter. These refer to the geographical level for which data were reported: s=State, r=Region, and c=City or metro. The abbreviation *ex* is used to mean *except* or *excluding*; *exp* stands for *expenditures*. For other abbreviations and further explanations, please see the Introduction.

Minneapolis-St. Paul, MN - continued

Item	Per	Value	Date	Ref.
Transportation				
Vehicle purchases (net outlay)	yr	3081	1999	30r
Vehicle rental, lease expenditures	yr	536	1999	30r
Utilities				
Electrical bill, average	mos	55.08	9/00	9s
Electricity, expenditures on	yr	841	1999	30r
Electricity, summer, 250 KWh	mos	21.30	2/96	97c
Electricity, summer, 500 KWh	mos	37.87	2/96	97c
Electricity, summer, 750 KWh	mos	54.45	2/96	97c
Electricity, summer, 1000 KWh	mos	71.02	2/96	97c
Electricity cost, average	KWh	5.80	9/00	9s
Utilities, fuels, and public services purchased	yr	2284	1999	30c
Water and other public services, expenditures on	yr	273	1999	30r
Weddings				
Wedding (national average cost)		19936	2000	33r
Wedding (regional average total cost)		16195	1997	110r
Attendants' gifts		321	1998	33r
Bridal attendants' apparel (5 persons)		824	2000	33r
Bride's headpiece/veil		173	1998	33r
Bride's wedding dress		859	1998	33r
Clergy, religious facility fee		242	1998	33r
Engagement ring		3177	1998	33r
Flowers		789	1998	33r
Groom's formalwear rental		99	2000	33r
Limousine		410	1998	33r
Marriage license cost		70.00	4/01	35s
Men's formalwear (ushers, best man)		469	2000	33r
Mother of bride apparel		241	2000	33r
Music		866	1998	33r
Photography and videography		1368	1998	33r
Rehearsal dinner		728	1998	33r
Wedding invitations and announcements		341	1998	33r
Wedding reception		7968	2000	33r
Wedding rings (bride and groom)		1060	1998	33r

Missoula, MT

Item	Per	Value	Date	Ref.
Composite, ACCRA index		101.60	3/01	4c
Alcoholic Beverages				
Beer, Heineken, 12-oz, ex deposit	6	7.05	3/01	4c
J & B Scotch	750-ml	22.31	3/01	4c
Wine, Livingston or Gallo, Chablis blanc	1.5 liter	6.52	3/01	4c
Appliances				
Appliance repair, service call, washing machine	min lab chg	43.67	3/01	4c
Banking and Money				
Mortgage rate, incl. points and orig. fee, 30-yr. conv. fixed or ARM	mos	6.97	3/01	4c
Clothing				
Boys' brief, cotton	3	5.49	3/01	4c
Shirt, man's dress shirt		31.37	3/01	4c
Slacks, man's "No Wrinkles" khaki		46.50	3/01	4c
Communications				
Newspaper subscription, daily and Sunday delivery	mos	16.09	3/01	4c
Phone line, single, business, field visit	inst.	61.40	12/97	17s
Phone line, single, business, no field visit	inst.	61.40	12/97	17s
Phone line, single, residence, field visit	inst.	25.00	12/97	17s
Phone line, single, residence, no field visit	inst.	25.00	12/97	17s
Postal rate, express mail, up to half-pound		12.45	7/01	108r
Postal rate, letter, first class, first ounce		0.34	7/01	108r
Postal rate, letter, two ounces		0.57	7/01	108r
Postal rate, post card		0.21	7/01	108r
Postal rate, priority mail, two pounds		3.95	7/01	108r
Postal rate, priority mail, up to one pound		3.50	7/01	108r
Telephone bill, business, basic rate	mos	38.69	12/97	18c
Telephone bill, family of three	mos	26.36	3/01	4c
Telephone bill, residential, basic rate	mos	13.84	12/97	18c

Missoula, MT - continued

Item	Per	Value	Date	Ref.
Education				
Board, 4-year private college/university	yr	2128	1996	38s
Board, 4-year public college/university	yr	3609	1996	38s
Room, 4-year private college/university	yr	1388	1996	38s
Room, 4-year public college/university	yr	1778	1996	38s
Total cost, 4-year private college/university	yr	11062	1996	38s
Total cost, 4-year public college/university	yr	7754	1996	38s
Tuition, 2-year public college/university, in state	yr	1382	1996	38s
Tuition, 4-year private college/university, in state	yr	7545	1996	38s
Tuition, 4-year public college/university	yr	2367	1996	38s
Energy and Fuels				
Energy, combined forms, 2400 sq ft	mos	93.87	3/01	4c
Energy, exc. electricity, 2400 sq ft	mos	55.45	3/01	4c
Gas, cooking, winter, 10 therms	mos	8.60	2/96	98c
Gas, cooking, winter, 30 therms	mos	16.91	2/96	98c
Gas, cooking, winter, 50 therms	mos	25.22	2/96	98c
Gas, heating, winter, average use	mos	80.76	2/96	98c
Gas, natural, commercial rate	1000 cf	5.54	11/00	88s
Gas, regular unleaded, cash, self-service	gal	1.59	3/01	4c
Entertainment				
Bowling, Saturday evening rate	line	1.75	3/01	4c
Monopoly game, Parker Brothers', No. 9	game	11.39	3/01	4c
Movie, first-run, Saturday, evening	adm.	6.25	3/01	4c
Tennis balls, yellow, Wilson or Penn, 3	can	2.51	3/01	4c
Funerals				
Total cost of funeral		5401.08	1/99	78r
Acknowledgement cards		33.64	1/99	78r
Casket		2170.43	1/99	78r
Cosmetology, hair, other preparation		136.32	1/99	78r
Embalming		319.13	1/99	78r
Funeral at funeral home		370.21	1/99	78r
Hearse (local)		161.04	1/99	78r
Professional service charges		963.15	1/99	78r
Service car/van		133.99	1/99	78r
Transfer of remains to funeral home		159.82	1/99	78r
Vault		778.07	1/99	78r
Visitation/viewing		175.28	1/99	78r
Groceries				
Groceries, ACCRA Index		114.20	3/01	4c
Antibiotic ointment, Polysporin	0.5 oz	4.69	3/01	4c
Baby food, strained vegetables or fruit, lowest price	4-4.5 oz	0.39	3/01	4c
Bananas	lb	0.71	3/01	4c
Beef or hamburger, ground	lb	1.73	3/01	4c
Bread, white	loaf	0.96	3/01	4c
Cheese, Kraft grated Parmesan	8 oz	4.96	3/01	4c
Chicken, whole fryer	lb	1.11	3/01	4c
Cigarettes, Winston, Kings	carton	31.45	3/01	4c
Coffee, vacuum-packed	13 oz	3.19	3/01	4c
Corn Flakes, Kellogg's or Post Toasties	18 oz	3.47	3/01	4c
Corn, frozen, whole kernel, lowest price	16 oz	1.35	3/01	4c
Eggs, Grade A or AA	dozen	1.21	3/01	4c
Lettuce, iceberg	head	0.96	3/01	4c
Margarine, Blue Bonnet or Parkay, stick	lb	0.75	3/01	4c
Milk, whole	1/2 gal	1.81	3/01	4c
Orange juice, Minute Maid frozen	12 oz	1.84	3/01	4c
Peaches, halves or slices, Hunt's, Del Monte, or Libby's	29 oz	1.79	3/01	4c
Peas, green, Del Monte or Green Giant	15 oz	0.84	3/01	4c
Potatoes, white or red	10 lb	2.14	3/01	4c
Sausage, Jimmy Dean/Owens pork	lb	4.52	3/01	4c
Shortening, vegetable, Crisco	3 lb	3.11	3/01	4c
Soft drink, Coca Cola, ex deposit	2 liter	1.01	3/01	4c
Steak, T-bone	lb	6.91	3/01	4c
Sugar, cane or beet	4 lbs	2.05	3/01	4c
Tomatoes, Hunt's or Del Monte	14.5 oz	0.98	3/01	4c
Tuna, chunk, light	6 oz	0.95	3/01	4c

Values are in dollars or fractions of dollars. In the column headed *Ref*, references are shown to sources. Each reference is followed by a letter. These refer to the geographical level for which data were reported: s=State, r=Region, and c=City or metro. The abbreviation *ex* is used to mean *except* or *excluding*; *exp* stands for *expenditures*. For other abbreviations and further explanations, please see the Introduction.

Missoula, MT - continued

Item	Per	Value	Date	Ref.
Goods and Services				
Miscellaneous goods and services, ACCRA Index		107.10	3/01	4c
Hunting license	yr	10.00	4/01	34s
Health Care				
Health care, ACCRA Index		102.20	3/01	4c
Cardiac catheterization, ave hospital/ physician charges		13700	1998	77s
Childbirth, Cesarean delivery		11587	1997	13r
Childbirth, vaginal delivery		6725	1997	13r
Dentist's fee, adult teeth cleaning and periodic oral exam	visit	79.75	3/01	4c
Doctor's fee, routine exam, established patient	visit	54.75	3/01	4c
Hospital care, private room	day	543.00	3/01	4c
Hysterectomy, laproscopically-assisted, ave hospital/physician charges		11400	1998	76s
Hysterectomy, vaginal, ave hospital and physician charges		8290	1998	76s
Medicaid dispensing fee		2.00-4.20	1999	87s
Household Goods				
Dishwashing powder, Cascade	50 oz	4.02	3/01	4c
Tissues, facial, Kleenex brand	175	1.54	3/01	4c
Housing				
Housing, ACCRA Index		93.40	3/01	4c
Home value, median		108000	2001	53s
House, 2400 sq ft, 8000 sq ft lot, new, urban, utilities	total	192333	3/01	4c
House payment, principal and interest, 25% down payment	mos	957	3/01	4c
Rent, apartment, 2 br, 1 1/2-2 baths, unfurn, 950 sq ft, water	mos	662	3/01	4c
Rental unit, 1 bedroom, with utilities	mos	393	4/01	41c
Rental unit, 2 bedroom, with utilities	mos	523	4/01	41c
Rental unit, 3 bedroom, with utilities	mos	674	4/01	41c
Rental unit, 4 bedroom, with utilities	mos	857	4/01	41c
Legal Fees				
Divorce, filing fee		230.00	4/01	35s
Driver's license fee	renew	16.00	1999	48s
Driver's license fee	orig	16.00	1999	48s
Fishing license	yr	17.00	4/01	34s
Personal Goods				
Shampoo, Alberto VO5	15 oz	1.34	3/01	4c
Toothpaste, Crest or Colgate	6-7 oz	2.41	3/01	4c
Personal Services				
Dry cleaning, man's 2-pc suit		7.76	3/01	4c
Man's haircut, barbershop, no styling		10.37	3/01	4c
Woman's shampoo, trim, blow-dry, no style-change		23.60	3/01	4c
Restaurant Food				
Chicken, fried, thigh and drumstick, KFC/ Church's		2.44	3/01	4c
Hamburger with cheese, McDonald's	1/4 lb	2.09	3/01	4c
Pizza, Pizza Hut or Pizza Inn	11-12 in	10.49	3/01	4c
Transportation				
Transportation, ACCRA Index		100.70	3/01	4c
Bus fare, one-way	trip	0.85	2000	1c
Bus fare, to central business district	1-way	0.85	3/01	4c
Diesel at the pump	gal	1.35	10/99	73s
Gasoline before-tax price (cents)	gal	126.00	10/00	43s
Tire balance, computer or spin balance, front	wheel	7.13	3/01	4c
Travel				
Hotel room	night	54.24	2/01	94s
Utilities				
Utilities, ACCRA Index		83.00	3/01	4c
Electrical bill, average	mos	52.58	9/00	9s

Missoula, MT - continued

Item	Per	Value	Date	Ref.
Utilities - continued				
Electricity and other, mixed, 2400 sq ft, new home	mos	38.42	3/01	4c
Electricity cost, average	KWh	5.92	9/00	9s
Weddings				
Wedding (national average cost)		19936	2000	33r
Attendants' gifts		321	1998	33r
Bridal attendants' apparel (5 persons)		824	2000	33r
Bride's headpiece/veil		173	1998	33r
Bride's wedding dress		859	1998	33r
Clergy, religious facility fee		242	1998	33r
Engagement ring		3177	1998	33r
Flowers		789	1998	33r
Groom's formalwear rental		99	2000	33r
Limousine		410	1998	33r
Marriage license cost		30.25	4/01	35s
Men's formalwear (ushers, best man)		469	2000	33r
Mother of bride apparel		241	2000	33r
Music		866	1998	33r
Photography and videography		1368	1998	33r
Rehearsal dinner		728	1998	33r
Wedding invitations and announcements		341	1998	33r
Wedding reception		7968	2000	33r
Wedding rings (bride and groom)		1060	1998	33r

Mobile, AL

Item	Per	Value	Date	Ref.
Composite, ACCRA index		94.80	3/01	4c
Alcoholic Beverages				
Alcoholic beverage purchases	yr	253	1999	30r
Beer, Heineken, 12-oz, ex deposit	6	7.38	3/01	4c
J & B Scotch	750-ml	23.99	3/01	4c
Malt beverages, all types, all sizes, any origin	16 oz	0.96	7/01	11r
Wine, Livingston or Gallo, Chablis blanc	1.5 liter	6.05	3/01	4c
Appliances				
Appliance repair, service call, washing machine	min lab chg	45.00	3/01	4c
Major appliances, expenditures on	yr	172	1999	30r
Small appliances, housewares, expenditures on	yr	81	1999	30r
Banking and Money				
Mortgage interest and charges paid	yr	2039	1999	30r
Mortgage principal paid on owned property	yr	1026	1999	30r
Mortgage rate, incl. points and orig. fee, 30-yr. conv. fixed or ARM	mos	6.76	3/01	4c
Vehicle finance charges paid	yr	365	1999	30r
Business Expenses				
Business travel, car rental	day	45	2001	3c
Business travel, food	day	46	2001	3c
Business travel, hotel	day	87	2001	3c
Charity				
Cash contributions, expenditures	yr	1127	1999	30r
Child Care				
Child raising cost, total, age 0-2	yr	8540	1999	60r
Child raising cost, total, age 3-5	yr	8780	1999	60r
Child raising cost, total, age 6-8	yr	8820	1999	60r
Child raising cost, total, age 9-11	yr	8800	1999	60r
Child raising cost, total, age 12-14	yr	9510	1999	60r
Child raising cost, total, age 15-17	yr	9740	1999	60r
Child's child care and education, age 0-2	yr	1380	1999	60r
Child's child care and education, age 3-5	yr	1520	1999	60r
Child's child care and education, age 6-8	yr	990	1999	60r
Child's child care and education, age 9-11	yr	650	1999	60r
Child's child care and education, age 12-14	yr	490	1999	60r
Child's child care and education, age 15-17	yr	840	1999	60r
Child's clothing, age 0-2	yr	480	1999	60r
Child's clothing, age 3-5	yr	470	1999	60r
Child's clothing, age 6-8	yr	520	1999	60r
Child's clothing, age 9-11	yr	570	1999	60r

Values are in dollars or fractions of dollars. In the column headed *Ref*, references are shown to sources. Each reference is followed by a letter. These refer to the geographical level for which data were reported: s=State, r=Region, and c=City or metro. The abbreviation *ex* is used to mean *except* or *excluding*; *exp* stands for *expenditures*. For other abbreviations and further explanations, please see the Introduction.

Item	Per	Value	Date	Ref.
Child Care				
Child's clothing, age 12-14	yr	950	1999	60r
Child's clothing, age 15-17	yr	850	1999	60r
Child's food, age 0-2	yr	1000	1999	60r
Child's food, age 3-5	yr	1160	1999	60r
Child's food, age 6-8	yr	1490	1999	60r
Child's food, age 9-11	yr	1770	1999	60r
Child's food, age 12-14	yr	1770	1999	60r
Child's food, age 15-17	yr	1980	1999	60r
Child's health care, age 0-2	yr	620	1999	60r
Child's health care, age 3-5	yr	590	1999	60r
Child's health care, age 6-8	yr	680	1999	60r
Child's health care, age 9-11	yr	720	1999	60r
Child's health care, age 12-14	yr	730	1999	60r
Child's health care, age 15-17	yr	760	1999	60r
Child's housing, age 0-2	yr	3070	1999	60r
Child's housing, age 3-5	yr	3050	1999	60r
Child's housing, age 6-8	yr	3010	1999	60r
Child's housing, age 9-11	yr	2850	1999	60r
Child's housing, age 12-14	yr	3040	1999	60r
Child's housing, age 15-17	yr	2650	1999	60r
Child's personal care, reading, age 0-2	yr	910	1999	60r
Child's personal care, reading, age 3-5	yr	930	1999	60r
Child's personal care, reading, age 6-8	yr	960	1999	60r
Child's personal care, reading, age 9-11	yr	1000	1999	60r
Child's personal care, reading, age 12-14	yr	1170	1999	60r
Child's personal care, reading, age 15-17	yr	950	1999	60r
Daycare	mos	319	1998	37c
Daycare, 3-year old, 5 days, 8 hrs/day	mos	319	1998	85c
Clothing				
Apparel and services purchases	yr	1610	1999	30r
Boys' brief, cotton	3	5.62	3/01	4c
Boys, 2 to 15, expenditures on	yr	89	1999	30r
Children under 2, expenditures on	yr	79	1999	30r
Footwear, expenditures on	yr	283	1999	30r
Girls, 2 to 15, expenditures on	yr	103	1999	30r
Men and boys, expenditures on	yr	351	1999	30r
Men, 16 and over, expenditures on	yr	262	1999	30r
Shirt, man's dress shirt		25.79	3/01	4c
Slacks, man's "No Wrinkles" khaki		33.39	3/01	4c
Women, 16 and over, expenditures on	yr	538	1999	30r
Communications				
Newspaper subscription, daily and Sunday delivery	mos	9.95	3/01	4c
Phone line, single, business, field visit	inst.	69.00	12/97	17s
Phone line, single, business, no field visit	inst.	69.00	12/97	17s
Phone line, single, residence, field visit	inst.	40.00	12/97	17s
Phone line, single, residence, no field visit	inst.	40.00	12/97	17s
Postage and stationery, expenditures on	yr	104	1999	30r
Postal rate, express mail, up to half-pound		12.45	7/01	108r
Postal rate, letter, first class, first ounce		0.34	7/01	108r
Postal rate, letter, two ounces		0.57	7/01	108r
Postal rate, post card		0.21	7/01	108r
Postal rate, priority mail, two pounds		3.95	7/01	108r
Postal rate, priority mail, up to one pound		3.50	7/01	108r
Telephone bill, business, basic rate	mos	40.71	12/97	18c
Telephone bill, family of three	mos	23.75	3/01	4c
Telephone bill, residential, basic rate	mos	16.30	12/97	18c
Telephone services, expenditures on	yr	860	1999	30r
Education				
Board, 4-year private college/university	yr	2256	1996	38s
Board, 4-year public college/university	yr	1739	1996	38s
Education expenditures	yr	431	1999	30r
Room, 4-year private college/university	yr	1799	1996	38s
Room, 4-year public college/university	yr	1757	1996	38s
Total cost, 4-year private college/university	yr	11635	1996	38s
Total cost, 4-year public college/university	yr	5737	1996	38s
Tuition, 2-year public college/university, in state	yr	1317	1996	38s
Tuition, 4-year private college/university, in state	yr	7580	1996	38s
Tuition, 4-year public college/university	yr	2240	1996	38s

Item	Per	Value	Date	Ref.
Energy and Fuels				
Electricity	KWh	0.09	7/01	11r
Electricity	500 KWhs	47.29	7/01	11r
Energy, combined forms, 2400 sq ft	mos	132.06	3/01	4c
Energy, exc. electricity, 2400 sq ft	mos	57.51	3/01	4c
Fuel oil #2	gal	1.43	7/01	11r
Fuel oil and other fuels, expenditures on	yr	45	1999	30r
Gas, cooking, winter, 10 therms	mos	14.30	2/96	98c
Gas, cooking, winter, 30 therms	mos	26.90	2/96	98c
Gas, cooking, winter, 50 therms	mos	38.65	2/96	98c
Gas, heating, winter, average use	mos	73.63	2/96	98c
Gas, natural, commercial rate	1000 cf	9.50	11/00	88s
Gas, regular unleaded, cash, self-service	gal	1.40	3/01	4c
Gasoline, all types	gal	1.60	7/01	11r
Gasoline, unleaded midgrade	gal	1.65	7/01	11r
Gasoline, unleaded premium	gal	1.74	7/01	11r
Natural gas, expenditures on	yr	164	1999	30r
Utility (piped) gas, therm		1.01	7/01	11r
Utility (piped) gas, 40 therms		44.29	7/01	11r
Utility (piped) gas, 100 therms		97.44	7/01	11r
Entertainment				
Bowling, Saturday evening rate	line	3.25	3/01	4c
Entertainment purchases	yr	1574	1999	30r
Fees and admissions paid	yr	371	1999	30r
Monopoly game, Parker Brothers', No. 9	game	10.56	3/01	4c
Movie, first-run, Saturday, evening	adm.	7.00	3/01	4c
Reading purchases	yr	121	1999	30r
Television, radios, sound equipment, expenditures on	yr	561	1999	30r
Tennis balls, yellow, Wilson or Penn, 3	can	2.48	3/01	4c
Groceries				
Groceries, ACCRA Index		93.80	3/01	4c
American processed cheese	lb	3.50	7/01	11r
Antibiotic ointment, Polysporin	0.5 oz	4.73	3/01	4c
Baby food, strained vegetables or fruit, lowest price	4-4.5 oz	0.36	3/01	4c
Bakery products, expenditures on	yr	261	1999	30r
Bananas	lb	0.53	3/01	4c
Bananas	lb	0.47	7/01	11r
Beans, dried, any type, all sizes	lb	0.63	7/01	11r
Beef for stew, boneless	lb	2.86	7/01	11r
Beef or hamburger, ground	lb	1.65	3/01	4c
Beef, expenditures on	yr	210	1999	30r
Bologna, all beef or mixed	lb	2.29	7/01	11r
Bread, French	lb	1.66	7/01	11r
Bread, white	loaf	0.86	3/01	4c
Bread, white, pan	lb	0.87	7/01	11r
Bread, whole wheat, pan	lb	1.38	7/01	11r
Broccoli	lb	1.04	7/01	11r
Butter, salted, grade AA, stick	lb	2.26	7/01	11r
Butter, yoghurt, cheese, etc, expenditures on	yr	170	1999	30r
Cabbage	lb	0.42	7/01	11r
Cereals and cereal products, expenditures on	yr	140	1999	30r
Cheddar cheese, natural	lb	3.75	7/01	11r
Cheese, Kraft grated Parmesan	8 oz	3.30	3/01	4c
Chicken breast, bone-in	lb	1.85	7/01	11r
Chicken legs, bone-in	lb	1.34	7/01	11r
Chicken, fresh, whole	lb	1.05	7/01	11r
Chicken, whole fryer	lb	0.86	3/01	4c
Chops, boneless,	lb	4.13	7/01	11r
Chuck roast, graded and ungraded, excl U.S. prime and choice	lb	2.35	7/01	11r
Chuck roast, U.S. choice, boneless	lb	2.67	7/01	11r
Cigarettes, Winston, Kings	carton	30.02	3/01	4c
Coffee, 100%, ground roast, all sizes	lb	2.88	7/01	11r
Coffee, instant, plain, regular, all sizes	16 oz	9.25	7/01	11r
Coffee, vacuum-packed	13 oz	2.25	3/01	4c
Cola, non diet,	2 liter	1.11	7/01	11r
Corn Flakes, Kellogg's or Post Toasties	18 oz	2.68	3/01	4c
Corn, frozen, whole kernel, lowest price	16 oz	1.02	3/01	4c

Values are in dollars or fractions of dollars. In the column headed *Ref*, references are shown to sources. Each reference is followed by a letter. These refer to the geographical level for which data were reported: s=State, r=Region, and c=City or metro. The abbreviation *ex* is used to mean *except* or *excluding*; *exp* stands for *expenditures*. For other abbreviations and further explanations, please see the Introduction.

Mobile, AL - continued

Item	Per	Value	Date	Ref.
Groceries				
Crackers, soda, salted	lb	1.70	7/01	11r
Dairy product purchases	yr	282	1999	30r
Eggs, expenditures on	yr	32	1999	30r
Eggs, Grade A or AA	dozen	1.19	3/01	4c
Fats and oils, expenditures on	yr	79	1999	30r
Fish and seafood, expenditures on	yr	99	1999	30r
Flour, white, all purpose	lb	0.32	7/01	11r
Food (excl fruit and vegetables), eaten at home, purchases	yr	815	1999	30r
Food cooked on trips, expenditures on	yr	36	1999	30r
Food purchases	yr	4533	1999	30r
Food purchases, eaten away from home	yr	1873	1999	30r
Food purchases, food eaten at home	yr	2660	1999	30r
Fresh fruits, expenditures on	yr	128	1999	30r
Fresh milk and cream, expenditures on	yr	112	1999	30r
Fresh vegetables, expenditures on	yr	131	1999	30r
Fruit and vegetable purchases	yr	438	1999	30r
Grapefruit	lb	0.59	7/01	11r
Grapes, Thompson, seedless	lb	2.12	7/01	11r
Ground beef, 100% beef	lb	1.76	7/01	11r
Ground beef, lean and extra lean	lb	2.60	7/01	11r
Ground chuck, 100% beef	lb	2.08	7/01	11r
Ham, boneless, excl canned	lb	2.71	7/01	11r
Ham, rump or shank half, bone-in, smoked	lb	2.19	7/01	11r
Ice cream, prepackaged, bulk, regular	1/2 gal	3.93	7/01	11r
Lemons	lb	1.32	7/01	11r
Lettuce, iceberg	head	0.95	3/01	4c
Lettuce, iceberg	lb	0.76	7/01	11r
Margarine, Blue Bonnet or Parkay, stick	lb	0.69	3/01	4c
Milk, fresh, low fat,	gal	2.75	7/01	11r
Milk, fresh, whole, fortified	gal	2.97	7/01	11r
Milk, whole	1/2 gal	1.79	3/01	4c
Nonalcoholic beverages, expenditures on	yr	228	1999	30r
Orange juice, frozen concentrate	16 oz	1.95	7/01	11r
Orange juice, Minute Maid frozen	12 oz	1.53	3/01	4c
Oranges, Navel	lb	0.73	7/01	11r
Oranges, Valencia	lb	0.55	7/01	11r
Peaches, halves or slices, Hunt's, Del Monte, or Libby's	29 oz	1.51	3/01	4c
Peanut butter, creamy, all sizes	lb	1.83	7/01	11r
Pears, Anjou	lb	0.98	7/01	11r
Peas, green, Del Monte or Green Giant	15 oz	0.62	3/01	4c
Pork chops, center cut, bone-in	lb	3.33	7/01	11r
Pork sausage, fresh, loose	lb	2.59	7/01	11r
Pork shoulder picnic, bone-in, smoked	lb	1.12	7/01	11r
Pork, expenditures on	yr	162	1999	30r
Potato chips	16 oz	3.59	7/01	11r
Potatoes, frozen, french fried	lb	1.00	7/01	11r
Potatoes, white or red	10 lb	2.67	3/01	4c
Potatoes, white, all types	lb	0.44	7/01	11r
Poultry, expenditures on	yr	137	1999	30r
Processed fruits, expenditures on	yr	97	1999	30r
Processed vegetables, expenditures on	yr	82	1999	30r
Rice, white, long grain, uncooked	lb	0.51	7/01	11r
Round roast, graded and ungraded, excl U.S. prime and choice	lb	2.96	7/01	11r
Round steak, graded and ungraded, excl U.S. prime and choice	lb	3.11	7/01	11r
Sausage, Jimmy Dean/Owens pork	lb	2.57	3/01	4c
Shortening, vegetable, Crisco	3 lb	2.94	3/01	4c
Sirloin steak, graded and ungraded, excl U.S. prime and choice	lb	4.23	7/01	11r
Soft drink, Coca Cola, ex deposit	2 liter	1.15	3/01	4c
Spaghetti and macaroni	lb	0.78	7/01	11r
Steak, round, U.S. choice, boneless	lb	3.56	7/01	11r
Steak, sirloin, U.S. choice, boneless	lb	5.65	7/01	11r
Steak, T-bone	lb	6.75	3/01	4c
Strawberries, dry pint	12 oz	1.50	7/01	11r
Sugar and other sweets, expenditures on	yr	99	1999	30r
Sugar, cane or beet	4 lbs	1.49	3/01	4c
Sugar, white, 33-80 ounce package	lb	0.39	7/01	11r
Sugar, white, all sizes	lb	0.42	7/01	11r

Mobile, AL - continued

Item	Per	Value	Date	Ref.
Groceries - continued				
Tobacco products and smoking supplies purchases	yr	288	1999	30r
Tomatoes, field grown	lb	1.43	7/01	11r
Tomatoes, Hunt's or Del Monte	14.5 oz	0.74	3/01	4c
Tuna, chunk, light	6 oz	0.47	3/01	4c
Tuna, light, chunk	lb	1.77	7/01	11r
Turkey, frozen, whole	lb	1.05	7/01	11r
Goods and Services				
Miscellaneous goods and services, ACCRA Index		98.60	3/01	4c
Hunting license	yr	16.00	4/01	34s
Health Care				
Health care, ACCRA Index		82.60	3/01	4c
Cardiac catheterization, ave hospital/ physician charges		15260	1998	77s
Childbirth, Cesarean delivery		11587	1997	13r
Childbirth, vaginal delivery		6725	1997	13r
Dentist's fee, adult teeth cleaning and periodic oral exam	visit	64.40	3/01	4c
Doctor's fee, routine exam, established patient	visit	49.60	3/01	4c
Drugs, expenditures on	yr	399	1999	30r
Health care purchases	yr	1971	1999	30r
Health insurance expenditures	yr	933	1999	30r
Hospital care, private room	day	281.80	3/01	4c
Hysterectomy, laproscopically-assisted, ave hospital/physician charges		16780	1998	76s
Hysterectomy, vaginal, ave hospital and physician charges		10990	1998	76s
Medicaid dispensing fee		5.40	1999	87s
Medical services expenditures	yr	547	1999	30r
Medical supplies, expenditures on	yr	91	1999	30r
Household Goods				
Dishwashing powder, Cascade	50 oz	3.07	3/01	4c
Floor coverings, expenditures on	yr	44	1999	30r
Furniture, expenditures on	yr	335	1999	30r
Household furnishings and equipment purchases	yr	1328	1999	30r
Household textiles, expenditures on	yr	89	1999	30r
Laundry and cleaning supplies, expenditures on	yr	113	1999	30r
Tissues, facial, Kleenex brand	175	1.31	3/01	4c
Housing				
Housing, ACCRA Index		88.10	3/01	4c
Home, 2200 sq ft, 4-br, 2-bath, 2-car garage, average		163100	2000	47c
Home price, existing, ave		160100	10/00	90r
Home value, median		115000	2001	53s
House, 2400 sq ft, 8000 sq ft lot, new, urban, utilities	total	192969	3/01	4c
House payment, principal and interest, 25% down payment	mos	940	3/01	4c
Household operation expenditures	yr	553	1999	30r
Housekeeping supplies purchases	yr	473	1999	30r
Housing, expenditures on	yr	10303	1999	30r
Maintenance, repairs, insurance expenditures	yr	699	1999	30r
Monthly rental value of owned home	mos	505	1999	30r
Owned dwellings, expenditures own	yr	3465	1999	30r
Rent expenditures	yr	1641	1999	30r
Rent, apartment, 2 br, 1 1/2-2 baths, unfurn, 950 sq ft, water	mos	529	3/01	4c
Rental unit, 1 bedroom, with utilities	mos	430	4/01	41c
Rental unit, 2 bedroom, with utilities	mos	493	4/01	41c
Rental unit, 3 bedroom, with utilities	mos	664	4/01	41c
Rental unit, 4 bedroom, with utilities	mos	779	4/01	41c
Shelter, expenditures on	yr	5467	1999	30r
Insurance and Pensions				
Life and other personal insurance purchases	yr	414	1999	30r

Values are in dollars or fractions of dollars. In the column headed *Ref*, references are shown to sources. Each reference is followed by a letter. These refer to the geographical level for which data were reported: s=State, r=Region, and c=City or metro. The abbreviation *ex* is used to mean *except* or *excluding*; *exp* stands for expenditures. For other abbreviations and further explanations, please see the Introduction.

Mobile, AL - continued

Item	Per	Value	Date	Ref.
Insurance and Pensions				
Pensions and Social Security, expenditures on	yr	2635	1999	30r
Personal insurance and pensions, expenditures on	yr	3048	1999	30r
Legal Fees				
Divorce, filing fee		146.00-193.00	4/01	35s
Driver's license fee	orig	18.50	1999	48s
Driver's license fee	renew	18.50	1999	48s
Personal Goods				
Personal care products and services purchases	yr	393	1999	30r
Shampoo, Alberto VO5	15 oz	1.08	3/01	4c
Toothpaste, Crest or Colgate	6-7 oz	2.40	3/01	4c
Personal Services				
Dry cleaning, man's 2-pc suit		6.51	3/01	4c
Man's haircut, barbershop, no styling		10.20	3/01	4c
Personal services, household, expenditures on	yr	258	1999	30r
Woman's shampoo, trim, blow-dry, no style-change		21.40	3/01	4c
Pets				
Pets, toys, and playground equipment, expenditures on	yr	306	1999	30r
Restaurant Food				
Chicken, fried, thigh and drumstick, KFC/Church's		2.39	3/01	4c
Hamburger with cheese, McDonald's	1/4 lb	1.97	3/01	4c
Pizza, Pizza Hut or Pizza Inn	11-12 in	9.59	3/01	4c
Taxes				
Federal income taxes paid	yr	2047	1999	30r
Personal taxes, expenditures on	yr	2554	1999	30r
Property taxes paid	yr	726	1999	30r
State and local income taxes paid	yr	363	1999	30r
Transportation				
Transportation, ACCRA Index		97.60	3/01	4c
Bus fare, to central business district	1-way	1.25	3/01	4c
Cars and trucks, new, expenditures on	yr	1648	1999	30r
Cars and trucks, used, expenditures on	yr	1651	1999	30r
Diesel at the pump	gal	1.19	10/99	73s
Gasoline and motor oil purchases	yr	1052	1999	30r
Gasoline before-tax price (cents)	gal	104.10	10/00	43s
Maintenance and repair expenditures	yr	621	1999	30r
Public transportation, expenditures on	yr	298	1999	30r
Tire balance, computer or spin balance, front	wheel	7.10	3/01	4c
Transportation purchases	yr	6738	1999	30r
Vehicle expenses, miscellaneous, purchases	yr	2033	1999	30r
Vehicle insurance payments	yr	696	1999	30r
Vehicle purchases (net outlay)	yr	3354	1999	30r
Vehicle rental, lease expenditures	yr	352	1999	30r
Utilities				
Utilities, ACCRA Index		108.30	3/01	4c
Electrical bill, average	mos	83.42	9/00	9s
Electricity, expenditures on	yr	1115	1999	30r
Electricity and other, mixed, 2400 sq ft, new home	mos	74.55	3/01	4c
Electricity cost, average	KWh	5.60	9/00	9s
Water and other public services, expenditures on	yr	298	1999	30r
Weddings				
Wedding (national average cost)		19936	2000	33r
Attendants' gifts		321	1998	33r
Bridal attendants' apparel (5 persons)		824	2000	33r
Bride's headpiece/veil		173	1998	33r
Bride's wedding dress		859	1998	33r
Clergy, religious facility fee		242	1998	33r
Engagement ring		3177	1998	33r

Mobile, AL - continued

Item	Per	Value	Date	Ref.
Weddings - continued				
Flowers		789	1998	33r
Groom's formalwear rental		99	2000	33r
Limousine		410	1998	33r
Marriage license cost		25.00	4/01	35s
Men's formalwear (ushers, best man)		469	2000	33r
Mother of bride apparel		241	2000	33r
Music		866	1998	33r
Photography and videography		1368	1998	33r
Rehearsal dinner		728	1998	33r
Wedding invitations and announcements		341	1998	33r
Wedding reception		7968	2000	33r
Wedding rings (bride and groom)		1060	1998	33r

Modesto, CA

Item	Per	Value	Date	Ref.
Average annual expenditures	yr	40662	1999	30r
Composite, ACCRA index		108.50	3/01	4c
Alcoholic Beverages				
Alcoholic beverage purchases	yr	372	1999	30r
Beer, Heineken, 12-oz, ex deposit	6	7.28	3/01	4c
J & B Scotch	750-ml	19.99	3/01	4c
Malt beverages, all types, all sizes, any origin	16 oz	0.94	7/01	11r
Wine, Livingston or Gallo, Chablis blanc	1.5 liter	5.01	3/01	4c
Wine, red and white table, all sizes, any origin	liter	6.00	7/01	11r
Appliances				
Appliance repair, service call, washing machine	min lab chg	45.99	3/01	4c
Major appliances, expenditures on	yr	167	1999	30r
Small appliances, housewares, expenditures on	yr	105	1999	30r
Banking and Money				
Mortgage interest and charges paid	yr	3368	1999	30r
Mortgage principal paid on owned property	yr	1677	1999	30r
Mortgage rate, incl. points and orig. fee, 30-yr. conv. fixed or ARM	mos	6.97	3/01	4c
Vehicle finance charges paid	yr	311	1999	30r
Charity				
Cash contributions, expenditures	yr	1344	1999	30r
Child Care				
Child raising cost, total, age 0-2	yr	9140	1999	60r
Child raising cost, total, age 3-5	yr	9370	1999	60r
Child raising cost, total, age 6-8	yr	9450	1999	60r
Child raising cost, total, age 9-11	yr	9470	1999	60r
Child raising cost, total, age 12-14	yr	10170	1999	60r
Child raising cost, total, age 15-17	yr	10360	1999	60r
Child's child care and education, age 0-2	yr	1250	1999	60r
Child's child care and education, age 3-5	yr	1380	1999	60r
Child's child care and education, age 6-8	yr	890	1999	60r
Child's child care and education, age 9-11	yr	580	1999	60r
Child's child care and education, age 12-14	yr	430	1999	60r
Child's child care and education, age 15-17	yr	730	1999	60r
Child's clothing, age 0-2	yr	430	1999	60r
Child's clothing, age 3-5	yr	420	1999	60r
Child's clothing, age 6-8	yr	470	1999	60r
Child's clothing, age 9-11	yr	520	1999	60r
Child's clothing, age 12-14	yr	870	1999	60r
Child's clothing, age 15-17	yr	770	1999	60r
Child's food, age 0-2	yr	1120	1999	60r
Child's food, age 3-5	yr	1280	1999	60r
Child's food, age 6-8	yr	1640	1999	60r
Child's food, age 9-11	yr	1930	1999	60r
Child's food, age 12-14	yr	1940	1999	60r
Child's food, age 15-17	yr	2150	1999	60r
Child's health care, age 0-2	yr	490	1999	60r
Child's health care, age 3-5	yr	470	1999	60r
Child's health care, age 6-8	yr	530	1999	60r
Child's health care, age 9-11	yr	570	1999	60r
Child's health care, age 12-14	yr	580	1999	60r

Values are in dollars or fractions of dollars. In the column headed *Ref*, references are shown to sources. Each reference is followed by a letter. These refer to the geographical level for which data were reported: s=State, r=Region, and c=City or metro. The abbreviation *ex* is used to mean *except* or *excluding*; *exp* stands for expenditures. For other abbreviations and further explanations, please see the Introduction.

Modesto, CA - continued

Item	Per	Value	Date	Ref.
Child Care				
Child's health care, age 15-17	yr	610	1999	60r
Child's housing, age 0-2	yr	3630	1999	60r
Child's housing, age 3-5	yr	3610	1999	60r
Child's housing, age 6-8	yr	3570	1999	60r
Child's housing, age 9-11	yr	3410	1999	60r
Child's housing, age 12-14	yr	3600	1999	60r
Child's housing, age 15-17	yr	3210	1999	60r
Child's personal care, reading, age 0-2	yr	1040	1999	60r
Child's personal care, reading, age 3-5	yr	1060	1999	60r
Child's personal care, reading, age 6-8	yr	1090	1999	60r
Child's personal care, reading, age 9-11	yr	1130	1999	60r
Child's personal care, reading, age 12-14	yr	1300	1999	60r
Child's personal care, reading, age 15-17	yr	1080	1999	60r
Clothing				
Apparel and services purchases	yr	1863	1999	30r
Boys' brief, cotton	3	6.62	3/01	4c
Boys, 2 to 15, expenditures on	yr	80	1999	30r
Children under 2, expenditures on	yr	74	1999	30r
Footwear, expenditures on	yr	307	1999	30r
Girls, 2 to 15, expenditures on	yr	101	1999	30r
Men and boys, expenditures on	yr	443	1999	30r
Men, 16 and over, expenditures on	yr	363	1999	30r
Shirt, man's dress shirt		30.87	3/01	4c
Slacks, man's "No Wrinkles" khaki		41.50	3/01	4c
Women, 16 and over, expenditures on	yr	594	1999	30r
Communications				
Cable modem installation, AT&T-BIS		150.00	6/99	103s
Cable modem installation, Charter		99.00-169.00	6/99	103s
Cable modem installation, Comcast		95.00	6/99	103s
Cable modem installation, Cox		99.00-174.95	6/99	103s
Cable modem installation, Media One		100.00	6/99	103s
Cable modem installation, Time Warner		75.00-225.00	6/99	103s
Cable modem rate, cable subscriber, AT&T-BIS	mos	39.95	6/99	103s
Cable modem rate, cable subscriber, Charter	mos	49.95-79.95	6/99	103s
Cable modem rate, cable subscriber, Comcast	mos	39.95	6/99	103s
Cable modem rate, cable subscriber, Cox	mos	29.95-44.95	6/99	103s
Cable modem rate, cable subscriber, Media One	mos	34.95-39.95	6/99	103s
Cable modem rate, cable subscriber, Time Warner	mos	39.95-49.95	6/99	103s
Cable modem rate, non-cable subscriber, Charter	mos	59.95-89.95	6/99	103s
Cable modem rate, non-cable subscriber, Comcast	mos	49.95	6/99	103s
Cable modem rate, non-cable subscriber, Cox	mos	42.95-54.95	6/99	103s
Cable modem rate, non-cable subscriber, Media One	mos	49.95	6/99	103s
Cable modem rate, non-cable subscriber, Time Warner	mos	39.95-54.95	6/99	103s
Newspaper subscription, daily and Sunday delivery	mos	12.08	3/01	4c
Phone line, single, business, field visit	inst.	70.75	12/97	17s
Phone line, single, business, no field visit	inst.	70.75	12/97	17s
Phone line, single, residence, field visit	inst.	34.75	12/97	17s
Phone line, single, residence, no field visit	inst.	34.75	12/97	17s
Postage and stationery, expenditures on	yr	150	1999	30r
Postal rate, express mail, up to half-pound		12.45	7/01	108r
Postal rate, letter, first class, first ounce		0.34	7/01	108r
Postal rate, letter, two ounces		0.57	7/01	108r
Postal rate, post card		0.21	7/01	108r
Postal rate, priority mail, two pounds		3.95	7/01	108r
Postal rate, priority mail, up to one pound		3.50	7/01	108r
Telephone bill, family of three	mos	22.17	3/01	4c

Modesto, CA - continued

Item	Per	Value	Date	Ref.
Communications - continued				
Telephone services, expenditures on	yr	825	1999	30r
Education				
Board, 4-year private college/university	yr	2970	1996	38s
Board, 4-year public college/university	yr	2516	1996	38s
Education expenditures	yr	676	1999	30r
Room, 4-year private college/university	yr	3196	1996	38s
Room, 4-year public college/university	yr	3031	1996	38s
Total cost, 4-year private college/university	yr	20143	1996	38s
Total cost, 4-year public college/university	yr	8213	1996	38s
Tuition, 2-year public college/university, in state	yr	362	1996	38s
Tuition, 4-year private college/university, in state	yr	13977	1996	38s
Tuition, 4-year public college/university	yr	2666	1996	38s
Energy and Fuels				
Electricity	500 KWhs	48.23	7/01	11r
Electricity	KWh	0.11	7/01	11r
Energy, combined forms, 2400 sq ft	mos	105.66	3/01	4c
Energy, exc. electricity, 2400 sq ft	mos	39.64	3/01	4c
Fuel oil and other fuels, expenditures on	yr	35	1999	30r
Gas, natural, commercial rate	1000 cf	8.74	11/00	88s
Gas, regular unleaded, cash, self-service	gal	1.60	3/01	4c
Gasoline, all types	gal	1.91	7/01	11r
Gasoline, unleaded premium	gal	2.05	7/01	11r
Gasoline, unleaded regular	gal	1.83	7/01	11r
Natural gas, expenditures on	yr	255	1999	30r
Utility (piped) gas, therm		0.98	7/01	11r
Utility (piped) gas, 40 therms		40.74	7/01	11r
Utility (piped) gas, 100 therms		96.80	7/01	11r
Entertainment				
Bowling, Saturday evening rate	line	4.00	3/01	4c
Entertainment purchases	yr	2139	1999	30r
Fees and admissions paid	yr	545	1999	30r
Monopoly game, Parker Brothers', No. 9	game	12.38	3/01	4c
Movie, first-run, Saturday, evening	adm.	7.58	3/01	4c
Television, radios, sound equipment, expenditures on	yr	624	1999	30r
Tennis balls, yellow, Wilson or Penn, 3	can	2.47	3/01	4c
Funerals				
Total cost of funeral		5401.08	1/99	78r
Acknowledgement cards		33.64	1/99	78r
Casket		2170.43	1/99	78r
Cosmetology, hair, other preparation		136.32	1/99	78r
Embalming		319.13	1/99	78r
Funeral at funeral home		370.21	1/99	78r
Hearse (local)		161.04	1/99	78r
Professional service charges		963.15	1/99	78r
Service car/van		133.99	1/99	78r
Transfer of remains to funeral home		159.82	1/99	78r
Vault		778.07	1/99	78r
Visitation/viewing		175.28	1/99	78r
Groceries				
Groceries, ACCRA Index		119.50	3/01	4c
Antibiotic ointment, Polysporin	0.5 oz	4.89	3/01	4c
Apples, red delicious	lb	0.84	7/01	11r
Baby food, strained vegetables or fruit, lowest price	4-4.5 oz	0.52	3/01	4c
Bacon, sliced	lb	3.38	7/01	11r
Bakery products, expenditures on	yr	299	1999	30r
Bananas	lb	0.61	3/01	4c
Bananas	lb	0.54	7/01	11r
Beans, dried, any type, all sizes	lb	0.76	7/01	11r
Beef or hamburger, ground	lb	1.86	3/01	4c
Beef, expenditures on	yr	222	1999	30r
Bread, white	loaf	1.27	3/01	4c
Bread, white, pan	lb	0.99	7/01	11r
Butter, yoghurt, cheese, etc, expenditures on	yr	211	1999	30r
Cereals and bakery product purchases	yr	466	1999	30r

Values are in dollars or fractions of dollars. In the column headed *Ref*, references are shown to sources. Each reference is followed by a letter. These refer to the geographical level for which data were reported: s=State, r=Region, and c=City or metro. The abbreviation *ex* is used to mean *except* or *excluding*; *exp* stands for *expenditures*. For other abbreviations and further explanations, please see the Introduction.

Modesto, CA - continued

Item	Per	Value	Date	Ref.
Groceries				
Cereals and cereal products, expenditures on	yr	168	1999	30r
Cheese, Kraft grated Parmesan	8 oz	4.25	3/01	4c
Chicken breast, bone-in	lb	2.45	7/01	11r
Chicken, fresh, whole	lb	1.19	7/01	11r
Chicken, whole fryer	lb	1.16	3/01	4c
Chops, boneless,	lb	4.00	7/01	11r
Chuck roast, graded and ungraded, excl U.S. prime and choice	lb	2.55	7/01	11r
Cigarettes, Winston, Kings	carton	37.63	3/01	4c
Coffee, 100%, ground roast, all sizes	lb	3.80	7/01	11r
Coffee, vacuum-packed	13 oz	3.17	3/01	4c
Cookies, chocolate chip	lb	2.83	7/01	11r
Corn Flakes, Kellogg's or Post Toasties	18 oz	3.25	3/01	4c
Corn, frozen, whole kernel, lowest price	16 oz	1.34	3/01	4c
Dairy product purchases	yr	341	1999	30r
Eggs, expenditures on	yr	39	1999	30r
Eggs, Grade A or AA	dozen	1.97	3/01	4c
Eggs, grade AA, large	dozen	1.23	7/01	11r
Fats and oils, expenditures on	yr	88	1999	30r
Fish and seafood, expenditures on	yr	121	1999	30r
Food (excl fruit and vegetables), eaten at home, purchases	yr	1001	1999	30r
Food cooked on trips, expenditures on	yr	64	1999	30r
Food purchases	yr	5312	1999	30r
Food purchases, eaten away from home	yr	2180	1999	30r
Food purchases, food eaten at home	yr	3132	1999	30r
Fresh fruits, expenditures on	yr	186	1999	30r
Fresh milk and cream, expenditures on	yr	130	1999	30r
Fresh vegetables, expenditures on	yr	177	1999	30r
Grapefruit	lb	0.68	7/01	11r
Grapes, Thompson, seedless	lb	2.42	7/01	11r
Ground beef, lean and extra lean	lb	2.46	7/01	11r
Ice cream, prepackaged, bulk, regular	1/2 gal	3.62	7/01	11r
Lettuce, iceberg	head	0.87	3/01	4c
Lettuce, iceberg	lb	0.63	7/01	11r
Margarine, Blue Bonnet or Parkay, stick	lb	1.05	3/01	4c
Meats, poultry, fish, and egg purchases	yr	761	1999	30r
Milk, fresh, low fat	gal	2.80	7/01	11r
Milk, fresh, whole, fortified	gal	2.88	7/01	11r
Milk, whole	1/2 gal	1.93	3/01	4c
Nonalcoholic beverages, expenditures on	yr	258	1999	30r
Orange juice, Minute Maid frozen	12 oz	1.74	3/01	4c
Oranges, Navel	lb	0.97	7/01	11r
Oranges, Valencia	lb	0.43	7/01	11r
Peaches	lb	1.38	7/01	11r
Peaches, halves or slices, Hunt's, Del Monte, or Libby's	29 oz	1.74	3/01	4c
Peanut butter, creamy, all sizes	lb	2.14	7/01	11r
Peas, green, Del Monte or Green Giant	15 oz	0.86	3/01	4c
Pork chops, center cut, bone-in	lb	3.83	7/01	11r
Pork, expenditures on	yr	141	1999	30r
Potatoes, white or red	10 lb	1.93	3/01	4c
Potatoes, white, all types	lb	0.37	7/01	11r
Poultry, expenditures on	yr	146	1999	30r
Processed fruits, expenditures on	yr	118	1999	30r
Processed vegetables, expenditures on	yr	81	1999	30r
Round roast, graded and ungraded, excl U.S. prime and choice	lb	3.07	7/01	11r
Round roast, U.S. choice, boneless	lb	3.37	7/01	11r
Round steak, graded and ungraded, excl U.S. prime and choice	lb	3.51	7/01	11r
Sausage, Jimmy Dean/Owens pork	lb	4.06	3/01	4c
Shortening, vegetable, Crisco	3 lb	3.62	3/01	4c
Sirloin steak, graded and ungraded, excl U.S. prime and choice	lb	4.67	7/01	11r
Soft drink, Coca Cola, ex deposit	2 liter	1.30	3/01	4c
Steak, sirloin, U.S. choice, boneless	lb	6.20	7/01	11r
Steak, T-bone	lb	6.99	3/01	4c
Strawberries, dry pint	12 oz	1.79	7/01	11r
Sugar and other sweets, expenditures on	yr	124	1999	30r
Sugar, cane or beet	4 lbs	1.70	3/01	4c

Modesto, CA - continued

Item	Per	Value	Date	Ref.
Groceries - continued				
Sugar, white, all sizes	lb	0.46	7/01	11r
Tobacco products and smoking supplies purchases	yr	217	1999	30r
Tomatoes, field grown	lb	1.17	7/01	11r
Tomatoes, Hunt's or Del Monte	14.5 oz	0.97	3/01	4c
Tuna, chunk, light	6 oz	0.81	3/01	4c
Tuna, light, chunk	lb	2.05	7/01	11r
Goods and Services				
Miscellaneous goods and services, ACCRA Index		109.20	3/01	4c
B&B Japanese maple (acer japonicum)	gal	39.99	4/00	93r
Boxwood (buxus)	2 gal	14.99-24.99	4/00	93r
Christmas tree, noble fir		40-60	2000	65s
Daylilly (hemerocallis)	gal	6.99-8.99	4/00	93r
Flat of annuals		16.68	4/00	93r
Fountain grass (pennisetum)	gal	7.99-11.99	4/00	93r
Hanging basket (10 in)		29.99	4/00	93r
Hardy geranium (geranium)	gal	6.99-11.99	4/00	93r
Hosta (hosta)	gal	6.99-18.99	4/00	93r
Lilac (syrubga vulgaris)	2 gal	14.99-17.99	4/00	93r
Miscellaneous purchases	yr	1070	1999	30r
Rhododendron (rhododendron)	2 gal	14.99	4/00	93r
Sage (salvia)	gal	6.99	4/00	93r
Wintercreeper euonymus (euonymus fortunei)	2 gal	14.99-22.99	4/00	93r
Hunting license	yr	29.95	4/01	34s
Health Care				
Health care, ACCRA Index		139.60	3/01	4c
Cardiac catheterization, ave hospital/ physician charges		24000	1998	77s
Childbirth, Cesarean delivery		11587	1997	13r
Childbirth, vaginal delivery		6725	1997	13r
Dentist's fee, adult teeth cleaning and periodic oral exam	visit	85.00	3/01	4c
Doctor's fee, routine exam, established patient	visit	61.50	3/01	4c
Drugs, expenditures on	yr	309	1999	30r
Health care purchases	yr	1869	1999	30r
Health insurance expenditures	yr	868	1999	30r
Hospital care, private room	day	1409.00	3/01	4c
Hysterectomy, laproscopically-assisted, ave hospital/physician charges		20760	1998	76s
Hysterectomy, vaginal, ave hospital and physician charges		14570	1998	76s
Medicaid dispensing fee		4.05	1999	87s
Medical services expenditures	yr	580	1999	30r
Medical supplies, expenditures on	yr	112	1999	30r
Household Goods				
Dishwashing powder, Cascade	50 oz	3.88	3/01	4c
Floor coverings, expenditures on	yr	49	1999	30r
Furniture, expenditures on	yr	444	1999	30r
Household furnishings and equipment purchases	yr	1768	1999	30r
Household textiles, expenditures on	yr	141	1999	30r
Laundry and cleaning supplies, expenditures on	yr	128	1999	30r
Tissues, facial, Kleenex brand	175	1.57	3/01	4c
Housing				
Housing, ACCRA Index		99.90	3/01	4c
Home price, existing, ave		239400	10/00	90r
Home value, median		215000	2001	53s
House, 2400 sq ft, 8000 sq ft lot, new, urban, utilities	total	200391	3/01	4c

Values are in dollars or fractions of dollars. In the column headed *Ref*, references are shown to sources. Each reference is followed by a letter. These refer to the geographical level for which data were reported: s=State, r=Region, and c=City or metro. The abbreviation *ex* is used to mean *except* or *excluding*; *exp* stands for *expenditures*. For other abbreviations and further explanations, please see the Introduction.

Modesto, CA - continued

Item	Per	Value	Date	Ref.
Housing				
House payment, principal and interest, 25% down payment	mos	997	3/01	4c
Household operation expenditures	yr	781	1999	30r
Housekeeping supplies purchases	yr	513	1999	30r
Lodging expenditures	yr	575	1999	30r
Maintenance, repairs, insurance expenditures	yr	939	1999	30r
Monthly rental value of owned home	mos	662	1999	30r
Owned dwellings, expenditures own	yr	5231	1999	30r
Rent expenditures	yr	2709	1999	30r
Rent, apartment, 2 br, 1 1/2-2 baths, unfurn, 950 sq ft, water	mos	780	3/01	4c
Rental unit, 1 bedroom, with utilities	mos	485	4/01	41c
Rental unit, 2 bedroom, with utilities	mos	592	4/01	41c
Rental unit, 3 bedroom, with utilities	mos	825	4/01	41c
Rental unit, 4 bedroom, with utilities	mos	972	4/01	41c
Shelter, expenditures on	yr	8516	1999	30r
Insurance and Pensions				
Life and other personal insurance purchases	yr	355	1999	30r
Pensions and Social Security, expenditures on	yr	3636	1999	30r
Legal Fees				
Divorce, filing fee		182.00	4/01	35s
Driver's license fee	orig	12.00	1999	48s
Driver's license fee	renew	15.00	1999	48s
Personal Goods				
Personal care products and services purchases	yr	449	1999	30r
Shampoo, Alberto VO5	15 oz	1.48	3/01	4c
Toothpaste, Crest or Colgate	6-7 oz	2.62	3/01	4c
Personal Services				
Dry cleaning, man's 2-pc suit		8.40	3/01	4c
Man's haircut, barbershop, no styling		8.80	3/01	4c
Personal services, household, expenditures on	yr	353	1999	30r
Woman's shampoo, trim, blow-dry, no style-change		29.25	3/01	4c
Pets				
Pets, toys, and playground equipment, expenditures on	yr	358	1999	30r
Restaurant Food				
Chicken, fried, thigh and drumstick, KFC/Church's		2.33	3/01	4c
Hamburger with cheese, McDonald's	1/4 lb	2.09	3/01	4c
Pizza, Pizza Hut or Pizza Inn	11-12 in	9.99	3/01	4c
Taxes				
Federal income taxes paid	yr	3200	1999	30r
Personal taxes, expenditures on	yr	4153	1999	30r
Property taxes paid	yr	923	1999	30r
State and local income taxes paid	yr	812	1999	30r
Transportation				
Transportation, ACCRA Index		113.10	3/01	4c
Cars and trucks, new, expenditures on	yr	1534	1999	30r
Cars and trucks, used, expenditures on	yr	1593	1999	30r
Diesel at the pump	gal	1.37	10/99	73s
Gasoline and motor oil purchases	yr	1129	1999	30r
Gasoline before-tax price (cents)	gal	128.80	10/00	43s
Maintenance and repair expenditures	yr	797	1999	30r
Public transportation, expenditures on	yr	530	1999	30r
Tire balance, computer or spin balance, front	wheel	8.89	3/01	4c
Transportation purchases	yr	7423	1999	30r
Vehicle expenses, miscellaneous, purchases	yr	2585	1999	30r
Vehicle insurance payments	yr	811	1999	30r
Vehicle purchases (net outlay)	yr	3180	1999	30r
Vehicle rental, lease expenditures	yr	666	1999	30r

Modesto, CA - continued

Item	Per	Value	Date	Ref.
Utilities				
Utilities, ACCRA Index		88.70	3/01	4c
Electrical bill, average	mos	58.66	9/00	9s
Electricity, expenditures on	yr	725	1999	30r
Electricity and other, mixed, 2400 sq ft, new home	mos	66.02	3/01	4c
Electricity cost, average	KWh	7.75	9/00	9s
Utilities, fuels, and public services purchased	yr	2179	1999	30r
Water and other public services, expenditures on	yr	339	1999	30r
Weddings				
Wedding (national average cost)		19936	2000	33r
Wedding (regional average total cost)		18918	1997	110r
Attendants' gifts		321	1998	33r
Bridal attendants' apparel (5 persons)		824	2000	33r
Bride's headpiece/veil		173	1998	33r
Bride's wedding dress		859	1998	33r
Clergy, religious facility fee		242	1998	33r
Engagement ring		3177	1998	33r
Flowers		789	1998	33r
Groom's formalwear rental		99	2000	33r
Limousine		410	1998	33r
Marriage license cost		50.00-80.00	4/01	35s
Men's formalwear (ushers, best man)		469	2000	33r
Mother of bride apparel		241	2000	33r
Music		866	1998	33r
Photography and videography		1368	1998	33r
Rehearsal dinner		728	1998	33r
Wedding invitations and announcements		341	1998	33r
Wedding reception		7968	2000	33r
Wedding rings (bride and groom)		1060	1998	33r

Monmouth-Ocean, NJ

Item	Per	Value	Date	Ref.
Average annual expenditures	yr	37971	1999	30r
Alcoholic Beverages				
Alcoholic beverage purchases	yr	368	1999	30r
Wine, red and white table, all sizes, any origin	liter	9.64	7/01	11r
Appliances				
Major appliances, expenditures on	yr	194	1999	30r
Small appliances, housewares, expenditures on	yr	93	1999	30r
Banking and Money				
Mortgage interest and charges paid	yr	2622	1999	30r
Mortgage principal paid on owned property	yr	1262	1999	30r
Vehicle finance charges paid	yr	240	1999	30r
Charity				
Cash contributions, expenditures	yr	1001	1999	30r
Child Care				
Child raising cost, total, age 0-2	yr	8670	1999	60r
Child raising cost, total, age 3-5	yr	8910	1999	60r
Child raising cost, total, age 6-8	yr	9040	1999	60r
Child raising cost, total, age 9-11	yr	9100	1999	60r
Child raising cost, total, age 12-14	yr	9890	1999	60r
Child raising cost, total, age 15-17	yr	10010	1999	60r
Child's child care and education, age 0-2	yr	1070	1999	60r
Child's child care and education, age 3-5	yr	1190	1999	60r
Child's child care and education, age 6-8	yr	740	1999	60r
Child's child care and education, age 9-11	yr	470	1999	60r
Child's child care and education, age 12-14	yr	350	1999	60r
Child's child care and education, age 15-17	yr	590	1999	60r
Child's clothing, age 0-2	yr	480	1999	60r
Child's clothing, age 3-5	yr	470	1999	60r
Child's clothing, age 6-8	yr	520	1999	60r
Child's clothing, age 9-11	yr	570	1999	60r
Child's clothing, age 12-14	yr	970	1999	60r
Child's clothing, age 15-17	yr	870	1999	60r

Values are in dollars or fractions of dollars. In the column headed *Ref*, references are shown to sources. Each reference is followed by a letter. These refer to the geographical level for which data were reported: s=State, r=Region, and c=City or metro. The abbreviation *ex* is used to mean *except* or *excluding*; *exp* stands for *expenditures*. For other abbreviations and further explanations, please see the Introduction.

Monmouth-Ocean, NJ - continued

Item	Per	Value	Date	Ref.
Child Care				
Child's food, age 0-2	yr	1130	1999	60r
Child's food, age 3-5	yr	1290	1999	60r
Child's food, age 6-8	yr	1640	1999	60r
Child's food, age 9-11	yr	1930	1999	60r
Child's food, age 12-14	yr	1940	1999	60r
Child's food, age 15-17	yr	2150	1999	60r
Child's health care, age 0-2	yr	550	1999	60r
Child's health care, age 3-5	yr	530	1999	60r
Child's health care, age 6-8	yr	610	1999	60r
Child's health care, age 9-11	yr	650	1999	60r
Child's health care, age 12-14	yr	660	1999	60r
Child's health care, age 15-17	yr	690	1999	60r
Child's housing, age 0-2	yr	3555	1999	60r
Child's housing, age 3-5	yr	3530	1999	60r
Child's housing, age 6-8	yr	3490	1999	60r
Child's housing, age 9-11	yr	3340	1999	60r
Child's housing, age 12-14	yr	3530	1999	60r
Child's housing, age 15-17	yr	3140	1999	60r
Child's personal care, reading, age 0-2	yr	920	1999	60r
Child's personal care, reading, age 3-5	yr	950	1999	60r
Child's personal care, reading, age 6-8	yr	980	1999	60r
Child's personal care, reading, age 9-11	yr	1020	1999	60r
Child's personal care, reading, age 12-14	yr	1190	1999	60r
Child's personal care, reading, age 15-17	yr	970	1999	60r
Clothing				
Apparel and services purchases	yr	1831	1999	30r
Boys, 2 to 15, expenditures on	yr	92	1999	30r
Children under 2, expenditures on	yr	63	1999	30r
Footwear, expenditures on	yr	300	1999	30r
Girls, 2 to 15, expenditures on	yr	101	1999	30r
Men and boys, expenditures on	yr	446	1999	30r
Men, 16 and over, expenditures on	yr	354	1999	30r
Women, 16 and over, expenditures on	yr	584	1999	30r
Communications				
Cable modem installation, Adelphi		54.90	6/99	103s
Cable modem installation, Comcast		95.00	6/99	103s
Cable modem rate, cable subscriber, Adelphi	mos	34.95	6/99	103s
Cable modem rate, cable subscriber, Comcast	mos	39.95	6/99	103s
Cable modem rate, non-cable subscriber, Adelphi	mos	44.95	6/99	103s
Cable modem rate, non-cable subscriber, Comcast	mos	49.95	6/99	103s
Phone line, single, business, field visit	inst.	98.50	12/97	17s
Phone line, single, business, no field visit	inst.	79.50	12/97	17s
Phone line, single, residence, field visit	inst.	56.50	12/97	17s
Phone line, single, residence, no field visit	inst.	42.00	12/97	17s
Postage and stationery, expenditures on	yr	138	1999	30r
Postal rate, express mail, up to half-pound		12.45	7/01	108r
Postal rate, letter, first class, first ounce		0.34	7/01	108r
Postal rate, letter, two ounces		0.57	7/01	108r
Postal rate, post card		0.21	7/01	108r
Postal rate, priority mail, two pounds		3.95	7/01	108r
Postal rate, priority mail, up to one pound		3.50	7/01	108r
Telephone services, expenditures on	yr	830	1999	30r
Education				
Board, 4-year private college/university	yr	2959	1996	38s
Board, 4-year public college/university	yr	2052	1996	38s
Education expenditures	yr	877	1999	30r
Room, 4-year private college/university	yr	3226	1996	38s
Room, 4-year public college/university	yr	3101	1996	38s
Total cost, 4-year private college/university	yr	19751	1996	38s
Total cost, 4-year public college/university	yr	9125	1996	38s
Tuition, 2-year public college/university, in state	yr	1878	1996	38s
Tuition, 4-year private college/university, in state	yr	13566	1996	38s
Tuition, 4-year public college/university	yr	3972	1996	38s

Monmouth-Ocean, NJ - continued

Item	Per	Value	Date	Ref.
Energy and Fuels				
Electricity	KWh	0.12	7/01	11r
Fuel oil #2	gal	1.31	7/01	11r
Fuel oil and other fuels, expenditures on	yr	207	1999	30r
Gas, natural, commercial rate	1000 cf	5.98	11/00	88s
Gasoline, all types	gal	1.80	7/01	11r
Gasoline, unleaded midgrade	gal	1.85	7/01	11r
Gasoline, unleaded premium	gal	1.91	7/01	11r
Gasoline, unleaded regular	gal	1.71	7/01	11r
Natural gas, expenditures on	yr	368	1999	30r
Utility (piped) gas, therm		1.08	7/01	11r
Utility (piped) gas, 40 therms		50.87	7/01	11r
Utility (piped) gas, 100 therms		111.06	7/01	11r
Entertainment				
Entertainment purchases	yr	1821	1999	30r
Fees and admissions paid	yr	511	1999	30r
Television, radios, sound equipment, expenditures on	yr	650	1999	30r
Funerals				
Total cost of funeral		5813.50	1/99	78r
Acknowledgement cards		28.32	1/99	78r
Casket		2082.20	1/99	78r
Cosmetology, hair, other preparation		169.59	1/99	78r
Embalming		465.60	1/99	78r
Funeral at funeral home		339.56	1/99	78r
Hearse (local)		183.96	1/99	78r
Professional service charges		1157.85	1/99	78r
Service car/van		100.41	1/99	78r
Transfer of remains to funeral home		158.66	1/99	78r
Vault		766.31	1/99	78r
Visitation/viewing		361.04	1/99	78r
Groceries				
Apples, red delicious	lb	0.95	7/01	11r
Bacon, sliced	lb	3.44	7/01	11r
Bakery products, expenditures on	yr	310	1999	30r
Bananas	lb	0.55	7/01	11r
Beef, expenditures on	yr	236	1999	30r
Bread, white, pan	lb	1.09	7/01	11r
Butter, yoghurt, cheese, etc, expenditures on	yr	214	1999	30r
Cereals and bakery product purchases	yr	474	1999	30r
Cereals and cereal products, expenditures on	yr	164	1999	30r
Chicken legs, bone-in	lb	1.23	7/01	11r
Chicken, fresh, whole	lb	1.13	7/01	11r
Chuck roast, U.S. choice, boneless	lb	2.79	7/01	11r
Coffee, 100%, ground roast, all sizes	lb	3.40	7/01	11r
Dairy product purchases	yr	342	1999	30r
Eggs, expenditures on	yr	34	1999	30r
Eggs, grade A, large	dozen	0.82	7/01	11r
Fats and oils, expenditures on	yr	80	1999	30r
Fish and seafood, expenditures on	yr	123	1999	30r
Food (excl fruit and vegetables), eaten at home, purchases	yr	838	1999	30r
Food cooked on trips, expenditures on	yr	48	1999	30r
Food purchases	yr	5314	1999	30r
Food purchases, eaten away from home	yr	2313	1999	30r
Food purchases, food eaten at home	yr	3001	1999	30r
Fresh fruits, expenditures on	yr	169	1999	30r
Fresh milk and cream, expenditures on	yr	128	1999	30r
Fresh vegetables, expenditures on	yr	164	1999	30r
Grapefruit	lb	0.67	7/01	11r
Grapes, Thompson, seedless	lb	2.18	7/01	11r
Ground beef, lean and extra lean	lb	2.66	7/01	11r
Ground chuck, 100% beef	lb	2.04	7/01	11r
Lettuce, iceberg	lb	0.76	7/01	11r
Meats, poultry, fish, and egg purchases	yr	808	1999	30r
Nonalcoholic beverages, expenditures on	yr	225	1999	30r
Orange juice, frozen concentrate	16 oz	1.88	7/01	11r
Oranges, Navel	lb	0.79	7/01	11r
Oranges, Valencia	lb	0.56	7/01	11r
Peaches	lb	1.16	7/01	11r
Peanut butter, creamy, all sizes	lb	2.01	7/01	11r

Values are in dollars or fractions of dollars. In the column headed *Ref*, references are shown to sources. Each reference is followed by a letter. These refer to the geographical level for which data were reported: s=State, r=Region, and c=City or metro. The abbreviation *ex* is used to mean *except* or *excluding*; *exp* stands for *expenditures*. For other abbreviations and further explanations, please see the Introduction.

Monmouth-Ocean, NJ - continued

Item	Per	Value	Date	Ref.
Groceries				
Pears, Anjou	lb	1.16	7/01	11r
Pork chops, center cut, bone-in	lb	3.57	7/01	11r
Pork, expenditures on	yr	146	1999	30r
Potato chips	16 oz	3.37	7/01	11r
Potatoes, white, all types	lb	0.42	7/01	11r
Poultry, expenditures on	yr	158	1999	30r
Processed fruits, expenditures on	yr	124	1999	30r
Processed vegetables, expenditures on	yr	82	1999	30r
Round roast, U.S. choice, boneless	lb	3.04	7/01	11r
Spaghetti and macaroni	lb	1.04	7/01	11r
Steak, sirloin, U.S. choice, boneless	lb	5.39	7/01	11r
Strawberries, dry pint	12 oz	1.51	7/01	11r
Sugar and other sweets, expenditures on	yr	110	1999	30r
Sugar, white, 33-80 ounce package	lb	0.46	7/01	11r
Sugar, white, all sizes	lb	0.47	7/01	11r
Tobacco products and smoking supplies purchases	yr	309	1999	30r
Yogurt, natural, fruit flavored	8 oz	0.79	7/01	11r
Goods and Services				
B&B Japanese maple (acer japonicum)	gal	38.99-125.00	4/00	93r
Boxwood (buxus)	2 gal	15.99-49.95	4/00	93r
Daylily (hemerocallis)	gal	4.95	4/00	93r
Flat of annuals		8.00-14.99	4/00	93r
Fountain grass (pennisetum)	gal	6.99-9.99	4/00	93r
Hanging basket (10 in)		12.95-19.99	4/00	93r
Hardy geranium (geranium)	gal	6.95-7.99	4/00	93r
Hosta (hosta)	gal	4.95	4/00	93r
Lilac (syrubga vulgaris)	2 gal	17.99-74.95	4/00	93r
Miscellaneous purchases	yr	872	1999	30r
Rhododendron (rhododendron)	2 gal	23.99-54.95	4/00	93r
Sage (salvia)	gal	6.95-7.99	4/00	93r
Wintercreeper euonymus (euonymus fortunei)	2 gal	14.99-23.95	4/00	93r
Hunting license	yr	22.50	4/01	34s
Health Care				
Cardiac catheterization, ave hospital/physician charges		14680	1998	77s
Childbirth, Cesarean delivery		14716	1997	13r
Childbirth, vaginal delivery		8541	1997	13r
Drugs, expenditures on	yr	296	1999	30r
Health care purchases	yr	1788	1999	30r
Health insurance expenditures	yr	875	1999	30r
Hysterectomy, laproscopically-assisted, ave hospital/physician charges		18330	1998	76s
Hysterectomy, vaginal, ave hospital and physician charges		13620	1998	76s
Medicaid dispensing fee		3.73-4.07	1999	87s
Medical services expenditures	yr	516	1999	30r
Medical supplies, expenditures on	yr	102	1999	30r
Plastic surgery, breast augmentation		4232	2000	7r
Plastic surgery, breast lift		4605	2000	7r
Plastic surgery, facelift		6964	2000	7r
Plastic surgery, hair transplantation		4193	2000	7r
Plastic surgery, lip augmentation		1675	2000	7r
Plastic surgery, lower body lift		6611	2000	7r
Plastic surgery, thigh lift		4751	2000	7r
Household Goods				
Floor coverings, expenditures on	yr	59	1999	30r
Furniture, expenditures on	yr	388	1999	30r
Household furnishings and equipment purchases	yr	1567	1999	30r

Monmouth-Ocean, NJ - continued

Item	Per	Value	Date	Ref.
Household Goods - continued				
Household textiles, expenditures on	yr	112	1999	30r
Laundry and cleaning supplies, expenditures on	yr	104	1999	30r
Housing				
Home price, existing, ave		180800	10/00	90r
Home value, median		213000	2001	53s
Household operation expenditures	yr	581	1999	30r
Housekeeping supplies purchases	yr	474	1999	30r
Lodging expenditures	yr	550	1999	30r
Maintenance, repairs, insurance expenditures	yr	835	1999	30r
Monthly rental value of owned home	mos	663	1999	30r
Owned dwellings, expenditures own	yr	5209	1999	30r
Rent expenditures	yr	2390	1999	30r
Rental unit, 1 bedroom, with utilities	mos	735	4/01	41c
Rental unit, 2 bedroom, with utilities	mos	933	4/01	41c
Rental unit, 3 bedroom, with utilities	mos	1240	4/01	41c
Rental unit, 4 bedroom, with utilities	mos	1454	4/01	41c
Shelter, expenditures on	yr	8149	1999	30r
Insurance and Pensions				
Auto insurance premium	yr	1292.76	1999	57s
Life and other personal insurance purchases	yr	424	1999	30r
Pensions and Social Security, expenditures on	yr	3037	1999	30r
Legal Fees				
Divorce, filing fee		65.00	4/01	35s
Driver's license fee	renew	15.00	1999	48s
Driver's license fee	orig	18.00	1999	48s
Fishing license	yr	22.50	4/01	34s
Personal Goods				
Personal care products and services purchases	yr	399	1999	30r
Personal Services				
Personal services, household, expenditures on	yr	271	1999	30r
Pets				
Pets, toys, and playground equipment, expenditures on	yr	325	1999	30r
Taxes				
Federal income taxes paid	yr	2606	1999	30r
Personal taxes, expenditures on	yr	3567	1999	30r
Property taxes paid	yr	1752	1999	30r
State and local income taxes paid	yr	694	1999	30r
Transportation				
Automobile insurance	yr	975.90	2000	79s
Cars and trucks, new, expenditures on	yr	1496	1999	30r
Cars and trucks, used, expenditures on	yr	1251	1999	30r
Diesel at the pump	gal	1.19	10/99	73s
Gasoline and motor oil purchases	yr	901	1999	30r
Gasoline before-tax price (cents)	gal	114.90	10/00	43s
Maintenance and repair expenditures	yr	618	1999	30r
Motorcycle license fee	orig	15.00	1999	49s
Motorcycle license fee	renew	13.00	1999	49s
Public transportation, expenditures on	yr	575	1999	30r
Transportation purchases	yr	6503	1999	30r
Vehicle expenses, miscellaneous, purchases	yr	2266	1999	30r
Vehicle insurance payments	yr	824	1999	30r
Vehicle purchases (net outlay)	yr	2761	1999	30r
Vehicle rental, lease expenditures	yr	584	1999	30r
Utilities				
Electrical bill, average	mos	74.08	9/00	9s
Electricity, expenditures on	yr	837	1999	30r
Electricity cost, average	KWh	8.91	9/00	9s
Utilities, fuels, and public services purchased	yr	2457	1999	30r
Water and other public services, expenditures on	yr	215	1999	30r

Values are in dollars or fractions of dollars. In the column headed *Ref*, references are shown to sources. Each reference is followed by a letter. These refer to the geographical level for which data were reported: s=State, r=Region, and c=City or metro. The abbreviation *ex* is used to mean *except* or *excluding*; *exp* stands for *expenditures*. For other abbreviations and further explanations, please see the Introduction.

Monmouth-Ocean, NJ - continued

Weddings

Item	Per	Value	Date	Ref.
Wedding (national average cost)		19936	2000	33r
Wedding (regional average total cost)		29454	1997	110r
Attendants' gifts		321	1998	33r
Bridal attendants' apparel (5 persons)		824	2000	33r
Bride's headpiece/veil		173	1998	33r
Bride's wedding dress		859	1998	33r
Clergy, religious facility fee		242	1998	33r
Engagement ring		3177	1998	33r
Flowers		789	1998	33r
Groom's formalwear rental		99	2000	33r
Limousine		410	1998	33r
Marriage license cost		28.00	4/01	35s
Men's formalwear (ushers, best man)		469	2000	33r
Mother of bride apparel		241	2000	33r
Music		866	1998	33r
Photography and videography		1368	1998	33r
Rehearsal dinner		728	1998	33r
Wedding invitations and announcements		341	1998	33r
Wedding reception		7968	2000	33r
Wedding rings (bride and groom)		1060	1998	33r

Monroe, LA

Item	Per	Value	Date	Ref.
Composite, ACCRA index		102.80	3/01	4c

Alcoholic Beverages

Item	Per	Value	Date	Ref.
Alcoholic beverage purchases	yr	253	1999	30r
Beer, Heineken, 12-oz, ex deposit	6	6.71	3/01	4c
J & B Scotch	750-ml	19.93	3/01	4c
Malt beverages, all types, all sizes, any origin	16 oz	0.96	7/01	11r
Wine, Livingston or Gallo, Chablis blanc	1.5 liter	5.45	3/01	4c

Appliances

Item	Per	Value	Date	Ref.
Appliance repair, service call, washing machine	min lab chg	41.00	3/01	4c
Major appliances, expenditures on	yr	172	1999	30r
Small appliances, housewares, expenditures on	yr	81	1999	30r

Banking and Money

Item	Per	Value	Date	Ref.
Mortgage interest and charges paid	yr	2039	1999	30r
Mortgage principal paid on owned property	yr	1026	1999	30r
Mortgage rate, incl. points and orig. fee, 30-yr. conv. fixed or ARM	mos	6.79	3/01	4c
Vehicle finance charges paid	yr	365	1999	30r

Charity

Item	Per	Value	Date	Ref.
Cash contributions, expenditures	yr	1127	1999	30r

Child Care

Item	Per	Value	Date	Ref.
Child raising cost, total, age 0-2	yr	8540	1999	60r
Child raising cost, total, age 3-5	yr	8780	1999	60r
Child raising cost, total, age 6-8	yr	8820	1999	60r
Child raising cost, total, age 9-11	yr	8800	1999	60r
Child raising cost, total, age 12-14	yr	9510	1999	60r
Child raising cost, total, age 15-17	yr	9740	1999	60r
Child's child care and education, age 0-2	yr	1380	1999	60r
Child's child care and education, age 3-5	yr	1520	1999	60r
Child's child care and education, age 6-8	yr	990	1999	60r
Child's child care and education, age 9-11	yr	650	1999	60r
Child's child care and education, age 12-14	yr	490	1999	60r
Child's child care and education, age 15-17	yr	840	1999	60r
Child's clothing, age 0-2	yr	480	1999	60r
Child's clothing, age 3-5	yr	470	1999	60r
Child's clothing, age 6-8	yr	520	1999	60r
Child's clothing, age 9-11	yr	570	1999	60r
Child's clothing, age 12-14	yr	950	1999	60r
Child's clothing, age 15-17	yr	850	1999	60r
Child's food, age 0-2	yr	1000	1999	60r
Child's food, age 3-5	yr	1160	1999	60r
Child's food, age 6-8	yr	1490	1999	60r
Child's food, age 9-11	yr	1770	1999	60r
Child's food, age 12-14	yr	1770	1999	60r
Child's food, age 15-17	yr	1980	1999	60r

Monroe, LA - continued

Child Care - continued

Item	Per	Value	Date	Ref.
Child's health care, age 0-2	yr	620	1999	60r
Child's health care, age 3-5	yr	590	1999	60r
Child's health care, age 6-8	yr	680	1999	60r
Child's health care, age 9-11	yr	720	1999	60r
Child's health care, age 12-14	yr	730	1999	60r
Child's health care, age 15-17	yr	760	1999	60r
Child's housing, age 0-2	yr	3070	1999	60r
Child's housing, age 3-5	yr	3050	1999	60r
Child's housing, age 6-8	yr	3010	1999	60r
Child's housing, age 9-11	yr	2850	1999	60r
Child's housing, age 12-14	yr	3040	1999	60r
Child's housing, age 15-17	yr	2650	1999	60r
Child's personal care, reading, age 0-2	yr	910	1999	60r
Child's personal care, reading, age 3-5	yr	930	1999	60r
Child's personal care, reading, age 6-8	yr	960	1999	60r
Child's personal care, reading, age 9-11	yr	1000	1999	60r
Child's personal care, reading, age 12-14	yr	1170	1999	60r
Child's personal care, reading, age 15-17	yr	950	1999	60r

Clothing

Item	Per	Value	Date	Ref.
Apparel and services purchases	yr	1610	1999	30r
Boys' brief, cotton	3	6.49	3/01	4c
Boys, 2 to 15, expenditures on	yr	89	1999	30r
Children under 2, expenditures on	yr	79	1999	30r
Footwear, expenditures on	yr	283	1999	30r
Girls, 2 to 15, expenditures on	yr	103	1999	30r
Men and boys, expenditures on	yr	351	1999	30r
Men, 16 and over, expenditures on	yr	262	1999	30r
Shirt, man's dress shirt		28.60	3/01	4c
Slacks, man's "No Wrinkles" khaki		40.60	3/01	4c
Women, 16 and over, expenditures on	yr	538	1999	30r

Communications

Item	Per	Value	Date	Ref.
Newspaper subscription, daily and Sunday delivery	mos	14.50	3/01	4c
Phone line, single, business, field visit	inst.	85.00	12/97	17s
Phone line, single, business, no field visit	inst.	85.00	12/97	17s
Phone line, single, residence, field visit	inst.	41.00	12/97	17s
Phone line, single, residence, no field visit	inst.	41.00	12/97	17s
Postage and stationery, expenditures on	yr	104	1999	30r
Postal rate, express mail, up to half-pound		12.45	7/01	108r
Postal rate, letter, first class, first ounce		0.34	7/01	108r
Postal rate, letter, two ounces		0.57	7/01	108r
Postal rate, post card		0.21	7/01	108r
Postal rate, priority mail, two pounds		3.95	7/01	108r
Postal rate, priority mail, up to one pound		3.50	7/01	108r
Telephone bill, family of three	mos	19.20	3/01	4c
Telephone services, expenditures on	yr	860	1999	30r

Education

Item	Per	Value	Date	Ref.
Board, 4-year private college/university	yr	2440	1996	38s
Board, 4-year public college/university	yr	1806	1996	38s
Education expenditures	yr	431	1999	30r
Room, 4-year private college/university	yr	2906	1996	38s
Room, 4-year public college/university	yr	1464	1996	38s
Total cost, 4-year private college/university	yr	17796	1996	38s
Total cost, 4-year public college/university	yr	5491	1996	38s
Tuition, 2-year public college/university, in state	yr	1031	1996	38s
Tuition, 4-year private college/university, in state	yr	12449	1996	38s
Tuition, 4-year public college/university	yr	2221	1996	38s

Energy and Fuels

Item	Per	Value	Date	Ref.
Electricity	KWh	0.09	7/01	11r
Electricity	500 KWhs	47.29	7/01	11r
Energy, combined forms, 2400 sq ft	mos	151.42	3/01	4c
Fuel oil #2	gal	1.43	7/01	11r
Fuel oil and other fuels, expenditures on	yr	45	1999	30r
Gas, natural, commercial rate	1000 cf	8.75	11/00	88s
Gas, regular unleaded, cash, self-service	gal	1.37	3/01	4c
Gasoline, all types	gal	1.60	7/01	11r
Gasoline, unleaded midgrade	gal	1.65	7/01	11r

Values are in dollars or fractions of dollars. In the column headed *Ref*, references are shown to sources. Each reference is followed by a letter. These refer to the geographical level for which data were reported: s=State, r=Region, and c=City or metro. The abbreviation *ex* is used to mean *except* or *excluding*; *exp* stands for expenditures. For other abbreviations and further explanations, please see the Introduction.

Monroe, LA - continued

Item	Per	Value	Date	Ref.
Energy and Fuels				
Gasoline, unleaded premium	gal	1.74	7/01	11r
Natural gas, expenditures on	yr	164	1999	30r
Utility (piped) gas, therm		1.01	7/01	11r
Utility (piped) gas, 40 therms		44.29	7/01	11r
Utility (piped) gas, 100 therms		97.44	7/01	11r
Entertainment				
Bowling, Saturday evening rate	line	2.95	3/01	4c
Entertainment purchases	yr	1574	1999	30r
Fees and admissions paid	yr	371	1999	30r
Monopoly game, Parker Brothers', No. 9	game	12.80	3/01	4c
Movie, first-run, Saturday, evening	adm.	5.37	3/01	4c
Reading purchases	yr	121	1999	30r
Television, radios, sound equipment, expenditures on	yr	561	1999	30r
Tennis balls, yellow, Wilson or Penn, 3	can	2.73	3/01	4c
Funerals				
Total cost of funeral		5842.28	1/99	78r
Acknowledgement cards		28.35	1/99	78r
Casket		2494.29	1/99	78r
Cosmetology, hair, other preparation		109.22	1/99	78r
Embalming		361.42	1/99	78r
Funeral at funeral home		349.20	1/99	78r
Hearse (local)		161.91	1/99	78r
Professional service charges		1116.50	1/99	78r
Service car/van		65.56	1/99	78r
Transfer of remains to funeral home		143.56	1/99	78r
Vault		785.25	1/99	78r
Visitation/viewing		227.02	1/99	78r
Groceries				
Groceries, ACCRA Index		92.80	3/01	4c
American processed cheese	lb	3.50	7/01	11r
Antibiotic ointment, Polysporin	0.5 oz	4.82	3/01	4c
Baby food, strained vegetables or fruit, lowest price	4-4.5 oz	0.39	3/01	4c
Bakery products, expenditures on	yr	261	1999	30r
Bananas	lb	0.42	3/01	4c
Bananas	lb	0.47	7/01	11r
Beans, dried, any type, all sizes	lb	0.63	7/01	11r
Beef for stew, boneless	lb	2.86	7/01	11r
Beef or hamburger, ground	lb	1.94	3/01	4c
Beef, expenditures on	yr	210	1999	30r
Bologna, all beef or mixed	lb	2.29	7/01	11r
Bread, French	lb	1.66	7/01	11r
Bread, white	loaf	0.87	3/01	4c
Bread, white, pan	lb	0.87	7/01	11r
Bread, whole wheat, pan	lb	1.38	7/01	11r
Broccoli	lb	1.04	7/01	11r
Butter, salted, grade AA, stick	lb	2.26	7/01	11r
Butter, yoghurt, cheese, etc, expenditures on	yr	170	1999	30r
Cabbage	lb	0.42	7/01	11r
Cereals and cereal products, expenditures on	yr	140	1999	30r
Cheddar cheese, natural	lb	3.75	7/01	11r
Cheese, Kraft grated Parmesan	8 oz	3.77	3/01	4c
Chicken breast, bone-in	lb	1.85	7/01	11r
Chicken legs, bone-in	lb	1.34	7/01	11r
Chicken, fresh, whole	lb	1.05	7/01	11r
Chicken, whole fryer	lb	0.73	3/01	4c
Chops, boneless,	lb	4.13	7/01	11r
Chuck roast, graded and ungraded, excl U.S. prime and choice	lb	2.35	7/01	11r
Chuck roast, U.S. choice, boneless	lb	2.67	7/01	11r
Cigarettes, Winston, Kings	carton	29.58	3/01	4c
Coffee, 100%, ground roast, all sizes	lb	2.88	7/01	11r
Coffee, instant, plain, regular, all sizes	16 oz	9.25	7/01	11r
Coffee, vacuum-packed	13 oz	2.25	3/01	4c
Cola, non diet,	2 liter	1.11	7/01	11r
Corn Flakes, Kellogg's or Post Toasties	18 oz	2.18	3/01	4c
Corn, frozen, whole kernel, lowest price	16 oz	1.01	3/01	4c
Crackers, soda, salted	lb	1.70	7/01	11r
Dairy product purchases	yr	282	1999	30r

Monroe, LA - continued

Item	Per	Value	Date	Ref.
Groceries - continued				
Eggs, expenditures on	yr	32	1999	30r
Eggs, Grade A or AA	dozen	1.05	3/01	4c
Fats and oils, expenditures on	yr	79	1999	30r
Fish and seafood, expenditures on	yr	99	1999	30r
Flour, white, all purpose	lb	0.32	7/01	11r
Food (excl fruit and vegetables), eaten at home, purchases	yr	815	1999	30r
Food cooked on trips, expenditures on	yr	36	1999	30r
Food purchases	yr	4533	1999	30r
Food purchases, eaten away from home	yr	1873	1999	30r
Food purchases, food eaten at home	yr	2660	1999	30r
Fresh fruits, expenditures on	yr	128	1999	30r
Fresh milk and cream, expenditures on	yr	112	1999	30r
Fresh vegetables, expenditures on	yr	131	1999	30r
Fruit and vegetable purchases	yr	438	1999	30r
Grapefruit	lb	0.59	7/01	11r
Grapes, Thompson, seedless	lb	2.12	7/01	11r
Ground beef, 100% beef	lb	1.76	7/01	11r
Ground beef, lean and extra lean	lb	2.60	7/01	11r
Ground chuck, 100% beef	lb	2.08	7/01	11r
Ham, boneless, excl canned	lb	2.71	7/01	11r
Ham, rump or shank half, bone-in, smoked	lb	2.19	7/01	11r
Ice cream, prepackaged, bulk, regular	1/2 gal	3.93	7/01	11r
Lemons	lb	1.32	7/01	11r
Lettuce, iceberg	head	1.13	3/01	4c
Lettuce, iceberg	lb	0.76	7/01	11r
Margarine, Blue Bonnet or Parkay, stick	lb	0.76	3/01	4c
Milk, fresh, low fat,	gal	2.75	7/01	11r
Milk, fresh, whole, fortified	gal	2.97	7/01	11r
Milk, whole	1/2 gal	1.60	3/01	4c
Nonalcoholic beverages, expenditures on	yr	228	1999	30r
Orange juice, frozen concentrate	16 oz	1.95	7/01	11r
Orange juice, Minute Maid frozen	12 oz	1.43	3/01	4c
Oranges, Navel	lb	0.73	7/01	11r
Oranges, Valencia	lb	0.55	7/01	11r
Peaches, halves or slices, Hunt's, Del Monte, or Libby's	29 oz	1.53	3/01	4c
Peanut butter, creamy, all sizes	lb	1.83	7/01	11r
Pears, Anjou	lb	0.98	7/01	11r
Peas, green, Del Monte or Green Giant	15 oz	0.65	3/01	4c
Pork chops, center cut, bone-in	lb	3.33	7/01	11r
Pork sausage, fresh, loose	lb	2.59	7/01	11r
Pork shoulder picnic, bone-in, smoked	lb	1.12	7/01	11r
Pork, expenditures on	yr	162	1999	30r
Potato chips	16 oz	3.59	7/01	11r
Potatoes, frozen, french fried	lb	1.00	7/01	11r
Potatoes, white or red	10 lb	2.66	3/01	4c
Potatoes, white, all types	lb	0.44	7/01	11r
Poultry, expenditures on	yr	137	1999	30r
Processed fruits, expenditures on	yr	97	1999	30r
Processed vegetables, expenditures on	yr	82	1999	30r
Rice, white, long grain, uncooked	lb	0.51	7/01	11r
Round roast, graded and ungraded, excl U.S. prime and choice	lb	2.96	7/01	11r
Round steak, graded and ungraded, excl U.S. prime and choice	lb	3.11	7/01	11r
Sausage, Jimmy Dean/Owens pork	lb	2.51	3/01	4c
Shortening, vegetable, Crisco	3 lb	2.81	3/01	4c
Sirloin steak, graded and ungraded, excl U.S. prime and choice	lb	4.23	7/01	11r
Soft drink, Coca Cola, ex deposit	2 liter	1.09	3/01	4c
Spaghetti and macaroni	lb	0.78	7/01	11r
Steak, round, U.S. choice, boneless	lb	3.56	7/01	11r
Steak, sirloin, U.S. choice, boneless	lb	5.65	7/01	11r
Steak, T-bone	lb	7.03	3/01	4c
Strawberries, dry pint	12 oz	1.50	7/01	11r
Sugar and other sweets, expenditures on	yr	99	1999	30r
Sugar, cane or beet	4 lbs	1.47	3/01	4c
Sugar, white, 33-80 ounce package	lb	0.39	7/01	11r
Sugar, white, all sizes	lb	0.42	7/01	11r
Tobacco products and smoking supplies purchases	yr	288	1999	30r

Values are in dollars or fractions of dollars. In the column headed *Ref*, references are shown to sources. Each reference is followed by a letter. These refer to the geographical level for which data were reported: s=State, r=Region, and c=City or metro. The abbreviation *ex* is used to mean *except* or *excluding*; *exp* stands for *expenditures*. For other abbreviations and further explanations, please see the Introduction.

Monroe, LA - continued

Item	Per	Value	Date	Ref.
Groceries				
Tomatoes, field grown	lb	1.43	7/01	11r
Tomatoes, Hunt's or Del Monte	14.5 oz	0.82	3/01	4c
Tuna, chunk, light	6 oz	0.58	3/01	4c
Tuna, light, chunk	lb	1.77	7/01	11r
Turkey, frozen, whole	lb	1.05	7/01	11r
Goods and Services				
Miscellaneous goods and services, ACCRA Index		103.80	3/01	4c
B&B Japanese maple (acer japonicum)	gal	79.98-99.00	4/00	93r
Boxwood (buxus)	2 gal	12.98-18.99	4/00	93r
Daylilly (hemerocallis)	gal	7.96-11.00	4/00	93r
Flat of annuals		13.99-27.99	4/00	93r
Fountain grass (pennisetum)	gal	6.96-9.00	4/00	93r
Hanging basket (10 in)		9.99-24.99	4/00	93r
Hardy geranium (geranium)	gal	5.96-8.00	4/00	93r
Hosta (hosta)	gal	8.96-12.99	4/00	93r
Lilac (syrubga vulgaris)	2 gal	13.00-19.99	4/00	93r
Rhododendron (rhododendron)	2 gal	12.98-29.99	4/00	93r
Sage (salvia)	gal	5.96-8.00	4/00	93r
Wintercreeper euonymus (euonymus fortunei)	2 gal	13.00-18.99	4/00	93r
Hunting license	yr	15.00	4/01	34s
Health Care				
Health care, ACCRA Index		89.20	3/01	4c
Cardiac catheterization, ave hospital/ physician charges		15650	1998	77s
Childbirth, Cesarean delivery		11587	1997	13r
Childbirth, vaginal delivery		6725	1997	13r
Dentist's fee, adult teeth cleaning and periodic oral exam	visit	64.57	3/01	4c
Doctor's fee, routine exam, established patient	visit	58.67	3/01	4c
Drugs, expenditures on	yr	399	1999	30r
Health care purchases	yr	1971	1999	30r
Health insurance expenditures	yr	933	1999	30r
Hospital care, private room	day	301.67	3/01	4c
Hysterectomy, laproscopically-assisted, ave hospital/physician charges		14600	1998	76s
Hysterectomy, vaginal, ave hospital and physician charges		10520	1998	76s
Medicaid dispensing fee		5.77	1999	87s
Medical services expenditures	yr	547	1999	30r
Medical supplies, expenditures on	yr	91	1999	30r
Household Goods				
Dishwashing powder, Cascade	50 oz	3.07	3/01	4c
Floor coverings, expenditures on	yr	44	1999	30r
Furniture, expenditures on	yr	335	1999	30r
Household furnishings and equipment purchases	yr	1328	1999	30r
Household textiles, expenditures on	yr	89	1999	30r
Laundry and cleaning supplies, expenditures on	yr	113	1999	30r
Tissues, facial, Kleenex brand	175	1.15	3/01	4c
Housing				
Housing, ACCRA Index		106.60	3/01	4c
Home price, existing, ave		160100	10/00	90r
Home value, median		108000	2001	53s
House, 2400 sq ft, 8000 sq ft lot, new, urban, utilities	total	242367	3/01	4c

Monroe, LA - continued

Item	Per	Value	Date	Ref.
Housing - continued				
House payment, principal and interest, 25% down payment	mos	1184	3/01	4c
Household operation expenditures	yr	553	1999	30r
Housekeeping supplies purchases	yr	473	1999	30r
Housing, expenditures on	yr	10303	1999	30r
Maintenance, repairs, insurance expenditures	yr	699	1999	30r
Monthly rental value of owned home	mos	505	1999	30r
Owned dwellings, expenditures own	yr	3465	1999	30r
Rent expenditures	yr	1641	1999	30r
Rent, apartment, 2 br, 1 1/2-2 baths, unfurn, 950 sq ft, water	mos	517	3/01	4c
Rental unit, 1 bedroom, with utilities	mos	343	4/01	41c
Rental unit, 2 bedroom, with utilities	mos	457	4/01	41c
Rental unit, 3 bedroom, with utilities	mos	616	4/01	41c
Rental unit, 4 bedroom, with utilities	mos	640	4/01	41c
Shelter, expenditures on	yr	5467	1999	30r
Insurance and Pensions				
Auto insurance premium	yr	965.15	1999	57s
Life and other personal insurance purchases	yr	414	1999	30r
Pensions and Social Security, expenditures on	yr	2635	1999	30r
Personal insurance and pensions, expenditures on	yr	3048	1999	30r
Legal Fees				
Divorce, filing fee		162.00	4/01	35s
Driver's license fee	renew	12.50	1999	48s
Driver's license fee	orig	18.00	1999	48s
Fishing license	yr	9.50	4/01	34s
Personal Goods				
Personal care products and services purchases	yr	393	1999	30r
Shampoo, Alberto VO5	15 oz	1.18	3/01	4c
Toothpaste, Crest or Colgate	6-7 oz	2.48	3/01	4c
Personal Services				
Dry cleaning, man's 2-pc suit		8.71	3/01	4c
Man's haircut, barbershop, no styling		13.50	3/01	4c
Personal services, household, expenditures on	yr	258	1999	30r
Woman's shampoo, trim, blow-dry, no style-change		21.33	3/01	4c
Pets				
Pets, toys, and playground equipment, expenditures on	yr	306	1999	30r
Restaurant Food				
Chicken, fried, thigh and drumstick, KFC/ Church's		2.11	3/01	4c
Hamburger with cheese, McDonald's	1/4 lb	2.02	3/01	4c
Pizza, Pizza Hut or Pizza Inn	11-12 in	9.49	3/01	4c
Taxes				
Federal income taxes paid	yr	2047	1999	30r
Personal taxes, expenditures on	yr	2554	1999	30r
Property taxes paid	yr	726	1999	30r
State and local income taxes paid	yr	363	1999	30r
Transportation				
Transportation, ACCRA Index		98.90	3/01	4c
Cars and trucks, new, expenditures on	yr	1648	1999	30r
Cars and trucks, used, expenditures on	yr	1651	1999	30r
Diesel at the pump	gal	1.19	10/99	73s
Gasoline and motor oil purchases	yr	1052	1999	30r
Gasoline before-tax price (cents)	gal	102.70	10/00	43s
Maintenance and repair expenditures	yr	621	1999	30r
Public transportation, expenditures on	yr	298	1999	30r
Tire balance, computer or spin balance, front	wheel	8.00	3/01	4c
Transportation purchases	yr	6738	1999	30r
Vehicle expenses, miscellaneous, purchases	yr	2033	1999	30r
Vehicle insurance payments	yr	696	1999	30r
Vehicle purchases (net outlay)	yr	3354	1999	30r

Values are in dollars or fractions of dollars. In the column headed *Ref*, references are shown to sources. Each reference is followed by a letter. These refer to the geographical level for which data were reported: s=State, r=Region, and c=City or metro. The abbreviation *ex* is used to mean *except* or *excluding*; *exp* stands for expenditures. For other abbreviations and further explanations, please see the Introduction.

Monroe, LA - continued

Item	Per	Value	Date	Ref.
Transportation				
Vehicle rental, lease expenditures	yr	352	1999	30r
Utilities				
Utilities, ACCRA Index		119.10	3/01	4c
Electrical bill, average	mos	87.50	9/00	9s
Electricity, 2400 sq ft, new home	mos	151.42	3/01	4c
Electricity, expenditures on	yr	1115	1999	30r
Electricity cost, average	KWh	6.35	9/00	9s
Water and other public services, expenditures on	yr	298	1999	30r
Weddings				
Wedding (national average cost)		19936	2000	33r
Attendants' gifts		321	1998	33r
Bridal attendants' apparel (5 persons)		824	2000	33r
Bride's headpiece/veil		173	1998	33r
Bride's wedding dress		859	1998	33r
Clergy, religious facility fee		242	1998	33r
Engagement ring		3177	1998	33r
Flowers		789	1998	33r
Groom's formalwear rental		99	2000	33r
Limousine		410	1998	33r
Marriage license cost		25.00	4/01	35s
Men's formalwear (ushers, best man)		469	2000	33r
Mother of bride apparel		241	2000	33r
Music		866	1998	33r
Photography and videography		1368	1998	33r
Rehearsal dinner		728	1998	33r
Wedding invitations and announcements		341	1998	33r
Wedding reception		7968	2000	33r
Wedding rings (bride and groom)		1060	1998	33r

Montgomery, AL

Item	Per	Value	Date	Ref.
Composite, ACCRA index		98.50	3/01	4c
Alcoholic Beverages				
Alcoholic beverage purchases	yr	253	1999	30r
Beer, Heineken, 12-oz, ex deposit	6	6.91	3/01	4c
J & B Scotch	750-ml	23.99	3/01	4c
Malt beverages, all types, all sizes, any origin	16 oz	0.96	7/01	11r
Wine, Livingston or Gallo, Chablis blanc	1.5 liter	6.77	3/01	4c
Appliances				
Appliance repair, service call, washing machine	min lab chg	42.99	3/01	4c
Major appliances, expenditures on	yr	172	1999	30r
Small appliances, housewares, expenditures on	yr	81	1999	30r
Banking and Money				
Mortgage interest and charges paid	yr	2039	1999	30r
Mortgage principal paid on owned property	yr	1026	1999	30r
Mortgage rate, incl. points and orig. fee, 30-yr. conv. fixed or ARM	mos	6.79	3/01	4c
Vehicle finance charges paid	yr	365	1999	30r
Charity				
Cash contributions, expenditures	yr	1127	1999	30r
Child Care				
Child raising cost, total, age 0-2	yr	8540	1999	60r
Child raising cost, total, age 3-5	yr	8780	1999	60r
Child raising cost, total, age 6-8	yr	8820	1999	60r
Child raising cost, total, age 9-11	yr	8800	1999	60r
Child raising cost, total, age 12-14	yr	9510	1999	60r
Child raising cost, total, age 15-17	yr	9740	1999	60r
Child's child care and education, age 0-2	yr	1380	1999	60r
Child's child care and education, age 3-5	yr	1520	1999	60r
Child's child care and education, age 6-8	yr	990	1999	60r
Child's child care and education, age 9-11	yr	650	1999	60r
Child's child care and education, age 12-14	yr	490	1999	60r
Child's child care and education, age 15-17	yr	840	1999	60r
Child's clothing, age 0-2	yr	480	1999	60r
Child's clothing, age 3-5	yr	470	1999	60r

Montgomery, AL - continued

Item	Per	Value	Date	Ref.
Child Care - continued				
Child's clothing, age 6-8	yr	520	1999	60r
Child's clothing, age 9-11	yr	570	1999	60r
Child's clothing, age 12-14	yr	950	1999	60r
Child's clothing, age 15-17	yr	850	1999	60r
Child's food, age 0-2	yr	1000	1999	60r
Child's food, age 3-5	yr	1160	1999	60r
Child's food, age 6-8	yr	1490	1999	60r
Child's food, age 9-11	yr	1770	1999	60r
Child's food, age 12-14	yr	1770	1999	60r
Child's food, age 15-17	yr	1980	1999	60r
Child's health care, age 0-2	yr	620	1999	60r
Child's health care, age 3-5	yr	590	1999	60r
Child's health care, age 6-8	yr	680	1999	60r
Child's health care, age 9-11	yr	720	1999	60r
Child's health care, age 12-14	yr	730	1999	60r
Child's health care, age 15-17	yr	760	1999	60r
Child's housing, age 0-2	yr	3070	1999	60r
Child's housing, age 3-5	yr	3050	1999	60r
Child's housing, age 6-8	yr	3010	1999	60r
Child's housing, age 9-11	yr	2850	1999	60r
Child's housing, age 12-14	yr	3040	1999	60r
Child's housing, age 15-17	yr	2650	1999	60r
Child's personal care, reading, age 0-2	yr	910	1999	60r
Child's personal care, reading, age 3-5	yr	930	1999	60r
Child's personal care, reading, age 6-8	yr	960	1999	60r
Child's personal care, reading, age 9-11	yr	1000	1999	60r
Child's personal care, reading, age 12-14	yr	1170	1999	60r
Child's personal care, reading, age 15-17	yr	950	1999	60r
Clothing				
Apparel and services purchases	yr	1610	1999	30r
Boys' brief, cotton	3	3.38	3/01	4c
Boys, 2 to 15, expenditures on	yr	89	1999	30r
Children under 2, expenditures on	yr	79	1999	30r
Footwear, expenditures on	yr	283	1999	30r
Girls, 2 to 15, expenditures on	yr	103	1999	30r
Men and boys, expenditures on	yr	351	1999	30r
Men, 16 and over, expenditures on	yr	262	1999	30r
Shirt, man's dress shirt		27.20	3/01	4c
Slacks, man's "No Wrinkles" khaki		34.39	3/01	4c
Women, 16 and over, expenditures on	yr	538	1999	30r
Communications				
Newspaper subscription, daily and Sunday delivery	mos	13.87	3/01	4c
Phone line, single, business, field visit	inst.	69.00	12/97	17s
Phone line, single, business, no field visit	inst.	69.00	12/97	17s
Phone line, single, residence, field visit	inst.	40.00	12/97	17s
Phone line, single, residence, no field visit	inst.	40.00	12/97	17s
Postage and stationery, expenditures on	yr	104	1999	30r
Postal rate, express mail, up to half-pound		12.45	7/01	108r
Postal rate, letter, first class, first ounce		0.34	7/01	108r
Postal rate, letter, two ounces		0.57	7/01	108r
Postal rate, post card		0.21	7/01	108r
Postal rate, priority mail, two pounds		3.95	7/01	108r
Postal rate, priority mail, up to one pound		3.50	7/01	108r
Telephone bill, family of three	mos	23.20	3/01	4c
Telephone services, expenditures on	yr	860	1999	30r
Education				
Board, 4-year private college/university	yr	2256	1996	38s
Board, 4-year public college/university	yr	1739	1996	38s
Education expenditures	yr	431	1999	30r
Room, 4-year private college/university	yr	1799	1996	38s
Room, 4-year public college/university	yr	1757	1996	38s
Total cost, 4-year private college/university	yr	11635	1996	38s
Total cost, 4-year public college/university	yr	5737	1996	38s
Tuition, 2-year public college/university, in state	yr	1317	1996	38s
Tuition, 4-year private college/university, in state	yr	7580	1996	38s
Tuition, 4-year public college/university	yr	2240	1996	38s

Values are in dollars or fractions of dollars. In the column headed *Ref*, references are shown to sources. Each reference is followed by a letter. These refer to the geographical level for which data were reported: s=State, r=Region, and c=City or metro. The abbreviation *ex* is used to mean *except* or *excluding*; *exp* stands for expenditures. For other abbreviations and further explanations, please see the Introduction.

Montgomery, AL - continued

Item	Per	Value	Date	Ref.
Energy and Fuels				
Electricity	500 KWhs	47.29	7/01	11r
Electricity	KWh	0.09	7/01	11r
Energy, combined forms, 2400 sq ft	mos	134.10	3/01	4c
Energy, exc. electricity, 2400 sq ft	mos	63.04	3/01	4c
Fuel oil #2	gal	1.43	7/01	11r
Fuel oil and other fuels, expenditures on	yr	45	1999	30r
Gas, natural, commercial rate	1000 cf	9.50	11/00	88s
Gas, regular unleaded, cash, self-service	gal	1.40	3/01	4c
Gasoline, all types	gal	1.60	7/01	11r
Gasoline, unleaded midgrade	gal	1.65	7/01	11r
Gasoline, unleaded premium	gal	1.74	7/01	11r
Natural gas, expenditures on	yr	164	1999	30r
Utility (piped) gas, therm		1.01	7/01	11r
Utility (piped) gas, 40 therms		44.29	7/01	11r
Utility (piped) gas, 100 therms		97.44	7/01	11r
Entertainment				
Bowling, Saturday evening rate	line	3.30	3/01	4c
Entertainment purchases	yr	1574	1999	30r
Fees and admissions paid	yr	371	1999	30r
Monopoly game, Parker Brothers', No. 9	game	11.79	3/01	4c
Movie, first-run, Saturday, evening	adm.	7.00	3/01	4c
Reading purchases	yr	121	1999	30r
Television, radios, sound equipment, expenditures on	yr	561	1999	30r
Tennis balls, yellow, Wilson or Penn, 3	can	2.05	3/01	4c
Groceries				
Groceries, ACCRA Index		96.80	3/01	4c
American processed cheese	lb	3.50	7/01	11r
Antibiotic ointment, Polysporin	0.5 oz	4.65	3/01	4c
Baby food, strained vegetables or fruit, lowest price	4-4.5 oz	0.37	3/01	4c
Bakery products, expenditures on	yr	261	1999	30r
Bananas	lb	0.54	3/01	4c
Bananas	lb	0.47	7/01	11r
Beans, dried, any type, all sizes	lb	0.63	7/01	11r
Beef for stew, boneless	lb	2.86	7/01	11r
Beef or hamburger, ground	lb	1.71	3/01	4c
Beef, expenditures on	yr	210	1999	30r
Bologna, all beef or mixed	lb	2.29	7/01	11r
Bread, French	lb	1.66	7/01	11r
Bread, white	loaf	0.93	3/01	4c
Bread, white, pan	lb	0.87	7/01	11r
Bread, whole wheat, pan	lb	1.38	7/01	11r
Broccoli	lb	1.04	7/01	11r
Butter, salted, grade AA, stick	lb	2.26	7/01	11r
Butter, yoghurt, cheese, etc, expenditures on	yr	170	1999	30r
Cabbage	lb	0.42	7/01	11r
Cereals and cereal products, expenditures on	yr	140	1999	30r
Cheddar cheese, natural	lb	3.75	7/01	11r
Cheese, Kraft grated Parmesan	8 oz	3.22	3/01	4c
Chicken breast, bone-in	lb	1.85	7/01	11r
Chicken legs, bone-in	lb	1.34	7/01	11r
Chicken, fresh, whole	lb	1.05	7/01	11r
Chicken, whole fryer	lb	0.89	3/01	4c
Chops, boneless,	lb	4.13	7/01	11r
Chuck roast, graded and ungraded, excl U.S. prime and choice	lb	2.35	7/01	11r
Chuck roast, U.S. choice, boneless	lb	2.67	7/01	11r
Cigarettes, Winston, Kings	carton	28.04	3/01	4c
Coffee, 100%, ground roast, all sizes	lb	2.88	7/01	11r
Coffee, instant, plain, regular, all sizes	16 oz	9.25	7/01	11r
Coffee, vacuum-packed	13 oz	2.19	3/01	4c
Cola, non diet	2 liter	1.11	7/01	11r
Corn Flakes, Kellogg's or Post Toasties	18 oz	3.19	3/01	4c
Corn, frozen, whole kernel, lowest price	16 oz	1.10	3/01	4c
Crackers, soda, salted	lb	1.70	7/01	11r
Dairy product purchases	yr	282	1999	30r
Eggs, expenditures on	yr	32	1999	30r
Eggs, Grade A or AA	dozen	1.23	3/01	4c

Item	Per	Value	Date	Ref.
Groceries - continued				
Fats and oils, expenditures on	yr	79	1999	30r
Fish and seafood, expenditures on	yr	99	1999	30r
Flour, white, all purpose	lb	0.32	7/01	11r
Food (excl fruit and vegetables), eaten at home, purchases	yr	815	1999	30r
Food cooked on trips, expenditures on	yr	36	1999	30r
Food purchases	yr	4533	1999	30r
Food purchases, eaten away from home	yr	1873	1999	30r
Food purchases, food eaten at home	yr	2660	1999	30r
Fresh fruits, expenditures on	yr	128	1999	30r
Fresh milk and cream, expenditures on	yr	112	1999	30r
Fresh vegetables, expenditures on	yr	131	1999	30r
Fruit and vegetable purchases	yr	438	1999	30r
Grapefruit	lb	0.59	7/01	11r
Grapes, Thompson, seedless	lb	2.12	7/01	11r
Ground beef, 100% beef	lb	1.76	7/01	11r
Ground beef, lean and extra lean	lb	2.60	7/01	11r
Ground chuck, 100% beef	lb	2.08	7/01	11r
Ham, boneless, excl canned	lb	2.71	7/01	11r
Ham, rump or shank half, bone-in, smoked	lb	2.19	7/01	11r
Ice cream, prepackaged, bulk, regular	1/2 gal	3.93	7/01	11r
Lemons	lb	1.32	7/01	11r
Lettuce, iceberg	head	1.02	3/01	4c
Lettuce, iceberg	lb	0.76	7/01	11r
Margarine, Blue Bonnet or Parkay, stick	lb	0.59	3/01	4c
Milk, fresh, low fat	gal	2.75	7/01	11r
Milk, fresh, whole, fortified	gal	2.97	7/01	11r
Milk, whole	1/2 gal	1.78	3/01	4c
Nonalcoholic beverages, expenditures on	yr	228	1999	30r
Orange juice, frozen concentrate	16 oz	1.95	7/01	11r
Orange juice, Minute Maid frozen	12 oz	1.75	3/01	4c
Oranges, Navel	lb	0.73	7/01	11r
Oranges, Valencia	lb	0.55	7/01	11r
Peaches, halves or slices, Hunt's, Del Monte, or Libby's	29 oz	1.63	3/01	4c
Peanut butter, creamy, all sizes	lb	1.83	7/01	11r
Pears, Anjou	lb	0.98	7/01	11r
Peas, green, Del Monte or Green Giant	15 oz	0.64	3/01	4c
Pork chops, center cut, bone-in	lb	3.33	7/01	11r
Pork sausage, fresh, loose	lb	2.59	7/01	11r
Pork shoulder picnic, bone-in, smoked	lb	1.12	7/01	11r
Pork, expenditures on	yr	162	1999	30r
Potato chips	16 oz	3.59	7/01	11r
Potatoes, frozen, french fried	lb	1.00	7/01	11r
Potatoes, white or red	10 lb	2.57	3/01	4c
Potatoes, white, all types	lb	0.44	7/01	11r
Poultry, expenditures on	yr	137	1999	30r
Processed fruits, expenditures on	yr	97	1999	30r
Processed vegetables, expenditures on	yr	82	1999	30r
Rice, white, long grain, uncooked	lb	0.51	7/01	11r
Round roast, graded and ungraded, excl U.S. prime and choice	lb	2.96	7/01	11r
Round steak, graded and ungraded, excl U.S. prime and choice	lb	3.11	7/01	11r
Sausage, Jimmy Dean/Owens pork	lb	2.52	3/01	4c
Shortening, vegetable, Crisco	3 lb	3.09	3/01	4c
Sirloin steak, graded and ungraded, excl U.S. prime and choice	lb	4.23	7/01	11r
Soft drink, Coca Cola, ex deposit	2 liter	1.11	3/01	4c
Spaghetti and macaroni	lb	0.78	7/01	11r
Steak, round, U.S. choice, boneless	lb	3.56	7/01	11r
Steak, sirloin, U.S. choice, boneless	lb	5.65	7/01	11r
Steak, T-bone	lb	6.89	3/01	4c
Strawberries, dry pint	12 oz	1.50	7/01	11r
Sugar and other sweets, expenditures on	yr	99	1999	30r
Sugar, cane or beet	4 lbs	1.49	3/01	4c
Sugar, white, 33-80 ounce package	lb	0.39	7/01	11r
Sugar, white, all sizes	lb	0.42	7/01	11r
Tobacco products and smoking supplies purchases	yr	288	1999	30r
Tomatoes, field grown	lb	1.43	7/01	11r
Tomatoes, Hunt's or Del Monte	14.5 oz	0.83	3/01	4c

Values are in dollars or fractions of dollars. In the column headed *Ref*, references are shown to sources. Each reference is followed by a letter. These refer to the geographical level for which data were reported: s=State, r=Region, and c=City or metro. The abbreviation *ex* is used to mean *except* or *excluding*; *exp* stands for *expenditures*. For other abbreviations and further explanations, please see the Introduction.

Montgomery, AL - continued

Item	Per	Value	Date	Ref.
Groceries				
Tuna, chunk, light	6 oz	0.43	3/01	4c
Tuna, light, chunk	lb	1.77	7/01	11r
Turkey, frozen, whole	lb	1.05	7/01	11r
Goods and Services				
Miscellaneous goods and services, ACCRA Index		99.10	3/01	4c
Hunting license	yr	16.00	4/01	34s
Health Care				
Health care, ACCRA Index		94.10	3/01	4c
Cardiac catheterization, ave hospital/ physician charges		15260	1998	77s
Childbirth, Cesarean delivery		11587	1997	13r
Childbirth, vaginal delivery		6725	1997	13r
Dentist's fee, adult teeth cleaning and periodic oral exam	visit	62.33	3/01	4c
Doctor's fee, routine exam, established patient	visit	52.33	3/01	4c
Drugs, expenditures on	yr	399	1999	30r
Health care purchases	yr	1971	1999	30r
Health insurance expenditures	yr	933	1999	30r
Hospital care, private room	day	598.08	3/01	4c
Hysterectomy, laproscopically-assisted, ave hospital/physician charges		16780	1998	76s
Hysterectomy, vaginal ave hospital and physician charges		10990	1998	76s
Medicaid dispensing fee		5.40	1999	87s
Medical services expenditures	yr	547	1999	30r
Medical supplies, expenditures on	yr	91	1999	30r
Household Goods				
Dishwashing powder, Cascade	50 oz	3.83	3/01	4c
Floor coverings, expenditures on	yr	44	1999	30r
Furniture, expenditures on	yr	335	1999	30r
Household furnishings and equipment purchases	yr	1328	1999	30r
Household textiles, expenditures on	yr	89	1999	30r
Laundry and cleaning supplies, expenditures on	yr	113	1999	30r
Tissues, facial, Kleenex brand	175	1.32	3/01	4c
Housing				
Housing, ACCRA Index		94.50	3/01	4c
Home, 2200 sq ft, 4-br, 2-bath, 2-car garage, average		140000	2000	47c
Home price, existing, ave		160100	10/00	90r
Home value, median		115000	2001	53s
House, 2400 sq ft, 8000 sq ft lot, new, urban, utilities	total	205000	3/01	4c
House payment, principal and interest, 25% down payment	mos	1001	3/01	4c
Household operation expenditures	yr	553	1999	30r
Housekeeping supplies purchases	yr	473	1999	30r
Housing, expenditures on	yr	10303	1999	30r
Maintenance, repairs, insurance expenditures	yr	699	1999	30r
Monthly rental value of owned home	mos	505	1999	30r
Owned dwellings, expenditures own	yr	3465	1999	30r
Rent expenditures	yr	1641	1999	30r
Rent, apartment, 2 br, 1 1/2-2 baths, unfurn, 950 sq ft, water	mos	586	3/01	4c
Rental unit, 1 bedroom, with utilities	mos	429	4/01	41c
Rental unit, 2 bedroom, with utilities	mos	507	4/01	41c
Rental unit, 3 bedroom, with utilities	mos	691	4/01	41c
Rental unit, 4 bedroom, with utilities	mos	832	4/01	41c
Shelter, expenditures on	yr	5467	1999	30r
Insurance and Pensions				
Life and other personal insurance purchases	yr	414	1999	30r
Pensions and Social Security, expenditures on	yr	2635	1999	30r
Personal insurance and pensions, expenditures on	yr	3048	1999	30r

Montgomery, AL - continued

Item	Per	Value	Date	Ref.
Legal Fees				
Divorce, filing fee		146.00- 193.00	4/01	35s
Driver's license fee	orig	18.50	1999	48s
Driver's license fee	renew	18.50	1999	48s
Personal Goods				
Personal care products and services purchases	yr	393	1999	30r
Shampoo, Alberto VO5	15 oz	1.15	3/01	4c
Toothpaste, Crest or Colgate	6-7 oz	2.49	3/01	4c
Personal Services				
Dry cleaning, man's 2-pc suit		5.13	3/01	4c
Man's haircut, barbershop, no styling		10.59	3/01	4c
Personal services, household, expenditures on	yr	258	1999	30r
Woman's shampoo, trim, blow-dry, no style-change		27.79	3/01	4c
Pets				
Pets, toys, and playground equipment, expenditures on	yr	306	1999	30r
Restaurant Food				
Chicken, fried, thigh and drumstick, KFC/ Church's		2.57	3/01	4c
Hamburger with cheese, McDonald's	1/4 lb	2.10	3/01	4c
Pizza, Pizza Hut or Pizza Inn	11-12 in	9.49	3/01	4c
Taxes				
Federal income taxes paid	yr	2047	1999	30r
Personal taxes, expenditures on	yr	2554	1999	30r
Property taxes paid	yr	726	1999	30r
State and local income taxes paid	yr	363	1999	30r
Transportation				
Transportation, ACCRA Index		104.10	3/01	4c
Bus fare, to central business district	1-way	1.50	3/01	4c
Cars and trucks, new, expenditures on	yr	1648	1999	30r
Cars and trucks, used, expenditures on	yr	1651	1999	30r
Diesel at the pump	gal	1.19	10/99	73s
Gasoline and motor oil purchases	yr	1052	1999	30r
Gasoline before-tax price (cents)	gal	104.10	10/00	43s
Maintenance and repair expenditures	yr	621	1999	30r
Public transportation, expenditures on	yr	298	1999	30r
Tire balance, computer or spin balance, front	wheel	7.98	3/01	4c
Transportation purchases	yr	6738	1999	30r
Vehicle expenses, miscellaneous, purchases	yr	2033	1999	30r
Vehicle insurance payments	yr	696	1999	30r
Vehicle purchases (net outlay)	yr	3354	1999	30r
Vehicle rental, lease expenditures	yr	352	1999	30r
Utilities				
Utilities, ACCRA Index		109.40	3/01	4c
Electrical bill, average	mos	83.42	9/00	9s
Electricity, expenditures on	yr	1115	1999	30r
Electricity and other, mixed, 2400 sq ft, new home	mos	71.06	3/01	4c
Electricity cost, average	KWh	5.60	9/00	9s
Water and other public services, expenditures on	yr	298	1999	30r
Weddings				
Wedding (national average cost)		19936	2000	33r
Attendants' gifts		321	1998	33r
Bridal attendants' apparel (5 persons)		824	2000	33r
Bride's headpiece/veil		173	1998	33r
Bride's wedding dress		859	1998	33r
Clergy, religious facility fee		242	1998	33r
Engagement ring		3177	1998	33r
Flowers		789	1998	33r
Groom's formalwear rental		99	2000	33r
Limousine		410	1998	33r
Marriage license cost		25.00	4/01	35s
Men's formalwear (ushers, best man)		469	2000	33r
Mother of bride apparel		241	2000	33r

Values are in dollars or fractions of dollars. In the column headed *Ref*, references are shown to sources. Each reference is followed by a letter. These refer to the geographical level for which data were reported: s=State, r=Region, and c=City or metro. The abbreviation *ex* is used to mean *except* or *excluding*; *exp* stands for *expenditures*. For other abbreviations and further explanations, please see the Introduction.

Montgomery, AL - continued

Item	Per	Value	Date	Ref.
Weddings				
Music		866	1998	33r
Photography and videography		1368	1998	33r
Rehearsal dinner		728	1998	33r
Wedding invitations and announcements		341	1998	33r
Wedding reception		7968	2000	33r
Wedding rings (bride and groom)		1060	1998	33r

Muncie, IN

Item	Per	Value	Date	Ref.
Average annual expenditures	yr	35369	1999	30r
Composite, ACCRA index		96.20	3/01	4c
Alcoholic Beverages				
Alcoholic beverage purchases	yr	304	1999	30r
Beer, Heineken, 12-oz, ex deposit	6	6.77	3/01	4c
J & B Scotch	750-ml	19.74	3/01	4c
Malt beverages, all types, all sizes, any origin	16 oz	0.93	7/01	11r
Wine, Livingston or Gallo, Chablis blanc	1.5 liter	4.37	3/01	4c
Wine, red and white table, all sizes, any origin	liter	7.04	7/01	11r
Appliances				
Appliance repair, service call, washing machine	min lab chg	51.33	3/01	4c
Major appliances, expenditures on	yr	165	1999	30r
Small appliances, housewares, expenditures on	yr	90	1999	30r
Banking and Money				
Mortgage interest and charges paid	yr	2277	1999	30r
Mortgage principal paid on owned property	yr	1230	1999	30r
Mortgage rate, incl. points and orig. fee, 30-yr. conv. fixed or ARM	mos	7.48	3/01	4c
Vehicle finance charges paid	yr	328	1999	30r
Charity				
Cash contributions, expenditures	yr	1126	1999	30r
Child Care				
Child raising cost, total, age 0-2	yr	7890	1999	60r
Child raising cost, total, age 3-5	yr	8130	1999	60r
Child raising cost, total, age 6-8	yr	8170	1999	60r
Child raising cost, total, age 9-11	yr	8190	1999	60r
Child raising cost, total, age 12-14	yr	8890	1999	60r
Child raising cost, total, age 15-17	yr	9050	1999	60r
Child's child care and education, age 0-2	yr	1240	1999	60r
Child's child care and education, age 3-5	yr	1370	1999	60r
Child's child care and education, age 6-8	yr	880	1999	60r
Child's child care and education, age 9-11	yr	570	1999	60r
Child's child care and education, age 12-14	yr	420	1999	60r
Child's child care and education, age 15-17	yr	720	1999	60r
Child's clothing, age 0-2	yr	410	1999	60r
Child's clothing, age 3-5	yr	400	1999	60r
Child's clothing, age 6-8	yr	450	1999	60r
Child's clothing, age 9-11	yr	500	1999	60r
Child's clothing, age 12-14	yr	840	1999	60r
Child's clothing, age 15-17	yr	740	1999	60r
Child's food, age 0-2	yr	960	1999	60r
Child's food, age 3-5	yr	1120	1999	60r
Child's food, age 6-8	yr	1430	1999	60r
Child's food, age 9-11	yr	1710	1999	60r
Child's food, age 12-14	yr	1710	1999	60r
Child's food, age 15-17	yr	1920	1999	60r
Child's health care, age 0-2	yr	520	1999	60r
Child's health care, age 3-5	yr	500	1999	60r
Child's health care, age 6-8	yr	570	1999	60r
Child's health care, age 9-11	yr	610	1999	60r
Child's health care, age 12-14	yr	630	1999	60r
Child's health care, age 15-17	yr	650	1999	60r
Child's housing, age 0-2	yr	2860	1999	60r
Child's housing, age 3-5	yr	2840	1999	60r
Child's housing, age 6-8	yr	2800	1999	60r
Child's housing, age 9-11	yr	2650	1999	60r
Child's housing, age 12-14	yr	2840	1999	60r

Muncie, IN - continued

Item	Per	Value	Date	Ref.
Child Care - continued				
Child's housing, age 15-17	yr	2440	1999	60r
Child's personal care, reading, age 0-2	yr	880	1999	60r
Child's personal care, reading, age 3-5	yr	900	1999	60r
Child's personal care, reading, age 6-8	yr	930	1999	60r
Child's personal care, reading, age 9-11	yr	970	1999	60r
Child's personal care, reading, age 12-14	yr	1150	1999	60r
Child's personal care, reading, age 15-17	yr	920	1999	60r
Clothing				
Apparel and services purchases	yr	1607	1999	30r
Boys' brief, cotton	3	3.77	3/01	4c
Boys, 2 to 15, expenditures on	yr	91	1999	30r
Children under 2, expenditures on	yr	59	1999	30r
Footwear, expenditures on	yr	285	1999	30r
Girls, 2 to 15, expenditures on	yr	116	1999	30r
Men and boys, expenditures on	yr	433	1999	30r
Men, 16 and over, expenditures on	yr	341	1999	30r
Shirt, man's dress shirt		24.74	3/01	4c
Slacks, man's "No Wrinkles" khaki		35.59	3/01	4c
Women, 16 and over, expenditures on	yr	490	1999	30r
Communications				
Newspaper subscription, daily and Sunday delivery	mos	14.13	3/01	4c
Phone line, single, business, field visit	inst.	59.00	12/97	17s
Phone line, single, business, no field visit	inst.	59.00	12/97	17s
Phone line, single, residence, field visit	inst.	47.00	12/97	17s
Phone line, single, residence, no field visit	inst.	47.00	12/97	17s
Postage and stationery, expenditures on	yr	140	1999	30r
Postal rate, express mail, up to half-pound		12.45	7/01	108r
Postal rate, letter, first class, first ounce		0.34	7/01	108r
Postal rate, letter, two ounces		0.57	7/01	108r
Postal rate, post card		0.21	7/01	108r
Postal rate, priority mail, two pounds		3.95	7/01	108r
Postal rate, priority mail, up to one pound		3.50	7/01	108r
Telephone bill, business, basic rate	mos	37.75	12/97	18c
Telephone bill, family of three	mos	19.20	3/01	4c
Telephone bill, residential, basic rate	mos	11.11	12/97	18c
Telephone services, expenditures on	yr	830	1999	30r
Education				
Board, 4-year private college/university	yr	2250	1996	38s
Board, 4-year public college/university	yr	2425	1996	38s
Education expenditures	yr	583	1999	30r
Room, 4-year private college/university	yr	1987	1996	38s
Room, 4-year public college/university	yr	1931	1996	38s
Total cost, 4-year private college/university	yr	16829	1996	38s
Total cost, 4-year public college/university	yr	7392	1996	38s
Tuition, 2-year public college/university, in state	yr	1937	1996	38s
Tuition, 4-year private college/university, in state	yr	12592	1996	38s
Tuition, 4-year public college/university	yr	3037	1996	38s
Energy and Fuels				
Electricity	500 KWhs	46.59	7/01	11r
Energy, combined forms, 2400 sq ft	mos	110.63	3/01	4c
Energy, exc. electricity, 2400 sq ft	mos	54.01	3/01	4c
Fuel oil #2	gal	1.27	7/01	11r
Fuel oil and other fuels, expenditures on	yr	68	1999	30r
Gas, cooking, winter, 10 therms	mos	14.67	2/96	98c
Gas, cooking, winter, 30 therms	mos	26.01	2/96	98c
Gas, cooking, winter, 50 therms	mos	36.99	2/96	98c
Gas, heating, winter, average use	mos	124.90	2/96	98c
Gas, natural, commercial rate	1000 cf	6.24	11/00	88s
Gas, regular unleaded, cash, self-service	gal	1.47	3/01	4c
Gasoline, unleaded midgrade	gal	1.79	7/01	11r
Gasoline, unleaded premium	gal	1.86	7/01	11r
Gasoline, unleaded regular	gal	1.58	7/01	11r
Natural gas, expenditures on	yr	389	1999	30r
Utility (piped) gas, therm		0.81	7/01	11r
Utility (piped) gas, 40 therms		38.01	7/01	11r
Utility (piped) gas, 100 therms		81.75	7/01	11r

Values are in dollars or fractions of dollars. In the column headed *Ref*, references are shown to sources. Each reference is followed by a letter. These refer to the geographical level for which data were reported: s=State, r=Region, and c=City or metro. The abbreviation *ex* is used to mean *except* or *excluding*; *exp* stands for *expenditures*. For other abbreviations and further explanations, please see the Introduction.

Muncie, IN - continued

Item	Per	Value	Date	Ref.
Entertainment				
Bowling, Saturday evening rate	line	2.33	3/01	4c
Entertainment purchases	yr	1984	1999	30r
Fees and admissions paid	yr	444	1999	30r
Monopoly game, Parker Brothers', No. 9	game	9.68	3/01	4c
Movie, first-run, Saturday, evening	adm.	6.00	3/01	4c
Television, radios, sound equipment, expenditures on	yr	580	1999	30r
Tennis balls, yellow, Wilson or Penn, 3	can	1.93	3/01	4c
Funerals				
Cosmetology, hair, other preparation		178.32	1/99	78r
Embalming		408.19	1/99	78r
Funeral at funeral home		362.13	1/99	78r
Professional service charges		1375.51	1/99	78r
Transfer of remains to funeral home		155.92	1/99	78r
Visitation/viewing		294.38	1/99	78r
Groceries				
Groceries, ACCRA Index		91.40	3/01	4c
Antibiotic ointment, Polysporin	0.5 oz	4.18	3/01	4c
Baby food, strained vegetables or fruit, lowest price	4-4.5 oz	0.37	3/01	4c
Bacon, sliced	lb	3.15	7/01	11r
Bakery products, expenditures on	yr	281	1999	30r
Bananas	lb	0.51	3/01	4c
Bananas	lb	0.48	7/01	11r
Beans, dried, any type, all sizes	lb	0.61	7/01	11r
Beef for stew, boneless	lb	3.08	7/01	11r
Beef or hamburger, ground	lb	1.56	3/01	4c
Beef, expenditures on	yr	217	1999	30r
Bologna, all beef or mixed	lb	2.52	7/01	11r
Bread, white	loaf	0.71	3/01	4c
Bread, white, pan	lb	1.06	7/01	11r
Broccoli	lb	0.91	7/01	11r
Butter, salted, grade AA, stick	lb	3.04	7/01	11r
Butter, yoghurt, cheese, etc, expenditures on	yr	183	1999	30r
Cereals and bakery product purchases	yr	430	1999	30r
Cereals and cereal products, expenditures on	yr	149	1999	30r
Cheese, Kraft grated Parmesan	8 oz	3.75	3/01	4c
Chicken, fresh, whole	lb	1.07	7/01	11r
Chicken, whole fryer	lb	1.04	3/01	4c
Chops, boneless,	lb	3.64	7/01	11r
Chuck roast, U.S. choice, boneless	lb	2.47	7/01	11r
Cigarettes, Winston, Kings	carton	28.79	3/01	4c
Coffee, 100%, ground roast, all sizes	lb	2.69	7/01	11r
Coffee, vacuum-packed	13 oz	2.47	3/01	4c
Cookies, chocolate chip	lb	2.87	7/01	11r
Corn Flakes, Kellogg's or Post Toasties	18 oz	1.83	3/01	4c
Corn, frozen, whole kernel, lowest price	16 oz	1.23	3/01	4c
Dairy product purchases	yr	304	1999	30r
Eggs, expenditures on	yr	26	1999	30r
Eggs, Grade A or AA	dozen	1.07	3/01	4c
Eggs, grade A, large	dozen	0.88	7/01	11r
Fats and oils, expenditures on	yr	75	1999	30r
Fish and seafood, expenditures on	yr	72	1999	30r
Food (excl fruit and vegetables), eaten at home, purchases	yr	887	1999	30r
Food cooked on trips, expenditures on	yr	44	1999	30r
Food purchases	yr	4802	1999	30r
Food purchases, eaten away from home	yr	2069	1999	30r
Food purchases, food eaten at home	yr	2733	1999	30r
Fresh fruits, expenditures on	yr	138	1999	30r
Fresh milk and cream, expenditures on	yr	120	1999	30r
Fresh vegetables, expenditures on	yr	126	1999	30r
Grapefruit	lb	0.66	7/01	11r
Grapes, Thompson, seedless	lb	1.64	7/01	11r
Ground beef, 100% beef	lb	1.64	7/01	11r
Ground beef, lean and extra lean	lb	2.16	7/01	11r
Ground chuck, 100% beef	lb	2.13	7/01	11r
Ham, boneless, excl canned	lb	2.62	7/01	11r
Ice cream, prepackaged, bulk, regular	1/2 gal	3.35	7/01	11r
Lemons	lb	1.19	7/01	11r

Muncie, IN - continued

Item	Per	Value	Date	Ref.
Groceries - continued				
Lettuce, iceberg	head	1.23	3/01	4c
Lettuce, iceberg	lb	0.73	7/01	11r
Margarine, Blue Bonnet or Parkay, stick	lb	0.65	3/01	4c
Margarine, soft, tubs	lb	0.89	7/01	11r
Meats, poultry, fish, and egg purchases	yr	671	1999	30r
Milk, fresh, whole, fortified	gal	2.71	7/01	11r
Milk, whole	1/2 gal	1.65	3/01	4c
Nonalcoholic beverages, expenditures on	yr	239	1999	30r
Orange juice, Minute Maid frozen	12 oz	1.65	3/01	4c
Oranges, Navel	lb	0.80	7/01	11r
Oranges, Valencia	lb	0.66	7/01	11r
Peaches, halves or slices, Hunt's, Del Monte, or Libby's	29 oz	1.32	3/01	4c
Pears, Anjou	lb	0.93	7/01	11r
Peas, green, Del Monte or Green Giant	15 oz	0.63	3/01	4c
Pork chops, center cut, bone-in	lb	3.63	7/01	11r
Pork, expenditures on	yr	150	1999	30r
Potato chips	16 oz	3.52	7/01	11r
Potatoes, frozen, french fried	lb	1.08	7/01	11r
Potatoes, white or red	10 lb	2.09	3/01	4c
Potatoes, white, all types	lb	0.33	7/01	11r
Poultry, expenditures on	yr	108	1999	30r
Processed fruits, expenditures on	yr	98	1999	30r
Processed vegetables, expenditures on	yr	80	1999	30r
Round roast, U.S. choice, boneless	lb	3.07	7/01	11r
Round steak, graded and ungraded, excl U.S. prime and choice	lb	3.41	7/01	11r
Sausage, Jimmy Dean/Owens pork	lb	2.95	3/01	4c
Shortening, vegetable oil blends	lb	1.13	7/01	11r
Shortening, vegetable, Crisco	3 lb	2.61	3/01	4c
Soft drink, Coca Cola, ex deposit	2 liter	1.18	3/01	4c
Spaghetti and macaroni	lb	0.80	7/01	11r
Steak, round, U.S. choice, boneless	lb	3.23	7/01	11r
Steak, T-bone	lb	6.05	3/01	4c
Steak, T-bone, U.S. choice, bone-in	lb	6.68	7/01	11r
Strawberries, dry pint	12 oz	1.32	7/01	11r
Sugar and other sweets, expenditures on	yr	114	1999	30r
Sugar, cane or beet	4 lbs	1.22	3/01	4c
Sugar, white, 33-80 ounce package	lb	0.42	7/01	11r
Sugar, white, all sizes	lb	0.43	7/01	11r
Tobacco products and smoking supplies purchases	yr	331	1999	30r
Tomatoes, field grown	lb	1.46	7/01	11r
Tomatoes, Hunt's or Del Monte	14.5 oz	0.86	3/01	4c
Tuna, chunk, light	6 oz	0.54	3/01	4c
Tuna, light, chunk	lb	1.80	7/01	11r
Turkey, frozen, whole	lb	1.15	7/01	11r
Goods and Services				
Miscellaneous goods and services, ACCRA Index		93.30	3/01	4c
B&B Japanese maple (acer japonicum)	gal	29.99-169.99	4/00	93r
Boxwood (buxus)	2 gal	18.99-39.99	4/00	93r
Daylilly (hemerocallis)	gal	4.99-25.00	4/00	93r
Flat of annuals		11.98-24.99	4/00	93r
Fountain grass (pennisetum)	gal	5.98-12.98	4/00	93r
Hanging basket (10 in)		12.99-27.99	4/00	93r
Hardy geranium (geranium)	gal	7.99-9.99	4/00	93r
Hosta (hosta)	gal	6.00-25.00	4/00	93r
Lilac (syrubga vulgaris)	2 gal	14.99-24.99	4/00	93r
Miscellaneous purchases	yr	865	1999	30r
Rhododendron (rhododendron)	2 gal	23.98-42.99	4/00	93r

Values are in dollars or fractions of dollars. In the column headed *Ref*, references are shown to sources. Each reference is followed by a letter. These refer to the geographical level for which data were reported: s=State, r=Region, and c=City or metro. The abbreviation *ex* is used to mean *except* or *excluding*; *exp* stands for *expenditures*. For other abbreviations and further explanations, please see the Introduction.

Muncie, IN - continued

Item	Per	Value	Date	Ref.
Goods and Services				
Sage (salvia)	gal	6.00-9.99	4/00	93r
Wintercreeper euonymus (euonymus fortunei)	2 gal	16.00-169.99	4/00	93r
Hunting license	yr	8.75	4/01	34s
Health Care				
Health care, ACCRA Index		92.20	3/01	4c
Cardiac catheterization, ave hospital/ physician charges		13380	1998	77s
Childbirth, Cesarean delivery		10722	1997	13r
Childbirth, vaginal delivery		6223	1997	13r
Dentist's fee, adult teeth cleaning and periodic oral exam	visit	65.60	3/01	4c
Doctor's fee, routine exam, established patient	visit	50.50	3/01	4c
Drugs, expenditures on	yr	394	1999	30r
Health care purchases	yr	2048	1999	30r
Health insurance expenditures	yr	978	1999	30r
Hospital care, private room	day	562.00	3/01	4c
Hysterectomy, laproscopically-assisted, ave hospital/physician charges		11310	1998	76s
Hysterectomy, vaginal, ave hospital and physician charges		9160	1998	76s
Medicaid dispensing fee		4.00	1999	87s
Medical services expenditures	yr	554	1999	30r
Medical supplies, expenditures on	yr	122	1999	30r
Plastic surgery, breast augmentation		3184	2000	7r
Plastic surgery, breast lift		3585	2000	7r
Plastic surgery, facelift		4999	2000	7r
Plastic surgery, hair transplantation		3105	2000	7r
Plastic surgery, lip augmentation		1290	2000	7r
Plastic surgery, lower body lift		8135	2000	7r
Plastic surgery, thigh lift		3839	2000	7r
Household Goods				
Dishwashing powder, Cascade	50 oz	3.05	3/01	4c
Floor coverings, expenditures on	yr	52	1999	30r
Furniture, expenditures on	yr	344	1999	30r
Household furnishings and equipment purchases	yr	1475	1999	30r
Household textiles, expenditures on	yr	109	1999	30r
Laundry and cleaning supplies, expenditures on	yr	134	1999	30r
Tissues, facial, Kleenex brand	175	1.05	3/01	4c
Housing				
Housing, ACCRA Index		102.30	3/01	4c
Home price, existing, ave		144400	10/00	90r
Home value, median		102000	2001	53s
House, 2400 sq ft, 8000 sq ft lot, new, urban, utilities	total	207430	3/01	4c
House payment, principal and interest, 25% down payment	mos	1085	3/01	4c
Household operation expenditures	yr	542	1999	30r
Housekeeping supplies purchases	yr	508	1999	30r
Lodging expenditures	yr	430	1999	30r
Maintenance, repairs, insurance expenditures	yr	853	1999	30r
Monthly rental value of owned home	mos	547	1999	30r
Owned dwellings, expenditures own	yr	4282	1999	30r
Rent expenditures	yr	1558	1999	30r
Rent, apartment, 2 br, 1 1/2-2 baths, unfurn, 950 sq ft, water	mos	630	3/01	4c
Rental unit, 1 bedroom, with utilities	mos	376	4/01	41c
Rental unit, 2 bedroom, with utilities	mos	446	4/01	41c
Rental unit, 3 bedroom, with utilities	mos	604	4/01	41c
Rental unit, 4 bedroom, with utilities	mos	713	4/01	41c
Shelter, expenditures on	yr	6270	1999	30r
Insurance and Pensions				
Life and other personal insurance purchases	yr	387	1999	30r
Pensions and Social Security, expenditures on	yr	2968	1999	30r

Muncie, IN - continued

Item	Per	Value	Date	Ref.
Legal Fees				
Divorce, filing fee		100.00	4/01	35s
Driver's license fee	renew	6.00	1999	48s
Driver's license fee	orig	6.00	1999	48s
Personal Goods				
Personal care products and services purchases	yr	385	1999	30r
Shampoo, Alberto VO5	15 oz	0.88	3/01	4c
Toothpaste, Crest or Colgate	6-7 oz	1.84	3/01	4c
Personal Services				
Dry cleaning, man's 2-pc suit		7.62	3/01	4c
Man's haircut, barbershop, no styling		9.60	3/01	4c
Personal services, household, expenditures on	yr	300	1999	30r
Woman's shampoo, trim, blow-dry, no style-change		22.38	3/01	4c
Pets				
Pets, toys, and playground equipment, expenditures on	yr	375	1999	30r
Restaurant Food				
Chicken, fried, thigh and drumstick, KFC/ Church's		2.54	3/01	4c
Hamburger with cheese, McDonald's	1/4 lb	1.99	3/01	4c
Pizza, Pizza Hut or Pizza Inn	11-12 in	8.99	3/01	4c
Taxes				
Federal income taxes paid	yr	2326	1999	30r
Personal taxes, expenditures on	yr	3223	1999	30r
Property taxes paid	yr	1152	1999	30r
State and local income taxes paid	yr	753	1999	30r
Transportation				
Transportation, ACCRA Index		103.20	3/01	4c
Bus fare, one-way	trip	0.50	2000	1c
Cars and trucks, new, expenditures on	yr	1280	1999	30r
Cars and trucks, used, expenditures on	yr	1763	1999	30r
Diesel at the pump	gal	1.17	10/99	73s
Gasoline and motor oil purchases	yr	1036	1999	30r
Gasoline before-tax price (cents)	gal	110.00	10/00	43s
Maintenance and repair expenditures	yr	594	1999	30r
Public transportation, expenditures on	yr	341	1999	30r
Tire balance, computer or spin balance, front	wheel	7.99	3/01	4c
Transportation purchases	yr	6617	1999	30r
Vehicle expenses, miscellaneous, purchases	yr	2159	1999	30r
Vehicle insurance payments	yr	701	1999	30r
Vehicle purchases (net outlay)	yr	3081	1999	30r
Vehicle rental, lease expenditures	yr	536	1999	30r
Utilities				
Utilities, ACCRA Index		90.30	3/01	4c
Electrical bill, average	mos	66.66	9/00	9s
Electricity, expenditures on	yr	841	1999	30r
Electricity and other, mixed, 2400 sq ft, new home	mos	56.62	3/01	4c
Electricity cost, average	KWh	5.00	9/00	9s
Utilities, fuels, and public services purchased	yr	2401	1999	30r
Water and other public services, expenditures on	yr	273	1999	30r
Weddings				
Wedding (national average cost)		19936	2000	33r
Wedding (regional average total cost)		16195	1997	110r
Attendants' gifts		321	1998	33r
Bridal attendants' apparel (5 persons)		824	2000	33r
Bride's headpiece/veil		173	1998	33r
Bride's wedding dress		859	1998	33r
Clergy, religious facility fee		242	1998	33r
Engagement ring		3177	1998	33r
Flowers		789	1998	33r
Groom's formalwear rental		99	2000	33r
Limousine		410	1998	33r
Marriage license cost		18.00	4/01	35s
Men's formalwear (ushers, best man)		469	2000	33r

Values are in dollars or fractions of dollars. In the column headed *Ref*, references are shown to sources. Each reference is followed by a letter. These refer to the geographical level for which data were reported: s=State, r=Region, and c=City or metro. The abbreviation *ex* is used to mean *except* or *excluding*; *exp* stands for *expenditures*. For other abbreviations and further explanations, please see the Introduction.

Muncie, IN - continued

Weddings

Item	Per	Value	Date	Ref.
Mother of bride apparel		241	2000	33r
Music		866	1998	33r
Photography and videography		1368	1998	33r
Rehearsal dinner		728	1998	33r
Wedding invitations and announcements		341	1998	33r
Wedding reception		7968	2000	33r
Wedding rings (bride and groom)		1060	1998	33r

Myrtle Beach, SC

Item	Per	Value	Date	Ref.
Composite, ACCRA index		98.30	3/01	4c
Alcoholic Beverages				
Alcoholic beverage purchases	yr	253	1999	30r
Beer, Heineken, 12-oz, ex deposit	6	7.24	3/01	4c
J & B Scotch	750-ml	20.46	3/01	4c
Malt beverages, all types, all sizes, any origin	16 oz	0.96	7/01	11r
Wine, Livingston or Gallo, Chablis blanc	1.5 liter	6.61	3/01	4c
Appliances				
Appliance repair, service call, washing machine	min lab chg	36.60	3/01	4c
Major appliances, expenditures on	yr	172	1999	30r
Small appliances, housewares, expenditures on	yr	81	1999	30r
Banking and Money				
Mortgage interest and charges paid	yr	2039	1999	30r
Mortgage principal paid on owned property	yr	1026	1999	30r
Mortgage rate, incl. points and orig. fee, 30-yr. conv. fixed or ARM	mos	7.17	3/01	4c
Vehicle finance charges paid	yr	365	1999	30r
Charity				
Cash contributions, expenditures	yr	1127	1999	30r
Child Care				
Child raising cost, total, age 0-2	yr	8540	1999	60r
Child raising cost, total, age 3-5	yr	8780	1999	60r
Child raising cost, total, age 6-8	yr	8820	1999	60r
Child raising cost, total, age 9-11	yr	8800	1999	60r
Child raising cost, total, age 12-14	yr	9510	1999	60r
Child raising cost, total, age 15-17	yr	9740	1999	60r
Child's child care and education, age 0-2	yr	1380	1999	60r
Child's child care and education, age 3-5	yr	1520	1999	60r
Child's child care and education, age 6-8	yr	990	1999	60r
Child's child care and education, age 9-11	yr	650	1999	60r
Child's child care and education, age 12-14	yr	490	1999	60r
Child's child care and education, age 15-17	yr	840	1999	60r
Child's clothing, age 0-2	yr	480	1999	60r
Child's clothing, age 3-5	yr	470	1999	60r
Child's clothing, age 6-8	yr	520	1999	60r
Child's clothing, age 9-11	yr	570	1999	60r
Child's clothing, age 12-14	yr	950	1999	60r
Child's clothing, age 15-17	yr	850	1999	60r
Child's food, age 0-2	yr	1000	1999	60r
Child's food, age 3-5	yr	1160	1999	60r
Child's food, age 6-8	yr	1490	1999	60r
Child's food, age 9-11	yr	1770	1999	60r
Child's food, age 12-14	yr	1770	1999	60r
Child's food, age 15-17	yr	1980	1999	60r
Child's health care, age 0-2	yr	620	1999	60r
Child's health care, age 3-5	yr	590	1999	60r
Child's health care, age 6-8	yr	680	1999	60r
Child's health care, age 9-11	yr	720	1999	60r
Child's health care, age 12-14	yr	730	1999	60r
Child's health care, age 15-17	yr	760	1999	60r
Child's housing, age 0-2	yr	3070	1999	60r
Child's housing, age 3-5	yr	3050	1999	60r
Child's housing, age 6-8	yr	3010	1999	60r
Child's housing, age 9-11	yr	2850	1999	60r
Child's housing, age 12-14	yr	3040	1999	60r
Child's housing, age 15-17	yr	2650	1999	60r
Child's personal care, reading, age 0-2	yr	910	1999	60r

Myrtle Beach, SC - continued

Item	Per	Value	Date	Ref.
Child Care - continued				
Child's personal care, reading, age 3-5	yr	930	1999	60r
Child's personal care, reading, age 6-8	yr	960	1999	60r
Child's personal care, reading, age 9-11	yr	1000	1999	60r
Child's personal care, reading, age 12-14	yr	1170	1999	60r
Child's personal care, reading, age 15-17	yr	950	1999	60r
Clothing				
Apparel and services purchases	yr	1610	1999	30r
Boys' brief, cotton	3	4.63	3/01	4c
Boys, 2 to 15, expenditures on	yr	89	1999	30r
Children under 2, expenditures on	yr	79	1999	30r
Footwear, expenditures on	yr	283	1999	30r
Girls, 2 to 15, expenditures on	yr	103	1999	30r
Men and boys, expenditures on	yr	351	1999	30r
Men, 16 and over, expenditures on	yr	262	1999	30r
Shirt, man's dress shirt		24.39	3/01	4c
Slacks, man's "No Wrinkles" khaki		38.66	3/01	4c
Women, 16 and over, expenditures on	yr	538	1999	30r
Communications				
Cable modem installation, Adelphi		54.90	6/99	103s
Cable modem installation, Comcast		95.00	6/99	103s
Cable modem installation, Intermedia		149.95	6/99	103s
Cable modem rate, cable subscriber, Adelphi	mos	34.95	6/99	103s
Cable modem rate, cable subscriber, Comcast	mos	39.95	6/99	103s
Cable modem rate, cable subscriber, Intermedia	mos	49.95	6/99	103s
Cable modem rate, non-cable subscriber, Adelphi	mos	44.95	6/99	103s
Cable modem rate, non-cable subscriber, Comcast	mos	49.95	6/99	103s
Cable modem rate, non-cable subscriber, Intermedia	mos	54.95	6/99	103s
Newspaper subscription, daily and Sunday delivery	mos	11.87	3/01	4c
Phone line, single, business, field visit	inst.	64.00	12/97	17s
Phone line, single, business, no field visit	inst.	64.00	12/97	17s
Phone line, single, residence, field visit	inst.	40.00	12/97	17s
Phone line, single, residence, no field visit	inst.	40.00	12/97	17s
Postage and stationery, expenditures on	yr	104	1999	30r
Postal rate, express mail, up to half-pound		12.45	7/01	108r
Postal rate, letter, first class, first ounce		0.34	7/01	108r
Postal rate, letter, two ounces		0.57	7/01	108r
Postal rate, post card		0.21	7/01	108r
Postal rate, priority mail, two pounds		3.95	7/01	108r
Postal rate, priority mail, up to one pound		3.50	7/01	108r
Telephone bill, family of three	mos	19.86	3/01	4c
Telephone services, expenditures on	yr	860	1999	30r
Education				
Board, 4-year private college/university	yr	1990	1996	38s
Board, 4-year public college/university	yr	1872	1996	38s
Education expenditures	yr	431	1999	30r
Room, 4-year private college/university	yr	1786	1996	38s
Room, 4-year public college/university	yr	1998	1996	38s
Total cost, 4-year private college/university	yr	13517	1996	38s
Total cost, 4-year public college/university	yr	6964	1996	38s
Tuition, 2-year public college/university, in state	yr	1071	1996	38s
Tuition, 4-year private college/university, in state	yr	9741	1996	38s
Tuition, 4-year public college/university	yr	3094	1996	38s
Energy and Fuels				
Electricity	500 KWhs	47.29	7/01	11r
Electricity	KWh	0.09	7/01	11r
Energy, combined forms, 2400 sq ft	mos	109.15	3/01	4c
Fuel oil #2	gal	1.43	7/01	11r
Fuel oil and other fuels, expenditures on	yr	45	1999	30r
Gas, natural, commercial rate	1000 cf	9.50	11/00	88s
Gas, regular unleaded, cash, self-service	gal	1.34	3/01	4c
Gasoline, all types	gal	1.60	7/01	11r

Values are in dollars or fractions of dollars. In the column headed *Ref*, references are shown to sources. Each reference is followed by a letter. These refer to the geographical level for which data were reported: s=State, r=Region, and c=City or metro. The abbreviation *ex* is used to mean *except* or *excluding*; *exp* stands for *expenditures*. For other abbreviations and further explanations, please see the Introduction.

Myrtle Beach, SC - continued

Item	Per	Value	Date	Ref.
Energy and Fuels				
Gasoline, unleaded midgrade	gal	1.65	7/01	11r
Gasoline, unleaded premium	gal	1.74	7/01	11r
Natural gas, expenditures on	yr	164	1999	30r
Utility (piped) gas, therm		1.01	7/01	11r
Utility (piped) gas, 40 therms		44.29	7/01	11r
Utility (piped) gas, 100 therms		97.44	7/01	11r
Entertainment				
Bowling, Saturday evening rate	line	3.09	3/01	4c
Entertainment purchases	yr	1574	1999	30r
Fees and admissions paid	yr	371	1999	30r
Monopoly game, Parker Brothers', No. 9	game	13.18	3/01	4c
Movie, first-run, Saturday, evening	adm.	6.94	3/01	4c
Reading purchases	yr	121	1999	30r
Television, radios, sound equipment, expenditures on	yr	561	1999	30r
Tennis balls, yellow, Wilson or Penn, 3	can	2.19	3/01	4c
Funerals				
Total cost of funeral		5922.53	1/99	78r
Acknowledgement cards		63.43	1/99	78r
Casket		2258.77	1/99	78r
Cosmetology, hair, other preparation		127.09	1/99	78r
Embalming		393.49	1/99	78r
Funeral at funeral home		367.50	1/99	78r
Hearse (local)		169.66	1/99	78r
Professional service charges		1211.32	1/99	78r
Service car/van		80.69	1/99	78r
Transfer of remains to funeral home		144.25	1/99	78r
Vault		803.50	1/99	78r
Visitation/viewing		302.83	1/99	78r
Groceries				
Groceries, ACCRA Index		104.50	3/01	4c
American processed cheese	lb	3.50	7/01	11r
Antibiotic ointment, Polysporin	0.5 oz	4.82	3/01	4c
Baby food, strained vegetables or fruit, lowest price	4-4.5 oz	0.49	3/01	4c
Bakery products, expenditures on	yr	261	1999	30r
Bananas	lb	0.58	3/01	4c
Bananas	lb	0.47	7/01	11r
Beans, dried, any type, all sizes	lb	0.63	7/01	11r
Beef for stew, boneless	lb	2.86	7/01	11r
Beef or hamburger, ground	lb	1.89	3/01	4c
Beef, expenditures on	yr	210	1999	30r
Bologna, all beef or mixed	lb	2.29	7/01	11r
Bread, French	lb	1.66	7/01	11r
Bread, white	loaf	1.10	3/01	4c
Bread, white, pan	lb	0.87	7/01	11r
Bread, whole wheat, pan	lb	1.38	7/01	11r
Broccoli	lb	1.04	7/01	11r
Butter, salted, grade AA, stick	lb	2.26	7/01	11r
Butter, yoghurt, cheese, etc, expenditures on	yr	170	1999	30r
Cabbage	lb	0.42	7/01	11r
Cereals and cereal products, expenditures on	yr	140	1999	30r
Cheddar cheese, natural	lb	3.75	7/01	11r
Cheese, Kraft grated Parmesan	8 oz	3.51	3/01	4c
Chicken breast, bone-in	lb	1.85	7/01	11r
Chicken legs, bone-in	lb	1.34	7/01	11r
Chicken, fresh, whole	lb	1.05	7/01	11r
Chicken, whole fryer	lb	0.99	3/01	4c
Chops, boneless,	lb	4.13	7/01	11r
Chuck roast, graded and ungraded, excl U.S. prime and choice	lb	2.35	7/01	11r
Chuck roast, U.S. choice, boneless	lb	2.67	7/01	11r
Cigarettes, Winston, Kings	carton	28.88	3/01	4c
Coffee, 100%, ground roast, all sizes	lb	2.88	7/01	11r
Coffee, instant, plain, regular, all sizes	16 oz	9.25	7/01	11r
Coffee, vacuum-packed	13 oz	2.41	3/01	4c
Cola, non diet,	2 liter	1.11	7/01	11r
Corn Flakes, Kellogg's or Post Toasties	18 oz	2.74	3/01	4c
Corn, frozen, whole kernel, lowest price	16 oz	0.97	3/01	4c
Crackers, soda, salted	lb	1.70	7/01	11r

Myrtle Beach, SC - continued

Item	Per	Value	Date	Ref.
Groceries - continued				
Dairy product purchases	yr	282	1999	30r
Eggs, expenditures on	yr	32	1999	30r
Eggs, Grade A or AA	dozen	1.33	3/01	4c
Fats and oils, expenditures on	yr	79	1999	30r
Fish and seafood, expenditures on	yr	99	1999	30r
Flour, white, all purpose	lb	0.32	7/01	11r
Food (excl fruit and vegetables), eaten at home, purchases	yr	815	1999	30r
Food cooked on trips, expenditures on	yr	36	1999	30r
Food purchases	yr	4533	1999	30r
Food purchases, eaten away from home	yr	1873	1999	30r
Food purchases, food eaten at home	yr	2660	1999	30r
Fresh fruits, expenditures on	yr	128	1999	30r
Fresh milk and cream, expenditures on	yr	112	1999	30r
Fresh vegetables, expenditures on	yr	131	1999	30r
Fruit and vegetable purchases	yr	438	1999	30r
Grapefruit	lb	0.59	7/01	11r
Grapes, Thompson, seedless	lb	2.12	7/01	11r
Ground beef, 100% beef	lb	1.76	7/01	11r
Ground beef, lean and extra lean	lb	2.60	7/01	11r
Ground chuck, 100% beef	lb	2.08	7/01	11r
Ham, boneless, excl canned	lb	2.71	7/01	11r
Ham, rump or shank half, bone-in, smoked	lb	2.19	7/01	11r
Ice cream, prepackaged, bulk, regular	1/2 gal	3.93	7/01	11r
Lemons	lb	1.32	7/01	11r
Lettuce, iceberg	head	1.01	3/01	4c
Lettuce, iceberg	lb	0.76	7/01	11r
Margarine, Blue Bonnet or Parkay, stick	lb	0.63	3/01	4c
Milk, fresh, low fat	gal	2.75	7/01	11r
Milk, fresh, whole, fortified	gal	2.97	7/01	11r
Milk, whole	1/2 gal	1.89	3/01	4c
Nonalcoholic beverages, expenditures on	yr	228	1999	30r
Orange juice, frozen concentrate	16 oz	1.95	7/01	11r
Orange juice, Minute Maid frozen	12 oz	1.47	3/01	4c
Oranges, Navel	lb	0.73	7/01	11r
Oranges, Valencia	lb	0.55	7/01	11r
Peaches, halves or slices, Hunt's, Del Monte, or Libby's	29 oz	1.59	3/01	4c
Peanut butter, creamy, all sizes	lb	1.83	7/01	11r
Pears, Anjou	lb	0.98	7/01	11r
Peas, green, Del Monte or Green Giant	15 oz	0.66	3/01	4c
Pork chops, center cut, bone-in	lb	3.33	7/01	11r
Pork sausage, fresh, loose	lb	2.59	7/01	11r
Pork shoulder picnic, bone-in, smoked	lb	1.12	7/01	11r
Pork, expenditures on	yr	162	1999	30r
Potato chips	16 oz	3.59	7/01	11r
Potatoes, frozen, french fried	lb	1.00	7/01	11r
Potatoes, white or red	10 lb	3.43	3/01	4c
Potatoes, white, all types	lb	0.44	7/01	11r
Poultry, expenditures on	yr	137	1999	30r
Processed fruits, expenditures on	yr	97	1999	30r
Processed vegetables, expenditures on	yr	82	1999	30r
Rice, white, long grain, uncooked	lb	0.51	7/01	11r
Round roast, graded and ungraded, excl U.S. prime and choice	lb	2.96	7/01	11r
Round steak, graded and ungraded, excl U.S. prime and choice	lb	3.11	7/01	11r
Sausage, Jimmy Dean/Owens pork	lb	3.37	3/01	4c
Shortening, vegetable, Crisco	3 lb	3.01	3/01	4c
Sirloin steak, graded and ungraded, excl U.S. prime and choice	lb	4.23	7/01	11r
Soft drink, Coca Cola, ex deposit	2 liter	1.37	3/01	4c
Spaghetti and macaroni	lb	0.78	7/01	11r
Steak, round, U.S. choice, boneless	lb	3.56	7/01	11r
Steak, sirloin, U.S. choice, boneless	lb	5.65	7/01	11r
Steak, T-bone	lb	7.11	3/01	4c
Strawberries, dry pint	12 oz	1.50	7/01	11r
Sugar and other sweets, expenditures on	yr	99	1999	30r
Sugar, cane or beet	4 lbs	1.42	3/01	4c
Sugar, white, 33-80 ounce package	lb	0.39	7/01	11r
Sugar, white, all sizes	lb	0.42	7/01	11r

Values are in dollars or fractions of dollars. In the column headed *Ref*, references are shown to sources. Each reference is followed by a letter. These refer to the geographical level for which data were reported: s=State, r=Region, and c=City or metro. The abbreviation *ex* is used to mean *except* or *excluding*; *exp* stands for expenditures. For other abbreviations and further explanations, please see the Introduction.

Myrtle Beach, SC - continued

Item	Per	Value	Date	Ref.
Groceries				
Tobacco products and smoking supplies purchases	yr	288	1999	30r
Tomatoes, field grown	lb	1.43	7/01	11r
Tomatoes, Hunt's or Del Monte	14.5 oz	0.86	3/01	4c
Tuna, chunk, light	6 oz	0.70	3/01	4c
Tuna, light, chunk	lb	1.77	7/01	11r
Turkey, frozen, whole	lb	1.05	7/01	11r
Goods and Services				
Miscellaneous goods and services, ACCRA Index		100.00	3/01	4c
B&B Japanese maple (acer japonicum)	gal	49.98-129.00	4/00	93r
Boxwood (buxus)	2 gal	12.99-16.99	4/00	93r
Daylilly (hemerocallis)	gal	4.99-8.99	4/00	93r
Flat of annuals		11.00-13.92	4/00	93r
Fountain grass (pennisetum)	gal	5.98-7.98	4/00	93r
Hanging basket (10 in)		7.99-14.98	4/00	93r
Hardy geranium (geranium)	gal	5.98-8.00	4/00	93r
Hosta (hosta)	gal	4.99-10.98	4/00	93r
Lilac (syrubga vulgaris)	2 gal	12.99-21.99	4/00	93r
Rhododendron (rhododendron)	2 gal	14.99-24.99	4/00	93r
Sage (salvia)	gal	5.98-6.99	4/00	93r
Wintercreeper euonymus (euonymus fortunei)	2 gal	7.99-89.99	4/00	93r
Hunting license	yr	12.00	4/01	34s
Health Care				
Health care, ACCRA Index		95.70	3/01	4c
Cardiac catheterization, ave hospital/physician charges		12360	1998	77s
Childbirth, Cesarean delivery		11587	1997	13r
Childbirth, vaginal delivery		6725	1997	13r
Dentist's fee, adult teeth cleaning and periodic oral exam	visit	63.40	3/01	4c
Doctor's fee, routine exam, established patient	visit	61.00	3/01	4c
Drugs, expenditures on	yr	399	1999	30r
Health care purchases	yr	1971	1999	30r
Health insurance expenditures	yr	933	1999	30r
Hospital care, private room	day	463.33	3/01	4c
Hysterectomy, laproscopically-assisted, ave hospital/physician charges		11920	1998	76s
Hysterectomy, vaginal, ave hospital and physician charges		4890	1998	76s
Medicaid dispensing fee		4.05	1999	87s
Medical services expenditures	yr	547	1999	30r
Medical supplies, expenditures on	yr	91	1999	30r
Plastic surgery, breast augmentation		2870	2000	7r
Plastic surgery, breast lift		3649	2000	7r
Plastic surgery, facelift		5008	2000	7r
Plastic surgery, hair transplantation		3425	2000	7r
Plastic surgery, lip augmentation		1227	2000	7r
Plastic surgery, lower body lift		4793	2000	7r
Plastic surgery, thigh lift		3862	2000	7r
Household Goods				
Dishwashing powder, Cascade	50 oz	3.16	3/01	4c
Floor coverings, expenditures on	yr	44	1999	30r
Furniture, expenditures on	yr	335	1999	30r
Household furnishings and equipment purchases	yr	1328	1999	30r
Household textiles, expenditures on	yr	89	1999	30r

Myrtle Beach, SC - continued

Item	Per	Value	Date	Ref.
Household Goods - continued				
Laundry and cleaning supplies, expenditures on	yr	113	1999	30r
Tissues, facial, Kleenex brand	175	1.29	3/01	4c
Housing				
Housing, ACCRA Index		97.80	3/01	4c
Home price, existing, ave		160100	10/00	90r
Home value, median		119000	2001	53s
House, 2400 sq ft, 8000 sq ft lot, new, urban, utilities	total	207430	3/01	4c
House payment, principal and interest, 25% down payment	mos	1053	3/01	4c
Household operation expenditures	yr	553	1999	30r
Housekeeping supplies purchases	yr	473	1999	30r
Housing, expenditures on	yr	10303	1999	30r
Maintenance, repairs, insurance expenditures	yr	699	1999	30r
Monthly rental value of owned home	mos	505	1999	30r
Owned dwellings, expenditures own	yr	3465	1999	30r
Rent expenditures	yr	1641	1999	30r
Rent, apartment, 2 br, 1 1/2-2 baths, unfurn, 950 sq ft, water	mos	562	3/01	4c
Rental unit, 1 bedroom, with utilities	mos	438	4/01	41c
Rental unit, 2 bedroom, with utilities	mos	561	4/01	41c
Rental unit, 3 bedroom, with utilities	mos	702	4/01	41c
Rental unit, 4 bedroom, with utilities	mos	786	4/01	41c
Shelter, expenditures on	yr	5467	1999	30r
Insurance and Pensions				
Auto insurance	yr	655.33	1998	86s
Life and other personal insurance purchases	yr	414	1999	30r
Pensions and Social Security, expenditures on	yr	2635	1999	30r
Personal insurance and pensions, expenditures on	yr	3048	1999	30r
Legal Fees				
Combination hunting and fishing license	yr	20.00	4/01	34s
Driver's license fee	renew	12.50	1999	48s
Driver's license fee	orig	12.50	1999	48s
Fishing license	yr	10.00	4/01	34s
Personal Goods				
Personal care products and services purchases	yr	393	1999	30r
Shampoo, Alberto VO5	15 oz	1.00	3/01	4c
Toothpaste, Crest or Colgate	6-7 oz	2.17	3/01	4c
Personal Services				
Dry cleaning, man's 2-pc suit		7.67	3/01	4c
Man's haircut, barbershop, no styling		9.59	3/01	4c
Personal services, household, expenditures on	yr	258	1999	30r
Woman's shampoo, trim, blow-dry, no style-change		24.20	3/01	4c
Pets				
Pets, toys, and playground equipment, expenditures on	yr	306	1999	30r
Restaurant Food				
Chicken, fried, thigh and drumstick, KFC/Church's		2.65	3/01	4c
Hamburger with cheese, McDonald's	1/4 lb	2.09	3/01	4c
Pizza, Pizza Hut or Pizza Inn	11-12 in	9.99	3/01	4c
Taxes				
Federal income taxes paid	yr	2047	1999	30r
Personal taxes, expenditures on	yr	2554	1999	30r
Property taxes paid	yr	726	1999	30r
State and local income taxes paid	yr	363	1999	30r
Transportation				
Transportation, ACCRA Index		92.30	3/01	4c
Cars and trucks, new, expenditures on	yr	1648	1999	30r
Cars and trucks, used, expenditures on	yr	1651	1999	30r

Values are in dollars or fractions of dollars. In the column headed *Ref*, references are shown to sources. Each reference is followed by a letter. These refer to the geographical level for which data were reported: s=State, r=Region, and c=City or metro. The abbreviation *ex* is used to mean *except* or *excluding*; *exp* stands for *expenditures*. For other abbreviations and further explanations, please see the Introduction.

Myrtle Beach, SC - continued

Item	Per	Value	Date	Ref.
Transportation				
Diesel at the pump	gal	1.13	10/99	73s
Gasoline and motor oil purchases	yr	1052	1999	30r
Gasoline before-tax price (cents)	gal	101.70	10/00	43s
Maintenance and repair expenditures	yr	621	1999	30r
Public transportation, expenditures on	yr	298	1999	30r
Tire balance, computer or spin balance, front	wheel	7.00	3/01	4c
Transportation purchases	yr	6738	1999	30r
Vehicle expenses, miscellaneous, purchases	yr	2033	1999	30r
Vehicle insurance payments	yr	696	1999	30r
Vehicle purchases (net outlay)	yr	3354	1999	30r
Vehicle rental, lease expenditures	yr	352	1999	30r
Utilities				
Utilities, ACCRA Index		89.70	3/01	4c
Electrical bill, average	mos	86.42	9/00	9s
Electricity, 2400 sq ft, new home	mos	109.15	3/01	4c
Electricity, expenditures on	yr	1115	1999	30r
Electricity cost, average	KWh	5.40	9/00	9s
Water and other public services, expenditures on	yr	298	1999	30r
Weddings				
Wedding (national average cost)		19936	2000	33r
Wedding (regional average total cost)		16293	1997	110r
Attendants' gifts		321	1998	33r
Bridal attendants' apparel (5 persons)		824	2000	33r
Bride's headpiece/veil		173	1998	33r
Bride's wedding dress		859	1998	33r
Clergy, religious facility fee		242	1998	33r
Engagement ring		3177	1998	33r
Flowers		789	1998	33r
Groom's formalwear rental		99	2000	33r
Limousine		410	1998	33r
Marriage license cost		25.00	4/01	35s
Men's formalwear (ushers, best man)		469	2000	33r
Mother of bride apparel		241	2000	33r
Music		866	1998	33r
Photography and videography		1368	1998	33r
Rehearsal dinner		728	1998	33r
Wedding invitations and announcements		341	1998	33r
Wedding reception		7968	2000	33r
Wedding rings (bride and groom)		1060	1998	33r

Naples, FL

Item	Per	Value	Date	Ref.
Alcoholic Beverages				
Alcoholic beverage purchases	yr	253	1999	30r
Malt beverages, all types, all sizes, any origin	16 oz	0.96	7/01	11r
Appliances				
Major appliances, expenditures on	yr	172	1999	30r
Small appliances, housewares, expenditures on	yr	81	1999	30r
Banking and Money				
Mortgage interest and charges paid	yr	2039	1999	30r
Mortgage principal paid on owned property	yr	1026	1999	30r
Vehicle finance charges paid	yr	365	1999	30r
Charity				
Cash contributions, expenditures	yr	1127	1999	30r
Child Care				
Child raising cost, total, age 0-2	yr	8540	1999	60r
Child raising cost, total, age 3-5	yr	8780	1999	60r
Child raising cost, total, age 6-8	yr	8820	1999	60r
Child raising cost, total, age 9-11	yr	8800	1999	60r
Child raising cost, total, age 12-14	yr	9510	1999	60r
Child raising cost, total, age 15-17	yr	9740	1999	60r
Child's child care and education, age 0-2	yr	1380	1999	60r
Child's child care and education, age 3-5	yr	1520	1999	60r
Child's child care and education, age 6-8	yr	990	1999	60r
Child's child care and education, age 9-11	yr	650	1999	60r
Child's child care and education, age 12-14	yr	490	1999	60r

Naples, FL - continued

Item	Per	Value	Date	Ref.
Child Care - continued				
Child's child care and education, age 15-17	yr	840	1999	60r
Child's clothing, age 0-2	yr	480	1999	60r
Child's clothing, age 3-5	yr	470	1999	60r
Child's clothing, age 6-8	yr	520	1999	60r
Child's clothing, age 9-11	yr	570	1999	60r
Child's clothing, age 12-14	yr	950	1999	60r
Child's clothing, age 15-17	yr	850	1999	60r
Child's food, age 0-2	yr	1000	1999	60r
Child's food, age 3-5	yr	1160	1999	60r
Child's food, age 6-8	yr	1490	1999	60r
Child's food, age 9-11	yr	1770	1999	60r
Child's food, age 12-14	yr	1770	1999	60r
Child's food, age 15-17	yr	1980	1999	60r
Child's health care, age 0-2	yr	620	1999	60r
Child's health care, age 3-5	yr	590	1999	60r
Child's health care, age 6-8	yr	680	1999	60r
Child's health care, age 9-11	yr	720	1999	60r
Child's health care, age 12-14	yr	730	1999	60r
Child's health care, age 15-17	yr	760	1999	60r
Child's housing, age 0-2	yr	3070	1999	60r
Child's housing, age 3-5	yr	3050	1999	60r
Child's housing, age 6-8	yr	3010	1999	60r
Child's housing, age 9-11	yr	2850	1999	60r
Child's housing, age 12-14	yr	3040	1999	60r
Child's housing, age 15-17	yr	2650	1999	60r
Child's personal care, reading, age 0-2	yr	910	1999	60r
Child's personal care, reading, age 3-5	yr	930	1999	60r
Child's personal care, reading, age 6-8	yr	960	1999	60r
Child's personal care, reading, age 9-11	yr	1000	1999	60r
Child's personal care, reading, age 12-14	yr	1170	1999	60r
Child's personal care, reading, age 15-17	yr	950	1999	60r
Clothing				
Apparel and services purchases	yr	1610	1999	30r
Boys, 2 to 15, expenditures on	yr	89	1999	30r
Children under 2, expenditures on	yr	79	1999	30r
Footwear, expenditures on	yr	283	1999	30r
Girls, 2 to 15, expenditures on	yr	103	1999	30r
Men and boys, expenditures on	yr	351	1999	30r
Men, 16 and over, expenditures on	yr	262	1999	30r
Women, 16 and over, expenditures on	yr	538	1999	30r
Communications				
Cable modem installation, Adelphi		54.90	6/99	103s
Cable modem installation, Comcast		95.00	6/99	103s
Cable modem installation, Media One		100.00	6/99	103s
Cable modem installation, Time Warner		75.00-225.00	6/99	103s
Cable modem rate, cable subscriber, Adelphi	mos	34.95	6/99	103s
Cable modem rate, cable subscriber, Comcast	mos	39.95	6/99	103s
Cable modem rate, cable subscriber, Media One	mos	34.95-39.95	6/99	103s
Cable modem rate, cable subscriber, Time Warner	mos	39.95-49.95	6/99	103s
Cable modem rate, non-cable subscriber, Adelphi	mos	44.95	6/99	103s
Cable modem rate, non-cable subscriber, Comcast	mos	49.95	6/99	103s
Cable modem rate, non-cable subscriber, Media One	mos	49.95	6/99	103s
Cable modem rate, non-cable subscriber, Time Warner	mos	39.95-54.95	6/99	103s
Phone line, single, business, field visit	inst.	56.00	12/97	17s
Phone line, single, business, no field visit	inst.	56.00	12/97	17s
Phone line, single, residence, field visit	inst.	40.00	12/97	17s
Phone line, single, residence, no field visit	inst.	40.00	12/97	17s
Postage and stationery, expenditures on	yr	104	1999	30r
Postal rate, express mail, up to half-pound		12.45	7/01	108r
Postal rate, letter, first class, first ounce		0.34	7/01	108r
Postal rate, letter, two ounces		0.57	7/01	108r
Postal rate, post card		0.21	7/01	108r
Postal rate, priority mail, two pounds		3.95	7/01	108r

Values are in dollars or fractions of dollars. In the column headed *Ref*, references are shown to sources. Each reference is followed by a letter. These refer to the geographical level for which data were reported: s=State, r=Region, and c=City or metro. The abbreviation *ex* is used to mean *except* or *excluding*; *exp* stands for *expenditures*. For other abbreviations and further explanations, please see the Introduction.

Naples, FL - continued

Item	Per	Value	Date	Ref.
Communications				
Postal rate, priority mail, up to one pound		3.50	7/01	108r
Telephone services, expenditures on	yr	860	1999	30r
Education				
Board, 4-year private college/university	yr	2236	1996	38s
Board, 4-year public college/university	yr	2295	1996	38s
Education expenditures	yr	431	1999	30r
Room, 4-year private college/university	yr	2428	1996	38s
Room, 4-year public college/university	yr	2193	1996	38s
Total cost, 4-year private college/university	yr	15028	1996	38s
Total cost, 4-year public college/university	yr	6254	1996	38s
Tuition, 2-year public college/university, in state	yr	1103	1996	38s
Tuition, 4-year private college/university, in state	yr	10364	1996	38s
Tuition, 4-year public college/university	yr	1767	1996	38s
Energy and Fuels				
Electricity	KWh	0.09	7/01	11r
Electricity	500 KWhs	47.29	7/01	11r
Fuel oil #2	gal	1.43	7/01	11r
Fuel oil and other fuels, expenditures on	yr	45	1999	30r
Gas, natural, commercial rate	1000 cf	8.44	11/00	88s
Gasoline, all types	gal	1.60	7/01	11r
Gasoline, unleaded midgrade	gal	1.65	7/01	11r
Gasoline, unleaded premium	gal	1.74	7/01	11r
Natural gas, expenditures on	yr	164	1999	30r
Utility (piped) gas, therm		1.01	7/01	11r
Utility (piped) gas, 40 therms		44.29	7/01	11r
Utility (piped) gas, 100 therms		97.44	7/01	11r
Entertainment				
Entertainment purchases	yr	1574	1999	30r
Fees and admissions paid	yr	371	1999	30r
Reading purchases	yr	121	1999	30r
Television, radios, sound equipment, expenditures on	yr	561	1999	30r
Funerals				
Total cost of funeral		5922.53	1/99	78r
Acknowledgement cards		63.43	1/99	78r
Casket		2258.77	1/99	78r
Cosmetology, hair, other preparation		127.09	1/99	78r
Embalming		393.49	1/99	78r
Funeral at funeral home		367.50	1/99	78r
Hearse (local)		169.66	1/99	78r
Professional service charges		1211.32	1/99	78r
Service car/van		80.69	1/99	78r
Transfer of remains to funeral home		144.25	1/99	78r
Vault		803.50	1/99	78r
Visitation/viewing		302.83	1/99	78r
Groceries				
American processed cheese	lb	3.50	7/01	11r
Bakery products, expenditures on	yr	261	1999	30r
Bananas	lb	0.47	7/01	11r
Beans, dried, any type, all sizes	lb	0.63	7/01	11r
Beef for stew, boneless	lb	2.86	7/01	11r
Beef, expenditures on	yr	210	1999	30r
Bologna, all beef or mixed	lb	2.29	7/01	11r
Bread, French	lb	1.66	7/01	11r
Bread, white, pan	lb	0.87	7/01	11r
Bread, whole wheat, pan	lb	1.38	7/01	11r
Broccoli	lb	1.04	7/01	11r
Butter, salted, grade AA, stick	lb	2.26	7/01	11r
Butter, yoghurt, cheese, etc, expenditures on	yr	170	1999	30r
Cabbage	lb	0.42	7/01	11r
Cereals and cereal products, expenditures on	yr	140	1999	30r
Cheddar cheese, natural	lb	3.75	7/01	11r
Chicken breast, bone-in	lb	1.85	7/01	11r
Chicken legs, bone-in	lb	1.34	7/01	11r
Chicken, fresh, whole	lb	1.05	7/01	11r

Naples, FL - continued

Item	Per	Value	Date	Ref.
Groceries - continued				
Chops, boneless,	lb	4.13	7/01	11r
Chuck roast, graded and ungraded, excl U.S. prime and choice	lb	2.35	7/01	11r
Chuck roast, U.S. choice, boneless	lb	2.67	7/01	11r
Coffee, 100%, ground roast, all sizes	lb	2.88	7/01	11r
Coffee, instant, plain, regular, all sizes	16 oz	9.25	7/01	11r
Cola, non diet	2 liter	1.11	7/01	11r
Crackers, soda, salted	lb	1.70	7/01	11r
Dairy product purchases	yr	282	1999	30r
Eggs, expenditures on	yr	32	1999	30r
Fats and oils, expenditures on	yr	79	1999	30r
Fish and seafood, expenditures on	yr	99	1999	30r
Flour, white, all purpose	lb	0.32	7/01	11r
Food (excl fruit and vegetables), eaten at home, purchases	yr	815	1999	30r
Food cooked on trips, expenditures on	yr	36	1999	30r
Food purchases	yr	4533	1999	30r
Food purchases, eaten away from home	yr	1873	1999	30r
Food purchases, food eaten at home	yr	2660	1999	30r
Fresh fruits, expenditures on	yr	128	1999	30r
Fresh milk and cream, expenditures on	yr	112	1999	30r
Fresh vegetables, expenditures on	yr	131	1999	30r
Fruit and vegetable purchases	yr	438	1999	30r
Grapefruit	lb	0.59	7/01	11r
Grapes, Thompson, seedless	lb	2.12	7/01	11r
Ground beef, 100% beef	lb	1.76	7/01	11r
Ground beef, lean and extra lean	lb	2.60	7/01	11r
Ground chuck, 100% beef	lb	2.08	7/01	11r
Ham, boneless, excl canned	lb	2.71	7/01	11r
Ham, rump or shank half, bone-in, smoked	lb	2.19	7/01	11r
Ice cream, prepackaged, bulk, regular	1/2 gal	3.93	7/01	11r
Lemons	lb	1.32	7/01	11r
Lettuce, iceberg	lb	0.76	7/01	11r
Milk, fresh, low fat,	gal	2.75	7/01	11r
Milk, fresh, whole, fortified	gal	2.97	7/01	11r
Nonalcoholic beverages, expenditures on	yr	228	1999	30r
Orange juice, frozen concentrate	16 oz	1.95	7/01	11r
Oranges, Navel	lb	0.73	7/01	11r
Oranges, Valencia	lb	0.55	7/01	11r
Peanut butter, creamy, all sizes	lb	1.83	7/01	11r
Pears, Anjou	lb	0.98	7/01	11r
Pork chops, center cut, bone-in	lb	3.33	7/01	11r
Pork sausage, fresh, loose	lb	2.59	7/01	11r
Pork shoulder picnic, bone-in, smoked	lb	1.12	7/01	11r
Pork, expenditures on	yr	162	1999	30r
Potato chips	16 oz	3.59	7/01	11r
Potatoes, frozen, french fried	lb	1.00	7/01	11r
Potatoes, white, all types	lb	0.44	7/01	11r
Poultry, expenditures on	yr	137	1999	30r
Processed fruits, expenditures on	yr	97	1999	30r
Processed vegetables, expenditures on	yr	82	1999	30r
Rice, white, long grain, uncooked	lb	0.51	7/01	11r
Round roast, graded and ungraded, excl U.S. prime and choice	lb	2.96	7/01	11r
Round steak, graded and ungraded, excl U.S. prime and choice	lb	3.11	7/01	11r
Sirloin steak, graded and ungraded, excl U.S. prime and choice	lb	4.23	7/01	11r
Spaghetti and macaroni	lb	0.78	7/01	11r
Steak, round, U.S. choice, boneless	lb	3.56	7/01	11r
Steak, sirloin, U.S. choice, boneless	lb	5.65	7/01	11r
Strawberries, dry pint	12 oz	1.50	7/01	11r
Sugar and other sweets, expenditures on	yr	99	1999	30r
Sugar, white, 33-80 ounce package	lb	0.39	7/01	11r
Sugar, white, all sizes	lb	0.42	7/01	11r
Tobacco products and smoking supplies purchases	yr	288	1999	30r
Tomatoes, field grown	lb	1.43	7/01	11r
Tuna, light, chunk	lb	1.77	7/01	11r
Turkey, frozen, whole	lb	1.05	7/01	11r

Values are in dollars or fractions of dollars. In the column headed *Ref*, references are shown to sources. Each reference is followed by a letter. These refer to the geographical level for which data were reported: s=State, r=Region, and c=City or metro. The abbreviation *ex* is used to mean *except* or *excluding*; *exp* stands for expenditures. For other abbreviations and further explanations, please see the Introduction.

Item	Per	Value	Date	Ref.
Goods and Services				
B&B Japanese maple (acer japonicum)	gal	49.98-129.00	4/00	93r
Boxwood (buxus)	2 gal	12.99-16.99	4/00	93r
Daylilly (hemerocallis)	gal	4.99-8.99	4/00	93r
Flat of annuals		11.00-13.92	4/00	93r
Fountain grass (pennisetum)	gal	5.98-7.98	4/00	93r
Hanging basket (10 in)		7.99-14.98	4/00	93r
Hardy geranium (geranium)	gal	5.98-8.00	4/00	93r
Hosta (hosta)	gal	4.99-10.98	4/00	93r
Lilac (syrubga vulgaris)	2 gal	12.99-21.99	4/00	93r
Rhododendron (rhododendron)	2 gal	14.99-24.99	4/00	93r
Sage (salvia)	gal	5.98-6.99	4/00	93r
Wintercreeper euonymus (euonymus fortunei)	2 gal	7.99-89.99	4/00	93r
Hunting license	yr	12.50	4/01	34s
Health Care				
Cardiac catheterization, ave hospital/ physician charges		15060	1998	77s
Childbirth, Cesarean delivery		11587	1997	13r
Childbirth, vaginal delivery		6725	1997	13r
Drugs, expenditures on	yr	399	1999	30r
Health care purchases	yr	1971	1999	30r
Health insurance expenditures	yr	933	1999	30r
Hysterectomy, laproscopically-assisted, ave hospital/physician charges		14760	1998	76s
Hysterectomy, vaginal, ave hospital and physician charges		11320	1998	76s
Medicaid dispensing fee		4.23	1999	87s
Medical services expenditures	yr	547	1999	30r
Medical supplies, expenditures on	yr	91	1999	30r
Plastic surgery, breast augmentation		2870	2000	7r
Plastic surgery, breast lift		3649	2000	7r
Plastic surgery, facelift		5008	2000	7r
Plastic surgery, hair transplantation		3425	2000	7r
Plastic surgery, lip augmentation		1227	2000	7r
Plastic surgery, lower body lift		4793	2000	7r
Plastic surgery, thigh lift		3862	2000	7r
Household Goods				
Floor coverings, expenditures on	yr	44	1999	30r
Furniture, expenditures on	yr	335	1999	30r
Household furnishings and equipment purchases	yr	1328	1999	30r
Household textiles, expenditures on	yr	89	1999	30r
Laundry and cleaning supplies, expenditures on	yr	113	1999	30r
Housing				
Home, 2200 sq ft, 4-br, 2-bath, 2-car garage, average		203750	2000	47c
Home price, existing, ave		160100	10/00	90r
Home value, median		104000	2001	53s
Household operation expenditures	yr	553	1999	30r
Housekeeping supplies purchases	yr	473	1999	30r
Housing, expenditures on	yr	10303	1999	30r
Maintenance, repairs, insurance expenditures	yr	699	1999	30r
Monthly rental value of owned home	mos	505	1999	30r
Owned dwellings, expenditures own	yr	3465	1999	30r
Rent expenditures	yr	1641	1999	30r
Rental unit, 1 bedroom, with utilities	mos	622	4/01	41c
Rental unit, 2 bedroom, with utilities	mos	749	4/01	41c
Rental unit, 3 bedroom, with utilities	mos	1041	4/01	41c

Item	Per	Value	Date	Ref.
Housing - continued				
Rental unit, 4 bedroom, with utilities	mos	1160	4/01	41c
Shelter, expenditures on	yr	5467	1999	30r
Insurance and Pensions				
Life and other personal insurance purchases	yr	414	1999	30r
Medigap health insurance, Plan H	yr	2887	2000	69s
Medigap health insurance, Plan I	yr	3302	2000	69s
Medigap health insurance, Plan J	yr	3889	2000	69s
Pensions and Social Security, expenditures on	yr	2635	1999	30r
Personal insurance and pensions, expenditures on	yr	3048	1999	30r
Legal Fees				
Divorce, filing fee		65.00-85.00	4/01	35s
Driver's license fee	orig	20.00	1999	48s
Driver's license fee	renew	15.00	1999	48s
Personal Goods				
Personal care products and services purchases	yr	393	1999	30r
Personal Services				
Personal services, household, expenditures on	yr	258	1999	30r
Pets				
Pets, toys, and playground equipment, expenditures on	yr	306	1999	30r
Taxes				
Federal income taxes paid	yr	2047	1999	30r
Personal taxes, expenditures on	yr	2554	1999	30r
Property taxes paid	yr	726	1999	30r
State and local income taxes paid	yr	363	1999	30r
Transportation				
Cars and trucks, new, expenditures on	yr	1648	1999	30r
Cars and trucks, used, expenditures on	yr	1651	1999	30r
Diesel at the pump	gal	1.26	10/99	73s
Gasoline and motor oil purchases	yr	1052	1999	30r
Gasoline before-tax price (cents)	gal	101.90	10/00	43s
Maintenance and repair expenditures	yr	621	1999	30r
Public transportation, expenditures on	yr	298	1999	30r
Transportation purchases	yr	6738	1999	30r
Vehicle expenses, miscellaneous, purchases	yr	2033	1999	30r
Vehicle insurance payments	yr	696	1999	30r
Vehicle purchases (net outlay)	yr	3354	1999	30r
Vehicle rental, lease expenditures	yr	352	1999	30r
Travel				
Hotel room	night	110.57	2/01	95s
Utilities				
Electrical bill, average	mos	86.33	9/00	9s
Electricity, expenditures on	yr	1115	1999	30r
Electricity cost, average	KWh	6.80	9/00	9s
Water and other public services, expenditures on	yr	298	1999	30r
Weddings				
Wedding (national average cost)		19936	2000	33r
Wedding (regional average total cost)		16293	1997	110r
Attendants' gifts		321	1998	33r
Bridal attendants' apparel (5 persons)		824	2000	33r
Bride's headpiece/veil		173	1998	33r
Bride's wedding dress		859	1998	33r
Clergy, religious facility fee		242	1998	33r
Engagement ring		3177	1998	33r
Flowers		789	1998	33r
Groom's formalwear rental		99	2000	33r
Limousine		410	1998	33r
Marriage license cost		56.00-88.50	4/01	35s
Men's formalwear (ushers, best man)		469	2000	33r
Mother of bride apparel		241	2000	33r

Values are in dollars or fractions of dollars. In the column headed *Ref*, references are shown to sources. Each reference is followed by a letter. These refer to the geographical level for which data were reported: s=State, r=Region, and c=City or metro. The abbreviation *ex* is used to mean *except* or *excluding*; *exp* stands for expenditures. For other abbreviations and further explanations, please see the Introduction.

Naples, FL - continued

Item	Per	Value	Date	Ref.
Weddings				
Music		866	1998	33r
Photography and videography		1368	1998	33r
Rehearsal dinner		728	1998	33r
Wedding invitations and announcements		341	1998	33r
Wedding reception		7968	2000	33r
Wedding rings (bride and groom)		1060	1998	33r

Nashua, NH

Item	Per	Value	Date	Ref.
Average annual expenditures	yr	37971	1999	30r
Alcoholic Beverages				
Alcoholic beverage purchases	yr	368	1999	30r
Wine, red and white table, all sizes, any origin	liter	9.64	7/01	11r
Appliances				
Major appliances, expenditures on	yr	194	1999	30r
Small appliances, housewares, expenditures on	yr	93	1999	30r
Banking and Money				
Mortgage interest and charges paid	yr	2622	1999	30r
Mortgage principal paid on owned property	yr	1262	1999	30r
Vehicle finance charges paid	yr	240	1999	30r
Charity				
Cash contributions, expenditures	yr	1001	1999	30r
Child Care				
Child raising cost, total, age 0-2	yr	8670	1999	60r
Child raising cost, total, age 3-5	yr	8910	1999	60r
Child raising cost, total, age 6-8	yr	9040	1999	60r
Child raising cost, total, age 9-11	yr	9100	1999	60r
Child raising cost, total, age 12-14	yr	9890	1999	60r
Child raising cost, total, age 15-17	yr	10010	1999	60r
Child's child care and education, age 0-2	yr	1070	1999	60r
Child's child care and education, age 3-5	yr	1190	1999	60r
Child's child care and education, age 6-8	yr	740	1999	60r
Child's child care and education, age 9-11	yr	470	1999	60r
Child's child care and education, age 12-14	yr	350	1999	60r
Child's child care and education, age 15-17	yr	590	1999	60r
Child's clothing, age 0-2	yr	480	1999	60r
Child's clothing, age 3-5	yr	470	1999	60r
Child's clothing, age 6-8	yr	520	1999	60r
Child's clothing, age 9-11	yr	570	1999	60r
Child's clothing, age 12-14	yr	970	1999	60r
Child's clothing, age 15-17	yr	870	1999	60r
Child's food, age 0-2	yr	1130	1999	60r
Child's food, age 3-5	yr	1290	1999	60r
Child's food, age 6-8	yr	1640	1999	60r
Child's food, age 9-11	yr	1930	1999	60r
Child's food, age 12-14	yr	1940	1999	60r
Child's food, age 15-17	yr	2150	1999	60r
Child's health care, age 0-2	yr	550	1999	60r
Child's health care, age 3-5	yr	530	1999	60r
Child's health care, age 6-8	yr	610	1999	60r
Child's health care, age 9-11	yr	650	1999	60r
Child's health care, age 12-14	yr	660	1999	60r
Child's health care, age 15-17	yr	690	1999	60r
Child's housing, age 0-2	yr	3555	1999	60r
Child's housing, age 3-5	yr	3530	1999	60r
Child's housing, age 6-8	yr	3490	1999	60r
Child's housing, age 9-11	yr	3340	1999	60r
Child's housing, age 12-14	yr	3530	1999	60r
Child's housing, age 15-17	yr	3140	1999	60r
Child's personal care, reading, age 0-2	yr	920	1999	60r
Child's personal care, reading, age 3-5	yr	950	1999	60r
Child's personal care, reading, age 6-8	yr	980	1999	60r
Child's personal care, reading, age 9-11	yr	1020	1999	60r
Child's personal care, reading, age 12-14	yr	1190	1999	60r
Child's personal care, reading, age 15-17	yr	970	1999	60r

Nashua, NH - continued

Item	Per	Value	Date	Ref.
Clothing				
Apparel and services purchases	yr	1831	1999	30r
Boys, 2 to 15, expenditures on	yr	92	1999	30r
Children under 2, expenditures on	yr	63	1999	30r
Footwear, expenditures on	yr	300	1999	30r
Girls, 2 to 15, expenditures on	yr	101	1999	30r
Men and boys, expenditures on	yr	446	1999	30r
Men, 16 and over, expenditures on	yr	354	1999	30r
Women, 16 and over, expenditures on	yr	584	1999	30r
Communications				
Cable modem installation, Media One		100.00	6/99	103s
Cable modem rate, cable subscriber, Media One	mos	34.95-39.95	6/99	103s
Cable modem rate, non-cable subscriber, Media One	mos	49.95	6/99	103s
Phone line, single, business, field visit	inst.	109.00	12/97	17s
Phone line, single, business, no field visit	inst.	75.00	12/97	17s
Phone line, single, residence, field visit	inst.	81.00	12/97	17s
Phone line, single, residence, no field visit	inst.	49.00	12/97	17s
Postage and stationery, expenditures on	yr	138	1999	30r
Postal rate, express mail, up to half-pound		12.45	7/01	108r
Postal rate, letter, first class, first ounce		0.34	7/01	108r
Postal rate, letter, two ounces		0.57	7/01	108r
Postal rate, post card		0.21	7/01	108r
Postal rate, priority mail, two pounds		3.95	7/01	108r
Postal rate, priority mail, up to one pound		3.50	7/01	108r
Telephone bill, business, basic rate	mos	44.67	12/97	18c
Telephone bill, residential, basic rate	mos	15.73	12/97	18c
Telephone services, expenditures on	yr	830	1999	30r
Education				
Board, 4-year private college/university	yr	3009	1996	38s
Board, 4-year public college/university	yr	1710	1996	38s
Education expenditures	yr	877	1999	30r
Room, 4-year private college/university	yr	3024	1996	38s
Room, 4-year public college/university	yr	2573	1996	38s
Total cost, 4-year private college/university	yr	21071	1996	38s
Total cost, 4-year public college/university	yr	8729	1996	38s
Tuition, 2-year public college/university, in state	yr	2420	1996	38s
Tuition, 4-year private college/university, in state	yr	15038	1996	38s
Tuition, 4-year public college/university	yr	4446	1996	38s
Energy and Fuels				
Electricity	KWh	0.12	7/01	11r
Fuel oil #2	gal	1.31	7/01	11r
Fuel oil and other fuels, expenditures on	yr	207	1999	30r
Gas, heating, winter, average use	mos	119.18	2/96	98c
Gasoline, all types	gal	1.80	7/01	11r
Gasoline, unleaded midgrade	gal	1.85	7/01	11r
Gasoline, unleaded premium	gal	1.91	7/01	11r
Gasoline, unleaded regular	gal	1.71	7/01	11r
Natural gas, expenditures on	yr	368	1999	30r
Utility (piped) gas, therm		1.08	7/01	11r
Utility (piped) gas, 40 therms		50.87	7/01	11r
Utility (piped) gas, 100 therms		111.06	7/01	11r
Entertainment				
Entertainment purchases	yr	1821	1999	30r
Fees and admissions paid	yr	511	1999	30r
Television, radios, sound equipment, expenditures on	yr	650	1999	30r
Funerals				
Total cost of funeral		5776.91	1/99	78r
Acknowledgement cards		14.47	1/99	78r
Casket		2090.19	1/99	78r
Cosmetology, hair, other preparation		132.92	1/99	78r
Embalming		377.33	1/99	78r
Funeral at funeral home		352.43	1/99	78r
Hearse (local)		185.55	1/99	78r
Professional service charges		1289.95	1/99	78r
Service car/van		87.42	1/99	78r

Values are in dollars or fractions of dollars. In the column headed *Ref*, references are shown to sources. Each reference is followed by a letter. These refer to the geographical level for which data were reported: s=State, r=Region, and c=City or metro. The abbreviation *ex* is used to mean *except* or *excluding*; *exp* stands for expenditures. For other abbreviations and further explanations, please see the Introduction.

Nashua, NH - continued

Item	Per	Value	Date	Ref.
Funerals				
Transfer of remains to funeral home		175.48	1/99	78r
Vault		729.40	1/99	78r
Visitation/viewing		341.76	1/99	78r
Groceries				
Apples, red delicious	lb	0.95	7/01	11r
Bacon, sliced	lb	3.44	7/01	11r
Bakery products, expenditures on	yr	310	1999	30r
Bananas	lb	0.55	7/01	11r
Beef, expenditures on	yr	236	1999	30r
Bread, white, pan	lb	1.09	7/01	11r
Butter, yoghurt, cheese, etc, expenditures on	yr	214	1999	30r
Cereals and bakery product purchases	yr	474	1999	30r
Cereals and cereal products, expenditures on	yr	164	1999	30r
Chicken legs, bone-in	lb	1.23	7/01	11r
Chicken, fresh, whole	lb	1.13	7/01	11r
Chuck roast, U.S. choice, boneless	lb	2.79	7/01	11r
Coffee, 100%, ground roast, all sizes	lb	3.40	7/01	11r
Dairy product purchases	yr	342	1999	30r
Eggs, expenditures on	yr	34	1999	30r
Eggs, grade A, large	dozen	0.82	7/01	11r
Fats and oils, expenditures on	yr	80	1999	30r
Fish and seafood, expenditures on	yr	123	1999	30r
Food (excl fruit and vegetables), eaten at home, purchases	yr	838	1999	30r
Food cooked on trips, expenditures on	yr	48	1999	30r
Food purchases	yr	5314	1999	30r
Food purchases, eaten away from home	yr	2313	1999	30r
Food purchases, food eaten at home	yr	3001	1999	30r
Fresh fruits, expenditures on	yr	169	1999	30r
Fresh milk and cream, expenditures on	yr	128	1999	30r
Fresh vegetables, expenditures on	yr	164	1999	30r
Grapefruit	lb	0.67	7/01	11r
Grapes, Thompson, seedless	lb	2.18	7/01	11r
Ground beef, lean and extra lean	lb	2.66	7/01	11r
Ground chuck, 100% beef	lb	2.04	7/01	11r
Lettuce, iceberg	lb	0.76	7/01	11r
Meats, poultry, fish, and egg purchases	yr	808	1999	30r
Nonalcoholic beverages, expenditures on	yr	225	1999	30r
Orange juice, frozen concentrate	16 oz	1.88	7/01	11r
Oranges, Navel	lb	0.79	7/01	11r
Oranges, Valencia	lb	0.56	7/01	11r
Peaches	lb	1.16	7/01	11r
Peanut butter, creamy, all sizes	lb	2.01	7/01	11r
Pears, Anjou	lb	1.16	7/01	11r
Pork chops, center cut, bone-in	lb	3.57	7/01	11r
Pork, expenditures on	yr	146	1999	30r
Potato chips	16 oz	3.37	7/01	11r
Potatoes, white, all types	lb	0.42	7/01	11r
Poultry, expenditures on	yr	158	1999	30r
Processed fruits, expenditures on	yr	124	1999	30r
Processed vegetables, expenditures on	yr	82	1999	30r
Round roast, U.S. choice, boneless	lb	3.04	7/01	11r
Spaghetti and macaroni	lb	1.04	7/01	11r
Steak, sirloin, U.S. choice, boneless	lb	5.39	7/01	11r
Strawberries, dry pint	12 oz	1.51	7/01	11r
Sugar and other sweets, expenditures on	yr	110	1999	30r
Sugar, white, 33-80 ounce package	lb	0.46	7/01	11r
Sugar, white, all sizes	lb	0.47	7/01	11r
Tobacco products and smoking supplies purchases	yr	309	1999	30r
Yogurt, natural, fruit flavored	8 oz	0.79	7/01	11r
Goods and Services				
B&B Japanese maple (acer japonicum)	gal	38.99-125.00	4/00	93r
Boxwood (buxus)	2 gal	15.99-49.95	4/00	93r
Daylily (hemerocallis)	gal	4.95	4/00	93r
Flat of annuals		8.00-14.99	4/00	93r

Nashua, NH - continued

Item	Per	Value	Date	Ref.
Goods and Services - continued				
Fountain grass (pennisetum)	gal	6.99-9.99	4/00	93r
Hanging basket (10 in)		12.95-19.99	4/00	93r
Hardy geranium (geranium)	gal	6.95-7.99	4/00	93r
Hosta (hosta)	gal	4.95	4/00	93r
Lilac (syrubga vulgaris)	2 gal	17.99-74.95	4/00	93r
Miscellaneous purchases	yr	872	1999	30r
Rhododendron (rhododendron)	2 gal	23.99-54.95	4/00	93r
Sage (salvia)	gal	6.95-7.99	4/00	93r
Wintercreeper euonymus (euonymus fortunei)	2 gal	14.99-23.95	4/00	93r
Hunting license	yr	15.50	4/01	34s
Health Care				
Cardiac catheterization, ave hospital/ physician charges		6880	1998	77s
Childbirth, Cesarean delivery		14716	1997	13r
Childbirth, vaginal delivery		8541	1997	13r
Drugs, expenditures on	yr	296	1999	30r
Health care purchases	yr	1788	1999	30r
Health insurance expenditures	yr	875	1999	30r
Hysterectomy, laproscopically-assisted, ave hospital/physician charges		13100	1998	76s
Hysterectomy, vaginal, ave hospital and physician charges		7610	1998	76s
Medicaid dispensing fee		2.50	1999	87s
Medical services expenditures	yr	516	1999	30r
Medical supplies, expenditures on	yr	102	1999	30r
Plastic surgery, breast augmentation		4232	2000	7r
Plastic surgery, breast lift		4605	2000	7r
Plastic surgery, facelift		6964	2000	7r
Plastic surgery, hair transplantation		4193	2000	7r
Plastic surgery, lip augmentation		1675	2000	7r
Plastic surgery, lower body lift		6611	2000	7r
Plastic surgery, thigh lift		4751	2000	7r
Household Goods				
Floor coverings, expenditures on	yr	59	1999	30r
Furniture, expenditures on	yr	388	1999	30r
Household furnishings and equipment purchases	yr	1567	1999	30r
Household textiles, expenditures on	yr	112	1999	30r
Laundry and cleaning supplies, expenditures on	yr	104	1999	30r
Housing				
Home, 2200 sq ft, 4-br, 2-bath, 2-car garage, average		190000	2000	47c
Home price, existing, ave		180800	10/00	90r
Home value, median		189000	2001	53s
Household operation expenditures	yr	581	1999	30r
Housekeeping supplies purchases	yr	474	1999	30r
Lodging expenditures	yr	550	1999	30r
Maintenance, repairs, insurance expenditures	yr	835	1999	30r
Monthly rental value of owned home	mos	663	1999	30r
Owned dwellings, expenditures own	yr	5209	1999	30r
Rent expenditures	yr	2390	1999	30r
Rental unit, 1 bedroom, with utilities	mos	673	4/01	41c
Rental unit, 2 bedroom, with utilities	mos	835	4/01	41c
Rental unit, 3 bedroom, with utilities	mos	1136	4/01	41c
Rental unit, 4 bedroom, with utilities	mos	1352	4/01	41c
Shelter, expenditures on	yr	8149	1999	30r
Insurance and Pensions				
Life and other personal insurance purchases	yr	424	1999	30r
Pensions and Social Security, expenditures on	yr	3037	1999	30r

Values are in dollars or fractions of dollars. In the column headed *Ref*, references are shown to sources. Each reference is followed by a letter. These refer to the geographical level for which data were reported: s=State, r=Region, and c=City or metro. The abbreviation *ex* is used to mean *except* or *excluding*; *exp* stands for expenditures. For other abbreviations and further explanations, please see the Introduction.

Nashua, NH - continued

Item	Per	Value	Date	Ref.
Legal Fees				
Combination hunting and fishing license	yr	31.50	4/01	34s
Divorce, filing fee		127.00	4/01	35s
Driver's license fee	orig	32.00	1999	48s
Driver's license fee	renew	32.00	1999	48s
Fishing license	yr	24.25	4/01	34s
Personal Goods				
Personal care products and services purchases	yr	399	1999	30r
Personal Services				
Personal services, household, expenditures on	yr	271	1999	30r
Pets				
Pets, toys, and playground equipment, expenditures on	yr	325	1999	30r
Taxes				
Federal income taxes paid	yr	2606	1999	30r
Personal taxes, expenditures on	yr	3567	1999	30r
Property taxes paid	yr	1752	1999	30r
State and local income taxes paid	yr	694	1999	30r
Transportation				
Cars and trucks, new, expenditures on	yr	1496	1999	30r
Cars and trucks, used, expenditures on	yr	1251	1999	30r
Diesel at the pump	gal	1.26	10/99	73s
Gasoline and motor oil purchases	yr	901	1999	30r
Gasoline before-tax price (cents)	gal	117.80	10/00	43s
Maintenance and repair expenditures	yr	618	1999	30r
Motorcycle license fee	orig	37.00	1999	49s
Motorcycle license fee	renew	37.00	1999	49s
Public transportation, expenditures on	yr	575	1999	30r
Transportation purchases	yr	6503	1999	30r
Vehicle expenses, miscellaneous, purchases	yr	2266	1999	30r
Vehicle insurance payments	yr	824	1999	30r
Vehicle purchases (net outlay)	yr	2761	1999	30r
Vehicle rental, lease expenditures	yr	584	1999	30r
Utilities				
Electrical bill, average	mos	77.50	9/00	9s
Electricity, expenditures on	yr	837	1999	30r
Electricity cost, average	KWh	11.80	9/00	9s
Utilities, fuels, and public services purchased	yr	2457	1999	30r
Water and other public services, expenditures on	yr	215	1999	30r
Weddings				
Wedding (national average cost)		19936	2000	33r
Wedding (regional average total cost)		29454	1997	110r
Attendants' gifts		321	1998	33r
Bridal attendants' apparel (5 persons)		824	2000	33r
Bride's headpiece/veil		173	1998	33r
Bride's wedding dress		859	1998	33r
Clergy, religious facility fee		242	1998	33r
Engagement ring		3177	1998	33r
Flowers		789	1998	33r
Groom's formalwear rental		99	2000	33r
Limousine		410	1998	33r
Marriage license cost		45.00-57.00	4/01	35s
Men's formalwear (ushers, best man)		469	2000	33r
Mother of bride apparel		241	2000	33r
Music		866	1998	33r
Photography and videography		1368	1998	33r
Rehearsal dinner		728	1998	33r
Wedding invitations and announcements		341	1998	33r
Wedding reception		7968	2000	33r
Wedding rings (bride and groom)		1060	1998	33r

Nashville, TN

Item	Per	Value	Date	Ref.
Alcoholic Beverages				
Alcoholic beverage purchases	yr	253	1999	30r
Malt beverages, all types, all sizes, any origin	16 oz	0.96	7/01	11r
Appliances				
Major appliances, expenditures on	yr	172	1999	30r
Small appliances, housewares, expenditures on	yr	81	1999	30r
Banking and Money				
Mortgage interest and charges paid	yr	2039	1999	30r
Mortgage principal paid on owned property	yr	1026	1999	30r
Vehicle finance charges paid	yr	365	1999	30r
Business Expenses				
Business travel, car rental	day	48	2001	3c
Business travel, food	day	53	2001	3c
Business travel, hotel	day	102	2001	3c
Charity				
Cash contributions, expenditures	yr	1127	1999	30r
Child Care				
Child raising cost, total, age 0-2	yr	8540	1999	60r
Child raising cost, total, age 3-5	yr	8780	1999	60r
Child raising cost, total, age 6-8	yr	8820	1999	60r
Child raising cost, total, age 9-11	yr	8800	1999	60r
Child raising cost, total, age 12-14	yr	9510	1999	60r
Child raising cost, total, age 15-17	yr	9740	1999	60r
Child's child care and education, age 0-2	yr	1380	1999	60r
Child's child care and education, age 3-5	yr	1520	1999	60r
Child's child care and education, age 6-8	yr	990	1999	60r
Child's child care and education, age 9-11	yr	650	1999	60r
Child's child care and education, age 12-14	yr	490	1999	60r
Child's child care and education, age 15-17	yr	840	1999	60r
Child's clothing, age 0-2	yr	480	1999	60r
Child's clothing, age 3-5	yr	470	1999	60r
Child's clothing, age 6-8	yr	520	1999	60r
Child's clothing, age 9-11	yr	570	1999	60r
Child's clothing, age 12-14	yr	950	1999	60r
Child's clothing, age 15-17	yr	850	1999	60r
Child's food, age 0-2	yr	1000	1999	60r
Child's food, age 3-5	yr	1160	1999	60r
Child's food, age 6-8	yr	1490	1999	60r
Child's food, age 9-11	yr	1770	1999	60r
Child's food, age 12-14	yr	1770	1999	60r
Child's food, age 15-17	yr	1980	1999	60r
Child's health care, age 0-2	yr	620	1999	60r
Child's health care, age 3-5	yr	590	1999	60r
Child's health care, age 6-8	yr	680	1999	60r
Child's health care, age 9-11	yr	720	1999	60r
Child's health care, age 12-14	yr	730	1999	60r
Child's health care, age 15-17	yr	760	1999	60r
Child's housing, age 0-2	yr	3070	1999	60r
Child's housing, age 3-5	yr	3050	1999	60r
Child's housing, age 6-8	yr	3010	1999	60r
Child's housing, age 9-11	yr	2850	1999	60r
Child's housing, age 12-14	yr	3040	1999	60r
Child's housing, age 15-17	yr	2650	1999	60r
Child's personal care, reading, age 0-2	yr	910	1999	60r
Child's personal care, reading, age 3-5	yr	930	1999	60r
Child's personal care, reading, age 6-8	yr	960	1999	60r
Child's personal care, reading, age 9-11	yr	1000	1999	60r
Child's personal care, reading, age 12-14	yr	1170	1999	60r
Child's personal care, reading, age 15-17	yr	950	1999	60r
Clothing				
Apparel and services purchases	yr	1610	1999	30r
Boys, 2 to 15, expenditures on	yr	89	1999	30r
Children under 2, expenditures on	yr	79	1999	30r
Footwear, expenditures on	yr	283	1999	30r
Girls, 2 to 15, expenditures on	yr	103	1999	30r
Men and boys, expenditures on	yr	351	1999	30r
Men, 16 and over, expenditures on	yr	262	1999	30r
Women, 16 and over, expenditures on	yr	538	1999	30r

Values are in dollars or fractions of dollars. In the column headed *Ref*, references are shown to sources. Each reference is followed by a letter. These refer to the geographical level for which data were reported: s=State, r=Region, and c=City or metro. The abbreviation *ex* is used to mean *except* or *excluding*; *exp* stands for *expenditures*. For other abbreviations and further explanations, please see the Introduction.

Nashville, TN - continued

Item	Per	Value	Date	Ref.
Communications				
Cable modem installation, Intermedia		149.95	6/99	103s
Cable modem installation, Time Warner		75.00-225.00	6/99	103s
Cable modem rate, cable subscriber, Intermedia	mos	49.95	6/99	103s
Cable modem rate, cable subscriber, Time Warner	mos	39.95-49.95	6/99	103s
Cable modem rate, non-cable subscriber, Intermedia	mos	54.95	6/99	103s
Cable modem rate, non-cable subscriber, Time Warner	mos	39.95-54.95	6/99	103s
Phone line, single, business, field visit	inst.	58.50	12/97	17s
Phone line, single, business, no field visit	inst.	58.50	12/97	17s
Phone line, single, residence, field visit	inst.	41.50	12/97	17s
Phone line, single, residence, no field visit	inst.	41.50	12/97	17s
Postage and stationery, expenditures on	yr	104	1999	30r
Postal rate, express mail, up to half-pound		12.45	7/01	108r
Postal rate, letter, first class, first ounce		0.34	7/01	108r
Postal rate, letter, two ounces		0.57	7/01	108r
Postal rate, post card		0.21	7/01	108r
Postal rate, priority mail, two pounds		3.95	7/01	108r
Postal rate, priority mail, up to one pound		3.50	7/01	108r
Telephone bill, business, basic rate	mos	39.70	12/97	18c
Telephone bill, residential, basic rate	mos	12.15	12/97	18c
Telephone services, expenditures on	yr	860	1999	30r
Education				
Board, 4-year private college/university	yr	2085	1996	38s
Board, 4-year public college/university	yr	1737	1996	38s
Education expenditures	yr	431	1999	30r
Room, 4-year private college/university	yr	2153	1996	38s
Room, 4-year public college/university	yr	1644	1996	38s
Total cost, 4-year private college/university	yr	14068	1996	38s
Total cost, 4-year public college/university	yr	5372	1996	38s
Tuition, 2-year public college/university, in state	yr	1022	1996	38s
Tuition, 4-year private college/university, in state	yr	9830	1996	38s
Tuition, 4-year public college/university	yr	1990	1996	38s
Energy and Fuels				
Electricity	KWh	0.09	7/01	11r
Electricity	500 KWhs	47.29	7/01	11r
Fuel oil #2	gal	1.43	7/01	11r
Fuel oil and other fuels, expenditures on	yr	45	1999	30r
Gas, cooking, winter, 10 therms	mos	12.15	2/96	98c
Gas, cooking, winter, 30 therms	mos	24.44	2/96	98c
Gas, cooking, winter, 50 therms	mos	36.74	2/96	98c
Gas, heating, winter, average use	mos	126.03	2/96	98c
Gas, natural, commercial rate	1000 cf	8.61	11/00	88s
Gasoline, all types	gal	1.60	7/01	11r
Gasoline, unleaded midgrade	gal	1.65	7/01	11r
Gasoline, unleaded premium	gal	1.74	7/01	11r
Natural gas, expenditures on	yr	164	1999	30r
Utility (piped) gas, therm		1.01	7/01	11r
Utility (piped) gas, 40 therms		44.29	7/01	11r
Utility (piped) gas, 100 therms		97.44	7/01	11r
Entertainment				
Entertainment purchases	yr	1574	1999	30r
Fees and admissions paid	yr	371	1999	30r
Reading purchases	yr	121	1999	30r
Television, radios, sound equipment, expenditures on	yr	561	1999	30r
Groceries				
American processed cheese	lb	3.50	7/01	11r
Bakery products, expenditures on	yr	261	1999	30r
Bananas	lb	0.47	7/01	11r
Beans, dried, any type, all sizes	lb	0.63	7/01	11r
Beef for stew, boneless	lb	2.86	7/01	11r
Beef, expenditures on	yr	210	1999	30r
Bologna, all beef or mixed	lb	2.29	7/01	11r

Nashville, TN - continued

Item	Per	Value	Date	Ref.
Groceries - continued				
Bread, French	lb	1.66	7/01	11r
Bread, white, pan	lb	0.87	7/01	11r
Bread, whole wheat, pan	lb	1.38	7/01	11r
Broccoli	lb	1.04	7/01	11r
Butter, salted, grade AA, stick	lb	2.26	7/01	11r
Butter, yoghurt, cheese, etc, expenditures on	yr	170	1999	30r
Cabbage	lb	0.42	7/01	11r
Cereals and cereal products, expenditures on	yr	140	1999	30r
Cheddar cheese, natural	lb	3.75	7/01	11r
Chicken breast, bone-in	lb	1.85	7/01	11r
Chicken legs, bone-in	lb	1.34	7/01	11r
Chicken, fresh, whole	lb	1.05	7/01	11r
Chops, boneless,	lb	4.13	7/01	11r
Chuck roast, graded and ungraded, excl U.S. prime and choice	lb	2.35	7/01	11r
Chuck roast, U.S. choice, boneless	lb	2.67	7/01	11r
Coffee, 100%, ground roast, all sizes	lb	2.88	7/01	11r
Coffee, instant, plain, regular, all sizes	16 oz	9.25	7/01	11r
Cola, non diet,	2 liter	1.11	7/01	11r
Crackers, soda, salted	lb	1.70	7/01	11r
Dairy product purchases	yr	282	1999	30r
Eggs, expenditures on	yr	32	1999	30r
Fats and oils, expenditures on	yr	79	1999	30r
Fish and seafood, expenditures on	yr	99	1999	30r
Flour, white, all purpose	lb	0.32	7/01	11r
Food (excl fruit and vegetables), eaten at home, purchases	yr	815	1999	30r
Food cooked on trips, expenditures on	yr	36	1999	30r
Food purchases	yr	4533	1999	30r
Food purchases, eaten away from home	yr	1873	1999	30r
Food purchases, food eaten at home	yr	2660	1999	30r
Fresh fruits, expenditures on	yr	128	1999	30r
Fresh milk and cream, expenditures on	yr	112	1999	30r
Fresh vegetables, expenditures on	yr	131	1999	30r
Fruit and vegetable purchases	yr	438	1999	30r
Grapefruit	lb	0.59	7/01	11r
Grapes, Thompson, seedless	lb	2.12	7/01	11r
Ground beef, 100% beef	lb	1.76	7/01	11r
Ground beef, lean and extra lean	lb	2.60	7/01	11r
Ground chuck, 100% beef	lb	2.08	7/01	11r
Ham, boneless, excl canned	lb	2.71	7/01	11r
Ham, rump or shank half, bone-in, smoked	lb	2.19	7/01	11r
Ice cream, prepackaged, bulk, regular	1/2 gal	3.93	7/01	11r
Lemons	lb	1.32	7/01	11r
Lettuce, iceberg	lb	0.76	7/01	11r
Milk, fresh, low fat	gal	2.75	7/01	11r
Milk, fresh, whole, fortified	gal	2.97	7/01	11r
Nonalcoholic beverages, expenditures on	yr	228	1999	30r
Orange juice, frozen concentrate	16 oz	1.95	7/01	11r
Oranges, Navel	lb	0.73	7/01	11r
Oranges, Valencia	lb	0.55	7/01	11r
Peanut butter, creamy, all sizes	lb	1.83	7/01	11r
Pears, Anjou	lb	0.98	7/01	11r
Pork chops, center cut, bone-in	lb	3.33	7/01	11r
Pork sausage, fresh, loose	lb	2.59	7/01	11r
Pork shoulder picnic, bone-in, smoked	lb	1.12	7/01	11r
Pork, expenditures on	yr	162	1999	30r
Potato chips	16 oz	3.59	7/01	11r
Potatoes, frozen, french fried	lb	1.00	7/01	11r
Potatoes, white, all types	lb	0.44	7/01	11r
Poultry, expenditures on	yr	137	1999	30r
Processed fruits, expenditures on	yr	97	1999	30r
Processed vegetables, expenditures on	yr	82	1999	30r
Rice, white, long grain, uncooked	lb	0.51	7/01	11r
Round roast, graded and ungraded, excl U.S. prime and choice	lb	2.96	7/01	11r
Round steak, graded and ungraded, excl U.S. prime and choice	lb	3.11	7/01	11r
Sirloin steak, graded and ungraded, excl U.S. prime and choice	lb	4.23	7/01	11r
Spaghetti and macaroni	lb	0.78	7/01	11r

Values are in dollars or fractions of dollars. In the column headed *Ref*, references are shown to sources. Each reference is followed by a letter. These refer to the geographical level for which data were reported: s=State, r=Region, and c=City or metro. The abbreviation *ex* is used to mean *except* or *excluding*; *exp* stands for *expenditures*. For other abbreviations and further explanations, please see the Introduction.

Nashville, TN - continued

Item	Per	Value	Date	Ref.
Groceries				
Steak, round, U.S. choice, boneless	lb	3.56	7/01	11r
Steak, sirloin, U.S. choice, boneless	lb	5.65	7/01	11r
Strawberries, dry pint	12 oz	1.50	7/01	11r
Sugar and other sweets, expenditures on	yr	99	1999	30r
Sugar, white, 33-80 ounce package	lb	0.39	7/01	11r
Sugar, white, all sizes	lb	0.42	7/01	11r
Tobacco products and smoking supplies purchases	yr	288	1999	30r
Tomatoes, field grown	lb	1.43	7/01	11r
Tuna, light, chunk	lb	1.77	7/01	11r
Turkey, frozen, whole	lb	1.05	7/01	11r
Health Care				
Cardiac catheterization, ave hospital/ physician charges		12170	1998	77s
Childbirth, Cesarean delivery		11587	1997	13r
Childbirth, vaginal delivery		6725	1997	13r
Drugs, expenditures on	yr	399	1999	30r
Health care purchases	yr	1971	1999	30r
Health insurance expenditures	yr	933	1999	30r
Home health care aide cost, licensed agency	hour	14	2000	82c
Hysterectomy, laproscopically-assisted, ave hospital/physician charges		13470	1998	76s
Hysterectomy, vaginal, ave hospital and physician charges		9530	1998	76s
Medical services expenditures	yr	547	1999	30r
Medical supplies, expenditures on	yr	91	1999	30r
Nursing home costs, private room	day	135	2000	82c
Nursing home stay, private room	day	135	2000	83c
Household Goods				
Floor coverings, expenditures on	yr	44	1999	30r
Furniture, expenditures on	yr	335	1999	30r
Household furnishings and equipment purchases	yr	1328	1999	30r
Household textiles, expenditures on	yr	89	1999	30r
Laundry and cleaning supplies, expenditures on	yr	113	1999	30r
Housing				
Home, 2200 sq ft, 4-br, 2-bath, 2-car garage, average		181133	2000	47c
Home price, existing, ave		160100	10/00	90r
Home value, median		112000	2001	53s
Household operation expenditures	yr	553	1999	30r
Housekeeping supplies purchases	yr	473	1999	30r
Housing, expenditures on	yr	10303	1999	30r
Maintenance, repairs, insurance expenditures	yr	699	1999	30r
Monthly rental value of owned home	mos	505	1999	30r
Owned dwellings, expenditures own	yr	3465	1999	30r
Rent expenditures	yr	1641	1999	30r
Rental unit, 1 bedroom, with utilities	mos	520	4/01	41c
Rental unit, 2 bedroom, with utilities	mos	641	4/01	41c
Rental unit, 3 bedroom, with utilities	mos	873	4/01	41c
Rental unit, 4 bedroom, with utilities	mos	979	4/01	41c
Shelter, expenditures on	yr	5467	1999	30r
Insurance and Pensions				
Life and other personal insurance purchases	yr	414	1999	30r
Pensions and Social Security, expenditures on	yr	2635	1999	30r
Personal insurance and pensions, expenditures on	yr	3048	1999	30r
Legal Fees				
Combination hunting and fishing license	yr	21.00	4/01	34s
Divorce, filing fee		64.00	4/01	35s
Driver's license fee	orig	17.50	1999	48s
Driver's license fee	renew	17.50	1999	48s
Personal Goods				
Personal care products and services purchases	yr	393	1999	30r

Nashville, TN - continued

Item	Per	Value	Date	Ref.
Personal Services				
Personal services, household, expenditures on	yr	258	1999	30r
Pets				
Pets, toys, and playground equipment, expenditures on	yr	306	1999	30r
Taxes				
Federal income taxes paid	yr	2047	1999	30r
Personal taxes, expenditures on	yr	2554	1999	30r
Property taxes paid	yr	726	1999	30r
State and local income taxes paid	yr	363	1999	30r
Transportation				
Cars and trucks, new, expenditures on	yr	1648	1999	30r
Cars and trucks, used, expenditures on	yr	1651	1999	30r
Diesel at the pump	gal	1.18	10/99	73s
Gasoline and motor oil purchases	yr	1052	1999	30r
Gasoline before-tax price (cents)	gal	102.50	10/00	43s
Maintenance and repair expenditures	yr	621	1999	30r
Public transportation, expenditures on	yr	298	1999	30r
Transportation purchases	yr	6738	1999	30r
Vehicle expenses, miscellaneous, purchases	yr	2033	1999	30r
Vehicle insurance payments	yr	696	1999	30r
Vehicle purchases (net outlay)	yr	3354	1999	30r
Vehicle rental, lease expenditures	yr	352	1999	30r
Utilities				
Electrical bill, average	mos	79.16	9/00	9s
Electricity, expenditures on	yr	1115	1999	30r
Electricity cost, average	KWh	5.60	9/00	9s
Water and other public services, expenditures on	yr	298	1999	30r
Weddings				
Wedding (national average cost)		19936	2000	33r
Attendants' gifts		321	1998	33r
Bridal attendants' apparel (5 persons)		824	2000	33r
Bride's headpiece/veil		173	1998	33r
Bride's wedding dress		859	1998	33r
Clergy, religious facility fee		242	1998	33r
Engagement ring		3177	1998	33r
Flowers		789	1998	33r
Groom's formalwear rental		99	2000	33r
Limousine		410	1998	33r
Marriage license cost		31.00	4/01	35s
Men's formalwear (ushers, best man)		469	2000	33r
Mother of bride apparel		241	2000	33r
Music		866	1998	33r
Photography and videography		1368	1998	33r
Rehearsal dinner		728	1998	33r
Wedding invitations and announcements		341	1998	33r
Wedding reception		7968	2000	33r
Wedding rings (bride and groom)		1060	1998	33r

Nashville-Franklin, TN

Item	Per	Value	Date	Ref.
Alcoholic Beverages				
Alcoholic beverage purchases	yr	253	1999	30r
Malt beverages, all types, all sizes, any origin	16 oz	0.96	7/01	11r
Appliances				
Major appliances, expenditures on	yr	172	1999	30r
Small appliances, housewares, expenditures on	yr	81	1999	30r
Banking and Money				
Mortgage interest and charges paid	yr	2039	1999	30r
Mortgage principal paid on owned property	yr	1026	1999	30r
Vehicle finance charges paid	yr	365	1999	30r
Charity				
Cash contributions, expenditures	yr	1127	1999	30r

Values are in dollars or fractions of dollars. In the column headed *Ref*, references are shown to sources. Each reference is followed by a letter. These refer to the geographical level for which data were reported: s=State, r=Region, and c=City or metro. The abbreviation *ex* is used to mean *except* or *excluding*; *exp* stands for *expenditures*. For other abbreviations and further explanations, please see the Introduction.

Nashville-Franklin, TN - continued

Item	Per	Value	Date	Ref.
Child Care				
Child raising cost, total, age 0-2	yr	8540	1999	60r
Child raising cost, total, age 3-5	yr	8780	1999	60r
Child raising cost, total, age 6-8	yr	8820	1999	60r
Child raising cost, total, age 9-11	yr	8800	1999	60r
Child raising cost, total, age 12-14	yr	9510	1999	60r
Child raising cost, total, age 15-17	yr	9740	1999	60r
Child's child care and education, age 0-2	yr	1380	1999	60r
Child's child care and education, age 3-5	yr	1520	1999	60r
Child's child care and education, age 6-8	yr	990	1999	60r
Child's child care and education, age 9-11	yr	650	1999	60r
Child's child care and education, age 12-14	yr	490	1999	60r
Child's child care and education, age 15-17	yr	840	1999	60r
Child's clothing, age 0-2	yr	480	1999	60r
Child's clothing, age 3-5	yr	470	1999	60r
Child's clothing, age 6-8	yr	520	1999	60r
Child's clothing, age 9-11	yr	570	1999	60r
Child's clothing, age 12-14	yr	950	1999	60r
Child's clothing, age 15-17	yr	850	1999	60r
Child's food, age 0-2	yr	1000	1999	60r
Child's food, age 3-5	yr	1160	1999	60r
Child's food, age 6-8	yr	1490	1999	60r
Child's food, age 9-11	yr	1770	1999	60r
Child's food, age 12-14	yr	1770	1999	60r
Child's food, age 15-17	yr	1980	1999	60r
Child's health care, age 0-2	yr	620	1999	60r
Child's health care, age 3-5	yr	590	1999	60r
Child's health care, age 6-8	yr	680	1999	60r
Child's health care, age 9-11	yr	720	1999	60r
Child's health care, age 12-14	yr	730	1999	60r
Child's health care, age 15-17	yr	760	1999	60r
Child's housing, age 0-2	yr	3070	1999	60r
Child's housing, age 3-5	yr	3050	1999	60r
Child's housing, age 6-8	yr	3010	1999	60r
Child's housing, age 9-11	yr	2850	1999	60r
Child's housing, age 12-14	yr	3040	1999	60r
Child's housing, age 15-17	yr	2650	1999	60r
Child's personal care, reading, age 0-2	yr	910	1999	60r
Child's personal care, reading, age 3-5	yr	930	1999	60r
Child's personal care, reading, age 6-8	yr	960	1999	60r
Child's personal care, reading, age 9-11	yr	1000	1999	60r
Child's personal care, reading, age 12-14	yr	1170	1999	60r
Child's personal care, reading, age 15-17	yr	950	1999	60r
Clothing				
Apparel and services purchases	yr	1610	1999	30r
Boys, 2 to 15, expenditures on	yr	89	1999	30r
Children under 2, expenditures on	yr	79	1999	30r
Footwear, expenditures on	yr	283	1999	30r
Girls, 2 to 15, expenditures on	yr	103	1999	30r
Men and boys, expenditures on	yr	351	1999	30r
Men, 16 and over, expenditures on	yr	262	1999	30r
Women, 16 and over, expenditures on	yr	538	1999	30r
Communications				
Cable modem installation, Intermedia		149.95	6/99	103s
Cable modem installation, Time Warner		75.00-225.00	6/99	103s
Cable modem rate, cable subscriber, Intermedia	mos	49.95	6/99	103s
Cable modem rate, cable subscriber, Time Warner	mos	39.95-49.95	6/99	103s
Cable modem rate, non-cable subscriber, Intermedia	mos	54.95	6/99	103s
Cable modem rate, non-cable subscriber, Time Warner	mos	39.95-54.95	6/99	103s
Phone line, single, business, field visit	inst.	58.50	12/97	17s
Phone line, single, business, no field visit	inst.	58.50	12/97	17s
Phone line, single, residence, field visit	inst.	41.50	12/97	17s
Phone line, single, residence, no field visit	inst.	41.50	12/97	17s
Postage and stationery, expenditures on	yr	104	1999	30r
Postal rate, express mail, up to half-pound		12.45	7/01	108r
Postal rate, letter, first class, first ounce		0.34	7/01	108r
Postal rate, letter, two ounces		0.57	7/01	108r

Nashville-Franklin, TN - continued

Item	Per	Value	Date	Ref.
Communications - continued				
Postal rate, post card		0.21	7/01	108r
Postal rate, priority mail, two pounds		3.95	7/01	108r
Postal rate, priority mail, up to one pound		3.50	7/01	108r
Telephone services, expenditures on	yr	860	1999	30r
Education				
Board, 4-year private college/university	yr	2085	1996	38s
Board, 4-year public college/university	yr	1737	1996	38s
Education expenditures	yr	431	1999	30r
Room, 4-year private college/university	yr	2153	1996	38s
Room, 4-year public college/university	yr	1644	1996	38s
Total cost, 4-year private college/university	yr	14068	1996	38s
Total cost, 4-year public college/university	yr	5372	1996	38s
Tuition, 2-year public college/university, in state	yr	1022	1996	38s
Tuition, 4-year private college/university, in state	yr	9830	1996	38s
Tuition, 4-year public college/university	yr	1990	1996	38s
Energy and Fuels				
Electricity	500 KWhs	47.29	7/01	11r
Electricity	KWh	0.09	7/01	11r
Fuel oil #2	gal	1.43	7/01	11r
Fuel oil and other fuels, expenditures on	yr	45	1999	30r
Gas, natural, commercial rate	1000 cf	8.61	11/00	88s
Gasoline, all types	gal	1.60	7/01	11r
Gasoline, unleaded midgrade	gal	1.65	7/01	11r
Gasoline, unleaded premium	gal	1.74	7/01	11r
Natural gas, expenditures on	yr	164	1999	30r
Utility (piped) gas, therm		1.01	7/01	11r
Utility (piped) gas, 40 therms		44.29	7/01	11r
Utility (piped) gas, 100 therms		97.44	7/01	11r
Entertainment				
Entertainment purchases	yr	1574	1999	30r
Fees and admissions paid	yr	371	1999	30r
Reading purchases	yr	121	1999	30r
Television, radios, sound equipment, expenditures on	yr	561	1999	30r
Groceries				
American processed cheese	lb	3.50	7/01	11r
Bakery products, expenditures on	yr	261	1999	30r
Bananas	lb	0.47	7/01	11r
Beans, dried, any type, all sizes	lb	0.63	7/01	11r
Beef for stew, boneless	lb	2.86	7/01	11r
Beef, expenditures on	yr	210	1999	30r
Bologna, all beef or mixed	lb	2.29	7/01	11r
Bread, French	lb	1.66	7/01	11r
Bread, white, pan	lb	0.87	7/01	11r
Bread, whole wheat, pan	lb	1.38	7/01	11r
Broccoli	lb	1.04	7/01	11r
Butter, salted, grade AA, stick	lb	2.26	7/01	11r
Butter, yoghurt, cheese, etc, expenditures on	yr	170	1999	30r
Cabbage	lb	0.42	7/01	11r
Cereals and cereal products, expenditures on	yr	140	1999	30r
Cheddar cheese, natural	lb	3.75	7/01	11r
Chicken breast, bone-in	lb	1.85	7/01	11r
Chicken legs, bone-in	lb	1.34	7/01	11r
Chicken, fresh, whole	lb	1.05	7/01	11r
Chops, boneless,	lb	4.13	7/01	11r
Chuck roast, graded and ungraded, excl U.S. prime and choice	lb	2.35	7/01	11r
Chuck roast, U.S. choice, boneless	lb	2.67	7/01	11r
Coffee, 100%, ground roast, all sizes	lb	2.88	7/01	11r
Coffee, instant, plain, regular, all sizes	16 oz	9.25	7/01	11r
Cola, non diet,	2 liter	1.11	7/01	11r
Crackers, soda, salted	lb	1.70	7/01	11r
Dairy product purchases	yr	282	1999	30r
Eggs, expenditures on	yr	32	1999	30r
Fats and oils, expenditures on	yr	79	1999	30r
Fish and seafood, expenditures on	yr	99	1999	30r

Values are in dollars or fractions of dollars. In the column headed *Ref*, references are shown to sources. Each reference is followed by a letter. These refer to the geographical level for which data were reported: s=State, r=Region, and c=City or metro. The abbreviation *ex* is used to mean *except* or *excluding*; *exp* stands for *expenditures*. For other abbreviations and further explanations, please see the Introduction.

Nashville-Franklin, TN - continued

Item	Per	Value	Date	Ref.
Groceries				
Flour, white, all purpose	lb	0.32	7/01	11r
Food (excl fruit and vegetables), eaten at home, purchases	yr	815	1999	30r
Food cooked on trips, expenditures on	yr	36	1999	30r
Food purchases	yr	4533	1999	30r
Food purchases, eaten away from home	yr	1873	1999	30r
Food purchases, food eaten at home	yr	2660	1999	30r
Fresh fruits, expenditures on	yr	128	1999	30r
Fresh milk and cream, expenditures on	yr	112	1999	30r
Fresh vegetables, expenditures on	yr	131	1999	30r
Fruit and vegetable purchases	yr	438	1999	30r
Grapefruit	lb	0.59	7/01	11r
Grapes, Thompson, seedless	lb	2.12	7/01	11r
Ground beef, 100% beef	lb	1.76	7/01	11r
Ground beef, lean and extra lean	lb	2.60	7/01	11r
Ground chuck, 100% beef	lb	2.08	7/01	11r
Ham, boneless, excl canned	lb	2.71	7/01	11r
Ham, rump or shank half, bone-in, smoked	lb	2.19	7/01	11r
Ice cream, prepackaged, bulk, regular	1/2 gal	3.93	7/01	11r
Lemons	lb	1.32	7/01	11r
Lettuce, iceberg	lb	0.76	7/01	11r
Milk, fresh, low fat,	gal	2.75	7/01	11r
Milk, fresh, whole, fortified	gal	2.97	7/01	11r
Nonalcoholic beverages, expenditures on	yr	228	1999	30r
Orange juice, frozen concentrate	16 oz	1.95	7/01	11r
Oranges, Navel	lb	0.73	7/01	11r
Oranges, Valencia	lb	0.55	7/01	11r
Peanut butter, creamy, all sizes	lb	1.83	7/01	11r
Pears, Anjou	lb	0.98	7/01	11r
Pork chops, center cut, bone-in	lb	3.33	7/01	11r
Pork sausage, fresh, loose	lb	2.59	7/01	11r
Pork shoulder picnic, bone-in, smoked	lb	1.12	7/01	11r
Pork, expenditures on	yr	162	1999	30r
Potato chips	16 oz	3.59	7/01	11r
Potatoes, frozen, french fried	lb	1.00	7/01	11r
Potatoes, white, all types	lb	0.44	7/01	11r
Poultry, expenditures on	yr	137	1999	30r
Processed fruits, expenditures on	yr	97	1999	30r
Processed vegetables, expenditures on	yr	82	1999	30r
Rice, white, long grain, uncooked	lb	0.51	7/01	11r
Round roast, graded and ungraded, excl U.S. prime and choice	lb	2.96	7/01	11r
Round steak, graded and ungraded, excl U.S. prime and choice	lb	3.11	7/01	11r
Sirloin steak, graded and ungraded, excl U.S. prime and choice	lb	4.23	7/01	11r
Spaghetti and macaroni	lb	0.78	7/01	11r
Steak, round, U.S. choice, boneless	lb	3.56	7/01	11r
Steak, sirloin, U.S. choice, boneless	lb	5.65	7/01	11r
Strawberries, dry pint	12 oz	1.50	7/01	11r
Sugar and other sweets, expenditures on	yr	99	1999	30r
Sugar, white, 33-80 ounce package	lb	0.39	7/01	11r
Sugar, white, all sizes	lb	0.42	7/01	11r
Tobacco products and smoking supplies purchases	yr	288	1999	30r
Tomatoes, field grown	lb	1.43	7/01	11r
Tuna, light, chunk	lb	1.77	7/01	11r
Turkey, frozen, whole	lb	1.05	7/01	11r
Health Care				
Cardiac catheterization, ave hospital/ physician charges		12170	1998	77s
Childbirth, Cesarean delivery		11587	1997	13r
Childbirth, vaginal delivery		6725	1997	13r
Drugs, expenditures on	yr	399	1999	30r
Health care purchases	yr	1971	1999	30r
Health insurance expenditures	yr	933	1999	30r
Hysterectomy, laproscopically-assisted, ave hospital/physician charges		13470	1998	76s
Hysterectomy, vaginal, ave hospital and physician charges		9530	1998	76s
Medical services expenditures	yr	547	1999	30r
Medical supplies, expenditures on	yr	91	1999	30r

Nashville-Franklin, TN - continued

Item	Per	Value	Date	Ref.
Household Goods				
Floor coverings, expenditures on	yr	44	1999	30r
Furniture, expenditures on	yr	335	1999	30r
Household furnishings and equipment purchases	yr	1328	1999	30r
Household textiles, expenditures on	yr	89	1999	30r
Laundry and cleaning supplies, expenditures on	yr	113	1999	30r
Housing				
Home price, existing, ave		160100	10/00	90r
Home value, median		112000	2001	53s
Household operation expenditures	yr	553	1999	30r
Housekeeping supplies purchases	yr	473	1999	30r
Housing, expenditures on	yr	10303	1999	30r
Maintenance, repairs, insurance expenditures	yr	699	1999	30r
Monthly rental value of owned home	mos	505	1999	30r
Owned dwellings, expenditures own	yr	3465	1999	30r
Rent expenditures	yr	1641	1999	30r
Shelter, expenditures on	yr	5467	1999	30r
Insurance and Pensions				
Life and other personal insurance purchases	yr	414	1999	30r
Pensions and Social Security, expenditures on	yr	2635	1999	30r
Personal insurance and pensions, expenditures on	yr	3048	1999	30r
Legal Fees				
Combination hunting and fishing license	yr	21.00	4/01	34s
Divorce, filing fee		64.00	4/01	35s
Driver's license fee	renew	17.50	1999	48s
Driver's license fee	orig	17.50	1999	48s
Personal Goods				
Personal care products and services purchases	yr	393	1999	30r
Personal Services				
Personal services, household, expenditures on	yr	258	1999	30r
Pets				
Pets, toys, and playground equipment, expenditures on	yr	306	1999	30r
Taxes				
Federal income taxes paid	yr	2047	1999	30r
Personal taxes, expenditures on	yr	2554	1999	30r
Property taxes paid	yr	726	1999	30r
State and local income taxes paid	yr	363	1999	30r
Transportation				
Bus fare, one-way	trip	1.45	2000	1c
Cars and trucks, new, expenditures on	yr	1648	1999	30r
Cars and trucks, used, expenditures on	yr	1651	1999	30r
Diesel at the pump	gal	1.18	10/99	73s
Gasoline and motor oil purchases	yr	1052	1999	30r
Gasoline before-tax price (cents)	gal	102.50	10/00	43s
Maintenance and repair expenditures	yr	621	1999	30r
Public transportation, expenditures on	yr	298	1999	30r
Transportation purchases	yr	6738	1999	30r
Vehicle expenses, miscellaneous, purchases	yr	2033	1999	30r
Vehicle insurance payments	yr	696	1999	30r
Vehicle purchases (net outlay)	yr	3354	1999	30r
Vehicle rental, lease expenditures	yr	352	1999	30r
Utilities				
Electrical bill, average	mos	79.16	9/00	9s
Electricity, expenditures on	yr	1115	1999	30r
Electricity cost, average	KWh	5.60	9/00	9s
Water and other public services, expenditures on	yr	298	1999	30r
Weddings				
Wedding (national average cost)		19936	2000	33r
Attendants' gifts		321	1998	33r

Values are in dollars or fractions of dollars. In the column headed *Ref*, references are shown to sources. Each reference is followed by a letter. These refer to the geographical level for which data were reported: s=State, r=Region, and c=City or metro. The abbreviation *ex* is used to mean *except* or *excluding*; *exp* stands for *expenditures*. For other abbreviations and further explanations, please see the Introduction.

Nashville-Franklin, TN - continued

Item	Per	Value	Date	Ref.
Weddings				
Bridal attendants' apparel (5 persons)		824	2000	33r
Bride's headpiece/veil		173	1998	33r
Bride's wedding dress		859	1998	33r
Clergy, religious facility fee		242	1998	33r
Engagement ring		3177	1998	33r
Flowers		789	1998	33r
Groom's formalwear rental		99	2000	33r
Limousine		410	1998	33r
Marriage license cost		31.00	4/01	35s
Men's formalwear (ushers, best man)		469	2000	33r
Mother of bride apparel		241	2000	33r
Music		866	1998	33r
Photography and videography		1368	1998	33r
Rehearsal dinner		728	1998	33r
Wedding invitations and announcements		341	1998	33r
Wedding reception		7968	2000	33r
Wedding rings (bride and groom)		1060	1998	33r

Nassau-Suffolk, NY

Item	Per	Value	Date	Ref.
Average annual expenditures	yr	37971	1999	30r
Alcoholic Beverages				
Alcoholic beverage purchases	yr	368	1999	30r
Wine, red and white table, all sizes, any origin	liter	9.64	7/01	11r
Appliances				
Major appliances, expenditures on	yr	194	1999	30r
Small appliances, housewares, expenditures on	yr	93	1999	30r
Banking and Money				
Mortgage interest and charges paid	yr	2622	1999	30r
Mortgage principal paid on owned property	yr	1262	1999	30r
Vehicle finance charges paid	yr	240	1999	30r
Charity				
Cash contributions, expenditures	yr	1001	1999	30r
Child Care				
Child raising cost, total, age 0-2	yr	8670	1999	60r
Child raising cost, total, age 3-5	yr	8910	1999	60r
Child raising cost, total, age 6-8	yr	9040	1999	60r
Child raising cost, total, age 9-11	yr	9100	1999	60r
Child raising cost, total, age 12-14	yr	9890	1999	60r
Child raising cost, total, age 15-17	yr	10010	1999	60r
Child's child care and education, age 0-2	yr	1070	1999	60r
Child's child care and education, age 3-5	yr	1190	1999	60r
Child's child care and education, age 6-8	yr	740	1999	60r
Child's child care and education, age 9-11	yr	470	1999	60r
Child's child care and education, age 12-14	yr	350	1999	60r
Child's child care and education, age 15-17	yr	590	1999	60r
Child's clothing, age 0-2	yr	480	1999	60r
Child's clothing, age 3-5	yr	470	1999	60r
Child's clothing, age 6-8	yr	520	1999	60r
Child's clothing, age 9-11	yr	570	1999	60r
Child's clothing, age 12-14	yr	970	1999	60r
Child's clothing, age 15-17	yr	870	1999	60r
Child's food, age 0-2	yr	1130	1999	60r
Child's food, age 3-5	yr	1290	1999	60r
Child's food, age 6-8	yr	1640	1999	60r
Child's food, age 9-11	yr	1930	1999	60r
Child's food, age 12-14	yr	1940	1999	60r
Child's food, age 15-17	yr	2150	1999	60r
Child's health care, age 0-2	yr	550	1999	60r
Child's health care, age 3-5	yr	530	1999	60r
Child's health care, age 6-8	yr	610	1999	60r
Child's health care, age 9-11	yr	650	1999	60r
Child's health care, age 12-14	yr	660	1999	60r
Child's health care, age 15-17	yr	690	1999	60r
Child's housing, age 0-2	yr	3555	1999	60r
Child's housing, age 3-5	yr	3530	1999	60r
Child's housing, age 6-8	yr	3490	1999	60r

Nassau-Suffolk, NY - continued

Item	Per	Value	Date	Ref.
Child Care - continued				
Child's housing, age 9-11	yr	3340	1999	60r
Child's housing, age 12-14	yr	3530	1999	60r
Child's housing, age 15-17	yr	3140	1999	60r
Child's personal care, reading, age 0-2	yr	920	1999	60r
Child's personal care, reading, age 3-5	yr	950	1999	60r
Child's personal care, reading, age 6-8	yr	980	1999	60r
Child's personal care, reading, age 9-11	yr	1020	1999	60r
Child's personal care, reading, age 12-14	yr	1190	1999	60r
Child's personal care, reading, age 15-17	yr	970	1999	60r
Nannies: criminal background check		74	1998	84s
Clothing				
Apparel and services purchases	yr	1831	1999	30r
Boys, 2 to 15, expenditures on	yr	92	1999	30r
Children under 2, expenditures on	yr	63	1999	30r
Footwear, expenditures on	yr	300	1999	30r
Girls, 2 to 15, expenditures on	yr	101	1999	30r
Men and boys, expenditures on	yr	446	1999	30r
Men, 16 and over, expenditures on	yr	354	1999	30r
Women, 16 and over, expenditures on	yr	584	1999	30r
Communications				
Cable modem installation, Adelphi		54.90	6/99	103s
Cable modem installation, Cablevision Systems		150.00	6/99	103s
Cable modem installation, Time Warner		75.00-225.00	6/99	103s
Cable modem rate, cable subscriber, Adelphi	mos	34.95	6/99	103s
Cable modem rate, cable subscriber, Cablevision Systems	mos	44.95	6/99	103s
Cable modem rate, cable subscriber, Century	mos	39.95	6/99	103s
Cable modem rate, cable subscriber, Time Warner	mos	39.95-49.95	6/99	103s
Cable modem rate, non-cable subscriber, Adelphi	mos	44.95	6/99	103s
Cable modem rate, non-cable subscriber, Cablevision Systems	mos	54.95	6/99	103s
Cable modem rate, non-cable subscriber, Time Warner	mos	39.95-54.95	6/99	103s
Phone line, single, business, field visit	inst.	142.76	12/97	17s
Phone line, single, business, no field visit	inst.	106.05	12/97	17s
Phone line, single, residence, field visit	inst.	102.78	12/97	17s
Phone line, single, residence, no field visit	inst.	55.00	12/97	17s
Postage and stationery, expenditures on	yr	138	1999	30r
Postal rate, express mail, up to half-pound		12.45	7/01	108r
Postal rate, letter, first class, first ounce		0.34	7/01	108r
Postal rate, letter, two ounces		0.57	7/01	108r
Postal rate, post card		0.21	7/01	108r
Postal rate, priority mail, two pounds		3.95	7/01	108r
Postal rate, priority mail, up to one pound		3.50	7/01	108r
Telephone services, expenditures on	yr	830	1999	30r
Education				
Board, 4-year private college/university	yr	3255	1996	38s
Board, 4-year public college/university	yr	2310	1996	38s
Education expenditures	yr	877	1999	30r
Room, 4-year private college/university	yr	3724	1996	38s
Room, 4-year public college/university	yr	2937	1996	38s
Total cost, 4-year private college/university	yr	20831	1996	38s
Total cost, 4-year public college/university	yr	8960	1996	38s
Tuition, 2-year public college/university, in state	yr	2427	1996	38s
Tuition, 4-year private college/university, in state	yr	13852	1996	38s
Tuition, 4-year public college/university	yr	3714	1996	38s
Energy and Fuels				
Electricity	KWh	0.12	7/01	11r
Fuel oil #2	gal	1.31	7/01	11r
Fuel oil and other fuels, expenditures on	yr	207	1999	30r
Gasoline, all types	gal	1.80	7/01	11r
Gasoline, unleaded midgrade	gal	1.85	7/01	11r
Gasoline, unleaded premium	gal	1.91	7/01	11r
Gasoline, unleaded regular	gal	1.71	7/01	11r

Values are in dollars or fractions of dollars. In the column headed *Ref*, references are shown to sources. Each reference is followed by a letter. These refer to the geographical level for which data were reported: s=State, r=Region, and c=City or metro. The abbreviation *ex* is used to mean *except* or *excluding*; *exp* stands for *expenditures*. For other abbreviations and further explanations, please see the Introduction.

Nassau-Suffolk, NY - continued

Item	Per	Value	Date	Ref.
Energy and Fuels				
Natural gas, expenditures on	yr	368	1999	30r
Utility (piped) gas, therm		1.08	7/01	11r
Utility (piped) gas, 40 therms		50.87	7/01	11r
Utility (piped) gas, 100 therms		111.06	7/01	11r
Entertainment				
Entertainment purchases	yr	1821	1999	30r
Fees and admissions paid	yr	511	1999	30r
Television, radios, sound equipment, expenditures on	yr	650	1999	30r
Funerals				
Total cost of funeral		5813.50	1/99	78r
Acknowledgement cards		28.32	1/99	78r
Casket		2082.20	1/99	78r
Cosmetology, hair, other preparation		169.59	1/99	78r
Embalming		465.60	1/99	78r
Funeral at funeral home		339.56	1/99	78r
Hearse (local)		183.96	1/99	78r
Professional service charges		1157.85	1/99	78r
Service car/van		100.41	1/99	78r
Transfer of remains to funeral home		158.66	1/99	78r
Vault		766.31	1/99	78r
Visitation/viewing		361.04	1/99	78r
Groceries				
Apples, red delicious	lb	0.95	7/01	11r
Bacon, sliced	lb	3.44	7/01	11r
Bakery products, expenditures on	yr	310	1999	30r
Bananas	lb	0.55	7/01	11r
Beef, expenditures on	yr	236	1999	30r
Bread, white, pan	lb	1.09	7/01	11r
Butter, yoghurt, cheese, etc, expenditures on	yr	214	1999	30r
Cereals and bakery product purchases	yr	474	1999	30r
Cereals and cereal products, expenditures on	yr	164	1999	30r
Chicken legs, bone-in	lb	1.23	7/01	11r
Chicken, fresh, whole	lb	1.13	7/01	11r
Chuck roast, U.S. choice, boneless	lb	2.79	7/01	11r
Coffee, 100%, ground roast, all sizes	lb	3.40	7/01	11r
Dairy product purchases	yr	342	1999	30r
Eggs, expenditures on	yr	34	1999	30r
Eggs, grade A, large	dozen	0.82	7/01	11r
Fats and oils, expenditures on	yr	80	1999	30r
Fish and seafood, expenditures on	yr	123	1999	30r
Food (excl fruit and vegetables), eaten at home, purchases	yr	838	1999	30r
Food cooked on trips, expenditures on	yr	48	1999	30r
Food purchases	yr	5314	1999	30r
Food purchases, eaten away from home	yr	2313	1999	30r
Food purchases, food eaten at home	yr	3001	1999	30r
Fresh fruits, expenditures on	yr	169	1999	30r
Fresh milk and cream, expenditures on	yr	128	1999	30r
Fresh vegetables, expenditures on	yr	164	1999	30r
Grapefruit	lb	0.67	7/01	11r
Grapes, Thompson, seedless	lb	2.18	7/01	11r
Ground beef, lean and extra lean	lb	2.66	7/01	11r
Ground chuck, 100% beef	lb	2.04	7/01	11r
Lettuce, iceberg	lb	0.76	7/01	11r
Meats, poultry, fish, and egg purchases	yr	808	1999	30r
Nonalcoholic beverages, expenditures on	yr	225	1999	30r
Orange juice, frozen concentrate	16 oz	1.88	7/01	11r
Oranges, Navel	lb	0.79	7/01	11r
Oranges, Valencia	lb	0.56	7/01	11r
Peaches	lb	1.16	7/01	11r
Peanut butter, creamy, all sizes	lb	2.01	7/01	11r
Pears, Anjou	lb	1.16	7/01	11r
Pork chops, center cut, bone-in	lb	3.57	7/01	11r
Pork, expenditures on	yr	146	1999	30r
Potato chips	16 oz	3.37	7/01	11r
Potatoes, white, all types	lb	0.42	7/01	11r
Poultry, expenditures on	yr	158	1999	30r
Processed fruits, expenditures on	yr	124	1999	30r
Processed vegetables, expenditures on	yr	82	1999	30r

Nassau-Suffolk, NY - continued

Item	Per	Value	Date	Ref.
Groceries - continued				
Round roast, U.S. choice, boneless	lb	3.04	7/01	11r
Spaghetti and macaroni	lb	1.04	7/01	11r
Steak, sirloin, U.S. choice, boneless	lb	5.39	7/01	11r
Strawberries, dry pint	12 oz	1.51	7/01	11r
Sugar and other sweets, expenditures on	yr	110	1999	30r
Sugar, white, 33-80 ounce package	lb	0.46	7/01	11r
Sugar, white, all sizes	lb	0.47	7/01	11r
Tobacco products and smoking supplies purchases	yr	309	1999	30r
Yogurt, natural, fruit flavored	8 oz	0.79	7/01	11r
Goods and Services				
B&B Japanese maple (acer japonicum)	gal	38.99-125.00	4/00	93r
Boxwood (buxus)	2 gal	15.99-49.95	4/00	93r
Daylilly (hemerocallis)	gal	4.95	4/00	93r
Flat of annuals		8.00-14.99	4/00	93r
Fountain grass (pennisetum)	gal	6.99-9.99	4/00	93r
Hanging basket (10 in)		12.95-19.99	4/00	93r
Hardy geranium (geranium)	gal	6.95-7.99	4/00	93r
Hosta (hosta)	gal	4.95	4/00	93r
Lilac (syrubga vulgaris)	2 gal	17.99-74.95	4/00	93r
Miscellaneous purchases	yr	872	1999	30r
Rhododendron (rhododendron)	2 gal	23.99-54.95	4/00	93r
Sage (salvia)	gal	6.95-7.99	4/00	93r
Wintercreeper euonymus (euonymus fortunei)	2 gal	14.99-23.95	4/00	93r
Hunting license	yr	11.00	4/01	34s
Health Care				
Cardiac catheterization, ave hospital/physician charges		12750	1998	77s
Childbirth, Cesarean delivery		14716	1997	13r
Childbirth, vaginal delivery		8541	1997	13r
Drugs, expenditures on	yr	296	1999	30r
Health care purchases	yr	1788	1999	30r
Health insurance expenditures	yr	875	1999	30r
Hysterectomy, laproscopically-assisted, ave hospital/physician charges		13460	1998	76s
Hysterectomy, vaginal, ave hospital and physician charges		10310	1998	76s
Medicaid dispensing fee		3.50-4.50	1999	87s
Medical services expenditures	yr	516	1999	30r
Medical supplies, expenditures on	yr	102	1999	30r
Plastic surgery, breast augmentation		4232	2000	7r
Plastic surgery, breast lift		4605	2000	7r
Plastic surgery, facelift		6964	2000	7r
Plastic surgery, hair transplantation		4193	2000	7r
Plastic surgery, lip augmentation		1675	2000	7r
Plastic surgery, lower body lift		6611	2000	7r
Plastic surgery, thigh lift		4751	2000	7r
Household Goods				
Floor coverings, expenditures on	yr	59	1999	30r
Furniture, expenditures on	yr	388	1999	30r
Household furnishings and equipment purchases	yr	1567	1999	30r
Household textiles, expenditures on	yr	112	1999	30r
Laundry and cleaning supplies, expenditures on	yr	104	1999	30r
Housing				
Home price, existing, ave		180800	10/00	90r
Home value, median		179000	2001	53s
Household operation expenditures	yr	581	1999	30r

Values are in dollars or fractions of dollars. In the column headed *Ref*, references are shown to sources. Each reference is followed by a letter. These refer to the geographical level for which data were reported: s=State, r=Region, and c=City or metro. The abbreviation *ex* is used to mean *except* or *excluding*; *exp* stands for *expenditures*. For other abbreviations and further explanations, please see the Introduction.

Nassau-Suffolk, NY - continued

Item	Per	Value	Date	Ref.
Housing				
Housekeeping supplies purchases	yr	474	1999	30r
Lodging expenditures	yr	550	1999	30r
Maintenance, repairs, insurance expenditures	yr	835	1999	30r
Monthly rental value of owned home	mos	663	1999	30r
Owned dwellings, expenditures own	yr	5209	1999	30r
Rent expenditures	yr	2390	1999	30r
Rental unit, 1 bedroom, with utilities	mos	962	4/01	41c
Rental unit, 2 bedroom, with utilities	mos	1173	4/01	41c
Rental unit, 3 bedroom, with utilities	mos	1633	4/01	41c
Rental unit, 4 bedroom, with utilities	mos	1749	4/01	41c
Shelter, expenditures on	yr	8149	1999	30r
Insurance and Pensions				
Auto insurance premium	yr	1113.55	1999	57s
Life and other personal insurance purchases	yr	424	1999	30r
Pensions and Social Security, expenditures on	yr	3037	1999	30r
Legal Fees				
Divorce, filing fee		270.00	4/01	35s
Driver's license fee	orig	25.00	1999	48s
Driver's license fee	renew	25.00	1999	48s
Fishing license	yr	14.00	4/01	34s
Personal Goods				
Personal care products and services purchases	yr	399	1999	30r
Personal Services				
Personal services, household, expenditures on	yr	271	1999	30r
Pets				
Pets, toys, and playground equipment, expenditures on	yr	325	1999	30r
Taxes				
Federal income taxes paid	yr	2606	1999	30r
Personal taxes, expenditures on	yr	3567	1999	30r
Property taxes paid	yr	1752	1999	30r
State and local income taxes paid	yr	694	1999	30r
Transportation				
Cars and trucks, new, expenditures on	yr	1496	1999	30r
Cars and trucks, used, expenditures on	yr	1251	1999	30r
Diesel at the pump	gal	1.33	10/99	73s
Gasoline and motor oil purchases	yr	901	1999	30r
Gasoline before-tax price (cents)	gal	110.70	10/00	43s
Maintenance and repair expenditures	yr	618	1999	30r
Public transportation, expenditures on	yr	575	1999	30r
Transportation purchases	yr	6503	1999	30r
Vehicle expenses, miscellaneous, purchases	yr	2266	1999	30r
Vehicle insurance payments	yr	824	1999	30r
Vehicle purchases (net outlay)	yr	2761	1999	30r
Vehicle rental, lease expenditures	yr	584	1999	30r
Travel				
Hotel room	night	139.88	2/01	95s
Utilities				
Electrical bill, average	mos	71.50	9/00	9s
Electricity, expenditures on	yr	837	1999	30r
Electricity cost, average	KWh	11.34	9/00	9s
Utilities, fuels, and public services purchased	yr	2457	1999	30r
Water and other public services, expenditures on	yr	215	1999	30r
Weddings				
Wedding (national average cost)		19936	2000	33r
Wedding (regional average total cost)		29454	1997	110r
Attendants' gifts		321	1998	33r
Bridal attendants' apparel (5 persons)		824	2000	33r
Bride's headpiece/veil		173	1998	33r
Bride's wedding dress		859	1998	33r
Clergy, religious facility fee		242	1998	33r
Engagement ring		3177	1998	33r

Nassau-Suffolk, NY - continued

Item	Per	Value	Date	Ref.
Weddings - continued				
Flowers		789	1998	33r
Groom's formalwear rental		99	2000	33r
Limousine		410	1998	33r
Marriage license cost		25.00	4/01	35s
Men's formalwear (ushers, best man)		469	2000	33r
Mother of bride apparel		241	2000	33r
Music		866	1998	33r
Photography and videography		1368	1998	33r
Rehearsal dinner		728	1998	33r
Wedding invitations and announcements		341	1998	33r
Wedding reception		7968	2000	33r
Wedding rings (bride and groom)		1060	1998	33r

New Bedford, MA

Item	Per	Value	Date	Ref.
Average annual expenditures	yr	37971	1999	30r
Alcoholic Beverages				
Alcoholic beverage purchases	yr	368	1999	30r
Wine, red and white table, all sizes, any origin	liter	9.64	7/01	11r
Appliances				
Major appliances, expenditures on	yr	194	1999	30r
Small appliances, housewares, expenditures on	yr	93	1999	30r
Banking and Money				
Mortgage interest and charges paid	yr	2622	1999	30r
Mortgage principal paid on owned property	yr	1262	1999	30r
Vehicle finance charges paid	yr	240	1999	30r
Charity				
Cash contributions, expenditures	yr	1001	1999	30r
Child Care				
Child raising cost, total, age 0-2	yr	8670	1999	60r
Child raising cost, total, age 3-5	yr	8910	1999	60r
Child raising cost, total, age 6-8	yr	9040	1999	60r
Child raising cost, total, age 9-11	yr	9100	1999	60r
Child raising cost, total, age 12-14	yr	9890	1999	60r
Child raising cost, total, age 15-17	yr	10010	1999	60r
Child's child care and education, age 0-2	yr	1070	1999	60r
Child's child care and education, age 3-5	yr	1190	1999	60r
Child's child care and education, age 6-8	yr	740	1999	60r
Child's child care and education, age 9-11	yr	470	1999	60r
Child's child care and education, age 12-14	yr	350	1999	60r
Child's child care and education, age 15-17	yr	590	1999	60r
Child's clothing, age 0-2	yr	480	1999	60r
Child's clothing, age 3-5	yr	470	1999	60r
Child's clothing, age 6-8	yr	520	1999	60r
Child's clothing, age 9-11	yr	570	1999	60r
Child's clothing, age 12-14	yr	970	1999	60r
Child's clothing, age 15-17	yr	870	1999	60r
Child's food, age 0-2	yr	1130	1999	60r
Child's food, age 3-5	yr	1290	1999	60r
Child's food, age 6-8	yr	1640	1999	60r
Child's food, age 9-11	yr	1930	1999	60r
Child's food, age 12-14	yr	1940	1999	60r
Child's food, age 15-17	yr	2150	1999	60r
Child's health care, age 0-2	yr	550	1999	60r
Child's health care, age 3-5	yr	530	1999	60r
Child's health care, age 6-8	yr	610	1999	60r
Child's health care, age 9-11	yr	650	1999	60r
Child's health care, age 12-14	yr	660	1999	60r
Child's health care, age 15-17	yr	690	1999	60r
Child's housing, age 0-2	yr	3555	1999	60r
Child's housing, age 3-5	yr	3530	1999	60r
Child's housing, age 6-8	yr	3490	1999	60r
Child's housing, age 9-11	yr	3340	1999	60r
Child's housing, age 12-14	yr	3530	1999	60r
Child's housing, age 15-17	yr	3140	1999	60r
Child's personal care, reading, age 0-2	yr	920	1999	60r
Child's personal care, reading, age 3-5	yr	950	1999	60r

Values are in dollars or fractions of dollars. In the column headed *Ref*, references are shown to sources. Each reference is followed by a letter. These refer to the geographical level for which data were reported: s=State, r=Region, and c=City or metro. The abbreviation *ex* is used to mean *except* or *excluding*; *exp* stands for *expenditures*. For other abbreviations and further explanations, please see the Introduction.

New Bedford, MA - continued

Item	Per	Value	Date	Ref.
Child Care				
Child's personal care, reading, age 6-8	yr	980	1999	60r
Child's personal care, reading, age 9-11	yr	1020	1999	60r
Child's personal care, reading, age 12-14	yr	1190	1999	60r
Child's personal care, reading, age 15-17	yr	970	1999	60r
Clothing				
Apparel and services purchases	yr	1831	1999	30r
Boys, 2 to 15, expenditures on	yr	92	1999	30r
Children under 2, expenditures on	yr	63	1999	30r
Footwear, expenditures on	yr	300	1999	30r
Girls, 2 to 15, expenditures on	yr	101	1999	30r
Men and boys, expenditures on	yr	446	1999	30r
Men, 16 and over, expenditures on	yr	354	1999	30r
Women, 16 and over, expenditures on	yr	584	1999	30r
Communications				
Cable modem installation, Adelphi		54.90	6/99	103s
Cable modem installation, Media One		100.00	6/99	103s
Cable modem rate, cable subscriber, Adelphi	mos	34.95	6/99	103s
Cable modem rate, cable subscriber, Media One	mos	34.95-39.95	6/99	103s
Cable modem rate, non-cable subscriber, Adelphi	mos	44.95	6/99	103s
Cable modem rate, non-cable subscriber, Media One	mos	49.95	6/99	103s
Phone line, single, business, field visit	inst.	120.52	12/97	17s
Phone line, single, business, no field visit	inst.	93.02	12/97	17s
Phone line, single, residence, field visit	inst.	64.57	12/97	17s
Phone line, single, residence, no field visit	inst.	37.07	12/97	17s
Postage and stationery, expenditures on	yr	138	1999	30r
Postal rate, express mail, up to half-pound		12.45	7/01	108r
Postal rate, letter, first class, first ounce		0.34	7/01	108r
Postal rate, letter, two ounces		0.57	7/01	108r
Postal rate, post card		0.21	7/01	108r
Postal rate, priority mail, two pounds		3.95	7/01	108r
Postal rate, priority mail, up to one pound		3.50	7/01	108r
Telephone services, expenditures on	yr	830	1999	30r
Education				
Board, 4-year private college/university	yr	3244	1996	38s
Board, 4-year public college/university	yr	2042	1996	38s
Education expenditures	yr	877	1999	30r
Room, 4-year private college/university	yr	3688	1996	38s
Room, 4-year public college/university	yr	2462	1996	38s
Total cost, 4-year private college/university	yr	23335	1996	38s
Total cost, 4-year public college/university	yr	8757	1996	38s
Tuition, 2-year public college/university, in state	yr	2359	1996	38s
Tuition, 4-year private college/university, in state	yr	16403	1996	38s
Tuition, 4-year public college/university	yr	4253	1996	38s
Energy and Fuels				
Electricity	KWh	0.12	7/01	11r
Fuel oil #2	gal	1.31	7/01	11r
Fuel oil and other fuels, expenditures on	yr	207	1999	30r
Gas, natural, commercial rate	1000 cf	10.82	11/00	88s
Gasoline, all types	gal	1.80	7/01	11r
Gasoline, unleaded midgrade	gal	1.85	7/01	11r
Gasoline, unleaded premium	gal	1.91	7/01	11r
Gasoline, unleaded regular	gal	1.71	7/01	11r
Natural gas, expenditures on	yr	368	1999	30r
Utility (piped) gas, therm		1.08	7/01	11r
Utility (piped) gas, 40 therms		50.87	7/01	11r
Utility (piped) gas, 100 therms		111.06	7/01	11r
Entertainment				
Entertainment purchases	yr	1821	1999	30r
Fees and admissions paid	yr	511	1999	30r
Television, radios, sound equipment, expenditures on	yr	650	1999	30r
Funerals				
Total cost of funeral		5776.91	1/99	78r
Acknowledgement cards		14.47	1/99	78r

New Bedford, MA - continued

Item	Per	Value	Date	Ref.
Funerals - continued				
Casket		2090.19	1/99	78r
Cosmetology, hair, other preparation		132.92	1/99	78r
Embalming		377.33	1/99	78r
Funeral at funeral home		352.43	1/99	78r
Hearse (local)		185.55	1/99	78r
Professional service charges		1289.95	1/99	78r
Service car/van		87.42	1/99	78r
Transfer of remains to funeral home		175.48	1/99	78r
Vault		729.40	1/99	78r
Visitation/viewing		341.76	1/99	78r
Groceries				
Apples, red delicious	lb	0.95	7/01	11r
Bacon, sliced	lb	3.44	7/01	11r
Bakery products, expenditures on	yr	310	1999	30r
Bananas	lb	0.55	7/01	11r
Beef, expenditures on	yr	236	1999	30r
Bread, white, pan	lb	1.09	7/01	11r
Butter, yoghurt, cheese, etc, expenditures on	yr	214	1999	30r
Cereals and bakery product purchases	yr	474	1999	30r
Cereals and cereal products, expenditures on	yr	164	1999	30r
Chicken legs, bone-in	lb	1.23	7/01	11r
Chicken, fresh, whole	lb	1.13	7/01	11r
Chuck roast, U.S. choice, boneless	lb	2.79	7/01	11r
Coffee, 100%, ground roast, all sizes	lb	3.40	7/01	11r
Dairy product purchases	yr	342	1999	30r
Eggs, expenditures on	yr	34	1999	30r
Eggs, grade A, large	dozen	0.82	7/01	11r
Fats and oils, expenditures on	yr	80	1999	30r
Fish and seafood, expenditures on	yr	123	1999	30r
Food (excl fruit and vegetables), eaten at home, purchases	yr	838	1999	30r
Food cooked on trips, expenditures on	yr	48	1999	30r
Food purchases	yr	5314	1999	30r
Food purchases, eaten away from home	yr	2313	1999	30r
Food purchases, food eaten at home	yr	3001	1999	30r
Fresh fruits, expenditures on	yr	169	1999	30r
Fresh milk and cream, expenditures on	yr	128	1999	30r
Fresh vegetables, expenditures on	yr	164	1999	30r
Grapefruit	lb	0.67	7/01	11r
Grapes, Thompson, seedless	lb	2.18	7/01	11r
Ground beef, lean and extra lean	lb	2.66	7/01	11r
Ground chuck, 100% beef	lb	2.04	7/01	11r
Lettuce, iceberg	lb	0.76	7/01	11r
Meats, poultry, fish, and egg purchases	yr	808	1999	30r
Nonalcoholic beverages, expenditures on	yr	225	1999	30r
Orange juice, frozen concentrate	16 oz	1.88	7/01	11r
Oranges, Navel	lb	0.79	7/01	11r
Oranges, Valencia	lb	0.56	7/01	11r
Peaches	lb	1.16	7/01	11r
Peanut butter, creamy, all sizes	lb	2.01	7/01	11r
Pears, Anjou	lb	1.16	7/01	11r
Pork chops, center cut, bone-in	lb	3.57	7/01	11r
Pork, expenditures on	yr	146	1999	30r
Potato chips	16 oz	3.37	7/01	11r
Potatoes, white, all types	lb	0.42	7/01	11r
Poultry, expenditures on	yr	158	1999	30r
Processed fruits, expenditures on	yr	124	1999	30r
Processed vegetables, expenditures on	yr	82	1999	30r
Round roast, U.S. choice, boneless	lb	3.04	7/01	11r
Spaghetti and macaroni	lb	1.04	7/01	11r
Steak, sirloin, U.S. choice, boneless	lb	5.39	7/01	11r
Strawberries, dry pint	12 oz	1.51	7/01	11r
Sugar and other sweets, expenditures on	yr	110	1999	30r
Sugar, white, 33-80 ounce package	lb	0.46	7/01	11r
Sugar, white, all sizes	lb	0.47	7/01	11r
Tobacco products and smoking supplies purchases	yr	309	1999	30r
Yogurt, natural, fruit flavored	8 oz	0.79	7/01	11r

Values are in dollars or fractions of dollars. In the column headed *Ref*, references are shown to sources. Each reference is followed by a letter. These refer to the geographical level for which data were reported: s=State, r=Region, and c=City or metro. The abbreviation *ex* is used to mean *except* or *excluding*; *exp* stands for expenditures. For other abbreviations and further explanations, please see the Introduction.

New Bedford, MA - continued

Item	Per	Value	Date	Ref.
Goods and Services				
B&B Japanese maple (acer japonicum)	gal	38.99-125.00	4/00	93r
Boxwood (buxus)	2 gal	15.99-49.95	4/00	93r
Daylilly (hemerocallis)	gal	4.95	4/00	93r
Flat of annuals		8.00-14.99	4/00	93r
Fountain grass (pennisetum)	gal	6.99-9.99	4/00	93r
Hanging basket (10 in)		12.95-19.99	4/00	93r
Hardy geranium (geranium)	gal	6.95-7.99	4/00	93r
Hosta (hosta)	gal	4.95	4/00	93r
Lilac (syrubga vulgaris)	2 gal	17.99-74.95	4/00	93r
Miscellaneous purchases	yr	872	1999	30r
Rhododendron (rhododendron)	2 gal	23.99-54.95	4/00	93r
Sage (salvia)	gal	6.95-7.99	4/00	93r
Wintercreeper euonymus (euonymus fortunei)	2 gal	14.99-23.95	4/00	93r
Hunting license	yr	27.50	4/01	34s
Health Care				
Cardiac catheterization, ave hospital/ physician charges		17080	1998	77s
Childbirth, Cesarean delivery		14716	1997	13r
Childbirth, vaginal delivery		8541	1997	13r
Drugs, expenditures on	yr	296	1999	30r
Health care purchases	yr	1788	1999	30r
Health insurance expenditures	yr	875	1999	30r
Hysterectomy, laproscopically-assisted, ave hospital/physician charges		13100	1998	76s
Hysterectomy, vaginal, ave hospital and physician charges		8780	1998	76s
Medicaid dispensing fee		3.00	1999	87s
Medical services expenditures	yr	516	1999	30r
Medical supplies, expenditures on	yr	102	1999	30r
Plastic surgery, breast augmentation		4232	2000	7r
Plastic surgery, breast lift		4605	2000	7r
Plastic surgery, facelift		6964	2000	7r
Plastic surgery, hair transplantation		4193	2000	7r
Plastic surgery, lip augmentation		1675	2000	7r
Plastic surgery, lower body lift		6611	2000	7r
Plastic surgery, thigh lift		4751	2000	7r
Household Goods				
Floor coverings, expenditures on	yr	59	1999	30r
Furniture, expenditures on	yr	388	1999	30r
Household furnishings and equipment purchases	yr	1567	1999	30r
Household textiles, expenditures on	yr	112	1999	30r
Laundry and cleaning supplies, expenditures on	yr	104	1999	30r
Housing				
Home price, existing, ave		180800	10/00	90r
Home value, median		261000	2001	53s
Household operation expenditures	yr	581	1999	30r
Housekeeping supplies purchases	yr	474	1999	30r
Lodging expenditures	yr	550	1999	30r
Maintenance, repairs, insurance expenditures	yr	835	1999	30r
Monthly rental value of owned home	mos	663	1999	30r
Owned dwellings, expenditures own	yr	5209	1999	30r
Rent expenditures	yr	2390	1999	30r
Rental unit, 1 bedroom, with utilities	mos	595	4/01	41c
Rental unit, 2 bedroom, with utilities	mos	677	4/01	41c
Rental unit, 3 bedroom, with utilities	mos	846	4/01	41c
Rental unit, 4 bedroom, with utilities	mos	950	4/01	41c
Shelter, expenditures on	yr	8149	1999	30r

New Bedford, MA - continued

Item	Per	Value	Date	Ref.
Insurance and Pensions				
Life and other personal insurance purchases	yr	424	1999	30r
Pensions and Social Security, expenditures on	yr	3037	1999	30r
Legal Fees				
Divorce, filing fee		100.00	4/01	35s
Driver's license fee	orig	33.75	1999	48s
Driver's license fee	renew	33.75	1999	48s
Fishing license	yr	27.50	4/01	34s
Personal Goods				
Personal care products and services purchases	yr	399	1999	30r
Personal Services				
Personal services, household, expenditures on	yr	271	1999	30r
Pets				
Pets, toys, and playground equipment, expenditures on	yr	325	1999	30r
Taxes				
Federal income taxes paid	yr	2606	1999	30r
Personal taxes, expenditures on	yr	3567	1999	30r
Property taxes paid	yr	1752	1999	30r
State and local income taxes paid	yr	694	1999	30r
Transportation				
Cars and trucks, new, expenditures on	yr	1496	1999	30r
Cars and trucks, used, expenditures on	yr	1251	1999	30r
Diesel at the pump	gal	1.32	10/99	73s
Gasoline and motor oil purchases	yr	901	1999	30r
Gasoline before-tax price (cents)	gal	118.70	10/00	43s
Maintenance and repair expenditures	yr	618	1999	30r
Public transportation, expenditures on	yr	575	1999	30r
Transportation purchases	yr	6503	1999	30r
Vehicle expenses, miscellaneous, purchases	yr	2266	1999	30r
Vehicle insurance payments	yr	824	1999	30r
Vehicle purchases (net outlay)	yr	2761	1999	30r
Vehicle rental, lease expenditures	yr	584	1999	30r
Travel				
Hotel room	night	111.15	2/01	95s
Utilities				
Electrical bill, average	mos	58.58	9/00	9s
Electricity, expenditures on	yr	837	1999	30r
Electricity, summer, 250 KWh	mos	37.43	2/96	97c
Electricity, summer, 500 KWh	mos	70.63	2/96	97c
Electricity, summer, 750 KWh	mos	103.84	2/96	97c
Electricity, summer, 1000 KWh	mos	137.04	2/96	97c
Electricity cost, average	KWh	8.90	9/00	9s
Utilities, fuels, and public services purchased	yr	2457	1999	30r
Water and other public services, expenditures on	yr	215	1999	30r
Weddings				
Wedding (national average cost)		19936	2000	33r
Wedding (regional average total cost)		29454	1997	110r
Attendants' gifts		321	1998	33r
Bridal attendants' apparel (5 persons)		824	2000	33r
Bride's headpiece/veil		173	1998	33r
Bride's wedding dress		859	1998	33r
Clergy, religious facility fee		242	1998	33r
Engagement ring		3177	1998	33r
Flowers		789	1998	33r
Groom's formalwear rental		99	2000	33r
Limousine		410	1998	33r
Marriage license cost		25.00	4/01	35s
Men's formalwear (ushers, best man)		469	2000	33r
Mother of bride apparel		241	2000	33r
Music		866	1998	33r
Photography and videography		1368	1998	33r
Rehearsal dinner		728	1998	33r
Wedding invitations and announcements		341	1998	33r

Values are in dollars or fractions of dollars. In the column headed *Ref*, references are shown to sources. Each reference is followed by a letter. These refer to the geographical level for which data were reported: s=State, r=Region, and c=City or metro. The abbreviation *ex* is used to mean *except* or *excluding*; *exp* stands for expenditures. For other abbreviations and further explanations, please see the Introduction.

New Bedford, MA - continued

Item	Per	Value	Date	Ref.
Weddings				
Wedding reception		7968	2000	33r
Wedding rings (bride and groom)		1060	1998	33r

New Haven-Meriden, CT

Item	Per	Value	Date	Ref.
Average annual expenditures	yr	37971	1999	30r
Alcoholic Beverages				
Alcoholic beverage purchases	yr	368	1999	30r
Wine, red and white table, all sizes, any origin	liter	9.64	7/01	11r
Appliances				
Major appliances, expenditures on	yr	194	1999	30r
Small appliances, housewares, expenditures on	yr	93	1999	30r
Banking and Money				
Mortgage interest and charges paid	yr	2622	1999	30r
Mortgage principal paid on owned property	yr	1262	1999	30r
Vehicle finance charges paid	yr	240	1999	30r
Charity				
Cash contributions, expenditures	yr	1001	1999	30r
Child Care				
Child raising cost, total, age 0-2	yr	8670	1999	60r
Child raising cost, total, age 3-5	yr	8910	1999	60r
Child raising cost, total, age 6-8	yr	9040	1999	60r
Child raising cost, total, age 9-11	yr	9100	1999	60r
Child raising cost, total, age 12-14	yr	9890	1999	60r
Child raising cost, total, age 15-17	yr	10010	1999	60r
Child's child care and education, age 0-2	yr	1070	1999	60r
Child's child care and education, age 3-5	yr	1190	1999	60r
Child's child care and education, age 6-8	yr	740	1999	60r
Child's child care and education, age 9-11	yr	470	1999	60r
Child's child care and education, age 12-14	yr	350	1999	60r
Child's child care and education, age 15-17	yr	590	1999	60r
Child's clothing, age 0-2	yr	480	1999	60r
Child's clothing, age 3-5	yr	470	1999	60r
Child's clothing, age 6-8	yr	520	1999	60r
Child's clothing, age 9-11	yr	570	1999	60r
Child's clothing, age 12-14	yr	970	1999	60r
Child's clothing, age 15-17	yr	870	1999	60r
Child's food, age 0-2	yr	1130	1999	60r
Child's food, age 3-5	yr	1290	1999	60r
Child's food, age 6-8	yr	1640	1999	60r
Child's food, age 9-11	yr	1930	1999	60r
Child's food, age 12-14	yr	1940	1999	60r
Child's food, age 15-17	yr	2150	1999	60r
Child's health care, age 0-2	yr	550	1999	60r
Child's health care, age 3-5	yr	530	1999	60r
Child's health care, age 6-8	yr	610	1999	60r
Child's health care, age 9-11	yr	650	1999	60r
Child's health care, age 12-14	yr	660	1999	60r
Child's health care, age 15-17	yr	690	1999	60r
Child's housing, age 0-2	yr	3555	1999	60r
Child's housing, age 3-5	yr	3530	1999	60r
Child's housing, age 6-8	yr	3490	1999	60r
Child's housing, age 9-11	yr	3340	1999	60r
Child's housing, age 12-14	yr	3530	1999	60r
Child's housing, age 15-17	yr	3140	1999	60r
Child's personal care, reading, age 0-2	yr	920	1999	60r
Child's personal care, reading, age 3-5	yr	950	1999	60r
Child's personal care, reading, age 6-8	yr	980	1999	60r
Child's personal care, reading, age 9-11	yr	1020	1999	60r
Child's personal care, reading, age 12-14	yr	1190	1999	60r
Child's personal care, reading, age 15-17	yr	970	1999	60r
Clothing				
Apparel and services purchases	yr	1831	1999	30r
Boys, 2 to 15, expenditures on	yr	92	1999	30r
Children under 2, expenditures on	yr	63	1999	30r
Footwear, expenditures on	yr	300	1999	30r

Item	Per	Value	Date	Ref.
Clothing - continued				
Girls, 2 to 15, expenditures on	yr	101	1999	30r
Men and boys, expenditures on	yr	446	1999	30r
Men, 16 and over, expenditures on	yr	354	1999	30r
Women, 16 and over, expenditures on	yr	584	1999	30r
Communications				
Cable modem installation, AT&T-BIS		150.00	6/99	103s
Cable modem installation, Cablevision Systems		150.00	6/99	103s
Cable modem installation, Cox		99.00-174.95	6/99	103s
Cable modem installation, Media One		100.00	6/99	103s
Cable modem rate, cable subscriber, AT&T-BIS	mos	39.95	6/99	103s
Cable modem rate, cable subscriber, Cablevision Systems	mos	44.95	6/99	103s
Cable modem rate, cable subscriber, Cox	mos	29.95-44.95	6/99	103s
Cable modem rate, cable subscriber, Media One	mos	34.95-39.95	6/99	103s
Cable modem rate, non-cable subscriber, Cablevision Systems	mos	54.95	6/99	103s
Cable modem rate, non-cable subscriber, Cox	mos	42.95-54.95	6/99	103s
Cable modem rate, non-cable subscriber, Media One	mos	49.95	6/99	103s
Phone line, single, business, field visit	inst.	65.00	12/97	17s
Phone line, single, business, no field visit	inst.	65.00	12/97	17s
Phone line, single, residence, field visit	inst.	45.00	12/97	17s
Phone line, single, residence, no field visit	inst.	45.00	12/97	17s
Postage and stationery, expenditures on	yr	138	1999	30r
Postal rate, express mail, up to half-pound		12.45	7/01	108r
Postal rate, letter, first class, first ounce		0.34	7/01	108r
Postal rate, letter, two ounces		0.57	7/01	108r
Postal rate, post card		0.21	7/01	108r
Postal rate, priority mail, two pounds		3.95	7/01	108r
Postal rate, priority mail, up to one pound		3.50	7/01	108r
Telephone services, expenditures on	yr	830	1999	30r
Education				
Board, 4-year private college/university	yr	2744	1996	38s
Board, 4-year public college/university	yr	2299	1996	38s
Education expenditures	yr	877	1999	30r
Room, 4-year private college/university	yr	3621	1996	38s
Room, 4-year public college/university	yr	2609	1996	38s
Total cost, 4-year private college/university	yr	23011	1996	38s
Total cost, 4-year public college/university	yr	8753	1996	38s
Tuition, 2-year public college/university, in state	yr	1646	1996	38s
Tuition, 4-year private college/university, in state	yr	16646	1996	38s
Tuition, 4-year public college/university	yr	3845	1996	38s
Energy and Fuels				
Electricity	KWh	0.12	7/01	11r
Fuel oil #2	gal	1.31	7/01	11r
Fuel oil and other fuels, expenditures on	yr	207	1999	30r
Gas, natural, commercial rate	1000 cf	7.08	11/00	88s
Gasoline, all types	gal	1.80	7/01	11r
Gasoline, unleaded midgrade	gal	1.85	7/01	11r
Gasoline, unleaded premium	gal	1.91	7/01	11r
Gasoline, unleaded regular	gal	1.71	7/01	11r
Natural gas, expenditures on	yr	368	1999	30r
Utility (piped) gas, therm		1.08	7/01	11r
Utility (piped) gas, 40 therms		50.87	7/01	11r
Utility (piped) gas, 100 therms		111.06	7/01	11r
Entertainment				
Entertainment purchases	yr	1821	1999	30r
Fees and admissions paid	yr	511	1999	30r
Hockey equipment, girls' hockey		800	2001	101s
Television, radios, sound equipment, expenditures on	yr	650	1999	30r

Values are in dollars or fractions of dollars. In the column headed *Ref*, references are shown to sources. Each reference is followed by a letter. These refer to the geographical level for which data were reported: s=State, r=Region, and c=City or metro. The abbreviation *ex* is used to mean *except* or *excluding*; *exp* stands for *expenditures*. For other abbreviations and further explanations, please see the Introduction.

New Haven-Meriden, CT - continued

Item	Per	Value	Date	Ref.
Funerals				
Total cost of funeral		5776.91	1/99	78r
Acknowledgement cards		14.47	1/99	78r
Casket		2090.19	1/99	78r
Cosmetology, hair, other preparation		132.92	1/99	78r
Embalming		377.33	1/99	78r
Funeral at funeral home		352.43	1/99	78r
Hearse (local)		185.55	1/99	78r
Professional service charges		1289.95	1/99	78r
Service car/van		87.42	1/99	78r
Transfer of remains to funeral home		175.48	1/99	78r
Vault		729.40	1/99	78r
Visitation/viewing		341.76	1/99	78r
Groceries				
Apples, red delicious	lb	0.95	7/01	11r
Bacon, sliced	lb	3.44	7/01	11r
Bakery products, expenditures on	yr	310	1999	30r
Bananas	lb	0.55	7/01	11r
Beef, expenditures on	yr	236	1999	30r
Bread, white, pan	lb	1.09	7/01	11r
Butter, yoghurt, cheese, etc, expenditures on	yr	214	1999	30r
Cereals and bakery product purchases	yr	474	1999	30r
Cereals and cereal products, expenditures on	yr	164	1999	30r
Chicken legs, bone-in	lb	1.23	7/01	11r
Chicken, fresh, whole	lb	1.13	7/01	11r
Chuck roast, U.S. choice, boneless	lb	2.79	7/01	11r
Coffee, 100%, ground roast, all sizes	lb	3.40	7/01	11r
Dairy product purchases	yr	342	1999	30r
Eggs, expenditures on	yr	34	1999	30r
Eggs, grade A, large	dozen	0.82	7/01	11r
Fats and oils, expenditures on	yr	80	1999	30r
Fish and seafood, expenditures on	yr	123	1999	30r
Food (excl fruit and vegetables), eaten at home, purchases	yr	838	1999	30r
Food cooked on trips, expenditures on	yr	48	1999	30r
Food purchases	yr	5314	1999	30r
Food purchases, eaten away from home	yr	2313	1999	30r
Food purchases, food eaten at home	yr	3001	1999	30r
Fresh fruits, expenditures on	yr	169	1999	30r
Fresh milk and cream, expenditures on	yr	128	1999	30r
Fresh vegetables, expenditures on	yr	164	1999	30r
Grapefruit	lb	0.67	7/01	11r
Grapes, Thompson, seedless	lb	2.18	7/01	11r
Ground beef, lean and extra lean	lb	2.66	7/01	11r
Ground chuck, 100% beef	lb	2.04	7/01	11r
Lettuce, iceberg	lb	0.76	7/01	11r
Meats, poultry, fish, and egg purchases	yr	808	1999	30r
Nonalcoholic beverages, expenditures on	yr	225	1999	30r
Orange juice, frozen concentrate	16 oz	1.88	7/01	11r
Oranges, Navel	lb	0.79	7/01	11r
Oranges, Valencia	lb	0.56	7/01	11r
Peaches	lb	1.16	7/01	11r
Peanut butter, creamy, all sizes	lb	2.01	7/01	11r
Pears, Anjou	lb	1.16	7/01	11r
Pork chops, center cut, bone-in	lb	3.57	7/01	11r
Pork, expenditures on	yr	146	1999	30r
Potato chips	16 oz	3.37	7/01	11r
Potatoes, white, all types	lb	0.42	7/01	11r
Poultry, expenditures on	yr	158	1999	30r
Processed fruits, expenditures on	yr	124	1999	30r
Processed vegetables, expenditures on	yr	82	1999	30r
Round roast, U.S. choice, boneless	lb	3.04	7/01	11r
Spaghetti and macaroni	lb	1.04	7/01	11r
Steak, sirloin, U.S. choice, boneless	lb	5.39	7/01	11r
Strawberries, dry pint	12 oz	1.51	7/01	11r
Sugar and other sweets, expenditures on	yr	110	1999	30r
Sugar, white, 33-80 ounce package	lb	0.46	7/01	11r
Sugar, white, all sizes	lb	0.47	7/01	11r
Tobacco products and smoking supplies purchases	yr	309	1999	30r
Yogurt, natural, fruit flavored	8 oz	0.79	7/01	11r

New Haven-Meriden, CT - continued

Item	Per	Value	Date	Ref.
Goods and Services				
B&B Japanese maple (acer japonicum)	gal	38.99-125.00	4/00	93r
Boxwood (buxus)	2 gal	15.99-49.95	4/00	93r
Daylily (hemerocallis)	gal	4.95	4/00	93r
Flat of annuals		8.00-14.99	4/00	93r
Fountain grass (pennisetum)	gal	6.99-9.99	4/00	93r
Hanging basket (10 in)		12.95-19.99	4/00	93r
Hardy geranium (geranium)	gal	6.95-7.99	4/00	93r
Hosta (hosta)	gal	4.95	4/00	93r
Lilac (syrubga vulgaris)	2 gal	17.99-74.95	4/00	93r
Miscellaneous purchases	yr	872	1999	30r
Rhododendron (rhododendron)	2 gal	23.99-54.95	4/00	93r
Sage (salvia)	gal	6.95-7.99	4/00	93r
Wintercreeper euonymus (euonymus fortunei)	2 gal	14.99-23.95	4/00	93r
Hunting license	yr	10.00	4/01	34s
Health Care				
Cardiac catheterization, ave hospital/ physician charges		14090	1998	77s
Childbirth, Cesarean delivery		14716	1997	13r
Childbirth, vaginal delivery		8541	1997	13r
Drugs, expenditures on	yr	296	1999	30r
Health care purchases	yr	1788	1999	30r
Health insurance expenditures	yr	875	1999	30r
Hysterectomy, laproscopically-assisted, ave hospital/physician charges		11610	1998	76s
Hysterectomy, vaginal, ave hospital and physician charges		12780	1998	76s
Medicaid dispensing fee		4.10	1999	87s
Medical services expenditures	yr	516	1999	30r
Medical supplies, expenditures on	yr	102	1999	30r
Plastic surgery, breast augmentation		4232	2000	7r
Plastic surgery, breast lift		4605	2000	7r
Plastic surgery, facelift		6964	2000	7r
Plastic surgery, hair transplantation		4193	2000	7r
Plastic surgery, lip augmentation		1675	2000	7r
Plastic surgery, lower body lift		6611	2000	7r
Plastic surgery, thigh lift		4751	2000	7r
Household Goods				
Floor coverings, expenditures on	yr	59	1999	30r
Furniture, expenditures on	yr	388	1999	30r
Household furnishings and equipment purchases	yr	1567	1999	30r
Household textiles, expenditures on	yr	112	1999	30r
Laundry and cleaning supplies, expenditures on	yr	104	1999	30r
Housing				
Home price, existing, ave		180800	10/00	90r
Home value, median		157000	2001	53s
Household operation expenditures	yr	581	1999	30r
Housekeeping supplies purchases	yr	474	1999	30r
Lodging expenditures	yr	550	1999	30r
Maintenance, repairs, insurance expenditures	yr	835	1999	30r
Monthly rental value of owned home	mos	663	1999	30r
Owned dwellings, expenditures own	yr	5209	1999	30r
Rent expenditures	yr	2390	1999	30r
Rental unit, 1 bedroom, with utilities	mos	674	4/01	41c
Rental unit, 2 bedroom, with utilities	mos	883	4/01	41c
Rental unit, 3 bedroom, with utilities	mos	1067	4/01	41c
Rental unit, 4 bedroom, with utilities	mos	1236	4/01	41c
Shelter, expenditures on	yr	8149	1999	30r

Values are in dollars or fractions of dollars. In the column headed *Ref*, references are shown to sources. Each reference is followed by a letter. These refer to the geographical level for which data were reported: s=State, r=Region, and c=City or metro. The abbreviation *ex* is used to mean *except* or *excluding*; *exp* stands for *expenditures*. For other abbreviations and further explanations, please see the Introduction.

New Haven-Meriden, CT - continued

Item	Per	Value	Date	Ref.
Insurance and Pensions				
Auto insurance premium	yr	982.00	1999	57s
Life and other personal insurance purchases	yr	424	1999	30r
Pensions and Social Security, expenditures on	yr	3037	1999	30r
Legal Fees				
Divorce, filing fee		150.00	4/01	35s
Driver's license fee	renew	28.50	1999	48s
Driver's license fee	orig	43.50	1999	48s
Personal Goods				
Personal care products and services purchases	yr	399	1999	30r
Personal Services				
Personal services, household, expenditures on	yr	271	1999	30r
Pets				
Pets, toys, and playground equipment, expenditures on	yr	325	1999	30r
Taxes				
Federal income taxes paid	yr	2606	1999	30r
Personal taxes, expenditures on	yr	3567	1999	30r
Property taxes paid	yr	1752	1999	30r
State and local income taxes paid	yr	694	1999	30r
Transportation				
Cars and trucks, new, expenditures on	yr	1496	1999	30r
Cars and trucks, used, expenditures on	yr	1251	1999	30r
Diesel at the pump	gal	1.36	10/99	73s
Gasoline and motor oil purchases	yr	901	1999	30r
Gasoline before-tax price (cents)	gal	117.10	10/00	43s
Maintenance and repair expenditures	yr	618	1999	30r
Public transportation, expenditures on	yr	575	1999	30r
Transportation purchases	yr	6503	1999	30r
Vehicle expenses, miscellaneous, purchases	yr	2266	1999	30r
Vehicle insurance payments	yr	824	1999	30r
Vehicle purchases (net outlay)	yr	2761	1999	30r
Vehicle rental, lease expenditures	yr	584	1999	30r
Utilities				
Electrical bill, average	mos	81.50	9/00	9s
Electricity, expenditures on	yr	837	1999	30r
Electricity cost, average	KWh	9.47	9/00	9s
Utilities, fuels, and public services purchased	yr	2457	1999	30r
Water and other public services, expenditures on	yr	215	1999	30r
Weddings				
Wedding (national average cost)		19936	2000	33r
Wedding (regional average total cost)		29454	1997	110r
Attendants' gifts		321	1998	33r
Bridal attendants' apparel (5 persons)		824	2000	33r
Bride's headpiece/veil		173	1998	33r
Bride's wedding dress		859	1998	33r
Clergy, religious facility fee		242	1998	33r
Engagement ring		3177	1998	33r
Flowers		789	1998	33r
Groom's formalwear rental		99	2000	33r
Limousine		410	1998	33r
Marriage license cost		30.00	4/01	35s
Men's formalwear (ushers, best man)		469	2000	33r
Mother of bride apparel		241	2000	33r
Music		866	1998	33r
Photography and videography		1368	1998	33r
Rehearsal dinner		728	1998	33r
Wedding invitations and announcements		341	1998	33r
Wedding reception		7968	2000	33r
Wedding rings (bride and groom)		1060	1998	33r

New London-Norwich, CT

Item	Per	Value	Date	Ref.
Average annual expenditures	yr	37971	1999	30r
Alcoholic Beverages				
Alcoholic beverage purchases	yr	368	1999	30r
Wine, red and white table, all sizes, any origin	liter	9.64	7/01	11r
Appliances				
Major appliances, expenditures on	yr	194	1999	30r
Small appliances, housewares, expenditures on	yr	93	1999	30r
Banking and Money				
Mortgage interest and charges paid	yr	2622	1999	30r
Mortgage principal paid on owned property	yr	1262	1999	30r
Vehicle finance charges paid	yr	240	1999	30r
Charity				
Cash contributions, expenditures	yr	1001	1999	30r
Child Care				
Child raising cost, total, age 0-2	yr	8670	1999	60r
Child raising cost, total, age 3-5	yr	8910	1999	60r
Child raising cost, total, age 6-8	yr	9040	1999	60r
Child raising cost, total, age 9-11	yr	9100	1999	60r
Child raising cost, total, age 12-14	yr	9890	1999	60r
Child raising cost, total, age 15-17	yr	10010	1999	60r
Child's child care and education, age 0-2	yr	1070	1999	60r
Child's child care and education, age 3-5	yr	1190	1999	60r
Child's child care and education, age 6-8	yr	740	1999	60r
Child's child care and education, age 9-11	yr	470	1999	60r
Child's child care and education, age 12-14	yr	350	1999	60r
Child's child care and education, age 15-17	yr	590	1999	60r
Child's clothing, age 0-2	yr	480	1999	60r
Child's clothing, age 3-5	yr	470	1999	60r
Child's clothing, age 6-8	yr	520	1999	60r
Child's clothing, age 9-11	yr	570	1999	60r
Child's clothing, age 12-14	yr	970	1999	60r
Child's clothing, age 15-17	yr	870	1999	60r
Child's food, age 0-2	yr	1130	1999	60r
Child's food, age 3-5	yr	1290	1999	60r
Child's food, age 6-8	yr	1640	1999	60r
Child's food, age 9-11	yr	1930	1999	60r
Child's food, age 12-14	yr	1940	1999	60r
Child's food, age 15-17	yr	2150	1999	60r
Child's health care, age 0-2	yr	550	1999	60r
Child's health care, age 3-5	yr	530	1999	60r
Child's health care, age 6-8	yr	610	1999	60r
Child's health care, age 9-11	yr	650	1999	60r
Child's health care, age 12-14	yr	660	1999	60r
Child's health care, age 15-17	yr	690	1999	60r
Child's housing, age 0-2	yr	3555	1999	60r
Child's housing, age 3-5	yr	3530	1999	60r
Child's housing, age 6-8	yr	3490	1999	60r
Child's housing, age 9-11	yr	3340	1999	60r
Child's housing, age 12-14	yr	3530	1999	60r
Child's housing, age 15-17	yr	3140	1999	60r
Child's personal care, reading, age 0-2	yr	920	1999	60r
Child's personal care, reading, age 3-5	yr	950	1999	60r
Child's personal care, reading, age 6-8	yr	980	1999	60r
Child's personal care, reading, age 9-11	yr	1020	1999	60r
Child's personal care, reading, age 12-14	yr	1190	1999	60r
Child's personal care, reading, age 15-17	yr	970	1999	60r
Clothing				
Apparel and services purchases	yr	1831	1999	30r
Boys, 2 to 15, expenditures on	yr	92	1999	30r
Children under 2, expenditures on	yr	63	1999	30r
Footwear, expenditures on	yr	300	1999	30r
Girls, 2 to 15, expenditures on	yr	101	1999	30r
Men and boys, expenditures on	yr	446	1999	30r
Men, 16 and over, expenditures on	yr	354	1999	30r
Women, 16 and over, expenditures on	yr	584	1999	30r
Communications				
Cable modem installation, AT&T-BIS		150.00	6/99	103s

Values are in dollars or fractions of dollars. In the column headed *Ref*, references are shown to sources. Each reference is followed by a letter. These refer to the geographical level for which data were reported: s=State, r=Region, and c=City or metro. The abbreviation *ex* is used to mean *except* or *excluding*; *exp* stands for *expenditures*. For other abbreviations and further explanations, please see the Introduction.

New London-Norwich, CT - continued

Item	Per	Value	Date	Ref.
Communications				
Cable modem installation, Cablevision Systems		150.00	6/99	103s
Cable modem installation, Cox		99.00-174.95	6/99	103s
Cable modem installation, Media One		100.00	6/99	103s
Cable modem rate, cable subscriber, AT&T-BIS	mos	39.95	6/99	103s
Cable modem rate, cable subscriber, Cablevision Systems	mos	44.95	6/99	103s
Cable modem rate, cable subscriber, Cox	mos	29.95-44.95	6/99	103s
Cable modem rate, cable subscriber, Media One	mos	34.95-39.95	6/99	103s
Cable modem rate, non-cable subscriber, Cablevision Systems	mos	54.95	6/99	103s
Cable modem rate, non-cable subscriber, Cox	mos	42.95-54.95	6/99	103s
Cable modem rate, non-cable subscriber, Media One	mos	49.95	6/99	103s
Phone line, single, business, field visit	inst.	65.00	12/97	17s
Phone line, single, business, no field visit	inst.	65.00	12/97	17s
Phone line, single, residence, field visit	inst.	45.00	12/97	17s
Phone line, single, residence, no field visit	inst.	45.00	12/97	17s
Postage and stationery, expenditures on	yr	138	1999	30r
Postal rate, express mail, up to half-pound		12.45	7/01	108r
Postal rate, letter, first class, first ounce		0.34	7/01	108r
Postal rate, letter, two ounces		0.57	7/01	108r
Postal rate, post card		0.21	7/01	108r
Postal rate, priority mail, two pounds		3.95	7/01	108r
Postal rate, priority mail, up to one pound		3.50	7/01	108r
Telephone services, expenditures on	yr	830	1999	30r
Education				
Board, 4-year private college/university	yr	2744	1996	38s
Board, 4-year public college/university	yr	2299	1996	38s
Education expenditures	yr	877	1999	30r
Room, 4-year private college/university	yr	3621	1996	38s
Room, 4-year public college/university	yr	2609	1996	38s
Total cost, 4-year private college/university	yr	23011	1996	38s
Total cost, 4-year public college/university	yr	8753	1996	38s
Tuition, 2-year public college/university, in state	yr	1646	1996	38s
Tuition, 4-year private college/university, in state	yr	16646	1996	38s
Tuition, 4-year public college/university	yr	3845	1996	38s
Energy and Fuels				
Electricity	KWh	0.12	7/01	11r
Fuel oil #2	gal	1.31	7/01	11r
Fuel oil and other fuels, expenditures on	yr	207	1999	30r
Gas, natural, commercial rate	1000 cf	7.08	11/00	88s
Gasoline, all types	gal	1.80	7/01	11r
Gasoline, unleaded midgrade	gal	1.85	7/01	11r
Gasoline, unleaded premium	gal	1.91	7/01	11r
Gasoline, unleaded regular	gal	1.71	7/01	11r
Natural gas, expenditures on	yr	368	1999	30r
Utility (piped) gas, therm		1.08	7/01	11r
Utility (piped) gas, 40 therms		50.87	7/01	11r
Utility (piped) gas, 100 therms		111.06	7/01	11r
Entertainment				
Entertainment purchases	yr	1821	1999	30r
Fees and admissions paid	yr	511	1999	30r
Hockey equipment, girls' hockey		800	2001	101s
Television, radios, sound equipment, expenditures on	yr	650	1999	30r
Funerals				
Total cost of funeral		5776.91	1/99	78r
Acknowledgement cards		14.47	1/99	78r
Casket		2090.19	1/99	78r
Cosmetology, hair, other preparation		132.92	1/99	78r
Embalming		377.33	1/99	78r
Funeral at funeral home		352.43	1/99	78r

New London-Norwich, CT - continued

Item	Per	Value	Date	Ref.
Funerals - continued				
Hearse (local)		185.55	1/99	78r
Professional service charges		1289.95	1/99	78r
Service car/van		87.42	1/99	78r
Transfer of remains to funeral home		175.48	1/99	78r
Vault		729.40	1/99	78r
Visitation/viewing		341.76	1/99	78r
Groceries				
Apples, red delicious	lb	0.95	7/01	11r
Bacon, sliced	lb	3.44	7/01	11r
Bakery products, expenditures on	yr	310	1999	30r
Bananas	lb	0.55	7/01	11r
Beef, expenditures on	yr	236	1999	30r
Bread, white, pan	lb	1.09	7/01	11r
Butter, yoghurt, cheese, etc, expenditures on	yr	214	1999	30r
Cereals and bakery product purchases	yr	474	1999	30r
Cereals and cereal products, expenditures on	yr	164	1999	30r
Chicken legs, bone-in	lb	1.23	7/01	11r
Chicken, fresh, whole	lb	1.13	7/01	11r
Chuck roast, U.S. choice, boneless	lb	2.79	7/01	11r
Coffee, 100%, ground roast, all sizes	lb	3.40	7/01	11r
Dairy product purchases	yr	342	1999	30r
Eggs, expenditures on	yr	34	1999	30r
Eggs, grade A, large	dozen	0.82	7/01	11r
Fats and oils, expenditures on	yr	80	1999	30r
Fish and seafood, expenditures on	yr	123	1999	30r
Food (excl fruit and vegetables), eaten at home, purchases	yr	838	1999	30r
Food cooked on trips, expenditures on	yr	48	1999	30r
Food purchases	yr	5314	1999	30r
Food purchases, eaten away from home	yr	2313	1999	30r
Food purchases, food eaten at home	yr	3001	1999	30r
Fresh fruits, expenditures on	yr	169	1999	30r
Fresh milk and cream, expenditures on	yr	128	1999	30r
Fresh vegetables, expenditures on	yr	164	1999	30r
Grapefruit	lb	0.67	7/01	11r
Grapes, Thompson, seedless	lb	2.18	7/01	11r
Ground beef, lean and extra lean	lb	2.66	7/01	11r
Ground chuck, 100% beef	lb	2.04	7/01	11r
Lettuce, iceberg	lb	0.76	7/01	11r
Meats, poultry, fish, and egg purchases	yr	808	1999	30r
Nonalcoholic beverages, expenditures on	yr	225	1999	30r
Orange juice, frozen concentrate	16 oz	1.88	7/01	11r
Oranges, Navel	lb	0.79	7/01	11r
Oranges, Valencia	lb	0.56	7/01	11r
Peaches	lb	1.16	7/01	11r
Peanut butter, creamy, all sizes	lb	2.01	7/01	11r
Pears, Anjou	lb	1.16	7/01	11r
Pork chops, center cut, bone-in	lb	3.57	7/01	11r
Pork, expenditures on	yr	146	1999	30r
Potato chips	16 oz	3.37	7/01	11r
Potatoes, white, all types	lb	0.42	7/01	11r
Poultry, expenditures on	yr	158	1999	30r
Processed fruits, expenditures on	yr	124	1999	30r
Processed vegetables, expenditures on	yr	82	1999	30r
Round roast, U.S. choice, boneless	lb	3.04	7/01	11r
Spaghetti and macaroni	lb	1.04	7/01	11r
Steak, sirloin, U.S. choice, boneless	lb	5.39	7/01	11r
Strawberries, dry pint	12 oz	1.51	7/01	11r
Sugar and other sweets, expenditures on	yr	110	1999	30r
Sugar, white, 33-80 ounce package	lb	0.46	7/01	11r
Sugar, white, all sizes	lb	0.47	7/01	11r
Tobacco products and smoking supplies purchases	yr	309	1999	30r
Yogurt, natural, fruit flavored	8 oz	0.79	7/01	11r
Goods and Services				
B&B Japanese maple (acer japonicum)	gal	38.99-125.00	4/00	93r
Boxwood (buxus)	2 gal	15.99-49.95	4/00	93r
Daylily (hemerocallis)	gal	4.95	4/00	93r

Values are in dollars or fractions of dollars. In the column headed *Ref*, references are shown to sources. Each reference is followed by a letter. These refer to the geographical level for which data were reported: s=State, r=Region, and c=City or metro. The abbreviation *ex* is used to mean *except* or *excluding*; *exp* stands for expenditures. For other abbreviations and further explanations, please see the Introduction.

New London-Norwich, CT - continued

Item	Per	Value	Date	Ref.
Goods and Services				
Flat of annuals		8.00-14.99	4/00	93r
Fountain grass (pennisetum)	gal	6.99-9.99	4/00	93r
Hanging basket (10 in)		12.95-19.99	4/00	93r
Hardy geranium (geranium)	gal	6.95-7.99	4/00	93r
Hosta (hosta)	gal	4.95	4/00	93r
Lilac (syrubga vulgaris)	2 gal	17.99-74.95	4/00	93r
Miscellaneous purchases	yr	872	1999	30r
Rhododendron (rhododendron)	2 gal	23.99-54.95	4/00	93r
Sage (salvia)	gal	6.95-7.99	4/00	93r
Wintercreeper euonymus (euonymus fortunei)	2 gal	14.99-23.95	4/00	93r
Hunting license	yr	10.00	4/01	34s
Health Care				
Cardiac catheterization, ave hospital/ physician charges		14090	1998	77s
Childbirth, Cesarean delivery		14716	1997	13r
Childbirth, vaginal delivery		8541	1997	13r
Drugs, expenditures on	yr	296	1999	30r
Health care purchases	yr	1788	1999	30r
Health insurance expenditures	yr	875	1999	30r
Hysterectomy, laproscopically-assisted, ave hospital/physician charges		11610	1998	76s
Hysterectomy, vaginal, ave hospital and physician charges		12780	1998	76s
Medicaid dispensing fee		4.10	1999	87s
Medical services expenditures	yr	516	1999	30r
Medical supplies, expenditures on	yr	102	1999	30r
Plastic surgery, breast augmentation		4232	2000	7r
Plastic surgery, breast lift		4605	2000	7r
Plastic surgery, facelift		6964	2000	7r
Plastic surgery, hair transplantation		4193	2000	7r
Plastic surgery, lip augmentation		1675	2000	7r
Plastic surgery, lower body lift		6611	2000	7r
Plastic surgery, thigh lift		4751	2000	7r
Household Goods				
Floor coverings, expenditures on	yr	59	1999	30r
Furniture, expenditures on	yr	388	1999	30r
Household furnishings and equipment purchases	yr	1567	1999	30r
Household textiles, expenditures on	yr	112	1999	30r
Laundry and cleaning supplies, expenditures on	yr	104	1999	30r
Housing				
Home price, existing, ave		180800	10/00	90r
Home value, median		157000	2001	53s
Household operation expenditures	yr	581	1999	30r
Housekeeping supplies purchases	yr	474	1999	30r
Lodging expenditures	yr	550	1999	30r
Maintenance, repairs, insurance expenditures	yr	835	1999	30r
Monthly rental value of owned home	mos	663	1999	30r
Owned dwellings, expenditures own	yr	5209	1999	30r
Rent expenditures	yr	2390	1999	30r
Rental unit, 1 bedroom, with utilities	mos	606	4/01	41c
Rental unit, 2 bedroom, with utilities	mos	738	4/01	41c
Rental unit, 3 bedroom, with utilities	mos	923	4/01	41c
Rental unit, 4 bedroom, with utilities	mos	1055	4/01	41c
Shelter, expenditures on	yr	8149	1999	30r
Insurance and Pensions				
Auto insurance premium	yr	982.00	1999	57s
Life and other personal insurance purchases	yr	424	1999	30r
Pensions and Social Security, expenditures on	yr	3037	1999	30r

New London-Norwich, CT - continued

Item	Per	Value	Date	Ref.
Legal Fees				
Divorce, filing fee		150.00	4/01	35s
Driver's license fee	renew	28.50	1999	48s
Driver's license fee	orig	43.50	1999	48s
Personal Goods				
Personal care products and services purchases	yr	399	1999	30r
Personal Services				
Personal services, household, expenditures on	yr	271	1999	30r
Pets				
Pets, toys, and playground equipment, expenditures on	yr	325	1999	30r
Taxes				
Federal income taxes paid	yr	2606	1999	30r
Personal taxes, expenditures on	yr	3567	1999	30r
Property taxes paid	yr	1752	1999	30r
State and local income taxes paid	yr	694	1999	30r
Transportation				
Cars and trucks, new, expenditures on	yr	1496	1999	30r
Cars and trucks, used, expenditures on	yr	1251	1999	30r
Diesel at the pump	gal	1.36	10/99	73s
Gasoline and motor oil purchases	yr	901	1999	30r
Gasoline before-tax price (cents)	gal	117.10	10/00	43s
Maintenance and repair expenditures	yr	618	1999	30r
Public transportation, expenditures on	yr	575	1999	30r
Transportation purchases	yr	6503	1999	30r
Vehicle expenses, miscellaneous, purchases	yr	2266	1999	30r
Vehicle insurance payments	yr	824	1999	30r
Vehicle purchases (net outlay)	yr	2761	1999	30r
Vehicle rental, lease expenditures	yr	584	1999	30r
Utilities				
Electrical bill, average	mos	81.50	9/00	9s
Electricity, expenditures on	yr	837	1999	30r
Electricity cost, average	KWh	9.47	9/00	9s
Utilities, fuels, and public services purchased	yr	2457	1999	30r
Water and other public services, expenditures on	yr	215	1999	30r
Weddings				
Wedding (national average cost)		19936	2000	33r
Wedding (regional average total cost)		29454	1997	110r
Attendants' gifts		321	1998	33r
Bridal attendants' apparel (5 persons)		824	2000	33r
Bride's headpiece/veil		173	1998	33r
Bride's wedding dress		859	1998	33r
Clergy, religious facility fee		242	1998	33r
Engagement ring		3177	1998	33r
Flowers		789	1998	33r
Groom's formalwear rental		99	2000	33r
Limousine		410	1998	33r
Marriage license cost		30.00	4/01	35s
Men's formalwear (ushers, best man)		469	2000	33r
Mother of bride apparel		241	2000	33r
Music		866	1998	33r
Photography and videography		1368	1998	33r
Rehearsal dinner		728	1998	33r
Wedding invitations and announcements		341	1998	33r
Wedding reception		7968	2000	33r
Wedding rings (bride and groom)		1060	1998	33r

New York, NY

Item	Per	Value	Date	Ref.
Average annual expenditures	yr	37971	1999	30r
Composite, ACCRA index		239.20	3/01	4c
Alcoholic Beverages				
Alcoholic beverage purchases	yr	405	1999	30c
Beer, Heineken, 12-oz, ex deposit	6	7.69	3/01	4c
J & B Scotch	750-ml	19.98	3/01	4c

Values are in dollars or fractions of dollars. In the column headed *Ref*, references are shown to sources. Each reference is followed by a letter. These refer to the geographical level for which data were reported: s=State, r=Region, and c=City or metro. The abbreviation *ex* is used to mean *except* or *excluding*; *exp* stands for expenditures. For other abbreviations and further explanations, please see the Introduction.

New York, NY - continued

Item	Per	Value	Date	Ref.
Alcoholic Beverages				
Wine, Livingston or Gallo, Chablis blanc	1.5 liter	6.59	3/01	4c
Wine, red and white table, all sizes, any origin	liter	9.64	7/01	11r
Appliances				
Appliance repair, service call, washing machine	min lab chg	74.97	3/01	4c
Major appliances, expenditures on	yr	194	1999	30r
Small appliances, housewares, expenditures on	yr	93	1999	30r
Banking and Money				
Mortgage interest and charges paid	yr	2622	1999	30r
Mortgage principal paid on owned property	yr	1262	1999	30r
Mortgage rate, incl. points and orig. fee, 30-yr. conv. fixed or ARM	mos	7.24	3/01	4c
Vehicle finance charges paid	yr	240	1999	30r
Business Expenses				
Business travel, car rental	day	83	2001	3c
Business travel, food	day	88	2001	3c
Business travel, hotel	day	237	2001	3c
Medical office space cost	sq ft	161.20	2001	31c
Office space, 2-4 storey building	sq ft	141.23	2001	31c
Office space, 5-10 storey building	sq ft	124.75	2001	31c
Office space, 11-20 storey building	sq ft	119.91	2001	31c
Charity				
Cash contributions, expenditures	yr	1022	1999	30c
Child Care				
Child raising cost, total, age 0-2	yr	8670	1999	60r
Child raising cost, total, age 3-5	yr	8910	1999	60r
Child raising cost, total, age 6-8	yr	9040	1999	60r
Child raising cost, total, age 9-11	yr	9100	1999	60r
Child raising cost, total, age 12-14	yr	9890	1999	60r
Child raising cost, total, age 15-17	yr	10010	1999	60r
Child's child care and education, age 0-2	yr	1070	1999	60r
Child's child care and education, age 3-5	yr	1190	1999	60r
Child's child care and education, age 6-8	yr	740	1999	60r
Child's child care and education, age 9-11	yr	470	1999	60r
Child's child care and education, age 12-14	yr	350	1999	60r
Child's child care and education, age 15-17	yr	590	1999	60r
Child's clothing, age 0-2	yr	480	1999	60r
Child's clothing, age 3-5	yr	470	1999	60r
Child's clothing, age 6-8	yr	520	1999	60r
Child's clothing, age 9-11	yr	570	1999	60r
Child's clothing, age 12-14	yr	970	1999	60r
Child's clothing, age 15-17	yr	870	1999	60r
Child's food, age 0-2	yr	1130	1999	60r
Child's food, age 3-5	yr	1290	1999	60r
Child's food, age 6-8	yr	1640	1999	60r
Child's food, age 9-11	yr	1930	1999	60r
Child's food, age 12-14	yr	1940	1999	60r
Child's food, age 15-17	yr	2150	1999	60r
Child's health care, age 0-2	yr	550	1999	60r
Child's health care, age 3-5	yr	530	1999	60r
Child's health care, age 6-8	yr	610	1999	60r
Child's health care, age 9-11	yr	650	1999	60r
Child's health care, age 12-14	yr	660	1999	60r
Child's health care, age 15-17	yr	690	1999	60r
Child's housing, age 0-2	yr	3555	1999	60r
Child's housing, age 3-5	yr	3530	1999	60r
Child's housing, age 6-8	yr	3490	1999	60r
Child's housing, age 9-11	yr	3340	1999	60r
Child's housing, age 12-14	yr	3530	1999	60r
Child's housing, age 15-17	yr	3140	1999	60r
Child's personal care, reading, age 0-2	yr	920	1999	60r
Child's personal care, reading, age 3-5	yr	950	1999	60r
Child's personal care, reading, age 6-8	yr	980	1999	60r
Child's personal care, reading, age 9-11	yr	1020	1999	60r
Child's personal care, reading, age 12-14	yr	1190	1999	60r
Child's personal care, reading, age 15-17	yr	970	1999	60r
Daycare	mos	661	1998	37c

New York, NY - continued

Item	Per	Value	Date	Ref.
Child Care - continued				
Daycare, 3-year old, 5 days, 8 hrs/day	mos	661	1998	85c
Nannies: criminal background check		74	1998	84s
Clothing				
Apparel and services purchases	yr	2327	1999	30c
Boys' brief, cotton	3	6.12	3/01	4c
Boys, 2 to 15, expenditures on	yr	92	1999	30r
Children under 2, expenditures on	yr	63	1999	30r
Footwear, expenditures on	yr	300	1999	30r
Girls, 2 to 15, expenditures on	yr	101	1999	30r
Men and boys, expenditures on	yr	446	1999	30r
Men, 16 and over, expenditures on	yr	354	1999	30r
Shirt, man's dress shirt		30.96	3/01	4c
Slacks, man's "No Wrinkles" khaki		52.48	3/01	4c
Women, 16 and over, expenditures on	yr	584	1999	30r
Communications				
Cable modem installation, Adelphi		54.90	6/99	103s
Cable modem installation, Cablevision Systems		150.00	6/99	103s
Cable modem installation, Time Warner		75.00-225.00	6/99	103s
Cable modem rate, cable subscriber, Adelphi	mos	34.95	6/99	103s
Cable modem rate, cable subscriber, Cablevision Systems	mos	44.95	6/99	103s
Cable modem rate, cable subscriber, Century	mos	39.95	6/99	103s
Cable modem rate, cable subscriber, Time Warner	mos	39.95-49.95	6/99	103s
Cable modem rate, non-cable subscriber, Adelphi	mos	44.95	6/99	103s
Cable modem rate, non-cable subscriber, Cablevision Systems	mos	54.95	6/99	103s
Cable modem rate, non-cable subscriber, Time Warner	mos	39.95-54.95	6/99	103s
Cellular phone service	mos	40.71	2/01	55c
Newspaper subscription, daily and Sunday delivery	mos	31.31	3/01	4c
Phone line, single, business, field visit	inst.	142.76	12/97	17s
Phone line, single, business, no field visit	inst.	106.05	12/97	17s
Phone line, single, residence, field visit	inst.	102.78	12/97	17s
Phone line, single, residence, no field visit	inst.	55.00	12/97	17s
Postage and stationery, expenditures on	yr	138	1999	30r
Postal rate, express mail, up to half-pound		12.45	7/01	108r
Postal rate, letter, first class, first ounce		0.34	7/01	108r
Postal rate, letter, two ounces		0.57	7/01	108r
Postal rate, post card		0.21	7/01	108r
Postal rate, priority mail, two pounds		3.95	7/01	108r
Postal rate, priority mail, up to one pound		3.50	7/01	108r
Telephone bill, family of three	mos	24.29	3/01	4c
Telephone services, expenditures on	yr	830	1999	30r
Wireless services	mos	42.84	1/00	42c
Education				
Board, 4-year private college/university	yr	3255	1996	38s
Board, 4-year public college/university	yr	2310	1996	38s
Education expenditures	yr	975	1999	30c
Room, 4-year private college/university	yr	3724	1996	38s
Room, 4-year public college/university	yr	2937	1996	38s
Total cost, 4-year private college/university	yr	20831	1996	38s
Total cost, 4-year public college/university	yr	8960	1996	38s
Tuition, 2-year public college/university, in state	yr	2427	1996	38s
Tuition, 4-year private college/university, in state	yr	13852	1996	38s
Tuition, 4-year public college/university	yr	3714	1996	38s
Energy and Fuels				
Electricity	KWh	0.12	7/01	11r
Energy, combined forms, 2400 sq ft	mos	211.56	3/01	4c
Energy, exc. electricity, 2400 sq ft	mos	97.65	3/01	4c
Fuel oil #2	gal	1.31	7/01	11r
Fuel oil and other fuels, expenditures on	yr	207	1999	30r
Gas, cooking, winter, 10 therms	mos	19.58	2/96	98c
Gas, cooking, winter, 30 therms	mos	38.11	2/96	98c

Values are in dollars or fractions of dollars. In the column headed *Ref*, references are shown to sources. Each reference is followed by a letter. These refer to the geographical level for which data were reported: s=State, r=Region, and c=City or metro. The abbreviation *ex* is used to mean *except* or *excluding*; *exp* stands for *expenditures*. For other abbreviations and further explanations, please see the Introduction.

New York, NY - continued

Item	Per	Value	Date	Ref.
Energy and Fuels				
Gas, cooking, winter, 50 therms	mos	56.73	2/96	98c
Gas, heating, winter, average use	mos	309.05	2/96	98c
Gas, regular unleaded, cash, self-service	gal	1.64	3/01	4c
Gasoline, all types	gal	1.80	7/01	11r
Gasoline, unleaded midgrade	gal	1.85	7/01	11r
Gasoline, unleaded premium	gal	1.91	7/01	11r
Gasoline, unleaded regular	gal	1.71	7/01	11r
Natural gas, expenditures on	yr	368	1999	30r
Utility (piped) gas, therm		1.08	7/01	11r
Utility (piped) gas, 40 therms		50.87	7/01	11r
Utility (piped) gas, 100 therms		111.06	7/01	11r
Entertainment				
Bowling, Saturday evening rate	line	6.95	3/01	4c
Broadway musical ticket		60.20	2/00	91c
Broadway play ticket		47.81	2/00	91c
Broadway show		85.00	2000	61c
Broadway show ticket (average)		58.55	2/00	91c
Entertainment purchases	yr	2007	1999	30c
Fees and admissions paid	yr	511	1999	30r
Major League baseball ticket		25.12	2000	16c
Major League baseball ticket		28.90	2000	105c
Monopoly game, Parker Brothers', No. 9	game	15.65	3/01	4c
Movie ticket, evening	person	9.50	1999	104c
Movie, first-run, Saturday, evening	adm.	9.50	3/01	4c
Reading purchases	yr	216	1999	30c
Television, radios, sound equipment, expenditures on	yr	650	1999	30r
Tennis balls, yellow, Wilson or Penn, 3	can	2.42	3/01	4c
World Series ticket (Yankee Stadium box seat)		160.00	2000	61c
Funerals				
Total cost of funeral		5813.50	1/99	78r
Acknowledgement cards		28.32	1/99	78r
Casket		2082.20	1/99	78r
Cosmetology, hair, other preparation		169.59	1/99	78r
Embalming		465.60	1/99	78r
Funeral at funeral home		339.56	1/99	78r
Hearse (local)		183.96	1/99	78r
Professional service charges		1157.85	1/99	78r
Service car/van		100.41	1/99	78r
Transfer of remains to funeral home		158.66	1/99	78r
Vault		766.31	1/99	78r
Visitation/viewing		361.04	1/99	78r
Groceries				
Groceries, ACCRA Index		141.60	3/01	4c
Antibiotic ointment, Polysporin	0.5 oz	4.95	3/01	4c
Apples	pound	0.87		29c
Apples, red delicious	lb	0.95	7/01	11r
Baby food, strained vegetables or fruit, lowest price	4-4.5 oz	0.59	3/01	4c
Bacon, sliced	lb	3.44	7/01	11r
Bakery products, expenditures on	yr	310	1999	30r
Bananas	lb	0.73	3/01	4c
Bananas	lb	0.55	7/01	11r
Beef or hamburger, ground	lb	2.75	3/01	4c
Beef, expenditures on	yr	236	1999	30r
Bread, white	loaf	1.08	3/01	4c
Bread, white, pan	lb	1.09	7/01	11r
Butter, yoghurt, cheese, etc, expenditures on	yr	214	1999	30r
Cereals and bakery product purchases	yr	474	1999	30r
Cereals and cereal products, expenditures on	yr	164	1999	30r
Cheese, Kraft grated Parmesan	8 oz	5.17	3/01	4c
Chicken legs, bone-in	lb	1.23	7/01	11r
Chicken, fresh, whole	lb	1.13	7/01	11r
Chicken, whole fryer	lb	1.33	3/01	4c
Chuck roast, U.S. choice, boneless	lb	2.79	7/01	11r
Cigarettes, Winston, Kings	carton	39.34	3/01	4c
Coca cola, 2l bottle		1.45	2000	106c
Coffee, 100%, ground roast, all sizes	lb	3.40	7/01	11r
Coffee, vacuum-packed	13 oz	4.11	3/01	4c

New York, NY - continued

Item	Per	Value	Date	Ref.
Groceries - continued				
Corn Flakes, Kellogg's or Post Toasties	18 oz	3.91	3/01	4c
Corn, frozen, whole kernel, lowest price	16 oz	1.65	3/01	4c
Dairy product purchases	yr	375	1999	30c
Eggs, expenditures on	yr	34	1999	30r
Eggs, Grade A or AA	dozen	1.57	3/01	4c
Eggs, grade A, large	dozen	0.82	7/01	11r
Fats and oils, expenditures on	yr	80	1999	30r
Fish and seafood, expenditures on	yr	123	1999	30r
Food (excl fruit and vegetables), eaten at home, purchases	yr	863	1999	30c
Food cooked on trips, expenditures on	yr	48	1999	30r
Food purchases	yr	6265	1999	30c
Food purchases, eaten away from home	yr	2891	1999	30c
Food purchases, food eaten at home	yr	3374	1999	30c
Fresh fruits, expenditures on	yr	169	1999	30r
Fresh milk and cream, expenditures on	yr	128	1999	30r
Fresh vegetables, expenditures on	yr	164	1999	30r
Fruit and vegetable purchases	yr	628	1999	30c
Grapefruit	lb	0.67	7/01	11r
Grapes, Thompson, seedless	lb	2.18	7/01	11r
Ground beef, lean and extra lean	lb	2.66	7/01	11r
Ground chuck, 100% beef	lb	2.04	7/01	11r
Juice (12-oz can)		1.81	2000	106c
Lettuce, iceberg	head	1.69	3/01	4c
Lettuce, iceberg	lb	0.76	7/01	11r
Margarine, Blue Bonnet or Parkay, stick	lb	1.87	3/01	4c
Meats, poultry, fish, and egg purchases	yr	808	1999	30r
Milk, whole	1/2 gal	1.74	3/01	4c
Nonalcoholic beverages, expenditures on	yr	225	1999	30r
Orange juice, frozen concentrate	16 oz	1.88	7/01	11r
Orange juice, Minute Maid frozen	12 oz	2.19	3/01	4c
Oranges, Navel	lb	0.79	7/01	11r
Oranges, Valencia	lb	0.56	7/01	11r
Peaches	lb	1.16	7/01	11r
Peaches, halves or slices, Hunt's, Del Monte, or Libby's	29 oz	2.03	3/01	4c
Peanut butter, creamy, all sizes	lb	2.01	7/01	11r
Pears, Anjou	lb	1.16	7/01	11r
Peas, green, Del Monte or Green Giant	15 oz	1.00	3/01	4c
Pork chops, center cut, bone-in	lb	3.57	7/01	11r
Pork, expenditures on	yr	146	1999	30r
Potato chips	16 oz	3.37	7/01	11r
Potatoes, white or red	10 lb	2.39	3/01	4c
Potatoes, white, all types	lb	0.42	7/01	11r
Poultry, expenditures on	yr	158	1999	30r
Processed fruits, expenditures on	yr	124	1999	30r
Processed vegetables, expenditures on	yr	82	1999	30r
Round roast, U.S. choice, boneless	lb	3.04	7/01	11r
Sausage, Jimmy Dean/Owens pork	lb	3.04	3/01	4c
Shortening, vegetable, Crisco	3 lb	4.70	3/01	4c
Soft drink, Coca Cola, ex deposit	2 liter	1.60	3/01	4c
Spaghetti and macaroni	lb	1.04	7/01	11r
Steak, sirloin, U.S. choice, boneless	lb	5.39	7/01	11r
Steak, T-bone	lb	8.35	3/01	4c
Strawberries, dry pint	12 oz	1.51	7/01	11r
Sugar and other sweets, expenditures on	yr	110	1999	30r
Sugar, cane or beet	4 lbs	2.49	3/01	4c
Sugar, white, 33-80 ounce package	lb	0.46	7/01	11r
Sugar, white, all sizes	lb	0.47	7/01	11r
Tobacco products and smoking supplies purchases	yr	304	1999	30c
Tomatoes, Hunt's or Del Monte	14.5 oz	1.25	3/01	4c
Tuna, chunk, light	6 oz	1.42	3/01	4c
Yogurt, natural, fruit flavored	8 oz	0.79	7/01	11r
Goods and Services				
Miscellaneous goods and services, ACCRA Index		139.80	3/01	4c
B&B Japanese maple (acer japonicum)	gal	38.99-125.00	4/00	93r
Beauty session (woman's trim, shampoo, blow dry)		42.00	2000	106c

Values are in dollars or fractions of dollars. In the column headed *Ref*, references are shown to sources. Each reference is followed by a letter. These refer to the geographical level for which data were reported: s=State, r=Region, and c=City or metro. The abbreviation *ex* is used to mean *except* or *excluding*; *exp* stands for expenditures. For other abbreviations and further explanations, please see the Introduction.

New York, NY - continued

Item	Per	Value	Date	Ref.
Goods and Services				
Boxwood (buxus)	2 gal	15.99- 49.95	4/00	93r
Daylilly (hemerocallis)	gal	4.95	4/00	93r
Flat of annuals		8.00- 14.99	4/00	93r
Fountain grass (pennisetum)	gal	6.99- 9.99	4/00	93r
Hanging basket (10 in)		12.95- 19.99	4/00	93r
Hardy geranium (geranium)	gal	6.95- 7.99	4/00	93r
Hosta (hosta)	gal	4.95	4/00	93r
Lilac (syrubga vulgaris)	2 gal	17.99- 74.95	4/00	93r
Miscellaneous purchases	yr	872	1999	30r
Rhododendron (rhododendron)	2 gal	23.99- 54.95	4/00	93r
Sage (salvia)	gal	6.95- 7.99	4/00	93r
Wintercreeper euonymus (euonymus fortunei)	2 gal	14.99- 23.95	4/00	93r
Hunting license	yr	11.00	4/01	34s
Health Care				
Health care, ACCRA Index		187.90	3/01	4c
Cardiac catheterization, ave hospital/ physician charges		12750	1998	77s
Childbirth, Cesarean delivery		14716	1997	13r
Childbirth, vaginal delivery		8541	1997	13r
Dentist's fee, adult teeth cleaning and periodic oral exam	visit	114.00	3/01	4c
Doctor's fee, routine exam, established patient	visit	97.00	3/01	4c
Drugs, expenditures on	yr	296	1999	30r
Health care purchases	yr	1863	1999	30c
Health insurance expenditures	yr	875	1999	30r
Home health care aide cost, licensed agency	hour	14	2000	82c
Hospital bed, semi private room	day	1359.00	2000	106c
Hospital care, private room	day	1760.80	3/01	4c
Hysterectomy, laproscopically-assisted, ave hospital/physician charges		13460	1998	76s
Hysterectomy, vaginal, ave hospital and physician charges		10310	1998	76s
Medicaid dispensing fee		3.50- 4.50	1999	87s
Medical services expenditures	yr	516	1999	30r
Medical supplies, expenditures on	yr	102	1999	30r
Nursing home care	day	295	2000	12c
Nursing home costs, private room	day	295	2000	82c
Nursing home costs, private room	day	200	2000	82c
Nursing home stay, private room	day	295	2000	83c
Plastic surgery, breast augmentation		4232	2000	7r
Plastic surgery, breast lift		4605	2000	7r
Plastic surgery, facelift		6964	2000	7r
Plastic surgery, hair transplantation		4193	2000	7r
Plastic surgery, lip augmentation		1675	2000	7r
Plastic surgery, lower body lift		6611	2000	7r
Plastic surgery, thigh lift		4751	2000	7r
Household Goods				
Dishwashing powder, Cascade	50 oz	4.11	3/01	4c
Floor coverings, expenditures on	yr	59	1999	30r
Furniture, expenditures on	yr	388	1999	30r
Household furnishings and equipment purchases	yr	1781	1999	30c
Household textiles, expenditures on	yr	112	1999	30r
Laundry and cleaning supplies, expenditures on	yr	104	1999	30r
Tissues, facial, Kleenex brand	175	1.88	3/01	4c
Housing				
Housing, ACCRA Index		485.20	3/01	4c
Apartment rent, 2 bedroom		2920.00	2000	106c
Home, suburban, 2,200 square feet		300300	2000	23c

New York, NY - continued

Item	Per	Value	Date	Ref.
Housing - continued				
Home price, existing, ave		180800	10/00	90r
Home purchase, 2,000 sq ft		820000	11/00	111c
Home value, median		179000	2001	53s
House, 2-story, 2,400 sq ft, 2-car garage, new		245800	2000	54c
House, 2400 sq ft, 8000 sq ft lot, new, urban, utilities	total	917800	3/01	4c
House payment, principal and interest, 25% down payment	mos	4693	3/01	4c
Household operation expenditures	yr	758	1999	30c
Housekeeping supplies purchases	yr	497	1999	30c
Housing, expenditures on	yr	16180	1999	30c
Lodging expenditures	yr	550	1999	30r
Maintenance, repairs, insurance expenditures	yr	835	1999	30r
Monthly rental value of owned home	mos	663	1999	30r
Owned dwellings, expenditures own	yr	6403	1999	30c
Rent expenditures	yr	3544	1999	30c
Rent, apartment, 2 br, 1 1/2-2 baths, unfurn, 950 sq ft, water	mos	4180	3/01	4c
Rental unit, 1 bedroom, with utilities	mos	836	4/01	41c
Rental unit, 2 bedroom, with utilities	mos	949	4/01	41c
Rental unit, 3 bedroom, with utilities	mos	1187	4/01	41c
Rental unit, 4 bedroom, with utilities	mos	1330	4/01	41c
Shelter, expenditures on	yr	10552	1999	30c
Single-family home, purchase price		221500	2000	19c
Insurance and Pensions				
Auto insurance premium	yr	1113.55	1999	57s
Life and other personal insurance purchases	yr	464	1999	30c
Pensions and Social Security, expenditures on	yr	3588	1999	30c
Personal insurance and pensions, expenditures on	yr	4052	1999	30c
Legal Fees				
Divorce, filing fee		270.00	4/01	35s
Driver's license fee	orig	25.00	1999	48s
Driver's license fee	renew	25.00	1999	48s
Fishing license	yr	14.00	4/01	34s
Parking in front of hydrant, fine		55	1998	20c
Parking in loading zone, fine		55	1998	20c
Parking meter violation, fine		55	1998	20c
Personal Goods				
Personal care products and services purchases	yr	485	1999	30c
Shampoo, Alberto VO5	15 oz	2.13	3/01	4c
Toothpaste, Crest or Colgate	6-7 oz	4.22	3/01	4c
Personal Services				
Dry cleaning, man's 2-pc suit		9.25	3/01	4c
Man's haircut, barbershop, no styling		19.00	3/01	4c
Personal services, household, expenditures on	yr	271	1999	30r
Woman's shampoo, trim, blow-dry, no style- change		49.00	3/01	4c
Pets				
Pets, toys, and playground equipment, expenditures on	yr	325	1999	30r
Restaurant Food				
Cheeseburger, 1/4-lb, large fries, medium soft drink, excl tax		5.68	1999	40c
Chicken, fried, thigh and drumstick, KFC/ Church's		2.99	3/01	4c
Hamburger with cheese, McDonald's	1/4 lb	2.99	3/01	4c
McDonald Quarterpounder		2.85	2000	106c
Pizza, Pizza Hut or Pizza Inn	11-12 in	10.16	3/01	4c
Taxes				
Federal income taxes paid	yr	2606	1999	30r
Personal taxes, expenditures on	yr	3567	1999	30r
Property taxes paid	yr	1752	1999	30r

Values are in dollars or fractions of dollars. In the column headed *Ref*, references are shown to sources. Each reference is followed by a letter. These refer to the geographical level for which data were reported: s=State, r=Region, and c=City or metro. The abbreviation *ex* is used to mean *except* or *excluding*; *exp* stands for *expenditures*. For other abbreviations and further explanations, please see the Introduction.

New York, NY - continued

Item	Per	Value	Date	Ref.
Taxes				
State and local income taxes paid	yr	694	1999	30r
Transportation				
Transportation, ACCRA Index		119.80	3/01	4c
Bus fare, one-way	trip	1.25	2000	1c
Bus fare, to central business district	1-way	1.50	3/01	4c
Cars and trucks, new, expenditures on	yr	1496	1999	30r
Cars and trucks, used, expenditures on	yr	1251	1999	30r
Commuter rail, one-way	trip	1.20-3.25	2000	2c
Diesel at the pump	gal	1.33	10/99	73s
Ferry boat transit fare, one-way	trip	2.00	2000	2c
Gasoline and motor oil purchases	yr	877	1999	30c
Gasoline before-tax price (cents)	gal	110.70	10/00	43s
Heavy rail transit fare, one-way	trip	1.00-1.50	2000	2c
Light rail transit fare, one-way	trip	1.00	2000	2c
Maintenance and repair expenditures	yr	618	1999	30r
Public transportation, expenditures on	yr	917	1999	30c
Subway token		1.50	2000	61c
Tire balance, computer or spin balance, front	wheel	9.40	3/01	4c
Transportation purchases	yr	6972	1999	30c
Vehicle expenses, miscellaneous, purchases	yr	2523	1999	30c
Vehicle insurance payments	yr	824	1999	30r
Vehicle purchases (net outlay)	yr	2655	1999	30c
Vehicle rental, lease expenditures	yr	584	1999	30r
Travel				
Car rental	day	85.50	2000	24c
Hotel rate, ave	day	226.00	1999	45c
Hotel room	night	139.88	2/01	95s
Hotel room, ave	night	225.11	2000	70c
Utilities				
Utilities, ACCRA Index		164.90	3/01	4c
Electrical bill, average	mos	71.50	9/00	9s
Electricity, expenditures on	yr	837	1999	30r
Electricity, summer, 250 KWh	mos	42.96	2/96	96c
Electricity, summer, 500 KWh	mos	78.75	2/96	96c
Electricity, summer, 750 KWh	mos	114.54	2/96	96c
Electricity, summer, 1000 KWh	mos	150.34	2/96	96c
Electricity and other, mixed, 2400 sq ft, new home	mos	113.91	3/01	4c
Electricity cost, average	KWh	11.34	9/00	9s
Utilities, fuels, and public services purchased	yr	2457	1999	30r
Water and other public services, expenditures on	yr	215	1999	30r
Water price	100 cf	1.25	2000	109c
Water price, dwelling unit	mos	24.53	2000	109c
Weddings				
Wedding (national average cost)		19936	2000	33r
Wedding (regional average total cost)		29454	1997	110r
Attendants' gifts		321	1998	33r
Bridal attendants' apparel (5 persons)		824	2000	33r
Bride's headpiece/veil		173	1998	33r
Bride's wedding dress		859	1998	33r
Clergy, religious facility fee		242	1998	33r
Engagement ring		3177	1998	33r
Flowers		789	1998	33r
Groom's formalwear rental		99	2000	33r
Limousine		410	1998	33r
Marriage license cost		25.00	4/01	35s
Men's formalwear (ushers, best man)		469	2000	33r
Mother of bride apparel		241	2000	33r
Music		866	1998	33r
Photography and videography		1368	1998	33r
Rehearsal dinner		728	1998	33r
Wedding invitations and announcements		341	1998	33r
Wedding reception		7968	2000	33r
Wedding rings (bride and groom)		1060	1998	33r

New York-Northeastern New Jersey, NY-NJ

Item	Per	Value	Date	Ref.
Average annual expenditures	yr	37971	1999	30r
Alcoholic Beverages				
Alcoholic beverage purchases	yr	368	1999	30r
Wine, red and white table, all sizes, any origin	liter	9.64	7/01	11r
Appliances				
Major appliances, expenditures on	yr	194	1999	30r
Small appliances, housewares, expenditures on	yr	93	1999	30r
Banking and Money				
Mortgage interest and charges paid	yr	2622	1999	30r
Mortgage principal paid on owned property	yr	1262	1999	30r
Vehicle finance charges paid	yr	240	1999	30r
Charity				
Cash contributions, expenditures	yr	1001	1999	30r
Child Care				
Child raising cost, total, age 0-2	yr	8670	1999	60r
Child raising cost, total, age 3-5	yr	8910	1999	60r
Child raising cost, total, age 6-8	yr	9040	1999	60r
Child raising cost, total, age 9-11	yr	9100	1999	60r
Child raising cost, total, age 12-14	yr	9890	1999	60r
Child raising cost, total, age 15-17	yr	10010	1999	60r
Child's child care and education, age 0-2	yr	1070	1999	60r
Child's child care and education, age 3-5	yr	1190	1999	60r
Child's child care and education, age 6-8	yr	740	1999	60r
Child's child care and education, age 9-11	yr	470	1999	60r
Child's child care and education, age 12-14	yr	350	1999	60r
Child's child care and education, age 15-17	yr	590	1999	60r
Child's clothing, age 0-2	yr	480	1999	60r
Child's clothing, age 3-5	yr	470	1999	60r
Child's clothing, age 6-8	yr	520	1999	60r
Child's clothing, age 9-11	yr	570	1999	60r
Child's clothing, age 12-14	yr	970	1999	60r
Child's clothing, age 15-17	yr	870	1999	60r
Child's food, age 0-2	yr	1130	1999	60r
Child's food, age 3-5	yr	1290	1999	60r
Child's food, age 6-8	yr	1640	1999	60r
Child's food, age 9-11	yr	1930	1999	60r
Child's food, age 12-14	yr	1940	1999	60r
Child's food, age 15-17	yr	2150	1999	60r
Child's health care, age 0-2	yr	550	1999	60r
Child's health care, age 3-5	yr	530	1999	60r
Child's health care, age 6-8	yr	610	1999	60r
Child's health care, age 9-11	yr	650	1999	60r
Child's health care, age 12-14	yr	660	1999	60r
Child's health care, age 15-17	yr	690	1999	60r
Child's housing, age 0-2	yr	3555	1999	60r
Child's housing, age 3-5	yr	3530	1999	60r
Child's housing, age 6-8	yr	3490	1999	60r
Child's housing, age 9-11	yr	3340	1999	60r
Child's housing, age 12-14	yr	3530	1999	60r
Child's housing, age 15-17	yr	3140	1999	60r
Child's personal care, reading, age 0-2	yr	920	1999	60r
Child's personal care, reading, age 3-5	yr	950	1999	60r
Child's personal care, reading, age 6-8	yr	980	1999	60r
Child's personal care, reading, age 9-11	yr	1020	1999	60r
Child's personal care, reading, age 12-14	yr	1190	1999	60r
Child's personal care, reading, age 15-17	yr	970	1999	60r
Nannies: criminal background check		74	1998	84s
Clothing				
Apparel and services purchases	yr	1831	1999	30r
Boys, 2 to 15, expenditures on	yr	92	1999	30r
Children under 2, expenditures on	yr	63	1999	30r
Footwear, expenditures on	yr	300	1999	30r
Girls, 2 to 15, expenditures on	yr	101	1999	30r
Men and boys, expenditures on	yr	446	1999	30r
Men, 16 and over, expenditures on	yr	354	1999	30r
Women, 16 and over, expenditures on	yr	584	1999	30r

Values are in dollars or fractions of dollars. In the column headed *Ref*, references are shown to sources. Each reference is followed by a letter. These refer to the geographical level for which data were reported: s=State, r=Region, and c=City or metro. The abbreviation *ex* is used to mean *except* or *excluding*; *exp* stands for *expenditures*. For other abbreviations and further explanations, please see the Introduction.

New York-Northeastern New Jersey, NY-NJ - continued

Item	Per	Value	Date	Ref.
Communications				
Cable modem installation, Adelphi		54.90	6/99	103s
Cable modem installation, Cablevision Systems		150.00	6/99	103s
Cable modem installation, Time Warner		75.00-225.00	6/99	103s
Cable modem rate, cable subscriber, Adelphi	mos	34.95	6/99	103s
Cable modem rate, cable subscriber, Cablevision Systems	mos	44.95	6/99	103s
Cable modem rate, cable subscriber, Century	mos	39.95	6/99	103s
Cable modem rate, cable subscriber, Time Warner	mos	39.95-49.95	6/99	103s
Cable modem rate, non-cable subscriber, Adelphi	mos	44.95	6/99	103s
Cable modem rate, non-cable subscriber, Cablevision Systems	mos	54.95	6/99	103s
Cable modem rate, non-cable subscriber, Time Warner	mos	39.95-54.95	6/99	103s
Phone line, single, business, field visit	inst.	142.76	12/97	17s
Phone line, single, business, no field visit	inst.	106.05	12/97	17s
Phone line, single, residence, field visit	inst.	102.78	12/97	17s
Phone line, single, residence, no field visit	inst.	55.00	12/97	17s
Postage and stationery, expenditures on	yr	138	1999	30r
Postal rate, express mail, up to half-pound		12.45	7/01	108r
Postal rate, letter, first class, first ounce		0.34	7/01	108r
Postal rate, letter, two ounces		0.57	7/01	108r
Postal rate, post card		0.21	7/01	108r
Postal rate, priority mail, two pounds		3.95	7/01	108r
Postal rate, priority mail, up to one pound		3.50	7/01	108r
Telephone services, expenditures on	yr	830	1999	30r
Education				
Board, 4-year private college/university	yr	3255	1996	38s
Board, 4-year public college/university	yr	2310	1996	38s
Education expenditures	yr	877	1999	30r
Room, 4-year private college/university	yr	3724	1996	38s
Room, 4-year public college/university	yr	2937	1996	38s
Total cost, 4-year private college/university	yr	20831	1996	38s
Total cost, 4-year public college/university	yr	8960	1996	38s
Tuition, 2-year public college/university, in state	yr	2427	1996	38s
Tuition, 4-year private college/university, in state	yr	13852	1996	38s
Tuition, 4-year public college/university	yr	3714	1996	38s
Energy and Fuels				
Electricity	KWh	0.12	7/01	11r
Electricity	500 KWhs	69.83	7/01	11c
Electricity	KWh	0.14	7/01	11c
Fuel oil #2	gal	1.31	7/01	11r
Fuel oil and other fuels, expenditures on	yr	207	1999	30r
Gasoline, all types	gal	1.90	7/01	11c
Gasoline, unleaded midgrade	gal	1.94	7/01	11c
Gasoline, unleaded premium	gal	1.91	7/01	11r
Gasoline, unleaded regular	gal	1.80	7/01	11c
Natural gas, expenditures on	yr	368	1999	30r
Utility (piped) gas, therm		1.08	7/01	11c
Utility (piped) gas, 40 therms		50.87	7/01	11r
Utility (piped) gas, 100 therms		109.49	7/01	11c
Entertainment				
Entertainment purchases	yr	1821	1999	30r
Fees and admissions paid	yr	511	1999	30r
Television, radios, sound equipment, expenditures on	yr	650	1999	30r
Funerals				
Total cost of funeral		5813.50	1/99	78r
Acknowledgement cards		28.32	1/99	78r
Casket		2082.20	1/99	78r
Cosmetology, hair, other preparation		169.59	1/99	78r
Embalming		465.60	1/99	78r
Funeral at funeral home		339.56	1/99	78r
Hearse (local)		183.96	1/99	78r

New York-Northeastern New Jersey, NY-NJ - continued

Item	Per	Value	Date	Ref.
Funerals - continued				
Professional service charges		1157.85	1/99	78r
Service car/van		100.41	1/99	78r
Transfer of remains to funeral home		158.66	1/99	78r
Vault		766.31	1/99	78r
Visitation/viewing		361.04	1/99	78r
Groceries				
Apples, red delicious	lb	0.95	7/01	11r
Bacon, sliced	lb	3.44	7/01	11r
Bakery products, expenditures on	yr	310	1999	30r
Bananas	lb	0.55	7/01	11r
Beef, expenditures on	yr	236	1999	30r
Bread, white, pan	lb	1.09	7/01	11r
Butter, yoghurt, cheese, etc, expenditures on	yr	214	1999	30r
Cereals and bakery product purchases	yr	474	1999	30r
Cereals and cereal products, expenditures on	yr	164	1999	30r
Chicken legs, bone-in	lb	1.23	7/01	11r
Chicken, fresh, whole	lb	1.13	7/01	11r
Chuck roast, U.S. choice, boneless	lb	2.79	7/01	11r
Coffee, 100%, ground roast, all sizes	lb	3.40	7/01	11r
Dairy product purchases	yr	342	1999	30r
Eggs, expenditures on	yr	34	1999	30r
Eggs, grade A, large	dozen	0.82	7/01	11r
Fats and oils, expenditures on	yr	80	1999	30r
Fish and seafood, expenditures on	yr	123	1999	30r
Food (excl fruit and vegetables), eaten at home, purchases	yr	838	1999	30r
Food cooked on trips, expenditures on	yr	48	1999	30r
Food purchases	yr	5314	1999	30r
Food purchases, eaten away from home	yr	2313	1999	30r
Food purchases, food eaten at home	yr	3001	1999	30r
Fresh fruits, expenditures on	yr	169	1999	30r
Fresh milk and cream, expenditures on	yr	128	1999	30r
Fresh vegetables, expenditures on	yr	164	1999	30r
Grapefruit	lb	0.67	7/01	11r
Grapes, Thompson, seedless	lb	2.18	7/01	11r
Ground beef, lean and extra lean	lb	2.66	7/01	11r
Ground chuck, 100% beef	lb	2.04	7/01	11r
Lettuce, iceberg	lb	0.76	7/01	11r
Meats, poultry, fish, and egg purchases	yr	808	1999	30r
Nonalcoholic beverages, expenditures on	yr	225	1999	30r
Orange juice, frozen concentrate	16 oz	1.88	7/01	11r
Oranges, Navel	lb	0.79	7/01	11r
Oranges, Valencia	lb	0.56	7/01	11r
Peaches	lb	1.16	7/01	11r
Peanut butter, creamy, all sizes	lb	2.01	7/01	11r
Pears, Anjou	lb	1.16	7/01	11r
Pork chops, center cut, bone-in	lb	3.57	7/01	11r
Pork, expenditures on	yr	146	1999	30r
Potato chips	16 oz	3.37	7/01	11r
Potatoes, white, all types	lb	0.42	7/01	11r
Poultry, expenditures on	yr	158	1999	30r
Processed fruits, expenditures on	yr	124	1999	30r
Processed vegetables, expenditures on	yr	82	1999	30r
Round roast, U.S. choice, boneless	lb	3.04	7/01	11r
Spaghetti and macaroni	lb	1.04	7/01	11r
Steak, sirloin, U.S. choice, boneless	lb	5.39	7/01	11r
Strawberries, dry pint	12 oz	1.51	7/01	11r
Sugar and other sweets, expenditures on	yr	110	1999	30r
Sugar, white, 33-80 ounce package	lb	0.46	7/01	11r
Sugar, white, all sizes	lb	0.47	7/01	11r
Tobacco products and smoking supplies purchases	yr	309	1999	30r
Yogurt, natural, fruit flavored	8 oz	0.79	7/01	11r
Goods and Services				
B&B Japanese maple (acer japonicum)	gal	38.99-125.00	4/00	93r
Boxwood (buxus)	2 gal	15.99-49.95	4/00	93r
Daylilly (hemerocallis)	gal	4.95	4/00	93r

Values are in dollars or fractions of dollars. In the column headed *Ref*, references are shown to sources. Each reference is followed by a letter. These refer to the geographical level for which data were reported: s=State, r=Region, and c=City or metro. The abbreviation *ex* is used to mean *except* or *excluding*; *exp* stands for expenditures. For other abbreviations and further explanations, please see the Introduction.

New York-Northeastern New Jersey, NY-NJ - continued

Item	Per	Value	Date	Ref.
Goods and Services				
Flat of annuals		8.00-14.99	4/00	93r
Fountain grass (pennisetum)	gal	6.99-9.99	4/00	93r
Hanging basket (10 in)		12.95-19.99	4/00	93r
Hardy geranium (geranium)	gal	6.95-7.99	4/00	93r
Hosta (hosta)	gal	4.95	4/00	93r
Lilac (syrubga vulgaris)	2 gal	17.99-74.95	4/00	93r
Miscellaneous purchases	yr	872	1999	30r
Rhododendron (rhododendron)	2 gal	23.99-54.95	4/00	93r
Sage (salvia)	gal	6.95-7.99	4/00	93r
Wintercreeper euonymus (euonymus fortunei)	2 gal	14.99-23.95	4/00	93r
Hunting license	yr	11.00	4/01	34s
Health Care				
Cardiac catheterization, ave hospital/physician charges		12750	1998	77s
Childbirth, Cesarean delivery		14716	1997	13r
Childbirth, vaginal delivery		8541	1997	13r
Drugs, expenditures on	yr	296	1999	30r
Health care purchases	yr	1788	1999	30r
Health insurance expenditures	yr	875	1999	30r
Hysterectomy, laproscopically-assisted, ave hospital/physician charges		13460	1998	76s
Hysterectomy, vaginal, ave hospital and physician charges		10310	1998	76s
Medicaid dispensing fee		3.50-4.50	1999	87s
Medical services expenditures	yr	516	1999	30r
Medical supplies, expenditures on	yr	102	1999	30r
Plastic surgery, breast augmentation		4232	2000	7r
Plastic surgery, breast lift		4605	2000	7r
Plastic surgery, facelift		6964	2000	7r
Plastic surgery, hair transplantation		4193	2000	7r
Plastic surgery, lip augmentation		1675	2000	7r
Plastic surgery, lower body lift		6611	2000	7r
Plastic surgery, thigh lift		4751	2000	7r
Household Goods				
Floor coverings, expenditures on	yr	59	1999	30r
Furniture, expenditures on	yr	388	1999	30r
Household furnishings and equipment purchases	yr	1567	1999	30r
Household textiles, expenditures on	yr	112	1999	30r
Laundry and cleaning supplies, expenditures on	yr	104	1999	30r
Housing				
Home price, existing, ave		180800	10/00	90r
Home value, median		179000	2001	53s
Household operation expenditures	yr	581	1999	30r
Housekeeping supplies purchases	yr	474	1999	30r
Lodging expenditures	yr	550	1999	30r
Maintenance, repairs, insurance expenditures	yr	835	1999	30r
Monthly rental value of owned home	mos	663	1999	30r
Owned dwellings, expenditures own	yr	5209	1999	30r
Rent expenditures	yr	2390	1999	30r
Shelter, expenditures on	yr	8149	1999	30r
Insurance and Pensions				
Auto insurance premium	yr	1113.55	1999	57s
Life and other personal insurance purchases	yr	424	1999	30r
Pensions and Social Security, expenditures on	yr	3037	1999	30r
Legal Fees				
Divorce, filing fee		270.00	4/01	35s

New York-Northeastern New Jersey, NY-NJ - continued

Item	Per	Value	Date	Ref.
Legal Fees - continued				
Driver's license fee	orig	25.00	1999	48s
Driver's license fee	renew	25.00	1999	48s
Fishing license	yr	14.00	4/01	34s
Personal Goods				
Personal care products and services purchases	yr	399	1999	30r
Personal Services				
Personal services, household, expenditures on	yr	271	1999	30r
Pets				
Pets, toys, and playground equipment, expenditures on	yr	325	1999	30r
Taxes				
Federal income taxes paid	yr	2606	1999	30r
Personal taxes, expenditures on	yr	3567	1999	30r
Property taxes paid	yr	1752	1999	30r
State and local income taxes paid	yr	694	1999	30r
Transportation				
Cars and trucks, new, expenditures on	yr	1496	1999	30r
Cars and trucks, used, expenditures on	yr	1251	1999	30r
Diesel at the pump	gal	1.33	10/99	73s
Gasoline and motor oil purchases	yr	901	1999	30r
Gasoline before-tax price (cents)	gal	110.70	10/00	43s
Maintenance and repair expenditures	yr	618	1999	30r
Public transportation, expenditures on	yr	575	1999	30r
Transportation purchases	yr	6503	1999	30r
Vehicle expenses, miscellaneous, purchases	yr	2266	1999	30r
Vehicle insurance payments	yr	824	1999	30r
Vehicle purchases (net outlay)	yr	2761	1999	30r
Vehicle rental, lease expenditures	yr	584	1999	30r
Travel				
Hotel room	night	139.88	2/01	95s
Utilities				
Electrical bill, average	mos	71.50	9/00	9s
Electricity, expenditures on	yr	837	1999	30r
Electricity cost, average	KWh	11.34	9/00	9s
Utilities, fuels, and public services purchased	yr	2457	1999	30r
Water and other public services, expenditures on	yr	215	1999	30r
Weddings				
Wedding (national average cost)		19936	2000	33r
Wedding (regional average total cost)		29454	1997	110r
Attendants' gifts		321	1998	33r
Bridal attendants' apparel (5 persons)		824	2000	33r
Bride's headpiece/veil		173	1998	33r
Bride's wedding dress		859	1998	33r
Clergy, religious facility fee		242	1998	33r
Engagement ring		3177	1998	33r
Flowers		789	1998	33r
Groom's formalwear rental		99	2000	33r
Limousine		410	1998	33r
Marriage license cost		25.00	4/01	35s
Men's formalwear (ushers, best man)		469	2000	33r
Mother of bride apparel		241	2000	33r
Music		866	1998	33r
Photography and videography		1368	1998	33r
Rehearsal dinner		728	1998	33r
Wedding invitations and announcements		341	1998	33r
Wedding reception		7968	2000	33r
Wedding rings (bride and groom)		1060	1998	33r

Newark, NJ

Item	Per	Value	Date	Ref.
Average annual expenditures	yr	37971	1999	30r

Values are in dollars or fractions of dollars. In the column headed *Ref*, references are shown to sources. Each reference is followed by a letter. These refer to the geographical level for which data were reported: s=State, r=Region, and c=City or metro. The abbreviation *ex* is used to mean *except* or *excluding*; *exp* stands for *expenditures*. For other abbreviations and further explanations, please see the Introduction.

Newark, NJ - continued

Item	Per	Value	Date	Ref.
Alcoholic Beverages				
Alcoholic beverage purchases	yr	368	1999	30r
Wine, red and white table, all sizes, any origin	liter	9.64	7/01	11r
Appliances				
Major appliances, expenditures on	yr	194	1999	30r
Small appliances, housewares, expenditures on	yr	93	1999	30r
Banking and Money				
Mortgage interest and charges paid	yr	2622	1999	30r
Mortgage principal paid on owned property	yr	1262	1999	30r
Vehicle finance charges paid	yr	240	1999	30r
Business Expenses				
Business travel, car rental	day	61	2001	3c
Business travel, food	day	49	2001	3c
Business travel, hotel	day	136	2001	3c
Charity				
Cash contributions, expenditures	yr	1001	1999	30r
Child Care				
Child raising cost, total, age 0-2	yr	8670	1999	60r
Child raising cost, total, age 3-5	yr	8910	1999	60r
Child raising cost, total, age 6-8	yr	9040	1999	60r
Child raising cost, total, age 9-11	yr	9100	1999	60r
Child raising cost, total, age 12-14	yr	9890	1999	60r
Child raising cost, total, age 15-17	yr	10010	1999	60r
Child's child care and education, age 0-2	yr	1070	1999	60r
Child's child care and education, age 3-5	yr	1190	1999	60r
Child's child care and education, age 6-8	yr	740	1999	60r
Child's child care and education, age 9-11	yr	470	1999	60r
Child's child care and education, age 12-14	yr	350	1999	60r
Child's child care and education, age 15-17	yr	590	1999	60r
Child's clothing, age 0-2	yr	480	1999	60r
Child's clothing, age 3-5	yr	470	1999	60r
Child's clothing, age 6-8	yr	520	1999	60r
Child's clothing, age 9-11	yr	570	1999	60r
Child's clothing, age 12-14	yr	970	1999	60r
Child's clothing, age 15-17	yr	870	1999	60r
Child's food, age 0-2	yr	1130	1999	60r
Child's food, age 3-5	yr	1290	1999	60r
Child's food, age 6-8	yr	1640	1999	60r
Child's food, age 9-11	yr	1930	1999	60r
Child's food, age 12-14	yr	1940	1999	60r
Child's food, age 15-17	yr	2150	1999	60r
Child's health care, age 0-2	yr	550	1999	60r
Child's health care, age 3-5	yr	530	1999	60r
Child's health care, age 6-8	yr	610	1999	60r
Child's health care, age 9-11	yr	650	1999	60r
Child's health care, age 12-14	yr	660	1999	60r
Child's health care, age 15-17	yr	690	1999	60r
Child's housing, age 0-2	yr	3555	1999	60r
Child's housing, age 3-5	yr	3530	1999	60r
Child's housing, age 6-8	yr	3490	1999	60r
Child's housing, age 9-11	yr	3340	1999	60r
Child's housing, age 12-14	yr	3530	1999	60r
Child's housing, age 15-17	yr	3140	1999	60r
Child's personal care, reading, age 0-2	yr	920	1999	60r
Child's personal care, reading, age 3-5	yr	950	1999	60r
Child's personal care, reading, age 6-8	yr	980	1999	60r
Child's personal care, reading, age 9-11	yr	1020	1999	60r
Child's personal care, reading, age 12-14	yr	1190	1999	60r
Child's personal care, reading, age 15-17	yr	970	1999	60r
Clothing				
Apparel and services purchases	yr	1831	1999	30r
Boys, 2 to 15, expenditures on	yr	92	1999	30r
Children under 2, expenditures on	yr	63	1999	30r
Footwear, expenditures on	yr	300	1999	30r
Girls, 2 to 15, expenditures on	yr	101	1999	30r
Men and boys, expenditures on	yr	446	1999	30r
Men, 16 and over, expenditures on	yr	354	1999	30r
Women, 16 and over, expenditures on	yr	584	1999	30r

Newark, NJ - continued

Item	Per	Value	Date	Ref.
Communications				
Cable modem installation, Adelphi		54.90	6/99	103s
Cable modem installation, Comcast		95.00	6/99	103s
Cable modem rate, cable subscriber, Adelphi	mos	34.95	6/99	103s
Cable modem rate, cable subscriber, Comcast	mos	39.95	6/99	103s
Cable modem rate, non-cable subscriber, Adelphi	mos	44.95	6/99	103s
Cable modem rate, non-cable subscriber, Comcast	mos	49.95	6/99	103s
Phone line, single, business, field visit	inst.	98.50	12/97	17s
Phone line, single, business, no field visit	inst.	79.50	12/97	17s
Phone line, single, residence, field visit	inst.	56.50	12/97	17s
Phone line, single, residence, no field visit	inst.	42.00	12/97	17s
Postage and stationery, expenditures on	yr	138	1999	30r
Postal rate, express mail, up to half-pound		12.45	7/01	108r
Postal rate, letter, first class, first ounce		0.34	7/01	108r
Postal rate, letter, two ounces		0.57	7/01	108r
Postal rate, post card		0.21	7/01	108r
Postal rate, priority mail, two pounds		3.95	7/01	108r
Postal rate, priority mail, up to one pound		3.50	7/01	108r
Telephone bill, business, basic rate	mos	12.96	12/97	18c
Telephone bill, residential, basic rate	mos	8.19	12/97	18c
Telephone services, expenditures on	yr	830	1999	30r
Education				
Board, 4-year private college/university	yr	2959	1996	38s
Board, 4-year public college/university	yr	2052	1996	38s
Education expenditures	yr	877	1999	30r
Room, 4-year private college/university	yr	3226	1996	38s
Room, 4-year public college/university	yr	3101	1996	38s
Total cost, 4-year private college/university	yr	19751	1996	38s
Total cost, 4-year public college/university	yr	9125	1996	38s
Tuition, 2-year public college/university, in state	yr	1878	1996	38s
Tuition, 4-year private college/university, in state	yr	13566	1996	38s
Tuition, 4-year public college/university	yr	3972	1996	38s
Energy and Fuels				
Electricity	KWh	0.12	7/01	11r
Fuel oil #2	gal	1.31	7/01	11r
Fuel oil and other fuels, expenditures on	yr	207	1999	30r
Gas, cooking, winter, 10 therms	mos	10.63	2/96	98c
Gas, cooking, winter, 30 therms	mos	21.08	2/96	98c
Gas, cooking, winter, 50 therms	mos	31.52	2/96	98c
Gas, heating, winter, average use	mos	124.02	2/96	98c
Gas, natural, commercial rate	1000 cf	5.98	11/00	88s
Gasoline, all types	gal	1.80	7/01	11r
Gasoline, unleaded midgrade	gal	1.85	7/01	11r
Gasoline, unleaded premium	gal	1.91	7/01	11r
Gasoline, unleaded regular	gal	1.71	7/01	11r
Natural gas, expenditures on	yr	368	1999	30r
Utility (piped) gas, therm		1.08	7/01	11r
Utility (piped) gas, 40 therms		50.87	7/01	11r
Utility (piped) gas, 100 therms		111.06	7/01	11r
Entertainment				
Entertainment purchases	yr	1821	1999	30r
Fees and admissions paid	yr	511	1999	30r
Television, radios, sound equipment, expenditures on	yr	650	1999	30r
Funerals				
Total cost of funeral		5813.50	1/99	78r
Acknowledgement cards		28.32	1/99	78r
Casket		2082.20	1/99	78r
Cosmetology, hair, other preparation		169.59	1/99	78r
Embalming		465.60	1/99	78r
Funeral at funeral home		339.56	1/99	78r
Hearse (local)		183.96	1/99	78r
Professional service charges		1157.85	1/99	78r
Service car/van		100.41	1/99	78r
Transfer of remains to funeral home		158.66	1/99	78r
Vault		766.31	1/99	78r

Values are in dollars or fractions of dollars. In the column headed *Ref*, references are shown to sources. Each reference is followed by a letter. These refer to the geographical level for which data were reported: s=State, r=Region, and c=City or metro. The abbreviation *ex* is used to mean *except* or *excluding*; *exp* stands for *expenditures*. For other abbreviations and further explanations, please see the Introduction.

Newark, NJ - continued

Item	Per	Value	Date	Ref.
Funerals				
Visitation/viewing		361.04	1/99	78r
Groceries				
Apples, red delicious	lb	0.95	7/01	11r
Bacon, sliced	lb	3.44	7/01	11r
Bakery products, expenditures on	yr	310	1999	30r
Bananas	lb	0.55	7/01	11r
Beef, expenditures on	yr	236	1999	30r
Bread, white, pan	lb	1.09	7/01	11r
Butter, yoghurt, cheese, etc, expenditures on	yr	214	1999	30r
Cereals and bakery product purchases	yr	474	1999	30r
Cereals and cereal products, expenditures on	yr	164	1999	30r
Chicken legs, bone-in	lb	1.23	7/01	11r
Chicken, fresh, whole	lb	1.13	7/01	11r
Chuck roast, U.S. choice, boneless	lb	2.79	7/01	11r
Coffee, 100%, ground roast, all sizes	lb	3.40	7/01	11r
Dairy product purchases	yr	342	1999	30r
Eggs, expenditures on	yr	34	1999	30r
Eggs, grade A, large	dozen	0.82	7/01	11r
Fats and oils, expenditures on	yr	80	1999	30r
Fish and seafood, expenditures on	yr	123	1999	30r
Food (excl fruit and vegetables), eaten at home, purchases	yr	838	1999	30r
Food cooked on trips, expenditures on	yr	48	1999	30r
Food purchases	yr	5314	1999	30r
Food purchases, eaten away from home	yr	2313	1999	30r
Food purchases, food eaten at home	yr	3001	1999	30r
Fresh fruits, expenditures on	yr	169	1999	30r
Fresh milk and cream, expenditures on	yr	128	1999	30r
Fresh vegetables, expenditures on	yr	164	1999	30r
Grapefruit	lb	0.67	7/01	11r
Grapes, Thompson, seedless	lb	2.18	7/01	11r
Ground beef, lean and extra lean	lb	2.66	7/01	11r
Ground chuck, 100% beef	lb	2.04	7/01	11r
Lettuce, iceberg	lb	0.76	7/01	11r
Meats, poultry, fish, and egg purchases	yr	808	1999	30r
Nonalcoholic beverages, expenditures on	yr	225	1999	30r
Orange juice, frozen concentrate	16 oz	1.88	7/01	11r
Oranges, Navel	lb	0.79	7/01	11r
Oranges, Valencia	lb	0.56	7/01	11r
Peaches	lb	1.16	7/01	11r
Peanut butter, creamy, all sizes	lb	2.01	7/01	11r
Pears, Anjou	lb	1.16	7/01	11r
Pork chops, center cut, bone-in	lb	3.57	7/01	11r
Pork, expenditures on	yr	146	1999	30r
Potato chips	16 oz	3.37	7/01	11r
Potatoes, white, all types	lb	0.42	7/01	11r
Poultry, expenditures on	yr	158	1999	30r
Processed fruits, expenditures on	yr	124	1999	30r
Processed vegetables, expenditures on	yr	82	1999	30r
Round roast, U.S. choice, boneless	lb	3.04	7/01	11r
Spaghetti and macaroni	lb	1.04	7/01	11r
Steak, sirloin, U.S. choice, boneless	lb	5.39	7/01	11r
Strawberries, dry pint	12 oz	1.51	7/01	11r
Sugar and other sweets, expenditures on	yr	110	1999	30r
Sugar, white, 33-80 ounce package	lb	0.46	7/01	11r
Sugar, white, all sizes	lb	0.47	7/01	11r
Tobacco products and smoking supplies purchases	yr	309	1999	30r
Yogurt, natural, fruit flavored	8 oz	0.79	7/01	11r
Goods and Services				
B&B Japanese maple (acer japonicum)	gal	38.99-125.00	4/00	93r
Boxwood (buxus)	2 gal	15.99-49.95	4/00	93r
Daylily (hemerocallis)	gal	4.95	4/00	93r
Flat of annuals		8.00-14.99	4/00	93r
Fountain grass (pennisetum)	gal	6.99-9.99	4/00	93r

Newark, NJ - continued

Item	Per	Value	Date	Ref.
Goods and Services - continued				
Hanging basket (10 in)		12.95-19.99	4/00	93r
Hardy geranium (geranium)	gal	6.95-7.99	4/00	93r
Hosta (hosta)	gal	4.95	4/00	93r
Lilac (syrubga vulgaris)	2 gal	17.99-74.95	4/00	93r
Miscellaneous purchases	yr	872	1999	30r
Rhododendron (rhododendron)	2 gal	23.99-54.95	4/00	93r
Sage (salvia)	gal	6.95-7.99	4/00	93r
Wintercreeper euonymus (euonymus fortunei)	2 gal	14.99-23.95	4/00	93r
Hunting license	yr	22.50	4/01	34s
Health Care				
Cardiac catheterization, ave hospital/ physician charges		14680	1998	77s
Childbirth, Cesarean delivery		14716	1997	13r
Childbirth, vaginal delivery		8541	1997	13r
Drugs, expenditures on	yr	296	1999	30r
Health care purchases	yr	1788	1999	30r
Health insurance expenditures	yr	875	1999	30r
Hysterectomy, laproscopically-assisted, ave hospital/physician charges		18330	1998	76s
Hysterectomy, vaginal, ave hospital and physician charges		13620	1998	76s
Medicaid dispensing fee		3.73-4.07	1999	87s
Medical services expenditures	yr	516	1999	30r
Medical supplies, expenditures on	yr	102	1999	30r
Nursing home costs, private room	day	228	2000	82c
Nursing home stay, private room	day	228	2000	81c
Plastic surgery, breast augmentation		4232	2000	7r
Plastic surgery, breast lift		4605	2000	7r
Plastic surgery, facelift		6964	2000	7r
Plastic surgery, hair transplantation		4193	2000	7r
Plastic surgery, lip augmentation		1675	2000	7r
Plastic surgery, lower body lift		6611	2000	7r
Plastic surgery, thigh lift		4751	2000	7r
Household Goods				
Floor coverings, expenditures on	yr	59	1999	30r
Furniture, expenditures on	yr	388	1999	30r
Household furnishings and equipment purchases	yr	1567	1999	30r
Household textiles, expenditures on	yr	112	1999	30r
Laundry and cleaning supplies, expenditures on	yr	104	1999	30r
Housing				
Home price, existing, ave		180800	10/00	90r
Home value, median		213000	2001	53s
Household operation expenditures	yr	581	1999	30r
Housekeeping supplies purchases	yr	474	1999	30r
Lodging expenditures	yr	550	1999	30r
Maintenance, repairs, insurance expenditures	yr	835	1999	30r
Monthly rental value of owned home	mos	663	1999	30r
Owned dwellings, expenditures own	yr	5209	1999	30r
Rent expenditures	yr	2390	1999	30r
Rental unit, 1 bedroom, with utilities	mos	724	4/01	41c
Rental unit, 2 bedroom, with utilities	mos	872	4/01	41c
Rental unit, 3 bedroom, with utilities	mos	1099	4/01	41c
Rental unit, 4 bedroom, with utilities	mos	1388	4/01	41c
Shelter, expenditures on	yr	8149	1999	30r
Insurance and Pensions				
Auto insurance premium	yr	1292.76	1999	57s
Life and other personal insurance purchases	yr	424	1999	30r
Pensions and Social Security, expenditures on	yr	3037	1999	30r

Values are in dollars or fractions of dollars. In the column headed *Ref*, references are shown to sources. Each reference is followed by a letter. These refer to the geographical level for which data were reported: s=State, r=Region, and c=City or metro. The abbreviation *ex* is used to mean *except* or *excluding*; *exp* stands for expenditures. For other abbreviations and further explanations, please see the Introduction.

Newark, NJ - continued

Item	Per	Value	Date	Ref.
Legal Fees				
Divorce, filing fee		65.00	4/01	35s
Driver's license fee	orig	18.00	1999	48s
Driver's license fee	renew	15.00	1999	48s
Fishing license	yr	22.50	4/01	34s
Personal Goods				
Personal care products and services purchases	yr	399	1999	30r
Personal Services				
Personal services, household, expenditures on	yr	271	1999	30r
Pets				
Pets, toys, and playground equipment, expenditures on	yr	325	1999	30r
Taxes				
Federal income taxes paid	yr	2606	1999	30r
Personal taxes, expenditures on	yr	3567	1999	30r
Property taxes paid	yr	1752	1999	30r
State and local income taxes paid	yr	694	1999	30r
Transportation				
Automobile insurance	yr	975.90	2000	79s
Cars and trucks, new, expenditures on	yr	1496	1999	30r
Cars and trucks, used, expenditures on	yr	1251	1999	30r
Diesel at the pump	gal	1.19	10/99	73s
Gasoline and motor oil purchases	yr	901	1999	30r
Gasoline before-tax price (cents)	gal	114.90	10/00	43s
Maintenance and repair expenditures	yr	618	1999	30r
Motorcycle license fee	orig	15.00	1999	49s
Motorcycle license fee	renew	13.00	1999	49s
Public transportation, expenditures on	yr	575	1999	30r
Transportation purchases	yr	6503	1999	30r
Vehicle expenses, miscellaneous, purchases	yr	2266	1999	30r
Vehicle insurance payments	yr	824	1999	30r
Vehicle purchases (net outlay)	yr	2761	1999	30r
Vehicle rental, lease expenditures	yr	584	1999	30r
Travel				
Car rental	day	85.00	2000	24c
Utilities				
Electrical bill, average	mos	74.08	9/00	9s
Electricity, expenditures on	yr	837	1999	30r
Electricity, summer, 250 KWh	mos	30.51	2/96	96c
Electricity, summer, 500 KWh	mos	58.77	2/96	96c
Electricity, summer, 750 KWh	mos	86.16	2/96	96c
Electricity, summer, 1000 KWh	mos	112.96	2/96	96c
Electricity cost, average	KWh	8.91	9/00	9s
Utilities, fuels, and public services purchased	yr	2457	1999	30r
Water and other public services, expenditures on	yr	215	1999	30r
Weddings				
Wedding (national average cost)		19936	2000	33r
Wedding (regional average total cost)		29454	1997	110r
Attendants' gifts		321	1998	33r
Bridal attendants' apparel (5 persons)		824	2000	33r
Bride's headpiece/veil		173	1998	33r
Bride's wedding dress		859	1998	33r
Clergy, religious facility fee		242	1998	33r
Engagement ring		3177	1998	33r
Flowers		789	1998	33r
Groom's formalwear rental		99	2000	33r
Limousine		410	1998	33r
Marriage license cost		28.00	4/01	35s
Men's formalwear (ushers, best man)		469	2000	33r
Mother of bride apparel		241	2000	33r
Music		866	1998	33r
Photography and videography		1368	1998	33r
Rehearsal dinner		728	1998	33r
Wedding invitations and announcements		341	1998	33r
Wedding reception		7968	2000	33r
Wedding rings (bride and groom)		1060	1998	33r

Newburgh, NY

Item	Per	Value	Date	Ref.
Average annual expenditures	yr	37971	1999	30r
Alcoholic Beverages				
Alcoholic beverage purchases	yr	368	1999	30r
Wine, red and white table, all sizes, any origin	liter	9.64	7/01	11r
Appliances				
Major appliances, expenditures on	yr	194	1999	30r
Small appliances, housewares, expenditures on	yr	93	1999	30r
Banking and Money				
Mortgage interest and charges paid	yr	2622	1999	30r
Mortgage principal paid on owned property	yr	1262	1999	30r
Vehicle finance charges paid	yr	240	1999	30r
Charity				
Cash contributions, expenditures	yr	1001	1999	30r
Child Care				
Child raising cost, total, age 0-2	yr	8670	1999	60r
Child raising cost, total, age 3-5	yr	8910	1999	60r
Child raising cost, total, age 6-8	yr	9040	1999	60r
Child raising cost, total, age 9-11	yr	9100	1999	60r
Child raising cost, total, age 12-14	yr	9890	1999	60r
Child raising cost, total, age 15-17	yr	10010	1999	60r
Child's child care and education, age 0-2	yr	1070	1999	60r
Child's child care and education, age 3-5	yr	1190	1999	60r
Child's child care and education, age 6-8	yr	740	1999	60r
Child's child care and education, age 9-11	yr	470	1999	60r
Child's child care and education, age 12-14	yr	350	1999	60r
Child's child care and education, age 15-17	yr	590	1999	60r
Child's clothing, age 0-2	yr	480	1999	60r
Child's clothing, age 3-5	yr	470	1999	60r
Child's clothing, age 6-8	yr	520	1999	60r
Child's clothing, age 9-11	yr	570	1999	60r
Child's clothing, age 12-14	yr	970	1999	60r
Child's clothing, age 15-17	yr	870	1999	60r
Child's food, age 0-2	yr	1130	1999	60r
Child's food, age 3-5	yr	1290	1999	60r
Child's food, age 6-8	yr	1640	1999	60r
Child's food, age 9-11	yr	1930	1999	60r
Child's food, age 12-14	yr	1940	1999	60r
Child's food, age 15-17	yr	2150	1999	60r
Child's health care, age 0-2	yr	550	1999	60r
Child's health care, age 3-5	yr	530	1999	60r
Child's health care, age 6-8	yr	610	1999	60r
Child's health care, age 9-11	yr	650	1999	60r
Child's health care, age 12-14	yr	660	1999	60r
Child's health care, age 15-17	yr	690	1999	60r
Child's housing, age 0-2	yr	3555	1999	60r
Child's housing, age 3-5	yr	3530	1999	60r
Child's housing, age 6-8	yr	3490	1999	60r
Child's housing, age 9-11	yr	3340	1999	60r
Child's housing, age 12-14	yr	3530	1999	60r
Child's housing, age 15-17	yr	3140	1999	60r
Child's personal care, reading, age 0-2	yr	920	1999	60r
Child's personal care, reading, age 3-5	yr	950	1999	60r
Child's personal care, reading, age 6-8	yr	980	1999	60r
Child's personal care, reading, age 9-11	yr	1020	1999	60r
Child's personal care, reading, age 12-14	yr	1190	1999	60r
Child's personal care, reading, age 15-17	yr	970	1999	60r
Nannies: criminal background check		74	1998	84s
Clothing				
Apparel and services purchases	yr	1831	1999	30r
Boys, 2 to 15, expenditures on	yr	92	1999	30r
Children under 2, expenditures on	yr	63	1999	30r
Footwear, expenditures on	yr	300	1999	30r
Girls, 2 to 15, expenditures on	yr	101	1999	30r
Men and boys, expenditures on	yr	446	1999	30r
Men, 16 and over, expenditures on	yr	354	1999	30r
Women, 16 and over, expenditures on	yr	584	1999	30r

Values are in dollars or fractions of dollars. In the column headed *Ref*, references are shown to sources. Each reference is followed by a letter. These refer to the geographical level for which data were reported: s=State, r=Region, and c=City or metro. The abbreviation *ex* is used to mean *except* or *excluding*; *exp* stands for *expenditures*. For other abbreviations and further explanations, please see the Introduction.

Newburgh, NY - continued

Item	Per	Value	Date	Ref.
Communications				
Cable modem installation, Adelphi		54.90	6/99	103s
Cable modem installation, Cablevision Systems		150.00	6/99	103s
Cable modem installation, Time Warner		75.00-225.00	6/99	103s
Cable modem rate, cable subscriber, Adelphi	mos	34.95	6/99	103s
Cable modem rate, cable subscriber, Cablevision Systems	mos	44.95	6/99	103s
Cable modem rate, cable subscriber, Century	mos	39.95	6/99	103s
Cable modem rate, cable subscriber, Time Warner	mos	39.95-49.95	6/99	103s
Cable modem rate, non-cable subscriber, Adelphi	mos	44.95	6/99	103s
Cable modem rate, non-cable subscriber, Cablevision Systems	mos	54.95	6/99	103s
Cable modem rate, non-cable subscriber, Time Warner	mos	39.95-54.95	6/99	103s
Phone line, single, business, field visit	inst.	142.76	12/97	17s
Phone line, single, business, no field visit	inst.	106.05	12/97	17s
Phone line, single, residence, field visit	inst.	102.78	12/97	17s
Phone line, single, residence, no field visit	inst.	55.00	12/97	17s
Postage and stationery, expenditures on	yr	138	1999	30r
Postal rate, express mail, up to half-pound		12.45	7/01	108r
Postal rate, letter, first class, first ounce		0.34	7/01	108r
Postal rate, letter, two ounces		0.57	7/01	108r
Postal rate, post card		0.21	7/01	108r
Postal rate, priority mail, two pounds		3.95	7/01	108r
Postal rate, priority mail, up to one pound		3.50	7/01	108r
Telephone services, expenditures on	yr	830	1999	30r
Education				
Board, 4-year private college/university	yr	3255	1996	38s
Board, 4-year public college/university	yr	2310	1996	38s
Education expenditures	yr	877	1999	30r
Room, 4-year private college/university	yr	3724	1996	38s
Room, 4-year public college/university	yr	2937	1996	38s
Total cost, 4-year private college/university	yr	20831	1996	38s
Total cost, 4-year public college/university	yr	8960	1996	38s
Tuition, 2-year public college/university, in state	yr	2427	1996	38s
Tuition, 4-year private college/university, in state	yr	13852	1996	38s
Tuition, 4-year public college/university	yr	3714	1996	38s
Energy and Fuels				
Electricity	KWh	0.12	7/01	11r
Fuel oil #2	gal	1.31	7/01	11r
Fuel oil and other fuels, expenditures on	yr	207	1999	30r
Gasoline, all types	gal	1.80	7/01	11r
Gasoline, unleaded midgrade	gal	1.85	7/01	11r
Gasoline, unleaded premium	gal	1.91	7/01	11r
Gasoline, unleaded regular	gal	1.71	7/01	11r
Natural gas, expenditures on	yr	368	1999	30r
Utility (piped) gas, therm		1.08	7/01	11r
Utility (piped) gas, 40 therms		50.87	7/01	11r
Utility (piped) gas, 100 therms		111.06	7/01	11r
Entertainment				
Entertainment purchases	yr	1821	1999	30r
Fees and admissions paid	yr	511	1999	30r
Television, radios, sound equipment, expenditures on	yr	650	1999	30r
Funerals				
Total cost of funeral		5813.50	1/99	78r
Acknowledgement cards		28.32	1/99	78r
Casket		2082.20	1/99	78r
Cosmetology, hair, other preparation		169.59	1/99	78r
Embalming		465.60	1/99	78r
Funeral at funeral home		339.56	1/99	78r
Hearse (local)		183.96	1/99	78r
Professional service charges		1157.85	1/99	78r
Service car/van		100.41	1/99	78r
Transfer of remains to funeral home		158.66	1/99	78r

Newburgh, NY - continued

Item	Per	Value	Date	Ref.
Funerals - continued				
Vault		766.31	1/99	78r
Visitation/viewing		361.04	1/99	78r
Groceries				
Apples, red delicious	lb	0.95	7/01	11r
Bacon, sliced	lb	3.44	7/01	11r
Bakery products, expenditures on	yr	310	1999	30r
Bananas	lb	0.55	7/01	11r
Beef, expenditures on	yr	236	1999	30r
Bread, white, pan	lb	1.09	7/01	11r
Butter, yoghurt, cheese, etc, expenditures on	yr	214	1999	30r
Cereals and bakery product purchases	yr	474	1999	30r
Cereals and cereal products, expenditures on	yr	164	1999	30r
Chicken legs, bone-in	lb	1.23	7/01	11r
Chicken, fresh, whole	lb	1.13	7/01	11r
Chuck roast, U.S. choice, boneless	lb	2.79	7/01	11r
Coffee, 100%, ground roast, all sizes	lb	3.40	7/01	11r
Dairy product purchases	yr	342	1999	30r
Eggs, expenditures on	yr	34	1999	30r
Eggs, grade A, large	dozen	0.82	7/01	11r
Fats and oils, expenditures on	yr	80	1999	30r
Fish and seafood, expenditures on	yr	123	1999	30r
Food (excl fruit and vegetables), eaten at home, purchases	yr	838	1999	30r
Food cooked on trips, expenditures on	yr	48	1999	30r
Food purchases	yr	5314	1999	30r
Food purchases, eaten away from home	yr	2313	1999	30r
Food purchases, food eaten at home	yr	3001	1999	30r
Fresh fruits, expenditures on	yr	169	1999	30r
Fresh milk and cream, expenditures on	yr	128	1999	30r
Fresh vegetables, expenditures on	yr	164	1999	30r
Grapefruit	lb	0.67	7/01	11r
Grapes, Thompson, seedless	lb	2.18	7/01	11r
Ground beef, lean and extra lean	lb	2.66	7/01	11r
Ground chuck, 100% beef	lb	2.04	7/01	11r
Lettuce, iceberg	lb	0.76	7/01	11r
Meats, poultry, fish, and egg purchases	yr	808	1999	30r
Nonalcoholic beverages, expenditures on	yr	225	1999	30r
Orange juice, frozen concentrate	16 oz	1.88	7/01	11r
Oranges, Navel	lb	0.79	7/01	11r
Oranges, Valencia	lb	0.56	7/01	11r
Peaches	lb	1.16	7/01	11r
Peanut butter, creamy, all sizes	lb	2.01	7/01	11r
Pears, Anjou	lb	1.16	7/01	11r
Pork chops, center cut, bone-in	lb	3.57	7/01	11r
Pork, expenditures on	yr	146	1999	30r
Potato chips	16 oz	3.37	7/01	11r
Potatoes, white, all types	lb	0.42	7/01	11r
Poultry, expenditures on	yr	158	1999	30r
Processed fruits, expenditures on	yr	124	1999	30r
Processed vegetables, expenditures on	yr	82	1999	30r
Round roast, U.S. choice, boneless	lb	3.04	7/01	11r
Spaghetti and macaroni	lb	1.04	7/01	11r
Steak, sirloin, U.S. choice, boneless	lb	5.39	7/01	11r
Strawberries, dry pint	12 oz	1.51	7/01	11r
Sugar and other sweets, expenditures on	yr	110	1999	30r
Sugar, white, 33-80 ounce package	lb	0.46	7/01	11r
Sugar, white, all sizes	lb	0.47	7/01	11r
Tobacco products and smoking supplies purchases	yr	309	1999	30r
Yogurt, natural, fruit flavored	8 oz	0.79	7/01	11r
Goods and Services				
B&B Japanese maple (acer japonicum)	gal	38.99-125.00	4/00	93r
Boxwood (buxus)	2 gal	15.99-49.95	4/00	93r
Daylily (hemerocallis)	gal	4.95	4/00	93r
Flat of annuals		8.00-14.99	4/00	93r
Fountain grass (pennisetum)	gal	6.99-9.99	4/00	93r

Values are in dollars or fractions of dollars. In the column headed *Ref*, references are shown to sources. Each reference is followed by a letter. These refer to the geographical level for which data were reported: s=State, r=Region, and c=City or metro. The abbreviation *ex* is used to mean *except* or *excluding*; *exp* stands for *expenditures*. For other abbreviations and further explanations, please see the Introduction.

Newburgh, NY - continued

Item	Per	Value	Date	Ref.
Goods and Services				
Hanging basket (10 in)		12.95-19.99	4/00	93r
Hardy geranium (geranium)	gal	6.95-7.99	4/00	93r
Hosta (hosta)	gal	4.95	4/00	93r
Lilac (syrubga vulgaris)	2 gal	17.99-74.95	4/00	93r
Miscellaneous purchases	yr	872	1999	30r
Rhododendron (rhododendron)	2 gal	23.99-54.95	4/00	93r
Sage (salvia)	gal	6.95-7.99	4/00	93r
Wintercreeper euonymus (euonymus fortunei)	2 gal	14.99-23.95	4/00	93r
Hunting license	yr	11.00	4/01	34s
Health Care				
Cardiac catheterization, ave hospital/ physician charges		12750	1998	77s
Childbirth, Cesarean delivery		14716	1997	13r
Childbirth, vaginal delivery		8541	1997	13r
Drugs, expenditures on	yr	296	1999	30r
Health care purchases	yr	1788	1999	30r
Health insurance expenditures	yr	875	1999	30r
Hysterectomy, laproscopically-assisted, ave hospital/physician charges		13460	1998	76s
Hysterectomy, vaginal, ave hospital and physician charges		10310	1998	76s
Medicaid dispensing fee		3.50-4.50	1999	87s
Medical services expenditures	yr	516	1999	30r
Medical supplies, expenditures on	yr	102	1999	30r
Plastic surgery, breast augmentation		4232	2000	7r
Plastic surgery, breast lift		4605	2000	7r
Plastic surgery, facelift		6964	2000	7r
Plastic surgery, hair transplantation		4193	2000	7r
Plastic surgery, lip augmentation		1675	2000	7r
Plastic surgery, lower body lift		6611	2000	7r
Plastic surgery, thigh lift		4751	2000	7r
Household Goods				
Floor coverings, expenditures on	yr	59	1999	30r
Furniture, expenditures on	yr	388	1999	30r
Household furnishings and equipment purchases	yr	1567	1999	30r
Household textiles, expenditures on	yr	112	1999	30r
Laundry and cleaning supplies, expenditures on	yr	104	1999	30r
Housing				
Home price, existing, ave		180800	10/00	90r
Home value, median		179000	2001	53s
Household operation expenditures	yr	581	1999	30r
Housekeeping supplies purchases	yr	474	1999	30r
Lodging expenditures	yr	550	1999	30r
Maintenance, repairs, insurance expenditures	yr	835	1999	30r
Monthly rental value of owned home	mos	663	1999	30r
Owned dwellings, expenditures own	yr	5209	1999	30r
Rent expenditures	yr	2390	1999	30r
Rental unit, 1 bedroom, with utilities	mos	618	4/01	41c
Rental unit, 2 bedroom, with utilities	mos	757	4/01	41c
Rental unit, 3 bedroom, with utilities	mos	960	4/01	41c
Rental unit, 4 bedroom, with utilities	mos	1095	4/01	41c
Shelter, expenditures on	yr	8149	1999	30r
Insurance and Pensions				
Auto insurance premium	yr	1113.55	1999	57s
Life and other personal insurance purchases	yr	424	1999	30r
Pensions and Social Security, expenditures on	yr	3037	1999	30r
Legal Fees				
Divorce, filing fee		270.00	4/01	35s

Newburgh, NY - continued

Item	Per	Value	Date	Ref.
Legal Fees - continued				
Driver's license fee	renew	25.00	1999	48s
Driver's license fee	orig	25.00	1999	48s
Fishing license	yr	14.00	4/01	34s
Personal Goods				
Personal care products and services purchases	yr	399	1999	30r
Personal Services				
Personal services, household, expenditures on	yr	271	1999	30r
Pets				
Pets, toys, and playground equipment, expenditures on	yr	325	1999	30r
Taxes				
Federal income taxes paid	yr	2606	1999	30r
Personal taxes, expenditures on	yr	3567	1999	30r
Property taxes paid	yr	1752	1999	30r
State and local income taxes paid	yr	694	1999	30r
Transportation				
Cars and trucks, new, expenditures on	yr	1496	1999	30r
Cars and trucks, used, expenditures on	yr	1251	1999	30r
Diesel at the pump	gal	1.33	10/99	73s
Gasoline and motor oil purchases	yr	901	1999	30r
Gasoline before-tax price (cents)	gal	110.70	10/00	43s
Maintenance and repair expenditures	yr	618	1999	30r
Public transportation, expenditures on	yr	575	1999	30r
Transportation purchases	yr	6503	1999	30r
Vehicle expenses, miscellaneous, purchases	yr	2266	1999	30r
Vehicle insurance payments	yr	824	1999	30r
Vehicle purchases (net outlay)	yr	2761	1999	30r
Vehicle rental, lease expenditures	yr	584	1999	30r
Travel				
Hotel room	night	139.88	2/01	95s
Utilities				
Electrical bill, average	mos	71.50	9/00	9s
Electricity, expenditures on	yr	837	1999	30r
Electricity cost, average	KWh	11.34	9/00	9s
Utilities, fuels, and public services purchased	yr	2457	1999	30r
Water and other public services, expenditures on	yr	215	1999	30r
Weddings				
Wedding (national average cost)		19936	2000	33r
Wedding (regional average total cost)		29454	1997	110r
Attendants' gifts		321	1998	33r
Bridal attendants' apparel (5 persons)		824	2000	33r
Bride's headpiece/veil		173	1998	33r
Bride's wedding dress		859	1998	33r
Clergy, religious facility fee		242	1998	33r
Engagement ring		3177	1998	33r
Flowers		789	1998	33r
Groom's formalwear rental		99	2000	33r
Limousine		410	1998	33r
Marriage license cost		25.00	4/01	35s
Men's formalwear (ushers, best man)		469	2000	33r
Mother of bride apparel		241	2000	33r
Music		866	1998	33r
Photography and videography		1368	1998	33r
Rehearsal dinner		728	1998	33r
Wedding invitations and announcements		341	1998	33r
Wedding reception		7968	2000	33r
Wedding rings (bride and groom)		1060	1998	33r

Norfolk-Virginia Beach-Newport News, VA-NC

Item	Per	Value	Date	Ref.
Alcoholic Beverages				
Alcoholic beverage purchases	yr	253	1999	30r
Malt beverages, all types, all sizes, any origin	16 oz	0.96	7/01	11r

Values are in dollars or fractions of dollars. In the column headed *Ref*, references are shown to sources. Each reference is followed by a letter. These refer to the geographical level for which data were reported: s=State, r=Region, and c=City or metro. The abbreviation *ex* is used to mean *except* or *excluding*; *exp* stands for *expenditures*. For other abbreviations and further explanations, please see the Introduction.

Norfolk-Virginia Beach-Newport News, VA-NC - continued

Item	Per	Value	Date	Ref.
Appliances				
Major appliances, expenditures on	yr	172	1999	30r
Small appliances, housewares, expenditures on	yr	81	1999	30r
Banking and Money				
Mortgage interest and charges paid	yr	2039	1999	30r
Mortgage principal paid on owned property	yr	1026	1999	30r
Vehicle finance charges paid	yr	365	1999	30r
Charity				
Cash contributions, expenditures	yr	1127	1999	30r
Child Care				
Child raising cost, total, age 0-2	yr	8540	1999	60r
Child raising cost, total, age 3-5	yr	8780	1999	60r
Child raising cost, total, age 6-8	yr	8820	1999	60r
Child raising cost, total, age 9-11	yr	8800	1999	60r
Child raising cost, total, age 12-14	yr	9510	1999	60r
Child raising cost, total, age 15-17	yr	9740	1999	60r
Child's child care and education, age 0-2	yr	1380	1999	60r
Child's child care and education, age 3-5	yr	1520	1999	60r
Child's child care and education, age 6-8	yr	990	1999	60r
Child's child care and education, age 9-11	yr	650	1999	60r
Child's child care and education, age 12-14	yr	490	1999	60r
Child's child care and education, age 15-17	yr	840	1999	60r
Child's clothing, age 0-2	yr	480	1999	60r
Child's clothing, age 3-5	yr	470	1999	60r
Child's clothing, age 6-8	yr	520	1999	60r
Child's clothing, age 9-11	yr	570	1999	60r
Child's clothing, age 12-14	yr	950	1999	60r
Child's clothing, age 15-17	yr	850	1999	60r
Child's food, age 0-2	yr	1000	1999	60r
Child's food, age 3-5	yr	1160	1999	60r
Child's food, age 6-8	yr	1490	1999	60r
Child's food, age 9-11	yr	1770	1999	60r
Child's food, age 12-14	yr	1770	1999	60r
Child's food, age 15-17	yr	1980	1999	60r
Child's health care, age 0-2	yr	620	1999	60r
Child's health care, age 3-5	yr	590	1999	60r
Child's health care, age 6-8	yr	680	1999	60r
Child's health care, age 9-11	yr	720	1999	60r
Child's health care, age 12-14	yr	730	1999	60r
Child's health care, age 15-17	yr	760	1999	60r
Child's housing, age 0-2	yr	3070	1999	60r
Child's housing, age 3-5	yr	3050	1999	60r
Child's housing, age 6-8	yr	3010	1999	60r
Child's housing, age 9-11	yr	2850	1999	60r
Child's housing, age 12-14	yr	3040	1999	60r
Child's housing, age 15-17	yr	2650	1999	60r
Child's personal care, reading, age 0-2	yr	910	1999	60r
Child's personal care, reading, age 3-5	yr	930	1999	60r
Child's personal care, reading, age 6-8	yr	960	1999	60r
Child's personal care, reading, age 9-11	yr	1000	1999	60r
Child's personal care, reading, age 12-14	yr	1170	1999	60r
Child's personal care, reading, age 15-17	yr	950	1999	60r
Clothing				
Apparel and services purchases	yr	1610	1999	30r
Boys, 2 to 15, expenditures on	yr	89	1999	30r
Children under 2, expenditures on	yr	79	1999	30r
Footwear, expenditures on	yr	283	1999	30r
Girls, 2 to 15, expenditures on	yr	103	1999	30r
Men and boys, expenditures on	yr	351	1999	30r
Men, 16 and over, expenditures on	yr	262	1999	30r
Women, 16 and over, expenditures on	yr	538	1999	30r
Communications				
Cable modem installation, Adelphi		54.90	6/99	103s
Cable modem installation, Comcast		95.00	6/99	103s
Cable modem installation, Cox		99.00-174.95	6/99	103s
Cable modem installation, Jones Intercable		100.00	6/99	103s
Cable modem rate, cable subscriber, Adelphi	mos	34.95	6/99	103s

Norfolk-Virginia Beach-Newport News, VA-NC - continued

Item	Per	Value	Date	Ref.
Communications - continued				
Cable modem rate, cable subscriber, Comcast	mos	39.95	6/99	103s
Cable modem rate, cable subscriber, Cox	mos	29.95-44.95	6/99	103s
Cable modem rate, cable subscriber, Jones Intercable	mos	29.95-39.95	6/99	103s
Cable modem rate, non-cable subscriber, Adelphi	mos	44.95	6/99	103s
Cable modem rate, non-cable subscriber, Comcast	mos	49.95	6/99	103s
Cable modem rate, non-cable subscriber, Cox	mos	42.95-54.95	6/99	103s
Phone line, single, business, field visit	inst.	64.00	12/97	17s
Phone line, single, business, no field visit	inst.	64.00	12/97	17s
Phone line, single, residence, field visit	inst.	38.50	12/97	17s
Phone line, single, residence, no field visit	inst.	38.50	12/97	17s
Postage and stationery, expenditures on	yr	104	1999	30r
Postal rate, express mail, up to half-pound		12.45	7/01	108r
Postal rate, letter, first class, first ounce		0.34	7/01	108r
Postal rate, letter, two ounces		0.57	7/01	108r
Postal rate, post card		0.21	7/01	108r
Postal rate, priority mail, two pounds		3.95	7/01	108r
Postal rate, priority mail, up to one pound		3.50	7/01	108r
Telephone services, expenditures on	yr	860	1999	30r
Education				
Board, 4-year private college/university	yr	2363	1996	38s
Board, 4-year public college/university	yr	2033	1996	38s
Education expenditures	yr	431	1999	30r
Room, 4-year private college/university	yr	2062	1996	38s
Room, 4-year public college/university	yr	2261	1996	38s
Total cost, 4-year private college/university	yr	15021	1996	38s
Total cost, 4-year public college/university	yr	8202	1996	38s
Tuition, 2-year public college/university, in state	yr	1433	1996	38s
Tuition, 4-year private college/university, in state	yr	10596	1996	38s
Tuition, 4-year public college/university	yr	3907	1996	38s
Energy and Fuels				
Electricity	KWh	0.09	7/01	11r
Electricity	500 KWhs	47.29	7/01	11r
Fuel oil #2	gal	1.43	7/01	11r
Fuel oil and other fuels, expenditures on	yr	45	1999	30r
Gas, natural, commercial rate	1000 cf	9.01	11/00	88s
Gasoline, all types	gal	1.60	7/01	11r
Gasoline, unleaded midgrade	gal	1.65	7/01	11r
Gasoline, unleaded premium	gal	1.74	7/01	11r
Natural gas, expenditures on	yr	164	1999	30r
Utility (piped) gas, therm		1.01	7/01	11r
Utility (piped) gas, 40 therms		44.29	7/01	11r
Utility (piped) gas, 100 therms		97.44	7/01	11r
Entertainment				
Entertainment purchases	yr	1574	1999	30r
Fees and admissions paid	yr	371	1999	30r
Reading purchases	yr	121	1999	30r
Television, radios, sound equipment, expenditures on	yr	561	1999	30r
Funerals				
Total cost of funeral		5922.53	1/99	78r
Acknowledgement cards		63.43	1/99	78r
Casket		2258.77	1/99	78r
Cosmetology, hair, other preparation		127.09	1/99	78r
Embalming		393.49	1/99	78r
Funeral at funeral home		367.50	1/99	78r
Hearse (local)		169.66	1/99	78r
Professional service charges		1211.32	1/99	78r
Service car/van		80.69	1/99	78r
Transfer of remains to funeral home		144.25	1/99	78r
Vault		803.50	1/99	78r
Visitation/viewing		302.83	1/99	78r

Values are in dollars or fractions of dollars. In the column headed *Ref*, references are shown to sources. Each reference is followed by a letter. These refer to the geographical level for which data were reported: s=State, r=Region, and c=City or metro. The abbreviation *ex* is used to mean *except* or *excluding*; *exp* stands for *expenditures*. For other abbreviations and further explanations, please see the Introduction.

Norfolk-Virginia Beach-Newport News, VA-NC - continued

Item	Per	Value	Date	Ref.
Groceries				
American processed cheese	lb	3.50	7/01	11r
Bakery products, expenditures on	yr	261	1999	30r
Bananas	lb	0.47	7/01	11r
Beans, dried, any type, all sizes	lb	0.63	7/01	11r
Beef for stew, boneless	lb	2.86	7/01	11r
Beef, expenditures on	yr	210	1999	30r
Bologna, all beef or mixed	lb	2.29	7/01	11r
Bread, French	lb	1.66	7/01	11r
Bread, white, pan	lb	0.87	7/01	11r
Bread, whole wheat, pan	lb	1.38	7/01	11r
Broccoli	lb	1.04	7/01	11r
Butter, salted, grade AA, stick	lb	2.26	7/01	11r
Butter, yoghurt, cheese, etc, expenditures on	yr	170	1999	30r
Cabbage	lb	0.42	7/01	11r
Cereals and cereal products, expenditures on	yr	140	1999	30r
Cheddar cheese, natural	lb	3.75	7/01	11r
Chicken breast, bone-in	lb	1.85	7/01	11r
Chicken legs, bone-in	lb	1.34	7/01	11r
Chicken, fresh, whole	lb	1.05	7/01	11r
Chops, boneless	lb	4.13	7/01	11r
Chuck roast, graded and ungraded, excl U.S. prime and choice	lb	2.35	7/01	11r
Chuck roast, U.S. choice, boneless	lb	2.67	7/01	11r
Coffee, 100%, ground roast, all sizes	lb	2.88	7/01	11r
Coffee, instant, plain, regular, all sizes	16 oz	9.25	7/01	11r
Cola, non diet,	2 liter	1.11	7/01	11r
Crackers, soda, salted	lb	1.70	7/01	11r
Dairy product purchases	yr	282	1999	30r
Eggs, expenditures on	yr	32	1999	30r
Fats and oils, expenditures on	yr	79	1999	30r
Fish and seafood, expenditures on	yr	99	1999	30r
Flour, white, all purpose	lb	0.32	7/01	11r
Food (excl fruit and vegetables), eaten at home, purchases	yr	815	1999	30r
Food cooked on trips, expenditures on	yr	36	1999	30r
Food purchases	yr	4533	1999	30r
Food purchases, eaten away from home	yr	1873	1999	30r
Food purchases, food eaten at home	yr	2660	1999	30r
Fresh fruits, expenditures on	yr	128	1999	30r
Fresh milk and cream, expenditures on	yr	112	1999	30r
Fresh vegetables, expenditures on	yr	131	1999	30r
Fruit and vegetable purchases	yr	438	1999	30r
Grapefruit	lb	0.59	7/01	11r
Grapes, Thompson, seedless	lb	2.12	7/01	11r
Ground beef, 100% beef	lb	1.76	7/01	11r
Ground beef, lean and extra lean	lb	2.60	7/01	11r
Ground chuck, 100% beef	lb	2.08	7/01	11r
Ham, boneless, excl canned	lb	2.71	7/01	11r
Ham, rump or shank half, bone-in, smoked	lb	2.19	7/01	11r
Ice cream, prepackaged, bulk, regular	1/2 gal	3.93	7/01	11r
Lemons	lb	1.32	7/01	11r
Lettuce, iceberg	lb	0.76	7/01	11r
Milk, fresh, low fat,	gal	2.75	7/01	11r
Milk, fresh, whole, fortified	gal	2.97	7/01	11r
Nonalcoholic beverages, expenditures on	yr	228	1999	30r
Orange juice, frozen concentrate	16 oz	1.95	7/01	11r
Oranges, Navel	lb	0.73	7/01	11r
Oranges, Valencia	lb	0.55	7/01	11r
Peanut butter, creamy, all sizes	lb	1.83	7/01	11r
Pears, Anjou	lb	0.98	7/01	11r
Pork chops, center cut, bone-in	lb	3.33	7/01	11r
Pork sausage, fresh, loose	lb	2.59	7/01	11r
Pork shoulder picnic, bone-in, smoked	lb	1.12	7/01	11r
Pork, expenditures on	yr	162	1999	30r
Potato chips	16 oz	3.59	7/01	11r
Potatoes, frozen, french fried	lb	1.00	7/01	11r
Potatoes, white, all types	lb	0.44	7/01	11r
Poultry, expenditures on	yr	137	1999	30r
Processed fruits, expenditures on	yr	97	1999	30r
Processed vegetables, expenditures on	yr	82	1999	30r
Rice, white, long grain, uncooked	lb	0.51	7/01	11r

Item	Per	Value	Date	Ref.
Groceries - continued				
Round roast, graded and ungraded, excl U.S. prime and choice	lb	2.96	7/01	11r
Round steak, graded and ungraded, excl U.S. prime and choice	lb	3.11	7/01	11r
Sirloin steak, graded and ungraded, excl U.S. prime and choice	lb	4.23	7/01	11r
Spaghetti and macaroni	lb	0.78	7/01	11r
Steak, round, U.S. choice, boneless	lb	3.56	7/01	11r
Steak, sirloin, U.S. choice, boneless	lb	5.65	7/01	11r
Strawberries, dry pint	12 oz	1.50	7/01	11r
Sugar and other sweets, expenditures on	yr	99	1999	30r
Sugar, white, 33-80 ounce package	lb	0.39	7/01	11r
Sugar, white, all sizes	lb	0.42	7/01	11r
Tobacco products and smoking supplies purchases	yr	288	1999	30r
Tomatoes, field grown	lb	1.43	7/01	11r
Tuna, light, chunk	lb	1.77	7/01	11r
Turkey, frozen, whole	lb	1.05	7/01	11r
Goods and Services				
B&B Japanese maple (acer japonicum)	gal	49.98-129.00	4/00	93r
Boxwood (buxus)	2 gal	12.99-16.99	4/00	93r
Daylily (hemerocallis)	gal	4.99-8.99	4/00	93r
Flat of annuals		11.00-13.92	4/00	93r
Fountain grass (pennisetum)	gal	5.98-7.98	4/00	93r
Hanging basket (10 in)		7.99-14.98	4/00	93r
Hardy geranium (geranium)	gal	5.98-8.00	4/00	93r
Hosta (hosta)	gal	4.99-10.98	4/00	93r
Lilac (syrubga vulgaris)	2 gal	12.99-21.99	4/00	93r
Rhododendron (rhododendron)	2 gal	14.99-24.99	4/00	93r
Sage (salvia)	gal	5.98-6.99	4/00	93r
Wintercreeper euonymus (euonymus fortunei)	2 gal	7.99-89.99	4/00	93r
Hunting license	yr	12.00	4/01	34s
Health Care				
Cardiac catheterization, ave hospital/physician charges		15370	1998	77s
Childbirth, Cesarean delivery		11587	1997	13r
Childbirth, vaginal delivery		6725	1997	13r
Drugs, expenditures on	yr	399	1999	30r
Health care purchases	yr	1971	1999	30r
Health insurance expenditures	yr	933	1999	30r
Hysterectomy, laproscopically-assisted, ave hospital/physician charges		15660	1998	76s
Hysterectomy, vaginal, ave hospital and physician charges		10260	1998	76s
Medicaid dispensing fee		4.25	1999	87s
Medical services expenditures	yr	547	1999	30r
Medical supplies, expenditures on	yr	91	1999	30r
Plastic surgery, breast augmentation		2870	2000	7r
Plastic surgery, breast lift		3649	2000	7r
Plastic surgery, facelift		5008	2000	7r
Plastic surgery, hair transplantation		3425	2000	7r
Plastic surgery, lip augmentation		1227	2000	7r
Plastic surgery, lower body lift		4793	2000	7r
Plastic surgery, thigh lift		3862	2000	7r
Household Goods				
Floor coverings, expenditures on	yr	44	1999	30r
Furniture, expenditures on	yr	335	1999	30r
Household furnishings and equipment purchases	yr	1328	1999	30r

Values are in dollars or fractions of dollars. In the column headed *Ref*, references are shown to sources. Each reference is followed by a letter. These refer to the geographical level for which data were reported: s=State, r=Region, and c=City or metro. The abbreviation *ex* is used to mean *except* or *excluding*; *exp* stands for expenditures. For other abbreviations and further explanations, please see the Introduction.

Norfolk-Virginia Beach-Newport News, VA-NC - continued

Item	Per	Value	Date	Ref.
Household Goods				
Household textiles, expenditures on	yr	89	1999	30r
Laundry and cleaning supplies, expenditures on	yr	113	1999	30r
Housing				
Home price, existing, ave		160100	10/00	90r
Home value, median		141000	2001	53s
Household operation expenditures	yr	553	1999	30r
Housekeeping supplies purchases	yr	473	1999	30r
Housing, expenditures on	yr	10303	1999	30r
Maintenance, repairs, insurance expenditures	yr	699	1999	30r
Monthly rental value of owned home	mos	505	1999	30r
Owned dwellings, expenditures own	yr	3465	1999	30r
Rent expenditures	yr	1641	1999	30r
Rental unit, 1 bedroom, with utilities	mos	496	4/01	41c
Rental unit, 2 bedroom, with utilities	mos	586	4/01	41c
Rental unit, 3 bedroom, with utilities	mos	817	4/01	41c
Rental unit, 4 bedroom, with utilities	mos	960	4/01	41c
Shelter, expenditures on	yr	5467	1999	30r
Insurance and Pensions				
Auto insurance premium	yr	628.58	1999	57s
Life and other personal insurance purchases	yr	414	1999	30r
Pensions and Social Security, expenditures on	yr	2635	1999	30r
Personal insurance and pensions, expenditures on	yr	3048	1999	30r
Legal Fees				
Divorce, filing fee		64.00	4/01	35s
Driver's license fee	orig	7.20	1999	48s
Driver's license fee	renew	7.20	1999	48s
Fishing license	yr	12.50	4/01	34s
Personal Goods				
Personal care products and services purchases	yr	393	1999	30r
Personal Services				
Personal services, household, expenditures on	yr	258	1999	30r
Pets				
Pets, toys, and playground equipment, expenditures on	yr	306	1999	30r
Taxes				
Federal income taxes paid	yr	2047	1999	30r
Personal taxes, expenditures on	yr	2554	1999	30r
Property taxes paid	yr	726	1999	30r
State and local income taxes paid	yr	363	1999	30r
Transportation				
Cars and trucks, new, expenditures on	yr	1648	1999	30r
Cars and trucks, used, expenditures on	yr	1651	1999	30r
Diesel at the pump	gal	1.14	10/99	73s
Gasoline and motor oil purchases	yr	1052	1999	30r
Gasoline before-tax price (cents)	gal	107.30	10/00	43s
Maintenance and repair expenditures	yr	621	1999	30r
Public transportation, expenditures on	yr	298	1999	30r
Transportation purchases	yr	6738	1999	30r
Vehicle expenses, miscellaneous, purchases	yr	2033	1999	30r
Vehicle insurance payments	yr	696	1999	30r
Vehicle purchases (net outlay)	yr	3354	1999	30r
Vehicle rental, lease expenditures	yr	352	1999	30r
Utilities				
Electrical bill, average	mos	82.17	9/00	9s
Electricity, expenditures on	yr	1115	1999	30r
Electricity cost, average	KWh	5.90	9/00	9s
Water and other public services, expenditures on	yr	298	1999	30r
Weddings				
Wedding (national average cost)		19936	2000	33r
Wedding (regional average total cost)		16293	1997	110r

Norfolk-Virginia Beach-Newport News, VA-NC - continued

Item	Per	Value	Date	Ref.
Weddings - continued				
Attendants' gifts		321	1998	33r
Bridal attendants' apparel (5 persons)		824	2000	33r
Bride's headpiece/veil		173	1998	33r
Bride's wedding dress		859	1998	33r
Clergy, religious facility fee		242	1998	33r
Engagement ring		3177	1998	33r
Flowers		789	1998	33r
Groom's formalwear rental		99	2000	33r
Limousine		410	1998	33r
Marriage license cost		30.00	4/01	35s
Men's formalwear (ushers, best man)		469	2000	33r
Mother of bride apparel		241	2000	33r
Music		866	1998	33r
Photography and videography		1368	1998	33r
Rehearsal dinner		728	1998	33r
Wedding invitations and announcements		341	1998	33r
Wedding reception		7968	2000	33r
Wedding rings (bride and groom)		1060	1998	33r

Oakland, CA

Item	Per	Value	Date	Ref.
Average annual expenditures	yr	40662	1999	30r
Alcoholic Beverages				
Alcoholic beverage purchases	yr	372	1999	30r
Malt beverages, all types, all sizes, any origin	16 oz	0.94	7/01	11r
Wine, red and white table, all sizes, any origin	liter	6.00	7/01	11r
Appliances				
Major appliances, expenditures on	yr	167	1999	30r
Small appliances, housewares, expenditures on	yr	105	1999	30r
Banking and Money				
Mortgage interest and charges paid	yr	3368	1999	30r
Mortgage principal paid on owned property	yr	1677	1999	30r
Vehicle finance charges paid	yr	311	1999	30r
Business Expenses				
Business travel, car rental	day	52	2001	3c
Business travel, food	day	53	2001	3c
Business travel, hotel	day	130	2001	3c
Office space, central business district, Class A	sq ft	25.92	3/99	74c
Charity				
Cash contributions, expenditures	yr	1344	1999	30r
Child Care				
Child care fee, one year old	week	209	5/99	26c
Child care fee, six year old	week	78	5/99	26c
Child care fee, three year old	week	132	5/99	26c
Child raising cost, total, age 0-2	yr	9140	1999	60r
Child raising cost, total, age 3-5	yr	9370	1999	60r
Child raising cost, total, age 6-8	yr	9450	1999	60r
Child raising cost, total, age 9-11	yr	9470	1999	60r
Child raising cost, total, age 12-14	yr	10170	1999	60r
Child raising cost, total, age 15-17	yr	10360	1999	60r
Child's child care and education, age 0-2	yr	1250	1999	60r
Child's child care and education, age 3-5	yr	1380	1999	60r
Child's child care and education, age 6-8	yr	890	1999	60r
Child's child care and education, age 9-11	yr	580	1999	60r
Child's child care and education, age 12-14	yr	430	1999	60r
Child's child care and education, age 15-17	yr	730	1999	60r
Child's clothing, age 0-2	yr	430	1999	60r
Child's clothing, age 3-5	yr	420	1999	60r
Child's clothing, age 6-8	yr	470	1999	60r
Child's clothing, age 9-11	yr	520	1999	60r
Child's clothing, age 12-14	yr	870	1999	60r
Child's clothing, age 15-17	yr	770	1999	60r
Child's food, age 0-2	yr	1120	1999	60r
Child's food, age 3-5	yr	1280	1999	60r
Child's food, age 6-8	yr	1640	1999	60r

Values are in dollars or fractions of dollars. In the column headed *Ref*, references are shown to sources. Each reference is followed by a letter. These refer to the geographical level for which data were reported: s=State, r=Region, and c=City or metro. The abbreviation *ex* is used to mean *except* or *excluding*; *exp* stands for *expenditures*. For other abbreviations and further explanations, please see the Introduction.

Oakland, CA - continued

Item	Per	Value	Date	Ref.
Child Care				
Child's food, age 9-11	yr	1930	1999	60r
Child's food, age 12-14	yr	1940	1999	60r
Child's food, age 15-17	yr	2150	1999	60r
Child's health care, age 0-2	yr	490	1999	60r
Child's health care, age 3-5	yr	470	1999	60r
Child's health care, age 6-8	yr	530	1999	60r
Child's health care, age 9-11	yr	570	1999	60r
Child's health care, age 12-14	yr	580	1999	60r
Child's health care, age 15-17	yr	610	1999	60r
Child's housing, age 0-2	yr	3630	1999	60r
Child's housing, age 3-5	yr	3610	1999	60r
Child's housing, age 6-8	yr	3570	1999	60r
Child's housing, age 9-11	yr	3410	1999	60r
Child's housing, age 12-14	yr	3600	1999	60r
Child's housing, age 15-17	yr	3210	1999	60r
Child's personal care, reading, age 0-2	yr	1040	1999	60r
Child's personal care, reading, age 3-5	yr	1060	1999	60r
Child's personal care, reading, age 6-8	yr	1090	1999	60r
Child's personal care, reading, age 9-11	yr	1130	1999	60r
Child's personal care, reading, age 12-14	yr	1300	1999	60r
Child's personal care, reading, age 15-17	yr	1080	1999	60r
Clothing				
Apparel and services purchases	yr	1863	1999	30r
Boys, 2 to 15, expenditures on	yr	80	1999	30r
Children under 2, expenditures on	yr	74	1999	30r
Footwear, expenditures on	yr	307	1999	30r
Girls, 2 to 15, expenditures on	yr	101	1999	30r
Men and boys, expenditures on	yr	443	1999	30r
Men, 16 and over, expenditures on	yr	363	1999	30r
Women, 16 and over, expenditures on	yr	594	1999	30r
Communications				
Cable modem installation, AT&T-BIS		150.00	6/99	103s
Cable modem installation, Charter		99.00-169.00	6/99	103s
Cable modem installation, Comcast		95.00	6/99	103s
Cable modem installation, Cox		99.00-174.95	6/99	103s
Cable modem installation, Media One		100.00	6/99	103s
Cable modem installation, Time Warner		75.00-225.00	6/99	103s
Cable modem rate, cable subscriber, AT&T-BIS	mos	39.95	6/99	103s
Cable modem rate, cable subscriber, Charter	mos	49.95-79.95	6/99	103s
Cable modem rate, cable subscriber, Comcast	mos	39.95	6/99	103s
Cable modem rate, cable subscriber, Cox	mos	29.95-44.95	6/99	103s
Cable modem rate, cable subscriber, Media One	mos	34.95-39.95	6/99	103s
Cable modem rate, cable subscriber, Time Warner	mos	39.95-49.95	6/99	103s
Cable modem rate, non-cable subscriber, Charter	mos	59.95-89.95	6/99	103s
Cable modem rate, non-cable subscriber, Comcast	mos	49.95	6/99	103s
Cable modem rate, non-cable subscriber, Cox	mos	42.95-54.95	6/99	103s
Cable modem rate, non-cable subscriber, Media One	mos	49.95	6/99	103s
Cable modem rate, non-cable subscriber, Time Warner	mos	39.95-54.95	6/99	103s
Phone line, single, business, field visit	inst.	70.75	12/97	17s
Phone line, single, business, no field visit	inst.	70.75	12/97	17s
Phone line, single, residence, field visit	inst.	34.75	12/97	17s
Phone line, single, residence, no field visit	inst.	34.75	12/97	17s
Postage and stationery, expenditures on	yr	150	1999	30r
Postal rate, express mail, up to half-pound		12.45	7/01	108r
Postal rate, letter, first class, first ounce		0.34	7/01	108r
Postal rate, letter, two ounces		0.57	7/01	108r
Postal rate, post card		0.21	7/01	108r

Oakland, CA - continued

Item	Per	Value	Date	Ref.
Communications - continued				
Postal rate, priority mail, two pounds		3.95	7/01	108r
Postal rate, priority mail, up to one pound		3.50	7/01	108r
Telephone services, expenditures on	yr	825	1999	30r
Education				
Board, 4-year private college/university	yr	2970	1996	38s
Board, 4-year public college/university	yr	2516	1996	38s
Education expenditures	yr	676	1999	30r
Room, 4-year private college/university	yr	3196	1996	38s
Room, 4-year public college/university	yr	3031	1996	38s
Total cost, 4-year private college/university	yr	20143	1996	38s
Total cost, 4-year public college/university	yr	8213	1996	38s
Tuition, 2-year public college/university, in state	yr	362	1996	38s
Tuition, 4-year private college/university, in state	yr	13977	1996	38s
Tuition, 4-year public college/university	yr	2666	1996	38s
Energy and Fuels				
Electricity	500 KWhs	48.23	7/01	11r
Electricity	KWh	0.11	7/01	11r
Fuel oil and other fuels, expenditures on	yr	35	1999	30r
Gas, natural, commercial rate	1000 cf	8.74	11/00	88s
Gasoline, all types	gal	1.91	7/01	11r
Gasoline, unleaded premium	gal	2.05	7/01	11r
Gasoline, unleaded regular	gal	1.83	7/01	11r
Natural gas, expenditures on	yr	255	1999	30r
Utility (piped) gas, therm		0.98	7/01	11r
Utility (piped) gas, 40 therms		40.74	7/01	11r
Utility (piped) gas, 100 therms		96.80	7/01	11r
Entertainment				
Entertainment purchases	yr	2139	1999	30r
Fees and admissions paid	yr	545	1999	30r
Television, radios, sound equipment, expenditures on	yr	624	1999	30r
Funerals				
Total cost of funeral		5401.08	1/99	78r
Acknowledgement cards		33.64	1/99	78r
Casket		2170.43	1/99	78r
Cosmetology, hair, other preparation		136.32	1/99	78r
Embalming		319.13	1/99	78r
Funeral at funeral home		370.21	1/99	78r
Hearse (local)		161.04	1/99	78r
Professional service charges		963.15	1/99	78r
Service car/van		133.99	1/99	78r
Transfer of remains to funeral home		159.82	1/99	78r
Vault		778.07	1/99	78r
Visitation/viewing		175.28	1/99	78r
Groceries				
Apples, red delicious	lb	0.84	7/01	11r
Bacon, sliced	lb	3.38	7/01	11r
Bakery products, expenditures on	yr	299	1999	30r
Bananas	lb	0.54	7/01	11r
Beans, dried, any type, all sizes	lb	0.76	7/01	11r
Beef, expenditures on	yr	222	1999	30r
Bread, white, pan	lb	0.99	7/01	11r
Butter, yoghurt, cheese, etc, expenditures on	yr	211	1999	30r
Cereals and bakery product purchases	yr	466	1999	30r
Cereals and cereal products, expenditures on	yr	168	1999	30r
Chicken breast, bone-in	lb	2.45	7/01	11r
Chicken, fresh, whole	lb	1.19	7/01	11r
Chops, boneless	lb	4.00	7/01	11r
Chuck roast, graded and ungraded, excl U.S. prime and choice	lb	2.55	7/01	11r
Coffee, 100%, ground roast, all sizes	lb	3.80	7/01	11r
Cookies, chocolate chip	lb	2.83	7/01	11r
Dairy product purchases	yr	341	1999	30r
Eggs, expenditures on	yr	39	1999	30r
Eggs, grade AA, large	dozen	1.23	7/01	11r

Values are in dollars or fractions of dollars. In the column headed *Ref*, references are shown to sources. Each reference is followed by a letter. These refer to the geographical level for which data were reported: s=State, r=Region, and c=City or metro. The abbreviation *ex* is used to mean *except* or *excluding*; *exp* stands for expenditures. For other abbreviations and further explanations, please see the Introduction.

Oakland, CA - continued

Item	Per	Value	Date	Ref.
Groceries				
Fats and oils, expenditures on	yr	88	1999	30r
Fish and seafood, expenditures on	yr	121	1999	30r
Food (excl fruit and vegetables), eaten at home, purchases	yr	1001	1999	30r
Food cooked on trips, expenditures on	yr	64	1999	30r
Food purchases	yr	5312	1999	30r
Food purchases, eaten away from home	yr	2180	1999	30r
Food purchases, food eaten at home	yr	3132	1999	30r
Fresh fruits, expenditures on	yr	186	1999	30r
Fresh milk and cream, expenditures on	yr	130	1999	30r
Fresh vegetables, expenditures on	yr	177	1999	30r
Grapefruit	lb	0.68	7/01	11r
Grapes, Thompson, seedless	lb	2.42	7/01	11r
Ground beef, lean and extra lean	lb	2.46	7/01	11r
Ice cream, prepackaged, bulk, regular	1/2 gal	3.62	7/01	11r
Lettuce, iceberg	lb	0.63	7/01	11r
Meats, poultry, fish, and egg purchases	yr	761	1999	30r
Milk, fresh, low fat,	gal	2.80	7/01	11r
Milk, fresh, whole, fortified	gal	2.88	7/01	11r
Nonalcoholic beverages, expenditures on	yr	258	1999	30r
Oranges, Navel	lb	0.97	7/01	11r
Oranges, Valencia	lb	0.43	7/01	11r
Peaches	lb	1.38	7/01	11r
Peanut butter, creamy, all sizes	lb	2.14	7/01	11r
Pork chops, center cut, bone-in	lb	3.83	7/01	11r
Pork, expenditures on	yr	141	1999	30r
Potatoes, white, all types	lb	0.37	7/01	11r
Poultry, expenditures on	yr	146	1999	30r
Processed fruits, expenditures on	yr	118	1999	30r
Processed vegetables, expenditures on	yr	81	1999	30r
Round roast, graded and ungraded, excl U.S. prime and choice	lb	3.07	7/01	11r
Round roast, U.S. choice, boneless	lb	3.37	7/01	11r
Round steak, graded and ungraded, excl U.S. prime and choice	lb	3.51	7/01	11r
Sirloin steak, graded and ungraded, excl U.S. prime and choice	lb	4.67	7/01	11r
Steak, sirloin, U.S. choice, boneless	lb	6.20	7/01	11r
Strawberries, dry pint	12 oz	1.79	7/01	11r
Sugar and other sweets, expenditures on	yr	124	1999	30r
Sugar, white, all sizes	lb	0.46	7/01	11r
Tobacco products and smoking supplies purchases	yr	217	1999	30r
Tomatoes, field grown	lb	1.17	7/01	11r
Tuna, light, chunk	lb	2.05	7/01	11r
Goods and Services				
B&B Japanese maple (acer japonicum)	gal	39.99	4/00	93r
Boxwood (buxus)	2 gal	14.99-24.99	4/00	93r
Christmas tree, noble fir		40-60	2000	65s
Daylilly (hemerocallis)	gal	6.99-8.99	4/00	93r
Flat of annuals		16.68	4/00	93r
Fountain grass (pennisetum)	gal	7.99-11.99	4/00	93r
Hanging basket (10 in)		29.99	4/00	93r
Hardy geranium (geranium)	gal	6.99-11.99	4/00	93r
Hosta (hosta)	gal	6.99-18.99	4/00	93r
Lilac (syrubga vulgaris)	2 gal	14.99-17.99	4/00	93r
Miscellaneous purchases	yr	1070	1999	30r
Rhododendron (rhododendron)	2 gal	14.99	4/00	93r
Sage (salvia)	gal	6.99	4/00	93r
Wintercreeper euonymus (euonymus fortunei)	2 gal	14.99-22.99	4/00	93r
Hunting license	yr	29.95	4/01	34s
Health Care				
Cardiac catheterization, ave hospital/ physician charges		24000	1998	77s

Oakland, CA - continued

Item	Per	Value	Date	Ref.
Health Care - continued				
Childbirth, Cesarean delivery		11587	1997	13r
Childbirth, vaginal delivery		6725	1997	13r
Drugs, expenditures on	yr	309	1999	30r
Health care purchases	yr	1869	1999	30r
Health insurance expenditures	yr	868	1999	30r
Hysterectomy, laproscopically-assisted, ave hospital/physician charges		20760	1998	76s
Hysterectomy, vaginal, ave hospital and physician charges		14570	1998	76s
Medicaid dispensing fee		4.05	1999	87s
Medical services expenditures	yr	580	1999	30r
Medical supplies, expenditures on	yr	112	1999	30r
Nursing home costs, private room	day	157	2000	82c
Nursing home stay, private room	day	157	2000	81c
Household Goods				
Floor coverings, expenditures on	yr	49	1999	30r
Furniture, expenditures on	yr	444	1999	30r
Household furnishings and equipment purchases	yr	1768	1999	30r
Household textiles, expenditures on	yr	141	1999	30r
Laundry and cleaning supplies, expenditures on	yr	128	1999	30r
Housing				
Home, 2200 sq ft, 4-br, 2-bath, 2-car garage, average		527250	2000	47c
Home price, existing, ave		239400	10/00	90r
Home value, median		215000	2001	53s
Household operation expenditures	yr	781	1999	30r
Housekeeping supplies purchases	yr	513	1999	30r
Lodging expenditures	yr	575	1999	30r
Maintenance, repairs, insurance expenditures	yr	939	1999	30r
Monthly rental value of owned home	mos	662	1999	30r
Owned dwellings, expenditures own	yr	5231	1999	30r
Rent expenditures	yr	2709	1999	30r
Rental unit, 1 bedroom, with utilities	mos	785	4/01	41c
Rental unit, 2 bedroom, with utilities	mos	985	4/01	41c
Rental unit, 3 bedroom, with utilities	mos	1350	4/01	41c
Rental unit, 4 bedroom, with utilities	mos	1613	4/01	41c
Shelter, expenditures on	yr	8516	1999	30r
Insurance and Pensions				
Life and other personal insurance purchases	yr	355	1999	30r
Pensions and Social Security, expenditures on	yr	3636	1999	30r
Legal Fees				
Divorce, filing fee		182.00	4/01	35s
Driver's license fee	orig	12.00	1999	48s
Driver's license fee	renew	15.00	1999	48s
Personal Goods				
Personal care products and services purchases	yr	449	1999	30r
Personal Services				
Personal services, household, expenditures on	yr	353	1999	30r
Pets				
Pets, toys, and playground equipment, expenditures on	yr	358	1999	30r
Taxes				
Federal income taxes paid	yr	3200	1999	30r
Personal taxes, expenditures on	yr	4153	1999	30r
Property taxes paid	yr	923	1999	30r
State and local income taxes paid	yr	812	1999	30r
Transportation				
Cars and trucks, new, expenditures on	yr	1534	1999	30r
Cars and trucks, used, expenditures on	yr	1593	1999	30r
Diesel at the pump	gal	1.37	10/99	73s
Gasoline and motor oil purchases	yr	1129	1999	30r

Values are in dollars or fractions of dollars. In the column headed *Ref*, references are shown to sources. Each reference is followed by a letter. These refer to the geographical level for which data were reported: s=State, r=Region, and c=City or metro. The abbreviation *ex* is used to mean *except* or *excluding*; *exp* stands for *expenditures*. For other abbreviations and further explanations, please see the Introduction.

Oakland, CA - continued

Item	Per	Value	Date	Ref.
Transportation				
Gasoline before-tax price (cents)	gal	128.80	10/00	43s
Maintenance and repair expenditures	yr	797	1999	30r
Public transportation, expenditures on	yr	530	1999	30r
Transportation purchases	yr	7423	1999	30r
Vehicle expenses, miscellaneous, purchases	yr	2585	1999	30r
Vehicle insurance payments	yr	811	1999	30r
Vehicle purchases (net outlay)	yr	3180	1999	30r
Vehicle rental, lease expenditures	yr	666	1999	30r
Utilities				
Electrical bill, average	mos	58.66	9/00	9s
Electricity, expenditures on	yr	725	1999	30r
Electricity cost, average	KWh	7.75	9/00	9s
Utilities, fuels, and public services purchased	yr	2179	1999	30r
Water and other public services, expenditures on	yr	339	1999	30r
Weddings				
Wedding (national average cost)		19936	2000	33r
Wedding (regional average total cost)		18918	1997	110r
Attendants' gifts		321	1998	33r
Bridal attendants' apparel (5 persons)		824	2000	33r
Bride's headpiece/veil		173	1998	33r
Bride's wedding dress		859	1998	33r
Clergy, religious facility fee		242	1998	33r
Engagement ring		3177	1998	33r
Flowers		789	1998	33r
Groom's formalwear rental		99	2000	33r
Limousine		410	1998	33r
Marriage license cost		50.00-80.00	4/01	35s
Men's formalwear (ushers, best man)		469	2000	33r
Mother of bride apparel		241	2000	33r
Music		866	1998	33r
Photography and videography		1368	1998	33r
Rehearsal dinner		728	1998	33r
Wedding invitations and announcements		341	1998	33r
Wedding reception		7968	2000	33r
Wedding rings (bride and groom)		1060	1998	33r

Ocala, FL

Item	Per	Value	Date	Ref.
Alcoholic Beverages				
Alcoholic beverage purchases	yr	253	1999	30r
Malt beverages, all types, all sizes, any origin	16 oz	0.96	7/01	11r
Appliances				
Major appliances, expenditures on	yr	172	1999	30r
Small appliances, housewares, expenditures on	yr	81	1999	30r
Banking and Money				
Mortgage interest and charges paid	yr	2039	1999	30r
Mortgage principal paid on owned property	yr	1026	1999	30r
Vehicle finance charges paid	yr	365	1999	30r
Charity				
Cash contributions, expenditures	yr	1127	1999	30r
Child Care				
Child raising cost, total, age 0-2	yr	8540	1999	60r
Child raising cost, total, age 3-5	yr	8780	1999	60r
Child raising cost, total, age 6-8	yr	8820	1999	60r
Child raising cost, total, age 9-11	yr	8800	1999	60r
Child raising cost, total, age 12-14	yr	9510	1999	60r
Child raising cost, total, age 15-17	yr	9740	1999	60r
Child's child care and education, age 0-2	yr	1380	1999	60r
Child's child care and education, age 3-5	yr	1520	1999	60r
Child's child care and education, age 6-8	yr	990	1999	60r
Child's child care and education, age 9-11	yr	650	1999	60r
Child's child care and education, age 12-14	yr	490	1999	60r
Child's child care and education, age 15-17	yr	840	1999	60r
Child's clothing, age 0-2	yr	480	1999	60r
Child's clothing, age 3-5	yr	470	1999	60r

Ocala, FL - continued

Item	Per	Value	Date	Ref.
Child Care - continued				
Child's clothing, age 6-8	yr	520	1999	60r
Child's clothing, age 9-11	yr	570	1999	60r
Child's clothing, age 12-14	yr	950	1999	60r
Child's clothing, age 15-17	yr	850	1999	60r
Child's food, age 0-2	yr	1000	1999	60r
Child's food, age 3-5	yr	1160	1999	60r
Child's food, age 6-8	yr	1490	1999	60r
Child's food, age 9-11	yr	1770	1999	60r
Child's food, age 12-14	yr	1770	1999	60r
Child's food, age 15-17	yr	1980	1999	60r
Child's health care, age 0-2	yr	620	1999	60r
Child's health care, age 3-5	yr	590	1999	60r
Child's health care, age 6-8	yr	680	1999	60r
Child's health care, age 9-11	yr	720	1999	60r
Child's health care, age 12-14	yr	730	1999	60r
Child's health care, age 15-17	yr	760	1999	60r
Child's housing, age 0-2	yr	3070	1999	60r
Child's housing, age 3-5	yr	3050	1999	60r
Child's housing, age 6-8	yr	3010	1999	60r
Child's housing, age 9-11	yr	2850	1999	60r
Child's housing, age 12-14	yr	3040	1999	60r
Child's housing, age 15-17	yr	2650	1999	60r
Child's personal care, reading, age 0-2	yr	910	1999	60r
Child's personal care, reading, age 3-5	yr	930	1999	60r
Child's personal care, reading, age 6-8	yr	960	1999	60r
Child's personal care, reading, age 9-11	yr	1000	1999	60r
Child's personal care, reading, age 12-14	yr	1170	1999	60r
Child's personal care, reading, age 15-17	yr	950	1999	60r
Clothing				
Apparel and services purchases	yr	1610	1999	30r
Boys, 2 to 15, expenditures on	yr	89	1999	30r
Children under 2, expenditures on	yr	79	1999	30r
Footwear, expenditures on	yr	283	1999	30r
Girls, 2 to 15, expenditures on	yr	103	1999	30r
Men and boys, expenditures on	yr	351	1999	30r
Men, 16 and over, expenditures on	yr	262	1999	30r
Women, 16 and over, expenditures on	yr	538	1999	30r
Communications				
Cable modem installation, Adelphi		54.90	6/99	103s
Cable modem installation, Comcast		95.00	6/99	103s
Cable modem installation, Media One		100.00	6/99	103s
Cable modem installation, Time Warner		75.00-225.00	6/99	103s
Cable modem rate, cable subscriber, Adelphi	mos	34.95	6/99	103s
Cable modem rate, cable subscriber, Comcast	mos	39.95	6/99	103s
Cable modem rate, cable subscriber, Media One	mos	34.95-39.95	6/99	103s
Cable modem rate, cable subscriber, Time Warner	mos	39.95-49.95	6/99	103s
Cable modem rate, non-cable subscriber, Adelphi	mos	44.95	6/99	103s
Cable modem rate, non-cable subscriber, Comcast	mos	49.95	6/99	103s
Cable modem rate, non-cable subscriber, Media One	mos	49.95	6/99	103s
Cable modem rate, non-cable subscriber, Time Warner	mos	39.95-54.95	6/99	103s
Phone line, single, business, field visit	inst.	56.00	12/97	17s
Phone line, single, business, no field visit	inst.	56.00	12/97	17s
Phone line, single, residence, field visit	inst.	40.00	12/97	17s
Phone line, single, residence, no field visit	inst.	40.00	12/97	17s
Postage and stationery, expenditures on	yr	104	1999	30r
Postal rate, express mail, up to half-pound		12.45	7/01	108r
Postal rate, letter, first class, first ounce		0.34	7/01	108r
Postal rate, letter, two ounces		0.57	7/01	108r
Postal rate, post card		0.21	7/01	108r
Postal rate, priority mail, two pounds		3.95	7/01	108r
Postal rate, priority mail, up to one pound		3.50	7/01	108r
Telephone services, expenditures on	yr	860	1999	30r

Values are in dollars or fractions of dollars. In the column headed *Ref*, references are shown to sources. Each reference is followed by a letter. These refer to the geographical level for which data were reported: s=State, r=Region, and c=City or metro. The abbreviation *ex* is used to mean *except* or *excluding*; *exp* stands for *expenditures*. For other abbreviations and further explanations, please see the Introduction.

Ocala, FL - continued

Item	Per	Value	Date	Ref.
Education				
Board, 4-year private college/university	yr	2236	1996	38s
Board, 4-year public college/university	yr	2295	1996	38s
Education expenditures	yr	431	1999	30r
Room, 4-year private college/university	yr	2428	1996	38s
Room, 4-year public college/university	yr	2193	1996	38s
Total cost, 4-year private college/university	yr	15028	1996	38s
Total cost, 4-year public college/university	yr	6254	1996	38s
Tuition, 2-year public college/university, in state	yr	1103	1996	38s
Tuition, 4-year private college/university, in state	yr	10364	1996	38s
Tuition, 4-year public college/university	yr	1767	1996	38s
Energy and Fuels				
Electricity	500 KWhs	47.29	7/01	11r
Electricity	KWh	0.09	7/01	11r
Fuel oil #2	gal	1.43	7/01	11r
Fuel oil and other fuels, expenditures on	yr	45	1999	30r
Gas, natural, commercial rate	1000 cf	8.44	11/00	88s
Gasoline, all types	gal	1.60	7/01	11r
Gasoline, unleaded midgrade	gal	1.65	7/01	11r
Gasoline, unleaded premium	gal	1.74	7/01	11r
Natural gas, expenditures on	yr	164	1999	30r
Utility (piped) gas, therm		1.01	7/01	11r
Utility (piped) gas, 40 therms		44.29	7/01	11r
Utility (piped) gas, 100 therms		97.44	7/01	11r
Entertainment				
Entertainment purchases	yr	1574	1999	30r
Fees and admissions paid	yr	371	1999	30r
Reading purchases	yr	121	1999	30r
Television, radios, sound equipment, expenditures on	yr	561	1999	30r
Funerals				
Total cost of funeral		5922.53	1/99	78r
Acknowledgement cards		63.43	1/99	78r
Casket		2258.77	1/99	78r
Cosmetology, hair, other preparation		127.09	1/99	78r
Embalming		393.49	1/99	78r
Funeral at funeral home		367.50	1/99	78r
Hearse (local)		169.66	1/99	78r
Professional service charges		1211.32	1/99	78r
Service car/van		80.69	1/99	78r
Transfer of remains to funeral home		144.25	1/99	78r
Vault		803.50	1/99	78r
Visitation/viewing		302.83	1/99	78r
Groceries				
American processed cheese	lb	3.50	7/01	11r
Bakery products, expenditures on	yr	261	1999	30r
Bananas	lb	0.47	7/01	11r
Beans, dried, any type, all sizes	lb	0.63	7/01	11r
Beef for stew, boneless	lb	2.86	7/01	11r
Beef, expenditures on	yr	210	1999	30r
Bologna, all beef or mixed	lb	2.29	7/01	11r
Bread, French	lb	1.66	7/01	11r
Bread, white, pan	lb	0.87	7/01	11r
Bread, whole wheat, pan	lb	1.38	7/01	11r
Broccoli	lb	1.04	7/01	11r
Butter, salted, grade AA, stick	lb	2.26	7/01	11r
Butter, yoghurt, cheese, etc, expenditures on	yr	170	1999	30r
Cabbage	lb	0.42	7/01	11r
Cereals and cereal products, expenditures on	yr	140	1999	30r
Cheddar cheese, natural	lb	3.75	7/01	11r
Chicken breast, bone-in	lb	1.85	7/01	11r
Chicken legs, bone-in	lb	1.34	7/01	11r
Chicken, fresh, whole	lb	1.05	7/01	11r
Chops, boneless,	lb	4.13	7/01	11r
Chuck roast, graded and ungraded, excl U.S. prime and choice	lb	2.35	7/01	11r
Chuck roast, U.S. choice, boneless	lb	2.67	7/01	11r

Ocala, FL - continued

Item	Per	Value	Date	Ref.
Groceries - continued				
Coffee, 100%, ground roast, all sizes	lb	2.88	7/01	11r
Coffee, instant, plain, regular, all sizes	16 oz	9.25	7/01	11r
Cola, non diet,	2 liter	1.11	7/01	11r
Crackers, soda, salted	lb	1.70	7/01	11r
Dairy product purchases	yr	282	1999	30r
Eggs, expenditures on	yr	32	1999	30r
Fats and oils, expenditures on	yr	79	1999	30r
Fish and seafood, expenditures on	yr	99	1999	30r
Flour, white, all purpose	lb	0.32	7/01	11r
Food (excl fruit and vegetables), eaten at home, purchases	yr	815	1999	30r
Food cooked on trips, expenditures on	yr	36	1999	30r
Food purchases	yr	4533	1999	30r
Food purchases, eaten away from home	yr	1873	1999	30r
Food purchases, food eaten at home	yr	2660	1999	30r
Fresh fruits, expenditures on	yr	128	1999	30r
Fresh milk and cream, expenditures on	yr	112	1999	30r
Fresh vegetables, expenditures on	yr	131	1999	30r
Fruit and vegetable purchases	yr	438	1999	30r
Grapefruit	lb	0.59	7/01	11r
Grapes, Thompson, seedless	lb	2.12	7/01	11r
Ground beef, 100% beef	lb	1.76	7/01	11r
Ground beef, lean and extra lean	lb	2.60	7/01	11r
Ground chuck, 100% beef	lb	2.08	7/01	11r
Ham, boneless, excl canned	lb	2.71	7/01	11r
Ham, rump or shank half, bone-in, smoked	lb	2.19	7/01	11r
Ice cream, prepackaged, bulk, regular	1/2 gal	3.93	7/01	11r
Lemons	lb	1.32	7/01	11r
Lettuce, iceberg	lb	0.76	7/01	11r
Milk, fresh, low fat,	gal	2.75	7/01	11r
Milk, fresh, whole, fortified	gal	2.97	7/01	11r
Nonalcoholic beverages, expenditures on	yr	228	1999	30r
Orange juice, frozen concentrate	16 oz	1.95	7/01	11r
Oranges, Navel	lb	0.73	7/01	11r
Oranges, Valencia	lb	0.55	7/01	11r
Peanut butter, creamy, all sizes	lb	1.83	7/01	11r
Pears, Anjou	lb	0.98	7/01	11r
Pork chops, center cut, bone-in	lb	3.33	7/01	11r
Pork sausage, fresh, loose	lb	2.59	7/01	11r
Pork shoulder picnic, bone-in, smoked	lb	1.12	7/01	11r
Pork, expenditures on	yr	162	1999	30r
Potato chips	16 oz	3.59	7/01	11r
Potatoes, frozen, french fried	lb	1.00	7/01	11r
Potatoes, white, all types	lb	0.44	7/01	11r
Poultry, expenditures on	yr	137	1999	30r
Processed fruits, expenditures on	yr	97	1999	30r
Processed vegetables, expenditures on	yr	82	1999	30r
Rice, white, long grain, uncooked	lb	0.51	7/01	11r
Round roast, graded and ungraded, excl U.S. prime and choice	lb	2.96	7/01	11r
Round steak, graded and ungraded, excl U.S. prime and choice	lb	3.11	7/01	11r
Sirloin steak, graded and ungraded, excl U.S. prime and choice	lb	4.23	7/01	11r
Spaghetti and macaroni	lb	0.78	7/01	11r
Steak, round, U.S. choice, boneless	lb	3.56	7/01	11r
Steak, sirloin, U.S. choice, boneless	lb	5.65	7/01	11r
Strawberries, dry pint	12 oz	1.50	7/01	11r
Sugar and other sweets, expenditures on	yr	99	1999	30r
Sugar, white, 33-80 ounce package	lb	0.39	7/01	11r
Sugar, white, all sizes	lb	0.42	7/01	11r
Tobacco products and smoking supplies purchases	yr	288	1999	30r
Tomatoes, field grown	lb	1.43	7/01	11r
Tuna, light, chunk	lb	1.77	7/01	11r
Turkey, frozen, whole	lb	1.05	7/01	11r
Goods and Services				
B&B Japanese maple (acer japonicum)	gal	49.98-129.00	4/00	93r
Boxwood (buxus)	2 gal	12.99-16.99	4/00	93r

Values are in dollars or fractions of dollars. In the column headed *Ref*, references are shown to sources. Each reference is followed by a letter. These refer to the geographical level for which data were reported: s=State, r=Region, and c=City or metro. The abbreviation *ex* is used to mean *except* or *excluding*; *exp* stands for expenditures. For other abbreviations and further explanations, please see the Introduction.

Ocala, FL - continued

Item	Per	Value	Date	Ref.
Goods and Services				
Daylilly (hemerocallis)	gal	4.99-8.99	4/00	93r
Flat of annuals		11.00-13.92	4/00	93r
Fountain grass (pennisetum)	gal	5.98-7.98	4/00	93r
Hanging basket (10 in)		7.99-14.98	4/00	93r
Hardy geranium (geranium)	gal	5.98-8.00	4/00	93r
Hosta (hosta)	gal	4.99-10.98	4/00	93r
Lilac (syrubga vulgaris)	2 gal	12.99-21.99	4/00	93r
Rhododendron (rhododendron)	2 gal	14.99-24.99	4/00	93r
Sage (salvia)	gal	5.98-6.99	4/00	93r
Wintercreeper euonymus (euonymus fortunei)	2 gal	7.99-89.99	4/00	93r
Hunting license	yr	12.50	4/01	34s
Health Care				
Cardiac catheterization, ave hospital/physician charges		15060	1998	77s
Childbirth, Cesarean delivery		11587	1997	13r
Childbirth, vaginal delivery		6725	1997	13r
Drugs, expenditures on	yr	399	1999	30r
Health care purchases	yr	1971	1999	30r
Health insurance expenditures	yr	933	1999	30r
Hysterectomy, laproscopically-assisted, ave hospital/physician charges		14760	1998	76s
Hysterectomy, vaginal, ave hospital and physician charges		11320	1998	76s
Medicaid dispensing fee		4.23	1999	87s
Medical services expenditures	yr	547	1999	30r
Medical supplies, expenditures on	yr	91	1999	30r
Plastic surgery, breast augmentation		2870	2000	7r
Plastic surgery, breast lift		3649	2000	7r
Plastic surgery, facelift		5008	2000	7r
Plastic surgery, hair transplantation		3425	2000	7r
Plastic surgery, lip augmentation		1227	2000	7r
Plastic surgery, lower body lift		4793	2000	7r
Plastic surgery, thigh lift		3862	2000	7r
Household Goods				
Floor coverings, expenditures on	yr	44	1999	30r
Furniture, expenditures on	yr	335	1999	30r
Household furnishings and equipment purchases	yr	1328	1999	30r
Household textiles, expenditures on	yr	89	1999	30r
Laundry and cleaning supplies, expenditures on	yr	113	1999	30r
Housing				
Home price, existing, ave		160100	10/00	90r
Home value, median		104000	2001	53s
Household operation expenditures	yr	553	1999	30r
Housekeeping supplies purchases	yr	473	1999	30r
Housing, expenditures on	yr	10303	1999	30r
Maintenance, repairs, insurance expenditures	yr	699	1999	30r
Monthly rental value of owned home	mos	505	1999	30r
Owned dwellings, expenditures own	yr	3465	1999	30r
Rent expenditures	yr	1641	1999	30r
Rental unit, 1 bedroom, with utilities	mos	451	4/01	41c
Rental unit, 2 bedroom, with utilities	mos	512	4/01	41c
Rental unit, 3 bedroom, with utilities	mos	672	4/01	41c
Rental unit, 4 bedroom, with utilities	mos	788	4/01	41c
Shelter, expenditures on	yr	5467	1999	30r
Insurance and Pensions				
Life and other personal insurance purchases	yr	414	1999	30r
Medigap health insurance, Plan H	yr	2887	2000	69s

Ocala, FL - continued

Item	Per	Value	Date	Ref.
Insurance and Pensions - continued				
Medigap health insurance, Plan I	yr	3302	2000	69s
Medigap health insurance, Plan J	yr	3889	2000	69s
Pensions and Social Security, expenditures on	yr	2635	1999	30r
Personal insurance and pensions, expenditures on	yr	3048	1999	30r
Legal Fees				
Divorce, filing fee		65.00-85.00	4/01	35s
Driver's license fee	renew	15.00	1999	48s
Driver's license fee	orig	20.00	1999	48s
Personal Goods				
Personal care products and services purchases	yr	393	1999	30r
Personal Services				
Personal services, household, expenditures on	yr	258	1999	30r
Pets				
Pets, toys, and playground equipment, expenditures on	yr	306	1999	30r
Taxes				
Federal income taxes paid	yr	2047	1999	30r
Personal taxes, expenditures on	yr	2554	1999	30r
Property taxes paid	yr	726	1999	30r
State and local income taxes paid	yr	363	1999	30r
Transportation				
Cars and trucks, new, expenditures on	yr	1648	1999	30r
Cars and trucks, used, expenditures on	yr	1651	1999	30r
Diesel at the pump	gal	1.26	10/99	73s
Gasoline and motor oil purchases	yr	1052	1999	30r
Gasoline before-tax price (cents)	gal	101.90	10/00	43s
Maintenance and repair expenditures	yr	621	1999	30r
Public transportation, expenditures on	yr	298	1999	30r
Transportation purchases	yr	6738	1999	30r
Vehicle expenses, miscellaneous, purchases	yr	2033	1999	30r
Vehicle insurance payments	yr	696	1999	30r
Vehicle purchases (net outlay)	yr	3354	1999	30r
Vehicle rental, lease expenditures	yr	352	1999	30r
Travel				
Hotel room	night	110.57	2/01	95s
Utilities				
Electrical bill, average	mos	86.33	9/00	9s
Electricity, expenditures on	yr	1115	1999	30r
Electricity cost, average	KWh	6.80	9/00	9s
Water and other public services, expenditures on	yr	298	1999	30r
Weddings				
Wedding (national average cost)		19936	2000	33r
Wedding (regional average total cost)		16293	1997	110r
Attendants' gifts		321	1998	33r
Bridal attendants' apparel (5 persons)		824	2000	33r
Bride's headpiece/veil		173	1998	33r
Bride's wedding dress		859	1998	33r
Clergy, religious facility fee		242	1998	33r
Engagement ring		3177	1998	33r
Flowers		789	1998	33r
Groom's formalwear rental		99	2000	33r
Limousine		410	1998	33r
Marriage license cost		56.00-88.50	4/01	35s
Men's formalwear (ushers, best man)		469	2000	33r
Mother of bride apparel		241	2000	33r
Music		866	1998	33r
Photography and videography		1368	1998	33r
Rehearsal dinner		728	1998	33r
Wedding invitations and announcements		341	1998	33r
Wedding reception		7968	2000	33r

Values are in dollars or fractions of dollars. In the column headed *Ref*, references are shown to sources. Each reference is followed by a letter. These refer to the geographical level for which data were reported: s=State, r=Region, and c=City or metro. The abbreviation *ex* is used to mean *except* or *excluding*; *exp* stands for *expenditures*. For other abbreviations and further explanations, please see the Introduction.

Ocala, FL - continued

Item	Per	Value	Date	Ref.
Weddings				
Wedding rings (bride and groom)		1060	1998	33r

Odessa-Midland, TX

Item	Per	Value	Date	Ref.
Alcoholic Beverages				
Alcoholic beverage purchases	yr	253	1999	30r
Malt beverages, all types, all sizes, any origin	16 oz	0.96	7/01	11r
Appliances				
Major appliances, expenditures on	yr	172	1999	30r
Small appliances, housewares, expenditures on	yr	81	1999	30r
Banking and Money				
Mortgage interest and charges paid	yr	2039	1999	30r
Mortgage principal paid on owned property	yr	1026	1999	30r
Vehicle finance charges paid	yr	365	1999	30r
Charity				
Cash contributions, expenditures	yr	1127	1999	30r
Child Care				
Child raising cost, total, age 0-2	yr	8540	1999	60r
Child raising cost, total, age 3-5	yr	8780	1999	60r
Child raising cost, total, age 6-8	yr	8820	1999	60r
Child raising cost, total, age 9-11	yr	8800	1999	60r
Child raising cost, total, age 12-14	yr	9510	1999	60r
Child raising cost, total, age 15-17	yr	9740	1999	60r
Child's child care and education, age 0-2	yr	1380	1999	60r
Child's child care and education, age 3-5	yr	1520	1999	60r
Child's child care and education, age 6-8	yr	990	1999	60r
Child's child care and education, age 9-11	yr	650	1999	60r
Child's child care and education, age 12-14	yr	490	1999	60r
Child's child care and education, age 15-17	yr	840	1999	60r
Child's clothing, age 0-2	yr	480	1999	60r
Child's clothing, age 3-5	yr	470	1999	60r
Child's clothing, age 6-8	yr	520	1999	60r
Child's clothing, age 9-11	yr	570	1999	60r
Child's clothing, age 12-14	yr	950	1999	60r
Child's clothing, age 15-17	yr	850	1999	60r
Child's food, age 0-2	yr	1000	1999	60r
Child's food, age 3-5	yr	1160	1999	60r
Child's food, age 6-8	yr	1490	1999	60r
Child's food, age 9-11	yr	1770	1999	60r
Child's food, age 12-14	yr	1770	1999	60r
Child's food, age 15-17	yr	1980	1999	60r
Child's health care, age 0-2	yr	620	1999	60r
Child's health care, age 3-5	yr	590	1999	60r
Child's health care, age 6-8	yr	680	1999	60r
Child's health care, age 9-11	yr	720	1999	60r
Child's health care, age 12-14	yr	730	1999	60r
Child's health care, age 15-17	yr	760	1999	60r
Child's housing, age 0-2	yr	3070	1999	60r
Child's housing, age 3-5	yr	3050	1999	60r
Child's housing, age 6-8	yr	3010	1999	60r
Child's housing, age 9-11	yr	2850	1999	60r
Child's housing, age 12-14	yr	3040	1999	60r
Child's housing, age 15-17	yr	2650	1999	60r
Child's personal care, reading, age 0-2	yr	910	1999	60r
Child's personal care, reading, age 3-5	yr	930	1999	60r
Child's personal care, reading, age 6-8	yr	960	1999	60r
Child's personal care, reading, age 9-11	yr	1000	1999	60r
Child's personal care, reading, age 12-14	yr	1170	1999	60r
Child's personal care, reading, age 15-17	yr	950	1999	60r
Clothing				
Apparel and services purchases	yr	1610	1999	30r
Boys, 2 to 15, expenditures on	yr	89	1999	30r
Children under 2, expenditures on	yr	79	1999	30r
Footwear, expenditures on	yr	283	1999	30r
Girls, 2 to 15, expenditures on	yr	103	1999	30r
Men and boys, expenditures on	yr	351	1999	30r
Men, 16 and over, expenditures on	yr	262	1999	30r

Odessa-Midland, TX - continued

Item	Per	Value	Date	Ref.
Clothing - continued				
Women, 16 and over, expenditures on	yr	538	1999	30r
Communications				
Cable modem installation, AT&T-BIS		150.00	6/99	103s
Cable modem installation, Marcus		499.00	6/99	103s
Cable modem installation, Time Warner		75.00-225.00	6/99	103s
Cable modem rate, cable subscriber, AT&T-BIS	mos	39.95	6/99	103s
Cable modem rate, cable subscriber, Marcus	mos	14.95-49.95	6/99	103s
Cable modem rate, cable subscriber, Time Warner	mos	39.95-49.95	6/99	103s
Cable modem rate, non-cable subscriber, Marcus	mos	60.95	6/99	103s
Cable modem rate, non-cable subscriber, Time Warner	mos	39.95-54.95	6/99	103s
Phone line, single, business, field visit	inst.	71.90	12/97	17s
Phone line, single, business, no field visit	inst.	57.30	12/97	17s
Phone line, single, residence, field visit	inst.	52.95	12/97	17s
Phone line, single, residence, no field visit	inst.	38.35	12/97	17s
Postage and stationery, expenditures on	yr	104	1999	30r
Postal rate, express mail, up to half-pound		12.45	7/01	108r
Postal rate, letter, first class, first ounce		0.34	7/01	108r
Postal rate, letter, two ounces		0.57	7/01	108r
Postal rate, post card		0.21	7/01	108r
Postal rate, priority mail, two pounds		3.95	7/01	108r
Postal rate, priority mail, up to one pound		3.50	7/01	108r
Telephone services, expenditures on	yr	860	1999	30r
Education				
Board, 4-year private college/university	yr	2198	1996	38s
Board, 4-year public college/university	yr	1759	1996	38s
Education expenditures	yr	431	1999	30r
Room, 4-year private college/university	yr	2000	1996	38s
Room, 4-year public college/university	yr	1885	1996	38s
Total cost, 4-year private college/university	yr	13156	1996	38s
Total cost, 4-year public college/university	yr	5464	1996	38s
Tuition, 2-year public college/university, in state	yr	771	1996	38s
Tuition, 4-year private college/university, in state	yr	8959	1996	38s
Tuition, 4-year public college/university	yr	1820	1996	38s
Energy and Fuels				
Electricity	KWh	0.09	7/01	11r
Electricity	500 KWhs	47.29	7/01	11r
Fuel oil #2	gal	1.43	7/01	11r
Fuel oil and other fuels, expenditures on	yr	45	1999	30r
Gas, natural, commercial rate	1000 cf	6.94	11/00	88s
Gasoline, all types	gal	1.60	7/01	11r
Gasoline, unleaded midgrade	gal	1.65	7/01	11r
Gasoline, unleaded premium	gal	1.74	7/01	11r
Natural gas, expenditures on	yr	164	1999	30r
Utility (piped) gas, therm		1.01	7/01	11r
Utility (piped) gas, 40 therms		44.29	7/01	11r
Utility (piped) gas, 100 therms		97.44	7/01	11r
Entertainment				
Entertainment purchases	yr	1574	1999	30r
Fees and admissions paid	yr	371	1999	30r
Reading purchases	yr	121	1999	30r
Television, radios, sound equipment, expenditures on	yr	561	1999	30r
Funerals				
Total cost of funeral		5842.28	1/99	78r
Acknowledgement cards		28.35	1/99	78r
Casket		2494.29	1/99	78r
Cosmetology, hair, other preparation		109.22	1/99	78r
Embalming		361.42	1/99	78r
Funeral at funeral home		349.20	1/99	78r
Hearse (local)		161.91	1/99	78r

Values are in dollars or fractions of dollars. In the column headed *Ref*, references are shown to sources. Each reference is followed by a letter. These refer to the geographical level for which data were reported: s=State, r=Region, and c=City or metro. The abbreviation *ex* is used to mean *except* or *excluding*; *exp* stands for *expenditures*. For other abbreviations and further explanations, please see the Introduction.

Odessa-Midland, TX - continued

Item	Per	Value	Date	Ref.
Funerals				
Professional service charges		1116.50	1/99	78r
Service car/van		65.56	1/99	78r
Transfer of remains to funeral home		143.56	1/99	78r
Vault		785.25	1/99	78r
Visitation/viewing		227.02	1/99	78r
Groceries				
American processed cheese	lb	3.50	7/01	11r
Bakery products, expenditures on	yr	261	1999	30r
Bananas	lb	0.47	7/01	11r
Beans, dried, any type, all sizes	lb	0.63	7/01	11r
Beef for stew, boneless	lb	2.86	7/01	11r
Beef, expenditures on	yr	210	1999	30r
Bologna, all beef or mixed	lb	2.29	7/01	11r
Bread, French	lb	1.66	7/01	11r
Bread, white, pan	lb	0.87	7/01	11r
Bread, whole wheat, pan	lb	1.38	7/01	11r
Broccoli	lb	1.04	7/01	11r
Butter, salted, grade AA, stick	lb	2.26	7/01	11r
Butter, yoghurt, cheese, etc, expenditures on	yr	170	1999	30r
Cabbage	lb	0.42	7/01	11r
Cereals and cereal products, expenditures on	yr	140	1999	30r
Cheddar cheese, natural	lb	3.75	7/01	11r
Chicken breast, bone-in	lb	1.85	7/01	11r
Chicken legs, bone-in	lb	1.34	7/01	11r
Chicken, fresh, whole	lb	1.05	7/01	11r
Chops, boneless	lb	4.13	7/01	11r
Chuck roast, graded and ungraded, excl U.S. prime and choice	lb	2.35	7/01	11r
Chuck roast, U.S. choice, boneless	lb	2.67	7/01	11r
Coffee, 100%, ground roast, all sizes	lb	2.88	7/01	11r
Coffee, instant, plain, regular, all sizes	16 oz	9.25	7/01	11r
Cola, non diet,	2 liter	1.11	7/01	11r
Crackers, soda, salted	lb	1.70	7/01	11r
Dairy product purchases	yr	282	1999	30r
Eggs, expenditures on	yr	32	1999	30r
Fats and oils, expenditures on	yr	79	1999	30r
Fish and seafood, expenditures on	yr	99	1999	30r
Flour, white, all purpose	lb	0.32	7/01	11r
Food (excl fruit and vegetables), eaten at home, purchases	yr	815	1999	30r
Food cooked on trips, expenditures on	yr	36	1999	30r
Food purchases	yr	4533	1999	30r
Food purchases, eaten away from home	yr	1873	1999	30r
Food purchases, food eaten at home	yr	2660	1999	30r
Fresh fruits, expenditures on	yr	128	1999	30r
Fresh milk and cream, expenditures on	yr	112	1999	30r
Fresh vegetables, expenditures on	yr	131	1999	30r
Fruit and vegetable purchases	yr	438	1999	30r
Grapefruit	lb	0.59	7/01	11r
Grapes, Thompson, seedless	lb	2.12	7/01	11r
Ground beef, 100% beef	lb	1.76	7/01	11r
Ground beef, lean and extra lean	lb	2.60	7/01	11r
Ground chuck, 100% beef	lb	2.08	7/01	11r
Ham, boneless, excl canned	lb	2.71	7/01	11r
Ham, rump or shank half, bone-in, smoked	lb	2.19	7/01	11r
Ice cream, prepackaged, bulk, regular	1/2 gal	3.93	7/01	11r
Lemons	lb	1.32	7/01	11r
Lettuce, iceberg	lb	0.76	7/01	11r
Milk, fresh, low fat,	gal	2.75	7/01	11r
Milk, fresh, whole, fortified	gal	2.97	7/01	11r
Nonalcoholic beverages, expenditures on	yr	228	1999	30r
Orange juice, frozen concentrate	16 oz	1.95	7/01	11r
Oranges, Navel	lb	0.73	7/01	11r
Oranges, Valencia	lb	0.55	7/01	11r
Peanut butter, creamy, all sizes	lb	1.83	7/01	11r
Pears, Anjou	lb	0.98	7/01	11r
Pork chops, center cut, bone-in	lb	3.33	7/01	11r
Pork sausage, fresh, loose	lb	2.59	7/01	11r
Pork shoulder picnic, bone-in, smoked	lb	1.12	7/01	11r
Pork, expenditures on	yr	162	1999	30r
Potato chips	16 oz	3.59	7/01	11r

Odessa-Midland, TX - continued

Item	Per	Value	Date	Ref.
Groceries - continued				
Potatoes, frozen, french fried	lb	1.00	7/01	11r
Potatoes, white, all types	lb	0.44	7/01	11r
Poultry, expenditures on	yr	137	1999	30r
Processed fruits, expenditures on	yr	97	1999	30r
Processed vegetables, expenditures on	yr	82	1999	30r
Rice, white, long grain, uncooked	lb	0.51	7/01	11r
Round roast, graded and ungraded, excl U.S. prime and choice	lb	2.96	7/01	11r
Round steak, graded and ungraded, excl U.S. prime and choice	lb	3.11	7/01	11r
Sirloin steak, graded and ungraded, excl U.S. prime and choice	lb	4.23	7/01	11r
Spaghetti and macaroni	lb	0.78	7/01	11r
Steak, round, U.S. choice, boneless	lb	3.56	7/01	11r
Steak, sirloin, U.S. choice, boneless	lb	5.65	7/01	11r
Strawberries, dry pint	12 oz	1.50	7/01	11r
Sugar and other sweets, expenditures on	yr	99	1999	30r
Sugar, white, 33-80 ounce package	lb	0.39	7/01	11r
Sugar, white, all sizes	lb	0.42	7/01	11r
Tobacco products and smoking supplies purchases	yr	288	1999	30r
Tomatoes, field grown	lb	1.43	7/01	11r
Tuna, light, chunk	lb	1.77	7/01	11r
Turkey, frozen, whole	lb	1.05	7/01	11r
Goods and Services				
B&B Japanese maple (acer japonicum)	gal	79.98-99.00	4/00	93r
Boxwood (buxus)	2 gal	12.98-18.99	4/00	93r
Christmas tree, noble fir		40-60	2000	65s
Daylilly (hemerocallis)	gal	7.96-11.00	4/00	93r
Flat of annuals		13.99-27.99	4/00	93r
Fountain grass (pennisetum)	gal	6.96-9.00	4/00	93r
Hanging basket (10 in)		9.99-24.99	4/00	93r
Hardy geranium (geranium)	gal	5.96-8.00	4/00	93r
Hosta (hosta)	gal	8.96-12.99	4/00	93r
Lilac (syrubga vulgaris)	2 gal	13.00-19.99	4/00	93r
Rhododendron (rhododendron)	2 gal	12.98-29.99	4/00	93r
Sage (salvia)	gal	5.96-8.00	4/00	93r
Wintercreeper euonymus (euonymus fortunei)	2 gal	13.00-18.99	4/00	93r
Hunting license	yr	19.00	4/01	34s
Health Care				
Cardiac catheterization, ave hospital/physician charges		20140	1998	77s
Childbirth, Cesarean delivery		11587	1997	13r
Childbirth, vaginal delivery		6725	1997	13r
Drugs, expenditures on	yr	399	1999	30r
Health care purchases	yr	1971	1999	30r
Health insurance expenditures	yr	933	1999	30r
Hysterectomy, laproscopically-assisted, ave hospital/physician charges		15700	1998	76s
Hysterectomy, vaginal, ave hospital and physician charges		12180	1998	76s
Medicaid dispensing fee		5.27	1999	87s
Medical services expenditures	yr	547	1999	30r
Medical supplies, expenditures on	yr	91	1999	30r
Household Goods				
Floor coverings, expenditures on	yr	44	1999	30r
Furniture, expenditures on	yr	335	1999	30r
Household furnishings and equipment purchases	yr	1328	1999	30r

Values are in dollars or fractions of dollars. In the column headed *Ref*, references are shown to sources. Each reference is followed by a letter. These refer to the geographical level for which data were reported: s=State, r=Region, and c=City or metro. The abbreviation *ex* is used to mean *except* or *excluding*; *exp* stands for *expenditures*. For other abbreviations and further explanations, please see the Introduction.

Odessa-Midland, TX - continued

Item	Per	Value	Date	Ref.
Household Goods				
Household textiles, expenditures on	yr	89	1999	30r
Laundry and cleaning supplies, expenditures on	yr	113	1999	30r
Housing				
Home price, existing, ave		160100	10/00	90r
Home value, median		112000	2001	53s
Household operation expenditures	yr	553	1999	30r
Housekeeping supplies purchases	yr	473	1999	30r
Housing, expenditures on	yr	10303	1999	30r
Maintenance, repairs, insurance expenditures	yr	699	1999	30r
Monthly rental value of owned home	mos	505	1999	30r
Owned dwellings, expenditures own	yr	3465	1999	30r
Rent expenditures	yr	1641	1999	30r
Rental unit, 1 bedroom, with utilities	mos	356	4/01	41c
Rental unit, 2 bedroom, with utilities	mos	475	4/01	41c
Rental unit, 3 bedroom, with utilities	mos	660	4/01	41c
Rental unit, 4 bedroom, with utilities	mos	765	4/01	41c
Shelter, expenditures on	yr	5467	1999	30r
Insurance and Pensions				
Life and other personal insurance purchases	yr	414	1999	30r
Pensions and Social Security, expenditures on	yr	2635	1999	30r
Personal insurance and pensions, expenditures on	yr	3048	1999	30r
Legal Fees				
Divorce, filing fee		150.00-200.00	4/01	35s
Driver's license fee	orig	24.00	1999	48s
Driver's license fee	renew	20.00	1999	48s
Fishing license	yr	19.00	4/01	34s
Personal Goods				
Personal care products and services purchases	yr	393	1999	30r
Personal Services				
Personal services, household, expenditures on	yr	258	1999	30r
Pets				
Pets, toys, and playground equipment, expenditures on	yr	306	1999	30r
Taxes				
Federal income taxes paid	yr	2047	1999	30r
Personal taxes, expenditures on	yr	2554	1999	30r
Property taxes paid	yr	726	1999	30r
State and local income taxes paid	yr	363	1999	30r
Transportation				
Cars and trucks, new, expenditures on	yr	1648	1999	30r
Cars and trucks, used, expenditures on	yr	1651	1999	30r
Diesel at the pump	gal	1.18	10/99	73s
Gasoline and motor oil purchases	yr	1052	1999	30r
Gasoline before-tax price (cents)	gal	101.30	10/00	43s
Maintenance and repair expenditures	yr	621	1999	30r
Public transportation, expenditures on	yr	298	1999	30r
Transportation purchases	yr	6738	1999	30r
Vehicle expenses, miscellaneous, purchases	yr	2033	1999	30r
Vehicle insurance payments	yr	696	1999	30r
Vehicle purchases (net outlay)	yr	3354	1999	30r
Vehicle rental, lease expenditures	yr	352	1999	30r
Utilities				
Electrical bill, average	mos	87.17	9/00	9s
Electricity, expenditures on	yr	1115	1999	30r
Electricity cost, average	KWh	6.48	9/00	9s
Water and other public services, expenditures on	yr	298	1999	30r
Weddings				
Wedding (national average cost)		19936	2000	33r
Attendants' gifts		321	1998	33r

Odessa-Midland, TX - continued

Item	Per	Value	Date	Ref.
Weddings - continued				
Bridal attendants' apparel (5 persons)		824	2000	33r
Bride's headpiece/veil		173	1998	33r
Bride's wedding dress		859	1998	33r
Clergy, religious facility fee		242	1998	33r
Engagement ring		3177	1998	33r
Flowers		789	1998	33r
Groom's formalwear rental		99	2000	33r
Limousine		410	1998	33r
Marriage license cost		36.00	4/01	35s
Men's formalwear (ushers, best man)		469	2000	33r
Mother of bride apparel		241	2000	33r
Music		866	1998	33r
Photography and videography		1368	1998	33r
Rehearsal dinner		728	1998	33r
Wedding invitations and announcements		341	1998	33r
Wedding reception		7968	2000	33r
Wedding rings (bride and groom)		1060	1998	33r

Oklahoma City, OK

Item	Per	Value	Date	Ref.
Composite, ACCRA index		94.10	3/01	4c
Alcoholic Beverages				
Alcoholic beverage purchases	yr	253	1999	30r
Beer, Heineken, 12-oz, ex deposit	6	7.39	3/01	4c
J & B Scotch	750-ml	17.00	3/01	4c
Malt beverages, all types, all sizes, any origin	16 oz	0.96	7/01	11r
Wine, Livingston or Gallo, Chablis blanc	1.5 liter	6.17	3/01	4c
Appliances				
Appliance repair, service call, washing machine	min lab chg	47.73	3/01	4c
Major appliances, expenditures on	yr	172	1999	30r
Small appliances, housewares, expenditures on	yr	81	1999	30r
Banking and Money				
Mortgage interest and charges paid	yr	2039	1999	30r
Mortgage principal paid on owned property	yr	1026	1999	30r
Mortgage rate, incl. points and orig. fee, 30-yr. conv. fixed or ARM	mos	7.02	3/01	4c
Vehicle finance charges paid	yr	365	1999	30r
Business Expenses				
Business travel, car rental	day	69	2001	3c
Business travel, food	day	40	2001	3c
Business travel, hotel	day	91	2001	3c
Charity				
Cash contributions, expenditures	yr	1127	1999	30r
Child Care				
Child raising cost, total, age 0-2	yr	8540	1999	60r
Child raising cost, total, age 3-5	yr	8780	1999	60r
Child raising cost, total, age 6-8	yr	8820	1999	60r
Child raising cost, total, age 9-11	yr	8800	1999	60r
Child raising cost, total, age 12-14	yr	9510	1999	60r
Child raising cost, total, age 15-17	yr	9740	1999	60r
Child's child care and education, age 0-2	yr	1380	1999	60r
Child's child care and education, age 3-5	yr	1520	1999	60r
Child's child care and education, age 6-8	yr	990	1999	60r
Child's child care and education, age 9-11	yr	650	1999	60r
Child's child care and education, age 12-14	yr	490	1999	60r
Child's child care and education, age 15-17	yr	840	1999	60r
Child's clothing, age 0-2	yr	480	1999	60r
Child's clothing, age 3-5	yr	470	1999	60r
Child's clothing, age 6-8	yr	520	1999	60r
Child's clothing, age 9-11	yr	570	1999	60r
Child's clothing, age 12-14	yr	950	1999	60r
Child's clothing, age 15-17	yr	850	1999	60r
Child's food, age 0-2	yr	1000	1999	60r
Child's food, age 3-5	yr	1160	1999	60r
Child's food, age 6-8	yr	1490	1999	60r
Child's food, age 9-11	yr	1770	1999	60r

Values are in dollars or fractions of dollars. In the column headed *Ref*, references are shown to sources. Each reference is followed by a letter. These refer to the geographical level for which data were reported: s=State, r=Region, and c=City or metro. The abbreviation *ex* is used to mean *except* or *excluding*; *exp* stands for expenditures. For other abbreviations and further explanations, please see the Introduction.

Oklahoma City, OK - continued

Item	Per	Value	Date	Ref.
Child Care				
Child's food, age 12-14	yr	1770	1999	60r
Child's food, age 15-17	yr	1980	1999	60r
Child's health care, age 0-2	yr	620	1999	60r
Child's health care, age 3-5	yr	590	1999	60r
Child's health care, age 6-8	yr	680	1999	60r
Child's health care, age 9-11	yr	720	1999	60r
Child's health care, age 12-14	yr	730	1999	60r
Child's health care, age 15-17	yr	760	1999	60r
Child's housing, age 0-2	yr	3070	1999	60r
Child's housing, age 3-5	yr	3050	1999	60r
Child's housing, age 6-8	yr	3010	1999	60r
Child's housing, age 9-11	yr	2850	1999	60r
Child's housing, age 12-14	yr	3040	1999	60r
Child's housing, age 15-17	yr	2650	1999	60r
Child's personal care, reading, age 0-2	yr	910	1999	60r
Child's personal care, reading, age 3-5	yr	930	1999	60r
Child's personal care, reading, age 6-8	yr	960	1999	60r
Child's personal care, reading, age 9-11	yr	1000	1999	60r
Child's personal care, reading, age 12-14	yr	1170	1999	60r
Child's personal care, reading, age 15-17	yr	950	1999	60r
Clothing				
Apparel and services purchases	yr	1610	1999	30r
Boys' brief, cotton	3	6.85	3/01	4c
Boys, 2 to 15, expenditures on	yr	89	1999	30r
Children under 2, expenditures on	yr	79	1999	30r
Footwear, expenditures on	yr	283	1999	30r
Girls, 2 to 15, expenditures on	yr	103	1999	30r
Men and boys, expenditures on	yr	351	1999	30r
Men, 16 and over, expenditures on	yr	262	1999	30r
Shirt, man's dress shirt		25.44	3/01	4c
Slacks, man's "No Wrinkles" khaki		38.83	3/01	4c
Women, 16 and over, expenditures on	yr	538	1999	30r
Communications				
Cable modem installation, Cox		99.00-174.95	6/99	103s
Cable modem rate, cable subscriber, Cox	mos	29.95-44.95	6/99	103s
Cable modem rate, non-cable subscriber, Cox	mos	42.95-54.95	6/99	103s
Newspaper subscription, daily and Sunday delivery	mos	12.60	3/01	4c
Phone line, single, business, field visit	inst.	82.75	12/97	17s
Phone line, single, business, no field visit	inst.	82.75	12/97	17s
Phone line, single, residence, field visit	inst.	44.45	12/97	17s
Phone line, single, residence, no field visit	inst.	44.45	12/97	17s
Postage and stationery, expenditures on	yr	104	1999	30r
Postal rate, express mail, up to half-pound		12.45	7/01	108r
Postal rate, letter, first class, first ounce		0.34	7/01	108r
Postal rate, letter, two ounces		0.57	7/01	108r
Postal rate, post card		0.21	7/01	108r
Postal rate, priority mail, two pounds		3.95	7/01	108r
Postal rate, priority mail, up to one pound		3.50	7/01	108r
Telephone bill, business, basic rate	mos	39.81	12/97	18c
Telephone bill, family of three	mos	21.05	3/01	4c
Telephone bill, residential, basic rate	mos	13.72	12/97	18c
Telephone services, expenditures on	yr	860	1999	30r
Education				
Board, 4-year private college/university	yr	1401	1996	38s
Board, 4-year public college/university	yr	61111	1996	38s
Education expenditures	yr	431	1999	30r
Room, 4-year private college/university	yr	8032	1996	38s
Room, 4-year public college/university	yr	8371	1996	38s
Total cost, 4-year private college/university	yr	7737	1996	38s
Total cost, 4-year public college/university	yr	4287	1996	38s
Tuition, 2-year public college/university, in state	yr	260	1996	38s
Tuition, 4-year private college/university, in state	yr	8311	1996	38s
Tuition, 4-year public college/university	yr	1839	1996	38s

Oklahoma City, OK - continued

Item	Per	Value	Date	Ref.
Energy and Fuels				
Electricity	KWh	0.09	7/01	11r
Electricity	500 KWhs	47.29	7/01	11r
Energy, combined forms, 2400 sq ft	mos	135.22	3/01	4c
Energy, exc. electricity, 2400 sq ft	mos	66.92	3/01	4c
Fuel oil #2	gal	1.43	7/01	11r
Fuel oil and other fuels, expenditures on	yr	45	1999	30r
Gas, cooking, winter, 10 therms	mos	11.64	2/96	98c
Gas, cooking, winter, 30 therms	mos	21.54	2/96	98c
Gas, cooking, winter, 50 therms	mos	28.55	2/96	98c
Gas, heating, winter, average use	mos	71.29	2/96	98c
Gas, natural, commercial rate	1000 cf	7.50	11/00	88s
Gas, regular unleaded, cash, self-service	gal	1.25	3/01	4c
Gasoline, all types	gal	1.60	7/01	11r
Gasoline, unleaded midgrade	gal	1.65	7/01	11r
Gasoline, unleaded premium	gal	1.74	7/01	11r
Natural gas, expenditures on	yr	164	1999	30r
Utility (piped) gas, therm		1.01	7/01	11r
Utility (piped) gas, 40 therms		44.29	7/01	11r
Utility (piped) gas, 100 therms		97.44	7/01	11r
Entertainment				
Bowling, Saturday evening rate	line	2.71	3/01	4c
Entertainment purchases	yr	1574	1999	30r
Fees and admissions paid	yr	371	1999	30r
Monopoly game, Parker Brothers', No. 9	game	10.75	3/01	4c
Movie, first-run, Saturday, evening	adm.	6.43	3/01	4c
Reading purchases	yr	121	1999	30r
Television, radios, sound equipment, expenditures on	yr	561	1999	30r
Tennis balls, yellow, Wilson or Penn, 3	can	2.12	3/01	4c
Funerals				
Total cost of funeral		5842.28	1/99	78r
Acknowledgement cards		28.35	1/99	78r
Casket		2494.29	1/99	78r
Cosmetology, hair, other preparation		109.22	1/99	78r
Embalming		361.42	1/99	78r
Funeral at funeral home		349.20	1/99	78r
Hearse (local)		161.91	1/99	78r
Professional service charges		1116.50	1/99	78r
Service car/van		65.56	1/99	78r
Transfer of remains to funeral home		143.56	1/99	78r
Vault		785.25	1/99	78r
Visitation/viewing		227.02	1/99	78r
Groceries				
Groceries, ACCRA Index		91.20	3/01	4c
American processed cheese	lb	3.50	7/01	11r
Antibiotic ointment, Polysporin	0.5 oz	4.48	3/01	4c
Baby food, strained vegetables or fruit, lowest price	4-4.5 oz	0.33	3/01	4c
Bakery products, expenditures on	yr	261	1999	30r
Bananas	lb	0.51	3/01	4c
Bananas	lb	0.47	7/01	11r
Beans, dried, any type, all sizes	lb	0.63	7/01	11r
Beef for stew, boneless	lb	2.86	7/01	11r
Beef or hamburger, ground	lb	1.40	3/01	4c
Beef, expenditures on	yr	210	1999	30r
Bologna, all beef or mixed	lb	2.29	7/01	11r
Bread, French	lb	1.66	7/01	11r
Bread, white	loaf	0.88	3/01	4c
Bread, white, pan	lb	0.87	7/01	11r
Bread, whole wheat, pan	lb	1.38	7/01	11r
Broccoli	lb	1.04	7/01	11r
Butter, salted, grade AA, stick	lb	2.26	7/01	11r
Butter, yoghurt, cheese, etc, expenditures on	yr	170	1999	30r
Cabbage	lb	0.42	7/01	11r
Cereals and cereal products, expenditures on	yr	140	1999	30r
Cheddar cheese, natural	lb	3.75	7/01	11r
Cheese, Kraft grated Parmesan	8 oz	3.23	3/01	4c
Chicken breast, bone-in	lb	1.85	7/01	11r
Chicken legs, bone-in	lb	1.34	7/01	11r

Values are in dollars or fractions of dollars. In the column headed *Ref*, references are shown to sources. Each reference is followed by a letter. These refer to the geographical level for which data were reported: s=State, r=Region, and c=City or metro. The abbreviation *ex* is used to mean *except* or *excluding*; *exp* stands for *expenditures*. For other abbreviations and further explanations, please see the Introduction.

Oklahoma City, OK - continued

Groceries

Item	Per	Value	Date	Ref.
Chicken, fresh, whole	lb	1.05	7/01	11r
Chicken, whole fryer	lb	0.87	3/01	4c
Chops, boneless,	lb	4.13	7/01	11r
Chuck roast, graded and ungraded, excl U.S. prime and choice	lb	2.35	7/01	11r
Chuck roast, U.S. choice, boneless	lb	2.67	7/01	11r
Cigarettes, Winston, Kings	carton	28.18	3/01	4c
Coffee, 100%, ground roast, all sizes	lb	2.88	7/01	11r
Coffee, instant, plain, regular, all sizes	16 oz	9.25	7/01	11r
Coffee, vacuum-packed	13 oz	2.43	3/01	4c
Cola, non diet,	2 liter	1.11	7/01	11r
Corn Flakes, Kellogg's or Post Toasties	18 oz	1.66	3/01	4c
Corn, frozen, whole kernel, lowest price	16 oz	1.06	3/01	4c
Crackers, soda, salted	lb	1.70	7/01	11r
Dairy product purchases	yr	282	1999	30r
Eggs, expenditures on	yr	32	1999	30r
Eggs, Grade A or AA	dozen	1.06	3/01	4c
Fats and oils, expenditures on	yr	79	1999	30r
Fish and seafood, expenditures on	yr	99	1999	30r
Flour, white, all purpose	lb	0.32	7/01	11r
Food (excl fruit and vegetables), eaten at home, purchases	yr	815	1999	30r
Food cooked on trips, expenditures on	yr	36	1999	30r
Food purchases	yr	4533	1999	30r
Food purchases, eaten away from home	yr	1873	1999	30r
Food purchases, food eaten at home	yr	2660	1999	30r
Fresh fruits, expenditures on	yr	128	1999	30r
Fresh milk and cream, expenditures on	yr	112	1999	30r
Fresh vegetables, expenditures on	yr	131	1999	30r
Fruit and vegetable purchases	yr	438	1999	30r
Grapefruit	lb	0.59	7/01	11r
Grapes, Thompson, seedless	lb	2.12	7/01	11r
Ground beef, 100% beef	lb	1.76	7/01	11r
Ground beef, lean and extra lean	lb	2.60	7/01	11r
Ground chuck, 100% beef	lb	2.08	7/01	11r
Ham, boneless, excl canned	lb	2.71	7/01	11r
Ham, rump or shank half, bone-in, smoked	lb	2.19	7/01	11r
Ice cream, prepackaged, bulk, regular	1/2 gal	3.93	7/01	11r
Lemons	lb	1.32	7/01	11r
Lettuce, iceberg	head	1.02	3/01	4c
Lettuce, iceberg	lb	0.76	7/01	11r
Margarine, Blue Bonnet or Parkay, stick	lb	0.78	3/01	4c
Milk, fresh, low fat,	gal	2.75	7/01	11r
Milk, fresh, whole, fortified	gal	2.97	7/01	11r
Milk, whole	1/2 gal	1.53	3/01	4c
Nonalcoholic beverages, expenditures on	yr	228	1999	30r
Orange juice, frozen concentrate	16 oz	1.95	7/01	11r
Orange juice, Minute Maid frozen	12 oz	1.60	3/01	4c
Oranges, Navel	lb	0.73	7/01	11r
Oranges, Valencia	lb	0.55	7/01	11r
Peaches, halves or slices, Hunt's, Del Monte, or Libby's	29 oz	1.51	3/01	4c
Peanut butter, creamy, all sizes	lb	1.83	7/01	11r
Pears, Anjou	lb	0.98	7/01	11r
Peas, green, Del Monte or Green Giant	15 oz	0.59	3/01	4c
Pork chops, center cut, bone-in	lb	3.33	7/01	11r
Pork sausage, fresh, loose	lb	2.59	7/01	11r
Pork shoulder picnic, bone-in, smoked	lb	1.12	7/01	11r
Pork, expenditures on	yr	162	1999	30r
Potato chips	16 oz	3.59	7/01	11r
Potatoes, frozen, french fried	lb	1.00	7/01	11r
Potatoes, white or red	10 lb	1.89	3/01	4c
Potatoes, white, all types	lb	0.44	7/01	11r
Poultry, expenditures on	yr	137	1999	30r
Processed fruits, expenditures on	yr	97	1999	30r
Processed vegetables, expenditures on	yr	82	1999	30r
Rice, white, long grain, uncooked	lb	0.51	7/01	11r
Round roast, graded and ungraded, excl U.S. prime and choice	lb	2.96	7/01	11r
Round steak, graded and ungraded, excl U.S. prime and choice	lb	3.11	7/01	11r
Sausage, Jimmy Dean/Owens pork	lb	2.41	3/01	4c

Oklahoma City, OK - continued

Groceries - continued

Item	Per	Value	Date	Ref.
Shortening, vegetable, Crisco	3 lb	2.83	3/01	4c
Sirloin steak, graded and ungraded, excl U.S. prime and choice	lb	4.23	7/01	11r
Soft drink, Coca Cola, ex deposit	2 liter	1.09	3/01	4c
Spaghetti and macaroni	lb	0.78	7/01	11r
Steak, round, U.S. choice, boneless	lb	3.56	7/01	11r
Steak, sirloin, U.S. choice, boneless	lb	5.65	7/01	11r
Steak, T-bone	lb	6.59	3/01	4c
Strawberries, dry pint	12 oz	1.50	7/01	11r
Sugar and other sweets, expenditures on	yr	99	1999	30r
Sugar, cane or beet	4 lbs	1.53	3/01	4c
Sugar, white, 33-80 ounce package	lb	0.39	7/01	11r
Sugar, white, all sizes	lb	0.42	7/01	11r
Tobacco products and smoking supplies purchases	yr	288	1999	30r
Tomatoes, field grown	lb	1.43	7/01	11r
Tomatoes, Hunt's or Del Monte	14.5 oz	0.84	3/01	4c
Tuna, chunk, light	6 oz	0.56	3/01	4c
Tuna, light, chunk	lb	1.77	7/01	11r
Turkey, frozen, whole	lb	1.05	7/01	11r

Goods and Services

Item	Per	Value	Date	Ref.
Miscellaneous goods and services, ACCRA Index		100.70	3/01	4c
B&B Japanese maple (acer japonicum)	gal	79.98-99.00	4/00	93r
Boxwood (buxus)	2 gal	12.98-18.99	4/00	93r
Daylilly (hemerocallis)	gal	7.96-11.00	4/00	93r
Flat of annuals		13.99-27.99	4/00	93r
Fountain grass (pennisetum)	gal	6.96-9.00	4/00	93r
Hanging basket (10 in)		9.99-24.99	4/00	93r
Hardy geranium (geranium)	gal	5.96-8.00	4/00	93r
Hosta (hosta)	gal	8.96-12.99	4/00	93r
Lilac (syrubga vulgaris)	2 gal	13.00-19.99	4/00	93r
Rhododendron (rhododendron)	2 gal	12.98-29.99	4/00	93r
Sage (salvia)	gal	5.96-8.00	4/00	93r
Wintercreeper euonymus (euonymus fortunei)	2 gal	13.00-18.99	4/00	93r
Hunting license	yr	12.50	4/01	34s

Health Care

Item	Per	Value	Date	Ref.
Health care, ACCRA Index		95.70	3/01	4c
Cardiac catheterization, ave hospital/physician charges		15750	1998	77s
Childbirth, Cesarean delivery		11587	1997	13r
Childbirth, vaginal delivery		6725	1997	13r
Dentist's fee, adult teeth cleaning and periodic oral exam	visit	78.80	3/01	4c
Doctor's fee, routine exam, established patient	visit	53.80	3/01	4c
Drugs, expenditures on	yr	399	1999	30r
Health care purchases	yr	1971	1999	30r
Health insurance expenditures	yr	933	1999	30r
Home health care aide cost, licensed agency	hour	14	2000	82c
Hospital care, private room	day	401.33	3/01	4c
Hysterectomy, laproscopically-assisted, ave hospital/physician charges		16080	1998	76s
Hysterectomy, vaginal, ave hospital and physician charges		8140	1998	76s
Medicaid dispensing fee		4.15	1999	87s
Medical services expenditures	yr	547	1999	30r
Medical supplies, expenditures on	yr	91	1999	30r
Nursing home costs, private room	day	134	2000	82c

Values are in dollars or fractions of dollars. In the column headed *Ref*, references are shown to sources. Each reference is followed by a letter. These refer to the geographical level for which data were reported: s=State, r=Region, and c=City or metro. The abbreviation *ex* is used to mean *except* or *excluding*; *exp* stands for *expenditures*. For other abbreviations and further explanations, please see the Introduction.

Oklahoma City, OK - continued

Item	Per	Value	Date	Ref.
Health Care				
Nursing home stay, private room	day	134	2000	83c
Household Goods				
Dishwashing powder, Cascade	50 oz	3.52	3/01	4c
Floor coverings, expenditures on	yr	44	1999	30r
Furniture, expenditures on	yr	335	1999	30r
Household furnishings and equipment purchases	yr	1328	1999	30r
Household textiles, expenditures on	yr	89	1999	30r
Laundry and cleaning supplies, expenditures on	yr	113	1999	30r
Tissues, facial, Kleenex brand	175	1.35	3/01	4c
Housing				
Housing, ACCRA Index		82.30	3/01	4c
Home, 2200 sq ft, 4-br, 2-bath, 2-car garage, average		135125	2000	47c
Home price, existing, ave		160100	10/00	90r
Home value, median		88000	2001	53s
House, 2400 sq ft, 8000 sq ft lot, new, urban, utilities	total	171109	3/01	4c
House payment, principal and interest, 25% down payment	mos	856	3/01	4c
Household operation expenditures	yr	553	1999	30r
Housekeeping supplies purchases	yr	473	1999	30r
Housing, expenditures on	yr	10303	1999	30r
Maintenance, repairs, insurance expenditures	yr	699	1999	30r
Monthly rental value of owned home	mos	505	1999	30r
Owned dwellings, expenditures own	yr	3465	1999	30r
Rent expenditures	yr	1641	1999	30r
Rent, apartment, 2 br, 1 1/2-2 baths, unfurn, 950 sq ft, water	mos	550	3/01	4c
Rental unit, 1 bedroom, with utilities	mos	366	4/01	41c
Rental unit, 2 bedroom, with utilities	mos	474	4/01	41c
Rental unit, 3 bedroom, with utilities	mos	659	4/01	41c
Rental unit, 4 bedroom, with utilities	mos	737	4/01	41c
Shelter, expenditures on	yr	5467	1999	30r
Insurance and Pensions				
Life and other personal insurance purchases	yr	414	1999	30r
Pensions and Social Security, expenditures on	yr	2635	1999	30r
Personal insurance and pensions, expenditures on	yr	3048	1999	30r
Legal Fees				
Combination hunting and fishing license	yr	21.00	4/01	34s
Divorce, filing fee		84.00	4/01	35s
Driver's license fee	renew	15.00	1999	48s
Driver's license fee	orig	15.00	1999	48s
Fishing license	yr	12.50	4/01	34s
Personal Goods				
Personal care products and services purchases	yr	393	1999	30r
Shampoo, Alberto VO5	15 oz	1.18	3/01	4c
Toothpaste, Crest or Colgate	6-7 oz	2.25	3/01	4c
Personal Services				
Dry cleaning, man's 2-pc suit		7.52	3/01	4c
Man's haircut, barbershop, no styling		8.70	3/01	4c
Personal services, household, expenditures on	yr	258	1999	30r
Woman's shampoo, trim, blow-dry, no style-change		24.00	3/01	4c
Pets				
Pets, toys, and playground equipment, expenditures on	yr	306	1999	30r
Restaurant Food				
Chicken, fried, thigh and drumstick, KFC/ Church's		2.85	3/01	4c
Hamburger with cheese, McDonald's	1/4 lb	1.87	3/01	4c
Pizza, Pizza Hut or Pizza Inn	11-12 in	9.19	3/01	4c

Oklahoma City, OK - continued

Item	Per	Value	Date	Ref.
Taxes				
Federal income taxes paid	yr	2047	1999	30r
Personal taxes, expenditures on	yr	2554	1999	30r
Property taxes paid	yr	726	1999	30r
State and local income taxes paid	yr	363	1999	30r
Transportation				
Transportation, ACCRA Index		97.00	3/01	4c
Bus fare, one-way	trip	1.00	2000	1c
Bus fare, to central business district	1-way	1.00	3/01	4c
Cars and trucks, new, expenditures on	yr	1648	1999	30r
Cars and trucks, used, expenditures on	yr	1651	1999	30r
Diesel at the pump	gal	1.13	10/99	73s
Gasoline and motor oil purchases	yr	1052	1999	30r
Gasoline before-tax price (cents)	gal	103.70	10/00	43s
Maintenance and repair expenditures	yr	621	1999	30r
Public transportation, expenditures on	yr	298	1999	30r
Tire balance, computer or spin balance, front	wheel	8.66	3/01	4c
Transportation purchases	yr	6738	1999	30r
Vehicle expenses, miscellaneous, purchases	yr	2033	1999	30r
Vehicle insurance payments	yr	696	1999	30r
Vehicle purchases (net outlay)	yr	3354	1999	30r
Vehicle rental, lease expenditures	yr	352	1999	30r
Travel				
Hotel room	night	55.28	2/01	94s
Hotel room, ave	night	56.52	2000	70c
Utilities				
Utilities, ACCRA Index		108.90	3/01	4c
Electrical bill, average	mos	67.33	9/00	9s
Electricity, expenditures on	yr	1115	1999	30r
Electricity, summer, 250 KWh	mos	25.67	2/96	96c
Electricity, summer, 500 KWh	mos	44.64	2/96	96c
Electricity, summer, 750 KWh	mos	63.61	2/96	96c
Electricity, summer, 1000 KWh	mos	82.58	2/96	96c
Electricity and other, mixed, 2400 sq ft, new home	mos	68.30	3/01	4c
Electricity cost, average	KWh	5.66	9/00	9s
Water and other public services, expenditures on	yr	298	1999	30r
Water price	100 cf	1.26	2000	109c
Water price, dwelling unit	mos	24.78	2000	109c
Weddings				
Wedding (national average cost)		19936	2000	33r
Attendants' gifts		321	1998	33r
Bridal attendants' apparel (5 persons)		824	2000	33r
Bride's headpiece/veil		173	1998	33r
Bride's wedding dress		859	1998	33r
Clergy, religious facility fee		242	1998	33r
Engagement ring		3177	1998	33r
Flowers		789	1998	33r
Groom's formalwear rental		99	2000	33r
Limousine		410	1998	33r
Marriage license cost		25.00	4/01	35s
Men's formalwear (ushers, best man)		469	2000	33r
Mother of bride apparel		241	2000	33r
Music		866	1998	33r
Photography and videography		1368	1998	33r
Rehearsal dinner		728	1998	33r
Wedding invitations and announcements		341	1998	33r
Wedding reception		7968	2000	33r
Wedding rings (bride and groom)		1060	1998	33r

Olympia, WA

Item	Per	Value	Date	Ref.
Average annual expenditures	yr	40662	1999	30r
Composite, ACCRA index		102.30	3/01	4c
Alcoholic Beverages				
Alcoholic beverage purchases	yr	372	1999	30r
Beer, Heineken, 12-oz, ex deposit	6	7.85	3/01	4c
J & B Scotch	750-ml	22.45	3/01	4c
Malt beverages, all types, all sizes, any origin	16 oz	0.94	7/01	11r

Values are in dollars or fractions of dollars. In the column headed *Ref*, references are shown to sources. Each reference is followed by a letter. These refer to the geographical level for which data were reported: s=State, r=Region, and c=City or metro. The abbreviation *ex* is used to mean *except* or *excluding*; *exp* stands for expenditures. For other abbreviations and further explanations, please see the Introduction.

Olympia, WA - continued

Item	Per	Value	Date	Ref.
Alcoholic Beverages				
Wine, Livingston or Gallo, Chablis blanc	1.5 liter	5.52	3/01	4c
Wine, red and white table, all sizes, any origin	liter	6.00	7/01	11r
Appliances				
Appliance repair, service call, washing machine	min lab chg	39.61	3/01	4c
Major appliances, expenditures on	yr	167	1999	30r
Small appliances, housewares, expenditures on	yr	105	1999	30r
Banking and Money				
Mortgage interest and charges paid	yr	3368	1999	30r
Mortgage principal paid on owned property	yr	1677	1999	30r
Mortgage rate, incl. points and orig. fee, 30-yr. conv. fixed or ARM	mos	6.77	3/01	4c
Vehicle finance charges paid	yr	311	1999	30r
Charity				
Cash contributions, expenditures	yr	1344	1999	30r
Child Care				
Child raising cost, total, age 0-2	yr	9140	1999	60r
Child raising cost, total, age 3-5	yr	9370	1999	60r
Child raising cost, total, age 6-8	yr	9450	1999	60r
Child raising cost, total, age 9-11	yr	9470	1999	60r
Child raising cost, total, age 12-14	yr	10170	1999	60r
Child raising cost, total, age 15-17	yr	10360	1999	60r
Child's child care and education, age 0-2	yr	1250	1999	60r
Child's child care and education, age 3-5	yr	1380	1999	60r
Child's child care and education, age 6-8	yr	890	1999	60r
Child's child care and education, age 9-11	yr	580	1999	60r
Child's child care and education, age 12-14	yr	430	1999	60r
Child's child care and education, age 15-17	yr	730	1999	60r
Child's clothing, age 0-2	yr	430	1999	60r
Child's clothing, age 3-5	yr	420	1999	60r
Child's clothing, age 6-8	yr	470	1999	60r
Child's clothing, age 9-11	yr	520	1999	60r
Child's clothing, age 12-14	yr	870	1999	60r
Child's clothing, age 15-17	yr	770	1999	60r
Child's food, age 0-2	yr	1120	1999	60r
Child's food, age 3-5	yr	1280	1999	60r
Child's food, age 6-8	yr	1640	1999	60r
Child's food, age 9-11	yr	1930	1999	60r
Child's food, age 12-14	yr	1940	1999	60r
Child's food, age 15-17	yr	2150	1999	60r
Child's health care, age 0-2	yr	490	1999	60r
Child's health care, age 3-5	yr	470	1999	60r
Child's health care, age 6-8	yr	530	1999	60r
Child's health care, age 9-11	yr	570	1999	60r
Child's health care, age 12-14	yr	580	1999	60r
Child's health care, age 15-17	yr	610	1999	60r
Child's housing, age 0-2	yr	3630	1999	60r
Child's housing, age 3-5	yr	3610	1999	60r
Child's housing, age 6-8	yr	3570	1999	60r
Child's housing, age 9-11	yr	3410	1999	60r
Child's housing, age 12-14	yr	3600	1999	60r
Child's housing, age 15-17	yr	3210	1999	60r
Child's personal care, reading, age 0-2	yr	1040	1999	60r
Child's personal care, reading, age 3-5	yr	1060	1999	60r
Child's personal care, reading, age 6-8	yr	1090	1999	60r
Child's personal care, reading, age 9-11	yr	1130	1999	60r
Child's personal care, reading, age 12-14	yr	1300	1999	60r
Child's personal care, reading, age 15-17	yr	1080	1999	60r
Clothing				
Apparel and services purchases	yr	1863	1999	30r
Boys' brief, cotton	3	5.49	3/01	4c
Boys, 2 to 15, expenditures on	yr	80	1999	30r
Children under 2, expenditures on	yr	74	1999	30r
Footwear, expenditures on	yr	307	1999	30r
Girls, 2 to 15, expenditures on	yr	101	1999	30r
Men and boys, expenditures on	yr	443	1999	30r
Men, 16 and over, expenditures on	yr	363	1999	30r

Olympia, WA - continued

Item	Per	Value	Date	Ref.
Clothing - continued				
Shirt, man's dress shirt		22.49	3/01	4c
Slacks, man's "No Wrinkles" khaki		37.66	3/01	4c
Women, 16 and over, expenditures on	yr	594	1999	30r
Communications				
Cable modem installation, AT&T-BIS		150.00	6/99	103s
Cable modem rate, cable subscriber, AT&T-BIS	mos	39.95	6/99	103s
Newspaper subscription, daily and Sunday delivery	mos	13.25	3/01	4c
Phone line, single, business, field visit	inst.	48.00	12/97	17s
Phone line, single, business, no field visit	inst.	48.00	12/97	17s
Phone line, single, residence, field visit	inst.	31.00	12/97	17s
Phone line, single, residence, no field visit	inst.	31.00	12/97	17s
Postage and stationery, expenditures on	yr	150	1999	30r
Postal rate, express mail, up to half-pound		12.45	7/01	108r
Postal rate, letter, first class, first ounce		0.34	7/01	108r
Postal rate, letter, two ounces		0.57	7/01	108r
Postal rate, post card		0.21	7/01	108r
Postal rate, priority mail, two pounds		3.95	7/01	108r
Postal rate, priority mail, up to one pound		3.50	7/01	108r
Telephone bill, family of three	mos	19.90	3/01	4c
Telephone services, expenditures on	yr	825	1999	30r
Education				
Board, 4-year private college/university	yr	2329	1996	38s
Board, 4-year public college/university	yr	2158	1996	38s
Education expenditures	yr	676	1999	30r
Room, 4-year private college/university	yr	2487	1996	38s
Room, 4-year public college/university	yr	2187	1996	38s
Total cost, 4-year private college/university	yr	18092	1996	38s
Total cost, 4-year public college/university	yr	7136	1996	38s
Tuition, 2-year public college/university, in state	yr	1369	1996	38s
Tuition, 4-year private college/university, in state	yr	13276	1996	38s
Tuition, 4-year public college/university	yr	2791	1996	38s
Energy and Fuels				
Electricity	KWh	0.11	7/01	11r
Electricity	500 KWhs	48.23	7/01	11r
Energy, combined forms, 2400 sq ft	mos	93.65	3/01	4c
Energy, exc. electricity, 2400 sq ft	mos	57.43	3/01	4c
Fuel oil and other fuels, expenditures on	yr	35	1999	30r
Gas, natural, commercial rate	1000 cf	6.89	11/00	88s
Gas, regular unleaded, cash, self-service	gal	1.53	3/01	4c
Gasoline, all types	gal	1.91	7/01	11r
Gasoline, unleaded premium	gal	2.05	7/01	11r
Gasoline, unleaded regular	gal	1.83	7/01	11r
Natural gas, expenditures on	yr	255	1999	30r
Utility (piped) gas, therm		0.98	7/01	11r
Utility (piped) gas, 40 therms		40.74	7/01	11r
Utility (piped) gas, 100 therms		96.80	7/01	11r
Entertainment				
Bowling, Saturday evening rate	line	2.47	3/01	4c
Entertainment purchases	yr	2139	1999	30r
Fees and admissions paid	yr	545	1999	30r
Monopoly game, Parker Brothers', No. 9	game	11.74	3/01	4c
Movie, first-run, Saturday, evening	adm.	7.25	3/01	4c
Television, radios, sound equipment, expenditures on	yr	624	1999	30r
Tennis balls, yellow, Wilson or Penn, 3	can	2.57	3/01	4c
Funerals				
Total cost of funeral		5401.08	1/99	78r
Acknowledgement cards		33.64	1/99	78r
Casket		2170.43	1/99	78r
Cosmetology, hair, other preparation		136.32	1/99	78r
Embalming		319.13	1/99	78r
Funeral at funeral home		370.21	1/99	78r
Hearse (local)		161.04	1/99	78r
Professional service charges		963.15	1/99	78r

Values are in dollars or fractions of dollars. In the column headed *Ref*, references are shown to sources. Each reference is followed by a letter. These refer to the geographical level for which data were reported: s=State, r=Region, and c=City or metro. The abbreviation *ex* is used to mean *except* or *excluding*; *exp* stands for *expenditures*. For other abbreviations and further explanations, please see the Introduction.

Olympia, WA - continued

Item	Per	Value	Date	Ref.
Funerals				
Service car/van		133.99	1/99	78r
Transfer of remains to funeral home		159.82	1/99	78r
Vault		778.07	1/99	78r
Visitation/viewing		175.28	1/99	78r
Groceries				
Groceries, ACCRA Index		106.60	3/01	4c
Antibiotic ointment, Polysporin	0.5 oz	4.71	3/01	4c
Apples, red delicious	lb	0.84	7/01	11r
Baby food, strained vegetables or fruit, lowest price	4-4.5 oz	0.33	3/01	4c
Bacon, sliced	lb	3.38	7/01	11r
Bakery products, expenditures on	yr	299	1999	30r
Bananas	lb	0.59	3/01	4c
Bananas	lb	0.54	7/01	11r
Beans, dried, any type, all sizes	lb	0.76	7/01	11r
Beef or hamburger, ground	lb	1.67	3/01	4c
Beef, expenditures on	yr	222	1999	30r
Bread, white	loaf	0.69	3/01	4c
Bread, white, pan	lb	0.99	7/01	11r
Butter, yoghurt, cheese, etc, expenditures on	yr	211	1999	30r
Cereals and bakery product purchases	yr	466	1999	30r
Cereals and cereal products, expenditures on	yr	168	1999	30r
Cheese, Kraft grated Parmesan	8 oz	4.43	3/01	4c
Chicken breast, bone-in	lb	2.45	7/01	11r
Chicken, fresh, whole	lb	1.19	7/01	11r
Chicken, whole fryer	lb	1.31	3/01	4c
Chops, boneless,	lb	4.00	7/01	11r
Chuck roast, graded and ungraded, excl U.S. prime and choice	lb	2.55	7/01	11r
Cigarettes, Winston, Kings	carton	40.37	3/01	4c
Coffee, 100%, ground roast, all sizes	lb	3.80	7/01	11r
Coffee, vacuum-packed	13 oz	3.21	3/01	4c
Cookies, chocolate chip	lb	2.83	7/01	11r
Corn Flakes, Kellogg's or Post Toasties	18 oz	2.74	3/01	4c
Corn, frozen, whole kernel, lowest price	16 oz	1.28	3/01	4c
Dairy product purchases	yr	341	1999	30r
Eggs, expenditures on	yr	39	1999	30r
Eggs, Grade A or AA	dozen	1.41	3/01	4c
Eggs, grade AA, large	dozen	1.23	7/01	11r
Fats and oils, expenditures on	yr	88	1999	30r
Fish and seafood, expenditures on	yr	121	1999	30r
Food (excl fruit and vegetables), eaten at home, purchases	yr	1001	1999	30r
Food cooked on trips, expenditures on	yr	64	1999	30r
Food purchases	yr	5312	1999	30r
Food purchases, eaten away from home	yr	2180	1999	30r
Food purchases, food eaten at home	yr	3132	1999	30r
Fresh fruits, expenditures on	yr	186	1999	30r
Fresh milk and cream, expenditures on	yr	130	1999	30r
Fresh vegetables, expenditures on	yr	177	1999	30r
Grapefruit	lb	0.68	7/01	11r
Grapes, Thompson, seedless	lb	2.42	7/01	11r
Ground beef, lean and extra lean	lb	2.46	7/01	11r
Ice cream, prepackaged, bulk, regular	1/2 gal	3.62	7/01	11r
Lettuce, iceberg	head	1.09	3/01	4c
Lettuce, iceberg	lb	0.63	7/01	11r
Margarine, Blue Bonnet or Parkay, stick	lb	0.81	3/01	4c
Meats, poultry, fish, and egg purchases	yr	761	1999	30r
Milk, fresh, low fat	gal	2.80	7/01	11r
Milk, fresh, whole, fortified	gal	2.88	7/01	11r
Milk, whole	1/2 gal	1.76	3/01	4c
Nonalcoholic beverages, expenditures on	yr	258	1999	30r
Orange juice, Minute Maid frozen	12 oz	1.40	3/01	4c
Oranges, Navel	lb	0.97	7/01	11r
Oranges, Valencia	lb	0.43	7/01	11r
Peaches	lb	1.38	7/01	11r
Peaches, halves or slices, Hunt's, Del Monte, or Libby's	29 oz	1.81	3/01	4c
Peanut butter, creamy, all sizes	lb	2.14	7/01	11r
Peas, green, Del Monte or Green Giant	15 oz	0.87	3/01	4c
Pork chops, center cut, bone-in	lb	3.83	7/01	11r

Olympia, WA - continued

Item	Per	Value	Date	Ref.
Groceries - continued				
Pork, expenditures on	yr	141	1999	30r
Potatoes, white or red	10 lb	2.05	3/01	4c
Potatoes, white, all types	lb	0.37	7/01	11r
Poultry, expenditures on	yr	146	1999	30r
Processed fruits, expenditures on	yr	118	1999	30r
Processed vegetables, expenditures on	yr	81	1999	30r
Round roast, graded and ungraded, excl U.S. prime and choice	lb	3.07	7/01	11r
Round roast, U.S. choice, boneless	lb	3.37	7/01	11r
Round steak, graded and ungraded, excl U.S. prime and choice	lb	3.51	7/01	11r
Sausage, Jimmy Dean/Owens pork	lb	4.40	3/01	4c
Shortening, vegetable, Crisco	3 lb	2.86	3/01	4c
Sirloin steak, graded and ungraded, excl U.S. prime and choice	lb	4.67	7/01	11r
Soft drink, Coca Cola, ex deposit	2 liter	1.21	3/01	4c
Steak, sirloin, U.S. choice, boneless	lb	6.20	7/01	11r
Steak, T-bone	lb	7.09	3/01	4c
Strawberries, dry pint	12 oz	1.79	7/01	11r
Sugar and other sweets, expenditures on	yr	124	1999	30r
Sugar, cane or beet	4 lbs	1.70	3/01	4c
Sugar, white, all sizes	lb	0.46	7/01	11r
Tobacco products and smoking supplies purchases	yr	217	1999	30r
Tomatoes, field grown	lb	1.17	7/01	11r
Tomatoes, Hunt's or Del Monte	14.5 oz	1.00	3/01	4c
Tuna, chunk, light	6 oz	0.72	3/01	4c
Tuna, light, chunk	lb	2.05	7/01	11r
Goods and Services				
Miscellaneous goods and services, ACCRA Index		104.10	3/01	4c
B&B Japanese maple (acer japonicum)	gal	39.99	4/00	93r
Boxwood (buxus)	2 gal	14.99-24.99	4/00	93r
Daylilly (hemerocallis)	gal	6.99-8.99	4/00	93r
Flat of annuals		16.68	4/00	93r
Fountain grass (pennisetum)	gal	7.99-11.99	4/00	93r
Hanging basket (10 in)		29.99	4/00	93r
Hardy geranium (geranium)	gal	6.99-11.99	4/00	93r
Hosta (hosta)	gal	6.99-18.99	4/00	93r
Lilac (syrubga vulgaris)	2 gal	14.99-17.99	4/00	93r
Miscellaneous purchases	yr	1070	1999	30r
Rhododendron (rhododendron)	2 gal	14.99	4/00	93r
Sage (salvia)	gal	6.99	4/00	93r
Wintercreeper euonymus (euonymus fortunei)	2 gal	14.99-22.99	4/00	93r
Hunting license	yr	30.00	4/01	34s
Health Care				
Health care, ACCRA Index		127.10	3/01	4c
Cardiac catheterization, ave hospital/physician charges		13290	1998	77s
Childbirth, Cesarean delivery		11587	1997	13r
Childbirth, vaginal delivery		6725	1997	13r
Dentist's fee, adult teeth cleaning and periodic oral exam	visit	111.63	3/01	4c
Doctor's fee, routine exam, established patient	visit	63.13	3/01	4c
Drugs, expenditures on	yr	309	1999	30r
Health care purchases	yr	1869	1999	30r
Health insurance expenditures	yr	868	1999	30r
Hospital care, private room	day	666.50	3/01	4c
Hysterectomy, laproscopically-assisted, ave hospital/physician charges		10960	1998	76s
Hysterectomy, vaginal, ave hospital and physician charges		9000	1998	76s

Values are in dollars or fractions of dollars. In the column headed *Ref*, references are shown to sources. Each reference is followed by a letter. These refer to the geographical level for which data were reported: s=State, r=Region, and c=City or metro. The abbreviation *ex* is used to mean *except* or *excluding*; *exp* stands for expenditures. For other abbreviations and further explanations, please see the Introduction.

Olympia, WA - continued

Item	Per	Value	Date	Ref.
Health Care				
Medicaid dispensing fee		3.98-4.92	1999	87s
Medical services expenditures	yr	580	1999	30r
Medical supplies, expenditures on	yr	112	1999	30r
Household Goods				
Dishwashing powder, Cascade	50 oz	3.65	3/01	4c
Floor coverings, expenditures on	yr	49	1999	30r
Furniture, expenditures on	yr	444	1999	30r
Household furnishings and equipment purchases	yr	1768	1999	30r
Household textiles, expenditures on	yr	141	1999	30r
Laundry and cleaning supplies, expenditures on	yr	128	1999	30r
Tissues, facial, Kleenex brand	175	1.28	3/01	4c
Housing				
Housing, ACCRA Index		99.20	3/01	4c
Home price, existing, ave		239400	10/00	90r
Home value, median		195000	2001	53s
House, 2400 sq ft, 8000 sq ft lot, new, urban, utilities	total	211880	3/01	4c
House payment, principal and interest, 25% down payment	mos	1033	3/01	4c
Household operation expenditures	yr	781	1999	30r
Housekeeping supplies purchases	yr	513	1999	30r
Lodging expenditures	yr	575	1999	30r
Maintenance, repairs, insurance expenditures	yr	939	1999	30r
Monthly rental value of owned home	mos	662	1999	30r
Owned dwellings, expenditures own	yr	5231	1999	30r
Rent expenditures	yr	2709	1999	30r
Rent, apartment, 2 br, 1 1/2-2 baths, unfurn, 950 sq ft, water	mos	662	3/01	4c
Rental unit, 1 bedroom, with utilities	mos	573	4/01	41c
Rental unit, 2 bedroom, with utilities	mos	716	4/01	41c
Rental unit, 3 bedroom, with utilities	mos	985	4/01	41c
Rental unit, 4 bedroom, with utilities	mos	1162	4/01	41c
Shelter, expenditures on	yr	8516	1999	30r
Insurance and Pensions				
Life and other personal insurance purchases	yr	355	1999	30r
Pensions and Social Security, expenditures on	yr	3636	1999	30r
Legal Fees				
Divorce, filing fee		100.00	4/01	35s
Driver's license fee	renew	14.00	1999	48s
Driver's license fee	orig	14.00	1999	48s
Fishing license	yr	20.00	4/01	34s
Personal Goods				
Personal care products and services purchases	yr	449	1999	30r
Shampoo, Alberto VO5	15 oz	1.25	3/01	4c
Toothpaste, Crest or Colgate	6-7 oz	2.35	3/01	4c
Personal Services				
Dry cleaning, man's 2-pc suit		9.58	3/01	4c
Man's haircut, barbershop, no styling		10.67	3/01	4c
Personal services, household, expenditures on	yr	353	1999	30r
Woman's shampoo, trim, blow-dry, no style-change		34.49	3/01	4c
Pets				
Pets, toys, and playground equipment, expenditures on	yr	358	1999	30r
Restaurant Food				
Chicken, fried, thigh and drumstick, KFC/Church's		3.01	3/01	4c
Hamburger with cheese, McDonald's	1/4 lb	2.26	3/01	4c
Pizza, Pizza Hut or Pizza Inn	11-12 in	9.99	3/01	4c

Olympia, WA - continued

Item	Per	Value	Date	Ref.
Taxes				
Federal income taxes paid	yr	3200	1999	30r
Personal taxes, expenditures on	yr	4153	1999	30r
Property taxes paid	yr	923	1999	30r
State and local income taxes paid	yr	812	1999	30r
Transportation				
Transportation, ACCRA Index		104.80	3/01	4c
Bus fare, one-way	trip	0.60	2000	1c
Bus fare, to central business district	1-way	0.60	3/01	4c
Cars and trucks, new, expenditures on	yr	1534	1999	30r
Cars and trucks, used, expenditures on	yr	1593	1999	30r
Diesel at the pump	gal	1.37	10/99	73s
Gasoline and motor oil purchases	yr	1129	1999	30r
Gasoline before-tax price (cents)	gal	127.10	10/00	43s
Maintenance and repair expenditures	yr	797	1999	30r
Public transportation, expenditures on	yr	530	1999	30r
Tire balance, computer or spin balance, front	wheel	8.94	3/01	4c
Transportation purchases	yr	7423	1999	30r
Vehicle expenses, miscellaneous, purchases	yr	2585	1999	30r
Vehicle insurance payments	yr	811	1999	30r
Vehicle purchases (net outlay)	yr	3180	1999	30r
Vehicle rental, lease expenditures	yr	666	1999	30r
Utilities				
Utilities, ACCRA Index		78.80	3/01	4c
Electrical bill, average	mos	58.33	9/00	9s
Electricity, expenditures on	yr	725	1999	30r
Electricity and other, mixed, 2400 sq ft, new home	mos	36.22	3/01	4c
Electricity cost, average	KWh	4.47	9/00	9s
Utilities, fuels, and public services purchased	yr	2179	1999	30r
Water and other public services, expenditures on	yr	339	1999	30r
Weddings				
Wedding (national average cost)		19936	2000	33r
Wedding (regional average total cost)		18918	1997	110r
Attendants' gifts		321	1998	33r
Bridal attendants' apparel (5 persons)		824	2000	33r
Bride's headpiece/veil		173	1998	33r
Bride's wedding dress		859	1998	33r
Clergy, religious facility fee		242	1998	33r
Engagement ring		3177	1998	33r
Flowers		789	1998	33r
Groom's formalwear rental		99	2000	33r
Limousine		410	1998	33r
Marriage license cost		52.00	4/01	35s
Men's formalwear (ushers, best man)		469	2000	33r
Mother of bride apparel		241	2000	33r
Music		866	1998	33r
Photography and videography		1368	1998	33r
Rehearsal dinner		728	1998	33r
Wedding invitations and announcements		341	1998	33r
Wedding reception		7968	2000	33r
Wedding rings (bride and groom)		1060	1998	33r

Omaha, NE

Item	Per	Value	Date	Ref.
Average annual expenditures	yr	35369	1999	30r
Composite, ACCRA index		95.40	3/01	4c
Alcoholic Beverages				
Alcoholic beverage purchases	yr	304	1999	30r
Beer, Heineken, 12-oz, ex deposit	6	7.19	3/01	4c
J & B Scotch	750-ml	20.55	3/01	4c
Malt beverages, all types, all sizes, any origin	16 oz	0.93	7/01	11r
Wine, Livingston or Gallo, Chablis blanc	1.5 liter	4.74	3/01	4c
Wine, red and white table, all sizes, any origin	liter	7.04	7/01	11r
Appliances				
Appliance repair, service call, washing machine	min lab chg	38.96	3/01	4c
Major appliances, expenditures on	yr	165	1999	30r

Values are in dollars or fractions of dollars. In the column headed *Ref*, references are shown to sources. Each reference is followed by a letter. These refer to the geographical level for which data were reported: s=State, r=Region, and c=City or metro. The abbreviation *ex* is used to mean *except* or *excluding*; *exp* stands for *expenditures*. For other abbreviations and further explanations, please see the Introduction.

Omaha, NE - continued

Item	Per	Value	Date	Ref.
Appliances				
Small appliances, housewares, expenditures on	yr	90	1999	30r
Banking and Money				
Mortgage interest and charges paid	yr	2277	1999	30r
Mortgage principal paid on owned property	yr	1230	1999	30r
Mortgage rate, incl. points and orig. fee, 30-yr. conv. fixed or ARM	mos	6.88	3/01	4c
Vehicle finance charges paid	yr	328	1999	30r
Business Expenses				
Business travel, car rental	day	49	2001	3c
Business travel, food	day	38	2001	3c
Business travel, hotel	day	101	2001	3c
Charity				
Cash contributions, expenditures	yr	1126	1999	30r
Child Care				
Child raising cost, total, age 0-2	yr	7890	1999	60r
Child raising cost, total, age 3-5	yr	8130	1999	60r
Child raising cost, total, age 6-8	yr	8170	1999	60r
Child raising cost, total, age 9-11	yr	8190	1999	60r
Child raising cost, total, age 12-14	yr	8890	1999	60r
Child raising cost, total, age 15-17	yr	9050	1999	60r
Child's child care and education, age 0-2	yr	1240	1999	60r
Child's child care and education, age 3-5	yr	1370	1999	60r
Child's child care and education, age 6-8	yr	880	1999	60r
Child's child care and education, age 9-11	yr	570	1999	60r
Child's child care and education, age 12-14	yr	420	1999	60r
Child's child care and education, age 15-17	yr	720	1999	60r
Child's clothing, age 0-2	yr	410	1999	60r
Child's clothing, age 3-5	yr	400	1999	60r
Child's clothing, age 6-8	yr	450	1999	60r
Child's clothing, age 9-11	yr	500	1999	60r
Child's clothing, age 12-14	yr	840	1999	60r
Child's clothing, age 15-17	yr	740	1999	60r
Child's food, age 0-2	yr	960	1999	60r
Child's food, age 3-5	yr	1120	1999	60r
Child's food, age 6-8	yr	1430	1999	60r
Child's food, age 9-11	yr	1710	1999	60r
Child's food, age 12-14	yr	1710	1999	60r
Child's food, age 15-17	yr	1920	1999	60r
Child's health care, age 0-2	yr	520	1999	60r
Child's health care, age 3-5	yr	500	1999	60r
Child's health care, age 6-8	yr	570	1999	60r
Child's health care, age 9-11	yr	610	1999	60r
Child's health care, age 12-14	yr	630	1999	60r
Child's health care, age 15-17	yr	650	1999	60r
Child's housing, age 0-2	yr	2860	1999	60r
Child's housing, age 3-5	yr	2840	1999	60r
Child's housing, age 6-8	yr	2800	1999	60r
Child's housing, age 9-11	yr	2650	1999	60r
Child's housing, age 12-14	yr	2840	1999	60r
Child's housing, age 15-17	yr	2440	1999	60r
Child's personal care, reading, age 0-2	yr	880	1999	60r
Child's personal care, reading, age 3-5	yr	900	1999	60r
Child's personal care, reading, age 6-8	yr	930	1999	60r
Child's personal care, reading, age 9-11	yr	970	1999	60r
Child's personal care, reading, age 12-14	yr	1150	1999	60r
Child's personal care, reading, age 15-17	yr	920	1999	60r
Clothing				
Apparel and services purchases	yr	1607	1999	30r
Boys' brief, cotton	3	3.64	3/01	4c
Boys, 2 to 15, expenditures on	yr	91	1999	30r
Children under 2, expenditures on	yr	59	1999	30r
Footwear, expenditures on	yr	285	1999	30r
Girls, 2 to 15, expenditures on	yr	116	1999	30r
Men and boys, expenditures on	yr	433	1999	30r
Men, 16 and over, expenditures on	yr	341	1999	30r
Shirt, man's dress shirt		24.19	3/01	4c
Slacks, man's "No Wrinkles" khaki		38.28	3/01	4c
Women, 16 and over, expenditures on	yr	490	1999	30r

Omaha, NE - continued

Item	Per	Value	Date	Ref.
Communications				
Cable modem installation, Cox		99.00-174.95	6/99	103s
Cable modem rate, cable subscriber, Cox	mos	29.95-44.95	6/99	103s
Cable modem rate, non-cable subscriber, Cox	mos	42.95-54.95	6/99	103s
Newspaper subscription, daily and Sunday delivery	mos	11.96	3/01	4c
Phone line, single, business, field visit	inst.	45.00	12/97	17s
Phone line, single, business, no field visit	inst.	45.00	12/97	17s
Phone line, single, residence, field visit	inst.	33.00	12/97	17s
Phone line, single, residence, no field visit	inst.	33.00	12/97	17s
Postage and stationery, expenditures on	yr	140	1999	30r
Postal rate, express mail, up to half-pound		12.45	7/01	108r
Postal rate, letter, first class, first ounce		0.34	7/01	108r
Postal rate, letter, two ounces		0.57	7/01	108r
Postal rate, post card		0.21	7/01	108r
Postal rate, priority mail, two pounds		3.95	7/01	108r
Postal rate, priority mail, up to one pound		3.50	7/01	108r
Telephone bill, business, basic rate	mos	37.55	12/97	18c
Telephone bill, family of three	mos	32.71	3/01	4c
Telephone bill, residential, basic rate	mos	16.35	12/97	18c
Telephone services, expenditures on	yr	830	1999	30r
Education				
Board, 4-year private college/university	yr	2003	1996	38s
Board, 4-year public college/university	yr	1892	1996	38s
Education expenditures	yr	583	1999	30r
Room, 4-year private college/university	yr	1801	1996	38s
Room, 4-year public college/university	yr	1422	1996	38s
Total cost, 4-year private college/university	yr	13234	1996	38s
Total cost, 4-year public college/university	yr	5497	1996	38s
Tuition, 2-year public college/university, in state	yr	1132	1996	38s
Tuition, 4-year private college/university, in state	yr	9430	1996	38s
Tuition, 4-year public college/university	yr	2182	1996	38s
Energy and Fuels				
Electricity	500 KWhs	46.59	7/01	11r
Energy, combined forms, 2400 sq ft	mos	144.87	3/01	4c
Energy, exc. electricity, 2400 sq ft	mos	92.03	3/01	4c
Fuel oil #2	gal	1.27	7/01	11r
Fuel oil and other fuels, expenditures on	yr	68	1999	30r
Gas, natural, commercial rate	1000 cf	6.59	11/00	88s
Gas, regular unleaded, cash, self-service	gal	1.38	3/01	4c
Gasoline, unleaded midgrade	gal	1.79	7/01	11r
Gasoline, unleaded premium	gal	1.86	7/01	11r
Gasoline, unleaded regular	gal	1.58	7/01	11r
Natural gas, expenditures on	yr	389	1999	30r
Utility (piped) gas, therm		0.81	7/01	11r
Utility (piped) gas, 40 therms		38.01	7/01	11r
Utility (piped) gas, 100 therms		81.75	7/01	11r
Entertainment				
Bowling, Saturday evening rate	line	2.38	3/01	4c
Entertainment purchases	yr	1984	1999	30r
Fees and admissions paid	yr	444	1999	30r
Monopoly game, Parker Brothers', No. 9	game	8.95	3/01	4c
Movie, first-run, Saturday, evening	adm.	6.61	3/01	4c
Television, radios, sound equipment, expenditures on	yr	580	1999	30r
Tennis balls, yellow, Wilson or Penn, 3	can	2.45	3/01	4c
Funerals				
Cosmetology, hair, other preparation		178.32	1/99	78r
Embalming		408.19	1/99	78r
Funeral at funeral home		362.13	1/99	78r
Professional service charges		1375.51	1/99	78r
Transfer of remains to funeral home		155.92	1/99	78r
Visitation/viewing		294.38	1/99	78r

Values are in dollars or fractions of dollars. In the column headed *Ref*, references are shown to sources. Each reference is followed by a letter. These refer to the geographical level for which data were reported: s=State, r=Region, and c=City or metro. The abbreviation *ex* is used to mean *except* or *excluding*; *exp* stands for *expenditures*. For other abbreviations and further explanations, please see the Introduction.

Omaha, NE - continued

Item	Per	Value	Date	Ref.
Groceries				
Groceries, ACCRA Index		93.80	3/01	4c
Antibiotic ointment, Polysporin	0.5 oz	4.76	3/01	4c
Baby food, strained vegetables or fruit, lowest price	4-4.5 oz	0.37	3/01	4c
Bacon, sliced	lb	3.15	7/01	11r
Bakery products, expenditures on	yr	281	1999	30r
Bananas	lb	0.43	3/01	4c
Bananas	lb	0.48	7/01	11r
Beans, dried, any type, all sizes	lb	0.61	7/01	11r
Beef for stew, boneless	lb	3.08	7/01	11r
Beef or hamburger, ground	lb	1.30	3/01	4c
Beef, expenditures on	yr	217	1999	30r
Bologna, all beef or mixed	lb	2.52	7/01	11r
Bread, white	loaf	1.03	3/01	4c
Bread, white, pan	lb	1.06	7/01	11r
Broccoli	lb	0.91	7/01	11r
Butter, salted, grade AA, stick	lb	3.04	7/01	11r
Butter, yoghurt, cheese, etc, expenditures on	yr	183	1999	30r
Cereals and bakery product purchases	yr	430	1999	30r
Cereals and cereal products, expenditures on	yr	149	1999	30r
Cheese, Kraft grated Parmesan	8 oz	3.62	3/01	4c
Chicken, fresh, whole	lb	1.07	7/01	11r
Chicken, whole fryer	lb	0.85	3/01	4c
Chops, boneless,	lb	3.64	7/01	11r
Chuck roast, U.S. choice, boneless	lb	2.47	7/01	11r
Cigarettes, Winston, Kings	carton	29.27	3/01	4c
Coffee, 100%, ground roast, all sizes	lb	2.69	7/01	11r
Coffee, vacuum-packed	13 oz	2.41	3/01	4c
Cookies, chocolate chip	lb	2.87	7/01	11r
Corn Flakes, Kellogg's or Post Toasties	18 oz	2.10	3/01	4c
Corn, frozen, whole kernel, lowest price	16 oz	1.11	3/01	4c
Dairy product purchases	yr	304	1999	30r
Eggs, expenditures on	yr	26	1999	30r
Eggs, Grade A or AA	dozen	1.03	3/01	4c
Eggs, grade A, large	dozen	0.88	7/01	11r
Fats and oils, expenditures on	yr	75	1999	30r
Fish and seafood, expenditures on	yr	72	1999	30r
Food (excl fruit and vegetables), eaten at home, purchases	yr	887	1999	30r
Food cooked on trips, expenditures on	yr	44	1999	30r
Food purchases	yr	4802	1999	30r
Food purchases, eaten away from home	yr	2069	1999	30r
Food purchases, food eaten at home	yr	2733	1999	30r
Fresh fruits, expenditures on	yr	138	1999	30r
Fresh milk and cream, expenditures on	yr	120	1999	30r
Fresh vegetables, expenditures on	yr	126	1999	30r
Grapefruit	lb	0.66	7/01	11r
Grapes, Thompson, seedless	lb	1.64	7/01	11r
Ground beef, 100% beef	lb	1.64	7/01	11r
Ground beef, lean and extra lean	lb	2.16	7/01	11r
Ground chuck, 100% beef	lb	2.13	7/01	11r
Ham, boneless, excl canned	lb	2.62	7/01	11r
Ice cream, prepackaged, bulk, regular	1/2 gal	3.35	7/01	11r
Lemons	lb	1.19	7/01	11r
Lettuce, iceberg	head	0.89	3/01	4c
Lettuce, iceberg	lb	0.73	7/01	11r
Margarine, Blue Bonnet or Parkay, stick	lb	0.68	3/01	4c
Margarine, soft, tubs	lb	0.89	7/01	11r
Meats, poultry, fish, and egg purchases	yr	671	1999	30r
Milk, fresh, whole, fortified	gal	2.71	7/01	11r
Milk, whole	1/2 gal	1.40	3/01	4c
Nonalcoholic beverages, expenditures on	yr	239	1999	30r
Orange juice, Minute Maid frozen	12 oz	1.66	3/01	4c
Oranges, Navel	lb	0.80	7/01	11r
Oranges, Valencia	lb	0.66	7/01	11r
Peaches, halves or slices, Hunt's, Del Monte, or Libby's	29 oz	1.62	3/01	4c
Pears, Anjou	lb	0.93	7/01	11r
Peas, green, Del Monte or Green Giant	15 oz	0.60	3/01	4c
Pork chops, center cut, bone-in	lb	3.63	7/01	11r
Pork, expenditures on	yr	150	1999	30r

Omaha, NE - continued

Item	Per	Value	Date	Ref.
Groceries - continued				
Potato chips	16 oz	3.52	7/01	11r
Potatoes, frozen, french fried	lb	1.08	7/01	11r
Potatoes, white or red	10 lb	2.26	3/01	4c
Potatoes, white, all types	lb	0.33	7/01	11r
Poultry, expenditures on	yr	108	1999	30r
Processed fruits, expenditures on	yr	98	1999	30r
Processed vegetables, expenditures on	yr	80	1999	30r
Round roast, U.S. choice, boneless	lb	3.07	7/01	11r
Round steak, graded and ungraded, excl U.S. prime and choice	lb	3.41	7/01	11r
Sausage, Jimmy Dean/Owens pork	lb	3.64	3/01	4c
Shortening, vegetable oil blends	lb	1.13	7/01	11r
Shortening, vegetable, Crisco	3 lb	2.68	3/01	4c
Soft drink, Coca Cola, ex deposit	2 liter	1.10	3/01	4c
Spaghetti and macaroni	lb	0.80	7/01	11r
Steak, round, U.S. choice, boneless	lb	3.23	7/01	11r
Steak, T-bone	lb	6.59	3/01	4c
Steak, T-bone, U.S. choice, bone-in	lb	6.68	7/01	11r
Strawberries, dry pint	12 oz	1.32	7/01	11r
Sugar and other sweets, expenditures on	yr	114	1999	30r
Sugar, cane or beet	4 lbs	1.43	3/01	4c
Sugar, white, 33-80 ounce package	lb	0.42	7/01	11r
Sugar, white, all sizes	lb	0.43	7/01	11r
Tobacco products and smoking supplies purchases	yr	331	1999	30r
Tomatoes, field grown	lb	1.46	7/01	11r
Tomatoes, Hunt's or Del Monte	14.5 oz	0.83	3/01	4c
Tuna, chunk, light	6 oz	0.52	3/01	4c
Tuna, light, chunk	lb	1.80	7/01	11r
Turkey, frozen, whole	lb	1.15	7/01	11r
Goods and Services				
Miscellaneous goods and services, ACCRA Index		95.00	3/01	4c
B&B Japanese maple (acer japonicum)	gal	29.99-169.99	4/00	93r
Boxwood (buxus)	2 gal	18.99-39.99	4/00	93r
Daylilly (hemerocallis)	gal	4.99-25.00	4/00	93r
Flat of annuals		11.98-24.99	4/00	93r
Fountain grass (pennisetum)	gal	5.98-12.98	4/00	93r
Hanging basket (10 in)		12.99-27.99	4/00	93r
Hardy geranium (geranium)	gal	7.99-9.99	4/00	93r
Hosta (hosta)	gal	6.00-25.00	4/00	93r
Lilac (syrubga vulgaris)	2 gal	14.99-24.99	4/00	93r
Miscellaneous purchases	yr	865	1999	30r
Rhododendron (rhododendron)	2 gal	23.98-42.99	4/00	93r
Sage (salvia)	gal	6.00-9.99	4/00	93r
Wintercreeper euonymus (euonymus fortunei)	2 gal	16.00-169.99	4/00	93r
Hunting license	yr	9.50	4/01	34s
Health Care				
Health care, ACCRA Index		96.80	3/01	4c
Cardiac catheterization, ave hospital/ physician charges		14740	1998	77s
Childbirth, Cesarean delivery		10722	1997	13r
Childbirth, vaginal delivery		6223	1997	13r
Dentist's fee, adult teeth cleaning and periodic oral exam	visit	72.40	3/01	4c
Doctor's fee, routine exam, established patient	visit	55.40	3/01	4c
Drugs, expenditures on	yr	394	1999	30r
Health care purchases	yr	2048	1999	30r

Values are in dollars or fractions of dollars. In the column headed *Ref*, references are shown to sources. Each reference is followed by a letter. These refer to the geographical level for which data were reported: s=State, r=Region, and c=City or metro. The abbreviation *ex* is used to mean *except* or *excluding*; *exp* stands for expenditures. For other abbreviations and further explanations, please see the Introduction.

Omaha, NE - continued

Item	Per	Value	Date	Ref.
Health Care				
Health insurance expenditures	yr	978	1999	30r
Home health care aide cost, licensed agency	hour	16	2000	82c
Hospital care, private room	day	472.14	3/01	4c
Hysterectomy, laproscopically-assisted, ave hospital/physician charges		10690	1998	76s
Hysterectomy, vaginal, ave hospital and physician charges		7730	1998	76s
Medicaid dispensing fee		2.85-5.05	1999	87s
Medical services expenditures	yr	554	1999	30r
Medical supplies, expenditures on	yr	122	1999	30r
Nursing home costs, private room	day	149	2000	82c
Nursing home stay, private room	day	149	2000	83c
Plastic surgery, breast augmentation		3184	2000	7r
Plastic surgery, breast lift		3585	2000	7r
Plastic surgery, facelift		4999	2000	7r
Plastic surgery, hair transplantation		3105	2000	7r
Plastic surgery, lip augmentation		1290	2000	7r
Plastic surgery, lower body lift		8135	2000	7r
Plastic surgery, thigh lift		3839	2000	7r
Household Goods				
Dishwashing powder, Cascade	50 oz	3.37	3/01	4c
Floor coverings, expenditures on	yr	52	1999	30r
Furniture, expenditures on	yr	344	1999	30r
Household furnishings and equipment purchases	yr	1475	1999	30r
Household textiles, expenditures on	yr	109	1999	30r
Laundry and cleaning supplies, expenditures on	yr	134	1999	30r
Tissues, facial, Kleenex brand	175	1.11	3/01	4c
Housing				
Housing, ACCRA Index		86.10	3/01	4c
Home price, existing, ave		144400	10/00	90r
Home value, median		108000	2001	53s
House, 2400 sq ft, 8000 sq ft lot, new, urban, utilities	total	179200	3/01	4c
House payment, principal and interest, 25% down payment	mos	883	3/01	4c
Household operation expenditures	yr	542	1999	30r
Housekeeping supplies purchases	yr	508	1999	30r
Lodging expenditures	yr	430	1999	30r
Maintenance, repairs, insurance expenditures	yr	853	1999	30r
Monthly rental value of owned home	mos	547	1999	30r
Owned dwellings, expenditures own	yr	4282	1999	30r
Rent expenditures	yr	1558	1999	30r
Rent, apartment, 2 br, 1 1/2-2 baths, unfurn, 950 sq ft, water	mos	611	3/01	4c
Rental unit, 1 bedroom, with utilities	mos	469	4/01	41c
Rental unit, 2 bedroom, with utilities	mos	593	4/01	41c
Rental unit, 3 bedroom, with utilities	mos	777	4/01	41c
Rental unit, 4 bedroom, with utilities	mos	872	4/01	41c
Shelter, expenditures on	yr	6270	1999	30r
Insurance and Pensions				
Auto insurance premium	yr	608.11	1999	57s
Life and other personal insurance purchases	yr	387	1999	30r
Pensions and Social Security, expenditures on	yr	2968	1999	30r
Legal Fees				
Combination hunting and fishing license	yr	21.75	4/01	34s
Divorce, filing fee		83.00	4/01	35s
Driver's license fee	renew	15.00	1999	48s
Driver's license fee	orig	15.00	1999	48s
Fishing license	yr	12.75	4/01	34s
Personal Goods				
Personal care products and services purchases	yr	385	1999	30r
Shampoo, Alberto VO5	15 oz	1.09	3/01	4c
Toothpaste, Crest or Colgate	6-7 oz	2.08	3/01	4c

Omaha, NE - continued

Item	Per	Value	Date	Ref.
Personal Services				
Dry cleaning, man's 2-pc suit		6.50	3/01	4c
Man's haircut, barbershop, no styling		10.93	3/01	4c
Personal services, household, expenditures on	yr	300	1999	30r
Woman's shampoo, trim, blow-dry, no style-change		23.40	3/01	4c
Pets				
Pets, toys, and playground equipment, expenditures on	yr	375	1999	30r
Restaurant Food				
Chicken, fried, thigh and drumstick, KFC/Church's		2.30	3/01	4c
Hamburger with cheese, McDonald's	1/4 lb	2.19	3/01	4c
Pizza, Pizza Hut or Pizza Inn	11-12 in	9.49	3/01	4c
Taxes				
Federal income taxes paid	yr	2326	1999	30r
Personal taxes, expenditures on	yr	3223	1999	30r
Property taxes paid	yr	1152	1999	30r
State and local income taxes paid	yr	753	1999	30r
Transportation				
Transportation, ACCRA Index		102.90	3/01	4c
Bus fare, one-way	trip	0.90	2000	1c
Bus fare, to central business district	1-way	1.25	3/01	4c
Cars and trucks, new, expenditures on	yr	1280	1999	30r
Cars and trucks, used, expenditures on	yr	1763	1999	30r
Diesel at the pump	gal	1.26	10/99	73s
Gasoline and motor oil purchases	yr	1036	1999	30r
Gasoline before-tax price (cents)	gal	111.50	10/00	43s
Maintenance and repair expenditures	yr	594	1999	30r
Motorcycle license fee	renew	3.75	1999	49s
Motorcycle license fee	orig	15.00	1999	49s
Public transportation, expenditures on	yr	341	1999	30r
Tire balance, computer or spin balance, front	wheel	8.41	3/01	4c
Transportation purchases	yr	6617	1999	30r
Vehicle expenses, miscellaneous, purchases	yr	2159	1999	30r
Vehicle insurance payments	yr	701	1999	30r
Vehicle purchases (net outlay)	yr	3081	1999	30r
Vehicle rental, lease expenditures	yr	536	1999	30r
Utilities				
Utilities, ACCRA Index		123.00	3/01	4c
Electrical bill, average	mos	60.00	9/00	9s
Electricity, expenditures on	yr	841	1999	30r
Electricity and other, mixed, 2400 sq ft, new home	mos	52.84	3/01	4c
Electricity cost, average	KWh	5.30	9/00	9s
Utilities, fuels, and public services purchased	yr	2401	1999	30r
Water and other public services, expenditures on	yr	273	1999	30r
Weddings				
Wedding (national average cost)		19936	2000	33r
Wedding (regional average total cost)		16195	1997	110r
Attendants' gifts		321	1998	33r
Bridal attendants' apparel (5 persons)		824	2000	33r
Bride's headpiece/veil		173	1998	33r
Bride's wedding dress		859	1998	33r
Clergy, religious facility fee		242	1998	33r
Engagement ring		3177	1998	33r
Flowers		789	1998	33r
Groom's formalwear rental		99	2000	33r
Limousine		410	1998	33r
Marriage license cost		15.00	4/01	35s
Men's formalwear (ushers, best man)		469	2000	33r
Mother of bride apparel		241	2000	33r
Music		866	1998	33r
Photography and videography		1368	1998	33r
Rehearsal dinner		728	1998	33r
Wedding invitations and announcements		341	1998	33r
Wedding reception		7968	2000	33r
Wedding rings (bride and groom)		1060	1998	33r

Values are in dollars or fractions of dollars. In the column headed *Ref*, references are shown to sources. Each reference is followed by a letter. These refer to the geographical level for which data were reported: s=State, r=Region, and c=City or metro. The abbreviation *ex* is used to mean *except* or *excluding*; *exp* stands for *expenditures*. For other abbreviations and further explanations, please see the Introduction.

Orange County, CA

Item	Per	Value	Date	Ref.
Average annual expenditures	yr	40662	1999	30r
Alcoholic Beverages				
Alcoholic beverage purchases	yr	372	1999	30r
Malt beverages, all types, all sizes, any origin	16 oz	0.94	7/01	11r
Wine, red and white table, all sizes, any origin	liter	6.00	7/01	11r
Appliances				
Major appliances, expenditures on	yr	167	1999	30r
Small appliances, housewares, expenditures on	yr	105	1999	30r
Banking and Money				
Mortgage interest and charges paid	yr	3368	1999	30r
Mortgage principal paid on owned property	yr	1677	1999	30r
Vehicle finance charges paid	yr	311	1999	30r
Business Expenses				
Office space, central business district, Class A	sq ft	29.40	3/99	74c
Charity				
Cash contributions, expenditures	yr	1344	1999	30r
Child Care				
Child raising cost, total, age 0-2	yr	9140	1999	60r
Child raising cost, total, age 3-5	yr	9370	1999	60r
Child raising cost, total, age 6-8	yr	9450	1999	60r
Child raising cost, total, age 9-11	yr	9470	1999	60r
Child raising cost, total, age 12-14	yr	10170	1999	60r
Child raising cost, total, age 15-17	yr	10360	1999	60r
Child's child care and education, age 0-2	yr	1250	1999	60r
Child's child care and education, age 3-5	yr	1380	1999	60r
Child's child care and education, age 6-8	yr	890	1999	60r
Child's child care and education, age 9-11	yr	580	1999	60r
Child's child care and education, age 12-14	yr	430	1999	60r
Child's child care and education, age 15-17	yr	730	1999	60r
Child's clothing, age 0-2	yr	430	1999	60r
Child's clothing, age 3-5	yr	420	1999	60r
Child's clothing, age 6-8	yr	470	1999	60r
Child's clothing, age 9-11	yr	520	1999	60r
Child's clothing, age 12-14	yr	870	1999	60r
Child's clothing, age 15-17	yr	770	1999	60r
Child's food, age 0-2	yr	1120	1999	60r
Child's food, age 3-5	yr	1280	1999	60r
Child's food, age 6-8	yr	1640	1999	60r
Child's food, age 9-11	yr	1930	1999	60r
Child's food, age 12-14	yr	1940	1999	60r
Child's food, age 15-17	yr	2150	1999	60r
Child's health care, age 0-2	yr	490	1999	60r
Child's health care, age 3-5	yr	470	1999	60r
Child's health care, age 6-8	yr	530	1999	60r
Child's health care, age 9-11	yr	570	1999	60r
Child's health care, age 12-14	yr	580	1999	60r
Child's health care, age 15-17	yr	610	1999	60r
Child's housing, age 0-2	yr	3630	1999	60r
Child's housing, age 3-5	yr	3610	1999	60r
Child's housing, age 6-8	yr	3570	1999	60r
Child's housing, age 9-11	yr	3410	1999	60r
Child's housing, age 12-14	yr	3600	1999	60r
Child's housing, age 15-17	yr	3210	1999	60r
Child's personal care, reading, age 0-2	yr	1040	1999	60r
Child's personal care, reading, age 3-5	yr	1060	1999	60r
Child's personal care, reading, age 6-8	yr	1090	1999	60r
Child's personal care, reading, age 9-11	yr	1130	1999	60r
Child's personal care, reading, age 12-14	yr	1300	1999	60r
Child's personal care, reading, age 15-17	yr	1080	1999	60r
Clothing				
Apparel and services purchases	yr	1863	1999	30r
Boys, 2 to 15, expenditures on	yr	80	1999	30r
Children under 2, expenditures on	yr	74	1999	30r
Footwear, expenditures on	yr	307	1999	30r
Girls, 2 to 15, expenditures on	yr	101	1999	30r
Men and boys, expenditures on	yr	443	1999	30r

Orange County, CA - continued

Item	Per	Value	Date	Ref.
Clothing - continued				
Men, 16 and over, expenditures on	yr	363	1999	30r
Women, 16 and over, expenditures on	yr	594	1999	30r
Communications				
Cable modem installation, AT&T-BIS		150.00	6/99	103s
Cable modem installation, Charter		99.00-169.00	6/99	103s
Cable modem installation, Comcast		95.00	6/99	103s
Cable modem installation, Cox		99.00-174.95	6/99	103s
Cable modem installation, Media One		100.00	6/99	103s
Cable modem installation, Time Warner		75.00-225.00	6/99	103s
Cable modem rate, cable subscriber, AT&T-BIS	mos	39.95	6/99	103s
Cable modem rate, cable subscriber, Charter	mos	49.95-79.95	6/99	103s
Cable modem rate, cable subscriber, Comcast	mos	39.95	6/99	103s
Cable modem rate, cable subscriber, Cox	mos	29.95-44.95	6/99	103s
Cable modem rate, cable subscriber, Media One	mos	34.95-39.95	6/99	103s
Cable modem rate, cable subscriber, Time Warner	mos	39.95-49.95	6/99	103s
Cable modem rate, non-cable subscriber, Charter	mos	59.95-89.95	6/99	103s
Cable modem rate, non-cable subscriber, Comcast	mos	49.95	6/99	103s
Cable modem rate, non-cable subscriber, Cox	mos	42.95-54.95	6/99	103s
Cable modem rate, non-cable subscriber, Media One	mos	49.95	6/99	103s
Cable modem rate, non-cable subscriber, Time Warner	mos	39.95-54.95	6/99	103s
Phone line, single, business, field visit	inst.	70.75	12/97	17s
Phone line, single, business, no field visit	inst.	70.75	12/97	17s
Phone line, single, residence, field visit	inst.	34.75	12/97	17s
Phone line, single, residence, no field visit	inst.	34.75	12/97	17s
Postage and stationery, expenditures on	yr	150	1999	30r
Postal rate, express mail, up to half-pound		12.45	7/01	108r
Postal rate, letter, first class, first ounce		0.34	7/01	108r
Postal rate, letter, two ounces		0.57	7/01	108r
Postal rate, post card		0.21	7/01	108r
Postal rate, priority mail, two pounds		3.95	7/01	108r
Postal rate, priority mail, up to one pound		3.50	7/01	108r
Telephone services, expenditures on	yr	825	1999	30r
Education				
Board, 4-year private college/university	yr	2970	1996	38s
Board, 4-year public college/university	yr	2516	1996	38s
Education expenditures	yr	676	1999	30r
Room, 4-year private college/university	yr	3196	1996	38s
Room, 4-year public college/university	yr	3031	1996	38s
Total cost, 4-year private college/university	yr	20143	1996	38s
Total cost, 4-year public college/university	yr	8213	1996	38s
Tuition, 2-year public college/university, in state	yr	362	1996	38s
Tuition, 4-year private college/university, in state	yr	13977	1996	38s
Tuition, 4-year public college/university	yr	2666	1996	38s
Energy and Fuels				
Electricity	KWh	0.11	7/01	11r
Electricity	500 KWhs	48.23	7/01	11r
Fuel oil and other fuels, expenditures on	yr	35	1999	30r
Gas, natural, commercial rate	1000 cf	8.74	11/00	88s
Gasoline, all types	gal	1.91	7/01	11r
Gasoline, unleaded premium	gal	2.05	7/01	11r
Gasoline, unleaded regular	gal	1.83	7/01	11r
Natural gas, expenditures on	yr	255	1999	30r
Utility (piped) gas, therm		0.98	7/01	11r
Utility (piped) gas, 40 therms		40.74	7/01	11r

Values are in dollars or fractions of dollars. In the column headed *Ref*, references are shown to sources. Each reference is followed by a letter. These refer to the geographical level for which data were reported: s=State, r=Region, and c=City or metro. The abbreviation *ex* is used to mean *except* or *excluding*; *exp* stands for *expenditures*. For other abbreviations and further explanations, please see the Introduction.

Orange County, CA - continued

Item	Per	Value	Date	Ref.
Energy and Fuels				
Utility (piped) gas, 100 therms		96.80	7/01	11r
Entertainment				
Entertainment purchases	yr	2139	1999	30r
Fees and admissions paid	yr	545	1999	30r
Television, radios, sound equipment, expenditures on	yr	624	1999	30r
Funerals				
Total cost of funeral		5401.08	1/99	78r
Acknowledgement cards		33.64	1/99	78r
Casket		2170.43	1/99	78r
Cosmetology, hair, other preparation		136.32	1/99	78r
Embalming		319.13	1/99	78r
Funeral at funeral home		370.21	1/99	78r
Hearse (local)		161.04	1/99	78r
Professional service charges		963.15	1/99	78r
Service car/van		133.99	1/99	78r
Transfer of remains to funeral home		159.82	1/99	78r
Vault		778.07	1/99	78r
Visitation/viewing		175.28	1/99	78r
Groceries				
Apples, red delicious	lb	0.84	7/01	11r
Bacon, sliced	lb	3.38	7/01	11r
Bakery products, expenditures on	yr	299	1999	30r
Bananas	lb	0.54	7/01	11r
Beans, dried, any type, all sizes	lb	0.76	7/01	11r
Beef, expenditures on	yr	222	1999	30r
Bread, white, pan	lb	0.99	7/01	11r
Butter, yoghurt, cheese, etc, expenditures on	yr	211	1999	30r
Cereals and bakery product purchases	yr	466	1999	30r
Cereals and cereal products, expenditures on	yr	168	1999	30r
Chicken breast, bone-in	lb	2.45	7/01	11r
Chicken, fresh, whole	lb	1.19	7/01	11r
Chops, boneless	lb	4.00	7/01	11r
Chuck roast, graded and ungraded, excl U.S. prime and choice	lb	2.55	7/01	11r
Coffee, 100%, ground roast, all sizes	lb	3.80	7/01	11r
Cookies, chocolate chip	lb	2.83	7/01	11r
Dairy product purchases	yr	341	1999	30r
Eggs, expenditures on	yr	39	1999	30r
Eggs, grade AA, large	dozen	1.23	7/01	11r
Fats and oils, expenditures on	yr	88	1999	30r
Fish and seafood, expenditures on	yr	121	1999	30r
Food (excl fruit and vegetables), eaten at home, purchases	yr	1001	1999	30r
Food cooked on trips, expenditures on	yr	64	1999	30r
Food purchases	yr	5312	1999	30r
Food purchases, eaten away from home	yr	2180	1999	30r
Food purchases, food eaten at home	yr	3132	1999	30r
Fresh fruits, expenditures on	yr	186	1999	30r
Fresh milk and cream, expenditures on	yr	130	1999	30r
Fresh vegetables, expenditures on	yr	177	1999	30r
Grapefruit	lb	0.68	7/01	11r
Grapes, Thompson, seedless	lb	2.42	7/01	11r
Ground beef, lean and extra lean	lb	2.46	7/01	11r
Ice cream, prepackaged, bulk, regular	1/2 gal	3.62	7/01	11r
Lettuce, iceberg	lb	0.63	7/01	11r
Meats, poultry, fish, and egg purchases	yr	761	1999	30r
Milk, fresh, low fat	gal	2.80	7/01	11r
Milk, fresh, whole, fortified	gal	2.88	7/01	11r
Nonalcoholic beverages, expenditures on	yr	258	1999	30r
Oranges, Navel	lb	0.97	7/01	11r
Oranges, Valencia	lb	0.43	7/01	11r
Peaches	lb	1.38	7/01	11r
Peanut butter, creamy, all sizes	lb	2.14	7/01	11r
Pork chops, center cut, bone-in	lb	3.83	7/01	11r
Pork, expenditures on	yr	141	1999	30r
Potatoes, white, all types	lb	0.37	7/01	11r
Poultry, expenditures on	yr	146	1999	30r
Processed fruits, expenditures on	yr	118	1999	30r
Processed vegetables, expenditures on	yr	81	1999	30r

Orange County, CA - continued

Item	Per	Value	Date	Ref.
Groceries - continued				
Round roast, graded and ungraded, excl U.S. prime and choice	lb	3.07	7/01	11r
Round roast, U.S. choice, boneless	lb	3.37	7/01	11r
Round steak, graded and ungraded, excl U.S. prime and choice	lb	3.51	7/01	11r
Sirloin steak, graded and ungraded, excl U.S. prime and choice	lb	4.67	7/01	11r
Steak, sirloin, U.S. choice, boneless	lb	6.20	7/01	11r
Strawberries, dry pint	12 oz	1.79	7/01	11r
Sugar and other sweets, expenditures on	yr	124	1999	30r
Sugar, white, all sizes	lb	0.46	7/01	11r
Tobacco products and smoking supplies purchases	yr	217	1999	30r
Tomatoes, field grown	lb	1.17	7/01	11r
Tuna, light, chunk	lb	2.05	7/01	11r
Goods and Services				
B&B Japanese maple (acer japonicum)	gal	39.99	4/00	93r
Boxwood (buxus)	2 gal	14.99-24.99	4/00	93r
Christmas tree, noble fir		40-60	2000	65s
Daylilly (hemerocallis)	gal	6.99-8.99	4/00	93r
Flat of annuals		16.68	4/00	93r
Fountain grass (pennisetum)	gal	7.99-11.99	4/00	93r
Hanging basket (10 in)		29.99	4/00	93r
Hardy geranium (geranium)	gal	6.99-11.99	4/00	93r
Hosta (hosta)	gal	6.99-18.99	4/00	93r
Lilac (syrubga vulgaris)	2 gal	14.99-17.99	4/00	93r
Miscellaneous purchases	yr	1070	1999	30r
Rhododendron (rhododendron)	2 gal	14.99	4/00	93r
Sage (salvia)	gal	6.99	4/00	93r
Wintercreeper euonymus (euonymus fortunei)	2 gal	14.99-22.99	4/00	93r
Hunting license	yr	29.95	4/01	34s
Health Care				
Cardiac catheterization, ave hospital/ physician charges		24000	1998	77s
Childbirth, Cesarean delivery		11587	1997	13r
Childbirth, vaginal delivery		6725	1997	13r
Drugs, expenditures on	yr	309	1999	30r
Health care purchases	yr	1869	1999	30r
Health insurance expenditures	yr	868	1999	30r
Hysterectomy, laproscopically-assisted, ave hospital/physician charges		20760	1998	76s
Hysterectomy, vaginal, ave hospital and physician charges		14570	1998	76s
Medicaid dispensing fee		4.05	1999	87s
Medical services expenditures	yr	580	1999	30r
Medical supplies, expenditures on	yr	112	1999	30r
Household Goods				
Floor coverings, expenditures on	yr	49	1999	30r
Furniture, expenditures on	yr	444	1999	30r
Household furnishings and equipment purchases	yr	1768	1999	30r
Household textiles, expenditures on	yr	141	1999	30r
Laundry and cleaning supplies, expenditures on	yr	128	1999	30r
Housing				
Home price, existing, ave		239400	10/00	90r
Home value, median		215000	2001	53s
Household operation expenditures	yr	781	1999	30r
Housekeeping supplies purchases	yr	513	1999	30r
Lodging expenditures	yr	575	1999	30r
Maintenance, repairs, insurance expenditures	yr	939	1999	30r
Monthly rental value of owned home	mos	662	1999	30r

Values are in dollars or fractions of dollars. In the column headed *Ref*, references are shown to sources. Each reference is followed by a letter. These refer to the geographical level for which data were reported: s=State, r=Region, and c=City or metro. The abbreviation *ex* is used to mean *except* or *excluding*; *exp* stands for expenditures. For other abbreviations and further explanations, please see the Introduction.

Orange County, CA - continued

Item	Per	Value	Date	Ref.
Housing				
Owned dwellings, expenditures own	yr	5231	1999	30r
Rent expenditures	yr	2709	1999	30r
Rental unit, 1 bedroom, with utilities	mos	792	4/01	41c
Rental unit, 2 bedroom, with utilities	mos	980	4/01	41c
Rental unit, 3 bedroom, with utilities	mos	1364	4/01	41c
Rental unit, 4 bedroom, with utilities	mos	1518	4/01	41c
Shelter, expenditures on	yr	8516	1999	30r
Single-family home, purchase price		300800	2000	19c
Insurance and Pensions				
Life and other personal insurance purchases	yr	355	1999	30r
Pensions and Social Security, expenditures on	yr	3636	1999	30r
Legal Fees				
Divorce, filing fee		182.00	4/01	35s
Driver's license fee	orig	12.00	1999	48s
Driver's license fee	renew	15.00	1999	48s
Personal Goods				
Personal care products and services purchases	yr	449	1999	30r
Personal Services				
Personal services, household, expenditures on	yr	353	1999	30r
Pets				
Pets, toys, and playground equipment, expenditures on	yr	358	1999	30r
Taxes				
Federal income taxes paid	yr	3200	1999	30r
Personal taxes, expenditures on	yr	4153	1999	30r
Property taxes paid	yr	923	1999	30r
State and local income taxes paid	yr	812	1999	30r
Transportation				
Cars and trucks, new, expenditures on	yr	1534	1999	30r
Cars and trucks, used, expenditures on	yr	1593	1999	30r
Diesel at the pump	gal	1.37	10/99	73s
Gasoline and motor oil purchases	yr	1129	1999	30r
Gasoline before-tax price (cents)	gal	128.80	10/00	43s
Maintenance and repair expenditures	yr	797	1999	30r
Public transportation, expenditures on	yr	530	1999	30r
Transportation purchases	yr	7423	1999	30r
Vehicle expenses, miscellaneous, purchases	yr	2585	1999	30r
Vehicle insurance payments	yr	811	1999	30r
Vehicle purchases (net outlay)	yr	3180	1999	30r
Vehicle rental, lease expenditures	yr	666	1999	30r
Utilities				
Electrical bill, average	mos	58.66	9/00	9s
Electricity, expenditures on	yr	725	1999	30r
Electricity cost, average	KWh	7.75	9/00	9s
Utilities, fuels, and public services purchased	yr	2179	1999	30r
Water and other public services, expenditures on	yr	339	1999	30r
Weddings				
Wedding (national average cost)		19936	2000	33r
Wedding (regional average total cost)		18918	1997	110r
Attendants' gifts		321	1998	33r
Bridal attendants' apparel (5 persons)		824	2000	33r
Bride's headpiece/veil		173	1998	33r
Bride's wedding dress		859	1998	33r
Clergy, religious facility fee		242	1998	33r
Engagement ring		3177	1998	33r
Flowers		789	1998	33r
Groom's formalwear rental		99	2000	33r
Limousine		410	1998	33r
Marriage license cost		50.00-80.00	4/01	35s
Men's formalwear (ushers, best man)		469	2000	33r
Mother of bride apparel		241	2000	33r
Music		866	1998	33r

Orange County, CA - continued

Item	Per	Value	Date	Ref.
Weddings - continued				
Photography and videography		1368	1998	33r
Rehearsal dinner		728	1998	33r
Wedding invitations and announcements		341	1998	33r
Wedding reception		7968	2000	33r
Wedding rings (bride and groom)		1060	1998	33r

Orlando, FL

Item	Per	Value	Date	Ref.
Composite, ACCRA index		99.10	3/01	4c
Alcoholic Beverages				
Alcoholic beverage purchases	yr	253	1999	30r
Beer, Heineken, 12-oz, ex deposit	6	6.73	3/01	4c
J & B Scotch	750-ml	20.96	3/01	4c
Malt beverages, all types, all sizes, any origin	16 oz	0.96	7/01	11r
Wine, Livingston or Gallo, Chablis blanc	1.5 liter	5.21	3/01	4c
Appliances				
Appliance repair, service call, washing machine	min lab chg	33.90	3/01	4c
Major appliances, expenditures on	yr	172	1999	30r
Small appliances, housewares, expenditures on	yr	81	1999	30r
Banking and Money				
Mortgage interest and charges paid	yr	2039	1999	30r
Mortgage principal paid on owned property	yr	1026	1999	30r
Mortgage rate, incl. points and orig. fee, 30-yr. conv. fixed or ARM	mos	6.96	3/01	4c
Vehicle finance charges paid	yr	365	1999	30r
Business Expenses				
Business travel, car rental	day	54	2001	3c
Business travel, food	day	47	2001	3c
Business travel, hotel	day	126	2001	3c
Charity				
Cash contributions, expenditures	yr	1127	1999	30r
Child Care				
Child care fee, one year old	week	96	5/99	26c
Child care fee, six year old	week	42	5/99	26c
Child care fee, three year old	week	81	5/99	26c
Child raising cost, total, age 0-2	yr	8540	1999	60r
Child raising cost, total, age 3-5	yr	8780	1999	60r
Child raising cost, total, age 6-8	yr	8820	1999	60r
Child raising cost, total, age 9-11	yr	8800	1999	60r
Child raising cost, total, age 12-14	yr	9510	1999	60r
Child raising cost, total, age 15-17	yr	9740	1999	60r
Child's child care and education, age 0-2	yr	1380	1999	60r
Child's child care and education, age 3-5	yr	1520	1999	60r
Child's child care and education, age 6-8	yr	990	1999	60r
Child's child care and education, age 9-11	yr	650	1999	60r
Child's child care and education, age 12-14	yr	490	1999	60r
Child's child care and education, age 15-17	yr	840	1999	60r
Child's clothing, age 0-2	yr	480	1999	60r
Child's clothing, age 3-5	yr	470	1999	60r
Child's clothing, age 6-8	yr	520	1999	60r
Child's clothing, age 9-11	yr	570	1999	60r
Child's clothing, age 12-14	yr	950	1999	60r
Child's clothing, age 15-17	yr	850	1999	60r
Child's food, age 0-2	yr	1000	1999	60r
Child's food, age 3-5	yr	1160	1999	60r
Child's food, age 6-8	yr	1490	1999	60r
Child's food, age 9-11	yr	1770	1999	60r
Child's food, age 12-14	yr	1770	1999	60r
Child's food, age 15-17	yr	1980	1999	60r
Child's health care, age 0-2	yr	620	1999	60r
Child's health care, age 3-5	yr	590	1999	60r
Child's health care, age 6-8	yr	680	1999	60r
Child's health care, age 9-11	yr	720	1999	60r
Child's health care, age 12-14	yr	730	1999	60r
Child's health care, age 15-17	yr	760	1999	60r
Child's housing, age 0-2	yr	3070	1999	60r

Values are in dollars or fractions of dollars. In the column headed *Ref*, references are shown to sources. Each reference is followed by a letter. These refer to the geographical level for which data were reported: s=State, r=Region, and c=City or metro. The abbreviation *ex* is used to mean *except* or *excluding*; *exp* stands for *expenditures*. For other abbreviations and further explanations, please see the Introduction.

Orlando, FL - continued

Item	Per	Value	Date	Ref.
Child Care				
Child's housing, age 3-5	yr	3050	1999	60r
Child's housing, age 6-8	yr	3010	1999	60r
Child's housing, age 9-11	yr	2850	1999	60r
Child's housing, age 12-14	yr	3040	1999	60r
Child's housing, age 15-17	yr	2650	1999	60r
Child's personal care, reading, age 0-2	yr	910	1999	60r
Child's personal care, reading, age 3-5	yr	930	1999	60r
Child's personal care, reading, age 6-8	yr	960	1999	60r
Child's personal care, reading, age 9-11	yr	1000	1999	60r
Child's personal care, reading, age 12-14	yr	1170	1999	60r
Child's personal care, reading, age 15-17	yr	950	1999	60r
Clothing				
Apparel and services purchases	yr	1610	1999	30r
Boys' brief, cotton	3	4.51	3/01	4c
Boys, 2 to 15, expenditures on	yr	89	1999	30r
Children under 2, expenditures on	yr	79	1999	30r
Footwear, expenditures on	yr	283	1999	30r
Girls, 2 to 15, expenditures on	yr	103	1999	30r
Men and boys, expenditures on	yr	351	1999	30r
Men, 16 and over, expenditures on	yr	262	1999	30r
Shirt, man's dress shirt		27.25	3/01	4c
Slacks, man's "No Wrinkles" khaki		35.99	3/01	4c
Women, 16 and over, expenditures on	yr	538	1999	30r
Communications				
Cable modem installation, Adelphi		54.90	6/99	103s
Cable modem installation, Comcast		95.00	6/99	103s
Cable modem installation, Media One		100.00	6/99	103s
Cable modem installation, Time Warner		75.00-225.00	6/99	103s
Cable modem rate, cable subscriber, Adelphi	mos	34.95	6/99	103s
Cable modem rate, cable subscriber, Comcast	mos	39.95	6/99	103s
Cable modem rate, cable subscriber, Media One	mos	34.95-39.95	6/99	103s
Cable modem rate, cable subscriber, Time Warner	mos	39.95-49.95	6/99	103s
Cable modem rate, non-cable subscriber, Adelphi	mos	44.95	6/99	103s
Cable modem rate, non-cable subscriber, Comcast	mos	49.95	6/99	103s
Cable modem rate, non-cable subscriber, Media One	mos	49.95	6/99	103s
Cable modem rate, non-cable subscriber, Time Warner	mos	39.95-54.95	6/99	103s
Newspaper subscription, daily and Sunday delivery	mos	16.75	3/01	4c
Phone line, single, business, field visit	inst.	56.00	12/97	17s
Phone line, single, business, no field visit	inst.	56.00	12/97	17s
Phone line, single, residence, field visit	inst.	40.00	12/97	17s
Phone line, single, residence, no field visit	inst.	40.00	12/97	17s
Postage and stationery, expenditures on	yr	104	1999	30r
Postal rate, express mail, up to half-pound		12.45	7/01	108r
Postal rate, letter, first class, first ounce		0.34	7/01	108r
Postal rate, letter, two ounces		0.57	7/01	108r
Postal rate, post card		0.21	7/01	108r
Postal rate, priority mail, two pounds		3.95	7/01	108r
Postal rate, priority mail, up to one pound		3.50	7/01	108r
Telephone bill, business, basic rate	mos	28.60	12/97	18c
Telephone bill, family of three	mos	20.63	3/01	4c
Telephone bill, residential, basic rate	mos	10.45	12/97	18c
Telephone services, expenditures on	yr	860	1999	30r
Education				
Board, 4-year private college/university	yr	2236	1996	38s
Board, 4-year public college/university	yr	2295	1996	38s
Education expenditures	yr	431	1999	30r
Room, 4-year private college/university	yr	2428	1996	38s
Room, 4-year public college/university	yr	2193	1996	38s
Total cost, 4-year private college/university	yr	15028	1996	38s
Total cost, 4-year public college/university	yr	6254	1996	38s
Tuition, 2-year public college/university, in state	yr	1103	1996	38s

Item	Per	Value	Date	Ref.
Education - continued				
Tuition, 4-year private college/university, in state	yr	10364	1996	38s
Tuition, 4-year public college/university	yr	1767	1996	38s
Energy and Fuels				
Electricity	KWh	0.09	7/01	11r
Electricity	500 KWhs	47.29	7/01	11r
Energy, combined forms, 2400 sq ft	mos	125.82	3/01	4c
Fuel oil #2	gal	1.43	7/01	11r
Fuel oil and other fuels, expenditures on	yr	45	1999	30r
Gas, natural, commercial rate	1000 cf	8.44	11/00	88s
Gas, regular unleaded, cash, self-service	gal	1.37	3/01	4c
Gasoline, all types	gal	1.60	7/01	11r
Gasoline, unleaded midgrade	gal	1.65	7/01	11r
Gasoline, unleaded premium	gal	1.74	7/01	11r
Natural gas, expenditures on	yr	164	1999	30r
Utility (piped) gas, therm		1.01	7/01	11r
Utility (piped) gas, 40 therms		44.29	7/01	11r
Utility (piped) gas, 100 therms		97.44	7/01	11r
Entertainment				
Bowling, Saturday evening rate	line	3.37	3/01	4c
Entertainment purchases	yr	1574	1999	30r
Fees and admissions paid	yr	371	1999	30r
Monopoly game, Parker Brothers', No. 9	game	10.15	3/01	4c
Movie ticket, evening	person	6.50	1999	104c
Movie, first-run, Saturday, evening	adm.	6.35	3/01	4c
Reading purchases	yr	121	1999	30r
Television, radios, sound equipment, expenditures on	yr	561	1999	30r
Tennis balls, yellow, Wilson or Penn, 3	can	2.54	3/01	4c
Funerals				
Total cost of funeral		5922.53	1/99	78r
Acknowledgement cards		63.43	1/99	78r
Casket		2258.77	1/99	78r
Cosmetology, hair, other preparation		127.09	1/99	78r
Embalming		393.49	1/99	78r
Funeral at funeral home		367.50	1/99	78r
Hearse (local)		169.66	1/99	78r
Professional service charges		1211.32	1/99	78r
Service car/van		80.69	1/99	78r
Transfer of remains to funeral home		144.25	1/99	78r
Vault		803.50	1/99	78r
Visitation/viewing		302.83	1/99	78r
Groceries				
Groceries, ACCRA Index		101.90	3/01	4c
American processed cheese	lb	3.50	7/01	11r
Antibiotic ointment, Polysporin	0.5 oz	4.54	3/01	4c
Baby food, strained vegetables or fruit, lowest price	4-4.5 oz	0.45	3/01	4c
Bakery products, expenditures on	yr	261	1999	30r
Bananas	lb	0.49	3/01	4c
Bananas	lb	0.47	7/01	11r
Beans, dried, any type, all sizes	lb	0.63	7/01	11r
Beef for stew, boneless	lb	2.86	7/01	11r
Beef or hamburger, ground	lb	1.59	3/01	4c
Beef, expenditures on	yr	210	1999	30r
Bologna, all beef or mixed	lb	2.29	7/01	11r
Bread, French	lb	1.66	7/01	11r
Bread, white	loaf	0.97	3/01	4c
Bread, white, pan	lb	0.87	7/01	11r
Bread, whole wheat, pan	lb	1.38	7/01	11r
Broccoli	lb	1.04	7/01	11r
Butter, salted, grade AA, stick	lb	2.26	7/01	11r
Butter, yoghurt, cheese, etc, expenditures on	yr	170	1999	30r
Cabbage	lb	0.42	7/01	11r
Cereals and cereal products, expenditures on	yr	140	1999	30r
Cheddar cheese, natural	lb	3.75	7/01	11r
Cheese, Kraft grated Parmesan	8 oz	3.51	3/01	4c
Chicken breast, bone-in	lb	1.85	7/01	11r

Values are in dollars or fractions of dollars. In the column headed *Ref*, references are shown to sources. Each reference is followed by a letter. These refer to the geographical level for which data were reported: s=State, r=Region, and c=City or metro. The abbreviation *ex* is used to mean *except* or *excluding*; *exp* stands for *expenditures*. For other abbreviations and further explanations, please see the Introduction.

Orlando, FL - continued

Item	Per	Value	Date	Ref.
Groceries				
Chicken legs, bone-in	lb	1.34	7/01	11r
Chicken, fresh, whole	lb	1.05	7/01	11r
Chicken, whole fryer	lb	1.05	3/01	4c
Chops, boneless,	lb	4.13	7/01	11r
Chuck roast, graded and ungraded, excl U.S. prime and choice	lb	2.35	7/01	11r
Chuck roast, U.S. choice, boneless	lb	2.67	7/01	11r
Cigarettes, Winston, Kings	carton	31.38	3/01	4c
Coffee, 100%, ground roast, all sizes	lb	2.88	7/01	11r
Coffee, instant, plain, regular, all sizes	16 oz	9.25	7/01	11r
Coffee, vacuum-packed	13 oz	2.61	3/01	4c
Cola, non diet,	2 liter	1.11	7/01	11r
Corn Flakes, Kellogg's or Post Toasties	18 oz	3.11	3/01	4c
Corn, frozen, whole kernel, lowest price	16 oz	1.22	3/01	4c
Crackers, soda, salted	lb	1.70	7/01	11r
Dairy product purchases	yr	282	1999	30r
Eggs, expenditures on	yr	32	1999	30r
Eggs, Grade A or AA	dozen	1.17	3/01	4c
Fats and oils, expenditures on	yr	79	1999	30r
Fish and seafood, expenditures on	yr	99	1999	30r
Flour, white, all purpose	lb	0.32	7/01	11r
Food (excl fruit and vegetables), eaten at home, purchases	yr	815	1999	30r
Food cooked on trips, expenditures on	yr	36	1999	30r
Food purchases	yr	4533	1999	30r
Food purchases, eaten away from home	yr	1873	1999	30r
Food purchases, food eaten at home	yr	2660	1999	30r
Fresh fruits, expenditures on	yr	128	1999	30r
Fresh milk and cream, expenditures on	yr	112	1999	30r
Fresh vegetables, expenditures on	yr	131	1999	30r
Fruit and vegetable purchases	yr	438	1999	30r
Grapefruit	lb	0.59	7/01	11r
Grapes, Thompson, seedless	lb	2.12	7/01	11r
Ground beef, 100% beef	lb	1.76	7/01	11r
Ground beef, lean and extra lean	lb	2.60	7/01	11r
Ground chuck, 100% beef	lb	2.08	7/01	11r
Ham, boneless, excl canned	lb	2.71	7/01	11r
Ham, rump or shank half, bone-in, smoked	lb	2.19	7/01	11r
Ice cream, prepackaged, bulk, regular	1/2 gal	3.93	7/01	11r
Lemons	lb	1.32	7/01	11r
Lettuce, iceberg	head	0.86	3/01	4c
Lettuce, iceberg	lb	0.76	7/01	11r
Margarine, Blue Bonnet or Parkay, stick	lb	0.73	3/01	4c
Milk, fresh, low fat,	gal	2.75	7/01	11r
Milk, fresh, whole, fortified	gal	2.97	7/01	11r
Milk, whole	1/2 gal	1.86	3/01	4c
Nonalcoholic beverages, expenditures on	yr	228	1999	30r
Orange juice, frozen concentrate	16 oz	1.95	7/01	11r
Orange juice, Minute Maid frozen	12 oz	1.46	3/01	4c
Oranges, Navel	lb	0.73	7/01	11r
Oranges, Valencia	lb	0.55	7/01	11r
Peaches, halves or slices, Hunt's, Del Monte, or Libby's	29 oz	1.56	3/01	4c
Peanut butter, creamy, all sizes	lb	1.83	7/01	11r
Pears, Anjou	lb	0.98	7/01	11r
Peas, green, Del Monte or Green Giant	15 oz	0.64	3/01	4c
Pork chops, center cut, bone-in	lb	3.33	7/01	11r
Pork sausage, fresh, loose	lb	2.59	7/01	11r
Pork shoulder picnic, bone-in, smoked	lb	1.12	7/01	11r
Pork, expenditures on	yr	162	1999	30r
Potato chips	16 oz	3.59	7/01	11r
Potatoes, frozen, french fried	lb	1.00	7/01	11r
Potatoes, white or red	10 lb	2.70	3/01	4c
Potatoes, white, all types	lb	0.44	7/01	11r
Poultry, expenditures on	yr	137	1999	30r
Processed fruits, expenditures on	yr	97	1999	30r
Processed vegetables, expenditures on	yr	82	1999	30r
Rice, white, long grain, uncooked	lb	0.51	7/01	11r
Round roast, graded and ungraded, excl U.S. prime and choice	lb	2.96	7/01	11r
Round steak, graded and ungraded, excl U.S. prime and choice	lb	3.11	7/01	11r

Orlando, FL - continued

Item	Per	Value	Date	Ref.
Groceries - continued				
Sausage, Jimmy Dean/Owens pork	lb	2.96	3/01	4c
Shortening, vegetable, Crisco	3 lb	3.34	3/01	4c
Sirloin steak, graded and ungraded, excl U.S. prime and choice	lb	4.23	7/01	11r
Soft drink, Coca Cola, ex deposit	2 liter	1.09	3/01	4c
Spaghetti and macaroni	lb	0.78	7/01	11r
Steak, round, U.S. choice, boneless	lb	3.56	7/01	11r
Steak, sirloin, U.S. choice, boneless	lb	5.65	7/01	11r
Steak, T-bone	lb	6.50	3/01	4c
Strawberries, dry pint	12 oz	1.50	7/01	11r
Sugar and other sweets, expenditures on	yr	99	1999	30r
Sugar, cane or beet	4 lbs	1.57	3/01	4c
Sugar, white, 33-80 ounce package	lb	0.39	7/01	11r
Sugar, white, all sizes	lb	0.42	7/01	11r
Tobacco products and smoking supplies purchases	yr	288	1999	30r
Tomatoes, field grown	lb	1.43	7/01	11r
Tomatoes, Hunt's or Del Monte	14.5 oz	0.75	3/01	4c
Tuna, chunk, light	6 oz	0.69	3/01	4c
Tuna, light, chunk	lb	1.77	7/01	11r
Turkey, frozen, whole	lb	1.05	7/01	11r
Goods and Services				
Miscellaneous goods and services, ACCRA Index		101.10	3/01	4c
B&B Japanese maple (acer japonicum)	gal	49.98-129.00	4/00	93r
Boxwood (buxus)	2 gal	12.99-16.99	4/00	93r
Daylilly (hemerocallis)	gal	4.99-8.99	4/00	93r
Flat of annuals		11.00-13.92	4/00	93r
Fountain grass (pennisetum)	gal	5.98-7.98	4/00	93r
Hanging basket (10 in)		7.99-14.98	4/00	93r
Hardy geranium (geranium)	gal	5.98-8.00	4/00	93r
Hosta (hosta)	gal	4.99-10.98	4/00	93r
Lilac (syrubga vulgaris)	2 gal	12.99-21.99	4/00	93r
Rhododendron (rhododendron)	2 gal	14.99-24.99	4/00	93r
Sage (salvia)	gal	5.98-6.99	4/00	93r
Wintercreeper euonymus (euonymus fortunei)	2 gal	7.99-89.99	4/00	93r
Hunting license	yr	12.50	4/01	34s
Health Care				
Health care, ACCRA Index		108.20	3/01	4c
Cardiac catheterization, ave hospital/ physician charges		15060	1998	77s
Childbirth, Cesarean delivery		11587	1997	13r
Childbirth, vaginal delivery		6725	1997	13r
Dentist's fee, adult teeth cleaning and periodic oral exam	visit	73.00	3/01	4c
Doctor's fee, routine exam, established patient	visit	58.40	3/01	4c
Drugs, expenditures on	yr	399	1999	30r
Health care purchases	yr	1971	1999	30r
Health insurance expenditures	yr	933	1999	30r
Home health care aide cost, licensed agency	hour	15	2000	82c
Hospital care, private room	day	754.30	3/01	4c
Hysterectomy, laproscopically-assisted, ave hospital/physician charges		14760	1998	76s
Hysterectomy, vaginal, ave hospital and physician charges		11320	1998	76s
Medicaid dispensing fee		4.23	1999	87s
Medical services expenditures	yr	547	1999	30r
Medical supplies, expenditures on	yr	91	1999	30r

Values are in dollars or fractions of dollars. In the column headed *Ref*, references are shown to sources. Each reference is followed by a letter. These refer to the geographical level for which data were reported: s=State, r=Region, and c=City or metro. The abbreviation *ex* is used to mean *except* or *excluding*; *exp* stands for expenditures. For other abbreviations and further explanations, please see the Introduction.

Orlando, FL - continued

Item	Per	Value	Date	Ref.
Health Care				
Nursing home costs, private room	day	125	2000	82c
Nursing home stay, private room	day	125	2000	83c
Plastic surgery, breast augmentation		2870	2000	7r
Plastic surgery, breast lift		3649	2000	7r
Plastic surgery, facelift		5008	2000	7r
Plastic surgery, hair transplantation		3425	2000	7r
Plastic surgery, lip augmentation		1227	2000	7r
Plastic surgery, lower body lift		4793	2000	7r
Plastic surgery, thigh lift		3862	2000	7r
Household Goods				
Dishwashing powder, Cascade	50 oz	3.45	3/01	4c
Floor coverings, expenditures on	yr	44	1999	30r
Furniture, expenditures on	yr	335	1999	30r
Household furnishings and equipment purchases	yr	1328	1999	30r
Household textiles, expenditures on	yr	89	1999	30r
Laundry and cleaning supplies, expenditures on	yr	113	1999	30r
Tissues, facial, Kleenex brand	175	1.40	3/01	4c
Housing				
Housing, ACCRA Index		93.90	3/01	4c
Home, 2200 sq ft, 4-br, 2-bath, 2-car garage, average		188450	2000	47c
Home price, existing, ave		160100	10/00	90r
Home value, median		104000	2001	53s
House, 2400 sq ft, 8000 sq ft lot, new, urban, utilities	total	191976	3/01	4c
House payment, principal and interest, 25% down payment	mos	954	3/01	4c
Household operation expenditures	yr	553	1999	30r
Housekeeping supplies purchases	yr	473	1999	30r
Housing, expenditures on	yr	10303	1999	30r
Maintenance, repairs, insurance expenditures	yr	699	1999	30r
Monthly rental value of owned home	mos	505	1999	30r
Owned dwellings, expenditures own	yr	3465	1999	30r
Rent expenditures	yr	1641	1999	30r
Rent, apartment, 2 br, 1 1/2-2 baths, unfurn, 950 sq ft, water	mos	691	3/01	4c
Rental unit, 1 bedroom, with utilities	mos	582	4/01	41c
Rental unit, 2 bedroom, with utilities	mos	694	4/01	41c
Rental unit, 3 bedroom, with utilities	mos	911	4/01	41c
Rental unit, 4 bedroom, with utilities	mos	1112	4/01	41c
Shelter, expenditures on	yr	5467	1999	30r
Insurance and Pensions				
Life and other personal insurance purchases	yr	414	1999	30r
Medigap health insurance, Plan H	yr	2887	2000	69s
Medigap health insurance, Plan I	yr	3302	2000	69s
Medigap health insurance, Plan J	yr	3889	2000	69s
Pensions and Social Security, expenditures on	yr	2635	1999	30r
Personal insurance and pensions, expenditures on	yr	3048	1999	30r
Legal Fees				
Divorce, filing fee		65.00-85.00	4/01	35s
Driver's license fee	orig	20.00	1999	48s
Driver's license fee	renew	15.00	1999	48s
Personal Goods				
Personal care products and services purchases	yr	393	1999	30r
Shampoo, Alberto VO5	15 oz	1.06	3/01	4c
Toothpaste, Crest or Colgate	6-7 oz	2.56	3/01	4c
Personal Services				
Dry cleaning, man's 2-pc suit		7.04	3/01	4c
Man's haircut, barbershop, no styling		8.20	3/01	4c
Personal services, household, expenditures on	yr	258	1999	30r

Orlando, FL - continued

Item	Per	Value	Date	Ref.
Personal Services - continued				
Woman's shampoo, trim, blow-dry, no style-change		33.10	3/01	4c
Pets				
Pets, toys, and playground equipment, expenditures on	yr	306	1999	30r
Restaurant Food				
Chicken, fried, thigh and drumstick, KFC/Church's		2.61	3/01	4c
Hamburger with cheese, McDonald's	1/4 lb	2.28	3/01	4c
Pizza, Pizza Hut or Pizza Inn	11-12 in	9.29	3/01	4c
Taxes				
Federal income taxes paid	yr	2047	1999	30r
Personal taxes, expenditures on	yr	2554	1999	30r
Property taxes paid	yr	726	1999	30r
State and local income taxes paid	yr	363	1999	30r
Transportation				
Transportation, ACCRA Index		95.30	3/01	4c
Bus fare, one-way	trip	1.00	2000	1c
Cars and trucks, new, expenditures on	yr	1648	1999	30r
Cars and trucks, used, expenditures on	yr	1651	1999	30r
Diesel at the pump	gal	1.26	10/99	73s
Gasoline and motor oil purchases	yr	1052	1999	30r
Gasoline before-tax price (cents)	gal	101.90	10/00	43s
Maintenance and repair expenditures	yr	621	1999	30r
Public transportation, expenditures on	yr	298	1999	30r
Tire balance, computer or spin balance, front	wheel	7.35	3/01	4c
Transportation purchases	yr	6738	1999	30r
Vehicle expenses, miscellaneous, purchases	yr	2033	1999	30r
Vehicle insurance payments	yr	696	1999	30r
Vehicle purchases (net outlay)	yr	3354	1999	30r
Vehicle rental, lease expenditures	yr	352	1999	30r
Travel				
Hotel room	night	110.57	2/01	95s
Hotel room, ave	night	87.93	2000	70c
Utilities				
Utilities, ACCRA Index		102.00	3/01	4c
Electrical bill, average	mos	86.33	9/00	9s
Electricity, 2400 sq ft, new home	mos	125.82	3/01	4c
Electricity, expenditures on	yr	1115	1999	30r
Electricity cost, average	KWh	6.80	9/00	9s
Water and other public services, expenditures on	yr	298	1999	30r
Weddings				
Wedding (national average cost)		19936	2000	33r
Wedding (regional average total cost)		16293	1997	110r
Attendants' gifts		321	1998	33r
Bridal attendants' apparel (5 persons)		824	2000	33r
Bride's headpiece/veil		173	1998	33r
Bride's wedding dress		859	1998	33r
Clergy, religious facility fee		242	1998	33r
Engagement ring		3177	1998	33r
Flowers		789	1998	33r
Groom's formalwear rental		99	2000	33r
Limousine		410	1998	33r
Marriage license cost		56.00-88.50	4/01	35s
Men's formalwear (ushers, best man)		469	2000	33r
Mother of bride apparel		241	2000	33r
Music		866	1998	33r
Photography and videography		1368	1998	33r
Rehearsal dinner		728	1998	33r
Wedding invitations and announcements		341	1998	33r
Wedding reception		7968	2000	33r
Wedding rings (bride and groom)		1060	1998	33r

Values are in dollars or fractions of dollars. In the column headed *Ref*, references are shown to sources. Each reference is followed by a letter. These refer to the geographical level for which data were reported: s=State, r=Region, and c=City or metro. The abbreviation *ex* is used to mean *except* or *excluding*; *exp* stands for *expenditures*. For other abbreviations and further explanations, please see the Introduction.

Owensboro, KY

Item	Per	Value	Date	Ref.
Alcoholic Beverages				
Alcoholic beverage purchases	yr	253	1999	30r
Malt beverages, all types, all sizes, any origin	16 oz	0.96	7/01	11r
Appliances				
Major appliances, expenditures on	yr	172	1999	30r
Small appliances, housewares, expenditures on	yr	81	1999	30r
Banking and Money				
Mortgage interest and charges paid	yr	2039	1999	30r
Mortgage principal paid on owned property	yr	1026	1999	30r
Vehicle finance charges paid	yr	365	1999	30r
Charity				
Cash contributions, expenditures	yr	1127	1999	30r
Child Care				
Child raising cost, total, age 0-2	yr	8540	1999	60r
Child raising cost, total, age 3-5	yr	8780	1999	60r
Child raising cost, total, age 6-8	yr	8820	1999	60r
Child raising cost, total, age 9-11	yr	8800	1999	60r
Child raising cost, total, age 12-14	yr	9510	1999	60r
Child raising cost, total, age 15-17	yr	9740	1999	60r
Child's child care and education, age 0-2	yr	1380	1999	60r
Child's child care and education, age 3-5	yr	1520	1999	60r
Child's child care and education, age 6-8	yr	990	1999	60r
Child's child care and education, age 9-11	yr	650	1999	60r
Child's child care and education, age 12-14	yr	490	1999	60r
Child's child care and education, age 15-17	yr	840	1999	60r
Child's clothing, age 0-2	yr	480	1999	60r
Child's clothing, age 3-5	yr	470	1999	60r
Child's clothing, age 6-8	yr	520	1999	60r
Child's clothing, age 9-11	yr	570	1999	60r
Child's clothing, age 12-14	yr	950	1999	60r
Child's clothing, age 15-17	yr	850	1999	60r
Child's food, age 0-2	yr	1000	1999	60r
Child's food, age 3-5	yr	1160	1999	60r
Child's food, age 6-8	yr	1490	1999	60r
Child's food, age 9-11	yr	1770	1999	60r
Child's food, age 12-14	yr	1770	1999	60r
Child's food, age 15-17	yr	1980	1999	60r
Child's health care, age 0-2	yr	620	1999	60r
Child's health care, age 3-5	yr	590	1999	60r
Child's health care, age 6-8	yr	680	1999	60r
Child's health care, age 9-11	yr	720	1999	60r
Child's health care, age 12-14	yr	730	1999	60r
Child's health care, age 15-17	yr	760	1999	60r
Child's housing, age 0-2	yr	3070	1999	60r
Child's housing, age 3-5	yr	3050	1999	60r
Child's housing, age 6-8	yr	3010	1999	60r
Child's housing, age 9-11	yr	2850	1999	60r
Child's housing, age 12-14	yr	3040	1999	60r
Child's housing, age 15-17	yr	2650	1999	60r
Child's personal care, reading, age 0-2	yr	910	1999	60r
Child's personal care, reading, age 3-5	yr	930	1999	60r
Child's personal care, reading, age 6-8	yr	960	1999	60r
Child's personal care, reading, age 9-11	yr	1000	1999	60r
Child's personal care, reading, age 12-14	yr	1170	1999	60r
Child's personal care, reading, age 15-17	yr	950	1999	60r
Clothing				
Apparel and services purchases	yr	1610	1999	30r
Boys, 2 to 15, expenditures on	yr	89	1999	30r
Children under 2, expenditures on	yr	79	1999	30r
Footwear, expenditures on	yr	283	1999	30r
Girls, 2 to 15, expenditures on	yr	103	1999	30r
Men and boys, expenditures on	yr	351	1999	30r
Men, 16 and over, expenditures on	yr	262	1999	30r
Women, 16 and over, expenditures on	yr	538	1999	30r
Communications				
Cable modem installation, Intermedia		149.95	6/99	103s
Cable modem rate, cable subscriber, Intermedia	mos	49.95	6/99	103s

Owensboro, KY - continued

Item	Per	Value	Date	Ref.
Communications - continued				
Cable modem rate, non-cable subscriber, Intermedia	mos	54.95	6/99	103s
Phone line, single, business, field visit	inst.	61.39	12/97	17s
Phone line, single, business, no field visit	inst.	61.39	12/97	17s
Phone line, single, residence, field visit	inst.	33.85	12/97	17s
Phone line, single, residence, no field visit	inst.	33.85	12/97	17s
Postage and stationery, expenditures on	yr	104	1999	30r
Postal rate, express mail, up to half-pound		12.45	7/01	108r
Postal rate, letter, first class, first ounce		0.34	7/01	108r
Postal rate, letter, two ounces		0.57	7/01	108r
Postal rate, post card		0.21	7/01	108r
Postal rate, priority mail, two pounds		3.95	7/01	108r
Postal rate, priority mail, up to one pound		3.50	7/01	108r
Telephone services, expenditures on	yr	860	1999	30r
Education				
Board, 4-year private college/university	yr	1985	1996	38s
Board, 4-year public college/university	yr	1767	1996	38s
Education expenditures	yr	431	1999	30r
Room, 4-year private college/university	yr	1711	1996	38s
Room, 4-year public college/university	yr	1527	1996	38s
Total cost, 4-year private college/university	yr	11192	1996	38s
Total cost, 4-year public college/university	yr	5455	1996	38s
Tuition, 2-year public college/university, in state	yr	1112	1996	38s
Tuition, 4-year private college/university, in state	yr	7497	1996	38s
Tuition, 4-year public college/university	yr	2161	1996	38s
Energy and Fuels				
Electricity	500 KWhs	47.29	7/01	11r
Electricity	KWh	0.09	7/01	11r
Fuel oil #2	gal	1.43	7/01	11r
Fuel oil and other fuels, expenditures on	yr	45	1999	30r
Gas, cooking, winter, 10 therms	mos	9.24	2/96	98c
Gas, cooking, winter, 30 therms	mos	17.51	2/96	98c
Gas, cooking, winter, 50 therms	mos	25.78	2/96	98c
Gas, heating, winter, average use	mos	77.48	2/96	98c
Gas, natural, commercial rate	1000 cf	8.25	11/00	88s
Gasoline, all types	gal	1.60	7/01	11r
Gasoline, unleaded midgrade	gal	1.65	7/01	11r
Gasoline, unleaded premium	gal	1.74	7/01	11r
Natural gas, expenditures on	yr	164	1999	30r
Utility (piped) gas, therm		1.01	7/01	11r
Utility (piped) gas, 40 therms		44.29	7/01	11r
Utility (piped) gas, 100 therms		97.44	7/01	11r
Entertainment				
Entertainment purchases	yr	1574	1999	30r
Fees and admissions paid	yr	371	1999	30r
Reading purchases	yr	121	1999	30r
Television, radios, sound equipment, expenditures on	yr	561	1999	30r
Groceries				
American processed cheese	lb	3.50	7/01	11r
Bakery products, expenditures on	yr	261	1999	30r
Bananas	lb	0.47	7/01	11r
Beans, dried, any type, all sizes	lb	0.63	7/01	11r
Beef for stew, boneless	lb	2.86	7/01	11r
Beef, expenditures on	yr	210	1999	30r
Bologna, all beef or mixed	lb	2.29	7/01	11r
Bread, French	lb	1.66	7/01	11r
Bread, white, pan	lb	0.87	7/01	11r
Bread, whole wheat, pan	lb	1.38	7/01	11r
Broccoli	lb	1.04	7/01	11r
Butter, salted, grade AA, stick	lb	2.26	7/01	11r
Butter, yoghurt, cheese, etc, expenditures on	yr	170	1999	30r
Cabbage	lb	0.42	7/01	11r
Cereals and cereal products, expenditures on	yr	140	1999	30r
Cheddar cheese, natural	lb	3.75	7/01	11r
Chicken breast, bone-in	lb	1.85	7/01	11r

Values are in dollars or fractions of dollars. In the column headed *Ref*, references are shown to sources. Each reference is followed by a letter. These refer to the geographical level for which data were reported: s=State, r=Region, and c=City or metro. The abbreviation *ex* is used to mean *except* or *excluding*; *exp* stands for *expenditures*. For other abbreviations and further explanations, please see the Introduction.

Owensboro, KY - continued

Item	Per	Value	Date	Ref.
Groceries				
Chicken legs, bone-in	lb	1.34	7/01	11r
Chicken, fresh, whole	lb	1.05	7/01	11r
Chops, boneless,	lb	4.13	7/01	11r
Chuck roast, graded and ungraded, excl U.S. prime and choice	lb	2.35	7/01	11r
Chuck roast, U.S. choice, boneless	lb	2.67	7/01	11r
Coffee, 100%, ground roast, all sizes	lb	2.88	7/01	11r
Coffee, instant, plain, regular, all sizes	16 oz	9.25	7/01	11r
Cola, non diet,	2 liter	1.11	7/01	11r
Crackers, soda, salted	lb	1.70	7/01	11r
Dairy product purchases	yr	282	1999	30r
Eggs, expenditures on	yr	32	1999	30r
Fats and oils, expenditures on	yr	79	1999	30r
Fish and seafood, expenditures on	yr	99	1999	30r
Flour, white, all purpose	lb	0.32	7/01	11r
Food (excl fruit and vegetables), eaten at home, purchases	yr	815	1999	30r
Food cooked on trips, expenditures on	yr	36	1999	30r
Food purchases	yr	4533	1999	30r
Food purchases, eaten away from home	yr	1873	1999	30r
Food purchases, food eaten at home	yr	2660	1999	30r
Fresh fruits, expenditures on	yr	128	1999	30r
Fresh milk and cream, expenditures on	yr	112	1999	30r
Fresh vegetables, expenditures on	yr	131	1999	30r
Fruit and vegetable purchases	yr	438	1999	30r
Grapefruit	lb	0.59	7/01	11r
Grapes, Thompson, seedless	lb	2.12	7/01	11r
Ground beef, 100% beef	lb	1.76	7/01	11r
Ground beef, lean and extra lean	lb	2.60	7/01	11r
Ground chuck, 100% beef	lb	2.08	7/01	11r
Ham, boneless, excl canned	lb	2.71	7/01	11r
Ham, rump or shank half, bone-in, smoked	lb	2.19	7/01	11r
Ice cream, prepackaged, bulk, regular	1/2 gal	3.93	7/01	11r
Lemons	lb	1.32	7/01	11r
Lettuce, iceberg	lb	0.76	7/01	11r
Milk, fresh, low fat	gal	2.75	7/01	11r
Milk, fresh, whole, fortified	gal	2.97	7/01	11r
Nonalcoholic beverages, expenditures on	yr	228	1999	30r
Orange juice, frozen concentrate	16 oz	1.95	7/01	11r
Oranges, Navel	lb	0.73	7/01	11r
Oranges, Valencia	lb	0.55	7/01	11r
Peanut butter, creamy, all sizes	lb	1.83	7/01	11r
Pears, Anjou	lb	0.98	7/01	11r
Pork chops, center cut, bone-in	lb	3.33	7/01	11r
Pork sausage, fresh, loose	lb	2.59	7/01	11r
Pork shoulder picnic, bone-in, smoked	lb	1.12	7/01	11r
Pork, expenditures on	yr	162	1999	30r
Potato chips	16 oz	3.59	7/01	11r
Potatoes, frozen, french fried	lb	1.00	7/01	11r
Potatoes, white, all types	lb	0.44	7/01	11r
Poultry, expenditures on	yr	137	1999	30r
Processed fruits, expenditures on	yr	97	1999	30r
Processed vegetables, expenditures on	yr	82	1999	30r
Rice, white, long grain, uncooked	lb	0.51	7/01	11r
Round roast, graded and ungraded, excl U.S. prime and choice	lb	2.96	7/01	11r
Round steak, graded and ungraded, excl U.S. prime and choice	lb	3.11	7/01	11r
Sirloin steak, graded and ungraded, excl U.S. prime and choice	lb	4.23	7/01	11r
Spaghetti and macaroni	lb	0.78	7/01	11r
Steak, round, U.S. choice, boneless	lb	3.56	7/01	11r
Steak, sirloin, U.S. choice, boneless	lb	5.65	7/01	11r
Strawberries, dry pint	12 oz	1.50	7/01	11r
Sugar and other sweets, expenditures on	yr	99	1999	30r
Sugar, white, 33-80 ounce package	lb	0.39	7/01	11r
Sugar, white, all sizes	lb	0.42	7/01	11r
Tobacco products and smoking supplies purchases	yr	288	1999	30r
Tomatoes, field grown	lb	1.43	7/01	11r
Tuna, light, chunk	lb	1.77	7/01	11r
Turkey, frozen, whole	lb	1.05	7/01	11r

Owensboro, KY - continued

Item	Per	Value	Date	Ref.
Goods and Services				
Hunting license	yr	15.00	4/01	34s
Health Care				
Cardiac catheterization, ave hospital/ physician charges		11480	1998	77s
Childbirth, Cesarean delivery		11587	1997	13r
Childbirth, vaginal delivery		6725	1997	13r
Drugs, expenditures on	yr	399	1999	30r
Health care purchases	yr	1971	1999	30r
Health insurance expenditures	yr	933	1999	30r
Hysterectomy, laproscopically-assisted, ave hospital/physician charges		12390	1998	76s
Hysterectomy, vaginal, ave hospital and physician charges		8440	1998	76s
Medicaid dispensing fee		4.75-5.75	1999	87s
Medical services expenditures	yr	547	1999	30r
Medical supplies, expenditures on	yr	91	1999	30r
Household Goods				
Floor coverings, expenditures on	yr	44	1999	30r
Furniture, expenditures on	yr	335	1999	30r
Household furnishings and equipment purchases	yr	1328	1999	30r
Household textiles, expenditures on	yr	89	1999	30r
Laundry and cleaning supplies, expenditures on	yr	113	1999	30r
Housing				
Home price, existing, ave		160100	10/00	90r
Home value, median		103000	2001	53s
Household operation expenditures	yr	553	1999	30r
Housekeeping supplies purchases	yr	473	1999	30r
Housing, expenditures on	yr	10303	1999	30r
Maintenance, repairs, insurance expenditures	yr	699	1999	30r
Monthly rental value of owned home	mos	505	1999	30r
Owned dwellings, expenditures own	yr	3465	1999	30r
Rent expenditures	yr	1641	1999	30r
Rental unit, 1 bedroom, with utilities	mos	316	4/01	41c
Rental unit, 2 bedroom, with utilities	mos	415	4/01	41c
Rental unit, 3 bedroom, with utilities	mos	557	4/01	41c
Rental unit, 4 bedroom, with utilities	mos	583	4/01	41c
Shelter, expenditures on	yr	5467	1999	30r
Insurance and Pensions				
Life and other personal insurance purchases	yr	414	1999	30r
Pensions and Social Security, expenditures on	yr	2635	1999	30r
Personal insurance and pensions, expenditures on	yr	3048	1999	30r
Legal Fees				
Combination hunting and fishing license	yr	22.50	4/01	34s
Driver's license fee	renew	10.00	1999	48s
Driver's license fee	orig	16.00	1999	48s
Fishing license	yr	15.00	4/01	34s
Personal Goods				
Personal care products and services purchases	yr	393	1999	30r
Personal Services				
Personal services, household, expenditures on	yr	258	1999	30r
Pets				
Pets, toys, and playground equipment, expenditures on	yr	306	1999	30r
Taxes				
Federal income taxes paid	yr	2047	1999	30r
Personal taxes, expenditures on	yr	2554	1999	30r
Property taxes paid	yr	726	1999	30r
State and local income taxes paid	yr	363	1999	30r

Values are in dollars or fractions of dollars. In the column headed *Ref*, references are shown to sources. Each reference is followed by a letter. These refer to the geographical level for which data were reported: s=State, r=Region, and c=City or metro. The abbreviation *ex* is used to mean *except* or *excluding*; *exp* stands for expenditures. For other abbreviations and further explanations, please see the Introduction.

Owensboro, KY - continued

Item	Per	Value	Date	Ref.
Transportation				
Bus fare, one-way	trip	1.00	2000	1c
Cars and trucks, new, expenditures on	yr	1648	1999	30r
Cars and trucks, used, expenditures on	yr	1651	1999	30r
Diesel at the pump	gal	1.15	10/99	73s
Gasoline and motor oil purchases	yr	1052	1999	30r
Gasoline before-tax price (cents)	gal	110.40	10/00	43s
Maintenance and repair expenditures	yr	621	1999	30r
Motorcycle license fee	orig	14.00	1999	49s
Motorcycle license fee	renew	3.00	1999	49s
Public transportation, expenditures on	yr	298	1999	30r
Transportation purchases	yr	6738	1999	30r
Vehicle expenses, miscellaneous, purchases	yr	2033	1999	30r
Vehicle insurance payments	yr	696	1999	30r
Vehicle purchases (net outlay)	yr	3354	1999	30r
Vehicle rental, lease expenditures	yr	352	1999	30r
Utilities				
Electrical bill, average	mos	60.42	9/00	9s
Electricity, expenditures on	yr	1115	1999	30r
Electricity cost, average	KWh	4.10	9/00	9s
Water and other public services, expenditures on	yr	298	1999	30r
Weddings				
Wedding (national average cost)		19936	2000	33r
Attendants' gifts		321	1998	33r
Bridal attendants' apparel (5 persons)		824	2000	33r
Bride's headpiece/veil		173	1998	33r
Bride's wedding dress		859	1998	33r
Clergy, religious facility fee		242	1998	33r
Engagement ring		3177	1998	33r
Flowers		789	1998	33r
Groom's formalwear rental		99	2000	33r
Limousine		410	1998	33r
Marriage license cost		34.50	4/01	35s
Men's formalwear (ushers, best man)		469	2000	33r
Mother of bride apparel		241	2000	33r
Music		866	1998	33r
Photography and videography		1368	1998	33r
Rehearsal dinner		728	1998	33r
Wedding invitations and announcements		341	1998	33r
Wedding reception		7968	2000	33r
Wedding rings (bride and groom)		1060	1998	33r

Panama City, FL

Item	Per	Value	Date	Ref.
Composite, ACCRA index		98.50	3/01	4c
Alcoholic Beverages				
Alcoholic beverage purchases	yr	253	1999	30r
Beer, Heineken, 12-oz, ex deposit	6	7.04	3/01	4c
J & B Scotch	750-ml	21.49	3/01	4c
Malt beverages, all types, all sizes, any origin	16 oz	0.96	7/01	11r
Wine, Livingston or Gallo, Chablis blanc	1.5 liter	6.81	3/01	4c
Appliances				
Appliance repair, service call, washing machine	min lab chg	33.49	3/01	4c
Major appliances, expenditures on	yr	172	1999	30r
Small appliances, housewares, expenditures on	yr	81	1999	30r
Banking and Money				
Mortgage interest and charges paid	yr	2039	1999	30r
Mortgage principal paid on owned property	yr	1026	1999	30r
Mortgage rate, incl. points and orig. fee, 30-yr. conv. fixed or ARM	mos	7.00	3/01	4c
Vehicle finance charges paid	yr	365	1999	30r
Charity				
Cash contributions, expenditures	yr	1127	1999	30r
Child Care				
Child raising cost, total, age 0-2	yr	8540	1999	60r
Child raising cost, total, age 3-5	yr	8780	1999	60r

Panama City, FL - continued

Item	Per	Value	Date	Ref.
Child Care - continued				
Child raising cost, total, age 6-8	yr	8820	1999	60r
Child raising cost, total, age 9-11	yr	8800	1999	60r
Child raising cost, total, age 12-14	yr	9510	1999	60r
Child raising cost, total, age 15-17	yr	9740	1999	60r
Child's child care and education, age 0-2	yr	1380	1999	60r
Child's child care and education, age 3-5	yr	1520	1999	60r
Child's child care and education, age 6-8	yr	990	1999	60r
Child's child care and education, age 9-11	yr	650	1999	60r
Child's child care and education, age 12-14	yr	490	1999	60r
Child's child care and education, age 15-17	yr	840	1999	60r
Child's clothing, age 0-2	yr	480	1999	60r
Child's clothing, age 3-5	yr	470	1999	60r
Child's clothing, age 6-8	yr	520	1999	60r
Child's clothing, age 9-11	yr	570	1999	60r
Child's clothing, age 12-14	yr	950	1999	60r
Child's clothing, age 15-17	yr	850	1999	60r
Child's food, age 0-2	yr	1000	1999	60r
Child's food, age 3-5	yr	1160	1999	60r
Child's food, age 6-8	yr	1490	1999	60r
Child's food, age 9-11	yr	1770	1999	60r
Child's food, age 12-14	yr	1770	1999	60r
Child's food, age 15-17	yr	1980	1999	60r
Child's health care, age 0-2	yr	620	1999	60r
Child's health care, age 3-5	yr	590	1999	60r
Child's health care, age 6-8	yr	680	1999	60r
Child's health care, age 9-11	yr	720	1999	60r
Child's health care, age 12-14	yr	730	1999	60r
Child's health care, age 15-17	yr	760	1999	60r
Child's housing, age 0-2	yr	3070	1999	60r
Child's housing, age 3-5	yr	3050	1999	60r
Child's housing, age 6-8	yr	3010	1999	60r
Child's housing, age 9-11	yr	2850	1999	60r
Child's housing, age 12-14	yr	3040	1999	60r
Child's housing, age 15-17	yr	2650	1999	60r
Child's personal care, reading, age 0-2	yr	910	1999	60r
Child's personal care, reading, age 3-5	yr	930	1999	60r
Child's personal care, reading, age 6-8	yr	960	1999	60r
Child's personal care, reading, age 9-11	yr	1000	1999	60r
Child's personal care, reading, age 12-14	yr	1170	1999	60r
Child's personal care, reading, age 15-17	yr	950	1999	60r
Clothing				
Apparel and services purchases	yr	1610	1999	30r
Boys' brief, cotton	3	4.58	3/01	4c
Boys, 2 to 15, expenditures on	yr	89	1999	30r
Children under 2, expenditures on	yr	79	1999	30r
Footwear, expenditures on	yr	283	1999	30r
Girls, 2 to 15, expenditures on	yr	103	1999	30r
Men and boys, expenditures on	yr	351	1999	30r
Men, 16 and over, expenditures on	yr	262	1999	30r
Shirt, man's dress shirt		27.16	3/01	4c
Slacks, man's "No Wrinkles" khaki		33.33	3/01	4c
Women, 16 and over, expenditures on	yr	538	1999	30r
Communications				
Cable modem installation, Adelphi		54.90	6/99	103s
Cable modem installation, Comcast		95.00	6/99	103s
Cable modem installation, Media One		100.00	6/99	103s
Cable modem installation, Time Warner		75.00-225.00	6/99	103s
Cable modem rate, cable subscriber, Adelphi	mos	34.95	6/99	103s
Cable modem rate, cable subscriber, Comcast	mos	39.95	6/99	103s
Cable modem rate, cable subscriber, Media One	mos	34.95-39.95	6/99	103s
Cable modem rate, cable subscriber, Time Warner	mos	39.95-49.95	6/99	103s
Cable modem rate, non-cable subscriber, Adelphi	mos	44.95	6/99	103s
Cable modem rate, non-cable subscriber, Comcast	mos	49.95	6/99	103s
Cable modem rate, non-cable subscriber, Media One	mos	49.95	6/99	103s

Values are in dollars or fractions of dollars. In the column headed *Ref*, references are shown to sources. Each reference is followed by a letter. These refer to the geographical level for which data were reported: s=State, r=Region, and c=City or metro. The abbreviation *ex* is used to mean *except* or *excluding*; *exp* stands for *expenditures*. For other abbreviations and further explanations, please see the Introduction.

Panama City, FL - continued

Item	Per	Value	Date	Ref.
Communications				
Cable modem rate, non-cable subscriber, Time Warner	mos	39.95-54.95	6/99	103s
Newspaper subscription, daily and Sunday delivery	mos	11.59	3/01	4c
Phone line, single, business, field visit	inst.	56.00	12/97	17s
Phone line, single, business, no field visit	inst.	56.00	12/97	17s
Phone line, single, residence, field visit	inst.	40.00	12/97	17s
Phone line, single, residence, no field visit	inst.	40.00	12/97	17s
Postage and stationery, expenditures on	yr	104	1999	30r
Postal rate, express mail, up to half-pound		12.45	7/01	108r
Postal rate, letter, first class, first ounce		0.34	7/01	108r
Postal rate, letter, two ounces		0.57	7/01	108r
Postal rate, post card		0.21	7/01	108r
Postal rate, priority mail, two pounds		3.95	7/01	108r
Postal rate, priority mail, up to one pound		3.50	7/01	108r
Telephone bill, family of three	mos	17.84	3/01	4c
Telephone services, expenditures on	yr	860	1999	30r
Education				
Board, 4-year private college/university	yr	2236	1996	38s
Board, 4-year public college/university	yr	2295	1996	38s
Education expenditures	yr	431	1999	30r
Room, 4-year private college/university	yr	2428	1996	38s
Room, 4-year public college/university	yr	2193	1996	38s
Total cost, 4-year private college/university	yr	15028	1996	38s
Total cost, 4-year public college/university	yr	6254	1996	38s
Tuition, 2-year public college/university, in state	yr	1103	1996	38s
Tuition, 4-year private college/university, in state	yr	10364	1996	38s
Tuition, 4-year public college/university	yr	1767	1996	38s
Energy and Fuels				
Electricity	500 KWhs	47.29	7/01	11r
Electricity	KWh	0.09	7/01	11r
Energy, combined forms, 2400 sq ft	mos	108.35	3/01	4c
Energy, exc. electricity, 2400 sq ft	mos	46.36	3/01	4c
Fuel oil #2	gal	1.43	7/01	11r
Fuel oil and other fuels, expenditures on	yr	45	1999	30r
Gas, natural, commercial rate	1000 cf	8.44	11/00	88s
Gas, regular unleaded, cash, self-service	gal	1.51	3/01	4c
Gasoline, all types	gal	1.60	7/01	11r
Gasoline, unleaded midgrade	gal	1.65	7/01	11r
Gasoline, unleaded premium	gal	1.74	7/01	11r
Natural gas, expenditures on	yr	164	1999	30r
Utility (piped) gas, therm		1.01	7/01	11r
Utility (piped) gas, 40 therms		44.29	7/01	11r
Utility (piped) gas, 100 therms		97.44	7/01	11r
Entertainment				
Bowling, Saturday evening rate	line	2.57	3/01	4c
Entertainment purchases	yr	1574	1999	30r
Fees and admissions paid	yr	371	1999	30r
Monopoly game, Parker Brothers', No. 9	game	11.82	3/01	4c
Movie, first-run, Saturday, evening	adm.	6.62	3/01	4c
Reading purchases	yr	121	1999	30r
Television, radios, sound equipment, expenditures on	yr	561	1999	30r
Tennis balls, yellow, Wilson or Penn, 3	can	2.51	3/01	4c
Funerals				
Total cost of funeral		5922.53	1/99	78r
Acknowledgement cards		63.43	1/99	78r
Casket		2258.77	1/99	78r
Cosmetology, hair, other preparation		127.09	1/99	78r
Embalming		393.49	1/99	78r
Funeral at funeral home		367.50	1/99	78r
Hearse (local)		169.66	1/99	78r
Professional service charges		1211.32	1/99	78r
Service car/van		80.69	1/99	78r
Transfer of remains to funeral home		144.25	1/99	78r
Vault		803.50	1/99	78r
Visitation/viewing		302.83	1/99	78r

Panama City, FL - continued

Item	Per	Value	Date	Ref.
Groceries				
Groceries, ACCRA Index		104.20	3/01	4c
American processed cheese	lb	3.50	7/01	11r
Antibiotic ointment, Polysporin	0.5 oz	4.80	3/01	4c
Baby food, strained vegetables or fruit, lowest price	4-4.5 oz	0.40	3/01	4c
Bakery products, expenditures on	yr	261	1999	30r
Bananas	lb	0.52	3/01	4c
Bananas	lb	0.47	7/01	11r
Beans, dried, any type, all sizes	lb	0.63	7/01	11r
Beef for stew, boneless	lb	2.86	7/01	11r
Beef or hamburger, ground	lb	1.41	3/01	4c
Beef, expenditures on	yr	210	1999	30r
Bologna, all beef or mixed	lb	2.29	7/01	11r
Bread, French	lb	1.66	7/01	11r
Bread, white	loaf	1.13	3/01	4c
Bread, white, pan	lb	0.87	7/01	11r
Bread, whole wheat, pan	lb	1.38	7/01	11r
Broccoli	lb	1.04	7/01	11r
Butter, salted, grade AA, stick	lb	2.26	7/01	11r
Butter, yoghurt, cheese, etc, expenditures on	yr	170	1999	30r
Cabbage	lb	0.42	7/01	11r
Cereals and cereal products, expenditures on	yr	140	1999	30r
Cheddar cheese, natural	lb	3.75	7/01	11r
Cheese, Kraft grated Parmesan	8 oz	3.47	3/01	4c
Chicken breast, bone-in	lb	1.85	7/01	11r
Chicken legs, bone-in	lb	1.34	7/01	11r
Chicken, fresh, whole	lb	1.05	7/01	11r
Chicken, whole fryer	lb	0.96	3/01	4c
Chops, boneless,	lb	4.13	7/01	11r
Chuck roast, graded and ungraded, excl U.S. prime and choice	lb	2.35	7/01	11r
Chuck roast, U.S. choice, boneless	lb	2.67	7/01	11r
Cigarettes, Winston, Kings	carton	30.71	3/01	4c
Coffee, 100%, ground roast, all sizes	lb	2.88	7/01	11r
Coffee, instant, plain, regular, all sizes	16 oz	9.25	7/01	11r
Coffee, vacuum-packed	13 oz	2.54	3/01	4c
Cola, non diet,	2 liter	1.11	7/01	11r
Corn Flakes, Kellogg's or Post Toasties	18 oz	3.01	3/01	4c
Corn, frozen, whole kernel, lowest price	16 oz	1.38	3/01	4c
Crackers, soda, salted	lb	1.70	7/01	11r
Dairy product purchases	yr	282	1999	30r
Eggs, expenditures on	yr	32	1999	30r
Eggs, Grade A or AA	dozen	1.19	3/01	4c
Fats and oils, expenditures on	yr	79	1999	30r
Fish and seafood, expenditures on	yr	99	1999	30r
Flour, white, all purpose	lb	0.32	7/01	11r
Food (excl fruit and vegetables), eaten at home, purchases	yr	815	1999	30r
Food cooked on trips, expenditures on	yr	36	1999	30r
Food purchases	yr	4533	1999	30r
Food purchases, eaten away from home	yr	1873	1999	30r
Food purchases, food eaten at home	yr	2660	1999	30r
Fresh fruits, expenditures on	yr	128	1999	30r
Fresh milk and cream, expenditures on	yr	112	1999	30r
Fresh vegetables, expenditures on	yr	131	1999	30r
Fruit and vegetable purchases	yr	438	1999	30r
Grapefruit	lb	0.59	7/01	11r
Grapes, Thompson, seedless	lb	2.12	7/01	11r
Ground beef, 100% beef	lb	1.76	7/01	11r
Ground beef, lean and extra lean	lb	2.60	7/01	11r
Ground chuck, 100% beef	lb	2.08	7/01	11r
Ham, boneless, excl canned	lb	2.71	7/01	11r
Ham, rump or shank half, bone-in, smoked	lb	2.19	7/01	11r
Ice cream, prepackaged, bulk, regular	1/2 gal	3.93	7/01	11r
Lemons	lb	1.32	7/01	11r
Lettuce, iceberg	head	1.04	3/01	4c
Lettuce, iceberg	lb	0.76	7/01	11r
Margarine, Blue Bonnet or Parkay, stick	lb	0.79	3/01	4c
Milk, fresh, low fat,	gal	2.75	7/01	11r
Milk, fresh, whole, fortified	gal	2.97	7/01	11r
Milk, whole	1/2 gal	1.84	3/01	4c

Values are in dollars or fractions of dollars. In the column headed *Ref*, references are shown to sources. Each reference is followed by a letter. These refer to the geographical level for which data were reported: s=State, r=Region, and c=City or metro. The abbreviation *ex* is used to mean *except* or *excluding*; *exp* stands for *expenditures*. For other abbreviations and further explanations, please see the Introduction.

Panama City, FL - continued

Item	Per	Value	Date	Ref.
Groceries				
Nonalcoholic beverages, expenditures on	yr	228	1999	30r
Orange juice, frozen concentrate	16 oz	1.95	7/01	11r
Orange juice, Minute Maid frozen	12 oz	1.61	3/01	4c
Oranges, Navel	lb	0.73	7/01	11r
Oranges, Valencia	lb	0.55	7/01	11r
Peaches, halves or slices, Hunt's, Del Monte, or Libby's	29 oz	1.62	3/01	4c
Peanut butter, creamy, all sizes	lb	1.83	7/01	11r
Pears, Anjou	lb	0.98	7/01	11r
Peas, green, Del Monte or Green Giant	15 oz	0.79	3/01	4c
Pork chops, center cut, bone-in	lb	3.33	7/01	11r
Pork sausage, fresh, loose	lb	2.59	7/01	11r
Pork shoulder picnic, bone-in, smoked	lb	1.12	7/01	11r
Pork, expenditures on	yr	162	1999	30r
Potato chips	16 oz	3.59	7/01	11r
Potatoes, frozen, french fried	lb	1.00	7/01	11r
Potatoes, white or red	10 lb	2.49	3/01	4c
Potatoes, white, all types	lb	0.44	7/01	11r
Poultry, expenditures on	yr	137	1999	30r
Processed fruits, expenditures on	yr	97	1999	30r
Processed vegetables, expenditures on	yr	82	1999	30r
Rice, white, long grain, uncooked	lb	0.51	7/01	11r
Round roast, graded and ungraded, excl U.S. prime and choice	lb	2.96	7/01	11r
Round steak, graded and ungraded, excl U.S. prime and choice	lb	3.11	7/01	11r
Sausage, Jimmy Dean/Owens pork	lb	3.06	3/01	4c
Shortening, vegetable, Crisco	3 lb	3.29	3/01	4c
Sirloin steak, graded and ungraded, excl U.S. prime and choice	lb	4.23	7/01	11r
Soft drink, Coca Cola, ex deposit	2 liter	1.09	3/01	4c
Spaghetti and macaroni	lb	0.78	7/01	11r
Steak, round, U.S. choice, boneless	lb	3.56	7/01	11r
Steak, sirloin, U.S. choice, boneless	lb	5.65	7/01	11r
Steak, T-bone	lb	7.04	3/01	4c
Strawberries, dry pint	12 oz	1.50	7/01	11r
Sugar and other sweets, expenditures on	yr	99	1999	30r
Sugar, cane or beet	4 lbs	1.49	3/01	4c
Sugar, white, 33-80 ounce package	lb	0.39	7/01	11r
Sugar, white, all sizes	lb	0.42	7/01	11r
Tobacco products and smoking supplies purchases	yr	288	1999	30r
Tomatoes, field grown	lb	1.43	7/01	11r
Tomatoes, Hunt's or Del Monte	14.5 oz	0.90	3/01	4c
Tuna, chunk, light	6 oz	0.84	3/01	4c
Tuna, light, chunk	lb	1.77	7/01	11r
Turkey, frozen, whole	lb	1.05	7/01	11r
Goods and Services				
Miscellaneous goods and services, ACCRA Index		98.10	3/01	4c
B&B Japanese maple (acer japonicum)	gal	49.98-129.00	4/00	93r
Boxwood (buxus)	2 gal	12.99-16.99	4/00	93r
Daylily (hemerocallis)	gal	4.99-8.99	4/00	93r
Flat of annuals		11.00-13.92	4/00	93r
Fountain grass (pennisetum)	gal	5.98-7.98	4/00	93r
Hanging basket (10 in)		7.99-14.98	4/00	93r
Hardy geranium (geranium)	gal	5.98-8.00	4/00	93r
Hosta (hosta)	gal	4.99-10.98	4/00	93r
Lilac (syrubga vulgaris)	2 gal	12.99-21.99	4/00	93r
Rhododendron (rhododendron)	2 gal	14.99-24.99	4/00	93r
Sage (salvia)	gal	5.98-6.99	4/00	93r

Panama City, FL - continued

Item	Per	Value	Date	Ref.
Goods and Services - continued				
Wintercreeper euonymus (euonymus fortunei)	2 gal	7.99-89.99	4/00	93r
Hunting license	yr	12.50	4/01	34s
Health Care				
Health care, ACCRA Index		103.00	3/01	4c
Cardiac catheterization, ave hospital/ physician charges		15060	1998	77s
Childbirth, Cesarean delivery		11587	1997	13r
Childbirth, vaginal delivery		6725	1997	13r
Dentist's fee, adult teeth cleaning and periodic oral exam	visit	66.60	3/01	4c
Doctor's fee, routine exam, established patient	visit	64.00	3/01	4c
Drugs, expenditures on	yr	399	1999	30r
Health care purchases	yr	1971	1999	30r
Health insurance expenditures	yr	933	1999	30r
Hospital care, private room	day	576.00	3/01	4c
Hysterectomy, laproscopically-assisted, ave hospital/physician charges		14760	1998	76s
Hysterectomy, vaginal, ave hospital and physician charges		11320	1998	76s
Medicaid dispensing fee		4.23	1999	87s
Medical services expenditures	yr	547	1999	30r
Medical supplies, expenditures on	yr	91	1999	30r
Plastic surgery, breast augmentation		2870	2000	7r
Plastic surgery, breast lift		3649	2000	7r
Plastic surgery, facelift		5008	2000	7r
Plastic surgery, hair transplantation		3425	2000	7r
Plastic surgery, lip augmentation		1227	2000	7r
Plastic surgery, lower body lift		4793	2000	7r
Plastic surgery, thigh lift		3862	2000	7r
Household Goods				
Dishwashing powder, Cascade	50 oz	3.57	3/01	4c
Floor coverings, expenditures on	yr	44	1999	30r
Furniture, expenditures on	yr	335	1999	30r
Household furnishings and equipment purchases	yr	1328	1999	30r
Household textiles, expenditures on	yr	89	1999	30r
Laundry and cleaning supplies, expenditures on	yr	113	1999	30r
Tissues, facial, Kleenex brand	175	1.43	3/01	4c
Housing				
Housing, ACCRA Index		95.60	3/01	4c
Home price, existing, ave		160100	10/00	90r
Home value, median		104000	2001	53s
House, 2400 sq ft, 8000 sq ft lot, new, urban, utilities	total	199841	3/01	4c
House payment, principal and interest, 25% down payment	mos	997	3/01	4c
Household operation expenditures	yr	553	1999	30r
Housekeeping supplies purchases	yr	473	1999	30r
Housing, expenditures on	yr	10303	1999	30r
Maintenance, repairs, insurance expenditures	yr	699	1999	30r
Monthly rental value of owned home	mos	505	1999	30r
Owned dwellings, expenditures own	yr	3465	1999	30r
Rent expenditures	yr	1641	1999	30r
Rent, apartment, 2 br, 1 1/2-2 baths, unfurn, 950 sq ft, water	mos	632	3/01	4c
Rental unit, 1 bedroom, with utilities	mos	451	4/01	41c
Rental unit, 2 bedroom, with utilities	mos	512	4/01	41c
Rental unit, 3 bedroom, with utilities	mos	653	4/01	41c
Rental unit, 4 bedroom, with utilities	mos	700	4/01	41c
Shelter, expenditures on	yr	5467	1999	30r
Insurance and Pensions				
Life and other personal insurance purchases	yr	414	1999	30r
Medigap health insurance, Plan H	yr	2887	2000	69s
Medigap health insurance, Plan I	yr	3302	2000	69s
Medigap health insurance, Plan J	yr	3889	2000	69s

Values are in dollars or fractions of dollars. In the column headed *Ref*, references are shown to sources. Each reference is followed by a letter. These refer to the geographical level for which data were reported: s=State, r=Region, and c=City or metro. The abbreviation *ex* is used to mean *except* or *excluding*; *exp* stands for *expenditures*. For other abbreviations and further explanations, please see the Introduction.

Panama City, FL - continued

Item	Per	Value	Date	Ref.
Insurance and Pensions				
Pensions and Social Security, expenditures on	yr	2635	1999	30r
Personal insurance and pensions, expenditures on	yr	3048	1999	30r
Legal Fees				
Divorce, filing fee		65.00-85.00	4/01	35s
Driver's license fee	renew	15.00	1999	48s
Driver's license fee	orig	20.00	1999	48s
Personal Goods				
Personal care products and services purchases	yr	393	1999	30r
Shampoo, Alberto VO5	15 oz	1.14	3/01	4c
Toothpaste, Crest or Colgate	6-7 oz	2.69	3/01	4c
Personal Services				
Dry cleaning, man's 2-pc suit		7.26	3/01	4c
Man's haircut, barbershop, no styling		7.80	3/01	4c
Personal services, household, expenditures on	yr	258	1999	30r
Woman's shampoo, trim, blow-dry, no style-change		19.99	3/01	4c
Pets				
Pets, toys, and playground equipment, expenditures on	yr	306	1999	30r
Restaurant Food				
Chicken, fried, thigh and drumstick, KFC/Church's		2.69	3/01	4c
Hamburger with cheese, McDonald's	1/4 lb	2.09	3/01	4c
Pizza, Pizza Hut or Pizza Inn	11-12 in	9.49	3/01	4c
Taxes				
Federal income taxes paid	yr	2047	1999	30r
Personal taxes, expenditures on	yr	2554	1999	30r
Property taxes paid	yr	726	1999	30r
State and local income taxes paid	yr	363	1999	30r
Transportation				
Transportation, ACCRA Index		105.50	3/01	4c
Cars and trucks, new, expenditures on	yr	1648	1999	30r
Cars and trucks, used, expenditures on	yr	1651	1999	30r
Diesel at the pump	gal	1.26	10/99	73s
Gasoline and motor oil purchases	yr	1052	1999	30r
Gasoline before-tax price (cents)	gal	101.90	10/00	43s
Maintenance and repair expenditures	yr	621	1999	30r
Public transportation, expenditures on	yr	298	1999	30r
Tire balance, computer or spin balance, front	wheel	8.15	3/01	4c
Transportation purchases	yr	6738	1999	30r
Vehicle expenses, miscellaneous, purchases	yr	2033	1999	30r
Vehicle insurance payments	yr	696	1999	30r
Vehicle purchases (net outlay)	yr	3354	1999	30r
Vehicle rental, lease expenditures	yr	352	1999	30r
Travel				
Hotel room	night	110.57	2/01	95s
Utilities				
Utilities, ACCRA Index		87.80	3/01	4c
Electrical bill, average	mos	86.33	9/00	9s
Electricity, expenditures on	yr	1115	1999	30r
Electricity and other, mixed, 2400 sq ft, new home	mos	61.99	3/01	4c
Electricity cost, average	KWh	6.80	9/00	9s
Water and other public services, expenditures on	yr	298	1999	30r
Weddings				
Wedding (national average cost)		19936	2000	33r
Wedding (regional average total cost)		16293	1997	110r
Attendants' gifts		321	1998	33r
Bridal attendants' apparel (5 persons)		824	2000	33r
Bride's headpiece/veil		173	1998	33r
Bride's wedding dress		859	1998	33r

Panama City, FL - continued

Item	Per	Value	Date	Ref.
Weddings - continued				
Clergy, religious facility fee		242	1998	33r
Engagement ring		3177	1998	33r
Flowers		789	1998	33r
Groom's formalwear rental		99	2000	33r
Limousine		410	1998	33r
Marriage license cost		56.00-88.50	4/01	35s
Men's formalwear (ushers, best man)		469	2000	33r
Mother of bride apparel		241	2000	33r
Music		866	1998	33r
Photography and videography		1368	1998	33r
Rehearsal dinner		728	1998	33r
Wedding invitations and announcements		341	1998	33r
Wedding reception		7968	2000	33r
Wedding rings (bride and groom)		1060	1998	33r

Parkersburg-Marietta, WV-OH

Item	Per	Value	Date	Ref.
Alcoholic Beverages				
Alcoholic beverage purchases	yr	253	1999	30r
Malt beverages, all types, all sizes, any origin	16 oz	0.96	7/01	11r
Appliances				
Major appliances, expenditures on	yr	172	1999	30r
Small appliances, housewares, expenditures on	yr	81	1999	30r
Banking and Money				
Mortgage interest and charges paid	yr	2039	1999	30r
Mortgage principal paid on owned property	yr	1026	1999	30r
Vehicle finance charges paid	yr	365	1999	30r
Charity				
Cash contributions, expenditures	yr	1127	1999	30r
Child Care				
Child raising cost, total, age 0-2	yr	8540	1999	60r
Child raising cost, total, age 3-5	yr	8780	1999	60r
Child raising cost, total, age 6-8	yr	8820	1999	60r
Child raising cost, total, age 9-11	yr	8800	1999	60r
Child raising cost, total, age 12-14	yr	9510	1999	60r
Child raising cost, total, age 15-17	yr	9740	1999	60r
Child's child care and education, age 0-2	yr	1380	1999	60r
Child's child care and education, age 3-5	yr	1520	1999	60r
Child's child care and education, age 6-8	yr	990	1999	60r
Child's child care and education, age 9-11	yr	650	1999	60r
Child's child care and education, age 12-14	yr	490	1999	60r
Child's child care and education, age 15-17	yr	840	1999	60r
Child's clothing, age 0-2	yr	480	1999	60r
Child's clothing, age 3-5	yr	470	1999	60r
Child's clothing, age 6-8	yr	520	1999	60r
Child's clothing, age 9-11	yr	570	1999	60r
Child's clothing, age 12-14	yr	950	1999	60r
Child's clothing, age 15-17	yr	850	1999	60r
Child's food, age 0-2	yr	1000	1999	60r
Child's food, age 3-5	yr	1160	1999	60r
Child's food, age 6-8	yr	1490	1999	60r
Child's food, age 9-11	yr	1770	1999	60r
Child's food, age 12-14	yr	1770	1999	60r
Child's food, age 15-17	yr	1980	1999	60r
Child's health care, age 0-2	yr	620	1999	60r
Child's health care, age 3-5	yr	590	1999	60r
Child's health care, age 6-8	yr	680	1999	60r
Child's health care, age 9-11	yr	720	1999	60r
Child's health care, age 12-14	yr	730	1999	60r
Child's health care, age 15-17	yr	760	1999	60r
Child's housing, age 0-2	yr	3070	1999	60r
Child's housing, age 3-5	yr	3050	1999	60r
Child's housing, age 6-8	yr	3010	1999	60r
Child's housing, age 9-11	yr	2850	1999	60r
Child's housing, age 12-14	yr	3040	1999	60r
Child's housing, age 15-17	yr	2650	1999	60r
Child's personal care, reading, age 0-2	yr	910	1999	60r

Values are in dollars or fractions of dollars. In the column headed *Ref*, references are shown to sources. Each reference is followed by a letter. These refer to the geographical level for which data were reported: s=State, r=Region, and c=City or metro. The abbreviation *ex* is used to mean *except* or *excluding*; *exp* stands for expenditures. For other abbreviations and further explanations, please see the Introduction.

Parkersburg-Marietta, WV-OH - continued

Item	Per	Value	Date	Ref.
Child Care				
Child's personal care, reading, age 3-5	yr	930	1999	60r
Child's personal care, reading, age 6-8	yr	960	1999	60r
Child's personal care, reading, age 9-11	yr	1000	1999	60r
Child's personal care, reading, age 12-14	yr	1170	1999	60r
Child's personal care, reading, age 15-17	yr	950	1999	60r
Clothing				
Apparel and services purchases	yr	1610	1999	30r
Boys, 2 to 15, expenditures on	yr	89	1999	30r
Children under 2, expenditures on	yr	79	1999	30r
Footwear, expenditures on	yr	283	1999	30r
Girls, 2 to 15, expenditures on	yr	103	1999	30r
Men and boys, expenditures on	yr	351	1999	30r
Men, 16 and over, expenditures on	yr	262	1999	30r
Women, 16 and over, expenditures on	yr	538	1999	30r
Communications				
Phone line, single, business, field visit	inst.	96.90	12/97	17s
Phone line, single, business, no field visit	inst.	96.90	12/97	17s
Phone line, single, residence, field visit	inst.	42.00	12/97	17s
Phone line, single, residence, no field visit	inst.	42.00	12/97	17s
Postage and stationery, expenditures on	yr	104	1999	30r
Postal rate, express mail, up to half-pound		12.45	7/01	108r
Postal rate, letter, first class, first ounce		0.34	7/01	108r
Postal rate, letter, two ounces		0.57	7/01	108r
Postal rate, post card		0.21	7/01	108r
Postal rate, priority mail, two pounds		3.95	7/01	108r
Postal rate, priority mail, up to one pound		3.50	7/01	108r
Telephone services, expenditures on	yr	860	1999	30r
Education				
Board, 4-year private college/university	yr	2370	1996	38s
Board, 4-year public college/university	yr	2133	1996	38s
Education expenditures	yr	431	1999	30r
Room, 4-year private college/university	yr	1853	1996	38s
Room, 4-year public college/university	yr	1970	1996	38s
Total cost, 4-year private college/university	yr	14231	1996	38s
Total cost, 4-year public college/university	yr	6128	1996	38s
Tuition, 2-year public college/university, in state	yr	1312	1996	38s
Tuition, 4-year private college/university, in state	yr	10008	1996	38s
Tuition, 4-year public college/university	yr	2024	1996	38s
Energy and Fuels				
Electricity	500 KWhs	47.29	7/01	11r
Electricity	KWh	0.09	7/01	11r
Fuel oil #2	gal	1.43	7/01	11r
Fuel oil and other fuels, expenditures on	yr	45	1999	30r
Gas, natural, commercial rate	1000 cf	6.75	11/00	88s
Gasoline, all types	gal	1.60	7/01	11r
Gasoline, unleaded midgrade	gal	1.65	7/01	11r
Gasoline, unleaded premium	gal	1.74	7/01	11r
Natural gas, expenditures on	yr	164	1999	30r
Utility (piped) gas, therm		1.01	7/01	11r
Utility (piped) gas, 40 therms		44.29	7/01	11r
Utility (piped) gas, 100 therms		97.44	7/01	11r
Entertainment				
Entertainment purchases	yr	1574	1999	30r
Fees and admissions paid	yr	371	1999	30r
Reading purchases	yr	121	1999	30r
Television, radios, sound equipment, expenditures on	yr	561	1999	30r
Funerals				
Total cost of funeral		5922.53	1/99	78r
Acknowledgement cards		63.43	1/99	78r
Casket		2258.77	1/99	78r
Cosmetology, hair, other preparation		127.09	1/99	78r
Embalming		393.49	1/99	78r
Funeral at funeral home		367.50	1/99	78r
Hearse (local)		169.66	1/99	78r
Professional service charges		1211.32	1/99	78r

Parkersburg-Marietta, WV-OH - continued

Item	Per	Value	Date	Ref.
Funerals - continued				
Service car/van		80.69	1/99	78r
Transfer of remains to funeral home		144.25	1/99	78r
Vault		803.50	1/99	78r
Visitation/viewing		302.83	1/99	78r
Groceries				
American processed cheese	lb	3.50	7/01	11r
Bakery products, expenditures on	yr	261	1999	30r
Bananas	lb	0.47	7/01	11r
Beans, dried, any type, all sizes	lb	0.63	7/01	11r
Beef for stew, boneless	lb	2.86	7/01	11r
Beef, expenditures on	yr	210	1999	30r
Bologna, all beef or mixed	lb	2.29	7/01	11r
Bread, French	lb	1.66	7/01	11r
Bread, white, pan	lb	0.87	7/01	11r
Bread, whole wheat, pan	lb	1.38	7/01	11r
Broccoli	lb	1.04	7/01	11r
Butter, salted, grade AA, stick	lb	2.26	7/01	11r
Butter, yoghurt, cheese, etc, expenditures on	yr	170	1999	30r
Cabbage	lb	0.42	7/01	11r
Cereals and cereal products, expenditures on	yr	140	1999	30r
Cheddar cheese, natural	lb	3.75	7/01	11r
Chicken breast, bone-in	lb	1.85	7/01	11r
Chicken legs, bone-in	lb	1.34	7/01	11r
Chicken, fresh, whole	lb	1.05	7/01	11r
Chops, boneless,	lb	4.13	7/01	11r
Chuck roast, graded and ungraded, excl U.S. prime and choice	lb	2.35	7/01	11r
Chuck roast, U.S. choice, boneless	lb	2.67	7/01	11r
Coffee, 100%, ground roast, all sizes	lb	2.88	7/01	11r
Coffee, instant, plain, regular, all sizes	16 oz	9.25	7/01	11r
Cola, non diet,	2 liter	1.11	7/01	11r
Crackers, soda, salted	lb	1.70	7/01	11r
Dairy product purchases	yr	282	1999	30r
Eggs, expenditures on	yr	32	1999	30r
Fats and oils, expenditures on	yr	79	1999	30r
Fish and seafood, expenditures on	yr	99	1999	30r
Flour, white, all purpose	lb	0.32	7/01	11r
Food (excl fruit and vegetables), eaten at home, purchases	yr	815	1999	30r
Food cooked on trips, expenditures on	yr	36	1999	30r
Food purchases	yr	4533	1999	30r
Food purchases, eaten away from home	yr	1873	1999	30r
Food purchases, food eaten at home	yr	2660	1999	30r
Fresh fruits, expenditures on	yr	128	1999	30r
Fresh milk and cream, expenditures on	yr	112	1999	30r
Fresh vegetables, expenditures on	yr	131	1999	30r
Fruit and vegetable purchases	yr	438	1999	30r
Grapefruit	lb	0.59	7/01	11r
Grapes, Thompson, seedless	lb	2.12	7/01	11r
Ground beef, 100% beef	lb	1.76	7/01	11r
Ground beef, lean and extra lean	lb	2.60	7/01	11r
Ground chuck, 100% beef	lb	2.08	7/01	11r
Ham, boneless, excl canned	lb	2.71	7/01	11r
Ham, rump or shank half, bone-in, smoked	lb	2.19	7/01	11r
Ice cream, prepackaged, bulk, regular	1/2 gal	3.93	7/01	11r
Lemons	lb	1.32	7/01	11r
Lettuce, iceberg	lb	0.76	7/01	11r
Milk, fresh, low fat,	gal	2.75	7/01	11r
Milk, fresh, whole, fortified	gal	2.97	7/01	11r
Nonalcoholic beverages, expenditures on	yr	228	1999	30r
Orange juice, frozen concentrate	16 oz	1.95	7/01	11r
Oranges, Navel	lb	0.73	7/01	11r
Oranges, Valencia	lb	0.55	7/01	11r
Peanut butter, creamy, all sizes	lb	1.83	7/01	11r
Pears, Anjou	lb	0.98	7/01	11r
Pork chops, center cut, bone-in	lb	3.33	7/01	11r
Pork sausage, fresh, loose	lb	2.59	7/01	11r
Pork shoulder picnic, bone-in, smoked	lb	1.12	7/01	11r
Pork, expenditures on	yr	162	1999	30r
Potato chips	16 oz	3.59	7/01	11r
Potatoes, frozen, french fried	lb	1.00	7/01	11r

Values are in dollars or fractions of dollars. In the column headed *Ref*, references are shown to sources. Each reference is followed by a letter. These refer to the geographical level for which data were reported: s=State, r=Region, and c=City or metro. The abbreviation *ex* is used to mean *except* or *excluding*; *exp* stands for expenditures. For other abbreviations and further explanations, please see the Introduction.

Parkersburg-Marietta, WV-OH - continued

Item	Per	Value	Date	Ref.
Groceries				
Potatoes, white, all types	lb	0.44	7/01	11r
Poultry, expenditures on	yr	137	1999	30r
Processed fruits, expenditures on	yr	97	1999	30r
Processed vegetables, expenditures on	yr	82	1999	30r
Rice, white, long grain, uncooked	lb	0.51	7/01	11r
Round roast, graded and ungraded, excl U.S. prime and choice	lb	2.96	7/01	11r
Round steak, graded and ungraded, excl U.S. prime and choice	lb	3.11	7/01	11r
Sirloin steak, graded and ungraded, excl U.S. prime and choice	lb	4.23	7/01	11r
Spaghetti and macaroni	lb	0.78	7/01	11r
Steak, round, U.S. choice, boneless	lb	3.56	7/01	11r
Steak, sirloin, U.S. choice, boneless	lb	5.65	7/01	11r
Strawberries, dry pint	12 oz	1.50	7/01	11r
Sugar and other sweets, expenditures on	yr	99	1999	30r
Sugar, white, 33-80 ounce package	lb	0.39	7/01	11r
Sugar, white, all sizes	lb	0.42	7/01	11r
Tobacco products and smoking supplies purchases	yr	288	1999	30r
Tomatoes, field grown	lb	1.43	7/01	11r
Tuna, light, chunk	lb	1.77	7/01	11r
Turkey, frozen, whole	lb	1.05	7/01	11r
Goods and Services				
B&B Japanese maple (acer japonicum)	gal	49.98-129.00	4/00	93r
Boxwood (buxus)	2 gal	12.99-16.99	4/00	93r
Daylilly (hemerocallis)	gal	4.99-8.99	4/00	93r
Flat of annuals		11.00-13.92	4/00	93r
Fountain grass (pennisetum)	gal	5.98-7.98	4/00	93r
Hanging basket (10 in)		7.99-14.98	4/00	93r
Hardy geranium (geranium)	gal	5.98-8.00	4/00	93r
Hosta (hosta)	gal	4.99-10.98	4/00	93r
Lilac (syrubga vulgaris)	2 gal	12.99-21.99	4/00	93r
Rhododendron (rhododendron)	2 gal	14.99-24.99	4/00	93r
Sage (salvia)	gal	5.98-6.99	4/00	93r
Wintercreeper euonymus (euonymus fortunei)	2 gal	7.99-89.99	4/00	93r
Hunting license	yr	11.00	4/01	34s
Health Care				
Cardiac catheterization, ave hospital/physician charges		10540	1998	77s
Childbirth, Cesarean delivery		11587	1997	13r
Childbirth, vaginal delivery		6725	1997	13r
Drugs, expenditures on	yr	399	1999	30r
Health care purchases	yr	1971	1999	30r
Health insurance expenditures	yr	933	1999	30r
Hysterectomy, laproscopically-assisted, ave hospital/physician charges		11620	1998	76s
Hysterectomy, vaginal, ave hospital and physician charges		8550	1998	76s
Medicaid dispensing fee		3.90-4.90	1999	87s
Medical services expenditures	yr	547	1999	30r
Medical supplies, expenditures on	yr	91	1999	30r
Plastic surgery, breast augmentation		2870	2000	7r
Plastic surgery, breast lift		3649	2000	7r
Plastic surgery, facelift		5008	2000	7r
Plastic surgery, hair transplantation		3425	2000	7r
Plastic surgery, lip augmentation		1227	2000	7r
Plastic surgery, lower body lift		4793	2000	7r

Parkersburg-Marietta, WV-OH - continued

Item	Per	Value	Date	Ref.
Health Care - continued				
Plastic surgery, thigh lift		3862	2000	7r
Household Goods				
Floor coverings, expenditures on	yr	44	1999	30r
Furniture, expenditures on	yr	335	1999	30r
Household furnishings and equipment purchases	yr	1328	1999	30r
Household textiles, expenditures on	yr	89	1999	30r
Laundry and cleaning supplies, expenditures on	yr	113	1999	30r
Housing				
Home price, existing, ave		160100	10/00	90r
Home value, median		93000	2001	53s
Household operation expenditures	yr	553	1999	30r
Housekeeping supplies purchases	yr	473	1999	30r
Housing, expenditures on	yr	10303	1999	30r
Maintenance, repairs, insurance expenditures	yr	699	1999	30r
Monthly rental value of owned home	mos	505	1999	30r
Owned dwellings, expenditures own	yr	3465	1999	30r
Rent expenditures	yr	1641	1999	30r
Rental unit, 1 bedroom, with utilities	mos	371	4/01	41c
Rental unit, 2 bedroom, with utilities	mos	424	4/01	41c
Rental unit, 3 bedroom, with utilities	mos	550	4/01	41c
Rental unit, 4 bedroom, with utilities	mos	597	4/01	41c
Shelter, expenditures on	yr	5467	1999	30r
Insurance and Pensions				
Life and other personal insurance purchases	yr	414	1999	30r
Pensions and Social Security, expenditures on	yr	2635	1999	30r
Personal insurance and pensions, expenditures on	yr	3048	1999	30r
Legal Fees				
Combination hunting and fishing license	yr	17.00	4/01	34s
Driver's license fee	orig	12.50	1999	48s
Driver's license fee	renew	12.50	1999	48s
Fishing license	yr	11.00	4/01	34s
Personal Goods				
Personal care products and services purchases	yr	393	1999	30r
Personal Services				
Personal services, household, expenditures on	yr	258	1999	30r
Pets				
Pets, toys, and playground equipment, expenditures on	yr	306	1999	30r
Taxes				
Federal income taxes paid	yr	2047	1999	30r
Personal taxes, expenditures on	yr	2554	1999	30r
Property taxes paid	yr	726	1999	30r
State and local income taxes paid	yr	363	1999	30r
Transportation				
Bus fare, one-way	trip	0.50	2000	1c
Cars and trucks, new, expenditures on	yr	1648	1999	30r
Cars and trucks, used, expenditures on	yr	1651	1999	30r
Diesel at the pump	gal	1.30	10/99	73s
Gasoline and motor oil purchases	yr	1052	1999	30r
Gasoline before-tax price (cents)	gal	108.80	10/00	43s
Maintenance and repair expenditures	yr	621	1999	30r
Public transportation, expenditures on	yr	298	1999	30r
Transportation purchases	yr	6738	1999	30r
Vehicle expenses, miscellaneous, purchases	yr	2033	1999	30r
Vehicle insurance payments	yr	696	1999	30r
Vehicle purchases (net outlay)	yr	3354	1999	30r
Vehicle rental, lease expenditures	yr	352	1999	30r
Utilities				
Electrical bill, average	mos	60.66	9/00	9s
Electricity, expenditures on	yr	1115	1999	30r

Values are in dollars or fractions of dollars. In the column headed *Ref*, references are shown to sources. Each reference is followed by a letter. These refer to the geographical level for which data were reported: s=State, r=Region, and c=City or metro. The abbreviation *ex* is used to mean *except* or *excluding*; *exp* stands for *expenditures*. For other abbreviations and further explanations, please see the Introduction.

Parkersburg-Marietta, WV-OH - continued

Item	Per	Value	Date	Ref.
Utilities				
Electricity, summer, 250 KWh	mos	19.56	2/96	96c
Electricity, summer, 500 KWh	mos	35.02	2/96	96c
Electricity, summer, 750 KWh	mos	50.48	2/96	96c
Electricity, summer, 1000 KWh	mos	65.94	2/96	96c
Electricity cost, average	KWh	5.20	9/00	9s
Water and other public services, expenditures on	yr	298	1999	30r
Weddings				
Wedding (national average cost)		19936	2000	33r
Wedding (regional average total cost)		16293	1997	110r
Attendants' gifts		321	1998	33r
Bridal attendants' apparel (5 persons)		824	2000	33r
Bride's headpiece/veil		173	1998	33r
Bride's wedding dress		859	1998	33r
Clergy, religious facility fee		242	1998	33r
Engagement ring		3177	1998	33r
Flowers		789	1998	33r
Groom's formalwear rental		99	2000	33r
Limousine		410	1998	33r
Marriage license cost		23.00	4/01	35s
Men's formalwear (ushers, best man)		469	2000	33r
Mother of bride apparel		241	2000	33r
Music		866	1998	33r
Photography and videography		1368	1998	33r
Rehearsal dinner		728	1998	33r
Wedding invitations and announcements		341	1998	33r
Wedding reception		7968	2000	33r
Wedding rings (bride and groom)		1060	1998	33r

Pensacola, FL

Item	Per	Value	Date	Ref.
Composite, ACCRA index		96.60	3/01	4c
Alcoholic Beverages				
Alcoholic beverage purchases	yr	253	1999	30r
Beer, Heineken, 12-oz, ex deposit	6	6.79	3/01	4c
J & B Scotch	750-ml	19.99	3/01	4c
Malt beverages, all types, all sizes, any origin	16 oz	0.96	7/01	11r
Wine, Livingston or Gallo, Chablis blanc	1.5 liter	6.09	3/01	4c
Appliances				
Appliance repair, service call, washing machine	min lab chg	38.40	3/01	4c
Major appliances, expenditures on	yr	172	1999	30r
Small appliances, housewares, expenditures on	yr	81	1999	30r
Banking and Money				
Mortgage interest and charges paid	yr	2039	1999	30r
Mortgage principal paid on owned property	yr	1026	1999	30r
Mortgage rate, incl. points and orig. fee, 30-yr. conv. fixed or ARM	mos	6.82	3/01	4c
Vehicle finance charges paid	yr	365	1999	30r
Charity				
Cash contributions, expenditures	yr	1127	1999	30r
Child Care				
Child raising cost, total, age 0-2	yr	8540	1999	60r
Child raising cost, total, age 3-5	yr	8780	1999	60r
Child raising cost, total, age 6-8	yr	8820	1999	60r
Child raising cost, total, age 9-11	yr	8800	1999	60r
Child raising cost, total, age 12-14	yr	9510	1999	60r
Child raising cost, total, age 15-17	yr	9740	1999	60r
Child's child care and education, age 0-2	yr	1380	1999	60r
Child's child care and education, age 3-5	yr	1520	1999	60r
Child's child care and education, age 6-8	yr	990	1999	60r
Child's child care and education, age 9-11	yr	650	1999	60r
Child's child care and education, age 12-14	yr	490	1999	60r
Child's child care and education, age 15-17	yr	840	1999	60r
Child's clothing, age 0-2	yr	480	1999	60r
Child's clothing, age 3-5	yr	470	1999	60r
Child's clothing, age 6-8	yr	520	1999	60r

Pensacola, FL - continued

Item	Per	Value	Date	Ref.
Child Care - continued				
Child's clothing, age 9-11	yr	570	1999	60r
Child's clothing, age 12-14	yr	950	1999	60r
Child's clothing, age 15-17	yr	850	1999	60r
Child's food, age 0-2	yr	1000	1999	60r
Child's food, age 3-5	yr	1160	1999	60r
Child's food, age 6-8	yr	1490	1999	60r
Child's food, age 9-11	yr	1770	1999	60r
Child's food, age 12-14	yr	1770	1999	60r
Child's food, age 15-17	yr	1980	1999	60r
Child's health care, age 0-2	yr	620	1999	60r
Child's health care, age 3-5	yr	590	1999	60r
Child's health care, age 6-8	yr	680	1999	60r
Child's health care, age 9-11	yr	720	1999	60r
Child's health care, age 12-14	yr	730	1999	60r
Child's health care, age 15-17	yr	760	1999	60r
Child's housing, age 0-2	yr	3070	1999	60r
Child's housing, age 3-5	yr	3050	1999	60r
Child's housing, age 6-8	yr	3010	1999	60r
Child's housing, age 9-11	yr	2850	1999	60r
Child's housing, age 12-14	yr	3040	1999	60r
Child's housing, age 15-17	yr	2650	1999	60r
Child's personal care, reading, age 0-2	yr	910	1999	60r
Child's personal care, reading, age 3-5	yr	930	1999	60r
Child's personal care, reading, age 6-8	yr	960	1999	60r
Child's personal care, reading, age 9-11	yr	1000	1999	60r
Child's personal care, reading, age 12-14	yr	1170	1999	60r
Child's personal care, reading, age 15-17	yr	950	1999	60r
Clothing				
Apparel and services purchases	yr	1610	1999	30r
Boys' brief, cotton	3	6.99	3/01	4c
Boys, 2 to 15, expenditures on	yr	89	1999	30r
Children under 2, expenditures on	yr	79	1999	30r
Footwear, expenditures on	yr	283	1999	30r
Girls, 2 to 15, expenditures on	yr	103	1999	30r
Men and boys, expenditures on	yr	351	1999	30r
Men, 16 and over, expenditures on	yr	262	1999	30r
Shirt, man's dress shirt		22.49	3/01	4c
Slacks, man's "No Wrinkles" khaki		28.99	3/01	4c
Women, 16 and over, expenditures on	yr	538	1999	30r
Communications				
Cable modem installation, Adelphi		54.90	6/99	103s
Cable modem installation, Comcast		95.00	6/99	103s
Cable modem installation, Media One		100.00	6/99	103s
Cable modem installation, Time Warner		75.00-225.00	6/99	103s
Cable modem rate, cable subscriber, Adelphi	mos	34.95	6/99	103s
Cable modem rate, cable subscriber, Comcast	mos	39.95	6/99	103s
Cable modem rate, cable subscriber, Media One	mos	34.95-39.95	6/99	103s
Cable modem rate, cable subscriber, Time Warner	mos	39.95-49.95	6/99	103s
Cable modem rate, non-cable subscriber, Adelphi	mos	44.95	6/99	103s
Cable modem rate, non-cable subscriber, Comcast	mos	49.95	6/99	103s
Cable modem rate, non-cable subscriber, Media One	mos	49.95	6/99	103s
Cable modem rate, non-cable subscriber, Time Warner	mos	39.95-54.95	6/99	103s
Newspaper subscription, daily and Sunday delivery	mos	18.65	3/01	4c
Phone line, single, business, field visit	inst.	56.00	12/97	17s
Phone line, single, business, no field visit	inst.	56.00	12/97	17s
Phone line, single, residence, field visit	inst.	40.00	12/97	17s
Phone line, single, residence, no field visit	inst.	40.00	12/97	17s
Postage and stationery, expenditures on	yr	104	1999	30r
Postal rate, express mail, up to half-pound		12.45	7/01	108r
Postal rate, letter, first class, first ounce		0.34	7/01	108r
Postal rate, letter, two ounces		0.57	7/01	108r
Postal rate, post card		0.21	7/01	108r

Values are in dollars or fractions of dollars. In the column headed *Ref*, references are shown to sources. Each reference is followed by a letter. These refer to the geographical level for which data were reported: s=State, r=Region, and c=City or metro. The abbreviation *ex* is used to mean *except* or *excluding*; *exp* stands for *expenditures*. For other abbreviations and further explanations, please see the Introduction.

Pensacola, FL - continued

Item	Per	Value	Date	Ref.
Communications				
Postal rate, priority mail, two pounds		3.95	7/01	108r
Postal rate, priority mail, up to one pound		3.50	7/01	108r
Telephone bill, family of three	mos	15.96	3/01	4c
Telephone services, expenditures on	yr	860	1999	30r
Education				
Board, 4-year private college/university	yr	2236	1996	38s
Board, 4-year public college/university	yr	2295	1996	38s
Education expenditures	yr	431	1999	30r
Room, 4-year private college/university	yr	2428	1996	38s
Room, 4-year public college/university	yr	2193	1996	38s
Total cost, 4-year private college/university	yr	15028	1996	38s
Total cost, 4-year public college/university	yr	6254	1996	38s
Tuition, 2-year public college/university, in state	yr	1103	1996	38s
Tuition, 4-year private college/university, in state	yr	10364	1996	38s
Tuition, 4-year public college/university	yr	1767	1996	38s
Energy and Fuels				
Electricity	500 KWhs	47.29	7/01	11r
Electricity	KWh	0.09	7/01	11r
Energy, combined forms, 2400 sq ft	mos	111.89	3/01	4c
Energy, exc. electricity, 2400 sq ft	mos	49.90	3/01	4c
Fuel oil #2	gal	1.43	7/01	11r
Fuel oil and other fuels, expenditures on	yr	45	1999	30r
Gas, natural, commercial rate	1000 cf	8.44	11/00	88s
Gas, regular unleaded, cash, self-service	gal	1.34	3/01	4c
Gasoline, all types	gal	1.60	7/01	11r
Gasoline, unleaded midgrade	gal	1.65	7/01	11r
Gasoline, unleaded premium	gal	1.74	7/01	11r
Natural gas, expenditures on	yr	164	1999	30r
Utility (piped) gas, therm		1.01	7/01	11r
Utility (piped) gas, 40 therms		44.29	7/01	11r
Utility (piped) gas, 100 therms		97.44	7/01	11r
Entertainment				
Bowling, Saturday evening rate	line	2.69	3/01	4c
Entertainment purchases	yr	1574	1999	30r
Fees and admissions paid	yr	371	1999	30r
Monopoly game, Parker Brothers', No. 9	game	11.15	3/01	4c
Movie, first-run, Saturday, evening	adm.	6.75	3/01	4c
Reading purchases	yr	121	1999	30r
Television, radios, sound equipment, expenditures on	yr	561	1999	30r
Tennis balls, yellow, Wilson or Penn, 3	can	2.39	3/01	4c
Funerals				
Total cost of funeral		5922.53	1/99	78r
Acknowledgement cards		63.43	1/99	78r
Casket		2258.77	1/99	78r
Cosmetology, hair, other preparation		127.09	1/99	78r
Embalming		393.49	1/99	78r
Funeral at funeral home		367.50	1/99	78r
Hearse (local)		169.66	1/99	78r
Professional service charges		1211.32	1/99	78r
Service car/van		80.69	1/99	78r
Transfer of remains to funeral home		144.25	1/99	78r
Vault		803.50	1/99	78r
Visitation/viewing		302.83	1/99	78r
Groceries				
Groceries, ACCRA Index		99.00	3/01	4c
American processed cheese	lb	3.50	7/01	11r
Antibiotic ointment, Polysporin	0.5 oz	4.69	3/01	4c
Baby food, strained vegetables or fruit, lowest price	4-4.5 oz	0.34	3/01	4c
Bakery products, expenditures on	yr	261	1999	30r
Bananas	lb	0.51	3/01	4c
Bananas	lb	0.47	7/01	11r
Beans, dried, any type, all sizes	lb	0.63	7/01	11r
Beef for stew, boneless	lb	2.86	7/01	11r
Beef or hamburger, ground	lb	1.54	3/01	4c

Item	Per	Value	Date	Ref.
Groceries - continued				
Beef, expenditures on	yr	210	1999	30r
Bologna, all beef or mixed	lb	2.29	7/01	11r
Bread, French	lb	1.66	7/01	11r
Bread, white	loaf	0.91	3/01	4c
Bread, white, pan	lb	0.87	7/01	11r
Bread, whole wheat, pan	lb	1.38	7/01	11r
Broccoli	lb	1.04	7/01	11r
Butter, salted, grade AA, stick	lb	2.26	7/01	11r
Butter, yoghurt, cheese, etc, expenditures on	yr	170	1999	30r
Cabbage	lb	0.42	7/01	11r
Cereals and cereal products, expenditures on	yr	140	1999	30r
Cheddar cheese, natural	lb	3.75	7/01	11r
Cheese, Kraft grated Parmesan	8 oz	3.51	3/01	4c
Chicken breast, bone-in	lb	1.85	7/01	11r
Chicken legs, bone-in	lb	1.34	7/01	11r
Chicken, fresh, whole	lb	1.05	7/01	11r
Chicken, whole fryer	lb	1.01	3/01	4c
Chops, boneless,	lb	4.13	7/01	11r
Chuck roast, graded and ungraded, excl U.S. prime and choice	lb	2.35	7/01	11r
Chuck roast, U.S. choice, boneless	lb	2.67	7/01	11r
Cigarettes, Winston, Kings	carton	31.06	3/01	4c
Coffee, 100%, ground roast, all sizes	lb	2.88	7/01	11r
Coffee, instant, plain, regular, all sizes	16 oz	9.25	7/01	11r
Coffee, vacuum-packed	13 oz	2.48	3/01	4c
Cola, non diet	2 liter	1.11	7/01	11r
Corn Flakes, Kellogg's or Post Toasties	18 oz	2.98	3/01	4c
Corn, frozen, whole kernel, lowest price	16 oz	1.01	3/01	4c
Crackers, soda, salted	lb	1.70	7/01	11r
Dairy product purchases	yr	282	1999	30r
Eggs, expenditures on	yr	32	1999	30r
Eggs, Grade A or AA	dozen	1.01	3/01	4c
Fats and oils, expenditures on	yr	79	1999	30r
Fish and seafood, expenditures on	yr	99	1999	30r
Flour, white, all purpose	lb	0.32	7/01	11r
Food (excl fruit and vegetables), eaten at home, purchases	yr	815	1999	30r
Food cooked on trips, expenditures on	yr	36	1999	30r
Food purchases	yr	4533	1999	30r
Food purchases, eaten away from home	yr	1873	1999	30r
Food purchases, food eaten at home	yr	2660	1999	30r
Fresh fruits, expenditures on	yr	128	1999	30r
Fresh milk and cream, expenditures on	yr	112	1999	30r
Fresh vegetables, expenditures on	yr	131	1999	30r
Fruit and vegetable purchases	yr	438	1999	30r
Grapefruit	lb	0.59	7/01	11r
Grapes, Thompson, seedless	lb	2.12	7/01	11r
Ground beef, 100% beef	lb	1.76	7/01	11r
Ground beef, lean and extra lean	lb	2.60	7/01	11r
Ground chuck, 100% beef	lb	2.08	7/01	11r
Ham, boneless, excl canned	lb	2.71	7/01	11r
Ham, rump or shank half, bone-in, smoked	lb	2.19	7/01	11r
Ice cream, prepackaged, bulk, regular	1/2 gal	3.93	7/01	11r
Lemons	lb	1.32	7/01	11r
Lettuce, iceberg	head	1.09	3/01	4c
Lettuce, iceberg	lb	0.76	7/01	11r
Margarine, Blue Bonnet or Parkay, stick	lb	0.75	3/01	4c
Milk, fresh, low fat,	gal	2.75	7/01	11r
Milk, fresh, whole, fortified	gal	2.97	7/01	11r
Milk, whole	1/2 gal	1.69	3/01	4c
Nonalcoholic beverages, expenditures on	yr	228	1999	30r
Orange juice, frozen concentrate	16 oz	1.95	7/01	11r
Orange juice, Minute Maid frozen	12 oz	1.80	3/01	4c
Oranges, Navel	lb	0.73	7/01	11r
Oranges, Valencia	lb	0.55	7/01	11r
Peaches, halves or slices, Hunt's, Del Monte, or Libby's	29 oz	1.54	3/01	4c
Peanut butter, creamy, all sizes	lb	1.83	7/01	11r
Pears, Anjou	lb	0.98	7/01	11r
Peas, green, Del Monte or Green Giant	15 oz	0.65	3/01	4c
Pork chops, center cut, bone-in	lb	3.33	7/01	11r

Values are in dollars or fractions of dollars. In the column headed *Ref*, references are shown to sources. Each reference is followed by a letter. These refer to the geographical level for which data were reported: s=State, r=Region, and c=City or metro. The abbreviation *ex* is used to mean *except* or *excluding*; *exp* stands for expenditures. For other abbreviations and further explanations, please see the Introduction.

Pensacola, FL - continued

Item	Per	Value	Date	Ref.
Groceries				
Pork sausage, fresh, loose	lb	2.59	7/01	11r
Pork shoulder picnic, bone-in, smoked	lb	1.12	7/01	11r
Pork, expenditures on	yr	162	1999	30r
Potato chips	16 oz	3.59	7/01	11r
Potatoes, frozen, french fried	lb	1.00	7/01	11r
Potatoes, white or red	10 lb	3.19	3/01	4c
Potatoes, white, all types	lb	0.44	7/01	11r
Poultry, expenditures on	yr	137	1999	30r
Processed fruits, expenditures on	yr	97	1999	30r
Processed vegetables, expenditures on	yr	82	1999	30r
Rice, white, long grain, uncooked	lb	0.51	7/01	11r
Round roast, graded and ungraded, excl U.S. prime and choice	lb	2.96	7/01	11r
Round steak, graded and ungraded, excl U.S. prime and choice	lb	3.11	7/01	11r
Sausage, Jimmy Dean/Owens pork	lb	2.69	3/01	4c
Shortening, vegetable, Crisco	3 lb	3.06	3/01	4c
Sirloin steak, graded and ungraded, excl U.S. prime and choice	lb	4.23	7/01	11r
Soft drink, Coca Cola, ex deposit	2 liter	1.08	3/01	4c
Spaghetti and macaroni	lb	0.78	7/01	11r
Steak, round, U.S. choice, boneless	lb	3.56	7/01	11r
Steak, sirloin, U.S. choice, boneless	lb	5.65	7/01	11r
Steak, T-bone	lb	6.71	3/01	4c
Strawberries, dry pint	12 oz	1.50	7/01	11r
Sugar and other sweets, expenditures on	yr	99	1999	30r
Sugar, cane or beet	4 lbs	1.48	3/01	4c
Sugar, white, 33-80 ounce package	lb	0.39	7/01	11r
Sugar, white, all sizes	lb	0.42	7/01	11r
Tobacco products and smoking supplies purchases	yr	288	1999	30r
Tomatoes, field grown	lb	1.43	7/01	11r
Tomatoes, Hunt's or Del Monte	14.5 oz	0.81	3/01	4c
Tuna, chunk, light	6 oz	0.58	3/01	4c
Tuna, light, chunk	lb	1.77	7/01	11r
Turkey, frozen, whole	lb	1.05	7/01	11r
Goods and Services				
Miscellaneous goods and services, ACCRA Index		98.20	3/01	4c
B&B Japanese maple (acer japonicum)	gal	49.98-129.00	4/00	93r
Boxwood (buxus)	2 gal	12.99-16.99	4/00	93r
Daylily (hemerocallis)	gal	4.99-8.99	4/00	93r
Flat of annuals		11.00-13.92	4/00	93r
Fountain grass (pennisetum)	gal	5.98-7.98	4/00	93r
Hanging basket (10 in)		7.99-14.98	4/00	93r
Hardy geranium (geranium)	gal	5.98-8.00	4/00	93r
Hosta (hosta)	gal	4.99-10.98	4/00	93r
Lilac (syrubga vulgaris)	2 gal	12.99-21.99	4/00	93r
Rhododendron (rhododendron)	2 gal	14.99-24.99	4/00	93r
Sage (salvia)	gal	5.98-6.99	4/00	93r
Wintercreeper euonymus (euonymus fortunei)	2 gal	7.99-89.99	4/00	93r
Hunting license	yr	12.50	4/01	34s
Health Care				
Health care, ACCRA Index		107.10	3/01	4c
Cardiac catheterization, ave hospital/ physician charges		15060	1998	77s
Childbirth, Cesarean delivery		11587	1997	13r
Childbirth, vaginal delivery		6725	1997	13r

Pensacola, FL - continued

Item	Per	Value	Date	Ref.
Health Care - continued				
Dentist's fee, adult teeth cleaning and periodic oral exam	visit	70.20	3/01	4c
Doctor's fee, routine exam, established patient	visit	64.50	3/01	4c
Drugs, expenditures on	yr	399	1999	30r
Health care purchases	yr	1971	1999	30r
Health insurance expenditures	yr	933	1999	30r
Home health care aide cost, licensed agency	hour	14	2000	82c
Hospital care, private room	day	642.67	3/01	4c
Hysterectomy, laproscopically-assisted, ave hospital/physician charges		14760	1998	76s
Hysterectomy, vaginal, ave hospital and physician charges		11320	1998	76s
Medicaid dispensing fee		4.23	1999	87s
Medical services expenditures	yr	547	1999	30r
Medical supplies, expenditures on	yr	91	1999	30r
Nursing home costs, private room	day	123	2000	82c
Nursing home stay, private room	day	123	2000	81c
Plastic surgery, breast augmentation		2870	2000	7r
Plastic surgery, breast lift		3649	2000	7r
Plastic surgery, facelift		5008	2000	7r
Plastic surgery, hair transplantation		3425	2000	7r
Plastic surgery, lip augmentation		1227	2000	7r
Plastic surgery, lower body lift		4793	2000	7r
Plastic surgery, thigh lift		3862	2000	7r
Household Goods				
Dishwashing powder, Cascade	50 oz	3.41	3/01	4c
Floor coverings, expenditures on	yr	44	1999	30r
Furniture, expenditures on	yr	335	1999	30r
Household furnishings and equipment purchases	yr	1328	1999	30r
Household textiles, expenditures on	yr	89	1999	30r
Laundry and cleaning supplies, expenditures on	yr	113	1999	30r
Tissues, facial, Kleenex brand	175	1.43	3/01	4c
Housing				
Housing, ACCRA Index		93.30	3/01	4c
Home, 2200 sq ft, 4-br, 2-bath, 2-car garage, average		156125	2000	47c
Home price, existing, ave		160100	10/00	90r
Home value, median		104000	2001	53s
House, 2400 sq ft, 8000 sq ft lot, new, urban, utilities	total	195560	3/01	4c
House payment, principal and interest, 25% down payment	mos	959	3/01	4c
Household operation expenditures	yr	553	1999	30r
Housekeeping supplies purchases	yr	473	1999	30r
Housing, expenditures on	yr	10303	1999	30r
Maintenance, repairs, insurance expenditures	yr	699	1999	30r
Monthly rental value of owned home	mos	505	1999	30r
Owned dwellings, expenditures own	yr	3465	1999	30r
Rent expenditures	yr	1641	1999	30r
Rent, apartment, 2 br, 1 1/2-2 baths, unfurn, 950 sq ft, water	mos	656	3/01	4c
Rental unit, 1 bedroom, with utilities	mos	451	4/01	41c
Rental unit, 2 bedroom, with utilities	mos	512	4/01	41c
Rental unit, 3 bedroom, with utilities	mos	684	4/01	41c
Rental unit, 4 bedroom, with utilities	mos	806	4/01	41c
Shelter, expenditures on	yr	5467	1999	30r
Insurance and Pensions				
Life and other personal insurance purchases	yr	414	1999	30r
Medigap health insurance, Plan H	yr	2887	2000	69s
Medigap health insurance, Plan I	yr	3302	2000	69s
Medigap health insurance, Plan J	yr	3889	2000	69s
Pensions and Social Security, expenditures on	yr	2635	1999	30r
Personal insurance and pensions, expenditures on	yr	3048	1999	30r

Values are in dollars or fractions of dollars. In the column headed *Ref*, references are shown to sources. Each reference is followed by a letter. These refer to the geographical level for which data were reported: s=State, r=Region, and c=City or metro. The abbreviation *ex* is used to mean *except* or *excluding*; *exp* stands for *expenditures*. For other abbreviations and further explanations, please see the Introduction.

Pensacola, FL - continued

Item	Per	Value	Date	Ref.
Legal Fees				
Divorce, filing fee		65.00-85.00	4/01	35s
Driver's license fee	renew	15.00	1999	48s
Driver's license fee	orig	20.00	1999	48s
Personal Goods				
Personal care products and services purchases	yr	393	1999	30r
Shampoo, Alberto VO5	15 oz	1.13	3/01	4c
Toothpaste, Crest or Colgate	6-7 oz	2.63	3/01	4c
Personal Services				
Dry cleaning, man's 2-pc suit		7.88	3/01	4c
Man's haircut, barbershop, no styling		11.95	3/01	4c
Personal services, household, expenditures on	yr	258	1999	30r
Woman's shampoo, trim, blow-dry, no style-change		23.66	3/01	4c
Pets				
Pets, toys, and playground equipment, expenditures on	yr	306	1999	30r
Restaurant Food				
Chicken, fried, thigh and drumstick, KFC/Church's		2.59	3/01	4c
Hamburger with cheese, McDonald's	1/4 lb	1.99	3/01	4c
Pizza, Pizza Hut or Pizza Inn	11-12 in	9.49	3/01	4c
Taxes				
Federal income taxes paid	yr	2047	1999	30r
Personal taxes, expenditures on	yr	2554	1999	30r
Property taxes paid	yr	726	1999	30r
State and local income taxes paid	yr	363	1999	30r
Transportation				
Transportation, ACCRA Index		97.40	3/01	4c
Bus fare, one-way	trip	1.00	2000	1c
Cars and trucks, new, expenditures on	yr	1648	1999	30r
Cars and trucks, used, expenditures on	yr	1651	1999	30r
Diesel at the pump	gal	1.26	10/99	73s
Gasoline and motor oil purchases	yr	1052	1999	30r
Gasoline before-tax price (cents)	gal	101.90	10/00	43s
Maintenance and repair expenditures	yr	621	1999	30r
Public transportation, expenditures on	yr	298	1999	30r
Tire balance, computer or spin balance, front	wheel	7.90	3/01	4c
Transportation purchases	yr	6738	1999	30r
Vehicle expenses, miscellaneous, purchases	yr	2033	1999	30r
Vehicle insurance payments	yr	696	1999	30r
Vehicle purchases (net outlay)	yr	3354	1999	30r
Vehicle rental, lease expenditures	yr	352	1999	30r
Travel				
Hotel room	night	110.57	2/01	95s
Utilities				
Utilities, ACCRA Index		89.20	3/01	4c
Electrical bill, average	mos	86.33	9/00	9s
Electricity, expenditures on	yr	1115	1999	30r
Electricity, summer, 250 KWh	mos	22.75	2/96	97c
Electricity, summer, 750 KWh	mos	54.39	2/96	97c
Electricity, summer, 1000 KWh	mos	69.80	2/96	97c
Electricity and other, mixed, 2400 sq ft, new home	mos	61.99	3/01	4c
Electricity cost, average	KWh	6.80	9/00	9s
Water and other public services, expenditures on	yr	298	1999	30r
Weddings				
Wedding (national average cost)		19936	2000	33r
Wedding (regional average total cost)		16293	1997	110r
Attendants' gifts		321	1998	33r
Bridal attendants' apparel (5 persons)		824	2000	33r
Bride's headpiece/veil		173	1998	33r
Bride's wedding dress		859	1998	33r
Clergy, religious facility fee		242	1998	33r

Pensacola, FL - continued

Item	Per	Value	Date	Ref.
Weddings - continued				
Engagement ring		3177	1998	33r
Flowers		789	1998	33r
Groom's formalwear rental		99	2000	33r
Limousine		410	1998	33r
Marriage license cost		56.00-88.50	4/01	35s
Men's formalwear (ushers, best man)		469	2000	33r
Mother of bride apparel		241	2000	33r
Music		866	1998	33r
Photography and videography		1368	1998	33r
Rehearsal dinner		728	1998	33r
Wedding invitations and announcements		341	1998	33r
Wedding reception		7968	2000	33r
Wedding rings (bride and groom)		1060	1998	33r

Peoria-Pekin, IL

Item	Per	Value	Date	Ref.
Average annual expenditures	yr	35369	1999	30r
Alcoholic Beverages				
Alcoholic beverage purchases	yr	304	1999	30r
Malt beverages, all types, all sizes, any origin	16 oz	0.93	7/01	11r
Wine, red and white table, all sizes, any origin	liter	7.04	7/01	11r
Appliances				
Major appliances, expenditures on	yr	165	1999	30r
Small appliances, housewares, expenditures on	yr	90	1999	30r
Banking and Money				
Mortgage interest and charges paid	yr	2277	1999	30r
Mortgage principal paid on owned property	yr	1230	1999	30r
Vehicle finance charges paid	yr	328	1999	30r
Charity				
Cash contributions, expenditures	yr	1126	1999	30r
Child Care				
Child raising cost, total, age 0-2	yr	7890	1999	60r
Child raising cost, total, age 3-5	yr	8130	1999	60r
Child raising cost, total, age 6-8	yr	8170	1999	60r
Child raising cost, total, age 9-11	yr	8190	1999	60r
Child raising cost, total, age 12-14	yr	8890	1999	60r
Child raising cost, total, age 15-17	yr	9050	1999	60r
Child's child care and education, age 0-2	yr	1240	1999	60r
Child's child care and education, age 3-5	yr	1370	1999	60r
Child's child care and education, age 6-8	yr	880	1999	60r
Child's child care and education, age 9-11	yr	570	1999	60r
Child's child care and education, age 12-14	yr	420	1999	60r
Child's child care and education, age 15-17	yr	720	1999	60r
Child's clothing, age 0-2	yr	410	1999	60r
Child's clothing, age 3-5	yr	400	1999	60r
Child's clothing, age 6-8	yr	450	1999	60r
Child's clothing, age 9-11	yr	500	1999	60r
Child's clothing, age 12-14	yr	840	1999	60r
Child's clothing, age 15-17	yr	740	1999	60r
Child's food, age 0-2	yr	960	1999	60r
Child's food, age 3-5	yr	1120	1999	60r
Child's food, age 6-8	yr	1430	1999	60r
Child's food, age 9-11	yr	1710	1999	60r
Child's food, age 12-14	yr	1710	1999	60r
Child's food, age 15-17	yr	1920	1999	60r
Child's health care, age 0-2	yr	520	1999	60r
Child's health care, age 3-5	yr	500	1999	60r
Child's health care, age 6-8	yr	570	1999	60r
Child's health care, age 9-11	yr	610	1999	60r
Child's health care, age 12-14	yr	630	1999	60r
Child's health care, age 15-17	yr	650	1999	60r
Child's housing, age 0-2	yr	2860	1999	60r
Child's housing, age 3-5	yr	2840	1999	60r
Child's housing, age 6-8	yr	2800	1999	60r
Child's housing, age 9-11	yr	2650	1999	60r
Child's housing, age 12-14	yr	2840	1999	60r

Values are in dollars or fractions of dollars. In the column headed *Ref*, references are shown to sources. Each reference is followed by a letter. These refer to the geographical level for which data were reported: s=State, r=Region, and c=City or metro. The abbreviation *ex* is used to mean *except* or *excluding*; *exp* stands for expenditures. For other abbreviations and further explanations, please see the Introduction.

Peoria-Pekin, IL - continued

Item	Per	Value	Date	Ref.
Child Care				
Child's housing, age 15-17	yr	2440	1999	60r
Child's personal care, reading, age 0-2	yr	880	1999	60r
Child's personal care, reading, age 3-5	yr	900	1999	60r
Child's personal care, reading, age 6-8	yr	930	1999	60r
Child's personal care, reading, age 9-11	yr	970	1999	60r
Child's personal care, reading, age 12-14	yr	1150	1999	60r
Child's personal care, reading, age 15-17	yr	920	1999	60r
Clothing				
Apparel and services purchases	yr	1607	1999	30r
Boys, 2 to 15, expenditures on	yr	91	1999	30r
Children under 2, expenditures on	yr	59	1999	30r
Footwear, expenditures on	yr	285	1999	30r
Girls, 2 to 15, expenditures on	yr	116	1999	30r
Men and boys, expenditures on	yr	433	1999	30r
Men, 16 and over, expenditures on	yr	341	1999	30r
Women, 16 and over, expenditures on	yr	490	1999	30r
Communications				
Cable modem installation, Adelphi		54.90	6/99	103s
Cable modem installation, AT&T-BIS		150.00	6/99	103s
Cable modem installation, Media One		100.00	6/99	103s
Cable modem rate, cable subscriber, Adelphi	mos	34.95	6/99	103s
Cable modem rate, cable subscriber, AT&T-BIS	mos	39.95	6/99	103s
Cable modem rate, cable subscriber, Media One	mos	34.95-39.95	6/99	103s
Cable modem rate, non-cable subscriber, Adelphi	mos	44.95	6/99	103s
Cable modem rate, non-cable subscriber, Media One	mos	49.95	6/99	103s
Phone line, single, business, field visit	inst.	52.35	12/97	17s
Phone line, single, business, no field visit	inst.	52.35	12/97	17s
Phone line, single, residence, field visit	inst.	55.00	12/97	17s
Phone line, single, residence, no field visit	inst.	55.00	12/97	17s
Postage and stationery, expenditures on	yr	140	1999	30r
Postal rate, express mail, up to half-pound		12.45	7/01	108r
Postal rate, letter, first class, first ounce		0.34	7/01	108r
Postal rate, letter, two ounces		0.57	7/01	108r
Postal rate, post card		0.21	7/01	108r
Postal rate, priority mail, two pounds		3.95	7/01	108r
Postal rate, priority mail, up to one pound		3.50	7/01	108r
Telephone services, expenditures on	yr	830	1999	30r
Education				
Board, 4-year private college/university	yr	2306	1996	38s
Board, 4-year public college/university	yr	2405	1996	38s
Education expenditures	yr	583	1999	30r
Room, 4-year private college/university	yr	2718	1996	38s
Room, 4-year public college/university	yr	2072	1996	38s
Total cost, 4-year private college/university	yr	16678	1996	38s
Total cost, 4-year public college/university	yr	7829	1996	38s
Tuition, 2-year public college/university, in state	yr	1232	1996	38s
Tuition, 4-year private college/university, in state	yr	11653	1996	38s
Tuition, 4-year public college/university	yr	3352	1996	38s
Energy and Fuels				
Electricity	500 KWhs	46.59	7/01	11r
Fuel oil #2	gal	1.27	7/01	11r
Fuel oil and other fuels, expenditures on	yr	68	1999	30r
Gas, natural, commercial rate	1000 cf	8.47	11/00	88s
Gasoline, unleaded midgrade	gal	1.79	7/01	11r
Gasoline, unleaded premium	gal	1.86	7/01	11r
Gasoline, unleaded regular	gal	1.58	7/01	11r
Natural gas, expenditures on	yr	389	1999	30r
Utility (piped) gas, therm		0.81	7/01	11r
Utility (piped) gas, 40 therms		38.01	7/01	11r
Utility (piped) gas, 100 therms		81.75	7/01	11r
Entertainment				
Entertainment purchases	yr	1984	1999	30r

Peoria-Pekin, IL - continued

Item	Per	Value	Date	Ref.
Entertainment - continued				
Fees and admissions paid	yr	444	1999	30r
Television, radios, sound equipment, expenditures on	yr	580	1999	30r
Funerals				
Cosmetology, hair, other preparation		178.32	1/99	78r
Embalming		408.19	1/99	78r
Funeral at funeral home		362.13	1/99	78r
Professional service charges		1375.51	1/99	78r
Transfer of remains to funeral home		155.92	1/99	78r
Visitation/viewing		294.38	1/99	78r
Groceries				
Bacon, sliced	lb	3.15	7/01	11r
Bakery products, expenditures on	yr	281	1999	30r
Bananas	lb	0.48	7/01	11r
Beans, dried, any type, all sizes	lb	0.61	7/01	11r
Beef for stew, boneless	lb	3.08	7/01	11r
Beef, expenditures on	yr	217	1999	30r
Bologna, all beef or mixed	lb	2.52	7/01	11r
Bread, white, pan	lb	1.06	7/01	11r
Broccoli	lb	0.91	7/01	11r
Butter, salted, grade AA, stick	lb	3.04	7/01	11r
Butter, yoghurt, cheese, etc, expenditures on	yr	183	1999	30r
Cereals and bakery product purchases	yr	430	1999	30r
Cereals and cereal products, expenditures on	yr	149	1999	30r
Chicken, fresh, whole	lb	1.07	7/01	11r
Chops, boneless,	lb	3.64	7/01	11r
Chuck roast, U.S. choice, boneless	lb	2.47	7/01	11r
Coffee, 100%, ground roast, all sizes	lb	2.69	7/01	11r
Cookies, chocolate chip	lb	2.87	7/01	11r
Dairy product purchases	yr	304	1999	30r
Eggs, expenditures on	yr	26	1999	30r
Eggs, grade A, large	dozen	0.88	7/01	11r
Fats and oils, expenditures on	yr	75	1999	30r
Fish and seafood, expenditures on	yr	72	1999	30r
Food (excl fruit and vegetables), eaten at home, purchases	yr	887	1999	30r
Food cooked on trips, expenditures on	yr	44	1999	30r
Food purchases	yr	4802	1999	30r
Food purchases, eaten away from home	yr	2069	1999	30r
Food purchases, food eaten at home	yr	2733	1999	30r
Fresh fruits, expenditures on	yr	138	1999	30r
Fresh milk and cream, expenditures on	yr	120	1999	30r
Fresh vegetables, expenditures on	yr	126	1999	30r
Grapefruit	lb	0.66	7/01	11r
Grapes, Thompson, seedless	lb	1.64	7/01	11r
Ground beef, 100% beef	lb	1.64	7/01	11r
Ground beef, lean and extra lean	lb	2.16	7/01	11r
Ground chuck, 100% beef	lb	2.13	7/01	11r
Ham, boneless, excl canned	lb	2.62	7/01	11r
Ice cream, prepackaged, bulk, regular	1/2 gal	3.35	7/01	11r
Lemons	lb	1.19	7/01	11r
Lettuce, iceberg	lb	0.73	7/01	11r
Margarine, soft, tubs	lb	0.89	7/01	11r
Meats, poultry, fish, and egg purchases	yr	671	1999	30r
Milk, fresh, whole, fortified	gal	2.71	7/01	11r
Nonalcoholic beverages, expenditures on	yr	239	1999	30r
Oranges, Navel	lb	0.80	7/01	11r
Oranges, Valencia	lb	0.66	7/01	11r
Pears, Anjou	lb	0.93	7/01	11r
Pork chops, center cut, bone-in	lb	3.63	7/01	11r
Pork, expenditures on	yr	150	1999	30r
Potato chips	16 oz	3.52	7/01	11r
Potatoes, frozen, french fried	lb	1.08	7/01	11r
Potatoes, white, all types	lb	0.33	7/01	11r
Poultry, expenditures on	yr	108	1999	30r
Processed fruits, expenditures on	yr	98	1999	30r
Processed vegetables, expenditures on	yr	80	1999	30r
Round roast, U.S. choice, boneless	lb	3.07	7/01	11r
Round steak, graded and ungraded, excl U.S. prime and choice	lb	3.41	7/01	11r

Values are in dollars or fractions of dollars. In the column headed *Ref*, references are shown to sources. Each reference is followed by a letter. These refer to the geographical level for which data were reported: s=State, r=Region, and c=City or metro. The abbreviation *ex* is used to mean *except* or *excluding*; *exp* stands for expenditures. For other abbreviations and further explanations, please see the Introduction.

Peoria-Pekin, IL - continued

Item	Per	Value	Date	Ref.
Groceries				
Shortening, vegetable oil blends	lb	1.13	7/01	11r
Spaghetti and macaroni	lb	0.80	7/01	11r
Steak, round, U.S. choice, boneless	lb	3.23	7/01	11r
Steak, T-bone, U.S. choice, bone-in	lb	6.68	7/01	11r
Strawberries, dry pint	12 oz	1.32	7/01	11r
Sugar and other sweets, expenditures on	yr	114	1999	30r
Sugar, white, 33-80 ounce package	lb	0.42	7/01	11r
Sugar, white, all sizes	lb	0.43	7/01	11r
Tobacco products and smoking supplies purchases	yr	331	1999	30r
Tomatoes, field grown	lb	1.46	7/01	11r
Tuna, light, chunk	lb	1.80	7/01	11r
Turkey, frozen, whole	lb	1.15	7/01	11r
Goods and Services				
B&B Japanese maple (acer japonicum)	gal	29.99-169.99	4/00	93r
Boxwood (buxus)	2 gal	18.99-39.99	4/00	93r
Daylilly (hemerocallis)	gal	4.99-25.00	4/00	93r
Flat of annuals		11.98-24.99	4/00	93r
Fountain grass (pennisetum)	gal	5.98-12.98	4/00	93r
Hanging basket (10 in)		12.99-27.99	4/00	93r
Hardy geranium (geranium)	gal	7.99-9.99	4/00	93r
Hosta (hosta)	gal	6.00-25.00	4/00	93r
Lilac (syrubga vulgaris)	2 gal	14.99-24.99	4/00	93r
Miscellaneous purchases	yr	865	1999	30r
Rhododendron (rhododendron)	2 gal	23.98-42.99	4/00	93r
Sage (salvia)	gal	6.00-9.99	4/00	93r
Wintercreeper euonymus (euonymus fortunei)	2 gal	16.00-169.99	4/00	93r
Hunting license	yr	7.50	4/01	34s
Health Care				
Cardiac catheterization, ave hospital/ physician charges		17690	1998	77s
Childbirth, Cesarean delivery		10722	1997	13r
Childbirth, vaginal delivery		6223	1997	13r
Drugs, expenditures on	yr	394	1999	30r
Health care purchases	yr	2048	1999	30r
Health insurance expenditures	yr	978	1999	30r
Hysterectomy, laproscopically-assisted, ave hospital/physician charges		15850	1998	76s
Hysterectomy, vaginal, ave hospital and physician charges		11810	1998	76s
Medicaid dispensing fee		3.69-15.45	1999	87s
Medical services expenditures	yr	554	1999	30r
Medical supplies, expenditures on	yr	122	1999	30r
Plastic surgery, breast augmentation		3184	2000	7r
Plastic surgery, breast lift		3585	2000	7r
Plastic surgery, facelift		4999	2000	7r
Plastic surgery, hair transplantation		3105	2000	7r
Plastic surgery, lip augmentation		1290	2000	7r
Plastic surgery, lower body lift		8135	2000	7r
Plastic surgery, thigh lift		3839	2000	7r
Household Goods				
Floor coverings, expenditures on	yr	52	1999	30r
Furniture, expenditures on	yr	344	1999	30r
Household furnishings and equipment purchases	yr	1475	1999	30r
Household textiles, expenditures on	yr	109	1999	30r
Laundry and cleaning supplies, expenditures on	yr	134	1999	30r

Peoria-Pekin, IL - continued

Item	Per	Value	Date	Ref.
Housing				
Home price, existing, ave		144400	10/00	90r
Home value, median		183000	2001	53s
Household operation expenditures	yr	542	1999	30r
Housekeeping supplies purchases	yr	508	1999	30r
Lodging expenditures	yr	430	1999	30r
Maintenance, repairs, insurance expenditures	yr	853	1999	30r
Monthly rental value of owned home	mos	547	1999	30r
Owned dwellings, expenditures own	yr	4282	1999	30r
Rent expenditures	yr	1558	1999	30r
Rental unit, 1 bedroom, with utilities	mos	423	4/01	41c
Rental unit, 2 bedroom, with utilities	mos	567	4/01	41c
Rental unit, 3 bedroom, with utilities	mos	755	4/01	41c
Rental unit, 4 bedroom, with utilities	mos	927	4/01	41c
Shelter, expenditures on	yr	6270	1999	30r
Insurance and Pensions				
Life and other personal insurance purchases	yr	387	1999	30r
Pensions and Social Security, expenditures on	yr	2968	1999	30r
Legal Fees				
Divorce, filing fee		100.00-150.00	4/01	35s
Driver's license fee	orig	10.00	1999	48s
Driver's license fee	renew	20.00	1999	48s
Personal Goods				
Personal care products and services purchases	yr	385	1999	30r
Personal Services				
Personal services, household, expenditures on	yr	300	1999	30r
Pets				
Pets, toys, and playground equipment, expenditures on	yr	375	1999	30r
Taxes				
Federal income taxes paid	yr	2326	1999	30r
Personal taxes, expenditures on	yr	3223	1999	30r
Property taxes paid	yr	1152	1999	30r
State and local income taxes paid	yr	753	1999	30r
Transportation				
Cars and trucks, new, expenditures on	yr	1280	1999	30r
Cars and trucks, used, expenditures on	yr	1763	1999	30r
Diesel at the pump	gal	1.33	10/99	73s
Gasoline and motor oil purchases	yr	1036	1999	30r
Gasoline before-tax price (cents)	gal	112.70	10/00	43s
Maintenance and repair expenditures	yr	594	1999	30r
Public transportation, expenditures on	yr	341	1999	30r
Transportation purchases	yr	6617	1999	30r
Vehicle expenses, miscellaneous, purchases	yr	2159	1999	30r
Vehicle insurance payments	yr	701	1999	30r
Vehicle purchases (net outlay)	yr	3081	1999	30r
Vehicle rental, lease expenditures	yr	536	1999	30r
Utilities				
Electrical bill, average	mos	63.08	9/00	9s
Electricity, expenditures on	yr	841	1999	30r
Electricity cost, average	KWh	6.49	9/00	9s
Utilities, fuels, and public services purchased	yr	2401	1999	30r
Water and other public services, expenditures on	yr	273	1999	30r
Weddings				
Wedding (national average cost)		19936	2000	33r
Wedding (regional average total cost)		16195	1997	110r
Attendants' gifts		321	1998	33r
Bridal attendants' apparel (5 persons)		824	2000	33r
Bride's headpiece/veil		173	1998	33r
Bride's wedding dress		859	1998	33r
Clergy, religious facility fee		242	1998	33r
Engagement ring		3177	1998	33r

Values are in dollars or fractions of dollars. In the column headed *Ref*, references are shown to sources. Each reference is followed by a letter. These refer to the geographical level for which data were reported: s=State, r=Region, and c=City or metro. The abbreviation *ex* is used to mean *except* or *excluding*; *exp* stands for *expenditures*. For other abbreviations and further explanations, please see the Introduction.

Peoria-Pekin, IL - continued

Item	Per	Value	Date	Ref.
Weddings				
Flowers		789	1998	33r
Groom's formalwear rental		99	2000	33r
Limousine		410	1998	33r
Marriage license cost		15.00-	4/01	35s
		20.00		
Men's formalwear (ushers, best man)		469	2000	33r
Mother of bride apparel		241	2000	33r
Music		866	1998	33r
Photography and videography		1368	1998	33r
Rehearsal dinner		728	1998	33r
Wedding invitations and announcements		341	1998	33r
Wedding reception		7968	2000	33r
Wedding rings (bride and groom)		1060	1998	33r

Philadelphia, PA

Item	Per	Value	Date	Ref.
Average annual expenditures	yr	37971	1999	30r
Composite, ACCRA index		121.70	3/01	4c
Alcoholic Beverages				
Alcoholic beverage purchases	yr	350	1999	30c
Beer, Heineken, 12-oz, ex deposit	6	7.24	3/01	4c
J & B Scotch	750-ml	22.99	3/01	4c
Wine, Livingston or Gallo, Chablis blanc	1.5 liter	6.99	3/01	4c
Wine, red and white table, all sizes, any origin	liter	9.64	7/01	11r
Appliances				
Appliance repair, service call, washing machine	min lab chg	45.00	3/01	4c
Major appliances, expenditures on	yr	194	1999	30r
Small appliances, housewares, expenditures on	yr	93	1999	30r
Banking and Money				
Mortgage interest and charges paid	yr	2622	1999	30r
Mortgage principal paid on owned property	yr	1262	1999	30r
Mortgage rate, incl. points and orig. fee, 30-yr. conv. fixed or ARM	mos	7.32	3/01	4c
Vehicle finance charges paid	yr	240	1999	30r
Business Expenses				
Business travel, car rental	day	59	2001	3c
Business travel, food	day	52	2001	3c
Business travel, hotel	day	154	2001	3c
Medical office space cost	sq ft	135.51	2001	31c
Office space, 2-4 storey building	sq ft	116.97	2001	31c
Office space, 5-10 storey building	sq ft	103.32	2001	31c
Office space, 11-20 storey building	sq ft	99.31	2001	31c
Office space, central business district, Class A	sq ft	24.53	3/99	74c
Office space, outside central business district, Class A	sq ft	22.08	3/99	74c
Charity				
Cash contributions, expenditures	yr	1093	1999	30c
Child Care				
Child raising cost, total, age 0-2	yr	8670	1999	60r
Child raising cost, total, age 3-5	yr	8910	1999	60r
Child raising cost, total, age 6-8	yr	9040	1999	60r
Child raising cost, total, age 9-11	yr	9100	1999	60r
Child raising cost, total, age 12-14	yr	9890	1999	60r
Child raising cost, total, age 15-17	yr	10010	1999	60r
Child's child care and education, age 0-2	yr	1070	1999	60r
Child's child care and education, age 3-5	yr	1190	1999	60r
Child's child care and education, age 6-8	yr	740	1999	60r
Child's child care and education, age 9-11	yr	470	1999	60r
Child's child care and education, age 12-14	yr	350	1999	60r
Child's child care and education, age 15-17	yr	590	1999	60r
Child's clothing, age 0-2	yr	480	1999	60r
Child's clothing, age 3-5	yr	470	1999	60r
Child's clothing, age 6-8	yr	520	1999	60r
Child's clothing, age 9-11	yr	570	1999	60r

Philadelphia, PA - continued

Item	Per	Value	Date	Ref.
Child Care - continued				
Child's clothing, age 12-14	yr	970	1999	60r
Child's clothing, age 15-17	yr	870	1999	60r
Child's food, age 0-2	yr	1130	1999	60r
Child's food, age 3-5	yr	1290	1999	60r
Child's food, age 6-8	yr	1640	1999	60r
Child's food, age 9-11	yr	1930	1999	60r
Child's food, age 12-14	yr	1940	1999	60r
Child's food, age 15-17	yr	2150	1999	60r
Child's health care, age 0-2	yr	550	1999	60r
Child's health care, age 3-5	yr	530	1999	60r
Child's health care, age 6-8	yr	610	1999	60r
Child's health care, age 9-11	yr	650	1999	60r
Child's health care, age 12-14	yr	660	1999	60r
Child's health care, age 15-17	yr	690	1999	60r
Child's housing, age 0-2	yr	3555	1999	60r
Child's housing, age 3-5	yr	3530	1999	60r
Child's housing, age 6-8	yr	3490	1999	60r
Child's housing, age 9-11	yr	3340	1999	60r
Child's housing, age 12-14	yr	3530	1999	60r
Child's housing, age 15-17	yr	3140	1999	60r
Child's personal care, reading, age 0-2	yr	920	1999	60r
Child's personal care, reading, age 3-5	yr	950	1999	60r
Child's personal care, reading, age 6-8	yr	980	1999	60r
Child's personal care, reading, age 9-11	yr	1020	1999	60r
Child's personal care, reading, age 12-14	yr	1190	1999	60r
Child's personal care, reading, age 15-17	yr	970	1999	60r
Clothing				
Apparel and services purchases	yr	1433	1999	30c
Boys' brief, cotton	3	5.94	3/01	4c
Boys, 2 to 15, expenditures on	yr	92	1999	30r
Children under 2, expenditures on	yr	63	1999	30r
Footwear, expenditures on	yr	300	1999	30r
Girls, 2 to 15, expenditures on	yr	101	1999	30r
Men and boys, expenditures on	yr	446	1999	30r
Men, 16 and over, expenditures on	yr	354	1999	30r
Shirt, man's dress shirt		32.00	3/01	4c
Slacks, man's "No Wrinkles" khaki		41.75	3/01	4c
Women, 16 and over, expenditures on	yr	584	1999	30r
Communications				
Cable modem installation, Adelphi		54.90	6/99	103s
Cable modem installation, Comcast		95.00	6/99	103s
Cable modem rate, cable subscriber, Adelphi	mos	34.95	6/99	103s
Cable modem rate, cable subscriber, Comcast	mos	39.95	6/99	103s
Cable modem rate, non-cable subscriber, Adelphi	mos	44.95	6/99	103s
Cable modem rate, non-cable subscriber, Comcast	mos	49.95	6/99	103s
Newspaper subscription, daily and Sunday delivery	mos	15.65	3/01	4c
Phone line, single, business, field visit	inst.	75.00	12/97	17s
Phone line, single, business, no field visit	inst.	75.00	12/97	17s
Phone line, single, residence, field visit	inst.	40.00	12/97	17s
Phone line, single, residence, no field visit	inst.	40.00	12/97	17s
Postage and stationery, expenditures on	yr	138	1999	30r
Postal rate, express mail, up to half-pound		12.45	7/01	108r
Postal rate, letter, first class, first ounce		0.34	7/01	108r
Postal rate, letter, two ounces		0.57	7/01	108r
Postal rate, post card		0.21	7/01	108r
Postal rate, priority mail, two pounds		3.95	7/01	108r
Postal rate, priority mail, up to one pound		3.50	7/01	108r
Telephone bill, business, basic rate	mos	19.20	12/97	18c
Telephone bill, family of three	mos	19.78	3/01	4c
Telephone bill, residential, basic rate	mos	6.85	12/97	18c
Telephone services, expenditures on	yr	830	1999	30r
Education				
Board, 4-year private college/university	yr	2822	1996	38s
Board, 4-year public college/university	yr	2174	1996	38s
Education expenditures	yr	1088	1999	30c
Room, 4-year private college/university	yr	2943	1996	38s
Room, 4-year public college/university	yr	2227	1996	38s

Values are in dollars or fractions of dollars. In the column headed *Ref*, references are shown to sources. Each reference is followed by a letter. These refer to the geographical level for which data were reported: s=State, r=Region, and c=City or metro. The abbreviation *ex* is used to mean *except* or *excluding*; *exp* stands for *expenditures*. For other abbreviations and further explanations, please see the Introduction.

Philadelphia, PA - continued

Item	Per	Value	Date	Ref.
Education				
Total cost, 4-year private college/university	yr	19876	1996	38s
Total cost, 4-year public college/university	yr	9124	1996	38s
Tuition, 2-year public college/university, in state	yr	1909	1996	38s
Tuition, 4-year private college/university, in state	yr	14111	1996	38s
Tuition, 4-year public college/university	yr	4723	1996	38s
Energy and Fuels				
Electricity	KWh	0.12	7/01	11r
Energy, combined forms, 2400 sq ft	mos	162.63	3/01	4c
Energy, exc. electricity, 2400 sq ft	mos	70.76	3/01	4c
Fuel oil #2	gal	1.31	7/01	11r
Fuel oil and other fuels, expenditures on	yr	207	1999	30r
Gas, natural, commercial rate	1000 cf	5.96	11/00	88s
Gas, regular unleaded, cash, self-service	gal	1.66	3/01	4c
Gasoline, all types	gal	1.80	7/01	11r
Gasoline, unleaded midgrade	gal	1.85	7/01	11r
Gasoline, unleaded premium	gal	1.91	7/01	11r
Gasoline, unleaded regular	gal	1.71	7/01	11r
Natural gas, expenditures on	yr	368	1999	30r
Utility (piped) gas, therm		1.08	7/01	11r
Utility (piped) gas, 40 therms		50.87	7/01	11r
Utility (piped) gas, 100 therms		111.06	7/01	11r
Entertainment				
Bowling, Saturday evening rate	line	2.94	3/01	4c
Entertainment purchases	yr	1721	1999	30c
Fees and admissions paid	yr	511	1999	30r
Monopoly game, Parker Brothers', No. 9	game	11.92	3/01	4c
Movie, first-run, Saturday, evening	adm.	7.50	3/01	4c
Reading purchases	yr	192	1999	30c
Television, radios, sound equipment, expenditures on	yr	650	1999	30r
Tennis balls, yellow, Wilson or Penn, 3	can	3.14	3/01	4c
Funerals				
Total cost of funeral		5813.50	1/99	78r
Acknowledgement cards		28.32	1/99	78r
Casket		2082.20	1/99	78r
Cosmetology, hair, other preparation		169.59	1/99	78r
Embalming		465.60	1/99	78r
Funeral at funeral home		339.56	1/99	78r
Hearse (local)		183.96	1/99	78r
Professional service charges		1157.85	1/99	78r
Service car/van		100.41	1/99	78r
Transfer of remains to funeral home		158.66	1/99	78r
Vault		766.31	1/99	78r
Visitation/viewing		361.04	1/99	78r
Groceries				
Groceries, ACCRA Index		104.80	3/01	4c
Antibiotic ointment, Polysporin	0.5 oz	5.04	3/01	4c
Apples, red delicious	lb	0.95	7/01	11r
Baby food, strained vegetables or fruit, lowest price	4-4.5 oz	0.47	3/01	4c
Bacon, sliced	lb	3.44	7/01	11r
Bakery products, expenditures on	yr	310	1999	30r
Bananas	lb	0.64	3/01	4c
Bananas	lb	0.55	7/01	11r
Beef or hamburger, ground	lb	1.67	3/01	4c
Beef, expenditures on	yr	236	1999	30r
Bread, white	loaf	0.86	3/01	4c
Bread, white, pan	lb	1.09	7/01	11r
Butter, yoghurt, cheese, etc, expenditures on	yr	214	1999	30r
Cereals and bakery product purchases	yr	474	1999	30r
Cereals and cereal products, expenditures on	yr	164	1999	30r
Cheese, Kraft grated Parmesan	8 oz	3.49	3/01	4c
Chicken legs, bone-in	lb	1.23	7/01	11r
Chicken, fresh, whole	lb	1.13	7/01	11r
Chicken, whole fryer	lb	1.04	3/01	4c
Chuck roast, U.S. choice, boneless	lb	2.79	7/01	11r
Cigarettes, Winston, Kings	carton	28.11	3/01	4c

Philadelphia, PA - continued

Item	Per	Value	Date	Ref.
Groceries - continued				
Coffee, 100%, ground roast, all sizes	lb	3.40	7/01	11r
Coffee, vacuum-packed	13 oz	3.10	3/01	4c
Corn Flakes, Kellogg's or Post Toasties	18 oz	2.85	3/01	4c
Corn, frozen, whole kernel, lowest price	16 oz	1.06	3/01	4c
Dairy product purchases	yr	291	1999	30c
Eggs, expenditures on	yr	34	1999	30r
Eggs, Grade A or AA	dozen	1.16	3/01	4c
Eggs, grade A, large	dozen	0.82	7/01	11r
Fats and oils, expenditures on	yr	80	1999	30r
Fish and seafood, expenditures on	yr	123	1999	30r
Food (excl fruit and vegetables), eaten at home, purchases	yr	681	1999	30c
Food cooked on trips, expenditures on	yr	48	1999	30r
Food purchases	yr	4753	1999	30c
Food purchases, eaten away from home	yr	2157	1999	30c
Food purchases, food eaten at home	yr	2596	1999	30c
Fresh fruits, expenditures on	yr	169	1999	30r
Fresh milk and cream, expenditures on	yr	128	1999	30r
Fresh vegetables, expenditures on	yr	164	1999	30r
Fruit and vegetable purchases	yr	474	1999	30c
Grapefruit	lb	0.67	7/01	11r
Grapes, Thompson, seedless	lb	2.18	7/01	11r
Ground beef, lean and extra lean	lb	2.66	7/01	11r
Ground chuck, 100% beef	lb	2.04	7/01	11r
Lettuce, iceberg	head	1.29	3/01	4c
Lettuce, iceberg	lb	0.76	7/01	11r
Margarine, Blue Bonnet or Parkay, stick	lb	0.86	3/01	4c
Meats, poultry, fish, and egg purchases	yr	808	1999	30r
Milk, whole	1/2 gal	1.42	3/01	4c
Nonalcoholic beverages, expenditures on	yr	225	1999	30r
Orange juice, frozen concentrate	16 oz	1.88	7/01	11r
Orange juice, Minute Maid frozen	12 oz	1.06	3/01	4c
Oranges, Navel	lb	0.79	7/01	11r
Oranges, Valencia	lb	0.56	7/01	11r
Peaches	lb	1.16	7/01	11r
Peaches, halves or slices, Hunt's, Del Monte, or Libby's	29 oz	1.72	3/01	4c
Peanut butter, creamy, all sizes	lb	2.01	7/01	11r
Pears, Anjou	lb	1.16	7/01	11r
Peas, green, Del Monte or Green Giant	15 oz	0.80	3/01	4c
Pork chops, center cut, bone-in	lb	3.57	7/01	11r
Pork, expenditures on	yr	146	1999	30r
Potato chips	16 oz	3.37	7/01	11r
Potatoes, white or red	10 lb	2.92	3/01	4c
Potatoes, white, all types	lb	0.42	7/01	11r
Poultry, expenditures on	yr	158	1999	30r
Processed fruits, expenditures on	yr	124	1999	30r
Processed vegetables, expenditures on	yr	82	1999	30r
Round roast, U.S. choice, boneless	lb	3.04	7/01	11r
Sausage, Jimmy Dean/Owens pork	lb	3.44	3/01	4c
Shortening, vegetable, Crisco	3 lb	2.92	3/01	4c
Soft drink, Coca Cola, ex deposit	2 liter	1.36	3/01	4c
Spaghetti and macaroni	lb	1.04	7/01	11r
Steak, sirloin, U.S. choice, boneless	lb	5.39	7/01	11r
Steak, T-bone	lb	6.52	3/01	4c
Strawberries, dry pint	12 oz	1.51	7/01	11r
Sugar and other sweets, expenditures on	yr	110	1999	30r
Sugar, cane or beet	4 lbs	1.94	3/01	4c
Sugar, white, 33-80 ounce package	lb	0.46	7/01	11r
Sugar, white, all sizes	lb	0.47	7/01	11r
Tobacco products and smoking supplies purchases	yr	260	1999	30c
Tomatoes, Hunt's or Del Monte	14.5 oz	0.92	3/01	4c
Tuna, chunk, light	6 oz	0.87	3/01	4c
Yogurt, natural, fruit flavored	8 oz	0.79	7/01	11r
Goods and Services				
Miscellaneous goods and services, ACCRA Index		113.60	3/01	4c
B&B Japanese maple (acer japonicum)	gal	38.99-125.00	4/00	93r
Boxwood (buxus)	2 gal	15.99-49.95	4/00	93r

Values are in dollars or fractions of dollars. In the column headed *Ref*, references are shown to sources. Each reference is followed by a letter. These refer to the geographical level for which data were reported: s=State, r=Region, and c=City or metro. The abbreviation *ex* is used to mean *except* or *excluding*; *exp* stands for expenditures. For other abbreviations and further explanations, please see the Introduction.

Philadelphia, PA - continued

Item	Per	Value	Date	Ref.
Goods and Services				
Daylilly (hemerocallis)	gal	4.95	4/00	93r
Flat of annuals		8.00-14.99	4/00	93r
Fountain grass (pennisetum)	gal	6.99-9.99	4/00	93r
Hanging basket (10 in)		12.95-19.99	4/00	93r
Hardy geranium (geranium)	gal	6.95-7.99	4/00	93r
Hosta (hosta)	gal	4.95	4/00	93r
Lilac (syrubga vulgaris)	2 gal	17.99-74.95	4/00	93r
Miscellaneous purchases	yr	872	1999	30r
Rhododendron (rhododendron)	2 gal	23.99-54.95	4/00	93r
Sage (salvia)	gal	6.95-7.99	4/00	93r
Wintercreeper euonymus (euonymus fortunei)	2 gal	14.99-23.95	4/00	93r
Hunting license	yr	20.00	4/01	34s
Health Care				
Health care, ACCRA Index		100.40	3/01	4c
Cardiac catheterization, ave hospital/ physician charges		13870	1998	77s
Childbirth, Cesarean delivery		14716	1997	13r
Childbirth, vaginal delivery		8541	1997	13r
Dentist's fee, adult teeth cleaning and periodic oral exam	visit	68.75	3/01	4c
Doctor's fee, routine exam, established patient	visit	58.75	3/01	4c
Drugs, expenditures on	yr	296	1999	30r
Health care purchases	yr	1781	1999	30c
Health insurance expenditures	yr	875	1999	30r
Home health care aide cost, licensed agency	hour	14	2000	82c
Hospital care, private room	day	548.00	3/01	4c
Hysterectomy, laproscopically-assisted, ave hospital/physician charges		14760	1998	76s
Hysterectomy, vaginal, ave hospital and physician charges		9270	1998	76s
Medicaid dispensing fee		4.00	1999	87s
Medical services expenditures	yr	516	1999	30r
Medical supplies, expenditures on	yr	102	1999	30r
Nursing home costs, private room	day	163	2000	82c
Nursing home stay, private room	day	163	2000	83c
Plastic surgery, breast augmentation		4232	2000	7r
Plastic surgery, breast lift		4605	2000	7r
Plastic surgery, facelift		6964	2000	7r
Plastic surgery, hair transplantation		4193	2000	7r
Plastic surgery, lip augmentation		1675	2000	7r
Plastic surgery, lower body lift		6611	2000	7r
Plastic surgery, thigh lift		4751	2000	7r
Household Goods				
Dishwashing powder, Cascade	50 oz	3.19	3/01	4c
Floor coverings, expenditures on	yr	59	1999	30r
Furniture, expenditures on	yr	388	1999	30r
Household furnishings and equipment purchases	yr	1709	1999	30c
Household textiles, expenditures on	yr	112	1999	30r
Laundry and cleaning supplies, expenditures on	yr	104	1999	30r
Tissues, facial, Kleenex brand	175	1.34	3/01	4c
Housing				
Housing, ACCRA Index		143.70	3/01	4c
Home price, existing, ave		180800	10/00	90r
Home value, median		115000	2001	53s
House, 2400 sq ft, 8000 sq ft lot, new, urban, utilities	total	301999	3/01	4c
House payment, principal and interest, 25% down payment	mos	1556	3/01	4c
Household operation expenditures	yr	518	1999	30c
Housekeeping supplies purchases	yr	477	1999	30c

Philadelphia, PA - continued

Item	Per	Value	Date	Ref.
Housing - continued				
Housing, expenditures on	yr	14783	1999	30c
Lodging expenditures	yr	550	1999	30r
Maintenance, repairs, insurance expenditures	yr	835	1999	30r
Monthly rental value of owned home	mos	663	1999	30r
Owned dwellings, expenditures own	yr	6615	1999	30c
Rent expenditures	yr	1875	1999	30c
Rent, apartment, 2 br, 1 1/2-2 baths, unfurn, 950 sq ft, water	mos	800	3/01	4c
Rental unit, 1 bedroom, with utilities	mos	611	4/01	41c
Rental unit, 2 bedroom, with utilities	mos	755	4/01	41c
Rental unit, 3 bedroom, with utilities	mos	945	4/01	41c
Rental unit, 4 bedroom, with utilities	mos	1185	4/01	41c
Shelter, expenditures on	yr	9239	1999	30c
Insurance and Pensions				
Life and other personal insurance purchases	yr	543	1999	30c
Pensions and Social Security, expenditures on	yr	3033	1999	30c
Personal insurance and pensions, expenditures on	yr	3576	1999	30c
Legal Fees				
Divorce, filing fee		65.00	4/01	35s
Driver's license fee	orig	29.00	1999	48s
Driver's license fee	renew	24.00	1999	48s
Fishing license	yr	17.00	4/01	34s
Personal Goods				
Personal care products and services purchases	yr	295	1999	30c
Shampoo, Alberto VO5	15 oz	1.29	3/01	4c
Toothpaste, Crest or Colgate	6-7 oz	2.75	3/01	4c
Personal Services				
Dry cleaning, man's 2-pc suit		9.22	3/01	4c
Man's haircut, barbershop, no styling		12.70	3/01	4c
Personal services, household, expenditures on	yr	271	1999	30r
Woman's shampoo, trim, blow-dry, no style-change		24.20	3/01	4c
Pets				
Pets, toys, and playground equipment, expenditures on	yr	325	1999	30r
Restaurant Food				
Chicken, fried, thigh and drumstick, KFC/ Church's		2.96	3/01	4c
Hamburger with cheese, McDonald's	1/4 lb	2.34	3/01	4c
Pizza, Pizza Hut or Pizza Inn	11-12 in	8.99	3/01	4c
Taxes				
Federal income taxes paid	yr	2606	1999	30r
Personal taxes, expenditures on	yr	3567	1999	30r
Property taxes paid	yr	1752	1999	30r
State and local income taxes paid	yr	694	1999	30r
Transportation				
Transportation, ACCRA Index		120.10	3/01	4c
Auto operation, annual cost		8715	2000	27c
Bus fare, one-way	trip	1.30	2000	1c
Bus fare, to central business district	1-way	1.60	3/01	4c
Cars and trucks, new, expenditures on	yr	1496	1999	30r
Cars and trucks, used, expenditures on	yr	1251	1999	30r
Commuter rail, one-way	trip	2.50	2000	2c
Diesel at the pump	gal	1.31	10/99	73s
Gasoline and motor oil purchases	yr	869	1999	30c
Gasoline before-tax price (cents)	gal	106.60	10/00	43s
Heavy rail transit fare, one-way	trip	0.85-1.60	2000	2c
Light rail transit fare, one-way	trip	1.60	2000	2c
Maintenance and repair expenditures	yr	618	1999	30r
Public transportation, expenditures on	yr	457	1999	30c
Tire balance, computer or spin balance, front	wheel	9.10	3/01	4c
Transportation purchases	yr	7896	1999	30c

Values are in dollars or fractions of dollars. In the column headed *Ref*, references are shown to sources. Each reference is followed by a letter. These refer to the geographical level for which data were reported: s=State, r=Region, and c=City or metro. The abbreviation *ex* is used to mean *except* or *excluding*; *exp* stands for expenditures. For other abbreviations and further explanations, please see the Introduction.

Philadelphia, PA - continued

Item	Per	Value	Date	Ref.
Transportation				
Trolley bus transit fare, one-way	trip	1.60	2000	2c
Vehicle expenses, miscellaneous, purchases	yr	2706	1999	30c
Vehicle insurance payments	yr	824	1999	30r
Vehicle purchases (net outlay)	yr	3865	1999	30c
Vehicle rental, lease expenditures	yr	584	1999	30r
Travel				
Hotel rate, ave	day	143.00	1999	45c
Hotel room, ave	night	145.00	2000	70c
Utilities				
Utilities, ACCRA Index		127.40	3/01	4c
Electrical bill, average	mos	69.16	9/00	9s
Electricity, expenditures on	yr	837	1999	30r
Electricity, summer, 250 KWh	mos	37.47	2/96	96c
Electricity, summer, 500 KWh	mos	69.84	2/96	96c
Electricity, summer, 750 KWh	mos	102.23	2/96	96c
Electricity, summer, 1000 KWh	mos	134.59	2/96	96c
Electricity and other, mixed, 2400 sq ft, new home	mos	91.87	3/01	4c
Electricity cost, average	KWh	5.08	9/00	9s
Utilities, fuels, and public services purchased	yr	2457	1999	30r
Water and other public services, expenditures on	yr	215	1999	30r
Weddings				
Wedding (national average cost)		19936	2000	33r
Wedding (regional average total cost)		29454	1997	110r
Attendants' gifts		321	1998	33r
Bridal attendants' apparel (5 persons)		824	2000	33r
Bride's headpiece/veil		173	1998	33r
Bride's wedding dress		859	1998	33r
Clergy, religious facility fee		242	1998	33r
Engagement ring		3177	1998	33r
Flowers		789	1998	33r
Groom's formalwear rental		99	2000	33r
Limousine		410	1998	33r
Marriage license cost		25.00-40.00	4/01	35s
Men's formalwear (ushers, best man)		469	2000	33r
Mother of bride apparel		241	2000	33r
Music		866	1998	33r
Photography and videography		1368	1998	33r
Rehearsal dinner		728	1998	33r
Wedding invitations and announcements		341	1998	33r
Wedding reception		7968	2000	33r
Wedding rings (bride and groom)		1060	1998	33r

Philadelphia-Wilmington-Atlantic City, PA

Item	Per	Value	Date	Ref.
Average annual expenditures	yr	37971	1999	30r
Alcoholic Beverages				
Alcoholic beverage purchases	yr	368	1999	30r
Wine, red and white table, all sizes, any origin	liter	9.64	7/01	11r
Appliances				
Major appliances, expenditures on	yr	194	1999	30r
Small appliances, housewares, expenditures on	yr	93	1999	30r
Banking and Money				
Mortgage interest and charges paid	yr	2622	1999	30r
Mortgage principal paid on owned property	yr	1262	1999	30r
Vehicle finance charges paid	yr	240	1999	30r
Charity				
Cash contributions, expenditures	yr	1001	1999	30r
Child Care				
Child raising cost, total, age 0-2	yr	8670	1999	60r
Child raising cost, total, age 3-5	yr	8910	1999	60r
Child raising cost, total, age 6-8	yr	9040	1999	60r
Child raising cost, total, age 9-11	yr	9100	1999	60r

Philadelphia-Wilmington-Atlantic City, PA - continued

Item	Per	Value	Date	Ref.
Child Care - continued				
Child raising cost, total, age 12-14	yr	9890	1999	60r
Child raising cost, total, age 15-17	yr	10010	1999	60r
Child's child care and education, age 0-2	yr	1070	1999	60r
Child's child care and education, age 3-5	yr	1190	1999	60r
Child's child care and education, age 6-8	yr	740	1999	60r
Child's child care and education, age 9-11	yr	470	1999	60r
Child's child care and education, age 12-14	yr	350	1999	60r
Child's child care and education, age 15-17	yr	590	1999	60r
Child's clothing, age 0-2	yr	480	1999	60r
Child's clothing, age 3-5	yr	470	1999	60r
Child's clothing, age 6-8	yr	520	1999	60r
Child's clothing, age 9-11	yr	570	1999	60r
Child's clothing, age 12-14	yr	970	1999	60r
Child's clothing, age 15-17	yr	870	1999	60r
Child's food, age 0-2	yr	1130	1999	60r
Child's food, age 3-5	yr	1290	1999	60r
Child's food, age 6-8	yr	1640	1999	60r
Child's food, age 9-11	yr	1930	1999	60r
Child's food, age 12-14	yr	1940	1999	60r
Child's food, age 15-17	yr	2150	1999	60r
Child's health care, age 0-2	yr	550	1999	60r
Child's health care, age 3-5	yr	530	1999	60r
Child's health care, age 6-8	yr	610	1999	60r
Child's health care, age 9-11	yr	650	1999	60r
Child's health care, age 12-14	yr	660	1999	60r
Child's health care, age 15-17	yr	690	1999	60r
Child's housing, age 0-2	yr	3555	1999	60r
Child's housing, age 3-5	yr	3530	1999	60r
Child's housing, age 6-8	yr	3490	1999	60r
Child's housing, age 9-11	yr	3340	1999	60r
Child's housing, age 12-14	yr	3530	1999	60r
Child's housing, age 15-17	yr	3140	1999	60r
Child's personal care, reading, age 0-2	yr	920	1999	60r
Child's personal care, reading, age 3-5	yr	950	1999	60r
Child's personal care, reading, age 6-8	yr	980	1999	60r
Child's personal care, reading, age 9-11	yr	1020	1999	60r
Child's personal care, reading, age 12-14	yr	1190	1999	60r
Child's personal care, reading, age 15-17	yr	970	1999	60r
Clothing				
Apparel and services purchases	yr	1831	1999	30r
Boys, 2 to 15, expenditures on	yr	92	1999	30r
Children under 2, expenditures on	yr	63	1999	30r
Footwear, expenditures on	yr	300	1999	30r
Girls, 2 to 15, expenditures on	yr	101	1999	30r
Men and boys, expenditures on	yr	446	1999	30r
Men, 16 and over, expenditures on	yr	354	1999	30r
Women, 16 and over, expenditures on	yr	584	1999	30r
Communications				
Cable modem installation, Adelphi		54.90	6/99	103s
Cable modem installation, Comcast		95.00	6/99	103s
Cable modem rate, cable subscriber, Adelphi	mos	34.95	6/99	103s
Cable modem rate, cable subscriber, Comcast	mos	39.95	6/99	103s
Cable modem rate, non-cable subscriber, Adelphi	mos	44.95	6/99	103s
Cable modem rate, non-cable subscriber, Comcast	mos	49.95	6/99	103s
Phone line, single, business, field visit	inst.	75.00	12/97	17s
Phone line, single, business, no field visit	inst.	75.00	12/97	17s
Phone line, single, residence, field visit	inst.	40.00	12/97	17s
Phone line, single, residence, no field visit	inst.	40.00	12/97	17s
Postage and stationery, expenditures on	yr	138	1999	30r
Postal rate, express mail, up to half-pound		12.45	7/01	108r
Postal rate, letter, first class, first ounce		0.34	7/01	108r
Postal rate, letter, two ounces		0.57	7/01	108r
Postal rate, post card		0.21	7/01	108r
Postal rate, priority mail, two pounds		3.95	7/01	108r
Postal rate, priority mail, up to one pound		3.50	7/01	108r
Telephone services, expenditures on	yr	830	1999	30r

Values are in dollars or fractions of dollars. In the column headed *Ref*, references are shown to sources. Each reference is followed by a letter. These refer to the geographical level for which data were reported: s=State, r=Region, and c=City or metro. The abbreviation *ex* is used to mean *except* or *excluding*; *exp* stands for *expenditures*. For other abbreviations and further explanations, please see the Introduction.

Philadelphia-Wilmington-Atlantic City, PA - continued

Item	Per	Value	Date	Ref.
Education				
Board, 4-year private college/university	yr	2822	1996	38s
Board, 4-year public college/university	yr	2174	1996	38s
Education expenditures	yr	877	1999	30r
Room, 4-year private college/university	yr	2943	1996	38s
Room, 4-year public college/university	yr	2227	1996	38s
Total cost, 4-year private college/university	yr	19876	1996	38s
Total cost, 4-year public college/university	yr	9124	1996	38s
Tuition, 2-year public college/university, in state	yr	1909	1996	38s
Tuition, 4-year private college/university, in state	yr	14111	1996	38s
Tuition, 4-year public college/university	yr	4723	1996	38s
Energy and Fuels				
Electricity	KWh	0.12	7/01	11r
Fuel oil #2	gal	1.31	7/01	11r
Fuel oil and other fuels, expenditures on	yr	207	1999	30r
Gas, natural, commercial rate	1000 cf	5.96	11/00	88s
Gasoline, all types	gal	1.80	7/01	11r
Gasoline, unleaded midgrade	gal	1.85	7/01	11r
Gasoline, unleaded premium	gal	1.91	7/01	11r
Gasoline, unleaded regular	gal	1.71	7/01	11r
Natural gas, expenditures on	yr	368	1999	30r
Utility (piped) gas, therm		1.08	7/01	11r
Utility (piped) gas, 40 therms		50.87	7/01	11r
Utility (piped) gas, 100 therms		111.06	7/01	11r
Entertainment				
Entertainment purchases	yr	1821	1999	30r
Fees and admissions paid	yr	511	1999	30r
Television, radios, sound equipment, expenditures on	yr	650	1999	30r
Funerals				
Total cost of funeral		5813.50	1/99	78r
Acknowledgement cards		28.32	1/99	78r
Casket		2082.20	1/99	78r
Cosmetology, hair, other preparation		169.59	1/99	78r
Embalming		465.60	1/99	78r
Funeral at funeral home		339.56	1/99	78r
Hearse (local)		183.96	1/99	78r
Professional service charges		1157.85	1/99	78r
Service car/van		100.41	1/99	78r
Transfer of remains to funeral home		158.66	1/99	78r
Vault		766.31	1/99	78r
Visitation/viewing		361.04	1/99	78r
Groceries				
Apples, red delicious	lb	0.95	7/01	11r
Bacon, sliced	lb	3.44	7/01	11r
Bakery products, expenditures on	yr	310	1999	30r
Bananas	lb	0.55	7/01	11r
Beef, expenditures on	yr	236	1999	30r
Bread, white, pan	lb	1.09	7/01	11r
Butter, yoghurt, cheese, etc, expenditures on	yr	214	1999	30r
Cereals and bakery product purchases	yr	474	1999	30r
Cereals and cereal products, expenditures on	yr	164	1999	30r
Chicken legs, bone-in	lb	1.23	7/01	11r
Chicken, fresh, whole	lb	1.13	7/01	11r
Chuck roast, U.S. choice, boneless	lb	2.79	7/01	11r
Coffee, 100%, ground roast, all sizes	lb	3.40	7/01	11r
Dairy product purchases	yr	342	1999	30r
Eggs, expenditures on	yr	34	1999	30r
Eggs, grade A, large	dozen	0.82	7/01	11r
Fats and oils, expenditures on	yr	80	1999	30r
Fish and seafood, expenditures on	yr	123	1999	30r
Food (excl fruit and vegetables), eaten at home, purchases	yr	838	1999	30r
Food cooked on trips, expenditures on	yr	48	1999	30r
Food purchases	yr	5314	1999	30r
Food purchases, eaten away from home	yr	2313	1999	30r
Food purchases, food eaten at home	yr	3001	1999	30r
Fresh fruits, expenditures on	yr	169	1999	30r

Philadelphia-Wilmington-Atlantic City, PA - continued

Item	Per	Value	Date	Ref.
Groceries - continued				
Fresh milk and cream, expenditures on	yr	128	1999	30r
Fresh vegetables, expenditures on	yr	164	1999	30r
Grapefruit	lb	0.67	7/01	11r
Grapes, Thompson, seedless	lb	2.18	7/01	11r
Ground beef, lean and extra lean	lb	2.66	7/01	11r
Ground chuck, 100% beef	lb	2.04	7/01	11r
Lettuce, iceberg	lb	0.76	7/01	11r
Meats, poultry, fish, and egg purchases	yr	808	1999	30r
Nonalcoholic beverages, expenditures on	yr	225	1999	30r
Orange juice, frozen concentrate	16 oz	1.88	7/01	11r
Oranges, Navel	lb	0.79	7/01	11r
Oranges, Valencia	lb	0.56	7/01	11r
Peaches	lb	1.16	7/01	11r
Peanut butter, creamy, all sizes	lb	2.01	7/01	11r
Pears, Anjou	lb	1.16	7/01	11r
Pork chops, center cut, bone-in	lb	3.57	7/01	11r
Pork, expenditures on	yr	146	1999	30r
Potato chips	16 oz	3.37	7/01	11r
Potatoes, white, all types	lb	0.42	7/01	11r
Poultry, expenditures on	yr	158	1999	30r
Processed fruits, expenditures on	yr	124	1999	30r
Processed vegetables, expenditures on	yr	82	1999	30r
Round roast, U.S. choice, boneless	lb	3.04	7/01	11r
Spaghetti and macaroni	lb	1.04	7/01	11r
Steak, sirloin, U.S. choice, boneless	lb	5.39	7/01	11r
Strawberries, dry pint	12 oz	1.51	7/01	11r
Sugar and other sweets, expenditures on	yr	110	1999	30r
Sugar, white, 33-80 ounce package	lb	0.46	7/01	11r
Sugar, white, all sizes	lb	0.47	7/01	11r
Tobacco products and smoking supplies purchases	yr	309	1999	30r
Yogurt, natural, fruit flavored	8 oz	0.79	7/01	11r
Goods and Services				
B&B Japanese maple (acer japonicum)	gal	38.99-125.00	4/00	93r
Boxwood (buxus)	2 gal	15.99-49.95	4/00	93r
Daylilly (hemerocallis)	gal	4.95	4/00	93r
Flat of annuals		8.00-14.99	4/00	93r
Fountain grass (pennisetum)	gal	6.99-9.99	4/00	93r
Hanging basket (10 in)		12.95-19.99	4/00	93r
Hardy geranium (geranium)	gal	6.95-7.99	4/00	93r
Hosta (hosta)	gal	4.95	4/00	93r
Lilac (syrubga vulgaris)	2 gal	17.99-74.95	4/00	93r
Miscellaneous purchases	yr	872	1999	30r
Rhododendron (rhododendron)	2 gal	23.99-54.95	4/00	93r
Sage (salvia)	gal	6.95-7.99	4/00	93r
Wintercreeper euonymus (euonymus fortunei)	2 gal	14.99-23.95	4/00	93r
Hunting license	yr	20.00	4/01	34s
Health Care				
Cardiac catheterization, ave hospital/ physician charges		13870	1998	77s
Childbirth, Cesarean delivery		14716	1997	13r
Childbirth, vaginal delivery		8541	1997	13r
Drugs, expenditures on	yr	296	1999	30r
Health care purchases	yr	1788	1999	30r
Health insurance expenditures	yr	875	1999	30r
Hysterectomy, laproscopically-assisted, ave hospital/physician charges		14760	1998	76s
Hysterectomy, vaginal, ave hospital and physician charges		9270	1998	76s
Medicaid dispensing fee		4.00	1999	87s
Medical services expenditures	yr	516	1999	30r

Values are in dollars or fractions of dollars. In the column headed *Ref*, references are shown to sources. Each reference is followed by a letter. These refer to the geographical level for which data were reported: s=State, r=Region, and c=City or metro. The abbreviation *ex* is used to mean *except* or *excluding*; *exp* stands for *expenditures*. For other abbreviations and further explanations, please see the Introduction.

Philadelphia-Wilmington-Atlantic City, PA - continued

Item	Per	Value	Date	Ref.
Health Care				
Medical supplies, expenditures on	yr	102	1999	30r
Plastic surgery, breast augmentation		4232	2000	7r
Plastic surgery, breast lift		4605	2000	7r
Plastic surgery, facelift		6964	2000	7r
Plastic surgery, hair transplantation		4193	2000	7r
Plastic surgery, lip augmentation		1675	2000	7r
Plastic surgery, lower body lift		6611	2000	7r
Plastic surgery, thigh lift		4751	2000	7r
Household Goods				
Floor coverings, expenditures on	yr	59	1999	30r
Furniture, expenditures on	yr	388	1999	30r
Household furnishings and equipment purchases	yr	1567	1999	30r
Household textiles, expenditures on	yr	112	1999	30r
Laundry and cleaning supplies, expenditures on	yr	104	1999	30r
Housing				
Home price, existing, ave		180800	10/00	90r
Home value, median		115000	2001	53s
Household operation expenditures	yr	581	1999	30r
Housekeeping supplies purchases	yr	474	1999	30r
Lodging expenditures	yr	550	1999	30r
Maintenance, repairs, insurance expenditures	yr	835	1999	30r
Monthly rental value of owned home	mos	663	1999	30r
Owned dwellings, expenditures own	yr	5209	1999	30r
Rent expenditures	yr	2390	1999	30r
Shelter, expenditures on	yr	8149	1999	30r
Insurance and Pensions				
Life and other personal insurance purchases	yr	424	1999	30r
Pensions and Social Security, expenditures on	yr	3037	1999	30r
Legal Fees				
Divorce, filing fee		65.00	4/01	35s
Driver's license fee	orig	29.00	1999	48s
Driver's license fee	renew	24.00	1999	48s
Fishing license	yr	17.00	4/01	34s
Personal Goods				
Personal care products and services purchases	yr	399	1999	30r
Personal Services				
Personal services, household, expenditures on	yr	271	1999	30r
Pets				
Pets, toys, and playground equipment, expenditures on	yr	325	1999	30r
Taxes				
Federal income taxes paid	yr	2606	1999	30r
Personal taxes, expenditures on	yr	3567	1999	30r
Property taxes paid	yr	1752	1999	30r
State and local income taxes paid	yr	694	1999	30r
Transportation				
Cars and trucks, new, expenditures on	yr	1496	1999	30r
Cars and trucks, used, expenditures on	yr	1251	1999	30r
Diesel at the pump	gal	1.31	10/99	73s
Gasoline and motor oil purchases	yr	901	1999	30r
Gasoline before-tax price (cents)	gal	106.60	10/00	43s
Household transportation expenditures	yr	6904	97-1998	102c
Maintenance and repair expenditures	yr	618	1999	30r
Public transportation, expenditures on	yr	575	1999	30r
Transportation purchases	yr	6503	1999	30r
Vehicle expenses, miscellaneous, purchases	yr	2266	1999	30r
Vehicle insurance payments	yr	824	1999	30r
Vehicle purchases (net outlay)	yr	2761	1999	30r
Vehicle rental, lease expenditures	yr	584	1999	30r

Philadelphia-Wilmington-Atlantic City, PA - continued

Item	Per	Value	Date	Ref.
Utilities				
Electrical bill, average	mos	69.16	9/00	9s
Electricity, expenditures on	yr	837	1999	30r
Electricity cost, average	KWh	5.08	9/00	9s
Utilities, fuels, and public services purchased	yr	2457	1999	30r
Water and other public services, expenditures on	yr	215	1999	30r
Weddings				
Wedding (national average cost)		19936	2000	33r
Wedding (regional average total cost)		29454	1997	110r
Attendants' gifts		321	1998	33r
Bridal attendants' apparel (5 persons)		824	2000	33r
Bride's headpiece/veil		173	1998	33r
Bride's wedding dress		859	1998	33r
Clergy, religious facility fee		242	1998	33r
Engagement ring		3177	1998	33r
Flowers		789	1998	33r
Groom's formalwear rental		99	2000	33r
Limousine		410	1998	33r
Marriage license cost		25.00-40.00	4/01	35s
Men's formalwear (ushers, best man)		469	2000	33r
Mother of bride apparel		241	2000	33r
Music		866	1998	33r
Photography and videography		1368	1998	33r
Rehearsal dinner		728	1998	33r
Wedding invitations and announcements		341	1998	33r
Wedding reception		7968	2000	33r
Wedding rings (bride and groom)		1060	1998	33r

Phoenix-Mesa, AZ

Item	Per	Value	Date	Ref.
Average annual expenditures	yr	40193	1999	30c
Composite, ACCRA index		100.20	3/01	4c
Alcoholic Beverages				
Alcoholic beverage purchases	yr	437	1999	30c
Beer, Heineken, 12-oz, ex deposit	6	7.69	3/01	4c
J & B Scotch	750-ml	18.34	3/01	4c
Wine, Livingston or Gallo, Chablis blanc	1.5 liter	5.22	3/01	4c
Appliances				
Appliance repair, service call, washing machine	min lab chg	42.80	3/01	4c
Banking and Money				
Mortgage rate, incl. points and orig. fee, 30-yr. conv. fixed or ARM	mos	7.09	3/01	4c
Business Expenses				
Business travel, car rental	day	53	2001	3c
Business travel, food	day	51	2001	3c
Business travel, hotel	day	129	2001	3c
Medical office space cost	sq ft	107.03	2001	31c
Office space, 2-4 storey building	sq ft	93.77	2001	31c
Office space, 5-10 storey building	sq ft	82.83	2001	31c
Office space, 11-20 storey building	sq ft	79.61	2001	31c
Charity				
Cash contributions, expenditures	yr	1552	1999	30c
Clothing				
Apparel and services purchases	yr	2057	1999	30c
Boys' brief, cotton	3	4.38	3/01	4c
Shirt, man's dress shirt		26.42	3/01	4c
Slacks, man's "No Wrinkles" khaki		37.14	3/01	4c
Communications				
Cable modem installation, Cox		99.00-174.95	6/99	103s
Cable modem rate, cable subscriber, Cox	mos	29.95-44.95	6/99	103s
Cable modem rate, non-cable subscriber, Cox	mos	42.95-54.95	6/99	103s

Values are in dollars or fractions of dollars. In the column headed *Ref*, references are shown to sources. Each reference is followed by a letter. These refer to the geographical level for which data were reported: s=State, r=Region, and c=City or metro. The abbreviation *ex* is used to mean *except* or *excluding*; *exp* stands for expenditures. For other abbreviations and further explanations, please see the Introduction.

Phoenix-Mesa, AZ - continued

Item	Per	Value	Date	Ref.
Communications				
Newspaper subscription, daily and Sunday delivery	mos	15.44	3/01	4c
Phone line, single, business, field visit	inst.	56.00	12/97	17s
Phone line, single, business, no field visit	inst.	56.00	12/97	17s
Phone line, single, residence, field visit	inst.	46.50	12/97	17s
Phone line, single, residence, no field visit	inst.	46.50	12/97	17s
Postal rate, express mail, up to half-pound		12.45	7/01	108r
Postal rate, letter, first class, first ounce		0.34	7/01	108r
Postal rate, letter, two ounces		0.57	7/01	108r
Postal rate, post card		0.21	7/01	108r
Postal rate, priority mail, two pounds		3.95	7/01	108r
Postal rate, priority mail, up to one pound		3.50	7/01	108r
Telephone bill, business, basic rate	mos	32.78	12/97	18c
Telephone bill, family of three	mos	20.65	3/01	4c
Telephone bill, residential, basic rate	mos	13.18	12/97	18c
Wireless services	mos	36.98	1/00	42c
Education				
Board, 4-year private college/university	yr	2143	1996	38s
Board, 4-year public college/university	yr	1815	1996	38s
Education expenditures	yr	535	1999	30c
Room, 4-year private college/university	yr	2012	1996	38s
Room, 4-year public college/university	yr	2257	1996	38s
Total cost, 4-year private college/university	yr	10934	1996	38s
Total cost, 4-year public college/university	yr	5998	1996	38s
Tuition, 2-year public college/university, in state	yr	764	1996	38s
Tuition, 4-year private college/university, in state	yr	6779	1996	38s
Tuition, 4-year public college/university	yr	1926	1996	38s
Energy and Fuels				
Energy, combined forms, 2400 sq ft	mos	112.59	3/01	4c
Gas, cooking, winter, 10 therms	mos	11.60	2/96	98c
Gas, cooking, winter, 30 therms	mos	23.80	2/96	98c
Gas, cooking, winter, 50 therms	mos	36.00	2/96	98c
Gas, heating, winter, average use	mos	42.10	2/96	98c
Gas, natural, commercial rate	1000 cf	8.12	11/00	88s
Gas, regular unleaded, cash, self-service	gal	1.48	3/01	4c
Entertainment				
Bowling, Saturday evening rate	line	3.29	3/01	4c
Entertainment purchases	yr	2036	1999	30c
Monopoly game, Parker Brothers', No. 9	game	10.41	3/01	4c
Movie, first-run, Saturday, evening	adm.	6.70	3/01	4c
Tennis balls, yellow, Wilson or Penn, 3	can	2.12	3/01	4c
Funerals				
Total cost of funeral		5401.08	1/99	78r
Acknowledgement cards		33.64	1/99	78r
Casket		2170.43	1/99	78r
Cosmetology, hair, other preparation		136.32	1/99	78r
Embalming		319.13	1/99	78r
Funeral at funeral home		370.21	1/99	78r
Hearse (local)		161.04	1/99	78r
Professional service charges		963.15	1/99	78r
Service car/van		133.99	1/99	78r
Transfer of remains to funeral home		159.82	1/99	78r
Vault		778.07	1/99	78r
Visitation/viewing		175.28	1/99	78r
Groceries				
Groceries, ACCRA Index		101.60	3/01	4c
Antibiotic ointment, Polysporin	0.5 oz	4.93	3/01	4c
Baby food, strained vegetables or fruit, lowest price	4-4.5 oz	0.34	3/01	4c
Bananas	lb	0.35	3/01	4c
Beef or hamburger, ground	lb	1.77	3/01	4c
Bread, white	loaf	0.94	3/01	4c
Cereals and bakery product purchases	yr	371	1999	30c
Cheese, Kraft grated Parmesan	8 oz	4.36	3/01	4c
Chicken, whole fryer	lb	0.95	3/01	4c
Cigarettes, Winston, Kings	carton	30.27	3/01	4c
Coffee, vacuum-packed	13 oz	2.81	3/01	4c

Phoenix-Mesa, AZ - continued

Item	Per	Value	Date	Ref.
Groceries - continued				
Corn Flakes, Kellogg's or Post Toasties	18 oz	3.12	3/01	4c
Corn, frozen, whole kernel, lowest price	16 oz	1.02	3/01	4c
Dairy product purchases	yr	334	1999	30c
Eggs, Grade A or AA	dozen	1.14	3/01	4c
Food (excl fruit and vegetables), eaten at home, purchases	yr	904	1999	30c
Food purchases	yr	4981	1999	30c
Food purchases, eaten away from home	yr	2311	1999	30c
Food purchases, food eaten at home	yr	2670	1999	30c
Lettuce, iceberg	head	0.97	3/01	4c
Margarine, Blue Bonnet or Parkay, stick	lb	0.94	3/01	4c
Meats, poultry, fish, and egg purchases	yr	607	1999	30c
Milk, whole	1/2 gal	1.74	3/01	4c
Orange juice, Minute Maid frozen	12 oz	1.70	3/01	4c
Peaches, halves or slices, Hunt's, Del Monte, or Libby's	29 oz	1.71	3/01	4c
Peas, green, Del Monte or Green Giant	15 oz	0.76	3/01	4c
Potatoes, white or red	10 lb	2.51	3/01	4c
Sausage, Jimmy Dean/Owens pork	lb	3.94	3/01	4c
Shortening, vegetable, Crisco	3 lb	3.82	3/01	4c
Soft drink, Coca Cola, ex deposit	2 liter	1.03	3/01	4c
Steak, T-bone	lb	5.41	3/01	4c
Sugar, cane or beet	4 lbs	1.54	3/01	4c
Tobacco products and smoking supplies purchases	yr	251	1999	30c
Tomatoes, Hunt's or Del Monte	14.5 oz	0.98	3/01	4c
Tuna, chunk, light	6 oz	0.58	3/01	4c
Goods and Services				
Miscellaneous goods and services, ACCRA Index		99.90	3/01	4c
Miscellaneous purchases	yr	967	1999	30c
Hunting license	yr	25.50	4/01	34s
Health Care				
Health care, ACCRA Index		118.60	3/01	4c
Cardiac catheterization, ave hospital/ physician charges		20100	1998	77s
Childbirth, Cesarean delivery		11587	1997	13r
Childbirth, vaginal delivery		6725	1997	13r
Dentist's fee, adult teeth cleaning and periodic oral exam	visit	86.37	3/01	4c
Doctor's fee, routine exam, established patient	visit	65.73	3/01	4c
Health care purchases	yr	2007	1999	30c
Home health care aide cost, licensed agency	hour	17	2000	82c
Hospital care, private room	day	709.70	3/01	4c
Hysterectomy, laproscopically-assisted, ave hospital/physician charges		19790	1998	76s
Hysterectomy, vaginal, ave hospital and physician charges		12130	1998	76s
Nursing home costs, private room	day	152	2000	82c
Nursing home stay, private room	day	152	2000	83c
Household Goods				
Dishwashing powder, Cascade	50 oz	3.40	3/01	4c
Household furnishings and equipment purchases	yr	1562	1999	30c
Tissues, facial, Kleenex brand	175	1.48	3/01	4c
Housing				
Housing, ACCRA Index		95.80	3/01	4c
Home, 2200 sq ft, 4-br, 2-bath, 2-car garage, average		194166	2000	47c
Home value, median		131000	2001	53s
House, 2400 sq ft, 8000 sq ft lot, new, urban, utilities	total	195491	3/01	4c
House payment, principal and interest, 25% down payment	mos	984	3/01	4c
Household operation expenditures	yr	669	1999	30c
Housekeeping supplies purchases	yr	479	1999	30c
Lodging expenditures	yr	496	1999	30c
Owned dwellings, expenditures own	yr	4691	1999	30c
Rent expenditures	yr	2538	1999	30c

Values are in dollars or fractions of dollars. In the column headed *Ref*, references are shown to sources. Each reference is followed by a letter. These refer to the geographical level for which data were reported: s=State, r=Region, and c=City or metro. The abbreviation *ex* is used to mean *except* or *excluding*; *exp* stands for *expenditures*. For other abbreviations and further explanations, please see the Introduction.

Phoenix-Mesa, AZ - continued

Item	Per	Value	Date	Ref.
Housing				
Rent, apartment, 2 br, 1 1/2-2 baths, unfurn, 950 sq ft, water	mos	675	3/01	4c
Rental unit, 1 bedroom, with utilities	mos	523	4/01	41c
Rental unit, 2 bedroom, with utilities	mos	656	4/01	41c
Rental unit, 3 bedroom, with utilities	mos	913	4/01	41c
Rental unit, 4 bedroom, with utilities	mos	1075	4/01	41c
Shelter, expenditures on	yr	7725	1999	30c
Insurance and Pensions				
Auto insurance premium	yr	901.65	1999	57s
Life and other personal insurance purchases	yr	336	1999	30c
Pensions and Social Security, expenditures on	yr	3290	1999	30c
Legal Fees				
Divorce, filing fee		64.00	4/01	35s
Driver's license fee	renew	17.50	1999	48s
Driver's license fee	orig	17.50	1999	48s
Personal Goods				
Personal care products and services purchases	yr	455	1999	30c
Shampoo, Alberto VO5	15 oz	1.24	3/01	4c
Toothpaste, Crest or Colgate	6-7 oz	2.07	3/01	4c
Personal Services				
Dry cleaning, man's 2-pc suit		8.60	3/01	4c
Man's haircut, barbershop, no styling		10.10	3/01	4c
Woman's shampoo, trim, blow-dry, no style-change		30.20	3/01	4c
Restaurant Food				
Chicken, fried, thigh and drumstick, KFC/Church's		2.33	3/01	4c
Hamburger with cheese, McDonald's	1/4 lb	2.23	3/01	4c
Pizza, Pizza Hut or Pizza Inn	11-12 in	9.29	3/01	4c
Transportation				
Transportation, ACCRA Index		107.80	3/01	4c
Bus fare, one-way	trip	1.35	2000	1c
Bus fare, to central business district	1-way	1.25	3/01	4c
Diesel at the pump	gal	1.27	10/99	73s
Gasoline and motor oil purchases	yr	1016	1999	30c
Gasoline before-tax price (cents)	gal	120.30	10/00	43s
Household transportation expenditures	yr	6826	97-1998	102c
Parking at airport, lowest rate	day	4.00	2000	46c
Public transportation, expenditures on	yr	464	1999	30c
Tire balance, computer or spin balance, front	wheel	8.63	3/01	4c
Transportation purchases	yr	8212	1999	30c
Vehicle expenses, miscellaneous, purchases	yr	2697	1999	30c
Travel				
Hotel room, ave	night	113.37	2000	70c
Utilities				
Utilities, ACCRA Index		92.60	3/01	4c
Electrical bill, average	mos	84.33	9/00	9s
Electricity, 2400 sq ft, new home	mos	112.59	3/01	4c
Electricity, summer, 250 KWh	mos	28.99	2/96	97c
Electricity, summer, 500 KWh	mos	50.47	2/96	97c
Electricity, summer, 750 KWh	mos	71.95	2/96	97c
Electricity, summer, 1000 KWh	mos	93.43	2/96	97c
Electricity cost, average	KWh	7.60	9/00	9s
Utilities, fuels, and public services purchased	yr	2458	1999	30c
Weddings				
Wedding (national average cost)		19936	2000	33r
Attendants' gifts		321	1998	33r
Bridal attendants' apparel (5 persons)		824	2000	33r
Bride's headpiece/veil		173	1998	33r
Bride's wedding dress		859	1998	33r
Clergy, religious facility fee		242	1998	33r
Engagement ring		3177	1998	33r
Flowers		789	1998	33r
Groom's formalwear rental		99	2000	33r
Limousine		410	1998	33r

Item	Per	Value	Date	Ref.
Weddings - continued				
Marriage license cost		50.00	4/01	35s
Men's formalwear (ushers, best man)		469	2000	33r
Mother of bride apparel		241	2000	33r
Music		866	1998	33r
Photography and videography		1368	1998	33r
Rehearsal dinner		728	1998	33r
Wedding invitations and announcements		341	1998	33r
Wedding reception		7968	2000	33r
Wedding rings (bride and groom)		1060	1998	33r

Pine Bluff, AR

Item	Per	Value	Date	Ref.
Alcoholic Beverages				
Alcoholic beverage purchases	yr	253	1999	30r
Malt beverages, all types, all sizes, any origin	16 oz	0.96	7/01	11r
Appliances				
Major appliances, expenditures on	yr	172	1999	30r
Small appliances, housewares, expenditures on	yr	81	1999	30r
Banking and Money				
Mortgage interest and charges paid	yr	2039	1999	30r
Mortgage principal paid on owned property	yr	1026	1999	30r
Vehicle finance charges paid	yr	365	1999	30r
Charity				
Cash contributions, expenditures	yr	1127	1999	30r
Child Care				
Child raising cost, total, age 0-2	yr	8540	1999	60r
Child raising cost, total, age 3-5	yr	8780	1999	60r
Child raising cost, total, age 6-8	yr	8820	1999	60r
Child raising cost, total, age 9-11	yr	8800	1999	60r
Child raising cost, total, age 12-14	yr	9510	1999	60r
Child raising cost, total, age 15-17	yr	9740	1999	60r
Child's child care and education, age 0-2	yr	1380	1999	60r
Child's child care and education, age 3-5	yr	1520	1999	60r
Child's child care and education, age 6-8	yr	990	1999	60r
Child's child care and education, age 9-11	yr	650	1999	60r
Child's child care and education, age 12-14	yr	490	1999	60r
Child's child care and education, age 15-17	yr	840	1999	60r
Child's clothing, age 0-2	yr	480	1999	60r
Child's clothing, age 3-5	yr	470	1999	60r
Child's clothing, age 6-8	yr	520	1999	60r
Child's clothing, age 9-11	yr	570	1999	60r
Child's clothing, age 12-14	yr	950	1999	60r
Child's clothing, age 15-17	yr	850	1999	60r
Child's food, age 0-2	yr	1000	1999	60r
Child's food, age 3-5	yr	1160	1999	60r
Child's food, age 6-8	yr	1490	1999	60r
Child's food, age 9-11	yr	1770	1999	60r
Child's food, age 12-14	yr	1770	1999	60r
Child's food, age 15-17	yr	1980	1999	60r
Child's health care, age 0-2	yr	620	1999	60r
Child's health care, age 3-5	yr	590	1999	60r
Child's health care, age 6-8	yr	680	1999	60r
Child's health care, age 9-11	yr	720	1999	60r
Child's health care, age 12-14	yr	730	1999	60r
Child's health care, age 15-17	yr	760	1999	60r
Child's housing, age 0-2	yr	3070	1999	60r
Child's housing, age 3-5	yr	3050	1999	60r
Child's housing, age 6-8	yr	3010	1999	60r
Child's housing, age 9-11	yr	2850	1999	60r
Child's housing, age 12-14	yr	3040	1999	60r
Child's housing, age 15-17	yr	2650	1999	60r
Child's personal care, reading, age 0-2	yr	910	1999	60r
Child's personal care, reading, age 3-5	yr	930	1999	60r
Child's personal care, reading, age 6-8	yr	960	1999	60r
Child's personal care, reading, age 9-11	yr	1000	1999	60r
Child's personal care, reading, age 12-14	yr	1170	1999	60r
Child's personal care, reading, age 15-17	yr	950	1999	60r

Values are in dollars or fractions of dollars. In the column headed *Ref*, references are shown to sources. Each reference is followed by a letter. These refer to the geographical level for which data were reported: s=State, r=Region, and c=City or metro. The abbreviation *ex* is used to mean *except* or *excluding*; *exp* stands for expenditures. For other abbreviations and further explanations, please see the Introduction.

Pine Bluff, AR - continued

Item	Per	Value	Date	Ref.
Clothing				
Apparel and services purchases	yr	1610	1999	30r
Boys, 2 to 15, expenditures on	yr	89	1999	30r
Children under 2, expenditures on	yr	79	1999	30r
Footwear, expenditures on	yr	283	1999	30r
Girls, 2 to 15, expenditures on	yr	103	1999	30r
Men and boys, expenditures on	yr	351	1999	30r
Men, 16 and over, expenditures on	yr	262	1999	30r
Women, 16 and over, expenditures on	yr	538	1999	30r
Communications				
Phone line, single, business, field visit	inst.	84.00	12/97	17s
Phone line, single, business, no field visit	inst.	84.00	12/97	17s
Phone line, single, residence, field visit	inst.	39.70	12/97	17s
Phone line, single, residence, no field visit	inst.	39.70	12/97	17s
Postage and stationery, expenditures on	yr	104	1999	30r
Postal rate, express mail, up to half-pound		12.45	7/01	108r
Postal rate, letter, first class, first ounce		0.34	7/01	108r
Postal rate, letter, two ounces		0.57	7/01	108r
Postal rate, post card		0.21	7/01	108r
Postal rate, priority mail, two pounds		3.95	7/01	108r
Postal rate, priority mail, up to one pound		3.50	7/01	108r
Telephone services, expenditures on	yr	860	1999	30r
Education				
Board, 4-year private college/university	yr	2121	1996	38s
Board, 4-year public college/university	yr	1423	1996	38s
Education expenditures	yr	431	1999	30r
Room, 4-year private college/university	yr	1488	1996	38s
Room, 4-year public college/university	yr	1613	1996	38s
Total cost, 4-year private college/university	yr	10183	1996	38s
Total cost, 4-year public college/university	yr	5064	1996	38s
Tuition, 2-year public college/university, in state	yr	903	1996	38s
Tuition, 4-year private college/university, in state	yr	6574	1996	38s
Tuition, 4-year public college/university	yr	2028	1996	38s
Energy and Fuels				
Electricity	KWh	0.09	7/01	11r
Electricity	500 KWhs	47.29	7/01	11r
Fuel oil #2	gal	1.43	7/01	11r
Fuel oil and other fuels, expenditures on	yr	45	1999	30r
Gasoline, all types	gal	1.60	7/01	11r
Gasoline, unleaded midgrade	gal	1.65	7/01	11r
Gasoline, unleaded premium	gal	1.74	7/01	11r
Natural gas, expenditures on	yr	164	1999	30r
Utility (piped) gas, therm		1.01	7/01	11r
Utility (piped) gas, 40 therms		44.29	7/01	11r
Utility (piped) gas, 100 therms		97.44	7/01	11r
Entertainment				
Entertainment purchases	yr	1574	1999	30r
Fees and admissions paid	yr	371	1999	30r
Reading purchases	yr	121	1999	30r
Television, radios, sound equipment, expenditures on	yr	561	1999	30r
Funerals				
Total cost of funeral		5842.28	1/99	78r
Acknowledgement cards		28.35	1/99	78r
Casket		2494.29	1/99	78r
Cosmetology, hair, other preparation		109.22	1/99	78r
Embalming		361.42	1/99	78r
Funeral at funeral home		349.20	1/99	78r
Hearse (local)		161.91	1/99	78r
Professional service charges		1116.50	1/99	78r
Service car/van		65.56	1/99	78r
Transfer of remains to funeral home		143.56	1/99	78r
Vault		785.25	1/99	78r
Visitation/viewing		227.02	1/99	78r
Groceries				
American processed cheese	lb	3.50	7/01	11r
Bakery products, expenditures on	yr	261	1999	30r

Pine Bluff, AR - continued

Item	Per	Value	Date	Ref.
Groceries - continued				
Bananas	lb	0.47	7/01	11r
Beans, dried, any type, all sizes	lb	0.63	7/01	11r
Beef for stew, boneless	lb	2.86	7/01	11r
Beef, expenditures on	yr	210	1999	30r
Bologna, all beef or mixed	lb	2.29	7/01	11r
Bread, French	lb	1.66	7/01	11r
Bread, white, pan	lb	0.87	7/01	11r
Bread, whole wheat, pan	lb	1.38	7/01	11r
Broccoli	lb	1.04	7/01	11r
Butter, salted, grade AA, stick	lb	2.26	7/01	11r
Butter, yoghurt, cheese, etc, expenditures on	yr	170	1999	30r
Cabbage	lb	0.42	7/01	11r
Cereals and cereal products, expenditures on	yr	140	1999	30r
Cheddar cheese, natural	lb	3.75	7/01	11r
Chicken breast, bone-in	lb	1.85	7/01	11r
Chicken legs, bone-in	lb	1.34	7/01	11r
Chicken, fresh, whole	lb	1.05	7/01	11r
Chops, boneless,	lb	4.13	7/01	11r
Chuck roast, graded and ungraded, excl U.S. prime and choice	lb	2.35	7/01	11r
Chuck roast, U.S. choice, boneless	lb	2.67	7/01	11r
Coffee, 100%, ground roast, all sizes	lb	2.88	7/01	11r
Coffee, instant, plain, regular, all sizes	16 oz	9.25	7/01	11r
Cola, non diet,	2 liter	1.11	7/01	11r
Crackers, soda, salted	lb	1.70	7/01	11r
Dairy product purchases	yr	282	1999	30r
Eggs, expenditures on	yr	32	1999	30r
Fats and oils, expenditures on	yr	79	1999	30r
Fish and seafood, expenditures on	yr	99	1999	30r
Flour, white, all purpose	lb	0.32	7/01	11r
Food (excl fruit and vegetables), eaten at home, purchases	yr	815	1999	30r
Food cooked on trips, expenditures on	yr	36	1999	30r
Food purchases	yr	4533	1999	30r
Food purchases, eaten away from home	yr	1873	1999	30r
Food purchases, food eaten at home	yr	2660	1999	30r
Fresh fruits, expenditures on	yr	128	1999	30r
Fresh milk and cream, expenditures on	yr	112	1999	30r
Fresh vegetables, expenditures on	yr	131	1999	30r
Fruit and vegetable purchases	yr	438	1999	30r
Grapefruit	lb	0.59	7/01	11r
Grapes, Thompson, seedless	lb	2.12	7/01	11r
Ground beef, 100% beef	lb	1.76	7/01	11r
Ground beef, lean and extra lean	lb	2.60	7/01	11r
Ground chuck, 100% beef	lb	2.08	7/01	11r
Ham, boneless, excl canned	lb	2.71	7/01	11r
Ham, rump or shank half, bone-in, smoked	lb	2.19	7/01	11r
Ice cream, prepackaged, bulk, regular	1/2 gal	3.93	7/01	11r
Lemons	lb	1.32	7/01	11r
Lettuce, iceberg	lb	0.76	7/01	11r
Milk, fresh, low fat,	gal	2.75	7/01	11r
Milk, fresh, whole, fortified	gal	2.97	7/01	11r
Nonalcoholic beverages, expenditures on	yr	228	1999	30r
Orange juice, frozen concentrate	16 oz	1.95	7/01	11r
Oranges, Navel	lb	0.73	7/01	11r
Oranges, Valencia	lb	0.55	7/01	11r
Peanut butter, creamy, all sizes	lb	1.83	7/01	11r
Pears, Anjou	lb	0.98	7/01	11r
Pork chops, center cut, bone-in	lb	3.33	7/01	11r
Pork sausage, fresh, loose	lb	2.59	7/01	11r
Pork shoulder picnic, bone-in, smoked	lb	1.12	7/01	11r
Pork, expenditures on	yr	162	1999	30r
Potato chips	16 oz	3.59	7/01	11r
Potatoes, frozen, french fried	lb	1.00	7/01	11r
Potatoes, white, all types	lb	0.44	7/01	11r
Poultry, expenditures on	yr	137	1999	30r
Processed fruits, expenditures on	yr	97	1999	30r
Processed vegetables, expenditures on	yr	82	1999	30r
Rice, white, long grain, uncooked	lb	0.51	7/01	11r
Round roast, graded and ungraded, excl U.S. prime and choice	lb	2.96	7/01	11r

Values are in dollars or fractions of dollars. In the column headed *Ref*, references are shown to sources. Each reference is followed by a letter. These refer to the geographical level for which data were reported: s=State, r=Region, and c=City or metro. The abbreviation *ex* is used to mean *except* or *excluding*; *exp* stands for *expenditures*. For other abbreviations and further explanations, please see the Introduction.

Pine Bluff, AR - continued

Item	Per	Value	Date	Ref.
Groceries				
Round steak, graded and ungraded, excl U.S. prime and choice	lb	3.11	7/01	11r
Sirloin steak, graded and ungraded, excl U.S. prime and choice	lb	4.23	7/01	11r
Spaghetti and macaroni	lb	0.78	7/01	11r
Steak, round, U.S. choice, boneless	lb	3.56	7/01	11r
Steak, sirloin, U.S. choice, boneless	lb	5.65	7/01	11r
Strawberries, dry pint	12 oz	1.50	7/01	11r
Sugar and other sweets, expenditures on	yr	99	1999	30r
Sugar, white, 33-80 ounce package	lb	0.39	7/01	11r
Sugar, white, all sizes	lb	0.42	7/01	11r
Tobacco products and smoking supplies purchases	yr	288	1999	30r
Tomatoes, field grown	lb	1.43	7/01	11r
Tuna, light, chunk	lb	1.77	7/01	11r
Turkey, frozen, whole	lb	1.05	7/01	11r
Goods and Services				
B&B Japanese maple (acer japonicum)	gal	79.98-99.00	4/00	93r
Boxwood (buxus)	2 gal	12.98-18.99	4/00	93r
Daylily (hemerocallis)	gal	7.96-11.00	4/00	93r
Flat of annuals		13.99-27.99	4/00	93r
Fountain grass (pennisetum)	gal	6.96-9.00	4/00	93r
Hanging basket (10 in)		9.99-24.99	4/00	93r
Hardy geranium (geranium)	gal	5.96-8.00	4/00	93r
Hosta (hosta)	gal	8.96-12.99	4/00	93r
Lilac (syrubga vulgaris)	2 gal	13.00-19.99	4/00	93r
Rhododendron (rhododendron)	2 gal	12.98-29.99	4/00	93r
Sage (salvia)	gal	5.96-8.00	4/00	93r
Wintercreeper euonymus (euonymus fortunei)	2 gal	13.00-18.99	4/00	93r
Hunting license	yr	25.00	4/01	34s
Health Care				
Cardiac catheterization, ave hospital/ physician charges		12240	1998	77s
Childbirth, Cesarean delivery		11587	1997	13r
Childbirth, vaginal delivery		6725	1997	13r
Drugs, expenditures on	yr	399	1999	30r
Health care purchases	yr	1971	1999	30r
Health insurance expenditures	yr	933	1999	30r
Hysterectomy, laproscopically-assisted, ave hospital/physician charges		10580	1998	76s
Hysterectomy, vaginal, ave hospital and physician charges		8270	1998	76s
Medicaid dispensing fee		5.51	1999	87s
Medical services expenditures	yr	547	1999	30r
Medical supplies, expenditures on	yr	91	1999	30r
Household Goods				
Floor coverings, expenditures on	yr	44	1999	30r
Furniture, expenditures on	yr	335	1999	30r
Household furnishings and equipment purchases	yr	1328	1999	30r
Household textiles, expenditures on	yr	89	1999	30r
Laundry and cleaning supplies, expenditures on	yr	113	1999	30r
Housing				
Home price, existing, ave		160100	10/00	90r
Home value, median		94000	2001	53s
Household operation expenditures	yr	553	1999	30r
Housekeeping supplies purchases	yr	473	1999	30r

Pine Bluff, AR - continued

Item	Per	Value	Date	Ref.
Housing - continued				
Housing, expenditures on	yr	10303	1999	30r
Maintenance, repairs, insurance expenditures	yr	699	1999	30r
Monthly rental value of owned home	mos	505	1999	30r
Owned dwellings, expenditures own	yr	3465	1999	30r
Rent expenditures	yr	1641	1999	30r
Rental unit, 1 bedroom, with utilities	mos	347	4/01	41c
Rental unit, 2 bedroom, with utilities	mos	456	4/01	41c
Rental unit, 3 bedroom, with utilities	mos	575	4/01	41c
Rental unit, 4 bedroom, with utilities	mos	746	4/01	41c
Shelter, expenditures on	yr	5467	1999	30r
Insurance and Pensions				
Life and other personal insurance purchases	yr	414	1999	30r
Pensions and Social Security, expenditures on	yr	2635	1999	30r
Personal insurance and pensions, expenditures on	yr	3048	1999	30r
Legal Fees				
Divorce, filing fee		100.00	4/01	35s
Driver's license fee	renew	14.00	1999	48s
Driver's license fee	orig	14.00	1999	48s
Personal Goods				
Personal care products and services purchases	yr	393	1999	30r
Personal Services				
Personal services, household, expenditures on	yr	258	1999	30r
Pets				
Pets, toys, and playground equipment, expenditures on	yr	306	1999	30r
Taxes				
Federal income taxes paid	yr	2047	1999	30r
Personal taxes, expenditures on	yr	2554	1999	30r
Property taxes paid	yr	726	1999	30r
State and local income taxes paid	yr	363	1999	30r
Transportation				
Cars and trucks, new, expenditures on	yr	1648	1999	30r
Cars and trucks, used, expenditures on	yr	1651	1999	30r
Diesel at the pump	gal	1.17	10/99	73s
Gasoline and motor oil purchases	yr	1052	1999	30r
Gasoline before-tax price (cents)	gal	102.60	10/00	43s
Maintenance and repair expenditures	yr	621	1999	30r
Public transportation, expenditures on	yr	298	1999	30r
Transportation purchases	yr	6738	1999	30r
Vehicle expenses, miscellaneous, purchases	yr	2033	1999	30r
Vehicle insurance payments	yr	696	1999	30r
Vehicle purchases (net outlay)	yr	3354	1999	30r
Vehicle rental, lease expenditures	yr	352	1999	30r
Utilities				
Electrical bill, average	mos	75.00	9/00	9s
Electricity, expenditures on	yr	1115	1999	30r
Electricity cost, average	KWh	5.70	9/00	9s
Water and other public services, expenditures on	yr	298	1999	30r
Weddings				
Wedding (national average cost)		19936	2000	33r
Attendants' gifts		321	1998	33r
Bridal attendants' apparel (5 persons)		824	2000	33r
Bride's headpiece/veil		173	1998	33r
Bride's wedding dress		859	1998	33r
Clergy, religious facility fee		242	1998	33r
Engagement ring		3177	1998	33r
Flowers		789	1998	33r
Groom's formalwear rental		99	2000	33r
Limousine		410	1998	33r
Marriage license cost		30.00	4/01	35s
Men's formalwear (ushers, best man)		469	2000	33r

Values are in dollars or fractions of dollars. In the column headed *Ref*, references are shown to sources. Each reference is followed by a letter. These refer to the geographical level for which data were reported: s=State, r=Region, and c=City or metro. The abbreviation *ex* is used to mean *except* or *excluding*; *exp* stands for *expenditures*. For other abbreviations and further explanations, please see the Introduction.

Pine Bluff, AR - continued

Item	Per	Value	Date	Ref.
Weddings				
Mother of bride apparel		241	2000	33r
Music		866	1998	33r
Photography and videography		1368	1998	33r
Rehearsal dinner		728	1998	33r
Wedding invitations and announcements		341	1998	33r
Wedding reception		7968	2000	33r
Wedding rings (bride and groom)		1060	1998	33r

Pittsburgh, PA

Item	Per	Value	Date	Ref.
Average annual expenditures	yr	37971	1999	30r
Composite, ACCRA index		109.50	3/01	4c
Alcoholic Beverages				
Alcoholic beverage purchases	yr	280	1999	30c
Beer, Heineken, 12-oz, ex deposit	6	8.94	3/01	4c
J & B Scotch	750-ml	22.99	3/01	4c
Wine, Livingston or Gallo, Chablis blanc	1.5 liter	6.99	3/01	4c
Wine, red and white table, all sizes, any origin	liter	9.64	7/01	11r
Appliances				
Appliance repair, service call, washing machine	min lab chg	31.49	3/01	4c
Major appliances, expenditures on	yr	194	1999	30r
Small appliances, housewares, expenditures on	yr	93	1999	30r
Banking and Money				
Mortgage interest and charges paid	yr	2622	1999	30r
Mortgage principal paid on owned property	yr	1262	1999	30r
Mortgage rate, incl. points and orig. fee, 30-yr. conv. fixed or ARM	mos	7.43	3/01	4c
Vehicle finance charges paid	yr	240	1999	30r
Business Expenses				
Business travel, car rental	day	46	2001	3c
Business travel, food	day	55	2001	3c
Business travel, hotel	day	94	2001	3c
Medical office space cost	sq ft	121.53	2001	31c
Office space, 2-4 storey building	sq ft	106.47	2001	31c
Office space, 5-10 storey building	sq ft	94.05	2001	31c
Office space, 11-20 storey building	sq ft	90.40	2001	31c
Charity				
Cash contributions, expenditures	yr	1408	1999	30c
Child Care				
Child raising cost, total, age 0-2	yr	8670	1999	60r
Child raising cost, total, age 3-5	yr	8910	1999	60r
Child raising cost, total, age 6-8	yr	9040	1999	60r
Child raising cost, total, age 9-11	yr	9100	1999	60r
Child raising cost, total, age 12-14	yr	9890	1999	60r
Child raising cost, total, age 15-17	yr	10010	1999	60r
Child's child care and education, age 0-2	yr	1070	1999	60r
Child's child care and education, age 3-5	yr	1190	1999	60r
Child's child care and education, age 6-8	yr	740	1999	60r
Child's child care and education, age 9-11	yr	470	1999	60r
Child's child care and education, age 12-14	yr	350	1999	60r
Child's child care and education, age 15-17	yr	590	1999	60r
Child's clothing, age 0-2	yr	480	1999	60r
Child's clothing, age 3-5	yr	470	1999	60r
Child's clothing, age 6-8	yr	520	1999	60r
Child's clothing, age 9-11	yr	570	1999	60r
Child's clothing, age 12-14	yr	970	1999	60r
Child's clothing, age 15-17	yr	870	1999	60r
Child's food, age 0-2	yr	1130	1999	60r
Child's food, age 3-5	yr	1290	1999	60r
Child's food, age 6-8	yr	1640	1999	60r
Child's food, age 9-11	yr	1930	1999	60r
Child's food, age 12-14	yr	1940	1999	60r
Child's food, age 15-17	yr	2150	1999	60r
Child's health care, age 0-2	yr	550	1999	60r
Child's health care, age 3-5	yr	530	1999	60r

Pittsburgh, PA - continued

Item	Per	Value	Date	Ref.
Child Care - continued				
Child's health care, age 6-8	yr	610	1999	60r
Child's health care, age 9-11	yr	650	1999	60r
Child's health care, age 12-14	yr	660	1999	60r
Child's health care, age 15-17	yr	690	1999	60r
Child's housing, age 0-2	yr	3555	1999	60r
Child's housing, age 3-5	yr	3530	1999	60r
Child's housing, age 6-8	yr	3490	1999	60r
Child's housing, age 9-11	yr	3340	1999	60r
Child's housing, age 12-14	yr	3530	1999	60r
Child's housing, age 15-17	yr	3140	1999	60r
Child's personal care, reading, age 0-2	yr	920	1999	60r
Child's personal care, reading, age 3-5	yr	950	1999	60r
Child's personal care, reading, age 6-8	yr	980	1999	60r
Child's personal care, reading, age 9-11	yr	1020	1999	60r
Child's personal care, reading, age 12-14	yr	1190	1999	60r
Child's personal care, reading, age 15-17	yr	970	1999	60r
Clothing				
Apparel and services purchases	yr	2331	1999	30c
Boys' brief, cotton	3	3.63	3/01	4c
Boys, 2 to 15, expenditures on	yr	92	1999	30r
Children under 2, expenditures on	yr	63	1999	30r
Footwear, expenditures on	yr	300	1999	30r
Girls, 2 to 15, expenditures on	yr	101	1999	30r
Men and boys, expenditures on	yr	446	1999	30r
Men, 16 and over, expenditures on	yr	354	1999	30r
Shirt, man's dress shirt		25.71	3/01	4c
Slacks, man's "No Wrinkles" khaki		46.22	3/01	4c
Women, 16 and over, expenditures on	yr	584	1999	30r
Communications				
Cable modem installation, Adelphi		54.90	6/99	103s
Cable modem installation, Comcast		95.00	6/99	103s
Cable modem rate, cable subscriber, Adelphi	mos	34.95	6/99	103s
Cable modem rate, cable subscriber, Comcast	mos	39.95	6/99	103s
Cable modem rate, non-cable subscriber, Adelphi	mos	44.95	6/99	103s
Cable modem rate, non-cable subscriber, Comcast	mos	49.95	6/99	103s
Newspaper subscription, daily and Sunday delivery	mos	11.74	3/01	4c
Phone line, single, business, field visit	inst.	75.00	12/97	17s
Phone line, single, business, no field visit	inst.	75.00	12/97	17s
Phone line, single, residence, field visit	inst.	40.00	12/97	17s
Phone line, single, residence, no field visit	inst.	40.00	12/97	17s
Postage and stationery, expenditures on	yr	138	1999	30r
Postal rate, express mail, up to half-pound		12.45	7/01	108r
Postal rate, letter, first class, first ounce		0.34	7/01	108r
Postal rate, letter, two ounces		0.57	7/01	108r
Postal rate, post card		0.21	7/01	108r
Postal rate, priority mail, two pounds		3.95	7/01	108r
Postal rate, priority mail, up to one pound		3.50	7/01	108r
Telephone bill, business, basic rate	mos	19.20	12/97	18c
Telephone bill, family of three	mos	20.13	3/01	4c
Telephone bill, residential, basic rate	mos	6.85	12/97	18c
Telephone services, expenditures on	yr	830	1999	30r
Education				
Board, 4-year private college/university	yr	2822	1996	38s
Board, 4-year public college/university	yr	2174	1996	38s
Education expenditures	yr	467	1999	30c
Room, 4-year private college/university	yr	2943	1996	38s
Room, 4-year public college/university	yr	2227	1996	38s
Total cost, 4-year private college/university	yr	19876	1996	38s
Total cost, 4-year public college/university	yr	9124	1996	38s
Tuition, 2-year public college/university, in state	yr	1909	1996	38s
Tuition, 4-year private college/university, in state	yr	14111	1996	38s
Tuition, 4-year public college/university	yr	4723	1996	38s

Values are in dollars or fractions of dollars. In the column headed *Ref*, references are shown to sources. Each reference is followed by a letter. These refer to the geographical level for which data were reported: s=State, r=Region, and c=City or metro. The abbreviation *ex* is used to mean *except* or *excluding*; *exp* stands for expenditures. For other abbreviations and further explanations, please see the Introduction.

Pittsburgh, PA - continued

Item	Per	Value	Date	Ref.
Energy and Fuels				
Electricity	KWh	0.12	7/01	11r
Energy, combined forms, 2400 sq ft	mos	184.41	3/01	4c
Energy, exc. electricity, 2400 sq ft	mos	95.59	3/01	4c
Fuel oil #2	gal	1.31	7/01	11r
Fuel oil and other fuels, expenditures on	yr	207	1999	30r
Gas, cooking, winter, 10 therms	mos	16.56	2/96	98c
Gas, cooking, winter, 30 therms	mos	27.58	2/96	98c
Gas, cooking, winter, 50 therms	mos	38.60	2/96	98c
Gas, heating, winter, average use	mos	123.35	2/96	98c
Gas, natural, commercial rate	1000 cf	5.96	11/00	88s
Gas, regular unleaded, cash, self-service	gal	1.39	3/01	4c
Gasoline, all types	gal	1.80	7/01	11r
Gasoline, unleaded midgrade	gal	1.85	7/01	11r
Gasoline, unleaded premium	gal	1.91	7/01	11r
Gasoline, unleaded regular	gal	1.71	7/01	11r
Natural gas, expenditures on	yr	368	1999	30r
Utility (piped) gas, therm		1.08	7/01	11r
Utility (piped) gas, 40 therms		50.87	7/01	11r
Utility (piped) gas, 100 therms		111.06	7/01	11r
Entertainment				
Bowling, Saturday evening rate	line	3.13	3/01	4c
Entertainment purchases	yr	1631	1999	30c
Fees and admissions paid	yr	511	1999	30r
Major League baseball ticket		21.48	2000	105c
Monopoly game, Parker Brothers', No. 9	game	10.49	3/01	4c
Movie, first-run, Saturday, evening	adm.	7.87	3/01	4c
Reading purchases	yr	181	1999	30c
Television, radios, sound equipment, expenditures on	yr	650	1999	30r
Tennis balls, yellow, Wilson or Penn, 3	can	2.93	3/01	4c
Funerals				
Total cost of funeral		5813.50	1/99	78r
Acknowledgement cards		28.32	1/99	78r
Casket		2082.20	1/99	78r
Cosmetology, hair, other preparation		169.59	1/99	78r
Embalming		465.60	1/99	78r
Funeral at funeral home		339.56	1/99	78r
Hearse (local)		183.96	1/99	78r
Professional service charges		1157.85	1/99	78r
Service car/van		100.41	1/99	78r
Transfer of remains to funeral home		158.66	1/99	78r
Vault		766.31	1/99	78r
Visitation/viewing		361.04	1/99	78r
Groceries				
Groceries, ACCRA Index		101.40	3/01	4c
Antibiotic ointment, Polysporin	0.5 oz	4.81	3/01	4c
Apples, red delicious	lb	0.95	7/01	11r
Baby food, strained vegetables or fruit, lowest price	4-4.5 oz	0.43	3/01	4c
Bacon, sliced	lb	3.44	7/01	11r
Bakery products, expenditures on	yr	310	1999	30r
Bananas	lb	0.41	3/01	4c
Bananas	lb	0.55	7/01	11r
Beef or hamburger, ground	lb	1.51	3/01	4c
Beef, expenditures on	yr	236	1999	30r
Bread, white	loaf	0.80	3/01	4c
Bread, white, pan	lb	1.09	7/01	11r
Butter, yoghurt, cheese, etc, expenditures on	yr	214	1999	30r
Cereals and bakery product purchases	yr	474	1999	30r
Cereals and cereal products, expenditures on	yr	164	1999	30r
Cheese, Kraft grated Parmesan	8 oz	3.69	3/01	4c
Chicken legs, bone-in	lb	1.23	7/01	11r
Chicken, fresh, whole	lb	1.13	7/01	11r
Chicken, whole fryer	lb	1.03	3/01	4c
Chuck roast, U.S. choice, boneless	lb	2.79	7/01	11r
Cigarettes, Winston, Kings	carton	29.87	3/01	4c
Coffee, 100%, ground roast, all sizes	lb	3.40	7/01	11r
Coffee, vacuum-packed	13 oz	2.77	3/01	4c
Corn Flakes, Kellogg's or Post Toasties	18 oz	2.74	3/01	4c
Corn, frozen, whole kernel, lowest price	16 oz	1.27	3/01	4c

Pittsburgh, PA - continued

Item	Per	Value	Date	Ref.
Groceries - continued				
Dairy product purchases	yr	331	1999	30c
Eggs, expenditures on	yr	34	1999	30r
Eggs, Grade A or AA	dozen	1.18	3/01	4c
Eggs, grade A, large	dozen	0.82	7/01	11r
Fats and oils, expenditures on	yr	80	1999	30r
Fish and seafood, expenditures on	yr	123	1999	30r
Food (excl fruit and vegetables), eaten at home, purchases	yr	846	1999	30c
Food cooked on trips, expenditures on	yr	48	1999	30r
Food purchases	yr	4981	1999	30c
Food purchases, eaten away from home	yr	2177	1999	30c
Food purchases, food eaten at home	yr	2803	1999	30c
Fresh fruits, expenditures on	yr	169	1999	30r
Fresh milk and cream, expenditures on	yr	128	1999	30r
Fresh vegetables, expenditures on	yr	164	1999	30r
Fruit and vegetable purchases	yr	447	1999	30c
Grapefruit	lb	0.67	7/01	11r
Grapes, Thompson, seedless	lb	2.18	7/01	11r
Ground beef, lean and extra lean	lb	2.66	7/01	11r
Ground chuck, 100% beef	lb	2.04	7/01	11r
Lettuce, iceberg	head	0.97	3/01	4c
Lettuce, iceberg	lb	0.76	7/01	11r
Margarine, Blue Bonnet or Parkay, stick	lb	0.90	3/01	4c
Meats, poultry, fish, and egg purchases	yr	808	1999	30r
Milk, whole	1/2 gal	1.56	3/01	4c
Nonalcoholic beverages, expenditures on	yr	225	1999	30r
Orange juice, frozen concentrate	16 oz	1.88	7/01	11r
Orange juice, Minute Maid frozen	12 oz	1.61	3/01	4c
Oranges, Navel	lb	0.79	7/01	11r
Oranges, Valencia	lb	0.56	7/01	11r
Peaches	lb	1.16	7/01	11r
Peaches, halves or slices, Hunt's, Del Monte, or Libby's	29 oz	1.67	3/01	4c
Peanut butter, creamy, all sizes	lb	2.01	7/01	11r
Pears, Anjou	lb	1.16	7/01	11r
Peas, green, Del Monte or Green Giant	15 oz	0.72	3/01	4c
Pork chops, center cut, bone-in	lb	3.57	7/01	11r
Pork, expenditures on	yr	146	1999	30r
Potato chips	16 oz	3.37	7/01	11r
Potatoes, white or red	10 lb	2.75	3/01	4c
Potatoes, white, all types	lb	0.42	7/01	11r
Poultry, expenditures on	yr	158	1999	30r
Processed fruits, expenditures on	yr	124	1999	30r
Processed vegetables, expenditures on	yr	82	1999	30r
Round roast, U.S. choice, boneless	lb	3.04	7/01	11r
Sausage, Jimmy Dean/Owens pork	lb	3.35	3/01	4c
Shortening, vegetable, Crisco	3 lb	3.41	3/01	4c
Soft drink, Coca Cola, ex deposit	2 liter	1.39	3/01	4c
Spaghetti and macaroni	lb	1.04	7/01	11r
Steak, sirloin, U.S. choice, boneless	lb	5.39	7/01	11r
Steak, T-bone	lb	6.73	3/01	4c
Strawberries, dry pint	12 oz	1.51	7/01	11r
Sugar and other sweets, expenditures on	yr	110	1999	30r
Sugar, cane or beet	4 lbs	1.63	3/01	4c
Sugar, white, 33-80 ounce package	lb	0.46	7/01	11r
Sugar, white, all sizes	lb	0.47	7/01	11r
Tobacco products and smoking supplies purchases	yr	296	1999	30c
Tomatoes, Hunt's or Del Monte	14.5 oz	0.91	3/01	4c
Tuna, chunk, light	6 oz	0.74	3/01	4c
Yogurt, natural, fruit flavored	8 oz	0.79	7/01	11r
Goods and Services				
Miscellaneous goods and services, ACCRA Index		104.40	3/01	4c
B&B Japanese maple (acer japonicum)	gal	38.99-125.00	4/00	93r
Boxwood (buxus)	2 gal	15.99-49.95	4/00	93r
Daylilly (hemerocallis)	gal	4.95	4/00	93r
Flat of annuals		8.00-14.99	4/00	93r

Values are in dollars or fractions of dollars. In the column headed *Ref*, references are shown as sources. Each reference is followed by a letter. These refer to the geographical level for which data were reported: s=State, r=Region, and c=City or metro. The abbreviation *ex* is used to mean *except* or *excluding*; *exp* stands for expenditures. For other abbreviations and further explanations, please see the Introduction.

Pittsburgh, PA - continued

Item	Per	Value	Date	Ref.
Goods and Services				
Fountain grass (pennisetum)	gal	6.99-9.99	4/00	93r
Hanging basket (10 in)		12.95-19.99	4/00	93r
Hardy geranium (geranium)	gal	6.95-7.99	4/00	93r
Hosta (hosta)	gal	4.95	4/00	93r
Lilac (syrubga vulgaris)	2 gal	17.99-74.95	4/00	93r
Miscellaneous purchases	yr	872	1999	30r
Rhododendron (rhododendron)	2 gal	23.99-54.95	4/00	93r
Sage (salvia)	gal	6.95-7.99	4/00	93r
Wintercreeper euonymus (euonymus fortunei)	2 gal	14.99-23.95	4/00	93r
Hunting license	yr	20.00	4/01	34s
Health Care				
Health care, ACCRA Index		94.80	3/01	4c
Cardiac catheterization, ave hospital/physician charges		13870	1998	77s
Childbirth, Cesarean delivery		14716	1997	13r
Childbirth, vaginal delivery		8541	1997	13r
Dentist's fee, adult teeth cleaning and periodic oral exam	visit	60.00	3/01	4c
Doctor's fee, routine exam, established patient	visit	47.00	3/01	4c
Drugs, expenditures on	yr	296	1999	30r
Health care purchases	yr	1932	1999	30c
Health insurance expenditures	yr	875	1999	30r
Hospital care, private room	day	731.00	3/01	4c
Hysterectomy, laproscopically-assisted, ave hospital/physician charges		14760	1998	76s
Hysterectomy, vaginal, ave hospital and physician charges		9270	1998	76s
Medicaid dispensing fee		4.00	1999	87s
Medical services expenditures	yr	516	1999	30r
Medical supplies, expenditures on	yr	102	1999	30r
Nursing home costs, private room	day	181	2000	82c
Nursing home stay, private room	day	181	2000	81c
Plastic surgery, breast augmentation		4232	2000	7r
Plastic surgery, breast lift		4605	2000	7r
Plastic surgery, facelift		6964	2000	7r
Plastic surgery, hair transplantation		4193	2000	7r
Plastic surgery, lip augmentation		1675	2000	7r
Plastic surgery, lower body lift		6611	2000	7r
Plastic surgery, thigh lift		4751	2000	7r
Household Goods				
Dishwashing powder, Cascade	50 oz	3.66	3/01	4c
Floor coverings, expenditures on	yr	59	1999	30r
Furniture, expenditures on	yr	388	1999	30r
Household furnishings and equipment purchases	yr	1535	1999	30c
Household textiles, expenditures on	yr	112	1999	30r
Laundry and cleaning supplies, expenditures on	yr	104	1999	30r
Tissues, facial, Kleenex brand	175	1.23	3/01	4c
Housing				
Housing, ACCRA Index		116.70	3/01	4c
Home, 2200 sq ft, 4-br, 2-bath, 2-car garage, average		176000	2000	47c
Home price, existing, ave		180800	10/00	90r
Home value, median		115000	2001	53s
House, 2400 sq ft, 8000 sq ft lot, new, urban, utilities	total	231600	3/01	4c
House payment, principal and interest, 25% down payment	mos	1206	3/01	4c
Household operation expenditures	yr	397	1999	30c
Housekeeping supplies purchases	yr	688	1999	30c
Housing, expenditures on	yr	9992	1999	30c
Lodging expenditures	yr	550	1999	30r

Pittsburgh, PA - continued

Item	Per	Value	Date	Ref.
Housing - continued				
Maintenance, repairs, insurance expenditures	yr	835	1999	30r
Monthly rental value of owned home	mos	663	1999	30r
Owned dwellings, expenditures own	yr	3080	1999	30c
Rent expenditures	yr	1587	1999	30c
Rent, apartment, 2 br, 1 1/2-2 baths, unfurn, 950 sq ft, water	mos	800	3/01	4c
Rental unit, 1 bedroom, with utilities	mos	476	4/01	41c
Rental unit, 2 bedroom, with utilities	mos	574	4/01	41c
Rental unit, 3 bedroom, with utilities	mos	719	4/01	41c
Rental unit, 4 bedroom, with utilities	mos	803	4/01	41c
Shelter, expenditures on	yr	4945	1999	30c
Insurance and Pensions				
Life and other personal insurance purchases	yr	1078	1999	30c
Pensions and Social Security, expenditures on	yr	2632	1999	30c
Personal insurance and pensions, expenditures on	yr	3710	1999	30c
Legal Fees				
Divorce, filing fee		65.00	4/01	35s
Driver's license fee	orig	29.00	1999	48s
Driver's license fee	renew	24.00	1999	48s
Fishing license	yr	17.00	4/01	34s
Personal Goods				
Personal care products and services purchases	yr	522	1999	30c
Shampoo, Alberto VO5	15 oz	1.33	3/01	4c
Toothpaste, Crest or Colgate	6-7 oz	2.87	3/01	4c
Personal Services				
Dry cleaning, man's 2-pc suit		8.22	3/01	4c
Man's haircut, barbershop, no styling		10.40	3/01	4c
Personal services, household, expenditures on	yr	271	1999	30r
Woman's shampoo, trim, blow-dry, no style-change		20.60	3/01	4c
Pets				
Pets, toys, and playground equipment, expenditures on	yr	325	1999	30r
Restaurant Food				
Chicken, fried, thigh and drumstick, KFC/Church's		2.69	3/01	4c
Hamburger with cheese, McDonald's	1/4 lb	2.11	3/01	4c
Pizza, Pizza Hut or Pizza Inn	11-12 in	8.99	3/01	4c
Taxes				
Federal income taxes paid	yr	2606	1999	30r
Personal taxes, expenditures on	yr	3567	1999	30r
Property taxes paid	yr	1752	1999	30r
State and local income taxes paid	yr	694	1999	30r
Transportation				
Transportation, ACCRA Index		100.00	3/01	4c
Bus fare, one-way	trip	1.20	2000	1c
Bus fare, to central business district	1-way	1.25	3/01	4c
Cars and trucks, new, expenditures on	yr	1496	1999	30r
Cars and trucks, used, expenditures on	yr	1251	1999	30r
Diesel at the pump	gal	1.31	10/99	73s
Gasoline and motor oil purchases	yr	862	1999	30c
Gasoline before-tax price (cents)	gal	106.60	10/00	43s
Light rail transit fare, one-way	trip	1.25	2000	2c
Maintenance and repair expenditures	yr	618	1999	30r
Public transportation, expenditures on	yr	307	1999	30c
Tire balance, computer or spin balance, front	wheel	7.68	3/01	4c
Transportation purchases	yr	5795	1999	30c
Vehicle expenses, miscellaneous, purchases	yr	2184	1999	30c
Vehicle insurance payments	yr	824	1999	30r
Vehicle purchases (net outlay)	yr	2443	1999	30c
Vehicle rental, lease expenditures	yr	584	1999	30r

Values are in dollars or fractions of dollars. In the column headed *Ref*, references are shown to sources. Each reference is followed by a letter. These refer to the geographical level for which data were reported: s=State, r=Region, and c=City or metro. The abbreviation *ex* is used to mean *except* or *excluding*; *exp* stands for *expenditures*. For other abbreviations and further explanations, please see the Introduction.

Pittsburgh, PA - continued

Item	Per	Value	Date	Ref.
Utilities				
Utilities, ACCRA Index		143.00	3/01	4c
Electrical bill, average	mos	69.16	9/00	9s
Electricity, expenditures on	yr	837	1999	30r
Electricity, summer, 250 KWh	mos	34.85	2/96	96c
Electricity, summer, 500 KWh	mos	63.33	2/96	96c
Electricity, summer, 750 KWh	mos	91.83	2/96	96c
Electricity, summer, 1000 KWh	mos	120.32	2/96	96c
Electricity and other, mixed, 2400 sq ft, new home	mos	88.82	3/01	4c
Electricity cost, average	KWh	5.08	9/00	9s
Utilities, fuels, and public services purchased	yr	2457	1999	30r
Water and other public services, expenditures on	yr	215	1999	30r
Water price	100 cf	2.97	2000	109c
Water price, dwelling unit	mos	58.24	2000	109c
Weddings				
Wedding (national average cost)		19936	2000	33r
Wedding (regional average total cost)		29454	1997	110r
Attendants' gifts		321	1998	33r
Bridal attendants' apparel (5 persons)		824	2000	33r
Bride's headpiece/veil		173	1998	33r
Bride's wedding dress		859	1998	33r
Clergy, religious facility fee		242	1998	33r
Engagement ring		3177	1998	33r
Flowers		789	1998	33r
Groom's formalwear rental		99	2000	33r
Limousine		410	1998	33r
Marriage license cost		25.00-40.00	4/01	35s
Men's formalwear (ushers, best man)		469	2000	33r
Mother of bride apparel		241	2000	33r
Music		866	1998	33r
Photography and videography		1368	1998	33r
Rehearsal dinner		728	1998	33r
Wedding invitations and announcements		341	1998	33r
Wedding reception		7968	2000	33r
Wedding rings (bride and groom)		1060	1998	33r

Pittsfield, MA

Item	Per	Value	Date	Ref.
Average annual expenditures	yr	37971	1999	30r
Alcoholic Beverages				
Alcoholic beverage purchases	yr	368	1999	30r
Wine, red and white table, all sizes, any origin	liter	9.64	7/01	11r
Appliances				
Major appliances, expenditures on	yr	194	1999	30r
Small appliances, housewares, expenditures on	yr	93	1999	30r
Banking and Money				
Mortgage interest and charges paid	yr	2622	1999	30r
Mortgage principal paid on owned property	yr	1262	1999	30r
Vehicle finance charges paid	yr	240	1999	30r
Charity				
Cash contributions, expenditures	yr	1001	1999	30r
Child Care				
Child raising cost, total, age 0-2	yr	8670	1999	60r
Child raising cost, total, age 3-5	yr	8910	1999	60r
Child raising cost, total, age 6-8	yr	9040	1999	60r
Child raising cost, total, age 9-11	yr	9100	1999	60r
Child raising cost, total, age 12-14	yr	9890	1999	60r
Child raising cost, total, age 15-17	yr	10010	1999	60r
Child's child care and education, age 0-2	yr	1070	1999	60r
Child's child care and education, age 3-5	yr	1190	1999	60r
Child's child care and education, age 6-8	yr	740	1999	60r
Child's child care and education, age 9-11	yr	470	1999	60r
Child's child care and education, age 12-14	yr	350	1999	60r
Child's child care and education, age 15-17	yr	590	1999	60r

Pittsfield, MA - continued

Item	Per	Value	Date	Ref.
Child Care - continued				
Child's clothing, age 0-2	yr	480	1999	60r
Child's clothing, age 3-5	yr	470	1999	60r
Child's clothing, age 6-8	yr	520	1999	60r
Child's clothing, age 9-11	yr	570	1999	60r
Child's clothing, age 12-14	yr	970	1999	60r
Child's clothing, age 15-17	yr	870	1999	60r
Child's food, age 0-2	yr	1130	1999	60r
Child's food, age 3-5	yr	1290	1999	60r
Child's food, age 6-8	yr	1640	1999	60r
Child's food, age 9-11	yr	1930	1999	60r
Child's food, age 12-14	yr	1940	1999	60r
Child's food, age 15-17	yr	2150	1999	60r
Child's health care, age 0-2	yr	550	1999	60r
Child's health care, age 3-5	yr	530	1999	60r
Child's health care, age 6-8	yr	610	1999	60r
Child's health care, age 9-11	yr	650	1999	60r
Child's health care, age 12-14	yr	660	1999	60r
Child's health care, age 15-17	yr	690	1999	60r
Child's housing, age 0-2	yr	3555	1999	60r
Child's housing, age 3-5	yr	3530	1999	60r
Child's housing, age 6-8	yr	3490	1999	60r
Child's housing, age 9-11	yr	3340	1999	60r
Child's housing, age 12-14	yr	3530	1999	60r
Child's housing, age 15-17	yr	3140	1999	60r
Child's personal care, reading, age 0-2	yr	920	1999	60r
Child's personal care, reading, age 3-5	yr	950	1999	60r
Child's personal care, reading, age 6-8	yr	980	1999	60r
Child's personal care, reading, age 9-11	yr	1020	1999	60r
Child's personal care, reading, age 12-14	yr	1190	1999	60r
Child's personal care, reading, age 15-17	yr	970	1999	60r
Clothing				
Apparel and services purchases	yr	1831	1999	30r
Boys, 2 to 15, expenditures on	yr	92	1999	30r
Children under 2, expenditures on	yr	63	1999	30r
Footwear, expenditures on	yr	300	1999	30r
Girls, 2 to 15, expenditures on	yr	101	1999	30r
Men and boys, expenditures on	yr	446	1999	30r
Men, 16 and over, expenditures on	yr	354	1999	30r
Women, 16 and over, expenditures on	yr	584	1999	30r
Communications				
Cable modem installation, Adelphi		54.90	6/99	103s
Cable modem installation, Media One		100.00	6/99	103s
Cable modem rate, cable subscriber, Adelphi	mos	34.95	6/99	103s
Cable modem rate, cable subscriber, Media One	mos	34.95-39.95	6/99	103s
Cable modem rate, non-cable subscriber, Adelphi	mos	44.95	6/99	103s
Cable modem rate, non-cable subscriber, Media One	mos	49.95	6/99	103s
Phone line, single, business, field visit	inst.	120.52	12/97	17s
Phone line, single, business, no field visit	inst.	93.02	12/97	17s
Phone line, single, residence, field visit	inst.	64.57	12/97	17s
Phone line, single, residence, no field visit	inst.	37.07	12/97	17s
Postage and stationery, expenditures on	yr	138	1999	30r
Postal rate, express mail, up to half-pound		12.45	7/01	108r
Postal rate, letter, first class, first ounce		0.34	7/01	108r
Postal rate, letter, two ounces		0.57	7/01	108r
Postal rate, post card		0.21	7/01	108r
Postal rate, priority mail, two pounds		3.95	7/01	108r
Postal rate, priority mail, up to one pound		3.50	7/01	108r
Telephone services, expenditures on	yr	830	1999	30r
Education				
Board, 4-year private college/university	yr	3244	1996	38s
Board, 4-year public college/university	yr	2042	1996	38s
Education expenditures	yr	877	1999	30r
Room, 4-year private college/university	yr	3688	1996	38s
Room, 4-year public college/university	yr	2462	1996	38s
Total cost, 4-year private college/university	yr	23335	1996	38s
Total cost, 4-year public college/university	yr	8757	1996	38s
Tuition, 2-year public college/university, in state	yr	2359	1996	38s

Values are in dollars or fractions of dollars. In the column headed *Ref*, references are shown to sources. Each reference is followed by a letter. These refer to the geographical level for which data were reported: s=State, r=Region, and c=City or metro. The abbreviation *ex* is used to mean *except* or *excluding*; *exp* stands for *expenditures*. For other abbreviations and further explanations, please see the Introduction.

Pittsfield, MA - continued

Item	Per	Value	Date	Ref.
Education				
Tuition, 4-year private college/university, in state	yr	16403	1996	38s
Tuition, 4-year public college/university	yr	4253	1996	38s
Energy and Fuels				
Electricity	KWh	0.12	7/01	11r
Fuel oil #2	gal	1.31	7/01	11r
Fuel oil and other fuels, expenditures on	yr	207	1999	30r
Gas, heating, winter, average use	mos	169.22	2/96	98c
Gas, natural, commercial rate	1000 cf	10.82	11/00	88s
Gasoline, all types	gal	1.80	7/01	11r
Gasoline, unleaded midgrade	gal	1.85	7/01	11r
Gasoline, unleaded premium	gal	1.91	7/01	11r
Gasoline, unleaded regular	gal	1.71	7/01	11r
Natural gas, expenditures on	yr	368	1999	30r
Utility (piped) gas, therm		1.08	7/01	11r
Utility (piped) gas, 40 therms		50.87	7/01	11r
Utility (piped) gas, 100 therms		111.06	7/01	11r
Entertainment				
Entertainment purchases	yr	1821	1999	30r
Fees and admissions paid	yr	511	1999	30r
Television, radios, sound equipment, expenditures on	yr	650	1999	30r
Funerals				
Total cost of funeral		5776.91	1/99	78r
Acknowledgement cards		14.47	1/99	78r
Casket		2090.19	1/99	78r
Cosmetology, hair, other preparation		132.92	1/99	78r
Embalming		377.33	1/99	78r
Funeral at funeral home		352.43	1/99	78r
Hearse (local)		185.55	1/99	78r
Professional service charges		1289.95	1/99	78r
Service car/van		87.42	1/99	78r
Transfer of remains to funeral home		175.48	1/99	78r
Vault		729.40	1/99	78r
Visitation/viewing		341.76	1/99	78r
Groceries				
Apples, red delicious	lb	0.95	7/01	11r
Bacon, sliced	lb	3.44	7/01	11r
Bakery products, expenditures on	yr	310	1999	30r
Bananas	lb	0.55	7/01	11r
Beef, expenditures on	yr	236	1999	30r
Bread, white, pan	lb	1.09	7/01	11r
Butter, yoghurt, cheese, etc, expenditures on	yr	214	1999	30r
Cereals and bakery product purchases	yr	474	1999	30r
Cereals and cereal products, expenditures on	yr	164	1999	30r
Chicken legs, bone-in	lb	1.23	7/01	11r
Chicken, fresh, whole	lb	1.13	7/01	11r
Chuck roast, U.S. choice, boneless	lb	2.79	7/01	11r
Coffee, 100%, ground roast, all sizes	lb	3.40	7/01	11r
Dairy product purchases	yr	342	1999	30r
Eggs, expenditures on	yr	34	1999	30r
Eggs, grade A, large	dozen	0.82	7/01	11r
Fats and oils, expenditures on	yr	80	1999	30r
Fish and seafood, expenditures on	yr	123	1999	30r
Food (excl fruit and vegetables), eaten at home, purchases	yr	838	1999	30r
Food cooked on trips, expenditures on	yr	48	1999	30r
Food purchases	yr	5314	1999	30r
Food purchases, eaten away from home	yr	2313	1999	30r
Food purchases, food eaten at home	yr	3001	1999	30r
Fresh fruits, expenditures on	yr	169	1999	30r
Fresh milk and cream, expenditures on	yr	128	1999	30r
Fresh vegetables, expenditures on	yr	164	1999	30r
Grapefruit	lb	0.67	7/01	11r
Grapes, Thompson, seedless	lb	2.18	7/01	11r
Ground beef, lean and extra lean	lb	2.66	7/01	11r
Ground chuck, 100% beef	lb	2.04	7/01	11r
Lettuce, iceberg	lb	0.76	7/01	11r
Meats, poultry, fish, and egg purchases	yr	808	1999	30r

Pittsfield, MA - continued

Item	Per	Value	Date	Ref.
Groceries - continued				
Nonalcoholic beverages, expenditures on	yr	225	1999	30r
Orange juice, frozen concentrate	16 oz	1.88	7/01	11r
Oranges, Navel	lb	0.79	7/01	11r
Oranges, Valencia	lb	0.56	7/01	11r
Peaches	lb	1.16	7/01	11r
Peanut butter, creamy, all sizes	lb	2.01	7/01	11r
Pears, Anjou	lb	1.16	7/01	11r
Pork chops, center cut, bone-in	lb	3.57	7/01	11r
Pork, expenditures on	yr	146	1999	30r
Potato chips	16 oz	3.37	7/01	11r
Potatoes, white, all types	lb	0.42	7/01	11r
Poultry, expenditures on	yr	158	1999	30r
Processed fruits, expenditures on	yr	124	1999	30r
Processed vegetables, expenditures on	yr	82	1999	30r
Round roast, U.S. choice, boneless	lb	3.04	7/01	11r
Spaghetti and macaroni	lb	1.04	7/01	11r
Steak, sirloin, U.S. choice, boneless	lb	5.39	7/01	11r
Strawberries, dry pint	12 oz	1.51	7/01	11r
Sugar and other sweets, expenditures on	yr	110	1999	30r
Sugar, white, 33-80 ounce package	lb	0.46	7/01	11r
Sugar, white, all sizes	lb	0.47	7/01	11r
Tobacco products and smoking supplies purchases	yr	309	1999	30r
Yogurt, natural, fruit flavored	8 oz	0.79	7/01	11r
Goods and Services				
B&B Japanese maple (acer japonicum)	gal	38.99-125.00	4/00	93r
Boxwood (buxus)	2 gal	15.99-49.95	4/00	93r
Daylily (hemerocallis)	gal	4.95	4/00	93r
Flat of annuals		8.00-14.99	4/00	93r
Fountain grass (pennisetum)	gal	6.99-9.99	4/00	93r
Hanging basket (10 in)		12.95-19.99	4/00	93r
Hardy geranium (geranium)	gal	6.95-7.99	4/00	93r
Hosta (hosta)	gal	4.95	4/00	93r
Lilac (syrubga vulgaris)	2 gal	17.99-74.95	4/00	93r
Miscellaneous purchases	yr	872	1999	30r
Rhododendron (rhododendron)	2 gal	23.99-54.95	4/00	93r
Sage (salvia)	gal	6.95-7.99	4/00	93r
Wintercreeper euonymus (euonymus fortunei)	2 gal	14.99-23.95	4/00	93r
Hunting license	yr	27.50	4/01	34s
Health Care				
Cardiac catheterization, ave hospital/ physician charges		17080	1998	77s
Childbirth, Cesarean delivery		14716	1997	13r
Childbirth, vaginal delivery		8541	1997	13r
Drugs, expenditures on	yr	296	1999	30r
Health care purchases	yr	1788	1999	30r
Health insurance expenditures	yr	875	1999	30r
Hysterectomy, laproscopically-assisted, ave hospital/physician charges		13100	1998	76s
Hysterectomy, vaginal, ave hospital and physician charges		8780	1998	76s
Medicaid dispensing fee		3.00	1999	87s
Medical services expenditures	yr	516	1999	30r
Medical supplies, expenditures on	yr	102	1999	30r
Plastic surgery, breast augmentation		4232	2000	7r
Plastic surgery, breast lift		4605	2000	7r
Plastic surgery, facelift		6964	2000	7r
Plastic surgery, hair transplantation		4193	2000	7r
Plastic surgery, lip augmentation		1675	2000	7r
Plastic surgery, lower body lift		6611	2000	7r
Plastic surgery, thigh lift		4751	2000	7r

Values are in dollars or fractions of dollars. In the column headed *Ref*, references are shown to sources. Each reference is followed by a letter. These refer to the geographical level for which data were reported: s=State, r=Region, and c=City or metro. The abbreviation *ex* is used to mean *except* or *excluding*; *exp* stands for *expenditures*. For other abbreviations and further explanations, please see the Introduction.

Pittsfield, MA - continued

Item	Per	Value	Date	Ref.
Household Goods				
Floor coverings, expenditures on	yr	59	1999	30r
Furniture, expenditures on	yr	388	1999	30r
Household furnishings and equipment purchases	yr	1567	1999	30r
Household textiles, expenditures on	yr	112	1999	30r
Laundry and cleaning supplies, expenditures on	yr	104	1999	30r
Housing				
Home price, existing, ave		180800	10/00	90r
Home value, median		261000	2001	53s
Household operation expenditures	yr	581	1999	30r
Housekeeping supplies purchases	yr	474	1999	30r
Lodging expenditures	yr	550	1999	30r
Maintenance, repairs, insurance expenditures	yr	835	1999	30r
Monthly rental value of owned home	mos	663	1999	30r
Owned dwellings, expenditures own	yr	5209	1999	30r
Rent expenditures	yr	2390	1999	30r
Rental unit, 1 bedroom, with utilities	mos	464	4/01	41c
Rental unit, 2 bedroom, with utilities	mos	571	4/01	41c
Rental unit, 3 bedroom, with utilities	mos	717	4/01	41c
Rental unit, 4 bedroom, with utilities	mos	888	4/01	41c
Shelter, expenditures on	yr	8149	1999	30r
Insurance and Pensions				
Life and other personal insurance purchases	yr	424	1999	30r
Pensions and Social Security, expenditures on	yr	3037	1999	30r
Legal Fees				
Divorce, filing fee		100.00	4/01	35s
Driver's license fee	orig	33.75	1999	48s
Driver's license fee	renew	33.75	1999	48s
Fishing license	yr	27.50	4/01	34s
Personal Goods				
Personal care products and services purchases	yr	399	1999	30r
Personal Services				
Personal services, household, expenditures on	yr	271	1999	30r
Pets				
Pets, toys, and playground equipment, expenditures on	yr	325	1999	30r
Taxes				
Federal income taxes paid	yr	2606	1999	30r
Personal taxes, expenditures on	yr	3567	1999	30r
Property taxes paid	yr	1752	1999	30r
State and local income taxes paid	yr	694	1999	30r
Transportation				
Cars and trucks, new, expenditures on	yr	1496	1999	30r
Cars and trucks, used, expenditures on	yr	1251	1999	30r
Diesel at the pump	gal	1.32	10/99	73s
Gasoline and motor oil purchases	yr	901	1999	30r
Gasoline before-tax price (cents)	gal	118.70	10/00	43s
Maintenance and repair expenditures	yr	618	1999	30r
Public transportation, expenditures on	yr	575	1999	30r
Transportation purchases	yr	6503	1999	30r
Vehicle expenses, miscellaneous, purchases	yr	2266	1999	30r
Vehicle insurance payments	yr	824	1999	30r
Vehicle purchases (net outlay)	yr	2761	1999	30r
Vehicle rental, lease expenditures	yr	584	1999	30r
Travel				
Hotel room	night	111.15	2/01	95s
Utilities				
Electrical bill, average	mos	58.58	9/00	9s
Electricity, expenditures on	yr	837	1999	30r
Electricity cost, average	KWh	8.90	9/00	9s
Utilities, fuels, and public services purchased	yr	2457	1999	30r

Pittsfield, MA - continued

Item	Per	Value	Date	Ref.
Utilities - continued				
Water and other public services, expenditures on	yr	215	1999	30r
Weddings				
Wedding (national average cost)		19936	2000	33r
Wedding (regional average total cost)		29454	1997	110r
Attendants' gifts		321	1998	33r
Bridal attendants' apparel (5 persons)		824	2000	33r
Bride's headpiece/veil		173	1998	33r
Bride's wedding dress		859	1998	33r
Clergy, religious facility fee		242	1998	33r
Engagement ring		3177	1998	33r
Flowers		789	1998	33r
Groom's formalwear rental		99	2000	33r
Limousine		410	1998	33r
Marriage license cost		25.00	4/01	35s
Men's formalwear (ushers, best man)		469	2000	33r
Mother of bride apparel		241	2000	33r
Music		866	1998	33r
Photography and videography		1368	1998	33r
Rehearsal dinner		728	1998	33r
Wedding invitations and announcements		341	1998	33r
Wedding reception		7968	2000	33r
Wedding rings (bride and groom)		1060	1998	33r

Pocatello, ID

Item	Per	Value	Date	Ref.
Composite, ACCRA index		98.20	3/01	4c
Alcoholic Beverages				
Beer, Heineken, 12-oz, ex deposit	6	8.32	3/01	4c
J & B Scotch	750-ml	21.95	3/01	4c
Wine, Livingston or Gallo, Chablis blanc	1.5 liter	5.53	3/01	4c
Appliances				
Appliance repair, service call, washing machine	min lab chg	36.00	3/01	4c
Banking and Money				
Mortgage rate, incl. points and orig. fee, 30-yr. conv. fixed or ARM	mos	6.89	3/01	4c
Clothing				
Boys' brief, cotton	3	4.44	3/01	4c
Shirt, man's dress shirt		29.75	3/01	4c
Slacks, man's "No Wrinkles" khaki		36.00	3/01	4c
Communications				
Newspaper subscription, daily and Sunday delivery	mos	9.75	3/01	4c
Phone line, single, business, field visit	inst.	47.50	12/97	17s
Phone line, single, business, no field visit	inst.	47.50	12/97	17s
Phone line, single, residence, field visit	inst.	28.50	12/97	17s
Phone line, single, residence, no field visit	inst.	28.50	12/97	17s
Postal rate, express mail, up to half-pound		12.45	7/01	108r
Postal rate, letter, first class, first ounce		0.34	7/01	108r
Postal rate, letter, two ounces		0.57	7/01	108r
Postal rate, post card		0.21	7/01	108r
Postal rate, priority mail, two pounds		3.95	7/01	108r
Postal rate, priority mail, up to one pound		3.50	7/01	108r
Telephone bill, family of three	mos	24.85	3/01	4c
Education				
Board, 4-year private college/university	yr	2035	1996	38s
Board, 4-year public college/university	yr	2098	1996	38s
Room, 4-year private college/university	yr	1430	1996	38s
Room, 4-year public college/university	yr	1541	1996	38s
Total cost, 4-year private college/university	yr	15307	1996	38s
Total cost, 4-year public college/university	yr	5321	1996	38s
Tuition, 2-year public college/university, in state	yr	991	1996	38s
Tuition, 4-year private college/university, in state	yr	11843	1996	38s
Tuition, 4-year public college/university	yr	1682	1996	38s

Values are in dollars or fractions of dollars. In the column headed *Ref*, references are shown to sources. Each reference is followed by a letter. These refer to the geographical level for which data were reported: s=State, r=Region, and c=City or metro. The abbreviation *ex* is used to mean *except* or *excluding*; *exp* stands for *expenditures*. For other abbreviations and further explanations, please see the Introduction.

Pocatello, ID - continued

Item	Per	Value	Date	Ref.
Energy and Fuels				
Energy, combined forms, 2400 sq ft	mos	106.05	3/01	4c
Energy, exc. electricity, 2400 sq ft	mos	70.85	3/01	4c
Gas, natural, commercial rate	1000 cf	6.71	11/00	88s
Gas, regular unleaded, cash, self-service	gal	1.39	3/01	4c
Entertainment				
Bowling, Saturday evening rate	line	2.20	3/01	4c
Monopoly game, Parker Brothers', No. 9	game	11.24	3/01	4c
Movie, first-run, Saturday, evening	adm.	6.50	3/01	4c
Tennis balls, yellow, Wilson or Penn, 3	can	2.99	3/01	4c
Funerals				
Total cost of funeral		5401.08	1/99	78r
Acknowledgement cards		33.64	1/99	78r
Casket		2170.43	1/99	78r
Cosmetology, hair, other preparation		136.32	1/99	78r
Embalming		319.13	1/99	78r
Funeral at funeral home		370.21	1/99	78r
Hearse (local)		161.04	1/99	78r
Professional service charges		963.15	1/99	78r
Service car/van		133.99	1/99	78r
Transfer of remains to funeral home		159.82	1/99	78r
Vault		778.07	1/99	78r
Visitation/viewing		175.28	1/99	78r
Groceries				
Groceries, ACCRA Index		100.20	3/01	4c
Antibiotic ointment, Polysporin	0.5 oz	4.91	3/01	4c
Baby food, strained vegetables or fruit, lowest price	4-4.5 oz	0.39	3/01	4c
Bananas	lb	0.43	3/01	4c
Beef or hamburger, ground	lb	1.76	3/01	4c
Bread, white	loaf	0.84	3/01	4c
Cheese, Kraft grated Parmesan	8 oz	3.74	3/01	4c
Chicken, whole fryer	lb	1.01	3/01	4c
Cigarettes, Winston, Kings	carton	28.53	3/01	4c
Coffee, vacuum-packed	13 oz	2.98	3/01	4c
Corn Flakes, Kellogg's or Post Toasties	18 oz	3.04	3/01	4c
Corn, frozen, whole kernel, lowest price	16 oz	1.14	3/01	4c
Eggs, Grade A or AA	dozen	1.12	3/01	4c
Lettuce, iceberg	head	0.83	3/01	4c
Margarine, Blue Bonnet or Parkay, stick	lb	0.57	3/01	4c
Milk, whole	1/2 gal	1.66	3/01	4c
Orange juice, Minute Maid frozen	12 oz	1.46	3/01	4c
Peaches, halves or slices, Hunt's, Del Monte, or Libby's	29 oz	1.64	3/01	4c
Peas, green, Del Monte or Green Giant	15 oz	0.63	3/01	4c
Potatoes, white or red	10 lb	2.04	3/01	4c
Sausage, Jimmy Dean/Owens pork	lb	3.97	3/01	4c
Shortening, vegetable, Crisco	3 lb	2.95	3/01	4c
Soft drink, Coca Cola, ex deposit	2 liter	1.39	3/01	4c
Steak, T-bone	lb	6.01	3/01	4c
Sugar, cane or beet	4 lbs	1.61	3/01	4c
Tomatoes, Hunt's or Del Monte	14.5 oz	0.79	3/01	4c
Tuna, chunk, light	6 oz	0.67	3/01	4c
Goods and Services				
Miscellaneous goods and services, ACCRA Index		102.60	3/01	4c
Hunting license	yr	11.50	4/01	34s
Health Care				
Health care, ACCRA Index		106.10	3/01	4c
Cardiac catheterization, ave hospital/ physician charges		14550	1998	77s
Childbirth, Cesarean delivery		11587	1997	13r
Childbirth, vaginal delivery		6725	1997	13r
Dentist's fee, adult teeth cleaning and periodic oral exam	visit	79.00	3/01	4c
Doctor's fee, routine exam, established patient	visit	60.00	3/01	4c
Hospital care, private room	day	558.00	3/01	4c
Hysterectomy, laproscopically-assisted, ave hospital/physician charges		10640	1998	76s

Pocatello, ID - continued

Item	Per	Value	Date	Ref.
Health Care - continued				
Hysterectomy, vaginal, ave hospital and physician charges		8560	1998	76s
Medicaid dispensing fee		4.94	1999	87s
Household Goods				
Dishwashing powder, Cascade	50 oz	3.86	3/01	4c
Tissues, facial, Kleenex brand	175	1.38	3/01	4c
Housing				
Housing, ACCRA Index		93.30	3/01	4c
Home value, median		112000	2001	53s
House, 2400 sq ft, 8000 sq ft lot, new, urban, utilities	total	210000	3/01	4c
House payment, principal and interest, 25% down payment	mos	1036	3/01	4c
Rent, apartment, 2 br, 1 1/2-2 baths, unfurn, 950 sq ft, water	mos	450	3/01	4c
Rental unit, 1 bedroom, with utilities	mos	329	4/01	41c
Rental unit, 2 bedroom, with utilities	mos	423	4/01	41c
Rental unit, 3 bedroom, with utilities	mos	576	4/01	41c
Rental unit, 4 bedroom, with utilities	mos	681	4/01	41c
Insurance and Pensions				
Auto insurance premium	yr	577.07	1999	57s
Legal Fees				
Driver's license fee	renew	20.50	1999	48s
Driver's license fee	orig	20.50	1999	48s
Personal Goods				
Shampoo, Alberto VO5	15 oz	1.29	3/01	4c
Toothpaste, Crest or Colgate	6-7 oz	3.08	3/01	4c
Personal Services				
Dry cleaning, man's 2-pc suit		7.35	3/01	4c
Man's haircut, barbershop, no styling		11.32	3/01	4c
Woman's shampoo, trim, blow-dry, no style-change		18.67	3/01	4c
Restaurant Food				
Chicken, fried, thigh and drumstick, KFC/ Church's		2.69	3/01	4c
Hamburger with cheese, McDonald's	1/4 lb	2.29	3/01	4c
Pizza, Pizza Hut or Pizza Inn	11-12 in	9.59	3/01	4c
Transportation				
Transportation, ACCRA Index		96.80	3/01	4c
Diesel at the pump	gal	1.33	10/99	73s
Gasoline before-tax price (cents)	gal	123.50	10/00	43s
Tire balance, computer or spin balance, front	wheel	7.44	3/01	4c
Utilities				
Utilities, ACCRA Index		90.60	3/01	4c
Electrical bill, average	mos	57.75	9/00	9s
Electricity and other, mixed, 2400 sq ft, new home	mos	35.20	3/01	4c
Electricity cost, average	KWh	4.10	9/00	9s
Weddings				
Wedding (national average cost)		19936	2000	33r
Attendants' gifts		321	1998	33r
Bridal attendants' apparel (5 persons)		824	2000	33r
Bride's headpiece/veil		173	1998	33r
Bride's wedding dress		859	1998	33r
Clergy, religious facility fee		242	1998	33r
Engagement ring		3177	1998	33r
Flowers		789	1998	33r
Groom's formalwear rental		99	2000	33r
Limousine		410	1998	33r
Marriage license cost		28.00	4/01	35s
Men's formalwear (ushers, best man)		469	2000	33r
Mother of bride apparel		241	2000	33r
Music		866	1998	33r
Photography and videography		1368	1998	33r
Rehearsal dinner		728	1998	33r
Wedding invitations and announcements		341	1998	33r
Wedding reception		7968	2000	33r

Values are in dollars or fractions of dollars. In the column headed *Ref*, references are shown to sources. Each reference is followed by a letter. These refer to the geographical level for which data were reported: s=State, r=Region, and c=City or metro. The abbreviation *ex* is used to mean *except* or *excluding*; *exp* stands for *expenditures*. For other abbreviations and further explanations, please see the Introduction.

Pocatello, ID - continued

Item	Per	Value	Date	Ref.
Weddings				
Wedding rings (bride and groom)		1060	1998	33r

Portland, ME

Item	Per	Value	Date	Ref.
Average annual expenditures	yr	37971	1999	30r
Alcoholic Beverages				
Alcoholic beverage purchases	yr	368	1999	30r
Wine, red and white table, all sizes, any origin	liter	9.64	7/01	11r
Appliances				
Major appliances, expenditures on	yr	194	1999	30r
Small appliances, housewares, expenditures on	yr	93	1999	30r
Banking and Money				
Mortgage interest and charges paid	yr	2622	1999	30r
Mortgage principal paid on owned property	yr	1262	1999	30r
Vehicle finance charges paid	yr	240	1999	30r
Charity				
Cash contributions, expenditures	yr	1001	1999	30r
Child Care				
Child raising cost, total, age 0-2	yr	8670	1999	60r
Child raising cost, total, age 3-5	yr	8910	1999	60r
Child raising cost, total, age 6-8	yr	9040	1999	60r
Child raising cost, total, age 9-11	yr	9100	1999	60r
Child raising cost, total, age 12-14	yr	9890	1999	60r
Child raising cost, total, age 15-17	yr	10010	1999	60r
Child's child care and education, age 0-2	yr	1070	1999	60r
Child's child care and education, age 3-5	yr	1190	1999	60r
Child's child care and education, age 6-8	yr	740	1999	60r
Child's child care and education, age 9-11	yr	470	1999	60r
Child's child care and education, age 12-14	yr	350	1999	60r
Child's child care and education, age 15-17	yr	590	1999	60r
Child's clothing, age 0-2	yr	480	1999	60r
Child's clothing, age 3-5	yr	470	1999	60r
Child's clothing, age 6-8	yr	520	1999	60r
Child's clothing, age 9-11	yr	570	1999	60r
Child's clothing, age 12-14	yr	970	1999	60r
Child's clothing, age 15-17	yr	870	1999	60r
Child's food, age 0-2	yr	1130	1999	60r
Child's food, age 3-5	yr	1290	1999	60r
Child's food, age 6-8	yr	1640	1999	60r
Child's food, age 9-11	yr	1930	1999	60r
Child's food, age 12-14	yr	1940	1999	60r
Child's food, age 15-17	yr	2150	1999	60r
Child's health care, age 0-2	yr	550	1999	60r
Child's health care, age 3-5	yr	530	1999	60r
Child's health care, age 6-8	yr	610	1999	60r
Child's health care, age 9-11	yr	650	1999	60r
Child's health care, age 12-14	yr	660	1999	60r
Child's health care, age 15-17	yr	690	1999	60r
Child's housing, age 0-2	yr	3555	1999	60r
Child's housing, age 3-5	yr	3530	1999	60r
Child's housing, age 6-8	yr	3490	1999	60r
Child's housing, age 9-11	yr	3340	1999	60r
Child's housing, age 12-14	yr	3530	1999	60r
Child's housing, age 15-17	yr	3140	1999	60r
Child's personal care, reading, age 0-2	yr	920	1999	60r
Child's personal care, reading, age 3-5	yr	950	1999	60r
Child's personal care, reading, age 6-8	yr	980	1999	60r
Child's personal care, reading, age 9-11	yr	1020	1999	60r
Child's personal care, reading, age 12-14	yr	1190	1999	60r
Child's personal care, reading, age 15-17	yr	970	1999	60r
Clothing				
Apparel and services purchases	yr	1831	1999	30r
Boys, 2 to 15, expenditures on	yr	92	1999	30r
Children under 2, expenditures on	yr	63	1999	30r
Footwear, expenditures on	yr	300	1999	30r
Girls, 2 to 15, expenditures on	yr	101	1999	30r

Portland, ME - continued

Item	Per	Value	Date	Ref.
Clothing - continued				
Men and boys, expenditures on	yr	446	1999	30r
Men, 16 and over, expenditures on	yr	354	1999	30r
Women, 16 and over, expenditures on	yr	584	1999	30r
Communications				
Cable modem installation, Time Warner		75.00-225.00	6/99	103s
Cable modem rate, cable subscriber, Time Warner	mos	39.95-49.95	6/99	103s
Cable modem rate, non-cable subscriber, Time Warner	mos	39.95-54.95	6/99	103s
Phone line, single, business, field visit	inst.	110.00	12/97	17s
Phone line, single, business, no field visit	inst.	75.00	12/97	17s
Phone line, single, residence, field visit	inst.	101.00	12/97	17s
Phone line, single, residence, no field visit	inst.	75.00	12/97	17s
Postage and stationery, expenditures on	yr	138	1999	30r
Postal rate, express mail, up to half-pound		12.45	7/01	108r
Postal rate, letter, first class, first ounce		0.34	7/01	108r
Postal rate, letter, two ounces		0.57	7/01	108r
Postal rate, post card		0.21	7/01	108r
Postal rate, priority mail, two pounds		3.95	7/01	108r
Postal rate, priority mail, up to one pound		3.50	7/01	108r
Telephone bill, business, basic rate	mos	34.21	12/97	18c
Telephone bill, residential, basic rate	mos	15.31	12/97	18c
Telephone services, expenditures on	yr	830	1999	30r
Education				
Board, 4-year private college/university	yr	2910	1996	38s
Board, 4-year public college/university	yr	2257	1996	38s
Education expenditures	yr	877	1999	30r
Room, 4-year private college/university	yr	2758	1996	38s
Room, 4-year public college/university	yr	2235	1996	38s
Total cost, 4-year private college/university	yr	21872	1996	38s
Total cost, 4-year public college/university	yr	7966	1996	38s
Tuition, 2-year public college/university, in state	yr	2381	1996	38s
Tuition, 4-year private college/university, in state	yr	16204	1996	38s
Tuition, 4-year public college/university	yr	3474	1996	38s
Energy and Fuels				
Electricity	KWh	0.12	7/01	11r
Fuel oil #2	gal	1.31	7/01	11r
Fuel oil and other fuels, expenditures on	yr	207	1999	30r
Gas, cooking, winter, 10 therms	mos	10.22	2/96	98c
Gas, cooking, winter, 30 therms	mos	26.69	2/96	98c
Gas, cooking, winter, 50 therms	mos	43.15	2/96	98c
Gas, heating, winter, average use	mos	114.55	2/96	98c
Gasoline, all types	gal	1.80	7/01	11r
Gasoline, unleaded midgrade	gal	1.85	7/01	11r
Gasoline, unleaded premium	gal	1.91	7/01	11r
Gasoline, unleaded regular	gal	1.71	7/01	11r
Natural gas, expenditures on	yr	368	1999	30r
Utility (piped) gas, therm		1.08	7/01	11r
Utility (piped) gas, 40 therms		50.87	7/01	11r
Utility (piped) gas, 100 therms		111.06	7/01	11r
Entertainment				
Entertainment purchases	yr	1821	1999	30r
Fees and admissions paid	yr	511	1999	30r
Television, radios, sound equipment, expenditures on	yr	650	1999	30r
Funerals				
Total cost of funeral		5776.91	1/99	78r
Acknowledgement cards		14.47	1/99	78r
Casket		2090.19	1/99	78r
Cosmetology, hair, other preparation		132.92	1/99	78r
Embalming		377.33	1/99	78r
Funeral at funeral home		352.43	1/99	78r
Hearse (local)		185.55	1/99	78r
Professional service charges		1289.95	1/99	78r
Service car/van		87.42	1/99	78r
Transfer of remains to funeral home		175.48	1/99	78r

Values are in dollars or fractions of dollars. In the column headed *Ref*, references are shown to sources. Each reference is followed by a letter. These refer to the geographical level for which data were reported: s=State, r=Region, and c=City or metro. The abbreviation *ex* is used to mean *except* or *excluding*; *exp* stands for *expenditures*. For other abbreviations and further explanations, please see the Introduction.

Portland, ME - continued

Item	Per	Value	Date	Ref.
Funerals				
Vault		729.40	1/99	78r
Visitation/viewing		341.76	1/99	78r
Groceries				
Apples, red delicious	lb	0.95	7/01	11r
Bacon, sliced	lb	3.44	7/01	11r
Bakery products, expenditures on	yr	310	1999	30r
Bananas	lb	0.55	7/01	11r
Beef, expenditures on	yr	236	1999	30r
Bread, white, pan	lb	1.09	7/01	11r
Butter, yoghurt, cheese, etc, expenditures on	yr	214	1999	30r
Cereals and bakery product purchases	yr	474	1999	30r
Cereals and cereal products, expenditures on	yr	164	1999	30r
Chicken legs, bone-in	lb	1.23	7/01	11r
Chicken, fresh, whole	lb	1.13	7/01	11r
Chuck roast, U.S. choice, boneless	lb	2.79	7/01	11r
Coffee, 100%, ground roast, all sizes	lb	3.40	7/01	11r
Dairy product purchases	yr	342	1999	30r
Eggs, expenditures on	yr	34	1999	30r
Eggs, grade A, large	dozen	0.82	7/01	11r
Fats and oils, expenditures on	yr	80	1999	30r
Fish and seafood, expenditures on	yr	123	1999	30r
Food (excl fruit and vegetables), eaten at home, purchases	yr	838	1999	30r
Food cooked on trips, expenditures on	yr	48	1999	30r
Food purchases	yr	5314	1999	30r
Food purchases, eaten away from home	yr	2313	1999	30r
Food purchases, food eaten at home	yr	3001	1999	30r
Fresh fruits, expenditures on	yr	169	1999	30r
Fresh milk and cream, expenditures on	yr	128	1999	30r
Fresh vegetables, expenditures on	yr	164	1999	30r
Grapefruit	lb	0.67	7/01	11r
Grapes, Thompson, seedless	lb	2.18	7/01	11r
Ground beef, lean and extra lean	lb	2.66	7/01	11r
Ground chuck, 100% beef	lb	2.04	7/01	11r
Lettuce, iceberg	lb	0.76	7/01	11r
Meats, poultry, fish, and egg purchases	yr	808	1999	30r
Nonalcoholic beverages, expenditures on	yr	225	1999	30r
Orange juice, frozen concentrate	16 oz	1.88	7/01	11r
Oranges, Navel	lb	0.79	7/01	11r
Oranges, Valencia	lb	0.56	7/01	11r
Peaches	lb	1.16	7/01	11r
Peanut butter, creamy, all sizes	lb	2.01	7/01	11r
Pears, Anjou	lb	1.16	7/01	11r
Pork chops, center cut, bone-in	lb	3.57	7/01	11r
Pork, expenditures on	yr	146	1999	30r
Potato chips	16 oz	3.37	7/01	11r
Potatoes, white, all types	lb	0.42	7/01	11r
Poultry, expenditures on	yr	158	1999	30r
Processed fruits, expenditures on	yr	124	1999	30r
Processed vegetables, expenditures on	yr	82	1999	30r
Round roast, U.S. choice, boneless	lb	3.04	7/01	11r
Spaghetti and macaroni	lb	1.04	7/01	11r
Steak, sirloin, U.S. choice, boneless	lb	5.39	7/01	11r
Strawberries, dry pint	12 oz	1.51	7/01	11r
Sugar and other sweets, expenditures on	yr	110	1999	30r
Sugar, white, 33-80 ounce package	lb	0.46	7/01	11r
Sugar, white, all sizes	lb	0.47	7/01	11r
Tobacco products and smoking supplies purchases	yr	309	1999	30r
Yogurt, natural, fruit flavored	8 oz	0.79	7/01	11r
Goods and Services				
B&B Japanese maple (acer japonicum)	gal	38.99-125.00	4/00	93r
Boxwood (buxus)	2 gal	15.99-49.95	4/00	93r
Daylilly (hemerocallis)	gal	4.95	4/00	93r
Flat of annuals		8.00-14.99	4/00	93r
Fountain grass (pennisetum)	gal	6.99-9.99	4/00	93r

Portland, ME - continued

Item	Per	Value	Date	Ref.
Goods and Services - continued				
Hanging basket (10 in)		12.95-19.99	4/00	93r
Hardy geranium (geranium)	gal	6.95-7.99	4/00	93r
Hosta (hosta)	gal	4.95	4/00	93r
Lilac (syrubga vulgaris)	2 gal	17.99-74.95	4/00	93r
Miscellaneous purchases	yr	872	1999	30r
Rhododendron (rhododendron)	2 gal	23.99-54.95	4/00	93r
Sage (salvia)	gal	6.95-7.99	4/00	93r
Wintercreeper euonymus (euonymus fortunei)	2 gal	14.99-23.95	4/00	93r
Hunting license	yr	19.00	4/01	34s
Health Care				
Cardiac catheterization, ave hospital/ physician charges		10740	1998	77s
Childbirth, Cesarean delivery		14716	1997	13r
Childbirth, vaginal delivery		8541	1997	13r
Drugs, expenditures on	yr	296	1999	30r
Health care purchases	yr	1788	1999	30r
Health insurance expenditures	yr	875	1999	30r
Hysterectomy, laproscopically-assisted, ave hospital/physician charges		11180	1998	76s
Hysterectomy, vaginal, ave hospital and physician charges		7810	1998	76s
Medicaid dispensing fee		3.35-5.35	1999	87s
Medical services expenditures	yr	516	1999	30r
Medical supplies, expenditures on	yr	102	1999	30r
Nursing home costs, private room	day	192	2000	82c
Nursing home stay, private room	day	192	2000	81c
Plastic surgery, breast augmentation		4232	2000	7r
Plastic surgery, breast lift		4605	2000	7r
Plastic surgery, facelift		6964	2000	7r
Plastic surgery, hair transplantation		4193	2000	7r
Plastic surgery, lip augmentation		1675	2000	7r
Plastic surgery, lower body lift		6611	2000	7r
Plastic surgery, thigh lift		4751	2000	7r
Household Goods				
Floor coverings, expenditures on	yr	59	1999	30r
Furniture, expenditures on	yr	388	1999	30r
Household furnishings and equipment purchases	yr	1567	1999	30r
Household textiles, expenditures on	yr	112	1999	30r
Laundry and cleaning supplies, expenditures on	yr	104	1999	30r
Housing				
Home, 2200 sq ft, 4-br, 2-bath, 2-car garage, average		199700	2000	47c
Home price, existing, ave		180800	10/00	90r
Home value, median		112000	2001	53s
Household operation expenditures	yr	581	1999	30r
Housekeeping supplies purchases	yr	474	1999	30r
Lodging expenditures	yr	550	1999	30r
Maintenance, repairs, insurance expenditures	yr	835	1999	30r
Monthly rental value of owned home	mos	663	1999	30r
Owned dwellings, expenditures own	yr	5209	1999	30r
Rent expenditures	yr	2390	1999	30r
Rental unit, 1 bedroom, with utilities	mos	497	4/01	41c
Rental unit, 2 bedroom, with utilities	mos	654	4/01	41c
Rental unit, 3 bedroom, with utilities	mos	818	4/01	41c
Rental unit, 4 bedroom, with utilities	mos	917	4/01	41c
Shelter, expenditures on	yr	8149	1999	30r
Insurance and Pensions				
Auto insurance premium	yr	542.81	1999	57s
Life and other personal insurance purchases	yr	424	1999	30r

Values are in dollars or fractions of dollars. In the column headed *Ref*, references are shown to sources. Each reference is followed by a letter. These refer to the geographical level for which data were reported: s=State, r=Region, and c=City or metro. The abbreviation *ex* is used to mean *except* or *excluding*; *exp* stands for *expenditures*. For other abbreviations and further explanations, please see the Introduction.

Portland, ME - continued

Item	Per	Value	Date	Ref.
Insurance and Pensions				
Pensions and Social Security, expenditures on	yr	3037	1999	30r
Legal Fees				
Combination hunting and fishing license	yr	36.00	4/01	34s
Divorce, filing fee	yr	60.00	4/01	35s
Driver's license fee	orig	35.00	1999	48s
Driver's license fee	renew	20.00	1999	48s
Fishing license	yr	19.00	4/01	34s
Personal Goods				
Personal care products and services purchases	yr	399	1999	30r
Personal Services				
Personal services, household, expenditures on	yr	271	1999	30r
Pets				
Pets, toys, and playground equipment, expenditures on	yr	325	1999	30r
Taxes				
Federal income taxes paid	yr	2606	1999	30r
Personal taxes, expenditures on	yr	3567	1999	30r
Property taxes paid	yr	1752	1999	30r
State and local income taxes paid	yr	694	1999	30r
Transportation				
Cars and trucks, new, expenditures on	yr	1496	1999	30r
Cars and trucks, used, expenditures on	yr	1251	1999	30r
Diesel at the pump	gal	1.32	10/99	73s
Gasoline and motor oil purchases	yr	901	1999	30r
Gasoline before-tax price (cents)	gal	117.60	10/00	43s
Maintenance and repair expenditures	yr	618	1999	30r
Public transportation, expenditures on	yr	575	1999	30r
Transportation purchases	yr	6503	1999	30r
Vehicle expenses, miscellaneous, purchases	yr	2266	1999	30r
Vehicle insurance payments	yr	824	1999	30r
Vehicle purchases (net outlay)	yr	2761	1999	30r
Vehicle rental, lease expenditures	yr	584	1999	30r
Utilities				
Electrical bill, average	mos	64.42	9/00	9s
Electricity, expenditures on	yr	837	1999	30r
Electricity, summer, 250 KWh	mos	28.90	2/96	97c
Electricity, summer, 500 KWh	mos	60.69	2/96	97c
Electricity, summer, 750 KWh	mos	96.81	2/96	97c
Electricity, summer, 1000 KWh	mos	132.93	2/96	97c
Electricity cost, average	KWh	10.12	9/00	9s
Utilities, fuels, and public services purchased	yr	2457	1999	30r
Water and other public services, expenditures on	yr	215	1999	30r
Weddings				
Wedding (national average cost)		19936	2000	33r
Wedding (regional average total cost)		29454	1997	110r
Attendants' gifts		321	1998	33r
Bridal attendants' apparel (5 persons)		824	2000	33r
Bride's headpiece/veil		173	1998	33r
Bride's wedding dress		859	1998	33r
Clergy, religious facility fee		242	1998	33r
Engagement ring		3177	1998	33r
Flowers		789	1998	33r
Groom's formalwear rental		99	2000	33r
Limousine		410	1998	33r
Marriage license cost		20.00	4/01	35s
Men's formalwear (ushers, best man)		469	2000	33r
Mother of bride apparel		241	2000	33r
Music		866	1998	33r
Photography and videography		1368	1998	33r
Rehearsal dinner		728	1998	33r
Wedding invitations and announcements		341	1998	33r
Wedding reception		7968	2000	33r
Wedding rings (bride and groom)		1060	1998	33r

Portland, OR

Item	Per	Value	Date	Ref.
Average annual expenditures	yr	43331	1999	30c
Composite, ACCRA index		104.20	3/01	4c
Alcoholic Beverages				
Alcoholic beverage purchases	yr	430	1999	30c
Beer, Heineken, 12-oz, ex deposit	6	7.29	3/01	4c
J & B Scotch	750-ml	22.95	3/01	4c
Malt beverages, all types, all sizes, any origin	16 oz	0.94	7/01	11r
Wine, Livingston or Gallo, Chablis blanc	1.5 liter	5.69	3/01	4c
Wine, red and white table, all sizes, any origin	liter	6.00	7/01	11r
Appliances				
Appliance repair, service call, washing machine	min lab chg	47.58	3/01	4c
Major appliances, expenditures on	yr	167	1999	30r
Small appliances, housewares, expenditures on	yr	105	1999	30r
Banking and Money				
Mortgage interest and charges paid	yr	3368	1999	30r
Mortgage principal paid on owned property	yr	1677	1999	30r
Mortgage rate, incl. points and orig. fee, 30-yr. conv. fixed or ARM	mos	6.81	3/01	4c
Vehicle finance charges paid	yr	311	1999	30r
Business Expenses				
Business travel, car rental	day	59	2001	3c
Business travel, food	day	52	2001	3c
Business travel, hotel	day	117	2001	3c
Medical office space cost	sq ft	127.88	2001	31c
Office space, 2-4 storey building	sq ft	112.04	2001	31c
Office space, 5-10 storey building	sq ft	98.96	2001	31c
Office space, 11-20 storey building	sq ft	95.12	2001	31c
Charity				
Cash contributions, expenditures	yr	2036	1999	30c
Child Care				
Child raising cost, total, age 0-2	yr	9140	1999	60r
Child raising cost, total, age 3-5	yr	9370	1999	60r
Child raising cost, total, age 6-8	yr	9450	1999	60r
Child raising cost, total, age 9-11	yr	9470	1999	60r
Child raising cost, total, age 12-14	yr	10170	1999	60r
Child raising cost, total, age 15-17	yr	10360	1999	60r
Child's child care and education, age 0-2	yr	1250	1999	60r
Child's child care and education, age 3-5	yr	1380	1999	60r
Child's child care and education, age 6-8	yr	890	1999	60r
Child's child care and education, age 9-11	yr	580	1999	60r
Child's child care and education, age 12-14	yr	430	1999	60r
Child's child care and education, age 15-17	yr	730	1999	60r
Child's clothing, age 0-2	yr	430	1999	60r
Child's clothing, age 3-5	yr	420	1999	60r
Child's clothing, age 6-8	yr	470	1999	60r
Child's clothing, age 9-11	yr	520	1999	60r
Child's clothing, age 12-14	yr	870	1999	60r
Child's clothing, age 15-17	yr	770	1999	60r
Child's food, age 0-2	yr	1120	1999	60r
Child's food, age 3-5	yr	1280	1999	60r
Child's food, age 6-8	yr	1640	1999	60r
Child's food, age 9-11	yr	1930	1999	60r
Child's food, age 12-14	yr	1940	1999	60r
Child's food, age 15-17	yr	2150	1999	60r
Child's health care, age 0-2	yr	490	1999	60r
Child's health care, age 3-5	yr	470	1999	60r
Child's health care, age 6-8	yr	530	1999	60r
Child's health care, age 9-11	yr	570	1999	60r
Child's health care, age 12-14	yr	580	1999	60r
Child's health care, age 15-17	yr	610	1999	60r
Child's housing, age 0-2	yr	3630	1999	60r
Child's housing, age 3-5	yr	3610	1999	60r
Child's housing, age 6-8	yr	3570	1999	60r
Child's housing, age 9-11	yr	3410	1999	60r
Child's housing, age 12-14	yr	3600	1999	60r
Child's housing, age 15-17	yr	3210	1999	60r
Child's personal care, reading, age 0-2	yr	1040	1999	60r

Values are in dollars or fractions of dollars. In the column headed *Ref*, references are shown to sources. Each reference is followed by a letter. These refer to the geographical level for which data were reported: s=State, r=Region, and c=City or metro. The abbreviation *ex* is used to mean *except* or *excluding*; *exp* stands for expenditures. For other abbreviations and further explanations, please see the Introduction.

Portland, OR - continued

Item	Per	Value	Date	Ref.
Child Care				
Child's personal care, reading, age 3-5	yr	1060	1999	60r
Child's personal care, reading, age 6-8	yr	1090	1999	60r
Child's personal care, reading, age 9-11	yr	1130	1999	60r
Child's personal care, reading, age 12-14	yr	1300	1999	60r
Child's personal care, reading, age 15-17	yr	1080	1999	60r
Daycare	mos	527	1998	37c
Daycare, 3-year old, 5 days, 8 hrs/day	mos	527	1998	85c
Clothing				
Apparel and services purchases	yr	1687	1999	30c
Boys' brief, cotton	3	5.55	3/01	4c
Boys, 2 to 15, expenditures on	yr	80	1999	30r
Children under 2, expenditures on	yr	74	1999	30r
Footwear, expenditures on	yr	307	1999	30r
Girls, 2 to 15, expenditures on	yr	101	1999	30r
Men and boys, expenditures on	yr	443	1999	30r
Men, 16 and over, expenditures on	yr	363	1999	30r
Shirt, man's dress shirt		25.59	3/01	4c
Slacks, man's "No Wrinkles" khaki		36.79	3/01	4c
Women, 16 and over, expenditures on	yr	594	1999	30r
Communications				
Newspaper subscription, daily and Sunday delivery	mos	13.04	3/01	4c
Phone line, single, business, field visit	inst.	31.00	12/97	17s
Phone line, single, business, no field visit	inst.	31.00	12/97	17s
Phone line, single, residence, field visit	inst.	12.00	12/97	17s
Phone line, single, residence, no field visit	inst.	12.00	12/97	17s
Postage and stationery, expenditures on	yr	150	1999	30r
Postal rate, express mail, up to half-pound		12.45	7/01	108r
Postal rate, letter, first class, first ounce		0.34	7/01	108r
Postal rate, letter, two ounces		0.57	7/01	108r
Postal rate, post card		0.21	7/01	108r
Postal rate, priority mail, two pounds		3.95	7/01	108r
Postal rate, priority mail, up to one pound		3.50	7/01	108r
Telephone bill, business, basic rate	mos	18.00	12/97	18c
Telephone bill, family of three	mos	20.92	3/01	4c
Telephone bill, residential, basic rate	mos	6.37	12/97	18c
Telephone services, expenditures on	yr	825	1999	30r
Education				
Board, 4-year private college/university	yr	2750	1996	38s
Board, 4-year public college/university	yr	2474	1996	38s
Education expenditures	yr	728	1999	30c
Room, 4-year private college/university	yr	2257	1996	38s
Room, 4-year public college/university	yr	1647	1996	38s
Total cost, 4-year private college/university	yr	18899	1996	38s
Total cost, 4-year public college/university	yr	7354	1996	38s
Tuition, 2-year public college/university, in state	yr	1338	1996	38s
Tuition, 4-year private college/university, in state	yr	13892	1996	38s
Tuition, 4-year public college/university	yr	3233	1996	38s
Energy and Fuels				
Electricity	500 KWhs	48.23	7/01	11r
Electricity	KWh	0.11	7/01	11r
Energy, combined forms, 2400 sq ft	mos	112.08	3/01	4c
Energy, exc. electricity, 2400 sq ft	mos	60.18	3/01	4c
Fuel oil and other fuels, expenditures on	yr	35	1999	30r
Gas, cooking, winter, 10 therms	mos	5.52	2/96	98c
Gas, cooking, winter, 30 therms	mos	16.57	2/96	98c
Gas, cooking, winter, 50 therms	mos	27.62	2/96	98c
Gas, heating, winter, average use	mos	141.00	2/96	98c
Gas, natural, commercial rate	1000 cf	7.55	11/00	88s
Gas, regular unleaded, cash, self-service	gal	1.58	3/01	4c
Gasoline, all types	gal	1.91	7/01	11r
Gasoline, unleaded premium	gal	2.05	7/01	11r
Gasoline, unleaded regular	gal	1.83	7/01	11r
Natural gas, expenditures on	yr	255	1999	30r
Utility (piped) gas, therm		0.98	7/01	11r
Utility (piped) gas, 40 therms		40.74	7/01	11r
Utility (piped) gas, 100 therms		96.80	7/01	11r

Portland, OR - continued

Item	Per	Value	Date	Ref.
Entertainment				
Bowling, Saturday evening rate	line	2.88	3/01	4c
Entertainment purchases	yr	2282	1999	30c
Fees and admissions paid	yr	545	1999	30r
Monopoly game, Parker Brothers', No. 9	game	11.77	3/01	4c
Movie, first-run, Saturday, evening	adm.	7.45	3/01	4c
Television, radios, sound equipment, expenditures on	yr	624	1999	30r
Tennis balls, yellow, Wilson or Penn, 3	can	2.63	3/01	4c
Funerals				
Total cost of funeral		5401.08	1/99	78r
Acknowledgement cards		33.64	1/99	78r
Casket		2170.43	1/99	78r
Cosmetology, hair, other preparation		136.32	1/99	78r
Embalming		319.13	1/99	78r
Funeral at funeral home		370.21	1/99	78r
Hearse (local)		161.04	1/99	78r
Professional service charges		963.15	1/99	78r
Service car/van		133.99	1/99	78r
Transfer of remains to funeral home		159.82	1/99	78r
Vault		778.07	1/99	78r
Visitation/viewing		175.28	1/99	78r
Groceries				
Groceries, ACCRA Index		103.70	3/01	4c
Antibiotic ointment, Polysporin	0.5 oz	4.53	3/01	4c
Apples, red delicious	lb	0.84	7/01	11r
Baby food, strained vegetables or fruit, lowest price	4-4.5 oz	0.37	3/01	4c
Bacon, sliced	lb	3.38	7/01	11r
Bakery products, expenditures on	yr	299	1999	30r
Bananas	lb	0.53	3/01	4c
Bananas	lb	0.54	7/01	11r
Beans, dried, any type, all sizes	lb	0.76	7/01	11r
Beef or hamburger, ground	lb	1.49	3/01	4c
Beef, expenditures on	yr	222	1999	30r
Bread, white	loaf	0.63	3/01	4c
Bread, white, pan	lb	0.99	7/01	11r
Butter, yoghurt, cheese, etc, expenditures on	yr	211	1999	30r
Cereals and bakery product purchases	yr	539	1999	30c
Cereals and cereal products, expenditures on	yr	168	1999	30r
Cheese, Kraft grated Parmesan	8 oz	4.35	3/01	4c
Chicken breast, bone-in	lb	2.45	7/01	11r
Chicken, fresh, whole	lb	1.19	7/01	11r
Chicken, whole fryer	lb	1.23	3/01	4c
Chops, boneless,	lb	4.00	7/01	11r
Chuck roast, graded and ungraded, excl U.S. prime and choice	lb	2.55	7/01	11r
Cigarettes, Winston, Kings	carton	34.45	3/01	4c
Coffee, 100%, ground roast, all sizes	lb	3.80	7/01	11r
Coffee, vacuum-packed	13 oz	3.65	3/01	4c
Cookies, chocolate chip	lb	2.83	7/01	11r
Corn Flakes, Kellogg's or Post Toasties	18 oz	2.79	3/01	4c
Corn, frozen, whole kernel, lowest price	16 oz	1.09	3/01	4c
Dairy product purchases	yr	397	1999	30c
Eggs, expenditures on	yr	39	1999	30r
Eggs, Grade A or AA	dozen	1.31	3/01	4c
Eggs, grade AA, large	dozen	1.23	7/01	11r
Fats and oils, expenditures on	yr	88	1999	30r
Fish and seafood, expenditures on	yr	121	1999	30r
Food (excl fruit and vegetables), eaten at home, purchases	yr	1182	1999	30c
Food cooked on trips, expenditures on	yr	64	1999	30r
Food purchases	yr	5855	1999	30c
Food purchases, eaten away from home	yr	2298	1999	30c
Food purchases, food eaten at home	yr	3557	1999	30c
Fresh fruits, expenditures on	yr	186	1999	30r
Fresh milk and cream, expenditures on	yr	130	1999	30r
Fresh vegetables, expenditures on	yr	177	1999	30r
Grapefruit	lb	0.68	7/01	11r
Grapes, Thompson, seedless	lb	2.42	7/01	11r
Ground beef, lean and extra lean	lb	2.46	7/01	11r

Values are in dollars or fractions of dollars. In the column headed *Ref*, references are shown to sources. Each reference is followed by a letter. These refer to the geographical level for which data were reported: s=State, r=Region, and c=City or metro. The abbreviation *ex* is used to mean *except* or *excluding*; *exp* stands for expenditures. For other abbreviations and further explanations, please see the Introduction.

Portland, OR - continued

Item	Per	Value	Date	Ref.
Groceries				
Ice cream, prepackaged, bulk, regular	1/2 gal	3.62	7/01	11r
Lettuce, iceberg	head	0.92	3/01	4c
Lettuce, iceberg	lb	0.63	7/01	11r
Margarine, Blue Bonnet or Parkay, stick	lb	0.57	3/01	4c
Meats, poultry, fish, and egg purchases	yr	770	1999	30c
Milk, fresh, low fat,	gal	2.80	7/01	11r
Milk, fresh, whole, fortified	gal	2.88	7/01	11r
Milk, whole	1/2 gal	2.03	3/01	4c
Nonalcoholic beverages, expenditures on	yr	258	1999	30r
Orange juice, Minute Maid frozen	12 oz	1.31	3/01	4c
Oranges, Navel	lb	0.97	7/01	11r
Oranges, Valencia	lb	0.43	7/01	11r
Peaches	lb	1.38	7/01	11r
Peaches, halves or slices, Hunt's, Del Monte, or Libby's	29 oz	1.59	3/01	4c
Peanut butter, creamy, all sizes	lb	2.14	7/01	11r
Peas, green, Del Monte or Green Giant	15 oz	0.89	3/01	4c
Pork chops, center cut, bone-in	lb	3.83	7/01	11r
Pork, expenditures on	yr	141	1999	30r
Potatoes, white or red	10 lb	1.81	3/01	4c
Potatoes, white, all types	lb	0.37	7/01	11r
Poultry, expenditures on	yr	146	1999	30r
Processed fruits, expenditures on	yr	118	1999	30r
Processed vegetables, expenditures on	yr	81	1999	30r
Round roast, graded and ungraded, excl U.S. prime and choice	lb	3.07	7/01	11r
Round roast, U.S. choice, boneless	lb	3.37	7/01	11r
Round steak, graded and ungraded, excl U.S. prime and choice	lb	3.51	7/01	11r
Sausage, Jimmy Dean/Owens pork	lb	4.56	3/01	4c
Shortening, vegetable, Crisco	3 lb	2.85	3/01	4c
Sirloin steak, graded and ungraded, excl U.S. prime and choice	lb	4.67	7/01	11r
Soft drink, Coca Cola, ex deposit	2 liter	1.21	3/01	4c
Steak, sirloin, U.S. choice, boneless	lb	6.20	7/01	11r
Steak, T-bone	lb	6.97	3/01	4c
Strawberries, dry pint	12 oz	1.79	7/01	11r
Sugar and other sweets, expenditures on	yr	124	1999	30r
Sugar, cane or beet	4 lbs	1.79	3/01	4c
Sugar, white, all sizes	lb	0.46	7/01	11r
Tobacco products and smoking supplies purchases	yr	256	1999	30c
Tomatoes, field grown	lb	1.17	7/01	11r
Tomatoes, Hunt's or Del Monte	14.5 oz	0.97	3/01	4c
Tuna, chunk, light	6 oz	0.56	3/01	4c
Tuna, light, chunk	lb	2.05	7/01	11r
Goods and Services				
Miscellaneous goods and services, ACCRA Index		106.70	3/01	4c
B&B Japanese maple (acer japonicum)	gal	39.99	4/00	93r
Boxwood (buxus)	2 gal	14.99-24.99	4/00	93r
Christmas tree, noble fir		20-25	2000	65s
Daylilly (hemerocallis)	gal	6.99-8.99	4/00	93r
Flat of annuals		16.68	4/00	93r
Fountain grass (pennisetum)	gal	7.99-11.99	4/00	93r
Hanging basket (10 in)		29.99	4/00	93r
Hardy geranium (geranium)	gal	6.99-11.99	4/00	93r
Hosta (hosta)	gal	6.99-18.99	4/00	93r
Lilac (syrubga vulgaris)	2 gal	14.99-17.99	4/00	93r
Miscellaneous purchases	yr	826	1999	30c
Rhododendron (rhododendron)	2 gal	14.99	4/00	93r
Sage (salvia)	gal	6.99	4/00	93r
Wintercreeper euonymus (euonymus fortunei)	2 gal	14.99-22.99	4/00	93r
Hunting license	yr	17.50	4/01	34s

Portland, OR - continued

Item	Per	Value	Date	Ref.
Health Care				
Health care, ACCRA Index		123.20	3/01	4c
Cardiac catheterization, ave hospital/ physician charges		10940	1998	77s
Childbirth, Cesarean delivery		11587	1997	13r
Childbirth, vaginal delivery		6725	1997	13r
Dentist's fee, adult teeth cleaning and periodic oral exam	visit	100.60	3/01	4c
Doctor's fee, routine exam, established patient	visit	71.36	3/01	4c
Drugs, expenditures on	yr	309	1999	30r
Health care purchases	yr	1837	1999	30c
Health insurance expenditures	yr	868	1999	30r
Hospital care, private room	day	573.80	3/01	4c
Hysterectomy, laproscopically-assisted, ave hospital/physician charges		11660	1998	76s
Hysterectomy, vaginal, ave hospital and physician charges		6680	1998	76s
Medicaid dispensing fee		3.80-4.16	1999	87s
Medical services expenditures	yr	580	1999	30r
Medical supplies, expenditures on	yr	112	1999	30r
Nursing home costs, private room	day	144	2000	82c
Nursing home stay, private room	day	144	2000	81c
Household Goods				
Dishwashing powder, Cascade	50 oz	3.70	3/01	4c
Floor coverings, expenditures on	yr	49	1999	30r
Furniture, expenditures on	yr	444	1999	30r
Household furnishings and equipment purchases	yr	1799	1999	30c
Household textiles, expenditures on	yr	141	1999	30r
Laundry and cleaning supplies, expenditures on	yr	128	1999	30r
Tissues, facial, Kleenex brand	175	1.49	3/01	4c
Housing				
Housing, ACCRA Index		98.00	3/01	4c
Home, 2200 sq ft, 4-br, 2-bath, 2-car garage, average		249125	2000	47c
Home price, existing, ave		239400	10/00	90r
Home value, median		149000	2001	53s
House, 2400 sq ft, 8000 sq ft lot, new, urban, utilities	total	202000	3/01	4c
House payment, principal and interest, 25% down payment	mos	989	3/01	4c
Household operation expenditures	yr	675	1999	30c
Housekeeping supplies purchases	yr	506	1999	30c
Lodging expenditures	yr	539	1999	30c
Maintenance, repairs, insurance expenditures	yr	939	1999	30r
Monthly rental value of owned home	mos	662	1999	30r
Owned dwellings, expenditures own	yr	5568	1999	30c
Rent expenditures	yr	2601	1999	30c
Rent, apartment, 2 br, 1 1/2-2 baths, unfurn, 950 sq ft, water	mos	734	3/01	4c
Shelter, expenditures on	yr	8708	1999	30c
Insurance and Pensions				
Life and other personal insurance purchases	yr	462	1999	30c
Pensions and Social Security, expenditures on	yr	4345	1999	30c
Legal Fees				
Combination hunting and fishing license	yr	33.75	4/01	34s
Divorce, filing fee		100.00-250.00	4/01	35s
Driver's license fee	renew	16.25	1999	48s
Driver's license fee	orig	26.25	1999	48s
Fishing license	yr	19.75	4/01	34s
Personal Goods				
Personal care products and services purchases	yr	424	1999	30c
Shampoo, Alberto VO5	15 oz	1.32	3/01	4c

Values are in dollars or fractions of dollars. In the column headed *Ref*, references are shown to sources. Each reference is followed by a letter. These refer to the geographical level for which data were reported: s=State, r=Region, and c=City or metro. The abbreviation *ex* is used to mean *except* or *excluding*; *exp* stands for expenditures. For other abbreviations and further explanations, please see the Introduction.

Portland, OR - continued

Item	Per	Value	Date	Ref.
Personal Goods				
Toothpaste, Crest or Colgate	6-7 oz	2.26	3/01	4c
Personal Services				
Dry cleaning, man's 2-pc suit		8.37	3/01	4c
Man's haircut, barbershop, no styling		10.30	3/01	4c
Personal services, household, expenditures on	yr	353	1999	30r
Woman's shampoo, trim, blow-dry, no style-change		30.00	3/01	4c
Pets				
Pets, toys, and playground equipment, expenditures on	yr	358	1999	30r
Restaurant Food				
Chicken, fried, thigh and drumstick, KFC/Church's		2.99	3/01	4c
Hamburger with cheese, McDonald's	1/4 lb	2.13	3/01	4c
Pizza, Pizza Hut or Pizza Inn	11-12 in	10.99	3/01	4c
Taxes				
Federal income taxes paid	yr	3200	1999	30r
Personal taxes, expenditures on	yr	4153	1999	30r
Property taxes paid	yr	923	1999	30r
State and local income taxes paid	yr	812	1999	30r
Transportation				
Transportation, ACCRA Index		113.60	3/01	4c
Bus fare, one-way	trip	0.85	2000	1c
Bus fare, to central business district	1-way	1.50	3/01	4c
Cars and trucks, new, expenditures on	yr	1534	1999	30r
Cars and trucks, used, expenditures on	yr	1593	1999	30r
Diesel at the pump	gal	1.16	10/99	73s
Gasoline and motor oil purchases	yr	1103	1999	30c
Gasoline before-tax price (cents)	gal	128.30	10/00	43s
Light rail transit fare, one-way	trip	1.10	2000	2c
Maintenance and repair expenditures	yr	797	1999	30r
Public transportation, expenditures on	yr	519	1999	30c
Tire balance, computer or spin balance, front	wheel	8.59	3/01	4c
Transportation purchases	yr	8117	1999	30c
Vehicle expenses, miscellaneous, purchases	yr	2373	1999	30c
Vehicle insurance payments	yr	811	1999	30r
Vehicle purchases (net outlay)	yr	3180	1999	30r
Vehicle rental, lease expenditures	yr	666	1999	30r
Travel				
Hotel room, ave	night	104.84	2000	70c
Utilities				
Utilities, ACCRA Index		92.40	3/01	4c
Electrical bill, average	mos	61.42	9/00	9s
Electricity, expenditures on	yr	725	1999	30r
Electricity, summer, 250 KWh	mos	20.01	2/96	96c
Electricity, summer, 500 KWh	mos	35.73	2/96	96c
Electricity, summer, 750 KWh	mos	51.87	2/96	96c
Electricity, summer, 1000 KWh	mos	68.01	2/96	96c
Electricity and other, mixed, 2400 sq ft, new home	mos	51.90	3/01	4c
Electricity cost, average	KWh	4.70	9/00	9s
Utilities, fuels, and public services purchased	yr	2160	1999	30c
Water and other public services, expenditures on	yr	339	1999	30r
Weddings				
Wedding (national average cost)		19936	2000	33r
Wedding (regional average total cost)		18918	1997	110r
Attendants' gifts		321	1998	33r
Bridal attendants' apparel (5 persons)		824	2000	33r
Bride's headpiece/veil		173	1998	33r
Bride's wedding dress		859	1998	33r
Clergy, religious facility fee		242	1998	33r
Engagement ring		3177	1998	33r
Flowers		789	1998	33r
Groom's formalwear rental		99	2000	33r
Limousine		410	1998	33r
Marriage license cost		60.00	4/01	35s

Portland, OR - continued

Item	Per	Value	Date	Ref.
Weddings - continued				
Men's formalwear (ushers, best man)		469	2000	33r
Mother of bride apparel		241	2000	33r
Music		866	1998	33r
Photography and videography		1368	1998	33r
Rehearsal dinner		728	1998	33r
Wedding invitations and announcements		341	1998	33r
Wedding reception		7968	2000	33r
Wedding rings (bride and groom)		1060	1998	33r

Portland-Vancouver, OR

Item	Per	Value	Date	Ref.
Average annual expenditures	yr	40662	1999	30r
Alcoholic Beverages				
Alcoholic beverage purchases	yr	372	1999	30r
Malt beverages, all types, all sizes, any origin	16 oz	0.94	7/01	11r
Wine, red and white table, all sizes, any origin	liter	6.00	7/01	11r
Appliances				
Major appliances, expenditures on	yr	167	1999	30r
Small appliances, housewares, expenditures on	yr	105	1999	30r
Banking and Money				
Mortgage interest and charges paid	yr	3368	1999	30r
Mortgage principal paid on owned property	yr	1677	1999	30r
Vehicle finance charges paid	yr	311	1999	30r
Charity				
Cash contributions, expenditures	yr	1344	1999	30r
Child Care				
Child raising cost, total, age 0-2	yr	9140	1999	60r
Child raising cost, total, age 3-5	yr	9370	1999	60r
Child raising cost, total, age 6-8	yr	9450	1999	60r
Child raising cost, total, age 9-11	yr	9470	1999	60r
Child raising cost, total, age 12-14	yr	10170	1999	60r
Child raising cost, total, age 15-17	yr	10360	1999	60r
Child's child care and education, age 0-2	yr	1250	1999	60r
Child's child care and education, age 3-5	yr	1380	1999	60r
Child's child care and education, age 6-8	yr	890	1999	60r
Child's child care and education, age 9-11	yr	580	1999	60r
Child's child care and education, age 12-14	yr	430	1999	60r
Child's child care and education, age 15-17	yr	730	1999	60r
Child's clothing, age 0-2	yr	430	1999	60r
Child's clothing, age 3-5	yr	420	1999	60r
Child's clothing, age 6-8	yr	470	1999	60r
Child's clothing, age 9-11	yr	520	1999	60r
Child's clothing, age 12-14	yr	870	1999	60r
Child's clothing, age 15-17	yr	770	1999	60r
Child's food, age 0-2	yr	1120	1999	60r
Child's food, age 3-5	yr	1280	1999	60r
Child's food, age 6-8	yr	1640	1999	60r
Child's food, age 9-11	yr	1930	1999	60r
Child's food, age 12-14	yr	1940	1999	60r
Child's food, age 15-17	yr	2150	1999	60r
Child's health care, age 0-2	yr	490	1999	60r
Child's health care, age 3-5	yr	470	1999	60r
Child's health care, age 6-8	yr	530	1999	60r
Child's health care, age 9-11	yr	570	1999	60r
Child's health care, age 12-14	yr	580	1999	60r
Child's health care, age 15-17	yr	610	1999	60r
Child's housing, age 0-2	yr	3630	1999	60r
Child's housing, age 3-5	yr	3610	1999	60r
Child's housing, age 6-8	yr	3570	1999	60r
Child's housing, age 9-11	yr	3410	1999	60r
Child's housing, age 12-14	yr	3600	1999	60r
Child's housing, age 15-17	yr	3210	1999	60r
Child's personal care, reading, age 0-2	yr	1040	1999	60r
Child's personal care, reading, age 3-5	yr	1060	1999	60r
Child's personal care, reading, age 6-8	yr	1090	1999	60r
Child's personal care, reading, age 9-11	yr	1130	1999	60r
Child's personal care, reading, age 12-14	yr	1300	1999	60r

Values are in dollars or fractions of dollars. In the column headed *Ref*, references are shown to sources. Each reference is followed by a letter. These refer to the geographical level for which data were reported: s=State, r=Region, and c=City or metro. The abbreviation *ex* is used to mean *except* or *excluding*; *exp* stands for expenditures. For other abbreviations and further explanations, please see the Introduction.

Portland-Vancouver, OR - continued

Item	Per	Value	Date	Ref.
Child Care				
Child's personal care, reading, age 15-17	yr	1080	1999	60r
Clothing				
Apparel and services purchases	yr	1863	1999	30r
Boys, 2 to 15, expenditures on	yr	80	1999	30r
Children under 2, expenditures on	yr	74	1999	30r
Footwear, expenditures on	yr	307	1999	30r
Girls, 2 to 15, expenditures on	yr	101	1999	30r
Men and boys, expenditures on	yr	443	1999	30r
Men, 16 and over, expenditures on	yr	363	1999	30r
Women, 16 and over, expenditures on	yr	594	1999	30r
Communications				
Phone line, single, business, field visit	inst.	31.00	12/97	17s
Phone line, single, business, no field visit	inst.	31.00	12/97	17s
Phone line, single, residence, field visit	inst.	12.00	12/97	17s
Phone line, single, residence, no field visit	inst.	12.00	12/97	17s
Postage and stationery, expenditures on	yr	150	1999	30r
Postal rate, express mail, up to half-pound		12.45	7/01	108r
Postal rate, letter, first class, first ounce		0.34	7/01	108r
Postal rate, letter, two ounces		0.57	7/01	108r
Postal rate, post card		0.21	7/01	108r
Postal rate, priority mail, two pounds		3.95	7/01	108r
Postal rate, priority mail, up to one pound		3.50	7/01	108r
Telephone services, expenditures on	yr	825	1999	30r
Education				
Board, 4-year private college/university	yr	2750	1996	38s
Board, 4-year public college/university	yr	2474	1996	38s
Education expenditures	yr	676	1999	30r
Room, 4-year private college/university	yr	2257	1996	38s
Room, 4-year public college/university	yr	1647	1996	38s
Total cost, 4-year private college/university	yr	18899	1996	38s
Total cost, 4-year public college/university	yr	7354	1996	38s
Tuition, 2-year public college/university, in state	yr	1338	1996	38s
Tuition, 4-year private college/university, in state	yr	13892	1996	38s
Tuition, 4-year public college/university	yr	3233	1996	38s
Energy and Fuels				
Electricity	500 KWhs	48.23	7/01	11r
Electricity	KWh	0.11	7/01	11r
Fuel oil and other fuels, expenditures on	yr	35	1999	30r
Gas, natural, commercial rate	1000 cf	7.55	11/00	88s
Gasoline, all types	gal	1.91	7/01	11r
Gasoline, unleaded premium	gal	2.05	7/01	11r
Gasoline, unleaded regular	gal	1.83	7/01	11r
Natural gas, expenditures on	yr	255	1999	30r
Utility (piped) gas, therm		0.98	7/01	11r
Utility (piped) gas, 40 therms		40.74	7/01	11r
Utility (piped) gas, 100 therms		96.80	7/01	11r
Entertainment				
Entertainment purchases	yr	2139	1999	30r
Fees and admissions paid	yr	545	1999	30r
Television, radios, sound equipment, expenditures on	yr	624	1999	30r
Funerals				
Total cost of funeral		5401.08	1/99	78r
Acknowledgement cards		33.64	1/99	78r
Casket		2170.43	1/99	78r
Cosmetology, hair, other preparation		136.32	1/99	78r
Embalming		319.13	1/99	78r
Funeral at funeral home		370.21	1/99	78r
Hearse (local)		161.04	1/99	78r
Professional service charges		963.15	1/99	78r
Service car/van		133.99	1/99	78r
Transfer of remains to funeral home		159.82	1/99	78r
Vault		778.07	1/99	78r
Visitation/viewing		175.28	1/99	78r

Portland-Vancouver, OR - continued

Item	Per	Value	Date	Ref.
Groceries				
Apples, red delicious	lb	0.84	7/01	11r
Bacon, sliced	lb	3.38	7/01	11r
Bakery products, expenditures on	yr	299	1999	30r
Bananas	lb	0.54	7/01	11r
Beans, dried, any type, all sizes	lb	0.76	7/01	11r
Beef, expenditures on	yr	222	1999	30r
Bread, white, pan	lb	0.99	7/01	11r
Butter, yoghurt, cheese, etc, expenditures on	yr	211	1999	30r
Cereals and bakery product purchases	yr	466	1999	30r
Cereals and cereal products, expenditures on	yr	168	1999	30r
Chicken breast, bone-in	lb	2.45	7/01	11r
Chicken, fresh, whole	lb	1.19	7/01	11r
Chops, boneless,	lb	4.00	7/01	11r
Chuck roast, graded and ungraded, excl U.S. prime and choice	lb	2.55	7/01	11r
Coffee, 100%, ground roast, all sizes	lb	3.80	7/01	11r
Cookies, chocolate chip	lb	2.83	7/01	11r
Dairy product purchases	yr	341	1999	30r
Eggs, expenditures on	yr	39	1999	30r
Eggs, grade AA, large	dozen	1.23	7/01	11r
Fats and oils, expenditures on	yr	88	1999	30r
Fish and seafood, expenditures on	yr	121	1999	30r
Food (excl fruit and vegetables), eaten at home, purchases	yr	1001	1999	30r
Food cooked on trips, expenditures on	yr	64	1999	30r
Food purchases	yr	5312	1999	30r
Food purchases, eaten away from home	yr	2180	1999	30r
Food purchases, food eaten at home	yr	3132	1999	30r
Fresh fruits, expenditures on	yr	186	1999	30r
Fresh milk and cream, expenditures on	yr	130	1999	30r
Fresh vegetables, expenditures on	yr	177	1999	30r
Grapefruit	lb	0.68	7/01	11r
Grapes, Thompson, seedless	lb	2.42	7/01	11r
Ground beef, lean and extra lean	lb	2.46	7/01	11r
Ice cream, prepackaged, bulk, regular	1/2 gal	3.62	7/01	11r
Lettuce, iceberg	lb	0.63	7/01	11r
Meats, poultry, fish, and egg purchases	yr	761	1999	30r
Milk, fresh, low fat,	gal	2.80	7/01	11r
Milk, fresh, whole, fortified	gal	2.88	7/01	11r
Nonalcoholic beverages, expenditures on	yr	258	1999	30r
Oranges, Navel	lb	0.97	7/01	11r
Oranges, Valencia	lb	0.43	7/01	11r
Peaches	lb	1.38	7/01	11r
Peanut butter, creamy, all sizes	lb	2.14	7/01	11r
Pork chops, center cut, bone-in	lb	3.83	7/01	11r
Pork, expenditures on	yr	141	1999	30r
Potatoes, white, all types	lb	0.37	7/01	11r
Poultry, expenditures on	yr	146	1999	30r
Processed fruits, expenditures on	yr	118	1999	30r
Processed vegetables, expenditures on	yr	81	1999	30r
Round roast, graded and ungraded, excl U.S. prime and choice	lb	3.07	7/01	11r
Round roast, U.S. choice, boneless	lb	3.37	7/01	11r
Round steak, graded and ungraded, excl U.S. prime and choice	lb	3.51	7/01	11r
Sirloin steak, graded and ungraded, excl U.S. prime and choice	lb	4.67	7/01	11r
Steak, sirloin, U.S. choice, boneless	lb	6.20	7/01	11r
Strawberries, dry pint	12 oz	1.79	7/01	11r
Sugar and other sweets, expenditures on	yr	124	1999	30r
Sugar, white, all sizes	lb	0.46	7/01	11r
Tobacco products and smoking supplies purchases	yr	217	1999	30r
Tomatoes, field grown	lb	1.17	7/01	11r
Tuna, light, chunk	lb	2.05	7/01	11r
Goods and Services				
B&B Japanese maple (acer japonicum)	gal	39.99	4/00	93r
Boxwood (buxus)	2 gal	14.99-24.99	4/00	93r
Christmas tree, noble fir		20-25	2000	65s

Values are in dollars or fractions of dollars. In the column headed *Ref*, references are shown to sources. Each reference is followed by a letter. These refer to the geographical level for which data were reported: s=State, r=Region, and c=City or metro. The abbreviation *ex* is used to mean *except* or *excluding*; *exp* stands for expenditures. For other abbreviations and further explanations, please see the Introduction.

Portland-Vancouver, OR - continued

Item	Per	Value	Date	Ref.
Goods and Services				
Daylily (hemerocallis)	gal	6.99-8.99	4/00	93r
Flat of annuals		16.68	4/00	93r
Fountain grass (pennisetum)	gal	7.99-11.99	4/00	93r
Hanging basket (10 in)		29.99	4/00	93r
Hardy geranium (geranium)	gal	6.99-11.99	4/00	93r
Hosta (hosta)	gal	6.99-18.99	4/00	93r
Lilac (syrubga vulgaris)	2 gal	14.99-17.99	4/00	93r
Miscellaneous purchases	yr	1070	1999	30r
Rhododendron (rhododendron)	2 gal	14.99	4/00	93r
Sage (salvia)	gal	6.99	4/00	93r
Wintercreeper euonymus (euonymus fortunei)	2 gal	14.99-22.99	4/00	93r
Hunting license	yr	17.50	4/01	34s
Health Care				
Cardiac catheterization, ave hospital/ physician charges		10940	1998	77s
Childbirth, Cesarean delivery		11587	1997	13r
Childbirth, vaginal delivery		6725	1997	13r
Drugs, expenditures on	yr	309	1999	30r
Health care purchases	yr	1869	1999	30r
Health insurance expenditures	yr	868	1999	30r
Hysterectomy, laproscopically-assisted, ave hospital/physician charges		11660	1998	76s
Hysterectomy, vaginal, ave hospital and physician charges		6680	1998	76s
Medicaid dispensing fee		3.80-4.16	1999	87s
Medical services expenditures	yr	580	1999	30r
Medical supplies, expenditures on	yr	112	1999	30r
Household Goods				
Floor coverings, expenditures on	yr	49	1999	30r
Furniture, expenditures on	yr	444	1999	30r
Household furnishings and equipment purchases	yr	1768	1999	30r
Household textiles, expenditures on	yr	141	1999	30r
Laundry and cleaning supplies, expenditures on	yr	128	1999	30r
Housing				
Home price, existing, ave		239400	10/00	90r
Home value, median		149000	2001	53s
Household operation expenditures	yr	781	1999	30r
Housekeeping supplies purchases	yr	513	1999	30r
Lodging expenditures	yr	575	1999	30r
Maintenance, repairs, insurance expenditures	yr	939	1999	30r
Monthly rental value of owned home	mos	662	1999	30r
Owned dwellings, expenditures own	yr	5231	1999	30r
Rent expenditures	yr	2709	1999	30r
Rental unit, 1 bedroom, with utilities	mos	592	4/01	41c
Rental unit, 2 bedroom, with utilities	mos	730	4/01	41c
Rental unit, 3 bedroom, with utilities	mos	1015	4/01	41c
Rental unit, 4 bedroom, with utilities	mos	1102	4/01	41c
Shelter, expenditures on	yr	8516	1999	30r
Insurance and Pensions				
Life and other personal insurance purchases	yr	355	1999	30r
Pensions and Social Security, expenditures on	yr	3636	1999	30r
Legal Fees				
Combination hunting and fishing license	yr	33.75	4/01	34s
Divorce, filing fee		100.00-250.00	4/01	35s
Driver's license fee	orig	26.25	1999	48s
Driver's license fee	renew	16.25	1999	48s
Fishing license	yr	19.75	4/01	34s

Portland-Vancouver, OR - continued

Item	Per	Value	Date	Ref.
Personal Goods				
Personal care products and services purchases	yr	449	1999	30r
Personal Services				
Personal services, household, expenditures on	yr	353	1999	30r
Pets				
Pets, toys, and playground equipment, expenditures on	yr	358	1999	30r
Taxes				
Federal income taxes paid	yr	3200	1999	30r
Personal taxes, expenditures on	yr	4153	1999	30r
Property taxes paid	yr	923	1999	30r
State and local income taxes paid	yr	812	1999	30r
Transportation				
Cars and trucks, new, expenditures on	yr	1534	1999	30r
Cars and trucks, used, expenditures on	yr	1593	1999	30r
Diesel at the pump	gal	1.16	10/99	73s
Gasoline and motor oil purchases	yr	1129	1999	30r
Gasoline before-tax price (cents)	gal	128.30	10/00	43s
Maintenance and repair expenditures	yr	797	1999	30r
Public transportation, expenditures on	yr	530	1999	30r
Transportation purchases	yr	7423	1999	30r
Vehicle expenses, miscellaneous, purchases	yr	2585	1999	30r
Vehicle insurance payments	yr	811	1999	30r
Vehicle purchases (net outlay)	yr	3180	1999	30r
Vehicle rental, lease expenditures	yr	666	1999	30r
Utilities				
Electrical bill, average	mos	61.42	9/00	9s
Electricity, expenditures on	yr	725	1999	30r
Electricity cost, average	KWh	4.70	9/00	9s
Utilities, fuels, and public services purchased	yr	2179	1999	30r
Water and other public services, expenditures on	yr	339	1999	30r
Weddings				
Wedding (national average cost)		19936	2000	33r
Wedding (regional average total cost)		18918	1997	110r
Attendants' gifts		321	1998	33r
Bridal attendants' apparel (5 persons)		824	2000	33r
Bride's headpiece/veil		173	1998	33r
Bride's wedding dress		859	1998	33r
Clergy, religious facility fee		242	1998	33r
Engagement ring		3177	1998	33r
Flowers		789	1998	33r
Groom's formalwear rental		99	2000	33r
Limousine		410	1998	33r
Marriage license cost		60.00	4/01	35s
Men's formalwear (ushers, best man)		469	2000	33r
Mother of bride apparel		241	2000	33r
Music		866	1998	33r
Photography and videography		1368	1998	33r
Rehearsal dinner		728	1998	33r
Wedding invitations and announcements		341	1998	33r
Wedding reception		7968	2000	33r
Wedding rings (bride and groom)		1060	1998	33r

Portsmouth-Rochester, NH

Item	Per	Value	Date	Ref.
Average annual expenditures	yr	37971	1999	30r
Alcoholic Beverages				
Alcoholic beverage purchases	yr	368	1999	30r
Wine, red and white table, all sizes, any origin	liter	9.64	7/01	11r
Appliances				
Major appliances, expenditures on	yr	194	1999	30r
Small appliances, housewares, expenditures on	yr	93	1999	30r

Values are in dollars or fractions of dollars. In the column headed *Ref*, references are shown to sources. Each reference is followed by a letter. These refer to the geographical level for which data were reported: s=State, r=Region, and c=City or metro. The abbreviation *ex* is used to mean *except* or *excluding*; *exp* stands for *expenditures*. For other abbreviations and further explanations, please see the Introduction.

Portsmouth-Rochester, NH - continued

Item	Per	Value	Date	Ref.
Banking and Money				
Mortgage interest and charges paid	yr	2622	1999	30r
Mortgage principal paid on owned property	yr	1262	1999	30r
Vehicle finance charges paid	yr	240	1999	30r
Charity				
Cash contributions, expenditures	yr	1001	1999	30r
Child Care				
Child raising cost, total, age 0-2	yr	8670	1999	60r
Child raising cost, total, age 3-5	yr	8910	1999	60r
Child raising cost, total, age 6-8	yr	9040	1999	60r
Child raising cost, total, age 9-11	yr	9100	1999	60r
Child raising cost, total, age 12-14	yr	9890	1999	60r
Child raising cost, total, age 15-17	yr	10010	1999	60r
Child's child care and education, age 0-2	yr	1070	1999	60r
Child's child care and education, age 3-5	yr	1190	1999	60r
Child's child care and education, age 6-8	yr	740	1999	60r
Child's child care and education, age 9-11	yr	470	1999	60r
Child's child care and education, age 12-14	yr	350	1999	60r
Child's child care and education, age 15-17	yr	590	1999	60r
Child's clothing, age 0-2	yr	480	1999	60r
Child's clothing, age 3-5	yr	470	1999	60r
Child's clothing, age 6-8	yr	520	1999	60r
Child's clothing, age 9-11	yr	570	1999	60r
Child's clothing, age 12-14	yr	970	1999	60r
Child's clothing, age 15-17	yr	870	1999	60r
Child's food, age 0-2	yr	1130	1999	60r
Child's food, age 3-5	yr	1290	1999	60r
Child's food, age 6-8	yr	1640	1999	60r
Child's food, age 9-11	yr	1930	1999	60r
Child's food, age 12-14	yr	1940	1999	60r
Child's food, age 15-17	yr	2150	1999	60r
Child's health care, age 0-2	yr	550	1999	60r
Child's health care, age 3-5	yr	530	1999	60r
Child's health care, age 6-8	yr	610	1999	60r
Child's health care, age 9-11	yr	650	1999	60r
Child's health care, age 12-14	yr	660	1999	60r
Child's health care, age 15-17	yr	690	1999	60r
Child's housing, age 0-2	yr	3555	1999	60r
Child's housing, age 3-5	yr	3530	1999	60r
Child's housing, age 6-8	yr	3490	1999	60r
Child's housing, age 9-11	yr	3340	1999	60r
Child's housing, age 12-14	yr	3530	1999	60r
Child's housing, age 15-17	yr	3140	1999	60r
Child's personal care, reading, age 0-2	yr	920	1999	60r
Child's personal care, reading, age 3-5	yr	950	1999	60r
Child's personal care, reading, age 6-8	yr	980	1999	60r
Child's personal care, reading, age 9-11	yr	1020	1999	60r
Child's personal care, reading, age 12-14	yr	1190	1999	60r
Child's personal care, reading, age 15-17	yr	970	1999	60r
Clothing				
Apparel and services purchases	yr	1831	1999	30r
Boys, 2 to 15, expenditures on	yr	92	1999	30r
Children under 2, expenditures on	yr	63	1999	30r
Footwear, expenditures on	yr	300	1999	30r
Girls, 2 to 15, expenditures on	yr	101	1999	30r
Men and boys, expenditures on	yr	446	1999	30r
Men, 16 and over, expenditures on	yr	354	1999	30r
Women, 16 and over, expenditures on	yr	584	1999	30r
Communications				
Cable modem installation, Media One		100.00	6/99	103s
Cable modem rate, cable subscriber, Media One	mos	34.95-39.95	6/99	103s
Cable modem rate, non-cable subscriber, Media One	mos	49.95	6/99	103s
Phone line, single, business, field visit	inst.	109.00	12/97	17s
Phone line, single, business, no field visit	inst.	75.00	12/97	17s
Phone line, single, residence, field visit	inst.	81.00	12/97	17s
Phone line, single, residence, no field visit	inst.	49.00	12/97	17s
Postage and stationery, expenditures on	yr	138	1999	30r
Postal rate, express mail, up to half-pound		12.45	7/01	108r
Postal rate, letter, first class, first ounce		0.34	7/01	108r

Portsmouth-Rochester, NH - continued

Item	Per	Value	Date	Ref.
Communications - continued				
Postal rate, letter, two ounces		0.57	7/01	108r
Postal rate, post card		0.21	7/01	108r
Postal rate, priority mail, two pounds		3.95	7/01	108r
Postal rate, priority mail, up to one pound		3.50	7/01	108r
Telephone services, expenditures on	yr	830	1999	30r
Education				
Board, 4-year private college/university	yr	3009	1996	38s
Board, 4-year public college/university	yr	1710	1996	38s
Education expenditures	yr	877	1999	30r
Room, 4-year private college/university	yr	3024	1996	38s
Room, 4-year public college/university	yr	2573	1996	38s
Total cost, 4-year private college/university	yr	21071	1996	38s
Total cost, 4-year public college/university	yr	8729	1996	38s
Tuition, 2-year public college/university, in state	yr	2420	1996	38s
Tuition, 4-year private college/university, in state	yr	15038	1996	38s
Tuition, 4-year public college/university	yr	4446	1996	38s
Energy and Fuels				
Electricity	KWh	0.12	7/01	11r
Fuel oil #2	gal	1.31	7/01	11r
Fuel oil and other fuels, expenditures on	yr	207	1999	30r
Gasoline, all types	gal	1.80	7/01	11r
Gasoline, unleaded midgrade	gal	1.85	7/01	11r
Gasoline, unleaded premium	gal	1.91	7/01	11r
Gasoline, unleaded regular	gal	1.71	7/01	11r
Natural gas, expenditures on	yr	368	1999	30r
Utility (piped) gas, therm		1.08	7/01	11r
Utility (piped) gas, 40 therms		50.87	7/01	11r
Utility (piped) gas, 100 therms		111.06	7/01	11r
Entertainment				
Entertainment purchases	yr	1821	1999	30r
Fees and admissions paid	yr	511	1999	30r
Television, radios, sound equipment, expenditures on	yr	650	1999	30r
Funerals				
Total cost of funeral		5776.91	1/99	78r
Acknowledgement cards		14.47	1/99	78r
Casket		2090.19	1/99	78r
Cosmetology, hair, other preparation		132.92	1/99	78r
Embalming		377.33	1/99	78r
Funeral at funeral home		352.43	1/99	78r
Hearse (local)		185.55	1/99	78r
Professional service charges		1289.95	1/99	78r
Service car/van		87.42	1/99	78r
Transfer of remains to funeral home		175.48	1/99	78r
Vault		729.40	1/99	78r
Visitation/viewing		341.76	1/99	78r
Groceries				
Apples, red delicious	lb	0.95	7/01	11r
Bacon, sliced	lb	3.44	7/01	11r
Bakery products, expenditures on	yr	310	1999	30r
Bananas	lb	0.55	7/01	11r
Beef, expenditures on	yr	236	1999	30r
Bread, white, pan	lb	1.09	7/01	11r
Butter, yoghurt, cheese, etc, expenditures on	yr	214	1999	30r
Cereals and bakery product purchases	yr	474	1999	30r
Cereals and cereal products, expenditures on	yr	164	1999	30r
Chicken legs, bone-in	lb	1.23	7/01	11r
Chicken, fresh, whole	lb	1.13	7/01	11r
Chuck roast, U.S. choice, boneless	lb	2.79	7/01	11r
Coffee, 100%, ground roast, all sizes	lb	3.40	7/01	11r
Dairy product purchases	yr	342	1999	30r
Eggs, expenditures on	yr	34	1999	30r
Eggs, grade A, large	dozen	0.82	7/01	11r
Fats and oils, expenditures on	yr	80	1999	30r
Fish and seafood, expenditures on	yr	123	1999	30r

Values are in dollars or fractions of dollars. In the column headed *Ref*, references are shown to sources. Each reference is followed by a letter. These refer to the geographical level for which data were reported: s=State, r=Region, and c=City or metro. The abbreviation *ex* is used to mean *except* or *excluding*; *exp* stands for expenditures. For other abbreviations and further explanations, please see the Introduction.

Portsmouth-Rochester, NH - continued

Item	Per	Value	Date	Ref.
Groceries				
Food (excl fruit and vegetables), eaten at home, purchases	yr	838	1999	30r
Food cooked on trips, expenditures on	yr	48	1999	30r
Food purchases	yr	5314	1999	30r
Food purchases, eaten away from home	yr	2313	1999	30r
Food purchases, food eaten at home	yr	3001	1999	30r
Fresh fruits, expenditures on	yr	169	1999	30r
Fresh milk and cream, expenditures on	yr	128	1999	30r
Fresh vegetables, expenditures on	yr	164	1999	30r
Grapefruit	lb	0.67	7/01	11r
Grapes, Thompson, seedless	lb	2.18	7/01	11r
Ground beef, lean and extra lean	lb	2.66	7/01	11r
Ground chuck, 100% beef	lb	2.04	7/01	11r
Lettuce, iceberg	lb	0.76	7/01	11r
Meats, poultry, fish, and egg purchases	yr	808	1999	30r
Nonalcoholic beverages, expenditures on	yr	225	1999	30r
Orange juice, frozen concentrate	16 oz	1.88	7/01	11r
Oranges, Navel	lb	0.79	7/01	11r
Oranges, Valencia	lb	0.56	7/01	11r
Peaches	lb	1.16	7/01	11r
Peanut butter, creamy, all sizes	lb	2.01	7/01	11r
Pears, Anjou	lb	1.16	7/01	11r
Pork chops, center cut, bone-in	lb	3.57	7/01	11r
Pork, expenditures on	yr	146	1999	30r
Potato chips	16 oz	3.37	7/01	11r
Potatoes, white, all types	lb	0.42	7/01	11r
Poultry, expenditures on	yr	158	1999	30r
Processed fruits, expenditures on	yr	124	1999	30r
Processed vegetables, expenditures on	yr	82	1999	30r
Round roast, U.S. choice, boneless	lb	3.04	7/01	11r
Spaghetti and macaroni	lb	1.04	7/01	11r
Steak, sirloin, U.S. choice, boneless	lb	5.39	7/01	11r
Strawberries, dry pint	12 oz	1.51	7/01	11r
Sugar and other sweets, expenditures on	yr	110	1999	30r
Sugar, white, 33-80 ounce package	lb	0.46	7/01	11r
Sugar, white, all sizes	lb	0.47	7/01	11r
Tobacco products and smoking supplies purchases	yr	309	1999	30r
Yogurt, natural, fruit flavored	8 oz	0.79	7/01	11r
Goods and Services				
B&B Japanese maple (acer japonicum)	gal	38.99-125.00	4/00	93r
Boxwood (buxus)	2 gal	15.99-49.95	4/00	93r
Daylilly (hemerocallis)	gal	4.95	4/00	93r
Flat of annuals		8.00-14.99	4/00	93r
Fountain grass (pennisetum)	gal	6.99-9.99	4/00	93r
Hanging basket (10 in)		12.95-19.99	4/00	93r
Hardy geranium (geranium)	gal	6.95-7.99	4/00	93r
Hosta (hosta)	gal	4.95	4/00	93r
Lilac (syrubga vulgaris)	2 gal	17.99-74.95	4/00	93r
Miscellaneous purchases	yr	872	1999	30r
Rhododendron (rhododendron)	2 gal	23.99-54.95	4/00	93r
Sage (salvia)	gal	6.95-7.99	4/00	93r
Wintercreeper euonymus (euonymus fortunei)	2 gal	14.99-23.95	4/00	93r
Hunting license	yr	15.50	4/01	34s
Health Care				
Cardiac catheterization, ave hospital/ physician charges		6880	1998	77s
Childbirth, Cesarean delivery		14716	1997	13r
Childbirth, vaginal delivery		8541	1997	13r
Drugs, expenditures on	yr	296	1999	30r
Health care purchases	yr	1788	1999	30r

Item	Per	Value	Date	Ref.
Health Care - continued				
Health insurance expenditures	yr	875	1999	30r
Hysterectomy, laproscopically-assisted, ave hospital/physician charges		13100	1998	76s
Hysterectomy, vaginal, ave hospital and physician charges		7610	1998	76s
Medicaid dispensing fee		2.50	1999	87s
Medical services expenditures	yr	516	1999	30r
Medical supplies, expenditures on	yr	102	1999	30r
Plastic surgery, breast augmentation		4232	2000	7r
Plastic surgery, breast lift		4605	2000	7r
Plastic surgery, facelift		6964	2000	7r
Plastic surgery, hair transplantation		4193	2000	7r
Plastic surgery, lip augmentation		1675	2000	7r
Plastic surgery, lower body lift		6611	2000	7r
Plastic surgery, thigh lift		4751	2000	7r
Household Goods				
Floor coverings, expenditures on	yr	59	1999	30r
Furniture, expenditures on	yr	388	1999	30r
Household furnishings and equipment purchases	yr	1567	1999	30r
Household textiles, expenditures on	yr	112	1999	30r
Laundry and cleaning supplies, expenditures on	yr	104	1999	30r
Housing				
Home price, existing, ave		180800	10/00	90r
Home value, median		189000	2001	53s
Household operation expenditures	yr	581	1999	30r
Housekeeping supplies purchases	yr	474	1999	30r
Lodging expenditures	yr	550	1999	30r
Maintenance, repairs, insurance expenditures	yr	835	1999	30r
Monthly rental value of owned home	mos	663	1999	30r
Owned dwellings, expenditures own	yr	5209	1999	30r
Rent expenditures	yr	2390	1999	30r
Rental unit, 1 bedroom, with utilities	mos	595	4/01	41c
Rental unit, 2 bedroom, with utilities	mos	765	4/01	41c
Rental unit, 3 bedroom, with utilities	mos	981	4/01	41c
Rental unit, 4 bedroom, with utilities	mos	1203	4/01	41c
Shelter, expenditures on	yr	8149	1999	30r
Insurance and Pensions				
Life and other personal insurance purchases	yr	424	1999	30r
Pensions and Social Security, expenditures on	yr	3037	1999	30r
Legal Fees				
Combination hunting and fishing license	yr	31.50	4/01	34s
Divorce, filing fee		127.00	4/01	35s
Driver's license fee	renew	32.00	1999	48s
Driver's license fee	orig	32.00	1999	48s
Fishing license	yr	24.25	4/01	34s
Personal Goods				
Personal care products and services purchases	yr	399	1999	30r
Personal Services				
Personal services, household, expenditures on	yr	271	1999	30r
Pets				
Pets, toys, and playground equipment, expenditures on	yr	325	1999	30r
Taxes				
Federal income taxes paid	yr	2606	1999	30r
Personal taxes, expenditures on	yr	3567	1999	30r
Property taxes paid	yr	1752	1999	30r
State and local income taxes paid	yr	694	1999	30r
Transportation				
Cars and trucks, new, expenditures on	yr	1496	1999	30r
Cars and trucks, used, expenditures on	yr	1251	1999	30r
Diesel at the pump	gal	1.26	10/99	73s

Values are in dollars or fractions of dollars. In the column headed *Ref*, references are shown to sources. Each reference is followed by a letter. These refer to the geographical level for which data were reported: s=State, r=Region, and c=City or metro. The abbreviation *ex* is used to mean *except* or *excluding*; *exp* stands for *expenditures*. For other abbreviations and further explanations, please see the Introduction.

Portsmouth-Rochester, NH - continued

Item	Per	Value	Date	Ref.
Transportation				
Gasoline and motor oil purchases	yr	901	1999	30r
Gasoline before-tax price (cents)	gal	117.80	10/00	43s
Maintenance and repair expenditures	yr	618	1999	30r
Motorcycle license fee	renew	37.00	1999	49s
Motorcycle license fee	orig	37.00	1999	49s
Public transportation, expenditures on	yr	575	1999	30r
Transportation purchases	yr	6503	1999	30r
Vehicle expenses, miscellaneous, purchases	yr	2266	1999	30r
Vehicle insurance payments	yr	824	1999	30r
Vehicle purchases (net outlay)	yr	2761	1999	30r
Vehicle rental, lease expenditures	yr	584	1999	30r
Utilities				
Electrical bill, average	mos	77.50	9/00	9s
Electricity, expenditures on	yr	837	1999	30r
Electricity cost, average	KWh	11.80	9/00	9s
Utilities, fuels, and public services purchased	yr	2457	1999	30r
Water and other public services, expenditures on	yr	215	1999	30r
Weddings				
Wedding (national average cost)		19936	2000	33r
Wedding (regional average total cost)		29454	1997	110r
Attendants' gifts		321	1998	33r
Bridal attendants' apparel (5 persons)		824	2000	33r
Bride's headpiece/veil		173	1998	33r
Bride's wedding dress		859	1998	33r
Clergy, religious facility fee		242	1998	33r
Engagement ring		3177	1998	33r
Flowers		789	1998	33r
Groom's formalwear rental		99	2000	33r
Limousine		410	1998	33r
Marriage license cost		45.00-57.00	4/01	35s
Men's formalwear (ushers, best man)		469	2000	33r
Mother of bride apparel		241	2000	33r
Music		866	1998	33r
Photography and videography		1368	1998	33r
Rehearsal dinner		728	1998	33r
Wedding invitations and announcements		341	1998	33r
Wedding reception		7968	2000	33r
Wedding rings (bride and groom)		1060	1998	33r

Providence-Fall River-Warwick, RI-MA

Item	Per	Value	Date	Ref.
Average annual expenditures	yr	37971	1999	30r
Alcoholic Beverages				
Alcoholic beverage purchases	yr	368	1999	30r
Wine, red and white table, all sizes, any origin	liter	9.64	7/01	11r
Appliances				
Major appliances, expenditures on	yr	194	1999	30r
Small appliances, housewares, expenditures on	yr	93	1999	30r
Banking and Money				
Mortgage interest and charges paid	yr	2622	1999	30r
Mortgage principal paid on owned property	yr	1262	1999	30r
Vehicle finance charges paid	yr	240	1999	30r
Charity				
Cash contributions, expenditures	yr	1001	1999	30r
Child Care				
Child raising cost, total, age 0-2	yr	8670	1999	60r
Child raising cost, total, age 3-5	yr	8910	1999	60r
Child raising cost, total, age 6-8	yr	9040	1999	60r
Child raising cost, total, age 9-11	yr	9100	1999	60r
Child raising cost, total, age 12-14	yr	9890	1999	60r
Child raising cost, total, age 15-17	yr	10010	1999	60r
Child's child care and education, age 0-2	yr	1070	1999	60r
Child's child care and education, age 3-5	yr	1190	1999	60r
Child's child care and education, age 6-8	yr	740	1999	60r

Item	Per	Value	Date	Ref.
Child Care - continued				
Child's child care and education, age 9-11	yr	470	1999	60r
Child's child care and education, age 12-14	yr	350	1999	60r
Child's child care and education, age 15-17	yr	590	1999	60r
Child's clothing, age 0-2	yr	480	1999	60r
Child's clothing, age 3-5	yr	470	1999	60r
Child's clothing, age 6-8	yr	520	1999	60r
Child's clothing, age 9-11	yr	570	1999	60r
Child's clothing, age 12-14	yr	970	1999	60r
Child's clothing, age 15-17	yr	870	1999	60r
Child's food, age 0-2	yr	1130	1999	60r
Child's food, age 3-5	yr	1290	1999	60r
Child's food, age 6-8	yr	1640	1999	60r
Child's food, age 9-11	yr	1930	1999	60r
Child's food, age 12-14	yr	1940	1999	60r
Child's food, age 15-17	yr	2150	1999	60r
Child's health care, age 0-2	yr	550	1999	60r
Child's health care, age 3-5	yr	530	1999	60r
Child's health care, age 6-8	yr	610	1999	60r
Child's health care, age 9-11	yr	650	1999	60r
Child's health care, age 12-14	yr	660	1999	60r
Child's health care, age 15-17	yr	690	1999	60r
Child's housing, age 0-2	yr	3555	1999	60r
Child's housing, age 3-5	yr	3530	1999	60r
Child's housing, age 6-8	yr	3490	1999	60r
Child's housing, age 9-11	yr	3340	1999	60r
Child's housing, age 12-14	yr	3530	1999	60r
Child's housing, age 15-17	yr	3140	1999	60r
Child's personal care, reading, age 0-2	yr	920	1999	60r
Child's personal care, reading, age 3-5	yr	950	1999	60r
Child's personal care, reading, age 6-8	yr	980	1999	60r
Child's personal care, reading, age 9-11	yr	1020	1999	60r
Child's personal care, reading, age 12-14	yr	1190	1999	60r
Child's personal care, reading, age 15-17	yr	970	1999	60r
Clothing				
Apparel and services purchases	yr	1831	1999	30r
Boys, 2 to 15, expenditures on	yr	92	1999	30r
Children under 2, expenditures on	yr	63	1999	30r
Footwear, expenditures on	yr	300	1999	30r
Girls, 2 to 15, expenditures on	yr	101	1999	30r
Men and boys, expenditures on	yr	446	1999	30r
Men, 16 and over, expenditures on	yr	354	1999	30r
Women, 16 and over, expenditures on	yr	584	1999	30r
Communications				
Cable modem installation, Cox		99.00-174.95	6/99	103s
Cable modem rate, cable subscriber, Cox	mos	29.95-44.95	6/99	103s
Cable modem rate, non-cable subscriber, Cox	mos	42.95-54.95	6/99	103s
Phone line, single, business, field visit	inst.	67.42	12/97	17s
Phone line, single, business, no field visit	inst.	44.61	12/97	17s
Phone line, single, residence, field visit	inst.	49.13	12/97	17s
Phone line, single, residence, no field visit	inst.	33.83	12/97	17s
Postage and stationery, expenditures on	yr	138	1999	30r
Postal rate, express mail, up to half-pound		12.45	7/01	108r
Postal rate, letter, first class, first ounce		0.34	7/01	108r
Postal rate, letter, two ounces		0.57	7/01	108r
Postal rate, post card		0.21	7/01	108r
Postal rate, priority mail, two pounds		3.95	7/01	108r
Postal rate, priority mail, up to one pound		3.50	7/01	108r
Telephone services, expenditures on	yr	830	1999	30r
Education				
Board, 4-year private college/university	yr	3072	1996	38s
Board, 4-year public college/university	yr	2561	1996	38s
Education expenditures	yr	877	1999	30r
Room, 4-year private college/university	yr	3613	1996	38s
Room, 4-year public college/university	yr	3029	1996	38s
Total cost, 4-year private college/university	yr	22075	1996	38s
Total cost, 4-year public college/university	yr	9446	1996	38s
Tuition, 2-year public college/university, in state	yr	1726	1996	38s

Values are in dollars or fractions of dollars. In the column headed *Ref*, references are shown to sources. Each reference is followed by a letter. These refer to the geographical level for which data were reported: s=State, r=Region, and c=City or metro. The abbreviation *ex* is used to mean *except* or *excluding*; *exp* stands for expenditures. For other abbreviations and further explanations, please see the Introduction.

Providence-Fall River-Warwick, RI-MA - continued

Item	Per	Value	Date	Ref.
Education				
Tuition, 4-year private college/university, in state	yr	15390	1996	38s
Tuition, 4-year public college/university	yr	3856	1996	38s
Energy and Fuels				
Electricity	KWh	0.12	7/01	11r
Fuel oil #2	gal	1.31	7/01	11r
Fuel oil and other fuels, expenditures on	yr	207	1999	30r
Gas, natural, commercial rate	1000 cf	9.70	11/00	88s
Gasoline, all types	gal	1.80	7/01	11r
Gasoline, unleaded midgrade	gal	1.85	7/01	11r
Gasoline, unleaded premium	gal	1.91	7/01	11r
Gasoline, unleaded regular	gal	1.71	7/01	11r
Natural gas, expenditures on	yr	368	1999	30r
Utility (piped) gas, therm		1.08	7/01	11r
Utility (piped) gas, 40 therms		50.87	7/01	11r
Utility (piped) gas, 100 therms		111.06	7/01	11r
Entertainment				
Entertainment purchases	yr	1821	1999	30r
Fees and admissions paid	yr	511	1999	30r
Television, radios, sound equipment, expenditures on	yr	650	1999	30r
Funerals				
Total cost of funeral		5776.91	1/99	78r
Acknowledgement cards		14.47	1/99	78r
Casket		2090.19	1/99	78r
Cosmetology, hair, other preparation		132.92	1/99	78r
Embalming		377.33	1/99	78r
Funeral at funeral home		352.43	1/99	78r
Hearse (local)		185.55	1/99	78r
Professional service charges		1289.95	1/99	78r
Service car/van		87.42	1/99	78r
Transfer of remains to funeral home		175.48	1/99	78r
Vault		729.40	1/99	78r
Visitation/viewing		341.76	1/99	78r
Groceries				
Apples, red delicious	lb	0.95	7/01	11r
Bacon, sliced	lb	3.44	7/01	11r
Bakery products, expenditures on	yr	310	1999	30r
Bananas	lb	0.55	7/01	11r
Beef, expenditures on	yr	236	1999	30r
Bread, white, pan	lb	1.09	7/01	11r
Butter, yoghurt, cheese, etc, expenditures on	yr	214	1999	30r
Cereals and bakery product purchases	yr	474	1999	30r
Cereals and cereal products, expenditures on	yr	164	1999	30r
Chicken legs, bone-in	lb	1.23	7/01	11r
Chicken, fresh, whole	lb	1.13	7/01	11r
Chuck roast, U.S. choice, boneless	lb	2.79	7/01	11r
Coffee, 100%, ground roast, all sizes	lb	3.40	7/01	11r
Dairy product purchases	yr	342	1999	30r
Eggs, expenditures on	yr	34	1999	30r
Eggs, grade A, large	dozen	0.82	7/01	11r
Fats and oils, expenditures on	yr	80	1999	30r
Fish and seafood, expenditures on	yr	123	1999	30r
Food (excl fruit and vegetables), eaten at home, purchases	yr	838	1999	30r
Food cooked on trips, expenditures on	yr	48	1999	30r
Food purchases	yr	5314	1999	30r
Food purchases, eaten away from home	yr	2313	1999	38s
Food purchases, food eaten at home	yr	3001	1999	30r
Fresh fruits, expenditures on	yr	169	1999	30r
Fresh milk and cream, expenditures on	yr	128	1999	30r
Fresh vegetables, expenditures on	yr	164	1999	30r
Grapefruit	lb	0.67	7/01	11r
Grapes, Thompson, seedless	lb	2.18	7/01	11r
Ground beef, lean and extra lean	lb	2.66	7/01	11r
Ground chuck, 100% beef	lb	2.04	7/01	11r
Lettuce, iceberg	lb	0.76	7/01	11r
Meats, poultry, fish, and egg purchases	yr	808	1999	30r
Nonalcoholic beverages, expenditures on	yr	225	1999	30r

Providence-Fall River-Warwick, RI-MA - continued

Item	Per	Value	Date	Ref.
Groceries - continued				
Orange juice, frozen concentrate	16 oz	1.88	7/01	11r
Oranges, Navel	lb	0.79	7/01	11r
Oranges, Valencia	lb	0.56	7/01	11r
Peaches	lb	1.16	7/01	11r
Peanut butter, creamy, all sizes	lb	2.01	7/01	11r
Pears, Anjou	lb	1.16	7/01	11r
Pork chops, center cut, bone-in	lb	3.57	7/01	11r
Pork, expenditures on	yr	146	1999	30r
Potato chips	16 oz	3.37	7/01	11r
Potatoes, white, all types	lb	0.42	7/01	11r
Poultry, expenditures on	yr	158	1999	30r
Processed fruits, expenditures on	yr	124	1999	30r
Processed vegetables, expenditures on	yr	82	1999	30r
Round roast, U.S. choice, boneless	lb	3.04	7/01	11r
Spaghetti and macaroni	lb	1.04	7/01	11r
Steak, sirloin, U.S. choice, boneless	lb	5.39	7/01	11r
Strawberries, dry pint	12 oz	1.51	7/01	11r
Sugar and other sweets, expenditures on	yr	110	1999	30r
Sugar, white, 33-80 ounce package	lb	0.46	7/01	11r
Sugar, white, all sizes	lb	0.47	7/01	11r
Tobacco products and smoking supplies purchases	yr	309	1999	30r
Yogurt, natural, fruit flavored	8 oz	0.79	7/01	11r
Goods and Services				
B&B Japanese maple (acer japonicum)	gal	38.99-125.00	4/00	93r
Boxwood (buxus)	2 gal	15.99-49.95	4/00	93r
Daylilly (hemerocallis)	gal	4.95	4/00	93r
Flat of annuals		8.00-14.99	4/00	93r
Fountain grass (pennisetum)	gal	6.99-9.99	4/00	93r
Hanging basket (10 in)		12.95-19.99	4/00	93r
Hardy geranium (geranium)	gal	6.95-7.99	4/00	93r
Hosta (hosta)	gal	4.95	4/00	93r
Lilac (syrubga vulgaris)	2 gal	17.99-74.95	4/00	93r
Miscellaneous purchases	yr	872	1999	30r
Rhododendron (rhododendron)	2 gal	23.99-54.95	4/00	93r
Sage (salvia)	gal	6.95-7.99	4/00	93r
Wintercreeper euonymus (euonymus fortunei)	2 gal	14.99-23.95	4/00	93r
Hunting license	yr	9.50	4/01	34s
Health Care				
Childbirth, Cesarean delivery		14716	1997	13r
Childbirth, vaginal delivery		8541	1997	13r
Drugs, expenditures on	yr	296	1999	30r
Health care purchases	yr	1788	1999	30r
Health insurance expenditures	yr	875	1999	30r
Hysterectomy, vaginal, ave hospital and physician charges		10280	1998	76s
Medicaid dispensing fee		2.85-3.40	1999	87s
Medical services expenditures	yr	516	1999	30r
Medical supplies, expenditures on	yr	102	1999	30r
Plastic surgery, breast augmentation		4232	2000	7r
Plastic surgery, breast lift		4605	2000	7r
Plastic surgery, facelift		6964	2000	7r
Plastic surgery, hair transplantation		4193	2000	7r
Plastic surgery, lip augmentation		1675	2000	7r
Plastic surgery, lower body lift		6611	2000	7r
Plastic surgery, thigh lift		4751	2000	7r
Household Goods				
Floor coverings, expenditures on	yr	59	1999	30r
Furniture, expenditures on	yr	388	1999	30r

Values are in dollars or fractions of dollars. In the column headed *Ref*, references are shown to sources. Each reference is followed by a letter. These refer to the geographical level for which data were reported: s=State, r=Region, and c=City or metro. The abbreviation *ex* is used to mean *except* or *excluding*; *exp* stands for expenditures. For other abbreviations and further explanations, please see the Introduction.

Providence-Fall River-Warwick, RI-MA - continued

Item	Per	Value	Date	Ref.
Household Goods				
Household furnishings and equipment purchases	yr	1567	1999	30r
Household textiles, expenditures on	yr	112	1999	30r
Laundry and cleaning supplies, expenditures on	yr	104	1999	30r
Housing				
Home price, existing, ave		180800	10/00	90r
Home value, median		160000	2001	53s
Household operation expenditures	yr	581	1999	30r
Housekeeping supplies purchases	yr	474	1999	30r
Lodging expenditures	yr	550	1999	30r
Maintenance, repairs, insurance expenditures	yr	835	1999	30r
Monthly rental value of owned home	mos	663	1999	30r
Owned dwellings, expenditures own	yr	5209	1999	30r
Rent expenditures	yr	2390	1999	30r
Rental unit, 1 bedroom, with utilities	mos	523	4/01	41c
Rental unit, 2 bedroom, with utilities	mos	628	4/01	41c
Rental unit, 3 bedroom, with utilities	mos	789	4/01	41c
Rental unit, 4 bedroom, with utilities	mos	972	4/01	41c
Shelter, expenditures on	yr	8149	1999	30r
Insurance and Pensions				
Auto insurance premium	yr	1000.45	1999	57s
Life and other personal insurance purchases	yr	424	1999	30r
Pensions and Social Security, expenditures on	yr	3037	1999	30r
Legal Fees				
Combination hunting and fishing license	yr	15.00	4/01	34s
Divorce, filing fee		100.00	4/01	35s
Driver's license fee	orig	30.00	1999	48s
Driver's license fee	renew	12.00	1999	48s
Fishing license	yr	9.50	4/01	34s
Personal Goods				
Personal care products and services purchases	yr	399	1999	30r
Personal Services				
Personal services, household, expenditures on	yr	271	1999	30r
Pets				
Pets, toys, and playground equipment, expenditures on	yr	325	1999	30r
Taxes				
Federal income taxes paid	yr	2606	1999	30r
Personal taxes, expenditures on	yr	3567	1999	30r
Property taxes paid	yr	1752	1999	30r
State and local income taxes paid	yr	694	1999	30r
Transportation				
Cars and trucks, new, expenditures on	yr	1496	1999	30r
Cars and trucks, used, expenditures on	yr	1251	1999	30r
Diesel at the pump	gal	1.40	10/99	73s
Gasoline and motor oil purchases	yr	901	1999	30r
Gasoline before-tax price (cents)	gal	112.50	10/00	43s
Maintenance and repair expenditures	yr	618	1999	30r
Motorcycle license fee	orig	1.00	1999	49s
Motorcycle license fee	renew	1.00	1999	49s
Public transportation, expenditures on	yr	575	1999	30r
Transportation purchases	yr	6503	1999	30r
Vehicle expenses, miscellaneous, purchases	yr	2266	1999	30r
Vehicle insurance payments	yr	824	1999	30r
Vehicle purchases (net outlay)	yr	2761	1999	30r
Vehicle rental, lease expenditures	yr	584	1999	30r
Utilities				
Electrical bill, average	mos	53.58	9/00	9s
Electricity, expenditures on	yr	837	1999	30r
Electricity cost, average	KWh	9.50	9/00	9s
Utilities, fuels, and public services purchased	yr	2457	1999	30r

Providence-Fall River-Warwick, RI-MA - continued

Item	Per	Value	Date	Ref.
Utilities - continued				
Water and other public services, expenditures on	yr	215	1999	30r
Weddings				
Wedding (national average cost)		19936	2000	33r
Wedding (regional average total cost)		29454	1997	110r
Attendants' gifts		321	1998	33r
Bridal attendants' apparel (5 persons)		824	2000	33r
Bride's headpiece/veil		173	1998	33r
Bride's wedding dress		859	1998	33r
Clergy, religious facility fee		242	1998	33r
Engagement ring		3177	1998	33r
Flowers		789	1998	33r
Groom's formalwear rental		99	2000	33r
Limousine		410	1998	33r
Marriage license cost		24.00	4/01	35s
Men's formalwear (ushers, best man)		469	2000	33r
Mother of bride apparel		241	2000	33r
Music		866	1998	33r
Photography and videography		1368	1998	33r
Rehearsal dinner		728	1998	33r
Wedding invitations and announcements		341	1998	33r
Wedding reception		7968	2000	33r
Wedding rings (bride and groom)		1060	1998	33r

Provo-Orem, UT

Item	Per	Value	Date	Ref.
Composite, ACCRA index		94.50	3/01	4c
Alcoholic Beverages				
Beer, Heineken, 12-oz, ex deposit	6	7.13	3/01	4c
J & B Scotch	750-ml	22.95	3/01	4c
Wine, Livingston or Gallo, Chablis blanc	1.5 liter	6.95	3/01	4c
Appliances				
Appliance repair, service call, washing machine	min lab chg	41.33	3/01	4c
Banking and Money				
Mortgage rate, incl. points and orig. fee, 30-yr. conv. fixed or ARM	mos	6.97	3/01	4c
Clothing				
Boys' brief, cotton	3	5.16	3/01	4c
Shirt, man's dress shirt		22.36	3/01	4c
Slacks, man's "No Wrinkles" khaki		29.99	3/01	4c
Communications				
Newspaper subscription, daily and Sunday delivery	mos	9.95	3/01	4c
Phone line, single, business, field visit	inst.	50.00	12/97	17s
Phone line, single, business, no field visit	inst.	50.00	12/97	17s
Phone line, single, residence, field visit	inst.	25.00	12/97	17s
Phone line, single, residence, no field visit	inst.	25.00	12/97	17s
Postal rate, express mail, up to half-pound		12.45	7/01	108r
Postal rate, letter, first class, first ounce		0.34	7/01	108r
Postal rate, letter, two ounces		0.57	7/01	108r
Postal rate, post card		0.21	7/01	108r
Postal rate, priority mail, two pounds		3.95	7/01	108r
Postal rate, priority mail, up to one pound		3.50	7/01	108r
Telephone bill, family of three	mos	22.24	3/01	4c
Education				
Board, 4-year private college/university	yr	3068	1996	38s
Board, 4-year public college/university	yr	1945	1996	38s
Room, 4-year private college/university	yr	1380	1996	38s
Room, 4-year public college/university	yr	1458	1996	38s
Total cost, 4-year private college/university	yr	7384	1996	38s
Total cost, 4-year public college/university	yr	5414	1996	38s
Tuition, 2-year public college/university, in state	yr	1375	1996	38s
Tuition, 4-year private college/university, in state	yr	2936	1996	38s
Tuition, 4-year public college/university	yr	2011	1996	38s

Values are in dollars or fractions of dollars. In the column headed *Ref*, references are shown to sources. Each reference is followed by a letter. These refer to the geographical level for which data were reported: s=State, r=Region, and c=City or metro. The abbreviation *ex* is used to mean *except* or *excluding*; *exp* stands for *expenditures*. For other abbreviations and further explanations, please see the Introduction.

Provo-Orem, UT - continued

Item	Per	Value	Date	Ref.
Energy and Fuels				
Energy, combined forms, 2400 sq ft	mos	103.48	3/01	4c
Energy, exc. electricity, 2400 sq ft	mos	56.05	3/01	4c
Gas, natural, commercial rate	1000 cf	5.42	11/00	88s
Gas, regular unleaded, cash, self-service	gal	1.39	3/01	4c
Entertainment				
Bowling, Saturday evening rate	line	2.68	3/01	4c
Monopoly game, Parker Brothers', No. 9	game	10.32	3/01	4c
Movie, first-run, Saturday, evening	adm.	6.58	3/01	4c
Tennis balls, yellow, Wilson or Penn, 3	can	2.32	3/01	4c
Funerals				
Total cost of funeral		5401.08	1/99	78r
Acknowledgement cards		33.64	1/99	78r
Casket		2170.43	1/99	78r
Cosmetology, hair, other preparation		136.32	1/99	78r
Embalming		319.13	1/99	78r
Funeral at funeral home		370.21	1/99	78r
Hearse (local)		161.04	1/99	78r
Professional service charges		963.15	1/99	78r
Service car/van		133.99	1/99	78r
Transfer of remains to funeral home		159.82	1/99	78r
Vault		778.07	1/99	78r
Visitation/viewing		175.28	1/99	78r
Groceries				
Groceries, ACCRA Index		110.30	3/01	4c
Antibiotic ointment, Polysporin	0.5 oz	4.99	3/01	4c
Baby food, strained vegetables or fruit, lowest price	4-4.5 oz	0.38	3/01	4c
Bananas	lb	0.73	3/01	4c
Beef or hamburger, ground	lb	1.85	3/01	4c
Bread, white	loaf	0.98	3/01	4c
Cheese, Kraft grated Parmesan	8 oz	4.19	3/01	4c
Chicken, whole fryer	lb	0.95	3/01	4c
Cigarettes, Winston, Kings	carton	32.23	3/01	4c
Coffee, vacuum-packed	13 oz	3.91	3/01	4c
Corn Flakes, Kellogg's or Post Toasties	18 oz	3.47	3/01	4c
Corn, frozen, whole kernel, lowest price	16 oz	1.20	3/01	4c
Eggs, Grade A or AA	dozen	1.09	3/01	4c
Lettuce, iceberg	head	0.89	3/01	4c
Margarine, Blue Bonnet or Parkay, stick	lb	0.60	3/01	4c
Milk, whole	1/2 gal	1.85	3/01	4c
Orange juice, Minute Maid frozen	12 oz	1.53	3/01	4c
Peaches, halves or slices, Hunt's, Del Monte, or Libby's	29 oz	1.77	3/01	4c
Peas, green, Del Monte or Green Giant	15 oz	0.73	3/01	4c
Potatoes, white or red	10 lb	2.39	3/01	4c
Sausage, Jimmy Dean/Owens pork	lb	3.88	3/01	4c
Shortening, vegetable, Crisco	3 lb	3.05	3/01	4c
Soft drink, Coca Cola, ex deposit	2 liter	0.99	3/01	4c
Steak, T-bone	lb	6.91	3/01	4c
Sugar, cane or beet	4 lbs	1.85	3/01	4c
Tomatoes, Hunt's or Del Monte	14.5 oz	0.94	3/01	4c
Tuna, chunk, light	6 oz	0.78	3/01	4c
Goods and Services				
Miscellaneous goods and services, ACCRA Index		96.70	3/01	4c
Hunting license	yr	17.00	4/01	34s
Health Care				
Health care, ACCRA Index		85.00	3/01	4c
Cardiac catheterization, ave hospital/ physician charges		17370	1998	77s
Childbirth, Cesarean delivery		11587	1997	13r
Childbirth, vaginal delivery		6725	1997	13r
Dentist's fee, adult teeth cleaning and periodic oral exam	visit	69.00	3/01	4c
Doctor's fee, routine exam, established patient	visit	46.67	3/01	4c
Hospital care, private room	day	321.00	3/01	4c
Hysterectomy, laproscopically-assisted, ave hospital/physician charges		11940	1998	76s

Provo-Orem, UT - continued

Item	Per	Value	Date	Ref.
Health Care - continued				
Hysterectomy, vaginal, ave hospital and physician charges		8530	1998	76s
Medicaid dispensing fee		3.90-4.40	1999	87s
Household Goods				
Dishwashing powder, Cascade	50 oz	3.86	3/01	4c
Tissues, facial, Kleenex brand	175	1.40	3/01	4c
Housing				
Housing, ACCRA Index		85.30	3/01	4c
Home value, median		134000	2001	53s
House, 2400 sq ft, 8000 sq ft lot, new, urban, utilities	total	172684	3/01	4c
House payment, principal and interest, 25% down payment	mos	859	3/01	4c
Rent, apartment, 2 br, 1 1/2-2 baths, unfurn, 950 sq ft, water	mos	645	3/01	4c
Rental unit, 1 bedroom, with utilities	mos	464	4/01	41c
Rental unit, 2 bedroom, with utilities	mos	574	4/01	41c
Rental unit, 3 bedroom, with utilities	mos	796	4/01	41c
Rental unit, 4 bedroom, with utilities	mos	941	4/01	41c
Legal Fees				
Combination hunting and fishing license	yr	32.00	4/01	34s
Divorce, filing fee		82.00	4/01	35s
Driver's license fee	orig	20.00	1999	48s
Driver's license fee	renew	13.50	1999	48s
Fishing license	yr	24.00	4/01	34s
Personal Goods				
Shampoo, Alberto VO5	15 oz	1.31	3/01	4c
Toothpaste, Crest or Colgate	6-7 oz	3.09	3/01	4c
Personal Services				
Dry cleaning, man's 2-pc suit		8.70	3/01	4c
Man's haircut, barbershop, no styling		9.17	3/01	4c
Woman's shampoo, trim, blow-dry, no style-change		27.50	3/01	4c
Restaurant Food				
Chicken, fried, thigh and drumstick, KFC/Church's		2.36	3/01	4c
Hamburger with cheese, McDonald's	1/4 lb	2.35	3/01	4c
Pizza, Pizza Hut or Pizza Inn	11-12 in	9.64	3/01	4c
Transportation				
Transportation, ACCRA Index		98.00	3/01	4c
Bus fare, one-way	trip	1.00	2000	1c
Diesel at the pump	gal	1.30	10/99	73s
Gasoline before-tax price (cents)	gal	115.90	10/00	43s
Tire balance, computer or spin balance, front	wheel	7.65	3/01	4c
Utilities				
Utilities, ACCRA Index		87.20	3/01	4c
Electrical bill, average	mos	44.08	9/00	9s
Electricity and other, mixed, 2400 sq ft, new home	mos	47.43	3/01	4c
Electricity cost, average	KWh	4.70	9/00	9s
Weddings				
Wedding (national average cost)		19936	2000	33r
Attendants' gifts		321	1998	33r
Bridal attendants' apparel (5 persons)		824	2000	33r
Bride's headpiece/veil		173	1998	33r
Bride's wedding dress		859	1998	33r
Clergy, religious facility fee		242	1998	33r
Engagement ring		3177	1998	33r
Flowers		789	1998	33r
Groom's formalwear rental		99	2000	33r
Limousine		410	1998	33r
Marriage license cost		40.00	4/01	35s
Men's formalwear (ushers, best man)		469	2000	33r
Mother of bride apparel		241	2000	33r
Music		866	1998	33r
Photography and videography		1368	1998	33r

Values are in dollars or fractions of dollars. In the column headed *Ref*, references are shown to sources. Each reference is followed by a letter. These refer to the geographical level for which data were reported: s=State, r=Region, and c=City or metro. The abbreviation *ex* is used to mean *except* or *excluding*; *exp* stands for expenditures. For other abbreviations and further explanations, please see the Introduction.

Provo-Orem, UT - continued

Item	Per	Value	Date	Ref.
Weddings				
Rehearsal dinner		728	1998	33r
Wedding invitations and announcements		341	1998	33r
Wedding reception		7968	2000	33r
Wedding rings (bride and groom)		1060	1998	33r

Pueblo, CO

Item	Per	Value	Date	Ref.
Composite, ACCRA index		91.80	3/01	4c
Alcoholic Beverages				
Beer, Heineken, 12-oz, ex deposit	6	6.99	3/01	4c
J & B Scotch	750-ml	22.11	3/01	4c
Wine, Livingston or Gallo, Chablis blanc	1.5 liter	4.86	3/01	4c
Appliances				
Appliance repair, service call, washing machine	min lab chg	23.36	3/01	4c
Banking and Money				
Mortgage rate, incl. points and orig. fee, 30-yr. conv. fixed or ARM	mos	7.02	3/01	4c
Clothing				
Boys' brief, cotton	3	5.37	3/01	4c
Shirt, man's dress shirt		26.00	3/01	4c
Slacks, man's "No Wrinkles" khaki		36.74	3/01	4c
Communications				
Cable modem installation, AT&T-BIS		150.00	6/99	103s
Cable modem rate, cable subscriber, AT&T-BIS	mos	39.95	6/99	103s
Newspaper subscription, daily and Sunday delivery	mos	9.00	3/01	4c
Phone line, single, business, field visit	inst.	70.00	12/97	17s
Phone line, single, business, no field visit	inst.	70.00	12/97	17s
Phone line, single, residence, field visit	inst.	35.00	12/97	17s
Phone line, single, residence, no field visit	inst.	35.00	12/97	17s
Postal rate, express mail, up to half-pound		12.45	7/01	108r
Postal rate, letter, first class, first ounce		0.34	7/01	108r
Postal rate, letter, two ounces		0.57	7/01	108r
Postal rate, post card		0.21	7/01	108r
Postal rate, priority mail, two pounds		3.95	7/01	108r
Postal rate, priority mail, up to one pound		3.50	7/01	108r
Telephone bill, business, basic rate	mos	37.31	12/97	18c
Telephone bill, family of three	mos	22.96	3/01	4c
Telephone bill, residential, basic rate	mos	14.87	12/97	18c
Education				
Board, 4-year private college/university	yr	2750	1996	38s
Board, 4-year public college/university	yr	2564	1996	38s
Room, 4-year private college/university	yr	2574	1996	38s
Room, 4-year public college/university	yr	2000	1996	38s
Total cost, 4-year private college/university	yr	17120	1996	38s
Total cost, 4-year public college/university	yr	7037	1996	38s
Tuition, 2-year public college/university, in state	yr	1340	1996	38s
Tuition, 4-year private college/university, in state	yr	11796	1996	38s
Tuition, 4-year public college/university	yr	2473	1996	38s
Energy and Fuels				
Energy, combined forms, 2400 sq ft	mos	107.98	3/01	4c
Energy, exc. electricity, 2400 sq ft	mos	59.01	3/01	4c
Gas, natural, commercial rate	1000 cf	6.42	11/00	88s
Gas, regular unleaded, cash, self-service	gal	1.30	3/01	4c
Entertainment				
Bowling, Saturday evening rate	line	2.42	3/01	4c
Monopoly game, Parker Brothers', No. 9	game	12.19	3/01	4c
Movie, first-run, Saturday, evening	adm.	6.75	3/01	4c
Tennis balls, yellow, Wilson or Penn, 3	can	2.19	3/01	4c
Funerals				
Total cost of funeral		5401.08	1/99	78r
Acknowledgement cards		33.64	1/99	78r
Casket		2170.43	1/99	78r

Pueblo, CO - continued

Item	Per	Value	Date	Ref.
Funerals - continued				
Cosmetology, hair, other preparation		136.32	1/99	78r
Embalming		319.13	1/99	78r
Funeral at funeral home		370.21	1/99	78r
Hearse (local)		161.04	1/99	78r
Professional service charges		963.15	1/99	78r
Service car/van		133.99	1/99	78r
Transfer of remains to funeral home		159.82	1/99	78r
Vault		778.07	1/99	78r
Visitation/viewing		175.28	1/99	78r
Groceries				
Groceries, ACCRA Index		110.90	3/01	4c
Antibiotic ointment, Polysporin	0.5 oz	5.73	3/01	4c
Baby food, strained vegetables or fruit, lowest price	4-4.5 oz	0.48	3/01	4c
Bacon	lb	3.99	5/99	8s
Bananas	lb	0.53	3/01	4c
Beef or hamburger, ground	lb	1.53	3/01	4c
Bread, white	loaf	1.04	3/01	4c
Bread, white, 20 oz loaf		0.64	5/99	8s
Cheddar cheese, mild	lb	3.59	5/99	8s
Cheerios, 10 oz box		2.99	5/99	8s
Cheese, Kraft grated Parmesan	8 oz	3.89	3/01	4c
Chicken, whole fryer	lb	1.01	3/01	4c
Cigarettes, Winston, Kings	carton	30.82	3/01	4c
Coffee, vacuum-packed	13 oz	3.59	3/01	4c
Corn Flakes, Kellogg's or Post Toasties	18 oz	3.23	3/01	4c
Corn oil, Mazola, 32 oz		2.75	5/99	8s
Corn, frozen, whole kernel, lowest price	16 oz	1.31	3/01	4c
Eggs, Grade A or AA	dozen	1.12	3/01	4c
Flour, all purpose	5 lb	1.69	5/99	8s
Grade A large eggs	doz	1.59	5/99	8s
Ground chuck	lb	1.99	5/99	8s
Lettuce, iceberg	head	1.33	3/01	4c
Margarine, Blue Bonnet or Parkay, stick	lb	0.75	3/01	4c
Mayonnaise, Kraft, 32 oz		2.50	5/99	8s
Milk, whole	1/2 gal	2.02	3/01	4c
Orange juice, Minute Maid frozen	12 oz	1.51	3/01	4c
Peaches, halves or slices, Hunt's, Del Monte, or Libby's	29 oz	2.00	3/01	4c
Peas, green, Del Monte or Green Giant	15 oz	0.81	3/01	4c
Potatoes, russet	5 lb	1.79	5/99	8s
Potatoes, white or red	10 lb	2.09	3/01	4c
Red Delicious apples	lb	1.39	5/99	8s
Sausage, Jimmy Dean/Owens pork	lb	3.77	3/01	4c
Shortening, vegetable, Crisco	3 lb	3.26	3/01	4c
Sirloin tip roast	lb	3.99	5/99	8s
Soft drink, Coca Cola, ex deposit	2 liter	1.14	3/01	4c
Steak, T-bone	lb	6.27	3/01	4c
Sugar, cane or beet	4 lbs	1.52	3/01	4c
Tomatoes, Hunt's or Del Monte	14.5 oz	0.92	3/01	4c
Tuna, chunk, light	6 oz	0.89	3/01	4c
Vegetable oil, Crisco, 32 oz		1.89	5/99	8s
Whole fryer	lb	1.99	5/99	8s
Whole milk	gal	0.89	5/99	8s
Goods and Services				
Miscellaneous goods and services, ACCRA Index		93.90	3/01	4c
Hunting license	yr	15.25	4/01	34s
Health Care				
Health care, ACCRA Index		103.50	3/01	4c
Cardiac catheterization, ave hospital/ physician charges		17910	1998	77s
Childbirth, Cesarean delivery		11587	1997	13r
Childbirth, vaginal delivery		6725	1997	13r
Dentist's fee, adult teeth cleaning and periodic oral exam	visit	63.80	3/01	4c
Doctor's fee, routine exam, established patient	visit	63.60	3/01	4c
Hospital care, private room	day	576.00	3/01	4c
Hysterectomy, laproscopically-assisted, ave hospital/physician charges		16210	1998	76s

Values are in dollars or fractions of dollars. In the column headed *Ref*, references are shown to sources. Each reference is followed by a letter. These refer to the geographical level for which data were reported: s=State, r=Region, and c=City or metro. The abbreviation *ex* is used to mean *except* or *excluding*; *exp* stands for *expenditures*. For other abbreviations and further explanations, please see the Introduction.

Pueblo, CO - continued

Item	Per	Value	Date	Ref.
Health Care				
Hysterectomy, vaginal, ave hospital and physician charges		11690	1998	76s
Medicaid dispensing fee		4.08	1999	87s
Household Goods				
Dishwashing powder, Cascade	50 oz	3.76	3/01	4c
Tissues, facial, Kleenex brand	175	1.56	3/01	4c
Housing				
Housing, ACCRA Index		78.10	3/01	4c
Home value, median		173000	2001	53s
House, 2400 sq ft, 8000 sq ft lot, new, urban, utilities	total	167025	3/01	4c
House payment, principal and interest, 25% down payment	mos	835	3/01	4c
Rent, apartment, 2 br, 1 1/2-2 baths, unfurn, 950 sq ft, water	mos	462	3/01	4c
Rental unit, 1 bedroom, with utilities	mos	449	4/01	41c
Rental unit, 2 bedroom, with utilities	mos	561	4/01	41c
Rental unit, 3 bedroom, with utilities	mos	755	4/01	41c
Rental unit, 4 bedroom, with utilities	mos	901	4/01	41c
Legal Fees				
Divorce, filing fee		65.00	4/01	35s
Driver's license fee	orig	15.00	1999	48s
Driver's license fee	renew	15.00	1999	48s
Personal Goods				
Shampoo, Alberto VO5	15 oz	1.09	3/01	4c
Toothpaste, Crest or Colgate	6-7 oz	2.23	3/01	4c
Personal Services				
Dry cleaning, man's 2-pc suit		6.78	3/01	4c
Man's haircut, barbershop, no styling		7.25	3/01	4c
Woman's shampoo, trim, blow-dry, no style-change		18.40	3/01	4c
Restaurant Food				
Chicken, fried, thigh and drumstick, KFC/ Church's		2.28	3/01	4c
Hamburger with cheese, McDonald's	1/4 lb	2.19	3/01	4c
Pizza, Pizza Hut or Pizza Inn	11-12 in	8.99	3/01	4c
Transportation				
Transportation, ACCRA Index		87.70	3/01	4c
Bus fare, to central business district	1-way	0.75	3/01	4c
Diesel at the pump	gal	1.28	10/99	73s
Gasoline before-tax price (cents)	gal	117.00	10/00	43s
Tire balance, computer or spin balance, front	wheel	6.83	3/01	4c
Travel				
Hotel room	night	118.98	2/01	95s
Utilities				
Utilities, ACCRA Index		90.80	3/01	4c
Electrical bill, average	mos	47.17	9/00	9s
Electricity, summer, 250 KWh	mos	20.88	2/96	97c
Electricity, summer, 500 KWh	mos	36.15	2/96	97c
Electricity, summer, 750 KWh	mos	51.43	2/96	97c
Electricity, summer, 1000 KWh	mos	65.37	2/96	97c
Electricity and other, mixed, 2400 sq ft, new home	mos	48.97	3/01	4c
Electricity cost, average	KWh	5.90	9/00	9s
Weddings				
Wedding (national average cost)		19936	2000	33r
Attendants' gifts		321	1998	33r
Bridal attendants' apparel (5 persons)		824	2000	33r
Bride's headpiece/veil		173	1998	33r
Bride's wedding dress		859	1998	33r
Clergy, religious facility fee		242	1998	33r
Engagement ring		3177	1998	33r
Flowers		789	1998	33r
Groom's formalwear rental		99	2000	33r
Limousine		410	1998	33r
Marriage license cost		20.00	4/01	35s
Men's formalwear (ushers, best man)		469	2000	33r

Pueblo, CO - continued

Item	Per	Value	Date	Ref.
Weddings - continued				
Mother of bride apparel		241	2000	33r
Music		866	1998	33r
Photography and videography		1368	1998	33r
Rehearsal dinner		728	1998	33r
Wedding invitations and announcements		341	1998	33r
Wedding reception		7968	2000	33r
Wedding rings (bride and groom)		1060	1998	33r

Punta Gorda, FL

Item	Per	Value	Date	Ref.
Alcoholic Beverages				
Alcoholic beverage purchases	yr	253	1999	30r
Malt beverages, all types, all sizes, any origin	16 oz	0.96	7/01	11r
Appliances				
Major appliances, expenditures on	yr	172	1999	30r
Small appliances, housewares, expenditures on	yr	81	1999	30r
Banking and Money				
Mortgage interest and charges paid	yr	2039	1999	30r
Mortgage principal paid on owned property	yr	1026	1999	30r
Vehicle finance charges paid	yr	365	1999	30r
Charity				
Cash contributions, expenditures	yr	1127	1999	30r
Child Care				
Child raising cost, total, age 0-2	yr	8540	1999	60r
Child raising cost, total, age 3-5	yr	8780	1999	60r
Child raising cost, total, age 6-8	yr	8820	1999	60r
Child raising cost, total, age 9-11	yr	8800	1999	60r
Child raising cost, total, age 12-14	yr	9510	1999	60r
Child raising cost, total, age 15-17	yr	9740	1999	60r
Child's child care and education, age 0-2	yr	1380	1999	60r
Child's child care and education, age 3-5	yr	1520	1999	60r
Child's child care and education, age 6-8	yr	990	1999	60r
Child's child care and education, age 9-11	yr	650	1999	60r
Child's child care and education, age 12-14	yr	490	1999	60r
Child's child care and education, age 15-17	yr	840	1999	60r
Child's clothing, age 0-2	yr	480	1999	60r
Child's clothing, age 3-5	yr	470	1999	60r
Child's clothing, age 6-8	yr	520	1999	60r
Child's clothing, age 9-11	yr	570	1999	60r
Child's clothing, age 12-14	yr	950	1999	60r
Child's clothing, age 15-17	yr	850	1999	60r
Child's food, age 0-2	yr	1000	1999	60r
Child's food, age 3-5	yr	1160	1999	60r
Child's food, age 6-8	yr	1490	1999	60r
Child's food, age 9-11	yr	1770	1999	60r
Child's food, age 12-14	yr	1770	1999	60r
Child's food, age 15-17	yr	1980	1999	60r
Child's health care, age 0-2	yr	620	1999	60r
Child's health care, age 3-5	yr	590	1999	60r
Child's health care, age 6-8	yr	680	1999	60r
Child's health care, age 9-11	yr	720	1999	60r
Child's health care, age 12-14	yr	730	1999	60r
Child's health care, age 15-17	yr	760	1999	60r
Child's housing, age 0-2	yr	3070	1999	60r
Child's housing, age 3-5	yr	3050	1999	60r
Child's housing, age 6-8	yr	3010	1999	60r
Child's housing, age 9-11	yr	2850	1999	60r
Child's housing, age 12-14	yr	3040	1999	60r
Child's housing, age 15-17	yr	2650	1999	60r
Child's personal care, reading, age 0-2	yr	910	1999	60r
Child's personal care, reading, age 3-5	yr	930	1999	60r
Child's personal care, reading, age 6-8	yr	960	1999	60r
Child's personal care, reading, age 9-11	yr	1000	1999	60r
Child's personal care, reading, age 12-14	yr	1170	1999	60r
Child's personal care, reading, age 15-17	yr	950	1999	60r
Clothing				
Apparel and services purchases	yr	1610	1999	30r

Values are in dollars or fractions of dollars. In the column headed *Ref*, references are shown to sources. Each reference is followed by a letter. These refer to the geographical level for which data were reported: s=State, r=Region, and c=City or metro. The abbreviation *ex* is used to mean *except* or *excluding*; *exp* stands for *expenditures*. For other abbreviations and further explanations, please see the Introduction.

Punta Gorda, FL - continued

Item	Per	Value	Date	Ref.
Clothing				
Boys, 2 to 15, expenditures on	yr	89	1999	30r
Children under 2, expenditures on	yr	79	1999	30r
Footwear, expenditures on	yr	283	1999	30r
Girls, 2 to 15, expenditures on	yr	103	1999	30r
Men and boys, expenditures on	yr	351	1999	30r
Men, 16 and over, expenditures on	yr	262	1999	30r
Women, 16 and over, expenditures on	yr	538	1999	30r
Communications				
Cable modem installation, Adelphi		54.90	6/99	103s
Cable modem installation, Comcast		95.00	6/99	103s
Cable modem installation, Media One		100.00	6/99	103s
Cable modem installation, Time Warner		75.00- 225.00	6/99	103s
Cable modem rate, cable subscriber, Adelphi	mos	34.95	6/99	103s
Cable modem rate, cable subscriber, Comcast	mos	39.95	6/99	103s
Cable modem rate, cable subscriber, Media One	mos	34.95- 39.95	6/99	103s
Cable modem rate, cable subscriber, Time Warner	mos	39.95- 49.95	6/99	103s
Cable modem rate, non-cable subscriber, Adelphi	mos	44.95	6/99	103s
Cable modem rate, non-cable subscriber, Comcast	mos	49.95	6/99	103s
Cable modem rate, non-cable subscriber, Media One	mos	49.95	6/99	103s
Cable modem rate, non-cable subscriber, Time Warner	mos	39.95- 54.95	6/99	103s
Phone line, single, business, field visit	inst.	56.00	12/97	17s
Phone line, single, business, no field visit	inst.	56.00	12/97	17s
Phone line, single, residence, field visit	inst.	40.00	12/97	17s
Phone line, single, residence, no field visit	inst.	40.00	12/97	17s
Postage and stationery, expenditures on	yr	104	1999	30r
Postal rate, express mail, up to half-pound		12.45	7/01	108r
Postal rate, letter, first class, first ounce		0.34	7/01	108r
Postal rate, letter, two ounces		0.57	7/01	108r
Postal rate, post card		0.21	7/01	108r
Postal rate, priority mail, two pounds		3.95	7/01	108r
Postal rate, priority mail, up to one pound		3.50	7/01	108r
Telephone services, expenditures on	yr	860	1999	30r
Education				
Board, 4-year private college/university	yr	2236	1996	38s
Board, 4-year public college/university	yr	2295	1996	38s
Education expenditures	yr	431	1999	30r
Room, 4-year private college/university	yr	2428	1996	38s
Room, 4-year public college/university	yr	2193	1996	38s
Total cost, 4-year private college/university	yr	15028	1996	38s
Total cost, 4-year public college/university	yr	6254	1996	38s
Tuition, 2-year public college/university, in state	yr	1103	1996	38s
Tuition, 4-year private college/university, in state	yr	10364	1996	38s
Tuition, 4-year public college/university	yr	1767	1996	38s
Energy and Fuels				
Electricity	KWh	0.09	7/01	11r
Electricity	500 KWhs	47.29	7/01	11r
Fuel oil #2	gal	1.43	7/01	11r
Fuel oil and other fuels, expenditures on	yr	45	1999	30r
Gas, natural, commercial rate	1000 cf	8.44	11/00	88s
Gasoline, all types	gal	1.60	7/01	11r
Gasoline, unleaded midgrade	gal	1.65	7/01	11r
Gasoline, unleaded premium	gal	1.74	7/01	11r
Natural gas, expenditures on	yr	164	1999	30r
Utility (piped) gas, therm		1.01	7/01	11r
Utility (piped) gas, 40 therms		44.29	7/01	11r
Utility (piped) gas, 100 therms		97.44	7/01	11r
Entertainment				
Entertainment purchases	yr	1574	1999	30r
Fees and admissions paid	yr	371	1999	30r

Punta Gorda, FL - continued

Item	Per	Value	Date	Ref.
Entertainment - continued				
Reading purchases	yr	121	1999	30r
Television, radios, sound equipment, expenditures on	yr	561	1999	30r
Funerals				
Total cost of funeral		5922.53	1/99	78r
Acknowledgement cards		63.43	1/99	78r
Casket		2258.77	1/99	78r
Cosmetology, hair, other preparation		127.09	1/99	78r
Embalming		393.49	1/99	78r
Funeral at funeral home		367.50	1/99	78r
Hearse (local)		169.66	1/99	78r
Professional service charges		1211.32	1/99	78r
Service car/van		80.69	1/99	78r
Transfer of remains to funeral home		144.25	1/99	78r
Vault		803.50	1/99	78r
Visitation/viewing		302.83	1/99	78r
Groceries				
American processed cheese	lb	3.50	7/01	11r
Bakery products, expenditures on	yr	261	1999	30r
Bananas	lb	0.47	7/01	11r
Beans, dried, any type, all sizes	lb	0.63	7/01	11r
Beef for stew, boneless	lb	2.86	7/01	11r
Beef, expenditures on	yr	210	1999	30r
Bologna, all beef or mixed	lb	2.29	7/01	11r
Bread, French	lb	1.66	7/01	11r
Bread, white, pan	lb	0.87	7/01	11r
Bread, whole wheat, pan	lb	1.38	7/01	11r
Broccoli	lb	1.04	7/01	11r
Butter, salted, grade AA, stick	lb	2.26	7/01	11r
Butter, yoghurt, cheese, etc, expenditures on	yr	170	1999	30r
Cabbage	lb	0.42	7/01	11r
Cereals and cereal products, expenditures on	yr	140	1999	30r
Cheddar cheese, natural	lb	3.75	7/01	11r
Chicken breast, bone-in	lb	1.85	7/01	11r
Chicken legs, bone-in	lb	1.34	7/01	11r
Chicken, fresh, whole	lb	1.05	7/01	11r
Chops, boneless,	lb	4.13	7/01	11r
Chuck roast, graded and ungraded, excl U.S. prime and choice	lb	2.35	7/01	11r
Chuck roast, U.S. choice, boneless	lb	2.67	7/01	11r
Coffee, 100%, ground roast, all sizes	lb	2.88	7/01	11r
Coffee, instant, plain, regular, all sizes	16 oz	9.25	7/01	11r
Cola, non diet,	2 liter	1.11	7/01	11r
Crackers, soda, salted	lb	1.70	7/01	11r
Dairy product purchases	yr	282	1999	30r
Eggs, expenditures on	yr	32	1999	30r
Fats and oils, expenditures on	yr	79	1999	30r
Fish and seafood, expenditures on	yr	99	1999	30r
Flour, white, all purpose	lb	0.32	7/01	11r
Food (excl fruit and vegetables), eaten at home, purchases	yr	815	1999	30r
Food cooked on trips, expenditures on	yr	36	1999	30r
Food purchases	yr	4533	1999	30r
Food purchases, eaten away from home	yr	1873	1999	30r
Food purchases, food eaten at home	yr	2660	1999	30r
Fresh fruits, expenditures on	yr	128	1999	30r
Fresh milk and cream, expenditures on	yr	112	1999	30r
Fresh vegetables, expenditures on	yr	131	1999	30r
Fruit and vegetable purchases	yr	438	1999	30r
Grapefruit	lb	0.59	7/01	11r
Grapes, Thompson, seedless	lb	2.12	7/01	11r
Ground beef, 100% beef	lb	1.76	7/01	11r
Ground beef, lean and extra lean	lb	2.60	7/01	11r
Ground chuck, 100% beef	lb	2.08	7/01	11r
Ham, boneless, excl canned	lb	2.71	7/01	11r
Ham, rump or shank half, bone-in, smoked	lb	2.19	7/01	11r
Ice cream, prepackaged, bulk, regular	1/2 gal	3.93	7/01	11r
Lemons	lb	1.32	7/01	11r
Lettuce, iceberg	lb	0.76	7/01	11r
Milk, fresh, low fat,	gal	2.75	7/01	11r

Values are in dollars or fractions of dollars. In the column headed *Ref*, references are shown to sources. Each reference is followed by a letter. These refer to the geographical level for which data were reported: s=State, r=Region, and c=City or metro. The abbreviation *ex* is used to mean *except* or *excluding*; *exp* stands for expenditures. For other abbreviations and further explanations, please see the Introduction.

Punta Gorda, FL - continued

Item	Per	Value	Date	Ref.
Groceries				
Milk, fresh, whole, fortified	gal	2.97	7/01	11r
Nonalcoholic beverages, expenditures on	yr	228	1999	30r
Orange juice, frozen concentrate	16 oz	1.95	7/01	11r
Oranges, Navel	lb	0.73	7/01	11r
Oranges, Valencia	lb	0.55	7/01	11r
Peanut butter, creamy, all sizes	lb	1.83	7/01	11r
Pears, Anjou	lb	0.98	7/01	11r
Pork chops, center cut, bone-in	lb	3.33	7/01	11r
Pork sausage, fresh, loose	lb	2.59	7/01	11r
Pork shoulder picnic, bone-in, smoked	lb	1.12	7/01	11r
Pork, expenditures on	yr	162	1999	30r
Potato chips	16 oz	3.59	7/01	11r
Potatoes, frozen, french fried	lb	1.00	7/01	11r
Potatoes, white, all types	lb	0.44	7/01	11r
Poultry, expenditures on	yr	137	1999	30r
Processed fruits, expenditures on	yr	97	1999	30r
Processed vegetables, expenditures on	yr	82	1999	30r
Rice, white, long grain, uncooked	lb	0.51	7/01	11r
Round roast, graded and ungraded, excl U.S. prime and choice	lb	2.96	7/01	11r
Round steak, graded and ungraded, excl U.S. prime and choice	lb	3.11	7/01	11r
Sirloin steak, graded and ungraded, excl U.S. prime and choice	lb	4.23	7/01	11r
Spaghetti and macaroni	lb	0.78	7/01	11r
Steak, round, U.S. choice, boneless	lb	3.56	7/01	11r
Steak, sirloin, U.S. choice, boneless	lb	5.65	7/01	11r
Strawberries, dry pint	12 oz	1.50	7/01	11r
Sugar and other sweets, expenditures on	yr	99	1999	30r
Sugar, white, 33-80 ounce package	lb	0.39	7/01	11r
Sugar, white, all sizes	lb	0.42	7/01	11r
Tobacco products and smoking supplies purchases	yr	288	1999	30r
Tomatoes, field grown	lb	1.43	7/01	11r
Tuna, light, chunk	lb	1.77	7/01	11r
Turkey, frozen, whole	lb	1.05	7/01	11r
Goods and Services				
B&B Japanese maple (acer japonicum)	gal	49.98-129.00	4/00	93r
Boxwood (buxus)	2 gal	12.99-16.99	4/00	93r
Daylilly (hemerocallis)	gal	4.99-8.99	4/00	93r
Flat of annuals		11.00-13.92	4/00	93r
Fountain grass (pennisetum)	gal	5.98-7.98	4/00	93r
Hanging basket (10 in)		7.99-14.98	4/00	93r
Hardy geranium (geranium)	gal	5.98-8.00	4/00	93r
Hosta (hosta)	gal	4.99-10.98	4/00	93r
Lilac (syrubga vulgaris)	2 gal	12.99-21.99	4/00	93r
Rhododendron (rhododendron)	2 gal	14.99-24.99	4/00	93r
Sage (salvia)	gal	5.98-6.99	4/00	93r
Wintercreeper euonymus (euonymus fortunei)	2 gal	7.99-89.99	4/00	93r
Hunting license	yr	12.50	4/01	34s
Health Care				
Cardiac catheterization, ave hospital/ physician charges		15060	1998	77s
Childbirth, Cesarean delivery		11587	1997	13r
Childbirth, vaginal delivery		6725	1997	13r
Drugs, expenditures on	yr	399	1999	30r
Health care purchases	yr	1971	1999	30r
Health insurance expenditures	yr	933	1999	30r

Punta Gorda, FL - continued

Item	Per	Value	Date	Ref.
Health Care - continued				
Hysterectomy, laproscopically-assisted, ave hospital/physician charges		14760	1998	76s
Hysterectomy, vaginal, ave hospital and physician charges		11320	1998	76s
Medicaid dispensing fee		4.23	1999	87s
Medical services expenditures	yr	547	1999	30r
Medical supplies, expenditures on	yr	91	1999	30r
Plastic surgery, breast augmentation		2870	2000	7r
Plastic surgery, breast lift		3649	2000	7r
Plastic surgery, facelift		5008	2000	7r
Plastic surgery, hair transplantation		3425	2000	7r
Plastic surgery, lip augmentation		1227	2000	7r
Plastic surgery, lower body lift		4793	2000	7r
Plastic surgery, thigh lift		3862	2000	7r
Household Goods				
Floor coverings, expenditures on	yr	44	1999	30r
Furniture, expenditures on	yr	335	1999	30r
Household furnishings and equipment purchases	yr	1328	1999	30r
Household textiles, expenditures on	yr	89	1999	30r
Laundry and cleaning supplies, expenditures on	yr	113	1999	30r
Housing				
Home price, existing, ave		160100	10/00	90r
Home value, median		104000	2001	53s
Household operation expenditures	yr	553	1999	30r
Housekeeping supplies purchases	yr	473	1999	30r
Housing, expenditures on	yr	10303	1999	30r
Maintenance, repairs, insurance expenditures	yr	699	1999	30r
Monthly rental value of owned home	mos	505	1999	30r
Owned dwellings, expenditures own	yr	3465	1999	30r
Rent expenditures	yr	1641	1999	30r
Rental unit, 1 bedroom, with utilities	mos	474	4/01	41c
Rental unit, 2 bedroom, with utilities	mos	631	4/01	41c
Rental unit, 3 bedroom, with utilities	mos	875	4/01	41c
Rental unit, 4 bedroom, with utilities	mos	1032	4/01	41c
Shelter, expenditures on	yr	5467	1999	30r
Insurance and Pensions				
Life and other personal insurance purchases	yr	414	1999	30r
Medigap health insurance, Plan H	yr	2887	2000	69s
Medigap health insurance, Plan I	yr	3302	2000	69s
Medigap health insurance, Plan J	yr	3889	2000	69s
Pensions and Social Security, expenditures on	yr	2635	1999	30r
Personal insurance and pensions, expenditures on	yr	3048	1999	30r
Legal Fees				
Divorce, filing fee		65.00-85.00	4/01	35s
Driver's license fee	orig	20.00	1999	48s
Driver's license fee	renew	15.00	1999	48s
Personal Goods				
Personal care products and services purchases	yr	393	1999	30r
Personal Services				
Personal services, household, expenditures on	yr	258	1999	30r
Pets				
Pets, toys, and playground equipment, expenditures on	yr	306	1999	30r
Taxes				
Federal income taxes paid	yr	2047	1999	30r
Personal taxes, expenditures on	yr	2554	1999	30r
Property taxes paid	yr	726	1999	30r
State and local income taxes paid	yr	363	1999	30r

Values are in dollars or fractions of dollars. In the column headed *Ref*, references are shown to sources. Each reference is followed by a letter. These refer to the geographical level for which data were reported: s=State, r=Region, and c=City or metro. The abbreviation *ex* is used to mean *except* or *excluding*; *exp* stands for expenditures. For other abbreviations and further explanations, please see the Introduction.

Punta Gorda, FL - continued

Item	Per	Value	Date	Ref.
Transportation				
Cars and trucks, new, expenditures on	yr	1648	1999	30r
Cars and trucks, used, expenditures on	yr	1651	1999	30r
Diesel at the pump	gal	1.26	10/99	73s
Gasoline and motor oil purchases	yr	1052	1999	30r
Gasoline before-tax price (cents)	gal	101.90	10/00	43s
Maintenance and repair expenditures	yr	621	1999	30r
Public transportation, expenditures on	yr	298	1999	30r
Transportation purchases	yr	6738	1999	30r
Vehicle expenses, miscellaneous, purchases	yr	2033	1999	30r
Vehicle insurance payments	yr	696	1999	30r
Vehicle purchases (net outlay)	yr	3354	1999	30r
Vehicle rental, lease expenditures	yr	352	1999	30r
Travel				
Hotel room	night	110.57	2/01	95s
Utilities				
Electrical bill, average	mos	86.33	9/00	9s
Electricity, expenditures on	yr	1115	1999	30r
Electricity cost, average	KWh	6.80	9/00	9s
Water and other public services, expenditures on	yr	298	1999	30r
Weddings				
Wedding (national average cost)		19936	2000	33r
Wedding (regional average total cost)		16293	1997	110r
Attendants' gifts		321	1998	33r
Bridal attendants' apparel (5 persons)		824	2000	33r
Bride's headpiece/veil		173	1998	33r
Bride's wedding dress		859	1998	33r
Clergy, religious facility fee		242	1998	33r
Engagement ring		3177	1998	33r
Flowers		789	1998	33r
Groom's formalwear rental		99	2000	33r
Limousine		410	1998	33r
Marriage license cost		56.00-88.50	4/01	35s
Men's formalwear (ushers, best man)		469	2000	33r
Mother of bride apparel		241	2000	33r
Music		866	1998	33r
Photography and videography		1368	1998	33r
Rehearsal dinner		728	1998	33r
Wedding invitations and announcements		341	1998	33r
Wedding reception		7968	2000	33r
Wedding rings (bride and groom)		1060	1998	33r

Racine, WI

Item	Per	Value	Date	Ref.
Average annual expenditures	yr	35369	1999	30r
Alcoholic Beverages				
Alcoholic beverage purchases	yr	304	1999	30r
Malt beverages, all types, all sizes, any origin	16 oz	0.93	7/01	11r
Wine, red and white table, all sizes, any origin	liter	7.04	7/01	11r
Appliances				
Major appliances, expenditures on	yr	165	1999	30r
Small appliances, housewares, expenditures on	yr	90	1999	30r
Banking and Money				
Mortgage interest and charges paid	yr	2277	1999	30r
Mortgage principal paid on owned property	yr	1230	1999	30r
Vehicle finance charges paid	yr	328	1999	30r
Charity				
Cash contributions, expenditures on	yr	1126	1999	30r
Child Care				
Child raising cost, total, age 0-2	yr	7890	1999	60r
Child raising cost, total, age 3-5	yr	8130	1999	60r
Child raising cost, total, age 6-8	yr	8170	1999	60r
Child raising cost, total, age 9-11	yr	8190	1999	60r
Child raising cost, total, age 12-14	yr	8890	1999	60r

Racine, WI - continued

Item	Per	Value	Date	Ref.
Child Care - continued				
Child raising cost, total, age 15-17	yr	9050	1999	60r
Child's child care and education, age 0-2	yr	1240	1999	60r
Child's child care and education, age 3-5	yr	1370	1999	60r
Child's child care and education, age 6-8	yr	880	1999	60r
Child's child care and education, age 9-11	yr	570	1999	60r
Child's child care and education, age 12-14	yr	420	1999	60r
Child's child care and education, age 15-17	yr	720	1999	60r
Child's clothing, age 0-2	yr	410	1999	60r
Child's clothing, age 3-5	yr	400	1999	60r
Child's clothing, age 6-8	yr	450	1999	60r
Child's clothing, age 9-11	yr	500	1999	60r
Child's clothing, age 12-14	yr	840	1999	60r
Child's clothing, age 15-17	yr	740	1999	60r
Child's food, age 0-2	yr	960	1999	60r
Child's food, age 3-5	yr	1120	1999	60r
Child's food, age 6-8	yr	1430	1999	60r
Child's food, age 9-11	yr	1710	1999	60r
Child's food, age 12-14	yr	1710	1999	60r
Child's food, age 15-17	yr	1920	1999	60r
Child's health care, age 0-2	yr	520	1999	60r
Child's health care, age 3-5	yr	500	1999	60r
Child's health care, age 6-8	yr	570	1999	60r
Child's health care, age 9-11	yr	610	1999	60r
Child's health care, age 12-14	yr	630	1999	60r
Child's health care, age 15-17	yr	650	1999	60r
Child's housing, age 0-2	yr	2860	1999	60r
Child's housing, age 3-5	yr	2840	1999	60r
Child's housing, age 6-8	yr	2800	1999	60r
Child's housing, age 9-11	yr	2650	1999	60r
Child's housing, age 12-14	yr	2840	1999	60r
Child's housing, age 15-17	yr	2440	1999	60r
Child's personal care, reading, age 0-2	yr	880	1999	60r
Child's personal care, reading, age 3-5	yr	900	1999	60r
Child's personal care, reading, age 6-8	yr	930	1999	60r
Child's personal care, reading, age 9-11	yr	970	1999	60r
Child's personal care, reading, age 12-14	yr	1150	1999	60r
Child's personal care, reading, age 15-17	yr	920	1999	60r
Clothing				
Apparel and services purchases	yr	1607	1999	30r
Boys, 2 to 15, expenditures on	yr	91	1999	30r
Children under 2, expenditures on	yr	59	1999	30r
Footwear, expenditures on	yr	285	1999	30r
Girls, 2 to 15, expenditures on	yr	116	1999	30r
Men and boys, expenditures on	yr	433	1999	30r
Men, 16 and over, expenditures on	yr	341	1999	30r
Women, 16 and over, expenditures on	yr	490	1999	30r
Communications				
Cable modem installation, Bresnan		99.95	6/99	103s
Cable modem installation, Marcus		499.00	6/99	103s
Cable modem rate, cable subscriber, Bresnan	mos	39.95	6/99	103s
Cable modem rate, cable subscriber, Marcus	mos	14.95-49.95	6/99	103s
Cable modem rate, non-cable subscriber, Bresnan	mos	49.95	6/99	103s
Cable modem rate, non-cable subscriber, Marcus	mos	60.95	6/99	103s
Phone line, single, business, field visit	inst.	64.65	12/97	17s
Phone line, single, business, no field visit	inst.	64.65	12/97	17s
Phone line, single, residence, field visit	inst.	33.05	12/97	17s
Phone line, single, residence, no field visit	inst.	33.05	12/97	17s
Postage and stationery, expenditures on	yr	140	1999	30r
Postal rate, express mail, up to half-pound		12.45	7/01	108r
Postal rate, letter, first class, first ounce		0.34	7/01	108r
Postal rate, letter, two ounces		0.57	7/01	108r
Postal rate, post card		0.21	7/01	108r
Postal rate, priority mail, two pounds		3.95	7/01	108r
Postal rate, priority mail, up to one pound		3.50	7/01	108r
Telephone bill, business, basic rate	mos	20.85	12/97	18c
Telephone bill, residential, basic rate	mos	5.40	12/97	18c
Telephone services, expenditures on	yr	830	1999	30r

Values are in dollars or fractions of dollars. In the column headed *Ref*, references are shown to sources. Each reference is followed by a letter. These refer to the geographical level for which data were reported: s=State, r=Region, and c=City or metro. The abbreviation *ex* is used to mean *except* or *excluding*; *exp* stands for expenditures. For other abbreviations and further explanations, please see the Introduction.

Racine, WI - continued

Item	Per	Value	Date	Ref.
Education				
Board, 4-year private college/university	yr	2271	1996	38s
Board, 4-year public college/university	yr	1527	1996	38s
Education expenditures	yr	583	1999	30r
Room, 4-year private college/university	yr	1812	1996	38s
Room, 4-year public college/university	yr	1706	1996	38s
Total cost, 4-year private college/university	yr	15652	1996	38s
Total cost, 4-year public college/university	yr	5847	1996	38s
Tuition, 2-year public college/university, in state	yr	1840	1996	38s
Tuition, 4-year private college/university, in state	yr	11569	1996	38s
Tuition, 4-year public college/university	yr	2614	1996	38s
Energy and Fuels				
Electricity	500 KWhs	46.59	7/01	11r
Fuel oil #2	gal	1.27	7/01	11r
Fuel oil and other fuels, expenditures on	yr	68	1999	30r
Gas, cooking, winter, 10 therms	mos	9.98	2/96	98c
Gas, cooking, winter, 30 therms	mos	18.94	2/96	98c
Gas, cooking, winter, 50 therms	mos	28.90	2/96	98c
Gas, heating, winter, average use	mos	87.62	2/96	98c
Gas, natural, commercial rate	1000 cf	7.32	11/00	88s
Gasoline, unleaded midgrade	gal	1.79	7/01	11r
Gasoline, unleaded premium	gal	1.86	7/01	11r
Gasoline, unleaded regular	gal	1.58	7/01	11r
Natural gas, expenditures on	yr	389	1999	30r
Utility (piped) gas, therm		0.81	7/01	11r
Utility (piped) gas, 40 therms		38.01	7/01	11r
Utility (piped) gas, 100 therms		81.75	7/01	11r
Entertainment				
Entertainment purchases	yr	1984	1999	30r
Fees and admissions paid	yr	444	1999	30r
Television, radios, sound equipment, expenditures on	yr	580	1999	30r
Funerals				
Cosmetology, hair, other preparation		178.32	1/99	78r
Embalming		408.19	1/99	78r
Funeral at funeral home		362.13	1/99	78r
Professional service charges		1375.51	1/99	78r
Transfer of remains to funeral home		155.92	1/99	78r
Visitation/viewing		294.38	1/99	78r
Groceries				
Bacon, sliced	lb	3.15	7/01	11r
Bakery products, expenditures on	yr	281	1999	30r
Bananas	lb	0.48	7/01	11r
Beans, dried, any type, all sizes	lb	0.61	7/01	11r
Beef for stew, boneless	lb	3.08	7/01	11r
Beef, expenditures on	yr	217	1999	30r
Bologna, all beef or mixed	lb	2.52	7/01	11r
Bread, white, pan	lb	1.06	7/01	11r
Broccoli	lb	0.91	7/01	11r
Butter, salted, grade AA, stick	lb	3.04	7/01	11r
Butter, yoghurt, cheese, etc, expenditures on	yr	183	1999	30r
Cereals and bakery product purchases	yr	430	1999	30r
Cereals and cereal products, expenditures on	yr	149	1999	30r
Chicken, fresh, whole	lb	1.07	7/01	11r
Chops, boneless,	lb	3.64	7/01	11r
Chuck roast, U.S. choice, boneless	lb	2.47	7/01	11r
Coffee, 100% ground roast, all sizes	lb	2.69	7/01	11r
Cookies, chocolate chip	lb	2.87	7/01	11r
Dairy product purchases	yr	304	1999	30r
Eggs, expenditures on	yr	26	1999	30r
Eggs, grade A, large	dozen	0.88	7/01	11r
Fats and oils, expenditures on	yr	75	1999	30r
Fish and seafood, expenditures on	yr	72	1999	30r
Food (excl fruit and vegetables), eaten at home, purchases	yr	887	1999	30r
Food cooked on trips, expenditures on	yr	44	1999	30r
Food purchases	yr	4802	1999	30r

Racine, WI - continued

Item	Per	Value	Date	Ref.
Groceries - continued				
Food purchases, eaten away from home	yr	2069	1999	30r
Food purchases, food eaten at home	yr	2733	1999	30r
Fresh fruits, expenditures on	yr	138	1999	30r
Fresh milk and cream, expenditures on	yr	120	1999	30r
Fresh vegetables, expenditures on	yr	126	1999	30r
Grapefruit	lb	0.66	7/01	11r
Grapes, Thompson, seedless	lb	1.64	7/01	11r
Ground beef, 100% beef	lb	1.64	7/01	11r
Ground beef, lean and extra lean	lb	2.16	7/01	11r
Ground chuck, 100% beef	lb	2.13	7/01	11r
Ham, boneless, excl canned	lb	2.62	7/01	11r
Ice cream, prepackaged, bulk, regular	1/2 gal	3.35	7/01	11r
Lemons	lb	1.19	7/01	11r
Lettuce, iceberg	lb	0.73	7/01	11r
Margarine, soft, tubs	lb	0.89	7/01	11r
Meats, poultry, fish, and egg purchases	yr	671	1999	30r
Milk, fresh, whole, fortified	gal	2.71	7/01	11r
Nonalcoholic beverages, expenditures on	yr	239	1999	30r
Oranges, Navel	lb	0.80	7/01	11r
Oranges, Valencia	lb	0.66	7/01	11r
Pears, Anjou	lb	0.93	7/01	11r
Pork chops, center cut, bone-in	lb	3.63	7/01	11r
Pork, expenditures on	yr	150	1999	30r
Potato chips	16 oz	3.52	7/01	11r
Potatoes, frozen, french fried	lb	1.08	7/01	11r
Potatoes, white, all types	lb	0.33	7/01	11r
Poultry, expenditures on	yr	108	1999	30r
Processed fruits, expenditures on	yr	98	1999	30r
Processed vegetables, expenditures on	yr	80	1999	30r
Round roast, U.S. choice, boneless	lb	3.07	7/01	11r
Round steak, graded and ungraded, excl U.S. prime and choice	lb	3.41	7/01	11r
Shortening, vegetable oil blends	lb	1.13	7/01	11r
Spaghetti and macaroni	lb	0.80	7/01	11r
Steak, round, U.S. choice, boneless	lb	3.23	7/01	11r
Steak, T-bone, U.S. choice, bone-in	lb	6.68	7/01	11r
Strawberries, dry pint	12 oz	1.32	7/01	11r
Sugar and other sweets, expenditures on	yr	114	1999	30r
Sugar, white, 33-80 ounce package	lb	0.42	7/01	11r
Sugar, white, all sizes	lb	0.43	7/01	11r
Tobacco products and smoking supplies purchases	yr	331	1999	30r
Tomatoes, field grown	lb	1.46	7/01	11r
Tuna, light, chunk	lb	1.80	7/01	11r
Turkey, frozen, whole	lb	1.15	7/01	11r
Goods and Services				
B&B Japanese maple (acer japonicum)	gal	29.99-169.99	4/00	93r
Boxwood (buxus)	2 gal	18.99-39.99	4/00	93r
Daylily (hemerocallis)	gal	4.99-25.00	4/00	93r
Flat of annuals		11.98-24.99	4/00	93r
Fountain grass (pennisetum)	gal	5.98-12.98	4/00	93r
Hanging basket (10 in)		12.99-27.99	4/00	93r
Hardy geranium (geranium)	gal	7.99-9.99	4/00	93r
Hosta (hosta)	gal	6.00-25.00	4/00	93r
Lilac (syrubga vulgaris)	2 gal	14.99-24.99	4/00	93r
Miscellaneous purchases	yr	865	1999	30r
Rhododendron (rhododendron)	2 gal	23.98-42.99	4/00	93r
Sage (salvia)	gal	6.00-9.99	4/00	93r
Wintercreeper euonymus (euonymus fortunei)	2 gal	16.00-169.99	4/00	93r
Hunting license	yr	14.00	4/01	34s

Values are in dollars or fractions of dollars. In the column headed *Ref*, references are shown to sources. Each reference is followed by a letter. These refer to the geographical level for which data were reported: s=State, r=Region, and c=City or metro. The abbreviation *ex* is used to mean *except* or *excluding*; *exp* stands for expenditures. For other abbreviations and further explanations, please see the Introduction.

Racine, WI - continued

Item	Per	Value	Date	Ref.
Health Care				
Cardiac catheterization, ave hospital/				
physician charges		13240	1998	77s
Childbirth, Cesarean delivery		10722	1997	13r
Childbirth, vaginal delivery		6223	1997	13r
Drugs, expenditures on	yr	394	1999	30r
Health care purchases	yr	2048	1999	30r
Health insurance expenditures	yr	978	1999	30r
Hysterectomy, laproscopically-assisted, ave				
hospital/physician charges		13270	1998	76s
Hysterectomy, vaginal, ave hospital and				
physician charges		9170	1998	76s
Laser eye surgery	eye	1950-2400	2000	63s
Medicaid dispensing fee		4.88-40.11	1999	87s
Medical services expenditures	yr	554	1999	30r
Medical supplies, expenditures on	yr	122	1999	30r
Plastic surgery, breast augmentation		3184	2000	7r
Plastic surgery, breast lift		3585	2000	7r
Plastic surgery, facelift		4999	2000	7r
Plastic surgery, hair transplantation		3105	2000	7r
Plastic surgery, lip augmentation		1290	2000	7r
Plastic surgery, lower body lift		8135	2000	7r
Plastic surgery, thigh lift		3839	2000	7r
Household Goods				
Floor coverings, expenditures on	yr	52	1999	30r
Furniture, expenditures on	yr	344	1999	30r
Household furnishings and equipment				
purchases	yr	1475	1999	30r
Household textiles, expenditures on	yr	109	1999	30r
Laundry and cleaning supplies, expenditures				
on	yr	134	1999	30r
Housing				
Home price, existing, ave		144400	10/00	90r
Home value, median		117000	2001	53s
Household operation expenditures	yr	542	1999	30r
Housekeeping supplies purchases	yr	508	1999	30r
Lodging expenditures	yr	430	1999	30r
Maintenance, repairs, insurance				
expenditures	yr	853	1999	30r
Monthly rental value of owned home	mos	547	1999	30r
Owned dwellings, expenditures own	yr	4282	1999	30r
Rent expenditures	yr	1558	1999	30r
Rental unit, 1 bedroom, with utilities	mos	425	4/01	41c
Rental unit, 2 bedroom, with utilities	mos	561	4/01	41c
Rental unit, 3 bedroom, with utilities	mos	724	4/01	41c
Rental unit, 4 bedroom, with utilities	mos	792	4/01	41c
Shelter, expenditures on	yr	6270	1999	30r
Insurance and Pensions				
Auto insurance premium	yr	603.84	1999	57s
Life and other personal insurance purchases	yr	387	1999	30r
Pensions and Social Security, expenditures				
on	yr	2968	1999	30r
Legal Fees				
Divorce, filing fee		142.00-150.00	4/01	35s
Driver's license fee	renew	12.00	1999	48s
Driver's license fee	orig	18.00	1999	48s
Fishing license	yr	14.00	4/01	34s
Personal Goods				
Personal care products and services				
purchases	yr	385	1999	30r
Personal Services				
Personal services, household, expenditures				
on	yr	300	1999	30r
Pets				
Pets, toys, and playground equipment,				
expenditures on	yr	375	1999	30r

Racine, WI - continued

Item	Per	Value	Date	Ref.
Taxes				
Federal income taxes paid	yr	2326	1999	30r
Personal taxes, expenditures on	yr	3223	1999	30r
Property taxes paid	yr	1152	1999	30r
State and local income taxes paid	yr	753	1999	30r
Transportation				
Cars and trucks, new, expenditures on	yr	1280	1999	30r
Cars and trucks, used, expenditures on	yr	1763	1999	30r
Diesel at the pump	gal	1.34	10/99	73s
Gasoline and motor oil purchases	yr	1036	1999	30r
Gasoline before-tax price (cents)	gal	113.40	10/00	43s
Maintenance and repair expenditures	yr	594	1999	30r
Public transportation, expenditures on	yr	341	1999	30r
Transportation purchases	yr	6617	1999	30r
Vehicle expenses, miscellaneous, purchases	yr	2159	1999	30r
Vehicle insurance payments	yr	701	1999	30r
Vehicle purchases (net outlay)	yr	3081	1999	30r
Vehicle rental, lease expenditures	yr	536	1999	30r
Utilities				
Electrical bill, average	mos	52.08	9/00	9s
Electricity, expenditures on	yr	841	1999	30r
Electricity cost, average	KWh	5.69	9/00	9s
Utilities, fuels, and public services purchased	yr	2401	1999	30r
Water and other public services,				
expenditures on	yr	273	1999	30r
Weddings				
Wedding (national average cost)		19936	2000	33r
Wedding (regional average total cost)		16195	1997	110r
Attendants' gifts		321	1998	33r
Bridal attendants' apparel (5 persons)		824	2000	33r
Bride's headpiece/veil		173	1998	33r
Bride's wedding dress		859	1998	33r
Clergy, religious facility fee		242	1998	33r
Engagement ring		3177	1998	33r
Flowers		789	1998	33r
Groom's formalwear rental		99	2000	33r
Limousine		410	1998	33r
Marriage license cost		50.00-60.00	4/01	35s
Men's formalwear (ushers, best man)		469	2000	33r
Mother of bride apparel		241	2000	33r
Music		866	1998	33r
Photography and videography		1368	1998	33r
Rehearsal dinner		728	1998	33r
Wedding invitations and announcements		341	1998	33r
Wedding reception		7968	2000	33r
Wedding rings (bride and groom)		1060	1998	33r

Raleigh-Durham-Chapel Hill, NC

Item	Per	Value	Date	Ref.
Alcoholic Beverages				
Alcoholic beverage purchases	yr	253	1999	30r
Malt beverages, all types, all sizes, any origin	16 oz	0.96	7/01	11r
Appliances				
Major appliances, expenditures on	yr	172	1999	30r
Small appliances, housewares, expenditures				
on	yr	81	1999	30r
Banking and Money				
Mortgage interest and charges paid	yr	2039	1999	30r
Mortgage principal paid on owned property	yr	1026	1999	30r
Vehicle finance charges paid	yr	365	1999	30r
Charity				
Cash contributions, expenditures	yr	1127	1999	30r
Child Care				
Child raising cost, total, age 0-2	yr	8540	1999	60r
Child raising cost, total, age 3-5	yr	8780	1999	60r
Child raising cost, total, age 6-8	yr	8820	1999	60r
Child raising cost, total, age 9-11	yr	8800	1999	60r

Values are in dollars or fractions of dollars. In the column headed *Ref*, references are shown to sources. Each reference is followed by a letter. These refer to the geographical level for which data were reported: s=State, r=Region, and c=City or metro. The abbreviation *ex* is used to mean *except* or *excluding*; *exp* stands for *expenditures*. For other abbreviations and further explanations, please see the Introduction.

Raleigh-Durham-Chapel Hill, NC - continued

Item	Per	Value	Date	Ref.
Child Care				
Child raising cost, total, age 12-14	yr	9510	1999	60r
Child raising cost, total, age 15-17	yr	9740	1999	60r
Child's child care and education, age 0-2	yr	1380	1999	60r
Child's child care and education, age 3-5	yr	1520	1999	60r
Child's child care and education, age 6-8	yr	990	1999	60r
Child's child care and education, age 9-11	yr	650	1999	60r
Child's child care and education, age 12-14	yr	490	1999	60r
Child's child care and education, age 15-17	yr	840	1999	60r
Child's clothing, age 0-2	yr	480	1999	60r
Child's clothing, age 3-5	yr	470	1999	60r
Child's clothing, age 6-8	yr	520	1999	60r
Child's clothing, age 9-11	yr	570	1999	60r
Child's clothing, age 12-14	yr	950	1999	60r
Child's clothing, age 15-17	yr	850	1999	60r
Child's food, age 0-2	yr	1000	1999	60r
Child's food, age 3-5	yr	1160	1999	60r
Child's food, age 6-8	yr	1490	1999	60r
Child's food, age 9-11	yr	1770	1999	60r
Child's food, age 12-14	yr	1770	1999	60r
Child's food, age 15-17	yr	1980	1999	60r
Child's health care, age 0-2	yr	620	1999	60r
Child's health care, age 3-5	yr	590	1999	60r
Child's health care, age 6-8	yr	680	1999	60r
Child's health care, age 9-11	yr	720	1999	60r
Child's health care, age 12-14	yr	730	1999	60r
Child's health care, age 15-17	yr	760	1999	60r
Child's housing, age 0-2	yr	3070	1999	60r
Child's housing, age 3-5	yr	3050	1999	60r
Child's housing, age 6-8	yr	3010	1999	60r
Child's housing, age 9-11	yr	2850	1999	60r
Child's housing, age 12-14	yr	3040	1999	60r
Child's housing, age 15-17	yr	2650	1999	60r
Child's personal care, reading, age 0-2	yr	910	1999	60r
Child's personal care, reading, age 3-5	yr	930	1999	60r
Child's personal care, reading, age 6-8	yr	960	1999	60r
Child's personal care, reading, age 9-11	yr	1000	1999	60r
Child's personal care, reading, age 12-14	yr	1170	1999	60r
Child's personal care, reading, age 15-17	yr	950	1999	60r
Clothing				
Apparel and services purchases	yr	1610	1999	30r
Boys, 2 to 15, expenditures on	yr	89	1999	30r
Children under 2, expenditures on	yr	79	1999	30r
Footwear, expenditures on	yr	283	1999	30r
Girls, 2 to 15, expenditures on	yr	103	1999	30r
Men and boys, expenditures on	yr	351	1999	30r
Men, 16 and over, expenditures on	yr	262	1999	30r
Women, 16 and over, expenditures on	yr	538	1999	30r
Communications				
Cable modem installation, Intermedia		149.95	6/99	103s
Cable modem installation, Time Warner		75.00-225.00	6/99	103s
Cable modem rate, cable subscriber, Intermedia	mos	49.95	6/99	103s
Cable modem rate, cable subscriber, Time Warner	mos	39.95-49.95	6/99	103s
Cable modem rate, non-cable subscriber, Intermedia	mos	54.95	6/99	103s
Cable modem rate, non-cable subscriber, Time Warner	mos	39.95-54.95	6/99	103s
Phone line, single, business, field visit	inst.	65.00	12/97	17s
Phone line, single, business, no field visit	inst.	65.00	12/97	17s
Phone line, single, residence, field visit	inst.	42.75	12/97	17s
Phone line, single, residence, no field visit	inst.	42.75	12/97	17s
Postage and stationery, expenditures on	yr	104	1999	30r
Postal rate, express mail, up to half-pound		12.45	7/01	108r
Postal rate, letter, first class, first ounce		0.34	7/01	108r
Postal rate, letter, two ounces		0.57	7/01	108r
Postal rate, post card		0.21	7/01	108r
Postal rate, priority mail, two pounds		3.95	7/01	108r
Postal rate, priority mail, up to one pound		3.50	7/01	108r
Telephone services, expenditures on	yr	860	1999	30r

Raleigh-Durham-Chapel Hill, NC - continued

Item	Per	Value	Date	Ref.
Education				
Board, 4-year private college/university	yr	2316	1996	38s
Board, 4-year public college/university	yr	1737	1996	38s
Education expenditures	yr	431	1999	30r
Room, 4-year private college/university	yr	2128	1996	38s
Room, 4-year public college/university	yr	1742	1996	38s
Total cost, 4-year private college/university	yr	15428	1996	38s
Total cost, 4-year public college/university	yr	5119	1996	38s
Tuition, 4-year private college/university, in state	yr	10984	1996	38s
Tuition, 4-year public college/university	yr	1639	1996	38s
Energy and Fuels				
Electricity	KWh	0.09	7/01	11r
Electricity	500 KWhs	47.29	7/01	11r
Fuel oil #2	gal	1.43	7/01	11r
Fuel oil and other fuels, expenditures on	yr	45	1999	30r
Gas, natural, commercial rate	1000 cf	9.25	11/00	88s
Gasoline, all types	gal	1.60	7/01	11r
Gasoline, unleaded midgrade	gal	1.65	7/01	11r
Gasoline, unleaded premium	gal	1.74	7/01	11r
Natural gas, expenditures on	yr	164	1999	30r
Utility (piped) gas, therm		1.01	7/01	11r
Utility (piped) gas, 40 therms		44.29	7/01	11r
Utility (piped) gas, 100 therms		97.44	7/01	11r
Entertainment				
Entertainment purchases	yr	1574	1999	30r
Fees and admissions paid	yr	371	1999	30r
Reading purchases	yr	121	1999	30r
Television, radios, sound equipment, expenditures on	yr	561	1999	30r
Funerals				
Total cost of funeral		5922.53	1/99	78r
Acknowledgement cards		63.43	1/99	78r
Casket		2258.77	1/99	78r
Cosmetology, hair, other preparation		127.09	1/99	78r
Embalming		393.49	1/99	78r
Funeral at funeral home		367.50	1/99	78r
Hearse (local)		169.66	1/99	78r
Professional service charges		1211.32	1/99	78r
Service car/van		80.69	1/99	78r
Transfer of remains to funeral home		144.25	1/99	78r
Vault		803.50	1/99	78r
Visitation/viewing		302.83	1/99	78r
Groceries				
American processed cheese	lb	3.50	7/01	11r
Bakery products, expenditures on	yr	261	1999	30r
Bananas	lb	0.47	7/01	11r
Beans, dried, any type, all sizes	lb	0.63	7/01	11r
Beef for stew, boneless	lb	2.86	7/01	11r
Beef, expenditures on	yr	210	1999	30r
Bologna, all beef or mixed	lb	2.29	7/01	11r
Bread, French	lb	1.66	7/01	11r
Bread, white, pan	lb	0.87	7/01	11r
Bread, whole wheat, pan	lb	1.38	7/01	11r
Broccoli	lb	1.04	7/01	11r
Butter, salted, grade AA, stick	lb	2.26	7/01	11r
Butter, yoghurt, cheese, etc, expenditures on	yr	170	1999	30r
Cabbage	lb	0.42	7/01	11r
Cereals and cereal products, expenditures on	yr	140	1999	30r
Cheddar cheese, natural	lb	3.75	7/01	11r
Chicken breast, bone-in	lb	1.85	7/01	11r
Chicken legs, bone-in	lb	1.34	7/01	11r
Chicken, fresh, whole	lb	1.05	7/01	11r
Chops, boneless,	lb	4.13	7/01	11r
Chuck roast, graded and ungraded, excl U.S. prime and choice	lb	2.35	7/01	11r
Chuck roast, U.S. choice, boneless	lb	2.67	7/01	11r
Coffee, 100%, ground roast, all sizes	lb	2.88	7/01	11r
Coffee, instant, plain, regular, all sizes	16 oz	9.25	7/01	11r

Values are in dollars or fractions of dollars. In the column headed *Ref*, references are shown to sources. Each reference is followed by a letter. These refer to the geographical level for which data were reported: s=State, r=Region, and c=City or metro. The abbreviation *ex* is used to mean *except* or *excluding*; *exp* stands for *expenditures*. For other abbreviations and further explanations, please see the Introduction.

Raleigh-Durham-Chapel Hill, NC - continued

Item	Per	Value	Date	Ref.
Groceries				
Cola, non diet,	2 liter	1.11	7/01	11r
Crackers, soda, salted	lb	1.70	7/01	11r
Dairy product purchases	yr	282	1999	30r
Eggs, expenditures on	yr	32	1999	30r
Fats and oils, expenditures on	yr	79	1999	30r
Fish and seafood, expenditures on	yr	99	1999	30r
Flour, white, all purpose	lb	0.32	7/01	11r
Food (excl fruit and vegetables), eaten at home, purchases	yr	815	1999	30r
Food cooked on trips, expenditures on	yr	36	1999	30r
Food purchases	yr	4533	1999	30r
Food purchases, eaten away from home	yr	1873	1999	30r
Food purchases, food eaten at home	yr	2660	1999	30r
Fresh fruits, expenditures on	yr	128	1999	30r
Fresh milk and cream, expenditures on	yr	112	1999	30r
Fresh vegetables, expenditures on	yr	131	1999	30r
Fruit and vegetable purchases	yr	438	1999	30r
Grapefruit	lb	0.59	7/01	11r
Grapes, Thompson, seedless	lb	2.12	7/01	11r
Ground beef, 100% beef	lb	1.76	7/01	11r
Ground beef, lean and extra lean	lb	2.60	7/01	11r
Ground chuck, 100% beef	lb	2.08	7/01	11r
Ham, boneless, excl canned	lb	2.71	7/01	11r
Ham, rump or shank half, bone-in, smoked	lb	2.19	7/01	11r
Ice cream, prepackaged, bulk, regular	1/2 gal	3.93	7/01	11r
Lemons	lb	1.32	7/01	11r
Lettuce, iceberg	lb	0.76	7/01	11r
Milk, fresh, low fat,	gal	2.75	7/01	11r
Milk, fresh, whole, fortified	gal	2.97	7/01	11r
Nonalcoholic beverages, expenditures on	yr	228	1999	30r
Orange juice, frozen concentrate	16 oz	1.95	7/01	11r
Oranges, Navel	lb	0.73	7/01	11r
Oranges, Valencia	lb	0.55	7/01	11r
Peanut butter, creamy, all sizes	lb	1.83	7/01	11r
Pears, Anjou	lb	0.98	7/01	11r
Pork chops, center cut, bone-in	lb	3.33	7/01	11r
Pork sausage, fresh, loose	lb	2.59	7/01	11r
Pork shoulder picnic, bone-in, smoked	lb	1.12	7/01	11r
Pork, expenditures on	yr	162	1999	30r
Potato chips	16 oz	3.59	7/01	11r
Potatoes, frozen, french fried	lb	1.00	7/01	11r
Potatoes, white, all types	lb	0.44	7/01	11r
Poultry, expenditures on	yr	137	1999	30r
Processed fruits, expenditures on	yr	97	1999	30r
Processed vegetables, expenditures on	yr	82	1999	30r
Rice, white, long grain, uncooked	lb	0.51	7/01	11r
Round roast, graded and ungraded, excl U.S. prime and choice	lb	2.96	7/01	11r
Round steak, graded and ungraded, excl U.S. prime and choice	lb	3.11	7/01	11r
Sirloin steak, graded and ungraded, excl U.S. prime and choice	lb	4.23	7/01	11r
Spaghetti and macaroni	lb	0.78	7/01	11r
Steak, round, U.S. choice, boneless	lb	3.56	7/01	11r
Steak, sirloin, U.S. choice, boneless	lb	5.65	7/01	11r
Strawberries, dry pint	12 oz	1.50	7/01	11r
Sugar and other sweets, expenditures on	yr	99	1999	30r
Sugar, white, 33-80 ounce package	lb	0.39	7/01	11r
Sugar, white, all sizes	lb	0.42	7/01	11r
Tobacco products and smoking supplies purchases	yr	288	1999	30r
Tomatoes, field grown	lb	1.43	7/01	11r
Tuna, light, chunk	lb	1.77	7/01	11r
Turkey, frozen, whole	lb	1.05	7/01	11r
Goods and Services				
B&B Japanese maple (acer japonicum)	gal	49.98-129.00	4/00	93r
Boxwood (buxus)	2 gal	12.99-16.99	4/00	93r
Daylily (hemerocallis)	gal	4.99-8.99	4/00	93r

Raleigh-Durham-Chapel Hill, NC - continued

Item	Per	Value	Date	Ref.
Goods and Services - continued				
Flat of annuals		11.00-13.92	4/00	93r
Fountain grass (pennisetum)	gal	5.98-7.98	4/00	93r
Hanging basket (10 in)		7.99-14.98	4/00	93r
Hardy geranium (geranium)	gal	5.98-8.00	4/00	93r
Hosta (hosta)	gal	4.99-10.98	4/00	93r
Lilac (syrubga vulgaris)	2 gal	12.99-21.99	4/00	93r
Rhododendron (rhododendron)	2 gal	14.99-24.99	4/00	93r
Sage (salvia)	gal	5.98-6.99	4/00	93r
Wintercreeper euonymus (euonymus fortunei)	2 gal	7.99-89.99	4/00	93r
Hunting license	yr	15.00	4/01	34s
Health Care				
Cardiac catheterization, ave hospital/ physician charges		12500	1998	77s
Childbirth, Cesarean delivery		11587	1997	13r
Childbirth, vaginal delivery		6725	1997	13r
Drugs, expenditures on	yr	399	1999	30r
Health care purchases	yr	1971	1999	30r
Health insurance expenditures	yr	933	1999	30r
Hysterectomy, laproscopically-assisted, ave hospital/physician charges		12260	1998	76s
Hysterectomy, vaginal, ave hospital and physician charges		8440	1998	76s
Medicaid dispensing fee		5.60	1999	87s
Medical services expenditures	yr	547	1999	30r
Medical supplies, expenditures on	yr	91	1999	30r
Plastic surgery, breast augmentation		2870	2000	7r
Plastic surgery, breast lift		3649	2000	7r
Plastic surgery, facelift		5008	2000	7r
Plastic surgery, hair transplantation		3425	2000	7r
Plastic surgery, lip augmentation		1227	2000	7r
Plastic surgery, lower body lift		4793	2000	7r
Plastic surgery, thigh lift		3862	2000	7r
Household Goods				
Floor coverings, expenditures on	yr	44	1999	30r
Furniture, expenditures on	yr	335	1999	30r
Household furnishings and equipment purchases	yr	1328	1999	30r
Household textiles, expenditures on	yr	89	1999	30r
Laundry and cleaning supplies, expenditures on	yr	113	1999	30r
Housing				
Home price, existing, ave		160100	10/00	90r
Home value, median		146000	2001	53s
Household operation expenditures	yr	553	1999	30r
Housekeeping supplies purchases	yr	473	1999	30r
Housing, expenditures on	yr	10303	1999	30r
Maintenance, repairs, insurance expenditures	yr	699	1999	30r
Monthly rental value of owned home	mos	505	1999	30r
Owned dwellings, expenditures own	yr	3465	1999	30r
Rent expenditures	yr	1641	1999	30r
Rental unit, 1 bedroom, with utilities	mos	643	4/01	41c
Rental unit, 2 bedroom, with utilities	mos	755	4/01	41c
Rental unit, 3 bedroom, with utilities	mos	1013	4/01	41c
Rental unit, 4 bedroom, with utilities	mos	1195	4/01	41c
Shelter, expenditures on	yr	5467	1999	30r
Insurance and Pensions				
Life and other personal insurance purchases	yr	414	1999	30r
Pensions and Social Security, expenditures on	yr	2635	1999	30r

Values are in dollars or fractions of dollars. In the column headed *Ref*, references are shown to sources. Each reference is followed by a letter. These refer to the geographical level for which data were reported: s=State, r=Region, and c=City or metro. The abbreviation *ex* is used to mean *except* or *excluding*; *exp* stands for expenditures. For other abbreviations and further explanations, please see the Introduction.

Raleigh-Durham-Chapel Hill, NC - continued

Item	Per	Value	Date	Ref.
Insurance and Pensions				
Personal insurance and pensions, expenditures on	yr	3048	1999	30r
Legal Fees				
Combination hunting and fishing license	yr	20.00	4/01	34s
Divorce, filing fee		80.00	4/01	35s
Driver's license fee	orig	10.00	1999	48s
Driver's license fee	renew	10.00	1999	48s
Fishing license	yr	15.00	4/01	34s
Personal Goods				
Personal care products and services purchases	yr	393	1999	30r
Personal Services				
Personal services, household, expenditures on	yr	258	1999	30r
Pets				
Pets, toys, and playground equipment, expenditures on	yr	306	1999	30r
Taxes				
Federal income taxes paid	yr	2047	1999	30r
Personal taxes, expenditures on	yr	2554	1999	30r
Property taxes paid	yr	726	1999	30r
State and local income taxes paid	yr	363	1999	30r
Transportation				
Cars and trucks, new, expenditures on	yr	1648	1999	30r
Cars and trucks, used, expenditures on	yr	1651	1999	30r
Diesel at the pump	gal	1.19	10/99	73s
Gasoline and motor oil purchases	yr	1052	1999	30r
Gasoline before-tax price (cents)	gal	103.20	10/00	43s
Maintenance and repair expenditures	yr	621	1999	30r
Motorcycle license fee	orig	1.50	1999	49s
Motorcycle license fee	renew	1.50	1999	49s
Public transportation, expenditures on	yr	298	1999	30r
Transportation purchases	yr	6738	1999	30r
Vehicle expenses, miscellaneous, purchases	yr	2033	1999	30r
Vehicle insurance payments	yr	696	1999	30r
Vehicle purchases (net outlay)	yr	3354	1999	30r
Vehicle rental, lease expenditures	yr	352	1999	30r
Utilities				
Electrical bill, average	mos	83.66	9/00	9s
Electricity, expenditures on	yr	1115	1999	30r
Electricity cost, average	KWh	6.40	9/00	9s
Water and other public services, expenditures on	yr	298	1999	30r
Weddings				
Wedding (national average cost)		19936	2000	33r
Wedding (regional average total cost)		16293	1997	110r
Attendants' gifts		321	1998	33r
Bridal attendants' apparel (5 persons)		824	2000	33r
Bride's headpiece/veil		173	1998	33r
Bride's wedding dress		859	1998	33r
Clergy, religious facility fee		242	1998	33r
Engagement ring		3177	1998	33r
Flowers		789	1998	33r
Groom's formalwear rental		99	2000	33r
Limousine		410	1998	33r
Marriage license cost		40.00	4/01	35s
Men's formalwear (ushers, best man)		469	2000	33r
Mother of bride apparel		241	2000	33r
Music		866	1998	33r
Photography and videography		1368	1998	33r
Rehearsal dinner		728	1998	33r
Wedding invitations and announcements		341	1998	33r
Wedding reception		7968	2000	33r
Wedding rings (bride and groom)		1060	1998	33r

Rapid City, SD

Item	Per	Value	Date	Ref.
Average annual expenditures	yr	35369	1999	30r
Alcoholic Beverages				
Alcoholic beverage purchases	yr	304	1999	30r
Malt beverages, all types, all sizes, any origin	16 oz	0.93	7/01	11r
Wine, red and white table, all sizes, any origin	liter	7.04	7/01	11r
Appliances				
Major appliances, expenditures on	yr	165	1999	30r
Small appliances, housewares, expenditures on	yr	90	1999	30r
Banking and Money				
Mortgage interest and charges paid	yr	2277	1999	30r
Mortgage principal paid on owned property	yr	1230	1999	30r
Vehicle finance charges paid	yr	328	1999	30r
Charity				
Cash contributions, expenditures	yr	1126	1999	30r
Child Care				
Child raising cost, total, age 0-2	yr	7890	1999	60r
Child raising cost, total, age 3-5	yr	8130	1999	60r
Child raising cost, total, age 6-8	yr	8170	1999	60r
Child raising cost, total, age 9-11	yr	8190	1999	60r
Child raising cost, total, age 12-14	yr	8890	1999	60r
Child raising cost, total, age 15-17	yr	9050	1999	60r
Child's child care and education, age 0-2	yr	1240	1999	60r
Child's child care and education, age 3-5	yr	1370	1999	60r
Child's child care and education, age 6-8	yr	880	1999	60r
Child's child care and education, age 9-11	yr	570	1999	60r
Child's child care and education, age 12-14	yr	420	1999	60r
Child's child care and education, age 15-17	yr	720	1999	60r
Child's clothing, age 0-2	yr	410	1999	60r
Child's clothing, age 3-5	yr	400	1999	60r
Child's clothing, age 6-8	yr	450	1999	60r
Child's clothing, age 9-11	yr	500	1999	60r
Child's clothing, age 12-14	yr	840	1999	60r
Child's clothing, age 15-17	yr	740	1999	60r
Child's food, age 0-2	yr	960	1999	60r
Child's food, age 3-5	yr	1120	1999	60r
Child's food, age 6-8	yr	1430	1999	60r
Child's food, age 9-11	yr	1710	1999	60r
Child's food, age 12-14	yr	1710	1999	60r
Child's food, age 15-17	yr	1920	1999	60r
Child's health care, age 0-2	yr	520	1999	60r
Child's health care, age 3-5	yr	500	1999	60r
Child's health care, age 6-8	yr	570	1999	60r
Child's health care, age 9-11	yr	610	1999	60r
Child's health care, age 12-14	yr	630	1999	60r
Child's health care, age 15-17	yr	650	1999	60r
Child's housing, age 0-2	yr	2860	1999	60r
Child's housing, age 3-5	yr	2840	1999	60r
Child's housing, age 6-8	yr	2800	1999	60r
Child's housing, age 9-11	yr	2650	1999	60r
Child's housing, age 12-14	yr	2840	1999	60r
Child's housing, age 15-17	yr	2440	1999	60r
Child's personal care, reading, age 0-2	yr	880	1999	60r
Child's personal care, reading, age 3-5	yr	900	1999	60r
Child's personal care, reading, age 6-8	yr	930	1999	60r
Child's personal care, reading, age 9-11	yr	970	1999	60r
Child's personal care, reading, age 12-14	yr	1150	1999	60r
Child's personal care, reading, age 15-17	yr	920	1999	60r
Clothing				
Apparel and services purchases	yr	1607	1999	30r
Boys, 2 to 15, expenditures on	yr	91	1999	30r
Children under 2, expenditures on	yr	59	1999	30r
Footwear, expenditures on	yr	285	1999	30r
Girls, 2 to 15, expenditures on	yr	116	1999	30r
Men and boys, expenditures on	yr	433	1999	30r
Men, 16 and over, expenditures on	yr	341	1999	30r
Women, 16 and over, expenditures on	yr	490	1999	30r

Values are in dollars or fractions of dollars. In the column headed *Ref*, references are shown to sources. Each reference is followed by a letter. These refer to the geographical level for which data were reported: s=State, r=Region, and c=City or metro. The abbreviation *ex* is used to mean *except* or *excluding*; *exp* stands for *expenditures*. For other abbreviations and further explanations, please see the Introduction.

Rapid City, SD - continued

Item	Per	Value	Date	Ref.
Communications				
Phone line, single, business, field visit	inst.	47.00	12/97	17s
Phone line, single, business, no field visit	inst.	47.00	12/97	17s
Phone line, single, residence, field visit	inst.	25.00	12/97	17s
Phone line, single, residence, no field visit	inst.	25.00	12/97	17s
Postage and stationery, expenditures on	yr	140	1999	30r
Postal rate, express mail, up to half-pound		12.45	7/01	108r
Postal rate, letter, first class, first ounce		0.34	7/01	108r
Postal rate, letter, two ounces		0.57	7/01	108r
Postal rate, post card		0.21	7/01	108r
Postal rate, priority mail, two pounds		3.95	7/01	108r
Postal rate, priority mail, up to one pound		3.50	7/01	108r
Telephone bill, business, basic rate	mos	36.60	12/97	18c
Telephone bill, residential, basic rate	mos	17.75	12/97	18c
Telephone services, expenditures on	yr	830	1999	30r
Education				
Board, 4-year private college/university	yr	2374	1996	38s
Board, 4-year public college/university	yr	1730	1996	38s
Education expenditures	yr	583	1999	30r
Room, 4-year private college/university	yr	1541	1996	38s
Room, 4-year public college/university	yr	1247	1996	38s
Total cost, 4-year private college/university	yr	13039	1996	38s
Total cost, 4-year public college/university	yr	5619	1996	38s
Tuition, 2-year public college/university, in state	yr	3430	1996	38s
Tuition, 4-year private college/university, in state	yr	9123	1996	38s
Tuition, 4-year public college/university	yr	2642	1996	38s
Energy and Fuels				
Electricity	500 KWhs	46.59	7/01	11r
Fuel oil #2	gal	1.27	7/01	11r
Fuel oil and other fuels, expenditures on	yr	68	1999	30r
Gas, cooking, winter, 10 therms	mos	11.48	2/96	98c
Gas, cooking, winter, 30 therms	mos	19.43	2/96	98c
Gas, cooking, winter, 50 therms	mos	27.38	2/96	98c
Gas, heating, winter, average use	mos	76.80	2/96	98c
Gasoline, unleaded midgrade	gal	1.79	7/01	11r
Gasoline, unleaded premium	gal	1.86	7/01	11r
Gasoline, unleaded regular	gal	1.58	7/01	11r
Natural gas, expenditures on	yr	389	1999	30r
Utility (piped) gas, therm		0.81	7/01	11r
Utility (piped) gas, 40 therms		38.01	7/01	11r
Utility (piped) gas, 100 therms		81.75	7/01	11r
Entertainment				
Entertainment purchases	yr	1984	1999	30r
Fees and admissions paid	yr	444	1999	30r
Television, radios, sound equipment, expenditures on	yr	580	1999	30r
Funerals				
Cosmetology, hair, other preparation		178.32	1/99	78r
Embalming		408.19	1/99	78r
Funeral at funeral home		362.13	1/99	78r
Professional service charges		1375.51	1/99	78r
Transfer of remains to funeral home		155.92	1/99	78r
Visitation/viewing		294.38	1/99	78r
Groceries				
Bacon, sliced	lb	3.15	7/01	11r
Bakery products, expenditures on	yr	281	1999	30r
Bananas	lb	0.48	7/01	11r
Beans, dried, any type, all sizes	lb	0.61	7/01	11r
Beef for stew, boneless	lb	3.08	7/01	11r
Beef, expenditures on	yr	217	1999	30r
Bologna, all beef or mixed	lb	2.52	7/01	11r
Bread, white, pan	lb	1.06	7/01	11r
Broccoli	lb	0.91	7/01	11r
Butter, salted, grade AA, stick	lb	3.04	7/01	11r
Butter, yoghurt, cheese, etc, expenditures on	yr	183	1999	30r
Cereals and bakery product purchases	yr	430	1999	30r

Rapid City, SD - continued

Item	Per	Value	Date	Ref.
Groceries - continued				
Cereals and cereal products, expenditures on	yr	149	1999	30r
Chicken, fresh, whole	lb	1.07	7/01	11r
Chops, boneless,	lb	3.64	7/01	11r
Chuck roast, U.S. choice, boneless	lb	2.47	7/01	11r
Coffee, 100%, ground roast, all sizes	lb	2.69	7/01	11r
Cookies, chocolate chip	lb	2.87	7/01	11r
Dairy product purchases	yr	304	1999	30r
Eggs, expenditures on	yr	26	1999	30r
Eggs, grade A, large	dozen	0.88	7/01	11r
Fats and oils, expenditures on	yr	75	1999	30r
Fish and seafood, expenditures on	yr	72	1999	30r
Food (excl fruit and vegetables), eaten at home, purchases	yr	887	1999	30r
Food cooked on trips, expenditures on	yr	44	1999	30r
Food purchases	yr	4802	1999	30r
Food purchases, eaten away from home	yr	2069	1999	30r
Food purchases, food eaten at home	yr	2733	1999	30r
Fresh fruits, expenditures on	yr	138	1999	30r
Fresh milk and cream, expenditures on	yr	120	1999	30r
Fresh vegetables, expenditures on	yr	126	1999	30r
Grapefruit	lb	0.66	7/01	11r
Grapes, Thompson, seedless	lb	1.64	7/01	11r
Ground beef, 100% beef	lb	1.64	7/01	11r
Ground beef, lean and extra lean	lb	2.16	7/01	11r
Ground chuck, 100% beef	lb	2.13	7/01	11r
Ham, boneless, excl canned	lb	2.62	7/01	11r
Ice cream, prepackaged, bulk, regular	1/2 gal	3.35	7/01	11r
Lemons	lb	1.19	7/01	11r
Lettuce, iceberg	lb	0.73	7/01	11r
Margarine, soft, tubs	lb	0.89	7/01	11r
Meats, poultry, fish, and egg purchases	yr	671	1999	30r
Milk, fresh, whole, fortified	gal	2.71	7/01	11r
Nonalcoholic beverages, expenditures on	yr	239	1999	30r
Oranges, Navel	lb	0.80	7/01	11r
Oranges, Valencia	lb	0.66	7/01	11r
Pears, Anjou	lb	0.93	7/01	11r
Pork chops, center cut, bone-in	lb	3.63	7/01	11r
Pork, expenditures on	yr	150	1999	30r
Potato chips	16 oz	3.52	7/01	11r
Potatoes, frozen, french fried	lb	1.08	7/01	11r
Potatoes, white, all types	lb	0.33	7/01	11r
Poultry, expenditures on	yr	108	1999	30r
Processed fruits, expenditures on	yr	98	1999	30r
Processed vegetables, expenditures on	yr	80	1999	30r
Round roast, U.S. choice, boneless	lb	3.07	7/01	11r
Round steak, graded and ungraded, excl U.S. prime and choice	lb	3.41	7/01	11r
Shortening, vegetable oil blends	lb	1.13	7/01	11r
Spaghetti and macaroni	lb	0.80	7/01	11r
Steak, round, U.S. choice, boneless	lb	3.23	7/01	11r
Steak, T-bone, U.S. choice, bone-in	lb	6.68	7/01	11r
Strawberries, dry pint	12 oz	1.32	7/01	11r
Sugar and other sweets, expenditures on	yr	114	1999	30r
Sugar, white, 33-80 ounce package	lb	0.42	7/01	11r
Sugar, white, all sizes	lb	0.43	7/01	11r
Tobacco products and smoking supplies purchases	yr	331	1999	30r
Tomatoes, field grown	lb	1.46	7/01	11r
Tuna, light, chunk	lb	1.80	7/01	11r
Turkey, frozen, whole	lb	1.15	7/01	11r
Goods and Services				
B&B Japanese maple (acer japonicum)	gal	29.99-169.99	4/00	93r
Boxwood (buxus)	2 gal	18.99-39.99	4/00	93r
Daylily (hemerocallis)	gal	4.99-25.00	4/00	93r
Flat of annuals		11.98-24.99	4/00	93r
Fountain grass (pennisetum)	gal	5.98-12.98	4/00	93r

Values are in dollars or fractions of dollars. In the column headed *Ref*, references are shown to sources. Each reference is followed by a letter. These refer to the geographical level for which data were reported: s=State, r=Region, and c=City or metro. The abbreviation *ex* is used to mean *except* or *excluding*; *exp* stands for expenditures. For other abbreviations and further explanations, please see the Introduction.

Rapid City, SD - continued

Item	Per	Value	Date	Ref.
Goods and Services				
Hanging basket (10 in)		12.99-27.99	4/00	93r
Hardy geranium (geranium)	gal	7.99-9.99	4/00	93r
Hosta (hosta)	gal	6.00-25.00	4/00	93r
Lilac (syrubga vulgaris)	2 gal	14.99-24.99	4/00	93r
Miscellaneous purchases	yr	865	1999	30r
Rhododendron (rhododendron)	2 gal	23.98-42.99	4/00	93r
Sage (salvia)	gal	6.00-9.99	4/00	93r
Wintercreeper euonymus (euonymus fortunei)	2 gal	16.00-169.99	4/00	93r
Hunting license	yr	27.00	4/01	34s
Health Care				
Cardiac catheterization, ave hospital/physician charges		16430	1998	77s
Childbirth, Cesarean delivery		10722	1997	13r
Childbirth, vaginal delivery		6223	1997	13r
Drugs, expenditures on	yr	394	1999	30r
Health care purchases	yr	2048	1999	30r
Health insurance expenditures	yr	978	1999	30r
Hysterectomy, vaginal, ave hospital and physician charges		9890	1998	76s
Medicaid dispensing fee		4.75-5.55	1999	87s
Medical services expenditures	yr	554	1999	30r
Medical supplies, expenditures on	yr	122	1999	30r
Plastic surgery, breast augmentation		3184	2000	7r
Plastic surgery, breast lift		3585	2000	7r
Plastic surgery, facelift		4999	2000	7r
Plastic surgery, hair transplantation		3105	2000	7r
Plastic surgery, lip augmentation		1290	2000	7r
Plastic surgery, lower body lift		8135	2000	7r
Plastic surgery, thigh lift		3839	2000	7r
Household Goods				
Floor coverings, expenditures on	yr	52	1999	30r
Furniture, expenditures on	yr	344	1999	30r
Household furnishings and equipment purchases	yr	1475	1999	30r
Household textiles, expenditures on	yr	109	1999	30r
Laundry and cleaning supplies, expenditures on	yr	134	1999	30r
Housing				
Home, 2200 sq ft, 4-br, 2-bath, 2-car garage, average		132425	2000	47c
Home price, existing, ave		144400	10/00	90r
Home value, median		94000	2001	53s
Household operation expenditures	yr	542	1999	30r
Housekeeping supplies purchases	yr	508	1999	30r
Lodging expenditures	yr	430	1999	30r
Maintenance, repairs, insurance expenditures	yr	853	1999	30r
Monthly rental value of owned home	mos	547	1999	30r
Owned dwellings, expenditures own	yr	4282	1999	30r
Rent expenditures	yr	1558	1999	30r
Rental unit, 1 bedroom, with utilities	mos	431	4/01	41c
Rental unit, 2 bedroom, with utilities	mos	574	4/01	41c
Rental unit, 3 bedroom, with utilities	mos	781	4/01	41c
Rental unit, 4 bedroom, with utilities	mos	945	4/01	41c
Shelter, expenditures on	yr	6270	1999	30r
Insurance and Pensions				
Auto insurance premium	yr	595.41	1999	57s
Life and other personal insurance purchases	yr	387	1999	30r
Pensions and Social Security, expenditures on	yr	2968	1999	30r

Rapid City, SD - continued

Item	Per	Value	Date	Ref.
Legal Fees				
Combination hunting and fishing license	yr	44.00	4/01	34s
Divorce, filing fee		50.00	4/01	35s
Driver's license fee	renew	5.00	1999	48s
Driver's license fee	orig	5.00	1999	48s
Fishing license	yr	21.00	4/01	34s
Personal Goods				
Personal care products and services purchases	yr	385	1999	30r
Personal Services				
Personal services, household, expenditures on	yr	300	1999	30r
Pets				
Pets, toys, and playground equipment, expenditures on	yr	375	1999	30r
Taxes				
Federal income taxes paid	yr	2326	1999	30r
Personal taxes, expenditures on	yr	3223	1999	30r
Property taxes paid	yr	1152	1999	30r
State and local income taxes paid	yr	753	1999	30r
Transportation				
Cars and trucks, new, expenditures on	yr	1280	1999	30r
Cars and trucks, used, expenditures on	yr	1763	1999	30r
Diesel at the pump	gal	1.28	10/99	73s
Gasoline and motor oil purchases	yr	1036	1999	30r
Gasoline before-tax price (cents)	gal	121.10	10/00	43s
Maintenance and repair expenditures	yr	594	1999	30r
Public transportation, expenditures on	yr	341	1999	30r
Transportation purchases	yr	6617	1999	30r
Vehicle expenses, miscellaneous, purchases	yr	2159	1999	30r
Vehicle insurance payments	yr	701	1999	30r
Vehicle purchases (net outlay)	yr	3081	1999	30r
Vehicle rental, lease expenditures	yr	536	1999	30r
Travel				
Hotel room	night	51.17	2/01	94s
Utilities				
Electrical bill, average	mos	64.08	9/00	9s
Electricity, expenditures on	yr	841	1999	30r
Electricity, summer, 250 KWh	mos	26.95	2/96	96c
Electricity, summer, 500 KWh	mos	46.40	2/96	96c
Electricity, summer, 750 KWh	mos	65.86	2/96	96c
Electricity, summer, 1000 KWh	mos	85.30	2/96	96c
Electricity cost, average	KWh	6.40	9/00	9s
Utilities, fuels, and public services purchased	yr	2401	1999	30r
Water and other public services, expenditures on	yr	273	1999	30r
Weddings				
Wedding (national average cost)		19936	2000	33r
Wedding (regional average total cost)		16195	1997	110r
Attendants' gifts		321	1998	33r
Bridal attendants' apparel (5 persons)		824	2000	33r
Bride's headpiece/veil		173	1998	33r
Bride's wedding dress		859	1998	33r
Clergy, religious facility fee		242	1998	33r
Engagement ring		3177	1998	33r
Flowers		789	1998	33r
Groom's formalwear rental		99	2000	33r
Limousine		410	1998	33r
Marriage license cost		40.00	4/01	35s
Men's formalwear (ushers, best man)		469	2000	33r
Mother of bride apparel		241	2000	33r
Music		866	1998	33r
Photography and videography		1368	1998	33r
Rehearsal dinner		728	1998	33r
Wedding invitations and announcements		341	1998	33r
Wedding reception		7968	2000	33r
Wedding rings (bride and groom)		1060	1998	33r

Values are in dollars or fractions of dollars. In the column headed *Ref*, references are shown to sources. Each reference is followed by a letter. These refer to the geographical level for which data were reported: s=State, r=Region, and c=City or metro. The abbreviation *ex* is used to mean *except* or *excluding*; *exp* stands for *expenditures*. For other abbreviations and further explanations, please see the Introduction.

Reading, PA

Item	Per	Value	Date	Ref.
Average annual expenditures	yr	37971	1999	30r
Alcoholic Beverages				
Alcoholic beverage purchases	yr	368	1999	30r
Wine, red and white table, all sizes, any origin	liter	9.64	7/01	11r
Appliances				
Major appliances, expenditures on	yr	194	1999	30r
Small appliances, housewares, expenditures on	yr	93	1999	30r
Banking and Money				
Mortgage interest and charges paid	yr	2622	1999	30r
Mortgage principal paid on owned property	yr	1262	1999	30r
Vehicle finance charges paid	yr	240	1999	30r
Charity				
Cash contributions, expenditures	yr	1001	1999	30r
Child Care				
Child raising cost, total, age 0-2	yr	8670	1999	60r
Child raising cost, total, age 3-5	yr	8910	1999	60r
Child raising cost, total, age 6-8	yr	9040	1999	60r
Child raising cost, total, age 9-11	yr	9100	1999	60r
Child raising cost, total, age 12-14	yr	9890	1999	60r
Child raising cost, total, age 15-17	yr	10010	1999	60r
Child's child care and education, age 0-2	yr	1070	1999	60r
Child's child care and education, age 3-5	yr	1190	1999	60r
Child's child care and education, age 6-8	yr	740	1999	60r
Child's child care and education, age 9-11	yr	470	1999	60r
Child's child care and education, age 12-14	yr	350	1999	60r
Child's child care and education, age 15-17	yr	590	1999	60r
Child's clothing, age 0-2	yr	480	1999	60r
Child's clothing, age 3-5	yr	470	1999	60r
Child's clothing, age 6-8	yr	520	1999	60r
Child's clothing, age 9-11	yr	570	1999	60r
Child's clothing, age 12-14	yr	970	1999	60r
Child's clothing, age 15-17	yr	870	1999	60r
Child's food, age 0-2	yr	1130	1999	60r
Child's food, age 3-5	yr	1290	1999	60r
Child's food, age 6-8	yr	1640	1999	60r
Child's food, age 9-11	yr	1930	1999	60r
Child's food, age 12-14	yr	1940	1999	60r
Child's food, age 15-17	yr	2150	1999	60r
Child's health care, age 0-2	yr	550	1999	60r
Child's health care, age 3-5	yr	530	1999	60r
Child's health care, age 6-8	yr	610	1999	60r
Child's health care, age 9-11	yr	650	1999	60r
Child's health care, age 12-14	yr	660	1999	60r
Child's health care, age 15-17	yr	690	1999	60r
Child's housing, age 0-2	yr	3555	1999	60r
Child's housing, age 3-5	yr	3530	1999	60r
Child's housing, age 6-8	yr	3490	1999	60r
Child's housing, age 9-11	yr	3340	1999	60r
Child's housing, age 12-14	yr	3530	1999	60r
Child's housing, age 15-17	yr	3140	1999	60r
Child's personal care, reading, age 0-2	yr	920	1999	60r
Child's personal care, reading, age 3-5	yr	950	1999	60r
Child's personal care, reading, age 6-8	yr	980	1999	60r
Child's personal care, reading, age 9-11	yr	1020	1999	60r
Child's personal care, reading, age 12-14	yr	1190	1999	60r
Child's personal care, reading, age 15-17	yr	970	1999	60r
Clothing				
Apparel and services purchases	yr	1831	1999	30r
Boys, 2 to 15, expenditures on	yr	92	1999	30r
Children under 2, expenditures on	yr	63	1999	30r
Footwear, expenditures on	yr	300	1999	30r
Girls, 2 to 15, expenditures on	yr	101	1999	30r
Men and boys, expenditures on	yr	446	1999	30r
Men, 16 and over, expenditures on	yr	354	1999	30r
Women, 16 and over, expenditures on	yr	584	1999	30r
Communications				
Cable modem installation, Adelphi		54.90	6/99	103s

Reading, PA - continued

Item	Per	Value	Date	Ref.
Communications - continued				
Cable modem installation, Comcast		95.00	6/99	103s
Cable modem rate, cable subscriber, Adelphi	mos	34.95	6/99	103s
Cable modem rate, cable subscriber, Comcast	mos	39.95	6/99	103s
Cable modem rate, non-cable subscriber, Adelphi	mos	44.95	6/99	103s
Cable modem rate, non-cable subscriber, Comcast	mos	49.95	6/99	103s
Phone line, single, business, field visit	inst.	75.00	12/97	17s
Phone line, single, business, no field visit	inst.	75.00	12/97	17s
Phone line, single, residence, field visit	inst.	40.00	12/97	17s
Phone line, single, residence, no field visit	inst.	40.00	12/97	17s
Postage and stationery, expenditures on	yr	138	1999	30r
Postal rate, express mail, up to half-pound		12.45	7/01	108r
Postal rate, letter, first class, first ounce		0.34	7/01	108r
Postal rate, letter, two ounces		0.57	7/01	108r
Postal rate, post card		0.21	7/01	108r
Postal rate, priority mail, two pounds		3.95	7/01	108r
Postal rate, priority mail, up to one pound		3.50	7/01	108r
Telephone services, expenditures on	yr	830	1999	30r
Education				
Board, 4-year private college/university	yr	2822	1996	38s
Board, 4-year public college/university	yr	2174	1996	38s
Education expenditures	yr	877	1999	30r
Room, 4-year private college/university	yr	2943	1996	38s
Room, 4-year public college/university	yr	2227	1996	38s
Total cost, 4-year private college/university	yr	19876	1996	38s
Total cost, 4-year public college/university	yr	9124	1996	38s
Tuition, 2-year public college/university, in state	yr	1909	1996	38s
Tuition, 4-year private college/university, in state	yr	14111	1996	38s
Tuition, 4-year public college/university	yr	4723	1996	38s
Energy and Fuels				
Electricity	KWh	0.12	7/01	11r
Fuel oil #2	gal	1.31	7/01	11r
Fuel oil and other fuels, expenditures on	yr	207	1999	30r
Gas, natural, commercial rate	1000 cf	5.96	11/00	88s
Gasoline, all types	gal	1.80	7/01	11r
Gasoline, unleaded midgrade	gal	1.85	7/01	11r
Gasoline, unleaded premium	gal	1.91	7/01	11r
Gasoline, unleaded regular	gal	1.71	7/01	11r
Natural gas, expenditures on	yr	368	1999	30r
Utility (piped) gas, therm		1.08	7/01	11r
Utility (piped) gas, 40 therms		50.87	7/01	11r
Utility (piped) gas, 100 therms		111.06	7/01	11r
Entertainment				
Entertainment purchases	yr	1821	1999	30r
Fees and admissions paid	yr	511	1999	30r
Television, radios, sound equipment, expenditures on	yr	650	1999	30r
Funerals				
Total cost of funeral		5813.50	1/99	78r
Acknowledgement cards		28.32	1/99	78r
Casket		2082.20	1/99	78r
Cosmetology, hair, other preparation		169.59	1/99	78r
Embalming		465.60	1/99	78r
Funeral at funeral home		339.56	1/99	78r
Hearse (local)		183.96	1/99	78r
Professional service charges		1157.85	1/99	78r
Service car/van		100.41	1/99	78r
Transfer of remains to funeral home		158.66	1/99	78r
Vault		766.31	1/99	78r
Visitation/viewing		361.04	1/99	78r
Groceries				
Apples, red delicious	lb	0.95	7/01	11r
Bacon, sliced	lb	3.44	7/01	11r
Bakery products, expenditures on	yr	310	1999	30r
Bananas	lb	0.55	7/01	11r

Values are in dollars or fractions of dollars. In the column headed *Ref*, references are shown to sources. Each reference is followed by a letter. These refer to the geographical level for which data were reported: s=State, r=Region, and c=City or metro. The abbreviation *ex* is used to mean *except* or *excluding*; *exp* stands for *expenditures*. For other abbreviations and further explanations, please see the Introduction.

Reading, PA - continued

Item	Per	Value	Date	Ref.
Groceries				
Beef, expenditures on	yr	236	1999	30r
Bread, white, pan	lb	1.09	7/01	11r
Butter, yoghurt, cheese, etc, expenditures on	yr	214	1999	30r
Cereals and bakery product purchases	yr	474	1999	30r
Cereals and cereal products, expenditures on	yr	164	1999	30r
Chicken legs, bone-in	lb	1.23	7/01	11r
Chicken, fresh, whole	lb	1.13	7/01	11r
Chuck roast, U.S. choice, boneless	lb	2.79	7/01	11r
Coffee, 100%, ground roast, all sizes	lb	3.40	7/01	11r
Dairy product purchases	yr	342	1999	30r
Eggs, expenditures on	yr	34	1999	30r
Eggs, grade A, large	dozen	0.82	7/01	11r
Fats and oils, expenditures on	yr	80	1999	30r
Fish and seafood, expenditures on	yr	123	1999	30r
Food (excl fruit and vegetables), eaten at home, purchases	yr	838	1999	30r
Food cooked on trips, expenditures on	yr	48	1999	30r
Food purchases	yr	5314	1999	30r
Food purchases, eaten away from home	yr	2313	1999	30r
Food purchases, food eaten at home	yr	3001	1999	30r
Fresh fruits, expenditures on	yr	169	1999	30r
Fresh milk and cream, expenditures on	yr	128	1999	30r
Fresh vegetables, expenditures on	yr	164	1999	30r
Grapefruit	lb	0.67	7/01	11r
Grapes, Thompson, seedless	lb	2.18	7/01	11r
Ground beef, lean and extra lean	lb	2.66	7/01	11r
Ground chuck, 100% beef	lb	2.04	7/01	11r
Lettuce, iceberg	lb	0.76	7/01	11r
Meats, poultry, fish, and egg purchases	yr	808	1999	30r
Nonalcoholic beverages, expenditures on	yr	225	1999	30r
Orange juice, frozen concentrate	16 oz	1.88	7/01	11r
Oranges, Navel	lb	0.79	7/01	11r
Oranges, Valencia	lb	0.56	7/01	11r
Peaches	lb	1.16	7/01	11r
Peanut butter, creamy, all sizes	lb	2.01	7/01	11r
Pears, Anjou	lb	1.16	7/01	11r
Pork chops, center cut, bone-in	lb	3.57	7/01	11r
Pork, expenditures on	yr	146	1999	30r
Potato chips	16 oz	3.37	7/01	11r
Potatoes, white, all types	lb	0.42	7/01	11r
Poultry, expenditures on	yr	158	1999	30r
Processed fruits, expenditures on	yr	124	1999	30r
Processed vegetables, expenditures on	yr	82	1999	30r
Round roast, U.S. choice, boneless	lb	3.04	7/01	11r
Spaghetti and macaroni	lb	1.04	7/01	11r
Steak, sirloin, U.S. choice, boneless	lb	5.39	7/01	11r
Strawberries, dry pint	12 oz	1.51	7/01	11r
Sugar and other sweets, expenditures on	yr	110	1999	30r
Sugar, white, 33-80 ounce package	lb	0.46	7/01	11r
Sugar, white, all sizes	lb	0.47	7/01	11r
Tobacco products and smoking supplies purchases	yr	309	1999	30r
Yogurt, natural, fruit flavored	8 oz	0.79	7/01	11r
Goods and Services				
B&B Japanese maple (acer japonicum)	gal	38.99-125.00	4/00	93r
Boxwood (buxus)	2 gal	15.99-49.95	4/00	93r
Daylily (hemerocallis)	gal	4.95	4/00	93r
Flat of annuals		8.00-14.99	4/00	93r
Fountain grass (pennisetum)	gal	6.99-9.99	4/00	93r
Hanging basket (10 in)		12.95-19.99	4/00	93r
Hardy geranium (geranium)	gal	6.95-7.99	4/00	93r
Hosta (hosta)	gal	4.95	4/00	93r
Lilac (syrubga vulgaris)	2 gal	17.99-74.95	4/00	93r
Miscellaneous purchases	yr	872	1999	30r

Reading, PA - continued

Item	Per	Value	Date	Ref.
Goods and Services - continued				
Rhododendron (rhododendron)	2 gal	23.99-54.95	4/00	93r
Sage (salvia)	gal	6.95-7.99	4/00	93r
Wintercreeper euonymus (euonymus fortunei)	2 gal	14.99-23.95	4/00	93r
Hunting license	yr	20.00	4/01	34s
Health Care				
Cardiac catheterization, ave hospital/physician charges		13870	1998	77s
Childbirth, Cesarean delivery		14716	1997	13r
Childbirth, vaginal delivery		8541	1997	13r
Drugs, expenditures on	yr	296	1999	30r
Health care purchases	yr	1788	1999	30r
Health insurance expenditures	yr	875	1999	30r
Hysterectomy, laproscopically-assisted, ave hospital/physician charges		14760	1998	76s
Hysterectomy, vaginal, ave hospital and physician charges		9270	1998	76s
Medicaid dispensing fee		4.00	1999	87s
Medical services expenditures	yr	516	1999	30r
Medical supplies, expenditures on	yr	102	1999	30r
Plastic surgery, breast augmentation		4232	2000	7r
Plastic surgery, breast lift		4605	2000	7r
Plastic surgery, facelift		6964	2000	7r
Plastic surgery, hair transplantation		4193	2000	7r
Plastic surgery, lip augmentation		1675	2000	7r
Plastic surgery, lower body lift		6611	2000	7r
Plastic surgery, thigh lift		4751	2000	7r
Household Goods				
Floor coverings, expenditures on	yr	59	1999	30r
Furniture, expenditures on	yr	388	1999	30r
Household furnishings and equipment purchases	yr	1567	1999	30r
Household textiles, expenditures on	yr	112	1999	30r
Laundry and cleaning supplies, expenditures on	yr	104	1999	30r
Housing				
Home, 2200 sq ft, 4-br, 2-bath, 2-car garage, average		142874	2000	47c
Home price, existing, ave		180800	10/00	90r
Home value, median		115000	2001	53s
Household operation expenditures	yr	581	1999	30r
Housekeeping supplies purchases	yr	474	1999	30r
Lodging expenditures	yr	550	1999	30r
Maintenance, repairs, insurance expenditures	yr	835	1999	30r
Monthly rental value of owned home	mos	663	1999	30r
Owned dwellings, expenditures own	yr	5209	1999	30r
Rent expenditures	yr	2390	1999	30r
Rental unit, 1 bedroom, with utilities	mos	448	4/01	41c
Rental unit, 2 bedroom, with utilities	mos	553	4/01	41c
Rental unit, 3 bedroom, with utilities	mos	691	4/01	41c
Rental unit, 4 bedroom, with utilities	mos	779	4/01	41c
Shelter, expenditures on	yr	8149	1999	30r
Insurance and Pensions				
Life and other personal insurance purchases	yr	424	1999	30r
Pensions and Social Security, expenditures on	yr	3037	1999	30r
Legal Fees				
Divorce, filing fee		65.00	4/01	35s
Driver's license fee	orig	29.00	1999	48s
Driver's license fee	renew	24.00	1999	48s
Fishing license	yr	17.00	4/01	34s
Personal Goods				
Personal care products and services purchases	yr	399	1999	30r

Values are in dollars or fractions of dollars. In the column headed *Ref*, references are shown to sources. Each reference is followed by a letter. These refer to the geographical level for which data were reported: s=State, r=Region, and c=City or metro. The abbreviation *ex* is used to mean *except* or *excluding*; *exp* stands for *expenditures*. For other abbreviations and further explanations, please see the Introduction.

Reading, PA - continued

Item	Per	Value	Date	Ref.
Personal Services				
Personal services, household, expenditures on	yr	271	1999	30r
Pets				
Pets, toys, and playground equipment, expenditures on	yr	325	1999	30r
Taxes				
Federal income taxes paid	yr	2606	1999	30r
Personal taxes, expenditures on	yr	3567	1999	30r
Property taxes paid	yr	1752	1999	30r
State and local income taxes paid	yr	694	1999	30r
Transportation				
Bus fare, one-way	trip	1.10	2000	1c
Cars and trucks, new, expenditures on	yr	1496	1999	30r
Cars and trucks, used, expenditures on	yr	1251	1999	30r
Diesel at the pump	gal	1.31	10/99	73s
Gasoline and motor oil purchases	yr	901	1999	30r
Gasoline before-tax price (cents)	gal	106.60	10/00	43s
Maintenance and repair expenditures	yr	618	1999	30r
Public transportation, expenditures on	yr	575	1999	30r
Transportation purchases	yr	6503	1999	30r
Vehicle expenses, miscellaneous, purchases	yr	2266	1999	30r
Vehicle insurance payments	yr	824	1999	30r
Vehicle purchases (net outlay)	yr	2761	1999	30r
Vehicle rental, lease expenditures	yr	584	1999	30r
Utilities				
Electrical bill, average	mos	69.16	9/00	9s
Electricity, expenditures on	yr	837	1999	30r
Electricity, summer, 250 KWh	mos	26.75	2/96	96c
Electricity, summer, 500 KWh	mos	46.88	2/96	96c
Electricity, summer, 750 KWh	mos	67.00	2/96	96c
Electricity, summer, 1000 KWh	mos	87.13	2/96	96c
Electricity cost, average	KWh	5.08	9/00	9s
Utilities, fuels, and public services purchased	yr	2457	1999	30r
Water and other public services, expenditures on	yr	215	1999	30r
Weddings				
Wedding (national average cost)		19936	2000	33r
Wedding (regional average total cost)		29454	1997	110r
Attendants' gifts		321	1998	33r
Bridal attendants' apparel (5 persons)		824	2000	33r
Bride's headpiece/veil		173	1998	33r
Bride's wedding dress		859	1998	33r
Clergy, religious facility fee		242	1998	33r
Engagement ring		3177	1998	33r
Flowers		789	1998	33r
Groom's formalwear rental		99	2000	33r
Limousine		410	1998	33r
Marriage license cost		25.00-40.00	4/01	35s
Men's formalwear (ushers, best man)		469	2000	33r
Mother of bride apparel		241	2000	33r
Music		866	1998	33r
Photography and videography		1368	1998	33r
Rehearsal dinner		728	1998	33r
Wedding invitations and announcements		341	1998	33r
Wedding reception		7968	2000	33r
Wedding rings (bride and groom)		1060	1998	33r

Redding, CA

Item	Per	Value	Date	Ref.
Average annual expenditures	yr	40662	1999	30r
Alcoholic Beverages				
Alcoholic beverage purchases	yr	372	1999	30r
Malt beverages, all types, all sizes, any origin	16 oz	0.94	7/01	11r
Wine, red and white table, all sizes, any origin	liter	6.00	7/01	11r

Redding, CA - continued

Item	Per	Value	Date	Ref.
Appliances				
Major appliances, expenditures on	yr	167	1999	30r
Small appliances, housewares, expenditures on	yr	105	1999	30r
Banking and Money				
Mortgage interest and charges paid	yr	3368	1999	30r
Mortgage principal paid on owned property	yr	1677	1999	30r
Vehicle finance charges paid	yr	311	1999	30r
Charity				
Cash contributions, expenditures	yr	1344	1999	30r
Child Care				
Child raising cost, total, age 0-2	yr	9140	1999	60r
Child raising cost, total, age 3-5	yr	9370	1999	60r
Child raising cost, total, age 6-8	yr	9450	1999	60r
Child raising cost, total, age 9-11	yr	9470	1999	60r
Child raising cost, total, age 12-14	yr	10170	1999	60r
Child raising cost, total, age 15-17	yr	10360	1999	60r
Child's child care and education, age 0-2	yr	1250	1999	60r
Child's child care and education, age 3-5	yr	1380	1999	60r
Child's child care and education, age 6-8	yr	890	1999	60r
Child's child care and education, age 9-11	yr	580	1999	60r
Child's child care and education, age 12-14	yr	430	1999	60r
Child's child care and education, age 15-17	yr	730	1999	60r
Child's clothing, age 0-2	yr	430	1999	60r
Child's clothing, age 3-5	yr	420	1999	60r
Child's clothing, age 6-8	yr	470	1999	60r
Child's clothing, age 9-11	yr	520	1999	60r
Child's clothing, age 12-14	yr	870	1999	60r
Child's clothing, age 15-17	yr	770	1999	60r
Child's food, age 0-2	yr	1120	1999	60r
Child's food, age 3-5	yr	1280	1999	60r
Child's food, age 6-8	yr	1640	1999	60r
Child's food, age 9-11	yr	1930	1999	60r
Child's food, age 12-14	yr	1940	1999	60r
Child's food, age 15-17	yr	2150	1999	60r
Child's health care, age 0-2	yr	490	1999	60r
Child's health care, age 3-5	yr	470	1999	60r
Child's health care, age 6-8	yr	530	1999	60r
Child's health care, age 9-11	yr	570	1999	60r
Child's health care, age 12-14	yr	580	1999	60r
Child's health care, age 15-17	yr	610	1999	60r
Child's housing, age 0-2	yr	3630	1999	60r
Child's housing, age 3-5	yr	3610	1999	60r
Child's housing, age 6-8	yr	3570	1999	60r
Child's housing, age 9-11	yr	3410	1999	60r
Child's housing, age 12-14	yr	3600	1999	60r
Child's housing, age 15-17	yr	3210	1999	60r
Child's personal care, reading, age 0-2	yr	1040	1999	60r
Child's personal care, reading, age 3-5	yr	1060	1999	60r
Child's personal care, reading, age 6-8	yr	1090	1999	60r
Child's personal care, reading, age 9-11	yr	1130	1999	60r
Child's personal care, reading, age 12-14	yr	1300	1999	60r
Child's personal care, reading, age 15-17	yr	1080	1999	60r
Clothing				
Apparel and services purchases	yr	1863	1999	30r
Boys, 2 to 15, expenditures on	yr	80	1999	30r
Children under 2, expenditures on	yr	74	1999	30r
Footwear, expenditures on	yr	307	1999	30r
Girls, 2 to 15, expenditures on	yr	101	1999	30r
Men and boys, expenditures on	yr	443	1999	30r
Men, 16 and over, expenditures on	yr	363	1999	30r
Women, 16 and over, expenditures on	yr	594	1999	30r
Communications				
Cable modem installation, AT&T-BIS		150.00	6/99	103s
Cable modem installation, Charter		99.00-169.00	6/99	103s
Cable modem installation, Comcast		95.00	6/99	103s
Cable modem installation, Cox		99.00-174.95	6/99	103s
Cable modem installation, Media One		100.00	6/99	103s

Values are in dollars or fractions of dollars. In the column headed *Ref*, references are shown to sources. Each reference is followed by a letter. These refer to the geographical level for which data were reported: s=State, r=Region, and c=City or metro. The abbreviation *ex* is used to mean *except* or *excluding*; *exp* stands for expenditures. For other abbreviations and further explanations, please see the Introduction.

Redding, CA - continued

Item	Per	Value	Date	Ref.
Communications				
Cable modem installation, Time Warner		75.00-225.00	6/99	103s
Cable modem rate, cable subscriber, AT&T-BIS	mos	39.95	6/99	103s
Cable modem rate, cable subscriber, Charter	mos	49.95-79.95	6/99	103s
Cable modem rate, cable subscriber, Comcast	mos	39.95	6/99	103s
Cable modem rate, cable subscriber, Cox	mos	29.95-44.95	6/99	103s
Cable modem rate, cable subscriber, Media One	mos	34.95-39.95	6/99	103s
Cable modem rate, cable subscriber, Time Warner	mos	39.95-49.95	6/99	103s
Cable modem rate, non-cable subscriber, Charter	mos	59.95-89.95	6/99	103s
Cable modem rate, non-cable subscriber, Comcast	mos	49.95	6/99	103s
Cable modem rate, non-cable subscriber, Cox	mos	42.95-54.95	6/99	103s
Cable modem rate, non-cable subscriber, Media One	mos	49.95	6/99	103s
Cable modem rate, non-cable subscriber, Time Warner	mos	39.95-54.95	6/99	103s
Phone line, single, business, field visit	inst.	70.75	12/97	17s
Phone line, single, business, no field visit	inst.	70.75	12/97	17s
Phone line, single, residence, field visit	inst.	34.75	12/97	17s
Phone line, single, residence, no field visit	inst.	34.75	12/97	17s
Postage and stationery, expenditures on	yr	150	1999	30r
Postal rate, express mail, up to half-pound		12.45	7/01	108r
Postal rate, letter, first class, first ounce		0.34	7/01	108r
Postal rate, letter, two ounces		0.57	7/01	108r
Postal rate, post card		0.21	7/01	108r
Postal rate, priority mail, two pounds		3.95	7/01	108r
Postal rate, priority mail, up to one pound		3.50	7/01	108r
Telephone services, expenditures on	yr	825	1999	30r
Education				
Board, 4-year private college/university	yr	2970	1996	38s
Board, 4-year public college/university	yr	2516	1996	38s
Education expenditures	yr	676	1999	30r
Room, 4-year private college/university	yr	3196	1996	38s
Room, 4-year public college/university	yr	3031	1996	38s
Total cost, 4-year private college/university	yr	20143	1996	38s
Total cost, 4-year public college/university	yr	8213	1996	38s
Tuition, 2-year public college/university, in state	yr	362	1996	38s
Tuition, 4-year private college/university, in state	yr	13977	1996	38s
Tuition, 4-year public college/university	yr	2666	1996	38s
Energy and Fuels				
Electricity	KWh	0.11	7/01	11r
Electricity	500 KWhs	48.23	7/01	11r
Fuel oil and other fuels, expenditures on	yr	35	1999	30r
Gas, natural, commercial rate	1000 cf	8.74	11/00	88s
Gasoline, all types	gal	1.91	7/01	11r
Gasoline, unleaded premium	gal	2.05	7/01	11r
Gasoline, unleaded regular	gal	1.83	7/01	11r
Natural gas, expenditures on	yr	255	1999	30r
Utility (piped) gas, therm		0.98	7/01	11r
Utility (piped) gas, 40 therms		40.74	7/01	11r
Utility (piped) gas, 100 therms		96.80	7/01	11r
Entertainment				
Entertainment purchases	yr	2139	1999	30r
Fees and admissions paid	yr	545	1999	30r
Television, radios, sound equipment, expenditures on	yr	624	1999	30r
Funerals				
Total cost of funeral		5401.08	1/99	78r
Acknowledgement cards		33.64	1/99	78r

Redding, CA - continued

Item	Per	Value	Date	Ref.
Funerals - continued				
Casket		2170.43	1/99	78r
Cosmetology, hair, other preparation		136.32	1/99	78r
Embalming		319.13	1/99	78r
Funeral at funeral home		370.21	1/99	78r
Hearse (local)		161.04	1/99	78r
Professional service charges		963.15	1/99	78r
Service car/van		133.99	1/99	78r
Transfer of remains to funeral home		159.82	1/99	78r
Vault		778.07	1/99	78r
Visitation/viewing		175.28	1/99	78r
Groceries				
Apples, red delicious	lb	0.84	7/01	11r
Bacon, sliced	lb	3.38	7/01	11r
Bakery products, expenditures on	yr	299	1999	30r
Bananas	lb	0.54	7/01	11r
Beans, dried, any type, all sizes	lb	0.76	7/01	11r
Beef, expenditures on	yr	222	1999	30r
Bread, white, pan	lb	0.99	7/01	11r
Butter, yoghurt, cheese, etc, expenditures on	yr	211	1999	30r
Cereals and bakery product purchases	yr	466	1999	30r
Cereals and cereal products, expenditures on	yr	168	1999	30r
Chicken breast, bone-in	lb	2.45	7/01	11r
Chicken, fresh, whole	lb	1.19	7/01	11r
Chops, boneless,	lb	4.00	7/01	11r
Chuck roast, graded and ungraded, excl U.S. prime and choice	lb	2.55	7/01	11r
Coffee, 100%, ground roast, all sizes	lb	3.80	7/01	11r
Cookies, chocolate chip	lb	2.83	7/01	11r
Dairy product purchases	yr	341	1999	30r
Eggs, expenditures on	yr	39	1999	30r
Eggs, grade AA, large	dozen	1.23	7/01	11r
Fats and oils, expenditures on	yr	88	1999	30r
Fish and seafood, expenditures on	yr	121	1999	30r
Food (excl fruit and vegetables), eaten at home, purchases	yr	1001	1999	30r
Food cooked on trips, expenditures on	yr	64	1999	30r
Food purchases	yr	5312	1999	30r
Food purchases, eaten away from home	yr	2180	1999	30r
Food purchases, food eaten at home	yr	3132	1999	30r
Fresh fruits, expenditures on	yr	186	1999	30r
Fresh milk and cream, expenditures on	yr	130	1999	30r
Fresh vegetables, expenditures on	yr	177	1999	30r
Grapefruit	lb	0.68	7/01	11r
Grapes, Thompson, seedless	lb	2.42	7/01	11r
Ground beef, lean and extra lean	lb	2.46	7/01	11r
Ice cream, prepackaged, bulk, regular	1/2 gal	3.62	7/01	11r
Lettuce, iceberg	lb	0.63	7/01	11r
Meats, poultry, fish, and egg purchases	yr	761	1999	30r
Milk, fresh, low fat	gal	2.80	7/01	11r
Milk, fresh, whole, fortified	gal	2.88	7/01	11r
Nonalcoholic beverages, expenditures on	yr	258	1999	30r
Oranges, Navel	lb	0.97	7/01	11r
Oranges, Valencia	lb	0.43	7/01	11r
Peaches	lb	1.38	7/01	11r
Peanut butter, creamy, all sizes	lb	2.14	7/01	11r
Pork chops, center cut, bone-in	lb	3.83	7/01	11r
Pork, expenditures on	yr	141	1999	30r
Potatoes, white, all types	lb	0.37	7/01	11r
Poultry, expenditures on	yr	146	1999	30r
Processed fruits, expenditures on	yr	118	1999	30r
Processed vegetables, expenditures on	yr	81	1999	30r
Round roast, graded and ungraded, excl U.S. prime and choice	lb	3.07	7/01	11r
Round roast, U.S. choice, boneless	lb	3.37	7/01	11r
Round steak, graded and ungraded, excl U.S. prime and choice	lb	3.51	7/01	11r
Sirloin steak, graded and ungraded, excl U.S. prime and choice	lb	4.67	7/01	11r
Steak, sirloin, U.S. choice, boneless	lb	6.20	7/01	11r
Strawberries, dry pint	12 oz	1.79	7/01	11r
Sugar and other sweets, expenditures on	yr	124	1999	30r

Values are in dollars or fractions of dollars. In the column headed *Ref*, references are shown to sources. Each reference is followed by a letter. These refer to the geographical level for which data were reported: s=State, r=Region, and c=City or metro. The abbreviation *ex* is used to mean *except* or *excluding*; *exp* stands for expenditures. For other abbreviations and further explanations, please see the Introduction.

Redding, CA - continued

Item	Per	Value	Date	Ref.
Groceries				
Sugar, white, all sizes	lb	0.46	7/01	11r
Tobacco products and smoking supplies purchases	yr	217	1999	30r
Tomatoes, field grown	lb	1.17	7/01	11r
Tuna, light, chunk	lb	2.05	7/01	11r
Goods and Services				
B&B Japanese maple (acer japonicum)	gal	39.99	4/00	93r
Boxwood (buxus)	2 gal	14.99-24.99	4/00	93r
Christmas tree, noble fir		40-60	2000	65s
Daylilly (hemerocallis)	gal	6.99-8.99	4/00	93r
Flat of annuals		16.68	4/00	93r
Fountain grass (pennisetum)	gal	7.99-11.99	4/00	93r
Hanging basket (10 in)		29.99	4/00	93r
Hardy geranium (geranium)	gal	6.99-11.99	4/00	93r
Hosta (hosta)	gal	6.99-18.99	4/00	93r
Lilac (syrubga vulgaris)	2 gal	14.99-17.99	4/00	93r
Miscellaneous purchases	yr	1070	1999	30r
Rhododendron (rhododendron)	2 gal	14.99	4/00	93r
Sage (salvia)	gal	6.99	4/00	93r
Wintercreeper euonymus (euonymus fortunei)	2 gal	14.99-22.99	4/00	93r
Hunting license	yr	29.95	4/01	34s
Health Care				
Cardiac catheterization, ave hospital/ physician charges		24000	1998	77s
Childbirth, Cesarean delivery		11587	1997	13r
Childbirth, vaginal delivery		6725	1997	13r
Drugs, expenditures on	yr	309	1999	30r
Health care purchases	yr	1869	1999	30r
Health insurance expenditures	yr	868	1999	30r
Hysterectomy, laproscopically-assisted, ave hospital/physician charges		20760	1998	76s
Hysterectomy, vaginal, ave hospital and physician charges		14570	1998	76s
Medicaid dispensing fee		4.05	1999	87s
Medical services expenditures	yr	580	1999	30r
Medical supplies, expenditures on	yr	112	1999	30r
Household Goods				
Floor coverings, expenditures on	yr	49	1999	30r
Furniture, expenditures on	yr	444	1999	30r
Household furnishings and equipment purchases	yr	1768	1999	30r
Household textiles, expenditures on	yr	141	1999	30r
Laundry and cleaning supplies, expenditures on	yr	128	1999	30r
Housing				
Home price, existing, ave		239400	10/00	90r
Home value, median		215000	2001	53s
Household operation expenditures	yr	781	1999	30r
Housekeeping supplies purchases	yr	513	1999	30r
Lodging expenditures	yr	575	1999	30r
Maintenance, repairs, insurance expenditures	yr	939	1999	30r
Monthly rental value of owned home	mos	662	1999	30r
Owned dwellings, expenditures own	yr	5231	1999	30r
Rent expenditures	yr	2709	1999	30r
Rental unit, 1 bedroom, with utilities	mos	429	4/01	41c
Rental unit, 2 bedroom, with utilities	mos	538	4/01	41c
Rental unit, 3 bedroom, with utilities	mos	747	4/01	41c
Rental unit, 4 bedroom, with utilities	mos	880	4/01	41c
Shelter, expenditures on	yr	8516	1999	30r
Insurance and Pensions				
Life and other personal insurance purchases	yr	355	1999	30r

Redding, CA - continued

Item	Per	Value	Date	Ref.
Insurance and Pensions - continued				
Pensions and Social Security, expenditures on	yr	3636	1999	30r
Legal Fees				
Divorce, filing fee		182.00	4/01	35s
Driver's license fee	renew	15.00	1999	48s
Driver's license fee	orig	12.00	1999	48s
Personal Goods				
Personal care products and services purchases	yr	449	1999	30r
Personal Services				
Personal services, household, expenditures on	yr	353	1999	30r
Pets				
Pets, toys, and playground equipment, expenditures on	yr	358	1999	30r
Taxes				
Federal income taxes paid	yr	3200	1999	30r
Personal taxes, expenditures on	yr	4153	1999	30r
Property taxes paid	yr	923	1999	30r
State and local income taxes paid	yr	812	1999	30r
Transportation				
Bus fare, one-way	trip	1.00	2000	1c
Cars and trucks, new, expenditures on	yr	1534	1999	30r
Cars and trucks, used, expenditures on	yr	1593	1999	30r
Diesel at the pump	gal	1.37	10/99	73s
Gasoline and motor oil purchases	yr	1129	1999	30r
Gasoline before-tax price (cents)	gal	128.80	10/00	43s
Maintenance and repair expenditures	yr	797	1999	30r
Public transportation, expenditures on	yr	530	1999	30r
Transportation purchases	yr	7423	1999	30r
Vehicle expenses, miscellaneous, purchases	yr	2585	1999	30r
Vehicle insurance payments	yr	811	1999	30r
Vehicle purchases (net outlay)	yr	3180	1999	30r
Vehicle rental, lease expenditures	yr	666	1999	30r
Utilities				
Electrical bill, average	mos	58.66	9/00	9s
Electricity, expenditures on	yr	725	1999	30r
Electricity cost, average	KWh	7.75	9/00	9s
Utilities, fuels, and public services purchased	yr	2179	1999	30r
Water and other public services, expenditures on	yr	339	1999	30r
Weddings				
Wedding (national average cost)		19936	2000	33r
Wedding (regional average total cost)		18918	1997	110r
Attendants' gifts		321	1998	33r
Bridal attendants' apparel (5 persons)		824	2000	33r
Bride's headpiece/veil		173	1998	33r
Bride's wedding dress		859	1998	33r
Clergy, religious facility fee		242	1998	33r
Engagement ring		3177	1998	33r
Flowers		789	1998	33r
Groom's formalwear rental		99	2000	33r
Limousine		410	1998	33r
Marriage license cost		50.00-80.00	4/01	35s
Men's formalwear (ushers, best man)		469	2000	33r
Mother of bride apparel		241	2000	33r
Music		866	1998	33r
Photography and videography		1368	1998	33r
Rehearsal dinner		728	1998	33r
Wedding invitations and announcements		341	1998	33r
Wedding reception		7968	2000	33r
Wedding rings (bride and groom)		1060	1998	33r

Values are in dollars or fractions of dollars. In the column headed *Ref*, references are shown to sources. Each reference is followed by a letter. These refer to the geographical level for which data were reported: s=State, r=Region, and c=City or metro. The abbreviation *ex* is used to mean *except* or *excluding*; *exp* stands for expenditures. For other abbreviations and further explanations, please see the Introduction.

Reno, NV

Item	Per	Value	Date	Ref.
Communications				
Cable modem installation, Cox		99.00-174.95	6/99	103s
Cable modem rate, cable subscriber, Cox	mos	29.95-44.95	6/99	103s
Cable modem rate, non-cable subscriber, Cox	mos	42.95-54.95	6/99	103s
Phone line, single, business, field visit	inst.	91.00	12/97	17s
Phone line, single, business, no field visit	inst.	74.00	12/97	17s
Phone line, single, residence, field visit	inst.	33.50	12/97	17s
Phone line, single, residence, no field visit	inst.	33.50	12/97	17s
Postal rate, express mail, up to half-pound		12.45	7/01	108r
Postal rate, letter, first class, first ounce		0.34	7/01	108r
Postal rate, letter, two ounces		0.57	7/01	108r
Postal rate, post card		0.21	7/01	108r
Postal rate, priority mail, two pounds		3.95	7/01	108r
Postal rate, priority mail, up to one pound		3.50	7/01	108r
Telephone bill, business, basic rate	mos	22.00	12/97	18c
Telephone bill, residential, basic rate	mos	10.75	12/97	18c
Education				
Board, 4-year public college/university	yr	2614	1996	38s
Room, 4-year private college/university	yr	3050	1996	38s
Room, 4-year public college/university	yr	3090	1996	38s
Total cost, 4-year public college/university	yr	7388	1996	38s
Tuition, 2-year public college/university, in state	yr	970	1996	38s
Tuition, 4-year private college/university, in state	yr	7841	1996	38s
Tuition, 4-year public college/university	yr	1684	1996	38s
Energy and Fuels				
Gas, cooking, winter, 10 therms	mos	9.05	2/96	98c
Gas, cooking, winter, 30 therms	mos	20.49	2/96	98c
Gas, cooking, winter, 50 therms	mos	31.95	2/96	98c
Gas, heating, winter, average use	mos	52.84	2/96	98c
Gas, natural, commercial rate	1000 cf	5.49	11/00	88s
Funerals				
Total cost of funeral		5401.08	1/99	78r
Acknowledgement cards		33.64	1/99	78r
Casket		2170.43	1/99	78r
Cosmetology, hair, other preparation		136.32	1/99	78r
Embalming		319.13	1/99	78r
Funeral at funeral home		370.21	1/99	78r
Hearse (local)		161.04	1/99	78r
Professional service charges		963.15	1/99	78r
Service car/van		133.99	1/99	78r
Transfer of remains to funeral home		159.82	1/99	78r
Vault		778.07	1/99	78r
Visitation/viewing		175.28	1/99	78r
Goods and Services				
Hunting license	yr	24.00	4/01	34s
Health Care				
Cardiac catheterization, ave hospital/ physician charges		26500	1998	77s
Childbirth, Cesarean delivery		11587	1997	13r
Childbirth, vaginal delivery		6725	1997	13r
Hysterectomy, laproscopically-assisted, ave hospital/physician charges		19670	1998	76s
Hysterectomy, vaginal, ave hospital and physician charges		15370	1998	76s
Medicaid dispensing fee		4.76	1999	87s
Housing				
Home, 2200 sq ft, 4-br, 2-bath, 2-car garage, average		224254	2000	47c
Home value, median		145000	2001	53s
Rental unit, 1 bedroom, with utilities	mos	570	4/01	41c
Rental unit, 2 bedroom, with utilities	mos	733	4/01	41c
Rental unit, 3 bedroom, with utilities	mos	1021	4/01	41c
Rental unit, 4 bedroom, with utilities	mos	1206	4/01	41c

Reno, NV - continued

Item	Per	Value	Date	Ref.
Insurance and Pensions				
Auto insurance premium	yr	956.06	1999	57s
Legal Fees				
Combination hunting and fishing license	yr	39.00	4/01	34s
Divorce, filing fee		64.00	4/01	35s
Driver's license fee	orig	20.50	1999	48s
Driver's license fee	renew	20.50	1999	48s
Fishing license	yr	21.00	4/01	34s
Transportation				
Bus fare, one-way	trip	1.25	2000	1c
Diesel at the pump	gal	1.37	10/99	73s
Gasoline before-tax price (cents)	gal	134.20	10/00	43s
Utilities				
Electrical bill, average	mos	65.50	9/00	9s
Electricity, summer, 250 KWh	mos	24.64	2/96	96c
Electricity, summer, 500 KWh	mos	46.22	2/96	96c
Electricity, summer, 750 KWh	mos	67.81	2/96	96c
Electricity, summer, 1000 KWh	mos	89.39	2/96	96c
Electricity cost, average	KWh	6.10	9/00	9s
Weddings				
Wedding (national average cost)		19936	2000	33r
Attendants' gifts		321	1998	33r
Bridal attendants' apparel (5 persons)		824	2000	33r
Bride's headpiece/veil		173	1998	33r
Bride's wedding dress		859	1998	33r
Clergy, religious facility fee		242	1998	33r
Engagement ring		3177	1998	33r
Flowers		789	1998	33r
Groom's formalwear rental		99	2000	33r
Limousine		410	1998	33r
Marriage license cost		35.00	4/01	35s
Men's formalwear (ushers, best man)		469	2000	33r
Mother of bride apparel		241	2000	33r
Music		866	1998	33r
Photography and videography		1368	1998	33r
Rehearsal dinner		728	1998	33r
Wedding invitations and announcements		341	1998	33r
Wedding reception		7968	2000	33r
Wedding rings (bride and groom)		1060	1998	33r

Richland-Kennewick-Pasco, WA

Item	Per	Value	Date	Ref.
Average annual expenditures	yr	40662	1999	30r
Composite, ACCRA index		98.70	3/01	4c
Alcoholic Beverages				
Alcoholic beverage purchases	yr	372	1999	30r
Beer, Heineken, 12-oz, ex deposit	6	7.74	3/01	4c
J & B Scotch	750-ml	22.45	3/01	4c
Malt beverages, all types, all sizes, any origin	16 oz	0.94	7/01	11r
Wine, Livingston or Gallo, Chablis blanc	1.5 liter	4.97	3/01	4c
Wine, red and white table, all sizes, any origin	liter	6.00	7/01	11r
Appliances				
Appliance repair, service call, washing machine	min lab chg	45.24	3/01	4c
Major appliances, expenditures on	yr	167	1999	30r
Small appliances, housewares, expenditures on	yr	105	1999	30r
Banking and Money				
Mortgage interest and charges paid	yr	3368	1999	30r
Mortgage principal paid on owned property	yr	1677	1999	30r
Mortgage rate, incl. points and orig. fee, 30-yr. conv. fixed or ARM	mos	7.00	3/01	4c
Vehicle finance charges paid	yr	311	1999	30r
Charity				
Cash contributions, expenditures	yr	1344	1999	30r

Values are in dollars or fractions of dollars. In the column headed *Ref*, references are shown to sources. Each reference is followed by a letter. These refer to the geographical level for which data were reported: s=State, r=Region, and c=City or metro. The abbreviation *ex* is used to mean *except* or *excluding*; *exp* stands for expenditures. For other abbreviations and further explanations, please see the Introduction.

Richland-Kennewick-Pasco, WA - continued

Item	Per	Value	Date	Ref.
Child Care				
Child raising cost, total, age 0-2	yr	9140	1999	60r
Child raising cost, total, age 3-5	yr	9370	1999	60r
Child raising cost, total, age 6-8	yr	9450	1999	60r
Child raising cost, total, age 9-11	yr	9470	1999	60r
Child raising cost, total, age 12-14	yr	10170	1999	60r
Child raising cost, total, age 15-17	yr	10360	1999	60r
Child's child care and education, age 0-2	yr	1250	1999	60r
Child's child care and education, age 3-5	yr	1380	1999	60r
Child's child care and education, age 6-8	yr	890	1999	60r
Child's child care and education, age 9-11	yr	580	1999	60r
Child's child care and education, age 12-14	yr	430	1999	60r
Child's child care and education, age 15-17	yr	730	1999	60r
Child's clothing, age 0-2	yr	430	1999	60r
Child's clothing, age 3-5	yr	420	1999	60r
Child's clothing, age 6-8	yr	470	1999	60r
Child's clothing, age 9-11	yr	520	1999	60r
Child's clothing, age 12-14	yr	870	1999	60r
Child's clothing, age 15-17	yr	770	1999	60r
Child's food, age 0-2	yr	1120	1999	60r
Child's food, age 3-5	yr	1280	1999	60r
Child's food, age 6-8	yr	1640	1999	60r
Child's food, age 9-11	yr	1930	1999	60r
Child's food, age 12-14	yr	1940	1999	60r
Child's food, age 15-17	yr	2150	1999	60r
Child's health care, age 0-2	yr	490	1999	60r
Child's health care, age 3-5	yr	470	1999	60r
Child's health care, age 6-8	yr	530	1999	60r
Child's health care, age 9-11	yr	570	1999	60r
Child's health care, age 12-14	yr	580	1999	60r
Child's health care, age 15-17	yr	610	1999	60r
Child's housing, age 0-2	yr	3630	1999	60r
Child's housing, age 3-5	yr	3610	1999	60r
Child's housing, age 6-8	yr	3570	1999	60r
Child's housing, age 9-11	yr	3410	1999	60r
Child's housing, age 12-14	yr	3600	1999	60r
Child's housing, age 15-17	yr	3210	1999	60r
Child's personal care, reading, age 0-2	yr	1040	1999	60r
Child's personal care, reading, age 3-5	yr	1060	1999	60r
Child's personal care, reading, age 6-8	yr	1090	1999	60r
Child's personal care, reading, age 9-11	yr	1130	1999	60r
Child's personal care, reading, age 12-14	yr	1300	1999	60r
Child's personal care, reading, age 15-17	yr	1080	1999	60r
Clothing				
Apparel and services purchases	yr	1863	1999	30r
Boys' brief, cotton	3	4.51	3/01	4c
Boys, 2 to 15, expenditures on	yr	80	1999	30r
Children under 2, expenditures on	yr	74	1999	30r
Footwear, expenditures on	yr	307	1999	30r
Girls, 2 to 15, expenditures on	yr	101	1999	30r
Men and boys, expenditures on	yr	443	1999	30r
Men, 16 and over, expenditures on	yr	363	1999	30r
Shirt, man's dress shirt		23.87	3/01	4c
Slacks, man's "No Wrinkles" khaki		35.99	3/01	4c
Women, 16 and over, expenditures on	yr	594	1999	30r
Communications				
Cable modem installation, AT&T-BIS		150.00	6/99	103s
Cable modem rate, cable subscriber, AT&T-BIS	mos	39.95	6/99	103s
Newspaper subscription, daily and Sunday delivery	mos	12.00	3/01	4c
Phone line, single, business, field visit	inst.	48.00	12/97	17s
Phone line, single, business, no field visit	inst.	48.00	12/97	17s
Phone line, single, residence, field visit	inst.	31.00	12/97	17s
Phone line, single, residence, no field visit	inst.	31.00	12/97	17s
Postage and stationery, expenditures on	yr	150	1999	30r
Postal rate, express mail, up to half-pound		12.45	7/01	108r
Postal rate, letter, first class, first ounce		0.34	7/01	108r
Postal rate, letter, two ounces		0.57	7/01	108r
Postal rate, post card		0.21	7/01	108r
Postal rate, priority mail, two pounds		3.95	7/01	108r
Postal rate, priority mail, up to one pound		3.50	7/01	108r

Richland-Kennewick-Pasco, WA - continued

Item	Per	Value	Date	Ref.
Communications - continued				
Telephone bill, family of three	mos	23.16	3/01	4c
Telephone services, expenditures on	yr	825	1999	30r
Education				
Board, 4-year private college/university	yr	2329	1996	38s
Board, 4-year public college/university	yr	2158	1996	38s
Education expenditures	yr	676	1999	30r
Room, 4-year private college/university	yr	2487	1996	38s
Room, 4-year public college/university	yr	2187	1996	38s
Total cost, 4-year private college/university	yr	18092	1996	38s
Total cost, 4-year public college/university	yr	7136	1996	38s
Tuition, 2-year public college/university, in state	yr	1369	1996	38s
Tuition, 4-year private college/university, in state	yr	13276	1996	38s
Tuition, 4-year public college/university	yr	2791	1996	38s
Energy and Fuels				
Electricity	500 KWhs	48.23	7/01	11r
Electricity	KWh	0.11	7/01	11r
Energy, combined forms, 2400 sq ft	mos	82.80	3/01	4c
Fuel oil and other fuels, expenditures on	yr	35	1999	30r
Gas, natural, commercial rate	1000 cf	6.89	11/00	88s
Gas, regular unleaded, cash, self-service	gal	1.56	3/01	4c
Gasoline, all types	gal	1.91	7/01	11r
Gasoline, unleaded premium	gal	2.05	7/01	11r
Gasoline, unleaded regular	gal	1.83	7/01	11r
Natural gas, expenditures on	yr	255	1999	30r
Utility (piped) gas, therm		0.98	7/01	11r
Utility (piped) gas, 40 therms		40.74	7/01	11r
Utility (piped) gas, 100 therms		96.80	7/01	11r
Entertainment				
Bowling, Saturday evening rate	line	2.09	3/01	4c
Entertainment purchases	yr	2139	1999	30r
Fees and admissions paid	yr	545	1999	30r
Monopoly game, Parker Brothers', No. 9	game	10.40	3/01	4c
Movie, first-run, Saturday, evening	adm.	6.88	3/01	4c
Television, radios, sound equipment, expenditures on	yr	624	1999	30r
Tennis balls, yellow, Wilson or Penn, 3	can	2.03	3/01	4c
Funerals				
Total cost of funeral		5401.08	1/99	78r
Acknowledgement cards		33.64	1/99	78r
Casket		2170.43	1/99	78r
Cosmetology, hair, other preparation		136.32	1/99	78r
Embalming		319.13	1/99	78r
Funeral at funeral home		370.21	1/99	78r
Hearse (local)		161.04	1/99	78r
Professional service charges		963.15	1/99	78r
Service car/van		133.99	1/99	78r
Transfer of remains to funeral home		159.82	1/99	78r
Vault		778.07	1/99	78r
Visitation/viewing		175.28	1/99	78r
Groceries				
Groceries, ACCRA Index		104.30	3/01	4c
Antibiotic ointment, Polysporin	0.5 oz	4.60	3/01	4c
Apples, red delicious	lb	0.84	7/01	11r
Baby food, strained vegetables or fruit, lowest price	4-4.5 oz	0.42	3/01	4c
Bacon, sliced	lb	3.38	7/01	11r
Bakery products, expenditures on	yr	299	1999	30r
Bananas	lb	0.59	3/01	4c
Bananas	lb	0.54	7/01	11r
Beans, dried, any type, all sizes	lb	0.76	7/01	11r
Beef or hamburger, ground	lb	1.73	3/01	4c
Beef, expenditures on	yr	222	1999	30r
Bread, white	loaf	0.76	3/01	4c
Bread, white, pan	lb	0.99	7/01	11r
Butter, yoghurt, cheese, etc, expenditures on	yr	211	1999	30r
Cereals and bakery product purchases	yr	466	1999	30r

Values are in dollars or fractions of dollars. In the column headed *Ref*, references are shown to sources. Each reference is followed by a letter. These refer to the geographical level for which data were reported: s=State, r=Region, and c=City or metro. The abbreviation *ex* is used to mean *except* or *excluding*; *exp* stands for *expenditures*. For other abbreviations and further explanations, please see the Introduction.

Richland-Kennewick-Pasco, WA - continued

Item	Per	Value	Date	Ref.
Groceries				
Cereals and cereal products, expenditures on	yr	168	1999	30r
Cheese, Kraft grated Parmesan	8 oz	4.04	3/01	4c
Chicken breast, bone-in	lb	2.45	7/01	11r
Chicken, fresh, whole	lb	1.19	7/01	11r
Chicken, whole fryer	lb	1.15	3/01	4c
Chops, boneless,	lb	4.00	7/01	11r
Chuck roast, graded and ungraded, excl U.S. prime and choice	lb	2.55	7/01	11r
Cigarettes, Winston, Kings	carton	35.35	3/01	4c
Coffee, 100%, ground roast, all sizes	lb	3.80	7/01	11r
Coffee, vacuum-packed	13 oz	3.17	3/01	4c
Cookies, chocolate chip	lb	2.83	7/01	11r
Corn Flakes, Kellogg's or Post Toasties	18 oz	2.97	3/01	4c
Corn, frozen, whole kernel, lowest price	16 oz	1.13	3/01	4c
Dairy product purchases	yr	341	1999	30r
Eggs, expenditures on	yr	39	1999	30r
Eggs, Grade A or AA	dozen	1.36	3/01	4c
Eggs, grade AA, large	dozen	1.23	7/01	11r
Fats and oils, expenditures on	yr	88	1999	30r
Fish and seafood, expenditures on	yr	121	1999	30r
Food (excl fruit and vegetables), eaten at home, purchases	yr	1001	1999	30r
Food cooked on trips, expenditures on	yr	64	1999	30r
Food purchases	yr	5312	1999	30r
Food purchases, eaten away from home	yr	2180	1999	30r
Food purchases, food eaten at home	yr	3132	1999	30r
Fresh fruits, expenditures on	yr	186	1999	30r
Fresh milk and cream, expenditures on	yr	130	1999	30r
Fresh vegetables, expenditures on	yr	177	1999	30r
Grapefruit	lb	0.68	7/01	11r
Grapes, Thompson, seedless	lb	2.42	7/01	11r
Ground beef, lean and extra lean	lb	2.46	7/01	11r
Ice cream, prepackaged, bulk, regular	1/2 gal	3.62	7/01	11r
Lettuce, iceberg	head	0.89	3/01	4c
Lettuce, iceberg	lb	0.63	7/01	11r
Margarine, Blue Bonnet or Parkay, stick	lb	0.73	3/01	4c
Meats, poultry, fish, and egg purchases	yr	761	1999	30r
Milk, fresh, low fat	gal	2.80	7/01	11r
Milk, fresh, whole, fortified	gal	2.88	7/01	11r
Milk, whole	1/2 gal	1.91	3/01	4c
Nonalcoholic beverages, expenditures on	yr	258	1999	30r
Orange juice, Minute Maid frozen	12 oz	1.45	3/01	4c
Oranges, Navel	lb	0.97	7/01	11r
Oranges, Valencia	lb	0.43	7/01	11r
Peaches	lb	1.38	7/01	11r
Peaches, halves or slices, Hunt's, Del Monte, or Libby's	29 oz	1.47	3/01	4c
Peanut butter, creamy, all sizes	lb	2.14	7/01	11r
Peas, green, Del Monte or Green Giant	15 oz	0.76	3/01	4c
Pork chops, center cut, bone-in	lb	3.83	7/01	11r
Pork, expenditures on	yr	141	1999	30r
Potatoes, white or red	10 lb	1.77	3/01	4c
Potatoes, white, all types	lb	0.37	7/01	11r
Poultry, expenditures on	yr	146	1999	30r
Processed fruits, expenditures on	yr	118	1999	30r
Processed vegetables, expenditures on	yr	81	1999	30r
Round roast, graded and ungraded, excl U.S. prime and choice	lb	3.07	7/01	11r
Round roast, U.S. choice, boneless	lb	3.37	7/01	11r
Round steak, graded and ungraded, excl U.S. prime and choice	lb	3.51	7/01	11r
Sausage, Jimmy Dean/Owens pork	lb	3.23	3/01	4c
Shortening, vegetable, Crisco	3 lb	2.84	3/01	4c
Sirloin steak, graded and ungraded, excl U.S. prime and choice	lb	4.67	7/01	11r
Soft drink, Coca Cola, ex deposit	2 liter	1.22	3/01	4c
Steak, sirloin, U.S. choice, boneless	lb	6.20	7/01	11r
Steak, T-bone	lb	6.57	3/01	4c
Strawberries, dry pint	12 oz	1.79	7/01	11r
Sugar and other sweets, expenditures on	yr	124	1999	30r
Sugar, cane or beet	4 lbs	1.59	3/01	4c

Item	Per	Value	Date	Ref.
Groceries - continued				
Sugar, white, all sizes	lb	0.46	7/01	11r
Tobacco products and smoking supplies purchases	yr	217	1999	30r
Tomatoes, field grown	lb	1.17	7/01	11r
Tomatoes, Hunt's or Del Monte	14.5 oz	0.96	3/01	4c
Tuna, chunk, light	6 oz	0.65	3/01	4c
Tuna, light, chunk	lb	2.05	7/01	11r
Goods and Services				
Miscellaneous goods and services, ACCRA Index		98.40	3/01	4c
B&B Japanese maple (acer japonicum)	gal	39.99	4/00	93r
Boxwood (buxus)	2 gal	14.99-24.99	4/00	93r
Daylilly (hemerocallis)	gal	6.99-8.99	4/00	93r
Flat of annuals		16.68	4/00	93r
Fountain grass (pennisetum)	gal	7.99-11.99	4/00	93r
Hanging basket (10 in)		29.99	4/00	93r
Hardy geranium (geranium)	gal	6.99-11.99	4/00	93r
Hosta (hosta)	gal	6.99-18.99	4/00	93r
Lilac (syrubga vulgaris)	2 gal	14.99-17.99	4/00	93r
Miscellaneous purchases	yr	1070	1999	30r
Rhododendron (rhododendron)	2 gal	14.99	4/00	93r
Sage (salvia)	gal	6.99	4/00	93r
Wintercreeper euonymus (euonymus fortunei)	2 gal	14.99-22.99	4/00	93r
Hunting license	yr	30.00	4/01	34s
Health Care				
Health care, ACCRA Index		122.80	3/01	4c
Cardiac catheterization, ave hospital/ physician charges		13290	1998	77s
Childbirth, Cesarean delivery		11587	1997	13r
Childbirth, vaginal delivery		6725	1997	13r
Dentist's fee, adult teeth cleaning and periodic oral exam	visit	112.38	3/01	4c
Doctor's fee, routine exam, established patient	visit	56.67	3/01	4c
Drugs, expenditures on	yr	309	1999	30r
Health care purchases	yr	1869	1999	30r
Health insurance expenditures	yr	868	1999	30r
Hospital care, private room	day	653.67	3/01	4c
Hysterectomy, laproscopically-assisted, ave hospital/physician charges		10960	1998	76s
Hysterectomy, vaginal, ave hospital and physician charges		9000	1998	76s
Medicaid dispensing fee		3.98-4.92	1999	87s
Medical services expenditures	yr	580	1999	30r
Medical supplies, expenditures on	yr	112	1999	30r
Household Goods				
Dishwashing powder, Cascade	50 oz	4.14	3/01	4c
Floor coverings, expenditures on	yr	49	1999	30r
Furniture, expenditures on	yr	444	1999	30r
Household furnishings and equipment purchases	yr	1768	1999	30r
Household textiles, expenditures on	yr	141	1999	30r
Laundry and cleaning supplies, expenditures on	yr	128	1999	30r
Tissues, facial, Kleenex brand	175	1.43	3/01	4c
Housing				
Housing, ACCRA Index		95.50	3/01	4c
Home price, existing, ave		239400	10/00	90r
Home value, median		195000	2001	53s
House, 2400 sq ft, 8000 sq ft lot, new, urban, utilities	total	192361	3/01	4c

Values are in dollars or fractions of dollars. In the column headed *Ref*, references are shown to sources. Each reference is followed by a letter. These refer to the geographical level for which data were reported: s=State, r=Region, and c=City or metro. The abbreviation *ex* is used to mean *except* or *excluding*; *exp* stands for *expenditures*. For other abbreviations and further explanations, please see the Introduction.

Richland-Kennewick-Pasco, WA - continued

Item	Per	Value	Date	Ref.
Housing				
House payment, principal and interest, 25% down payment	mos	960	3/01	4c
Household operation expenditures	yr	781	1999	30r
Housekeeping supplies purchases	yr	513	1999	30r
Lodging expenditures	yr	575	1999	30r
Maintenance, repairs, insurance expenditures	yr	939	1999	30r
Monthly rental value of owned home	mos	662	1999	30r
Owned dwellings, expenditures own	yr	5231	1999	30r
Rent expenditures	yr	2709	1999	30r
Rent, apartment, 2 br, 1 1/2-2 baths, unfurn, 950 sq ft, water	mos	729	3/01	4c
Rental unit, 1 bedroom, with utilities	mos	639	4/01	41c
Rental unit, 2 bedroom, with utilities	mos	809	4/01	41c
Rental unit, 3 bedroom, with utilities	mos	1123	4/01	41c
Rental unit, 4 bedroom, with utilities	mos	1327	4/01	41c
Shelter, expenditures on	yr	8516	1999	30r
Insurance and Pensions				
Life and other personal insurance purchases	yr	355	1999	30r
Pensions and Social Security, expenditures on	yr	3636	1999	30r
Legal Fees				
Divorce, filing fee		100.00	4/01	35s
Driver's license fee	renew	14.00	1999	48s
Driver's license fee	orig	14.00	1999	48s
Fishing license	yr	20.00	4/01	34s
Personal Goods				
Personal care products and services purchases	yr	449	1999	30r
Shampoo, Alberto VO5	15 oz	1.20	3/01	4c
Toothpaste, Crest or Colgate	6-7 oz	2.29	3/01	4c
Personal Services				
Dry cleaning, man's 2-pc suit		8.84	3/01	4c
Man's haircut, barbershop, no styling		9.80	3/01	4c
Personal services, household, expenditures on	yr	353	1999	30r
Woman's shampoo, trim, blow-dry, no style-change		27.80	3/01	4c
Pets				
Pets, toys, and playground equipment, expenditures on	yr	358	1999	30r
Restaurant Food				
Chicken, fried, thigh and drumstick, KFC/Church's		2.39	3/01	4c
Hamburger with cheese, McDonald's	1/4 lb	2.35	3/01	4c
Pizza, Pizza Hut or Pizza Inn	11-12 in	10.79	3/01	4c
Taxes				
Federal income taxes paid	yr	3200	1999	30r
Personal taxes, expenditures on	yr	4153	1999	30r
Property taxes paid	yr	923	1999	30r
State and local income taxes paid	yr	812	1999	30r
Transportation				
Transportation, ACCRA Index		108.00	3/01	4c
Bus fare, one-way	trip	0.50	2000	1c
Cars and trucks, new, expenditures on	yr	1534	1999	30r
Cars and trucks, used, expenditures on	yr	1593	1999	30r
Diesel at the pump	gal	1.37	10/99	73s
Gasoline and motor oil purchases	yr	1129	1999	30r
Gasoline before-tax price (cents)	gal	127.10	10/00	43s
Maintenance and repair expenditures	yr	797	1999	30r
Public transportation, expenditures on	yr	530	1999	30r
Tire balance, computer or spin balance, front	wheel	8.24	3/01	4c
Transportation purchases	yr	7423	1999	30r
Vehicle expenses, miscellaneous, purchases	yr	2585	1999	30r
Vehicle insurance payments	yr	811	1999	30r
Vehicle purchases (net outlay)	yr	3180	1999	30r
Vehicle rental, lease expenditures	yr	666	1999	30r

Richland-Kennewick-Pasco, WA - continued

Item	Per	Value	Date	Ref.
Utilities				
Utilities, ACCRA Index		73.10	3/01	4c
Electrical bill, average	mos	58.33	9/00	9s
Electricity, 2400 sq ft, new home	mos	82.80	3/01	4c
Electricity, expenditures on	yr	725	1999	30r
Electricity cost, average	KWh	4.47	9/00	9s
Utilities, fuels, and public services purchased	yr	2179	1999	30r
Water and other public services, expenditures on	yr	339	1999	30r
Weddings				
Wedding (national average cost)		19936	2000	33r
Wedding (regional average total cost)		18918	1997	110r
Attendants' gifts		321	1998	33r
Bridal attendants' apparel (5 persons)		824	2000	33r
Bride's headpiece/veil		173	1998	33r
Bride's wedding dress		859	1998	33r
Clergy, religious facility fee		242	1998	33r
Engagement ring		3177	1998	33r
Flowers		789	1998	33r
Groom's formalwear rental		99	2000	33r
Limousine		410	1998	33r
Marriage license cost		52.00	4/01	35s
Men's formalwear (ushers, best man)		469	2000	33r
Mother of bride apparel		241	2000	33r
Music		866	1998	33r
Photography and videography		1368	1998	33r
Rehearsal dinner		728	1998	33r
Wedding invitations and announcements		341	1998	33r
Wedding reception		7968	2000	33r
Wedding rings (bride and groom)		1060	1998	33r

Richmond-Petersburg, VA

Item	Per	Value	Date	Ref.
Alcoholic Beverages				
Alcoholic beverage purchases	yr	253	1999	30r
Malt beverages, all types, all sizes, any origin	16 oz	0.96	7/01	11r
Appliances				
Major appliances, expenditures on	yr	172	1999	30r
Small appliances, housewares, expenditures on	yr	81	1999	30r
Banking and Money				
Mortgage interest and charges paid	yr	2039	1999	30r
Mortgage principal paid on owned property	yr	1026	1999	30r
Vehicle finance charges paid	yr	365	1999	30r
Charity				
Cash contributions, expenditures	yr	1127	1999	30r
Child Care				
Child raising cost, total, age 0-2	yr	8540	1999	60r
Child raising cost, total, age 3-5	yr	8780	1999	60r
Child raising cost, total, age 6-8	yr	8820	1999	60r
Child raising cost, total, age 9-11	yr	8800	1999	60r
Child raising cost, total, age 12-14	yr	9510	1999	60r
Child raising cost, total, age 15-17	yr	9740	1999	60r
Child's child care and education, age 0-2	yr	1380	1999	60r
Child's child care and education, age 3-5	yr	1520	1999	60r
Child's child care and education, age 6-8	yr	990	1999	60r
Child's child care and education, age 9-11	yr	650	1999	60r
Child's child care and education, age 12-14	yr	490	1999	60r
Child's child care and education, age 15-17	yr	840	1999	60r
Child's clothing, age 0-2	yr	480	1999	60r
Child's clothing, age 3-5	yr	470	1999	60r
Child's clothing, age 6-8	yr	520	1999	60r
Child's clothing, age 9-11	yr	570	1999	60r
Child's clothing, age 12-14	yr	950	1999	60r
Child's clothing, age 15-17	yr	850	1999	60r
Child's food, age 0-2	yr	1000	1999	60r
Child's food, age 3-5	yr	1160	1999	60r
Child's food, age 6-8	yr	1490	1999	60r
Child's food, age 9-11	yr	1770	1999	60r

Values are in dollars or fractions of dollars. In the column headed *Ref*, references are shown to sources. Each reference is followed by a letter. These refer to the geographical level for which data were reported: s=State, r=Region, and c=City or metro. The abbreviation *ex* is used to mean *except* or *excluding*; *exp* stands for *expenditures*. For other abbreviations and further explanations, please see the Introduction.

Richmond-Petersburg, VA - continued

Item	Per	Value	Date	Ref.
Child Care				
Child's food, age 12-14	yr	1770	1999	60r
Child's food, age 15-17	yr	1980	1999	60r
Child's health care, age 0-2	yr	620	1999	60r
Child's health care, age 3-5	yr	590	1999	60r
Child's health care, age 6-8	yr	680	1999	60r
Child's health care, age 9-11	yr	720	1999	60r
Child's health care, age 12-14	yr	730	1999	60r
Child's health care, age 15-17	yr	760	1999	60r
Child's housing, age 0-2	yr	3070	1999	60r
Child's housing, age 3-5	yr	3050	1999	60r
Child's housing, age 6-8	yr	3010	1999	60r
Child's housing, age 9-11	yr	2850	1999	60r
Child's housing, age 12-14	yr	3040	1999	60r
Child's housing, age 15-17	yr	2650	1999	60r
Child's personal care, reading, age 0-2	yr	910	1999	60r
Child's personal care, reading, age 3-5	yr	930	1999	60r
Child's personal care, reading, age 6-8	yr	960	1999	60r
Child's personal care, reading, age 9-11	yr	1000	1999	60r
Child's personal care, reading, age 12-14	yr	1170	1999	60r
Child's personal care, reading, age 15-17	yr	950	1999	60r
Clothing				
Apparel and services purchases	yr	1610	1999	30r
Boys, 2 to 15, expenditures on	yr	89	1999	30r
Children under 2, expenditures on	yr	79	1999	30r
Footwear, expenditures on	yr	283	1999	30r
Girls, 2 to 15, expenditures on	yr	103	1999	30r
Men and boys, expenditures on	yr	351	1999	30r
Men, 16 and over, expenditures on	yr	262	1999	30r
Women, 16 and over, expenditures on	yr	538	1999	30r
Communications				
Cable modem installation, Adelphi		54.90	6/99	103s
Cable modem installation, Comcast		95.00	6/99	103s
Cable modem installation, Cox		99.00-174.95	6/99	103s
Cable modem installation, Jones Intercable		100.00	6/99	103s
Cable modem rate, cable subscriber, Adelphi	mos	34.95	6/99	103s
Cable modem rate, cable subscriber, Comcast	mos	39.95	6/99	103s
Cable modem rate, cable subscriber, Cox	mos	29.95-44.95	6/99	103s
Cable modem rate, cable subscriber, Jones Intercable	mos	29.95-39.95	6/99	103s
Cable modem rate, non-cable subscriber, Adelphi	mos	44.95	6/99	103s
Cable modem rate, non-cable subscriber, Comcast	mos	49.95	6/99	103s
Cable modem rate, non-cable subscriber, Cox	mos	42.95-54.95	6/99	103s
Phone line, single, business, field visit	inst.	64.00	12/97	17s
Phone line, single, business, no field visit	inst.	64.00	12/97	17s
Phone line, single, residence, field visit	inst.	38.50	12/97	17s
Phone line, single, residence, no field visit	inst.	38.50	12/97	17s
Postage and stationery, expenditures on	yr	104	1999	30r
Postal rate, express mail, up to half-pound		12.45	7/01	108r
Postal rate, letter, first class, first ounce		0.34	7/01	108r
Postal rate, letter, two ounces		0.57	7/01	108r
Postal rate, post card		0.21	7/01	108r
Postal rate, priority mail, two pounds		3.95	7/01	108r
Postal rate, priority mail, up to one pound		3.50	7/01	108r
Telephone services, expenditures on	yr	860	1999	30r
Education				
Board, 4-year private college/university	yr	2363	1996	38s
Board, 4-year public college/university	yr	2033	1996	38s
Education expenditures	yr	431	1999	30r
Room, 4-year private college/university	yr	2062	1996	38s
Room, 4-year public college/university	yr	2261	1996	38s
Total cost, 4-year private college/university	yr	15021	1996	38s
Total cost, 4-year public college/university	yr	8202	1996	38s
Tuition, 2-year public college/university, in state	yr	1433	1996	38s

Richmond-Petersburg, VA - continued

Item	Per	Value	Date	Ref.
Education - continued				
Tuition, 4-year private college/university, in state	yr	10596	1996	38s
Tuition, 4-year public college/university	yr	3907	1996	38s
Energy and Fuels				
Electricity	KWh	0.09	7/01	11r
Electricity	500 KWhs	47.29	7/01	11r
Fuel oil #2	gal	1.43	7/01	11r
Fuel oil and other fuels, expenditures on	yr	45	1999	30r
Gas, natural, commercial rate	1000 cf	9.01	11/00	88s
Gasoline, all types	gal	1.60	7/01	11r
Gasoline, unleaded midgrade	gal	1.65	7/01	11r
Gasoline, unleaded premium	gal	1.74	7/01	11r
Natural gas, expenditures on	yr	164	1999	30r
Utility (piped) gas, therm		1.01	7/01	11r
Utility (piped) gas, 40 therms		44.29	7/01	11r
Utility (piped) gas, 100 therms		97.44	7/01	11r
Entertainment				
Entertainment purchases	yr	1574	1999	30r
Fees and admissions paid	yr	371	1999	30r
Reading purchases	yr	121	1999	30r
Television, radios, sound equipment, expenditures on	yr	561	1999	30r
Funerals				
Total cost of funeral		5922.53	1/99	78r
Acknowledgement cards		63.43	1/99	78r
Casket		2258.77	1/99	78r
Cosmetology, hair, other preparation		127.09	1/99	78r
Embalming		393.49	1/99	78r
Funeral at funeral home		367.50	1/99	78r
Hearse (local)		169.66	1/99	78r
Professional service charges		1211.32	1/99	78r
Service car/van		80.69	1/99	78r
Transfer of remains to funeral home		144.25	1/99	78r
Vault		803.50	1/99	78r
Visitation/viewing		302.83	1/99	78r
Groceries				
American processed cheese	lb	3.50	7/01	11r
Bakery products, expenditures on	yr	261	1999	30r
Bananas	lb	0.47	7/01	11r
Beans, dried, any type, all sizes	lb	0.63	7/01	11r
Beef for stew, boneless	lb	2.86	7/01	11r
Beef, expenditures on	yr	210	1999	30r
Bologna, all beef or mixed	lb	2.29	7/01	11r
Bread, French	lb	1.66	7/01	11r
Bread, white, pan	lb	0.87	7/01	11r
Bread, whole wheat, pan	lb	1.38	7/01	11r
Broccoli	lb	1.04	7/01	11r
Butter, salted, grade AA, stick	lb	2.26	7/01	11r
Butter, yoghurt, cheese, etc, expenditures on	yr	170	1999	30r
Cabbage	lb	0.42	7/01	11r
Cereals and cereal products, expenditures on	yr	140	1999	30r
Cheddar cheese, natural	lb	3.75	7/01	11r
Chicken breast, bone-in	lb	1.85	7/01	11r
Chicken legs, bone-in	lb	1.34	7/01	11r
Chicken, fresh, whole	lb	1.05	7/01	11r
Chops, boneless	lb	4.13	7/01	11r
Chuck roast, graded and ungraded, excl U.S. prime and choice	lb	2.35	7/01	11r
Chuck roast, U.S. choice, boneless	lb	2.67	7/01	11r
Coffee, 100%, ground roast, all sizes	lb	2.88	7/01	11r
Coffee, instant, plain, regular, all sizes	16 oz	9.25	7/01	11r
Cola, non diet	2 liter	1.11	7/01	11r
Crackers, soda, salted	lb	1.70	7/01	11r
Dairy product purchases	yr	282	1999	30r
Eggs, expenditures on	yr	32	1999	30r
Fats and oils, expenditures on	yr	79	1999	30r
Fish and seafood, expenditures on	yr	99	1999	30r
Flour, white, all purpose	lb	0.32	7/01	11r

Values are in dollars or fractions of dollars. In the column headed *Ref*, references are shown to sources. Each reference is followed by a letter. These refer to the geographical level for which data were reported: s=State, r=Region, and c=City or metro. The abbreviation *ex* is used to mean *except* or *excluding*; *exp* stands for *expenditures*. For other abbreviations and further explanations, please see the Introduction.

Richmond-Petersburg, VA - continued

Item	Per	Value	Date	Ref.
Groceries				
Food (excl fruit and vegetables), eaten at home, purchases	yr	815	1999	30r
Food cooked on trips, expenditures on	yr	36	1999	30r
Food purchases	yr	4533	1999	30r
Food purchases, eaten away from home	yr	1873	1999	30r
Food purchases, food eaten at home	yr	2660	1999	30r
Fresh fruits, expenditures on	yr	128	1999	30r
Fresh milk and cream, expenditures on	yr	112	1999	30r
Fresh vegetables, expenditures on	yr	131	1999	30r
Fruit and vegetable purchases	yr	438	1999	30r
Grapefruit	lb	0.59	7/01	11r
Grapes, Thompson, seedless	lb	2.12	7/01	11r
Ground beef, 100% beef	lb	1.76	7/01	11r
Ground beef, lean and extra lean	lb	2.60	7/01	11r
Ground chuck, 100% beef	lb	2.08	7/01	11r
Ham, boneless, excl canned	lb	2.71	7/01	11r
Ham, rump or shank half, bone-in, smoked	lb	2.19	7/01	11r
Ice cream, prepackaged, bulk, regular	1/2 gal	3.93	7/01	11r
Lemons	lb	1.32	7/01	11r
Lettuce, iceberg	lb	0.76	7/01	11r
Milk, fresh, low fat,	gal	2.75	7/01	11r
Milk, fresh, whole, fortified	gal	2.97	7/01	11r
Nonalcoholic beverages, expenditures on	yr	228	1999	30r
Orange juice, frozen concentrate	16 oz	1.95	7/01	11r
Oranges, Navel	lb	0.73	7/01	11r
Oranges, Valencia	lb	0.55	7/01	11r
Peanut butter, creamy, all sizes	lb	1.83	7/01	11r
Pears, Anjou	lb	0.98	7/01	11r
Pork chops, center cut, bone-in	lb	3.33	7/01	11r
Pork sausage, fresh, loose	lb	2.59	7/01	11r
Pork shoulder picnic, bone-in, smoked	lb	1.12	7/01	11r
Pork, expenditures on	yr	162	1999	30r
Potato chips	16 oz	3.59	7/01	11r
Potatoes, frozen, french fried	lb	1.00	7/01	11r
Potatoes, white, all types	lb	0.44	7/01	11r
Poultry, expenditures on	yr	137	1999	30r
Processed fruits, expenditures on	yr	97	1999	30r
Processed vegetables, expenditures on	yr	82	1999	30r
Rice, white, long grain, uncooked	lb	0.51	7/01	11r
Round roast, graded and ungraded, excl U.S. prime and choice	lb	2.96	7/01	11r
Round steak, graded and ungraded, excl U.S. prime and choice	lb	3.11	7/01	11r
Sirloin steak, graded and ungraded, excl U.S. prime and choice	lb	4.23	7/01	11r
Spaghetti and macaroni	lb	0.78	7/01	11r
Steak, round, U.S. choice, boneless	lb	3.56	7/01	11r
Steak, sirloin, U.S. choice, boneless	lb	5.65	7/01	11r
Strawberries, dry pint	12 oz	1.50	7/01	11r
Sugar and other sweets, expenditures on	yr	99	1999	30r
Sugar, white, 33-80 ounce package	lb	0.39	7/01	11r
Sugar, white, all sizes	lb	0.42	7/01	11r
Tobacco products and smoking supplies purchases	yr	288	1999	30r
Tomatoes, field grown	lb	1.43	7/01	11r
Tuna, light, chunk	lb	1.77	7/01	11r
Turkey, frozen, whole	lb	1.05	7/01	11r
Goods and Services				
B&B Japanese maple (acer japonicum)	gal	49.98-129.00	4/00	93r
Boxwood (buxus)	2 gal	12.99-16.99	4/00	93r
Daylilly (hemerocallis)	gal	4.99-8.99	4/00	93r
Flat of annuals		11.00-13.92	4/00	93r
Fountain grass (pennisetum)	gal	5.98-7.98	4/00	93r
Hanging basket (10 in)		7.99-14.98	4/00	93r
Hardy geranium (geranium)	gal	5.98-8.00	4/00	93r

Richmond-Petersburg, VA - continued

Item	Per	Value	Date	Ref.
Goods and Services - continued				
Hosta (hosta)	gal	4.99-10.98	4/00	93r
Lilac (syrubga vulgaris)	2 gal	12.99-21.99	4/00	93r
Rhododendron (rhododendron)	2 gal	14.99-24.99	4/00	93r
Sage (salvia)	gal	5.98-6.99	4/00	93r
Wintercreeper euonymus (euonymus fortunei)	2 gal	7.99-89.99	4/00	93r
Hunting license	yr	12.00	4/01	34s
Health Care				
Cardiac catheterization, ave hospital/ physician charges		15370	1998	77s
Childbirth, Cesarean delivery		11587	1997	13r
Childbirth, vaginal delivery		6725	1997	13r
Drugs, expenditures on	yr	399	1999	30r
Health care purchases	yr	1971	1999	30r
Health insurance expenditures	yr	933	1999	30r
Hysterectomy, laproscopically-assisted, ave hospital/physician charges		15660	1998	76s
Hysterectomy, vaginal, ave hospital and physician charges		10260	1998	76s
Medicaid dispensing fee		4.25	1999	87s
Medical services expenditures	yr	547	1999	30r
Medical supplies, expenditures on	yr	91	1999	30r
Plastic surgery, breast augmentation		2870	2000	7r
Plastic surgery, breast lift		3649	2000	7r
Plastic surgery, facelift		5008	2000	7r
Plastic surgery, hair transplantation		3425	2000	7r
Plastic surgery, lip augmentation		1227	2000	7r
Plastic surgery, lower body lift		4793	2000	7r
Plastic surgery, thigh lift		3862	2000	7r
Household Goods				
Floor coverings, expenditures on	yr	44	1999	30r
Furniture, expenditures on	yr	335	1999	30r
Household furnishings and equipment purchases	yr	1328	1999	30r
Household textiles, expenditures on	yr	89	1999	30r
Laundry and cleaning supplies, expenditures on	yr	113	1999	30r
Housing				
Home price, existing, ave		160100	10/00	90r
Home value, median		141000	2001	53s
Household operation expenditures	yr	553	1999	30r
Housekeeping supplies purchases	yr	473	1999	30r
Housing, expenditures on	yr	10303	1999	30r
Maintenance, repairs, insurance expenditures	yr	699	1999	30r
Monthly rental value of owned home	mos	505	1999	30r
Owned dwellings, expenditures own	yr	3465	1999	30r
Rent expenditures	yr	1641	1999	30r
Rental unit, 1 bedroom, with utilities	mos	542	4/01	41c
Rental unit, 2 bedroom, with utilities	mos	631	4/01	41c
Rental unit, 3 bedroom, with utilities	mos	878	4/01	41c
Rental unit, 4 bedroom, with utilities	mos	1036	4/01	41c
Shelter, expenditures on	yr	5467	1999	30r
Insurance and Pensions				
Auto insurance premium	yr	628.58	1999	57s
Life and other personal insurance purchases	yr	414	1999	30r
Pensions and Social Security, expenditures on	yr	2635	1999	30r
Personal insurance and pensions, expenditures on	yr	3048	1999	30r
Legal Fees				
Divorce, filing fee		64.00	4/01	35s
Driver's license fee	renew	7.20	1999	48s
Driver's license fee	orig	7.20	1999	48s
Fishing license	yr	12.50	4/01	34s

Values are in dollars or fractions of dollars. In the column headed *Ref*, references are shown to sources. Each reference is followed by a letter. These refer to the geographical level for which data were reported: s=State, r=Region, and c=City or metro. The abbreviation *ex* is used to mean *except* or *excluding*; *exp* stands for expenditures. For other abbreviations and further explanations, please see the Introduction.

Richmond-Petersburg, VA - continued

Item	Per	Value	Date	Ref.
Personal Goods				
Personal care products and services purchases	yr	393	1999	30r
Personal Services				
Personal services, household, expenditures on	yr	258	1999	30r
Pets				
Pets, toys, and playground equipment, expenditures on	yr	306	1999	30r
Taxes				
Federal income taxes paid	yr	2047	1999	30r
Personal taxes, expenditures on	yr	2554	1999	30r
Property taxes paid	yr	726	1999	30r
State and local income taxes paid	yr	363	1999	30r
Transportation				
Cars and trucks, new, expenditures on	yr	1648	1999	30r
Cars and trucks, used, expenditures on	yr	1651	1999	30r
Diesel at the pump	gal	1.14	10/99	73s
Gasoline and motor oil purchases	yr	1052	1999	30r
Gasoline before-tax price (cents)	gal	107.30	10/00	43s
Maintenance and repair expenditures	yr	621	1999	30r
Public transportation, expenditures on	yr	298	1999	30r
Transportation purchases	yr	6738	1999	30r
Vehicle expenses, miscellaneous, purchases	yr	2033	1999	30r
Vehicle insurance payments	yr	696	1999	30r
Vehicle purchases (net outlay)	yr	3354	1999	30r
Vehicle rental, lease expenditures	yr	352	1999	30r
Utilities				
Electrical bill, average	mos	82.17	9/00	9s
Electricity, expenditures on	yr	1115	1999	30r
Electricity cost, average	KWh	5.90	9/00	9s
Water and other public services, expenditures on	yr	298	1999	30r
Weddings				
Wedding (national average cost)		19936	2000	33r
Wedding (regional average total cost)		16293	1997	110r
Attendants' gifts		321	1998	33r
Bridal attendants' apparel (5 persons)		824	2000	33r
Bride's headpiece/veil		173	1998	33r
Bride's wedding dress		859	1998	33r
Clergy, religious facility fee		242	1998	33r
Engagement ring		3177	1998	33r
Flowers		789	1998	33r
Groom's formalwear rental		99	2000	33r
Limousine		410	1998	33r
Marriage license cost		30.00	4/01	35s
Men's formalwear (ushers, best man)		469	2000	33r
Mother of bride apparel		241	2000	33r
Music		866	1998	33r
Photography and videography		1368	1998	33r
Rehearsal dinner		728	1998	33r
Wedding invitations and announcements		341	1998	33r
Wedding reception		7968	2000	33r
Wedding rings (bride and groom)		1060	1998	33r

Riverside-San Bernardino, CA

Item	Per	Value	Date	Ref.
Average annual expenditures	yr	40662	1999	30r
Alcoholic Beverages				
Alcoholic beverage purchases	yr	372	1999	30r
Malt beverages, all types, all sizes, any origin	16 oz	0.94	7/01	11r
Wine, red and white table, all sizes, any origin	liter	6.00	7/01	11r
Appliances				
Major appliances, expenditures on	yr	167	1999	30r
Small appliances, housewares, expenditures on	yr	105	1999	30r

Riverside-San Bernardino, CA - continued

Item	Per	Value	Date	Ref.
Banking and Money				
Mortgage interest and charges paid	yr	3368	1999	30r
Mortgage principal paid on owned property	yr	1677	1999	30r
Vehicle finance charges paid	yr	311	1999	30r
Charity				
Cash contributions, expenditures	yr	1344	1999	30r
Child Care				
Child raising cost, total, age 0-2	yr	9140	1999	60r
Child raising cost, total, age 3-5	yr	9370	1999	60r
Child raising cost, total, age 6-8	yr	9450	1999	60r
Child raising cost, total, age 9-11	yr	9470	1999	60r
Child raising cost, total, age 12-14	yr	10170	1999	60r
Child raising cost, total, age 15-17	yr	10360	1999	60r
Child's child care and education, age 0-2	yr	1250	1999	60r
Child's child care and education, age 3-5	yr	1380	1999	60r
Child's child care and education, age 6-8	yr	890	1999	60r
Child's child care and education, age 9-11	yr	580	1999	60r
Child's child care and education, age 12-14	yr	430	1999	60r
Child's child care and education, age 15-17	yr	730	1999	60r
Child's clothing, age 0-2	yr	430	1999	60r
Child's clothing, age 3-5	yr	420	1999	60r
Child's clothing, age 6-8	yr	470	1999	60r
Child's clothing, age 9-11	yr	520	1999	60r
Child's clothing, age 12-14	yr	870	1999	60r
Child's clothing, age 15-17	yr	770	1999	60r
Child's food, age 0-2	yr	1120	1999	60r
Child's food, age 3-5	yr	1280	1999	60r
Child's food, age 6-8	yr	1640	1999	60r
Child's food, age 9-11	yr	1930	1999	60r
Child's food, age 12-14	yr	1940	1999	60r
Child's food, age 15-17	yr	2150	1999	60r
Child's health care, age 0-2	yr	490	1999	60r
Child's health care, age 3-5	yr	470	1999	60r
Child's health care, age 6-8	yr	530	1999	60r
Child's health care, age 9-11	yr	570	1999	60r
Child's health care, age 12-14	yr	580	1999	60r
Child's health care, age 15-17	yr	610	1999	60r
Child's housing, age 0-2	yr	3630	1999	60r
Child's housing, age 3-5	yr	3610	1999	60r
Child's housing, age 6-8	yr	3570	1999	60r
Child's housing, age 9-11	yr	3410	1999	60r
Child's housing, age 12-14	yr	3600	1999	60r
Child's housing, age 15-17	yr	3210	1999	60r
Child's personal care, reading, age 0-2	yr	1040	1999	60r
Child's personal care, reading, age 3-5	yr	1060	1999	60r
Child's personal care, reading, age 6-8	yr	1090	1999	60r
Child's personal care, reading, age 9-11	yr	1130	1999	60r
Child's personal care, reading, age 12-14	yr	1300	1999	60r
Child's personal care, reading, age 15-17	yr	1080	1999	60r
Clothing				
Apparel and services purchases	yr	1863	1999	30r
Boys, 2 to 15, expenditures on	yr	80	1999	30r
Children under 2, expenditures on	yr	74	1999	30r
Footwear, expenditures on	yr	307	1999	30r
Girls, 2 to 15, expenditures on	yr	101	1999	30r
Men and boys, expenditures on	yr	443	1999	30r
Men, 16 and over, expenditures on	yr	363	1999	30r
Women, 16 and over, expenditures on	yr	594	1999	30r
Communications				
Cable modem installation, AT&T-BIS		150.00	6/99	103s
Cable modem installation, Charter		99.00-169.00	6/99	103s
Cable modem installation, Comcast		95.00	6/99	103s
Cable modem installation, Cox		99.00-174.95	6/99	103s
Cable modem installation, Media One		100.00	6/99	103s
Cable modem installation, Time Warner		75.00-225.00	6/99	103s
Cable modem rate, cable subscriber, AT&T-BIS	mos	39.95	6/99	103s

Values are in dollars or fractions of dollars. In the column headed *Ref*, references are shown to sources. Each reference is followed by a letter. These refer to the geographical level for which data were reported: s=State, r=Region, and c=City or metro. The abbreviation *ex* is used to mean *except* or *excluding*; *exp* stands for *expenditures*. For other abbreviations and further explanations, please see the Introduction.

Riverside-San Bernardino, CA - continued

Item	Per	Value	Date	Ref.
Communications				
Cable modem rate, cable subscriber, Charter	mos	49.95-79.95	6/99	103s
Cable modem rate, cable subscriber, Comcast	mos	39.95	6/99	103s
Cable modem rate, cable subscriber, Cox	mos	29.95-44.95	6/99	103s
Cable modem rate, cable subscriber, Media One	mos	34.95-39.95	6/99	103s
Cable modem rate, cable subscriber, Time Warner	mos	39.95-49.95	6/99	103s
Cable modem rate, non-cable subscriber, Charter	mos	59.95-89.95	6/99	103s
Cable modem rate, non-cable subscriber, Comcast	mos	49.95	6/99	103s
Cable modem rate, non-cable subscriber, Cox	mos	42.95-54.95	6/99	103s
Cable modem rate, non-cable subscriber, Media One	mos	49.95	6/99	103s
Cable modem rate, non-cable subscriber, Time Warner	mos	39.95-54.95	6/99	103s
Phone line, single, business, field visit	inst.	70.75	12/97	17s
Phone line, single, business, no field visit	inst.	70.75	12/97	17s
Phone line, single, residence, field visit	inst.	34.75	12/97	17s
Phone line, single, residence, no field visit	inst.	34.75	12/97	17s
Postage and stationery, expenditures on	yr	150	1999	30r
Postal rate, express mail, up to half-pound		12.45	7/01	108r
Postal rate, letter, first class, first ounce		0.34	7/01	108r
Postal rate, letter, two ounces		0.57	7/01	108r
Postal rate, post card		0.21	7/01	108r
Postal rate, priority mail, two pounds		3.95	7/01	108r
Postal rate, priority mail, up to one pound		3.50	7/01	108r
Telephone services, expenditures on	yr	825	1999	30r
Education				
Board, 4-year private college/university	yr	2970	1996	38s
Board, 4-year public college/university	yr	2516	1996	38s
Education expenditures	yr	676	1999	30r
Room, 4-year private college/university	yr	3196	1996	38s
Room, 4-year public college/university	yr	3031	1996	38s
Total cost, 4-year private college/university	yr	20143	1996	38s
Total cost, 4-year public college/university	yr	8213	1996	38s
Tuition, 2-year public college/university, in state	yr	362	1996	38s
Tuition, 4-year private college/university, in state	yr	13977	1996	38s
Tuition, 4-year public college/university	yr	2666	1996	38s
Energy and Fuels				
Electricity	KWh	0.11	7/01	11r
Electricity	500 KWhs	48.23	7/01	11r
Fuel oil and other fuels, expenditures on	yr	35	1999	30r
Gas, natural, commercial rate	1000 cf	8.74	11/00	88s
Gasoline, all types	gal	1.91	7/01	11r
Gasoline, unleaded premium	gal	2.05	7/01	11r
Gasoline, unleaded regular	gal	1.83	7/01	11r
Natural gas, expenditures on	yr	255	1999	30r
Utility (piped) gas, therm		0.98	7/01	11r
Utility (piped) gas, 40 therms		40.74	7/01	11r
Utility (piped) gas, 100 therms		96.80	7/01	11r
Entertainment				
Entertainment purchases	yr	2139	1999	30r
Fees and admissions paid	yr	545	1999	30r
Television, radios, sound equipment, expenditures on	yr	624	1999	30r
Funerals				
Total cost of funeral		5401.08	1/99	78r
Acknowledgement cards		33.64	1/99	78r
Casket		2170.43	1/99	78r
Cosmetology, hair, other preparation		136.32	1/99	78r
Embalming		319.13	1/99	78r
Funeral at funeral home		370.21	1/99	78r

Riverside-San Bernardino, CA - continued

Item	Per	Value	Date	Ref.
Funerals - continued				
Hearse (local)		161.04	1/99	78r
Professional service charges		963.15	1/99	78r
Service car/van		133.99	1/99	78r
Transfer of remains to funeral home		159.82	1/99	78r
Vault		778.07	1/99	78r
Visitation/viewing		175.28	1/99	78r
Groceries				
Apples, red delicious	lb	0.84	7/01	11r
Bacon, sliced	lb	3.38	7/01	11r
Bakery products, expenditures on	yr	299	1999	30r
Bananas	lb	0.54	7/01	11r
Beans, dried, any type, all sizes	lb	0.76	7/01	11r
Beef, expenditures on	yr	222	1999	30r
Bread, white, pan	lb	0.99	7/01	11r
Butter, yoghurt, cheese, etc, expenditures on	yr	211	1999	30r
Cereals and bakery product purchases	yr	466	1999	30r
Cereals and cereal products, expenditures on	yr	168	1999	30r
Chicken breast, bone-in	lb	2.45	7/01	11r
Chicken, fresh, whole	lb	1.19	7/01	11r
Chops, boneless,	lb	4.00	7/01	11r
Chuck roast, graded and ungraded, excl U.S. prime and choice	lb	2.55	7/01	11r
Coffee, 100%, ground roast, all sizes	lb	3.80	7/01	11r
Cookies, chocolate chip	lb	2.83	7/01	11r
Dairy product purchases	yr	341	1999	30r
Eggs, expenditures on	yr	39	1999	30r
Eggs, grade AA, large	dozen	1.23	7/01	11r
Fats and oils, expenditures on	yr	88	1999	30r
Fish and seafood, expenditures on	yr	121	1999	30r
Food (excl fruit and vegetables), eaten at home, purchases	yr	1001	1999	30r
Food cooked on trips, expenditures on	yr	64	1999	30r
Food purchases	yr	5312	1999	30r
Food purchases, eaten away from home	yr	2180	1999	30r
Food purchases, food eaten at home	yr	3132	1999	30r
Fresh fruits, expenditures on	yr	186	1999	30r
Fresh milk and cream, expenditures on	yr	130	1999	30r
Fresh vegetables, expenditures on	yr	177	1999	30r
Grapefruit	lb	0.68	7/01	11r
Grapes, Thompson, seedless	lb	2.42	7/01	11r
Ground beef, lean and extra lean	lb	2.46	7/01	11r
Ice cream, prepackaged, bulk, regular	1/2 gal	3.62	7/01	11r
Lettuce, iceberg	lb	0.63	7/01	11r
Meats, poultry, fish, and egg purchases	yr	761	1999	30r
Milk, fresh, low fat,	gal	2.80	7/01	11r
Milk, fresh, whole, fortified	gal	2.88	7/01	11r
Nonalcoholic beverages, expenditures on	yr	258	1999	30r
Oranges, Navel	lb	0.97	7/01	11r
Oranges, Valencia	lb	0.43	7/01	11r
Peaches	lb	1.38	7/01	11r
Peanut butter, creamy, all sizes	lb	2.14	7/01	11r
Pork chops, center cut, bone-in	lb	3.83	7/01	11r
Pork, expenditures on	yr	141	1999	30r
Potatoes, white, all types	lb	0.37	7/01	11r
Poultry, expenditures on	yr	146	1999	30r
Processed fruits, expenditures on	yr	118	1999	30r
Processed vegetables, expenditures on	yr	81	1999	30r
Round roast, graded and ungraded, excl U.S. prime and choice	lb	3.07	7/01	11r
Round roast, U.S. choice, boneless	lb	3.37	7/01	11r
Round steak, graded and ungraded, excl U.S. prime and choice	lb	3.51	7/01	11r
Sirloin steak, graded and ungraded, excl U.S. prime and choice	lb	4.67	7/01	11r
Steak, sirloin, U.S. choice, boneless	lb	6.20	7/01	11r
Strawberries, dry pint	12 oz	1.79	7/01	11r
Sugar and other sweets, expenditures on	yr	124	1999	30r
Sugar, white, all sizes	lb	0.46	7/01	11r
Tobacco products and smoking supplies purchases	yr	217	1999	30r
Tomatoes, field grown	lb	1.17	7/01	11r

Values are in dollars or fractions of dollars. In the column headed *Ref*, references are shown to sources. Each reference is followed by a letter. These refer to the geographical level for which data were reported: s=State, r=Region, and c=City or metro. The abbreviation *ex* is used to mean *except* or *excluding*; *exp* stands for *expenditures*. For other abbreviations and further explanations, please see the Introduction.

Riverside-San Bernardino, CA - continued

Item	Per	Value	Date	Ref.
Groceries				
Tuna, light, chunk	lb	2.05	7/01	11r
Goods and Services				
B&B Japanese maple (acer japonicum)	gal	39.99	4/00	93r
Boxwood (buxus)	2 gal	14.99-24.99	4/00	93r
Christmas tree, noble fir		40-60	2000	65s
Daylilly (hemerocallis)	gal	6.99-8.99	4/00	93r
Flat of annuals		16.68	4/00	93r
Fountain grass (pennisetum)	gal	7.99-11.99	4/00	93r
Hanging basket (10 in)		29.99	4/00	93r
Hardy geranium (geranium)	gal	6.99-11.99	4/00	93r
Hosta (hosta)	gal	6.99-18.99	4/00	93r
Lilac (syrubga vulgaris)	2 gal	14.99-17.99	4/00	93r
Miscellaneous purchases	yr	1070	1999	30r
Rhododendron (rhododendron)	2 gal	14.99	4/00	93r
Sage (salvia)	gal	6.99	4/00	93r
Wintercreeper euonymus (euonymus fortunei)	2 gal	14.99-22.99	4/00	93r
Hunting license	yr	29.95	4/01	34s
Health Care				
Cardiac catheterization, ave hospital/ physician charges		24000	1998	77s
Childbirth, Cesarean delivery		11587	1997	13r
Childbirth, vaginal delivery		6725	1997	13r
Drugs, expenditures on	yr	309	1999	30r
Health care purchases	yr	1869	1999	30r
Health insurance expenditures	yr	868	1999	30r
Hysterectomy, laproscopically-assisted, ave hospital/physician charges		20760	1998	76s
Hysterectomy, vaginal, ave hospital and physician charges		14570	1998	76s
Medicaid dispensing fee		4.05	1999	87s
Medical services expenditures	yr	580	1999	30r
Medical supplies, expenditures on	yr	112	1999	30r
Household Goods				
Floor coverings, expenditures on	yr	49	1999	30r
Furniture, expenditures on	yr	444	1999	30r
Household furnishings and equipment purchases	yr	1768	1999	30r
Household textiles, expenditures on	yr	141	1999	30r
Laundry and cleaning supplies, expenditures on	yr	128	1999	30r
Housing				
Home price, existing, ave		239400	10/00	90r
Home value, median		215000	2001	53s
Household operation expenditures	yr	781	1999	30r
Housekeeping supplies purchases	yr	513	1999	30r
Lodging expenditures	yr	575	1999	30r
Maintenance, repairs, insurance expenditures	yr	939	1999	30r
Monthly rental value of owned home	mos	662	1999	30r
Owned dwellings, expenditures own	yr	5231	1999	30r
Rent expenditures	yr	2709	1999	30r
Rental unit, 1 bedroom, with utilities	mos	508	4/01	41c
Rental unit, 2 bedroom, with utilities	mos	621	4/01	41c
Rental unit, 3 bedroom, with utilities	mos	861	4/01	41c
Rental unit, 4 bedroom, with utilities	mos	1018	4/01	41c
Shelter, expenditures on	yr	8516	1999	30r
Insurance and Pensions				
Life and other personal insurance purchases	yr	355	1999	30r
Pensions and Social Security, expenditures on	yr	3636	1999	30r

Riverside-San Bernardino, CA - continued

Item	Per	Value	Date	Ref.
Legal Fees				
Divorce, filing fee		182.00	4/01	35s
Driver's license fee	renew	15.00	1999	48s
Driver's license fee	orig	12.00	1999	48s
Personal Goods				
Personal care products and services purchases	yr	449	1999	30r
Personal Services				
Personal services, household, expenditures on	yr	353	1999	30r
Pets				
Pets, toys, and playground equipment, expenditures on	yr	358	1999	30r
Taxes				
Federal income taxes paid	yr	3200	1999	30r
Personal taxes, expenditures on	yr	4153	1999	30r
Property taxes paid	yr	923	1999	30r
State and local income taxes paid	yr	812	1999	30r
Transportation				
Cars and trucks, new, expenditures on	yr	1534	1999	30r
Cars and trucks, used, expenditures on	yr	1593	1999	30r
Diesel at the pump	gal	1.37	10/99	73s
Gasoline and motor oil purchases	yr	1129	1999	30r
Gasoline before-tax price (cents)	gal	128.80	10/00	43s
Maintenance and repair expenditures	yr	797	1999	30r
Public transportation, expenditures on	yr	530	1999	30r
Transportation purchases	yr	7423	1999	30r
Vehicle expenses, miscellaneous, purchases	yr	2585	1999	30r
Vehicle insurance payments	yr	811	1999	30r
Vehicle purchases (net outlay)	yr	3180	1999	30r
Vehicle rental, lease expenditures	yr	666	1999	30r
Utilities				
Electrical bill, average	mos	58.66	9/00	9s
Electricity, expenditures on	yr	725	1999	30r
Electricity cost, average	KWh	7.75	9/00	9s
Utilities, fuels, and public services purchased	yr	2179	1999	30r
Water and other public services, expenditures on	yr	339	1999	30r
Weddings				
Wedding (national average cost)		19936	2000	33r
Wedding (regional average total cost)		18918	1997	110r
Attendants' gifts		321	1998	33r
Bridal attendants' apparel (5 persons)		824	2000	33r
Bride's headpiece/veil		173	1998	33r
Bride's wedding dress		859	1998	33r
Clergy, religious facility fee		242	1998	33r
Engagement ring		3177	1998	33r
Flowers		789	1998	33r
Groom's formalwear rental		99	2000	33r
Limousine		410	1998	33r
Marriage license cost		50.00-80.00	4/01	35s
Men's formalwear (ushers, best man)		469	2000	33r
Mother of bride apparel		241	2000	33r
Music		866	1998	33r
Photography and videography		1368	1998	33r
Rehearsal dinner		728	1998	33r
Wedding invitations and announcements		341	1998	33r
Wedding reception		7968	2000	33r
Wedding rings (bride and groom)		1060	1998	33r

Roanoke, VA

Item	Per	Value	Date	Ref.
Composite, ACCRA index		90.00	3/01	4c
Alcoholic Beverages				
Alcoholic beverage purchases	yr	253	1999	30r
Beer, Heineken, 12-oz, ex deposit	6	6.82	3/01	4c
J & B Scotch	750-ml	20.95	3/01	4c

Values are in dollars or fractions of dollars. In the column headed *Ref*, references are shown to sources. Each reference is followed by a letter. These refer to the geographical level for which data were reported: s=State, r=Region, and c=City or metro. The abbreviation *ex* is used to mean *except* or *excluding*; *exp* stands for expenditures. For other abbreviations and further explanations, please see the Introduction.

Roanoke, VA - continued

Item	Per	Value	Date	Ref.
Alcoholic Beverages				
Malt beverages, all types, all sizes, any origin	16 oz	0.96	7/01	11r
Wine, Livingston or Gallo, Chablis blanc	1.5 liter	5.47	3/01	4c
Appliances				
Appliance repair, service call, washing machine	min lab chg	38.71	3/01	4c
Major appliances, expenditures on	yr	172	1999	30r
Small appliances, housewares, expenditures on	yr	81	1999	30r
Banking and Money				
Mortgage interest and charges paid	yr	2039	1999	30r
Mortgage principal paid on owned property	yr	1026	1999	30r
Mortgage rate, incl. points and orig. fee, 30-yr. conv. fixed or ARM	mos	6.80	3/01	4c
Vehicle finance charges paid	yr	365	1999	30r
Business Expenses				
Business travel, car rental	day	39	2001	3c
Business travel, food	day	42	2001	3c
Business travel, hotel	day	87	2001	3c
Charity				
Cash contributions, expenditures	yr	1127	1999	30r
Child Care				
Child raising cost, total, age 0-2	yr	8540	1999	60r
Child raising cost, total, age 3-5	yr	8780	1999	60r
Child raising cost, total, age 6-8	yr	8820	1999	60r
Child raising cost, total, age 9-11	yr	8800	1999	60r
Child raising cost, total, age 12-14	yr	9510	1999	60r
Child raising cost, total, age 15-17	yr	9740	1999	60r
Child's child care and education, age 0-2	yr	1380	1999	60r
Child's child care and education, age 3-5	yr	1520	1999	60r
Child's child care and education, age 6-8	yr	990	1999	60r
Child's child care and education, age 9-11	yr	650	1999	60r
Child's child care and education, age 12-14	yr	490	1999	60r
Child's child care and education, age 15-17	yr	840	1999	60r
Child's clothing, age 0-2	yr	480	1999	60r
Child's clothing, age 3-5	yr	470	1999	60r
Child's clothing, age 6-8	yr	520	1999	60r
Child's clothing, age 9-11	yr	570	1999	60r
Child's clothing, age 12-14	yr	950	1999	60r
Child's clothing, age 15-17	yr	850	1999	60r
Child's food, age 0-2	yr	1000	1999	60r
Child's food, age 3-5	yr	1160	1999	60r
Child's food, age 6-8	yr	1490	1999	60r
Child's food, age 9-11	yr	1770	1999	60r
Child's food, age 12-14	yr	1770	1999	60r
Child's food, age 15-17	yr	1980	1999	60r
Child's health care, age 0-2	yr	620	1999	60r
Child's health care, age 3-5	yr	590	1999	60r
Child's health care, age 6-8	yr	680	1999	60r
Child's health care, age 9-11	yr	720	1999	60r
Child's health care, age 12-14	yr	730	1999	60r
Child's health care, age 15-17	yr	760	1999	60r
Child's housing, age 0-2	yr	3070	1999	60r
Child's housing, age 3-5	yr	3050	1999	60r
Child's housing, age 6-8	yr	3010	1999	60r
Child's housing, age 9-11	yr	2850	1999	60r
Child's housing, age 12-14	yr	3040	1999	60r
Child's housing, age 15-17	yr	2650	1999	60r
Child's personal care, reading, age 0-2	yr	910	1999	60r
Child's personal care, reading, age 3-5	yr	930	1999	60r
Child's personal care, reading, age 6-8	yr	960	1999	60r
Child's personal care, reading, age 9-11	yr	1000	1999	60r
Child's personal care, reading, age 12-14	yr	1170	1999	60r
Child's personal care, reading, age 15-17	yr	950	1999	60r
Clothing				
Apparel and services purchases	yr	1610	1999	30r
Boys' brief, cotton	3	3.83	3/01	4c
Boys, 2 to 15, expenditures on	yr	89	1999	30r
Children under 2, expenditures on	yr	79	1999	30r
Footwear, expenditures on	yr	283	1999	30r

Roanoke, VA - continued

Item	Per	Value	Date	Ref.
Clothing - continued				
Girls, 2 to 15, expenditures on	yr	103	1999	30r
Men and boys, expenditures on	yr	351	1999	30r
Men, 16 and over, expenditures on	yr	262	1999	30r
Shirt, man's dress shirt		20.39	3/01	4c
Slacks, man's "No Wrinkles" khaki		34.28	3/01	4c
Women, 16 and over, expenditures on	yr	538	1999	30r
Communications				
Cable modem installation, Adelphi		54.90	6/99	103s
Cable modem installation, Comcast		95.00	6/99	103s
Cable modem installation, Cox		99.00-174.95	6/99	103s
Cable modem installation, Jones Intercable		100.00	6/99	103s
Cable modem rate, cable subscriber, Adelphi	mos	34.95	6/99	103s
Cable modem rate, cable subscriber, Comcast	mos	39.95	6/99	103s
Cable modem rate, cable subscriber, Cox	mos	29.95-44.95	6/99	103s
Cable modem rate, cable subscriber, Jones Intercable	mos	29.95-39.95	6/99	103s
Cable modem rate, non-cable subscriber, Adelphi	mos	44.95	6/99	103s
Cable modem rate, non-cable subscriber, Comcast	mos	49.95	6/99	103s
Cable modem rate, non-cable subscriber, Cox	mos	42.95-54.95	6/99	103s
Newspaper subscription, daily and Sunday delivery	mos	12.13	3/01	4c
Phone line, single, business, field visit	inst.	64.00	12/97	17s
Phone line, single, business, no field visit	inst.	64.00	12/97	17s
Phone line, single, residence, field visit	inst.	38.50	12/97	17s
Phone line, single, residence, no field visit	inst.	38.50	12/97	17s
Postage and stationery, expenditures on	yr	104	1999	30r
Postal rate, express mail, up to half-pound		12.45	7/01	108r
Postal rate, letter, first class, first ounce		0.34	7/01	108r
Postal rate, letter, two ounces		0.57	7/01	108r
Postal rate, post card		0.21	7/01	108r
Postal rate, priority mail, two pounds		3.95	7/01	108r
Postal rate, priority mail, up to one pound		3.50	7/01	108r
Telephone bill, family of three	mos	25.20	3/01	4c
Telephone services, expenditures on	yr	860	1999	30r
Education				
Board, 4-year private college/university	yr	2363	1996	38s
Board, 4-year public college/university	yr	2033	1996	38s
Education expenditures	yr	431	1999	30r
Room, 4-year private college/university	yr	2062	1996	38s
Room, 4-year public college/university	yr	2261	1996	38s
Total cost, 4-year private college/university	yr	15021	1996	38s
Total cost, 4-year public college/university	yr	8202	1996	38s
Tuition, 2-year public college/university, in state	yr	1433	1996	38s
Tuition, 4-year private college/university, in state	yr	10596	1996	38s
Tuition, 4-year public college/university	yr	3907	1996	38s
Energy and Fuels				
Electricity	500 KWhs	47.29	7/01	11r
Electricity	KWh	0.09	7/01	11r
Energy, combined forms, 2400 sq ft	mos	78.44	3/01	4c
Fuel oil #2	gal	1.43	7/01	11r
Fuel oil and other fuels, expenditures on	yr	45	1999	30r
Gas, cooking, winter, 10 therms	mos	14.09	2/96	98c
Gas, cooking, winter, 30 therms	mos	25.78	2/96	98c
Gas, cooking, winter, 50 therms	mos	37.46	2/96	98c
Gas, heating, winter, average use	mos	120.71	2/96	98c
Gas, natural, commercial rate	1000 cf	9.01	11/00	88s
Gas, regular unleaded, cash, self-service	gal	1.27	3/01	4c
Gasoline, all types	gal	1.60	7/01	11r
Gasoline, unleaded midgrade	gal	1.65	7/01	11r
Gasoline, unleaded premium	gal	1.74	7/01	11r
Natural gas, expenditures on	yr	164	1999	30r
Utility (piped) gas, therm		1.01	7/01	11r

Values are in dollars or fractions of dollars. In the column headed *Ref*, references are shown to sources. Each reference is followed by a letter. These refer to the geographical level for which data were reported: s=State, r=Region, and c=City or metro. The abbreviation *ex* is used to mean *except* or *excluding*; *exp* stands for *expenditures*. For other abbreviations and further explanations, please see the Introduction.

Roanoke, VA - continued

Item	Per	Value	Date	Ref.
Energy and Fuels				
Utility (piped) gas, 40 therms		44.29	7/01	11r
Utility (piped) gas, 100 therms		97.44	7/01	11r
Entertainment				
Bowling, Saturday evening rate	line	2.90	3/01	4c
Entertainment purchases	yr	1574	1999	30r
Fees and admissions paid	yr	371	1999	30r
Monopoly game, Parker Brothers', No. 9	game	9.72	3/01	4c
Movie, first-run, Saturday, evening	adm.	6.75	3/01	4c
Reading purchases	yr	121	1999	30r
Television, radios, sound equipment, expenditures on	yr	561	1999	30r
Tennis balls, yellow, Wilson or Penn, 3	can	2.28	3/01	4c
Funerals				
Total cost of funeral		5922.53	1/99	78r
Acknowledgement cards		63.43	1/99	78r
Casket		2258.77	1/99	78r
Cosmetology, hair, other preparation		127.09	1/99	78r
Embalming		393.49	1/99	78r
Funeral at funeral home		367.50	1/99	78r
Hearse (local)		169.66	1/99	78r
Professional service charges		1211.32	1/99	78r
Service car/van		80.69	1/99	78r
Transfer of remains to funeral home		144.25	1/99	78r
Vault		803.50	1/99	78r
Visitation/viewing		302.83	1/99	78r
Groceries				
Groceries, ACCRA Index		93.40	3/01	4c
American processed cheese	lb	3.50	7/01	11r
Antibiotic ointment, Polysporin	0.5 oz	4.55	3/01	4c
Baby food, strained vegetables or fruit, lowest price	4-4.5 oz	0.41	3/01	4c
Bakery products, expenditures on	yr	261	1999	30r
Bananas	lb	0.52	3/01	4c
Bananas	lb	0.47	7/01	11r
Beans, dried, any type, all sizes	lb	0.63	7/01	11r
Beef for stew, boneless	lb	2.86	7/01	11r
Beef or hamburger, ground	lb	1.70	3/01	4c
Beef, expenditures on	yr	210	1999	30r
Bologna, all beef or mixed	lb	2.29	7/01	11r
Bread, French	lb	1.66	7/01	11r
Bread, white	loaf	0.86	3/01	4c
Bread, white, pan	lb	0.87	7/01	11r
Bread, whole wheat, pan	lb	1.38	7/01	11r
Broccoli	lb	1.04	7/01	11r
Butter, salted, grade AA, stick	lb	2.26	7/01	11r
Butter, yoghurt, cheese, etc, expenditures on	yr	170	1999	30r
Cabbage	lb	0.42	7/01	11r
Cereals and cereal products, expenditures on	yr	140	1999	30r
Cheddar cheese, natural	lb	3.75	7/01	11r
Cheese, Kraft grated Parmesan	8 oz	3.44	3/01	4c
Chicken breast, bone-in	lb	1.85	7/01	11r
Chicken legs, bone-in	lb	1.34	7/01	11r
Chicken, fresh, whole	lb	1.05	7/01	11r
Chicken, whole fryer	lb	1.02	3/01	4c
Chops, boneless,	lb	4.13	7/01	11r
Chuck roast, graded and ungraded, excl U.S. prime and choice	lb	2.35	7/01	11r
Chuck roast, U.S. choice, boneless	lb	2.67	7/01	11r
Cigarettes, Winston, Kings	carton	26.68	3/01	4c
Coffee, 100%, ground roast, all sizes	lb	2.88	7/01	11r
Coffee, instant, plain, regular, all sizes	16 oz	9.25	7/01	11r
Coffee, vacuum-packed	13 oz	1.92	7/01	4c
Cola, non diet,	2 liter	1.11	7/01	11r
Corn Flakes, Kellogg's or Post Toasties	18 oz	2.53	3/01	4c
Corn, frozen, whole kernel, lowest price	16 oz	1.06	3/01	4c
Crackers, soda, salted	lb	1.70	7/01	11r
Dairy product purchases	yr	282	1999	30r
Eggs, expenditures on	yr	32	1999	30r
Eggs, Grade A or AA	dozen	1.33	3/01	4c
Fats and oils, expenditures on	yr	79	1999	30r

Roanoke, VA - continued

Item	Per	Value	Date	Ref.
Groceries - continued				
Fish and seafood, expenditures on	yr	99	1999	30r
Flour, white, all purpose	lb	0.32	7/01	11r
Food (excl fruit and vegetables), eaten at home, purchases	yr	815	1999	30r
Food cooked on trips, expenditures on	yr	36	1999	30r
Food purchases	yr	4533	1999	30r
Food purchases, eaten away from home	yr	1873	1999	30r
Food purchases, food eaten at home	yr	2660	1999	30r
Fresh fruits, expenditures on	yr	128	1999	30r
Fresh milk and cream, expenditures on	yr	112	1999	30r
Fresh vegetables, expenditures on	yr	131	1999	30r
Fruit and vegetable purchases	yr	438	1999	30r
Grapefruit	lb	0.59	7/01	11r
Grapes, Thompson, seedless	lb	2.12	7/01	11r
Ground beef, 100% beef	lb	1.76	7/01	11r
Ground beef, lean and extra lean	lb	2.60	7/01	11r
Ground chuck, 100% beef	lb	2.08	7/01	11r
Ham, boneless, excl canned	lb	2.71	7/01	11r
Ham, rump or shank half, bone-in, smoked	lb	2.19	7/01	11r
Ice cream, prepackaged, bulk, regular	1/2 gal	3.93	7/01	11r
Lemons	lb	1.32	7/01	11r
Lettuce, iceberg	head	1.15	3/01	4c
Lettuce, iceberg	lb	0.76	7/01	11r
Margarine, Blue Bonnet or Parkay, stick	lb	0.71	3/01	4c
Milk, fresh, low fat,	gal	2.75	7/01	11r
Milk, fresh, whole, fortified	gal	2.97	7/01	11r
Milk, whole	1/2 gal	1.80	3/01	4c
Nonalcoholic beverages, expenditures on	yr	228	1999	30r
Orange juice, frozen concentrate	16 oz	1.95	7/01	11r
Orange juice, Minute Maid frozen	12 oz	1.39	3/01	4c
Oranges, Navel	lb	0.73	7/01	11r
Oranges, Valencia	lb	0.55	7/01	11r
Peaches, halves or slices, Hunt's, Del Monte, or Libby's	29 oz	1.59	3/01	4c
Peanut butter, creamy, all sizes	lb	1.83	7/01	11r
Pears, Anjou	lb	0.98	7/01	11r
Peas, green, Del Monte or Green Giant	15 oz	0.64	3/01	4c
Pork chops, center cut, bone-in	lb	3.33	7/01	11r
Pork sausage, fresh, loose	lb	2.59	7/01	11r
Pork shoulder picnic, bone-in, smoked	lb	1.12	7/01	11r
Pork, expenditures on	yr	162	1999	30r
Potato chips	16 oz	3.59	7/01	11r
Potatoes, frozen, french fried	lb	1.00	7/01	11r
Potatoes, white or red	10 lb	2.61	3/01	4c
Potatoes, white, all types	lb	0.44	7/01	11r
Poultry, expenditures on	yr	137	1999	30r
Processed fruits, expenditures on	yr	97	1999	30r
Processed vegetables, expenditures on	yr	82	1999	30r
Rice, white, long grain, uncooked	lb	0.51	7/01	11r
Round roast, graded and ungraded, excl U.S. prime and choice	lb	2.96	7/01	11r
Round steak, graded and ungraded, excl U.S. prime and choice	lb	3.11	7/01	11r
Sausage, Jimmy Dean/Owens pork	lb	3.29	3/01	4c
Shortening, vegetable, Crisco	3 lb	3.07	3/01	4c
Sirloin steak, graded and ungraded, excl U.S. prime and choice	lb	4.23	7/01	11r
Soft drink, Coca Cola, ex deposit	2 liter	1.14	3/01	4c
Spaghetti and macaroni	lb	0.78	7/01	11r
Steak, round, U.S. choice, boneless	lb	3.56	7/01	11r
Steak, sirloin, U.S. choice, boneless	lb	5.65	7/01	11r
Steak, T-bone	lb	6.06	3/01	4c
Strawberries, dry pint	12 oz	1.50	7/01	11r
Sugar and other sweets, expenditures on	yr	99	1999	30r
Sugar, cane or beet	4 lbs	1.20	3/01	4c
Sugar, white, 33-80 ounce package	lb	0.39	7/01	11r
Sugar, white, all sizes	lb	0.42	7/01	11r
Tobacco products and smoking supplies purchases	yr	288	1999	30r
Tomatoes, field grown	lb	1.43	7/01	11r
Tomatoes, Hunt's or Del Monte	14.5 oz	0.77	3/01	4c
Tuna, chunk, light	6 oz	0.40	3/01	4c

Values are in dollars or fractions of dollars. In the column headed *Ref*, references are shown to sources. Each reference is followed by a letter. These refer to the geographical level for which data were reported: s=State, r=Region, and c=City or metro. The abbreviation *ex* is used to mean *except* or *excluding*; *exp* stands for expenditures. For other abbreviations and further explanations, please see the Introduction.

Roanoke, VA - continued

Item	Per	Value	Date	Ref.
Groceries				
Tuna, light, chunk	lb	1.77	7/01	11r
Turkey, frozen, whole	lb	1.05	7/01	11r
Goods and Services				
Miscellaneous goods and services, ACCRA Index		93.30	3/01	4c
B&B Japanese maple (acer japonicum)	gal	49.98-129.00	4/00	93r
Boxwood (buxus)	2 gal	12.99-16.99	4/00	93r
Daylilly (hemerocallis)	gal	4.99-8.99	4/00	93r
Flat of annuals		11.00-13.92	4/00	93r
Fountain grass (pennisetum)	gal	5.98-7.98	4/00	93r
Hanging basket (10 in)		7.99-14.98	4/00	93r
Hardy geranium (geranium)	gal	5.98-8.00	4/00	93r
Hosta (hosta)	gal	4.99-10.98	4/00	93r
Lilac (syrubga vulgaris)	2 gal	12.99-21.99	4/00	93r
Rhododendron (rhododendron)	2 gal	14.99-24.99	4/00	93r
Sage (salvia)	gal	5.98-6.99	4/00	93r
Wintercreeper euonymus (euonymus fortunei)	2 gal	7.99-89.99	4/00	93r
Hunting license	yr	12.00	4/01	34s
Health Care				
Health care, ACCRA Index		93.70	3/01	4c
Cardiac catheterization, ave hospital/ physician charges		15370	1998	77s
Childbirth, Cesarean delivery		11587	1997	13r
Childbirth, vaginal delivery		6725	1997	13r
Dentist's fee, adult teeth cleaning and periodic oral exam	visit	64.83	3/01	4c
Doctor's fee, routine exam, established patient	visit	62.40	3/01	4c
Drugs, expenditures on	yr	399	1999	30r
Health care purchases	yr	1971	1999	30r
Health insurance expenditures	yr	933	1999	30r
Hospital care, private room	day	382.33	3/01	4c
Hysterectomy, laproscopically-assisted, ave hospital/physician charges		15660	1998	76s
Hysterectomy, vaginal, ave hospital and physician charges		10260	1998	76s
Medicaid dispensing fee		4.25	1999	87s
Medical services expenditures	yr	547	1999	30r
Medical supplies, expenditures on	yr	91	1999	30r
Plastic surgery, breast augmentation		2870	2000	7r
Plastic surgery, breast lift		3649	2000	7r
Plastic surgery, facelift		5008	2000	7r
Plastic surgery, hair transplantation		3425	2000	7r
Plastic surgery, lip augmentation		1227	2000	7r
Plastic surgery, lower body lift		4793	2000	7r
Plastic surgery, thigh lift		3862	2000	7r
Household Goods				
Dishwashing powder, Cascade	50 oz	2.88	3/01	4c
Floor coverings, expenditures on	yr	44	1999	30r
Furniture, expenditures on	yr	335	1999	30r
Household furnishings and equipment purchases	yr	1328	1999	30r
Household textiles, expenditures on	yr	89	1999	30r
Laundry and cleaning supplies, expenditures on	yr	113	1999	30r
Tissues, facial, Kleenex brand	175	1.24	3/01	4c

Roanoke, VA - continued

Item	Per	Value	Date	Ref.
Housing				
Housing, ACCRA Index		90.40	3/01	4c
Home price, existing, ave		160100	10/00	90r
Home value, median		141000	2001	53s
House, 2400 sq ft, 8000 sq ft lot, new, urban, utilities	total	194735	3/01	4c
House payment, principal and interest, 25% down payment	mos	952	3/01	4c
Household operation expenditures	yr	553	1999	30r
Housekeeping supplies purchases	yr	473	1999	30r
Housing, expenditures on	yr	10303	1999	30r
Maintenance, repairs, insurance expenditures	yr	699	1999	30r
Monthly rental value of owned home	mos	505	1999	30r
Owned dwellings, expenditures own	yr	3465	1999	30r
Rent expenditures	yr	1641	1999	30r
Rent, apartment, 2 br, 1 1/2-2 baths, unfurn, 950 sq ft, water	mos	573	3/01	4c
Rental unit, 1 bedroom, with utilities	mos	373	4/01	41c
Rental unit, 2 bedroom, with utilities	mos	484	4/01	41c
Rental unit, 3 bedroom, with utilities	mos	621	4/01	41c
Rental unit, 4 bedroom, with utilities	mos	773	4/01	41c
Shelter, expenditures on	yr	5467	1999	30r
Insurance and Pensions				
Auto insurance premium	yr	628.58	1999	57s
Life and other personal insurance purchases	yr	414	1999	30r
Pensions and Social Security, expenditures on	yr	2635	1999	30r
Personal insurance and pensions, expenditures on	yr	3048	1999	30r
Legal Fees				
Divorce, filing fee		64.00	4/01	35s
Driver's license fee	orig	7.20	1999	48s
Driver's license fee	renew	7.20	1999	48s
Fishing license	yr	12.50	4/01	34s
Personal Goods				
Personal care products and services purchases	yr	393	1999	30r
Shampoo, Alberto VO5	15 oz	0.99	3/01	4c
Toothpaste, Crest or Colgate	6-7 oz	2.07	3/01	4c
Personal Services				
Dry cleaning, man's 2-pc suit		7.81	3/01	4c
Man's haircut, barbershop, no styling		9.80	3/01	4c
Personal services, household, expenditures on	yr	258	1999	30r
Woman's shampoo, trim, blow-dry, no style-change		24.17	3/01	4c
Pets				
Pets, toys, and playground equipment, expenditures on	yr	306	1999	30r
Restaurant Food				
Chicken, fried, thigh and drumstick, KFC/Church's		2.50	3/01	4c
Hamburger with cheese, McDonald's	1/4 lb	2.09	3/01	4c
Pizza, Pizza Hut or Pizza Inn	11-12 in	9.75	3/01	4c
Taxes				
Federal income taxes paid	yr	2047	1999	30r
Personal taxes, expenditures on	yr	2554	1999	30r
Property taxes paid	yr	726	1999	30r
State and local income taxes paid	yr	363	1999	30r
Transportation				
Transportation, ACCRA Index		85.40	3/01	4c
Cars and trucks, new, expenditures on	yr	1648	1999	30r
Cars and trucks, used, expenditures on	yr	1651	1999	30r
Diesel at the pump	gal	1.14	10/99	73s
Gasoline and motor oil purchases	yr	1052	1999	30r
Gasoline before-tax price (cents)	gal	107.30	10/00	43s
Maintenance and repair expenditures	yr	621	1999	30r
Public transportation, expenditures on	yr	298	1999	30r

Values are in dollars or fractions of dollars. In the column headed *Ref*, references are shown to sources. Each reference is followed by a letter. These refer to the geographical level for which data were reported: s=State, r=Region, and c=City or metro. The abbreviation *ex* is used to mean *except* or *excluding*; *exp* stands for *expenditures*. For other abbreviations and further explanations, please see the Introduction.

Roanoke, VA - continued

Item	Per	Value	Date	Ref.
Transportation				
Tire balance, computer or spin balance, front	wheel	6.24	3/01	4c
Transportation purchases	yr	6738	1999	30r
Vehicle expenses, miscellaneous, purchases	yr	2033	1999	30r
Vehicle insurance payments	yr	696	1999	30r
Vehicle purchases (net outlay)	yr	3354	1999	30r
Vehicle rental, lease expenditures	yr	352	1999	30r
Utilities				
Utilities, ACCRA Index		71.40	3/01	4c
Electrical bill, average	mos	82.17	9/00	9s
Electricity, 2400 sq ft, new home	mos	78.44	3/01	4c
Electricity, expenditures on	yr	1115	1999	30r
Electricity cost, average	KWh	5.90	9/00	9s
Water and other public services, expenditures on	yr	298	1999	30r
Weddings				
Wedding (national average cost)		19936	2000	33r
Wedding (regional average total cost)		16293	1997	110r
Attendants' gifts		321	1998	33r
Bridal attendants' apparel (5 persons)		824	2000	33r
Bride's headpiece/veil		173	1998	33r
Bride's wedding dress		859	1998	33r
Clergy, religious facility fee		242	1998	33r
Engagement ring		3177	1998	33r
Flowers		789	1998	33r
Groom's formalwear rental		99	2000	33r
Limousine		410	1998	33r
Marriage license cost		30.00	4/01	35s
Men's formalwear (ushers, best man)		469	2000	33r
Mother of bride apparel		241	2000	33r
Music		866	1998	33r
Photography and videography		1368	1998	33r
Rehearsal dinner		728	1998	33r
Wedding invitations and announcements		341	1998	33r
Wedding reception		7968	2000	33r
Wedding rings (bride and groom)		1060	1998	33r

Rochester, MN

Item	Per	Value	Date	Ref.
Average annual expenditures	yr	35369	1999	30r
Composite, ACCRA index		103.80	3/01	4c
Alcoholic Beverages				
Alcoholic beverage purchases	yr	304	1999	30r
Beer, Heineken, 12-oz, ex deposit	6	6.52	3/01	4c
J & B Scotch	750-ml	21.05	3/01	4c
Malt beverages, all types, all sizes, any origin	16 oz	0.93	7/01	11r
Wine, Livingston or Gallo, Chablis blanc	1.5 liter	5.58	3/01	4c
Wine, red and white table, all sizes, any origin	liter	7.04	7/01	11r
Appliances				
Appliance repair, service call, washing machine	min lab chg	47.69	3/01	4c
Major appliances, expenditures on	yr	165	1999	30r
Small appliances, housewares, expenditures on	yr	90	1999	30r
Banking and Money				
Mortgage interest and charges paid	yr	2277	1999	30r
Mortgage principal paid on owned property	yr	1230	1999	30r
Mortgage rate, incl. points and orig. fee, 30-yr. conv. fixed or ARM	mos	7.36	3/01	4c
Vehicle finance charges paid	yr	328	1999	30r
Charity				
Cash contributions, expenditures	yr	1126	1999	30r
Child Care				
Child raising cost, total, age 0-2	yr	7890	1999	60r
Child raising cost, total, age 3-5	yr	8130	1999	60r
Child raising cost, total, age 6-8	yr	8170	1999	60r
Child raising cost, total, age 9-11	yr	8190	1999	60r
Child raising cost, total, age 12-14	yr	8890	1999	60r

Rochester, MN - continued

Item	Per	Value	Date	Ref.
Child Care - continued				
Child raising cost, total, age 15-17	yr	9050	1999	60r
Child's child care and education, age 0-2	yr	1240	1999	60r
Child's child care and education, age 3-5	yr	1370	1999	60r
Child's child care and education, age 6-8	yr	880	1999	60r
Child's child care and education, age 9-11	yr	570	1999	60r
Child's child care and education, age 12-14	yr	420	1999	60r
Child's child care and education, age 15-17	yr	720	1999	60r
Child's clothing, age 0-2	yr	410	1999	60r
Child's clothing, age 3-5	yr	400	1999	60r
Child's clothing, age 6-8	yr	450	1999	60r
Child's clothing, age 9-11	yr	500	1999	60r
Child's clothing, age 12-14	yr	840	1999	60r
Child's clothing, age 15-17	yr	740	1999	60r
Child's food, age 0-2	yr	960	1999	60r
Child's food, age 3-5	yr	1120	1999	60r
Child's food, age 6-8	yr	1430	1999	60r
Child's food, age 9-11	yr	1710	1999	60r
Child's food, age 12-14	yr	1710	1999	60r
Child's food, age 15-17	yr	1920	1999	60r
Child's health care, age 0-2	yr	520	1999	60r
Child's health care, age 3-5	yr	500	1999	60r
Child's health care, age 6-8	yr	570	1999	60r
Child's health care, age 9-11	yr	610	1999	60r
Child's health care, age 12-14	yr	630	1999	60r
Child's health care, age 15-17	yr	650	1999	60r
Child's housing, age 0-2	yr	2860	1999	60r
Child's housing, age 3-5	yr	2840	1999	60r
Child's housing, age 6-8	yr	2800	1999	60r
Child's housing, age 9-11	yr	2650	1999	60r
Child's housing, age 12-14	yr	2840	1999	60r
Child's housing, age 15-17	yr	2440	1999	60r
Child's personal care, reading, age 0-2	yr	880	1999	60r
Child's personal care, reading, age 3-5	yr	900	1999	60r
Child's personal care, reading, age 6-8	yr	930	1999	60r
Child's personal care, reading, age 9-11	yr	970	1999	60r
Child's personal care, reading, age 12-14	yr	1150	1999	60r
Child's personal care, reading, age 15-17	yr	920	1999	60r
Clothing				
Apparel and services purchases	yr	1607	1999	30r
Boys' brief, cotton	3	4.63	3/01	4c
Boys, 2 to 15, expenditures on	yr	91	1999	30r
Children under 2, expenditures on	yr	59	1999	30r
Footwear, expenditures on	yr	285	1999	30r
Girls, 2 to 15, expenditures on	yr	116	1999	30r
Men and boys, expenditures on	yr	433	1999	30r
Men, 16 and over, expenditures on	yr	341	1999	30r
Shirt, man's dress shirt		28.84	3/01	4c
Slacks, man's "No Wrinkles" khaki		45.63	3/01	4c
Women, 16 and over, expenditures on	yr	490	1999	30r
Communications				
Cable modem installation, Media One		100.00	6/99	103s
Cable modem rate, cable subscriber, Media One	mos	34.95-39.95	6/99	103s
Cable modem rate, non-cable subscriber, Media One	mos	49.95	6/99	103s
Newspaper subscription, daily and Sunday delivery	mos	13.31	3/01	4c
Phone line, single, business, field visit	inst.	45.00	12/97	17s
Phone line, single, business, no field visit	inst.	45.00	12/97	17s
Phone line, single, residence, field visit	inst.	16.25	12/97	17s
Phone line, single, residence, no field visit	inst.	16.25	12/97	17s
Postage and stationery, expenditures on	yr	140	1999	30r
Postal rate, express mail, up to half-pound		12.45	7/01	108r
Postal rate, letter, first class, first ounce		0.34	7/01	108r
Postal rate, letter, two ounces		0.57	7/01	108r
Postal rate, post card		0.21	7/01	108r
Postal rate, priority mail, two pounds		3.95	7/01	108r
Postal rate, priority mail, up to one pound		3.50	7/01	108r
Telephone bill, business, basic rate	mos	34.61	12/97	18c
Telephone bill, family of three	mos	25.53	3/01	4c
Telephone bill, residential, basic rate	mos	13.96	12/97	18c

Values are in dollars or fractions of dollars. In the column headed *Ref*, references are shown to sources. Each reference is followed by a letter. These refer to the geographical level for which data were reported: s=State, r=Region, and c=City or metro. The abbreviation *ex* is used to mean *except* or *excluding*; *exp* stands for expenditures. For other abbreviations and further explanations, please see the Introduction.

Rochester, MN - continued

Item	Per	Value	Date	Ref.
Communications				
Telephone services, expenditures on	yr	830	1999	30r
Education				
Board, 4-year private college/university	yr	2267	1996	38s
Board, 4-year public college/university	yr	1474	1996	38s
Education expenditures	yr	583	1999	30r
Room, 4-year private college/university	yr	2058	1996	38s
Room, 4-year public college/university	yr	2022	1996	38s
Total cost, 4-year private college/university	yr	17222	1996	38s
Total cost, 4-year public college/university	yr	6712	1996	38s
Tuition, 2-year public college/university, in state	yr	2065	1996	38s
Tuition, 4-year private college/university, in state	yr	12897	1996	38s
Tuition, 4-year public college/university	yr	3216	1996	38s
Energy and Fuels				
Electricity	500 KWhs	46.59	7/01	11r
Energy, combined forms, 2400 sq ft	mos	169.25	3/01	4c
Energy, exc. electricity, 2400 sq ft	mos	119.71	3/01	4c
Fuel oil #2	gal	1.27	7/01	11r
Fuel oil and other fuels, expenditures on	yr	68	1999	30r
Gas, cooking, winter, 10 therms	mos	10.27	2/96	98c
Gas, cooking, winter, 30 therms	mos	18.81	2/96	98c
Gas, cooking, winter, 50 therms	mos	27.37	2/96	98c
Gas, heating, winter, average use	mos	100.69	2/96	98c
Gas, natural, commercial rate	1000 cf	6.86	11/00	88s
Gas, regular unleaded, cash, self-service	gal	1.60	3/01	4c
Gasoline, unleaded midgrade	gal	1.79	7/01	11r
Gasoline, unleaded premium	gal	1.86	7/01	11r
Gasoline, unleaded regular	gal	1.58	7/01	11r
Natural gas, expenditures on	yr	389	1999	30r
Utility (piped) gas, therm		0.81	7/01	11r
Utility (piped) gas, 40 therms		38.01	7/01	11r
Utility (piped) gas, 100 therms		81.75	7/01	11r
Entertainment				
Bowling, Saturday evening rate	line	2.75	3/01	4c
Entertainment purchases	yr	1984	1999	30r
Fees and admissions paid	yr	444	1999	30r
Monopoly game, Parker Brothers', No. 9	game	11.69	3/01	4c
Movie, first-run, Saturday, evening	adm.	6.50	3/01	4c
Television, radios, sound equipment, expenditures on	yr	580	1999	30r
Tennis balls, yellow, Wilson or Penn, 3	can	2.87	3/01	4c
Funerals				
Cosmetology, hair, other preparation		178.32	1/99	78r
Embalming		408.19	1/99	78r
Funeral at funeral home		362.13	1/99	78r
Professional service charges		1375.51	1/99	78r
Transfer of remains to funeral home		155.92	1/99	78r
Visitation/viewing		294.38	1/99	78r
Groceries				
Groceries, ACCRA Index		97.50	3/01	4c
Antibiotic ointment, Polysporin	0.5 oz	4.44	3/01	4c
Baby food, strained vegetables or fruit, lowest price	4-4.5 oz	0.45	3/01	4c
Bacon, sliced	lb	3.15	7/01	11r
Bakery products, expenditures on	yr	281	1999	30r
Bananas	lb	0.38	3/01	4c
Bananas	lb	0.48	7/01	11r
Beans, dried, any type, all sizes	lb	0.61	7/01	11r
Beef for stew, boneless	lb	3.08	7/01	11r
Beef or hamburger, ground	lb	1.18	3/01	4c
Beef, expenditures on	yr	217	1999	30r
Bologna, all beef or mixed	lb	2.52	7/01	11r
Bread, white	loaf	0.92	3/01	4c
Bread, white, pan	lb	1.06	7/01	11r
Broccoli	lb	0.91	7/01	11r
Butter, salted, grade AA, stick	lb	3.04	7/01	11r
Butter, yoghurt, cheese, etc, expenditures on	yr	183	1999	30r

Rochester, MN - continued

Item	Per	Value	Date	Ref.
Groceries - continued				
Cereals and bakery product purchases	yr	430	1999	30r
Cereals and cereal products, expenditures on	yr	149	1999	30r
Cheese, Kraft grated Parmesan	8 oz	3.52	3/01	4c
Chicken, fresh, whole	lb	1.07	7/01	11r
Chicken, whole fryer	lb	1.10	3/01	4c
Chops, boneless,	lb	3.64	7/01	11r
Chuck roast, U.S. choice, boneless	lb	2.47	7/01	11r
Cigarettes, Winston, Kings	carton	30.02	3/01	4c
Coffee, 100%, ground roast, all sizes	lb	2.69	7/01	11r
Coffee, vacuum-packed	13 oz	2.54	3/01	4c
Cookies, chocolate chip	lb	2.87	7/01	11r
Corn Flakes, Kellogg's or Post Toasties	18 oz	2.31	3/01	4c
Corn, frozen, whole kernel, lowest price	16 oz	0.95	3/01	4c
Dairy product purchases	yr	304	1999	30r
Eggs, expenditures on	yr	26	1999	30r
Eggs, Grade A or AA	dozen	0.84	3/01	4c
Eggs, grade A, large	dozen	0.88	7/01	11r
Fats and oils, expenditures on	yr	75	1999	30r
Fish and seafood, expenditures on	yr	72	1999	30r
Food (excl fruit and vegetables), eaten at home, purchases	yr	887	1999	30r
Food cooked on trips, expenditures on	yr	44	1999	30r
Food purchases	yr	4802	1999	30r
Food purchases, eaten away from home	yr	2069	1999	30r
Food purchases, food eaten at home	yr	2733	1999	30r
Fresh fruits, expenditures on	yr	138	1999	30r
Fresh milk and cream, expenditures on	yr	120	1999	30r
Fresh vegetables, expenditures on	yr	126	1999	30r
Grapefruit	lb	0.66	7/01	11r
Grapes, Thompson, seedless	lb	1.64	7/01	11r
Ground beef, 100% beef	lb	1.64	7/01	11r
Ground beef, lean and extra lean	lb	2.16	7/01	11r
Ground chuck, 100% beef	lb	2.13	7/01	11r
Ham, boneless, excl canned	lb	2.62	7/01	11r
Ice cream, prepackaged, bulk, regular	1/2 gal	3.35	7/01	11r
Lemons	lb	1.19	7/01	11r
Lettuce, iceberg	head	0.97	3/01	4c
Lettuce, iceberg	lb	0.73	7/01	11r
Margarine, Blue Bonnet or Parkay, stick	lb	0.93	3/01	4c
Margarine, soft, tubs	lb	0.89	7/01	11r
Meats, poultry, fish, and egg purchases	yr	671	1999	30r
Milk, fresh, whole, fortified	gal	2.71	7/01	11r
Milk, whole	1/2 gal	1.44	3/01	4c
Nonalcoholic beverages, expenditures on	yr	239	1999	30r
Orange juice, Minute Maid frozen	12 oz	1.42	3/01	4c
Oranges, Navel	lb	0.80	7/01	11r
Oranges, Valencia	lb	0.66	7/01	11r
Peaches, halves or slices, Hunt's, Del Monte, or Libby's	29 oz	1.65	3/01	4c
Pears, Anjou	lb	0.93	7/01	11r
Peas, green, Del Monte or Green Giant	15 oz	0.64	3/01	4c
Pork chops, center cut, bone-in	lb	3.63	7/01	11r
Pork, expenditures on	yr	150	1999	30r
Potato chips	16 oz	3.52	7/01	11r
Potatoes, frozen, french fried	lb	1.08	7/01	11r
Potatoes, white or red	10 lb	1.92	3/01	4c
Potatoes, white, all types	lb	0.33	7/01	11r
Poultry, expenditures on	yr	108	1999	30r
Processed fruits, expenditures on	yr	98	1999	30r
Processed vegetables, expenditures on	yr	80	1999	30r
Round roast, U.S. choice, boneless	lb	3.07	7/01	11r
Round steak, graded and ungraded, excl U.S. prime and choice	lb	3.41	7/01	11r
Sausage, Jimmy Dean/Owens pork	lb	3.55	7/01	11r
Shortening, vegetable oil blends	lb	1.13	7/01	11r
Shortening, vegetable, Crisco	3 lb	3.03	3/01	4c
Soft drink, Coca Cola, ex deposit	2 liter	1.21	3/01	4c
Spaghetti and macaroni	lb	0.80	7/01	11r
Steak, round, U.S. choice, boneless	lb	3.23	7/01	11r
Steak, T-bone	lb	6.87	3/01	4c
Steak, T-bone, U.S. choice, bone-in	lb	6.68	7/01	11r

Values are in dollars or fractions of dollars. In the column headed *Ref*, references are shown to sources. Each reference is followed by a letter. These refer to the geographical level for which data were reported: s=State, r=Region, and c=City or metro. The abbreviation *ex* is used to mean *except* or *excluding*; *exp* stands for expenditures. For other abbreviations and further explanations, please see the Introduction.

Rochester, MN - continued

Item	Per	Value	Date	Ref.
Groceries				
Strawberries, dry pint	12 oz	1.32	7/01	11r
Sugar and other sweets, expenditures on	yr	114	1999	30r
Sugar, cane or beet	4 lbs	1.28	3/01	4c
Sugar, white, 33-80 ounce package	lb	0.42	7/01	11r
Sugar, white, all sizes	lb	0.43	7/01	11r
Tobacco products and smoking supplies purchases	yr	331	1999	30r
Tomatoes, field grown	lb	1.46	7/01	11r
Tomatoes, Hunt's or Del Monte	14.5 oz	0.88	3/01	4c
Tuna, chunk, light	6 oz	0.76	3/01	4c
Tuna, light, chunk	lb	1.80	7/01	11r
Turkey, frozen, whole	lb	1.15	7/01	11r
Goods and Services				
Miscellaneous goods and services, ACCRA Index		104.70	3/01	4c
B&B Japanese maple (acer japonicum)	gal	29.99-169.99	4/00	93r
Boxwood (buxus)	2 gal	18.99-39.99	4/00	93r
Daylilly (hemerocallis)	gal	4.99-25.00	4/00	93r
Flat of annuals		11.98-24.99	4/00	93r
Fountain grass (pennisetum)	gal	5.98-12.98	4/00	93r
Hanging basket (10 in)		12.99-27.99	4/00	93r
Hardy geranium (geranium)	gal	7.99-9.99	4/00	93r
Hosta (hosta)	gal	6.00-25.00	4/00	93r
Lilac (syrubga vulgaris)	2 gal	14.99-24.99	4/00	93r
Miscellaneous purchases	yr	865	1999	30r
Rhododendron (rhododendron)	2 gal	23.98-42.99	4/00	93r
Sage (salvia)	gal	6.00-9.99	4/00	93r
Wintercreeper euonymus (euonymus fortunei)	2 gal	16.00-169.99	4/00	93r
Hunting license	yr	17.00	4/01	34s
Health Care				
Health care, ACCRA Index		115.70	3/01	4c
Cardiac catheterization, ave hospital/ physician charges		19020	1998	77s
Childbirth, Cesarean delivery		10722	1997	13r
Childbirth, vaginal delivery		6223	1997	13r
Dentist's fee, adult teeth cleaning and periodic oral exam	visit	76.86	3/01	4c
Doctor's fee, routine exam, established patient	visit	72.08	3/01	4c
Drugs, expenditures on	yr	394	1999	30r
Health care purchases	yr	2048	1999	30r
Health insurance expenditures	yr	978	1999	30r
Hospital care, private room	day	682.67	3/01	4c
Hysterectomy, laproscopically-assisted, ave hospital/physician charges		15580	1998	76s
Hysterectomy, vaginal, ave hospital and physician charges		10690	1998	76s
Medicaid dispensing fee		3.65	1999	87s
Medical services expenditures	yr	554	1999	30r
Medical supplies, expenditures on	yr	122	1999	30r
Plastic surgery, breast augmentation		3184	2000	7r
Plastic surgery, breast lift		3585	2000	7r
Plastic surgery, facelift		4999	2000	7r
Plastic surgery, hair transplantation		3105	2000	7r
Plastic surgery, lip augmentation		1290	2000	7r
Plastic surgery, lower body lift		8135	2000	7r
Plastic surgery, thigh lift		3839	2000	7r

Rochester, MN - continued

Item	Per	Value	Date	Ref.
Household Goods				
Dishwashing powder, Cascade	50 oz	3.88	3/01	4c
Floor coverings, expenditures on	yr	52	1999	30r
Furniture, expenditures on	yr	344	1999	30r
Household furnishings and equipment purchases	yr	1475	1999	30r
Household textiles, expenditures on	yr	109	1999	30r
Laundry and cleaning supplies, expenditures on	yr	134	1999	30r
Tissues, facial, Kleenex brand	175	1.10	3/01	4c
Housing				
Housing, ACCRA Index		93.20	3/01	4c
Home, 2200 sq ft, 4-br, 2-bath, 2-car garage, average		169900	2000	47c
Home price, existing, ave		144400	10/00	90r
Home value, median		135000	2001	53s
House, 2400 sq ft, 8000 sq ft lot, new, urban, utilities	total	183720	3/01	4c
House payment, principal and interest, 25% down payment	mos	950	3/01	4c
Household operation expenditures	yr	542	1999	30r
Housekeeping supplies purchases	yr	508	1999	30r
Lodging expenditures	yr	430	1999	30r
Maintenance, repairs, insurance expenditures	yr	853	1999	30r
Monthly rental value of owned home	mos	547	1999	30r
Owned dwellings, expenditures own	yr	4282	1999	30r
Rent expenditures	yr	1558	1999	30r
Rent, apartment, 2 br, 1 1/2-2 baths, unfurn, 950 sq ft, water	mos	675	3/01	4c
Rental unit, 1 bedroom, with utilities	mos	466	4/01	41c
Rental unit, 2 bedroom, with utilities	mos	610	4/01	41c
Rental unit, 3 bedroom, with utilities	mos	843	4/01	41c
Rental unit, 4 bedroom, with utilities	mos	947	4/01	41c
Shelter, expenditures on	yr	6270	1999	30r
Insurance and Pensions				
Life and other personal insurance purchases	yr	387	1999	30r
Pensions and Social Security, expenditures on	yr	2968	1999	30r
Legal Fees				
Divorce, filing fee		122.00	4/01	35s
Driver's license fee	renew	13.00	1999	48s
Driver's license fee	orig	16.00	1999	48s
Fishing license	yr	18.00	4/01	34s
Personal Goods				
Personal care products and services purchases	yr	385	1999	30r
Shampoo, Alberto VO5	15 oz	1.11	3/01	4c
Toothpaste, Crest or Colgate	6-7 oz	1.95	3/01	4c
Personal Services				
Dry cleaning, man's 2-pc suit		8.75	3/01	4c
Man's haircut, barbershop, no styling		11.99	3/01	4c
Personal services, household, expenditures on	yr	300	1999	30r
Woman's shampoo, trim, blow-dry, no style-change		22.40	3/01	4c
Pets				
Pets, toys, and playground equipment, expenditures on	yr	375	1999	30r
Restaurant Food				
Chicken, fried, thigh and drumstick, KFC/ Church's		2.22	3/01	4c
Hamburger with cheese, McDonald's	1/4 lb	2.10	3/01	4c
Pizza, Pizza Hut or Pizza Inn	11-12 in	9.35	3/01	4c
Taxes				
Federal income taxes paid	yr	2326	1999	30r
Personal taxes, expenditures on	yr	3223	1999	30r
Property taxes paid	yr	1152	1999	30r
State and local income taxes paid	yr	753	1999	30r

Values are in dollars or fractions of dollars. In the column headed *Ref*, references are shown as sources. Each reference is followed by a letter. These refer to the geographical level for which data were reported: s=State, r=Region, and c=City or metro. The abbreviation *ex* is used to mean *except* or *excluding*; *exp* stands for *expenditures*. For other abbreviations and further explanations, please see the Introduction.

Rochester, MN - continued

Item	Per	Value	Date	Ref.
Transportation				
Transportation, ACCRA Index		109.60	3/01	4c
Cars and trucks, new, expenditures on	yr	1280	1999	30r
Cars and trucks, used, expenditures on	yr	1763	1999	30r
Diesel at the pump	gal	1.28	10/99	73s
Gasoline and motor oil purchases	yr	1036	1999	30r
Gasoline before-tax price (cents)	gal	117.20	10/00	43s
Maintenance and repair expenditures	yr	594	1999	30r
Motorcycle license fee	orig	16.00	1999	49s
Motorcycle license fee	renew	13.00	1999	49s
Public transportation, expenditures on	yr	341	1999	30r
Tire balance, computer or spin balance, front	wheel	8.21	3/01	4c
Transportation purchases	yr	6617	1999	30r
Vehicle expenses, miscellaneous, purchases	yr	2159	1999	30r
Vehicle insurance payments	yr	701	1999	30r
Vehicle purchases (net outlay)	yr	3081	1999	30r
Vehicle rental, lease expenditures	yr	536	1999	30r
Utilities				
Utilities, ACCRA Index		135.70	3/01	4c
Electrical bill, average	mos	55.08	9/00	9s
Electricity, expenditures on	yr	841	1999	30r
Electricity and other, mixed, 2400 sq ft, new home	mos	49.54	3/01	4c
Electricity cost, average	KWh	5.80	9/00	9s
Utilities, fuels, and public services purchased	yr	2401	1999	30r
Water and other public services, expenditures on	yr	273	1999	30r
Weddings				
Wedding (national average cost)		19936	2000	33r
Wedding (regional average total cost)		16195	1997	110r
Attendants' gifts		321	1998	33r
Bridal attendants' apparel (5 persons)		824	2000	33r
Bride's headpiece/veil		173	1998	33r
Bride's wedding dress		859	1998	33r
Clergy, religious facility fee		242	1998	33r
Engagement ring		3177	1998	33r
Flowers		789	1998	33r
Groom's formalwear rental		99	2000	33r
Limousine		410	1998	33r
Marriage license cost		70.00	4/01	35s
Men's formalwear (ushers, best man)		469	2000	33r
Mother of bride apparel		241	2000	33r
Music		866	1998	33r
Photography and videography		1368	1998	33r
Rehearsal dinner		728	1998	33r
Wedding invitations and announcements		341	1998	33r
Wedding reception		7968	2000	33r
Wedding rings (bride and groom)		1060	1998	33r

Rochester, NY

Item	Per	Value	Date	Ref.
Average annual expenditures	yr	37971	1999	30r
Alcoholic Beverages				
Alcoholic beverage purchases	yr	368	1999	30r
Wine, red and white table, all sizes, any origin	liter	9.64	7/01	11r
Appliances				
Major appliances, expenditures on	yr	194	1999	30r
Small appliances, housewares, expenditures on	yr	93	1999	30r
Banking and Money				
Mortgage interest and charges paid	yr	2622	1999	30r
Mortgage principal paid on owned property	yr	1262	1999	30r
Vehicle finance charges paid	yr	240	1999	30r
Business Expenses				
Business travel, car rental	day	48	2001	3c
Business travel, food	day	58	2001	3c
Business travel, hotel	day	101	2001	3c

Rochester, NY - continued

Item	Per	Value	Date	Ref.
Charity				
Cash contributions, expenditures	yr	1001	1999	30r
Child Care				
Child raising cost, total, age 0-2	yr	8670	1999	60r
Child raising cost, total, age 3-5	yr	8910	1999	60r
Child raising cost, total, age 6-8	yr	9040	1999	60r
Child raising cost, total, age 9-11	yr	9100	1999	60r
Child raising cost, total, age 12-14	yr	9890	1999	60r
Child raising cost, total, age 15-17	yr	10010	1999	60r
Child's child care and education, age 0-2	yr	1070	1999	60r
Child's child care and education, age 3-5	yr	1190	1999	60r
Child's child care and education, age 6-8	yr	740	1999	60r
Child's child care and education, age 9-11	yr	470	1999	60r
Child's child care and education, age 12-14	yr	350	1999	60r
Child's child care and education, age 15-17	yr	590	1999	60r
Child's clothing, age 0-2	yr	480	1999	60r
Child's clothing, age 3-5	yr	470	1999	60r
Child's clothing, age 6-8	yr	520	1999	60r
Child's clothing, age 9-11	yr	570	1999	60r
Child's clothing, age 12-14	yr	970	1999	60r
Child's clothing, age 15-17	yr	870	1999	60r
Child's food, age 0-2	yr	1130	1999	60r
Child's food, age 3-5	yr	1290	1999	60r
Child's food, age 6-8	yr	1640	1999	60r
Child's food, age 9-11	yr	1930	1999	60r
Child's food, age 12-14	yr	1940	1999	60r
Child's food, age 15-17	yr	2150	1999	60r
Child's health care, age 0-2	yr	550	1999	60r
Child's health care, age 3-5	yr	530	1999	60r
Child's health care, age 6-8	yr	610	1999	60r
Child's health care, age 9-11	yr	650	1999	60r
Child's health care, age 12-14	yr	660	1999	60r
Child's health care, age 15-17	yr	690	1999	60r
Child's housing, age 0-2	yr	3555	1999	60r
Child's housing, age 3-5	yr	3530	1999	60r
Child's housing, age 6-8	yr	3490	1999	60r
Child's housing, age 9-11	yr	3340	1999	60r
Child's housing, age 12-14	yr	3530	1999	60r
Child's housing, age 15-17	yr	3140	1999	60r
Child's personal care, reading, age 0-2	yr	920	1999	60r
Child's personal care, reading, age 3-5	yr	950	1999	60r
Child's personal care, reading, age 6-8	yr	980	1999	60r
Child's personal care, reading, age 9-11	yr	1020	1999	60r
Child's personal care, reading, age 12-14	yr	1190	1999	60r
Child's personal care, reading, age 15-17	yr	970	1999	60r
Nannies: criminal background check		74	1998	84s
Clothing				
Apparel and services purchases	yr	1831	1999	30r
Boys, 2 to 15, expenditures on	yr	92	1999	30r
Children under 2, expenditures on	yr	63	1999	30r
Footwear, expenditures on	yr	300	1999	30r
Girls, 2 to 15, expenditures on	yr	101	1999	30r
Men and boys, expenditures on	yr	446	1999	30r
Men, 16 and over, expenditures on	yr	354	1999	30r
Women, 16 and over, expenditures on	yr	584	1999	30r
Communications				
Cable modem installation, Adelphi		54.90	6/99	103s
Cable modem installation, Cablevision Systems		150.00	6/99	103s
Cable modem installation, Time Warner		75.00-225.00	6/99	103s
Cable modem rate, cable subscriber, Adelphi	mos	34.95	6/99	103s
Cable modem rate, cable subscriber, Cablevision Systems	mos	44.95	6/99	103s
Cable modem rate, cable subscriber, Century	mos	39.95	6/99	103s
Cable modem rate, cable subscriber, Time Warner	mos	39.95-49.95	6/99	103s
Cable modem rate, non-cable subscriber, Adelphi	mos	44.95	6/99	103s
Cable modem rate, non-cable subscriber, Cablevision Systems	mos	54.95	6/99	103s

Values are in dollars or fractions of dollars. In the column headed *Ref*, references are shown to sources. Each reference is followed by a letter. These refer to the geographical level for which data were reported: s=State, r=Region, and c=City or metro. The abbreviation *ex* is used to mean *except* or *excluding*; *exp* stands for expenditures. For other abbreviations and further explanations, please see the Introduction.

Rochester, NY - continued

Item	Per	Value	Date	Ref.
Communications				
Cable modem rate, non-cable subscriber, Time Warner	mos	39.95-54.95	6/99	103s
Phone line, single, business, field visit	inst.	142.76	12/97	17s
Phone line, single, business, no field visit	inst.	106.05	12/97	17s
Phone line, single, residence, field visit	inst.	102.78	12/97	17s
Phone line, single, residence, no field visit	inst.	55.00	12/97	17s
Postage and stationery, expenditures on	yr	138	1999	30r
Postal rate, express mail, up to half-pound		12.45	7/01	108r
Postal rate, letter, first class, first ounce		0.34	7/01	108r
Postal rate, letter, two ounces		0.57	7/01	108r
Postal rate, post card		0.21	7/01	108r
Postal rate, priority mail, two pounds		3.95	7/01	108r
Postal rate, priority mail, up to one pound		3.50	7/01	108r
Telephone services, expenditures on	yr	830	1999	30r
Education				
Board, 4-year private college/university	yr	3255	1996	38s
Board, 4-year public college/university	yr	2310	1996	38s
Education expenditures	yr	877	1999	30r
Room, 4-year private college/university	yr	3724	1996	38s
Room, 4-year public college/university	yr	2937	1996	38s
Total cost, 4-year private college/university	yr	20831	1996	38s
Total cost, 4-year public college/university	yr	8960	1996	38s
Tuition, 2-year public college/university, in state	yr	2427	1996	38s
Tuition, 4-year private college/university, in state	yr	13852	1996	38s
Tuition, 4-year public college/university	yr	3714	1996	38s
Energy and Fuels				
Electricity	KWh	0.12	7/01	11r
Fuel oil #2	gal	1.31	7/01	11r
Fuel oil and other fuels, expenditures on	yr	207	1999	30r
Gas, cooking, winter, 10 therms	mos	13.04	2/96	98c
Gas, cooking, winter, 30 therms	mos	28.27	2/96	98c
Gas, cooking, winter, 50 therms	mos	43.51	2/96	98c
Gas, heating, winter, average use	mos	186.00	2/96	98c
Gasoline, all types	gal	1.80	7/01	11r
Gasoline, unleaded midgrade	gal	1.85	7/01	11r
Gasoline, unleaded premium	gal	1.91	7/01	11r
Gasoline, unleaded regular	gal	1.71	7/01	11r
Natural gas, expenditures on	yr	368	1999	30r
Utility (piped) gas, therm		1.08	7/01	11r
Utility (piped) gas, 40 therms		50.87	7/01	11r
Utility (piped) gas, 100 therms		111.06	7/01	11r
Entertainment				
Entertainment purchases	yr	1821	1999	30r
Fees and admissions paid	yr	511	1999	30r
Television, radios, sound equipment, expenditures on	yr	650	1999	30r
Funerals				
Total cost of funeral		5813.50	1/99	78r
Acknowledgement cards		28.32	1/99	78r
Casket		2082.20	1/99	78r
Cosmetology, hair, other preparation		169.59	1/99	78r
Embalming		465.60	1/99	78r
Funeral at funeral home		339.56	1/99	78r
Hearse (local)		183.96	1/99	78r
Professional service charges		1157.85	1/99	78r
Service car/van		100.41	1/99	78r
Transfer of remains to funeral home		158.66	1/99	78r
Vault		766.31	1/99	78r
Visitation/viewing		361.04	1/99	78r
Groceries				
Apples, red delicious	lb	0.95	7/01	11r
Bacon, sliced	lb	3.44	7/01	11r
Bakery products, expenditures on	yr	310	1999	30r
Bananas	lb	0.55	7/01	11r
Beef, expenditures on	yr	236	1999	30r
Bread, white, pan	lb	1.09	7/01	11r
Butter, yoghurt, cheese, etc, expenditures on	yr	214	1999	30r

Rochester, NY - continued

Item	Per	Value	Date	Ref.
Groceries - continued				
Cereals and bakery product purchases	yr	474	1999	30r
Cereals and cereal products, expenditures on	yr	164	1999	30r
Chicken legs, bone-in	lb	1.23	7/01	11r
Chicken, fresh, whole	lb	1.13	7/01	11r
Chuck roast, U.S. choice, boneless	lb	2.79	7/01	11r
Coffee, 100%, ground roast, all sizes	lb	3.40	7/01	11r
Dairy product purchases	yr	342	1999	30r
Eggs, expenditures on	yr	34	1999	30r
Eggs, grade A, large	dozen	0.82	7/01	11r
Fats and oils, expenditures on	yr	80	1999	30r
Fish and seafood, expenditures on	yr	123	1999	30r
Food (excl fruit and vegetables), eaten at home, purchases	yr	838	1999	30r
Food cooked on trips, expenditures on	yr	48	1999	30r
Food purchases	yr	5314	1999	30r
Food purchases, eaten away from home	yr	2313	1999	30r
Food purchases, food eaten at home	yr	3001	1999	30r
Fresh fruits, expenditures on	yr	169	1999	30r
Fresh milk and cream, expenditures on	yr	128	1999	30r
Fresh vegetables, expenditures on	yr	164	1999	30r
Grapefruit	lb	0.67	7/01	11r
Grapes, Thompson, seedless	lb	2.18	7/01	11r
Ground beef, lean and extra lean	lb	2.66	7/01	11r
Ground chuck, 100% beef	lb	2.04	7/01	11r
Lettuce, iceberg	lb	0.76	7/01	11r
Meats, poultry, fish, and egg purchases	yr	808	1999	30r
Nonalcoholic beverages, expenditures on	yr	225	1999	30r
Orange juice, frozen concentrate	16 oz	1.88	7/01	11r
Oranges, Navel	lb	0.79	7/01	11r
Oranges, Valencia	lb	0.56	7/01	11r
Peaches	lb	1.16	7/01	11r
Peanut butter, creamy, all sizes	lb	2.01	7/01	11r
Pears, Anjou	lb	1.16	7/01	11r
Pork chops, center cut, bone-in	lb	3.57	7/01	11r
Pork, expenditures on	yr	146	1999	30r
Potato chips	16 oz	3.37	7/01	11r
Potatoes, white, all types	lb	0.42	7/01	11r
Poultry, expenditures on	yr	158	1999	30r
Processed fruits, expenditures on	yr	124	1999	30r
Processed vegetables, expenditures on	yr	82	1999	30r
Round roast, U.S. choice, boneless	lb	3.04	7/01	11r
Spaghetti and macaroni	lb	1.04	7/01	11r
Steak, sirloin, U.S. choice, boneless	lb	5.39	7/01	11r
Strawberries, dry pint	12 oz	1.51	7/01	11r
Sugar and other sweets, expenditures on	yr	110	1999	30r
Sugar, white, 33-80 ounce package	lb	0.46	7/01	11r
Sugar, white, all sizes	lb	0.47	7/01	11r
Tobacco products and smoking supplies purchases	yr	309	1999	30r
Yogurt, natural, fruit flavored	8 oz	0.79	7/01	11r
Goods and Services				
B&B Japanese maple (acer japonicum)	gal	38.99-125.00	4/00	93r
Boxwood (buxus)	2 gal	15.99-49.95	4/00	93r
Daylily (hemerocallis)	gal	4.95	4/00	93r
Flat of annuals		8.00-14.99	4/00	93r
Fountain grass (pennisetum)	gal	6.99-9.99	4/00	93r
Hanging basket (10 in)		12.95-19.99	4/00	93r
Hardy geranium (geranium)	gal	6.95-7.99	4/00	93r
Hosta (hosta)	gal	4.95	4/00	93r
Lilac (syrubga vulgaris)	2 gal	17.99-74.95	4/00	93r
Miscellaneous purchases	yr	872	1999	30r
Rhododendron (rhododendron)	2 gal	23.99-54.95	4/00	93r

Values are in dollars or fractions of dollars. In the column headed *Ref*, references are shown to sources. Each reference is followed by a letter. These refer to the geographical level for which data were reported: s=State, r=Region, and c=City or metro. The abbreviation *ex* is used to mean *except* or *excluding*; *exp* stands for *expenditures*. For other abbreviations and further explanations, please see the Introduction.

Rochester, NY - continued

Item	Per	Value	Date	Ref.
Goods and Services				
Sage (salvia)	gal	6.95-7.99	4/00	93r
Wintercreeper euonymus (euonymus fortunei)	2 gal	14.99-23.95	4/00	93r
Hunting license	yr	11.00	4/01	34s
Health Care				
Cardiac catheterization, ave hospital/physician charges		12750	1998	77s
Childbirth, Cesarean delivery		14716	1997	13r
Childbirth, vaginal delivery		8541	1997	13r
Drugs, expenditures on	yr	296	1999	30r
Health care purchases	yr	1788	1999	30r
Health insurance expenditures	yr	875	1999	30r
Hysterectomy, laproscopically-assisted, ave hospital/physician charges		13460	1998	76s
Hysterectomy, vaginal, ave hospital and physician charges		10310	1998	76s
Medicaid dispensing fee		3.50-4.50	1999	87s
Medical services expenditures	yr	516	1999	30r
Medical supplies, expenditures on	yr	102	1999	30r
Nursing home costs, private room	day	187	2000	82c
Nursing home stay, private room	day	187	2000	81c
Plastic surgery, breast augmentation		4232	2000	7r
Plastic surgery, breast lift		4605	2000	7r
Plastic surgery, facelift		6964	2000	7r
Plastic surgery, hair transplantation		4193	2000	7r
Plastic surgery, lip augmentation		1675	2000	7r
Plastic surgery, lower body lift		6611	2000	7r
Plastic surgery, thigh lift		4751	2000	7r
Household Goods				
Floor coverings, expenditures on	yr	59	1999	30r
Furniture, expenditures on	yr	388	1999	30r
Household furnishings and equipment purchases	yr	1567	1999	30r
Household textiles, expenditures on	yr	112	1999	30r
Laundry and cleaning supplies, expenditures on	yr	104	1999	30r
Housing				
Home, 2200 sq ft, 4-br, 2-bath, 2-car garage, average		204600	2000	47c
Home price, existing, ave		180800	10/00	90r
Home value, median		179000	2001	53s
Household operation expenditures	yr	581	1999	30r
Housekeeping supplies purchases	yr	474	1999	30r
Lodging expenditures	yr	550	1999	30r
Maintenance, repairs, insurance expenditures	yr	835	1999	30r
Monthly rental value of owned home	mos	663	1999	30r
Owned dwellings, expenditures own	yr	5209	1999	30r
Rent expenditures	yr	2390	1999	30r
Rental unit, 1 bedroom, with utilities	mos	504	4/01	41c
Rental unit, 2 bedroom, with utilities	mos	612	4/01	41c
Rental unit, 3 bedroom, with utilities	mos	785	4/01	41c
Rental unit, 4 bedroom, with utilities	mos	858	4/01	41c
Shelter, expenditures on	yr	8149	1999	30r
Insurance and Pensions				
Auto insurance premium	yr	1113.55	1999	57s
Life and other personal insurance purchases	yr	424	1999	30r
Pensions and Social Security, expenditures on	yr	3037	1999	30r
Legal Fees				
Divorce, filing fee		270.00	4/01	35s
Driver's license fee	renew	25.00	1999	48s
Driver's license fee	orig	25.00	1999	48s
Fishing license	yr	14.00	4/01	34s
Personal Goods				
Personal care products and services purchases	yr	399	1999	30r

Rochester, NY - continued

Item	Per	Value	Date	Ref.
Personal Services				
Personal services, household, expenditures on	yr	271	1999	30r
Pets				
Pets, toys, and playground equipment, expenditures on	yr	325	1999	30r
Taxes				
Federal income taxes paid	yr	2606	1999	30r
Personal taxes, expenditures on	yr	3567	1999	30r
Property taxes paid	yr	1752	1999	30r
State and local income taxes paid	yr	694	1999	30r
Transportation				
Bus fare, one-way	trip	1.25	2000	1c
Cars and trucks, new, expenditures on	yr	1496	1999	30r
Cars and trucks, used, expenditures on	yr	1251	1999	30r
Diesel at the pump	gal	1.33	10/99	73s
Gasoline and motor oil purchases	yr	901	1999	30r
Gasoline before-tax price (cents)	gal	110.70	10/00	43s
Maintenance and repair expenditures	yr	618	1999	30r
Public transportation, expenditures on	yr	575	1999	30r
Transportation purchases	yr	6503	1999	30r
Vehicle expenses, miscellaneous, purchases	yr	2266	1999	30r
Vehicle insurance payments	yr	824	1999	30r
Vehicle purchases (net outlay)	yr	2761	1999	30r
Vehicle rental, lease expenditures	yr	584	1999	30r
Travel				
Hotel room	night	139.88	2/01	95s
Utilities				
Electrical bill, average	mos	71.50	9/00	9s
Electricity, expenditures on	yr	837	1999	30r
Electricity, summer, 250 KWh	mos	36.31	2/96	96c
Electricity, summer, 500 KWh	mos	62.90	2/96	96c
Electricity, summer, 750 KWh	mos	89.50	2/96	96c
Electricity, summer, 1000 KWh	mos	116.10	2/96	96c
Electricity cost, average	KWh	11.34	9/00	9s
Utilities, fuels, and public services purchased	yr	2457	1999	30r
Water and other public services, expenditures on	yr	215	1999	30r
Weddings				
Wedding (national average cost)		19936	2000	33r
Wedding (regional average total cost)		29454	1997	110r
Attendants' gifts		321	1998	33r
Bridal attendants' apparel (5 persons)		824	2000	33r
Bride's headpiece/veil		173	1998	33r
Bride's wedding dress		859	1998	33r
Clergy, religious facility fee		242	1998	33r
Engagement ring		3177	1998	33r
Flowers		789	1998	33r
Groom's formalwear rental		99	2000	33r
Limousine		410	1998	33r
Marriage license cost		25.00	4/01	35s
Men's formalwear (ushers, best man)		469	2000	33r
Mother of bride apparel		241	2000	33r
Music		866	1998	33r
Photography and videography		1368	1998	33r
Rehearsal dinner		728	1998	33r
Wedding invitations and announcements		341	1998	33r
Wedding reception		7968	2000	33r
Wedding rings (bride and groom)		1060	1998	33r

Rockford, IL

Item	Per	Value	Date	Ref.
Average annual expenditures	yr	35369	1999	30r
Composite, ACCRA index		105.00	3/01	4c
Alcoholic Beverages				
Alcoholic beverage purchases	yr	304	1999	30r
Beer, Heineken, 12-oz, ex deposit	6	7.11	3/01	4c
J & B Scotch	750-ml	18.63	3/01	4c
Malt beverages, all types, all sizes, any origin	16 oz	0.93	7/01	11r

Values are in dollars or fractions of dollars. In the column headed *Ref*, references are shown to sources. Each reference is followed by a letter. These refer to the geographical level for which data were reported: s=State, r=Region, and c=City or metro. The abbreviation *ex* is used to mean *except* or *excluding*; *exp* stands for *expenditures*. For other abbreviations and further explanations, please see the Introduction.

Rockford, IL - continued

Item	Per	Value	Date	Ref.
Alcoholic Beverages				
Wine, Livingston or Gallo, Chablis blanc	1.5 liter	5.20	3/01	4c
Wine, red and white table, all sizes, any origin	liter	7.04	7/01	11r
Appliances				
Appliance repair, service call, washing machine	min lab chg	50.39	3/01	4c
Major appliances, expenditures on	yr	165	1999	30r
Small appliances, housewares, expenditures on	yr	90	1999	30r
Banking and Money				
Mortgage interest and charges paid	yr	2277	1999	30r
Mortgage principal paid on owned property	yr	1230	1999	30r
Mortgage rate, incl. points and orig. fee, 30-yr. conv. fixed or ARM	mos	7.39	3/01	4c
Vehicle finance charges paid	yr	328	1999	30r
Charity				
Cash contributions, expenditures	yr	1126	1999	30r
Child Care				
Child raising cost, total, age 0-2	yr	7890	1999	60r
Child raising cost, total, age 3-5	yr	8130	1999	60r
Child raising cost, total, age 6-8	yr	8170	1999	60r
Child raising cost, total, age 9-11	yr	8190	1999	60r
Child raising cost, total, age 12-14	yr	8890	1999	60r
Child raising cost, total, age 15-17	yr	9050	1999	60r
Child's child care and education, age 0-2	yr	1240	1999	60r
Child's child care and education, age 3-5	yr	1370	1999	60r
Child's child care and education, age 6-8	yr	880	1999	60r
Child's child care and education, age 9-11	yr	570	1999	60r
Child's child care and education, age 12-14	yr	420	1999	60r
Child's child care and education, age 15-17	yr	720	1999	60r
Child's clothing, age 0-2	yr	410	1999	60r
Child's clothing, age 3-5	yr	400	1999	60r
Child's clothing, age 6-8	yr	450	1999	60r
Child's clothing, age 9-11	yr	500	1999	60r
Child's clothing, age 12-14	yr	840	1999	60r
Child's clothing, age 15-17	yr	740	1999	60r
Child's food, age 0-2	yr	960	1999	60r
Child's food, age 3-5	yr	1120	1999	60r
Child's food, age 6-8	yr	1430	1999	60r
Child's food, age 9-11	yr	1710	1999	60r
Child's food, age 12-14	yr	1710	1999	60r
Child's food, age 15-17	yr	1920	1999	60r
Child's health care, age 0-2	yr	520	1999	60r
Child's health care, age 3-5	yr	500	1999	60r
Child's health care, age 6-8	yr	570	1999	60r
Child's health care, age 9-11	yr	610	1999	60r
Child's health care, age 12-14	yr	630	1999	60r
Child's health care, age 15-17	yr	650	1999	60r
Child's housing, age 0-2	yr	2860	1999	60r
Child's housing, age 3-5	yr	2840	1999	60r
Child's housing, age 6-8	yr	2800	1999	60r
Child's housing, age 9-11	yr	2650	1999	60r
Child's housing, age 12-14	yr	2840	1999	60r
Child's housing, age 15-17	yr	2440	1999	60r
Child's personal care, reading, age 0-2	yr	880	1999	60r
Child's personal care, reading, age 3-5	yr	900	1999	60r
Child's personal care, reading, age 6-8	yr	930	1999	60r
Child's personal care, reading, age 9-11	yr	970	1999	60r
Child's personal care, reading, age 12-14	yr	1150	1999	60r
Child's personal care, reading, age 15-17	yr	920	1999	60r
Clothing				
Apparel and services purchases	yr	1607	1999	30r
Boys' brief, cotton	3	4.12	3/01	4c
Boys, 2 to 15, expenditures on	yr	91	1999	30r
Children under 2, expenditures on	yr	59	1999	30r
Footwear, expenditures on	yr	285	1999	30r
Girls, 2 to 15, expenditures on	yr	116	1999	30r
Men and boys, expenditures on	yr	433	1999	30r
Men, 16 and over, expenditures on	yr	341	1999	30r

Rockford, IL - continued

Item	Per	Value	Date	Ref.
Clothing - continued				
Shirt, man's dress shirt		26.59	3/01	4c
Slacks, man's "No Wrinkles" khaki		37.79	3/01	4c
Women, 16 and over, expenditures on	yr	490	1999	30r
Communications				
Cable modem installation, Adelphi		54.90	6/99	103s
Cable modem installation, AT&T-BIS		150.00	6/99	103s
Cable modem installation, Media One		100.00	6/99	103s
Cable modem rate, cable subscriber, Adelphi	mos	34.95	6/99	103s
Cable modem rate, cable subscriber, AT&T-BIS	mos	39.95	6/99	103s
Cable modem rate, cable subscriber, Media One	mos	34.95-39.95	6/99	103s
Cable modem rate, non-cable subscriber, Adelphi	mos	44.95	6/99	103s
Cable modem rate, non-cable subscriber, Media One	mos	49.95	6/99	103s
Newspaper subscription, daily and Sunday delivery	mos	15.22	3/01	4c
Phone line, single, business, field visit	inst.	52.35	12/97	17s
Phone line, single, business, no field visit	inst.	52.35	12/97	17s
Phone line, single, residence, field visit	inst.	55.00	12/97	17s
Phone line, single, residence, no field visit	inst.	55.00	12/97	17s
Postage and stationery, expenditures on	yr	140	1999	30r
Postal rate, express mail, up to half-pound		12.45	7/01	108r
Postal rate, letter, first class, first ounce		0.34	7/01	108r
Postal rate, letter, two ounces		0.57	7/01	108r
Postal rate, post card		0.21	7/01	108r
Postal rate, priority mail, two pounds		3.95	7/01	108r
Postal rate, priority mail, up to one pound		3.50	7/01	108r
Telephone bill, business, basic rate	mos	11.87	12/97	18c
Telephone bill, family of three	mos	18.98	3/01	4c
Telephone bill, residential, basic rate	mos	9.00	12/97	18c
Telephone services, expenditures on	yr	830	1999	30r
Education				
Board, 4-year private college/university	yr	2306	1996	38s
Board, 4-year public college/university	yr	2405	1996	38s
Education expenditures	yr	583	1999	30r
Room, 4-year private college/university	yr	2718	1996	38s
Room, 4-year public college/university	yr	2072	1996	38s
Total cost, 4-year private college/university	yr	16678	1996	38s
Total cost, 4-year public college/university	yr	7829	1996	38s
Tuition, 2-year public college/university, in state	yr	1232	1996	38s
Tuition, 4-year private college/university, in state	yr	11653	1996	38s
Tuition, 4-year public college/university	yr	3352	1996	38s
Energy and Fuels				
Electricity	500 KWhs	46.59	7/01	11r
Energy, combined forms, 2400 sq ft	mos	169.91	3/01	4c
Energy, exc. electricity, 2400 sq ft	mos	104.54	3/01	4c
Fuel oil #2	gal	1.27	7/01	11r
Fuel oil and other fuels, expenditures on	yr	68	1999	30r
Gas, natural, commercial rate	1000 cf	8.47	11/00	88s
Gas, regular unleaded, cash, self-service	gal	1.40	3/01	4c
Gasoline, unleaded midgrade	gal	1.79	7/01	11r
Gasoline, unleaded premium	gal	1.86	7/01	11r
Gasoline, unleaded regular	gal	1.58	7/01	11r
Natural gas, expenditures on	yr	389	1999	30r
Utility (piped) gas, therm		0.81	7/01	11r
Utility (piped) gas, 40 therms		38.01	7/01	11r
Utility (piped) gas, 100 therms		81.75	7/01	11r
Entertainment				
Bowling, Saturday evening rate	line	2.75	3/01	4c
Entertainment purchases	yr	1984	1999	30r
Fees and admissions paid	yr	444	1999	30r
Monopoly game, Parker Brothers', No. 9	game	12.58	3/01	4c
Movie, first-run, Saturday, evening	adm.	6.67	3/01	4c
Television, radios, sound equipment, expenditures on	yr	580	1999	30r

Values are in dollars or fractions of dollars. In the column headed *Ref*, references are shown to sources. Each reference is followed by a letter. These refer to the geographical level for which data were reported: s=State, r=Region, and c=City or metro. The abbreviation *ex* is used to mean *except* or *excluding*; *exp* stands for expenditures. For other abbreviations and further explanations, please see the Introduction.

Rockford, IL - continued

Item	Per	Value	Date	Ref.
Entertainment				
Tennis balls, yellow, Wilson or Penn, 3	can	2.39	3/01	4c
Funerals				
Cosmetology, hair, other preparation		178.32	1/99	78r
Embalming		408.19	1/99	78r
Funeral at funeral home		362.13	1/99	78r
Professional service charges		1375.51	1/99	78r
Transfer of remains to funeral home		155.92	1/99	78r
Visitation/viewing		294.38	1/99	78r
Groceries				
Groceries, ACCRA Index		104.10	3/01	4c
Antibiotic ointment, Polysporin	0.5 oz	5.01	3/01	4c
Baby food, strained vegetables or fruit, lowest price	4-4.5 oz	0.51	3/01	4c
Bacon, sliced	lb	3.15	7/01	11r
Bakery products, expenditures on	yr	281	1999	30r
Bananas	lb	0.52	3/01	4c
Bananas	lb	0.48	7/01	11r
Beans, dried, any type, all sizes	lb	0.61	7/01	11r
Beef for stew, boneless	lb	3.08	7/01	11r
Beef or hamburger, ground	lb	1.53	3/01	4c
Beef, expenditures on	yr	217	1999	30r
Bologna, all beef or mixed	lb	2.52	7/01	11r
Bread, white	loaf	0.97	3/01	4c
Bread, white, pan	lb	1.06	7/01	11r
Broccoli	lb	0.91	7/01	11r
Butter, salted, grade AA, stick	lb	3.04	7/01	11r
Butter, yoghurt, cheese, etc, expenditures on	yr	183	1999	30r
Cereals and bakery product purchases	yr	430	1999	30r
Cereals and cereal products, expenditures on	yr	149	1999	30r
Cheese, Kraft grated Parmesan	8 oz	3.84	3/01	4c
Chicken, fresh, whole	lb	1.07	7/01	11r
Chicken, whole fryer	lb	1.03	3/01	4c
Chops, boneless,	lb	3.64	7/01	11r
Chuck roast, U.S. choice, boneless	lb	2.47	7/01	11r
Cigarettes, Winston, Kings	carton	35.03	3/01	4c
Coffee, 100%, ground roast, all sizes	lb	2.69	7/01	11r
Coffee, vacuum-packed	13 oz	2.58	3/01	4c
Cookies, chocolate chip	lb	2.87	7/01	11r
Corn Flakes, Kellogg's or Post Toasties	18 oz	2.79	3/01	4c
Corn, frozen, whole kernel, lowest price	16 oz	1.08	3/01	4c
Dairy product purchases	yr	304	1999	30r
Eggs, expenditures on	yr	26	1999	30r
Eggs, Grade A or AA	dozen	1.00	3/01	4c
Eggs, grade A, large	dozen	0.88	7/01	11r
Fats and oils, expenditures on	yr	75	1999	30r
Fish and seafood, expenditures on	yr	72	1999	30r
Food (excl fruit and vegetables), eaten at home, purchases	yr	887	1999	30r
Food cooked on trips, expenditures on	yr	44	1999	30r
Food purchases	yr	4802	1999	30r
Food purchases, eaten away from home	yr	2069	1999	30r
Food purchases, food eaten at home	yr	2733	1999	30r
Fresh fruits, expenditures on	yr	138	1999	30r
Fresh milk and cream, expenditures on	yr	120	1999	30r
Fresh vegetables, expenditures on	yr	126	1999	30r
Grapefruit	lb	0.66	7/01	11r
Grapes, Thompson, seedless	lb	1.64	7/01	11r
Ground beef, 100% beef	lb	1.64	7/01	11r
Ground beef, lean and extra lean	lb	2.16	7/01	11r
Ground chuck, 100% beef	lb	2.13	7/01	11r
Ham, boneless, excl canned	lb	2.62	7/01	11r
Ice cream, prepackaged, bulk, regular	1/2 gal	3.35	7/01	11r
Lemons	lb	1.19	7/01	11r
Lettuce, iceberg	head	1.07	3/01	4c
Lettuce, iceberg	lb	0.73	7/01	11r
Margarine, Blue Bonnet or Parkay, stick	lb	1.05	3/01	4c
Margarine, soft, tubs	lb	0.89	7/01	11r
Meats, poultry, fish, and egg purchases	yr	671	1999	30r
Milk, fresh, whole, fortified	gal	2.71	7/01	11r
Milk, whole	1/2 gal	1.71	3/01	4c

Rockford, IL - continued

Item	Per	Value	Date	Ref.
Groceries - continued				
Nonalcoholic beverages, expenditures on	yr	239	1999	30r
Orange juice, Minute Maid frozen	12 oz	1.56	3/01	4c
Oranges, Navel	lb	0.80	7/01	11r
Oranges, Valencia	lb	0.66	7/01	11r
Peaches, halves or slices, Hunt's, Del Monte, or Libby's	29 oz	1.62	3/01	4c
Pears, Anjou	lb	0.93	7/01	11r
Peas, green, Del Monte or Green Giant	15 oz	0.80	3/01	4c
Pork chops, center cut, bone-in	lb	3.63	7/01	11r
Pork, expenditures on	yr	150	1999	30r
Potato chips	16 oz	3.52	7/01	11r
Potatoes, frozen, french fried	lb	1.08	7/01	11r
Potatoes, white or red	10 lb	2.95	3/01	4c
Potatoes, white, all types	lb	0.33	7/01	11r
Poultry, expenditures on	yr	108	1999	30r
Processed fruits, expenditures on	yr	98	1999	30r
Processed vegetables, expenditures on	yr	80	1999	30r
Round roast, U.S. choice, boneless	lb	3.07	7/01	11r
Round steak, graded and ungraded, excl U.S. prime and choice	lb	3.41	7/01	11r
Sausage, Jimmy Dean/Owens pork	lb	3.17	3/01	4c
Shortening, vegetable oil blends	lb	1.13	7/01	11r
Shortening, vegetable, Crisco	3 lb	2.89	3/01	4c
Soft drink, Coca Cola, ex deposit	2 liter	1.15	3/01	4c
Spaghetti and macaroni	lb	0.80	7/01	11r
Steak, round, U.S. choice, boneless	lb	3.23	7/01	11r
Steak, T-bone	lb	4.77	3/01	4c
Steak, T-bone, U.S. choice, bone-in	lb	6.68	7/01	11r
Strawberries, dry pint	12 oz	1.32	7/01	11r
Sugar and other sweets, expenditures on	yr	114	1999	30r
Sugar, cane or beet	4 lbs	1.77	3/01	4c
Sugar, white, 33-80 ounce package	lb	0.42	7/01	11r
Sugar, white, all sizes	lb	0.43	7/01	11r
Tobacco products and smoking supplies purchases	yr	331	1999	30r
Tomatoes, field grown	lb	1.46	7/01	11r
Tomatoes, Hunt's or Del Monte	14.5 oz	0.94	3/01	4c
Tuna, chunk, light	6 oz	0.71	3/01	4c
Tuna, light, chunk	lb	1.80	7/01	11r
Turkey, frozen, whole	lb	1.15	7/01	11r
Goods and Services				
Miscellaneous goods and services, ACCRA Index		101.20	3/01	4c
B&B Japanese maple (acer japonicum)	gal	29.99-169.99	4/00	93r
Boxwood (buxus)	2 gal	18.99-39.99	4/00	93r
Daylilly (hemerocallis)	gal	4.99-25.00	4/00	93r
Flat of annuals		11.98-24.99	4/00	93r
Fountain grass (pennisetum)	gal	5.98-12.98	4/00	93r
Hanging basket (10 in)		12.99-27.99	4/00	93r
Hardy geranium (geranium)	gal	7.99-9.99	4/00	93r
Hosta (hosta)	gal	6.00-25.00	4/00	93r
Lilac (syrubga vulgaris)	2 gal	14.99-24.99	4/00	93r
Miscellaneous purchases	yr	865	1999	30r
Rhododendron (rhododendron)	2 gal	23.98-42.99	4/00	93r
Sage (salvia)	gal	6.00-9.99	4/00	93r
Wintercreeper euonymus (euonymus fortunei)	2 gal	16.00-169.99	4/00	93r
Hunting license	yr	7.50	4/01	34s

Values are in dollars or fractions of dollars. In the column headed *Ref*, references are shown to sources. Each reference is followed by a letter. These refer to the geographical level for which data were reported: s=State, r=Region, and c=City or metro. The abbreviation *ex* is used to mean *except* or *excluding*; *exp* stands for *expenditures*. For other abbreviations and further explanations, please see the Introduction.

Rockford, IL - continued

Item	Per	Value	Date	Ref.
Health Care				
Health care, ACCRA Index		105.90	3/01	4c
Cardiac catheterization, ave hospital/ physician charges		17690	1998	77s
Childbirth, Cesarean delivery		10722	1997	13r
Childbirth, vaginal delivery		6223	1997	13r
Dentist's fee, adult teeth cleaning and periodic oral exam	visit	74.75	3/01	4c
Doctor's fee, routine exam, established patient	visit	61.43	3/01	4c
Drugs, expenditures on	yr	394	1999	30r
Health care purchases	yr	2048	1999	30r
Health insurance expenditures	yr	978	1999	30r
Hospital care, private room	day	577.17	3/01	4c
Hysterectomy, laproscopically-assisted, ave hospital/physician charges		15850	1998	76s
Hysterectomy, vaginal, ave hospital and physician charges		11810	1998	76s
Medicaid dispensing fee		3.69-15.45	1999	87s
Medical services expenditures	yr	554	1999	30r
Medical supplies, expenditures on	yr	122	1999	30r
Plastic surgery, breast augmentation		3184	2000	7r
Plastic surgery, breast lift		3585	2000	7r
Plastic surgery, facelift		4999	2000	7r
Plastic surgery, hair transplantation		3105	2000	7r
Plastic surgery, lip augmentation		1290	2000	7r
Plastic surgery, lower body lift		8135	2000	7r
Plastic surgery, thigh lift		3839	2000	7r
Household Goods				
Dishwashing powder, Cascade	50 oz	2.91	3/01	4c
Floor coverings, expenditures on	yr	52	1999	30r
Furniture, expenditures on	yr	344	1999	30r
Household furnishings and equipment purchases	yr	1475	1999	30r
Household textiles, expenditures on	yr	109	1999	30r
Laundry and cleaning supplies, expenditures on	yr	134	1999	30r
Tissues, facial, Kleenex brand	175	1.30	3/01	4c
Housing				
Housing, ACCRA Index		101.90	3/01	4c
Home, 2200 sq ft, 4-br, 2-bath, 2-car garage, average		147333	2000	47c
Home price, existing, ave		144400	10/00	90r
Home value, median		183000	2001	53s
House, 2400 sq ft, 8000 sq ft lot, new, urban, utilities	total	194012	3/01	4c
House payment, principal and interest, 25% down payment	mos	1007	3/01	4c
Household operation expenditures	yr	542	1999	30r
Housekeeping supplies purchases	yr	508	1999	30r
Lodging expenditures	yr	430	1999	30r
Maintenance, repairs, insurance expenditures	yr	853	1999	30r
Monthly rental value of owned home	mos	547	1999	30r
Owned dwellings, expenditures own	yr	4282	1999	30r
Rent expenditures	yr	1558	1999	30r
Rent, apartment, 2 br, 1 1/2-2 baths, unfurn, 950 sq ft, water	mos	822	3/01	4c
Rental unit, 1 bedroom, with utilities	mos	471	4/01	41c
Rental unit, 2 bedroom, with utilities	mos	574	4/01	41c
Rental unit, 3 bedroom, with utilities	mos	721	4/01	41c
Rental unit, 4 bedroom, with utilities	mos	841	4/01	41c
Shelter, expenditures on	yr	6270	1999	30r
Insurance and Pensions				
Life and other personal insurance purchases	yr	387	1999	30r
Pensions and Social Security, expenditures on	yr	2968	1999	30r
Legal Fees				
Divorce, filing fee		100.00-150.00	4/01	35s

Rockford, IL - continued

Item	Per	Value	Date	Ref.
Legal Fees - continued				
Driver's license fee	renew	20.00	1999	48s
Driver's license fee	orig	10.00	1999	48s
Personal Goods				
Personal care products and services purchases	yr	385	1999	30r
Shampoo, Alberto VO5	15 oz	1.37	3/01	4c
Toothpaste, Crest or Colgate	6-7 oz	2.59	3/01	4c
Personal Services				
Dry cleaning, man's 2-pc suit		8.70	3/01	4c
Man's haircut, barbershop, no styling		8.00	3/01	4c
Personal services, household, expenditures on	yr	300	1999	30r
Woman's shampoo, trim, blow-dry, no style-change		30.40	3/01	4c
Pets				
Pets, toys, and playground equipment, expenditures on	yr	375	1999	30r
Restaurant Food				
Chicken, fried, thigh and drumstick, KFC/ Church's		2.55	3/01	4c
Hamburger with cheese, McDonald's	1/4 lb	1.99	3/01	4c
Pizza, Pizza Hut or Pizza Inn	11-12 in	8.99	3/01	4c
Taxes				
Federal income taxes paid	yr	2326	1999	30r
Personal taxes, expenditures on	yr	3223	1999	30r
Property taxes paid	yr	1152	1999	30r
State and local income taxes paid	yr	753	1999	30r
Transportation				
Transportation, ACCRA Index		106.00	3/01	4c
Bus fare, to central business district	1-way	1.00	3/01	4c
Cars and trucks, new, expenditures on	yr	1280	1999	30r
Cars and trucks, used, expenditures on	yr	1763	1999	30r
Diesel at the pump	gal	1.33	10/99	73s
Gasoline and motor oil purchases	yr	1036	1999	30r
Gasoline before-tax price (cents)	gal	112.70	10/00	43s
Maintenance and repair expenditures	yr	594	1999	30r
Public transportation, expenditures on	yr	341	1999	30r
Tire balance, computer or spin balance, front	wheel	9.43	3/01	4c
Transportation purchases	yr	6617	1999	30r
Vehicle expenses, miscellaneous, purchases	yr	2159	1999	30r
Vehicle insurance payments	yr	701	1999	30r
Vehicle purchases (net outlay)	yr	3081	1999	30r
Vehicle rental, lease expenditures	yr	536	1999	30r
Utilities				
Utilities, ACCRA Index		132.10	3/01	4c
Electrical bill, average	mos	63.08	9/00	9s
Electricity, expenditures on	yr	841	1999	30r
Electricity and other, mixed, 2400 sq ft, new home	mos	65.37	3/01	4c
Electricity cost, average	KWh	6.49	9/00	9s
Utilities, fuels, and public services purchased	yr	2401	1999	30r
Water and other public services, expenditures on	yr	273	1999	30r
Weddings				
Wedding (national average cost)		19936	2000	33r
Wedding (regional average total cost)		16195	1997	110r
Attendants' gifts		321	1998	33r
Bridal attendants' apparel (5 persons)		824	2000	33r
Bride's headpiece/veil		173	1998	33r
Bride's wedding dress		859	1998	33r
Clergy, religious facility fee		242	1998	33r
Engagement ring		3177	1998	33r
Flowers		789	1998	33r
Groom's formalwear rental		99	2000	33r
Limousine		410	1998	33r
Marriage license cost		15.00-20.00	4/01	35s
Men's formalwear (ushers, best man)		469	2000	33r

Values are in dollars or fractions of dollars. In the column headed *Ref*, references are shown to sources. Each reference is followed by a letter. These refer to the geographical level for which data were reported: s=State, r=Region, and c=City or metro. The abbreviation *ex* is used to mean *except* or *excluding*; *exp* stands for expenditures. For other abbreviations and further explanations, please see the Introduction.

Rockford, IL - continued

Item	Per	Value	Date	Ref.
Weddings				
Mother of bride apparel		241	2000	33r
Music		866	1998	33r
Photography and videography		1368	1998	33r
Rehearsal dinner		728	1998	33r
Wedding invitations and announcements		341	1998	33r
Wedding reception		7968	2000	33r
Wedding rings (bride and groom)		1060	1998	33r

Rocky Mount, NC

Item	Per	Value	Date	Ref.
Composite, ACCRA index		99.50	3/01	4c
Alcoholic Beverages				
Alcoholic beverage purchases	yr	253	1999	30r
Beer, Heineken, 12-oz, ex deposit	6	6.70	3/01	4c
J & B Scotch	750-ml	20.75	3/01	4c
Malt beverages, all types, all sizes, any origin	16 oz	0.96	7/01	11r
Wine, Livingston or Gallo, Chablis blanc	1.5 liter	5.91	3/01	4c
Appliances				
Appliance repair, service call, washing machine	min lab chg	46.80	3/01	4c
Major appliances, expenditures on	yr	172	1999	30r
Small appliances, housewares, expenditures on	yr	81	1999	30r
Banking and Money				
Mortgage interest and charges paid	yr	2039	1999	30r
Mortgage principal paid on owned property	yr	1026	1999	30r
Mortgage rate, incl. points and orig. fee, 30-yr. conv. fixed or ARM	mos	7.09	3/01	4c
Vehicle finance charges paid	yr	365	1999	30r
Charity				
Cash contributions, expenditures	yr	1127	1999	30r
Child Care				
Child raising cost, total, age 0-2	yr	8540	1999	60r
Child raising cost, total, age 3-5	yr	8780	1999	60r
Child raising cost, total, age 6-8	yr	8820	1999	60r
Child raising cost, total, age 9-11	yr	8800	1999	60r
Child raising cost, total, age 12-14	yr	9510	1999	60r
Child raising cost, total, age 15-17	yr	9740	1999	60r
Child's child care and education, age 0-2	yr	1380	1999	60r
Child's child care and education, age 3-5	yr	1520	1999	60r
Child's child care and education, age 6-8	yr	990	1999	60r
Child's child care and education, age 9-11	yr	650	1999	60r
Child's child care and education, age 12-14	yr	490	1999	60r
Child's child care and education, age 15-17	yr	840	1999	60r
Child's clothing, age 0-2	yr	480	1999	60r
Child's clothing, age 3-5	yr	470	1999	60r
Child's clothing, age 6-8	yr	520	1999	60r
Child's clothing, age 9-11	yr	570	1999	60r
Child's clothing, age 12-14	yr	950	1999	60r
Child's clothing, age 15-17	yr	850	1999	60r
Child's food, age 0-2	yr	1000	1999	60r
Child's food, age 3-5	yr	1160	1999	60r
Child's food, age 6-8	yr	1490	1999	60r
Child's food, age 9-11	yr	1770	1999	60r
Child's food, age 12-14	yr	1770	1999	60r
Child's food, age 15-17	yr	1980	1999	60r
Child's health care, age 0-2	yr	620	1999	60r
Child's health care, age 3-5	yr	590	1999	60r
Child's health care, age 6-8	yr	680	1999	60r
Child's health care, age 9-11	yr	720	1999	60r
Child's health care, age 12-14	yr	730	1999	60r
Child's health care, age 15-17	yr	760	1999	60r
Child's housing, age 0-2	yr	3070	1999	60r
Child's housing, age 3-5	yr	3050	1999	60r
Child's housing, age 6-8	yr	3010	1999	60r
Child's housing, age 9-11	yr	2850	1999	60r
Child's housing, age 12-14	yr	3040	1999	60r
Child's housing, age 15-17	yr	2650	1999	60r
Child's personal care, reading, age 0-2	yr	910	1999	60r

Rocky Mount, NC - continued

Item	Per	Value	Date	Ref.
Child Care - continued				
Child's personal care, reading, age 3-5	yr	930	1999	60r
Child's personal care, reading, age 6-8	yr	960	1999	60r
Child's personal care, reading, age 9-11	yr	1000	1999	60r
Child's personal care, reading, age 12-14	yr	1170	1999	60r
Child's personal care, reading, age 15-17	yr	950	1999	60r
Clothing				
Apparel and services purchases	yr	1610	1999	30r
Boys' brief, cotton	3	5.24	3/01	4c
Boys, 2 to 15, expenditures on	yr	89	1999	30r
Children under 2, expenditures on	yr	79	1999	30r
Footwear, expenditures on	yr	283	1999	30r
Girls, 2 to 15, expenditures on	yr	103	1999	30r
Men and boys, expenditures on	yr	351	1999	30r
Men, 16 and over, expenditures on	yr	262	1999	30r
Shirt, man's dress shirt		30.87	3/01	4c
Slacks, man's "No Wrinkles" khaki		29.73	3/01	4c
Women, 16 and over, expenditures on	yr	538	1999	30r
Communications				
Cable modem installation, Intermedia		149.95	6/99	103s
Cable modem installation, Time Warner		75.00-225.00	6/99	103s
Cable modem rate, cable subscriber, Intermedia	mos	49.95	6/99	103s
Cable modem rate, cable subscriber, Time Warner	mos	39.95-49.95	6/99	103s
Cable modem rate, non-cable subscriber, Intermedia	mos	54.95	6/99	103s
Cable modem rate, non-cable subscriber, Time Warner	mos	39.95-54.95	6/99	103s
Newspaper subscription, daily and Sunday delivery	mos	9.99	3/01	4c
Phone line, single, business, field visit	inst.	65.00	12/97	17s
Phone line, single, business, no field visit	inst.	65.00	12/97	17s
Phone line, single, residence, field visit	inst.	42.75	12/97	17s
Phone line, single, residence, no field visit	inst.	42.75	12/97	17s
Postage and stationery, expenditures on	yr	104	1999	30r
Postal rate, express mail, up to half-pound		12.45	7/01	108r
Postal rate, letter, first class, first ounce		0.34	7/01	108r
Postal rate, letter, two ounces		0.57	7/01	108r
Postal rate, post card		0.21	7/01	108r
Postal rate, priority mail, two pounds		3.95	7/01	108r
Postal rate, priority mail, up to one pound		3.50	7/01	108r
Telephone bill, family of three	mos	19.96	3/01	4c
Telephone services, expenditures on	yr	860	1999	30r
Education				
Board, 4-year private college/university	yr	2316	1996	38s
Board, 4-year public college/university	yr	1737	1996	38s
Education expenditures	yr	431	1999	30r
Room, 4-year private college/university	yr	2128	1996	38s
Room, 4-year public college/university	yr	1742	1996	38s
Total cost, 4-year private college/university	yr	15428	1996	38s
Total cost, 4-year public college/university	yr	5119	1996	38s
Tuition, 4-year private college/university, in state	yr	10984	1996	38s
Tuition, 4-year public college/university	yr	1639	1996	38s
Energy and Fuels				
Electricity	KWh	0.09	7/01	11r
Electricity	500 KWhs	47.29	7/01	11r
Energy, combined forms, 2400 sq ft	mos	134.71	3/01	4c
Fuel oil #2	gal	1.43	7/01	11r
Fuel oil and other fuels, expenditures on	yr	45	1999	30r
Gas, natural, commercial rate	1000 cf	9.25	11/00	88s
Gas, regular unleaded, cash, self-service	gal	1.35	3/01	4c
Gasoline, all types	gal	1.60	7/01	11r
Gasoline, unleaded midgrade	gal	1.65	7/01	11r
Gasoline, unleaded premium	gal	1.74	7/01	11r
Natural gas, expenditures on	yr	164	1999	30r
Utility (piped) gas, therm		1.01	7/01	11r
Utility (piped) gas, 40 therms		44.29	7/01	11r

Values are in dollars or fractions of dollars. In the column headed *Ref*, references are shown to sources. Each reference is followed by a letter. These refer to the geographical level for which data were reported: s=State, r=Region, and c=City or metro. The abbreviation *ex* is used to mean *except* or *excluding*; *exp* stands for expenditures. For other abbreviations and further explanations, please see the Introduction.

Rocky Mount, NC - continued

Item	Per	Value	Date	Ref.
Energy and Fuels				
Utility (piped) gas, 100 therms		97.44	7/01	11r
Entertainment				
Bowling, Saturday evening rate	line	3.75	3/01	4c
Entertainment purchases	yr	1574	1999	30r
Fees and admissions paid	yr	371	1999	30r
Monopoly game, Parker Brothers', No. 9	game	8.66	3/01	4c
Movie, first-run, Saturday, evening	adm.	6.25	3/01	4c
Reading purchases	yr	121	1999	30r
Television, radios, sound equipment, expenditures on	yr	561	1999	30r
Tennis balls, yellow, Wilson or Penn, 3	can	2.09	3/01	4c
Funerals				
Total cost of funeral		5922.53	1/99	78r
Acknowledgement cards		63.43	1/99	78r
Casket		2258.77	1/99	78r
Cosmetology, hair, other preparation		127.09	1/99	78r
Embalming		393.49	1/99	78r
Funeral at funeral home		367.50	1/99	78r
Hearse (local)		169.66	1/99	78r
Professional service charges		1211.32	1/99	78r
Service car/van		80.69	1/99	78r
Transfer of remains to funeral home		144.25	1/99	78r
Vault		803.50	1/99	78r
Visitation/viewing		302.83	1/99	78r
Groceries				
Groceries, ACCRA Index		102.40	3/01	4c
American processed cheese	lb	3.50	7/01	11r
Antibiotic ointment, Polysporin	0.5 oz	4.18	3/01	4c
Baby food, strained vegetables or fruit, lowest price	4-4.5 oz	0.43	3/01	4c
Bakery products, expenditures on	yr	261	1999	30r
Bananas	lb	0.45	3/01	4c
Bananas	lb	0.47	7/01	11r
Beans, dried, any type, all sizes	lb	0.63	7/01	11r
Beef for stew, boneless	lb	2.86	7/01	11r
Beef or hamburger, ground	lb	2.09	3/01	4c
Beef, expenditures on	yr	210	1999	30r
Bologna, all beef or mixed	lb	2.29	7/01	11r
Bread, French	lb	1.66	7/01	11r
Bread, white	loaf	0.96	3/01	4c
Bread, white, pan	lb	0.87	7/01	11r
Bread, whole wheat, pan	lb	1.38	7/01	11r
Broccoli	lb	1.04	7/01	11r
Butter, salted, grade AA, stick	lb	2.26	7/01	11r
Butter, yoghurt, cheese, etc, expenditures on	yr	170	1999	30r
Cabbage	lb	0.42	7/01	11r
Cereals and cereal products, expenditures on	yr	140	1999	30r
Cheddar cheese, natural	lb	3.75	7/01	11r
Cheese, Kraft grated Parmesan	8 oz	3.19	3/01	4c
Chicken breast, bone-in	lb	1.85	7/01	11r
Chicken legs, bone-in	lb	1.34	7/01	11r
Chicken, fresh, whole	lb	1.05	7/01	11r
Chicken, whole fryer	lb	1.05	3/01	4c
Chops, boneless	lb	4.13	7/01	11r
Chuck roast, graded and ungraded, excl U.S. prime and choice	lb	2.35	7/01	11r
Chuck roast, U.S. choice, boneless	lb	2.67	7/01	11r
Cigarettes, Winston, Kings	carton	26.16	3/01	4c
Coffee, 100%, ground roast, all sizes	lb	2.88	7/01	11r
Coffee, instant, plain, regular, all sizes	16 oz	9.25	7/01	11r
Coffee, vacuum-packed	13 oz	2.11	3/01	4c
Cola, non diet	2 liter	1.11	7/01	11r
Corn Flakes, Kellogg's or Post Toasties	18 oz	2.76	3/01	4c
Corn, frozen, whole kernel, lowest price	16 oz	1.18	3/01	4c
Crackers, soda, salted	lb	1.70	7/01	11r
Dairy product purchases	yr	282	1999	30r
Eggs, expenditures on	yr	32	1999	30r
Eggs, Grade A or AA	dozen	1.48	3/01	4c
Fats and oils, expenditures on	yr	79	1999	30r
Fish and seafood, expenditures on	yr	99	1999	30r

Rocky Mount, NC - continued

Item	Per	Value	Date	Ref.
Groceries - continued				
Flour, white, all purpose	lb	0.32	7/01	11r
Food (excl fruit and vegetables), eaten at home, purchases	yr	815	1999	30r
Food cooked on trips, expenditures on	yr	36	1999	30r
Food purchases	yr	4533	1999	30r
Food purchases, eaten away from home	yr	1873	1999	30r
Food purchases, food eaten at home	yr	2660	1999	30r
Fresh fruits, expenditures on	yr	128	1999	30r
Fresh milk and cream, expenditures on	yr	112	1999	30r
Fresh vegetables, expenditures on	yr	131	1999	30r
Fruit and vegetable purchases	yr	438	1999	30r
Grapefruit	lb	0.59	7/01	11r
Grapes, Thompson, seedless	lb	2.12	7/01	11r
Ground beef, 100% beef	lb	1.76	7/01	11r
Ground beef, lean and extra lean	lb	2.60	7/01	11r
Ground chuck, 100% beef	lb	2.08	7/01	11r
Ham, boneless, excl canned	lb	2.71	7/01	11r
Ham, rump or shank half, bone-in, smoked	lb	2.19	7/01	11r
Ice cream, prepackaged, bulk, regular	1/2 gal	3.93	7/01	11r
Lemons	lb	1.32	7/01	11r
Lettuce, iceberg	head	1.17	3/01	4c
Lettuce, iceberg	lb	0.76	7/01	11r
Margarine, Blue Bonnet or Parkay, stick	lb	0.69	3/01	4c
Milk, fresh, low fat,	gal	2.75	7/01	11r
Milk, fresh, whole, fortified	gal	2.97	7/01	11r
Milk, whole	1/2 gal	1.85	3/01	4c
Nonalcoholic beverages, expenditures on	yr	228	1999	30r
Orange juice, frozen concentrate	16 oz	1.95	7/01	11r
Orange juice, Minute Maid frozen	12 oz	1.92	3/01	4c
Oranges, Navel	lb	0.73	7/01	11r
Oranges, Valencia	lb	0.55	7/01	11r
Peaches, halves or slices, Hunt's, Del Monte, or Libby's	29 oz	1.57	3/01	4c
Peanut butter, creamy, all sizes	lb	1.83	7/01	11r
Pears, Anjou	lb	0.98	7/01	11r
Peas, green, Del Monte or Green Giant	15 oz	0.62	3/01	4c
Pork chops, center cut, bone-in	lb	3.33	7/01	11r
Pork sausage, fresh, loose	lb	2.59	7/01	11r
Pork shoulder picnic, bone-in, smoked	lb	1.12	7/01	11r
Pork, expenditures on	yr	162	1999	30r
Potato chips	16 oz	3.59	7/01	11r
Potatoes, frozen, french fried	lb	1.00	7/01	11r
Potatoes, white or red	10 lb	2.69	3/01	4c
Potatoes, white, all types	lb	0.44	7/01	11r
Poultry, expenditures on	yr	137	1999	30r
Processed fruits, expenditures on	yr	97	1999	30r
Processed vegetables, expenditures on	yr	82	1999	30r
Rice, white, long grain, uncooked	lb	0.51	7/01	11r
Round roast, graded and ungraded, excl U.S. prime and choice	lb	2.96	7/01	11r
Round steak, graded and ungraded, excl U.S. prime and choice	lb	3.11	7/01	11r
Sausage, Jimmy Dean/Owens pork	lb	3.25	3/01	4c
Shortening, vegetable, Crisco	3 lb	2.93	3/01	4c
Sirloin steak, graded and ungraded, excl U.S. prime and choice	lb	4.23	7/01	11r
Soft drink, Coca Cola, ex deposit	2 liter	1.19	3/01	4c
Spaghetti and macaroni	lb	0.78	7/01	11r
Steak, round, U.S. choice, boneless	lb	3.56	7/01	11r
Steak, sirloin, U.S. choice, boneless	lb	5.65	7/01	11r
Steak, T-bone	lb	6.99	3/01	4c
Strawberries, dry pint	12 oz	1.50	7/01	11r
Sugar and other sweets, expenditures on	yr	99	1999	30r
Sugar, cane or beet	4 lbs	1.53	3/01	4c
Sugar, white, 33-80 ounce package	lb	0.39	7/01	11r
Sugar, white, all sizes	lb	0.42	7/01	11r
Tobacco products and smoking supplies purchases	yr	288	1999	30r
Tomatoes, field grown	lb	1.43	7/01	11r
Tomatoes, Hunt's or Del Monte	14.5 oz	0.91	3/01	4c
Tuna, chunk, light	6 oz	0.89	3/01	4c
Tuna, light, chunk	lb	1.77	7/01	11r

Values are in dollars or fractions of dollars. In the column headed *Ref*, references are shown to sources. Each reference is followed by a letter. These refer to the geographical level for which data were reported: s=State, r=Region, and c=City or metro. The abbreviation *ex* is used to mean *except* or *excluding*; *exp* stands for *expenditures*. For other abbreviations and further explanations, please see the Introduction.

Rocky Mount, NC - continued

Item	Per	Value	Date	Ref.
Groceries				
Turkey, frozen, whole	lb	1.05	7/01	11r
Goods and Services				
Miscellaneous goods and services, ACCRA Index		98.90	3/01	4c
B&B Japanese maple (acer japonicum)	gal	49.98-129.00	4/00	93r
Boxwood (buxus)	2 gal	12.99-16.99	4/00	93r
Daylilly (hemerocallis)	gal	4.99-8.99	4/00	93r
Flat of annuals		11.00-13.92	4/00	93r
Fountain grass (pennisetum)	gal	5.98-7.98	4/00	93r
Hanging basket (10 in)		7.99-14.98	4/00	93r
Hardy geranium (geranium)	gal	5.98-8.00	4/00	93r
Hosta (hosta)	gal	4.99-10.98	4/00	93r
Lilac (syrubga vulgaris)	2 gal	12.99-21.99	4/00	93r
Rhododendron (rhododendron)	2 gal	14.99-24.99	4/00	93r
Sage (salvia)	gal	5.98-6.99	4/00	93r
Wintercreeper euonymus (euonymus fortunei)	2 gal	7.99-89.99	4/00	93r
Hunting license	yr	15.00	4/01	34s
Health Care				
Health care, ACCRA Index		99.40	3/01	4c
Cardiac catheterization, ave hospital/ physician charges		12500	1998	77s
Childbirth, Cesarean delivery		11587	1997	13r
Childbirth, vaginal delivery		6725	1997	13r
Dentist's fee, adult teeth cleaning and periodic oral exam	visit	82.00	3/01	4c
Doctor's fee, routine exam, established patient	visit	63.80	3/01	4c
Drugs, expenditures on	yr	399	1999	30r
Health care purchases	yr	1971	1999	30r
Health insurance expenditures	yr	933	1999	30r
Hospital care, private room	day	307.00	3/01	4c
Hysterectomy, laproscopically-assisted, ave hospital/physician charges		12260	1998	76s
Hysterectomy, vaginal, ave hospital and physician charges		8440	1998	76s
Medicaid dispensing fee		5.60	1999	87s
Medical services expenditures	yr	547	1999	30r
Medical supplies, expenditures on	yr	91	1999	30r
Plastic surgery, breast augmentation		2870	2000	7r
Plastic surgery, breast lift		3649	2000	7r
Plastic surgery, facelift		5008	2000	7r
Plastic surgery, hair transplantation		3425	2000	7r
Plastic surgery, lip augmentation		1227	2000	7r
Plastic surgery, lower body lift		4793	2000	7r
Plastic surgery, thigh lift		3862	2000	7r
Household Goods				
Dishwashing powder, Cascade	50 oz	3.19	3/01	4c
Floor coverings, expenditures on	yr	44	1999	30r
Furniture, expenditures on	yr	335	1999	30r
Household furnishings and equipment purchases	yr	1328	1999	30r
Household textiles, expenditures on	yr	89	1999	30r
Laundry and cleaning supplies, expenditures on	yr	113	1999	30r
Tissues, facial, Kleenex brand	175	1.29	3/01	4c
Housing				
Housing, ACCRA Index		96.10	3/01	4c
Home price, existing, ave		160100	10/00	90r

Rocky Mount, NC - continued

Item	Per	Value	Date	Ref.
Housing - continued				
Home value, median		146000	2001	53s
House, 2400 sq ft, 8000 sq ft lot, new, urban, utilities	total	203000	3/01	4c
House payment, principal and interest, 25% down payment	mos	1022	3/01	4c
Household operation expenditures	yr	553	1999	30r
Housekeeping supplies purchases	yr	473	1999	30r
Housing, expenditures on	yr	10303	1999	30r
Maintenance, repairs, insurance expenditures	yr	699	1999	30r
Monthly rental value of owned home	mos	505	1999	30r
Owned dwellings, expenditures own	yr	3465	1999	30r
Rent expenditures	yr	1641	1999	30r
Rent, apartment, 2 br, 1 1/2-2 baths, unfurn, 950 sq ft, water	mos	584	3/01	4c
Rental unit, 1 bedroom, with utilities	mos	361	4/01	41c
Rental unit, 2 bedroom, with utilities	mos	438	4/01	41c
Rental unit, 3 bedroom, with utilities	mos	581	4/01	41c
Rental unit, 4 bedroom, with utilities	mos	641	4/01	41c
Shelter, expenditures on	yr	5467	1999	30r
Insurance and Pensions				
Life and other personal insurance purchases	yr	414	1999	30r
Pensions and Social Security, expenditures on	yr	2635	1999	30r
Personal insurance and pensions, expenditures on	yr	3048	1999	30r
Legal Fees				
Combination hunting and fishing license	yr	20.00	4/01	34s
Divorce, filing fee		80.00	4/01	35s
Driver's license fee	renew	10.00	1999	48s
Driver's license fee	orig	10.00	1999	48s
Fishing license	yr	15.00	4/01	34s
Personal Goods				
Personal care products and services purchases	yr	393	1999	30r
Shampoo, Alberto VO5	15 oz	1.11	3/01	4c
Toothpaste, Crest or Colgate	6-7 oz	2.13	3/01	4c
Personal Services				
Dry cleaning, man's 2-pc suit		7.73	3/01	4c
Man's haircut, barbershop, no styling		10.20	3/01	4c
Personal services, household, expenditures on	yr	258	1999	30r
Woman's shampoo, trim, blow-dry, no style-change		22.79	3/01	4c
Pets				
Pets, toys, and playground equipment, expenditures on	yr	306	1999	30r
Restaurant Food				
Chicken, fried, thigh and drumstick, KFC/ Church's		2.58	3/01	4c
Hamburger with cheese, McDonald's	1/4 lb	2.09	3/01	4c
Pizza, Pizza Hut or Pizza Inn	11-12 in	9.57	3/01	4c
Taxes				
Federal income taxes paid	yr	2047	1999	30r
Personal taxes, expenditures on	yr	2554	1999	30r
Property taxes paid	yr	726	1999	30r
State and local income taxes paid	yr	363	1999	30r
Transportation				
Transportation, ACCRA Index		100.10	3/01	4c
Cars and trucks, new, expenditures on	yr	1648	1999	30r
Cars and trucks, used, expenditures on	yr	1651	1999	30r
Diesel at the pump	gal	1.19	10/99	73s
Gasoline and motor oil purchases	yr	1052	1999	30r
Gasoline before-tax price (cents)	gal	103.20	10/00	43s
Maintenance and repair expenditures	yr	621	1999	30r
Motorcycle license fee	orig	1.50	1999	49s
Motorcycle license fee	renew	1.50	1999	49s
Public transportation, expenditures on	yr	298	1999	30r

Values are in dollars or fractions of dollars. In the column headed *Ref*, references are shown to sources. Each reference is followed by a letter. These refer to the geographical level for which data were reported: s=State, r=Region, and c=City or metro. The abbreviation *ex* is used to mean *except* or *excluding*; *exp* stands for expenditures. For other abbreviations and further explanations, please see the Introduction.

Rocky Mount, NC - continued

Item	Per	Value	Date	Ref.
Transportation				
Tire balance, computer or spin balance, front	wheel	8.40	3/01	4c
Transportation purchases	yr	6738	1999	30r
Vehicle expenses, miscellaneous, purchases	yr	2033	1999	30r
Vehicle insurance payments	yr	696	1999	30r
Vehicle purchases (net outlay)	yr	3354	1999	30r
Vehicle rental, lease expenditures	yr	352	1999	30r
Utilities				
Utilities, ACCRA Index		107.80	3/01	4c
Electrical bill, average	mos	83.66	9/00	9s
Electricity, 2400 sq ft, new home	mos	134.71	3/01	4c
Electricity, expenditures on	yr	1115	1999	30r
Electricity cost, average	KWh	6.40	9/00	9s
Water and other public services, expenditures on	yr	298	1999	30r
Weddings				
Wedding (national average cost)		19936	2000	33r
Wedding (regional average total cost)		16293	1997	110r
Attendants' gifts		321	1998	33r
Bridal attendants' apparel (5 persons)		824	2000	33r
Bride's headpiece/veil		173	1998	33r
Bride's wedding dress		859	1998	33r
Clergy, religious facility fee		242	1998	33r
Engagement ring		3177	1998	33r
Flowers		789	1998	33r
Groom's formalwear rental		99	2000	33r
Limousine		410	1998	33r
Marriage license cost		40.00	4/01	35s
Men's formalwear (ushers, best man)		469	2000	33r
Mother of bride apparel		241	2000	33r
Music		866	1998	33r
Photography and videography		1368	1998	33r
Rehearsal dinner		728	1998	33r
Wedding invitations and announcements		341	1998	33r
Wedding reception		7968	2000	33r
Wedding rings (bride and groom)		1060	1998	33r

Sacramento, CA

Item	Per	Value	Date	Ref.
Average annual expenditures	yr	40662	1999	30r
Composite, ACCRA index		116.60	3/01	4c
Alcoholic Beverages				
Alcoholic beverage purchases	yr	372	1999	30r
Beer, Heineken, 12-oz, ex deposit	6	6.95	3/01	4c
J & B Scotch	750-ml	20.99	3/01	4c
Malt beverages, all types, all sizes, any origin	16 oz	0.94	7/01	11r
Wine, Livingston or Gallo, Chablis blanc	1.5 liter	4.91	3/01	4c
Wine, red and white table, all sizes, any origin	liter	6.00	7/01	11r
Appliances				
Appliance repair, service call, washing machine	min lab chg	39.80	3/01	4c
Major appliances, expenditures on	yr	167	1999	30r
Small appliances, housewares, expenditures on	yr	105	1999	30r
Banking and Money				
Mortgage interest and charges paid	yr	3368	1999	30r
Mortgage principal paid on owned property	yr	1677	1999	30r
Mortgage rate, incl. points and orig. fee, 30-yr. conv. fixed or ARM	mos	7.05	3/01	4c
Vehicle finance charges paid	yr	311	1999	30r
Business Expenses				
Business travel, car rental	day	56	2001	3c
Business travel, food	day	53	2001	3c
Business travel, hotel	day	121	2001	3c
Charity				
Cash contributions, expenditures	yr	1344	1999	30r

Sacramento, CA - continued

Item	Per	Value	Date	Ref.
Child Care				
Child raising cost, total, age 0-2	yr	9140	1999	60r
Child raising cost, total, age 3-5	yr	9370	1999	60r
Child raising cost, total, age 6-8	yr	9450	1999	60r
Child raising cost, total, age 9-11	yr	9470	1999	60r
Child raising cost, total, age 12-14	yr	10170	1999	60r
Child raising cost, total, age 15-17	yr	10360	1999	60r
Child's child care and education, age 0-2	yr	1250	1999	60r
Child's child care and education, age 3-5	yr	1380	1999	60r
Child's child care and education, age 6-8	yr	890	1999	60r
Child's child care and education, age 9-11	yr	580	1999	60r
Child's child care and education, age 12-14	yr	430	1999	60r
Child's child care and education, age 15-17	yr	730	1999	60r
Child's clothing, age 0-2	yr	430	1999	60r
Child's clothing, age 3-5	yr	420	1999	60r
Child's clothing, age 6-8	yr	470	1999	60r
Child's clothing, age 9-11	yr	520	1999	60r
Child's clothing, age 12-14	yr	870	1999	60r
Child's clothing, age 15-17	yr	770	1999	60r
Child's food, age 0-2	yr	1120	1999	60r
Child's food, age 3-5	yr	1280	1999	60r
Child's food, age 6-8	yr	1640	1999	60r
Child's food, age 9-11	yr	1930	1999	60r
Child's food, age 12-14	yr	1940	1999	60r
Child's food, age 15-17	yr	2150	1999	60r
Child's health care, age 0-2	yr	490	1999	60r
Child's health care, age 3-5	yr	470	1999	60r
Child's health care, age 6-8	yr	530	1999	60r
Child's health care, age 9-11	yr	570	1999	60r
Child's health care, age 12-14	yr	580	1999	60r
Child's health care, age 15-17	yr	610	1999	60r
Child's housing, age 0-2	yr	3630	1999	60r
Child's housing, age 3-5	yr	3610	1999	60r
Child's housing, age 6-8	yr	3570	1999	60r
Child's housing, age 9-11	yr	3410	1999	60r
Child's housing, age 12-14	yr	3600	1999	60r
Child's housing, age 15-17	yr	3210	1999	60r
Child's personal care, reading, age 0-2	yr	1040	1999	60r
Child's personal care, reading, age 3-5	yr	1060	1999	60r
Child's personal care, reading, age 6-8	yr	1090	1999	60r
Child's personal care, reading, age 9-11	yr	1130	1999	60r
Child's personal care, reading, age 12-14	yr	1300	1999	60r
Child's personal care, reading, age 15-17	yr	1080	1999	60r
Clothing				
Apparel and services purchases	yr	1863	1999	30r
Boys' brief, cotton	3	5.79	3/01	4c
Boys, 2 to 15, expenditures on	yr	80	1999	30r
Children under 2, expenditures on	yr	74	1999	30r
Footwear, expenditures on	yr	307	1999	30r
Girls, 2 to 15, expenditures on	yr	101	1999	30r
Men and boys, expenditures on	yr	443	1999	30r
Men, 16 and over, expenditures on	yr	363	1999	30r
Shirt, man's dress shirt		26.40	3/01	4c
Slacks, man's "No Wrinkles" khaki		33.59	3/01	4c
Women, 16 and over, expenditures on	yr	594	1999	30r
Communications				
Cable modem installation, AT&T-BIS		150.00	6/99	103s
Cable modem installation, Charter		99.00-169.00	6/99	103s
Cable modem installation, Comcast		95.00	6/99	103s
Cable modem installation, Cox		99.00-174.95	6/99	103s
Cable modem installation, Media One		100.00	6/99	103s
Cable modem installation, Time Warner		75.00-225.00	6/99	103s
Cable modem rate, cable subscriber, AT&T-BIS	mos	39.95	6/99	103s
Cable modem rate, cable subscriber, Charter	mos	49.95-79.95	6/99	103s
Cable modem rate, cable subscriber, Comcast	mos	39.95	6/99	103s

Values are in dollars or fractions of dollars. In the column headed *Ref*, references are shown to sources. Each reference is followed by a letter. These refer to the geographical level for which data were reported: s=State, r=Region, and c=City or metro. The abbreviation *ex* is used to mean *except* or *excluding*; *exp* stands for expenditures. For other abbreviations and further explanations, please see the Introduction.

Sacramento, CA - continued

Item	Per	Value	Date	Ref.
Communications				
Cable modem rate, cable subscriber, Cox	mos	29.95-44.95	6/99	103s
Cable modem rate, cable subscriber, Media One	mos	34.95-39.95	6/99	103s
Cable modem rate, cable subscriber, Time Warner	mos	39.95-49.95	6/99	103s
Cable modem rate, non-cable subscriber, Charter	mos	59.95-89.95	6/99	103s
Cable modem rate, non-cable subscriber, Comcast	mos	49.95	6/99	103s
Cable modem rate, non-cable subscriber, Cox	mos	42.95-54.95	6/99	103s
Cable modem rate, non-cable subscriber, Media One	mos	49.95	6/99	103s
Cable modem rate, non-cable subscriber, Time Warner	mos	39.95-54.95	6/99	103s
Newspaper subscription, daily and Sunday delivery	mos	12.87	3/01	4c
Phone line, single, business, field visit	inst.	70.75	12/97	17s
Phone line, single, business, no field visit	inst.	70.75	12/97	17s
Phone line, single, residence, field visit	inst.	34.75	12/97	17s
Phone line, single, residence, no field visit	inst.	34.75	12/97	17s
Postage and stationery, expenditures on	yr	150	1999	30r
Postal rate, express mail, up to half-pound		12.45	7/01	108r
Postal rate, letter, first class, first ounce		0.34	7/01	108r
Postal rate, letter, two ounces		0.57	7/01	108r
Postal rate, post card		0.21	7/01	108r
Postal rate, priority mail, two pounds		3.95	7/01	108r
Postal rate, priority mail, up to one pound		3.50	7/01	108r
Telephone bill, family of three	mos	17.69	3/01	4c
Telephone services, expenditures on	yr	825	1999	30r
Wireless services	mos	37.15	1/00	42c
Education				
Board, 4-year private college/university	yr	2970	1996	38s
Board, 4-year public college/university	yr	2516	1996	38s
Education expenditures	yr	676	1999	30r
Room, 4-year private college/university	yr	3196	1996	38s
Room, 4-year public college/university	yr	3031	1996	38s
Total cost, 4-year private college/university	yr	20143	1996	38s
Total cost, 4-year public college/university	yr	8213	1996	38s
Tuition, 2-year public college/university, in state	yr	362	1996	38s
Tuition, 4-year private college/university, in state	yr	13977	1996	38s
Tuition, 4-year public college/university	yr	2666	1996	38s
Energy and Fuels				
Electricity	KWh	0.11	7/01	11r
Electricity	500 KWhs	48.23	7/01	11r
Energy, combined forms, 2400 sq ft	mos	139.22	3/01	4c
Energy, exc. electricity, 2400 sq ft	mos	17.04	3/01	4c
Fuel oil and other fuels, expenditures on	yr	35	1999	30r
Gas, natural, commercial rate	1000 cf	8.74	11/00	88s
Gas, regular unleaded, cash, self-service	gal	1.65	3/01	4c
Gasoline, all types	gal	1.91	7/01	11r
Gasoline, unleaded premium	gal	2.05	7/01	11r
Gasoline, unleaded regular	gal	1.83	7/01	11r
Natural gas, expenditures on	yr	255	1999	30r
Utility (piped) gas, therm		0.98	7/01	11r
Utility (piped) gas, 40 therms		40.74	7/01	11r
Utility (piped) gas, 100 therms		96.80	7/01	11r
Entertainment				
Bowling, Saturday evening rate	line	3.19	3/01	4c
Entertainment purchases	yr	2139	1999	30r
Fees and admissions paid	yr	545	1999	30r
Monopoly game, Parker Brothers', No. 9	game	9.10	3/01	4c
Movie, first-run, Saturday, evening	adm.	8.50	3/01	4c
Television, radios, sound equipment, expenditures on	yr	624	1999	30r
Tennis balls, yellow, Wilson or Penn, 3	can	2.50	3/01	4c

Sacramento, CA - continued

Item	Per	Value	Date	Ref.
Funerals				
Total cost of funeral		5401.08	1/99	78r
Acknowledgement cards		33.64	1/99	78r
Casket		2170.43	1/99	78r
Cosmetology, hair, other preparation		136.32	1/99	78r
Embalming		319.13	1/99	78r
Funeral at funeral home		370.21	1/99	78r
Hearse (local)		161.04	1/99	78r
Professional service charges		963.15	1/99	78r
Service car/van		133.99	1/99	78r
Transfer of remains to funeral home		159.82	1/99	78r
Vault		778.07	1/99	78r
Visitation/viewing		175.28	1/99	78r
Groceries				
Groceries, ACCRA Index		121.90	3/01	4c
Antibiotic ointment, Polysporin	0.5 oz	5.32	3/01	4c
Apples, red delicious	lb	0.84	7/01	11r
Baby food, strained vegetables or fruit, lowest price	4-4.5 oz	0.49	3/01	4c
Bacon, sliced	lb	3.38	7/01	11r
Bakery products, expenditures on	yr	299	1999	30r
Bananas	lb	0.59	3/01	4c
Bananas	lb	0.54	7/01	11r
Beans, dried, any type, all sizes	lb	0.76	7/01	11r
Beef or hamburger, ground	lb	1.71	3/01	4c
Beef, expenditures on	yr	222	1999	30r
Bread, white	loaf	1.24	3/01	4c
Bread, white, pan	lb	0.99	7/01	11r
Butter, yoghurt, cheese, etc, expenditures on	yr	211	1999	30r
Cereals and bakery product purchases	yr	466	1999	30r
Cereals and cereal products, expenditures on	yr	168	1999	30r
Cheese, Kraft grated Parmesan	8 oz	4.43	3/01	4c
Chicken breast, bone-in	lb	2.45	7/01	11r
Chicken, fresh, whole	lb	1.19	7/01	11r
Chicken, whole fryer	lb	1.13	3/01	4c
Chops, boneless,	lb	4.00	7/01	11r
Chuck roast, graded and ungraded, excl U.S. prime and choice	lb	2.55	7/01	11r
Cigarettes, Winston, Kings	carton	38.52	3/01	4c
Coffee, 100%, ground roast, all sizes	lb	3.80	7/01	11r
Coffee, vacuum-packed	13 oz	3.72	3/01	4c
Cookies, chocolate chip	lb	2.83	7/01	11r
Corn Flakes, Kellogg's or Post Toasties	18 oz	3.56	3/01	4c
Corn, frozen, whole kernel, lowest price	16 oz	1.54	3/01	4c
Dairy product purchases	yr	341	1999	30r
Eggs, expenditures on	yr	39	1999	30r
Eggs, Grade A or AA	dozen	1.73	3/01	4c
Eggs, grade AA, large	dozen	1.23	7/01	11r
Fats and oils, expenditures on	yr	88	1999	30r
Fish and seafood, expenditures on	yr	121	1999	30r
Food (excl fruit and vegetables), eaten at home, purchases	yr	1001	1999	30r
Food cooked on trips, expenditures on	yr	64	1999	30r
Food purchases	yr	5312	1999	30r
Food purchases, eaten away from home	yr	2180	1999	30r
Food purchases, food eaten at home	yr	3132	1999	30r
Fresh fruits, expenditures on	yr	186	1999	30r
Fresh milk and cream, expenditures on	yr	130	1999	30r
Fresh vegetables, expenditures on	yr	177	1999	30r
Grapefruit	lb	0.68	7/01	11r
Grapes, Thompson, seedless	lb	2.42	7/01	11r
Ground beef, lean and extra lean	lb	2.46	7/01	11r
Ice cream, prepackaged, bulk, regular	1/2 gal	3.62	7/01	11r
Lettuce, iceberg	head	0.93	3/01	4c
Lettuce, iceberg	lb	0.63	7/01	11r
Margarine, Blue Bonnet or Parkay, stick	lb	0.99	3/01	4c
Meats, poultry, fish, and egg purchases	yr	761	1999	30r
Milk, fresh, low fat	gal	2.80	7/01	11r
Milk, fresh, whole, fortified	gal	2.88	7/01	11r
Milk, whole	1/2 gal	2.17	3/01	4c
Nonalcoholic beverages, expenditures on	yr	258	1999	30r
Orange juice, Minute Maid frozen	12 oz	1.71	3/01	4c

Values are in dollars or fractions of dollars. In the column headed *Ref*, references are shown to sources. Each reference is followed by a letter. These refer to the geographical level for which data were reported: s=State, r=Region, and c=City or metro. The abbreviation *ex* is used to mean *except* or *excluding*; *exp* stands for expenditures. For other abbreviations and further explanations, please see the Introduction.

Sacramento, CA - continued

Item	Per	Value	Date	Ref.
Groceries				
Oranges, Navel	lb	0.97	7/01	11r
Oranges, Valencia	lb	0.43	7/01	11r
Peaches	lb	1.38	7/01	11r
Peaches, halves or slices, Hunt's, Del Monte, or Libby's	29 oz	1.93	3/01	4c
Peanut butter, creamy, all sizes	lb	2.14	7/01	11r
Peas, green, Del Monte or Green Giant	15 oz	0.96	3/01	4c
Pork chops, center cut, bone-in	lb	3.83	7/01	11r
Pork, expenditures on	yr	141	1999	30r
Potatoes, white or red	10 lb	2.27	3/01	4c
Potatoes, white, all types	lb	0.37	7/01	11r
Poultry, expenditures on	yr	146	1999	30r
Processed fruits, expenditures on	yr	118	1999	30r
Processed vegetables, expenditures on	yr	81	1999	30r
Round roast, graded and ungraded, excl U.S. prime and choice	lb	3.07	7/01	11r
Round roast, U.S. choice, boneless	lb	3.37	7/01	11r
Round steak, graded and ungraded, excl U.S. prime and choice	lb	3.51	7/01	11r
Sausage, Jimmy Dean/Owens pork	lb	4.49	3/01	4c
Shortening, vegetable, Crisco	3 lb	3.57	3/01	4c
Sirloin steak, graded and ungraded, excl U.S. prime and choice	lb	4.67	7/01	11r
Soft drink, Coca Cola, ex deposit	2 liter	1.33	3/01	4c
Steak, sirloin, U.S. choice, boneless	lb	6.20	7/01	11r
Steak, T-bone	lb	6.79	3/01	4c
Strawberries, dry pint	12 oz	1.79	7/01	11r
Sugar and other sweets, expenditures on	yr	124	1999	30r
Sugar, cane or beet	4 lbs	1.79	3/01	4c
Sugar, white, all sizes	lb	0.46	7/01	11r
Tobacco products and smoking supplies purchases	yr	217	1999	30r
Tomatoes, field grown	lb	1.17	7/01	11r
Tomatoes, Hunt's or Del Monte	14.5 oz	1.09	3/01	4c
Tuna, chunk, light	6 oz	0.83	3/01	4c
Tuna, light, chunk	lb	2.05	7/01	11r
Goods and Services				
Miscellaneous goods and services, ACCRA Index		101.40	3/01	4c
B&B Japanese maple (acer japonicum)	gal	39.99	4/00	93r
Boxwood (buxus)	2 gal	14.99-24.99	4/00	93r
Christmas tree, noble fir		40-60	2000	65s
Daylilly (hemerocallis)	gal	6.99-8.99	4/00	93r
Flat of annuals		16.68	4/00	93r
Fountain grass (pennisetum)	gal	7.99-11.99	4/00	93r
Hanging basket (10 in)		29.99	4/00	93r
Hardy geranium (geranium)	gal	6.99-11.99	4/00	93r
Hosta (hosta)	gal	6.99-18.99	4/00	93r
Lilac (syrubga vulgaris)	2 gal	14.99-17.99	4/00	93r
Miscellaneous purchases	yr	1070	1999	30r
Rhododendron (rhododendron)	2 gal	14.99	4/00	93r
Sage (salvia)	gal	6.99	4/00	93r
Wintercreeper euonymus (euonymus fortunei)	2 gal	14.99-22.99	4/00	93r
Hunting license	yr	29.95	4/01	34s
Health Care				
Health care, ACCRA Index		153.00	3/01	4c
Cardiac catheterization, ave hospital/physician charges		24000	1998	77s
Childbirth, Cesarean delivery		11587	1997	13r
Childbirth, vaginal delivery		6725	1997	13r
Dentist's fee, adult teeth cleaning and periodic oral exam	visit	104.00	3/01	4c
Doctor's fee, routine exam, established patient	visit	60.20	3/01	4c

Sacramento, CA - continued

Item	Per	Value	Date	Ref.
Health Care - continued				
Drugs, expenditures on	yr	309	1999	30r
Health care purchases	yr	1869	1999	30r
Health insurance expenditures	yr	868	1999	30r
Hospital care, private room	day	1520.40	3/01	4c
Hysterectomy, laproscopically-assisted, ave hospital/physician charges		20760	1998	76s
Hysterectomy, vaginal, ave hospital and physician charges		14570	1998	76s
Medicaid dispensing fee		4.05	1999	87s
Medical services expenditures	yr	580	1999	30r
Medical supplies, expenditures on	yr	112	1999	30r
Household Goods				
Dishwashing powder, Cascade	50 oz	3.51	3/01	4c
Floor coverings, expenditures on	yr	49	1999	30r
Furniture, expenditures on	yr	444	1999	30r
Household furnishings and equipment purchases	yr	1768	1999	30r
Household textiles, expenditures on	yr	141	1999	30r
Laundry and cleaning supplies, expenditures on	yr	128	1999	30r
Tissues, facial, Kleenex brand	175	1.61	3/01	4c
Housing				
Housing, ACCRA Index		127.60	3/01	4c
Home, 2200 sq ft, 4-br, 2-bath, 2-car garage, average		294833	2000	47c
Home price, existing, ave		239400	10/00	90r
Home value, median		215000	2001	53s
House, 2400 sq ft, 8000 sq ft lot, new, urban, utilities	total	280000	3/01	4c
House payment, principal and interest, 25% down payment	mos	1404	3/01	4c
Household operation expenditures	yr	781	1999	30r
Housekeeping supplies purchases	yr	513	1999	30r
Lodging expenditures	yr	575	1999	30r
Maintenance, repairs, insurance expenditures	yr	939	1999	30r
Monthly rental value of owned home	mos	662	1999	30r
Owned dwellings, expenditures own	yr	5231	1999	30r
Rent expenditures	yr	2709	1999	30r
Rent, apartment, 2 br, 1 1/2-2 baths, unfurn, 950 sq ft, water	mos	652	3/01	4c
Rental unit, 1 bedroom, with utilities	mos	515	4/01	41c
Rental unit, 2 bedroom, with utilities	mos	645	4/01	41c
Rental unit, 3 bedroom, with utilities	mos	894	4/01	41c
Rental unit, 4 bedroom, with utilities	mos	1054	4/01	41c
Shelter, expenditures on	yr	8516	1999	30r
Insurance and Pensions				
Life and other personal insurance purchases	yr	355	1999	30r
Pensions and Social Security, expenditures on	yr	3636	1999	30r
Legal Fees				
Divorce, filing fee		182.00	4/01	35s
Driver's license fee	orig	12.00	1999	48s
Driver's license fee	renew	15.00	1999	48s
Personal Goods				
Personal care products and services purchases	yr	449	1999	30r
Shampoo, Alberto VO5	15 oz	1.58	3/01	4c
Toothpaste, Crest or Colgate	6-7 oz	1.95	3/01	4c
Personal Services				
Dry cleaning, man's 2-pc suit		8.05	3/01	4c
Man's haircut, barbershop, no styling		10.20	3/01	4c
Personal services, household, expenditures on	yr	353	1999	30r
Woman's shampoo, trim, blow-dry, no style-change		30.00	3/01	4c

Values are in dollars or fractions of dollars. In the column headed *Ref*, references are shown to sources. Each reference is followed by a letter. These refer to the geographical level for which data were reported: s=State, r=Region, and c=City or metro. The abbreviation *ex* is used to mean *except* or *excluding*; *exp* stands for *expenditures*. For other abbreviations and further explanations, please see the Introduction.

Sacramento, CA - continued

Item	Per	Value	Date	Ref.
Pets				
Pets, toys, and playground equipment, expenditures on	yr	358	1999	30r
Restaurant Food				
Chicken, fried, thigh and drumstick, KFC/ Church's		2.37	3/01	4c
Hamburger with cheese, McDonald's	1/4 lb	2.17	3/01	4c
Pizza, Pizza Hut or Pizza Inn	11-12 in	9.99	3/01	4c
Taxes				
Federal income taxes paid	yr	3200	1999	30r
Personal taxes, expenditures on	yr	4153	1999	30r
Property taxes paid	yr	923	1999	30r
State and local income taxes paid	yr	812	1999	30r
Transportation				
Transportation, ACCRA Index		114.80	3/01	4c
Bus fare, one-way	trip	1.25	2000	1c
Bus fare, to central business district	1-way	1.50	3/01	4c
Cars and trucks, new, expenditures on	yr	1534	1999	30r
Cars and trucks, used, expenditures on	yr	1593	1999	30r
Diesel at the pump	gal	1.37	10/99	73s
Gasoline and motor oil purchases	yr	1129	1999	30r
Gasoline before-tax price (cents)	gal	128.80	10/00	43s
Light rail transit fare, one-way	trip	1.25	2000	2c
Maintenance and repair expenditures	yr	797	1999	30r
Public transportation, expenditures on	yr	530	1999	30r
Tire balance, computer or spin balance, front	wheel	8.30	3/01	4c
Transportation purchases	yr	7423	1999	30r
Vehicle expenses, miscellaneous, purchases	yr	2585	1999	30r
Vehicle insurance payments	yr	811	1999	30r
Vehicle purchases (net outlay)	yr	3180	1999	30r
Vehicle rental, lease expenditures	yr	666	1999	30r
Utilities				
Utilities, ACCRA Index		109.60	3/01	4c
Electrical bill, average	mos	58.66	9/00	9s
Electricity, expenditures on	yr	725	1999	30r
Electricity and other, mixed, 2400 sq ft, new home	mos	122.18	3/01	4c
Electricity cost, average	KWh	7.75	9/00	9s
Utilities, fuels, and public services purchased	yr	2179	1999	30r
Water and other public services, expenditures on	yr	339	1999	30r
Weddings				
Wedding (national average cost)		19936	2000	33r
Wedding (regional average total cost)		18918	1997	110r
Attendants' gifts		321	1998	33r
Bridal attendants' apparel (5 persons)		824	2000	33r
Bride's headpiece/veil		173	1998	33r
Bride's wedding dress		859	1998	33r
Clergy, religious facility fee		242	1998	33r
Engagement ring		3177	1998	33r
Flowers		789	1998	33r
Groom's formalwear rental		99	2000	33r
Limousine		410	1998	33r
Marriage license cost		50.00-80.00	4/01	35s
Men's formalwear (ushers, best man)		469	2000	33r
Mother of bride apparel		241	2000	33r
Music		866	1998	33r
Photography and videography		1368	1998	33r
Rehearsal dinner		728	1998	33r
Wedding invitations and announcements		341	1998	33r
Wedding reception		7968	2000	33r
Wedding rings (bride and groom)		1060	1998	33r

Saginaw-Bay City-Midland, MI

Item	Per	Value	Date	Ref.
Average annual expenditures	yr	35369	1999	30r
Alcoholic Beverages				
Alcoholic beverage purchases	yr	304	1999	30r
Malt beverages, all types, all sizes, any origin	16 oz	0.93	7/01	11r
Wine, red and white table, all sizes, any origin	liter	7.04	7/01	11r
Appliances				
Major appliances, expenditures on	yr	165	1999	30r
Small appliances, housewares, expenditures on	yr	90	1999	30r
Banking and Money				
Mortgage interest and charges paid	yr	2277	1999	30r
Mortgage principal paid on owned property	yr	1230	1999	30r
Vehicle finance charges paid	yr	328	1999	30r
Charity				
Cash contributions, expenditures	yr	1126	1999	30r
Child Care				
Child raising cost, total, age 0-2	yr	7890	1999	60r
Child raising cost, total, age 3-5	yr	8130	1999	60r
Child raising cost, total, age 6-8	yr	8170	1999	60r
Child raising cost, total, age 9-11	yr	8190	1999	60r
Child raising cost, total, age 12-14	yr	8890	1999	60r
Child raising cost, total, age 15-17	yr	9050	1999	60r
Child's child care and education, age 0-2	yr	1240	1999	60r
Child's child care and education, age 3-5	yr	1370	1999	60r
Child's child care and education, age 6-8	yr	880	1999	60r
Child's child care and education, age 9-11	yr	570	1999	60r
Child's child care and education, age 12-14	yr	420	1999	60r
Child's child care and education, age 15-17	yr	720	1999	60r
Child's clothing, age 0-2	yr	410	1999	60r
Child's clothing, age 3-5	yr	400	1999	60r
Child's clothing, age 6-8	yr	450	1999	60r
Child's clothing, age 9-11	yr	500	1999	60r
Child's clothing, age 12-14	yr	840	1999	60r
Child's clothing, age 15-17	yr	740	1999	60r
Child's food, age 0-2	yr	960	1999	60r
Child's food, age 3-5	yr	1120	1999	60r
Child's food, age 6-8	yr	1430	1999	60r
Child's food, age 9-11	yr	1710	1999	60r
Child's food, age 12-14	yr	1710	1999	60r
Child's food, age 15-17	yr	1920	1999	60r
Child's health care, age 0-2	yr	520	1999	60r
Child's health care, age 3-5	yr	500	1999	60r
Child's health care, age 6-8	yr	570	1999	60r
Child's health care, age 9-11	yr	610	1999	60r
Child's health care, age 12-14	yr	630	1999	60r
Child's health care, age 15-17	yr	650	1999	60r
Child's housing, age 0-2	yr	2860	1999	60r
Child's housing, age 3-5	yr	2840	1999	60r
Child's housing, age 6-8	yr	2800	1999	60r
Child's housing, age 9-11	yr	2650	1999	60r
Child's housing, age 12-14	yr	2840	1999	60r
Child's housing, age 15-17	yr	2440	1999	60r
Child's personal care, reading, age 0-2	yr	880	1999	60r
Child's personal care, reading, age 3-5	yr	900	1999	60r
Child's personal care, reading, age 6-8	yr	930	1999	60r
Child's personal care, reading, age 9-11	yr	970	1999	60r
Child's personal care, reading, age 12-14	yr	1150	1999	60r
Child's personal care, reading, age 15-17	yr	920	1999	60r
Clothing				
Apparel and services purchases	yr	1607	1999	30r
Boys, 2 to 15, expenditures on	yr	91	1999	30r
Children under 2, expenditures on	yr	59	1999	30r
Footwear, expenditures on	yr	285	1999	30r
Girls, 2 to 15, expenditures on	yr	116	1999	30r
Men and boys, expenditures on	yr	433	1999	30r
Men, 16 and over, expenditures on	yr	341	1999	30r
Women, 16 and over, expenditures on	yr	490	1999	30r

Values are in dollars or fractions of dollars. In the column headed *Ref*, references are shown to sources. Each reference is followed by a letter. These refer to the geographical level for which data were reported: s=State, r=Region, and c=City or metro. The abbreviation *ex* is used to mean *except* or *excluding*; *exp* stands for *expenditures*. For other abbreviations and further explanations, please see the Introduction.

Saginaw-Bay City-Midland, MI - continued

Item	Per	Value	Date	Ref.
Communications				
Cable modem installation, Bresnan		99.95	6/99	103s
Cable modem installation, Comcast		95.00	6/99	103s
Cable modem installation, Media One		100.00	6/99	103s
Cable modem rate, cable subscriber, Bresnan	mos	39.95	6/99	103s
Cable modem rate, cable subscriber, Comcast	mos	39.95	6/99	103s
Cable modem rate, cable subscriber, Media One	mos	34.95-39.95	6/99	103s
Cable modem rate, non-cable subscriber, Bresnan	mos	49.95	6/99	103s
Cable modem rate, non-cable subscriber, Comcast	mos	49.95	6/99	103s
Cable modem rate, non-cable subscriber, Media One	mos	49.95	6/99	103s
Phone line, single, business, field visit	inst.	42.00	12/97	17s
Phone line, single, business, no field visit	inst.	42.00	12/97	17s
Phone line, single, residence, field visit	inst.	42.00	12/97	17s
Phone line, single, residence, no field visit	inst.	42.00	12/97	17s
Postage and stationery, expenditures on	yr	140	1999	30r
Postal rate, express mail, up to half-pound		12.45	7/01	108r
Postal rate, letter, first class, first ounce		0.34	7/01	108r
Postal rate, letter, two ounces		0.57	7/01	108r
Postal rate, post card		0.21	7/01	108r
Postal rate, priority mail, two pounds		3.95	7/01	108r
Postal rate, priority mail, up to one pound		3.50	7/01	108r
Telephone services, expenditures on	yr	830	1999	30r
Education				
Board, 4-year private college/university	yr	2182	1996	38s
Board, 4-year public college/university	yr	2276	1996	38s
Education expenditures	yr	583	1999	30r
Room, 4-year private college/university	yr	1974	1996	38s
Room, 4-year public college/university	yr	2024	1996	38s
Total cost, 4-year private college/university	yr	13331	1996	38s
Total cost, 4-year public college/university	yr	8195	1996	38s
Tuition, 2-year public college/university, in state	yr	1529	1996	38s
Tuition, 4-year private college/university, in state	yr	9176	1996	38s
Tuition, 4-year public college/university	yr	3895	1996	38s
Energy and Fuels				
Electricity	500 KWhs	46.59	7/01	11r
Fuel oil #2	gal	1.27	7/01	11r
Fuel oil and other fuels, expenditures on	yr	68	1999	30r
Gas, natural, commercial rate	1000 cf	4.91	11/00	88s
Gasoline, unleaded midgrade	gal	1.79	7/01	11r
Gasoline, unleaded premium	gal	1.86	7/01	11r
Gasoline, unleaded regular	gal	1.58	7/01	11r
Natural gas, expenditures on	yr	389	1999	30r
Utility (piped) gas, therm		0.81	7/01	11r
Utility (piped) gas, 40 therms		38.01	7/01	11r
Utility (piped) gas, 100 therms		81.75	7/01	11r
Entertainment				
Entertainment purchases	yr	1984	1999	30r
Fees and admissions paid	yr	444	1999	30r
Television, radios, sound equipment, expenditures on	yr	580	1999	30r
Funerals				
Cosmetology, hair, other preparation		178.32	1/99	78r
Embalming		408.19	1/99	78r
Funeral at funeral home		362.13	1/99	78r
Professional service charges		1375.51	1/99	78r
Transfer of remains to funeral home		155.92	1/99	78r
Visitation/viewing		294.38	1/99	78r
Groceries				
Bacon, sliced	lb	3.15	7/01	11r
Bakery products, expenditures on	yr	281	1999	30r
Bananas	lb	0.48	7/01	11r

Saginaw-Bay City-Midland, MI - continued

Item	Per	Value	Date	Ref.
Groceries - continued				
Beans, dried, any type, all sizes	lb	0.61	7/01	11r
Beef for stew, boneless	lb	3.08	7/01	11r
Beef, expenditures on	yr	217	1999	30r
Bologna, all beef or mixed	lb	2.52	7/01	11r
Bread, white, pan	lb	1.06	7/01	11r
Broccoli	lb	0.91	7/01	11r
Butter, salted, grade AA, stick	lb	3.04	7/01	11r
Butter, yoghurt, cheese, etc, expenditures on	yr	183	1999	30r
Cereals and bakery product purchases	yr	430	1999	30r
Cereals and cereal products, expenditures on	yr	149	1999	30r
Chicken, fresh, whole	lb	1.07	7/01	11r
Chops, boneless,	lb	3.64	7/01	11r
Chuck roast, U.S. choice, boneless	lb	2.47	7/01	11r
Coffee, 100%, ground roast, all sizes	lb	2.69	7/01	11r
Cookies, chocolate chip	lb	2.87	7/01	11r
Dairy product purchases	yr	304	1999	30r
Eggs, expenditures on	yr	26	1999	30r
Eggs, grade A, large	dozen	0.88	7/01	11r
Fats and oils, expenditures on	yr	75	1999	30r
Fish and seafood, expenditures on	yr	72	1999	30r
Food (excl fruit and vegetables), eaten at home, purchases	yr	887	1999	30r
Food cooked on trips, expenditures on	yr	44	1999	30r
Food purchases	yr	4802	1999	30r
Food purchases, eaten away from home	yr	2069	1999	30r
Food purchases, food eaten at home	yr	2733	1999	30r
Fresh fruits, expenditures on	yr	138	1999	30r
Fresh milk and cream, expenditures on	yr	120	1999	30r
Fresh vegetables, expenditures on	yr	126	1999	30r
Grapefruit	lb	0.66	7/01	11r
Grapes, Thompson, seedless	lb	1.64	7/01	11r
Ground beef, 100% beef	lb	1.64	7/01	11r
Ground beef, lean and extra lean	lb	2.16	7/01	11r
Ground chuck, 100% beef	lb	2.13	7/01	11r
Ham, boneless, excl canned	lb	2.62	7/01	11r
Ice cream, prepackaged, bulk, regular	1/2 gal	3.35	7/01	11r
Lemons	lb	1.19	7/01	11r
Lettuce, iceberg	lb	0.73	7/01	11r
Margarine, soft, tubs	lb	0.89	7/01	11r
Meats, poultry, fish, and egg purchases	yr	671	1999	30r
Milk, fresh, whole, fortified	gal	2.71	7/01	11r
Nonalcoholic beverages, expenditures on	yr	239	1999	30r
Oranges, Navel	lb	0.80	7/01	11r
Oranges, Valencia	lb	0.66	7/01	11r
Pears, Anjou	lb	0.93	7/01	11r
Pork chops, center cut, bone-in	lb	3.63	7/01	11r
Pork, expenditures on	yr	150	1999	30r
Potato chips	16 oz	3.52	7/01	11r
Potatoes, frozen, french fried	lb	1.08	7/01	11r
Potatoes, white, all types	lb	0.33	7/01	11r
Poultry, expenditures on	yr	108	1999	30r
Processed fruits, expenditures on	yr	98	1999	30r
Processed vegetables, expenditures on	yr	80	1999	30r
Round roast, U.S. choice, boneless	lb	3.07	7/01	11r
Round steak, graded and ungraded, excl U.S. prime and choice	lb	3.41	7/01	11r
Shortening, vegetable oil blends	lb	1.13	7/01	11r
Spaghetti and macaroni	lb	0.80	7/01	11r
Steak, round, U.S. choice, boneless	lb	3.23	7/01	11r
Steak, T-bone, U.S. choice, bone-in	lb	6.68	7/01	11r
Strawberries, dry pint	12 oz	1.32	7/01	11r
Sugar and other sweets, expenditures on	yr	114	1999	30r
Sugar, white, 33-80 ounce package	lb	0.42	7/01	11r
Sugar, white, all sizes	lb	0.43	7/01	11r
Tobacco products and smoking supplies purchases	yr	331	1999	30r
Tomatoes, field grown	lb	1.46	7/01	11r
Tuna, light, chunk	lb	1.80	7/01	11r
Turkey, frozen, whole	lb	1.15	7/01	11r

Values are in dollars or fractions of dollars. In the column headed *Ref*, references are shown to sources. Each reference is followed by a letter. These refer to the geographical level for which data were reported: s=State, r=Region, and c=City or metro. The abbreviation *ex* is used to mean *except* or *excluding*; *exp* stands for expenditures. For other abbreviations and further explanations, please see the Introduction.

Saginaw-Bay City-Midland, MI - continued

Item	Per	Value	Date	Ref.
Goods and Services				
B&B Japanese maple (acer japonicum)	gal	29.99-169.99	4/00	93r
Boxwood (buxus)	2 gal	18.99-39.99	4/00	93r
Daylilly (hemerocallis)	gal	4.99-25.00	4/00	93r
Flat of annuals		11.98-24.99	4/00	93r
Fountain grass (pennisetum)	gal	5.98-12.98	4/00	93r
Hanging basket (10 in)		12.99-27.99	4/00	93r
Hardy geranium (geranium)	gal	7.99-9.99	4/00	93r
Hosta (hosta)	gal	6.00-25.00	4/00	93r
Lilac (syrubga vulgaris)	2 gal	14.99-24.99	4/00	93r
Miscellaneous purchases	yr	865	1999	30r
Rhododendron (rhododendron)	2 gal	23.98-42.99	4/00	93r
Sage (salvia)	gal	6.00-9.99	4/00	93r
Snowblower, single stage		400-600	12/00	99s
Wintercreeper euonymus (euonymus fortunei)	2 gal	16.00-169.99	4/00	93r
Hunting license	yr	14.00	4/01	34s
Health Care				
Cardiac catheterization, ave hospital/ physician charges		11830	1998	77s
Childbirth, Cesarean delivery		10722	1997	13r
Childbirth, vaginal delivery		6223	1997	13r
Drugs, expenditures on	yr	394	1999	30r
Health care purchases	yr	2048	1999	30r
Health insurance expenditures	yr	978	1999	30r
Hysterectomy, laproscopically-assisted, ave hospital/physician charges		13820	1998	76s
Hysterectomy, vaginal, ave hospital and physician charges		8780	1998	76s
Medicaid dispensing fee		3.72	1999	87s
Medical services expenditures	yr	554	1999	30r
Medical supplies, expenditures on	yr	122	1999	30r
Plastic surgery, breast augmentation		3184	2000	7r
Plastic surgery, breast lift		3585	2000	7r
Plastic surgery, facelift		4999	2000	7r
Plastic surgery, hair transplantation		3105	2000	7r
Plastic surgery, lip augmentation		1290	2000	7r
Plastic surgery, lower body lift		8135	2000	7r
Plastic surgery, thigh lift		3839	2000	7r
Household Goods				
Floor coverings, expenditures on	yr	52	1999	30r
Furniture, expenditures on	yr	344	1999	30r
Household furnishings and equipment purchases	yr	1475	1999	30r
Household textiles, expenditures on	yr	109	1999	30r
Laundry and cleaning supplies, expenditures on	yr	134	1999	30r
Housing				
Home price, existing, ave		144400	10/00	90r
Home value, median		135000	2001	53s
Household operation expenditures	yr	542	1999	30r
Housekeeping supplies purchases	yr	508	1999	30r
Lodging expenditures	yr	430	1999	30r
Maintenance, repairs, insurance expenditures	yr	853	1999	30r
Monthly rental value of owned home	mos	547	1999	30r
Owned dwellings, expenditures own	yr	4282	1999	30r
Rent expenditures	yr	1558	1999	30r
Rental unit, 1 bedroom, with utilities	mos	388	4/01	41c
Rental unit, 2 bedroom, with utilities	mos	516	4/01	41c
Rental unit, 3 bedroom, with utilities	mos	644	4/01	41c

Saginaw-Bay City-Midland, MI - continued

Item	Per	Value	Date	Ref.
Housing - continued				
Rental unit, 4 bedroom, with utilities	mos	722	4/01	41c
Shelter, expenditures on	yr	6270	1999	30r
Insurance and Pensions				
Life and other personal insurance purchases	yr	387	1999	30r
Pensions and Social Security, expenditures on	yr	2968	1999	30r
Legal Fees				
Divorce, filing fee		65.00	4/01	35s
Driver's license fee	orig	20.00	1999	48s
Driver's license fee	renew	5.00	1999	48s
Fishing license	yr	14.00	4/01	34s
Personal Goods				
Personal care products and services purchases	yr	385	1999	30r
Personal Services				
Personal services, household, expenditures on	yr	300	1999	30r
Pets				
Pets, toys, and playground equipment, expenditures on	yr	375	1999	30r
Taxes				
Federal income taxes paid	yr	2326	1999	30r
Personal taxes, expenditures on	yr	3223	1999	30r
Property taxes paid	yr	1152	1999	30r
State and local income taxes paid	yr	753	1999	30r
Transportation				
Cars and trucks, new, expenditures on	yr	1280	1999	30r
Cars and trucks, used, expenditures on	yr	1763	1999	30r
Diesel at the pump	gal	1.19	10/99	73s
Gasoline and motor oil purchases	yr	1036	1999	30r
Gasoline before-tax price (cents)	gal	111.50	10/00	43s
Maintenance and repair expenditures	yr	594	1999	30r
Public transportation, expenditures on	yr	341	1999	30r
Transportation purchases	yr	6617	1999	30r
Vehicle expenses, miscellaneous, purchases	yr	2159	1999	30r
Vehicle insurance payments	yr	701	1999	30r
Vehicle purchases (net outlay)	yr	3081	1999	30r
Vehicle rental, lease expenditures	yr	536	1999	30r
Utilities				
Electrical bill, average	mos	55.00	9/00	9s
Electricity, expenditures on	yr	841	1999	30r
Electricity cost, average	KWh	7.00	9/00	9s
Utilities, fuels, and public services purchased	yr	2401	1999	30r
Water and other public services, expenditures on	yr	273	1999	30r
Weddings				
Wedding (national average cost)		19936	2000	33r
Wedding (regional average total cost)		16195	1997	110r
Attendants' gifts		321	1998	33r
Bridal attendants' apparel (5 persons)		824	2000	33r
Bride's headpiece/veil		173	1998	33r
Bride's wedding dress		859	1998	33r
Clergy, religious facility fee		242	1998	33r
Engagement ring		3177	1998	33r
Flowers		789	1998	33r
Groom's formalwear rental		99	2000	33r
Limousine		410	1998	33r
Marriage license cost		20.00	4/01	35s
Men's formalwear (ushers, best man)		469	2000	33r
Mother of bride apparel		241	2000	33r
Music		866	1998	33r
Photography and videography		1368	1998	33r
Rehearsal dinner		728	1998	33r
Wedding invitations and announcements		341	1998	33r
Wedding reception		7968	2000	33r
Wedding rings (bride and groom)		1060	1998	33r

Values are in dollars or fractions of dollars. In the column headed *Ref*, references are shown to sources. Each reference is followed by a letter. These refer to the geographical level for which data were reported: s=State, r=Region, and c=City or metro. The abbreviation *ex* is used to mean *except* or *excluding*; *exp* stands for *expenditures*. For other abbreviations and further explanations, please see the Introduction.

Saint Cloud, MN

Item	Per	Value	Date	Ref.
Average annual expenditures	yr	35369	1999	30r
Composite, ACCRA index		101.70	3/01	4c
Alcoholic Beverages				
Alcoholic beverage purchases	yr	304	1999	30r
Beer, Heineken, 12-oz, ex deposit	6	6.74	3/01	4c
J & B Scotch	750-ml	16.12	3/01	4c
Malt beverages, all types, all sizes, any origin	16 oz	0.93	7/01	11r
Wine, Livingston or Gallo, Chablis blanc	1.5 liter	4.49	3/01	4c
Wine, red and white table, all sizes, any origin	liter	7.04	7/01	11r
Appliances				
Appliance repair, service call, washing machine	min lab chg	41.13	3/01	4c
Major appliances, expenditures on	yr	165	1999	30r
Small appliances, housewares, expenditures on	yr	90	1999	30r
Banking and Money				
Mortgage interest and charges paid	yr	2277	1999	30r
Mortgage principal paid on owned property	yr	1230	1999	30r
Mortgage rate, incl. points and orig. fee, 30-yr. conv. fixed or ARM	mos	7.20	3/01	4c
Vehicle finance charges paid	yr	328	1999	30r
Charity				
Cash contributions, expenditures	yr	1126	1999	30r
Child Care				
Child raising cost, total, age 0-2	yr	7890	1999	60r
Child raising cost, total, age 3-5	yr	8130	1999	60r
Child raising cost, total, age 6-8	yr	8170	1999	60r
Child raising cost, total, age 9-11	yr	8190	1999	60r
Child raising cost, total, age 12-14	yr	8890	1999	60r
Child raising cost, total, age 15-17	yr	9050	1999	60r
Child's child care and education, age 0-2	yr	1240	1999	60r
Child's child care and education, age 3-5	yr	1370	1999	60r
Child's child care and education, age 6-8	yr	880	1999	60r
Child's child care and education, age 9-11	yr	570	1999	60r
Child's child care and education, age 12-14	yr	420	1999	60r
Child's child care and education, age 15-17	yr	720	1999	60r
Child's clothing, age 0-2	yr	410	1999	60r
Child's clothing, age 3-5	yr	400	1999	60r
Child's clothing, age 6-8	yr	450	1999	60r
Child's clothing, age 9-11	yr	500	1999	60r
Child's clothing, age 12-14	yr	840	1999	60r
Child's clothing, age 15-17	yr	740	1999	60r
Child's food, age 0-2	yr	960	1999	60r
Child's food, age 3-5	yr	1120	1999	60r
Child's food, age 6-8	yr	1430	1999	60r
Child's food, age 9-11	yr	1710	1999	60r
Child's food, age 12-14	yr	1710	1999	60r
Child's food, age 15-17	yr	1920	1999	60r
Child's health care, age 0-2	yr	520	1999	60r
Child's health care, age 3-5	yr	500	1999	60r
Child's health care, age 6-8	yr	570	1999	60r
Child's health care, age 9-11	yr	610	1999	60r
Child's health care, age 12-14	yr	630	1999	60r
Child's health care, age 15-17	yr	650	1999	60r
Child's housing, age 0-2	yr	2860	1999	60r
Child's housing, age 3-5	yr	2840	1999	60r
Child's housing, age 6-8	yr	2800	1999	60r
Child's housing, age 9-11	yr	2650	1999	60r
Child's housing, age 12-14	yr	2840	1999	60r
Child's housing, age 15-17	yr	2440	1999	60r
Child's personal care, reading, age 0-2	yr	880	1999	60r
Child's personal care, reading, age 3-5	yr	900	1999	60r
Child's personal care, reading, age 6-8	yr	930	1999	60r
Child's personal care, reading, age 9-11	yr	970	1999	60r
Child's personal care, reading, age 12-14	yr	1150	1999	60r
Child's personal care, reading, age 15-17	yr	920	1999	60r
Clothing				
Apparel and services purchases	yr	1607	1999	30r
Boys' brief, cotton	3	3.98	3/01	4c

Saint Cloud, MN - continued

Item	Per	Value	Date	Ref.
Clothing - continued				
Boys, 2 to 15, expenditures on	yr	91	1999	30r
Children under 2, expenditures on	yr	59	1999	30r
Footwear, expenditures on	yr	285	1999	30r
Girls, 2 to 15, expenditures on	yr	116	1999	30r
Men and boys, expenditures on	yr	433	1999	30r
Men, 16 and over, expenditures on	yr	341	1999	30r
Shirt, man's dress shirt		38.83	3/01	4c
Slacks, man's "No Wrinkles" khaki		31.66	3/01	4c
Women, 16 and over, expenditures on	yr	490	1999	30r
Communications				
Cable modem installation, Media One		100.00	6/99	103s
Cable modem rate, cable subscriber, Media One	mos	34.95-39.95	6/99	103s
Cable modem rate, non-cable subscriber, Media One	mos	49.95	6/99	103s
Newspaper subscription, daily and Sunday delivery	mos	15.22	3/01	4c
Phone line, single, business, field visit	inst.	45.00	12/97	17s
Phone line, single, business, no field visit	inst.	45.00	12/97	17s
Phone line, single, residence, field visit	inst.	16.25	12/97	17s
Phone line, single, residence, no field visit	inst.	16.25	12/97	17s
Postage and stationery, expenditures on	yr	140	1999	30r
Postal rate, express mail, up to half-pound		12.45	7/01	108r
Postal rate, letter, first class, first ounce		0.34	7/01	108r
Postal rate, letter, two ounces		0.57	7/01	108r
Postal rate, post card		0.21	7/01	108r
Postal rate, priority mail, two pounds		3.95	7/01	108r
Postal rate, priority mail, up to one pound		3.50	7/01	108r
Telephone bill, family of three	mos	26.23	3/01	4c
Telephone services, expenditures on	yr	830	1999	30r
Education				
Board, 4-year private college/university	yr	2267	1996	38s
Board, 4-year public college/university	yr	1474	1996	38s
Education expenditures	yr	583	1999	30r
Room, 4-year private college/university	yr	2058	1996	38s
Room, 4-year public college/university	yr	2022	1996	38s
Total cost, 4-year private college/university	yr	17222	1996	38s
Total cost, 4-year public college/university	yr	6712	1996	38s
Tuition, 2-year public college/university, in state	yr	2065	1996	38s
Tuition, 4-year private college/university, in state	yr	12897	1996	38s
Tuition, 4-year public college/university	yr	3216	1996	38s
Energy and Fuels				
Electricity	500 KWhs	46.59	7/01	11r
Energy, combined forms, 2400 sq ft	mos	164.34	3/01	4c
Energy, exc. electricity, 2400 sq ft	mos	109.96	3/01	4c
Fuel oil #2	gal	1.27	7/01	11r
Fuel oil and other fuels, expenditures on	yr	68	1999	30r
Gas, natural, commercial rate	1000 cf	6.86	11/00	88s
Gas, regular unleaded, cash, self-service	gal	1.61	3/01	4c
Gasoline, unleaded midgrade	gal	1.79	7/01	11r
Gasoline, unleaded premium	gal	1.86	7/01	11r
Gasoline, unleaded regular	gal	1.58	7/01	11r
Natural gas, expenditures on	yr	389	1999	30r
Utility (piped) gas, therm		0.81	7/01	11r
Utility (piped) gas, 40 therms		38.01	7/01	11r
Utility (piped) gas, 100 therms		81.75	7/01	11r
Entertainment				
Bowling, Saturday evening rate	line	2.88	3/01	4c
Entertainment purchases	yr	1984	1999	30r
Fees and admissions paid	yr	444	1999	30r
Monopoly game, Parker Brothers', No. 9	game	7.92	3/01	4c
Movie, first-run, Saturday, evening	adm.	6.50	3/01	4c
Television, radios, sound equipment, expenditures on	yr	580	1999	30r
Tennis balls, yellow, Wilson or Penn, 3	can	3.19	3/01	4c

Values are in dollars or fractions of dollars. In the column headed *Ref*, references are shown to sources. Each reference is followed by a letter. These refer to the geographical level for which data were reported: s=State, r=Region, and c=City or metro. The abbreviation *ex* is used to mean *except* or *excluding*; *exp* stands for *expenditures*. For other abbreviations and further explanations, please see the Introduction.

Saint Cloud, MN - continued

Item	Per	Value	Date	Ref.
Funerals				
Cosmetology, hair, other preparation		178.32	1/99	78r
Embalming		408.19	1/99	78r
Funeral at funeral home		362.13	1/99	78r
Professional service charges		1375.51	1/99	78r
Transfer of remains to funeral home		155.92	1/99	78r
Visitation/viewing		294.38	1/99	78r
Groceries				
Groceries, ACCRA Index		99.90	3/01	4c
Antibiotic ointment, Polysporin	0.5 oz	4.86	3/01	4c
Baby food, strained vegetables or fruit, lowest price	4-4.5 oz	0.53	3/01	4c
Bacon, sliced	lb	3.15	7/01	11r
Bakery products, expenditures on	yr	281	1999	30r
Bananas	lb	0.49	3/01	4c
Bananas	lb	0.48	7/01	11r
Beans, dried, any type, all sizes	lb	0.61	7/01	11r
Beef for stew, boneless	lb	3.08	7/01	11r
Beef or hamburger, ground	lb	1.93	3/01	4c
Beef, expenditures on	yr	217	1999	30r
Bologna, all beef or mixed	lb	2.52	7/01	11r
Bread, white	loaf	0.88	3/01	4c
Bread, white, pan	lb	1.06	7/01	11r
Broccoli	lb	0.91	7/01	11r
Butter, salted, grade AA, stick	lb	3.04	7/01	11r
Butter, yoghurt, cheese, etc, expenditures on	yr	183	1999	30r
Cereals and bakery product purchases	yr	430	1999	30r
Cereals and cereal products, expenditures on	yr	149	1999	30r
Cheese, Kraft grated Parmesan	8 oz	3.20	3/01	4c
Chicken, fresh, whole	lb	1.07	7/01	11r
Chicken, whole fryer	lb	1.11	3/01	4c
Chops, boneless,	lb	3.64	7/01	11r
Chuck roast, U.S. choice, boneless	lb	2.47	7/01	11r
Cigarettes, Winston, Kings	carton	29.63	3/01	4c
Coffee, 100%, ground roast, all sizes	lb	2.69	7/01	11r
Coffee, vacuum-packed	13 oz	2.47	3/01	4c
Cookies, chocolate chip	lb	2.87	7/01	11r
Corn Flakes, Kellogg's or Post Toasties	18 oz	2.27	3/01	4c
Corn, frozen, whole kernel, lowest price	16 oz	0.97	3/01	4c
Dairy product purchases	yr	304	1999	30r
Eggs, expenditures on	yr	26	1999	30r
Eggs, Grade A or AA	dozen	0.80	3/01	4c
Eggs, grade A, large	dozen	0.88	7/01	11r
Fats and oils, expenditures on	yr	75	1999	30r
Fish and seafood, expenditures on	yr	72	1999	30r
Food (excl fruit and vegetables), eaten at home, purchases	yr	887	1999	30r
Food cooked on trips, expenditures on	yr	44	1999	30r
Food purchases	yr	4802	1999	30r
Food purchases, eaten away from home	yr	2069	1999	30r
Food purchases, food eaten at home	yr	2733	1999	30r
Fresh fruits, expenditures on	yr	138	1999	30r
Fresh milk and cream, expenditures on	yr	120	1999	30r
Fresh vegetables, expenditures on	yr	126	1999	30r
Grapefruit	lb	0.66	7/01	11r
Grapes, Thompson, seedless	lb	1.64	7/01	11r
Ground beef, 100% beef	lb	1.64	7/01	11r
Ground beef, lean and extra lean	lb	2.16	7/01	11r
Ground chuck, 100% beef	lb	2.13	7/01	11r
Ham, boneless, excl canned	lb	2.62	7/01	11r
Ice cream, prepackaged, bulk, regular	1/2 gal	3.35	7/01	11r
Lemons	lb	1.19	7/01	11r
Lettuce, iceberg	head	0.86	3/01	4c
Lettuce, iceberg	lb	0.73	7/01	11r
Margarine, Blue Bonnet or Parkay, stick	lb	0.83	3/01	4c
Margarine, soft, tubs	lb	0.89	7/01	11r
Meats, poultry, fish, and egg purchases	yr	671	1999	30r
Milk, fresh, whole, fortified	gal	2.71	7/01	11r
Milk, whole	1/2 gal	1.81	3/01	4c
Nonalcoholic beverages, expenditures on	yr	239	1999	30r
Orange juice, Minute Maid frozen	12 oz	1.35	3/01	4c
Oranges, Navel	lb	0.80	7/01	11r

Saint Cloud, MN - continued

Item	Per	Value	Date	Ref.
Groceries - continued				
Oranges, Valencia	lb	0.66	7/01	11r
Peaches, halves or slices, Hunt's, Del Monte, or Libby's	29 oz	1.56	3/01	4c
Pears, Anjou	lb	0.93	7/01	11r
Peas, green, Del Monte or Green Giant	15 oz	0.75	3/01	4c
Pork chops, center cut, bone-in	lb	3.63	7/01	11r
Pork, expenditures on	yr	150	1999	30r
Potato chips	16 oz	3.52	7/01	11r
Potatoes, frozen, french fried	lb	1.08	7/01	11r
Potatoes, white or red	10 lb	1.87	3/01	4c
Potatoes, white, all types	lb	0.33	7/01	11r
Poultry, expenditures on	yr	108	1999	30r
Processed fruits, expenditures on	yr	98	1999	30r
Processed vegetables, expenditures on	yr	80	1999	30r
Round roast, U.S. choice, boneless	lb	3.07	7/01	11r
Round steak, graded and ungraded, excl U.S. prime and choice	lb	3.41	7/01	11r
Sausage, Jimmy Dean/Owens pork	lb	3.88	3/01	4c
Shortening, vegetable oil blends	lb	1.13	7/01	11r
Shortening, vegetable, Crisco	3 lb	2.82	3/01	4c
Soft drink, Coca Cola, ex deposit	2 liter	1.16	3/01	4c
Spaghetti and macaroni	lb	0.80	7/01	11r
Steak, round, U.S. choice, boneless	lb	3.23	7/01	11r
Steak, T-bone	lb	6.11	3/01	4c
Steak, T-bone, U.S. choice, bone-in	lb	6.68	7/01	11r
Strawberries, dry pint	12 oz	1.32	7/01	11r
Sugar and other sweets, expenditures on	yr	114	1999	30r
Sugar, cane or beet	4 lbs	1.57	3/01	4c
Sugar, white, 33-80 ounce package	lb	0.42	7/01	11r
Sugar, white, all sizes	lb	0.43	7/01	11r
Tobacco products and smoking supplies purchases	yr	331	1999	30r
Tomatoes, field grown	lb	1.46	7/01	11r
Tomatoes, Hunt's or Del Monte	14.5 oz	0.85	3/01	4c
Tuna, chunk, light	6 oz	0.57	3/01	4c
Tuna, light, chunk	lb	1.80	7/01	11r
Turkey, frozen, whole	lb	1.15	7/01	11r
Goods and Services				
Miscellaneous goods and services, ACCRA Index		104.00	3/01	4c
B&B Japanese maple (acer japonicum)	gal	29.99-169.99	4/00	93r
Boxwood (buxus)	2 gal	18.99-39.99	4/00	93r
Daylily (hemerocallis)	gal	4.99-25.00	4/00	93r
Flat of annuals		11.98-24.99	4/00	93r
Fountain grass (pennisetum)	gal	5.98-12.98	4/00	93r
Hanging basket (10 in)		12.99-27.99	4/00	93r
Hardy geranium (geranium)	gal	7.99-9.99	4/00	93r
Hosta (hosta)	gal	6.00-25.00	4/00	93r
Lilac (syrubga vulgaris)	2 gal	14.99-24.99	4/00	93r
Miscellaneous purchases	yr	865	1999	30r
Rhododendron (rhododendron)	2 gal	23.98-42.99	4/00	93r
Sage (salvia)	gal	6.00-9.99	4/00	93r
Wintercreeper euonymus (euonymus fortunei)	2 gal	16.00-169.99	4/00	93r
Hunting license	yr	17.00	4/01	34s
Health Care				
Health care, ACCRA Index		106.00	3/01	4c
Cardiac catheterization, ave hospital/ physician charges		19020	1998	77s
Childbirth, Cesarean delivery		10722	1997	13r

Values are in dollars or fractions of dollars. In the column headed *Ref*, references are shown to sources. Each reference is followed by a letter. These refer to the geographical level for which data were reported: s=State, r=Region, and c=City or metro. The abbreviation *ex* is used to mean *except* or *excluding*; *exp* stands for *expenditures*. For other abbreviations and further explanations, please see the Introduction.

Saint Cloud, MN - continued

Item	Per	Value	Date	Ref.
Health Care				
Childbirth, vaginal delivery		6223	1997	13r
Dentist's fee, adult teeth cleaning and periodic oral exam	visit	72.75	3/01	4c
Doctor's fee, routine exam, established patient	visit	61.50	3/01	4c
Drugs, expenditures on	yr	394	1999	30r
Health care purchases	yr	2048	1999	30r
Health insurance expenditures	yr	978	1999	30r
Hospital care, private room	day	618.00	3/01	4c
Hysterectomy, laproscopically-assisted, ave hospital/physician charges		15580	1998	76s
Hysterectomy, vaginal, ave hospital and physician charges		10690	1998	76s
Medicaid dispensing fee		3.65	1999	87s
Medical services expenditures	yr	554	1999	30r
Medical supplies, expenditures on	yr	122	1999	30r
Plastic surgery, breast augmentation		3184	2000	7r
Plastic surgery, breast lift		3585	2000	7r
Plastic surgery, facelift		4999	2000	7r
Plastic surgery, hair transplantation		3105	2000	7r
Plastic surgery, lip augmentation		1290	2000	7r
Plastic surgery, lower body lift		8135	2000	7r
Plastic surgery, thigh lift		3839	2000	7r
Household Goods				
Dishwashing powder, Cascade	50 oz	3.88	3/01	4c
Floor coverings, expenditures on	yr	52	1999	30r
Furniture, expenditures on	yr	344	1999	30r
Household furnishings and equipment purchases	yr	1475	1999	30r
Household textiles, expenditures on	yr	109	1999	30r
Laundry and cleaning supplies, expenditures on	yr	134	1999	30r
Tissues, facial, Kleenex brand	175	1.14	3/01	4c
Housing				
Housing, ACCRA Index		85.90	3/01	4c
Home price, existing, ave		144400	10/00	90r
Home value, median		135000	2001	53s
House, 2400 sq ft, 8000 sq ft lot, new, urban, utilities	total	175800	3/01	4c
House payment, principal and interest, 25% down payment	mos	895	3/01	4c
Household operation expenditures	yr	542	1999	30r
Housekeeping supplies purchases	yr	508	1999	30r
Lodging expenditures	yr	430	1999	30r
Maintenance, repairs, insurance expenditures	yr	853	1999	30r
Monthly rental value of owned home	mos	547	1999	30r
Owned dwellings, expenditures own	yr	4282	1999	30r
Rent expenditures	yr	1558	1999	30r
Rent, apartment, 2 br, 1 1/2-2 baths, unfurn, 950 sq ft, water	mos	571	3/01	4c
Rental unit, 1 bedroom, with utilities	mos	427	4/01	41c
Rental unit, 2 bedroom, with utilities	mos	505	4/01	41c
Rental unit, 3 bedroom, with utilities	mos	637	4/01	41c
Rental unit, 4 bedroom, with utilities	mos	813	4/01	41c
Shelter, expenditures on	yr	6270	1999	30r
Insurance and Pensions				
Life and other personal insurance purchases	yr	387	1999	30r
Pensions and Social Security, expenditures on	yr	2968	1999	30r
Legal Fees				
Divorce, filing fee		122.00	4/01	35s
Driver's license fee	renew	13.00	1999	48s
Driver's license fee	orig	16.00	1999	48s
Fishing license	yr	18.00	4/01	34s
Personal Goods				
Personal care products and services purchases	yr	385	1999	30r
Shampoo, Alberto VO5	15 oz	1.17	3/01	4c

Saint Cloud, MN - continued

Item	Per	Value	Date	Ref.
Personal Goods - continued				
Toothpaste, Crest or Colgate	6-7 oz	2.32	3/01	4c
Personal Services				
Dry cleaning, man's 2-pc suit		8.23	3/01	4c
Man's haircut, barbershop, no styling		11.99	3/01	4c
Personal services, household, expenditures on	yr	300	1999	30r
Woman's shampoo, trim, blow-dry, no style-change		21.00	3/01	4c
Pets				
Pets, toys, and playground equipment, expenditures on	yr	375	1999	30r
Restaurant Food				
Chicken, fried, thigh and drumstick, KFC/Church's		2.38	3/01	4c
Hamburger with cheese, McDonald's	1/4 lb	2.09	3/01	4c
Pizza, Pizza Hut or Pizza Inn	11-12 in	9.99	3/01	4c
Taxes				
Federal income taxes paid	yr	2326	1999	30r
Personal taxes, expenditures on	yr	3223	1999	30r
Property taxes paid	yr	1152	1999	30r
State and local income taxes paid	yr	753	1999	30r
Transportation				
Transportation, ACCRA Index		113.80	3/01	4c
Cars and trucks, new, expenditures on	yr	1280	1999	30r
Cars and trucks, used, expenditures on	yr	1763	1999	30r
Diesel at the pump	gal	1.28	10/99	73s
Gasoline and motor oil purchases	yr	1036	1999	30r
Gasoline before-tax price (cents)	gal	117.20	10/00	43s
Maintenance and repair expenditures	yr	594	1999	30r
Motorcycle license fee	orig	16.00	1999	49s
Motorcycle license fee	renew	13.00	1999	49s
Public transportation, expenditures on	yr	341	1999	30r
Tire balance, computer or spin balance, front	wheel	8.89	3/01	4c
Transportation purchases	yr	6617	1999	30r
Vehicle expenses, miscellaneous, purchases	yr	2159	1999	30r
Vehicle insurance payments	yr	701	1999	30r
Vehicle purchases (net outlay)	yr	3081	1999	30r
Vehicle rental, lease expenditures	yr	536	1999	30r
Utilities				
Utilities, ACCRA Index		132.70	3/01	4c
Electrical bill, average	mos	55.08	9/00	9s
Electricity, expenditures on	yr	841	1999	30r
Electricity and other, mixed, 2400 sq ft, new home	mos	54.38	3/01	4c
Electricity cost, average	KWh	5.80	9/00	9s
Utilities, fuels, and public services purchased	yr	2401	1999	30r
Water and other public services, expenditures on	yr	273	1999	30r
Weddings				
Wedding (national average cost)		19936	2000	33r
Wedding (regional average total cost)		16195	1997	110r
Attendants' gifts		321	1998	33r
Bridal attendants' apparel (5 persons)		824	2000	33r
Bride's headpiece/veil		173	1998	33r
Bride's wedding dress		859	1998	33r
Clergy, religious facility fee		242	1998	33r
Engagement ring		3177	1998	33r
Flowers		789	1998	33r
Groom's formalwear rental		99	2000	33r
Limousine		410	1998	33r
Marriage license cost		70.00	4/01	35s
Men's formalwear (ushers, best man)		469	2000	33r
Mother of bride apparel		241	2000	33r
Music		866	1998	33r
Photography and videography		1368	1998	33r
Rehearsal dinner		728	1998	33r
Wedding invitations and announcements		341	1998	33r
Wedding reception		7968	2000	33r

Values are in dollars or fractions of dollars. In the column headed *Ref*, references are shown to sources. Each reference is followed by a letter. These refer to the geographical level for which data were reported: s=State, r=Region, and c=City or metro. The abbreviation *ex* is used to mean *except* or *excluding*; *exp* stands for expenditures. For other abbreviations and further explanations, please see the Introduction.

Saint Cloud, MN - continued

Item	Per	Value	Date	Ref.
Weddings				
Wedding rings (bride and groom)		1060	1998	33r

Saint Joseph, MO

Item	Per	Value	Date	Ref.
Average annual expenditures	yr	35369	1999	30r
Composite, ACCRA index		94.20	3/01	4c
Alcoholic Beverages				
Alcoholic beverage purchases	yr	304	1999	30r
Beer, Heineken, 12-oz, ex deposit	6	6.92	3/01	4c
J & B Scotch	750-ml	19.29	3/01	4c
Malt beverages, all types, all sizes, any origin	16 oz	0.93	7/01	11r
Wine, Livingston or Gallo, Chablis blanc	1.5 liter	5.90	3/01	4c
Wine, red and white table, all sizes, any origin	liter	7.04	7/01	11r
Appliances				
Appliance repair, service call, washing machine	min lab chg	37.33	3/01	4c
Major appliances, expenditures on	yr	165	1999	30r
Small appliances, housewares, expenditures on	yr	90	1999	30r
Banking and Money				
Mortgage interest and charges paid	yr	2277	1999	30r
Mortgage principal paid on owned property	yr	1230	1999	30r
Mortgage rate, incl. points and orig. fee, 30-yr. conv. fixed or ARM	mos	7.04	3/01	4c
Vehicle finance charges paid	yr	328	1999	30r
Charity				
Cash contributions, expenditures	yr	1126	1999	30r
Child Care				
Child raising cost, total, age 0-2	yr	7890	1999	60r
Child raising cost, total, age 3-5	yr	8130	1999	60r
Child raising cost, total, age 6-8	yr	8170	1999	60r
Child raising cost, total, age 9-11	yr	8190	1999	60r
Child raising cost, total, age 12-14	yr	8890	1999	60r
Child raising cost, total, age 15-17	yr	9050	1999	60r
Child's child care and education, age 0-2	yr	1240	1999	60r
Child's child care and education, age 3-5	yr	1370	1999	60r
Child's child care and education, age 6-8	yr	880	1999	60r
Child's child care and education, age 9-11	yr	570	1999	60r
Child's child care and education, age 12-14	yr	420	1999	60r
Child's child care and education, age 15-17	yr	720	1999	60r
Child's clothing, age 0-2	yr	410	1999	60r
Child's clothing, age 3-5	yr	400	1999	60r
Child's clothing, age 6-8	yr	450	1999	60r
Child's clothing, age 9-11	yr	500	1999	60r
Child's clothing, age 12-14	yr	840	1999	60r
Child's clothing, age 15-17	yr	740	1999	60r
Child's food, age 0-2	yr	960	1999	60r
Child's food, age 3-5	yr	1120	1999	60r
Child's food, age 6-8	yr	1430	1999	60r
Child's food, age 9-11	yr	1710	1999	60r
Child's food, age 12-14	yr	1710	1999	60r
Child's food, age 15-17	yr	1920	1999	60r
Child's health care, age 0-2	yr	520	1999	60r
Child's health care, age 3-5	yr	500	1999	60r
Child's health care, age 6-8	yr	570	1999	60r
Child's health care, age 9-11	yr	610	1999	60r
Child's health care, age 12-14	yr	630	1999	60r
Child's health care, age 15-17	yr	650	1999	60r
Child's housing, age 0-2	yr	2860	1999	60r
Child's housing, age 3-5	yr	2840	1999	60r
Child's housing, age 6-8	yr	2800	1999	60r
Child's housing, age 9-11	yr	2650	1999	60r
Child's housing, age 12-14	yr	2840	1999	60r
Child's housing, age 15-17	yr	2440	1999	60r
Child's personal care, reading, age 0-2	yr	880	1999	60r
Child's personal care, reading, age 3-5	yr	900	1999	60r
Child's personal care, reading, age 6-8	yr	930	1999	60r
Child's personal care, reading, age 9-11	yr	970	1999	60r

Saint Joseph, MO - continued

Item	Per	Value	Date	Ref.
Child Care - continued				
Child's personal care, reading, age 12-14	yr	1150	1999	60r
Child's personal care, reading, age 15-17	yr	920	1999	60r
Clothing				
Apparel and services purchases	yr	1607	1999	30r
Boys' brief, cotton	3	3.97	3/01	4c
Boys, 2 to 15, expenditures on	yr	91	1999	30r
Children under 2, expenditures on	yr	59	1999	30r
Footwear, expenditures on	yr	285	1999	30r
Girls, 2 to 15, expenditures on	yr	116	1999	30r
Men and boys, expenditures on	yr	433	1999	30r
Men, 16 and over, expenditures on	yr	341	1999	30r
Shirt, man's dress shirt		29.75	3/01	4c
Slacks, man's "No Wrinkles" khaki		39.00	3/01	4c
Women, 16 and over, expenditures on	yr	490	1999	30r
Communications				
Newspaper subscription, daily and Sunday delivery	mos	13.00	3/01	4c
Phone line, single, business, field visit	inst.	52.25	12/97	17s
Phone line, single, business, no field visit	inst.	52.25	12/97	17s
Phone line, single, residence, field visit	inst.	36.50	12/97	17s
Phone line, single, residence, no field visit	inst.	36.50	12/97	17s
Postage and stationery, expenditures on	yr	140	1999	30r
Postal rate, express mail, up to half-pound		12.45	7/01	108r
Postal rate, letter, first class, first ounce		0.34	7/01	108r
Postal rate, letter, two ounces		0.57	7/01	108r
Postal rate, post card		0.21	7/01	108r
Postal rate, priority mail, two pounds		3.95	7/01	108r
Postal rate, priority mail, up to one pound		3.50	7/01	108r
Telephone bill, business, basic rate	mos	23.10	12/97	18c
Telephone bill, family of three	mos	15.26	3/01	4c
Telephone bill, residential, basic rate	mos	9.10	12/97	18c
Telephone services, expenditures on	yr	830	1999	30r
Education				
Board, 4-year private college/university	yr	2387	1996	38s
Board, 4-year public college/university	yr	1713	1996	38s
Education expenditures	yr	583	1999	30r
Room, 4-year private college/university	yr	2162	1996	38s
Room, 4-year public college/university	yr	2022	1996	38s
Total cost, 4-year private college/university	yr	14116	1996	38s
Total cost, 4-year public college/university	yr	6750	1996	38s
Tuition, 2-year public college/university, in state	yr	1255	1996	38s
Tuition, 4-year private college/university, in state	yr	9566	1996	38s
Tuition, 4-year public college/university	yr	3015	1996	38s
Energy and Fuels				
Electricity	500 KWhs	46.59	7/01	11r
Energy, combined forms, 2400 sq ft	mos	115.87	3/01	4c
Energy, exc. electricity, 2400 sq ft	mos	64.06	3/01	4c
Fuel oil #2	gal	1.27	7/01	11r
Fuel oil and other fuels, expenditures on	yr	68	1999	30r
Gas, natural, commercial rate	1000 cf	8.38	11/00	88s
Gas, regular unleaded, cash, self-service	gal	1.30	3/01	4c
Gasoline, unleaded midgrade	gal	1.79	7/01	11r
Gasoline, unleaded premium	gal	1.86	7/01	11r
Gasoline, unleaded regular	gal	1.58	7/01	11r
Natural gas, expenditures on	yr	389	1999	30r
Utility (piped) gas, therm		0.81	7/01	11r
Utility (piped) gas, 40 therms		38.01	7/01	11r
Utility (piped) gas, 100 therms		81.75	7/01	11r
Entertainment				
Bowling, Saturday evening rate	line	3.03	3/01	4c
Entertainment purchases	yr	1984	1999	30r
Fees and admissions paid	yr	444	1999	30r
Monopoly game, Parker Brothers', No. 9	game	10.37	3/01	4c
Movie, first-run, Saturday, evening	adm.	6.25	3/01	4c
Television, radios, sound equipment, expenditures on	yr	580	1999	30r

Values are in dollars or fractions of dollars. In the column headed *Ref*, references are shown to sources. Each reference is followed by a letter. These refer to the geographical level for which data were reported: s=State, r=Region, and c=City or metro. The abbreviation *ex* is used to mean *except* or *excluding*; *exp* stands for expenditures. For other abbreviations and further explanations, please see the Introduction.

Saint Joseph, MO - continued

Item	Per	Value	Date	Ref.
Entertainment				
Tennis balls, yellow, Wilson or Penn, 3	can	2.13	3/01	4c
Funerals				
Cosmetology, hair, other preparation		178.32	1/99	78r
Embalming		408.19	1/99	78r
Funeral at funeral home		362.13	1/99	78r
Professional service charges		1375.51	1/99	78r
Transfer of remains to funeral home		155.92	1/99	78r
Visitation/viewing		294.38	1/99	78r
Groceries				
Groceries, ACCRA Index		89.20	3/01	4c
Antibiotic ointment, Polysporin	0.5 oz	5.09	3/01	4c
Baby food, strained vegetables or fruit, lowest price	4-4.5 oz	0.42	3/01	4c
Bacon, sliced	lb	3.15	7/01	11r
Bakery products, expenditures on	yr	281	1999	30r
Bananas	lb	0.45	3/01	4c
Bananas	lb	0.48	7/01	11r
Beans, dried, any type, all sizes	lb	0.61	7/01	11r
Beef for stew, boneless	lb	3.08	7/01	11r
Beef or hamburger, ground	lb	1.29	3/01	4c
Beef, expenditures on	yr	217	1999	30r
Bologna, all beef or mixed	lb	2.52	7/01	11r
Bread, white	loaf	0.74	3/01	4c
Bread, white, pan	lb	1.06	7/01	11r
Broccoli	lb	0.91	7/01	11r
Butter, salted, grade AA, stick	lb	3.04	7/01	11r
Butter, yoghurt, cheese, etc, expenditures on	yr	183	1999	30r
Cereals and bakery product purchases	yr	430	1999	30r
Cereals and cereal products, expenditures on	yr	149	1999	30r
Cheese, Kraft grated Parmesan	8 oz	3.16	3/01	4c
Chicken, fresh, whole	lb	1.07	7/01	11r
Chicken, whole fryer	lb	0.91	3/01	4c
Chops, boneless,	lb	3.64	7/01	11r
Chuck roast, U.S. choice, boneless	lb	2.47	7/01	11r
Cigarettes, Winston, Kings	carton	29.39	3/01	4c
Coffee, 100%, ground roast, all sizes	lb	2.69	7/01	11r
Coffee, vacuum-packed	13 oz	2.43	3/01	4c
Cookies, chocolate chip	lb	2.87	7/01	11r
Corn Flakes, Kellogg's or Post Toasties	18 oz	1.71	3/01	4c
Corn, frozen, whole kernel, lowest price	16 oz	1.11	3/01	4c
Dairy product purchases	yr	304	1999	30r
Eggs, expenditures on	yr	26	1999	30r
Eggs, Grade A or AA	dozen	1.06	3/01	4c
Eggs, grade A, large	dozen	0.88	7/01	11r
Fats and oils, expenditures on	yr	75	1999	30r
Fish and seafood, expenditures on	yr	72	1999	30r
Food (excl fruit and vegetables), eaten at home, purchases	yr	887	1999	30r
Food cooked on trips, expenditures on	yr	44	1999	30r
Food purchases	yr	4802	1999	30r
Food purchases, eaten away from home	yr	2069	1999	30r
Food purchases, food eaten at home	yr	2733	1999	30r
Fresh fruits, expenditures on	yr	138	1999	30r
Fresh milk and cream, expenditures on	yr	120	1999	30r
Fresh vegetables, expenditures on	yr	126	1999	30r
Grapefruit	lb	0.66	7/01	11r
Grapes, Thompson, seedless	lb	1.64	7/01	11r
Ground beef, 100% beef	lb	1.64	7/01	11r
Ground beef, lean and extra lean	lb	2.16	7/01	11r
Ground chuck, 100% beef	lb	2.13	7/01	11r
Ham, boneless, excl canned	lb	2.62	7/01	11r
Ice cream, prepackaged, bulk, regular	1/2 gal	3.35	7/01	11r
Lemons	lb	1.19	7/01	11r
Lettuce, iceberg	head	0.94	3/01	4c
Lettuce, iceberg	lb	0.73	7/01	11r
Margarine, Blue Bonnet or Parkay, stick	lb	0.83	3/01	4c
Margarine, soft, tubs	lb	0.89	7/01	11r
Meats, poultry, fish, and egg purchases	yr	671	1999	30r
Milk, fresh, whole, fortified	gal	2.71	7/01	11r
Milk, whole	1/2 gal	1.48	3/01	4c

Saint Joseph, MO - continued

Item	Per	Value	Date	Ref.
Groceries - continued				
Nonalcoholic beverages, expenditures on	yr	239	1999	30r
Orange juice, Minute Maid frozen	12 oz	1.52	3/01	4c
Oranges, Navel	lb	0.80	7/01	11r
Oranges, Valencia	lb	0.66	7/01	11r
Peaches, halves or slices, Hunt's, Del Monte, or Libby's	29 oz	1.59	3/01	4c
Pears, Anjou	lb	0.93	7/01	11r
Peas, green, Del Monte or Green Giant	15 oz	0.73	3/01	4c
Pork chops, center cut, bone-in	lb	3.63	7/01	11r
Pork, expenditures on	yr	150	1999	30r
Potato chips	16 oz	3.52	7/01	11r
Potatoes, frozen, french fried	lb	1.08	7/01	11r
Potatoes, white or red	10 lb	1.74	3/01	4c
Potatoes, white, all types	lb	0.33	7/01	11r
Poultry, expenditures on	yr	108	1999	30r
Processed fruits, expenditures on	yr	98	1999	30r
Processed vegetables, expenditures on	yr	80	1999	30r
Round roast, U.S. choice, boneless	lb	3.07	7/01	11r
Round steak, graded and ungraded, excl U.S. prime and choice	lb	3.41	7/01	11r
Sausage, Jimmy Dean/Owens pork	lb	3.00	3/01	4c
Shortening, vegetable oil blends	lb	1.13	7/01	11r
Shortening, vegetable, Crisco	3 lb	2.71	3/01	4c
Soft drink, Coca Cola, ex deposit	2 liter	1.14	3/01	4c
Spaghetti and macaroni	lb	0.80	7/01	11r
Steak, round, U.S. choice, boneless	lb	3.23	7/01	11r
Steak, T-bone	lb	5.56	3/01	4c
Steak, T-bone, U.S. choice, bone-in	lb	6.68	7/01	11r
Strawberries, dry pint	12 oz	1.32	7/01	11r
Sugar and other sweets, expenditures on	yr	114	1999	30r
Sugar, cane or beet	4 lbs	1.35	3/01	4c
Sugar, white, 33-80 ounce package	lb	0.42	7/01	11r
Sugar, white, all sizes	lb	0.43	7/01	11r
Tobacco products and smoking supplies purchases	yr	331	1999	30r
Tomatoes, field grown	lb	1.46	7/01	11r
Tomatoes, Hunt's or Del Monte	14.5 oz	0.84	3/01	4c
Tuna, chunk, light	6 oz	0.46	3/01	4c
Tuna, light, chunk	lb	1.80	7/01	11r
Turkey, frozen, whole	lb	1.15	7/01	11r
Goods and Services				
Miscellaneous goods and services, ACCRA Index		100.40	3/01	4c
B&B Japanese maple (acer japonicum)	gal	29.99-169.99	4/00	93r
Boxwood (buxus)	2 gal	18.99-39.99	4/00	93r
Daylilly (hemerocallis)	gal	4.99-25.00	4/00	93r
Flat of annuals		11.98-24.99	4/00	93r
Fountain grass (pennisetum)	gal	5.98-12.98	4/00	93r
Hanging basket (10 in)		12.99-27.99	4/00	93r
Hardy geranium (geranium)	gal	7.99-9.99	4/00	93r
Hosta (hosta)	gal	6.00-25.00	4/00	93r
Lilac (syrubga vulgaris)	2 gal	14.99-24.99	4/00	93r
Miscellaneous purchases	yr	865	1999	30r
Rhododendron (rhododendron)	2 gal	23.98-42.99	4/00	93r
Sage (salvia)	gal	6.00-9.99	4/00	93r
Wintercreeper euonymus (euonymus fortunei)	2 gal	16.00-169.99	4/00	93r
Hunting license	yr	9.00	4/01	34s

Values are in dollars or fractions of dollars. In the column headed *Ref*, references are shown to sources. Each reference is followed by a letter. These refer to the geographical level for which data were reported: s=State, r=Region, and c=City or metro. The abbreviation *ex* is used to mean *except* or *excluding*; *exp* stands for *expenditures*. For other abbreviations and further explanations, please see the Introduction.

Saint Joseph, MO - continued

Item	Per	Value	Date	Ref.
Health Care				
Health care, ACCRA Index		99.40	3/01	4c
Cardiac catheterization, ave hospital/ physician charges		13930	1998	77s
Childbirth, Cesarean delivery		10722	1997	13r
Childbirth, vaginal delivery		6223	1997	13r
Dentist's fee, adult teeth cleaning and periodic oral exam	visit	65.40	3/01	4c
Doctor's fee, routine exam, established patient	visit	57.00	3/01	4c
Drugs, expenditures on	yr	394	1999	30r
Health care purchases	yr	2048	1999	30r
Health insurance expenditures	yr	978	1999	30r
Hospital care, private room	day	595.00	3/01	4c
Hysterectomy, laproscopically-assisted, ave hospital/physician charges		11300	1998	76s
Hysterectomy, vaginal, ave hospital and physician charges		9200	1998	76s
Medicaid dispensing fee		4.09	1999	87s
Medical services expenditures	yr	554	1999	30r
Medical supplies, expenditures on	yr	122	1999	30r
Plastic surgery, breast augmentation		3184	2000	7r
Plastic surgery, breast lift		3585	2000	7r
Plastic surgery, facelift		4999	2000	7r
Plastic surgery, hair transplantation		3105	2000	7r
Plastic surgery, lip augmentation		1290	2000	7r
Plastic surgery, lower body lift		8135	2000	7r
Plastic surgery, thigh lift		3839	2000	7r
Household Goods				
Dishwashing powder, Cascade	50 oz	3.15	3/01	4c
Floor coverings, expenditures on	yr	52	1999	30r
Furniture, expenditures on	yr	344	1999	30r
Household furnishings and equipment purchases	yr	1475	1999	30r
Household textiles, expenditures on	yr	109	1999	30r
Laundry and cleaning supplies, expenditures on	yr	134	1999	30r
Tissues, facial, Kleenex brand	175	1.14	3/01	4c
Housing				
Housing, ACCRA Index		90.00	3/01	4c
Home price, existing, ave		144400	10/00	90r
Home value, median		89000	2001	53s
House, 2400 sq ft, 8000 sq ft lot, new, urban, utilities	total	186800	3/01	4c
House payment, principal and interest, 25% down payment	mos	936	3/01	4c
Household operation expenditures	yr	542	1999	30r
Housekeeping supplies purchases	yr	508	1999	30r
Lodging expenditures	yr	430	1999	30r
Maintenance, repairs, insurance expenditures	yr	853	1999	30r
Monthly rental value of owned home	mos	547	1999	30r
Owned dwellings, expenditures own	yr	4282	1999	30r
Rent expenditures	yr	1558	1999	30r
Rent, apartment, 2 br, 1 1/2-2 baths, unfurn, 950 sq ft, water	mos	602	3/01	4c
Rental unit, 1 bedroom, with utilities	mos	302	4/01	41c
Rental unit, 2 bedroom, with utilities	mos	403	4/01	41c
Rental unit, 3 bedroom, with utilities	mos	509	4/01	41c
Rental unit, 4 bedroom, with utilities	mos	565	4/01	41c
Shelter, expenditures on	yr	6270	1999	30r
Insurance and Pensions				
Life and other personal insurance purchases	yr	387	1999	30r
Pensions and Social Security, expenditures on	yr	2968	1999	30r
Legal Fees				
Driver's license fee	orig	15.00	1999	48s
Driver's license fee	renew	15.00	1999	48s
Fishing license	yr	11.00	4/01	34s

Saint Joseph, MO - continued

Item	Per	Value	Date	Ref.
Personal Goods				
Personal care products and services purchases	yr	385	1999	30r
Shampoo, Alberto VO5	15 oz	0.98	3/01	4c
Toothpaste, Crest or Colgate	6-7 oz	2.26	3/01	4c
Personal Services				
Dry cleaning, man's 2-pc suit		6.48	3/01	4c
Man's haircut, barbershop, no styling		8.75	3/01	4c
Personal services, household, expenditures on	yr	300	1999	30r
Woman's shampoo, trim, blow-dry, no style-change		22.20	3/01	4c
Pets				
Pets, toys, and playground equipment, expenditures on	yr	375	1999	30r
Restaurant Food				
Chicken, fried, thigh and drumstick, KFC/ Church's		2.69	3/01	4c
Hamburger with cheese, McDonald's	1/4 lb	2.32	3/01	4c
Pizza, Pizza Hut or Pizza Inn	11-12 in	9.69	3/01	4c
Taxes				
Federal income taxes paid	yr	2326	1999	30r
Personal taxes, expenditures on	yr	3223	1999	30r
Property taxes paid	yr	1152	1999	30r
State and local income taxes paid	yr	753	1999	30r
Transportation				
Transportation, ACCRA Index		92.70	3/01	4c
Cars and trucks, new, expenditures on	yr	1280	1999	30r
Cars and trucks, used, expenditures on	yr	1763	1999	30r
Diesel at the pump	gal	1.16	10/99	73s
Gasoline and motor oil purchases	yr	1036	1999	30r
Gasoline before-tax price (cents)	gal	108.50	10/00	43s
Maintenance and repair expenditures	yr	594	1999	30r
Public transportation, expenditures on	yr	341	1999	30r
Tire balance, computer or spin balance, front	wheel	7.37	3/01	4c
Transportation purchases	yr	6617	1999	30r
Vehicle expenses, miscellaneous, purchases	yr	2159	1999	30r
Vehicle insurance payments	yr	701	1999	30r
Vehicle purchases (net outlay)	yr	3081	1999	30r
Vehicle rental, lease expenditures	yr	536	1999	30r
Utilities				
Utilities, ACCRA Index		91.50	3/01	4c
Electrical bill, average	mos	68.50	9/00	9s
Electricity, expenditures on	yr	841	1999	30r
Electricity, summer, 250 KWh	mos	20.38	2/96	97c
Electricity, summer, 500 KWh	mos	35.03	2/96	97c
Electricity, summer, 750 KWh	mos	48.16	2/96	97c
Electricity, summer, 1000 KWh	mos	59.02	2/96	97c
Electricity and other, mixed, 2400 sq ft, new home	mos	51.81	3/01	4c
Electricity cost, average	KWh	6.00	9/00	9s
Utilities, fuels, and public services purchased	yr	2401	1999	30r
Water and other public services, expenditures on	yr	273	1999	30r
Weddings				
Wedding (national average cost)		19936	2000	33r
Wedding (regional average total cost)		16195	1997	110r
Attendants' gifts		321	1998	33r
Bridal attendants' apparel (5 persons)		824	2000	33r
Bride's headpiece/veil		173	1998	33r
Bride's wedding dress		859	1998	33r
Clergy, religious facility fee		242	1998	33r
Engagement ring		3177	1998	33r
Flowers		789	1998	33r
Groom's formalwear rental		99	2000	33r
Limousine		410	1998	33r
Marriage license cost		50.00	4/01	35s
Men's formalwear (ushers, best man)		469	2000	33r
Mother of bride apparel		241	2000	33r

Values are in dollars or fractions of dollars. In the column headed *Ref*, references are shown to sources. Each reference is followed by a letter. These refer to the geographical level for which data were reported: s=State, r=Region, and c=City or metro. The abbreviation *ex* is used to mean *except* or *excluding*; *exp* stands for expenditures. For other abbreviations and further explanations, please see the Introduction.

Saint Joseph, MO - continued

Item	Per	Value	Date	Ref.
Weddings				
Music		866	1998	33r
Photography and videography		1368	1998	33r
Rehearsal dinner		728	1998	33r
Wedding invitations and announcements		341	1998	33r
Wedding reception		7968	2000	33r
Wedding rings (bride and groom)		1060	1998	33r

Saint Louis, MO-IL

Item	Per	Value	Date	Ref.
Average annual expenditures	yr	35369	1999	30r
Composite, ACCRA index		96.60	3/01	4c
Alcoholic Beverages				
Alcoholic beverage purchases	yr	222	1999	30c
Beer, Heineken, 12-oz, ex deposit	6	6.33	3/01	4c
J & B Scotch	750-ml	18.43	3/01	4c
Malt beverages, all types, all sizes, any origin	16 oz	0.93	7/01	11r
Wine, Livingston or Gallo, Chablis blanc	1.5 liter	5.32	3/01	4c
Wine, red and white table, all sizes, any origin	liter	7.04	7/01	11r
Appliances				
Appliance repair, service call, washing machine	min lab chg	37.23	3/01	4c
Major appliances, expenditures on	yr	165	1999	30r
Small appliances, housewares, expenditures on	yr	90	1999	30r
Banking and Money				
Mortgage interest and charges paid	yr	2277	1999	30r
Mortgage principal paid on owned property	yr	1230	1999	30r
Mortgage rate, incl. points and orig. fee, 30-yr. conv. fixed or ARM	mos	7.03	3/01	4c
Vehicle finance charges paid	yr	328	1999	30r
Business Expenses				
Business travel, car rental	day	42	2001	3c
Business travel, food	day	62	2001	3c
Business travel, hotel	day	102	2001	3c
Medical office space cost	sq ft	123.69	2001	31c
Office space, 2-4 storey building	sq ft	108.36	2001	31c
Office space, 5-10 storey building	sq ft	95.72	2001	31c
Office space, 11-20 storey building	sq ft	92.00	2001	31c
Charity				
Cash contributions, expenditures	yr	1294	1999	30c
Child Care				
Child raising cost, total, age 0-2	yr	7890	1999	60r
Child raising cost, total, age 3-5	yr	8130	1999	60r
Child raising cost, total, age 6-8	yr	8170	1999	60r
Child raising cost, total, age 9-11	yr	8190	1999	60r
Child raising cost, total, age 12-14	yr	8890	1999	60r
Child raising cost, total, age 15-17	yr	9050	1999	60r
Child's child care and education, age 0-2	yr	1240	1999	60r
Child's child care and education, age 3-5	yr	1370	1999	60r
Child's child care and education, age 6-8	yr	880	1999	60r
Child's child care and education, age 9-11	yr	570	1999	60r
Child's child care and education, age 12-14	yr	420	1999	60r
Child's child care and education, age 15-17	yr	720	1999	60r
Child's clothing, age 0-2	yr	410	1999	60r
Child's clothing, age 3-5	yr	400	1999	60r
Child's clothing, age 6-8	yr	450	1999	60r
Child's clothing, age 9-11	yr	500	1999	60r
Child's clothing, age 12-14	yr	840	1999	60r
Child's clothing, age 15-17	yr	740	1999	60r
Child's food, age 0-2	yr	960	1999	60r
Child's food, age 3-5	yr	1120	1999	60r
Child's food, age 6-8	yr	1430	1999	60r
Child's food, age 9-11	yr	1710	1999	60r
Child's food, age 12-14	yr	1710	1999	60r
Child's food, age 15-17	yr	1920	1999	60r
Child's health care, age 0-2	yr	520	1999	60r
Child's health care, age 3-5	yr	500	1999	60r

Saint Louis, MO-IL - continued

Item	Per	Value	Date	Ref.
Child Care - continued				
Child's health care, age 6-8	yr	570	1999	60r
Child's health care, age 9-11	yr	610	1999	60r
Child's health care, age 12-14	yr	630	1999	60r
Child's health care, age 15-17	yr	650	1999	60r
Child's housing, age 0-2	yr	2860	1999	60r
Child's housing, age 3-5	yr	2840	1999	60r
Child's housing, age 6-8	yr	2800	1999	60r
Child's housing, age 9-11	yr	2650	1999	60r
Child's housing, age 12-14	yr	2840	1999	60r
Child's housing, age 15-17	yr	2440	1999	60r
Child's personal care, reading, age 0-2	yr	880	1999	60r
Child's personal care, reading, age 3-5	yr	900	1999	60r
Child's personal care, reading, age 6-8	yr	930	1999	60r
Child's personal care, reading, age 9-11	yr	970	1999	60r
Child's personal care, reading, age 12-14	yr	1150	1999	60r
Child's personal care, reading, age 15-17	yr	920	1999	60r
Clothing				
Apparel and services purchases	yr	1911	1999	30c
Boys' brief, cotton	3	3.50	3/01	4c
Boys, 2 to 15, expenditures on	yr	91	1999	30r
Children under 2, expenditures on	yr	59	1999	30r
Footwear, expenditures on	yr	285	1999	30r
Girls, 2 to 15, expenditures on	yr	116	1999	30r
Men and boys, expenditures on	yr	433	1999	30r
Men, 16 and over, expenditures on	yr	341	1999	30r
Shirt, man's dress shirt		28.53	3/01	4c
Slacks, man's "No Wrinkles" khaki		46.08	3/01	4c
Women, 16 and over, expenditures on	yr	490	1999	30r
Communications				
Newspaper subscription, daily and Sunday delivery	mos	17.50	3/01	4c
Phone line, single, business, field visit	inst.	52.25	12/97	17s
Phone line, single, business, no field visit	inst.	52.25	12/97	17s
Phone line, single, residence, field visit	inst.	36.50	12/97	17s
Phone line, single, residence, no field visit	inst.	36.50	12/97	17s
Postage and stationery, expenditures on	yr	140	1999	30r
Postal rate, express mail, up to half-pound		12.45	7/01	108r
Postal rate, letter, first class, first ounce		0.34	7/01	108r
Postal rate, letter, two ounces		0.57	7/01	108r
Postal rate, post card		0.21	7/01	108r
Postal rate, priority mail, two pounds		3.95	7/01	108r
Postal rate, priority mail, up to one pound		3.50	7/01	108r
Telephone bill, business, basic rate	mos	33.55	12/97	18c
Telephone bill, family of three	mos	20.18	3/01	4c
Telephone bill, residential, basic rate	mos	11.35	12/97	18c
Telephone services, expenditures on	yr	830	1999	30r
Education				
Board, 4-year private college/university	yr	2387	1996	38s
Board, 4-year public college/university	yr	1713	1996	38s
Education expenditures	yr	508	1999	30c
Room, 4-year private college/university	yr	2162	1996	38s
Room, 4-year public college/university	yr	2022	1996	38s
Total cost, 4-year private college/university	yr	14116	1996	38s
Total cost, 4-year public college/university	yr	6750	1996	38s
Tuition, 2-year public college/university, in state	yr	1255	1996	38s
Tuition, 4-year private college/university, in state	yr	9566	1996	38s
Tuition, 4-year public college/university	yr	3015	1996	38s
Energy and Fuels				
Electricity	500 KWhs	46.59	7/01	11r
Energy, combined forms, 2400 sq ft	mos	109.95	3/01	4c
Energy, exc. electricity, 2400 sq ft	mos	45.41	3/01	4c
Fuel oil #2	gal	1.27	7/01	11r
Fuel oil and other fuels, expenditures on	yr	68	1999	30r
Gas, cooking, winter, 10 therms	mos	15.80	2/96	98c
Gas, cooking, winter, 30 therms	mos	25.41	2/96	98c
Gas, cooking, winter, 50 therms	mos	35.02	2/96	98c
Gas, heating, winter, average use	mos	87.30	2/96	98c

Values are in dollars or fractions of dollars. In the column headed *Ref*, references are shown to sources. Each reference is followed by a letter. These refer to the geographical level for which data were reported: s=State, r=Region, and c=City or metro. The abbreviation *ex* is used to mean *except* or *excluding*; *exp* stands for *expenditures*. For other abbreviations and further explanations, please see the Introduction.

Saint Louis, MO-IL - continued

Item	Per	Value	Date	Ref.
Energy and Fuels				
Gas, natural, commercial rate	1000 cf	8.38	11/00	88s
Gas, regular unleaded, cash, self-service	gal	1.47	3/01	4c
Gasoline, unleaded midgrade	gal	1.79	7/01	11r
Gasoline, unleaded premium	gal	1.86	7/01	11r
Gasoline, unleaded regular	gal	1.58	7/01	11r
Natural gas, expenditures on	yr	389	1999	30r
Utility (piped) gas, therm		0.81	7/01	11r
Utility (piped) gas, 40 therms		38.01	7/01	11r
Utility (piped) gas, 100 therms		81.75	7/01	11r
Entertainment				
Bowling, Saturday evening rate	line	2.94	3/01	4c
Entertainment purchases	yr	1640	1999	30c
Fees and admissions paid	yr	444	1999	30r
Monopoly game, Parker Brothers', No. 9	game	10.60	3/01	4c
Movie, first-run, Saturday, evening	adm.	6.95	3/01	4c
Reading purchases	yr	140	1999	30c
Television, radios, sound equipment, expenditures on	yr	580	1999	30r
Tennis balls, yellow, Wilson or Penn, 3	can	2.17	3/01	4c
Funerals				
Cosmetology, hair, other preparation		178.32	1/99	78r
Embalming		408.19	1/99	78r
Funeral at funeral home		362.13	1/99	78r
Professional service charges		1375.51	1/99	78r
Transfer of remains to funeral home		155.92	1/99	78r
Visitation/viewing		294.38	1/99	78r
Groceries				
Groceries, ACCRA Index		94.30	3/01	4c
Antibiotic ointment, Polysporin	0.5 oz	4.61	3/01	4c
Baby food, strained vegetables or fruit, lowest price	4-4.5 oz	0.39	3/01	4c
Bacon, sliced	lb	3.15	7/01	11r
Bakery products, expenditures on	yr	281	1999	30r
Bananas	lb	0.57	3/01	4c
Bananas	lb	0.48	7/01	11r
Beans, dried, any type, all sizes	lb	0.61	7/01	11r
Beef for stew, boneless	lb	3.08	7/01	11r
Beef or hamburger, ground	lb	1.38	3/01	4c
Beef, expenditures on	yr	217	1999	30r
Bologna, all beef or mixed	lb	2.52	7/01	11r
Bread, white	loaf	0.95	3/01	4c
Bread, white, pan	lb	1.06	7/01	11r
Broccoli	lb	0.91	7/01	11r
Butter, salted, grade AA, stick	lb	3.04	7/01	11r
Butter, yoghurt, cheese, etc, expenditures on	yr	183	1999	30r
Cereals and bakery product purchases	yr	430	1999	30r
Cereals and cereal products, expenditures on	yr	149	1999	30r
Cheese, Kraft grated Parmesan	8 oz	3.94	3/01	4c
Chicken, fresh, whole	lb	1.07	7/01	11r
Chicken, whole fryer	lb	0.83	3/01	4c
Chops, boneless,	lb	3.64	7/01	11r
Chuck roast, U.S. choice, boneless	lb	2.47	7/01	11r
Cigarettes, Winston, Kings	carton	28.01	3/01	4c
Coffee, 100%, ground roast, all sizes	lb	2.69	7/01	11r
Coffee, vacuum-packed	13 oz	2.94	3/01	4c
Cookies, chocolate chip	lb	2.87	7/01	11r
Corn Flakes, Kellogg's or Post Toasties	18 oz	1.92	3/01	4c
Corn, frozen, whole kernel, lowest price	16 oz	1.10	3/01	4c
Dairy product purchases	yr	314	1999	30c
Eggs, expenditures on	yr	26	1999	30r
Eggs, Grade A or AA	dozen	0.88	3/01	4c
Eggs, grade A, large	dozen	0.88	7/01	11r
Fats and oils, expenditures on	yr	75	1999	30r
Fish and seafood, expenditures on	yr	72	1999	30r
Food (excl fruit and vegetables), eaten at home, purchases	yr	931	1999	30c
Food cooked on trips, expenditures on	yr	44	1999	30r
Food purchases	yr	5270	1999	30c
Food purchases, eaten away from home	yr	2078	1999	30c
Food purchases, food eaten at home	yr	3193	1999	30c

Item	Per	Value	Date	Ref.
Groceries - continued				
Fresh fruits, expenditures on	yr	138	1999	30r
Fresh milk and cream, expenditures on	yr	120	1999	30r
Fresh vegetables, expenditures on	yr	126	1999	30r
Fruit and vegetable purchases	yr	536	1999	30c
Grapefruit	lb	0.66	7/01	11r
Grapes, Thompson, seedless	lb	1.64	7/01	11r
Ground beef, 100% beef	lb	1.64	7/01	11r
Ground beef, lean and extra lean	lb	2.16	7/01	11r
Ground chuck, 100% beef	lb	2.13	7/01	11r
Ham, boneless, excl canned	lb	2.62	7/01	11r
Ice cream, prepackaged, bulk, regular	1/2 gal	3.35	7/01	11r
Lemons	lb	1.19	7/01	11r
Lettuce, iceberg	head	0.94	3/01	4c
Lettuce, iceberg	lb	0.73	7/01	11r
Margarine, Blue Bonnet or Parkay, stick	lb	0.69	3/01	4c
Margarine, soft, tubs	lb	0.89	7/01	11r
Meats, poultry, fish, and egg purchases	yr	671	1999	30r
Milk, fresh, whole, fortified	gal	2.71	7/01	11r
Milk, whole	1/2 gal	1.72	3/01	4c
Nonalcoholic beverages, expenditures on	yr	239	1999	30r
Orange juice, Minute Maid frozen	12 oz	1.57	3/01	4c
Oranges, Navel	lb	0.80	7/01	11r
Oranges, Valencia	lb	0.66	7/01	11r
Peaches, halves or slices, Hunt's, Del Monte, or Libby's	29 oz	1.66	3/01	4c
Pears, Anjou	lb	0.93	7/01	11r
Peas, green, Del Monte or Green Giant	15 oz	0.66	3/01	4c
Pork chops, center cut, bone-in	lb	3.63	7/01	11r
Pork, expenditures on	yr	150	1999	30r
Potato chips	16 oz	3.52	7/01	11r
Potatoes, frozen, french fried	lb	1.08	7/01	11r
Potatoes, white or red	10 lb	2.13	3/01	4c
Potatoes, white, all types	lb	0.33	7/01	11r
Poultry, expenditures on	yr	108	1999	30r
Processed fruits, expenditures on	yr	98	1999	30r
Processed vegetables, expenditures on	yr	80	1999	30r
Round roast, U.S. choice, boneless	lb	3.07	7/01	11r
Round steak, graded and ungraded, excl U.S. prime and choice	lb	3.41	7/01	11r
Sausage, Jimmy Dean/Owens pork	lb	2.27	3/01	4c
Shortening, vegetable oil blends	lb	1.13	7/01	11r
Shortening, vegetable, Crisco	3 lb	3.03	3/01	4c
Soft drink, Coca Cola, ex deposit	2 liter	0.95	3/01	4c
Spaghetti and macaroni	lb	0.80	7/01	11r
Steak, round, U.S. choice, boneless	lb	3.23	7/01	11r
Steak, T-bone	lb	5.88	3/01	4c
Steak, T-bone, U.S. choice, bone-in	lb	6.68	7/01	11r
Strawberries, dry pint	12 oz	1.32	7/01	11r
Sugar and other sweets, expenditures on	yr	114	1999	30r
Sugar, cane or beet	4 lbs	1.43	3/01	4c
Sugar, white, 33-80 ounce package	lb	0.42	7/01	11r
Sugar, white, all sizes	lb	0.43	7/01	11r
Tobacco products and smoking supplies purchases	yr	233	1999	30c
Tomatoes, field grown	lb	1.46	7/01	11r
Tomatoes, Hunt's or Del Monte	14.5 oz	0.89	3/01	4c
Tuna, chunk, light	6 oz	0.72	3/01	4c
Tuna, light, chunk	lb	1.80	7/01	11r
Turkey, frozen, whole	lb	1.15	7/01	11r
Goods and Services				
Miscellaneous goods and services, ACCRA Index		101.80	3/01	4c
B&B Japanese maple (acer japonicum)	gal	29.99-169.99	4/00	93r
Boxwood (buxus)	2 gal	18.99-39.99	4/00	93r
Daylily (hemerocallis)	gal	4.99-25.00	4/00	93r
Flat of annuals		11.98-24.99	4/00	93r
Fountain grass (pennisetum)	gal	5.98-12.98	4/00	93r

Values are in dollars or fractions of dollars. In the column headed *Ref*, references are shown to sources. Each reference is followed by a letter. These refer to the geographical level for which data were reported: s=State, r=Region, and c=City or metro. The abbreviation *ex* is used to mean *except* or *excluding*; *exp* stands for *expenditures*. For other abbreviations and further explanations, please see the Introduction.

Saint Louis, MO-IL - continued

Item	Per	Value	Date	Ref.
Goods and Services				
Hanging basket (10 in)		12.99-27.99	4/00	93r
Hardy geranium (geranium)	gal	7.99-9.99	4/00	93r
Hosta (hosta)	gal	6.00-25.00	4/00	93r
Lilac (syrubga vulgaris)	2 gal	14.99-24.99	4/00	93r
Miscellaneous purchases	yr	865	1999	30r
Rhododendron (rhododendron)	2 gal	23.98-42.99	4/00	93r
Sage (salvia)	gal	6.00-9.99	4/00	93r
Wintercreeper euonymus (euonymus fortunei)	2 gal	16.00-169.99	4/00	93r
Hunting license	yr	9.00	4/01	34s
Health Care				
Health care, ACCRA Index		104.70	3/01	4c
Cardiac catheterization, ave hospital/ physician charges		13930	1998	77s
Childbirth, Cesarean delivery		10722	1997	13r
Childbirth, vaginal delivery		6223	1997	13r
Dentist's fee, adult teeth cleaning and periodic oral exam	visit	69.60	3/01	4c
Doctor's fee, routine exam, established patient	visit	70.00	3/01	4c
Drugs, expenditures on	yr	394	1999	30r
Health care purchases	yr	1985	1999	30c
Health insurance expenditures	yr	978	1999	30r
Home health care aide cost, licensed agency	hour	19	2000	82c
Hospital care, private room	day	491.50	3/01	4c
Hysterectomy, laproscopically-assisted, ave hospital/physician charges		11300	1998	76s
Hysterectomy, vaginal, ave hospital and physician charges		9200	1998	76s
Medicaid dispensing fee		4.09	1999	87s
Medical services expenditures	yr	554	1999	30r
Medical supplies, expenditures on	yr	122	1999	30r
Nursing home costs, private room	day	138	2000	82c
Nursing home stay, private room	day	138	2000	83c
Plastic surgery, breast augmentation		3184	2000	7r
Plastic surgery, breast lift		3585	2000	7r
Plastic surgery, facelift		4999	2000	7r
Plastic surgery, hair transplantation		3105	2000	7r
Plastic surgery, lip augmentation		1290	2000	7r
Plastic surgery, lower body lift		8135	2000	7r
Plastic surgery, thigh lift		3839	2000	7r
Household Goods				
Dishwashing powder, Cascade	50 oz	2.84	3/01	4c
Floor coverings, expenditures on	yr	52	1999	30r
Furniture, expenditures on	yr	344	1999	30r
Household furnishings and equipment purchases	yr	1115	1999	30c
Household textiles, expenditures on	yr	109	1999	30r
Laundry and cleaning supplies, expenditures on	yr	134	1999	30r
Tissues, facial, Kleenex brand	175	1.23	3/01	4c
Housing				
Housing, ACCRA Index		88.70	3/01	4c
Home, 2200 sq ft, 4-br, 2-bath, 2-car garage, average		192550	2000	47c
Home price, existing, ave		144400	10/00	90r
Home value, median		89000	2001	53s
House, 2400 sq ft, 8000 sq ft lot, new, urban, utilities	total	178707	3/01	4c
House payment, principal and interest, 25% down payment	mos	895	3/01	4c
Household operation expenditures	yr	745	1999	30c
Housekeeping supplies purchases	yr	328	1999	30c
Housing, expenditures on	yr	11304	1999	30c
Lodging expenditures	yr	430	1999	30r

Saint Louis, MO-IL - continued

Item	Per	Value	Date	Ref.
Housing - continued				
Maintenance, repairs, insurance expenditures	yr	853	1999	30r
Monthly rental value of owned home	mos	547	1999	30r
Owned dwellings, expenditures own	yr	4539	1999	30c
Rent expenditures	yr	1589	1999	30c
Rent, apartment, 2 br, 1 1/2-2 baths, unfurn, 950 sq ft, water	mos	668	3/01	4c
Rental unit, 1 bedroom, with utilities	mos	400	4/01	41c
Rental unit, 2 bedroom, with utilities	mos	519	4/01	41c
Rental unit, 3 bedroom, with utilities	mos	676	4/01	41c
Rental unit, 4 bedroom, with utilities	mos	747	4/01	41c
Shelter, expenditures on	yr	6435	1999	30c
Insurance and Pensions				
Life and other personal insurance purchases	yr	361	1999	30c
Pensions and Social Security, expenditures on	yr	3016	1999	30c
Personal insurance and pensions, expenditures on	yr	3377	1999	30c
Legal Fees				
Driver's license fee	orig	15.00	1999	48s
Driver's license fee	renew	15.00	1999	48s
Fishing license	yr	11.00	4/01	34s
Personal Goods				
Personal care products and services purchases	yr	342	1999	30c
Shampoo, Alberto VO5	15 oz	1.27	3/01	4c
Toothpaste, Crest or Colgate	6-7 oz	2.21	3/01	4c
Personal Services				
Dry cleaning, man's 2-pc suit		7.13	3/01	4c
Man's haircut, barbershop, no styling		11.10	3/01	4c
Personal services, household, expenditures on	yr	300	1999	30r
Woman's shampoo, trim, blow-dry, no style-change		24.40	3/01	4c
Pets				
Pets, toys, and playground equipment, expenditures on	yr	375	1999	30r
Restaurant Food				
Cheeseburger, 1/4-lb, large fries, medium soft drink, excl tax		4.49	1999	40c
Chicken, fried, thigh and drumstick, KFC/ Church's		2.56	3/01	4c
Hamburger with cheese, McDonald's	1/4 lb	2.09	3/01	4c
Pizza, Pizza Hut or Pizza Inn	11-12 in	8.78	3/01	4c
Taxes				
Federal income taxes paid	yr	2326	1999	30r
Personal taxes, expenditures on	yr	3223	1999	30r
Property taxes paid	yr	1152	1999	30r
State and local income taxes paid	yr	753	1999	30r
Transportation				
Transportation, ACCRA Index		105.70	3/01	4c
Bus fare, one-way	trip	1.25	2000	1c
Bus fare, to central business district	1-way	1.25	3/01	4c
Cars and trucks, new, expenditures on	yr	1280	1999	30r
Cars and trucks, used, expenditures on	yr	1763	1999	30r
Diesel at the pump	gal	1.16	10/99	73s
Gasoline and motor oil purchases	yr	970	1999	30c
Gasoline before-tax price (cents)	gal	108.50	10/00	43s
Light rail transit fare, one-way	trip	1.25	2000	2c
Maintenance and repair expenditures	yr	594	1999	30r
Public transportation, expenditures on	yr	294	1999	30c
Tire balance, computer or spin balance, front	wheel	8.26	3/01	4c
Transportation purchases	yr	7014	1999	30c
Vehicle expenses, miscellaneous, purchases	yr	2168	1999	30c
Vehicle insurance payments	yr	701	1999	30r
Vehicle purchases (net outlay)	yr	3582	1999	30c
Vehicle rental, lease expenditures	yr	536	1999	30r

Values are in dollars or fractions of dollars. In the column headed *Ref*, references are shown as sources. Each reference is followed by a letter. These refer to the geographical level for which data were reported: s=State, r=Region, and c=City or metro. The abbreviation *ex* is used to mean *except* or *excluding*; *exp* stands for expenditures. For other abbreviations and further explanations, please see the Introduction.

Saint Louis, MO-IL - continued

Item	Per	Value	Date	Ref.
Travel				
Car rental	day	79.50	2000	24c
Hotel room, ave	night	87.53	2000	70c
Utilities				
Utilities, ACCRA Index		90.50	3/01	4c
Electrical bill, average	mos	68.50	9/00	9s
Electricity, expenditures on	yr	841	1999	30r
Electricity, summer, 250 KWh	mos	21.66	2/96	97c
Electricity, summer, 500 KWh	mos	3732	2/96	97c
Electricity, summer, 750 KWh	mos	52.97	2/96	97c
Electricity, summer, 1000 KWh	mos	68.63	2/96	97c
Electricity and other, mixed, 2400 sq ft, new home	mos	64.54	3/01	4c
Electricity cost, average	KWh	6.00	9/00	9s
Utilities, fuels, and public services purchased	yr	2401	1999	30r
Water and other public services, expenditures on	yr	273	1999	30r
Water price	100 cf	0.93	2000	109c
Water price, dwelling unit	mos	18.34	2000	109c
Weddings				
Wedding (national average cost)		19936	2000	33r
Wedding (regional average total cost)		16195	1997	110r
Attendants' gifts		321	1998	33r
Bridal attendants' apparel (5 persons)		824	2000	33r
Bride's headpiece/veil		173	1998	33r
Bride's wedding dress		859	1998	33r
Clergy, religious facility fee		242	1998	33r
Engagement ring		3177	1998	33r
Flowers		789	1998	33r
Groom's formalwear rental		99	2000	33r
Limousine		410	1998	33r
Marriage license cost		50.00	4/01	35s
Men's formalwear (ushers, best man)		469	2000	33r
Mother of bride apparel		241	2000	33r
Music		866	1998	33r
Photography and videography		1368	1998	33r
Rehearsal dinner		728	1998	33r
Wedding invitations and announcements		341	1998	33r
Wedding reception		7968	2000	33r
Wedding rings (bride and groom)		1060	1998	33r

Salem, OR

Item	Per	Value	Date	Ref.
Average annual expenditures	yr	40662	1999	30r
Composite, ACCRA index		102.30	3/01	4c
Alcoholic Beverages				
Alcoholic beverage purchases	yr	372	1999	30r
Beer, Heineken, 12-oz, ex deposit	6	7.66	3/01	4c
J & B Scotch	750-ml	22.95	3/01	4c
Malt beverages, all types, all sizes, any origin	16 oz	0.94	7/01	11r
Wine, Livingston or Gallo, Chablis blanc	1.5 liter	5.65	3/01	4c
Wine, red and white table, all sizes, any origin	liter	6.00	7/01	11r
Appliances				
Appliance repair, service call, washing machine	min lab chg	48.66	3/01	4c
Major appliances, expenditures on	yr	167	1999	30r
Small appliances, housewares, expenditures on	yr	105	1999	30r
Banking and Money				
Mortgage interest and charges paid	yr	3368	1999	30r
Mortgage principal paid on owned property	yr	1677	1999	30r
Mortgage rate, incl. points and orig. fee, 30-yr. conv. fixed or ARM	mos	7.02	3/01	4c
Vehicle finance charges paid	yr	311	1999	30r
Charity				
Cash contributions, expenditures	yr	1344	1999	30r

Salem, OR - continued

Item	Per	Value	Date	Ref.
Child Care				
Child raising cost, total, age 0-2	yr	9140	1999	60r
Child raising cost, total, age 3-5	yr	9370	1999	60r
Child raising cost, total, age 6-8	yr	9450	1999	60r
Child raising cost, total, age 9-11	yr	9470	1999	60r
Child raising cost, total, age 12-14	yr	10170	1999	60r
Child raising cost, total, age 15-17	yr	10360	1999	60r
Child's child care and education, age 0-2	yr	1250	1999	60r
Child's child care and education, age 3-5	yr	1380	1999	60r
Child's child care and education, age 6-8	yr	890	1999	60r
Child's child care and education, age 9-11	yr	580	1999	60r
Child's child care and education, age 12-14	yr	430	1999	60r
Child's child care and education, age 15-17	yr	730	1999	60r
Child's clothing, age 0-2	yr	430	1999	60r
Child's clothing, age 3-5	yr	420	1999	60r
Child's clothing, age 6-8	yr	470	1999	60r
Child's clothing, age 9-11	yr	520	1999	60r
Child's clothing, age 12-14	yr	870	1999	60r
Child's clothing, age 15-17	yr	770	1999	60r
Child's food, age 0-2	yr	1120	1999	60r
Child's food, age 3-5	yr	1280	1999	60r
Child's food, age 6-8	yr	1640	1999	60r
Child's food, age 9-11	yr	1930	1999	60r
Child's food, age 12-14	yr	1940	1999	60r
Child's food, age 15-17	yr	2150	1999	60r
Child's health care, age 0-2	yr	490	1999	60r
Child's health care, age 3-5	yr	470	1999	60r
Child's health care, age 6-8	yr	530	1999	60r
Child's health care, age 9-11	yr	570	1999	60r
Child's health care, age 12-14	yr	580	1999	60r
Child's health care, age 15-17	yr	610	1999	60r
Child's housing, age 0-2	yr	3630	1999	60r
Child's housing, age 3-5	yr	3610	1999	60r
Child's housing, age 6-8	yr	3570	1999	60r
Child's housing, age 9-11	yr	3410	1999	60r
Child's housing, age 12-14	yr	3600	1999	60r
Child's housing, age 15-17	yr	3210	1999	60r
Child's personal care, reading, age 0-2	yr	1040	1999	60r
Child's personal care, reading, age 3-5	yr	1060	1999	60r
Child's personal care, reading, age 6-8	yr	1090	1999	60r
Child's personal care, reading, age 9-11	yr	1130	1999	60r
Child's personal care, reading, age 12-14	yr	1300	1999	60r
Child's personal care, reading, age 15-17	yr	1080	1999	60r
Clothing				
Apparel and services purchases	yr	1863	1999	30r
Boys' brief, cotton	3	4.95	3/01	4c
Boys, 2 to 15, expenditures on	yr	80	1999	30r
Children under 2, expenditures on	yr	74	1999	30r
Footwear, expenditures on	yr	307	1999	30r
Girls, 2 to 15, expenditures on	yr	101	1999	30r
Men and boys, expenditures on	yr	443	1999	30r
Men, 16 and over, expenditures on	yr	363	1999	30r
Shirt, man's dress shirt		31.30	3/01	4c
Slacks, man's "No Wrinkles" khaki		32.49	3/01	4c
Women, 16 and over, expenditures on	yr	594	1999	30r
Communications				
Newspaper subscription, daily and Sunday delivery	mos	14.00	3/01	4c
Phone line, single, business, field visit	inst.	31.00	12/97	17s
Phone line, single, business, no field visit	inst.	31.00	12/97	17s
Phone line, single, residence, field visit	inst.	12.00	12/97	17s
Phone line, single, residence, no field visit	inst.	12.00	12/97	17s
Postage and stationery, expenditures on	yr	150	1999	30r
Postal rate, express mail, up to half-pound		12.45	7/01	108r
Postal rate, letter, first class, first ounce		0.34	7/01	108r
Postal rate, letter, two ounces		0.57	7/01	108r
Postal rate, post card		0.21	7/01	108r
Postal rate, priority mail, two pounds		3.95	7/01	108r
Postal rate, priority mail, up to one pound		3.50	7/01	108r
Telephone bill, business, basic rate	mos	18.00	12/97	18c
Telephone bill, family of three	mos	22.35	3/01	4c
Telephone bill, residential, basic rate	mos	6.37	12/97	18c

Values are in dollars or fractions of dollars. In the column headed *Ref*, references are shown to sources. Each reference is followed by a letter. These refer to the geographical level for which data were reported: s=State, r=Region, and c=City or metro. The abbreviation *ex* is used to mean *except* or *excluding*; *exp* stands for expenditures. For other abbreviations and further explanations, please see the Introduction.

Salem, OR - continued

Item	Per	Value	Date	Ref.
Communications				
Telephone services, expenditures on	yr	825	1999	30r
Education				
Board, 4-year private college/university	yr	2750	1996	38s
Board, 4-year public college/university	yr	2474	1996	38s
Education expenditures	yr	676	1999	30r
Room, 4-year private college/university	yr	2257	1996	38s
Room, 4-year public college/university	yr	1647	1996	38s
Total cost, 4-year private college/university	yr	18899	1996	38s
Total cost, 4-year public college/university	yr	7354	1996	38s
Tuition, 2-year public college/university, in state	yr	1338	1996	38s
Tuition, 4-year private college/university, in state	yr	13892	1996	38s
Tuition, 4-year public college/university	yr	3233	1996	38s
Energy and Fuels				
Electricity	500 KWhs	48.23	7/01	11r
Electricity	KWh	0.11	7/01	11r
Energy, combined forms, 2400 sq ft	mos	101.88	3/01	4c
Energy, exc. electricity, 2400 sq ft	mos	61.77	3/01	4c
Fuel oil and other fuels, expenditures on	yr	35	1999	30r
Gas, natural, commercial rate	1000 cf	7.55	11/00	88s
Gas, regular unleaded, cash, self-service	gal	1.49	3/01	4c
Gasoline, all types	gal	1.91	7/01	11r
Gasoline, unleaded premium	gal	2.05	7/01	11r
Gasoline, unleaded regular	gal	1.83	7/01	11r
Natural gas, expenditures on	yr	255	1999	30r
Utility (piped) gas, therm		0.98	7/01	11r
Utility (piped) gas, 40 therms		40.74	7/01	11r
Utility (piped) gas, 100 therms		96.80	7/01	11r
Entertainment				
Bowling, Saturday evening rate	line	3.25	3/01	4c
Entertainment purchases	yr	2139	1999	30r
Fees and admissions paid	yr	545	1999	30r
Monopoly game, Parker Brothers', No. 9	game	11.12	3/01	4c
Movie, first-run, Saturday, evening	adm.	7.75	3/01	4c
Television, radios, sound equipment, expenditures on	yr	624	1999	30r
Tennis balls, yellow, Wilson or Penn, 3	can	2.37	3/01	4c
Funerals				
Total cost of funeral		5401.08	1/99	78r
Acknowledgement cards		33.64	1/99	78r
Casket		2170.43	1/99	78r
Cosmetology, hair, other preparation		136.32	1/99	78r
Embalming		319.13	1/99	78r
Funeral at funeral home		370.21	1/99	78r
Hearse (local)		161.04	1/99	78r
Professional service charges		963.15	1/99	78r
Service car/van		133.99	1/99	78r
Transfer of remains to funeral home		159.82	1/99	78r
Vault		778.07	1/99	78r
Visitation/viewing		175.28	1/99	78r
Groceries				
Groceries, ACCRA Index		100.20	3/01	4c
Antibiotic ointment, Polysporin	0.5 oz	4.64	3/01	4c
Apples, red delicious	lb	0.84	7/01	11r
Baby food, strained vegetables or fruit, lowest price	4-4.5 oz	0.35	3/01	4c
Bacon, sliced	lb	3.38	7/01	11r
Bakery products, expenditures on	yr	299	1999	30r
Bananas	lb	0.59	3/01	4c
Bananas	lb	0.54	7/01	11r
Beans, dried, any type, all sizes	lb	0.76	7/01	11r
Beef or hamburger, ground	lb	1.61	3/01	4c
Beef, expenditures on	yr	222	1999	30r
Bread, white	loaf	0.75	3/01	4c
Bread, white, pan	lb	0.99	7/01	11r
Butter, yoghurt, cheese, etc, expenditures on	yr	211	1999	30r
Cereals and bakery product purchases	yr	466	1999	30r

Salem, OR - continued

Item	Per	Value	Date	Ref.
Groceries - continued				
Cereals and cereal products, expenditures on	yr	168	1999	30r
Cheese, Kraft grated Parmesan	8 oz	3.84	3/01	4c
Chicken breast, bone-in	lb	2.45	7/01	11r
Chicken, fresh, whole	lb	1.19	7/01	11r
Chicken, whole fryer	lb	1.09	3/01	4c
Chops, boneless,	lb	4.00	7/01	11r
Chuck roast, graded and ungraded, excl U.S. prime and choice	lb	2.55	7/01	11r
Cigarettes, Winston, Kings	carton	34.22	3/01	4c
Coffee, 100%, ground roast, all sizes	lb	3.80	7/01	11r
Coffee, vacuum-packed	13 oz	3.04	3/01	4c
Cookies, chocolate chip	lb	2.83	7/01	11r
Corn Flakes, Kellogg's or Post Toasties	18 oz	2.67	3/01	4c
Corn, frozen, whole kernel, lowest price	16 oz	1.09	3/01	4c
Dairy product purchases	yr	341	1999	30r
Eggs, expenditures on	yr	39	1999	30r
Eggs, Grade A or AA	dozen	1.31	3/01	4c
Eggs, grade AA, large	dozen	1.23	7/01	11r
Fats and oils, expenditures on	yr	88	1999	30r
Fish and seafood, expenditures on	yr	121	1999	30r
Food (excl fruit and vegetables), eaten at home, purchases	yr	1001	1999	30r
Food cooked on trips, expenditures on	yr	64	1999	30r
Food purchases	yr	5312	1999	30r
Food purchases, eaten away from home	yr	2180	1999	30r
Food purchases, food eaten at home	yr	3132	1999	30r
Fresh fruits, expenditures on	yr	186	1999	30r
Fresh milk and cream, expenditures on	yr	130	1999	30r
Fresh vegetables, expenditures on	yr	177	1999	30r
Grapefruit	lb	0.68	7/01	11r
Grapes, Thompson, seedless	lb	2.42	7/01	11r
Ground beef, lean and extra lean	lb	2.46	7/01	11r
Ice cream, prepackaged, bulk, regular	1/2 gal	3.62	7/01	11r
Lettuce, iceberg	head	0.85	3/01	4c
Lettuce, iceberg	lb	0.63	7/01	11r
Margarine, Blue Bonnet or Parkay, stick	lb	0.59	3/01	4c
Meats, poultry, fish, and egg purchases	yr	761	1999	30r
Milk, fresh, low fat	gal	2.80	7/01	11r
Milk, fresh, whole, fortified	gal	2.88	7/01	11r
Milk, whole	1/2 gal	1.82	3/01	4c
Nonalcoholic beverages, expenditures on	yr	258	1999	30r
Orange juice, Minute Maid frozen	12 oz	1.31	3/01	4c
Oranges, Navel	lb	0.97	7/01	11r
Oranges, Valencia	lb	0.43	7/01	11r
Peaches	lb	1.38	7/01	11r
Peaches, halves or slices, Hunt's, Del Monte, or Libby's	29 oz	1.65	3/01	4c
Peanut butter, creamy, all sizes	lb	2.14	7/01	11r
Peas, green, Del Monte or Green Giant	15 oz	0.87	3/01	4c
Pork chops, center cut, bone-in	lb	3.83	7/01	11r
Pork, expenditures on	yr	141	1999	30r
Potatoes, white or red	10 lb	1.94	3/01	4c
Potatoes, white, all types	lb	0.37	7/01	11r
Poultry, expenditures on	yr	146	1999	30r
Processed fruits, expenditures on	yr	118	1999	30r
Processed vegetables, expenditures on	yr	81	1999	30r
Round roast, graded and ungraded, excl U.S. prime and choice	lb	3.07	7/01	11r
Round roast, U.S. choice, boneless	lb	3.37	7/01	11r
Round steak, graded and ungraded, excl U.S. prime and choice	lb	3.51	7/01	11r
Sausage, Jimmy Dean/Owens pork	lb	3.98	3/01	4c
Shortening, vegetable, Crisco	3 lb	2.80	3/01	4c
Sirloin steak, graded and ungraded, excl U.S. prime and choice	lb	4.67	7/01	11r
Soft drink, Coca Cola, ex deposit	2 liter	0.99	3/01	4c
Steak, sirloin, U.S. choice, boneless	lb	6.20	7/01	11r
Steak, T-bone	lb	5.81	3/01	4c
Strawberries, dry pint	12 oz	1.79	7/01	11r
Sugar and other sweets, expenditures on	yr	124	1999	30r
Sugar, cane or beet	4 lbs	1.84	3/01	4c

Values are in dollars or fractions of dollars. In the column headed *Ref*, references are shown to sources. Each reference is followed by a letter. These refer to the geographical level for which data were reported: s=State, r=Region, and c=City or metro. The abbreviation *ex* is used to mean *except* or *excluding*; *exp* stands for expenditures. For other abbreviations and further explanations, please see the Introduction.

Salem, OR - continued

Item	Per	Value	Date	Ref.
Groceries				
Sugar, white, all sizes	lb	0.46	7/01	11r
Tobacco products and smoking supplies purchases	yr	217	1999	30r
Tomatoes, field grown	lb	1.17	7/01	11r
Tomatoes, Hunt's or Del Monte	14.5 oz	0.85	3/01	4c
Tuna, chunk, light	6 oz	0.68	3/01	4c
Tuna, light, chunk	lb	2.05	7/01	11r
Goods and Services				
Miscellaneous goods and services, ACCRA Index		107.80	3/01	4c
B&B Japanese maple (acer japonicum)	gal	39.99	4/00	93r
Boxwood (buxus)	2 gal	14.99-24.99	4/00	93r
Christmas tree, noble fir		20-25	2000	65s
Daylilly (hemerocallis)	gal	6.99-8.99	4/00	93r
Flat of annuals		16.68	4/00	93r
Fountain grass (pennisetum)	gal	7.99-11.99	4/00	93r
Hanging basket (10 in)		29.99	4/00	93r
Hardy geranium (geranium)	gal	6.99-11.99	4/00	93r
Hosta (hosta)	gal	6.99-18.99	4/00	93r
Lilac (syrubga vulgaris)	2 gal	14.99-17.99	4/00	93r
Miscellaneous purchases	yr	1070	1999	30r
Rhododendron (rhododendron)	2 gal	14.99	4/00	93r
Sage (salvia)	gal	6.99	4/00	93r
Wintercreeper euonymus (euonymus fortunei)	2 gal	14.99-22.99	4/00	93r
Hunting license	yr	17.50	4/01	34s
Health Care				
Health care, ACCRA Index		120.80	3/01	4c
Cardiac catheterization, ave hospital/physician charges		10940	1998	77s
Childbirth, Cesarean delivery		11587	1997	13r
Childbirth, vaginal delivery		6725	1997	13r
Dentist's fee, adult teeth cleaning and periodic oral exam	visit	107.00	3/01	4c
Doctor's fee, routine exam, established patient	visit	66.20	3/01	4c
Drugs, expenditures on	yr	309	1999	30r
Health care purchases	yr	1869	1999	30r
Health insurance expenditures	yr	868	1999	30r
Hospital care, private room	day	500.00	3/01	4c
Hysterectomy, laproscopically-assisted, ave hospital/physician charges		11660	1998	76s
Hysterectomy, vaginal, ave hospital and physician charges		6680	1998	76s
Medicaid dispensing fee		3.80-4.16	1999	87s
Medical services expenditures	yr	580	1999	30r
Medical supplies, expenditures on	yr	112	1999	30r
Household Goods				
Dishwashing powder, Cascade	50 oz	3.62	3/01	4c
Floor coverings, expenditures on	yr	49	1999	30r
Furniture, expenditures on	yr	444	1999	30r
Household furnishings and equipment purchases	yr	1768	1999	30r
Household textiles, expenditures on	yr	141	1999	30r
Laundry and cleaning supplies, expenditures on	yr	128	1999	30r
Tissues, facial, Kleenex brand	175	1.42	3/01	4c
Housing				
Housing, ACCRA Index		99.70	3/01	4c
Home, 2200 sq ft, 4-br, 2-bath, 2-car garage, average		187467	2000	47c
Home price, existing, ave		239400	10/00	90r
Home value, median		149000	2001	53s

Salem, OR - continued

Item	Per	Value	Date	Ref.
Housing - continued				
House, 2400 sq ft, 8000 sq ft lot, new, urban, utilities	total	215116	3/01	4c
House payment, principal and interest, 25% down payment	mos	1075	3/01	4c
Household operation expenditures	yr	781	1999	30r
Housekeeping supplies purchases	yr	513	1999	30r
Lodging expenditures	yr	575	1999	30r
Maintenance, repairs, insurance expenditures	yr	939	1999	30r
Monthly rental value of owned home	mos	662	1999	30r
Owned dwellings, expenditures own	yr	5231	1999	30r
Rent expenditures	yr	2709	1999	30r
Rent, apartment, 2 br, 1 1/2-2 baths, unfurn, 950 sq ft, water	mos	566	3/01	4c
Rental unit, 1 bedroom, with utilities	mos	480	4/01	41c
Rental unit, 2 bedroom, with utilities	mos	615	4/01	41c
Rental unit, 3 bedroom, with utilities	mos	846	4/01	41c
Rental unit, 4 bedroom, with utilities	mos	886	4/01	41c
Shelter, expenditures on	yr	8516	1999	30r
Insurance and Pensions				
Life and other personal insurance purchases	yr	355	1999	30r
Pensions and Social Security, expenditures on	yr	3636	1999	30r
Legal Fees				
Combination hunting and fishing license	yr	33.75	4/01	34s
Divorce, filing fee		100.00-250.00	4/01	35s
Driver's license fee	orig	26.25	1999	48s
Driver's license fee	renew	16.25	1999	48s
Fishing license	yr	19.75	4/01	34s
Personal Goods				
Personal care products and services purchases	yr	449	1999	30r
Shampoo, Alberto VO5	15 oz	1.08	3/01	4c
Toothpaste, Crest or Colgate	6-7 oz	2.51	3/01	4c
Personal Services				
Dry cleaning, man's 2-pc suit		9.38	3/01	4c
Man's haircut, barbershop, no styling		11.40	3/01	4c
Personal services, household, expenditures on	yr	353	1999	30r
Woman's shampoo, trim, blow-dry, no style-change		29.99	3/01	4c
Pets				
Pets, toys, and playground equipment, expenditures on	yr	358	1999	30r
Restaurant Food				
Chicken, fried, thigh and drumstick, KFC/Church's		3.14	3/01	4c
Hamburger with cheese, McDonald's	1/4 lb	2.24	3/01	4c
Pizza, Pizza Hut or Pizza Inn	11-12 in	9.99	3/01	4c
Taxes				
Federal income taxes paid	yr	3200	1999	30r
Personal taxes, expenditures on	yr	4153	1999	30r
Property taxes paid	yr	923	1999	30r
State and local income taxes paid	yr	812	1999	30r
Transportation				
Transportation, ACCRA Index		98.30	3/01	4c
Bus fare, one-way	trip	0.75	2000	1c
Bus fare, to central business district	1-way	0.75	3/01	4c
Cars and trucks, new, expenditures on	yr	1534	1999	30r
Cars and trucks, used, expenditures on	yr	1593	1999	30r
Diesel at the pump	gal	1.16	10/99	73s
Gasoline and motor oil purchases	yr	1129	1999	30r
Gasoline before-tax price (cents)	gal	128.30	10/00	43s
Maintenance and repair expenditures	yr	797	1999	30r
Public transportation, expenditures on	yr	530	1999	30r
Tire balance, computer or spin balance, front	wheel	7.60	3/01	4c
Transportation purchases	yr	7423	1999	30r

Values are in dollars or fractions of dollars. In the column headed *Ref*, references are shown to sources. Each reference is followed by a letter. These refer to the geographical level for which data were reported: s=State, r=Region, and c=City or metro. The abbreviation *ex* is used to mean *except* or *excluding*; *exp* stands for *expenditures*. For other abbreviations and further explanations, please see the Introduction.

Salem, OR - continued

Item	Per	Value	Date	Ref.
Transportation				
Vehicle expenses, miscellaneous, purchases	yr	2585	1999	30r
Vehicle insurance payments	yr	811	1999	30r
Vehicle purchases (net outlay)	yr	3180	1999	30r
Vehicle rental, lease expenditures	yr	666	1999	30r
Utilities				
Utilities, ACCRA Index		86.10	3/01	4c
Electrical bill, average	mos	61.42	9/00	9s
Electricity, expenditures on	yr	725	1999	30r
Electricity and other, mixed, 2400 sq ft, new home	mos	40.11	3/01	4c
Electricity cost, average	KWh	4.70	9/00	9s
Utilities, fuels, and public services purchased	yr	2179	1999	30r
Water and other public services, expenditures on	yr	339	1999	30r
Weddings				
Wedding (national average cost)		19936	2000	33r
Wedding (regional average total cost)		18918	1997	110r
Attendants' gifts		321	1998	33r
Bridal attendants' apparel (5 persons)		824	2000	33r
Bride's headpiece/veil		173	1998	33r
Bride's wedding dress		859	1998	33r
Clergy, religious facility fee		242	1998	33r
Engagement ring		3177	1998	33r
Flowers		789	1998	33r
Groom's formalwear rental		99	2000	33r
Limousine		410	1998	33r
Marriage license cost		60.00	4/01	35s
Men's formalwear (ushers, best man)		469	2000	33r
Mother of bride apparel		241	2000	33r
Music		866	1998	33r
Photography and videography		1368	1998	33r
Rehearsal dinner		728	1998	33r
Wedding invitations and announcements		341	1998	33r
Wedding reception		7968	2000	33r
Wedding rings (bride and groom)		1060	1998	33r

Salinas, CA

Item	Per	Value	Date	Ref.
Average annual expenditures	yr	40662	1999	30r
Alcoholic Beverages				
Alcoholic beverage purchases	yr	372	1999	30r
Malt beverages, all types, all sizes, any origin	16 oz	0.94	7/01	11r
Wine, red and white table, all sizes, any origin	liter	6.00	7/01	11r
Appliances				
Major appliances, expenditures on	yr	167	1999	30r
Small appliances, housewares, expenditures on	yr	105	1999	30r
Banking and Money				
Mortgage interest and charges paid	yr	3368	1999	30r
Mortgage principal paid on owned property	yr	1677	1999	30r
Vehicle finance charges paid	yr	311	1999	30r
Charity				
Cash contributions, expenditures	yr	1344	1999	30r
Child Care				
Child raising cost, total, age 0-2	yr	9140	1999	60r
Child raising cost, total, age 3-5	yr	9370	1999	60r
Child raising cost, total, age 6-8	yr	9450	1999	60r
Child raising cost, total, age 9-11	yr	9470	1999	60r
Child raising cost, total, age 12-14	yr	10170	1999	60r
Child raising cost, total, age 15-17	yr	10360	1999	60r
Child's child care and education, age 0-2	yr	1250	1999	60r
Child's child care and education, age 3-5	yr	1380	1999	60r
Child's child care and education, age 6-8	yr	890	1999	60r
Child's child care and education, age 9-11	yr	580	1999	60r
Child's child care and education, age 12-14	yr	430	1999	60r
Child's child care and education, age 15-17	yr	730	1999	60r
Child's clothing, age 0-2	yr	430	1999	60r

Salinas, CA - continued

Item	Per	Value	Date	Ref.
Child Care - continued				
Child's clothing, age 3-5	yr	420	1999	60r
Child's clothing, age 6-8	yr	470	1999	60r
Child's clothing, age 9-11	yr	520	1999	60r
Child's clothing, age 12-14	yr	870	1999	60r
Child's clothing, age 15-17	yr	770	1999	60r
Child's food, age 0-2	yr	1120	1999	60r
Child's food, age 3-5	yr	1280	1999	60r
Child's food, age 6-8	yr	1640	1999	60r
Child's food, age 9-11	yr	1930	1999	60r
Child's food, age 12-14	yr	1940	1999	60r
Child's food, age 15-17	yr	2150	1999	60r
Child's health care, age 0-2	yr	490	1999	60r
Child's health care, age 3-5	yr	470	1999	60r
Child's health care, age 6-8	yr	530	1999	60r
Child's health care, age 9-11	yr	570	1999	60r
Child's health care, age 12-14	yr	580	1999	60r
Child's health care, age 15-17	yr	610	1999	60r
Child's housing, age 0-2	yr	3630	1999	60r
Child's housing, age 3-5	yr	3610	1999	60r
Child's housing, age 6-8	yr	3570	1999	60r
Child's housing, age 9-11	yr	3410	1999	60r
Child's housing, age 12-14	yr	3600	1999	60r
Child's housing, age 15-17	yr	3210	1999	60r
Child's personal care, reading, age 0-2	yr	1040	1999	60r
Child's personal care, reading, age 3-5	yr	1060	1999	60r
Child's personal care, reading, age 6-8	yr	1090	1999	60r
Child's personal care, reading, age 9-11	yr	1130	1999	60r
Child's personal care, reading, age 12-14	yr	1300	1999	60r
Child's personal care, reading, age 15-17	yr	1080	1999	60r
Clothing				
Apparel and services purchases	yr	1863	1999	30r
Boys, 2 to 15, expenditures on	yr	80	1999	30r
Children under 2, expenditures on	yr	74	1999	30r
Footwear, expenditures on	yr	307	1999	30r
Girls, 2 to 15, expenditures on	yr	101	1999	30r
Men and boys, expenditures on	yr	443	1999	30r
Men, 16 and over, expenditures on	yr	363	1999	30r
Women, 16 and over, expenditures on	yr	594	1999	30r
Communications				
Cable modem installation, AT&T-BIS		150.00	6/99	103s
Cable modem installation, Charter		99.00-169.00	6/99	103s
Cable modem installation, Comcast		95.00	6/99	103s
Cable modem installation, Cox		99.00-174.95	6/99	103s
Cable modem installation, Media One		100.00	6/99	103s
Cable modem installation, Time Warner		75.00-225.00	6/99	103s
Cable modem rate, cable subscriber, AT&T-BIS	mos	39.95	6/99	103s
Cable modem rate, cable subscriber, Charter	mos	49.95-79.95	6/99	103s
Cable modem rate, cable subscriber, Comcast	mos	39.95	6/99	103s
Cable modem rate, cable subscriber, Cox	mos	29.95-44.95	6/99	103s
Cable modem rate, cable subscriber, Media One	mos	34.95-39.95	6/99	103s
Cable modem rate, cable subscriber, Time Warner	mos	39.95-49.95	6/99	103s
Cable modem rate, non-cable subscriber, Charter	mos	59.95-89.95	6/99	103s
Cable modem rate, non-cable subscriber, Comcast	mos	49.95	6/99	103s
Cable modem rate, non-cable subscriber, Cox	mos	42.95-54.95	6/99	103s
Cable modem rate, non-cable subscriber, Media One	mos	49.95	6/99	103s
Cable modem rate, non-cable subscriber, Time Warner	mos	39.95-54.95	6/99	103s
Phone line, single, business, field visit	inst.	70.75	12/97	17s

Values are in dollars or fractions of dollars. In the column headed *Ref*, references are shown to sources. Each reference is followed by a letter. These refer to the geographical level for which data were reported: s=State, r=Region, and c=City or metro. The abbreviation *ex* is used to mean *except* or *excluding*; *exp* stands for *expenditures*. For other abbreviations and further explanations, please see the Introduction.

Salinas, CA - continued

Item	Per	Value	Date	Ref.
Communications				
Phone line, single, business, no field visit	inst.	70.75	12/97	17s
Phone line, single, residence, field visit	inst.	34.75	12/97	17s
Phone line, single, residence, no field visit	inst.	34.75	12/97	17s
Postage and stationery, expenditures on	yr	150	1999	30r
Postal rate, express mail, up to half-pound		12.45	7/01	108r
Postal rate, letter, first class, first ounce		0.34	7/01	108r
Postal rate, letter, two ounces		0.57	7/01	108r
Postal rate, post card		0.21	7/01	108r
Postal rate, priority mail, two pounds		3.95	7/01	108r
Postal rate, priority mail, up to one pound		3.50	7/01	108r
Telephone services, expenditures on	yr	825	1999	30r
Education				
Board, 4-year private college/university	yr	2970	1996	38s
Board, 4-year public college/university	yr	2516	1996	38s
Education expenditures	yr	676	1999	30r
Room, 4-year private college/university	yr	3196	1996	38s
Room, 4-year public college/university	yr	3031	1996	38s
Total cost, 4-year private college/university	yr	20143	1996	38s
Total cost, 4-year public college/university	yr	8213	1996	38s
Tuition, 2-year public college/university, in state	yr	362	1996	38s
Tuition, 4-year private college/university, in state	yr	13977	1996	38s
Tuition, 4-year public college/university	yr	2666	1996	38s
Energy and Fuels				
Electricity	KWh	0.11	7/01	11r
Electricity	500 KWhs	48.23	7/01	11r
Fuel oil and other fuels, expenditures on	yr	35	1999	30r
Gas, natural, commercial rate	1000 cf	8.74	11/00	88s
Gasoline, all types	gal	1.91	7/01	11r
Gasoline, unleaded premium	gal	2.05	7/01	11r
Gasoline, unleaded regular	gal	1.83	7/01	11r
Natural gas, expenditures on	yr	255	1999	30r
Utility (piped) gas, therm		0.98	7/01	11r
Utility (piped) gas, 40 therms		40.74	7/01	11r
Utility (piped) gas, 100 therms		96.80	7/01	11r
Entertainment				
Entertainment purchases	yr	2139	1999	30r
Fees and admissions paid	yr	545	1999	30r
Television, radios, sound equipment, expenditures on	yr	624	1999	30r
Funerals				
Total cost of funeral		5401.08	1/99	78r
Acknowledgement cards		33.64	1/99	78r
Casket		2170.43	1/99	78r
Cosmetology, hair, other preparation		136.32	1/99	78r
Embalming		319.13	1/99	78r
Funeral at funeral home		370.21	1/99	78r
Hearse (local)		161.04	1/99	78r
Professional service charges		963.15	1/99	78r
Service car/van		133.99	1/99	78r
Transfer of remains to funeral home		159.82	1/99	78r
Vault		778.07	1/99	78r
Visitation/viewing		175.28	1/99	78r
Groceries				
Apples, red delicious	lb	0.84	7/01	11r
Bacon, sliced	lb	3.38	7/01	11r
Bakery products, expenditures on	yr	299	1999	30r
Bananas	lb	0.54	7/01	11r
Beans, dried, any type, all sizes	lb	0.76	7/01	11r
Beef, expenditures on	yr	222	1999	30r
Bread, white, pan	lb	0.99	7/01	11r
Butter, yoghurt, cheese, etc, expenditures on	yr	211	1999	30r
Cereals and bakery product purchases	yr	466	1999	30r
Cereals and cereal products, expenditures on	yr	168	1999	30r
Chicken breast, bone-in	lb	2.45	7/01	11r
Chicken, fresh, whole	lb	1.19	7/01	11r

Salinas, CA - continued

Item	Per	Value	Date	Ref.
Groceries - continued				
Chops, boneless,	lb	4.00	7/01	11r
Chuck roast, graded and ungraded, excl U.S. prime and choice	lb	2.55	7/01	11r
Coffee, 100%, ground roast, all sizes	lb	3.80	7/01	11r
Cookies, chocolate chip	lb	2.83	7/01	11r
Dairy product purchases	yr	341	1999	30r
Eggs, expenditures on	yr	39	1999	30r
Eggs, grade AA, large	dozen	1.23	7/01	11r
Fats and oils, expenditures on	yr	88	1999	30r
Fish and seafood, expenditures on	yr	121	1999	30r
Food (excl fruit and vegetables), eaten at home, purchases	yr	1001	1999	30r
Food cooked on trips, expenditures on	yr	64	1999	30r
Food purchases	yr	5312	1999	30r
Food purchases, eaten away from home	yr	2180	1999	30r
Food purchases, food eaten at home	yr	3132	1999	30r
Fresh fruits, expenditures on	yr	186	1999	30r
Fresh milk and cream, expenditures on	yr	130	1999	30r
Fresh vegetables, expenditures on	yr	177	1999	30r
Grapefruit	lb	0.68	7/01	11r
Grapes, Thompson, seedless	lb	2.42	7/01	11r
Ground beef, lean and extra lean	lb	2.46	7/01	11r
Ice cream, prepackaged, bulk, regular	1/2 gal	3.62	7/01	11r
Lettuce, iceberg	lb	0.63	7/01	11r
Meats, poultry, fish, and egg purchases	yr	761	1999	30r
Milk, fresh, low fat	gal	2.80	7/01	11r
Milk, fresh, whole, fortified	gal	2.88	7/01	11r
Nonalcoholic beverages, expenditures on	yr	258	1999	30r
Oranges, Navel	lb	0.97	7/01	11r
Oranges, Valencia	lb	0.43	7/01	11r
Peaches	lb	1.38	7/01	11r
Peanut butter, creamy, all sizes	lb	2.14	7/01	11r
Pork chops, center cut, bone-in	lb	3.83	7/01	11r
Pork, expenditures on	yr	141	1999	30r
Potatoes, white, all types	lb	0.37	7/01	11r
Poultry, expenditures on	yr	146	1999	30r
Processed fruits, expenditures on	yr	118	1999	30r
Processed vegetables, expenditures on	yr	81	1999	30r
Round roast, graded and ungraded, excl U.S. prime and choice	lb	3.07	7/01	11r
Round roast, U.S. choice, boneless	lb	3.37	7/01	11r
Round steak, graded and ungraded, excl U.S. prime and choice	lb	3.51	7/01	11r
Sirloin steak, graded and ungraded, excl U.S. prime and choice	lb	4.67	7/01	11r
Steak, sirloin, U.S. choice, boneless	lb	6.20	7/01	11r
Strawberries, dry pint	12 oz	1.79	7/01	11r
Sugar and other sweets, expenditures on	yr	124	1999	30r
Sugar, white, all sizes	lb	0.46	7/01	11r
Tobacco products and smoking supplies purchases	yr	217	1999	30r
Tomatoes, field grown	lb	1.17	7/01	11r
Tuna, light, chunk	lb	2.05	7/01	11r
Goods and Services				
B&B Japanese maple (acer japonicum)	gal	39.99	4/00	93r
Boxwood (buxus)	2 gal	14.99-24.99	4/00	93r
Christmas tree, noble fir		40-60	2000	65s
Daylilly (hemerocallis)	gal	6.99-8.99	4/00	93r
Flat of annuals		16.68	4/00	93r
Fountain grass (pennisetum)	gal	7.99-11.99	4/00	93r
Hanging basket (10 in)		29.99	4/00	93r
Hardy geranium (geranium)	gal	6.99-11.99	4/00	93r
Hosta (hosta)	gal	6.99-18.99	4/00	93r
Lilac (syrubga vulgaris)	2 gal	14.99-17.99	4/00	93r
Miscellaneous purchases	yr	1070	1999	30r
Rhododendron (rhododendron)	2 gal	14.99	4/00	93r

Values are in dollars or fractions of dollars. In the column headed *Ref*, references are shown to sources. Each reference is followed by a letter. These refer to the geographical level for which data were reported: s=State, r=Region, and c=City or metro. The abbreviation *ex* is used to mean *except* or *excluding*; *exp* stands for *expenditures*. For other abbreviations and further explanations, please see the Introduction.

Salinas, CA - continued

Item	Per	Value	Date	Ref.
Goods and Services				
Sage (salvia)	gal	6.99	4/00	93r
Wintercreeper euonymus (euonymus fortunei)	2 gal	14.99-22.99	4/00	93r
Hunting license	yr	29.95	4/01	34s
Health Care				
Cardiac catheterization, ave hospital/physician charges		24000	1998	77s
Childbirth, Cesarean delivery		11587	1997	13r
Childbirth, vaginal delivery		6725	1997	13r
Drugs, expenditures on	yr	309	1999	30r
Health care purchases	yr	1869	1999	30r
Health insurance expenditures	yr	868	1999	30r
Hysterectomy, laproscopically-assisted, ave hospital/physician charges		20760	1998	76s
Hysterectomy, vaginal, ave hospital and physician charges		14570	1998	76s
Medicaid dispensing fee		4.05	1999	87s
Medical services expenditures	yr	580	1999	30r
Medical supplies, expenditures on	yr	112	1999	30r
Household Goods				
Floor coverings, expenditures on	yr	49	1999	30r
Furniture, expenditures on	yr	444	1999	30r
Household furnishings and equipment purchases	yr	1768	1999	30r
Household textiles, expenditures on	yr	141	1999	30r
Laundry and cleaning supplies, expenditures on	yr	128	1999	30r
Housing				
Home price, existing, ave		239400	10/00	90r
Home value, median		215000	2001	53s
Household operation expenditures	yr	781	1999	30r
Housekeeping supplies purchases	yr	513	1999	30r
Lodging expenditures	yr	575	1999	30r
Maintenance, repairs, insurance expenditures	yr	939	1999	30r
Monthly rental value of owned home	mos	662	1999	30r
Owned dwellings, expenditures own	yr	5231	1999	30r
Rent expenditures	yr	2709	1999	30r
Rental unit, 1 bedroom, with utilities	mos	641	4/01	41c
Rental unit, 2 bedroom, with utilities	mos	773	4/01	41c
Rental unit, 3 bedroom, with utilities	mos	1074	4/01	41c
Rental unit, 4 bedroom, with utilities	mos	1127	4/01	41c
Shelter, expenditures on	yr	8516	1999	30r
Insurance and Pensions				
Life and other personal insurance purchases	yr	355	1999	30r
Pensions and Social Security, expenditures on	yr	3636	1999	30r
Legal Fees				
Divorce, filing fee		182.00	4/01	35s
Driver's license fee	orig	12.00	1999	48s
Driver's license fee	renew	15.00	1999	48s
Personal Goods				
Personal care products and services purchases	yr	449	1999	30r
Personal Services				
Personal services, household, expenditures on	yr	353	1999	30r
Pets				
Pets, toys, and playground equipment, expenditures on	yr	358	1999	30r
Taxes				
Federal income taxes paid	yr	3200	1999	30r
Personal taxes, expenditures on	yr	4153	1999	30r
Property taxes paid	yr	923	1999	30r
State and local income taxes paid	yr	812	1999	30r

Salinas, CA - continued

Item	Per	Value	Date	Ref.
Transportation				
Bus fare, one-way	trip	1.50	2000	1c
Cars and trucks, new, expenditures on	yr	1534	1999	30r
Cars and trucks, used, expenditures on	yr	1593	1999	30r
Diesel at the pump	gal	1.37	10/99	73s
Gasoline and motor oil purchases	yr	1129	1999	30r
Gasoline before-tax price (cents)	gal	128.80	10/00	43s
Maintenance and repair expenditures	yr	797	1999	30r
Public transportation, expenditures on	yr	530	1999	30r
Transportation purchases	yr	7423	1999	30r
Vehicle expenses, miscellaneous, purchases	yr	2585	1999	30r
Vehicle insurance payments	yr	811	1999	30r
Vehicle purchases (net outlay)	yr	3180	1999	30r
Vehicle rental, lease expenditures	yr	666	1999	30r
Utilities				
Electrical bill, average	mos	58.66	9/00	9s
Electricity, expenditures on	yr	725	1999	30r
Electricity cost, average	KWh	7.75	9/00	9s
Utilities, fuels, and public services purchased	yr	2179	1999	30r
Water and other public services, expenditures on	yr	339	1999	30r
Weddings				
Wedding (national average cost)		19936	2000	33r
Wedding (regional average total cost)		18918	1997	110r
Attendants' gifts		321	1998	33r
Bridal attendants' apparel (5 persons)		824	2000	33r
Bride's headpiece/veil		173	1998	33r
Bride's wedding dress		859	1998	33r
Clergy, religious facility fee		242	1998	33r
Engagement ring		3177	1998	33r
Flowers		789	1998	33r
Groom's formalwear rental		99	2000	33r
Limousine		410	1998	33r
Marriage license cost		50.00-80.00	4/01	35s
Men's formalwear (ushers, best man)		469	2000	33r
Mother of bride apparel		241	2000	33r
Music		866	1998	33r
Photography and videography		1368	1998	33r
Rehearsal dinner		728	1998	33r
Wedding invitations and announcements		341	1998	33r
Wedding reception		7968	2000	33r
Wedding rings (bride and groom)		1060	1998	33r

Salt Lake City-Ogden, UT

Item	Per	Value	Date	Ref.
Composite, ACCRA index		99.00	3/01	4c
Alcoholic Beverages				
Beer, Heineken, 12-oz, ex deposit	6	6.43	3/01	4c
J & B Scotch	750-ml	22.95	3/01	4c
Wine, Livingston or Gallo, Chablis blanc	1.5 liter	6.95	3/01	4c
Appliances				
Appliance repair, service call, washing machine	min lab chg	31.79	3/01	4c
Banking and Money				
Mortgage rate, incl. points and orig. fee, 30-yr. conv. fixed or ARM	mos	7.07	3/01	4c
Business Expenses				
Business travel, car rental	day	50	2001	3c
Business travel, food	day	48	2001	3c
Business travel, hotel	day	103	2001	3c
Clothing				
Boys' brief, cotton	3	4.59	3/01	4c
Shirt, man's dress shirt		27.09	3/01	4c
Slacks, man's "No Wrinkles" khaki		34.47	3/01	4c
Communications				
Newspaper subscription, daily and Sunday delivery	mos	10.04	3/01	4c

Values are in dollars or fractions of dollars. In the column headed *Ref*, references are shown to sources. Each reference is followed by a letter. These refer to the geographical level for which data were reported: s=State, r=Region, and c=City or metro. The abbreviation *ex* is used to mean *except* or *excluding*; *exp* stands for *expenditures*. For other abbreviations and further explanations, please see the Introduction.

Salt Lake City-Ogden, UT - continued

Item	Per	Value	Date	Ref.
Communications				
Phone line, single, business, field visit	inst.	50.00	12/97	17s
Phone line, single, business, no field visit	inst.	50.00	12/97	17s
Phone line, single, residence, field visit	inst.	25.00	12/97	17s
Phone line, single, residence, no field visit	inst.	25.00	12/97	17s
Postal rate, express mail, up to half-pound		12.45	7/01	108r
Postal rate, letter, first class, first ounce		0.34	7/01	108r
Postal rate, letter, two ounces		0.57	7/01	108r
Postal rate, post card		0.21	7/01	108r
Postal rate, priority mail, two pounds		3.95	7/01	108r
Postal rate, priority mail, up to one pound		3.50	7/01	108r
Telephone bill, business, basic rate	mos	25.22	12/97	18c
Telephone bill, family of three	mos	21.81	3/01	4c
Telephone bill, residential, basic rate	mos	16.58	12/97	18c
Education				
Board, 4-year private college/university	yr	3068	1996	38s
Board, 4-year public college/university	yr	1945	1996	38s
Room, 4-year private college/university	yr	1380	1996	38s
Room, 4-year public college/university	yr	1458	1996	38s
Total cost, 4-year private college/university	yr	7384	1996	38s
Total cost, 4-year public college/university	yr	5414	1996	38s
Tuition, 2-year public college/university, in state	yr	1375	1996	38s
Tuition, 4-year private college/university, in state	yr	2936	1996	38s
Tuition, 4-year public college/university	yr	2011	1996	38s
Energy and Fuels				
Energy, combined forms, 2400 sq ft	mos	102.01	3/01	4c
Energy, exc. electricity, 2400 sq ft	mos	59.47	3/01	4c
Gas, cooking, winter, 10 therms	mos	9.06	2/96	98c
Gas, cooking, winter, 30 therms	mos	17.17	2/96	98c
Gas, cooking, winter, 50 therms	mos	25.28	2/96	98c
Gas, heating, winter, average use	mos	71.91	2/96	98c
Gas, natural, commercial rate	1000 cf	5.42	11/00	88s
Gas, regular unleaded, cash, self-service	gal	1.37	3/01	4c
Entertainment				
Bowling, Saturday evening rate	line	1.91	3/01	4c
Monopoly game, Parker Brothers', No. 9	game	10.72	3/01	4c
Movie, first-run, Saturday, evening	adm.	7.35	3/01	4c
Tennis balls, yellow, Wilson or Penn, 3	can	2.12	3/01	4c
Funerals				
Total cost of funeral		5401.08	1/99	78r
Acknowledgement cards		33.64	1/99	78r
Casket		2170.43	1/99	78r
Cosmetology, hair, other preparation		136.32	1/99	78r
Embalming		319.13	1/99	78r
Funeral at funeral home		370.21	1/99	78r
Hearse (local)		161.04	1/99	78r
Professional service charges		963.15	1/99	78r
Service car/van		133.99	1/99	78r
Transfer of remains to funeral home		159.82	1/99	78r
Vault		778.07	1/99	78r
Visitation/viewing		175.28	1/99	78r
Groceries				
Groceries, ACCRA Index		112.60	3/01	4c
Antibiotic ointment, Polysporin	0.5 oz	4.19	3/01	4c
Baby food, strained vegetables or fruit, lowest price	4-4.5 oz	0.36	3/01	4c
Bananas	lb	0.71	3/01	4c
Beef or hamburger, ground	lb	1.96	3/01	4c
Bread, white	loaf	1.17	3/01	4c
Cheese, Kraft grated Parmesan	8 oz	3.53	3/01	4c
Chicken, whole fryer	lb	1.19	3/01	4c
Cigarettes, Winston, Kings	carton	32.86	3/01	4c
Coffee, vacuum-packed	13 oz	3.53	3/01	4c
Corn Flakes, Kellogg's or Post Toasties	18 oz	3.56	3/01	4c
Corn, frozen, whole kernel, lowest price	16 oz	1.47	3/01	4c
Eggs, Grade A or AA	dozen	1.11	3/01	4c
Lettuce, iceberg	head	1.11	3/01	4c
Margarine, Blue Bonnet or Parkay, stick	lb	0.69	3/01	4c

Salt Lake City-Ogden, UT - continued

Item	Per	Value	Date	Ref.
Groceries - continued				
Milk, whole	1/2 gal	2.03	3/01	4c
Orange juice, Minute Maid frozen	12 oz	1.61	3/01	4c
Peaches, halves or slices, Hunt's, Del Monte, or Libby's	29 oz	1.89	3/01	4c
Peas, green, Del Monte or Green Giant	15 oz	0.83	3/01	4c
Potatoes, white or red	10 lb	2.07	3/01	4c
Sausage, Jimmy Dean/Owens pork	lb	2.89	3/01	4c
Shortening, vegetable, Crisco	3 lb	3.09	3/01	4c
Soft drink, Coca Cola, ex deposit	2 liter	1.17	3/01	4c
Steak, T-bone	lb	6.35	3/01	4c
Sugar, cane or beet	4 lbs	1.77	3/01	4c
Tomatoes, Hunt's or Del Monte	14.5 oz	1.01	3/01	4c
Tuna, chunk, light	6 oz	0.92	3/01	4c
Goods and Services				
Miscellaneous goods and services, ACCRA Index		98.20	3/01	4c
Hunting license	yr	17.00	4/01	34s
Health Care				
Health care, ACCRA Index		94.00	3/01	4c
Cardiac catheterization, ave hospital/ physician charges		17370	1998	77s
Childbirth, Cesarean delivery		11587	1997	13r
Childbirth, vaginal delivery		6725	1997	13r
Dentist's fee, adult teeth cleaning and periodic oral exam	visit	72.20	3/01	4c
Doctor's fee, routine exam, established patient	visit	50.25	3/01	4c
Hospital care, private room	day	523.80	3/01	4c
Hysterectomy, laproscopically-assisted, ave hospital/physician charges		11940	1998	76s
Hysterectomy, vaginal, ave hospital and physician charges		8530	1998	76s
Medicaid dispensing fee		3.90-4.40	1999	87s
Nursing home costs, private room	day	135	2000	82c
Nursing home stay, private room	day	135	2000	81c
Household Goods				
Dishwashing powder, Cascade	50 oz	3.81	3/01	4c
Tissues, facial, Kleenex brand	175	1.26	3/01	4c
Housing				
Housing, ACCRA Index		97.30	3/01	4c
Home, 2200 sq ft, 4-br, 2-bath, 2-car garage, average		163362	2000	47c
Home value, median		134000	2001	53s
House, 2400 sq ft, 8000 sq ft lot, new, urban, utilities	total	190500	3/01	4c
House payment, principal and interest, 25% down payment	mos	957	3/01	4c
Rent, apartment, 2 br, 1 1/2-2 baths, unfurn, 950 sq ft, water	mos	797	3/01	4c
Rental unit, 1 bedroom, with utilities	mos	520	4/01	41c
Rental unit, 2 bedroom, with utilities	mos	660	4/01	41c
Rental unit, 3 bedroom, with utilities	mos	918	4/01	41c
Rental unit, 4 bedroom, with utilities	mos	1076	4/01	41c
Legal Fees				
Combination hunting and fishing license	yr	32.00	4/01	34s
Divorce, filing fee		82.00	4/01	35s
Driver's license fee	orig	20.00	1999	48s
Driver's license fee	renew	13.50	1999	48s
Fishing license	yr	24.00	4/01	34s
Personal Goods				
Shampoo, Alberto VO5	15 oz	1.63	3/01	4c
Toothpaste, Crest or Colgate	6-7 oz	2.69	3/01	4c
Personal Services				
Dry cleaning, man's 2-pc suit		9.85	3/01	4c
Man's haircut, barbershop, no styling		11.40	3/01	4c
Woman's shampoo, trim, blow-dry, no style-change		25.39	3/01	4c

Values are in dollars or fractions of dollars. In the column headed *Ref*, references are shown to sources. Each reference is followed by a letter. These refer to the geographical level for which data were reported: s=State, r=Region, and c=City or metro. The abbreviation *ex* is used to mean *except* or *excluding*; *exp* stands for *expenditures*. For other abbreviations and further explanations, please see the Introduction.

Salt Lake City-Ogden, UT - continued

Item	Per	Value	Date	Ref.
Restaurant Food				
Chicken, fried, thigh and drumstick, KFC/ Church's		2.79	3/01	4c
Hamburger with cheese, McDonald's	1/4 lb	2.09	3/01	4c
Pizza, Pizza Hut or Pizza Inn	11-12 in	8.99	3/01	4c
Transportation				
Transportation, ACCRA Index		97.80	3/01	4c
Bus fare, one-way	trip	1.00	2000	1c
Bus fare, to central business district	1-way	1.00	3/01	4c
Diesel at the pump	gal	1.30	10/99	73s
Gasoline before-tax price (cents)	gal	115.90	10/00	43s
Tire balance, computer or spin balance, front	wheel	7.89	3/01	4c
Travel				
Hotel room, ave	night	75.69	2000	70c
Utilities				
Utilities, ACCRA Index		85.90	3/01	4c
Electrical bill, average	mos	44.08	9/00	9s
Electricity, summer, 250 KWh	mos	18.10	2/96	96c
Electricity, summer, 500 KWh	mos	35.20	2/96	96c
Electricity, summer, 750 KWh	mos	52.29	2/96	96c
Electricity, summer, 1000 KWh	mos	63.39	2/96	96c
Electricity and other, mixed, 2400 sq ft, new home	mos	42.54	3/01	4c
Electricity cost, average	KWh	4.70	9/00	9s
Water price	100 cf	0.53	2000	109c
Water price, dwelling unit	mos	10.33	2000	109c
Weddings				
Wedding (national average cost)		19936	2000	33r
Attendants' gifts		321	1998	33r
Bridal attendants' apparel (5 persons)		824	2000	33r
Bride's headpiece/veil		173	1998	33r
Bride's wedding dress		859	1998	33r
Clergy, religious facility fee		242	1998	33r
Engagement ring		3177	1998	33r
Flowers		789	1998	33r
Groom's formalwear rental		99	2000	33r
Limousine		410	1998	33r
Marriage license cost		40.00	4/01	35s
Men's formalwear (ushers, best man)		469	2000	33r
Mother of bride apparel		241	2000	33r
Music		866	1998	33r
Photography and videography		1368	1998	33r
Rehearsal dinner		728	1998	33r
Wedding invitations and announcements		341	1998	33r
Wedding reception		7968	2000	33r
Wedding rings (bride and groom)		1060	1998	33r

San Angelo, TX

Item	Per	Value	Date	Ref.
Composite, ACCRA index		91.50	3/01	4c
Alcoholic Beverages				
Alcoholic beverage purchases	yr	253	1999	30r
Beer, Heineken, 12-oz, ex deposit	6	6.86	3/01	4c
J & B Scotch	750-ml	22.27	3/01	4c
Malt beverages, all types, all sizes, any origin	16 oz	0.96	7/01	11r
Wine, Livingston or Gallo, Chablis blanc	1.5 liter	7.47	3/01	4c
Appliances				
Appliance repair, service call, washing machine	min lab chg	39.15	3/01	4c
Major appliances, expenditures on	yr	172	1999	30r
Small appliances, housewares, expenditures on	yr	81	1999	30r
Banking and Money				
Mortgage interest and charges paid	yr	2039	1999	30r
Mortgage principal paid on owned property	yr	1026	1999	30r
Mortgage rate, incl. points and orig. fee, 30-yr. conv. fixed or ARM	mos	6.85	3/01	4c
Vehicle finance charges paid	yr	365	1999	30r

San Angelo, TX - continued

Item	Per	Value	Date	Ref.
Charity				
Cash contributions, expenditures	yr	1127	1999	30r
Child Care				
Child raising cost, total, age 0-2	yr	8540	1999	60r
Child raising cost, total, age 3-5	yr	8780	1999	60r
Child raising cost, total, age 6-8	yr	8820	1999	60r
Child raising cost, total, age 9-11	yr	8800	1999	60r
Child raising cost, total, age 12-14	yr	9510	1999	60r
Child raising cost, total, age 15-17	yr	9740	1999	60r
Child's child care and education, age 0-2	yr	1380	1999	60r
Child's child care and education, age 3-5	yr	1520	1999	60r
Child's child care and education, age 6-8	yr	990	1999	60r
Child's child care and education, age 9-11	yr	650	1999	60r
Child's child care and education, age 12-14	yr	490	1999	60r
Child's child care and education, age 15-17	yr	840	1999	60r
Child's clothing, age 0-2	yr	480	1999	60r
Child's clothing, age 3-5	yr	470	1999	60r
Child's clothing, age 6-8	yr	520	1999	60r
Child's clothing, age 9-11	yr	570	1999	60r
Child's clothing, age 12-14	yr	950	1999	60r
Child's clothing, age 15-17	yr	850	1999	60r
Child's food, age 0-2	yr	1000	1999	60r
Child's food, age 3-5	yr	1160	1999	60r
Child's food, age 6-8	yr	1490	1999	60r
Child's food, age 9-11	yr	1770	1999	60r
Child's food, age 12-14	yr	1770	1999	60r
Child's food, age 15-17	yr	1980	1999	60r
Child's health care, age 0-2	yr	620	1999	60r
Child's health care, age 3-5	yr	590	1999	60r
Child's health care, age 6-8	yr	680	1999	60r
Child's health care, age 9-11	yr	720	1999	60r
Child's health care, age 12-14	yr	730	1999	60r
Child's health care, age 15-17	yr	760	1999	60r
Child's housing, age 0-2	yr	3070	1999	60r
Child's housing, age 3-5	yr	3050	1999	60r
Child's housing, age 6-8	yr	3010	1999	60r
Child's housing, age 9-11	yr	2850	1999	60r
Child's housing, age 12-14	yr	3040	1999	60r
Child's housing, age 15-17	yr	2650	1999	60r
Child's personal care, reading, age 0-2	yr	910	1999	60r
Child's personal care, reading, age 3-5	yr	930	1999	60r
Child's personal care, reading, age 6-8	yr	960	1999	60r
Child's personal care, reading, age 9-11	yr	1000	1999	60r
Child's personal care, reading, age 12-14	yr	1170	1999	60r
Child's personal care, reading, age 15-17	yr	950	1999	60r
Clothing				
Apparel and services purchases	yr	1610	1999	30r
Boys' brief, cotton	3	4.32	3/01	4c
Boys, 2 to 15, expenditures on	yr	89	1999	30r
Children under 2, expenditures on	yr	79	1999	30r
Footwear, expenditures on	yr	283	1999	30r
Girls, 2 to 15, expenditures on	yr	103	1999	30r
Men and boys, expenditures on	yr	351	1999	30r
Men, 16 and over, expenditures on	yr	262	1999	30r
Shirt, man's dress shirt		25.83	3/01	4c
Slacks, man's "No Wrinkles" khaki		38.75	3/01	4c
Women, 16 and over, expenditures on	yr	538	1999	30r
Communications				
Cable modem installation, AT&T-BIS		150.00	6/99	103s
Cable modem installation, Marcus		499.00	6/99	103s
Cable modem installation, Time Warner		75.00-225.00	6/99	103s
Cable modem rate, cable subscriber, AT&T-BIS	mos	39.95	6/99	103s
Cable modem rate, cable subscriber, Marcus	mos	14.95-49.95	6/99	103s
Cable modem rate, cable subscriber, Time Warner	mos	39.95-49.95	6/99	103s
Cable modem rate, non-cable subscriber, Marcus	mos	60.95	6/99	103s
Cable modem rate, non-cable subscriber, Time Warner	mos	39.95-54.95	6/99	103s

Values are in dollars or fractions of dollars. In the column headed *Ref*, references are shown to sources. Each reference is followed by a letter. These refer to the geographical level for which data were reported: s=State, r=Region, and c=City or metro. The abbreviation *ex* is used to mean *except* or *excluding*; *exp* stands for expenditures. For other abbreviations and further explanations, please see the Introduction.

San Angelo, TX - continued

Item	Per	Value	Date	Ref.
Communications				
Newspaper subscription, daily and Sunday delivery	mos	14.95	3/01	4c
Phone line, single, business, field visit	inst.	71.90	12/97	17s
Phone line, single, business, no field visit	inst.	57.30	12/97	17s
Phone line, single, residence, field visit	inst.	52.95	12/97	17s
Phone line, single, residence, no field visit	inst.	38.35	12/97	17s
Postage and stationery, expenditures on	yr	104	1999	30r
Postal rate, express mail, up to half-pound		12.45	7/01	108r
Postal rate, letter, first class, first ounce		0.34	7/01	108r
Postal rate, letter, two ounces		0.57	7/01	108r
Postal rate, post card		0.21	7/01	108r
Postal rate, priority mail, two pounds		3.95	7/01	108r
Postal rate, priority mail, up to one pound		3.50	7/01	108r
Telephone bill, family of three	mos	19.23	3/01	4c
Telephone services, expenditures on	yr	860	1999	30r
Education				
Board, 4-year private college/university	yr	2198	1996	38s
Board, 4-year public college/university	yr	1759	1996	38s
Education expenditures	yr	431	1999	30r
Room, 4-year private college/university	yr	2000	1996	38s
Room, 4-year public college/university	yr	1885	1996	38s
Total cost, 4-year private college/university	yr	13156	1996	38s
Total cost, 4-year public college/university	yr	5464	1996	38s
Tuition, 2-year public college/university, in state	yr	771	1996	38s
Tuition, 4-year private college/university, in state	yr	8959	1996	38s
Tuition, 4-year public college/university	yr	1820	1996	38s
Energy and Fuels				
Electricity	KWh	0.09	7/01	11r
Electricity	500 KWhs	47.29	7/01	11r
Energy, combined forms, 2400 sq ft	mos	99.61	3/01	4c
Energy, exc. electricity, 2400 sq ft	mos	45.94	3/01	4c
Fuel oil #2	gal	1.43	7/01	11r
Fuel oil and other fuels, expenditures on	yr	45	1999	30r
Gas, natural, commercial rate	1000 cf	6.94	11/00	88s
Gas, regular unleaded, cash, self-service	gal	1.31	3/01	4c
Gasoline, all types	gal	1.60	7/01	11r
Gasoline, unleaded midgrade	gal	1.65	7/01	11r
Gasoline, unleaded premium	gal	1.74	7/01	11r
Natural gas, expenditures on	yr	164	1999	30r
Utility (piped) gas, therm		1.01	7/01	11r
Utility (piped) gas, 40 therms		44.29	7/01	11r
Utility (piped) gas, 100 therms		97.44	7/01	11r
Entertainment				
Bowling, Saturday evening rate	line	2.63	3/01	4c
Entertainment purchases	yr	1574	1999	30r
Fees and admissions paid	yr	371	1999	30r
Monopoly game, Parker Brothers', No. 9	game	13.15	3/01	4c
Movie, first-run, Saturday, evening	adm.	5.63	3/01	4c
Reading purchases	yr	121	1999	30r
Television, radios, sound equipment, expenditures on	yr	561	1999	30r
Tennis balls, yellow, Wilson or Penn, 3	can	2.36	3/01	4c
Funerals				
Total cost of funeral		5842.28	1/99	78r
Acknowledgement cards		28.35	1/99	78r
Casket		2494.29	1/99	78r
Cosmetology, hair, other preparation		109.22	1/99	78r
Embalming		361.42	1/99	78r
Funeral at funeral home		349.20	1/99	78r
Hearse (local)		161.91	1/99	78r
Professional service charges		1116.50	1/99	78r
Service car/van		65.56	1/99	78r
Transfer of remains to funeral home		143.56	1/99	78r
Vault		785.25	1/99	78r
Visitation/viewing		227.02	1/99	78r

San Angelo, TX - continued

Item	Per	Value	Date	Ref.
Groceries				
Groceries, ACCRA Index		88.60	3/01	4c
American processed cheese	lb	3.50	7/01	11r
Antibiotic ointment, Polysporin	0.5 oz	4.76	3/01	4c
Baby food, strained vegetables or fruit, lowest price	4-4.5 oz	0.25	3/01	4c
Bakery products, expenditures on	yr	261	1999	30r
Bananas	lb	0.44	3/01	4c
Bananas	lb	0.47	7/01	11r
Beans, dried, any type, all sizes	lb	0.63	7/01	11r
Beef for stew, boneless	lb	2.86	7/01	11r
Beef or hamburger, ground	lb	1.14	3/01	4c
Beef, expenditures on	yr	210	1999	30r
Bologna, all beef or mixed	lb	2.29	7/01	11r
Bread, French	lb	1.66	7/01	11r
Bread, white	loaf	0.71	3/01	4c
Bread, white, pan	lb	0.87	7/01	11r
Bread, whole wheat, pan	lb	1.38	7/01	11r
Broccoli	lb	1.04	7/01	11r
Butter, salted, grade AA, stick	lb	2.26	7/01	11r
Butter, yoghurt, cheese, etc, expenditures on	yr	170	1999	30r
Cabbage	lb	0.42	7/01	11r
Cereals and cereal products, expenditures on	yr	140	1999	30r
Cheddar cheese, natural	lb	3.75	7/01	11r
Cheese, Kraft grated Parmesan	8 oz	3.83	3/01	4c
Chicken breast, bone-in	lb	1.85	7/01	11r
Chicken legs, bone-in	lb	1.34	7/01	11r
Chicken, fresh, whole	lb	1.05	7/01	11r
Chicken, whole fryer	lb	0.78	3/01	4c
Chops, boneless,	lb	4.13	7/01	11r
Chuck roast, graded and ungraded, excl U.S. prime and choice	lb	2.35	7/01	11r
Chuck roast, U.S. choice, boneless	lb	2.67	7/01	11r
Cigarettes, Winston, Kings	carton	29.37	3/01	4c
Coffee, 100%, ground roast, all sizes	lb	2.88	7/01	11r
Coffee, instant, plain, regular, all sizes	16 oz	9.25	7/01	11r
Coffee, vacuum-packed	13 oz	2.40	3/01	4c
Cola, non diet	2 liter	1.11	7/01	11r
Corn Flakes, Kellogg's or Post Toasties	18 oz	2.44	3/01	4c
Corn, frozen, whole kernel, lowest price	16 oz	0.89	3/01	4c
Crackers, soda, salted	lb	1.70	7/01	11r
Dairy product purchases	yr	282	1999	30r
Eggs, expenditures on	yr	32	1999	30r
Eggs, Grade A or AA	dozen	0.92	3/01	4c
Fats and oils, expenditures on	yr	79	1999	30r
Fish and seafood, expenditures on	yr	99	1999	30r
Flour, white, all purpose	lb	0.32	7/01	11r
Food (excl fruit and vegetables), eaten at home, purchases	yr	815	1999	30r
Food cooked on trips, expenditures on	yr	36	1999	30r
Food purchases	yr	4533	1999	30r
Food purchases, eaten away from home	yr	1873	1999	30r
Food purchases, food eaten at home	yr	2660	1999	30r
Fresh fruits, expenditures on	yr	128	1999	30r
Fresh milk and cream, expenditures on	yr	112	1999	30r
Fresh vegetables, expenditures on	yr	131	1999	30r
Fruit and vegetable purchases	yr	438	1999	30r
Grapefruit	lb	0.59	7/01	11r
Grapes, Thompson, seedless	lb	2.12	7/01	11r
Ground beef, 100% beef	lb	1.76	7/01	11r
Ground beef, lean and extra lean	lb	2.60	7/01	11r
Ground chuck, 100% beef	lb	2.08	7/01	11r
Ham, boneless, excl canned	lb	2.71	7/01	11r
Ham, rump or shank half, bone-in, smoked	lb	2.19	7/01	11r
Ice cream, prepackaged, bulk, regular	1/2 gal	3.93	7/01	11r
Lemons	lb	1.32	7/01	11r
Lettuce, iceberg	head	1.18	3/01	4c
Lettuce, iceberg	lb	0.76	7/01	11r
Margarine, Blue Bonnet or Parkay, stick	lb	0.74	3/01	4c
Milk, fresh, low fat	gal	2.75	7/01	11r
Milk, fresh, whole, fortified	gal	2.97	7/01	11r
Milk, whole	1/2 gal	1.47	3/01	4c

Values are in dollars or fractions of dollars. In the column headed *Ref*, references are shown to sources. Each reference is followed by a letter. These refer to the geographical level for which data were reported: s=State, r=Region, and c=City or metro. The abbreviation *ex* is used to mean *except* or *excluding*; *exp* stands for *expenditures*. For other abbreviations and further explanations, please see the Introduction.

San Angelo, TX - continued

Item	Per	Value	Date	Ref.
Groceries				
Nonalcoholic beverages, expenditures on	yr	228	1999	30r
Orange juice, frozen concentrate	16 oz	1.95	7/01	11r
Orange juice, Minute Maid frozen	12 oz	1.45	3/01	4c
Oranges, Navel	lb	0.73	7/01	11r
Oranges, Valencia	lb	0.55	7/01	11r
Peaches, halves or slices, Hunt's, Del Monte, or Libby's	29 oz	1.69	3/01	4c
Peanut butter, creamy, all sizes	lb	1.83	7/01	11r
Pears, Anjou	lb	0.98	7/01	11r
Peas, green, Del Monte or Green Giant	15 oz	0.63	3/01	4c
Pork chops, center cut, bone-in	lb	3.33	7/01	11r
Pork sausage, fresh, loose	lb	2.59	7/01	11r
Pork shoulder picnic, bone-in, smoked	lb	1.12	7/01	11r
Pork, expenditures on	yr	162	1999	30r
Potato chips	16 oz	3.59	7/01	11r
Potatoes, frozen, french fried	lb	1.00	7/01	11r
Potatoes, white or red	10 lb	2.75	3/01	4c
Potatoes, white, all types	lb	0.44	7/01	11r
Poultry, expenditures on	yr	137	1999	30r
Processed fruits, expenditures on	yr	97	1999	30r
Processed vegetables, expenditures on	yr	82	1999	30r
Rice, white, long grain, uncooked	lb	0.51	7/01	11r
Round roast, graded and ungraded, excl U.S. prime and choice	lb	2.96	7/01	11r
Round steak, graded and ungraded, excl U.S. prime and choice	lb	3.11	7/01	11r
Sausage, Jimmy Dean/Owens pork	lb	2.45	3/01	4c
Shortening, vegetable, Crisco	3 lb	2.93	3/01	4c
Sirloin steak, graded and ungraded, excl U.S. prime and choice	lb	4.23	7/01	11r
Soft drink, Coca Cola, ex deposit	2 liter	1.49	3/01	4c
Spaghetti and macaroni	lb	0.78	7/01	11r
Steak, round, U.S. choice, boneless	lb	3.56	7/01	11r
Steak, sirloin, U.S. choice, boneless	lb	5.65	7/01	11r
Steak, T-bone	lb	5.06	3/01	4c
Strawberries, dry pint	12 oz	1.50	7/01	11r
Sugar and other sweets, expenditures on	yr	99	1999	30r
Sugar, cane or beet	4 lbs	1.32	3/01	4c
Sugar, white, 33-80 ounce package	lb	0.39	7/01	11r
Sugar, white, all sizes	lb	0.42	7/01	11r
Tobacco products and smoking supplies purchases	yr	288	1999	30r
Tomatoes, field grown	lb	1.43	7/01	11r
Tomatoes, Hunt's or Del Monte	14.5 oz	0.94	3/01	4c
Tuna, chunk, light	6 oz	0.68	3/01	4c
Tuna, light, chunk	lb	1.77	7/01	11r
Turkey, frozen, whole	lb	1.05	7/01	11r
Goods and Services				
Miscellaneous goods and services, ACCRA Index		100.80	3/01	4c
B&B Japanese maple (acer japonicum)	gal	79.98-99.00	4/00	93r
Boxwood (buxus)	2 gal	12.98-18.99	4/00	93r
Christmas tree, noble fir		40-60	2000	65s
Daylily (hemerocallis)	gal	7.96-11.00	4/00	93r
Flat of annuals		13.99-27.99	4/00	93r
Fountain grass (pennisetum)	gal	6.96-9.00	4/00	93r
Hanging basket (10 in)		9.99-24.99	4/00	93r
Hardy geranium (geranium)	gal	5.96-8.00	4/00	93r
Hosta (hosta)	gal	8.96-12.99	4/00	93r
Lilac (syrubga vulgaris)	2 gal	13.00-19.99	4/00	93r
Rhododendron (rhododendron)	2 gal	12.98-29.99	4/00	93r

San Angelo, TX - continued

Item	Per	Value	Date	Ref.
Goods and Services - continued				
Sage (salvia)	gal	5.96-8.00	4/00	93r
Wintercreeper euonymus (euonymus fortunei)	2 gal	13.00-18.99	4/00	93r
Hunting license	yr	19.00	4/01	34s
Health Care				
Health care, ACCRA Index		98.00	3/01	4c
Cardiac catheterization, ave hospital/physician charges		20140	1998	77s
Childbirth, Cesarean delivery		11587	1997	13r
Childbirth, vaginal delivery		6725	1997	13r
Dentist's fee, adult teeth cleaning and periodic oral exam	visit	68.25	3/01	4c
Doctor's fee, routine exam, established patient	visit	64.00	3/01	4c
Drugs, expenditures on	yr	399	1999	30r
Health care purchases	yr	1971	1999	30r
Health insurance expenditures	yr	933	1999	30r
Hospital care, private room	day	413.00	3/01	4c
Hysterectomy, laproscopically-assisted, ave hospital/physician charges		15700	1998	76s
Hysterectomy, vaginal, ave hospital and physician charges		12180	1998	76s
Medicaid dispensing fee		5.27	1999	87s
Medical services expenditures	yr	547	1999	30r
Medical supplies, expenditures on	yr	91	1999	30r
Household Goods				
Dishwashing powder, Cascade	50 oz	3.11	3/01	4c
Floor coverings, expenditures on	yr	44	1999	30r
Furniture, expenditures on	yr	335	1999	30r
Household furnishings and equipment purchases	yr	1328	1999	30r
Household textiles, expenditures on	yr	89	1999	30r
Laundry and cleaning supplies, expenditures on	yr	113	1999	30r
Tissues, facial, Kleenex brand	175	1.18	3/01	4c
Housing				
Housing, ACCRA Index		81.70	3/01	4c
Home price, existing, ave		160100	10/00	90r
Home value, median		112000	2001	53s
House, 2400 sq ft, 8000 sq ft lot, new, urban, utilities	total	175167	3/01	4c
House payment, principal and interest, 25% down payment	mos	861	3/01	4c
Household operation expenditures	yr	553	1999	30r
Housekeeping supplies purchases	yr	473	1999	30r
Housing, expenditures on	yr	10303	1999	30r
Maintenance, repairs, insurance expenditures	yr	699	1999	30r
Monthly rental value of owned home	mos	505	1999	30r
Owned dwellings, expenditures own	yr	3465	1999	30r
Rent expenditures	yr	1641	1999	30r
Rent, apartment, 2 br, 1 1/2-2 baths, unfurn, 950 sq ft, water	mos	520	3/01	4c
Rental unit, 1 bedroom, with utilities	mos	365	4/01	41c
Rental unit, 2 bedroom, with utilities	mos	443	4/01	41c
Rental unit, 3 bedroom, with utilities	mos	608	4/01	41c
Rental unit, 4 bedroom, with utilities	mos	717	4/01	41c
Shelter, expenditures on	yr	5467	1999	30r
Insurance and Pensions				
Life and other personal insurance purchases	yr	414	1999	30r
Pensions and Social Security, expenditures on	yr	2635	1999	30r
Personal insurance and pensions, expenditures on	yr	3048	1999	30r
Legal Fees				
Divorce, filing fee		150.00-200.00	4/01	35s
Driver's license fee	renew	20.00	1999	48s

Values are in dollars or fractions of dollars. In the column headed *Ref*, references are shown to sources. Each reference is followed by a letter. These refer to the geographical level for which data were reported: s=State, r=Region, and c=City or metro. The abbreviation *ex* is used to mean *except* or *excluding*; *exp* stands for *expenditures*. For other abbreviations and further explanations, please see the Introduction.

San Angelo, TX - continued

Item	Per	Value	Date	Ref.
Legal Fees				
Driver's license fee	orig	24.00	1999	48s
Fishing license	yr	19.00	4/01	34s
Personal Goods				
Personal care products and services purchases	yr	393	1999	30r
Shampoo, Alberto VO5	15 oz	1.13	3/01	4c
Toothpaste, Crest or Colgate	6-7 oz	2.08	3/01	4c
Personal Services				
Dry cleaning, man's 2-pc suit		6.71	3/01	4c
Man's haircut, barbershop, no styling		8.25	3/01	4c
Personal services, household, expenditures on	yr	258	1999	30r
Woman's shampoo, trim, blow-dry, no style-change		24.25	3/01	4c
Pets				
Pets, toys, and playground equipment, expenditures on	yr	306	1999	30r
Restaurant Food				
Chicken, fried, thigh and drumstick, KFC/Church's		2.89	3/01	4c
Hamburger with cheese, McDonald's	1/4 lb	1.99	3/01	4c
Pizza, Pizza Hut or Pizza Inn	11-12 in	9.99	3/01	4c
Taxes				
Federal income taxes paid	yr	2047	1999	30r
Personal taxes, expenditures on	yr	2554	1999	30r
Property taxes paid	yr	726	1999	30r
State and local income taxes paid	yr	363	1999	30r
Transportation				
Transportation, ACCRA Index		96.50	3/01	4c
Cars and trucks, new, expenditures on	yr	1648	1999	30r
Cars and trucks, used, expenditures on	yr	1651	1999	30r
Diesel at the pump	gal	1.18	10/99	73s
Gasoline and motor oil purchases	yr	1052	1999	30r
Gasoline before-tax price (cents)	gal	101.30	10/00	43s
Maintenance and repair expenditures	yr	621	1999	30r
Public transportation, expenditures on	yr	298	1999	30r
Tire balance, computer or spin balance, front	wheel	8.00	3/01	4c
Transportation purchases	yr	6738	1999	30r
Vehicle expenses, miscellaneous, purchases	yr	2033	1999	30r
Vehicle insurance payments	yr	696	1999	30r
Vehicle purchases (net outlay)	yr	3354	1999	30r
Vehicle rental, lease expenditures	yr	352	1999	30r
Utilities				
Utilities, ACCRA Index		82.50	3/01	4c
Electrical bill, average	mos	87.17	9/00	9s
Electricity, expenditures on	yr	1115	1999	30r
Electricity and other, mixed, 2400 sq ft, new home	mos	53.67	3/01	4c
Electricity cost, average	KWh	6.48	9/00	9s
Water and other public services, expenditures on	yr	298	1999	30r
Weddings				
Wedding (national average cost)		19936	2000	33r
Attendants' gifts		321	1998	33r
Bridal attendants' apparel (5 persons)		824	2000	33r
Bride's headpiece/veil		173	1998	33r
Bride's wedding dress		859	1998	33r
Clergy, religious facility fee		242	1998	33r
Engagement ring		3177	1998	33r
Flowers		789	1998	33r
Groom's formalwear rental		99	2000	33r
Limousine		410	1998	33r
Marriage license cost		36.00	4/01	35s
Men's formalwear (ushers, best man)		469	2000	33r
Mother of bride apparel		241	2000	33r
Music		866	1998	33r
Photography and videography		1368	1998	33r
Rehearsal dinner		728	1998	33r

San Angelo, TX - continued

Item	Per	Value	Date	Ref.
Weddings - continued				
Wedding invitations and announcements		341	1998	33r
Wedding reception		7968	2000	33r
Wedding rings (bride and groom)		1060	1998	33r

San Antonio, TX

Item	Per	Value	Date	Ref.
Composite, ACCRA index		90.10	3/01	4c
Alcoholic Beverages				
Alcoholic beverage purchases	yr	253	1999	30r
Beer, Heineken, 12-oz, ex deposit	6	6.70	3/01	4c
J & B Scotch	750-ml	22.09	3/01	4c
Malt beverages, all types, all sizes, any origin	16 oz	0.96	7/01	11r
Wine, Livingston or Gallo, Chablis blanc	1.5 liter	6.24	3/01	4c
Appliances				
Appliance repair, service call, washing machine	min lab chg	45.90	3/01	4c
Major appliances, expenditures on	yr	172	1999	30r
Small appliances, housewares, expenditures on	yr	81	1999	30r
Banking and Money				
Mortgage interest and charges paid	yr	2039	1999	30r
Mortgage principal paid on owned property	yr	1026	1999	30r
Mortgage rate, incl. points and orig. fee, 30-yr. conv. fixed or ARM	mos	6.82	3/01	4c
Vehicle finance charges paid	yr	365	1999	30r
Business Expenses				
Business travel, car rental	day	47	2001	3c
Business travel, food	day	52	2001	3c
Business travel, hotel	day	117	2001	3c
Charity				
Cash contributions, expenditures	yr	1127	1999	30r
Child Care				
Child raising cost, total, age 0-2	yr	8540	1999	60r
Child raising cost, total, age 3-5	yr	8780	1999	60r
Child raising cost, total, age 6-8	yr	8820	1999	60r
Child raising cost, total, age 9-11	yr	8800	1999	60r
Child raising cost, total, age 12-14	yr	9510	1999	60r
Child raising cost, total, age 15-17	yr	9740	1999	60r
Child's child care and education, age 0-2	yr	1380	1999	60r
Child's child care and education, age 3-5	yr	1520	1999	60r
Child's child care and education, age 6-8	yr	990	1999	60r
Child's child care and education, age 9-11	yr	650	1999	60r
Child's child care and education, age 12-14	yr	490	1999	60r
Child's child care and education, age 15-17	yr	840	1999	60r
Child's clothing, age 0-2	yr	480	1999	60r
Child's clothing, age 3-5	yr	470	1999	60r
Child's clothing, age 6-8	yr	520	1999	60r
Child's clothing, age 9-11	yr	570	1999	60r
Child's clothing, age 12-14	yr	950	1999	60r
Child's clothing, age 15-17	yr	850	1999	60r
Child's food, age 0-2	yr	1000	1999	60r
Child's food, age 3-5	yr	1160	1999	60r
Child's food, age 6-8	yr	1490	1999	60r
Child's food, age 9-11	yr	1770	1999	60r
Child's food, age 12-14	yr	1770	1999	60r
Child's food, age 15-17	yr	1980	1999	60r
Child's health care, age 0-2	yr	620	1999	60r
Child's health care, age 3-5	yr	590	1999	60r
Child's health care, age 6-8	yr	680	1999	60r
Child's health care, age 9-11	yr	720	1999	60r
Child's health care, age 12-14	yr	730	1999	60r
Child's health care, age 15-17	yr	760	1999	60r
Child's housing, age 0-2	yr	3070	1999	60r
Child's housing, age 3-5	yr	3050	1999	60r
Child's housing, age 6-8	yr	3010	1999	60r
Child's housing, age 9-11	yr	2850	1999	60r
Child's housing, age 12-14	yr	3040	1999	60r
Child's housing, age 15-17	yr	2650	1999	60r

Values are in dollars or fractions of dollars. In the column headed *Ref*, references are shown to sources. Each reference is followed by a letter. These refer to the geographical level for which data were reported: s=State, r=Region, and c=City or metro. The abbreviation *ex* is used to mean *except* or *excluding*; *exp* stands for *expenditures*. For other abbreviations and further explanations, please see the Introduction.

San Antonio, TX - continued

Item	Per	Value	Date	Ref.
Child Care				
Child's personal care, reading, age 0-2	yr	910	1999	60r
Child's personal care, reading, age 3-5	yr	930	1999	60r
Child's personal care, reading, age 6-8	yr	960	1999	60r
Child's personal care, reading, age 9-11	yr	1000	1999	60r
Child's personal care, reading, age 12-14	yr	1170	1999	60r
Child's personal care, reading, age 15-17	yr	950	1999	60r
Clothing				
Apparel and services purchases	yr	1610	1999	30r
Boys' brief, cotton	3	5.29	3/01	4c
Boys, 2 to 15, expenditures on	yr	89	1999	30r
Children under 2, expenditures on	yr	79	1999	30r
Footwear, expenditures on	yr	283	1999	30r
Girls, 2 to 15, expenditures on	yr	103	1999	30r
Men and boys, expenditures on	yr	351	1999	30r
Men, 16 and over, expenditures on	yr	262	1999	30r
Shirt, man's dress shirt		25.99	3/01	4c
Slacks, man's "No Wrinkles" khaki		31.58	3/01	4c
Women, 16 and over, expenditures on	yr	538	1999	30r
Communications				
Cable modem installation, AT&T-BIS		150.00	6/99	103s
Cable modem installation, Marcus		499.00	6/99	103s
Cable modem installation, Time Warner		75.00-225.00	6/99	103s
Cable modem rate, cable subscriber, AT&T-BIS	mos	39.95	6/99	103s
Cable modem rate, cable subscriber, Marcus	mos	14.95-49.95	6/99	103s
Cable modem rate, cable subscriber, Time Warner	mos	39.95-49.95	6/99	103s
Cable modem rate, non-cable subscriber, Marcus	mos	60.95	6/99	103s
Cable modem rate, non-cable subscriber, Time Warner	mos	39.95-54.95	6/99	103s
Newspaper subscription, daily and Sunday delivery	mos	14.73	3/01	4c
Phone line, single, business, field visit	inst.	71.90	12/97	17s
Phone line, single, business, no field visit	inst.	57.30	12/97	17s
Phone line, single, residence, field visit	inst.	52.95	12/97	17s
Phone line, single, residence, no field visit	inst.	38.35	12/97	17s
Postage and stationery, expenditures on	yr	104	1999	30r
Postal rate, express mail, up to half-pound		12.45	7/01	108r
Postal rate, letter, first class, first ounce		0.34	7/01	108r
Postal rate, letter, two ounces		0.57	7/01	108r
Postal rate, post card		0.21	7/01	108r
Postal rate, priority mail, two pounds		3.95	7/01	108r
Postal rate, priority mail, up to one pound		3.50	7/01	108r
Telephone bill, business, basic rate	mos	23.10	12/97	18c
Telephone bill, family of three	mos	18.40	3/01	4c
Telephone bill, residential, basic rate	mos	9.85	12/97	18c
Telephone services, expenditures on	yr	860	1999	30r
Education				
Board, 4-year private college/university	yr	2198	1996	38s
Board, 4-year public college/university	yr	1759	1996	38s
Education expenditures	yr	431	1999	30r
Room, 4-year private college/university	yr	2000	1996	38s
Room, 4-year public college/university	yr	1885	1996	38s
Total cost, 4-year private college/university	yr	13156	1996	38s
Total cost, 4-year public college/university	yr	5464	1996	38s
Tuition, 2-year public college/university, in state	yr	771	1996	38s
Tuition, 4-year private college/university, in state	yr	8959	1996	38s
Tuition, 4-year public college/university	yr	1820	1996	38s
Energy and Fuels				
Electricity	KWh	0.09	7/01	11r
Electricity	500 KWhs	47.29	7/01	11r
Energy, combined forms, 2400 sq ft	mos	97.17	3/01	4c
Energy, exc. electricity, 2400 sq ft	mos	22.53	3/01	4c
Fuel oil #2	gal	1.43	7/01	11r

San Antonio, TX - continued

Item	Per	Value	Date	Ref.
Energy and Fuels - continued				
Fuel oil and other fuels, expenditures on	yr	45	1999	30r
Gas, natural, commercial rate	1000 cf	6.94	11/00	88s
Gas, regular unleaded, cash, self-service	gal	1.30	3/01	4c
Gasoline, all types	gal	1.60	7/01	11r
Gasoline, unleaded midgrade	gal	1.65	7/01	11r
Gasoline, unleaded premium	gal	1.74	7/01	11r
Natural gas, expenditures on	yr	164	1999	30r
Utility (piped) gas, therm		1.01	7/01	11r
Utility (piped) gas, 40 therms		44.29	7/01	11r
Utility (piped) gas, 100 therms		97.44	7/01	11r
Entertainment				
Bowling, Saturday evening rate	line	3.20	3/01	4c
Entertainment purchases	yr	1574	1999	30r
Fees and admissions paid	yr	371	1999	30r
Monopoly game, Parker Brothers', No. 9	game	11.74	3/01	4c
Movie, first-run, Saturday, evening	adm.	7.15	3/01	4c
Reading purchases	yr	121	1999	30r
Sea-World ticket price	day	33.95	2000	71c
Television, radios, sound equipment, expenditures on	yr	561	1999	30r
Tennis balls, yellow, Wilson or Penn, 3	can	2.12	3/01	4c
Funerals				
Total cost of funeral		5842.28	1/99	78r
Acknowledgement cards		28.35	1/99	78r
Casket		2494.29	1/99	78r
Cosmetology, hair, other preparation		109.22	1/99	78r
Embalming		361.42	1/99	78r
Funeral at funeral home		349.20	1/99	78r
Hearse (local)		161.91	1/99	78r
Professional service charges		1116.50	1/99	78r
Service car/van		65.56	1/99	78r
Transfer of remains to funeral home		143.56	1/99	78r
Vault		785.25	1/99	78r
Visitation/viewing		227.02	1/99	78r
Groceries				
Groceries, ACCRA Index		86.70	3/01	4c
American processed cheese	lb	3.50	7/01	11r
Antibiotic ointment, Polysporin	0.5 oz	4.43	3/01	4c
Baby food, strained vegetables or fruit, lowest price	4-4.5 oz	0.26	3/01	4c
Bakery products, expenditures on	yr	261	1999	30r
Bananas	lb	0.35	3/01	4c
Bananas	lb	0.47	7/01	11r
Beans, dried, any type, all sizes	lb	0.63	7/01	11r
Beef for stew, boneless	lb	2.86	7/01	11r
Beef or hamburger, ground	lb	1.69	3/01	4c
Beef, expenditures on	yr	210	1999	30r
Bologna, all beef or mixed	lb	2.29	7/01	11r
Bread, French	lb	1.66	7/01	11r
Bread, white	loaf	0.72	3/01	4c
Bread, white, pan	lb	0.87	7/01	11r
Bread, whole wheat, pan	lb	1.38	7/01	11r
Broccoli	lb	1.04	7/01	11r
Butter, salted, grade AA, stick	lb	2.26	7/01	11r
Butter, yoghurt, cheese, etc, expenditures on	yr	170	1999	30r
Cabbage	lb	0.42	7/01	11r
Cereals and cereal products, expenditures on	yr	140	1999	30r
Cheddar cheese, natural	lb	3.75	7/01	11r
Cheese, Kraft grated Parmesan	8 oz	3.95	3/01	4c
Chicken breast, bone-in	lb	1.85	7/01	11r
Chicken legs, bone-in	lb	1.34	7/01	11r
Chicken, fresh, whole	lb	1.05	7/01	11r
Chicken, whole fryer	lb	0.73	3/01	4c
Chops, boneless,	lb	4.13	7/01	11r
Chuck roast, graded and ungraded, excl U.S. prime and choice	lb	2.35	7/01	11r
Chuck roast, U.S. choice, boneless	lb	2.67	7/01	11r
Cigarettes, Winston, Kings	carton	33.03	3/01	4c
Coffee, 100%, ground roast, all sizes	lb	2.88	7/01	11r
Coffee, instant, plain, regular, all sizes	16 oz	9.25	7/01	11r

Values are in dollars or fractions of dollars. In the column headed *Ref*, references are shown to sources. Each reference is followed by a letter. These refer to the geographical level for which data were reported: s=State, r=Region, and c=City or metro. The abbreviation *ex* is used to mean *except* or *excluding*; *exp* stands for *expenditures*. For other abbreviations and further explanations, please see the Introduction.

San Antonio, TX - continued

Item	Per	Value	Date	Ref.
Groceries				
Coffee, vacuum-packed	13 oz	2.62	3/01	4c
Cola, non diet,	2 liter	1.11	7/01	11r
Corn Flakes, Kellogg's or Post Toasties	18 oz	2.08	3/01	4c
Corn, frozen, whole kernel, lowest price	16 oz	1.12	3/01	4c
Crackers, soda, salted	lb	1.70	7/01	11r
Dairy product purchases	yr	282	1999	30r
Eggs, expenditures on	yr	32	1999	30r
Eggs, Grade A or AA	dozen	1.07	3/01	4c
Fats and oils, expenditures on	yr	79	1999	30r
Fish and seafood, expenditures on	yr	99	1999	30r
Flour, white, all purpose	lb	0.32	7/01	11r
Food (excl fruit and vegetables), eaten at home, purchases	yr	815	1999	30r
Food cooked on trips, expenditures on	yr	36	1999	30r
Food purchases	yr	4533	1999	30r
Food purchases, eaten away from home	yr	1873	1999	30r
Food purchases, food eaten at home	yr	2660	1999	30r
Fresh fruits, expenditures on	yr	128	1999	30r
Fresh milk and cream, expenditures on	yr	112	1999	30r
Fresh vegetables, expenditures on	yr	131	1999	30r
Fruit and vegetable purchases	yr	438	1999	30r
Grapefruit	lb	0.59	7/01	11r
Grapes, Thompson, seedless	lb	2.12	7/01	11r
Ground beef, 100% beef	lb	1.76	7/01	11r
Ground beef, lean and extra lean	lb	2.60	7/01	11r
Ground chuck, 100% beef	lb	2.08	7/01	11r
Ham, boneless, excl canned	lb	2.71	7/01	11r
Ham, rump or shank half, bone-in, smoked	lb	2.19	7/01	11r
Ice cream, prepackaged, bulk, regular	1/2 gal	3.93	7/01	11r
Lemons	lb	1.32	7/01	11r
Lettuce, iceberg	head	0.83	3/01	4c
Lettuce, iceberg	lb	0.76	7/01	11r
Margarine, Blue Bonnet or Parkay, stick	lb	0.80	3/01	4c
Milk, fresh, low fat,	gal	2.75	7/01	11r
Milk, fresh, whole, fortified	gal	2.97	7/01	11r
Milk, whole	1/2 gal	1.54	3/01	4c
Nonalcoholic beverages, expenditures on	yr	228	1999	30r
Orange juice, frozen concentrate	16 oz	1.95	7/01	11r
Orange juice, Minute Maid frozen	12 oz	1.23	3/01	4c
Oranges, Navel	lb	0.73	7/01	11r
Oranges, Valencia	lb	0.55	7/01	11r
Peaches, halves or slices, Hunt's, Del Monte, or Libby's	29 oz	1.50	3/01	4c
Peanut butter, creamy, all sizes	lb	1.83	7/01	11r
Pears, Anjou	lb	0.98	7/01	11r
Peas, green, Del Monte or Green Giant	15 oz	0.66	3/01	4c
Pork chops, center cut, bone-in	lb	3.33	7/01	11r
Pork sausage, fresh, loose	lb	2.59	7/01	11r
Pork shoulder picnic, bone-in, smoked	lb	1.12	7/01	11r
Pork, expenditures on	yr	162	1999	30r
Potato chips	16 oz	3.59	7/01	11r
Potatoes, frozen, french fried	lb	1.00	7/01	11r
Potatoes, white or red	10 lb	2.32	3/01	4c
Potatoes, white, all types	lb	0.44	7/01	11r
Poultry, expenditures on	yr	137	1999	30r
Processed fruits, expenditures on	yr	97	1999	30r
Processed vegetables, expenditures on	yr	82	1999	30r
Rice, white, long grain, uncooked	lb	0.51	7/01	11r
Round roast, graded and ungraded, excl U.S. prime and choice	lb	2.96	7/01	11r
Round steak, graded and ungraded, excl U.S. prime and choice	lb	3.11	7/01	11r
Sausage, Jimmy Dean/Owens pork	lb	2.57	3/01	4c
Shortening, vegetable, Crisco	3 lb	2.76	3/01	4c
Sirloin steak, graded and ungraded, excl U.S. prime and choice	lb	4.23	7/01	11r
Soft drink, Coca Cola, ex deposit	2 liter	1.16	3/01	4c
Spaghetti and macaroni	lb	0.78	7/01	11r
Steak, round, U.S. choice, boneless	lb	3.56	7/01	11r
Steak, sirloin, U.S. choice, boneless	lb	5.65	7/01	11r
Steak, T-bone	lb	5.23	3/01	4c
Strawberries, dry pint	12 oz	1.50	7/01	11r

San Antonio, TX - continued

Item	Per	Value	Date	Ref.
Groceries - continued				
Sugar and other sweets, expenditures on	yr	99	1999	30r
Sugar, cane or beet	4 lbs	1.47	3/01	4c
Sugar, white, 33-80 ounce package	lb	0.39	7/01	11r
Sugar, white, all sizes	lb	0.42	7/01	11r
Tobacco products and smoking supplies purchases	yr	288	1999	30r
Tomatoes, field grown	lb	1.43	7/01	11r
Tomatoes, Hunt's or Del Monte	14.5 oz	0.72	3/01	4c
Tuna, chunk, light	6 oz	0.43	3/01	4c
Tuna, light, chunk	lb	1.77	7/01	11r
Turkey, frozen, whole	lb	1.05	7/01	11r
Goods and Services				
Miscellaneous goods and services, ACCRA Index		99.90	3/01	4c
B&B Japanese maple (acer japonicum)	gal	79.98-99.00	4/00	93r
Boxwood (buxus)	2 gal	12.98-18.99	4/00	93r
Christmas tree, noble fir		40-60	2000	65s
Daylilly (hemerocallis)	gal	7.96-11.00	4/00	93r
Flat of annuals		13.99-27.99	4/00	93r
Fountain grass (pennisetum)	gal	6.96-9.00	4/00	93r
Hanging basket (10 in)		9.99-24.99	4/00	93r
Hardy geranium (geranium)	gal	5.96-8.00	4/00	93r
Hosta (hosta)	gal	8.96-12.99	4/00	93r
Lilac (syrubga vulgaris)	2 gal	13.00-19.99	4/00	93r
Rhododendron (rhododendron)	2 gal	12.98-29.99	4/00	93r
Sage (salvia)	gal	5.96-8.00	4/00	93r
Wintercreeper euonymus (euonymus fortunei)	2 gal	13.00-18.99	4/00	93r
Hunting license	yr	19.00	4/01	34s
Health Care				
Health care, ACCRA Index		89.30	3/01	4c
Cardiac catheterization, ave hospital/ physician charges		20140	1998	77s
Childbirth, Cesarean delivery		11587	1997	13r
Childbirth, vaginal delivery		6725	1997	13r
Dentist's fee, adult teeth cleaning and periodic oral exam	visit	60.40	3/01	4c
Doctor's fee, routine exam, established patient	visit	54.80	3/01	4c
Drugs, expenditures on	yr	399	1999	30r
Health care purchases	yr	1971	1999	30r
Health insurance expenditures	yr	933	1999	30r
Home health care aide cost, licensed agency	hour	12	2000	82c
Hospital care, private room	day	459.00	3/01	4c
Hysterectomy, laproscopically-assisted, ave hospital/physician charges		15700	1998	76s
Hysterectomy, vaginal, ave hospital and physician charges		12180	1998	76s
Medicaid dispensing fee		5.27	1999	87s
Medical services expenditures	yr	547	1999	30r
Medical supplies, expenditures on	yr	91	1999	30r
Nursing home costs, private room	day	114	2000	82c
Nursing home stay, private room	day	114	2000	83c
Household Goods				
Dishwashing powder, Cascade	50 oz	3.09	3/01	4c
Floor coverings, expenditures on	yr	44	1999	30r
Furniture, expenditures on	yr	335	1999	30r
Household furnishings and equipment purchases	yr	1328	1999	30r
Household textiles, expenditures on	yr	89	1999	30r

Values are in dollars or fractions of dollars. In the column headed *Ref*, references are shown to sources. Each reference is followed by a letter. These refer to the geographical level for which data were reported: s=State, r=Region, and c=City or metro. The abbreviation *ex* is used to mean *except* or *excluding*; *exp* stands for expenditures. For other abbreviations and further explanations, please see the Introduction.

San Antonio, TX - continued

Item	Per	Value	Date	Ref.
Household Goods				
Laundry and cleaning supplies, expenditures on	yr	113	1999	30r
Tissues, facial, Kleenex brand	175	1.23	3/01	4c
Housing				
Housing, ACCRA Index		84.20	3/01	4c
Home, 2200 sq ft, 4-br, 2-bath, 2-car garage, average		193225	2000	47c
Home, suburban, 2,200 square feet		122600	2000	23c
Home price, existing, ave		160100	10/00	90r
Home value, median		112000	2001	53s
House, 2400 sq ft, 8000 sq ft lot, new, urban, utilities	total	173691	3/01	4c
House payment, principal and interest, 25% down payment	mos	851	3/01	4c
Household operation expenditures	yr	553	1999	30r
Housekeeping supplies purchases	yr	473	1999	30r
Housing, expenditures on	yr	10303	1999	30r
Maintenance, repairs, insurance expenditures	yr	699	1999	30r
Monthly rental value of owned home	mos	505	1999	30r
Owned dwellings, expenditures own	yr	3465	1999	30r
Rent expenditures	yr	1641	1999	30r
Rent, apartment, 2 br, 1 1/2-2 baths, unfurn, 950 sq ft, water	mos	630	3/01	4c
Rental unit, 1 bedroom, with utilities	mos	434	4/01	41c
Rental unit, 2 bedroom, with utilities	mos	561	4/01	41c
Rental unit, 3 bedroom, with utilities	mos	781	4/01	41c
Rental unit, 4 bedroom, with utilities	mos	923	4/01	41c
Shelter, expenditures on	yr	5467	1999	30r
Insurance and Pensions				
Life and other personal insurance purchases	yr	414	1999	30r
Pensions and Social Security, expenditures on	yr	2635	1999	30r
Personal insurance and pensions, expenditures on	yr	3048	1999	30r
Legal Fees				
Divorce, filing fee		150.00-200.00	4/01	35s
Driver's license fee	orig	24.00	1999	48s
Driver's license fee	renew	20.00	1999	48s
Fishing license	yr	19.00	4/01	34s
Personal Goods				
Personal care products and services purchases	yr	393	1999	30r
Shampoo, Alberto VO5	15 oz	1.04	3/01	4c
Toothpaste, Crest or Colgate	6-7 oz	2.28	3/01	4c
Personal Services				
Dry cleaning, man's 2-pc suit		7.56	3/01	4c
Man's haircut, barbershop, no styling		7.60	3/01	4c
Personal services, household, expenditures on	yr	258	1999	30r
Woman's shampoo, trim, blow-dry, no style-change		29.40	3/01	4c
Pets				
Pets, toys, and playground equipment, expenditures on	yr	306	1999	30r
Restaurant Food				
Chicken, fried, thigh and drumstick, KFC/Church's		2.47	3/01	4c
Hamburger with cheese, McDonald's	1/4 lb	2.22	3/01	4c
Pizza, Pizza Hut or Pizza Inn	11-12 in	9.79	3/01	4c
Taxes				
Federal income taxes paid	yr	2047	1999	30r
Personal taxes, expenditures on	yr	2554	1999	30r
Property taxes paid	yr	726	1999	30r
State and local income taxes paid	yr	363	1999	30r

San Antonio, TX - continued

Item	Per	Value	Date	Ref.
Transportation				
Transportation, ACCRA Index		88.20	3/01	4c
Bus fare, one-way	trip	0.75	2000	1c
Bus fare, to central business district	1-way	1.58	3/01	4c
Cars and trucks, new, expenditures on	yr	1648	1999	30r
Cars and trucks, used, expenditures on	yr	1651	1999	30r
Diesel at the pump	gal	1.18	10/99	73s
Gasoline and motor oil purchases	yr	1052	1999	30r
Gasoline before-tax price (cents)	gal	101.30	10/00	43s
Maintenance and repair expenditures	yr	621	1999	30r
Public transportation, expenditures on	yr	298	1999	30r
Tire balance, computer or spin balance, front	wheel	5.20	3/01	4c
Transportation purchases	yr	6738	1999	30r
Vehicle expenses, miscellaneous, purchases	yr	2033	1999	30r
Vehicle insurance payments	yr	696	1999	30r
Vehicle purchases (net outlay)	yr	3354	1999	30r
Vehicle rental, lease expenditures	yr	352	1999	30r
Utilities				
Utilities, ACCRA Index		80.30	3/01	4c
Electrical bill, average	mos	87.17	9/00	9s
Electricity, expenditures on	yr	1115	1999	30r
Electricity and other, mixed, 2400 sq ft, new home	mos	74.64	3/01	4c
Electricity cost, average	KWh	6.48	9/00	9s
Water and other public services, expenditures on	yr	298	1999	30r
Weddings				
Wedding (national average cost)		19936	2000	33r
Attendants' gifts		321	1998	33r
Bridal attendants' apparel (5 persons)		824	2000	33r
Bride's headpiece/veil		173	1998	33r
Bride's wedding dress		859	1998	33r
Clergy, religious facility fee		242	1998	33r
Engagement ring		3177	1998	33r
Flowers		789	1998	33r
Groom's formalwear rental		99	2000	33r
Limousine		410	1998	33r
Marriage license cost		36.00	4/01	35s
Men's formalwear (ushers, best man)		469	2000	33r
Mother of bride apparel		241	2000	33r
Music		866	1998	33r
Photography and videography		1368	1998	33r
Rehearsal dinner		728	1998	33r
Wedding invitations and announcements		341	1998	33r
Wedding reception		7968	2000	33r
Wedding rings (bride and groom)		1060	1998	33r

San Diego, CA

Item	Per	Value	Date	Ref.
Average annual expenditures	yr	44235	1999	30c
Composite, ACCRA index		127.00	3/01	4c
Alcoholic Beverages				
Alcoholic beverage purchases	yr	462	1999	30c
Beer, Heineken, 12-oz, ex deposit	6	7.20	3/01	4c
J & B Scotch	750-ml	19.11	3/01	4c
Malt beverages, all types, all sizes, any origin	16 oz	0.94	7/01	11r
Wine, Livingston or Gallo, Chablis blanc	1.5 liter	5.89	3/01	4c
Wine, red and white table, all sizes, any origin	liter	6.00	7/01	11r
Appliances				
Appliance repair, service call, washing machine	min lab chg	45.32	3/01	4c
Major appliances, expenditures on	yr	167	1999	30r
Small appliances, housewares, expenditures on	yr	105	1999	30r
Banking and Money				
Mortgage interest and charges paid	yr	3368	1999	30r
Mortgage principal paid on owned property	yr	1677	1999	30r
Mortgage rate, incl. points and orig. fee, 30-yr. conv. fixed or ARM	mos	6.81	3/01	4c

Values are in dollars or fractions of dollars. In the column headed *Ref*, references are shown to sources. Each reference is followed by a letter. These refer to the geographical level for which data were reported: s=State, r=Region, and c=City or metro. The abbreviation *ex* is used to mean *except* or *excluding*; *exp* stands for *expenditures*. For other abbreviations and further explanations, please see the Introduction.

San Diego, CA - continued

Item	Per	Value	Date	Ref.
Banking and Money				
Vehicle finance charges paid	yr	311	1999	30r
Business Expenses				
Business travel, car rental	day	54	2001	3c
Business travel, food	day	56	2001	3c
Business travel, hotel	day	143	2001	3c
Medical office space cost	sq ft	127.40	2001	31c
Office space, 2-4 storey building	sq ft	111.62	2001	31c
Office space, 5-10 storey building	sq ft	98.59	2001	31c
Office space, 11-20 storey building	sq ft	94.77	2001	31c
Charity				
Cash contributions, expenditures	yr	842	1999	30c
Child Care				
Child raising cost, total, age 0-2	yr	9140	1999	60r
Child raising cost, total, age 3-5	yr	9370	1999	60r
Child raising cost, total, age 6-8	yr	9450	1999	60r
Child raising cost, total, age 9-11	yr	9470	1999	60r
Child raising cost, total, age 12-14	yr	10170	1999	60r
Child raising cost, total, age 15-17	yr	10360	1999	60r
Child's child care and education, age 0-2	yr	1250	1999	60r
Child's child care and education, age 3-5	yr	1380	1999	60r
Child's child care and education, age 6-8	yr	890	1999	60r
Child's child care and education, age 9-11	yr	580	1999	60r
Child's child care and education, age 12-14	yr	430	1999	60r
Child's child care and education, age 15-17	yr	730	1999	60r
Child's clothing, age 0-2	yr	430	1999	60r
Child's clothing, age 3-5	yr	420	1999	60r
Child's clothing, age 6-8	yr	470	1999	60r
Child's clothing, age 9-11	yr	520	1999	60r
Child's clothing, age 12-14	yr	870	1999	60r
Child's clothing, age 15-17	yr	770	1999	60r
Child's food, age 0-2	yr	1120	1999	60r
Child's food, age 3-5	yr	1280	1999	60r
Child's food, age 6-8	yr	1640	1999	60r
Child's food, age 9-11	yr	1930	1999	60r
Child's food, age 12-14	yr	1940	1999	60r
Child's food, age 15-17	yr	2150	1999	60r
Child's health care, age 0-2	yr	490	1999	60r
Child's health care, age 3-5	yr	470	1999	60r
Child's health care, age 6-8	yr	530	1999	60r
Child's health care, age 9-11	yr	570	1999	60r
Child's health care, age 12-14	yr	580	1999	60r
Child's health care, age 15-17	yr	610	1999	60r
Child's housing, age 0-2	yr	3630	1999	60r
Child's housing, age 3-5	yr	3610	1999	60r
Child's housing, age 6-8	yr	3570	1999	60r
Child's housing, age 9-11	yr	3410	1999	60r
Child's housing, age 12-14	yr	3600	1999	60r
Child's housing, age 15-17	yr	3210	1999	60r
Child's personal care, reading, age 0-2	yr	1040	1999	60r
Child's personal care, reading, age 3-5	yr	1060	1999	60r
Child's personal care, reading, age 6-8	yr	1090	1999	60r
Child's personal care, reading, age 9-11	yr	1130	1999	60r
Child's personal care, reading, age 12-14	yr	1300	1999	60r
Child's personal care, reading, age 15-17	yr	1080	1999	60r
Clothing				
Apparel and services purchases	yr	2018	1999	30c
Boys' brief, cotton	3	6.00	3/01	4c
Boys, 2 to 15, expenditures on	yr	80	1999	30r
Children under 2, expenditures on	yr	74	1999	30r
Footwear, expenditures on	yr	307	1999	30r
Girls, 2 to 15, expenditures on	yr	101	1999	30r
Men and boys, expenditures on	yr	443	1999	30r
Men, 16 and over, expenditures on	yr	363	1999	30r
Shirt, man's dress shirt		29.08	3/01	4c
Slacks, man's "No Wrinkles" khaki		35.99	3/01	4c
Women, 16 and over, expenditures on	yr	594	1999	30r
Communications				
Cable modem installation, AT&T-BIS		150.00	6/99	103s

San Diego, CA - continued

Item	Per	Value	Date	Ref.
Communications - continued				
Cable modem installation, Charter		99.00-169.00	6/99	103s
Cable modem installation, Comcast		95.00	6/99	103s
Cable modem installation, Cox		99.00-174.95	6/99	103s
Cable modem installation, Media One		100.00	6/99	103s
Cable modem installation, Time Warner		75.00-225.00	6/99	103s
Cable modem rate, cable subscriber, AT&T-BIS	mos	39.95	6/99	103s
Cable modem rate, cable subscriber, Charter	mos	49.95-79.95	6/99	103s
Cable modem rate, cable subscriber, Comcast	mos	39.95	6/99	103s
Cable modem rate, cable subscriber, Cox	mos	29.95-44.95	6/99	103s
Cable modem rate, cable subscriber, Media One	mos	34.95-39.95	6/99	103s
Cable modem rate, cable subscriber, Time Warner	mos	39.95-49.95	6/99	103s
Cable modem rate, non-cable subscriber, Charter	mos	59.95-89.95	6/99	103s
Cable modem rate, non-cable subscriber, Comcast	mos	49.95	6/99	103s
Cable modem rate, non-cable subscriber, Cox	mos	42.95-54.95	6/99	103s
Cable modem rate, non-cable subscriber, Media One	mos	49.95	6/99	103s
Cable modem rate, non-cable subscriber, Time Warner	mos	39.95-54.95	6/99	103s
Newspaper subscription, daily and Sunday delivery	mos	13.00	3/01	4c
Phone line, single, business, field visit	inst.	70.75	12/97	17s
Phone line, single, business, no field visit	inst.	70.75	12/97	17s
Phone line, single, residence, field visit	inst.	34.75	12/97	17s
Phone line, single, residence, no field visit	inst.	34.75	12/97	17s
Postage and stationery, expenditures on	yr	150	1999	30r
Postal rate, express mail, up to half-pound		12.45	7/01	108r
Postal rate, letter, first class, first ounce		0.34	7/01	108r
Postal rate, letter, two ounces		0.57	7/01	108r
Postal rate, post card		0.21	7/01	108r
Postal rate, priority mail, two pounds		3.95	7/01	108r
Postal rate, priority mail, up to one pound		3.50	7/01	108r
Telephone bill, business, basic rate	mos	10.32	12/97	18c
Telephone bill, family of three	mos	27.80	3/01	4c
Telephone bill, residential, basic rate	mos	3.00	12/97	18c
Telephone services, expenditures on	yr	825	1999	30r
Wireless services	mos	42.48	1/00	42c
Education				
Board, 4-year private college/university	yr	2970	1996	38s
Board, 4-year public college/university	yr	2516	1996	38s
Education expenditures	yr	398	1999	30c
Room, 4-year private college/university	yr	3196	1996	38s
Room, 4-year public college/university	yr	3031	1996	38s
Total cost, 4-year private college/university	yr	20143	1996	38s
Total cost, 4-year public college/university	yr	8213	1996	38s
Tuition, 2-year public college/university, in state	yr	362	1996	38s
Tuition, 4-year private college/university, in state	yr	13977	1996	38s
Tuition, 4-year public college/university	yr	2666	1996	38s
Energy and Fuels				
Electricity	KWh	0.11	7/01	11r
Electricity	500 KWhs	48.23	7/01	11r
Energy, combined forms, 2400 sq ft	mos	128.05	3/01	4c
Energy, exc. electricity, 2400 sq ft	mos	70.99	3/01	4c
Fuel oil and other fuels, expenditures on	yr	35	1999	30r
Gas, cooking, winter, 10 therms	mos	6.12	2/96	98c
Gas, cooking, winter, 30 therms	mos	18.35	2/96	98c
Gas, cooking, winter, 50 therms	mos	32.19	2/96	98c

Values are in dollars or fractions of dollars. In the column headed *Ref*, references are shown to sources. Each reference is followed by a letter. These refer to the geographical level for which data were reported: s=State, r=Region, and c=City or metro. The abbreviation *ex* is used to mean *except* or *excluding*; *exp* stands for *expenditures*. For other abbreviations and further explanations, please see the Introduction.

San Diego, CA - continued

Item	Per	Value	Date	Ref.
Energy and Fuels				
Gas, heating, winter, average use	mos	33.85	2/96	98c
Gas, natural, commercial rate	1000 cf	8.74	11/00	88s
Gas, regular unleaded, cash, self-service	gal	1.76	3/01	4c
Gasoline, all types	gal	1.91	7/01	11r
Gasoline, unleaded premium	gal	2.05	7/01	11r
Gasoline, unleaded regular	gal	1.83	7/01	11r
Natural gas, expenditures on	yr	255	1999	30r
Utility (piped) gas, therm		0.98	7/01	11r
Utility (piped) gas, 40 therms		40.74	7/01	11r
Utility (piped) gas, 100 therms		96.80	7/01	11r
Entertainment				
Bowling, Saturday evening rate	line	3.03	3/01	4c
Entertainment purchases	yr	2684	1999	30c
Fees and admissions paid	yr	545	1999	30r
Monopoly game, Parker Brothers', No. 9	game	12.99	3/01	4c
Movie, first-run, Saturday, evening	adm.	8.30	3/01	4c
Television, radios, sound equipment, expenditures on	yr	624	1999	30r
Tennis balls, yellow, Wilson or Penn, 3	can	2.29	3/01	4c
Funerals				
Total cost of funeral		5401.08	1/99	78r
Acknowledgement cards		33.64	1/99	78r
Casket		2170.43	1/99	78r
Cosmetology, hair, other preparation		136.32	1/99	78r
Embalming		319.13	1/99	78r
Funeral at funeral home		370.21	1/99	78r
Hearse (local)		161.04	1/99	78r
Professional service charges		963.15	1/99	78r
Service car/van		133.99	1/99	78r
Transfer of remains to funeral home		159.82	1/99	78r
Vault		778.07	1/99	78r
Visitation/viewing		175.28	1/99	78r
Groceries				
Groceries, ACCRA Index		120.00	3/01	4c
Antibiotic ointment, Polysporin	0.5 oz	5.00	3/01	4c
Apples, red delicious	lb	0.84	7/01	11r
Baby food, strained vegetables or fruit, lowest price	4-4.5 oz	0.52	3/01	4c
Bacon, sliced	lb	3.38	7/01	11r
Bakery products, expenditures on	yr	299	1999	30r
Bananas	lb	0.64	3/01	4c
Bananas	lb	0.54	7/01	11r
Beans, dried, any type, all sizes	lb	0.76	7/01	11r
Beef or hamburger, ground	lb	2.20	3/01	4c
Beef, expenditures on	yr	222	1999	30r
Bread, white	loaf	1.26	3/01	4c
Bread, white, pan	lb	0.99	7/01	11r
Butter, yoghurt, cheese, etc, expenditures on	yr	211	1999	30r
Cereals and bakery product purchases	yr	444	1999	30c
Cereals and cereal products, expenditures on	yr	168	1999	30r
Cheese, Kraft grated Parmesan	8 oz	4.06	3/01	4c
Chicken breast, bone-in	lb	2.45	7/01	11r
Chicken, fresh, whole	lb	1.19	7/01	11r
Chicken, whole fryer	lb	1.06	3/01	4c
Chops, boneless,	lb	4.00	7/01	11r
Chuck roast, graded and ungraded, excl U.S. prime and choice	lb	2.55	7/01	11r
Cigarettes, Winston, Kings	carton	36.79	3/01	4c
Coffee, 100%, ground roast, all sizes	lb	3.80	7/01	11r
Coffee, vacuum-packed	13 oz	3.54	3/01	4c
Cookies, chocolate chip	lb	2.83	7/01	11r
Corn Flakes, Kellogg's or Post Toasties	18 oz	3.08	3/01	4c
Corn, frozen, whole kernel, lowest price	16 oz	1.09	3/01	4c
Dairy product purchases	yr	304	1999	30c
Eggs, expenditures on	yr	39	1999	30r
Eggs, Grade A or AA	dozen	2.01	3/01	4c
Eggs, grade AA, large	dozen	1.23	7/01	11r
Fats and oils, expenditures on	yr	88	1999	30r
Fish and seafood, expenditures on	yr	121	1999	30r

San Diego, CA - continued

Item	Per	Value	Date	Ref.
Groceries - continued				
Food (excl fruit and vegetables), eaten at home, purchases	yr	901	1999	30c
Food cooked on trips, expenditures on	yr	64	1999	30r
Food purchases	yr	5292	1999	30c
Food purchases, eaten away from home	yr	2443	1999	30c
Food purchases, food eaten at home	yr	2849	1999	30c
Fresh fruits, expenditures on	yr	186	1999	30r
Fresh milk and cream, expenditures on	yr	130	1999	30r
Fresh vegetables, expenditures on	yr	177	1999	30r
Grapefruit	lb	0.68	7/01	11r
Grapes, Thompson, seedless	lb	2.42	7/01	11r
Ground beef, lean and extra lean	lb	2.46	7/01	11r
Ice cream, prepackaged, bulk, regular	1/2 gal	3.62	7/01	11r
Lettuce, iceberg	head	0.99	3/01	4c
Lettuce, iceberg	lb	0.63	7/01	11r
Margarine, Blue Bonnet or Parkay, stick	lb	0.79	3/01	4c
Meats, poultry, fish, and egg purchases	yr	671	1999	30c
Milk, fresh, low fat	gal	2.80	7/01	11r
Milk, fresh, whole, fortified	gal	2.88	7/01	11r
Milk, whole	1/2 gal	2.30	3/01	4c
Nonalcoholic beverages, expenditures on	yr	258	1999	30r
Orange juice, Minute Maid frozen	12 oz	1.72	3/01	4c
Oranges, Navel	lb	0.97	7/01	11r
Oranges, Valencia	lb	0.43	7/01	11r
Peaches	lb	1.38	7/01	11r
Peaches, halves or slices, Hunt's, Del Monte, or Libby's	29 oz	1.44	3/01	4c
Peanut butter, creamy, all sizes	lb	2.14	7/01	11r
Peas, green, Del Monte or Green Giant	15 oz	0.85	3/01	4c
Pork chops, center cut, bone-in	lb	3.83	7/01	11r
Pork, expenditures on	yr	141	1999	30r
Potatoes, white or red	10 lb	2.49	3/01	4c
Potatoes, white, all types	lb	0.37	7/01	11r
Poultry, expenditures on	yr	146	1999	30r
Processed fruits, expenditures on	yr	118	1999	30r
Processed vegetables, expenditures on	yr	81	1999	30r
Round roast, graded and ungraded, excl U.S. prime and choice	lb	3.07	7/01	11r
Round roast, U.S. choice, boneless	lb	3.37	7/01	11r
Round steak, graded and ungraded, excl U.S. prime and choice	lb	3.51	7/01	11r
Sausage, Jimmy Dean/Owens pork	lb	3.44	3/01	4c
Shortening, vegetable, Crisco	3 lb	3.64	3/01	4c
Sirloin steak, graded and ungraded, excl U.S. prime and choice	lb	4.67	7/01	11r
Soft drink, Coca Cola, ex deposit	2 liter	1.27	3/01	4c
Steak, sirloin, U.S. choice, boneless	lb	6.20	7/01	11r
Steak, T-bone	lb	8.19	3/01	4c
Strawberries, dry pint	12 oz	1.79	7/01	11r
Sugar and other sweets, expenditures on	yr	124	1999	30r
Sugar, cane or beet	4 lbs	1.89	3/01	4c
Sugar, white, all sizes	lb	0.46	7/01	11r
Tobacco products and smoking supplies purchases	yr	166	1999	30c
Tomatoes, field grown	lb	1.17	7/01	11r
Tomatoes, Hunt's or Del Monte	14.5 oz	0.96	3/01	4c
Tuna, chunk, light	6 oz	0.92	3/01	4c
Tuna, light, chunk	lb	2.05	7/01	11r
Goods and Services				
Miscellaneous goods and services, ACCRA Index		106.90	3/01	4c
B&B Japanese maple (acer japonicum)	gal	39.99	4/00	93r
Boxwood (buxus)	2 gal	14.99-24.99	4/00	93r
Christmas tree, noble fir		40-60	2000	65s
Daylilly (hemerocallis)	gal	6.99-8.99	4/00	93r
Flat of annuals		16.68	4/00	93r
Fountain grass (pennisetum)	gal	7.99-11.99	4/00	93r
Hanging basket (10 in)		29.99	4/00	93r

Values are in dollars or fractions of dollars. In the column headed *Ref*, references are shown to sources. Each reference is followed by a letter. These refer to the geographical level for which data were reported: s=State, r=Region, and c=City or metro. The abbreviation *ex* is used to mean *except* or *excluding*; *exp* stands for *expenditures*. For other abbreviations and further explanations, please see the Introduction.

San Diego, CA - continued

Item	Per	Value	Date	Ref.
Goods and Services				
Hardy geranium (geranium)	gal	6.99-11.99	4/00	93r
Hosta (hosta)	gal	6.99-18.99	4/00	93r
Lilac (syrubga vulgaris)	2 gal	14.99-17.99	4/00	93r
Miscellaneous purchases	yr	898	1999	30c
Rhododendron (rhododendron)	2 gal	14.99	4/00	93r
Sage (salvia)	gal	6.99	4/00	93r
Wintercreeper euonymus (euonymus fortunei)	2 gal	14.99-22.99	4/00	93r
Hunting license	yr	29.95	4/01	34s
Health Care				
Health care, ACCRA Index		122.20	3/01	4c
Cardiac catheterization, ave hospital/physician charges		24000	1998	77s
Childbirth, Cesarean delivery		11587	1997	13r
Childbirth, vaginal delivery		6725	1997	13r
Dentist's fee, adult teeth cleaning and periodic oral exam	visit	91.14	3/01	4c
Doctor's fee, routine exam, established patient	visit	58.17	3/01	4c
Drugs, expenditures on	yr	309	1999	30r
Health care purchases	yr	1850	1999	30c
Health insurance expenditures	yr	868	1999	30r
Hospital care, private room	day	874.83	3/01	4c
Hysterectomy, laproscopically-assisted, ave hospital/physician charges		20760	1998	76s
Hysterectomy, vaginal, ave hospital and physician charges		14570	1998	76s
Medicaid dispensing fee		4.05	1999	87s
Medical services expenditures	yr	580	1999	30r
Medical supplies, expenditures on	yr	112	1999	30r
Nursing home costs, private room	day	149	2000	82c
Nursing home stay, private room	day	149	2000	81c
Household Goods				
Dishwashing powder, Cascade	50 oz	3.57	3/01	4c
Floor coverings, expenditures on	yr	49	1999	30r
Furniture, expenditures on	yr	444	1999	30r
Household furnishings and equipment purchases	yr	2327	1999	30c
Household textiles, expenditures on	yr	141	1999	30r
Laundry and cleaning supplies, expenditures on	yr	128	1999	30r
Tissues, facial, Kleenex brand	175	1.38	3/01	4c
Housing				
Housing, ACCRA Index		164.50	3/01	4c
Home, 2200 sq ft, 4-br, 2-bath, 2-car garage, average		390500	2000	47c
Home, suburban, 2,200 square feet		312300	2000	23c
Home price, existing, ave		239400	10/00	90r
Home value, median		215000	2001	53s
House, 2400 sq ft, 8000 sq ft lot, new, urban, utilities	total	340000	3/01	4c
House payment, principal and interest, 25% down payment	mos	1665	3/01	4c
Household operation expenditures	yr	990	1999	30c
Housekeeping supplies purchases	yr	514	1999	30c
Lodging expenditures	yr	600	1999	30c
Maintenance, repairs, insurance expenditures	yr	939	1999	30r
Monthly rental value of owned home	mos	662	1999	30r
Owned dwellings, expenditures own	yr	6105	1999	30c
Rent expenditures	yr	3756	1999	30c
Rent, apartment, 2 br, 1 1/2-2 baths, unfurn, 950 sq ft, water	mos	1224	3/01	4c
Rental unit, 1 bedroom, with utilities	mos	670	4/01	41c
Rental unit, 2 bedroom, with utilities	mos	839	4/01	41c
Rental unit, 3 bedroom, with utilities	mos	1167	4/01	41c
Rental unit, 4 bedroom, with utilities	mos	1376	4/01	41c
Shelter, expenditures on	yr	10461	1999	30c

San Diego, CA - continued

Item	Per	Value	Date	Ref.
Housing - continued				
Single-family home, purchase price		251400	2000	19c
Insurance and Pensions				
Life and other personal insurance purchases	yr	452	1999	30c
Pensions and Social Security, expenditures on	yr	3618	1999	30c
Legal Fees				
Divorce, filing fee		182.00	4/01	35s
Driver's license fee	orig	12.00	1999	48s
Driver's license fee	renew	15.00	1999	48s
Personal Goods				
Personal care products and services purchases	yr	544	1999	30c
Shampoo, Alberto VO5	15 oz	1.48	3/01	4c
Toothpaste, Crest or Colgate	6-7 oz	2.87	3/01	4c
Personal Services				
Dry cleaning, man's 2-pc suit		7.31	3/01	4c
Man's haircut, barbershop, no styling		9.38	3/01	4c
Personal services, household, expenditures on	yr	353	1999	30r
Woman's shampoo, trim, blow-dry, no style-change		33.14	3/01	4c
Pets				
Pets, toys, and playground equipment, expenditures on	yr	358	1999	30r
Restaurant Food				
Chicken, fried, thigh and drumstick, KFC/Church's		2.43	3/01	4c
Hamburger with cheese, McDonald's	1/4 lb	2.39	3/01	4c
Pizza, Pizza Hut or Pizza Inn	11-12 in	9.99	3/01	4c
Taxes				
Federal income taxes paid	yr	3200	1999	30r
Personal taxes, expenditures on	yr	4153	1999	30r
Property taxes paid	yr	923	1999	30r
State and local income taxes paid	yr	812	1999	30r
Transportation				
Transportation, ACCRA Index		116.80	3/01	4c
Bus fare, one-way	trip	1.55	2000	1c
Bus fare, to central business district	1-way	1.75	3/01	4c
Cars and trucks, new, expenditures on	yr	1534	1999	30r
Cars and trucks, used, expenditures on	yr	1593	1999	30r
Commuter rail, one-way	trip	3.00	2000	2c
Diesel at the pump	gal	1.37	10/99	73s
Gasoline and motor oil purchases	yr	1177	1999	30c
Gasoline before-tax price (cents)	gal	128.80	10/00	43s
Light rail transit fare, one-way	trip	1.00	2000	2c
Maintenance and repair expenditures	yr	797	1999	30r
Public transportation, expenditures on	yr	637	1999	30c
Tire balance, computer or spin balance, front	wheel	7.33	3/01	4c
Transportation purchases	yr	8550	1999	30c
Vehicle expenses, miscellaneous, purchases	yr	2748	1999	30c
Vehicle insurance payments	yr	811	1999	30r
Vehicle purchases (net outlay)	yr	3180	1999	30r
Vehicle rental, lease expenditures	yr	666	1999	30r
Travel				
Hotel room, ave	night	135.50	2000	70c
Utilities				
Utilities, ACCRA Index		108.10	3/01	4c
Electrical bill, average	mos	58.66	9/00	9s
Electricity, expenditures on	yr	725	1999	30r
Electricity, summer, 250 KWh	mos	25.73	2/96	97c
Electricity, summer, 500 KWh	mos	57.97	2/96	97c
Electricity, summer, 750 KWh	mos	90.21	2/96	97c
Electricity, summer, 1000 KWh	mos	122.45	2/96	97c
Electricity and other, mixed, 2400 sq ft, new home	mos	57.06	3/01	4c
Electricity cost, average	KWh	7.75	9/00	9s
Utilities, fuels, and public services purchased	yr	1977	1999	30c

Values are in dollars or fractions of dollars. In the column headed *Ref*, references are shown to sources. Each reference is followed by a letter. These refer to the geographical level for which data were reported: s=State, r=Region, and c=City or metro. The abbreviation *ex* is used to mean *except* or *excluding*; *exp* stands for *expenditures*. For other abbreviations and further explanations, please see the Introduction.

San Diego, CA - continued

Item	Per	Value	Date	Ref.
Utilities				
Water and other public services, expenditures on	yr	339	1999	30r
Weddings				
Wedding (national average cost)		19936	2000	33r
Wedding (regional average total cost)		18918	1997	110r
Attendants' gifts		321	1998	33r
Bridal attendants' apparel (5 persons)		824	2000	33r
Bride's headpiece/veil		173	1998	33r
Bride's wedding dress		859	1998	33r
Clergy, religious facility fee		242	1998	33r
Engagement ring		3177	1998	33r
Flowers		789	1998	33r
Groom's formalwear rental		99	2000	33r
Limousine		410	1998	33r
Marriage license cost		50.00-80.00	4/01	35s
Men's formalwear (ushers, best man)		469	2000	33r
Mother of bride apparel		241	2000	33r
Music		866	1998	33r
Photography and videography		1368	1998	33r
Rehearsal dinner		728	1998	33r
Wedding invitations and announcements		341	1998	33r
Wedding reception		7968	2000	33r
Wedding rings (bride and groom)		1060	1998	33r

San Francisco, CA

Item	Per	Value	Date	Ref.
Average annual expenditures	yr	40662	1999	30r
Composite, ACCRA index		179.80	3/01	4c
Alcoholic Beverages				
Alcoholic beverage purchases	yr	516	1999	30c
Beer, Heineken, 12-oz, ex deposit	6	7.91	4c	
J & B Scotch	750-ml	20.69	3/01	4c
Malt beverages, all types, all sizes, any origin	16 oz	0.94	7/01	11r
Wine, Livingston or Gallo, Chablis blanc	1.5 liter	4.69	3/01	4c
Wine, red and white table, all sizes, any origin	liter	6.00	7/01	11r
Appliances				
Appliance repair, service call, washing machine	min lab chg	41.09	3/01	4c
Major appliances, expenditures on	yr	167	1999	30r
Small appliances, housewares, expenditures on	yr	105	1999	30r
Banking and Money				
Mortgage interest and charges paid	yr	3368	1999	30r
Mortgage principal paid on owned property	yr	1677	1999	30r
Mortgage rate, incl. points and orig. fee, 30-yr. conv. fixed or ARM	mos	7.21	3/01	4c
Vehicle finance charges paid	yr	311	1999	30r
Business Expenses				
Business travel, car rental	day	50	2001	3c
Business travel, food	day	64	2001	3c
Business travel, hotel	day	204	2001	3c
Medical office space cost	sq ft	146.94	2001	31c
Office space, 2-4 storey building	sq ft	128.73	2001	31c
Office space, 5-10 storey building	sq ft	113.71	2001	31c
Office space, 11-20 storey building	sq ft	109.30	2001	31c
Office space, central business district, Class A	sq ft	46.08	3/99	74c
Office space, outside central business district, Class A	sq ft	34.44	3/99	74c
Charity				
Cash contributions, expenditures	yr	2056	1999	30c
Child Care				
Child raising cost, total, age 0-2	yr	9140	1999	60r
Child raising cost, total, age 3-5	yr	9370	1999	60r
Child raising cost, total, age 6-8	yr	9450	1999	60r
Child raising cost, total, age 9-11	yr	9470	1999	60r

San Francisco, CA - continued

Item	Per	Value	Date	Ref.
Child Care - continued				
Child raising cost, total, age 12-14	yr	10170	1999	60r
Child raising cost, total, age 15-17	yr	10360	1999	60r
Child's child care and education, age 0-2	yr	1250	1999	60r
Child's child care and education, age 3-5	yr	1380	1999	60r
Child's child care and education, age 6-8	yr	890	1999	60r
Child's child care and education, age 9-11	yr	580	1999	60r
Child's child care and education, age 12-14	yr	430	1999	60r
Child's child care and education, age 15-17	yr	730	1999	60r
Child's clothing, age 0-2	yr	430	1999	60r
Child's clothing, age 3-5	yr	420	1999	60r
Child's clothing, age 6-8	yr	470	1999	60r
Child's clothing, age 9-11	yr	520	1999	60r
Child's clothing, age 12-14	yr	870	1999	60r
Child's clothing, age 15-17	yr	770	1999	60r
Child's food, age 0-2	yr	1120	1999	60r
Child's food, age 3-5	yr	1280	1999	60r
Child's food, age 6-8	yr	1640	1999	60r
Child's food, age 9-11	yr	1930	1999	60r
Child's food, age 12-14	yr	1940	1999	60r
Child's food, age 15-17	yr	2150	1999	60r
Child's health care, age 0-2	yr	490	1999	60r
Child's health care, age 3-5	yr	470	1999	60r
Child's health care, age 6-8	yr	530	1999	60r
Child's health care, age 9-11	yr	570	1999	60r
Child's health care, age 12-14	yr	580	1999	60r
Child's health care, age 15-17	yr	610	1999	60r
Child's housing, age 0-2	yr	3630	1999	60r
Child's housing, age 3-5	yr	3610	1999	60r
Child's housing, age 6-8	yr	3570	1999	60r
Child's housing, age 9-11	yr	3410	1999	60r
Child's housing, age 12-14	yr	3600	1999	60r
Child's housing, age 15-17	yr	3210	1999	60r
Child's personal care, reading, age 0-2	yr	1040	1999	60r
Child's personal care, reading, age 3-5	yr	1060	1999	60r
Child's personal care, reading, age 6-8	yr	1090	1999	60r
Child's personal care, reading, age 9-11	yr	1130	1999	60r
Child's personal care, reading, age 12-14	yr	1300	1999	60r
Child's personal care, reading, age 15-17	yr	1080	1999	60r
Daycare	mos	543	1998	37c
Daycare, 3-year old, 5 days, 8 hrs/day	mos	543	1998	85c
Clothing				
Apparel and services purchases	yr	2444	1999	30c
Boys' brief, cotton	3	5.59	3/01	4c
Boys, 2 to 15, expenditures on	yr	80	1999	30r
Children under 2, expenditures on	yr	74	1999	30r
Footwear, expenditures on	yr	307	1999	30r
Girls, 2 to 15, expenditures on	yr	101	1999	30r
Men and boys, expenditures on	yr	443	1999	30r
Men, 16 and over, expenditures on	yr	363	1999	30r
Shirt, man's dress shirt		30.30	3/01	4c
Slacks, man's "No Wrinkles" khaki		32.74	3/01	4c
Women, 16 and over, expenditures on	yr	594	1999	30r
Communications				
Cable modem installation, AT&T-BIS		150.00	6/99	103s
Cable modem installation, Charter		99.00-169.00	6/99	103s
Cable modem installation, Comcast		95.00	6/99	103s
Cable modem installation, Cox		99.00-174.95	6/99	103s
Cable modem installation, Media One		100.00	6/99	103s
Cable modem installation, Time Warner		75.00-225.00	6/99	103s
Cable modem rate, cable subscriber, AT&T-BIS	mos	39.95	6/99	103s
Cable modem rate, cable subscriber, Charter	mos	49.95-79.95	6/99	103s
Cable modem rate, cable subscriber, Comcast	mos	39.95	6/99	103s
Cable modem rate, cable subscriber, Cox	mos	29.95-44.95	6/99	103s

Values are in dollars or fractions of dollars. In the column headed *Ref*, references are shown to sources. Each reference is followed by a letter. These refer to the geographical level for which data were reported: s=State, r=Region, and c=City or metro. The abbreviation *ex* is used to mean *except* or *excluding*; *exp* stands for expenditures. For other abbreviations and further explanations, please see the Introduction.

San Francisco, CA - continued

Item	Per	Value	Date	Ref.
Communications				
Cable modem rate, cable subscriber, Media One	mos	34.95-39.95	6/99	103s
Cable modem rate, cable subscriber, Time Warner	mos	39.95-49.95	6/99	103s
Cable modem rate, non-cable subscriber, Charter	mos	59.95-89.95	6/99	103s
Cable modem rate, non-cable subscriber, Comcast	mos	49.95	6/99	103s
Cable modem rate, non-cable subscriber, Cox	mos	42.95-54.95	6/99	103s
Cable modem rate, non-cable subscriber, Media One	mos	49.95	6/99	103s
Cable modem rate, non-cable subscriber, Time Warner	mos	39.95-54.95	6/99	103s
Cellular phone service	mos	44.24	2/01	55c
Cellular phone service	mos	45.84	2001	25c
Newspaper subscription, daily and Sunday delivery	mos	16.68	3/01	4c
Phone line, single, business, field visit	inst.	70.75	12/97	17s
Phone line, single, business, no field visit	inst.	70.75	12/97	17s
Phone line, single, residence, field visit	inst.	34.75	12/97	17s
Phone line, single, residence, no field visit	inst.	34.75	12/97	17s
Postage and stationery, expenditures on	yr	150	1999	30r
Postal rate, express mail, up to half-pound		12.45	7/01	108r
Postal rate, letter, first class, first ounce		0.34	7/01	108r
Postal rate, letter, two ounces		0.57	7/01	108r
Postal rate, post card		0.21	7/01	108r
Postal rate, priority mail, two pounds		3.95	7/01	108r
Postal rate, priority mail, up to one pound		3.50	7/01	108r
Telephone bill, business, basic rate	mos	10.32	12/97	18c
Telephone bill, family of three	mos	22.10	3/01	4c
Telephone bill, residential, basic rate	mos	3.00	12/97	18c
Telephone services, expenditures on	yr	825	1999	30r
Wireless services	mos	42.43	1/00	42c
Education				
Board, 4-year private college/university	yr	2970	1996	38s
Board, 4-year public college/university	yr	2516	1996	38s
Education expenditures	yr	875	1999	30c
Room, 4-year private college/university	yr	3196	1996	38s
Room, 4-year public college/university	yr	3031	1996	38s
Total cost, 4-year private college/university	yr	20143	1996	38s
Total cost, 4-year public college/university	yr	8213	1996	38s
Tuition, 2-year public college/university, in state	yr	362	1996	38s
Tuition, 4-year private college/university, in state	yr	13977	1996	38s
Tuition, 4-year public college/university	yr	2666	1996	38s
Energy and Fuels				
Electricity	KWh	0.11	7/01	11r
Electricity	500 KWhs	48.23	7/01	11r
Energy, combined forms, 2400 sq ft	mos	170.14	3/01	4c
Energy, exc. electricity, 2400 sq ft	mos	97.57	3/01	4c
Fuel oil and other fuels, expenditures on	yr	35	1999	30r
Gas, natural, commercial rate	1000 cf	8.74	11/00	88s
Gas, regular unleaded, cash, self-service	gal	1.85	3/01	4c
Gasoline, all types	gal	1.91	7/01	11r
Gasoline, unleaded premium	gal	2.05	7/01	11r
Gasoline, unleaded regular	gal	1.83	7/01	11r
Natural gas, expenditures on	yr	255	1999	30r
Utility (piped) gas, therm		0.98	7/01	11r
Utility (piped) gas, 40 therms		40.74	7/01	11r
Utility (piped) gas, 100 therms		96.80	7/01	11r
Entertainment				
Bowling, Saturday evening rate	line	3.65	3/01	4c
Entertainment purchases	yr	2395	1999	30c
Fees and admissions paid	yr	545	1999	30r
Major League baseball ticket		21.24	2000	16c
Monopoly game, Parker Brothers', No. 9	game	14.38	3/01	4c
Movie, first-run, Saturday, evening	adm.	8.60	3/01	4c
Reading purchases	yr	257	1999	30c

San Francisco, CA - continued

Item	Per	Value	Date	Ref.
Entertainment - continued				
Television, radios, sound equipment, expenditures on	yr	624	1999	30r
Tennis balls, yellow, Wilson or Penn, 3	can	3.17	3/01	4c
Funerals				
Total cost of funeral		5401.08	1/99	78r
Acknowledgement cards		33.64	1/99	78r
Casket		2170.43	1/99	78r
Cosmetology, hair, other preparation		136.32	1/99	78r
Embalming		319.13	1/99	78r
Funeral at funeral home		370.21	1/99	78r
Hearse (local)		161.04	1/99	78r
Professional service charges		963.15	1/99	78r
Service car/van		133.99	1/99	78r
Transfer of remains to funeral home		159.82	1/99	78r
Vault		778.07	1/99	78r
Visitation/viewing		175.28	1/99	78r
Groceries				
Groceries, ACCRA Index		118.90	3/01	4c
Antibiotic ointment, Polysporin	0.5 oz	5.65	3/01	4c
Apples	pound	0.91		29c
Apples, red delicious	lb	0.84	7/01	11r
Baby food, strained vegetables or fruit, lowest price	4-4.5 oz	0.48	3/01	4c
Bacon, sliced	lb	3.38	7/01	11r
Bakery products, expenditures on	yr	299	1999	30r
Bananas	lb	0.59	3/01	4c
Bananas	lb	0.54	7/01	11r
Beans, dried, any type, all sizes	lb	0.76	7/01	11r
Beef or hamburger, ground	lb	1.91	3/01	4c
Beef, expenditures on	yr	222	1999	30r
Bread, white	loaf	1.09	3/01	4c
Bread, white, pan	lb	0.99	7/01	11r
Butter, yoghurt, cheese, etc, expenditures on	yr	211	1999	30r
Cereals and bakery product purchases	yr	466	1999	30r
Cereals and cereal products, expenditures on	yr	168	1999	30r
Cheese, Kraft grated Parmesan	8 oz	4.49	3/01	4c
Chicken breast, bone-in	lb	2.45	7/01	11r
Chicken, fresh, whole	lb	1.19	7/01	11r
Chicken, whole fryer	lb	0.81	3/01	4c
Chops, boneless,	lb	4.00	7/01	11r
Chuck roast, graded and ungraded, excl U.S. prime and choice	lb	2.55	7/01	11r
Cigarettes, Winston, Kings	carton	42.14	3/01	4c
Coffee, 100%, ground roast, all sizes	lb	3.80	7/01	11r
Coffee, vacuum-packed	13 oz	3.62	3/01	4c
Cookies, chocolate chip	lb	2.83	7/01	11r
Corn Flakes, Kellogg's or Post Toasties	18 oz	3.77	3/01	4c
Corn, frozen, whole kernel, lowest price	16 oz	1.99	3/01	4c
Dairy product purchases	yr	409	1999	30c
Eggs, expenditures on	yr	39	1999	30r
Eggs, Grade A or AA	dozen	2.31	3/01	4c
Eggs, grade AA, large	dozen	1.23	7/01	11r
Fats and oils, expenditures on	yr	88	1999	30r
Fish and seafood, expenditures on	yr	121	1999	30r
Food (excl fruit and vegetables), eaten at home, purchases	yr	1304	1999	30c
Food cooked on trips, expenditures on	yr	64	1999	30r
Food purchases	yr	6963	1999	30c
Food purchases, eaten away from home	yr	2749	1999	30c
Food purchases, food eaten at home	yr	4214	1999	30c
Fresh fruits, expenditures on	yr	186	1999	30r
Fresh milk and cream, expenditures on	yr	130	1999	30r
Fresh vegetables, expenditures on	yr	177	1999	30r
Fruit and vegetable purchases	yr	794	1999	30c
Grapefruit	lb	0.68	7/01	11r
Grapes, Thompson, seedless	lb	2.42	7/01	11r
Ground beef, lean and extra lean	lb	2.46	7/01	11r
Ice cream, prepackaged, bulk, regular	1/2 gal	3.62	7/01	11r
Lettuce, iceberg	head	0.97	3/01	4c
Lettuce, iceberg	lb	0.63	7/01	11r

Values are in dollars or fractions of dollars. In the column headed *Ref*, references are shown to sources. Each reference is followed by a letter. These refer to the geographical level for which data were reported: s=State, r=Region, and c=City or metro. The abbreviation *ex* is used to mean *except* or *excluding*; *exp* stands for *expenditures*. For other abbreviations and further explanations, please see the Introduction.

San Francisco, CA - continued

Item	Per	Value	Date	Ref.
Groceries				
Margarine, Blue Bonnet or Parkay, stick	lb	1.23	3/01	4c
Meats, poultry, fish, and egg purchases	yr	761	1999	30r
Milk, fresh, low fat,	gal	2.80	7/01	11r
Milk, fresh, whole, fortified	gal	2.88	7/01	11r
Milk, whole	1/2 gal	2.30	3/01	4c
Nonalcoholic beverages, expenditures on	yr	258	1999	30r
Orange juice, Minute Maid frozen	12 oz	1.27	3/01	4c
Oranges, Navel	lb	0.97	7/01	11r
Oranges, Valencia	lb	0.43	7/01	11r
Peaches	lb	1.38	7/01	11r
Peaches, halves or slices, Hunt's, Del Monte, or Libby's	29 oz	1.99	3/01	4c
Peanut butter, creamy, all sizes	lb	2.14	7/01	11r
Peas, green, Del Monte or Green Giant	15 oz	1.02	3/01	4c
Pork chops, center cut, bone-in	lb	3.83	7/01	11r
Pork, expenditures on	yr	141	1999	30r
Potatoes, white or red	10 lb	1.89	3/01	4c
Potatoes, white, all types	lb	0.37	7/01	11r
Poultry, expenditures on	yr	146	1999	30r
Processed fruits, expenditures on	yr	118	1999	30r
Processed vegetables, expenditures on	yr	81	1999	30r
Round roast, graded and ungraded, excl U.S. prime and choice	lb	3.07	7/01	11r
Round roast, U.S. choice, boneless	lb	3.37	7/01	11r
Round steak, graded and ungraded, excl U.S. prime and choice	lb	3.51	7/01	11r
Sausage, Jimmy Dean/Owens pork	lb	4.76	3/01	4c
Shortening, vegetable, Crisco	3 lb	3.85	3/01	4c
Sirloin steak, graded and ungraded, excl U.S. prime and choice	lb	4.67	7/01	11r
Soft drink, Coca Cola, ex deposit	2 liter	1.25	3/01	4c
Steak, sirloin, U.S. choice, boneless	lb	6.20	7/01	11r
Steak, T-bone	lb	6.79	3/01	4c
Strawberries, dry pint	12 oz	1.79	7/01	11r
Sugar and other sweets, expenditures on	yr	124	1999	30r
Sugar, cane or beet	4 lbs	1.49	3/01	4c
Sugar, white, all sizes	lb	0.46	7/01	11r
Tobacco products and smoking supplies purchases	yr	192	1999	30c
Tomatoes, field grown	lb	1.17	7/01	11r
Tomatoes, Hunt's or Del Monte	14.5 oz	1.35	3/01	4c
Tuna, chunk, light	6 oz	0.83	3/01	4c
Tuna, light, chunk	lb	2.05	7/01	11r
Goods and Services				
Miscellaneous goods and services, ACCRA Index		111.10	3/01	4c
B&B Japanese maple (acer japonicum)	gal	39.99	4/00	93r
Boxwood (buxus)	2 gal	14.99-24.99	4/00	93r
Christmas tree, noble fir		40-60	2000	65s
Daylilly (hemerocallis)	gal	6.99-8.99	4/00	93r
Flat of annuals		16.68		93r
Fountain grass (pennisetum)	gal	7.99-11.99	4/00	93r
Hanging basket (10 in)		29.99	4/00	93r
Hardy geranium (geranium)	gal	6.99-11.99	4/00	93r
Hosta (hosta)	gal	6.99-18.99	4/00	93r
Lilac (syrubga vulgaris)	2 gal	14.99-17.99	4/00	93r
Miscellaneous purchases	yr	1070	1999	30r
Rhododendron (rhododendron)	2 gal	14.99	4/00	93r
Sage (salvia)	gal	6.99	4/00	93r
Wintercreeper euonymus (euonymus fortunei)	2 gal	14.99-22.99	4/00	93r
Hunting license	yr	29.95	4/01	34s
Health Care				
Health care, ACCRA Index		170.50	3/01	4c

San Francisco, CA - continued

Item	Per	Value	Date	Ref.
Health Care - continued				
Cardiac catheterization, ave hospital/ physician charges		24000	1998	77s
Childbirth, Cesarean delivery		11587	1997	13r
Childbirth, vaginal delivery		6725	1997	13r
Dentist's fee, adult teeth cleaning and periodic oral exam	visit	108.56	3/01	4c
Doctor's fee, routine exam, established patient	visit	74.10	3/01	4c
Drugs, expenditures on	yr	309	1999	30r
Health care purchases	yr	1792	1999	30c
Health insurance expenditures	yr	868	1999	30r
Home health care aide cost, licensed agency	hour	17	2000	82c
Hospital care, private room	day	1692.38	3/01	4c
Hysterectomy, laproscopically-assisted, ave hospital/physician charges		20760	1998	76s
Hysterectomy, vaginal, ave hospital and physician charges		14570	1998	76s
Medicaid dispensing fee		4.05	1999	87s
Medical services expenditures	yr	580	1999	30r
Medical supplies, expenditures on	yr	112	1999	30r
Nursing home costs, private room	day	169	2000	82c
Nursing home stay, private room	day	169	2000	83c
Household Goods				
Dishwashing powder, Cascade	50 oz	3.33	3/01	4c
Floor coverings, expenditures on	yr	49	1999	30r
Furniture, expenditures on	yr	444	1999	30r
Household furnishings and equipment purchases	yr	2232	1999	30c
Household textiles, expenditures on	yr	141	1999	30r
Laundry and cleaning supplies, expenditures on	yr	128	1999	30r
Tissues, facial, Kleenex brand	175	1.15	3/01	4c
Housing				
Housing, ACCRA Index		328.40	3/01	4c
Home, 2200 sq ft, 4-br, 2-bath, 2-car garage, average		759250	2000	47c
Home, suburban, 2,200 square feet		567400	2000	23c
Home price, existing, ave		239400	10/00	90r
Home purchase, 2,000 sq ft		550000	11/00	111c
Home value, median		215000	2001	53s
House, 2-story, 2,400 sq ft, 2-car garage, new		250500	2000	54c
House, 2400 sq ft, 8000 sq ft lot, new, urban, utilities	total	656000	3/01	4c
House payment, principal and interest, 25% down payment	mos	3344	3/01	4c
Household operation expenditures	yr	1128	1999	30c
Housekeeping supplies purchases	yr	620	1999	30c
Housing, expenditures on	yr	18059	1999	30c
Lodging expenditures	yr	575	1999	30r
Maintenance, repairs, insurance expenditures	yr	939	1999	30r
Monthly rental value of owned home	mos	662	1999	30r
Owned dwellings, expenditures own	yr	7377	1999	30c
Rent expenditures	yr	3818	1999	30c
Rent, apartment, 2 br, 1 1/2-2 baths, unfurn, 950 sq ft, water	mos	2390	3/01	4c
Rental unit, 1 bedroom, with utilities	mos	1154	4/01	41c
Rental unit, 2 bedroom, with utilities	mos	1459	4/01	41c
Rental unit, 3 bedroom, with utilities	mos	2001	4/01	41c
Rental unit, 4 bedroom, with utilities	mos	2118	4/01	41c
Shelter, expenditures on	yr	11886	1999	30c
Single-family home, purchase price		418600	2000	19c
Insurance and Pensions				
Life and other personal insurance purchases	yr	330	1999	30c
Pensions and Social Security, expenditures on	yr	5257	1999	30c
Personal insurance and pensions, expenditures on	yr	5587	1999	30c

Values are in dollars or fractions of dollars. In the column headed *Ref*, references are shown to sources. Each reference is followed by a letter. These refer to the geographical level for which data were reported: s=State, r=Region, and c=City or metro. The abbreviation *ex* is used to mean *except* or *excluding*; *exp* stands for expenditures. For other abbreviations and further explanations, please see the Introduction.

San Francisco, CA - continued

Item	Per	Value	Date	Ref.
Legal Fees				
Divorce, filing fee		182.00	4/01	35s
Driver's license fee	renew	15.00	1999	48s
Driver's license fee	orig	12.00	1999	48s
Parking in front of hydrant, fine		33	1998	20c
Parking in loading zone, fine		25	1998	20c
Parking meter violation, fine		25	1998	20c
Personal Goods				
Personal care products and services purchases	yr	558	1999	30c
Shampoo, Alberto VO5	15 oz	1.59	3/01	4c
Toothpaste, Crest or Colgate	6-7 oz	2.56	3/01	4c
Personal Services				
Dry cleaning, man's 2-pc suit		7.87	3/01	4c
Man's haircut, barbershop, no styling		12.71	3/01	4c
Personal services, household, expenditures on	yr	353	1999	30r
Woman's shampoo, trim, blow-dry, no style-change		34.00	3/01	4c
Pets				
Kennel charges, dog	night	15-20	2001	66c
Pets, toys, and playground equipment, expenditures on	yr	358	1999	30r
Restaurant Food				
Cheeseburger, 1/4-lb, large fries, medium soft drink, excl tax		4.83	1999	40c
Chicken, fried, thigh and drumstick, KFC/Church's		2.37	3/01	4c
Hamburger with cheese, McDonald's	1/4 lb	2.40	3/01	4c
Pizza, Pizza Hut or Pizza Inn	11-12 in	9.99	3/01	4c
Taxes				
Federal income taxes paid	yr	3200	1999	30r
Personal taxes, expenditures on	yr	4153	1999	30r
Property taxes paid	yr	923	1999	30r
State and local income taxes paid	yr	812	1999	30r
Transportation				
Transportation, ACCRA Index		129.30	3/01	4c
Bus fare, one-way	trip	1.30	2000	1c
Bus fare, to central business district	1-way	1.00	3/01	4c
Cars and trucks, new, expenditures on	yr	1534	1999	30r
Cars and trucks, used, expenditures on	yr	1593	1999	30r
Commuter rail, one-way	trip	1.25	2000	2c
Diesel at the pump	gal	1.37	10/99	73s
Ferry boat transit fare, one-way	trip	2.85	2000	2c
Gasoline and motor oil purchases	yr	1232	1999	30c
Gasoline before-tax price (cents)	gal	128.80	10/00	43s
Heavy rail transit fare, one-way	trip	1.10	2000	2c
Light rail transit fare, one-way	trip	1.00	2000	2c
Maintenance and repair expenditures	yr	797	1999	30r
Parking at airport, lowest rate	day	14.00	2000	46c
Public transportation, expenditures on	yr	836	1999	30c
Tire balance, computer or spin balance, front	wheel	10.79	3/01	4c
Transportation purchases	yr	8186	1999	30c
Trolley bus transit fare, one-way	trip	1.00	2000	2c
Vehicle expenses, miscellaneous, purchases	yr	2954	1999	30c
Vehicle insurance payments	yr	811	1999	30r
Vehicle purchases (net outlay)	yr	3164	1999	30c
Vehicle rental, lease expenditures	yr	666	1999	30r
Travel				
Hotel rate, ave	day	153.63	1999	45c
Utilities				
Utilities, ACCRA Index		134.20	3/01	4c
Electrical bill, average	mos	58.66	9/00	9s
Electricity, 1000 KWh	mos	125.00	1/00	80c
Electricity, expenditures on	yr	725	1999	30r
Electricity and other, mixed, 2400 sq ft, new home	mos	72.57	3/01	4c
Electricity cost, average	KWh	7.75	9/00	9s
Utilities, fuels, and public services purchased	yr	2179	1999	30r

San Francisco, CA - continued

Item	Per	Value	Date	Ref.
Utilities - continued				
Water and other public services, expenditures on	yr	339	1999	30r
Weddings				
Wedding (national average cost)		19936	2000	33r
Wedding (regional average total cost)		18918	1997	110r
Attendants' gifts		321	1998	33r
Bridal attendants' apparel (5 persons)		824	1998	33r
Bride's headpiece/veil		173	1998	33r
Bride's wedding dress		859	1998	33r
Clergy, religious facility fee		242	1998	33r
Engagement ring		3177	1998	33r
Flowers		789	1998	33r
Groom's formalwear rental		99	2000	33r
Limousine		410	1998	33r
Marriage license cost		50.00-80.00	4/01	35s
Men's formalwear (ushers, best man)		469	2000	33r
Mother of bride apparel		241	2000	33r
Music		866	1998	33r
Photography and videography		1368	1998	33r
Rehearsal dinner		728	1998	33r
Wedding invitations and announcements		341	1998	33r
Wedding reception		7968	2000	33r
Wedding rings (bride and groom)		1060	1998	33r

San Francisco-Oakland-San Jose, CA

Item	Per	Value	Date	Ref.
Average annual expenditures	yr	40662	1999	30r
Alcoholic Beverages				
Alcoholic beverage purchases	yr	372	1999	30r
Malt beverages, all types, all sizes, any origin	16 oz	0.94	7/01	11r
Wine, red and white table, all sizes, any origin	liter	6.00	7/01	11r
Appliances				
Major appliances, expenditures on	yr	167	1999	30r
Small appliances, housewares, expenditures on	yr	105	1999	30r
Banking and Money				
Mortgage interest and charges paid	yr	3368	1999	30r
Mortgage principal paid on owned property	yr	1677	1999	30r
Vehicle finance charges paid	yr	311	1999	30r
Charity				
Cash contributions, expenditures	yr	1344	1999	30r
Child Care				
Child raising cost, total, age 0-2	yr	9140	1999	60r
Child raising cost, total, age 3-5	yr	9370	1999	60r
Child raising cost, total, age 6-8	yr	9450	1999	60r
Child raising cost, total, age 9-11	yr	9470	1999	60r
Child raising cost, total, age 12-14	yr	10170	1999	60r
Child raising cost, total, age 15-17	yr	10360	1999	60r
Child's child care and education, age 0-2	yr	1250	1999	60r
Child's child care and education, age 3-5	yr	1380	1999	60r
Child's child care and education, age 6-8	yr	890	1999	60r
Child's child care and education, age 9-11	yr	580	1999	60r
Child's child care and education, age 12-14	yr	430	1999	60r
Child's child care and education, age 15-17	yr	730	1999	60r
Child's clothing, age 0-2	yr	430	1999	60r
Child's clothing, age 3-5	yr	420	1999	60r
Child's clothing, age 6-8	yr	470	1999	60r
Child's clothing, age 9-11	yr	520	1999	60r
Child's clothing, age 12-14	yr	870	1999	60r
Child's clothing, age 15-17	yr	770	1999	60r
Child's food, age 0-2	yr	1120	1999	60r
Child's food, age 3-5	yr	1280	1999	60r
Child's food, age 6-8	yr	1640	1999	60r
Child's food, age 9-11	yr	1930	1999	60r
Child's food, age 12-14	yr	1940	1999	60r
Child's food, age 15-17	yr	2150	1999	60r

Values are in dollars or fractions of dollars. In the column headed *Ref*, references are shown to sources. Each reference is followed by a letter. These refer to the geographical level for which data were reported: s=State, r=Region, and c=City or metro. The abbreviation *ex* is used to mean *except* or *excluding*; *exp* stands for *expenditures*. For other abbreviations and further explanations, please see the Introduction.

San Francisco-Oakland-San Jose, CA - continued

Item	Per	Value	Date	Ref.
Child Care				
Child's health care, age 0-2	yr	490	1999	60r
Child's health care, age 3-5	yr	470	1999	60r
Child's health care, age 6-8	yr	530	1999	60r
Child's health care, age 9-11	yr	570	1999	60r
Child's health care, age 12-14	yr	580	1999	60r
Child's health care, age 15-17	yr	610	1999	60r
Child's housing, age 0-2	yr	3630	1999	60r
Child's housing, age 3-5	yr	3610	1999	60r
Child's housing, age 6-8	yr	3570	1999	60r
Child's housing, age 9-11	yr	3410	1999	60r
Child's housing, age 12-14	yr	3600	1999	60r
Child's housing, age 15-17	yr	3210	1999	60r
Child's personal care, reading, age 0-2	yr	1040	1999	60r
Child's personal care, reading, age 3-5	yr	1060	1999	60r
Child's personal care, reading, age 6-8	yr	1090	1999	60r
Child's personal care, reading, age 9-11	yr	1130	1999	60r
Child's personal care, reading, age 12-14	yr	1300	1999	60r
Child's personal care, reading, age 15-17	yr	1080	1999	60r
Clothing				
Apparel and services purchases	yr	1863	1999	30r
Boys, 2 to 15, expenditures on	yr	80	1999	30r
Children under 2, expenditures on	yr	74	1999	30r
Footwear, expenditures on	yr	307	1999	30r
Girls, 2 to 15, expenditures on	yr	101	1999	30r
Men and boys, expenditures on	yr	443	1999	30r
Men, 16 and over, expenditures on	yr	363	1999	30r
Women, 16 and over, expenditures on	yr	594	1999	30r
Communications				
Cable modem installation, AT&T-BIS		150.00	6/99	103s
Cable modem installation, Charter		99.00-169.00	6/99	103s
Cable modem installation, Comcast		95.00	6/99	103s
Cable modem installation, Cox		99.00-174.95	6/99	103s
Cable modem installation, Media One		100.00	6/99	103s
Cable modem installation, Time Warner		75.00-225.00	6/99	103s
Cable modem rate, cable subscriber, AT&T-BIS	mos	39.95	6/99	103s
Cable modem rate, cable subscriber, Charter	mos	49.95-79.95	6/99	103s
Cable modem rate, cable subscriber, Comcast	mos	39.95	6/99	103s
Cable modem rate, cable subscriber, Cox	mos	29.95-44.95	6/99	103s
Cable modem rate, cable subscriber, Media One	mos	34.95-39.95	6/99	103s
Cable modem rate, cable subscriber, Time Warner	mos	39.95-49.95	6/99	103s
Cable modem rate, non-cable subscriber, Charter	mos	59.95-89.95	6/99	103s
Cable modem rate, non-cable subscriber, Comcast	mos	49.95	6/99	103s
Cable modem rate, non-cable subscriber, Cox	mos	42.95-54.95	6/99	103s
Cable modem rate, non-cable subscriber, Media One	mos	49.95	6/99	103s
Cable modem rate, non-cable subscriber, Time Warner	mos	39.95-54.95	6/99	103s
Phone line, single, business, field visit	inst.	70.75	12/97	17s
Phone line, single, business, no field visit	inst.	70.75	12/97	17s
Phone line, single, residence, field visit	inst.	34.75	12/97	17s
Phone line, single, residence, no field visit	inst.	34.75	12/97	17s
Postage and stationery, expenditures on	yr	150	1999	30r
Postal rate, express mail, up to half-pound		12.45	7/01	108r
Postal rate, letter, first class, first ounce		0.34	7/01	108r
Postal rate, letter, two ounces		0.57	7/01	108r
Postal rate, post card		0.21	7/01	108r
Postal rate, priority mail, two pounds		3.95	7/01	108r
Postal rate, priority mail, up to one pound		3.50	7/01	108r
Telephone services, expenditures on	yr	825	1999	30r

San Francisco-Oakland-San Jose, CA - continued

Item	Per	Value	Date	Ref.
Education				
Board, 4-year private college/university	yr	2970	1996	38s
Board, 4-year public college/university	yr	2516	1996	38s
Education expenditures	yr	676	1999	30r
Room, 4-year private college/university	yr	3196	1996	38s
Room, 4-year public college/university	yr	3031	1996	38s
Total cost, 4-year private college/university	yr	20143	1996	38s
Total cost, 4-year public college/university	yr	8213	1996	38s
Tuition, 2-year public college/university, in state	yr	362	1996	38s
Tuition, 4-year private college/university, in state	yr	13977	1996	38s
Tuition, 4-year public college/university	yr	2666	1996	38s
Energy and Fuels				
Electricity	KWh	0.11	7/01	11r
Electricity	500 KWhs	64.18	7/01	11c
Electricity	KWh	0.17	7/01	11c
Electricity	500 KWhs	48.23	7/01	11r
Fuel oil and other fuels, expenditures on	yr	35	1999	30r
Gas, natural, commercial rate	1000 cf	8.74	11/00	88s
Gasoline, all types	gal	2.01	7/01	11c
Gasoline, unleaded midgrade	gal	2.08	7/01	11c
Gasoline, unleaded premium	gal	2.05	7/01	11r
Gasoline, unleaded regular	gal	1.94	7/01	11c
Natural gas, expenditures on	yr	255	1999	30r
Utility (piped) gas, therm		0.93	7/01	11c
Utility (piped) gas, 40 therms		40.74	7/01	11r
Utility (piped) gas, 100 therms		95.55	7/01	11c
Entertainment				
Entertainment purchases	yr	2139	1999	30r
Fees and admissions paid	yr	545	1999	30r
Television, radios, sound equipment, expenditures on	yr	624	1999	30r
Funerals				
Total cost of funeral		5401.08	1/99	78r
Acknowledgement cards		33.64	1/99	78r
Casket		2170.43	1/99	78r
Cosmetology, hair, other preparation		136.32	1/99	78r
Embalming		319.13	1/99	78r
Funeral at funeral home		370.21	1/99	78r
Hearse (local)		161.04	1/99	78r
Professional service charges		963.15	1/99	78r
Service car/van		133.99	1/99	78r
Transfer of remains to funeral home		159.82	1/99	78r
Vault		778.07	1/99	78r
Visitation/viewing		175.28	1/99	78r
Groceries				
Apples, red delicious	lb	0.84	7/01	11r
Bacon, sliced	lb	3.38	7/01	11r
Bakery products, expenditures on	yr	299	1999	30r
Bananas	lb	0.54	7/01	11r
Beans, dried, any type, all sizes	lb	0.76	7/01	11r
Beef, expenditures on	yr	222	1999	30r
Bread, white, pan	lb	0.99	7/01	11r
Butter, yoghurt, cheese, etc, expenditures on	yr	211	1999	30r
Cereals and bakery product purchases	yr	466	1999	30r
Cereals and cereal products, expenditures on	yr	168	1999	30r
Chicken breast, bone-in	lb	2.45	7/01	11r
Chicken, fresh, whole	lb	1.19	7/01	11r
Chops, boneless,	lb	4.00	7/01	11r
Chuck roast, graded and ungraded, excl U.S. prime and choice	lb	2.55	7/01	11r
Coffee, 100%, ground roast, all sizes	lb	3.80	7/01	11r
Cookies, chocolate chip	lb	2.83	7/01	11r
Dairy product purchases	yr	341	1999	30r
Eggs, expenditures on	yr	39	1999	30r
Eggs, grade AA, large	dozen	1.23	7/01	11r
Fats and oils, expenditures on	yr	88	1999	30r

Values are in dollars or fractions of dollars. In the column headed *Ref*, references are shown to sources. Each reference is followed by a letter. These refer to the geographical level for which data were reported: s=State, r=Region, and c=City or metro. The abbreviation *ex* is used to mean *except* or *excluding*; *exp* stands for *expenditures*. For other abbreviations and further explanations, please see the Introduction.

San Francisco-Oakland-San Jose, CA - continued

Item	Per	Value	Date	Ref.
Groceries				
Fish and seafood, expenditures on	yr	121	1999	30r
Food (excl fruit and vegetables), eaten at home, purchases	yr	1001	1999	30r
Food cooked on trips, expenditures on	yr	64	1999	30r
Food purchases	yr	5312	1999	30r
Food purchases, eaten away from home	yr	2180	1999	30r
Food purchases, food eaten at home	yr	3132	1999	30r
Fresh fruits, expenditures on	yr	186	1999	30r
Fresh milk and cream, expenditures on	yr	130	1999	30r
Fresh vegetables, expenditures on	yr	177	1999	30r
Grapefruit	lb	0.68	7/01	11r
Grapes, Thompson, seedless	lb	2.42	7/01	11r
Ground beef, lean and extra lean	lb	2.46	7/01	11r
Ice cream, prepackaged, bulk, regular	1/2 gal	3.62	7/01	11r
Lettuce, iceberg	lb	0.63	7/01	11r
Meats, poultry, fish, and egg purchases	yr	761	1999	30r
Milk, fresh, low fat	gal	2.80	7/01	11r
Milk, fresh, whole, fortified	gal	2.88	7/01	11r
Nonalcoholic beverages, expenditures on	yr	258	1999	30r
Oranges, Navel	lb	0.97	7/01	11r
Oranges, Valencia	lb	0.43	7/01	11r
Peaches	lb	1.38	7/01	11r
Peanut butter, creamy, all sizes	lb	2.14	7/01	11r
Pork chops, center cut, bone-in	lb	3.83	7/01	11r
Pork, expenditures on	yr	141	1999	30r
Potatoes, white, all types	lb	0.37	7/01	11r
Poultry, expenditures on	yr	146	1999	30r
Processed fruits, expenditures on	yr	118	1999	30r
Processed vegetables, expenditures on	yr	81	1999	30r
Round roast, graded and ungraded, excl U.S. prime and choice	lb	3.07	7/01	11r
Round roast, U.S. choice, boneless	lb	3.37	7/01	11r
Round steak, graded and ungraded, excl U.S. prime and choice	lb	3.51	7/01	11r
Sirloin steak, graded and ungraded, excl U.S. prime and choice	lb	4.67	7/01	11r
Steak, sirloin, U.S. choice, boneless	lb	6.20	7/01	11r
Strawberries, dry pint	12 oz	1.79	7/01	11r
Sugar and other sweets, expenditures on	yr	124	1999	30r
Sugar, white, all sizes	lb	0.46	7/01	11r
Tobacco products and smoking supplies purchases	yr	217	1999	30r
Tomatoes, field grown	lb	1.17	7/01	11r
Tuna, light, chunk	lb	2.05	7/01	11r
Goods and Services				
B&B Japanese maple (acer japonicum)	gal	39.99	4/00	93r
Boxwood (buxus)	2 gal	14.99-24.99	4/00	93r
Christmas tree, noble fir		40-60	2000	65s
Daylilly (hemerocallis)	gal	6.99-8.99	4/00	93r
Flat of annuals		16.68	4/00	93r
Fountain grass (pennisetum)	gal	7.99-11.99	4/00	93r
Hanging basket (10 in)		29.99	4/00	93r
Hardy geranium (geranium)	gal	6.99-11.99	4/00	93r
Hosta (hosta)	gal	6.99-18.99	4/00	93r
Lilac (syrubga vulgaris)	2 gal	14.99-17.99	4/00	93r
Miscellaneous purchases	yr	1070	1999	30r
Rhododendron (rhododendron)	2 gal	14.99	4/00	93r
Sage (salvia)	gal	6.99	4/00	93r
Wintercreeper euonymus (euonymus fortunei)	2 gal	14.99-22.99	4/00	93r
Hunting license	yr	29.95	4/01	34s
Health Care				
Cardiac catheterization, ave hospital/physician charges		24000	1998	77s
Childbirth, Cesarean delivery		11587	1997	13r

San Francisco-Oakland-San Jose, CA - continued

Item	Per	Value	Date	Ref.
Health Care - continued				
Childbirth, vaginal delivery		6725	1997	13r
Drugs, expenditures on	yr	309	1999	30r
Health care purchases	yr	1869	1999	30r
Health insurance expenditures	yr	868	1999	30r
Hysterectomy, laproscopically-assisted, ave hospital/physician charges		20760	1998	76s
Hysterectomy, vaginal, ave hospital and physician charges		14570	1998	76s
Medicaid dispensing fee		4.05	1999	87s
Medical services expenditures	yr	580	1999	30r
Medical supplies, expenditures on	yr	112	1999	30r
Household Goods				
Floor coverings, expenditures on	yr	49	1999	30r
Furniture, expenditures on	yr	444	1999	30r
Household furnishings and equipment purchases	yr	1768	1999	30r
Household textiles, expenditures on	yr	141	1999	30r
Laundry and cleaning supplies, expenditures on	yr	128	1999	30r
Housing				
Home price, existing, ave		239400	10/00	90r
Home value, median		215000	2001	53s
Household operation expenditures	yr	781	1999	30r
Housekeeping supplies purchases	yr	513	1999	30r
Lodging expenditures	yr	575	1999	30r
Maintenance, repairs, insurance expenditures	yr	939	1999	30r
Monthly rental value of owned home	mos	662	1999	30r
Owned dwellings, expenditures own	yr	5231	1999	30r
Rent expenditures	yr	2709	1999	30r
Shelter, expenditures on	yr	8516	1999	30r
Insurance and Pensions				
Life and other personal insurance purchases	yr	355	1999	30r
Pensions and Social Security, expenditures on	yr	3636	1999	30r
Legal Fees				
Divorce, filing fee		182.00	4/01	35s
Driver's license fee	renew	15.00	1999	48s
Driver's license fee	orig	12.00	1999	48s
Personal Goods				
Personal care products and services purchases	yr	449	1999	30r
Personal Services				
Personal services, household, expenditures on	yr	353	1999	30r
Pets				
Pets, toys, and playground equipment, expenditures on	yr	358	1999	30r
Taxes				
Federal income taxes paid	yr	3200	1999	30r
Personal taxes, expenditures on	yr	4153	1999	30r
Property taxes paid	yr	923	1999	30r
State and local income taxes paid	yr	812	1999	30r
Transportation				
Cars and trucks, new, expenditures on	yr	1534	1999	30r
Cars and trucks, used, expenditures on	yr	1593	1999	30r
Diesel at the pump	gal	1.37	10/99	73s
Gasoline and motor oil purchases	yr	1129	1999	30r
Gasoline before-tax price (cents)	gal	128.80	10/00	43s
Maintenance and repair expenditures	yr	797	1999	30r
Public transportation, expenditures on	yr	530	1999	30r
Transportation purchases	yr	7423	1999	30r
Vehicle expenses, miscellaneous, purchases	yr	2585	1999	30r
Vehicle insurance payments	yr	811	1999	30r
Vehicle purchases (net outlay)	yr	3180	1999	30r
Vehicle rental, lease expenditures	yr	666	1999	30r

Values are in dollars or fractions of dollars. In the column headed *Ref*, references are shown to sources. Each reference is followed by a letter. These refer to the geographical level for which data were reported: s=State, r=Region, and c=City or metro. The abbreviation *ex* is used to mean *except* or *excluding*; *exp* stands for expenditures. For other abbreviations and further explanations, please see the Introduction.

San Francisco-Oakland-San Jose, CA - continued

Item	Per	Value	Date	Ref.
Utilities				
Electrical bill, average	mos	58.66	9/00	9s
Electricity, expenditures on	yr	725	1999	30r
Electricity cost, average	KWh	7.75	9/00	9s
Utilities, fuels, and public services purchased	yr	2179	1999	30r
Water and other public services, expenditures on	yr	339	1999	30r
Weddings				
Wedding (national average cost)		19936	2000	33r
Wedding (regional average total cost)		18918	1997	110r
Attendants' gifts		321	1998	33r
Bridal attendants' apparel (5 persons)		824	2000	33r
Bride's headpiece/veil		173	1998	33r
Bride's wedding dress		859	1998	33r
Clergy, religious facility fee		242	1998	33r
Engagement ring		3177	1998	33r
Flowers		789	1998	33r
Groom's formalwear rental		99	2000	33r
Limousine		410	1998	33r
Marriage license cost		50.00-80.00	4/01	35s
Men's formalwear (ushers, best man)		469	2000	33r
Mother of bride apparel		241	2000	33r
Music		866	1998	33r
Photography and videography		1368	1998	33r
Rehearsal dinner		728	1998	33r
Wedding invitations and announcements		341	1998	33r
Wedding reception		7968	2000	33r
Wedding rings (bride and groom)		1060	1998	33r

San Jose, CA

Item	Per	Value	Date	Ref.
Average annual expenditures	yr	40662	1999	30r
Alcoholic Beverages				
Alcoholic beverage purchases	yr	372	1999	30r
Malt beverages, all types, all sizes, any origin	16 oz	0.94	7/01	11r
Wine, red and white table, all sizes, any origin	liter	6.00	7/01	11r
Appliances				
Major appliances, expenditures on	yr	167	1999	30r
Small appliances, housewares, expenditures on	yr	105	1999	30r
Banking and Money				
Mortgage interest and charges paid	yr	3368	1999	30r
Mortgage principal paid on owned property	yr	1677	1999	30r
Vehicle finance charges paid	yr	311	1999	30r
Business Expenses				
Business travel, car rental	day	52	2001	3c
Business travel, food	day	55	2001	3c
Business travel, hotel	day	184	2001	3c
Office space, central business district, Class A	sq ft	36.60	3/99	74c
Office space, outside central business district, Class A	sq ft	37.56	3/99	74c
Charity				
Cash contributions, expenditures	yr	1344	1999	30r
Child Care				
Child raising cost, total, age 0-2	yr	9140	1999	60r
Child raising cost, total, age 3-5	yr	9370	1999	60r
Child raising cost, total, age 6-8	yr	9450	1999	60r
Child raising cost, total, age 9-11	yr	9470	1999	60r
Child raising cost, total, age 12-14	yr	10170	1999	60r
Child raising cost, total, age 15-17	yr	10360	1999	60r
Child's child care and education, age 0-2	yr	1250	1999	60r
Child's child care and education, age 3-5	yr	1380	1999	60r
Child's child care and education, age 6-8	yr	890	1999	60r
Child's child care and education, age 9-11	yr	580	1999	60r
Child's child care and education, age 12-14	yr	430	1999	60r
Child's child care and education, age 15-17	yr	730	1999	60r

San Jose, CA - continued

Item	Per	Value	Date	Ref.
Child Care - continued				
Child's clothing, age 0-2	yr	430	1999	60r
Child's clothing, age 3-5	yr	420	1999	60r
Child's clothing, age 6-8	yr	470	1999	60r
Child's clothing, age 9-11	yr	520	1999	60r
Child's clothing, age 12-14	yr	870	1999	60r
Child's clothing, age 15-17	yr	770	1999	60r
Child's food, age 0-2	yr	1120	1999	60r
Child's food, age 3-5	yr	1280	1999	60r
Child's food, age 6-8	yr	1640	1999	60r
Child's food, age 9-11	yr	1930	1999	60r
Child's food, age 12-14	yr	1940	1999	60r
Child's food, age 15-17	yr	2150	1999	60r
Child's health care, age 0-2	yr	490	1999	60r
Child's health care, age 3-5	yr	470	1999	60r
Child's health care, age 6-8	yr	530	1999	60r
Child's health care, age 9-11	yr	570	1999	60r
Child's health care, age 12-14	yr	580	1999	60r
Child's health care, age 15-17	yr	610	1999	60r
Child's housing, age 0-2	yr	3630	1999	60r
Child's housing, age 3-5	yr	3610	1999	60r
Child's housing, age 6-8	yr	3570	1999	60r
Child's housing, age 9-11	yr	3410	1999	60r
Child's housing, age 12-14	yr	3600	1999	60r
Child's housing, age 15-17	yr	3210	1999	60r
Child's personal care, reading, age 0-2	yr	1040	1999	60r
Child's personal care, reading, age 3-5	yr	1060	1999	60r
Child's personal care, reading, age 6-8	yr	1090	1999	60r
Child's personal care, reading, age 9-11	yr	1130	1999	60r
Child's personal care, reading, age 12-14	yr	1300	1999	60r
Child's personal care, reading, age 15-17	yr	1080	1999	60r
Clothing				
Apparel and services purchases	yr	1863	1999	30r
Boys, 2 to 15, expenditures on	yr	80	1999	30r
Children under 2, expenditures on	yr	74	1999	30r
Footwear, expenditures on	yr	307	1999	30r
Girls, 2 to 15, expenditures on	yr	101	1999	30r
Men and boys, expenditures on	yr	443	1999	30r
Men, 16 and over, expenditures on	yr	363	1999	30r
Women, 16 and over, expenditures on	yr	594	1999	30r
Communications				
Cable modem installation, AT&T-BIS		150.00	6/99	103s
Cable modem installation, Charter		99.00-169.00	6/99	103s
Cable modem installation, Comcast		95.00	6/99	103s
Cable modem installation, Cox		99.00-174.95	6/99	103s
Cable modem installation, Media One		100.00	6/99	103s
Cable modem installation, Time Warner		75.00-225.00	6/99	103s
Cable modem rate, cable subscriber, AT&T-BIS	mos	39.95	6/99	103s
Cable modem rate, cable subscriber, Charter	mos	49.95-79.95	6/99	103s
Cable modem rate, cable subscriber, Comcast	mos	39.95	6/99	103s
Cable modem rate, cable subscriber, Cox	mos	29.95-44.95	6/99	103s
Cable modem rate, cable subscriber, Media One	mos	34.95-39.95	6/99	103s
Cable modem rate, cable subscriber, Time Warner	mos	39.95-49.95	6/99	103s
Cable modem rate, non-cable subscriber, Charter	mos	59.95-89.95	6/99	103s
Cable modem rate, non-cable subscriber, Comcast	mos	49.95	6/99	103s
Cable modem rate, non-cable subscriber, Cox	mos	42.95-54.95	6/99	103s
Cable modem rate, non-cable subscriber, Media One	mos	49.95	6/99	103s
Cable modem rate, non-cable subscriber, Time Warner	mos	39.95-54.95	6/99	103s

Values are in dollars or fractions of dollars. In the column headed *Ref*, references are shown to sources. Each reference is followed by a letter. These refer to the geographical level for which data were reported: s=State, r=Region, and c=City or metro. The abbreviation *ex* is used to mean *except* or *excluding*; *exp* stands for *expenditures*. For other abbreviations and further explanations, please see the Introduction.

San Jose, CA - continued

Item	Per	Value	Date	Ref.
Communications				
Phone line, single, business, field visit	inst.	70.75	12/97	17s
Phone line, single, business, no field visit	inst.	70.75	12/97	17s
Phone line, single, residence, field visit	inst.	34.75	12/97	17s
Phone line, single, residence, no field visit	inst.	34.75	12/97	17s
Postage and stationery, expenditures on	yr	150	1999	30r
Postal rate, express mail, up to half-pound		12.45	7/01	108r
Postal rate, letter, first class, first ounce		0.34	7/01	108r
Postal rate, letter, two ounces		0.57	7/01	108r
Postal rate, post card		0.21	7/01	108r
Postal rate, priority mail, two pounds		3.95	7/01	108r
Postal rate, priority mail, up to one pound		3.50	7/01	108r
Telephone bill, business, basic rate	mos	10.32	12/97	18c
Telephone bill, residential, basic rate	mos	3.00	12/97	18c
Telephone services, expenditures on	yr	825	1999	30r
Education				
Board, 4-year private college/university	yr	2970	1996	38s
Board, 4-year public college/university	yr	2516	1996	38s
Education expenditures	yr	676	1999	30r
Room, 4-year private college/university	yr	3196	1996	38s
Room, 4-year public college/university	yr	3031	1996	38s
Total cost, 4-year private college/university	yr	20143	1996	38s
Total cost, 4-year public college/university	yr	8213	1996	38s
Tuition, 2-year public college/university, in state	yr	362	1996	38s
Tuition, 4-year private college/university, in state	yr	13977	1996	38s
Tuition, 4-year public college/university	yr	2666	1996	38s
Energy and Fuels				
Electricity	KWh	0.11	7/01	11r
Electricity	500 KWhs	48.23	7/01	11r
Fuel oil and other fuels, expenditures on	yr	35	1999	30r
Gas, cooking, winter, 10 therms	mos	5.40	2/96	98c
Gas, cooking, winter, 30 therms	mos	16.20	2/96	98c
Gas, cooking, winter, 50 therms	mos	26.47	2/96	98c
Gas, heating, winter, average use	mos	45.13	2/96	98c
Gas, natural, commercial rate	1000 cf	8.74	11/00	88s
Gasoline, all types	gal	1.91	7/01	11r
Gasoline, unleaded premium	gal	2.05	7/01	11r
Gasoline, unleaded regular	gal	1.83	7/01	11r
Natural gas, expenditures on	yr	255	1999	30r
Utility (piped) gas, therm		0.98	7/01	11r
Utility (piped) gas, 40 therms		40.74	7/01	11r
Utility (piped) gas, 100 therms		96.80	7/01	11r
Entertainment				
Entertainment purchases	yr	2139	1999	30r
Fees and admissions paid	yr	545	1999	30r
First-run film ticket		8.50	1999	68c
Television, radios, sound equipment, expenditures on	yr	624	1999	30r
Funerals				
Total cost of funeral		5401.08	1/99	78r
Acknowledgement cards		33.64	1/99	78r
Casket		2170.43	1/99	78r
Cosmetology, hair, other preparation		136.32	1/99	78r
Embalming		319.13	1/99	78r
Funeral at funeral home		370.21	1/99	78r
Hearse (local)		161.04	1/99	78r
Professional service charges		963.15	1/99	78r
Service car/van		133.99	1/99	78r
Transfer of remains to funeral home		159.82	1/99	78r
Vault		778.07	1/99	78r
Visitation/viewing		175.28	1/99	78r
Groceries				
Apples, red delicious	lb	0.84	7/01	11r
Bacon, sliced	lb	3.38	7/01	11r
Bakery products, expenditures on	yr	299	1999	30r
Bananas	lb	0.54	7/01	11r
Beans, dried, any type, all sizes	lb	0.76	7/01	11r

San Jose, CA - continued

Item	Per	Value	Date	Ref.
Groceries - continued				
Beef, expenditures on	yr	222	1999	30r
Bread, white, pan	lb	0.99	7/01	11r
Butter, yoghurt, cheese, etc, expenditures on	yr	211	1999	30r
Cereals and bakery product purchases	yr	466	1999	30r
Cereals and cereal products, expenditures on	yr	168	1999	30r
Chicken breast, bone-in	lb	2.45	7/01	11r
Chicken, fresh, whole	lb	1.19	7/01	11r
Chops, boneless,	lb	4.00	7/01	11r
Chuck roast, graded and ungraded, excl U.S. prime and choice	lb	2.55	7/01	11r
Coffee, 100%, ground roast, all sizes	lb	3.80	7/01	11r
Cookies, chocolate chip	lb	2.83	7/01	11r
Dairy product purchases	yr	341	1999	30r
Eggs, expenditures on	yr	39	1999	30r
Eggs, grade AA, large	dozen	1.23	7/01	11r
Fats and oils, expenditures on	yr	88	1999	30r
Fish and seafood, expenditures on	yr	121	1999	30r
Food (excl fruit and vegetables), eaten at home, purchases	yr	1001	1999	30r
Food cooked on trips, expenditures on	yr	64	1999	30r
Food purchases	yr	5312	1999	30r
Food purchases, eaten away from home	yr	2180	1999	30r
Food purchases, food eaten at home	yr	3132	1999	30r
Fresh fruits, expenditures on	yr	186	1999	30r
Fresh milk and cream, expenditures on	yr	130	1999	30r
Fresh vegetables, expenditures on	yr	177	1999	30r
Grapefruit	lb	0.68	7/01	11r
Grapes, Thompson, seedless	lb	2.42	7/01	11r
Ground beef, lean and extra lean	lb	2.46	7/01	11r
Ice cream, prepackaged, bulk, regular	1/2 gal	3.62	7/01	11r
Lettuce, iceberg	lb	0.63	7/01	11r
Meats, poultry, fish, and egg purchases	yr	761	1999	30r
Milk, fresh, low fat	gal	2.80	7/01	11r
Milk, fresh, whole, fortified	gal	2.88	7/01	11r
Nonalcoholic beverages, expenditures on	yr	258	1999	30r
Oranges, Navel	lb	0.97	7/01	11r
Oranges, Valencia	lb	0.43	7/01	11r
Peaches	lb	1.38	7/01	11r
Peanut butter, creamy, all sizes	lb	2.14	7/01	11r
Pork chops, center cut, bone-in	lb	3.83	7/01	11r
Pork, expenditures on	yr	141	1999	30r
Potatoes, white, all types	lb	0.37	7/01	11r
Poultry, expenditures on	yr	146	1999	30r
Processed fruits, expenditures on	yr	118	1999	30r
Processed vegetables, expenditures on	yr	81	1999	30r
Round roast, graded and ungraded, excl U.S. prime and choice	lb	3.07	7/01	11r
Round roast, U.S. choice, boneless	lb	3.37	7/01	11r
Round steak, graded and ungraded, excl U.S. prime and choice	lb	3.51	7/01	11r
Sirloin steak, graded and ungraded, excl U.S. prime and choice	lb	4.67	7/01	11r
Steak, sirloin, U.S. choice, boneless	lb	6.20	7/01	11r
Strawberries, dry pint	12 oz	1.79	7/01	11r
Sugar and other sweets, expenditures on	yr	124	1999	30r
Sugar, white, all sizes	lb	0.46	7/01	11r
Tobacco products and smoking supplies purchases	yr	217	1999	30r
Tomatoes, field grown	lb	1.17	7/01	11r
Tuna, light, chunk	lb	2.05	7/01	11r
Goods and Services				
B&B Japanese maple (acer japonicum)	gal	39.99	4/00	93r
Boxwood (buxus)	2 gal	14.99-24.99	4/00	93r
Christmas tree, noble fir		40-60	2000	65s
Daylily (hemerocallis)	gal	6.99-8.99	4/00	93r
Flat of annuals		16.68	4/00	93r
Fountain grass (pennisetum)	gal	7.99-11.99	4/00	93r
Hanging basket (10 in)		29.99	4/00	93r

Values are in dollars or fractions of dollars. In the column headed *Ref*, references are shown to sources. Each reference is followed by a letter. These refer to the geographical level for which data were reported: s=State, r=Region, and c=City or metro. The abbreviation *ex* is used to mean *except* or *excluding*; *exp* stands for expenditures. For other abbreviations and further explanations, please see the Introduction.

San Jose, CA - continued

Item	Per	Value	Date	Ref.
Goods and Services				
Hardy geranium (geranium)	gal	6.99-11.99	4/00	93r
Hosta (hosta)	gal	6.99-18.99	4/00	93r
Lilac (syrubga vulgaris)	2 gal	14.99-17.99	4/00	93r
Miscellaneous purchases	yr	1070	1999	30r
Rhododendron (rhododendron)	2 gal	14.99	4/00	93r
Sage (salvia)	gal	6.99	4/00	93r
Wintercreeper euonymus (euonymus fortunei)	2 gal	14.99-22.99	4/00	93r
Hunting license	yr	29.95	4/01	34s
Health Care				
Cardiac catheterization, ave hospital/physician charges		24000	1998	77s
Childbirth, Cesarean delivery		11587	1997	13r
Childbirth, vaginal delivery		6725	1997	13r
Drugs, expenditures on	yr	309	1999	30r
Health care purchases	yr	1869	1999	30r
Health insurance expenditures	yr	868	1999	30r
Hysterectomy, laproscopically-assisted, ave hospital/physician charges		20760	1998	76s
Hysterectomy, vaginal, ave hospital and physician charges		14570	1998	76s
Medicaid dispensing fee		4.05	1999	87s
Medical services expenditures	yr	580	1999	30r
Medical supplies, expenditures on	yr	112	1999	30r
Household Goods				
Floor coverings, expenditures on	yr	49	1999	30r
Furniture, expenditures on	yr	444	1999	30r
Household furnishings and equipment purchases	yr	1768	1999	30r
Household textiles, expenditures on	yr	141	1999	30r
Laundry and cleaning supplies, expenditures on	yr	128	1999	30r
Housing				
Home, 2200 sq ft, 4-br, 2-bath, 2-car garage, average		528750	2000	47c
Home, suburban, 2,200 square feet		708600	2000	23c
Home price, existing, ave		239400	10/00	90r
Home value, median		215000	2001	53s
Household operation expenditures	yr	781	1999	30r
Housekeeping supplies purchases	yr	513	1999	30r
Lodging expenditures	yr	575	1999	30r
Maintenance, repairs, insurance expenditures	yr	939	1999	30r
Monthly rental value of owned home	mos	662	1999	30r
Owned dwellings, expenditures own	yr	5231	1999	30r
Rent expenditures	yr	2709	1999	30r
Rental unit, 1 bedroom, with utilities	mos	1058	4/01	41c
Rental unit, 2 bedroom, with utilities	mos	1308	4/01	41c
Rental unit, 3 bedroom, with utilities	mos	1792	4/01	41c
Rental unit, 4 bedroom, with utilities	mos	2013	4/01	41c
Shelter, expenditures on	yr	8516	1999	30r
Insurance and Pensions				
Auto insurance, no teens	yr	1100	1999	68c
Life and other personal insurance purchases	yr	355	1999	30r
Pensions and Social Security, expenditures on	yr	3636	1999	30r
Legal Fees				
Divorce, filing fee		182.00	4/01	35s
Driver's license fee	renew	15.00	1999	48s
Driver's license fee	orig	12.00	1999	48s
Personal Goods				
Personal care products and services purchases	yr	449	1999	30r

San Jose, CA - continued

Item	Per	Value	Date	Ref.
Personal Services				
Personal services, household, expenditures on	yr	353	1999	30r
Pets				
Pets, toys, and playground equipment, expenditures on	yr	358	1999	30r
Restaurant Food				
Fine restaurant meal		28.49	1999	68c
Taxes				
Federal income taxes paid	yr	3200	1999	30r
Personal taxes, expenditures on	yr	4153	1999	30r
Property taxes paid	yr	923	1999	30r
State and local income taxes paid	yr	812	1999	30r
Transportation				
Bus fare, one-way	trip	1.25	2000	1c
Cars and trucks, new, expenditures on	yr	1534	1999	30r
Cars and trucks, used, expenditures on	yr	1593	1999	30r
Diesel at the pump	gal	1.37	10/99	73s
Gasoline and motor oil purchases	yr	1129	1999	30r
Gasoline before-tax price (cents)	gal	128.80	10/00	43s
Light rail transit fare, one-way	trip	1.25	2000	2c
Maintenance and repair expenditures	yr	797	1999	30r
Public transportation, expenditures on	yr	530	1999	30r
Transportation purchases	yr	7423	1999	30r
Vehicle expenses, miscellaneous, purchases	yr	2585	1999	30r
Vehicle insurance payments	yr	811	1999	30r
Vehicle purchases (net outlay)	yr	3180	1999	30r
Vehicle rental, lease expenditures	yr	666	1999	30r
Utilities				
Electrical bill, average	mos	58.66	9/00	9s
Electricity, expenditures on	yr	725	1999	30r
Electricity, summer, 250 KWh	mos	33.96	2/96	97c
Electricity, summer, 500 KWh	mos	70.55	2/96	97c
Electricity, summer, 750 KWh	mos	108.84	2/96	97c
Electricity, summer, 1000 KWh	mos	147.12	2/96	97c
Electricity cost, average	KWh	7.75	9/00	9s
Utilities, fuels, and public services purchased	yr	2179	1999	30r
Water and other public services, expenditures on	yr	339	1999	30r
Weddings				
Wedding (national average cost)		19936	2000	33r
Wedding (regional average total cost)		18918	1997	110r
Attendants' gifts		321	1998	33r
Bridal attendants' apparel (5 persons)		824	2000	33r
Bride's headpiece/veil		173	1998	33r
Bride's wedding dress		859	1998	33r
Clergy, religious facility fee		242	1998	33r
Engagement ring		3177	1998	33r
Flowers		789	1998	33r
Groom's formalwear rental		99	2000	33r
Limousine		410	1998	33r
Marriage license cost		50.00-80.00	4/01	35s
Men's formalwear (ushers, best man)		469	2000	33r
Mother of bride apparel		241	2000	33r
Music		866	1998	33r
Photography and videography		1368	1998	33r
Rehearsal dinner		728	1998	33r
Wedding invitations and announcements		341	1998	33r
Wedding reception		7968	2000	33r
Wedding rings (bride and groom)		1060	1998	33r

San Luis Obispo-Atascadero-Paso Robles, CA

Item	Per	Value	Date	Ref.
Average annual expenditures	yr	40662	1999	30r
Alcoholic Beverages				
Alcoholic beverage purchases	yr	372	1999	30r
Malt beverages, all types, all sizes, any origin	16 oz	0.94	7/01	11r

Values are in dollars or fractions of dollars. In the column headed *Ref*, references are shown to sources. Each reference is followed by a letter. These refer to the geographical level for which data were reported: s=State, r=Region, and c=City or metro. The abbreviation *ex* is used to mean *except* or *excluding*; *exp* stands for *expenditures*. For other abbreviations and further explanations, please see the Introduction.

San Luis Obispo-Atascadero-Paso Robles, CA - continued

Item	Per	Value	Date	Ref.
Alcoholic Beverages				
Wine, red and white table, all sizes, any origin	liter	6.00	7/01	11r
Appliances				
Major appliances, expenditures on	yr	167	1999	30r
Small appliances, housewares, expenditures on	yr	105	1999	30r
Banking and Money				
Mortgage interest and charges paid	yr	3368	1999	30r
Mortgage principal paid on owned property	yr	1677	1999	30r
Vehicle finance charges paid	yr	311	1999	30r
Charity				
Cash contributions, expenditures	yr	1344	1999	30r
Child Care				
Child raising cost, total, age 0-2	yr	9140	1999	60r
Child raising cost, total, age 3-5	yr	9370	1999	60r
Child raising cost, total, age 6-8	yr	9450	1999	60r
Child raising cost, total, age 9-11	yr	9470	1999	60r
Child raising cost, total, age 12-14	yr	10170	1999	60r
Child raising cost, total, age 15-17	yr	10360	1999	60r
Child's child care and education, age 0-2	yr	1250	1999	60r
Child's child care and education, age 3-5	yr	1380	1999	60r
Child's child care and education, age 6-8	yr	890	1999	60r
Child's child care and education, age 9-11	yr	580	1999	60r
Child's child care and education, age 12-14	yr	430	1999	60r
Child's child care and education, age 15-17	yr	730	1999	60r
Child's clothing, age 0-2	yr	430	1999	60r
Child's clothing, age 3-5	yr	420	1999	60r
Child's clothing, age 6-8	yr	470	1999	60r
Child's clothing, age 9-11	yr	520	1999	60r
Child's clothing, age 12-14	yr	870	1999	60r
Child's clothing, age 15-17	yr	770	1999	60r
Child's food, age 0-2	yr	1120	1999	60r
Child's food, age 3-5	yr	1280	1999	60r
Child's food, age 6-8	yr	1640	1999	60r
Child's food, age 9-11	yr	1930	1999	60r
Child's food, age 12-14	yr	1940	1999	60r
Child's food, age 15-17	yr	2150	1999	60r
Child's health care, age 0-2	yr	490	1999	60r
Child's health care, age 3-5	yr	470	1999	60r
Child's health care, age 6-8	yr	530	1999	60r
Child's health care, age 9-11	yr	570	1999	60r
Child's health care, age 12-14	yr	580	1999	60r
Child's health care, age 15-17	yr	610	1999	60r
Child's housing, age 0-2	yr	3630	1999	60r
Child's housing, age 3-5	yr	3610	1999	60r
Child's housing, age 6-8	yr	3570	1999	60r
Child's housing, age 9-11	yr	3410	1999	60r
Child's housing, age 12-14	yr	3600	1999	60r
Child's housing, age 15-17	yr	3210	1999	60r
Child's personal care, reading, age 0-2	yr	1040	1999	60r
Child's personal care, reading, age 3-5	yr	1060	1999	60r
Child's personal care, reading, age 6-8	yr	1090	1999	60r
Child's personal care, reading, age 9-11	yr	1130	1999	60r
Child's personal care, reading, age 12-14	yr	1300	1999	60r
Child's personal care, reading, age 15-17	yr	1080	1999	60r
Clothing				
Apparel and services purchases	yr	1863	1999	30r
Boys, 2 to 15, expenditures on	yr	80	1999	30r
Children under 2, expenditures on	yr	74	1999	30r
Footwear, expenditures on	yr	307	1999	30r
Girls, 2 to 15, expenditures on	yr	101	1999	30r
Men and boys, expenditures on	yr	443	1999	30r
Men, 16 and over, expenditures on	yr	363	1999	30r
Women, 16 and over, expenditures on	yr	594	1999	30r
Communications				
Cable modem installation, AT&T-BIS		150.00	6/99	103s
Cable modem installation, Charter		99.00-169.00	6/99	103s
Cable modem installation, Comcast		95.00	6/99	103s

San Luis Obispo-Atascadero-Paso Robles, CA - continued

Item	Per	Value	Date	Ref.
Communications - continued				
Cable modem installation, Cox		99.00-174.95	6/99	103s
Cable modem installation, Media One		100.00	6/99	103s
Cable modem installation, Time Warner		75.00-225.00	6/99	103s
Cable modem rate, cable subscriber, AT&T-BIS	mos	39.95	6/99	103s
Cable modem rate, cable subscriber, Charter	mos	49.95-79.95	6/99	103s
Cable modem rate, cable subscriber, Comcast	mos	39.95	6/99	103s
Cable modem rate, cable subscriber, Cox	mos	29.95-44.95	6/99	103s
Cable modem rate, cable subscriber, Media One	mos	34.95-39.95	6/99	103s
Cable modem rate, cable subscriber, Time Warner	mos	39.95-49.95	6/99	103s
Cable modem rate, non-cable subscriber, Charter	mos	59.95-89.95	6/99	103s
Cable modem rate, non-cable subscriber, Comcast	mos	49.95	6/99	103s
Cable modem rate, non-cable subscriber, Cox	mos	42.95-54.95	6/99	103s
Cable modem rate, non-cable subscriber, Media One	mos	49.95	6/99	103s
Cable modem rate, non-cable subscriber, Time Warner	mos	39.95-54.95	6/99	103s
Phone line, single, business, field visit	inst.	70.75	12/97	17s
Phone line, single, business, no field visit	inst.	70.75	12/97	17s
Phone line, single, residence, field visit	inst.	34.75	12/97	17s
Phone line, single, residence, no field visit	inst.	34.75	12/97	17s
Postage and stationery, expenditures on	yr	150	1999	30r
Postal rate, express mail, up to half-pound		12.45	7/01	108r
Postal rate, letter, first class, first ounce		0.34	7/01	108r
Postal rate, letter, two ounces		0.57	7/01	108r
Postal rate, post card		0.21	7/01	108r
Postal rate, priority mail, two pounds		3.95	7/01	108r
Postal rate, priority mail, up to one pound		3.50	7/01	108r
Telephone services, expenditures on	yr	825	1999	30r
Education				
Board, 4-year private college/university	yr	2970	1996	38s
Board, 4-year public college/university	yr	2516	1996	38s
Education expenditures	yr	676	1999	30r
Room, 4-year private college/university	yr	3196	1996	38s
Room, 4-year public college/university	yr	3031	1996	38s
Total cost, 4-year private college/university	yr	20143	1996	38s
Total cost, 4-year public college/university	yr	8213	1996	38s
Tuition, 2-year public college/university, in state	yr	362	1996	38s
Tuition, 4-year private college/university, in state	yr	13977	1996	38s
Tuition, 4-year public college/university	yr	2666	1996	38s
Energy and Fuels				
Electricity	KWh	0.11	7/01	11r
Electricity	500 KWhs	48.23	7/01	11r
Fuel oil and other fuels, expenditures on	yr	35	1999	30r
Gas, natural, commercial rate	1000 cf	8.74	11/00	88s
Gasoline, all types	gal	1.91	7/01	11r
Gasoline, unleaded premium	gal	2.05	7/01	11r
Gasoline, unleaded regular	gal	1.83	7/01	11r
Natural gas, expenditures on	yr	255	1999	30r
Utility (piped) gas, therm		0.98	7/01	11r
Utility (piped) gas, 40 therms		40.74	7/01	11r
Utility (piped) gas, 100 therms		96.80	7/01	11r
Entertainment				
Entertainment purchases	yr	2139	1999	30r
Fees and admissions paid	yr	545	1999	30r
Television, radios, sound equipment, expenditures on	yr	624	1999	30r

Values are in dollars or fractions of dollars. In the column headed *Ref*, references are shown to sources. Each reference is followed by a letter. These refer to the geographical level for which data were reported: s=State, r=Region, and c=City or metro. The abbreviation *ex* is used to mean *except* or *excluding*; *exp* stands for *expenditures*. For other abbreviations and further explanations, please see the Introduction.

San Luis Obispo-Atascadero-Paso Robles, CA - continued

Item	Per	Value	Date	Ref.
Funerals				
Total cost of funeral		5401.08	1/99	78r
Acknowledgement cards		33.64	1/99	78r
Casket		2170.43	1/99	78r
Cosmetology, hair, other preparation		136.32	1/99	78r
Embalming		319.13	1/99	78r
Funeral at funeral home		370.21	1/99	78r
Hearse (local)		161.04	1/99	78r
Professional service charges		963.15	1/99	78r
Service car/van		133.99	1/99	78r
Transfer of remains to funeral home		159.82	1/99	78r
Vault		778.07	1/99	78r
Visitation/viewing		175.28	1/99	78r
Groceries				
Apples, red delicious	lb	0.84	7/01	11r
Bacon, sliced	lb	3.38	7/01	11r
Bakery products, expenditures on	yr	299	1999	30r
Bananas	lb	0.54	7/01	11r
Beans, dried, any type, all sizes	lb	0.76	7/01	11r
Beef, expenditures on	yr	222	1999	30r
Bread, white, pan	lb	0.99	7/01	11r
Butter, yoghurt, cheese, etc, expenditures on	yr	211	1999	30r
Cereals and bakery product purchases	yr	466	1999	30r
Cereals and cereal products, expenditures on	yr	168	1999	30r
Chicken breast, bone-in	lb	2.45	7/01	11r
Chicken, fresh, whole	lb	1.19	7/01	11r
Chops, boneless,	lb	4.00	7/01	11r
Chuck roast, graded and ungraded, excl U.S. prime and choice	lb	2.55	7/01	11r
Coffee, 100%, ground roast, all sizes	lb	3.80	7/01	11r
Cookies, chocolate chip	lb	2.83	7/01	11r
Dairy product purchases	yr	341	1999	30r
Eggs, expenditures on	yr	39	1999	30r
Eggs, grade AA, large	dozen	1.23	7/01	11r
Fats and oils, expenditures on	yr	88	1999	30r
Fish and seafood, expenditures on	yr	121	1999	30r
Food (excl fruit and vegetables), eaten at home, purchases	yr	1001	1999	30r
Food cooked on trips, expenditures on	yr	64	1999	30r
Food purchases	yr	5312	1999	30r
Food purchases, eaten away from home	yr	2180	1999	30r
Food purchases, food eaten at home	yr	3132	1999	30r
Fresh fruits, expenditures on	yr	186	1999	30r
Fresh milk and cream, expenditures on	yr	130	1999	30r
Fresh vegetables, expenditures on	yr	177	1999	30r
Grapefruit	lb	0.68	7/01	11r
Grapes, Thompson, seedless	lb	2.42	7/01	11r
Ground beef, lean and extra lean	lb	2.46	7/01	11r
Ice cream, prepackaged, bulk, regular	1/2 gal	3.62	7/01	11r
Lettuce, iceberg	lb	0.63	7/01	11r
Meats, poultry, fish, and egg purchases	yr	761	1999	30r
Milk, fresh, low fat,	gal	2.80	7/01	11r
Milk, fresh, whole, fortified	gal	2.88	7/01	11r
Nonalcoholic beverages, expenditures on	yr	258	1999	30r
Oranges, Navel	lb	0.97	7/01	11r
Oranges, Valencia	lb	0.43	7/01	11r
Peaches	lb	1.38	7/01	11r
Peanut butter, creamy, all sizes	lb	2.14	7/01	11r
Pork chops, center cut, bone-in	lb	3.83	7/01	11r
Pork, expenditures on	yr	141	1999	30r
Potatoes, white, all types	lb	0.37	7/01	11r
Poultry, expenditures on	yr	146	1999	30r
Processed fruits, expenditures on	yr	118	1999	30r
Processed vegetables, expenditures on	yr	81	1999	30r
Round roast, graded and ungraded, excl U.S. prime and choice	lb	3.07	7/01	11r
Round roast, U.S. choice, boneless	lb	3.37	7/01	11r
Round steak, graded and ungraded, excl U.S. prime and choice	lb	3.51	7/01	11r
Sirloin steak, graded and ungraded, excl U.S. prime and choice	lb	4.67	7/01	11r
Steak, sirloin, U.S. choice, boneless	lb	6.20	7/01	11r

San Luis Obispo-Atascadero-Paso Robles, CA - continued

Item	Per	Value	Date	Ref.
Groceries - continued				
Strawberries, dry pint	12 oz	1.79	7/01	11r
Sugar and other sweets, expenditures on	yr	124	1999	30r
Sugar, white, all sizes	lb	0.46	7/01	11r
Tobacco products and smoking supplies purchases	yr	217	1999	30r
Tomatoes, field grown	lb	1.17	7/01	11r
Tuna, light, chunk	lb	2.05	7/01	11r
Goods and Services				
B&B Japanese maple (acer japonicum)	gal	39.99	4/00	93r
Boxwood (buxus)	2 gal	14.99-24.99	4/00	93r
Christmas tree, noble fir		40-60	2000	65s
Daylilly (hemerocallis)	gal	6.99-8.99	4/00	93r
Flat of annuals		16.68	4/00	93r
Fountain grass (pennisetum)	gal	7.99-11.99	4/00	93r
Hanging basket (10 in)		29.99	4/00	93r
Hardy geranium (geranium)	gal	6.99-11.99	4/00	93r
Hosta (hosta)	gal	6.99-18.99	4/00	93r
Lilac (syrubga vulgaris)	2 gal	14.99-17.99	4/00	93r
Miscellaneous purchases	yr	1070	1999	30r
Rhododendron (rhododendron)	2 gal	14.99	4/00	93r
Sage (salvia)	gal	6.99	4/00	93r
Wintercreeper euonymus (euonymus fortunei)	2 gal	14.99-22.99	4/00	93r
Hunting license	yr	29.95	4/01	34s
Health Care				
Cardiac catheterization, ave hospital/ physician charges		24000	1998	77s
Childbirth, Cesarean delivery		11587	1997	13r
Childbirth, vaginal delivery		6725	1997	13r
Drugs, expenditures on	yr	309	1999	30r
Health care purchases	yr	1869	1999	30r
Health insurance expenditures	yr	868	1999	30r
Hysterectomy, laproscopically-assisted, ave hospital/physician charges		20760	1998	76s
Hysterectomy, vaginal, ave hospital and physician charges		14570	1998	76s
Medicaid dispensing fee		4.05	1999	87s
Medical services expenditures	yr	580	1999	30r
Medical supplies, expenditures on	yr	112	1999	30r
Household Goods				
Floor coverings, expenditures on	yr	49	1999	30r
Furniture, expenditures on	yr	444	1999	30r
Household furnishings and equipment purchases	yr	1768	1999	30r
Household textiles, expenditures on	yr	141	1999	30r
Laundry and cleaning supplies, expenditures on	yr	128	1999	30r
Housing				
Home price, existing, ave		239400	10/00	90r
Home value, median		215000	2001	53s
Household operation expenditures	yr	781	1999	30r
Housekeeping supplies purchases	yr	513	1999	30r
Lodging expenditures	yr	575	1999	30r
Maintenance, repairs, insurance expenditures	yr	939	1999	30r
Monthly rental value of owned home	mos	662	1999	30r
Owned dwellings, expenditures own	yr	5231	1999	30r
Rent expenditures	yr	2709	1999	30r
Rental unit, 1 bedroom, with utilities	mos	593	4/01	41c
Rental unit, 2 bedroom, with utilities	mos	752	4/01	41c
Rental unit, 3 bedroom, with utilities	mos	1045	4/01	41c
Rental unit, 4 bedroom, with utilities	mos	1234	4/01	41c
Shelter, expenditures on	yr	8516	1999	30r

Values are in dollars or fractions of dollars. In the column headed *Ref*, references are shown to sources. Each reference is followed by a letter. These refer to the geographical level for which data were reported: s=State, r=Region, and c=City or metro. The abbreviation *ex* is used to mean *except* or *excluding*; *exp* stands for *expenditures*. For other abbreviations and further explanations, please see the Introduction.

San Luis Obispo-Atascadero-Paso Robles, CA - continued

Item	Per	Value	Date	Ref.
Insurance and Pensions				
Life and other personal insurance purchases	yr	355	1999	30r
Pensions and Social Security, expenditures on	yr	3636	1999	30r
Legal Fees				
Divorce, filing fee		182.00	4/01	35s
Driver's license fee	renew	15.00	1999	48s
Driver's license fee	orig	12.00	1999	48s
Personal Goods				
Personal care products and services purchases	yr	449	1999	30r
Personal Services				
Personal services, household, expenditures on	yr	353	1999	30r
Pets				
Pets, toys, and playground equipment, expenditures on	yr	358	1999	30r
Taxes				
Federal income taxes paid	yr	3200	1999	30r
Personal taxes, expenditures on	yr	4153	1999	30r
Property taxes paid	yr	923	1999	30r
State and local income taxes paid	yr	812	1999	30r
Transportation				
Cars and trucks, new, expenditures on	yr	1534	1999	30r
Cars and trucks, used, expenditures on	yr	1593	1999	30r
Diesel at the pump	gal	1.37	10/99	73s
Gasoline and motor oil purchases	yr	1129	1999	30r
Gasoline before-tax price (cents)	gal	128.80	10/00	43s
Maintenance and repair expenditures	yr	797	1999	30r
Public transportation, expenditures on	yr	530	1999	30r
Transportation purchases	yr	7423	1999	30r
Vehicle expenses, miscellaneous, purchases	yr	2585	1999	30r
Vehicle insurance payments	yr	811	1999	30r
Vehicle purchases (net outlay)	yr	3180	1999	30r
Vehicle rental, lease expenditures	yr	666	1999	30r
Utilities				
Electrical bill, average	mos	58.66	9/00	9s
Electricity, expenditures on	yr	725	1999	30r
Electricity cost, average	KWh	7.75	9/00	9s
Utilities, fuels, and public services purchased	yr	2179	1999	30r
Water and other public services, expenditures on	yr	339	1999	30r
Weddings				
Wedding (national average cost)		19936	2000	33r
Wedding (regional average total cost)		18918	1997	110r
Attendants' gifts		321	1998	33r
Bridal attendants' apparel (5 persons)		824	2000	33r
Bride's headpiece/veil		173	1998	33r
Bride's wedding dress		859	1998	33r
Clergy, religious facility fee		242	1998	33r
Engagement ring		3177	1998	33r
Flowers		789	1998	33r
Groom's formalwear rental		99	2000	33r
Limousine		410	1998	33r
Marriage license cost		50.00- 80.00	4/01	35s
Men's formalwear (ushers, best man)		469	2000	33r
Mother of bride apparel		241	2000	33r
Music		866	1998	33r
Photography and videography		1368	1998	33r
Rehearsal dinner		728	1998	33r
Wedding invitations and announcements		341	1998	33r
Wedding reception		7968	2000	33r
Wedding rings (bride and groom)		1060	1998	33r

Santa Barbara-Santa Maria-Lompoc, CA

Item	Per	Value	Date	Ref.
Average annual expenditures	yr	40662	1999	30r
Alcoholic Beverages				
Alcoholic beverage purchases	yr	372	1999	30r
Malt beverages, all types, all sizes, any origin	16 oz	0.94	7/01	11r
Wine, red and white table, all sizes, any origin	liter	6.00	7/01	11r
Appliances				
Major appliances, expenditures on	yr	167	1999	30r
Small appliances, housewares, expenditures on	yr	105	1999	30r
Banking and Money				
Mortgage interest and charges paid	yr	3368	1999	30r
Mortgage principal paid on owned property	yr	1677	1999	30r
Vehicle finance charges paid	yr	311	1999	30r
Charity				
Cash contributions, expenditures	yr	1344	1999	30r
Child Care				
Child raising cost, total, age 0-2	yr	9140	1999	60r
Child raising cost, total, age 3-5	yr	9370	1999	60r
Child raising cost, total, age 6-8	yr	9450	1999	60r
Child raising cost, total, age 9-11	yr	9470	1999	60r
Child raising cost, total, age 12-14	yr	10170	1999	60r
Child raising cost, total, age 15-17	yr	10360	1999	60r
Child's child care and education, age 0-2	yr	1250	1999	60r
Child's child care and education, age 3-5	yr	1380	1999	60r
Child's child care and education, age 6-8	yr	890	1999	60r
Child's child care and education, age 9-11	yr	580	1999	60r
Child's child care and education, age 12-14	yr	430	1999	60r
Child's child care and education, age 15-17	yr	730	1999	60r
Child's clothing, age 0-2	yr	430	1999	60r
Child's clothing, age 3-5	yr	420	1999	60r
Child's clothing, age 6-8	yr	470	1999	60r
Child's clothing, age 9-11	yr	520	1999	60r
Child's clothing, age 12-14	yr	870	1999	60r
Child's clothing, age 15-17	yr	770	1999	60r
Child's food, age 0-2	yr	1120	1999	60r
Child's food, age 3-5	yr	1280	1999	60r
Child's food, age 6-8	yr	1640	1999	60r
Child's food, age 9-11	yr	1930	1999	60r
Child's food, age 12-14	yr	1940	1999	60r
Child's food, age 15-17	yr	2150	1999	60r
Child's health care, age 0-2	yr	490	1999	60r
Child's health care, age 3-5	yr	470	1999	60r
Child's health care, age 6-8	yr	530	1999	60r
Child's health care, age 9-11	yr	570	1999	60r
Child's health care, age 12-14	yr	580	1999	60r
Child's health care, age 15-17	yr	610	1999	60r
Child's housing, age 0-2	yr	3630	1999	60r
Child's housing, age 3-5	yr	3610	1999	60r
Child's housing, age 6-8	yr	3570	1999	60r
Child's housing, age 9-11	yr	3410	1999	60r
Child's housing, age 12-14	yr	3600	1999	60r
Child's housing, age 15-17	yr	3210	1999	60r
Child's personal care, reading, age 0-2	yr	1040	1999	60r
Child's personal care, reading, age 3-5	yr	1060	1999	60r
Child's personal care, reading, age 6-8	yr	1090	1999	60r
Child's personal care, reading, age 9-11	yr	1130	1999	60r
Child's personal care, reading, age 12-14	yr	1300	1999	60r
Child's personal care, reading, age 15-17	yr	1080	1999	60r
Clothing				
Apparel and services purchases	yr	1863	1999	30r
Boys, 2 to 15, expenditures on	yr	80	1999	30r
Children under 2, expenditures on	yr	74	1999	30r
Footwear, expenditures on	yr	307	1999	30r
Girls, 2 to 15, expenditures on	yr	101	1999	30r
Men and boys, expenditures on	yr	443	1999	30r
Men, 16 and over, expenditures on	yr	363	1999	30r
Women, 16 and over, expenditures on	yr	594	1999	30r

Values are in dollars or fractions of dollars. In the column headed *Ref*, references are shown to sources. Each reference is followed by a letter. These refer to the geographical level for which data were reported: s=State, r=Region, and c=City or metro. The abbreviation *ex* is used to mean *except* or *excluding*; *exp* stands for *expenditures*. For other abbreviations and further explanations, please see the Introduction.

Santa Barbara-Santa Maria-Lompoc, CA - continued

Item	Per	Value	Date	Ref.
Communications				
Cable modem installation, AT&T-BIS		150.00	6/99	103s
Cable modem installation, Charter		99.00-169.00	6/99	103s
Cable modem installation, Comcast		95.00	6/99	103s
Cable modem installation, Cox		99.00-174.95	6/99	103s
Cable modem installation, Media One		100.00	6/99	103s
Cable modem installation, Time Warner		75.00-225.00	6/99	103s
Cable modem rate, cable subscriber, AT&T-BIS	mos	39.95	6/99	103s
Cable modem rate, cable subscriber, Charter	mos	49.95-79.95	6/99	103s
Cable modem rate, cable subscriber, Comcast	mos	39.95	6/99	103s
Cable modem rate, cable subscriber, Cox	mos	29.95-44.95	6/99	103s
Cable modem rate, cable subscriber, Media One	mos	34.95-39.95	6/99	103s
Cable modem rate, cable subscriber, Time Warner	mos	39.95-49.95	6/99	103s
Cable modem rate, non-cable subscriber, Charter	mos	59.95-89.95	6/99	103s
Cable modem rate, non-cable subscriber, Comcast	mos	49.95	6/99	103s
Cable modem rate, non-cable subscriber, Cox	mos	42.95-54.95	6/99	103s
Cable modem rate, non-cable subscriber, Media One	mos	49.95	6/99	103s
Cable modem rate, non-cable subscriber, Time Warner	mos	39.95-54.95	6/99	103s
Phone line, single, business, field visit	inst.	70.75	12/97	17s
Phone line, single, business, no field visit	inst.	70.75	12/97	17s
Phone line, single, residence, field visit	inst.	34.75	12/97	17s
Phone line, single, residence, no field visit	inst.	34.75	12/97	17s
Postage and stationery, expenditures on	yr	150	1999	30r
Postal rate, express mail, up to half-pound		12.45	7/01	108r
Postal rate, letter, first class, first ounce		0.34	7/01	108r
Postal rate, letter, two ounces		0.57	7/01	108r
Postal rate, post card		0.21	7/01	108r
Postal rate, priority mail, two pounds		3.95	7/01	108r
Postal rate, priority mail, up to one pound		3.50	7/01	108r
Telephone services, expenditures on	yr	825	1999	30r
Education				
Board, 4-year private college/university	yr	2970	1996	38s
Board, 4-year public college/university	yr	2516	1996	38s
Education expenditures	yr	676	1999	30r
Room, 4-year private college/university	yr	3196	1996	38s
Room, 4-year public college/university	yr	3031	1996	38s
Total cost, 4-year private college/university	yr	20143	1996	38s
Total cost, 4-year public college/university	yr	8213	1996	38s
Tuition, 2-year public college/university, in state	yr	362	1996	38s
Tuition, 4-year private college/university, in state	yr	13977	1996	38s
Tuition, 4-year public college/university	yr	2666	1996	38s
Energy and Fuels				
Electricity	KWh	0.11	7/01	11r
Electricity	500 KWhs	48.23	7/01	11r
Fuel oil and other fuels, expenditures on	yr	35	1999	30r
Gas, natural, commercial rate	1000 cf	8.74	11/00	88s
Gasoline, all types	gal	1.91	7/01	11r
Gasoline, unleaded premium	gal	2.05	7/01	11r
Gasoline, unleaded regular	gal	1.83	7/01	11r
Natural gas, expenditures on	yr	255	1999	30r
Utility (piped) gas, therm		0.98	7/01	11r
Utility (piped) gas, 40 therms		40.74	7/01	11r
Utility (piped) gas, 100 therms		96.80	7/01	11r

Santa Barbara-Santa Maria-Lompoc, CA - continued

Item	Per	Value	Date	Ref.
Entertainment				
Entertainment purchases	yr	2139	1999	30r
Fees and admissions paid	yr	545	1999	30r
Television, radios, sound equipment, expenditures on	yr	624	1999	30r
Funerals				
Total cost of funeral		5401.08	1/99	78r
Acknowledgement cards		33.64	1/99	78r
Casket		2170.43	1/99	78r
Cosmetology, hair, other preparation		136.32	1/99	78r
Embalming		319.13	1/99	78r
Funeral at funeral home		370.21	1/99	78r
Hearse (local)		161.04	1/99	78r
Professional service charges		963.15	1/99	78r
Service car/van		133.99	1/99	78r
Transfer of remains to funeral home		159.82	1/99	78r
Vault		778.07	1/99	78r
Visitation/viewing		175.28	1/99	78r
Groceries				
Apples, red delicious	lb	0.84	7/01	11r
Bacon, sliced	lb	3.38	7/01	11r
Bakery products, expenditures on	yr	299	1999	30r
Bananas	lb	0.54	7/01	11r
Beans, dried, any type, all sizes	lb	0.76	7/01	11r
Beef, expenditures on	yr	222	1999	30r
Bread, white, pan	lb	0.99	7/01	11r
Butter, yoghurt, cheese, etc, expenditures on	yr	211	1999	30r
Cereals and bakery product purchases	yr	466	1999	30r
Cereals and cereal products, expenditures on	yr	168	1999	30r
Chicken breast, bone-in	lb	2.45	7/01	11r
Chicken, fresh, whole	lb	1.19	7/01	11r
Chops, boneless,	lb	4.00	7/01	11r
Chuck roast, graded and ungraded, excl U.S. prime and choice	lb	2.55	7/01	11r
Coffee, 100%, ground roast, all sizes	lb	3.80	7/01	11r
Cookies, chocolate chip	lb	2.83	7/01	11r
Dairy product purchases	yr	341	1999	30r
Eggs, expenditures on	yr	39	1999	30r
Eggs, grade AA, large	dozen	1.23	7/01	11r
Fats and oils, expenditures on	yr	88	1999	30r
Fish and seafood, expenditures on	yr	121	1999	30r
Food (excl fruit and vegetables), eaten at home, purchases	yr	1001	1999	30r
Food cooked on trips, expenditures on	yr	64	1999	30r
Food purchases	yr	5312	1999	30r
Food purchases, eaten away from home	yr	2180	1999	30r
Food purchases, food eaten at home	yr	3132	1999	30r
Fresh fruits, expenditures on	yr	186	1999	30r
Fresh milk and cream, expenditures on	yr	130	1999	30r
Fresh vegetables, expenditures on	yr	177	1999	30r
Grapefruit	lb	0.68	7/01	11r
Grapes, Thompson, seedless	lb	2.42	7/01	11r
Ground beef, lean and extra lean	lb	2.46	7/01	11r
Ice cream, prepackaged, bulk, regular	1/2 gal	3.62	7/01	11r
Lettuce, iceberg	lb	0.63	7/01	11r
Meats, poultry, fish, and egg purchases	yr	761	1999	30r
Milk, fresh, low fat,	gal	2.80	7/01	11r
Milk, fresh, whole, fortified	gal	2.88	7/01	11r
Nonalcoholic beverages, expenditures on	yr	258	1999	30r
Oranges, Navel	lb	0.97	7/01	11r
Oranges, Valencia	lb	0.43	7/01	11r
Peaches	lb	1.38	7/01	11r
Peanut butter, creamy, all sizes	lb	2.14	7/01	11r
Pork chops, center cut, bone-in	lb	3.83	7/01	11r
Pork, expenditures on	yr	141	1999	30r
Potatoes, white, all types	lb	0.37	7/01	11r
Poultry, expenditures on	yr	146	1999	30r
Processed fruits, expenditures on	yr	118	1999	30r
Processed vegetables, expenditures on	yr	81	1999	30r
Round roast, graded and ungraded, excl U.S. prime and choice	lb	3.07	7/01	11r

Values are in dollars or fractions of dollars. In the column headed *Ref*, references are shown to sources. Each reference is followed by a letter. These refer to the geographical level for which data were reported: s=State, r=Region, and c=City or metro. The abbreviation *ex* is used to mean *except* or *excluding*; *exp* stands for *expenditures*. For other abbreviations and further explanations, please see the Introduction.

Santa Barbara-Santa Maria-Lompoc, CA - continued

Item	Per	Value	Date	Ref.
Groceries				
Round roast, U.S. choice, boneless	lb	3.37	7/01	11r
Round steak, graded and ungraded, excl U.S. prime and choice	lb	3.51	7/01	11r
Sirloin steak, graded and ungraded, excl U.S. prime and choice	lb	4.67	7/01	11r
Steak, sirloin, U.S. choice, boneless	lb	6.20	7/01	11r
Strawberries, dry pint	12 oz	1.79	7/01	11r
Sugar and other sweets, expenditures on	yr	124	1999	30r
Sugar, white, all sizes	lb	0.46	7/01	11r
Tobacco products and smoking supplies purchases	yr	217	1999	30r
Tomatoes, field grown	lb	1.17	7/01	11r
Tuna, light, chunk	lb	2.05	7/01	11r
Goods and Services				
B&B Japanese maple (acer japonicum)	gal	39.99	4/00	93r
Boxwood (buxus)	2 gal	14.99-24.99	4/00	93r
Christmas tree, noble fir		40-60	2000	65s
Daylilly (hemerocallis)	gal	6.99-8.99	4/00	93r
Flat of annuals		16.68	4/00	93r
Fountain grass (pennisetum)	gal	7.99-11.99	4/00	93r
Hanging basket (10 in)		29.99	4/00	93r
Hardy geranium (geranium)	gal	6.99-11.99	4/00	93r
Hosta (hosta)	gal	6.99-18.99	4/00	93r
Lilac (syrubga vulgaris)	2 gal	14.99-17.99	4/00	93r
Miscellaneous purchases	yr	1070	1999	30r
Rhododendron (rhododendron)	2 gal	14.99	4/00	93r
Sage (salvia)	gal	6.99	4/00	93r
Wintercreeper euonymus (euonymus fortunei)	2 gal	14.99-22.99	4/00	93r
Hunting license	yr	29.95	4/01	34s
Health Care				
Cardiac catheterization, ave hospital/ physician charges		24000	1998	77s
Childbirth, Cesarean delivery		11587	1997	13r
Childbirth, vaginal delivery		6725	1997	13r
Drugs, expenditures on	yr	309	1999	30r
Health care purchases	yr	1869	1999	30r
Health insurance expenditures	yr	868	1999	30r
Hysterectomy, laproscopically-assisted, ave hospital/physician charges		20760	1998	76s
Hysterectomy, vaginal, ave hospital and physician charges		14570	1998	76s
Medicaid dispensing fee		4.05	1999	87s
Medical services expenditures	yr	580	1999	30r
Medical supplies, expenditures on	yr	112	1999	30r
Household Goods				
Floor coverings, expenditures on	yr	49	1999	30r
Furniture, expenditures on	yr	444	1999	30r
Household furnishings and equipment purchases	yr	1768	1999	30r
Household textiles, expenditures on	yr	141	1999	30r
Laundry and cleaning supplies, expenditures on	yr	128	1999	30r
Housing				
Home price, existing, ave		239400	10/00	90r
Home value, median		215000	2001	53s
Household operation expenditures	yr	781	1999	30r
Housekeeping supplies purchases	yr	513	1999	30r
Lodging expenditures	yr	575	1999	30r
Maintenance, repairs, insurance expenditures	yr	939	1999	30r
Monthly rental value of owned home	mos	662	1999	30r
Owned dwellings, expenditures own	yr	5231	1999	30r
Rent expenditures	yr	2709	1999	30r

Santa Barbara-Santa Maria-Lompoc, CA - continued

Item	Per	Value	Date	Ref.
Housing - continued				
Rental unit, 1 bedroom, with utilities	mos	708	4/01	41c
Rental unit, 2 bedroom, with utilities	mos	897	4/01	41c
Rental unit, 3 bedroom, with utilities	mos	1250	4/01	41c
Rental unit, 4 bedroom, with utilities	mos	1411	4/01	41c
Shelter, expenditures on	yr	8516	1999	30r
Insurance and Pensions				
Life and other personal insurance purchases	yr	355	1999	30r
Pensions and Social Security, expenditures on	yr	3636	1999	30r
Legal Fees				
Divorce, filing fee		182.00	4/01	35s
Driver's license fee	orig	12.00	1999	48s
Driver's license fee	renew	15.00	1999	48s
Personal Goods				
Personal care products and services purchases	yr	449	1999	30r
Personal Services				
Personal services, household, expenditures on	yr	353	1999	30r
Pets				
Pets, toys, and playground equipment, expenditures on	yr	358	1999	30r
Taxes				
Federal income taxes paid	yr	3200	1999	30r
Personal taxes, expenditures on	yr	4153	1999	30r
Property taxes paid	yr	923	1999	30r
State and local income taxes paid	yr	812	1999	30r
Transportation				
Cars and trucks, new, expenditures on	yr	1534	1999	30r
Cars and trucks, used, expenditures on	yr	1593	1999	30r
Diesel at the pump	gal	1.37	10/99	73s
Gasoline and motor oil purchases	yr	1129	1999	30r
Gasoline before-tax price (cents)	gal	128.80	10/00	43s
Maintenance and repair expenditures	yr	797	1999	30r
Public transportation, expenditures on	yr	530	1999	30r
Transportation purchases	yr	7423	1999	30r
Vehicle expenses, miscellaneous, purchases	yr	2585	1999	30r
Vehicle insurance payments	yr	811	1999	30r
Vehicle purchases (net outlay)	yr	3180	1999	30r
Vehicle rental, lease expenditures	yr	666	1999	30r
Utilities				
Electrical bill, average	mos	58.66	9/00	9s
Electricity, expenditures on	yr	725	1999	30r
Electricity cost, average	KWh	7.75	9/00	9s
Utilities, fuels, and public services purchased	yr	2179	1999	30r
Water and other public services, expenditures on	yr	339	1999	30r
Weddings				
Wedding (national average cost)		19936	2000	33r
Wedding (regional average total cost)		18918	1997	110r
Attendants' gifts		321	1998	33r
Bridal attendants' apparel (5 persons)		824	2000	33r
Bride's headpiece/veil		173	1998	33r
Bride's wedding dress		859	1998	33r
Clergy, religious facility fee		242	1998	33r
Engagement ring		3177	1998	33r
Flowers		789	1998	33r
Groom's formalwear rental		99	2000	33r
Limousine		410	1998	33r
Marriage license cost		50.00-80.00	4/01	35s
Men's formalwear (ushers, best man)		469	2000	33r
Mother of bride apparel		241	2000	33r
Music		866	1998	33r
Photography and videography		1368	1998	33r
Rehearsal dinner		728	1998	33r
Wedding invitations and announcements		341	1998	33r

Values are in dollars or fractions of dollars. In the column headed *Ref*, references are shown to sources. Each reference is followed by a letter. These refer to the geographical level for which data were reported: s=State, r=Region, and c=City or metro. The abbreviation *ex* is used to mean *except* or *excluding*; *exp* stands for *expenditures*. For other abbreviations and further explanations, please see the Introduction.

Santa Barbara-Santa Maria-Lompoc, CA - continued

Item	Per	Value	Date	Ref.
Weddings				
Wedding reception		7968	2000	33r
Wedding rings (bride and groom)		1060	1998	33r

Santa Cruz-Watsonville, CA

Item	Per	Value	Date	Ref.
Average annual expenditures	yr	40662	1999	30r
Alcoholic Beverages				
Alcoholic beverage purchases	yr	372	1999	30r
Malt beverages, all types, all sizes, any origin	16 oz	0.94	7/01	11r
Wine, red and white table, all sizes, any origin	liter	6.00	7/01	11r
Appliances				
Major appliances, expenditures on	yr	167	1999	30r
Small appliances, housewares, expenditures on	yr	105	1999	30r
Banking and Money				
Mortgage interest and charges paid	yr	3368	1999	30r
Mortgage principal paid on owned property	yr	1677	1999	30r
Vehicle finance charges paid	yr	311	1999	30r
Charity				
Cash contributions, expenditures	yr	1344	1999	30r
Child Care				
Child raising cost, total, age 0-2	yr	9140	1999	60r
Child raising cost, total, age 3-5	yr	9370	1999	60r
Child raising cost, total, age 6-8	yr	9450	1999	60r
Child raising cost, total, age 9-11	yr	9470	1999	60r
Child raising cost, total, age 12-14	yr	10170	1999	60r
Child raising cost, total, age 15-17	yr	10360	1999	60r
Child's child care and education, age 0-2	yr	1250	1999	60r
Child's child care and education, age 3-5	yr	1380	1999	60r
Child's child care and education, age 6-8	yr	890	1999	60r
Child's child care and education, age 9-11	yr	580	1999	60r
Child's child care and education, age 12-14	yr	430	1999	60r
Child's child care and education, age 15-17	yr	730	1999	60r
Child's clothing, age 0-2	yr	430	1999	60r
Child's clothing, age 3-5	yr	420	1999	60r
Child's clothing, age 6-8	yr	470	1999	60r
Child's clothing, age 9-11	yr	520	1999	60r
Child's clothing, age 12-14	yr	870	1999	60r
Child's clothing, age 15-17	yr	770	1999	60r
Child's food, age 0-2	yr	1120	1999	60r
Child's food, age 3-5	yr	1280	1999	60r
Child's food, age 6-8	yr	1640	1999	60r
Child's food, age 9-11	yr	1930	1999	60r
Child's food, age 12-14	yr	1940	1999	60r
Child's food, age 15-17	yr	2150	1999	60r
Child's health care, age 0-2	yr	490	1999	60r
Child's health care, age 3-5	yr	470	1999	60r
Child's health care, age 6-8	yr	530	1999	60r
Child's health care, age 9-11	yr	570	1999	60r
Child's health care, age 12-14	yr	580	1999	60r
Child's health care, age 15-17	yr	610	1999	60r
Child's housing, age 0-2	yr	3630	1999	60r
Child's housing, age 3-5	yr	3610	1999	60r
Child's housing, age 6-8	yr	3570	1999	60r
Child's housing, age 9-11	yr	3410	1999	60r
Child's housing, age 12-14	yr	3600	1999	60r
Child's housing, age 15-17	yr	3210	1999	60r
Child's personal care, reading, age 0-2	yr	1040	1999	60r
Child's personal care, reading, age 3-5	yr	1060	1999	60r
Child's personal care, reading, age 6-8	yr	1090	1999	60r
Child's personal care, reading, age 9-11	yr	1130	1999	60r
Child's personal care, reading, age 12-14	yr	1300	1999	60r
Child's personal care, reading, age 15-17	yr	1080	1999	60r
Clothing				
Apparel and services purchases	yr	1863	1999	30r
Boys, 2 to 15, expenditures on	yr	80	1999	30r
Children under 2, expenditures on	yr	74	1999	30r

Santa Cruz-Watsonville, CA - continued

Item	Per	Value	Date	Ref.
Clothing - continued				
Footwear, expenditures on	yr	307	1999	30r
Girls, 2 to 15, expenditures on	yr	101	1999	30r
Men and boys, expenditures on	yr	443	1999	30r
Men, 16 and over, expenditures on	yr	363	1999	30r
Women, 16 and over, expenditures on	yr	594	1999	30r
Communications				
Cable modem installation, AT&T-BIS		150.00	6/99	103s
Cable modem installation, Charter		99.00-169.00	6/99	103s
Cable modem installation, Comcast		95.00	6/99	103s
Cable modem installation, Cox		99.00-174.95	6/99	103s
Cable modem installation, Media One		100.00	6/99	103s
Cable modem installation, Time Warner		75.00-225.00	6/99	103s
Cable modem rate, cable subscriber, AT&T-BIS	mos	39.95	6/99	103s
Cable modem rate, cable subscriber, Charter	mos	49.95-79.95	6/99	103s
Cable modem rate, cable subscriber, Comcast	mos	39.95	6/99	103s
Cable modem rate, cable subscriber, Cox	mos	29.95-44.95	6/99	103s
Cable modem rate, cable subscriber, Media One	mos	34.95-39.95	6/99	103s
Cable modem rate, cable subscriber, Time Warner	mos	39.95-49.95	6/99	103s
Cable modem rate, non-cable subscriber, Charter	mos	59.95-89.95	6/99	103s
Cable modem rate, non-cable subscriber, Comcast	mos	49.95	6/99	103s
Cable modem rate, non-cable subscriber, Cox	mos	42.95-54.95	6/99	103s
Cable modem rate, non-cable subscriber, Media One	mos	49.95	6/99	103s
Cable modem rate, non-cable subscriber, Time Warner	mos	39.95-54.95	6/99	103s
Phone line, single, business, field visit	inst.	70.75	12/97	17s
Phone line, single, business, no field visit	inst.	70.75	12/97	17s
Phone line, single, residence, field visit	inst.	34.75	12/97	17s
Phone line, single, residence, no field visit	inst.	34.75	12/97	17s
Postage and stationery, expenditures on	yr	150	1999	30r
Postal rate, express mail, up to half-pound		12.45	7/01	108r
Postal rate, letter, first class, first ounce		0.34	7/01	108r
Postal rate, letter, two ounces		0.57	7/01	108r
Postal rate, post card		0.21	7/01	108r
Postal rate, priority mail, two pounds		3.95	7/01	108r
Postal rate, priority mail, up to one pound		3.50	7/01	108r
Telephone services, expenditures on	yr	825	1999	30r
Education				
Board, 4-year private college/university	yr	2970	1996	38s
Board, 4-year public college/university	yr	2516	1996	38s
Education expenditures	yr	676	1999	30r
Room, 4-year private college/university	yr	3196	1996	38s
Room, 4-year public college/university	yr	3031	1996	38s
Total cost, 4-year private college/university	yr	20143	1996	38s
Total cost, 4-year public college/university	yr	8213	1996	38s
Tuition, 2-year public college/university, in state	yr	362	1996	38s
Tuition, 4-year private college/university, in state	yr	13977	1996	38s
Tuition, 4-year public college/university	yr	2666	1996	38s
Energy and Fuels				
Electricity	KWh	0.11	7/01	11r
Electricity	500 KWhs	48.23	7/01	11r
Fuel oil and other fuels, expenditures on	yr	35	1999	30r
Gas, natural, commercial rate	1000 cf	8.74	11/00	88s
Gasoline, all types	gal	1.91	7/01	11r
Gasoline, unleaded premium	gal	2.05	7/01	11r
Gasoline, unleaded regular	gal	1.83	7/01	11r

Values are in dollars or fractions of dollars. In the column headed *Ref*, references are shown to sources. Each reference is followed by a letter. These refer to the geographical level for which data were reported: s=State, r=Region, and c=City or metro. The abbreviation *ex* is used to mean *except* or *excluding*; *exp* stands for *expenditures*. For other abbreviations and further explanations, please see the Introduction.

Santa Cruz-Watsonville, CA - continued

Item	Per	Value	Date	Ref.
Energy and Fuels				
Natural gas, expenditures on	yr	255	1999	30r
Utility (piped) gas, therm		0.98	7/01	11r
Utility (piped) gas, 40 therms		40.74	7/01	11r
Utility (piped) gas, 100 therms		96.80	7/01	11r
Entertainment				
Entertainment purchases	yr	2139	1999	30r
Fees and admissions paid	yr	545	1999	30r
Television, radios, sound equipment, expenditures on	yr	624	1999	30r
Funerals				
Total cost of funeral		5401.08	1/99	78r
Acknowledgement cards		33.64	1/99	78r
Casket		2170.43	1/99	78r
Cosmetology, hair, other preparation		136.32	1/99	78r
Embalming		319.13	1/99	78r
Funeral at funeral home		370.21	1/99	78r
Hearse (local)		161.04	1/99	78r
Professional service charges		963.15	1/99	78r
Service car/van		133.99	1/99	78r
Transfer of remains to funeral home		159.82	1/99	78r
Vault		778.07	1/99	78r
Visitation/viewing		175.28	1/99	78r
Groceries				
Apples, red delicious	lb	0.84	7/01	11r
Bacon, sliced	lb	3.38	7/01	11r
Bakery products, expenditures on	yr	299	1999	30r
Bananas	lb	0.54	7/01	11r
Beans, dried, any type, all sizes	lb	0.76	7/01	11r
Beef, expenditures on	yr	222	1999	30r
Bread, white, pan	lb	0.99	7/01	11r
Butter, yoghurt, cheese, etc, expenditures on	yr	211	1999	30r
Cereals and bakery product purchases	yr	466	1999	30r
Cereals and cereal products, expenditures on	yr	168	1999	30r
Chicken breast, bone-in	lb	2.45	7/01	11r
Chicken, fresh, whole	lb	1.19	7/01	11r
Chops, boneless,	lb	4.00	7/01	11r
Chuck roast, graded and ungraded, excl U.S. prime and choice	lb	2.55	7/01	11r
Coffee, 100%, ground roast, all sizes	lb	3.80	7/01	11r
Cookies, chocolate chip	lb	2.83	7/01	11r
Dairy product purchases	yr	341	1999	30r
Eggs, expenditures on	yr	39	1999	30r
Eggs, grade AA, large	dozen	1.23	7/01	11r
Fats and oils, expenditures on	yr	88	1999	30r
Fish and seafood, expenditures on	yr	121	1999	30r
Food (excl fruit and vegetables), eaten at home, purchases	yr	1001	1999	30r
Food cooked on trips, expenditures on	yr	64	1999	30r
Food purchases	yr	5312	1999	30r
Food purchases, eaten away from home	yr	2180	1999	30r
Food purchases, food eaten at home	yr	3132	1999	30r
Fresh fruits, expenditures on	yr	186	1999	30r
Fresh milk and cream, expenditures on	yr	130	1999	30r
Fresh vegetables, expenditures on	yr	177	1999	30r
Grapefruit	lb	0.68	7/01	11r
Grapes, Thompson, seedless	lb	2.42	7/01	11r
Ground beef, lean and extra lean	lb	2.46	7/01	11r
Ice cream, prepackaged, bulk, regular	1/2 gal	3.62	7/01	11r
Lettuce, iceberg	lb	0.63	7/01	11r
Meats, poultry, fish, and egg purchases	yr	761	1999	30r
Milk, fresh, low fat,	gal	2.80	7/01	11r
Milk, fresh, whole, fortified	gal	2.88	7/01	11r
Nonalcoholic beverages, expenditures on	yr	258	1999	30r
Oranges, Navel	lb	0.97	7/01	11r
Oranges, Valencia	lb	0.43	7/01	11r
Peaches	lb	1.38	7/01	11r
Peanut butter, creamy, all sizes	lb	2.14	7/01	11r
Pork chops, center cut, bone-in	lb	3.83	7/01	11r
Pork, expenditures on	yr	141	1999	30r
Potatoes, white, all types	lb	0.37	7/01	11r

Item	Per	Value	Date	Ref.
Groceries - continued				
Poultry, expenditures on	yr	146	1999	30r
Processed fruits, expenditures on	yr	118	1999	30r
Processed vegetables, expenditures on	yr	81	1999	30r
Round roast, graded and ungraded, excl U.S. prime and choice	lb	3.07	7/01	11r
Round roast, U.S. choice, boneless	lb	3.37	7/01	11r
Round steak, graded and ungraded, excl U.S. prime and choice	lb	3.51	7/01	11r
Sirloin steak, graded and ungraded, excl U.S. prime and choice	lb	4.67	7/01	11r
Steak, sirloin, U.S. choice, boneless	lb	6.20	7/01	11r
Strawberries, dry pint	12 oz	1.79	7/01	11r
Sugar and other sweets, expenditures on	yr	124	1999	30r
Sugar, white, all sizes	lb	0.46	7/01	11r
Tobacco products and smoking supplies purchases	yr	217	1999	30r
Tomatoes, field grown	lb	1.17	7/01	11r
Tuna, light, chunk	lb	2.05	7/01	11r
Goods and Services				
B&B Japanese maple (acer japonicum)	gal	39.99	4/00	93r
Boxwood (buxus)	2 gal	14.99-24.99	4/00	93r
Christmas tree, noble fir		40-60	2000	65s
Daylilly (hemerocallis)	gal	6.99-8.99	4/00	93r
Flat of annuals		16.68		93r
Fountain grass (pennisetum)	gal	7.99-11.99	4/00	93r
Hanging basket (10 in)		29.99	4/00	93r
Hardy geranium (geranium)	gal	6.99-11.99	4/00	93r
Hosta (hosta)	gal	6.99-18.99	4/00	93r
Lilac (syrubga vulgaris)	2 gal	14.99-17.99	4/00	93r
Miscellaneous purchases	yr	1070	1999	30r
Rhododendron (rhododendron)	2 gal	14.99	4/00	93r
Sage (salvia)	gal	6.99	4/00	93r
Wintercreeper euonymus (euonymus fortunei)	2 gal	14.99-22.99	4/00	93r
Hunting license	yr	29.95	4/01	34s
Health Care				
Cardiac catheterization, ave hospital/physician charges		24000	1998	77s
Childbirth, Cesarean delivery		11587	1997	13r
Childbirth, vaginal delivery		6725	1997	13r
Drugs, expenditures on	yr	309	1999	30r
Health care purchases	yr	1869	1999	30r
Health insurance expenditures	yr	868	1999	30r
Hysterectomy, laproscopically-assisted, ave hospital/physician charges		20760	1998	76s
Hysterectomy, vaginal, ave hospital and physician charges		14570	1998	76s
Medicaid dispensing fee		4.05	1999	87s
Medical services expenditures	yr	580	1999	30r
Medical supplies, expenditures on	yr	112	1999	30r
Household Goods				
Floor coverings, expenditures on	yr	49	1999	30r
Furniture, expenditures on	yr	444	1999	30r
Household furnishings and equipment purchases	yr	1768	1999	30r
Household textiles, expenditures on	yr	141	1999	30r
Laundry and cleaning supplies, expenditures on	yr	128	1999	30r
Housing				
Home price, existing, ave		239400	10/00	90r
Home value, median		215000	2001	53s
Household operation expenditures	yr	781	1999	30r
Housekeeping supplies purchases	yr	513	1999	30r
Lodging expenditures	yr	575	1999	30r

Values are in dollars or fractions of dollars. In the column headed *Ref*, references are shown to sources. Each reference is followed by a letter. These refer to the geographical level for which data were reported: s=State, r=Region, and c=City or metro. The abbreviation *ex* is used to mean *except* or *excluding*; *exp* stands for *expenditures*. For other abbreviations and further explanations, please see the Introduction.

Santa Cruz-Watsonville, CA - continued

Item	Per	Value	Date	Ref.
Housing				
Maintenance, repairs, insurance expenditures	yr	939	1999	30r
Monthly rental value of owned home	mos	662	1999	30r
Owned dwellings, expenditures own	yr	5231	1999	30r
Rent expenditures	yr	2709	1999	30r
Rental unit, 1 bedroom, with utilities	mos	817	4/01	41c
Rental unit, 2 bedroom, with utilities	mos	1091	4/01	41c
Rental unit, 3 bedroom, with utilities	mos	1517	4/01	41c
Rental unit, 4 bedroom, with utilities	mos	1777	4/01	41c
Shelter, expenditures on	yr	8516	1999	30r
Insurance and Pensions				
Life and other personal insurance purchases	yr	355	1999	30r
Pensions and Social Security, expenditures on	yr	3636	1999	30r
Legal Fees				
Divorce, filing fee		182.00	4/01	35s
Driver's license fee	renew	15.00	1999	48s
Driver's license fee	orig	12.00	1999	48s
Personal Goods				
Personal care products and services purchases	yr	449	1999	30r
Personal Services				
Personal services, household, expenditures on	yr	353	1999	30r
Pets				
Pets, toys, and playground equipment, expenditures on	yr	358	1999	30r
Taxes				
Federal income taxes paid	yr	3200	1999	30r
Personal taxes, expenditures on	yr	4153	1999	30r
Property taxes paid	yr	923	1999	30r
State and local income taxes paid	yr	812	1999	30r
Transportation				
Cars and trucks, new, expenditures on	yr	1534	1999	30r
Cars and trucks, used, expenditures on	yr	1593	1999	30r
Diesel at the pump	gal	1.37	10/99	73s
Gasoline and motor oil purchases	yr	1129	1999	30r
Gasoline before-tax price (cents)	gal	128.80	10/00	43s
Maintenance and repair expenditures	yr	797	1999	30r
Public transportation, expenditures on	yr	530	1999	30r
Transportation purchases	yr	7423	1999	30r
Vehicle expenses, miscellaneous, purchases	yr	2585	1999	30r
Vehicle insurance payments	yr	811	1999	30r
Vehicle purchases (net outlay)	yr	3180	1999	30r
Vehicle rental, lease expenditures	yr	666	1999	30r
Utilities				
Electrical bill, average	mos	58.66	9/00	9s
Electricity, expenditures on	yr	725	1999	30r
Electricity cost, average	KWh	7.75	9/00	9s
Utilities, fuels and public services purchased	yr	2179	1999	30r
Water and other public services, expenditures on	yr	339	1999	30r
Weddings				
Wedding (national average cost)		19936	2000	33r
Wedding (regional average total cost)		18918	1997	110r
Attendants' gifts		321	1998	33r
Bridal attendants' apparel (5 persons)		824	2000	33r
Bride's headpiece/veil		173	1998	33r
Bride's wedding dress		859	1998	33r
Clergy, religious facility fee		242	1998	33r
Engagement ring		3177	1998	33r
Flowers		789	1998	33r
Groom's formalwear rental		99	2000	33r
Limousine		410	1998	33r
Marriage license cost		50.00-80.00	4/01	35s
Men's formalwear (ushers, best man)		469	2000	33r

Santa Cruz-Watsonville, CA - continued

Item	Per	Value	Date	Ref.
Weddings - continued				
Mother of bride apparel		241	2000	33r
Music		866	1998	33r
Photography and videography		1368	1998	33r
Rehearsal dinner		728	1998	33r
Wedding invitations and announcements		341	1998	33r
Wedding reception		7968	2000	33r
Wedding rings (bride and groom)		1060	1998	33r

Santa Fe, NM

Item	Per	Value	Date	Ref.
Composite, ACCRA index		118.10	3/01	4c
Alcoholic Beverages				
Beer, Heineken, 12-oz, ex deposit	6	7.56	3/01	4c
J & B Scotch	750-ml	19.99	3/01	4c
Wine, Livingston or Gallo, Chablis blanc	1.5 liter	6.66	3/01	4c
Appliances				
Appliance repair, service call, washing machine	min lab chg	49.67	3/01	4c
Banking and Money				
Mortgage rate, incl. points and orig. fee, 30-yr. conv. fixed or ARM	mos	7.34	3/01	4c
Clothing				
Boys' brief, cotton	3	3.78	3/01	4c
Shirt, man's dress shirt		29.00	3/01	4c
Slacks, man's "No Wrinkles" khaki		41.99	3/01	4c
Communications				
Newspaper subscription, daily and Sunday delivery	mos	12.72	3/01	4c
Phone line, single, business, field visit	inst.	53.95	12/97	17s
Phone line, single, business, no field visit	inst.	53.95	12/97	17s
Phone line, single, residence, field visit	inst.	30.00	12/97	17s
Phone line, single, residence, no field visit	inst.	30.00	12/97	17s
Postal rate, express mail, up to half-pound		12.45	7/01	108r
Postal rate, letter, first class, first ounce		0.34	7/01	108r
Postal rate, letter, two ounces		0.57	7/01	108r
Postal rate, post card		0.21	7/01	108r
Postal rate, priority mail, two pounds		3.95	7/01	108r
Postal rate, priority mail, up to one pound		3.50	7/01	108r
Telephone bill, business, basic rate	mos	45.55	12/97	18c
Telephone bill, family of three	mos	18.13	3/01	4c
Telephone bill, residential, basic rate	mos	14.54	12/97	18c
Education				
Board, 4-year private college/university	yr	2282	1996	38s
Board, 4-year public college/university	yr	1854	1996	38s
Room, 4-year private college/university	yr	2289	1996	38s
Room, 4-year public college/university	yr	1504	1996	38s
Total cost, 4-year private college/university	yr	14355	1996	38s
Total cost, 4-year public college/university	yr	5298	1996	38s
Tuition, 2-year public college/university, in state	yr	690	1996	38s
Tuition, 4-year private college/university, in state	yr	9784	1996	38s
Tuition, 4-year public college/university	yr	1940	1996	38s
Energy and Fuels				
Energy, combined forms, 2400 sq ft	mos	106.77	3/01	4c
Energy, exc. electricity, 2400 sq ft	mos	43.99	3/01	4c
Gas, regular unleaded, cash, self-service	gal	1.59	3/01	4c
Entertainment				
Bowling, Saturday evening rate	line	2.95	3/01	4c
Monopoly game, Parker Brothers', No. 9	game	9.66	3/01	4c
Movie, first-run, Saturday, evening	adm.	7.00	3/01	4c
Tennis balls, yellow, Wilson or Penn, 3	can	1.86	3/01	4c
Funerals				
Total cost of funeral		5401.08	1/99	78r
Acknowledgement cards		33.64	1/99	78r
Casket		2170.43	1/99	78r
Cosmetology, hair, other preparation		136.32	1/99	78r

Values are in dollars or fractions of dollars. In the column headed *Ref*, references are shown to sources. Each reference is followed by a letter. These refer to the geographical level for which data were reported: s=State, r=Region, and c=City or metro. The abbreviation *ex* is used to mean *except* or *excluding*; *exp* stands for expenditures. For other abbreviations and further explanations, please see the Introduction.

Santa Fe, NM - continued

Item	Per	Value	Date	Ref.
Funerals				
Embalming		319.13	1/99	78r
Funeral at funeral home		370.21	1/99	78r
Hearse (local)		161.04	1/99	78r
Professional service charges		963.15	1/99	78r
Service car/van		133.99	1/99	78r
Transfer of remains to funeral home		159.82	1/99	78r
Vault		778.07	1/99	78r
Visitation/viewing		175.28	1/99	78r
Groceries				
Groceries, ACCRA Index		106.10	3/01	4c
Antibiotic ointment, Polysporin	0.5 oz	4.73	3/01	4c
Baby food, strained vegetables or fruit, lowest price	4-4.5 oz	0.31	3/01	4c
Bananas	lb	0.59	3/01	4c
Beef or hamburger, ground	lb	1.66	3/01	4c
Bread, white	loaf	0.99	3/01	4c
Cheese, Kraft grated Parmesan	8 oz	3.82	3/01	4c
Chicken, whole fryer	lb	1.19	3/01	4c
Cigarettes, Winston, Kings	carton	25.98	3/01	4c
Coffee, vacuum-packed	13 oz	3.03	3/01	4c
Corn Flakes, Kellogg's or Post Toasties	18 oz	2.52	3/01	4c
Corn, frozen, whole kernel, lowest price	16 oz	1.06	3/01	4c
Eggs, Grade A or AA	dozen	1.29	3/01	4c
Lettuce, iceberg	head	1.22	3/01	4c
Margarine, Blue Bonnet or Parkay, stick	lb	1.12	3/01	4c
Milk, whole	1/2 gal	1.39	3/01	4c
Orange juice, Minute Maid frozen	12 oz	1.86	3/01	4c
Peaches, halves or slices, Hunt's, Del Monte, or Libby's	29 oz	1.69	3/01	4c
Peas, green, Del Monte or Green Giant	15 oz	0.72	3/01	4c
Potatoes, white or red	10 lb	1.79	3/01	4c
Sausage, Jimmy Dean/Owens pork	lb	3.95	3/01	4c
Shortening, vegetable, Crisco	3 lb	4.02	3/01	4c
Soft drink, Coca Cola, ex deposit	2 liter	1.16	3/01	4c
Steak, T-bone	lb	6.32	3/01	4c
Sugar, cane or beet	4 lbs	1.72	3/01	4c
Tomatoes, Hunt's or Del Monte	14.5 oz	0.89	3/01	4c
Tuna, chunk, light	6 oz	1.02	3/01	4c
Goods and Services				
Miscellaneous goods and services, ACCRA Index		104.70	3/01	4c
Hunting license	yr	25.00	4/01	34s
Health Care				
Health care, ACCRA Index		126.60	3/01	4c
Cardiac catheterization, ave hospital/ physician charges		15920	1998	77s
Childbirth, Cesarean delivery		11587	1997	13r
Childbirth, vaginal delivery		6725	1997	13r
Dentist's fee, adult teeth cleaning and periodic oral exam	visit	96.75	3/01	4c
Doctor's fee, routine exam, established patient	visit	86.30	3/01	4c
Hospital care, private room	day	450.00	3/01	4c
Hysterectomy, laproscopically-assisted, ave hospital/physician charges		11750	1998	76s
Hysterectomy, vaginal, ave hospital and physician charges		8980	1998	76s
Medicaid dispensing fee		4.00	1999	87s
Household Goods				
Dishwashing powder, Cascade	50 oz	3.00	3/01	4c
Tissues, facial, Kleenex brand	175	1.37	3/01	4c
Housing				
Housing, ACCRA Index		150.00	3/01	4c
Home value, median		119000	2001	53s
House, 2400 sq ft, 8000 sq ft lot, new, urban, utilities	total	318250	3/01	4c
House payment, principal and interest, 25% down payment	mos	1642	3/01	4c

Santa Fe, NM - continued

Item	Per	Value	Date	Ref.
Housing - continued				
Rent, apartment, 2 br, 1 1/2-2 baths, unfurn, 950 sq ft, water	mos	790	3/01	4c
Rental unit, 1 bedroom, with utilities	mos	607	4/01	41c
Rental unit, 2 bedroom, with utilities	mos	749	4/01	41c
Rental unit, 3 bedroom, with utilities	mos	1006	4/01	41c
Rental unit, 4 bedroom, with utilities	mos	1139	4/01	41c
Legal Fees				
Combination hunting and fishing license	yr	37.50	4/01	34s
Driver's license fee	orig	10.00	1999	48s
Driver's license fee	renew	10.00	1999	48s
Fishing license	yr	25.00	4/01	34s
Personal Goods				
Shampoo, Alberto VO5	15 oz	1.07	3/01	4c
Toothpaste, Crest or Colgate	6-7 oz	2.32	3/01	4c
Personal Services				
Dry cleaning, man's 2-pc suit		9.05	3/01	4c
Man's haircut, barbershop, no styling		11.49	3/01	4c
Woman's shampoo, trim, blow-dry, no style-change		27.75	3/01	4c
Restaurant Food				
Chicken, fried, thigh and drumstick, KFC/ Church's		2.98	3/01	4c
Hamburger with cheese, McDonald's	1/4 lb	2.32	3/01	4c
Pizza, Pizza Hut or Pizza Inn	11-12 in	9.55	3/01	4c
Transportation				
Transportation, ACCRA Index		113.30	3/01	4c
Diesel at the pump	gal	1.22	10/99	73s
Gasoline before-tax price (cents)	gal	115.20	10/00	43s
Tire balance, computer or spin balance, front	wheel	9.00	3/01	4c
Utilities				
Utilities, ACCRA Index		86.90	3/01	4c
Electrical bill, average	mos	46.92	9/00	9s
Electricity and other, mixed, 2400 sq ft, new home	mos	62.78	3/01	4c
Electricity cost, average	KWh	6.30	9/00	9s
Weddings				
Wedding (national average cost)		19936	2000	33r
Attendants' gifts		321	1998	33r
Bridal attendants' apparel (5 persons)		824	2000	33r
Bride's headpiece/veil		173	1998	33r
Bride's wedding dress		859	1998	33r
Clergy, religious facility fee		242	1998	33r
Engagement ring		3177	1998	33r
Flowers		789	1998	33r
Groom's formalwear rental		99	2000	33r
Limousine		410	1998	33r
Marriage license cost		25.00	4/01	35s
Men's formalwear (ushers, best man)		469	2000	33r
Mother of bride apparel		241	2000	33r
Music		866	1998	33r
Photography and videography		1368	1998	33r
Rehearsal dinner		728	1998	33r
Wedding invitations and announcements		341	1998	33r
Wedding reception		7968	2000	33r
Wedding rings (bride and groom)		1060	1998	33r

Santa Rosa, CA

Item	Per	Value	Date	Ref.
Average annual expenditures	yr	40662	1999	30r
Alcoholic Beverages				
Alcoholic beverage purchases	yr	372	1999	30r
Malt beverages, all types, all sizes, any origin	16 oz	0.94	7/01	11r
Wine, red and white table, all sizes, any origin	liter	6.00	7/01	11r
Appliances				
Major appliances, expenditures on	yr	167	1999	30r

Values are in dollars or fractions of dollars. In the column headed *Ref*, references are shown to sources. Each reference is followed by a letter. These refer to the geographical level for which data were reported: s=State, r=Region, and c=City or metro. The abbreviation *ex* is used to mean *except* or *excluding*; *exp* stands for *expenditures*. For other abbreviations and further explanations, please see the Introduction.

Santa Rosa, CA - continued

Item	Per	Value	Date	Ref.
Appliances				
Small appliances, housewares, expenditures on	yr	105	1999	30r
Banking and Money				
Mortgage interest and charges paid	yr	3368	1999	30r
Mortgage principal paid on owned property	yr	1677	1999	30r
Vehicle finance charges paid	yr	311	1999	30r
Charity				
Cash contributions, expenditures	yr	1344	1999	30r
Child Care				
Child raising cost, total, age 0-2	yr	9140	1999	60r
Child raising cost, total, age 3-5	yr	9370	1999	60r
Child raising cost, total, age 6-8	yr	9450	1999	60r
Child raising cost, total, age 9-11	yr	9470	1999	60r
Child raising cost, total, age 12-14	yr	10170	1999	60r
Child raising cost, total, age 15-17	yr	10360	1999	60r
Child's child care and education, age 0-2	yr	1250	1999	60r
Child's child care and education, age 3-5	yr	1380	1999	60r
Child's child care and education, age 6-8	yr	890	1999	60r
Child's child care and education, age 9-11	yr	580	1999	60r
Child's child care and education, age 12-14	yr	430	1999	60r
Child's child care and education, age 15-17	yr	730	1999	60r
Child's clothing, age 0-2	yr	430	1999	60r
Child's clothing, age 3-5	yr	420	1999	60r
Child's clothing, age 6-8	yr	470	1999	60r
Child's clothing, age 9-11	yr	520	1999	60r
Child's clothing, age 12-14	yr	870	1999	60r
Child's clothing, age 15-17	yr	770	1999	60r
Child's food, age 0-2	yr	1120	1999	60r
Child's food, age 3-5	yr	1280	1999	60r
Child's food, age 6-8	yr	1640	1999	60r
Child's food, age 9-11	yr	1930	1999	60r
Child's food, age 12-14	yr	1940	1999	60r
Child's food, age 15-17	yr	2150	1999	60r
Child's health care, age 0-2	yr	490	1999	60r
Child's health care, age 3-5	yr	470	1999	60r
Child's health care, age 6-8	yr	530	1999	60r
Child's health care, age 9-11	yr	570	1999	60r
Child's health care, age 12-14	yr	580	1999	60r
Child's health care, age 15-17	yr	610	1999	60r
Child's housing, age 0-2	yr	3630	1999	60r
Child's housing, age 3-5	yr	3610	1999	60r
Child's housing, age 6-8	yr	3570	1999	60r
Child's housing, age 9-11	yr	3410	1999	60r
Child's housing, age 12-14	yr	3600	1999	60r
Child's housing, age 15-17	yr	3210	1999	60r
Child's personal care, reading, age 0-2	yr	1040	1999	60r
Child's personal care, reading, age 3-5	yr	1060	1999	60r
Child's personal care, reading, age 6-8	yr	1090	1999	60r
Child's personal care, reading, age 9-11	yr	1130	1999	60r
Child's personal care, reading, age 12-14	yr	1300	1999	60r
Child's personal care, reading, age 15-17	yr	1080	1999	60r
Clothing				
Apparel and services purchases	yr	1863	1999	30r
Boys, 2 to 15, expenditures on	yr	80	1999	30r
Children under 2, expenditures on	yr	74	1999	30r
Footwear, expenditures on	yr	307	1999	30r
Girls, 2 to 15, expenditures on	yr	101	1999	30r
Men and boys, expenditures on	yr	443	1999	30r
Men, 16 and over, expenditures on	yr	363	1999	30r
Women, 16 and over, expenditures on	yr	594	1999	30r
Communications				
Cable modem installation, AT&T-BIS		150.00	6/99	103s
Cable modem installation, Charter		99.00-169.00	6/99	103s
Cable modem installation, Comcast		95.00	6/99	103s
Cable modem installation, Cox		99.00-174.95	6/99	103s
Cable modem installation, Media One		100.00	6/99	103s

Item	Per	Value	Date	Ref.
Communications - continued				
Cable modem installation, Time Warner		75.00-225.00	6/99	103s
Cable modem rate, cable subscriber, AT&T-BIS	mos	39.95	6/99	103s
Cable modem rate, cable subscriber, Charter	mos	49.95-79.95	6/99	103s
Cable modem rate, cable subscriber, Comcast	mos	39.95	6/99	103s
Cable modem rate, cable subscriber, Cox	mos	29.95-44.95	6/99	103s
Cable modem rate, cable subscriber, Media One	mos	34.95-39.95	6/99	103s
Cable modem rate, cable subscriber, Time Warner	mos	39.95-49.95	6/99	103s
Cable modem rate, non-cable subscriber, Charter	mos	59.95-89.95	6/99	103s
Cable modem rate, non-cable subscriber, Comcast	mos	49.95	6/99	103s
Cable modem rate, non-cable subscriber, Cox	mos	42.95-54.95	6/99	103s
Cable modem rate, non-cable subscriber, Media One	mos	49.95	6/99	103s
Cable modem rate, non-cable subscriber, Time Warner	mos	39.95-54.95	6/99	103s
Phone line, single, business, field visit	inst.	70.75	12/97	17s
Phone line, single, business, no field visit	inst.	70.75	12/97	17s
Phone line, single, residence, field visit	inst.	34.75	12/97	17s
Phone line, single, residence, no field visit	inst.	34.75	12/97	17s
Postage and stationery, expenditures on	yr	150	1999	30r
Postal rate, express mail, up to half-pound		12.45	7/01	108r
Postal rate, letter, first class, first ounce		0.34	7/01	108r
Postal rate, letter, two ounces		0.57	7/01	108r
Postal rate, post card		0.21	7/01	108r
Postal rate, priority mail, two pounds		3.95	7/01	108r
Postal rate, priority mail, up to one pound		3.50	7/01	108r
Telephone services, expenditures on	yr	825	1999	30r
Education				
Board, 4-year private college/university	yr	2970	1996	38s
Board, 4-year public college/university	yr	2516	1996	38s
Education expenditures	yr	676	1999	30r
Room, 4-year private college/university	yr	3196	1996	38s
Room, 4-year public college/university	yr	3031	1996	38s
Total cost, 4-year private college/university	yr	20143	1996	38s
Total cost, 4-year public college/university	yr	8213	1996	38s
Tuition, 2-year public college/university, in state	yr	362	1996	38s
Tuition, 4-year private college/university, in state	yr	13977	1996	38s
Tuition, 4-year public college/university	yr	2666	1996	38s
Energy and Fuels				
Electricity	KWh	0.11	7/01	11r
Electricity	500 KWhs	48.23	7/01	11r
Fuel oil and other fuels, expenditures on	yr	35	1999	30r
Gas, natural, commercial rate	1000 cf	8.74	11/00	88s
Gasoline, all types	gal	1.91	7/01	11r
Gasoline, unleaded premium	gal	2.05	7/01	11r
Gasoline, unleaded regular	gal	1.83	7/01	11r
Natural gas, expenditures on	yr	255	1999	30r
Utility (piped) gas, therm		0.98	7/01	11r
Utility (piped) gas, 40 therms		40.74	7/01	11r
Utility (piped) gas, 100 therms		96.80	7/01	11r
Entertainment				
Entertainment purchases	yr	2139	1999	30r
Fees and admissions paid	yr	545	1999	30r
Television, radios, sound equipment, expenditures on	yr	624	1999	30r
Funerals				
Total cost of funeral		5401.08	1/99	78r
Acknowledgement cards		33.64	1/99	78r

Values are in dollars or fractions of dollars. In the column headed *Ref*, references are shown to sources. Each reference is followed by a letter. These refer to the geographical level for which data were reported: s=State, r=Region, and c=City or metro. The abbreviation *ex* is used to mean *except* or *excluding*; *exp* stands for expenditures. For other abbreviations and further explanations, please see the Introduction.

Santa Rosa, CA - continued

Item	Per	Value	Date	Ref.
Funerals				
Casket		2170.43	1/99	78r
Cosmetology, hair, other preparation		136.32	1/99	78r
Embalming		319.13	1/99	78r
Funeral at funeral home		370.21	1/99	78r
Hearse (local)		161.04	1/99	78r
Professional service charges		963.15	1/99	78r
Service car/van		133.99	1/99	78r
Transfer of remains to funeral home		159.82	1/99	78r
Vault		778.07	1/99	78r
Visitation/viewing		175.28	1/99	78r
Groceries				
Apples, red delicious	lb	0.84	7/01	11r
Bacon, sliced	lb	3.38	7/01	11r
Bakery products, expenditures on	yr	299	1999	30r
Bananas	lb	0.54	7/01	11r
Beans, dried, any type, all sizes	lb	0.76	7/01	11r
Beef, expenditures on	yr	222	1999	30r
Bread, white, pan	lb	0.99	7/01	11r
Butter, yoghurt, cheese, etc, expenditures on	yr	211	1999	30r
Cereals and bakery product purchases	yr	466	1999	30r
Cereals and cereal products, expenditures on	yr	168	1999	30r
Chicken breast, bone-in	lb	2.45	7/01	11r
Chicken, fresh, whole	lb	1.19	7/01	11r
Chops, boneless,	lb	4.00	7/01	11r
Chuck roast, graded and ungraded, excl U.S. prime and choice	lb	2.55	7/01	11r
Coffee, 100%, ground roast, all sizes	lb	3.80	7/01	11r
Cookies, chocolate chip	lb	2.83	7/01	11r
Dairy product purchases	yr	341	1999	30r
Eggs, expenditures on	yr	39	1999	30r
Eggs, grade AA, large	dozen	1.23	7/01	11r
Fats and oils, expenditures on	yr	88	1999	30r
Fish and seafood, expenditures on	yr	121	1999	30r
Food (excl fruit and vegetables), eaten at home, purchases	yr	1001	1999	30r
Food cooked on trips, expenditures on	yr	64	1999	30r
Food purchases	yr	5312	1999	30r
Food purchases, eaten away from home	yr	2180	1999	30r
Food purchases, food eaten at home	yr	3132	1999	30r
Fresh fruits, expenditures on	yr	186	1999	30r
Fresh milk and cream, expenditures on	yr	130	1999	30r
Fresh vegetables, expenditures on	yr	177	1999	30r
Grapefruit	lb	0.68	7/01	11r
Grapes, Thompson, seedless	lb	2.42	7/01	11r
Ground beef, lean and extra lean	lb	2.46	7/01	11r
Ice cream, prepackaged, bulk, regular	1/2 gal	3.62	7/01	11r
Lettuce, iceberg	lb	0.63	7/01	11r
Meats, poultry, fish, and egg purchases	yr	761	1999	30r
Milk, fresh, low fat,	gal	2.80	7/01	11r
Milk, fresh, whole, fortified	gal	2.88	7/01	11r
Nonalcoholic beverages, expenditures on	yr	258	1999	30r
Oranges, Navel	lb	0.97	7/01	11r
Oranges, Valencia	lb	0.43	7/01	11r
Peaches	lb	1.38	7/01	11r
Peanut butter, creamy, all sizes	lb	2.14	7/01	11r
Pork chops, center cut, bone-in	lb	3.83	7/01	11r
Pork, expenditures on	yr	141	1999	30r
Potatoes, white, all types	lb	0.37	7/01	11r
Poultry, expenditures on	yr	146	1999	30r
Processed fruits, expenditures on	yr	118	1999	30r
Processed vegetables, expenditures on	yr	81	1999	30r
Round roast, graded and ungraded, excl U.S. prime and choice	lb	3.07	7/01	11r
Round roast, U.S. choice, boneless	lb	3.37	7/01	11r
Round steak, graded and ungraded, excl U.S. prime and choice	lb	3.51	7/01	11r
Sirloin steak, graded and ungraded, excl U.S. prime and choice	lb	4.67	7/01	11r
Steak, sirloin, U.S. choice, boneless	lb	6.20	7/01	11r
Strawberries, dry pint	12 oz	1.79	7/01	11r
Sugar and other sweets, expenditures on	yr	124	1999	30r

Santa Rosa, CA - continued

Item	Per	Value	Date	Ref.
Groceries - continued				
Sugar, white, all sizes	lb	0.46	7/01	11r
Tobacco products and smoking supplies purchases	yr	217	1999	30r
Tomatoes, field grown	lb	1.17	7/01	11r
Tuna, light, chunk	lb	2.05	7/01	11r
Goods and Services				
B&B Japanese maple (acer japonicum)	gal	39.99	4/00	93r
Boxwood (buxus)	2 gal	14.99-24.99	4/00	93r
Christmas tree, noble fir		40-60	2000	65s
Daylilly (hemerocallis)	gal	6.99-8.99	4/00	93r
Flat of annuals		16.68	4/00	93r
Fountain grass (pennisetum)	gal	7.99-11.99	4/00	93r
Hanging basket (10 in)		29.99	4/00	93r
Hardy geranium (geranium)	gal	6.99-11.99	4/00	93r
Hosta (hosta)	gal	6.99-18.99	4/00	93r
Lilac (syrubga vulgaris)	2 gal	14.99-17.99	4/00	93r
Miscellaneous purchases	yr	1070	1999	30r
Rhododendron (rhododendron)	2 gal	14.99	4/00	93r
Sage (salvia)	gal	6.99	4/00	93r
Wintercreeper euonymus (euonymus fortunei)	2 gal	14.99-22.99	4/00	93r
Hunting license	yr	29.95	4/01	34s
Health Care				
Cardiac catheterization, ave hospital/ physician charges		24000	1998	77s
Childbirth, Cesarean delivery		11587	1997	13r
Childbirth, vaginal delivery		6725	1997	13r
Drugs, expenditures on	yr	309	1999	30r
Health care purchases	yr	1869	1999	30r
Health insurance expenditures	yr	868	1999	30r
Hysterectomy, laproscopically-assisted, ave hospital/physician charges		20760	1998	76s
Hysterectomy, vaginal, ave hospital and physician charges		14570	1998	76s
Medicaid dispensing fee		4.05	1999	87s
Medical services expenditures	yr	580	1999	30r
Medical supplies, expenditures on	yr	112	1999	30r
Household Goods				
Floor coverings, expenditures on	yr	49	1999	30r
Furniture, expenditures on	yr	444	1999	30r
Household furnishings and equipment purchases	yr	1768	1999	30r
Household textiles, expenditures on	yr	141	1999	30r
Laundry and cleaning supplies, expenditures on	yr	128	1999	30r
Housing				
Home, 2200 sq ft, 4-br, 2-bath, 2-car garage, average		298500	2000	47c
Home price, existing, ave		239400	10/00	90r
Home value, median		215000	2001	53s
Household operation expenditures	yr	781	1999	30r
Housekeeping supplies purchases	yr	513	1999	30r
Lodging expenditures	yr	575	1999	30r
Maintenance, repairs, insurance expenditures	yr	939	1999	30r
Monthly rental value of owned home	mos	662	1999	30r
Owned dwellings, expenditures own	yr	5231	1999	30r
Rent expenditures	yr	2709	1999	30r
Rental unit, 1 bedroom, with utilities	mos	730	4/01	41c
Rental unit, 2 bedroom, with utilities	mos	946	4/01	41c
Rental unit, 3 bedroom, with utilities	mos	1315	4/01	41c
Rental unit, 4 bedroom, with utilities	mos	1552	4/01	41c
Shelter, expenditures on	yr	8516	1999	30r

Values are in dollars or fractions of dollars. In the column headed *Ref*, references are shown to sources. Each reference is followed by a letter. These refer to the geographical level for which data were reported: s=State, r=Region, and c=City or metro. The abbreviation *ex* is used to mean *except* or *excluding*; *exp* stands for *expenditures*. For other abbreviations and further explanations, please see the Introduction.

Santa Rosa, CA - continued

Item	Per	Value	Date	Ref.
Insurance and Pensions				
Life and other personal insurance purchases	yr	355	1999	30r
Pensions and Social Security, expenditures on	yr	3636	1999	30r
Legal Fees				
Divorce, filing fee		182.00	4/01	35s
Driver's license fee	renew	15.00	1999	48s
Driver's license fee	orig	12.00	1999	48s
Personal Goods				
Personal care products and services purchases	yr	449	1999	30r
Personal Services				
Personal services, household, expenditures on	yr	353	1999	30r
Pets				
Pets, toys, and playground equipment, expenditures on	yr	358	1999	30r
Taxes				
Federal income taxes paid	yr	3200	1999	30r
Personal taxes, expenditures on	yr	4153	1999	30r
Property taxes paid	yr	923	1999	30r
State and local income taxes paid	yr	812	1999	30r
Transportation				
Cars and trucks, new, expenditures on	yr	1534	1999	30r
Cars and trucks, used, expenditures on	yr	1593	1999	30r
Diesel at the pump	gal	1.37	10/99	73s
Gasoline and motor oil purchases	yr	1129	1999	30r
Gasoline before-tax price (cents)	gal	128.80	10/00	43s
Maintenance and repair expenditures	yr	797	1999	30r
Public transportation, expenditures on	yr	530	1999	30r
Transportation purchases	yr	7423	1999	30r
Vehicle expenses, miscellaneous, purchases	yr	2585	1999	30r
Vehicle insurance payments	yr	811	1999	30r
Vehicle purchases (net outlay)	yr	3180	1999	30r
Vehicle rental, lease expenditures	yr	666	1999	30r
Utilities				
Electrical bill, average	mos	58.66	9/00	9s
Electricity, expenditures on	yr	725	1999	30r
Electricity cost, average	KWh	7.75	9/00	9s
Utilities, fuels, and public services purchased	yr	2179	1999	30r
Water and other public services, expenditures on	yr	339	1999	30r
Weddings				
Wedding (national average cost)		19936	2000	33r
Wedding (regional average total cost)		18918	1997	110r
Attendants' gifts		321	1998	33r
Bridal attendants' apparel (5 persons)		824	2000	33r
Bride's headpiece/veil		173	1998	33r
Bride's wedding dress		859	1998	33r
Clergy, religious facility fee		242	1998	33r
Engagement ring		3177	1998	33r
Flowers		789	1998	33r
Groom's formalwear rental		99	2000	33r
Limousine		410	1998	33r
Marriage license cost		50.00-80.00	4/01	35s
Men's formalwear (ushers, best man)		469	2000	33r
Mother of bride apparel		241	2000	33r
Music		866	1998	33r
Photography and videography		1368	1998	33r
Rehearsal dinner		728	1998	33r
Wedding invitations and announcements		341	1998	33r
Wedding reception		7968	2000	33r
Wedding rings (bride and groom)		1060	1998	33r

Sarasota-Brandenton, FL

Item	Per	Value	Date	Ref.
Alcoholic Beverages				
Alcoholic beverage purchases	yr	253	1999	30r
Malt beverages, all types, all sizes, any origin	16 oz	0.96	7/01	11r
Appliances				
Major appliances, expenditures on	yr	172	1999	30r
Small appliances, housewares, expenditures on	yr	81	1999	30r
Banking and Money				
Mortgage interest and charges paid	yr	2039	1999	30r
Mortgage principal paid on owned property	yr	1026	1999	30r
Vehicle finance charges paid	yr	365	1999	30r
Charity				
Cash contributions, expenditures	yr	1127	1999	30r
Child Care				
Child raising cost, total, age 0-2	yr	8540	1999	60r
Child raising cost, total, age 3-5	yr	8780	1999	60r
Child raising cost, total, age 6-8	yr	8820	1999	60r
Child raising cost, total, age 9-11	yr	8800	1999	60r
Child raising cost, total, age 12-14	yr	9510	1999	60r
Child raising cost, total, age 15-17	yr	9740	1999	60r
Child's child care and education, age 0-2	yr	1380	1999	60r
Child's child care and education, age 3-5	yr	1520	1999	60r
Child's child care and education, age 6-8	yr	990	1999	60r
Child's child care and education, age 9-11	yr	650	1999	60r
Child's child care and education, age 12-14	yr	490	1999	60r
Child's child care and education, age 15-17	yr	840	1999	60r
Child's clothing, age 0-2	yr	480	1999	60r
Child's clothing, age 3-5	yr	470	1999	60r
Child's clothing, age 6-8	yr	520	1999	60r
Child's clothing, age 9-11	yr	570	1999	60r
Child's clothing, age 12-14	yr	950	1999	60r
Child's clothing, age 15-17	yr	850	1999	60r
Child's food, age 0-2	yr	1000	1999	60r
Child's food, age 3-5	yr	1160	1999	60r
Child's food, age 6-8	yr	1490	1999	60r
Child's food, age 9-11	yr	1770	1999	60r
Child's food, age 12-14	yr	1770	1999	60r
Child's food, age 15-17	yr	1980	1999	60r
Child's health care, age 0-2	yr	620	1999	60r
Child's health care, age 3-5	yr	590	1999	60r
Child's health care, age 6-8	yr	680	1999	60r
Child's health care, age 9-11	yr	720	1999	60r
Child's health care, age 12-14	yr	730	1999	60r
Child's health care, age 15-17	yr	760	1999	60r
Child's housing, age 0-2	yr	3070	1999	60r
Child's housing, age 3-5	yr	3050	1999	60r
Child's housing, age 6-8	yr	3010	1999	60r
Child's housing, age 9-11	yr	2850	1999	60r
Child's housing, age 12-14	yr	3040	1999	60r
Child's housing, age 15-17	yr	2650	1999	60r
Child's personal care, reading, age 0-2	yr	910	1999	60r
Child's personal care, reading, age 3-5	yr	930	1999	60r
Child's personal care, reading, age 6-8	yr	960	1999	60r
Child's personal care, reading, age 9-11	yr	1000	1999	60r
Child's personal care, reading, age 12-14	yr	1170	1999	60r
Child's personal care, reading, age 15-17	yr	950	1999	60r
Clothing				
Apparel and services purchases	yr	1610	1999	30r
Boys, 2 to 15, expenditures on	yr	89	1999	30r
Children under 2, expenditures on	yr	79	1999	30r
Footwear, expenditures on	yr	283	1999	30r
Girls, 2 to 15, expenditures on	yr	103	1999	30r
Men and boys, expenditures on	yr	351	1999	30r
Men, 16 and over, expenditures on	yr	262	1999	30r
Women, 16 and over, expenditures on	yr	538	1999	30r
Communications				
Cable modem installation, Adelphi		54.90	6/99	103s
Cable modem installation, Comcast		95.00	6/99	103s
Cable modem installation, Media One		100.00	6/99	103s

Values are in dollars or fractions of dollars. In the column headed *Ref*, references are shown to sources. Each reference is followed by a letter. These refer to the geographical level for which data were reported: s=State, r=Region, and c=City or metro. The abbreviation *ex* is used to mean *except* or *excluding*; *exp* stands for expenditures. For other abbreviations and further explanations, please see the Introduction.

Sarasota-Brandenton, FL - continued

Item	Per	Value	Date	Ref.
Communications				
Cable modem installation, Time Warner		75.00-225.00	6/99	103s
Cable modem rate, cable subscriber, Adelphi	mos	34.95	6/99	103s
Cable modem rate, cable subscriber, Comcast	mos	39.95	6/99	103s
Cable modem rate, cable subscriber, Media One	mos	34.95-39.95	6/99	103s
Cable modem rate, cable subscriber, Time Warner	mos	39.95-49.95	6/99	103s
Cable modem rate, non-cable subscriber, Adelphi	mos	44.95	6/99	103s
Cable modem rate, non-cable subscriber, Comcast	mos	49.95	6/99	103s
Cable modem rate, non-cable subscriber, Media One	mos	49.95	6/99	103s
Cable modem rate, non-cable subscriber, Time Warner	mos	39.95-54.95	6/99	103s
Phone line, single, business, field visit	inst.	56.00	12/97	17s
Phone line, single, business, no field visit	inst.	56.00	12/97	17s
Phone line, single, residence, field visit	inst.	40.00	12/97	17s
Phone line, single, residence, no field visit	inst.	40.00	12/97	17s
Postage and stationery, expenditures on	yr	104	1999	30r
Postal rate, express mail, up to half-pound		12.45	7/01	108r
Postal rate, letter, first class, first ounce		0.34	7/01	108r
Postal rate, letter, two ounces		0.57	7/01	108r
Postal rate, post card		0.21	7/01	108r
Postal rate, priority mail, two pounds		3.95	7/01	108r
Postal rate, priority mail, up to one pound		3.50	7/01	108r
Telephone services, expenditures on	yr	860	1999	30r
Education				
Board, 4-year private college/university	yr	2236	1996	38s
Board, 4-year public college/university	yr	2295	1996	38s
Education expenditures	yr	431	1999	30r
Room, 4-year private college/university	yr	2428	1996	38s
Room, 4-year public college/university	yr	2193	1996	38s
Total cost, 4-year private college/university	yr	15028	1996	38s
Total cost, 4-year public college/university	yr	6254	1996	38s
Tuition, 2-year public college/university, in state	yr	1103	1996	38s
Tuition, 4-year private college/university, in state	yr	10364	1996	38s
Tuition, 4-year public college/university	yr	1767	1996	38s
Energy and Fuels				
Electricity	KWh	0.09	7/01	11r
Electricity	500 KWhs	47.29	7/01	11r
Fuel oil #2	gal	1.43	7/01	11r
Fuel oil and other fuels, expenditures on	yr	45	1999	30r
Gas, natural, commercial rate	1000 cf	8.44	11/00	88s
Gasoline, all types	gal	1.60	7/01	11r
Gasoline, unleaded midgrade	gal	1.65	7/01	11r
Gasoline, unleaded premium	gal	1.74	7/01	11r
Natural gas, expenditures on	yr	164	1999	30r
Utility (piped) gas, therm		1.01	7/01	11r
Utility (piped) gas, 40 therms		44.29	7/01	11r
Utility (piped) gas, 100 therms		97.44	7/01	11r
Entertainment				
Entertainment purchases	yr	1574	1999	30r
Fees and admissions paid	yr	371	1999	30r
Reading purchases	yr	121	1999	30r
Television, radios, sound equipment, expenditures on	yr	561	1999	30r
Funerals				
Total cost of funeral		5922.53	1/99	78r
Acknowledgement cards		63.43	1/99	78r
Casket		2258.77	1/99	78r
Cosmetology, hair, other preparation		127.09	1/99	78r
Embalming		393.49	1/99	78r
Funeral at funeral home		367.50	1/99	78r
Hearse (local)		169.66	1/99	78r

Sarasota-Brandenton, FL - continued

Item	Per	Value	Date	Ref.
Funerals - continued				
Professional service charges		1211.32	1/99	78r
Service car/van		80.69	1/99	78r
Transfer of remains to funeral home		144.25	1/99	78r
Vault		803.50	1/99	78r
Visitation/viewing		302.83	1/99	78r
Groceries				
American processed cheese	lb	3.50	7/01	11r
Bakery products, expenditures on	yr	261	1999	30r
Bananas	lb	0.47	7/01	11r
Beans, dried, any type, all sizes	lb	0.63	7/01	11r
Beef for stew, boneless	lb	2.86	7/01	11r
Beef, expenditures on	yr	210	1999	30r
Bologna, all beef or mixed	lb	2.29	7/01	11r
Bread, French	lb	1.66	7/01	11r
Bread, white, pan	lb	0.87	7/01	11r
Bread, whole wheat, pan	lb	1.38	7/01	11r
Broccoli	lb	1.04	7/01	11r
Butter, salted, grade AA, stick	lb	2.26	7/01	11r
Butter, yoghurt, cheese, etc, expenditures on	yr	170	1999	30r
Cabbage	lb	0.42	7/01	11r
Cereals and cereal products, expenditures on	yr	140	1999	30r
Cheddar cheese, natural	lb	3.75	7/01	11r
Chicken breast, bone-in	lb	1.85	7/01	11r
Chicken legs, bone-in	lb	1.34	7/01	11r
Chicken, fresh, whole	lb	1.05	7/01	11r
Chops, boneless,	lb	4.13	7/01	11r
Chuck roast, graded and ungraded, excl U.S. prime and choice	lb	2.35	7/01	11r
Chuck roast, U.S. choice, boneless	lb	2.67	7/01	11r
Coffee, 100%, ground roast, all sizes	lb	2.88	7/01	11r
Coffee, instant, plain, regular, all sizes	16 oz	9.25	7/01	11r
Cola, non diet,	2 liter	1.11	7/01	11r
Crackers, soda, salted	lb	1.70	7/01	11r
Dairy product purchases	yr	282	1999	30r
Eggs, expenditures on	yr	32	1999	30r
Fats and oils, expenditures on	yr	79	1999	30r
Fish and seafood, expenditures on	yr	99	1999	30r
Flour, white, all purpose	lb	0.32	7/01	11r
Food (excl fruit and vegetables), eaten at home, purchases	yr	815	1999	30r
Food cooked on trips, expenditures on	yr	36	1999	30r
Food purchases	yr	4533	1999	30r
Food purchases, eaten away from home	yr	1873	1999	30r
Food purchases, food eaten at home	yr	2660	1999	30r
Fresh fruits, expenditures on	yr	128	1999	30r
Fresh milk and cream, expenditures on	yr	112	1999	30r
Fresh vegetables, expenditures on	yr	131	1999	30r
Fruit and vegetable purchases	yr	438	1999	30r
Grapefruit	lb	0.59	7/01	11r
Grapes, Thompson, seedless	lb	2.12	7/01	11r
Ground beef, 100% beef	lb	1.76	7/01	11r
Ground beef, lean and extra lean	lb	2.60	7/01	11r
Ground chuck, 100% beef	lb	2.08	7/01	11r
Ham, boneless, excl canned	lb	2.71	7/01	11r
Ham, rump or shank half, bone-in, smoked	lb	2.19	7/01	11r
Ice cream, prepackaged, bulk, regular	1/2 gal	3.93	7/01	11r
Lemons	lb	1.32	7/01	11r
Lettuce, iceberg	lb	0.76	7/01	11r
Milk, fresh, low fat,	gal	2.75	7/01	11r
Milk, fresh, whole, fortified	gal	2.97	7/01	11r
Nonalcoholic beverages, expenditures on	yr	228	1999	30r
Orange juice, frozen concentrate	16 oz	1.95	7/01	11r
Oranges, Navel	lb	0.73	7/01	11r
Oranges, Valencia	lb	0.55	7/01	11r
Peanut butter, creamy, all sizes	lb	1.83	7/01	11r
Pears, Anjou	lb	0.98	7/01	11r
Pork chops, center cut, bone-in	lb	3.33	7/01	11r
Pork sausage, fresh, loose	lb	2.59	7/01	11r
Pork shoulder picnic, bone-in, smoked	lb	1.12	7/01	11r
Pork, expenditures on	yr	162	1999	30r
Potato chips	16 oz	3.59	7/01	11r

Values are in dollars or fractions of dollars. In the column headed *Ref*, references are shown as sources. Each reference is followed by a letter. These refer to the geographical level for which data were reported: s=State, r=Region, and c=City or metro. The abbreviation *ex* is used to mean *except* or *excluding*; *exp* stands for *expenditures*. For other abbreviations and further explanations, please see the Introduction.

Sarasota-Brandenton, FL - continued

Item	Per	Value	Date	Ref.
Groceries				
Potatoes, frozen, french fried	lb	1.00	7/01	11r
Potatoes, white, all types	lb	0.44	7/01	11r
Poultry, expenditures on	yr	137	1999	30r
Processed fruits, expenditures on	yr	97	1999	30r
Processed vegetables, expenditures on	yr	82	1999	30r
Rice, white, long grain, uncooked	lb	0.51	7/01	11r
Round roast, graded and ungraded, excl U.S. prime and choice	lb	2.96	7/01	11r
Round steak, graded and ungraded, excl U.S. prime and choice	lb	3.11	7/01	11r
Sirloin steak, graded and ungraded, excl U.S. prime and choice	lb	4.23	7/01	11r
Spaghetti and macaroni	lb	0.78	7/01	11r
Steak, round, U.S. choice, boneless	lb	3.56	7/01	11r
Steak, sirloin, U.S. choice, boneless	lb	5.65	7/01	11r
Strawberries, dry pint	12 oz	1.50	7/01	11r
Sugar and other sweets, expenditures on	yr	99	1999	30r
Sugar, white, 33-80 ounce package	lb	0.39	7/01	11r
Sugar, white, all sizes	lb	0.42	7/01	11r
Tobacco products and smoking supplies purchases	yr	288	1999	30r
Tomatoes, field grown	lb	1.43	7/01	11r
Tuna, light, chunk	lb	1.77	7/01	11r
Turkey, frozen, whole	lb	1.05	7/01	11r
Goods and Services				
B&B Japanese maple (acer japonicum)	gal	49.98-129.00	4/00	93r
Boxwood (buxus)	2 gal	12.99-16.99	4/00	93r
Daylilly (hemerocallis)	gal	4.99-8.99	4/00	93r
Flat of annuals		11.00-13.92	4/00	93r
Fountain grass (pennisetum)	gal	5.98-7.98	4/00	93r
Hanging basket (10 in)		7.99-14.98	4/00	93r
Hardy geranium (geranium)	gal	5.98-8.00	4/00	93r
Hosta (hosta)	gal	4.99-10.98	4/00	93r
Lilac (syrubga vulgaris)	2 gal	12.99-21.99	4/00	93r
Rhododendron (rhododendron)	2 gal	14.99-24.99	4/00	93r
Sage (salvia)	gal	5.98-6.99	4/00	93r
Wintercreeper euonymus (euonymus fortunei)	2 gal	7.99-89.99	4/00	93r
Hunting license	yr	12.50	4/01	34s
Health Care				
Cardiac catheterization, ave hospital/physician charges		15060	1998	77s
Childbirth, Cesarean delivery		11587	1997	13r
Childbirth, vaginal delivery		6725	1997	13r
Drugs, expenditures on	yr	399	1999	30r
Health care purchases	yr	1971	1999	30r
Health insurance expenditures	yr	933	1999	30r
Hysterectomy, laproscopically-assisted, ave hospital/physician charges		14760	1998	76s
Hysterectomy, vaginal, ave hospital and physician charges		11320	1998	76s
Medicaid dispensing fee		4.23	1999	87s
Medical services expenditures	yr	547	1999	30r
Medical supplies, expenditures on	yr	91	1999	30r
Plastic surgery, breast augmentation		2870	2000	7r
Plastic surgery, breast lift		3649	2000	7r
Plastic surgery, facelift		5008	2000	7r
Plastic surgery, hair transplantation		3425	2000	7r
Plastic surgery, lip augmentation		1227	2000	7r
Plastic surgery, lower body lift		4793	2000	7r

Sarasota-Brandenton, FL - continued

Item	Per	Value	Date	Ref.
Health Care - continued				
Plastic surgery, thigh lift		3862	2000	7r
Household Goods				
Floor coverings, expenditures on	yr	44	1999	30r
Furniture, expenditures on	yr	335	1999	30r
Household furnishings and equipment purchases	yr	1328	1999	30r
Household textiles, expenditures on	yr	89	1999	30r
Laundry and cleaning supplies, expenditures on	yr	113	1999	30r
Housing				
Home price, existing, ave		160100	10/00	90r
Home value, median		104000	2001	53s
Household operation expenditures	yr	553	1999	30r
Housekeeping supplies purchases	yr	473	1999	30r
Housing, expenditures on	yr	10303	1999	30r
Maintenance, repairs, insurance expenditures	yr	699	1999	30r
Monthly rental value of owned home	mos	505	1999	30r
Owned dwellings, expenditures own	yr	3465	1999	30r
Rent expenditures	yr	1641	1999	30r
Rental unit, 1 bedroom, with utilities	mos	526	4/01	41c
Rental unit, 2 bedroom, with utilities	mos	669	4/01	41c
Rental unit, 3 bedroom, with utilities	mos	860	4/01	41c
Rental unit, 4 bedroom, with utilities	mos	936	4/01	41c
Shelter, expenditures on	yr	5467	1999	30r
Insurance and Pensions				
Life and other personal insurance purchases	yr	414	1999	30r
Medigap health insurance, Plan H	yr	2887	2000	69s
Medigap health insurance, Plan I	yr	3302	2000	69s
Medigap health insurance, Plan J	yr	3889	2000	69s
Pensions and Social Security, expenditures on	yr	2635	1999	30r
Personal insurance and pensions, expenditures on	yr	3048	1999	30r
Legal Fees				
Divorce, filing fee		65.00-85.00	4/01	35s
Driver's license fee	renew	15.00	1999	48s
Driver's license fee	orig	20.00	1999	48s
Personal Goods				
Personal care products and services purchases	yr	393	1999	30r
Personal Services				
Personal services, household, expenditures on	yr	258	1999	30r
Pets				
Pets, toys, and playground equipment, expenditures on	yr	306	1999	30r
Taxes				
Federal income taxes paid	yr	2047	1999	30r
Personal taxes, expenditures on	yr	2554	1999	30r
Property taxes paid	yr	726	1999	30r
State and local income taxes paid	yr	363	1999	30r
Transportation				
Cars and trucks, new, expenditures on	yr	1648	1999	30r
Cars and trucks, used, expenditures on	yr	1651	1999	30r
Diesel at the pump	gal	1.26	10/99	73s
Gasoline and motor oil purchases	yr	1052	1999	30r
Gasoline before-tax price (cents)	gal	101.90	10/00	43s
Maintenance and repair expenditures	yr	621	1999	30r
Public transportation, expenditures on	yr	298	1999	30r
Transportation purchases	yr	6738	1999	30r
Vehicle expenses, miscellaneous, purchases	yr	2033	1999	30r
Vehicle insurance payments	yr	696	1999	30r
Vehicle purchases (net outlay)	yr	3354	1999	30r
Vehicle rental, lease expenditures	yr	352	1999	30r

Values are in dollars or fractions of dollars. In the column headed *Ref*, references are shown to sources. Each reference is followed by a letter. These refer to the geographical level for which data were reported: s=State, r=Region, and c=City or metro. The abbreviation *ex* is used to mean *except* or *excluding*; *exp* stands for *expenditures*. For other abbreviations and further explanations, please see the Introduction.

Sarasota-Brandenton, FL - continued

Item	Per	Value	Date	Ref.
Travel				
Hotel room	night	110.57	2/01	95s
Utilities				
Electrical bill, average	mos	86.33	9/00	9s
Electricity, expenditures on	yr	1115	1999	30r
Electricity cost, average	KWh	6.80	9/00	9s
Water and other public services, expenditures on	yr	298	1999	30r
Weddings				
Wedding (national average cost)		19936	2000	33r
Wedding (regional average total cost)		16293	1997	110r
Attendants' gifts		321	1998	33r
Bridal attendants' apparel (5 persons)		824	2000	33r
Bride's headpiece/veil		173	1998	33r
Bride's wedding dress		859	1998	33r
Clergy, religious facility fee		242	1998	33r
Engagement ring		3177	1998	33r
Flowers		789	1998	33r
Groom's formalwear rental		99	2000	33r
Limousine		410	1998	33r
Marriage license cost		56.00-88.50	4/01	35s
Men's formalwear (ushers, best man)		469	2000	33r
Mother of bride apparel		241	2000	33r
Music		866	1998	33r
Photography and videography		1368	1998	33r
Rehearsal dinner		728	1998	33r
Wedding invitations and announcements		341	1998	33r
Wedding reception		7968	2000	33r
Wedding rings (bride and groom)		1060	1998	33r

Savannah, GA

Item	Per	Value	Date	Ref.
Composite, ACCRA index		103.00	3/01	4c
Alcoholic Beverages				
Alcoholic beverage purchases	yr	253	1999	30r
Beer, Heineken, 12-oz, ex deposit	6	7.57	3/01	4c
J & B Scotch	750-ml	21.07	3/01	4c
Malt beverages, all types, all sizes, any origin	16 oz	0.96	7/01	11r
Wine, Livingston or Gallo, Chablis blanc	1.5 liter	5.87	3/01	4c
Appliances				
Appliance repair, service call, washing machine	min lab chg	47.86	3/01	4c
Major appliances, expenditures on	yr	172	1999	30r
Small appliances, housewares, expenditures on	yr	81	1999	30r
Banking and Money				
Mortgage interest and charges paid	yr	2039	1999	30r
Mortgage principal paid on owned property	yr	1026	1999	30r
Mortgage rate, incl. points and orig. fee, 30-yr. conv. fixed or ARM	mos	6.82	3/01	4c
Vehicle finance charges paid	yr	365	1999	30r
Business Expenses				
Business travel, car rental	day	45	2001	3c
Business travel, food	day	48	2001	3c
Business travel, hotel	day	102	2001	3c
Charity				
Cash contributions, expenditures	yr	1127	1999	30r
Child Care				
Child raising cost, total, age 0-2	yr	8540	1999	60r
Child raising cost, total, age 3-5	yr	8780	1999	60r
Child raising cost, total, age 6-8	yr	8820	1999	60r
Child raising cost, total, age 9-11	yr	8800	1999	60r
Child raising cost, total, age 12-14	yr	9510	1999	60r
Child raising cost, total, age 15-17	yr	9740	1999	60r
Child's child care and education, age 0-2	yr	1380	1999	60r
Child's child care and education, age 3-5	yr	1520	1999	60r
Child's child care and education, age 6-8	yr	990	1999	60r

Savannah, GA - continued

Item	Per	Value	Date	Ref.
Child Care - continued				
Child's child care and education, age 9-11	yr	650	1999	60r
Child's child care and education, age 12-14	yr	490	1999	60r
Child's child care and education, age 15-17	yr	840	1999	60r
Child's clothing, age 0-2	yr	480	1999	60r
Child's clothing, age 3-5	yr	470	1999	60r
Child's clothing, age 6-8	yr	520	1999	60r
Child's clothing, age 9-11	yr	570	1999	60r
Child's clothing, age 12-14	yr	950	1999	60r
Child's clothing, age 15-17	yr	850	1999	60r
Child's food, age 0-2	yr	1000	1999	60r
Child's food, age 3-5	yr	1160	1999	60r
Child's food, age 6-8	yr	1490	1999	60r
Child's food, age 9-11	yr	1770	1999	60r
Child's food, age 12-14	yr	1770	1999	60r
Child's food, age 15-17	yr	1980	1999	60r
Child's health care, age 0-2	yr	620	1999	60r
Child's health care, age 3-5	yr	590	1999	60r
Child's health care, age 6-8	yr	680	1999	60r
Child's health care, age 9-11	yr	720	1999	60r
Child's health care, age 12-14	yr	730	1999	60r
Child's health care, age 15-17	yr	760	1999	60r
Child's housing, age 0-2	yr	3070	1999	60r
Child's housing, age 3-5	yr	3050	1999	60r
Child's housing, age 6-8	yr	3010	1999	60r
Child's housing, age 9-11	yr	2850	1999	60r
Child's housing, age 12-14	yr	3040	1999	60r
Child's housing, age 15-17	yr	2650	1999	60r
Child's personal care, reading, age 0-2	yr	910	1999	60r
Child's personal care, reading, age 3-5	yr	930	1999	60r
Child's personal care, reading, age 6-8	yr	960	1999	60r
Child's personal care, reading, age 9-11	yr	1000	1999	60r
Child's personal care, reading, age 12-14	yr	1170	1999	60r
Child's personal care, reading, age 15-17	yr	950	1999	60r
Clothing				
Apparel and services purchases	yr	1610	1999	30r
Boys' brief, cotton	3	4.38	3/01	4c
Boys, 2 to 15, expenditures on	yr	89	1999	30r
Children under 2, expenditures on	yr	79	1999	30r
Footwear, expenditures on	yr	283	1999	30r
Girls, 2 to 15, expenditures on	yr	103	1999	30r
Men and boys, expenditures on	yr	351	1999	30r
Men, 16 and over, expenditures on	yr	262	1999	30r
Shirt, man's dress shirt		29.00	3/01	4c
Slacks, man's "No Wrinkles" khaki		44.20	3/01	4c
Women, 16 and over, expenditures on	yr	538	1999	30r
Communications				
Cable modem installation, Charter		99.00-169.00	6/99	103s
Cable modem installation, Comcast		95.00	6/99	103s
Cable modem installation, Intermedia		149.95	6/99	103s
Cable modem installation, Media One		100.00	6/99	103s
Cable modem rate, cable subscriber, Charter	mos	49.95-79.95	6/99	103s
Cable modem rate, cable subscriber, Comcast	mos	39.95	6/99	103s
Cable modem rate, cable subscriber, Intermedia	mos	49.95	6/99	103s
Cable modem rate, cable subscriber, Media One	mos	34.95-39.95	6/99	103s
Cable modem rate, non-cable subscriber, Charter	mos	59.95-89.95	6/99	103s
Cable modem rate, non-cable subscriber, Comcast	mos	49.95	6/99	103s
Cable modem rate, non-cable subscriber, Intermedia	mos	54.95	6/99	103s
Cable modem rate, non-cable subscriber, Media One	mos	49.95	6/99	103s
Newspaper subscription, daily and Sunday delivery	mos	13.00	3/01	4c
Phone line, single, business, field visit	inst.	58.25	12/97	17s
Phone line, single, business, no field visit	inst.	58.25	12/97	17s

Values are in dollars or fractions of dollars. In the column headed *Ref*, references are shown to sources. Each reference is followed by a letter. These refer to the geographical level for which data were reported: s=State, r=Region, and c=City or metro. The abbreviation *ex* is used to mean *except* or *excluding*; *exp* stands for *expenditures*. For other abbreviations and further explanations, please see the Introduction.

Savannah, GA - continued

Item	Per	Value	Date	Ref.
Communications				
Phone line, single, residence, field visit	inst.	42.50	12/97	17s
Phone line, single, residence, no field visit	inst.	42.50	12/97	17s
Postage and stationery, expenditures on	yr	104	1999	30r
Postal rate, express mail, up to half-pound		12.45	7/01	108r
Postal rate, letter, first class, first ounce		0.34	7/01	108r
Postal rate, letter, two ounces		0.57	7/01	108r
Postal rate, post card		0.21	7/01	108r
Postal rate, priority mail, two pounds		3.95	7/01	108r
Postal rate, priority mail, up to one pound		3.50	7/01	108r
Telephone bill, family of three	mos	25.42	3/01	4c
Telephone services, expenditures on	yr	860	1999	30r
Education				
Board, 4-year private college/university	yr	2267	1996	38s
Board, 4-year public college/university	yr	1877	1996	38s
Education expenditures	yr	431	1999	30r
Room, 4-year private college/university	yr	2719	1996	38s
Room, 4-year public college/university	yr	1712	1996	38s
Total cost, 4-year private college/university	yr	15194	1996	38s
Total cost, 4-year public college/university	yr	5691	1996	38s
Tuition, 2-year public college/university, in state	yr	1062	1996	38s
Tuition, 4-year private college/university, in state	yr	10208	1996	38s
Tuition, 4-year public college/university	yr	2103	1996	38s
Energy and Fuels				
Electricity	KWh	0.09	7/01	11r
Electricity	500 KWhs	47.29	7/01	11r
Energy, combined forms, 2400 sq ft	mos	109.67	3/01	4c
Fuel oil #2	gal	1.43	7/01	11r
Fuel oil and other fuels, expenditures on	yr	45	1999	30r
Gas, regular unleaded, cash, self-service	gal	1.40	3/01	4c
Gasoline, all types	gal	1.60	7/01	11r
Gasoline, unleaded midgrade	gal	1.65	7/01	11r
Gasoline, unleaded premium	gal	1.74	7/01	11r
Natural gas, expenditures on	yr	164	1999	30r
Utility (piped) gas, therm		1.01	7/01	11r
Utility (piped) gas, 40 therms		44.29	7/01	11r
Utility (piped) gas, 100 therms		97.44	7/01	11r
Entertainment				
Bowling, Saturday evening rate	line	3.70	3/01	4c
Entertainment purchases	yr	1574	1999	30r
Fees and admissions paid	yr	371	1999	30r
Monopoly game, Parker Brothers', No. 9	game	10.54	3/01	4c
Movie, first-run, Saturday, evening	adm.	7.00	3/01	4c
Reading purchases	yr	121	1999	30r
Television, radios, sound equipment, expenditures on	yr	561	1999	30r
Tennis balls, yellow, Wilson or Penn, 3	can	2.05	3/01	4c
Funerals				
Total cost of funeral		5922.53	1/99	78r
Acknowledgement cards		63.43	1/99	78r
Casket		2258.77	1/99	78r
Cosmetology, hair, other preparation		127.09	1/99	78r
Embalming		393.49	1/99	78r
Funeral at funeral home		367.50	1/99	78r
Hearse (local)		169.66	1/99	78r
Professional service charges		1211.32	1/99	78r
Service car/van		80.69	1/99	78r
Transfer of remains to funeral home		144.25	1/99	78r
Vault		803.50	1/99	78r
Visitation/viewing		302.83	1/99	78r
Groceries				
Groceries, ACCRA Index		103.50	3/01	4c
American processed cheese	lb	3.50	7/01	11r
Antibiotic ointment, Polysporin	0.5 oz	4.98	3/01	4c
Baby food, strained vegetables or fruit, lowest price	4-4.5 oz	0.45	3/01	4c
Bakery products, expenditures on	yr	261	1999	30r

Savannah, GA - continued

Item	Per	Value	Date	Ref.
Groceries - continued				
Bananas	lb	0.52	3/01	4c
Bananas	lb	0.47	7/01	11r
Beans, dried, any type, all sizes	lb	0.63	7/01	11r
Beef for stew, boneless	lb	2.86	7/01	11r
Beef or hamburger, ground	lb	1.84	3/01	4c
Beef, expenditures on	yr	210	1999	30r
Bologna, all beef or mixed	lb	2.29	7/01	11r
Bread, French	lb	1.66	7/01	11r
Bread, white	loaf	1.12	3/01	4c
Bread, white, pan	lb	0.87	7/01	11r
Bread, whole wheat, pan	lb	1.38	7/01	11r
Broccoli	lb	1.04	7/01	11r
Butter, salted, grade AA, stick	lb	2.26	7/01	11r
Butter, yoghurt, cheese, etc, expenditures on	yr	170	1999	30r
Cabbage	lb	0.42	7/01	11r
Cereals and cereal products, expenditures on	yr	140	1999	30r
Cheddar cheese, natural	lb	3.75	7/01	11r
Cheese, Kraft grated Parmesan	8 oz	3.68	3/01	4c
Chicken breast, bone-in	lb	1.85	7/01	11r
Chicken legs, bone-in	lb	1.34	7/01	11r
Chicken, fresh, whole	lb	1.05	7/01	11r
Chicken, whole fryer	lb	0.99	3/01	4c
Chops, boneless,	lb	4.13	7/01	11r
Chuck roast, graded and ungraded, excl U.S. prime and choice	lb	2.35	7/01	11r
Chuck roast, U.S. choice, boneless	lb	2.67	7/01	11r
Cigarettes, Winston, Kings	carton	27.46	3/01	4c
Coffee, 100%, ground roast, all sizes	lb	2.88	7/01	11r
Coffee, instant, plain, regular, all sizes	16 oz	9.25	7/01	11r
Coffee, vacuum-packed	13 oz	2.48	3/01	4c
Cola, non diet,	2 liter	1.11	7/01	11r
Corn Flakes, Kellogg's or Post Toasties	18 oz	2.69	3/01	4c
Corn, frozen, whole kernel, lowest price	16 oz	1.15	3/01	4c
Crackers, soda, salted	lb	1.70	7/01	11r
Dairy product purchases	yr	282	1999	30r
Eggs, expenditures on	yr	32	1999	30r
Eggs, Grade A or AA	dozen	1.29	3/01	4c
Fats and oils, expenditures on	yr	79	1999	30r
Fish and seafood, expenditures on	yr	99	1999	30r
Flour, white, all purpose	lb	0.32	7/01	11r
Food (excl fruit and vegetables), eaten at home, purchases	yr	815	1999	30r
Food cooked on trips, expenditures on	yr	36	1999	30r
Food purchases	yr	4533	1999	30r
Food purchases, eaten away from home	yr	1873	1999	30r
Food purchases, food eaten at home	yr	2660	1999	30r
Fresh fruits, expenditures on	yr	128	1999	30r
Fresh milk and cream, expenditures on	yr	112	1999	30r
Fresh vegetables, expenditures on	yr	131	1999	30r
Fruit and vegetable purchases	yr	438	1999	30r
Grapefruit	lb	0.59	7/01	11r
Grapes, Thompson, seedless	lb	2.12	7/01	11r
Ground beef, 100% beef	lb	1.76	7/01	11r
Ground beef, lean and extra lean	lb	2.60	7/01	11r
Ground chuck, 100% beef	lb	2.08	7/01	11r
Ham, boneless, excl canned	lb	2.71	7/01	11r
Ham, rump or shank half, bone-in, smoked	lb	2.19	7/01	11r
Ice cream, prepackaged, bulk, regular	1/2 gal	3.93	7/01	11r
Lemons	lb	1.32	7/01	11r
Lettuce, iceberg	head	0.99	3/01	4c
Lettuce, iceberg	lb	0.76	7/01	11r
Margarine, Blue Bonnet or Parkay, stick	lb	0.82	3/01	4c
Milk, fresh, low fat,	gal	2.75	7/01	11r
Milk, fresh, whole, fortified	gal	2.97	7/01	11r
Milk, whole	1/2 gal	1.93	3/01	4c
Nonalcoholic beverages, expenditures on	yr	228	1999	30r
Orange juice, frozen concentrate	16 oz	1.95	7/01	11r
Orange juice, Minute Maid frozen	12 oz	1.48	3/01	4c
Oranges, Navel	lb	0.73	7/01	11r
Oranges, Valencia	lb	0.55	7/01	11r

Values are in dollars or fractions of dollars. In the column headed *Ref*, references are shown to sources. Each reference is followed by a letter. These refer to the geographical level for which data were reported: s=State, r=Region, and c=City or metro. The abbreviation *ex* is used to mean *except* or *excluding*; *exp* stands for *expenditures*. For other abbreviations and further explanations, please see the Introduction.

Savannah, GA - continued

Item	Per	Value	Date	Ref.
Groceries				
Peaches, halves or slices, Hunt's, Del Monte, or Libby's	29 oz	1.54	3/01	4c
Peanut butter, creamy, all sizes	lb	1.83	7/01	11r
Pears, Anjou	lb	0.98	7/01	11r
Peas, green, Del Monte or Green Giant	15 oz	0.69	3/01	4c
Pork chops, center cut, bone-in	lb	3.33	7/01	11r
Pork sausage, fresh, loose	lb	2.59	7/01	11r
Pork shoulder picnic, bone-in, smoked	lb	1.12	7/01	11r
Pork, expenditures on	yr	162	1999	30r
Potato chips	16 oz	3.59	7/01	11r
Potatoes, frozen, french fried	lb	1.00	7/01	11r
Potatoes, white or red	10 lb	3.11	3/01	4c
Potatoes, white, all types	lb	0.44	7/01	11r
Poultry, expenditures on	yr	137	1999	30r
Processed fruits, expenditures on	yr	97	1999	30r
Processed vegetables, expenditures on	yr	82	1999	30r
Rice, white, long grain, uncooked	lb	0.51	7/01	11r
Round roast, graded and ungraded, excl U.S. prime and choice	lb	2.96	7/01	11r
Round steak, graded and ungraded, excl U.S. prime and choice	lb	3.11	7/01	11r
Sausage, Jimmy Dean/Owens pork	lb	3.40	3/01	4c
Shortening, vegetable, Crisco	3 lb	3.06	3/01	4c
Sirloin steak, graded and ungraded, excl U.S. prime and choice	lb	4.23	7/01	11r
Soft drink, Coca Cola, ex deposit	2 liter	1.41	3/01	4c
Spaghetti and macaroni	lb	0.78	7/01	11r
Steak, round, U.S. choice, boneless	lb	3.56	7/01	11r
Steak, sirloin, U.S. choice, boneless	lb	5.65	7/01	11r
Steak, T-bone	lb	6.78	3/01	4c
Strawberries, dry pint	12 oz	1.50	7/01	11r
Sugar and other sweets, expenditures on	yr	99	1999	30r
Sugar, cane or beet	4 lbs	1.44	3/01	4c
Sugar, white, 33-80 ounce package	lb	0.39	7/01	11r
Sugar, white, all sizes	lb	0.42	7/01	11r
Tobacco products and smoking supplies purchases	yr	288	1999	30r
Tomatoes, field grown	lb	1.43	7/01	11r
Tomatoes, Hunt's or Del Monte	14.5 oz	0.79	3/01	4c
Tuna, chunk, light	6 oz	0.50	3/01	4c
Tuna, light, chunk	lb	1.77	7/01	11r
Turkey, frozen, whole	lb	1.05	7/01	11r
Goods and Services				
Miscellaneous goods and services, ACCRA Index		104.80	3/01	4c
B&B Japanese maple (acer japonicum)	gal	49.98-129.00	4/00	93r
Boxwood (buxus)	2 gal	12.99-16.99	4/00	93r
Daylily (hemerocallis)	gal	4.99-8.99	4/00	93r
Flat of annuals		11.00-13.92	4/00	93r
Fountain grass (pennisetum)	gal	5.98-7.98	4/00	93r
Hanging basket (10 in)		7.99-14.98	4/00	93r
Hardy geranium (geranium)	gal	5.98-8.00	4/00	93r
Hosta (hosta)	gal	4.99-10.98	4/00	93r
Lilac (syrubga vulgaris)	2 gal	12.99-21.99	4/00	93r
Rhododendron (rhododendron)	2 gal	14.99-24.99	4/00	93r
Sage (salvia)	gal	5.98-6.99	4/00	93r
Wintercreeper euonymus (euonymus fortunei)	2 gal	7.99-89.99	4/00	93r
Hunting license	yr	10.00	4/01	34s

Savannah, GA - continued

Item	Per	Value	Date	Ref.
Health Care				
Health care, ACCRA Index		94.30	3/01	4c
Cardiac catheterization, ave hospital/physician charges		14190	1998	77s
Childbirth, Cesarean delivery		11587	1997	13r
Childbirth, vaginal delivery		6725	1997	13r
Dentist's fee, adult teeth cleaning and periodic oral exam	visit	69.00	3/01	4c
Doctor's fee, routine exam, established patient	visit	55.00	3/01	4c
Drugs, expenditures on	yr	399	1999	30r
Health care purchases	yr	1971	1999	30r
Health insurance expenditures	yr	933	1999	30r
Home health care aide cost, licensed agency	hour	12	2000	82c
Hospital care, private room	day	441.00	3/01	4c
Hysterectomy, laproscopically-assisted, ave hospital/physician charges		16760	1998	76s
Hysterectomy, vaginal, ave hospital and physician charges		11160	1998	76s
Medicaid dispensing fee		4.63	1999	87s
Medical services expenditures	yr	547	1999	30r
Medical supplies, expenditures on	yr	91	1999	30r
Nursing home costs, private room	day	103	2000	82c
Nursing home stay, private room	day	103	2000	81c
Plastic surgery, breast augmentation		2870	2000	7r
Plastic surgery, breast lift		3649	2000	7r
Plastic surgery, facelift		5008	2000	7r
Plastic surgery, hair transplantation		3425	2000	7r
Plastic surgery, lip augmentation		1227	2000	7r
Plastic surgery, lower body lift		4793	2000	7r
Plastic surgery, thigh lift		3862	2000	7r
Household Goods				
Dishwashing powder, Cascade	50 oz	3.43	3/01	4c
Floor coverings, expenditures on	yr	44	1999	30r
Furniture, expenditures on	yr	335	1999	30r
Household furnishings and equipment purchases	yr	1328	1999	30r
Household textiles, expenditures on	yr	89	1999	30r
Laundry and cleaning supplies, expenditures on	yr	113	1999	30r
Tissues, facial, Kleenex brand	175	1.36	3/01	4c
Housing				
Housing, ACCRA Index		107.30	3/01	4c
Home, 2200 sq ft, 4-br, 2-bath, 2-car garage, average		145250	2000	47c
Home price, existing, ave		160100	10/00	90r
Home value, median		131000	2001	53s
House, 2400 sq ft, 8000 sq ft lot, new, urban, utilities	total	236169	3/01	4c
House payment, principal and interest, 25% down payment	mos	1157	3/01	4c
Household operation expenditures	yr	553	1999	30r
Housekeeping supplies purchases	yr	473	1999	30r
Housing, expenditures on	yr	10303	1999	30r
Maintenance, repairs, insurance expenditures	yr	699	1999	30r
Monthly rental value of owned home	mos	505	1999	30r
Owned dwellings, expenditures own	yr	3465	1999	30r
Rent expenditures	yr	1641	1999	30r
Rent, apartment, 2 br, 1 1/2-2 baths, unfurn, 950 sq ft, water	mos	611	3/01	4c
Rental unit, 1 bedroom, with utilities	mos	461	4/01	41c
Rental unit, 2 bedroom, with utilities	mos	536	4/01	41c
Rental unit, 3 bedroom, with utilities	mos	723	4/01	41c
Rental unit, 4 bedroom, with utilities	mos	752	4/01	41c
Shelter, expenditures on	yr	5467	1999	30r
Insurance and Pensions				
Life and other personal insurance purchases	yr	414	1999	30r
Pensions and Social Security, expenditures on	yr	2635	1999	30r
Personal insurance and pensions, expenditures on	yr	3048	1999	30r

Values are in dollars or fractions of dollars. In the column headed *Ref*, references are shown to sources. Each reference is followed by a letter. These refer to the geographical level for which data were reported: s=State, r=Region, and c=City or metro. The abbreviation *ex* is used to mean *except* or *excluding*; *exp* stands for *expenditures*. For other abbreviations and further explanations, please see the Introduction.

Savannah, GA - continued

Item	Per	Value	Date	Ref.
Legal Fees				
Divorce, filing fee		65.00- 85.00	4/01	35s
Driver's license fee	renew	15.00	1999	48s
Driver's license fee	orig	16.50	1999	48s
Personal Goods				
Personal care products and services purchases	yr	393	1999	30r
Shampoo, Alberto VO5	15 oz	1.14	3/01	4c
Toothpaste, Crest or Colgate	6-7 oz	2.45	3/01	4c
Personal Services				
Dry cleaning, man's 2-pc suit		7.94	3/01	4c
Man's haircut, barbershop, no styling		9.28	3/01	4c
Personal services, household, expenditures on	yr	258	1999	30r
Woman's shampoo, trim, blow-dry, no style- change		26.86	3/01	4c
Pets				
Pets, toys, and playground equipment, expenditures on	yr	306	1999	30r
Restaurant Food				
Chicken, fried, thigh and drumstick, KFC/ Church's		2.62	3/01	4c
Hamburger with cheese, McDonald's	1/4 lb	2.09	3/01	4c
Pizza, Pizza Hut or Pizza Inn	11-12 in	9.49	3/01	4c
Taxes				
Federal income taxes paid	yr	2047	1999	30r
Personal taxes, expenditures on	yr	2554	1999	30r
Property taxes paid	yr	726	1999	30r
State and local income taxes paid	yr	363	1999	30r
Transportation				
Transportation, ACCRA Index		95.60	3/01	4c
Bus fare, one-way	trip	0.75	2000	1c
Cars and trucks, new, expenditures on	yr	1648	1999	30r
Cars and trucks, used, expenditures on	yr	1651	1999	30r
Diesel at the pump	gal	1.10	10/99	73s
Gasoline and motor oil purchases	yr	1052	1999	30r
Gasoline before-tax price (cents)	gal	102.00	10/00	43s
Maintenance and repair expenditures	yr	621	1999	30r
Public transportation, expenditures on	yr	298	1999	30r
Tire balance, computer or spin balance, front	wheel	7.10	3/01	4c
Transportation purchases	yr	6738	1999	30r
Vehicle expenses, miscellaneous, purchases	yr	2033	1999	30r
Vehicle insurance payments	yr	696	1999	30r
Vehicle purchases (net outlay)	yr	3354	1999	30r
Vehicle rental, lease expenditures	yr	352	1999	30r
Utilities				
Utilities, ACCRA Index		93.60	3/01	4c
Electrical bill, average	mos	79.83	9/00	9s
Electricity, 2400 sq ft, new home	mos	109.67	3/01	4c
Electricity, expenditures on	yr	1115	1999	30r
Electricity, summer, 250 KWh	mos	22.25	2/96	97c
Electricity, summer, 500 KWh	mos	39.28	2/96	97c
Electricity, summer, 750 KWh	mos	56.33	2/96	97c
Electricity, summer, 1000 KWh	mos	67.94	2/96	97c
Electricity cost, average	KWh	6.10	9/00	9s
Water and other public services, expenditures on	yr	298	1999	30r
Weddings				
Wedding (national average cost)		19936	2000	33r
Wedding (regional average total cost)		16293	1997	110r
Attendants' gifts		321	1998	33r
Bridal attendants' apparel (5 persons)		824	2000	33r
Bride's headpiece/veil		173	1998	33r
Bride's wedding dress		859	1998	33r
Clergy, religious facility fee		242	1998	33r
Engagement ring		3177	1998	33r
Flowers		789	1998	33r
Groom's formalwear rental		99	2000	33r

Savannah, GA - continued

Item	Per	Value	Date	Ref.
Weddings - continued				
Limousine		410	1998	33r
Marriage license cost		40.00	4/01	35s
Men's formalwear (ushers, best man)		469	2000	33r
Mother of bride apparel		241	2000	33r
Music		866	1998	33r
Photography and videography		1368	1998	33r
Rehearsal dinner		728	1998	33r
Wedding invitations and announcements		341	1998	33r
Wedding reception		7968	2000	33r
Wedding rings (bride and groom)		1060	1998	33r

Scranton-Wilkes-Barre-Hazleton, PA

Item	Per	Value	Date	Ref.
Average annual expenditures	yr	37971	1999	30r
Alcoholic Beverages				
Alcoholic beverage purchases	yr	368	1999	30r
Wine, red and white table, all sizes, any origin	liter	9.64	7/01	11r
Appliances				
Major appliances, expenditures on	yr	194	1999	30r
Small appliances, housewares, expenditures on	yr	93	1999	30r
Banking and Money				
Mortgage interest and charges paid	yr	2622	1999	30r
Mortgage principal paid on owned property	yr	1262	1999	30r
Vehicle finance charges paid	yr	240	1999	30r
Charity				
Cash contributions, expenditures	yr	1001	1999	30r
Child Care				
Child raising cost, total, age 0-2	yr	8670	1999	60r
Child raising cost, total, age 3-5	yr	8910	1999	60r
Child raising cost, total, age 6-8	yr	9040	1999	60r
Child raising cost, total, age 9-11	yr	9100	1999	60r
Child raising cost, total, age 12-14	yr	9890	1999	60r
Child raising cost, total, age 15-17	yr	10010	1999	60r
Child's child care and education, age 0-2	yr	1070	1999	60r
Child's child care and education, age 3-5	yr	1190	1999	60r
Child's child care and education, age 6-8	yr	740	1999	60r
Child's child care and education, age 9-11	yr	470	1999	60r
Child's child care and education, age 12-14	yr	350	1999	60r
Child's child care and education, age 15-17	yr	590	1999	60r
Child's clothing, age 0-2	yr	480	1999	60r
Child's clothing, age 3-5	yr	470	1999	60r
Child's clothing, age 6-8	yr	520	1999	60r
Child's clothing, age 9-11	yr	570	1999	60r
Child's clothing, age 12-14	yr	970	1999	60r
Child's clothing, age 15-17	yr	870	1999	60r
Child's food, age 0-2	yr	1130	1999	60r
Child's food, age 3-5	yr	1290	1999	60r
Child's food, age 6-8	yr	1640	1999	60r
Child's food, age 9-11	yr	1930	1999	60r
Child's food, age 12-14	yr	1940	1999	60r
Child's food, age 15-17	yr	2150	1999	60r
Child's health care, age 0-2	yr	550	1999	60r
Child's health care, age 3-5	yr	530	1999	60r
Child's health care, age 6-8	yr	610	1999	60r
Child's health care, age 9-11	yr	650	1999	60r
Child's health care, age 12-14	yr	660	1999	60r
Child's health care, age 15-17	yr	690	1999	60r
Child's housing, age 0-2	yr	3555	1999	60r
Child's housing, age 3-5	yr	3530	1999	60r
Child's housing, age 6-8	yr	3490	1999	60r
Child's housing, age 9-11	yr	3340	1999	60r
Child's housing, age 12-14	yr	3530	1999	60r
Child's housing, age 15-17	yr	3140	1999	60r
Child's personal care, reading, age 0-2	yr	920	1999	60r
Child's personal care, reading, age 3-5	yr	950	1999	60r
Child's personal care, reading, age 6-8	yr	980	1999	60r
Child's personal care, reading, age 9-11	yr	1020	1999	60r

Values are in dollars or fractions of dollars. In the column headed *Ref*, references are shown to sources. Each reference is followed by a letter. These refer to the geographical level for which data were reported: s=State, r=Region, and c=City or metro. The abbreviation *ex* is used to mean *except* or *excluding*; *exp* stands for expenditures. For other abbreviations and further explanations, please see the Introduction.

Scranton-Wilkes-Barre-Hazleton, PA - continued

Item	Per	Value	Date	Ref.
Child Care				
Child's personal care, reading, age 12-14	yr	1190	1999	60r
Child's personal care, reading, age 15-17	yr	970	1999	60r
Clothing				
Apparel and services purchases	yr	1831	1999	30r
Boys, 2 to 15, expenditures on	yr	92	1999	30r
Children under 2, expenditures on	yr	63	1999	30r
Footwear, expenditures on	yr	300	1999	30r
Girls, 2 to 15, expenditures on	yr	101	1999	30r
Men and boys, expenditures on	yr	446	1999	30r
Men, 16 and over, expenditures on	yr	354	1999	30r
Women, 16 and over, expenditures on	yr	584	1999	30r
Communications				
Cable modem installation, Adelphi		54.90	6/99	103s
Cable modem installation, Comcast		95.00	6/99	103s
Cable modem rate, cable subscriber, Adelphi	mos	34.95	6/99	103s
Cable modem rate, cable subscriber, Comcast	mos	39.95	6/99	103s
Cable modem rate, non-cable subscriber, Adelphi	mos	44.95	6/99	103s
Cable modem rate, non-cable subscriber, Comcast	mos	49.95	6/99	103s
Phone line, single, business, field visit	inst.	75.00	12/97	17s
Phone line, single, business, no field visit	inst.	75.00	12/97	17s
Phone line, single, residence, field visit	inst.	40.00	12/97	17s
Phone line, single, residence, no field visit	inst.	40.00	12/97	17s
Postage and stationery, expenditures on	yr	138	1999	30r
Postal rate, express mail, up to half-pound		12.45	7/01	108r
Postal rate, letter, first class, first ounce		0.34	7/01	108r
Postal rate, letter, two ounces		0.57	7/01	108r
Postal rate, post card		0.21	7/01	108r
Postal rate, priority mail, two pounds		3.95	7/01	108r
Postal rate, priority mail, up to one pound		3.50	7/01	108r
Telephone services, expenditures on	yr	830	1999	30r
Education				
Board, 4-year private college/university	yr	2822	1996	38s
Board, 4-year public college/university	yr	2174	1996	38s
Education expenditures	yr	877	1999	30r
Room, 4-year private college/university	yr	2943	1996	38s
Room, 4-year public college/university	yr	2227	1996	38s
Total cost, 4-year private college/university	yr	19876	1996	38s
Total cost, 4-year public college/university	yr	9124	1996	38s
Tuition, 2-year public college/university, in state	yr	1909	1996	38s
Tuition, 4-year private college/university, in state	yr	14111	1996	38s
Tuition, 4-year public college/university	yr	4723	1996	38s
Energy and Fuels				
Electricity	KWh	0.12	7/01	11r
Fuel oil #2	gal	1.31	7/01	11r
Fuel oil and other fuels, expenditures on	yr	207	1999	30r
Gas, natural, commercial rate	1000 cf	5.96	11/00	88s
Gasoline, all types	gal	1.80	7/01	11r
Gasoline, unleaded midgrade	gal	1.85	7/01	11r
Gasoline, unleaded premium	gal	1.91	7/01	11r
Gasoline, unleaded regular	gal	1.71	7/01	11r
Natural gas, expenditures on	yr	368	1999	30r
Utility (piped) gas, therm		1.08	7/01	11r
Utility (piped) gas, 40 therms		50.87	7/01	11r
Utility (piped) gas, 100 therms		111.06	7/01	11r
Entertainment				
Entertainment purchases	yr	1821	1999	30r
Fees and admissions paid	yr	511	1999	30r
Television, radios, sound equipment, expenditures on	yr	650	1999	30r
Funerals				
Total cost of funeral		5813.50	1/99	78r
Acknowledgement cards		28.32	1/99	78r
Casket		2082.20	1/99	78r
Cosmetology, hair, other preparation		169.59	1/99	78r

Scranton-Wilkes-Barre-Hazleton, PA - continued

Item	Per	Value	Date	Ref.
Funerals - continued				
Embalming		465.60	1/99	78r
Funeral at funeral home		339.56	1/99	78r
Hearse (local)		183.96	1/99	78r
Professional service charges		1157.85	1/99	78r
Service car/van		100.41	1/99	78r
Transfer of remains to funeral home		158.66	1/99	78r
Vault		766.31	1/99	78r
Visitation/viewing		361.04	1/99	78r
Groceries				
Apples, red delicious	lb	0.95	7/01	11r
Bacon, sliced	lb	3.44	7/01	11r
Bakery products, expenditures on	yr	310	1999	30r
Bananas	lb	0.55	7/01	11r
Beef, expenditures on	yr	236	1999	30r
Bread, white, pan	lb	1.09	7/01	11r
Butter, yoghurt, cheese, etc, expenditures on	yr	214	1999	30r
Cereals and bakery product purchases	yr	474	1999	30r
Cereals and cereal products, expenditures on	yr	164	1999	30r
Chicken legs, bone-in	lb	1.23	7/01	11r
Chicken, fresh, whole	lb	1.13	7/01	11r
Chuck roast, U.S. choice, boneless	lb	2.79	7/01	11r
Coffee, 100%, ground roast, all sizes	lb	3.40	7/01	11r
Dairy product purchases	yr	342	1999	30r
Eggs, expenditures on	yr	34	1999	30r
Eggs, grade A, large	dozen	0.82	7/01	11r
Fats and oils, expenditures on	yr	80	1999	30r
Fish and seafood, expenditures on	yr	123	1999	30r
Food (excl fruit and vegetables), eaten at home, purchases	yr	838	1999	30r
Food cooked on trips, expenditures on	yr	48	1999	30r
Food purchases	yr	5314	1999	30r
Food purchases, eaten away from home	yr	2313	1999	30r
Food purchases, food eaten at home	yr	3001	1999	30r
Fresh fruits, expenditures on	yr	169	1999	30r
Fresh milk and cream, expenditures on	yr	128	1999	30r
Fresh vegetables, expenditures on	yr	164	1999	30r
Grapefruit	lb	0.67	7/01	11r
Grapes, Thompson, seedless	lb	2.18	7/01	11r
Ground beef, lean and extra lean	lb	2.66	7/01	11r
Ground chuck, 100% beef	lb	2.04	7/01	11r
Lettuce, iceberg	lb	0.76	7/01	11r
Meats, poultry, fish, and egg purchases	yr	808	1999	30r
Nonalcoholic beverages, expenditures on	yr	225	1999	30r
Orange juice, frozen concentrate	16 oz	1.88	7/01	11r
Oranges, Navel	lb	0.79	7/01	11r
Oranges, Valencia	lb	0.56	7/01	11r
Peaches	lb	1.16	7/01	11r
Peanut butter, creamy, all sizes	lb	2.01	7/01	11r
Pears, Anjou	lb	1.16	7/01	11r
Pork chops, center cut, bone-in	lb	3.57	7/01	11r
Pork, expenditures on	yr	146	1999	30r
Potato chips	16 oz	3.37	7/01	11r
Potatoes, white, all types	lb	0.42	7/01	11r
Poultry, expenditures on	yr	158	1999	30r
Processed fruits, expenditures on	yr	124	1999	30r
Processed vegetables, expenditures on	yr	82	1999	30r
Round roast, U.S. choice, boneless	lb	3.04	7/01	11r
Spaghetti and macaroni	lb	1.04	7/01	11r
Steak, sirloin, U.S. choice, boneless	lb	5.39	7/01	11r
Strawberries, dry pint	12 oz	1.51	7/01	11r
Sugar and other sweets, expenditures on	yr	110	1999	30r
Sugar, white, 33-80 ounce package	lb	0.46	7/01	11r
Sugar, white, all sizes	lb	0.47	7/01	11r
Tobacco products and smoking supplies purchases	yr	309	1999	30r
Yogurt, natural, fruit flavored	8 oz	0.79	7/01	11r
Goods and Services				
B&B Japanese maple (acer japonicum)	gal	38.99-125.00	4/00	93r

Values are in dollars or fractions of dollars. In the column headed *Ref*, references are shown to sources. Each reference is followed by a letter. These refer to the geographical level for which data were reported: s=State, r=Region, and c=City or metro. The abbreviation *ex* is used to mean *except* or *excluding*; *exp* stands for *expenditures*. For other abbreviations and further explanations, please see the Introduction.

Scranton-Wilkes-Barre-Hazleton, PA - continued

Item	Per	Value	Date	Ref.
Goods and Services				
Boxwood (buxus)	2 gal	15.99-49.95	4/00	93r
Daylilly (hemerocallis)	gal	4.95	4/00	93r
Flat of annuals		8.00-14.99	4/00	93r
Fountain grass (pennisetum)	gal	6.99-9.99	4/00	93r
Hanging basket (10 in)		12.95-19.99	4/00	93r
Hardy geranium (geranium)	gal	6.95-7.99	4/00	93r
Hosta (hosta)	gal	4.95	4/00	93r
Lilac (syrubga vulgaris)	2 gal	17.99-74.95	4/00	93r
Miscellaneous purchases	yr	872	1999	30r
Rhododendron (rhododendron)	2 gal	23.99-54.95	4/00	93r
Sage (salvia)	gal	6.95-7.99	4/00	93r
Wintercreeper euonymus (euonymus fortunei)	2 gal	14.99-23.95	4/00	93r
Hunting license	yr	20.00	4/01	34s
Health Care				
Cardiac catheterization, ave hospital/physician charges		13870	1998	77s
Childbirth, Cesarean delivery		14716	1997	13r
Childbirth, vaginal delivery		8541	1997	13r
Drugs, expenditures on	yr	296	1999	30r
Health care purchases	yr	1788	1999	30r
Health insurance expenditures	yr	875	1999	30r
Hysterectomy, laproscopically-assisted, ave hospital/physician charges		14760	1998	76s
Hysterectomy, vaginal, ave hospital and physician charges		9270	1998	76s
Medicaid dispensing fee		4.00	1999	87s
Medical services expenditures	yr	516	1999	30r
Medical supplies, expenditures on	yr	102	1999	30r
Plastic surgery, breast augmentation		4232	2000	7r
Plastic surgery, breast lift		4605	2000	7r
Plastic surgery, facelift		6964	2000	7r
Plastic surgery, hair transplantation		4193	2000	7r
Plastic surgery, lip augmentation		1675	2000	7r
Plastic surgery, lower body lift		6611	2000	7r
Plastic surgery, thigh lift		4751	2000	7r
Household Goods				
Floor coverings, expenditures on	yr	59	1999	30r
Furniture, expenditures on	yr	388	1999	30r
Household furnishings and equipment purchases	yr	1567	1999	30r
Household textiles, expenditures on	yr	112	1999	30r
Laundry and cleaning supplies, expenditures on	yr	104	1999	30r
Housing				
Home price, existing, ave		180800	10/00	90r
Home value, median		115000	2001	53s
Household operation expenditures	yr	581	1999	30r
Housekeeping supplies purchases	yr	474	1999	30r
Lodging expenditures	yr	550	1999	30r
Maintenance, repairs, insurance expenditures	yr	835	1999	30r
Monthly rental value of owned home	mos	663	1999	30r
Owned dwellings, expenditures own	yr	5209	1999	30r
Rent expenditures	yr	2390	1999	30r
Rental unit, 1 bedroom, with utilities	mos	408	4/01	41c
Rental unit, 2 bedroom, with utilities	mos	489	4/01	41c
Rental unit, 3 bedroom, with utilities	mos	610	4/01	41c
Rental unit, 4 bedroom, with utilities	mos	737	4/01	41c
Shelter, expenditures on	yr	8149	1999	30r

Scranton-Wilkes-Barre-Hazleton, PA - continued

Item	Per	Value	Date	Ref.
Insurance and Pensions				
Life and other personal insurance purchases	yr	424	1999	30r
Pensions and Social Security, expenditures on	yr	3037	1999	30r
Legal Fees				
Divorce, filing fee		65.00	4/01	35s
Driver's license fee	orig	29.00	1999	48s
Driver's license fee	renew	24.00	1999	48s
Fishing license	yr	17.00	4/01	34s
Personal Goods				
Personal care products and services purchases	yr	399	1999	30r
Personal Services				
Personal services, household, expenditures on	yr	271	1999	30r
Pets				
Pets, toys, and playground equipment, expenditures on	yr	325	1999	30r
Taxes				
Federal income taxes paid	yr	2606	1999	30r
Personal taxes, expenditures on	yr	3567	1999	30r
Property taxes paid	yr	1752	1999	30r
State and local income taxes paid	yr	694	1999	30r
Transportation				
Cars and trucks, new, expenditures on	yr	1496	1999	30r
Cars and trucks, used, expenditures on	yr	1251	1999	30r
Diesel at the pump	gal	1.31	10/99	73s
Gasoline and motor oil purchases	yr	901	1999	30r
Gasoline before-tax price (cents)	gal	106.60	10/00	43s
Maintenance and repair expenditures	yr	618	1999	30r
Public transportation, expenditures on	yr	575	1999	30r
Transportation purchases	yr	6503	1999	30r
Vehicle expenses, miscellaneous, purchases	yr	2266	1999	30r
Vehicle insurance payments	yr	824	1999	30r
Vehicle purchases (net outlay)	yr	2761	1999	30r
Vehicle rental, lease expenditures	yr	584	1999	30r
Utilities				
Electrical bill, average	mos	69.16	9/00	9s
Electricity, expenditures on	yr	837	1999	30r
Electricity cost, average	KWh	5.08	9/00	9s
Utilities, fuels, and public services purchased	yr	2457	1999	30r
Water and other public services, expenditures on	yr	215	1999	30r
Weddings				
Wedding (national average cost)		19936	2000	33r
Wedding (regional average total cost)		29454	1997	110r
Attendants' gifts		321	1998	33r
Bridal attendants' apparel (5 persons)		824	2000	33r
Bride's headpiece/veil		173	1998	33r
Bride's wedding dress		859	1998	33r
Clergy, religious facility fee		242	1998	33r
Engagement ring		3177	1998	33r
Flowers		789	1998	33r
Groom's formalwear rental		99	2000	33r
Limousine		410	1998	33r
Marriage license cost		25.00-40.00	4/01	35s
Men's formalwear (ushers, best man)		469	2000	33r
Mother of bride apparel		241	2000	33r
Music		866	1998	33r
Photography and videography		1368	1998	33r
Rehearsal dinner		728	1998	33r
Wedding invitations and announcements		341	1998	33r
Wedding reception		7968	2000	33r
Wedding rings (bride and groom)		1060	1998	33r

Values are in dollars or fractions of dollars. In the column headed *Ref*, references are shown to sources. Each reference is followed by a letter. These refer to the geographical level for which data were reported: s=State, r=Region, and c=City or metro. The abbreviation *ex* is used to mean *except* or *excluding*; *exp* stands for expenditures. For other abbreviations and further explanations, please see the Introduction.

Seattle-Bellevue-Everett, WA

Item	Per	Value	Date	Ref.
Average annual expenditures	yr	44078	1999	30c
Alcoholic Beverages				
Alcoholic beverage purchases	yr	541	1999	30c
Malt beverages, all types, all sizes, any origin	16 oz	0.94	7/01	11r
Wine, red and white table, all sizes, any origin	liter	6.00	7/01	11r
Appliances				
Major appliances, expenditures on	yr	167	1999	30r
Small appliances, housewares, expenditures on	yr	105	1999	30r
Banking and Money				
Mortgage interest and charges paid	yr	3368	1999	30r
Mortgage principal paid on owned property	yr	1677	1999	30r
Vehicle finance charges paid	yr	311	1999	30r
Business Expenses				
Business travel, car rental	day	68	2001	3c
Business travel, food	day	65	2001	3c
Business travel, hotel	day	117	2001	3c
Medical office space cost	sq ft	125.12	2001	31c
Office space, 2-4 storey building	sq ft	109.62	2001	31c
Office space, 5-10 storey building	sq ft	96.83	2001	31c
Office space, 11-20 storey building	sq ft	93.07	2001	31c
Office space, central business district, Class A	sq ft	31.65	3/99	74c
Office space, outside central business district, Class A	sq ft	18.08	3/99	74c
Charity				
Cash contributions, expenditures	yr	879	1999	30c
Child Care				
Child raising cost, total, age 0-2	yr	9140	1999	60r
Child raising cost, total, age 3-5	yr	9370	1999	60r
Child raising cost, total, age 6-8	yr	9450	1999	60r
Child raising cost, total, age 9-11	yr	9470	1999	60r
Child raising cost, total, age 12-14	yr	10170	1999	60r
Child raising cost, total, age 15-17	yr	10360	1999	60r
Child's child care and education, age 0-2	yr	1250	1999	60r
Child's child care and education, age 3-5	yr	1380	1999	60r
Child's child care and education, age 6-8	yr	890	1999	60r
Child's child care and education, age 9-11	yr	580	1999	60r
Child's child care and education, age 12-14	yr	430	1999	60r
Child's child care and education, age 15-17	yr	730	1999	60r
Child's clothing, age 0-2	yr	430	1999	60r
Child's clothing, age 3-5	yr	420	1999	60r
Child's clothing, age 6-8	yr	470	1999	60r
Child's clothing, age 9-11	yr	520	1999	60r
Child's clothing, age 12-14	yr	870	1999	60r
Child's clothing, age 15-17	yr	770	1999	60r
Child's food, age 0-2	yr	1120	1999	60r
Child's food, age 3-5	yr	1280	1999	60r
Child's food, age 6-8	yr	1640	1999	60r
Child's food, age 9-11	yr	1930	1999	60r
Child's food, age 12-14	yr	1940	1999	60r
Child's food, age 15-17	yr	2150	1999	60r
Child's health care, age 0-2	yr	490	1999	60r
Child's health care, age 3-5	yr	470	1999	60r
Child's health care, age 6-8	yr	530	1999	60r
Child's health care, age 9-11	yr	570	1999	60r
Child's health care, age 12-14	yr	580	1999	60r
Child's health care, age 15-17	yr	610	1999	60r
Child's housing, age 0-2	yr	3630	1999	60r
Child's housing, age 3-5	yr	3610	1999	60r
Child's housing, age 6-8	yr	3570	1999	60r
Child's housing, age 9-11	yr	3410	1999	60r
Child's housing, age 12-14	yr	3600	1999	60r
Child's housing, age 15-17	yr	3210	1999	60r
Child's personal care, reading, age 0-2	yr	1040	1999	60r
Child's personal care, reading, age 3-5	yr	1060	1999	60r
Child's personal care, reading, age 6-8	yr	1090	1999	60r
Child's personal care, reading, age 9-11	yr	1130	1999	60r
Child's personal care, reading, age 12-14	yr	1300	1999	60r

Seattle-Bellevue-Everett, WA - continued

Item	Per	Value	Date	Ref.
Child Care - continued				
Child's personal care, reading, age 15-17	yr	1080	1999	60r
Clothing				
Apparel and services purchases	yr	1932	1999	30c
Boys, 2 to 15, expenditures on	yr	80	1999	30r
Children under 2, expenditures on	yr	74	1999	30r
Footwear, expenditures on	yr	307	1999	30r
Girls, 2 to 15, expenditures on	yr	101	1999	30r
Men and boys, expenditures on	yr	443	1999	30r
Men, 16 and over, expenditures on	yr	363	1999	30r
Women, 16 and over, expenditures on	yr	594	1999	30r
Communications				
Cable modem installation, AT&T-BIS		150.00	6/99	103s
Cable modem rate, cable subscriber, AT&T-BIS	mos	39.95	6/99	103s
Phone line, single, business, field visit	inst.	48.00	12/97	17s
Phone line, single, business, no field visit	inst.	48.00	12/97	17s
Phone line, single, residence, field visit	inst.	31.00	12/97	17s
Phone line, single, residence, no field visit	inst.	31.00	12/97	17s
Postage and stationery, expenditures on	yr	150	1999	30r
Postal rate, express mail, up to half-pound		12.45	7/01	108r
Postal rate, letter, first class, first ounce		0.34	7/01	108r
Postal rate, letter, two ounces		0.57	7/01	108r
Postal rate, post card		0.21	7/01	108r
Postal rate, priority mail, two pounds		3.95	7/01	108r
Postal rate, priority mail, up to one pound		3.50	7/01	108r
Telephone bill, business, basic rate	mos	18.60	12/97	18c
Telephone bill, residential, basic rate	mos	8.95	12/97	18c
Telephone services, expenditures on	yr	825	1999	30r
Wireless services	mos	38.19	1/00	42c
Education				
Board, 4-year private college/university	yr	2329	1996	38s
Board, 4-year public college/university	yr	2158	1996	38s
Education expenditures	yr	618	1999	30c
Room, 4-year private college/university	yr	2487	1996	38s
Room, 4-year public college/university	yr	2187	1996	38s
Total cost, 4-year private college/university	yr	18092	1996	38s
Total cost, 4-year public college/university	yr	7136	1996	38s
Tuition, 2-year public college/university, in state	yr	1369	1996	38s
Tuition, 4-year private college/university, in state	yr	13276	1996	38s
Tuition, 4-year public college/university	yr	2791	1996	38s
Energy and Fuels				
Electricity	500 KWhs	48.23	7/01	11r
Electricity	KWh	0.11	7/01	11r
Electricity	500 KWhs	32.07	7/01	11c
Electricity	KWh	0.07	7/01	11c
Fuel oil and other fuels, expenditures on	yr	35	1999	30r
Gas, cooking, winter, 10 therms	mos	9.40	2/96	98c
Gas, cooking, winter, 30 therms	mos	19.20	2/96	98c
Gas, cooking, winter, 50 therms	mos	29.01	2/96	98c
Gas, heating, winter, average use	mos	87.91	2/96	98c
Gas, natural, commercial rate	1000 cf	6.89	11/00	88s
Gasoline, all types	gal	1.68	7/01	11c
Gasoline, unleaded midgrade	gal	1.73	7/01	11c
Gasoline, unleaded premium	gal	2.05	7/01	11r
Gasoline, unleaded regular	gal	1.62	7/01	11c
Natural gas, expenditures on	yr	255	1999	30r
Utility (piped) gas, therm		1.05	7/01	11c
Utility (piped) gas, 40 therms		40.74	7/01	11r
Utility (piped) gas, 100 therms		103.10	7/01	11c
Entertainment				
Entertainment purchases	yr	3060	1999	30c
Fees and admissions paid	yr	545	1999	30r
Major League baseball ticket		26.31	2000	16c
Television, radios, sound equipment, expenditures on	yr	624	1999	30r

Values are in dollars or fractions of dollars. In the column headed *Ref*, references are shown to sources. Each reference is followed by a letter. These refer to the geographical level for which data were reported: s=State, r=Region, and c=City or metro. The abbreviation *ex* is used to mean *except* or *excluding*; *exp* stands for *expenditures*. For other abbreviations and further explanations, please see the Introduction.

Seattle-Bellevue-Everett, WA - continued

Item	Per	Value	Date	Ref.
Funerals				
Total cost of funeral		5401.08	1/99	78r
Acknowledgement cards		33.64	1/99	78r
Casket		2170.43	1/99	78r
Cosmetology, hair, other preparation		136.32	1/99	78r
Embalming		319.13	1/99	78r
Funeral at funeral home		370.21	1/99	78r
Funeral, traditional, average		2661	2000	32c
Hearse (local)		161.04	1/99	78r
Professional service charges		963.15	1/99	78r
Service car/van		133.99	1/99	78r
Transfer of remains to funeral home		159.82	1/99	78r
Vault		778.07	1/99	78r
Visitation/viewing		175.28	1/99	78r
Groceries				
Apples, red delicious	lb	0.84	7/01	11r
Bacon, sliced	lb	3.38	7/01	11r
Bakery products, expenditures on	yr	299	1999	30r
Bananas	lb	0.54	7/01	11r
Beans, dried, any type, all sizes	lb	0.76	7/01	11r
Beef, expenditures on	yr	222	1999	30r
Bread, white, pan	lb	0.99	7/01	11r
Butter, yoghurt, cheese, etc, expenditures on	yr	211	1999	30r
Cereals and bakery product purchases	yr	545	1999	30c
Cereals and cereal products, expenditures on	yr	168	1999	30r
Chicken breast, bone-in	lb	2.45	7/01	11r
Chicken, fresh, whole	lb	1.19	7/01	11r
Chops, boneless,	lb	4.00	7/01	11r
Chuck roast, graded and ungraded, excl U.S. prime and choice	lb	2.55	7/01	11r
Coffee, 100%, ground roast, all sizes	lb	3.80	7/01	11r
Cookies, chocolate chip	lb	2.83	7/01	11r
Dairy product purchases	yr	362	1999	30c
Eggs, expenditures on	yr	39	1999	30r
Eggs, grade AA, large	dozen	1.23	7/01	11r
Fats and oils, expenditures on	yr	88	1999	30r
Fish and seafood, expenditures on	yr	121	1999	30r
Food (excl fruit and vegetables), eaten at home, purchases	yr	1133	1999	30c
Food cooked on trips, expenditures on	yr	64	1999	30r
Food purchases	yr	6080	1999	30c
Food purchases, eaten away from home	yr	2594	1999	30c
Food purchases, food eaten at home	yr	3486	1999	30c
Fresh fruits, expenditures on	yr	186	1999	30r
Fresh milk and cream, expenditures on	yr	130	1999	30r
Fresh vegetables, expenditures on	yr	177	1999	30r
Grapefruit	lb	0.68	7/01	11r
Grapes, Thompson, seedless	lb	2.42	7/01	11r
Ground beef, lean and extra lean	lb	2.46	7/01	11r
Ice cream, prepackaged, bulk, regular	1/2 gal	3.62	7/01	11r
Lettuce, iceberg	lb	0.63	7/01	11r
Meats, poultry, fish, and egg purchases	yr	805	1999	30c
Milk, fresh, low fat,	gal	2.80	7/01	11r
Milk, fresh, whole, fortified	gal	2.88	7/01	11r
Nonalcoholic beverages, expenditures on	yr	258	1999	30r
Oranges, Navel	lb	0.97	7/01	11r
Oranges, Valencia	lb	0.43	7/01	11r
Peaches	lb	1.38	7/01	11r
Peanut butter, creamy, all sizes	lb	2.14	7/01	11r
Pork chops, center cut, bone-in	lb	3.83	7/01	11r
Pork, expenditures on	yr	141	1999	30r
Potatoes, white, all types	lb	0.37	7/01	11r
Poultry, expenditures on	yr	146	1999	30r
Processed fruits, expenditures on	yr	118	1999	30r
Processed vegetables, expenditures on	yr	81	1999	30r
Round roast, graded and ungraded, excl U.S. prime and choice	lb	3.07	7/01	11r
Round roast, U.S. choice, boneless	lb	3.37	7/01	11r
Round steak, graded and ungraded, excl U.S. prime and choice	lb	3.51	7/01	11r
Sirloin steak, graded and ungraded, excl U.S. prime and choice	lb	4.67	7/01	11r

Seattle-Bellevue-Everett, WA - continued

Item	Per	Value	Date	Ref.
Groceries - continued				
Steak, sirloin, U.S. choice, boneless	lb	6.20	7/01	11r
Strawberries, dry pint	12 oz	1.79	7/01	11r
Sugar and other sweets, expenditures on	yr	124	1999	30r
Sugar, white, all sizes	lb	0.46	7/01	11r
Tobacco products and smoking supplies purchases	yr	311	1999	30c
Tomatoes, field grown	lb	1.17	7/01	11r
Tuna, light, chunk	lb	2.05	7/01	11r
Goods and Services				
B&B Japanese maple (acer japonicum)	gal	39.99	4/00	93r
Boxwood (buxus)	2 gal	14.99-24.99	4/00	93r
Daylilly (hemerocallis)	gal	6.99-8.99	4/00	93r
Flat of annuals		16.68	4/00	93r
Fountain grass (pennisetum)	gal	7.99-11.99	4/00	93r
Hanging basket (10 in)		29.99	4/00	93r
Hardy geranium (geranium)	gal	6.99-11.99	4/00	93r
Hosta (hosta)	gal	6.99-18.99	4/00	93r
Lilac (syrubga vulgaris)	2 gal	14.99-17.99	4/00	93r
Miscellaneous purchases	yr	1101	1999	30c
Rhododendron (rhododendron)	2 gal	14.99	4/00	93r
Sage (salvia)	gal	6.99	4/00	93r
Wintercreeper euonymus (euonymus fortunei)	2 gal	14.99-22.99	4/00	93r
Hunting license	yr	30.00	4/01	34s
Health Care				
Cardiac catheterization, ave hospital/physician charges		13290	1998	77s
Childbirth, Cesarean delivery		11587	1997	13r
Childbirth, vaginal delivery		6725	1997	13r
Drugs, expenditures on	yr	309	1999	30r
Health care purchases	yr	1931	1999	30c
Health insurance expenditures	yr	868	1999	30r
Home health care aide cost, licensed agency	hour	19	2000	82c
Hysterectomy, laproscopically-assisted, ave hospital/physician charges		10960	1998	76s
Hysterectomy, vaginal, ave hospital and physician charges		9000	1998	76s
Medicaid dispensing fee		3.98-4.92	1999	87s
Medical services expenditures	yr	580	1999	30r
Medical supplies, expenditures on	yr	112	1999	30r
Nursing home costs, private room	day	174	2000	82c
Nursing home stay, private room	day	174	2000	83c
Household Goods				
Floor coverings, expenditures on	yr	49	1999	30r
Furniture, expenditures on	yr	444	1999	30r
Household furnishings and equipment purchases	yr	1890	1999	30c
Household textiles, expenditures on	yr	141	1999	30r
Laundry and cleaning supplies, expenditures on	yr	128	1999	30r
Housing				
Home, 2200 sq ft, 4-br, 2-bath, 2-car garage, average		303633	2000	47c
Home, suburban, 2,200 square feet		278800	2000	23c
Home price, existing, ave		239400	10/00	90r
Home value, median		195000	2001	53s
Household operation expenditures	yr	666	1999	30c
Housekeeping supplies purchases	yr	693	1999	30c
Lodging expenditures	yr	766	1999	30c
Maintenance, repairs, insurance expenditures	yr	939	1999	30r
Monthly rental value of owned home	mos	662	1999	30r
Owned dwellings, expenditures own	yr	6160	1999	30c

Values are in dollars or fractions of dollars. In the column headed *Ref*, references are shown to sources. Each reference is followed by a letter. These refer to the geographical level for which data were reported: s=State, r=Region, and c=City or metro. The abbreviation *ex* is used to mean *except* or *excluding*; *exp* stands for *expenditures*. For other abbreviations and further explanations, please see the Introduction.

Seattle-Bellevue-Everett, WA - continued

Item	Per	Value	Date	Ref.
Housing				
Rent expenditures	yr	2461	1999	30c
Rental unit, 1 bedroom, with utilities	mos	572	4/01	41c
Rental unit, 2 bedroom, with utilities	mos	685	4/01	41c
Rental unit, 3 bedroom, with utilities	mos	954	4/01	41c
Rental unit, 4 bedroom, with utilities	mos	1119	4/01	41c
Shelter, expenditures on	yr	9387	1999	30c
Single-family home, purchase price		226100	2000	19c
Insurance and Pensions				
Life and other personal insurance purchases	yr	427	1999	30c
Pensions and Social Security, expenditures on	yr	3872	1999	30c
Legal Fees				
Divorce, filing fee		100.00	4/01	35s
Driver's license fee	renew	14.00	1999	48s
Driver's license fee	orig	14.00	1999	48s
Fishing license	yr	20.00	4/01	34s
Personal Goods				
Personal care products and services purchases	yr	522	1999	30c
Personal Services				
Navel piercing	ea	45	1999	58c
Personal services, household, expenditures on	yr	353	1999	30r
Tatooing	hour	100	1999	58c
Tongue piercing	ea	60	1999	58c
Pets				
Pets, toys, and playground equipment, expenditures on	yr	358	1999	30r
Restaurant Food				
Cheeseburger, 1/4-lb, large fries, medium soft drink, excl tax		4.82	1999	40c
Taxes				
Federal income taxes paid	yr	3200	1999	30r
Personal taxes, expenditures on	yr	4153	1999	30r
Property taxes paid	yr	923	1999	30r
State and local income taxes paid	yr	812	1999	30r
Transportation				
Bus fare, one-way	trip	1.00	2000	1c
Cars and trucks, new, expenditures on	yr	1534	1999	30r
Cars and trucks, used, expenditures on	yr	1593	1999	30r
Commuter rail, one-way	trip	2.00	2000	2c
Diesel at the pump	gal	1.37	10/99	73s
Ferry boat transit fare, one-way	trip	3.70	2000	2c
Gasoline and motor oil purchases	yr	1216	1999	30c
Gasoline before-tax price (cents)	gal	127.10	10/00	43s
Light rail transit fare, one-way	trip	1.00	2000	2c
Maintenance and repair expenditures	yr	797	1999	30r
Monorail transit fare, one-way	trip	1.25	2000	2c
Public transportation, expenditures on	yr	725	1999	30c
Transportation purchases	yr	7650	1999	30c
Trolley bus transit fare, one-way	trip	1.00	2000	2c
Vehicle expenses, miscellaneous, purchases	yr	2843	1999	30c
Vehicle insurance payments	yr	811	1999	30r
Vehicle purchases (net outlay)	yr	3180	1999	30r
Vehicle rental, lease expenditures	yr	666	1999	30r
Utilities				
Electrical bill, average	mos	58.33	9/00	9s
Electricity, expenditures on	yr	725	1999	30r
Electricity bill	mos	39	2000	75c
Electricity cost, average	KWh	4.47	9/00	9s
Utilities, fuels, and public services purchased	yr	2263	1999	30c
Water and other public services, expenditures on	yr	339	1999	30r
Weddings				
Wedding (national average cost)		19936	2000	33r
Wedding (regional average total cost)		18918	1997	110r
Attendants' gifts		321	1998	33r

Seattle-Bellevue-Everett, WA - continued

Item	Per	Value	Date	Ref.
Weddings - continued				
Bridal attendants' apparel (5 persons)		824	2000	33r
Bride's headpiece/veil		173	1998	33r
Bride's wedding dress		859	1998	33r
Clergy, religious facility fee		242	1998	33r
Engagement ring		3177	1998	33r
Flowers		789	1998	33r
Groom's formalwear rental		99	2000	33r
Limousine		410	1998	33r
Marriage license cost		52.00	4/01	35s
Men's formalwear (ushers, best man)		469	2000	33r
Mother of bride apparel		241	2000	33r
Music		866	1998	33r
Photography and videography		1368	1998	33r
Rehearsal dinner		728	1998	33r
Wedding invitations and announcements		341	1998	33r
Wedding reception		7968	2000	33r
Wedding rings (bride and groom)		1060	1998	33r

Sharon, PA

Item	Per	Value	Date	Ref.
Average annual expenditures	yr	37971	1999	30r
Alcoholic Beverages				
Alcoholic beverage purchases	yr	368	1999	30r
Wine, red and white table, all sizes, any origin	liter	9.64	7/01	11r
Appliances				
Major appliances, expenditures on	yr	194	1999	30r
Small appliances, housewares, expenditures on	yr	93	1999	30r
Banking and Money				
Mortgage interest and charges paid	yr	2622	1999	30r
Mortgage principal paid on owned property	yr	1262	1999	30r
Vehicle finance charges paid	yr	240	1999	30r
Charity				
Cash contributions, expenditures	yr	1001	1999	30r
Child Care				
Child raising cost, total, age 0-2	yr	8670	1999	60r
Child raising cost, total, age 3-5	yr	8910	1999	60r
Child raising cost, total, age 6-8	yr	9040	1999	60r
Child raising cost, total, age 9-11	yr	9100	1999	60r
Child raising cost, total, age 12-14	yr	9890	1999	60r
Child raising cost, total, age 15-17	yr	10010	1999	60r
Child's child care and education, age 0-2	yr	1070	1999	60r
Child's child care and education, age 3-5	yr	1190	1999	60r
Child's child care and education, age 6-8	yr	740	1999	60r
Child's child care and education, age 9-11	yr	470	1999	60r
Child's child care and education, age 12-14	yr	350	1999	60r
Child's child care and education, age 15-17	yr	590	1999	60r
Child's clothing, age 0-2	yr	480	1999	60r
Child's clothing, age 3-5	yr	470	1999	60r
Child's clothing, age 6-8	yr	520	1999	60r
Child's clothing, age 9-11	yr	570	1999	60r
Child's clothing, age 12-14	yr	970	1999	60r
Child's clothing, age 15-17	yr	870	1999	60r
Child's food, age 0-2	yr	1130	1999	60r
Child's food, age 3-5	yr	1290	1999	60r
Child's food, age 6-8	yr	1640	1999	60r
Child's food, age 9-11	yr	1930	1999	60r
Child's food, age 12-14	yr	1940	1999	60r
Child's food, age 15-17	yr	2150	1999	60r
Child's health care, age 0-2	yr	550	1999	60r
Child's health care, age 3-5	yr	530	1999	60r
Child's health care, age 6-8	yr	610	1999	60r
Child's health care, age 9-11	yr	650	1999	60r
Child's health care, age 12-14	yr	660	1999	60r
Child's health care, age 15-17	yr	690	1999	60r
Child's housing, age 0-2	yr	3555	1999	60r
Child's housing, age 3-5	yr	3530	1999	60r
Child's housing, age 6-8	yr	3490	1999	60r

Values are in dollars or fractions of dollars. In the column headed *Ref*, references are shown to sources. Each reference is followed by a letter. These refer to the geographical level for which data were reported: s=State, r=Region, and c=City or metro. The abbreviation *ex* is used to mean *except* or *excluding*; *exp* stands for *expenditures*. For other abbreviations and further explanations, please see the Introduction.

Sharon, PA - continued

Item	Per	Value	Date	Ref.
Child Care				
Child's housing, age 9-11	yr	3340	1999	60r
Child's housing, age 12-14	yr	3530	1999	60r
Child's housing, age 15-17	yr	3140	1999	60r
Child's personal care, reading, age 0-2	yr	920	1999	60r
Child's personal care, reading, age 3-5	yr	950	1999	60r
Child's personal care, reading, age 6-8	yr	980	1999	60r
Child's personal care, reading, age 9-11	yr	1020	1999	60r
Child's personal care, reading, age 12-14	yr	1190	1999	60r
Child's personal care, reading, age 15-17	yr	970	1999	60r
Clothing				
Apparel and services purchases	yr	1831	1999	30r
Boys, 2 to 15, expenditures on	yr	92	1999	30r
Children under 2, expenditures on	yr	63	1999	30r
Footwear, expenditures on	yr	300	1999	30r
Girls, 2 to 15, expenditures on	yr	101	1999	30r
Men and boys, expenditures on	yr	446	1999	30r
Men, 16 and over, expenditures on	yr	354	1999	30r
Women, 16 and over, expenditures on	yr	584	1999	30r
Communications				
Cable modem installation, Adelphi		54.90	6/99	103s
Cable modem installation, Comcast		95.00	6/99	103s
Cable modem rate, cable subscriber, Adelphi	mos	34.95	6/99	103s
Cable modem rate, cable subscriber, Comcast	mos	39.95	6/99	103s
Cable modem rate, non-cable subscriber, Adelphi	mos	44.95	6/99	103s
Cable modem rate, non-cable subscriber, Comcast	mos	49.95	6/99	103s
Phone line, single, business, field visit	inst.	75.00	12/97	17s
Phone line, single, business, no field visit	inst.	75.00	12/97	17s
Phone line, single, residence, field visit	inst.	40.00	12/97	17s
Phone line, single, residence, no field visit	inst.	40.00	12/97	17s
Postage and stationery, expenditures on	yr	138	1999	30r
Postal rate, express mail, up to half-pound		12.45	7/01	108r
Postal rate, letter, first class, first ounce		0.34	7/01	108r
Postal rate, letter, two ounces		0.57	7/01	108r
Postal rate, post card		0.21	7/01	108r
Postal rate, priority mail, two pounds		3.95	7/01	108r
Postal rate, priority mail, up to one pound		3.50	7/01	108r
Telephone services, expenditures on	yr	830	1999	30r
Education				
Board, 4-year private college/university	yr	2822	1996	38s
Board, 4-year public college/university	yr	2174	1996	38s
Education expenditures	yr	877	1999	30r
Room, 4-year private college/university	yr	2943	1996	38s
Room, 4-year public college/university	yr	2227	1996	38s
Total cost, 4-year private college/university	yr	19876	1996	38s
Total cost, 4-year public college/university	yr	9124	1996	38s
Tuition, 2-year public college/university, in state	yr	1909	1996	38s
Tuition, 4-year private college/university, in state	yr	14111	1996	38s
Tuition, 4-year public college/university	yr	4723	1996	38s
Energy and Fuels				
Electricity	KWh	0.12	7/01	11r
Fuel oil #2	gal	1.31	7/01	11r
Fuel oil and other fuels, expenditures on	yr	207	1999	30r
Gas, natural, commercial rate	1000 cf	5.96	11/00	88s
Gasoline, all types	gal	1.80	7/01	11r
Gasoline, unleaded midgrade	gal	1.85	7/01	11r
Gasoline, unleaded premium	gal	1.91	7/01	11r
Gasoline, unleaded regular	gal	1.71	7/01	11r
Natural gas, expenditures on	yr	368	1999	30r
Utility (piped) gas, therm		1.08	7/01	11r
Utility (piped) gas, 40 therms		50.87	7/01	11r
Utility (piped) gas, 100 therms		111.06	7/01	11r
Entertainment				
Entertainment purchases	yr	1821	1999	30r
Fees and admissions paid	yr	511	1999	30r

Sharon, PA - continued

Item	Per	Value	Date	Ref.
Entertainment - continued				
Television, radios, sound equipment, expenditures on	yr	650	1999	30r
Funerals				
Total cost of funeral		5813.50	1/99	78r
Acknowledgement cards		28.32	1/99	78r
Casket		2082.20	1/99	78r
Cosmetology, hair, other preparation		169.59	1/99	78r
Embalming		465.60	1/99	78r
Funeral at funeral home		339.56	1/99	78r
Hearse (local)		183.96	1/99	78r
Professional service charges		1157.85	1/99	78r
Service car/van		100.41	1/99	78r
Transfer of remains to funeral home		158.66	1/99	78r
Vault		766.31	1/99	78r
Visitation/viewing		361.04	1/99	78r
Groceries				
Apples, red delicious	lb	0.95	7/01	11r
Bacon, sliced	lb	3.44	7/01	11r
Bakery products, expenditures on	yr	310	1999	30r
Bananas	lb	0.55	7/01	11r
Beef, expenditures on	yr	236	1999	30r
Bread, white, pan	lb	1.09	7/01	11r
Butter, yoghurt, cheese, etc, expenditures on	yr	214	1999	30r
Cereals and bakery product purchases	yr	474	1999	30r
Cereals and cereal products, expenditures on	yr	164	1999	30r
Chicken legs, bone-in	lb	1.23	7/01	11r
Chicken, fresh, whole	lb	1.13	7/01	11r
Chuck roast, U.S. choice, boneless	lb	2.79	7/01	11r
Coffee, 100%, ground roast, all sizes	lb	3.40	7/01	11r
Dairy product purchases	yr	342	1999	30r
Eggs, expenditures on	yr	34	1999	30r
Eggs, grade A, large	dozen	0.82	7/01	11r
Fats and oils, expenditures on	yr	80	1999	30r
Fish and seafood, expenditures on	yr	123	1999	30r
Food (excl fruit and vegetables), eaten at home, purchases	yr	838	1999	30r
Food cooked on trips, expenditures on	yr	48	1999	30r
Food purchases	yr	5314	1999	30r
Food purchases, eaten away from home	yr	2313	1999	30r
Food purchases, food eaten at home	yr	3001	1999	30r
Fresh fruits, expenditures on	yr	169	1999	30r
Fresh milk and cream, expenditures on	yr	128	1999	30r
Fresh vegetables, expenditures on	yr	164	1999	30r
Grapefruit	lb	0.67	7/01	11r
Grapes, Thompson, seedless	lb	2.18	7/01	11r
Ground beef, lean and extra lean	lb	2.66	7/01	11r
Ground chuck, 100% beef	lb	2.04	7/01	11r
Lettuce, iceberg	lb	0.76	7/01	11r
Meats, poultry, fish, and egg purchases	yr	808	1999	30r
Nonalcoholic beverages, expenditures on	yr	225	1999	30r
Orange juice, frozen concentrate	16 oz	1.88	7/01	11r
Oranges, Navel	lb	0.79	7/01	11r
Oranges, Valencia	lb	0.56	7/01	11r
Peaches	lb	1.16	7/01	11r
Peanut butter, creamy, all sizes	lb	2.01	7/01	11r
Pears, Anjou	lb	1.16	7/01	11r
Pork chops, center cut, bone-in	lb	3.57	7/01	11r
Pork, expenditures on	yr	146	1999	30r
Potato chips	16 oz	3.37	7/01	11r
Potatoes, white, all types	lb	0.42	7/01	11r
Poultry, expenditures on	yr	158	1999	30r
Processed fruits, expenditures on	yr	124	1999	30r
Processed vegetables, expenditures on	yr	82	1999	30r
Round roast, U.S. choice, boneless	lb	3.04	7/01	11r
Spaghetti and macaroni	lb	1.04	7/01	11r
Steak, sirloin, U.S. choice, boneless	lb	5.39	7/01	11r
Strawberries, dry pint	12 oz	1.51	7/01	11r
Sugar and other sweets, expenditures on	yr	110	1999	30r
Sugar, white, 33-80 ounce package	lb	0.46	7/01	11r
Sugar, white, all sizes	lb	0.47	7/01	11r

Values are in dollars or fractions of dollars. In the column headed *Ref*, references are shown to sources. Each reference is followed by a letter. These refer to the geographical level for which data were reported: s=State, r=Region, and c=City or metro. The abbreviation *ex* is used to mean *except* or *excluding*; *exp* stands for *expenditures*. For other abbreviations and further explanations, please see the Introduction.

Sharon, PA - continued

Item	Per	Value	Date	Ref.
Groceries				
Tobacco products and smoking supplies purchases	yr	309	1999	30r
Yogurt, natural, fruit flavored	8 oz	0.79	7/01	11r
Goods and Services				
B&B Japanese maple (acer japonicum)	gal	38.99-125.00	4/00	93r
Boxwood (buxus)	2 gal	15.99-49.95	4/00	93r
Daylilly (hemerocallis)	gal	4.95	4/00	93r
Flat of annuals		8.00-14.99	4/00	93r
Fountain grass (pennisetum)	gal	6.99-9.99	4/00	93r
Hanging basket (10 in)		12.95-19.99	4/00	93r
Hardy geranium (geranium)	gal	6.95-7.99	4/00	93r
Hosta (hosta)	gal	4.95	4/00	93r
Lilac (syrubga vulgaris)	2 gal	17.99-74.95	4/00	93r
Miscellaneous purchases	yr	872	1999	30r
Rhododendron (rhododendron)	2 gal	23.99-54.95	4/00	93r
Sage (salvia)	gal	6.95-7.99	4/00	93r
Wintercreeper euonymus (euonymus fortunei)	2 gal	14.99-23.95	4/00	93r
Hunting license	yr	20.00	4/01	34s
Health Care				
Cardiac catheterization, ave hospital/ physician charges		13870	1998	77s
Childbirth, Cesarean delivery		14716	1997	13r
Childbirth, vaginal delivery		8541	1997	13r
Drugs, expenditures on	yr	296	1999	30r
Health care purchases	yr	1788	1999	30r
Health insurance expenditures	yr	875	1999	30r
Hysterectomy, laproscopically-assisted, ave hospital/physician charges		14760	1998	76s
Hysterectomy, vaginal, ave hospital and physician charges		9270	1998	76s
Medicaid dispensing fee		4.00	1999	87s
Medical services expenditures	yr	516	1999	30r
Medical supplies, expenditures on	yr	102	1999	30r
Plastic surgery, breast augmentation		4232	2000	7r
Plastic surgery, breast lift		4605	2000	7r
Plastic surgery, facelift		6964	2000	7r
Plastic surgery, hair transplantation		4193	2000	7r
Plastic surgery, lip augmentation		1675	2000	7r
Plastic surgery, lower body lift		6611	2000	7r
Plastic surgery, thigh lift		4751	2000	7r
Household Goods				
Floor coverings, expenditures on	yr	59	1999	30r
Furniture, expenditures on	yr	388	1999	30r
Household furnishings and equipment purchases	yr	1567	1999	30r
Household textiles, expenditures on	yr	112	1999	30r
Laundry and cleaning supplies, expenditures on	yr	104	1999	30r
Housing				
Home price, existing, ave		180800	10/00	90r
Home value, median		115000	2001	53s
Household operation expenditures	yr	581	1999	30r
Housekeeping supplies purchases	yr	474	1999	30r
Lodging expenditures	yr	550	1999	30r
Maintenance, repairs, insurance expenditures	yr	835	1999	30r
Monthly rental value of owned home	mos	663	1999	30r
Owned dwellings, expenditures own	yr	5209	1999	30r
Rent expenditures	yr	2390	1999	30r
Rental unit, 1 bedroom, with utilities	mos	371	4/01	41c

Sharon, PA - continued

Item	Per	Value	Date	Ref.
Housing - continued				
Rental unit, 2 bedroom, with utilities	mos	446	4/01	41c
Rental unit, 3 bedroom, with utilities	mos	579	4/01	41c
Rental unit, 4 bedroom, with utilities	mos	647	4/01	41c
Shelter, expenditures on	yr	8149	1999	30r
Insurance and Pensions				
Life and other personal insurance purchases	yr	424	1999	30r
Pensions and Social Security, expenditures on	yr	3037	1999	30r
Legal Fees				
Divorce, filing fee		65.00	4/01	35s
Driver's license fee	renew	24.00	1999	48s
Driver's license fee	orig	29.00	1999	48s
Fishing license	yr	17.00	4/01	34s
Personal Goods				
Personal care products and services purchases	yr	399	1999	30r
Personal Services				
Personal services, household, expenditures on	yr	271	1999	30r
Pets				
Pets, toys, and playground equipment, expenditures on	yr	325	1999	30r
Taxes				
Federal income taxes paid	yr	2606	1999	30r
Personal taxes, expenditures on	yr	3567	1999	30r
Property taxes paid	yr	1752	1999	30r
State and local income taxes paid	yr	694	1999	30r
Transportation				
Cars and trucks, new, expenditures on	yr	1496	1999	30r
Cars and trucks, used, expenditures on	yr	1251	1999	30r
Diesel at the pump	gal	1.31	10/99	73s
Gasoline and motor oil purchases	yr	901	1999	30r
Gasoline before-tax price (cents)	gal	106.60	10/00	43s
Maintenance and repair expenditures	yr	618	1999	30r
Public transportation, expenditures on	yr	575	1999	30r
Transportation purchases	yr	6503	1999	30r
Vehicle expenses, miscellaneous, purchases	yr	2266	1999	30r
Vehicle insurance payments	yr	824	1999	30r
Vehicle purchases (net outlay)	yr	2761	1999	30r
Vehicle rental, lease expenditures	yr	584	1999	30r
Utilities				
Electrical bill, average	mos	69.16	9/00	9s
Electricity, expenditures on	yr	837	1999	30r
Electricity cost, average	KWh	5.08	9/00	9s
Utilities, fuels, and public services purchased	yr	2457	1999	30r
Water and other public services, expenditures on	yr	215	1999	30r
Weddings				
Wedding (national average cost)		19936	2000	33r
Wedding (regional average total cost)		29454	1997	110r
Attendants' gifts		321	1998	33r
Bridal attendants' apparel (5 persons)		824	2000	33r
Bride's headpiece/veil		173	1998	33r
Bride's wedding dress		859	1998	33r
Clergy, religious facility fee		242	1998	33r
Engagement ring		3177	1998	33r
Flowers		789	1998	33r
Groom's formalwear rental		99	2000	33r
Limousine		410	1998	33r
Marriage license cost		25.00-40.00	4/01	35s
Men's formalwear (ushers, best man)		469	2000	33r
Mother of bride apparel		241	2000	33r
Music		866	1998	33r
Photography and videography		1368	1998	33r
Rehearsal dinner		728	1998	33r
Wedding invitations and announcements		341	1998	33r

Values are in dollars or fractions of dollars. In the column headed *Ref*, references are shown to sources. Each reference is followed by a letter. These refer to the geographical level for which data were reported: s=State, r=Region, and c=City or metro. The abbreviation *ex* is used to mean *except* or *excluding*; *exp* stands for *expenditures*. For other abbreviations and further explanations, please see the Introduction.

Sharon, PA - continued

Item	Per	Value	Date	Ref.
Weddings				
Wedding reception		7968	2000	33r
Wedding rings (bride and groom)		1060	1998	33r

Sheboygan, WI

Item	Per	Value	Date	Ref.
Average annual expenditures	yr	35369	1999	30r
Composite, ACCRA index		97.00	3/01	4c
Alcoholic Beverages				
Alcoholic beverage purchases	yr	304	1999	30r
Beer, Heineken, 12-oz, ex deposit	6	6.76	3/01	4c
J & B Scotch	750-ml	17.29	3/01	4c
Malt beverages, all types, all sizes, any origin	16 oz	0.93	7/01	11r
Wine, Livingston or Gallo, Chablis blanc	1.5 liter	4.31	3/01	4c
Wine, red and white table, all sizes, any origin	liter	7.04	7/01	11r
Appliances				
Appliance repair, service call, washing machine	min lab chg	39.98	3/01	4c
Major appliances, expenditures on	yr	165	1999	30r
Small appliances, housewares, expenditures on	yr	90	1999	30r
Banking and Money				
Mortgage interest and charges paid	yr	2277	1999	30r
Mortgage principal paid on owned property	yr	1230	1999	30r
Mortgage rate, incl. points and orig. fee, 30-yr. conv. fixed or ARM	mos	7.15	3/01	4c
Vehicle finance charges paid	yr	328	1999	30r
Charity				
Cash contributions, expenditures	yr	1126	1999	30r
Child Care				
Child raising cost, total, age 0-2	yr	7890	1999	60r
Child raising cost, total, age 3-5	yr	8130	1999	60r
Child raising cost, total, age 6-8	yr	8170	1999	60r
Child raising cost, total, age 9-11	yr	8190	1999	60r
Child raising cost, total, age 12-14	yr	8890	1999	60r
Child raising cost, total, age 15-17	yr	9050	1999	60r
Child's child care and education, age 0-2	yr	1240	1999	60r
Child's child care and education, age 3-5	yr	1370	1999	60r
Child's child care and education, age 6-8	yr	880	1999	60r
Child's child care and education, age 9-11	yr	570	1999	60r
Child's child care and education, age 12-14	yr	420	1999	60r
Child's child care and education, age 15-17	yr	720	1999	60r
Child's clothing, age 0-2	yr	410	1999	60r
Child's clothing, age 3-5	yr	400	1999	60r
Child's clothing, age 6-8	yr	450	1999	60r
Child's clothing, age 9-11	yr	500	1999	60r
Child's clothing, age 12-14	yr	840	1999	60r
Child's clothing, age 15-17	yr	740	1999	60r
Child's food, age 0-2	yr	960	1999	60r
Child's food, age 3-5	yr	1120	1999	60r
Child's food, age 6-8	yr	1430	1999	60r
Child's food, age 9-11	yr	1710	1999	60r
Child's food, age 12-14	yr	1710	1999	60r
Child's food, age 15-17	yr	1920	1999	60r
Child's health care, age 0-2	yr	520	1999	60r
Child's health care, age 3-5	yr	500	1999	60r
Child's health care, age 6-8	yr	570	1999	60r
Child's health care, age 9-11	yr	610	1999	60r
Child's health care, age 12-14	yr	630	1999	60r
Child's health care, age 15-17	yr	650	1999	60r
Child's housing, age 0-2	yr	2860	1999	60r
Child's housing, age 3-5	yr	2840	1999	60r
Child's housing, age 6-8	yr	2800	1999	60r
Child's housing, age 9-11	yr	2650	1999	60r
Child's housing, age 12-14	yr	2840	1999	60r
Child's housing, age 15-17	yr	2440	1999	60r
Child's personal care, reading, age 0-2	yr	880	1999	60r
Child's personal care, reading, age 3-5	yr	900	1999	60r
Child's personal care, reading, age 6-8	yr	930	1999	60r

Item	Per	Value	Date	Ref.
Child Care - continued				
Child's personal care, reading, age 9-11	yr	970	1999	60r
Child's personal care, reading, age 12-14	yr	1150	1999	60r
Child's personal care, reading, age 15-17	yr	920	1999	60r
Clothing				
Apparel and services purchases	yr	1607	1999	30r
Boys' brief, cotton	3	3.60	3/01	4c
Boys, 2 to 15, expenditures on	yr	91	1999	30r
Children under 2, expenditures on	yr	59	1999	30r
Footwear, expenditures on	yr	285	1999	30r
Girls, 2 to 15, expenditures on	yr	116	1999	30r
Men and boys, expenditures on	yr	433	1999	30r
Men, 16 and over, expenditures on	yr	341	1999	30r
Shirt, man's dress shirt		22.08	3/01	4c
Slacks, man's "No Wrinkles" khaki		35.66	3/01	4c
Women, 16 and over, expenditures on	yr	490	1999	30r
Communications				
Cable modem installation, Bresnan		99.95	6/99	103s
Cable modem installation, Marcus		499.00	6/99	103s
Cable modem rate, cable subscriber, Bresnan	mos	39.95	6/99	103s
Cable modem rate, cable subscriber, Marcus	mos	14.95-49.95	6/99	103s
Cable modem rate, non-cable subscriber, Bresnan	mos	49.95	6/99	103s
Cable modem rate, non-cable subscriber, Marcus	mos	60.95	6/99	103s
Newspaper subscription, daily and Sunday delivery	mos	15.22	3/01	4c
Phone line, single, business, field visit	inst.	64.65	12/97	17s
Phone line, single, business, no field visit	inst.	64.65	12/97	17s
Phone line, single, residence, field visit	inst.	33.05	12/97	17s
Phone line, single, residence, no field visit	inst.	33.05	12/97	17s
Postage and stationery, expenditures on	yr	140	1999	30r
Postal rate, express mail, up to half-pound		12.45	7/01	108r
Postal rate, letter, first class, first ounce		0.34	7/01	108r
Postal rate, letter, two ounces		0.57	7/01	108r
Postal rate, post card		0.21	7/01	108r
Postal rate, priority mail, two pounds		3.95	7/01	108r
Postal rate, priority mail, up to one pound		3.50	7/01	108r
Telephone bill, family of three	mos	16.43	3/01	4c
Telephone services, expenditures on	yr	830	1999	30r
Education				
Board, 4-year private college/university	yr	2271	1996	38s
Board, 4-year public college/university	yr	1527	1996	38s
Education expenditures	yr	583	1999	30r
Room, 4-year private college/university	yr	1812	1996	38s
Room, 4-year public college/university	yr	1706	1996	38s
Total cost, 4-year private college/university	yr	15652	1996	38s
Total cost, 4-year public college/university	yr	5847	1996	38s
Tuition, 2-year public college/university, in state	yr	1840	1996	38s
Tuition, 4-year private college/university, in state	yr	11569	1996	38s
Tuition, 4-year public college/university	yr	2614	1996	38s
Energy and Fuels				
Electricity	500 KWhs	46.59	7/01	11r
Energy, combined forms, 2400 sq ft	mos	154.91	3/01	4c
Energy, exc. electricity, 2400 sq ft	mos	110.58	3/01	4c
Fuel oil #2	gal	1.27	7/01	11r
Fuel oil and other fuels, expenditures on	yr	68	1999	30r
Gas, natural, commercial rate	1000 cf	7.32	11/00	88s
Gas, regular unleaded, cash, self-service	gal	1.51	3/01	4c
Gasoline, unleaded midgrade	gal	1.79	7/01	11r
Gasoline, unleaded premium	gal	1.86	7/01	11r
Gasoline, unleaded regular	gal	1.58	7/01	11r
Natural gas, expenditures on	yr	389	1999	30r
Utility (piped) gas, therm		0.81	7/01	11r
Utility (piped) gas, 40 therms		38.01	7/01	11r
Utility (piped) gas, 100 therms		81.75	7/01	11r

Values are in dollars or fractions of dollars. In the column headed *Ref*, references are shown to sources. Each reference is followed by a letter. These refer to the geographical level for which data were reported: s=State, r=Region, and c=City or metro. The abbreviation *ex* is used to mean *except* or *excluding*; *exp* stands for *expenditures*. For other abbreviations and further explanations, please see the Introduction.

Sheboygan, WI - continued

Item	Per	Value	Date	Ref.
Entertainment				
Bowling, Saturday evening rate	line	2.26	3/01	4c
Entertainment purchases	yr	1984	1999	30r
Fees and admissions paid	yr	444	1999	30r
Monopoly game, Parker Brothers', No. 9	game	11.24	3/01	4c
Movie, first-run, Saturday, evening	adm.	7.25	3/01	4c
Television, radios, sound equipment, expenditures on	yr	580	1999	30r
Tennis balls, yellow, Wilson or Penn, 3	can	2.18	3/01	4c
Funerals				
Cosmetology, hair, other preparation		178.32	1/99	78r
Embalming		408.19	1/99	78r
Funeral at funeral home		362.13	1/99	78r
Professional service charges		1375.51	1/99	78r
Transfer of remains to funeral home		155.92	1/99	78r
Visitation/viewing		294.38	1/99	78r
Groceries				
Groceries, ACCRA Index		95.00	3/01	4c
Antibiotic ointment, Polysporin	0.5 oz	4.44	3/01	4c
Baby food, strained vegetables or fruit, lowest price	4-4.5 oz	0.49	3/01	4c
Bacon, sliced	lb	3.15	7/01	11r
Bakery products, expenditures on	yr	281	1999	30r
Bananas	lb	0.44	3/01	4c
Bananas	lb	0.48	7/01	11r
Beans, dried, any type, all sizes	lb	0.61	7/01	11r
Beef for stew, boneless	lb	3.08	7/01	11r
Beef or hamburger, ground	lb	1.78	3/01	4c
Beef, expenditures on	yr	217	1999	30r
Bologna, all beef or mixed	lb	2.52	7/01	11r
Bread, white	loaf	0.78	3/01	4c
Bread, white, pan	lb	1.06	7/01	11r
Broccoli	lb	0.91	7/01	11r
Butter, salted, grade AA, stick	lb	3.04	7/01	11r
Butter, yoghurt, cheese, etc, expenditures on	yr	183	1999	30r
Cereals and bakery product purchases	yr	430	1999	30r
Cereals and cereal products, expenditures on	yr	149	1999	30r
Cheese, Kraft grated Parmesan	8 oz	3.20	3/01	4c
Chicken, fresh, whole	lb	1.07	7/01	11r
Chicken, whole fryer	lb	1.08	3/01	4c
Chops, boneless,	lb	3.64	7/01	11r
Chuck roast, U.S. choice, boneless	lb	2.47	7/01	11r
Cigarettes, Winston, Kings	carton	31.45	3/01	4c
Coffee, 100%, ground roast, all sizes	lb	2.69	7/01	11r
Coffee, vacuum-packed	13 oz	2.28	3/01	4c
Cookies, chocolate chip	lb	2.87	7/01	11r
Corn Flakes, Kellogg's or Post Toasties	18 oz	2.34	3/01	4c
Corn, frozen, whole kernel, lowest price	16 oz	1.09	3/01	4c
Dairy product purchases	yr	304	1999	30r
Eggs, expenditures on	yr	26	1999	30r
Eggs, Grade A or AA	dozen	0.93	3/01	4c
Eggs, grade A, large	dozen	0.88	7/01	11r
Fats and oils, expenditures on	yr	75	1999	30r
Fish and seafood, expenditures on	yr	72	1999	30r
Food (excl fruit and vegetables), eaten at home, purchases	yr	887	1999	30r
Food cooked on trips, expenditures on	yr	44	1999	30r
Food purchases	yr	4802	1999	30r
Food purchases, eaten away from home	yr	2069	1999	30r
Food purchases, food eaten at home	yr	2733	1999	30r
Fresh fruits, expenditures on	yr	138	1999	30r
Fresh milk and cream, expenditures on	yr	120	1999	30r
Fresh vegetables, expenditures on	yr	126	1999	30r
Grapefruit	lb	0.66	7/01	11r
Grapes, Thompson, seedless	lb	1.64	7/01	11r
Ground beef, 100% beef	lb	1.64	7/01	11r
Ground beef, lean and extra lean	lb	2.16	7/01	11r
Ground chuck, 100% beef	lb	2.13	7/01	11r
Ham, boneless, excl canned	lb	2.62	7/01	11r
Ice cream, prepackaged, bulk, regular	1/2 gal	3.35	7/01	11r
Lemons	lb	1.19	7/01	11r

Sheboygan, WI - continued

Item	Per	Value	Date	Ref.
Groceries - continued				
Lettuce, iceberg	head	1.08	3/01	4c
Lettuce, iceberg	lb	0.73	7/01	11r
Margarine, Blue Bonnet or Parkay, stick	lb	0.69	3/01	4c
Margarine, soft, tubs	lb	0.89	7/01	11r
Meats, poultry, fish, and egg purchases	yr	671	1999	30r
Milk, fresh, whole, fortified	gal	2.71	7/01	11r
Milk, whole	1/2 gal	1.67	3/01	4c
Nonalcoholic beverages, expenditures on	yr	239	1999	30r
Orange juice, Minute Maid frozen	12 oz	1.32	3/01	4c
Oranges, Navel	lb	0.80	7/01	11r
Oranges, Valencia	lb	0.66	7/01	11r
Peaches, halves or slices, Hunt's, Del Monte, or Libby's	29 oz	1.62	3/01	4c
Pears, Anjou	lb	0.93	7/01	11r
Peas, green, Del Monte or Green Giant	15 oz	0.76	3/01	4c
Pork chops, center cut, bone-in	lb	3.63	7/01	11r
Pork, expenditures on	yr	150	1999	30r
Potato chips	16 oz	3.52	7/01	11r
Potatoes, frozen, french fried	lb	1.08	7/01	11r
Potatoes, white or red	10 lb	1.82	3/01	4c
Potatoes, white, all types	lb	0.33	7/01	11r
Poultry, expenditures on	yr	108	1999	30r
Processed fruits, expenditures on	yr	98	1999	30r
Processed vegetables, expenditures on	yr	80	1999	30r
Round roast, U.S. choice, boneless	lb	3.07	7/01	11r
Round steak, graded and ungraded, excl U.S. prime and choice	lb	3.41	7/01	11r
Sausage, Jimmy Dean/Owens pork	lb	2.96	3/01	4c
Shortening, vegetable oil blends	lb	1.13	7/01	11r
Shortening, vegetable, Crisco	3 lb	2.90	3/01	4c
Soft drink, Coca Cola, ex deposit	2 liter	0.94	3/01	4c
Spaghetti and macaroni	lb	0.80	7/01	11r
Steak, round, U.S. choice, boneless	lb	3.23	7/01	11r
Steak, T-bone	lb	7.06	3/01	4c
Steak, T-bone, U.S. choice, bone-in	lb	6.68	7/01	11r
Strawberries, dry pint	12 oz	1.32	7/01	11r
Sugar and other sweets, expenditures on	yr	114	1999	30r
Sugar, cane or beet	4 lbs	1.61	3/01	4c
Sugar, white, 33-80 ounce package	lb	0.42	7/01	11r
Sugar, white, all sizes	lb	0.43	7/01	11r
Tobacco products and smoking supplies purchases	yr	331	1999	30r
Tomatoes, field grown	lb	1.46	7/01	11r
Tomatoes, Hunt's or Del Monte	14.5 oz	0.84	3/01	4c
Tuna, chunk, light	6 oz	0.45	3/01	4c
Tuna, light, chunk	lb	1.80	7/01	11r
Turkey, frozen, whole	lb	1.15	7/01	11r
Goods and Services				
Miscellaneous goods and services, ACCRA Index		93.20	3/01	4c
B&B Japanese maple (acer japonicum)	gal	29.99-169.99	4/00	93r
Boxwood (buxus)	2 gal	18.99-39.99	4/00	93r
Daylilly (hemerocallis)	gal	4.99-25.00	4/00	93r
Flat of annuals		11.98-24.99	4/00	93r
Fountain grass (pennisetum)	gal	5.98-12.98	4/00	93r
Hanging basket (10 in)		12.99-27.99	4/00	93r
Hardy geranium (geranium)	gal	7.99-9.99	4/00	93r
Hosta (hosta)	gal	6.00-25.00	4/00	93r
Lilac (syrubga vulgaris)	2 gal	14.99-24.99	4/00	93r
Miscellaneous purchases	yr	865	1999	30r
Rhododendron (rhododendron)	2 gal	23.98-42.99	4/00	93r

Values are in dollars or fractions of dollars. In the column headed *Ref*, references are shown to sources. Each reference is followed by a letter. These refer to the geographical level for which data were reported: s=State, r=Region, and c=City or metro. The abbreviation *ex* is used to mean *except* or *excluding*; *exp* stands for *expenditures*. For other abbreviations and further explanations, please see the Introduction.

Sheboygan, WI - continued

Item	Per	Value	Date	Ref.
Goods and Services				
Sage (salvia)	gal	6.00-9.99	4/00	93r
Wintercreeper euonymus (euonymus fortunei)	2 gal	16.00-169.99	4/00	93r
Hunting license	yr	14.00	4/01	34s
Health Care				
Health care, ACCRA Index		100.10	3/01	4c
Cardiac catheterization, ave hospital/physician charges		13240	1998	77s
Childbirth, Cesarean delivery		10722	1997	13r
Childbirth, vaginal delivery		6223	1997	13r
Dentist's fee, adult teeth cleaning and periodic oral exam	visit	72.75	3/01	4c
Doctor's fee, routine exam, established patient	visit	66.50	3/01	4c
Drugs, expenditures on	yr	394	1999	30r
Health care purchases	yr	2048	1999	30r
Health insurance expenditures	yr	978	1999	30r
Hospital care, private room	day	390.00	3/01	4c
Hysterectomy, laproscopically-assisted, ave hospital/physician charges		13270	1998	76s
Hysterectomy, vaginal, ave hospital and physician charges		9170	1998	76s
Laser eye surgery	eye	1950-2400	2000	63s
Medicaid dispensing fee		4.88-40.11	1999	87s
Medical services expenditures	yr	554	1999	30r
Medical supplies, expenditures on	yr	122	1999	30r
Plastic surgery, breast augmentation		3184	2000	7r
Plastic surgery, breast lift		3585	2000	7r
Plastic surgery, facelift		4999	2000	7r
Plastic surgery, hair transplantation		3105	2000	7r
Plastic surgery, lip augmentation		1290	2000	7r
Plastic surgery, lower body lift		8135	2000	7r
Plastic surgery, thigh lift		3839	2000	7r
Household Goods				
Dishwashing powder, Cascade	50 oz	3.44	3/01	4c
Floor coverings, expenditures on	yr	52	1999	30r
Furniture, expenditures on	yr	344	1999	30r
Household furnishings and equipment purchases	yr	1475	1999	30r
Household textiles, expenditures on	yr	109	1999	30r
Laundry and cleaning supplies, expenditures on	yr	134	1999	30r
Tissues, facial, Kleenex brand	175	1.29	3/01	4c
Housing				
Housing, ACCRA Index		90.40	3/01	4c
Home price, existing, ave		144400	10/00	90r
Home value, median		117000	2001	53s
House, 2400 sq ft, 8000 sq ft lot, new, urban, utilities	total	177900	3/01	4c
House payment, principal and interest, 25% down payment	mos	901	3/01	4c
Household operation expenditures	yr	542	1999	30r
Housekeeping supplies purchases	yr	508	1999	30r
Lodging expenditures	yr	430	1999	30r
Maintenance, repairs, insurance expenditures	yr	853	1999	30r
Monthly rental value of owned home	mos	547	1999	30r
Owned dwellings, expenditures own	yr	4282	1999	30r
Rent expenditures	yr	1558	1999	30r
Rent, apartment, 2 br, 1 1/2-2 baths, unfurn, 950 sq ft, water	mos	708	3/01	4c
Rental unit, 1 bedroom, with utilities	mos	399	4/01	41c
Rental unit, 2 bedroom, with utilities	mos	487	4/01	41c
Rental unit, 3 bedroom, with utilities	mos	609	4/01	41c
Rental unit, 4 bedroom, with utilities	mos	756	4/01	41c
Shelter, expenditures on	yr	6270	1999	30r

Sheboygan, WI - continued

Item	Per	Value	Date	Ref.
Insurance and Pensions				
Auto insurance premium	yr	603.84	1999	57s
Life and other personal insurance purchases	yr	387	1999	30r
Pensions and Social Security, expenditures on	yr	2968	1999	30r
Legal Fees				
Divorce, filing fee		142.00-150.00	4/01	35s
Driver's license fee	orig	18.00	1999	48s
Driver's license fee	renew	12.00	1999	48s
Fishing license	yr	14.00	4/01	34s
Personal Goods				
Personal care products and services purchases	yr	385	1999	30r
Shampoo, Alberto VO5	15 oz	1.06	3/01	4c
Toothpaste, Crest or Colgate	6-7 oz	2.65	3/01	4c
Personal Services				
Dry cleaning, man's 2-pc suit		9.23	3/01	4c
Man's haircut, barbershop, no styling		10.10	3/01	4c
Personal services, household, expenditures on	yr	300	1999	30r
Woman's shampoo, trim, blow-dry, no style-change		22.50	3/01	4c
Pets				
Pets, toys, and playground equipment, expenditures on	yr	375	1999	30r
Restaurant Food				
Chicken, fried, thigh and drumstick, KFC/Church's		2.29	3/01	4c
Hamburger with cheese, McDonald's	1/4 lb	1.99	3/01	4c
Pizza, Pizza Hut or Pizza Inn	11-12 in	8.99	3/01	4c
Taxes				
Federal income taxes paid	yr	2326	1999	30r
Personal taxes, expenditures on	yr	3223	1999	30r
Property taxes paid	yr	1152	1999	30r
State and local income taxes paid	yr	753	1999	30r
Transportation				
Transportation, ACCRA Index		111.60	3/01	4c
Cars and trucks, new, expenditures on	yr	1280	1999	30r
Cars and trucks, used, expenditures on	yr	1763	1999	30r
Diesel at the pump	gal	1.34	10/99	73s
Gasoline and motor oil purchases	yr	1036	1999	30r
Gasoline before-tax price (cents)	gal	113.40	10/00	43s
Maintenance and repair expenditures	yr	594	1999	30r
Public transportation, expenditures on	yr	341	1999	30r
Tire balance, computer or spin balance, front	wheel	9.25	3/01	4c
Transportation purchases	yr	6617	1999	30r
Vehicle expenses, miscellaneous, purchases	yr	2159	1999	30r
Vehicle insurance payments	yr	701	1999	30r
Vehicle purchases (net outlay)	yr	3081	1999	30r
Vehicle rental, lease expenditures	yr	536	1999	30r
Utilities				
Utilities, ACCRA Index		119.90	3/01	4c
Electrical bill, average	mos	52.08	9/00	9s
Electricity, expenditures on	yr	841	1999	30r
Electricity and other, mixed, 2400 sq ft, new home	mos	44.33	3/01	4c
Electricity cost, average	KWh	5.69	9/00	9s
Utilities, fuels, and public services purchased	yr	2401	1999	30r
Water and other public services, expenditures on	yr	273	1999	30r
Weddings				
Wedding (national average cost)		19936	2000	33r
Wedding (regional average total cost)		16195	1997	110r
Attendants' gifts		321	1998	33r
Bridal attendants' apparel (5 persons)		824	2000	33r
Bride's headpiece/veil		173	1998	33r
Bride's wedding dress		859	1998	33r

Values are in dollars or fractions of dollars. In the column headed *Ref*, references are shown to sources. Each reference is followed by a letter. These refer to the geographical level for which data were reported: s=State, r=Region, and c=City or metro. The abbreviation *ex* is used to mean *except* or *excluding*; *exp* stands for *expenditures*. For other abbreviations and further explanations, please see the Introduction.

Sheboygan, WI - continued

Item	Per	Value	Date	Ref.
Weddings				
Clergy, religious facility fee		242	1998	33r
Engagement ring		3177	1998	33r
Flowers		789	1998	33r
Groom's formalwear rental		99	2000	33r
Limousine		410	1998	33r
Marriage license cost		50.00-60.00	4/01	35s
Men's formalwear (ushers, best man)		469	2000	33r
Mother of bride apparel		241	2000	33r
Music		866	1998	33r
Photography and videography		1368	1998	33r
Rehearsal dinner		728	1998	33r
Wedding invitations and announcements		341	1998	33r
Wedding reception		7968	2000	33r
Wedding rings (bride and groom)		1060	1998	33r

Sherman-Denison, TX

Item	Per	Value	Date	Ref.
Composite, ACCRA index		96.20	3/01	4c
Alcoholic Beverages				
Alcoholic beverage purchases	yr	253	1999	30r
Beer, Heineken, 12-oz, ex deposit	6	7.01	3/01	4c
J & B Scotch	750-ml	22.69	3/01	4c
Malt beverages, all types, all sizes, any origin	16 oz	0.96	7/01	11r
Wine, Livingston or Gallo, Chablis blanc	1.5 liter	6.67	3/01	4c
Appliances				
Appliance repair, service call, washing machine	min lab chg	42.50	3/01	4c
Major appliances, expenditures on	yr	172	1999	30r
Small appliances, housewares, expenditures on	yr	81	1999	30r
Banking and Money				
Mortgage interest and charges paid	yr	2039	1999	30r
Mortgage principal paid on owned property	yr	1026	1999	30r
Mortgage rate, incl. points and orig. fee, 30-yr. conv. fixed or ARM	mos	7.23	3/01	4c
Vehicle finance charges paid	yr	365	1999	30r
Charity				
Cash contributions, expenditures	yr	1127	1999	30r
Child Care				
Child raising cost, total, age 0-2	yr	8540	1999	60r
Child raising cost, total, age 3-5	yr	8780	1999	60r
Child raising cost, total, age 6-8	yr	8820	1999	60r
Child raising cost, total, age 9-11	yr	8800	1999	60r
Child raising cost, total, age 12-14	yr	9510	1999	60r
Child raising cost, total, age 15-17	yr	9740	1999	60r
Child's child care and education, age 0-2	yr	1380	1999	60r
Child's child care and education, age 3-5	yr	1520	1999	60r
Child's child care and education, age 6-8	yr	990	1999	60r
Child's child care and education, age 9-11	yr	650	1999	60r
Child's child care and education, age 12-14	yr	490	1999	60r
Child's child care and education, age 15-17	yr	840	1999	60r
Child's clothing, age 0-2	yr	480	1999	60r
Child's clothing, age 3-5	yr	470	1999	60r
Child's clothing, age 6-8	yr	520	1999	60r
Child's clothing, age 9-11	yr	570	1999	60r
Child's clothing, age 12-14	yr	950	1999	60r
Child's clothing, age 15-17	yr	850	1999	60r
Child's food, age 0-2	yr	1000	1999	60r
Child's food, age 3-5	yr	1160	1999	60r
Child's food, age 6-8	yr	1490	1999	60r
Child's food, age 9-11	yr	1770	1999	60r
Child's food, age 12-14	yr	1770	1999	60r
Child's food, age 15-17	yr	1980	1999	60r
Child's health care, age 0-2	yr	620	1999	60r
Child's health care, age 3-5	yr	590	1999	60r
Child's health care, age 6-8	yr	680	1999	60r
Child's health care, age 9-11	yr	720	1999	60r
Child's health care, age 12-14	yr	730	1999	60r

Sherman-Denison, TX - continued

Item	Per	Value	Date	Ref.
Child Care - continued				
Child's health care, age 15-17	yr	760	1999	60r
Child's housing, age 0-2	yr	3070	1999	60r
Child's housing, age 3-5	yr	3050	1999	60r
Child's housing, age 6-8	yr	3010	1999	60r
Child's housing, age 9-11	yr	2850	1999	60r
Child's housing, age 12-14	yr	3040	1999	60r
Child's housing, age 15-17	yr	2650	1999	60r
Child's personal care, reading, age 0-2	yr	910	1999	60r
Child's personal care, reading, age 3-5	yr	930	1999	60r
Child's personal care, reading, age 6-8	yr	960	1999	60r
Child's personal care, reading, age 9-11	yr	1000	1999	60r
Child's personal care, reading, age 12-14	yr	1170	1999	60r
Child's personal care, reading, age 15-17	yr	950	1999	60r
Clothing				
Apparel and services purchases	yr	1610	1999	30r
Boys' brief, cotton	3	3.78	3/01	4c
Boys, 2 to 15, expenditures on	yr	89	1999	30r
Children under 2, expenditures on	yr	79	1999	30r
Footwear, expenditures on	yr	283	1999	30r
Girls, 2 to 15, expenditures on	yr	103	1999	30r
Men and boys, expenditures on	yr	351	1999	30r
Men, 16 and over, expenditures on	yr	262	1999	30r
Shirt, man's dress shirt		26.24	3/01	4c
Slacks, man's "No Wrinkles" khaki		35.99	3/01	4c
Women, 16 and over, expenditures on	yr	538	1999	30r
Communications				
Cable modem installation, AT&T-BIS		150.00	6/99	103s
Cable modem installation, Marcus		499.00	6/99	103s
Cable modem installation, Time Warner		75.00-225.00	6/99	103s
Cable modem rate, cable subscriber, AT&T-BIS	mos	39.95	6/99	103s
Cable modem rate, cable subscriber, Marcus	mos	14.95-49.95	6/99	103s
Cable modem rate, cable subscriber, Time Warner	mos	39.95-49.95	6/99	103s
Cable modem rate, non-cable subscriber, Marcus	mos	60.95	6/99	103s
Cable modem rate, non-cable subscriber, Time Warner	mos	39.95-54.95	6/99	103s
Newspaper subscription, daily and Sunday delivery	mos	13.00	3/01	4c
Phone line, single, business, field visit	inst.	71.90	12/97	17s
Phone line, single, business, no field visit	inst.	57.30	12/97	17s
Phone line, single, residence, field visit	inst.	52.95	12/97	17s
Phone line, single, residence, no field visit	inst.	38.35	12/97	17s
Postage and stationery, expenditures on	yr	104	1999	30r
Postal rate, express mail, up to half-pound		12.45	7/01	108r
Postal rate, letter, first class, first ounce		0.34	7/01	108r
Postal rate, letter, two ounces		0.57	7/01	108r
Postal rate, post card		0.21	7/01	108r
Postal rate, priority mail, two pounds		3.95	7/01	108r
Postal rate, priority mail, up to one pound		3.50	7/01	108r
Telephone bill, family of three	mos	25.28	3/01	4c
Telephone services, expenditures on	yr	860	1999	30r
Education				
Board, 4-year private college/university	yr	2198	1996	38s
Board, 4-year public college/university	yr	1759	1996	38s
Education expenditures	yr	431	1999	30r
Room, 4-year private college/university	yr	2000	1996	38s
Room, 4-year public college/university	yr	1885	1996	38s
Total cost, 4-year private college/university	yr	13156	1996	38s
Total cost, 4-year public college/university	yr	5464	1996	38s
Tuition, 2-year public college/university, in state	yr	771	1996	38s
Tuition, 4-year private college/university, in state	yr	8959	1996	38s
Tuition, 4-year public college/university	yr	1820	1996	38s

Values are in dollars or fractions of dollars. In the column headed *Ref*, references are shown to sources. Each reference is followed by a letter. These refer to the geographical level for which data were reported: s=State, r=Region, and c=City or metro. The abbreviation *ex* is used to mean *except* or *excluding*; *exp* stands for expenditures. For other abbreviations and further explanations, please see the Introduction.

Sherman-Denison, TX - continued

Item	Per	Value	Date	Ref.
Energy and Fuels				
Electricity	KWh	0.09	7/01	11r
Electricity	500 KWhs	47.29	7/01	11r
Energy, combined forms, 2400 sq ft	mos	125.88	3/01	4c
Energy, exc. electricity, 2400 sq ft	mos	40.23	3/01	4c
Fuel oil #2	gal	1.43	7/01	11r
Fuel oil and other fuels, expenditures on	yr	45	1999	30r
Gas, natural, commercial rate	1000 cf	6.94	11/00	88s
Gas, regular unleaded, cash, self-service	gal	1.34	3/01	4c
Gasoline, all types	gal	1.60	7/01	11r
Gasoline, unleaded midgrade	gal	1.65	7/01	11r
Gasoline, unleaded premium	gal	1.74	7/01	11r
Natural gas, expenditures on	yr	164	1999	30r
Utility (piped) gas, therm		1.01	7/01	11r
Utility (piped) gas, 40 therms		44.29	7/01	11r
Utility (piped) gas, 100 therms		97.44	7/01	11r
Entertainment				
Bowling, Saturday evening rate	line	2.75	3/01	4c
Entertainment purchases	yr	1574	1999	30r
Fees and admissions paid	yr	371	1999	30r
Monopoly game, Parker Brothers', No. 9	game	12.20	3/01	4c
Movie, first-run, Saturday, evening	adm.	5.50	3/01	4c
Reading purchases	yr	121	1999	30r
Television, radios, sound equipment, expenditures on	yr	561	1999	30r
Tennis balls, yellow, Wilson or Penn, 3	can	2.74	3/01	4c
Funerals				
Total cost of funeral		5842.28	1/99	78r
Acknowledgement cards		28.35	1/99	78r
Casket		2494.29	1/99	78r
Cosmetology, hair, other preparation		109.22	1/99	78r
Embalming		361.42	1/99	78r
Funeral at funeral home		349.20	1/99	78r
Hearse (local)		161.91	1/99	78r
Professional service charges		1116.50	1/99	78r
Service car/van		65.56	1/99	78r
Transfer of remains to funeral home		143.56	1/99	78r
Vault		785.25	1/99	78r
Visitation/viewing		227.02	1/99	78r
Groceries				
Groceries, ACCRA Index		93.20	3/01	4c
American processed cheese	lb	3.50	7/01	11r
Antibiotic ointment, Polysporin	0.5 oz	4.70	3/01	4c
Baby food, strained vegetables or fruit, lowest price	4-4.5 oz	0.35	3/01	4c
Bakery products, expenditures on	yr	261	1999	30r
Bananas	lb	0.42	3/01	4c
Bananas	lb	0.47	7/01	11r
Beans, dried, any type, all sizes	lb	0.63	7/01	11r
Beef for stew, boneless	lb	2.86	7/01	11r
Beef or hamburger, ground	lb	1.70	3/01	4c
Beef, expenditures on	yr	210	1999	30r
Bologna, all beef or mixed	lb	2.29	7/01	11r
Bread, French	lb	1.66	7/01	11r
Bread, white	loaf	0.85	3/01	4c
Bread, white, pan	lb	0.87	7/01	11r
Bread, whole wheat, pan	lb	1.38	7/01	11r
Broccoli	lb	1.04	7/01	11r
Butter, salted, grade AA, stick	lb	2.26	7/01	11r
Butter, yoghurt, cheese, etc, expenditures on	yr	170	1999	30r
Cabbage	lb	0.42	7/01	11r
Cereals and cereal products, expenditures on	yr	140	1999	30r
Cheddar cheese, natural	lb	3.75	7/01	11r
Cheese, Kraft grated Parmesan	8 oz	3.90	3/01	4c
Chicken breast, bone-in	lb	1.85	7/01	11r
Chicken legs, bone-in	lb	1.34	7/01	11r
Chicken, fresh, whole	lb	1.05	7/01	11r
Chicken, whole fryer	lb	0.86	3/01	4c
Chops, boneless,	lb	4.13	7/01	11r

Sherman-Denison, TX - continued

Item	Per	Value	Date	Ref.
Groceries - continued				
Chuck roast, graded and ungraded, excl U.S. prime and choice	lb	2.35	7/01	11r
Chuck roast, U.S. choice, boneless	lb	2.67	7/01	11r
Cigarettes, Winston, Kings	carton	30.71	3/01	4c
Coffee, 100%, ground roast, all sizes	lb	2.88	7/01	11r
Coffee, instant, plain, regular, all sizes	16 oz	9.25	7/01	11r
Coffee, vacuum-packed	13 oz	2.32	3/01	4c
Cola, non diet,	2 liter	1.11	7/01	11r
Corn Flakes, Kellogg's or Post Toasties	18 oz	2.18	3/01	4c
Corn, frozen, whole kernel, lowest price	16 oz	1.10	3/01	4c
Crackers, soda, salted	lb	1.70	7/01	11r
Dairy product purchases	yr	282	1999	30r
Eggs, expenditures on	yr	32	1999	30r
Eggs, Grade A or AA	dozen	1.09	3/01	4c
Fats and oils, expenditures on	yr	79	1999	30r
Fish and seafood, expenditures on	yr	99	1999	30r
Flour, white, all purpose	lb	0.32	7/01	11r
Food (excl fruit and vegetables), eaten at home, purchases	yr	815	1999	30r
Food cooked on trips, expenditures on	yr	36	1999	30r
Food purchases	yr	4533	1999	30r
Food purchases, eaten away from home	yr	1873	1999	30r
Food purchases, food eaten at home	yr	2660	1999	30r
Fresh fruits, expenditures on	yr	128	1999	30r
Fresh milk and cream, expenditures on	yr	112	1999	30r
Fresh vegetables, expenditures on	yr	131	1999	30r
Fruit and vegetable purchases	yr	438	1999	30r
Grapefruit	lb	0.59	7/01	11r
Grapes, Thompson, seedless	lb	2.12	7/01	11r
Ground beef, 100% beef	lb	1.76	7/01	11r
Ground beef, lean and extra lean	lb	2.60	7/01	11r
Ground chuck, 100% beef	lb	2.08	7/01	11r
Ham, boneless, excl canned	lb	2.71	7/01	11r
Ham, rump or shank half, bone-in, smoked	lb	2.19	7/01	11r
Ice cream, prepackaged, bulk, regular	1/2 gal	3.93	7/01	11r
Lemons	lb	1.32	7/01	11r
Lettuce, iceberg	head	1.16	3/01	4c
Lettuce, iceberg	lb	0.76	7/01	11r
Margarine, Blue Bonnet or Parkay, stick	lb	0.66	3/01	4c
Milk, fresh, low fat,	gal	2.75	7/01	11r
Milk, fresh, whole, fortified	gal	2.97	7/01	11r
Milk, whole	1/2 gal	1.54	3/01	4c
Nonalcoholic beverages, expenditures on	yr	228	1999	30r
Orange juice, frozen concentrate	16 oz	1.95	7/01	11r
Orange juice, Minute Maid frozen	12 oz	1.44	3/01	4c
Oranges, Navel	lb	0.73	7/01	11r
Oranges, Valencia	lb	0.55	7/01	11r
Peaches, halves or slices, Hunt's, Del Monte, or Libby's	29 oz	1.43	3/01	4c
Peanut butter, creamy, all sizes	lb	1.83	7/01	11r
Pears, Anjou	lb	0.98	7/01	11r
Peas, green, Del Monte or Green Giant	15 oz	0.65	3/01	4c
Pork chops, center cut, bone-in	lb	3.33	7/01	11r
Pork sausage, fresh, loose	lb	2.59	7/01	11r
Pork shoulder picnic, bone-in, smoked	lb	1.12	7/01	11r
Pork, expenditures on	yr	162	1999	30r
Potato chips	16 oz	3.59	7/01	11r
Potatoes, frozen, french fried	lb	1.00	7/01	11r
Potatoes, white or red	10 lb	2.98	3/01	4c
Potatoes, white, all types	lb	0.44	7/01	11r
Poultry, expenditures on	yr	137	1999	30r
Processed fruits, expenditures on	yr	97	1999	30r
Processed vegetables, expenditures on	yr	82	1999	30r
Rice, white, long grain, uncooked	lb	0.51	7/01	11r
Round roast, graded and ungraded, excl U.S. prime and choice	lb	2.96	7/01	11r
Round steak, graded and ungraded, excl U.S. prime and choice	lb	3.11	7/01	11r
Sausage, Jimmy Dean/Owens pork	lb	2.90	3/01	4c
Shortening, vegetable, Crisco	3 lb	2.53	3/01	4c
Sirloin steak, graded and ungraded, excl U.S. prime and choice	lb	4.23	7/01	11r

Values are in dollars or fractions of dollars. In the column headed *Ref*, references are shown to sources. Each reference is followed by a letter. These refer to the geographical level for which data were reported: s=State, r=Region, and c=City or metro. The abbreviation *ex* is used to mean *except* or *excluding*; *exp* stands for expenditures. For other abbreviations and further explanations, please see the Introduction.

Sherman-Denison, TX - continued

Item	Per	Value	Date	Ref.
Groceries				
Soft drink, Coca Cola, ex deposit	2 liter	1.28	3/01	4c
Spaghetti and macaroni	lb	0.78	7/01	11r
Steak, round, U.S. choice, boneless	lb	3.56	7/01	11r
Steak, sirloin, U.S. choice, boneless	lb	5.65	7/01	11r
Steak, T-bone	lb	5.82	3/01	4c
Strawberries, dry pint	12 oz	1.50	7/01	11r
Sugar and other sweets, expenditures on	yr	99	1999	30r
Sugar, cane or beet	4 lbs	1.46	3/01	4c
Sugar, white, 33-80 ounce package	lb	0.39	7/01	11r
Sugar, white, all sizes	lb	0.42	7/01	11r
Tobacco products and smoking supplies purchases	yr	288	1999	30r
Tomatoes, field grown	lb	1.43	7/01	11r
Tomatoes, Hunt's or Del Monte	14.5 oz	0.83	3/01	4c
Tuna, chunk, light	6 oz	0.64	3/01	4c
Tuna, light, chunk	lb	1.77	7/01	11r
Turkey, frozen, whole	lb	1.05	7/01	11r
Goods and Services				
Miscellaneous goods and services, ACCRA Index		98.70	3/01	4c
B&B Japanese maple (acer japonicum)	gal	79.98-99.00	4/00	93r
Boxwood (buxus)	2 gal	12.98-18.99	4/00	93r
Christmas tree, noble fir		40-60	2000	65s
Daylilly (hemerocallis)	gal	7.96-11.00	4/00	93r
Flat of annuals		13.99-27.99	4/00	93r
Fountain grass (pennisetum)	gal	6.96-9.00	4/00	93r
Hanging basket (10 in)		9.99-24.99	4/00	93r
Hardy geranium (geranium)	gal	5.96-8.00	4/00	93r
Hosta (hosta)	gal	8.96-12.99	4/00	93r
Lilac (syrubga vulgaris)	2 gal	13.00-19.99	4/00	93r
Rhododendron (rhododendron)	2 gal	12.98-29.99	4/00	93r
Sage (salvia)	gal	5.96-8.00	4/00	93r
Wintercreeper euonymus (euonymus fortunei)	2 gal	13.00-18.99	4/00	93r
Hunting license	yr	19.00	4/01	34s
Health Care				
Health care, ACCRA Index		104.20	3/01	4c
Cardiac catheterization, ave hospital/ physician charges		20140	1998	77s
Childbirth, Cesarean delivery		11587	1997	13r
Childbirth, vaginal delivery		6725	1997	13r
Dentist's fee, adult teeth cleaning and periodic oral exam	visit	82.87	3/01	4c
Doctor's fee, routine exam, established patient	visit	61.20	3/01	4c
Drugs, expenditures on	yr	399	1999	30r
Health care purchases	yr	1971	1999	30r
Health insurance expenditures	yr	933	1999	30r
Hospital care, private room	day	443.33	3/01	4c
Hysterectomy, laproscopically-assisted, ave hospital/physician charges		15700	1998	76s
Hysterectomy, vaginal, ave hospital and physician charges		12180	1998	76s
Medicaid dispensing fee		5.27	1999	87s
Medical services expenditures	yr	547	1999	30r
Medical supplies, expenditures on	yr	91	1999	30r
Household Goods				
Dishwashing powder, Cascade	50 oz	3.11	3/01	4c
Floor coverings, expenditures on	yr	44	1999	30r
Furniture, expenditures on	yr	335	1999	30r

Sherman-Denison, TX - continued

Item	Per	Value	Date	Ref.
Household Goods - continued				
Household furnishings and equipment purchases	yr	1328	1999	30r
Household textiles, expenditures on	yr	89	1999	30r
Laundry and cleaning supplies, expenditures on	yr	113	1999	30r
Tissues, facial, Kleenex brand	175	1.24	3/01	4c
Housing				
Housing, ACCRA Index		89.30	3/01	4c
Home price, existing, ave		160100	10/00	90r
Home value, median		112000	2001	53s
House, 2400 sq ft, 8000 sq ft lot, new, urban, utilities	total	183667	3/01	4c
House payment, principal and interest, 25% down payment	mos	938	3/01	4c
Household operation expenditures	yr	553	1999	30r
Housekeeping supplies purchases	yr	473	1999	30r
Housing, expenditures on	yr	10303	1999	30r
Maintenance, repairs, insurance expenditures	yr	699	1999	30r
Monthly rental value of owned home	mos	505	1999	30r
Owned dwellings, expenditures own	yr	3465	1999	30r
Rent expenditures	yr	1641	1999	30r
Rent, apartment, 2 br, 1 1/2-2 baths, unfurn, 950 sq ft, water	mos	574	3/01	4c
Rental unit, 1 bedroom, with utilities	mos	391	4/01	41c
Rental unit, 2 bedroom, with utilities	mos	472	4/01	41c
Rental unit, 3 bedroom, with utilities	mos	603	4/01	41c
Rental unit, 4 bedroom, with utilities	mos	721	4/01	41c
Shelter, expenditures on	yr	5467	1999	30r
Insurance and Pensions				
Life and other personal insurance purchases	yr	414	1999	30r
Pensions and Social Security, expenditures on	yr	2635	1999	30r
Personal insurance and pensions, expenditures on	yr	3048	1999	30r
Legal Fees				
Divorce, filing fee		150.00-200.00	4/01	35s
Driver's license fee	orig	24.00	1999	48s
Driver's license fee	renew	20.00	1999	48s
Fishing license	yr	19.00	4/01	34s
Personal Goods				
Personal care products and services purchases	yr	393	1999	30r
Shampoo, Alberto VO5	15 oz	1.08	3/01	4c
Toothpaste, Crest or Colgate	6-7 oz	2.28	3/01	4c
Personal Services				
Dry cleaning, man's 2-pc suit		5.65	3/01	4c
Man's haircut, barbershop, no styling		8.11	3/01	4c
Personal services, household, expenditures on	yr	258	1999	30r
Woman's shampoo, trim, blow-dry, no style-change		20.60	3/01	4c
Pets				
Pets, toys, and playground equipment, expenditures on	yr	306	1999	30r
Restaurant Food				
Chicken, fried, thigh and drumstick, KFC/ Church's		2.37	3/01	4c
Hamburger with cheese, McDonald's	1/4 lb	2.49	3/01	4c
Pizza, Pizza Hut or Pizza Inn	11-12 in	8.69	3/01	4c
Taxes				
Federal income taxes paid	yr	2047	1999	30r
Personal taxes, expenditures on	yr	2554	1999	30r
Property taxes paid	yr	726	1999	30r
State and local income taxes paid	yr	363	1999	30r

Values are in dollars or fractions of dollars. In the column headed *Ref*, references are shown to sources. Each reference is followed by a letter. These refer to the geographical level for which data were reported: s=State, r=Region, and c=City or metro. The abbreviation *ex* is used to mean *except* or *excluding*; *exp* stands for expenditures. For other abbreviations and further explanations, please see the Introduction.

Sherman-Denison, TX - continued

Item	Per	Value	Date	Ref.
Transportation				
Transportation, ACCRA Index		101.60	3/01	4c
Cars and trucks, new, expenditures on	yr	1648	1999	30r
Cars and trucks, used, expenditures on	yr	1651	1999	30r
Diesel at the pump	gal	1.18	10/99	73s
Gasoline and motor oil purchases	yr	1052	1999	30r
Gasoline before-tax price (cents)	gal	101.30	10/00	43s
Maintenance and repair expenditures	yr	621	1999	30r
Public transportation, expenditures on	yr	298	1999	30r
Tire balance, computer or spin balance, front	wheel	8.75	3/01	4c
Transportation purchases	yr	6738	1999	30r
Vehicle expenses, miscellaneous, purchases	yr	2033	1999	30r
Vehicle insurance payments	yr	696	1999	30r
Vehicle purchases (net outlay)	yr	3354	1999	30r
Vehicle rental, lease expenditures	yr	352	1999	30r
Utilities				
Utilities, ACCRA Index		104.90	3/01	4c
Electrical bill, average	mos	87.17	9/00	9s
Electricity, expenditures on	yr	1115	1999	30r
Electricity and other, mixed, 2400 sq ft, new home	mos	85.65	3/01	4c
Electricity cost, average	KWh	6.48	9/00	9s
Water and other public services, expenditures on	yr	298	1999	30r
Weddings				
Wedding (national average cost)		19936	2000	33r
Attendants' gifts		321	1998	33r
Bridal attendants' apparel (5 persons)		824	2000	33r
Bride's headpiece/veil		173	1998	33r
Bride's wedding dress		859	1998	33r
Clergy, religious facility fee		242	1998	33r
Engagement ring		3177	1998	33r
Flowers		789	1998	33r
Groom's formalwear rental		99	2000	33r
Limousine		410	1998	33r
Marriage license cost		36.00	4/01	35s
Men's formalwear (ushers, best man)		469	2000	33r
Mother of bride apparel		241	2000	33r
Music		866	1998	33r
Photography and videography		1368	1998	33r
Rehearsal dinner		728	1998	33r
Wedding invitations and announcements		341	1998	33r
Wedding reception		7968	2000	33r
Wedding rings (bride and groom)		1060	1998	33r

Shreveport-Bossier City, LA

Item	Per	Value	Date	Ref.
Composite, ACCRA index		91.30	12/00	5c
Alcoholic Beverages				
Alcoholic beverage purchases	yr	253	1999	30r
Beer, Heineken, 12-oz, ex deposit	6	6.84	12/00	5c
J & B Scotch	750-ml	18.59	12/00	5c
Malt beverages, all types, all sizes, any origin	16 oz	0.96	7/01	11r
Wine, Livingston or Gallo, Chablis blanc	1.5 liter	5.95	12/00	5c
Appliances				
Appliance repair, service call, washing machine	min lab chg	40.40	12/00	5c
Major appliances, expenditures on	yr	172	1999	30r
Small appliances, housewares, expenditures on	yr	81	1999	30r
Banking and Money				
Mortgage interest and charges paid	yr	2039	1999	30r
Mortgage principal paid on owned property	yr	1026	1999	30r
Mortgage rate, incl. points and orig. fee, 30-yr. conv. fixed or ARM	mos	7.91	12/00	5c
Vehicle finance charges paid	yr	365	1999	30r
Business Expenses				
Business travel, car rental	day	63	2001	3c
Business travel, food	day	42	2001	3c

Shreveport-Bossier City, LA - continued

Item	Per	Value	Date	Ref.
Business Expenses - continued				
Business travel, hotel	day	70	2001	3c
Charity				
Cash contributions, expenditures	yr	1127	1999	30r
Child Care				
Child raising cost, total, age 0-2	yr	8540	1999	60r
Child raising cost, total, age 3-5	yr	8780	1999	60r
Child raising cost, total, age 6-8	yr	8820	1999	60r
Child raising cost, total, age 9-11	yr	8800	1999	60r
Child raising cost, total, age 12-14	yr	9510	1999	60r
Child raising cost, total, age 15-17	yr	9740	1999	60r
Child's child care and education, age 0-2	yr	1380	1999	60r
Child's child care and education, age 3-5	yr	1520	1999	60r
Child's child care and education, age 6-8	yr	990	1999	60r
Child's child care and education, age 9-11	yr	650	1999	60r
Child's child care and education, age 12-14	yr	490	1999	60r
Child's child care and education, age 15-17	yr	840	1999	60r
Child's clothing, age 0-2	yr	480	1999	60r
Child's clothing, age 3-5	yr	470	1999	60r
Child's clothing, age 6-8	yr	520	1999	60r
Child's clothing, age 9-11	yr	570	1999	60r
Child's clothing, age 12-14	yr	950	1999	60r
Child's clothing, age 15-17	yr	850	1999	60r
Child's food, age 0-2	yr	1000	1999	60r
Child's food, age 3-5	yr	1160	1999	60r
Child's food, age 6-8	yr	1490	1999	60r
Child's food, age 9-11	yr	1770	1999	60r
Child's food, age 12-14	yr	1770	1999	60r
Child's food, age 15-17	yr	1980	1999	60r
Child's health care, age 0-2	yr	620	1999	60r
Child's health care, age 3-5	yr	590	1999	60r
Child's health care, age 6-8	yr	680	1999	60r
Child's health care, age 9-11	yr	720	1999	60r
Child's health care, age 12-14	yr	730	1999	60r
Child's health care, age 15-17	yr	760	1999	60r
Child's housing, age 0-2	yr	3070	1999	60r
Child's housing, age 3-5	yr	3050	1999	60r
Child's housing, age 6-8	yr	3010	1999	60r
Child's housing, age 9-11	yr	2850	1999	60r
Child's housing, age 12-14	yr	3040	1999	60r
Child's housing, age 15-17	yr	2650	1999	60r
Child's personal care, reading, age 0-2	yr	910	1999	60r
Child's personal care, reading, age 3-5	yr	930	1999	60r
Child's personal care, reading, age 6-8	yr	960	1999	60r
Child's personal care, reading, age 9-11	yr	1000	1999	60r
Child's personal care, reading, age 12-14	yr	1170	1999	60r
Child's personal care, reading, age 15-17	yr	950	1999	60r
Clothing				
Apparel and services purchases	yr	1610	1999	30r
Boys' brief, cotton	3	4.01	12/00	5c
Boys, 2 to 15, expenditures on	yr	89	1999	30r
Children under 2, expenditures on	yr	79	1999	30r
Footwear, expenditures on	yr	283	1999	30r
Girls, 2 to 15, expenditures on	yr	103	1999	30r
Men and boys, expenditures on	yr	351	1999	30r
Men, 16 and over, expenditures on	yr	262	1999	30r
Shirt, man's dress shirt		28.20	12/00	5c
Slacks, man's "No Wrinkles" khaki		34.80	12/00	5c
Women, 16 and over, expenditures on	yr	538	1999	30r
Communications				
Newspaper subscription, daily and Sunday delivery	mos	14.25	12/00	5c
Phone line, single, business, field visit	inst.	85.00	12/97	17s
Phone line, single, business, no field visit	inst.	85.00	12/97	17s
Phone line, single, residence, field visit	inst.	41.00	12/97	17s
Phone line, single, residence, no field visit	inst.	41.00	12/97	17s
Postage and stationery, expenditures on	yr	104	1999	30r
Postal rate, express mail, up to half-pound		12.45	7/01	108r
Postal rate, letter, first class, first ounce		0.34	7/01	108r
Postal rate, letter, two ounces		0.57	7/01	108r
Postal rate, post card		0.21	7/01	108r

Values are in dollars or fractions of dollars. In the column headed *Ref*, references are shown to sources. Each reference is followed by a letter. These refer to the geographical level for which data were reported: s=State, r=Region, and c=City or metro. The abbreviation *ex* is used to mean *except* or *excluding*; *exp* stands for expenditures. For other abbreviations and further explanations, please see the Introduction.

Shreveport-Bossier City, LA - continued

Item	Per	Value	Date	Ref.
Communications				
Postal rate, priority mail, two pounds		3.95	7/01	108r
Postal rate, priority mail, up to one pound		3.50	7/01	108r
Telephone bill, business, basic rate	mos	36.76	12/97	18c
Telephone bill, family of three	mos	21.68	12/00	5c
Telephone bill, residential, basic rate	mos	12.64	12/97	18c
Telephone services, expenditures on	yr	860	1999	30r
Education				
Board, 4-year private college/university	yr	2440	1996	38s
Board, 4-year public college/university	yr	1806	1996	38s
Education expenditures	yr	431	1999	30r
Room, 4-year private college/university	yr	2906	1996	38s
Room, 4-year public college/university	yr	1464	1996	38s
Total cost, 4-year private college/university	yr	17796	1996	38s
Total cost, 4-year public college/university	yr	5491	1996	38s
Tuition, 2-year public college/university, in state	yr	1031	1996	38s
Tuition, 4-year private college/university, in state	yr	12449	1996	38s
Tuition, 4-year public college/university	yr	2221	1996	38s
Energy and Fuels				
Electricity	KWh	0.09	7/01	11r
Electricity	500 KWhs	47.29	7/01	11r
Energy, combined forms, 2400 sq ft	mos	99.64	12/00	5c
Fuel oil #2	gal	1.43	7/01	11r
Fuel oil and other fuels, expenditures on	yr	45	1999	30r
Gas, cooking, winter, 10 therms	mos	11.27	2/96	98c
Gas, cooking, winter, 30 therms	mos	24.02	2/96	98c
Gas, cooking, winter, 50 therms	mos	36.77	2/96	98c
Gas, heating, winter, average use	mos	91.46	2/96	98c
Gas, natural, commercial rate	1000 cf	8.75	11/00	88s
Gas, regular unleaded, cash, self-service	gal	1.37	12/00	5c
Gasoline, all types	gal	1.60	7/01	11r
Gasoline, unleaded midgrade	gal	1.65	7/01	11r
Gasoline, unleaded premium	gal	1.74	7/01	11r
Natural gas, expenditures on	yr	164	1999	30r
Utility (piped) gas, therm		1.01	7/01	11r
Utility (piped) gas, 40 therms		44.29	7/01	11r
Utility (piped) gas, 100 therms		97.44	7/01	11r
Entertainment				
Bowling, Saturday evening rate	line	3.13	12/00	5c
Entertainment purchases	yr	1574	1999	30r
Fees and admissions paid	yr	371	1999	30r
Monopoly game, Parker Brothers', No. 9	game	12.86	12/00	5c
Movie, first-run, Saturday, evening	adm.	6.25	12/00	5c
Reading purchases	yr	121	1999	30r
Television, radios, sound equipment, expenditures on	yr	561	1999	30r
Tennis balls, yellow, Wilson or Penn, 3	can	2.10	12/00	5c
Funerals				
Total cost of funeral		5842.28	1/99	78r
Acknowledgement cards		28.35	1/99	78r
Casket		2494.29	1/99	78r
Cosmetology, hair, other preparation		109.22	1/99	78r
Embalming		361.42	1/99	78r
Funeral at funeral home		349.20	1/99	78r
Hearse (local)		161.91	1/99	78r
Professional service charges		1116.50	1/99	78r
Service car/van		65.56	1/99	78r
Transfer of remains to funeral home		143.56	1/99	78r
Vault		785.25	1/99	78r
Visitation/viewing		227.02	1/99	78r
Groceries				
Groceries, ACCRA Index		89.00	12/00	5c
American processed cheese	lb	3.50	7/01	11r
Antibiotic ointment, Polysporin	0.5 oz	4.34	12/00	5c
Baby food, strained vegetables or fruit, lowest price	4-4.5 oz	0.30	12/00	5c
Bakery products, expenditures on	yr	261	1999	30r

Shreveport-Bossier City, LA - continued

Item	Per	Value	Date	Ref.
Groceries - continued				
Bananas	lb	0.47	7/01	11r
Bananas	lb	0.46	12/00	5c
Beans, dried, any type, all sizes	lb	0.63	7/01	11r
Beef for stew, boneless	lb	2.86	7/01	11r
Beef or hamburger, ground	lb	1.31	12/00	5c
Beef, expenditures on	yr	210	1999	30r
Bologna, all beef or mixed	lb	2.29	7/01	11r
Bread, French	lb	1.66	7/01	11r
Bread, white	loaf	0.66	12/00	5c
Bread, white, pan	lb	0.87	7/01	11r
Bread, whole wheat, pan	lb	1.38	7/01	11r
Broccoli	lb	1.04	7/01	11r
Butter, salted, grade AA, stick	lb	2.26	7/01	11r
Butter, yoghurt, cheese, etc, expenditures on	yr	170	1999	30r
Cabbage	lb	0.42	7/01	11r
Cereals and cereal products, expenditures on	yr	140	1999	30r
Cheddar cheese, natural	lb	3.75	7/01	11r
Cheese, Kraft grated Parmesan	8 oz	3.49	12/00	5c
Chicken breast, bone-in	lb	1.85	7/01	11r
Chicken legs, bone-in	lb	1.34	7/01	11r
Chicken, fresh, whole	lb	1.05	7/01	11r
Chicken, whole fryer	lb	0.81	12/00	5c
Chops, boneless,	lb	4.13	7/01	11r
Chuck roast, graded and ungraded, excl U.S. prime and choice	lb	2.35	7/01	11r
Chuck roast, U.S. choice, boneless	lb	2.67	7/01	11r
Cigarettes, Winston, Kings	carton	27.53	12/00	5c
Coffee, 100%, ground roast, all sizes	lb	2.88	7/01	11r
Coffee, instant, plain, regular, all sizes	16 oz	9.25	7/01	11r
Coffee, vacuum-packed	13 oz	2.37	12/00	5c
Cola, non diet,	2 liter	1.11	7/01	11r
Corn Flakes, Kellogg's or Post Toasties	18 oz	2.46	12/00	5c
Corn, frozen, whole kernel, lowest price	16 oz	1.00	12/00	5c
Crackers, soda, salted	lb	1.70	7/01	11r
Dairy product purchases	yr	282	1999	30r
Eggs, expenditures on	yr	32	1999	30r
Eggs, Grade A or AA	dozen	0.83	12/00	5c
Fats and oils, expenditures on	yr	79	1999	30r
Fish and seafood, expenditures on	yr	99	1999	30r
Flour, white, all purpose	lb	0.32	7/01	11r
Food (excl fruit and vegetables), eaten at home, purchases	yr	815	1999	30r
Food cooked on trips, expenditures on	yr	36	1999	30r
Food purchases	yr	4533	1999	30r
Food purchases, eaten away from home	yr	1873	1999	30r
Food purchases, food eaten at home	yr	2660	1999	30r
Fresh fruits, expenditures on	yr	128	1999	30r
Fresh milk and cream, expenditures on	yr	112	1999	30r
Fresh vegetables, expenditures on	yr	131	1999	30r
Fruit and vegetable purchases	yr	438	1999	30r
Grapefruit	lb	0.59	7/01	11r
Grapes, Thompson, seedless	lb	2.12	7/01	11r
Ground beef, 100% beef	lb	1.76	7/01	11r
Ground beef, lean and extra lean	lb	2.60	7/01	11r
Ground chuck, 100% beef	lb	2.08	7/01	11r
Ham, boneless, excl canned	lb	2.71	7/01	11r
Ham, rump or shank half, bone-in, smoked	lb	2.19	7/01	11r
Ice cream, prepackaged, bulk, regular	1/2 gal	3.93	7/01	11r
Lemons	lb	1.32	7/01	11r
Lettuce, iceberg	lb	0.76	7/01	11r
Lettuce, iceberg	head	1.09	12/00	5c
Margarine, Blue Bonnet or Parkay, stick	lb	0.73	12/00	5c
Milk, fresh, low fat,	gal	2.75	7/01	11r
Milk, fresh, whole, fortified	gal	2.97	7/01	11r
Milk, whole	1/2 gal	1.77	12/00	5c
Nonalcoholic beverages, expenditures on	yr	228	1999	30r
Orange juice, frozen concentrate	16 oz	1.95	7/01	11r
Orange juice, Minute Maid frozen	12 oz	1.51	12/00	5c
Oranges, Navel	lb	0.73	7/01	11r
Oranges, Valencia	lb	0.55	7/01	11r

Values are in dollars or fractions of dollars. In the column headed *Ref*, references are shown to sources. Each reference is followed by a letter. These refer to the geographical level for which data were reported: s=State, r=Region, and c=City or metro. The abbreviation *ex* is used to mean *except* or *excluding*; *exp* stands for *expenditures*. For other abbreviations and further explanations, please see the Introduction.

Shreveport-Bossier City, LA - continued

Item	Per	Value	Date	Ref.
Groceries				
Peaches, halves or slices, Hunt's, Del Monte, or Libby's	29 oz	1.58	12/00	5c
Peanut butter, creamy, all sizes	lb	1.83	7/01	11r
Pears, Anjou	lb	0.98	7/01	11r
Peas, green, Del Monte or Green Giant	15 oz	0.55	12/00	5c
Pork chops, center cut, bone-in	lb	3.33	7/01	11r
Pork sausage, fresh, loose	lb	2.59	7/01	11r
Pork shoulder picnic, bone-in, smoked	lb	1.12	7/01	11r
Pork, expenditures on	yr	162	1999	30r
Potato chips	16 oz	3.59	7/01	11r
Potatoes, frozen, french fried	lb	1.00	7/01	11r
Potatoes, white or red	10 lb	2.70	12/00	5c
Potatoes, white, all types	lb	0.44	7/01	11r
Poultry, expenditures on	yr	137	1999	30r
Processed fruits, expenditures on	yr	97	1999	30r
Processed vegetables, expenditures on	yr	82	1999	30r
Rice, white, long grain, uncooked	lb	0.51	7/01	11r
Round roast, graded and ungraded, excl U.S. prime and choice	lb	2.96	7/01	11r
Round steak, graded and ungraded, excl U.S. prime and choice	lb	3.11	7/01	11r
Sausage, Jimmy Dean/Owens pork	lb	2.83	12/00	5c
Shortening, vegetable, Crisco	3 lb	2.75	12/00	5c
Sirloin steak, graded and ungraded, excl U.S. prime and choice	lb	4.23	7/01	11r
Soft drink, Coca Cola, ex deposit	2 liter	1.01	12/00	5c
Spaghetti and macaroni	lb	0.78	7/01	11r
Steak, round, U.S. choice, boneless	lb	3.56	7/01	11r
Steak, sirloin, U.S. choice, boneless	lb	5.65	7/01	11r
Steak, T-bone	lb	6.43	12/00	5c
Strawberries, dry pint	12 oz	1.50	7/01	11r
Sugar and other sweets, expenditures on	yr	99	1999	30r
Sugar, cane or beet	4 lbs	1.35	12/00	5c
Sugar, white, 33-80 ounce package	lb	0.39	7/01	11r
Sugar, white, all sizes	lb	0.42	7/01	11r
Tobacco products and smoking supplies purchases	yr	288	1999	30r
Tomatoes, field grown	lb	1.43	7/01	11r
Tomatoes, Hunt's or Del Monte	14.5 oz	0.80	12/00	5c
Tuna, chunk, light	6 oz	0.53	12/00	5c
Tuna, light, chunk	lb	1.77	7/01	11r
Turkey, frozen, whole	lb	1.05	7/01	11r
Goods and Services				
Miscellaneous goods and services, ACCRA Index		97.50	12/00	5c
B&B Japanese maple (acer japonicum)	gal	79.98-99.00	4/00	93r
Boxwood (buxus)	2 gal	12.98-18.99	4/00	93r
Daylilly (hemerocallis)	gal	7.96-11.00	4/00	93r
Flat of annuals		13.99-27.99	4/00	93r
Fountain grass (pennisetum)	gal	6.96-9.00	4/00	93r
Hanging basket (10 in)		9.99-24.99	4/00	93r
Hardy geranium (geranium)	gal	5.96-8.00	4/00	93r
Hosta (hosta)	gal	8.96-12.99	4/00	93r
Lilac (syrubga vulgaris)	2 gal	13.00-19.99	4/00	93r
Rhododendron (rhododendron)	2 gal	12.98-29.99	4/00	93r
Sage (salvia)	gal	5.96-8.00	4/00	93r
Wintercreeper euonymus (euonymus fortunei)	2 gal	13.00-18.99	4/00	93r
Hunting license	yr	15.00	4/01	34s

Shreveport-Bossier City, LA - continued

Item	Per	Value	Date	Ref.
Health Care				
Health care, ACCRA Index		89.80	12/00	5c
Cardiac catheterization, ave hospital/physician charges		15650	1998	77s
Childbirth, Cesarean delivery		11587	1997	13r
Childbirth, vaginal delivery		6725	1997	13r
Dentist's fee, adult teeth cleaning and periodic oral exam	visit	62.00	12/00	5c
Doctor's fee, routine exam, established patient	visit	52.00	12/00	5c
Drugs, expenditures on	yr	399	1999	30r
Health care purchases	yr	1971	1999	30r
Health insurance expenditures	yr	933	1999	30r
Hospital care, private room	day	446.60	12/00	5c
Hysterectomy, laproscopically-assisted, ave hospital/physician charges		14600	1998	76s
Hysterectomy, vaginal, ave hospital and physician charges		10520	1998	76s
Medicaid dispensing fee		5.77	1999	87s
Medical services expenditures	yr	547	1999	30r
Medical supplies, expenditures on	yr	91	1999	30r
Household Goods				
Dishwashing powder, Cascade	50 oz	2.80	12/00	5c
Floor coverings, expenditures on	yr	44	1999	30r
Furniture, expenditures on	yr	335	1999	30r
Household furnishings and equipment purchases	yr	1328	1999	30r
Household textiles, expenditures on	yr	89	1999	30r
Laundry and cleaning supplies, expenditures on	yr	113	1999	30r
Tissues, facial, Kleenex brand	175	1.20	12/00	5c
Housing				
Housing, ACCRA Index		85.90	12/00	5c
Home, 2200 sq ft, 4-br, 2-bath, 2-car garage, average		183375	2000	47c
Home price, existing, ave		160100	10/00	90r
Home value, median		108000	2001	53s
House, 2400 sq ft, 8000 sq ft lot, new, urban, utilities	total	180000	12/00	5c
House payment, principal and interest, 25% down payment	mos	982	12/00	5c
Household operation expenditures	yr	553	1999	30r
Housekeeping supplies purchases	yr	473	1999	30r
Housing, expenditures on	yr	10303	1999	30r
Maintenance, repairs, insurance expenditures	yr	699	1999	30r
Monthly rental value of owned home	mos	505	1999	30r
Owned dwellings, expenditures own	yr	3465	1999	30r
Rent expenditures	yr	1641	1999	30r
Rent, apartment, 2 br, 1 1/2-2 baths, unfurn, 950 sq ft, water	mos	557	12/00	5c
Rental unit, 1 bedroom, with utilities	mos	392	4/01	41c
Rental unit, 2 bedroom, with utilities	mos	492	4/01	41c
Rental unit, 3 bedroom, with utilities	mos	658	4/01	41c
Rental unit, 4 bedroom, with utilities	mos	808	4/01	41c
Shelter, expenditures on	yr	5467	1999	30r
Insurance and Pensions				
Auto insurance premium	yr	965.15	1999	57s
Life and other personal insurance purchases	yr	414	1999	30r
Pensions and Social Security, expenditures on	yr	2635	1999	30r
Personal insurance and pensions, expenditures on	yr	3048	1999	30r
Legal Fees				
Divorce, filing fee		162.00	4/01	35s
Driver's license fee	renew	12.50	1999	48s
Driver's license fee	orig	18.00	1999	48s
Fishing license	yr	9.50	4/01	34s

Values are in dollars or fractions of dollars. In the column headed *Ref*, references are shown to sources. Each reference is followed by a letter. These refer to the geographical level for which data were reported: s=State, r=Region, and c=City or metro. The abbreviation *ex* is used to mean *except* or *excluding*; *exp* stands for *expenditures*. For other abbreviations and further explanations, please see the Introduction.

Shreveport-Bossier City, LA - continued

Item	Per	Value	Date	Ref.
Personal Goods				
Personal care products and services purchases	yr	393	1999	30r
Shampoo, Alberto VO5	15 oz	1.14	12/00	5c
Toothpaste, Crest or Colgate	6-7 oz	2.43	12/00	5c
Personal Services				
Dry cleaning, man's 2-pc suit		7.36	12/00	5c
Man's haircut, barbershop, no styling		8.00	12/00	5c
Personal services, household, expenditures on	yr	258	1999	30r
Woman's shampoo, trim, blow-dry, no style-change		25.60	12/00	5c
Pets				
Pets, toys, and playground equipment, expenditures on	yr	306	1999	30r
Restaurant Food				
Chicken, fried, thigh and drumstick, KFC/ Church's		2.23	12/00	5c
Hamburger with cheese, McDonald's	1/4 lb	2.13	12/00	5c
Pizza, Pizza Hut or Pizza Inn	11-12 in	8.99	12/00	5c
Taxes				
Federal income taxes paid	yr	2047	1999	30r
Personal taxes, expenditures on	yr	2554	1999	30r
Property taxes paid	yr	726	1999	30r
State and local income taxes paid	yr	363	1999	30r
Transportation				
Transportation, ACCRA Index		91.20	12/00	5c
Cars and trucks, new, expenditures on	yr	1648	1999	30r
Cars and trucks, used, expenditures on	yr	1651	1999	30r
Diesel at the pump	gal	1.19	10/99	73s
Gasoline and motor oil purchases	yr	1052	1999	30r
Gasoline before-tax price (cents)	gal	102.70	10/00	43s
Maintenance and repair expenditures	yr	621	1999	30r
Public transportation, expenditures on	yr	298	1999	30r
Tire balance, computer or spin balance, front	wheel	7.09	12/00	5c
Transportation purchases	yr	6738	1999	30r
Vehicle expenses, miscellaneous, purchases	yr	2033	1999	30r
Vehicle insurance payments	yr	696	1999	30r
Vehicle purchases (net outlay)	yr	3354	1999	30r
Vehicle rental, lease expenditures	yr	352	1999	30r
Utilities				
Utilities, ACCRA Index		90.40	12/00	5c
Electrical bill, average	mos	87.50	9/00	9s
Electricity, 2400 sq ft, new home	mos	99.64	12/00	5c
Electricity, expenditures on	yr	1115	1999	30r
Electricity, summer, 250 KWh	mos	18.61	2/96	97c
Electricity, summer, 500 KWh	mos	33.22	2/96	97c
Electricity, summer, 750 KWh	mos	47.83	2/96	97c
Electricity, summer, 1000 KWh	mos	62.43	2/96	97c
Electricity cost, average	KWh	6.35	9/00	9s
Water and other public services, expenditures on	yr	298	1999	30r
Weddings				
Wedding (national average cost)		19936	2000	33r
Attendants' gifts		321	1998	33r
Bridal attendants' apparel (5 persons)		824	2000	33r
Bride's headpiece/veil		173	1998	33r
Bride's wedding dress		859	1998	33r
Clergy, religious facility fee		242	1998	33r
Engagement ring		3177	1998	33r
Flowers		789	1998	33r
Groom's formalwear rental		99	2000	33r
Limousine		410	1998	33r
Marriage license cost		25.00	4/01	35s
Men's formalwear (ushers, best man)		469	2000	33r
Mother of bride apparel		241	2000	33r
Music		866	1998	33r
Photography and videography		1368	1998	33r
Rehearsal dinner		728	1998	33r

Shreveport-Bossier City, LA - continued

Item	Per	Value	Date	Ref.
Weddings - continued				
Wedding invitations and announcements		341	1998	33r
Wedding reception		7968	2000	33r
Wedding rings (bride and groom)		1060	1998	33r

Sioux City, IA

Item	Per	Value	Date	Ref.
Average annual expenditures	yr	35369	1999	30r
Alcoholic Beverages				
Alcoholic beverage purchases	yr	304	1999	30r
Malt beverages, all types, all sizes, any origin	16 oz	0.93	7/01	11r
Wine, red and white table, all sizes, any origin	liter	7.04	7/01	11r
Appliances				
Major appliances, expenditures on	yr	165	1999	30r
Small appliances, housewares, expenditures on	yr	90	1999	30r
Banking and Money				
Mortgage interest and charges paid	yr	2277	1999	30r
Mortgage principal paid on owned property	yr	1230	1999	30r
Vehicle finance charges paid	yr	328	1999	30r
Charity				
Cash contributions, expenditures	yr	1126	1999	30r
Child Care				
Child raising cost, total, age 0-2	yr	7890	1999	60r
Child raising cost, total, age 3-5	yr	8130	1999	60r
Child raising cost, total, age 6-8	yr	8170	1999	60r
Child raising cost, total, age 9-11	yr	8190	1999	60r
Child raising cost, total, age 12-14	yr	8890	1999	60r
Child raising cost, total, age 15-17	yr	9050	1999	60r
Child's child care and education, age 0-2	yr	1240	1999	60r
Child's child care and education, age 3-5	yr	1370	1999	60r
Child's child care and education, age 6-8	yr	880	1999	60r
Child's child care and education, age 9-11	yr	570	1999	60r
Child's child care and education, age 12-14	yr	420	1999	60r
Child's child care and education, age 15-17	yr	720	1999	60r
Child's clothing, age 0-2	yr	410	1999	60r
Child's clothing, age 3-5	yr	400	1999	60r
Child's clothing, age 6-8	yr	450	1999	60r
Child's clothing, age 9-11	yr	500	1999	60r
Child's clothing, age 12-14	yr	840	1999	60r
Child's clothing, age 15-17	yr	740	1999	60r
Child's food, age 0-2	yr	960	1999	60r
Child's food, age 3-5	yr	1120	1999	60r
Child's food, age 6-8	yr	1430	1999	60r
Child's food, age 9-11	yr	1710	1999	60r
Child's food, age 12-14	yr	1710	1999	60r
Child's food, age 15-17	yr	1920	1999	60r
Child's health care, age 0-2	yr	520	1999	60r
Child's health care, age 3-5	yr	500	1999	60r
Child's health care, age 6-8	yr	570	1999	60r
Child's health care, age 9-11	yr	610	1999	60r
Child's health care, age 12-14	yr	630	1999	60r
Child's health care, age 15-17	yr	650	1999	60r
Child's housing, age 0-2	yr	2860	1999	60r
Child's housing, age 3-5	yr	2840	1999	60r
Child's housing, age 6-8	yr	2800	1999	60r
Child's housing, age 9-11	yr	2650	1999	60r
Child's housing, age 12-14	yr	2840	1999	60r
Child's housing, age 15-17	yr	2440	1999	60r
Child's personal care, reading, age 0-2	yr	880	1999	60r
Child's personal care, reading, age 3-5	yr	900	1999	60r
Child's personal care, reading, age 6-8	yr	930	1999	60r
Child's personal care, reading, age 9-11	yr	970	1999	60r
Child's personal care, reading, age 12-14	yr	1150	1999	60r
Child's personal care, reading, age 15-17	yr	920	1999	60r
Clothing				
Apparel and services purchases	yr	1607	1999	30r
Boys, 2 to 15, expenditures on	yr	91	1999	30r

Values are in dollars or fractions of dollars. In the column headed *Ref*, references are shown to sources. Each reference is followed by a letter. These refer to the geographical level for which data were reported: s=State, r=Region, and c=City or metro. The abbreviation *ex* is used to mean *except* or *excluding*; *exp* stands for *expenditures*. For other abbreviations and further explanations, please see the Introduction.

Item	Per	Value	Date	Ref.
Clothing				
Children under 2, expenditures on	yr	59	1999	30r
Footwear, expenditures on	yr	285	1999	30r
Girls, 2 to 15, expenditures on	yr	116	1999	30r
Men and boys, expenditures on	yr	433	1999	30r
Men, 16 and over, expenditures on	yr	341	1999	30r
Women, 16 and over, expenditures on	yr	490	1999	30r
Communications				
Phone line, single, business, field visit	inst.	50.00	12/97	17s
Phone line, single, business, no field visit	inst.	50.00	12/97	17s
Phone line, single, residence, field visit	inst.	35.00	12/97	17s
Phone line, single, residence, no field visit	inst.	35.00	12/97	17s
Postage and stationery, expenditures on	yr	140	1999	30r
Postal rate, express mail, up to half-pound		12.45	7/01	108r
Postal rate, letter, first class, first ounce		0.34	7/01	108r
Postal rate, letter, two ounces		0.57	7/01	108r
Postal rate, post card		0.21	7/01	108r
Postal rate, priority mail, two pounds		3.95	7/01	108r
Postal rate, priority mail, up to one pound		3.50	7/01	108r
Telephone bill, business, basic rate	mos	30.15	12/97	18c
Telephone bill, residential, basic rate	mos	12.05	12/97	18c
Telephone services, expenditures on	yr	830	1999	30r
Education				
Board, 4-year private college/university	yr	2138	1996	38s
Board, 4-year public college/university	yr	1688	1996	38s
Education expenditures	yr	583	1999	30r
Room, 4-year private college/university	yr	1864	1996	38s
Room, 4-year public college/university	yr	1693	1996	38s
Total cost, 4-year private college/university	yr	15934	1996	38s
Total cost, 4-year public college/university	yr	5945	1996	38s
Tuition, 2-year public college/university, in state	yr	1782	1996	38s
Tuition, 4-year private college/university, in state	yr	11932	1996	38s
Tuition, 4-year public college/university	yr	2565	1996	38s
Energy and Fuels				
Electricity	500 KWhs	46.59	7/01	11r
Fuel oil #2	gal	1.27	7/01	11r
Fuel oil and other fuels, expenditures on	yr	68	1999	30r
Gas, natural, commercial rate	1000 cf	7.18	11/00	88s
Gasoline, unleaded midgrade	gal	1.79	7/01	11r
Gasoline, unleaded premium	gal	1.86	7/01	11r
Gasoline, unleaded regular	gal	1.58	7/01	11r
Natural gas, expenditures on	yr	389	1999	30r
Utility (piped) gas, therm		0.81	7/01	11r
Utility (piped) gas, 40 therms		38.01	7/01	11r
Utility (piped) gas, 100 therms		81.75	7/01	11r
Entertainment				
Entertainment purchases	yr	1984	1999	30r
Fees and admissions paid	yr	444	1999	30r
Television, radios, sound equipment, expenditures on	yr	580	1999	30r
Funerals				
Cosmetology, hair, other preparation		178.32	1/99	78r
Embalming		408.19	1/99	78r
Funeral at funeral home		362.13	1/99	78r
Professional service charges		1375.51	1/99	78r
Transfer of remains to funeral home		155.92	1/99	78r
Visitation/viewing		294.38	1/99	78r
Groceries				
Bacon, sliced	lb	3.15	7/01	11r
Bakery products, expenditures on	yr	281	1999	30r
Bananas	lb	0.48	7/01	11r
Beans, dried, any type, all sizes	lb	0.61	7/01	11r
Beef for stew, boneless	lb	3.08	7/01	11r
Beef, expenditures on	yr	217	1999	30r
Bologna, all beef or mixed	lb	2.52	7/01	11r
Bread, white, pan	lb	1.06	7/01	11r
Broccoli	lb	0.91	7/01	11r

Item	Per	Value	Date	Ref.
Groceries - continued				
Butter, salted, grade AA, stick	lb	3.04	7/01	11r
Butter, yoghurt, cheese, etc, expenditures on	yr	183	1999	30r
Cereals and bakery product purchases	yr	430	1999	30r
Cereals and cereal products, expenditures on	yr	149	1999	30r
Chicken, fresh, whole	lb	1.07	7/01	11r
Chops, boneless	lb	3.64	7/01	11r
Chuck roast, U.S. choice, boneless	lb	2.47	7/01	11r
Coffee, 100%, ground roast, all sizes	lb	2.69	7/01	11r
Cookies, chocolate chip	lb	2.87	7/01	11r
Dairy product purchases	yr	304	1999	30r
Eggs, expenditures on	yr	26	1999	30r
Eggs, grade A, large	dozen	0.88	7/01	11r
Fats and oils, expenditures on	yr	75	1999	30r
Fish and seafood, expenditures on	yr	72	1999	30r
Food (excl fruit and vegetables), eaten at home, purchases	yr	887	1999	30r
Food cooked on trips, expenditures on	yr	44	1999	30r
Food purchases	yr	4802	1999	30r
Food purchases, eaten away from home	yr	2069	1999	30r
Food purchases, food eaten at home	yr	2733	1999	30r
Fresh fruits, expenditures on	yr	138	1999	30r
Fresh milk and cream, expenditures on	yr	120	1999	30r
Fresh vegetables, expenditures on	yr	126	1999	30r
Grapefruit	lb	0.66	7/01	11r
Grapes, Thompson, seedless	lb	1.64	7/01	11r
Ground beef, 100% beef	lb	1.64	7/01	11r
Ground beef, lean and extra lean	lb	2.16	7/01	11r
Ground chuck, 100% beef	lb	2.13	7/01	11r
Ham, boneless, excl canned	lb	2.62	7/01	11r
Ice cream, prepackaged, bulk, regular	1/2 gal	3.35	7/01	11r
Lemons	lb	1.19	7/01	11r
Lettuce, iceberg	lb	0.73	7/01	11r
Margarine, soft, tubs	lb	0.89	7/01	11r
Meats, poultry, fish, and egg purchases	yr	671	1999	30r
Milk, fresh, whole, fortified	gal	2.71	7/01	11r
Nonalcoholic beverages, expenditures on	yr	239	1999	30r
Oranges, Navel	lb	0.80	7/01	11r
Oranges, Valencia	lb	0.66	7/01	11r
Pears, Anjou	lb	0.93	7/01	11r
Pork chops, center cut, bone-in	lb	3.63	7/01	11r
Pork, expenditures on	yr	150	1999	30r
Potato chips	16 oz	3.52	7/01	11r
Potatoes, frozen, french fried	lb	1.08	7/01	11r
Potatoes, white, all types	lb	0.33	7/01	11r
Poultry, expenditures on	yr	108	1999	30r
Processed fruits, expenditures on	yr	98	1999	30r
Processed vegetables, expenditures on	yr	80	1999	30r
Round roast, U.S. choice, boneless	lb	3.07	7/01	11r
Round steak, graded and ungraded, excl U.S. prime and choice	lb	3.41	7/01	11r
Shortening, vegetable oil blends	lb	1.13	7/01	11r
Spaghetti and macaroni	lb	0.80	7/01	11r
Steak, round, U.S. choice, boneless	lb	3.23	7/01	11r
Steak, T-bone, U.S. choice, bone-in	lb	6.68	7/01	11r
Strawberries, dry pint	12 oz	1.32	7/01	11r
Sugar and other sweets, expenditures on	yr	114	1999	30r
Sugar, white, 33-80 ounce package	lb	0.42	7/01	11r
Sugar, white, all sizes	lb	0.43	7/01	11r
Tobacco products and smoking supplies purchases	yr	331	1999	30r
Tomatoes, field grown	lb	1.46	7/01	11r
Tuna, light, chunk	lb	1.80	7/01	11r
Turkey, frozen, whole	lb	1.15	7/01	11r
Goods and Services				
B&B Japanese maple (acer japonicum)	gal	29.99-169.99	4/00	93r
Boxwood (buxus)	2 gal	18.99-39.99	4/00	93r
Daylily (hemerocallis)	gal	4.99-25.00	4/00	93r

Values are in dollars or fractions of dollars. In the column headed *Ref*, references are shown to sources. Each reference is followed by a letter. These refer to the geographical level for which data were reported: s=State, r=Region, and c=City or metro. The abbreviation *ex* is used to mean *except* or *excluding*; *exp* stands for *expenditures*. For other abbreviations and further explanations, please see the Introduction.

Sioux City, IA - continued

Item	Per	Value	Date	Ref.
Goods and Services				
Flat of annuals		11.98-24.99	4/00	93r
Fountain grass (pennisetum)	gal	5.98-12.98	4/00	93r
Hanging basket (10 in)		12.99-27.99	4/00	93r
Hardy geranium (geranium)	gal	7.99-9.99	4/00	93r
Hosta (hosta)	gal	6.00-25.00	4/00	93r
Lilac (syrubga vulgaris)	2 gal	14.99-24.99	4/00	93r
Miscellaneous purchases	yr	865	1999	30r
Rhododendron (rhododendron)	2 gal	23.98-42.99	4/00	93r
Sage (salvia)	gal	6.00-9.99	4/00	93r
Wintercreeper euonymus (euonymus fortunei)	2 gal	16.00-169.99	4/00	93r
Hunting license	yr	16.00	4/01	34s
Health Care				
Cardiac catheterization, ave hospital/ physician charges		8810	1998	77s
Childbirth, Cesarean delivery		10722	1997	13r
Childbirth, vaginal delivery		6223	1997	13r
Drugs, expenditures on	yr	394	1999	30r
Health care purchases	yr	2048	1999	30r
Health insurance expenditures	yr	978	1999	30r
Hysterectomy, laproscopically-assisted, ave hospital/physician charges		8620	1998	76s
Hysterectomy, vaginal, ave hospital and physician charges		6630	1998	76s
Medicaid dispensing fee		4.10-6.38	1999	87s
Medical services expenditures	yr	554	1999	30r
Medical supplies, expenditures on	yr	122	1999	30r
Plastic surgery, breast augmentation		3184	2000	7r
Plastic surgery, breast lift		3585	2000	7r
Plastic surgery, facelift		4999	2000	7r
Plastic surgery, hair transplantation		3105	2000	7r
Plastic surgery, lip augmentation		1290	2000	7r
Plastic surgery, lower body lift		8135	2000	7r
Plastic surgery, thigh lift		3839	2000	7r
Household Goods				
Floor coverings, expenditures on	yr	52	1999	30r
Furniture, expenditures on	yr	344	1999	30r
Household furnishings and equipment purchases	yr	1475	1999	30r
Household textiles, expenditures on	yr	109	1999	30r
Laundry and cleaning supplies, expenditures on	yr	134	1999	30r
Housing				
Home, 2200 sq ft, 4-br, 2-bath, 2-car garage, average		108000	2000	47c
Home price, existing, ave		144400	10/00	90r
Home value, median		100000	2001	53s
Household operation expenditures	yr	542	1999	30r
Housekeeping supplies purchases	yr	508	1999	30r
Lodging expenditures	yr	430	1999	30r
Maintenance, repairs, insurance expenditures	yr	853	1999	30r
Monthly rental value of owned home	mos	547	1999	30r
Owned dwellings, expenditures own	yr	4282	1999	30r
Rent expenditures	yr	1558	1999	30r
Rental unit, 1 bedroom, with utilities	mos	419	4/01	41c
Rental unit, 2 bedroom, with utilities	mos	522	4/01	41c
Rental unit, 3 bedroom, with utilities	mos	651	4/01	41c
Rental unit, 4 bedroom, with utilities	mos	744	4/01	41c
Shelter, expenditures on	yr	6270	1999	30r

Sioux City, IA - continued

Item	Per	Value	Date	Ref.
Insurance and Pensions				
Auto insurance premium	yr	520.76	1999	57s
Life and other personal insurance purchases	yr	387	1999	30r
Pensions and Social Security, expenditures on	yr	2968	1999	30r
Legal Fees				
Divorce, filing fee		110.00	4/01	35s
Driver's license fee	orig	16.00	1999	48s
Driver's license fee	renew	16.00	1999	48s
Personal Goods				
Personal care products and services purchases	yr	385	1999	30r
Personal Services				
Personal services, household, expenditures on	yr	300	1999	30r
Pets				
Pets, toys, and playground equipment, expenditures on	yr	375	1999	30r
Taxes				
Federal income taxes paid	yr	2326	1999	30r
Personal taxes, expenditures on	yr	3223	1999	30r
Property taxes paid	yr	1152	1999	30r
State and local income taxes paid	yr	753	1999	30r
Transportation				
Cars and trucks, new, expenditures on	yr	1280	1999	30r
Cars and trucks, used, expenditures on	yr	1763	1999	30r
Diesel at the pump	gal	1.25	10/99	73s
Gasoline and motor oil purchases	yr	1036	1999	30r
Gasoline before-tax price (cents)	gal	112.30	10/00	43s
Maintenance and repair expenditures	yr	594	1999	30r
Public transportation, expenditures on	yr	341	1999	30r
Transportation purchases	yr	6617	1999	30r
Vehicle expenses, miscellaneous, purchases	yr	2159	1999	30r
Vehicle insurance payments	yr	701	1999	30r
Vehicle purchases (net outlay)	yr	3081	1999	30r
Vehicle rental, lease expenditures	yr	536	1999	30r
Utilities				
Electrical bill, average	mos	67.25	9/00	9s
Electricity, expenditures on	yr	841	1999	30r
Electricity, summer, 250 KWh	mos	26.21	2/96	97c
Electricity, summer, 500 KWh	mos	43.76	2/96	97c
Electricity, summer, 750 KWh	mos	61.30	2/96	97c
Electricity, summer, 1000 KWh	mos	78.85	2/96	97c
Electricity cost, average	KWh	5.90	9/00	9s
Utilities, fuels, and public services purchased	yr	2401	1999	30r
Water and other public services, expenditures on	yr	273	1999	30r
Weddings				
Wedding (national average cost)		19936	2000	33r
Wedding (regional average total cost)		16195	1997	110r
Attendants' gifts		321	1998	33r
Bridal attendants' apparel (5 persons)		824	2000	33r
Bride's headpiece/veil		173	1998	33r
Bride's wedding dress		859	1998	33r
Clergy, religious facility fee		242	1998	33r
Engagement ring		3177	1998	33r
Flowers		789	1998	33r
Groom's formalwear rental		99	2000	33r
Limousine		410	1998	33r
Marriage license cost		30.00	4/01	35s
Men's formalwear (ushers, best man)		469	2000	33r
Mother of bride apparel		241	2000	33r
Music		866	1998	33r
Photography and videography		1368	1998	33r
Rehearsal dinner		728	1998	33r
Wedding invitations and announcements		341	1998	33r
Wedding reception		7968	2000	33r
Wedding rings (bride and groom)		1060	1998	33r

Values are in dollars or fractions of dollars. In the column headed *Ref*, references are shown to sources. Each reference is followed by a letter. These refer to the geographical level for which data were reported: s=State, r=Region, and c=City or metro. The abbreviation *ex* is used to mean *except* or *excluding*; *exp* stands for *expenditures*. For other abbreviations and further explanations, please see the Introduction.

Sioux Falls, SD

Item	Per	Value	Date	Ref.
Average annual expenditures	yr	35369	1999	30r
Composite, ACCRA index		99.70	3/01	4c
Alcoholic Beverages				
Alcoholic beverage purchases	yr	304	1999	30r
Beer, Heineken, 12-oz, ex deposit	6	6.79	3/01	4c
J & B Scotch	750-ml	18.19	3/01	4c
Malt beverages, all types, all sizes, any origin	16 oz	0.93	7/01	11r
Wine, Livingston or Gallo, Chablis blanc	1.5 liter	5.97	3/01	4c
Wine, red and white table, all sizes, any origin	liter	7.04	7/01	11r
Appliances				
Appliance repair, service call, washing machine	min lab chg	45.00	3/01	4c
Major appliances, expenditures on	yr	165	1999	30r
Small appliances, housewares, expenditures on	yr	90	1999	30r
Banking and Money				
Mortgage interest and charges paid	yr	2277	1999	30r
Mortgage principal paid on owned property	yr	1230	1999	30r
Mortgage rate, incl. points and orig. fee, 30-yr. conv. fixed or ARM	mos	6.93	3/01	4c
Vehicle finance charges paid	yr	328	1999	30r
Charity				
Cash contributions, expenditures	yr	1126	1999	30r
Child Care				
Child raising cost, total, age 0-2	yr	7890	1999	60r
Child raising cost, total, age 3-5	yr	8130	1999	60r
Child raising cost, total, age 6-8	yr	8170	1999	60r
Child raising cost, total, age 9-11	yr	8190	1999	60r
Child raising cost, total, age 12-14	yr	8890	1999	60r
Child raising cost, total, age 15-17	yr	9050	1999	60r
Child's child care and education, age 0-2	yr	1240	1999	60r
Child's child care and education, age 3-5	yr	1370	1999	60r
Child's child care and education, age 6-8	yr	880	1999	60r
Child's child care and education, age 9-11	yr	570	1999	60r
Child's child care and education, age 12-14	yr	420	1999	60r
Child's child care and education, age 15-17	yr	720	1999	60r
Child's clothing, age 0-2	yr	410	1999	60r
Child's clothing, age 3-5	yr	400	1999	60r
Child's clothing, age 6-8	yr	450	1999	60r
Child's clothing, age 9-11	yr	500	1999	60r
Child's clothing, age 12-14	yr	840	1999	60r
Child's clothing, age 15-17	yr	740	1999	60r
Child's food, age 0-2	yr	960	1999	60r
Child's food, age 3-5	yr	1120	1999	60r
Child's food, age 6-8	yr	1430	1999	60r
Child's food, age 9-11	yr	1710	1999	60r
Child's food, age 12-14	yr	1710	1999	60r
Child's food, age 15-17	yr	1920	1999	60r
Child's health care, age 0-2	yr	520	1999	60r
Child's health care, age 3-5	yr	500	1999	60r
Child's health care, age 6-8	yr	570	1999	60r
Child's health care, age 9-11	yr	610	1999	60r
Child's health care, age 12-14	yr	630	1999	60r
Child's health care, age 15-17	yr	650	1999	60r
Child's housing, age 0-2	yr	2860	1999	60r
Child's housing, age 3-5	yr	2840	1999	60r
Child's housing, age 6-8	yr	2800	1999	60r
Child's housing, age 9-11	yr	2650	1999	60r
Child's housing, age 12-14	yr	2840	1999	60r
Child's housing, age 15-17	yr	2440	1999	60r
Child's personal care, reading, age 0-2	yr	880	1999	60r
Child's personal care, reading, age 3-5	yr	900	1999	60r
Child's personal care, reading, age 6-8	yr	930	1999	60r
Child's personal care, reading, age 9-11	yr	970	1999	60r
Child's personal care, reading, age 12-14	yr	1150	1999	60r
Child's personal care, reading, age 15-17	yr	920	1999	60r
Clothing				
Apparel and services purchases	yr	1607	1999	30r
Boys' brief, cotton	3	4.17	3/01	4c

Sioux Falls, SD - continued

Item	Per	Value	Date	Ref.
Clothing - continued				
Boys, 2 to 15, expenditures on	yr	91	1999	30r
Children under 2, expenditures on	yr	59	1999	30r
Footwear, expenditures on	yr	285	1999	30r
Girls, 2 to 15, expenditures on	yr	116	1999	30r
Men and boys, expenditures on	yr	433	1999	30r
Men, 16 and over, expenditures on	yr	341	1999	30r
Shirt, man's dress shirt		27.39	3/01	4c
Slacks, man's "No Wrinkles" khaki		38.19	3/01	4c
Women, 16 and over, expenditures on	yr	490	1999	30r
Communications				
Newspaper subscription, daily and Sunday delivery	mos	15.22	3/01	4c
Phone line, single, business, field visit	inst.	47.00	12/97	17s
Phone line, single, business, no field visit	inst.	47.00	12/97	17s
Phone line, single, residence, field visit	inst.	25.00	12/97	17s
Phone line, single, residence, no field visit	inst.	25.00	12/97	17s
Postage and stationery, expenditures on	yr	140	1999	30r
Postal rate, express mail, up to half-pound		12.45	7/01	108r
Postal rate, letter, first class, first ounce		0.34	7/01	108r
Postal rate, letter, two ounces		0.57	7/01	108r
Postal rate, post card		0.21	7/01	108r
Postal rate, priority mail, two pounds		3.95	7/01	108r
Postal rate, priority mail, up to one pound		3.50	7/01	108r
Telephone bill, business, basic rate	mos	38.40	12/97	18c
Telephone bill, family of three	mos	26.92	3/01	4c
Telephone bill, residential, basic rate	mos	18.25	12/97	18c
Telephone services, expenditures on	yr	830	1999	30r
Education				
Board, 4-year private college/university	yr	2374	1996	38s
Board, 4-year public college/university	yr	1730	1996	38s
Education expenditures	yr	583	1999	30r
Room, 4-year private college/university	yr	1541	1996	38s
Room, 4-year public college/university	yr	1247	1996	38s
Total cost, 4-year private college/university	yr	13039	1996	38s
Total cost, 4-year public college/university	yr	5619	1996	38s
Tuition, 2-year public college/university, in state	yr	3430	1996	38s
Tuition, 4-year private college/university, in state	yr	9123	1996	38s
Tuition, 4-year public college/university	yr	2642	1996	38s
Energy and Fuels				
Electricity	500 KWhs	46.59	7/01	11r
Energy, combined forms, 2400 sq ft	mos	170.43	3/01	4c
Energy, exc. electricity, 2400 sq ft	mos	115.74	3/01	4c
Fuel oil #2	gal	1.27	7/01	11r
Fuel oil and other fuels, expenditures on	yr	68	1999	30r
Gas, cooking, winter, 10 therms	mos	6.79	2/96	98c
Gas, cooking, winter, 30 therms	mos	16.17	2/96	98c
Gas, cooking, winter, 50 therms	mos	25.56	2/96	98c
Gas, heating, winter, average use	mos	78.63	2/96	98c
Gas, regular unleaded, cash, self-service	gal	1.46	3/01	4c
Gasoline, unleaded midgrade	gal	1.79	7/01	11r
Gasoline, unleaded premium	gal	1.86	7/01	11r
Gasoline, unleaded regular	gal	1.58	7/01	11r
Natural gas, expenditures on	yr	389	1999	30r
Utility (piped) gas, therm		0.81	7/01	11r
Utility (piped) gas, 40 therms		38.01	7/01	11r
Utility (piped) gas, 100 therms		81.75	7/01	11r
Entertainment				
Bowling, Saturday evening rate	line	2.61	3/01	4c
Entertainment purchases	yr	1984	1999	30r
Fees and admissions paid	yr	444	1999	30r
Monopoly game, Parker Brothers', No. 9	game	10.30	3/01	4c
Movie, first-run, Saturday, evening	adm.	6.75	3/01	4c
Television, radios, sound equipment, expenditures on	yr	580	1999	30r
Tennis balls, yellow, Wilson or Penn, 3	can	1.97	3/01	4c

Values are in dollars or fractions of dollars. In the column headed *Ref*, references are shown to sources. Each reference is followed by a letter. These refer to the geographical level for which data were reported: s=State, r=Region, and c=City or metro. The abbreviation *ex* is used to mean *except* or *excluding*; *exp* stands for *expenditures*. For other abbreviations and further explanations, please see the Introduction.

Sioux Falls, SD - continued

Item	Per	Value	Date	Ref.
Funerals				
Cosmetology, hair, other preparation		178.32	1/99	78r
Embalming		408.19	1/99	78r
Funeral at funeral home		362.13	1/99	78r
Professional service charges		1375.51	1/99	78r
Transfer of remains to funeral home		155.92	1/99	78r
Visitation/viewing		294.38	1/99	78r
Groceries				
Groceries, ACCRA Index		100.20	3/01	4c
Antibiotic ointment, Polysporin	0.5 oz	4.21	3/01	4c
Baby food, strained vegetables or fruit, lowest price	4-4.5 oz	0.45	3/01	4c
Bacon, sliced	lb	3.15	7/01	11r
Bakery products, expenditures on	yr	281	1999	30r
Bananas	lb	0.47	3/01	4c
Bananas	lb	0.48	7/01	11r
Beans, dried, any type, all sizes	lb	0.61	7/01	11r
Beef for stew, boneless	lb	3.08	7/01	11r
Beef or hamburger, ground	lb	1.31	3/01	4c
Beef, expenditures on	yr	217	1999	30r
Bologna, all beef or mixed	lb	2.52	7/01	11r
Bread, white	loaf	1.06	3/01	4c
Bread, white, pan	lb	1.06	7/01	11r
Broccoli	lb	0.91	7/01	11r
Butter, salted, grade AA, stick	lb	3.04	7/01	11r
Butter, yoghurt, cheese, etc, expenditures on	yr	183	1999	30r
Cereals and bakery product purchases	yr	430	1999	30r
Cereals and cereal products, expenditures on	yr	149	1999	30r
Cheese, Kraft grated Parmesan	8 oz	4.17	3/01	4c
Chicken, fresh, whole	lb	1.07	7/01	11r
Chicken, whole fryer	lb	0.87	3/01	4c
Chops, boneless,	lb	3.64	7/01	11r
Chuck roast, U.S. choice, boneless	lb	2.47	7/01	11r
Cigarettes, Winston, Kings	carton	29.42	3/01	4c
Coffee, 100%, ground roast, all sizes	lb	2.69	7/01	11r
Coffee, vacuum-packed	13 oz	2.31	3/01	4c
Cookies, chocolate chip	lb	2.87	7/01	11r
Corn Flakes, Kellogg's or Post Toasties	18 oz	1.91	3/01	4c
Corn, frozen, whole kernel, lowest price	16 oz	1.24	3/01	4c
Dairy product purchases	yr	304	1999	30r
Eggs, expenditures on	yr	26	1999	30r
Eggs, Grade A or AA	dozen	1.18	3/01	4c
Eggs, grade A, large	dozen	0.88	7/01	11r
Fats and oils, expenditures on	yr	75	1999	30r
Fish and seafood, expenditures on	yr	72	1999	30r
Food (excl fruit and vegetables), eaten at home, purchases	yr	887	1999	30r
Food cooked on trips, expenditures on	yr	44	1999	30r
Food purchases	yr	4802	1999	30r
Food purchases, eaten away from home	yr	2069	1999	30r
Food purchases, food eaten at home	yr	2733	1999	30r
Fresh fruits, expenditures on	yr	138	1999	30r
Fresh milk and cream, expenditures on	yr	120	1999	30r
Fresh vegetables, expenditures on	yr	126	1999	30r
Grapefruit	lb	0.66	7/01	11r
Grapes, Thompson, seedless	lb	1.64	7/01	11r
Ground beef, 100% beef	lb	1.64	7/01	11r
Ground beef, lean and extra lean	lb	2.16	7/01	11r
Ground chuck, 100% beef	lb	2.13	7/01	11r
Ham, boneless, excl canned	lb	2.62	7/01	11r
Ice cream, prepackaged, bulk, regular	1/2 gal	3.35	7/01	11r
Lemons	lb	1.19	7/01	11r
Lettuce, iceberg	head	1.11	3/01	4c
Lettuce, iceberg	lb	0.73	7/01	11r
Margarine, Blue Bonnet or Parkay, stick	lb	0.76	3/01	4c
Margarine, soft, tubs	lb	0.89	7/01	11r
Meats, poultry, fish, and egg purchases	yr	671	1999	30r
Milk, fresh, whole, fortified	gal	2.71	7/01	11r
Milk, whole	1/2 gal	1.50	3/01	4c
Nonalcoholic beverages, expenditures on	yr	239	1999	30r
Orange juice, Minute Maid frozen	12 oz	1.79	3/01	4c
Oranges, Navel	lb	0.80	7/01	11r

Sioux Falls, SD - continued

Item	Per	Value	Date	Ref.
Groceries - continued				
Oranges, Valencia	lb	0.66	7/01	11r
Peaches, halves or slices, Hunt's, Del Monte, or Libby's	29 oz	1.60	3/01	4c
Pears, Anjou	lb	0.93	7/01	11r
Peas, green, Del Monte or Green Giant	15 oz	0.72	3/01	4c
Pork chops, center cut, bone-in	lb	3.63	7/01	11r
Pork, expenditures on	yr	150	1999	30r
Potato chips	16 oz	3.52	7/01	11r
Potatoes, frozen, french fried	lb	1.08	7/01	11r
Potatoes, white or red	10 lb	2.31	3/01	4c
Potatoes, white, all types	lb	0.33	7/01	11r
Poultry, expenditures on	yr	108	1999	30r
Processed fruits, expenditures on	yr	98	1999	30r
Processed vegetables, expenditures on	yr	80	1999	30r
Round roast, U.S. choice, boneless	lb	3.07	7/01	11r
Round steak, graded and ungraded, excl U.S. prime and choice	lb	3.41	7/01	11r
Sausage, Jimmy Dean/Owens pork	lb	4.10	3/01	4c
Shortening, vegetable oil blends	lb	1.13	7/01	11r
Shortening, vegetable, Crisco	3 lb	2.84	3/01	4c
Soft drink, Coca Cola, ex deposit	2 liter	1.35	3/01	4c
Spaghetti and macaroni	lb	0.80	7/01	11r
Steak, round, U.S. choice, boneless	lb	3.23	7/01	11r
Steak, T-bone	lb	6.43	3/01	4c
Steak, T-bone, U.S. choice, bone-in	lb	6.68	7/01	11r
Strawberries, dry pint	12 oz	1.32	7/01	11r
Sugar and other sweets, expenditures on	yr	114	1999	30r
Sugar, cane or beet	4 lbs	1.44	3/01	4c
Sugar, white, 33-80 ounce package	lb	0.42	7/01	11r
Sugar, white, all sizes	lb	0.43	7/01	11r
Tobacco products and smoking supplies purchases	yr	331	1999	30r
Tomatoes, field grown	lb	1.46	7/01	11r
Tomatoes, Hunt's or Del Monte	14.5 oz	0.84	3/01	4c
Tuna, chunk, light	6 oz	0.63	3/01	4c
Tuna, light, chunk	lb	1.80	7/01	11r
Turkey, frozen, whole	lb	1.15	7/01	11r
Goods and Services				
Miscellaneous goods and services, ACCRA Index		97.60	3/01	4c
B&B Japanese maple (acer japonicum)	gal	29.99-169.99	4/00	93r
Boxwood (buxus)	2 gal	18.99-39.99	4/00	93r
Daylily (hemerocallis)	gal	4.99-25.00	4/00	93r
Flat of annuals		11.98-24.99	4/00	93r
Fountain grass (pennisetum)	gal	5.98-12.98	4/00	93r
Hanging basket (10 in)		12.99-27.99	4/00	93r
Hardy geranium (geranium)	gal	7.99-9.99	4/00	93r
Hosta (hosta)	gal	6.00-25.00	4/00	93r
Lilac (syrubga vulgaris)	2 gal	14.99-24.99	4/00	93r
Miscellaneous purchases	yr	865	1999	30r
Rhododendron (rhododendron)	2 gal	23.98-42.99	4/00	93r
Sage (salvia)	gal	6.00-9.99	4/00	93r
Wintercreeper euonymus (euonymus fortunei)	2 gal	16.00-169.99	4/00	93r
Hunting license	yr	27.00	4/01	34s
Health Care				
Health care, ACCRA Index		95.10	3/01	4c
Cardiac catheterization, ave hospital/ physician charges		16430	1998	77s
Childbirth, Cesarean delivery		10722	1997	13r

Values are in dollars or fractions of dollars. In the column headed *Ref*, references are shown to sources. Each reference is followed by a letter. These refer to the geographical level for which data were reported: s=State, r=Region, and c=City or metro. The abbreviation *ex* is used to mean *except* or *excluding*; *exp* stands for expenditures. For other abbreviations and further explanations, please see the Introduction.

Sioux Falls, SD - continued

Item	Per	Value	Date	Ref.
Health Care				
Childbirth, vaginal delivery		6223	1997	13r
Dentist's fee, adult teeth cleaning and periodic oral exam	visit	71.38	3/01	4c
Doctor's fee, routine exam, established patient	visit	56.00	3/01	4c
Drugs, expenditures on	yr	394	1999	30r
Health care purchases	yr	2048	1999	30r
Health insurance expenditures	yr	978	1999	30r
Hospital care, private room	day	467.00	3/01	4c
Hysterectomy, vaginal, ave hospital and physician charges		9890	1998	76s
Medicaid dispensing fee		4.75-5.55	1999	87s
Medical services expenditures	yr	554	1999	30r
Medical supplies, expenditures on	yr	122	1999	30r
Plastic surgery, breast augmentation		3184	2000	7r
Plastic surgery, breast lift		3585	2000	7r
Plastic surgery, facelift		4999	2000	7r
Plastic surgery, hair transplantation		3105	2000	7r
Plastic surgery, lip augmentation		1290	2000	7r
Plastic surgery, lower body lift		8135	2000	7r
Plastic surgery, thigh lift		3839	2000	7r
Household Goods				
Dishwashing powder, Cascade	50 oz	3.52	3/01	4c
Floor coverings, expenditures on	yr	52	1999	30r
Furniture, expenditures on	yr	344	1999	30r
Household furnishings and equipment purchases	yr	1475	1999	30r
Household textiles, expenditures on	yr	109	1999	30r
Laundry and cleaning supplies, expenditures on	yr	134	1999	30r
Tissues, facial, Kleenex brand	175	1.26	3/01	4c
Housing				
Housing, ACCRA Index		91.10	3/01	4c
Home, 2200 sq ft, 4-br, 2-bath, 2-car garage, average		166500	2000	47c
Home price, existing, ave		144400	10/00	90r
Home value, median		94000	2001	53s
House, 2400 sq ft, 8000 sq ft lot, new, urban, utilities	total	189730	3/01	4c
House payment, principal and interest, 25% down payment	mos	940	3/01	4c
Household operation expenditures	yr	542	1999	30r
Housekeeping supplies purchases	yr	508	1999	30r
Lodging expenditures	yr	430	1999	30r
Maintenance, repairs, insurance expenditures	yr	853	1999	30r
Monthly rental value of owned home	mos	547	1999	30r
Owned dwellings, expenditures own	yr	4282	1999	30r
Rent expenditures	yr	1558	1999	30r
Rent, apartment, 2 br, 1 1/2-2 baths, unfurn, 950 sq ft, water	mos	631	3/01	4c
Rental unit, 1 bedroom, with utilities	mos	484	4/01	41c
Rental unit, 2 bedroom, with utilities	mos	614	4/01	41c
Rental unit, 3 bedroom, with utilities	mos	777	4/01	41c
Rental unit, 4 bedroom, with utilities	mos	892	4/01	41c
Shelter, expenditures on	yr	6270	1999	30r
Insurance and Pensions				
Auto insurance premium	yr	595.41	1999	57s
Life and other personal insurance purchases	yr	387	1999	30r
Pensions and Social Security, expenditures on	yr	2968	1999	30r
Legal Fees				
Combination hunting and fishing license	yr	44.00	4/01	34s
Divorce, filing fee		50.00	4/01	35s
Driver's license fee	orig	5.00	1999	48s
Driver's license fee	renew	5.00	1999	48s
Fishing license	yr	21.00	4/01	34s

Sioux Falls, SD - continued

Item	Per	Value	Date	Ref.
Personal Goods				
Personal care products and services purchases	yr	385	1999	30r
Shampoo, Alberto VO5	15 oz	1.16	3/01	4c
Toothpaste, Crest or Colgate	6-7 oz	1.94	3/01	4c
Personal Services				
Dry cleaning, man's 2-pc suit		7.97	3/01	4c
Man's haircut, barbershop, no styling		10.85	3/01	4c
Personal services, household, expenditures on	yr	300	1999	30r
Woman's shampoo, trim, blow-dry, no style-change		22.00	3/01	4c
Pets				
Pets, toys, and playground equipment, expenditures on	yr	375	1999	30r
Restaurant Food				
Chicken, fried, thigh and drumstick, KFC/Church's		2.30	3/01	4c
Hamburger with cheese, McDonald's	1/4 lb	2.19	3/01	4c
Pizza, Pizza Hut or Pizza Inn	11-12 in	8.89	3/01	4c
Taxes				
Federal income taxes paid	yr	2326	1999	30r
Personal taxes, expenditures on	yr	3223	1999	30r
Property taxes paid	yr	1152	1999	30r
State and local income taxes paid	yr	753	1999	30r
Transportation				
Transportation, ACCRA Index		101.60	3/01	4c
Auto operation, annual cost		6171	2000	27c
Cars and trucks, new, expenditures on	yr	1280	1999	30r
Cars and trucks, used, expenditures on	yr	1763	1999	30r
Diesel at the pump	gal	1.28	10/99	73s
Gasoline and motor oil purchases	yr	1036	1999	30r
Gasoline before-tax price (cents)	gal	121.10	10/00	43s
Maintenance and repair expenditures	yr	594	1999	30r
Public transportation, expenditures on	yr	341	1999	30r
Tire balance, computer or spin balance, front	wheel	7.80	3/01	4c
Transportation purchases	yr	6617	1999	30r
Vehicle expenses, miscellaneous, purchases	yr	2159	1999	30r
Vehicle insurance payments	yr	701	1999	30r
Vehicle purchases (net outlay)	yr	3081	1999	30r
Vehicle rental, lease expenditures	yr	536	1999	30r
Travel				
Car rental	day	44.00	2000	52c
Hotel room	night	51.17	2/01	94s
Utilities				
Utilities, ACCRA Index		137.50	3/01	4c
Electrical bill, average	mos	64.08	9/00	9s
Electricity, expenditures on	yr	841	1999	30r
Electricity, summer, 250 KWh	mos	23.73	2/96	96c
Electricity, summer, 500 KWh	mos	38.90	2/96	96c
Electricity, summer, 750 KWh	mos	54.08	2/96	96c
Electricity, summer, 1000 KWh	mos	69.25	2/96	96c
Electricity and other, mixed, 2400 sq ft, new home	mos	54.69	3/01	4c
Electricity cost, average	KWh	6.40	9/00	9s
Utilities, fuels, and public services purchased	yr	2401	1999	30r
Water and other public services, expenditures on	yr	273	1999	30r
Weddings				
Wedding (national average cost)		19936	2000	33r
Wedding (regional average total cost)		16195	1997	110r
Attendants' gifts		321	1998	33r
Bridal attendants' apparel (5 persons)		824	2000	33r
Bride's headpiece/veil		173	1998	33r
Bride's wedding dress		859	1998	33r
Clergy, religious facility fee		242	1998	33r
Engagement ring		3177	1998	33r
Flowers		789	1998	33r
Groom's formalwear rental		99	2000	33r

Values are in dollars or fractions of dollars. In the column headed *Ref*, references are shown to sources. Each reference is followed by a letter. These refer to the geographical level for which data were reported: s=State, r=Region, and c=City or metro. The abbreviation *ex* is used to mean *except* or *excluding*; *exp* stands for *expenditures*. For other abbreviations and further explanations, please see the Introduction.

Sioux Falls, SD - continued

Item	Per	Value	Date	Ref.
Weddings				
Limousine		410	1998	33r
Marriage license cost		40.00	4/01	35s
Men's formalwear (ushers, best man)		469	2000	33r
Mother of bride apparel		241	2000	33r
Music		866	1998	33r
Photography and videography		1368	1998	33r
Rehearsal dinner		728	1998	33r
Wedding invitations and announcements		341	1998	33r
Wedding reception		7968	2000	33r
Wedding rings (bride and groom)		1060	1998	33r

South Bend, IN

Item	Per	Value	Date	Ref.
Average annual expenditures	yr	35369	1999	30r
Composite, ACCRA index		93.90	3/01	4c
Alcoholic Beverages				
Alcoholic beverage purchases	yr	304	1999	30r
Beer, Heineken, 12-oz, ex deposit	6	7.32	3/01	4c
J & B Scotch	750-ml	19.15	3/01	4c
Malt beverages, all types, all sizes, any origin	16 oz	0.93	7/01	11r
Wine, Livingston or Gallo, Chablis blanc	1.5 liter	4.30	3/01	4c
Wine, red and white table, all sizes, any origin	liter	7.04	7/01	11r
Appliances				
Appliance repair, service call, washing machine	min lab chg	42.47	3/01	4c
Major appliances, expenditures on	yr	165	1999	30r
Small appliances, housewares, expenditures on	yr	90	1999	30r
Banking and Money				
Mortgage interest and charges paid	yr	2277	1999	30r
Mortgage principal paid on owned property	yr	1230	1999	30r
Mortgage rate, incl. points and orig. fee, 30-yr. conv. fixed or ARM	mos	7.11	3/01	4c
Vehicle finance charges paid	yr	328	1999	30r
Charity				
Cash contributions, expenditures	yr	1126	1999	30r
Child Care				
Child raising cost, total, age 0-2	yr	7890	1999	60r
Child raising cost, total, age 3-5	yr	8130	1999	60r
Child raising cost, total, age 6-8	yr	8170	1999	60r
Child raising cost, total, age 9-11	yr	8190	1999	60r
Child raising cost, total, age 12-14	yr	8890	1999	60r
Child raising cost, total, age 15-17	yr	9050	1999	60r
Child's child care and education, age 0-2	yr	1240	1999	60r
Child's child care and education, age 3-5	yr	1370	1999	60r
Child's child care and education, age 6-8	yr	880	1999	60r
Child's child care and education, age 9-11	yr	570	1999	60r
Child's child care and education, age 12-14	yr	420	1999	60r
Child's child care and education, age 15-17	yr	720	1999	60r
Child's clothing, age 0-2	yr	410	1999	60r
Child's clothing, age 3-5	yr	400	1999	60r
Child's clothing, age 6-8	yr	450	1999	60r
Child's clothing, age 9-11	yr	500	1999	60r
Child's clothing, age 12-14	yr	840	1999	60r
Child's clothing, age 15-17	yr	740	1999	60r
Child's food, age 0-2	yr	960	1999	60r
Child's food, age 3-5	yr	1120	1999	60r
Child's food, age 6-8	yr	1430	1999	60r
Child's food, age 9-11	yr	1710	1999	60r
Child's food, age 12-14	yr	1710	1999	60r
Child's food, age 15-17	yr	1920	1999	60r
Child's health care, age 0-2	yr	520	1999	60r
Child's health care, age 3-5	yr	500	1999	60r
Child's health care, age 6-8	yr	570	1999	60r
Child's health care, age 9-11	yr	610	1999	60r
Child's health care, age 12-14	yr	630	1999	60r
Child's health care, age 15-17	yr	650	1999	60r
Child's housing, age 0-2	yr	2860	1999	60r

South Bend, IN - continued

Item	Per	Value	Date	Ref.
Child Care - continued				
Child's housing, age 3-5	yr	2840	1999	60r
Child's housing, age 6-8	yr	2800	1999	60r
Child's housing, age 9-11	yr	2650	1999	60r
Child's housing, age 12-14	yr	2840	1999	60r
Child's housing, age 15-17	yr	2440	1999	60r
Child's personal care, reading, age 0-2	yr	880	1999	60r
Child's personal care, reading, age 3-5	yr	900	1999	60r
Child's personal care, reading, age 6-8	yr	930	1999	60r
Child's personal care, reading, age 9-11	yr	970	1999	60r
Child's personal care, reading, age 12-14	yr	1150	1999	60r
Child's personal care, reading, age 15-17	yr	920	1999	60r
Clothing				
Apparel and services purchases	yr	1607	1999	30r
Boys' brief, cotton	3	3.00	3/01	4c
Boys, 2 to 15, expenditures on	yr	91	1999	30r
Children under 2, expenditures on	yr	59	1999	30r
Footwear, expenditures on	yr	285	1999	30r
Girls, 2 to 15, expenditures on	yr	116	1999	30r
Men and boys, expenditures on	yr	433	1999	30r
Men, 16 and over, expenditures on	yr	341	1999	30r
Shirt, man's dress shirt		25.59	3/01	4c
Slacks, man's "No Wrinkles" khaki		31.51	3/01	4c
Women, 16 and over, expenditures on	yr	490	1999	30r
Communications				
Newspaper subscription, daily and Sunday delivery	mos	11.77	3/01	4c
Phone line, single, business, field visit	inst.	59.00	12/97	17s
Phone line, single, business, no field visit	inst.	59.00	12/97	17s
Phone line, single, residence, field visit	inst.	47.00	12/97	17s
Phone line, single, residence, no field visit	inst.	47.00	12/97	17s
Postage and stationery, expenditures on	yr	140	1999	30r
Postal rate, express mail, up to half-pound		12.45	7/01	108r
Postal rate, letter, first class, first ounce		0.34	7/01	108r
Postal rate, letter, two ounces		0.57	7/01	108r
Postal rate, post card		0.21	7/01	108r
Postal rate, priority mail, two pounds		3.95	7/01	108r
Postal rate, priority mail, up to one pound		3.50	7/01	108r
Telephone bill, family of three	mos	23.49	3/01	4c
Telephone services, expenditures on	yr	830	1999	30r
Education				
Board, 4-year private college/university	yr	2250	1996	38s
Board, 4-year public college/university	yr	2425	1996	38s
Education expenditures	yr	583	1999	30r
Room, 4-year private college/university	yr	1987	1996	38s
Room, 4-year public college/university	yr	1931	1996	38s
Total cost, 4-year private college/university	yr	16829	1996	38s
Total cost, 4-year public college/university	yr	7392	1996	38s
Tuition, 2-year public college/university, in state	yr	1937	1996	38s
Tuition, 4-year private college/university, in state	yr	12592	1996	38s
Tuition, 4-year public college/university	yr	3037	1996	38s
Energy and Fuels				
Electricity	500 KWhs	46.59	7/01	11r
Energy, combined forms, 2400 sq ft	mos	129.34	3/01	4c
Energy, exc. electricity, 2400 sq ft	mos	79.99	3/01	4c
Fuel oil #2	gal	1.27	7/01	11r
Fuel oil and other fuels, expenditures on	yr	68	1999	30r
Gas, natural, commercial rate	1000 cf	6.24	11/00	88s
Gas, regular unleaded, cash, self-service	gal	1.33	3/01	4c
Gasoline, unleaded midgrade	gal	1.79	7/01	11r
Gasoline, unleaded premium	gal	1.86	7/01	11r
Gasoline, unleaded regular	gal	1.58	7/01	11r
Natural gas, expenditures on	yr	389	1999	30r
Utility (piped) gas, therm		0.81	7/01	11r
Utility (piped) gas, 40 therms		38.01	7/01	11r
Utility (piped) gas, 100 therms		81.75	7/01	11r

Values are in dollars or fractions of dollars. In the column headed *Ref*, references are shown to sources. Each reference is followed by a letter. These refer to the geographical level for which data were reported: s=State, r=Region, and c=City or metro. The abbreviation *ex* is used to mean *except* or *excluding*; *exp* stands for expenditures. For other abbreviations and further explanations, please see the Introduction.

South Bend, IN - continued

Item	Per	Value	Date	Ref.
Entertainment				
Bowling, Saturday evening rate	line	2.75	3/01	4c
Entertainment purchases	yr	1984	1999	30r
Fees and admissions paid	yr	444	1999	30r
Monopoly game, Parker Brothers', No. 9	game	9.97	3/01	4c
Movie, first-run, Saturday, evening	adm.	6.50	3/01	4c
Television, radios, sound equipment, expenditures on	yr	580	1999	30r
Tennis balls, yellow, Wilson or Penn, 3	can	2.16	3/01	4c
Funerals				
Cosmetology, hair, other preparation		178.32	1/99	78r
Embalming		408.19	1/99	78r
Funeral at funeral home		362.13	1/99	78r
Professional service charges		1375.51	1/99	78r
Transfer of remains to funeral home		155.92	1/99	78r
Visitation/viewing		294.38	1/99	78r
Groceries				
Groceries, ACCRA Index		89.50	3/01	4c
Antibiotic ointment, Polysporin	0.5 oz	4.29	3/01	4c
Baby food, strained vegetables or fruit, lowest price	4-4.5 oz	0.45	3/01	4c
Bacon, sliced	lb	3.15	7/01	11r
Bakery products, expenditures on	yr	281	1999	30r
Bananas	lb	0.49	3/01	4c
Bananas	lb	0.48	7/01	11r
Beans, dried, any type, all sizes	lb	0.61	7/01	11r
Beef for stew, boneless	lb	3.08	7/01	11r
Beef or hamburger, ground	lb	1.42	3/01	4c
Beef, expenditures on	yr	217	1999	30r
Bologna, all beef or mixed	lb	2.52	7/01	11r
Bread, white	loaf	0.83	3/01	4c
Bread, white, pan	lb	1.06	7/01	11r
Broccoli	lb	0.91	7/01	11r
Butter, salted, grade AA, stick	lb	3.04	7/01	11r
Butter, yoghurt, cheese, etc, expenditures on	yr	183	1999	30r
Cereals and bakery product purchases	yr	430	1999	30r
Cereals and cereal products, expenditures on	yr	149	1999	30r
Cheese, Kraft grated Parmesan	8 oz	3.80	3/01	4c
Chicken, fresh, whole	lb	1.07	7/01	11r
Chicken, whole fryer	lb	0.97	3/01	4c
Chops, boneless,	lb	3.64	7/01	11r
Chuck roast, U.S. choice, boneless	lb	2.47	7/01	11r
Cigarettes, Winston, Kings	carton	27.37	3/01	4c
Coffee, 100%, ground roast, all sizes	lb	2.69	7/01	11r
Coffee, vacuum-packed	13 oz	2.29	3/01	4c
Cookies, chocolate chip	lb	2.87	7/01	11r
Corn Flakes, Kellogg's or Post Toasties	18 oz	1.86	3/01	4c
Corn, frozen, whole kernel, lowest price	16 oz	1.02	3/01	4c
Dairy product purchases	yr	304	1999	30r
Eggs, expenditures on	yr	26	1999	30r
Eggs, Grade A or AA	dozen	1.14	3/01	4c
Eggs, grade A, large	dozen	0.88	7/01	11r
Fats and oils, expenditures on	yr	75	1999	30r
Fish and seafood, expenditures on	yr	72	1999	30r
Food (excl fruit and vegetables), eaten at home, purchases	yr	887	1999	30r
Food cooked on trips, expenditures on	yr	44	1999	30r
Food purchases	yr	4802	1999	30r
Food purchases, eaten away from home	yr	2069	1999	30r
Food purchases, food eaten at home	yr	2733	1999	30r
Fresh fruits, expenditures on	yr	138	1999	30r
Fresh milk and cream, expenditures on	yr	120	1999	30r
Fresh vegetables, expenditures on	yr	126	1999	30r
Grapefruit	lb	0.66	7/01	11r
Grapes, Thompson, seedless	lb	1.64	7/01	11r
Ground beef, 100% beef	lb	1.64	7/01	11r
Ground beef, lean and extra lean	lb	2.16	7/01	11r
Ground chuck, 100% beef	lb	2.13	7/01	11r
Ham, boneless, excl canned	lb	2.62	7/01	11r
Ice cream, prepackaged, bulk, regular	1/2 gal	3.35	7/01	11r
Lemons	lb	1.19	7/01	11r

South Bend, IN - continued

Item	Per	Value	Date	Ref.
Groceries - continued				
Lettuce, iceberg	head	0.95	3/01	4c
Lettuce, iceberg	lb	0.73	7/01	11r
Margarine, Blue Bonnet or Parkay, stick	lb	0.64	3/01	4c
Margarine, soft, tubs	lb	0.89	7/01	11r
Meats, poultry, fish, and egg purchases	yr	671	1999	30r
Milk, fresh, whole, fortified	gal	2.71	7/01	11r
Milk, whole	1/2 gal	1.48	3/01	4c
Nonalcoholic beverages, expenditures on	yr	239	1999	30r
Orange juice, Minute Maid frozen	12 oz	1.33	3/01	4c
Oranges, Navel	lb	0.80	7/01	11r
Oranges, Valencia	lb	0.66	7/01	11r
Peaches, halves or slices, Hunt's, Del Monte, or Libby's	29 oz	1.44	3/01	4c
Pears, Anjou	lb	0.93	7/01	11r
Peas, green, Del Monte or Green Giant	15 oz	0.48	3/01	4c
Pork chops, center cut, bone-in	lb	3.63	7/01	11r
Pork, expenditures on	yr	150	1999	30r
Potato chips	16 oz	3.52	7/01	11r
Potatoes, frozen, french fried	lb	1.08	7/01	11r
Potatoes, white or red	10 lb	2.19	3/01	4c
Potatoes, white, all types	lb	0.33	7/01	11r
Poultry, expenditures on	yr	108	1999	30r
Processed fruits, expenditures on	yr	98	1999	30r
Processed vegetables, expenditures on	yr	80	1999	30r
Round roast, U.S. choice, boneless	lb	3.07	7/01	11r
Round steak, graded and ungraded, excl U.S. prime and choice	lb	3.41	7/01	11r
Sausage, Jimmy Dean/Owens pork	lb	2.95	3/01	4c
Shortening, vegetable oil blends	lb	1.13	7/01	11r
Shortening, vegetable, Crisco	3 lb	2.49	3/01	4c
Soft drink, Coca Cola, ex deposit	2 liter	1.11	3/01	4c
Spaghetti and macaroni	lb	0.80	7/01	11r
Steak, round, U.S. choice, boneless	lb	3.23	7/01	11r
Steak, T-bone	lb	6.11	3/01	4c
Steak, T-bone, U.S. choice, bone-in	lb	6.68	7/01	11r
Strawberries, dry pint	12 oz	1.32	7/01	11r
Sugar and other sweets, expenditures on	yr	114	1999	30r
Sugar, cane or beet	4 lbs	1.25	3/01	4c
Sugar, white, 33-80 ounce package	lb	0.42	7/01	11r
Sugar, white, all sizes	lb	0.43	7/01	11r
Tobacco products and smoking supplies purchases	yr	331	1999	30r
Tomatoes, field grown	lb	1.46	7/01	11r
Tomatoes, Hunt's or Del Monte	14.5 oz	0.70	3/01	4c
Tuna, chunk, light	6 oz	0.51	3/01	4c
Tuna, light, chunk	lb	1.80	7/01	11r
Turkey, frozen, whole	lb	1.15	7/01	11r
Goods and Services				
Miscellaneous goods and services, ACCRA Index		94.10	3/01	4c
B&B Japanese maple (acer japonicum)	gal	29.99-169.99	4/00	93r
Boxwood (buxus)	2 gal	18.99-39.99	4/00	93r
Daylilly (hemerocallis)	gal	4.99-25.00	4/00	93r
Flat of annuals		11.98-24.99	4/00	93r
Fountain grass (pennisetum)	gal	5.98-12.98	4/00	93r
Hanging basket (10 in)		12.99-27.99	4/00	93r
Hardy geranium (geranium)	gal	7.99-9.99	4/00	93r
Hosta (hosta)	gal	6.00-25.00	4/00	93r
Lilac (syrubga vulgaris)	2 gal	14.99-24.99	4/00	93r
Miscellaneous purchases	yr	865	1999	30r
Rhododendron (rhododendron)	2 gal	23.98-42.99	4/00	93r

Values are in dollars or fractions of dollars. In the column headed *Ref*, references are shown to sources. Each reference is followed by a letter. These refer to the geographical level for which data were reported: s=State, r=Region, and c=City or metro. The abbreviation *ex* is used to mean *except* or *excluding*; *exp* stands for expenditures. For other abbreviations and further explanations, please see the Introduction.

South Bend, IN - continued

Item	Per	Value	Date	Ref.
Goods and Services				
Sage (salvia)	gal	6.00-9.99	4/00	93r
Wintercreeper euonymus (euonymus fortunei)	2 gal	16.00-169.99	4/00	93r
Hunting license	yr	8.75	4/01	34s
Health Care				
Health care, ACCRA Index		97.90	3/01	4c
Cardiac catheterization, ave hospital/ physician charges		13380	1998	77s
Childbirth, Cesarean delivery		10722	1997	13r
Childbirth, vaginal delivery		6223	1997	13r
Dentist's fee, adult teeth cleaning and periodic oral exam	visit	64.40	3/01	4c
Doctor's fee, routine exam, established patient	visit	50.40	3/01	4c
Drugs, expenditures on	yr	394	1999	30r
Health care purchases	yr	2048	1999	30r
Health insurance expenditures	yr	978	1999	30r
Hospital care, private room	day	735.33	3/01	4c
Hysterectomy, laproscopically-assisted, ave hospital/physician charges		11310	1998	76s
Hysterectomy, vaginal, ave hospital and physician charges		9160	1998	76s
Medicaid dispensing fee		4.00	1999	87s
Medical services expenditures	yr	554	1999	30r
Medical supplies, expenditures on	yr	122	1999	30r
Plastic surgery, breast augmentation		3184	2000	7r
Plastic surgery, breast lift		3585	2000	7r
Plastic surgery, facelift		4999	2000	7r
Plastic surgery, hair transplantation		3105	2000	7r
Plastic surgery, lip augmentation		1290	2000	7r
Plastic surgery, lower body lift		8135	2000	7r
Plastic surgery, thigh lift		3839	2000	7r
Household Goods				
Dishwashing powder, Cascade	50 oz	2.63	3/01	4c
Floor coverings, expenditures on	yr	52	1999	30r
Furniture, expenditures on	yr	344	1999	30r
Household furnishings and equipment purchases	yr	1475	1999	30r
Household textiles, expenditures on	yr	109	1999	30r
Laundry and cleaning supplies, expenditures on	yr	134	1999	30r
Tissues, facial, Kleenex brand	175	1.14	3/01	4c
Housing				
Housing, ACCRA Index		92.80	3/01	4c
Home, 2200 sq ft, 4-br, 2-bath, 2-car garage, average		146483	2000	47c
Home price, existing, ave		144400	10/00	90r
Home value, median		102000	2001	53s
House, 2400 sq ft, 8000 sq ft lot, new, urban, utilities	total	191042	3/01	4c
House payment, principal and interest, 25% down payment	mos	964	3/01	4c
Household operation expenditures	yr	542	1999	30r
Housekeeping supplies purchases	yr	508	1999	30r
Lodging expenditures	yr	430	1999	30r
Maintenance, repairs, insurance expenditures	yr	853	1999	30r
Monthly rental value of owned home	mos	547	1999	30r
Owned dwellings, expenditures own	yr	4282	1999	30r
Rent expenditures	yr	1558	1999	30r
Rent, apartment, 2 br, 1 1/2-2 baths, unfurn, 950 sq ft, water	mos	626	3/01	4c
Rental unit, 1 bedroom, with utilities	mos	434	4/01	41c
Rental unit, 2 bedroom, with utilities	mos	570	4/01	41c
Rental unit, 3 bedroom, with utilities	mos	712	4/01	41c
Rental unit, 4 bedroom, with utilities	mos	799	4/01	41c
Shelter, expenditures on	yr	6270	1999	30r

South Bend, IN - continued

Item	Per	Value	Date	Ref.
Insurance and Pensions				
Life and other personal insurance purchases	yr	387	1999	30r
Pensions and Social Security, expenditures on	yr	2968	1999	30r
Legal Fees				
Divorce, filing fee		100.00	4/01	35s
Driver's license fee	renew	6.00	1999	48s
Driver's license fee	orig	6.00	1999	48s
Personal Goods				
Personal care products and services purchases	yr	385	1999	30r
Shampoo, Alberto VO5	15 oz	0.98	3/01	4c
Toothpaste, Crest or Colgate	6-7 oz	2.09	3/01	4c
Personal Services				
Dry cleaning, man's 2-pc suit		7.44	3/01	4c
Man's haircut, barbershop, no styling		12.00	3/01	4c
Personal services, household, expenditures on	yr	300	1999	30r
Woman's shampoo, trim, blow-dry, no style-change		28.00	3/01	4c
Pets				
Pets, toys, and playground equipment, expenditures on	yr	375	1999	30r
Restaurant Food				
Chicken, fried, thigh and drumstick, KFC/ Church's		2.66	3/01	4c
Hamburger with cheese, McDonald's	1/4 lb	2.13	3/01	4c
Pizza, Pizza Hut or Pizza Inn	11-12 in	8.99	3/01	4c
Taxes				
Federal income taxes paid	yr	2326	1999	30r
Personal taxes, expenditures on	yr	3223	1999	30r
Property taxes paid	yr	1152	1999	30r
State and local income taxes paid	yr	753	1999	30r
Transportation				
Transportation, ACCRA Index		91.50	3/01	4c
Bus fare, one-way	trip	0.75	2000	1c
Bus fare, to central business district	1-way	0.75	3/01	4c
Cars and trucks, new, expenditures on	yr	1280	1999	30r
Cars and trucks, used, expenditures on	yr	1763	1999	30r
Diesel at the pump	gal	1.17	10/99	73s
Gasoline and motor oil purchases	yr	1036	1999	30r
Gasoline before-tax price (cents)	gal	110.00	10/00	43s
Maintenance and repair expenditures	yr	594	1999	30r
Public transportation, expenditures on	yr	341	1999	30r
Tire balance, computer or spin balance, front	wheel	7.40	3/01	4c
Transportation purchases	yr	6617	1999	30r
Vehicle expenses, miscellaneous, purchases	yr	2159	1999	30r
Vehicle insurance payments	yr	701	1999	30r
Vehicle purchases (net outlay)	yr	3081	1999	30r
Vehicle rental, lease expenditures	yr	536	1999	30r
Utilities				
Utilities, ACCRA Index		106.20	3/01	4c
Electrical bill, average	mos	66.66	9/00	9s
Electricity, expenditures on	yr	841	1999	30r
Electricity and other, mixed, 2400 sq ft, new home	mos	49.35	3/01	4c
Electricity cost, average	KWh	5.00	9/00	9s
Utilities, fuels, and public services purchased	yr	2401	1999	30r
Water and other public services, expenditures on	yr	273	1999	30r
Weddings				
Wedding (national average cost)		19936	2000	33r
Wedding (regional average total cost)		16195	1997	110r
Attendants' gifts		321	1998	33r
Bridal attendants' apparel (5 persons)		824	2000	33r
Bride's headpiece/veil		173	1998	33r
Bride's wedding dress		859	1998	33r
Clergy, religious facility fee		242	1998	33r

Values are in dollars or fractions of dollars. In the column headed *Ref*, references are shown to sources. Each reference is followed by a letter. These refer to the geographical level for which data were reported: s=State, r=Region, and c=City or metro. The abbreviation *ex* is used to mean *except* or *excluding*; *exp* stands for expenditures. For other abbreviations and further explanations, please see the Introduction.

South Bend, IN - continued

Weddings

Item	Per	Value	Date	Ref.
Engagement ring		3177	1998	33r
Flowers		789	1998	33r
Groom's formalwear rental		99	2000	33r
Limousine		410	1998	33r
Marriage license cost		18.00	4/01	35s
Men's formalwear (ushers, best man)		469	2000	33r
Mother of bride apparel		241	2000	33r
Music		866	1998	33r
Photography and videography		1368	1998	33r
Rehearsal dinner		728	1998	33r
Wedding invitations and announcements		341	1998	33r
Wedding reception		7968	2000	33r
Wedding rings (bride and groom)		1060	1998	33r

Spokane, WA

Item	Per	Value	Date	Ref.
Average annual expenditures	yr	40662	1999	30r
Composite, ACCRA index		101.20	3/01	4c
Alcoholic Beverages				
Alcoholic beverage purchases	yr	372	1999	30r
Beer, Heineken, 12-oz, ex deposit	6	7.57	3/01	4c
J & B Scotch	750-ml	22.45	3/01	4c
Malt beverages, all types, all sizes, any origin	16 oz	0.94	7/01	11r
Wine, Livingston or Gallo, Chablis blanc	1.5 liter	5.31	3/01	4c
Wine, red and white table, all sizes, any origin	liter	6.00	7/01	11r
Appliances				
Appliance repair, service call, washing machine	min lab chg	48.57	3/01	4c
Major appliances, expenditures on	yr	167	1999	30r
Small appliances, housewares, expenditures on	yr	105	1999	30r
Banking and Money				
Mortgage interest and charges paid	yr	3368	1999	30r
Mortgage principal paid on owned property	yr	1677	1999	30r
Mortgage rate, incl. points and orig. fee, 30-yr. conv. fixed or ARM	mos	6.88	3/01	4c
Vehicle finance charges paid	yr	311	1999	30r
Business Expenses				
Business travel, car rental	day	44	2001	3c
Business travel, food	day	49	2001	3c
Business travel, hotel	day	77	2001	3c
Charity				
Cash contributions, expenditures	yr	1344	1999	30r
Child Care				
Child raising cost, total, age 0-2	yr	9140	1999	60r
Child raising cost, total, age 3-5	yr	9370	1999	60r
Child raising cost, total, age 6-8	yr	9450	1999	60r
Child raising cost, total, age 9-11	yr	9470	1999	60r
Child raising cost, total, age 12-14	yr	10170	1999	60r
Child raising cost, total, age 15-17	yr	10360	1999	60r
Child's child care and education, age 0-2	yr	1250	1999	60r
Child's child care and education, age 3-5	yr	1380	1999	60r
Child's child care and education, age 6-8	yr	890	1999	60r
Child's child care and education, age 9-11	yr	580	1999	60r
Child's child care and education, age 12-14	yr	430	1999	60r
Child's child care and education, age 15-17	yr	730	1999	60r
Child's clothing, age 0-2	yr	430	1999	60r
Child's clothing, age 3-5	yr	420	1999	60r
Child's clothing, age 6-8	yr	470	1999	60r
Child's clothing, age 9-11	yr	520	1999	60r
Child's clothing, age 12-14	yr	870	1999	60r
Child's clothing, age 15-17	yr	770	1999	60r
Child's food, age 0-2	yr	1120	1999	60r
Child's food, age 3-5	yr	1280	1999	60r
Child's food, age 6-8	yr	1640	1999	60r
Child's food, age 9-11	yr	1930	1999	60r
Child's food, age 12-14	yr	1940	1999	60r

Spokane, WA - continued

Item	Per	Value	Date	Ref.
Child Care - continued				
Child's food, age 15-17	yr	2150	1999	60r
Child's health care, age 0-2	yr	490	1999	60r
Child's health care, age 3-5	yr	470	1999	60r
Child's health care, age 6-8	yr	530	1999	60r
Child's health care, age 9-11	yr	570	1999	60r
Child's health care, age 12-14	yr	580	1999	60r
Child's health care, age 15-17	yr	610	1999	60r
Child's housing, age 0-2	yr	3630	1999	60r
Child's housing, age 3-5	yr	3610	1999	60r
Child's housing, age 6-8	yr	3570	1999	60r
Child's housing, age 9-11	yr	3410	1999	60r
Child's housing, age 12-14	yr	3600	1999	60r
Child's housing, age 15-17	yr	3210	1999	60r
Child's personal care, reading, age 0-2	yr	1040	1999	60r
Child's personal care, reading, age 3-5	yr	1060	1999	60r
Child's personal care, reading, age 6-8	yr	1090	1999	60r
Child's personal care, reading, age 9-11	yr	1130	1999	60r
Child's personal care, reading, age 12-14	yr	1300	1999	60r
Child's personal care, reading, age 15-17	yr	1080	1999	60r
Clothing				
Apparel and services purchases	yr	1863	1999	30r
Boys' brief, cotton	3	5.47	3/01	4c
Boys, 2 to 15, expenditures on	yr	80	1999	30r
Children under 2, expenditures on	yr	74	1999	30r
Footwear, expenditures on	yr	307	1999	30r
Girls, 2 to 15, expenditures on	yr	101	1999	30r
Men and boys, expenditures on	yr	443	1999	30r
Men, 16 and over, expenditures on	yr	363	1999	30r
Shirt, man's dress shirt		29.12	3/01	4c
Slacks, man's "No Wrinkles" khaki		35.59	3/01	4c
Women, 16 and over, expenditures on	yr	594	1999	30r
Communications				
Cable modem installation, AT&T-BIS		150.00	6/99	103s
Cable modem rate, cable subscriber, AT&T-BIS	mos	39.95	6/99	103s
Newspaper subscription, daily and Sunday delivery	mos	12.42	3/01	4c
Phone line, single, business, field visit	inst.	48.00	12/97	17s
Phone line, single, business, no field visit	inst.	48.00	12/97	17s
Phone line, single, residence, field visit	inst.	31.00	12/97	17s
Phone line, single, residence, no field visit	inst.	31.00	12/97	17s
Postage and stationery, expenditures on	yr	150	1999	30r
Postal rate, express mail, up to half-pound		12.45	7/01	108r
Postal rate, letter, first class, first ounce		0.34	7/01	108r
Postal rate, letter, two ounces		0.57	7/01	108r
Postal rate, post card		0.21	7/01	108r
Postal rate, priority mail, two pounds		3.95	7/01	108r
Postal rate, priority mail, up to one pound		3.50	7/01	108r
Telephone bill, business, basic rate	mos	18.60	12/97	18c
Telephone bill, family of three	mos	19.95	3/01	4c
Telephone bill, residential, basic rate	mos	8.95	12/97	18c
Telephone services, expenditures on	yr	825	1999	30r
Education				
Board, 4-year private college/university	yr	2329	1996	38s
Board, 4-year public college/university	yr	2158	1996	38s
Education expenditures	yr	676	1999	30r
Room, 4-year private college/university	yr	2487	1996	38s
Room, 4-year public college/university	yr	2187	1996	38s
Total cost, 4-year private college/university	yr	18092	1996	38s
Total cost, 4-year public college/university	yr	7136	1996	38s
Tuition, 2-year public college/university, in state	yr	1369	1996	38s
Tuition, 4-year private college/university, in state	yr	13276	1996	38s
Tuition, 4-year public college/university	yr	2791	1996	38s
Energy and Fuels				
Electricity	500 KWhs	48.23	7/01	11r
Electricity	KWh	0.11	7/01	11r
Energy, combined forms, 2400 sq ft	mos	83.97	3/01	4c

Values are in dollars or fractions of dollars. In the column headed *Ref*, references are shown to sources. Each reference is followed by a letter. These refer to the geographical level for which data were reported: s=State, r=Region, and c=City or metro. The abbreviation *ex* is used to mean *except* or *excluding*; *exp* stands for *expenditures*. For other abbreviations and further explanations, please see the Introduction.

Spokane, WA - continued

Item	Per	Value	Date	Ref.
Energy and Fuels				
Energy, exc. electricity, 2400 sq ft	mos	54.17	3/01	4c
Fuel oil and other fuels, expenditures on	yr	35	1999	30r
Gas, cooking, winter, 10 therms	mos	6.96	2/96	98c
Gas, cooking, winter, 30 therms	mos	14.38	2/96	98c
Gas, cooking, winter, 50 therms	mos	21.80	2/96	98c
Gas, heating, winter, average use	mos	63.01	2/96	98c
Gas, natural, commercial rate	1000 cf	6.89	11/00	88s
Gas, regular unleaded, cash, self-service	gal	1.45	3/01	4c
Gasoline, all types	gal	1.91	7/01	11r
Gasoline, unleaded premium	gal	2.05	7/01	11r
Gasoline, unleaded regular	gal	1.83	7/01	11r
Natural gas, expenditures on	yr	255	1999	30r
Utility (piped) gas, therm		0.98	7/01	11r
Utility (piped) gas, 40 therms		40.74	7/01	11r
Utility (piped) gas, 100 therms		96.80	7/01	11r
Entertainment				
Bowling, Saturday evening rate	line	2.55	3/01	4c
Entertainment purchases	yr	2139	1999	30r
Fees and admissions paid	yr	545	1999	30r
Monopoly game, Parker Brothers', No. 9	game	10.96	3/01	4c
Movie, first-run, Saturday, evening	adm.	6.88	3/01	4c
Television, radios, sound equipment, expenditures on	yr	624	1999	30r
Tennis balls, yellow, Wilson or Penn, 3	can	2.57	3/01	4c
Funerals				
Total cost of funeral		5401.08	1/99	78r
Acknowledgement cards		33.64	1/99	78r
Casket		2170.43	1/99	78r
Cosmetology, hair, other preparation		136.32	1/99	78r
Embalming		319.13	1/99	78r
Funeral at funeral home		370.21	1/99	78r
Hearse (local)		161.04	1/99	78r
Professional service charges		963.15	1/99	78r
Service car/van		133.99	1/99	78r
Transfer of remains to funeral home		159.82	1/99	78r
Vault		778.07	1/99	78r
Visitation/viewing		175.28	1/99	78r
Groceries				
Groceries, ACCRA Index		108.80	3/01	4c
Antibiotic ointment, Polysporin	0.5 oz	5.04	3/01	4c
Apples, red delicious	lb	0.84	7/01	11r
Baby food, strained vegetables or fruit, lowest price	4-4.5 oz	0.42	3/01	4c
Bacon, sliced	lb	3.38	7/01	11r
Bakery products, expenditures on	yr	299	1999	30r
Bananas	lb	0.53	3/01	4c
Bananas	lb	0.54	7/01	11r
Beans, dried, any type, all sizes	lb	0.76	7/01	11r
Beef or hamburger, ground	lb	1.61	3/01	4c
Beef, expenditures on	yr	222	1999	30r
Bread, white	loaf	0.82	3/01	4c
Bread, white, pan	lb	0.99	7/01	11r
Butter, yoghurt, cheese, etc, expenditures on	yr	211	1999	30r
Cereals and bakery product purchases	yr	466	1999	30r
Cereals and cereal products, expenditures on	yr	168	1999	30r
Cheese, Kraft grated Parmesan	8 oz	4.50	3/01	4c
Chicken breast, bone-in	lb	2.45	7/01	11r
Chicken, fresh, whole	lb	1.19	7/01	11r
Chicken, whole fryer	lb	1.17	3/01	4c
Chops, boneless,	lb	4.00	7/01	11r
Chuck roast, graded and ungraded, excl U.S. prime and choice	lb	2.55	7/01	11r
Cigarettes, Winston, Kings	carton	39.31	3/01	4c
Coffee, 100%, ground roast, all sizes	lb	3.80	7/01	11r
Coffee, vacuum-packed	13 oz	3.16	3/01	4c
Cookies, chocolate chip	lb	2.83	7/01	11r
Corn Flakes, Kellogg's or Post Toasties	18 oz	3.01	3/01	4c
Corn, frozen, whole kernel, lowest price	16 oz	1.12	3/01	4c
Dairy product purchases	yr	341	1999	30r
Eggs, expenditures on	yr	39	1999	30r

Spokane, WA - continued

Item	Per	Value	Date	Ref.
Groceries - continued				
Eggs, Grade A or AA	dozen	1.37	3/01	4c
Eggs, grade AA, large	dozen	1.23	7/01	11r
Fats and oils, expenditures on	yr	88	1999	30r
Fish and seafood, expenditures on	yr	121	1999	30r
Food (excl fruit and vegetables), eaten at home, purchases	yr	1001	1999	30r
Food cooked on trips, expenditures on	yr	64	1999	30r
Food purchases	yr	5312	1999	30r
Food purchases, eaten away from home	yr	2180	1999	30r
Food purchases, food eaten at home	yr	3132	1999	30r
Fresh fruits, expenditures on	yr	186	1999	30r
Fresh milk and cream, expenditures on	yr	130	1999	30r
Fresh vegetables, expenditures on	yr	177	1999	30r
Grapefruit	lb	0.68	7/01	11r
Grapes, Thompson, seedless	lb	2.42	7/01	11r
Ground beef, lean and extra lean	lb	2.46	7/01	11r
Ice cream, prepackaged, bulk, regular	1/2 gal	3.62	7/01	11r
Lettuce, iceberg	head	0.96	3/01	4c
Lettuce, iceberg	lb	0.63	7/01	11r
Margarine, Blue Bonnet or Parkay, stick	lb	0.74	3/01	4c
Meats, poultry, fish, and egg purchases	yr	761	1999	30r
Milk, fresh, low fat	gal	2.80	7/01	11r
Milk, fresh, whole, fortified	gal	2.88	7/01	11r
Milk, whole	1/2 gal	2.07	3/01	4c
Nonalcoholic beverages, expenditures on	yr	258	1999	30r
Orange juice, Minute Maid frozen	12 oz	1.58	3/01	4c
Oranges, Navel	lb	0.97	7/01	11r
Oranges, Valencia	lb	0.43	7/01	11r
Peaches	lb	1.38	7/01	11r
Peaches, halves or slices, Hunt's, Del Monte, or Libby's	29 oz	1.47	3/01	4c
Peanut butter, creamy, all sizes	lb	2.14	7/01	11r
Peas, green, Del Monte or Green Giant	15 oz	0.79	3/01	4c
Pork chops, center cut, bone-in	lb	3.83	7/01	11r
Pork, expenditures on	yr	141	1999	30r
Potatoes, white or red	10 lb	1.87	3/01	4c
Potatoes, white, all types	lb	0.37	7/01	11r
Poultry, expenditures on	yr	146	1999	30r
Processed fruits, expenditures on	yr	118	1999	30r
Processed vegetables, expenditures on	yr	81	1999	30r
Round roast, graded and ungraded, excl U.S. prime and choice	lb	3.07	7/01	11r
Round roast, U.S. choice, boneless	lb	3.37	7/01	11r
Round steak, graded and ungraded, excl U.S. prime and choice	lb	3.51	7/01	11r
Sausage, Jimmy Dean/Owens pork	lb	4.10	3/01	4c
Shortening, vegetable, Crisco	3 lb	2.87	3/01	4c
Sirloin steak, graded and ungraded, excl U.S. prime and choice	lb	4.67	7/01	11r
Soft drink, Coca Cola, ex deposit	2 liter	1.41	3/01	4c
Steak, sirloin, U.S. choice, boneless	lb	6.20	7/01	11r
Steak, T-bone	lb	6.49	3/01	4c
Strawberries, dry pint	12 oz	1.79	7/01	11r
Sugar and other sweets, expenditures on	yr	124	1999	30r
Sugar, cane or beet	4 lbs	1.52	3/01	4c
Sugar, white, all sizes	lb	0.46	7/01	11r
Tobacco products and smoking supplies purchases	yr	217	1999	30r
Tomatoes, field grown	lb	1.17	7/01	11r
Tomatoes, Hunt's or Del Monte	14.5 oz	0.88	3/01	4c
Tuna, chunk, light	6 oz	0.80	3/01	4c
Tuna, light, chunk	lb	2.05	7/01	11r
Goods and Services				
Miscellaneous goods and services, ACCRA Index		106.80	3/01	4c
B&B Japanese maple (acer japonicum)	gal	39.99	4/00	93r
Boxwood (buxus)	2 gal	14.99-24.99	4/00	93r
Daylilly (hemerocallis)	gal	6.99-8.99	4/00	93r
Flat of annuals		16.68	4/00	93r

Values are in dollars or fractions of dollars. In the column headed *Ref*, references are shown to sources. Each reference is followed by a letter. These refer to the geographical level for which data were reported: s=State, r=Region, and c=City or metro. The abbreviation *ex* is used to mean *except* or *excluding*; *exp* stands for expenditures. For other abbreviations and further explanations, please see the Introduction.

Spokane, WA - continued

Item	Per	Value	Date	Ref.
Goods and Services				
Fountain grass (pennisetum)	gal	7.99-11.99	4/00	93r
Hanging basket (10 in)		29.99	4/00	93r
Hardy geranium (geranium)	gal	6.99-11.99	4/00	93r
Hosta (hosta)	gal	6.99-18.99	4/00	93r
Lilac (syrubga vulgaris)	2 gal	14.99-17.99	4/00	93r
Miscellaneous purchases	yr	1070	1999	30r
Rhododendron (rhododendron)	2 gal	14.99	4/00	93r
Sage (salvia)	gal	6.99	4/00	93r
Wintercreeper euonymus (euonymus fortunei)	2 gal	14.99-22.99	4/00	93r
Hunting license	yr	30.00	4/01	34s
Health Care				
Health care, ACCRA Index		118.10	3/01	4c
Cardiac catheterization, ave hospital/ physician charges		13290	1998	77s
Childbirth, Cesarean delivery		11587	1997	13r
Childbirth, vaginal delivery		6725	1997	13r
Dentist's fee, adult teeth cleaning and periodic oral exam	visit	103.67	3/01	4c
Doctor's fee, routine exam, established patient	visit	57.71	3/01	4c
Drugs, expenditures on	yr	309	1999	30r
Health care purchases	yr	1869	1999	30r
Health insurance expenditures	yr	868	1999	30r
Hospital care, private room	day	591.00	3/01	4c
Hysterectomy, laproscopically-assisted, ave hospital/physician charges		10960	1998	76s
Hysterectomy, vaginal, ave hospital and physician charges		9000	1998	76s
Medicaid dispensing fee		3.98-4.92	1999	87s
Medical services expenditures	yr	580	1999	30r
Medical supplies, expenditures on	yr	112	1999	30r
Household Goods				
Dishwashing powder, Cascade	50 oz	3.87	3/01	4c
Floor coverings, expenditures on	yr	49	1999	30r
Furniture, expenditures on	yr	444	1999	30r
Household furnishings and equipment purchases	yr	1768	1999	30r
Household textiles, expenditures on	yr	141	1999	30r
Laundry and cleaning supplies, expenditures on	yr	128	1999	30r
Tissues, facial, Kleenex brand	175	1.48	3/01	4c
Housing				
Housing, ACCRA Index		96.40	3/01	4c
Home, 2200 sq ft, 4-br, 2-bath, 2-car garage, average		163962	2000	47c
Home price, existing, ave		239400	10/00	90r
Home value, median		195000	2001	53s
House, 2400 sq ft, 8000 sq ft lot, new, urban, utilities	total	206581	3/01	4c
House payment, principal and interest, 25% down payment	mos	1018	3/01	4c
Household operation expenditures	yr	781	1999	30r
Housekeeping supplies purchases	yr	513	1999	30r
Lodging expenditures	yr	575	1999	30r
Maintenance, repairs, insurance expenditures	yr	939	1999	30r
Monthly rental value of owned home	mos	662	1999	30r
Owned dwellings, expenditures own	yr	5231	1999	30r
Rent expenditures	yr	2709	1999	30r
Rent, apartment, 2 br, 1 1/2-2 baths, unfurn, 950 sq ft, water	mos	605	3/01	4c
Rental unit, 1 bedroom, with utilities	mos	436	4/01	41c
Rental unit, 2 bedroom, with utilities	mos	527	4/01	41c
Rental unit, 3 bedroom, with utilities	mos	716	4/01	41c
Rental unit, 4 bedroom, with utilities	mos	801	4/01	41c

Spokane, WA - continued

Item	Per	Value	Date	Ref.
Housing - continued				
Shelter, expenditures on	yr	8516	1999	30r
Insurance and Pensions				
Life and other personal insurance purchases	yr	355	1999	30r
Pensions and Social Security, expenditures on	yr	3636	1999	30r
Legal Fees				
Divorce, filing fee		100.00	4/01	35s
Driver's license fee	renew	14.00	1999	48s
Driver's license fee	orig	14.00	1999	48s
Fishing license	yr	20.00	4/01	34s
Personal Goods				
Personal care products and services purchases	yr	449	1999	30r
Shampoo, Alberto VO5	15 oz	1.17	3/01	4c
Toothpaste, Crest or Colgate	6-7 oz	2.41	3/01	4c
Personal Services				
Dry cleaning, man's 2-pc suit		8.95	3/01	4c
Man's haircut, barbershop, no styling		9.57	3/01	4c
Personal services, household, expenditures on	yr	353	1999	30r
Woman's shampoo, trim, blow-dry, no style-change		22.67	3/01	4c
Pets				
Pets, toys, and playground equipment, expenditures on	yr	358	1999	30r
Restaurant Food				
Chicken, fried, thigh and drumstick, KFC/ Church's		2.99	3/01	4c
Hamburger with cheese, McDonald's	1/4 lb	2.29	3/01	4c
Pizza, Pizza Hut or Pizza Inn	11-12 in	11.29	3/01	4c
Taxes				
Federal income taxes paid	yr	3200	1999	30r
Personal taxes, expenditures on	yr	4153	1999	30r
Property taxes paid	yr	923	1999	30r
State and local income taxes paid	yr	812	1999	30r
Transportation				
Transportation, ACCRA Index		98.80	3/01	4c
Bus fare, one-way	trip	0.75	2000	1c
Bus fare, to central business district	1-way	0.75	3/01	4c
Cars and trucks, new, expenditures on	yr	1534	1999	30r
Cars and trucks, used, expenditures on	yr	1593	1999	30r
Diesel at the pump	gal	1.37	10/99	73s
Gasoline and motor oil purchases	yr	1129	1999	30r
Gasoline before-tax price (cents)	gal	127.10	10/00	43s
Maintenance and repair expenditures	yr	797	1999	30r
Public transportation, expenditures on	yr	530	1999	30r
Tire balance, computer or spin balance, front	wheel	8.02	3/01	4c
Transportation purchases	yr	7423	1999	30r
Vehicle expenses, miscellaneous, purchases	yr	2585	1999	30r
Vehicle insurance payments	yr	811	1999	30r
Vehicle purchases (net outlay)	yr	3180	1999	30r
Vehicle rental, lease expenditures	yr	666	1999	30r
Utilities				
Utilities, ACCRA Index		71.90	3/01	4c
Electrical bill, average	mos	58.33	9/00	9s
Electricity, expenditures on	yr	725	1999	30r
Electricity, summer, 250 KWh	mos	13.15	2/96	96c
Electricity, summer, 500 KWh	mos	23.20	2/96	96c
Electricity, summer, 750 KWh	mos	34.45	2/96	96c
Electricity, summer, 1000 KWh	mos	45.62	2/96	96c
Electricity and other, mixed, 2400 sq ft, new home	mos	29.80	3/01	4c
Electricity cost, average	KWh	4.47	9/00	9s
Utilities, fuels, and public services purchased	yr	2179	1999	30r
Water and other public services, expenditures on	yr	339	1999	30r

Values are in dollars or fractions of dollars. In the column headed *Ref*, references are shown to sources. Each reference is followed by a letter. These refer to the geographical level for which data were reported: s=State, r=Region, and c=City or metro. The abbreviation *ex* is used to mean *except* or *excluding*; *exp* stands for expenditures. For other abbreviations and further explanations, please see the Introduction.

Spokane, WA - continued

Item	Per	Value	Date	Ref.
Weddings				
Wedding (national average cost)		19936	2000	33r
Wedding (regional average total cost)		18918	1997	110r
Attendants' gifts		321	1998	33r
Bridal attendants' apparel (5 persons)		824	2000	33r
Bride's headpiece/veil		173	1998	33r
Bride's wedding dress		859	1998	33r
Clergy, religious facility fee		242	1998	33r
Engagement ring		3177	1998	33r
Flowers		789	1998	33r
Groom's formalwear rental		99	2000	33r
Limousine		410	1998	33r
Marriage license cost		52.00	4/01	35s
Men's formalwear (ushers, best man)		469	2000	33r
Mother of bride apparel		241	2000	33r
Music		866	1998	33r
Photography and videography		1368	1998	33r
Rehearsal dinner		728	1998	33r
Wedding invitations and announcements		341	1998	33r
Wedding reception		7968	2000	33r
Wedding rings (bride and groom)		1060	1998	33r

Springfield, IL

Item	Per	Value	Date	Ref.
Average annual expenditures	yr	35369	1999	30r
Composite, ACCRA index		94.70	3/01	4c
Alcoholic Beverages				
Alcoholic beverage purchases	yr	304	1999	30r
Beer, Heineken, 12-oz, ex deposit	6	6.33	3/01	4c
J & B Scotch	750-ml	18.21	3/01	4c
Malt beverages, all types, all sizes, any origin	16 oz	0.93	7/01	11r
Wine, Livingston or Gallo, Chablis blanc	1.5 liter	4.55	3/01	4c
Wine, red and white table, all sizes, any origin	liter	7.04	7/01	11r
Appliances				
Appliance repair, service call, washing machine	min lab chg	19.20	3/01	4c
Major appliances, expenditures on	yr	165	1999	30r
Small appliances, housewares, expenditures on	yr	90	1999	30r
Banking and Money				
Mortgage interest and charges paid	yr	2277	1999	30r
Mortgage principal paid on owned property	yr	1230	1999	30r
Mortgage rate, incl. points and orig. fee, 30-yr. conv. fixed or ARM	mos	7.03	3/01	4c
Vehicle finance charges paid	yr	328	1999	30r
Charity				
Cash contributions, expenditures	yr	1126	1999	30r
Child Care				
Child raising cost, total, age 0-2	yr	7890	1999	60r
Child raising cost, total, age 3-5	yr	8130	1999	60r
Child raising cost, total, age 6-8	yr	8170	1999	60r
Child raising cost, total, age 9-11	yr	8190	1999	60r
Child raising cost, total, age 12-14	yr	8890	1999	60r
Child raising cost, total, age 15-17	yr	9050	1999	60r
Child's child care and education, age 0-2	yr	1240	1999	60r
Child's child care and education, age 3-5	yr	1370	1999	60r
Child's child care and education, age 6-8	yr	880	1999	60r
Child's child care and education, age 9-11	yr	570	1999	60r
Child's child care and education, age 12-14	yr	420	1999	60r
Child's child care and education, age 15-17	yr	720	1999	60r
Child's clothing, age 0-2	yr	410	1999	60r
Child's clothing, age 3-5	yr	400	1999	60r
Child's clothing, age 6-8	yr	450	1999	60r
Child's clothing, age 9-11	yr	500	1999	60r
Child's clothing, age 12-14	yr	840	1999	60r
Child's clothing, age 15-17	yr	740	1999	60r
Child's food, age 0-2	yr	960	1999	60r
Child's food, age 3-5	yr	1120	1999	60r
Child's food, age 6-8	yr	1430	1999	60r

Item	Per	Value	Date	Ref.
Child Care - continued				
Child's food, age 9-11	yr	1710	1999	60r
Child's food, age 12-14	yr	1710	1999	60r
Child's food, age 15-17	yr	1920	1999	60r
Child's health care, age 0-2	yr	520	1999	60r
Child's health care, age 3-5	yr	500	1999	60r
Child's health care, age 6-8	yr	570	1999	60r
Child's health care, age 9-11	yr	610	1999	60r
Child's health care, age 12-14	yr	630	1999	60r
Child's health care, age 15-17	yr	650	1999	60r
Child's housing, age 0-2	yr	2860	1999	60r
Child's housing, age 3-5	yr	2840	1999	60r
Child's housing, age 6-8	yr	2800	1999	60r
Child's housing, age 9-11	yr	2650	1999	60r
Child's housing, age 12-14	yr	2840	1999	60r
Child's housing, age 15-17	yr	2440	1999	60r
Child's personal care, reading, age 0-2	yr	880	1999	60r
Child's personal care, reading, age 3-5	yr	900	1999	60r
Child's personal care, reading, age 6-8	yr	930	1999	60r
Child's personal care, reading, age 9-11	yr	970	1999	60r
Child's personal care, reading, age 12-14	yr	1150	1999	60r
Child's personal care, reading, age 15-17	yr	920	1999	60r
Daycare	mos	332	1998	37c
Daycare, 3-year old, 5 days, 8 hrs/day	mos	332	1998	85c
Clothing				
Apparel and services purchases	yr	1607	1999	30r
Boys' brief, cotton	3	4.71	3/01	4c
Boys, 2 to 15, expenditures on	yr	91	1999	30r
Children under 2, expenditures on	yr	59	1999	30r
Footwear, expenditures on	yr	285	1999	30r
Girls, 2 to 15, expenditures on	yr	116	1999	30r
Men and boys, expenditures on	yr	433	1999	30r
Men, 16 and over, expenditures on	yr	341	1999	30r
Shirt, man's dress shirt		23.79	3/01	4c
Slacks, man's "No Wrinkles" khaki		29.99	3/01	4c
Women, 16 and over, expenditures on	yr	490	1999	30r
Communications				
Cable modem installation, Adelphi		54.90	6/99	103s
Cable modem installation, AT&T-BIS		150.00	6/99	103s
Cable modem installation, Media One		100.00	6/99	103s
Cable modem rate, cable subscriber, Adelphi	mos	34.95	6/99	103s
Cable modem rate, cable subscriber, AT&T-BIS	mos	39.95	6/99	103s
Cable modem rate, cable subscriber, Media One	mos	34.95-39.95	6/99	103s
Cable modem rate, non-cable subscriber, Adelphi	mos	44.95	6/99	103s
Cable modem rate, non-cable subscriber, Media One	mos	49.95	6/99	103s
Newspaper subscription, daily and Sunday delivery	mos	14.00	3/01	4c
Phone line, single, business, field visit	inst.	52.35	12/97	17s
Phone line, single, business, no field visit	inst.	52.35	12/97	17s
Phone line, single, residence, field visit	inst.	55.00	12/97	17s
Phone line, single, residence, no field visit	inst.	55.00	12/97	17s
Postage and stationery, expenditures on	yr	140	1999	30r
Postal rate, express mail, up to half-pound		12.45	7/01	108r
Postal rate, letter, first class, first ounce		0.34	7/01	108r
Postal rate, letter, two ounces		0.57	7/01	108r
Postal rate, post card		0.21	7/01	108r
Postal rate, priority mail, two pounds		3.95	7/01	108r
Postal rate, priority mail, up to one pound		3.50	7/01	108r
Telephone bill, business, basic rate	mos	11.87	12/97	18c
Telephone bill, family of three	mos	19.50	3/01	4c
Telephone bill, residential, basic rate	mos	9.00	12/97	18c
Telephone services, expenditures on	yr	830	1999	30r
Education				
Board, 4-year private college/university	yr	2306	1996	38s
Board, 4-year public college/university	yr	2405	1996	38s
Education expenditures	yr	583	1999	30r
Room, 4-year private college/university	yr	2718	1996	38s
Room, 4-year public college/university	yr	2072	1996	38s

Values are in dollars or fractions of dollars. In the column headed *Ref*, references are shown to sources. Each reference is followed by a letter. These refer to the geographical level for which data were reported: s=State, r=Region, and c=City or metro. The abbreviation *ex* is used to mean *except* or *excluding*; *exp* stands for expenditures. For other abbreviations and further explanations, please see the Introduction.

Springfield, IL - continued

Item	Per	Value	Date	Ref.
Education				
Total cost, 4-year private college/university	yr	16678	1996	38s
Total cost, 4-year public college/university	yr	7829	1996	38s
Tuition, 2-year public college/university, in state	yr	1232	1996	38s
Tuition, 4-year private college/university, in state	yr	11653	1996	38s
Tuition, 4-year public college/university	yr	3352	1996	38s
Energy and Fuels				
Electricity	500 KWhs	46.59	7/01	11r
Energy, combined forms, 2400 sq ft	mos	139.01	3/01	4c
Energy, exc. electricity, 2400 sq ft	mos	90.35	3/01	4c
Fuel oil #2	gal	1.27	7/01	11r
Fuel oil and other fuels, expenditures on	yr	68	1999	30r
Gas, natural, commercial rate	1000 cf	8.47	11/00	88s
Gas, regular unleaded, cash, self-service	gal	1.43	3/01	4c
Gasoline, unleaded midgrade	gal	1.79	7/01	11r
Gasoline, unleaded premium	gal	1.86	7/01	11r
Gasoline, unleaded regular	gal	1.58	7/01	11r
Natural gas, expenditures on	yr	389	1999	30r
Utility (piped) gas, therm		0.81	7/01	11r
Utility (piped) gas, 40 therms		38.01	7/01	11r
Utility (piped) gas, 100 therms		81.75	7/01	11r
Entertainment				
Bowling, Saturday evening rate	line	2.83	3/01	4c
Entertainment purchases	yr	1984	1999	30r
Fees and admissions paid	yr	444	1999	30r
Monopoly game, Parker Brothers', No. 9	game	11.17	3/01	4c
Movie, first-run, Saturday, evening	adm.	7.00	3/01	4c
Television, radios, sound equipment, expenditures on	yr	580	1999	30r
Tennis balls, yellow, Wilson or Penn, 3	can	2.43	3/01	4c
Funerals				
Cosmetology, hair, other preparation		178.32	1/99	78s
Embalming		408.19	1/99	78r
Funeral at funeral home		362.13	1/99	78r
Professional service charges		1375.51	1/99	78r
Transfer of remains to funeral home		155.92	1/99	78r
Visitation/viewing		294.38	1/99	78r
Groceries				
Groceries, ACCRA Index		95.20	3/01	4c
Antibiotic ointment, Polysporin	0.5 oz	4.65	3/01	4c
Baby food, strained vegetables or fruit, lowest price	4-4.5 oz	0.36	3/01	4c
Bacon, sliced	lb	3.15	7/01	11r
Bakery products, expenditures on	yr	281	1999	30r
Bananas	lb	0.51	3/01	4c
Bananas	lb	0.48	7/01	11r
Beans, dried, any type, all sizes	lb	0.61	7/01	11r
Beef for stew, boneless	lb	3.08	7/01	11r
Beef or hamburger, ground	lb	1.58	3/01	4c
Beef, expenditures on	yr	217	1999	30r
Bologna, all beef or mixed	lb	2.52	7/01	11r
Bread, white	loaf	0.93	3/01	4c
Bread, white, pan	lb	1.06	7/01	11r
Broccoli	lb	0.91	7/01	11r
Butter, salted, grade AA, stick	lb	3.04	7/01	11r
Butter, yoghurt, cheese, etc, expenditures on	yr	183	1999	30r
Cereals and bakery product purchases	yr	430	1999	30r
Cereals and cereal products, expenditures on	yr	149	1999	30r
Cheese, Kraft grated Parmesan	8 oz	3.40	3/01	4c
Chicken, fresh, whole	lb	1.07	7/01	11r
Chicken, whole fryer	lb	1.01	3/01	4c
Chops, boneless,	lb	3.64	7/01	11r
Chuck roast, U.S. choice, boneless	lb	2.47	7/01	11r
Cigarettes, Winston, Kings	carton	32.67	3/01	4c
Coffee, 100%, ground roast, all sizes	lb	2.69	7/01	11r
Coffee, vacuum-packed	13 oz	2.31	3/01	4c
Cookies, chocolate chip	lb	2.87	7/01	11r

Springfield, IL - continued

Item	Per	Value	Date	Ref.
Groceries - continued				
Corn Flakes, Kellogg's or Post Toasties	18 oz	2.02	3/01	4c
Corn, frozen, whole kernel, lowest price	16 oz	1.00	3/01	4c
Dairy product purchases	yr	304	1999	30r
Eggs, expenditures on	yr	26	1999	30r
Eggs, Grade A or AA	dozen	1.10	3/01	4c
Eggs, grade A, large	dozen	0.88	7/01	11r
Fats and oils, expenditures on	yr	75	1999	30r
Fish and seafood, expenditures on	yr	72	1999	30r
Food (excl fruit and vegetables), eaten at home, purchases	yr	887	1999	30r
Food cooked on trips, expenditures on	yr	44	1999	30r
Food purchases	yr	4802	1999	30r
Food purchases, eaten away from home	yr	2069	1999	30r
Food purchases, food eaten at home	yr	2733	1999	30r
Fresh fruits, expenditures on	yr	138	1999	30r
Fresh milk and cream, expenditures on	yr	120	1999	30r
Fresh vegetables, expenditures on	yr	126	1999	30r
Grapefruit	lb	0.66	7/01	11r
Grapes, Thompson, seedless	lb	1.64	7/01	11r
Ground beef, 100% beef	lb	1.64	7/01	11r
Ground beef, lean and extra lean	lb	2.16	7/01	11r
Ground chuck, 100% beef	lb	2.13	7/01	11r
Ham, boneless, excl canned	lb	2.62	7/01	11r
Ice cream, prepackaged, bulk, regular	1/2 gal	3.35	7/01	11r
Lemons	lb	1.19	7/01	11r
Lettuce, iceberg	head	0.95	3/01	4c
Lettuce, iceberg	lb	0.73	7/01	11r
Margarine, Blue Bonnet or Parkay, stick	lb	0.67	3/01	4c
Margarine, soft, tubs	lb	0.89	7/01	11r
Meats, poultry, fish, and egg purchases	yr	671	1999	30r
Milk, fresh, whole, fortified	gal	2.71	7/01	11r
Milk, whole	1/2 gal	1.87	3/01	4c
Nonalcoholic beverages, expenditures on	yr	239	1999	30r
Orange juice, Minute Maid frozen	12 oz	1.54	3/01	4c
Oranges, Navel	lb	0.80	7/01	11r
Oranges, Valencia	lb	0.66	7/01	11r
Peaches, halves or slices, Hunt's, Del Monte, or Libby's	29 oz	1.56	3/01	4c
Pears, Anjou	lb	0.93	7/01	11r
Peas, green, Del Monte or Green Giant	15 oz	0.56	3/01	4c
Pork chops, center cut, bone-in	lb	3.63	7/01	11r
Pork, expenditures on	yr	150	1999	30r
Potato chips	16 oz	3.52	7/01	11r
Potatoes, frozen, french fried	lb	1.08	7/01	11r
Potatoes, white or red	10 lb	2.71	3/01	4c
Potatoes, white, all types	lb	0.33	7/01	11r
Poultry, expenditures on	yr	108	1999	30r
Processed fruits, expenditures on	yr	98	1999	30r
Processed vegetables, expenditures on	yr	80	1999	30r
Round roast, U.S. choice, boneless	lb	3.07	7/01	11r
Round steak, graded and ungraded, excl U.S. prime and choice	lb	3.41	7/01	11r
Sausage, Jimmy Dean/Owens pork	lb	3.39	3/01	4c
Shortening, vegetable oil blends	lb	1.13	7/01	11r
Shortening, vegetable, Crisco	3 lb	2.99	3/01	4c
Soft drink, Coca Cola, ex deposit	2 liter	1.09	3/01	4c
Spaghetti and macaroni	lb	0.80	7/01	11r
Steak, round, U.S. choice, boneless	lb	3.23	7/01	11r
Steak, T-bone	lb	6.55	3/01	4c
Steak, T-bone, U.S. choice, bone-in	lb	6.68	7/01	11r
Strawberries, dry pint	12 oz	1.32	7/01	11r
Sugar and other sweets, expenditures on	yr	114	1999	30r
Sugar, cane or beet	4 lbs	1.29	3/01	4c
Sugar, white, 33-80 ounce package	lb	0.42	7/01	11r
Sugar, white, all sizes	lb	0.43	7/01	11r
Tobacco products and smoking supplies purchases	yr	331	1999	30r
Tomatoes, field grown	lb	1.46	7/01	11r
Tomatoes, Hunt's or Del Monte	14.5 oz	0.81	3/01	4c
Tuna, chunk, light	6 oz	0.54	3/01	4c
Tuna, light, chunk	lb	1.80	7/01	11r
Turkey, frozen, whole	lb	1.15	7/01	11r

Values are in dollars or fractions of dollars. In the column headed *Ref*, references are shown to sources. Each reference is followed by a letter. These refer to the geographical level for which data were reported: s=State, r=Region, and c=City or metro. The abbreviation *ex* is used to mean *except* or *excluding*; *exp* stands for *expenditures*. For other abbreviations and further explanations, please see the Introduction.

Item	Per	Value	Date	Ref.
Goods and Services				
Miscellaneous goods and services, ACCRA Index		93.60	3/01	4c
B&B Japanese maple (acer japonicum)	gal	29.99-169.99	4/00	93r
Boxwood (buxus)	2 gal	18.99-39.99	4/00	93r
Daylilly (hemerocallis)	gal	4.99-25.00	4/00	93r
Flat of annuals		11.98-24.99	4/00	93r
Fountain grass (pennisetum)	gal	5.98-12.98	4/00	93r
Hanging basket (10 in)		12.99-27.99	4/00	93r
Hardy geranium (geranium)	gal	7.99-9.99	4/00	93r
Hosta (hosta)	gal	6.00-25.00	4/00	93r
Lilac (syrubga vulgaris)	2 gal	14.99-24.99	4/00	93r
Miscellaneous purchases	yr	865	1999	30r
Rhododendron (rhododendron)	2 gal	23.98-42.99	4/00	93r
Sage (salvia)	gal	6.00-9.99	4/00	93r
Wintercreeper euonymus (euonymus fortunei)	2 gal	16.00-169.99	4/00	93r
Hunting license	yr	7.50	4/01	34s
Health Care				
Health care, ACCRA Index		100.90	3/01	4c
Cardiac catheterization, ave hospital/ physician charges		17690	1998	77s
Childbirth, Cesarean delivery		10722	1997	13r
Childbirth, vaginal delivery		6223	1997	13r
Dentist's fee, adult teeth cleaning and periodic oral exam	visit	70.80	3/01	4c
Doctor's fee, routine exam, established patient	visit	57.40	3/01	4c
Drugs, expenditures on	yr	394	1999	30r
Health care purchases	yr	2048	1999	30r
Health insurance expenditures	yr	978	1999	30r
Hospital care, private room	day	585.00	3/01	4c
Hysterectomy, laproscopically-assisted, ave hospital/physician charges		15850	1998	76s
Hysterectomy, vaginal, ave hospital and physician charges		11810	1998	76s
Medicaid dispensing fee		3.69-15.45	1999	87s
Medical services expenditures	yr	554	1999	30r
Medical supplies, expenditures on	yr	122	1999	30r
Plastic surgery, breast augmentation		3184	2000	7r
Plastic surgery, breast lift		3585	2000	7r
Plastic surgery, facelift		4999	2000	7r
Plastic surgery, hair transplantation		3105	2000	7r
Plastic surgery, lip augmentation		1290	2000	7r
Plastic surgery, lower body lift		8135	2000	7r
Plastic surgery, thigh lift		3839	2000	7r
Household Goods				
Dishwashing powder, Cascade	50 oz	3.07	3/01	4c
Floor coverings, expenditures on	yr	52	1999	30r
Furniture, expenditures on	yr	344	1999	30r
Household furnishings and equipment purchases	yr	1475	1999	30r
Household textiles, expenditures on	yr	109	1999	30r
Laundry and cleaning supplies, expenditures on	yr	134	1999	30r
Tissues, facial, Kleenex brand	175	1.12	3/01	4c
Housing				
Housing, ACCRA Index		89.60	3/01	4c
Home, 2200 sq ft, 4-br, 2-bath, 2-car garage, average		139000	2000	47c

Item	Per	Value	Date	Ref.
Housing - continued				
Home price, existing, ave		144400	10/00	90r
Home value, median		183000	2001	53s
House, 2400 sq ft, 8000 sq ft lot, new, urban, utilities	total	184000	3/01	4c
House payment, principal and interest, 25% down payment	mos	920	3/01	4c
Household operation expenditures	yr	542	1999	30r
Housekeeping supplies purchases	yr	508	1999	30r
Lodging expenditures	yr	430	1999	30r
Maintenance, repairs, insurance expenditures	yr	853	1999	30r
Monthly rental value of owned home	mos	547	1999	30r
Owned dwellings, expenditures own	yr	4282	1999	30r
Rent expenditures	yr	1558	1999	30r
Rent, apartment, 2 br, 1 1/2-2 baths, unfurn, 950 sq ft, water	mos	631	3/01	4c
Rental unit, 1 bedroom, with utilities	mos	393	4/01	41c
Rental unit, 2 bedroom, with utilities	mos	524	4/01	41c
Rental unit, 3 bedroom, with utilities	mos	697	4/01	41c
Rental unit, 4 bedroom, with utilities	mos	793	4/01	41c
Shelter, expenditures on	yr	6270	1999	30r
Insurance and Pensions				
Life and other personal insurance purchases	yr	387	1999	30r
Pensions and Social Security, expenditures on	yr	2968	1999	30r
Legal Fees				
Divorce, filing fee		100.00-150.00	4/01	35s
Driver's license fee	orig	10.00	1999	48s
Driver's license fee	renew	20.00	1999	48s
Personal Goods				
Personal care products and services purchases	yr	385	1999	30r
Shampoo, Alberto VO5	15 oz	0.92	3/01	4c
Toothpaste, Crest or Colgate	6-7 oz	2.12	3/01	4c
Personal Services				
Dry cleaning, man's 2-pc suit		7.20	3/01	4c
Man's haircut, barbershop, no styling		9.80	3/01	4c
Personal services, household, expenditures on	yr	300	1999	30r
Woman's shampoo, trim, blow-dry, no style-change		30.00	3/01	4c
Pets				
Pets, toys, and playground equipment, expenditures on	yr	375	1999	30r
Restaurant Food				
Chicken, fried, thigh and drumstick, KFC/ Church's		2.44	3/01	4c
Hamburger with cheese, McDonald's	1/4 lb	2.29	3/01	4c
Pizza, Pizza Hut or Pizza Inn	11-12 in	9.49	3/01	4c
Taxes				
Federal income taxes paid	yr	2326	1999	30r
Personal taxes, expenditures on	yr	3223	1999	30r
Property taxes paid	yr	1152	1999	30r
State and local income taxes paid	yr	753	1999	30r
Transportation				
Transportation, ACCRA Index		95.70	3/01	4c
Bus fare, one-way	trip	0.75	2000	1c
Bus fare, to central business district	1-way	0.75	3/01	4c
Cars and trucks, new, expenditures on	yr	1280	1999	30r
Cars and trucks, used, expenditures on	yr	1763	1999	30r
Diesel at the pump	gal	1.33	10/99	73s
Gasoline and motor oil purchases	yr	1036	1999	30r
Gasoline before-tax price (cents)	gal	112.70	10/00	43s
Maintenance and repair expenditures	yr	594	1999	30r
Public transportation, expenditures on	yr	341	1999	30r
Tire balance, computer or spin balance, front	wheel	7.50	3/01	4c
Transportation purchases	yr	6617	1999	30r

Values are in dollars or fractions of dollars. In the column headed *Ref*, references are shown to sources. Each reference is followed by a letter. These refer to the geographical level for which data were reported: s=State, r=Region, and c=City or metro. The abbreviation *ex* is used to mean *except* or *excluding*; *exp* stands for *expenditures*. For other abbreviations and further explanations, please see the Introduction.

Springfield, IL - continued

Item	Per	Value	Date	Ref.
Transportation				
Vehicle expenses, miscellaneous, purchases	yr	2159	1999	30r
Vehicle insurance payments	yr	701	1999	30r
Vehicle purchases (net outlay)	yr	3081	1999	30r
Vehicle rental, lease expenditures	yr	536	1999	30r
Utilities				
Utilities, ACCRA Index		110.60	3/01	4c
Electrical bill, average	mos	63.08	9/00	9s
Electricity, expenditures on	yr	841	1999	30r
Electricity and other, mixed, 2400 sq ft, new home	mos	48.66	3/01	4c
Electricity cost, average	KWh	6.49	9/00	9s
Utilities, fuels, and public services purchased	yr	2401	1999	30r
Water and other public services, expenditures on	yr	273	1999	30r
Weddings				
Wedding (national average cost)		19936	2000	33r
Wedding (regional average total cost)		16195	1997	110r
Attendants' gifts		321	1998	33r
Bridal attendants' apparel (5 persons)		824	2000	33r
Bride's headpiece/veil		173	1998	33r
Bride's wedding dress		859	1998	33r
Clergy, religious facility fee		242	1998	33r
Engagement ring		3177	1998	33r
Flowers		789	1998	33r
Groom's formalwear rental		99	2000	33r
Limousine		410	1998	33r
Marriage license cost		15.00-20.00	4/01	35s
Men's formalwear (ushers, best man)		469	2000	33r
Mother of bride apparel		241	2000	33r
Music		866	1998	33r
Photography and videography		1368	1998	33r
Rehearsal dinner		728	1998	33r
Wedding invitations and announcements		341	1998	33r
Wedding reception		7968	2000	33r
Wedding rings (bride and groom)		1060	1998	33r

Springfield, MA

Item	Per	Value	Date	Ref.
Average annual expenditures	yr	37971	1999	30r
Alcoholic Beverages				
Alcoholic beverage purchases	yr	368	1999	30r
Wine, red and white table, all sizes, any origin	liter	9.64	7/01	11r
Appliances				
Major appliances, expenditures on	yr	194	1999	30r
Small appliances, housewares, expenditures on	yr	93	1999	30r
Banking and Money				
Mortgage interest and charges paid	yr	2622	1999	30r
Mortgage principal paid on owned property	yr	1262	1999	30r
Vehicle finance charges paid	yr	240	1999	30r
Charity				
Cash contributions, expenditures	yr	1001	1999	30r
Child Care				
Child raising cost, total, age 0-2	yr	8670	1999	60r
Child raising cost, total, age 3-5	yr	8910	1999	60r
Child raising cost, total, age 6-8	yr	9040	1999	60r
Child raising cost, total, age 9-11	yr	9100	1999	60r
Child raising cost, total, age 12-14	yr	9890	1999	60r
Child raising cost, total, age 15-17	yr	10010	1999	60r
Child's child care and education, age 0-2	yr	1070	1999	60r
Child's child care and education, age 3-5	yr	1190	1999	60r
Child's child care and education, age 6-8	yr	740	1999	60r
Child's child care and education, age 9-11	yr	470	1999	60r
Child's child care and education, age 12-14	yr	350	1999	60r
Child's child care and education, age 15-17	yr	590	1999	60r
Child's clothing, age 0-2	yr	480	1999	60r

Springfield, MA - continued

Item	Per	Value	Date	Ref.
Child Care - continued				
Child's clothing, age 3-5	yr	470	1999	60r
Child's clothing, age 6-8	yr	520	1999	60r
Child's clothing, age 9-11	yr	570	1999	60r
Child's clothing, age 12-14	yr	970	1999	60r
Child's clothing, age 15-17	yr	870	1999	60r
Child's food, age 0-2	yr	1130	1999	60r
Child's food, age 3-5	yr	1290	1999	60r
Child's food, age 6-8	yr	1640	1999	60r
Child's food, age 9-11	yr	1930	1999	60r
Child's food, age 12-14	yr	1940	1999	60r
Child's food, age 15-17	yr	2150	1999	60r
Child's health care, age 0-2	yr	550	1999	60r
Child's health care, age 3-5	yr	530	1999	60r
Child's health care, age 6-8	yr	610	1999	60r
Child's health care, age 9-11	yr	650	1999	60r
Child's health care, age 12-14	yr	660	1999	60r
Child's health care, age 15-17	yr	690	1999	60r
Child's housing, age 0-2	yr	3555	1999	60r
Child's housing, age 3-5	yr	3530	1999	60r
Child's housing, age 6-8	yr	3490	1999	60r
Child's housing, age 9-11	yr	3340	1999	60r
Child's housing, age 12-14	yr	3530	1999	60r
Child's housing, age 15-17	yr	3140	1999	60r
Child's personal care, reading, age 0-2	yr	920	1999	60r
Child's personal care, reading, age 3-5	yr	950	1999	60r
Child's personal care, reading, age 6-8	yr	980	1999	60r
Child's personal care, reading, age 9-11	yr	1020	1999	60r
Child's personal care, reading, age 12-14	yr	1190	1999	60r
Child's personal care, reading, age 15-17	yr	970	1999	60r
Clothing				
Apparel and services purchases	yr	1831	1999	30r
Boys, 2 to 15, expenditures on	yr	92	1999	30r
Children under 2, expenditures on	yr	63	1999	30r
Footwear, expenditures on	yr	300	1999	30r
Girls, 2 to 15, expenditures on	yr	101	1999	30r
Men and boys, expenditures on	yr	446	1999	30r
Men, 16 and over, expenditures on	yr	354	1999	30r
Women, 16 and over, expenditures on	yr	584	1999	30r
Communications				
Cable modem installation, Adelphi		54.90	6/99	103s
Cable modem installation, Media One		100.00	6/99	103s
Cable modem rate, cable subscriber, Adelphi	mos	34.95	6/99	103s
Cable modem rate, cable subscriber, Media One	mos	34.95-39.95	6/99	103s
Cable modem rate, non-cable subscriber, Adelphi	mos	44.95	6/99	103s
Cable modem rate, non-cable subscriber, Media One	mos	49.95	6/99	103s
Phone line, single, business, field visit	inst.	120.52	12/97	17s
Phone line, single, business, no field visit	inst.	93.02	12/97	17s
Phone line, single, residence, field visit	inst.	64.57	12/97	17s
Phone line, single, residence, no field visit	inst.	37.07	12/97	17s
Postage and stationery, expenditures on	yr	138	1999	30r
Postal rate, express mail, up to half-pound		12.45	7/01	108r
Postal rate, letter, first class, first ounce		0.34	7/01	108r
Postal rate, letter, two ounces		0.57	7/01	108r
Postal rate, post card		0.21	7/01	108r
Postal rate, priority mail, two pounds		3.95	7/01	108r
Postal rate, priority mail, up to one pound		3.50	7/01	108r
Telephone bill, business, basic rate	mos	39.77	12/97	18c
Telephone bill, residential, basic rate	mos	16.85	12/97	18c
Telephone services, expenditures on	yr	830	1999	30r
Education				
Board, 4-year private college/university	yr	3244	1996	38s
Board, 4-year public college/university	yr	2042	1996	38s
Education expenditures	yr	877	1999	30r
Room, 4-year private college/university	yr	3688	1996	38s
Room, 4-year public college/university	yr	2462	1996	38s
Total cost, 4-year private college/university	yr	23335	1996	38s
Total cost, 4-year public college/university	yr	8757	1996	38s

Values are in dollars or fractions of dollars. In the column headed *Ref*, references are shown to sources. Each reference is followed by a letter. These refer to the geographical level for which data were reported: s=State, r=Region, and c=City or metro. The abbreviation *ex* is used to mean *except* or *excluding*; *exp* stands for *expenditures*. For other abbreviations and further explanations, please see the Introduction.

Springfield, MA - continued

Item	Per	Value	Date	Ref.
Education				
Tuition, 2-year public college/university, in state	yr	2359	1996	38s
Tuition, 4-year private college/university, in state	yr	16403	1996	38s
Tuition, 4-year public college/university	yr	4253	1996	38s
Energy and Fuels				
Electricity	KWh	0.12	7/01	11r
Fuel oil #2	gal	1.31	7/01	11r
Fuel oil and other fuels, expenditures on	yr	207	1999	30r
Gas, heating, winter, average use	mos	152.87	2/96	98c
Gas, natural, commercial rate	1000 cf	10.82	11/00	88s
Gasoline, all types	gal	1.80	7/01	11r
Gasoline, unleaded midgrade	gal	1.85	7/01	11r
Gasoline, unleaded premium	gal	1.91	7/01	11r
Gasoline, unleaded regular	gal	1.71	7/01	11r
Natural gas, expenditures on	yr	368	1999	30r
Utility (piped) gas, therm		1.08	7/01	11r
Utility (piped) gas, 40 therms		50.87	7/01	11r
Utility (piped) gas, 100 therms		111.06	7/01	11r
Entertainment				
Entertainment purchases	yr	1821	1999	30r
Fees and admissions paid	yr	511	1999	30r
Television, radios, sound equipment, expenditures on	yr	650	1999	30r
Funerals				
Total cost of funeral		5776.91	1/99	78r
Acknowledgement cards		14.47	1/99	78r
Casket		2090.19	1/99	78r
Cosmetology, hair, other preparation		132.92	1/99	78r
Embalming		377.33	1/99	78r
Funeral at funeral home		352.43	1/99	78r
Hearse (local)		185.55	1/99	78r
Professional service charges		1289.95	1/99	78r
Service car/van		87.42	1/99	78r
Transfer of remains to funeral home		175.48	1/99	78r
Vault		729.40	1/99	78r
Visitation/viewing		341.76	1/99	78r
Groceries				
Apples, red delicious	lb	0.95	7/01	11r
Bacon, sliced	lb	3.44	7/01	11r
Bakery products, expenditures on	yr	310	1999	30r
Bananas	lb	0.55	7/01	11r
Beef, expenditures on	yr	236	1999	30r
Bread, white, pan	lb	1.09	7/01	11r
Butter, yoghurt, cheese, etc, expenditures on	yr	214	1999	30r
Cereals and bakery product purchases	yr	474	1999	30r
Cereals and cereal products, expenditures on	yr	164	1999	30r
Chicken legs, bone-in	lb	1.23	7/01	11r
Chicken, fresh, whole	lb	1.13	7/01	11r
Chuck roast, U.S. choice, boneless	lb	2.79	7/01	11r
Coffee, 100%, ground roast, all sizes	lb	3.40	7/01	11r
Dairy product purchases	yr	342	1999	30r
Eggs, expenditures on	yr	34	1999	30r
Eggs, grade A, large	dozen	0.82	7/01	11r
Fats and oils, expenditures on	yr	80	1999	30r
Fish and seafood, expenditures on	yr	123	1999	30r
Food (excl fruit and vegetables), eaten at home, purchases	yr	838	1999	30r
Food cooked on trips, expenditures on	yr	48	1999	30r
Food purchases	yr	5314	1999	30r
Food purchases, eaten away from home	yr	2313	1999	30r
Food purchases, food eaten at home	yr	3001	1999	30r
Fresh fruits, expenditures on	yr	169	1999	30r
Fresh milk and cream, expenditures on	yr	128	1999	30r
Fresh vegetables, expenditures on	yr	164	1999	30r
Grapefruit	lb	0.67	7/01	11r
Grapes, Thompson, seedless	lb	2.18	7/01	11r
Ground beef, lean and extra lean	lb	2.66	7/01	11r
Ground chuck, 100% beef	lb	2.04	7/01	11r

Springfield, MA - continued

Item	Per	Value	Date	Ref.
Groceries - continued				
Lettuce, iceberg	lb	0.76	7/01	11r
Meats, poultry, fish, and egg purchases	yr	808	1999	30r
Nonalcoholic beverages, expenditures on	yr	225	1999	30r
Orange juice, frozen concentrate	16 oz	1.88	7/01	11r
Oranges, Navel	lb	0.79	7/01	11r
Oranges, Valencia	lb	0.56	7/01	11r
Peaches	lb	1.16	7/01	11r
Peanut butter, creamy, all sizes	lb	2.01	7/01	11r
Pears, Anjou	lb	1.16	7/01	11r
Pork chops, center cut, bone-in	lb	3.57	7/01	11r
Pork, expenditures on	yr	146	1999	30r
Potato chips	16 oz	3.37	7/01	11r
Potatoes, white, all types	lb	0.42	7/01	11r
Poultry, expenditures on	yr	158	1999	30r
Processed fruits, expenditures on	yr	124	1999	30r
Processed vegetables, expenditures on	yr	82	1999	30r
Round roast, U.S. choice, boneless	lb	3.04	7/01	11r
Spaghetti and macaroni	lb	1.04	7/01	11r
Steak, sirloin, U.S. choice, boneless	lb	5.39	7/01	11r
Strawberries, dry pint	12 oz	1.51	7/01	11r
Sugar and other sweets, expenditures on	yr	110	1999	30r
Sugar, white, 33-80 ounce package	lb	0.46	7/01	11r
Sugar, white, all sizes	lb	0.47	7/01	11r
Tobacco products and smoking supplies purchases	yr	309	1999	30r
Yogurt, natural, fruit flavored	8 oz	0.79	7/01	11r
Goods and Services				
B&B Japanese maple (acer japonicum)	gal	38.99-125.00	4/00	93r
Boxwood (buxus)	2 gal	15.99-49.95	4/00	93r
Daylilly (hemerocallis)	gal	4.95	4/00	93r
Flat of annuals		8.00-14.99	4/00	93r
Fountain grass (pennisetum)	gal	6.99-9.99	4/00	93r
Hanging basket (10 in)		12.95-19.99	4/00	93r
Hardy geranium (geranium)	gal	6.95-7.99	4/00	93r
Hosta (hosta)	gal	4.95	4/00	93r
Lilac (syrubga vulgaris)	2 gal	17.99-74.95	4/00	93r
Miscellaneous purchases	yr	872	1999	30r
Rhododendron (rhododendron)	2 gal	23.99-54.95	4/00	93r
Sage (salvia)	gal	6.95-7.99	4/00	93r
Wintercreeper euonymus (euonymus fortunei)	2 gal	14.99-23.95	4/00	93r
Hunting license	yr	27.50	4/01	34s
Health Care				
Cardiac catheterization, ave hospital/physician charges		17080	1998	77s
Childbirth, Cesarean delivery		14716	1997	13r
Childbirth, vaginal delivery		8541	1997	13r
Drugs, expenditures on	yr	296	1999	30r
Health care purchases	yr	1788	1999	30r
Health insurance expenditures	yr	875	1999	30r
Hysterectomy, laproscopically-assisted, ave hospital/physician charges		13100	1998	76s
Hysterectomy, vaginal, ave hospital and physician charges		8780	1998	76s
Medicaid dispensing fee		3.00	1999	87s
Medical services expenditures	yr	516	1999	30r
Medical supplies, expenditures on	yr	102	1999	30r
Nursing home costs, private room	day	181	2000	82c
Nursing home stay, private room	day	181	2000	81c
Plastic surgery, breast augmentation		4232	2000	7r
Plastic surgery, breast lift		4605	2000	7r
Plastic surgery, facelift		6964	2000	7r

Values are in dollars or fractions of dollars. In the column headed *Ref*, references are shown to sources. Each reference is followed by a letter. These refer to the geographical level for which data were reported: s=State, r=Region, and c=City or metro. The abbreviation *ex* is used to mean *except* or *excluding*; *exp* stands for *expenditures*. For other abbreviations and further explanations, please see the Introduction.

Springfield, MA - continued

Item	Per	Value	Date	Ref.
Health Care				
Plastic surgery, hair transplantation		4193	2000	7r
Plastic surgery, lip augmentation		1675	2000	7r
Plastic surgery, lower body lift		6611	2000	7r
Plastic surgery, thigh lift		4751	2000	7r
Household Goods				
Floor coverings, expenditures on	yr	59	1999	30r
Furniture, expenditures on	yr	388	1999	30r
Household furnishings and equipment purchases	yr	1567	1999	30r
Household textiles, expenditures on	yr	112	1999	30r
Laundry and cleaning supplies, expenditures on	yr	104	1999	30r
Housing				
Home, 2200 sq ft, 4-br, 2-bath, 2-car garage, average		193171	2000	47c
Home price, existing, ave		180800	10/00	90r
Home value, median		261000	2001	53s
Household operation expenditures	yr	581	1999	30r
Housekeeping supplies purchases	yr	474	1999	30r
Lodging expenditures	yr	550	1999	30r
Maintenance, repairs, insurance expenditures	yr	835	1999	30r
Monthly rental value of owned home	mos	663	1999	30r
Owned dwellings, expenditures own	yr	5209	1999	30r
Rent expenditures	yr	2390	1999	30r
Rental unit, 1 bedroom, with utilities	mos	503	4/01	41c
Rental unit, 2 bedroom, with utilities	mos	635	4/01	41c
Rental unit, 3 bedroom, with utilities	mos	793	4/01	41c
Rental unit, 4 bedroom, with utilities	mos	976	4/01	41c
Shelter, expenditures on	yr	8149	1999	30r
Insurance and Pensions				
Life and other personal insurance purchases	yr	424	1999	30r
Pensions and Social Security, expenditures on	yr	3037	1999	30r
Legal Fees				
Divorce, filing fee		100.00	4/01	35s
Driver's license fee	orig	33.75	1999	48s
Driver's license fee	renew	33.75	1999	48s
Fishing license	yr	27.50	4/01	34s
Personal Goods				
Personal care products and services purchases	yr	399	1999	30r
Personal Services				
Personal services, household, expenditures on	yr	271	1999	30r
Pets				
Pets, toys, and playground equipment, expenditures on	yr	325	1999	30r
Taxes				
Federal income taxes paid	yr	2606	1999	30r
Personal taxes, expenditures on	yr	3567	1999	30r
Property taxes paid	yr	1752	1999	30r
State and local income taxes paid	yr	694	1999	30r
Transportation				
Cars and trucks, new, expenditures on	yr	1496	1999	30r
Cars and trucks, used, expenditures on	yr	1251	1999	30r
Diesel at the pump	gal	1.32	10/99	73s
Gasoline and motor oil purchases	yr	901	1999	30r
Gasoline before-tax price (cents)	gal	118.70	10/00	43s
Maintenance and repair expenditures	yr	618	1999	30r
Public transportation, expenditures on	yr	575	1999	30r
Transportation purchases	yr	6503	1999	30r
Vehicle expenses, miscellaneous, purchases	yr	2266	1999	30r
Vehicle insurance payments	yr	824	1999	30r
Vehicle purchases (net outlay)	yr	2761	1999	30r
Vehicle rental, lease expenditures	yr	584	1999	30r

Springfield, MA - continued

Item	Per	Value	Date	Ref.
Travel				
Hotel room	night	111.15	2/01	95s
Utilities				
Electrical bill, average	mos	58.58	9/00	9s
Electricity, expenditures on	yr	837	1999	30r
Electricity, summer, 250 KWh	mos	36.29	2/96	97c
Electricity, summer, 500 KWh	mos	63.20	2/96	97c
Electricity, summer, 750 KWh	mos	90.11	2/96	97c
Electricity, summer, 1000 KWh	mos	117.01	2/96	97c
Electricity cost, average	KWh	8.90	9/00	9s
Utilities, fuels, and public services purchased	yr	2457	1999	30r
Water and other public services, expenditures on	yr	215	1999	30r
Weddings				
Wedding (national average cost)		19936	2000	33r
Wedding (regional average total cost)		29454	1997	110r
Attendants' gifts		321	1998	33r
Bridal attendants' apparel (5 persons)		824	2000	33r
Bride's headpiece/veil		173	1998	33r
Bride's wedding dress		859	1998	33r
Clergy, religious facility fee		242	1998	33r
Engagement ring		3177	1998	33r
Flowers		789	1998	33r
Groom's formalwear rental		99	2000	33r
Limousine		410	1998	33r
Marriage license cost		25.00	4/01	35s
Men's formalwear (ushers, best man)		469	2000	33r
Mother of bride apparel		241	2000	33r
Music		866	1998	33r
Photography and videography		1368	1998	33r
Rehearsal dinner		728	1998	33r
Wedding invitations and announcements		341	1998	33r
Wedding reception		7968	2000	33r
Wedding rings (bride and groom)		1060	1998	33r

Springfield, MO

Item	Per	Value	Date	Ref.
Average annual expenditures	yr	35369	1999	30r
Composite, ACCRA index		92.10	3/01	4c
Alcoholic Beverages				
Alcoholic beverage purchases	yr	304	1999	30r
Beer, Heineken, 12-oz, ex deposit	6	6.95	3/01	4c
J & B Scotch	750-ml	19.43	3/01	4c
Malt beverages, all types, all sizes, any origin	16 oz	0.93	7/01	11r
Wine, Livingston or Gallo, Chablis blanc	1.5 liter	5.70	3/01	4c
Wine, red and white table, all sizes, any origin	liter	7.04	7/01	11r
Appliances				
Appliance repair, service call, washing machine	min lab chg	40.74	3/01	4c
Major appliances, expenditures on	yr	165	1999	30r
Small appliances, housewares, expenditures on	yr	90	1999	30r
Banking and Money				
Mortgage interest and charges paid	yr	2277	1999	30r
Mortgage principal paid on owned property	yr	1230	1999	30r
Mortgage rate, incl. points and orig. fee, 30-yr. conv. fixed or ARM	mos	7.18	3/01	4c
Vehicle finance charges paid	yr	328	1999	30r
Business Expenses				
Business travel, car rental	day	47	2001	3c
Business travel, food	day	41	2001	3c
Business travel, hotel	day	80	2001	3c
Charity				
Cash contributions, expenditures	yr	1126	1999	30r
Child Care				
Child raising cost, total, age 0-2	yr	7890	1999	60r
Child raising cost, total, age 3-5	yr	8130	1999	60r

Values are in dollars or fractions of dollars. In the column headed *Ref*, references are shown to sources. Each reference is followed by a letter. These refer to the geographical level for which data were reported: s=State, r=Region, and c=City or metro. The abbreviation *ex* is used to mean *except* or *excluding*; *exp* stands for expenditures. For other abbreviations and further explanations, please see the Introduction.

Springfield, MO - continued

Item	Per	Value	Date	Ref.
Child Care				
Child raising cost, total, age 6-8	yr	8170	1999	60r
Child raising cost, total, age 9-11	yr	8190	1999	60r
Child raising cost, total, age 12-14	yr	8890	1999	60r
Child raising cost, total, age 15-17	yr	9050	1999	60r
Child's child care and education, age 0-2	yr	1240	1999	60r
Child's child care and education, age 3-5	yr	1370	1999	60r
Child's child care and education, age 6-8	yr	880	1999	60r
Child's child care and education, age 9-11	yr	570	1999	60r
Child's child care and education, age 12-14	yr	420	1999	60r
Child's child care and education, age 15-17	yr	720	1999	60r
Child's clothing, age 0-2	yr	410	1999	60r
Child's clothing, age 3-5	yr	400	1999	60r
Child's clothing, age 6-8	yr	450	1999	60r
Child's clothing, age 9-11	yr	500	1999	60r
Child's clothing, age 12-14	yr	840	1999	60r
Child's clothing, age 15-17	yr	740	1999	60r
Child's food, age 0-2	yr	960	1999	60r
Child's food, age 3-5	yr	1120	1999	60r
Child's food, age 6-8	yr	1430	1999	60r
Child's food, age 9-11	yr	1710	1999	60r
Child's food, age 12-14	yr	1710	1999	60r
Child's food, age 15-17	yr	1920	1999	60r
Child's health care, age 0-2	yr	520	1999	60r
Child's health care, age 3-5	yr	500	1999	60r
Child's health care, age 6-8	yr	570	1999	60r
Child's health care, age 9-11	yr	610	1999	60r
Child's health care, age 12-14	yr	630	1999	60r
Child's health care, age 15-17	yr	650	1999	60r
Child's housing, age 0-2	yr	2860	1999	60r
Child's housing, age 3-5	yr	2840	1999	60r
Child's housing, age 6-8	yr	2800	1999	60r
Child's housing, age 9-11	yr	2650	1999	60r
Child's housing, age 12-14	yr	2840	1999	60r
Child's housing, age 15-17	yr	2440	1999	60r
Child's personal care, reading, age 0-2	yr	880	1999	60r
Child's personal care, reading, age 3-5	yr	900	1999	60r
Child's personal care, reading, age 6-8	yr	930	1999	60r
Child's personal care, reading, age 9-11	yr	970	1999	60r
Child's personal care, reading, age 12-14	yr	1150	1999	60r
Child's personal care, reading, age 15-17	yr	920	1999	60r
Clothing				
Apparel and services purchases	yr	1607	1999	30r
Boys' brief, cotton	3	3.25	3/01	4c
Boys, 2 to 15, expenditures on	yr	91	1999	30r
Children under 2, expenditures on	yr	59	1999	30r
Footwear, expenditures on	yr	285	1999	30r
Girls, 2 to 15, expenditures on	yr	116	1999	30r
Men and boys, expenditures on	yr	433	1999	30r
Men, 16 and over, expenditures on	yr	341	1999	30r
Shirt, man's dress shirt		26.37	3/01	4c
Slacks, man's "No Wrinkles" khaki		31.98	3/01	4c
Women, 16 and over, expenditures on	yr	490	1999	30r
Communications				
Newspaper subscription, daily and Sunday delivery	mos	14.13	3/01	4c
Phone line, single, business, field visit	inst.	52.25	12/97	17s
Phone line, single, business, no field visit	inst.	52.25	12/97	17s
Phone line, single, residence, field visit	inst.	36.50	12/97	17s
Phone line, single, residence, no field visit	inst.	36.50	12/97	17s
Postage and stationery, expenditures on	yr	140	1999	30r
Postal rate, express mail, up to half-pound		12.45	7/01	108r
Postal rate, letter, first class, first ounce		0.34	7/01	108r
Postal rate, letter, two ounces		0.57	7/01	108r
Postal rate, post card		0.21	7/01	108r
Postal rate, priority mail, two pounds		3.95	7/01	108r
Postal rate, priority mail, up to one pound		3.50	7/01	108r
Telephone bill, business, basic rate	mos	25.70	12/97	18c
Telephone bill, family of three	mos	18.28	3/01	4c
Telephone bill, residential, basic rate	mos	10.10	12/97	18c
Telephone services, expenditures on	yr	830	1999	30r

Springfield, MO - continued

Item	Per	Value	Date	Ref.
Education				
Board, 4-year private college/university	yr	2387	1996	38s
Board, 4-year public college/university	yr	1713	1996	38s
Education expenditures	yr	583	1999	30r
Room, 4-year private college/university	yr	2162	1996	38s
Room, 4-year public college/university	yr	2022	1996	38s
Total cost, 4-year private college/university	yr	14116	1996	38s
Total cost, 4-year public college/university	yr	6750	1996	38s
Tuition, 2-year public college/university, in state	yr	1255	1996	38s
Tuition, 4-year private college/university, in state	yr	9566	1996	38s
Tuition, 4-year public college/university	yr	3015	1996	38s
Energy and Fuels				
Electricity	500 KWhs	46.59	7/01	11r
Energy, combined forms, 2400 sq ft	mos	95.51	3/01	4c
Energy, exc. electricity, 2400 sq ft	mos	51.64	3/01	4c
Fuel oil #2	gal	1.27	7/01	11r
Fuel oil and other fuels, expenditures on	yr	68	1999	30r
Gas, natural, commercial rate	1000 cf	8.38	11/00	88s
Gas, regular unleaded, cash, self-service	gal	1.30	3/01	4c
Gasoline, unleaded midgrade	gal	1.79	7/01	11r
Gasoline, unleaded premium	gal	1.86	7/01	11r
Gasoline, unleaded regular	gal	1.58	7/01	11r
Natural gas, expenditures on	yr	389	1999	30r
Utility (piped) gas, therm		0.81	7/01	11r
Utility (piped) gas, 40 therms		38.01	7/01	11r
Utility (piped) gas, 100 therms		81.75	7/01	11r
Entertainment				
Bowling, Saturday evening rate	line	2.36	3/01	4c
Entertainment purchases	yr	1984	1999	30r
Fees and admissions paid	yr	444	1999	30r
Monopoly game, Parker Brothers', No. 9	game	7.89	3/01	4c
Movie, first-run, Saturday, evening	adm.	7.00	3/01	4c
Television, radios, sound equipment, expenditures on	yr	580	1999	30r
Tennis balls, yellow, Wilson or Penn, 3	can	1.96	3/01	4c
Funerals				
Cosmetology, hair, other preparation		178.32	1/99	78r
Embalming		408.19	1/99	78r
Funeral at funeral home		362.13	1/99	78r
Professional service charges		1375.51	1/99	78r
Transfer of remains to funeral home		155.92	1/99	78r
Visitation/viewing		294.38	1/99	78r
Groceries				
Groceries, ACCRA Index		100.40	3/01	4c
Antibiotic ointment, Polysporin	0.5 oz	4.10	3/01	4c
Baby food, strained vegetables or fruit, lowest price	4-4.5 oz	0.44	3/01	4c
Bacon, sliced	lb	3.15	7/01	11r
Bakery products, expenditures on	yr	281	1999	30r
Bananas	lb	0.45	3/01	4c
Bananas	lb	0.48	7/01	11r
Beans, dried, any type, all sizes	lb	0.61	7/01	11r
Beef for stew, boneless	lb	3.08	7/01	11r
Beef or hamburger, ground	lb	1.24	3/01	4c
Beef, expenditures on	yr	217	1999	30r
Bologna, all beef or mixed	lb	2.52	7/01	11r
Bread, white	loaf	1.13	3/01	4c
Bread, white, pan	lb	1.06	7/01	11r
Broccoli	lb	0.91	7/01	11r
Butter, salted, grade AA, stick	lb	3.04	7/01	11r
Butter, yoghurt, cheese, etc, expenditures on	yr	183	1999	30r
Cereals and bakery product purchases	yr	430	1999	30r
Cereals and cereal products, expenditures on	yr	149	1999	30r
Cheese, Kraft grated Parmesan	8 oz	3.83	3/01	4c
Chicken, fresh, whole	lb	1.07	7/01	11r
Chicken, whole fryer	lb	1.03	3/01	4c
Chops, boneless,	lb	3.64	7/01	11r

Values are in dollars or fractions of dollars. In the column headed *Ref*, references are shown to sources. Each reference is followed by a letter. These refer to the geographical level for which data were reported: s=State, r=Region, and c=City or metro. The abbreviation *ex* is used to mean *except* or *excluding*; *exp* stands for expenditures. For other abbreviations and further explanations, please see the Introduction.

Springfield, MO - continued

Groceries

Item	Per	Value	Date	Ref.
Chuck roast, U.S. choice, boneless	lb	2.47	7/01	11r
Cigarettes, Winston, Kings	carton	29.22	3/01	4c
Coffee, 100%, ground roast, all sizes	lb	2.69	7/01	11r
Coffee, vacuum-packed	13 oz	2.97	3/01	4c
Cookies, chocolate chip	lb	2.87	7/01	11r
Corn Flakes, Kellogg's or Post Toasties	18 oz	2.10	3/01	4c
Corn, frozen, whole kernel, lowest price	16 oz	1.05	3/01	4c
Dairy product purchases	yr	304	1999	30r
Eggs, expenditures on	yr	26	1999	30r
Eggs, Grade A or AA	dozen	1.01	3/01	4c
Eggs, grade A, large	dozen	0.88	7/01	11r
Fats and oils, expenditures on	yr	75	1999	30r
Fish and seafood, expenditures on	yr	72	1999	30r
Food (excl fruit and vegetables), eaten at home, purchases	yr	887	1999	30r
Food cooked on trips, expenditures on	yr	44	1999	30r
Food purchases	yr	4802	1999	30r
Food purchases, eaten away from home	yr	2069	1999	30r
Food purchases, food eaten at home	yr	2733	1999	30r
Fresh fruits, expenditures on	yr	138	1999	30r
Fresh milk and cream, expenditures on	yr	120	1999	30r
Fresh vegetables, expenditures on	yr	126	1999	30r
Grapefruit	lb	0.66	7/01	11r
Grapes, Thompson, seedless	lb	1.64	7/01	11r
Ground beef, 100% beef	lb	1.64	7/01	11r
Ground beef, lean and extra lean	lb	2.16	7/01	11r
Ground chuck, 100% beef	lb	2.13	7/01	11r
Ham, boneless, excl canned	lb	2.62	7/01	11r
Ice cream, prepackaged, bulk, regular	1/2 gal	3.35	7/01	11r
Lemons	lb	1.19	7/01	11r
Lettuce, iceberg	head	0.97	3/01	4c
Lettuce, iceberg	lb	0.73	7/01	11r
Margarine, Blue Bonnet or Parkay, stick	lb	0.75	3/01	4c
Margarine, soft, tubs	lb	0.89	7/01	11r
Meats, poultry, fish, and egg purchases	yr	671	1999	30r
Milk, fresh, whole, fortified	gal	2.71	7/01	11r
Milk, whole	1/2 gal	1.59	3/01	4c
Nonalcoholic beverages, expenditures on	yr	239	1999	30r
Orange juice, Minute Maid frozen	12 oz	1.64	3/01	4c
Oranges, Navel	lb	0.80	7/01	11r
Oranges, Valencia	lb	0.66	7/01	11r
Peaches, halves or slices, Hunt's, Del Monte, or Libby's	29 oz	1.88	3/01	4c
Pears, Anjou	lb	0.93	7/01	11r
Peas, green, Del Monte or Green Giant	15 oz	0.75	3/01	4c
Pork chops, center cut, bone-in	lb	3.63	7/01	11r
Pork, expenditures on	yr	150	1999	30r
Potato chips	16 oz	3.52	7/01	11r
Potatoes, frozen, french fried	lb	1.08	7/01	11r
Potatoes, white or red	10 lb	2.39	3/01	4c
Potatoes, white, all types	lb	0.33	7/01	11r
Poultry, expenditures on	yr	108	1999	30r
Processed fruits, expenditures on	yr	98	1999	30r
Processed vegetables, expenditures on	yr	80	1999	30r
Round roast, U.S. choice, boneless	lb	3.07	7/01	11r
Round steak, graded and ungraded, excl U.S. prime and choice	lb	3.41	7/01	11r
Sausage, Jimmy Dean/Owens pork	lb	3.04	3/01	4c
Shortening, vegetable oil blends	lb	1.13	7/01	11r
Shortening, vegetable, Crisco	3 lb	2.82	3/01	4c
Soft drink, Coca Cola, ex deposit	2 liter	1.22	3/01	4c
Spaghetti and macaroni	lb	0.80	7/01	11r
Steak, round, U.S. choice, boneless	lb	3.23	7/01	11r
Steak, T-bone	lb	5.46	3/01	4c
Steak, T-bone, U.S. choice, bone-in	lb	6.68	7/01	11r
Strawberries, dry pint	12 oz	1.32	7/01	11r
Sugar and other sweets, expenditures on	yr	114	1999	30r
Sugar, cane or beet	4 lbs	1.63	3/01	4c
Sugar, white, 33-80 ounce package	lb	0.42	7/01	11r
Sugar, white, all sizes	lb	0.43	7/01	11r
Tobacco products and smoking supplies purchases	yr	331	1999	30r

Springfield, MO - continued

Groceries - continued

Item	Per	Value	Date	Ref.
Tomatoes, field grown	lb	1.46	7/01	11r
Tomatoes, Hunt's or Del Monte	14.5 oz	0.97	3/01	4c
Tuna, chunk, light	6 oz	0.64	3/01	4c
Tuna, light, chunk	lb	1.80	7/01	11r
Turkey, frozen, whole	lb	1.15	7/01	11r

Goods and Services

Item	Per	Value	Date	Ref.
Miscellaneous goods and services, ACCRA Index		92.10	3/01	4c
B&B Japanese maple (acer japonicum)	gal	29.99-169.99	4/00	93r
Boxwood (buxus)	2 gal	18.99-39.99		93r
Daylily (hemerocallis)	gal	4.99-25.00	4/00	93r
Flat of annuals		11.98-24.99	4/00	93r
Fountain grass (pennisetum)	gal	5.98-12.98	4/00	93r
Hanging basket (10 in)		12.99-27.99	4/00	93r
Hardy geranium (geranium)	gal	7.99-9.99	4/00	93r
Hosta (hosta)	gal	6.00-25.00	4/00	93r
Lilac (syrubga vulgaris)	2 gal	14.99-24.99	4/00	93r
Miscellaneous purchases	yr	865	1999	30r
Rhododendron (rhododendron)	2 gal	23.98-42.99	4/00	93r
Sage (salvia)	gal	6.00-9.99	4/00	93r
Wintercreeper euonymus (euonymus fortunei)	2 gal	16.00-169.99	4/00	93r
Hunting license	yr	9.00	4/01	34s

Health Care

Item	Per	Value	Date	Ref.
Health care, ACCRA Index		99.70	3/01	4c
Cardiac catheterization, ave hospital/physician charges		13930	1998	77s
Childbirth, Cesarean delivery		10722	1997	13r
Childbirth, vaginal delivery		6223	1997	13r
Dentist's fee, adult teeth cleaning and periodic oral exam	visit	77.50	3/01	4c
Doctor's fee, routine exam, established patient	visit	55.94	3/01	4c
Drugs, expenditures on	yr	394	1999	30r
Health care purchases	yr	2048	1999	30r
Health insurance expenditures	yr	978	1999	30r
Hospital care, private room	day	520.00	3/01	4c
Hysterectomy, laproscopically-assisted, ave hospital/physician charges		11300	1998	76s
Hysterectomy, vaginal, ave hospital and physician charges		9200	1998	76s
Medicaid dispensing fee		4.09	1999	87s
Medical services expenditures	yr	554	1999	30r
Medical supplies, expenditures on	yr	122	1999	30r
Plastic surgery, breast augmentation		3184	2000	7r
Plastic surgery, breast lift		3585	2000	7r
Plastic surgery, facelift		4999	2000	7r
Plastic surgery, hair transplantation		3105	2000	7r
Plastic surgery, lip augmentation		1290	2000	7r
Plastic surgery, lower body lift		8135	2000	7r
Plastic surgery, thigh lift		3839	2000	7r

Household Goods

Item	Per	Value	Date	Ref.
Dishwashing powder, Cascade	50 oz	3.54	3/01	4c
Floor coverings, expenditures on	yr	52	1999	30r
Furniture, expenditures on	yr	344	1999	30r
Household furnishings and equipment purchases	yr	1475	1999	30r
Household textiles, expenditures on	yr	109	1999	30r
Laundry and cleaning supplies, expenditures on	yr	134	1999	30r

Values are in dollars or fractions of dollars. In the column headed *Ref*, references are shown to sources. Each reference is followed by a letter. These refer to the geographical level for which data were reported: s=State, r=Region, and c=City or metro. The abbreviation *ex* is used to mean *except* or *excluding*; *exp* stands for expenditures. For other abbreviations and further explanations, please see the Introduction.

Springfield, MO - continued

Item	Per	Value	Date	Ref.
Household Goods				
Tissues, facial, Kleenex brand	175	1.26	3/01	4c
Housing				
Housing, ACCRA Index		89.70	3/01	4c
Home price, existing, ave		144400	10/00	90r
Home value, median		89000	2001	53s
House, 2400 sq ft, 8000 sq ft lot, new, urban, utilities	total	186500	3/01	4c
House payment, principal and interest, 25% down payment	mos	947	3/01	4c
Household operation expenditures	yr	542	1999	30r
Housekeeping supplies purchases	yr	508	1999	30r
Lodging expenditures	yr	430	1999	30r
Maintenance, repairs, insurance expenditures	yr	853	1999	30r
Monthly rental value of owned home	mos	547	1999	30r
Owned dwellings, expenditures own	yr	4282	1999	30r
Rent expenditures	yr	1558	1999	30r
Rent, apartment, 2 br, 1 1/2-2 baths, unfurn, 950 sq ft, water	mos	565	3/01	4c
Rental unit, 1 bedroom, with utilities	mos	345	4/01	41c
Rental unit, 2 bedroom, with utilities	mos	446	4/01	41c
Rental unit, 3 bedroom, with utilities	mos	616	4/01	41c
Rental unit, 4 bedroom, with utilities	mos	641	4/01	41c
Shelter, expenditures on	yr	6270	1999	30r
Insurance and Pensions				
Life and other personal insurance purchases	yr	387	1999	30r
Pensions and Social Security, expenditures on	yr	2968	1999	30r
Legal Fees				
Driver's license fee	orig	15.00	1999	48s
Driver's license fee	renew	15.00	1999	48s
Fishing license	yr	11.00	4/01	34s
Personal Goods				
Personal care products and services purchases	yr	385	1999	30r
Shampoo, Alberto VO5	15 oz	0.98	3/01	4c
Toothpaste, Crest or Colgate	6-7 oz	2.53	3/01	4c
Personal Services				
Dry cleaning, man's 2-pc suit		6.45	3/01	4c
Man's haircut, barbershop, no styling		9.50	3/01	4c
Personal services, household, expenditures on	yr	300	1999	30r
Woman's shampoo, trim, blow-dry, no style-change		23.63	3/01	4c
Pets				
Pets, toys, and playground equipment, expenditures on	yr	375	1999	30r
Restaurant Food				
Chicken, fried, thigh and drumstick, KFC/Church's		2.59	3/01	4c
Hamburger with cheese, McDonald's	1/4 lb	2.19	3/01	4c
Pizza, Pizza Hut or Pizza Inn	11-12 in	7.99	3/01	4c
Taxes				
Federal income taxes paid	yr	2326	1999	30r
Personal taxes, expenditures on	yr	3223	1999	30r
Property taxes paid	yr	1152	1999	30r
State and local income taxes paid	yr	753	1999	30r
Transportation				
Transportation, ACCRA Index		92.10	3/01	4c
Bus fare, one-way	trip	0.75	2000	1c
Bus fare, to central business district	1-way	0.75	3/01	4c
Cars and trucks, new, expenditures on	yr	1280	1999	30r
Cars and trucks, used, expenditures on	yr	1763	1999	30r
Diesel at the pump	gal	1.16	10/99	73s
Gasoline and motor oil purchases	yr	1036	1999	30r
Gasoline before-tax price (cents)	gal	108.50	10/00	43s
Maintenance and repair expenditures	yr	594	1999	30r

Springfield, MO - continued

Item	Per	Value	Date	Ref.
Transportation - continued				
Public transportation, expenditures on	yr	341	1999	30r
Tire balance, computer or spin balance, front	wheel	7.75	3/01	4c
Transportation purchases	yr	6617	1999	30r
Vehicle expenses, miscellaneous, purchases	yr	2159	1999	30r
Vehicle insurance payments	yr	701	1999	30r
Vehicle purchases (net outlay)	yr	3081	1999	30r
Vehicle rental, lease expenditures	yr	536	1999	30r
Utilities				
Utilities, ACCRA Index		79.00	3/01	4c
Electrical bill, average	mos	68.50	9/00	9s
Electricity, expenditures on	yr	841	1999	30r
Electricity and other, mixed, 2400 sq ft, new home	mos	43.87	3/01	4c
Electricity cost, average	KWh	6.00	9/00	9s
Utilities, fuels, and public services purchased	yr	2401	1999	30r
Water and other public services, expenditures on	yr	273	1999	30r
Weddings				
Wedding (national average cost)		19936	2000	33r
Wedding (regional average total cost)		16195	1997	110r
Attendants' gifts		321	1998	33r
Bridal attendants' apparel (5 persons)		824	2000	33r
Bride's headpiece/veil		173	1998	33r
Bride's wedding dress		859	1998	33r
Clergy, religious facility fee		242	1998	33r
Engagement ring		3177	1998	33r
Flowers		789	1998	33r
Groom's formalwear rental		99	2000	33r
Limousine		410	1998	33r
Marriage license cost		50.00	4/01	35s
Men's formalwear (ushers, best man)		469	2000	33r
Mother of bride apparel		241	2000	33r
Music		866	1998	33r
Photography and videography		1368	1998	33r
Rehearsal dinner		728	1998	33r
Wedding invitations and announcements		341	1998	33r
Wedding reception		7968	2000	33r
Wedding rings (bride and groom)		1060	1998	33r

Stamford-Norwalk, CT

Item	Per	Value	Date	Ref.
Average annual expenditures	yr	37971	1999	30r
Alcoholic Beverages				
Alcoholic beverage purchases	yr	368	1999	30r
Wine, red and white table, all sizes, any origin	liter	9.64	7/01	11r
Appliances				
Major appliances, expenditures on	yr	194	1999	30r
Small appliances, housewares, expenditures on	yr	93	1999	30r
Banking and Money				
Mortgage interest and charges paid	yr	2622	1999	30r
Mortgage principal paid on owned property	yr	1262	1999	30r
Vehicle finance charges paid	yr	240	1999	30r
Charity				
Cash contributions, expenditures	yr	1001	1999	30r
Child Care				
Child raising cost, total, age 0-2	yr	8670	1999	60r
Child raising cost, total, age 3-5	yr	8910	1999	60r
Child raising cost, total, age 6-8	yr	9040	1999	60r
Child raising cost, total, age 9-11	yr	9100	1999	60r
Child raising cost, total, age 12-14	yr	9890	1999	60r
Child raising cost, total, age 15-17	yr	10010	1999	60r
Child's child care and education, age 0-2	yr	1070	1999	60r
Child's child care and education, age 3-5	yr	1190	1999	60r
Child's child care and education, age 6-8	yr	740	1999	60r
Child's child care and education, age 9-11	yr	470	1999	60r
Child's child care and education, age 12-14	yr	350	1999	60r

Values are in dollars or fractions of dollars. In the column headed *Ref*, references are shown to sources. Each reference is followed by a letter. These refer to the geographical level for which data were reported: s=State, r=Region, and c=City or metro. The abbreviation *ex* is used to mean *except* or *excluding*; *exp* stands for *expenditures*. For other abbreviations and further explanations, please see the Introduction.

Stamford-Norwalk, CT - continued

Item	Per	Value	Date	Ref.
Child Care				
Child's child care and education, age 15-17	yr	590	1999	60r
Child's clothing, age 0-2	yr	480	1999	60r
Child's clothing, age 3-5	yr	470	1999	60r
Child's clothing, age 6-8	yr	520	1999	60r
Child's clothing, age 9-11	yr	570	1999	60r
Child's clothing, age 12-14	yr	970	1999	60r
Child's clothing, age 15-17	yr	870	1999	60r
Child's food, age 0-2	yr	1130	1999	60r
Child's food, age 3-5	yr	1290	1999	60r
Child's food, age 6-8	yr	1640	1999	60r
Child's food, age 9-11	yr	1930	1999	60r
Child's food, age 12-14	yr	1940	1999	60r
Child's food, age 15-17	yr	2150	1999	60r
Child's health care, age 0-2	yr	550	1999	60r
Child's health care, age 3-5	yr	530	1999	60r
Child's health care, age 6-8	yr	610	1999	60r
Child's health care, age 9-11	yr	650	1999	60r
Child's health care, age 12-14	yr	660	1999	60r
Child's health care, age 15-17	yr	690	1999	60r
Child's housing, age 0-2	yr	3555	1999	60r
Child's housing, age 3-5	yr	3530	1999	60r
Child's housing, age 6-8	yr	3490	1999	60r
Child's housing, age 9-11	yr	3340	1999	60r
Child's housing, age 12-14	yr	3530	1999	60r
Child's housing, age 15-17	yr	3140	1999	60r
Child's personal care, reading, age 0-2	yr	920	1999	60r
Child's personal care, reading, age 3-5	yr	950	1999	60r
Child's personal care, reading, age 6-8	yr	980	1999	60r
Child's personal care, reading, age 9-11	yr	1020	1999	60r
Child's personal care, reading, age 12-14	yr	1190	1999	60r
Child's personal care, reading, age 15-17	yr	970	1999	60r
Clothing				
Apparel and services purchases	yr	1831	1999	30r
Boys, 2 to 15, expenditures on	yr	92	1999	30r
Children under 2, expenditures on	yr	63	1999	30r
Footwear, expenditures on	yr	300	1999	30r
Girls, 2 to 15, expenditures on	yr	101	1999	30r
Men and boys, expenditures on	yr	446	1999	30r
Men, 16 and over, expenditures on	yr	354	1999	30r
Women, 16 and over, expenditures on	yr	584	1999	30r
Communications				
Cable modem installation, AT&T-BIS		150.00	6/99	103s
Cable modem installation, Cablevision Systems		150.00	6/99	103s
Cable modem installation, Cox		99.00-174.95	6/99	103s
Cable modem installation, Media One		100.00	6/99	103s
Cable modem rate, cable subscriber, AT&T-BIS	mos	39.95	6/99	103s
Cable modem rate, cable subscriber, Cablevision Systems	mos	44.95	6/99	103s
Cable modem rate, cable subscriber, Cox	mos	29.95-44.95	6/99	103s
Cable modem rate, cable subscriber, Media One	mos	34.95-39.95	6/99	103s
Cable modem rate, non-cable subscriber, Cablevision Systems	mos	54.95	6/99	103s
Cable modem rate, non-cable subscriber, Cox	mos	42.95-54.95	6/99	103s
Cable modem rate, non-cable subscriber, Media One	mos	49.95	6/99	103s
Phone line, single, business, field visit	inst.	65.00	12/97	17s
Phone line, single, business, no field visit	inst.	65.00	12/97	17s
Phone line, single, residence, field visit	inst.	45.00	12/97	17s
Phone line, single, residence, no field visit	inst.	45.00	12/97	17s
Postage and stationery, expenditures on	yr	138	1999	30r
Postal rate, express mail, up to half-pound		12.45	7/01	108r
Postal rate, letter, first class, first ounce		0.34	7/01	108r
Postal rate, letter, two ounces		0.57	7/01	108r
Postal rate, post card		0.21	7/01	108r
Postal rate, priority mail, two pounds		3.95	7/01	108r

Stamford-Norwalk, CT - continued

Item	Per	Value	Date	Ref.
Communications - continued				
Postal rate, priority mail, up to one pound		3.50	7/01	108r
Telephone services, expenditures on	yr	830	1999	30r
Education				
Board, 4-year private college/university	yr	2744	1996	38s
Board, 4-year public college/university	yr	2299	1996	38s
Education expenditures	yr	877	1999	30r
Room, 4-year private college/university	yr	3621	1996	38s
Room, 4-year public college/university	yr	2609	1996	38s
Total cost, 4-year private college/university	yr	23011	1996	38s
Total cost, 4-year public college/university	yr	8753	1996	38s
Tuition, 2-year public college/university, in state	yr	1646	1996	38s
Tuition, 4-year private college/university, in state	yr	16646	1996	38s
Tuition, 4-year public college/university	yr	3845	1996	38s
Energy and Fuels				
Electricity	KWh	0.12	7/01	11r
Fuel oil #2	gal	1.31	7/01	11r
Fuel oil and other fuels, expenditures on	yr	207	1999	30r
Gas, natural, commercial rate	1000 cf	7.08	11/00	88s
Gasoline, all types	gal	1.80	7/01	11r
Gasoline, unleaded midgrade	gal	1.85	7/01	11r
Gasoline, unleaded premium	gal	1.91	7/01	11r
Gasoline, unleaded regular	gal	1.71	7/01	11r
Natural gas, expenditures on	yr	368	1999	30r
Utility (piped) gas, therm		1.08	7/01	11r
Utility (piped) gas, 40 therms		50.87	7/01	11r
Utility (piped) gas, 100 therms		111.06	7/01	11r
Entertainment				
Entertainment purchases	yr	1821	1999	30r
Fees and admissions paid	yr	511	1999	30r
Hockey equipment, girls' hockey		800	2001	101s
Television, radios, sound equipment, expenditures on	yr	650	1999	30r
Funerals				
Total cost of funeral		5776.91	1/99	78r
Acknowledgement cards		14.47	1/99	78r
Casket		2090.19	1/99	78r
Cosmetology, hair, other preparation		132.92	1/99	78r
Embalming		377.33	1/99	78r
Funeral at funeral home		352.43	1/99	78r
Hearse (local)		185.55	1/99	78r
Professional service charges		1289.95	1/99	78r
Service car/van		87.42	1/99	78r
Transfer of remains to funeral home		175.48	1/99	78r
Vault		729.40	1/99	78r
Visitation/viewing		341.76	1/99	78r
Groceries				
Apples, red delicious	lb	0.95	7/01	11r
Bacon, sliced	lb	3.44	7/01	11r
Bakery products, expenditures on	yr	310	1999	30r
Bananas	lb	0.55	7/01	11r
Beef, expenditures on	yr	236	1999	30r
Bread, white, pan	lb	1.09	7/01	11r
Butter, yoghurt, cheese, etc, expenditures on	yr	214	1999	30r
Cereals and bakery product purchases	yr	474	1999	30r
Cereals and cereal products, expenditures on	yr	164	1999	30r
Chicken legs, bone-in	lb	1.23	7/01	11r
Chicken, fresh, whole	lb	1.13	7/01	11r
Chuck roast, U.S. choice, boneless	lb	2.79	7/01	11r
Coffee, 100%, ground roast, all sizes	lb	3.40	7/01	11r
Dairy product purchases	yr	342	1999	30r
Eggs, expenditures on	yr	34	1999	30r
Eggs, grade A, large	dozen	0.82	7/01	11r
Fats and oils, expenditures on	yr	80	1999	30r
Fish and seafood, expenditures on	yr	123	1999	30r
Food (excl fruit and vegetables), eaten at home, purchases	yr	838	1999	30r

Values are in dollars or fractions of dollars. In the column headed *Ref*, references are shown to sources. Each reference is followed by a letter. These refer to the geographical level for which data were reported: s=State, r=Region, and c=City or metro. The abbreviation *ex* is used to mean *except* or *excluding*; *exp* stands for *expenditures*. For other abbreviations and further explanations, please see the Introduction.

Stamford-Norwalk, CT - continued

Item	Per	Value	Date	Ref.
Groceries				
Food cooked on trips, expenditures on	yr	48	1999	30r
Food purchases	yr	5314	1999	30r
Food purchases, eaten away from home	yr	2313	1999	30r
Food purchases, food eaten at home	yr	3001	1999	30r
Fresh fruits, expenditures on	yr	169	1999	30r
Fresh milk and cream, expenditures on	yr	128	1999	30r
Fresh vegetables, expenditures on	yr	164	1999	30r
Grapefruit	lb	0.67	7/01	11r
Grapes, Thompson, seedless	lb	2.18	7/01	11r
Ground beef, lean and extra lean	lb	2.66	7/01	11r
Ground chuck, 100% beef	lb	2.04	7/01	11r
Lettuce, iceberg	lb	0.76	7/01	11r
Meats, poultry, fish, and egg purchases	yr	808	1999	30r
Nonalcoholic beverages, expenditures on	yr	225	1999	30r
Orange juice, frozen concentrate	16 oz	1.88	7/01	11r
Oranges, Navel	lb	0.79	7/01	11r
Oranges, Valencia	lb	0.56	7/01	11r
Peaches	lb	1.16	7/01	11r
Peanut butter, creamy, all sizes	lb	2.01	7/01	11r
Pears, Anjou	lb	1.16	7/01	11r
Pork chops, center cut, bone-in	lb	3.57	7/01	11r
Pork, expenditures on	yr	146	1999	30r
Potato chips	16 oz	3.37	7/01	11r
Potatoes, white, all types	lb	0.42	7/01	11r
Poultry, expenditures on	yr	158	1999	30r
Processed fruits, expenditures on	yr	124	1999	30r
Processed vegetables, expenditures on	yr	82	1999	30r
Round roast, U.S. choice, boneless	lb	3.04	7/01	11r
Spaghetti and macaroni	lb	1.04	7/01	11r
Steak, sirloin, U.S. choice, boneless	lb	5.39	7/01	11r
Strawberries, dry pint	12 oz	1.51	7/01	11r
Sugar and other sweets, expenditures on	yr	110	1999	30r
Sugar, white, 33-80 ounce package	lb	0.46	7/01	11r
Sugar, white, all sizes	lb	0.47	7/01	11r
Tobacco products and smoking supplies purchases	yr	309	1999	30r
Yogurt, natural, fruit flavored	8 oz	0.79	7/01	11r
Goods and Services				
B&B Japanese maple (acer japonicum)	gal	38.99-125.00	4/00	93r
Boxwood (buxus)	2 gal	15.99-49.95	4/00	93r
Daylily (hemerocallis)	gal	4.95	4/00	93r
Flat of annuals		8.00-14.99	4/00	93r
Fountain grass (pennisetum)	gal	6.99-9.99	4/00	93r
Hanging basket (10 in)		12.95-19.99	4/00	93r
Hardy geranium (geranium)	gal	6.95-7.99	4/00	93r
Hosta (hosta)	gal	4.95	4/00	93r
Lilac (syrubga vulgaris)	2 gal	17.99-74.95	4/00	93r
Miscellaneous purchases	yr	872	1999	30r
Rhododendron (rhododendron)	2 gal	23.99-54.95	4/00	93r
Sage (salvia)	gal	6.95-7.99	4/00	93r
Wintercreeper euonymus (euonymus fortunei)	2 gal	14.99-23.95	4/00	93r
Hunting license	yr	10.00	4/01	34s
Health Care				
Cardiac catheterization, ave hospital/physician charges		14090	1998	77s
Childbirth, Cesarean delivery		14716	1997	13r
Childbirth, vaginal delivery		8541	1997	13r
Drugs, expenditures on	yr	296	1999	30r
Health care purchases	yr	1788	1999	30r
Health insurance expenditures	yr	875	1999	30r

Stamford-Norwalk, CT - continued

Item	Per	Value	Date	Ref.
Health Care - continued				
Hysterectomy, laproscopically-assisted, ave hospital/physician charges		11610	1998	76s
Hysterectomy, vaginal, ave hospital and physician charges		12780	1998	76s
Medicaid dispensing fee		4.10	1999	87s
Medical services expenditures	yr	516	1999	30r
Medical supplies, expenditures on	yr	102	1999	30r
Plastic surgery, breast augmentation		4232	2000	7r
Plastic surgery, breast lift		4605	2000	7r
Plastic surgery, facelift		6964	2000	7r
Plastic surgery, hair transplantation		4193	2000	7r
Plastic surgery, lip augmentation		1675	2000	7r
Plastic surgery, lower body lift		6611	2000	7r
Plastic surgery, thigh lift		4751	2000	7r
Household Goods				
Floor coverings, expenditures on	yr	59	1999	30r
Furniture, expenditures on	yr	388	1999	30r
Household furnishings and equipment purchases	yr	1567	1999	30r
Household textiles, expenditures on	yr	112	1999	30r
Laundry and cleaning supplies, expenditures on	yr	104	1999	30r
Housing				
Home price, existing, ave		180800	10/00	90r
Home value, median		157000	2001	53s
Household operation expenditures	yr	581	1999	30r
Housekeeping supplies purchases	yr	474	1999	30r
Lodging expenditures	yr	550	1999	30r
Maintenance, repairs, insurance expenditures	yr	835	1999	30r
Monthly rental value of owned home	mos	663	1999	30r
Owned dwellings, expenditures own	yr	5209	1999	30r
Rent expenditures	yr	2390	1999	30r
Rental unit, 1 bedroom, with utilities	mos	964	4/01	41c
Rental unit, 2 bedroom, with utilities	mos	1176	4/01	41c
Rental unit, 3 bedroom, with utilities	mos	1576	4/01	41c
Rental unit, 4 bedroom, with utilities	mos	1741	4/01	41c
Shelter, expenditures on	yr	8149	1999	30r
Insurance and Pensions				
Auto insurance premium	yr	982.00	1999	57s
Life and other personal insurance purchases	yr	424	1999	30r
Pensions and Social Security, expenditures on	yr	3037	1999	30r
Legal Fees				
Divorce, filing fee		150.00	4/01	35s
Driver's license fee	renew	28.50	1999	48s
Driver's license fee	orig	43.50	1999	48s
Personal Goods				
Personal care products and services purchases	yr	399	1999	30r
Personal Services				
Personal services, household, expenditures on	yr	271	1999	30r
Pets				
Pets, toys, and playground equipment, expenditures on	yr	325	1999	30r
Taxes				
Federal income taxes paid	yr	2606	1999	30r
Personal taxes, expenditures on	yr	3567	1999	30r
Property taxes paid	yr	1752	1999	30r
State and local income taxes paid	yr	694	1999	30r
Transportation				
Cars and trucks, new, expenditures on	yr	1496	1999	30r
Cars and trucks, used, expenditures on	yr	1251	1999	30r
Diesel at the pump	gal	1.36	10/99	73s
Gasoline and motor oil purchases	yr	901	1999	30r
Gasoline before-tax price (cents)	gal	117.10	10/00	43s

Values are in dollars or fractions of dollars. In the column headed *Ref*, references are shown to sources. Each reference is followed by a letter. These refer to the geographical level for which data were reported: s=State, r=Region, and c=City or metro. The abbreviation *ex* is used to mean *except* or *excluding*; *exp* stands for expenditures. For other abbreviations and further explanations, please see the Introduction.

Stamford-Norwalk, CT - continued

Item	Per	Value	Date	Ref.
Transportation				
Maintenance and repair expenditures	yr	618	1999	30r
Public transportation, expenditures on	yr	575	1999	30r
Transportation purchases	yr	6503	1999	30r
Vehicle expenses, miscellaneous, purchases	yr	2266	1999	30r
Vehicle insurance payments	yr	824	1999	30r
Vehicle purchases (net outlay)	yr	2761	1999	30r
Vehicle rental, lease expenditures	yr	584	1999	30r
Utilities				
Electrical bill, average	mos	81.50	9/00	9s
Electricity, expenditures on	yr	837	1999	30r
Electricity cost, average	KWh	9.47	9/00	9s
Utilities, fuels, and public services purchased	yr	2457	1999	30r
Water and other public services, expenditures on	yr	215	1999	30r
Weddings				
Wedding (national average cost)		19936	2000	33r
Wedding (regional average total cost)		29454	1997	110r
Attendants' gifts		321	1998	33r
Bridal attendants' apparel (5 persons)		824	2000	33r
Bride's headpiece/veil		173	1998	33r
Bride's wedding dress		859	1998	33r
Clergy, religious facility fee		242	1998	33r
Engagement ring		3177	1998	33r
Flowers		789	1998	33r
Groom's formalwear rental		99	2000	33r
Limousine		410	1998	33r
Marriage license cost		30.00	4/01	35s
Men's formalwear (ushers, best man)		469	2000	33r
Mother of bride apparel		241	2000	33r
Music		866	1998	33r
Photography and videography		1368	1998	33r
Rehearsal dinner		728	1998	33r
Wedding invitations and announcements		341	1998	33r
Wedding reception		7968	2000	33r
Wedding rings (bride and groom)		1060	1998	33r

State College, PA

Item	Per	Value	Date	Ref.
Average annual expenditures	yr	37971	1999	30r
Alcoholic Beverages				
Alcoholic beverage purchases	yr	368	1999	30r
Wine, red and white table, all sizes, any origin	liter	9.64	7/01	11r
Appliances				
Major appliances, expenditures on	yr	194	1999	30r
Small appliances, housewares, expenditures on	yr	93	1999	30r
Banking and Money				
Mortgage interest and charges paid	yr	2622	1999	30r
Mortgage principal paid on owned property	yr	1262	1999	30r
Vehicle finance charges paid	yr	240	1999	30r
Charity				
Cash contributions, expenditures	yr	1001	1999	30r
Child Care				
Child raising cost, total, age 0-2	yr	8670	1999	60r
Child raising cost, total, age 3-5	yr	8910	1999	60r
Child raising cost, total, age 6-8	yr	9040	1999	60r
Child raising cost, total, age 9-11	yr	9100	1999	60r
Child raising cost, total, age 12-14	yr	9890	1999	60r
Child raising cost, total, age 15-17	yr	10010	1999	60r
Child's child care and education, age 0-2	yr	1070	1999	60r
Child's child care and education, age 3-5	yr	1190	1999	60r
Child's child care and education, age 6-8	yr	740	1999	60r
Child's child care and education, age 9-11	yr	470	1999	60r
Child's child care and education, age 12-14	yr	350	1999	60r
Child's child care and education, age 15-17	yr	590	1999	60r
Child's clothing, age 0-2	yr	480	1999	60r
Child's clothing, age 3-5	yr	470	1999	60r

State College, PA - continued

Item	Per	Value	Date	Ref.
Child Care - continued				
Child's clothing, age 6-8	yr	520	1999	60r
Child's clothing, age 9-11	yr	570	1999	60r
Child's clothing, age 12-14	yr	970	1999	60r
Child's clothing, age 15-17	yr	870	1999	60r
Child's food, age 0-2	yr	1130	1999	60r
Child's food, age 3-5	yr	1290	1999	60r
Child's food, age 6-8	yr	1640	1999	60r
Child's food, age 9-11	yr	1930	1999	60r
Child's food, age 12-14	yr	1940	1999	60r
Child's food, age 15-17	yr	2150	1999	60r
Child's health care, age 0-2	yr	550	1999	60r
Child's health care, age 3-5	yr	530	1999	60r
Child's health care, age 6-8	yr	610	1999	60r
Child's health care, age 9-11	yr	650	1999	60r
Child's health care, age 12-14	yr	660	1999	60r
Child's health care, age 15-17	yr	690	1999	60r
Child's housing, age 0-2	yr	3555	1999	60r
Child's housing, age 3-5	yr	3530	1999	60r
Child's housing, age 6-8	yr	3490	1999	60r
Child's housing, age 9-11	yr	3340	1999	60r
Child's housing, age 12-14	yr	3530	1999	60r
Child's housing, age 15-17	yr	3140	1999	60r
Child's personal care, reading, age 0-2	yr	920	1999	60r
Child's personal care, reading, age 3-5	yr	950	1999	60r
Child's personal care, reading, age 6-8	yr	980	1999	60r
Child's personal care, reading, age 9-11	yr	1020	1999	60r
Child's personal care, reading, age 12-14	yr	1190	1999	60r
Child's personal care, reading, age 15-17	yr	970	1999	60r
Clothing				
Apparel and services purchases	yr	1831	1999	30r
Boys, 2 to 15, expenditures on	yr	92	1999	30r
Children under 2, expenditures on	yr	63	1999	30r
Footwear, expenditures on	yr	300	1999	30r
Girls, 2 to 15, expenditures on	yr	101	1999	30r
Men and boys, expenditures on	yr	446	1999	30r
Men, 16 and over, expenditures on	yr	354	1999	30r
Women, 16 and over, expenditures on	yr	584	1999	30r
Communications				
Cable modem installation, Adelphi		54.90	6/99	103s
Cable modem installation, Comcast		95.00	6/99	103s
Cable modem rate, cable subscriber, Adelphi	mos	34.95	6/99	103s
Cable modem rate, cable subscriber, Comcast	mos	39.95	6/99	103s
Cable modem rate, non-cable subscriber, Adelphi	mos	44.95	6/99	103s
Cable modem rate, non-cable subscriber, Comcast	mos	49.95	6/99	103s
Phone line, single, business, field visit	inst.	75.00	12/97	17s
Phone line, single, business, no field visit	inst.	75.00	12/97	17s
Phone line, single, residence, field visit	inst.	40.00	12/97	17s
Phone line, single, residence, no field visit	inst.	40.00	12/97	17s
Postage and stationery, expenditures on	yr	138	1999	30r
Postal rate, express mail, up to half-pound		12.45	7/01	108r
Postal rate, letter, first class, first ounce		0.34	7/01	108r
Postal rate, letter, two ounces		0.57	7/01	108r
Postal rate, post card		0.21	7/01	108r
Postal rate, priority mail, two pounds		3.95	7/01	108r
Postal rate, priority mail, up to one pound		3.50	7/01	108r
Telephone services, expenditures on	yr	830	1999	30r
Education				
Board, 4-year private college/university	yr	2822	1996	38s
Board, 4-year public college/university	yr	2174	1996	38s
Education expenditures	yr	877	1999	30r
Room, 4-year private college/university	yr	2943	1996	38s
Room, 4-year public college/university	yr	2227	1996	38s
Total cost, 4-year private college/university	yr	19876	1996	38s
Total cost, 4-year public college/university	yr	9124	1996	38s
Tuition, 2-year public college/university, in state	yr	1909	1996	38s
Tuition, 4-year private college/university, in state	yr	14111	1996	38s

Values are in dollars or fractions of dollars. In the column headed *Ref*, references are shown to sources. Each reference is followed by a letter. These refer to the geographical level for which data were reported: s=State, r=Region, and c=City or metro. The abbreviation *ex* is used to mean *except* or *excluding*; *exp* stands for expenditures. For other abbreviations and further explanations, please see the Introduction.

State College, PA - continued

Item	Per	Value	Date	Ref.
Education				
Tuition, 4-year public college/university	yr	4723	1996	38s
Energy and Fuels				
Electricity	KWh	0.12	7/01	11r
Fuel oil #2	gal	1.31	7/01	11r
Fuel oil and other fuels, expenditures on	yr	207	1999	30r
Gas, natural, commercial rate	1000 cf	5.96	11/00	88s
Gasoline, all types	gal	1.80	7/01	11r
Gasoline, unleaded midgrade	gal	1.85	7/01	11r
Gasoline, unleaded premium	gal	1.91	7/01	11r
Gasoline, unleaded regular	gal	1.71	7/01	11r
Natural gas, expenditures on	yr	368	1999	30r
Utility (piped) gas, therm		1.08	7/01	11r
Utility (piped) gas, 40 therms		50.87	7/01	11r
Utility (piped) gas, 100 therms		111.06	7/01	11r
Entertainment				
Entertainment purchases	yr	1821	1999	30r
Fees and admissions paid	yr	511	1999	30r
Television, radios, sound equipment, expenditures on	yr	650	1999	30r
Funerals				
Total cost of funeral		5813.50	1/99	78r
Acknowledgement cards		28.32	1/99	78r
Casket		2082.20	1/99	78r
Cosmetology, hair, other preparation		169.59	1/99	78r
Embalming		465.60	1/99	78r
Funeral at funeral home		339.56	1/99	78r
Hearse (local)		183.96	1/99	78r
Professional service charges		1157.85	1/99	78r
Service car/van		100.41	1/99	78r
Transfer of remains to funeral home		158.66	1/99	78r
Vault		766.31	1/99	78r
Visitation/viewing		361.04	1/99	78r
Groceries				
Apples, red delicious	lb	0.95	7/01	11r
Bacon, sliced	lb	3.44	7/01	11r
Bakery products, expenditures on	yr	310	1999	30r
Bananas	lb	0.55	7/01	11r
Beef, expenditures on	yr	236	1999	30r
Bread, white, pan	lb	1.09	7/01	11r
Butter, yoghurt, cheese, etc, expenditures on	yr	214	1999	30r
Cereals and bakery product purchases	yr	474	1999	30r
Cereals and cereal products, expenditures on	yr	164	1999	30r
Chicken legs, bone-in	lb	1.23	7/01	11r
Chicken, fresh, whole	lb	1.13	7/01	11r
Chuck roast, U.S. choice, boneless	lb	2.79	7/01	11r
Coffee, 100%, ground roast, all sizes	lb	3.40	7/01	11r
Dairy product purchases	yr	342	1999	30r
Eggs, expenditures on	yr	34	1999	30r
Eggs, grade A, large	dozen	0.82	7/01	11r
Fats and oils, expenditures on	yr	80	1999	30r
Fish and seafood, expenditures on	yr	123	1999	30r
Food (excl fruit and vegetables), eaten at home, purchases	yr	838	1999	30r
Food cooked on trips, expenditures on	yr	48	1999	30r
Food purchases	yr	5314	1999	30r
Food purchases, eaten away from home	yr	2313	1999	30r
Food purchases, food eaten at home	yr	3001	1999	30r
Fresh fruits, expenditures on	yr	169	1999	30r
Fresh milk and cream, expenditures on	yr	128	1999	30r
Fresh vegetables, expenditures on	yr	164	1999	30r
Grapefruit	lb	0.67	7/01	11r
Grapes, Thompson, seedless	lb	2.18	7/01	11r
Ground beef, lean and extra lean	lb	2.66	7/01	11r
Ground chuck, 100% beef	lb	2.04	7/01	11r
Lettuce, iceberg	lb	0.76	7/01	11r
Meats, poultry, fish, and egg purchases	yr	808	1999	30r
Nonalcoholic beverages, expenditures on	yr	225	1999	30r
Orange juice, frozen concentrate	16 oz	1.88	7/01	11r
Oranges, Navel	lb	0.79	7/01	11r

State College, PA - continued

Item	Per	Value	Date	Ref.
Groceries - continued				
Oranges, Valencia	lb	0.56	7/01	11r
Peaches	lb	1.16	7/01	11r
Peanut butter, creamy, all sizes	lb	2.01	7/01	11r
Pears, Anjou	lb	1.16	7/01	11r
Pork chops, center cut, bone-in	lb	3.57	7/01	11r
Pork, expenditures on	yr	146	1999	30r
Potato chips	16 oz	3.37	7/01	11r
Potatoes, white, all types	lb	0.42	7/01	11r
Poultry, expenditures on	yr	158	1999	30r
Processed fruits, expenditures on	yr	124	1999	30r
Processed vegetables, expenditures on	yr	82	1999	30r
Round roast, U.S. choice, boneless	lb	3.04	7/01	11r
Spaghetti and macaroni	lb	1.04	7/01	11r
Steak, sirloin, U.S. choice, boneless	lb	5.39	7/01	11r
Strawberries, dry pint	12 oz	1.51	7/01	11r
Sugar and other sweets, expenditures on	yr	110	1999	30r
Sugar, white, 33-80 ounce package	lb	0.46	7/01	11r
Sugar, white, all sizes	lb	0.47	7/01	11r
Tobacco products and smoking supplies purchases	yr	309	1999	30r
Yogurt, natural, fruit flavored	8 oz	0.79	7/01	11r
Goods and Services				
B&B Japanese maple (acer japonicum)	gal	38.99-125.00	4/00	93r
Boxwood (buxus)	2 gal	15.99-49.95	4/00	93r
Daylilly (hemerocallis)	gal	4.95	4/00	93r
Flat of annuals		8.00-14.99	4/00	93r
Fountain grass (pennisetum)	gal	6.99-9.99	4/00	93r
Hanging basket (10 in)		12.95-19.99	4/00	93r
Hardy geranium (geranium)	gal	6.95-7.99	4/00	93r
Hosta (hosta)	gal	4.95	4/00	93r
Lilac (syrubga vulgaris)	2 gal	17.99-74.95	4/00	93r
Miscellaneous purchases	yr	872	1999	30r
Rhododendron (rhododendron)	2 gal	23.99-54.95	4/00	93r
Sage (salvia)	gal	6.95-7.99	4/00	93r
Wintercreeper euonymus (euonymus fortunei)	2 gal	14.99-23.95	4/00	93r
Hunting license	yr	20.00	4/01	34s
Health Care				
Cardiac catheterization, ave hospital/ physician charges		13870	1998	77s
Childbirth, Cesarean delivery		14716	1997	13r
Childbirth, vaginal delivery		8541	1997	13r
Drugs, expenditures on	yr	296	1999	30r
Health care purchases	yr	1788	1999	30r
Health insurance expenditures	yr	875	1999	30r
Hysterectomy, laproscopically-assisted, ave hospital/physician charges		14760	1998	76s
Hysterectomy, vaginal, ave hospital and physician charges		9270	1998	76s
Medicaid dispensing fee		4.00	1999	87s
Medical services expenditures	yr	516	1999	30r
Medical supplies, expenditures on	yr	102	1999	30r
Plastic surgery, breast augmentation		4232	2000	7r
Plastic surgery, breast lift		4605	2000	7r
Plastic surgery, facelift		6964	2000	7r
Plastic surgery, hair transplantation		4193	2000	7r
Plastic surgery, lip augmentation		1675	2000	7r
Plastic surgery, lower body lift		6611	2000	7r
Plastic surgery, thigh lift		4751	2000	7r
Household Goods				
Floor coverings, expenditures on	yr	59	1999	30r
Furniture, expenditures on	yr	388	1999	30r

Values are in dollars or fractions of dollars. In the column headed *Ref*, references are shown to sources. Each reference is followed by a letter. These refer to the geographical level for which data were reported: s=State, r=Region, and c=City or metro. The abbreviation *ex* is used to mean *except* or *excluding*; *exp* stands for *expenditures*. For other abbreviations and further explanations, please see the Introduction.

State College, PA - continued

Item	Per	Value	Date	Ref.
Household Goods				
Household furnishings and equipment purchases	yr	1567	1999	30r
Household textiles, expenditures on	yr	112	1999	30r
Laundry and cleaning supplies, expenditures on	yr	104	1999	30r
Housing				
Home price, existing, ave		180800	10/00	90r
Home value, median		115000	2001	53s
Household operation expenditures	yr	581	1999	30r
Housekeeping supplies purchases	yr	474	1999	30r
Lodging expenditures	yr	550	1999	30r
Maintenance, repairs, insurance expenditures	yr	835	1999	30r
Monthly rental value of owned home	mos	663	1999	30r
Owned dwellings, expenditures own	yr	5209	1999	30r
Rent expenditures	yr	2390	1999	30r
Rental unit, 1 bedroom, with utilities	mos	513	4/01	41c
Rental unit, 2 bedroom, with utilities	mos	635	4/01	41c
Rental unit, 3 bedroom, with utilities	mos	832	4/01	41c
Rental unit, 4 bedroom, with utilities	mos	890	4/01	41c
Shelter, expenditures on	yr	8149	1999	30r
Insurance and Pensions				
Life and other personal insurance purchases	yr	424	1999	30r
Pensions and Social Security, expenditures on	yr	3037	1999	30r
Legal Fees				
Divorce, filing fee		65.00	4/01	35s
Driver's license fee	orig	29.00	1999	48s
Driver's license fee	renew	24.00	1999	48s
Fishing license	yr	17.00	4/01	34s
Personal Goods				
Personal care products and services purchases	yr	399	1999	30r
Personal Services				
Personal services, household, expenditures on	yr	271	1999	30r
Pets				
Pets, toys, and playground equipment, expenditures on	yr	325	1999	30r
Taxes				
Federal income taxes paid	yr	2606	1999	30r
Personal taxes, expenditures on	yr	3567	1999	30r
Property taxes paid	yr	1752	1999	30r
State and local income taxes paid	yr	694	1999	30r
Transportation				
Bus fare, one-way	trip	1.00	2000	1c
Cars and trucks, new, expenditures on	yr	1496	1999	30r
Cars and trucks, used, expenditures on	yr	1251	1999	30r
Diesel at the pump	gal	1.31	10/99	73s
Gasoline and motor oil purchases	yr	901	1999	30r
Gasoline before-tax price (cents)	gal	106.60	10/00	43s
Maintenance and repair expenditures	yr	618	1999	30r
Public transportation, expenditures on	yr	575	1999	30r
Transportation purchases	yr	6503	1999	30r
Vehicle expenses, miscellaneous, purchases	yr	2266	1999	30r
Vehicle insurance payments	yr	824	1999	30r
Vehicle purchases (net outlay)	yr	2761	1999	53r
Vehicle rental, lease expenditures	yr	584	1999	30r
Utilities				
Electrical bill, average	mos	69.16	9/00	9s
Electricity, expenditures on	yr	837	1999	30r
Electricity cost, average	KWh	5.08	9/00	9s
Utilities, fuels, and public services purchased	yr	2457	1999	30r
Water and other public services, expenditures on	yr	215	1999	30r

State College, PA - continued

Item	Per	Value	Date	Ref.
Weddings				
Wedding (national average cost)		19936	2000	33r
Wedding (regional average total cost)		29454	1997	110r
Attendants' gifts		321	1998	33r
Bridal attendants' apparel (5 persons)		824	2000	33r
Bride's headpiece/veil		173	1998	33r
Bride's wedding dress		859	1998	33r
Clergy, religious facility fee		242	1998	33r
Engagement ring		3177	1998	33r
Flowers		789	1998	33r
Groom's formalwear rental		99	2000	33r
Limousine		410	1998	33r
Marriage license cost		25.00-40.00	4/01	35s
Men's formalwear (ushers, best man)		469	2000	33r
Mother of bride apparel		241	2000	33r
Music		866	1998	33r
Photography and videography		1368	1998	33r
Rehearsal dinner		728	1998	33r
Wedding invitations and announcements		341	1998	33r
Wedding reception		7968	2000	33r
Wedding rings (bride and groom)		1060	1998	33r

Steubenville-Weirton, OH

Item	Per	Value	Date	Ref.
Average annual expenditures	yr	35369	1999	30r
Alcoholic Beverages				
Alcoholic beverage purchases	yr	304	1999	30r
Malt beverages, all types, all sizes, any origin	16 oz	0.93	7/01	11r
Wine, red and white table, all sizes, any origin	liter	7.04	7/01	11r
Appliances				
Major appliances, expenditures on	yr	165	1999	30r
Small appliances, housewares, expenditures on	yr	90	1999	30r
Banking and Money				
Mortgage interest and charges paid	yr	2277	1999	30r
Mortgage principal paid on owned property	yr	1230	1999	30r
Vehicle finance charges paid	yr	328	1999	30r
Charity				
Cash contributions, expenditures	yr	1126	1999	30r
Child Care				
Child raising cost, total, age 0-2	yr	7890	1999	60r
Child raising cost, total, age 3-5	yr	8130	1999	60r
Child raising cost, total, age 6-8	yr	8170	1999	60r
Child raising cost, total, age 9-11	yr	8190	1999	60r
Child raising cost, total, age 12-14	yr	8890	1999	60r
Child raising cost, total, age 15-17	yr	9050	1999	60r
Child's child care and education, age 0-2	yr	1240	1999	60r
Child's child care and education, age 3-5	yr	1370	1999	60r
Child's child care and education, age 6-8	yr	880	1999	60r
Child's child care and education, age 9-11	yr	570	1999	60r
Child's child care and education, age 12-14	yr	420	1999	60r
Child's child care and education, age 15-17	yr	720	1999	60r
Child's clothing, age 0-2	yr	410	1999	60r
Child's clothing, age 3-5	yr	400	1999	60r
Child's clothing, age 6-8	yr	450	1999	60r
Child's clothing, age 9-11	yr	500	1999	60r
Child's clothing, age 12-14	yr	840	1999	60r
Child's clothing, age 15-17	yr	740	1999	60r
Child's food, age 0-2	yr	960	1999	60r
Child's food, age 3-5	yr	1120	1999	60r
Child's food, age 6-8	yr	1430	1999	60r
Child's food, age 9-11	yr	1710	1999	60r
Child's food, age 12-14	yr	1710	1999	60r
Child's food, age 15-17	yr	1920	1999	60r
Child's health care, age 0-2	yr	520	1999	60r
Child's health care, age 3-5	yr	500	1999	60r
Child's health care, age 6-8	yr	570	1999	60r
Child's health care, age 9-11	yr	610	1999	60r

Values are in dollars or fractions of dollars. In the column headed *Ref*, references are shown to sources. Each reference is followed by a letter. These refer to the geographical level for which data were reported: s=State, r=Region, and c=City or metro. The abbreviation *ex* is used to mean *except* or *excluding*; *exp* stands for expenditures. For other abbreviations and further explanations, please see the Introduction.

Steubenville-Weirton, OH - continued

Item	Per	Value	Date	Ref.
Child Care				
Child's health care, age 12-14	yr	630	1999	60r
Child's health care, age 15-17	yr	650	1999	60r
Child's housing, age 0-2	yr	2860	1999	60r
Child's housing, age 3-5	yr	2840	1999	60r
Child's housing, age 6-8	yr	2800	1999	60r
Child's housing, age 9-11	yr	2650	1999	60r
Child's housing, age 12-14	yr	2840	1999	60r
Child's housing, age 15-17	yr	2440	1999	60r
Child's personal care, reading, age 0-2	yr	880	1999	60r
Child's personal care, reading, age 3-5	yr	900	1999	60r
Child's personal care, reading, age 6-8	yr	930	1999	60r
Child's personal care, reading, age 9-11	yr	970	1999	60r
Child's personal care, reading, age 12-14	yr	1150	1999	60r
Child's personal care, reading, age 15-17	yr	920	1999	60r
Clothing				
Apparel and services purchases	yr	1607	1999	30r
Boys, 2 to 15, expenditures on	yr	91	1999	30r
Children under 2, expenditures on	yr	59	1999	30r
Footwear, expenditures on	yr	285	1999	30r
Girls, 2 to 15, expenditures on	yr	116	1999	30r
Men and boys, expenditures on	yr	433	1999	30r
Men, 16 and over, expenditures on	yr	341	1999	30r
Women, 16 and over, expenditures on	yr	490	1999	30r
Communications				
Cable modem installation, Adelphi		54.90	6/99	103s
Cable modem installation, Media One		100.00	6/99	103s
Cable modem installation, Time Warner		75.00-225.00	6/99	103s
Cable modem rate, cable subscriber, Adelphi	mos	34.95	6/99	103s
Cable modem rate, cable subscriber, Media One	mos	34.95-39.95	6/99	103s
Cable modem rate, cable subscriber, Time Warner	mos	39.95-49.95	6/99	103s
Cable modem rate, non-cable subscriber, Adelphi	mos	44.95	6/99	103s
Cable modem rate, non-cable subscriber, Media One	mos	49.95	6/99	103s
Cable modem rate, non-cable subscriber, Time Warner	mos	39.95-54.95	6/99	103s
Phone line, single, business, field visit	inst.	56.32	12/97	17s
Phone line, single, business, no field visit	inst.	56.32	12/97	17s
Phone line, single, residence, field visit	inst.	31.10	12/97	17s
Phone line, single, residence, no field visit	inst.	31.10	12/97	17s
Postage and stationery, expenditures on	yr	140	1999	30r
Postal rate, express mail, up to half-pound		12.45	7/01	108r
Postal rate, letter, first class, first ounce		0.34	7/01	108r
Postal rate, letter, two ounces		0.57	7/01	108r
Postal rate, post card		0.21	7/01	108r
Postal rate, priority mail, two pounds		3.95	7/01	108r
Postal rate, priority mail, up to one pound		3.50	7/01	108r
Telephone services, expenditures on	yr	830	1999	30r
Education				
Board, 4-year private college/university	yr	2414	1996	38s
Board, 4-year public college/university	yr	2181	1996	38s
Education expenditures	yr	583	1999	30r
Room, 4-year private college/university	yr	2349	1996	38s
Room, 4-year public college/university	yr	2386	1996	38s
Total cost, 4-year private college/university	yr	17139	1996	38s
Total cost, 4-year public college/university	yr	8169	1996	38s
Tuition, 2-year public college/university, in state	yr	2261	1996	38s
Tuition, 4-year private college/university, in state	yr	12377	1996	38s
Tuition, 4-year public college/university	yr	3603	1996	38s
Energy and Fuels				
Electricity	500 KWhs	46.59	7/01	11r
Fuel oil #2	gal	1.27	7/01	11r
Fuel oil and other fuels, expenditures on	yr	68	1999	30r
Gas, natural, commercial rate	1000 cf	8.65	11/00	88s

Steubenville-Weirton, OH - continued

Item	Per	Value	Date	Ref.
Energy and Fuels - continued				
Gasoline, unleaded midgrade	gal	1.79	7/01	11r
Gasoline, unleaded premium	gal	1.86	7/01	11r
Gasoline, unleaded regular	gal	1.58	7/01	11r
Natural gas, expenditures on	yr	389	1999	30r
Utility (piped) gas, therm		0.81	7/01	11r
Utility (piped) gas, 40 therms		38.01	7/01	11r
Utility (piped) gas, 100 therms		81.75	7/01	11r
Entertainment				
Entertainment purchases	yr	1984	1999	30r
Fees and admissions paid	yr	444	1999	30r
Television, radios, sound equipment, expenditures on	yr	580	1999	30r
Funerals				
Cosmetology, hair, other preparation		178.32	1/99	78r
Embalming		408.19	1/99	78r
Funeral at funeral home		362.13	1/99	78r
Professional service charges		1375.51	1/99	78r
Transfer of remains to funeral home		155.92	1/99	78r
Visitation/viewing		294.38	1/99	78r
Groceries				
Bacon, sliced	lb	3.15	7/01	11r
Bakery products, expenditures on	yr	281	1999	30r
Bananas	lb	0.48	7/01	11r
Beans, dried, any type, all sizes	lb	0.61	7/01	11r
Beef for stew, boneless	lb	3.08	7/01	11r
Beef, expenditures on	yr	217	1999	30r
Bologna, all beef or mixed	lb	2.52	7/01	11r
Bread, white, pan	lb	1.06	7/01	11r
Broccoli	lb	0.91	7/01	11r
Butter, salted, grade AA, stick	lb	3.04	7/01	11r
Butter, yoghurt, cheese, etc, expenditures on	yr	183	1999	30r
Cereals and bakery product purchases	yr	430	1999	30r
Cereals and cereal products, expenditures on	yr	149	1999	30r
Chicken, fresh, whole	lb	1.07	7/01	11r
Chops, boneless,	lb	3.64	7/01	11r
Chuck roast, U.S. choice, boneless	lb	2.47	7/01	11r
Coffee, 100%, ground roast, all sizes	lb	2.69	7/01	11r
Cookies, chocolate chip	lb	2.87	7/01	11r
Dairy product purchases	yr	304	1999	30r
Eggs, expenditures on	yr	26	1999	30r
Eggs, grade A, large	dozen	0.88	7/01	11r
Fats and oils, expenditures on	yr	75	1999	30r
Fish and seafood, expenditures on	yr	72	1999	30r
Food (excl fruit and vegetables), eaten at home, purchases	yr	887	1999	30r
Food cooked on trips, expenditures on	yr	44	1999	30r
Food purchases	yr	4802	1999	30r
Food purchases, eaten away from home	yr	2069	1999	30r
Food purchases, food eaten at home	yr	2733	1999	30r
Fresh fruits, expenditures on	yr	138	1999	30r
Fresh milk and cream, expenditures on	yr	120	1999	30r
Fresh vegetables, expenditures on	yr	126	1999	30r
Grapefruit	lb	0.66	7/01	11r
Grapes, Thompson, seedless	lb	1.64	7/01	11r
Ground beef, 100% beef	lb	1.64	7/01	11r
Ground beef, lean and extra lean	lb	2.16	7/01	11r
Ground chuck, 100% beef	lb	2.13	7/01	11r
Ham, boneless, excl canned	lb	2.62	7/01	11r
Ice cream, prepackaged, bulk, regular	1/2 gal	3.35	7/01	11r
Lemons	lb	1.19	7/01	11r
Lettuce, iceberg	lb	0.73	7/01	11r
Margarine, soft, tubs	lb	0.89	7/01	11r
Meats, poultry, fish, and egg purchases	yr	671	1999	30r
Milk, fresh, whole, fortified	gal	2.71	7/01	11r
Nonalcoholic beverages, expenditures on	yr	239	1999	30r
Oranges, Navel	lb	0.80	7/01	11r
Oranges, Valencia	lb	0.66	7/01	11r
Pears, Anjou	lb	0.93	7/01	11r
Pork chops, center cut, bone-in	lb	3.63	7/01	11r
Pork, expenditures on	yr	150	1999	30r

Values are in dollars or fractions of dollars. In the column headed *Ref*, references are shown to sources. Each reference is followed by a letter. These refer to the geographical level for which data were reported: s=State, r=Region, and c=City or metro. The abbreviation *ex* is used to mean *except* or *excluding*; *exp* stands for *expenditures*. For other abbreviations and further explanations, please see the Introduction.

Steubenville-Weirton, OH - continued

Item	Per	Value	Date	Ref.
Groceries				
Potato chips	16 oz	3.52	7/01	11r
Potatoes, frozen, french fried	lb	1.08	7/01	11r
Potatoes, white, all types	lb	0.33	7/01	11r
Poultry, expenditures on	yr	108	1999	30r
Processed fruits, expenditures on	yr	98	1999	30r
Processed vegetables, expenditures on	yr	80	1999	30r
Round roast, U.S. choice, boneless	lb	3.07	7/01	11r
Round steak, graded and ungraded, excl U.S. prime and choice	lb	3.41	7/01	11r
Shortening, vegetable oil blends	lb	1.13	7/01	11r
Spaghetti and macaroni	lb	0.80	7/01	11r
Steak, round, U.S. choice, boneless	lb	3.23	7/01	11r
Steak, T-bone, U.S. choice, bone-in	lb	6.68	7/01	11r
Strawberries, dry pint	12 oz	1.32	7/01	11r
Sugar and other sweets, expenditures on	yr	114	1999	30r
Sugar, white, 33-80 ounce package	lb	0.42	7/01	11r
Sugar, white, all sizes	lb	0.43	7/01	11r
Tobacco products and smoking supplies purchases	yr	331	1999	30r
Tomatoes, field grown	lb	1.46	7/01	11r
Tuna, light, chunk	lb	1.80	7/01	11r
Turkey, frozen, whole	lb	1.15	7/01	11r
Goods and Services				
B&B Japanese maple (acer japonicum)	gal	29.99-169.99	4/00	93r
Boxwood (buxus)	2 gal	18.99-39.99	4/00	93r
Daylily (hemerocallis)	gal	4.99-25.00	4/00	93r
Flat of annuals		11.98-24.99	4/00	93r
Fountain grass (pennisetum)	gal	5.98-12.98	4/00	93r
Hanging basket (10 in)		12.99-27.99	4/00	93r
Hardy geranium (geranium)	gal	7.99-9.99	4/00	93r
Hosta (hosta)	gal	6.00-25.00	4/00	93r
Lilac (syrubga vulgaris)	2 gal	14.99-24.99	4/00	93r
Miscellaneous purchases	yr	865	1999	30r
Rhododendron (rhododendron)	2 gal	23.98-42.99	4/00	93r
Sage (salvia)	gal	6.00-9.99	4/00	93r
Wintercreeper euonymus (euonymus fortunei)	2 gal	16.00-169.99	4/00	93r
Hunting license	yr	15.00	4/01	34s
Health Care				
Cardiac catheterization, ave hospital/ physician charges		11760	1998	77s
Childbirth, Cesarean delivery		10722	1997	13r
Childbirth, vaginal delivery		6223	1997	13r
Drugs, expenditures on	yr	394	1999	30r
Health care purchases	yr	2048	1999	30r
Health insurance expenditures	yr	978	1999	30r
Hysterectomy, laproscopically-assisted, ave hospital/physician charges		11730	1998	76s
Hysterectomy, vaginal, ave hospital and physician charges		9640	1998	76s
Medicaid dispensing fee		3.70	1999	87s
Medical services expenditures	yr	554	1999	30r
Medical supplies, expenditures on	yr	122	1999	30r
Plastic surgery, breast augmentation		3184	2000	7r
Plastic surgery, breast lift		3585	2000	7r
Plastic surgery, facelift		4999	2000	7r
Plastic surgery, hair transplantation		3105	2000	7r
Plastic surgery, lip augmentation		1290	2000	7r
Plastic surgery, lower body lift		8135	2000	7r
Plastic surgery, thigh lift		3839	2000	7r

Steubenville-Weirton, OH - continued

Item	Per	Value	Date	Ref.
Household Goods				
Floor coverings, expenditures on	yr	52	1999	30r
Furniture, expenditures on	yr	344	1999	30r
Household furnishings and equipment purchases	yr	1475	1999	30r
Household textiles, expenditures on	yr	109	1999	30r
Laundry and cleaning supplies, expenditures on	yr	134	1999	30r
Housing				
Home price, existing, ave		144400	10/00	90r
Home value, median		96000	2001	53s
Household operation expenditures	yr	542	1999	30r
Housekeeping supplies purchases	yr	508	1999	30r
Lodging expenditures	yr	430	1999	30r
Maintenance, repairs, insurance expenditures	yr	853	1999	30r
Monthly rental value of owned home	mos	547	1999	30r
Owned dwellings, expenditures own	yr	4282	1999	30r
Rent expenditures	yr	1558	1999	30r
Rental unit, 1 bedroom, with utilities	mos	344	4/01	41c
Rental unit, 2 bedroom, with utilities	mos	431	4/01	41c
Rental unit, 3 bedroom, with utilities	mos	549	4/01	41c
Rental unit, 4 bedroom, with utilities	mos	613	4/01	41c
Shelter, expenditures on	yr	6270	1999	30r
Insurance and Pensions				
Life and other personal insurance purchases	yr	387	1999	30r
Pensions and Social Security, expenditures on	yr	2968	1999	30r
Legal Fees				
Divorce, filing fee		100.00	4/01	35s
Driver's license fee	renew	14.50	1999	48s
Driver's license fee	orig	14.50	1999	48s
Fishing license	yr	15.00	4/01	34s
Personal Goods				
Personal care products and services purchases	yr	385	1999	30r
Personal Services				
Personal services, household, expenditures on	yr	300	1999	30r
Pets				
Pets, toys, and playground equipment, expenditures on	yr	375	1999	30r
Taxes				
Federal income taxes paid	yr	2326	1999	30r
Personal taxes, expenditures on	yr	3223	1999	30r
Property taxes paid	yr	1152	1999	30r
State and local income taxes paid	yr	753	1999	30r
Transportation				
Cars and trucks, new, expenditures on	yr	1280	1999	30r
Cars and trucks, used, expenditures on	yr	1763	1999	30r
Diesel at the pump	gal	1.25	10/99	73s
Gasoline and motor oil purchases	yr	1036	1999	30r
Gasoline before-tax price (cents)	gal	109.50	10/00	43s
Maintenance and repair expenditures	yr	594	1999	30r
Public transportation, expenditures on	yr	341	1999	30r
Transportation purchases	yr	6617	1999	30r
Vehicle expenses, miscellaneous, purchases	yr	2159	1999	30r
Vehicle insurance payments	yr	701	1999	30r
Vehicle purchases (net outlay)	yr	3081	1999	30r
Vehicle rental, lease expenditures	yr	536	1999	30r
Utilities				
Electrical bill, average	mos	72.83	9/00	9s
Electricity, expenditures on	yr	841	1999	30r
Electricity cost, average	KWh	6.59	9/00	9s
Utilities, fuels, and public services purchased	yr	2401	1999	30r
Water and other public services, expenditures on	yr	273	1999	30r

Values are in dollars or fractions of dollars. In the column headed *Ref*, references are shown to sources. Each reference is followed by a letter. These refer to the geographical level for which data were reported: s=State, r=Region, and c=City or metro. The abbreviation *ex* is used to mean *except* or *excluding*; *exp* stands for *expenditures*. For other abbreviations and further explanations, please see the Introduction.

Steubenville-Weirton, OH - continued

Item	Per	Value	Date	Ref.
Weddings				
Wedding (national average cost)		19936	2000	33r
Wedding (regional average total cost)		16195	1997	110r
Attendants' gifts		321	1998	33r
Bridal attendants' apparel (5 persons)		824	2000	33r
Bride's headpiece/veil		173	1998	33r
Bride's wedding dress		859	1998	33r
Clergy, religious facility fee		242	1998	33r
Engagement ring		3177	1998	33r
Flowers		789	1998	33r
Groom's formalwear rental		99	2000	33r
Limousine		410	1998	33r
Marriage license cost		45.00	4/01	35s
Men's formalwear (ushers, best man)		469	2000	33r
Mother of bride apparel		241	2000	33r
Music		866	1998	33r
Photography and videography		1368	1998	33r
Rehearsal dinner		728	1998	33r
Wedding invitations and announcements		341	1998	33r
Wedding reception		7968	2000	33r
Wedding rings (bride and groom)		1060	1998	33r

Stockton-Lodi, CA

Item	Per	Value	Date	Ref.
Average annual expenditures	yr	40662	1999	30r
Alcoholic Beverages				
Alcoholic beverage purchases	yr	372	1999	30r
Malt beverages, all types, all sizes, any origin	16 oz	0.94	7/01	11r
Wine, red and white table, all sizes, any origin	liter	6.00	7/01	11r
Appliances				
Major appliances, expenditures on	yr	167	1999	30r
Small appliances, housewares, expenditures on	yr	105	1999	30r
Banking and Money				
Mortgage interest and charges paid	yr	3368	1999	30r
Mortgage principal paid on owned property	yr	1677	1999	30r
Vehicle finance charges paid	yr	311	1999	30r
Charity				
Cash contributions, expenditures	yr	1344	1999	30r
Child Care				
Child raising cost, total, age 0-2	yr	9140	1999	60r
Child raising cost, total, age 3-5	yr	9370	1999	60r
Child raising cost, total, age 6-8	yr	9450	1999	60r
Child raising cost, total, age 9-11	yr	9470	1999	60r
Child raising cost, total, age 12-14	yr	10170	1999	60r
Child raising cost, total, age 15-17	yr	10360	1999	60r
Child's child care and education, age 0-2	yr	1250	1999	60r
Child's child care and education, age 3-5	yr	1380	1999	60r
Child's child care and education, age 6-8	yr	890	1999	60r
Child's child care and education, age 9-11	yr	580	1999	60r
Child's child care and education, age 12-14	yr	430	1999	60r
Child's child care and education, age 15-17	yr	730	1999	60r
Child's clothing, age 0-2	yr	430	1999	60r
Child's clothing, age 3-5	yr	420	1999	60r
Child's clothing, age 6-8	yr	470	1999	60r
Child's clothing, age 9-11	yr	520	1999	60r
Child's clothing, age 12-14	yr	870	1999	60r
Child's clothing, age 15-17	yr	770	1999	60r
Child's food, age 0-2	yr	1120	1999	60r
Child's food, age 3-5	yr	1280	1999	60r
Child's food, age 6-8	yr	1640	1999	60r
Child's food, age 9-11	yr	1930	1999	60r
Child's food, age 12-14	yr	1940	1999	60r
Child's food, age 15-17	yr	2150	1999	60r
Child's health care, age 0-2	yr	490	1999	60r
Child's health care, age 3-5	yr	470	1999	60r
Child's health care, age 6-8	yr	530	1999	60r
Child's health care, age 9-11	yr	570	1999	60r
Child's health care, age 12-14	yr	580	1999	60r

Item	Per	Value	Date	Ref.
Child Care - continued				
Child's health care, age 15-17	yr	610	1999	60r
Child's housing, age 0-2	yr	3630	1999	60r
Child's housing, age 3-5	yr	3610	1999	60r
Child's housing, age 6-8	yr	3570	1999	60r
Child's housing, age 9-11	yr	3410	1999	60r
Child's housing, age 12-14	yr	3600	1999	60r
Child's housing, age 15-17	yr	3210	1999	60r
Child's personal care, reading, age 0-2	yr	1040	1999	60r
Child's personal care, reading, age 3-5	yr	1060	1999	60r
Child's personal care, reading, age 6-8	yr	1090	1999	60r
Child's personal care, reading, age 9-11	yr	1130	1999	60r
Child's personal care, reading, age 12-14	yr	1300	1999	60r
Child's personal care, reading, age 15-17	yr	1080	1999	60r
Clothing				
Apparel and services purchases	yr	1863	1999	30r
Boys, 2 to 15, expenditures on	yr	80	1999	30r
Children under 2, expenditures on	yr	74	1999	30r
Footwear, expenditures on	yr	307	1999	30r
Girls, 2 to 15, expenditures on	yr	101	1999	30r
Men and boys, expenditures on	yr	443	1999	30r
Men, 16 and over, expenditures on	yr	363	1999	30r
Women, 16 and over, expenditures on	yr	594	1999	30r
Communications				
Cable modem installation, AT&T-BIS		150.00	6/99	103s
Cable modem installation, Charter		99.00-169.00	6/99	103s
Cable modem installation, Comcast		95.00	6/99	103s
Cable modem installation, Cox		99.00-174.95	6/99	103s
Cable modem installation, Media One		100.00	6/99	103s
Cable modem installation, Time Warner		75.00-225.00	6/99	103s
Cable modem rate, cable subscriber, AT&T-BIS	mos	39.95	6/99	103s
Cable modem rate, cable subscriber, Charter	mos	49.95-79.95	6/99	103s
Cable modem rate, cable subscriber, Comcast	mos	39.95	6/99	103s
Cable modem rate, cable subscriber, Cox	mos	29.95-44.95	6/99	103s
Cable modem rate, cable subscriber, Media One	mos	34.95-39.95	6/99	103s
Cable modem rate, cable subscriber, Time Warner	mos	39.95-49.95	6/99	103s
Cable modem rate, non-cable subscriber, Charter	mos	59.95-89.95	6/99	103s
Cable modem rate, non-cable subscriber, Comcast	mos	49.95	6/99	103s
Cable modem rate, non-cable subscriber, Cox	mos	42.95-54.95	6/99	103s
Cable modem rate, non-cable subscriber, Media One	mos	49.95	6/99	103s
Cable modem rate, non-cable subscriber, Time Warner	mos	39.95-54.95	6/99	103s
Phone line, single, business, field visit	inst.	70.75	12/97	17s
Phone line, single, business, no field visit	inst.	70.75	12/97	17s
Phone line, single, residence, field visit	inst.	34.75	12/97	17s
Phone line, single, residence, no field visit	inst.	34.75	12/97	17s
Postage and stationery, expenditures on	yr	150	1999	30r
Postal rate, express mail, up to half-pound		12.45	7/01	108r
Postal rate, letter, first class, first ounce		0.34	7/01	108r
Postal rate, letter, two ounces		0.57	7/01	108r
Postal rate, post card		0.21	7/01	108r
Postal rate, priority mail, two pounds		3.95	7/01	108r
Postal rate, priority mail, up to one pound		3.50	7/01	108r
Telephone services, expenditures on	yr	825	1999	30r
Education				
Board, 4-year private college/university	yr	2970	1996	38s
Board, 4-year public college/university	yr	2516	1996	38s
Education expenditures	yr	676	1999	30r
Room, 4-year private college/university	yr	3196	1996	38s

Values are in dollars or fractions of dollars. In the column headed *Ref*, references are shown to sources. Each reference is followed by a letter. These refer to the geographical level for which data were reported: s=State, r=Region, and c=City or metro. The abbreviation *ex* is used to mean *except* or *excluding*; *exp* stands for *expenditures*. For other abbreviations and further explanations, please see the Introduction.

Stockton-Lodi, CA - continued

Item	Per	Value	Date	Ref.
Education				
Room, 4-year public college/university	yr	3031	1996	38s
Total cost, 4-year private college/university	yr	20143	1996	38s
Total cost, 4-year public college/university	yr	8213	1996	38s
Tuition, 2-year public college/university, in state	yr	362	1996	38s
Tuition, 4-year private college/university, in state	yr	13977	1996	38s
Tuition, 4-year public college/university	yr	2666	1996	38s
Energy and Fuels				
Electricity	KWh	0.11	7/01	11r
Electricity	500 KWhs	48.23	7/01	11r
Fuel oil and other fuels, expenditures on	yr	35	1999	30r
Gas, natural, commercial rate	1000 cf	8.74	11/00	88s
Gasoline, all types	gal	1.91	7/01	11r
Gasoline, unleaded premium	gal	2.05	7/01	11r
Gasoline, unleaded regular	gal	1.83	7/01	11r
Natural gas, expenditures on	yr	255	1999	30r
Utility (piped) gas, therm		0.98	7/01	11r
Utility (piped) gas, 40 therms		40.74	7/01	11r
Utility (piped) gas, 100 therms		96.80	7/01	11r
Entertainment				
Entertainment purchases	yr	2139	1999	30r
Fees and admissions paid	yr	545	1999	30r
Television, radios, sound equipment, expenditures on	yr	624	1999	30r
Funerals				
Total cost of funeral		5401.08	1/99	78r
Acknowledgement cards		33.64	1/99	78r
Casket		2170.43	1/99	78r
Cosmetology, hair, other preparation		136.32	1/99	78r
Embalming		319.13	1/99	78r
Funeral at funeral home		370.21	1/99	78r
Hearse (local)		161.04	1/99	78r
Professional service charges		963.15	1/99	78r
Service car/van		133.99	1/99	78r
Transfer of remains to funeral home		159.82	1/99	78r
Vault		778.07	1/99	78r
Visitation/viewing		175.28	1/99	78r
Groceries				
Apples, red delicious	lb	0.84	7/01	11r
Bacon, sliced	lb	3.38	7/01	11r
Bakery products, expenditures on	yr	299	1999	30r
Bananas	lb	0.54	7/01	11r
Beans, dried, any type, all sizes	lb	0.76	7/01	11r
Beef, expenditures on	yr	222	1999	30r
Bread, white, pan	lb	0.99	7/01	11r
Butter, yoghurt, cheese, etc, expenditures on	yr	211	1999	30r
Cereals and bakery product purchases	yr	466	1999	30r
Cereals and cereal products, expenditures on	yr	168	1999	30r
Chicken breast, bone-in	lb	2.45	7/01	11r
Chicken, fresh, whole	lb	1.19	7/01	11r
Chops, boneless,	lb	4.00	7/01	11r
Chuck roast, graded and ungraded, excl U.S. prime and choice	lb	2.55	7/01	11r
Coffee, 100%, ground roast, all sizes	lb	3.80	7/01	11r
Cookies, chocolate chip	lb	2.83	7/01	11r
Dairy product purchases	yr	341	1999	30r
Eggs, expenditures on	yr	39	1999	30r
Eggs, grade AA, large	dozen	1.23	7/01	11r
Fats and oils, expenditures on	yr	88	1999	30r
Fish and seafood, expenditures on	yr	121	1999	30r
Food (excl fruit and vegetables), eaten at home, purchases	yr	1001	1999	30r
Food cooked on trips, expenditures on	yr	64	1999	30r
Food purchases	yr	5312	1999	30r
Food purchases, eaten away from home	yr	2180	1999	30r
Food purchases, food eaten at home	yr	3132	1999	30r
Fresh fruits, expenditures on	yr	186	1999	30r

Stockton-Lodi, CA - continued

Item	Per	Value	Date	Ref.
Groceries - continued				
Fresh milk and cream, expenditures on	yr	130	1999	30r
Fresh vegetables, expenditures on	yr	177	1999	30r
Grapefruit	lb	0.68	7/01	11r
Grapes, Thompson, seedless	lb	2.42	7/01	11r
Ground beef, lean and extra lean	lb	2.46	7/01	11r
Ice cream, prepackaged, bulk, regular	1/2 gal	3.62	7/01	11r
Lettuce, iceberg	lb	0.63	7/01	11r
Meats, poultry, fish, and egg purchases	yr	761	1999	30r
Milk, fresh, low fat	gal	2.80	7/01	11r
Milk, fresh, whole, fortified	gal	2.88	7/01	11r
Nonalcoholic beverages, expenditures on	yr	258	1999	30r
Oranges, Navel	lb	0.97	7/01	11r
Oranges, Valencia	lb	0.43	7/01	11r
Peaches	lb	1.38	7/01	11r
Peanut butter, creamy, all sizes	lb	2.14	7/01	11r
Pork chops, center cut, bone-in	lb	3.83	7/01	11r
Pork, expenditures on	yr	141	1999	30r
Potatoes, white, all types	lb	0.37	7/01	11r
Poultry, expenditures on	yr	146	1999	30r
Processed fruits, expenditures on	yr	118	1999	30r
Processed vegetables, expenditures on	yr	81	1999	30r
Round roast, graded and ungraded, excl U.S. prime and choice	lb	3.07	7/01	11r
Round roast, U.S. choice, boneless	lb	3.37	7/01	11r
Round steak, graded and ungraded, excl U.S. prime and choice	lb	3.51	7/01	11r
Sirloin steak, graded and ungraded, excl U.S. prime and choice	lb	4.67	7/01	11r
Steak, sirloin, U.S. choice, boneless	lb	6.20	7/01	11r
Strawberries, dry pint	12 oz	1.79	7/01	11r
Sugar and other sweets, expenditures on	yr	124	1999	30r
Sugar, white, all sizes	lb	0.46	7/01	11r
Tobacco products and smoking supplies purchases	yr	217	1999	30r
Tomatoes, field grown	lb	1.17	7/01	11r
Tuna, light, chunk	lb	2.05	7/01	11r
Goods and Services				
B&B Japanese maple (acer japonicum)	gal	39.99	4/00	93r
Boxwood (buxus)	2 gal	14.99-24.99	4/00	93r
Christmas tree, noble fir		40-60	2000	65s
Daylilly (hemerocallis)	gal	6.99-8.99	4/00	93r
Flat of annuals		16.68	4/00	93r
Fountain grass (pennisetum)	gal	7.99-11.99	4/00	93r
Hanging basket (10 in)		29.99	4/00	93r
Hardy geranium (geranium)	gal	6.99-11.99	4/00	93r
Hosta (hosta)	gal	6.99-18.99	4/00	93r
Lilac (syrubga vulgaris)	2 gal	14.99-17.99	4/00	93r
Miscellaneous purchases	yr	1070	1999	30r
Rhododendron (rhododendron)	2 gal	14.99	4/00	93r
Sage (salvia)	gal	6.99	4/00	93r
Wintercreeper euonymus (euonymus fortunei)	2 gal	14.99-22.99	4/00	93r
Hunting license	yr	29.95	4/01	34s
Health Care				
Cardiac catheterization, ave hospital/ physician charges		24000	1998	77s
Childbirth, Cesarean delivery		11587	1997	13r
Childbirth, vaginal delivery		6725	1997	13r
Drugs, expenditures on	yr	309	1999	30r
Health care purchases	yr	1869	1999	30r
Health insurance expenditures	yr	868	1999	30r
Hysterectomy, laproscopically-assisted, ave hospital/physician charges		20760	1998	76s
Hysterectomy, vaginal, ave hospital and physician charges		14570	1998	76s

Values are in dollars or fractions of dollars. In the column headed *Ref*, references are shown to sources. Each reference is followed by a letter. These refer to the geographical level for which data were reported: s=State, r=Region, and c=City or metro. The abbreviation *ex* is used to mean *except* or *excluding*; *exp* stands for expenditures. For other abbreviations and further explanations, please see the Introduction.

Stockton-Lodi, CA - continued

Item	Per	Value	Date	Ref.
Health Care				
Medicaid dispensing fee		4.05	1999	87s
Medical services expenditures	yr	580	1999	30r
Medical supplies, expenditures on	yr	112	1999	30r
Household Goods				
Floor coverings, expenditures on	yr	49	1999	30r
Furniture, expenditures on	yr	444	1999	30r
Household furnishings and equipment purchases	yr	1768	1999	30r
Household textiles, expenditures on	yr	141	1999	30r
Laundry and cleaning supplies, expenditures on	yr	128	1999	30r
Housing				
Home price, existing, ave		239400	10/00	90r
Home value, median		215000	2001	53s
Household operation expenditures	yr	781	1999	30r
Housekeeping supplies purchases	yr	513	1999	30r
Lodging expenditures	yr	575	1999	30r
Maintenance, repairs, insurance expenditures	yr	939	1999	30r
Monthly rental value of owned home	mos	662	1999	30r
Owned dwellings, expenditures own	yr	5231	1999	30r
Rent expenditures	yr	2709	1999	30r
Rental unit, 1 bedroom, with utilities	mos	477	4/01	41c
Rental unit, 2 bedroom, with utilities	mos	613	4/01	41c
Rental unit, 3 bedroom, with utilities	mos	853	4/01	41c
Rental unit, 4 bedroom, with utilities	mos	1006	4/01	41c
Shelter, expenditures on	yr	8516	1999	30r
Insurance and Pensions				
Life and other personal insurance purchases	yr	355	1999	30r
Pensions and Social Security, expenditures on	yr	3636	1999	30r
Legal Fees				
Divorce, filing fee		182.00	4/01	35s
Driver's license fee	renew	15.00	1999	48s
Driver's license fee	orig	12.00	1999	48s
Personal Goods				
Personal care products and services purchases	yr	449	1999	30r
Personal Services				
Personal services, household, expenditures on	yr	353	1999	30r
Pets				
Pets, toys, and playground equipment, expenditures on	yr	358	1999	30r
Taxes				
Federal income taxes paid	yr	3200	1999	30r
Personal taxes, expenditures on	yr	4153	1999	30r
Property taxes paid	yr	923	1999	30r
State and local income taxes paid	yr	812	1999	30r
Transportation				
Cars and trucks, new, expenditures on	yr	1534	1999	30r
Cars and trucks, used, expenditures on	yr	1593	1999	30r
Diesel at the pump	gal	1.37	10/99	73s
Gasoline and motor oil purchases	yr	1129	1999	30r
Gasoline before-tax price (cents)	gal	128.80	10/00	43s
Maintenance and repair expenditures	yr	797	1999	30r
Public transportation, expenditures on	yr	530	1999	30r
Transportation purchases	yr	7423	1999	30r
Vehicle expenses, miscellaneous, purchases	yr	2585	1999	30r
Vehicle insurance payments	yr	811	1999	30r
Vehicle purchases (net outlay)	yr	3180	1999	30r
Vehicle rental, lease expenditures	yr	666	1999	30r
Utilities				
Electrical bill, average	mos	58.66	9/00	9s
Electricity, expenditures on	yr	725	1999	30r
Electricity cost, average	KWh	7.75	9/00	9s
Utilities, fuels, and public services purchased	yr	2179	1999	30r

Stockton-Lodi, CA - continued

Item	Per	Value	Date	Ref.
Utilities - continued				
Water and other public services, expenditures on	yr	339	1999	30r
Weddings				
Wedding (national average cost)		19936	2000	33r
Wedding (regional average total cost)		18918	1997	110r
Attendants' gifts		321	1998	33r
Bridal attendants' apparel (5 persons)		824	2000	33r
Bride's headpiece/veil		173	1998	33r
Bride's wedding dress		859	1998	33r
Clergy, religious facility fee		242	1998	33r
Engagement ring		3177	1998	33r
Flowers		789	1998	33r
Groom's formalwear rental		99	2000	33r
Limousine		410	1998	33r
Marriage license cost		50.00-80.00	4/01	35s
Men's formalwear (ushers, best man)		469	2000	33r
Mother of bride apparel		241	2000	33r
Music		866	1998	33r
Photography and videography		1368	1998	33r
Rehearsal dinner		728	1998	33r
Wedding invitations and announcements		341	1998	33r
Wedding reception		7968	2000	33r
Wedding rings (bride and groom)		1060	1998	33r

Sumter, SC

Item	Per	Value	Date	Ref.
Composite, ACCRA index		95.30	3/01	4c
Alcoholic Beverages				
Alcoholic beverage purchases	yr	253	1999	30r
Beer, Heineken, 12-oz, ex deposit	6	6.86	3/01	4c
J & B Scotch	750-ml	21.01	3/01	4c
Malt beverages, all types, all sizes, any origin	16 oz	0.96	7/01	11r
Wine, Livingston or Gallo, Chablis blanc	1.5 liter	6.04	3/01	4c
Appliances				
Appliance repair, service call, washing machine	min lab chg	47.50	3/01	4c
Major appliances, expenditures on	yr	172	1999	30r
Small appliances, housewares, expenditures on	yr	81	1999	30r
Banking and Money				
Mortgage interest and charges paid	yr	2039	1999	30r
Mortgage principal paid on owned property	yr	1026	1999	30r
Mortgage rate, incl. points and orig. fee, 30-yr. conv. fixed or ARM	mos	6.93	3/01	4c
Vehicle finance charges paid	yr	365	1999	30r
Charity				
Cash contributions, expenditures	yr	1127	1999	30r
Child Care				
Child raising cost, total, age 0-2	yr	8540	1999	60r
Child raising cost, total, age 3-5	yr	8780	1999	60r
Child raising cost, total, age 6-8	yr	8820	1999	60r
Child raising cost, total, age 9-11	yr	8800	1999	60r
Child raising cost, total, age 12-14	yr	9510	1999	60r
Child raising cost, total, age 15-17	yr	9740	1999	60r
Child's child care and education, age 0-2	yr	1380	1999	60r
Child's child care and education, age 3-5	yr	1520	1999	60r
Child's child care and education, age 6-8	yr	990	1999	60r
Child's child care and education, age 9-11	yr	650	1999	60r
Child's child care and education, age 12-14	yr	490	1999	60r
Child's child care and education, age 15-17	yr	840	1999	60r
Child's clothing, age 0-2	yr	480	1999	60r
Child's clothing, age 3-5	yr	470	1999	60r
Child's clothing, age 6-8	yr	520	1999	60r
Child's clothing, age 9-11	yr	570	1999	60r
Child's clothing, age 12-14	yr	950	1999	60r
Child's clothing, age 15-17	yr	850	1999	60r
Child's food, age 0-2	yr	1000	1999	60r

Values are in dollars or fractions of dollars. In the column headed *Ref*, references are shown to sources. Each reference is followed by a letter. These refer to the geographical level for which data were reported: s=State, r=Region, and c=City or metro. The abbreviation *ex* is used to mean *except* or *excluding*; *exp* stands for *expenditures*. For other abbreviations and further explanations, please see the Introduction.

Sumter, SC - continued

Item	Per	Value	Date	Ref.
Child Care				
Child's food, age 3-5	yr	1160	1999	60r
Child's food, age 6-8	yr	1490	1999	60r
Child's food, age 9-11	yr	1770	1999	60r
Child's food, age 12-14	yr	1770	1999	60r
Child's food, age 15-17	yr	1980	1999	60r
Child's health care, age 0-2	yr	620	1999	60r
Child's health care, age 3-5	yr	590	1999	60r
Child's health care, age 6-8	yr	680	1999	60r
Child's health care, age 9-11	yr	720	1999	60r
Child's health care, age 12-14	yr	730	1999	60r
Child's health care, age 15-17	yr	760	1999	60r
Child's housing, age 0-2	yr	3070	1999	60r
Child's housing, age 3-5	yr	3050	1999	60r
Child's housing, age 6-8	yr	3010	1999	60r
Child's housing, age 9-11	yr	2850	1999	60r
Child's housing, age 12-14	yr	3040	1999	60r
Child's housing, age 15-17	yr	2650	1999	60r
Child's personal care, reading, age 0-2	yr	910	1999	60r
Child's personal care, reading, age 3-5	yr	930	1999	60r
Child's personal care, reading, age 6-8	yr	960	1999	60r
Child's personal care, reading, age 9-11	yr	1000	1999	60r
Child's personal care, reading, age 12-14	yr	1170	1999	60r
Child's personal care, reading, age 15-17	yr	950	1999	60r
Clothing				
Apparel and services purchases	yr	1610	1999	30r
Boys' brief, cotton	3	6.63	3/01	4c
Boys, 2 to 15, expenditures on	yr	89	1999	30r
Children under 2, expenditures on	yr	79	1999	30r
Footwear, expenditures on	yr	283	1999	30r
Girls, 2 to 15, expenditures on	yr	103	1999	30r
Men and boys, expenditures on	yr	351	1999	30r
Men, 16 and over, expenditures on	yr	262	1999	30r
Shirt, man's dress shirt		32.00	3/01	4c
Slacks, man's "No Wrinkles" khaki		33.49	3/01	4c
Women, 16 and over, expenditures on	yr	538	1999	30r
Communications				
Cable modem installation, Adelphi		54.90	6/99	103s
Cable modem installation, Comcast		95.00	6/99	103s
Cable modem installation, Intermedia		149.95	6/99	103s
Cable modem rate, cable subscriber, Adelphi	mos	34.95	6/99	103s
Cable modem rate, cable subscriber, Comcast	mos	39.95	6/99	103s
Cable modem rate, cable subscriber, Intermedia	mos	49.95	6/99	103s
Cable modem rate, non-cable subscriber, Adelphi	mos	44.95	6/99	103s
Cable modem rate, non-cable subscriber, Comcast	mos	49.95	6/99	103s
Cable modem rate, non-cable subscriber, Intermedia	mos	54.95	6/99	103s
Newspaper subscription, daily and Sunday delivery	mos	14.32	3/01	4c
Phone line, single, business, field visit	inst.	64.00	12/97	17s
Phone line, single, business, no field visit	inst.	64.00	12/97	17s
Phone line, single, residence, field visit	inst.	40.00	12/97	17s
Phone line, single, residence, no field visit	inst.	40.00	12/97	17s
Postage and stationery, expenditures on	yr	104	1999	30r
Postal rate, express mail, up to half-pound		12.45	7/01	108r
Postal rate, letter, first class, first ounce		0.34	7/01	108r
Postal rate, letter, two ounces		0.57	7/01	108r
Postal rate, post card		0.21	7/01	108r
Postal rate, priority mail, two pounds		3.95	7/01	108r
Postal rate, priority mail, up to one pound		3.50	7/01	108r
Telephone bill, family of three	mos	23.28	3/01	4c
Telephone services, expenditures on	yr	860	1999	30r
Education				
Board, 4-year private college/university	yr	1990	1996	38s
Board, 4-year public college/university	yr	1872	1996	38s
Education expenditures	yr	431	1999	30r
Room, 4-year private college/university	yr	1786	1996	38s
Room, 4-year public college/university	yr	1998	1996	38s

Sumter, SC - continued

Item	Per	Value	Date	Ref.
Education - continued				
Total cost, 4-year private college/university	yr	13517	1996	38s
Total cost, 4-year public college/university	yr	6964	1996	38s
Tuition, 2-year public college/university, in state	yr	1071	1996	38s
Tuition, 4-year private college/university, in state	yr	9741	1996	38s
Tuition, 4-year public college/university	yr	3094	1996	38s
Energy and Fuels				
Electricity	500 KWhs	47.29	7/01	11r
Electricity	KWh	0.09	7/01	11r
Energy, combined forms, 2400 sq ft	mos	106.59	3/01	4c
Fuel oil #2	gal	1.43	7/01	11r
Fuel oil and other fuels, expenditures on	yr	45	1999	30r
Gas, natural, commercial rate	1000 cf	9.50	11/00	88s
Gas, regular unleaded, cash, self-service	gal	1.35	3/01	4c
Gasoline, all types	gal	1.60	7/01	11r
Gasoline, unleaded midgrade	gal	1.65	7/01	11r
Gasoline, unleaded premium	gal	1.74	7/01	11r
Natural gas, expenditures on	yr	164	1999	30r
Utility (piped) gas, therm		1.01	7/01	11r
Utility (piped) gas, 40 therms		44.29	7/01	11r
Utility (piped) gas, 100 therms		97.44	7/01	11r
Entertainment				
Bowling, Saturday evening rate	line	3.00	3/01	4c
Entertainment purchases	yr	1574	1999	30r
Fees and admissions paid	yr	371	1999	30r
Monopoly game, Parker Brothers', No. 9	game	9.43	3/01	4c
Movie, first-run, Saturday, evening	adm.	6.37	3/01	4c
Reading purchases	yr	121	1999	30r
Television, radios, sound equipment, expenditures on	yr	561	1999	30r
Tennis balls, yellow, Wilson or Penn, 3	can	2.07	3/01	4c
Funerals				
Total cost of funeral		5922.53	1/99	78r
Acknowledgement cards		63.43	1/99	78r
Casket		2258.77	1/99	78r
Cosmetology, hair, other preparation		127.09	1/99	78r
Embalming		393.49	1/99	78r
Funeral at funeral home		367.50	1/99	78r
Hearse (local)		169.66	1/99	78r
Professional service charges		1211.32	1/99	78r
Service car/van		80.69	1/99	78r
Transfer of remains to funeral home		144.25	1/99	78r
Vault		803.50	1/99	78r
Visitation/viewing		302.83	1/99	78r
Groceries				
Groceries, ACCRA Index		101.80	3/01	4c
American processed cheese	lb	3.50	7/01	11r
Antibiotic ointment, Polysporin	0.5 oz	4.75	3/01	4c
Baby food, strained vegetables or fruit, lowest price	4-4.5 oz	0.45	3/01	4c
Bakery products, expenditures on	yr	261	1999	30r
Bananas	lb	0.56	3/01	4c
Bananas	lb	0.47	7/01	11r
Beans, dried, any type, all sizes	lb	0.63	7/01	11r
Beef for stew, boneless	lb	2.86	7/01	11r
Beef or hamburger, ground	lb	1.79	3/01	4c
Beef, expenditures on	yr	210	1999	30r
Bologna, all beef or mixed	lb	2.29	7/01	11r
Bread, French	lb	1.66	7/01	11r
Bread, white	loaf	1.11	3/01	4c
Bread, white, pan	lb	0.87	7/01	11r
Bread, whole wheat, pan	lb	1.38	7/01	11r
Broccoli	lb	1.04	7/01	11r
Butter, salted, grade AA, stick	lb	2.26	7/01	11r
Butter, yoghurt, cheese, etc, expenditures on	yr	170	1999	30r
Cabbage	lb	0.42	7/01	11r
Cereals and cereal products, expenditures on	yr	140	1999	30r

Values are in dollars or fractions of dollars. In the column headed *Ref*, references are shown to sources. Each reference is followed by a letter. These refer to the geographical level for which data were reported: s=State, r=Region, and c=City or metro. The abbreviation *ex* is used to mean *except* or *excluding*; *exp* stands for *expenditures*. For other abbreviations and further explanations, please see the Introduction.

Sumter, SC - continued

Item	Per	Value	Date	Ref.
Groceries				
Cheddar cheese, natural	lb	3.75	7/01	11r
Cheese, Kraft grated Parmesan	8 oz	3.51	3/01	4c
Chicken breast, bone-in	lb	1.85	7/01	11r
Chicken legs, bone-in	lb	1.34	7/01	11r
Chicken, fresh, whole	lb	1.05	7/01	11r
Chicken, whole fryer	lb	0.99	3/01	4c
Chops, boneless,	lb	4.13	7/01	11r
Chuck roast, graded and ungraded, excl U.S. prime and choice	lb	2.35	7/01	11r
Chuck roast, U.S. choice, boneless	lb	2.67	7/01	11r
Cigarettes, Winston, Kings	carton	24.92	3/01	4c
Coffee, 100%, ground roast, all sizes	lb	2.88	7/01	11r
Coffee, instant, plain, regular, all sizes	16 oz	9.25	7/01	11r
Coffee, vacuum-packed	13 oz	2.29	3/01	4c
Cola, non diet,	2 liter	1.11	7/01	11r
Corn Flakes, Kellogg's or Post Toasties	18 oz	2.89	3/01	4c
Corn, frozen, whole kernel, lowest price	16 oz	1.22	3/01	4c
Crackers, soda, salted	lb	1.70	7/01	11r
Dairy product purchases	yr	282	1999	30r
Eggs, expenditures on	yr	32	1999	30r
Eggs, Grade A or AA	dozen	1.24	3/01	4c
Fats and oils, expenditures on	yr	79	1999	30r
Fish and seafood, expenditures on	yr	99	1999	30r
Flour, white, all purpose	lb	0.32	7/01	11r
Food (excl fruit and vegetables), eaten at home, purchases	yr	815	1999	30r
Food cooked on trips, expenditures on	yr	36	1999	30r
Food purchases	yr	4533	1999	30r
Food purchases, eaten away from home	yr	1873	1999	30r
Food purchases, food eaten at home	yr	2660	1999	30r
Fresh fruits, expenditures on	yr	128	1999	30r
Fresh milk and cream, expenditures on	yr	112	1999	30r
Fresh vegetables, expenditures on	yr	131	1999	30r
Fruit and vegetable purchases	yr	438	1999	30r
Grapefruit	lb	0.59	7/01	11r
Grapes, Thompson, seedless	lb	2.12	7/01	11r
Ground beef, 100% beef	lb	1.76	7/01	11r
Ground beef, lean and extra lean	lb	2.60	7/01	11r
Ground chuck, 100% beef	lb	2.08	7/01	11r
Ham, boneless, excl canned	lb	2.71	7/01	11r
Ham, rump or shank half, bone-in, smoked	lb	2.19	7/01	11r
Ice cream, prepackaged, bulk, regular	1/2 gal	3.93	7/01	11r
Lemons	lb	1.32	7/01	11r
Lettuce, iceberg	head	1.19	3/01	4c
Lettuce, iceberg	lb	0.76	7/01	11r
Margarine, Blue Bonnet or Parkay, stick	lb	0.70	3/01	4c
Milk, fresh, low fat	gal	2.75	7/01	11r
Milk, fresh, whole, fortified	gal	2.97	7/01	11r
Milk, whole	1/2 gal	1.94	3/01	4c
Nonalcoholic beverages, expenditures on	yr	228	1999	30r
Orange juice, frozen concentrate	16 oz	1.95	7/01	11r
Orange juice, Minute Maid frozen	12 oz	1.66	3/01	4c
Oranges, Navel	lb	0.73	7/01	11r
Oranges, Valencia	lb	0.55	7/01	11r
Peaches, halves or slices, Hunt's, Del Monte, or Libby's	29 oz	1.47	3/01	4c
Peanut butter, creamy, all sizes	lb	1.83	7/01	11r
Pears, Anjou	lb	0.98	7/01	11r
Peas, green, Del Monte or Green Giant	15 oz	0.63	3/01	4c
Pork chops, center cut, bone-in	lb	3.33	7/01	11r
Pork sausage, fresh, loose	lb	2.59	7/01	11r
Pork shoulder picnic, bone-in, smoked	lb	1.12	7/01	11r
Pork, expenditures on	yr	162	1999	30r
Potato chips	16 oz	3.59	7/01	11r
Potatoes, frozen, french fried	lb	1.00	7/01	11r
Potatoes, white or red	10 lb	2.94	3/01	4c
Potatoes, white, all types	lb	0.44	7/01	11r
Poultry, expenditures on	yr	137	1999	30r
Processed fruits, expenditures on	yr	97	1999	30r
Processed vegetables, expenditures on	yr	82	1999	30r
Rice, white, long grain, uncooked	lb	0.51	7/01	11r

Sumter, SC - continued

Item	Per	Value	Date	Ref.
Groceries - continued				
Round roast, graded and ungraded, excl U.S. prime and choice	lb	2.96	7/01	11r
Round steak, graded and ungraded, excl U.S. prime and choice	lb	3.11	7/01	11r
Sausage, Jimmy Dean/Owens pork	lb	3.36	3/01	4c
Shortening, vegetable, Crisco	3 lb	3.09	3/01	4c
Sirloin steak, graded and ungraded, excl U.S. prime and choice	lb	4.23	7/01	11r
Soft drink, Coca Cola, ex deposit	2 liter	1.01	3/01	4c
Spaghetti and macaroni	lb	0.78	7/01	11r
Steak, round, U.S. choice, boneless	lb	3.56	7/01	11r
Steak, sirloin, U.S. choice, boneless	lb	5.65	7/01	11r
Steak, T-bone	lb	6.44	3/01	4c
Strawberries, dry pint	12 oz	1.50	7/01	11r
Sugar and other sweets, expenditures on	yr	99	1999	30r
Sugar, cane or beet	4 lbs	1.56	3/01	4c
Sugar, white, 33-80 ounce package	lb	0.39	7/01	11r
Sugar, white, all sizes	lb	0.42	7/01	11r
Tobacco products and smoking supplies purchases	yr	288	1999	30r
Tomatoes, field grown	lb	1.43	7/01	11r
Tomatoes, Hunt's or Del Monte	14.5 oz	0.86	3/01	4c
Tuna, chunk, light	6 oz	0.54	3/01	4c
Tuna, light, chunk	lb	1.77	7/01	11r
Turkey, frozen, whole	lb	1.05	7/01	11r
Goods and Services				
Miscellaneous goods and services, ACCRA Index		101.10	3/01	4c
B&B Japanese maple (acer japonicum)	gal	49.98-129.00	4/00	93r
Boxwood (buxus)	2 gal	12.99-16.99	4/00	93r
Daylilly (hemerocallis)	gal	4.99-8.99	4/00	93r
Flat of annuals		11.00-13.92	4/00	93r
Fountain grass (pennisetum)	gal	5.98-7.98	4/00	93r
Hanging basket (10 in)		7.99-14.98	4/00	93r
Hardy geranium (geranium)	gal	5.98-8.00	4/00	93r
Hosta (hosta)	gal	4.99-10.98	4/00	93r
Lilac (syrubga vulgaris)	2 gal	12.99-21.99	4/00	93r
Rhododendron (rhododendron)	2 gal	14.99-24.99	4/00	93r
Sage (salvia)	gal	5.98-6.99	4/00	93r
Wintercreeper euonymus (euonymus fortunei)	2 gal	7.99-89.99	4/00	93r
Hunting license	yr	12.00	4/01	34s
Health Care				
Health care, ACCRA Index		96.20	3/01	4c
Cardiac catheterization, ave hospital/physician charges		12360	1998	77s
Childbirth, Cesarean delivery		11587	1997	13r
Childbirth, vaginal delivery		6725	1997	13r
Dentist's fee, adult teeth cleaning and periodic oral exam	visit	75.00	3/01	4c
Doctor's fee, routine exam, established patient	visit	57.50	3/01	4c
Drugs, expenditures on	yr	399	1999	30r
Health care purchases	yr	1971	1999	30r
Health insurance expenditures	yr	933	1999	30r
Hospital care, private room	day	383.00	3/01	4c
Hysterectomy, laproscopically-assisted, ave hospital/physician charges		11920	1998	76s
Hysterectomy, vaginal, ave hospital and physician charges		4890	1998	76s

Values are in dollars or fractions of dollars. In the column headed *Ref*, references are shown to sources. Each reference is followed by a letter. These refer to the geographical level for which data were reported: s=State, r=Region, and c=City or metro. The abbreviation *ex* is used to mean *except* or *excluding*; *exp* stands for expenditures. For other abbreviations and further explanations, please see the Introduction.

Sumter, SC - continued

Item	Per	Value	Date	Ref.
Health Care				
Medicaid dispensing fee		4.05	1999	87s
Medical services expenditures	yr	547	1999	30r
Medical supplies, expenditures on	yr	91	1999	30r
Plastic surgery, breast augmentation		2870	2000	7r
Plastic surgery, breast lift		3649	2000	7r
Plastic surgery, facelift		5008	2000	7r
Plastic surgery, hair transplantation		3425	2000	7r
Plastic surgery, lip augmentation		1227	2000	7r
Plastic surgery, lower body lift		4793	2000	7r
Plastic surgery, thigh lift		3862	2000	7r
Household Goods				
Dishwashing powder, Cascade	50 oz	3.33	3/01	4c
Floor coverings, expenditures on	yr	44	1999	30r
Furniture, expenditures on	yr	335	1999	30r
Household furnishings and equipment purchases	yr	1328	1999	30r
Household textiles, expenditures on	yr	89	1999	30r
Laundry and cleaning supplies, expenditures on	yr	113	1999	30r
Tissues, facial, Kleenex brand	175	1.20	3/01	4c
Housing				
Housing, ACCRA Index		86.40	3/01	4c
Home price, existing, ave		160100	10/00	90r
Home value, median		119000	2001	53s
House, 2400 sq ft, 8000 sq ft lot, new, urban, utilities	total	189098	3/01	4c
House payment, principal and interest, 25% down payment	mos	937	3/01	4c
Household operation expenditures	yr	553	1999	30r
Housekeeping supplies purchases	yr	473	1999	30r
Housing, expenditures on	yr	10303	1999	30r
Maintenance, repairs, insurance expenditures	yr	699	1999	30r
Monthly rental value of owned home	mos	505	1999	30r
Owned dwellings, expenditures own	yr	3465	1999	30r
Rent expenditures	yr	1641	1999	30r
Rent, apartment, 2 br, 1 1/2-2 baths, unfurn, 950 sq ft, water	mos	478	3/01	4c
Rental unit, 1 bedroom, with utilities	mos	390	4/01	41c
Rental unit, 2 bedroom, with utilities	mos	442	4/01	41c
Rental unit, 3 bedroom, with utilities	mos	605	4/01	41c
Rental unit, 4 bedroom, with utilities	mos	719	4/01	41c
Shelter, expenditures on	yr	5467	1999	30r
Insurance and Pensions				
Auto insurance	yr	655.33	1998	86s
Life and other personal insurance purchases	yr	414	1999	30r
Pensions and Social Security, expenditures on	yr	2635	1999	30r
Personal insurance and pensions, expenditures on	yr	3048	1999	30r
Legal Fees				
Combination hunting and fishing license	yr	20.00	4/01	34s
Driver's license fee	orig	12.50	1999	48s
Driver's license fee	renew	12.50	1999	48s
Fishing license	yr	10.00	4/01	34s
Personal Goods				
Personal care products and services purchases	yr	393	1999	30r
Shampoo, Alberto VO5	15 oz	1.04	3/01	4c
Toothpaste, Crest or Colgate	6-7 oz	2.34	3/01	4c
Personal Services				
Dry cleaning, man's 2-pc suit		7.81	3/01	4c
Man's haircut, barbershop, no styling		14.00	3/01	4c
Personal services, household, expenditures on	yr	258	1999	30r
Woman's shampoo, trim, blow-dry, no style-change		24.00	3/01	4c

Sumter, SC - continued

Item	Per	Value	Date	Ref.
Pets				
Pets, toys, and playground equipment, expenditures on	yr	306	1999	30r
Restaurant Food				
Chicken, fried, thigh and drumstick, KFC/Church's		2.24	3/01	4c
Hamburger with cheese, McDonald's	1/4 lb	2.09	3/01	4c
Pizza, Pizza Hut or Pizza Inn	11-12 in	8.59	3/01	4c
Taxes				
Federal income taxes paid	yr	2047	1999	30r
Personal taxes, expenditures on	yr	2554	1999	30r
Property taxes paid	yr	726	1999	30r
State and local income taxes paid	yr	363	1999	30r
Transportation				
Transportation, ACCRA Index		94.10	3/01	4c
Cars and trucks, new, expenditures on	yr	1648	1999	30r
Cars and trucks, used, expenditures on	yr	1651	1999	30r
Diesel at the pump	gal	1.13	10/99	73s
Gasoline and motor oil purchases	yr	1052	1999	30r
Gasoline before-tax price (cents)	gal	101.70	10/00	43s
Maintenance and repair expenditures	yr	621	1999	30r
Public transportation, expenditures on	yr	298	1999	30r
Tire balance, computer or spin balance, front	wheel	7.25	3/01	4c
Transportation purchases	yr	6738	1999	30r
Vehicle expenses, miscellaneous, purchases	yr	2033	1999	30r
Vehicle insurance payments	yr	696	1999	30r
Vehicle purchases (net outlay)	yr	3354	1999	30r
Vehicle rental, lease expenditures	yr	352	1999	30r
Utilities				
Utilities, ACCRA Index		90.00	3/01	4c
Electrical bill, average	mos	86.42	9/00	9s
Electricity, 2400 sq ft, new home	mos	106.59	3/01	4c
Electricity, expenditures on	yr	1115	1999	30r
Electricity cost, average	KWh	5.40	9/00	9s
Water and other public services, expenditures on	yr	298	1999	30r
Weddings				
Wedding (national average cost)		19936	2000	33r
Wedding (regional average total cost)		16293	1997	110r
Attendants' gifts		321	1998	33r
Bridal attendants' apparel (5 persons)		824	2000	33r
Bride's headpiece/veil		173	1998	33r
Bride's wedding dress		859	1998	33r
Clergy, religious facility fee		242	1998	33r
Engagement ring		3177	1998	33r
Flowers		789	1998	33r
Groom's formalwear rental		99	2000	33r
Limousine		410	1998	33r
Marriage license cost		25.00	4/01	35s
Men's formalwear (ushers, best man)		469	2000	33r
Mother of bride apparel		241	2000	33r
Music		866	1998	33r
Photography and videography		1368	1998	33r
Rehearsal dinner		728	1998	33r
Wedding invitations and announcements		341	1998	33r
Wedding reception		7968	2000	33r
Wedding rings (bride and groom)		1060	1998	33r

Syracuse, NY

Item	Per	Value	Date	Ref.
Average annual expenditures	yr	37971	1999	30r
Composite, ACCRA index		101.40	3/01	4c
Alcoholic Beverages				
Alcoholic beverage purchases	yr	368	1999	30r
Beer, Heineken, 12-oz, ex deposit	6	6.99	3/01	4c
J & B Scotch	750-ml	18.36	3/01	4c
Wine, Livingston or Gallo, Chablis blanc	1.5 liter	5.99	3/01	4c
Wine, red and white table, all sizes, any origin	liter	9.64	7/01	11r

Values are in dollars or fractions of dollars. In the column headed *Ref*, references are shown to sources. Each reference is followed by a letter. These refer to the geographical level for which data were reported: s=State, r=Region, and c=City or metro. The abbreviation *ex* is used to mean *except* or *excluding*; *exp* stands for expenditures. For other abbreviations and further explanations, please see the Introduction.

Syracuse, NY - continued

Item	Per	Value	Date	Ref.
Appliances				
Appliance repair, service call, washing machine	min lab chg	41.49	3/01	4c
Major appliances, expenditures on	yr	194	1999	30r
Small appliances, housewares, expenditures on	yr	93	1999	30r
Banking and Money				
Mortgage interest and charges paid	yr	2622	1999	30r
Mortgage principal paid on owned property	yr	1262	1999	30r
Mortgage rate, incl. points and orig. fee, 30-yr. conv. fixed or ARM	mos	7.08	3/01	4c
Vehicle finance charges paid	yr	240	1999	30r
Business Expenses				
Business travel, car rental	day	60	2001	3c
Business travel, food	day	40	2001	3c
Business travel, hotel	day	90	2001	3c
Charity				
Cash contributions, expenditures	yr	1001	1999	30r
Child Care				
Child raising cost, total, age 0-2	yr	8670	1999	60r
Child raising cost, total, age 3-5	yr	8910	1999	60r
Child raising cost, total, age 6-8	yr	9040	1999	60r
Child raising cost, total, age 9-11	yr	9100	1999	60r
Child raising cost, total, age 12-14	yr	9890	1999	60r
Child raising cost, total, age 15-17	yr	10010	1999	60r
Child's child care and education, age 0-2	yr	1070	1999	60r
Child's child care and education, age 3-5	yr	1190	1999	60r
Child's child care and education, age 6-8	yr	740	1999	60r
Child's child care and education, age 9-11	yr	470	1999	60r
Child's child care and education, age 12-14	yr	350	1999	60r
Child's child care and education, age 15-17	yr	590	1999	60r
Child's clothing, age 0-2	yr	480	1999	60r
Child's clothing, age 3-5	yr	470	1999	60r
Child's clothing, age 6-8	yr	520	1999	60r
Child's clothing, age 9-11	yr	570	1999	60r
Child's clothing, age 12-14	yr	970	1999	60r
Child's clothing, age 15-17	yr	870	1999	60r
Child's food, age 0-2	yr	1130	1999	60r
Child's food, age 3-5	yr	1290	1999	60r
Child's food, age 6-8	yr	1640	1999	60r
Child's food, age 9-11	yr	1930	1999	60r
Child's food, age 12-14	yr	1940	1999	60r
Child's food, age 15-17	yr	2150	1999	60r
Child's health care, age 0-2	yr	550	1999	60r
Child's health care, age 3-5	yr	530	1999	60r
Child's health care, age 6-8	yr	610	1999	60r
Child's health care, age 9-11	yr	650	1999	60r
Child's health care, age 12-14	yr	660	1999	60r
Child's health care, age 15-17	yr	690	1999	60r
Child's housing, age 0-2	yr	3555	1999	60r
Child's housing, age 3-5	yr	3530	1999	60r
Child's housing, age 6-8	yr	3490	1999	60r
Child's housing, age 9-11	yr	3340	1999	60r
Child's housing, age 12-14	yr	3530	1999	60r
Child's housing, age 15-17	yr	3140	1999	60r
Child's personal care, reading, age 0-2	yr	920	1999	60r
Child's personal care, reading, age 3-5	yr	950	1999	60r
Child's personal care, reading, age 6-8	yr	980	1999	60r
Child's personal care, reading, age 9-11	yr	1020	1999	60r
Child's personal care, reading, age 12-14	yr	1190	1999	60r
Child's personal care, reading, age 15-17	yr	970	1999	60r
Nannies: criminal background check		74	1998	84s
Clothing				
Apparel and services purchases	yr	1831	1999	30r
Boys' brief, cotton	3	4.01	3/01	4c
Boys, 2 to 15, expenditures on	yr	92	1999	30r
Children under 2, expenditures on	yr	63	1999	30r
Footwear, expenditures on	yr	300	1999	30r
Girls, 2 to 15, expenditures on	yr	101	1999	30r
Men and boys, expenditures on	yr	446	1999	30r

Syracuse, NY - continued

Item	Per	Value	Date	Ref.
Clothing - continued				
Men, 16 and over, expenditures on	yr	354	1999	30r
Shirt, man's dress shirt		25.49	3/01	4c
Slacks, man's "No Wrinkles" khaki		33.74	3/01	4c
Women, 16 and over, expenditures on	yr	584	1999	30r
Communications				
Cable modem installation, Adelphi		54.90	6/99	103s
Cable modem installation, Cablevision Systems		150.00	6/99	103s
Cable modem installation, Time Warner		75.00-225.00	6/99	103s
Cable modem rate, cable subscriber, Adelphi	mos	34.95	6/99	103s
Cable modem rate, cable subscriber, Cablevision Systems	mos	44.95	6/99	103s
Cable modem rate, cable subscriber, Century	mos	39.95	6/99	103s
Cable modem rate, cable subscriber, Time Warner	mos	39.95-49.95	6/99	103s
Cable modem rate, non-cable subscriber, Adelphi	mos	44.95	6/99	103s
Cable modem rate, non-cable subscriber, Cablevision Systems	mos	54.95	6/99	103s
Cable modem rate, non-cable subscriber, Time Warner	mos	39.95-54.95	6/99	103s
Newspaper subscription, daily and Sunday delivery	mos	16.74	3/01	4c
Phone line, single, business, field visit	inst.	142.76	12/97	17s
Phone line, single, business, no field visit	inst.	106.05	12/97	17s
Phone line, single, residence, field visit	inst.	102.78	12/97	17s
Phone line, single, residence, no field visit	inst.	55.00	12/97	17s
Postage and stationery, expenditures on	yr	138	1999	30r
Postal rate, express mail, up to half-pound		12.45	7/01	108r
Postal rate, letter, first class, first ounce		0.34	7/01	108r
Postal rate, letter, two ounces		0.57	7/01	108r
Postal rate, post card		0.21	7/01	108r
Postal rate, priority mail, two pounds		3.95	7/01	108r
Postal rate, priority mail, up to one pound		3.50	7/01	108r
Telephone bill, business, basic rate	mos	16.23	12/97	18c
Telephone bill, family of three	mos	29.68	3/01	4c
Telephone bill, residential, basic rate	mos	20.16	12/97	18c
Telephone services, expenditures on	yr	830	1999	30r
Education				
Board, 4-year private college/university	yr	3255	1996	38s
Board, 4-year public college/university	yr	2310	1996	38s
Education expenditures	yr	877	1999	30r
Room, 4-year private college/university	yr	3724	1996	38s
Room, 4-year public college/university	yr	2937	1996	38s
Total cost, 4-year private college/university	yr	20831	1996	38s
Total cost, 4-year public college/university	yr	8960	1996	38s
Tuition, 2-year public college/university, in state	yr	2427	1996	38s
Tuition, 4-year private college/university, in state	yr	13852	1996	38s
Tuition, 4-year public college/university	yr	3714	1996	38s
Energy and Fuels				
Electricity	KWh	0.12	7/01	11r
Energy, combined forms, 2400 sq ft	mos	174.16	3/01	4c
Energy, exc. electricity, 2400 sq ft	mos	102.02	3/01	4c
Fuel oil #2	gal	1.31	7/01	11r
Fuel oil and other fuels, expenditures on	yr	207	1999	30r
Gas, cooking, winter, 10 therms	mos	14.91	2/96	98c
Gas, cooking, winter, 30 therms	mos	31.66	2/96	98c
Gas, cooking, winter, 50 therms	mos	45.84	2/96	98c
Gas, heating, winter, average use	mos	167.85	2/96	98c
Gas, regular unleaded, cash, self-service	gal	1.46	3/01	4c
Gasoline, all types	gal	1.80	7/01	11r
Gasoline, unleaded midgrade	gal	1.85	7/01	11r
Gasoline, unleaded premium	gal	1.91	7/01	11r
Gasoline, unleaded regular	gal	1.71	7/01	11r
Natural gas, expenditures on	yr	368	1999	30r
Utility (piped) gas, therm		1.08	7/01	11r
Utility (piped) gas, 40 therms		50.87	7/01	11r
Utility (piped) gas, 100 therms		111.06	7/01	11r

Values are in dollars or fractions of dollars. In the column headed *Ref*, references are shown to sources. Each reference is followed by a letter. These refer to the geographical level for which data were reported: s=State, r=Region, and c=City or metro. The abbreviation *ex* is used to mean *except* or *excluding*; *exp* stands for *expenditures*. For other abbreviations and further explanations, please see the Introduction.

Syracuse, NY - continued

Item	Per	Value	Date	Ref.
Entertainment				
Bowling, Saturday evening rate	line	2.39	3/01	4c
Entertainment purchases	yr	1821	1999	30r
Fees and admissions paid	yr	511	1999	30r
Monopoly game, Parker Brothers', No. 9	game	11.17	3/01	4c
Movie, first-run, Saturday, evening	adm.	8.19	3/01	4c
Television, radios, sound equipment, expenditures on	yr	650	1999	30r
Tennis balls, yellow, Wilson or Penn, 3	can	2.13	3/01	4c
Funerals				
Total cost of funeral		5813.50	1/99	78r
Acknowledgement cards		28.32	1/99	78r
Casket		2082.20	1/99	78r
Cosmetology, hair, other preparation		169.59	1/99	78r
Embalming		465.60	1/99	78r
Funeral at funeral home		339.56	1/99	78r
Hearse (local)		183.96	1/99	78r
Professional service charges		1157.85	1/99	78r
Service car/van		100.41	1/99	78r
Transfer of remains to funeral home		158.66	1/99	78r
Vault		766.31	1/99	78r
Visitation/viewing		361.04	1/99	78r
Groceries				
Groceries, ACCRA Index		109.00	3/01	4c
Antibiotic ointment, Polysporin	0.5 oz	4.07	3/01	4c
Apples, red delicious	lb	0.95	7/01	11r
Baby food, strained vegetables or fruit, lowest price	4-4.5 oz	0.51	3/01	4c
Bacon, sliced	lb	3.44	7/01	11r
Bakery products, expenditures on	yr	310	1999	30r
Bananas	lb	0.50	3/01	4c
Bananas	lb	0.55	7/01	11r
Beef or hamburger, ground	lb	1.75	3/01	4c
Beef, expenditures on	yr	236	1999	30r
Bread, white	loaf	0.87	3/01	4c
Bread, white, pan	lb	1.09	7/01	11r
Butter, yoghurt, cheese, etc, expenditures on	yr	214	1999	30r
Cereals and bakery product purchases	yr	474	1999	30r
Cereals and cereal products, expenditures on	yr	164	1999	30r
Cheese, Kraft grated Parmesan	8 oz	4.05	3/01	4c
Chicken legs, bone-in	lb	1.23	7/01	11r
Chicken, fresh, whole	lb	1.13	7/01	11r
Chicken, whole fryer	lb	1.01	3/01	4c
Chuck roast, U.S. choice, boneless	lb	2.79	7/01	11r
Cigarettes, Winston, Kings	carton	39.96	3/01	4c
Coffee, 100%, ground roast, all sizes	lb	3.40	7/01	11r
Coffee, vacuum-packed	13 oz	2.55	3/01	4c
Corn Flakes, Kellogg's or Post Toasties	18 oz	2.95	3/01	4c
Corn, frozen, whole kernel, lowest price	16 oz	1.17	3/01	4c
Dairy product purchases	yr	342	1999	30r
Eggs, expenditures on	yr	34	1999	30r
Eggs, Grade A or AA	dozen	1.03	3/01	4c
Eggs, grade A, large	dozen	0.82	7/01	11r
Fats and oils, expenditures on	yr	80	1999	30r
Fish and seafood, expenditures on	yr	123	1999	30r
Food (excl fruit and vegetables), eaten at home, purchases	yr	838	1999	30r
Food cooked on trips, expenditures on	yr	48	1999	30r
Food purchases	yr	5314	1999	30r
Food purchases, eaten away from home	yr	2313	1999	30r
Food purchases, food eaten at home	yr	3001	1999	30r
Fresh fruits, expenditures on	yr	169	1999	30r
Fresh milk and cream, expenditures on	yr	128	1999	30r
Fresh vegetables, expenditures on	yr	164	1999	30r
Grapefruit	lb	0.67	7/01	11r
Grapes, Thompson, seedless	lb	2.18	7/01	11r
Ground beef, lean and extra lean	lb	2.66	7/01	11r
Ground chuck, 100% beef	lb	2.04	7/01	11r
Lettuce, iceberg	head	1.19	3/01	4c
Lettuce, iceberg	lb	0.76	7/01	11r
Margarine, Blue Bonnet or Parkay, stick	lb	0.98	3/01	4c

Syracuse, NY - continued

Item	Per	Value	Date	Ref.
Groceries - continued				
Meats, poultry, fish, and egg purchases	yr	808	1999	30r
Milk, whole	1/2 gal	1.46	3/01	4c
Nonalcoholic beverages, expenditures on	yr	225	1999	30r
Orange juice, frozen concentrate	16 oz	1.88	7/01	11r
Orange juice, Minute Maid frozen	12 oz	1.75	3/01	4c
Oranges, Navel	lb	0.79	7/01	11r
Oranges, Valencia	lb	0.56	7/01	11r
Peaches	lb	1.16	7/01	11r
Peaches, halves or slices, Hunt's, Del Monte, or Libby's	29 oz	1.81	3/01	4c
Peanut butter, creamy, all sizes	lb	2.01	7/01	11r
Pears, Anjou	lb	1.16	7/01	11r
Peas, green, Del Monte or Green Giant	15 oz	0.71	3/01	4c
Pork chops, center cut, bone-in	lb	3.57	7/01	11r
Pork, expenditures on	yr	146	1999	30r
Potato chips	16 oz	3.37	7/01	11r
Potatoes, white or red	10 lb	2.41	3/01	4c
Potatoes, white, all types	lb	0.42	7/01	11r
Poultry, expenditures on	yr	158	1999	30r
Processed fruits, expenditures on	yr	124	1999	30r
Processed vegetables, expenditures on	yr	82	1999	30r
Round roast, U.S. choice, boneless	lb	3.04	7/01	11r
Sausage, Jimmy Dean/Owens pork	lb	4.26	3/01	4c
Shortening, vegetable, Crisco	3 lb	3.37	3/01	4c
Soft drink, Coca Cola, ex deposit	2 liter	1.31	3/01	4c
Spaghetti and macaroni	lb	1.04	7/01	11r
Steak, sirloin, U.S. choice, boneless	lb	5.39	7/01	11r
Steak, T-bone	lb	6.97	3/01	4c
Strawberries, dry pint	12 oz	1.51	7/01	11r
Sugar and other sweets, expenditures on	yr	110	1999	30r
Sugar, cane or beet	4 lbs	1.30	3/01	4c
Sugar, white, 33-80 ounce package	lb	0.46	7/01	11r
Sugar, white, all sizes	lb	0.47	7/01	11r
Tobacco products and smoking supplies purchases	yr	309	1999	30r
Tomatoes, Hunt's or Del Monte	14.5 oz	0.97	3/01	4c
Tuna, chunk, light	6 oz	0.78	3/01	4c
Yogurt, natural, fruit flavored	8 oz	0.79	7/01	11r
Goods and Services				
Miscellaneous goods and services, ACCRA Index		98.10	3/01	4c
B&B Japanese maple (acer japonicum)	gal	38.99-125.00	4/00	93r
Boxwood (buxus)	2 gal	15.99-49.95	4/00	93r
Daylilly (hemerocallis)	gal	4.95	4/00	93r
Flat of annuals		8.00-14.99	4/00	93r
Fountain grass (pennisetum)	gal	6.99-9.99	4/00	93r
Hanging basket (10 in)		12.95-19.99	4/00	93r
Hardy geranium (geranium)	gal	6.95-7.99	4/00	93r
Hosta (hosta)	gal	4.95	4/00	93r
Lilac (syrubga vulgaris)	2 gal	17.99-74.95	4/00	93r
Miscellaneous purchases	yr	872	1999	30r
Rhododendron (rhododendron)	2 gal	23.99-54.95	4/00	93r
Sage (salvia)	gal	6.95-7.99	4/00	93r
Wintercreeper euonymus (euonymus fortunei)	2 gal	14.99-23.95	4/00	93r
Hunting license	yr	11.00	4/01	34s
Health Care				
Health care, ACCRA Index		100.70	3/01	4c
Cardiac catheterization, ave hospital/physician charges		12750	1998	77s
Childbirth, Cesarean delivery		14716	1997	13r
Childbirth, vaginal delivery		8541	1997	13r

Values are in dollars or fractions of dollars. In the column headed *Ref*, references are shown to sources. Each reference is followed by a letter. These refer to the geographical level for which data were reported: s=State, r=Region, and c=City or metro. The abbreviation *ex* is used to mean *except* or *excluding*; *exp* stands for *expenditures*. For other abbreviations and further explanations, please see the Introduction.

Syracuse, NY - continued

Item	Per	Value	Date	Ref.
Health Care				
Dentist's fee, adult teeth cleaning and periodic oral exam	visit	66.20	3/01	4c
Doctor's fee, routine exam, established patient	visit	57.60	3/01	4c
Drugs, expenditures on	yr	296	1999	30r
Health care purchases	yr	1788	1999	30r
Health insurance expenditures	yr	875	1999	30r
Hospital care, private room	day	679.67	3/01	4c
Hysterectomy, laproscopically-assisted, ave hospital/physician charges		13460	1998	76s
Hysterectomy, vaginal, ave hospital and physician charges		10310	1998	76s
Medicaid dispensing fee		3.50-4.50	1999	87s
Medical services expenditures	yr	516	1999	30r
Medical supplies, expenditures on	yr	102	1999	30r
Nursing home costs, private room	day	196	2000	82c
Nursing home stay, private room	day	196	2000	81c
Plastic surgery, breast augmentation		4232	2000	7r
Plastic surgery, breast lift		4605	2000	7r
Plastic surgery, facelift		6964	2000	7r
Plastic surgery, hair transplantation		4193	2000	7r
Plastic surgery, lip augmentation		1675	2000	7r
Plastic surgery, lower body lift		6611	2000	7r
Plastic surgery, thigh lift		4751	2000	7r
Household Goods				
Dishwashing powder, Cascade	50 oz	3.40	3/01	4c
Floor coverings, expenditures on	yr	59	1999	30r
Furniture, expenditures on	yr	388	1999	30r
Household furnishings and equipment purchases	yr	1567	1999	30r
Household textiles, expenditures on	yr	112	1999	30r
Laundry and cleaning supplies, expenditures on	yr	104	1999	30r
Tissues, facial, Kleenex brand	175	1.55	3/01	4c
Housing				
Housing, ACCRA Index		87.80	3/01	4c
Home price, existing, ave		180800	10/00	90r
Home value, median		179000	2001	53s
House, 2400 sq ft, 8000 sq ft lot, new, urban, utilities	total	187200	3/01	4c
House payment, principal and interest, 25% down payment	mos	941	3/01	4c
Household operation expenditures	yr	581	1999	30r
Housekeeping supplies purchases	yr	474	1999	30r
Lodging expenditures	yr	550	1999	30r
Maintenance, repairs, insurance expenditures	yr	835	1999	30r
Monthly rental value of owned home	mos	663	1999	30r
Owned dwellings, expenditures own	yr	5209	1999	30r
Rent expenditures	yr	2390	1999	30r
Rent, apartment, 2 br, 1 1/2-2 baths, unfurn, 950 sq ft, water	mos	515	3/01	4c
Rental unit, 1 bedroom, with utilities	mos	464	4/01	41c
Rental unit, 2 bedroom, with utilities	mos	575	4/01	41c
Rental unit, 3 bedroom, with utilities	mos	734	4/01	41c
Rental unit, 4 bedroom, with utilities	mos	814	4/01	41c
Shelter, expenditures on	yr	8149	1999	30r
Insurance and Pensions				
Auto insurance premium	yr	1113.55	1999	57s
Life and other personal insurance purchases	yr	424	1999	30r
Pensions and Social Security, expenditures on	yr	3037	1999	30r
Legal Fees				
Divorce, filing fee		270.00	4/01	35s
Driver's license fee	renew	25.00	1999	48s
Driver's license fee	orig	25.00	1999	48s
Fishing license	yr	14.00	4/01	34s

Syracuse, NY - continued

Item	Per	Value	Date	Ref.
Personal Goods				
Personal care products and services purchases	yr	399	1999	30r
Shampoo, Alberto VO5	15 oz	1.12	3/01	4c
Toothpaste, Crest or Colgate	6-7 oz	2.46	3/01	4c
Personal Services				
Dry cleaning, man's 2-pc suit		8.56	3/01	4c
Man's haircut, barbershop, no styling		8.25	3/01	4c
Personal services, household, expenditures on	yr	271	1999	30r
Woman's shampoo, trim, blow-dry, no style-change		20.40	3/01	4c
Pets				
Pets, toys, and playground equipment, expenditures on	yr	325	1999	30r
Restaurant Food				
Chicken, fried, thigh and drumstick, KFC/Church's		2.79	3/01	4c
Hamburger with cheese, McDonald's	1/4 lb	2.06	3/01	4c
Pizza, Pizza Hut or Pizza Inn	11-12 in	9.49	3/01	4c
Taxes				
Federal income taxes paid	yr	2606	1999	30r
Personal taxes, expenditures on	yr	3567	1999	30r
Property taxes paid	yr	1752	1999	30r
State and local income taxes paid	yr	694	1999	30r
Transportation				
Transportation, ACCRA Index		106.20	3/01	4c
Bus fare, one-way	trip	1.00	2000	1c
Bus fare, to central business district	1-way	1.00	3/01	4c
Cars and trucks, new, expenditures on	yr	1496	1999	30r
Cars and trucks, used, expenditures on	yr	1251	1999	30r
Diesel at the pump	gal	1.33	10/99	73s
Gasoline and motor oil purchases	yr	901	1999	30r
Gasoline before-tax price (cents)	gal	110.70	10/00	43s
Maintenance and repair expenditures	yr	618	1999	30r
Public transportation, expenditures on	yr	575	1999	30r
Tire balance, computer or spin balance, front	wheel	8.99	3/01	4c
Transportation purchases	yr	6503	1999	30r
Vehicle expenses, miscellaneous, purchases	yr	2266	1999	30r
Vehicle insurance payments	yr	824	1999	30r
Vehicle purchases (net outlay)	yr	2761	1999	30r
Vehicle rental, lease expenditures	yr	584	1999	30r
Travel				
Hotel room	night	139.88	2/01	95s
Utilities				
Utilities, ACCRA Index		141.80	3/01	4c
Electrical bill, average	mos	71.50	9/00	9s
Electricity, expenditures on	yr	837	1999	30r
Electricity and other, mixed, 2400 sq ft, new home	mos	72.14	3/01	4c
Electricity cost, average	KWh	11.34	9/00	9s
Utilities, fuels, and public services purchased	yr	2457	1999	30r
Water and other public services, expenditures on	yr	215	1999	30r
Weddings				
Wedding (national average cost)		19936	2000	33r
Wedding (regional average total cost)		29454	1997	110r
Attendants' gifts		321	1998	33r
Bridal attendants' apparel (5 persons)		824	2000	33r
Bride's headpiece/veil		173	1998	33r
Bride's wedding dress		859	1998	33r
Clergy, religious facility fee		242	1998	33r
Engagement ring		3177	1998	33r
Flowers		789	1998	33r
Groom's formalwear rental		99	2000	33r
Limousine		410	1998	33r
Marriage license cost		25.00	4/01	35s
Men's formalwear (ushers, best man)		469	2000	33r
Mother of bride apparel		241	2000	33r

Values are in dollars or fractions of dollars. In the column headed *Ref*, references are shown to sources. Each reference is followed by a letter. These refer to the geographical level for which data were reported: s=State, r=Region, and c=City or metro. The abbreviation *ex* is used to mean *except* or *excluding*; *exp* stands for expenditures. For other abbreviations and further explanations, please see the Introduction.

Syracuse, NY - continued

Item	Per	Value	Date	Ref.
Weddings				
Music		866	1998	33r
Photography and videography		1368	1998	33r
Rehearsal dinner		728	1998	33r
Wedding invitations and announcements		341	1998	33r
Wedding reception		7968	2000	33r
Wedding rings (bride and groom)		1060	1998	33r

Tacoma, WA

Item	Per	Value	Date	Ref.
Average annual expenditures	yr	40662	1999	30r
Composite, ACCRA index		101.40	3/01	4c
Alcoholic Beverages				
Alcoholic beverage purchases	yr	372	1999	30r
Beer, Heineken, 12-oz, ex deposit	6	7.73	3/01	4c
J & B Scotch	750-ml	22.45	3/01	4c
Malt beverages, all types, all sizes, any origin	16 oz	0.94	7/01	11r
Wine, Livingston or Gallo, Chablis blanc	1.5 liter	5.89	3/01	4c
Wine, red and white table, all sizes, any origin	liter	6.00	7/01	11r
Appliances				
Appliance repair, service call, washing machine	min lab chg	45.97	3/01	4c
Major appliances, expenditures on	yr	167	1999	30r
Small appliances, housewares, expenditures on	yr	105	1999	30r
Banking and Money				
Mortgage interest and charges paid	yr	3368	1999	30r
Mortgage principal paid on owned property	yr	1677	1999	30r
Mortgage rate, incl. points and orig. fee, 30-yr. conv. fixed or ARM	mos	6.73	3/01	4c
Vehicle finance charges paid	yr	311	1999	30r
Charity				
Cash contributions, expenditures	yr	1344	1999	30r
Child Care				
Child raising cost, total, age 0-2	yr	9140	1999	60r
Child raising cost, total, age 3-5	yr	9370	1999	60r
Child raising cost, total, age 6-8	yr	9450	1999	60r
Child raising cost, total, age 9-11	yr	9470	1999	60r
Child raising cost, total, age 12-14	yr	10170	1999	60r
Child raising cost, total, age 15-17	yr	10360	1999	60r
Child's child care and education, age 0-2	yr	1250	1999	60r
Child's child care and education, age 3-5	yr	1380	1999	60r
Child's child care and education, age 6-8	yr	890	1999	60r
Child's child care and education, age 9-11	yr	580	1999	60r
Child's child care and education, age 12-14	yr	430	1999	60r
Child's child care and education, age 15-17	yr	730	1999	60r
Child's clothing, age 0-2	yr	430	1999	60r
Child's clothing, age 3-5	yr	420	1999	60r
Child's clothing, age 6-8	yr	470	1999	60r
Child's clothing, age 9-11	yr	520	1999	60r
Child's clothing, age 12-14	yr	870	1999	60r
Child's clothing, age 15-17	yr	770	1999	60r
Child's food, age 0-2	yr	1120	1999	60r
Child's food, age 3-5	yr	1280	1999	60r
Child's food, age 6-8	yr	1640	1999	60r
Child's food, age 9-11	yr	1930	1999	60r
Child's food, age 12-14	yr	1940	1999	60r
Child's food, age 15-17	yr	2150	1999	60r
Child's health care, age 0-2	yr	490	1999	60r
Child's health care, age 3-5	yr	470	1999	60r
Child's health care, age 6-8	yr	530	1999	60r
Child's health care, age 9-11	yr	570	1999	60r
Child's health care, age 12-14	yr	580	1999	60r
Child's health care, age 15-17	yr	610	1999	60r
Child's housing, age 0-2	yr	3630	1999	60r
Child's housing, age 3-5	yr	3610	1999	60r
Child's housing, age 6-8	yr	3570	1999	60r
Child's housing, age 9-11	yr	3410	1999	60r
Child's housing, age 12-14	yr	3600	1999	60r

Tacoma, WA - continued

Item	Per	Value	Date	Ref.
Child Care - continued				
Child's housing, age 15-17	yr	3210	1999	60r
Child's personal care, reading, age 0-2	yr	1040	1999	60r
Child's personal care, reading, age 3-5	yr	1060	1999	60r
Child's personal care, reading, age 6-8	yr	1090	1999	60r
Child's personal care, reading, age 9-11	yr	1130	1999	60r
Child's personal care, reading, age 12-14	yr	1300	1999	60r
Child's personal care, reading, age 15-17	yr	1080	1999	60r
Clothing				
Apparel and services purchases	yr	1863	1999	30r
Boys' brief, cotton	3	5.49	3/01	4c
Boys, 2 to 15, expenditures on	yr	80	1999	30r
Children under 2, expenditures on	yr	74	1999	30r
Footwear, expenditures on	yr	307	1999	30r
Girls, 2 to 15, expenditures on	yr	101	1999	30r
Men and boys, expenditures on	yr	443	1999	30r
Men, 16 and over, expenditures on	yr	363	1999	30r
Shirt, man's dress shirt		19.66	3/01	4c
Slacks, man's "No Wrinkles" khaki		41.80	3/01	4c
Women, 16 and over, expenditures on	yr	594	1999	30r
Communications				
Cable modem installation, AT&T-BIS		150.00	6/99	103s
Cable modem rate, cable subscriber, AT&T-BIS	mos	39.95	6/99	103s
Newspaper subscription, daily and Sunday delivery	mos	10.50	3/01	4c
Phone line, single, business, field visit	inst.	48.00	12/97	17s
Phone line, single, business, no field visit	inst.	48.00	12/97	17s
Phone line, single, residence, field visit	inst.	31.00	12/97	17s
Phone line, single, residence, no field visit	inst.	31.00	12/97	17s
Postage and stationery, expenditures on	yr	150	1999	30r
Postal rate, express mail, up to half-pound		12.45	7/01	108r
Postal rate, letter, first class, first ounce		0.34	7/01	108r
Postal rate, letter, two ounces		0.57	7/01	108r
Postal rate, post card		0.21	7/01	108r
Postal rate, priority mail, two pounds		3.95	7/01	108r
Postal rate, priority mail, up to one pound		3.50	7/01	108r
Telephone bill, business, basic rate	mos	18.60	12/97	18c
Telephone bill, family of three	mos	20.25	3/01	4c
Telephone bill, residential, basic rate	mos	8.95	12/97	18c
Telephone services, expenditures on	yr	825	1999	30r
Education				
Board, 4-year private college/university	yr	2329	1996	38s
Board, 4-year public college/university	yr	2158	1996	38s
Education expenditures	yr	676	1999	30r
Room, 4-year private college/university	yr	2487	1996	38s
Room, 4-year public college/university	yr	2187	1996	38s
Total cost, 4-year private college/university	yr	18092	1996	38s
Total cost, 4-year public college/university	yr	7136	1996	38s
Tuition, 2-year public college/university, in state	yr	1369	1996	38s
Tuition, 4-year private college/university, in state	yr	13276	1996	38s
Tuition, 4-year public college/university	yr	2791	1996	38s
Energy and Fuels				
Electricity	500 KWhs	48.23	7/01	11r
Electricity	KWh	0.11	7/01	11r
Energy, combined forms, 2400 sq ft	mos	95.45	4c	
Energy, exc. electricity, 2400 sq ft	mos	57.61	3/01	4c
Fuel oil and other fuels, expenditures on	yr	35	1999	30r
Gas, natural, commercial rate	1000 cf	6.89	11/00	88s
Gas, regular unleaded, cash, self-service	gal	1.60	3/01	4c
Gasoline, all types	gal	1.91	7/01	11r
Gasoline, unleaded premium	gal	2.05	7/01	11r
Gasoline, unleaded regular	gal	1.83	7/01	11r
Natural gas, expenditures on	yr	255	1999	30r
Utility (piped) gas, therm		0.98	7/01	11r
Utility (piped) gas, 40 therms		40.74	7/01	11r
Utility (piped) gas, 100 therms		96.80	7/01	11r

Values are in dollars or fractions of dollars. In the column headed *Ref*, references are shown to sources. Each reference is followed by a letter. These refer to the geographical level for which data were reported: s=State, r=Region, and c=City or metro. The abbreviation *ex* is used to mean *except* or *excluding*; *exp* stands for *expenditures*. For other abbreviations and further explanations, please see the Introduction.

Tacoma, WA - continued

Item	Per	Value	Date	Ref.
Entertainment				
Bowling, Saturday evening rate	line	2.57	3/01	4c
Entertainment purchases	yr	2139	1999	30r
Fees and admissions paid	yr	545	1999	30r
Monopoly game, Parker Brothers', No. 9	game	9.97	3/01	4c
Movie, first-run, Saturday, evening	adm.	7.30	3/01	4c
Television, radios, sound equipment, expenditures on	yr	624	1999	30r
Tennis balls, yellow, Wilson or Penn, 3	can	2.65	3/01	4c
Funerals				
Total cost of funeral		5401.08	1/99	78r
Acknowledgement cards		33.64	1/99	78r
Casket		2170.43	1/99	78r
Cosmetology, hair, other preparation		136.32	1/99	78r
Embalming		319.13	1/99	78r
Funeral at funeral home		370.21	1/99	78r
Hearse (local)		161.04	1/99	78r
Professional service charges		963.15	1/99	78r
Service car/van		133.99	1/99	78r
Transfer of remains to funeral home		159.82	1/99	78r
Vault		778.07	1/99	78r
Visitation/viewing		175.28	1/99	78r
Groceries				
Groceries, ACCRA Index		114.00	3/01	4c
Antibiotic ointment, Polysporin	0.5 oz	4.59	3/01	4c
Apples, red delicious	lb	0.84	7/01	11r
Baby food, strained vegetables or fruit, lowest price	4-4.5 oz	0.35	3/01	4c
Bacon, sliced	lb	3.38	7/01	11r
Bakery products, expenditures on	yr	299	1999	30r
Bananas	lb	0.79	3/01	4c
Bananas	lb	0.54	7/01	11r
Beans, dried, any type, all sizes	lb	0.76	7/01	11r
Beef or hamburger, ground	lb	1.85	3/01	4c
Beef, expenditures on	yr	222	1999	30r
Bread, white	loaf	0.70	3/01	4c
Bread, white, pan	lb	0.99	7/01	11r
Butter, yoghurt, cheese, etc, expenditures on	yr	211	1999	30r
Cereals and bakery product purchases	yr	466	1999	30r
Cereals and cereal products, expenditures on	yr	168	1999	30r
Cheese, Kraft grated Parmesan	8 oz	4.67	3/01	4c
Chicken breast, bone-in	lb	2.45	7/01	11r
Chicken, fresh, whole	lb	1.19	7/01	11r
Chicken, whole fryer	lb	1.29	3/01	4c
Chops, boneless,	lb	4.00	7/01	11r
Chuck roast, graded and ungraded, excl U.S. prime and choice	lb	2.55	7/01	11r
Cigarettes, Winston, Kings	carton	38.47	3/01	4c
Coffee, 100%, ground roast, all sizes	lb	3.80	7/01	11r
Coffee, vacuum-packed	13 oz	3.79	3/01	4c
Cookies, chocolate chip	lb	2.83	7/01	11r
Corn Flakes, Kellogg's or Post Toasties	18 oz	2.88	3/01	4c
Corn, frozen, whole kernel, lowest price	16 oz	1.47	3/01	4c
Dairy product purchases	yr	341	1999	30r
Eggs, expenditures on	yr	39	1999	30r
Eggs, Grade A or AA	dozen	1.07	3/01	4c
Eggs, grade AA, large	dozen	1.23	7/01	11r
Fats and oils, expenditures on	yr	88	1999	30r
Fish and seafood, expenditures on	yr	121	1999	30r
Food (excl fruit and vegetables), eaten at home, purchases	yr	1001	1999	30r
Food cooked on trips, expenditures on	yr	64	1999	30r
Food purchases	yr	5312	1999	30r
Food purchases, eaten away from home	yr	2180	1999	30r
Food purchases, food eaten at home	yr	3132	1999	30r
Fresh fruits, expenditures on	yr	186	1999	30r
Fresh milk and cream, expenditures on	yr	130	1999	30r
Fresh vegetables, expenditures on	yr	177	1999	30r
Grapefruit	lb	0.68	7/01	11r
Grapes, Thompson, seedless	lb	2.42	7/01	11r
Ground beef, lean and extra lean	lb	2.46	7/01	11r

Tacoma, WA - continued

Item	Per	Value	Date	Ref.
Groceries - continued				
Ice cream, prepackaged, bulk, regular	1/2 gal	3.62	7/01	11r
Lettuce, iceberg	head	1.39	3/01	4c
Lettuce, iceberg	lb	0.63	7/01	11r
Margarine, Blue Bonnet or Parkay, stick	lb	0.95	3/01	4c
Meats, poultry, fish, and egg purchases	yr	761	1999	30r
Milk, fresh, low fat,	gal	2.80	7/01	11r
Milk, fresh, whole, fortified	gal	2.88	7/01	11r
Milk, whole	1/2 gal	1.95	3/01	4c
Nonalcoholic beverages, expenditures on	yr	258	1999	30r
Orange juice, Minute Maid frozen	12 oz	1.47	3/01	4c
Oranges, Navel	lb	0.97	7/01	11r
Oranges, Valencia	lb	0.43	7/01	11r
Peaches	lb	1.38	7/01	11r
Peaches, halves or slices, Hunt's, Del Monte, or Libby's	29 oz	1.93	3/01	4c
Peanut butter, creamy, all sizes	lb	2.14	7/01	11r
Peas, green, Del Monte or Green Giant	15 oz	0.93	3/01	4c
Pork chops, center cut, bone-in	lb	3.83	7/01	11r
Pork, expenditures on	yr	141	1999	30r
Potatoes, white or red	10 lb	2.15	3/01	4c
Potatoes, white, all types	lb	0.37	7/01	11r
Poultry, expenditures on	yr	146	1999	30r
Processed fruits, expenditures on	yr	118	1999	30r
Processed vegetables, expenditures on	yr	81	1999	30r
Round roast, graded and ungraded, excl U.S. prime and choice	lb	3.07	7/01	11r
Round roast, U.S. choice, boneless	lb	3.37	7/01	11r
Round steak, graded and ungraded, excl U.S. prime and choice	lb	3.51	7/01	11r
Sausage, Jimmy Dean/Owens pork	lb	3.34	3/01	4c
Shortening, vegetable, Crisco	3 lb	2.92	3/01	4c
Sirloin steak, graded and ungraded, excl U.S. prime and choice	lb	4.67	7/01	11r
Soft drink, Coca Cola, ex deposit	2 liter	1.17	3/01	4c
Steak, sirloin, U.S. choice, boneless	lb	6.20	7/01	11r
Steak, T-bone	lb	7.19	3/01	4c
Strawberries, dry pint	12 oz	1.79	7/01	11r
Sugar and other sweets, expenditures on	yr	124	1999	30r
Sugar, cane or beet	4 lbs	1.87	3/01	4c
Sugar, white, all sizes	lb	0.46	7/01	11r
Tobacco products and smoking supplies purchases	yr	217	1999	30r
Tomatoes, field grown	lb	1.17	7/01	11r
Tomatoes, Hunt's or Del Monte	14.5 oz	0.93	3/01	4c
Tuna, chunk, light	6 oz	0.93	3/01	4c
Tuna, light, chunk	lb	2.05	7/01	11r
Goods and Services				
Miscellaneous goods and services, ACCRA Index		101.80	3/01	4c
B&B Japanese maple (acer japonicum)	gal	39.99	4/00	93r
Boxwood (buxus)	2 gal	14.99-24.99	4/00	93r
Daylilly (hemerocallis)	gal	6.99-8.99	4/00	93r
Flat of annuals		16.68	4/00	93r
Fountain grass (pennisetum)	gal	7.99-11.99	4/00	93r
Hanging basket (10 in)		29.99	4/00	93r
Hardy geranium (geranium)	gal	6.99-11.99	4/00	93r
Hosta (hosta)	gal	6.99-18.99	4/00	93r
Lilac (syrubga vulgaris)	2 gal	14.99-17.99	4/00	93r
Miscellaneous purchases	yr	1070	1999	30r
Rhododendron (rhododendron)	2 gal	14.99	4/00	93r
Sage (salvia)	gal	6.99	4/00	93r
Wintercreeper euonymus (euonymus fortunei)	2 gal	14.99-22.99	4/00	93r
Hunting license	yr	30.00	4/01	34s

Values are in dollars or fractions of dollars. In the column headed *Ref*, references are shown to sources. Each reference is followed by a letter. These refer to the geographical level for which data were reported: s=State, r=Region, and c=City or metro. The abbreviation *ex* is used to mean *except* or *excluding*; *exp* stands for expenditures. For other abbreviations and further explanations, please see the Introduction.

Tacoma, WA - continued

Item	Per	Value	Date	Ref.
Health Care				
Health care, ACCRA Index		123.50	3/01	4c
Cardiac catheterization, ave hospital/ physician charges		13290	1998	77s
Childbirth, Cesarean delivery		11587	1997	13r
Childbirth, vaginal delivery		6725	1997	13r
Dentist's fee, adult teeth cleaning and periodic oral exam	visit	123.63	3/01	4c
Doctor's fee, routine exam, established patient	visit	63.60	3/01	4c
Drugs, expenditures on	yr	309	1999	30r
Health care purchases	yr	1869	1999	30r
Health insurance expenditures	yr	868	1999	30r
Hospital care, private room	day	397.29	3/01	4c
Hysterectomy, laproscopically-assisted, ave hospital/physician charges		10960	1998	76s
Hysterectomy, vaginal, ave hospital and physician charges		9000	1998	76s
Medicaid dispensing fee		3.98-4.92	1999	87s
Medical services expenditures	yr	580	1999	30r
Medical supplies, expenditures on	yr	112	1999	30r
Household Goods				
Dishwashing powder, Cascade	50 oz	4.24	3/01	4c
Floor coverings, expenditures on	yr	49	1999	30r
Furniture, expenditures on	yr	444	1999	30r
Household furnishings and equipment purchases	yr	1768	1999	30r
Household textiles, expenditures on	yr	141	1999	30r
Laundry and cleaning supplies, expenditures on	yr	128	1999	30r
Tissues, facial, Kleenex brand	175	1.51	3/01	4c
Housing				
Housing, ACCRA Index		93.60	3/01	4c
Home, 2200 sq ft, 4-br, 2-bath, 2-car garage, average		196000	2000	47c
Home price, existing, ave		239400	10/00	90r
Home value, median		195000	2001	53s
House, 2400 sq ft, 8000 sq ft lot, new, urban, utilities	total	195048	3/01	4c
House payment, principal and interest, 25% down payment	mos	947	3/01	4c
Household operation expenditures	yr	781	1999	30r
Housekeeping supplies purchases	yr	513	1999	30r
Lodging expenditures	yr	575	1999	30r
Maintenance, repairs, insurance expenditures	yr	939	1999	30r
Monthly rental value of owned home	mos	662	1999	30r
Owned dwellings, expenditures own	yr	5231	1999	30r
Rent expenditures	yr	2709	1999	30r
Rent, apartment, 2 br, 1 1/2-2 baths, unfurn, 950 sq ft, water	mos	697	3/01	4c
Rental unit, 1 bedroom, with utilities	mos	482	4/01	41c
Rental unit, 2 bedroom, with utilities	mos	642	4/01	41c
Rental unit, 3 bedroom, with utilities	mos	893	4/01	41c
Rental unit, 4 bedroom, with utilities	mos	1009	4/01	41c
Shelter, expenditures on	yr	8516	1999	30r
Insurance and Pensions				
Life and other personal insurance purchases	yr	355	1999	30r
Pensions and Social Security, expenditures on	yr	3636	1999	30r
Legal Fees				
Divorce, filing fee		100.00	4/01	35s
Driver's license fee	orig	14.00	1999	48s
Driver's license fee	renew	14.00	1999	48s
Fishing license	yr	20.00	4/01	34s
Personal Goods				
Personal care products and services purchases	yr	449	1999	30r
Shampoo, Alberto VO5	15 oz	1.47	3/01	4c

Tacoma, WA - continued

Item	Per	Value	Date	Ref.
Personal Goods - continued				
Toothpaste, Crest or Colgate	6-7 oz	3.23	3/01	4c
Personal Services				
Dry cleaning, man's 2-pc suit		8.40	3/01	4c
Man's haircut, barbershop, no styling		10.29	3/01	4c
Personal services, household, expenditures on	yr	353	1999	30r
Woman's shampoo, trim, blow-dry, no style-change		32.80	3/01	4c
Pets				
Pets, toys, and playground equipment, expenditures on	yr	358	1999	30r
Restaurant Food				
Chicken, fried, thigh and drumstick, KFC/ Church's		2.34	3/01	4c
Hamburger with cheese, McDonald's	1/4 lb	2.15	3/01	4c
Pizza, Pizza Hut or Pizza Inn	11-12 in	10.19	3/01	4c
Taxes				
Federal income taxes paid	yr	3200	1999	30r
Personal taxes, expenditures on	yr	4153	1999	30r
Property taxes paid	yr	923	1999	30r
State and local income taxes paid	yr	812	1999	30r
Transportation				
Transportation, ACCRA Index		107.20	3/01	4c
Bus fare, one-way	trip	1.05	2000	1c
Cars and trucks, new, expenditures on	yr	1534	1999	30r
Cars and trucks, used, expenditures on	yr	1593	1999	30r
Diesel at the pump	gal	1.37	10/99	73s
Gasoline and motor oil purchases	yr	1129	1999	30r
Gasoline before-tax price (cents)	gal	127.10	10/00	43s
Maintenance and repair expenditures	yr	797	1999	30r
Public transportation, expenditures on	yr	530	1999	30r
Tire balance, computer or spin balance, front	wheel	7.80	3/01	4c
Transportation purchases	yr	7423	1999	30r
Vehicle expenses, miscellaneous, purchases	yr	2585	1999	30r
Vehicle insurance payments	yr	811	1999	30r
Vehicle purchases (net outlay)	yr	3180	1999	30r
Vehicle rental, lease expenditures	yr	666	1999	30r
Utilities				
Utilities, ACCRA Index		80.30	3/01	4c
Electrical bill, average	mos	58.33	9/00	9s
Electricity, expenditures on	yr	725	1999	30r
Electricity and other, mixed, 2400 sq ft, new home	mos	37.84	3/01	4c
Electricity bill	mos	31	2000	75c
Electricity cost, average	KWh	4.47	9/00	9s
Utilities, fuels, and public services purchased	yr	2179	1999	30r
Water and other public services, expenditures on	yr	339	1999	30r
Weddings				
Wedding (national average cost)		19936	2000	33r
Wedding (regional average total cost)		18918	1997	110r
Attendants' gifts		321	1998	33r
Bridal attendants' apparel (5 persons)		824	2000	33r
Bride's headpiece/veil		173	1998	33r
Bride's wedding dress		859	1998	33r
Clergy, religious facility fee		242	1998	33r
Engagement ring		3177	1998	33r
Flowers		789	1998	33r
Groom's formalwear rental		99	2000	33r
Limousine		410	1998	33r
Marriage license cost		52.00	4/01	35s
Men's formalwear (ushers, best man)		469	2000	33r
Mother of bride apparel		241	2000	33r
Music		866	1998	33r
Photography and videography		1368	1998	33r
Rehearsal dinner		728	1998	33r
Wedding invitations and announcements		341	1998	33r
Wedding reception		7968	2000	33r

Values are in dollars or fractions of dollars. In the column headed *Ref*, references are shown to sources. Each reference is followed by a letter. These refer to the geographical level for which data were reported: s=State, r=Region, and c=City or metro. The abbreviation *ex* is used to mean *except* or *excluding*; *exp* stands for expenditures. For other abbreviations and further explanations, please see the Introduction.

Tacoma, WA - continued

Item	Per	Value	Date	Ref.
Weddings				
Wedding rings (bride and groom)		1060	1998	33r

Tallahassee, FL

Item	Per	Value	Date	Ref.
Composite, ACCRA index		108.10	3/01	4c
Alcoholic Beverages				
Alcoholic beverage purchases	yr	253	1999	30r
Beer, Heineken, 12-oz, ex deposit	6	6.89	3/01	4c
J & B Scotch	750-ml	20.99	3/01	4c
Malt beverages, all types, all sizes, any origin	16 oz	0.96	7/01	11r
Wine, Livingston or Gallo, Chablis blanc	1.5 liter	5.57	3/01	4c
Appliances				
Appliance repair, service call, washing machine	min lab chg	48.08	3/01	4c
Major appliances, expenditures on	yr	172	1999	30r
Small appliances, housewares, expenditures on	yr	81	1999	30r
Banking and Money				
Mortgage interest and charges paid	yr	2039	1999	30r
Mortgage principal paid on owned property	yr	1026	1999	30r
Mortgage rate, incl. points and orig. fee, 30-yr. conv. fixed or ARM	mos	7.05	3/01	4c
Vehicle finance charges paid	yr	365	1999	30r
Business Expenses				
Business travel, car rental	day	73	2001	3c
Business travel, food	day	42	2001	3c
Business travel, hotel	day	93	2001	3c
Charity				
Cash contributions, expenditures	yr	1127	1999	30r
Child Care				
Child raising cost, total, age 0-2	yr	8540	1999	60r
Child raising cost, total, age 3-5	yr	8780	1999	60r
Child raising cost, total, age 6-8	yr	8820	1999	60r
Child raising cost, total, age 9-11	yr	8800	1999	60r
Child raising cost, total, age 12-14	yr	9510	1999	60r
Child raising cost, total, age 15-17	yr	9740	1999	60r
Child's child care and education, age 0-2	yr	1380	1999	60r
Child's child care and education, age 3-5	yr	1520	1999	60r
Child's child care and education, age 6-8	yr	990	1999	60r
Child's child care and education, age 9-11	yr	650	1999	60r
Child's child care and education, age 12-14	yr	490	1999	60r
Child's child care and education, age 15-17	yr	840	1999	60r
Child's clothing, age 0-2	yr	480	1999	60r
Child's clothing, age 3-5	yr	470	1999	60r
Child's clothing, age 6-8	yr	520	1999	60r
Child's clothing, age 9-11	yr	570	1999	60r
Child's clothing, age 12-14	yr	950	1999	60r
Child's clothing, age 15-17	yr	850	1999	60r
Child's food, age 0-2	yr	1000	1999	60r
Child's food, age 3-5	yr	1160	1999	60r
Child's food, age 6-8	yr	1490	1999	60r
Child's food, age 9-11	yr	1770	1999	60r
Child's food, age 12-14	yr	1770	1999	60r
Child's food, age 15-17	yr	1980	1999	60r
Child's health care, age 0-2	yr	620	1999	60r
Child's health care, age 3-5	yr	590	1999	60r
Child's health care, age 6-8	yr	680	1999	60r
Child's health care, age 9-11	yr	720	1999	60r
Child's health care, age 12-14	yr	730	1999	60r
Child's health care, age 15-17	yr	760	1999	60r
Child's housing, age 0-2	yr	3070	1999	60r
Child's housing, age 3-5	yr	3050	1999	60r
Child's housing, age 6-8	yr	3010	1999	60r
Child's housing, age 9-11	yr	2850	1999	60r
Child's housing, age 12-14	yr	3040	1999	60r
Child's housing, age 15-17	yr	2650	1999	60r
Child's personal care, reading, age 0-2	yr	910	1999	60r
Child's personal care, reading, age 3-5	yr	930	1999	60r

Tallahassee, FL - continued

Item	Per	Value	Date	Ref.
Child Care - continued				
Child's personal care, reading, age 6-8	yr	960	1999	60r
Child's personal care, reading, age 9-11	yr	1000	1999	60r
Child's personal care, reading, age 12-14	yr	1170	1999	60r
Child's personal care, reading, age 15-17	yr	950	1999	60r
Clothing				
Apparel and services purchases	yr	1610	1999	30r
Boys' brief, cotton	3	6.98	3/01	4c
Boys, 2 to 15, expenditures on	yr	89	1999	30r
Children under 2, expenditures on	yr	79	1999	30r
Footwear, expenditures on	yr	283	1999	30r
Girls, 2 to 15, expenditures on	yr	103	1999	30r
Men and boys, expenditures on	yr	351	1999	30r
Men, 16 and over, expenditures on	yr	262	1999	30r
Shirt, man's dress shirt		28.41	3/01	4c
Slacks, man's "No Wrinkles" khaki		44.67	3/01	4c
Women, 16 and over, expenditures on	yr	538	1999	30r
Communications				
Cable modem installation, Adelphi		54.90	6/99	103s
Cable modem installation, Comcast		95.00	6/99	103s
Cable modem installation, Media One		100.00	6/99	103s
Cable modem installation, Time Warner		75.00-225.00	6/99	103s
Cable modem rate, cable subscriber, Adelphi	mos	34.95	6/99	103s
Cable modem rate, cable subscriber, Comcast	mos	39.95	6/99	103s
Cable modem rate, cable subscriber, Media One	mos	34.95-39.95	6/99	103s
Cable modem rate, cable subscriber, Time Warner	mos	39.95-49.95	6/99	103s
Cable modem rate, non-cable subscriber, Adelphi	mos	44.95	6/99	103s
Cable modem rate, non-cable subscriber, Comcast	mos	49.95	6/99	103s
Cable modem rate, non-cable subscriber, Media One	mos	49.95	6/99	103s
Cable modem rate, non-cable subscriber, Time Warner	mos	39.95-54.95	6/99	103s
Newspaper subscription, daily and Sunday delivery	mos	13.09	3/01	4c
Phone line, single, business, field visit	inst.	56.00	12/97	17s
Phone line, single, business, no field visit	inst.	56.00	12/97	17s
Phone line, single, residence, field visit	inst.	40.00	12/97	17s
Phone line, single, residence, no field visit	inst.	40.00	12/97	17s
Postage and stationery, expenditures on	yr	104	1999	30r
Postal rate, express mail, up to half-pound		12.45	7/01	108r
Postal rate, letter, first class, first ounce		0.34	7/01	108r
Postal rate, letter, two ounces		0.57	7/01	108r
Postal rate, post card		0.21	7/01	108r
Postal rate, priority mail, two pounds		3.95	7/01	108r
Postal rate, priority mail, up to one pound		3.50	7/01	108r
Telephone bill, family of three	mos	20.07	3/01	4c
Telephone services, expenditures on	yr	860	1999	30r
Education				
Board, 4-year private college/university	yr	2236	1996	38s
Board, 4-year public college/university	yr	2295	1996	38s
Education expenditures	yr	431	1999	30r
Room, 4-year private college/university	yr	2428	1996	38s
Room, 4-year public college/university	yr	2193	1996	38s
Total cost, 4-year private college/university	yr	15028	1996	38s
Total cost, 4-year public college/university	yr	6254	1996	38s
Tuition, 2-year public college/university, in state	yr	1103	1996	38s
Tuition, 4-year private college/university, in state	yr	10364	1996	38s
Tuition, 4-year public college/university	yr	1767	1996	38s
Energy and Fuels				
Electricity	KWh	0.09	7/01	11r
Electricity	500 KWhs	47.29	7/01	11r
Energy, combined forms, 2400 sq ft	mos	138.51	3/01	4c

Values are in dollars or fractions of dollars. In the column headed *Ref*, references are shown to sources. Each reference is followed by a letter. These refer to the geographical level for which data were reported: s=State, r=Region, and c=City or metro. The abbreviation *ex* is used to mean *except* or *excluding*; *exp* stands for expenditures. For other abbreviations and further explanations, please see the Introduction.

Tallahassee, FL - continued

Item	Per	Value	Date	Ref.
Energy and Fuels				
Fuel oil #2	gal	1.43	7/01	11r
Fuel oil and other fuels, expenditures on	yr	45	1999	30r
Gas, natural, commercial rate	1000 cf	8.44	11/00	88s
Gas, regular unleaded, cash, self-service	gal	1.44	3/01	4c
Gasoline, all types	gal	1.60	7/01	11r
Gasoline, unleaded midgrade	gal	1.65	7/01	11r
Gasoline, unleaded premium	gal	1.74	7/01	11r
Natural gas, expenditures on	yr	164	1999	30r
Utility (piped) gas, therm		1.01	7/01	11r
Utility (piped) gas, 40 therms		44.29	7/01	11r
Utility (piped) gas, 100 therms		97.44	7/01	11r
Entertainment				
Bowling, Saturday evening rate	line	3.15	3/01	4c
Entertainment purchases	yr	1574	1999	30r
Fees and admissions paid	yr	371	1999	30r
Monopoly game, Parker Brothers', No. 9	game	12.14	3/01	4c
Movie, first-run, Saturday, evening	adm.	6.75	3/01	4c
Reading purchases	yr	121	1999	30r
Television, radios, sound equipment, expenditures on	yr	561	1999	30r
Tennis balls, yellow, Wilson or Penn, 3	can	2.67	3/01	4c
Funerals				
Total cost of funeral		5922.53	1/99	78r
Acknowledgement cards		63.43	1/99	78r
Casket		2258.77	1/99	78r
Cosmetology, hair, other preparation		127.09	1/99	78r
Embalming		393.49	1/99	78r
Funeral at funeral home		367.50	1/99	78r
Hearse (local)		169.66	1/99	78r
Professional service charges		1211.32	1/99	78r
Service car/van		80.69	1/99	78r
Transfer of remains to funeral home		144.25	1/99	78r
Vault		803.50	1/99	78r
Visitation/viewing		302.83	1/99	78r
Groceries				
Groceries, ACCRA Index		110.20	3/01	4c
American processed cheese	lb	3.50	7/01	11r
Antibiotic ointment, Polysporin	0.5 oz	4.86	3/01	4c
Baby food, strained vegetables or fruit, lowest price	4-4.5 oz	0.49	3/01	4c
Bakery products, expenditures on	yr	261	1999	30r
Bananas	lb	0.49	3/01	4c
Bananas	lb	0.47	7/01	11r
Beans, dried, any type, all sizes	lb	0.63	7/01	11r
Beef for stew, boneless	lb	2.86	7/01	11r
Beef or hamburger, ground	lb	1.77	3/01	4c
Beef, expenditures on	yr	210	1999	30r
Bologna, all beef or mixed	lb	2.29	7/01	11r
Bread, French	lb	1.66	7/01	11r
Bread, white	loaf	1.15	3/01	4c
Bread, white, pan	lb	0.87	7/01	11r
Bread, whole wheat, pan	lb	1.38	7/01	11r
Broccoli	lb	1.04	7/01	11r
Butter, salted, grade AA, stick	lb	2.26	7/01	11r
Butter, yoghurt, cheese, etc, expenditures on	yr	170	1999	30r
Cabbage	lb	0.42	7/01	11r
Cereals and cereal products, expenditures on	yr	140	1999	30r
Cheddar cheese, natural	lb	3.75	7/01	11r
Cheese, Kraft grated Parmesan	8 oz	3.19	3/01	4c
Chicken breast, bone-in	lb	1.85	7/01	11r
Chicken legs, bone-in	lb	1.34	7/01	11r
Chicken, fresh, whole	lb	1.05	7/01	11r
Chicken, whole fryer	lb	0.99	3/01	4c
Chops, boneless,	lb	4.13	7/01	11r
Chuck roast, graded and ungraded, excl U.S. prime and choice	lb	2.35	7/01	11r
Chuck roast, U.S. choice, boneless	lb	2.67	7/01	11r
Cigarettes, Winston, Kings	carton	32.04	3/01	4c
Coffee, 100%, ground roast, all sizes	lb	2.88	7/01	11r
Coffee, instant, plain, regular, all sizes	16 oz	9.25	7/01	11r

Tallahassee, FL - continued

Item	Per	Value	Date	Ref.
Groceries - continued				
Coffee, vacuum-packed	13 oz	2.76	3/01	4c
Cola, non diet,	2 liter	1.11	7/01	11r
Corn Flakes, Kellogg's or Post Toasties	18 oz	3.09	3/01	4c
Corn, frozen, whole kernel, lowest price	16 oz	1.21	3/01	4c
Crackers, soda, salted	lb	1.70	7/01	11r
Dairy product purchases	yr	282	1999	30r
Eggs, expenditures on	yr	32	1999	30r
Eggs, Grade A or AA	dozen	1.21	3/01	4c
Fats and oils, expenditures on	yr	79	1999	30r
Fish and seafood, expenditures on	yr	99	1999	30r
Flour, white, all purpose	lb	0.32	7/01	11r
Food (excl fruit and vegetables), eaten at home, purchases	yr	815	1999	30r
Food cooked on trips, expenditures on	yr	36	1999	30r
Food purchases	yr	4533	1999	30r
Food purchases, eaten away from home	yr	1873	1999	30r
Food purchases, food eaten at home	yr	2660	1999	30r
Fresh fruits, expenditures on	yr	128	1999	30r
Fresh milk and cream, expenditures on	yr	112	1999	30r
Fresh vegetables, expenditures on	yr	131	1999	30r
Fruit and vegetable purchases	yr	438	1999	30r
Grapefruit	lb	0.59	7/01	11r
Grapes, Thompson, seedless	lb	2.12	7/01	11r
Ground beef, 100% beef	lb	1.76	7/01	11r
Ground beef, lean and extra lean	lb	2.60	7/01	11r
Ground chuck, 100% beef	lb	2.08	7/01	11r
Ham, boneless, excl canned	lb	2.71	7/01	11r
Ham, rump or shank half, bone-in, smoked	lb	2.19	7/01	11r
Ice cream, prepackaged, bulk, regular	1/2 gal	3.93	7/01	11r
Lemons	lb	1.32	7/01	11r
Lettuce, iceberg	head	1.07	3/01	4c
Lettuce, iceberg	lb	0.76	7/01	11r
Margarine, Blue Bonnet or Parkay, stick	lb	0.97	3/01	4c
Milk, fresh, low fat,	gal	2.75	7/01	11r
Milk, fresh, whole, fortified	gal	2.97	7/01	11r
Milk, whole	1/2 gal	1.89	3/01	4c
Nonalcoholic beverages, expenditures on	yr	228	1999	30r
Orange juice, frozen concentrate	16 oz	1.95	7/01	11r
Orange juice, Minute Maid frozen	12 oz	1.92	3/01	4c
Oranges, Navel	lb	0.73	7/01	11r
Oranges, Valencia	lb	0.55	7/01	11r
Peaches, halves or slices, Hunt's, Del Monte, or Libby's	29 oz	1.62	3/01	4c
Peanut butter, creamy, all sizes	lb	1.83	7/01	11r
Pears, Anjou	lb	0.98	7/01	11r
Peas, green, Del Monte or Green Giant	15 oz	0.67	3/01	4c
Pork chops, center cut, bone-in	lb	3.33	7/01	11r
Pork sausage, fresh, loose	lb	2.59	7/01	11r
Pork shoulder picnic, bone-in, smoked	lb	1.12	7/01	11r
Pork, expenditures on	yr	162	1999	30r
Potato chips	16 oz	3.59	7/01	11r
Potatoes, frozen, french fried	lb	1.00	7/01	11r
Potatoes, white or red	10 lb	3.51	3/01	4c
Potatoes, white, all types	lb	0.44	7/01	11r
Poultry, expenditures on	yr	137	1999	30r
Processed fruits, expenditures on	yr	97	1999	30r
Processed vegetables, expenditures on	yr	82	1999	30r
Rice, white, long grain, uncooked	lb	0.51	7/01	11r
Round roast, graded and ungraded, excl U.S. prime and choice	lb	2.96	7/01	11r
Round steak, graded and ungraded, excl U.S. prime and choice	lb	3.11	7/01	11r
Sausage, Jimmy Dean/Owens pork	lb	3.16	3/01	4c
Shortening, vegetable, Crisco	3 lb	3.32	3/01	4c
Sirloin steak, graded and ungraded, excl U.S. prime and choice	lb	4.23	7/01	11r
Soft drink, Coca Cola, ex deposit	2 liter	1.41	3/01	4c
Spaghetti and macaroni	lb	0.78	7/01	11r
Steak, round, U.S. choice, boneless	lb	3.56	7/01	11r
Steak, sirloin, U.S. choice, boneless	lb	5.65	7/01	11r
Steak, T-bone	lb	7.42	3/01	4c
Strawberries, dry pint	12 oz	1.50	7/01	11r

Values are in dollars or fractions of dollars. In the column headed *Ref*, references are shown to sources. Each reference is followed by a letter. These refer to the geographical level for which data were reported: s=State, r=Region, and c=City or metro. The abbreviation *ex* is used to mean *except* or *excluding*; *exp* stands for *expenditures*. For other abbreviations and further explanations, please see the Introduction.

Tallahassee, FL - continued

Item	Per	Value	Date	Ref.
Groceries				
Sugar and other sweets, expenditures on	yr	99	1999	30r
Sugar, cane or beet	4 lbs	1.59	3/01	4c
Sugar, white, 33-80 ounce package	lb	0.39	7/01	11r
Sugar, white, all sizes	lb	0.42	7/01	11r
Tobacco products and smoking supplies purchases	yr	288	1999	30r
Tomatoes, field grown	lb	1.43	7/01	11r
Tomatoes, Hunt's or Del Monte	14.5 oz	0.91	3/01	4c
Tuna, chunk, light	6 oz	0.67	3/01	4c
Tuna, light, chunk	lb	1.77	7/01	11r
Turkey, frozen, whole	lb	1.05	7/01	11r
Goods and Services				
Miscellaneous goods and services, ACCRA Index		108.50	3/01	4c
B&B Japanese maple (acer japonicum)	gal	49.98-129.00	4/00	93r
Boxwood (buxus)	2 gal	12.99-16.99	4/00	93r
Daylily (hemerocallis)	gal	4.99-8.99	4/00	93r
Flat of annuals		11.00-13.92	4/00	93r
Fountain grass (pennisetum)	gal	5.98-7.98	4/00	93r
Hanging basket (10 in)		7.99-14.98	4/00	93r
Hardy geranium (geranium)	gal	5.98-8.00	4/00	93r
Hosta (hosta)	gal	4.99-10.98	4/00	93r
Lilac (syrubga vulgaris)	2 gal	12.99-21.99	4/00	93r
Rhododendron (rhododendron)	2 gal	14.99-24.99	4/00	93r
Sage (salvia)	gal	5.98-6.99	4/00	93r
Wintercreeper euonymus (euonymus fortunei)	2 gal	7.99-89.99	4/00	93r
Hunting license	yr	12.50	4/01	34s
Health Care				
Health care, ACCRA Index		103.80	3/01	4c
Cardiac catheterization, ave hospital/physician charges		15060	1998	77s
Childbirth, Cesarean delivery		11587	1997	13r
Childbirth, vaginal delivery		6725	1997	13r
Dentist's fee, adult teeth cleaning and periodic oral exam	visit	68.17	3/01	4c
Doctor's fee, routine exam, established patient	visit	62.17	3/01	4c
Drugs, expenditures on	yr	399	1999	30r
Health care purchases	yr	1971	1999	30r
Health insurance expenditures	yr	933	1999	30r
Hospital care, private room	day	608.00	3/01	4c
Hysterectomy, laproscopically-assisted, ave hospital/physician charges		14760	1998	76s
Hysterectomy, vaginal, ave hospital and physician charges		11320	1998	76s
Medicaid dispensing fee		4.23	1999	87s
Medical services expenditures	yr	547	1999	30r
Medical supplies, expenditures on	yr	91	1999	30r
Plastic surgery, breast augmentation		2870	2000	7r
Plastic surgery, breast lift		3649	2000	7r
Plastic surgery, facelift		5008	2000	7r
Plastic surgery, hair transplantation		3425	2000	7r
Plastic surgery, lip augmentation		1227	2000	7r
Plastic surgery, lower body lift		4793	2000	7r
Plastic surgery, thigh lift		3862	2000	7r
Household Goods				
Dishwashing powder, Cascade	50 oz	3.36	3/01	4c
Floor coverings, expenditures on	yr	44	1999	30r
Furniture, expenditures on	yr	335	1999	30r

Tallahassee, FL - continued

Item	Per	Value	Date	Ref.
Household Goods - continued				
Household furnishings and equipment purchases	yr	1328	1999	30r
Household textiles, expenditures on	yr	89	1999	30r
Laundry and cleaning supplies, expenditures on	yr	113	1999	30r
Tissues, facial, Kleenex brand	175	1.40	3/01	4c
Housing				
Housing, ACCRA Index		107.80	3/01	4c
Home, 2200 sq ft, 4-br, 2-bath, 2-car garage, average		172350	2000	47c
Home price, existing, ave		160100	10/00	90r
Home value, median		104000	2001	53s
House, 2400 sq ft, 8000 sq ft lot, new, urban, utilities	total	223583	3/01	4c
House payment, principal and interest, 25% down payment	mos	1122	3/01	4c
Household operation expenditures	yr	553	1999	30r
Housekeeping supplies purchases	yr	473	1999	30r
Housing, expenditures on	yr	10303	1999	30r
Maintenance, repairs, insurance expenditures	yr	699	1999	30r
Monthly rental value of owned home	mos	505	1999	30r
Owned dwellings, expenditures own	yr	3465	1999	30r
Rent expenditures	yr	1641	1999	30r
Rent, apartment, 2 br, 1 1/2-2 baths, unfurn, 950 sq ft, water	mos	722	3/01	4c
Rental unit, 1 bedroom, with utilities	mos	468	4/01	41c
Rental unit, 2 bedroom, with utilities	mos	616	4/01	41c
Rental unit, 3 bedroom, with utilities	mos	805	4/01	41c
Rental unit, 4 bedroom, with utilities	mos	970	4/01	41c
Shelter, expenditures on	yr	5467	1999	30r
Insurance and Pensions				
Life and other personal insurance purchases	yr	414	1999	30r
Medigap health insurance, Plan H	yr	2887	2000	69s
Medigap health insurance, Plan I	yr	3302	2000	69s
Medigap health insurance, Plan J	yr	3889	2000	69s
Pensions and Social Security, expenditures on	yr	2635	1999	30r
Personal insurance and pensions, expenditures on	yr	3048	1999	30r
Legal Fees				
Divorce, filing fee		65.00-85.00	4/01	35s
Driver's license fee	orig	20.00	1999	48s
Driver's license fee	renew	15.00	1999	48s
Personal Goods				
Personal care products and services purchases	yr	393	1999	30r
Shampoo, Alberto VO5	15 oz	1.04	3/01	4c
Toothpaste, Crest or Colgate	6-7 oz	2.47	3/01	4c
Personal Services				
Dry cleaning, man's 2-pc suit		7.89	3/01	4c
Man's haircut, barbershop, no styling		10.91	3/01	4c
Personal services, household, expenditures on	yr	258	1999	30r
Woman's shampoo, trim, blow-dry, no style-change		27.33	3/01	4c
Pets				
Pets, toys, and playground equipment, expenditures on	yr	306	1999	30r
Restaurant Food				
Chicken, fried, thigh and drumstick, KFC/Church's		2.59	3/01	4c
Hamburger with cheese, McDonald's	1/4 lb	2.09	3/01	4c
Pizza, Pizza Hut or Pizza Inn	11-12 in	9.49	3/01	4c
Taxes				
Federal income taxes paid	yr	2047	1999	30r
Personal taxes, expenditures on	yr	2554	1999	30r

Values are in dollars or fractions of dollars. In the column headed *Ref*, references are shown to sources. Each reference is followed by a letter. These refer to the geographical level for which data were reported: s=State, r=Region, and c=City or metro. The abbreviation *ex* is used to mean *except* or *excluding*; *exp* stands for *expenditures*. For other abbreviations and further explanations, please see the Introduction.

Tallahassee, FL - continued

Taxes

Item	Per	Value	Date	Ref.
Property taxes paid	yr	726	1999	30r
State and local income taxes paid	yr	363	1999	30r

Transportation

Item	Per	Value	Date	Ref.
Transportation, ACCRA Index		104.30	3/01	4c
Cars and trucks, new, expenditures on	yr	1648	1999	30r
Cars and trucks, used, expenditures on	yr	1651	1999	30r
Diesel at the pump	gal	1.26	10/99	73s
Gasoline and motor oil purchases	yr	1052	1999	30r
Gasoline before-tax price (cents)	gal	101.90	10/00	43s
Maintenance and repair expenditures	yr	621	1999	30r
Public transportation, expenditures on	yr	298	1999	30r
Tire balance, computer or spin balance, front	wheel	8.50	3/01	4c
Transportation purchases	yr	6738	1999	30r
Vehicle expenses, miscellaneous, purchases	yr	2033	1999	30r
Vehicle insurance payments	yr	696	1999	30r
Vehicle purchases (net outlay)	yr	3354	1999	30r
Vehicle rental, lease expenditures	yr	352	1999	30r

Travel

Item	Per	Value	Date	Ref.
Hotel room	night	110.57	2/01	95s

Utilities

Item	Per	Value	Date	Ref.
Utilities, ACCRA Index		110.60	3/01	4c
Electrical bill, average	mos	86.33	9/00	9s
Electricity, 2400 sq ft, new home	mos	138.51	3/01	4c
Electricity, expenditures on	yr	1115	1999	30r
Electricity cost, average	KWh	6.80	9/00	9s
Water and other public services, expenditures on	yr	298	1999	30r

Weddings

Item	Per	Value	Date	Ref.
Wedding (national average cost)		19936	2000	33r
Wedding (regional average total cost)		16293	1997	110r
Attendants' gifts		321	1998	33r
Bridal attendants' apparel (5 persons)		824	2000	33r
Bride's headpiece/veil		173	1998	33r
Bride's wedding dress		859	1998	33r
Clergy, religious facility fee		242	1998	33r
Engagement ring		3177	1998	33r
Flowers		789	1998	33r
Groom's formalwear rental		99	2000	33r
Limousine		410	1998	33r
Marriage license cost		56.00-88.50	4/01	35s
Men's formalwear (ushers, best man)		469	2000	33r
Mother of bride apparel		241	2000	33r
Music		866	1998	33r
Photography and videography		1368	1998	33r
Rehearsal dinner		728	1998	33r
Wedding invitations and announcements		341	1998	33r
Wedding reception		7968	2000	33r
Wedding rings (bride and groom)		1060	1998	33r

Tampa-St. Petersburg-Clearwater, FL

Item	Per	Value	Date	Ref.
Average annual expenditures	yr	32932	1999	30c
Composite, ACCRA index		98.40	3/01	4c

Alcoholic Beverages

Item	Per	Value	Date	Ref.
Alcoholic beverage purchases	yr	405	1999	30c
Beer, Heineken, 12-oz, ex deposit	6	6.48	3/01	4c
J & B Scotch	750-ml	20.43	3/01	4c
Malt beverages, all types, all sizes, any origin	16 oz	0.96	7/01	11r
Wine, Livingston or Gallo, Chablis blanc	1.5 liter	5.29	3/01	4c

Appliances

Item	Per	Value	Date	Ref.
Appliance repair, service call, washing machine	min lab chg	38.49	3/01	4c
Major appliances, expenditures on	yr	172	1999	30r
Small appliances, housewares, expenditures on	yr	81	1999	30r

Banking and Money

Item	Per	Value	Date	Ref.
Mortgage interest and charges paid	yr	2039	1999	30r
Mortgage principal paid on owned property	yr	1026	1999	30r
Mortgage rate, incl. points and orig. fee, 30-yr. conv. fixed or ARM	mos	7.02	3/01	4c
Vehicle finance charges paid	yr	365	1999	30r

Business Expenses

Item	Per	Value	Date	Ref.
Business travel, car rental	day	43	2001	3c
Business travel, food	day	48	2001	3c
Business travel, hotel	day	114	2001	3c
Office space, central business district, Class A	sq ft	20.72	3/99	74c

Charity

Item	Per	Value	Date	Ref.
Cash contributions, expenditures	yr	834	1999	30c

Child Care

Item	Per	Value	Date	Ref.
Child raising cost, total, age 0-2	yr	8540	1999	60r
Child raising cost, total, age 3-5	yr	8780	1999	60r
Child raising cost, total, age 6-8	yr	8820	1999	60r
Child raising cost, total, age 9-11	yr	8800	1999	60r
Child raising cost, total, age 12-14	yr	9510	1999	60r
Child raising cost, total, age 15-17	yr	9740	1999	60r
Child's child care and education, age 0-2	yr	1380	1999	60r
Child's child care and education, age 3-5	yr	1520	1999	60r
Child's child care and education, age 6-8	yr	990	1999	60r
Child's child care and education, age 9-11	yr	650	1999	60r
Child's child care and education, age 12-14	yr	490	1999	60r
Child's child care and education, age 15-17	yr	840	1999	60r
Child's clothing, age 0-2	yr	480	1999	60r
Child's clothing, age 3-5	yr	470	1999	60r
Child's clothing, age 6-8	yr	520	1999	60r
Child's clothing, age 9-11	yr	570	1999	60r
Child's clothing, age 12-14	yr	950	1999	60r
Child's clothing, age 15-17	yr	850	1999	60r
Child's food, age 0-2	yr	1000	1999	60r
Child's food, age 3-5	yr	1160	1999	60r
Child's food, age 6-8	yr	1490	1999	60r
Child's food, age 9-11	yr	1770	1999	60r
Child's food, age 12-14	yr	1770	1999	60r
Child's food, age 15-17	yr	1980	1999	60r
Child's health care, age 0-2	yr	620	1999	60r
Child's health care, age 3-5	yr	590	1999	60r
Child's health care, age 6-8	yr	680	1999	60r
Child's health care, age 9-11	yr	720	1999	60r
Child's health care, age 12-14	yr	730	1999	60r
Child's health care, age 15-17	yr	760	1999	60r
Child's housing, age 0-2	yr	3070	1999	60r
Child's housing, age 3-5	yr	3050	1999	60r
Child's housing, age 6-8	yr	3010	1999	60r
Child's housing, age 9-11	yr	2850	1999	60r
Child's housing, age 12-14	yr	3040	1999	60r
Child's housing, age 15-17	yr	2650	1999	60r
Child's personal care, reading, age 0-2	yr	910	1999	60r
Child's personal care, reading, age 3-5	yr	930	1999	60r
Child's personal care, reading, age 6-8	yr	960	1999	60r
Child's personal care, reading, age 9-11	yr	1000	1999	60r
Child's personal care, reading, age 12-14	yr	1170	1999	60r
Child's personal care, reading, age 15-17	yr	950	1999	60r
Daycare	mos	260	1998	37c
Daycare, 3-year old, 5 days, 8 hrs/day	mos	260	1998	85c

Clothing

Item	Per	Value	Date	Ref.
Apparel and services purchases	yr	1330	1999	30c
Boys' brief, cotton	3	5.56	3/01	4c
Boys, 2 to 15, expenditures on	yr	89	1999	30r
Children under 2, expenditures on	yr	79	1999	30r
Footwear, expenditures on	yr	283	1999	30r
Girls, 2 to 15, expenditures on	yr	103	1999	30r
Men and boys, expenditures on	yr	351	1999	30r
Men, 16 and over, expenditures on	yr	262	1999	30r
Shirt, man's dress shirt		27.15	3/01	4c
Slacks, man's "No Wrinkles" khaki		35.29	3/01	4c
Women, 16 and over, expenditures on	yr	538	1999	30r

Values are in dollars or fractions of dollars. In the column headed *Ref*, references are shown to sources. Each reference is followed by a letter. These refer to the geographical level for which data were reported: s=State, r=Region, and c=City or metro. The abbreviation *ex* is used to mean *except* or *excluding*; *exp* stands for expenditures. For other abbreviations and further explanations, please see the Introduction.

Tampa-St. Petersburg-Clearwater, FL - continued

Item	Per	Value	Date	Ref.
Communications				
Cable modem installation, Adelphi		54.90	6/99	103s
Cable modem installation, Comcast		95.00	6/99	103s
Cable modem installation, Media One		100.00	6/99	103s
Cable modem installation, Time Warner		75.00-225.00	6/99	103s
Cable modem rate, cable subscriber, Adelphi	mos	34.95	6/99	103s
Cable modem rate, cable subscriber, Comcast	mos	39.95	6/99	103s
Cable modem rate, cable subscriber, Media One	mos	34.95-39.95	6/99	103s
Cable modem rate, cable subscriber, Time Warner	mos	39.95-49.95	6/99	103s
Cable modem rate, non-cable subscriber, Adelphi	mos	44.95	6/99	103s
Cable modem rate, non-cable subscriber, Comcast	mos	49.95	6/99	103s
Cable modem rate, non-cable subscriber, Media One	mos	49.95	6/99	103s
Cable modem rate, non-cable subscriber, Time Warner	mos	39.95-54.95	6/99	103s
Newspaper subscription, daily and Sunday delivery	mos	11.60	3/01	4c
Phone line, single, business, field visit	inst.	56.00	12/97	17s
Phone line, single, business, no field visit	inst.	56.00	12/97	17s
Phone line, single, residence, field visit	inst.	40.00	12/97	17s
Phone line, single, residence, no field visit	inst.	40.00	12/97	17s
Postage and stationery, expenditures on	yr	104	1999	30r
Postal rate, express mail, up to half-pound		12.45	7/01	108r
Postal rate, letter, first class, first ounce		0.34	7/01	108r
Postal rate, letter, two ounces		0.57	7/01	108r
Postal rate, post card		0.21	7/01	108r
Postal rate, priority mail, two pounds		3.95	7/01	108r
Postal rate, priority mail, up to one pound		3.50	7/01	108r
Telephone bill, family of three	mos	18.52	3/01	4c
Telephone services, expenditures on	yr	860	1999	30r
Education				
Board, 4-year private college/university	yr	2236	1996	38s
Board, 4-year public college/university	yr	2295	1996	38s
Education expenditures	yr	392	1999	30c
Room, 4-year private college/university	yr	2428	1996	38s
Room, 4-year public college/university	yr	2193	1996	38s
Total cost, 4-year private college/university	yr	15028	1996	38s
Total cost, 4-year public college/university	yr	6254	1996	38s
Tuition, 2-year public college/university, in state	yr	1103	1996	38s
Tuition, 4-year private college/university, in state	yr	10364	1996	38s
Tuition, 4-year public college/university	yr	1767	1996	38s
Energy and Fuels				
Electricity	KWh	0.09	7/01	11r
Electricity	500 KWhs	47.29	7/01	11r
Energy, combined forms, 2400 sq ft	mos	121.51	3/01	4c
Fuel oil #2	gal	1.43	7/01	11r
Fuel oil and other fuels, expenditures on	yr	45	1999	30r
Gas, natural, commercial rate	1000 cf	8.44	11/00	88s
Gas, regular unleaded, cash, self-service	gal	1.37	3/01	4c
Gasoline, all types	gal	1.60	7/01	11r
Gasoline, unleaded midgrade	gal	1.65	7/01	11r
Gasoline, unleaded premium	gal	1.74	7/01	11r
Natural gas, expenditures on	yr	164	1999	30r
Utility (piped) gas, therm		1.01	7/01	11r
Utility (piped) gas, 40 therms		44.29	7/01	11r
Utility (piped) gas, 100 therms		97.44	7/01	11r
Entertainment				
Bowling, Saturday evening rate	line	2.92	3/01	4c
Entertainment purchases	yr	1471	1999	30c
Fees and admissions paid	yr	371	1999	30r
Monopoly game, Parker Brothers', No. 9	game	9.53	3/01	4c
Movie, first-run, Saturday, evening	adm.	6.93	3/01	4c
Reading purchases	yr	121	1999	30r

Tampa-St. Petersburg-Clearwater, FL - continued

Item	Per	Value	Date	Ref.
Entertainment - continued				
Television, radios, sound equipment, expenditures on	yr	561	1999	30r
Tennis balls, yellow, Wilson or Penn, 3	can	2.57	3/01	4c
Funerals				
Total cost of funeral		5922.53	1/99	78r
Acknowledgement cards		63.43	1/99	78r
Casket		2258.77	1/99	78r
Cosmetology, hair, other preparation		127.09	1/99	78r
Embalming		393.49	1/99	78r
Funeral at funeral home		367.50	1/99	78r
Hearse (local)		169.66	1/99	78r
Professional service charges		1211.32	1/99	78r
Service car/van		80.69	1/99	78r
Transfer of remains to funeral home		144.25	1/99	78r
Vault		803.50	1/99	78r
Visitation/viewing		302.83	1/99	78r
Groceries				
Groceries, ACCRA Index		98.60	3/01	4c
American processed cheese	lb	3.50	7/01	11r
Antibiotic ointment, Polysporin	0.5 oz	4.29	3/01	4c
Baby food, strained vegetables or fruit, lowest price	4-4.5 oz	0.43	3/01	4c
Bakery products, expenditures on	yr	261	1999	30r
Bananas	lb	0.48	3/01	4c
Bananas	lb	0.47	7/01	11r
Beans, dried, any type, all sizes	lb	0.63	7/01	11r
Beef for stew, boneless	lb	2.86	7/01	11r
Beef or hamburger, ground	lb	1.77	3/01	4c
Beef, expenditures on	yr	210	1999	30r
Bologna, all beef or mixed	lb	2.29	7/01	11r
Bread, French	lb	1.66	7/01	11r
Bread, white	loaf	0.99	3/01	4c
Bread, white, pan	lb	0.87	7/01	11r
Bread, whole wheat, pan	lb	1.38	7/01	11r
Broccoli	lb	1.04	7/01	11r
Butter, salted, grade AA, stick	lb	2.26	7/01	11r
Butter, yoghurt, cheese, etc, expenditures on	yr	170	1999	30r
Cabbage	lb	0.42	7/01	11r
Cereals and bakery product purchases	yr	398	1999	30c
Cereals and cereal products, expenditures on	yr	140	1999	30r
Cheddar cheese, natural	lb	3.75	7/01	11r
Cheese, Kraft grated Parmesan	8 oz	3.35	3/01	4c
Chicken breast, bone-in	lb	1.85	7/01	11r
Chicken legs, bone-in	lb	1.34	7/01	11r
Chicken, fresh, whole	lb	1.05	7/01	11r
Chicken, whole fryer	lb	1.02	3/01	4c
Chops, boneless	lb	4.13	7/01	11r
Chuck roast, graded and ungraded, excl U.S. prime and choice	lb	2.35	7/01	11r
Chuck roast, U.S. choice, boneless	lb	2.67	7/01	11r
Cigarettes, Winston, Kings	carton	25.21	3/01	4c
Coffee, 100%, ground roast, all sizes	lb	2.88	7/01	11r
Coffee, instant, plain, regular, all sizes	16 oz	9.25	7/01	11r
Coffee, vacuum-packed	13 oz	2.39	3/01	4c
Cola, non diet	2 liter	1.11	7/01	11r
Corn Flakes, Kellogg's or Post Toasties	18 oz	2.95	3/01	4c
Corn, frozen, whole kernel, lowest price	16 oz	0.90	3/01	4c
Crackers, soda, salted	lb	1.70	7/01	11r
Dairy product purchases	yr	295	1999	30c
Eggs, expenditures on	yr	32	1999	30r
Eggs, Grade A or AA	dozen	1.29	3/01	4c
Fats and oils, expenditures on	yr	79	1999	30r
Fish and seafood, expenditures on	yr	99	1999	30r
Flour, white, all purpose	lb	0.32	7/01	11r
Food (excl fruit and vegetables), eaten at home, purchases	yr	825	1999	30c
Food cooked on trips, expenditures on	yr	36	1999	30r
Food purchases	yr	4750	1999	30c
Food purchases, eaten away from home	yr	2009	1999	30c
Food purchases, food eaten at home	yr	2741	1999	30c

Values are in dollars or fractions of dollars. In the column headed *Ref*, references are shown to sources. Each reference is followed by a letter. These refer to the geographical level for which data were reported: s=State, r=Region, and c=City or metro. The abbreviation *ex* is used to mean *except* or *excluding*; *exp* stands for *expenditures*. For other abbreviations and further explanations, please see the Introduction.

Tampa-St. Petersburg-Clearwater, FL - continued

Item	Per	Value	Date	Ref.
Groceries				
Fresh fruits, expenditures on	yr	128	1999	30r
Fresh milk and cream, expenditures on	yr	112	1999	30r
Fresh vegetables, expenditures on	yr	131	1999	30r
Fruit and vegetable purchases	yr	438	1999	30r
Grapefruit	lb	0.59	7/01	11r
Grapes, Thompson, seedless	lb	2.12	7/01	11r
Ground beef, 100% beef	lb	1.76	7/01	11r
Ground beef, lean and extra lean	lb	2.60	7/01	11r
Ground chuck, 100% beef	lb	2.08	7/01	11r
Ham, boneless, excl canned	lb	2.71	7/01	11r
Ham, rump or shank half, bone-in, smoked	lb	2.19	7/01	11r
Ice cream, prepackaged, bulk, regular	1/2 gal	3.93	7/01	11r
Lemons	lb	1.32	7/01	11r
Lettuce, iceberg	head	0.75	3/01	4c
Lettuce, iceberg	lb	0.76	7/01	11r
Margarine, Blue Bonnet or Parkay, stick	lb	0.75	3/01	4c
Meats, poultry, fish, and egg purchases	yr	786	1999	30c
Milk, fresh, low fat	gal	2.75	7/01	11r
Milk, fresh, whole, fortified	gal	2.97	7/01	11r
Milk, whole	1/2 gal	1.87	3/01	4c
Nonalcoholic beverages, expenditures on	yr	228	1999	30r
Orange juice, frozen concentrate	16 oz	1.95	7/01	11r
Orange juice, Minute Maid frozen	12 oz	1.38	3/01	4c
Oranges, Navel	lb	0.73	7/01	11r
Oranges, Valencia	lb	0.55	7/01	11r
Peaches, halves or slices, Hunt's, Del Monte, or Libby's	29 oz	1.51	3/01	4c
Peanut butter, creamy, all sizes	lb	1.83	7/01	11r
Pears, Anjou	lb	0.98	7/01	11r
Peas, green, Del Monte or Green Giant	15 oz	0.63	3/01	4c
Pork chops, center cut, bone-in	lb	3.33	7/01	11r
Pork sausage, fresh, loose	lb	2.59	7/01	11r
Pork shoulder picnic, bone-in, smoked	lb	1.12	7/01	11r
Pork, expenditures on	yr	162	1999	30r
Potato chips	16 oz	3.59	7/01	11r
Potatoes, frozen, french fried	lb	1.00	7/01	11r
Potatoes, white or red	10 lb	3.10	3/01	4c
Potatoes, white, all types	lb	0.44	7/01	11r
Poultry, expenditures on	yr	137	1999	30r
Processed fruits, expenditures on	yr	97	1999	30r
Processed vegetables, expenditures on	yr	82	1999	30r
Rice, white, long grain, uncooked	lb	0.51	7/01	11r
Round roast, graded and ungraded, excl U.S. prime and choice	lb	2.96	7/01	11r
Round steak, graded and ungraded, excl U.S. prime and choice	lb	3.11	7/01	11r
Sausage, Jimmy Dean/Owens pork	lb	3.10	3/01	4c
Shortening, vegetable, Crisco	3 lb	3.04	3/01	4c
Sirloin steak, graded and ungraded, excl U.S. prime and choice	lb	4.23	7/01	11r
Soft drink, Coca Cola, ex deposit	2 liter	1.27	3/01	4c
Spaghetti and macaroni	lb	0.78	7/01	11r
Steak, round, U.S. choice, boneless	lb	3.56	7/01	11r
Steak, sirloin, U.S. choice, boneless	lb	5.65	7/01	11r
Steak, T-bone	lb	6.96	3/01	4c
Strawberries, dry pint	12 oz	1.50	7/01	11r
Sugar and other sweets, expenditures on	yr	99	1999	30r
Sugar, cane or beet	4 lbs	1.44	3/01	4c
Sugar, white, 33-80 ounce package	lb	0.39	7/01	11r
Sugar, white, all sizes	lb	0.42	7/01	11r
Tobacco products and smoking supplies purchases	yr	284	1999	30c
Tomatoes, field grown	lb	1.43	7/01	11r
Tomatoes, Hunt's or Del Monte	14.5 oz	0.79	3/01	4c
Tuna, chunk, light	6 oz	0.60	3/01	4c
Tuna, light, chunk	lb	1.77	7/01	11r
Turkey, frozen, whole	lb	1.05	7/01	11r
Goods and Services				
Miscellaneous goods and services, ACCRA Index		97.70	3/01	4c
B&B Japanese maple (acer japonicum)	gal	49.98-129.00	4/00	93r

Tampa-St. Petersburg-Clearwater, FL - continued

Item	Per	Value	Date	Ref.
Goods and Services - continued				
Boxwood (buxus)	2 gal	12.99-16.99	4/00	93r
Daylilly (hemerocallis)	gal	4.99-8.99	4/00	93r
Flat of annuals		11.00-13.92	4/00	93r
Fountain grass (pennisetum)	gal	5.98-7.98	4/00	93r
Hanging basket (10 in)		7.99-14.98	4/00	93r
Hardy geranium (geranium)	gal	5.98-8.00	4/00	93r
Hosta (hosta)	gal	4.99-10.98	4/00	93r
Lilac (syrubga vulgaris)	2 gal	12.99-21.99	4/00	93r
Miscellaneous purchases	yr	707	1999	30c
Rhododendron (rhododendron)	2 gal	14.99-24.99	4/00	93r
Sage (salvia)	gal	5.98-6.99	4/00	93r
Wintercreeper euonymus (euonymus fortunei)	2 gal	7.99-89.99	4/00	93r
Hunting license	yr	12.50	4/01	34s
Health Care				
Health care, ACCRA Index		101.80	3/01	4c
Cardiac catheterization, ave hospital/ physician charges		15060	1998	77s
Childbirth, Cesarean delivery		11587	1997	13r
Childbirth, vaginal delivery		6725	1997	13r
Dentist's fee, adult teeth cleaning and periodic oral exam	visit	77.70	3/01	4c
Doctor's fee, routine exam, established patient	visit	55.80	3/01	4c
Drugs, expenditures on	yr	399	1999	30r
Health care purchases	yr	2294	1999	30c
Health insurance expenditures	yr	933	1999	30r
Home health care aide cost, licensed agency	hour	16	2000	82c
Hospital care, private room	day	569.29	3/01	4c
Hysterectomy, laproscopically-assisted, ave hospital/physician charges		14760	1998	76s
Hysterectomy, vaginal, ave hospital and physician charges		11320	1998	76s
Medicaid dispensing fee		4.23	1999	87s
Medical services expenditures	yr	547	1999	30r
Medical supplies, expenditures on	yr	91	1999	30r
Nursing home costs, private room	day	128	2000	82c
Nursing home stay, private room	day	128	2000	83c
Plastic surgery, breast augmentation		2870	2000	7r
Plastic surgery, breast lift		3649	2000	7r
Plastic surgery, facelift		5008	2000	7r
Plastic surgery, hair transplantation		3425	2000	7r
Plastic surgery, lip augmentation		1227	2000	7r
Plastic surgery, lower body lift		4793	2000	7r
Plastic surgery, thigh lift		3862	2000	7r
Household Goods				
Dishwashing powder, Cascade	50 oz	2.85	3/01	4c
Floor coverings, expenditures on	yr	44	1999	30r
Furniture, expenditures on	yr	335	1999	30r
Household furnishings and equipment purchases	yr	1240	1999	30c
Household textiles, expenditures on	yr	89	1999	30r
Laundry and cleaning supplies, expenditures on	yr	113	1999	30r
Tissues, facial, Kleenex brand	175	1.36	3/01	4c
Housing				
Housing, ACCRA Index		97.90	3/01	4c
Home, 2200 sq ft, 4-br, 2-bath, 2-car garage, average		181000	2000	47c
Home price, existing, ave		160100	10/00	90r
Home value, median		104000	2001	53s

Values are in dollars or fractions of dollars. In the column headed *Ref*, references are shown to sources. Each reference is followed by a letter. These refer to the geographical level for which data were reported: s=State, r=Region, and c=City or metro. The abbreviation *ex* is used to mean *except* or *excluding*; *exp* stands for *expenditures*. For other abbreviations and further explanations, please see the Introduction.

Tampa-St. Petersburg-Clearwater, FL - continued

Item	Per	Value	Date	Ref.
Housing				
House, 2400 sq ft, 8000 sq ft lot, new, urban, utilities	total	188560	3/01	4c
House payment, principal and interest, 25% down payment	mos	943	3/01	4c
Household operation expenditures	yr	639	1999	30c
Housekeeping supplies purchases	yr	449	1999	30c
Housing, expenditures on	yr	10303	1999	30r
Lodging expenditures	yr	550	1999	30c
Maintenance, repairs, insurance expenditures	yr	699	1999	30r
Monthly rental value of owned home	mos	505	1999	30r
Owned dwellings, expenditures own	yr	3836	1999	30c
Rent expenditures	yr	1873	1999	30c
Rent, apartment, 2 br, 1 1/2-2 baths, unfurn, 950 sq ft, water	mos	854	3/01	4c
Rental unit, 1 bedroom, with utilities	mos	524	4/01	41c
Rental unit, 2 bedroom, with utilities	mos	649	4/01	41c
Rental unit, 3 bedroom, with utilities	mos	862	4/01	41c
Rental unit, 4 bedroom, with utilities	mos	1045	4/01	41c
Shelter, expenditures on	yr	6258	1999	30c
Insurance and Pensions				
Life and other personal insurance purchases	yr	324	1999	30c
Medigap health insurance, Plan H	yr	2887	2000	69s
Medigap health insurance, Plan I	yr	3302	2000	69s
Medigap health insurance, Plan J	yr	3889	2000	69s
Pensions and Social Security, expenditures on	yr	2702	1999	30c
Personal insurance and pensions, expenditures on	yr	3048	1999	30r
Legal Fees				
Divorce, filing fee		65.00-85.00	4/01	35s
Driver's license fee	renew	15.00	1999	48s
Driver's license fee	orig	20.00	1999	48s
Personal Goods				
Personal care products and services purchases	yr	292	1999	30c
Shampoo, Alberto VO5	15 oz	1.01	3/01	4c
Toothpaste, Crest or Colgate	6-7 oz	2.36	3/01	4c
Personal Services				
Dry cleaning, man's 2-pc suit		7.14	3/01	4c
Man's haircut, barbershop, no styling		9.92	3/01	4c
Personal services, household, expenditures on	yr	258	1999	30r
Woman's shampoo, trim, blow-dry, no style-change		27.00	3/01	4c
Pets				
Pets, toys, and playground equipment, expenditures on	yr	306	1999	30r
Restaurant Food				
Chicken, fried, thigh and drumstick, KFC/Church's		2.31	3/01	4c
Hamburger with cheese, McDonald's	1/4 lb	1.99	3/01	4c
Pizza, Pizza Hut or Pizza Inn	11-12 in	9.14	3/01	4c
Taxes				
Federal income taxes paid	yr	2047	1999	30r
Personal taxes, expenditures on	yr	2554	1999	30r
Property taxes paid	yr	726	1999	30r
State and local income taxes paid	yr	363	1999	30r
Transportation				
Transportation, ACCRA Index		100.80	3/01	4c
Bus fare, one-way	trip	0.85	2000	1c
Bus fare, to central business district	1-way	1.15	3/01	4c
Cars and trucks, new, expenditures on	yr	1648	1999	30r
Cars and trucks, used, expenditures on	yr	1651	1999	30r
Diesel at the pump	gal	1.26	10/99	73s
Gasoline and motor oil purchases	yr	900	1999	30c
Gasoline before-tax price (cents)	gal	101.90	10/00	43s

Tampa-St. Petersburg-Clearwater, FL - continued

Item	Per	Value	Date	Ref.
Transportation - continued				
Household transportation expenditures	yr	5864	97-1998	102c
Maintenance and repair expenditures	yr	621	1999	30r
Public transportation, expenditures on	yr	411	1999	30c
Tire balance, computer or spin balance, front	wheel	8.23	3/01	4c
Transportation purchases	yr	5986	1999	30c
Vehicle expenses, miscellaneous, purchases	yr	2074	1999	30c
Vehicle insurance payments	yr	696	1999	30r
Vehicle purchases (net outlay)	yr	3354	1999	30r
Vehicle rental, lease expenditures	yr	352	1999	30r
Travel				
Hotel room	night	110.57	2/01	95s
Utilities				
Utilities, ACCRA Index		97.60	3/01	4c
Electrical bill, average	mos	86.33	9/00	9s
Electricity, 2400 sq ft, new home	mos	121.51	3/01	4c
Electricity, expenditures on	yr	1115	1999	30r
Electricity, summer, 250 KWh	mos	26.94	2/96	97c
Electricity, summer, 500 KWh	mos	45.15	2/96	97c
Electricity, summer, 750 KWh	mos	63.38	2/96	97c
Electricity, summer, 1000 KWh	mos	81.58	2/96	97c
Electricity cost, average	KWh	6.80	9/00	9s
Utilities, fuels, and public services purchased	yr	2457	1999	30c
Water and other public services, expenditures on	yr	298	1999	30r
Weddings				
Wedding (national average cost)		19936	2000	33r
Wedding (regional average total cost)		16293	1997	110r
Attendants' gifts		321	1998	33r
Bridal attendants' apparel (5 persons)		824	2000	33r
Bride's headpiece/veil		173	1998	33r
Bride's wedding dress		859	1998	33r
Clergy, religious facility fee		242	1998	33r
Engagement ring		3177	1998	33r
Flowers		789	1998	33r
Groom's formalwear rental		99	2000	33r
Limousine		410	1998	33r
Marriage license cost		56.00-88.50	4/01	35s
Men's formalwear (ushers, best man)		469	2000	33r
Mother of bride apparel		241	2000	33r
Music		866	1998	33r
Photography and videography		1368	1998	33r
Rehearsal dinner		728	1998	33r
Wedding invitations and announcements		341	1998	33r
Wedding reception		7968	2000	33r
Wedding rings (bride and groom)		1060	1998	33r

Terre Haute, IN

Item	Per	Value	Date	Ref.
Average annual expenditures	yr	35369	1999	30r
Alcoholic Beverages				
Alcoholic beverage purchases	yr	304	1999	30r
Malt beverages, all types, all sizes, any origin	16 oz	0.93	7/01	11r
Wine, red and white table, all sizes, any origin	liter	7.04	7/01	11r
Appliances				
Major appliances, expenditures on	yr	165	1999	30r
Small appliances, housewares, expenditures on	yr	90	1999	30r
Banking and Money				
Mortgage interest and charges paid	yr	2277	1999	30r
Mortgage principal paid on owned property	yr	1230	1999	30r
Vehicle finance charges paid	yr	328	1999	30r
Charity				
Cash contributions, expenditures	yr	1126	1999	30r

Values are in dollars or fractions of dollars. In the column headed *Ref*, references are shown to sources. Each reference is followed by a letter. These refer to the geographical level for which data were reported: s=State, r=Region, and c=City or metro. The abbreviation *ex* is used to mean *except* or *excluding*; *exp* stands for expenditures. For other abbreviations and further explanations, please see the Introduction.

Terre Haute, IN - continued

Item	Per	Value	Date	Ref.
Child Care				
Child raising cost, total, age 0-2	yr	7890	1999	60r
Child raising cost, total, age 3-5	yr	8130	1999	60r
Child raising cost, total, age 6-8	yr	8170	1999	60r
Child raising cost, total, age 9-11	yr	8190	1999	60r
Child raising cost, total, age 12-14	yr	8890	1999	60r
Child raising cost, total, age 15-17	yr	9050	1999	60r
Child's child care and education, age 0-2	yr	1240	1999	60r
Child's child care and education, age 3-5	yr	1370	1999	60r
Child's child care and education, age 6-8	yr	880	1999	60r
Child's child care and education, age 9-11	yr	570	1999	60r
Child's child care and education, age 12-14	yr	420	1999	60r
Child's child care and education, age 15-17	yr	720	1999	60r
Child's clothing, age 0-2	yr	410	1999	60r
Child's clothing, age 3-5	yr	400	1999	60r
Child's clothing, age 6-8	yr	450	1999	60r
Child's clothing, age 9-11	yr	500	1999	60r
Child's clothing, age 12-14	yr	840	1999	60r
Child's clothing, age 15-17	yr	740	1999	60r
Child's food, age 0-2	yr	960	1999	60r
Child's food, age 3-5	yr	1120	1999	60r
Child's food, age 6-8	yr	1430	1999	60r
Child's food, age 9-11	yr	1710	1999	60r
Child's food, age 12-14	yr	1710	1999	60r
Child's food, age 15-17	yr	1920	1999	60r
Child's health care, age 0-2	yr	520	1999	60r
Child's health care, age 3-5	yr	500	1999	60r
Child's health care, age 6-8	yr	570	1999	60r
Child's health care, age 9-11	yr	610	1999	60r
Child's health care, age 12-14	yr	630	1999	60r
Child's health care, age 15-17	yr	650	1999	60r
Child's housing, age 0-2	yr	2860	1999	60r
Child's housing, age 3-5	yr	2840	1999	60r
Child's housing, age 6-8	yr	2800	1999	60r
Child's housing, age 9-11	yr	2650	1999	60r
Child's housing, age 12-14	yr	2840	1999	60r
Child's housing, age 15-17	yr	2440	1999	60r
Child's personal care, reading, age 0-2	yr	880	1999	60r
Child's personal care, reading, age 3-5	yr	900	1999	60r
Child's personal care, reading, age 6-8	yr	930	1999	60r
Child's personal care, reading, age 9-11	yr	970	1999	60r
Child's personal care, reading, age 12-14	yr	1150	1999	60r
Child's personal care, reading, age 15-17	yr	920	1999	60r
Clothing				
Apparel and services purchases	yr	1607	1999	30r
Boys, 2 to 15, expenditures on	yr	91	1999	30r
Children under 2, expenditures on	yr	59	1999	30r
Footwear, expenditures on	yr	285	1999	30r
Girls, 2 to 15, expenditures on	yr	116	1999	30r
Men and boys, expenditures on	yr	433	1999	30r
Men, 16 and over, expenditures on	yr	341	1999	30r
Women, 16 and over, expenditures on	yr	490	1999	30r
Communications				
Phone line, single, business, field visit	inst.	59.00	12/97	17s
Phone line, single, business, no field visit	inst.	59.00	12/97	17s
Phone line, single, residence, field visit	inst.	47.00	12/97	17s
Phone line, single, residence, no field visit	inst.	47.00	12/97	17s
Postage and stationery, expenditures on	yr	140	1999	30r
Postal rate, express mail, up to half-pound		12.45	7/01	108r
Postal rate, letter, first class, first ounce		0.34	7/01	108r
Postal rate, letter, two ounces		0.57	7/01	108r
Postal rate, post card		0.21	7/01	108r
Postal rate, priority mail, two pounds		3.95	7/01	108r
Postal rate, priority mail, up to one pound		3.50	7/01	108r
Telephone services, expenditures on	yr	830	1999	30r
Education				
Board, 4-year private college/university	yr	2250	1996	38s
Board, 4-year public college/university	yr	2425	1996	38s
Education expenditures	yr	583	1999	30r
Room, 4-year private college/university	yr	1987	1996	38s
Room, 4-year public college/university	yr	1931	1996	38s
Total cost, 4-year private college/university	yr	16829	1996	38s

Terre Haute, IN - continued

Item	Per	Value	Date	Ref.
Education - continued				
Total cost, 4-year public college/university	yr	7392	1996	38s
Tuition, 2-year public college/university, in state	yr	1937	1996	38s
Tuition, 4-year private college/university, in state	yr	12592	1996	38s
Tuition, 4-year public college/university	yr	3037	1996	38s
Energy and Fuels				
Electricity	500 KWhs	46.59	7/01	11r
Fuel oil #2	gal	1.27	7/01	11r
Fuel oil and other fuels, expenditures on	yr	68	1999	30r
Gas, natural, commercial rate	1000 cf	6.24	11/00	88s
Gasoline, unleaded midgrade	gal	1.79	7/01	11r
Gasoline, unleaded premium	gal	1.86	7/01	11r
Gasoline, unleaded regular	gal	1.58	7/01	11r
Natural gas, expenditures on	yr	389	1999	30r
Utility (piped) gas, therm		0.81	7/01	11r
Utility (piped) gas, 40 therms		38.01	7/01	11r
Utility (piped) gas, 100 therms		81.75	7/01	11r
Entertainment				
Entertainment purchases	yr	1984	1999	30r
Fees and admissions paid	yr	444	1999	30r
Television, radios, sound equipment, expenditures on	yr	580	1999	30r
Funerals				
Cosmetology, hair, other preparation		178.32	1/99	78r
Embalming		408.19	1/99	78r
Funeral at funeral home		362.13	1/99	78r
Professional service charges		1375.51	1/99	78r
Transfer of remains to funeral home		155.92	1/99	78r
Visitation/viewing		294.38	1/99	78r
Groceries				
Bacon, sliced	lb	3.15	7/01	11r
Bakery products, expenditures on	yr	281	1999	30r
Bananas	lb	0.48	7/01	11r
Beans, dried, any type, all sizes	lb	0.61	7/01	11r
Beef for stew, boneless	lb	3.08	7/01	11r
Beef, expenditures on	yr	217	1999	30r
Bologna, all beef or mixed	lb	2.52	7/01	11r
Bread, white, pan	lb	1.06	7/01	11r
Broccoli	lb	0.91	7/01	11r
Butter, salted, grade AA, stick	lb	3.04	7/01	11r
Butter, yoghurt, cheese, etc, expenditures on	yr	183	1999	30r
Cereals and bakery product purchases	yr	430	1999	30r
Cereals and cereal products, expenditures on	yr	149	1999	30r
Chicken, fresh, whole	lb	1.07	7/01	11r
Chops, boneless,	lb	3.64	7/01	11r
Chuck roast, U.S. choice, boneless	lb	2.47	7/01	11r
Coffee, 100%, ground roast, all sizes	lb	2.69	7/01	11r
Cookies, chocolate chip	lb	2.87	7/01	11r
Dairy product purchases	yr	304	1999	30r
Eggs, expenditures on	yr	26	1999	30r
Eggs, grade A, large	dozen	0.88	7/01	11r
Fats and oils, expenditures on	yr	75	1999	30r
Fish and seafood, expenditures on	yr	72	1999	30r
Food (excl fruit and vegetables), eaten at home, purchases	yr	887	1999	30r
Food cooked on trips, expenditures on	yr	44	1999	30r
Food purchases	yr	4802	1999	30r
Food purchases, eaten away from home	yr	2069	1999	30r
Food purchases, food eaten at home	yr	2733	1999	30r
Fresh fruits, expenditures on	yr	138	1999	30r
Fresh milk and cream, expenditures on	yr	120	1999	30r
Fresh vegetables, expenditures on	yr	126	1999	30r
Grapefruit	lb	0.66	7/01	11r
Grapes, Thompson, seedless	lb	1.64	7/01	11r
Ground beef, 100% beef	lb	1.64	7/01	11r
Ground beef, lean and extra lean	lb	2.16	7/01	11r
Ground chuck, 100% beef	lb	2.13	7/01	11r

Values are in dollars or fractions of dollars. In the column headed *Ref*, references are shown to sources. Each reference is followed by a letter. These refer to the geographical level for which data were reported: s=State, r=Region, and c=City or metro. The abbreviation *ex* is used to mean *except* or *excluding*; *exp* stands for *expenditures*. For other abbreviations and further explanations, please see the Introduction.

Terre Haute, IN - continued

Item	Per	Value	Date	Ref.
Groceries				
Ham, boneless, excl canned	lb	2.62	7/01	11r
Ice cream, prepackaged, bulk, regular	1/2 gal	3.35	7/01	11r
Lemons	lb	1.19	7/01	11r
Lettuce, iceberg	lb	0.73	7/01	11r
Margarine, soft, tubs	lb	0.89	7/01	11r
Meats, poultry, fish, and egg purchases	yr	671	1999	30r
Milk, fresh, whole, fortified	gal	2.71	7/01	11r
Nonalcoholic beverages, expenditures on	yr	239	1999	30r
Oranges, Navel	lb	0.80	7/01	11r
Oranges, Valencia	lb	0.66	7/01	11r
Pears, Anjou	lb	0.93	7/01	11r
Pork chops, center cut, bone-in	lb	3.63	7/01	11r
Pork, expenditures on	yr	150	1999	30r
Potato chips	16 oz	3.52	7/01	11r
Potatoes, frozen, french fried	lb	1.08	7/01	11r
Potatoes, white, all types	lb	0.33	7/01	11r
Poultry, expenditures on	yr	108	1999	30r
Processed fruits, expenditures on	yr	98	1999	30r
Processed vegetables, expenditures on	yr	80	1999	30r
Round roast, U.S. choice, boneless	lb	3.07	7/01	11r
Round steak, graded and ungraded, excl U.S. prime and choice	lb	3.41	7/01	11r
Shortening, vegetable oil blends	lb	1.13	7/01	11r
Spaghetti and macaroni	lb	0.80	7/01	11r
Steak, round, U.S. choice, boneless	lb	3.23	7/01	11r
Steak, T-bone, U.S. choice, bone-in	lb	6.68	7/01	11r
Strawberries, dry pint	12 oz	1.32	7/01	11r
Sugar and other sweets, expenditures on	yr	114	1999	30r
Sugar, white, 33-80 ounce package	lb	0.42	7/01	11r
Sugar, white, all sizes	lb	0.43	7/01	11r
Tobacco products and smoking supplies purchases	yr	331	1999	30r
Tomatoes, field grown	lb	1.46	7/01	11r
Tuna, light, chunk	lb	1.80	7/01	11r
Turkey, frozen, whole	lb	1.15	7/01	11r
Goods and Services				
B&B Japanese maple (acer japonicum)	gal	29.99-169.99	4/00	93r
Boxwood (buxus)	2 gal	18.99-39.99	4/00	93r
Daylilly (hemerocallis)	gal	4.99-25.00	4/00	93r
Flat of annuals		11.98-24.99	4/00	93r
Fountain grass (pennisetum)	gal	5.98-12.98	4/00	93r
Hanging basket (10 in)		12.99-27.99	4/00	93r
Hardy geranium (geranium)	gal	7.99-9.99	4/00	93r
Hosta (hosta)	gal	6.00-25.00	4/00	93r
Lilac (syrubga vulgaris)	2 gal	14.99-24.99	4/00	93r
Miscellaneous purchases	yr	865	1999	30r
Rhododendron (rhododendron)	2 gal	23.98-42.99	4/00	93r
Sage (salvia)	gal	6.00-9.99	4/00	93r
Wintercreeper euonymus (euonymus fortunei)	2 gal	16.00-169.99	4/00	93r
Hunting license	yr	8.75	4/01	34s
Health Care				
Cardiac catheterization, ave hospital/physician charges		13380	1998	77s
Childbirth, Cesarean delivery		10722	1997	13r
Childbirth, vaginal delivery		6223	1997	13r
Drugs, expenditures on	yr	394	1999	30r
Health care purchases	yr	2048	1999	30r
Health insurance expenditures	yr	978	1999	30r

Terre Haute, IN - continued

Item	Per	Value	Date	Ref.
Health Care - continued				
Hysterectomy, laproscopically-assisted, ave hospital/physician charges		11310	1998	76s
Hysterectomy, vaginal, ave hospital and physician charges		9160	1998	76s
Medicaid dispensing fee		4.00	1999	87s
Medical services expenditures	yr	554	1999	30r
Medical supplies, expenditures on	yr	122	1999	30r
Plastic surgery, breast augmentation		3184	2000	7r
Plastic surgery, breast lift		3585	2000	7r
Plastic surgery, facelift		4999	2000	7r
Plastic surgery, hair transplantation		3105	2000	7r
Plastic surgery, lip augmentation		1290	2000	7r
Plastic surgery, lower body lift		8135	2000	7r
Plastic surgery, thigh lift		3839	2000	7r
Household Goods				
Floor coverings, expenditures on	yr	52	1999	30r
Furniture, expenditures on	yr	344	1999	30r
Household furnishings and equipment purchases	yr	1475	1999	30r
Household textiles, expenditures on	yr	109	1999	30r
Laundry and cleaning supplies, expenditures on	yr	134	1999	30r
Housing				
Home price, existing, ave		144400	10/00	90r
Home value, median		102000	2001	53s
Household operation expenditures	yr	542	1999	30r
Housekeeping supplies purchases	yr	508	1999	30r
Lodging expenditures	yr	430	1999	30r
Maintenance, repairs, insurance expenditures	yr	853	1999	30r
Monthly rental value of owned home	mos	547	1999	30r
Owned dwellings, expenditures own	yr	4282	1999	30r
Rent expenditures	yr	1558	1999	30r
Rental unit, 1 bedroom, with utilities	mos	344	4/01	41c
Rental unit, 2 bedroom, with utilities	mos	439	4/01	41c
Rental unit, 3 bedroom, with utilities	mos	547	4/01	41c
Rental unit, 4 bedroom, with utilities	mos	611	4/01	41c
Shelter, expenditures on	yr	6270	1999	30r
Insurance and Pensions				
Life and other personal insurance purchases	yr	387	1999	30r
Pensions and Social Security, expenditures on	yr	2968	1999	30r
Legal Fees				
Divorce, filing fee		100.00	4/01	35s
Driver's license fee	orig	6.00	1999	48s
Driver's license fee	renew	6.00	1999	48s
Personal Goods				
Personal care products and services purchases	yr	385	1999	30r
Personal Services				
Personal services, household, expenditures on	yr	300	1999	30r
Pets				
Pets, toys, and playground equipment, expenditures on	yr	375	1999	30r
Taxes				
Federal income taxes paid	yr	2326	1999	30r
Personal taxes, expenditures on	yr	3223	1999	30r
Property taxes paid	yr	1152	1999	30r
State and local income taxes paid	yr	753	1999	30r
Transportation				
Cars and trucks, new, expenditures on	yr	1280	1999	30r
Cars and trucks, used, expenditures on	yr	1763	1999	30r
Diesel at the pump	gal	1.17	10/99	73s
Gasoline and motor oil purchases	yr	1036	1999	30r
Gasoline before-tax price (cents)	gal	110.00	10/00	43s
Maintenance and repair expenditures	yr	594	1999	30r

Values are in dollars or fractions of dollars. In the column headed *Ref*, references are shown to sources. Each reference is followed by a letter. These refer to the geographical level for which data were reported: s=State, r=Region, and c=City or metro. The abbreviation *ex* is used to mean *except* or *excluding*; *exp* stands for *expenditures*. For other abbreviations and further explanations, please see the Introduction.

Terre Haute, IN - continued

Item	Per	Value	Date	Ref.
Transportation				
Public transportation, expenditures on	yr	341	1999	30r
Transportation purchases	yr	6617	1999	30r
Vehicle expenses, miscellaneous, purchases	yr	2159	1999	30r
Vehicle insurance payments	yr	701	1999	30r
Vehicle purchases (net outlay)	yr	3081	1999	30r
Vehicle rental, lease expenditures	yr	536	1999	30r
Utilities				
Electrical bill, average	mos	66.66	9/00	9s
Electricity, expenditures on	yr	841	1999	30r
Electricity, summer, 250 KWh	mos	26.09	2/96	97c
Electricity, summer, 500 KWh	mos	39.45	2/96	97c
Electricity, summer, 750 KWh	mos	51.41	2/96	97c
Electricity, summer, 1000 KWh	mos	63.37	2/96	97c
Electricity cost, average	KWh	5.00	9/00	9s
Utilities, fuels, and public services purchased	yr	2401	1999	30r
Water and other public services, expenditures on	yr	273	1999	30r
Weddings				
Wedding (national average cost)		19936	2000	33r
Wedding (regional average total cost)		16195	1997	110r
Attendants' gifts		321	1998	33r
Bridal attendants' apparel (5 persons)		824	2000	33r
Bride's headpiece/veil		173	1998	33r
Bride's wedding dress		859	1998	33r
Clergy, religious facility fee		242	1998	33r
Engagement ring		3177	1998	33r
Flowers		789	1998	33r
Groom's formalwear rental		99	2000	33r
Limousine		410	1998	33r
Marriage license cost		18.00	4/01	35s
Men's formalwear (ushers, best man)		469	2000	33r
Mother of bride apparel		241	2000	33r
Music		866	1998	33r
Photography and videography		1368	1998	33r
Rehearsal dinner		728	1998	33r
Wedding invitations and announcements		341	1998	33r
Wedding reception		7968	2000	33r
Wedding rings (bride and groom)		1060	1998	33r

Texarcana, TX-AR

Item	Per	Value	Date	Ref.
Alcoholic Beverages				
Alcoholic beverage purchases	yr	253	1999	30r
Malt beverages, all types, all sizes, any origin	16 oz	0.96	7/01	11r
Appliances				
Major appliances, expenditures on	yr	172	1999	30r
Small appliances, housewares, expenditures on	yr	81	1999	30r
Banking and Money				
Mortgage interest and charges paid	yr	2039	1999	30r
Mortgage principal paid on owned property	yr	1026	1999	30r
Vehicle finance charges paid	yr	365	1999	30r
Charity				
Cash contributions, expenditures	yr	1127	1999	30r
Child Care				
Child raising cost, total, age 0-2	yr	8540	1999	60r
Child raising cost, total, age 3-5	yr	8780	1999	60r
Child raising cost, total, age 6-8	yr	8820	1999	60r
Child raising cost, total, age 9-11	yr	8800	1999	60r
Child raising cost, total, age 12-14	yr	9510	1999	60r
Child raising cost, total, age 15-17	yr	9740	1999	60r
Child's child care and education, age 0-2	yr	1380	1999	60r
Child's child care and education, age 3-5	yr	1520	1999	60r
Child's child care and education, age 6-8	yr	990	1999	60r
Child's child care and education, age 9-11	yr	650	1999	60r
Child's child care and education, age 12-14	yr	490	1999	60r
Child's child care and education, age 15-17	yr	840	1999	60r
Child's clothing, age 0-2	yr	480	1999	60r

Item	Per	Value	Date	Ref.
Child Care - continued				
Child's clothing, age 3-5	yr	470	1999	60r
Child's clothing, age 6-8	yr	520	1999	60r
Child's clothing, age 9-11	yr	570	1999	60r
Child's clothing, age 12-14	yr	950	1999	60r
Child's clothing, age 15-17	yr	850	1999	60r
Child's food, age 0-2	yr	1000	1999	60r
Child's food, age 3-5	yr	1160	1999	60r
Child's food, age 6-8	yr	1490	1999	60r
Child's food, age 9-11	yr	1770	1999	60r
Child's food, age 12-14	yr	1770	1999	60r
Child's food, age 15-17	yr	1980	1999	60r
Child's health care, age 0-2	yr	620	1999	60r
Child's health care, age 3-5	yr	590	1999	60r
Child's health care, age 6-8	yr	680	1999	60r
Child's health care, age 9-11	yr	720	1999	60r
Child's health care, age 12-14	yr	730	1999	60r
Child's health care, age 15-17	yr	760	1999	60r
Child's housing, age 0-2	yr	3070	1999	60r
Child's housing, age 3-5	yr	3050	1999	60r
Child's housing, age 6-8	yr	3010	1999	60r
Child's housing, age 9-11	yr	2850	1999	60r
Child's housing, age 12-14	yr	3040	1999	60r
Child's housing, age 15-17	yr	2650	1999	60r
Child's personal care, reading, age 0-2	yr	910	1999	60r
Child's personal care, reading, age 3-5	yr	930	1999	60r
Child's personal care, reading, age 6-8	yr	960	1999	60r
Child's personal care, reading, age 9-11	yr	1000	1999	60r
Child's personal care, reading, age 12-14	yr	1170	1999	60r
Child's personal care, reading, age 15-17	yr	950	1999	60r
Clothing				
Apparel and services purchases	yr	1610	1999	30r
Boys, 2 to 15, expenditures on	yr	89	1999	30r
Children under 2, expenditures on	yr	79	1999	30r
Footwear, expenditures on	yr	283	1999	30r
Girls, 2 to 15, expenditures on	yr	103	1999	30r
Men and boys, expenditures on	yr	351	1999	30r
Men, 16 and over, expenditures on	yr	262	1999	30r
Women, 16 and over, expenditures on	yr	538	1999	30r
Communications				
Cable modem installation, AT&T-BIS		150.00	6/99	103s
Cable modem installation, Marcus		499.00	6/99	103s
Cable modem installation, Time Warner		75.00-225.00	6/99	103s
Cable modem rate, cable subscriber, AT&T-BIS	mos	39.95	6/99	103s
Cable modem rate, cable subscriber, Marcus	mos	14.95-49.95	6/99	103s
Cable modem rate, cable subscriber, Time Warner	mos	39.95-49.95	6/99	103s
Cable modem rate, non-cable subscriber, Marcus	mos	60.95	6/99	103s
Cable modem rate, non-cable subscriber, Time Warner	mos	39.95-54.95	6/99	103s
Phone line, single, business, field visit	inst.	71.90	12/97	17s
Phone line, single, business, no field visit	inst.	57.30	12/97	17s
Phone line, single, residence, field visit	inst.	52.95	12/97	17s
Phone line, single, residence, no field visit	inst.	38.35	12/97	17s
Postage and stationery, expenditures on	yr	104	1999	30r
Postal rate, express mail, up to half-pound		12.45	7/01	108r
Postal rate, letter, first class, first ounce		0.34	7/01	108r
Postal rate, letter, two ounces		0.57	7/01	108r
Postal rate, post card		0.21	7/01	108r
Postal rate, priority mail, two pounds		3.95	7/01	108r
Postal rate, priority mail, up to one pound		3.50	7/01	108r
Telephone services, expenditures on	yr	860	1999	30r
Education				
Board, 4-year private college/university	yr	2198	1996	38s
Board, 4-year public college/university	yr	1759	1996	38s
Education expenditures	yr	431	1999	30r
Room, 4-year private college/university	yr	2000	1996	38s
Room, 4-year public college/university	yr	1885	1996	38s

Values are in dollars or fractions of dollars. In the column headed *Ref*, references are shown to sources. Each reference is followed by a letter. These refer to the geographical level for which data were reported: s=State, r=Region, and c=City or metro. The abbreviation *ex* is used to mean *except* or *excluding*; *exp* stands for expenditures. For other abbreviations and further explanations, please see the Introduction.

Texarcana, TX-AR - continued

Item	Per	Value	Date	Ref.
Education				
Total cost, 4-year private college/university	yr	13156	1996	38s
Total cost, 4-year public college/university	yr	5464	1996	38s
Tuition, 2-year public college/university, in state	yr	771	1996	38s
Tuition, 4-year private college/university, in state	yr	8959	1996	38s
Tuition, 4-year public college/university	yr	1820	1996	38s
Energy and Fuels				
Electricity	KWh	0.09	7/01	11r
Electricity	500 KWhs	47.29	7/01	11r
Fuel oil #2	gal	1.43	7/01	11r
Fuel oil and other fuels, expenditures on	yr	45	1999	30r
Gas, natural, commercial rate	1000 cf	6.94	11/00	88s
Gasoline, all types	gal	1.60	7/01	11r
Gasoline, unleaded midgrade	gal	1.65	7/01	11r
Gasoline, unleaded premium	gal	1.74	7/01	11r
Natural gas, expenditures on	yr	164	1999	30r
Utility (piped) gas, therm		1.01	7/01	11r
Utility (piped) gas, 40 therms		44.29	7/01	11r
Utility (piped) gas, 100 therms		97.44	7/01	11r
Entertainment				
Entertainment purchases	yr	1574	1999	30r
Fees and admissions paid	yr	371	1999	30r
Reading purchases	yr	121	1999	30r
Television, radios, sound equipment, expenditures on	yr	561	1999	30r
Funerals				
Total cost of funeral		5842.28	1/99	78r
Acknowledgement cards		28.35	1/99	78r
Casket		2494.29	1/99	78r
Cosmetology, hair, other preparation		109.22	1/99	78r
Embalming		361.42	1/99	78r
Funeral at funeral home		349.20	1/99	78r
Hearse (local)		161.91	1/99	78r
Professional service charges		1116.50	1/99	78r
Service car/van		65.56	1/99	78r
Transfer of remains to funeral home		143.56	1/99	78r
Vault		785.25	1/99	78r
Visitation/viewing		227.02	1/99	78r
Groceries				
American processed cheese	lb	3.50	7/01	11r
Bakery products, expenditures on	yr	261	1999	30r
Bananas	lb	0.47	7/01	11r
Beans, dried, any type, all sizes	lb	0.63	7/01	11r
Beef for stew, boneless	lb	2.86	7/01	11r
Beef, expenditures on	yr	210	1999	30r
Bologna, all beef or mixed	lb	2.29	7/01	11r
Bread, French	lb	1.66	7/01	11r
Bread, white, pan	lb	0.87	7/01	11r
Bread, whole wheat, pan	lb	1.38	7/01	11r
Broccoli	lb	1.04	7/01	11r
Butter, salted, grade AA, stick	lb	2.26	7/01	11r
Butter, yoghurt, cheese, etc, expenditures on	yr	170	1999	30r
Cabbage	lb	0.42	7/01	11r
Cereals and cereal products, expenditures on	yr	140	1999	30r
Cheddar cheese, natural	lb	3.75	7/01	11r
Chicken breast, bone-in	lb	1.85	7/01	11r
Chicken legs, bone-in	lb	1.34	7/01	11r
Chicken, fresh, whole	lb	1.05	7/01	11r
Chops, boneless,	lb	4.13	7/01	11r
Chuck roast, graded and ungraded, excl U.S. prime and choice	lb	2.35	7/01	11r
Chuck roast, U.S. choice, boneless	lb	2.67	7/01	11r
Coffee, 100%, ground roast, all sizes	lb	2.88	7/01	11r
Coffee, instant, plain, regular, all sizes	16 oz	9.25	7/01	11r
Cola, non diet,	2 liter	1.11	7/01	11r
Crackers, soda, salted	lb	1.70	7/01	11r
Dairy product purchases	yr	282	1999	30r

Texarcana, TX-AR - continued

Item	Per	Value	Date	Ref.
Groceries - continued				
Eggs, expenditures on	yr	32	1999	30r
Fats and oils, expenditures on	yr	79	1999	30r
Fish and seafood, expenditures on	yr	99	1999	30r
Flour, white, all purpose	lb	0.32	7/01	11r
Food (excl fruit and vegetables), eaten at home, purchases	yr	815	1999	30r
Food cooked on trips, expenditures on	yr	36	1999	30r
Food purchases	yr	4533	1999	30r
Food purchases, eaten away from home	yr	1873	1999	30r
Food purchases, food eaten at home	yr	2660	1999	30r
Fresh fruits, expenditures on	yr	128	1999	30r
Fresh milk and cream, expenditures on	yr	112	1999	30r
Fresh vegetables, expenditures on	yr	131	1999	30r
Fruit and vegetable purchases	yr	438	1999	30r
Grapefruit	lb	0.59	7/01	11r
Grapes, Thompson, seedless	lb	2.12	7/01	11r
Ground beef, 100% beef	lb	1.76	7/01	11r
Ground beef, lean and extra lean	lb	2.60	7/01	11r
Ground chuck, 100% beef	lb	2.08	7/01	11r
Ham, boneless, excl canned	lb	2.71	7/01	11r
Ham, rump or shank half, bone-in, smoked	lb	2.19	7/01	11r
Ice cream, prepackaged, bulk, regular	1/2 gal	3.93	7/01	11r
Lemons	lb	1.32	7/01	11r
Lettuce, iceberg	lb	0.76	7/01	11r
Milk, fresh, low fat	gal	2.75	7/01	11r
Milk, fresh, whole, fortified	gal	2.97	7/01	11r
Nonalcoholic beverages, expenditures on	yr	228	1999	30r
Orange juice, frozen concentrate	16 oz	1.95	7/01	11r
Oranges, Navel	lb	0.73	7/01	11r
Oranges, Valencia	lb	0.55	7/01	11r
Peanut butter, creamy, all sizes	lb	1.83	7/01	11r
Pears, Anjou	lb	0.98	7/01	11r
Pork chops, center cut, bone-in	lb	3.33	7/01	11r
Pork sausage, fresh, loose	lb	2.59	7/01	11r
Pork shoulder picnic, bone-in, smoked	lb	1.12	7/01	11r
Pork, expenditures on	yr	162	1999	30r
Potato chips	16 oz	3.59	7/01	11r
Potatoes, frozen, french fried	lb	1.00	7/01	11r
Potatoes, white, all types	lb	0.44	7/01	11r
Poultry, expenditures on	yr	137	1999	30r
Processed fruits, expenditures on	yr	97	1999	30r
Processed vegetables, expenditures on	yr	82	1999	30r
Rice, white, long grain, uncooked	lb	0.51	7/01	11r
Round roast, graded and ungraded, excl U.S. prime and choice	lb	2.96	7/01	11r
Round steak, graded and ungraded, excl U.S. prime and choice	lb	3.11	7/01	11r
Sirloin steak, graded and ungraded, excl U.S. prime and choice	lb	4.23	7/01	11r
Spaghetti and macaroni	lb	0.78	7/01	11r
Steak, round, U.S. choice, boneless	lb	3.56	7/01	11r
Steak, sirloin, U.S. choice, boneless	lb	5.65	7/01	11r
Strawberries, dry pint	12 oz	1.50	7/01	11r
Sugar and other sweets, expenditures on	yr	99	1999	30r
Sugar, white, 33-80 ounce package	lb	0.39	7/01	11r
Sugar, white, all sizes	lb	0.42	7/01	11r
Tobacco products and smoking supplies purchases	yr	288	1999	30r
Tomatoes, field grown	lb	1.43	7/01	11r
Tuna, light, chunk	lb	1.77	7/01	11r
Turkey, frozen, whole	lb	1.05	7/01	11r
Goods and Services				
B&B Japanese maple (acer japonicum)	gal	79.98-99.00	4/00	93r
Boxwood (buxus)	2 gal	12.98-18.99	4/00	93r
Christmas tree, noble fir		40-60	2000	65s
Daylilly (hemerocallis)	gal	7.96-11.00	4/00	93r
Flat of annuals		13.99-27.99	4/00	93r

Values are in dollars or fractions of dollars. In the column headed *Ref*, references are shown to sources. Each reference is followed by a letter. These refer to the geographical level for which data were reported: s=State, r=Region, and c=City or metro. The abbreviation *ex* is used to mean *except* or *excluding*; *exp* stands for *expenditures*. For other abbreviations and further explanations, please see the Introduction.

Texarcana, TX-AR - continued

Item	Per	Value	Date	Ref.
Goods and Services				
Fountain grass (pennisetum)	gal	6.96-9.00	4/00	93r
Hanging basket (10 in)		9.99-24.99	4/00	93r
Hardy geranium (geranium)	gal	5.96-8.00	4/00	93r
Hosta (hosta)	gal	8.96-12.99	4/00	93r
Lilac (syrubga vulgaris)	2 gal	13.00-19.99	4/00	93r
Rhododendron (rhododendron)	2 gal	12.98-29.99	4/00	93r
Sage (salvia)	gal	5.96-8.00	4/00	93r
Wintercreeper euonymus (euonymus fortunei)	2 gal	13.00-18.99	4/00	93r
Hunting license	yr	19.00	4/01	34s
Health Care				
Cardiac catheterization, ave hospital/ physician charges		20140	1998	77s
Childbirth, Cesarean delivery		11587	1997	13r
Childbirth, vaginal delivery		6725	1997	13r
Drugs, expenditures on	yr	399	1999	30r
Health care purchases	yr	1971	1999	30r
Health insurance expenditures	yr	933	1999	30r
Hysterectomy, laproscopically-assisted, ave hospital/physician charges		15700	1998	76s
Hysterectomy, vaginal, ave hospital and physician charges		12180	1998	76s
Medicaid dispensing fee		5.27	1999	87s
Medical services expenditures	yr	547	1999	30r
Medical supplies, expenditures on	yr	91	1999	30r
Household Goods				
Floor coverings, expenditures on	yr	44	1999	30r
Furniture, expenditures on	yr	335	1999	30r
Household furnishings and equipment purchases	yr	1328	1999	30r
Household textiles, expenditures on	yr	89	1999	30r
Laundry and cleaning supplies, expenditures on	yr	113	1999	30r
Housing				
Home price, existing, ave		160100	10/00	90r
Home value, median		112000	2001	53s
Household operation expenditures	yr	553	1999	30r
Housekeeping supplies purchases	yr	473	1999	30r
Housing, expenditures on	yr	10303	1999	30r
Maintenance, repairs, insurance expenditures	yr	699	1999	30r
Monthly rental value of owned home	mos	505	1999	30r
Owned dwellings, expenditures own	yr	3465	1999	30r
Rent expenditures	yr	1641	1999	30r
Rental unit, 1 bedroom, with utilities	mos	380	4/01	41c
Rental unit, 2 bedroom, with utilities	mos	464	4/01	41c
Rental unit, 3 bedroom, with utilities	mos	612	4/01	41c
Rental unit, 4 bedroom, with utilities	mos	649	4/01	41c
Shelter, expenditures on	yr	5467	1999	30r
Insurance and Pensions				
Life and other personal insurance purchases	yr	414	1999	30r
Pensions and Social Security, expenditures on	yr	2635	1999	30r
Personal insurance and pensions, expenditures on	yr	3048	1999	30r
Legal Fees				
Divorce, filing fee		150.00-200.00	4/01	35s
Driver's license fee	orig	24.00	1999	48s
Driver's license fee	renew	20.00	1999	48s
Fishing license	yr	19.00	4/01	34s

Texarcana, TX-AR - continued

Item	Per	Value	Date	Ref.
Personal Goods				
Personal care products and services purchases	yr	393	1999	30r
Personal Services				
Personal services, household, expenditures on	yr	258	1999	30r
Pets				
Pets, toys, and playground equipment, expenditures on	yr	306	1999	30r
Taxes				
Federal income taxes paid	yr	2047	1999	30r
Personal taxes, expenditures on	yr	2554	1999	30r
Property taxes paid	yr	726	1999	30r
State and local income taxes paid	yr	363	1999	30r
Transportation				
Cars and trucks, new, expenditures on	yr	1648	1999	30r
Cars and trucks, used, expenditures on	yr	1651	1999	30r
Diesel at the pump	gal	1.18	10/99	73s
Gasoline and motor oil purchases	yr	1052	1999	30r
Gasoline before-tax price (cents)	gal	101.30	10/00	43s
Maintenance and repair expenditures	yr	621	1999	30r
Public transportation, expenditures on	yr	298	1999	30r
Transportation purchases	yr	6738	1999	30r
Vehicle expenses, miscellaneous, purchases	yr	2033	1999	30r
Vehicle insurance payments	yr	696	1999	30r
Vehicle purchases (net outlay)	yr	3354	1999	30r
Vehicle rental, lease expenditures	yr	352	1999	30r
Utilities				
Electrical bill, average	mos	87.17	9/00	9s
Electricity, expenditures on	yr	1115	1999	30r
Electricity cost, average	KWh	6.48	9/00	9s
Water and other public services, expenditures on	yr	298	1999	30r
Weddings				
Wedding (national average cost)		19936	2000	33r
Attendants' gifts		321	1998	33r
Bridal attendants' apparel (5 persons)		824	2000	33r
Bride's headpiece/veil		173	1998	33r
Bride's wedding dress		859	1998	33r
Clergy, religious facility fee		242	1998	33r
Engagement ring		3177	1998	33r
Flowers		789	1998	33r
Groom's formalwear rental		99	2000	33r
Limousine		410	1998	33r
Marriage license cost		36.00	4/01	35s
Men's formalwear (ushers, best man)		469	2000	33r
Mother of bride apparel		241	2000	33r
Music		866	1998	33r
Photography and videography		1368	1998	33r
Rehearsal dinner		728	1998	33r
Wedding invitations and announcements		341	1998	33r
Wedding reception		7968	2000	33r
Wedding rings (bride and groom)		1060	1998	33r

Toledo, OH

Item	Per	Value	Date	Ref.
Average annual expenditures	yr	35369	1999	30r
Composite, ACCRA index		101.60	3/01	4c
Alcoholic Beverages				
Alcoholic beverage purchases	yr	304	1999	30r
Beer, Heineken, 12-oz, ex deposit	6	7.49	3/01	4c
J & B Scotch	750-ml	21.40	3/01	4c
Malt beverages, all types, all sizes, any origin	16 oz	0.93	7/01	11r
Wine, Livingston or Gallo, Chablis blanc	1.5 liter	6.49	3/01	4c
Wine, red and white table, all sizes, any origin	liter	7.04	7/01	11r

Values are in dollars or fractions of dollars. In the column headed *Ref*, references are shown to sources. Each reference is followed by a letter. These refer to the geographical level for which data were reported: s=State, r=Region, and c=City or metro. The abbreviation *ex* is used to mean *except* or *excluding*; *exp* stands for expenditures. For other abbreviations and further explanations, please see the Introduction.

Toledo, OH - continued

Item	Per	Value	Date	Ref.
Appliances				
Appliance repair, service call, washing machine	min lab chg	54.26	3/01	4c
Major appliances, expenditures on	yr	165	1999	30r
Small appliances, housewares, expenditures on	yr	90	1999	30r
Banking and Money				
Mortgage interest and charges paid	yr	2277	1999	30r
Mortgage principal paid on owned property	yr	1230	1999	30r
Mortgage rate, incl. points and orig. fee, 30-yr. conv. fixed or ARM	mos	7.33	3/01	4c
Vehicle finance charges paid	yr	328	1999	30r
Business Expenses				
Business travel, car rental	day	55	2001	3c
Business travel, food	day	42	2001	3c
Business travel, hotel	day	91	2001	3c
Charity				
Cash contributions, expenditures	yr	1126	1999	30r
Child Care				
Child raising cost, total, age 0-2	yr	7890	1999	60r
Child raising cost, total, age 3-5	yr	8130	1999	60r
Child raising cost, total, age 6-8	yr	8170	1999	60r
Child raising cost, total, age 9-11	yr	8190	1999	60r
Child raising cost, total, age 12-14	yr	8890	1999	60r
Child raising cost, total, age 15-17	yr	9050	1999	60r
Child's child care and education, age 0-2	yr	1240	1999	60r
Child's child care and education, age 3-5	yr	1370	1999	60r
Child's child care and education, age 6-8	yr	880	1999	60r
Child's child care and education, age 9-11	yr	570	1999	60r
Child's child care and education, age 12-14	yr	420	1999	60r
Child's child care and education, age 15-17	yr	720	1999	60r
Child's clothing, age 0-2	yr	410	1999	60r
Child's clothing, age 3-5	yr	400	1999	60r
Child's clothing, age 6-8	yr	450	1999	60r
Child's clothing, age 9-11	yr	500	1999	60r
Child's clothing, age 12-14	yr	840	1999	60r
Child's clothing, age 15-17	yr	740	1999	60r
Child's food, age 0-2	yr	960	1999	60r
Child's food, age 3-5	yr	1120	1999	60r
Child's food, age 6-8	yr	1430	1999	60r
Child's food, age 9-11	yr	1710	1999	60r
Child's food, age 12-14	yr	1710	1999	60r
Child's food, age 15-17	yr	1920	1999	60r
Child's health care, age 0-2	yr	520	1999	60r
Child's health care, age 3-5	yr	500	1999	60r
Child's health care, age 6-8	yr	570	1999	60r
Child's health care, age 9-11	yr	610	1999	60r
Child's health care, age 12-14	yr	630	1999	60r
Child's health care, age 15-17	yr	650	1999	60r
Child's housing, age 0-2	yr	2860	1999	60r
Child's housing, age 3-5	yr	2840	1999	60r
Child's housing, age 6-8	yr	2800	1999	60r
Child's housing, age 9-11	yr	2650	1999	60r
Child's housing, age 12-14	yr	2840	1999	60r
Child's housing, age 15-17	yr	2440	1999	60r
Child's personal care, reading, age 0-2	yr	880	1999	60r
Child's personal care, reading, age 3-5	yr	900	1999	60r
Child's personal care, reading, age 6-8	yr	930	1999	60r
Child's personal care, reading, age 9-11	yr	970	1999	60r
Child's personal care, reading, age 12-14	yr	1150	1999	60r
Child's personal care, reading, age 15-17	yr	920	1999	60r
Clothing				
Apparel and services purchases	yr	1607	1999	30r
Boys' brief, cotton	3	6.98	3/01	4c
Boys, 2 to 15, expenditures on	yr	91	1999	30r
Children under 2, expenditures on	yr	59	1999	30r
Footwear, expenditures on	yr	285	1999	30r
Girls, 2 to 15, expenditures on	yr	116	1999	30r
Men and boys, expenditures on	yr	433	1999	30r
Men, 16 and over, expenditures on	yr	341	1999	30r

Toledo, OH - continued

Item	Per	Value	Date	Ref.
Clothing - continued				
Shirt, man's dress shirt		24.95	3/01	4c
Slacks, man's "No Wrinkles" khaki		31.79	3/01	4c
Women, 16 and over, expenditures on	yr	490	1999	30r
Communications				
Cable modem installation, Adelphi		54.90	6/99	103s
Cable modem installation, Media One		100.00	6/99	103s
Cable modem installation, Time Warner		75.00-225.00	6/99	103s
Cable modem rate, cable subscriber, Adelphi	mos	34.95	6/99	103s
Cable modem rate, cable subscriber, Media One	mos	34.95-39.95	6/99	103s
Cable modem rate, cable subscriber, Time Warner	mos	39.95-49.95	6/99	103s
Cable modem rate, non-cable subscriber, Adelphi	mos	44.95	6/99	103s
Cable modem rate, non-cable subscriber, Media One	mos	49.95	6/99	103s
Cable modem rate, non-cable subscriber, Time Warner	mos	39.95-54.95	6/99	103s
Newspaper subscription, daily and Sunday delivery	mos	11.30	3/01	4c
Phone line, single, business, field visit	inst.	56.32	12/97	17s
Phone line, single, business, no field visit	inst.	56.32	12/97	17s
Phone line, single, residence, field visit	inst.	31.10	12/97	17s
Phone line, single, residence, no field visit	inst.	31.10	12/97	17s
Postage and stationery, expenditures on	yr	140	1999	30r
Postal rate, express mail, up to half-pound		12.45	7/01	108r
Postal rate, letter, first class, first ounce		0.34	7/01	108r
Postal rate, letter, two ounces		0.57	7/01	108r
Postal rate, post card		0.21	7/01	108r
Postal rate, priority mail, two pounds		3.95	7/01	108r
Postal rate, priority mail, up to one pound		3.50	7/01	108r
Telephone bill, family of three	mos	19.27	3/01	4c
Telephone services, expenditures on	yr	830	1999	30r
Education				
Board, 4-year private college/university	yr	2414	1996	38s
Board, 4-year public college/university	yr	2181	1996	38s
Education expenditures	yr	583	1999	30r
Room, 4-year private college/university	yr	2349	1996	38s
Room, 4-year public college/university	yr	2386	1996	38s
Total cost, 4-year private college/university	yr	17139	1996	38s
Total cost, 4-year public college/university	yr	8169	1996	38s
Tuition, 2-year public college/university, in state	yr	2261	1996	38s
Tuition, 4-year private college/university, in state	yr	12377	1996	38s
Tuition, 4-year public college/university	yr	3603	1996	38s
Energy and Fuels				
Electricity	500 KWhs	46.59	7/01	11r
Energy, combined forms, 2400 sq ft	mos	158.41	3/01	4c
Energy, exc. electricity, 2400 sq ft	mos	68.07	3/01	4c
Fuel oil #2	gal	1.27	7/01	11r
Fuel oil and other fuels, expenditures on	yr	68	1999	30r
Gas, natural, commercial rate	1000 cf	8.65	11/00	88s
Gas, regular unleaded, cash, self-service	gal	1.35	3/01	4c
Gasoline, unleaded midgrade	gal	1.79	7/01	11r
Gasoline, unleaded premium	gal	1.86	7/01	11r
Gasoline, unleaded regular	gal	1.58	7/01	11r
Natural gas, expenditures on	yr	389	1999	30r
Utility (piped) gas, therm		0.81	7/01	11r
Utility (piped) gas, 40 therms		38.01	7/01	11r
Utility (piped) gas, 100 therms		81.75	7/01	11r
Entertainment				
Bowling, Saturday evening rate	line	2.71	3/01	4c
Entertainment purchases	yr	1984	1999	30r
Fees and admissions paid	yr	444	1999	30r
Monopoly game, Parker Brothers', No. 9	game	10.39	3/01	4c
Movie, first-run, Saturday, evening	adm.	8.50	3/01	4c

Values are in dollars or fractions of dollars. In the column headed *Ref*, references are shown to sources. Each reference is followed by a letter. These refer to the geographical level for which data were reported: s=State, r=Region, and c=City or metro. The abbreviation *ex* is used to mean *except* or *excluding*; *exp* stands for *expenditures*. For other abbreviations and further explanations, please see the Introduction.

Toledo, OH - continued

Item	Per	Value	Date	Ref.
Entertainment				
Television, radios, sound equipment, expenditures on	yr	580	1999	30r
Tennis balls, yellow, Wilson or Penn, 3	can	1.99	3/01	4c
Funerals				
Cosmetology, hair, other preparation		178.32	1/99	78r
Embalming		408.19	1/99	78r
Funeral at funeral home		362.13	1/99	78r
Professional service charges		1375.51	1/99	78r
Transfer of remains to funeral home		155.92	1/99	78r
Visitation/viewing		294.38	1/99	78r
Groceries				
Groceries, ACCRA Index		110.50	3/01	4c
Antibiotic ointment, Polysporin	0.5 oz	4.55	3/01	4c
Baby food, strained vegetables or fruit, lowest price	4-4.5 oz	0.44	3/01	4c
Bacon, sliced	lb	3.15	7/01	11r
Bakery products, expenditures on	yr	281	1999	30r
Bananas	lb	0.57	3/01	4c
Bananas	lb	0.48	7/01	11r
Beans, dried, any type, all sizes	lb	0.61	7/01	11r
Beef for stew, boneless	lb	3.08	7/01	11r
Beef or hamburger, ground	lb	1.79	3/01	4c
Beef, expenditures on	yr	217	1999	30r
Bologna, all beef or mixed	lb	2.52	7/01	11r
Bread, white	loaf	1.09	3/01	4c
Bread, white, pan	lb	1.06	7/01	11r
Broccoli	lb	0.91	7/01	11r
Butter, salted, grade AA, stick	lb	3.04	7/01	11r
Butter, yoghurt, cheese, etc, expenditures on	yr	183	1999	30r
Cereals and bakery product purchases	yr	430	1999	30r
Cereals and cereal products, expenditures on	yr	149	1999	30r
Cheese, Kraft grated Parmesan	8 oz	3.92	3/01	4c
Chicken, fresh, whole	lb	1.07	7/01	11r
Chicken, whole fryer	lb	1.13	3/01	4c
Chops, boneless	lb	3.64	7/01	11r
Chuck roast, U.S. choice, boneless	lb	2.47	7/01	11r
Cigarettes, Winston, Kings	carton	29.31	3/01	4c
Coffee, 100%, ground roast, all sizes	lb	2.69	7/01	11r
Coffee, vacuum-packed	13 oz	3.29	3/01	4c
Cookies, chocolate chip	lb	2.87	7/01	11r
Corn Flakes, Kellogg's or Post Toasties	18 oz	3.27	3/01	4c
Corn, frozen, whole kernel, lowest price	16 oz	1.04	3/01	4c
Dairy product purchases	yr	304	1999	30r
Eggs, expenditures on	yr	26	1999	30r
Eggs, Grade A or AA	dozen	1.07	3/01	4c
Eggs, grade A, large	dozen	0.88	7/01	11r
Fats and oils, expenditures on	yr	75	1999	30r
Fish and seafood, expenditures on	yr	72	1999	30r
Food (excl fruit and vegetables), eaten at home, purchases	yr	887	1999	30r
Food cooked on trips, expenditures on	yr	44	1999	30r
Food purchases	yr	4802	1999	30r
Food purchases, eaten away from home	yr	2069	1999	30r
Food purchases, food eaten at home	yr	2733	1999	30r
Fresh fruits, expenditures on	yr	138	1999	30r
Fresh milk and cream, expenditures on	yr	120	1999	30r
Fresh vegetables, expenditures on	yr	126	1999	30r
Grapefruit	lb	0.66	7/01	11r
Grapes, Thompson, seedless	lb	1.64	7/01	11r
Ground beef, 100% beef	lb	1.64	7/01	11r
Ground beef, lean and extra lean	lb	2.16	7/01	11r
Ground chuck, 100% beef	lb	2.13	7/01	11r
Ham, boneless, excl canned	lb	2.62	7/01	11r
Ice cream, prepackaged, bulk, regular	1/2 gal	3.35	7/01	11r
Lemons	lb	1.19	7/01	11r
Lettuce, iceberg	head	1.05	3/01	4c
Lettuce, iceberg	lb	0.73	7/01	11r
Margarine, Blue Bonnet or Parkay, stick	lb	0.91	3/01	4c
Margarine, soft, tubs	lb	0.89	7/01	11r
Meats, poultry, fish, and egg purchases	yr	671	1999	30r

Toledo, OH - continued

Item	Per	Value	Date	Ref.
Groceries - continued				
Milk, fresh, whole, fortified	gal	2.71	7/01	11r
Milk, whole	1/2 gal	1.89	3/01	4c
Nonalcoholic beverages, expenditures on	yr	239	1999	30r
Orange juice, Minute Maid frozen	12 oz	1.66	3/01	4c
Oranges, Navel	lb	0.80	7/01	11r
Oranges, Valencia	lb	0.66	7/01	11r
Peaches, halves or slices, Hunt's, Del Monte, or Libby's	29 oz	1.87	3/01	4c
Pears, Anjou	lb	0.93	7/01	11r
Peas, green, Del Monte or Green Giant	15 oz	0.86	3/01	4c
Pork chops, center cut, bone-in	lb	3.63	7/01	11r
Pork, expenditures on	yr	150	1999	30r
Potato chips	16 oz	3.52	7/01	11r
Potatoes, frozen, french fried	lb	1.08	7/01	11r
Potatoes, white or red	10 lb	2.59	3/01	4c
Potatoes, white, all types	lb	0.33	7/01	11r
Poultry, expenditures on	yr	108	1999	30r
Processed fruits, expenditures on	yr	98	1999	30r
Processed vegetables, expenditures on	yr	80	1999	30r
Round roast, U.S. choice, boneless	lb	3.07	7/01	11r
Round steak, graded and ungraded, excl U.S. prime and choice	lb	3.41	7/01	11r
Sausage, Jimmy Dean/Owens pork	lb	2.81	3/01	4c
Shortening, vegetable oil blends	lb	1.13	7/01	11r
Shortening, vegetable, Crisco	3 lb	3.65	3/01	4c
Soft drink, Coca Cola, ex deposit	2 liter	1.29	3/01	4c
Spaghetti and macaroni	lb	0.80	7/01	11r
Steak, round, U.S. choice, boneless	lb	3.23	7/01	11r
Steak, T-bone	lb	6.96	3/01	4c
Steak, T-bone, U.S. choice, bone-in	lb	6.68	7/01	11r
Strawberries, dry pint	12 oz	1.32	7/01	11r
Sugar and other sweets, expenditures on	yr	114	1999	30r
Sugar, cane or beet	4 lbs	1.87	3/01	4c
Sugar, white, 33-80 ounce package	lb	0.42	7/01	11r
Sugar, white, all sizes	lb	0.43	7/01	11r
Tobacco products and smoking supplies purchases	yr	331	1999	30r
Tomatoes, field grown	lb	1.46	7/01	11r
Tomatoes, Hunt's or Del Monte	14.5 oz	0.99	3/01	4c
Tuna, chunk, light	6 oz	0.59	3/01	4c
Tuna, light, chunk	lb	1.80	7/01	11r
Turkey, frozen, whole	lb	1.15	7/01	11r
Goods and Services				
Miscellaneous goods and services, ACCRA Index		100.00	3/01	4c
B&B Japanese maple (acer japonicum)	gal	29.99-169.99	4/00	93r
Boxwood (buxus)	2 gal	18.99-39.99	4/00	93r
Daylilly (hemerocallis)	gal	4.99-25.00	4/00	93r
Flat of annuals		11.98-24.99	4/00	93r
Fountain grass (pennisetum)	gal	5.98-12.98	4/00	93r
Hanging basket (10 in)		12.99-27.99	4/00	93r
Hardy geranium (geranium)	gal	7.99-9.99	4/00	93r
Hosta (hosta)	gal	6.00-25.00	4/00	93r
Lilac (syrubga vulgaris)	2 gal	14.99-24.99	4/00	93r
Miscellaneous purchases	yr	865	1999	30r
Rhododendron (rhododendron)	2 gal	23.98-42.99	4/00	93r
Sage (salvia)	gal	6.00-9.99	4/00	93r
Wintercreeper euonymus (euonymus fortunei)	2 gal	16.00-169.99	4/00	93r
Hunting license	yr	15.00	4/01	34s

Values are in dollars or fractions of dollars. In the column headed *Ref*, references are shown to sources. Each reference is followed by a letter. These refer to the geographical level for which data were reported: s=State, r=Region, and c=City or metro. The abbreviation *ex* is used to mean *except* or *excluding*; *exp* stands for expenditures. For other abbreviations and further explanations, please see the Introduction.

Toledo, OH - continued

Item	Per	Value	Date	Ref.
Health Care				
Health care, ACCRA Index		104.10	3/01	4c
Cardiac catheterization, ave hospital/ physician charges		11760	1998	77s
Childbirth, Cesarean delivery		10722	1997	13r
Childbirth, vaginal delivery		6223	1997	13r
Dentist's fee, adult teeth cleaning and periodic oral exam	visit	70.60	3/01	4c
Doctor's fee, routine exam, established patient	visit	67.90	3/01	4c
Drugs, expenditures on	yr	394	1999	30r
Health care purchases	yr	2048	1999	30r
Health insurance expenditures	yr	978	1999	30r
Home health care aide cost, licensed agency	hour	15	2000	82c
Hospital care, private room	day	503.71	3/01	4c
Hysterectomy, laproscopically-assisted, ave hospital/physician charges		11730	1998	76s
Hysterectomy, vaginal, ave hospital and physician charges		9640	1998	76s
Medicaid dispensing fee		3.70	1999	87s
Medical services expenditures	yr	554	1999	30r
Medical supplies, expenditures on	yr	122	1999	30r
Nursing home costs, private room	day	128	2000	82c
Nursing home stay, private room	day	128	2000	81c
Plastic surgery, breast augmentation		3184	2000	7r
Plastic surgery, breast lift		3585	2000	7r
Plastic surgery, facelift		4999	2000	7r
Plastic surgery, hair transplantation		3105	2000	7r
Plastic surgery, lip augmentation		1290	2000	7r
Plastic surgery, lower body lift		8135	2000	7r
Plastic surgery, thigh lift		3839	2000	7r
Household Goods				
Dishwashing powder, Cascade	50 oz	4.02	3/01	4c
Floor coverings, expenditures on	yr	52	1999	30r
Furniture, expenditures on	yr	344	1999	30r
Household furnishings and equipment purchases	yr	1475	1999	30r
Household textiles, expenditures on	yr	109	1999	30r
Laundry and cleaning supplies, expenditures on	yr	134	1999	30r
Tissues, facial, Kleenex brand	175	1.48	3/01	4c
Housing				
Housing, ACCRA Index		91.60	3/01	4c
Home, 2200 sq ft, 4-br, 2-bath, 2-car garage, average		209995	2000	47c
Home price, existing, ave		144400	10/00	90r
Home value, median		96000	2001	53s
House, 2400 sq ft, 8000 sq ft lot, new, urban, utilities	total	192820	3/01	4c
House payment, principal and interest, 25% down payment	mos	994	3/01	4c
Household operation expenditures	yr	542	1999	30r
Housekeeping supplies purchases	yr	508	1999	30r
Lodging expenditures	yr	430	1999	30r
Maintenance, repairs, insurance expenditures	yr	853	1999	30r
Monthly rental value of owned home	mos	547	1999	30r
Owned dwellings, expenditures own	yr	4282	1999	30r
Rent expenditures	yr	1558	1999	30r
Rent, apartment, 2 br, 1 1/2-2 baths, unfurn, 950 sq ft, water	mos	506	3/01	4c
Rental unit, 1 bedroom, with utilities	mos	444	4/01	41c
Rental unit, 2 bedroom, with utilities	mos	542	4/01	41c
Rental unit, 3 bedroom, with utilities	mos	698	4/01	41c
Rental unit, 4 bedroom, with utilities	mos	758	4/01	41c
Shelter, expenditures on	yr	6270	1999	30r
Insurance and Pensions				
Life and other personal insurance purchases	yr	387	1999	30r
Pensions and Social Security, expenditures on	yr	2968	1999	30r

Toledo, OH - continued

Item	Per	Value	Date	Ref.
Legal Fees				
Divorce, filing fee		100.00	4/01	35s
Driver's license fee	renew	14.50	1999	48s
Driver's license fee	orig	14.50	1999	48s
Fishing license	yr	15.00	4/01	34s
Personal Goods				
Personal care products and services purchases	yr	385	1999	30r
Shampoo, Alberto VO5	15 oz	1.11	3/01	4c
Toothpaste, Crest or Colgate	6-7 oz	2.27	3/01	4c
Personal Services				
Dry cleaning, man's 2-pc suit		8.76	3/01	4c
Man's haircut, barbershop, no styling		10.90	3/01	4c
Personal services, household, expenditures on	yr	300	1999	30r
Woman's shampoo, trim, blow-dry, no style-change		28.75	3/01	4c
Pets				
Pets, toys, and playground equipment, expenditures on	yr	375	1999	30r
Restaurant Food				
Chicken, fried, thigh and drumstick, KFC/ Church's		2.46	3/01	4c
Hamburger with cheese, McDonald's	1/4 lb	2.29	3/01	4c
Pizza, Pizza Hut or Pizza Inn	11-12 in	7.99	3/01	4c
Taxes				
Federal income taxes paid	yr	2326	1999	30r
Personal taxes, expenditures on	yr	3223	1999	30r
Property taxes paid	yr	1152	1999	30r
State and local income taxes paid	yr	753	1999	30r
Transportation				
Transportation, ACCRA Index		101.50	3/01	4c
Bus fare, one-way	trip	0.75	2000	1c
Bus fare, to central business district	1-way	0.85	3/01	4c
Cars and trucks, new, expenditures on	yr	1280	1999	30r
Cars and trucks, used, expenditures on	yr	1763	1999	30r
Diesel at the pump	gal	1.25	10/99	73s
Gasoline and motor oil purchases	yr	1036	1999	30r
Gasoline before-tax price (cents)	gal	109.50	10/00	43s
Maintenance and repair expenditures	yr	594	1999	30r
Public transportation, expenditures on	yr	341	1999	30r
Tire balance, computer or spin balance, front	wheel	9.17	3/01	4c
Transportation purchases	yr	6617	1999	30r
Vehicle expenses, miscellaneous, purchases	yr	2159	1999	30r
Vehicle insurance payments	yr	701	1999	30r
Vehicle purchases (net outlay)	yr	3081	1999	30r
Vehicle rental, lease expenditures	yr	536	1999	30r
Utilities				
Utilities, ACCRA Index		124.10	3/01	4c
Electrical bill, average	mos	72.83	9/00	9s
Electricity, expenditures on	yr	841	1999	30r
Electricity, summer, 250 KWh	mos	30.49	2/96	96c
Electricity, summer, 500 KWh	mos	57.02	2/96	96c
Electricity, summer, 750 KWh	mos	83.54	2/96	96c
Electricity, summer, 1000 KWh	mos	110.07	2/96	96c
Electricity and other, mixed, 2400 sq ft, new home	mos	90.34	3/01	4c
Electricity cost, average	KWh	6.59	9/00	9s
Utilities, fuels, and public services purchased	yr	2401	1999	30r
Water and other public services, expenditures on	yr	273	1999	30r
Weddings				
Wedding (national average cost)		19936	2000	33r
Wedding (regional average total cost)		16195	1997	110r
Attendants' gifts		321	1998	33r
Bridal attendants' apparel (5 persons)		824	2000	33r
Bride's headpiece/veil		173	1998	33r
Bride's wedding dress		859	1998	33r
Clergy, religious facility fee		242	1998	33r

Values are in dollars or fractions of dollars. In the column headed *Ref*, references are shown to sources. Each reference is followed by a letter. These refer to the geographical level for which data were reported: s=State, r=Region, and c=City or metro. The abbreviation *ex* is used to mean *except* or *excluding*; *exp* stands for expenditures. For other abbreviations and further explanations, please see the Introduction.

Toledo, OH - continued

Item	Per	Value	Date	Ref.
Weddings				
Engagement ring		3177	1998	33r
Flowers		789	1998	33r
Groom's formalwear rental		99	2000	33r
Limousine		410	1998	33r
Marriage license cost		45.00	4/01	35s
Men's formalwear (ushers, best man)		469	2000	33r
Mother of bride apparel		241	2000	33r
Music		866	1998	33r
Photography and videography		1368	1998	33r
Rehearsal dinner		728	1998	33r
Wedding invitations and announcements		341	1998	33r
Wedding reception		7968	2000	33r
Wedding rings (bride and groom)		1060	1998	33r

Topeka, KS

Item	Per	Value	Date	Ref.
Average annual expenditures	yr	35369	1999	30r
Composite, ACCRA index		97.50	3/01	4c
Alcoholic Beverages				
Alcoholic beverage purchases	yr	304	1999	30r
Beer, Heineken, 12-oz, ex deposit	6	7.30	3/01	4c
J & B Scotch	750-ml	21.29	3/01	4c
Malt beverages, all types, all sizes, any origin	16 oz	0.93	7/01	11r
Wine, Livingston or Gallo, Chablis blanc	1.5 liter	6.33	3/01	4c
Wine, red and white table, all sizes, any origin	liter	7.04	7/01	11r
Appliances				
Appliance repair, service call, washing machine	min lab chg	35.00	3/01	4c
Major appliances, expenditures on	yr	165	1999	30r
Small appliances, housewares, expenditures on	yr	90	1999	30r
Banking and Money				
Mortgage interest and charges paid	yr	2277	1999	30r
Mortgage principal paid on owned property	yr	1230	1999	30r
Mortgage rate, incl. points and orig. fee, 30-yr. conv. fixed or ARM	mos	7.07	3/01	4c
Vehicle finance charges paid	yr	328	1999	30r
Charity				
Cash contributions, expenditures	yr	1126	1999	30r
Child Care				
Child raising cost, total, age 0-2	yr	7890	1999	60r
Child raising cost, total, age 3-5	yr	8130	1999	60r
Child raising cost, total, age 6-8	yr	8170	1999	60r
Child raising cost, total, age 9-11	yr	8190	1999	60r
Child raising cost, total, age 12-14	yr	8890	1999	60r
Child raising cost, total, age 15-17	yr	9050	1999	60r
Child's child care and education, age 0-2	yr	1240	1999	60r
Child's child care and education, age 3-5	yr	1370	1999	60r
Child's child care and education, age 6-8	yr	880	1999	60r
Child's child care and education, age 9-11	yr	570	1999	60r
Child's child care and education, age 12-14	yr	420	1999	60r
Child's child care and education, age 15-17	yr	720	1999	60r
Child's clothing, age 0-2	yr	410	1999	60r
Child's clothing, age 3-5	yr	400	1999	60r
Child's clothing, age 6-8	yr	450	1999	60r
Child's clothing, age 9-11	yr	500	1999	60r
Child's clothing, age 12-14	yr	840	1999	60r
Child's clothing, age 15-17	yr	740	1999	60r
Child's food, age 0-2	yr	960	1999	60r
Child's food, age 3-5	yr	1120	1999	60r
Child's food, age 6-8	yr	1430	1999	60r
Child's food, age 9-11	yr	1710	1999	60r
Child's food, age 12-14	yr	1710	1999	60r
Child's food, age 15-17	yr	1920	1999	60r
Child's health care, age 0-2	yr	520	1999	60r
Child's health care, age 3-5	yr	500	1999	60r
Child's health care, age 6-8	yr	570	1999	60r
Child's health care, age 9-11	yr	610	1999	60r

Topeka, KS - continued

Item	Per	Value	Date	Ref.
Child Care - continued				
Child's health care, age 12-14	yr	630	1999	60r
Child's health care, age 15-17	yr	650	1999	60r
Child's housing, age 0-2	yr	2860	1999	60r
Child's housing, age 3-5	yr	2840	1999	60r
Child's housing, age 6-8	yr	2800	1999	60r
Child's housing, age 9-11	yr	2650	1999	60r
Child's housing, age 12-14	yr	2840	1999	60r
Child's housing, age 15-17	yr	2440	1999	60r
Child's personal care, reading, age 0-2	yr	880	1999	60r
Child's personal care, reading, age 3-5	yr	900	1999	60r
Child's personal care, reading, age 6-8	yr	930	1999	60r
Child's personal care, reading, age 9-11	yr	970	1999	60r
Child's personal care, reading, age 12-14	yr	1150	1999	60r
Child's personal care, reading, age 15-17	yr	920	1999	60r
Clothing				
Apparel and services purchases	yr	1607	1999	30r
Boys' brief, cotton	3	3.53	3/01	4c
Boys, 2 to 15, expenditures on	yr	91	1999	30r
Children under 2, expenditures on	yr	59	1999	30r
Footwear, expenditures on	yr	285	1999	30r
Girls, 2 to 15, expenditures on	yr	116	1999	30r
Men and boys, expenditures on	yr	433	1999	30r
Men, 16 and over, expenditures on	yr	341	1999	30r
Shirt, man's dress shirt		23.57	3/01	4c
Slacks, man's "No Wrinkles" khaki		37.20	3/01	4c
Women, 16 and over, expenditures on	yr	490	1999	30r
Communications				
Newspaper subscription, daily and Sunday delivery	mos	12.58	3/01	4c
Phone line, single, business, field visit	inst.	57.40	12/97	17s
Phone line, single, business, no field visit	inst.	57.40	12/97	17s
Phone line, single, residence, field visit	inst.	39.00	12/97	17s
Phone line, single, residence, no field visit	inst.	39.00	12/97	17s
Postage and stationery, expenditures on	yr	140	1999	30r
Postal rate, express mail, up to half-pound		12.45	7/01	108r
Postal rate, letter, first class, first ounce		0.34	7/01	108r
Postal rate, letter, two ounces		0.57	7/01	108r
Postal rate, post card		0.21	7/01	108r
Postal rate, priority mail, two pounds		3.95	7/01	108r
Postal rate, priority mail, up to one pound		3.50	7/01	108r
Telephone bill, business, basic rate	mos	22.33	12/97	18c
Telephone bill, family of three	mos	23.79	3/01	4c
Telephone bill, residential, basic rate	mos	11.27	12/97	18c
Telephone services, expenditures on	yr	830	1999	30r
Education				
Board, 4-year private college/university	yr	2183	1996	38s
Board, 4-year public college/university	yr	1841	1996	38s
Education expenditures	yr	583	1999	30r
Room, 4-year private college/university	yr	1582	1996	38s
Room, 4-year public college/university	yr	1731	1996	38s
Total cost, 4-year private college/university	yr	12400	1996	38s
Total cost, 4-year public college/university	yr	5691	1996	38s
Tuition, 2-year public college/university, in state	yr	1147	1996	38s
Tuition, 4-year private college/university, in state	yr	8634	1996	38s
Tuition, 4-year public college/university	yr	2120	1996	38s
Energy and Fuels				
Electricity	500 KWhs	46.59	7/01	11r
Energy, combined forms, 2400 sq ft	mos	126.43	3/01	4c
Energy, exc. electricity, 2400 sq ft	mos	83.19	3/01	4c
Fuel oil #2	gal	1.27	7/01	11r
Fuel oil and other fuels, expenditures on	yr	68	1999	30r
Gas, regular unleaded, cash, self-service	gal	1.32	3/01	4c
Gasoline, unleaded midgrade	gal	1.79	7/01	11r
Gasoline, unleaded premium	gal	1.86	7/01	11r
Gasoline, unleaded regular	gal	1.58	7/01	11r
Natural gas, expenditures on	yr	389	1999	30r
Utility (piped) gas, therm		0.81	7/01	11r

Values are in dollars or fractions of dollars. In the column headed *Ref*, references are shown to sources. Each reference is followed by a letter. These refer to the geographical level for which data were reported: s=State, r=Region, and c=City or metro. The abbreviation *ex* is used to mean *except* or *excluding*; *exp* stands for *expenditures*. For other abbreviations and further explanations, please see the Introduction.

Topeka, KS - continued

Item	Per	Value	Date	Ref.
Energy and Fuels				
Utility (piped) gas, 40 therms		38.01	7/01	11r
Utility (piped) gas, 100 therms		81.75	7/01	11r
Entertainment				
Bowling, Saturday evening rate	line	3.05	3/01	4c
Entertainment purchases	yr	1984	1999	30r
Fees and admissions paid	yr	444	1999	30r
Monopoly game, Parker Brothers', No. 9	game	11.22	3/01	4c
Movie, first-run, Saturday, evening	adm.	6.25	3/01	4c
Television, radios, sound equipment, expenditures on	yr	580	1999	30r
Tennis balls, yellow, Wilson or Penn, 3	can	3.13	3/01	4c
Funerals				
Cosmetology, hair, other preparation		178.32	1/99	78r
Embalming		408.19	1/99	78r
Funeral at funeral home		362.13	1/99	78r
Professional service charges		1375.51	1/99	78r
Transfer of remains to funeral home		155.92	1/99	78r
Visitation/viewing		294.38	1/99	78r
Groceries				
Groceries, ACCRA Index		95.10	3/01	4c
Antibiotic ointment, Polysporin	0.5 oz	4.95	3/01	4c
Baby food, strained vegetables or fruit, lowest price	4-4.5 oz	0.42	3/01	4c
Bacon, sliced	lb	3.15	7/01	11r
Bakery products, expenditures on	yr	281	1999	30r
Bananas	lb	0.46	3/01	4c
Bananas	lb	0.48	7/01	11r
Beans, dried, any type, all sizes	lb	0.61	7/01	11r
Beef for stew, boneless	lb	3.08	7/01	11r
Beef or hamburger, ground	lb	1.31	3/01	4c
Beef, expenditures on	yr	217	1999	30r
Bologna, all beef or mixed	lb	2.52	7/01	11r
Bread, white	loaf	1.05	3/01	4c
Bread, white, pan	lb	1.06	7/01	11r
Broccoli	lb	0.91	7/01	11r
Butter, salted, grade AA, stick	lb	3.04	7/01	11r
Butter, yoghurt, cheese, etc, expenditures on	yr	183	1999	30r
Cereals and bakery product purchases	yr	430	1999	30r
Cereals and cereal products, expenditures on	yr	149	1999	30r
Cheese, Kraft grated Parmesan	8 oz	3.57	3/01	4c
Chicken, fresh, whole	lb	1.07	7/01	11r
Chicken, whole fryer	lb	0.86	3/01	4c
Chops, boneless	lb	3.64	7/01	11r
Chuck roast, U.S. choice, boneless	lb	2.47	7/01	11r
Cigarettes, Winston, Kings	carton	29.86	3/01	4c
Coffee, 100%, ground roast, all sizes	lb	2.69	7/01	11r
Coffee, vacuum-packed	13 oz	2.16	3/01	4c
Cookies, chocolate chip	lb	2.87	7/01	11r
Corn Flakes, Kellogg's or Post Toasties	18 oz	2.14	3/01	4c
Corn, frozen, whole kernel, lowest price	16 oz	1.08	3/01	4c
Dairy product purchases	yr	304	1999	30r
Eggs, expenditures on	yr	26	1999	30r
Eggs, Grade A or AA	dozen	1.02	3/01	4c
Eggs, grade A, large	dozen	0.88	7/01	11r
Fats and oils, expenditures on	yr	75	1999	30r
Fish and seafood, expenditures on	yr	72	1999	30r
Food (excl fruit and vegetables), eaten at home, purchases	yr	887	1999	30r
Food cooked on trips, expenditures on	yr	44	1999	30r
Food purchases	yr	4802	1999	30r
Food purchases, eaten away from home	yr	2069	1999	30r
Food purchases, food eaten at home	yr	2733	1999	30r
Fresh fruits, expenditures on	yr	138	1999	30r
Fresh milk and cream, expenditures on	yr	120	1999	30r
Fresh vegetables, expenditures on	yr	126	1999	30r
Grapefruit	lb	0.66	7/01	11r
Grapes, Thompson, seedless	lb	1.64	7/01	11r
Ground beef, 100% beef	lb	1.64	7/01	11r
Ground beef, lean and extra lean	lb	2.16	7/01	11r
Ground chuck, 100% beef	lb	2.13	7/01	11r

Topeka, KS - continued

Item	Per	Value	Date	Ref.
Groceries - continued				
Ham, boneless, excl canned	lb	2.62	7/01	11r
Ice cream, prepackaged, bulk, regular	1/2 gal	3.35	7/01	11r
Lemons	lb	1.19	7/01	11r
Lettuce, iceberg	head	0.99	3/01	4c
Lettuce, iceberg	lb	0.73	7/01	11r
Margarine, Blue Bonnet or Parkay, stick	lb	0.64	3/01	4c
Margarine, soft, tubs	lb	0.89	7/01	11r
Meats, poultry, fish, and egg purchases	yr	671	1999	30r
Milk, fresh, whole, fortified	gal	2.71	7/01	11r
Milk, whole	1/2 gal	1.64	3/01	4c
Nonalcoholic beverages, expenditures on	yr	239	1999	30r
Orange juice, Minute Maid frozen	12 oz	1.75	3/01	4c
Oranges, Navel	lb	0.80	7/01	11r
Oranges, Valencia	lb	0.66	7/01	11r
Peaches, halves or slices, Hunt's, Del Monte, or Libby's	29 oz	1.70	3/01	4c
Pears, Anjou	lb	0.93	7/01	11r
Peas, green, Del Monte or Green Giant	15 oz	0.74	3/01	4c
Pork chops, center cut, bone-in	lb	3.63	7/01	11r
Pork, expenditures on	yr	150	1999	30r
Potato chips	16 oz	3.52	7/01	11r
Potatoes, frozen, french fried	lb	1.08	7/01	11r
Potatoes, white or red	10 lb	1.89	3/01	4c
Potatoes, white, all types	lb	0.33	7/01	11r
Poultry, expenditures on	yr	108	1999	30r
Processed fruits, expenditures on	yr	98	1999	30r
Processed vegetables, expenditures on	yr	80	1999	30r
Round roast, U.S. choice, boneless	lb	3.07	7/01	11r
Round steak, graded and ungraded, excl U.S. prime and choice	lb	3.41	7/01	11r
Sausage, Jimmy Dean/Owens pork	lb	2.98	3/01	4c
Shortening, vegetable oil blends	lb	1.13	7/01	11r
Shortening, vegetable, Crisco	3 lb	2.69	3/01	4c
Soft drink, Coca Cola, ex deposit	2 liter	1.10	3/01	4c
Spaghetti and macaroni	lb	0.80	7/01	11r
Steak, round, U.S. choice, boneless	lb	3.23	7/01	11r
Steak, T-bone	lb	6.27	3/01	4c
Steak, T-bone, U.S. choice, bone-in	lb	6.68	7/01	11r
Strawberries, dry pint	12 oz	1.32	7/01	11r
Sugar and other sweets, expenditures on	yr	114	1999	30r
Sugar, cane or beet	4 lbs	1.57	3/01	4c
Sugar, white, 33-80 ounce package	lb	0.42	7/01	11r
Sugar, white, all sizes	lb	0.43	7/01	11r
Tobacco products and smoking supplies purchases	yr	331	1999	30r
Tomatoes, field grown	lb	1.46	7/01	11r
Tomatoes, Hunt's or Del Monte	14.5 oz	0.92	3/01	4c
Tuna, chunk, light	6 oz	0.46	3/01	4c
Tuna, light, chunk	lb	1.80	7/01	11r
Turkey, frozen, whole	lb	1.15	7/01	11r
Goods and Services				
Miscellaneous goods and services, ACCRA Index		99.50	3/01	4c
B&B Japanese maple (acer japonicum)	gal	29.99-169.99	4/00	93r
Boxwood (buxus)	2 gal	18.99-39.99	4/00	93r
Daylily (hemerocallis)	gal	4.99-25.00	4/00	93r
Flat of annuals		11.98-24.99	4/00	93r
Fountain grass (pennisetum)	gal	5.98-12.98	4/00	93r
Hanging basket (10 in)		12.99-27.99	4/00	93r
Hardy geranium (geranium)	gal	7.99-9.99	4/00	93r
Hosta (hosta)	gal	6.00-25.00	4/00	93r
Lilac (syrubga vulgaris)	2 gal	14.99-24.99	4/00	93r
Miscellaneous purchases	yr	865	1999	30r

Values are in dollars or fractions of dollars. In the column headed *Ref*, references are shown to sources. Each reference is followed by a letter. These refer to the geographical level for which data were reported: s=State, r=Region, and c=City or metro. The abbreviation *ex* is used to mean *except* or *excluding*; *exp* stands for *expenditures*. For other abbreviations and further explanations, please see the Introduction.

Topeka, KS - continued

Item	Per	Value	Date	Ref.
Goods and Services				
Rhododendron (rhododendron)	2 gal	23.98-42.99	4/00	93r
Sage (salvia)	gal	6.00-9.99	4/00	93r
Wintercreeper euonymus (euonymus fortunei)	2 gal	16.00-169.99	4/00	93r
Hunting license	yr	15.50	4/01	34s
Health Care				
Health care, ACCRA Index		91.90	3/01	4c
Cardiac catheterization, ave hospital/physician charges		11230	1998	77s
Childbirth, Cesarean delivery		10722	1997	13r
Childbirth, vaginal delivery		6223	1997	13r
Dentist's fee, adult teeth cleaning and periodic oral exam	visit	67.60	3/01	4c
Doctor's fee, routine exam, established patient	visit	53.83	3/01	4c
Drugs, expenditures on	yr	394	1999	30r
Health care purchases	yr	2048	1999	30r
Health insurance expenditures	yr	978	1999	30r
Hospital care, private room	day	413.50	3/01	4c
Hysterectomy, laproscopically-assisted, ave hospital/physician charges		9610	1998	76s
Hysterectomy, vaginal, ave hospital and physician charges		6500	1998	76s
Medicaid dispensing fee		4.94	1999	87s
Medical services expenditures	yr	554	1999	30r
Medical supplies, expenditures on	yr	122	1999	30r
Plastic surgery, breast augmentation		3184	2000	7r
Plastic surgery, breast lift		3585	2000	7r
Plastic surgery, facelift		4999	2000	7r
Plastic surgery, hair transplantation		3105	2000	7r
Plastic surgery, lip augmentation		1290	2000	7r
Plastic surgery, lower body lift		8135	2000	7r
Plastic surgery, thigh lift		3839	2000	7r
Household Goods				
Dishwashing powder, Cascade	50 oz	3.43	3/01	4c
Floor coverings, expenditures on	yr	52	1999	30r
Furniture, expenditures on	yr	344	1999	30r
Household furnishings and equipment purchases	yr	1475	1999	30r
Household textiles, expenditures on	yr	109	1999	30r
Laundry and cleaning supplies, expenditures on	yr	134	1999	30r
Tissues, facial, Kleenex brand	175	1.36	3/01	4c
Housing				
Housing, ACCRA Index		95.70	3/01	4c
Home, 2200 sq ft, 4-br, 2-bath, 2-car garage, average		132500	2000	47c
Home price, existing, ave		144400	10/00	90r
Home value, median		112000	2001	53s
House, 2400 sq ft, 8000 sq ft lot, new, urban, utilities	total	197930	3/01	4c
House payment, principal and interest, 25% down payment	mos	995	3/01	4c
Household operation expenditures	yr	542	1999	30r
Housekeeping supplies purchases	yr	508	1999	30r
Lodging expenditures	yr	430	1999	30r
Maintenance, repairs, insurance expenditures	yr	853	1999	30r
Monthly rental value of owned home	mos	547	1999	30r
Owned dwellings, expenditures own	yr	4282	1999	30r
Rent expenditures	yr	1558	1999	30r
Rent, apartment, 2 br, 1 1/2-2 baths, unfurn, 950 sq ft, water	mos	644	3/01	4c
Rental unit, 1 bedroom, with utilities	mos	389	4/01	41c
Rental unit, 2 bedroom, with utilities	mos	507	4/01	41c
Rental unit, 3 bedroom, with utilities	mos	685	4/01	41c
Rental unit, 4 bedroom, with utilities	mos	772	4/01	41c
Shelter, expenditures on	yr	6270	1999	30r

Topeka, KS - continued

Item	Per	Value	Date	Ref.
Insurance and Pensions				
Life and other personal insurance purchases	yr	387	1999	30r
Pensions and Social Security, expenditures on	yr	2968	1999	30r
Legal Fees				
Combination hunting and fishing license	yr	30.50	4/01	34s
Divorce, filing fee		100.00	4/01	35s
Driver's license fee	renew	18.00	1999	48s
Driver's license fee	orig	18.00	1999	48s
Fishing license	yr	15.50	4/01	34s
Personal Goods				
Personal care products and services purchases	yr	385	1999	30r
Shampoo, Alberto VO5	15 oz	1.15	3/01	4c
Toothpaste, Crest or Colgate	6-7 oz	2.39	3/01	4c
Personal Services				
Dry cleaning, man's 2-pc suit		7.90	3/01	4c
Man's haircut, barbershop, no styling		9.50	3/01	4c
Personal services, household, expenditures on	yr	300	1999	30r
Woman's shampoo, trim, blow-dry, no style-change		27.20	3/01	4c
Pets				
Pets, toys, and playground equipment, expenditures on	yr	375	1999	30r
Restaurant Food				
Chicken, fried, thigh and drumstick, KFC/Church's		2.45	3/01	4c
Hamburger with cheese, McDonald's	1/4 lb	2.21	3/01	4c
Pizza, Pizza Hut or Pizza Inn	11-12 in	9.49	3/01	4c
Taxes				
Federal income taxes paid	yr	2326	1999	30r
Personal taxes, expenditures on	yr	3223	1999	30r
Property taxes paid	yr	1152	1999	30r
State and local income taxes paid	yr	753	1999	30r
Transportation				
Transportation, ACCRA Index		97.40	3/01	4c
Bus fare, one-way	trip	0.75	2000	1c
Bus fare, to central business district	1-way	0.80	3/01	4c
Cars and trucks, new, expenditures on	yr	1280	1999	30r
Cars and trucks, used, expenditures on	yr	1763	1999	30r
Diesel at the pump	gal	1.24	10/99	73s
Gasoline and motor oil purchases	yr	1036	1999	30r
Gasoline before-tax price (cents)	gal	108.00	10/00	43s
Maintenance and repair expenditures	yr	594	1999	30r
Public transportation, expenditures on	yr	341	1999	30r
Tire balance, computer or spin balance, front	wheel	8.60	3/01	4c
Transportation purchases	yr	6617	1999	30r
Vehicle expenses, miscellaneous, purchases	yr	2159	1999	30r
Vehicle insurance payments	yr	701	1999	30r
Vehicle purchases (net outlay)	yr	3081	1999	30r
Vehicle rental, lease expenditures	yr	536	1999	30r
Utilities				
Utilities, ACCRA Index		104.40	3/01	4c
Electrical bill, average	mos	64.66	9/00	9s
Electricity, expenditures on	yr	841	1999	30r
Electricity, summer, 250 KWh	mos	19.54	2/96	97c
Electricity, summer, 500 KWh	mos	34.92	2/96	97c
Electricity, summer, 750 KWh	mos	50.30	2/96	97c
Electricity, summer, 1000 KWh	mos	65.69	2/96	97c
Electricity and other, mixed, 2400 sq ft, new home	mos	43.24	3/01	4c
Electricity cost, average	KWh	6.30	9/00	9s
Utilities, fuels, and public services purchased	yr	2401	1999	30r
Water and other public services, expenditures on	yr	273	1999	30r

Values are in dollars or fractions of dollars. In the column headed *Ref*, references are shown to sources. Each reference is followed by a letter. These refer to the geographical level for which data were reported: s=State, r=Region, and c=City or metro. The abbreviation *ex* is used to mean *except* or *excluding*; *exp* stands for *expenditures*. For other abbreviations and further explanations, please see the Introduction.

Topeka, KS - continued

Item	Per	Value	Date	Ref.
Weddings				
Wedding (national average cost)		19936	2000	33r
Wedding (regional average total cost)		16195	1997	110r
Attendants' gifts		321	1998	33r
Bridal attendants' apparel (5 persons)		824	2000	33r
Bride's headpiece/veil		173	1998	33r
Bride's wedding dress		859	1998	33r
Clergy, religious facility fee		242	1998	33r
Engagement ring		3177	1998	33r
Flowers		789	1998	33r
Groom's formalwear rental		99	2000	33r
Limousine		410	1998	33r
Marriage license cost		50.00	4/01	35s
Men's formalwear (ushers, best man)		469	2000	33r
Mother of bride apparel		241	2000	33r
Music		866	1998	33r
Photography and videography		1368	1998	33r
Rehearsal dinner		728	1998	33r
Wedding invitations and announcements		341	1998	33r
Wedding reception		7968	2000	33r
Wedding rings (bride and groom)		1060	1998	33r

Trenton, NJ

Item	Per	Value	Date	Ref.
Average annual expenditures	yr	37971	1999	30r
Alcoholic Beverages				
Alcoholic beverage purchases	yr	368	1999	30r
Wine, red and white table, all sizes, any origin	liter	9.64	7/01	11r
Appliances				
Major appliances, expenditures on	yr	194	1999	30r
Small appliances, housewares, expenditures on	yr	93	1999	30r
Banking and Money				
Mortgage interest and charges paid	yr	2622	1999	30r
Mortgage principal paid on owned property	yr	1262	1999	30r
Vehicle finance charges paid	yr	240	1999	30r
Charity				
Cash contributions, expenditures	yr	1001	1999	30r
Child Care				
Child raising cost, total, age 0-2	yr	8670	1999	60r
Child raising cost, total, age 3-5	yr	8910	1999	60r
Child raising cost, total, age 6-8	yr	9040	1999	60r
Child raising cost, total, age 9-11	yr	9100	1999	60r
Child raising cost, total, age 12-14	yr	9890	1999	60r
Child raising cost, total, age 15-17	yr	10010	1999	60r
Child's child care and education, age 0-2	yr	1070	1999	60r
Child's child care and education, age 3-5	yr	1190	1999	60r
Child's child care and education, age 6-8	yr	740	1999	60r
Child's child care and education, age 9-11	yr	470	1999	60r
Child's child care and education, age 12-14	yr	350	1999	60r
Child's child care and education, age 15-17	yr	590	1999	60r
Child's clothing, age 0-2	yr	480	1999	60r
Child's clothing, age 3-5	yr	470	1999	60r
Child's clothing, age 6-8	yr	520	1999	60r
Child's clothing, age 9-11	yr	570	1999	60r
Child's clothing, age 12-14	yr	970	1999	60r
Child's clothing, age 15-17	yr	870	1999	60r
Child's food, age 0-2	yr	1130	1999	60r
Child's food, age 3-5	yr	1290	1999	60r
Child's food, age 6-8	yr	1640	1999	60r
Child's food, age 9-11	yr	1930	1999	60r
Child's food, age 12-14	yr	1940	1999	60r
Child's food, age 15-17	yr	2150	1999	60r
Child's health care, age 0-2	yr	550	1999	60r
Child's health care, age 3-5	yr	530	1999	60r
Child's health care, age 6-8	yr	610	1999	60r
Child's health care, age 9-11	yr	650	1999	60r
Child's health care, age 12-14	yr	660	1999	60r
Child's health care, age 15-17	yr	690	1999	60r

Trenton, NJ - continued

Item	Per	Value	Date	Ref.
Child Care - continued				
Child's housing, age 0-2	yr	3555	1999	60r
Child's housing, age 3-5	yr	3530	1999	60r
Child's housing, age 6-8	yr	3490	1999	60r
Child's housing, age 9-11	yr	3340	1999	60r
Child's housing, age 12-14	yr	3530	1999	60r
Child's housing, age 15-17	yr	3140	1999	60r
Child's personal care, reading, age 0-2	yr	920	1999	60r
Child's personal care, reading, age 3-5	yr	950	1999	60r
Child's personal care, reading, age 6-8	yr	980	1999	60r
Child's personal care, reading, age 9-11	yr	1020	1999	60r
Child's personal care, reading, age 12-14	yr	1190	1999	60r
Child's personal care, reading, age 15-17	yr	970	1999	60r
Clothing				
Apparel and services purchases	yr	1831	1999	30r
Boys, 2 to 15, expenditures on	yr	92	1999	30r
Children under 2, expenditures on	yr	63	1999	30r
Footwear, expenditures on	yr	300	1999	30r
Girls, 2 to 15, expenditures on	yr	101	1999	30r
Men and boys, expenditures on	yr	446	1999	30r
Men, 16 and over, expenditures on	yr	354	1999	30r
Women, 16 and over, expenditures on	yr	584	1999	30r
Communications				
Cable modem installation, Adelphi		54.90	6/99	103s
Cable modem installation, Comcast		95.00	6/99	103s
Cable modem rate, cable subscriber, Adelphi	mos	34.95	6/99	103s
Cable modem rate, cable subscriber, Comcast	mos	39.95	6/99	103s
Cable modem rate, non-cable subscriber, Adelphi	mos	44.95	6/99	103s
Cable modem rate, non-cable subscriber, Comcast	mos	49.95	6/99	103s
Phone line, single, business, field visit	inst.	98.50	12/97	17s
Phone line, single, business, no field visit	inst.	79.50	12/97	17s
Phone line, single, residence, field visit	inst.	56.50	12/97	17s
Phone line, single, residence, no field visit	inst.	42.00	12/97	17s
Postage and stationery, expenditures on	yr	138	1999	30r
Postal rate, express mail, up to half-pound		12.45	7/01	108r
Postal rate, letter, first class, first ounce		0.34	7/01	108r
Postal rate, letter, two ounces		0.57	7/01	108r
Postal rate, post card		0.21	7/01	108r
Postal rate, priority mail, two pounds		3.95	7/01	108r
Postal rate, priority mail, up to one pound		3.50	7/01	108r
Telephone services, expenditures on	yr	830	1999	30r
Education				
Board, 4-year private college/university	yr	2959	1996	38s
Board, 4-year public college/university	yr	2052	1996	38s
Education expenditures	yr	877	1999	30r
Room, 4-year private college/university	yr	3226	1996	38s
Room, 4-year public college/university	yr	3101	1996	38s
Total cost, 4-year private college/university	yr	19751	1996	38s
Total cost, 4-year public college/university	yr	9125	1996	38s
Tuition, 2-year public college/university, in state	yr	1878	1996	38s
Tuition, 4-year private college/university, in state	yr	13566	1996	38s
Tuition, 4-year public college/university	yr	3972	1996	38s
Energy and Fuels				
Electricity	KWh	0.12	7/01	11r
Fuel oil #2	gal	1.31	7/01	11r
Fuel oil and other fuels, expenditures on	yr	207	1999	30r
Gas, natural, commercial rate	1000 cf	5.98	11/00	88s
Gasoline, all types	gal	1.80	7/01	11r
Gasoline, unleaded midgrade	gal	1.85	7/01	11r
Gasoline, unleaded premium	gal	1.91	7/01	11r
Gasoline, unleaded regular	gal	1.71	7/01	11r
Natural gas, expenditures on	yr	368	1999	30r
Utility (piped) gas, therm		1.08	7/01	11r
Utility (piped) gas, 40 therms		50.87	7/01	11r
Utility (piped) gas, 100 therms		111.06	7/01	11r

Values are in dollars or fractions of dollars. In the column headed *Ref*, references are shown to sources. Each reference is followed by a letter. These refer to the geographical level for which data were reported: s=State, r=Region, and c=City or metro. The abbreviation *ex* is used to mean *except* or *excluding*; *exp* stands for expenditures. For other abbreviations and further explanations, please see the Introduction.

Trenton, NJ - continued

Item	Per	Value	Date	Ref.
Entertainment				
Entertainment purchases	yr	1821	1999	30r
Fees and admissions paid	yr	511	1999	30r
Television, radios, sound equipment, expenditures on	yr	650	1999	30r
Funerals				
Total cost of funeral		5813.50	1/99	78r
Acknowledgement cards		28.32	1/99	78r
Casket		2082.20	1/99	78r
Cosmetology, hair, other preparation		169.59	1/99	78r
Embalming		465.60	1/99	78r
Funeral at funeral home		339.56	1/99	78r
Hearse (local)		183.96	1/99	78r
Professional service charges		1157.85	1/99	78r
Service car/van		100.41	1/99	78r
Transfer of remains to funeral home		158.66	1/99	78r
Vault		766.31	1/99	78r
Visitation/viewing		361.04	1/99	78r
Groceries				
Apples, red delicious	lb	0.95	7/01	11r
Bacon, sliced	lb	3.44	7/01	11r
Bakery products, expenditures on	yr	310	1999	30r
Bananas	lb	0.55	7/01	11r
Beef, expenditures on	yr	236	1999	30r
Bread, white, pan	lb	1.09	7/01	11r
Butter, yoghurt, cheese, etc, expenditures on	yr	214	1999	30r
Cereals and bakery product purchases	yr	474	1999	30r
Cereals and cereal products, expenditures on	yr	164	1999	30r
Chicken legs, bone-in	lb	1.23	7/01	11r
Chicken, fresh, whole	lb	1.13	7/01	11r
Chuck roast, U.S. choice, boneless	lb	2.79	7/01	11r
Coffee, 100%, ground roast, all sizes	lb	3.40	7/01	11r
Dairy product purchases	yr	342	1999	30r
Eggs, expenditures on	yr	34	1999	30r
Eggs, grade A, large	dozen	0.82	7/01	11r
Fats and oils, expenditures on	yr	80	1999	30r
Fish and seafood, expenditures on	yr	123	1999	30r
Food (excl fruit and vegetables), eaten at home, purchases	yr	838	1999	30r
Food cooked on trips, expenditures on	yr	48	1999	30r
Food purchases	yr	5314	1999	30r
Food purchases, eaten away from home	yr	2313	1999	30r
Food purchases, food eaten at home	yr	3001	1999	30r
Fresh fruits, expenditures on	yr	169	1999	30r
Fresh milk and cream, expenditures on	yr	128	1999	30r
Fresh vegetables, expenditures on	yr	164	1999	30r
Grapefruit	lb	0.67	7/01	11r
Grapes, Thompson, seedless	lb	2.18	7/01	11r
Ground beef, lean and extra lean	lb	2.66	7/01	11r
Ground chuck, 100% beef	lb	2.04	7/01	11r
Lettuce, iceberg	lb	0.76	7/01	11r
Meats, poultry, fish, and egg purchases	yr	808	1999	30r
Nonalcoholic beverages, expenditures on	yr	225	1999	30r
Orange juice, frozen concentrate	16 oz	1.88	7/01	11r
Oranges, Navel	lb	0.79	7/01	11r
Oranges, Valencia	lb	0.56	7/01	11r
Peaches	lb	1.16	7/01	11r
Peanut butter, creamy, all sizes	lb	2.01	7/01	11r
Pears, Anjou	lb	1.16	7/01	11r
Pork chops, center cut, bone-in	lb	3.57	7/01	11r
Pork, expenditures on	yr	146	1999	30r
Potato chips	16 oz	3.37	7/01	11r
Potatoes, white, all types	lb	0.42	7/01	11r
Poultry, expenditures on	yr	158	1999	30r
Processed fruits, expenditures on	yr	124	1999	30r
Processed vegetables, expenditures on	yr	82	1999	30r
Round roast, U.S. choice, boneless	lb	3.04	7/01	11r
Spaghetti and macaroni	lb	1.04	7/01	11r
Steak, sirloin, U.S. choice, boneless	lb	5.39	7/01	11r
Strawberries, dry pint	12 oz	1.51	7/01	11r
Sugar and other sweets, expenditures on	yr	110	1999	30r

Trenton, NJ - continued

Item	Per	Value	Date	Ref.
Groceries - continued				
Sugar, white, 33-80 ounce package	lb	0.46	7/01	11r
Sugar, white, all sizes	lb	0.47	7/01	11r
Tobacco products and smoking supplies purchases	yr	309	1999	30r
Yogurt, natural, fruit flavored	8 oz	0.79	7/01	11r
Goods and Services				
B&B Japanese maple (acer japonicum)	gal	38.99-125.00	4/00	93r
Boxwood (buxus)	2 gal	15.99-49.95	4/00	93r
Daylilly (hemerocallis)	gal	4.95	4/00	93r
Flat of annuals		8.00-14.99	4/00	93r
Fountain grass (pennisetum)	gal	6.99-9.99	4/00	93r
Hanging basket (10 in)		12.95-19.99	4/00	93r
Hardy geranium (geranium)	gal	6.95-7.99	4/00	93r
Hosta (hosta)	gal	4.95	4/00	93r
Lilac (syrubga vulgaris)	2 gal	17.99-74.95	4/00	93r
Miscellaneous purchases	yr	872	1999	30r
Rhododendron (rhododendron)	2 gal	23.99-54.95	4/00	93r
Sage (salvia)	gal	6.95-7.99	4/00	93r
Wintercreeper euonymus (euonymus fortunei)	2 gal	14.99-23.95	4/00	93r
Hunting license	yr	22.50	4/01	34s
Health Care				
Cardiac catheterization, ave hospital/physician charges		14680	1998	77s
Childbirth, Cesarean delivery		14716	1997	13r
Childbirth, vaginal delivery		8541	1997	13r
Drugs, expenditures on	yr	296	1999	30r
Health care purchases	yr	1788	1999	30r
Health insurance expenditures	yr	875	1999	30r
Hysterectomy, laproscopically-assisted, ave hospital/physician charges		18330	1998	76s
Hysterectomy, vaginal, ave hospital and physician charges		13620	1998	76s
Medicaid dispensing fee		3.73-4.07	1999	87s
Medical services expenditures	yr	516	1999	30r
Medical supplies, expenditures on	yr	102	1999	30r
Nursing home costs, private room	day	195	2000	82c
Nursing home stay, private room	day	195	2000	81c
Plastic surgery, breast augmentation		4232	2000	7r
Plastic surgery, breast lift		4605	2000	7r
Plastic surgery, facelift		6964	2000	7r
Plastic surgery, hair transplantation		4193	2000	7r
Plastic surgery, lip augmentation		1675	2000	7r
Plastic surgery, lower body lift		6611	2000	7r
Plastic surgery, thigh lift		4751	2000	7r
Household Goods				
Floor coverings, expenditures on	yr	59	1999	30r
Furniture, expenditures on	yr	388	1999	30r
Household furnishings and equipment purchases	yr	1567	1999	30r
Household textiles, expenditures on	yr	112	1999	30r
Laundry and cleaning supplies, expenditures on	yr	104	1999	30r
Housing				
Home price, existing, ave		180800	10/00	90r
Home value, median		213000	2001	53s
Household operation expenditures	yr	581	1999	30r
Housekeeping supplies purchases	yr	474	1999	30r
Lodging expenditures	yr	550	1999	30r

Values are in dollars or fractions of dollars. In the column headed *Ref*, references are shown to sources. Each reference is followed by a letter. These refer to the geographical level for which data were reported: s=State, r=Region, and c=City or metro. The abbreviation *ex* is used to mean *except* or *excluding*; *exp* stands for *expenditures*. For other abbreviations and further explanations, please see the Introduction.

Trenton, NJ - continued

Item	Per	Value	Date	Ref.
Housing				
Maintenance, repairs, insurance expenditures	yr	835	1999	30r
Monthly rental value of owned home	mos	663	1999	30r
Owned dwellings, expenditures own	yr	5209	1999	30r
Rent expenditures	yr	2390	1999	30r
Rental unit, 1 bedroom, with utilities	mos	707	4/01	41c
Rental unit, 2 bedroom, with utilities	mos	862	4/01	41c
Rental unit, 3 bedroom, with utilities	mos	1167	4/01	41c
Rental unit, 4 bedroom, with utilities	mos	1409	4/01	41c
Shelter, expenditures on	yr	8149	1999	30r
Insurance and Pensions				
Auto insurance premium	yr	1292.76	1999	57s
Life and other personal insurance purchases	yr	424	1999	30r
Pensions and Social Security, expenditures on	yr	3037	1999	30r
Legal Fees				
Divorce, filing fee		65.00	4/01	35s
Driver's license fee	orig	18.00	1999	48s
Driver's license fee	renew	15.00	1999	48s
Fishing license	yr	22.50	4/01	34s
Personal Goods				
Personal care products and services purchases	yr	399	1999	30r
Personal Services				
Personal services, household, expenditures on	yr	271	1999	30r
Pets				
Pets, toys, and playground equipment, expenditures on	yr	325	1999	30r
Taxes				
Federal income taxes paid	yr	2606	1999	30r
Personal taxes, expenditures on	yr	3567	1999	30r
Property taxes paid	yr	1752	1999	30r
State and local income taxes paid	yr	694	1999	30r
Transportation				
Automobile insurance	yr	975.90	2000	79s
Bus fare, one-way	trip	1.00	2000	1c
Cars and trucks, new, expenditures on	yr	1496	1999	30r
Cars and trucks, used, expenditures on	yr	1251	1999	30r
Diesel at the pump	gal	1.19	10/99	73s
Gasoline and motor oil purchases	yr	901	1999	30r
Gasoline before-tax price (cents)	gal	114.90	10/00	43s
Maintenance and repair expenditures	yr	618	1999	30r
Motorcycle license fee	orig	15.00	1999	49s
Motorcycle license fee	renew	13.00	1999	49s
Public transportation, expenditures on	yr	575	1999	30r
Transportation purchases	yr	6503	1999	30r
Vehicle expenses, miscellaneous, purchases	yr	2266	1999	30r
Vehicle insurance payments	yr	824	1999	30r
Vehicle purchases (net outlay)	yr	2761	1999	30r
Vehicle rental, lease expenditures	yr	584	1999	30r
Utilities				
Electrical bill, average	mos	74.08	9/00	9s
Electricity, expenditures on	yr	837	1999	30r
Electricity cost, average	KWh	8.91	9/00	9s
Utilities, fuels, and public services purchased	yr	2457	1999	30r
Water and other public services, expenditures on	yr	215	1999	30r
Weddings				
Wedding (national average cost)		19936	2000	33r
Wedding (regional average total cost)		29454	1997	110r
Attendants' gifts		321	1998	33r
Bridal attendants' apparel (5 persons)		824	2000	33r
Bride's headpiece/veil		173	1998	33r
Bride's wedding dress		859	1998	33r
Clergy, religious facility fee		242	1998	33r
Engagement ring		3177	1998	33r

Trenton, NJ - continued

Item	Per	Value	Date	Ref.
Weddings - continued				
Flowers		789	1998	33r
Groom's formalwear rental		99	2000	33r
Limousine		410	1998	33r
Marriage license cost		28.00	4/01	35s
Men's formalwear (ushers, best man)		469	2000	33r
Mother of bride apparel		241	2000	33r
Music		866	1998	33r
Photography and videography		1368	1998	33r
Rehearsal dinner		728	1998	33r
Wedding invitations and announcements		341	1998	33r
Wedding reception		7968	2000	33r
Wedding rings (bride and groom)		1060	1998	33r

Tucson, AZ

Item	Per	Value	Date	Ref.
Composite, ACCRA index		99.90	3/01	4c
Alcoholic Beverages				
Beer, Heineken, 12-oz, ex deposit	6	7.69	3/01	4c
J & B Scotch	750-ml	19.29	3/01	4c
Wine, Livingston or Gallo, Chablis blanc	1.5 liter	5.73	3/01	4c
Appliances				
Appliance repair, service call, washing machine	min lab chg	35.38	3/01	4c
Banking and Money				
Mortgage rate, incl. points and orig. fee, 30-yr. conv. fixed or ARM	mos	6.77	3/01	4c
Business Expenses				
Business travel, car rental	day	55	2001	3c
Business travel, food	day	42	2001	3c
Business travel, hotel	day	127	2001	3c
Clothing				
Boys' brief, cotton	3	4.19	3/01	4c
Shirt, man's dress shirt		27.99	3/01	4c
Slacks, man's "No Wrinkles" khaki		35.74	3/01	4c
Communications				
Cable modem installation, Cox		99.00-174.95	6/99	103s
Cable modem rate, cable subscriber, Cox	mos	29.95-44.95	6/99	103s
Cable modem rate, non-cable subscriber, Cox	mos	42.95-54.95	6/99	103s
Newspaper subscription, daily and Sunday delivery	mos	12.61	3/01	4c
Phone line, single, business, field visit	inst.	56.00	12/97	17s
Phone line, single, business, no field visit	inst.	56.00	12/97	17s
Phone line, single, residence, field visit	inst.	46.50	12/97	17s
Phone line, single, residence, no field visit	inst.	46.50	12/97	17s
Postal rate, express mail, up to half-pound		12.45	7/01	108r
Postal rate, letter, first class, first ounce		0.34	7/01	108r
Postal rate, letter, two ounces		0.57	7/01	108r
Postal rate, post card		0.21	7/01	108r
Postal rate, priority mail, two pounds		3.95	7/01	108r
Postal rate, priority mail, up to one pound		3.50	7/01	108r
Telephone bill, business, basic rate	mos	32.78	12/97	18c
Telephone bill, family of three	mos	19.91	3/01	4c
Telephone bill, residential, basic rate	mos	13.18	12/97	18c
Education				
Board, 4-year private college/university	yr	2143	1996	38s
Board, 4-year public college/university	yr	1815	1996	38s
Room, 4-year private college/university	yr	2012	1996	38s
Room, 4-year public college/university	yr	2257	1996	38s
Total cost, 4-year private college/university	yr	10934	1996	38s
Total cost, 4-year public college/university	yr	5998	1996	38s
Tuition, 2-year public college/university, in state	yr	764	1996	38s
Tuition, 4-year private college/university, in state	yr	6779	1996	38s
Tuition, 4-year public college/university	yr	1926	1996	38s

Values are in dollars or fractions of dollars. In the column headed *Ref*, references are shown to sources. Each reference is followed by a letter. These refer to the geographical level for which data were reported: s=State, r=Region, and c=City or metro. The abbreviation *ex* is used to mean *except* or *excluding*; *exp* stands for *expenditures*. For other abbreviations and further explanations, please see the Introduction.

Tucson, AZ - continued

Item	Per	Value	Date	Ref.
Energy and Fuels				
Energy, combined forms, 2400 sq ft	mos	130.73	3/01	4c
Energy, exc. electricity, 2400 sq ft	mos	42.53	3/01	4c
Gas, cooking, winter, 10 therms	mos	11.64	2/96	98c
Gas, cooking, winter, 30 therms	mos	23.92	2/96	98c
Gas, cooking, winter, 50 therms	mos	36.19	2/96	98c
Gas, heating, winter, average use	mos	42.94	2/96	98c
Gas, natural, commercial rate	1000 cf	8.12	11/00	88s
Gas, regular unleaded, cash, self-service	gal	1.50	3/01	4c
Entertainment				
Bowling, Saturday evening rate	line	3.20	3/01	4c
Monopoly game, Parker Brothers', No. 9	game	9.45	3/01	4c
Movie, first-run, Saturday, evening	adm.	7.62	3/01	4c
Tennis balls, yellow, Wilson or Penn, 3	can	2.42	3/01	4c
Funerals				
Total cost of funeral		5401.08	1/99	78r
Acknowledgement cards		33.64	1/99	78r
Casket		2170.43	1/99	78r
Cosmetology, hair, other preparation		136.32	1/99	78r
Embalming		319.13	1/99	78r
Funeral at funeral home		370.21	1/99	78r
Hearse (local)		161.04	1/99	78r
Professional service charges		963.15	1/99	78r
Service car/van		133.99	1/99	78r
Transfer of remains to funeral home		159.82	1/99	78r
Vault		778.07	1/99	78r
Visitation/viewing		175.28	1/99	78r
Groceries				
Groceries, ACCRA Index		104.50	3/01	4c
Antibiotic ointment, Polysporin	0.5 oz	4.91	3/01	4c
Baby food, strained vegetables or fruit, lowest price	4-4.5 oz	0.37	3/01	4c
Bananas	lb	0.45	3/01	4c
Beef or hamburger, ground	lb	1.77	3/01	4c
Bread, white	loaf	0.87	3/01	4c
Cheese, Kraft grated Parmesan	8 oz	4.43	3/01	4c
Chicken, whole fryer	lb	0.97	3/01	4c
Cigarettes, Winston, Kings	carton	29.53	3/01	4c
Coffee, vacuum-packed	13 oz	2.97	3/01	4c
Corn Flakes, Kellogg's or Post Toasties	18 oz	3.01	3/01	4c
Corn, frozen, whole kernel, lowest price	16 oz	1.15	3/01	4c
Eggs, Grade A or AA	dozen	1.16	3/01	4c
Lettuce, iceberg	head	0.97	3/01	4c
Margarine, Blue Bonnet or Parkay, stick	lb	0.88	3/01	4c
Milk, whole	1/2 gal	1.93	3/01	4c
Orange juice, Minute Maid frozen	12 oz	1.65	3/01	4c
Peaches, halves or slices, Hunt's, Del Monte, or Libby's	29 oz	1.72	3/01	4c
Peas, green, Del Monte or Green Giant	15 oz	0.85	3/01	4c
Potatoes, white or red	10 lb	2.53	3/01	4c
Sausage, Jimmy Dean/Owens pork	lb	4.17	3/01	4c
Shortening, vegetable, Crisco	3 lb	3.87	3/01	4c
Soft drink, Coca Cola, ex deposit	2 liter	1.15	3/01	4c
Steak, T-bone	lb	5.75	3/01	4c
Sugar, cane or beet	4 lbs	1.91	3/01	4c
Tomatoes, Hunt's or Del Monte	14.5 oz	0.95	3/01	4c
Tuna, chunk, light	6 oz	0.65	3/01	4c
Goods and Services				
Miscellaneous goods and services, ACCRA Index		98.60	3/01	4c
Hunting license	yr	25.50	4/01	34s
Health Care				
Health care, ACCRA Index		103.20	3/01	4c
Cardiac catheterization, ave hospital/ physician charges		20100	1998	77s
Childbirth, Cesarean delivery		11587	1997	13r
Childbirth, vaginal delivery		6725	1997	13r
Dentist's fee, adult teeth cleaning and periodic oral exam	visit	73.40	3/01	4c

Tucson, AZ - continued

Item	Per	Value	Date	Ref.
Health Care - continued				
Doctor's fee, routine exam, established patient	visit	50.40	3/01	4c
Home health care aide cost, licensed agency	hour	15	2000	82c
Hospital care, private room	day	720.00	3/01	4c
Hysterectomy, laproscopically-assisted, ave hospital/physician charges		19790	1998	76s
Hysterectomy, vaginal, ave hospital and physician charges		12130	1998	76s
Nursing home costs, private room	day	149	2000	82c
Nursing home stay, private room	day	149	2000	83c
Household Goods				
Dishwashing powder, Cascade	50 oz	2.98	3/01	4c
Tissues, facial, Kleenex brand	175	1.56	3/01	4c
Housing				
Housing, ACCRA Index		95.50	3/01	4c
Home, 2200 sq ft, 4-br, 2-bath, 2-car garage, average		189167	2000	47c
Home value, median		131000	2001	53s
House, 2-story, 2,400 sq ft, 2-car garage, new		136700	2000	54c
House, 2400 sq ft, 8000 sq ft lot, new, urban, utilities	total	195828	3/01	4c
House payment, principal and interest, 25% down payment	mos	955	3/01	4c
Rent, apartment, 2 br, 1 1/2-2 baths, unfurn, 950 sq ft, water	mos	740	3/01	4c
Rental unit, 1 bedroom, with utilities	mos	470	4/01	41c
Rental unit, 2 bedroom, with utilities	mos	625	4/01	41c
Rental unit, 3 bedroom, with utilities	mos	869	4/01	41c
Rental unit, 4 bedroom, with utilities	mos	1025	4/01	41c
Insurance and Pensions				
Auto insurance premium	yr	901.65	1999	57s
Legal Fees				
Divorce, filing fee		64.00	4/01	35s
Driver's license fee	orig	17.50	1999	48s
Driver's license fee	renew	17.50	1999	48s
Personal Goods				
Shampoo, Alberto VO5	15 oz	1.31	3/01	4c
Toothpaste, Crest or Colgate	6-7 oz	2.13	3/01	4c
Personal Services				
Dry cleaning, man's 2-pc suit		8.76	3/01	4c
Man's haircut, barbershop, no styling		10.49	3/01	4c
Woman's shampoo, trim, blow-dry, no style-change		26.25	3/01	4c
Restaurant Food				
Chicken, fried, thigh and drumstick, KFC/ Church's		1.99	3/01	4c
Hamburger with cheese, McDonald's	1/4 lb	2.19	3/01	4c
Pizza, Pizza Hut or Pizza Inn	11-12 in	9.79	3/01	4c
Transportation				
Transportation, ACCRA Index		103.00	3/01	4c
Bus fare, one-way	trip	0.85	2000	1c
Bus fare, to central business district	1-way	1.00	3/01	4c
Diesel at the pump	gal	1.27	10/99	73s
Gasoline before-tax price (cents)	gal	120.30	10/00	43s
Tire balance, computer or spin balance, front	wheel	8.00	3/01	4c
Utilities				
Utilities, ACCRA Index		105.00	3/01	4c
Electrical bill, average	mos	84.33	9/00	9s
Electricity, summer, 250 KWh	mos	25.69	2/96	97c
Electricity, summer, 500 KWh	mos	46.28	2/96	97c
Electricity, summer, 750 KWh	mos	66.86	2/96	97c
Electricity, summer, 1000 KWh	mos	87.44	2/96	97c
Electricity and other, mixed, 2400 sq ft, new home	mos	88.20	3/01	4c
Electricity cost, average	KWh	7.60	9/00	9s

Values are in dollars or fractions of dollars. In the column headed *Ref*, references are shown to sources. Each reference is followed by a letter. These refer to the geographical level for which data were reported: s=State, r=Region, and c=City or metro. The abbreviation *ex* is used to mean *except* or *excluding*; *exp* stands for *expenditures*. For other abbreviations and further explanations, please see the Introduction.

Tucson, AZ - continued

Item	Per	Value	Date	Ref.
Weddings				
Wedding (national average cost)		19936	2000	33r
Attendants' gifts		321	1998	33r
Bridal attendants' apparel (5 persons)		824	2000	33r
Bride's headpiece/veil		173	1998	33r
Bride's wedding dress		859	1998	33r
Clergy, religious facility fee		242	1998	33r
Engagement ring		3177	1998	33r
Flowers		789	1998	33r
Groom's formalwear rental		99	2000	33r
Limousine		410	1998	33r
Marriage license cost		50.00	4/01	35s
Men's formalwear (ushers, best man)		469	2000	33r
Mother of bride apparel		241	2000	33r
Music		866	1998	33r
Photography and videography		1368	1998	33r
Rehearsal dinner		728	1998	33r
Wedding invitations and announcements		341	1998	33r
Wedding reception		7968	2000	33r
Wedding rings (bride and groom)		1060	1998	33r

Tulsa, OK

Item	Per	Value	Date	Ref.
Composite, ACCRA index		94.10	3/01	4c
Alcoholic Beverages				
Alcoholic beverage purchases	yr	253	1999	30r
Beer, Heineken, 12-oz, ex deposit	6	7.17	3/01	4c
J & B Scotch	750-ml	17.89	3/01	4c
Malt beverages, all types, all sizes, any origin	16 oz	0.96	7/01	11r
Wine, Livingston or Gallo, Chablis blanc	1.5 liter	6.13	3/01	4c
Appliances				
Appliance repair, service call, washing machine	min lab chg	38.80	3/01	4c
Major appliances, expenditures on	yr	172	1999	30r
Small appliances, housewares, expenditures on	yr	81	1999	30r
Banking and Money				
Mortgage interest and charges paid	yr	2039	1999	30r
Mortgage principal paid on owned property	yr	1026	1999	30r
Mortgage rate, incl. points and orig. fee, 30-yr. conv. fixed or ARM	mos	7.00	3/01	4c
Vehicle finance charges paid	yr	365	1999	30r
Business Expenses				
Business travel, car rental	day	51	2001	3c
Business travel, food	day	44	2001	3c
Business travel, hotel	day	92	2001	3c
Charity				
Cash contributions, expenditures	yr	1127	1999	30r
Child Care				
Child raising cost, total, age 0-2	yr	8540	1999	60r
Child raising cost, total, age 3-5	yr	8780	1999	60r
Child raising cost, total, age 6-8	yr	8820	1999	60r
Child raising cost, total, age 9-11	yr	8800	1999	60r
Child raising cost, total, age 12-14	yr	9510	1999	60r
Child raising cost, total, age 15-17	yr	9740	1999	60r
Child's child care and education, age 0-2	yr	1380	1999	60r
Child's child care and education, age 3-5	yr	1520	1999	60r
Child's child care and education, age 6-8	yr	990	1999	60r
Child's child care and education, age 9-11	yr	650	1999	60r
Child's child care and education, age 12-14	yr	490	1999	60r
Child's child care and education, age 15-17	yr	840	1999	60r
Child's clothing, age 0-2	yr	480	1999	60r
Child's clothing, age 3-5	yr	470	1999	60r
Child's clothing, age 6-8	yr	520	1999	60r
Child's clothing, age 9-11	yr	570	1999	60r
Child's clothing, age 12-14	yr	950	1999	60r
Child's clothing, age 15-17	yr	850	1999	60r
Child's food, age 0-2	yr	1000	1999	60r
Child's food, age 3-5	yr	1160	1999	60r

Tulsa, OK - continued

Item	Per	Value	Date	Ref.
Child Care - continued				
Child's food, age 6-8	yr	1490	1999	60r
Child's food, age 9-11	yr	1770	1999	60r
Child's food, age 12-14	yr	1770	1999	60r
Child's food, age 15-17	yr	1980	1999	60r
Child's health care, age 0-2	yr	620	1999	60r
Child's health care, age 3-5	yr	590	1999	60r
Child's health care, age 6-8	yr	680	1999	60r
Child's health care, age 9-11	yr	720	1999	60r
Child's health care, age 12-14	yr	730	1999	60r
Child's health care, age 15-17	yr	760	1999	60r
Child's housing, age 0-2	yr	3070	1999	60r
Child's housing, age 3-5	yr	3050	1999	60r
Child's housing, age 6-8	yr	3010	1999	60r
Child's housing, age 9-11	yr	2850	1999	60r
Child's housing, age 12-14	yr	3040	1999	60r
Child's housing, age 15-17	yr	2650	1999	60r
Child's personal care, reading, age 0-2	yr	910	1999	60r
Child's personal care, reading, age 3-5	yr	930	1999	60r
Child's personal care, reading, age 6-8	yr	960	1999	60r
Child's personal care, reading, age 9-11	yr	1000	1999	60r
Child's personal care, reading, age 12-14	yr	1170	1999	60r
Child's personal care, reading, age 15-17	yr	950	1999	60r
Clothing				
Apparel and services purchases	yr	1610	1999	30r
Boys' brief, cotton	3	5.27	3/01	4c
Boys, 2 to 15, expenditures on	yr	89	1999	30r
Children under 2, expenditures on	yr	79	1999	30r
Footwear, expenditures on	yr	283	1999	30r
Girls, 2 to 15, expenditures on	yr	103	1999	30r
Men and boys, expenditures on	yr	351	1999	30r
Men, 16 and over, expenditures on	yr	262	1999	30r
Shirt, man's dress shirt		25.53	3/01	4c
Slacks, man's "No Wrinkles" khaki		30.69	3/01	4c
Women, 16 and over, expenditures on	yr	538	1999	30r
Communications				
Cable modem installation, Cox		99.00-174.95	6/99	103s
Cable modem rate, cable subscriber, Cox	mos	29.95-44.95	6/99	103s
Cable modem rate, non-cable subscriber, Cox	mos	42.95-54.95	6/99	103s
Newspaper subscription, daily and Sunday delivery	mos	15.00	3/01	4c
Phone line, single, business, field visit	inst.	82.75	12/97	17s
Phone line, single, business, no field visit	inst.	82.75	12/97	17s
Phone line, single, residence, field visit	inst.	44.45	12/97	17s
Phone line, single, residence, no field visit	inst.	44.45	12/97	17s
Postage and stationery, expenditures on	yr	104	1999	30r
Postal rate, express mail, up to half-pound		12.45	7/01	108r
Postal rate, letter, first class, first ounce		0.34	7/01	108r
Postal rate, letter, two ounces		0.57	7/01	108r
Postal rate, post card		0.21	7/01	108r
Postal rate, priority mail, two pounds		3.95	7/01	108r
Postal rate, priority mail, up to one pound		3.50	7/01	108r
Telephone bill, family of three	mos	18.88	3/01	4c
Telephone services, expenditures on	yr	860	1999	30r
Education				
Board, 4-year private college/university	yr	1401	1996	38s
Board, 4-year public college/university	yr	61111	1996	38s
Education expenditures	yr	431	1999	30r
Room, 4-year private college/university	yr	8032	1996	38s
Room, 4-year public college/university	yr	8371	1996	38s
Total cost, 4-year private college/university	yr	7737	1996	38s
Total cost, 4-year public college/university	yr	4287	1996	38s
Tuition, 2-year public college/university, in state	yr	260	1996	38s
Tuition, 4-year private college/university, in state	yr	8311	1996	38s
Tuition, 4-year public college/university	yr	1839	1996	38s

Values are in dollars or fractions of dollars. In the column headed *Ref*, references are shown to sources. Each reference is followed by a letter. These refer to the geographical level for which data were reported: s=State, r=Region, and c=City or metro. The abbreviation *ex* is used to mean *except* or *excluding*; *exp* stands for *expenditures*. For other abbreviations and further explanations, please see the Introduction.

Tulsa, OK - continued

Item	Per	Value	Date	Ref.
Energy and Fuels				
Electricity	KWh	0.09	7/01	11r
Electricity	500 KWhs	47.29	7/01	11r
Energy, combined forms, 2400 sq ft	mos	125.03	3/01	4c
Energy, exc. electricity, 2400 sq ft	mos	63.83	3/01	4c
Fuel oil #2	gal	1.43	7/01	11r
Fuel oil and other fuels, expenditures on	yr	45	1999	30r
Gas, natural, commercial rate	1000 cf	7.50	11/00	88s
Gas, regular unleaded, cash, self-service	gal	1.28	3/01	4c
Gasoline, all types	gal	1.60	7/01	11r
Gasoline, unleaded midgrade	gal	1.65	7/01	11r
Gasoline, unleaded premium	gal	1.74	7/01	11r
Natural gas, expenditures on	yr	164	1999	30r
Utility (piped) gas, therm		1.01	7/01	11r
Utility (piped) gas, 40 therms		44.29	7/01	11r
Utility (piped) gas, 100 therms		97.44	7/01	11r
Entertainment				
Bowling, Saturday evening rate	line	3.00	3/01	4c
Entertainment purchases	yr	1574	1999	30r
Fees and admissions paid	yr	371	1999	30r
Monopoly game, Parker Brothers', No. 9	game	9.83	3/01	4c
Movie, first-run, Saturday, evening	adm.	6.75	3/01	4c
Reading purchases	yr	121	1999	30r
Television, radios, sound equipment, expenditures on	yr	561	1999	30r
Tennis balls, yellow, Wilson or Penn, 3	can	2.77	3/01	4c
Funerals				
Total cost of funeral		5842.28	1/99	78r
Acknowledgement cards		28.35	1/99	78r
Casket		2494.29	1/99	78r
Cosmetology, hair, other preparation		109.22	1/99	78r
Embalming		361.42	1/99	78r
Funeral at funeral home		349.20	1/99	78r
Hearse (local)		161.91	1/99	78r
Professional service charges		1116.50	1/99	78r
Service car/van		65.56	1/99	78r
Transfer of remains to funeral home		143.56	1/99	78r
Vault		785.25	1/99	78r
Visitation/viewing		227.02	1/99	78r
Groceries				
Groceries, ACCRA Index		102.20	3/01	4c
American processed cheese	lb	3.50	7/01	11r
Antibiotic ointment, Polysporin	0.5 oz	4.53	3/01	4c
Baby food, strained vegetables or fruit, lowest price	4-4.5 oz	0.48	3/01	4c
Bakery products, expenditures on	yr	261	1999	30r
Bananas	lb	0.54	3/01	4c
Bananas	lb	0.47	7/01	11r
Beans, dried, any type, all sizes	lb	0.63	7/01	11r
Beef for stew, boneless	lb	2.86	7/01	11r
Beef or hamburger, ground	lb	1.51	3/01	4c
Beef, expenditures on	yr	210	1999	30r
Bologna, all beef or mixed	lb	2.29	7/01	11r
Bread, French	lb	1.66	7/01	11r
Bread, white	loaf	0.86	3/01	4c
Bread, white, pan	lb	0.87	7/01	11r
Bread, whole wheat, pan	lb	1.38	7/01	11r
Broccoli	lb	1.04	7/01	11r
Butter, salted, grade AA, stick	lb	2.26	7/01	11r
Butter, yoghurt, cheese, etc, expenditures on	yr	170	1999	30r
Cabbage	lb	0.42	7/01	11r
Cereals and cereal products, expenditures on	yr	140	1999	30r
Cheddar cheese, natural	lb	3.75	7/01	11r
Cheese, Kraft grated Parmesan	8 oz	3.41	3/01	4c
Chicken breast, bone-in	lb	1.85	7/01	11r
Chicken legs, bone-in	lb	1.34	7/01	11r
Chicken, fresh, whole	lb	1.05	7/01	11r
Chicken, whole fryer	lb	0.83	3/01	4c
Chops, boneless,	lb	4.13	7/01	11r

Tulsa, OK - continued

Item	Per	Value	Date	Ref.
Groceries - continued				
Chuck roast, graded and ungraded, excl U.S. prime and choice	lb	2.35	7/01	11r
Chuck roast, U.S. choice, boneless	lb	2.67	7/01	11r
Cigarettes, Winston, Kings	carton	29.41	3/01	4c
Coffee, 100%, ground roast, all sizes	lb	2.88	7/01	11r
Coffee, instant, plain, regular, all sizes	16 oz	9.25	7/01	11r
Coffee, vacuum-packed	13 oz	2.79	3/01	4c
Cola, non diet	2 liter	1.11	7/01	11r
Corn Flakes, Kellogg's or Post Toasties	18 oz	3.24	3/01	4c
Corn, frozen, whole kernel, lowest price	16 oz	1.39	3/01	4c
Crackers, soda, salted	lb	1.70	7/01	11r
Dairy product purchases	yr	282	1999	30r
Eggs, expenditures on	yr	32	1999	30r
Eggs, Grade A or AA	dozen	0.94	3/01	4c
Fats and oils, expenditures on	yr	79	1999	30r
Fish and seafood, expenditures on	yr	99	1999	30r
Flour, white, all purpose	lb	0.32	7/01	11r
Food (excl fruit and vegetables), eaten at home, purchases	yr	815	1999	30r
Food cooked on trips, expenditures on	yr	36	1999	30r
Food purchases	yr	4533	1999	30r
Food purchases, eaten away from home	yr	1873	1999	30r
Food purchases, food eaten at home	yr	2660	1999	30r
Fresh fruits, expenditures on	yr	128	1999	30r
Fresh milk and cream, expenditures on	yr	112	1999	30r
Fresh vegetables, expenditures on	yr	131	1999	30r
Fruit and vegetable purchases	yr	438	1999	30r
Grapefruit	lb	0.59	7/01	11r
Grapes, Thompson, seedless	lb	2.12	7/01	11r
Ground beef, 100% beef	lb	1.76	7/01	11r
Ground beef, lean and extra lean	lb	2.60	7/01	11r
Ground chuck, 100% beef	lb	2.08	7/01	11r
Ham, boneless, excl canned	lb	2.71	7/01	11r
Ham, rump or shank half, bone-in, smoked	lb	2.19	7/01	11r
Ice cream, prepackaged, bulk, regular	1/2 gal	3.93	7/01	11r
Lemons	lb	1.32	7/01	11r
Lettuce, iceberg	head	1.17	3/01	4c
Lettuce, iceberg	lb	0.76	7/01	11r
Margarine, Blue Bonnet or Parkay, stick	lb	1.04	3/01	4c
Milk, fresh, low fat,	gal	2.75	7/01	11r
Milk, fresh, whole, fortified	gal	2.97	7/01	11r
Milk, whole	1/2 gal	1.67	3/01	4c
Nonalcoholic beverages, expenditures on	yr	228	1999	30r
Orange juice, frozen concentrate	16 oz	1.95	7/01	11r
Orange juice, Minute Maid frozen	12 oz	1.52	3/01	4c
Oranges, Navel	lb	0.73	7/01	11r
Oranges, Valencia	lb	0.55	7/01	11r
Peaches, halves or slices, Hunt's, Del Monte, or Libby's	29 oz	1.62	3/01	4c
Peanut butter, creamy, all sizes	lb	1.83	7/01	11r
Pears, Anjou	lb	0.98	7/01	11r
Peas, green, Del Monte or Green Giant	15 oz	0.64	3/01	4c
Pork chops, center cut, bone-in	lb	3.33	7/01	11r
Pork sausage, fresh, loose	lb	2.59	7/01	11r
Pork shoulder picnic, bone-in, smoked	lb	1.12	7/01	11r
Pork, expenditures on	yr	162	1999	30r
Potato chips	16 oz	3.59	7/01	11r
Potatoes, frozen, french fried	lb	1.00	7/01	11r
Potatoes, white or red	10 lb	2.35	3/01	4c
Potatoes, white, all types	lb	0.44	7/01	11r
Poultry, expenditures on	yr	137	1999	30r
Processed fruits, expenditures on	yr	97	1999	30r
Processed vegetables, expenditures on	yr	82	1999	30r
Rice, white, long grain, uncooked	lb	0.51	7/01	11r
Round roast, graded and ungraded, excl U.S. prime and choice	lb	2.96	7/01	11r
Round steak, graded and ungraded, excl U.S. prime and choice	lb	3.11	7/01	11r
Sausage, Jimmy Dean/Owens pork	lb	2.79	3/01	4c
Shortening, vegetable, Crisco	3 lb	2.74	3/01	4c
Sirloin steak, graded and ungraded, excl U.S. prime and choice	lb	4.23	7/01	11r

Values are in dollars or fractions of dollars. In the column headed *Ref*, references are shown to sources. Each reference is followed by a letter. These refer to the geographical level for which data were reported: s=State, r=Region, and c=City or metro. The abbreviation *ex* is used to mean *except* or *excluding*; *exp* stands for *expenditures*. For other abbreviations and further explanations, please see the Introduction.

Tulsa, OK - continued

Item	Per	Value	Date	Ref.
Groceries				
Soft drink, Coca Cola, ex deposit	2 liter	1.09	3/01	4c
Spaghetti and macaroni	lb	0.78	7/01	11r
Steak, round, U.S. choice, boneless	lb	3.56	7/01	11r
Steak, sirloin, U.S. choice, boneless	lb	5.65	7/01	11r
Steak, T-bone	lb	7.02	3/01	4c
Strawberries, dry pint	12 oz	1.50	7/01	11r
Sugar and other sweets, expenditures on	yr	99	1999	30r
Sugar, cane or beet	4 lbs	1.69	3/01	4c
Sugar, white, 33-80 ounce package	lb	0.39	7/01	11r
Sugar, white, all sizes	lb	0.42	7/01	11r
Tobacco products and smoking supplies purchases	yr	288	1999	30r
Tomatoes, field grown	lb	1.43	7/01	11r
Tomatoes, Hunt's or Del Monte	14.5 oz	0.89	3/01	4c
Tuna, chunk, light	6 oz	0.75	3/01	4c
Tuna, light, chunk	lb	1.77	7/01	11r
Turkey, frozen, whole	lb	1.05	7/01	11r
Goods and Services				
Miscellaneous goods and services, ACCRA Index		98.50	3/01	4c
B&B Japanese maple (acer japonicum)	gal	79.98-99.00	4/00	93r
Boxwood (buxus)	2 gal	12.98-18.99	4/00	93r
Daylily (hemerocallis)	gal	7.96-11.00	4/00	93r
Flat of annuals		13.99-27.99	4/00	93r
Fountain grass (pennisetum)	gal	6.96-9.00	4/00	93r
Hanging basket (10 in)		9.99-24.99	4/00	93r
Hardy geranium (geranium)	gal	5.96-8.00	4/00	93r
Hosta (hosta)	gal	8.96-12.99	4/00	93r
Lilac (syrubga vulgaris)	2 gal	13.00-19.99	4/00	93r
Rhododendron (rhododendron)	2 gal	12.98-29.99	4/00	93r
Sage (salvia)	gal	5.96-8.00	4/00	93r
Wintercreeper euonymus (euonymus fortunei)	2 gal	13.00-18.99	4/00	93r
Hunting license	yr	12.50	4/01	34s
Health Care				
Health care, ACCRA Index		101.60	3/01	4c
Cardiac catheterization, ave hospital/ physician charges		15750	1998	77s
Childbirth, Cesarean delivery		11587	1997	13r
Childbirth, vaginal delivery		6725	1997	13r
Dentist's fee, adult teeth cleaning and periodic oral exam	visit	77.00	3/01	4c
Doctor's fee, routine exam, established patient	visit	62.80	3/01	4c
Drugs, expenditures on	yr	399	1999	30r
Health care purchases	yr	1971	1999	30r
Health insurance expenditures	yr	933	1999	30r
Hospital care, private room	day	432.50	3/01	4c
Hysterectomy, laproscopically-assisted, ave hospital/physician charges		16080	1998	76s
Hysterectomy, vaginal, ave hospital and physician charges		8140	1998	76s
Medicaid dispensing fee		4.15	1999	87s
Medical services expenditures	yr	547	1999	30r
Medical supplies, expenditures on	yr	91	1999	30r
Household Goods				
Dishwashing powder, Cascade	50 oz	3.19	3/01	4c
Floor coverings, expenditures on	yr	44	1999	30r
Furniture, expenditures on	yr	335	1999	30r

Tulsa, OK - continued

Item	Per	Value	Date	Ref.
Household Goods - continued				
Household furnishings and equipment purchases	yr	1328	1999	30r
Household textiles, expenditures on	yr	89	1999	30r
Laundry and cleaning supplies, expenditures on	yr	113	1999	30r
Tissues, facial, Kleenex brand	175	1.45	3/01	4c
Housing				
Housing, ACCRA Index		82.80	3/01	4c
Home, 2200 sq ft, 4-br, 2-bath, 2-car garage, average		129950	2000	47c
Home price, existing, ave		160100	10/00	90r
Home value, median		88000	2001	53s
House, 2400 sq ft, 8000 sq ft lot, new, urban, utilities	total	170000	3/01	4c
House payment, principal and interest, 25% down payment	mos	849	3/01	4c
Household operation expenditures	yr	553	1999	30r
Housekeeping supplies purchases	yr	473	1999	30r
Housing, expenditures on	yr	10303	1999	30r
Maintenance, repairs, insurance expenditures	yr	699	1999	30r
Monthly rental value of owned home	mos	505	1999	30r
Owned dwellings, expenditures own	yr	3465	1999	30r
Rent expenditures	yr	1641	1999	30r
Rent, apartment, 2 br, 1 1/2-2 baths, unfurn, 950 sq ft, water	mos	586	3/01	4c
Rental unit, 1 bedroom, with utilities	mos	402	4/01	41c
Rental unit, 2 bedroom, with utilities	mos	527	4/01	41c
Rental unit, 3 bedroom, with utilities	mos	733	4/01	41c
Rental unit, 4 bedroom, with utilities	mos	865	4/01	41c
Shelter, expenditures on	yr	5467	1999	30r
Insurance and Pensions				
Life and other personal insurance purchases	yr	414	1999	30r
Pensions and Social Security, expenditures on	yr	2635	1999	30r
Personal insurance and pensions, expenditures on	yr	3048	1999	30r
Legal Fees				
Combination hunting and fishing license	yr	21.00	4/01	34s
Divorce, filing fee		84.00	4/01	35s
Driver's license fee	renew	15.00	1999	48s
Driver's license fee	orig	15.00	1999	48s
Fishing license	yr	12.50	4/01	34s
Personal Goods				
Personal care products and services purchases	yr	393	1999	30r
Shampoo, Alberto VO5	15 oz	1.04	3/01	4c
Toothpaste, Crest or Colgate	6-7 oz	2.48	3/01	4c
Personal Services				
Dry cleaning, man's 2-pc suit		8.23	3/01	4c
Man's haircut, barbershop, no styling		9.00	3/01	4c
Personal services, household, expenditures on	yr	258	1999	30r
Woman's shampoo, trim, blow-dry, no style-change		22.30	3/01	4c
Pets				
Pets, toys, and playground equipment, expenditures on	yr	306	1999	30r
Restaurant Food				
Chicken, fried, thigh and drumstick, KFC/ Church's		2.55	3/01	4c
Hamburger with cheese, McDonald's	1/4 lb	2.07	3/01	4c
Pizza, Pizza Hut or Pizza Inn	11-12 in	9.79	3/01	4c
Taxes				
Federal income taxes paid	yr	2047	1999	30r
Personal taxes, expenditures on	yr	2554	1999	30r
Property taxes paid	yr	726	1999	30r
State and local income taxes paid	yr	363	1999	30r

Values are in dollars or fractions of dollars. In the column headed *Ref*, references are shown to sources. Each reference is followed by a letter. These refer to the geographical level for which data were reported: s=State, r=Region, and c=City or metro. The abbreviation *ex* is used to mean *except* or *excluding*; *exp* stands for expenditures. For other abbreviations and further explanations, please see the Introduction.

Tulsa, OK - continued

Item	Per	Value	Date	Ref.
Transportation				
Transportation, ACCRA Index		89.40	3/01	4c
Cars and trucks, new, expenditures on	yr	1648	1999	30r
Cars and trucks, used, expenditures on	yr	1651	1999	30r
Diesel at the pump	gal	1.13	10/99	73s
Gasoline and motor oil purchases	yr	1052	1999	30r
Gasoline before-tax price (cents)	gal	103.70	10/00	43s
Maintenance and repair expenditures	yr	621	1999	30r
Public transportation, expenditures on	yr	298	1999	30r
Tire balance, computer or spin balance, front	wheel	6.90	3/01	4c
Transportation purchases	yr	6738	1999	30r
Vehicle expenses, miscellaneous, purchases	yr	2033	1999	30r
Vehicle insurance payments	yr	696	1999	30r
Vehicle purchases (net outlay)	yr	3354	1999	30r
Vehicle rental, lease expenditures	yr	352	1999	30r
Travel				
Hotel room	night	55.28	2/01	94s
Utilities				
Utilities, ACCRA Index		100.30	3/01	4c
Electrical bill, average	mos	67.33	9/00	9s
Electricity, expenditures on	yr	1115	1999	30r
Electricity, summer, 250 KWh	mos	21.59	2/96	96c
Electricity, summer, 500 KWh	mos	35.53	2/96	96c
Electricity, summer, 750 KWh	mos	49.47	2/96	96c
Electricity, summer, 1000 KWh	mos	63.41	2/96	96c
Electricity and other, mixed, 2400 sq ft, new home	mos	61.20	3/01	4c
Electricity cost, average	KWh	5.66	9/00	9s
Water and other public services, expenditures on	yr	298	1999	30r
Weddings				
Wedding (national average cost)		19936	2000	33r
Attendants' gifts		321	1998	33r
Bridal attendants' apparel (5 persons)		824	2000	33r
Bride's headpiece/veil		173	1998	33r
Bride's wedding dress		859	1998	33r
Clergy, religious facility fee		242	1998	33r
Engagement ring		3177	1998	33r
Flowers		789	1998	33r
Groom's formalwear rental		99	2000	33r
Limousine		410	1998	33r
Marriage license cost		25.00	4/01	35s
Men's formalwear (ushers, best man)		469	2000	33r
Mother of bride apparel		241	2000	33r
Music		866	1998	33r
Photography and videography		1368	1998	33r
Rehearsal dinner		728	1998	33r
Wedding invitations and announcements		341	1998	33r
Wedding reception		7968	2000	33r
Wedding rings (bride and groom)		1060	1998	33r

Tuscaloosa, AL

Item	Per	Value	Date	Ref.
Composite, ACCRA index		98.40	3/01	4c
Alcoholic Beverages				
Alcoholic beverage purchases	yr	253	1999	30r
Beer, Heineken, 12-oz, ex deposit	6	7.62	3/01	4c
J & B Scotch	750-ml	23.99	3/01	4c
Malt beverages, all types, all sizes, any origin	16 oz	0.96	7/01	11r
Wine, Livingston or Gallo, Chablis blanc	1.5 liter	6.08	3/01	4c
Appliances				
Appliance repair, service call, washing machine	min lab chg	51.25	3/01	4c
Major appliances, expenditures on	yr	172	1999	30r
Small appliances, housewares, expenditures on	yr	81	1999	30r
Banking and Money				
Mortgage interest and charges paid	yr	2039	1999	30r
Mortgage principal paid on owned property	yr	1026	1999	30r

Tuscaloosa, AL - continued

Item	Per	Value	Date	Ref.
Banking and Money - continued				
Mortgage rate, incl. points and orig. fee, 30-yr. conv. fixed or ARM	mos	6.85	3/01	4c
Vehicle finance charges paid	yr	365	1999	30r
Charity				
Cash contributions, expenditures	yr	1127	1999	30r
Child Care				
Child raising cost, total, age 0-2	yr	8540	1999	60r
Child raising cost, total, age 3-5	yr	8780	1999	60r
Child raising cost, total, age 6-8	yr	8820	1999	60r
Child raising cost, total, age 9-11	yr	8800	1999	60r
Child raising cost, total, age 12-14	yr	9510	1999	60r
Child raising cost, total, age 15-17	yr	9740	1999	60r
Child's child care and education, age 0-2	yr	1380	1999	60r
Child's child care and education, age 3-5	yr	1520	1999	60r
Child's child care and education, age 6-8	yr	990	1999	60r
Child's child care and education, age 9-11	yr	650	1999	60r
Child's child care and education, age 12-14	yr	490	1999	60r
Child's child care and education, age 15-17	yr	840	1999	60r
Child's clothing, age 0-2	yr	480	1999	60r
Child's clothing, age 3-5	yr	470	1999	60r
Child's clothing, age 6-8	yr	520	1999	60r
Child's clothing, age 9-11	yr	570	1999	60r
Child's clothing, age 12-14	yr	950	1999	60r
Child's clothing, age 15-17	yr	850	1999	60r
Child's food, age 0-2	yr	1000	1999	60r
Child's food, age 3-5	yr	1160	1999	60r
Child's food, age 6-8	yr	1490	1999	60r
Child's food, age 9-11	yr	1770	1999	60r
Child's food, age 12-14	yr	1770	1999	60r
Child's food, age 15-17	yr	1980	1999	60r
Child's health care, age 0-2	yr	620	1999	60r
Child's health care, age 3-5	yr	590	1999	60r
Child's health care, age 6-8	yr	680	1999	60r
Child's health care, age 9-11	yr	720	1999	60r
Child's health care, age 12-14	yr	730	1999	60r
Child's health care, age 15-17	yr	760	1999	60r
Child's housing, age 0-2	yr	3070	1999	60r
Child's housing, age 3-5	yr	3050	1999	60r
Child's housing, age 6-8	yr	3010	1999	60r
Child's housing, age 9-11	yr	2850	1999	60r
Child's housing, age 12-14	yr	3040	1999	60r
Child's housing, age 15-17	yr	2650	1999	60r
Child's personal care, reading, age 0-2	yr	910	1999	60r
Child's personal care, reading, age 3-5	yr	930	1999	60r
Child's personal care, reading, age 6-8	yr	960	1999	60r
Child's personal care, reading, age 9-11	yr	1000	1999	60r
Child's personal care, reading, age 12-14	yr	1170	1999	60r
Child's personal care, reading, age 15-17	yr	950	1999	60r
Clothing				
Apparel and services purchases	yr	1610	1999	30r
Boys' brief, cotton	3	5.99	3/01	4c
Boys, 2 to 15, expenditures on	yr	89	1999	30r
Children under 2, expenditures on	yr	79	1999	30r
Footwear, expenditures on	yr	283	1999	30r
Girls, 2 to 15, expenditures on	yr	103	1999	30r
Men and boys, expenditures on	yr	351	1999	30r
Men, 16 and over, expenditures on	yr	262	1999	30r
Shirt, man's dress shirt		26.24	3/01	4c
Slacks, man's "No Wrinkles" khaki		39.25	3/01	4c
Women, 16 and over, expenditures on	yr	538	1999	30r
Communications				
Newspaper subscription, daily and Sunday delivery	mos	12.35	3/01	4c
Phone line, single, business, field visit	inst.	69.00	12/97	17s
Phone line, single, business, no field visit	inst.	69.00	12/97	17s
Phone line, single, residence, field visit	inst.	40.00	12/97	17s
Phone line, single, residence, no field visit	inst.	40.00	12/97	17s
Postage and stationery, expenditures on	yr	104	1999	30r
Postal rate, express mail, up to half-pound		12.45	7/01	108r
Postal rate, letter, first class, first ounce		0.34	7/01	108r

Values are in dollars or fractions of dollars. In the column headed *Ref*, references are shown to sources. Each reference is followed by a letter. These refer to the geographical level for which data were reported: s=State, r=Region, and c=City or metro. The abbreviation *ex* is used to mean *except* or *excluding*; *exp* stands for *expenditures*. For other abbreviations and further explanations, please see the Introduction.

Tuscaloosa, AL - continued

Item	Per	Value	Date	Ref.
Communications				
Postal rate, letter, two ounces		0.57	7/01	108r
Postal rate, post card		0.21	7/01	108r
Postal rate, priority mail, two pounds		3.95	7/01	108r
Postal rate, priority mail, up to one pound		3.50	7/01	108r
Telephone bill, family of three	mos	19.95	3/01	4c
Telephone services, expenditures on	yr	860	1999	30r
Education				
Board, 4-year private college/university	yr	2256	1996	38s
Board, 4-year public college/university	yr	1739	1996	38s
Education expenditures	yr	431	1999	30r
Room, 4-year private college/university	yr	1799	1996	38s
Room, 4-year public college/university	yr	1757	1996	38s
Total cost, 4-year private college/university	yr	11635	1996	38s
Total cost, 4-year public college/university	yr	5737	1996	38s
Tuition, 2-year public college/university, in state	yr	1317	1996	38s
Tuition, 4-year private college/university, in state	yr	7580	1996	38s
Tuition, 4-year public college/university	yr	2240	1996	38s
Energy and Fuels				
Electricity	500 KWhs	47.29	7/01	11r
Electricity	KWh	0.09	7/01	11r
Energy, combined forms, 2400 sq ft	mos	111.47	3/01	4c
Fuel oil #2	gal	1.43	7/01	11r
Fuel oil and other fuels, expenditures on	yr	45	1999	30r
Gas, natural, commercial rate	1000 cf	9.50	11/00	88s
Gas, regular unleaded, cash, self-service	gal	1.30	3/01	4c
Gasoline, all types	gal	1.60	7/01	11r
Gasoline, unleaded midgrade	gal	1.65	7/01	11r
Gasoline, unleaded premium	gal	1.74	7/01	11r
Natural gas, expenditures on	yr	164	1999	30r
Utility (piped) gas, therm		1.01	7/01	11r
Utility (piped) gas, 40 therms		44.29	7/01	11r
Utility (piped) gas, 100 therms		97.44	7/01	11r
Entertainment				
Bowling, Saturday evening rate	line	2.62	3/01	4c
Entertainment purchases	yr	1574	1999	30r
Fees and admissions paid	yr	371	1999	30r
Monopoly game, Parker Brothers', No. 9	game	10.74	3/01	4c
Movie, first-run, Saturday, evening	adm.	6.88	3/01	4c
Reading purchases	yr	121	1999	30r
Television, radios, sound equipment, expenditures on	yr	561	1999	30r
Tennis balls, yellow, Wilson or Penn, 3	can	2.75	3/01	4c
Groceries				
Groceries, ACCRA Index		97.30	3/01	4c
American processed cheese	lb	3.50	7/01	11r
Antibiotic ointment, Polysporin	0.5 oz	4.63	3/01	4c
Baby food, strained vegetables or fruit, lowest price	4-4.5 oz	0.35	3/01	4c
Bakery products, expenditures on	yr	261	1999	30r
Bananas	lb	0.55	3/01	4c
Bananas	lb	0.47	7/01	11r
Beans, dried, any type, all sizes	lb	0.63	7/01	11r
Beef for stew, boneless	lb	2.86	7/01	11r
Beef or hamburger, ground	lb	1.57	3/01	4c
Beef, expenditures on	yr	210	1999	30r
Bologna, all beef or mixed	lb	2.29	7/01	11r
Bread, French	lb	1.66	7/01	11r
Bread, white	loaf	0.96	3/01	4c
Bread, white, pan	lb	0.87	7/01	11r
Bread, whole wheat, pan	lb	1.38	7/01	11r
Broccoli	lb	1.04	7/01	11r
Butter, salted, grade AA, stick	lb	2.26	7/01	11r
Butter, yoghurt, cheese, etc, expenditures on	yr	170	1999	30r
Cabbage	lb	0.42	7/01	11r
Cereals and cereal products, expenditures on	yr	140	1999	30r
Cheddar cheese, natural	lb	3.75	7/01	11r

Tuscaloosa, AL - continued

Item	Per	Value	Date	Ref.
Groceries - continued				
Cheese, Kraft grated Parmesan	8 oz	3.47	3/01	4c
Chicken breast, bone-in	lb	1.85	7/01	11r
Chicken legs, bone-in	lb	1.34	7/01	11r
Chicken, fresh, whole	lb	1.05	7/01	11r
Chicken, whole fryer	lb	0.93	3/01	4c
Chops, boneless,	lb	4.13	7/01	11r
Chuck roast, graded and ungraded, excl U.S. prime and choice	lb	2.35	7/01	11r
Chuck roast, U.S. choice, boneless	lb	2.67	7/01	11r
Cigarettes, Winston, Kings	carton	26.75	3/01	4c
Coffee, 100%, ground roast, all sizes	lb	2.88	7/01	11r
Coffee, instant, plain, regular, all sizes	16 oz	9.25	7/01	11r
Coffee, vacuum-packed	13 oz	2.64	3/01	4c
Cola, non diet,	2 liter	1.11	7/01	11r
Corn Flakes, Kellogg's or Post Toasties	18 oz	2.96	3/01	4c
Corn, frozen, whole kernel, lowest price	16 oz	1.16	3/01	4c
Crackers, soda, salted	lb	1.70	7/01	11r
Dairy product purchases	yr	282	1999	30r
Eggs, expenditures on	yr	32	1999	30r
Eggs, Grade A or AA	dozen	1.18	3/01	4c
Fats and oils, expenditures on	yr	79	1999	30r
Fish and seafood, expenditures on	yr	99	1999	30r
Flour, white, all purpose	lb	0.32	7/01	11r
Food (excl fruit and vegetables), eaten at home, purchases	yr	815	1999	30r
Food cooked on trips, expenditures on	yr	36	1999	30r
Food purchases	yr	4533	1999	30r
Food purchases, eaten away from home	yr	1873	1999	30r
Food purchases, food eaten at home	yr	2660	1999	30r
Fresh fruits, expenditures on	yr	128	1999	30r
Fresh milk and cream, expenditures on	yr	112	1999	30r
Fresh vegetables, expenditures on	yr	131	1999	30r
Fruit and vegetable purchases	yr	438	1999	30r
Grapefruit	lb	0.59	7/01	11r
Grapes, Thompson, seedless	lb	2.12	7/01	11r
Ground beef, 100% beef	lb	1.76	7/01	11r
Ground beef, lean and extra lean	lb	2.60	7/01	11r
Ground chuck, 100% beef	lb	2.08	7/01	11r
Ham, boneless, excl canned	lb	2.71	7/01	11r
Ham, rump or shank half, bone-in, smoked	lb	2.19	7/01	11r
Ice cream, prepackaged, bulk, regular	1/2 gal	3.93	7/01	11r
Lemons	lb	1.32	7/01	11r
Lettuce, iceberg	head	0.95	3/01	4c
Lettuce, iceberg	lb	0.76	7/01	11r
Margarine, Blue Bonnet or Parkay, stick	lb	0.64	3/01	4c
Milk, fresh, low fat,	gal	2.75	7/01	11r
Milk, fresh, whole, fortified	gal	2.97	7/01	11r
Milk, whole	1/2 gal	1.90	3/01	4c
Nonalcoholic beverages, expenditures on	yr	228	1999	30r
Orange juice, frozen concentrate	16 oz	1.95	7/01	11r
Orange juice, Minute Maid frozen	12 oz	1.58	3/01	4c
Oranges, Navel	lb	0.73	7/01	11r
Oranges, Valencia	lb	0.55	7/01	11r
Peaches, halves or slices, Hunt's, Del Monte, or Libby's	29 oz	1.55	3/01	4c
Peanut butter, creamy, all sizes	lb	1.83	7/01	11r
Pears, Anjou	lb	0.98	7/01	11r
Peas, green, Del Monte or Green Giant	15 oz	0.77	3/01	4c
Pork chops, center cut, bone-in	lb	3.33	7/01	11r
Pork sausage, fresh, loose	lb	2.59	7/01	11r
Pork shoulder picnic, bone-in, smoked	lb	1.12	7/01	11r
Pork, expenditures on	yr	162	1999	30r
Potato chips	16 oz	3.59	7/01	11r
Potatoes, frozen, french fried	lb	1.00	7/01	11r
Potatoes, white or red	10 lb	2.96	3/01	4c
Potatoes, white, all types	lb	0.44	7/01	11r
Poultry, expenditures on	yr	137	1999	30r
Processed fruits, expenditures on	yr	97	1999	30r
Processed vegetables, expenditures on	yr	82	1999	30r
Rice, white, long grain, uncooked	lb	0.51	7/01	11r
Round roast, graded and ungraded, excl U.S. prime and choice	lb	2.96	7/01	11r

Values are in dollars or fractions of dollars. In the column headed *Ref*, references are shown to sources. Each reference is followed by a letter. These refer to the geographical level for which data were reported: s=State, r=Region, and c=City or metro. The abbreviation *ex* is used to mean *except* or *excluding*; *exp* stands for *expenditures*. For other abbreviations and further explanations, please see the Introduction.

Tuscaloosa, AL - continued

Item	Per	Value	Date	Ref.
Groceries				
Round steak, graded and ungraded, excl U.S. prime and choice	lb	3.11	7/01	11r
Sausage, Jimmy Dean/Owens pork	lb	2.58	3/01	4c
Shortening, vegetable, Crisco	3 lb	3.00	3/01	4c
Sirloin steak, graded and ungraded, excl U.S. prime and choice	lb	4.23	7/01	11r
Soft drink, Coca Cola, ex deposit	2 liter	1.05	3/01	4c
Spaghetti and macaroni	lb	0.78	7/01	11r
Steak, round, U.S. choice, boneless	lb	3.56	7/01	11r
Steak, sirloin, U.S. choice, boneless	lb	5.65	7/01	11r
Steak, T-bone	lb	7.19	3/01	4c
Strawberries, dry pint	12 oz	1.50	7/01	11r
Sugar and other sweets, expenditures on	yr	99	1999	30r
Sugar, cane or beet	4 lbs	1.56	3/01	4c
Sugar, white, 33-80 ounce package	lb	0.39	7/01	11r
Sugar, white, all sizes	lb	0.42	7/01	11r
Tobacco products and smoking supplies purchases	yr	288	1999	30r
Tomatoes, field grown	lb	1.43	7/01	11r
Tomatoes, Hunt's or Del Monte	14.5 oz	0.79	3/01	4c
Tuna, chunk, light	6 oz	0.43	3/01	4c
Tuna, light, chunk	lb	1.77	7/01	11r
Turkey, frozen, whole	lb	1.05	7/01	11r
Goods and Services				
Miscellaneous goods and services, ACCRA Index		105.00	3/01	4c
Hunting license	yr	16.00	4/01	34s
Health Care				
Health care, ACCRA Index		98.40	3/01	4c
Cardiac catheterization, ave hospital/ physician charges		15260	1998	77s
Childbirth, Cesarean delivery		11587	1997	13r
Childbirth, vaginal delivery		6725	1997	13r
Dentist's fee, adult teeth cleaning and periodic oral exam	visit	71.20	3/01	4c
Doctor's fee, routine exam, established patient	visit	52.57	3/01	4c
Drugs, expenditures on	yr	399	1999	30r
Health care purchases	yr	1971	1999	30r
Health insurance expenditures	yr	933	1999	30r
Hospital care, private room	day	595.00	3/01	4c
Hysterectomy, laproscopically-assisted, ave hospital/physician charges		16780	1998	76s
Hysterectomy, vaginal, ave hospital and physician charges		10990	1998	76s
Medicaid dispensing fee		5.40	1999	87s
Medical services expenditures	yr	547	1999	30r
Medical supplies, expenditures on	yr	91	1999	30r
Household Goods				
Dishwashing powder, Cascade	50 oz	3.41	3/01	4c
Floor coverings, expenditures on	yr	44	1999	30r
Furniture, expenditures on	yr	335	1999	30r
Household furnishings and equipment purchases	yr	1328	1999	30r
Household textiles, expenditures on	yr	89	1999	30r
Laundry and cleaning supplies, expenditures on	yr	113	1999	30r
Tissues, facial, Kleenex brand	175	1.36	3/01	4c
Housing				
Housing, ACCRA Index		93.80	3/01	4c
Home price, existing, ave		160100	10/00	90r
Home value, median		115000	2001	53s
House, 2400 sq ft, 8000 sq ft lot, new, urban, utilities	total	189558	3/01	4c
House payment, principal and interest, 25% down payment	mos	931	3/01	4c
Household operation expenditures	yr	553	1999	30r
Housekeeping supplies purchases	yr	473	1999	30r
Housing, expenditures on	yr	10303	1999	30r

Tuscaloosa, AL - continued

Item	Per	Value	Date	Ref.
Housing - continued				
Maintenance, repairs, insurance expenditures	yr	699	1999	30r
Monthly rental value of owned home	mos	505	1999	30r
Owned dwellings, expenditures own	yr	3465	1999	30r
Rent expenditures	yr	1641	1999	30r
Rent, apartment, 2 br, 1 1/2-2 baths, unfurn, 950 sq ft, water	mos	744	3/01	4c
Rental unit, 1 bedroom, with utilities	mos	371	4/01	41c
Rental unit, 2 bedroom, with utilities	mos	493	4/01	41c
Rental unit, 3 bedroom, with utilities	mos	678	4/01	41c
Rental unit, 4 bedroom, with utilities	mos	717	4/01	41c
Shelter, expenditures on	yr	5467	1999	30r
Insurance and Pensions				
Life and other personal insurance purchases	yr	414	1999	30r
Pensions and Social Security, expenditures on	yr	2635	1999	30r
Personal insurance and pensions, expenditures on	yr	3048	1999	30r
Legal Fees				
Divorce, filing fee		146.00-193.00	4/01	35s
Driver's license fee	renew	18.50	1999	48s
Driver's license fee	orig	18.50	1999	48s
Personal Goods				
Personal care products and services purchases	yr	393	1999	30r
Shampoo, Alberto VO5	15 oz	1.13	3/01	4c
Toothpaste, Crest or Colgate	6-7 oz	2.62	3/01	4c
Personal Services				
Dry cleaning, man's 2-pc suit		8.54	3/01	4c
Man's haircut, barbershop, no styling		15.00	3/01	4c
Personal services, household, expenditures on	yr	258	1999	30r
Woman's shampoo, trim, blow-dry, no style-change		29.92	3/01	4c
Pets				
Pets, toys, and playground equipment, expenditures on	yr	306	1999	30r
Restaurant Food				
Chicken, fried, thigh and drumstick, KFC/ Church's		2.26	3/01	4c
Hamburger with cheese, McDonald's	1/4 lb	2.19	3/01	4c
Pizza, Pizza Hut or Pizza Inn	11-12 in	9.49	3/01	4c
Taxes				
Federal income taxes paid	yr	2047	1999	30r
Personal taxes, expenditures on	yr	2554	1999	30r
Property taxes paid	yr	726	1999	30r
State and local income taxes paid	yr	363	1999	30r
Transportation				
Transportation, ACCRA Index		97.00	3/01	4c
Cars and trucks, new, expenditures on	yr	1648	1999	30r
Cars and trucks, used, expenditures on	yr	1651	1999	30r
Diesel at the pump	gal	1.19	10/99	73s
Gasoline and motor oil purchases	yr	1052	1999	30r
Gasoline before-tax price (cents)	gal	104.10	10/00	43s
Maintenance and repair expenditures	yr	621	1999	30r
Public transportation, expenditures on	yr	298	1999	30r
Tire balance, computer or spin balance, front	wheel	8.17	3/01	4c
Transportation purchases	yr	6738	1999	30r
Vehicle expenses, miscellaneous, purchases	yr	2033	1999	30r
Vehicle insurance payments	yr	696	1999	30r
Vehicle purchases (net outlay)	yr	3354	1999	30r
Vehicle rental, lease expenditures	yr	352	1999	30r
Utilities				
Utilities, ACCRA Index		91.40	3/01	4c
Electrical bill, average	mos	83.42	9/00	9s
Electricity, 2400 sq ft, new home	mos	111.47	3/01	4c

Values are in dollars or fractions of dollars. In the column headed *Ref*, references are shown to sources. Each reference is followed by a letter. These refer to the geographical level for which data were reported: s=State, r=Region, and c=City or metro. The abbreviation *ex* is used to mean *except* or *excluding*; *exp* stands for expenditures. For other abbreviations and further explanations, please see the Introduction.

Tuscaloosa, AL - continued

Item	Per	Value	Date	Ref.
Utilities				
Electricity, expenditures on	yr	1115	1999	30r
Electricity cost, average	KWh	5.60	9/00	9s
Water and other public services, expenditures on	yr	298	1999	30r
Weddings				
Wedding (national average cost)		19936	2000	33r
Attendants' gifts		321	1998	33r
Bridal attendants' apparel (5 persons)		824	2000	33r
Bride's headpiece/veil		173	1998	33r
Bride's wedding dress		859	1998	33r
Clergy, religious facility fee		242	1998	33r
Engagement ring		3177	1998	33r
Flowers		789	1998	33r
Groom's formalwear rental		99	2000	33r
Limousine		410	1998	33r
Marriage license cost		25.00	4/01	35s
Men's formalwear (ushers, best man)		469	2000	33r
Mother of bride apparel		241	2000	33r
Music		866	1998	33r
Photography and videography		1368	1998	33r
Rehearsal dinner		728	1998	33r
Wedding invitations and announcements		341	1998	33r
Wedding reception		7968	2000	33r
Wedding rings (bride and groom)		1060	1998	33r

Tyler, TX

Item	Per	Value	Date	Ref.
Composite, ACCRA index		90.90	12/00	5c
Alcoholic Beverages				
Alcoholic beverage purchases	yr	253	1999	30r
Beer, Heineken, 12-oz, ex deposit	6	6.84	12/00	5c
J & B Scotch	750-ml	24.32	12/00	5c
Malt beverages, all types, all sizes, any origin	16 oz	0.96	7/01	11r
Wine, Livingston or Gallo, Chablis blanc	1.5 liter	6.34	12/00	5c
Appliances				
Appliance repair, service call, washing machine	min lab chg	43.58	12/00	5c
Major appliances, expenditures on	yr	172	1999	30r
Small appliances, housewares, expenditures on	yr	81	1999	30r
Banking and Money				
Mortgage interest and charges paid	yr	2039	1999	30r
Mortgage principal paid on owned property	yr	1026	1999	30r
Mortgage rate, incl. points and orig. fee, 30-yr. conv. fixed or ARM	mos	7.82	12/00	5c
Vehicle finance charges paid	yr	365	1999	30r
Charity				
Cash contributions, expenditures	yr	1127	1999	30r
Child Care				
Child raising cost, total, age 0-2	yr	8540	1999	60r
Child raising cost, total, age 3-5	yr	8780	1999	60r
Child raising cost, total, age 6-8	yr	8820	1999	60r
Child raising cost, total, age 9-11	yr	8800	1999	60r
Child raising cost, total, age 12-14	yr	9510	1999	60r
Child raising cost, total, age 15-17	yr	9740	1999	60r
Child's child care and education, age 0-2	yr	1380	1999	60r
Child's child care and education, age 3-5	yr	1520	1999	60r
Child's child care and education, age 6-8	yr	990	1999	60r
Child's child care and education, age 9-11	yr	650	1999	60r
Child's child care and education, age 12-14	yr	490	1999	60r
Child's child care and education, age 15-17	yr	840	1999	60r
Child's clothing, age 0-2	yr	480	1999	60r
Child's clothing, age 3-5	yr	470	1999	60r
Child's clothing, age 6-8	yr	520	1999	60r
Child's clothing, age 9-11	yr	570	1999	60r
Child's clothing, age 12-14	yr	950	1999	60r
Child's clothing, age 15-17	yr	850	1999	60r
Child's food, age 0-2	yr	1000	1999	60r

Tyler, TX - continued

Item	Per	Value	Date	Ref.
Child Care - continued				
Child's food, age 3-5	yr	1160	1999	60r
Child's food, age 6-8	yr	1490	1999	60r
Child's food, age 9-11	yr	1770	1999	60r
Child's food, age 12-14	yr	1770	1999	60r
Child's food, age 15-17	yr	1980	1999	60r
Child's health care, age 0-2	yr	620	1999	60r
Child's health care, age 3-5	yr	590	1999	60r
Child's health care, age 6-8	yr	680	1999	60r
Child's health care, age 9-11	yr	720	1999	60r
Child's health care, age 12-14	yr	730	1999	60r
Child's health care, age 15-17	yr	760	1999	60r
Child's housing, age 0-2	yr	3070	1999	60r
Child's housing, age 3-5	yr	3050	1999	60r
Child's housing, age 6-8	yr	3010	1999	60r
Child's housing, age 9-11	yr	2850	1999	60r
Child's housing, age 12-14	yr	3040	1999	60r
Child's housing, age 15-17	yr	2650	1999	60r
Child's personal care, reading, age 0-2	yr	910	1999	60r
Child's personal care, reading, age 3-5	yr	930	1999	60r
Child's personal care, reading, age 6-8	yr	960	1999	60r
Child's personal care, reading, age 9-11	yr	1000	1999	60r
Child's personal care, reading, age 12-14	yr	1170	1999	60r
Child's personal care, reading, age 15-17	yr	950	1999	60r
Clothing				
Apparel and services purchases	yr	1610	1999	30r
Boys' brief, cotton	3	5.99	12/00	5c
Boys, 2 to 15, expenditures on	yr	89	1999	30r
Children under 2, expenditures on	yr	79	1999	30r
Footwear, expenditures on	yr	283	1999	30r
Girls, 2 to 15, expenditures on	yr	103	1999	30r
Men and boys, expenditures on	yr	351	1999	30r
Men, 16 and over, expenditures on	yr	262	1999	30r
Shirt, man's dress shirt		25.87	12/00	5c
Slacks, man's "No Wrinkles" khaki		28.24	12/00	5c
Women, 16 and over, expenditures on	yr	538	1999	30r
Communications				
Cable modem installation, AT&T-BIS		150.00	6/99	103s
Cable modem installation, Marcus		499.00	6/99	103s
Cable modem installation, Time Warner		75.00-225.00	6/99	103s
Cable modem rate, cable subscriber, AT&T-BIS	mos	39.95	6/99	103s
Cable modem rate, cable subscriber, Marcus	mos	14.95-49.95	6/99	103s
Cable modem rate, cable subscriber, Time Warner	mos	39.95-49.95	6/99	103s
Cable modem rate, non-cable subscriber, Marcus	mos	60.95	6/99	103s
Cable modem rate, non-cable subscriber, Time Warner	mos	39.95-54.95	6/99	103s
Newspaper subscription, daily and Sunday delivery	mos	7.50	12/00	5c
Phone line, single, business, field visit	inst.	71.90	12/97	17s
Phone line, single, business, no field visit	inst.	57.30	12/97	17s
Phone line, single, residence, field visit	inst.	52.95	12/97	17s
Phone line, single, residence, no field visit	inst.	38.35	12/97	17s
Postage and stationery, expenditures on	yr	104	1999	30r
Postal rate, express mail, up to half-pound		12.45	7/01	108r
Postal rate, letter, first class, first ounce		0.34	7/01	108r
Postal rate, letter, two ounces		0.57	7/01	108r
Postal rate, post card		0.21	7/01	108r
Postal rate, priority mail, two pounds		3.95	7/01	108r
Postal rate, priority mail, up to one pound		3.50	7/01	108r
Telephone bill, family of three	mos	15.76	12/00	5c
Telephone services, expenditures on	yr	860	1999	30r
Education				
Board, 4-year private college/university	yr	2198	1996	38s
Board, 4-year public college/university	yr	1759	1996	38s
Education expenditures	yr	431	1999	30r
Room, 4-year private college/university	yr	2000	1996	38s
Room, 4-year public college/university	yr	1885	1996	38s

Values are in dollars or fractions of dollars. In the column headed *Ref*, references are shown to sources. Each reference is followed by a letter. These refer to the geographical level for which data were reported: s=State, r=Region, and c=City or metro. The abbreviation *ex* is used to mean *except* or *excluding*; *exp* stands for expenditures. For other abbreviations and further explanations, please see the Introduction.

Tyler, TX - continued

Item	Per	Value	Date	Ref.
Education				
Total cost, 4-year private college/university	yr	13156	1996	38s
Total cost, 4-year public college/university	yr	5464	1996	38s
Tuition, 2-year public college/university, in state	yr	771	1996	38s
Tuition, 4-year private college/university, in state	yr	8959	1996	38s
Tuition, 4-year public college/university	yr	1820	1996	38s
Energy and Fuels				
Electricity	KWh	0.09	7/01	11r
Electricity	500 KWhs	47.29	7/01	11r
Energy, combined forms, 2400 sq ft	mos	124.71	12/00	5c
Energy, exc. electricity, 2400 sq ft	mos	41.19	12/00	5c
Fuel oil #2	gal	1.43	7/01	11r
Fuel oil and other fuels, expenditures on	yr	45	1999	30r
Gas, natural, commercial rate	1000 cf	6.94	11/00	88s
Gas, regular unleaded, cash, self-service	gal	1.38	12/00	5c
Gasoline, all types	gal	1.60	7/01	11r
Gasoline, unleaded midgrade	gal	1.65	7/01	11r
Gasoline, unleaded premium	gal	1.74	7/01	11r
Natural gas, expenditures on	yr	164	1999	30r
Utility (piped) gas, therm		1.01	7/01	11r
Utility (piped) gas, 40 therms		44.29	7/01	11r
Utility (piped) gas, 100 therms		97.44	7/01	11r
Entertainment				
Bowling, Saturday evening rate	line	2.75	12/00	5c
Entertainment purchases	yr	1574	1999	30r
Fees and admissions paid	yr	371	1999	30r
Monopoly game, Parker Brothers', No. 9	game	11.49	12/00	5c
Movie, first-run, Saturday, evening	adm.	6.63	12/00	5c
Reading purchases	yr	121	1999	30r
Television, radios, sound equipment, expenditures on	yr	561	1999	30r
Tennis balls, yellow, Wilson or Penn, 3	can	2.51	12/00	5c
Funerals				
Total cost of funeral		5842.28	1/99	78r
Acknowledgement cards		28.35	1/99	78r
Casket		2494.29	1/99	78r
Cosmetology, hair, other preparation		109.22	1/99	78r
Embalming		361.42	1/99	78r
Funeral at funeral home		349.20	1/99	78r
Hearse (local)		161.91	1/99	78r
Professional service charges		1116.50	1/99	78r
Service car/van		65.56	1/99	78r
Transfer of remains to funeral home		143.56	1/99	78r
Vault		785.25	1/99	78r
Visitation/viewing		227.02	1/99	78r
Groceries				
Groceries, ACCRA Index		90.90	12/00	5c
American processed cheese	lb	3.50	7/01	11r
Antibiotic ointment, Polysporin	0.5 oz	4.42	12/00	5c
Baby food, strained vegetables or fruit, lowest price	4-4.5 oz	0.30	12/00	5c
Bakery products, expenditures on	yr	261	1999	30r
Bananas	lb	0.47	7/01	11r
Bananas	lb	0.45	12/00	5c
Beans, dried, any type, all sizes	lb	0.63	7/01	11r
Beef for stew, boneless	lb	2.86	7/01	11r
Beef or hamburger, ground	lb	1.66	12/00	5c
Beef, expenditures on	yr	210	1999	30r
Bologna, all beef or mixed	lb	2.29	7/01	11r
Bread, French	lb	1.66	7/01	11r
Bread, white	loaf	0.76	12/00	5c
Bread, white, pan	lb	0.87	7/01	11r
Bread, whole wheat, pan	lb	1.38	7/01	11r
Broccoli	lb	1.04	7/01	11r
Butter, salted, grade AA, stick	lb	2.26	7/01	11r
Butter, yoghurt, cheese, etc, expenditures on	yr	170	1999	30r
Cabbage	lb	0.42	7/01	11r

Tyler, TX - continued

Item	Per	Value	Date	Ref.
Groceries - continued				
Cereals and cereal products, expenditures on	yr	140	1999	30r
Cheddar cheese, natural	lb	3.75	7/01	11r
Cheese, Kraft grated Parmesan	8 oz	3.18	12/00	5c
Chicken breast, bone-in	lb	1.85	7/01	11r
Chicken legs, bone-in	lb	1.34	7/01	11r
Chicken, fresh, whole	lb	1.05	7/01	11r
Chicken, whole fryer	lb	0.73	12/00	5c
Chops, boneless,	lb	4.13	7/01	11r
Chuck roast, graded and ungraded, excl U.S. prime and choice	lb	2.35	7/01	11r
Chuck roast, U.S. choice, boneless	lb	2.67	7/01	11r
Cigarettes, Winston, Kings	carton	31.56	12/00	5c
Coffee, 100%, ground roast, all sizes	lb	2.88	7/01	11r
Coffee, instant, plain, regular, all sizes	16 oz	9.25	7/01	11r
Coffee, vacuum-packed	13 oz	2.11	12/00	5c
Cola, non diet	2 liter	1.11	7/01	11r
Corn Flakes, Kellogg's or Post Toasties	18 oz	2.54	12/00	5c
Corn, frozen, whole kernel, lowest price	16 oz	1.05	12/00	5c
Crackers, soda, salted	lb	1.70	7/01	11r
Dairy product purchases	yr	282	1999	30r
Eggs, expenditures on	yr	32	1999	30r
Eggs, Grade A or AA	dozen	0.74	12/00	5c
Fats and oils, expenditures on	yr	79	1999	30r
Fish and seafood, expenditures on	yr	99	1999	30r
Flour, white, all purpose	lb	0.32	7/01	11r
Food (excl fruit and vegetables), eaten at home, purchases	yr	815	1999	30r
Food cooked on trips, expenditures on	yr	36	1999	30r
Food purchases	yr	4533	1999	30r
Food purchases, eaten away from home	yr	1873	1999	30r
Food purchases, food eaten at home	yr	2660	1999	30r
Fresh fruits, expenditures on	yr	128	1999	30r
Fresh milk and cream, expenditures on	yr	112	1999	30r
Fresh vegetables, expenditures on	yr	131	1999	30r
Fruit and vegetable purchases	yr	438	1999	30r
Grapefruit	lb	0.59	7/01	11r
Grapes, Thompson, seedless	lb	2.12	7/01	11r
Ground beef, 100% beef	lb	1.76	7/01	11r
Ground beef, lean and extra lean	lb	2.60	7/01	11r
Ground chuck, 100% beef	lb	2.08	7/01	11r
Ham, boneless, excl canned	lb	2.71	7/01	11r
Ham, rump or shank half, bone-in, smoked	lb	2.19	7/01	11r
Ice cream, prepackaged, bulk, regular	1/2 gal	3.93	7/01	11r
Lemons	lb	1.32	7/01	11r
Lettuce, iceberg	lb	0.76	7/01	11r
Lettuce, iceberg	head	1.06	12/00	5c
Margarine, Blue Bonnet or Parkay, stick	lb	0.71	12/00	5c
Milk, fresh, low fat,	gal	2.75	7/01	11r
Milk, fresh, whole, fortified	gal	2.97	7/01	11r
Milk, whole	1/2 gal	1.78	12/00	5c
Nonalcoholic beverages, expenditures on	yr	228	1999	30r
Orange juice, frozen concentrate	16 oz	1.95	7/01	11r
Orange juice, Minute Maid frozen	12 oz	1.47	12/00	5c
Oranges, Navel	lb	0.73	7/01	11r
Oranges, Valencia	lb	0.55	7/01	11r
Peaches, halves or slices, Hunt's, Del Monte, or Libby's	29 oz	1.61	12/00	5c
Peanut butter, creamy, all sizes	lb	1.83	7/01	11r
Pears, Anjou	lb	0.98	7/01	11r
Peas, green, Del Monte or Green Giant	15 oz	0.52	12/00	5c
Pork chops, center cut, bone-in	lb	3.33	7/01	11r
Pork sausage, fresh, loose	lb	2.59	7/01	11r
Pork shoulder picnic, bone-in, smoked	lb	1.12	7/01	11r
Pork, expenditures on	yr	162	1999	30r
Potato chips	16 oz	3.59	7/01	11r
Potatoes, frozen, french fried	lb	1.00	7/01	11r
Potatoes, white or red	10 lb	3.37	12/00	5c
Potatoes, white, all types	lb	0.44	7/01	11r
Poultry, expenditures on	yr	137	1999	30r
Processed fruits, expenditures on	yr	97	1999	30r
Processed vegetables, expenditures on	yr	82	1999	30r

Values are in dollars or fractions of dollars. In the column headed *Ref*, references are shown to sources. Each reference is followed by a letter. These refer to the geographical level for which data were reported: s=State, r=Region, and c=City or metro. The abbreviation *ex* is used to mean *except* or *excluding*; *exp* stands for expenditures. For other abbreviations and further explanations, please see the Introduction.

Tyler, TX - continued

Item	Per	Value	Date	Ref.
Groceries				
Rice, white, long grain, uncooked	lb	0.51	7/01	11r
Round roast, graded and ungraded, excl U.S. prime and choice	lb	2.96	7/01	11r
Round steak, graded and ungraded, excl U.S. prime and choice	lb	3.11	7/01	11r
Sausage, Jimmy Dean/Owens pork	lb	2.75	12/00	5c
Shortening, vegetable, Crisco	3 lb	2.71	12/00	5c
Sirloin steak, graded and ungraded, excl U.S. prime and choice	lb	4.23	7/01	11r
Soft drink, Coca Cola, ex deposit	2 liter	1.13	12/00	5c
Spaghetti and macaroni	lb	0.78	7/01	11r
Steak, round, U.S. choice, boneless	lb	3.56	7/01	11r
Steak, sirloin, U.S. choice, boneless	lb	5.65	7/01	11r
Steak, T-bone	lb	6.23	12/00	5c
Strawberries, dry pint	12 oz	1.50	7/01	11r
Sugar and other sweets, expenditures on	yr	99	1999	30r
Sugar, cane or beet	4 lbs	1.38	12/00	5c
Sugar, white, 33-80 ounce package	lb	0.39	7/01	11r
Sugar, white, all sizes	lb	0.42	7/01	11r
Tobacco products and smoking supplies purchases	yr	288	1999	30r
Tomatoes, field grown	lb	1.43	7/01	11r
Tomatoes, Hunt's or Del Monte	14.5 oz	0.92	12/00	5c
Tuna, chunk, light	6 oz	0.55	12/00	5c
Tuna, light, chunk	lb	1.77	7/01	11r
Turkey, frozen, whole	lb	1.05	7/01	11r
Goods and Services				
Miscellaneous goods and services, ACCRA Index		96.00	12/00	5c
B&B Japanese maple (acer japonicum)	gal	79.98-99.00	4/00	93r
Boxwood (buxus)	2 gal	12.98-18.99	4/00	93r
Christmas tree, noble fir		40-60	2000	65s
Daylilly (hemerocallis)	gal	7.96-11.00	4/00	93r
Flat of annuals		13.99-27.99	4/00	93r
Fountain grass (pennisetum)	gal	6.96-9.00	4/00	93r
Hanging basket (10 in)		9.99-24.99	4/00	93r
Hardy geranium (geranium)	gal	5.96-8.00	4/00	93r
Hosta (hosta)	gal	8.96-12.99	4/00	93r
Lilac (syrubga vulgaris)	2 gal	13.00-19.99	4/00	93r
Rhododendron (rhododendron)	2 gal	12.98-29.99	4/00	93r
Sage (salvia)	gal	5.96-8.00	4/00	93r
Wintercreeper euonymus (euonymus fortunei)	2 gal	13.00-18.99	4/00	93r
Hunting license	yr	19.00	4/01	34s
Health Care				
Health care, ACCRA Index		95.30	12/00	5c
Cardiac catheterization, ave hospital/ physician charges		20140	1998	77s
Childbirth, Cesarean delivery		11587	1997	13r
Childbirth, vaginal delivery		6725	1997	13r
Dentist's fee, adult teeth cleaning and periodic oral exam	visit	66.00	12/00	5c
Doctor's fee, routine exam, established patient	visit	47.20	12/00	5c
Drugs, expenditures on	yr	399	1999	30r
Health care purchases	yr	1971	1999	30r
Health insurance expenditures	yr	933	1999	30r
Hospital care, private room	day	622.67	12/00	5c
Hysterectomy, laproscopically-assisted, ave hospital/physician charges		15700	1998	76s

Tyler, TX - continued

Item	Per	Value	Date	Ref.
Health Care - continued				
Hysterectomy, vaginal, ave hospital and physician charges		12180	1998	76s
Medicaid dispensing fee		5.27	1999	87s
Medical services expenditures	yr	547	1999	30r
Medical supplies, expenditures on	yr	91	1999	30r
Household Goods				
Dishwashing powder, Cascade	50 oz	2.64	12/00	5c
Floor coverings, expenditures on	yr	44	1999	30r
Furniture, expenditures on	yr	335	1999	30r
Household furnishings and equipment purchases	yr	1328	1999	30r
Household textiles, expenditures on	yr	89	1999	30r
Laundry and cleaning supplies, expenditures on	yr	113	1999	30r
Tissues, facial, Kleenex brand	175	1.18	12/00	5c
Housing				
Housing, ACCRA Index		80.10	12/00	5c
Home price, existing, ave		160100	10/00	90r
Home value, median		112000	2001	53s
House, 2400 sq ft, 8000 sq ft lot, new, urban, utilities	total	162500	12/00	5c
House payment, principal and interest, 25% down payment	mos	879	12/00	5c
Household operation expenditures	yr	553	1999	30r
Housekeeping supplies purchases	yr	473	1999	30r
Housing, expenditures on	yr	10303	1999	30r
Maintenance, repairs, insurance expenditures	yr	699	1999	30r
Monthly rental value of owned home	mos	505	1999	30r
Owned dwellings, expenditures own	yr	3465	1999	30r
Rent expenditures	yr	1641	1999	30r
Rent, apartment, 2 br, 1 1/2-2 baths, unfurn, 950 sq ft, water	mos	608	12/00	5c
Rental unit, 1 bedroom, with utilities	mos	395	4/01	41c
Rental unit, 2 bedroom, with utilities	mos	482	4/01	41c
Rental unit, 3 bedroom, with utilities	mos	668	4/01	41c
Rental unit, 4 bedroom, with utilities	mos	707	4/01	41c
Shelter, expenditures on	yr	5467	1999	30r
Insurance and Pensions				
Life and other personal insurance purchases	yr	414	1999	30r
Pensions and Social Security, expenditures on	yr	2635	1999	30r
Personal insurance and pensions, expenditures on	yr	3048	1999	30r
Legal Fees				
Divorce, filing fee		150.00-200.00	4/01	35s
Driver's license fee	orig	24.00	1999	48s
Driver's license fee	renew	20.00	1999	48s
Fishing license	yr	19.00	4/01	34s
Personal Goods				
Personal care products and services purchases	yr	393	1999	30r
Shampoo, Alberto VO5	15 oz	1.08	12/00	5c
Toothpaste, Crest or Colgate	6-7 oz	2.21	12/00	5c
Personal Services				
Dry cleaning, man's 2-pc suit		6.60	12/00	5c
Man's haircut, barbershop, no styling		10.90	12/00	5c
Personal services, household, expenditures on	yr	258	1999	30r
Woman's shampoo, trim, blow-dry, no style-change		26.40	12/00	5c
Pets				
Pets, toys, and playground equipment, expenditures on	yr	306	1999	30r
Restaurant Food				
Chicken, fried, thigh and drumstick, KFC/ Church's		2.19	12/00	5c

Values are in dollars or fractions of dollars. In the column headed *Ref*, references are shown to sources. Each reference is followed by a letter. These refer to the geographical level for which data were reported: s=State, r=Region, and c=City or metro. The abbreviation *ex* is used to mean *except* or *excluding*; *exp* stands for expenditures. For other abbreviations and further explanations, please see the Introduction.

Tyler, TX - continued

Item	Per	Value	Date	Ref.
Restaurant Food				
Hamburger with cheese, McDonald's	1/4 lb	1.99	12/00	5c
Pizza, Pizza Hut or Pizza Inn	11-12 in	9.84	12/00	5c
Taxes				
Federal income taxes paid	yr	2047	1999	30r
Personal taxes, expenditures on	yr	2554	1999	30r
Property taxes paid	yr	726	1999	30r
State and local income taxes paid	yr	363	1999	30r
Transportation				
Transportation, ACCRA Index		89.80	12/00	5c
Cars and trucks, new, expenditures on	yr	1648	1999	30r
Cars and trucks, used, expenditures on	yr	1651	1999	30r
Diesel at the pump	gal	1.18	10/99	73s
Gasoline and motor oil purchases	yr	1052	1999	30r
Gasoline before-tax price (cents)	gal	101.30	10/00	43s
Maintenance and repair expenditures	yr	621	1999	30r
Public transportation, expenditures on	yr	298	1999	30r
Tire balance, computer or spin balance, front	wheel	6.79	12/00	5c
Transportation purchases	yr	6738	1999	30r
Vehicle expenses, miscellaneous, purchases	yr	2033	1999	30r
Vehicle insurance payments	yr	696	1999	30r
Vehicle purchases (net outlay)	yr	3354	1999	30r
Vehicle rental, lease expenditures	yr	352	1999	30r
Utilities				
Utilities, ACCRA Index		105.90	12/00	5c
Electrical bill, average	mos	87.17	9/00	9s
Electricity, expenditures on	yr	1115	1999	30r
Electricity and other, mixed, 2400 sq ft, new home	mos	83.52	12/00	5c
Electricity cost, average	KWh	6.48	9/00	9s
Water and other public services, expenditures on	yr	298	1999	30r
Weddings				
Wedding (national average cost)		19936	2000	33r
Attendants' gifts		321	1998	33r
Bridal attendants' apparel (5 persons)		824	2000	33r
Bride's headpiece/veil		173	1998	33r
Bride's wedding dress		859	1998	33r
Clergy, religious facility fee		242	1998	33r
Engagement ring		3177	1998	33r
Flowers		789	1998	33r
Groom's formalwear rental		99	2000	33r
Limousine		410	1998	33r
Marriage license cost		36.00	4/01	35s
Men's formalwear (ushers, best man)		469	2000	33r
Mother of bride apparel		241	2000	33r
Music		866	1998	33r
Photography and videography		1368	1998	33r
Rehearsal dinner		728	1998	33r
Wedding invitations and announcements		341	1998	33r
Wedding reception		7968	2000	33r
Wedding rings (bride and groom)		1060	1998	33r

Utica-Rome, NY

Item	Per	Value	Date	Ref.
Average annual expenditures	yr	37971	1999	30r
Alcoholic Beverages				
Alcoholic beverage purchases	yr	368	1999	30r
Wine, red and white table, all sizes, any origin	liter	9.64	7/01	11r
Appliances				
Major appliances, expenditures on	yr	194	1999	30r
Small appliances, housewares, expenditures on	yr	93	1999	30r
Banking and Money				
Mortgage interest and charges paid	yr	2622	1999	30r
Mortgage principal paid on owned property	yr	1262	1999	30r
Vehicle finance charges paid	yr	240	1999	30r

Utica-Rome, NY - continued

Item	Per	Value	Date	Ref.
Charity				
Cash contributions, expenditures	yr	1001	1999	30r
Child Care				
Child raising cost, total, age 0-2	yr	8670	1999	60r
Child raising cost, total, age 3-5	yr	8910	1999	60r
Child raising cost, total, age 6-8	yr	9040	1999	60r
Child raising cost, total, age 9-11	yr	9100	1999	60r
Child raising cost, total, age 12-14	yr	9890	1999	60r
Child raising cost, total, age 15-17	yr	10010	1999	60r
Child's child care and education, age 0-2	yr	1070	1999	60r
Child's child care and education, age 3-5	yr	1190	1999	60r
Child's child care and education, age 6-8	yr	740	1999	60r
Child's child care and education, age 9-11	yr	470	1999	60r
Child's child care and education, age 12-14	yr	350	1999	60r
Child's child care and education, age 15-17	yr	590	1999	60r
Child's clothing, age 0-2	yr	480	1999	60r
Child's clothing, age 3-5	yr	470	1999	60r
Child's clothing, age 6-8	yr	520	1999	60r
Child's clothing, age 9-11	yr	570	1999	60r
Child's clothing, age 12-14	yr	970	1999	60r
Child's clothing, age 15-17	yr	870	1999	60r
Child's food, age 0-2	yr	1130	1999	60r
Child's food, age 3-5	yr	1290	1999	60r
Child's food, age 6-8	yr	1640	1999	60r
Child's food, age 9-11	yr	1930	1999	60r
Child's food, age 12-14	yr	1940	1999	60r
Child's food, age 15-17	yr	2150	1999	60r
Child's health care, age 0-2	yr	550	1999	60r
Child's health care, age 3-5	yr	530	1999	60r
Child's health care, age 6-8	yr	610	1999	60r
Child's health care, age 9-11	yr	650	1999	60r
Child's health care, age 12-14	yr	660	1999	60r
Child's health care, age 15-17	yr	690	1999	60r
Child's housing, age 0-2	yr	3555	1999	60r
Child's housing, age 3-5	yr	3530	1999	60r
Child's housing, age 6-8	yr	3490	1999	60r
Child's housing, age 9-11	yr	3340	1999	60r
Child's housing, age 12-14	yr	3530	1999	60r
Child's housing, age 15-17	yr	3140	1999	60r
Child's personal care, reading, age 0-2	yr	920	1999	60r
Child's personal care, reading, age 3-5	yr	950	1999	60r
Child's personal care, reading, age 6-8	yr	980	1999	60r
Child's personal care, reading, age 9-11	yr	1020	1999	60r
Child's personal care, reading, age 12-14	yr	1190	1999	60r
Child's personal care, reading, age 15-17	yr	970	1999	60r
Nannies: criminal background check		74	1998	84s
Clothing				
Apparel and services purchases	yr	1831	1999	30r
Boys, 2 to 15, expenditures on	yr	92	1999	30r
Children under 2, expenditures on	yr	63	1999	30r
Footwear, expenditures on	yr	300	1999	30r
Girls, 2 to 15, expenditures on	yr	101	1999	30r
Men and boys, expenditures on	yr	446	1999	30r
Men, 16 and over, expenditures on	yr	354	1999	30r
Women, 16 and over, expenditures on	yr	584	1999	30r
Communications				
Cable modem installation, Adelphi		54.90	6/99	103s
Cable modem installation, Cablevision Systems		150.00	6/99	103s
Cable modem installation, Time Warner		75.00-225.00	6/99	103s
Cable modem rate, cable subscriber, Adelphi	mos	34.95	6/99	103s
Cable modem rate, cable subscriber, Cablevision Systems	mos	44.95	6/99	103s
Cable modem rate, cable subscriber, Century	mos	39.95	6/99	103s
Cable modem rate, cable subscriber, Time Warner	mos	39.95-49.95	6/99	103s
Cable modem rate, non-cable subscriber, Adelphi	mos	44.95	6/99	103s
Cable modem rate, non-cable subscriber, Cablevision Systems	mos	54.95	6/99	103s

Values are in dollars or fractions of dollars. In the column headed *Ref*, references are shown to sources. Each reference is followed by a letter. These refer to the geographical level for which data were reported: s=State, r=Region, and c=City or metro. The abbreviation *ex* is used to mean *except* or *excluding*; *exp* stands for expenditures. For other abbreviations and further explanations, please see the Introduction.

Utica-Rome, NY - continued

Item	Per	Value	Date	Ref.
Communications				
Cable modem rate, non-cable subscriber, Time Warner	mos	39.95- 54.95	6/99	103s
Phone line, single, business, field visit	inst.	142.76	12/97	17s
Phone line, single, business, no field visit	inst.	106.05	12/97	17s
Phone line, single, residence, field visit	inst.	102.78	12/97	17s
Phone line, single, residence, no field visit	inst.	55.00	12/97	17s
Postage and stationery, expenditures on	yr	138	1999	30r
Postal rate, express mail, up to half-pound		12.45	7/01	108r
Postal rate, letter, first class, first ounce		0.34	7/01	108r
Postal rate, letter, two ounces		0.57	7/01	108r
Postal rate, post card		0.21	7/01	108r
Postal rate, priority mail, two pounds		3.95	7/01	108r
Postal rate, priority mail, up to one pound		3.50	7/01	108r
Telephone services, expenditures on	yr	830	1999	30r
Education				
Board, 4-year private college/university	yr	3255	1996	38s
Board, 4-year public college/university	yr	2310	1996	38s
Education expenditures	yr	877	1999	30r
Room, 4-year private college/university	yr	3724	1996	38s
Room, 4-year public college/university	yr	2937	1996	38s
Total cost, 4-year private college/university	yr	20831	1996	38s
Total cost, 4-year public college/university	yr	8960	1996	38s
Tuition, 2-year public college/university, in state	yr	2427	1996	38s
Tuition, 4-year private college/university, in state	yr	13852	1996	38s
Tuition, 4-year public college/university	yr	3714	1996	38s
Energy and Fuels				
Electricity	KWh	0.12	7/01	11r
Fuel oil #2	gal	1.31	7/01	11r
Fuel oil and other fuels, expenditures on	yr	207	1999	30r
Gasoline, all types	gal	1.80	7/01	11r
Gasoline, unleaded midgrade	gal	1.85	7/01	11r
Gasoline, unleaded premium	gal	1.91	7/01	11r
Gasoline, unleaded regular	gal	1.71	7/01	11r
Natural gas, expenditures on	yr	368	1999	30r
Utility (piped) gas, therm		1.08	7/01	11r
Utility (piped) gas, 40 therms		50.87	7/01	11r
Utility (piped) gas, 100 therms		111.06	7/01	11r
Entertainment				
Entertainment purchases	yr	1821	1999	30r
Fees and admissions paid	yr	511	1999	30r
Television, radios, sound equipment, expenditures on	yr	650	1999	30r
Funerals				
Total cost of funeral		5813.50	1/99	78r
Acknowledgement cards		28.32	1/99	78r
Casket		2082.20	1/99	78r
Cosmetology, hair, other preparation		169.59	1/99	78r
Embalming		465.60	1/99	78r
Funeral at funeral home		339.56	1/99	78r
Hearse (local)		183.96	1/99	78r
Professional service charges		1157.85	1/99	78r
Service car/van		100.41	1/99	78r
Transfer of remains to funeral home		158.66	1/99	78r
Vault		766.31	1/99	78r
Visitation/viewing		361.04	1/99	78r
Groceries				
Apples, red delicious	lb	0.95	7/01	11r
Bacon, sliced	lb	3.44	7/01	11r
Bakery products, expenditures on	yr	310	1999	30r
Bananas	lb	0.55	7/01	11r
Beef, expenditures on	yr	236	1999	30r
Bread, white, pan	lb	1.09	7/01	11r
Butter, yoghurt, cheese, etc, expenditures on	yr	214	1999	30r
Cereals and bakery product purchases	yr	474	1999	30r
Cereals and cereal products, expenditures on	yr	164	1999	30r
Chicken legs, bone-in	lb	1.23	7/01	11r

Utica-Rome, NY - continued

Item	Per	Value	Date	Ref.
Groceries - continued				
Chicken, fresh, whole	lb	1.13	7/01	11r
Chuck roast, U.S. choice, boneless	lb	2.79	7/01	11r
Coffee, 100%, ground roast, all sizes	lb	3.40	7/01	11r
Dairy product purchases	yr	342	1999	30r
Eggs, expenditures on	yr	34	1999	30r
Eggs, grade A, large	dozen	0.82	7/01	11r
Fats and oils, expenditures on	yr	80	1999	30r
Fish and seafood, expenditures on	yr	123	1999	30r
Food (excl fruit and vegetables), eaten at home, purchases	yr	838	1999	30r
Food cooked on trips, expenditures on	yr	48	1999	30r
Food purchases	yr	5314	1999	30r
Food purchases, eaten away from home	yr	2313	1999	30r
Food purchases, food eaten at home	yr	3001	1999	30r
Fresh fruits, expenditures on	yr	169	1999	30r
Fresh milk and cream, expenditures on	yr	128	1999	30r
Fresh vegetables, expenditures on	yr	164	1999	30r
Grapefruit	lb	0.67	7/01	11r
Grapes, Thompson, seedless	lb	2.18	7/01	11r
Ground beef, lean and extra lean	lb	2.66	7/01	11r
Ground chuck, 100% beef	lb	2.04	7/01	11r
Lettuce, iceberg	lb	0.76	7/01	11r
Meats, poultry, fish, and egg purchases	yr	808	1999	30r
Nonalcoholic beverages, expenditures on	yr	225	1999	30r
Orange juice, frozen concentrate	16 oz	1.88	7/01	11r
Oranges, Navel	lb	0.79	7/01	11r
Oranges, Valencia	lb	0.56	7/01	11r
Peaches	lb	1.16	7/01	11r
Peanut butter, creamy, all sizes	lb	2.01	7/01	11r
Pears, Anjou	lb	1.16	7/01	11r
Pork chops, center cut, bone-in	lb	3.57	7/01	11r
Pork, expenditures on	yr	146	1999	30r
Potato chips	16 oz	3.37	7/01	11r
Potatoes, white, all types	lb	0.42	7/01	11r
Poultry, expenditures on	yr	158	1999	30r
Processed fruits, expenditures on	yr	124	1999	30r
Processed vegetables, expenditures on	yr	82	1999	30r
Round roast, U.S. choice, boneless	lb	3.04	7/01	11r
Spaghetti and macaroni	lb	1.04	7/01	11r
Steak, sirloin, U.S. choice, boneless	lb	5.39	7/01	11r
Strawberries, dry pint	12 oz	1.51	7/01	11r
Sugar and other sweets, expenditures on	yr	110	1999	30r
Sugar, white, 33-80 ounce package	lb	0.46	7/01	11r
Sugar, white, all sizes	lb	0.47	7/01	11r
Tobacco products and smoking supplies purchases	yr	309	1999	30r
Yogurt, natural, fruit flavored	8 oz	0.79	7/01	11r
Goods and Services				
B&B Japanese maple (acer japonicum)	gal	38.99- 125.00	4/00	93r
Boxwood (buxus)	2 gal	15.99- 49.95	4/00	93r
Daylily (hemerocallis)	gal	4.95	4/00	93r
Flat of annuals		8.00- 14.99	4/00	93r
Fountain grass (pennisetum)	gal	6.99- 9.99	4/00	93r
Hanging basket (10 in)		12.95- 19.99	4/00	93r
Hardy geranium (geranium)	gal	6.95- 7.99	4/00	93r
Hosta (hosta)	gal	4.95	4/00	93r
Lilac (syrubga vulgaris)	2 gal	17.99- 74.95	4/00	93r
Miscellaneous purchases	yr	872	1999	30r
Rhododendron (rhododendron)	2 gal	23.99- 54.95	4/00	93r
Sage (salvia)	gal	6.95- 7.99	4/00	93r
Wintercreeper euonymus (euonymus fortunei)	2 gal	14.99- 23.95	4/00	93r
Hunting license	yr	11.00	4/01	34s

Values are in dollars or fractions of dollars. In the column headed *Ref*, references are shown to sources. Each reference is followed by a letter. These refer to the geographical level for which data were reported: s=State, r=Region, and c=City or metro. The abbreviation *ex* is used to mean *except* or *excluding*; *exp* stands for *expenditures*. For other abbreviations and further explanations, please see the Introduction.

Utica-Rome, NY - continued

Item	Per	Value	Date	Ref.
Health Care				
Cardiac catheterization, ave hospital/ physician charges		12750	1998	77s
Childbirth, Cesarean delivery		14716	1997	13r
Childbirth, vaginal delivery		8541	1997	13r
Drugs, expenditures on	yr	296	1999	30r
Health care purchases	yr	1788	1999	30r
Health insurance expenditures	yr	875	1999	30r
Hysterectomy, laproscopically-assisted, ave hospital/physician charges		13460	1998	76s
Hysterectomy, vaginal, ave hospital and physician charges		10310	1998	76s
Medicaid dispensing fee		3.50-4.50	1999	87s
Medical services expenditures	yr	516	1999	30r
Medical supplies, expenditures on	yr	102	1999	30r
Plastic surgery, breast augmentation		4232	2000	7r
Plastic surgery, breast lift		4605	2000	7r
Plastic surgery, facelift		6964	2000	7r
Plastic surgery, hair transplantation		4193	2000	7r
Plastic surgery, lip augmentation		1675	2000	7r
Plastic surgery, lower body lift		6611	2000	7r
Plastic surgery, thigh lift		4751	2000	7r
Household Goods				
Floor coverings, expenditures on	yr	59	1999	30r
Furniture, expenditures on	yr	388	1999	30r
Household furnishings and equipment purchases	yr	1567	1999	30r
Household textiles, expenditures on	yr	112	1999	30r
Laundry and cleaning supplies, expenditures on	yr	104	1999	30r
Housing				
Home price, existing, ave		180800	10/00	90r
Home value, median		179000	2001	53s
Household operation expenditures	yr	581	1999	30r
Housekeeping supplies purchases	yr	474	1999	30r
Lodging expenditures	yr	550	1999	30r
Maintenance, repairs, insurance expenditures	yr	835	1999	30r
Monthly rental value of owned home	mos	663	1999	30r
Owned dwellings, expenditures own	yr	5209	1999	30r
Rent expenditures	yr	2390	1999	30r
Rental unit, 1 bedroom, with utilities	mos	403	4/01	41c
Rental unit, 2 bedroom, with utilities	mos	484	4/01	41c
Rental unit, 3 bedroom, with utilities	mos	686	4/01	41c
Rental unit, 4 bedroom, with utilities	mos	715	4/01	41c
Shelter, expenditures on	yr	8149	1999	30r
Insurance and Pensions				
Auto insurance premium	yr	1113.55	1999	57s
Life and other personal insurance purchases	yr	424	1999	30r
Pensions and Social Security, expenditures on	yr	3037	1999	30r
Legal Fees				
Divorce, filing fee		270.00	4/01	35s
Driver's license fee	renew	25.00	1999	48s
Driver's license fee	orig	25.00	1999	48s
Fishing license	yr	14.00	4/01	34s
Personal Goods				
Personal care products and services purchases	yr	399	1999	30r
Personal Services				
Personal services, household, expenditures on	yr	271	1999	30r
Pets				
Pets, toys, and playground equipment, expenditures on	yr	325	1999	30r
Taxes				
Federal income taxes paid	yr	2606	1999	30r
Personal taxes, expenditures on	yr	3567	1999	30r

Utica-Rome, NY - continued

Item	Per	Value	Date	Ref.
Taxes - continued				
Property taxes paid	yr	1752	1999	30r
State and local income taxes paid	yr	694	1999	30r
Transportation				
Cars and trucks, new, expenditures on	yr	1496	1999	30r
Cars and trucks, used, expenditures on	yr	1251	1999	30r
Diesel at the pump	gal	1.33	10/99	73s
Gasoline and motor oil purchases	yr	901	1999	30r
Gasoline before-tax price (cents)	gal	110.70	10/00	43s
Maintenance and repair expenditures	yr	618	1999	30r
Public transportation, expenditures on	yr	575	1999	30r
Transportation purchases	yr	6503	1999	30r
Vehicle expenses, miscellaneous, purchases	yr	2266	1999	30r
Vehicle insurance payments	yr	824	1999	30r
Vehicle purchases (net outlay)	yr	2761	1999	30r
Vehicle rental, lease expenditures	yr	584	1999	30r
Travel				
Hotel room	night	139.88	2/01	95s
Utilities				
Electrical bill, average	mos	71.50	9/00	9s
Electricity, expenditures on	yr	837	1999	30r
Electricity cost, average	KWh	11.34	9/00	9s
Utilities, fuels, and public services purchased	yr	2457	1999	30r
Water and other public services, expenditures on	yr	215	1999	30r
Weddings				
Wedding (national average cost)		19936	2000	33r
Wedding (regional average total cost)		29454	1997	110r
Attendants' gifts		321	1998	33r
Bridal attendants' apparel (5 persons)		824	2000	33r
Bride's headpiece/veil		173	1998	33r
Bride's wedding dress		859	1998	33r
Clergy, religious facility fee		242	1998	33r
Engagement ring		3177	1998	33r
Flowers		789	1998	33r
Groom's formalwear rental		99	2000	33r
Limousine		410	1998	33r
Marriage license cost		25.00	4/01	35s
Men's formalwear (ushers, best man)		469	2000	33r
Mother of bride apparel		241	2000	33r
Music		866	1998	33r
Photography and videography		1368	1998	33r
Rehearsal dinner		728	1998	33r
Wedding invitations and announcements		341	1998	33r
Wedding reception		7968	2000	33r
Wedding rings (bride and groom)		1060	1998	33r

Vallejo-Fairfield-Napa, CA

Item	Per	Value	Date	Ref.
Average annual expenditures	yr	40662	1999	30r
Alcoholic Beverages				
Alcoholic beverage purchases	yr	372	1999	30r
Malt beverages, all types, all sizes, any origin	16 oz	0.94	7/01	11r
Wine, red and white table, all sizes, any origin	liter	6.00	7/01	11r
Appliances				
Major appliances, expenditures on	yr	167	1999	30r
Small appliances, housewares, expenditures on	yr	105	1999	30r
Banking and Money				
Mortgage interest and charges paid	yr	3368	1999	30r
Mortgage principal paid on owned property	yr	1677	1999	30r
Vehicle finance charges paid	yr	311	1999	30r
Charity				
Cash contributions, expenditures	yr	1344	1999	30r
Child Care				
Child raising cost, total, age 0-2	yr	9140	1999	60r
Child raising cost, total, age 3-5	yr	9370	1999	60r

Values are in dollars or fractions of dollars. In the column headed *Ref*, references are shown to sources. Each reference is followed by a letter. These refer to the geographical level for which data were reported: s=State, r=Region, and c=City or metro. The abbreviation *ex* is used to mean *except* or *excluding*; *exp* stands for *expenditures*. For other abbreviations and further explanations, please see the Introduction.

Vallejo-Fairfield-Napa, CA - continued

Item	Per	Value	Date	Ref.
Child Care				
Child raising cost, total, age 6-8	yr	9450	1999	60r
Child raising cost, total, age 9-11	yr	9470	1999	60r
Child raising cost, total, age 12-14	yr	10170	1999	60r
Child raising cost, total, age 15-17	yr	10360	1999	60r
Child's child care and education, age 0-2	yr	1250	1999	60r
Child's child care and education, age 3-5	yr	1380	1999	60r
Child's child care and education, age 6-8	yr	890	1999	60r
Child's child care and education, age 9-11	yr	580	1999	60r
Child's child care and education, age 12-14	yr	430	1999	60r
Child's child care and education, age 15-17	yr	730	1999	60r
Child's clothing, age 0-2	yr	430	1999	60r
Child's clothing, age 3-5	yr	420	1999	60r
Child's clothing, age 6-8	yr	470	1999	60r
Child's clothing, age 9-11	yr	520	1999	60r
Child's clothing, age 12-14	yr	870	1999	60r
Child's clothing, age 15-17	yr	770	1999	60r
Child's food, age 0-2	yr	1120	1999	60r
Child's food, age 3-5	yr	1280	1999	60r
Child's food, age 6-8	yr	1640	1999	60r
Child's food, age 9-11	yr	1930	1999	60r
Child's food, age 12-14	yr	1940	1999	60r
Child's food, age 15-17	yr	2150	1999	60r
Child's health care, age 0-2	yr	490	1999	60r
Child's health care, age 3-5	yr	470	1999	60r
Child's health care, age 6-8	yr	530	1999	60r
Child's health care, age 9-11	yr	570	1999	60r
Child's health care, age 12-14	yr	580	1999	60r
Child's health care, age 15-17	yr	610	1999	60r
Child's housing, age 0-2	yr	3630	1999	60r
Child's housing, age 3-5	yr	3610	1999	60r
Child's housing, age 6-8	yr	3570	1999	60r
Child's housing, age 9-11	yr	3410	1999	60r
Child's housing, age 12-14	yr	3600	1999	60r
Child's housing, age 15-17	yr	3210	1999	60r
Child's personal care, reading, age 0-2	yr	1040	1999	60r
Child's personal care, reading, age 3-5	yr	1060	1999	60r
Child's personal care, reading, age 6-8	yr	1090	1999	60r
Child's personal care, reading, age 9-11	yr	1130	1999	60r
Child's personal care, reading, age 12-14	yr	1300	1999	60r
Child's personal care, reading, age 15-17	yr	1080	1999	60r
Clothing				
Apparel and services purchases	yr	1863	1999	30r
Boys, 2 to 15, expenditures on	yr	80	1999	30r
Children under 2, expenditures on	yr	74	1999	30r
Footwear, expenditures on	yr	307	1999	30r
Girls, 2 to 15, expenditures on	yr	101	1999	30r
Men and boys, expenditures on	yr	443	1999	30r
Men, 16 and over, expenditures on	yr	363	1999	30r
Women, 16 and over, expenditures on	yr	594	1999	30r
Communications				
Cable modem installation, AT&T-BIS		150.00	6/99	103s
Cable modem installation, Charter		99.00-169.00	6/99	103s
Cable modem installation, Comcast		95.00	6/99	103s
Cable modem installation, Cox		99.00-174.95	6/99	103s
Cable modem installation, Media One		100.00	6/99	103s
Cable modem installation, Time Warner		75.00-225.00	6/99	103s
Cable modem rate, cable subscriber, AT&T-BIS	mos	39.95	6/99	103s
Cable modem rate, cable subscriber, Charter	mos	49.95-79.95	6/99	103s
Cable modem rate, cable subscriber, Comcast	mos	39.95	6/99	103s
Cable modem rate, cable subscriber, Cox	mos	29.95-44.95	6/99	103s
Cable modem rate, cable subscriber, Media One	mos	34.95-39.95	6/99	103s
Cable modem rate, cable subscriber, Time Warner	mos	39.95-49.95	6/99	103s

Vallejo-Fairfield-Napa, CA - continued

Item	Per	Value	Date	Ref.
Communications - continued				
Cable modem rate, non-cable subscriber, Charter	mos	59.95-89.95	6/99	103s
Cable modem rate, non-cable subscriber, Comcast	mos	49.95	6/99	103s
Cable modem rate, non-cable subscriber, Cox	mos	42.95-54.95	6/99	103s
Cable modem rate, non-cable subscriber, Media One	mos	49.95	6/99	103s
Cable modem rate, non-cable subscriber, Time Warner	mos	39.95-54.95	6/99	103s
Phone line, single, business, field visit	inst.	70.75	12/97	17s
Phone line, single, business, no field visit	inst.	70.75	12/97	17s
Phone line, single, residence, field visit	inst.	34.75	12/97	17s
Phone line, single, residence, no field visit	inst.	34.75	12/97	17s
Postage and stationery, expenditures on	yr	150	1999	30r
Postal rate, express mail, up to half-pound		12.45	7/01	108r
Postal rate, letter, first class, first ounce		0.34	7/01	108r
Postal rate, letter, two ounces		0.57	7/01	108r
Postal rate, post card		0.21	7/01	108r
Postal rate, priority mail, two pounds		3.95	7/01	108r
Postal rate, priority mail, up to one pound		3.50	7/01	108r
Telephone services, expenditures on	yr	825	1999	30r
Education				
Board, 4-year private college/university	yr	2970	1996	38s
Board, 4-year public college/university	yr	2516	1996	38s
Education expenditures	yr	676	1999	30r
Room, 4-year private college/university	yr	3196	1996	38s
Room, 4-year public college/university	yr	3031	1996	38s
Total cost, 4-year private college/university	yr	20143	1996	38s
Total cost, 4-year public college/university	yr	8213	1996	38s
Tuition, 2-year public college/university, in state	yr	362	1996	38s
Tuition, 4-year private college/university, in state	yr	13977	1996	38s
Tuition, 4-year public college/university	yr	2666	1996	38s
Energy and Fuels				
Electricity	KWh	0.11	7/01	11r
Electricity	500 KWhs	48.23	7/01	11r
Fuel oil and other fuels, expenditures on	yr	35	1999	30r
Gas, natural, commercial rate	1000 cf	8.74	11/00	88s
Gasoline, all types	gal	1.91	7/01	11r
Gasoline, unleaded premium	gal	2.05	7/01	11r
Gasoline, unleaded regular	gal	1.83	7/01	11r
Natural gas, expenditures on	yr	255	1999	30r
Utility (piped) gas, therm		0.98	7/01	11r
Utility (piped) gas, 40 therms		40.74	7/01	11r
Utility (piped) gas, 100 therms		96.80	7/01	11r
Entertainment				
Entertainment purchases	yr	2139	1999	30r
Fees and admissions paid	yr	545	1999	30r
Television, radios, sound equipment, expenditures on	yr	624	1999	30r
Funerals				
Total cost of funeral		5401.08	1/99	78r
Acknowledgement cards		33.64	1/99	78r
Casket		2170.43	1/99	78r
Cosmetology, hair, other preparation		136.32	1/99	78r
Embalming		319.13	1/99	78r
Funeral at funeral home		370.21	1/99	78r
Hearse (local)		161.04	1/99	78r
Professional service charges		963.15	1/99	78r
Service car/van		133.99	1/99	78r
Transfer of remains to funeral home		159.82	1/99	78r
Vault		778.07	1/99	78r
Visitation/viewing		175.28	1/99	78r
Groceries				
Apples, red delicious	lb	0.84	7/01	11r
Bacon, sliced	lb	3.38	7/01	11r

Values are in dollars or fractions of dollars. In the column headed *Ref*, references are shown to sources. Each reference is followed by a letter. These refer to the geographical level for which data were reported: s=State, r=Region, and c=City or metro. The abbreviation *ex* is used to mean *except* or *excluding*; *exp* stands for *expenditures*. For other abbreviations and further explanations, please see the Introduction.

Vallejo-Fairfield-Napa, CA - continued

Item	Per	Value	Date	Ref.
Groceries				
Bakery products, expenditures on	yr	299	1999	30r
Bananas	lb	0.54	7/01	11r
Beans, dried, any type, all sizes	lb	0.76	7/01	11r
Beef, expenditures on	yr	222	1999	30r
Bread, white, pan	lb	0.99	7/01	11r
Butter, yoghurt, cheese, etc, expenditures on	yr	211	1999	30r
Cereals and bakery product purchases	yr	466	1999	30r
Cereals and cereal products, expenditures on	yr	168	1999	30r
Chicken breast, bone-in	lb	2.45	7/01	11r
Chicken, fresh, whole	lb	1.19	7/01	11r
Chops, boneless,	lb	4.00	7/01	11r
Chuck roast, graded and ungraded, excl U.S. prime and choice	lb	2.55	7/01	11r
Coffee, 100%, ground roast, all sizes	lb	3.80	7/01	11r
Cookies, chocolate chip	lb	2.83	7/01	11r
Dairy product purchases	yr	341	1999	30r
Eggs, expenditures on	yr	39	1999	30r
Eggs, grade AA, large	dozen	1.23	7/01	11r
Fats and oils, expenditures on	yr	88	1999	30r
Fish and seafood, expenditures on	yr	121	1999	30r
Food (excl fruit and vegetables), eaten at home, purchases	yr	1001	1999	30r
Food cooked on trips, expenditures on	yr	64	1999	30r
Food purchases	yr	5312	1999	30r
Food purchases, eaten away from home	yr	2180	1999	30r
Food purchases, food eaten at home	yr	3132	1999	30r
Fresh fruits, expenditures on	yr	186	1999	30r
Fresh milk and cream, expenditures on	yr	130	1999	30r
Fresh vegetables, expenditures on	yr	177	1999	30r
Grapefruit	lb	0.68	7/01	11r
Grapes, Thompson, seedless	lb	2.42	7/01	11r
Ground beef, lean and extra lean	lb	2.46	7/01	11r
Ice cream, prepackaged, bulk, regular	1/2 gal	3.62	7/01	11r
Lettuce, iceberg	lb	0.63	7/01	11r
Meats, poultry, fish, and egg purchases	yr	761	1999	30r
Milk, fresh, low fat,	gal	2.80	7/01	11r
Milk, fresh, whole, fortified	gal	2.88	7/01	11r
Nonalcoholic beverages, expenditures on	yr	258	1999	30r
Oranges, Navel	lb	0.97	7/01	11r
Oranges, Valencia	lb	0.43	7/01	11r
Peaches	lb	1.38	7/01	11r
Peanut butter, creamy, all sizes	lb	2.14	7/01	11r
Pork chops, center cut, bone-in	lb	3.83	7/01	11r
Pork, expenditures on	yr	141	1999	30r
Potatoes, white, all types	lb	0.37	7/01	11r
Poultry, expenditures on	yr	146	1999	30r
Processed fruits, expenditures on	yr	118	1999	30r
Processed vegetables, expenditures on	yr	81	1999	30r
Round roast, graded and ungraded, excl U.S. prime and choice	lb	3.07	7/01	11r
Round roast, U.S. choice, boneless	lb	3.37	7/01	11r
Round steak, graded and ungraded, excl U.S. prime and choice	lb	3.51	7/01	11r
Sirloin steak, graded and ungraded, excl U.S. prime and choice	lb	4.67	7/01	11r
Steak, sirloin, U.S. choice, boneless	lb	6.20	7/01	11r
Strawberries, dry pint	12 oz	1.79	7/01	11r
Sugar and other sweets, expenditures on	yr	124	1999	30r
Sugar, white, all sizes	lb	0.46	7/01	11r
Tobacco products and smoking supplies purchases	yr	217	1999	30r
Tomatoes, field grown	lb	1.17	7/01	11r
Tuna, light, chunk	lb	2.05	7/01	11r
Goods and Services				
B&B Japanese maple (acer japonicum)	gal	39.99	4/00	93r
Boxwood (buxus)	2 gal	14.99-24.99	4/00	93r
Christmas tree, noble fir		40-60	2000	65s
Daylily (hemerocallis)	gal	6.99-8.99	4/00	93r
Flat of annuals		16.68	4/00	93r

Vallejo-Fairfield-Napa, CA - continued

Item	Per	Value	Date	Ref.
Goods and Services - continued				
Fountain grass (pennisetum)	gal	7.99-11.99	4/00	93r
Hanging basket (10 in)		29.99	4/00	93r
Hardy geranium (geranium)	gal	6.99-11.99	4/00	93r
Hosta (hosta)	gal	6.99-18.99	4/00	93r
Lilac (syrubga vulgaris)	2 gal	14.99-17.99	4/00	93r
Miscellaneous purchases	yr	1070	1999	30r
Rhododendron (rhododendron)	2 gal	14.99	4/00	93r
Sage (salvia)	gal	6.99	4/00	93r
Wintercreeper euonymus (euonymus fortunei)	2 gal	14.99-22.99	4/00	93r
Hunting license	yr	29.95	4/01	34s
Health Care				
Cardiac catheterization, ave hospital/ physician charges		24000	1998	77s
Childbirth, Cesarean delivery		11587	1997	13r
Childbirth, vaginal delivery		6725	1997	13r
Drugs, expenditures on	yr	309	1999	30r
Health care purchases	yr	1869	1999	30r
Health insurance expenditures	yr	868	1999	30r
Hysterectomy, laproscopically-assisted, ave hospital/physician charges		20760	1998	76s
Hysterectomy, vaginal, ave hospital and physician charges		14570	1998	76s
Medicaid dispensing fee		4.05	1999	87s
Medical services expenditures	yr	580	1999	30r
Medical supplies, expenditures on	yr	112	1999	30r
Household Goods				
Floor coverings, expenditures on	yr	49	1999	30r
Furniture, expenditures on	yr	444	1999	30r
Household furnishings and equipment purchases	yr	1768	1999	30r
Household textiles, expenditures on	yr	141	1999	30r
Laundry and cleaning supplies, expenditures on	yr	128	1999	30r
Housing				
Home price, existing, ave		239400	10/00	90r
Home value, median		215000	2001	53s
Household operation expenditures	yr	781	1999	30r
Housekeeping supplies purchases	yr	513	1999	30r
Lodging expenditures	yr	575	1999	30r
Maintenance, repairs, insurance expenditures	yr	939	1999	30r
Monthly rental value of owned home	mos	662	1999	30r
Owned dwellings, expenditures own	yr	5231	1999	30r
Rent expenditures	yr	2709	1999	30r
Rental unit, 1 bedroom, with utilities	mos	703	4/01	41c
Rental unit, 2 bedroom, with utilities	mos	857	4/01	41c
Rental unit, 3 bedroom, with utilities	mos	1190	4/01	41c
Rental unit, 4 bedroom, with utilities	mos	1405	4/01	41c
Shelter, expenditures on	yr	8516	1999	30r
Insurance and Pensions				
Life and other personal insurance purchases	yr	355	1999	30r
Pensions and Social Security, expenditures on	yr	3636	1999	30r
Legal Fees				
Divorce, filing fee		182.00	4/01	35s
Driver's license fee	renew	15.00	1999	48s
Driver's license fee	orig	12.00	1999	48s
Personal Goods				
Personal care products and services purchases	yr	449	1999	30r
Personal Services				
Personal services, household, expenditures on	yr	353	1999	30r

Values are in dollars or fractions of dollars. In the column headed *Ref*, references are shown to sources. Each reference is followed by a letter. These refer to the geographical level for which data were reported: s=State, r=Region, and c=City or metro. The abbreviation *ex* is used to mean *except* or *excluding*; *exp* stands for *expenditures*. For other abbreviations and further explanations, please see the Introduction.

Vallejo-Fairfield-Napa, CA - continued

Item	Per	Value	Date	Ref.
Pets				
Pets, toys, and playground equipment, expenditures on	yr	358	1999	30r
Taxes				
Federal income taxes paid	yr	3200	1999	30r
Personal taxes, expenditures on	yr	4153	1999	30r
Property taxes paid	yr	923	1999	30r
State and local income taxes paid	yr	812	1999	30r
Transportation				
Cars and trucks, new, expenditures on	yr	1534	1999	30r
Cars and trucks, used, expenditures on	yr	1593	1999	30r
Diesel at the pump	gal	1.37	10/99	73s
Gasoline and motor oil purchases	yr	1129	1999	30r
Gasoline before-tax price (cents)	gal	128.80	10/00	43s
Maintenance and repair expenditures	yr	797	1999	30r
Public transportation, expenditures on	yr	530	1999	30r
Transportation purchases	yr	7423	1999	30r
Vehicle expenses, miscellaneous, purchases	yr	2585	1999	30r
Vehicle insurance payments	yr	811	1999	30r
Vehicle purchases (net outlay)	yr	3180	1999	30r
Vehicle rental, lease expenditures	yr	666	1999	30r
Utilities				
Electrical bill, average	mos	58.66	9/00	9s
Electricity, expenditures on	yr	725	1999	30r
Electricity cost, average	KWh	7.75	9/00	9s
Utilities, fuels, and public services purchased	yr	2179	1999	30r
Water and other public services, expenditures on	yr	339	1999	30r
Weddings				
Wedding (national average cost)		19936	2000	33r
Wedding (regional average total cost)		18918	1997	110r
Attendants' gifts		321	1998	33r
Bridal attendants' apparel (5 persons)		824	2000	33r
Bride's headpiece/veil		173	1998	33r
Bride's wedding dress		859	1998	33r
Clergy, religious facility fee		242	1998	33r
Engagement ring		3177	1998	33r
Flowers		789	1998	33r
Groom's formalwear rental		99	2000	33r
Limousine		410	1998	33r
Marriage license cost		50.00-80.00	4/01	35s
Men's formalwear (ushers, best man)		469	2000	33r
Mother of bride apparel		241	2000	33r
Music		866	1998	33r
Photography and videography		1368	1998	33r
Rehearsal dinner		728	1998	33r
Wedding invitations and announcements		341	1998	33r
Wedding reception		7968	2000	33r
Wedding rings (bride and groom)		1060	1998	33r

Ventura, CA

Item	Per	Value	Date	Ref.
Average annual expenditures	yr	40662	1999	30r
Alcoholic Beverages				
Alcoholic beverage purchases	yr	372	1999	30r
Malt beverages, all types, all sizes, any origin	16 oz	0.94	7/01	11r
Wine, red and white table, all sizes, any origin	liter	6.00	7/01	11r
Appliances				
Major appliances, expenditures on	yr	167	1999	30r
Small appliances, housewares, expenditures on	yr	105	1999	30r
Banking and Money				
Mortgage interest and charges paid	yr	3368	1999	30r
Mortgage principal paid on owned property	yr	1677	1999	30r
Vehicle finance charges paid	yr	311	1999	30r

Ventura, CA - continued

Item	Per	Value	Date	Ref.
Charity				
Cash contributions, expenditures	yr	1344	1999	30r
Child Care				
Child raising cost, total, age 0-2	yr	9140	1999	60r
Child raising cost, total, age 3-5	yr	9370	1999	60r
Child raising cost, total, age 6-8	yr	9450	1999	60r
Child raising cost, total, age 9-11	yr	9470	1999	60r
Child raising cost, total, age 12-14	yr	10170	1999	60r
Child raising cost, total, age 15-17	yr	10360	1999	60r
Child's child care and education, age 0-2	yr	1250	1999	60r
Child's child care and education, age 3-5	yr	1380	1999	60r
Child's child care and education, age 6-8	yr	890	1999	60r
Child's child care and education, age 9-11	yr	580	1999	60r
Child's child care and education, age 12-14	yr	430	1999	60r
Child's child care and education, age 15-17	yr	730	1999	60r
Child's clothing, age 0-2	yr	430	1999	60r
Child's clothing, age 3-5	yr	420	1999	60r
Child's clothing, age 6-8	yr	470	1999	60r
Child's clothing, age 9-11	yr	520	1999	60r
Child's clothing, age 12-14	yr	870	1999	60r
Child's clothing, age 15-17	yr	770	1999	60r
Child's food, age 0-2	yr	1120	1999	60r
Child's food, age 3-5	yr	1280	1999	60r
Child's food, age 6-8	yr	1640	1999	60r
Child's food, age 9-11	yr	1930	1999	60r
Child's food, age 12-14	yr	1940	1999	60r
Child's food, age 15-17	yr	2150	1999	60r
Child's health care, age 0-2	yr	490	1999	60r
Child's health care, age 3-5	yr	470	1999	60r
Child's health care, age 6-8	yr	530	1999	60r
Child's health care, age 9-11	yr	570	1999	60r
Child's health care, age 12-14	yr	580	1999	60r
Child's health care, age 15-17	yr	610	1999	60r
Child's housing, age 0-2	yr	3630	1999	60r
Child's housing, age 3-5	yr	3610	1999	60r
Child's housing, age 6-8	yr	3570	1999	60r
Child's housing, age 9-11	yr	3410	1999	60r
Child's housing, age 12-14	yr	3600	1999	60r
Child's housing, age 15-17	yr	3210	1999	60r
Child's personal care, reading, age 0-2	yr	1040	1999	60r
Child's personal care, reading, age 3-5	yr	1060	1999	60r
Child's personal care, reading, age 6-8	yr	1090	1999	60r
Child's personal care, reading, age 9-11	yr	1130	1999	60r
Child's personal care, reading, age 12-14	yr	1300	1999	60r
Child's personal care, reading, age 15-17	yr	1080	1999	60r
Clothing				
Apparel and services purchases	yr	1863	1999	30r
Boys, 2 to 15, expenditures on	yr	80	1999	30r
Children under 2, expenditures on	yr	74	1999	30r
Footwear, expenditures on	yr	307	1999	30r
Girls, 2 to 15, expenditures on	yr	101	1999	30r
Men and boys, expenditures on	yr	443	1999	30r
Men, 16 and over, expenditures on	yr	363	1999	30r
Women, 16 and over, expenditures on	yr	594	1999	30r
Communications				
Cable modem installation, AT&T-BIS		150.00	6/99	103s
Cable modem installation, Charter		99.00-169.00	6/99	103s
Cable modem installation, Comcast		95.00	6/99	103s
Cable modem installation, Cox		99.00-174.95	6/99	103s
Cable modem installation, Media One		100.00	6/99	103s
Cable modem installation, Time Warner		75.00-225.00	6/99	103s
Cable modem rate, cable subscriber, AT&T-BIS	mos	39.95	6/99	103s
Cable modem rate, cable subscriber, Charter	mos	49.95-79.95	6/99	103s
Cable modem rate, cable subscriber, Comcast	mos	39.95	6/99	103s
Cable modem rate, cable subscriber, Cox	mos	29.95-44.95	6/99	103s

Values are in dollars or fractions of dollars. In the column headed *Ref*, references are shown to sources. Each reference is followed by a letter. These refer to the geographical level for which data were reported: s=State, r=Region, and c=City or metro. The abbreviation *ex* is used to mean *except* or *excluding*; *exp* stands for expenditures. For other abbreviations and further explanations, please see the Introduction.

Ventura, CA - continued

Item	Per	Value	Date	Ref.
Communications				
Cable modem rate, cable subscriber, Media One	mos	34.95-39.95	6/99	103s
Cable modem rate, cable subscriber, Time Warner	mos	39.95-49.95	6/99	103s
Cable modem rate, non-cable subscriber, Charter	mos	59.95-89.95	6/99	103s
Cable modem rate, non-cable subscriber, Comcast	mos	49.95	6/99	103s
Cable modem rate, non-cable subscriber, Cox	mos	42.95-54.95	6/99	103s
Cable modem rate, non-cable subscriber, Media One	mos	49.95	6/99	103s
Cable modem rate, non-cable subscriber, Time Warner	mos	39.95-54.95	6/99	103s
Phone line, single, business, field visit	inst.	70.75	12/97	17s
Phone line, single, business, no field visit	inst.	70.75	12/97	17s
Phone line, single, residence, field visit	inst.	34.75	12/97	17s
Phone line, single, residence, no field visit	inst.	34.75	12/97	17s
Postage and stationery, expenditures on	yr	150	1999	30r
Postal rate, express mail, up to half-pound		12.45	7/01	108r
Postal rate, letter, first class, first ounce		0.34	7/01	108r
Postal rate, letter, two ounces		0.57	7/01	108r
Postal rate, post card		0.21	7/01	108r
Postal rate, priority mail, two pounds		3.95	7/01	108r
Postal rate, priority mail, up to one pound		3.50	7/01	108r
Telephone services, expenditures on	yr	825	1999	30r
Education				
Board, 4-year private college/university	yr	2970	1996	38s
Board, 4-year public college/university	yr	2516	1996	38s
Education expenditures	yr	676	1999	30r
Room, 4-year private college/university	yr	3196	1996	38s
Room, 4-year public college/university	yr	3031	1996	38s
Total cost, 4-year private college/university	yr	20143	1996	38s
Total cost, 4-year public college/university	yr	8213	1996	38s
Tuition, 2-year public college/university, in state	yr	362	1996	38s
Tuition, 4-year private college/university, in state	yr	13977	1996	38s
Tuition, 4-year public college/university	yr	2666	1996	38s
Energy and Fuels				
Electricity	KWh	0.11	7/01	11r
Electricity	500 KWhs	48.23	7/01	11r
Fuel oil and other fuels, expenditures on	yr	35	1999	30r
Gas, natural, commercial rate	1000 cf	8.74	11/00	88s
Gasoline, all types	gal	1.91	7/01	11r
Gasoline, unleaded premium	gal	2.05	7/01	11r
Gasoline, unleaded regular	gal	1.83	7/01	11r
Natural gas, expenditures on	yr	255	1999	30r
Utility (piped) gas, therm		0.98	7/01	11r
Utility (piped) gas, 40 therms		40.74	7/01	11r
Utility (piped) gas, 100 therms		96.80	7/01	11r
Entertainment				
Entertainment purchases	yr	2139	1999	30r
Fees and admissions paid	yr	545	1999	30r
Television, radios, sound equipment, expenditures on	yr	624	1999	30r
Funerals				
Total cost of funeral		5401.08	1/99	78r
Acknowledgement cards		33.64	1/99	78r
Casket		2170.43	1/99	78r
Cosmetology, hair, other preparation		136.32	1/99	78r
Embalming		319.13	1/99	78r
Funeral at funeral home		370.21	1/99	78r
Hearse (local)		161.04	1/99	78r
Professional service charges		963.15	1/99	78r
Service car/van		133.99	1/99	78r
Transfer of remains to funeral home		159.82	1/99	78r
Vault		778.07	1/99	78r
Visitation/viewing		175.28	1/99	78r

Ventura, CA - continued

Item	Per	Value	Date	Ref.
Groceries				
Apples, red delicious	lb	0.84	7/01	11r
Bacon, sliced	lb	3.38	7/01	11r
Bakery products, expenditures on	yr	299	1999	30r
Bananas	lb	0.54	7/01	11r
Beans, dried, any type, all sizes	lb	0.76	7/01	11r
Beef, expenditures on	yr	222	1999	30r
Bread, white, pan	lb	0.99	7/01	11r
Butter, yoghurt, cheese, etc, expenditures on	yr	211	1999	30r
Cereals and bakery product purchases	yr	466	1999	30r
Cereals and cereal products, expenditures on	yr	168	1999	30r
Chicken breast, bone-in	lb	2.45	7/01	11r
Chicken, fresh, whole	lb	1.19	7/01	11r
Chops, boneless,	lb	4.00	7/01	11r
Chuck roast, graded and ungraded, excl U.S. prime and choice	lb	2.55	7/01	11r
Coffee, 100%, ground roast, all sizes	lb	3.80	7/01	11r
Cookies, chocolate chip	lb	2.83	7/01	11r
Dairy product purchases	yr	341	1999	30r
Eggs, expenditures on	yr	39	1999	30r
Eggs, grade AA, large	dozen	1.23	7/01	11r
Fats and oils, expenditures on	yr	88	1999	30r
Fish and seafood, expenditures on	yr	121	1999	30r
Food (excl fruit and vegetables), eaten at home, purchases	yr	1001	1999	30r
Food cooked on trips, expenditures on	yr	64	1999	30r
Food purchases	yr	5312	1999	30r
Food purchases, eaten away from home	yr	2180	1999	30r
Food purchases, food eaten at home	yr	3132	1999	30r
Fresh fruits, expenditures on	yr	186	1999	30r
Fresh milk and cream, expenditures on	yr	130	1999	30r
Fresh vegetables, expenditures on	yr	177	1999	30r
Grapefruit	lb	0.68	7/01	11r
Grapes, Thompson, seedless	lb	2.42	7/01	11r
Ground beef, lean and extra lean	lb	2.46	7/01	11r
Ice cream, prepackaged, bulk, regular	1/2 gal	3.62	7/01	11r
Lettuce, iceberg	lb	0.63	7/01	11r
Meats, poultry, fish, and egg purchases	yr	761	1999	30r
Milk, fresh, low fat,	gal	2.80	7/01	11r
Milk, fresh, whole, fortified	gal	2.88	7/01	11r
Nonalcoholic beverages, expenditures on	yr	258	1999	30r
Oranges, Navel	lb	0.97	7/01	11r
Oranges, Valencia	lb	0.43	7/01	11r
Peaches	lb	1.38	7/01	11r
Peanut butter, creamy, all sizes	lb	2.14	7/01	11r
Pork chops, center cut, bone-in	lb	3.83	7/01	11r
Pork, expenditures on	yr	141	1999	30r
Potatoes, white, all types	lb	0.37	7/01	11r
Poultry, expenditures on	yr	146	1999	30r
Processed fruits, expenditures on	yr	118	1999	30r
Processed vegetables, expenditures on	yr	81	1999	30r
Round roast, graded and ungraded, excl U.S. prime and choice	lb	3.07	7/01	11r
Round roast, U.S. choice, boneless	lb	3.37	7/01	11r
Round steak, graded and ungraded, excl U.S. prime and choice	lb	3.51	7/01	11r
Sirloin steak, graded and ungraded, excl U.S. prime and choice	lb	4.67	7/01	11r
Steak, sirloin, U.S. choice, boneless	lb	6.20	7/01	11r
Strawberries, dry pint	12 oz	1.79	7/01	11r
Sugar and other sweets, expenditures on	yr	124	1999	30r
Sugar, white, all sizes	lb	0.46	7/01	11r
Tobacco products and smoking supplies purchases	yr	217	1999	30r
Tomatoes, field grown	lb	1.17	7/01	11r
Tuna, light, chunk	lb	2.05	7/01	11r
Goods and Services				
B&B Japanese maple (acer japonicum)	gal	39.99	4/00	93r
Boxwood (buxus)	2 gal	14.99-24.99	4/00	93r
Christmas tree, noble fir		40-60	2000	65s

Values are in dollars or fractions of dollars. In the column headed *Ref*, references are shown to sources. Each reference is followed by a letter. These refer to the geographical level for which data were reported: s=State, r=Region, and c=City or metro. The abbreviation *ex* is used to mean *except* or *excluding*; *exp* stands for *expenditures*. For other abbreviations and further explanations, please see the Introduction.

Ventura, CA - continued

Item	Per	Value	Date	Ref.
Goods and Services				
Daylilly (hemerocallis)	gal	6.99-8.99	4/00	93r
Flat of annuals		16.68	4/00	93r
Fountain grass (pennisetum)	gal	7.99-11.99	4/00	93r
Hanging basket (10 in)		29.99	4/00	93r
Hardy geranium (geranium)	gal	6.99-11.99	4/00	93r
Hosta (hosta)	gal	6.99-18.99	4/00	93r
Lilac (syrubga vulgaris)	2 gal	14.99-17.99	4/00	93r
Miscellaneous purchases	yr	1070	1999	30r
Rhododendron (rhododendron)	2 gal	14.99	4/00	93r
Sage (salvia)	gal	6.99	4/00	93r
Wintercreeper euonymus (euonymus fortunei)	2 gal	14.99-22.99	4/00	93r
Hunting license	yr	29.95	4/01	34s
Health Care				
Cardiac catheterization, ave hospital/physician charges		24000	1998	77s
Childbirth, Cesarean delivery		11587	1997	13r
Childbirth, vaginal delivery		6725	1997	13r
Drugs, expenditures on	yr	309	1999	30r
Health care purchases	yr	1869	1999	30r
Health insurance expenditures	yr	868	1999	30r
Hysterectomy, laproscopically-assisted, ave hospital/physician charges		20760	1998	76s
Hysterectomy, vaginal, ave hospital and physician charges		14570	1998	76s
Medicaid dispensing fee		4.05	1999	87s
Medical services expenditures	yr	580	1999	30r
Medical supplies, expenditures on	yr	112	1999	30r
Household Goods				
Floor coverings, expenditures on	yr	49	1999	30r
Furniture, expenditures on	yr	444	1999	30r
Household furnishings and equipment purchases	yr	1768	1999	30r
Household textiles, expenditures on	yr	141	1999	30r
Laundry and cleaning supplies, expenditures on	yr	128	1999	30r
Housing				
Home price, existing, ave		239400	10/00	90r
Home value, median		215000	2001	53s
Household operation expenditures	yr	781	1999	30r
Housekeeping supplies purchases	yr	513	1999	30r
Lodging expenditures	yr	575	1999	30r
Maintenance, repairs, insurance expenditures	yr	939	1999	30r
Monthly rental value of owned home	mos	662	1999	30r
Owned dwellings, expenditures own	yr	5231	1999	30r
Rent expenditures	yr	2709	1999	30r
Rental unit, 1 bedroom, with utilities	mos	655	4/01	41c
Rental unit, 2 bedroom, with utilities	mos	829	4/01	41c
Rental unit, 3 bedroom, with utilities	mos	1103	4/01	41c
Rental unit, 4 bedroom, with utilities	mos	1284	4/01	41c
Shelter, expenditures on	yr	8516	1999	30r
Insurance and Pensions				
Life and other personal insurance purchases	yr	355	1999	30r
Pensions and Social Security, expenditures on	yr	3636	1999	30r
Legal Fees				
Divorce, filing fee		182.00	4/01	35s
Driver's license fee	orig	12.00	1999	48s
Driver's license fee	renew	15.00	1999	48s
Personal Goods				
Personal care products and services purchases	yr	449	1999	30r

Ventura, CA - continued

Item	Per	Value	Date	Ref.
Personal Services				
Personal services, household, expenditures on	yr	353	1999	30r
Pets				
Pets, toys, and playground equipment, expenditures on	yr	358	1999	30r
Taxes				
Federal income taxes paid	yr	3200	1999	30r
Personal taxes, expenditures on	yr	4153	1999	30r
Property taxes paid	yr	923	1999	30r
State and local income taxes paid	yr	812	1999	30r
Transportation				
Cars and trucks, new, expenditures on	yr	1534	1999	30r
Cars and trucks, used, expenditures on	yr	1593	1999	30r
Diesel at the pump	gal	1.37	10/99	73s
Gasoline and motor oil purchases	yr	1129	1999	30r
Gasoline before-tax price (cents)	gal	128.80	10/00	43s
Maintenance and repair expenditures	yr	797	1999	30r
Public transportation, expenditures on	yr	530	1999	30r
Transportation purchases	yr	7423	1999	30r
Vehicle expenses, miscellaneous, purchases	yr	2585	1999	30r
Vehicle insurance payments	yr	811	1999	30r
Vehicle purchases (net outlay)	yr	3180	1999	30r
Vehicle rental, lease expenditures	yr	666	1999	30r
Utilities				
Electrical bill, average	mos	58.66	9/00	9s
Electricity, expenditures on	yr	725	1999	30r
Electricity cost, average	KWh	7.75	9/00	9s
Utilities, fuels, and public services purchased	yr	2179	1999	30r
Water and other public services, expenditures on	yr	339	1999	30r
Weddings				
Wedding (national average cost)		19936	2000	33r
Wedding (regional average total cost)		18918	1997	110r
Attendants' gifts		321	1998	33r
Bridal attendants' apparel (5 persons)		824	2000	33r
Bride's headpiece/veil		173	1998	33r
Bride's wedding dress		859	1998	33r
Clergy, religious facility fee		242	1998	33r
Engagement ring		3177	1998	33r
Flowers		789	1998	33r
Groom's formalwear rental		99	2000	33r
Limousine		410	1998	33r
Marriage license cost		50.00-80.00	4/01	35s
Men's formalwear (ushers, best man)		469	2000	33r
Mother of bride apparel		241	2000	33r
Music		866	1998	33r
Photography and videography		1368	1998	33r
Rehearsal dinner		728	1998	33r
Wedding invitations and announcements		341	1998	33r
Wedding reception		7968	2000	33r
Wedding rings (bride and groom)		1060	1998	33r

Victoria, TX

Item	Per	Value	Date	Ref.
Composite, ACCRA index		87.60	3/01	4c
Alcoholic Beverages				
Alcoholic beverage purchases	yr	253	1999	30r
Beer, Heineken, 12-oz, ex deposit	6	6.35	3/01	4c
J & B Scotch	750-ml	19.78	3/01	4c
Malt beverages, all types, all sizes, any origin	16 oz	0.96	7/01	11r
Wine, Livingston or Gallo, Chablis blanc	1.5 liter	4.53	3/01	4c
Appliances				
Appliance repair, service call, washing machine	min lab chg	32.50	3/01	4c
Major appliances, expenditures on	yr	172	1999	30r
Small appliances, housewares, expenditures on	yr	81	1999	30r

Values are in dollars or fractions of dollars. In the column headed *Ref*, references are shown as sources. Each reference is followed by a letter. These refer to the geographical level for which data were reported: s=State, r=Region, and c=City or metro. The abbreviation *ex* is used to mean *except* or *excluding*; *exp* stands for *expenditures*. For other abbreviations and further explanations, please see the Introduction.

Victoria, TX - continued

Item	Per	Value	Date	Ref.
Banking and Money				
Mortgage interest and charges paid	yr	2039	1999	30r
Mortgage principal paid on owned property	yr	1026	1999	30r
Mortgage rate, incl. points and orig. fee, 30-yr. conv. fixed or ARM	mos	7.13	3/01	4c
Vehicle finance charges paid	yr	365	1999	30r
Charity				
Cash contributions, expenditures	yr	1127	1999	30r
Child Care				
Child raising cost, total, age 0-2	yr	8540	1999	60r
Child raising cost, total, age 3-5	yr	8780	1999	60r
Child raising cost, total, age 6-8	yr	8820	1999	60r
Child raising cost, total, age 9-11	yr	8800	1999	60r
Child raising cost, total, age 12-14	yr	9510	1999	60r
Child raising cost, total, age 15-17	yr	9740	1999	60r
Child's child care and education, age 0-2	yr	1380	1999	60r
Child's child care and education, age 3-5	yr	1520	1999	60r
Child's child care and education, age 6-8	yr	990	1999	60r
Child's child care and education, age 9-11	yr	650	1999	60r
Child's child care and education, age 12-14	yr	490	1999	60r
Child's child care and education, age 15-17	yr	840	1999	60r
Child's clothing, age 0-2	yr	480	1999	60r
Child's clothing, age 3-5	yr	470	1999	60r
Child's clothing, age 6-8	yr	520	1999	60r
Child's clothing, age 9-11	yr	570	1999	60r
Child's clothing, age 12-14	yr	950	1999	60r
Child's clothing, age 15-17	yr	850	1999	60r
Child's food, age 0-2	yr	1000	1999	60r
Child's food, age 3-5	yr	1160	1999	60r
Child's food, age 6-8	yr	1490	1999	60r
Child's food, age 9-11	yr	1770	1999	60r
Child's food, age 12-14	yr	1770	1999	60r
Child's food, age 15-17	yr	1980	1999	60r
Child's health care, age 0-2	yr	620	1999	60r
Child's health care, age 3-5	yr	590	1999	60r
Child's health care, age 6-8	yr	680	1999	60r
Child's health care, age 9-11	yr	720	1999	60r
Child's health care, age 12-14	yr	730	1999	60r
Child's health care, age 15-17	yr	760	1999	60r
Child's housing, age 0-2	yr	3070	1999	60r
Child's housing, age 3-5	yr	3050	1999	60r
Child's housing, age 6-8	yr	3010	1999	60r
Child's housing, age 9-11	yr	2850	1999	60r
Child's housing, age 12-14	yr	3040	1999	60r
Child's housing, age 15-17	yr	2650	1999	60r
Child's personal care, reading, age 0-2	yr	910	1999	60r
Child's personal care, reading, age 3-5	yr	930	1999	60r
Child's personal care, reading, age 6-8	yr	960	1999	60r
Child's personal care, reading, age 9-11	yr	1000	1999	60r
Child's personal care, reading, age 12-14	yr	1170	1999	60r
Child's personal care, reading, age 15-17	yr	950	1999	60r
Clothing				
Apparel and services purchases	yr	1610	1999	30r
Boys' brief, cotton	3	2.96	3/01	4c
Boys, 2 to 15, expenditures on	yr	89	1999	30r
Children under 2, expenditures on	yr	79	1999	30r
Footwear, expenditures on	yr	283	1999	30r
Girls, 2 to 15, expenditures on	yr	103	1999	30r
Men and boys, expenditures on	yr	351	1999	30r
Men, 16 and over, expenditures on	yr	262	1999	30r
Shirt, man's dress shirt		24.00	3/01	4c
Slacks, man's "No Wrinkles" khaki		29.50	3/01	4c
Women, 16 and over, expenditures on	yr	538	1999	30r
Communications				
Cable modem installation, AT&T-BIS		150.00	6/99	103s
Cable modem installation, Marcus		499.00	6/99	103s
Cable modem installation, Time Warner		75.00-225.00	6/99	103s
Cable modem rate, cable subscriber, AT&T-BIS	mos	39.95	6/99	103s

Victoria, TX - continued

Item	Per	Value	Date	Ref.
Communications - continued				
Cable modem rate, cable subscriber, Marcus	mos	14.95-49.95	6/99	103s
Cable modem rate, cable subscriber, Time Warner	mos	39.95-49.95	6/99	103s
Cable modem rate, non-cable subscriber, Marcus	mos	60.95	6/99	103s
Cable modem rate, non-cable subscriber, Time Warner	mos	39.95-54.95	6/99	103s
Newspaper subscription, daily and Sunday delivery	mos	10.00	3/01	4c
Phone line, single, business, field visit	inst.	71.90	12/97	17s
Phone line, single, business, no field visit	inst.	57.30	12/97	17s
Phone line, single, residence, field visit	inst.	52.95	12/97	17s
Phone line, single, residence, no field visit	inst.	38.35	12/97	17s
Postage and stationery, expenditures on	yr	104	1999	30r
Postal rate, express mail, up to half-pound		12.45	7/01	108r
Postal rate, letter, first class, first ounce		0.34	7/01	108r
Postal rate, letter, two ounces		0.57	7/01	108r
Postal rate, post card		0.21	7/01	108r
Postal rate, priority mail, two pounds		3.95	7/01	108r
Postal rate, priority mail, up to one pound		3.50	7/01	108r
Telephone bill, family of three	mos	16.30	3/01	4c
Telephone services, expenditures on	yr	860	1999	30r
Education				
Board, 4-year private college/university	yr	2198	1996	38s
Board, 4-year public college/university	yr	1759	1996	38s
Education expenditures	yr	431	1999	30r
Room, 4-year private college/university	yr	2000	1996	38s
Room, 4-year public college/university	yr	1885	1996	38s
Total cost, 4-year private college/university	yr	13156	1996	38s
Total cost, 4-year public college/university	yr	5464	1996	38s
Tuition, 2-year public college/university, in state	yr	771	1996	38s
Tuition, 4-year private college/university, in state	yr	8959	1996	38s
Tuition, 4-year public college/university	yr	1820	1996	38s
Energy and Fuels				
Electricity	KWh	0.09	7/01	11r
Electricity	500 KWhs	47.29	7/01	11r
Energy, combined forms, 2400 sq ft	mos	138.77	3/01	4c
Energy, exc. electricity, 2400 sq ft	mos	38.58	3/01	4c
Fuel oil #2	gal	1.43	7/01	11r
Fuel oil and other fuels, expenditures on	yr	45	1999	30r
Gas, natural, commercial rate	1000 cf	6.94	11/00	88s
Gas, regular unleaded, cash, self-service	gal	1.37	3/01	4c
Gasoline, all types	gal	1.60	7/01	11r
Gasoline, unleaded midgrade	gal	1.65	7/01	11r
Gasoline, unleaded premium	gal	1.74	7/01	11r
Natural gas, expenditures on	yr	164	1999	30r
Utility (piped) gas, therm		1.01	7/01	11r
Utility (piped) gas, 40 therms		44.29	7/01	11r
Utility (piped) gas, 100 therms		97.44	7/01	11r
Entertainment				
Bowling, Saturday evening rate	line	2.30	3/01	4c
Entertainment purchases	yr	1574	1999	30r
Fees and admissions paid	yr	371	1999	30r
Monopoly game, Parker Brothers', No. 9	game	9.95	3/01	4c
Movie, first-run, Saturday, evening	adm.	5.75	3/01	4c
Reading purchases	yr	121	1999	30r
Television, radios, sound equipment, expenditures on	yr	561	1999	30r
Tennis balls, yellow, Wilson or Penn, 3	can	2.00	3/01	4c
Funerals				
Total cost of funeral		5842.28	1/99	78r
Acknowledgement cards		28.35	1/99	78r
Casket		2494.29	1/99	78r
Cosmetology, hair, other preparation		109.22	1/99	78r
Embalming		361.42	1/99	78r
Funeral at funeral home		349.20	1/99	78r

Values are in dollars or fractions of dollars. In the column headed *Ref*, references are shown to sources. Each reference is followed by a letter. These refer to the geographical level for which data were reported: s=State, r=Region, and c=City or metro. The abbreviation *ex* is used to mean *except* or *excluding*; *exp* stands for *expenditures*. For other abbreviations and further explanations, please see the Introduction.

Victoria, TX - continued

Item	Per.	Value	Date	Ref.
Funerals				
Hearse (local)		161.91	1/99	78r
Professional service charges		1116.50	1/99	78r
Service car/van		65.56	1/99	78r
Transfer of remains to funeral home		143.56	1/99	78r
Vault		785.25	1/99	78r
Visitation/viewing		227.02	1/99	78r
Groceries				
Groceries, ACCRA Index		77.60	3/01	4c
American processed cheese	lb	3.50	7/01	11r
Antibiotic ointment, Polysporin	0.5 oz	4.39	3/01	4c
Baby food, strained vegetables or fruit, lowest price	4-4.5 oz	0.21	3/01	4c
Bakery products, expenditures on	yr	261	1999	30r
Bananas	lb	0.27	3/01	4c
Bananas	lb	0.47	7/01	11r
Beans, dried, any type, all sizes	lb	0.63	7/01	11r
Beef for stew, boneless	lb	2.86	7/01	11r
Beef or hamburger, ground	lb	0.93	3/01	4c
Beef, expenditures on	yr	210	1999	30r
Bologna, all beef or mixed	lb	2.29	7/01	11r
Bread, French	lb	1.66	7/01	11r
Bread, white	loaf	0.55	3/01	4c
Bread, white, pan	lb	0.87	7/01	11r
Bread, whole wheat, pan	lb	1.38	7/01	11r
Broccoli	lb	1.04	7/01	11r
Butter, salted, grade AA, stick	lb	2.26	7/01	11r
Butter, yoghurt, cheese, etc, expenditures on	yr	170	1999	30r
Cabbage	lb	0.42	7/01	11r
Cereals and cereal products, expenditures on	yr	140	1999	30r
Cheddar cheese, natural	lb	3.75	7/01	11r
Cheese, Kraft grated Parmesan	8 oz	3.33	3/01	4c
Chicken breast, bone-in	lb	1.85	7/01	11r
Chicken legs, bone-in	lb	1.34	7/01	11r
Chicken, fresh, whole	lb	1.05	7/01	11r
Chicken, whole fryer	lb	0.60	3/01	4c
Chops, boneless,	lb	4.13	7/01	11r
Chuck roast, graded and ungraded, excl U.S. prime and choice	lb	2.35	7/01	11r
Chuck roast, U.S. choice, boneless	lb	2.67	7/01	11r
Cigarettes, Winston, Kings	carton	33.98	3/01	4c
Coffee, 100%, ground roast, all sizes	lb	2.88	7/01	11r
Coffee, instant, plain, regular, all sizes	16 oz	9.25	7/01	11r
Coffee, vacuum-packed	13 oz	2.28	3/01	4c
Cola, non diet,	2 liter	1.11	7/01	11r
Corn Flakes, Kellogg's or Post Toasties	18 oz	1.89	3/01	4c
Corn, frozen, whole kernel, lowest price	16 oz	0.93	3/01	4c
Crackers, soda, salted	lb	1.70	7/01	11r
Dairy product purchases	yr	282	1999	30r
Eggs, expenditures on	yr	32	1999	30r
Eggs, Grade A or AA	dozen	0.97	3/01	4c
Fats and oils, expenditures on	yr	79	1999	30r
Fish and seafood, expenditures on	yr	99	1999	30r
Flour, white, all purpose	lb	0.32	7/01	11r
Food (excl fruit and vegetables), eaten at home, purchases	yr	815	1999	30r
Food cooked on trips, expenditures on	yr	36	1999	30r
Food purchases	yr	4533	1999	30r
Food purchases, eaten away from home	yr	1873	1999	30r
Food purchases, food eaten at home	yr	2660	1999	30r
Fresh fruits, expenditures on	yr	128	1999	30r
Fresh milk and cream, expenditures on	yr	112	1999	30r
Fresh vegetables, expenditures on	yr	131	1999	30r
Fruit and vegetable purchases	yr	438	1999	30r
Grapefruit	lb	0.59	7/01	11r
Grapes, Thompson, seedless	lb	2.12	7/01	11r
Ground beef, 100% beef	lb	1.76	7/01	11r
Ground beef, lean and extra lean	lb	2.60	7/01	11r
Ground chuck, 100% beef	lb	2.08	7/01	11r
Ham, boneless, excl canned	lb	2.71	7/01	11r
Ham, rump or shank half, bone-in, smoked	lb	2.19	7/01	11r
Ice cream, prepackaged, bulk, regular	1/2 gal	3.93	7/01	11r

Victoria, TX - continued

Item	Per	Value	Date	Ref.
Groceries - continued				
Lemons	lb	1.32	7/01	11r
Lettuce, iceberg	head	0.95	3/01	4c
Lettuce, iceberg	lb	0.76	7/01	11r
Margarine, Blue Bonnet or Parkay, stick	lb	0.71	3/01	4c
Milk, fresh, low fat	gal	2.75	7/01	11r
Milk, fresh, whole, fortified	gal	2.97	7/01	11r
Milk, whole	1/2 gal	1.52	3/01	4c
Nonalcoholic beverages, expenditures on	yr	228	1999	30r
Orange juice, frozen concentrate	16 oz	1.95	7/01	11r
Orange juice, Minute Maid frozen	12 oz	1.31	3/01	4c
Oranges, Navel	lb	0.73	7/01	11r
Oranges, Valencia	lb	0.55	7/01	11r
Peaches, halves or slices, Hunt's, Del Monte, or Libby's	29 oz	1.46	3/01	4c
Peanut butter, creamy, all sizes	lb	1.83	7/01	11r
Pears, Anjou	lb	0.98	7/01	11r
Peas, green, Del Monte or Green Giant	15 oz	0.53	3/01	4c
Pork chops, center cut, bone-in	lb	3.33	7/01	11r
Pork sausage, fresh, loose	lb	2.59	7/01	11r
Pork shoulder picnic, bone-in, smoked	lb	1.12	7/01	11r
Pork, expenditures on	yr	162	1999	30r
Potato chips	16 oz	3.59	7/01	11r
Potatoes, frozen, french fried	lb	1.00	7/01	11r
Potatoes, white or red	10 lb	2.13	3/01	4c
Potatoes, white, all types	lb	0.44	7/01	11r
Poultry, expenditures on	yr	137	1999	30r
Processed fruits, expenditures on	yr	97	1999	30r
Processed vegetables, expenditures on	yr	82	1999	30r
Rice, white, long grain, uncooked	lb	0.51	7/01	11r
Round roast, graded and ungraded, excl U.S. prime and choice	lb	2.96	7/01	11r
Round steak, graded and ungraded, excl U.S. prime and choice	lb	3.11	7/01	11r
Sausage, Jimmy Dean/Owens pork	lb	2.52	3/01	4c
Shortening, vegetable, Crisco	3 lb	2.67	3/01	4c
Sirloin steak, graded and ungraded, excl U.S. prime and choice	lb	4.23	7/01	11r
Soft drink, Coca Cola, ex deposit	2 liter	1.01	3/01	4c
Spaghetti and macaroni	lb	0.78	7/01	11r
Steak, round, U.S. choice, boneless	lb	3.56	7/01	11r
Steak, sirloin, U.S. choice, boneless	lb	5.65	7/01	11r
Steak, T-bone	lb	6.06	3/01	4c
Strawberries, dry pint	12 oz	1.50	7/01	11r
Sugar and other sweets, expenditures on	yr	99	1999	30r
Sugar, cane or beet	4 lbs	1.18	3/01	4c
Sugar, white, 33-80 ounce package	lb	0.39	7/01	11r
Sugar, white, all sizes	lb	0.42	7/01	11r
Tobacco products and smoking supplies purchases	yr	288	1999	30r
Tomatoes, field grown	lb	1.43	7/01	11r
Tomatoes, Hunt's or Del Monte	14.5 oz	0.76	3/01	4c
Tuna, chunk, light	6 oz	0.41	3/01	4c
Tuna, light, chunk	lb	1.77	7/01	11r
Turkey, frozen, whole	lb	1.05	7/01	11r
Goods and Services				
Miscellaneous goods and services, ACCRA Index		87.80	3/01	4c
B&B Japanese maple (acer japonicum)	gal	79.98-99.00	4/00	93r
Boxwood (buxus)	2 gal	12.98-18.99	4/00	93r
Christmas tree, noble fir		40-60	2000	65s
Daylilly (hemerocallis)	gal	7.96-11.00	4/00	93r
Flat of annuals		13.99-27.99	4/00	93r
Fountain grass (pennisetum)	gal	6.96-9.00	4/00	93r
Hanging basket (10 in)		9.99-24.99	4/00	93r
Hardy geranium (geranium)	gal	5.96-8.00	4/00	93r

Values are in dollars or fractions of dollars. In the column headed *Ref*, references are shown to sources. Each reference is followed by a letter. These refer to the geographical level for which data were reported: s=State, r=Region, and c=City or metro. The abbreviation *ex* is used to mean *except* or *excluding*; *exp* stands for *expenditures*. For other abbreviations and further explanations, please see the Introduction.

Victoria, TX - continued

Item	Per	Value	Date	Ref.
Goods and Services				
Hosta (hosta)	gal	8.96-12.99	4/00	93r
Lilac (syrubga vulgaris)	2 gal	13.00-19.99	4/00	93r
Rhododendron (rhododendron)	2 gal	12.98-29.99	4/00	93r
Sage (salvia)	gal	5.96-8.00	4/00	93r
Wintercreeper euonymus (euonymus fortunei)	2 gal	13.00-18.99	4/00	93r
Hunting license	yr	19.00	4/01	34s
Health Care				
Health care, ACCRA Index		88.30	3/01	4c
Cardiac catheterization, ave hospital/ physician charges		20140	1998	77s
Childbirth, Cesarean delivery		11587	1997	13r
Childbirth, vaginal delivery		6725	1997	13r
Dentist's fee, adult teeth cleaning and periodic oral exam	visit	69.33	3/01	4c
Doctor's fee, routine exam, established patient	visit	51.00	3/01	4c
Drugs, expenditures on	yr	399	1999	30r
Health care purchases	yr	1971	1999	30r
Health insurance expenditures	yr	933	1999	30r
Hospital care, private room	day	376.00	3/01	4c
Hysterectomy, laproscopically-assisted, ave hospital/physician charges		15700	1998	76s
Hysterectomy, vaginal, ave hospital and physician charges		12180	1998	76s
Medicaid dispensing fee		5.27	1999	87s
Medical services expenditures	yr	547	1999	30r
Medical supplies, expenditures on	yr	91	1999	30r
Household Goods				
Dishwashing powder, Cascade	50 oz	2.89	3/01	4c
Floor coverings, expenditures on	yr	44	1999	30r
Furniture, expenditures on	yr	335	1999	30r
Household furnishings and equipment purchases	yr	1328	1999	30r
Household textiles, expenditures on	yr	89	1999	30r
Laundry and cleaning supplies, expenditures on	yr	113	1999	30r
Tissues, facial, Kleenex brand	175	1.06	3/01	4c
Housing				
Housing, ACCRA Index		84.40	3/01	4c
Home price, existing, ave		160100	10/00	90r
Home value, median		112000	2001	53s
House, 2400 sq ft, 8000 sq ft lot, new, urban, utilities	total	172320	3/01	4c
House payment, principal and interest, 25% down payment	mos	871	3/01	4c
Household operation expenditures	yr	553	1999	30r
Housekeeping supplies purchases	yr	473	1999	30r
Housing, expenditures on	yr	10303	1999	30r
Maintenance, repairs, insurance expenditures	yr	699	1999	30r
Monthly rental value of owned home	mos	505	1999	30r
Owned dwellings, expenditures own	yr	3465	1999	30r
Rent expenditures	yr	1641	1999	30r
Rent, apartment, 2 br, 1 1/2-2 baths, unfurn, 950 sq ft, water	mos	584	3/01	4c
Rental unit, 1 bedroom, with utilities	mos	358	4/01	41c
Rental unit, 2 bedroom, with utilities	mos	452	4/01	41c
Rental unit, 3 bedroom, with utilities	mos	627	4/01	41c
Rental unit, 4 bedroom, with utilities	mos	707	4/01	41c
Shelter, expenditures on	yr	5467	1999	30r
Insurance and Pensions				
Life and other personal insurance purchases	yr	414	1999	30r
Pensions and Social Security, expenditures on	yr	2635	1999	30r

Victoria, TX - continued

Item	Per	Value	Date	Ref.
Insurance and Pensions - continued				
Personal insurance and pensions, expenditures on	yr	3048	1999	30r
Legal Fees				
Divorce, filing fee		150.00-200.00	4/01	35s
Driver's license fee	orig	24.00	1999	48s
Driver's license fee	renew	20.00	1999	48s
Fishing license	yr	19.00	4/01	34s
Personal Goods				
Personal care products and services purchases	yr	393	1999	30r
Shampoo, Alberto VO5	15 oz	0.95	3/01	4c
Toothpaste, Crest or Colgate	6-7 oz	2.06	3/01	4c
Personal Services				
Dry cleaning, man's 2-pc suit		6.51	3/01	4c
Man's haircut, barbershop, no styling		9.32	3/01	4c
Personal services, household, expenditures on	yr	258	1999	30r
Woman's shampoo, trim, blow-dry, no style-change		16.98	3/01	4c
Pets				
Pets, toys, and playground equipment, expenditures on	yr	306	1999	30r
Restaurant Food				
Chicken, fried, thigh and drumstick, KFC/ Church's		2.25	3/01	4c
Hamburger with cheese, McDonald's	1/4 lb	2.26	3/01	4c
Pizza, Pizza Hut or Pizza Inn	11-12 in	9.99	3/01	4c
Taxes				
Federal income taxes paid	yr	2047	1999	30r
Personal taxes, expenditures on	yr	2554	1999	30r
Property taxes paid	yr	726	1999	30r
State and local income taxes paid	yr	363	1999	30r
Transportation				
Transportation, ACCRA Index		95.10	3/01	4c
Cars and trucks, new, expenditures on	yr	1648	1999	30r
Cars and trucks, used, expenditures on	yr	1651	1999	30r
Diesel at the pump	gal	1.18	10/99	73s
Gasoline and motor oil purchases	yr	1052	1999	30r
Gasoline before-tax price (cents)	gal	101.30	10/00	43s
Maintenance and repair expenditures	yr	621	1999	30r
Public transportation, expenditures on	yr	298	1999	30r
Tire balance, computer or spin balance, front	wheel	7.24	3/01	4c
Transportation purchases	yr	6738	1999	30r
Vehicle expenses, miscellaneous, purchases	yr	2033	1999	30r
Vehicle insurance payments	yr	696	1999	30r
Vehicle purchases (net outlay)	yr	3354	1999	30r
Vehicle rental, lease expenditures	yr	352	1999	30r
Utilities				
Utilities, ACCRA Index		108.40	3/01	4c
Electrical bill, average	mos	87.17	9/00	9s
Electricity, expenditures on	yr	1115	1999	30r
Electricity and other, mixed, 2400 sq ft, new home	mos	100.19	3/01	4c
Electricity cost, average	KWh	6.48	9/00	9s
Water and other public services, expenditures on	yr	298	1999	30r
Weddings				
Wedding (national average cost)		19936	2000	33r
Attendants' gifts		321	1998	33r
Bridal attendants' apparel (5 persons)		824	2000	33r
Bride's headpiece/veil		173	1998	33r
Bride's wedding dress		859	1998	33r
Clergy, religious facility fee		242	1998	33r
Engagement ring		3177	1998	33r
Flowers		789	1998	33r
Groom's formalwear rental		99	2000	33r

Values are in dollars or fractions of dollars. In the column headed *Ref*, references are shown to sources. Each reference is followed by a letter. These refer to the geographical level for which data were reported: s=State, r=Region, and c=City or metro. The abbreviation *ex* is used to mean *except* or *excluding*; *exp* stands for expenditures. For other abbreviations and further explanations, please see the Introduction.

Victoria, TX - continued

Item	Per	Value	Date	Ref.
Weddings				
Limousine		410	1998	33r
Marriage license cost		36.00	4/01	35s
Men's formalwear (ushers, best man)		469	2000	33r
Mother of bride apparel		241	2000	33r
Music		866	1998	33r
Photography and videography		1368	1998	33r
Rehearsal dinner		728	1998	33r
Wedding invitations and announcements		341	1998	33r
Wedding reception		7968	2000	33r
Wedding rings (bride and groom)		1060	1998	33r

Vineland-Millville-Bridgeton, NJ

Item	Per	Value	Date	Ref.
Average annual expenditures	yr	37971	1999	30r
Alcoholic Beverages				
Alcoholic beverage purchases	yr	368	1999	30r
Wine, red and white table, all sizes, any origin	liter	9.64	7/01	11r
Appliances				
Major appliances, expenditures on	yr	194	1999	30r
Small appliances, housewares, expenditures on	yr	93	1999	30r
Banking and Money				
Mortgage interest and charges paid	yr	2622	1999	30r
Mortgage principal paid on owned property	yr	1262	1999	30r
Vehicle finance charges paid	yr	240	1999	30r
Charity				
Cash contributions, expenditures	yr	1001	1999	30r
Child Care				
Child raising cost, total, age 0-2	yr	8670	1999	60r
Child raising cost, total, age 3-5	yr	8910	1999	60r
Child raising cost, total, age 6-8	yr	9040	1999	60r
Child raising cost, total, age 9-11	yr	9100	1999	60r
Child raising cost, total, age 12-14	yr	9890	1999	60r
Child raising cost, total, age 15-17	yr	10010	1999	60r
Child's child care and education, age 0-2	yr	1070	1999	60r
Child's child care and education, age 3-5	yr	1190	1999	60r
Child's child care and education, age 6-8	yr	740	1999	60r
Child's child care and education, age 9-11	yr	470	1999	60r
Child's child care and education, age 12-14	yr	350	1999	60r
Child's child care and education, age 15-17	yr	590	1999	60r
Child's clothing, age 0-2	yr	480	1999	60r
Child's clothing, age 3-5	yr	470	1999	60r
Child's clothing, age 6-8	yr	520	1999	60r
Child's clothing, age 9-11	yr	570	1999	60r
Child's clothing, age 12-14	yr	970	1999	60r
Child's clothing, age 15-17	yr	870	1999	60r
Child's food, age 0-2	yr	1130	1999	60r
Child's food, age 3-5	yr	1290	1999	60r
Child's food, age 6-8	yr	1640	1999	60r
Child's food, age 9-11	yr	1930	1999	60r
Child's food, age 12-14	yr	1940	1999	60r
Child's food, age 15-17	yr	2150	1999	60r
Child's health care, age 0-2	yr	550	1999	60r
Child's health care, age 3-5	yr	530	1999	60r
Child's health care, age 6-8	yr	610	1999	60r
Child's health care, age 9-11	yr	650	1999	60r
Child's health care, age 12-14	yr	660	1999	60r
Child's health care, age 15-17	yr	690	1999	60r
Child's housing, age 0-2	yr	3555	1999	60r
Child's housing, age 3-5	yr	3530	1999	60r
Child's housing, age 6-8	yr	3490	1999	60r
Child's housing, age 9-11	yr	3340	1999	60r
Child's housing, age 12-14	yr	3530	1999	60r
Child's housing, age 15-17	yr	3140	1999	60r
Child's personal care, reading, age 0-2	yr	920	1999	60r
Child's personal care, reading, age 3-5	yr	950	1999	60r
Child's personal care, reading, age 6-8	yr	980	1999	60r
Child's personal care, reading, age 9-11	yr	1020	1999	60r

Vineland-Millville-Bridgeton, NJ - continued

Item	Per	Value	Date	Ref.
Child Care - continued				
Child's personal care, reading, age 12-14	yr	1190	1999	60r
Child's personal care, reading, age 15-17	yr	970	1999	60r
Clothing				
Apparel and services purchases	yr	1831	1999	30r
Boys, 2 to 15, expenditures on	yr	92	1999	30r
Children under 2, expenditures on	yr	63	1999	30r
Footwear, expenditures on	yr	300	1999	30r
Girls, 2 to 15, expenditures on	yr	101	1999	30r
Men and boys, expenditures on	yr	446	1999	30r
Men, 16 and over, expenditures on	yr	354	1999	30r
Women, 16 and over, expenditures on	yr	584	1999	30r
Communications				
Cable modem installation, Adelphi		54.90	6/99	103s
Cable modem installation, Comcast		95.00	6/99	103s
Cable modem rate, cable subscriber, Adelphi	mos	34.95	6/99	103s
Cable modem rate, cable subscriber, Comcast	mos	39.95	6/99	103s
Cable modem rate, non-cable subscriber, Adelphi	mos	44.95	6/99	103s
Cable modem rate, non-cable subscriber, Comcast	mos	49.95	6/99	103s
Phone line, single, business, field visit	inst.	98.50	12/97	17s
Phone line, single, business, no field visit	inst.	79.50	12/97	17s
Phone line, single, residence, field visit	inst.	56.50	12/97	17s
Phone line, single, residence, no field visit	inst.	42.00	12/97	17s
Postage and stationery, expenditures on	yr	138	1999	30r
Postal rate, express mail, up to half-pound		12.45	7/01	108r
Postal rate, letter, first class, first ounce		0.34	7/01	108r
Postal rate, letter, two ounces		0.57	7/01	108r
Postal rate, post card		0.21	7/01	108r
Postal rate, priority mail, two pounds		3.95	7/01	108r
Postal rate, priority mail, up to one pound		3.50	7/01	108r
Telephone services, expenditures on	yr	830	1999	30r
Education				
Board, 4-year private college/university	yr	2959	1996	38s
Board, 4-year public college/university	yr	2052	1996	38s
Education expenditures	yr	877	1999	30r
Room, 4-year private college/university	yr	3226	1996	38s
Room, 4-year public college/university	yr	3101	1996	38s
Total cost, 4-year private college/university	yr	19751	1996	38s
Total cost, 4-year public college/university	yr	9125	1996	38s
Tuition, 2-year public college/university, in state	yr	1878	1996	38s
Tuition, 4-year private college/university, in state	yr	13566	1996	38s
Tuition, 4-year public college/university	yr	3972	1996	38s
Energy and Fuels				
Electricity	KWh	0.12	7/01	11r
Fuel oil #2	gal	1.31	7/01	11r
Fuel oil and other fuels, expenditures on	yr	207	1999	30r
Gas, natural, commercial rate	1000 cf	5.98	11/00	88s
Gasoline, all types	gal	1.80	7/01	11r
Gasoline, unleaded midgrade	gal	1.85	7/01	11r
Gasoline, unleaded premium	gal	1.91	7/01	11r
Gasoline, unleaded regular	gal	1.71	7/01	11r
Natural gas, expenditures on	yr	368	1999	30r
Utility (piped) gas, therm		1.08	7/01	11r
Utility (piped) gas, 40 therms		50.87	7/01	11r
Utility (piped) gas, 100 therms		111.06	7/01	11r
Entertainment				
Entertainment purchases	yr	1821	1999	30r
Fees and admissions paid	yr	511	1999	30r
Television, radios, sound equipment, expenditures on	yr	650	1999	30r
Funerals				
Total cost of funeral		5813.50	1/99	78r
Acknowledgement cards		28.32	1/99	78r
Casket		2082.20	1/99	78r
Cosmetology, hair, other preparation		169.59	1/99	78r

Values are in dollars or fractions of dollars. In the column headed *Ref*, references are shown to sources. Each reference is followed by a letter. These refer to the geographical level for which data were reported: s=State, r=Region, and c=City or metro. The abbreviation *ex* is used to mean *except* or *excluding*; *exp* stands for expenditures. For other abbreviations and further explanations, please see the Introduction.

Vineland-Millville-Bridgeton, NJ - continued

Item	Per	Value	Date	Ref.
Funerals				
Embalming		465.60	1/99	78r
Funeral at funeral home		339.56	1/99	78r
Hearse (local)		183.96	1/99	78r
Professional service charges		1157.85	1/99	78r
Service car/van		100.41	1/99	78r
Transfer of remains to funeral home		158.66	1/99	78r
Vault		766.31	1/99	78r
Visitation/viewing		361.04	1/99	78r
Groceries				
Apples, red delicious	lb	0.95	7/01	11r
Bacon, sliced	lb	3.44	7/01	11r
Bakery products, expenditures on	yr	310	1999	30r
Bananas	lb	0.55	7/01	11r
Beef, expenditures on	yr	236	1999	30r
Bread, white, pan	lb	1.09	7/01	11r
Butter, yoghurt, cheese, etc, expenditures on	yr	214	1999	30r
Cereals and bakery product purchases	yr	474	1999	30r
Cereals and cereal products, expenditures on	yr	164	1999	30r
Chicken legs, bone-in	lb	1.23	7/01	11r
Chicken, fresh, whole	lb	1.13	7/01	11r
Chuck roast, U.S. choice, boneless	lb	2.79	7/01	11r
Coffee, 100%, ground roast, all sizes	lb	3.40	7/01	11r
Dairy product purchases	yr	342	1999	30r
Eggs, expenditures on	yr	34	1999	30r
Eggs, grade A, large	dozen	0.82	7/01	11r
Fats and oils, expenditures on	yr	80	1999	30r
Fish and seafood, expenditures on	yr	123	1999	30r
Food (excl fruit and vegetables), eaten at home, purchases	yr	838	1999	30r
Food cooked on trips, expenditures on	yr	48	1999	30r
Food purchases	yr	5314	1999	30r
Food purchases, eaten away from home	yr	2313	1999	30r
Food purchases, food eaten at home	yr	3001	1999	30r
Fresh fruits, expenditures on	yr	169	1999	30r
Fresh milk and cream, expenditures on	yr	128	1999	30r
Fresh vegetables, expenditures on	yr	164	1999	30r
Grapefruit	lb	0.67	7/01	11r
Grapes, Thompson, seedless	lb	2.18	7/01	11r
Ground beef, lean and extra lean	lb	2.66	7/01	11r
Ground chuck, 100% beef	lb	2.04	7/01	11r
Lettuce, iceberg	lb	0.76	7/01	11r
Meats, poultry, fish, and egg purchases	yr	808	1999	30r
Nonalcoholic beverages, expenditures on	yr	225	1999	30r
Orange juice, frozen concentrate	16 oz	1.88	7/01	11r
Oranges, Navel	lb	0.79	7/01	11r
Oranges, Valencia	lb	0.56	7/01	11r
Peaches	lb	1.16	7/01	11r
Peanut butter, creamy, all sizes	lb	2.01	7/01	11r
Pears, Anjou	lb	1.16	7/01	11r
Pork chops, center cut, bone-in	lb	3.57	7/01	11r
Pork, expenditures on	yr	146	1999	30r
Potato chips	16 oz	3.37	7/01	11r
Potatoes, white, all types	lb	0.42	7/01	11r
Poultry, expenditures on	yr	158	1999	30r
Processed fruits, expenditures on	yr	124	1999	30r
Processed vegetables, expenditures on	yr	82	1999	30r
Round roast, U.S. choice, boneless	lb	3.04	7/01	11r
Spaghetti and macaroni	lb	1.04	7/01	11r
Steak, sirloin, U.S. choice, boneless	lb	5.39	7/01	11r
Strawberries, dry pint	12 oz	1.51	7/01	11r
Sugar and other sweets, expenditures on	yr	110	1999	30r
Sugar, white, 33-80 ounce package	lb	0.46	7/01	11r
Sugar, white, all sizes	lb	0.47	7/01	11r
Tobacco products and smoking supplies purchases	yr	309	1999	30r
Yogurt, natural, fruit flavored	8 oz	0.79	7/01	11r
Goods and Services				
B&B Japanese maple (acer japonicum)	gal	38.99-125.00	4/00	93r

Vineland-Millville-Bridgeton, NJ - continued

Item	Per	Value	Date	Ref.
Goods and Services - continued				
Boxwood (buxus)	2 gal	15.99-49.95	4/00	93r
Daylilly (hemerocallis)	gal	4.95	4/00	93r
Flat of annuals		8.00-14.99	4/00	93r
Fountain grass (pennisetum)	gal	6.99-9.99	4/00	93r
Hanging basket (10 in)		12.95-19.99		
Hardy geranium (geranium)	gal	6.95-7.99	4/00	93r
Hosta (hosta)	gal	4.95	4/00	93r
Lilac (syrubga vulgaris)	2 gal	17.99-74.95	4/00	93r
Miscellaneous purchases	yr	872	1999	30r
Rhododendron (rhododendron)	2 gal	23.99-54.95	4/00	93r
Sage (salvia)	gal	6.95-7.99	4/00	93r
Wintercreeper euonymus (euonymus fortunei)	2 gal	14.99-23.95	4/00	93r
Hunting license	yr	22.50	4/01	34s
Health Care				
Cardiac catheterization, ave hospital/ physician charges		14680	1998	77s
Childbirth, Cesarean delivery		14716	1997	13r
Childbirth, vaginal delivery		8541	1997	13r
Drugs, expenditures on	yr	296	1999	30r
Health care purchases	yr	1788	1999	30r
Health insurance expenditures	yr	875	1999	30r
Hysterectomy, laproscopically-assisted, ave hospital/physician charges		18330	1998	76s
Hysterectomy, vaginal, ave hospital and physician charges		13620	1998	76s
Medicaid dispensing fee		3.73-4.07	1999	87s
Medical services expenditures	yr	516	1999	30r
Medical supplies, expenditures on	yr	102	1999	30r
Plastic surgery, breast augmentation		4232	2000	7r
Plastic surgery, breast lift		4605	2000	7r
Plastic surgery, facelift		6964	2000	7r
Plastic surgery, hair transplantation		4193	2000	7r
Plastic surgery, lip augmentation		1675	2000	7r
Plastic surgery, lower body lift		6611	2000	7r
Plastic surgery, thigh lift		4751	2000	7r
Household Goods				
Floor coverings, expenditures on	yr	59	1999	30r
Furniture, expenditures on	yr	388	1999	30r
Household furnishings and equipment purchases	yr	1567	1999	30r
Household textiles, expenditures on	yr	112	1999	30r
Laundry and cleaning supplies, expenditures on	yr	104	1999	30r
Housing				
Home price, existing, ave		180800	10/00	90r
Home value, median		213000	2001	53s
Household operation expenditures	yr	581	1999	30r
Housekeeping supplies purchases	yr	474	1999	30r
Lodging expenditures	yr	550	1999	30r
Maintenance, repairs, insurance expenditures	yr	835	1999	30r
Monthly rental value of owned home	mos	663	1999	30r
Owned dwellings, expenditures own	yr	5209	1999	30r
Rent expenditures	yr	2390	1999	30r
Rental unit, 1 bedroom, with utilities	mos	600	4/01	41c
Rental unit, 2 bedroom, with utilities	mos	723	4/01	41c
Rental unit, 3 bedroom, with utilities	mos	902	4/01	41c
Rental unit, 4 bedroom, with utilities	mos	1014	4/01	41c
Shelter, expenditures on	yr	8149	1999	30r

Values are in dollars or fractions of dollars. In the column headed *Ref*, references are shown to sources. Each reference is followed by a letter. These refer to the geographical level for which data were reported: s=State, r=Region, and c=City or metro. The abbreviation *ex* is used to mean *except* or *excluding*; *exp* stands for *expenditures*. For other abbreviations and further explanations, please see the Introduction.

Vineland-Millville-Bridgeton, NJ - continued

Item	Per	Value	Date	Ref.
Insurance and Pensions				
Auto insurance premium	yr	1292.76	1999	57s
Life and other personal insurance purchases	yr	424	1999	30r
Pensions and Social Security, expenditures on	yr	3037	1999	30r
Legal Fees				
Divorce, filing fee		65.00	4/01	35s
Driver's license fee	orig	18.00	1999	48s
Driver's license fee	renew	15.00	1999	48s
Fishing license	yr	22.50	4/01	34s
Personal Goods				
Personal care products and services purchases	yr	399	1999	30r
Personal Services				
Personal services, household, expenditures on	yr	271	1999	30r
Pets				
Pets, toys, and playground equipment, expenditures on	yr	325	1999	30r
Taxes				
Federal income taxes paid	yr	2606	1999	30r
Personal taxes, expenditures on	yr	3567	1999	30r
Property taxes paid	yr	1752	1999	30r
State and local income taxes paid	yr	694	1999	30r
Transportation				
Automobile insurance	yr	975.90	2000	79s
Cars and trucks, new, expenditures on	yr	1496	1999	30r
Cars and trucks, used, expenditures on	yr	1251	1999	30r
Diesel at the pump	gal	1.19	10/99	73s
Gasoline and motor oil purchases	yr	901	1999	30r
Gasoline before-tax price (cents)	gal	114.90	10/00	43s
Maintenance and repair expenditures	yr	618	1999	30r
Motorcycle license fee	orig	15.00	1999	49s
Motorcycle license fee	renew	13.00	1999	49s
Public transportation, expenditures on	yr	575	1999	30r
Transportation purchases	yr	6503	1999	30r
Vehicle expenses, miscellaneous, purchases	yr	2266	1999	30r
Vehicle insurance payments	yr	824	1999	30r
Vehicle purchases (net outlay)	yr	2761	1999	30r
Vehicle rental, lease expenditures	yr	584	1999	30r
Utilities				
Electrical bill, average	mos	74.08	9/00	9s
Electricity, expenditures on	yr	837	1999	30r
Electricity cost, average	KWh	8.91	9/00	9s
Utilities, fuels, and public services purchased	yr	2457	1999	30r
Water and other public services, expenditures on	yr	215	1999	30r
Weddings				
Wedding (national average cost)		19936	2000	33r
Wedding (regional average total cost)		29454	1997	110r
Attendants' gifts		321	1998	33r
Bridal attendants' apparel (5 persons)		824	2000	33r
Bride's headpiece/veil		173	1998	33r
Bride's wedding dress		859	1998	33r
Clergy, religious facility fee		242	1998	33r
Engagement ring		3177	1998	33r
Flowers		789	1998	33r
Groom's formalwear rental		99	2000	33r
Limousine		410	1998	33r
Marriage license cost		28.00	4/01	35s
Men's formalwear (ushers, best man)		469	2000	33r
Mother of bride apparel		241	2000	33r
Music		866	1998	33r
Photography and videography		1368	1998	33r
Rehearsal dinner		728	1998	33r
Wedding invitations and announcements		341	1998	33r
Wedding reception		7968	2000	33r
Wedding rings (bride and groom)		1060	1998	33r

Visalia-Tulare-Porterville, CA

Item	Per	Value	Date	Ref.
Average annual expenditures	yr	40662	1999	30r
Alcoholic Beverages				
Alcoholic beverage purchases	yr	372	1999	30r
Malt beverages, all types, all sizes, any origin	16 oz	0.94	7/01	11r
Wine, red and white table, all sizes, any origin	liter	6.00	7/01	11r
Appliances				
Major appliances, expenditures on	yr	167	1999	30r
Small appliances, housewares, expenditures on	yr	105	1999	30r
Banking and Money				
Mortgage interest and charges paid	yr	3368	1999	30r
Mortgage principal paid on owned property	yr	1677	1999	30r
Vehicle finance charges paid	yr	311	1999	30r
Charity				
Cash contributions, expenditures	yr	1344	1999	30r
Child Care				
Child raising cost, total, age 0-2	yr	9140	1999	60r
Child raising cost, total, age 3-5	yr	9370	1999	60r
Child raising cost, total, age 6-8	yr	9450	1999	60r
Child raising cost, total, age 9-11	yr	9470	1999	60r
Child raising cost, total, age 12-14	yr	10170	1999	60r
Child raising cost, total, age 15-17	yr	10360	1999	60r
Child's child care and education, age 0-2	yr	1250	1999	60r
Child's child care and education, age 3-5	yr	1380	1999	60r
Child's child care and education, age 6-8	yr	890	1999	60r
Child's child care and education, age 9-11	yr	580	1999	60r
Child's child care and education, age 12-14	yr	430	1999	60r
Child's child care and education, age 15-17	yr	730	1999	60r
Child's clothing, age 0-2	yr	430	1999	60r
Child's clothing, age 3-5	yr	420	1999	60r
Child's clothing, age 6-8	yr	470	1999	60r
Child's clothing, age 9-11	yr	520	1999	60r
Child's clothing, age 12-14	yr	870	1999	60r
Child's clothing, age 15-17	yr	770	1999	60r
Child's food, age 0-2	yr	1120	1999	60r
Child's food, age 3-5	yr	1280	1999	60r
Child's food, age 6-8	yr	1640	1999	60r
Child's food, age 9-11	yr	1930	1999	60r
Child's food, age 12-14	yr	1940	1999	60r
Child's food, age 15-17	yr	2150	1999	60r
Child's health care, age 0-2	yr	490	1999	60r
Child's health care, age 3-5	yr	470	1999	60r
Child's health care, age 6-8	yr	530	1999	60r
Child's health care, age 9-11	yr	570	1999	60r
Child's health care, age 12-14	yr	580	1999	60r
Child's health care, age 15-17	yr	610	1999	60r
Child's housing, age 0-2	yr	3630	1999	60r
Child's housing, age 3-5	yr	3610	1999	60r
Child's housing, age 6-8	yr	3570	1999	60r
Child's housing, age 9-11	yr	3410	1999	60r
Child's housing, age 12-14	yr	3600	1999	60r
Child's housing, age 15-17	yr	3210	1999	60r
Child's personal care, reading, age 0-2	yr	1040	1999	60r
Child's personal care, reading, age 3-5	yr	1060	1999	60r
Child's personal care, reading, age 6-8	yr	1090	1999	60r
Child's personal care, reading, age 9-11	yr	1130	1999	60r
Child's personal care, reading, age 12-14	yr	1300	1999	60r
Child's personal care, reading, age 15-17	yr	1080	1999	60r
Clothing				
Apparel and services purchases	yr	1863	1999	30r
Boys, 2 to 15, expenditures on	yr	80	1999	30r
Children under 2, expenditures on	yr	74	1999	30r
Footwear, expenditures on	yr	307	1999	30r
Girls, 2 to 15, expenditures on	yr	101	1999	30r
Men and boys, expenditures on	yr	443	1999	30r
Men, 16 and over, expenditures on	yr	363	1999	30r
Women, 16 and over, expenditures on	yr	594	1999	30r

Values are in dollars or fractions of dollars. In the column headed *Ref*, references are shown to sources. Each reference is followed by a letter. These refer to the geographical level for which data were reported: s=State, r=Region, and c=City or metro. The abbreviation *ex* is used to mean *except* or *excluding*; *exp* stands for *expenditures*. For other abbreviations and further explanations, please see the Introduction.

Visalia-Tulare-Porterville, CA - continued

Item	Per	Value	Date	Ref.
Communications				
Cable modem installation, AT&T-BIS		150.00	6/99	103s
Cable modem installation, Charter		99.00-169.00	6/99	103s
Cable modem installation, Comcast		95.00	6/99	103s
Cable modem installation, Cox		99.00-174.95	6/99	103s
Cable modem installation, Media One		100.00	6/99	103s
Cable modem installation, Time Warner		75.00-225.00	6/99	103s
Cable modem rate, cable subscriber, AT&T-BIS	mos	39.95	6/99	103s
Cable modem rate, cable subscriber, Charter	mos	49.95-79.95	6/99	103s
Cable modem rate, cable subscriber, Comcast	mos	39.95	6/99	103s
Cable modem rate, cable subscriber, Cox	mos	29.95-44.95	6/99	103s
Cable modem rate, cable subscriber, Media One	mos	34.95-39.95	6/99	103s
Cable modem rate, cable subscriber, Time Warner	mos	39.95-49.95	6/99	103s
Cable modem rate, non-cable subscriber, Charter	mos	59.95-89.95	6/99	103s
Cable modem rate, non-cable subscriber, Comcast	mos	49.95	6/99	103s
Cable modem rate, non-cable subscriber, Cox	mos	42.95-54.95	6/99	103s
Cable modem rate, non-cable subscriber, Media One	mos	49.95	6/99	103s
Cable modem rate, non-cable subscriber, Time Warner	mos	39.95-54.95	6/99	103s
Phone line, single, business, field visit	inst.	70.75	12/97	17s
Phone line, single, business, no field visit	inst.	70.75	12/97	17s
Phone line, single, residence, field visit	inst.	34.75	12/97	17s
Phone line, single, residence, no field visit	inst.	34.75	12/97	17s
Postage and stationery, expenditures on	yr	150	1999	30r
Postal rate, express mail, up to half-pound		12.45	7/01	108r
Postal rate, letter, first class, first ounce		0.34	7/01	108r
Postal rate, letter, two ounces		0.57	7/01	108r
Postal rate, post card		0.21	7/01	108r
Postal rate, priority mail, two pounds		3.95	7/01	108r
Postal rate, priority mail, up to one pound		3.50	7/01	108r
Telephone services, expenditures on	yr	825	1999	30r
Education				
Board, 4-year private college/university	yr	2970	1996	38s
Board, 4-year public college/university	yr	2516	1996	38s
Education expenditures	yr	676	1999	30r
Room, 4-year private college/university	yr	3196	1996	38s
Room, 4-year public college/university	yr	3031	1996	38s
Total cost, 4-year private college/university	yr	20143	1996	38s
Total cost, 4-year public college/university	yr	8213	1996	38s
Tuition, 2-year public college/university, in state	yr	362	1996	38s
Tuition, 4-year private college/university, in state	yr	13977	1996	38s
Tuition, 4-year public college/university	yr	2666	1996	38s
Energy and Fuels				
Electricity	KWh	0.11	7/01	11r
Electricity	500 KWhs	48.23	7/01	11r
Fuel oil and other fuels, expenditures on	yr	35	1999	30r
Gas, natural, commercial rate	1000 cf	8.74	11/00	88s
Gasoline, all types	gal	1.91	7/01	11r
Gasoline, unleaded premium	gal	2.05	7/01	11r
Gasoline, unleaded regular	gal	1.83	7/01	11r
Natural gas, expenditures on	yr	255	1999	30r
Utility (piped) gas, therm		0.98	7/01	11r
Utility (piped) gas, 40 therms		40.74	7/01	11r
Utility (piped) gas, 100 therms		96.80	7/01	11r

Visalia-Tulare-Porterville, CA - continued

Item	Per	Value	Date	Ref.
Entertainment				
Entertainment purchases	yr	2139	1999	30r
Fees and admissions paid	yr	545	1999	30r
Television, radios, sound equipment, expenditures on	yr	624	1999	30r
Funerals				
Total cost of funeral		5401.08	1/99	78r
Acknowledgement cards		33.64	1/99	78r
Casket		2170.43	1/99	78r
Cosmetology, hair, other preparation		136.32	1/99	78r
Embalming		319.13	1/99	78r
Funeral at funeral home		370.21	1/99	78r
Hearse (local)		161.04	1/99	78r
Professional service charges		963.15	1/99	78r
Service car/van		133.99	1/99	78r
Transfer of remains to funeral home		159.82	1/99	78r
Vault		778.07	1/99	78r
Visitation/viewing		175.28	1/99	78r
Groceries				
Apples, red delicious	lb	0.84	7/01	11r
Bacon, sliced	lb	3.38	7/01	11r
Bakery products, expenditures on	yr	299	1999	30r
Bananas	lb	0.54	7/01	11r
Beans, dried, any type, all sizes	lb	0.76	7/01	11r
Beef, expenditures on	yr	222	1999	30r
Bread, white, pan	lb	0.99	7/01	11r
Butter, yoghurt, cheese, etc, expenditures on	yr	211	1999	30r
Cereals and bakery product purchases	yr	466	1999	30r
Cereals and cereal products, expenditures on	yr	168	1999	30r
Chicken breast, bone-in	lb	2.45	7/01	11r
Chicken, fresh, whole	lb	1.19	7/01	11r
Chops, boneless,	lb	4.00	7/01	11r
Chuck roast, graded and ungraded, excl U.S. prime and choice	lb	2.55	7/01	11r
Coffee, 100%, ground roast, all sizes	lb	3.80	7/01	11r
Cookies, chocolate chip	lb	2.83	7/01	11r
Dairy product purchases	yr	341	1999	30r
Eggs, expenditures on	yr	39	1999	30r
Eggs, grade AA, large	dozen	1.23	7/01	11r
Fats and oils, expenditures on	yr	88	1999	30r
Fish and seafood, expenditures on	yr	121	1999	30r
Food (excl fruit and vegetables), eaten at home, purchases	yr	1001	1999	30r
Food cooked on trips, expenditures on	yr	64	1999	30r
Food purchases	yr	5312	1999	30r
Food purchases, eaten away from home	yr	2180	1999	30r
Food purchases, food eaten at home	yr	3132	1999	30r
Fresh fruits, expenditures on	yr	186	1999	30r
Fresh milk and cream, expenditures on	yr	130	1999	30r
Fresh vegetables, expenditures on	yr	177	1999	30r
Grapefruit	lb	0.68	7/01	11r
Grapes, Thompson, seedless	lb	2.42	7/01	11r
Ground beef, lean and extra lean	lb	2.46	7/01	11r
Ice cream, prepackaged, bulk, regular	1/2 gal	3.62	7/01	11r
Lettuce, iceberg	lb	0.63	7/01	11r
Meats, poultry, fish, and egg purchases	yr	761	1999	30r
Milk, fresh, low fat	gal	2.80	7/01	11r
Milk, fresh, whole, fortified	gal	2.88	7/01	11r
Nonalcoholic beverages, expenditures on	yr	258	1999	30r
Oranges, Navel	lb	0.97	7/01	11r
Oranges, Valencia	lb	0.43	7/01	11r
Peaches	lb	1.38	7/01	11r
Peanut butter, creamy, all sizes	lb	2.14	7/01	11r
Pork chops, center cut, bone-in	lb	3.83	7/01	11r
Pork, expenditures on	yr	141	1999	30r
Potatoes, white, all types	lb	0.37	7/01	11r
Poultry, expenditures on	yr	146	1999	30r
Processed fruits, expenditures on	yr	118	1999	30r
Processed vegetables, expenditures on	yr	81	1999	30r
Round roast, graded and ungraded, excl U.S. prime and choice	lb	3.07	7/01	11r

Values are in dollars or fractions of dollars. In the column headed *Ref*, references are shown to sources. Each reference is followed by a letter. These refer to the geographical level for which data were reported: s=State, r=Region, and c=City or metro. The abbreviation *ex* is used to mean *except* or *excluding*; *exp* stands for *expenditures*. For other abbreviations and further explanations, please see the Introduction.

Visalia-Tulare-Porterville, CA - continued

Item	Per	Value	Date	Ref.
Groceries				
Round roast, U.S. choice, boneless	lb	3.37	7/01	11r
Round steak, graded and ungraded, excl U.S. prime and choice	lb	3.51	7/01	11r
Sirloin steak, graded and ungraded, excl U.S. prime and choice	lb	4.67	7/01	11r
Steak, sirloin, U.S. choice, boneless	lb	6.20	7/01	11r
Strawberries, dry pint	12 oz	1.79	7/01	11r
Sugar and other sweets, expenditures on	yr	124	1999	30r
Sugar, white, all sizes	lb	0.46	7/01	11r
Tobacco products and smoking supplies purchases	yr	217	1999	30r
Tomatoes, field grown	lb	1.17	7/01	11r
Tuna, light, chunk	lb	2.05	7/01	11r
Goods and Services				
B&B Japanese maple (acer japonicum)	gal	39.99	4/00	93r
Boxwood (buxus)	2 gal	14.99-24.99	4/00	93r
Christmas tree, noble fir		40-60	2000	65s
Daylilly (hemerocallis)	gal	6.99-8.99	4/00	93r
Flat of annuals		16.68	4/00	93r
Fountain grass (pennisetum)	gal	7.99-11.99	4/00	93r
Hanging basket (10 in)		29.99	4/00	93r
Hardy geranium (geranium)	gal	6.99-11.99	4/00	93r
Hosta (hosta)	gal	6.99-18.99	4/00	93r
Lilac (syrubga vulgaris)	2 gal	14.99-17.99	4/00	93r
Miscellaneous purchases	yr	1070	1999	30r
Rhododendron (rhododendron)	2 gal	14.99	4/00	93r
Sage (salvia)	gal	6.99	4/00	93r
Wintercreeper euonymus (euonymus fortunei)	2 gal	14.99-22.99	4/00	93r
Hunting license	yr	29.95	4/01	34s
Health Care				
Cardiac catheterization, ave hospital/physician charges		24000	1998	77s
Childbirth, Cesarean delivery		11587	1997	13r
Childbirth, vaginal delivery		6725	1997	13r
Drugs, expenditures on	yr	309	1999	30r
Health care purchases	yr	1869	1999	30r
Health insurance expenditures	yr	868	1999	30r
Hysterectomy, laproscopically-assisted, ave hospital/physician charges		20760	1998	76s
Hysterectomy, vaginal, ave hospital and physician charges		14570	1998	76s
Medicaid dispensing fee		4.05	1999	87s
Medical services expenditures	yr	580	1999	30r
Medical supplies, expenditures on	yr	112	1999	30r
Household Goods				
Floor coverings, expenditures on	yr	49	1999	30r
Furniture, expenditures on	yr	444	1999	30r
Household furnishings and equipment purchases	yr	1768	1999	30r
Household textiles, expenditures on	yr	141	1999	30r
Laundry and cleaning supplies, expenditures on	yr	128	1999	30r
Housing				
Home price, existing, ave		239400	10/00	90r
Home value, median		215000	2001	53s
Household operation expenditures	yr	781	1999	30r
Housekeeping supplies purchases	yr	513	1999	30r
Lodging expenditures	yr	575	1999	30r
Maintenance, repairs, insurance expenditures	yr	939	1999	30r
Monthly rental value of owned home	mos	662	1999	30r
Owned dwellings, expenditures own	yr	5231	1999	30r
Rent expenditures	yr	2709	1999	30r

Visalia-Tulare-Porterville, CA - continued

Item	Per	Value	Date	Ref.
Housing - continued				
Rental unit, 1 bedroom, with utilities	mos	402	4/01	41c
Rental unit, 2 bedroom, with utilities	mos	524	4/01	41c
Rental unit, 3 bedroom, with utilities	mos	731	4/01	41c
Rental unit, 4 bedroom, with utilities	mos	834	4/01	41c
Shelter, expenditures on	yr	8516	1999	30r
Insurance and Pensions				
Life and other personal insurance purchases	yr	355	1999	30r
Pensions and Social Security, expenditures on	yr	3636	1999	30r
Legal Fees				
Divorce, filing fee		182.00	4/01	35s
Driver's license fee	renew	15.00	1999	48s
Driver's license fee	orig	12.00	1999	48s
Personal Goods				
Personal care products and services purchases	yr	449	1999	30r
Personal Services				
Personal services, household, expenditures on	yr	353	1999	30r
Pets				
Pets, toys, and playground equipment, expenditures on	yr	358	1999	30r
Taxes				
Federal income taxes paid	yr	3200	1999	30r
Personal taxes, expenditures on	yr	4153	1999	30r
Property taxes paid	yr	923	1999	30r
State and local income taxes paid	yr	812	1999	30r
Transportation				
Cars and trucks, new, expenditures on	yr	1534	1999	30r
Cars and trucks, used, expenditures on	yr	1593	1999	30r
Diesel at the pump	gal	1.37	10/99	73s
Gasoline and motor oil purchases	yr	1129	1999	30r
Gasoline before-tax price (cents)	gal	128.80	10/00	43s
Maintenance and repair expenditures	yr	797	1999	30r
Public transportation, expenditures on	yr	530	1999	30r
Transportation purchases	yr	7423	1999	30r
Vehicle expenses, miscellaneous, purchases	yr	2585	1999	30r
Vehicle insurance payments	yr	811	1999	30r
Vehicle purchases (net outlay)	yr	3180	1999	30r
Vehicle rental, lease expenditures	yr	666	1999	30r
Utilities				
Electrical bill, average	mos	58.66	9/00	9s
Electricity, expenditures on	yr	725	1999	30r
Electricity cost, average	KWh	7.75	9/00	9s
Utilities, fuels, and public services purchased	yr	2179	1999	30r
Water and other public services, expenditures on	yr	339	1999	30r
Weddings				
Wedding (national average cost)		19936	2000	33r
Wedding (regional average total cost)		18918	1997	110r
Attendants' gifts		321	1998	33r
Bridal attendants' apparel (5 persons)		824	2000	33r
Bride's headpiece/veil		173	1998	33r
Bride's wedding dress		859	1998	33r
Clergy, religious facility fee		242	1998	33r
Engagement ring		3177	1998	33r
Flowers		789	1998	33r
Groom's formalwear rental		99	2000	33r
Limousine		410	1998	33r
Marriage license cost		50.00-80.00	4/01	35s
Men's formalwear (ushers, best man)		469	2000	33r
Mother of bride apparel		241	2000	33r
Music		866	1998	33r
Photography and videography		1368	1998	33r
Rehearsal dinner		728	1998	33r
Wedding invitations and announcements		341	1998	33r

Values are in dollars or fractions of dollars. In the column headed *Ref*, references are shown to sources. Each reference is followed by a letter. These refer to the geographical level for which data were reported: s=State, r=Region, and c=City or metro. The abbreviation *ex* is used to mean *except* or *excluding*; *exp* stands for expenditures. For other abbreviations and further explanations, please see the Introduction.

Visalia-Tulare-Porterville, CA - continued

Item	Per	Value	Date	Ref.
Weddings				
Wedding reception		7968	2000	33r
Wedding rings (bride and groom)		1060	1998	33r

Waco, TX

Item	Per	Value	Date	Ref.
Composite, ACCRA index		93.50	3/01	4c
Alcoholic Beverages				
Alcoholic beverage purchases	yr	253	1999	30r
Beer, Heineken, 12-oz, ex deposit	6	7.01	3/01	4c
J & B Scotch	750-ml	19.78	3/01	4c
Malt beverages, all types, all sizes, any origin	16 oz	0.96	7/01	11r
Wine, Livingston or Gallo, Chablis blanc	1.5 liter	4.99	3/01	4c
Appliances				
Appliance repair, service call, washing machine	min lab chg	53.00	3/01	4c
Major appliances, expenditures on	yr	172	1999	30r
Small appliances, housewares, expenditures on	yr	81	1999	30r
Banking and Money				
Mortgage interest and charges paid	yr	2039	1999	30r
Mortgage principal paid on owned property	yr	1026	1999	30r
Mortgage rate, incl. points and orig. fee, 30-yr. conv. fixed or ARM	mos	7.19	3/01	4c
Vehicle finance charges paid	yr	365	1999	30r
Charity				
Cash contributions, expenditures	yr	1127	1999	30r
Child Care				
Child raising cost, total, age 0-2	yr	8540	1999	60r
Child raising cost, total, age 3-5	yr	8780	1999	60r
Child raising cost, total, age 6-8	yr	8820	1999	60r
Child raising cost, total, age 9-11	yr	8800	1999	60r
Child raising cost, total, age 12-14	yr	9510	1999	60r
Child raising cost, total, age 15-17	yr	9740	1999	60r
Child's child care and education, age 0-2	yr	1380	1999	60r
Child's child care and education, age 3-5	yr	1520	1999	60r
Child's child care and education, age 6-8	yr	990	1999	60r
Child's child care and education, age 9-11	yr	650	1999	60r
Child's child care and education, age 12-14	yr	490	1999	60r
Child's child care and education, age 15-17	yr	840	1999	60r
Child's clothing, age 0-2	yr	480	1999	60r
Child's clothing, age 3-5	yr	470	1999	60r
Child's clothing, age 6-8	yr	520	1999	60r
Child's clothing, age 9-11	yr	570	1999	60r
Child's clothing, age 12-14	yr	950	1999	60r
Child's clothing, age 15-17	yr	850	1999	60r
Child's food, age 0-2	yr	1000	1999	60r
Child's food, age 3-5	yr	1160	1999	60r
Child's food, age 6-8	yr	1490	1999	60r
Child's food, age 9-11	yr	1770	1999	60r
Child's food, age 12-14	yr	1770	1999	60r
Child's food, age 15-17	yr	1980	1999	60r
Child's health care, age 0-2	yr	620	1999	60r
Child's health care, age 3-5	yr	590	1999	60r
Child's health care, age 6-8	yr	680	1999	60r
Child's health care, age 9-11	yr	720	1999	60r
Child's health care, age 12-14	yr	730	1999	60r
Child's health care, age 15-17	yr	760	1999	60r
Child's housing, age 0-2	yr	3070	1999	60r
Child's housing, age 3-5	yr	3050	1999	60r
Child's housing, age 6-8	yr	3010	1999	60r
Child's housing, age 9-11	yr	2850	1999	60r
Child's housing, age 12-14	yr	3040	1999	60r
Child's housing, age 15-17	yr	2650	1999	60r
Child's personal care, reading, age 0-2	yr	910	1999	60r
Child's personal care, reading, age 3-5	yr	930	1999	60r
Child's personal care, reading, age 6-8	yr	960	1999	60r
Child's personal care, reading, age 9-11	yr	1000	1999	60r
Child's personal care, reading, age 12-14	yr	1170	1999	60r
Child's personal care, reading, age 15-17	yr	950	1999	60r

Waco, TX - continued

Item	Per	Value	Date	Ref.
Clothing				
Apparel and services purchases	yr	1610	1999	30r
Boys' brief, cotton	3	6.62	3/01	4c
Boys, 2 to 15, expenditures on	yr	89	1999	30r
Children under 2, expenditures on	yr	79	1999	30r
Footwear, expenditures on	yr	283	1999	30r
Girls, 2 to 15, expenditures on	yr	103	1999	30r
Men and boys, expenditures on	yr	351	1999	30r
Men, 16 and over, expenditures on	yr	262	1999	30r
Shirt, man's dress shirt		30.00	3/01	4c
Slacks, man's "No Wrinkles" khaki		40.00	3/01	4c
Women, 16 and over, expenditures on	yr	538	1999	30r
Communications				
Cable modem installation, AT&T-BIS		150.00	6/99	103s
Cable modem installation, Marcus		499.00	6/99	103s
Cable modem installation, Time Warner		75.00-225.00	6/99	103s
Cable modem rate, cable subscriber, AT&T-BIS	mos	39.95	6/99	103s
Cable modem rate, cable subscriber, Marcus	mos	14.95-49.95	6/99	103s
Cable modem rate, cable subscriber, Time Warner	mos	39.95-49.95	6/99	103s
Cable modem rate, non-cable subscriber, Marcus	mos	60.95	6/99	103s
Cable modem rate, non-cable subscriber, Time Warner	mos	39.95-54.95	6/99	103s
Newspaper subscription, daily and Sunday delivery	mos	12.00	3/01	4c
Phone line, single, business, field visit	inst.	71.90	12/97	17s
Phone line, single, business, no field visit	inst.	57.30	12/97	17s
Phone line, single, residence, field visit	inst.	52.95	12/97	17s
Phone line, single, residence, no field visit	inst.	38.35	12/97	17s
Postage and stationery, expenditures on	yr	104	1999	30r
Postal rate, express mail, up to half-pound		12.45	7/01	108r
Postal rate, letter, first class, first ounce		0.34	7/01	108r
Postal rate, letter, two ounces		0.57	7/01	108r
Postal rate, post card		0.21	7/01	108r
Postal rate, priority mail, two pounds		3.95	7/01	108r
Postal rate, priority mail, up to one pound		3.50	7/01	108r
Telephone bill, family of three	mos	16.70	3/01	4c
Telephone services, expenditures on	yr	860	1999	30r
Education				
Board, 4-year private college/university	yr	2198	1996	38s
Board, 4-year public college/university	yr	1759	1996	38s
Education expenditures	yr	431	1999	30r
Room, 4-year private college/university	yr	2000	1996	38s
Room, 4-year public college/university	yr	1885	1996	38s
Total cost, 4-year private college/university	yr	13156	1996	38s
Total cost, 4-year public college/university	yr	5464	1996	38s
Tuition, 2-year public college/university, in state	yr	771	1996	38s
Tuition, 4-year private college/university, in state	yr	8959	1996	38s
Tuition, 4-year public college/university	yr	1820	1996	38s
Energy and Fuels				
Electricity	KWh	0.09	7/01	11r
Electricity	500 KWhs	47.29	7/01	11r
Energy, combined forms, 2400 sq ft	mos	123.48	3/01	4c
Fuel oil #2	gal	1.43	7/01	11r
Fuel oil and other fuels, expenditures on	yr	45	1999	30r
Gas, natural, commercial rate	1000 cf	6.94	11/00	88s
Gas, regular unleaded, cash, self-service	gal	1.27	3/01	4c
Gasoline, all types	gal	1.60	7/01	11r
Gasoline, unleaded midgrade	gal	1.65	7/01	11r
Gasoline, unleaded premium	gal	1.74	7/01	11r
Natural gas, expenditures on	yr	164	1999	30r
Utility (piped) gas, therm		1.01	7/01	11r
Utility (piped) gas, 40 therms		44.29	7/01	11r
Utility (piped) gas, 100 therms		97.44	7/01	11r

Values are in dollars or fractions of dollars. In the column headed *Ref*, references are shown to sources. Each reference is followed by a letter. These refer to the geographical level for which data were reported: s=State, r=Region, and c=City or metro. The abbreviation *ex* is used to mean *except* or *excluding*; *exp* stands for *expenditures*. For other abbreviations and further explanations, please see the Introduction.

Waco, TX - continued

Item	Per	Value	Date	Ref.
Entertainment				
Bowling, Saturday evening rate	line	2.50	3/01	4c
Entertainment purchases	yr	1574	1999	30r
Fees and admissions paid	yr	371	1999	30r
Monopoly game, Parker Brothers', No. 9	game	10.46	3/01	4c
Movie, first-run, Saturday, evening	adm.	6.50	3/01	4c
Reading purchases	yr	121	1999	30r
Television, radios, sound equipment, expenditures on	yr	561	1999	30r
Tennis balls, yellow, Wilson or Penn, 3	can	2.38	3/01	4c
Funerals				
Total cost of funeral		5842.28	1/99	78r
Acknowledgement cards		28.35	1/99	78r
Casket		2494.29	1/99	78r
Cosmetology, hair, other preparation		109.22	1/99	78r
Embalming		361.42	1/99	78r
Funeral at funeral home		349.20	1/99	78r
Hearse (local)		161.91	1/99	78r
Professional service charges		1116.50	1/99	78r
Service car/van		65.56	1/99	78r
Transfer of remains to funeral home		143.56	1/99	78r
Vault		785.25	1/99	78r
Visitation/viewing		227.02	1/99	78r
Groceries				
Groceries, ACCRA Index		86.70	3/01	4c
American processed cheese	lb	3.50	7/01	11r
Antibiotic ointment, Polysporin	0.5 oz	4.58	3/01	4c
Baby food, strained vegetables or fruit, lowest price	4-4.5 oz	0.30	3/01	4c
Bakery products, expenditures on	yr	261	1999	30r
Bananas	lb	0.40	3/01	4c
Bananas	lb	0.47	7/01	11r
Beans, dried, any type, all sizes	lb	0.63	7/01	11r
Beef for stew, boneless	lb	2.86	7/01	11r
Beef or hamburger, ground	lb	1.13	4/01	4c
Beef, expenditures on	yr	210	1999	30r
Bologna, all beef or mixed	lb	2.29	7/01	11r
Bread, French	lb	1.66	7/01	11r
Bread, white	loaf	0.67	3/01	4c
Bread, white, pan	lb	0.87	7/01	11r
Bread, whole wheat, pan	lb	1.38	7/01	11r
Broccoli	lb	1.04	7/01	11r
Butter, salted, grade AA, stick	lb	2.26	7/01	11r
Butter, yoghurt, cheese, etc, expenditures on	yr	170	1999	30r
Cabbage	lb	0.42	7/01	11r
Cereals and cereal products, expenditures on	yr	140	1999	30r
Cheddar cheese, natural	lb	3.75	7/01	11r
Cheese, Kraft grated Parmesan	8 oz	3.43	3/01	4c
Chicken breast, bone-in	lb	1.85	7/01	11r
Chicken legs, bone-in	lb	1.34	7/01	11r
Chicken, fresh, whole	lb	1.05	7/01	11r
Chicken, whole fryer	lb	0.56	3/01	4c
Chops, boneless,	lb	4.13	7/01	11r
Chuck roast, graded and ungraded, excl U.S. prime and choice	lb	2.35	7/01	11r
Chuck roast, U.S. choice, boneless	lb	2.67	7/01	11r
Cigarettes, Winston, Kings	carton	32.56	3/01	4c
Coffee, 100%, ground roast, all sizes	lb	2.88	7/01	11r
Coffee, instant, plain, regular, all sizes	16 oz	9.25	7/01	11r
Coffee, vacuum-packed	13 oz	2.43	3/01	4c
Cola, non diet	2 liter	1.11	7/01	11r
Corn Flakes, Kellogg's or Post Toasties	18 oz	2.63	3/01	4c
Corn, frozen, whole kernel, lowest price	16 oz	1.15	3/01	4c
Crackers, soda, salted	lb	1.70	7/01	11r
Dairy product purchases	yr	282	1999	30r
Eggs, expenditures on	yr	32	1999	30r
Eggs, Grade A or AA	dozen	0.81	3/01	4c
Fats and oils, expenditures on	yr	79	1999	30r
Fish and seafood, expenditures on	yr	99	1999	30r
Flour, white, all purpose	lb	0.32	7/01	11r

Waco, TX - continued

Item	Per	Value	Date	Ref.
Groceries - continued				
Food (excl fruit and vegetables), eaten at home, purchases	yr	815	1999	30r
Food cooked on trips, expenditures on	yr	36	1999	30r
Food purchases	yr	4533	1999	30r
Food purchases, eaten away from home	yr	1873	1999	30r
Food purchases, food eaten at home	yr	2660	1999	30r
Fresh fruits, expenditures on	yr	128	1999	30r
Fresh milk and cream, expenditures on	yr	112	1999	30r
Fresh vegetables, expenditures on	yr	131	1999	30r
Fruit and vegetable purchases	yr	438	1999	30r
Grapefruit	lb	0.59	7/01	11r
Grapes, Thompson, seedless	lb	2.12	7/01	11r
Ground beef, 100% beef	lb	1.76	7/01	11r
Ground beef, lean and extra lean	lb	2.60	7/01	11r
Ground chuck, 100% beef	lb	2.08	7/01	11r
Ham, boneless, excl canned	lb	2.71	7/01	11r
Ham, rump or shank half, bone-in, smoked	lb	2.19	7/01	11r
Ice cream, prepackaged, bulk, regular	1/2 gal	3.93	7/01	11r
Lemons	lb	1.32	7/01	11r
Lettuce, iceberg	head	0.92	3/01	4c
Lettuce, iceberg	lb	0.76	7/01	11r
Margarine, Blue Bonnet or Parkay, stick	lb	0.63	3/01	4c
Milk, fresh, low fat,	gal	2.75	7/01	11r
Milk, fresh, whole, fortified	gal	2.97	7/01	11r
Milk, whole	1/2 gal	1.61	3/01	4c
Nonalcoholic beverages, expenditures on	yr	228	1999	30r
Orange juice, frozen concentrate	16 oz	1.95	7/01	11r
Orange juice, Minute Maid frozen	12 oz	1.49	3/01	4c
Oranges, Navel	lb	0.73	7/01	11r
Oranges, Valencia	lb	0.55	7/01	11r
Peaches, halves or slices, Hunt's, Del Monte, or Libby's	29 oz	1.63	3/01	4c
Peanut butter, creamy, all sizes	lb	1.83	7/01	11r
Pears, Anjou	lb	0.98	7/01	11r
Peas, green, Del Monte or Green Giant	15 oz	0.65	3/01	4c
Pork chops, center cut, bone-in	lb	3.33	7/01	11r
Pork sausage, fresh, loose	lb	2.59	7/01	11r
Pork shoulder picnic, bone-in, smoked	lb	1.12	7/01	11r
Pork, expenditures on	yr	162	1999	30r
Potato chips	16 oz	3.59	7/01	11r
Potatoes, frozen, french fried	lb	1.00	7/01	11r
Potatoes, white or red	10 lb	2.07	3/01	4c
Potatoes, white, all types	lb	0.44	7/01	11r
Poultry, expenditures on	yr	137	1999	30r
Processed fruits, expenditures on	yr	97	1999	30r
Processed vegetables, expenditures on	yr	82	1999	30r
Rice, white, long grain, uncooked	lb	0.51	7/01	11r
Round roast, graded and ungraded, excl U.S. prime and choice	lb	2.96	7/01	11r
Round steak, graded and ungraded, excl U.S. prime and choice	lb	3.11	7/01	11r
Sausage, Jimmy Dean/Owens pork	lb	2.87	3/01	4c
Shortening, vegetable, Crisco	3 lb	2.74	3/01	4c
Sirloin steak, graded and ungraded, excl U.S. prime and choice	lb	4.23	7/01	11r
Soft drink, Coca Cola, ex deposit	2 liter	1.15	3/01	4c
Spaghetti and macaroni	lb	0.78	7/01	11r
Steak, round, U.S. choice, boneless	lb	3.56	7/01	11r
Steak, sirloin, U.S. choice, boneless	lb	5.65	7/01	11r
Steak, T-bone	lb	5.69	3/01	4c
Strawberries, dry pint	12 oz	1.50	7/01	11r
Sugar and other sweets, expenditures on	yr	99	1999	30r
Sugar, cane or beet	4 lbs	1.44	3/01	4c
Sugar, white, 33-80 ounce package	lb	0.39	7/01	11r
Sugar, white, all sizes	lb	0.42	7/01	11r
Tobacco products and smoking supplies purchases	yr	288	1999	30r
Tomatoes, field grown	lb	1.43	7/01	11r
Tomatoes, Hunt's or Del Monte	14.5 oz	0.86	3/01	4c
Tuna, chunk, light	6 oz	0.50	3/01	4c
Tuna, light, chunk	lb	1.77	7/01	11r
Turkey, frozen, whole	lb	1.05	7/01	11r

Values are in dollars or fractions of dollars. In the column headed *Ref*, references are shown to sources. Each reference is followed by a letter. These refer to the geographical level for which data were reported: s=State, r=Region, and c=City or metro. The abbreviation *ex* is used to mean *except* or *excluding*; *exp* stands for *expenditures*. For other abbreviations and further explanations, please see the Introduction.

Waco, TX - continued

Item	Per	Value	Date	Ref.
Goods and Services				
Miscellaneous goods and services, ACCRA Index		101.80	3/01	4c
B&B Japanese maple (acer japonicum)	gal	79.98-99.00	4/00	93r
Boxwood (buxus)	2 gal	12.98-18.99	4/00	93r
Christmas tree, noble fir		40-60	2000	65s
Daylilly (hemerocallis)	gal	7.96-11.00	4/00	93r
Flat of annuals		13.99-27.99	4/00	93r
Fountain grass (pennisetum)	gal	6.96-9.00	4/00	93r
Hanging basket (10 in)		9.99-24.99	4/00	93r
Hardy geranium (geranium)	gal	5.96-8.00	4/00	93r
Hosta (hosta)	gal	8.96-12.99	4/00	93r
Lilac (syrubga vulgaris)	2 gal	13.00-19.99	4/00	93r
Rhododendron (rhododendron)	2 gal	12.98-29.99	4/00	93r
Sage (salvia)	gal	5.96-8.00	4/00	93r
Wintercreeper euonymus (euonymus fortunei)	2 gal	13.00-18.99	4/00	93r
Hunting license	yr	19.00	4/01	34s
Health Care				
Health care, ACCRA Index		95.20	3/01	4c
Cardiac catheterization, ave hospital/ physician charges		20140	1998	77s
Childbirth, Cesarean delivery		11587	1997	13r
Childbirth, vaginal delivery		6725	1997	13r
Dentist's fee, adult teeth cleaning and periodic oral exam	visit	69.67	3/01	4c
Doctor's fee, routine exam, established patient	visit	61.50	3/01	4c
Drugs, expenditures on	yr	399	1999	30r
Health care purchases	yr	1971	1999	30r
Health insurance expenditures	yr	933	1999	30r
Hospital care, private room	day	372.00	3/01	4c
Hysterectomy, laproscopically-assisted, ave hospital/physician charges		15700	1998	76s
Hysterectomy, vaginal, ave hospital and physician charges		12180	1998	76s
Medicaid dispensing fee		5.27	1999	87s
Medical services expenditures	yr	547	1999	30r
Medical supplies, expenditures on	yr	91	1999	30r
Household Goods				
Dishwashing powder, Cascade	50 oz	3.27	3/01	4c
Floor coverings, expenditures on	yr	44	1999	30r
Furniture, expenditures on	yr	335	1999	30r
Household furnishings and equipment purchases	yr	1328	1999	30r
Household textiles, expenditures on	yr	89	1999	30r
Laundry and cleaning supplies, expenditures on	yr	113	1999	30r
Tissues, facial, Kleenex brand	175	1.18	3/01	4c
Housing				
Housing, ACCRA Index		85.30	3/01	4c
Home price, existing, ave		160100	10/00	90r
Home value, median		112000	2001	53s
House, 2400 sq ft, 8000 sq ft lot, new, urban, utilities	total	170703	3/01	4c
House payment, principal and interest, 25% down payment	mos	868	3/01	4c
Household operation expenditures	yr	553	1999	30r
Housekeeping supplies purchases	yr	473	1999	30r
Housing, expenditures on	yr	10303	1999	30r

Waco, TX - continued

Item	Per	Value	Date	Ref.
Housing - continued				
Maintenance, repairs, insurance expenditures	yr	699	1999	30r
Monthly rental value of owned home	mos	505	1999	30r
Owned dwellings, expenditures own	yr	3465	1999	30r
Rent expenditures	yr	1641	1999	30r
Rent, apartment, 2 br, 1 1/2-2 baths, unfurn, 950 sq ft, water	mos	623	3/01	4c
Rental unit, 1 bedroom, with utilities	mos	381	4/01	41c
Rental unit, 2 bedroom, with utilities	mos	502	4/01	41c
Rental unit, 3 bedroom, with utilities	mos	667	4/01	41c
Rental unit, 4 bedroom, with utilities	mos	703	4/01	41c
Shelter, expenditures on	yr	5467	1999	30r
Insurance and Pensions				
Life and other personal insurance purchases	yr	414	1999	30r
Pensions and Social Security, expenditures on	yr	2635	1999	30r
Personal insurance and pensions, expenditures on	yr	3048	1999	30r
Legal Fees				
Divorce, filing fee		150.00-200.00	4/01	35s
Driver's license fee	orig	24.00	1999	48s
Driver's license fee	renew	20.00	1999	48s
Fishing license	yr	19.00	4/01	34s
Personal Goods				
Personal care products and services purchases	yr	393	1999	30r
Shampoo, Alberto VO5	15 oz	1.04	3/01	4c
Toothpaste, Crest or Colgate	6-7 oz	2.11	3/01	4c
Personal Services				
Dry cleaning, man's 2-pc suit		6.17	3/01	4c
Man's haircut, barbershop, no styling		9.95	3/01	4c
Personal services, household, expenditures on	yr	258	1999	30r
Woman's shampoo, trim, blow-dry, no style-change		24.97	3/01	4c
Pets				
Pets, toys, and playground equipment, expenditures on	yr	306	1999	30r
Restaurant Food				
Chicken, fried, thigh and drumstick, KFC/ Church's		2.45	3/01	4c
Hamburger with cheese, McDonald's	1/4 lb	1.89	3/01	4c
Pizza, Pizza Hut or Pizza Inn	11-12 in	8.99	3/01	4c
Taxes				
Federal income taxes paid	yr	2047	1999	30r
Personal taxes, expenditures on	yr	2554	1999	30r
Property taxes paid	yr	726	1999	30r
State and local income taxes paid	yr	363	1999	30r
Transportation				
Transportation, ACCRA Index		95.70	3/01	4c
Bus fare, one-way	trip	0.75	2000	1c
Cars and trucks, new, expenditures on	yr	1648	1999	30r
Cars and trucks, used, expenditures on	yr	1651	1999	30r
Diesel at the pump	gal	1.18	10/99	73s
Gasoline and motor oil purchases	yr	1052	1999	30r
Gasoline before-tax price (cents)	gal	101.30	10/00	43s
Maintenance and repair expenditures	yr	621	1999	30r
Public transportation, expenditures on	yr	298	1999	30r
Tire balance, computer or spin balance, front	wheel	8.12	3/01	4c
Transportation purchases	yr	6738	1999	30r
Vehicle expenses, miscellaneous, purchases	yr	2033	1999	30r
Vehicle insurance payments	yr	696	1999	30r
Vehicle purchases (net outlay)	yr	3354	1999	30r
Vehicle rental, lease expenditures	yr	352	1999	30r

Values are in dollars or fractions of dollars. In the column headed *Ref*, references are shown to sources. Each reference is followed by a letter. These refer to the geographical level for which data were reported: s=State, r=Region, and c=City or metro. The abbreviation *ex* is used to mean *except* or *excluding*; *exp* stands for *expenditures*. For other abbreviations and further explanations, please see the Introduction.

Waco, TX - continued

Item	Per	Value	Date	Ref.
Utilities				
Utilities, ACCRA Index		97.80	3/01	4c
Electrical bill, average	mos	87.17	9/00	9s
Electricity, 2400 sq ft, new home	mos	123.48	3/01	4c
Electricity, expenditures on	yr	1115	1999	30r
Electricity cost, average	KWh	6.48	9/00	9s
Water and other public services, expenditures on	yr	298	1999	30r
Weddings				
Wedding (national average cost)		19936	2000	33r
Attendants' gifts		321	1998	33r
Bridal attendants' apparel (5 persons)		824	2000	33r
Bride's headpiece/veil		173	1998	33r
Bride's wedding dress		859	1998	33r
Clergy, religious facility fee		242	1998	33r
Engagement ring		3177	1998	33r
Flowers		789	1998	33r
Groom's formalwear rental		99	2000	33r
Limousine		410	1998	33r
Marriage license cost		36.00	4/01	35s
Men's formalwear (ushers, best man)		469	2000	33r
Mother of bride apparel		241	2000	33r
Music		866	1998	33r
Photography and videography		1368	1998	33r
Rehearsal dinner		728	1998	33r
Wedding invitations and announcements		341	1998	33r
Wedding reception		7968	2000	33r
Wedding rings (bride and groom)		1060	1998	33r

Wasau, WI

Item	Per	Value	Date	Ref.
Average annual expenditures	yr	35369	1999	30r
Alcoholic Beverages				
Alcoholic beverage purchases	yr	304	1999	30r
Malt beverages, all types, all sizes, any origin	16 oz	0.93	7/01	11r
Wine, red and white table, all sizes, any origin	liter	7.04	7/01	11r
Appliances				
Major appliances, expenditures on	yr	165	1999	30r
Small appliances, housewares, expenditures on	yr	90	1999	30r
Banking and Money				
Mortgage interest and charges paid	yr	2277	1999	30r
Mortgage principal paid on owned property	yr	1230	1999	30r
Vehicle finance charges paid	yr	328	1999	30r
Charity				
Cash contributions, expenditures	yr	1126	1999	30r
Child Care				
Child raising cost, total, age 0-2	yr	7890	1999	60r
Child raising cost, total, age 3-5	yr	8130	1999	60r
Child raising cost, total, age 6-8	yr	8170	1999	60r
Child raising cost, total, age 9-11	yr	8190	1999	60r
Child raising cost, total, age 12-14	yr	8890	1999	60r
Child raising cost, total, age 15-17	yr	9050	1999	60r
Child's child care and education, age 0-2	yr	1240	1999	60r
Child's child care and education, age 3-5	yr	1370	1999	60r
Child's child care and education, age 6-8	yr	880	1999	60r
Child's child care and education, age 9-11	yr	570	1999	60r
Child's child care and education, age 12-14	yr	420	1999	60r
Child's child care and education, age 15-17	yr	720	1999	60r
Child's clothing, age 0-2	yr	410	1999	60r
Child's clothing, age 3-5	yr	400	1999	60r
Child's clothing, age 6-8	yr	450	1999	60r
Child's clothing, age 9-11	yr	500	1999	60r
Child's clothing, age 12-14	yr	840	1999	60r
Child's clothing, age 15-17	yr	740	1999	60r
Child's food, age 0-2	yr	960	1999	60r
Child's food, age 3-5	yr	1120	1999	60r
Child's food, age 6-8	yr	1430	1999	60r

Item	Per	Value	Date	Ref.
Child Care - continued				
Child's food, age 9-11	yr	1710	1999	60r
Child's food, age 12-14	yr	1710	1999	60r
Child's food, age 15-17	yr	1920	1999	60r
Child's health care, age 0-2	yr	520	1999	60r
Child's health care, age 3-5	yr	500	1999	60r
Child's health care, age 6-8	yr	570	1999	60r
Child's health care, age 9-11	yr	610	1999	60r
Child's health care, age 12-14	yr	630	1999	60r
Child's health care, age 15-17	yr	650	1999	60r
Child's housing, age 0-2	yr	2860	1999	60r
Child's housing, age 3-5	yr	2840	1999	60r
Child's housing, age 6-8	yr	2800	1999	60r
Child's housing, age 9-11	yr	2650	1999	60r
Child's housing, age 12-14	yr	2840	1999	60r
Child's housing, age 15-17	yr	2440	1999	60r
Child's personal care, reading, age 0-2	yr	880	1999	60r
Child's personal care, reading, age 3-5	yr	900	1999	60r
Child's personal care, reading, age 6-8	yr	930	1999	60r
Child's personal care, reading, age 9-11	yr	970	1999	60r
Child's personal care, reading, age 12-14	yr	1150	1999	60r
Child's personal care, reading, age 15-17	yr	920	1999	60r
Clothing				
Apparel and services purchases	yr	1607	1999	30r
Boys, 2 to 15, expenditures on	yr	91	1999	30r
Children under 2, expenditures on	yr	59	1999	30r
Footwear, expenditures on	yr	285	1999	30r
Girls, 2 to 15, expenditures on	yr	116	1999	30r
Men and boys, expenditures on	yr	433	1999	30r
Men, 16 and over, expenditures on	yr	341	1999	30r
Women, 16 and over, expenditures on	yr	490	1999	30r
Communications				
Cable modem installation, Bresnan		99.95	6/99	103s
Cable modem installation, Marcus		499.00	6/99	103s
Cable modem rate, cable subscriber, Bresnan	mos	39.95	6/99	103s
Cable modem rate, cable subscriber, Marcus	mos	14.95-49.95	6/99	103s
Cable modem rate, non-cable subscriber, Bresnan	mos	49.95	6/99	103s
Cable modem rate, non-cable subscriber, Marcus	mos	60.95	6/99	103s
Phone line, single, business, field visit	inst.	64.65	12/97	17s
Phone line, single, business, no field visit	inst.	64.65	12/97	17s
Phone line, single, residence, field visit	inst.	33.05	12/97	17s
Phone line, single, residence, no field visit	inst.	33.05	12/97	17s
Postage and stationery, expenditures on	yr	140	1999	30r
Postal rate, express mail, up to half-pound		12.45	7/01	108r
Postal rate, letter, first class, first ounce		0.34	7/01	108r
Postal rate, letter, two ounces		0.57	7/01	108r
Postal rate, post card		0.21	7/01	108r
Postal rate, priority mail, two pounds		3.95	7/01	108r
Postal rate, priority mail, up to one pound		3.50	7/01	108r
Telephone services, expenditures on	yr	830	1999	30r
Education				
Board, 4-year private college/university	yr	2271	1996	38s
Board, 4-year public college/university	yr	1527	1996	38s
Education expenditures	yr	583	1999	30r
Room, 4-year private college/university	yr	1812	1996	38s
Room, 4-year public college/university	yr	1706	1996	38s
Total cost, 4-year private college/university	yr	15652	1996	38s
Total cost, 4-year public college/university	yr	5847	1996	38s
Tuition, 2-year public college/university, in state	yr	1840	1996	38s
Tuition, 4-year private college/university, in state	yr	11569	1996	38s
Tuition, 4-year public college/university	yr	2614	1996	38s
Energy and Fuels				
Electricity	500 KWhs	46.59	7/01	11r
Fuel oil #2	gal	1.27	7/01	11r

Values are in dollars or fractions of dollars. In the column headed *Ref*, references are shown to sources. Each reference is followed by a letter. These refer to the geographical level for which data were reported: s=State, r=Region, and c=City or metro. The abbreviation *ex* is used to mean *except* or *excluding*; *exp* stands for *expenditures*. For other abbreviations and further explanations, please see the Introduction.

Wasau, WI - continued

Item	Per	Value	Date	Ref.
Energy and Fuels				
Fuel oil and other fuels, expenditures on	yr	68	1999	30r
Gas, natural, commercial rate	1000 cf	7.32	11/00	88s
Gasoline, unleaded midgrade	gal	1.79	7/01	11r
Gasoline, unleaded premium	gal	1.86	7/01	11r
Gasoline, unleaded regular	gal	1.58	7/01	11r
Natural gas, expenditures on	yr	389	1999	30r
Utility (piped) gas, therm		0.81	7/01	11r
Utility (piped) gas, 40 therms		38.01	7/01	11r
Utility (piped) gas, 100 therms		81.75	7/01	11r
Entertainment				
Entertainment purchases	yr	1984	1999	30r
Fees and admissions paid	yr	444	1999	30r
Television, radios, sound equipment, expenditures on	yr	580	1999	30r
Funerals				
Cosmetology, hair, other preparation		178.32	1/99	78r
Embalming		408.19	1/99	78r
Funeral at funeral home		362.13	1/99	78r
Professional service charges		1375.51	1/99	78r
Transfer of remains to funeral home		155.92	1/99	78r
Visitation/viewing		294.38	1/99	78r
Groceries				
Bacon, sliced	lb	3.15	7/01	11r
Bakery products, expenditures on	yr	281	1999	30r
Bananas	lb	0.48	7/01	11r
Beans, dried, any type, all sizes	lb	0.61	7/01	11r
Beef for stew, boneless	lb	3.08	7/01	11r
Beef, expenditures on	yr	217	1999	30r
Bologna, all beef or mixed	lb	2.52	7/01	11r
Bread, white, pan	lb	1.06	7/01	11r
Broccoli	lb	0.91	7/01	11r
Butter, salted, grade AA, stick	lb	3.04	7/01	11r
Butter, yoghurt, cheese, etc, expenditures on	yr	183	1999	30r
Cereals and bakery product purchases	yr	430	1999	30r
Cereals and cereal products, expenditures on	yr	149	1999	30r
Chicken, fresh, whole	lb	1.07	7/01	11r
Chops, boneless,	lb	3.64	7/01	11r
Chuck roast, U.S. choice, boneless	lb	2.47	7/01	11r
Coffee, 100%, ground roast, all sizes	lb	2.69	7/01	11r
Cookies, chocolate chip	lb	2.87	7/01	11r
Dairy product purchases	yr	304	1999	30r
Eggs, expenditures on	yr	26	1999	30r
Eggs, grade A, large	dozen	0.88	7/01	11r
Fats and oils, expenditures on	yr	75	1999	30r
Fish and seafood, expenditures on	yr	72	1999	30r
Food (excl fruit and vegetables), eaten at home, purchases	yr	887	1999	30r
Food cooked on trips, expenditures on	yr	44	1999	30r
Food purchases	yr	4802	1999	30r
Food purchases, eaten away from home	yr	2069	1999	30r
Food purchases, food eaten at home	yr	2733	1999	30r
Fresh fruits, expenditures on	yr	138	1999	30r
Fresh milk and cream, expenditures on	yr	120	1999	30r
Fresh vegetables, expenditures on	yr	126	1999	30r
Grapefruit	lb	0.66	7/01	11r
Grapes, Thompson, seedless	lb	1.64	7/01	11r
Ground beef, 100% beef	lb	1.64	7/01	11r
Ground beef, lean and extra lean	lb	2.16	7/01	11r
Ground chuck, 100% beef	lb	2.13	7/01	11r
Ham, boneless, excl canned	lb	2.62	7/01	11r
Ice cream, prepackaged, bulk, regular	1/2 gal	3.35	7/01	11r
Lemons	lb	1.19	7/01	11r
Lettuce, iceberg	lb	0.73	7/01	11r
Margarine, soft, tubs	lb	0.89	7/01	11r
Meats, poultry, fish, and egg purchases	yr	671	1999	30r
Milk, fresh, whole, fortified	gal	2.71	7/01	11r
Nonalcoholic beverages, expenditures on	yr	239	1999	30r
Oranges, Navel	lb	0.80	7/01	11r
Oranges, Valencia	lb	0.66	7/01	11r
Pears, Anjou	lb	0.93	7/01	11r

Wasau, WI - continued

Item	Per	Value	Date	Ref.
Groceries - continued				
Pork chops, center cut, bone-in	lb	3.63	7/01	11r
Pork, expenditures on	yr	150	1999	30r
Potato chips	16 oz	3.52	7/01	11r
Potatoes, frozen, french fried	lb	1.08	7/01	11r
Potatoes, white, all types	lb	0.33	7/01	11r
Poultry, expenditures on	yr	108	1999	30r
Processed fruits, expenditures on	yr	98	1999	30r
Processed vegetables, expenditures on	yr	80	1999	30r
Round roast, U.S. choice, boneless	lb	3.07	7/01	11r
Round steak, graded and ungraded, excl U.S. prime and choice	lb	3.41	7/01	11r
Shortening, vegetable oil blends	lb	1.13	7/01	11r
Spaghetti and macaroni	lb	0.80	7/01	11r
Steak, round, U.S. choice, boneless	lb	3.23	7/01	11r
Steak, T-bone, U.S. choice, bone-in	lb	6.68	7/01	11r
Strawberries, dry pint	12 oz	1.32	7/01	11r
Sugar and other sweets, expenditures on	yr	114	1999	30r
Sugar, white, 33-80 ounce package	lb	0.42	7/01	11r
Sugar, white, all sizes	lb	0.43	7/01	11r
Tobacco products and smoking supplies purchases	yr	331	1999	30r
Tomatoes, field grown	lb	1.46	7/01	11r
Tuna, light, chunk	lb	1.80	7/01	11r
Turkey, frozen, whole	lb	1.15	7/01	11r
Goods and Services				
B&B Japanese maple (acer japonicum)	gal	29.99-169.99	4/00	93r
Boxwood (buxus)	2 gal	18.99-39.99	4/00	93r
Daylilly (hemerocallis)	gal	4.99-25.00	4/00	93r
Flat of annuals		11.98-24.99	4/00	93r
Fountain grass (pennisetum)	gal	5.98-12.98	4/00	93r
Hanging basket (10 in)		12.99-27.99	4/00	93r
Hardy geranium (geranium)	gal	7.99-9.99	4/00	93r
Hosta (hosta)	gal	6.00-25.00	4/00	93r
Lilac (syrubga vulgaris)	2 gal	14.99-24.99	4/00	93r
Miscellaneous purchases	yr	865	1999	30r
Rhododendron (rhododendron)	2 gal	23.98-42.99	4/00	93r
Sage (salvia)	gal	6.00-9.99	4/00	93r
Wintercreeper euonymus (euonymus fortunei)	2 gal	16.00-169.99	4/00	93r
Hunting license	yr	14.00	4/01	34s
Health Care				
Cardiac catheterization, ave hospital/ physician charges		13240	1998	77s
Childbirth, Cesarean delivery		10722	1997	13r
Childbirth, vaginal delivery		6223	1997	13r
Drugs, expenditures on	yr	394	1999	30r
Health care purchases	yr	2048	1999	30r
Health insurance expenditures	yr	978	1999	30r
Hysterectomy, laproscopically-assisted, ave hospital/physician charges		13270	1998	76s
Hysterectomy, vaginal, ave hospital and physician charges		9170	1998	76s
Laser eye surgery	eye	1950-2400	2000	63s
Medicaid dispensing fee		4.88-40.11	1999	87s
Medical services expenditures	yr	554	1999	30r
Medical supplies, expenditures on	yr	122	1999	30r
Plastic surgery, breast augmentation		3184	2000	7r
Plastic surgery, breast lift		3585	2000	7r

Values are in dollars or fractions of dollars. In the column headed *Ref*, references are shown to sources. Each reference is followed by a letter. These refer to the geographical level for which data were reported: s=State, r=Region, and c=City or metro. The abbreviation *ex* is used to mean *except* or *excluding*; *exp* stands for *expenditures*. For other abbreviations and further explanations, please see the Introduction.

Wasau, WI - continued

Item	Per	Value	Date	Ref.
Health Care				
Plastic surgery, facelift		4999	2000	7r
Plastic surgery, hair transplantation		3105	2000	7r
Plastic surgery, lip augmentation		1290	2000	7r
Plastic surgery, lower body lift		8135	2000	7r
Plastic surgery, thigh lift		3839	2000	7r
Household Goods				
Floor coverings, expenditures on	yr	52	1999	30r
Furniture, expenditures on	yr	344	1999	30r
Household furnishings and equipment purchases	yr	1475	1999	30r
Household textiles, expenditures on	yr	109	1999	30r
Laundry and cleaning supplies, expenditures on	yr	134	1999	30r
Housing				
Home price, existing, ave		144400	10/00	90r
Home value, median		117000	2001	53s
Household operation expenditures	yr	542	1999	30r
Housekeeping supplies purchases	yr	508	1999	30r
Lodging expenditures	yr	430	1999	30r
Maintenance, repairs, insurance expenditures	yr	853	1999	30r
Monthly rental value of owned home	mos	547	1999	30r
Owned dwellings, expenditures own	yr	4282	1999	30r
Rent expenditures	yr	1558	1999	30r
Rental unit, 1 bedroom, with utilities	mos	394	4/01	41c
Rental unit, 2 bedroom, with utilities	mos	492	4/01	41c
Rental unit, 3 bedroom, with utilities	mos	672	4/01	41c
Rental unit, 4 bedroom, with utilities	mos	745	4/01	41c
Shelter, expenditures on	yr	6270	1999	30r
Insurance and Pensions				
Auto insurance premium	yr	603.84	1999	57s
Life and other personal insurance purchases	yr	387	1999	30r
Pensions and Social Security, expenditures on	yr	2968	1999	30r
Legal Fees				
Divorce, filing fee		142.00-150.00	4/01	35s
Driver's license fee	renew	12.00	1999	48s
Driver's license fee	orig	18.00	1999	48s
Fishing license	yr	14.00	4/01	34s
Personal Goods				
Personal care products and services purchases	yr	385	1999	30r
Personal Services				
Personal services, household, expenditures on	yr	300	1999	30r
Pets				
Pets, toys, and playground equipment, expenditures on	yr	375	1999	30r
Taxes				
Federal income taxes paid	yr	2326	1999	30r
Personal taxes, expenditures on	yr	3223	1999	30r
Property taxes paid	yr	1152	1999	30r
State and local income taxes paid	yr	753	1999	30r
Transportation				
Cars and trucks, new, expenditures on	yr	1280	1999	30r
Cars and trucks, used, expenditures on	yr	1763	1999	30r
Diesel at the pump	gal	1.34	10/99	73s
Gasoline and motor oil purchases	yr	1036	1999	30r
Gasoline before-tax price (cents)	gal	113.40	10/00	43s
Maintenance and repair expenditures	yr	594	1999	30r
Public transportation, expenditures on	yr	341	1999	30r
Transportation purchases	yr	6617	1999	30r
Vehicle expenses, miscellaneous, purchases	yr	2159	1999	30r
Vehicle insurance payments	yr	701	1999	30r
Vehicle purchases (net outlay)	yr	3081	1999	30r
Vehicle rental, lease expenditures	yr	536	1999	30r

Wasau, WI - continued

Item	Per	Value	Date	Ref.
Utilities				
Electrical bill, average	mos	52.08	9/00	9s
Electricity, expenditures on	yr	841	1999	30r
Electricity cost, average	KWh	5.69	9/00	9s
Utilities, fuels, and public services purchased	yr	2401	1999	30r
Water and other public services, expenditures on	yr	273	1999	30r
Weddings				
Wedding (national average cost)		19936	2000	33r
Wedding (regional average total cost)		16195	1997	110r
Attendants' gifts		321	1998	33r
Bridal attendants' apparel (5 persons)		824	2000	33r
Bride's headpiece/veil		173	1998	33r
Bride's wedding dress		859	1998	33r
Clergy, religious facility fee		242	1998	33r
Engagement ring		3177	1998	33r
Flowers		789	1998	33r
Groom's formalwear rental		99	2000	33r
Limousine		410	1998	33r
Marriage license cost		50.00-60.00	4/01	35s
Men's formalwear (ushers, best man)		469	2000	33r
Mother of bride apparel		241	2000	33r
Music		866	1998	33r
Photography and videography		1368	1998	33r
Rehearsal dinner		728	1998	33r
Wedding invitations and announcements		341	1998	33r
Wedding reception		7968	2000	33r
Wedding rings (bride and groom)		1060	1998	33r

Washington, DC-MD-VA-WV

Item	Per	Value	Date	Ref.
Composite, ACCRA index		112.90	3/01	4c
Alcoholic Beverages				
Alcoholic beverage purchases	yr	419	1999	30c
Beer, Heineken, 12-oz, ex deposit	6	6.99	3/01	4c
J & B Scotch	750-ml	19.68	3/01	4c
Malt beverages, all types, all sizes, any origin	16 oz	0.96	7/01	11r
Wine, Livingston or Gallo, Chablis blanc	1.5 liter	6.34	3/01	4c
Appliances				
Appliance repair, service call, washing machine	min lab chg	49.48	3/01	4c
Major appliances, expenditures on	yr	172	1999	30r
Small appliances, housewares, expenditures on	yr	81	1999	30r
Banking and Money				
Mortgage interest and charges paid	yr	2039	1999	30r
Mortgage principal paid on owned property	yr	1026	1999	30r
Mortgage rate, incl. points and orig. fee, 30-yr. conv. fixed or ARM	mos	6.68	3/01	4c
Vehicle finance charges paid	yr	365	1999	30r
Business Expenses				
Business travel, car rental	day	69	2001	3c
Business travel, food	day	70	2001	3c
Business travel, hotel	day	184	2001	3c
Medical office space cost	sq ft	113.62	2001	31c
Office space, 2-4 storey building	sq ft	99.54	2001	31c
Office space, 5-10 storey building	sq ft	87.93	2001	31c
Office space, 11-20 storey building	sq ft	84.51	2001	31c
Charity				
Cash contributions, expenditures	yr	1366	1999	30c
Child Care				
Child raising cost, total, age 0-2	yr	8540	1999	60r
Child raising cost, total, age 3-5	yr	8780	1999	60r
Child raising cost, total, age 6-8	yr	8820	1999	60r
Child raising cost, total, age 9-11	yr	8800	1999	60r
Child raising cost, total, age 12-14	yr	9510	1999	60r
Child raising cost, total, age 15-17	yr	9740	1999	60r
Child's child care and education, age 0-2	yr	1380	1999	60r

Values are in dollars or fractions of dollars. In the column headed *Ref*, references are shown to sources. Each reference is followed by a letter. These refer to the geographical level for which data were reported: s=State, r=Region, and c=City or metro. The abbreviation *ex* is used to mean *except* or *excluding*; *exp* stands for *expenditures*. For other abbreviations and further explanations, please see the Introduction.

Washington, DC-MD-VA-WV - continued

Item	Per	Value	Date	Ref.
Child Care				
Child's child care and education, age 3-5	yr	1520	1999	60r
Child's child care and education, age 6-8	yr	990	1999	60r
Child's child care and education, age 9-11	yr	650	1999	60r
Child's child care and education, age 12-14	yr	490	1999	60r
Child's child care and education, age 15-17	yr	840	1999	60r
Child's clothing, age 0-2	yr	480	1999	60r
Child's clothing, age 3-5	yr	470	1999	60r
Child's clothing, age 6-8	yr	520	1999	60r
Child's clothing, age 9-11	yr	570	1999	60r
Child's clothing, age 12-14	yr	950	1999	60r
Child's clothing, age 15-17	yr	850	1999	60r
Child's food, age 0-2	yr	1000	1999	60r
Child's food, age 3-5	yr	1160	1999	60r
Child's food, age 6-8	yr	1490	1999	60r
Child's food, age 9-11	yr	1770	1999	60r
Child's food, age 12-14	yr	1770	1999	60r
Child's food, age 15-17	yr	1980	1999	60r
Child's health care, age 0-2	yr	620	1999	60r
Child's health care, age 3-5	yr	590	1999	60r
Child's health care, age 6-8	yr	680	1999	60r
Child's health care, age 9-11	yr	720	1999	60r
Child's health care, age 12-14	yr	730	1999	60r
Child's health care, age 15-17	yr	760	1999	60r
Child's housing, age 0-2	yr	3070	1999	60r
Child's housing, age 3-5	yr	3050	1999	60r
Child's housing, age 6-8	yr	3010	1999	60r
Child's housing, age 9-11	yr	2850	1999	60r
Child's housing, age 12-14	yr	3040	1999	60r
Child's housing, age 15-17	yr	2650	1999	60r
Child's personal care, reading, age 0-2	yr	910	1999	60r
Child's personal care, reading, age 3-5	yr	930	1999	60r
Child's personal care, reading, age 6-8	yr	960	1999	60r
Child's personal care, reading, age 9-11	yr	1000	1999	60r
Child's personal care, reading, age 12-14	yr	1170	1999	60r
Child's personal care, reading, age 15-17	yr	950	1999	60r
Daycare	mos	631	1998	37c
Daycare, 3-year old, 5 days, 8 hrs/day	mos	631	1998	85c
Infant care, federal child care center	yr	10000	2001	15c
Clothing				
Apparel and services purchases	yr	2279	1999	30c
Boys' brief, cotton	3	5.99	3/01	4c
Boys, 2 to 15, expenditures on	yr	89	1999	30r
Children under 2, expenditures on	yr	79	1999	30r
Footwear, expenditures on	yr	283	1999	30r
Girls, 2 to 15, expenditures on	yr	103	1999	30r
Men and boys, expenditures on	yr	351	1999	30r
Men, 16 and over, expenditures on	yr	262	1999	30r
Shirt, man's dress shirt		27.19	3/01	4c
Slacks, man's "No Wrinkles" khaki		38.89	3/01	4c
Women, 16 and over, expenditures on	yr	538	1999	30r
Communications				
Newspaper subscription, daily and Sunday delivery	mos	12.78	3/01	4c
Phone line, single, business, field visit	inst.	83.25	12/97	17c
Phone line, single, business, no field visit	inst.	83.25	12/97	17c
Phone line, single, residence, field visit	inst.	30.76	12/97	17c
Phone line, single, residence, no field visit	inst.	30.76	12/97	17c
Postage and stationery, expenditures on	yr	104	1999	30r
Postal rate, express mail, up to half-pound		12.45	7/01	108r
Postal rate, letter, first class, first ounce		0.34	7/01	108r
Postal rate, letter, two ounces		0.57	7/01	108r
Postal rate, post card		0.21	7/01	108r
Postal rate, priority mail, two pounds		3.95	7/01	108r
Postal rate, priority mail, up to one pound		3.50	7/01	108r
Telephone bill, business, basic rate	mos	14.15	12/97	18c
Telephone bill, family of three	mos	22.30	3/01	4c
Telephone bill, residential, basic rate	mos	7.45	12/97	18c
Telephone services, expenditures on	yr	860	1999	30r
Wireless services	mos	41.64	1/00	42c

Washington, DC-MD-VA-WV - continued

Item	Per	Value	Date	Ref.
Education				
Board, 4-year private college/university	yr	2740	1996	38s
Education expenditures	yr	856	1999	30c
Room, 4-year private college/university	yr	3917	1996	38s
Total cost, 4-year private college/university	yr	21337	1996	38s
Tuition, 4-year private college/university, in state	yr	14681	1996	38s
Tuition, 4-year public college/university	yr	1118	1996	38s
Energy and Fuels				
Electricity	500 KWhs	47.29	7/01	11r
Electricity	KWh	0.09	7/01	11r
Energy, combined forms, 2400 sq ft	mos	101.92	3/01	4c
Energy, exc. electricity, 2400 sq ft	mos	37.96	3/01	4c
Fuel oil #2	gal	1.43	7/01	11r
Fuel oil and other fuels, expenditures on	yr	45	1999	30r
Gas, cooking, winter, 10 therms	mos	12.93	2/96	98c
Gas, cooking, winter, 30 therms	mos	28.88	2/96	98c
Gas, cooking, winter, 50 therms	mos	44.84	2/96	98c
Gas, heating, winter, average use	mos	168.56	2/96	98c
Gas, natural, commercial rate	1000 cf	11.64	11/00	88c
Gas, regular unleaded, cash, self-service	gal	1.56	3/01	4c
Gasoline, all types	gal	1.60	7/01	11r
Gasoline, unleaded midgrade	gal	1.65	7/01	11r
Gasoline, unleaded premium	gal	1.74	7/01	11r
Natural gas, expenditures on	yr	164	1999	30r
Utility (piped) gas, therm		1.01	7/01	11r
Utility (piped) gas, 40 therms		44.29	7/01	11r
Utility (piped) gas, 100 therms		97.44	7/01	11r
Entertainment				
Bowling, Saturday evening rate	line	3.56	3/01	4c
Entertainment purchases	yr	2261	1999	30c
Fees and admissions paid	yr	371	1999	30r
Monopoly game, Parker Brothers', No. 9	game	11.09	3/01	4c
Movie, first-run, Saturday, evening	adm.	7.90	3/01	4c
Reading purchases	yr	244	1999	30c
Television, radios, sound equipment, expenditures on	yr	561	1999	30r
Tennis balls, yellow, Wilson or Penn, 3	can	2.30	3/01	4c
Funerals				
Total cost of funeral		5922.53	1/99	78r
Acknowledgement cards		63.43	1/99	78r
Casket		2258.77	1/99	78r
Cosmetology, hair, other preparation		127.09	1/99	78r
Embalming		393.49	1/99	78r
Funeral at funeral home		367.50	1/99	78r
Hearse (local)		169.66	1/99	78r
Professional service charges		1211.32	1/99	78r
Service car/van		80.69	1/99	78r
Transfer of remains to funeral home		144.25	1/99	78r
Vault		803.50	1/99	78r
Visitation/viewing		302.83	1/99	78r
Groceries				
Groceries, ACCRA Index		113.20	3/01	4c
American processed cheese	lb	3.50	7/01	11r
Antibiotic ointment, Polysporin	0.5 oz	4.45	3/01	4c
Baby food, strained vegetables or fruit, lowest price	4-4.5 oz	0.47	3/01	4c
Bakery products, expenditures on	yr	261	1999	30r
Bananas	lb	0.59	3/01	4c
Bananas	lb	0.47	7/01	11r
Beans, dried, any type, all sizes	lb	0.63	7/01	11r
Beef for stew, boneless	lb	2.86	7/01	11r
Beef or hamburger, ground	lb	2.20	3/01	4c
Beef, expenditures on	yr	210	1999	30r
Bologna, all beef or mixed	lb	2.29	7/01	11r
Box of cereal		3.71	2000	39c
Bread, French	lb	1.66	7/01	11r
Bread, white	loaf	0.70	3/01	4c
Bread, white, pan	lb	0.87	7/01	11r
Bread, whole wheat, pan	lb	1.38	7/01	11r

Values are in dollars or fractions of dollars. In the column headed *Ref*, references are shown to sources. Each reference is followed by a letter. These refer to the geographical level for which data were reported: s=State, r=Region, and c=City or metro. The abbreviation *ex* is used to mean *except* or *excluding*; *exp* stands for *expenditures*. For other abbreviations and further explanations, please see the Introduction.

Washington, DC-MD-VA-WV - continued

Item	Per	Value	Date	Ref.
Groceries				
Broccoli	lb	1.04	7/01	11r
Butter, salted, grade AA, stick	lb	2.26	7/01	11r
Butter, yoghurt, cheese, etc, expenditures on	yr	170	1999	30r
Cabbage	lb	0.42	7/01	11r
Cereals and cereal products, expenditures on	yr	140	1999	30r
Cheddar cheese	lb	5.91	2000	39c
Cheddar cheese, natural	lb	3.75	7/01	11r
Cheese, Kraft grated Parmesan	8 oz	4.57	3/01	4c
Chicken breast, bone-in	lb	1.85	7/01	11r
Chicken legs, bone-in	lb	1.34	7/01	11r
Chicken, fresh, whole	lb	1.05	7/01	11r
Chicken, whole fryer	lb	1.31	3/01	4c
Chops, boneless,	lb	4.13	7/01	11r
Chuck roast, graded and ungraded, excl U.S. prime and choice	lb	2.35	7/01	11r
Chuck roast, U.S. choice, boneless	lb	2.67	7/01	11r
Cigarettes, Winston, Kings	carton	28.73	3/01	4c
Coffee, 100%, ground roast, all sizes	lb	2.88	7/01	11r
Coffee, instant, plain, regular, all sizes	16 oz	9.25	7/01	11r
Coffee, vacuum-packed	13 oz	2.77	3/01	4c
Cola, non diet	2 liter	1.11	7/01	11r
Corn Flakes, Kellogg's or Post Toasties	18 oz	3.40	3/01	4c
Corn, frozen, whole kernel, lowest price	16 oz	1.55	3/01	4c
Crackers, soda, salted	lb	1.70	7/01	11r
Dairy product purchases	yr	291	1999	30c
Eggs, expenditures on	yr	32	1999	30r
Eggs, Grade A or AA	dozen	1.60	3/01	4c
Fats and oils, expenditures on	yr	79	1999	30r
Fish and seafood, expenditures on	yr	99	1999	30r
Flour, white, all purpose	lb	0.32	7/01	11r
Food (excl fruit and vegetables), eaten at home, purchases	yr	906	1999	30c
Food cooked on trips, expenditures on	yr	36	1999	30r
Food purchases	yr	5358	1999	30c
Food purchases, eaten away from home	yr	2451	1999	30c
Food purchases, food eaten at home	yr	2907	1999	30c
Fresh fruits, expenditures on	yr	128	1999	30r
Fresh milk and cream, expenditures on	yr	112	1999	30r
Fresh vegetables, expenditures on	yr	131	1999	30r
Fruit and vegetable purchases	yr	602	1999	30c
Grapefruit	lb	0.59	7/01	11r
Grapes, Thompson, seedless	lb	2.12	7/01	11r
Ground beef, 100% beef	lb	1.76	7/01	11r
Ground beef, lean and extra lean	lb	2.60	7/01	11r
Ground chuck, 100% beef	lb	2.08	7/01	11r
Ham, boneless, excl canned	lb	2.71	7/01	11r
Ham, rump or shank half, bone-in, smoked	lb	2.19	7/01	11r
Head of lettuce		1.29	2000	39c
Ice cream, prepackaged, bulk, regular	1/2 gal	3.93	7/01	11r
Lemons	lb	1.32	7/01	11r
Lettuce, iceberg	head	1.49	3/01	4c
Lettuce, iceberg	lb	0.76	7/01	11r
Loaf of bread		1.39	2000	39c
Margarine, Blue Bonnet or Parkay, stick	lb	1.09	3/01	4c
Milk, fresh, low fat,	gal	2.75	7/01	11r
Milk, fresh, whole, fortified	gal	2.97	7/01	11r
Milk, whole	1/2 gal	1.56	3/01	4c
Nonalcoholic beverages, expenditures on	yr	228	1999	30r
Orange juice, frozen concentrate	16 oz	1.95	7/01	11r
Orange juice, Minute Maid frozen	12 oz	1.76	3/01	4c
Oranges, Navel	lb	0.73	7/01	11r
Oranges, Valencia	lb	0.55	7/01	11r
Peaches, halves or slices, Hunt's, Del Monte, or Libby's	29 oz	1.67	3/01	4c
Peanut butter, creamy, all sizes	lb	1.83	7/01	11r
Pears, Anjou	lb	0.98	7/01	11r
Peas, green, Del Monte or Green Giant	15 oz	0.78	3/01	4c
Pork chops, center cut, bone-in	lb	3.33	7/01	11r
Pork sausage, fresh, loose	lb	2.59	7/01	11r
Pork shoulder picnic, bone-in, smoked	lb	1.12	7/01	11r
Pork, expenditures on	yr	162	1999	30r

Washington, DC-MD-VA-WV - continued

Item	Per	Value	Date	Ref.
Groceries - continued				
Potato chips	16 oz	3.59	7/01	11r
Potato chips	9 oz	1.99	2000	39c
Potatoes, frozen, french fried	lb	1.00	7/01	11r
Potatoes, white or red	10 lb	3.52	3/01	4c
Potatoes, white, all types	lb	0.44	7/01	11r
Poultry, expenditures on	yr	137	1999	30r
Processed fruits, expenditures on	yr	97	1999	30r
Processed vegetables, expenditures on	yr	82	1999	30r
Rice, white, long grain, uncooked	lb	0.51	7/01	11r
Round roast, graded and ungraded, excl U.S. prime and choice	lb	2.96	7/01	11r
Round steak, graded and ungraded, excl U.S. prime and choice	lb	3.11	7/01	11r
Sausage, Jimmy Dean/Owens pork	lb	3.69	3/01	4c
Shortening, vegetable, Crisco	3 lb	3.50	3/01	4c
Sirloin steak	lb	4.39	2000	39c
Sirloin steak, graded and ungraded, excl U.S. prime and choice	lb	4.23	7/01	11r
Soft drink, Coca Cola, ex deposit	2 liter	1.31	3/01	4c
Spaghetti and macaroni	lb	0.78	7/01	11r
Steak, round, U.S. choice, boneless	lb	3.56	7/01	11r
Steak, sirloin, U.S. choice, boneless	lb	5.65	7/01	11r
Steak, T-bone	lb	9.21	3/01	4c
Strawberries, dry pint	12 oz	1.50	7/01	11r
Sugar and other sweets, expenditures on	yr	99	1999	30r
Sugar, cane or beet	4 lbs	1.58	3/01	4c
Sugar, white, 33-80 ounce package	lb	0.39	7/01	11r
Sugar, white, all sizes	lb	0.42	7/01	11r
Tobacco products and smoking supplies purchases	yr	228	1999	30c
Tomatoes, field grown	lb	1.43	7/01	11r
Tomatoes, Hunt's or Del Monte	14.5 oz	0.83	3/01	4c
Tuna, chunk, light	6 oz	0.86	3/01	4c
Tuna, light, chunk	lb	1.77	7/01	11r
Turkey, frozen, whole	lb	1.05	7/01	11r
Goods and Services				
Miscellaneous goods and services, ACCRA Index		107.90	3/01	4c
B&B Japanese maple (acer japonicum)	gal	49.98-129.00	4/00	93r
Boxwood (buxus)	2 gal	12.99-16.99	4/00	93r
Daylily (hemerocallis)	gal	4.99-8.99	4/00	93r
Flat of annuals		11.00-13.92	4/00	93r
Fountain grass (pennisetum)	gal	5.98-7.98	4/00	93r
Hanging basket (10 in)		7.99-14.98	4/00	93r
Hardy geranium (geranium)	gal	5.98-8.00	4/00	93r
Hosta (hosta)	gal	4.99-10.98	4/00	93r
Lilac (syrubga vulgaris)	2 gal	12.99-21.99	4/00	93r
Rhododendron (rhododendron)	2 gal	14.99-24.99	4/00	93r
Sage (salvia)	gal	5.98-6.99	4/00	93r
Wintercreeper euonymus (euonymus fortunei)	2 gal	7.99-89.99	4/00	93r
Health Care				
Health care, ACCRA Index		118.60	3/01	4c
Childbirth, Cesarean delivery		11587	1997	13r
Childbirth, vaginal delivery		6725	1997	13r
Dentist's fee, adult teeth cleaning and periodic oral exam	visit	92.50	3/01	4c
Doctor's fee, routine exam, established patient	visit	72.00	3/01	4c
Drugs, expenditures on	yr	399	1999	30r

Values are in dollars or fractions of dollars. In the column headed *Ref*, references are shown to sources. Each reference is followed by a letter. These refer to the geographical level for which data were reported: s=State, r=Region, and c=City or metro. The abbreviation *ex* is used to mean *except* or *excluding*; *exp* stands for expenditures. For other abbreviations and further explanations, please see the Introduction.

Washington, DC-MD-VA-WV - continued

Item	Per	Value	Date	Ref.
Health Care				
Health care purchases	yr	2202	1999	30c
Health insurance expenditures	yr	933	1999	30r
Home health care aide cost, licensed agency	hour	16	2000	82c
Hospital care, private room	day	550.15	3/01	4c
Hysterectomy, laproscopically-assisted, ave hospital/physician charges		16500	1998	76s
Hysterectomy, vaginal, ave hospital and physician charges		12540	1998	76s
Medicaid dispensing fee		3.75	1999	87s
Medical services expenditures	yr	547	1999	30r
Medical supplies, expenditures on	yr	91	1999	30r
Nursing home costs, private room	day	165	2000	82c
Nursing home stay, private room	day	165	2000	83c
Plastic surgery, breast augmentation		2870	2000	7r
Plastic surgery, breast lift		3649	2000	7r
Plastic surgery, facelift		5008	2000	7r
Plastic surgery, hair transplantation		3425	2000	7r
Plastic surgery, lip augmentation		1227	2000	7r
Plastic surgery, lower body lift		4793	2000	7r
Plastic surgery, thigh lift		3862	2000	7r
Household Goods				
Dishwashing powder, Cascade	50 oz	2.94	3/01	4c
Floor coverings, expenditures on	yr	44	1999	30r
Furniture, expenditures on	yr	335	1999	30r
Household furnishings and equipment purchases	yr	1981	1999	30c
Household textiles, expenditures on	yr	89	1999	30r
Laundry and cleaning supplies, expenditures on	yr	113	1999	30r
Tissues, facial, Kleenex brand	175	1.56	3/01	4c
Housing				
Housing, ACCRA Index		124.90	3/01	4c
Home, 2200 sq ft, 4-br, 2-bath, 2-car garage, average		398375	2000	47c
Home, suburban, 2,200 square feet		332100	2000	23c
Home price, existing, ave		160100	10/00	90r
Home value, median		176000	2001	53s
House, 2400 sq ft, 8000 sq ft lot, new, urban, utilities	total	250378	3/01	4c
House payment, principal and interest, 25% down payment	mos	1209	3/01	4c
Household operation expenditures	yr	815	1999	30c
Housekeeping supplies purchases	yr	473	1999	30c
Housing, expenditures on	yr	16381	1999	30c
Maintenance, repairs, insurance expenditures	yr	699	1999	30r
Monthly rental value of owned home	mos	505	1999	30r
Owned dwellings, expenditures own	yr	6501	1999	30c
Rent expenditures	yr	3052	1999	30c
Rent, apartment, 2 br, 1 1/2-2 baths, unfurn, 950 sq ft, water	mos	1074	3/01	4c
Rental unit, 1 bedroom, with utilities	mos	735	4/01	41c
Rental unit, 2 bedroom, with utilities	mos	863	4/01	41c
Rental unit, 3 bedroom, with utilities	mos	1176	4/01	41c
Rental unit, 4 bedroom, with utilities	mos	1418	4/01	41c
Shelter, expenditures on	yr	10472	1999	30c
Insurance and Pensions				
Auto insurance premium	yr	1180.30	1999	57s
Life and other personal insurance purchases	yr	674	1999	30c
Pensions and Social Security, expenditures on	yr	4679	1999	30c
Personal insurance and pensions, expenditures on	yr	5353	1999	30c
Legal Fees				
Divorce, filing fee		80.00	4/01	35s
Driver's license fee	orig	20.00	1999	48s
Driver's license fee	renew	20.00	1999	48s

Washington, DC-MD-VA-WV - continued

Item	Per	Value	Date	Ref.
Personal Goods				
Personal care products and services purchases	yr	640	1999	30c
Shampoo, Alberto VO5	15 oz	1.44	3/01	4c
Toothpaste, Crest or Colgate	6-7 oz	2.19	3/01	4c
Personal Services				
Dry cleaning, man's 2-pc suit		7.55	3/01	4c
Man's haircut, barbershop, no styling		11.50	3/01	4c
Personal services, household, expenditures on	yr	258	1999	30r
Woman's shampoo, trim, blow-dry, no style-change		33.20	3/01	4c
Pets				
Pets, toys, and playground equipment, expenditures on	yr	306	1999	30r
Restaurant Food				
Cheeseburger, 1/4-lb, large fries, medium soft drink, excl tax		4.97	1999	40c
Chicken, fried, thigh and drumstick, KFC/Church's		2.81	3/01	4c
Hamburger with cheese, McDonald's	1/4 lb	2.25	3/01	4c
Pizza, Pizza Hut or Pizza Inn	11-12 in	9.99	3/01	4c
Taxes				
Federal income taxes paid	yr	2047	1999	30r
Personal taxes, expenditures on	yr	2554	1999	30r
Property taxes paid	yr	726	1999	30r
State and local income taxes paid	yr	363	1999	30r
Transportation				
Transportation, ACCRA Index		114.20	3/01	4c
Bus fare, one-way	trip	0.80	2000	1c
Bus fare, to central business district	1-way	1.60	3/01	4c
Cars and trucks, new, expenditures on	yr	1648	1999	30r
Cars and trucks, used, expenditures on	yr	1651	1999	30r
Commuter rail, one-way	trip	3.60	2000	2c
Gasoline and motor oil purchases	yr	1040	1999	30c
Heavy rail transit fare, one-way	trip	1.10	2000	2c
Maintenance and repair expenditures	yr	621	1999	30r
Public transportation, expenditures on	yr	755	1999	30c
Tire balance, computer or spin balance, front	wheel	8.67	3/01	4c
Transportation purchases	yr	8171	1999	30c
Vehicle expenses, miscellaneous, purchases	yr	2463	1999	30c
Vehicle insurance payments	yr	696	1999	30r
Vehicle purchases (net outlay)	yr	3914	1999	30c
Vehicle purchases (net outlay)	yr	3354	1999	30r
Vehicle rental, lease expenditures	yr	352	1999	30r
Travel				
Hotel rate, ave	day	140.62	1999	45c
Utilities				
Utilities, ACCRA Index		86.10	3/01	4c
Electrical bill, average	mos	56.50	9/00	9s
Electricity, expenditures on	yr	1115	1999	30r
Electricity, summer, 250 KWh	mos	12.79	2/96	97c
Electricity, summer, 500 KWh	mos	28.70	2/96	97c
Electricity, summer, 750 KWh	mos	50.25	2/96	97c
Electricity, summer, 1000 KWh	mos	71.81	2/96	97c
Electricity and other, mixed, 2400 sq ft, new home	mos	63.96	3/01	4c
Electricity cost, average	KWh	7.60	9/00	9s
Water and other public services, expenditures on	yr	298	1999	30r
Water price	100 cf	1.38	2000	109c
Water price, dwelling unit	mos	27.08	2000	109c
Weddings				
Wedding (national average cost)		19936	2000	33r
Wedding (regional average total cost)		16293	1997	110r
Attendants' gifts		321	1998	33r
Bridal attendants' apparel (5 persons)		824	2000	33r
Bride's headpiece/veil		173	1998	33r
Bride's wedding dress		859	1998	33r

Values are in dollars or fractions of dollars. In the column headed *Ref*, references are shown to sources. Each reference is followed by a letter. These refer to the geographical level for which data were reported: s=State, r=Region, and c=City or metro. The abbreviation *ex* is used to mean *except* or *excluding*; *exp* stands for expenditures. For other abbreviations and further explanations, please see the Introduction.

Item	Per	Value	Date	Ref.
Weddings				
Clergy, religious facility fee		242	1998	33r
Engagement ring		3177	1998	33r
Flowers		789	1998	33r
Groom's formalwear rental		99	2000	33r
Limousine		410	1998	33r
Marriage license cost		35.00	4/01	35s
Men's formalwear (ushers, best man)		469	2000	33r
Mother of bride apparel		241	2000	33r
Music		866	1998	33r
Photography and videography		1368	1998	33r
Rehearsal dinner		728	1998	33r
Wedding invitations and announcements		341	1998	33r
Wedding reception		7968	2000	33r
Wedding rings (bride and groom)		1060	1998	33r

Waterbury, CT

Item	Per	Value	Date	Ref.
Average annual expenditures	yr	37971	1999	30r
Alcoholic Beverages				
Alcoholic beverage purchases	yr	368	1999	30r
Wine, red and white table, all sizes, any origin	liter	9.64	7/01	11r
Appliances				
Major appliances, expenditures on	yr	194	1999	30r
Small appliances, housewares, expenditures on	yr	93	1999	30r
Banking and Money				
Mortgage interest and charges paid	yr	2622	1999	30r
Mortgage principal paid on owned property	yr	1262	1999	30r
Vehicle finance charges paid	yr	240	1999	30r
Charity				
Cash contributions, expenditures	yr	1001	1999	30r
Child Care				
Child raising cost, total, age 0-2	yr	8670	1999	60r
Child raising cost, total, age 3-5	yr	8910	1999	60r
Child raising cost, total, age 6-8	yr	9040	1999	60r
Child raising cost, total, age 9-11	yr	9100	1999	60r
Child raising cost, total, age 12-14	yr	9890	1999	60r
Child raising cost, total, age 15-17	yr	10010	1999	60r
Child's child care and education, age 0-2	yr	1070	1999	60r
Child's child care and education, age 3-5	yr	1190	1999	60r
Child's child care and education, age 6-8	yr	740	1999	60r
Child's child care and education, age 9-11	yr	470	1999	60r
Child's child care and education, age 12-14	yr	350	1999	60r
Child's child care and education, age 15-17	yr	590	1999	60r
Child's clothing, age 0-2	yr	480	1999	60r
Child's clothing, age 3-5	yr	470	1999	60r
Child's clothing, age 6-8	yr	520	1999	60r
Child's clothing, age 9-11	yr	570	1999	60r
Child's clothing, age 12-14	yr	970	1999	60r
Child's clothing, age 15-17	yr	870	1999	60r
Child's food, age 0-2	yr	1130	1999	60r
Child's food, age 3-5	yr	1290	1999	60r
Child's food, age 6-8	yr	1640	1999	60r
Child's food, age 9-11	yr	1930	1999	60r
Child's food, age 12-14	yr	1940	1999	60r
Child's food, age 15-17	yr	2150	1999	60r
Child's health care, age 0-2	yr	550	1999	60r
Child's health care, age 3-5	yr	530	1999	60r
Child's health care, age 6-8	yr	610	1999	60r
Child's health care, age 9-11	yr	650	1999	60r
Child's health care, age 12-14	yr	660	1999	60r
Child's health care, age 15-17	yr	690	1999	60r
Child's housing, age 0-2	yr	3555	1999	60r
Child's housing, age 3-5	yr	3530	1999	60r
Child's housing, age 6-8	yr	3490	1999	60r
Child's housing, age 9-11	yr	3340	1999	60r
Child's housing, age 12-14	yr	3530	1999	60r
Child's housing, age 15-17	yr	3140	1999	60r

Item	Per	Value	Date	Ref.
Child Care - continued				
Child's personal care, reading, age 0-2	yr	920	1999	60r
Child's personal care, reading, age 3-5	yr	950	1999	60r
Child's personal care, reading, age 6-8	yr	980	1999	60r
Child's personal care, reading, age 9-11	yr	1020	1999	60r
Child's personal care, reading, age 12-14	yr	1190	1999	60r
Child's personal care, reading, age 15-17	yr	970	1999	60r
Clothing				
Apparel and services purchases	yr	1831	1999	30r
Boys, 2 to 15, expenditures on	yr	92	1999	30r
Children under 2, expenditures on	yr	63	1999	30r
Footwear, expenditures on	yr	300	1999	30r
Girls, 2 to 15, expenditures on	yr	101	1999	30r
Men and boys, expenditures on	yr	446	1999	30r
Men, 16 and over, expenditures on	yr	354	1999	30r
Women, 16 and over, expenditures on	yr	584	1999	30r
Communications				
Cable modem installation, AT&T-BIS		150.00	6/99	103s
Cable modem installation, Cablevision Systems		150.00	6/99	103s
Cable modem installation, Cox		99.00-174.95	6/99	103s
Cable modem installation, Media One		100.00	6/99	103s
Cable modem rate, cable subscriber, AT&T-BIS	mos	39.95	6/99	103s
Cable modem rate, cable subscriber, Cablevision Systems	mos	44.95	6/99	103s
Cable modem rate, cable subscriber, Cox	mos	29.95-44.95	6/99	103s
Cable modem rate, cable subscriber, Media One	mos	34.95-39.95	6/99	103s
Cable modem rate, non-cable subscriber, Cablevision Systems	mos	54.95	6/99	103s
Cable modem rate, non-cable subscriber, Cox	mos	42.95-54.95	6/99	103s
Cable modem rate, non-cable subscriber, Media One	mos	49.95	6/99	103s
Phone line, single, business, field visit	inst.	65.00	12/97	17s
Phone line, single, business, no field visit	inst.	65.00	12/97	17s
Phone line, single, residence, field visit	inst.	45.00	12/97	17s
Phone line, single, residence, no field visit	inst.	45.00	12/97	17s
Postage and stationery, expenditures on	yr	138	1999	30r
Postal rate, express mail, up to half-pound		12.45	7/01	108r
Postal rate, letter, first class, first ounce		0.34	7/01	108r
Postal rate, letter, two ounces		0.57	7/01	108r
Postal rate, post card		0.21	7/01	108r
Postal rate, priority mail, two pounds		3.95	7/01	108r
Postal rate, priority mail, up to one pound		3.50	7/01	108r
Telephone bill, business, basic rate	mos	36.43	12/97	18c
Telephone bill, residential, basic rate	mos	13.53	12/97	18c
Telephone services, expenditures on	yr	830	1999	30r
Education				
Board, 4-year private college/university	yr	2744	1996	38s
Board, 4-year public college/university	yr	2299	1996	38s
Education expenditures	yr	877	1999	30r
Room, 4-year private college/university	yr	3621	1996	38s
Room, 4-year public college/university	yr	2609	1996	38s
Total cost, 4-year private college/university	yr	23011	1996	38s
Total cost, 4-year public college/university	yr	8753	1996	38s
Tuition, 2-year public college/university, in state	yr	1646	1996	38s
Tuition, 4-year private college/university, in state	yr	16646	1996	38s
Tuition, 4-year public college/university	yr	3845	1996	38s
Energy and Fuels				
Electricity	KWh	0.12	7/01	11r
Fuel oil #2	gal	1.31	7/01	11r
Fuel oil and other fuels, expenditures on	yr	207	1999	30r
Gas, cooking, winter, 10 therms	mos	17.20	2/96	98c
Gas, cooking, winter, 30 therms	mos	35.41	2/96	98c
Gas, cooking, winter, 50 therms	mos	53.62	2/96	98c

Values are in dollars or fractions of dollars. In the column headed *Ref*, references are shown to sources. Each reference is followed by a letter. These refer to the geographical level for which data were reported: s=State, r=Region, and c=City or metro. The abbreviation *ex* is used to mean *except* or *excluding*; *exp* stands for *expenditures*. For other abbreviations and further explanations, please see the Introduction.

Waterbury, CT - continued

Item	Per	Value	Date	Ref.
Energy and Fuels				
Gas, heating, winter, average use	mos	177.80	2/96	98c
Gas, natural, commercial rate	1000 cf	7.08	11/00	88s
Gasoline, all types	gal	1.80	7/01	11r
Gasoline, unleaded midgrade	gal	1.85	7/01	11r
Gasoline, unleaded premium	gal	1.91	7/01	11r
Gasoline, unleaded regular	gal	1.71	7/01	11r
Natural gas, expenditures on	yr	368	1999	30r
Utility (piped) gas, therm		1.08	7/01	11r
Utility (piped) gas, 40 therms		50.87	7/01	11r
Utility (piped) gas, 100 therms		111.06	7/01	11r
Entertainment				
Entertainment purchases	yr	1821	1999	30r
Fees and admissions paid	yr	511	1999	30r
Hockey equipment, girls' hockey		800	2001	101s
Television, radios, sound equipment, expenditures on	yr	650	1999	30r
Funerals				
Total cost of funeral		5776.91	1/99	78r
Acknowledgement cards		14.47	1/99	78r
Casket		2090.19	1/99	78r
Cosmetology, hair, other preparation		132.92	1/99	78r
Embalming		377.33	1/99	78r
Funeral at funeral home		352.43	1/99	78r
Hearse (local)		185.55	1/99	78r
Professional service charges		1289.95	1/99	78r
Service car/van		87.42	1/99	78r
Transfer of remains to funeral home		175.48	1/99	78r
Vault		729.40	1/99	78r
Visitation/viewing		341.76	1/99	78r
Groceries				
Apples, red delicious	lb	0.95	7/01	11r
Bacon, sliced	lb	3.44	7/01	11r
Bakery products, expenditures on	yr	310	1999	30r
Bananas	lb	0.55	7/01	11r
Beef, expenditures on	yr	236	1999	30r
Bread, white, pan	lb	1.09	7/01	11r
Butter, yoghurt, cheese, etc, expenditures on	yr	214	1999	30r
Cereals and bakery product purchases	yr	474	1999	30r
Cereals and cereal products, expenditures on	yr	164	1999	30r
Chicken legs, bone-in	lb	1.23	7/01	11r
Chicken, fresh, whole	lb	1.13	7/01	11r
Chuck roast, U.S. choice, boneless	lb	2.79	7/01	11r
Coffee, 100%, ground roast, all sizes	lb	3.40	7/01	11r
Dairy product purchases	yr	342	1999	30r
Eggs, expenditures on	yr	34	1999	30r
Eggs, grade A, large	dozen	0.82	7/01	11r
Fats and oils, expenditures on	yr	80	1999	30r
Fish and seafood, expenditures on	yr	123	1999	30r
Food (excl fruit and vegetables), eaten at home, purchases	yr	838	1999	30r
Food cooked on trips, expenditures on	yr	48	1999	30r
Food purchases	yr	5314	1999	30r
Food purchases, eaten away from home	yr	2313	1999	30r
Food purchases, food eaten at home	yr	3001	1999	30r
Fresh fruits, expenditures on	yr	169	1999	30r
Fresh milk and cream, expenditures on	yr	128	1999	30r
Fresh vegetables, expenditures on	yr	164	1999	30r
Grapefruit	lb	0.67	7/01	11r
Grapes, Thompson, seedless	lb	2.18	7/01	11r
Ground beef, lean and extra lean	lb	2.66	7/01	11r
Ground chuck, 100% beef	lb	2.04	7/01	11r
Lettuce, iceberg	lb	0.76	7/01	11r
Meats, poultry, fish, and egg purchases	yr	808	1999	30r
Nonalcoholic beverages, expenditures on	yr	225	1999	30r
Orange juice, frozen concentrate	16 oz	1.88	7/01	11r
Oranges, Navel	lb	0.79	7/01	11r
Oranges, Valencia	lb	0.56	7/01	11r
Peaches	lb	1.16	7/01	11r
Peanut butter, creamy, all sizes	lb	2.01	7/01	11r
Pears, Anjou	lb	1.16	7/01	11r

Waterbury, CT - continued

Item	Per	Value	Date	Ref.
Groceries - continued				
Pork chops, center cut, bone-in	lb	3.57	7/01	11r
Pork, expenditures on	yr	146	1999	30r
Potato chips	16 oz	3.37	7/01	11r
Potatoes, white, all types	lb	0.42	7/01	11r
Poultry, expenditures on	yr	158	1999	30r
Processed fruits, expenditures on	yr	124	1999	30r
Processed vegetables, expenditures on	yr	82	1999	30r
Round roast, U.S. choice, boneless	lb	3.04	7/01	11r
Spaghetti and macaroni	lb	1.04	7/01	11r
Steak, sirloin, U.S. choice, boneless	lb	5.39	7/01	11r
Strawberries, dry pint	12 oz	1.51	7/01	11r
Sugar and other sweets, expenditures on	yr	110	1999	30r
Sugar, white, 33-80 ounce package	lb	0.46	7/01	11r
Sugar, white, all sizes	lb	0.47	7/01	11r
Tobacco products and smoking supplies purchases	yr	309	1999	30r
Yogurt, natural, fruit flavored	8 oz	0.79	7/01	11r
Goods and Services				
B&B Japanese maple (acer japonicum)	gal	38.99-125.00	4/00	93r
Boxwood (buxus)	2 gal	15.99-49.95	4/00	93r
Daylilly (hemerocallis)	gal	4.95	4/00	93r
Flat of annuals		8.00-14.99	4/00	93r
Fountain grass (pennisetum)	gal	6.99-9.99	4/00	93r
Hanging basket (10 in)		12.95-19.99	4/00	93r
Hardy geranium (geranium)	gal	6.95-7.99	4/00	93r
Hosta (hosta)	gal	4.95	4/00	93r
Lilac (syrubga vulgaris)	2 gal	17.99-74.95	4/00	93r
Miscellaneous purchases	yr	872	1999	30r
Rhododendron (rhododendron)	2 gal	23.99-54.95	4/00	93r
Sage (salvia)	gal	6.95-7.99	4/00	93r
Wintercreeper euonymus (euonymus fortunei)	2 gal	14.99-23.95	4/00	93r
Hunting license	yr	10.00	4/01	34s
Health Care				
Cardiac catheterization, ave hospital/ physician charges		14090	1998	77s
Childbirth, Cesarean delivery		14716	1997	13r
Childbirth, vaginal delivery		8541	1997	13r
Drugs, expenditures on	yr	296	1999	30r
Health care purchases	yr	1788	1999	30r
Health insurance expenditures	yr	875	1999	30r
Hysterectomy, laproscopically-assisted, ave hospital/physician charges		11610	1998	76s
Hysterectomy, vaginal, ave hospital and physician charges		12780	1998	76s
Medicaid dispensing fee		4.10	1999	87s
Medical services expenditures	yr	516	1999	30r
Medical supplies, expenditures on	yr	102	1999	30r
Plastic surgery, breast augmentation		4232	2000	7r
Plastic surgery, breast lift		4605	2000	7r
Plastic surgery, facelift		6964	2000	7r
Plastic surgery, hair transplantation		4193	2000	7r
Plastic surgery, lip augmentation		1675	2000	7r
Plastic surgery, lower body lift		6611	2000	7r
Plastic surgery, thigh lift		4751	2000	7r
Household Goods				
Floor coverings, expenditures on	yr	59	1999	30r
Furniture, expenditures on	yr	388	1999	30r
Household furnishings and equipment purchases	yr	1567	1999	30r
Household textiles, expenditures on	yr	112	1999	30r

Values are in dollars or fractions of dollars. In the column headed *Ref*, references are shown to sources. Each reference is followed by a letter. These refer to the geographical level for which data were reported: s=State, r=Region, and c=City or metro. The abbreviation *ex* is used to mean *except* or *excluding*; *exp* stands for *expenditures*. For other abbreviations and further explanations, please see the Introduction.

Waterbury, CT - continued

Item	Per	Value	Date	Ref.
Household Goods				
Laundry and cleaning supplies, expenditures on	yr	104	1999	30r
Housing				
Home price, existing, ave		180800	10/00	90r
Home value, median		157000	2001	53s
Household operation expenditures	yr	581	1999	30r
Housekeeping supplies purchases	yr	474	1999	30r
Lodging expenditures	yr	550	1999	30r
Maintenance, repairs, insurance expenditures	yr	835	1999	30r
Monthly rental value of owned home	mos	663	1999	30r
Owned dwellings, expenditures own	yr	5209	1999	30r
Rent expenditures	yr	2390	1999	30r
Rental unit, 1 bedroom, with utilities	mos	630	4/01	41c
Rental unit, 2 bedroom, with utilities	mos	781	4/01	41c
Rental unit, 3 bedroom, with utilities	mos	973	4/01	41c
Rental unit, 4 bedroom, with utilities	mos	1091	4/01	41c
Shelter, expenditures on	yr	8149	1999	30r
Insurance and Pensions				
Auto insurance premium	yr	982.00	1999	57s
Life and other personal insurance purchases	yr	424	1999	30r
Pensions and Social Security, expenditures on	yr	3037	1999	30r
Legal Fees				
Divorce, filing fee		150.00	4/01	35s
Driver's license fee	renew	28.50	1999	48s
Driver's license fee	orig	43.50	1999	48s
Personal Goods				
Personal care products and services purchases	yr	399	1999	30r
Personal Services				
Personal services, household, expenditures on	yr	271	1999	30r
Pets				
Pets, toys, and playground equipment, expenditures on	yr	325	1999	30r
Taxes				
Federal income taxes paid	yr	2606	1999	30r
Personal taxes, expenditures on	yr	3567	1999	30r
Property taxes paid	yr	1752	1999	30r
State and local income taxes paid	yr	694	1999	30r
Transportation				
Cars and trucks, new, expenditures on	yr	1496	1999	30r
Cars and trucks, used, expenditures on	yr	1251	1999	30r
Diesel at the pump	gal	1.36	10/99	73s
Gasoline and motor oil purchases	yr	901	1999	30r
Gasoline before-tax price (cents)	gal	117.10	10/00	43s
Maintenance and repair expenditures	yr	618	1999	30r
Public transportation, expenditures on	yr	575	1999	30r
Transportation purchases	yr	6503	1999	30r
Vehicle expenses, miscellaneous, purchases	yr	2266	1999	30r
Vehicle insurance payments	yr	824	1999	30r
Vehicle purchases (net outlay)	yr	2761	1999	30r
Vehicle rental, lease expenditures	yr	584	1999	30r
Utilities				
Electrical bill, average	mos	81.50	9/00	9s
Electricity, expenditures on	yr	837	1999	30r
Electricity cost, average	KWh	9.47	9/00	9s
Utilities, fuels, and public services purchased	yr	2457	1999	30r
Water and other public services, expenditures on	yr	215	1999	30r
Weddings				
Wedding (national average cost)		19936	2000	33r
Wedding (regional average total cost)		29454	1997	110r
Attendants' gifts		321	1998	33r
Bridal attendants' apparel (5 persons)		824	2000	33r
Bride's headpiece/veil		173	1998	33r

Waterbury, CT - continued

Item	Per	Value	Date	Ref.
Weddings - continued				
Bride's wedding dress		859	1998	33r
Clergy, religious facility fee		242	1998	33r
Engagement ring		3177	1998	33r
Flowers		789	1998	33r
Groom's formalwear rental		99	2000	33r
Limousine		410	1998	33r
Marriage license cost		30.00	4/01	35s
Men's formalwear (ushers, best man)		469	2000	33r
Mother of bride apparel		241	2000	33r
Music		866	1998	33r
Photography and videography		1368	1998	33r
Rehearsal dinner		728	1998	33r
Wedding invitations and announcements		341	1998	33r
Wedding reception		7968	2000	33r
Wedding rings (bride and groom)		1060	1998	33r

Waterloo-Cedar Falls, IA

Item	Per	Value	Date	Ref.
Average annual expenditures	yr	35369	1999	30r
Composite, ACCRA index		97.60	3/01	4c
Alcoholic Beverages				
Alcoholic beverage purchases	yr	304	1999	30r
Beer, Heineken, 12-oz, ex deposit	6	7.15	3/01	4c
J & B Scotch	750-ml	21.55	3/01	4c
Malt beverages, all types, all sizes, any origin	16 oz	0.93	7/01	11r
Wine, Livingston or Gallo, Chablis blanc	1.5 liter	5.25	3/01	4c
Wine, red and white table, all sizes, any origin	liter	7.04	7/01	11r
Appliances				
Appliance repair, service call, washing machine	min lab chg	36.90	3/01	4c
Major appliances, expenditures on	yr	165	1999	30r
Small appliances, housewares, expenditures on	yr	90	1999	30r
Banking and Money				
Mortgage interest and charges paid	yr	2277	1999	30r
Mortgage principal paid on owned property	yr	1230	1999	30r
Mortgage rate, incl. points and orig. fee, 30-yr. conv. fixed or ARM	mos	6.82	3/01	4c
Vehicle finance charges paid	yr	328	1999	30r
Charity				
Cash contributions, expenditures	yr	1126	1999	30r
Child Care				
Child raising cost, total, age 0-2	yr	7890	1999	60r
Child raising cost, total, age 3-5	yr	8130	1999	60r
Child raising cost, total, age 6-8	yr	8170	1999	60r
Child raising cost, total, age 9-11	yr	8190	1999	60r
Child raising cost, total, age 12-14	yr	8890	1999	60r
Child raising cost, total, age 15-17	yr	9050	1999	60r
Child's child care and education, age 0-2	yr	1240	1999	60r
Child's child care and education, age 3-5	yr	1370	1999	60r
Child's child care and education, age 6-8	yr	880	1999	60r
Child's child care and education, age 9-11	yr	570	1999	60r
Child's child care and education, age 12-14	yr	420	1999	60r
Child's child care and education, age 15-17	yr	720	1999	60r
Child's clothing, age 0-2	yr	410	1999	60r
Child's clothing, age 3-5	yr	400	1999	60r
Child's clothing, age 6-8	yr	450	1999	60r
Child's clothing, age 9-11	yr	500	1999	60r
Child's clothing, age 12-14	yr	840	1999	60r
Child's clothing, age 15-17	yr	740	1999	60r
Child's food, age 0-2	yr	960	1999	60r
Child's food, age 3-5	yr	1120	1999	60r
Child's food, age 6-8	yr	1430	1999	60r
Child's food, age 9-11	yr	1710	1999	60r
Child's food, age 12-14	yr	1710	1999	60r
Child's food, age 15-17	yr	1920	1999	60r
Child's health care, age 0-2	yr	520	1999	60r
Child's health care, age 3-5	yr	500	1999	60r

Values are in dollars or fractions of dollars. In the column headed *Ref*, references are shown to sources. Each reference is followed by a letter. These refer to the geographical level for which data were reported: s=State, r=Region, and c=City or metro. The abbreviation *ex* is used to mean *except* or *excluding*; *exp* stands for *expenditures*. For other abbreviations and further explanations, please see the Introduction.

Waterloo-Cedar Falls, IA - continued

Item	Per	Value	Date	Ref.
Child Care				
Child's health care, age 6-8	yr	570	1999	60r
Child's health care, age 9-11	yr	610	1999	60r
Child's health care, age 12-14	yr	630	1999	60r
Child's health care, age 15-17	yr	650	1999	60r
Child's housing, age 0-2	yr	2860	1999	60r
Child's housing, age 3-5	yr	2840	1999	60r
Child's housing, age 6-8	yr	2800	1999	60r
Child's housing, age 9-11	yr	2650	1999	60r
Child's housing, age 12-14	yr	2840	1999	60r
Child's housing, age 15-17	yr	2440	1999	60r
Child's personal care, reading, age 0-2	yr	880	1999	60r
Child's personal care, reading, age 3-5	yr	900	1999	60r
Child's personal care, reading, age 6-8	yr	930	1999	60r
Child's personal care, reading, age 9-11	yr	970	1999	60r
Child's personal care, reading, age 12-14	yr	1150	1999	60r
Child's personal care, reading, age 15-17	yr	920	1999	60r
Clothing				
Apparel and services purchases	yr	1607	1999	30r
Boys' brief, cotton	3	3.75	3/01	4c
Boys, 2 to 15, expenditures on	yr	91	1999	30r
Children under 2, expenditures on	yr	59	1999	30r
Footwear, expenditures on	yr	285	1999	30r
Girls, 2 to 15, expenditures on	yr	116	1999	30r
Men and boys, expenditures on	yr	433	1999	30r
Men, 16 and over, expenditures on	yr	341	1999	30r
Shirt, man's dress shirt		29.70	3/01	4c
Slacks, man's "No Wrinkles" khaki		41.00	3/01	4c
Women, 16 and over, expenditures on	yr	490	1999	30r
Communications				
Newspaper subscription, daily and Sunday delivery	mos	21.74	3/01	4c
Phone line, single, business, field visit	inst.	50.00	12/97	17s
Phone line, single, business, no field visit	inst.	50.00	12/97	17s
Phone line, single, residence, field visit	inst.	35.00	12/97	17s
Phone line, single, residence, no field visit	inst.	35.00	12/97	17s
Postage and stationery, expenditures on	yr	140	1999	30r
Postal rate, express mail, up to half-pound		12.45	7/01	108r
Postal rate, letter, first class, first ounce		0.34	7/01	108r
Postal rate, letter, two ounces		0.57	7/01	108r
Postal rate, post card		0.21	7/01	108r
Postal rate, priority mail, two pounds		3.95	7/01	108r
Postal rate, priority mail, up to one pound		3.50	7/01	108r
Telephone bill, family of three	mos	19.64	3/01	4c
Telephone services, expenditures on	yr	830	1999	30r
Education				
Board, 4-year private college/university	yr	2138	1996	38s
Board, 4-year public college/university	yr	1688	1996	38s
Education expenditures	yr	583	1999	30r
Room, 4-year private college/university	yr	1864	1996	38s
Room, 4-year public college/university	yr	1693	1996	38s
Total cost, 4-year private college/university	yr	15934	1996	38s
Total cost, 4-year public college/university	yr	5945	1996	38s
Tuition, 2-year public college/university, in state	yr	1782	1996	38s
Tuition, 4-year private college/university, in state	yr	11932	1996	38s
Tuition, 4-year public college/university	yr	2565	1996	38s
Energy and Fuels				
Electricity	500 KWhs	46.59	7/01	11r
Energy, combined forms, 2400 sq ft	mos	153.17	3/01	4c
Energy, exc. electricity, 2400 sq ft	mos	107.32	3/01	4c
Fuel oil #2	gal	1.27	7/01	11r
Fuel oil and other fuels, expenditures on	yr	68	1999	30r
Gas, natural, commercial rate	1000 cf	7.18	11/00	88s
Gas, regular unleaded, cash, self-service	gal	1.37	3/01	4c
Gasoline, unleaded midgrade	gal	1.79	7/01	11r
Gasoline, unleaded premium	gal	1.86	7/01	11r
Gasoline, unleaded regular	gal	1.58	7/01	11r
Natural gas, expenditures on	yr	389	1999	30r

Waterloo-Cedar Falls, IA - continued

Item	Per	Value	Date	Ref.
Energy and Fuels - continued				
Utility (piped) gas, therm		0.81	7/01	11r
Utility (piped) gas, 40 therms		38.01	7/01	11r
Utility (piped) gas, 100 therms		81.75	7/01	11r
Entertainment				
Bowling, Saturday evening rate	line	2.67	3/01	4c
Entertainment purchases	yr	1984	1999	30r
Fees and admissions paid	yr	444	1999	30r
Monopoly game, Parker Brothers', No. 9	game	10.47	3/01	4c
Movie, first-run, Saturday, evening	adm.	6.25	3/01	4c
Television, radios, sound equipment, expenditures on	yr	580	1999	30r
Tennis balls, yellow, Wilson or Penn, 3	can	2.07	3/01	4c
Funerals				
Cosmetology, hair, other preparation		178.32	1/99	78r
Embalming		408.19	1/99	78r
Funeral at funeral home		362.13	1/99	78r
Professional service charges		1375.51	1/99	78r
Transfer of remains to funeral home		155.92	1/99	78r
Visitation/viewing		294.38	1/99	78r
Groceries				
Groceries, ACCRA Index		91.60	3/01	4c
Antibiotic ointment, Polysporin	0.5 oz	4.74	3/01	4c
Baby food, strained vegetables or fruit, lowest price	4-4.5 oz	0.42	3/01	4c
Bacon, sliced	lb	3.15	7/01	11r
Bakery products, expenditures on	yr	281	1999	30r
Bananas	lb	0.42	3/01	4c
Bananas	lb	0.48	7/01	11r
Beans, dried, any type, all sizes	lb	0.61	7/01	11r
Beef for stew, boneless	lb	3.08	7/01	11r
Beef or hamburger, ground	lb	1.48	3/01	4c
Beef, expenditures on	yr	217	1999	30r
Bologna, all beef or mixed	lb	2.52	7/01	11r
Bread, white	loaf	0.89	3/01	4c
Bread, white, pan	lb	1.06	7/01	11r
Broccoli	lb	0.91	7/01	11r
Butter, salted, grade AA, stick	lb	3.04	7/01	11r
Butter, yoghurt, cheese, etc, expenditures on	yr	183	1999	30r
Cereals and bakery product purchases	yr	430	1999	30r
Cereals and cereal products, expenditures on	yr	149	1999	30r
Cheese, Kraft grated Parmesan	8 oz	3.75	3/01	4c
Chicken, fresh, whole	lb	1.07	7/01	11r
Chicken, whole fryer	lb	0.83	3/01	4c
Chops, boneless,	lb	3.64	7/01	11r
Chuck roast, U.S. choice, boneless	lb	2.47	7/01	11r
Cigarettes, Winston, Kings	carton	30.15	3/01	4c
Coffee, 100%, ground roast, all sizes	lb	2.69	7/01	11r
Coffee, vacuum-packed	13 oz	2.25	3/01	4c
Cookies, chocolate chip	lb	2.87	7/01	11r
Corn Flakes, Kellogg's or Post Toasties	18 oz	2.07	3/01	4c
Corn, frozen, whole kernel, lowest price	16 oz	1.06	3/01	4c
Dairy product purchases	yr	304	1999	30r
Eggs, expenditures on	yr	26	1999	30r
Eggs, Grade A or AA	dozen	1.08	3/01	4c
Eggs, grade A, large	dozen	0.88	7/01	11r
Fats and oils, expenditures on	yr	75	1999	30r
Fish and seafood, expenditures on	yr	72	1999	30r
Food (excl fruit and vegetables), eaten at home, purchases	yr	887	1999	30r
Food cooked on trips, expenditures on	yr	44	1999	30r
Food purchases	yr	4802	1999	30r
Food purchases, eaten away from home	yr	2069	1999	30r
Food purchases, food eaten at home	yr	2733	1999	30r
Fresh fruits, expenditures on	yr	138	1999	30r
Fresh milk and cream, expenditures on	yr	120	1999	30r
Fresh vegetables, expenditures on	yr	126	1999	30r
Grapefruit	lb	0.66	7/01	11r
Grapes, Thompson, seedless	lb	1.64	7/01	11r
Ground beef, 100% beef	lb	1.64	7/01	11r
Ground beef, lean and extra lean	lb	2.16	7/01	11r

Values are in dollars or fractions of dollars. In the column headed *Ref*, references are shown to sources. Each reference is followed by a letter. These refer to the geographical level for which data were reported: s=State, r=Region, and c=City or metro. The abbreviation *ex* is used to mean *except* or *excluding*; *exp* stands for *expenditures*. For other abbreviations and further explanations, please see the Introduction.

Waterloo-Cedar Falls, IA - continued

Item	Per	Value	Date	Ref.
Groceries				
Ground chuck, 100% beef	lb	2.13	7/01	11r
Ham, boneless, excl canned	lb	2.62	7/01	11r
Ice cream, prepackaged, bulk, regular	1/2 gal	3.35	7/01	11r
Lemons	lb	1.19	7/01	11r
Lettuce, iceberg	head	0.91	3/01	4c
Lettuce, iceberg	lb	0.73	7/01	11r
Margarine, Blue Bonnet or Parkay, stick	lb	0.50	3/01	4c
Margarine, soft, tubs	lb	0.89	7/01	11r
Meats, poultry, fish, and egg purchases	yr	671	1999	30r
Milk, fresh, whole, fortified	gal	2.71	7/01	11r
Milk, whole	1/2 gal	1.41	3/01	4c
Nonalcoholic beverages, expenditures on	yr	239	1999	30r
Orange juice, Minute Maid frozen	12 oz	1.56	3/01	4c
Oranges, Navel	lb	0.80	7/01	11r
Oranges, Valencia	lb	0.66	7/01	11r
Peaches, halves or slices, Hunt's, Del Monte, or Libby's	29 oz	1.55	3/01	4c
Pears, Anjou	lb	0.93	7/01	11r
Peas, green, Del Monte or Green Giant	15 oz	0.74	3/01	4c
Pork chops, center cut, bone-in	lb	3.63	7/01	11r
Pork, expenditures on	yr	150	1999	30r
Potato chips	16 oz	3.52	7/01	11r
Potatoes, frozen, french fried	lb	1.08	7/01	11r
Potatoes, white or red	10 lb	2.23	3/01	4c
Potatoes, white, all types	lb	0.33	7/01	11r
Poultry, expenditures on	yr	108	1999	30r
Processed fruits, expenditures on	yr	98	1999	30r
Processed vegetables, expenditures on	yr	80	1999	30r
Round roast, U.S. choice, boneless	lb	3.07	7/01	11r
Round steak, graded and ungraded, excl U.S. prime and choice	lb	3.41	7/01	11r
Sausage, Jimmy Dean/Owens pork	lb	3.00	3/01	4c
Shortening, vegetable oil blends	lb	1.13	7/01	11r
Shortening, vegetable, Crisco	3 lb	2.69	3/01	4c
Soft drink, Coca Cola, ex deposit	2 liter	1.17	3/01	4c
Spaghetti and macaroni	lb	0.80	7/01	11r
Steak, round, U.S. choice, boneless	lb	3.23	7/01	11r
Steak, T-bone	lb	6.42	3/01	4c
Steak, T-bone, U.S. choice, bone-in	lb	6.68	7/01	11r
Strawberries, dry pint	12 oz	1.32	7/01	11r
Sugar and other sweets, expenditures on	yr	114	1999	30r
Sugar, cane or beet	4 lbs	1.44	3/01	4c
Sugar, white, 33-80 ounce package	lb	0.42	7/01	11r
Sugar, white, all sizes	lb	0.43	7/01	11r
Tobacco products and smoking supplies purchases	yr	331	1999	30r
Tomatoes, field grown	lb	1.46	7/01	11r
Tomatoes, Hunt's or Del Monte	14.5 oz	0.81	3/01	4c
Tuna, chunk, light	6 oz	0.56	3/01	4c
Tuna, light, chunk	lb	1.80	7/01	11r
Turkey, frozen, whole	lb	1.15	7/01	11r
Goods and Services				
Miscellaneous goods and services, ACCRA Index		99.10	3/01	4c
B&B Japanese maple (acer japonicum)	gal	29.99-169.99	4/00	93r
Boxwood (buxus)	2 gal	18.99-39.99	4/00	93r
Daylily (hemerocallis)	gal	4.99-25.00	4/00	93r
Flat of annuals		11.98-24.99	4/00	93r
Fountain grass (pennisetum)	gal	5.98-12.98	4/00	93r
Hanging basket (10 in)		12.99-27.99	4/00	93r
Hardy geranium (geranium)	gal	7.99-9.99	4/00	93r
Hosta (hosta)	gal	6.00-25.00	4/00	93r
Lilac (syrubga vulgaris)	2 gal	14.99-24.99	4/00	93r

Waterloo-Cedar Falls, IA - continued

Item	Per	Value	Date	Ref.
Goods and Services - continued				
Miscellaneous purchases	yr	865	1999	30r
Rhododendron (rhododendron)	2 gal	23.98-42.99	4/00	93r
Sage (salvia)	gal	6.00-9.99	4/00	93r
Wintercreeper euonymus (euonymus fortunei)	2 gal	16.00-169.99	4/00	93r
Hunting license	yr	16.00	4/01	34s
Health Care				
Health care, ACCRA Index		93.00	3/01	4c
Cardiac catheterization, ave hospital/ physician charges		8810	1998	77s
Childbirth, Cesarean delivery		10722	1997	13r
Childbirth, vaginal delivery		6223	1997	13r
Dentist's fee, adult teeth cleaning and periodic oral exam	visit	61.20	3/01	4c
Doctor's fee, routine exam, established patient	visit	55.60	3/01	4c
Drugs, expenditures on	yr	394	1999	30r
Health care purchases	yr	2048	1999	30r
Health insurance expenditures	yr	978	1999	30r
Hospital care, private room	day	518.62	3/01	4c
Hysterectomy, laproscopically-assisted, ave hospital/physician charges		8620	1998	76s
Hysterectomy, vaginal, ave hospital and physician charges		6630	1998	76s
Medicaid dispensing fee		4.10-6.38	1999	87s
Medical services expenditures	yr	554	1999	30r
Medical supplies, expenditures on	yr	122	1999	30r
Plastic surgery, breast augmentation		3184	2000	7r
Plastic surgery, breast lift		3585	2000	7r
Plastic surgery, facelift		4999	2000	7r
Plastic surgery, hair transplantation		3105	2000	7r
Plastic surgery, lip augmentation		1290	2000	7r
Plastic surgery, lower body lift		8135	2000	7r
Plastic surgery, thigh lift		3839	2000	7r
Household Goods				
Dishwashing powder, Cascade	50 oz	3.31	3/01	4c
Floor coverings, expenditures on	yr	52	1999	30r
Furniture, expenditures on	yr	344	1999	30r
Household furnishings and equipment purchases	yr	1475	1999	30r
Household textiles, expenditures on	yr	109	1999	30r
Laundry and cleaning supplies, expenditures on	yr	134	1999	30r
Tissues, facial, Kleenex brand	175	1.07	3/01	4c
Housing				
Housing, ACCRA Index		91.90	3/01	4c
Home price, existing, ave		144400	10/00	90r
Home value, median		100000	2001	53s
House, 2400 sq ft, 8000 sq ft lot, new, urban, utilities	total	198394	3/01	4c
House payment, principal and interest, 25% down payment	mos	972	3/01	4c
Household operation expenditures	yr	542	1999	30r
Housekeeping supplies purchases	yr	508	1999	30r
Lodging expenditures	yr	430	1999	30r
Maintenance, repairs, insurance expenditures	yr	853	1999	30r
Monthly rental value of owned home	mos	547	1999	30r
Owned dwellings, expenditures own	yr	4282	1999	30r
Rent expenditures	yr	1558	1999	30r
Rent, apartment, 2 br, 1 1/2-2 baths, unfurn, 950 sq ft, water	mos	571	3/01	4c
Rental unit, 1 bedroom, with utilities	mos	418	4/01	41c
Rental unit, 2 bedroom, with utilities	mos	522	4/01	41c
Rental unit, 3 bedroom, with utilities	mos	695	4/01	41c
Rental unit, 4 bedroom, with utilities	mos	817	4/01	41c
Shelter, expenditures on	yr	6270	1999	30r

Values are in dollars or fractions of dollars. In the column headed *Ref*, references are shown to sources. Each reference is followed by a letter. These refer to the geographical level for which data were reported: s=State, r=Region, and c=City or metro. The abbreviation *ex* is used to mean *except* or *excluding; exp* stands for *expenditures.* For other abbreviations and further explanations, please see the Introduction.

Waterloo-Cedar Falls, IA - continued

Item	Per	Value	Date	Ref.
Insurance and Pensions				
Auto insurance premium	yr	520.76	1999	57s
Life and other personal insurance purchases	yr	387	1999	30r
Pensions and Social Security, expenditures on	yr	2968	1999	30r
Legal Fees				
Divorce, filing fee		110.00	4/01	35s
Driver's license fee	orig	16.00	1999	48s
Driver's license fee	renew	16.00	1999	48s
Personal Goods				
Personal care products and services purchases	yr	385	1999	30r
Shampoo, Alberto VO5	15 oz	1.01	3/01	4c
Toothpaste, Crest or Colgate	6-7 oz	1.90	3/01	4c
Personal Services				
Dry cleaning, man's 2-pc suit		6.80	3/01	4c
Man's haircut, barbershop, no styling		9.59	3/01	4c
Personal services, household, expenditures on	yr	300	1999	30r
Woman's shampoo, trim, blow-dry, no style-change		16.80	3/01	4c
Pets				
Pets, toys, and playground equipment, expenditures on	yr	375	1999	30r
Restaurant Food				
Chicken, fried, thigh and drumstick, KFC/Church's		2.46	3/01	4c
Hamburger with cheese, McDonald's	1/4 lb	2.09	3/01	4c
Pizza, Pizza Hut or Pizza Inn	11-12 in	8.99	3/01	4c
Taxes				
Federal income taxes paid	yr	2326	1999	30r
Personal taxes, expenditures on	yr	3223	1999	30r
Property taxes paid	yr	1152	1999	30r
State and local income taxes paid	yr	753	1999	30r
Transportation				
Transportation, ACCRA Index		101.60	3/01	4c
Bus fare, to central business district	1-way	1.50	3/01	4c
Cars and trucks, new, expenditures on	yr	1280	1999	30r
Cars and trucks, used, expenditures on	yr	1763	1999	30r
Diesel at the pump	gal	1.25	10/99	73s
Gasoline and motor oil purchases	yr	1036	1999	30r
Gasoline before-tax price (cents)	gal	112.30	10/00	43s
Maintenance and repair expenditures	yr	594	1999	30r
Public transportation, expenditures on	yr	341	1999	30r
Tire balance, computer or spin balance, front	wheel	7.69	3/01	4c
Transportation purchases	yr	6617	1999	30r
Vehicle expenses, miscellaneous, purchases	yr	2159	1999	30r
Vehicle insurance payments	yr	701	1999	30r
Vehicle purchases (net outlay)	yr	3081	1999	30r
Vehicle rental, lease expenditures	yr	536	1999	30r
Utilities				
Utilities, ACCRA Index		120.70	3/01	4c
Electrical bill, average	mos	67.25	9/00	9s
Electricity, expenditures on	yr	841	1999	30r
Electricity and other, mixed, 2400 sq ft, new home	mos	45.85	3/01	4c
Electricity cost, average	KWh	5.90	9/00	9s
Utilities, fuels, and public services purchased	yr	2401	1999	30r
Water and other public services, expenditures on	yr	273	1999	30r
Weddings				
Wedding (national average cost)		19936	2000	33r
Wedding (regional average total cost)		16195	1997	110r
Attendants' gifts		321	1998	33r
Bridal attendants' apparel (5 persons)		824	2000	33r
Bride's headpiece/veil		173	1998	33r
Bride's wedding dress		859	1998	33r
Clergy, religious facility fee		242	1998	33r

Waterloo-Cedar Falls, IA - continued

Item	Per	Value	Date	Ref.
Weddings - continued				
Engagement ring		3177	1998	33r
Flowers		789	1998	33r
Groom's formalwear rental		99	2000	33r
Limousine		410	1998	33r
Marriage license cost		30.00	4/01	35s
Men's formalwear (ushers, best man)		469	2000	33r
Mother of bride apparel		241	2000	33r
Music		866	1998	33r
Photography and videography		1368	1998	33r
Rehearsal dinner		728	1998	33r
Wedding invitations and announcements		341	1998	33r
Wedding reception		7968	2000	33r
Wedding rings (bride and groom)		1060	1998	33r

West Palm Beach-Boca Raton, FL

Item	Per	Value	Date	Ref.
Alcoholic Beverages				
Alcoholic beverage purchases	yr	253	1999	30r
Malt beverages, all types, all sizes, any origin	16 oz	0.96	7/01	11r
Appliances				
Major appliances, expenditures on	yr	172	1999	30r
Small appliances, housewares, expenditures on	yr	81	1999	30r
Banking and Money				
Mortgage interest and charges paid	yr	2039	1999	30r
Mortgage principal paid on owned property	yr	1026	1999	30r
Vehicle finance charges paid	yr	365	1999	30r
Charity				
Cash contributions, expenditures	yr	1127	1999	30r
Child Care				
Child raising cost, total, age 0-2	yr	8540	1999	60r
Child raising cost, total, age 3-5	yr	8780	1999	60r
Child raising cost, total, age 6-8	yr	8820	1999	60r
Child raising cost, total, age 9-11	yr	8800	1999	60r
Child raising cost, total, age 12-14	yr	9510	1999	60r
Child raising cost, total, age 15-17	yr	9740	1999	60r
Child's child care and education, age 0-2	yr	1380	1999	60r
Child's child care and education, age 3-5	yr	1520	1999	60r
Child's child care and education, age 6-8	yr	990	1999	60r
Child's child care and education, age 9-11	yr	650	1999	60r
Child's child care and education, age 12-14	yr	490	1999	60r
Child's child care and education, age 15-17	yr	840	1999	60r
Child's clothing, age 0-2	yr	480	1999	60r
Child's clothing, age 3-5	yr	470	1999	60r
Child's clothing, age 6-8	yr	520	1999	60r
Child's clothing, age 9-11	yr	570	1999	60r
Child's clothing, age 12-14	yr	950	1999	60r
Child's clothing, age 15-17	yr	850	1999	60r
Child's food, age 0-2	yr	1000	1999	60r
Child's food, age 3-5	yr	1160	1999	60r
Child's food, age 6-8	yr	1490	1999	60r
Child's food, age 9-11	yr	1770	1999	60r
Child's food, age 12-14	yr	1770	1999	60r
Child's food, age 15-17	yr	1980	1999	60r
Child's health care, age 0-2	yr	620	1999	60r
Child's health care, age 3-5	yr	590	1999	60r
Child's health care, age 6-8	yr	680	1999	60r
Child's health care, age 9-11	yr	720	1999	60r
Child's health care, age 12-14	yr	730	1999	60r
Child's health care, age 15-17	yr	760	1999	60r
Child's housing, age 0-2	yr	3070	1999	60r
Child's housing, age 3-5	yr	3050	1999	60r
Child's housing, age 6-8	yr	3010	1999	60r
Child's housing, age 9-11	yr	2850	1999	60r
Child's housing, age 12-14	yr	3040	1999	60r
Child's housing, age 15-17	yr	2650	1999	60r
Child's personal care, reading, age 0-2	yr	910	1999	60r
Child's personal care, reading, age 3-5	yr	930	1999	60r
Child's personal care, reading, age 6-8	yr	960	1999	60r

Values are in dollars or fractions of dollars. In the column headed *Ref*, references are shown to sources. Each reference is followed by a letter. These refer to the geographical level for which data were reported: s=State, r=Region, and c=City or metro. The abbreviation *ex* is used to mean *except* or *excluding*; *exp* stands for expenditures. For other abbreviations and further explanations, please see the Introduction.

West Palm Beach-Boca Raton, FL - continued

Item	Per	Value	Date	Ref.
Child Care				
Child's personal care, reading, age 9-11	yr	1000	1999	60r
Child's personal care, reading, age 12-14	yr	1170	1999	60r
Child's personal care, reading, age 15-17	yr	950	1999	60r
Clothing				
Apparel and services purchases	yr	1610	1999	30r
Boys, 2 to 15, expenditures on	yr	89	1999	30r
Children under 2, expenditures on	yr	79	1999	30r
Footwear, expenditures on	yr	283	1999	30r
Girls, 2 to 15, expenditures on	yr	103	1999	30r
Men and boys, expenditures on	yr	351	1999	30r
Men, 16 and over, expenditures on	yr	262	1999	30r
Women, 16 and over, expenditures on	yr	538	1999	30r
Communications				
Cable modem installation, Adelphi		54.90	6/99	103s
Cable modem installation, Comcast		95.00	6/99	103s
Cable modem installation, Media One		100.00	6/99	103s
Cable modem installation, Time Warner		75.00-225.00	6/99	103s
Cable modem rate, cable subscriber, Adelphi	mos	34.95	6/99	103s
Cable modem rate, cable subscriber, Comcast	mos	39.95	6/99	103s
Cable modem rate, cable subscriber, Media One	mos	34.95-39.95	6/99	103s
Cable modem rate, cable subscriber, Time Warner	mos	39.95-49.95	6/99	103s
Cable modem rate, non-cable subscriber, Adelphi	mos	44.95	6/99	103s
Cable modem rate, non-cable subscriber, Comcast	mos	49.95	6/99	103s
Cable modem rate, non-cable subscriber, Media One	mos	49.95	6/99	103s
Cable modem rate, non-cable subscriber, Time Warner	mos	39.95-54.95	6/99	103s
Phone line, single, business, field visit	inst.	56.00	12/97	17s
Phone line, single, business, no field visit	inst.	56.00	12/97	17s
Phone line, single, residence, field visit	inst.	40.00	12/97	17s
Phone line, single, residence, no field visit	inst.	40.00	12/97	17s
Postage and stationery, expenditures on	yr	104	1999	30r
Postal rate, express mail, up to half-pound		12.45	7/01	108r
Postal rate, letter, first class, first ounce		0.34	7/01	108r
Postal rate, letter, two ounces		0.57	7/01	108r
Postal rate, post card		0.21	7/01	108r
Postal rate, priority mail, two pounds		3.95	7/01	108r
Postal rate, priority mail, up to one pound		3.50	7/01	108r
Telephone services, expenditures on	yr	860	1999	30r
Education				
Board, 4-year private college/university	yr	2236	1996	38s
Board, 4-year public college/university	yr	2295	1996	38s
Education expenditures	yr	431	1999	30r
Room, 4-year private college/university	yr	2428	1996	38s
Room, 4-year public college/university	yr	2193	1996	38s
Total cost, 4-year private college/university	yr	15028	1996	38s
Total cost, 4-year public college/university	yr	6254	1996	38s
Tuition, 2-year public college/university, in state	yr	1103	1996	38s
Tuition, 4-year private college/university, in state	yr	10364	1996	38s
Tuition, 4-year public college/university	yr	1767	1996	38s
Energy and Fuels				
Electricity	500 KWhs	47.29	7/01	11r
Electricity	KWh	0.09	7/01	11r
Fuel oil #2	gal	1.43	7/01	11r
Fuel oil and other fuels, expenditures on	yr	45	1999	30r
Gas, natural, commercial rate	1000 cf	8.44	11/00	88s
Gasoline, all types	gal	1.60	7/01	11r
Gasoline, unleaded midgrade	gal	1.65	7/01	11r
Gasoline, unleaded premium	gal	1.74	7/01	11r
Natural gas, expenditures on	yr	164	1999	30r
Utility (piped) gas, therm		1.01	7/01	11r

West Palm Beach-Boca Raton, FL - continued

Item	Per	Value	Date	Ref.
Energy and Fuels - continued				
Utility (piped) gas, 40 therms		44.29	7/01	11r
Utility (piped) gas, 100 therms		97.44	7/01	11r
Entertainment				
Entertainment purchases	yr	1574	1999	30r
Fees and admissions paid	yr	371	1999	30r
Reading purchases	yr	121	1999	30r
Television, radios, sound equipment, expenditures on	yr	561	1999	30r
Funerals				
Total cost of funeral		5922.53	1/99	78r
Acknowledgement cards		63.43	1/99	78r
Casket		2258.77	1/99	78r
Cosmetology, hair, other preparation		127.09	1/99	78r
Embalming		393.49	1/99	78r
Funeral at funeral home		367.50	1/99	78r
Hearse (local)		169.66	1/99	78r
Professional service charges		1211.32	1/99	78r
Service car/van		80.69	1/99	78r
Transfer of remains to funeral home		144.25	1/99	78r
Vault		803.50	1/99	78r
Visitation/viewing		302.83	1/99	78r
Groceries				
American processed cheese	lb	3.50	7/01	11r
Bakery products, expenditures on	yr	261	1999	30r
Bananas	lb	0.47	7/01	11r
Beans, dried, any type, all sizes	lb	0.63	7/01	11r
Beef for stew, boneless	lb	2.86	7/01	11r
Beef, expenditures on	yr	210	1999	30r
Bologna, all beef or mixed	lb	2.29	7/01	11r
Bread, French	lb	1.66	7/01	11r
Bread, white, pan	lb	0.87	7/01	11r
Bread, whole wheat, pan	lb	1.38	7/01	11r
Broccoli	lb	1.04	7/01	11r
Butter, salted, grade AA, stick	lb	2.26	7/01	11r
Butter, yoghurt, cheese, etc, expenditures on	yr	170	1999	30r
Cabbage	lb	0.42	7/01	11r
Cereals and cereal products, expenditures on	yr	140	1999	30r
Cheddar cheese, natural	lb	3.75	7/01	11r
Chicken breast, bone-in	lb	1.85	7/01	11r
Chicken legs, bone-in	lb	1.34	7/01	11r
Chicken, fresh, whole	lb	1.05	7/01	11r
Chops, boneless,	lb	4.13	7/01	11r
Chuck roast, graded and ungraded, excl U.S. prime and choice	lb	2.35	7/01	11r
Chuck roast, U.S. choice, boneless	lb	2.67	7/01	11r
Coffee, 100%, ground roast, all sizes	lb	2.88	7/01	11r
Coffee, instant, plain, regular, all sizes	16 oz	9.25	7/01	11r
Cola, non diet,	2 liter	1.11	7/01	11r
Crackers, soda, salted	lb	1.70	7/01	11r
Dairy product purchases	yr	282	1999	30r
Eggs, expenditures on	yr	32	1999	30r
Fats and oils, expenditures on	yr	79	1999	30r
Fish and seafood, expenditures on	yr	99	1999	30r
Flour, white, all purpose	lb	0.32	7/01	11r
Food (excl fruit and vegetables), eaten at home, purchases	yr	815	1999	30r
Food cooked on trips, expenditures on	yr	36	1999	30r
Food purchases	yr	4533	1999	30r
Food purchases, eaten away from home	yr	1873	1999	30r
Food purchases, food eaten at home	yr	2660	1999	30r
Fresh fruits, expenditures on	yr	128	1999	30r
Fresh milk and cream, expenditures on	yr	112	1999	30r
Fresh vegetables, expenditures on	yr	131	1999	30r
Fruit and vegetable purchases	yr	438	1999	30r
Grapefruit	lb	0.59	7/01	11r
Grapes, Thompson, seedless	lb	2.12	7/01	11r
Ground beef, 100% beef	lb	1.76	7/01	11r
Ground beef, lean and extra lean	lb	2.60	7/01	11r
Ground chuck, 100% beef	lb	2.08	7/01	11r
Ham, boneless, excl canned	lb	2.71	7/01	11r

Values are in dollars or fractions of dollars. In the column headed *Ref*, references are shown to sources. Each reference is followed by a letter. These refer to the geographical level for which data were reported: s=State, r=Region, and c=City or metro. The abbreviation *ex* is used to mean *except* or *excluding*; *exp* stands for *expenditures*. For other abbreviations and further explanations, please see the Introduction.

West Palm Beach-Boca Raton, FL - continued

Item	Per	Value	Date	Ref.
Groceries				
Ham, rump or shank half, bone-in, smoked	lb	2.19	7/01	11r
Ice cream, prepackaged, bulk, regular	1/2 gal	3.93	7/01	11r
Lemons	lb	1.32	7/01	11r
Lettuce, iceberg	lb	0.76	7/01	11r
Milk, fresh, low fat,	gal	2.75	7/01	11r
Milk, fresh, whole, fortified	gal	2.97	7/01	11r
Nonalcoholic beverages, expenditures on	yr	228	1999	30r
Orange juice, frozen concentrate	16 oz	1.95	7/01	11r
Oranges, Navel	lb	0.73	7/01	11r
Oranges, Valencia	lb	0.55	7/01	11r
Peanut butter, creamy, all sizes	lb	1.83	7/01	11r
Pears, Anjou	lb	0.98	7/01	11r
Pork chops, center cut, bone-in	lb	3.33	7/01	11r
Pork sausage, fresh, loose	lb	2.59	7/01	11r
Pork shoulder picnic, bone-in, smoked	lb	1.12	7/01	11r
Pork, expenditures on	yr	162	1999	30r
Potato chips	16 oz	3.59	7/01	11r
Potatoes, frozen, french fried	lb	1.00	7/01	11r
Potatoes, white, all types	lb	0.44	7/01	11r
Poultry, expenditures on	yr	137	1999	30r
Processed fruits, expenditures on	yr	97	1999	30r
Processed vegetables, expenditures on	yr	82	1999	30r
Rice, white, long grain, uncooked	lb	0.51	7/01	11r
Round roast, graded and ungraded, excl U.S. prime and choice	lb	2.96	7/01	11r
Round steak, graded and ungraded, excl U.S. prime and choice	lb	3.11	7/01	11r
Sirloin steak, graded and ungraded, excl U.S. prime and choice	lb	4.23	7/01	11r
Spaghetti and macaroni	lb	0.78	7/01	11r
Steak, round, U.S. choice, boneless	lb	3.56	7/01	11r
Steak, sirloin, U.S. choice, boneless	lb	5.65	7/01	11r
Strawberries, dry pint	12 oz	1.50	7/01	11r
Sugar and other sweets, expenditures on	yr	99	1999	30r
Sugar, white, 33-80 ounce package	lb	0.39	7/01	11r
Sugar, white, all sizes	lb	0.42	7/01	11r
Tobacco products and smoking supplies purchases	yr	288	1999	30r
Tomatoes, field grown	lb	1.43	7/01	11r
Tuna, light, chunk	lb	1.77	7/01	11r
Turkey, frozen, whole	lb	1.05	7/01	11r
Goods and Services				
B&B Japanese maple (acer japonicum)	gal	49.98-129.00	4/00	93r
Boxwood (buxus)	2 gal	12.99-16.99	4/00	93r
Daylily (hemerocallis)	gal	4.99-8.99	4/00	93r
Flat of annuals		11.00-13.92	4/00	93r
Fountain grass (pennisetum)	gal	5.98-7.98	4/00	93r
Hanging basket (10 in)		7.99-14.98	4/00	93r
Hardy geranium (geranium)	gal	5.98-8.00	4/00	93r
Hosta (hosta)	gal	4.99-10.98	4/00	93r
Lilac (syrubga vulgaris)	2 gal	12.99-21.99	4/00	93r
Rhododendron (rhododendron)	2 gal	14.99-24.99	4/00	93r
Sage (salvia)	gal	5.98-6.99	4/00	93r
Wintercreeper euonymus (euonymus fortunei)	2 gal	7.99-89.99	4/00	93r
Hunting license	yr	12.50	4/01	34s
Health Care				
Cardiac catheterization, ave hospital/ physician charges		15060	1998	77s
Childbirth, Cesarean delivery		11587	1997	13r

West Palm Beach-Boca Raton, FL - continued

Item	Per	Value	Date	Ref.
Health Care - continued				
Childbirth, vaginal delivery		6725	1997	13r
Drugs, expenditures on	yr	399	1999	30r
Health care purchases	yr	1971	1999	30r
Health insurance expenditures	yr	933	1999	30r
Hysterectomy, laproscopically-assisted, ave hospital/physician charges		14760	1998	76s
Hysterectomy, vaginal, ave hospital and physician charges		11320	1998	76s
Medicaid dispensing fee		4.23	1999	87s
Medical services expenditures	yr	547	1999	30r
Medical supplies, expenditures on	yr	91	1999	30r
Plastic surgery, breast augmentation		2870	2000	7r
Plastic surgery, breast lift		3649	2000	7r
Plastic surgery, facelift		5008	2000	7r
Plastic surgery, hair transplantation		3425	2000	7r
Plastic surgery, lip augmentation		1227	2000	7r
Plastic surgery, lower body lift		4793	2000	7r
Plastic surgery, thigh lift		3862	2000	7r
Household Goods				
Floor coverings, expenditures on	yr	44	1999	30r
Furniture, expenditures on	yr	335	1999	30r
Household furnishings and equipment purchases	yr	1328	1999	30r
Household textiles, expenditures on	yr	89	1999	30r
Laundry and cleaning supplies, expenditures on	yr	113	1999	30r
Housing				
Home price, existing, ave		160100	10/00	90r
Home value, median		104000	2001	53s
Household operation expenditures	yr	553	1999	30r
Housekeeping supplies purchases	yr	473	1999	30r
Housing, expenditures on	yr	10303	1999	30r
Maintenance, repairs, insurance expenditures	yr	699	1999	30r
Monthly rental value of owned home	mos	505	1999	30r
Owned dwellings, expenditures own	yr	3465	1999	30r
Rent expenditures	yr	1641	1999	30r
Rental unit, 1 bedroom, with utilities	mos	591	4/01	41c
Rental unit, 2 bedroom, with utilities	mos	731	4/01	41c
Rental unit, 3 bedroom, with utilities	mos	971	4/01	41c
Rental unit, 4 bedroom, with utilities	mos	1202	4/01	41c
Shelter, expenditures on	yr	5467	1999	30r
Insurance and Pensions				
Life and other personal insurance purchases	yr	414	1999	30r
Medigap health insurance, Plan H	yr	2887	2000	69s
Medigap health insurance, Plan I	yr	3302	2000	69s
Medigap health insurance, Plan J	yr	3889	2000	69s
Pensions and Social Security, expenditures on	yr	2635	1999	30r
Personal insurance and pensions, expenditures on	yr	3048	1999	30r
Legal Fees				
Divorce, filing fee		65.00-85.00	4/01	35s
Driver's license fee	orig	20.00	1999	48s
Driver's license fee	renew	15.00	1999	48s
Personal Goods				
Personal care products and services purchases	yr	393	1999	30r
Personal Services				
Personal services, household, expenditures on	yr	258	1999	30r
Pets				
Pets, toys, and playground equipment, expenditures on	yr	306	1999	30r
Taxes				
Federal income taxes paid	yr	2047	1999	30r
Personal taxes, expenditures on	yr	2554	1999	30r

Values are in dollars or fractions of dollars. In the column headed *Ref*, references are shown to sources. Each reference is followed by a letter. These refer to the geographical level for which data were reported: s=State, r=Region, and c=City or metro. The abbreviation *ex* is used to mean *except* or *excluding; exp* stands for expenditures. For other abbreviations and further explanations, please see the Introduction.

West Palm Beach-Boca Raton, FL - continued

Item	Per	Value	Date	Ref.
Taxes				
Property taxes paid	yr	726	1999	30r
State and local income taxes paid	yr	363	1999	30r
Transportation				
Bus fare, one-way	trip	1.00	2000	1c
Cars and trucks, new, expenditures on	yr	1648	1999	30r
Cars and trucks, used, expenditures on	yr	1651	1999	30r
Diesel at the pump	gal	1.26	10/99	73s
Gasoline and motor oil purchases	yr	1052	1999	30r
Gasoline before-tax price (cents)	gal	101.90	10/00	43s
Maintenance and repair expenditures	yr	621	1999	30r
Public transportation, expenditures on	yr	298	1999	30r
Transportation purchases	yr	6738	1999	30r
Vehicle expenses, miscellaneous, purchases	yr	2033	1999	30r
Vehicle insurance payments	yr	696	1999	30r
Vehicle purchases (net outlay)	yr	3354	1999	30r
Vehicle rental, lease expenditures	yr	352	1999	30r
Travel				
Hotel room	night	110.57	2/01	95s
Utilities				
Electrical bill, average	mos	86.33	9/00	9s
Electricity, expenditures on	yr	1115	1999	30r
Electricity cost, average	KWh	6.80	9/00	9s
Water and other public services, expenditures on	yr	298	1999	30r
Weddings				
Wedding (national average cost)		19936	2000	33r
Wedding (regional average total cost)		16293	1997	110r
Attendants' gifts		321	1998	33r
Bridal attendants' apparel (5 persons)		824	2000	33r
Bride's headpiece/veil		173	1998	33r
Bride's wedding dress		859	1998	33r
Clergy, religious facility fee		242	1998	33r
Engagement ring		3177	1998	33r
Flowers		789	1998	33r
Groom's formalwear rental		99	2000	33r
Limousine		410	1998	33r
Marriage license cost		56.00-88.50	4/01	35s
Men's formalwear (ushers, best man)		469	2000	33r
Mother of bride apparel		241	2000	33r
Music		866	1998	33r
Photography and videography		1368	1998	33r
Rehearsal dinner		728	1998	33r
Wedding invitations and announcements		341	1998	33r
Wedding reception		7968	2000	33r
Wedding rings (bride and groom)		1060	1998	33r

Wheeling, WV

Item	Per	Value	Date	Ref.
Alcoholic Beverages				
Alcoholic beverage purchases	yr	253	1999	30r
Malt beverages, all types, all sizes, any origin	16 oz	0.96	7/01	11r
Appliances				
Major appliances, expenditures on	yr	172	1999	30r
Small appliances, housewares, expenditures on	yr	81	1999	30r
Banking and Money				
Mortgage interest and charges paid	yr	2039	1999	30r
Mortgage principal paid on owned property	yr	1026	1999	30r
Vehicle finance charges paid	yr	365	1999	30r
Charity				
Cash contributions, expenditures	yr	1127	1999	30r
Child Care				
Child raising cost, total, age 0-2	yr	8540	1999	60r
Child raising cost, total, age 3-5	yr	8780	1999	60r
Child raising cost, total, age 6-8	yr	8820	1999	60r
Child raising cost, total, age 9-11	yr	8800	1999	60r

Wheeling, WV - continued

Item	Per	Value	Date	Ref.
Child Care - continued				
Child raising cost, total, age 12-14	yr	9510	1999	60r
Child raising cost, total, age 15-17	yr	9740	1999	60r
Child's child care and education, age 0-2	yr	1380	1999	60r
Child's child care and education, age 3-5	yr	1520	1999	60r
Child's child care and education, age 6-8	yr	990	1999	60r
Child's child care and education, age 9-11	yr	650	1999	60r
Child's child care and education, age 12-14	yr	490	1999	60r
Child's child care and education, age 15-17	yr	840	1999	60r
Child's clothing, age 0-2	yr	480	1999	60r
Child's clothing, age 3-5	yr	470	1999	60r
Child's clothing, age 6-8	yr	520	1999	60r
Child's clothing, age 9-11	yr	570	1999	60r
Child's clothing, age 12-14	yr	950	1999	60r
Child's clothing, age 15-17	yr	850	1999	60r
Child's food, age 0-2	yr	1000	1999	60r
Child's food, age 3-5	yr	1160	1999	60r
Child's food, age 6-8	yr	1490	1999	60r
Child's food, age 9-11	yr	1770	1999	60r
Child's food, age 12-14	yr	1770	1999	60r
Child's food, age 15-17	yr	1980	1999	60r
Child's health care, age 0-2	yr	620	1999	60r
Child's health care, age 3-5	yr	590	1999	60r
Child's health care, age 6-8	yr	680	1999	60r
Child's health care, age 9-11	yr	720	1999	60r
Child's health care, age 12-14	yr	730	1999	60r
Child's health care, age 15-17	yr	760	1999	60r
Child's housing, age 0-2	yr	3070	1999	60r
Child's housing, age 3-5	yr	3050	1999	60r
Child's housing, age 6-8	yr	3010	1999	60r
Child's housing, age 9-11	yr	2850	1999	60r
Child's housing, age 12-14	yr	3040	1999	60r
Child's housing, age 15-17	yr	2650	1999	60r
Child's personal care, reading, age 0-2	yr	910	1999	60r
Child's personal care, reading, age 3-5	yr	930	1999	60r
Child's personal care, reading, age 6-8	yr	960	1999	60r
Child's personal care, reading, age 9-11	yr	1000	1999	60r
Child's personal care, reading, age 12-14	yr	1170	1999	60r
Child's personal care, reading, age 15-17	yr	950	1999	60r
Clothing				
Apparel and services purchases	yr	1610	1999	30r
Boys, 2 to 15, expenditures on	yr	89	1999	30r
Children under 2, expenditures on	yr	79	1999	30r
Footwear, expenditures on	yr	283	1999	30r
Girls, 2 to 15, expenditures on	yr	103	1999	30r
Men and boys, expenditures on	yr	351	1999	30r
Men, 16 and over, expenditures on	yr	262	1999	30r
Women, 16 and over, expenditures on	yr	538	1999	30r
Communications				
Phone line, single, business, field visit	inst.	96.90	12/97	17s
Phone line, single, business, no field visit	inst.	96.90	12/97	17s
Phone line, single, residence, field visit	inst.	42.00	12/97	17s
Phone line, single, residence, no field visit	inst.	42.00	12/97	17s
Postage and stationery, expenditures on	yr	104	1999	30r
Postal rate, express mail, up to half-pound		12.45	7/01	108r
Postal rate, letter, first class, first ounce		0.34	7/01	108r
Postal rate, letter, two ounces		0.57	7/01	108r
Postal rate, post card		0.21	7/01	108r
Postal rate, priority mail, two pounds		3.95	7/01	108r
Postal rate, priority mail, up to one pound		3.50	7/01	108r
Telephone bill, business, basic rate	mos	24.50	12/97	18c
Telephone bill, residential, basic rate	mos	36.15	12/97	18c
Telephone services, expenditures on	yr	860	1999	30r
Education				
Board, 4-year private college/university	yr	2370	1996	38s
Board, 4-year public college/university	yr	2133	1996	38s
Education expenditures	yr	431	1999	30r
Room, 4-year private college/university	yr	1853	1996	38s
Room, 4-year public college/university	yr	1970	1996	38s
Total cost, 4-year private college/university	yr	14231	1996	38s
Total cost, 4-year public college/university	yr	6128	1996	38s

Values are in dollars or fractions of dollars. In the column headed *Ref*, references are shown to sources. Each reference is followed by a letter. These refer to the geographical level for which data were reported: s=State, r=Region, and c=City or metro. The abbreviation *ex* is used to mean *except* or *excluding*; *exp* stands for *expenditures*. For other abbreviations and further explanations, please see the Introduction.

Wheeling, WV - continued

Item	Per	Value	Date	Ref.
Education				
Tuition, 2-year public college/university, in state	yr	1312	1996	38s
Tuition, 4-year private college/university, in state	yr	10008	1996	38s
Tuition, 4-year public college/university	yr	2024	1996	38s
Energy and Fuels				
Electricity	500 KWhs	47.29	7/01	11r
Electricity	KWh	0.09	7/01	11r
Fuel oil #2	gal	1.43	7/01	11r
Fuel oil and other fuels, expenditures on	yr	45	1999	30r
Gas, natural, commercial rate	1000 cf	6.75	11/00	88s
Gasoline, all types	gal	1.60	7/01	11r
Gasoline, unleaded midgrade	gal	1.65	7/01	11r
Gasoline, unleaded premium	gal	1.74	7/01	11r
Natural gas, expenditures on	yr	164	1999	30r
Utility (piped) gas, therm		1.01	7/01	11r
Utility (piped) gas, 40 therms		44.29	7/01	11r
Utility (piped) gas, 100 therms		97.44	7/01	11r
Entertainment				
Entertainment purchases	yr	1574	1999	30r
Fees and admissions paid	yr	371	1999	30r
Reading purchases	yr	121	1999	30r
Television, radios, sound equipment, expenditures on	yr	561	1999	30r
Funerals				
Total cost of funeral		5922.53	1/99	78r
Acknowledgement cards		63.43	1/99	78r
Casket		2258.77	1/99	78r
Cosmetology, hair, other preparation		127.09	1/99	78r
Embalming		393.49	1/99	78r
Funeral at funeral home		367.50	1/99	78r
Hearse (local)		169.66	1/99	78r
Professional service charges		1211.32	1/99	78r
Service car/van		80.69	1/99	78r
Transfer of remains to funeral home		144.25	1/99	78r
Vault		803.50	1/99	78r
Visitation/viewing		302.83	1/99	78r
Groceries				
American processed cheese	lb	3.50	7/01	11r
Bakery products, expenditures on	yr	261	1999	30r
Bananas	lb	0.47	7/01	11r
Beans, dried, any type, all sizes	lb	0.63	7/01	11r
Beef for stew, boneless	lb	2.86	7/01	11r
Beef, expenditures on	yr	210	1999	30r
Bologna, all beef or mixed	lb	2.29	7/01	11r
Bread, French	lb	1.66	7/01	11r
Bread, white, pan	lb	0.87	7/01	11r
Bread, whole wheat, pan	lb	1.38	7/01	11r
Broccoli	lb	1.04	7/01	11r
Butter, salted, grade AA, stick	lb	2.26	7/01	11r
Butter, yoghurt, cheese, etc, expenditures on	yr	170	1999	30r
Cabbage	lb	0.42	7/01	11r
Cereals and cereal products, expenditures on	yr	140	1999	30r
Cheddar cheese, natural	lb	3.75	7/01	11r
Chicken breast, bone-in	lb	1.85	7/01	11r
Chicken legs, bone-in	lb	1.34	7/01	11r
Chicken, fresh, whole	lb	1.05	7/01	11r
Chops, boneless,	lb	4.13	7/01	11r
Chuck roast, graded and ungraded, excl U.S. prime and choice	lb	2.35	7/01	11r
Chuck roast, U.S. choice, boneless	lb	2.67	7/01	11r
Coffee, 100%, ground roast, all sizes	lb	2.88	7/01	11r
Coffee, instant, plain, regular, all sizes	16 oz	9.25	7/01	11r
Cola, non diet,	2 liter	1.11	7/01	11r
Crackers, soda, salted	lb	1.70	7/01	11r
Dairy product purchases	yr	282	1999	30r
Eggs, expenditures on	yr	32	1999	30r
Fats and oils, expenditures on	yr	79	1999	30r

Wheeling, WV - continued

Item	Per	Value	Date	Ref.
Groceries - continued				
Fish and seafood, expenditures on	yr	99	1999	30r
Flour, white, all purpose	lb	0.32	7/01	11r
Food (excl fruit and vegetables), eaten at home, purchases	yr	815	1999	30r
Food cooked on trips, expenditures on	yr	36	1999	30r
Food purchases	yr	4533	1999	30r
Food purchases, eaten away from home	yr	1873	1999	30r
Food purchases, food eaten at home	yr	2660	1999	30r
Fresh fruits, expenditures on	yr	128	1999	30r
Fresh milk and cream, expenditures on	yr	112	1999	30r
Fresh vegetables, expenditures on	yr	131	1999	30r
Fruit and vegetable purchases	yr	438	1999	30r
Grapefruit	lb	0.59	7/01	11r
Grapes, Thompson, seedless	lb	2.12	7/01	11r
Ground beef, 100% beef	lb	1.76	7/01	11r
Ground beef, lean and extra lean	lb	2.60	7/01	11r
Ground chuck, 100% beef	lb	2.08	7/01	11r
Ham, boneless, excl canned	lb	2.71	7/01	11r
Ham, rump or shank half, bone-in, smoked	lb	2.19	7/01	11r
Ice cream, prepackaged, bulk, regular	1/2 gal	3.93	7/01	11r
Lemons	lb	1.32	7/01	11r
Lettuce, iceberg	lb	0.76	7/01	11r
Milk, fresh, low fat,	gal	2.75	7/01	11r
Milk, fresh, whole, fortified	gal	2.97	7/01	11r
Nonalcoholic beverages, expenditures on	yr	228	1999	30r
Orange juice, frozen concentrate	16 oz	1.95	7/01	11r
Oranges, Navel	lb	0.73	7/01	11r
Oranges, Valencia	lb	0.55	7/01	11r
Peanut butter, creamy, all sizes	lb	1.83	7/01	11r
Pears, Anjou	lb	0.98	7/01	11r
Pork chops, center cut, bone-in	lb	3.33	7/01	11r
Pork sausage, fresh, loose	lb	2.59	7/01	11r
Pork shoulder picnic, bone-in, smoked	lb	1.12	7/01	11r
Pork, expenditures on	yr	162	1999	30r
Potato chips	16 oz	3.59	7/01	11r
Potatoes, frozen, french fried	lb	1.00	7/01	11r
Potatoes, white, all types	lb	0.44	7/01	11r
Poultry, expenditures on	yr	137	1999	30r
Processed fruits, expenditures on	yr	97	1999	30r
Processed vegetables, expenditures on	yr	82	1999	30r
Rice, white, long grain, uncooked	lb	0.51	7/01	11r
Round roast, graded and ungraded, excl U.S. prime and choice	lb	2.96	7/01	11r
Round steak, graded and ungraded, excl U.S. prime and choice	lb	3.11	7/01	11r
Sirloin steak, graded and ungraded, excl U.S. prime and choice	lb	4.23	7/01	11r
Spaghetti and macaroni	lb	0.78	7/01	11r
Steak, round, U.S. choice, boneless	lb	3.56	7/01	11r
Steak, sirloin, U.S. choice, boneless	lb	5.65	7/01	11r
Strawberries, dry pint	12 oz	1.50	7/01	11r
Sugar and other sweets, expenditures on	yr	99	1999	30r
Sugar, white, 33-80 ounce package	lb	0.39	7/01	11r
Sugar, white, all sizes	lb	0.42	7/01	11r
Tobacco products and smoking supplies purchases	yr	288	1999	30r
Tomatoes, field grown	lb	1.43	7/01	11r
Tuna, light, chunk	lb	1.77	7/01	11r
Turkey, frozen, whole	lb	1.05	7/01	11r
Goods and Services				
B&B Japanese maple (acer japonicum)	gal	49.98-129.00	4/00	93r
Boxwood (buxus)	2 gal	12.99-16.99	4/00	93r
Daylilly (hemerocallis)	gal	4.99-8.99	4/00	93r
Flat of annuals		11.00-13.92	4/00	93r
Fountain grass (pennisetum)	gal	5.98-7.98	4/00	93r
Hanging basket (10 in)		7.99-14.98	4/00	93r

Values are in dollars or fractions of dollars. In the column headed *Ref*, references are shown to sources. Each reference is followed by a letter. These refer to the geographical level for which data were reported: s=State, r=Region, and c=City or metro. The abbreviation *ex* is used to mean *except* or *excluding*; *exp* stands for *expenditures*. For other abbreviations and further explanations, please see the Introduction.

Wheeling, WV - continued

Item	Per	Value	Date	Ref.
Goods and Services				
Hardy geranium (geranium)	gal	5.98-8.00	4/00	93r
Hosta (hosta)	gal	4.99-10.98	4/00	93r
Lilac (syrubga vulgaris)	2 gal	12.99-21.99	4/00	93r
Rhododendron (rhododendron)	2 gal	14.99-24.99	4/00	93r
Sage (salvia)	gal	5.98-6.99	4/00	93r
Wintercreeper euonymus (euonymus fortunei)	2 gal	7.99-89.99	4/00	93r
Hunting license	yr	11.00	4/01	34s
Health Care				
Cardiac catheterization, ave hospital/physician charges		10540	1998	77s
Childbirth, Cesarean delivery		11587	1997	13r
Childbirth, vaginal delivery		6725	1997	13r
Drugs, expenditures on	yr	399	1999	30r
Health care purchases	yr	1971	1999	30r
Health insurance expenditures	yr	933	1999	30r
Hysterectomy, laproscopically-assisted, ave hospital/physician charges		11620	1998	76s
Hysterectomy, vaginal, ave hospital and physician charges		8550	1998	76s
Medicaid dispensing fee		3.90-4.90	1999	87s
Medical services expenditures	yr	547	1999	30r
Medical supplies, expenditures on	yr	91	1999	30r
Plastic surgery, breast augmentation		2870	2000	7r
Plastic surgery, breast lift		3649	2000	7r
Plastic surgery, facelift		5008	2000	7r
Plastic surgery, hair transplantation		3425	2000	7r
Plastic surgery, lip augmentation		1227	2000	7r
Plastic surgery, lower body lift		4793	2000	7r
Plastic surgery, thigh lift		3862	2000	7r
Household Goods				
Floor coverings, expenditures on	yr	44	1999	30r
Furniture, expenditures on	yr	335	1999	30r
Household furnishings and equipment purchases	yr	1328	1999	30r
Household textiles, expenditures on	yr	89	1999	30r
Laundry and cleaning supplies, expenditures on	yr	113	1999	30r
Housing				
Home price, existing, ave		160100	10/00	90r
Home value, median		93000	2001	53s
Household operation expenditures	yr	553	1999	30r
Housekeeping supplies purchases	yr	473	1999	30r
Housing, expenditures on	yr	10303	1999	30r
Maintenance, repairs, insurance expenditures	yr	699	1999	30r
Monthly rental value of owned home	mos	505	1999	30r
Owned dwellings, expenditures own	yr	3465	1999	30r
Rent expenditures	yr	1641	1999	30r
Rental unit, 1 bedroom, with utilities	mos	349	4/01	41c
Rental unit, 2 bedroom, with utilities	mos	431	4/01	41c
Rental unit, 3 bedroom, with utilities	mos	549	4/01	41c
Rental unit, 4 bedroom, with utilities	mos	613	4/01	41c
Shelter, expenditures on	yr	5467	1999	30r
Insurance and Pensions				
Life and other personal insurance purchases	yr	414	1999	30r
Pensions and Social Security, expenditures on	yr	2635	1999	30r
Personal insurance and pensions, expenditures on	yr	3048	1999	30r
Legal Fees				
Combination hunting and fishing license	yr	17.00	4/01	34s
Driver's license fee	renew	12.50	1999	48s

Wheeling, WV - continued

Item	Per	Value	Date	Ref.
Legal Fees - continued				
Driver's license fee	orig	12.50	1999	48s
Fishing license	yr	11.00	4/01	34s
Personal Goods				
Personal care products and services purchases	yr	393	1999	30r
Personal Services				
Personal services, household, expenditures on	yr	258	1999	30r
Pets				
Pets, toys, and playground equipment, expenditures on	yr	306	1999	30r
Taxes				
Federal income taxes paid	yr	2047	1999	30r
Personal taxes, expenditures on	yr	2554	1999	30r
Property taxes paid	yr	726	1999	30r
State and local income taxes paid	yr	363	1999	30r
Transportation				
Cars and trucks, new, expenditures on	yr	1648	1999	30r
Cars and trucks, used, expenditures on	yr	1651	1999	30r
Diesel at the pump	gal	1.30	10/99	73s
Gasoline and motor oil purchases	yr	1052	1999	30r
Gasoline before-tax price (cents)	gal	108.80	10/00	43s
Maintenance and repair expenditures	yr	621	1999	30r
Public transportation, expenditures on	yr	298	1999	30r
Transportation purchases	yr	6738	1999	30r
Vehicle expenses, miscellaneous, purchases	yr	2033	1999	30r
Vehicle insurance payments	yr	696	1999	30r
Vehicle purchases (net outlay)	yr	3354	1999	30r
Vehicle rental, lease expenditures	yr	352	1999	30r
Utilities				
Electrical bill, average	mos	60.66	9/00	9s
Electricity, expenditures on	yr	1115	1999	30r
Electricity, summer, 250 KWh	mos	21.62	2/96	96s
Electricity, summer, 500 KWh	mos	38.93	2/96	96s
Electricity, summer, 750 KWh	mos	55.12	2/96	96s
Electricity, summer, 1000 KWh	mos	71.41	2/96	96s
Electricity cost, average	KWh	5.20	9/00	9s
Water and other public services, expenditures on	yr	298	1999	30r
Weddings				
Wedding (national average cost)		19936	2000	33r
Wedding (regional average total cost)		16293	1997	110r
Attendants' gifts		321	1998	33r
Bridal attendants' apparel (5 persons)		824	2000	33r
Bride's headpiece/veil		173	1998	33r
Bride's wedding dress		859	1998	33r
Clergy, religious facility fee		242	1998	33r
Engagement ring		3177	1998	33r
Flowers		789	1998	33r
Groom's formalwear rental		99	2000	33r
Limousine		410	1998	33r
Marriage license cost		23.00	4/01	35s
Men's formalwear (ushers, best man)		469	2000	33r
Mother of bride apparel		241	2000	33r
Music		866	1999	33r
Photography and videography		1368	1998	33r
Rehearsal dinner		728	1998	33r
Wedding invitations and announcements		341	1998	33r
Wedding reception		7968	2000	33r
Wedding rings (bride and groom)		1060	1998	33r

Wichita, KS

Item	Per	Value	Date	Ref.
Average annual expenditures	yr	35369	1999	30r
Composite, ACCRA index		100.40	12/00	5c

Values are in dollars or fractions of dollars. In the column headed *Ref*, references are shown to sources. Each reference is followed by a letter. These refer to the geographical level for which data were reported: s=State, r=Region, and c=City or metro. The abbreviation *ex* is used to mean *except* or *excluding*; *exp* stands for *expenditures*. For other abbreviations and further explanations, please see the Introduction.

Wichita, KS - continued

Item	Per	Value	Date	Ref.
Alcoholic Beverages				
Alcoholic beverage purchases	yr	304	1999	30r
Beer, Heineken, 12-oz, ex deposit	6	7.24	12/00	5c
J & B Scotch	750-ml	21.30	12/00	5c
Malt beverages, all types, all sizes, any origin	16 oz	0.93	7/01	11r
Wine, Livingston or Gallo, Chablis blanc	1.5 liter	6.36	12/00	5c
Wine, red and white table, all sizes, any origin	liter	7.04	7/01	11r
Appliances				
Appliance repair, service call, washing machine	min lab chg	41.56	12/00	5c
Major appliances, expenditures on	yr	165	1999	30r
Small appliances, housewares, expenditures on	yr	90	1999	30r
Banking and Money				
Mortgage interest and charges paid	yr	2277	1999	30r
Mortgage principal paid on owned property	yr	1230	1999	30r
Mortgage rate, incl. points and orig. fee, 30-yr. conv. fixed or ARM	mos	7.84	12/00	5c
Vehicle finance charges paid	yr	328	1999	30r
Business Expenses				
Business travel, car rental	day	61	2001	3c
Business travel, food	day	42	2001	3c
Business travel, hotel	day	103	2001	3c
Charity				
Cash contributions, expenditures	yr	1126	1999	30r
Child Care				
Child raising cost, total, age 0-2	yr	7890	1999	60r
Child raising cost, total, age 3-5	yr	8130	1999	60r
Child raising cost, total, age 6-8	yr	8170	1999	60r
Child raising cost, total, age 9-11	yr	8190	1999	60r
Child raising cost, total, age 12-14	yr	8890	1999	60r
Child raising cost, total, age 15-17	yr	9050	1999	60r
Child's child care and education, age 0-2	yr	1240	1999	60r
Child's child care and education, age 3-5	yr	1370	1999	60r
Child's child care and education, age 6-8	yr	880	1999	60r
Child's child care and education, age 9-11	yr	570	1999	60r
Child's child care and education, age 12-14	yr	420	1999	60r
Child's child care and education, age 15-17	yr	720	1999	60r
Child's clothing, age 0-2	yr	410	1999	60r
Child's clothing, age 3-5	yr	400	1999	60r
Child's clothing, age 6-8	yr	450	1999	60r
Child's clothing, age 9-11	yr	500	1999	60r
Child's clothing, age 12-14	yr	840	1999	60r
Child's clothing, age 15-17	yr	740	1999	60r
Child's food, age 0-2	yr	960	1999	60r
Child's food, age 3-5	yr	1120	1999	60r
Child's food, age 6-8	yr	1430	1999	60r
Child's food, age 9-11	yr	1710	1999	60r
Child's food, age 12-14	yr	1710	1999	60r
Child's food, age 15-17	yr	1920	1999	60r
Child's health care, age 0-2	yr	520	1999	60r
Child's health care, age 3-5	yr	500	1999	60r
Child's health care, age 6-8	yr	570	1999	60r
Child's health care, age 9-11	yr	610	1999	60r
Child's health care, age 12-14	yr	630	1999	60r
Child's health care, age 15-17	yr	650	1999	60r
Child's housing, age 0-2	yr	2860	1999	60r
Child's housing, age 3-5	yr	2840	1999	60r
Child's housing, age 6-8	yr	2800	1999	60r
Child's housing, age 9-11	yr	2650	1999	60r
Child's housing, age 12-14	yr	2840	1999	60r
Child's housing, age 15-17	yr	2440	1999	60r
Child's personal care, reading, age 0-2	yr	880	1999	60r
Child's personal care, reading, age 3-5	yr	900	1999	60r
Child's personal care, reading, age 6-8	yr	930	1999	60r
Child's personal care, reading, age 9-11	yr	970	1999	60r
Child's personal care, reading, age 12-14	yr	1150	1999	60r
Child's personal care, reading, age 15-17	yr	920	1999	60r

Wichita, KS - continued

Item	Per	Value	Date	Ref.
Clothing				
Apparel and services purchases	yr	1607	1999	30r
Boys' brief, cotton	3	4.19	12/00	5c
Boys, 2 to 15, expenditures on	yr	91	1999	30r
Children under 2, expenditures on	yr	59	1999	30r
Footwear, expenditures on	yr	285	1999	30r
Girls, 2 to 15, expenditures on	yr	116	1999	30r
Men and boys, expenditures on	yr	433	1999	30r
Men, 16 and over, expenditures on	yr	341	1999	30r
Shirt, man's dress shirt		28.50	12/00	5c
Slacks, man's "No Wrinkles" khaki		41.94	12/00	5c
Women, 16 and over, expenditures on	yr	490	1999	30r
Communications				
Newspaper subscription, daily and Sunday delivery	mos	16.04	12/00	5c
Phone line, single, business, field visit	inst.	57.40	12/97	17s
Phone line, single, business, no field visit	inst.	57.40	12/97	17s
Phone line, single, residence, field visit	inst.	39.00	12/97	17s
Phone line, single, residence, no field visit	inst.	39.00	12/97	17s
Postage and stationery, expenditures on	yr	140	1999	30r
Postal rate, express mail, up to half-pound		12.45	7/01	108r
Postal rate, letter, first class, first ounce		0.34	7/01	108r
Postal rate, letter, two ounces		0.57	7/01	108r
Postal rate, post card		0.21	7/01	108r
Postal rate, priority mail, two pounds		3.95	7/01	108r
Postal rate, priority mail, up to one pound		3.50	7/01	108r
Telephone bill, business, basic rate	mos	25.02	12/97	18c
Telephone bill, family of three	mos	25.10	12/00	5c
Telephone bill, residential, basic rate	mos	11.72	12/97	18c
Telephone services, expenditures on	yr	830	1999	30r
Education				
Board, 4-year private college/university	yr	2183	1996	38s
Board, 4-year public college/university	yr	1841	1996	38s
Education expenditures	yr	583	1999	30r
Room, 4-year private college/university	yr	1582	1996	38s
Room, 4-year public college/university	yr	1731	1996	38s
Total cost, 4-year private college/university	yr	12400	1996	38s
Total cost, 4-year public college/university	yr	5691	1996	38s
Tuition, 2-year public college/university, in state	yr	1147	1996	38s
Tuition, 4-year private college/university, in state	yr	8634	1996	38s
Tuition, 4-year public college/university	yr	2120	1996	38s
Energy and Fuels				
Electricity	500 KWhs	46.59	7/01	11r
Energy, combined forms, 2400 sq ft	mos	125.79	12/00	5c
Energy, exc. electricity, 2400 sq ft	mos	57.13	12/00	5c
Fuel oil #2	gal	1.27	7/01	11r
Fuel oil and other fuels, expenditures on	yr	68	1999	30r
Gas, cooking, winter, 10 therms	mos	9.78	2/96	98c
Gas, cooking, winter, 30 therms	mos	19.35	2/96	98c
Gas, cooking, winter, 50 therms	mos	28.92	2/96	98c
Gas, heating, winter, average use	mos	124.50	2/96	98c
Gas, regular unleaded, cash, self-service	gal	1.35	12/00	5c
Gasoline, unleaded midgrade	gal	1.79	7/01	11r
Gasoline, unleaded premium	gal	1.86	7/01	11r
Gasoline, unleaded regular	gal	1.58	7/01	11r
Natural gas, expenditures on	yr	389	1999	30r
Utility (piped) gas, therm		0.81	7/01	11r
Utility (piped) gas, 40 therms		38.01	7/01	11r
Utility (piped) gas, 100 therms		81.75	7/01	11r
Entertainment				
Bowling, Saturday evening rate	line	3.03	12/00	5c
Entertainment purchases	yr	1984	1999	30r
Fees and admissions paid	yr	444	1999	30r
Monopoly game, Parker Brothers', No. 9	game	9.92	12/00	5c
Movie, first-run, Saturday, evening	adm.	6.42	12/00	5c
Television, radios, sound equipment, expenditures on	yr	580	1999	30r
Tennis balls, yellow, Wilson or Penn, 3	can	2.74	12/00	5c

Values are in dollars or fractions of dollars. In the column headed *Ref*, references are shown to sources. Each reference is followed by a letter. These refer to the geographical level for which data were reported: s=State, r=Region, and c=City or metro. The abbreviation *ex* is used to mean *except* or *excluding*; *exp* stands for *expenditures*. For other abbreviations and further explanations, please see the Introduction.

Wichita, KS

American Cost of Living Survey, 3rd Edition

Wichita, KS - continued

Item	Per	Value	Date	Ref.
Funerals				
Cosmetology, hair, other preparation		178.32	1/99	78r
Embalming		408.19	1/99	78r
Funeral at funeral home		362.13	1/99	78r
Professional service charges		1375.51	1/99	78r
Transfer of remains to funeral home		155.92	1/99	78r
Visitation/viewing		294.38	1/99	78r
Groceries				
Groceries, ACCRA Index		97.70	12/00	5c
Antibiotic ointment, Polysporin	0.5 oz	4.69	12/00	5c
Baby food, strained vegetables or fruit, lowest price	4-4.5 oz	0.40	12/00	5c
Bacon, sliced	lb	3.15	7/01	11r
Bakery products, expenditures on	yr	281	1999	30r
Bananas	lb	0.48	7/01	11r
Bananas	lb	0.52	12/00	5c
Beans, dried, any type, all sizes	lb	0.61	7/01	11r
Beef for stew, boneless	lb	3.08	7/01	11r
Beef or hamburger, ground	lb	1.31	12/00	5c
Beef, expenditures on	yr	217	1999	30r
Bologna, all beef or mixed	lb	2.52	7/01	11r
Bread, white	loaf	1.03	12/00	5c
Bread, white, pan	lb	1.06	7/01	11r
Broccoli	lb	0.91	7/01	11r
Butter, salted, grade AA, stick	lb	3.04	7/01	11r
Butter, yoghurt, cheese, etc, expenditures on	yr	183	1999	30r
Cereals and bakery product purchases	yr	430	1999	30r
Cereals and cereal products, expenditures on	yr	149	1999	30r
Cheese, Kraft grated Parmesan	8 oz	3.33	12/00	5c
Chicken, fresh, whole	lb	1.07	7/01	11r
Chicken, whole fryer	lb	0.86	12/00	5c
Chops, boneless,	lb	3.64	7/01	11r
Chuck roast, U.S. choice, boneless	lb	2.47	7/01	11r
Cigarettes, Winston, Kings	carton	27.89	12/00	5c
Coffee, 100%, ground roast, all sizes	lb	2.69	7/01	11r
Coffee, vacuum-packed	13 oz	2.52	12/00	5c
Cookies, chocolate chip	lb	2.87	7/01	11r
Corn Flakes, Kellogg's or Post Toasties	18 oz	2.42	12/00	5c
Corn, frozen, whole kernel, lowest price	16 oz	1.04	12/00	5c
Dairy product purchases	yr	304	1999	30r
Eggs, expenditures on	yr	26	1999	30r
Eggs, Grade A or AA	dozen	0.98	12/00	5c
Eggs, grade A, large	dozen	0.88	7/01	11r
Fats and oils, expenditures on	yr	75	1999	30r
Fish and seafood, expenditures on	yr	72	1999	30r
Food (excl fruit and vegetables), eaten at home, purchases	yr	887	1999	30r
Food cooked on trips, expenditures on	yr	44	1999	30r
Food purchases	yr	4802	1999	30r
Food purchases, eaten away from home	yr	2069	1999	30r
Food purchases, food eaten at home	yr	2733	1999	30r
Fresh fruits, expenditures on	yr	138	1999	30r
Fresh milk and cream, expenditures on	yr	120	1999	30r
Fresh vegetables, expenditures on	yr	126	1999	30r
Grapefruit	lb	0.66	7/01	11r
Grapes, Thompson, seedless	lb	1.64	7/01	11r
Ground beef, 100% beef	lb	1.64	7/01	11r
Ground beef, lean and extra lean	lb	2.16	7/01	11r
Ground chuck, 100% beef	lb	2.13	7/01	11r
Ham, boneless, excl canned	lb	2.62	7/01	11r
Ice cream, prepackaged, bulk, regular	1/2 gal	3.35	7/01	11r
Lemons	lb	1.19	7/01	11r
Lettuce, iceberg	lb	0.73	7/01	11r
Lettuce, iceberg	head	1.19	12/00	5c
Margarine, Blue Bonnet or Parkay, stick	lb	0.67	12/00	5c
Margarine, soft, tubs	lb	0.89	7/01	11r
Meats, poultry, fish, and egg purchases	yr	671	1999	30r
Milk, fresh, whole, fortified	gal	2.71	7/01	11r
Milk, whole	1/2 gal	1.70	12/00	5c
Nonalcoholic beverages, expenditures on	yr	239	1999	30r
Orange juice, Minute Maid frozen	12 oz	1.69	12/00	5c
Oranges, Navel	lb	0.80	7/01	11r

Wichita, KS - continued

Item	Per	Value	Date	Ref.
Groceries - continued				
Oranges, Valencia	lb	0.66	7/01	11r
Peaches, halves or slices, Hunt's, Del Monte, or Libby's	29 oz	1.70	12/00	5c
Pears, Anjou	lb	0.93	7/01	11r
Peas, green, Del Monte or Green Giant	15 oz	0.79	12/00	5c
Pork chops, center cut, bone-in	lb	3.63	7/01	11r
Pork, expenditures on	yr	150	1999	30r
Potato chips	16 oz	3.52	7/01	11r
Potatoes, frozen, french fried	lb	1.08	7/01	11r
Potatoes, white or red	10 lb	2.15	12/00	5c
Potatoes, white, all types	lb	0.33	7/01	11r
Poultry, expenditures on	yr	108	1999	30r
Processed fruits, expenditures on	yr	98	1999	30r
Processed vegetables, expenditures on	yr	80	1999	30r
Round roast, U.S. choice, boneless	lb	3.07	7/01	11r
Round steak, graded and ungraded, excl U.S. prime and choice	lb	3.41	7/01	11r
Sausage, Jimmy Dean/Owens pork	lb	2.94	12/00	5c
Shortening, vegetable oil blends	lb	1.13	7/01	11r
Shortening, vegetable, Crisco	3 lb	2.79	12/00	5c
Soft drink, Coca Cola, ex deposit	2 liter	1.14	12/00	5c
Spaghetti and macaroni	lb	0.80	7/01	11r
Steak, round, U.S. choice, boneless	lb	3.23	7/01	11r
Steak, T-bone	lb	6.71	12/00	5c
Steak, T-bone, U.S. choice, bone-in	lb	6.68	7/01	11r
Strawberries, dry pint	12 oz	1.32	7/01	11r
Sugar and other sweets, expenditures on	yr	114	1999	30r
Sugar, cane or beet	4 lbs	1.45	12/00	5c
Sugar, white, 33-80 ounce package	lb	0.42	7/01	11r
Sugar, white, all sizes	lb	0.43	7/01	11r
Tobacco products and smoking supplies purchases	yr	331	1999	30r
Tomatoes, field grown	lb	1.46	7/01	11r
Tomatoes, Hunt's or Del Monte	14.5 oz	0.97	12/00	5c
Tuna, chunk, light	6 oz	0.67	12/00	5c
Tuna, light, chunk	lb	1.80	7/01	11r
Turkey, frozen, whole	lb	1.15	7/01	11r
Goods and Services				
Miscellaneous goods and services, ACCRA Index		102.00	12/00	5c
B&B Japanese maple (acer japonicum)	gal	29.99-169.99	4/00	93r
Boxwood (buxus)	2 gal	18.99-39.99	4/00	93r
Daylily (hemerocallis)	gal	4.99-25.00	4/00	93r
Flat of annuals		11.98-24.99	4/00	93r
Fountain grass (pennisetum)	gal	5.98-12.98	4/00	93r
Hanging basket (10 in)		12.99-27.99	4/00	93r
Hardy geranium (geranium)	gal	7.99-9.99	4/00	93r
Hosta (hosta)	gal	6.00-25.00	4/00	93r
Lilac (syrubga vulgaris)	2 gal	14.99-24.99	4/00	93r
Miscellaneous purchases	yr	865	1999	30r
Rhododendron (rhododendron)	2 gal	23.98-42.99	4/00	93r
Sage (salvia)	gal	6.00-9.99	4/00	93r
Wintercreeper euonymus (euonymus fortunei)	2 gal	16.00-169.99	4/00	93r
Hunting license	yr	15.50	4/01	34s
Health Care				
Health care, ACCRA Index		106.30	12/00	5c
Cardiac catheterization, ave hospital/ physician charges		11230	1998	77s
Childbirth, Cesarean delivery		10722	1997	13r

Values are in dollars or fractions of dollars. In the column headed *Ref*, references are shown to sources. Each reference is followed by a letter. These refer to the geographical level for which data were reported: s=State, r=Region, and c=City or metro. The abbreviation *ex* is used to mean *except* or *excluding*; *exp* stands for expenditures. For other abbreviations and further explanations, please see the Introduction.

Wichita, KS - continued

Item	Per	Value	Date	Ref.
Health Care				
Childbirth, vaginal delivery		6223	1997	13r
Dentist's fee, adult teeth cleaning and periodic oral exam	visit	72.80	12/00	5c
Doctor's fee, routine exam, established patient	visit	55.90	12/00	5c
Drugs, expenditures on	yr	394	1999	30r
Health care purchases	yr	2048	1999	30r
Health insurance expenditures	yr	978	1999	30r
Hospital care, private room	day	665.67	12/00	5c
Hysterectomy, laproscopically-assisted, ave hospital/physician charges		9610	1998	76s
Hysterectomy, vaginal, ave hospital and physician charges		6500	1998	76s
Medicaid dispensing fee		4.94	1999	87s
Medical services expenditures	yr	554	1999	30r
Medical supplies, expenditures on	yr	122	1999	30r
Plastic surgery, breast augmentation		3184	2000	7r
Plastic surgery, breast lift		3585	2000	7r
Plastic surgery, facelift		4999	2000	7r
Plastic surgery, hair transplantation		3105	2000	7r
Plastic surgery, lip augmentation		1290	2000	7r
Plastic surgery, lower body lift		8135	2000	7r
Plastic surgery, thigh lift		3839	2000	7r
Household Goods				
Dishwashing powder, Cascade	50 oz	2.83	12/00	5c
Floor coverings, expenditures on	yr	52	1999	30r
Furniture, expenditures on	yr	344	1999	30r
Household furnishings and equipment purchases	yr	1475	1999	30r
Household textiles, expenditures on	yr	109	1999	30r
Laundry and cleaning supplies, expenditures on	yr	134	1999	30r
Tissues, facial, Kleenex brand	175	1.20	12/00	5c
Housing				
Housing, ACCRA Index		95.60	12/00	5c
Home, 2200 sq ft, 4-br, 2-bath, 2-car garage, average		173000	2000	47c
Home price, existing, ave		144400	10/00	90r
Home value, median		112000	2001	53s
House, 2400 sq ft, 8000 sq ft lot, new, urban, utilities	total	207000	12/00	5c
House payment, principal and interest, 25% down payment	mos	1122	12/00	5c
Household operation expenditures	yr	542	1999	30r
Housekeeping supplies purchases	yr	508	1999	30r
Lodging expenditures	yr	430	1999	30r
Maintenance, repairs, insurance expenditures	yr	853	1999	30r
Monthly rental value of owned home	mos	547	1999	30r
Owned dwellings, expenditures own	yr	4282	1999	30r
Rent expenditures	yr	1558	1999	30r
Rent, apartment, 2 br, 1 1/2-2 baths, unfurn, 950 sq ft, water	mos	548	12/00	5c
Rental unit, 1 bedroom, with utilities	mos	399	4/01	41c
Rental unit, 2 bedroom, with utilities	mos	534	4/01	41c
Rental unit, 3 bedroom, with utilities	mos	722	4/01	41c
Rental unit, 4 bedroom, with utilities	mos	780	4/01	41c
Shelter, expenditures on	yr	6270	1999	30r
Insurance and Pensions				
Life and other personal insurance purchases	yr	387	1999	30r
Pensions and Social Security, expenditures on	yr	2968	1999	30r
Legal Fees				
Combination hunting and fishing license	yr	30.50	4/01	34s
Divorce, filing fee		100.00	4/01	35s
Driver's license fee	renew	18.00	1999	48s
Driver's license fee	orig	18.00	1999	48s
Fishing license	yr	15.50	4/01	34s

Wichita, KS - continued

Item	Per	Value	Date	Ref.
Personal Goods				
Personal care products and services purchases	yr	385	1999	30r
Shampoo, Alberto VO5	15 oz	1.15	12/00	5c
Toothpaste, Crest or Colgate	6-7 oz	2.00	12/00	5c
Personal Services				
Dry cleaning, man's 2-pc suit		8.46	12/00	5c
Man's haircut, barbershop, no styling		11.19	12/00	5c
Personal services, household, expenditures on	yr	300	1999	30r
Woman's shampoo, trim, blow-dry, no style-change		26.88	12/00	5c
Pets				
Pets, toys, and playground equipment, expenditures on	yr	375	1999	30r
Restaurant Food				
Chicken, fried, thigh and drumstick, KFC/Church's		2.14	12/00	5c
Hamburger with cheese, McDonald's	1/4 lb	2.09	12/00	5c
Pizza, Pizza Hut or Pizza Inn	11-12 in	8.99	12/00	5c
Taxes				
Federal income taxes paid	yr	2326	1999	30r
Personal taxes, expenditures on	yr	3223	1999	30r
Property taxes paid	yr	1152	1999	30r
State and local income taxes paid	yr	753	1999	30r
Transportation				
Transportation, ACCRA Index		99.70	12/00	5c
Bus fare, to central business district	1-way	1.00	12/00	5c
Cars and trucks, new, expenditures on	yr	1280	1999	30r
Cars and trucks, used, expenditures on	yr	1763	1999	30r
Diesel at the pump	gal	1.24	10/99	73s
Gasoline and motor oil purchases	yr	1036	1999	30r
Gasoline before-tax price (cents)	gal	108.00	10/00	43s
Maintenance and repair expenditures	yr	594	1999	30r
Public transportation, expenditures on	yr	341	1999	30r
Tire balance, computer or spin balance, front	wheel	8.90	12/00	5c
Transportation purchases	yr	6617	1999	30r
Vehicle expenses, miscellaneous, purchases	yr	2159	1999	30r
Vehicle insurance payments	yr	701	1999	30r
Vehicle purchases (net outlay)	yr	3081	1999	30r
Vehicle rental, lease expenditures	yr	536	1999	30r
Utilities				
Utilities, ACCRA Index		112.70	12/00	5c
Electrical bill, average	mos	64.66	9/00	9s
Electricity, expenditures on	yr	841	1999	30r
Electricity, summer, 250 KWh	mos	31.11	2/96	97c
Electricity, summer, 500 KWh	mos	53.58	2/96	97c
Electricity, summer, 750 KWh	mos	76.06	2/96	97c
Electricity, summer, 1000 KWh	mos	98.54	2/96	97c
Electricity and other, mixed, 2400 sq ft, new home	mos	68.66	12/00	5c
Electricity cost, average	KWh	6.30	9/00	9s
Utilities, fuels, and public services purchased	yr	2401	1999	30r
Water and other public services, expenditures on	yr	273	1999	30r
Water price	100 cf	1.06	2000	109c
Water price, dwelling unit	mos	20.89	2000	109c
Weddings				
Wedding (national average cost)		19936	2000	33r
Wedding (regional average total cost)		16195	1997	110r
Attendants' gifts		321	1998	33r
Bridal attendants' apparel (5 persons)		824	2000	33r
Bride's headpiece/veil		173	1998	33r
Bride's wedding dress		859	1998	33r
Clergy, religious facility fee		242	1998	33r
Engagement ring		3177	1998	33r
Flowers		789	1998	33r
Groom's formalwear rental		99	2000	33r
Limousine		410	1998	33r

Values are in dollars or fractions of dollars. In the column headed *Ref*, references are shown to sources. Each reference is followed by a letter. These refer to the geographical level for which data were reported: s=State, r=Region, and c=City or metro. The abbreviation *ex* is used to mean *except* or *excluding*; *exp* stands for *expenditures*. For other abbreviations and further explanations, please see the Introduction.

Wichita, KS - continued

Item	Per	Value	Date	Ref.
Weddings				
Marriage license cost		50.00	4/01	35s
Men's formalwear (ushers, best man)		469	2000	33r
Mother of bride apparel		241	2000	33r
Music		866	1998	33r
Photography and videography		1368	1998	33r
Rehearsal dinner		728	1998	33r
Wedding invitations and announcements		341	1998	33r
Wedding reception		7968	2000	33r
Wedding rings (bride and groom)		1060	1998	33r

Wichita Falls, TX

Item	Per	Value	Date	Ref.
Alcoholic Beverages				
Alcoholic beverage purchases	yr	253	1999	30r
Malt beverages, all types, all sizes, any origin	16 oz	0.96	7/01	11r
Appliances				
Major appliances, expenditures on	yr	172	1999	30r
Small appliances, housewares, expenditures on	yr	81	1999	30r
Banking and Money				
Mortgage interest and charges paid	yr	2039	1999	30r
Mortgage principal paid on owned property	yr	1026	1999	30r
Vehicle finance charges paid	yr	365	1999	30r
Charity				
Cash contributions, expenditures	yr	1127	1999	30r
Child Care				
Child raising cost, total, age 0-2	yr	8540	1999	60r
Child raising cost, total, age 3-5	yr	8780	1999	60r
Child raising cost, total, age 6-8	yr	8820	1999	60r
Child raising cost, total, age 9-11	yr	8800	1999	60r
Child raising cost, total, age 12-14	yr	9510	1999	60r
Child raising cost, total, age 15-17	yr	9740	1999	60r
Child's child care and education, age 0-2	yr	1380	1999	60r
Child's child care and education, age 3-5	yr	1520	1999	60r
Child's child care and education, age 6-8	yr	990	1999	60r
Child's child care and education, age 9-11	yr	650	1999	60r
Child's child care and education, age 12-14	yr	490	1999	60r
Child's child care and education, age 15-17	yr	840	1999	60r
Child's clothing, age 0-2	yr	480	1999	60r
Child's clothing, age 3-5	yr	470	1999	60r
Child's clothing, age 6-8	yr	520	1999	60r
Child's clothing, age 9-11	yr	570	1999	60r
Child's clothing, age 12-14	yr	950	1999	60r
Child's clothing, age 15-17	yr	850	1999	60r
Child's food, age 0-2	yr	1000	1999	60r
Child's food, age 3-5	yr	1160	1999	60r
Child's food, age 6-8	yr	1490	1999	60r
Child's food, age 9-11	yr	1770	1999	60r
Child's food, age 12-14	yr	1770	1999	60r
Child's food, age 15-17	yr	1980	1999	60r
Child's health care, age 0-2	yr	620	1999	60r
Child's health care, age 3-5	yr	590	1999	60r
Child's health care, age 6-8	yr	680	1999	60r
Child's health care, age 9-11	yr	720	1999	60r
Child's health care, age 12-14	yr	730	1999	60r
Child's health care, age 15-17	yr	760	1999	60r
Child's housing, age 0-2	yr	3070	1999	60r
Child's housing, age 3-5	yr	3050	1999	60r
Child's housing, age 6-8	yr	3010	1999	60r
Child's housing, age 9-11	yr	2850	1999	60r
Child's housing, age 12-14	yr	3040	1999	60r
Child's housing, age 15-17	yr	2650	1999	60r
Child's personal care, reading, age 0-2	yr	910	1999	60r
Child's personal care, reading, age 3-5	yr	930	1999	60r
Child's personal care, reading, age 6-8	yr	960	1999	60r
Child's personal care, reading, age 9-11	yr	1000	1999	60r
Child's personal care, reading, age 12-14	yr	1170	1999	60r
Child's personal care, reading, age 15-17	yr	950	1999	60r

Wichita Falls, TX - continued

Item	Per	Value	Date	Ref.
Clothing				
Apparel and services purchases	yr	1610	1999	30r
Boys, 2 to 15, expenditures on	yr	89	1999	30r
Children under 2, expenditures on	yr	79	1999	30r
Footwear, expenditures on	yr	283	1999	30r
Girls, 2 to 15, expenditures on	yr	103	1999	30r
Men and boys, expenditures on	yr	351	1999	30r
Men, 16 and over, expenditures on	yr	262	1999	30r
Women, 16 and over, expenditures on	yr	538	1999	30r
Communications				
Cable modem installation, AT&T-BIS		150.00	6/99	103s
Cable modem installation, Marcus		499.00	6/99	103s
Cable modem installation, Time Warner		75.00-225.00	6/99	103s
Cable modem rate, cable subscriber, AT&T-BIS	mos	39.95	6/99	103s
Cable modem rate, cable subscriber, Marcus	mos	14.95-49.95	6/99	103s
Cable modem rate, cable subscriber, Time Warner	mos	39.95-49.95	6/99	103s
Cable modem rate, non-cable subscriber, Marcus	mos	60.95	6/99	103s
Cable modem rate, non-cable subscriber, Time Warner	mos	39.95-54.95	6/99	103s
Phone line, single, business, field visit	inst.	71.90	12/97	17s
Phone line, single, business, no field visit	inst.	57.30	12/97	17s
Phone line, single, residence, field visit	inst.	52.95	12/97	17s
Phone line, single, residence, no field visit	inst.	38.35	12/97	17s
Postage and stationery, expenditures on	yr	104	1999	30r
Postal rate, express mail, up to half-pound		12.45	7/01	108r
Postal rate, letter, first class, first ounce		0.34	7/01	108r
Postal rate, letter, two ounces		0.57	7/01	108r
Postal rate, post card		0.21	7/01	108r
Postal rate, priority mail, two pounds		3.95	7/01	108r
Postal rate, priority mail, up to one pound		3.50	7/01	108r
Telephone services, expenditures on	yr	860	1999	30r
Education				
Board, 4-year private college/university	yr	2198	1996	38s
Board, 4-year public college/university	yr	1759	1996	38s
Education expenditures	yr	431	1999	30r
Room, 4-year private college/university	yr	2000	1996	38s
Room, 4-year public college/university	yr	1885	1996	38s
Total cost, 4-year private college/university	yr	13156	1996	38s
Total cost, 4-year public college/university	yr	5464	1996	38s
Tuition, 2-year public college/university, in state	yr	771	1996	38s
Tuition, 4-year private college/university, in state	yr	8959	1996	38s
Tuition, 4-year public college/university	yr	1820	1996	38s
Energy and Fuels				
Electricity	KWh	0.09	7/01	11r
Electricity	500 KWhs	47.29	7/01	11r
Fuel oil #2	gal	1.43	7/01	11r
Fuel oil and other fuels, expenditures on	yr	45	1999	30r
Gas, natural, commercial rate	1000 cf	6.94	11/00	88s
Gasoline, all types	gal	1.60	7/01	11r
Gasoline, unleaded midgrade	gal	1.65	7/01	11r
Gasoline, unleaded premium	gal	1.74	7/01	11r
Natural gas, expenditures on	yr	164	1999	30r
Utility (piped) gas, therm		1.01	7/01	11r
Utility (piped) gas, 40 therms		44.29	7/01	11r
Utility (piped) gas, 100 therms		97.44	7/01	11r
Entertainment				
Entertainment purchases	yr	1574	1999	30r
Fees and admissions paid	yr	371	1999	30r
Reading purchases	yr	121	1999	30r
Television, radios, sound equipment, expenditures on	yr	561	1999	30r

Values are in dollars or fractions of dollars. In the column headed *Ref*, references are shown to sources. Each reference is followed by a letter. These refer to the geographical level for which data were reported: s=State, r=Region, and c=City or metro. The abbreviation *ex* is used to mean *except* or *excluding*; *exp* stands for expenditures. For other abbreviations and further explanations, please see the Introduction.

Wichita Falls, TX - continued

Item	Per	Value	Date	Ref.
Funerals				
Total cost of funeral		5842.28	1/99	78r
Acknowledgement cards		28.35	1/99	78r
Casket		2494.29	1/99	78r
Cosmetology, hair, other preparation		109.22	1/99	78r
Embalming		361.42	1/99	78r
Funeral at funeral home		349.20	1/99	78r
Hearse (local)		161.91	1/99	78r
Professional service charges		1116.50	1/99	78r
Service car/van		65.56	1/99	78r
Transfer of remains to funeral home		143.56	1/99	78r
Vault		785.25	1/99	78r
Visitation/viewing		227.02	1/99	78r
Groceries				
American processed cheese	lb	3.50	7/01	11r
Bakery products, expenditures on	yr	261	1999	30r
Bananas	lb	0.47	7/01	11r
Beans, dried, any type, all sizes	lb	0.63	7/01	11r
Beef for stew, boneless	lb	2.86	7/01	11r
Beef, expenditures on	yr	210	1999	30r
Bologna, all beef or mixed	lb	2.29	7/01	11r
Bread, French	lb	1.66	7/01	11r
Bread, white, pan	lb	0.87	7/01	11r
Bread, whole wheat, pan	lb	1.38	7/01	11r
Broccoli	lb	1.04	7/01	11r
Butter, salted, grade AA, stick	lb	2.26	7/01	11r
Butter, yoghurt, cheese, etc, expenditures on	yr	170	1999	30r
Cabbage	lb	0.42	7/01	11r
Cereals and cereal products, expenditures on	yr	140	1999	30r
Cheddar cheese, natural	lb	3.75	7/01	11r
Chicken breast, bone-in	lb	1.85	7/01	11r
Chicken legs, bone-in	lb	1.34	7/01	11r
Chicken, fresh, whole	lb	1.05	7/01	11r
Chops, boneless	lb	4.13	7/01	11r
Chuck roast, graded and ungraded, excl U.S. prime and choice	lb	2.35	7/01	11r
Chuck roast, U.S. choice, boneless	lb	2.67	7/01	11r
Coffee, 100% ground roast, all sizes	lb	2.88	7/01	11r
Coffee, instant, plain, regular, all sizes	16 oz	9.25	7/01	11r
Cola, non diet,	2 liter	1.11	7/01	11r
Crackers, soda, salted	lb	1.70	7/01	11r
Dairy product purchases	yr	282	1999	30r
Eggs, expenditures on	yr	32	1999	30r
Fats and oils, expenditures on	yr	79	1999	30r
Fish and seafood, expenditures on	yr	99	1999	30r
Flour, white, all purpose	lb	0.32	7/01	11r
Food (excl fruit and vegetables), eaten at home, purchases	yr	815	1999	30r
Food cooked on trips, expenditures on	yr	36	1999	30r
Food purchases	yr	4533	1999	30r
Food purchases, eaten away from home	yr	1873	1999	30r
Food purchases, food eaten at home	yr	2660	1999	30r
Fresh fruits, expenditures on	yr	128	1999	30r
Fresh milk and cream, expenditures on	yr	112	1999	30r
Fresh vegetables, expenditures on	yr	131	1999	30r
Fruit and vegetable purchases	yr	438	1999	30r
Grapefruit	lb	0.59	7/01	11r
Grapes, Thompson, seedless	lb	2.12	7/01	11r
Ground beef, 100% beef	lb	1.76	7/01	11r
Ground beef, lean and extra lean	lb	2.60	7/01	11r
Ground chuck, 100% beef	lb	2.08	7/01	11r
Ham, boneless, excl canned	lb	2.71	7/01	11r
Ham, rump or shank half, bone-in, smoked	lb	2.19	7/01	11r
Ice cream, prepackaged, bulk, regular	1/2 gal	3.93	7/01	11r
Lemons	lb	1.32	7/01	11r
Lettuce, iceberg	lb	0.76	7/01	11r
Milk, fresh, low fat,	gal	2.75	7/01	11r
Milk, fresh, whole, fortified	gal	2.97	7/01	11r
Nonalcoholic beverages, expenditures on	yr	228	1999	30r
Orange juice, frozen concentrate	16 oz	1.95	7/01	11r
Oranges, Navel	lb	0.73	7/01	11r
Oranges, Valencia	lb	0.55	7/01	11r

Wichita Falls, TX - continued

Item	Per	Value	Date	Ref.
Groceries - continued				
Peanut butter, creamy, all sizes	lb	1.83	7/01	11r
Pears, Anjou	lb	0.98	7/01	11r
Pork chops, center cut, bone-in	lb	3.33	7/01	11r
Pork sausage, fresh, loose	lb	2.59	7/01	11r
Pork shoulder picnic, bone-in, smoked	lb	1.12	7/01	11r
Pork, expenditures on	yr	162	1999	30r
Potato chips	16 oz	3.59	7/01	11r
Potatoes, frozen, french fried	lb	1.00	7/01	11r
Potatoes, white, all types	lb	0.44	7/01	11r
Poultry, expenditures on	yr	137	1999	30r
Processed fruits, expenditures on	yr	97	1999	30r
Processed vegetables, expenditures on	yr	82	1999	30r
Rice, white, long grain, uncooked	lb	0.51	7/01	11r
Round roast, graded and ungraded, excl U.S. prime and choice	lb	2.96	7/01	11r
Round steak, graded and ungraded, excl U.S. prime and choice	lb	3.11	7/01	11r
Sirloin steak, graded and ungraded, excl U.S. prime and choice	lb	4.23	7/01	11r
Spaghetti and macaroni	lb	0.78	7/01	11r
Steak, round, U.S. choice, boneless	lb	3.56	7/01	11r
Steak, sirloin, U.S. choice, boneless	lb	5.65	7/01	11r
Strawberries, dry pint	12 oz	1.50	7/01	11r
Sugar and other sweets, expenditures on	yr	99	1999	30r
Sugar, white, 33-80 ounce package	lb	0.39	7/01	11r
Sugar, white, all sizes	lb	0.42	7/01	11r
Tobacco products and smoking supplies purchases	yr	288	1999	30r
Tomatoes, field grown	lb	1.43	7/01	11r
Tuna, light, chunk	lb	1.77	7/01	11r
Turkey, frozen, whole	lb	1.05	7/01	11r
Goods and Services				
B&B Japanese maple (acer japonicum)	gal	79.98-99.00	4/00	93r
Boxwood (buxus)	2 gal	12.98-18.99	4/00	93r
Christmas tree, noble fir		40-60	2000	65s
Daylilly (hemerocallis)	gal	7.96-11.00	4/00	93r
Flat of annuals		13.99-27.99	4/00	93r
Fountain grass (pennisetum)	gal	6.96-9.00	4/00	93r
Hanging basket (10 in)		9.99-24.99	4/00	93r
Hardy geranium (geranium)	gal	5.96-8.00	4/00	93r
Hosta (hosta)	gal	8.96-12.99	4/00	93r
Lilac (syrubga vulgaris)	2 gal	13.00-19.99	4/00	93r
Rhododendron (rhododendron)	2 gal	12.98-29.99	4/00	93r
Sage (salvia)	gal	5.96-8.00	4/00	93r
Wintercreeper euonymus (euonymus fortunei)	2 gal	13.00-18.99	4/00	93r
Hunting license	yr	19.00	4/01	34s
Health Care				
Cardiac catheterization, ave hospital/physician charges		20140	1998	77s
Childbirth, Cesarean delivery		11587	1997	13r
Childbirth, vaginal delivery		6725	1997	13r
Drugs, expenditures on	yr	399	1999	30r
Health care purchases	yr	1971	1999	30r
Health insurance expenditures	yr	933	1999	30r
Hysterectomy, laproscopically-assisted, ave hospital/physician charges		15700	1998	76s
Hysterectomy, vaginal, ave hospital and physician charges		12180	1998	76s
Medicaid dispensing fee		5.27	1999	87s

Values are in dollars or fractions of dollars. In the column headed *Ref*, references are shown to sources. Each reference is followed by a letter. These refer to the geographical level for which data were reported: s=State, r=Region, and c=City or metro. The abbreviation *ex* is used to mean *except* or *excluding*; *exp* stands for *expenditures*. For other abbreviations and further explanations, please see the Introduction.

Wichita Falls, TX - continued

Item	Per	Value	Date	Ref.
Health Care				
Medical services expenditures	yr	547	1999	30r
Medical supplies, expenditures on	yr	91	1999	30r
Household Goods				
Floor coverings, expenditures on	yr	44	1999	30r
Furniture, expenditures on	yr	335	1999	30r
Household furnishings and equipment purchases	yr	1328	1999	30r
Household textiles, expenditures on	yr	89	1999	30r
Laundry and cleaning supplies, expenditures on	yr	113	1999	30r
Housing				
Home price, existing, ave		160100	10/00	90r
Home value, median		112000	2001	53s
Household operation expenditures	yr	553	1999	30r
Housekeeping supplies purchases	yr	473	1999	30r
Housing, expenditures on	yr	10303	1999	30r
Maintenance, repairs, insurance expenditures	yr	699	1999	30r
Monthly rental value of owned home	mos	505	1999	30r
Owned dwellings, expenditures own	yr	3465	1999	30r
Rent expenditures	yr	1641	1999	30r
Rental unit, 1 bedroom, with utilities	mos	383	4/01	41c
Rental unit, 2 bedroom, with utilities	mos	462	4/01	41c
Rental unit, 3 bedroom, with utilities	mos	615	4/01	41c
Rental unit, 4 bedroom, with utilities	mos	725	4/01	41c
Shelter, expenditures on	yr	5467	1999	30r
Insurance and Pensions				
Life and other personal insurance purchases	yr	414	1999	30r
Pensions and Social Security, expenditures on	yr	2635	1999	30r
Personal insurance and pensions, expenditures on	yr	3048	1999	30r
Legal Fees				
Divorce, filing fee		150.00-200.00	4/01	35s
Driver's license fee	renew	20.00	1999	48s
Driver's license fee	orig	24.00	1999	48s
Fishing license	yr	19.00	4/01	34s
Personal Goods				
Personal care products and services purchases	yr	393	1999	30r
Personal Services				
Personal services, household, expenditures on	yr	258	1999	30r
Pets				
Pets, toys, and playground equipment, expenditures on	yr	306	1999	30r
Taxes				
Federal income taxes paid	yr	2047	1999	30r
Personal taxes, expenditures on	yr	2554	1999	30r
Property taxes paid	yr	726	1999	30r
State and local income taxes paid	yr	363	1999	30r
Transportation				
Cars and trucks, new, expenditures on	yr	1648	1999	30r
Cars and trucks, used, expenditures on	yr	1651	1999	30r
Diesel at the pump	gal	1.18	10/99	73s
Gasoline and motor oil purchases	yr	1052	1999	30r
Gasoline before-tax price (cents)	gal	101.30	10/00	43s
Maintenance and repair expenditures	yr	621	1999	30r
Public transportation, expenditures on	yr	298	1999	30r
Transportation purchases	yr	6738	1999	30r
Vehicle expenses, miscellaneous, purchases	yr	2033	1999	30r
Vehicle insurance payments	yr	696	1999	30r
Vehicle purchases (net outlay)	yr	3354	1999	30r
Vehicle rental, lease expenditures	yr	352	1999	30r

Wichita Falls, TX - continued

Item	Per	Value	Date	Ref.
Utilities				
Electrical bill, average	mos	87.17	9/00	9s
Electricity, expenditures on	yr	1115	1999	30r
Electricity cost, average	KWh	6.48	9/00	9s
Water and other public services, expenditures on	yr	298	1999	30r
Weddings				
Wedding (national average cost)		19936	2000	33r
Attendants' gifts		321	1998	33r
Bridal attendants' apparel (5 persons)		824	2000	33r
Bride's headpiece/veil		173	1998	33r
Bride's wedding dress		859	1998	33r
Clergy, religious facility fee		242	1998	33r
Engagement ring		3177	1998	33r
Flowers		789	1998	33r
Groom's formalwear rental		99	2000	33r
Limousine		410	1998	33r
Marriage license cost		36.00	4/01	35s
Men's formalwear (ushers, best man)		469	2000	33r
Mother of bride apparel		241	2000	33r
Music		866	1998	33r
Photography and videography		1368	1998	33r
Rehearsal dinner		728	1998	33r
Wedding invitations and announcements		341	1998	33r
Wedding reception		7968	2000	33r
Wedding rings (bride and groom)		1060	1998	33r

Williamsport, PA

Item	Per	Value	Date	Ref.
Average annual expenditures	yr	37971	1999	30r
Alcoholic Beverages				
Alcoholic beverage purchases	yr	368	1999	30r
Wine, red and white table, all sizes, any origin	liter	9.64	7/01	11r
Appliances				
Major appliances, expenditures on	yr	194	1999	30r
Small appliances, housewares, expenditures on	yr	93	1999	30r
Banking and Money				
Mortgage interest and charges paid	yr	2622	1999	30r
Mortgage principal paid on owned property	yr	1262	1999	30r
Vehicle finance charges paid	yr	240	1999	30r
Charity				
Cash contributions, expenditures	yr	1001	1999	30r
Child Care				
Child raising cost, total, age 0-2	yr	8670	1999	60r
Child raising cost, total, age 3-5	yr	8910	1999	60r
Child raising cost, total, age 6-8	yr	9040	1999	60r
Child raising cost, total, age 9-11	yr	9100	1999	60r
Child raising cost, total, age 12-14	yr	9890	1999	60r
Child raising cost, total, age 15-17	yr	10010	1999	60r
Child's child care and education, age 0-2	yr	1070	1999	60r
Child's child care and education, age 3-5	yr	1190	1999	60r
Child's child care and education, age 6-8	yr	740	1999	60r
Child's child care and education, age 9-11	yr	470	1999	60r
Child's child care and education, age 12-14	yr	350	1999	60r
Child's child care and education, age 15-17	yr	590	1999	60r
Child's clothing, age 0-2	yr	480	1999	60r
Child's clothing, age 3-5	yr	470	1999	60r
Child's clothing, age 6-8	yr	520	1999	60r
Child's clothing, age 9-11	yr	570	1999	60r
Child's clothing, age 12-14	yr	970	1999	60r
Child's clothing, age 15-17	yr	870	1999	60r
Child's food, age 0-2	yr	1130	1999	60r
Child's food, age 3-5	yr	1290	1999	60r
Child's food, age 6-8	yr	1640	1999	60r
Child's food, age 9-11	yr	1930	1999	60r
Child's food, age 12-14	yr	1940	1999	60r
Child's food, age 15-17	yr	2150	1999	60r

Values are in dollars or fractions of dollars. In the column headed *Ref*, references are shown to sources. Each reference is followed by a letter. These refer to the geographical level for which data were reported: s=State, r=Region, and c=City or metro. The abbreviation *ex* is used to mean *except* or *excluding*; *exp* stands for *expenditures*. For other abbreviations and further explanations, please see the Introduction.

Williamsport, PA - continued

Item	Per	Value	Date	Ref.
Child Care				
Child's health care, age 0-2	yr	550	1999	60r
Child's health care, age 3-5	yr	530	1999	60r
Child's health care, age 6-8	yr	610	1999	60r
Child's health care, age 9-11	yr	650	1999	60r
Child's health care, age 12-14	yr	660	1999	60r
Child's health care, age 15-17	yr	690	1999	60r
Child's housing, age 0-2	yr	3555	1999	60r
Child's housing, age 3-5	yr	3530	1999	60r
Child's housing, age 6-8	yr	3490	1999	60r
Child's housing, age 9-11	yr	3340	1999	60r
Child's housing, age 12-14	yr	3530	1999	60r
Child's housing, age 15-17	yr	3140	1999	60r
Child's personal care, reading, age 0-2	yr	920	1999	60r
Child's personal care, reading, age 3-5	yr	950	1999	60r
Child's personal care, reading, age 6-8	yr	980	1999	60r
Child's personal care, reading, age 9-11	yr	1020	1999	60r
Child's personal care, reading, age 12-14	yr	1190	1999	60r
Child's personal care, reading, age 15-17	yr	970	1999	60r
Clothing				
Apparel and services purchases	yr	1831	1999	30r
Boys, 2 to 15, expenditures on	yr	92	1999	30r
Children under 2, expenditures on	yr	63	1999	30r
Footwear, expenditures on	yr	300	1999	30r
Girls, 2 to 15, expenditures on	yr	101	1999	30r
Men and boys, expenditures on	yr	446	1999	30r
Men, 16 and over, expenditures on	yr	354	1999	30r
Women, 16 and over, expenditures on	yr	584	1999	30r
Communications				
Cable modem installation, Adelphi		54.90	6/99	103s
Cable modem installation, Comcast		95.00	6/99	103s
Cable modem rate, cable subscriber, Adelphi	mos	34.95	6/99	103s
Cable modem rate, cable subscriber, Comcast	mos	39.95	6/99	103s
Cable modem rate, non-cable subscriber, Adelphi	mos	44.95	6/99	103s
Cable modem rate, non-cable subscriber, Comcast	mos	49.95	6/99	103s
Phone line, single, business, field visit	inst.	75.00	12/97	17s
Phone line, single, business, no field visit	inst.	75.00	12/97	17s
Phone line, single, residence, field visit	inst.	40.00	12/97	17s
Phone line, single, residence, no field visit	inst.	40.00	12/97	17s
Postage and stationery, expenditures on	yr	138	1999	30r
Postal rate, express mail, up to half-pound		12.45	7/01	108r
Postal rate, letter, first class, first ounce		0.34	7/01	108r
Postal rate, letter, two ounces		0.57	7/01	108r
Postal rate, post card		0.21	7/01	108r
Postal rate, priority mail, two pounds		3.95	7/01	108r
Postal rate, priority mail, up to one pound		3.50	7/01	108r
Telephone services, expenditures on	yr	830	1999	30r
Education				
Board, 4-year private college/university	yr	2822	1996	38s
Board, 4-year public college/university	yr	2174	1996	38s
Education expenditures	yr	877	1999	30r
Room, 4-year private college/university	yr	2943	1996	38s
Room, 4-year public college/university	yr	2227	1996	38s
Total cost, 4-year private college/university	yr	19876	1996	38s
Total cost, 4-year public college/university	yr	9124	1996	38s
Tuition, 2-year public college/university, in state	yr	1909	1996	38s
Tuition, 4-year private college/university, in state	yr	14111	1996	38s
Tuition, 4-year public college/university	yr	4723	1996	38s
Energy and Fuels				
Electricity	KWh	0.12	7/01	11r
Fuel oil #2	gal	1.31	7/01	11r
Fuel oil and other fuels, expenditures on	yr	207	1999	30r
Gas, natural, commercial rate	1000 cf	5.96	11/00	88s
Gasoline, all types	gal	1.80	7/01	11r
Gasoline, unleaded midgrade	gal	1.85	7/01	11r
Gasoline, unleaded premium	gal	1.91	7/01	11r

Williamsport, PA - continued

Item	Per	Value	Date	Ref.
Energy and Fuels - continued				
Gasoline, unleaded regular	gal	1.71	7/01	11r
Natural gas, expenditures on	yr	368	1999	30r
Utility (piped) gas, therm		1.08	7/01	11r
Utility (piped) gas, 40 therms		50.87	7/01	11r
Utility (piped) gas, 100 therms		111.06	7/01	11r
Entertainment				
Entertainment purchases	yr	1821	1999	30r
Fees and admissions paid	yr	511	1999	30r
Television, radios, sound equipment, expenditures on	yr	650	1999	30r
Funerals				
Total cost of funeral		5813.50	1/99	78r
Acknowledgement cards		28.32	1/99	78r
Casket		2082.20	1/99	78r
Cosmetology, hair, other preparation		169.59	1/99	78r
Embalming		465.60	1/99	78r
Funeral at funeral home		339.56	1/99	78r
Hearse (local)		183.96	1/99	78r
Professional service charges		1157.85	1/99	78r
Service car/van		100.41	1/99	78r
Transfer of remains to funeral home		158.66	1/99	78r
Vault		766.31	1/99	78r
Visitation/viewing		361.04	1/99	78r
Groceries				
Apples, red delicious	lb	0.95	7/01	11r
Bacon, sliced	lb	3.44	7/01	11r
Bakery products, expenditures on	yr	310	1999	30r
Bananas	lb	0.55	7/01	11r
Beef, expenditures on	yr	236	1999	30r
Bread, white, pan	lb	1.09	7/01	11r
Butter, yoghurt, cheese, etc, expenditures on	yr	214	1999	30r
Cereals and bakery product purchases	yr	474	1999	30r
Cereals and cereal products, expenditures on	yr	164	1999	30r
Chicken legs, bone-in	lb	1.23	7/01	11r
Chicken, fresh, whole	lb	1.13	7/01	11r
Chuck roast, U.S. choice, boneless	lb	2.79	7/01	11r
Coffee, 100%, ground roast, all sizes	lb	3.40	7/01	11r
Dairy product purchases	yr	342	1999	30r
Eggs, expenditures on	yr	34	1999	30r
Eggs, grade A, large	dozen	0.82	7/01	11r
Fats and oils, expenditures on	yr	80	1999	30r
Fish and seafood, expenditures on	yr	123	1999	30r
Food (excl fruit and vegetables), eaten at home, purchases	yr	838	1999	30r
Food cooked on trips, expenditures on	yr	48	1999	30r
Food purchases	yr	5314	1999	30r
Food purchases, eaten away from home	yr	2313	1999	30r
Food purchases, food eaten at home	yr	3001	1999	30r
Fresh fruits, expenditures on	yr	169	1999	30r
Fresh milk and cream, expenditures on	yr	128	1999	30r
Fresh vegetables, expenditures on	yr	164	1999	30r
Grapefruit	lb	0.67	7/01	11r
Grapes, Thompson, seedless	lb	2.18	7/01	11r
Ground beef, lean and extra lean	lb	2.66	7/01	11r
Ground chuck, 100% beef	lb	2.04	7/01	11r
Lettuce, iceberg	lb	0.76	7/01	11r
Meats, poultry, fish, and egg purchases	yr	808	1999	30r
Nonalcoholic beverages, expenditures on	yr	225	1999	30r
Orange juice, frozen concentrate	16 oz	1.88	7/01	11r
Oranges, Navel	lb	0.79	7/01	11r
Oranges, Valencia	lb	0.56	7/01	11r
Peaches	lb	1.16	7/01	11r
Peanut butter, creamy, all sizes	lb	2.01	7/01	11r
Pears, Anjou	lb	1.16	7/01	11r
Pork chops, center cut, bone-in	lb	3.57	7/01	11r
Pork, expenditures on	yr	146	1999	30r
Potato chips	16 oz	3.37	7/01	11r
Potatoes, white, all types	lb	0.42	7/01	11r
Poultry, expenditures on	yr	158	1999	30r
Processed fruits, expenditures on	yr	124	1999	30r

Values are in dollars or fractions of dollars. In the column headed *Ref*, references are shown to sources. Each reference is followed by a letter. These refer to the geographical level for which data were reported: s=State, r=Region, and c=City or metro. The abbreviation *ex* is used to mean *except* or *excluding*; *exp* stands for *expenditures*. For other abbreviations and further explanations, please see the Introduction.

Williamsport, PA - continued

Item	Per	Value	Date	Ref.
Groceries				
Processed vegetables, expenditures on	yr	82	1999	30r
Round roast, U.S. choice, boneless	lb	3.04	7/01	11r
Spaghetti and macaroni	lb	1.04	7/01	11r
Steak, sirloin, U.S. choice, boneless	lb	5.39	7/01	11r
Strawberries, dry pint	12 oz	1.51	7/01	11r
Sugar and other sweets, expenditures on	yr	110	1999	30r
Sugar, white, 33-80 ounce package	lb	0.46	7/01	11r
Sugar, white, all sizes	lb	0.47	7/01	11r
Tobacco products and smoking supplies purchases	yr	309	1999	30r
Yogurt, natural, fruit flavored	8 oz	0.79	7/01	11r
Goods and Services				
B&B Japanese maple (acer japonicum)	gal	38.99- 125.00	4/00	93r
Boxwood (buxus)	2 gal	15.99- 49.95	4/00	93r
Daylilly (hemerocallis)	gal	4.95	4/00	93r
Flat of annuals		8.00- 14.99	4/00	93r
Fountain grass (pennisetum)	gal	6.99- 9.99	4/00	93r
Hanging basket (10 in)		12.95- 19.99	4/00	93r
Hardy geranium (geranium)	gal	6.95- 7.99	4/00	93r
Hosta (hosta)	gal	4.95	4/00	93r
Lilac (syrubga vulgaris)	2 gal	17.99- 74.95	4/00	93r
Miscellaneous purchases	yr	872	1999	30r
Rhododendron (rhododendron)	2 gal	23.99- 54.95	4/00	93r
Sage (salvia)	gal	6.95- 7.99	4/00	93r
Wintercreeper euonymus (euonymus fortunei)	2 gal	14.99- 23.95	4/00	93r
Hunting license	yr	20.00	4/01	34s
Health Care				
Cardiac catheterization, ave hospital/ physician charges		13870	1998	77s
Childbirth, Cesarean delivery		14716	1997	13r
Childbirth, vaginal delivery		8541	1997	13r
Drugs, expenditures on	yr	296	1999	30r
Health care purchases	yr	1788	1999	30r
Health insurance expenditures	yr	875	1999	30r
Hysterectomy, laproscopically-assisted, ave hospital/physician charges		14760	1998	76s
Hysterectomy, vaginal, ave hospital and physician charges		9270	1998	76s
Medicaid dispensing fee		4.00	1999	87s
Medical services expenditures	yr	516	1999	30r
Medical supplies, expenditures on	yr	102	1999	30r
Plastic surgery, breast augmentation		4232	2000	7r
Plastic surgery, breast lift		4605	2000	7r
Plastic surgery, facelift		6964	2000	7r
Plastic surgery, hair transplantation		4193	2000	7r
Plastic surgery, lip augmentation		1675	2000	7r
Plastic surgery, lower body lift		6611	2000	7r
Plastic surgery, thigh lift		4751	2000	7r
Household Goods				
Floor coverings, expenditures on	yr	59	1999	30r
Furniture, expenditures on	yr	388	1999	30r
Household furnishings and equipment purchases	yr	1567	1999	30r
Household textiles, expenditures on	yr	112	1999	30r
Laundry and cleaning supplies, expenditures on	yr	104	1999	30r
Housing				
Home price, existing, ave		180800	10/00	90r
Home value, median		115000	2001	53s
Household operation expenditures	yr	581	1999	30r

Williamsport, PA - continued

Item	Per	Value	Date	Ref.
Housing - continued				
Housekeeping supplies purchases	yr	474	1999	30r
Lodging expenditures	yr	550	1999	30r
Maintenance, repairs, insurance expenditures	yr	835	1999	30r
Monthly rental value of owned home	mos	663	1999	30r
Owned dwellings, expenditures own	yr	5209	1999	30r
Rent expenditures	yr	2390	1999	30r
Rental unit, 1 bedroom, with utilities	mos	373	4/01	41c
Rental unit, 2 bedroom, with utilities	mos	448	4/01	41c
Rental unit, 3 bedroom, with utilities	mos	579	4/01	41c
Rental unit, 4 bedroom, with utilities	mos	647	4/01	41c
Shelter, expenditures on	yr	8149	1999	30r
Insurance and Pensions				
Life and other personal insurance purchases	yr	424	1999	30r
Pensions and Social Security, expenditures on	yr	3037	1999	30r
Legal Fees				
Divorce, filing fee		65.00	4/01	35s
Driver's license fee	renew	24.00	1999	48s
Driver's license fee	orig	29.00	1999	48s
Fishing license	yr	17.00	4/01	34s
Personal Goods				
Personal care products and services purchases	yr	399	1999	30r
Personal Services				
Personal services, household, expenditures on	yr	271	1999	30r
Pets				
Pets, toys, and playground equipment, expenditures on	yr	325	1999	30r
Taxes				
Federal income taxes paid	yr	2606	1999	30r
Personal taxes, expenditures on	yr	3567	1999	30r
Property taxes paid	yr	1752	1999	30r
State and local income taxes paid	yr	694	1999	30r
Transportation				
Bus fare, one-way	trip	1.00	2000	1c
Cars and trucks, new, expenditures on	yr	1496	1999	30r
Cars and trucks, used, expenditures on	yr	1251	1999	30r
Diesel at the pump	gal	1.31	10/99	73s
Gasoline and motor oil purchases	yr	901	1999	30r
Gasoline before-tax price (cents)	gal	106.60	10/00	43s
Maintenance and repair expenditures	yr	618	1999	30r
Public transportation, expenditures on	yr	575	1999	30r
Transportation purchases	yr	6503	1999	30r
Vehicle expenses, miscellaneous, purchases	yr	2266	1999	30r
Vehicle insurance payments	yr	824	1999	30r
Vehicle purchases (net outlay)	yr	2761	1999	30r
Vehicle rental, lease expenditures	yr	584	1999	30r
Utilities				
Electrical bill, average	mos	69.16	9/00	9s
Electricity, expenditures on	yr	837	1999	30r
Electricity cost, average	KWh	5.08	9/00	9s
Utilities, fuels, and public services purchased	yr	2457	1999	30r
Water and other public services, expenditures on	yr	215	1999	30r
Weddings				
Wedding (national average cost)		19936	2000	33r
Wedding (regional average total cost)		29454	1997	110r
Attendants' gifts		321	1998	33r
Bridal attendants' apparel (5 persons)		824	2000	33r
Bride's headpiece/veil		173	1998	33r
Bride's wedding dress		859	1998	33r
Clergy, religious facility fee		242	1998	33r
Engagement ring		3177	1998	33r
Flowers		789	1998	33r
Groom's formalwear rental		99	2000	33r

Values are in dollars or fractions of dollars. In the column headed *Ref*, references are shown to sources. Each reference is followed by a letter. These refer to the geographical level for which data were reported: s=State, r=Region, and c=City or metro. The abbreviation *ex* is used to mean *except* or *excluding*; *exp* stands for expenditures. For other abbreviations and further explanations, please see the Introduction.

Williamsport, PA - continued

Item	Per	Value	Date	Ref.
Weddings				
Limousine		410	1998	33r
Marriage license cost		25.00- 40.00	4/01	35s
Men's formalwear (ushers, best man)		469	2000	33r
Mother of bride apparel		241	2000	33r
Music		866	1998	33r
Photography and videography		1368	1998	33r
Rehearsal dinner		728	1998	33r
Wedding invitations and announcements		341	1998	33r
Wedding reception		7968	2000	33r
Wedding rings (bride and groom)		1060	1998	33r

Wilmington, DE

Item	Per	Value	Date	Ref.
Composite, ACCRA index		109.70	3/01	4c
Composite, ACCRA index		110.70	12/00	5c
Alcoholic Beverages				
Alcoholic beverage purchases	yr	253	1999	30r
Beer, Heineken, 12-oz, ex deposit	6	6.71	3/01	4c
Beer, Heineken, 12-oz, ex deposit	6	6.80	12/00	5c
J & B Scotch	750-ml	17.41	3/01	4c
J & B Scotch	750-ml	17.41	12/00	5c
Malt beverages, all types, all sizes, any origin	16 oz	0.96	7/01	11r
Wine, Livingston or Gallo, Chablis blanc	1.5 liter	6.45	3/01	4c
Wine, Livingston or Gallo, Chablis blanc	1.5 liter	6.44	12/00	5c
Appliances				
Appliance repair, service call, washing machine	min lab chg	44.98	3/01	4c
Appliance repair, service call, washing machine	min lab chg	44.98	12/00	5c
Major appliances, expenditures on	yr	172	1999	30r
Small appliances, housewares, expenditures on	yr	81	1999	30r
Banking and Money				
Mortgage interest and charges paid	yr	2039	1999	30r
Mortgage principal paid on owned property	yr	1026	1999	30r
Mortgage rate, incl. points and orig. fee, 30-yr. conv. fixed or ARM	mos	7.21	3/01	4c
Mortgage rate, incl. points and orig. fee, 30-yr. conv. fixed or ARM	mos	7.63	12/00	5c
Vehicle finance charges paid	yr	365	1999	30r
Business Expenses				
Business travel, car rental	day	64	2001	3c
Business travel, food	day	44	2001	3c
Business travel, hotel	day	107	2001	3c
Charity				
Cash contributions, expenditures	yr	1127	1999	30r
Child Care				
Child raising cost, total, age 0-2	yr	8540	1999	60r
Child raising cost, total, age 3-5	yr	8780	1999	60r
Child raising cost, total, age 6-8	yr	8820	1999	60r
Child raising cost, total, age 9-11	yr	8800	1999	60r
Child raising cost, total, age 12-14	yr	9510	1999	60r
Child raising cost, total, age 15-17	yr	9740	1999	60r
Child's child care and education, age 0-2	yr	1380	1999	60r
Child's child care and education, age 3-5	yr	1520	1999	60r
Child's child care and education, age 6-8	yr	990	1999	60r
Child's child care and education, age 9-11	yr	650	1999	60r
Child's child care and education, age 12-14	yr	490	1999	60r
Child's child care and education, age 15-17	yr	840	1999	60r
Child's clothing, age 0-2	yr	480	1999	60r
Child's clothing, age 3-5	yr	470	1999	60r
Child's clothing, age 6-8	yr	520	1999	60r
Child's clothing, age 9-11	yr	570	1999	60r
Child's clothing, age 12-14	yr	950	1999	60r
Child's clothing, age 15-17	yr	850	1999	60r
Child's food, age 0-2	yr	1000	1999	60r
Child's food, age 3-5	yr	1160	1999	60r

Wilmington, DE - continued

Item	Per	Value	Date	Ref.
Child Care - continued				
Child's food, age 6-8	yr	1490	1999	60r
Child's food, age 9-11	yr	1770	1999	60r
Child's food, age 12-14	yr	1770	1999	60r
Child's food, age 15-17	yr	1980	1999	60r
Child's health care, age 0-2	yr	620	1999	60r
Child's health care, age 3-5	yr	590	1999	60r
Child's health care, age 6-8	yr	680	1999	60r
Child's health care, age 9-11	yr	720	1999	60r
Child's health care, age 12-14	yr	730	1999	60r
Child's health care, age 15-17	yr	760	1999	60r
Child's housing, age 0-2	yr	3070	1999	60r
Child's housing, age 3-5	yr	3050	1999	60r
Child's housing, age 6-8	yr	3010	1999	60r
Child's housing, age 9-11	yr	2850	1999	60r
Child's housing, age 12-14	yr	3040	1999	60r
Child's housing, age 15-17	yr	2650	1999	60r
Child's personal care, reading, age 0-2	yr	910	1999	60r
Child's personal care, reading, age 3-5	yr	930	1999	60r
Child's personal care, reading, age 6-8	yr	960	1999	60r
Child's personal care, reading, age 9-11	yr	1000	1999	60r
Child's personal care, reading, age 12-14	yr	1170	1999	60r
Child's personal care, reading, age 15-17	yr	950	1999	60r
Daycare	mos	540	1998	37c
Daycare, 3-year old, 5 days, 8 hrs/day	mos	540	1998	85c
Clothing				
Apparel and services purchases	yr	1610	1999	30r
Boys' brief, cotton	3	4.19	3/01	4c
Boys' brief, cotton	3	4.19	12/00	5c
Boys, 2 to 15, expenditures on	yr	89	1999	30r
Children under 2, expenditures on	yr	79	1999	30r
Footwear, expenditures on	yr	283	1999	30r
Girls, 2 to 15, expenditures on	yr	103	1999	30r
Men and boys, expenditures on	yr	351	1999	30r
Men, 16 and over, expenditures on	yr	262	1999	30r
Shirt, man's dress shirt		25.62	3/01	4c
Shirt, man's dress shirt		29.37	12/00	5c
Slacks, man's "No Wrinkles" khaki		38.75	3/01	4c
Slacks, man's "No Wrinkles" khaki		45.50	12/00	5c
Women, 16 and over, expenditures on	yr	538	1999	30r
Communications				
Newspaper subscription, daily and Sunday delivery	mos	15.44	3/01	4c
Newspaper subscription, daily and Sunday delivery	mos	15.38	12/00	5c
Phone line, single, business, field visit	inst.	60.94	12/97	17s
Phone line, single, business, no field visit	inst.	60.94	12/97	17s
Phone line, single, residence, field visit	inst.	35.96	12/97	17s
Phone line, single, residence, no field visit	inst.	35.96	12/97	17s
Postage and stationery, expenditures on	yr	104	1999	30r
Postal rate, express mail, up to half-pound		12.45	7/01	108r
Postal rate, letter, first class, first ounce		0.34	7/01	108r
Postal rate, letter, two ounces		0.57	7/01	108r
Postal rate, post card		0.21	7/01	108r
Postal rate, priority mail, two pounds		3.95	7/01	108r
Postal rate, priority mail, up to one pound		3.50	7/01	108r
Telephone bill, business, basic rate	mos	4.55	12/97	18c
Telephone bill, family of three	mos	17.52	3/01	4c
Telephone bill, family of three	mos	16.16	12/00	5c
Telephone bill, residential, basic rate	mos	2.25	12/97	18c
Telephone services, expenditures on	yr	860	1999	30r
Education				
Board, 4-year private college/university	yr	1443	1996	38s
Board, 4-year public college/university	yr	2101	1996	38s
Education expenditures	yr	431	1999	30r
Room, 4-year private college/university	yr	2701	1996	38s
Room, 4-year public college/university	yr	2407	1996	38s
Total cost, 4-year private college/university	yr	11518	1996	38s
Total cost, 4-year public college/university	yr	8489	1996	38s
Tuition, 2-year public college/university, in state	yr	1266	1996	38s

Values are in dollars or fractions of dollars. In the column headed *Ref*, references are shown to sources. Each reference is followed by a letter. These refer to the geographical level for which data were reported: s=State, r=Region, and c=City or metro. The abbreviation *ex* is used to mean *except* or *excluding*; *exp* stands for *expenditures*. For other abbreviations and further explanations, please see the Introduction.

Wilmington, DE - continued

Item	Per	Value	Date	Ref.
Education				
Tuition, 4-year private college/university, in state	yr	7373	1996	38s
Tuition, 4-year public college/university	yr	3981	1996	38s
Energy and Fuels				
Electricity	KWh	0.09	7/01	11r
Electricity	500 KWhs	47.29	7/01	11r
Energy, combined forms, 2400 sq ft	mos	157.60	3/01	4c
Energy, combined forms, 2400 sq ft	mos	157.60	12/00	5c
Fuel oil #2	gal	1.43	7/01	11r
Fuel oil and other fuels, expenditures on	yr	45	1999	30r
Gas, cooking, winter, 10 therms	mos	9.84	2/96	98c
Gas, cooking, winter, 30 therms	mos	22.59	2/96	98c
Gas, cooking, winter, 50 therms	mos	35.34	2/96	98c
Gas, heating, winter, average use	mos	132.77	2/96	98c
Gas, natural, commercial rate	1000 cf	7.37	11/00	88s
Gas, regular unleaded, cash, self-service	gal	1.50	3/01	4c
Gas, regular unleaded, cash, self-service	gal	1.58	12/00	5c
Gasoline, all types	gal	1.60	7/01	11r
Gasoline, unleaded midgrade	gal	1.65	7/01	11r
Gasoline, unleaded premium	gal	1.74	7/01	11r
Natural gas, expenditures on	yr	164	1999	30r
Utility (piped) gas, therm		1.01	7/01	11r
Utility (piped) gas, 40 therms		44.29	7/01	11r
Utility (piped) gas, 100 therms		97.44	7/01	11r
Entertainment				
Bowling, Saturday evening rate	line	3.88	3/01	4c
Bowling, Saturday evening rate	line	3.88	12/00	5c
Entertainment purchases	yr	1574	1999	30r
Fees and admissions paid	yr	371	1999	30r
Monopoly game, Parker Brothers', No. 9	game	11.69	3/01	4c
Monopoly game, Parker Brothers', No. 9	game	11.68	12/00	5c
Movie, first-run, Saturday, evening	adm.	6.58	3/01	4c
Movie, first-run, Saturday, evening	adm.	6.58	12/00	5c
Reading purchases	yr	121	1999	30r
Television, radios, sound equipment, expenditures on	yr	561	1999	30r
Tennis balls, yellow, Wilson or Penn, 3	can	2.03	3/01	4c
Tennis balls, yellow, Wilson or Penn, 3	can	2.03	12/00	5c
Funerals				
Total cost of funeral		5922.53	1/99	78r
Acknowledgement cards		63.43	1/99	78r
Casket		2258.77	1/99	78r
Cosmetology, hair, other preparation		127.09	1/99	78r
Embalming		393.49	1/99	78r
Funeral at funeral home		367.50	1/99	78r
Hearse (local)		169.66	1/99	78r
Professional service charges		1211.32	1/99	78r
Service car/van		80.69	1/99	78r
Transfer of remains to funeral home		144.25	1/99	78r
Vault		803.50	1/99	78r
Visitation/viewing		302.83	1/99	78r
Groceries				
Groceries, ACCRA Index		109.40	3/01	4c
Groceries, ACCRA Index		109.70	12/00	5c
American processed cheese	lb	3.50	7/01	11r
Antibiotic ointment, Polysporin	0.5 oz	5.05	3/01	4c
Antibiotic ointment, Polysporin	0.5 oz	5.05	12/00	5c
Baby food, strained vegetables or fruit, lowest price	4-4.5 oz	0.46	3/01	4c
Baby food, strained vegetables or fruit, lowest price	4-4.5 oz	0.46	12/00	5c
Bakery products, expenditures on	yr	261	1999	30r
Bananas	lb	0.55	3/01	4c
Bananas	lb	0.47	7/01	11r
Bananas	lb	0.43	12/00	5c
Beans, dried, any type, all sizes	lb	0.63	7/01	11r
Beef for stew, boneless	lb	2.86	7/01	11r
Beef or hamburger, ground	lb	1.87	3/01	4c
Beef or hamburger, ground	lb	1.67	12/00	5c

Wilmington, DE - continued

Item	Per	Value	Date	Ref.
Groceries - continued				
Beef, expenditures on	yr	210	1999	30r
Bologna, all beef or mixed	lb	2.29	7/01	11r
Bread, French	lb	1.66	7/01	11r
Bread, white	loaf	0.83	3/01	4c
Bread, white	loaf	0.97	12/00	5c
Bread, white, pan	lb	0.87	7/01	11r
Bread, whole wheat, pan	lb	1.38	7/01	11r
Broccoli	lb	1.04	7/01	11r
Butter, salted, grade AA, stick	lb	2.26	7/01	11r
Butter, yoghurt, cheese, etc, expenditures on	yr	170	1999	30r
Cabbage	lb	0.42	7/01	11r
Cereals and cereal products, expenditures on	yr	140	1999	30r
Cheddar cheese, natural	lb	3.75	7/01	11r
Cheese, Kraft grated Parmesan	8 oz	4.77	3/01	4c
Cheese, Kraft grated Parmesan	8 oz	4.37	12/00	5c
Chicken breast, bone-in	lb	1.85	7/01	11r
Chicken legs, bone-in	lb	1.34	7/01	11r
Chicken, fresh, whole	lb	1.05	7/01	11r
Chicken, whole fryer	lb	1.27	3/01	4c
Chicken, whole fryer	lb	1.03	12/00	5c
Chops, boneless,	lb	4.13	7/01	11r
Chuck roast, graded and ungraded, excl U.S. prime and choice	lb	2.35	7/01	11r
Chuck roast, U.S. choice, boneless	lb	2.67	7/01	11r
Cigarettes, Winston, Kings	carton	28.65	3/01	4c
Cigarettes, Winston, Kings	carton	27.95	12/00	5c
Coffee, 100%, ground roast, all sizes	lb	2.88	7/01	11r
Coffee, instant, plain, regular, all sizes	16 oz	9.25	7/01	11r
Coffee, vacuum-packed	13 oz	2.53	3/01	4c
Coffee, vacuum-packed	13 oz	2.91	12/00	5c
Cola, non diet,	2 liter	1.11	7/01	11r
Corn Flakes, Kellogg's or Post Toasties	18 oz	3.37	3/01	4c
Corn Flakes, Kellogg's or Post Toasties	18 oz	3.03	12/00	5c
Corn, frozen, whole kernel, lowest price	16 oz	1.35	3/01	4c
Corn, frozen, whole kernel, lowest price	16 oz	1.15	12/00	5c
Crackers, soda, salted	lb	1.70	7/01	11r
Dairy product purchases	yr	282	1999	30r
Eggs, expenditures on	yr	32	1999	30r
Eggs, Grade A or AA	dozen	1.31	3/01	4c
Eggs, Grade A or AA	dozen	1.14	12/00	5c
Fats and oils, expenditures on	yr	79	1999	30r
Fish and seafood, expenditures on	yr	99	1999	30r
Flour, white, all purpose	lb	0.32	7/01	11r
Food (excl fruit and vegetables), eaten at home, purchases	yr	815	1999	30r
Food cooked on trips, expenditures on	yr	36	1999	30r
Food purchases	yr	4533	1999	30r
Food purchases, eaten away from home	yr	1873	1999	30r
Food purchases, food eaten at home	yr	2660	1999	30r
Fresh fruits, expenditures on	yr	128	1999	30r
Fresh milk and cream, expenditures on	yr	112	1999	30r
Fresh vegetables, expenditures on	yr	131	1999	30r
Fruit and vegetable purchases	yr	438	1999	30r
Grapefruit	lb	0.59	7/01	11r
Grapes, Thompson, seedless	lb	2.12	7/01	11r
Ground beef, 100% beef	lb	1.76	7/01	11r
Ground beef, lean and extra lean	lb	2.60	7/01	11r
Ground chuck, 100% beef	lb	2.08	7/01	11r
Ham, boneless, excl canned	lb	2.71	7/01	11r
Ham, rump or shank half, bone-in, smoked	lb	2.19	7/01	11r
Ice cream, prepackaged, bulk, regular	1/2 gal	3.93	7/01	11r
Lemons	lb	1.32	7/01	11r
Lettuce, iceberg	head	1.29	3/01	4c
Lettuce, iceberg	lb	0.76	7/01	11r
Lettuce, iceberg	head	1.27	12/00	5c
Margarine, Blue Bonnet or Parkay, stick	lb	1.10	3/01	4c
Margarine, Blue Bonnet or Parkay, stick	lb	1.16	12/00	5c
Milk, fresh, low fat,	gal	2.75	7/01	11r
Milk, fresh, whole, fortified	gal	2.97	7/01	11r
Milk, whole	1/2 gal	1.72	3/01	4c
Milk, whole	1/2 gal	1.68	12/00	5c

Values are in dollars or fractions of dollars. In the column headed *Ref*, references are shown to sources. Each reference is followed by a letter. These refer to the geographical level for which data were reported: s=State, r=Region, and c=City or metro. The abbreviation *ex* is used to mean *except* or *excluding*; *exp* stands for expenditures. For other abbreviations and further explanations, please see the Introduction.

Wilmington, DE - continued

Item	Per	Value	Date	Ref.
Groceries				
Nonalcoholic beverages, expenditures on	yr	228	1999	30r
Orange juice, frozen concentrate	16 oz	1.95	7/01	11r
Orange juice, Minute Maid frozen	12 oz	1.93	3/01	4c
Orange juice, Minute Maid frozen	12 oz	1.89	12/00	5c
Oranges, Navel	lb	0.73	7/01	11r
Oranges, Valencia	lb	0.55	7/01	11r
Peaches, halves or slices, Hunt's, Del Monte, or Libby's	29 oz	1.65	3/01	4c
Peaches, halves or slices, Hunt's, Del Monte, or Libby's	29 oz	1.69	12/00	5c
Peanut butter, creamy, all sizes	lb	1.83	7/01	11r
Pears, Anjou	lb	0.98	7/01	11r
Peas, green, Del Monte or Green Giant	15 oz	0.80	3/01	4c
Peas, green, Del Monte or Green Giant	15 oz	0.73	12/00	5c
Pork chops, center cut, bone-in	lb	3.33	7/01	11r
Pork sausage, fresh, loose	lb	2.59	7/01	11r
Pork shoulder picnic, bone-in, smoked	lb	1.12	7/01	11r
Pork, expenditures on	yr	162	1999	30r
Potato chips	16 oz	3.59	7/01	11r
Potatoes, frozen, french fried	lb	1.00	7/01	11r
Potatoes, white or red	10 lb	2.69	3/01	4c
Potatoes, white or red	10 lb	2.59	12/00	5c
Potatoes, white, all types	lb	0.44	7/01	11r
Poultry, expenditures on	yr	137	1999	30r
Processed fruits, expenditures on	yr	97	1999	30r
Processed vegetables, expenditures on	yr	82	1999	30r
Rice, white, long grain, uncooked	lb	0.51	7/01	11r
Round roast, graded and ungraded, excl U.S. prime and choice	lb	2.96	7/01	11r
Round steak, graded and ungraded, excl U.S. prime and choice	lb	3.11	7/01	11r
Sausage, Jimmy Dean/Owens pork	lb	3.02	3/01	4c
Sausage, Jimmy Dean/Owens pork	lb	4.08	12/00	5c
Shortening, vegetable, Crisco	3 lb	3.73	3/01	4c
Shortening, vegetable, Crisco	3 lb	3.73	12/00	5c
Sirloin steak, graded and ungraded, excl U.S. prime and choice	lb	4.23	7/01	11r
Soft drink, Coca Cola, ex deposit	2 liter	1.09	3/01	4c
Soft drink, Coca Cola, ex deposit	2 liter	0.97	12/00	5c
Spaghetti and macaroni	lb	0.78	7/01	11r
Steak, round, U.S. choice, boneless	lb	3.56	7/01	11r
Steak, sirloin, U.S. choice, boneless	lb	5.65	7/01	11r
Steak, T-bone	lb	6.73	3/01	4c
Steak, T-bone	lb	7.19	12/00	5c
Strawberries, dry pint	12 oz	1.50	7/01	11r
Sugar and other sweets, expenditures on	yr	99	1999	30r
Sugar, cane or beet	4 lbs	2.10	3/01	4c
Sugar, cane or beet	4 lbs	1.97	12/00	5c
Sugar, white, 33-80 ounce package	lb	0.39	7/01	11r
Sugar, white, all sizes	lb	0.42	7/01	11r
Tobacco products and smoking supplies purchases	yr	288	1999	30r
Tomatoes, field grown	lb	1.43	7/01	11r
Tomatoes, Hunt's or Del Monte	14.5 oz	0.99	3/01	4c
Tomatoes, Hunt's or Del Monte	14.5 oz	0.99	12/00	5c
Tuna, chunk, light	6 oz	0.70	3/01	4c
Tuna, chunk, light	6 oz	0.67	12/00	5c
Tuna, light, chunk	lb	1.77	7/01	11r
Turkey, frozen, whole	lb	1.05	7/01	11r
Goods and Services				
Miscellaneous goods and services, ACCRA Index		102.90	3/01	4c
Miscellaneous goods and services, ACCRA Index		106.90	12/00	5c
B&B Japanese maple (acer japonicum)	gal	49.98-129.00	4/00	93r
Boxwood (buxus)	2 gal	12.99-16.99	4/00	93r
Daylilly (hemerocallis)	gal	4.99-8.99	4/00	93r
Flat of annuals		11.00-13.92	4/00	93r

Wilmington, DE - continued

Item	Per	Value	Date	Ref.
Goods and Services - continued				
Fountain grass (pennisetum)	gal	5.98-7.98	4/00	93r
Hanging basket (10 in)		7.99-14.98	4/00	93r
Hardy geranium (geranium)	gal	5.98-8.00	4/00	93r
Hosta (hosta)	gal	4.99-10.98	4/00	93r
Lilac (syrubga vulgaris)	2 gal	12.99-21.99	4/00	93r
Rhododendron (rhododendron)	2 gal	14.99-24.99	4/00	93r
Sage (salvia)	gal	5.98-6.99	4/00	93r
Wintercreeper euonymus (euonymus fortunei)	2 gal	7.99-89.99	4/00	93r
Hunting license	yr	12.50	4/01	34s
Health Care				
Health care, ACCRA Index		117.40	3/01	4c
Health care, ACCRA Index		120.10	12/00	5c
Cardiac catheterization, ave hospital/ physician charges		14610	1998	77s
Childbirth, Cesarean delivery		11587	1997	13r
Childbirth, vaginal delivery		6725	1997	13r
Dentist's fee, adult teeth cleaning and periodic oral exam	visit	103.75	3/01	4c
Dentist's fee, adult teeth cleaning and periodic oral exam	visit	103.75	12/00	5c
Doctor's fee, routine exam, established patient	visit	57.50	3/01	4c
Doctor's fee, routine exam, established patient	visit	57.50	12/00	5c
Drugs, expenditures on	yr	399	1999	30r
Health care purchases	yr	1971	1999	30r
Health insurance expenditures	yr	933	1999	30r
Hospital care, private room	day	571.50	3/01	4c
Hospital care, private room	day	571.50	12/00	5c
Hysterectomy, laproscopically-assisted, ave hospital/physician charges		12750	1998	76s
Hysterectomy, vaginal, ave hospital and physician charges		7150	1998	76s
Medicaid dispensing fee		3.65	1999	87s
Medical services expenditures	yr	547	1999	30r
Medical supplies, expenditures on	yr	91	1999	30r
Plastic surgery, breast augmentation		2870	2000	7r
Plastic surgery, breast lift		3649	2000	7r
Plastic surgery, facelift		5008	2000	7r
Plastic surgery, hair transplantation		3425	2000	7r
Plastic surgery, lip augmentation		1227	2000	7r
Plastic surgery, lower body lift		4793	2000	7r
Plastic surgery, thigh lift		3862	2000	7r
Household Goods				
Dishwashing powder, Cascade	50 oz	2.89	3/01	4c
Dishwashing powder, Cascade	50 oz	2.99	12/00	5c
Floor coverings, expenditures on	yr	44	1999	30r
Furniture, expenditures on	yr	335	1999	30r
Household furnishings and equipment purchases	yr	1328	1999	30r
Household textiles, expenditures on	yr	89	1999	30r
Laundry and cleaning supplies, expenditures on	yr	113	1999	30r
Tissues, facial, Kleenex brand	175	1.59	3/01	4c
Tissues, facial, Kleenex brand	175	1.57	12/00	5c
Housing				
Housing, ACCRA Index		115.40	3/01	4c
Housing, ACCRA Index		111.40	12/00	5c
Home, 2200 sq ft, 4-br, 2-bath, 2-car garage, average		193675	2000	47c
Home price, existing, ave		160100	10/00	90r
Home value, median		181000	2001	53s

Values are in dollars or fractions of dollars. In the column headed *Ref*, references are shown to sources. Each reference is followed by a letter. These refer to the geographical level for which data were reported: s=State, r=Region, and c=City or metro. The abbreviation *ex* is used to mean *except* or *excluding*; *exp* stands for *expenditures*. For other abbreviations and further explanations, please see the Introduction.

Wilmington, DE - continued

Item	Per	Value	Date	Ref.
Housing				
House, 2400 sq ft, 8000 sq ft lot, new, urban, utilities	total	241333	3/01	4c
House, 2400 sq ft, 8000 sq ft lot, new, urban, utilities	total	241333	12/00	5c
House payment, principal and interest, 25% down payment	mos	1229	3/01	4c
House payment, principal and interest, 25% down payment	mos	1282	12/00	5c
Household operation expenditures	yr	553	1999	30r
Housekeeping supplies purchases	yr	473	1999	30r
Housing, expenditures on	yr	10303	1999	30r
Maintenance, repairs, insurance expenditures	yr	699	1999	30r
Monthly rental value of owned home	mos	505	1999	30r
Owned dwellings, expenditures own	yr	3465	1999	30r
Rent expenditures	yr	1641	1999	30r
Rent, apartment, 2 br, 1 1/2-2 baths, unfurn, 950 sq ft, water	mos	699	3/01	4c
Rent, apartment, 2 br, 1 1/2-2 baths, unfurn, 950 sq ft, water	mos	701	12/00	5c
Shelter, expenditures on	yr	5467	1999	30r
Insurance and Pensions				
Life and other personal insurance purchases	yr	414	1999	30r
Pensions and Social Security, expenditures on	yr	2635	1999	30r
Personal insurance and pensions, expenditures on	yr	3048	1999	30r
Legal Fees				
Divorce, filing fee		75.00	4/01	35s
Driver's license fee	renew	12.50	1999	48s
Driver's license fee	orig	12.50	1999	48s
Personal Goods				
Personal care products and services purchases	yr	393	1999	30r
Shampoo, Alberto VO5	15 oz	1.14	3/01	4c
Shampoo, Alberto VO5	15 oz	1.06	12/00	5c
Toothpaste, Crest or Colgate	6-7 oz	2.02	3/01	4c
Toothpaste, Crest or Colgate	6-7 oz	1.94	12/00	5c
Personal Services				
Dry cleaning, man's 2-pc suit		7.05	3/01	4c
Dry cleaning, man's 2-pc suit		7.05	12/00	5c
Man's haircut, barbershop, no styling		9.75	3/01	4c
Man's haircut, barbershop, no styling		9.75	12/00	5c
Personal services, household, expenditures on	yr	258	1999	30r
Woman's shampoo, trim, blow-dry, no style-change		19.00	3/01	4c
Woman's shampoo, trim, blow-dry, no style-change		19.00	12/00	5c
Pets				
Pets, toys, and playground equipment, expenditures on	yr	306	1999	30r
Restaurant Food				
Chicken, fried, thigh and drumstick, KFC/Church's		2.79	3/01	4c
Chicken, fried, thigh and drumstick, KFC/Church's		2.79	12/00	5c
Hamburger with cheese, McDonald's	1/4 lb	2.25	3/01	4c
Hamburger with cheese, McDonald's	1/4 lb	2.25	12/00	5c
Pizza, Pizza Hut or Pizza Inn	11-12 in	10.79	3/01	4c
Pizza, Pizza Hut or Pizza Inn	11-12 in	10.79	12/00	5c
Taxes				
Federal income taxes paid	yr	2047	1999	30r
Personal taxes, expenditures on	yr	2554	1999	30r
Property taxes paid	yr	726	1999	30r
State and local income taxes paid	yr	363	1999	30r

Wilmington, DE - continued

Item	Per	Value	Date	Ref.
Transportation				
Transportation, ACCRA Index		102.40	3/01	4c
Transportation, ACCRA Index		102.00	12/00	5c
Bus fare, one-way	trip	1.15	2000	1c
Cars and trucks, new, expenditures on	yr	1648	1999	30r
Cars and trucks, used, expenditures on	yr	1651	1999	30r
Diesel at the pump	gal	1.26	10/99	73s
Gasoline and motor oil purchases	yr	1052	1999	30r
Gasoline before-tax price (cents)	gal	112.60	10/00	43s
Maintenance and repair expenditures	yr	621	1999	30r
Motorcycle license fee	orig	5.00	1999	49s
Motorcycle license fee	renew	5.00	1999	49s
Public transportation, expenditures on	yr	298	1999	30r
Tire balance, computer or spin balance, front	wheel	7.60	3/01	4c
Tire balance, computer or spin balance, front	wheel	7.60	12/00	5c
Transportation purchases	yr	6738	1999	30r
Vehicle expenses, miscellaneous, purchases	yr	2033	1999	30r
Vehicle insurance payments	yr	696	1999	30r
Vehicle purchases (net outlay)	yr	3354	1999	30r
Vehicle rental, lease expenditures	yr	352	1999	30r
Utilities				
Utilities, ACCRA Index		122.40	3/01	4c
Utilities, ACCRA Index		131.40	12/00	5c
Electrical bill, average	mos	81.50	9/00	9s
Electricity, 2400 sq ft, new home	mos	157.60	3/01	4c
Electricity, 2400 sq ft, new home	mos	157.60	12/00	5c
Electricity, expenditures on	yr	1115	1999	30r
Electricity, summer, 250 KWh	mos	27.63	2/96	97c
Electricity, summer, 500 KWh	mos	50.43	2/96	97c
Electricity, summer, 750 KWh	mos	71.03	2/96	97c
Electricity, summer, 1000 KWh	mos	91.63	2/96	97c
Electricity cost, average	KWh	6.60	9/00	9s
Water and other public services, expenditures on	yr	298	1999	30r
Weddings				
Wedding (national average cost)		19936	2000	33r
Wedding (regional average total cost)		16293	1997	110r
Attendants' gifts		321	1998	33r
Bridal attendants' apparel (5 persons)		824	2000	33r
Bride's headpiece/veil		173	1998	33r
Bride's wedding dress		859	1998	33r
Clergy, religious facility fee		242	1998	33r
Engagement ring		3177	1998	33r
Flowers		789	1998	33r
Groom's formalwear rental		99	2000	33r
Limousine		410	1998	33r
Marriage license cost		35.00	4/01	35s
Men's formalwear (ushers, best man)		469	2000	33r
Mother of bride apparel		241	2000	33r
Music		866	1998	33r
Photography and videography		1368	1998	33r
Rehearsal dinner		728	1998	33r
Wedding invitations and announcements		341	1998	33r
Wedding reception		7968	2000	33r
Wedding rings (bride and groom)		1060	1998	33r

Wilmington, NC

Item	Per	Value	Date	Ref.
Composite, ACCRA index		105.20	12/00	5c
Alcoholic Beverages				
Alcoholic beverage purchases	yr	253	1999	30r
Beer, Heineken, 12-oz, ex deposit	6	7.08	12/00	5c
J & B Scotch	750-ml	20.75	12/00	5c
Malt beverages, all types, all sizes, any origin	16 oz	0.96	7/01	11r
Wine, Livingston or Gallo, Chablis blanc	1.5 liter	6.06	12/00	5c
Appliances				
Appliance repair, service call, washing machine	min lab chg	42.70	12/00	5c
Major appliances, expenditures on	yr	172	1999	30r
Small appliances, housewares, expenditures on	yr	81	1999	30r

Values are in dollars or fractions of dollars. In the column headed *Ref*, references are shown to sources. Each reference is followed by a letter. These refer to the geographical level for which data were reported: s=State, r=Region, and c=City or metro. The abbreviation *ex* is used to mean *except* or *excluding*; *exp* stands for expenditures. For other abbreviations and further explanations, please see the Introduction.

Wilmington, NC - continued

Item	Per	Value	Date	Ref.
Banking and Money				
Mortgage interest and charges paid	yr	2039	1999	30r
Mortgage principal paid on owned property	yr	1026	1999	30r
Mortgage rate, incl. points and orig. fee, 30-yr. conv. fixed or ARM	mos	7.92	12/00	5c
Vehicle finance charges paid	yr	365	1999	30r
Charity				
Cash contributions, expenditures	yr	1127	1999	30r
Child Care				
Child raising cost, total, age 0-2	yr	8540	1999	60r
Child raising cost, total, age 3-5	yr	8780	1999	60r
Child raising cost, total, age 6-8	yr	8820	1999	60r
Child raising cost, total, age 9-11	yr	8800	1999	60r
Child raising cost, total, age 12-14	yr	9510	1999	60r
Child raising cost, total, age 15-17	yr	9740	1999	60r
Child's child care and education, age 0-2	yr	1380	1999	60r
Child's child care and education, age 3-5	yr	1520	1999	60r
Child's child care and education, age 6-8	yr	990	1999	60r
Child's child care and education, age 9-11	yr	650	1999	60r
Child's child care and education, age 12-14	yr	490	1999	60r
Child's child care and education, age 15-17	yr	840	1999	60r
Child's clothing, age 0-2	yr	480	1999	60r
Child's clothing, age 3-5	yr	470	1999	60r
Child's clothing, age 6-8	yr	520	1999	60r
Child's clothing, age 9-11	yr	570	1999	60r
Child's clothing, age 12-14	yr	950	1999	60r
Child's clothing, age 15-17	yr	850	1999	60r
Child's food, age 0-2	yr	1000	1999	60r
Child's food, age 3-5	yr	1160	1999	60r
Child's food, age 6-8	yr	1490	1999	60r
Child's food, age 9-11	yr	1770	1999	60r
Child's food, age 12-14	yr	1770	1999	60r
Child's food, age 15-17	yr	1980	1999	60r
Child's health care, age 0-2	yr	620	1999	60r
Child's health care, age 3-5	yr	590	1999	60r
Child's health care, age 6-8	yr	680	1999	60r
Child's health care, age 9-11	yr	720	1999	60r
Child's health care, age 12-14	yr	730	1999	60r
Child's health care, age 15-17	yr	760	1999	60r
Child's housing, age 0-2	yr	3070	1999	60r
Child's housing, age 3-5	yr	3050	1999	60r
Child's housing, age 6-8	yr	3010	1999	60r
Child's housing, age 9-11	yr	2850	1999	60r
Child's housing, age 12-14	yr	3040	1999	60r
Child's housing, age 15-17	yr	2650	1999	60r
Child's personal care, reading, age 0-2	yr	910	1999	60r
Child's personal care, reading, age 3-5	yr	930	1999	60r
Child's personal care, reading, age 6-8	yr	960	1999	60r
Child's personal care, reading, age 9-11	yr	1000	1999	60r
Child's personal care, reading, age 12-14	yr	1170	1999	60r
Child's personal care, reading, age 15-17	yr	950	1999	60r
Clothing				
Apparel and services purchases	yr	1610	1999	30r
Boys' brief, cotton	3	4.14	12/00	5c
Boys, 2 to 15, expenditures on	yr	89	1999	30r
Children under 2, expenditures on	yr	79	1999	30r
Footwear, expenditures on	yr	283	1999	30r
Girls, 2 to 15, expenditures on	yr	103	1999	30r
Men and boys, expenditures on	yr	351	1999	30r
Men, 16 and over, expenditures on	yr	262	1999	30r
Shirt, man's dress shirt		30.00	12/00	5c
Slacks, man's "No Wrinkles" khaki		48.00	12/00	5c
Women, 16 and over, expenditures on	yr	538	1999	30r
Communications				
Cable modem installation, Intermedia		149.95	6/99	103s
Cable modem installation, Time Warner		75.00-225.00	6/99	103s
Cable modem rate, cable subscriber, Intermedia	mos	49.95	6/99	103s
Cable modem rate, cable subscriber, Time Warner	mos	39.95-49.95	6/99	103s

Wilmington, NC - continued

Item	Per	Value	Date	Ref.
Communications - continued				
Cable modem rate, non-cable subscriber, Intermedia	mos	54.95	6/99	103s
Cable modem rate, non-cable subscriber, Time Warner	mos	39.95-54.95	6/99	103s
Newspaper subscription, daily and Sunday delivery	mos	10.99	12/00	5c
Phone line, single, business, field visit	inst.	65.00	12/97	17s
Phone line, single, business, no field visit	inst.	65.00	12/97	17s
Phone line, single, residence, field visit	inst.	42.75	12/97	17s
Phone line, single, residence, no field visit	inst.	42.75	12/97	17s
Postage and stationery, expenditures on	yr	104	1999	30r
Postal rate, express mail, up to half-pound		12.45	7/01	108r
Postal rate, letter, first class, first ounce		0.34	7/01	108r
Postal rate, letter, two ounces		0.57	7/01	108r
Postal rate, post card		0.21	7/01	108r
Postal rate, priority mail, two pounds		3.95	7/01	108r
Postal rate, priority mail, up to one pound		3.50	7/01	108r
Telephone bill, family of three	mos	17.86	12/00	5c
Telephone services, expenditures on	yr	860	1999	30r
Education				
Board, 4-year private college/university	yr	2316	1996	38s
Board, 4-year public college/university	yr	1737	1996	38s
Education expenditures	yr	431	1999	30r
Room, 4-year private college/university	yr	2128	1996	38s
Room, 4-year public college/university	yr	1742	1996	38s
Total cost, 4-year private college/university	yr	15428	1996	38s
Total cost, 4-year public college/university	yr	5119	1996	38s
Tuition, 4-year private college/university, in state	yr	10984	1996	38s
Tuition, 4-year public college/university	yr	1639	1996	38s
Energy and Fuels				
Electricity	500 KWhs	47.29	7/01	11r
Electricity	KWh	0.09	7/01	11r
Energy, combined forms, 2400 sq ft	mos	117.62	12/00	5c
Fuel oil #2	gal	1.43	7/01	11r
Fuel oil and other fuels, expenditures on	yr	45	1999	30r
Gas, natural, commercial rate	1000 cf	9.25	11/00	88s
Gas, regular unleaded, cash, self-service	gal	1.47	12/00	5c
Gasoline, all types	gal	1.60	7/01	11r
Gasoline, unleaded midgrade	gal	1.65	7/01	11r
Gasoline, unleaded premium	gal	1.74	7/01	11r
Natural gas, expenditures on	yr	164	1999	30r
Utility (piped) gas, therm		1.01	7/01	11r
Utility (piped) gas, 40 therms		44.29	7/01	11r
Utility (piped) gas, 100 therms		97.44	7/01	11r
Entertainment				
Bowling, Saturday evening rate	line	3.08	12/00	5c
Entertainment purchases	yr	1574	1999	30r
Fees and admissions paid	yr	371	1999	30r
Monopoly game, Parker Brothers', No. 9	game	10.59	12/00	5c
Movie, first-run, Saturday, evening	adm.	6.67	12/00	5c
Reading purchases	yr	121	1999	30r
Television, radios, sound equipment, expenditures on	yr	561	1999	30r
Tennis balls, yellow, Wilson or Penn, 3	can	1.94	12/00	5c
Funerals				
Total cost of funeral		5922.53	1/99	78r
Acknowledgement cards		63.43	1/99	78r
Casket		2258.77	1/99	78r
Cosmetology, hair, other preparation		127.09	1/99	78r
Embalming		393.49	1/99	78r
Funeral at funeral home		367.50	1/99	78r
Hearse (local)		169.66	1/99	78r
Professional service charges		1211.32	1/99	78r
Service car/van		80.69	1/99	78r
Transfer of remains to funeral home		144.25	1/99	78r
Vault		803.50	1/99	78r
Visitation/viewing		302.83	1/99	78r

Values are in dollars or fractions of dollars. In the column headed *Ref*, references are shown to sources. Each reference is followed by a letter. These refer to the geographical level for which data were reported: s=State, r=Region, and c=City or metro. The abbreviation *ex* is used to mean *except* or *excluding*; *exp* stands for *expenditures*. For other abbreviations and further explanations, please see the Introduction.

Wilmington, NC - continued

Item	Per	Value	Date	Ref.
Groceries				
Groceries, ACCRA Index		107.20	12/00	5c
American processed cheese	lb	3.50	7/01	11r
Antibiotic ointment, Polysporin	0.5 oz	4.22	12/00	5c
Baby food, strained vegetables or fruit,				
lowest price	4-4.5 oz	0.46	12/00	5c
Bakery products, expenditures on	yr	261	1999	30r
Bananas	lb	0.47	7/01	11r
Bananas	lb	0.58	12/00	5c
Beans, dried, any type, all sizes	lb	0.63	7/01	11r
Beef for stew, boneless	lb	2.86	7/01	11r
Beef or hamburger, ground	lb	1.82	12/00	5c
Beef, expenditures on	yr	210	1999	30r
Bologna, all beef or mixed	lb	2.29	7/01	11r
Bread, French	lb	1.66	7/01	11r
Bread, white	loaf	1.05	12/00	5c
Bread, white, pan	lb	0.87	7/01	11r
Bread, whole wheat, pan	lb	1.38	7/01	11r
Broccoli	lb	1.04	7/01	11r
Butter, salted, grade AA, stick	lb	2.26	7/01	11r
Butter, yoghurt, cheese, etc, expenditures on	yr	170	1999	30r
Cabbage	lb	0.42	7/01	11r
Cereals and cereal products, expenditures				
on	yr	140	1999	30r
Cheddar cheese, natural	lb	3.75	7/01	11r
Cheese, Kraft grated Parmesan	8 oz	3.29	12/00	5c
Chicken breast, bone-in	lb	1.85	7/01	11r
Chicken legs, bone-in	lb	1.34	7/01	11r
Chicken, fresh, whole	lb	1.05	7/01	11r
Chicken, whole fryer	lb	1.02	12/00	5c
Chops, boneless,	lb	4.13	7/01	11r
Chuck roast, graded and ungraded, excl U.S.				
prime and choice	lb	2.35	7/01	11r
Chuck roast, U.S. choice, boneless	lb	2.67	7/01	11r
Cigarettes, Winston, Kings	carton	27.12	12/00	5c
Coffee, 100%, ground roast, all sizes	lb	2.88	7/01	11r
Coffee, instant, plain, regular, all sizes	16 oz	9.25	7/01	11r
Coffee, vacuum-packed	13 oz	2.52	12/00	5c
Cola, non diet	2 liter	1.11	7/01	11r
Corn Flakes, Kellogg's or Post Toasties	18 oz	2.86	12/00	5c
Corn, frozen, whole kernel, lowest price	16 oz	1.09	12/00	5c
Crackers, soda, salted	lb	1.70	7/01	11r
Dairy product purchases	yr	282	1999	30r
Eggs, expenditures on	yr	32	1999	30r
Eggs, Grade A or AA	dozen	1.09	12/00	5c
Fats and oils, expenditures on	yr	79	1999	30r
Fish and seafood, expenditures on	yr	99	1999	30r
Flour, white, all purpose	lb	0.32	7/01	11r
Food (excl fruit and vegetables), eaten at				
home, purchases	yr	815	1999	30r
Food cooked on trips, expenditures on	yr	36	1999	30r
Food purchases	yr	4533	1999	30r
Food purchases, eaten away from home	yr	1873	1999	30r
Food purchases, food eaten at home	yr	2660	1999	30r
Fresh fruits, expenditures on	yr	128	1999	30r
Fresh milk and cream, expenditures on	yr	112	1999	30r
Fresh vegetables, expenditures on	yr	131	1999	30r
Fruit and vegetable purchases	yr	438	1999	30r
Grapefruit	lb	0.59	7/01	11r
Grapes, Thompson, seedless	lb	2.12	7/01	11r
Ground beef, 100% beef	lb	1.76	7/01	11r
Ground beef, lean and extra lean	lb	2.60	7/01	11r
Ground chuck, 100% beef	lb	2.08	7/01	11r
Ham, boneless, excl canned	lb	2.71	7/01	11r
Ham, rump or shank half, bone-in, smoked	lb	2.19	7/01	11r
Ice cream, prepackaged, bulk, regular	1/2 gal	3.93	7/01	11r
Lemons	lb	1.32	7/01	11r
Lettuce, iceberg	lb	0.76	7/01	11r
Lettuce, iceberg	head	1.04	12/00	5c
Margarine, Blue Bonnet or Parkay, stick	lb	1.22	12/00	5c
Milk, fresh, low fat	gal	2.75	7/01	11r
Milk, fresh, whole, fortified	gal	2.97	7/01	11r
Milk, whole	1/2 gal	1.89	12/00	5c

Wilmington, NC - continued

Item	Per	Value	Date	Ref.
Groceries - continued				
Nonalcoholic beverages, expenditures on	yr	228	1999	30r
Orange juice, frozen concentrate	16 oz	1.95	7/01	11r
Orange juice, Minute Maid frozen	12 oz	1.72	12/00	5c
Oranges, Navel	lb	0.73	7/01	11r
Oranges, Valencia	lb	0.55	7/01	11r
Peaches, halves or slices, Hunt's, Del Monte,				
or Libby's	29 oz	1.59	12/00	5c
Peanut butter, creamy, all sizes	lb	1.83	7/01	11r
Pears, Anjou	lb	0.98	7/01	11r
Peas, green, Del Monte or Green Giant	15 oz	0.67	12/00	5c
Pork chops, center cut, bone-in	lb	3.33	7/01	11r
Pork sausage, fresh, loose	lb	2.59	7/01	11r
Pork shoulder picnic, bone-in, smoked	lb	1.12	7/01	11r
Pork, expenditures on	yr	162	1999	30r
Potato chips	16 oz	3.59	7/01	11r
Potatoes, frozen, french fried	lb	1.00	7/01	11r
Potatoes, white or red	10 lb	3.32	12/00	5c
Potatoes, white, all types	lb	0.44	7/01	11r
Poultry, expenditures on	yr	137	1999	30r
Processed fruits, expenditures on	yr	97	1999	30r
Processed vegetables, expenditures on	yr	82	1999	30r
Rice, white, long grain, uncooked	lb	0.51	7/01	11r
Round roast, graded and ungraded, excl U.S.				
prime and choice	lb	2.96	7/01	11r
Round steak, graded and ungraded, excl				
U.S. prime and choice	lb	3.11	7/01	11r
Sausage, Jimmy Dean/Owens pork	lb	3.49	12/00	5c
Shortening, vegetable, Crisco	3 lb	3.09	12/00	5c
Sirloin steak, graded and ungraded, excl U.S.				
prime and choice	lb	4.23	7/01	11r
Soft drink, Coca Cola, ex deposit	2 liter	1.09	12/00	5c
Spaghetti and macaroni	lb	0.78	7/01	11r
Steak, round, U.S. choice, boneless	lb	3.56	7/01	11r
Steak, sirloin, U.S. choice, boneless	lb	5.65	7/01	11r
Steak, T-bone	lb	7.32	12/00	5c
Strawberries, dry pint	12 oz	1.50	7/01	11r
Sugar and other sweets, expenditures on	yr	99	1999	30r
Sugar, cane or beet	4 lbs	1.76	12/00	5c
Sugar, white, 33-80 ounce package	lb	0.39	7/01	11r
Sugar, white, all sizes	lb	0.42	7/01	11r
Tobacco products and smoking supplies				
purchases	yr	288	1999	30r
Tomatoes, field grown	lb	1.43	7/01	11r
Tomatoes, Hunt's or Del Monte	14.5 oz	0.96	12/00	5c
Tuna, chunk, light	6 oz	0.69	12/00	5c
Tuna, light, chunk	lb	1.77	7/01	11r
Turkey, frozen, whole	lb	1.05	7/01	11r
Goods and Services				
Miscellaneous goods and services, ACCRA				
Index		103.00	12/00	5c
B&B Japanese maple (acer japonicum)	gal	49.98-129.00	4/00	93r
Boxwood (buxus)	2 gal	12.99-16.99	4/00	93r
Daylilly (hemerocallis)	gal	4.99-8.99	4/00	93r
Flat of annuals		11.00-13.92	4/00	93r
Fountain grass (pennisetum)	gal	5.98-7.98	4/00	93r
Hanging basket (10 in)		7.99-14.98	4/00	93r
Hardy geranium (geranium)	gal	5.98-8.00	4/00	93r
Hosta (hosta)	gal	4.99-10.98	4/00	93r
Lilac (syrubga vulgaris)	2 gal	12.99-21.99	4/00	93r
Rhododendron (rhododendron)	2 gal	14.99-24.99	4/00	93r
Sage (salvia)	gal	5.98-6.99	4/00	93r

Values are in dollars or fractions of dollars. In the column headed *Ref*, references are shown as sources. Each reference is followed by a letter. These refer to the geographical level for which data were reported: s=State, r=Region, and c=City or metro. The abbreviation *ex* is used to mean *except* or *excluding*; *exp* stands for expenditures. For other abbreviations and further explanations, please see the Introduction.

Wilmington, NC - continued

Item	Per	Value	Date	Ref.
Goods and Services				
Wintercreeper euonymus (euonymus fortunei)	2 gal	7.99-89.99	4/00	93r
Hunting license	yr	15.00	4/01	34s
Health Care				
Health care, ACCRA Index		96.20	12/00	5c
Cardiac catheterization, ave hospital/ physician charges		12500	1998	77s
Childbirth, Cesarean delivery		11587	1997	13r
Childbirth, vaginal delivery		6725	1997	13r
Dentist's fee, adult teeth cleaning and periodic oral exam	visit	67.25	12/00	5c
Doctor's fee, routine exam, established patient	visit	64.40	12/00	5c
Drugs, expenditures on	yr	399	1999	30r
Health care purchases	yr	1971	1999	30r
Health insurance expenditures	yr	933	1999	30r
Hospital care, private room	day	343.00	12/00	5c
Hysterectomy, laproscopically-assisted, ave hospital/physician charges		12260	1998	76s
Hysterectomy, vaginal, ave hospital and physician charges		8440	1998	76s
Medicaid dispensing fee		5.60	1999	87s
Medical services expenditures	yr	547	1999	30r
Medical supplies, expenditures on	yr	91	1999	30r
Plastic surgery, breast augmentation		2870	2000	7r
Plastic surgery, breast lift		3649	2000	7r
Plastic surgery, facelift		5008	2000	7r
Plastic surgery, hair transplantation		3425	2000	7r
Plastic surgery, lip augmentation		1227	2000	7r
Plastic surgery, lower body lift		4793	2000	7r
Plastic surgery, thigh lift		3862	2000	7r
Household Goods				
Dishwashing powder, Cascade	50 oz	2.49	12/00	5c
Floor coverings, expenditures on	yr	44	1999	30r
Furniture, expenditures on	yr	335	1999	30r
Household furnishings and equipment purchases	yr	1328	1999	30r
Household textiles, expenditures on	yr	89	1999	30r
Laundry and cleaning supplies, expenditures on	yr	113	1999	30r
Tissues, facial, Kleenex brand	175	1.32	12/00	5c
Housing				
Housing, ACCRA Index		115.20	12/00	5c
Home, 2200 sq ft, 4-br, 2-bath, 2-car garage, average		169975	2000	47c
Home price, existing, ave		160100	10/00	90r
Home value, median		146000	2001	53s
House, 2400 sq ft, 8000 sq ft lot, new, urban, utilities	total	246000	12/00	5c
House payment, principal and interest, 25% down payment	mos	1343	12/00	5c
Household operation expenditures	yr	553	1999	30r
Housekeeping supplies purchases	yr	473	1999	30r
Housing, expenditures on	yr	10303	1999	30r
Maintenance, repairs, insurance expenditures	yr	699	1999	30r
Monthly rental value of owned home	mos	505	1999	30r
Owned dwellings, expenditures own	yr	3465	1999	30r
Rent expenditures	yr	1641	1999	30r
Rent, apartment, 2 br, 1 1/2-2 baths, unfurn, 950 sq ft, water	mos	684	12/00	5c
Rental unit, 1 bedroom, with utilities	mos	502	4/01	41c
Rental unit, 2 bedroom, with utilities	mos	615	4/01	41c
Rental unit, 3 bedroom, with utilities	mos	842	4/01	41c
Rental unit, 4 bedroom, with utilities	mos	1004	4/01	41c
Shelter, expenditures on	yr	5467	1999	30r
Insurance and Pensions				
Life and other personal insurance purchases	yr	414	1999	30r
Pensions and Social Security, expenditures on	yr	2635	1999	30r

Wilmington, NC - continued

Item	Per	Value	Date	Ref.
Insurance and Pensions - continued				
Personal insurance and pensions, expenditures on	yr	3048	1999	30r
Legal Fees				
Combination hunting and fishing license	yr	20.00	4/01	34s
Divorce, filing fee		80.00	4/01	35s
Driver's license fee	renew	10.00	1999	48s
Driver's license fee	orig	10.00	1999	48s
Fishing license	yr	15.00	4/01	34s
Personal Goods				
Personal care products and services purchases	yr	393	1999	30r
Shampoo, Alberto VO5	15 oz	0.94	12/00	5c
Toothpaste, Crest or Colgate	6-7 oz	1.95	12/00	5c
Personal Services				
Dry cleaning, man's 2-pc suit		7.79	12/00	5c
Man's haircut, barbershop, no styling		10.00	12/00	5c
Personal services, household, expenditures on	yr	258	1999	30r
Woman's shampoo, trim, blow-dry, no style-change		27.60	12/00	5c
Pets				
Pets, toys, and playground equipment, expenditures on	yr	306	1999	30r
Restaurant Food				
Chicken, fried, thigh and drumstick, KFC/Church's		2.69	12/00	5c
Hamburger with cheese, McDonald's	1/4 lb	2.11	12/00	5c
Pizza, Pizza Hut or Pizza Inn	11-12 in	8.81	12/00	5c
Taxes				
Federal income taxes paid	yr	2047	1999	30r
Personal taxes, expenditures on	yr	2554	1999	30r
Property taxes paid	yr	726	1999	30r
State and local income taxes paid	yr	363	1999	30r
Transportation				
Transportation, ACCRA Index		88.50	12/00	5c
Bus fare, to central business district	1-way	1.00	12/00	5c
Cars and trucks, new, expenditures on	yr	1648	1999	30r
Cars and trucks, used, expenditures on	yr	1651	1999	30r
Diesel at the pump	gal	1.19	10/99	73s
Gasoline and motor oil purchases	yr	1052	1999	30r
Gasoline before-tax price (cents)	gal	103.20	10/00	43s
Maintenance and repair expenditures	yr	621	1999	30r
Motorcycle license fee	orig	1.50	1999	49s
Motorcycle license fee	renew	1.50	1999	49s
Public transportation, expenditures on	yr	298	1999	30r
Tire balance, computer or spin balance, front	wheel	5.75	12/00	5c
Transportation purchases	yr	6738	1999	30r
Vehicle expenses, miscellaneous, purchases	yr	2033	1999	30r
Vehicle insurance payments	yr	696	1999	30r
Vehicle purchases (net outlay)	yr	3354	1999	30r
Vehicle rental, lease expenditures	yr	352	1999	30r
Utilities				
Utilities, ACCRA Index		101.80	12/00	5c
Electrical bill, average	mos	83.66	9/00	9s
Electricity, 2400 sq ft, new home	mos	117.62	12/00	5c
Electricity, expenditures on	yr	1115	1999	30r
Electricity cost, average	KWh	6.40	9/00	9s
Water and other public services, expenditures on	yr	298	1999	30r
Weddings				
Wedding (national average cost)		19936	2000	33r
Wedding (regional average total cost)		16293	1997	110r
Attendants' gifts		321	1998	33r
Bridal attendants' apparel (5 persons)		824	2000	33r
Bride's headpiece/veil		173	1998	33r
Bride's wedding dress		859	1998	33r
Clergy, religious facility fee		242	1998	33r

Values are in dollars or fractions of dollars. In the column headed *Ref*, references are shown to sources. Each reference is followed by a letter. These refer to the geographical level for which data were reported: s=State, r=Region, and c=City or metro. The abbreviation *ex* is used to mean *except* or *excluding*; *exp* stands for *expenditures*. For other abbreviations and further explanations, please see the Introduction.

Wilmington, NC - continued

Item	Per	Value	Date	Ref.
Weddings				
Engagement ring		3177	1998	33r
Flowers		789	1998	33r
Groom's formalwear rental		99	2000	33r
Limousine		410	1998	33r
Marriage license cost		40.00	4/01	35s
Men's formalwear (ushers, best man)		469	2000	33r
Mother of bride apparel		241	2000	33r
Music		866	1998	33r
Photography and videography		1368	1998	33r
Rehearsal dinner		728	1998	33r
Wedding invitations and announcements		341	1998	33r
Wedding reception		7968	2000	33r
Wedding rings (bride and groom)		1060	1998	33r

Wilmington-Newark, DE-MD

Item	Per	Value	Date	Ref.
Alcoholic Beverages				
Alcoholic beverage purchases	yr	253	1999	30r
Malt beverages, all types, all sizes, any origin	16 oz	0.96	7/01	11r
Appliances				
Major appliances, expenditures on	yr	172	1999	30r
Small appliances, housewares, expenditures on	yr	81	1999	30r
Banking and Money				
Mortgage interest and charges paid	yr	2039	1999	30r
Mortgage principal paid on owned property	yr	1026	1999	30r
Vehicle finance charges paid	yr	365	1999	30r
Charity				
Cash contributions, expenditures	yr	1127	1999	30r
Child Care				
Child raising cost, total, age 0-2	yr	8540	1999	60r
Child raising cost, total, age 3-5	yr	8780	1999	60r
Child raising cost, total, age 6-8	yr	8820	1999	60r
Child raising cost, total, age 9-11	yr	8800	1999	60r
Child raising cost, total, age 12-14	yr	9510	1999	60r
Child raising cost, total, age 15-17	yr	9740	1999	60r
Child's child care and education, age 0-2	yr	1380	1999	60r
Child's child care and education, age 3-5	yr	1520	1999	60r
Child's child care and education, age 6-8	yr	990	1999	60r
Child's child care and education, age 9-11	yr	650	1999	60r
Child's child care and education, age 12-14	yr	490	1999	60r
Child's child care and education, age 15-17	yr	840	1999	60r
Child's clothing, age 0-2	yr	480	1999	60r
Child's clothing, age 3-5	yr	470	1999	60r
Child's clothing, age 6-8	yr	520	1999	60r
Child's clothing, age 9-11	yr	570	1999	60r
Child's clothing, age 12-14	yr	950	1999	60r
Child's clothing, age 15-17	yr	850	1999	60r
Child's food, age 0-2	yr	1000	1999	60r
Child's food, age 3-5	yr	1160	1999	60r
Child's food, age 6-8	yr	1490	1999	60r
Child's food, age 9-11	yr	1770	1999	60r
Child's food, age 12-14	yr	1770	1999	60r
Child's food, age 15-17	yr	1980	1999	60r
Child's health care, age 0-2	yr	620	1999	60r
Child's health care, age 3-5	yr	590	1999	60r
Child's health care, age 6-8	yr	680	1999	60r
Child's health care, age 9-11	yr	720	1999	60r
Child's health care, age 12-14	yr	730	1999	60r
Child's health care, age 15-17	yr	760	1999	60r
Child's housing, age 0-2	yr	3070	1999	60r
Child's housing, age 3-5	yr	3050	1999	60r
Child's housing, age 6-8	yr	3010	1999	60r
Child's housing, age 9-11	yr	2850	1999	60r
Child's housing, age 12-14	yr	3040	1999	60r
Child's housing, age 15-17	yr	2650	1999	60r
Child's personal care, reading, age 0-2	yr	910	1999	60r
Child's personal care, reading, age 3-5	yr	930	1999	60r
Child's personal care, reading, age 6-8	yr	960	1999	60r

Item	Per	Value	Date	Ref.
Child Care - continued				
Child's personal care, reading, age 9-11	yr	1000	1999	60r
Child's personal care, reading, age 12-14	yr	1170	1999	60r
Child's personal care, reading, age 15-17	yr	950	1999	60r
Clothing				
Apparel and services purchases	yr	1610	1999	30r
Boys, 2 to 15, expenditures on	yr	89	1999	30r
Children under 2, expenditures on	yr	79	1999	30r
Footwear, expenditures on	yr	283	1999	30r
Girls, 2 to 15, expenditures on	yr	103	1999	30r
Men and boys, expenditures on	yr	351	1999	30r
Men, 16 and over, expenditures on	yr	262	1999	30r
Women, 16 and over, expenditures on	yr	538	1999	30r
Communications				
Phone line, single, business, field visit	inst.	60.94	12/97	17s
Phone line, single, business, no field visit	inst.	60.94	12/97	17s
Phone line, single, residence, field visit	inst.	35.96	12/97	17s
Phone line, single, residence, no field visit	inst.	35.96	12/97	17s
Postage and stationery, expenditures on	yr	104	1999	30r
Postal rate, express mail, up to half-pound		12.45	7/01	108r
Postal rate, letter, first class, first ounce		0.34	7/01	108r
Postal rate, letter, two ounces		0.57	7/01	108r
Postal rate, post card		0.21	7/01	108r
Postal rate, priority mail, two pounds		3.95	7/01	108r
Postal rate, priority mail, up to one pound		3.50	7/01	108r
Telephone services, expenditures on	yr	860	1999	30r
Education				
Board, 4-year private college/university	yr	1443	1996	38s
Board, 4-year public college/university	yr	2101	1996	38s
Education expenditures	yr	431	1999	30r
Room, 4-year private college/university	yr	2701	1996	38s
Room, 4-year public college/university	yr	2407	1996	38s
Total cost, 4-year private college/university	yr	11518	1996	38s
Total cost, 4-year public college/university	yr	8489	1996	38s
Tuition, 2-year public college/university, in state	yr	1266	1996	38s
Tuition, 4-year private college/university, in state	yr	7373	1996	38s
Tuition, 4-year public college/university	yr	3981	1996	38s
Energy and Fuels				
Electricity	500 KWhs	47.29	7/01	11r
Electricity	KWh	0.09	7/01	11r
Fuel oil #2	gal	1.43	7/01	11r
Fuel oil and other fuels, expenditures on	yr	45	1999	30r
Gas, natural, commercial rate	1000 cf	7.37	11/00	88s
Gasoline, all types	gal	1.60	7/01	11r
Gasoline, unleaded midgrade	gal	1.65	7/01	11r
Gasoline, unleaded premium	gal	1.74	7/01	11r
Natural gas, expenditures on	yr	164	1999	30r
Utility (piped) gas, therm		1.01	7/01	11r
Utility (piped) gas, 40 therms		44.29	7/01	11r
Utility (piped) gas, 100 therms		97.44	7/01	11r
Entertainment				
Entertainment purchases	yr	1574	1999	30r
Fees and admissions paid	yr	371	1999	30r
Reading purchases	yr	121	1999	30r
Television, radios, sound equipment, expenditures on	yr	561	1999	30r
Funerals				
Total cost of funeral		5922.53	1/99	78r
Acknowledgement cards		63.43	1/99	78r
Casket		2258.77	1/99	78r
Cosmetology, hair, other preparation		127.09	1/99	78r
Embalming		393.49	1/99	78r
Funeral at funeral home		367.50	1/99	78r
Hearse (local)		169.66	1/99	78r
Professional service charges		1211.32	1/99	78r
Service car/van		80.69	1/99	78r
Transfer of remains to funeral home		144.25	1/99	78r

Values are in dollars or fractions of dollars. In the column headed *Ref*, references are shown to sources. Each reference is followed by a letter. These refer to the geographical level for which data were reported: s=State, r=Region, and c=City or metro. The abbreviation *ex* is used to mean *except* or *excluding*; *exp* stands for *expenditures*. For other abbreviations and further explanations, please see the Introduction.

Wilmington-Newark, DE-MD - continued

Item	Per	Value	Date	Ref.
Funerals				
Vault		803.50	1/99	78r
Visitation/viewing		302.83	1/99	78r
Groceries				
American processed cheese	lb	3.50	7/01	11r
Bakery products, expenditures on	yr	261	1999	30r
Bananas	lb	0.47	7/01	11r
Beans, dried, any type, all sizes	lb	0.63	7/01	11r
Beef for stew, boneless	lb	2.86	7/01	11r
Beef, expenditures on	yr	210	1999	30r
Bologna, all beef or mixed	lb	2.29	7/01	11r
Bread, French	lb	1.66	7/01	11r
Bread, white, pan	lb	0.87	7/01	11r
Bread, whole wheat, pan	lb	1.38	7/01	11r
Broccoli	lb	1.04	7/01	11r
Butter, salted, grade AA, stick	lb	2.26	7/01	11r
Butter, yoghurt, cheese, etc, expenditures on	yr	170	1999	30r
Cabbage	lb	0.42	7/01	11r
Cereals and cereal products, expenditures on	yr	140	1999	30r
Cheddar cheese, natural	lb	3.75	7/01	11r
Chicken breast, bone-in	lb	1.85	7/01	11r
Chicken legs, bone-in	lb	1.34	7/01	11r
Chicken, fresh, whole	lb	1.05	7/01	11r
Chops, boneless,	lb	4.13	7/01	11r
Chuck roast, graded and ungraded, excl U.S. prime and choice	lb	2.35	7/01	11r
Chuck roast, U.S. choice, boneless	lb	2.67	7/01	11r
Coffee, 100%, ground roast, all sizes	lb	2.88	7/01	11r
Coffee, instant, plain, regular, all sizes	16 oz	9.25	7/01	11r
Cola, non diet,	2 liter	1.11	7/01	11r
Crackers, soda, salted	lb	1.70	7/01	11r
Dairy product purchases	yr	282	1999	30r
Eggs, expenditures on	yr	32	1999	30r
Fats and oils, expenditures on	yr	79	1999	30r
Fish and seafood, expenditures on	yr	99	1999	30r
Flour, white, all purpose	lb	0.32	7/01	11r
Food (excl fruit and vegetables), eaten at home, purchases	yr	815	1999	30r
Food cooked on trips, expenditures on	yr	36	1999	30r
Food purchases	yr	4533	1999	30r
Food purchases, eaten away from home	yr	1873	1999	30r
Food purchases, food eaten at home	yr	2660	1999	30r
Fresh fruits, expenditures on	yr	128	1999	30r
Fresh milk and cream, expenditures on	yr	112	1999	30r
Fresh vegetables, expenditures on	yr	131	1999	30r
Fruit and vegetable purchases	yr	438	1999	30r
Grapefruit	lb	0.59	7/01	11r
Grapes, Thompson, seedless	lb	2.12	7/01	11r
Ground beef, 100% beef	lb	1.76	7/01	11r
Ground beef, lean and extra lean	lb	2.60	7/01	11r
Ground chuck, 100% beef	lb	2.08	7/01	11r
Ham, boneless, excl canned	lb	2.71	7/01	11r
Ham, rump or shank half, bone-in, smoked	lb	2.19	7/01	11r
Ice cream, prepackaged, bulk, regular	1/2 gal	3.93	7/01	11r
Lemons	lb	1.32	7/01	11r
Lettuce, iceberg	lb	0.76	7/01	11r
Milk, fresh, low fat,	gal	2.75	7/01	11r
Milk, fresh, whole, fortified	gal	2.97	7/01	11r
Nonalcoholic beverages, expenditures on	yr	228	1999	30r
Orange juice, frozen concentrate	16 oz	1.95	7/01	11r
Oranges, Navel	lb	0.73	7/01	11r
Oranges, Valencia	lb	0.55	7/01	11r
Peanut butter, creamy, all sizes	lb	1.83	7/01	11r
Pears, Anjou	lb	0.98	7/01	11r
Pork chops, center cut, bone-in	lb	3.33	7/01	11r
Pork sausage, fresh, loose	lb	2.59	7/01	11r
Pork shoulder picnic, bone-in, smoked	lb	1.12	7/01	11r
Pork, expenditures on	yr	162	1999	30r
Potato chips	16 oz	3.59	7/01	11r
Potatoes, frozen, french fried	lb	1.00	7/01	11r
Potatoes, white, all types	lb	0.44	7/01	11r
Poultry, expenditures on	yr	137	1999	30r

Wilmington-Newark, DE-MD - continued

Item	Per	Value	Date	Ref.
Groceries - continued				
Processed fruits, expenditures on	yr	97	1999	30r
Processed vegetables, expenditures on	yr	82	1999	30r
Rice, white, long grain, uncooked	lb	0.51	7/01	11r
Round roast, graded and ungraded, excl U.S. prime and choice	lb	2.96	7/01	11r
Round steak, graded and ungraded, excl U.S. prime and choice	lb	3.11	7/01	11r
Sirloin steak, graded and ungraded, excl U.S. prime and choice	lb	4.23	7/01	11r
Spaghetti and macaroni	lb	0.78	7/01	11r
Steak, round, U.S. choice, boneless	lb	3.56	7/01	11r
Steak, sirloin, U.S. choice, boneless	lb	5.65	7/01	11r
Strawberries, dry pint	12 oz	1.50	7/01	11r
Sugar and other sweets, expenditures on	yr	99	1999	30r
Sugar, white, 33-80 ounce package	lb	0.39	7/01	11r
Sugar, white, all sizes	lb	0.42	7/01	11r
Tobacco products and smoking supplies purchases	yr	288	1999	30r
Tomatoes, field grown	lb	1.43	7/01	11r
Tuna, light, chunk	lb	1.77	7/01	11r
Turkey, frozen, whole	lb	1.05	7/01	11r
Goods and Services				
B&B Japanese maple (acer japonicum)	gal	49.98-129.00	4/00	93r
Boxwood (buxus)	2 gal	12.99-16.99	4/00	93r
Daylilly (hemerocallis)	gal	4.99-8.99	4/00	93r
Flat of annuals		11.00-13.92	4/00	93r
Fountain grass (pennisetum)	gal	5.98-7.98	4/00	93r
Hanging basket (10 in)		7.99-14.98	4/00	93r
Hardy geranium (geranium)	gal	5.98-8.00	4/00	93r
Hosta (hosta)	gal	4.99-10.98	4/00	93r
Lilac (syrubga vulgaris)	2 gal	12.99-21.99	4/00	93r
Rhododendron (rhododendron)	2 gal	14.99-24.99	4/00	93r
Sage (salvia)	gal	5.98-6.99	4/00	93r
Wintercreeper euonymus (euonymus fortunei)	2 gal	7.99-89.99	4/00	93r
Hunting license	yr	12.50	4/01	34s
Health Care				
Cardiac catheterization, ave hospital/physician charges		14610	1998	77s
Childbirth, Cesarean delivery		11587	1997	13r
Childbirth, vaginal delivery		6725	1997	13r
Drugs, expenditures on	yr	399	1999	30r
Health care purchases	yr	1971	1999	30r
Health insurance expenditures	yr	933	1999	30r
Hysterectomy, laproscopically-assisted, ave hospital/physician charges		12750	1998	76s
Hysterectomy, vaginal, ave hospital and physician charges		7150	1998	76s
Medicaid dispensing fee		3.65	1999	87s
Medical services expenditures	yr	547	1999	30r
Medical supplies, expenditures on	yr	91	1999	30r
Plastic surgery, breast augmentation		2870	2000	7r
Plastic surgery, breast lift		3649	2000	7r
Plastic surgery, facelift		5008	2000	7r
Plastic surgery, hair transplantation		3425	2000	7r
Plastic surgery, lip augmentation		1227	2000	7r
Plastic surgery, lower body lift		4793	2000	7r
Plastic surgery, thigh lift		3862	2000	7r

Values are in dollars or fractions of dollars. In the column headed *Ref*, references are shown to sources. Each reference is followed by a letter. These refer to the geographical level for which data were reported: s=State, r=Region, and c=City or metro. The abbreviation *ex* is used to mean *except* or *excluding*; *exp* stands for *expenditures*. For other abbreviations and further explanations, please see the Introduction.

Wilmington-Newark, DE-MD - continued

Item	Per	Value	Date	Ref.
Household Goods				
Floor coverings, expenditures on	yr	44	1999	30r
Furniture, expenditures on	yr	335	1999	30r
Household furnishings and equipment purchases	yr	1328	1999	30r
Household textiles, expenditures on	yr	89	1999	30r
Laundry and cleaning supplies, expenditures on	yr	113	1999	30r
Housing				
Home price, existing, ave		160100	10/00	90r
Home value, median		181000	2001	53s
Household operation expenditures	yr	553	1999	30r
Housekeeping supplies purchases	yr	473	1999	30r
Housing, expenditures on	yr	10303	1999	30r
Maintenance, repairs, insurance expenditures	yr	699	1999	30r
Monthly rental value of owned home	mos	505	1999	30r
Owned dwellings, expenditures own	yr	3465	1999	30r
Rent expenditures	yr	1641	1999	30r
Rental unit, 1 bedroom, with utilities	mos	603	4/01	41c
Rental unit, 2 bedroom, with utilities	mos	703	4/01	41c
Rental unit, 3 bedroom, with utilities	mos	954	4/01	41c
Rental unit, 4 bedroom, with utilities	mos	1153	4/01	41c
Shelter, expenditures on	yr	5467	1999	30r
Insurance and Pensions				
Life and other personal insurance purchases	yr	414	1999	30r
Pensions and Social Security, expenditures on	yr	2635	1999	30r
Personal insurance and pensions, expenditures on	yr	3048	1999	30r
Legal Fees				
Divorce, filing fee		75.00	4/01	35s
Driver's license fee	orig	12.50	1999	48s
Driver's license fee	renew	12.50	1999	48s
Personal Goods				
Personal care products and services purchases	yr	393	1999	30r
Personal Services				
Personal services, household, expenditures on	yr	258	1999	30r
Pets				
Pets, toys, and playground equipment, expenditures on	yr	306	1999	30r
Taxes				
Federal income taxes paid	yr	2047	1999	30r
Personal taxes, expenditures on	yr	2554	1999	30r
Property taxes paid	yr	726	1999	30r
State and local income taxes paid	yr	363	1999	30r
Transportation				
Cars and trucks, new, expenditures on	yr	1648	1999	30r
Cars and trucks, used, expenditures on	yr	1651	1999	30r
Diesel at the pump	gal	1.26	10/99	73s
Gasoline and motor oil purchases	yr	1052	1999	30r
Gasoline before-tax price (cents)	gal	112.60	10/00	43s
Maintenance and repair expenditures	yr	621	1999	30r
Motorcycle license fee	renew	5.00	1999	49s
Motorcycle license fee	orig	5.00	1999	49s
Public transportation, expenditures on	yr	298	1999	30r
Transportation purchases	yr	6738	1999	30r
Vehicle expenses, miscellaneous, purchases	yr	2033	1999	30r
Vehicle insurance payments	yr	696	1999	30r
Vehicle purchases (net outlay)	yr	3354	1999	30r
Vehicle rental, lease expenditures	yr	352	1999	30r
Utilities				
Electrical bill, average	mos	81.50	9/00	9s
Electricity, expenditures on	yr	1115	1999	30r
Electricity cost, average	KWh	6.60	9/00	9s

Wilmington-Newark, DE-MD - continued

Item	Per	Value	Date	Ref.
Utilities - continued				
Water and other public services, expenditures on	yr	298	1999	30r
Weddings				
Wedding (national average cost)		19936	2000	33r
Wedding (regional average total cost)		16293	1997	110r
Attendants' gifts		321	1998	33r
Bridal attendants' apparel (5 persons)		824	2000	33r
Bride's headpiece/veil		173	1998	33r
Bride's wedding dress		859	1998	33r
Clergy, religious facility fee		242	1998	33r
Engagement ring		3177	1998	33r
Flowers		789	1998	33r
Groom's formalwear rental		99	2000	33r
Limousine		410	1998	33r
Marriage license cost		35.00	4/01	35s
Men's formalwear (ushers, best man)		469	2000	33r
Mother of bride apparel		241	2000	33r
Music		866	1998	33r
Photography and videography		1368	1998	33r
Rehearsal dinner		728	1998	33r
Wedding invitations and announcements		341	1998	33r
Wedding reception		7968	2000	33r
Wedding rings (bride and groom)		1060	1998	33r

Worcester, CT

Item	Per	Value	Date	Ref.
Average annual expenditures	yr	37971	1999	30r
Alcoholic Beverages				
Alcoholic beverage purchases	yr	368	1999	30r
Wine, red and white table, all sizes, any origin	liter	9.64	7/01	11r
Appliances				
Major appliances, expenditures on	yr	194	1999	30r
Small appliances, housewares, expenditures on	yr	93	1999	30r
Banking and Money				
Mortgage interest and charges paid	yr	2622	1999	30r
Mortgage principal paid on owned property	yr	1262	1999	30r
Vehicle finance charges paid	yr	240	1999	30r
Charity				
Cash contributions, expenditures	yr	1001	1999	30r
Child Care				
Child raising cost, total, age 0-2	yr	8670	1999	60r
Child raising cost, total, age 3-5	yr	8910	1999	60r
Child raising cost, total, age 6-8	yr	9040	1999	60r
Child raising cost, total, age 9-11	yr	9100	1999	60r
Child raising cost, total, age 12-14	yr	9890	1999	60r
Child raising cost, total, age 15-17	yr	10010	1999	60r
Child's child care and education, age 0-2	yr	1070	1999	60r
Child's child care and education, age 3-5	yr	1190	1999	60r
Child's child care and education, age 6-8	yr	740	1999	60r
Child's child care and education, age 9-11	yr	470	1999	60r
Child's child care and education, age 12-14	yr	350	1999	60r
Child's child care and education, age 15-17	yr	590	1999	60r
Child's clothing, age 0-2	yr	480	1999	60r
Child's clothing, age 3-5	yr	470	1999	60r
Child's clothing, age 6-8	yr	520	1999	60r
Child's clothing, age 9-11	yr	570	1999	60r
Child's clothing, age 12-14	yr	970	1999	60r
Child's clothing, age 15-17	yr	870	1999	60r
Child's food, age 0-2	yr	1130	1999	60r
Child's food, age 3-5	yr	1290	1999	60r
Child's food, age 6-8	yr	1640	1999	60r
Child's food, age 9-11	yr	1930	1999	60r
Child's food, age 12-14	yr	1940	1999	60r
Child's food, age 15-17	yr	2150	1999	60r
Child's health care, age 0-2	yr	550	1999	60r
Child's health care, age 3-5	yr	530	1999	60r

Values are in dollars or fractions of dollars. In the column headed *Ref*, references are shown to sources. Each reference is followed by a letter. These refer to the geographical level for which data were reported: s=State, r=Region, and c=City or metro. The abbreviation *ex* is used to mean *except* or *excluding*; *exp* stands for expenditures. For other abbreviations and further explanations, please see the Introduction.

Worcester, CT - continued

Item	Per	Value	Date	Ref.
Child Care				
Child's health care, age 6-8	yr	610	1999	60r
Child's health care, age 9-11	yr	650	1999	60r
Child's health care, age 12-14	yr	660	1999	60r
Child's health care, age 15-17	yr	690	1999	60r
Child's housing, age 0-2	yr	3555	1999	60r
Child's housing, age 3-5	yr	3530	1999	60r
Child's housing, age 6-8	yr	3490	1999	60r
Child's housing, age 9-11	yr	3340	1999	60r
Child's housing, age 12-14	yr	3530	1999	60r
Child's housing, age 15-17	yr	3140	1999	60r
Child's personal care, reading, age 0-2	yr	920	1999	60r
Child's personal care, reading, age 3-5	yr	950	1999	60r
Child's personal care, reading, age 6-8	yr	980	1999	60r
Child's personal care, reading, age 9-11	yr	1020	1999	60r
Child's personal care, reading, age 12-14	yr	1190	1999	60r
Child's personal care, reading, age 15-17	yr	970	1999	60r
Clothing				
Apparel and services purchases	yr	1831	1999	30r
Boys, 2 to 15, expenditures on	yr	92	1999	30r
Children under 2, expenditures on	yr	63	1999	30r
Footwear, expenditures on	yr	300	1999	30r
Girls, 2 to 15, expenditures on	yr	101	1999	30r
Men and boys, expenditures on	yr	446	1999	30r
Men, 16 and over, expenditures on	yr	354	1999	30r
Women, 16 and over, expenditures on	yr	584	1999	30r
Communications				
Cable modem installation, AT&T-BIS		150.00	6/99	103s
Cable modem installation, Cablevision Systems		150.00	6/99	103s
Cable modem installation, Cox		99.00-174.95	6/99	103s
Cable modem installation, Media One		100.00	6/99	103s
Cable modem rate, cable subscriber, AT&T-BIS	mos	39.95	6/99	103s
Cable modem rate, cable subscriber, Cablevision Systems	mos	44.95	6/99	103s
Cable modem rate, cable subscriber, Cox	mos	29.95-44.95	6/99	103s
Cable modem rate, cable subscriber, Media One	mos	34.95-39.95	6/99	103s
Cable modem rate, non-cable subscriber, Cablevision Systems	mos	54.95	6/99	103s
Cable modem rate, non-cable subscriber, Cox	mos	42.95-54.95	6/99	103s
Cable modem rate, non-cable subscriber, Media One	mos	49.95	6/99	103s
Phone line, single, business, field visit	inst.	65.00	12/97	17s
Phone line, single, business, no field visit	inst.	65.00	12/97	17s
Phone line, single, residence, field visit	inst.	45.00	12/97	17s
Phone line, single, residence, no field visit	inst.	45.00	12/97	17s
Postage and stationery, expenditures on	yr	138	1999	30r
Postal rate, express mail, up to half-pound		12.45	7/01	108r
Postal rate, letter, first class, first ounce		0.34	7/01	108r
Postal rate, letter, two ounces		0.57	7/01	108r
Postal rate, post card		0.21	7/01	108r
Postal rate, priority mail, two pounds		3.95	7/01	108r
Postal rate, priority mail, up to one pound		3.50	7/01	108r
Telephone services, expenditures on	yr	830	1999	30r
Education				
Board, 4-year private college/university	yr	2744	1996	38s
Board, 4-year public college/university	yr	2299	1996	38s
Education expenditures	yr	877	1999	30r
Room, 4-year private college/university	yr	3621	1996	38s
Room, 4-year public college/university	yr	2609	1996	38s
Total cost, 4-year private college/university	yr	23011	1996	38s
Total cost, 4-year public college/university	yr	8753	1996	38s
Tuition, 2-year public college/university, in state	yr	1646	1996	38s
Tuition, 4-year private college/university, in state	yr	16646	1996	38s
Tuition, 4-year public college/university	yr	3845	1996	38s

Worcester, CT - continued

Item	Per	Value	Date	Ref.
Energy and Fuels				
Electricity	KWh	0.12	7/01	11r
Fuel oil #2	gal	1.31	7/01	11r
Fuel oil and other fuels, expenditures on	yr	207	1999	30r
Gas, natural, commercial rate	1000 cf	7.08	11/00	88s
Gasoline, all types	gal	1.80	7/01	11r
Gasoline, unleaded midgrade	gal	1.85	7/01	11r
Gasoline, unleaded premium	gal	1.91	7/01	11r
Gasoline, unleaded regular	gal	1.71	7/01	11r
Natural gas, expenditures on	yr	368	1999	30r
Utility (piped) gas, therm		1.08	7/01	11r
Utility (piped) gas, 40 therms		50.87	7/01	11r
Utility (piped) gas, 100 therms		111.06	7/01	11r
Entertainment				
Entertainment purchases	yr	1821	1999	30r
Fees and admissions paid	yr	511	1999	30r
Hockey equipment, girls' hockey		800	2001	101s
Television, radios, sound equipment, expenditures on	yr	650	1999	30r
Funerals				
Total cost of funeral		5776.91	1/99	78r
Acknowledgement cards		14.47	1/99	78r
Casket		2090.19	1/99	78r
Cosmetology, hair, other preparation		132.92	1/99	78r
Embalming		377.33	1/99	78r
Funeral at funeral home		352.43	1/99	78r
Hearse (local)		185.55	1/99	78r
Professional service charges		1289.95	1/99	78r
Service car/van		87.42	1/99	78r
Transfer of remains to funeral home		175.48	1/99	78r
Vault		729.40	1/99	78r
Visitation/viewing		341.76	1/99	78r
Groceries				
Apples, red delicious	lb	0.95	7/01	11r
Bacon, sliced	lb	3.44	7/01	11r
Bakery products, expenditures on	yr	310	1999	30r
Bananas	lb	0.55	7/01	11r
Beef, expenditures on	yr	236	1999	30r
Bread, white, pan	lb	1.09	7/01	11r
Butter, yoghurt, cheese, etc, expenditures on	yr	214	1999	30r
Cereals and bakery product purchases	yr	474	1999	30r
Cereals and cereal products, expenditures on	yr	164	1999	30r
Chicken legs, bone-in	lb	1.23	7/01	11r
Chicken, fresh, whole	lb	1.13	7/01	11r
Chuck roast, U.S. choice, boneless	lb	2.79	7/01	11r
Coffee, 100%, ground roast, all sizes	lb	3.40	7/01	11r
Dairy product purchases	yr	342	1999	30r
Eggs, expenditures on	yr	34	1999	30r
Eggs, grade A, large	dozen	0.82	7/01	11r
Fats and oils, expenditures on	yr	80	1999	30r
Fish and seafood, expenditures on	yr	123	1999	30r
Food (excl fruit and vegetables), eaten at home, purchases	yr	838	1999	30r
Food cooked on trips, expenditures on	yr	48	1999	30r
Food purchases	yr	5314	1999	30r
Food purchases, eaten away from home	yr	2313	1999	30r
Food purchases, food eaten at home	yr	3001	1999	30r
Fresh fruits, expenditures on	yr	169	1999	30r
Fresh milk and cream, expenditures on	yr	128	1999	30r
Fresh vegetables, expenditures on	yr	164	1999	30r
Grapefruit	lb	0.67	7/01	11r
Grapes, Thompson, seedless	lb	2.18	7/01	11r
Ground beef, lean and extra lean	lb	2.66	7/01	11r
Ground chuck, 100% beef	lb	2.04	7/01	11r
Lettuce, iceberg	lb	0.76	7/01	11r
Meats, poultry, fish, and egg purchases	yr	808	1999	30r
Nonalcoholic beverages, expenditures on	yr	225	1999	30r
Orange juice, frozen concentrate	16 oz	1.88	7/01	11r
Oranges, Navel	lb	0.79	7/01	11r
Oranges, Valencia	lb	0.56	7/01	11r
Peaches	lb	1.16	7/01	11r

Values are in dollars or fractions of dollars. In the column headed *Ref*, references are shown to sources. Each reference is followed by a letter. These refer to the geographical level for which data were reported: s=State, r=Region, and c=City or metro. The abbreviation *ex* is used to mean *except* or *excluding*; *exp* stands for *expenditures*. For other abbreviations and further explanations, please see the Introduction.

Worcester, CT - continued

Item	Per	Value	Date	Ref.
Groceries				
Peanut butter, creamy, all sizes	lb	2.01	7/01	11r
Pears, Anjou	lb	1.16	7/01	11r
Pork chops, center cut, bone-in	lb	3.57	7/01	11r
Pork, expenditures on	yr	146	1999	30r
Potato chips	16 oz	3.37	7/01	11r
Potatoes, white, all types	lb	0.42	7/01	11r
Poultry, expenditures on	yr	158	1999	30r
Processed fruits, expenditures on	yr	124	1999	30r
Processed vegetables, expenditures on	yr	82	1999	30r
Round roast, U.S. choice, boneless	lb	3.04	7/01	11r
Spaghetti and macaroni	lb	1.04	7/01	11r
Steak, sirloin, U.S. choice, boneless	lb	5.39	7/01	11r
Strawberries, dry pint	12 oz	1.51	7/01	11r
Sugar and other sweets, expenditures on	yr	110	1999	30r
Sugar, white, 33-80 ounce package	lb	0.46	7/01	11r
Sugar, white, all sizes	lb	0.47	7/01	11r
Tobacco products and smoking supplies purchases	yr	309	1999	30r
Yogurt, natural, fruit flavored	8 oz	0.79	7/01	11r
Goods and Services				
B&B Japanese maple (acer japonicum)	gal	38.99-125.00	4/00	93r
Boxwood (buxus)	2 gal	15.99-49.95	4/00	93r
Daylilly (hemerocallis)	gal	4.95	4/00	93r
Flat of annuals		8.00-14.99	4/00	93r
Fountain grass (pennisetum)	gal	6.99-9.99	4/00	93r
Hanging basket (10 in)		12.95-19.99	4/00	93r
Hardy geranium (geranium)	gal	6.95-7.99	4/00	93r
Hosta (hosta)	gal	4.95	4/00	93r
Lilac (syrubga vulgaris)	2 gal	17.99-74.95	4/00	93r
Miscellaneous purchases	yr	872	1999	30r
Rhododendron (rhododendron)	2 gal	23.99-54.95	4/00	93r
Sage (salvia)	gal	6.95-7.99	4/00	93r
Wintercreeper euonymus (euonymus fortunei)	2 gal	14.99-23.95	4/00	93r
Hunting license	yr	10.00	4/01	34s
Health Care				
Cardiac catheterization, ave hospital/physician charges		14090	1998	77s
Childbirth, Cesarean delivery		14716	1997	13r
Childbirth, vaginal delivery		8541	1997	13r
Drugs, expenditures on	yr	296	1999	30r
Health care purchases	yr	1788	1999	30r
Health insurance expenditures	yr	875	1999	30r
Hysterectomy, laproscopically-assisted, ave hospital/physician charges		11610	1998	76s
Hysterectomy, vaginal, ave hospital and physician charges		12780	1998	76s
Medicaid dispensing fee		4.10	1999	87s
Medical services expenditures	yr	516	1999	30r
Medical supplies, expenditures on	yr	102	1999	30r
Plastic surgery, breast augmentation		4232	2000	7r
Plastic surgery, breast lift		4605	2000	7r
Plastic surgery, facelift		6964	2000	7r
Plastic surgery, hair transplantation		4193	2000	7r
Plastic surgery, lip augmentation		1675	2000	7r
Plastic surgery, lower body lift		6611	2000	7r
Plastic surgery, thigh lift		4751	2000	7r
Household Goods				
Floor coverings, expenditures on	yr	59	1999	30r
Furniture, expenditures on	yr	388	1999	30r
Household furnishings and equipment purchases	yr	1567	1999	30r

Worcester, CT - continued

Item	Per	Value	Date	Ref.
Household Goods - continued				
Household textiles, expenditures on	yr	112	1999	30r
Laundry and cleaning supplies, expenditures on	yr	104	1999	30r
Housing				
Home price, existing, ave		180800	10/00	90r
Home value, median		157000	2001	53s
Household operation expenditures	yr	581	1999	30r
Housekeeping supplies purchases	yr	474	1999	30r
Lodging expenditures	yr	550	1999	30r
Maintenance, repairs, insurance expenditures	yr	835	1999	30r
Monthly rental value of owned home	mos	663	1999	30r
Owned dwellings, expenditures own	yr	5209	1999	30r
Rent expenditures	yr	2390	1999	30r
Rental unit, 1 bedroom, with utilities	mos	546	4/01	41c
Rental unit, 2 bedroom, with utilities	mos	681	4/01	41c
Rental unit, 3 bedroom, with utilities	mos	850	4/01	41c
Rental unit, 4 bedroom, with utilities	mos	953	4/01	41c
Shelter, expenditures on	yr	8149	1999	30r
Insurance and Pensions				
Auto insurance premium	yr	982.00	1999	57s
Life and other personal insurance purchases	yr	424	1999	30r
Pensions and Social Security, expenditures on	yr	3037	1999	30r
Legal Fees				
Divorce, filing fee		150.00	4/01	35s
Driver's license fee	renew	28.50	1999	48s
Driver's license fee	orig	43.50	1999	48s
Personal Goods				
Personal care products and services purchases	yr	399	1999	30r
Personal Services				
Personal services, household, expenditures on	yr	271	1999	30r
Pets				
Pets, toys, and playground equipment, expenditures on	yr	325	1999	30r
Taxes				
Federal income taxes paid	yr	2606	1999	30r
Personal taxes, expenditures on	yr	3567	1999	30r
Property taxes paid	yr	1752	1999	30r
State and local income taxes paid	yr	694	1999	30r
Transportation				
Cars and trucks, new, expenditures on	yr	1496	1999	30r
Cars and trucks, used, expenditures on	yr	1251	1999	30r
Diesel at the pump	gal	1.36	10/99	73s
Gasoline and motor oil purchases	yr	901	1999	30r
Gasoline before-tax price (cents)	gal	117.10	10/00	43s
Maintenance and repair expenditures	yr	618	1999	30r
Public transportation, expenditures on	yr	575	1999	30r
Transportation purchases	yr	6503	1999	30r
Vehicle expenses, miscellaneous, purchases	yr	2266	1999	30r
Vehicle insurance payments	yr	824	1999	30r
Vehicle purchases (net outlay)	yr	2761	1999	30r
Vehicle rental, lease expenditures	yr	584	1999	30r
Utilities				
Electrical bill, average	mos	81.50	9/00	9s
Electricity, expenditures on	yr	837	1999	30r
Electricity cost, average	KWh	9.47	9/00	9s
Utilities, fuels, and public services purchased	yr	2457	1999	30r
Water and other public services, expenditures on	yr	215	1999	30r
Weddings				
Wedding (national average cost)		19936	2000	33r
Wedding (regional average total cost)		29454	1997	110r
Attendants' gifts		321	1998	33r
Bridal attendants' apparel (5 persons)		824	2000	33r

Values are in dollars or fractions of dollars. In the column headed *Ref*, references are shown to sources. Each reference is followed by a letter. These refer to the geographical level for which data were reported: s=State, r=Region, and c=City or metro. The abbreviation *ex* is used to mean *except* or *excluding*; *exp* stands for expenditures. For other abbreviations and further explanations, please see the Introduction.

Worcester, CT - continued

Item	Per	Value	Date	Ref.
Weddings				
Bride's headpiece/veil		173	1998	33r
Bride's wedding dress		859	1998	33r
Clergy, religious facility fee		242	1998	33r
Engagement ring		3177	1998	33r
Flowers		789	1998	33r
Groom's formalwear rental		99	2000	33r
Limousine		410	1998	33r
Marriage license cost		30.00	4/01	35s
Men's formalwear (ushers, best man)		469	2000	33r
Mother of bride apparel		241	2000	33r
Music		866	1998	33r
Photography and videography		1368	1998	33r
Rehearsal dinner		728	1998	33r
Wedding invitations and announcements		341	1998	33r
Wedding reception		7968	2000	33r
Wedding rings (bride and groom)		1060	1998	33r

Yakima, WA

Item	Per	Value	Date	Ref.
Average annual expenditures	yr	40662	1999	30r
Composite, ACCRA index		101.70	3/01	4c
Alcoholic Beverages				
Alcoholic beverage purchases	yr	372	1999	30r
Beer, Heineken, 12-oz, ex deposit	6	7.44	3/01	4c
J & B Scotch	750-ml	22.45	3/01	4c
Malt beverages, all types, all sizes, any origin	16 oz	0.94	7/01	11r
Wine, Livingston or Gallo, Chablis blanc	1.5 liter	5.29	3/01	4c
Wine, red and white table, all sizes, any origin	liter	6.00	7/01	11r
Appliances				
Appliance repair, service call, washing machine	min lab chg	44.13	3/01	4c
Major appliances, expenditures on	yr	167	1999	30r
Small appliances, housewares, expenditures on	yr	105	1999	30r
Banking and Money				
Mortgage interest and charges paid	yr	3368	1999	30r
Mortgage principal paid on owned property	yr	1677	1999	30r
Mortgage rate, incl. points and orig. fee, 30-yr. conv. fixed or ARM	mos	6.90	3/01	4c
Vehicle finance charges paid	yr	311	1999	30r
Charity				
Cash contributions, expenditures	yr	1344	1999	30r
Child Care				
Child raising cost, total, age 0-2	yr	9140	1999	60r
Child raising cost, total, age 3-5	yr	9370	1999	60r
Child raising cost, total, age 6-8	yr	9450	1999	60r
Child raising cost, total, age 9-11	yr	9470	1999	60r
Child raising cost, total, age 12-14	yr	10170	1999	60r
Child raising cost, total, age 15-17	yr	10360	1999	60r
Child's child care and education, age 0-2	yr	1250	1999	60r
Child's child care and education, age 3-5	yr	1380	1999	60r
Child's child care and education, age 6-8	yr	890	1999	60r
Child's child care and education, age 9-11	yr	580	1999	60r
Child's child care and education, age 12-14	yr	430	1999	60r
Child's child care and education, age 15-17	yr	730	1999	60r
Child's clothing, age 0-2	yr	430	1999	60r
Child's clothing, age 3-5	yr	420	1999	60r
Child's clothing, age 6-8	yr	470	1999	60r
Child's clothing, age 9-11	yr	520	1999	60r
Child's clothing, age 12-14	yr	870	1999	60r
Child's clothing, age 15-17	yr	770	1999	60r
Child's food, age 0-2	yr	1120	1999	60r
Child's food, age 3-5	yr	1280	1999	60r
Child's food, age 6-8	yr	1640	1999	60r
Child's food, age 9-11	yr	1930	1999	60r
Child's food, age 12-14	yr	1940	1999	60r
Child's food, age 15-17	yr	2150	1999	60r
Child's health care, age 0-2	yr	490	1999	60r

Yakima, WA - continued

Item	Per	Value	Date	Ref.
Child Care - continued				
Child's health care, age 3-5	yr	470	1999	60r
Child's health care, age 6-8	yr	530	1999	60r
Child's health care, age 9-11	yr	570	1999	60r
Child's health care, age 12-14	yr	580	1999	60r
Child's health care, age 15-17	yr	610	1999	60r
Child's housing, age 0-2	yr	3630	1999	60r
Child's housing, age 3-5	yr	3610	1999	60r
Child's housing, age 6-8	yr	3570	1999	60r
Child's housing, age 9-11	yr	3410	1999	60r
Child's housing, age 12-14	yr	3600	1999	60r
Child's housing, age 15-17	yr	3210	1999	60r
Child's personal care, reading, age 0-2	yr	1040	1999	60r
Child's personal care, reading, age 3-5	yr	1060	1999	60r
Child's personal care, reading, age 6-8	yr	1090	1999	60r
Child's personal care, reading, age 9-11	yr	1130	1999	60r
Child's personal care, reading, age 12-14	yr	1300	1999	60r
Child's personal care, reading, age 15-17	yr	1080	1999	60r
Clothing				
Apparel and services purchases	yr	1863	1999	30r
Boys' brief, cotton	3	3.98	3/01	4c
Boys, 2 to 15, expenditures on	yr	80	1999	30r
Children under 2, expenditures on	yr	74	1999	30r
Footwear, expenditures on	yr	307	1999	30r
Girls, 2 to 15, expenditures on	yr	101	1999	30r
Men and boys, expenditures on	yr	443	1999	30r
Men, 16 and over, expenditures on	yr	363	1999	30r
Shirt, man's dress shirt		30.99	3/01	4c
Slacks, man's "No Wrinkles" khaki		33.49	3/01	4c
Women, 16 and over, expenditures on	yr	594	1999	30r
Communications				
Cable modem installation, AT&T-BIS		150.00	6/99	103s
Cable modem rate, cable subscriber, AT&T-BIS	mos	39.95	6/99	103s
Newspaper subscription, daily and Sunday delivery	mos	10.50	3/01	4c
Phone line, single, business, field visit	inst.	48.00	12/97	17s
Phone line, single, business, no field visit	inst.	48.00	12/97	17s
Phone line, single, residence, field visit	inst.	31.00	12/97	17s
Phone line, single, residence, no field visit	inst.	31.00	12/97	17s
Postage and stationery, expenditures on	yr	150	1999	30r
Postal rate, express mail, up to half-pound		12.45	7/01	108r
Postal rate, letter, first class, first ounce		0.34	7/01	108r
Postal rate, letter, two ounces		0.57	7/01	108r
Postal rate, post card		0.21	7/01	108r
Postal rate, priority mail, two pounds		3.95	7/01	108r
Postal rate, priority mail, up to one pound		3.50	7/01	108r
Telephone bill, family of three	mos	17.62	3/01	4c
Telephone services, expenditures on	yr	825	1999	30r
Education				
Board, 4-year private college/university	yr	2329	1996	38s
Board, 4-year public college/university	yr	2158	1996	38s
Education expenditures	yr	676	1999	30r
Room, 4-year private college/university	yr	2487	1996	38s
Room, 4-year public college/university	yr	2187	1996	38s
Total cost, 4-year private college/university	yr	18092	1996	38s
Total cost, 4-year public college/university	yr	7136	1996	38s
Tuition, 2-year public college/university, in state	yr	1369	1996	38s
Tuition, 4-year private college/university, in state	yr	13276	1996	38s
Tuition, 4-year public college/university	yr	2791	1996	38s
Energy and Fuels				
Electricity	500 KWhs	48.23	7/01	11r
Electricity	KWh	0.11	7/01	11r
Energy, combined forms, 2400 sq ft	mos	93.32	3/01	4c
Fuel oil and other fuels, expenditures on	yr	35	1999	30r
Gas, natural, commercial rate	1000 cf	6.89	11/00	88s
Gas, regular unleaded, cash, self-service	gal	1.49	3/01	4c
Gasoline, all types	gal	1.91	7/01	11r

Values are in dollars or fractions of dollars. In the column headed *Ref*, references are shown to sources. Each reference is followed by a letter. These refer to the geographical level for which data were reported: s=State, r=Region, and c=City or metro. The abbreviation *ex* is used to mean *except* or *excluding*; *exp* stands for *expenditures*. For other abbreviations and further explanations, please see the Introduction.

Yakima, WA - continued

Item	Per	Value	Date	Ref.
Energy and Fuels				
Gasoline, unleaded premium	gal	2.05	7/01	11r
Gasoline, unleaded regular	gal	1.83	7/01	11r
Natural gas, expenditures on	yr	255	1999	30r
Utility (piped) gas, therm		0.98	7/01	11r
Utility (piped) gas, 40 therms		40.74	7/01	11r
Utility (piped) gas, 100 therms		96.80	7/01	11r
Entertainment				
Bowling, Saturday evening rate	line	2.67	3/01	4c
Entertainment purchases	yr	2139	1999	30r
Fees and admissions paid	yr	545	1999	30r
Monopoly game, Parker Brothers', No. 9	game	10.98	3/01	4c
Movie, first-run, Saturday, evening	adm.	7.50	3/01	4c
Television, radios, sound equipment, expenditures on	yr	624	1999	30r
Tennis balls, yellow, Wilson or Penn, 3	can	2.24	3/01	4c
Funerals				
Total cost of funeral		5401.08	1/99	78r
Acknowledgement cards		33.64	1/99	78r
Casket		2170.43	1/99	78r
Cosmetology, hair, other preparation		136.32	1/99	78r
Embalming		319.13	1/99	78r
Funeral at funeral home		370.21	1/99	78r
Hearse (local)		161.04	1/99	78r
Professional service charges		963.15	1/99	78r
Service car/van		133.99	1/99	78r
Transfer of remains to funeral home		159.82	1/99	78r
Vault		778.07	1/99	78r
Visitation/viewing		175.28	1/99	78r
Groceries				
Groceries, ACCRA Index		103.50	3/01	4c
Antibiotic ointment, Polysporin	0.5 oz	4.56	3/01	4c
Apples, red delicious	lb	0.84	7/01	11r
Baby food, strained vegetables or fruit, lowest price	4-4.5 oz	0.33	3/01	4c
Bacon, sliced	lb	3.38	7/01	11r
Bakery products, expenditures on	yr	299	1999	30r
Bananas	lb	0.76	3/01	4c
Bananas	lb	0.54	7/01	11r
Beans, dried, any type, all sizes	lb	0.76	7/01	11r
Beef or hamburger, ground	lb	1.49	3/01	4c
Beef, expenditures on	yr	222	1999	30r
Bread, white	loaf	0.98	3/01	4c
Bread, white, pan	lb	0.99	7/01	11r
Butter, yoghurt, cheese, etc, expenditures on	yr	211	1999	30r
Cereals and bakery product purchases	yr	466	1999	30r
Cereals and cereal products, expenditures on	yr	168	1999	30r
Cheese, Kraft grated Parmesan	8 oz	4.13	3/01	4c
Chicken breast, bone-in	lb	2.45	7/01	11r
Chicken, fresh, whole	lb	1.19	7/01	11r
Chicken, whole fryer	lb	1.02	3/01	4c
Chops, boneless,	lb	4.00	7/01	11r
Chuck roast, graded and ungraded, excl U.S. prime and choice	lb	2.55	7/01	11r
Cigarettes, Winston, Kings	carton	35.39	3/01	4c
Coffee, 100%, ground roast, all sizes	lb	3.80	7/01	11r
Coffee, vacuum-packed	13 oz	2.79	3/01	4c
Cookies, chocolate chip	lb	2.83	7/01	11r
Corn Flakes, Kellogg's or Post Toasties	18 oz	2.36	3/01	4c
Corn, frozen, whole kernel, lowest price	16 oz	1.06	3/01	4c
Dairy product purchases	yr	341	1999	30r
Eggs, expenditures on	yr	39	1999	30r
Eggs, Grade A or AA	dozen	1.16	3/01	4c
Eggs, grade AA, large	dozen	1.23	7/01	11r
Fats and oils, expenditures on	yr	88	1999	30r
Fish and seafood, expenditures on	yr	121	1999	30r
Food (excl fruit and vegetables), eaten at home, purchases	yr	1001	1999	30r
Food cooked on trips, expenditures on	yr	64	1999	30r
Food purchases	yr	5312	1999	30r
Food purchases, eaten away from home	yr	2180	1999	30r

Yakima, WA - continued

Item	Per	Value	Date	Ref.
Groceries - continued				
Food purchases, food eaten at home	yr	3132	1999	30r
Fresh fruits, expenditures on	yr	186	1999	30r
Fresh milk and cream, expenditures on	yr	130	1999	30r
Fresh vegetables, expenditures on	yr	177	1999	30r
Grapefruit	lb	0.68	7/01	11r
Grapes, Thompson, seedless	lb	2.42	7/01	11r
Ground beef, lean and extra lean	lb	2.46	7/01	11r
Ice cream, prepackaged, bulk, regular	1/2 gal	3.62	7/01	11r
Lettuce, iceberg	head	1.06	3/01	4c
Lettuce, iceberg	lb	0.63	7/01	11r
Margarine, Blue Bonnet or Parkay, stick	lb	0.55	3/01	4c
Meats, poultry, fish, and egg purchases	yr	761	1999	30r
Milk, fresh, low fat,	gal	2.80	7/01	11r
Milk, fresh, whole, fortified	gal	2.88	7/01	11r
Milk, whole	1/2 gal	1.89	3/01	4c
Nonalcoholic beverages, expenditures on	yr	258	1999	30r
Orange juice, Minute Maid frozen	12 oz	1.23	3/01	4c
Oranges, Navel	lb	0.97	7/01	11r
Oranges, Valencia	lb	0.43	7/01	11r
Peaches	lb	1.38	7/01	11r
Peaches, halves or slices, Hunt's, Del Monte, or Libby's	29 oz	1.44	3/01	4c
Peanut butter, creamy, all sizes	lb	2.14	7/01	11r
Peas, green, Del Monte or Green Giant	15 oz	0.75	3/01	4c
Pork chops, center cut, bone-in	lb	3.83	7/01	11r
Pork, expenditures on	yr	141	1999	30r
Potatoes, white or red	10 lb	2.05	3/01	4c
Potatoes, white, all types	lb	0.37	7/01	11r
Poultry, expenditures on	yr	146	1999	30r
Processed fruits, expenditures on	yr	118	1999	30r
Processed vegetables, expenditures on	yr	81	1999	30r
Round roast, graded and ungraded, excl U.S. prime and choice	lb	3.07	7/01	11r
Round roast, U.S. choice, boneless	lb	3.37	7/01	11r
Round steak, graded and ungraded, excl U.S. prime and choice	lb	3.51	7/01	11r
Sausage, Jimmy Dean/Owens pork	lb	4.47	3/01	4c
Shortening, vegetable, Crisco	3 lb	2.89	3/01	4c
Sirloin steak, graded and ungraded, excl U.S. prime and choice	lb	4.67	7/01	11r
Soft drink, Coca Cola, ex deposit	2 liter	1.16	3/01	4c
Steak, sirloin, U.S. choice, boneless	lb	6.20	7/01	11r
Steak, T-bone	lb	6.07	3/01	4c
Strawberries, dry pint	12 oz	1.79	7/01	11r
Sugar and other sweets, expenditures on	yr	124	1999	30r
Sugar, cane or beet	4 lbs	1.76	3/01	4c
Sugar, white, all sizes	lb	0.46	7/01	11r
Tobacco products and smoking supplies purchases	yr	217	1999	30r
Tomatoes, field grown	lb	1.17	7/01	11r
Tomatoes, Hunt's or Del Monte	14.5 oz	0.65	3/01	4c
Tuna, chunk, light	6 oz	0.79	3/01	4c
Tuna, light, chunk	lb	2.05	7/01	11r
Goods and Services				
Miscellaneous goods and services, ACCRA Index		100.60	3/01	4c
B&B Japanese maple (acer japonicum)	gal	39.99	4/00	93r
Boxwood (buxus)	2 gal	14.99-24.99	4/00	93r
Daylily (hemerocallis)	gal	6.99-8.99	4/00	93r
Flat of annuals		16.68	4/00	93r
Fountain grass (pennisetum)	gal	7.99-11.99	4/00	93r
Hanging basket (10 in)		29.99	4/00	93r
Hardy geranium (geranium)	gal	6.99-11.99	4/00	93r
Hosta (hosta)	gal	6.99-18.99	4/00	93r
Lilac (syrubga vulgaris)	2 gal	14.99-17.99	4/00	93r
Miscellaneous purchases	yr	1070	1999	30r

Values are in dollars or fractions of dollars. In the column headed *Ref*, references are shown to sources. Each reference is followed by a letter. These refer to the geographical level for which data were reported: s=State, r=Region, and c=City or metro. The abbreviation *ex* is used to mean *except* or *excluding*; *exp* stands for expenditures. For other abbreviations and further explanations, please see the Introduction.

Yakima, WA - continued

Item	Per	Value	Date	Ref.
Goods and Services				
Rhododendron (rhododendron)	2 gal	14.99	4/00	93r
Sage (salvia)	gal	6.99	4/00	93r
Wintercreeper euonymus (euonymus fortunei)	2 gal	14.99-22.99	4/00	93r
Hunting license	yr	30.00	4/01	34s
Health Care				
Health care, ACCRA Index		127.60	3/01	4c
Cardiac catheterization, ave hospital/ physician charges		13290	1998	77s
Childbirth, Cesarean delivery		11587	1997	13r
Childbirth, vaginal delivery		6725	1997	13r
Dentist's fee, adult teeth cleaning and periodic oral exam	visit	118.50	3/01	4c
Doctor's fee, routine exam, established patient	visit	56.50	3/01	4c
Drugs, expenditures on	yr	309	1999	30r
Health care purchases	yr	1869	1999	30r
Health insurance expenditures	yr	868	1999	30r
Hospital care, private room	day	710.00	3/01	4c
Hysterectomy, laproscopically-assisted, ave hospital/physician charges		10960	1998	76s
Hysterectomy, vaginal, ave hospital and physician charges		9000	1998	76s
Medicaid dispensing fee		3.98-4.92	1999	87s
Medical services expenditures	yr	580	1999	30r
Medical supplies, expenditures on	yr	112	1999	30r
Household Goods				
Dishwashing powder, Cascade	50 oz	3.41	3/01	4c
Floor coverings, expenditures on	yr	49	1999	30r
Furniture, expenditures on	yr	444	1999	30r
Household furnishings and equipment purchases	yr	1768	1999	30r
Household textiles, expenditures on	yr	141	1999	30r
Laundry and cleaning supplies, expenditures on	yr	128	1999	30r
Tissues, facial, Kleenex brand	175	1.39	3/01	4c
Housing				
Housing, ACCRA Index		107.00	3/01	4c
Home price, existing, ave		239400	10/00	90r
Home value, median		195000	2001	53s
House, 2400 sq ft, 8000 sq ft lot, new, urban, utilities	total	191833	3/01	4c
House payment, principal and interest, 25% down payment	mos	1115	3/01	4c
Household operation expenditures	yr	781	1999	30r
Housekeeping supplies purchases	yr	513	1999	30r
Lodging expenditures	yr	575	1999	30r
Maintenance, repairs, insurance expenditures	yr	939	1999	30r
Monthly rental value of owned home	mos	662	1999	30r
Owned dwellings, expenditures own	yr	5231	1999	30r
Rent expenditures	yr	2709	1999	30r
Rent, apartment, 2 br, 1 1/2-2 baths, unfurn, 950 sq ft, water	mos	712	3/01	4c
Rental unit, 1 bedroom, with utilities	mos	444	4/01	41c
Rental unit, 2 bedroom, with utilities	mos	551	4/01	41c
Rental unit, 3 bedroom, with utilities	mos	739	4/01	41c
Rental unit, 4 bedroom, with utilities	mos	771	4/01	41c
Shelter, expenditures on	yr	8516	1999	30r
Insurance and Pensions				
Life and other personal insurance purchases	yr	355	1999	30r
Pensions and Social Security, expenditures on	yr	3636	1999	30r
Legal Fees				
Divorce, filing fee		100.00	4/01	35s
Driver's license fee	orig	14.00	1999	48s
Driver's license fee	renew	14.00	1999	48s
Fishing license	yr	20.00	4/01	34s

Yakima, WA - continued

Item	Per	Value	Date	Ref.
Personal Goods				
Personal care products and services purchases	yr	449	1999	30r
Shampoo, Alberto VO5	15 oz	1.04	3/01	4c
Toothpaste, Crest or Colgate	6-7 oz	1.97	3/01	4c
Personal Services				
Dry cleaning, man's 2-pc suit		7.38	3/01	4c
Man's haircut, barbershop, no styling		9.00	3/01	4c
Personal services, household, expenditures on	yr	353	1999	30r
Woman's shampoo, trim, blow-dry, no style-change		23.75	3/01	4c
Pets				
Pets, toys, and playground equipment, expenditures on	yr	358	1999	30r
Restaurant Food				
Chicken, fried, thigh and drumstick, KFC/ Church's		2.40	3/01	4c
Hamburger with cheese, McDonald's	1/4 lb	2.29	3/01	4c
Pizza, Pizza Hut or Pizza Inn	11-12 in	10.79	3/01	4c
Taxes				
Federal income taxes paid	yr	3200	1999	30r
Personal taxes, expenditures on	yr	4153	1999	30r
Property taxes paid	yr	923	1999	30r
State and local income taxes paid	yr	812	1999	30r
Transportation				
Transportation, ACCRA Index		93.90	3/01	4c
Bus fare, to central business district	1-way	0.50	3/01	4c
Cars and trucks, new, expenditures on	yr	1534	1999	30r
Cars and trucks, used, expenditures on	yr	1593	1999	30r
Diesel at the pump	gal	1.37	10/99	73s
Gasoline and motor oil purchases	yr	1129	1999	30r
Gasoline before-tax price (cents)	gal	127.10	10/00	43s
Maintenance and repair expenditures	yr	797	1999	30r
Public transportation, expenditures on	yr	530	1999	30r
Tire balance, computer or spin balance, front	wheel	7.19	3/01	4c
Transportation purchases	yr	7423	1999	30r
Vehicle expenses, miscellaneous, purchases	yr	2585	1999	30r
Vehicle insurance payments	yr	811	1999	30r
Vehicle purchases (net outlay)	yr	3180	1999	30r
Vehicle rental, lease expenditures	yr	666	1999	30r
Utilities				
Utilities, ACCRA Index		77.10	3/01	4c
Electrical bill, average	mos	58.33	9/00	9s
Electricity, 2400 sq ft, new home	mos	93.32	3/01	4c
Electricity, expenditures on	yr	725	1999	30r
Electricity, summer, 250 KWh	mos	13.80	2/96	96c
Electricity, summer, 500 KWh	mos	23.86	2/96	96c
Electricity, summer, 750 KWh	mos	35.68	2/96	96c
Electricity, summer, 1000 KWh	mos	48.67	2/96	96c
Electricity cost, average	KWh	4.47	9/00	9s
Utilities, fuels, and public services purchased	yr	2179	1999	30r
Water and other public services, expenditures on	yr	339	1999	30r
Weddings				
Wedding (national average cost)		19936	2000	33r
Wedding (regional average total cost)		18918	1997	110r
Attendants' gifts		321	1998	33r
Bridal attendants' apparel (5 persons)		824	2000	33r
Bride's headpiece/veil		173	1998	33r
Bride's wedding dress		859	1998	33r
Clergy, religious facility fee		242	1998	33r
Engagement ring		3177	1998	33r
Flowers		789	1998	33r
Groom's formalwear rental		99	2000	33r
Limousine		410	1998	33r
Marriage license cost		52.00	4/01	35s
Men's formalwear (ushers, best man)		469	2000	33r
Mother of bride apparel		241	2000	33r

Values are in dollars or fractions of dollars. In the column headed *Ref*, references are shown to sources. Each reference is followed by a letter. These refer to the geographical level for which data were reported: s=State, r=Region, and c=City or metro. The abbreviation *ex* is used to mean *except* or *excluding*; *exp* stands for expenditures. For other abbreviations and further explanations, please see the Introduction.

Yakima, WA - continued

Item	Per	Value	Date	Ref.
Weddings				
Music		866	1998	33r
Photography and videography		1368	1998	33r
Rehearsal dinner		728	1998	33r
Wedding invitations and announcements		341	1998	33r
Wedding reception		7968	2000	33r
Wedding rings (bride and groom)		1060	1998	33r

Yolo, CA

Item	Per	Value	Date	Ref.
Average annual expenditures	yr	40662	1999	30r
Alcoholic Beverages				
Alcoholic beverage purchases	yr	372	1999	30r
Malt beverages, all types, all sizes, any origin	16 oz	0.94	7/01	11r
Wine, red and white table, all sizes, any origin	liter	6.00	7/01	11r
Appliances				
Major appliances, expenditures on	yr	167	1999	30r
Small appliances, housewares, expenditures on	yr	105	1999	30r
Banking and Money				
Mortgage interest and charges paid	yr	3368	1999	30r
Mortgage principal paid on owned property	yr	1677	1999	30r
Vehicle finance charges paid	yr	311	1999	30r
Charity				
Cash contributions, expenditures	yr	1344	1999	30r
Child Care				
Child raising cost, total, age 0-2	yr	9140	1999	60r
Child raising cost, total, age 3-5	yr	9370	1999	60r
Child raising cost, total, age 6-8	yr	9450	1999	60r
Child raising cost, total, age 9-11	yr	9470	1999	60r
Child raising cost, total, age 12-14	yr	10170	1999	60r
Child raising cost, total, age 15-17	yr	10360	1999	60r
Child's child care and education, age 0-2	yr	1250	1999	60r
Child's child care and education, age 3-5	yr	1380	1999	60r
Child's child care and education, age 6-8	yr	890	1999	60r
Child's child care and education, age 9-11	yr	580	1999	60r
Child's child care and education, age 12-14	yr	430	1999	60r
Child's child care and education, age 15-17	yr	730	1999	60r
Child's clothing, age 0-2	yr	430	1999	60r
Child's clothing, age 3-5	yr	420	1999	60r
Child's clothing, age 6-8	yr	470	1999	60r
Child's clothing, age 9-11	yr	520	1999	60r
Child's clothing, age 12-14	yr	870	1999	60r
Child's clothing, age 15-17	yr	770	1999	60r
Child's food, age 0-2	yr	1120	1999	60r
Child's food, age 3-5	yr	1280	1999	60r
Child's food, age 6-8	yr	1640	1999	60r
Child's food, age 9-11	yr	1930	1999	60r
Child's food, age 12-14	yr	1940	1999	60r
Child's food, age 15-17	yr	2150	1999	60r
Child's health care, age 0-2	yr	490	1999	60r
Child's health care, age 3-5	yr	470	1999	60r
Child's health care, age 6-8	yr	530	1999	60r
Child's health care, age 9-11	yr	570	1999	60r
Child's health care, age 12-14	yr	580	1999	60r
Child's health care, age 15-17	yr	610	1999	60r
Child's housing, age 0-2	yr	3630	1999	60r
Child's housing, age 3-5	yr	3610	1999	60r
Child's housing, age 6-8	yr	3570	1999	60r
Child's housing, age 9-11	yr	3410	1999	60r
Child's housing, age 12-14	yr	3600	1999	60r
Child's housing, age 15-17	yr	3210	1999	60r
Child's personal care, reading, age 0-2	yr	1040	1999	60r
Child's personal care, reading, age 3-5	yr	1060	1999	60r
Child's personal care, reading, age 6-8	yr	1090	1999	60r
Child's personal care, reading, age 9-11	yr	1130	1999	60r
Child's personal care, reading, age 12-14	yr	1300	1999	60r
Child's personal care, reading, age 15-17	yr	1080	1999	60r

Yolo, CA - continued

Item	Per	Value	Date	Ref.
Clothing				
Apparel and services purchases	yr	1863	1999	30r
Boys, 2 to 15, expenditures on	yr	80	1999	30r
Children under 2, expenditures on	yr	74	1999	30r
Footwear, expenditures on	yr	307	1999	30r
Girls, 2 to 15, expenditures on	yr	101	1999	30r
Men and boys, expenditures on	yr	443	1999	30r
Men, 16 and over, expenditures on	yr	363	1999	30r
Women, 16 and over, expenditures on	yr	594	1999	30r
Communications				
Cable modem installation, AT&T-BIS		150.00	6/99	103s
Cable modem installation, Charter		99.00-169.00	6/99	103s
Cable modem installation, Comcast		95.00	6/99	103s
Cable modem installation, Cox		99.00-174.95	6/99	103s
Cable modem installation, Media One		100.00	6/99	103s
Cable modem installation, Time Warner		75.00-225.00	6/99	103s
Cable modem rate, cable subscriber, AT&T-BIS	mos	39.95	6/99	103s
Cable modem rate, cable subscriber, Charter	mos	49.95-79.95	6/99	103s
Cable modem rate, cable subscriber, Comcast	mos	39.95	6/99	103s
Cable modem rate, cable subscriber, Cox	mos	29.95-44.95	6/99	103s
Cable modem rate, cable subscriber, Media One	mos	34.95-39.95	6/99	103s
Cable modem rate, cable subscriber, Time Warner	mos	39.95-49.95	6/99	103s
Cable modem rate, non-cable subscriber, Charter	mos	59.95-89.95	6/99	103s
Cable modem rate, non-cable subscriber, Comcast	mos	49.95	6/99	103s
Cable modem rate, non-cable subscriber, Cox	mos	42.95-54.95	6/99	103s
Cable modem rate, non-cable subscriber, Media One	mos	49.95	6/99	103s
Cable modem rate, non-cable subscriber, Time Warner	mos	39.95-54.95	6/99	103s
Phone line, single, business, field visit	inst.	70.75	12/97	17s
Phone line, single, business, no field visit	inst.	70.75	12/97	17s
Phone line, single, residence, field visit	inst.	34.75	12/97	17s
Phone line, single, residence, no field visit	inst.	34.75	12/97	17s
Postage and stationery, expenditures on	yr	150	1999	30r
Postal rate, express mail, up to half-pound		12.45	7/01	108r
Postal rate, letter, first class, first ounce		0.34	7/01	108r
Postal rate, letter, two ounces		0.57	7/01	108r
Postal rate, post card		0.21	7/01	108r
Postal rate, priority mail, two pounds		3.95	7/01	108r
Postal rate, priority mail, up to one pound		3.50	7/01	108r
Telephone services, expenditures on	yr	825	1999	30r
Education				
Board, 4-year private college/university	yr	2970	1996	38s
Board, 4-year public college/university	yr	2516	1996	38s
Education expenditures	yr	676	1999	30r
Room, 4-year private college/university	yr	3196	1996	38s
Room, 4-year public college/university	yr	3031	1996	38s
Total cost, 4-year private college/university	yr	20143	1996	38s
Total cost, 4-year public college/university	yr	8213	1996	38s
Tuition, 2-year public college/university, in state	yr	362	1996	38s
Tuition, 4-year private college/university, in state	yr	13977	1996	38s
Tuition, 4-year public college/university	yr	2666	1996	38s
Energy and Fuels				
Electricity	KWh	0.11	7/01	11r
Electricity	500 KWhs	48.23	7/01	11r
Fuel oil and other fuels, expenditures on	yr	35	1999	30r
Gas, natural, commercial rate	1000 cf	8.74	11/00	88s

Values are in dollars or fractions of dollars. In the column headed *Ref*, references are shown to sources. Each reference is followed by a letter. These refer to the geographical level for which data were reported: s=State, r=Region, and c=City or metro. The abbreviation *ex* is used to mean *except* or *excluding*; *exp* stands for *expenditures*. For other abbreviations and further explanations, please see the Introduction.

Yolo, CA - continued

Item	Per	Value	Date	Ref.
Energy and Fuels				
Gasoline, all types	gal	1.91	7/01	11r
Gasoline, unleaded premium	gal	2.05	7/01	11r
Gasoline, unleaded regular	gal	1.83	7/01	11r
Natural gas, expenditures on	yr	255	1999	30r
Utility (piped) gas, therm		0.98	7/01	11r
Utility (piped) gas, 40 therms		40.74	7/01	11r
Utility (piped) gas, 100 therms		96.80	7/01	11r
Entertainment				
Entertainment purchases	yr	2139	1999	30r
Fees and admissions paid	yr	545	1999	30r
Television, radios, sound equipment, expenditures on	yr	624	1999	30r
Funerals				
Total cost of funeral		5401.08	1/99	78r
Acknowledgement cards		33.64	1/99	78r
Casket		2170.43	1/99	78r
Cosmetology, hair, other preparation		136.32	1/99	78r
Embalming		319.13	1/99	78r
Funeral at funeral home		370.21	1/99	78r
Hearse (local)		161.04	1/99	78r
Professional service charges		963.15	1/99	78r
Service car/van		133.99	1/99	78r
Transfer of remains to funeral home		159.82	1/99	78r
Vault		778.07	1/99	78r
Visitation/viewing		175.28	1/99	78r
Groceries				
Apples, red delicious	lb	0.84	7/01	11r
Bacon, sliced	lb	3.38	7/01	11r
Bakery products, expenditures on	yr	299	1999	30r
Bananas	lb	0.54	7/01	11r
Beans, dried, any type, all sizes	lb	0.76	7/01	11r
Beef, expenditures on	yr	222	1999	30r
Bread, white, pan	lb	0.99	7/01	11r
Butter, yoghurt, cheese, etc, expenditures on	yr	211	1999	30r
Cereals and bakery product purchases	yr	466	1999	30r
Cereals and cereal products, expenditures on	yr	168	1999	30r
Chicken breast, bone-in	lb	2.45	7/01	11r
Chicken, fresh, whole	lb	1.19	7/01	11r
Chops, boneless,	lb	4.00	7/01	11r
Chuck roast, graded and ungraded, excl U.S. prime and choice	lb	2.55	7/01	11r
Coffee, 100%, ground roast, all sizes	lb	3.80	7/01	11r
Cookies, chocolate chip	lb	2.83	7/01	11r
Dairy product purchases	yr	341	1999	30r
Eggs, expenditures on	yr	39	1999	30r
Eggs, grade AA, large	dozen	1.23	7/01	11r
Fats and oils, expenditures on	yr	88	1999	30r
Fish and seafood, expenditures on	yr	121	1999	30r
Food (excl fruit and vegetables), eaten at home, purchases	yr	1001	1999	30r
Food cooked on trips, expenditures on	yr	64	1999	30r
Food purchases	yr	5312	1999	30r
Food purchases, eaten away from home	yr	2180	1999	30r
Food purchases, food eaten at home	yr	3132	1999	30r
Fresh fruits, expenditures on	yr	186	1999	30r
Fresh milk and cream, expenditures on	yr	130	1999	30r
Fresh vegetables, expenditures on	yr	177	1999	30r
Grapefruit	lb	0.68	7/01	11r
Grapes, Thompson, seedless	lb	2.42	7/01	11r
Ground beef, lean and extra lean	lb	2.46	7/01	11r
Ice cream, prepackaged, bulk, regular	1/2 gal	3.62	7/01	11r
Lettuce, iceberg	lb	0.63	7/01	11r
Meats, poultry, fish, and egg purchases	yr	761	1999	30r
Milk, fresh, low fat,	gal	2.80	7/01	11r
Milk, fresh, whole, fortified	gal	2.88	7/01	11r
Nonalcoholic beverages, expenditures on	yr	258	1999	30r
Oranges, Navel	lb	0.97	7/01	11r
Oranges, Valencia	lb	0.43	7/01	11r
Peaches	lb	1.38	7/01	11r
Peanut butter, creamy, all sizes	lb	2.14	7/01	11r

Yolo, CA - continued

Item	Per	Value	Date	Ref.
Groceries - continued				
Pork chops, center cut, bone-in	lb	3.83	7/01	11r
Pork, expenditures on	yr	141	1999	30r
Potatoes, white, all types	lb	0.37	7/01	11r
Poultry, expenditures on	yr	146	1999	30r
Processed fruits, expenditures on	yr	118	1999	30r
Processed vegetables, expenditures on	yr	81	1999	30r
Round roast, graded and ungraded, excl U.S. prime and choice	lb	3.07	7/01	11r
Round roast, U.S. choice, boneless	lb	3.37	7/01	11r
Round steak, graded and ungraded, excl U.S. prime and choice	lb	3.51	7/01	11r
Sirloin steak, graded and ungraded, excl U.S. prime and choice	lb	4.67	7/01	11r
Steak, sirloin, U.S. choice, boneless	lb	6.20	7/01	11r
Strawberries, dry pint	12 oz	1.79	7/01	11r
Sugar and other sweets, expenditures on	yr	124	1999	30r
Sugar, white, all sizes	lb	0.46	7/01	11r
Tobacco products and smoking supplies purchases	yr	217	1999	30r
Tomatoes, field grown	lb	1.17	7/01	11r
Tuna, light, chunk	lb	2.05	7/01	11r
Goods and Services				
B&B Japanese maple (acer japonicum)	gal	39.99	4/00	93r
Boxwood (buxus)	2 gal	14.99-24.99	4/00	93r
Christmas tree, noble fir		40-60	2000	65s
Daylilly (hemerocallis)	gal	6.99-8.99	4/00	93r
Flat of annuals		16.68	4/00	93r
Fountain grass (pennisetum)	gal	7.99-11.99	4/00	93r
Hanging basket (10 in)		29.99	4/00	93r
Hardy geranium (geranium)	gal	6.99-11.99	4/00	93r
Hosta (hosta)	gal	6.99-18.99	4/00	93r
Lilac (syrubga vulgaris)	2 gal	14.99-17.99	4/00	93r
Miscellaneous purchases	yr	1070	1999	30r
Rhododendron (rhododendron)	2 gal	14.99	4/00	93r
Sage (salvia)	gal	6.99	4/00	93r
Wintercreeper euonymus (euonymus fortunei)	2 gal	14.99-22.99	4/00	93r
Hunting license	yr	29.95	4/01	34s
Health Care				
Cardiac catheterization, ave hospital/ physician charges		24000	1998	77s
Childbirth, Cesarean delivery		11587	1997	13r
Childbirth, vaginal delivery		6725	1997	13r
Drugs, expenditures on	yr	309	1999	30r
Health care purchases	yr	1869	1999	30r
Health insurance expenditures	yr	868	1999	30r
Hysterectomy, laproscopically-assisted, ave hospital/physician charges		20760	1998	76s
Hysterectomy, vaginal, ave hospital and physician charges		14570	1998	76s
Medicaid dispensing fee		4.05	1999	87s
Medical services expenditures	yr	580	1999	30r
Medical supplies, expenditures on	yr	112	1999	30r
Household Goods				
Floor coverings, expenditures on	yr	49	1999	30r
Furniture, expenditures on	yr	444	1999	30r
Household furnishings and equipment purchases	yr	1768	1999	30r
Household textiles, expenditures on	yr	141	1999	30r
Laundry and cleaning supplies, expenditures on	yr	128	1999	30r
Housing				
Home price, existing, ave		239400	10/00	90r
Home value, median		215000	2001	53s

Values are in dollars or fractions of dollars. In the column headed *Ref*, references are shown to sources. Each reference is followed by a letter. These refer to the geographical level for which data were reported: s=State, r=Region, and c=City or metro. The abbreviation *ex* is used to mean *except* or *excluding*; *exp* stands for expenditures. For other abbreviations and further explanations, please see the Introduction.

Yolo, CA - continued

Item	Per	Value	Date	Ref.
Housing				
Household operation expenditures	yr	781	1999	30r
Housekeeping supplies purchases	yr	513	1999	30r
Lodging expenditures	yr	575	1999	30r
Maintenance, repairs, insurance expenditures	yr	939	1999	30r
Monthly rental value of owned home	mos	662	1999	30r
Owned dwellings, expenditures own	yr	5231	1999	30r
Rent expenditures	yr	2709	1999	30r
Rental unit, 1 bedroom, with utilities	mos	556	4/01	41c
Rental unit, 2 bedroom, with utilities	mos	688	4/01	41c
Rental unit, 3 bedroom, with utilities	mos	953	4/01	41c
Rental unit, 4 bedroom, with utilities	mos	1126	4/01	41c
Shelter, expenditures on	yr	8516	1999	30r
Insurance and Pensions				
Life and other personal insurance purchases	yr	355	1999	30r
Pensions and Social Security, expenditures on	yr	3636	1999	30r
Legal Fees				
Divorce, filing fee		182.00	4/01	35s
Driver's license fee	renew	15.00	1999	48s
Driver's license fee	orig	12.00	1999	48s
Personal Goods				
Personal care products and services purchases	yr	449	1999	30r
Personal Services				
Personal services, household, expenditures on	yr	353	1999	30r
Pets				
Pets, toys, and playground equipment, expenditures on	yr	358	1999	30r
Taxes				
Federal income taxes paid	yr	3200	1999	30r
Personal taxes, expenditures on	yr	4153	1999	30r
Property taxes paid	yr	923	1999	30r
State and local income taxes paid	yr	812	1999	30r
Transportation				
Cars and trucks, new, expenditures on	yr	1534	1999	30r
Cars and trucks, used, expenditures on	yr	1593	1999	30r
Diesel at the pump	gal	1.37	10/99	73s
Gasoline and motor oil purchases	yr	1129	1999	30r
Gasoline before-tax price (cents)	gal	128.80	10/00	43s
Maintenance and repair expenditures	yr	797	1999	30r
Public transportation, expenditures on	yr	530	1999	30r
Transportation purchases	yr	7423	1999	30r
Vehicle expenses, miscellaneous, purchases	yr	2585	1999	30r
Vehicle insurance payments	yr	811	1999	30r
Vehicle purchases (net outlay)	yr	3180	1999	30r
Vehicle rental, lease expenditures	yr	666	1999	30r
Utilities				
Electrical bill, average	mos	58.66	9/00	9s
Electricity, expenditures on	yr	725	1999	30r
Electricity cost, average	KWh	7.75	9/00	9s
Utilities, fuels, and public services purchased	yr	2179	1999	30r
Water and other public services, expenditures on	yr	339	1999	30r
Weddings				
Wedding (national average cost)		19936	2000	33r
Wedding (regional average total cost)		18918	1997	110r
Attendants' gifts		321	1998	33r
Bridal attendants' apparel (5 persons)		824	2000	33r
Bride's headpiece/veil		173	1998	33r
Bride's wedding dress		859	1998	33r
Clergy, religious facility fee		242	1998	33r
Engagement ring		3177	1998	33r
Flowers		789	1998	33r
Groom's formalwear rental		99	2000	33r
Limousine		410	1998	33r

Yolo, CA - continued

Item	Per	Value	Date	Ref.
Weddings - continued				
Marriage license cost		50.00-80.00	4/01	35s
Men's formalwear (ushers, best man)		469	2000	33r
Mother of bride apparel		241	2000	33r
Music		866	1998	33r
Photography and videography		1368	1998	33r
Rehearsal dinner		728	1998	33r
Wedding invitations and announcements		341	1998	33r
Wedding reception		7968	2000	33r
Wedding rings (bride and groom)		1060	1998	33r

York, PA

Item	Per	Value	Date	Ref.
Average annual expenditures	yr	37971	1999	30r
Alcoholic Beverages				
Alcoholic beverage purchases	yr	368	1999	30r
Wine, red and white table, all sizes, any origin	liter	9.64	7/01	11r
Appliances				
Major appliances, expenditures on	yr	194	1999	30r
Small appliances, housewares, expenditures on	yr	93	1999	30r
Banking and Money				
Mortgage interest and charges paid	yr	2622	1999	30r
Mortgage principal paid on owned property	yr	1262	1999	30r
Vehicle finance charges paid	yr	240	1999	30r
Charity				
Cash contributions, expenditures	yr	1001	1999	30r
Child Care				
Child raising cost, total, age 0-2	yr	8670	1999	60r
Child raising cost, total, age 3-5	yr	8910	1999	60r
Child raising cost, total, age 6-8	yr	9040	1999	60r
Child raising cost, total, age 9-11	yr	9100	1999	60r
Child raising cost, total, age 12-14	yr	9890	1999	60r
Child raising cost, total, age 15-17	yr	10010	1999	60r
Child's child care and education, age 0-2	yr	1070	1999	60r
Child's child care and education, age 3-5	yr	1190	1999	60r
Child's child care and education, age 6-8	yr	740	1999	60r
Child's child care and education, age 9-11	yr	470	1999	60r
Child's child care and education, age 12-14	yr	350	1999	60r
Child's child care and education, age 15-17	yr	590	1999	60r
Child's clothing, age 0-2	yr	480	1999	60r
Child's clothing, age 3-5	yr	470	1999	60r
Child's clothing, age 6-8	yr	520	1999	60r
Child's clothing, age 9-11	yr	570	1999	60r
Child's clothing, age 12-14	yr	970	1999	60r
Child's clothing, age 15-17	yr	870	1999	60r
Child's food, age 0-2	yr	1130	1999	60r
Child's food, age 3-5	yr	1290	1999	60r
Child's food, age 6-8	yr	1640	1999	60r
Child's food, age 9-11	yr	1930	1999	60r
Child's food, age 12-14	yr	1940	1999	60r
Child's food, age 15-17	yr	2150	1999	60r
Child's health care, age 0-2	yr	550	1999	60r
Child's health care, age 3-5	yr	530	1999	60r
Child's health care, age 6-8	yr	610	1999	60r
Child's health care, age 9-11	yr	650	1999	60r
Child's health care, age 12-14	yr	660	1999	60r
Child's health care, age 15-17	yr	690	1999	60r
Child's housing, age 0-2	yr	3555	1999	60r
Child's housing, age 3-5	yr	3530	1999	60r
Child's housing, age 6-8	yr	3490	1999	60r
Child's housing, age 9-11	yr	3340	1999	60r
Child's housing, age 12-14	yr	3530	1999	60r
Child's housing, age 15-17	yr	3140	1999	60r
Child's personal care, reading, age 0-2	yr	920	1999	60r
Child's personal care, reading, age 3-5	yr	950	1999	60r
Child's personal care, reading, age 6-8	yr	980	1999	60r
Child's personal care, reading, age 9-11	yr	1020	1999	60r

Values are in dollars or fractions of dollars. In the column headed *Ref*, references are shown to sources. Each reference is followed by a letter. These refer to the geographical level for which data were reported: s=State, r=Region, and c=City or metro. The abbreviation *ex* is used to mean *except* or *excluding*; *exp* stands for expenditures. For other abbreviations and further explanations, please see the Introduction.

York, PA - continued

Item	Per	Value	Date	Ref.
Child Care				
Child's personal care, reading, age 12-14	yr	1190	1999	60r
Child's personal care, reading, age 15-17	yr	970	1999	60r
Clothing				
Apparel and services purchases	yr	1831	1999	30r
Boys, 2 to 15, expenditures on	yr	92	1999	30r
Children under 2, expenditures on	yr	63	1999	30r
Footwear, expenditures on	yr	300	1999	30r
Girls, 2 to 15, expenditures on	yr	101	1999	30r
Men and boys, expenditures on	yr	446	1999	30r
Men, 16 and over, expenditures on	yr	354	1999	30r
Women, 16 and over, expenditures on	yr	584	1999	30r
Communications				
Cable modem installation, Adelphi		54.90	6/99	103s
Cable modem installation, Comcast		95.00	6/99	103s
Cable modem rate, cable subscriber, Adelphi	mos	34.95	6/99	103s
Cable modem rate, cable subscriber, Comcast	mos	39.95	6/99	103s
Cable modem rate, non-cable subscriber, Adelphi	mos	44.95	6/99	103s
Cable modem rate, non-cable subscriber, Comcast	mos	49.95	6/99	103s
Phone line, single, business, field visit	inst.	75.00	12/97	17s
Phone line, single, business, no field visit	inst.	75.00	12/97	17s
Phone line, single, residence, field visit	inst.	40.00	12/97	17s
Phone line, single, residence, no field visit	inst.	40.00	12/97	17s
Postage and stationery, expenditures on	yr	138	1999	30r
Postal rate, express mail, up to half-pound		12.45	7/01	108r
Postal rate, letter, first class, first ounce		0.34	7/01	108r
Postal rate, letter, two ounces		0.57	7/01	108r
Postal rate, post card		0.21	7/01	108r
Postal rate, priority mail, two pounds		3.95	7/01	108r
Postal rate, priority mail, up to one pound		3.50	7/01	108r
Telephone services, expenditures on	yr	830	1999	30r
Education				
Board, 4-year private college/university	yr	2822	1996	38s
Board, 4-year public college/university	yr	2174	1996	38s
Education expenditures	yr	877	1999	30r
Room, 4-year private college/university	yr	2943	1996	38s
Room, 4-year public college/university	yr	2227	1996	38s
Total cost, 4-year private college/university	yr	19876	1996	38s
Total cost, 4-year public college/university	yr	9124	1996	38s
Tuition, 2-year public college/university, in state	yr	1909	1996	38s
Tuition, 4-year private college/university, in state	yr	14111	1996	38s
Tuition, 4-year public college/university	yr	4723	1996	38s
Energy and Fuels				
Electricity	KWh	0.12	7/01	11r
Fuel oil #2	gal	1.31	7/01	11r
Fuel oil and other fuels, expenditures on	yr	207	1999	30r
Gas, natural, commercial rate	1000 cf	5.96	11/00	88s
Gasoline, all types	gal	1.80	7/01	11r
Gasoline, unleaded midgrade	gal	1.85	7/01	11r
Gasoline, unleaded premium	gal	1.91	7/01	11r
Gasoline, unleaded regular	gal	1.71	7/01	11r
Natural gas, expenditures on	yr	368	1999	30r
Utility (piped) gas, therm		1.08	7/01	11r
Utility (piped) gas, 40 therms		50.87	7/01	11r
Utility (piped) gas, 100 therms		111.06	7/01	11r
Entertainment				
Entertainment purchases	yr	1821	1999	30r
Fees and admissions paid	yr	511	1999	30r
Television, radios, sound equipment, expenditures on	yr	650	1999	30r
Funerals				
Total cost of funeral		5813.50	1/99	78r
Acknowledgement cards		28.32	1/99	78r
Casket		2082.20	1/99	78r
Cosmetology, hair, other preparation		169.59	1/99	78r

York, PA - continued

Item	Per	Value	Date	Ref.
Funerals - continued				
Embalming		465.60	1/99	78r
Funeral at funeral home		339.56	1/99	78r
Hearse (local)		183.96	1/99	78r
Professional service charges		1157.85	1/99	78r
Service car/van		100.41	1/99	78r
Transfer of remains to funeral home		158.66	1/99	78r
Vault		766.31	1/99	78r
Visitation/viewing		361.04	1/99	78r
Groceries				
Apples, red delicious	lb	0.95	7/01	11r
Bacon, sliced	lb	3.44	7/01	11r
Bakery products, expenditures on	yr	310	1999	30r
Bananas	lb	0.55	7/01	11r
Beef, expenditures on	yr	236	1999	30r
Bread, white, pan	lb	1.09	7/01	11r
Butter, yoghurt, cheese, etc, expenditures on	yr	214	1999	30r
Cereals and bakery product purchases	yr	474	1999	30r
Cereals and cereal products, expenditures on	yr	164	1999	30r
Chicken legs, bone-in	lb	1.23	7/01	11r
Chicken, fresh, whole	lb	1.13	7/01	11r
Chuck roast, U.S. choice, boneless	lb	2.79	7/01	11r
Coffee, 100%, ground roast, all sizes	lb	3.40	7/01	11r
Dairy product purchases	yr	342	1999	30r
Eggs, expenditures on	yr	34	1999	30r
Eggs, grade A, large	dozen	0.82	7/01	11r
Fats and oils, expenditures on	yr	80	1999	30r
Fish and seafood, expenditures on	yr	123	1999	30r
Food (excl fruit and vegetables), eaten at home, purchases	yr	838	1999	30r
Food cooked on trips, expenditures on	yr	48	1999	30r
Food purchases	yr	5314	1999	30r
Food purchases, eaten away from home	yr	2313	1999	30r
Food purchases, food eaten at home	yr	3001	1999	30r
Fresh fruits, expenditures on	yr	169	1999	30r
Fresh milk and cream, expenditures on	yr	128	1999	30r
Fresh vegetables, expenditures on	yr	164	1999	30r
Grapefruit	lb	0.67	7/01	11r
Grapes, Thompson, seedless	lb	2.18	7/01	11r
Ground beef, lean and extra lean	lb	2.66	7/01	11r
Ground chuck, 100% beef	lb	2.04	7/01	11r
Lettuce, iceberg	lb	0.76	7/01	11r
Meats, poultry, fish, and egg purchases	yr	808	1999	30r
Nonalcoholic beverages, expenditures on	yr	225	1999	30r
Orange juice, frozen concentrate	16 oz	1.88	7/01	11r
Oranges, Navel	lb	0.79	7/01	11r
Oranges, Valencia	lb	0.56	7/01	11r
Peaches	lb	1.16	7/01	11r
Peanut butter, creamy, all sizes	lb	2.01	7/01	11r
Pears, Anjou	lb	1.16	7/01	11r
Pork chops, center cut, bone-in	lb	3.57	7/01	11r
Pork, expenditures on	yr	146	1999	30r
Potato chips	16 oz	3.37	7/01	11r
Potatoes, white, all types	lb	0.42	7/01	11r
Poultry, expenditures on	yr	158	1999	30r
Processed fruits, expenditures on	yr	124	1999	30r
Processed vegetables, expenditures on	yr	82	1999	30r
Round roast, U.S. choice, boneless	lb	3.04	7/01	11r
Spaghetti and macaroni	lb	1.04	7/01	11r
Steak, sirloin, U.S. choice, boneless	lb	5.39	7/01	11r
Strawberries, dry pint	12 oz	1.51	7/01	11r
Sugar and other sweets, expenditures on	yr	110	1999	30r
Sugar, white, 33-80 ounce package	lb	0.46	7/01	11r
Sugar, white, all sizes	lb	0.47	7/01	11r
Tobacco products and smoking supplies purchases	yr	309	1999	30r
Yogurt, natural, fruit flavored	8 oz	0.79	7/01	11r
Goods and Services				
B&B Japanese maple (acer japonicum)	gal	38.99-125.00	4/00	93r

Values are in dollars or fractions of dollars. In the column headed *Ref*, references are shown to sources. Each reference is followed by a letter. These refer to the geographical level for which data were reported: s=State, r=Region, and c=City or metro. The abbreviation *ex* is used to mean *except* or *excluding*; *exp* stands for expenditures. For other abbreviations and further explanations, please see the Introduction.

York, PA - continued

Item	Per	Value	Date	Ref.
Goods and Services				
Boxwood (buxus)	2 gal	15.99-49.95	4/00	93r
Daylilly (hemerocallis)	gal	4.95	4/00	93r
Flat of annuals		8.00-14.99	4/00	93r
Fountain grass (pennisetum)	gal	6.99-9.99	4/00	93r
Hanging basket (10 in)		12.95-19.99	4/00	93r
Hardy geranium (geranium)	gal	6.95-7.99	4/00	93r
Hosta (hosta)	gal	4.95	4/00	93r
Lilac (syrubga vulgaris)	2 gal	17.99-74.95	4/00	93r
Miscellaneous purchases	yr	872	1999	30r
Rhododendron (rhododendron)	2 gal	23.99-54.95	4/00	93r
Sage (salvia)	gal	6.95-7.99	4/00	93r
Wintercreeper euonymus (euonymus fortunei)	2 gal	14.99-23.95	4/00	93r
Hunting license	yr	20.00	4/01	34s
Health Care				
Cardiac catheterization, ave hospital/physician charges		13870	1998	77s
Childbirth, Cesarean delivery		14716	1997	13r
Childbirth, vaginal delivery		8541	1997	13r
Drugs, expenditures on	yr	296	1999	30r
Health care purchases	yr	1788	1999	30r
Health insurance expenditures	yr	875	1999	30r
Hysterectomy, laproscopically-assisted, ave hospital/physician charges		14760	1998	76s
Hysterectomy, vaginal, ave hospital and physician charges		9270	1998	76s
Medicaid dispensing fee		4.00	1999	87s
Medical services expenditures	yr	516	1999	30r
Medical supplies, expenditures on	yr	102	1999	30r
Plastic surgery, breast augmentation		4232	2000	7r
Plastic surgery, breast lift		4605	2000	7r
Plastic surgery, facelift		6964	2000	7r
Plastic surgery, hair transplantation		4193	2000	7r
Plastic surgery, lip augmentation		1675	2000	7r
Plastic surgery, lower body lift		6611	2000	7r
Plastic surgery, thigh lift		4751	2000	7r
Household Goods				
Floor coverings, expenditures on	yr	59	1999	30r
Furniture, expenditures on	yr	388	1999	30r
Household furnishings and equipment purchases	yr	1567	1999	30r
Household textiles, expenditures on	yr	112	1999	30r
Laundry and cleaning supplies, expenditures on	yr	104	1999	30r
Housing				
Home, 2200 sq ft, 4-br, 2-bath, 2-car garage, average		151000	2000	47c
Home price, existing, ave		180800	10/00	90r
Home value, median		115000	2001	53s
Household operation expenditures	yr	581	1999	30r
Housekeeping supplies purchases	yr	474	1999	30r
Lodging expenditures	yr	550	1999	30r
Maintenance, repairs, insurance expenditures	yr	835	1999	30r
Monthly rental value of owned home	mos	663	1999	30r
Owned dwellings, expenditures own	yr	5209	1999	30r
Rent expenditures	yr	2390	1999	30r
Rental unit, 1 bedroom, with utilities	mos	446	4/01	41c
Rental unit, 2 bedroom, with utilities	mos	553	4/01	41c
Rental unit, 3 bedroom, with utilities	mos	690	4/01	41c
Rental unit, 4 bedroom, with utilities	mos	772	4/01	41c
Shelter, expenditures on	yr	8149	1999	30r

York, PA - continued

Item	Per	Value	Date	Ref.
Insurance and Pensions				
Life and other personal insurance purchases	yr	424	1999	30r
Pensions and Social Security, expenditures on	yr	3037	1999	30r
Legal Fees				
Divorce, filing fee		65.00	4/01	35s
Driver's license fee	orig	29.00	1999	48s
Driver's license fee	renew	24.00	1999	48s
Fishing license	yr	17.00	4/01	34s
Personal Goods				
Personal care products and services purchases	yr	399	1999	30r
Personal Services				
Personal services, household, expenditures on	yr	271	1999	30r
Pets				
Pets, toys, and playground equipment, expenditures on	yr	325	1999	30r
Taxes				
Federal income taxes paid	yr	2606	1999	30r
Personal taxes, expenditures on	yr	3567	1999	30r
Property taxes paid	yr	1752	1999	30r
State and local income taxes paid	yr	694	1999	30r
Transportation				
Bus fare, one-way	trip	1.00	2000	1c
Cars and trucks, new, expenditures on	yr	1496	1999	30r
Cars and trucks, used, expenditures on	yr	1251	1999	30r
Diesel at the pump	gal	1.31	10/99	73s
Gasoline and motor oil purchases	yr	901	1999	30r
Gasoline before-tax price (cents)	gal	106.60	10/00	43s
Maintenance and repair expenditures	yr	618	1999	30r
Public transportation, expenditures on	yr	575	1999	30r
Transportation purchases	yr	6503	1999	30r
Vehicle expenses, miscellaneous, purchases	yr	2266	1999	30r
Vehicle insurance payments	yr	824	1999	30r
Vehicle purchases (net outlay)	yr	2761	1999	30r
Vehicle rental, lease expenditures	yr	584	1999	30r
Utilities				
Electrical bill, average	mos	69.16	9/00	9s
Electricity, expenditures on	yr	837	1999	30r
Electricity cost, average	KWh	5.08	9/00	9s
Utilities, fuels, and public services purchased	yr	2457	1999	30r
Water and other public services, expenditures on	yr	215	1999	30r
Weddings				
Wedding (national average cost)		19936	2000	33r
Wedding (regional average total cost)		29454	1997	110r
Attendants' gifts		321	1998	33r
Bridal attendants' apparel (5 persons)		824	2000	33r
Bride's headpiece/veil		173	1998	33r
Bride's wedding dress		859	1998	33r
Clergy, religious facility fee		242	1998	33r
Engagement ring		3177	1998	33r
Flowers		789	1998	33r
Groom's formalwear rental		99	2000	33r
Limousine		410	1998	33r
Marriage license cost		25.00-40.00	4/01	35s
Men's formalwear (ushers, best man)		469	2000	33r
Mother of bride apparel		241	2000	33r
Music		866	1998	33r
Photography and videography		1368	1998	33r
Rehearsal dinner		728	1998	33r
Wedding invitations and announcements		341	1998	33r
Wedding reception		7968	2000	33r
Wedding rings (bride and groom)		1060	1998	33r

Values are in dollars or fractions of dollars. In the column headed *Ref*, references are shown to sources. Each reference is followed by a letter. These refer to the geographical level for which data were reported: s=State, r=Region, and c=City or metro. The abbreviation *ex* is used to mean *except* or *excluding*; *exp* stands for expenditures. For other abbreviations and further explanations, please see the Introduction.

Youngstown-Warren, OH

Item	Per	Value	Date	Ref.
Average annual expenditures	yr	35369	1999	30r
Composite, ACCRA index		94.70	3/01	4c
Alcoholic Beverages				
Alcoholic beverage purchases	yr	304	1999	30r
Beer, Heineken, 12-oz, ex deposit	6	7.65	3/01	4c
J & B Scotch	750-ml	21.35	3/01	4c
Malt beverages, all types, all sizes, any origin	16 oz	0.93	7/01	11r
Wine, Livingston or Gallo, Chablis blanc	1.5 liter	5.69	3/01	4c
Wine, red and white table, all sizes, any origin	liter	7.04	7/01	11r
Appliances				
Appliance repair, service call, washing machine	min lab chg	33.60	3/01	4c
Major appliances, expenditures on	yr	165	1999	30r
Small appliances, housewares, expenditures on	yr	90	1999	30r
Banking and Money				
Mortgage interest and charges paid	yr	2277	1999	30r
Mortgage principal paid on owned property	yr	1230	1999	30r
Mortgage rate, incl. points and orig. fee, 30-yr. conv. fixed or ARM	mos	7.24	3/01	4c
Vehicle finance charges paid	yr	328	1999	30r
Charity				
Cash contributions, expenditures	yr	1126	1999	30r
Child Care				
Child raising cost, total, age 0-2	yr	7890	1999	60r
Child raising cost, total, age 3-5	yr	8130	1999	60r
Child raising cost, total, age 6-8	yr	8170	1999	60r
Child raising cost, total, age 9-11	yr	8190	1999	60r
Child raising cost, total, age 12-14	yr	8890	1999	60r
Child raising cost, total, age 15-17	yr	9050	1999	60r
Child's child care and education, age 0-2	yr	1240	1999	60r
Child's child care and education, age 3-5	yr	1370	1999	60r
Child's child care and education, age 6-8	yr	880	1999	60r
Child's child care and education, age 9-11	yr	570	1999	60r
Child's child care and education, age 12-14	yr	420	1999	60r
Child's child care and education, age 15-17	yr	720	1999	60r
Child's clothing, age 0-2	yr	410	1999	60r
Child's clothing, age 3-5	yr	400	1999	60r
Child's clothing, age 6-8	yr	450	1999	60r
Child's clothing, age 9-11	yr	500	1999	60r
Child's clothing, age 12-14	yr	840	1999	60r
Child's clothing, age 15-17	yr	740	1999	60r
Child's food, age 0-2	yr	960	1999	60r
Child's food, age 3-5	yr	1120	1999	60r
Child's food, age 6-8	yr	1430	1999	60r
Child's food, age 9-11	yr	1710	1999	60r
Child's food, age 12-14	yr	1710	1999	60r
Child's food, age 15-17	yr	1920	1999	60r
Child's health care, age 0-2	yr	520	1999	60r
Child's health care, age 3-5	yr	500	1999	60r
Child's health care, age 6-8	yr	570	1999	60r
Child's health care, age 9-11	yr	610	1999	60r
Child's health care, age 12-14	yr	630	1999	60r
Child's health care, age 15-17	yr	650	1999	60r
Child's housing, age 0-2	yr	2860	1999	60r
Child's housing, age 3-5	yr	2840	1999	60r
Child's housing, age 6-8	yr	2800	1999	60r
Child's housing, age 9-11	yr	2650	1999	60r
Child's housing, age 12-14	yr	2840	1999	60r
Child's housing, age 15-17	yr	2440	1999	60r
Child's personal care, reading, age 0-2	yr	880	1999	60r
Child's personal care, reading, age 3-5	yr	900	1999	60r
Child's personal care, reading, age 6-8	yr	930	1999	60r
Child's personal care, reading, age 9-11	yr	970	1999	60r
Child's personal care, reading, age 12-14	yr	1150	1999	60r
Child's personal care, reading, age 15-17	yr	920	1999	60r
Clothing				
Apparel and services purchases	yr	1607	1999	30r
Boys' brief, cotton	3	3.53	3/01	4c

Youngstown-Warren, OH - continued

Item	Per	Value	Date	Ref.
Clothing - continued				
Boys, 2 to 15, expenditures on	yr	91	1999	30r
Children under 2, expenditures on	yr	59	1999	30r
Footwear, expenditures on	yr	285	1999	30r
Girls, 2 to 15, expenditures on	yr	116	1999	30r
Men and boys, expenditures on	yr	433	1999	30r
Men, 16 and over, expenditures on	yr	341	1999	30r
Shirt, man's dress shirt		30.80	3/01	4c
Slacks, man's "No Wrinkles" khaki		36.79	3/01	4c
Women, 16 and over, expenditures on	yr	490	1999	30r
Communications				
Cable modem installation, Adelphi		54.90	6/99	103s
Cable modem installation, Media One		100.00	6/99	103s
Cable modem installation, Time Warner		75.00-225.00	6/99	103s
Cable modem rate, cable subscriber, Adelphi	mos	34.95	6/99	103s
Cable modem rate, cable subscriber, Media One	mos	34.95-39.95	6/99	103s
Cable modem rate, cable subscriber, Time Warner	mos	39.95-49.95	6/99	103s
Cable modem rate, non-cable subscriber, Adelphi	mos	44.95	6/99	103s
Cable modem rate, non-cable subscriber, Media One	mos	49.95	6/99	103s
Cable modem rate, non-cable subscriber, Time Warner	mos	39.95-54.95	6/99	103s
Newspaper subscription, daily and Sunday delivery	mos	9.75	3/01	4c
Phone line, single, business, field visit	inst.	56.32	12/97	17s
Phone line, single, business, no field visit	inst.	56.32	12/97	17s
Phone line, single, residence, field visit	inst.	31.10	12/97	17s
Phone line, single, residence, no field visit	inst.	31.10	12/97	17s
Postage and stationery, expenditures on	yr	140	1999	30r
Postal rate, express mail, up to half-pound		12.45	7/01	108r
Postal rate, letter, first class, first ounce		0.34	7/01	108r
Postal rate, letter, two ounces		0.57	7/01	108r
Postal rate, post card		0.21	7/01	108r
Postal rate, priority mail, two pounds		3.95	7/01	108r
Postal rate, priority mail, up to one pound		3.50	7/01	108r
Telephone bill, family of three	mos	19.73	3/01	4c
Telephone services, expenditures on	yr	830	1999	30r
Education				
Board, 4-year private college/university	yr	2414	1996	38s
Board, 4-year public college/university	yr	2181	1996	38s
Education expenditures	yr	583	1999	30r
Room, 4-year private college/university	yr	2349	1996	38s
Room, 4-year public college/university	yr	2386	1996	38s
Total cost, 4-year private college/university	yr	17139	1996	38s
Total cost, 4-year public college/university	yr	8169	1996	38s
Tuition, 2-year public college/university, in state	yr	2261	1996	38s
Tuition, 4-year private college/university, in state	yr	12377	1996	38s
Tuition, 4-year public college/university	yr	3603	1996	38s
Energy and Fuels				
Electricity	500 KWhs	46.59	7/01	11r
Energy, combined forms, 2400 sq ft	mos	154.64	3/01	4c
Energy, exc. electricity, 2400 sq ft	mos	73.99	3/01	4c
Fuel oil #2	gal	1.27	7/01	11r
Fuel oil and other fuels, expenditures on	yr	68	1999	30r
Gas, natural, commercial rate	1000 cf	8.65	11/00	88s
Gas, regular unleaded, cash, self-service	gal	1.26	3/01	4c
Gasoline, unleaded midgrade	gal	1.79	7/01	11r
Gasoline, unleaded premium	gal	1.86	7/01	11r
Gasoline, unleaded regular	gal	1.58	7/01	11r
Natural gas, expenditures on	yr	389	1999	30r
Utility (piped) gas, therm		0.81	7/01	11r
Utility (piped) gas, 40 therms		38.01	7/01	11r
Utility (piped) gas, 100 therms		81.75	7/01	11r

Values are in dollars or fractions of dollars. In the column headed *Ref*, references are shown to sources. Each reference is followed by a letter. These refer to the geographical level for which data were reported: s=State, r=Region, and c=City or metro. The abbreviation *ex* is used to mean *except* or *excluding*; *exp* stands for *expenditures*. For other abbreviations and further explanations, please see the Introduction.

Youngstown-Warren, OH - continued

Item	Per	Value	Date	Ref.
Entertainment				
Bowling, Saturday evening rate	line	2.54	3/01	4c
Entertainment purchases	yr	1984	1999	30r
Fees and admissions paid	yr	444	1999	30r
Monopoly game, Parker Brothers', No. 9	game	8.75	3/01	4c
Movie, first-run, Saturday, evening	adm.	7.00	3/01	4c
Television, radios, sound equipment, expenditures on	yr	580	1999	30r
Tennis balls, yellow, Wilson or Penn, 3	can	2.12	3/01	4c
Funerals				
Cosmetology, hair, other preparation		178.32	1/99	78r
Embalming		408.19	1/99	78r
Funeral at funeral home		362.13	1/99	78r
Professional service charges		1375.51	1/99	78r
Transfer of remains to funeral home		155.92	1/99	78r
Visitation/viewing		294.38	1/99	78r
Groceries				
Groceries, ACCRA Index		103.30	3/01	4c
Antibiotic ointment, Polysporin	0.5 oz	4.24	3/01	4c
Baby food, strained vegetables or fruit, lowest price	4-4.5 oz	0.43	3/01	4c
Bacon, sliced	lb	3.15	7/01	11r
Bakery products, expenditures on	yr	281	1999	30r
Bananas	lb	0.44	3/01	4c
Bananas	lb	0.48	7/01	11r
Beans, dried, any type, all sizes	lb	0.61	7/01	11r
Beef for stew, boneless	lb	3.08	7/01	11r
Beef or hamburger, ground	lb	1.67	3/01	4c
Beef, expenditures on	yr	217	1999	30r
Bologna, all beef or mixed	lb	2.52	7/01	11r
Bread, white	loaf	0.97	3/01	4c
Bread, white, pan	lb	1.06	7/01	11r
Broccoli	lb	0.91	7/01	11r
Butter, salted, grade AA, stick	lb	3.04	7/01	11r
Butter, yoghurt, cheese, etc, expenditures on	yr	183	1999	30r
Cereals and bakery product purchases	yr	430	1999	30r
Cereals and cereal products, expenditures on	yr	149	1999	30r
Cheese, Kraft grated Parmesan	8 oz	3.99	3/01	4c
Chicken, fresh, whole	lb	1.07	7/01	11r
Chicken, whole fryer	lb	1.25	3/01	4c
Chops, boneless,	lb	3.64	7/01	11r
Chuck roast, U.S. choice, boneless	lb	2.47	7/01	11r
Cigarettes, Winston, Kings	carton	27.88	3/01	4c
Coffee, 100%, ground roast, all sizes	lb	2.69	7/01	11r
Coffee, vacuum-packed	13 oz	2.54	3/01	4c
Cookies, chocolate chip	lb	2.87	7/01	11r
Corn Flakes, Kellogg's or Post Toasties	18 oz	2.89	3/01	4c
Corn, frozen, whole kernel, lowest price	16 oz	1.33	3/01	4c
Dairy product purchases	yr	304	1999	30r
Eggs, expenditures on	yr	26	1999	30r
Eggs, Grade A or AA	dozen	1.21	3/01	4c
Eggs, grade A, large	dozen	0.88	7/01	11r
Fats and oils, expenditures on	yr	75	1999	30r
Fish and seafood, expenditures on	yr	72	1999	30r
Food (excl fruit and vegetables), eaten at home, purchases	yr	887	1999	30r
Food cooked on trips, expenditures on	yr	44	1999	30r
Food purchases	yr	4802	1999	30r
Food purchases, eaten away from home	yr	2069	1999	30r
Food purchases, food eaten at home	yr	2733	1999	30r
Fresh fruits, expenditures on	yr	138	1999	30r
Fresh milk and cream, expenditures on	yr	120	1999	30r
Fresh vegetables, expenditures on	yr	126	1999	30r
Grapefruit	lb	0.66	7/01	11r
Grapes, Thompson, seedless	lb	1.64	7/01	11r
Ground beef, 100% beef	lb	1.64	7/01	11r
Ground beef, lean and extra lean	lb	2.16	7/01	11r
Ground chuck, 100% beef	lb	2.13	7/01	11r
Ham, boneless, excl canned	lb	2.62	7/01	11r
Ice cream, prepackaged, bulk, regular	1/2 gal	3.35	7/01	11r
Lemons	lb	1.19	7/01	11r

Youngstown-Warren, OH - continued

Item	Per	Value	Date	Ref.
Groceries - continued				
Lettuce, iceberg	head	0.67	3/01	4c
Lettuce, iceberg	lb	0.73	7/01	11r
Margarine, Blue Bonnet or Parkay, stick	lb	0.97	3/01	4c
Margarine, soft, tubs	lb	0.89	7/01	11r
Meats, poultry, fish, and egg purchases	yr	671	1999	30r
Milk, fresh, whole, fortified	gal	2.71	7/01	11r
Milk, whole	1/2 gal	1.42	3/01	4c
Nonalcoholic beverages, expenditures on	yr	239	1999	30r
Orange juice, Minute Maid frozen	12 oz	1.43	3/01	4c
Oranges, Navel	lb	0.80	7/01	11r
Oranges, Valencia	lb	0.66	7/01	11r
Peaches, halves or slices, Hunt's, Del Monte, or Libby's	29 oz	1.69	3/01	4c
Pears, Anjou	lb	0.93	7/01	11r
Peas, green, Del Monte or Green Giant	15 oz	0.53	3/01	4c
Pork chops, center cut, bone-in	lb	3.63	7/01	11r
Pork, expenditures on	yr	150	1999	30r
Potato chips	16 oz	3.52	7/01	11r
Potatoes, frozen, french fried	lb	1.08	7/01	11r
Potatoes, white or red	10 lb	2.83	3/01	4c
Potatoes, white, all types	lb	0.33	7/01	11r
Poultry, expenditures on	yr	108	1999	30r
Processed fruits, expenditures on	yr	98	1999	30r
Processed vegetables, expenditures on	yr	80	1999	30r
Round roast, U.S. choice, boneless	lb	3.07	7/01	11r
Round steak, graded and ungraded, excl U.S. prime and choice	lb	3.41	7/01	11r
Sausage, Jimmy Dean/Owens pork	lb	3.61	3/01	4c
Shortening, vegetable oil blends	lb	1.13	7/01	11r
Shortening, vegetable, Crisco	3 lb	3.41	3/01	4c
Soft drink, Coca Cola, ex deposit	2 liter	1.35	3/01	4c
Spaghetti and macaroni	lb	0.80	7/01	11r
Steak, round, U.S. choice, boneless	lb	3.23	7/01	11r
Steak, T-bone	lb	7.47	3/01	4c
Steak, T-bone, U.S. choice, bone-in	lb	6.68	7/01	11r
Strawberries, dry pint	12 oz	1.32	7/01	11r
Sugar and other sweets, expenditures on	yr	114	1999	30r
Sugar, cane or beet	4 lbs	1.57	3/01	4c
Sugar, white, 33-80 ounce package	lb	0.42	7/01	11r
Sugar, white, all sizes	lb	0.43	7/01	11r
Tobacco products and smoking supplies purchases	yr	331	1999	30r
Tomatoes, field grown	lb	1.46	7/01	11r
Tomatoes, Hunt's or Del Monte	14.5 oz	0.84	3/01	4c
Tuna, chunk, light	6 oz	0.78	3/01	4c
Tuna, light, chunk	lb	1.80	7/01	11r
Turkey, frozen, whole	lb	1.15	7/01	11r
Goods and Services				
Miscellaneous goods and services, ACCRA Index		96.10	3/01	4c
B&B Japanese maple (acer japonicum)	gal	29.99-169.99	4/00	93r
Boxwood (buxus)	2 gal	18.99-39.99	4/00	93r
Daylily (hemerocallis)	gal	4.99-25.00	4/00	93r
Flat of annuals		11.98-24.99	4/00	93r
Fountain grass (pennisetum)	gal	5.98-12.98	4/00	93r
Hanging basket (10 in)		12.99-27.99	4/00	93r
Hardy geranium (geranium)	gal	7.99-9.99	4/00	93r
Hosta (hosta)	gal	6.00-25.00	4/00	93r
Lilac (syrubga vulgaris)	2 gal	14.99-24.99	4/00	93r
Miscellaneous purchases	yr	865	1999	30r
Rhododendron (rhododendron)	2 gal	23.98-42.99	4/00	93r

Values are in dollars or fractions of dollars. In the column headed *Ref*, references are shown to sources. Each reference is followed by a letter. These refer to the geographical level for which data were reported: s=State, r=Region, and c=City or metro. The abbreviation *ex* is used to mean *except* or *excluding*; *exp* stands for expenditures. For other abbreviations and further explanations, please see the Introduction.

Youngstown-Warren, OH - continued

Item	Per	Value	Date	Ref.
Goods and Services				
Sage (salvia)	gal	6.00-9.99	4/00	93r
Wintercreeper euonymus (euonymus fortunei)	2 gal	16.00-169.99	4/00	93r
Hunting license	yr	15.00	4/01	34s
Health Care				
Health care, ACCRA Index		84.80	3/01	4c
Cardiac catheterization, ave hospital/physician charges		11760	1998	77s
Childbirth, Cesarean delivery		10722	1997	13r
Childbirth, vaginal delivery		6223	1997	13r
Dentist's fee, adult teeth cleaning and periodic oral exam	visit	63.20	3/01	4c
Doctor's fee, routine exam, established patient	visit	50.00	3/01	4c
Drugs, expenditures on	yr	394	1999	30r
Health care purchases	yr	2048	1999	30r
Health insurance expenditures	yr	978	1999	30r
Hospital care, private room	day	386.75	3/01	4c
Hysterectomy, laproscopically-assisted, ave hospital/physician charges		11730	1998	76s
Hysterectomy, vaginal, ave hospital and physician charges		9640	1998	76s
Medicaid dispensing fee		3.70	1999	87s
Medical services expenditures	yr	554	1999	30r
Medical supplies, expenditures on	yr	122	1999	30r
Plastic surgery, breast augmentation		3184	2000	7r
Plastic surgery, breast lift		3585	2000	7r
Plastic surgery, facelift		4999	2000	7r
Plastic surgery, hair transplantation		3105	2000	7r
Plastic surgery, lip augmentation		1290	2000	7r
Plastic surgery, lower body lift		8135	2000	7r
Plastic surgery, thigh lift		3839	2000	7r
Household Goods				
Dishwashing powder, Cascade	50 oz	3.29	3/01	4c
Floor coverings, expenditures on	yr	52	1999	30r
Furniture, expenditures on	yr	344	1999	30r
Household furnishings and equipment purchases	yr	1475	1999	30r
Household textiles, expenditures on	yr	109	1999	30r
Laundry and cleaning supplies, expenditures on	yr	134	1999	30r
Tissues, facial, Kleenex brand	175	1.25	3/01	4c
Housing				
Housing, ACCRA Index		86.00	3/01	4c
Home price, existing, ave		144400	10/00	90r
Home value, median		96000	2001	53s
House, 2400 sq ft, 8000 sq ft lot, new, urban, utilities	total	180000	3/01	4c
House payment, principal and interest, 25% down payment	mos	920	3/01	4c
Household operation expenditures	yr	542	1999	30r
Housekeeping supplies purchases	yr	508	1999	30r
Lodging expenditures	yr	430	1999	30r
Maintenance, repairs, insurance expenditures	yr	853	1999	30r
Monthly rental value of owned home	mos	547	1999	30r
Owned dwellings, expenditures own	yr	4282	1999	30r
Rent expenditures	yr	1558	1999	30r
Rent, apartment, 2 br, 1 1/2-2 baths, unfurn, 950 sq ft, water	mos	509	3/01	4c
Rental unit, 1 bedroom, with utilities	mos	403	4/01	41c
Rental unit, 2 bedroom, with utilities	mos	505	4/01	41c
Rental unit, 3 bedroom, with utilities	mos	634	4/01	41c
Rental unit, 4 bedroom, with utilities	mos	722	4/01	41c
Shelter, expenditures on	yr	6270	1999	30r
Insurance and Pensions				
Life and other personal insurance purchases	yr	387	1999	30r
Pensions and Social Security, expenditures on	yr	2968	1999	30r

Youngstown-Warren, OH - continued

Item	Per	Value	Date	Ref.
Legal Fees				
Divorce, filing fee		100.00	4/01	35s
Driver's license fee	orig	14.50	1999	48s
Driver's license fee	renew	14.50	1999	48s
Fishing license	yr	15.00	4/01	34s
Personal Goods				
Personal care products and services purchases	yr	385	1999	30r
Shampoo, Alberto VO5	15 oz	0.98	3/01	4c
Toothpaste, Crest or Colgate	6-7 oz	2.05	3/01	4c
Personal Services				
Dry cleaning, man's 2-pc suit		7.20	3/01	4c
Man's haircut, barbershop, no styling		10.20	3/01	4c
Personal services, household, expenditures on	yr	300	1999	30r
Woman's shampoo, trim, blow-dry, no style-change		21.65	3/01	4c
Pets				
Pets, toys, and playground equipment, expenditures on	yr	375	1999	30r
Restaurant Food				
Chicken, fried, thigh and drumstick, KFC/Church's		2.75	3/01	4c
Hamburger with cheese, McDonald's	1/4 lb	2.19	3/01	4c
Pizza, Pizza Hut or Pizza Inn	11-12 in	7.99	3/01	4c
Taxes				
Federal income taxes paid	yr	2326	1999	30r
Personal taxes, expenditures on	yr	3223	1999	30r
Property taxes paid	yr	1152	1999	30r
State and local income taxes paid	yr	753	1999	30r
Transportation				
Transportation, ACCRA Index		83.60	3/01	4c
Bus fare, one-way	trip	0.85	2000	1c
Cars and trucks, new, expenditures on	yr	1280	1999	30r
Cars and trucks, used, expenditures on	yr	1763	1999	30r
Diesel at the pump	gal	1.25	10/99	73s
Gasoline and motor oil purchases	yr	1036	1999	30r
Gasoline before-tax price (cents)	gal	109.50	10/00	43s
Maintenance and repair expenditures	yr	594	1999	30r
Public transportation, expenditures on	yr	341	1999	30r
Tire balance, computer or spin balance, front	wheel	5.99	3/01	4c
Transportation purchases	yr	6617	1999	30r
Vehicle expenses, miscellaneous, purchases	yr	2159	1999	30r
Vehicle insurance payments	yr	701	1999	30r
Vehicle purchases (net outlay)	yr	3081	1999	30r
Vehicle rental, lease expenditures	yr	536	1999	30r
Travel				
Car rental	day	84.50	2000	24c
Utilities				
Utilities, ACCRA Index		121.80	3/01	4c
Electrical bill, average	mos	72.83	9/00	9s
Electricity, expenditures on	yr	841	1999	30r
Electricity and other, mixed, 2400 sq ft, new home	mos	80.65	3/01	4c
Electricity cost, average	KWh	6.59	9/00	9s
Utilities, fuels, and public services purchased	yr	2401	1999	30r
Water and other public services, expenditures on	yr	273	1999	30r
Weddings				
Wedding (national average cost)		19936	2000	33r
Wedding (regional average total cost)		16195	1997	110r
Attendants' gifts		321	1998	33r
Bridal attendants' apparel (5 persons)		824	2000	33r
Bride's headpiece/veil		173	1998	33r
Bride's wedding dress		859	1998	33r
Clergy, religious facility fee		242	1998	33r
Engagement ring		3177	1998	33r
Flowers		789	1998	33r

Values are in dollars or fractions of dollars. In the column headed *Ref*, references are shown to sources. Each reference is followed by a letter. These refer to the geographical level for which data were reported: s=State, r=Region, and c=City or metro. The abbreviation *ex* is used to mean *except* or *excluding*; *exp* stands for expenditures. For other abbreviations and further explanations, please see the Introduction.

Youngstown-Warren, OH - continued

Item	Per	Value	Date	Ref.
Weddings				
Groom's formalwear rental		99	2000	33r
Limousine		410	1998	33r
Marriage license cost		45.00	4/01	35s
Men's formalwear (ushers, best man)		469	2000	33r
Mother of bride apparel		241	2000	33r
Music		866	1998	33r
Photography and videography		1368	1998	33r
Rehearsal dinner		728	1998	33r
Wedding invitations and announcements		341	1998	33r
Wedding reception		7968	2000	33r
Wedding rings (bride and groom)		1060	1998	33r

Yuba City, CA

Item	Per	Value	Date	Ref.
Average annual expenditures	yr	40662	1999	30r
Alcoholic Beverages				
Alcoholic beverage purchases	yr	372	1999	30r
Malt beverages, all types, all sizes, any origin	16 oz	0.94	7/01	11r
Wine, red and white table, all sizes, any origin	liter	6.00	7/01	11r
Appliances				
Major appliances, expenditures on	yr	167	1999	30r
Small appliances, housewares, expenditures on	yr	105	1999	30r
Banking and Money				
Mortgage interest and charges paid	yr	3368	1999	30r
Mortgage principal paid on owned property	yr	1677	1999	30r
Vehicle finance charges paid	yr	311	1999	30r
Charity				
Cash contributions, expenditures	yr	1344	1999	30r
Child Care				
Child raising cost, total, age 0-2	yr	9140	1999	60r
Child raising cost, total, age 3-5	yr	9370	1999	60r
Child raising cost, total, age 6-8	yr	9450	1999	60r
Child raising cost, total, age 9-11	yr	9470	1999	60r
Child raising cost, total, age 12-14	yr	10170	1999	60r
Child raising cost, total, age 15-17	yr	10360	1999	60r
Child's child care and education, age 0-2	yr	1250	1999	60r
Child's child care and education, age 3-5	yr	1380	1999	60r
Child's child care and education, age 6-8	yr	890	1999	60r
Child's child care and education, age 9-11	yr	580	1999	60r
Child's child care and education, age 12-14	yr	430	1999	60r
Child's child care and education, age 15-17	yr	730	1999	60r
Child's clothing, age 0-2	yr	430	1999	60r
Child's clothing, age 3-5	yr	420	1999	60r
Child's clothing, age 6-8	yr	470	1999	60r
Child's clothing, age 9-11	yr	520	1999	60r
Child's clothing, age 12-14	yr	870	1999	60r
Child's clothing, age 15-17	yr	770	1999	60r
Child's food, age 0-2	yr	1120	1999	60r
Child's food, age 3-5	yr	1280	1999	60r
Child's food, age 6-8	yr	1640	1999	60r
Child's food, age 9-11	yr	1930	1999	60r
Child's food, age 12-14	yr	1940	1999	60r
Child's food, age 15-17	yr	2150	1999	60r
Child's health care, age 0-2	yr	490	1999	60r
Child's health care, age 3-5	yr	470	1999	60r
Child's health care, age 6-8	yr	530	1999	60r
Child's health care, age 9-11	yr	570	1999	60r
Child's health care, age 12-14	yr	580	1999	60r
Child's health care, age 15-17	yr	610	1999	60r
Child's housing, age 0-2	yr	3630	1999	60r
Child's housing, age 3-5	yr	3610	1999	60r
Child's housing, age 6-8	yr	3570	1999	60r
Child's housing, age 9-11	yr	3410	1999	60r
Child's housing, age 12-14	yr	3600	1999	60r
Child's housing, age 15-17	yr	3210	1999	60r
Child's personal care, reading, age 0-2	yr	1040	1999	60r
Child's personal care, reading, age 3-5	yr	1060	1999	60r

Yuba City, CA - continued

Item	Per	Value	Date	Ref.
Child Care - continued				
Child's personal care, reading, age 6-8	yr	1090	1999	60r
Child's personal care, reading, age 9-11	yr	1130	1999	60r
Child's personal care, reading, age 12-14	yr	1300	1999	60r
Child's personal care, reading, age 15-17	yr	1080	1999	60r
Clothing				
Apparel and services purchases	yr	1863	1999	30r
Boys, 2 to 15, expenditures on	yr	80	1999	30r
Children under 2, expenditures on	yr	74	1999	30r
Footwear, expenditures on	yr	307	1999	30r
Girls, 2 to 15, expenditures on	yr	101	1999	30r
Men and boys, expenditures on	yr	443	1999	30r
Men, 16 and over, expenditures on	yr	363	1999	30r
Women, 16 and over, expenditures on	yr	594	1999	30r
Communications				
Cable modem installation, AT&T-BIS		150.00	6/99	103s
Cable modem installation, Charter		99.00-169.00	6/99	103s
Cable modem installation, Comcast		95.00	6/99	103s
Cable modem installation, Cox		99.00-174.95	6/99	103s
Cable modem installation, Media One		100.00	6/99	103s
Cable modem installation, Time Warner		75.00-225.00	6/99	103s
Cable modem rate, cable subscriber, AT&T-BIS	mos	39.95	6/99	103s
Cable modem rate, cable subscriber, Charter	mos	49.95-79.95	6/99	103s
Cable modem rate, cable subscriber, Comcast	mos	39.95	6/99	103s
Cable modem rate, cable subscriber, Cox	mos	29.95-44.95	6/99	103s
Cable modem rate, cable subscriber, Media One	mos	34.95-39.95	6/99	103s
Cable modem rate, cable subscriber, Time Warner	mos	39.95-49.95	6/99	103s
Cable modem rate, non-cable subscriber, Charter	mos	59.95-89.95	6/99	103s
Cable modem rate, non-cable subscriber, Comcast	mos	49.95	6/99	103s
Cable modem rate, non-cable subscriber, Cox	mos	42.95-54.95	6/99	103s
Cable modem rate, non-cable subscriber, Media One	mos	49.95	6/99	103s
Cable modem rate, non-cable subscriber, Time Warner	mos	39.95-54.95	6/99	103s
Phone line, single, business, field visit	inst.	70.75	12/97	17s
Phone line, single, business, no field visit	inst.	70.75	12/97	17s
Phone line, single, residence, field visit	inst.	34.75	12/97	17s
Phone line, single, residence, no field visit	inst.	34.75	12/97	17s
Postage and stationery, expenditures on	yr	150	1999	30r
Postal rate, express mail, up to half-pound		12.45	7/01	108r
Postal rate, letter, first class, first ounce		0.34	7/01	108r
Postal rate, letter, two ounces		0.57	7/01	108r
Postal rate, post card		0.21	7/01	108r
Postal rate, priority mail, two pounds		3.95	7/01	108r
Postal rate, priority mail, up to one pound		3.50	7/01	108r
Telephone services, expenditures on	yr	825	1999	30r
Education				
Board, 4-year private college/university	yr	2970	1996	38s
Board, 4-year public college/university	yr	2516	1996	38s
Education expenditures	yr	676	1999	30r
Room, 4-year private college/university	yr	3196	1996	38s
Room, 4-year public college/university	yr	3031	1996	38s
Total cost, 4-year private college/university	yr	20143	1996	38s
Total cost, 4-year public college/university	yr	8213	1996	38s
Tuition, 2-year public college/university, in state	yr	362	1996	38s
Tuition, 4-year private college/university, in state	yr	13977	1996	38s
Tuition, 4-year public college/university	yr	2666	1996	38s

Values are in dollars or fractions of dollars. In the column headed *Ref*, references are shown to sources. Each reference is followed by a letter. These refer to the geographical level for which data were reported: s=State, r=Region, and c=City or metro. The abbreviation *ex* is used to mean *except* or *excluding*; *exp* stands for *expenditures*. For other abbreviations and further explanations, please see the Introduction.

Yuba City, CA - continued

Item	Per	Value	Date	Ref.
Energy and Fuels				
Electricity	KWh	0.11	7/01	11r
Electricity	500 KWhs	48.23	7/01	11r
Fuel oil and other fuels, expenditures on	yr	35	1999	30r
Gas, natural, commercial rate	1000 cf	8.74	11/00	88s
Gasoline, all types	gal	1.91	7/01	11r
Gasoline, unleaded premium	gal	2.05	7/01	11r
Gasoline, unleaded regular	gal	1.83	7/01	11r
Natural gas, expenditures on	yr	255	1999	30r
Utility (piped) gas, therm		0.98	7/01	11r
Utility (piped) gas, 40 therms		40.74	7/01	11r
Utility (piped) gas, 100 therms		96.80	7/01	11r
Entertainment				
Entertainment purchases	yr	2139	1999	30r
Fees and admissions paid	yr	545	1999	30r
Television, radios, sound equipment, expenditures on	yr	624	1999	30r
Funerals				
Total cost of funeral		5401.08	1/99	78r
Acknowledgement cards		33.64	1/99	78r
Casket		2170.43	1/99	78r
Cosmetology, hair, other preparation		136.32	1/99	78r
Embalming		319.13	1/99	78r
Funeral at funeral home		370.21	1/99	78r
Hearse (local)		161.04	1/99	78r
Professional service charges		963.15	1/99	78r
Service car/van		133.99	1/99	78r
Transfer of remains to funeral home		159.82	1/99	78r
Vault		778.07	1/99	78r
Visitation/viewing		175.28	1/99	78r
Groceries				
Apples, red delicious	lb	0.84	7/01	11r
Bacon, sliced	lb	3.38	7/01	11r
Bakery products, expenditures on	yr	299	1999	30r
Bananas	lb	0.54	7/01	11r
Beans, dried, any type, all sizes	lb	0.76	7/01	11r
Beef, expenditures on	yr	222	1999	30r
Bread, white, pan	lb	0.99	7/01	11r
Butter, yoghurt, cheese, etc, expenditures on	yr	211	1999	30r
Cereals and bakery product purchases	yr	466	1999	30r
Cereals and cereal products, expenditures on	yr	168	1999	30r
Chicken breast, bone-in	lb	2.45	7/01	11r
Chicken, fresh, whole	lb	1.19	7/01	11r
Chops, boneless,	lb	4.00	7/01	11r
Chuck roast, graded and ungraded, excl U.S. prime and choice	lb	2.55	7/01	11r
Coffee, 100%, ground roast, all sizes	lb	3.80	7/01	11r
Cookies, chocolate chip	lb	2.83	7/01	11r
Dairy product purchases	yr	341	1999	30r
Eggs, expenditures on	yr	39	1999	30r
Eggs, grade AA, large	dozen	1.23	7/01	11r
Fats and oils, expenditures on	yr	88	1999	30r
Fish and seafood, expenditures on	yr	121	1999	30r
Food (excl fruit and vegetables), eaten at home, purchases	yr	1001	1999	30r
Food cooked on trips, expenditures on	yr	64	1999	30r
Food purchases	yr	5312	1999	30r
Food purchases, eaten away from home	yr	2180	1999	30r
Food purchases, food eaten at home	yr	3132	1999	30r
Fresh fruits, expenditures on	yr	186	1999	30r
Fresh milk and cream, expenditures on	yr	130	1999	30r
Fresh vegetables, expenditures on	yr	177	1999	30r
Grapefruit	lb	0.68	7/01	11r
Grapes, Thompson, seedless	lb	2.42	7/01	11r
Ground beef, lean and extra lean	lb	2.46	7/01	11r
Ice cream, prepackaged, bulk, regular	1/2 gal	3.62	7/01	11r
Lettuce, iceberg	lb	0.63	7/01	11r
Meats, poultry, fish, and egg purchases	yr	761	1999	30r
Milk, fresh, low fat	gal	2.80	7/01	11r
Milk, fresh, whole, fortified	gal	2.88	7/01	11r

Yuba City, CA - continued

Item	Per	Value	Date	Ref.
Groceries - continued				
Nonalcoholic beverages, expenditures on	yr	258	1999	30r
Oranges, Navel	lb	0.97	7/01	11r
Oranges, Valencia	lb	0.43	7/01	11r
Peaches	lb	1.38	7/01	11r
Peanut butter, creamy, all sizes	lb	2.14	7/01	11r
Pork chops, center cut, bone-in	lb	3.83	7/01	11r
Pork, expenditures on	yr	141	1999	30r
Potatoes, white, all types	lb	0.37	7/01	11r
Poultry, expenditures on	yr	146	1999	30r
Processed fruits, expenditures on	yr	118	1999	30r
Processed vegetables, expenditures on	yr	81	1999	30r
Round roast, graded and ungraded, excl U.S. prime and choice	lb	3.07	7/01	11r
Round roast, U.S. choice, boneless	lb	3.37	7/01	11r
Round steak, graded and ungraded, excl U.S. prime and choice	lb	3.51	7/01	11r
Sirloin steak, graded and ungraded, excl U.S. prime and choice	lb	4.67	7/01	11r
Steak, sirloin, U.S. choice, boneless	lb	6.20	7/01	11r
Strawberries, dry pint	12 oz	1.79	7/01	11r
Sugar and other sweets, expenditures on	yr	124	1999	30r
Sugar, white, all sizes	lb	0.46	7/01	11r
Tobacco products and smoking supplies purchases	yr	217	1999	30r
Tomatoes, field grown	lb	1.17	7/01	11r
Tuna, light, chunk	lb	2.05	7/01	11r
Goods and Services				
B&B Japanese maple (acer japonicum)	gal	39.99	4/00	93r
Boxwood (buxus)	2 gal	14.99-24.99	4/00	93r
Christmas tree, noble fir		40-60	2000	65s
Daylilly (hemerocallis)	gal	6.99-8.99	4/00	93r
Flat of annuals		16.68	4/00	93r
Fountain grass (pennisetum)	gal	7.99-11.99	4/00	93r
Hanging basket (10 in)		29.99	4/00	93r
Hardy geranium (geranium)	gal	6.99-11.99	4/00	93r
Hosta (hosta)	gal	6.99-18.99	4/00	93r
Lilac (syrubga vulgaris)	2 gal	14.99-17.99	4/00	93r
Miscellaneous purchases	yr	1070	1999	30r
Rhododendron (rhododendron)	2 gal	14.99	4/00	93r
Sage (salvia)	gal	6.99	4/00	93r
Wintercreeper euonymus (euonymus fortunei)	2 gal	14.99-22.99	4/00	93r
Hunting license	yr	29.95	4/01	34s
Health Care				
Cardiac catheterization, ave hospital/ physician charges		24000	1998	77s
Childbirth, Cesarean delivery		11587	1997	13r
Childbirth, vaginal delivery		6725	1997	13r
Drugs, expenditures on	yr	309	1999	30r
Health care purchases	yr	1869	1999	30r
Health insurance expenditures	yr	868	1999	30r
Hysterectomy, laproscopically-assisted, ave hospital/physician charges		20760	1998	76s
Hysterectomy, vaginal, ave hospital and physician charges		14570	1998	76s
Medicaid dispensing fee		4.05	1999	87s
Medical services expenditures	yr	580	1999	30r
Medical supplies, expenditures on	yr	112	1999	30r
Household Goods				
Floor coverings, expenditures on	yr	49	1999	30r
Furniture, expenditures on	yr	444	1999	30r
Household furnishings and equipment purchases	yr	1768	1999	30r
Household textiles, expenditures on	yr	141	1999	30r

Values are in dollars or fractions of dollars. In the column headed *Ref*, references are shown to sources. Each reference is followed by a letter. These refer to the geographical level for which data were reported: s=State, r=Region, and c=City or metro. The abbreviation *ex* is used to mean *except* or *excluding*; *exp* stands for *expenditures*. For other abbreviations and further explanations, please see the Introduction.

Yuba City, CA - continued

Item	Per	Value	Date	Ref.
Household Goods				
Laundry and cleaning supplies, expenditures on	yr	128	1999	30r
Housing				
Home price, existing, ave		239400	10/00	90r
Home value, median		215000	2001	53s
Household operation expenditures	yr	781	1999	30r
Housekeeping supplies purchases	yr	513	1999	30r
Lodging expenditures	yr	575	1999	30r
Maintenance, repairs, insurance expenditures	yr	939	1999	30r
Monthly rental value of owned home	mos	662	1999	30r
Owned dwellings, expenditures own	yr	5231	1999	30r
Rent expenditures	yr	2709	1999	30r
Rental unit, 1 bedroom, with utilities	mos	393	4/01	41c
Rental unit, 2 bedroom, with utilities	mos	505	4/01	41c
Rental unit, 3 bedroom, with utilities	mos	704	4/01	41c
Rental unit, 4 bedroom, with utilities	mos	814	4/01	41c
Shelter, expenditures on	yr	8516	1999	30r
Insurance and Pensions				
Life and other personal insurance purchases	yr	355	1999	30r
Pensions and Social Security, expenditures on	yr	3636	1999	30r
Legal Fees				
Divorce, filing fee		182.00	4/01	35s
Driver's license fee	orig	12.00	1999	48s
Driver's license fee	renew	15.00	1999	48s
Personal Goods				
Personal care products and services purchases	yr	449	1999	30r
Personal Services				
Personal services, household, expenditures on	yr	353	1999	30r
Pets				
Pets, toys, and playground equipment, expenditures on	yr	358	1999	30r
Taxes				
Federal income taxes paid	yr	3200	1999	30r
Personal taxes, expenditures on	yr	4153	1999	30r
Property taxes paid	yr	923	1999	30r
State and local income taxes paid	yr	812	1999	30r
Transportation				
Cars and trucks, new, expenditures on	yr	1534	1999	30r
Cars and trucks, used, expenditures on	yr	1593	1999	30r
Diesel at the pump	gal	1.37	10/99	73s
Gasoline and motor oil purchases	yr	1129	1999	30r
Gasoline before-tax price (cents)	gal	128.80	10/00	43s
Maintenance and repair expenditures	yr	797	1999	30r
Public transportation, expenditures on	yr	530	1999	30r
Transportation purchases	yr	7423	1999	30r
Vehicle expenses, miscellaneous, purchases	yr	2585	1999	30r
Vehicle insurance payments	yr	811	1999	30r
Vehicle purchases (net outlay)	yr	3180	1999	30r
Vehicle rental, lease expenditures	yr	666	1999	30r
Utilities				
Electrical bill, average	mos	58.66	9/00	9s
Electricity, expenditures on	yr	725	1999	30r
Electricity cost, average	KWh	7.75	9/00	9s
Utilities, fuels, and public services purchased	yr	2179	1999	30r
Water and other public services, expenditures on	yr	339	1999	30r
Weddings				
Wedding (national average cost)		19936	2000	33r
Wedding (regional average total cost)		18918	1997	110r
Attendants' gifts		321	1998	33r
Bridal attendants' apparel (5 persons)		824	2000	33r
Bride's headpiece/veil		173	1998	33r
Bride's wedding dress		859	1998	33r

Yuba City, CA - continued

Item	Per	Value	Date	Ref.
Weddings - continued				
Clergy, religious facility fee		242	1998	33r
Engagement ring		3177	1998	33r
Flowers		789	1998	33r
Groom's formalwear rental		99	2000	33r
Limousine		410	1998	33r
Marriage license cost		50.00-80.00	4/01	35s
Men's formalwear (ushers, best man)		469	2000	33r
Mother of bride apparel		241	2000	33r
Music		866	1998	33r
Photography and videography		1368	1998	33r
Rehearsal dinner		728	1998	33r
Wedding invitations and announcements		341	1998	33r
Wedding reception		7968	2000	33r
Wedding rings (bride and groom)		1060	1998	33r

Yuma, AZ

Item	Per	Value	Date	Ref.
Composite, ACCRA index		98.00	3/01	4c
Alcoholic Beverages				
Beer, Heineken, 12-oz, ex deposit	6	6.82	3/01	4c
J & B Scotch	750-ml	18.89	3/01	4c
Wine, Livingston or Gallo, Chablis blanc	1.5 liter	5.74	3/01	4c
Appliances				
Appliance repair, service call, washing machine	min lab chg	42.50	3/01	4c
Banking and Money				
Mortgage rate, incl. points and orig. fee, 30-yr. conv. fixed or ARM	mos	6.97	3/01	4c
Clothing				
Boys' brief, cotton	3	2.72	3/01	4c
Shirt, man's dress shirt		26.46	3/01	4c
Slacks, man's "No Wrinkles" khaki		31.74	3/01	4c
Communications				
Cable modem installation, Cox		99.00-174.95	6/99	103s
Cable modem rate, cable subscriber, Cox	mos	29.95-44.95	6/99	103s
Cable modem rate, non-cable subscriber, Cox	mos	42.95-54.95	6/99	103s
Newspaper subscription, daily and Sunday delivery	mos	15.44	3/01	4c
Phone line, single, business, field visit	inst.	56.00	12/97	17s
Phone line, single, business, no field visit	inst.	56.00	12/97	17s
Phone line, single, residence, field visit	inst.	46.50	12/97	17s
Phone line, single, residence, no field visit	inst.	46.50	12/97	17s
Postal rate, express mail, up to half-pound		12.45	7/01	108r
Postal rate, letter, first class, first ounce		0.34	7/01	108r
Postal rate, letter, two ounces		0.57	7/01	108r
Postal rate, post card		0.21	7/01	108r
Postal rate, priority mail, two pounds		3.95	7/01	108r
Postal rate, priority mail, up to one pound		3.50	7/01	108r
Telephone bill, business, basic rate	mos	32.78	12/97	18c
Telephone bill, family of three	mos	19.88	3/01	4c
Telephone bill, residential, basic rate	mos	13.18	12/97	18c
Education				
Board, 4-year private college/university	yr	2143	1996	38s
Board, 4-year public college/university	yr	1815	1996	38s
Room, 4-year private college/university	yr	2012	1996	38s
Room, 4-year public college/university	yr	2257	1996	38s
Total cost, 4-year private college/university	yr	10934	1996	38s
Total cost, 4-year public college/university	yr	5998	1996	38s
Tuition, 2-year public college/university, in state	yr	764	1996	38s
Tuition, 4-year private college/university, in state	yr	6779	1996	38s
Tuition, 4-year public college/university	yr	1926	1996	38s

Values are in dollars or fractions of dollars. In the column headed *Ref*, references are shown to sources. Each reference is followed by a letter. These refer to the geographical level for which data were reported: s=State, r=Region, and c=City or metro. The abbreviation *ex* is used to mean *except* or *excluding; exp* stands for *expenditures*. For other abbreviations and further explanations, please see the Introduction.

Yuma, AZ - continued

Item	Per	Value	Date	Ref.
Energy and Fuels				
Energy, combined forms, 2400 sq ft	mos	167.73	3/01	4c
Gas, natural, commercial rate	1000 cf	8.12	11/00	88s
Gas, regular unleaded, cash, self-service	gal	1.54	3/01	4c
Entertainment				
Bowling, Saturday evening rate	line	2.16	3/01	4c
Monopoly game, Parker Brothers', No. 9	game	8.91	3/01	4c
Movie, first-run, Saturday, evening	adm.	6.50	3/01	4c
Tennis balls, yellow, Wilson or Penn, 3	can	2.16	3/01	4c
Funerals				
Total cost of funeral		5401.08	1/99	78r
Acknowledgement cards		33.64	1/99	78r
Casket		2170.43	1/99	78r
Cosmetology, hair, other preparation		136.32	1/99	78r
Embalming		319.13	1/99	78r
Funeral at funeral home		370.21	1/99	78r
Hearse (local)		161.04	1/99	78r
Professional service charges		963.15	1/99	78r
Service car/van		133.99	1/99	78r
Transfer of remains to funeral home		159.82	1/99	78r
Vault		778.07	1/99	78r
Visitation/viewing		175.28	1/99	78r
Groceries				
Groceries, ACCRA Index		105.30	3/01	4c
Antibiotic ointment, Polysporin	0.5 oz	4.66	3/01	4c
Baby food, strained vegetables or fruit, lowest price	4-4.5 oz	0.35	3/01	4c
Bananas	lb	0.51	3/01	4c
Beef or hamburger, ground	lb	1.19	3/01	4c
Bread, white	loaf	0.99	3/01	4c
Cheese, Kraft grated Parmesan	8 oz	3.71	3/01	4c
Chicken, whole fryer	lb	1.09	3/01	4c
Cigarettes, Winston, Kings	carton	26.16	3/01	4c
Coffee, vacuum-packed	13 oz	3.41	3/01	4c
Corn Flakes, Kellogg's or Post Toasties	18 oz	3.27	3/01	4c
Corn, frozen, whole kernel, lowest price	16 oz	1.27	3/01	4c
Eggs, Grade A or AA	dozen	0.97	3/01	4c
Lettuce, iceberg	head	0.89	3/01	4c
Margarine, Blue Bonnet or Parkay, stick	lb	0.91	3/01	4c
Milk, whole	1/2 gal	1.93	3/01	4c
Orange juice, Minute Maid frozen	12 oz	1.69	3/01	4c
Peaches, halves or slices, Hunt's, Del Monte, or Libby's	29 oz	1.70	3/01	4c
Peas, green, Del Monte or Green Giant	15 oz	0.69	3/01	4c
Potatoes, white or red	10 lb	1.99	3/01	4c
Sausage, Jimmy Dean/Owens pork	lb	4.69	3/01	4c
Shortening, vegetable, Crisco	3 lb	3.85	3/01	4c
Soft drink, Coca Cola, ex deposit	2 liter	1.23	3/01	4c
Steak, T-bone	lb	4.97	3/01	4c
Sugar, cane or beet	4 lbs	1.93	3/01	4c
Tomatoes, Hunt's or Del Monte	14.5 oz	0.85	3/01	4c
Tuna, chunk, light	6 oz	0.81	3/01	4c
Goods and Services				
Miscellaneous goods and services, ACCRA Index		93.00	3/01	4c
Hunting license	yr	25.50	4/01	34s
Health Care				
Health care, ACCRA Index		100.30	3/01	4c
Cardiac catheterization, ave hospital/ physician charges		20100	1998	77s
Childbirth, Cesarean delivery		11587	1997	13r
Childbirth, vaginal delivery		6725	1997	13r
Dentist's fee, adult teeth cleaning and periodic oral exam	visit	67.50	3/01	4c
Doctor's fee, routine exam, established patient	visit	59.00	3/01	4c
Hospital care, private room	day	586.00	3/01	4c
Hysterectomy, laproscopically-assisted, ave hospital/physician charges		19790	1998	76s

Yuma, AZ - continued

Item	Per	Value	Date	Ref.
Health Care - continued				
Hysterectomy, vaginal, ave hospital and physician charges		12130	1998	76s
Household Goods				
Dishwashing powder, Cascade	50 oz	3.23	3/01	4c
Tissues, facial, Kleenex brand	175	1.15	3/01	4c
Housing				
Housing, ACCRA Index		86.90	3/01	4c
Home value, median		131000	2001	53s
House, 2400 sq ft, 8000 sq ft lot, new, urban, utilities	total	179500	3/01	4c
House payment, principal and interest, 25% down payment	mos	902	3/01	4c
Rent, apartment, 2 br, 1 1/2-2 baths, unfurn, 950 sq ft, water	mos	587	3/01	4c
Rental unit, 1 bedroom, with utilities	mos	438	4/01	41c
Rental unit, 2 bedroom, with utilities	mos	583	4/01	41c
Rental unit, 3 bedroom, with utilities	mos	810	4/01	41c
Rental unit, 4 bedroom, with utilities	mos	816	4/01	41c
Insurance and Pensions				
Auto insurance premium	yr	901.65	1999	57s
Legal Fees				
Divorce, filing fee		64.00	4/01	35s
Driver's license fee	renew	17.50	1999	48s
Driver's license fee	orig	17.50	1999	48s
Personal Goods				
Shampoo, Alberto VO5	15 oz	1.03	3/01	4c
Toothpaste, Crest or Colgate	6-7 oz	2.39	3/01	4c
Personal Services				
Dry cleaning, man's 2-pc suit		7.48	3/01	4c
Man's haircut, barbershop, no styling		7.70	3/01	4c
Woman's shampoo, trim, blow-dry, no style-change		24.25	3/01	4c
Restaurant Food				
Chicken, fried, thigh and drumstick, KFC/ Church's		2.18	3/01	4c
Hamburger with cheese, McDonald's	1/4 lb	2.28	3/01	4c
Pizza, Pizza Hut or Pizza Inn	11-12 in	9.79	3/01	4c
Transportation				
Transportation, ACCRA Index		106.40	3/01	4c
Diesel at the pump	gal	1.27	10/99	73s
Gasoline before-tax price (cents)	gal	120.30	10/00	43s
Tire balance, computer or spin balance, front	wheel	8.10	3/01	4c
Utilities				
Utilities, ACCRA Index		131.10	3/01	4c
Electrical bill, average	mos	84.33	9/00	9s
Electricity, 2400 sq ft, new home	mos	167.73	3/01	4c
Electricity cost, average	KWh	7.60	9/00	9s
Weddings				
Wedding (national average cost)		19936	2000	33r
Attendants' gifts		321	1998	33r
Bridal attendants' apparel (5 persons)		824	2000	33r
Bride's headpiece/veil		173	1998	33r
Bride's wedding dress		859	1998	33r
Clergy, religious facility fee		242	1998	33r
Engagement ring		3177	1998	33r
Flowers		789	1998	33r
Groom's formalwear rental		99	2000	33r
Limousine		410	1998	33r
Marriage license cost		50.00	4/01	35s
Men's formalwear (ushers, best man)		469	2000	33r
Mother of bride apparel		241	2000	33r
Music		866	1998	33r
Photography and videography		1368	1998	33r
Rehearsal dinner		728	1998	33r
Wedding invitations and announcements		341	1998	33r
Wedding reception		7968	2000	33r
Wedding rings (bride and groom)		1060	1998	33r

Values are in dollars or fractions of dollars. In the column headed *Ref*, references are shown to sources. Each reference is followed by a letter. These refer to the geographical level for which data were reported: s=State, r=Region, and c=City or metro. The abbreviation *ex* is used to mean *except* or *excluding*; *exp* stands for *expenditures*. For other abbreviations and further explanations, please see the Introduction.

LIST OF SOURCES

This section shows all sources used in *American Cost of Living Survey*, 3rd Edition. Numberals in bold on the left are found in the data tables in the column marked Ref. Notes to the data are also provided as shown in the source.

1   *2000 APTA Transit Fare Summary.* Washington, D.C.: American Public Transit Association (APTA), 2001. *Notes:* Figures for bus fare in Chicago, Cincinnati, Cleveland, Dallas, Minneapolis, Norfolk, VA, Philadelphia, Pittsburgh, Riverside, CA, and Sarasota, FL are averages of fares charged by two bus systems. Phoenix data are averages of three systems; San Diego and Seattle are averages of four, New York City, San Franciso, and Washington, DC, are averages of six, and Los Angeles an average of 11 systems. All average fares are rounded to the nearest nickel.

2   *2000 APTA Transit Fare Summary.* Washington, D.C.: American Public Transit Association (APTA), 2001.

3   "2001 T&E Benchmarks in 100 Cities: Hotel Prices Lift Total Per Diems," Institute of Management & Administration, April 2001.

4   *ACCRA Cost of Living Index*, First Quarter 2001, Arlington, VA: American Chambers of Commerce Research Association (ACCRA).

5   *ACCRA Cost of Living Index*, Fourth Quarter 2000, Arlington, VA: American Chambers of Commerce Research Association (ACCRA).

6   AHFC Rental Market Survey, July 28, 2000, Alaska Housing Finance Corporation.

7   "ASAPS 2000 Statistics on Cosmetic Surgery," American Society for Aesthetic Plastic Surgery, Inc., www.surgery.org, 2001.

8   Aven, Paula, "Behind sky-high grocery prices," *Denver Business Journal*, June 18, 1999, p 3a.

9   "Average monthly electric bills, rates," *USA Today*, February 1, 2001, p. 3b. Data for Maine are for 1999.

10   "Average Per Diem Travel Cost," *TradeshowWeek*, November 13, 2000, p. A3.

11   *Average Price Data (AP) Survey*, U.S. Department of Labor, Bureau of Labor Statistics, Washington, DC 20402.

12   "Average SNF cost per day is $153," *McKnight's Long-Term Care News*, August 25, 2000. Cost in New York City is for a private room.

13   "Baby Bills," *Special Delivery,* Vol. 21, No. 2, Summer 1998, p. 13. Data for South, West, and Moutain regions estimated by the editor based on information in the source.

14   Baker, Jim, "Lawrence, Kan., Dog Day Care Business Is Part of Growing Trend," *Knight-Ridder/Tribune Business News*, November 7, 2000.

15   Barr, Stephen, "Child Care Subsidy Program Has Strong Beginning — but OMB Reports Drawbacks," *The Washington Post*, April 2, 2001, p. b2.

16   "Baseball Ticket Prices Soar Out of the Park," *Insight*, May 8, 2000, p. 33. New York data are an average of Yankee Stadium and Shea Stadium.

17   *Bell Operating Companies Exchange Service Telephone Rates,December 31, 1997. Washington, D.C.: National Association of Regulatory Utility Commissioners (NARUC), 1997. Notes:* Idaho, Kentucky, and Ohio rates are the average of two service providers.

18   *Bell Operating Companies Exchange Service Telephone Rates,December 31, 1997. Washington, D.C.: National Association of Regulatory Utility Commissioners (NARUC), 1997. Notes:* The basic rate is the fixed monthly rate for the access line and a fixed monthly rate for a usage package which includes an unlimited number of local calls. In all cases shown, rates are for a single party. In*California*, a flat rate is not available. The measured rate includes the first 30 direct dial local calls; no calls are included for business. Rates are 4 cents for the initial minute, 1.5 cents for each additional minute.*Illinois* has no fixed rates for metropolitan areas. Data shown are measured rate base prices. *Chicago* rates are an average of two "area" rates. Data for*Kansas* are averages of several zones.*New York City* has only measured rates of 10.6 cents per message for residental; the business rate is 8 cents for the first three minutes and 0.13 cents for each additional minute. Cities in the state of*Washington* are on measured rates, with a base rate and then 2.5 cents for the initial minute and 1 cent for each additional minute.

19   "Beware of high mortgages in hot markets," *Medical Economics*, December 18, 2000, p. 12.

20   "Big ticket items," *The Boston Globe*, August 28, 1998, p. B8.

21   Boucher, John, "The Cost of Living in Alaska," *Alaska Economic Trends*, June 2000.

22   "Business Expense," *ABA Journal*, June 1999, p. 16.

23　　"California dreamin'? Get ready for high living costs," *Medical Economics*, July 10, 2000, from Runzheimer International, p. 23.

24　　"Car rental rates: Some of the priciest are surprises," *The Christian Science Monitor*, February 28, 2001, p. 24, from Runzheimer International.

25　　"Cell phones get cheaper in Detroit," *Crain's Detroit Business*, February 19, 2001, p. 12.

26　　"Child care fees rising slowly," *Child Care Information Exchange*, September 1999, p. 82.

27　　"Cities where it is most expensive to own a vehicle" and "Cities where it is least expensive to own a vehicle," *USA Today*, October 17-18, 2000, p. 1. Data from Runzheimer International. *Notes:* Data based on a four- year, 60,000 mile trad-in cycle. Costs of fuel, depreciation, maintenance, insurance, registration, etc., are included.

28　　"Cold Spots," *The Wall Street Journal*, January 19, 2001, p. W4.

29　　"Comparing apples to apples," *USA Today*, September 12, 2000, p. 1, from Runzheimer International.

30　　*Consumer Expenditure (CE) Survey*, U.S. Department of Labor, Bureau of Labor Statistics, Washington, DC 20402.

31　　"Cost comparisons per square foot in select metro areas," *Building Design & Construction*, February 2001, p. 23.

32　　"The cost of dying," *Puget Sound Business Journal*, October 20,2000, p. 2. Data collected by People's Memorial Assocation, Seattle.

33　　Data extrapolated from "Wedding Love & Money," *BRIDE's Magazine*, May 1998, based on a commissioned study titled "American Marriage Today." Data have been updated for inflation, 1998 to 2000 using the GDP chained price index for Personal Consumption Expenditures. Data are based on a survey of national average data for upscale respondents; actual national data may be lower.

34　　Data obtained from government sources in each state. *Notes:* Hunting licenses are typically for small game. Additional licenses or stamps are usually required for turkey, deer, and other larger mammals. Fishing licenses are typically for freshwater sports fishing unless the state issued both fresh and saltwater licenses automatically.

35　　Data obtained from state and local sources.

36　　Davis, William A., "Coming full cycle," *The Boston Globe*, August 8, 1998, p. C5.

37   "Daycare Costs for Relocating Parents Can Easily Double from One Location to the Next," *Relocation Journal*, March 1999, from Runzheimer International. *Notes:* Data are based on monthly fees for a three- year old, 5 days a week, for 8 hours. Data from for-profit daycare centers.

38   "Fall Enrollment" and "Institutional Characteristics" surveys, National Center for Education Statistics, Integrated Postsecondary Education Data System (IPEDS), U.S. Department of Education, September 1996.

39   "Farmers' share of food dollar," *Wallaces Farmer*, May 2000, p. 9.

40   "Fast-food price menu," *USA Today*, April 7, 1999, p. B1, from Runzheimer International.

41   *Federal Register*, April 28, 2000. Department of Housing and Urban Development. 24 CFR Part 888. Notice of Proposed Fiscal Year (FY) 2001 Fair Market Rents (FMRs). *Notes:* Value are determined by survey and represent the 40th percentile rent, defined as "the dollar amount below which 40 percent of the standard quality rental housing units rent." The values shown are, therefore, somewhat lower than median rents. All types of rental properties are included. The survey excludes recently built units. Utilities exclude telephone service.

42   Fennelly, Rita, "Prices Decreasing for S.D. Cell Phone Customers," *San Diego Business Journal*, February 28, 2000, p. 23.

43   "Gas Prices Dipping: Florida Prices Remain Among Nation's Lowest, Notes FPMA," *PR Newswire*, January 5, 2001.

44   Gaston, Janice, "Raze the Roof," *Winston-Salem Journal*, March 24, 2001, p. e1.

45   "Health of the Lodging Industry Exeeds Last Year's Forecast," *Travel Agent*, October 9, 2000, from PKF Consulting.

46   Hendricks, Gary, "Some parking rates going up," *Atlanta Journal- Constitution*, October 2, 2000, p. d3.

47   "Here's how house prices stack up from city to city," *USA Today*, August 2, 2000, p. 6B, from Caldwell-Banker.

48   *Highway Statistics 1999*, Office of Highway Policy Information / Federal Highway Administration, U.S. Department of Commerce, Washington, D.C. *Notes:* Where data were available for periods shorter and/or longer than 4 or 5 years, the data closest to a 4-5 year term was used.

49   *Highway Statistics 1999*, Office of Highway Policy Information / Federal Highway Administration, U.S. Department of Commerce, Washington, D.C.

50   "Home Sales Poised to Soar," *Rocky Mountain News*, March 31, 2001, p. 3b.

51   "Home sales start hitting the ceiling," *Business North Carolina*, February 2001, p. 73.

52   "Honolulu has cheapest car rental rates; Cleveland, most expensive," *USA Today*, March 21, 2001, p. 1. from Runzheimer International. *Notes:* Data for an intermediate automobile. Taxes, optional items, and miscellaneous fees are excluded.

53   "House values soar," *USA Today*, May 4, 2001, p. 3B.

54   Kadlec, Daniel, "House Guess," *Time*, December 4, 2000, from State Farm Insurance.

55   Kanell, Michael E., "Atlanta Rings up Cheapest Cellular Use," *The Atlanta Journal-Constitution*, March 29, 2001, p. D1, from Econ One Research, Inc.

56   Karlen, Neal, "What's Doing in St. Paul," *The New York Times*, January 7, 2001, p. 14, from Runzheimer International. *Notes:* Meal includes tip but excludes drinks. Hotel includes taxes.

57   Kelly, Dennis, "Driving Down Rates," *Best's Review*, September 1999, p. 101. Data from National Association of Insurance Commissioners.

58   Kim, Nancy J., "Body Images," *Puget Sound Business Journal*, April 5, 1999, www.amcity.com/seattle.stories.smallb1.html.

59   LeDuc, Doug, "Number of homes sold in 2000 dips," *Fort Wayne News- Sentinel*, March 5, 2001, p. 1b.

60   Lino, Mark.*Expenditures on Children by Families, 1999 Annual Report*, U.S. Department of Agriculture, Center for Nutrition Policy and Promotion, Miscellaneous Publication No. 1528-1999, 2000. *Notes:* Data are for costs experienced by husband-wife families earning, on average, $49,000 a year.

61   "Looking back to '56," *The New York Times*, October 21, 2000, p. b21.

62   Malchow, Aaron, "Districts get serious about teacher housing," *The Business Journal*, December 2000.

63   Manning, Joe, "Eye surgery enter price war," *Milwaukee Journal Sentinel*, July 31, 2000, p. 1.

64   Marcus, Mary Brophy

65   Martinis, Cheryl, "Dealers Scramble for Oregon's Finest Christmas Trees, Which Fetch No-ble a Sum," *Knight-Ridder/Tribune Business News*, November 28, 2000.

66   Materna, Jessica, "Let the dogs out," *San Francisco Business Times*, January 19, 2001, p. 15.

67   Mauch, Rich, "In Texas, high school hockey continues to grow," *Knight- Ridder/Tribute News Services*, April 14, 2000.

68   McCollum, Charlie, "How Costs Compare With Other Cities'," *San Jose Mercury News*, Au-gust 15, 1999.

69   McVicar, Nancy, "Increase in Prescription Drug Prices Drives Up Medigap Costs," *South Florida Sun-Sentinel*, March 27, 2001. *Notes: Plans H, I, and J provide some coverage for prescription drugs.*

70   Meyer, Harvey, "Sold Out: Coping with the Seller's Market," *Associations and Meetings*, Oc-tober 2000, p. 36, from PKF Consulting.

71   Monroe, Melissa S., "San Antonio, Texas-Area Theme Parks Raise Admission Costs," *San Antonio Express-News*, January 12, 2001.

72   "More for your Dollar," The Wall Street Journal, December 22, 2000, p. b4.

73   *Motortruck*, December 1999, p. 24.

74   "Moving Downtown? Office Rental Rates Moving Up, Says C&W," *Facilities Design & Man-agement*, August 1999, p. 21.

75   Moving.com, http://www.moving.com, February 28, 2001 Data cover the monthly electric bills for a 2,000 sq ft home.

76   Mushinski, Margaret, "Average Charges for Three Types of Hysterectomy Procedures: United States, 1998," *Statistical Bulletin-Metropolitan Life Insurance Company*, April-June 2000, p. 27.

77   Mushinski, Margaret, "Cardiac Catheterizations: Average Inpatient Charges, 1998," *Statisti-cal Bulletin-Metropolitan Life Insurance Company*, April-June 2000, p. 10.

78   National Funeral Directors Association (NFDA). Data are from a survey of 2,600 NFDA members from which 829 questionnaires were returned. Unpublished data courtesy of NFDA. NFDA's website is www.nfda.org.

79   Newman, Richard, "Allstate Cuts Rates in New Jersey to Attract New Car- Insurance Customers," *The Record*, Hackensack, NJ, April 13, 2001.

80   "Northwest dragged into Calif. crisis," *USA Today*, January 26, 2001, p. 3a.

81   "Nursing Care Costs Vary Greatly by Region: Study," *Provider* October 2000, p. 17. Data from MetLife Mature Market Institute.

82   "Nursing Home Cost Average $153 Per Day in U.S." Press Release, July 24, 2000. MetLife Mature Market Institute, Westport, CT.

83   "Nursing home costs vary by state," *Medical Economics*, September 18, 2000, p. 22, from MetLife Mature Market Institute.

84   "N.Y. law allows child care checks," *The Boston Globe*, August 4, 1998, p. A4.

85   Olenchek, Christina, "Milwaukee day care costs on upper end of scale," *The Business Journal-Milwaukee*, July 21, 2000, p. 5, from Runzheimer International.

86   Parker, Jim, "South Carolina Car Insurance Rates Rise Quickly," *Knight- Ridder/Tribune Business News*, January 17, 2001.

87   "Pharmacy Payment and Patient Cost Sharing," *Drugtopics.com*, www.drugtopics.com/medicaid.html, acquired July 5, 2000, from state program administrators as reported in the 1999 National Pharmaceutical Council survey.

88   "Ranking of Gas Utility Prices by State, Commercial," *Energy User News*, April 2001, p. 36.

89   Rawls, Linda, "Chrimstmas Tree Shopping Already Brisk," *The Palm Beach Post*, November 25, 2000, p. 10b.

90   *Real Estate Outlook*, National Association of Realtors, February 2001, p. 15. By permission.

91   "Reba, Bebe lift biz," *Variety*, February 26-March 4, 2001.

92   Rebchook, John, "Record $8.77 Billion in Homes Sold," *Rocky Mountain News*, October 28, 2000, p. 1B.

93   "Regional Garden Center Price Ranges for Basic Plant Material," *American Nurseryman*, August 1, 2000, p. 47.

94   Reilly, Shannon, "Business travel," *USA Today*, April 10, 2001, p. B1, from American Express Consulting.

95   Reilly, Shannon, "Business travel," *USA Today*, April 11, 2001, p. B1, from American Express Consulting.

96   *Residential Electric Bills, Summer 1996.Washington, D.C.: National Association of Regulatory Utility Commissioners (NARUC), 1996. Notes:* Data for Vermont and West Virginia are a state average.

97   *Residential Electric Bills, Winter 1995-96.* Washington, D.C.: National Association of Regulatory Utility Commissioners (NARUC), 1996.

98   "Residential Gas Bills, Winter 1995-96," National Association of Regulatory Utility Commissioners, Washington, DC, May 16, 1997. *Notes:* Data for Pittsburgh are an average of rates for two companies.

99   Rios, Brenda, "Snowblowers ease winter workouts," *Detroit Free Press*, December 15, 2000.

100   "Scary movie prices," *U.S. News & World Report*, March 12, 2001.

101   Scherer, Ron, "More female skaters trade sequeins for a stick," *The Christian Science Monitor*, January 24, 2001, p. 3.

102   Simmons, Kelly, "Suburban sprawl driving u cost of living in metro area," *The Atlanta Journal and Constitution*, November 30, 2000.

103   "Sixth Annual Report on Competition in Video Markets," Federal Communications Commission, January 14, 2000, p. B-10.

104   "Sticker shock at Manhattan's theaters," *The Christian Science Monitor*, March 8, 1999, p. 3.

105   "Tale of Two Cities," *The Wall Street Journal*, April 11, 2000, p. B1.

106   Thomas, Scott, "Price is right WNY," *Business First of Buffalo*, Febuary 16, 1998, p. 2.

107   *Travel Holiday*, December 2000/January 2001 and May 2000.

108　United States Postal Services, http://new.usps.com, July 1, 2001.

109　"Water Rates Vary Widely Across U.S.," *U.S. Water News*, March 2000, cited on watercenter.unl.edu/apr00/water.html. *Notes:* Data derived from a survey that priced the cost of 220,200 gallons of water consumed in a month serving a commercial unit, e.g., 15 units of an apartment block. Values shown are calculated by the editors from data reported.

110　"Wedding Love & Money," *BRIDE's Magazine*, May 1998, based on a commissioned study titled "American Marriage Today." *Notes:* Data are based on a survey of upscale respondents; actual regional data may be lower. The national average in 1997 was $19,104.

111　Wells, Tish, "30 most expensive U.S. housing markets," Knight-Ridder/Tribune Information Services, from Yahoo! Real Estate home purchase costs, November 15, 2000.

112　Wotapka, Dawn, "A New Way to Shop for Plants," *The News & Observer*, March 30, 2001.